The Oxford Spanish
Desk Dictionary

The Oxford Spanish Desk Dictionary

Second Edition

Spanish ····> English
English ····> Spanish

Chief editors
Carol Styles Carvajal
Jane Horwood

OXFORD
UNIVERSITY PRESS

OXFORD
UNIVERSITY PRESS

Great Clarendon Street, Oxford OX2 6DP

Oxford University Press is a department of the University of Oxford.
It furthers the University's objective of excellence in research, scholarship,
and education by publishing worldwide in

Oxford New York

Auckland Bangkok Buenos Aires Cape Town Chennai
Dar es Salaam Delhi Hong Kong Istanbul Karachi Kolkata
Kuala Lumpur Madrid Melbourne Mexico City Mumbai Nairobi
São Paulo Shanghai Singapore Taipei Tokyo Toronto

and an associated company in Berlin

Oxford is a registered trade mark of Oxford University Press
in the UK and in certain other countries

Published in the United States
by Oxford University Press Inc., New York

© Oxford University Press 1997, 2001

The moral rights of the author have been asserted
Database right Oxford University Press (maker)

First published 1997
Second edition 2001

British Library Cataloguing in Publication Data
Data available

Library of Congress Cataloging in Publication Data
Data available

ISBN 0-19-521829-9

10 9 8 7 6 5 4 3

Designed by Information Design Unit, Newport Pagnell
Typeset in Nimrod, Arial and Meta by Tradespools
Printed in Great Britain by Clays Ltd, Bungay Suffolk

Preface / Prólogo

This major new edition of the *Oxford Spanish Desk Dictionary* has been enlarged and extensively revised and updated to meet the needs of both the general and school user. New words and phrases reflect scientific and technological innovations, as well as changes in politics, culture, and society.

Combining the authority of the *Oxford Spanish Dictionary* with the convenience of a smaller format and quick-access layout, this easy-to-use pocket dictionary is the ideal reference tool for all those requiring quick and reliable answers to their translation questions. It provides clear guidance on selecting the most appropriate translation, numerous examples to help with problems of usage and construction, and precise information on grammar, style, and pronunciation.

For this edition the principal changes to the use of accents in Spanish recently introduced by the *Real Academia de la Lengua Española* have been adopted, and **ch** and **ll** are alphabetized within the letters **c** and **l** rather than treated as separate letters.

Included as special features are an A-Z of Spanish-speaking countries, a calendar of traditions, festivals, and holidays, and a guide to letter writing, including sample letters and practical tips about key differences between Spanish and English letter styles and layout, and a glossary explaining grammatical terms used in the dictionary.

Geared to the needs of a wide range of users, from the student at intermediate level and above to the enthusiastic tourist or business professional, the *Oxford Spanish Desk Dictionary* is an invaluable practical resource for learners of Spanish at the start of the twenty-first century.

Esta importante nueva edición del *Diccionario Oxford Compact* ha sido ampliada, exhaustivamente revisada y actualizada a fin de satisfacer las necesidades tanto del usuario en general como del escolar. Nuevas palabras y frases reflejan las novedades producidas en el campo científico y técnico como también los cambios que se han experimentado en el plano político, cultural y social.

Al combinarse la autoridad del *Diccionario Oxford* con la comodidad del formato más pequeño y un diseño de acceso rápido, este diccionario compacto y fácil de usar es un instrumento ideal de referencia para todos aquellos que necesiten una respuesta rápida y fiable para las preguntas que surjan al traducir. Proporciona una guía clara para seleccionar la traducción más apropiada, incluye numerosos ejemplos que ayudan con los problemas de uso y construcción, como también información precisa sobre gramática, estilo y pronunciación.

En esta edición se han adoptado las principales modificaciones sobre acentuación introducidas últimamente por la Real Academia de la Lengua Española, asimismo la **ch** y **ll** ya no aparecen como letras independientes dentro del orden alfabético.

Como característica relevante, se incluye información enciclopédica y cultural sobre España y Latinoamérica, una lista desde la A a la Z con las diferentes instituciones, organismos, etc., de la vida y cultura británicas y estadounidenses, y un calendario con los días festivos, fiestas y tradiciones en Gran Bretaña y Estados Unidos. Además contiene una guía para la redacción de cartas, con ejemplos y datos prácticos sobre las diferencias fundamentales entre el español y el inglés en cuanto al estilo y composición de una carta, y también un glosario con los términos gramaticales usados en el diccionario.

El *Diccionario Compact Oxford* ha sido preparado teniendo en cuenta las necesidades de una gran variedad de usuarios, desde el estudiante de un nivel intermedio y superior, al turista entusiasta o el profesional de los negocios, y es un inapreciable instrumento práctico de trabajo para los que aprenden el español moderno e idiomático a comienzos del siglo veintiuno.

List of contributors / Lista de colaboradores

Chief Editors/Dirección editorial
Carol Styles Carvajal
Jane Horwood

Data input/Entrada de datos
Anne McConnell
Marianne Selby-Smith
Anna Cotgreave
Sarah Hawker

Días festivos, fiestas y tradiciones en Gran Bretaña y EEUU
La vida y cultura británicas y estadounidenses desde la 'A' a la 'Z'

Ella Associates
Valerie Grundy

Ana Cristina Llompart
Mónica Bossons

Calendar of traditions, festivals, and holidays in Spanish-speaking countries

Ella Associates
Valerie Grundy

Josephine Grundy

Contents / Índice

Proprietary names / Marcas registradas

This dictionary includes some words which have, or are asserted to have, proprietary status as trademarks or otherwise. Their inclusion does not imply that they have acquired for legal purposes a non-proprietary or general significance, nor is any other judgment implied concerning their legal status. In cases where the editorial staff have some evidence that a word has proprietary status this is indicated in the entry for that word by the symbol ®, but no judgment concerning the legal status of such words is made or implied thereby.

Este diccionario incluye palabras que constituyen, o se afirma que constituyen, marcas registradas o nombres comerciales. Su inclusión no significa que a efectos legales hayan dejado de tener ese carácter, ni supone un pronunciamiento respecto de su situación legal.

Cuando al editor le consta que una palabra es una marca registrada o un nombre comercial, esto se indica por medio del símbolo ®, lo que tampoco supone un pronunciamiento acerca de la situación legal de esa palabra.

Structure of a Spanish–English entry

Headword •————— **acertijo** *m* riddle, puzzle
Vocablo cabeza de
artículo

Variant form of •————— **achichincle**, **achichinque** *mf* (Méx fam &
headword   pey) hanger-on (colloq & pej)
Variante del vocablo
cabeza de artículo
                                acomodar [A1] *vt* **1** (adaptar, amoldar) to adapt   •— **Sense divisions**
                                2 ⟨huésped⟩ to put ... up **3** **(a)** (AmL) (arreglar) to   Divisiones
                                arrange; (poner) to put **(b)** (fam) ⟨persona⟩ (en   correspondientes a las
                                puesto): **su tío lo acomodó en su sección** his uncle   distintas acepciones
                                fixed him up with a job in his department

                                acomplejado -da *adj*: **es muy ~** he's full of
                                complexes; **está ~ por su gordura** he has a
                                complex about being fat
A change of part of •——— ■ *m,f*: **es un ~** he's a mass of complexes
speech within an entry   **acomplejar** [A1] *vt* to give ... a complex
is marked by a box ■   ■ **acomplejarse** *v pron* to get a complex
Todo cambio de categoría
gramatical dentro de una
entrada se indica con el
símbolo ■
                                acondicionar [A1] *vt* **(a)** ⟨vivienda/local⟩ to   •— **Part of speech**
                                equip, fit out **(b)** (Col) ⟨carro⟩ to soup up   Función gramatical
                                aconsejable *adj* advisable

Irregular plural form •——— **acusetas** *mf* (*pl* ~), **acusete -ta** *m,f* (fam)
Plurales irregulares   tattletale (AmE colloq), telltale (BrE colloq)

                                adecuar [A1] *or* [A18] *vt* **~ algo A algo** to   •— **Every verb has a**
                                adapt sth ᴛᴏ sth   **reference to the verb**
                                                                                               tables on p. 967
                                                                                               Cada verbo se remite a
                                                                                               la tabla de
                                                                                               conjugaciones en la
                                                                                               página 967

The use of ser or estar •— **agarrado¹ -da** *adj* **(a)** [ѕᴇʀ] (fam) (tacaño)
with adjectives is   tightfisted (colloq) **(b)** [ᴇѕᴛᴀʀ] (CS fam) (enamorado)
marked when necessary   in love
El uso de ser o estar con   ■ *m,f* (fam) (tacaño) skinflint (colloq), tightwad (AmE
adjetivos se indica donde   colloq)
es necesario

                                águila *f‡* **(a)** (ave) eagle; **ser un ~** to be very   •— **The part of speech** *f‡*
                                sharp **(b)** (Méx) (de moneda) ≈ heads (*pl*); **¿~ o**   **indicates a feminine**
                                sol? heads or tails?   **noun that takes the**
                                                                                               masculine article in
                                                                                               the singular
                                                                                               La función gramatical
                                                                                               f‡ indica un sustantivo
                                                                                               femenino usado con el
                                                                                               artículo masculino en el
                                                                                               singular

Structure of a Spanish–English entry

Pronominal verb
Verbo pronominal

■ **apretujarse** *v pron* to squash *o* squeeze together

aprobación *f* (de proyecto de ley, moción) passing; (de préstamo, acuerdo, plan) approval, endorsement; (de actuación, conducta) approval

● **Sense indicators**
Indicadores semánticos

Field labels
Indicadores de campo semántico

arco *m* [1] (Arquit) arch; (Anat) arch; (Mat) arc; ~ **de triunfo** triumphal arch; ~ **iris** rainbow [2] (AmL) (en fútbol) goal [3] (a) (Arm, Dep) bow (b) (de violín) bow

arete *m* (Col, Méx) earring

● **Regional labels**
Indicadores de uso regional

armario *m* (a) (para ropa — mueble) wardrobe; (— empotrado) closet (AmE), wardrobe (BrE) (b) (de cocina) cupboard; (de cuarto de baño) cabinet

Stylistic labels
Indicadores de estilo

armatoste *m* (fam) huge great thing (colloq)

ascendencia *f* (a) (linaje) descent, ancestry; **es de ~ francesa** he is of French descent (b) (origen) origin(s); **su ~ humilde** her humble origins

● **Examples**
Ejemplos

**Idioms and proverbs
appear in bold italics**
Los modismos y los proverbios aparecen en negritas cursivas

ascua *f‡* ember; *estar en/tener a algn en ~s* (fam) to be on/to keep sb on tenterhooks

aspereza *f* [1] (a) (de superficie, piel) roughness (b) (de sabor) sharpness; (de voz, clima) harshness [2] (parte áspera): **usar papel de lija para quitar las ~s** use sandpaper to remove any roughness; *limar ~s* to smooth things over

aviso *m* [1] (a) (notificación) notice; Ⓢ **aviso al público** notice to the public; **dio ~ a la policía** he notified *o* informed the police …

● Ⓢ **indicates the use of the headword in signs, notices, warnings, etc**
El símbolo Ⓢ indica el uso del vocablo cabeza de artículo en letreros, anuncios, advertencias, etc.

Structure of a Spanish–English entry

Universally valid translation(s) followed by regional alternative(s)
Traducción universalmente válida seguida de alternativas regionales

balancín *m* (de niños) seesaw, teeter-totter (AmE)

balompié *m* soccer, football (BrE)

Words often used with the headword, shown to help select the correct translation for each context
Palabras que suelen acompañar al vocablo cabeza de artículo y que ayudan a elegir la traducción que corresponde a cada contexto

bancario -ria *adj* ‹interés/préstamo› bank (*before n*); ‹sector› banking (*before n*)

bañar [A1] *vt* ① ‹niño/enfermo› to bath, give ... a bath ② ‹pulsera/cubierto› to plate

bifurcarse [A2] *v pron* «camino» to fork, diverge (frml); «vía férrea» to diverge

bancario -ria *adj* ‹interés/préstamo› bank (*before n*); ‹sector› banking (*before n*)

● **Nouns modified by an adjective**
Sustantivos calificados por un adjetivo

bañar [A1] *vt* ① ‹niño/enfermo› to bath, give ... a bath ② ‹pulsera/cubierto› to plate

● **Objects of a verb**
Complementos de un verbo

bifurcarse [A2] *v pron* «camino» to fork, diverge (frml); «vía férrea» to diverge

● **Subjects of a verb appear in double angled parentheses**
Los posibles sujetos de un verbo aparecen entre paréntesis angulares dobles

The sign ≈ is used to indicate approximate equivalence
El símbolo ≈ indica un equivalente aproximado en la lengua de destino

canciller *m* (a) (jefe de estado) chancellor (b) (AmS) (ministro) ≈ Secretary of State (*in US*), ≈ Foreign Secretary (*in UK*)

Structure of a Spanish–English entry

Grammatical constructions in which the headword commonly occurs are indicated by small capitals
Las construcciones gramaticales en las que suele aparecer el vocablo cabeza de artículo se destacan mediante versalitas

■ **cansarse** *v pron* **(a)** (fatigarse) to tire oneself out; **se le cansa la vista** her eyes get tired **(b)** (aburrirse) to get bored; **~se DE algo/algn** to get tired OF sth/sb, get bored WITH sth/sb, **~se DE hacer algo** to get tired OF doing sth

carnet /kar'ne/ *m* (*pl* **-nets**) ▶ CARNÉ

ceder [E1] *vt* **1** **(a)** ⟨derecho⟩ to transfer, assign; ⟨territorio⟩ to cede; ⟨puesto/título⟩ (voluntariamente) to hand over; (a la fuerza) to give up; **~ el poder** to hand over power; **me cedió el asiento** he let me have his seat; ▶ PASO 1B **(b)** ⟨balón/pelota⟩ to pass

An arrow directs the user to another entry with the same meaning or to where a compound, idiomatic expression, or other useful expression is to be found
Se utiliza una flecha para remitir al usuario a una variante sinónima o a otro artículo donde aparece un compuesto, un modismo u otro uso de interés

'ver tb' directs the user to a headword where additional information is to be found
'ver tb' remite al usuario a otro artículo donde se hallará información complementaria

chiva *f* **1** (AmL) (barba) goatee **2** (Col) (bus) rural o country bus **3** (Col period) (primicia) scoop, exclusive **4** (Chi fam) (mentira) cock-and-bull story (colloq); *ver tb* CHIVO **5** **chivas** *fpl* (Méx fam) (cachivaches) junk (colloq)

Estructura del artículo Inglés–Español

Vocablo cabeza de artículo
Headword

alligator /'æləgeɪtər ‖'ælɪgeɪtə(r)/ *n* aligátor *m*

all: **~-important** /'ɔ:lɪm'pɔ:rtn̩t ‖,ɔ:lɪm'pɔ:tn̩t/ *adj* de suma importancia; **~-night** /'ɔ:l'naɪt/ *adj* ⟨party/show⟩ que dura toda la noche; ⟨café/store⟩ que está abierto toda la noche

Nombres compuestos
Compounds

La transcripción fonética aparece inmediatamente después del vocablo cabeza de artículo [ver página xxi]
Pronunciation is shown immediately after the headword [see p. xxi]

allocate /'æləkeɪt/ *vt* asignar; (distribute) repartir; **$3 million has been ~d for research** se han destinado tres millones de dólares a la investigación

Variante del vocablo cabeza de artículo
Variant form of a headword

amoeba, (AmE also) **ameba** /ə'miːbə/ *n* ameba *f*, amiba *f*

answer¹ /'ænsər ‖'ɑːnsə(r)/ *n* [1] **(a)** (reply) respuesta *f*, contestación *f*; in ~ to your question para contestar tu pregunta **(b)** (response): her ~ to his rudeness was to ignore it respondió a su grosería ignorándola; Britain's ~ to Elvis Presley el Elvis Presley británico [2] **(a)** (in exam, test, quiz) respuesta *f* **(b)** (solution) solución *f*; ~ TO sth solución DE algo

Divisiones correspondientes a las distintas acepciones
Sense divisions

Los verbos con partícula aparecen al final del artículo correspondiente
Phrasal verbs appear at the end of the root word entry

answer² *vt* [1] **(a)** (reply to) ‹person/letter› contestar ...
■ **answer back** [1] [*v + adv*] (rudely) contestar [2] [*v + o + adv*] to ~ sb back contestarle mal *or* de mala manera a algn
■ **answer for** [*v + prep + o*] (accept responsibility for) ‹conduct/consequences› responder de; his parents have a lot to ~ for sus padres tienen mucha culpa

appreciate /ə'priːʃieɪt/ *vt* **(a)** (value) ‹food/ novel› apreciar **(b)** (be grateful for) agradecer* **(c)** (understand) ‹danger/difficulties› darse* cuenta de; I ~ that, but ... lo comprendo, pero ...
■ ~ *vi* «shares/property» (re)valorizarse*

Todo cambio de categoría gramatical de un verbo se indica con el símbolo ■
A change of part of speech of a verb is marked by a box ■

Función gramatical
Part of speech

approximate /ə'prɑːksəmət ‖ə'prɒksɪmət/ *adj* aproximado
approximately /ə'prɑːksəmətli ‖ə'prɒksɪmətli/ *adv* aproximadamente

artery /'ɑːrtəri ‖'ɑːtəri/ *n* (*pl* -**ries**) arteria *f*
auditorium /ˌɔːdə'tɔːriəm ‖ˌɔːdɪ'tɔːriəm/ *n* (*pl* -**riums** *or* -**ria** /-riə/) auditorio *m*

Inflexiones irregulares
Irregular inflections

El comparativo y el superlativo del adjetivo
Comparative and superlative forms of an adjective

baggy /'bægi/ *adj* -**gier**, -**giest** ancho, guango (Méx)

Estructura del artículo Inglés–Español

bang² *vt* **(a)** (strike) golpear **(b)** (slam): he ~ed the door dio un portazo (fam)
■ ~ *vi* **(a)** (strike) to ~ on sth golpear algo; to ~ INTO sth darse* CONTRA algo **(b)** (slam) «door» cerrarse* de un golpe

■ **bear out** [v + o + adv, v + adv + o] ‹theory› confirmar
■ **bear up** [v + adv]: she bore up well under the strain sobrellevó muy bien la situación

beg /beg/ **-gg-** *vt* 1 ‹money/food› pedir*, mendigar* 2 (fml) **(a)** (entreat) ‹person› suplicarle* a, rogarle* a **(b)** (ask for) ‹forgiveness› suplicar*, rogar*
■ ~ *vi* «beggar» pedir*, mendigar*; to ~ for mercy pedir* or suplicar* clemencia

belief /bə'li:f ‖ br'li:f/ *n* **(a)** (conviction, opinion) creencia *f* **(b)** (confidence) ~ IN sb/sth confianza *f* or fe *f* EN algn/algo **(c)** (Relig) fe *f*

belt¹ /belt/ *n* 1 (Clothing) cinturón *m* 2 (Mech Eng) correa *f*

Biro®, **biro** /'baɪrəʊ ‖ 'baɪərəʊ/ *n* (*pl* **biros**) (BrE) bolígrafo *m*, birome *f* (RPl), esfero *m* (Col), lápiz *m* de pasta (Chi), boli *m* (Esp fam)

Estructura del artículo Inglés–Español

bitch /bɪtʃ/ n **1** (female dog) perra f **2** (spiteful woman) (AmE vulg, BrE sl) bruja f (fam), arpía f (fam), cabrona f (Esp, Méx vulg)

• **Indicadores de estilo**
Stylistic labels

Ejemplos
Examples

bounce² n **(a)** (action) rebote m, pique m (AmL) **(b)** (springiness, vitality): **this shampoo puts the ~ back into your hair** este champú les da nueva vida a sus cabellos; **she's full of ~** es una persona llena de vida

breath /breθ/ n aliento m; **to have bad ~** tener* mal aliento; **to take a ~** aspirar, inspirar; **take a deep ~** respire hondo; **out of ~** sin aliento; **to hold one's ~** contener* la respiración; **to take sb's ~ away** dejar a algn sin habla

• **Los modismos y los proverbios aparecen en negritas cursivas**
Idioms and proverbs appear in bold italics

El símbolo ⑤ indica el uso del vocablo cabeza de artículo en letreros, anuncios, advertencias, etc.
⑤ indicates the use of the headword in signs, notices, warnings, etc

customer /ˈkʌstəmər ‖ˈkʌstəmə(r)/ n cliente, -ta m,f; (before n) ⑤ **customer services** información y reclamaciones

Palabras que suelen acompañar al vocablo cabeza de artículo y que ayudan a elegir la traducción que corresponde a cada contexto
Words often used with the headword, shown to help select the correct translation for each context

dump¹ /dʌmp/ n **1** (place for waste) vertedero m (de basura), basural m (AmL), tiradero m (Méx) ...

• **Traducción universalmente válida seguida de alternativas regionales**
Universal Spanish translation followed by regional alternatives

ease² vt **1** **(a)** (relieve) ⟨pain⟩ calmar, aliviar; ⟨tension⟩ hacer* disminuir, aliviar; ⟨burden⟩ aligerar; **to ~ sb's mind** tranquilizar* a algn **(b)** (make easier) ⟨situation⟩ paliar; ⟨transition⟩ facilitar; **to ~ the way for sth** preparar el terreno para algo
■ **ease off** [v + adv] «rain» amainar; «pain» aliviarse, calmarse; «pressure/traffic» disminuir*

efficient /ɪˈfɪʃənt/ adj ⟨person/system⟩ eficiente; ⟨machine/engine⟩ de buen rendimiento

ease² vt **1** **(a)** (relieve) ⟨pain⟩ calmar, aliviar; ⟨tension⟩ hacer* disminuir, aliviar; ⟨burden⟩ aligerar; **to ~ sb's mind** tranquilizar* a algn **(b)** (make easier) ⟨situation⟩ paliar; ⟨transition⟩ facilitar; **to ~ the way for sth** preparar el terreno para algo

• **Complementos de un verbo**
Objects of a verb

■ **ease off** [v + adv] «rain» amainar; «pain» aliviarse, calmarse; «pressure/traffic» disminuir*

• **Los posibles sujetos de un verbo aparecen entre paréntesis angulares dobles**
Subjects of a verb appear in double angled brackets

efficient /ɪˈfɪʃənt/ adj ⟨person/system⟩ eficiente; ⟨machine/engine⟩ de buen rendimiento

• **Sustantivos calificados por un adjetivo**
Nouns modified by an adjective

Inland Revenue /'mlənd/ *n* (in UK) the ~ ~
≈ Hacienda, ≈ la Dirección General Impositiva
(*en RPl*), ≈ Impuestos Internos (*en Chi*)

● El símbolo ≈ indica un equivalente aproximado en la lengua de destino
The sign ≈ is used to indicate approximate equivalence

Se utiliza una flecha ● para remitir al usuario a una variante sinónima o a otro artículo donde aparece un compuesto, un modismo u otro uso de interés
An arrow directs the user to another entry with the same meaning or to where a compound, idiomatic expression, or other useful expression is to be found

inmost /'ınməʊst/ *adj* ▶ INNERMOST
jersey /'dʒərzi ‖'dʒɜːzi/ *n* (*pl* -seys) ① (a)
(sports shirt) camiseta *f* (b) (Tex) jersey *m* (c) (BrE)
▶ SWEATER ② Jersey (la isla de) Jersey

jetsam /'dʒetsəm/ *n* echazón *f*; *see also* FLOTSAM

● 'see also' remite al usuario a otro artículo donde se hallará información complementaria
'see also' directs the user to a headword where additional information is to be found

The pronunciation of Spanish

Symbols used in this dictionary

The pronunciation of Spanish words is directly represented by their written form and therefore phonetic transcriptions have only been supplied for loan words which retain their original spelling.

Consonants and semi-vowels

Symbol	Example	Approximation
/b/	**boca** /'boka/ **vaso** /'baso/	English *b* in *bin* but without the aspiration that follows it.
/β/	**cabo** /'kaβo/ **ave** /'aβe/	Very soft *b*, produced with the lips hardly meeting.
/d/	**dolor** /do'lor/	English *d* in *den*.
/ð/	**cada** /'kaða/	English *th* in *rather*.
/f/	**fino** /'fino/	English *f* in *feat*.
/g/	**gota** /'gota/	English *g* in *goat*.
/ɣ/	**pago** /'paɣo/ **largo** /'larɣo/	Very soft continuous sound, not punctuated like /g/.
/ʝ/	**mayo** /'maʝo/ **llave** /'ʝaβe/	English *y* in *yet*. For regional variants see points 7 and 14 of **General Rules of Spanish Pronunciation** on page xviii.
/j/	**tiene** /'tjene/	English *y* in *yet*.
/k/	**cama** /'kama/ **cuna** /'kuna/ **quiso** /'kiso/ **kilo** /'kilo/	English *c* in *cap* but without the aspiration that follows it.
/l/	**lago** /'laɣo/	English *l* in *lid*.

Symbol	Example	Approximation
/m/	**mono** /'mono/	English *m* in *most*.
/n/	**no** /no/	English *n* in *nib*.
/ŋ/	banco /'baŋko/	English *ng* in *song*.
/ɲ/	**año** /'aɲo/	Like *gn* in French *soigné*, similar to the *ni* in *onion*.
/p/	**peso** /'peso/	English *p* in *spin*.
/r/	**aro** /'aro/ **árbol** /'arβol/	A single flap with a curved tongue against the palate.
/rr/	**rato** /'rrato/ **parra** /'parra/	A rolled '*r*' as found in some Scottish accents.
/s/	**asa** /'asa/ **celo** /'selo/ **cinco** /'siŋko/ **azote** /a'sote/ (Latin-American Spanish)	English *s* in *stop*.
/θ/	**celo** /'θelo/ **cinco** /'θiŋko/ **azote** /a'θote/ (European Spanish)	English *th* in *thin*.
/t/	**todo** /'toðo/	English *t* in *step*.
/tʃ/	**chapa** /'tʃapa/	English *ch* in *church*.
/w/	**cuatro** /'kwatro/	English *w*.
/x/	**jota** /'xota/ **general** /xene'ral/ **gigante** /xi'ɣante/	*ch* in Scottish *loch*.
/z/	**desde** /'dezðe/	English *s* in *is*.

Vowels

None of the five Spanish vowels corresponds exactly to an English vowel.

Symbol	Example	Approximation
/a/	**casa** /'kasa/	Shorter than *a* in *father*.
/e/	**seco** /'seko/	English *e* in *pen*.
/i/	**fin** /fin/	Between English *ee* in *seen* and *i* in *sin*.
/o/	**oro** /'oro/	Shorter than English *o* in *rose*.
/u/	**uña** /'uɲa/	Between English *oo* in *boot* and *oo* in *foot*.

The stress mark

When phonetic transcriptions of Spanish headwords are given in the dictionary, the symbol ' precedes the syllable that carries the stress:

footing /'futin/

For information about where other words should be stressed, see the section **Stress** on the next page.

General rules of Spanish pronunciation

Consonants

1 The letters *b* and *v* are pronounced in exactly the same way: /b/ when at the beginning of an utterance or after *m* or *n* (**barco** /'barko/, **vaca** /'baka/, **ambos** /'ambos/), and /β/ in all other contexts (**rabo** /'rraβo/, **ave** /'aβe/, **árbol** /'arβol/).

2 *C* is pronounced /k/ when followed by a consonant other than *h* or by *a*, *o* or *u* (**acto** /'akto/, **casa** /'kasa/, **coma** /'koma/). When it is followed by *e* or

i, it is pronounced /s/ in Latin America and parts of southern Spain and /θ/ in the rest of Spain (**cero** /'sero/, /'θero/; **cinco** /'siŋko/, /'θiŋko/).

3 *D* is pronounced /d/ when it occurs at the beginning of an utterance or after *n* or *l* (**digo** /'diɣo/, **anda** /'anda/) and /ð/ in all other contexts (**hada** /'aða/, **arde** /'arðe/). It is often not pronounced at all at the end of a word (**libertad** /liβer'ta(ð)/, **Madrid** /ma'ðri(ð)/).

4 *G* is pronounced /x/ when followed by *e* or *i* (**gitano** /xi'tano/, **auge** /'awxe/). When followed by *a, o, u, ue* or *ui* it is pronounced /g/ if at the beginning of an utterance or after *n* (**gato** /'gato/, **gula** /'gula/, **tango** /'taŋgo/, **guiso** /'giso/) and /ɣ/ in all other contexts (**hago** /'aɣo/, **trague** /'traɣe/). Note that the *u* is not pronounced in the combinations *gue* and *gui*, unless it is written with a diaeresis (**paragüero** /para'ɣwero/, **agüita** /a'ɣwita/).

5 *H* is mute in Spanish, (**huevo** /'weβo/, **almohada** /almo'aða/) except in the combination *ch*, which is pronounced /tʃ/ (**chico** /'tʃiko/, **leche** /'letʃe/).

6 *J* is always pronounced /x/ (**jamón** /xa'mon/, **jefe** /'xefe/).

7 The pronunciation of *ll* varies greatly throughout the Spanish-speaking world.

a It is pronounced rather like the *y* in English *yes* by the majority of speakers, who do not distinguish between the pronunciation of *ll* and that of *y* (e.g. between *haya* and *halla*). The sound is pronounced slightly more emphatically when at the beginning of an utterance.

b In some areas, particularly Bolivia, parts of Chile, Peru and Castile in Spain, the distinction between *ll* and *y* has been preserved. In these areas *ll* is pronounced similarly to *lli* in *million*.

c In the River Plate area *ll* is pronounced /ʒ/ (as in English *measure*), sometimes tending toward /ʃ/ (as in *shop*).

8 *Ñ* is always pronounced /ɲ/.

9 *Q* is pronounced /k/, and the *u* that always follows it is silent (**quema** /'kema/, **quiso** /'kiso/).

10 *R* is pronounced /r/ when it occurs between vowels or in syllable-final position (**aro** /'aro/, **barco** /'barko/, **cantar** /kan'tar/). It is pronounced /rr/ when in initial position (**rama** /'rrama/). The double consonant *rr* is always pronounced /rr/.

11 *S* is pronounced /s/ but it is aspirated by speakers in many regions when it occurs in syllable-final position (**hasta** /'ahta/, **los cuatro** /loh'kwatro/). In other regions it is voiced when followed by a voiced consonant (**mismo** /'mɪzmo/, **los dos** /loz'ðos/).

12 *V* see 1 above.

13 *X* is pronounced /ks/, although there is a marked tendency to render it as /s/ before consonants (**extra** /'ekstra/, /'estra/).

In some words derived from Nahuatl and other Indian languages it is pronounced /x/ (**México** /'mexiko/) and in others it is pronounced /s/ (**Xochimilco** /sotʃi'milko/).

14 When followed by a vowel within the same syllable *y* is pronounced rather like the *y* in English *yes* (slightly more emphatically when at the beginning of an utterance). In the River Plate area it is pronounced /ʒ/ (as in English *measure*), sometimes tending toward /ʃ/ (as in *shop*).

As the conjunction *y* and in syllable-final position, *y* is pronounced /i/.

15 *Z* is pronounced /s/ in Latin America and parts of southern Spain and /θ/ in the rest of Spain.

Stress

When no phonetic transcription is given for a Spanish headword, the following rules determine where it should be stressed:

1 If there is no written accent:

a a word is stressed on the penultimate syllable if it ends in a vowel, or in *n* or *s*:
   arma /'arma/
   ponen /'ponen/
   mariposas /mari'posas/

b words which end in a consonant other than *n* or *s* are stressed on the last syllable:
   cantar /kan'tar/
   delantal /delan'tal/
   maguey /ma'ɣei/

2 If a word is not stressed in accordance with the above rules, the written accent indicates the syllable where the emphasis is to be placed:
balcón /bal'kon/
salí /sa'li/
carácter /ka'rakter/

It should be noted that unstressed vowels have the same quality as stressed vowels and are not noticeably weakened as they are in

English. For example, there is no perceptible difference between any of the e's in *entenderé* or between the a's in *Panamá*.

Combinations of vowels

A combination of a strong vowel (*a*, *e* or *o*) and a weak vowel (*i* or *u*) or of two weak vowels forms a diphthong and is therefore pronounced as one syllable. The stress falls on the strong vowel if there is one. In a combination of two weak vowels, it falls on the second element:

cuando /'kwando/ *stressed on the* /a/
aula /'awla/ *stressed on the* /a/
viudo /'bjuðo/ *stressed on the* /u/

A combination of two strong vowels does not form a diphthong and the vowels retain their separate values. They count as two separate syllables for the purposes of applying the above rules on stress:

faena /fa'ena/ *stressed on the* /e/
polea /po'lea/ *stressed on the* /e/

La pronunciación del inglés

La transcripción fonética que sigue a cada palabra cabeza de artículo corresponde a la pronunciación norteamericana de uso más extendido en los Estados Unidos. Se ha incluido la pronunciación británica (precedida por el símbolo ‖) únicamente en aquellos casos en que esta difiere sustancialmente de la pronunciación norteamericana. Ejemplo:

address[1] /'ædres ‖ ə'dres/
induce /ɪn'du:s ‖ ɪn'dju:s/

Se reconoce la validez de muchas variantes regionales, tanto norteamericanas como británicas, pero estas no se han incluido por razones de espacio.

Los símbolos empleados en las transcripciones son los del Alfabeto Fonético Internacional (AFI). Estos se enumeran a continuación, seguidos de un ejemplo y una breve aproximación o descripción del sonido que representan. Estas descripciones no siguen criterios fonéticos estrictos.

Consonantes y semivocales

Símbolo	Ejemplo	Aproximación
/b/	**bat** /bæt/	Sonido más explosivo que el de una *b* inicial española.
/d/	**dig** /dɪg/	Sonido más explosivo que el de una *d* inicial española.
/dʒ/	**jam** /dʒæm/	Similar a una *ch* pero más cercano al sonido inicial de *Giuseppe* en italiano.
/f/	**fit** /fɪt/	Como la *f* española.
/g/	**good** /gʊd/	Sonido más explosivo que el de una *g* inicial española.

Símbolo	Ejemplo	Aproximación
/h/	**hat** /hæt/	Sonido de aspiración más suave que la *j* española, articulado como si se estuviera intentando empañar un espejo con el aliento.
/hw/	**wheel** /hwi:l/	Una /w/ con la aspiración de la /h/ (muchos hablantes no distinguen entre /hw/ y /w/ y pronuncian *whale* de la misma manera que *wail*).
/j/	**yes** /jes/	Como la *y* española en *yema* y *yo* (excepto en el español rioplatense).

La pronunciación del inglés

Símbolo	Ejemplo	Aproximación
/k/	cat /kæt/	Sonido más explosivo que el de una c española en *cama* o *acto*.
/l/	lid /lɪd/	Como la l española.
/l̩/	tidal /'taɪdl̩/	l alargada y resonante.
/m/	mat /mæt/	Como la m española.
/n/	nib /nɪb/	Como la n española.
/n̩/	threaten /'θretn̩/	n alargada y resonante.
/ŋ/	sing /sɪŋ/	Como la n española en *banco* o *anca*.
/p/	pet /pet/	Sonido más explosivo que el de una p española.
/r/	rat /ræt/	Entre la r y la rr españolas, pronunciado con la punta de la lengua curvada hacia atrás y sin llegar a tocar el paladar.
/s/	sip /sɪp/	Como la s española.
/ʃ/	ship /ʃɪp/	Sonido similar al de la interjección ¡sh!, utilizada para pedir silencio (ver también /tʃ/).
/t/	tip /tɪp/	Sonido más explosivo que el de una t española.
/tʃ/	chin /tʃɪn/	Como la ch española.
/θ/	thin /θɪn/	Como la c o la z del español europeo en *cinco* o *zapato*.

Símbolo	Ejemplo	Aproximación
/ð/	the /ðə/	Sonido similar a una d intervocálica española como la de *cada* o *modo*.
/v/	van /væn/	Sonido sonoro que se produce con los incisivos superiores sobre el labio inferior.
/w/	win /wɪn/	Similar al sonido inicial de *huevo*.
/x/	loch /lɑːx/	Como la j española.
/z/	zip /zɪp/	s sonora (con zumbido).
/ʒ/	vision /'vɪʒən/	Sonido similar al de la y o la ll del español rioplatense en *yo* o *llave*, o al de la j francesa en *je* (ver también /dʒ/).

Vocales y diptongos

El símbolo : indica que la vocal precedente es larga

Símbolo	Ejemplo	Aproximación
/ɑː/	father /'fɑːðər/	Sonido más largo que el de una a española.
/æ/	fat /fæt/	Sonido que se obtiene al pronunciar una a española con los labios en la posición de pronunciar una e.
/ʌ/	cup /kʌp/	Sonido más breve que la a española y que se pronuncia en la parte posterior de la boca.

La pronunciación del inglés

Símbolo	Ejemplo	Aproximación
/e/	**met** /met/	Sonido parecido a la e española en *mesa*.
/ə/	**abet** /ə'bet/	Sonido similar al de la e francesa en *je* (ver también /əʊ/).
/ɜ:/	**fur** /fɜ:r/	Sonido que se obtiene al pronunciar una e española con los labios en la posición de pronunciar una o.
/ɪ/	**bit** /bɪt/	Sonido más breve que el de la i española.
/i:/	**beat** /bi:t/	Sonido más largo que el de la i española.
/i/	**very** /'veri/	Sonido similar al de la i española en *papi*.
/ɔ:/	**paw** /pɔ:/	Sonido más largo que el de la o española.
/u:/	**boot** /bu:t/	Sonido más largo que el de una u española.
/ʊ/	**book** /bʊk/	Sonido más breve que el de la u española.
/aɪ/	**fine** /faɪn/	Como ai en las palabras españolas *aire*, *baile*.
/aʊ/	**now** /naʊ/	Como au en las palabras españolas *pausa*, *flauta*.
/eɪ/	**fate** /feɪt/	Como ei en las palabras españolas *peine*, *aceite*.

Símbolo	Ejemplo	Aproximación
/əʊ/	**goat** /gəʊt/	Como una o pronunciada sin redondear demasiado los labios.
/ɔɪ/	**boil** /bɔɪl/	Como oy en *voy*, *coypu*.
/uə/	**sexual** /'sekʃuəl/	Como una u pronunciada sin redondear demasiado los labios y seguida de una /ə/.

Símbolos adicionales utilizados en la transcripción de sonidos vocálicos británicos

Símbolo	Ejemplo	Aproximación
/ɒ/	**dog** /dɒg/	Similar a una o española.
/eə/	**fair** /feə(r)/	Como una e española seguida de /ə/.
/ɪə/	**near** /nɪə(r)/	Como una i española seguida de /ə/.
/ʊə/	**tour** /tʊə(r)/	Como una u española pronunciada sin redondear demasiado los labios y seguida de /ə/.

Acentuación

El símbolo ' precede a la sílaba sobre la cual recae el acento tónico primario:
ago /ə'gəʊ/
dinosaur /'daɪnəsɔ:r/

El símbolo ˌ precede a la sílaba sobre la cual recae el acento tónico secundario:
blackmailer /'blækˌmeɪlər/

Abbreviations and labels / Abreviaturas e indicadores

adjetivo	adj	adjective	Correspondencia	Corresp	Correspondence
adjetivo invariable	adj inv	invariable adjective	numerable	count	countable
			Costa Rica	CR	Costa Rica
Administración	Adm	Administration	uso criticado	crit	criticized usage
adverbio	adv	adverb	Cono Sur	CS	Southern Cone
Espacio	Aerosp	Aerospace	Cuba	Cu	Cuba
Agricultura	Agr	Agriculture	Cocina	Culin	Cookery
América Central	AmC	Central America	anticuado	dated	dated
inglés norteamericano	AmE	American English	artículo definido	def art	definite article
América Latina	AmL	Latin America	Odontología	Dent	Dentistry
América del Sur	AmS	South America	Deporte	Dep	Sport
Anatomía	Anat	Anatomy	Derecho	Der	Law
Andes	Andes	Andes	dialecto	dial	dialect
anticuado	ant	dated	Ecuador	Ec	Ecuador
Antropología	Anthrop	Anthropology	Comunidad Europea	EC	European Community
arcaico	arc, arch	archaic	Ecología	Ecol	Ecology
Arqueología	Archeol	Archeology	Economía	Econ	Economics
Arquitectura	Archit	Architecture	Educación	Educ	Education
argot	arg	slang	Electricidad	Elec	Electricity
Argentina	Arg	Argentina	Electrónica	Electrón, Electron	Electronics
Armas	Arm	Arms			
Arqueología	Arqueol	Archeology	enfático	enf	emphatic
Arquitectura	Arquit	Architecture	Ingeniería	Eng	Engineering
artículo	art	article	Equitación	Equ	Equestrianism
Arte	Arte, Art	Art	especialmente	esp	especially
Astrología	Astrol	Astrology	España	Esp	Spain
Astronomía	Astron	Astronomy	Espacio	Espac	Aerospace
Audio	Audio	Audio	Espectáculos	Espec	Entertainment
Automovilismo	Auto	Cars	eufemismo	euf, euph	euphemism
Aviación	Aviac, Aviat	Aviation	excepto	exc	excluding
			femenino	f	feminine
Biblia	Bib	Bible	*véase página ix*	f‡	*see page ix*
Biología	Biol	Biology	familiar	fam	colloquial
Bolivia	Bol	Bolivia	Farmacología	Farm	Pharmacology
Botánica	Bot	Botany	Ferrocarriles	Ferr	Railways
inglés británico	BrE	British English	Filosofía	Fil	Philosophy
causativo	caus	causative	Finanzas	Fin	Finance
Química	Chem	Chemistry	Física	Fís	Physics
Chile	Chi	Chile	Fisco	Fisco	Tax
Cine	Cin	Cinema	Fisiología	Fisiol	Physiology
Ingeniería civil	Civil Eng	Civil Engineering	Fotografía	Fot	Photography
Indumentaria	Clothing	Clothing	femenino plural	fpl	feminine plural
Cocina	Coc	Cookery	frase hecha	fr hecha	set phrase
Colombia	Col	Colombia	formal	frml	formal
familiar	colloq	colloquial	Juegos	Games	Games
Comercio	Com	Business	generalmente	gen	generally
Informática	Comput	Computing	Geografía	Geog	Geography
conjunción	conj	conjunction	Geología	Geol	Geology
Construcción	Const	Building	gerundio	ger	gerund

Gobierno	**Gob, Govt**	Government
Historia	**Hist**	History
Horticultura	**Hort**	Horticulture
humorístico	**hum**	humorous
Imprenta e Industria editorial	**Impr**	Printing and Publishing
artículo indefinido	**indef art**	indefinite article
Indumentaria	**Indum**	Clothing
Informática	**Inf**	Computing
Ingeniería	**Ing**	Engineering
interjección	**interj**	exclamation
irónico	**iró, iro**	ironical
lenguaje periodístico	**journ**	journalese
Periodismo	**Journ**	Journalism
Juegos	**Jueg**	Games
Relaciones Laborales	**Lab Rel**	Labor Relations
Derecho	**Law**	Law
Ocio	**Leisure**	Leisure
lenguaje infantil	**leng infantil**	used to or by children
Lingüística	**Ling**	Linguistics
Literatura	**Lit**	Literature
literario	**liter**	literary
locución	**loc**	phrase
locución adjetiva	**loc adj**	adjectival phrase
locución adverbial	**loc adv**	adverbial phrase
locución preposicional	**loc prep**	prepositional phrase
masculino	**m**	masculine
Márketing	**Marketing**	Marketing
Matemáticas	**Mat, Math**	Mathematics
Mecánica	**Mec, Mech Eng**	Mechanical Engineering
Medicina	**Med**	Medicine
Metalurgia	**Metal, Metall**	Metallurgy
Meteorología	**Meteo**	Meteorology
México	**Méx**	Mexico
masculino y femenino	**mf**	masculine and feminine
masculino, femenino	**m, f**	masculine, feminine
Militar	**Mil**	Military
Minería	**Min**	Mining
Mitología	**Mit**	Mythology
masculino plural	**mpl**	masculine plural
Música	**Mús, Mus**	Music
Mitología	**Myth**	Mythology
nombre, sustantivo	**n**	noun
Náutica	**Náut, Naut**	Nautical
negativo	**neg**	negative
Ocultismo	**Occult**	Occult
Ocio	**Ocio**	Leisure
Odontología	**Odont**	Dentistry
Óptica	**Ópt, Opt**	Optics
Panamá	**Pan**	Panama
Paraguay	**Par**	Paraguay
participio pasado	**past p**	past participle
peyorativo	**pej**	pejorative
Perú	**Per**	Peru
lenguaje periodístico	**period**	journalese
Periodismo	**Period**	Journalism
peyorativo	**pey**	pejorative
Farmacología	**Pharm**	Pharmacology
Filosofía	**Phil**	Philosophy
Fotografía	**Phot**	Photography
Física	**Phys**	Physics
Fisiología	**Physiol**	Physiology
plural	**pl**	plural
sustantivo plural	**pl n**	plural noun
poético	**poet**	poetic
Política	**Pol**	Politics
Correo	**Post**	Post
participio pasado	**pp**	past participle
prefijo	**pref**	prefix
preposición	**prep**	preposition
participio presente	**pres p**	present participle
Imprenta	**Print**	Printing
pronombre	**pron**	pronoun
pronombre demostrativo	**pron dem**	demonstrative pronoun
pronombre personal	**pron pers**	personal pronoun
pronombre relativo	**pron rel**	relative pronoun
Psicología	**Psic, Psych**	Psychology
Industria editorial	**Publ**	Publishing
Química	**Quím**	Chemistry
marca registrada	**®**	registered trademark
Radio	**Rad**	Radio
Ferrocarriles	**Rail**	Railways
recíproco	**recipr**	reciprocal
reflexivo	**refl**	reflexive
Religión	**Relig**	Religion
Relaciones Laborales	**Rels Labs**	Labor Relations
Río de la Plata	**RPl**	River Plate area
inglés de Escocia	**Scot**	Scottish English
Servicios Sociales	**Servs Socs**	Social Administration
singular	**sing**	singular
argot	**sl**	slang
Servicios Sociales	**Soc Adm**	Social Administration
Sociología	**Sociol**	Sociology
Deporte	**Sport**	Sport

Abbreviations and labels /Abreviaturas e indicadores xxvi

sufijo	**suf, suff**	suffix
Tauromaquia	**Taur**	Bullfighting
Fisco	**Tax**	Tax
también	**tb**	also
Teatro	**Teatr**	Theater
Tecnología	**Tec, Tech**	Technology
lenguaje técnico	**téc, tech**	technical language
Telecomunicaciones	**Telec**	Telecommunications
Textiles	**Tex**	Textiles
Teatro	**Theat**	Theater
Turismo	**Tourism**	Tourism
Transporte	**Transp**	Transport
Televisión	**TV**	Television
no numerable	**uncount**	uncountable

Uruguay	**Ur**	Uruguay
verbo	**v**	verb
verbo auxiliar	**v aux**	auxiliary verb
verbo	**vb**	verb
Venezuela	**Ven**	Venezuela
Veterinaria	**Vet, Vet Sci**	Veterinary Science
verbo intransitivo	**vi**	intransitive verb
Video	**Video**	Video
verbo impersonal	**v impers**	impersonal verb
Vinicultura	**Vin**	Wine
verbo modal	**v mod**	modal verb
verbo pronominal	**v pron**	pronominal verb
verbo transitivo	**vt**	transitive verb
vulgar	**vulg**	vulgar
Zoología	**Zool**	Zoology

A, a *f* (*pl* **aes**) (*read as* /a/) *the letter* A, a

a *prep*

■ **Nota** La preposición *a* suele emplearse precedida de ciertos verbos como *empezar, ir, oler, sonar* etc, en cuyo caso ver bajo el respectivo verbo. No se traduce cuando introduce el complemento directo de persona (ser humano, pronombres personales que lo representan, como *quien, alguien, algún* etc) o un nombre con un objeto o animal personalizado: *amo a mi patria* = I love my country, *paseo a mi perro* = I walk my dog. En los casos en que precede al artículo definido *el* para formar la contracción *al*, ver bajo la siguiente entrada, donde también se encontrarán otros ejemplos y usos de *a*.

1 (a) (indicando dirección) to; **voy a México/la tienda** I'm going to Mexico/to the shop; **voy a casa** I'm going home; **se cayó al río** she fell into the river **(b)** (indicando posición): **estaban sentados a la mesa** they were sitting at the table; **a orillas del Ebro** on the banks of the Ebro; **se sentó al sol** he sat in the sun; **se sentó a mi derecha** he sat down on my right **(c)** (indicando distancia): **a diez kilómetros de aquí** ten kilometers from here

2 (a) (señalando hora, momento) at; **a las ocho** at eight o'clock; **a la hora de comer** at lunch time; **¿a qué hora vengo?** what time shall I come?; **a mediados de abril** in mid-April; **al día siguiente** the next *o* following day **(b)** (señalando fecha): **hoy estamos a lunes/a 20** today is Monday/it's the 20th today **(c)** **al + INF**: **se cayó al bajar del tren** she fell as she was getting off the train; **al enterarse de la noticia** when he learnt *o* on learning the news **(d)** (indicando distancia en el tiempo): **a escasos minutos de su llegada** (después) a few minutes after she arrived; (antes) a few minutes before she arrived; **de lunes a viernes** (from) Monday to Friday

3 (en relaciones de proporción, equivalencia): **tres veces al día** three times a day; **sale a 100 pesetas cada uno** it works out at 100 pesetas each; **a 100 kilómetros por hora** (at) 100 kilometers per hour; **nos ganaron cinco a tres** they beat us five three *o* (AmE) five to three

4 (indicando modo, medio, estilo): **a pie/a caballo** on foot/on horseback; **a crédito** on credit; **funciona a pilas** it runs on batteries; **a mano** by hand; **a rayas** striped; **vestirse a lo punk** to wear punk clothes

5 (a) (introduciendo el complemento directo de persona): **¿viste a José?** did you see José?; **no he leído a Freud** I haven't read (any) Freud **(b)** (introduciendo el complemento indirecto) to; **le escribió una carta a su padre** he wrote a letter to his father, he wrote his father a letter; **dáselo a ella** give it to her; **les enseña inglés a mis hijos** she teaches my children English; **le echó (la) llave a la puerta** she locked the door **(c)** (indicando procedencia): **se lo compré a una gitana** I bought it from *o* (colloq) off a gipsy

abadía *f* (monasterio) abbey; (dignidad) abbacy

abajo *adv* **1 (a)** (lugar, parte): **aquí ～** down here; **en el estante de ～** (el siguiente) on the shelf below; (el último) on the bottom shelf; **más ～** further down; **por ～** underneath; **la parte de ～** the bottom (part) **(b)** (en un edificio) downstairs; **los vecinos de ～** the people downstairs **(c)** (en una escala, jerarquía): **del jefe para ～** from the boss down *o* downward(s); **de 20 años para ～** 20 or under

2 (expresando dirección, movimiento) down; **escaleras ～** down the street/stairs; **tire hacia ～** pull down *o* downward(s); **desde ～** from below

3 **～ abajo de** (AmL) under; **～ de la cama** under the bed

4 (en interjecciones) down with; **¡～ la dictadura!** down with the dictatorship!

abalanzarse [A4] *v pron*: **se abalanzaron hacia las salidas** they rushed toward(s) the exits; **～ SOBRE algn/algo** to leap ON sb/sth

abandonado -da *adj* **1** [ESTAR] (deshabitado) deserted **2** [ESTAR] 〈niño/perro/coche〉 abandoned **3** [ESTAR] (desatendido, descuidado) 〈jardín/parque〉 neglected

abandonar [A1] *vt* **1 (a)** (frml) 〈lugar〉 to leave **(b)** 〈familia/bebé〉 to leave, abandon; 〈marido/amante〉 to leave; 〈coche/barco〉 to abandon; **los abandonó a su suerte** he abandoned them to their fate **2** «fuerzas» to desert **3 (a)** 〈actividad/propósito/esperanza〉 to give up; **～ los estudios** to drop out of school/college **(b)** (Dep) 〈carrera/partido〉 to retire from, pull out of
■ ～ *vi* (Dep) **(a)** (en carrera, competición) to pull out **(b)** (en ajedrez) to resign; (en boxeo, lucha) to concede defeat
■ **abandonarse** *v pron* **1** (entregarse) **～se a algo** 〈a vicios/placeres〉 to abandon oneself TO sth **2** (en el aspecto personal) to let oneself go

abandono *m* **1 (a)** (de una persona) abandonment; **～ del hogar** desertion **2** (Dep) (antes de la carrera, competición) withdrawal; (iniciada la carrera, competición) retirement; (en ajedrez) resignation **3** (descuido, desatención) neglect

abanicar [A2] *vt/vi* to fan
■ **abanicarse** *v pron* to fan oneself

abanico *m* (utensilio) fan

abaratar [A1] *vt* 〈precios/costos〉 to reduce; 〈producto〉 to make ... cheaper, reduce the price of
■ **abaratarse** *v pron* «costos» to drop, come down; «producto» to become cheaper, come down in price

abarcar [A2] *vt* **(a)** 〈temas/materias〉 to cover; 〈superficie/territorio〉 span, cover; 〈siglos/generaciones〉 to span; **la conversación abarcó varios temas** the conversation ranged over many topics **(b)** (dar abasto con) 〈trabajos/actividades〉 to cope with; **quien mucho abarca poco aprieta** you shouldn't bite off more than you can chew **(c)** (con los brazos, la mano) to encircle

abarrotado -da adj crammed, packed; ~ DE algo ‹de gente› packed o crammed WITH sth

abarrotar [A1] vt ‹sala/teatro› to pack

abarrotería f (Méx) grocery store (AmE), grocer's (shop) (BrE)

abarrotero -ra m,f (Chi, Méx) (tendero) storekeeper (AmE), shopkeeper (BrE)

abarrotes mpl (AmL exc RPl) (comestibles) groceries (pl); (tienda) grocery store (AmE), grocer's (shop) (BrE)

abastecedor -dora m,f supplier

abastecer [E3] vt to supply; ~ a algn DE algo to supply sb WITH sth
■ **abastecerse** v pron ~se DE algo (obtener) to obtain sth; (almacenar) to stock up WITH sth

abastecimiento m supply

abasto m (a) (aprovisionamiento) supply; no dar ~: no dan ~ con el trabajo they can't cope with all the work (b) (provisiones) tb ~s mpl basic provisions (pl) (esp foodstuffs)

abatible adj ‹respaldo› reclining (before n); (hacia adelante) folding (before n)

abatido -da adj [ESTAR] (deprimido, triste) depressed; (desanimado) downhearted, dispirited

abatir [I1] vt 1 (derribar) ‹pájaro/avión› to bring down; ‹muro/edificio› to knock down; ‹árbol› to fell; fue abatido a tiros he was gunned down 2 (deprimir, entristecer): la enfermedad lo abatió mucho his illness made him feel very low; no te dejes ~ por las preocupaciones don't let your worries get you down 3 ‹asiento› to recline
■ **abatirse** v pron 1 (deprimirse) to get depressed 2 (frml) ~se SOBRE algo/algn ‹pájaro/avión› to swoop down ON sth/sb; ‹desgracia› to befall sth/sb (frml); el caos se abatió sobre el país the country was plunged into chaos

abdicación f abdication

abdicar [A2] vi «soberano» to abdicate; ~ EN algn to abdicate in FAVOR OF sb
■ ~ vt ‹trono/corona› to give up, abdicate

abdomen m abdomen

abdominal adj abdominal
■ m sit-up

abecedario m alphabet

abedul m birch

abeja f bee; ~ obrera/reina worker/queen bee

abejorro m bumblebee

aberración f (disparate, extravío) outrage; robarle a un ciego es una ~ stealing from sb who's blind is outrageous

abertura f (en general) opening; (agujero) hole; (rendija) gap; (corte, tajo) slit

abeto m fir (tree)

abierto¹ -ta adj 1 (a) ‹ventana/boca› open; está ~ it's open; con los ojos muy ~s with eyes wide open; un sobre ~ an unsealed envelope; los espacios ~s de la ciudad the city's open spaces (b) [ESTAR] ‹válvula› open; dejaste la llave ~ you left the faucet (AmE) o (BrE) tap running (c) (desabrochado) undone (d) ‹herida› open; ‹madera/ costura› split 2 [ESTAR] ‹comercio/museo› open

3 (Ling) ‹vocal› open 4 (a) [SER] (espontáneo) open (b) (receptivo) open-minded; ~ A algo open TO sth 5 (manifiesto, directo) open

abierto² m (Dep) open (tournament)

abismante adj (Andes) ‹valentía› extraordinary; ‹belleza› breathtaking; ‹cifra/ cantidad› staggering

abismo m abyss; hay un profundo ~ entre ellos there's a deep rift between them

ablandar [A1] vt ‹cera/cuero› to soften; ‹carne› to tenderize (b) ‹persona› to soften; ‹corazón› to melt
■ **ablandarse** v pron (a) «cera/cuero» to soften (b) «persona» to soften up; «mirada» to soften

abnegación f self-denial, abnegation (frml)

abnegado -da adj self-sacrificing, selfless

abofetear [A1] vt to slap

abogacía f law; ejercer la ~ to practice law

abogado -da m,f (en general) lawyer, solicitor (in UK); (ante un tribunal superior) attorney (in US), barrister (in UK); ~ defensor defense lawyer (AmE), defence counsel (BrE); ~ del diablo devil's advocate

abolición f abolition

abolir [I32] vt to abolish

abolladura f dent

abollar [A1] vt ‹coche/cacerola› to dent
■ **abollarse** v pron to get dented

abombado -da adj 1 ‹superficie› convex; ‹techo› domed 2 (AmL fam) (atontado) dopey (colloq), dozy (colloq) 3 (AmS) (en mal estado) ‹alimento›: esta carne está abombada this meat has gone bad o (BrE) is off

abombarse [A1] v pron (AmS) to go bad, go off

abominable adj abominable

abominar [A1] vt to detest, abominate (frml)

abonado -da m,f (del teléfono, a revista) subscriber; (del gas) consumer, customer; (a espectáculo, transporte) season-ticket holder

abonar [A1] vt 1 ‹tierra/campo› to fertilize 2 (a) (frml) (pagar) ‹cantidad/honorarios› to pay; el cheque se lo ~án en caja you can cash the check at the cash desk (b) (depositar) to credit; hemos abonado la cantidad en su cuenta we have credited your account with the amount (c) (Andes, Méx) (dar a cuenta) to give ... on account
■ **abonarse** v pron ~se A algo ‹a espectáculo› to buy a season ticket FOR sth; ‹a revista› to subscribe TO sth

abono m 1 (Agr) fertilizer 2 (para espectáculos, transporte) season ticket 3 (frml) (a) (pago) payment (b) (en una cuenta) credit (c) (Andes, Méx) (cuota) installment*

abordar [A1] vt 1 (a) (encarar) ‹problema› to tackle, deal with (b) (plantear) ‹tema/asunto› to raise 2 ‹persona› to approach; (agresivamente) to accost 3 (Méx) «pasajero» ‹barco/avión› to board; ‹automóvil› to get into
■ ~ vi (Méx) (subir a bordo) to board

aborigen adj aboriginal, indigenous
■ mf aborigine, aboriginal

aborrecer [E3] *vt* **(a)** ⟨*persona/actividad*⟩ to detest, loathe **(b)** ⟨*crías*⟩ to reject

aborrecible *adj* loathsome, detestable

abortar [A1] *vi* (Med) (de forma espontánea) to have a miscarriage, miscarry; (de forma provocada) to have an abortion, abort
■ ~ *vt* ⟨*maniobra/aterrizaje*⟩ to abort

aborto *m* (Med) (espontáneo) miscarriage; (provocado) abortion

abotagado -da *adj* ⟨*cara*⟩ swollen; ⟨*cuerpo*⟩ bloated

abotonar [A1] *vt* to button up, do up
■ **abotonarse** *v pron* ⟨*chaqueta/camisa*⟩ to button up, do up

abrasador -dora *adj* burning (*before n*)

abrasar [A1] *vt* **(a)** (quemar) to burn; **murieron abrasados** they were burned to death **(b)** «*bebida*» to scald, burn; «*comida*» to burn
■ ~ *vi* «*sol*» to burn, scorch
■ **abrasarse** *v pron* «*bosque*» to be burned (down); «*planta*» to get scorched; **nos abrasábamos bajo el sol** we were sweltering under the sun

abrasivo -va *adj/m* abrasive

abrazar [A4] *vt* ⟨*persona*⟩ to hug; (con más sentimiento) to embrace; **abrázame fuerte** hold me tight
■ **abrazarse** *v pron* (*recípr*) to hug each other; (con más sentimiento) to embrace each other; ~**se A algn/algo** to hold on *o* cling TO sb/sth

abrazo *m* hug; (con más sentimiento) embrace; **me dio un** ~ he gave me a hug, he hugged/embraced me; **dale un** ~ **de mi parte** give my love to her; **un** ~**, Miguel** (en cartas) best wishes, Miguel, regards, Miguel; (más íntimo) love, Miguel

abrebotellas *m* (*pl* ~) bottle opener

abrecartas *m* (*pl* ~) letter opener

abrelatas *m* (*pl* ~) can opener, tin opener (BrE)

abreviar [A1] *vt* ⟨*permanencia/visita*⟩ to cut short; ⟨*plazo*⟩ to shorten; ⟨*texto/artículo*⟩ to abridge; ⟨*palabra*⟩ to shorten
■ ~ *vi*: **abreviando ...** in short ...

abreviatura *f* abbreviation

abridor *m* (de botellas) bottle opener; (de latas) can opener, tin opener (BrE)

abrigado -da *adj* **(a)** [ESTAR] ⟨*lugar*⟩ sheltered **(b)** [ESTAR] ⟨*persona*⟩: **¿estás bien** ~ **con esas mantas?** are you warm enough with those blankets?; **está demasiado** ~ he has too many clothes on; **iba bien** ~ he was wrapped up warm **(c)** [SER] (RPl, Ven) ⟨*ropa*⟩ warm

abrigador -dora *adj* [SER] (Andes, Méx) ⟨*ropa*⟩ warm

abrigar [A3] *vt* **1** (con ropa) to wrap ... up warm; **el pañuelo me abriga el cuello** the scarf keeps my neck warm **2** ⟨*idea/esperanza*⟩ to cherish; ⟨*sospecha/duda*⟩ to harbor*, entertain
■ ~ *vi* «*ropa*» to be warm
■ **abrigarse** *v pron* (*refl*) to wrap up warm

abrigo *m* **1** **(a)** (prenda) coat **(b)** (calor que brinda la ropa): **necesita más** ~ she needs to be wrapped up more warmly; **con una manta no tengo suficiente** ~ I'm not warm enough with one blanket; **ropa de** ~ warm clothes **2** (refugio,

protección) shelter; **al** ~ **de la lluvia/los árboles** sheltered from the rain/under the trees; **al** ~ **de la lumbre** by the fireside

abril *m* April; *para ejemplos ver* ENERO

abrillantar [A1] *vt* to polish

abrir [I33] *vt* **1** (en general) to open; ⟨*paraguas*⟩ to open, put up; ⟨*mapa*⟩ to open out, unfold; ⟨*cortinas*⟩ (en general) to draw back; ⟨*persianas*⟩ to raise, pull up; ⟨*cremallera*⟩ to undo
2 ⟨*llave/gas*⟩ to turn on; ⟨*válvula*⟩ to open; ⟨*cerradura*⟩ to unlock
3 **(a)** ⟨*zanja/túnel*⟩ to dig; ⟨*agujero*⟩ to make **(b)** (fam) ⟨*paciente*⟩ to open ... up (colloq)
4 **(a)** ⟨*comercio/museo*⟩ (para el quehacer diario) to open; (inaugurar) to open (up); **¿a qué hora abren la taquilla?** what time does the box office open? **(b)** ⟨*carretera/aeropuerto*⟩ to open; ⟨*frontera*⟩ to open (up)
5 **(a)** (iniciar) ⟨*cuenta bancaria*⟩ to open; ⟨*negocio*⟩ to start, set up; ⟨*suscripción*⟩ to take out; ⟨*investigación*⟩ to begin, set up; **no han abierto la matrícula aún** registration hasn't begun yet; ~ **fuego** to open fire **(b)** ⟨*acto/debate/baile*⟩ to open **(c)** ⟨*desfile/cortejo*⟩ to head, lead **(d)** ⟨*paréntesis/comillas*⟩ to open
6 ⟨*apetito*⟩ to whet
■ **abrirse** *v pron* **1** **(a)** «*puerta/ventana*» to open; ~**se A algo** ⟨*a jardín/corredor*⟩ to open ONTO sth **(b)** «*flor/almeja*» to open; «*paracaídas*» to open
2 (*refl*) ⟨*chaqueta/cremallera*⟩ to undo
3 **(a)** «*porvenir*» to lie ahead; «*perspectivas*» to open up; **con este descubrimiento se abren nuevos horizontes** this discovery opens up new horizons **(b)** «*período/era*» to begin

abrochar [A1] *vt* ⟨*chaqueta/botón*⟩ to fasten, do up; ⟨*collar/cinturón de seguridad*⟩ to fasten
■ **abrocharse** *v pron* ⟨*chaqueta/botón*⟩ to fasten, do up; ⟨*collar/cinturón de seguridad*⟩ to fasten

abrumador -dora *adj* **(a)** ⟨*victoria/mayoría*⟩ overwhelming **(b)** ⟨*trabajo/tarea*⟩ exhausting

abrumar [A1] *vt* to overwhelm; ~ **a algn CON algo** ⟨*con problemas/quejas*⟩ to wear sb out WITH sth; **la** ~**on con sus atenciones** she was overwhelmed by their kindness

abrupto -ta *adj* **(a)** ⟨*camino/pendiente*⟩ steep; ⟨*terreno*⟩ rough **(b)** ⟨*tono*⟩ abrupt **(c)** ⟨*cambio/descenso*⟩ abrupt, sudden

absentismo *m* (Esp) absenteeism; ~ **escolar** (Esp) truancy, absenteeism

absolución *f* **(a)** (Relig) absolution **(b)** (Der) acquittal

absolutamente *adv* totally, absolutely; **no se ve** ~ **nada** you can't see a thing; ~ **nadie** not a soul; **¿estás segura?** — ~ are you sure? — absolutely *o* I'm positive

absoluto -ta *adj* **1** ⟨*monarca/poder*⟩ absolute **2** **(a)** (total) total, absolute, complete; **tengo la absoluta certeza** I am absolutely convinced **(b)** **en absoluto** (*loc adv*): **¿te gustó?** — **en** ~ did you like it? — no, not at all; **no lo consentiré en** ~ there is absolutely no way I will agree to it

absolver [E11] *vt* **(a)** (Relig) to absolve **(b)** (Der) ⟨*acusado*⟩ to acquit, find ... not guilty

absorbente *adj* **1** ⟨*esponja/papel*⟩ absorbent **2** ⟨*persona*⟩ demanding; ⟨*hobby/tarea*⟩ time-consuming; ⟨*profesión*⟩ demanding

absorber [E1] *vt* **(a)** ⟨*líquido/ruido/calor*⟩ to absorb **(b)** ⟨*tiempo*⟩ to occupy, take up; ⟨*recursos/energía*⟩ to absorb

absorción *f* (de líquido, calor, ruido) absorption

absorto -ta *adj* engrossed, absorbed

abstemio -mia *adj* teetotal
■ *m,f* teetotaler*

abstención *f* abstention

abstencionismo *m* abstentionism

abstenerse [E27] *v pron* **(a)** (en votación) to abstain **(b)** (frml) (no hacer): ~ DE hacer algo to refrain FROM doing sth **(c)** (privarse de): ~ del alcohol to avoid alcohol

abstinencia *f* abstinence

abstracto -ta *adj* abstract

abstraerse [E23] *v pron* ~se DE algo ⟨*de pensamiento/preocupación*⟩ to block out FROM sth

abstraído -da *adj*: estar ~ en algo to be absorbed in sth; lo noté como ~ he seemed rather preoccupied

absuelto -ta *pp*: ▶ ABSOLVER

absurdo -da *adj* absurd, ridiculous

abuchear [A1] *vt* to boo

abucheo *m* booing

abuelito -ta *m,f* (*m*) grandpa (colloq), granddad (colloq); (*f*) grandma (colloq), granny (colloq)

abuelo -la *m,f* **1** (pariente) (*m*) grandfather; (*f*) grandmother; mis ~s my grandparents; ¡cuéntaselo a tu abuela! (fam) pull the other one! (colloq) **2** (fam) (persona mayor) (*m*) old man, old guy (colloq); (*f*) old woman, old lady; ¡oiga ~! hey, granddad! (colloq)

abultado -da *adj* ⟨*ojos/vientre*⟩ bulging; ⟨*labios*⟩ thick; ⟨*cartera*⟩ bulging **(b)** ⟨abundante⟩ ⟨*deuda/suma*⟩ enormous, huge **(c)** ⟨exagerado⟩ ⟨*cifra/cantidad*⟩ inflated

abultar [A1] *vi* **(a)** (formar un bulto) to make a bulge **(b)** (ocupar lugar) to be bulky
■ ~ *vt* ⟨*cifras/resultados*⟩ to inflate

abundancia *f* **1** (gran cantidad) abundance; la ~ de peces the abundance of fish; hay comida en ~ there's an abundance of food; darse en ~ to be plentiful **2** (riqueza): tiempos de ~ times of plenty; viven en la ~ they're well-off; nadar en la ~ to be rolling in money (colloq)

abundante *adj* ⟨*reservas/cosecha*⟩ plentiful, abundant; la pesca es ~ the fishing is good; aguas ~s en especies marinas waters which abound in marine life

abundar [A1] *vi* **(a)** (existir en gran número o cantidad) ⟨*especie/mineral*⟩ to be abundant **(b)** (tener mucho) ~ EN algo to abound o be rich IN sth

aburrido -da *adj* **1** [ESTAR] ⟨*persona*⟩ **(a)** (sin entretenimiento) bored; estoy muy ~ I'm bored stiff **(b)** (harto) fed up; ~ DE algo tired OF sth, fed up WITH sth; ~ DE hacer algo tired OF doing sth **2** [SER] ⟨*película/persona*⟩ boring; ⟨*trabajo*⟩ boring, tedious
■ *m,f* bore

aburridor -dora *adj* (AmL) ▶ ABURRIDO 2

aburrimiento *m* **(a)** (estado) boredom **(b)** (cosa aburrida): ¡qué ~! what a bore!

aburrir [I1] *vt* to bore
■ **aburrirse** *v pron* **(a)** (por falta de entretenimiento)

to get bored **(b)** (hartarse) ~se DE algo/algn to get tired OF o fed up WITH sth/sb; ~se DE hacer algo to get tired OF doing sth

abusador -dora *adj* (aprovechado) ⟨*comerciante*⟩ opportunist; ¡qué ~ eres! you really take advantage of the situation!
■ *m,f*: estos comerciantes son unos ~es these shopkeepers really take advantage; es un ~ con sus padres he takes advantage of his parents

abusar [A1] *vi* **1** **(a)** (aprovecharse): es muy hospitalaria pero no abuses she's very hospitable but don't take advantage of her; ~ DE algo ⟨*de autoridad/posición/generosidad*⟩ to abuse sth; no quisiera ~ de su amabilidad I don't want to impose (on you); ~ DE algn ⟨*de padres/amigo*⟩ to take advantage OF sb **(b)** (sexualmente) ~ DE algn to sexually abuse sb **2** (usar en exceso): abusa de los tranquilizantes he takes too many tranquilizers; no se debe ~ del alcohol alcohol should be drunk in moderation

abusivo -va *adj* ⟨*precio/interés*⟩ outrageous

abuso *m* **(a)** (uso excesivo) abuse; ~ de autoridad abuse of authority; el ~ en la bebida excessive drinking; ~s deshonestos indecent assault; ~ sexual infantil child abuse **(b)** (de hospitalidad, generosidad): espero no lo considere un ~ I hope you don't think it an imposition; ¡qué ~ de confianza! (fam) what a nerve! (colloq) **(c)** (injusticia) outrage; ¡esto es un ~! this is outrageous!; prestarse a ~s to lay itself open to abuse

abusón -sona *adj/m,f* (Esp, Méx fam) ▶ ABUSADOR

acá *adv* **1** (en el espacio) here; ¡ven ~! come here!; ya viene para ~ he's on his way over; nos pasamos el día de ~ para allá we spent the whole day going to and fro; un poquito más ~ a little closer o nearer (to me) **2** (en el tiempo): del verano (para) ~ since the summer

acabado¹ -da *adj* [ESTAR] **(a)** ⟨*trabajo*⟩ finished; son todos productos muy bien ~s they are all well-finished products **(b)** ⟨*persona*⟩ finished

acabado² *m* finish

acabar [A1] *vi* **1** **(a)** «*reunión/película*» to finish, end; «*persona*» to finish; «*novios*» to split up; ya casi acabo I've nearly finished **(b)** (en un estado, situación) to end up; acabó en la cárcel he ended up in jail; (+ compl) acabamos cansadísimos by the end we were exhausted; ese chico va a ~ mal that boy will come to no good; la película acabó bien the movie had a happy ending; ~án aceptándolo o por aceptarlo they'll end up accepting it; ~ DE algo to end up AS sth; acabó de camarero he ended up (working) as a waiter **(c)** (rematar) ~ EN algo to end IN sth **2** **acabar con (a)** ~ CON algo (terminar) ⟨*con libro/tarea*⟩ to finish WITH sth; ⟨*con bombones/bebidas*⟩ to finish off sth; ⟨*con salud/carrera*⟩ to ruin sth; ⟨*con sueldo/herencia*⟩ to fritter away sth; ⟨*con abuso/problema*⟩ to put an end TO sth **(b)** (fam) ~ CON algn (pelearse) to finish WITH sb; (matar) to do away WITH sb (colloq); este niño va a ~ conmigo this child will be the death of me **3** **acabar de (a)** (terminar) ~ DE hacer algo to finish doing sth; cuando acabes de leerlo when you've finished reading it **(b)** (para referirse a acción reciente): acaba de salir she's just gone out; acababa de meterme en la cama cuando … I had

just got into bed when ... **(c)** (llegar a): **no acabo de entenderlo** I just don't understand; **no acababa de gustarle** she wasn't totally happy about it
■ ~ *vt* ⟨*trabajo/libro*⟩ to finish; ⟨*curso/carrera*⟩ to finish, complete
■ **acabarse** *v pron* **1** (terminarse) «*provisiones/comida*» to run out; «*problema*» to be over; «*reunión/fiesta/curso*» to end; «*proyecto*» to finish, come to an end; «*año*» to come to an end; **se nos acabó el café** we ran out of coffee; **se le ~on las fuerzas** he ran out of energy; **un trabajo que no se acaba nunca** a never-ending *o* an endless task; **¡esto se acabó!** that's it!
2 (*enf*) (comer) to finish (up)

acabose *m* (fam): **¡esto es el ~!** this is the end *o* limit! (colloq)

academia *f* **(a)** (sociedad) academy **(b)** (Educ) school; **~ de conductores** *or* (AmL) **choferes** driving school; **~ de idiomas** language school

académico -ca *adj* ⟨*estudios/año*⟩ academic (*before n*); ⟨*estilo/lenguaje*⟩ academic
■ *m,f* academician

acalorado -da *adj* **1** [SER] ⟨*discusión/riña*⟩ heated **2** [ESTAR] ⟨*persona*⟩ (enfadado) worked up; (con calor) hot

acalorarse [A1] *v pron* (enfadarse) to get worked up; (sofocarse) to get hot

acampada *f* camp; **ir de ~** to go camping

acampanado -da *adj* ⟨*falda/pantalones*⟩ flared

acampante *mf* camper

acampar [A1] *vi* to camp

acantilado *m* cliff

acaparador -dora *adj* (egoísta) selfish, greedy; (posesivo) possessive
■ *m,f* **(a)** (de productos) hoarder **(b)** (persona egoísta) selfish person

acaparar [A1] *vt* **(a)** ⟨*productos/existencias*⟩ to hoard, stockpile **(b)** ⟨*interés/atención*⟩ to capture; **el trabajo acapara todo su tiempo** work takes up all his time

acaramelado -da *adj* **(a)** ⟨*pareja*⟩: **estaban ~s** they were hugging and kissing **(b)** ⟨*voz*⟩ sugary **(c)** (Coc) toffee-coated; ⟨*molde*⟩ coated with caramel

acariciar [A1] *vt* ⟨*persona*⟩ to caress; ⟨*mejilla/pelo*⟩ to stroke, caress; ⟨*perro/gato*⟩ to stroke

acarrear [A1] *vt* **(a)** ⟨*problema*⟩ to give rise to, lead to; **esto le acarreó problemas** this caused her problems **(b)** ⟨*materiales/paquetes*⟩ to carry

acaso *adv* **1** (en preguntas): **¿~ no te lo dije?** I told you, didn't I?; **¿~ tengo yo la culpa?** is it <u>my</u> fault? **2** (en locs) **por si acaso** just in case; **si acaso** (quizás) maybe, perhaps; (en caso de que) if

acatar [A1] *vt* ⟨*leyes/orden*⟩ to obey, comply with

acatarrado -da *adj*: **estar ~** to have a cold

acatarrarse [A1] *v pron* (resfriarse) to catch a cold

acceder [E1] *vi* **1** (consentir) to agree; **~ A algo** to agree TO sth **2** (entrar) **~ A algo** gain access TO sth; (Inf) to access sth

accesible *adj* **(a)** ⟨*lugar*⟩ accessible; ⟨*persona*⟩ approachable; ⟨*precio*⟩ affordable **(b)** ⟨*novela/lenguaje*⟩ accessible

acceso *m* **1** **(a)** (a un lugar) access; **rutas de ~** approach roads **(b)** (a persona, información) access **(c)** (Inf) access **2** (a un curso) entrance; **pruebas de ~** entrance examinations; **curso de ~** preparatory course

accesorio *m* accessory (Cin, Teatr) prop; **~s del vestir** accessories; **~s de baño** bathroom fittings

accidentado -da *adj* **1** **(a)** ⟨*viaje*⟩ eventful; ⟨*historia*⟩ turbulent; ⟨*carrera/pasado*⟩ checkered* (*before n*); ⟨*vida*⟩ troubled **(b)** ⟨*terreno*⟩ rough, rugged; ⟨*costa*⟩ broken **2** ⟨*persona*⟩ hurt, injured
■ *m,f*: **llevaron a los ~s al hospital** those injured *o* hurt in the accident were taken to hospital

accidental *adj* ⟨*encuentro*⟩ chance (*before n*), accidental; ⟨*circunstancias*⟩ coincidental

accidente *m* **1** (percance) accident; **tener** *or* **sufrir un ~** to have an accident; **~ aéreo** plane crash; **~ de circulación/tráfico** traffic *o* road accident; **~ laboral** industrial accident **2** (hecho fortuito) coincidence; **por ~** by chance **3** (del terreno) unevenness; **~ geográfico** geographical feature

acción *f* **1** (acto, hecho) act; **acciones dignas de elogio** praiseworthy acts *o* actions; **hacer una buena ~** to do a good deed; **~ de gracias** thanksgiving **2** **(a)** (actividad) action; **poner algo en ~** to put sth into action; **novela de ~** adventure story; **una película llena de ~** an action-packed movie *o* (BrE) film **(b)** (Mil) action **(c)** (Cin, Lit) (trama) action, plot **3** **(a)** (Der) action, lawsuit **(b)** (Fin) share; **acciones** shares, stock **4** (Per) (de una rifa) ticket

accionar [A1] *vt* ⟨*palanca*⟩ to pull; ⟨*mecanismo/dispositivo*⟩ activate, trigger

accionista *mf* stockholder, shareholder

acebo *m* holly; (árbol) holly tree

acechar [A1] *vt* ⟨*enemigo/presa*⟩ to lie in wait for; **el peligro que nos acecha** the danger that lies ahead of us

acecho *m*: **al ~** lying in wait

aceite *m* oil; **~ lubricante** lubricating oil; **~ de oliva/girasol** olive/sunflower oil; **~ de ricino** castor oil

aceitera *f* (Tec) oilcan; (Coc) cruet

aceitoso -sa *adj* oily

aceituna *f* olive; **~s rellenas/sin hueso** stuffed/pitted olives

aceitunado -da *adj* olive (*before n*)

aceleración *f* acceleration

acelerado -da *adj* ⟨*curso*⟩ intensive, crash (*before n*); **a paso ~** at a brisk pace

acelerador *m* (Auto) accelerator

acelerar [A1] *vt* **(a)** ⟨*coche/motor*⟩: **aceleró el coche** (en marcha) he accelerated; (sin desplazarse) he revved the engine *o* car (up) **(b)** ⟨*proceso/cambio*⟩ to speed up; ⟨*paso*⟩ to quicken
■ ~ *vi* **(a)** (Auto) to accelerate **(b)** (fam) (darse prisa) to hurry (up)

acelgas *fpl* Swiss chard

acento *m* **(a)** (Ling) (tilde) accent; (de intensidad) stress, accent **(b)** (énfasis) emphasis **(c)** (dejo, pronunciación) accent; **tiene ~ francés** he has a French accent

acentuado -da *adj* **(a)** ⟨*palabra/sílaba*⟩ accented **(b)** ⟨*diferencia/cambio*⟩ marked, distinct

acentuar [A18] *vt* **(a)** (Ling) (al hablar) to stress, accent; (al escribir) to accent **(b)** (intensificar, hacer resaltar) to accentuate, emphasize
■ **acentuarse** *v pron* ‹diferencias/problemas› to become accentuated

acepción *f* sense, meaning

aceptable *adj* acceptable, passable

aceptación *f* **(a)** (éxito) success; **de gran ~ entre los jóvenes** very popular *o* successful with young people **(b)** (acción) acceptance

aceptar [A1] *vt* ‹excusas/invitación/cargo› to accept; ‹términos/condiciones› to agree to; **aceptan cheques** they take checks; **aceptó venir** she agreed to come; **no acepto que me digas eso** I won't have you saying that to me

acequia *f* irrigation ditch *o* channel

acera *f* sidewalk (AmE), pavement (BrE)

acerca de *loc prep* about

acercamiento *m* (entre posturas, países) rapprochement; (entre personas): **ese incidente produjo un ~ entre ellos** that incident brought them closer together

acercar [A2] *vt* ⓵ **(a)** (aproximar) to bring ... closer *o* nearer; **~on la mesa a la puerta** they moved the table closer *o* nearer to the door; **acercó las manos al fuego** he held his hands closer to the fire; **¿puedes ~me ese libro?** can you pass *o* give me that book? **(b)** (unir) ‹posturas/países› to bring ... closer
⓶ (llevar): **me acercó a la parada** she gave me a ride (AmE) *o* (BrE) lift to the bus stop
■ **acercarse** *v pron* **(a)** (aproximarse) to approach, to get closer *o* nearer; **acércate más** (acercándose al hablante) come *o* get closer *o* nearer; (alejándose del hablante) go *o* get closer *o* nearer; **se le ~on dos policías** two policemen came up to *o* approached him **(b)** «amigos/países» to draw *o* come closer together **(c)** «hora/momento» to draw near, approach; **ahora que se acerca la Navidad** now that Christmas is coming

acero *m* (Metal) steel; **~ inoxidable** stainless steel

acérrimo -ma *adj* ‹partidario/defensor› staunch; ‹enemigo› bitter

acertado -da *adj* ‹comentario› pertinent; ‹solución/elección› good

acertante *adj* winning (before n)
■ *m,f* winner

acertar [A5] *vt* ‹respuesta/resultado› to get ... right; **a ver si aciertas quién es** see if you can guess who it is
■ **~** *vi* ⓵ **(a)** (dar, pegar): **~le ᴀ algo** to hit sth; **tiró pero no le acertó** he shot at it but (he) missed **(b)** (atinar) to be right; **acertaste con el regalo** your present was perfect ⓶ (lograr) **~ ᴀ hacer algo** to manage to do sth

acertijo *m* riddle, puzzle

acetona *f* (Quím) acetone; (quitaesmaltes) nail-polish remover

achacar [A2] *vt*: **~le la culpa a algn** to lay *o* put the blame on sb

achaques *mpl* ailments (pl); **mis acostumbrados ~** my usual aches and pains

achatar [A1] *vt* to flatten

achicar [A2] *vt* ⓵ **(a)** ‹chaqueta/vestido› to take in **(b)** ‹persona› to intimidate, daunt ⓶ ‹agua› to bail out
■ **achicarse** *v pron* **(a)** (de tamaño) to shrink **(b)** (amilanarse) to be intimidated, be daunted

achicharrante *adj* (fam) ‹sol› scorching; **hizo un calor ~** it was scorching

achicharrar [A1] *vt* (fam) **(a)** ‹carne/comida› to burn ... to a cinder (colloq) **(b)** «sol» ‹planta› to scorch; **hace un sol que te achicharra** the sun is scorching hot
■ **achicharrarse** *v pron* (fam) **(a)** «persona» to fry (colloq); «planta» to get scorched **(b)** «carne/comida» to be burned to a crisp (colloq)

achichincle, achichinque *mf* (Méx fam & pey) hanger-on (colloq & pej)

achicopalar [A1] *vt* (Col, Méx fam) to intimidate
■ **achicopalarse** *v pron* (Col, Méx fam) to feel intimidated

achicoria *f* chicory

achinado -da *adj* ‹ojos› slanting

achiote *m* (AmL) annatto

achispado -da *adj* (fam) tipsy (colloq)

achuras *fpl* (RPl) offal

acicalarse [A1] *v pron* to dress up, get dressed up

acicate *m* **(a)** (estímulo) incentive **(b)** (espuela) spur

acidez *f* (Quím) acidity; (Med) (en el estómago) acidity; (en el esófago) heartburn

ácido¹ -da *adj* **(a)** ‹sabor› acid; ‹fruta› acid, tart, sharp; ‹vino› sharp **(b)** ‹carácter/tono› acid, caustic

ácido² *m* **(a)** (Quím) acid **(b)** (arg) (droga) acid (sl)

acierta, aciertas, etc ▶ ᴀᴄᴇʀᴛᴀʀ

acierto *m* **(a)** (decisión correcta) good decision, good *o* wise move **(b)** (respuesta correcta) correct answer

acitronar [A1] *vt* (Méx) to fry ... until golden brown

aclamación *f* acclaim

aclamar [A1] *vt* to acclaim, applaud

aclaración *f* explanation; **quisiera hacer una ~** I'd like to make one thing clear

aclarado *m* (Esp) rinse

aclarar [A1] *v impers* **(a)** (amanecer): **aclara temprano** it gets light early; **cuando nos levantamos estaba aclarando** dawn *o* day was breaking when we got up **(b)** (escampar) to clear up
■ **~** *vi* **(a)** «día» (empezar) to break, dawn **(b)** «tiempo/día» (escampar) to clear up
■ **~** *vt* ⓵ (quitar color a) to lighten

AmC	Central America	Arg	Argentina	Cu	Cuba	Per Peru
AmL	Latin America	Bol	Bolivia	Ec	Ecuador	RPI River Plate Area
AmS	South America	Chi	Chile	Esp	Spain	Ur Uruguay
Andes	Andean Region	CS	Southern Cone	Méx	Mexico	Ven Venezuela

[2] ⟨ideas⟩ to get ... straight; ⟨duda⟩ to clear up, clarify; **quiero ~ que ...** I want to make it clear that ...

[3] (Esp) ⟨ropa/vajilla⟩ to rinse

■ **aclararse** *v pron* [1] **~se la voz** to clear one's throat

[2] (Esp fam) (entender) to understand; *a ver si nos aclaramos* let's see if we can sort things out *o* get things straight

aclimatarse [A1] *v pron* to acclimatize, get *o* become acclimatized

acné *m or f* acne

acobardar [A1] *vt* ⟨persona⟩ to unnerve, intimidate

■ **acobardarse** *v pron* to lose one's nerve; **~se ante el peligro** to lose one's nerve in the face of danger

acogedor -dora *adj* ⟨casa/habitación⟩ cozy*, welcoming; ⟨ambiente⟩ warm, friendly

acoger [E6] *vt* **(a)** ⟨huérfano/anciano⟩ to take in; ⟨refugiado⟩ to accept, admit **(b)** ⟨propuesta/persona⟩ to receive; **acogieron la noticia con satisfacción** the news was well received

■ **acogerse** *v pron* **~se a algo** ⟨a la ley⟩ to have recourse TO sth; ⟨a un régimen⟩ to opt FOR sth

acogida *f* **(a)** (de persona) welcome; (de noticia, propuesta) reception **(b)** (de huérfano) taking in; (de refugiado) acceptance

acolchar, acolchonar [A1] *vt* ⟨bata/tela⟩ to quilt; ⟨pared/puerta⟩ to pad

acomedido -da *adj* (Chi, Méx, Per) obliging, helpful

acomedirse [I14] *v pron* (Méx) to offer to help

acometer [E1] *vi* to attack; **~ CONTRA algo/algn** to attack sth/sb

acomodado -da *adj* [1] ⟨familia/gente⟩ well-off, well-to-do; **de posición acomodada** well-off, well-to-do [2] (CS, Méx fam) (que tiene palanca): **estar ~** to have contacts *o* connections

acomodador -dora *m,f* (*m*) usher; (*f*) usherette

acomodar [A1] *vt* [1] (adaptar, amoldar) to adapt [2] ⟨huésped⟩ to put ... up [3] **(a)** (AmL) (arreglar) to arrange; (poner) to put **(b)** (fam) ⟨persona⟩ (en puesto): **su tío lo acomodó en su sección** his uncle fixed him up with a job in his department

■ **acomodarse** *v pron* **(a)** (ponerse cómodo) to make oneself comfortable **(b)** (adaptarse, amoldarse) **~se A algo** to adapt TO sth **(c)** (AmL) (arreglarse) ⟨ropa/anteojos⟩ to adjust

acompañado -da *adj* accompanied; **bien/mal ~** in good/bad company; **vino ~ de un amigo** he came with a friend

acompañamiento *m* **(a)** (Mús) accompaniment **(b)** (Coc) accompaniment; **¿con qué ~ lo quiere?** what would you like it served with?

acompañar [A1] *vt* [1] **(a)** (a un lugar) to go with, accompany (frml); **acompáñalo hasta la puerta** see him to the door, see him out; **la acompañé a su casa** I walked her home; **¿me acompañas?** will you come with me? **(b)** (hacer compañía) to keep ... company **(c)** (Mús) to accompany [2] (frml) (adjuntar) to enclose; **acompañado de un certificado médico** accompanied by a medical certificate

acomplejado -da *adj*: **es muy ~** he's full of complexes; **está ~ por su gordura** he has a complex about being fat

■ *m,f*: **es un ~** he's a mass of complexes

acomplejar [A1] *vt* to give ... a complex

■ **acomplejarse** *v pron* to get a complex

acondicionador *m* **(a)** *tb* **~ de pelo** (hair) conditioner **(b)** **~ de aire** air conditioner

acondicionamiento *m* fitting-out

acondicionar [A1] *vt* **(a)** ⟨vivienda/local⟩ to equip, fit out **(b)** (Col) ⟨carro⟩ to soup up

aconsejable *adj* advisable

aconsejar [A1] *vt* to advise; **~le a algn hacer algo/que haga algo** to advise sb to do sth; **has sido mal aconsejado** you've been given bad advice; **necesito que alguien me aconseje** I need some advice

acontecer [E3] *vi* (*en 3ª pers*) (frml) to take place, occur (frml); **los sucesos acontecidos ayer** the events which took place *o* occurred yesterday;

■ *m*: **el diario ~** everyday events *o* occurrences

acontecimiento *m* event; **adelantarse a los ~s** to jump the gun

acoplar [A1] *vt* **(a)** ⟨piezas⟩ to fit *o* put together **(b)** (Elec) to connect **(c)** (Ferr) to couple

acorazado *m* battleship

acordar [A10] *vt* ⟨términos⟩ to agree; ⟨precio/fecha⟩ to agree (on)

■ ~ *vi* (Andes) (recordar) **~le a algn DE hacer algo/que haga algo** to remind sb to do sth

■ **acordarse** *v pron* to remember; **si mal no me acuerdo** if I remember right; **~se DE algn/algo** to remember sb/sth; **no quiero ni ~me** I don't even want to think about it; **~se DE hacer algo** (de una acción que hay/había que realizar) to remember to do sth; (de una acción que ya se realizó) to remember *o* recall doing sth; **se acordó de haberlo visto allí** she remembered *o* recalled seeing him there; **~se (DE) QUE ...** to remember THAT ...

acorde *adj* (en armonía) ⟨sonidos⟩ harmonious; **colores ~s** colors that go *o* blend well together; **con un salario ~** with a salary to match; **~ CON** *or* **A algo** appropriate TO sth, in keeping WITH sth

■ *m* (Mús) chord

acordeón *m* [1] (Mús) accordion [2] (Méx fam) (para un examen) crib

acordeonista *mf* accordionist

acordonar [A1] *vt* **(a)** ⟨lugar⟩ to cordon off **(b)** ⟨zapatos⟩ to lace (up)

acorralar [A1] *vt* **(a)** ⟨animal/fugitivo⟩ to corner **(b)** ⟨ganado⟩ to round up

acortar [A1] *vt* ⟨falda/vestido⟩ to shorten; ⟨texto/artículo⟩ to cut, shorten; ⟨vacaciones/permanencia⟩ to cut short; ⟨película/carrera⟩ to reduce the length of; ⟨distancia⟩ to reduce; **~ camino** to take a short cut

■ **acortarse** *v pron* to get shorter

acosar [A1] *vt* **(a)** ⟨persona⟩ to hound; (sexualmente) to harass; **me ~on con preguntas** they plagued *o* bombarded me with questions **(b)** ⟨presa⟩ to hound, pursue relentlessly

acosijar [A1] *vt* (Méx) to badger, pester

acoso *m* **(a)** (de persona) hounding, harassment; **~ sexual** sexual harassment **(b)** (de presa) hounding, relentless pursuit

acostar [A10] vt ⟨persona⟩ to put ... to bed
■ **acostarse** v pron (a) (irse a dormir) to go to bed
(b) (tenderse, tumbarse) to lie down; **~se boca
abajo** to lie face down (c) (tener relaciones sexuales)
to go to bed together, sleep together; **~se CON
algn** to go to bed with sb, sleep with sb

acostumbrado -da adj (a) (habituado): **está
mal ~** he's got into bad habits; **~ A algo/hacer
algo** used TO sth/doing sth; **estamos ~s a cenar
temprano** we're used to having dinner early; **está
~ a que le sirvan** he's used to being served (b)
(habitual) customary, usual

acostumbrar [A1] vt **~ a algn A algo/hacer
algo** to get sb used TO sth/doing sth
■ **~** vi: **~ A hacer algo** to be accustomed TO doing
sth, be in the habit of doing sth
■ **acostumbrarse** v pron **~se A algo/algn** to
get used TO sth/sb; **~se A hacer algo** to get used
TO doing sth

acotación f (en texto) marginal note, annotation

acotamiento m (Méx) shoulder (AmE), hard
shoulder (BrE)

acrecentar [A5] vt to increase
■ **acrecentarse** v pron to increase, grow

acreditado -da adj (a) ⟨establecimiento/
marca⟩ reputable, well-known (b) ⟨diplomático/
periodista⟩ accredited; ⟨agente/representante⟩
authorized, official

acreditar [A1] vt ① ⟨diplomático/periodista⟩ to
accredit; ⟨representante⟩ to authorize ② (frml) (a)
(probar, avalar) ⟨pago⟩ to prove; **este libro lo
acredita como un gran pensador** this book
confirms him as a great thinker (b) (dar renombre):
con la calidad que lo acredita with the quality for
which it's renowned ③ (Fin) to credit

acreedor -dora m,f creditor

acribillar [A1] vt (a) (llenar de agujeros): **lo ~on
a balazos** they riddled him with bullets (b)
(asediar): **me ~on a preguntas** they fired a barrage
of questions at me

acrílico m acrylic

acristalar [A1] vt to glaze

acrobacia f (arte) acrobatics; **hacer ~s** to
perform acrobatics; **~ aérea** aerobatics

acróbata mf acrobat

acta f‡ (de reunión) minutes (pl); **levantar (el) ~**
to take (the) minutes; **~ de defunción** (Col, Méx,
Ven) entry in the register of deaths; **~ de
matrimonio/nacimiento** (Méx) marriage/birth
certificate; **~ notarial** notarial deed

actitud f (disposición) attitude; **adoptar una ~
firme (con algn)** to be firm (with sb)

activar [A1] vt (a) (agilizar) ⟨proceso/crecimiento⟩
to speed up; ⟨economía/producción⟩ to stimulate;
⟨circulación⟩ to stimulate; ⟨negociaciones⟩ to give
fresh impetus to (b) (poner en funcionamiento)
⟨alarma⟩ to activate, trigger; ⟨dispositivo⟩ to
activate; ⟨máquina⟩ to set ... in motion
■ **activarse** v pron «alarma» to go off;
«dispositivo» to start working

actividad f activity; **un volcán en ~** an active
volcano

activista mf activist

activo¹ -va adj active

activo² m assets (pl)

acto m ① (a) (acción) act; **morir en ~ de
servicio** «soldado» to die on active service;
«policía/bombero» to die in the course of one's
duty; **~ sexual** sexual act (frml) (b) (en locs) **acto
seguido** immediately after; **en el acto** ⟨morir⟩
instantly; ⟨acudir⟩ immediately; **lo despidieron
en el ~** he was fired on the spot ② (a)
(ceremonia) ceremony (b) (Teatr) act

actor m actor

actriz f actress

actuación f (a) (acción) action (b) (Cin, Dep,
Teatr) performance; **la ~ es pésima** the acting is
appalling (c) (conducta) conduct (d) (recital, sesión)
performance, concert

actual adj ⟨ley/situación/dirección⟩ present,
current; **en el Chile ~** in present-day Chile; **en el
mundo ~** in the modern world, in today's world

actualidad f (a) (tiempo presente): **en la ~**
currently, at present; **la ~ cubana** the current
situation in Cuba (b) (de tema, noticia) topicality;
las noticias de ~ today's (o this week's etc) news;
un tema de ~ (period) a topical subject; **sucesos
de ~** current affairs

actualizar [A4] vt ⟨salarios/pensiones/
legislación⟩ to bring ... up to date; ⟨información/
manual⟩ to update; (Inf) ⟨software⟩ to upgrade

actualmente adv (hoy en día) nowadays; (en
este momento) at present; **se encuentra ~ en
Suecia** she is currently in Sweden, she is in
Sweden at present

actuar [A18] vi (a) «persona» (obrar) to act;
forma de ~ behavior*; (b) «medicamento» to
work, act (c) «actor» to act; «torero» to
perform; **¿quién actúa en esa película?** who's in
the movie?

acuarela f watercolor*

acuario m aquarium

Acuario m (signo) Aquarius; **es (de) ~** he's an
Aquarius o Aquarian
■ mf (persona) tb **acuario** Aquarian, Aquarius

acuático -ca adj aquatic

acuatizaje m: landing on water

acuatizar [A4] vi to land on water

acuchillar [A1] vt ⟨persona⟩ to stab

acudir [I1] vi ① (frml) (ir) to go; (venir) to come;
nadie acudió en su ayuda nobody went/came to
his aid; **~ A algo** ⟨a cita⟩ to arrive FOR sth; ⟨a
reunión⟩ to attend sth; **la policía acudió al lugar
de los hechos** the police arrived at the scene (of
the incident) ② (recurrir) **~ A algn** to turn TO sb;
no tenía a quien ~ he had nobody to turn to

acueducto m aqueduct

acuerdo m (a) (arreglo, pacto) agreement; **llegar
a un ~** to reach an agreement; **~ de paz** peace
agreement o (frml) accord (b) **estar de ~** to agree;
ponerse de ~ to come to o reach an agreement;
estar de ~ EN algo to agree ON something; **estar
de ~ CON algn/algo** to agree WITH sb/sth;
¿mañana a las ocho? — de ~ (indep) tomorrow
at eight? — OK o all right (c) **de ~ con** or **a** in
accordance with

acuesta, acuestas, etc ▶ ACOSTAR

acumulación f accumulation

acumular [A1] vt ⟨riquezas/poder⟩ to
accumulate; ⟨experiencia⟩ to gain

■ **acumularse** *v pron* «*trabajo*» to pile up, mount up; «*intereses*» to accumulate; «*deudas*» to mount up; «*polvo*» to accumulate

acunar [A1] *vt* to rock

acuñar [A1] *vt* ‹*moneda*› to mint; ‹*frase/palabra*› to coin

acuoso -sa *adj* watery

acupuntura *f* acupuncture

acupunturista *mf* acupuncturist

acurrucarse [A2] *v pron* to curl up

acusación *f* (a) (imputación) accusation (b) (Der) charge

acusado -da *m,f*: el/la ~ the accused, the defendant

acusador -dora *adj* accusing, accusatory (frml); **una mirada** ~ an accusing look
■ *m,f* prosecuting attorney (AmE), prosecuting counsel (BrE)

acusar [A1] *vt* 1 (a) (culpar) to accuse; ~ a algn DE algo to accuse sb of sth; **me acusan de haber mentido** they accuse me of lying (b) (Der) ~ a algn DE algo to charge sb WITH sth (c) (fam) (delatar) to tell on (colloq) 2 (reconocer): ~ **recibo de algo** (Corresp) to acknowledge receipt of sth

acusetas *mf* (*pl* ~), **acusete -ta** *m,f* (fam) tattletale (AmE colloq), telltale (BrE colloq)

acústica *f* (ciencia) acoustics; (de local) acoustics (*pl*)

acústico -ca *adj* acoustic

adaptable *adj* adaptable

adaptación *f* (a) (proceso) adaptation, adjustment (b) (cosa adaptada) adaptation; **la ~ cinematográfica** the screen version

adaptador *m* adaptor

adaptar [A1] *vt* ‹*cortinas/vestido*› to alter; ‹*habitación*› to convert; ‹*pieza/motor*› to adapt; ‹*obra/novela*› to adapt; (Inf) to convert
■ **adaptarse** *v pron* to adapt; ~**se** A **algo/hacer algo** to adapt TO sth/doing sth; **un coche que se adapta a cualquier terreno** a car which is well suited to any terrain

a. de C. (= antes de Cristo) BC, before Christ

adecentar [A1] *vt* ‹*habitación*› to tidy up

adecuado -da *adj* (a) (apropiado) ‹*vestido/regalo*› suitable; ‹*momento*› right; ‹*medios*› adequate; **la persona adecuada para el cargo** the right person for the job (b) (aceptable) adequate

adecuar [A1] *or* [A18] *vt* ~ **algo** A **algo** to adapt sth TO sth

adefesio *m* (cosa) eyesore; (persona): **es un** ~ he's so ugly; **ir hecho un** ~ to look a sight *o* fright (colloq)

adelantado -da *adj* 1 (a) (desarrollado) ‹*país*› advanced (b) (aventajado): **va muy** ~ **en sus estudios** he is doing very well in his studies; **va** ~ **para su edad** he's advanced for his age 2 [ESTAR] ‹*reloj*› fast 3 (Com, Fin): **pago** ~ payment in advance; **por** ~ in advance 4 (avanzado): **las obras están muy adelantadas** construction is already well underway; **vamos bastante** ~**s** we're quite far ahead with it 5 (Dep) ‹*pase*› forward

adelantamiento *m* passing maneuver (AmE), overtaking manoeuvre (BrE)

adelantar [A1] *vt* 1 (a) ‹*fecha/viaje*› to bring forward (b) ‹*pieza/ficha*› to move ... forward 2 (sobrepasar) to overtake, pass 3 (a) ‹*reloj*› to put ... forward (b) ‹*balón*› to pass ... forward (c) ‹*trabajo*› to get on with 4 (conseguir) to gain; **con llorar no adelantas nada** crying won't get you anywhere
■ ~ *vi* 1 (a) (avanzar) to make progress (b) «*reloj*» to gain 2 (Auto) to pass, overtake (BrE)
■ **adelantarse** *v pron* 1 (a) (avanzar) to move forward (b) (ir delante) to go ahead; **se adelantó para comprar las entradas** she went (on) ahead to buy the tickets 2 (a) «*cosecha*» to be early; «*verano/frío*» to arrive early (b) «*reloj*» to gain 3 (anticiparse): **se adelantó a su época** he was ahead of his time; ~**se a los acontecimientos** to jump the gun; **yo iba a pagar, pero él se me adelantó** I was going to pay, but he beat me to it

adelante *adv* 1 (en el espacio) (a) (expresando dirección, movimiento) forward; **para/hacia** ~ forward; **seguir** ~ to go on; **¡**~**!** (*como interj*) (autorizando la entrada) come in!; (ordenando marchar) forward! (b) (lugar, posición): **se sentó** ~ (en coche) she sat in front; (en clase, cine) she sat at the front; **más** ~ **la calle se bifurca** further on, the road forks; **la parte de** ~ the front 2 (en el tiempo): **más** ~ later; **(de ahora) en** ~ from now on; **de hoy en** ~ as of *o* from today 3 **adelante de** (*loc prep*) (AmL) in front of

adelanto *m* 1 (avance) step forward; **los** ~**s de la ciencia** the advances of science 2 (del sueldo) advance; (depósito) deposit 3 (en el tiempo): **llegó con un poco de** ~ he/she/it arrived slightly early

adelgazamiento *m* slimming

adelgazante *adj* weight-reducing (*before n*), slimming (*before n*) (BrE)

adelgazar [A4] *vt* ‹*caderas/cintura*› to slim down; ‹*kilos*› to lose
■ ~ *vi* to lose weight

ademán *m* (expresión) expression; (movimiento, gesto) gesture; **hizo** ~ **de levantarse** he made as if to get up

además *adv* 1 (a) (también) as well, too; ~ **habla ruso** she speaks Russian as well *o* too (b) (lo que es más) what's more (c) (por otra parte) anyway, besides; ~ **¿a mí qué me importa?** anyway, what do I care? 2 **además de** besides, apart from; ~ **de hacerte mal, engorda** besides *o* apart from being bad for you, it's also fattening; ~ **de hacerlos, los diseña** he designs them as well as making them

adentro *adv* 1 (a) (expresando dirección, movimiento): **vamos para** ~ let's go in *o* inside; **ven aquí** ~ come in here (b) (lugar, parte) inside; [*European Spanish prefers* DENTRO *in many of these examples*] **¡qué calor hace aquí** ~**!** it's so hot in here!; **¿comemos** ~**?** shall we eat indoors *o* inside?; **la parte de** ~ the inside 2 **adentro de** (AmL) in, inside

adentros *mpl*: **dije para mis** ~ I said to myself; **se rió para sus** ~**s** he chuckled to himself

adepto -ta *adj*: **ser** ~ A **algo** ‹*a secta*› to be a follower OF sth; ‹*a partido*› to be a supporter OF sth
■ *m,f* (de secta) follower; (de partido) supporter

aderezar [A4] *vt* ⟨*guiso*⟩ to season; ⟨*ensalada*⟩ to dress

aderezo *m* (de guiso) seasoning; (de ensalada) dressing

adherencia *f* **(a)** (acción) adherence **(b)** (Auto) grip, roadholding **(c)** (Med) adhesion

adherente *adj* adhesive

adherir [I11] *vt* to stick
■ **adherirse** *v pron* **(a)** (pegarse) to stick **(b)** (unirse) ~se A algo ⟨*a propuesta/causa*⟩ to give one's support TO sth; ⟨*a movimiento/partido*⟩ to join sth

adhesión *f* **(a)** (a una superficie) adhesion **(b)** (apoyo) support **(c)** (a una organización) joining

adhesivo¹ -va *adj* adhesive, sticky

adhesivo² *m* (sustancia) adhesive; (lámina, estampa) sticker

adicción *f* addiction; ~ a la heroína heroin addiction

adición *f* **(a)** (Mat) addition **(b)** (RPl) (cuenta) check (AmE), bill (BrE)

adicional *adj* additional; **una cantidad** ~ a supplement

adicto -ta *adj* (a la bebida, la droga) addicted; ~ A algo addicted TO sth
■ *m,f* addict; **los** ~**s a la cocaína** cocaine addicts

adiestrar [A1] *vt* to train

adinerado -da *adj* wealthy, moneyed

adiós *m/interj* (al despedirse) goodbye, bye (colloq); (al pasar) hello; ▶ DECIR² *vt* 3B

aditivo *m* additive

adivinanza *f* riddle; **jugar a las** ~**s** to play at guessing riddles

adivinar [A1] *vt* **(a)** (por conjeturas, al azar) to guess **(b)** (por magia) to foretell, predict
■ ~ *vi* to guess

adivino -na *m,f* fortune-teller

adjetivo¹ -va *adj* adjectival

adjetivo² *m* adjective

adjudicación *f* **(a)** (de premio, contrato) awarding; (de viviendas) allocation **(b)** (en subasta) sale

adjudicar [A2] *vt* **(a)** ⟨*premio/contrato*⟩ to award; ⟨*vivienda*⟩ to allot, allocate **(b)** (en subasta): **le** ~**on la alfombra al anticuario** the carpet was sold to o went to the antique dealer; **¡adjudicado!** sold!

adjuntar [A1] *vt* to enclose

adjunto -ta *adj* **(a)** ⟨*director*⟩ deputy (*before n*); **profesor** ~ associate professor (AmE), senior lecturer (BrE) **(b)** ⟨*lista/copia*⟩ enclosed, attached

administración *f* ⟨**1**⟩ **(a)** (de empresa, bienes) management **(b)** (Pol) administration; ~ **pública** civil service ⟨**2**⟩ **(a)** (conjunto de personas) management **(b)** (oficina, departamento) administration

administrador -dora *m,f* (de empresa) manager, administrator; (de bienes) administrator

administrar [A1] *vt* **(a)** ⟨*empresa/bienes*⟩ to manage, administer (frml) **(b)** (frml) (dar) ⟨*sacramentos/medicamento*⟩ to give
■ **administrarse** *v pron*: ~**se bien/mal** to manage one's money well/badly

administrativo -va *adj* administrative
■ *m,f* administrative assistant (o officer *etc*); (con funciones más rutinarias) clerk

admirable *adj* admirable

admiración *f* **(a)** (respeto) admiration **(b)** (sorpresa) amazement

admirador -dora *m,f* **(a)** (de persona) admirer, fan **(b)** (hum) (pretendiente) admirer (hum)

admirar [A1] *vt* **(a)** (respetar) ⟨*persona/cualidad*⟩ to admire **(b)** (contemplar) to admire **(c)** (sorprender) to amaze
■ **admirarse** *v pron* ~**se DE algo** to be amazed AT o ABOUT sth

admisible *adj* ⟨*comportamiento*⟩ admissible, acceptable; ⟨*excusa*⟩ acceptable

admisión *f* admission; **examen** or **prueba de** ~ entrance examination o test

admitir [I11] *vt* ⟨**1**⟩ **(a)** (aceptar) to accept; **❸ se admiten tarjetas de crédito** we take o accept credit cards **(b)** (permitir) to allow **(c)** (reconocer) to admit ⟨**2**⟩ (dar cabida a) ⟨*local*⟩ to hold

ADN *m* (= **ácido desoxirribonucleico**) DNA

adobar [A1] *vt* ⟨*carne/pescado*⟩ (condimentar) to marinade; (para conservar) to pickle; (para curar) to cure

adobe *m* adobe

adobo *m* (condimento) marinade; (para conservar) pickle

adoctrinar [A1] *vt* to indoctrinate

adolecer [E3] *vi* ~ DE algo ⟨*de enfermedad/defecto*⟩ to suffer FROM sth

adolescencia *f* adolescence; **durante su** ~ (when he was) in his teens, in adolescence (frml)

adolescente *adj* adolescent; **tiene dos hijos** ~**s** she has two teenage o adolescent children
■ *mf* (en contextos no técnicos) teenager; (Med, Psic) adolescent

adolorido -da *adj* (esp AmL) ▶ DOLORIDO A

adonde *adv* where; **el lugar** ~ **se dirigían** the place where o to which they were going

adónde *adv* where

adondequiera *adv*: ~ **que vayas** wherever you go

adopción *f* adoption

adoptar [A1] *vt* **(a)** ⟨*actitud/costumbre*⟩ to adopt; ⟨*decisión/medida/posición*⟩ to take **(b)** ⟨*niño/nacionalidad*⟩ to adopt

adoptivo -va *adj* **(a)** ⟨*hijo*⟩ adopted; ⟨*padres*⟩ adoptive **(b)** ⟨*patria/país*⟩ adopted

adoquín *m* **(a)** (de piedra) paving stone; (ovalado) cobblestone **(b)** (Per) (helado) Popsicle® (AmE), ice lolly (BrE)

adorable *adj* adorable

adoración f (a) (de persona) adoration (b) (de deidad) adoration, worship

adorar [A1] vt (a) ⟨persona/cosa⟩ to adore (b) ⟨deidad⟩ to worship, adore

adormecer [E3] vt (a) ⟨persona⟩ to make ... sleepy o drowsy; ⟨sentidos⟩ to numb, dull (b) ⟨pierna/mano⟩ to numb
■ **adormecerse** v pron to fall asleep, doze off

adormecimiento m (a) (somnolencia) sleepiness, drowsiness (b) (de un miembro) numbness

adormilarse [A1] v pron to doze

adornar [A1] vt (a) ⟨habitación/sombrero/comida⟩ to decorate (b) ⟨relato/discurso⟩ to embellish (c) «flores/banderas» to adorn
■ **adornarse** v pron (refl) ⟨cabeza/pelo⟩ to adorn

adorno m (a) (objeto) ornament; los ~s de Navidad the Christmas decorations (b) (decoración) adornment; de ~ for decoration

adosado -da adj ~ A algo fixed TO sth; ▶ CASA 1A

adosar [A1] vt (a) ⟨armario/escritorio⟩ ~ algo A algo to fix sth TO sth (b) (Méx) ⟨documento⟩ to enclose, attach

adquiera, adquirió, etc ▶ ADQUIRIR

adquirir [I13] vt ⟨casa/coche⟩ to acquire, obtain; (comprar) to purchase, buy; ⟨conocimientos/colección/fortuna⟩ to acquire; ⟨fama⟩ to attain, achieve; ⟨experiencia⟩ to gain; ~ malas costumbres to get into bad habits

adquisición f acquisition; (compra) purchase

adquisitivo -va adj purchasing

adrede adv on purpose, deliberately

adrenalina f adrenaline

aduana f customs; libre de derechos de ~ duty free

aduanero -ra adj customs (before n)
■ m,f customs officer

adulación f flattery

adulador -dora adj flattering
■ m,f flatterer

adular [A1] vt to flatter

adulterar [A1] vt ⟨alimento/vino⟩ to adulterate; ⟨información⟩ to falsify

adulterio m adultery

adulto -ta adj (a) ⟨persona/animal⟩ adult (before n) (b) ⟨reacción/opinión⟩ adult
■ m,f adult

adusto -ta adj ⟨persona/expresión⟩ austere, severe; ⟨paisaje⟩ bleak, harsh

advenedizo -za adj upstart (before n)
■ m,f social climber

adverbio m adverb

adversario -ria adj opposing (before n)
■ m,f opponent, adversary

adversidad f adversity; en la ~ in adversity

adverso -sa adj ⟨circunstancias/resultado⟩ adverse

advertencia f warning; que les sirva de ~ let it be a warning to them

advertir [I11] vt (a) (avisar) to warn; ¡te lo advierto! I'm warning you!; ~le A algn DE algo to warn sb ABOUT sth; le advertí que tuviera cuidado I warned him to be careful; te advierto que no me sorprendió nada I must say I wasn't at all surprised (b) (notar) to notice

adviento m Advent

advierta, advirtió, etc ▶ ADVERTIR

adyacente adj adjacent

aéreo -rea adj ⟨vista⟩ aerial; ⟨tráfico⟩ air (before n)

aerobic /e'roβik/ m, (Méx) **aerobics** mpl aerobics

aerodeslizador m (Náut) hovercraft

aerodinámica f aerodynamics

aerodinámico -ca adj aerodynamic

aeródromo m aerodrome, airfield

aeroespacial adj aerospace (before n)

aerograma m aerogram, air (mail) letter

aerolínea f airline

aeromodelismo m model airplane making

aeromozo -za m,f (AmL) flight attendant

aeronáutica f (a) (ciencia) aeronautics (b) (RPl) (aviación militar) air force

aeronáutico -ca adj aeronautic, aeronautical

aeronave f (a) (globo dirigible) airship (b) (frml) (avión) airliner, aircraft

aeroplano m (ant) airplane, aeroplane (BrE)

aeropuerto m airport

aerosol m aerosol, spray can

afable adj affable

afán m [1] (a) (anhelo) eagerness; su ~ de aventuras his thirst for adventure; ~ DE hacer algo eagerness TO do sth; su ~ de agradar their eagerness to please; tiene ~ de aprender she's eager to learn (b) (empeño) effort [2] (Col fam) (prisa) hurry

afanado -da adj [1] [ESTAR] ⟨persona⟩ busy [2] [ESTAR] (Col, Per fam) (con prisa) in a hurry

afanarse [A1] v pron (esforzarse) to work, toil; ~se EN or POR hacer algo to strive TO do sth

afear [A1] vt (a) ⟨persona⟩ to make ... look ugly; ⟨paisaje⟩ to spoil (b) ⟨conducta⟩ to criticize
■ **afearse** v pron to lose one's looks

afectación f affectation

afectado -da adj (a) ⟨gestos/acento⟩ affected (b) ⟨área/órgano⟩ affected; está afectado de una grave enfermedad (frml) he is suffering from a serious disease

afectar [A1] vt [1] (a) (tener efecto en) to affect; esto nos afecta a todos this affects us all (b) (afligir) to affect (frml); la noticia lo afectó mucho the news upset him terribly [2] (fingir) ⟨admiración/indiferencia⟩ to affect, feign

afectísimo -ma adj (Corresp) (frml): suyo ~ yours truly

afectivo -va adj emotional

afecto m (cariño) affection; tenerle ~ a algn to be fond of sb; tomarle ~ a algn to grow fond of sb

afectuoso -sa adj ⟨persona⟩ affectionate; recibe un ~ saludo (Corresp) with warm o kind regards

afeitadora f shaver, electric razor

afeitar [A1] vt ⟨persona/cabeza⟩ to shave; ⟨barba⟩ to shave off
■ **afeitarse** v pron (refl) to shave; se afeitó la barba he shaved off his beard

··· afeminado ···> agarrar

afeminado -da *adj* effeminate

aferrarse [A1] *v pron:* ~**se A** algo/algn to cling (ON) TO sth/sb

affmo. affma. (Corresp) (frml) = **afectísimo, -ma**

Afganistán *m* Afghanistan

afgano -na *adj/m,f* Afghan

afianzar [A4] *vt* ⟨posición/postura⟩ to consolidate
■ **afianzarse** *v pron* «prestigio/sistema» to become consolidated

afiche *m* (esp AmL) poster

afición *f* **(a)** (inclinación, gusto) love, liking; ~ a la lectura/música love of reading/music **(b)** (pasatiempo) hobby **(c)** (Dep, Taur): la ~ the fans (*pl*)

aficionado -da *adj* [SER] **(a)** (entusiasta) ~ A algo fond OF o keen ON sth **(b)** (no profesional) amateur
■ *m,f* **(a)** (entusiasta) enthusiast; **para los** ~s al **bricolaje** for do-it-yourself enthusiasts; **un** ~ a la **música** a music lover; **los** ~s al tenis/fútbol tennis/football fans **(b)** (no profesional) amateur

aficionarse [A1] *v pron* ~**se A** algo to become interested IN sth

afilado -da *adj* **1** **(a)** ⟨borde/cuchillo⟩ sharp **(b)** ⟨nariz⟩ pointed; ⟨rasgos⟩ sharp; ⟨dedos⟩ long **2** (mordaz) ⟨lengua⟩ sharp; ⟨pluma⟩ biting

afilar [A1] *vt* ⟨navaja/cuchillo⟩ to sharpen, hone

afiliación *f* affiliation

afiliado -da *m,f* member

afiliarse [A1] *v pron* ~**se A** algo ⟨a partido/sindicato⟩ to become a member OF sth, to join sth; ⟨a sistema⟩ to join sth

afín *adj* ⟨temas/lenguas⟩ related; ⟨culturas/ideologías⟩ similar; ⟨intereses⟩ common; **ideas afines a las nuestras** ideas which have a lot in common with our own

afinación *f* tuning

afinar [A1] *vt* **1** **(a)** ⟨instrumento⟩ to tune **(b)** ⟨coche⟩ to tune up; ⟨motor⟩ to tune **2** ⟨punta⟩ to sharpen

afinidad *f* (entre personas, caracteres) affinity; **no tengo ninguna** ~ **con él** I have nothing in common with him

afirmación *f* (declaración) statement, assertion; (respuesta positiva) affirmation

afirmar [A1] *vt* **1** (aseverar) to state, declare, assert (frml); **no lo afirmó ni lo negó** she neither confirmed nor denied it **2** ⟨escalera⟩ to steady
■ ~ *vi*: afirmó con la cabeza he nodded
■ **afirmarse** *v pron* (físicamente) to steady oneself; ~**se EN** algo/algn to hold ON to sth/sb

afirmativo -va *adj* ⟨respuesta/frase⟩ affirmative

afligido -da *adj* distressed

afligir [I7] *vt* **(a)** (afectar) to afflict **(b)** (apenar) to upset
■ **afligirse** *v pron* to get upset

aflojar [A1] *vt* **1** ⟨cinturón/tornillo⟩ to loosen; ⟨cuerda/riendas⟩ to slacken; ⟨presión/tensión⟩ to ease; ⟨marcha/paso⟩ to slow **2** (fam) ⟨dinero⟩ to hand over **3** (AmL) ⟨motor⟩ to run in
■ ~ *vi* ⟨tormenta⟩ to ease off; ⟨fiebre/viento⟩ to drop; ⟨calor⟩ to let up; ⟨tensión/presión⟩ to ease off

aflojarse *v pron* **(a)** (refl) ⟨cinturón⟩ to loosen **(b)** «tornillo/tuerca» to come o work loose

afónico -ca *adj:* estar ~ to have lost one's voice; **quedarse** ~ to lose one's voice

afortunadamente *adv* fortunately, luckily

afortunado *adj* ⟨persona⟩ lucky, fortunate; ⟨encuentro/coincidencia⟩ happy, fortunate; **una elección poco afortunada** a rather unfortunate choice

África *f* tb el ~ Africa

África del Sur *f* South Africa

africano -na *adj/m,f* African

afrikaans *m* Afrikaans

afrikaner *adj/mf* (*pl* **-ners**) Afrikaner

afrodisíaco¹ -ca *adj* aphrodisiac

afrodisíaco² *m* aphrodisiac

afrontar [A1] *vt* ⟨problema/responsabilidad⟩ to face up to; ⟨desafío/peligro⟩ to face

afuera *adv* **1** **(a)** (expresando dirección, movimiento) outside; **ven aquí** ~ come out here; **¡~!** get out of here! **(b)** (lugar, parte) outside; [*European Spanish prefers* FUERA *in many of these examples*] **aquí** ~ **se está muy bien** it's really nice out here; **comimos** ~ (en el jardín) we ate outside o outdoors; (en un restaurante) we ate out; **por** ~ **es rojo** it's red on the outside **2** **afuera de** (AmL): **¿qué haces** ~ **de la cama?** what are you doing out of bed?; ~ **del edificio** outside the building

afueras *fpl:* las ~ the outskirts

agachar [A1] *vt* ⟨cabeza⟩ to lower
■ **agacharse** *v pron* **(a)** (ponerse en cuclillas) to crouch down; (inclinarse) to bend down **(b)** (AmL fam) (rebajarse) to eat humble pie o (AmE) crow (colloq)

agallas *fpl* (fam) (valor) guts (*pl*) (colloq); **con** ~**s** gutsy (colloq); **hay que tener** ~**s** it takes guts (colloq)

agarrado¹ -da *adj* **(a)** [SER] (fam) (tacaño) tightfisted (colloq) **(b)** [ESTAR] (CS fam) (enamorado) in love
■ *m,f* (fam) (tacaño) skinflint (colloq), tightwad (AmE colloq)

agarrado² *adv:* bailar ~ to dance closely

agarrar [A1] *vt* **1** (sujetar) to grab, get hold of; **me agarró del brazo** (para apoyar) she took hold of my arm; (con violencia, rapidez) she grabbed me by the arm **2** (esp AmL) ⟨objeto⟩ (tomar) to take; (atajar) to catch; **agarra un papel y toma nota** get a piece of paper and take this down **3** (AmL) (pescar, atrapar) to catch; **si lo agarro, lo mato** if I get o lay my hands on him, I'll kill him **4** (esp AmL) (adquirir) ⟨resfriado/pulmonía⟩ to catch; ⟨costumbre/vicio⟩ to pick up; ⟨ritmo⟩ to get into; ⟨velocidad⟩ to gather, pick up; ~**le cariño a** algn to grow fond of sb; **le agarró asco** he got sick of it; **le he agarrado odio** I've come to hate him **5** (AmL) (entender) ⟨indirecta/chiste⟩ to get
■ ~ *vi* **1** (asir, sujetar): **toma, agarra** here, hold this; **agarra por ahí** take hold of that part **2** «planta/injerto» to take; «tornillo» to grip, catch; «ruedas» to grip; «tinte» to take
■ **agarrarse** *v pron* **1** (asirse) to hold on; **agárrate bien** o **fuerte** hold on tight; ~**se A** o **DE** algo to hold on TO sth; **iban agarrados del brazo** they were walking along arm in arm

2 ⟨*dedo/manga*⟩ to catch; **me agarré el dedo en el cajón** I caught my finger in the drawer **3** (esp AmL) ⟨*resfriado/pulmonía*⟩ to catch; **~se una borrachera** to get drunk; **~se un disgusto/ una rabieta** to get upset/into a temper **4** (AmL fam) (pelearse) to get into a fight; **se ~on a patadas** they started kicking each other; **~se CON algn** to have a set-to WITH sb (colloq)

agarre *m* (de neumático) grip; (de coche) roadholding

agarrotar [A1] *vt* ⟨*piernas/músculos*⟩ to make ... stiff
■ **agarrotarse** *v pron* **(a)** «*manos/músculos*» to stiffen up; **tengo las manos agarrotadas** my hands are stiff **(b)** «*motor/máquina*» to seize up

agazaparse [A1] *v pron* «*animal*» to crouch; «*persona*» to crouch (down)

agencia *f* (oficina) office; (sucursal) branch; **~ de colocaciones** employment agency *o* bureau (*generally for domestic staff*); **~ de prensa** *or* **de noticias** press *o* news agency; **~ de viajes** travel agent's, travel agency; **~ matrimonial** marriage bureau

agenda *f* (libreta) appointment book (AmE), diary (BrE); (programa) agenda; **~ de bolsillo** pocket diary; **~ de trabajo** engagement book

agente *mf* **1** (Com, Fin) agent; **~ de bolsa** stockbroker; **~ de publicidad** advertising agent; **~ de seguros** insurance broker; **~ de viajes** travel agent **2** (frml) (funcionario) employee; **~ de policía** police officer; **~ de tráfico** *or* (Arg, Méx) de tránsito** ≈traffic policeman (*in US*), ≈traffic warden (*in UK*); **~ secreto** secret agent

ágil *adj* ⟨*persona/movimiento*⟩ agile; ⟨*estilo/ programa*⟩ lively

agilidad *f* (de persona) agility; (de estilo) liveliness

agilizar [A4] *vt* ⟨*gestiones/proceso*⟩ to speed up; ⟨*pensamiento*⟩ to sharpen; ⟨*ritmo/presentación*⟩ to make ... livelier *o* more dynamic

agitación *f* **(a)** (nerviosismo) agitation **(b)** (de calle, ciudad) bustle

agitado -da *adj* **(a)** ⟨*mar*⟩ rough, choppy **(b)** ⟨*día/vida*⟩ hectic, busy **(c)** ⟨*persona*⟩ worked up, agitated

agitador -dora *m,f* (persona) agitator

agitar [A1] *vt* **(a)** ⟨*líquido/botella*⟩ to shake **(b)** ⟨*brazo/pañuelo*⟩ to wave; ⟨*alas*⟩ to flap
■ **agitarse** *v pron* **(a)** «*mar*» to get rough; «*barca*» to toss; «*toldo*» to flap **(b)** (inquietarse) to get worked up

aglomeración *f* **(a)** (de gente): **se produjo una ~ a la entrada** people crowded at the entrance; **para evitar las aglomeraciones** to avoid crowding; **las aglomeraciones urbanas** the built-up urban areas **(b)** (de tráfico) buildup

aglomerarse [A1] *v pron* to crowd (together)

agnóstico -ca *adj/m,f* agnostic

agobiado -da *adj* [ESTAR] **~ DE algo** ⟨*de trabajo*⟩ snowed under WITH sth; ⟨*de deudas*⟩ overwhelmed WITH sth; **estaba agobiada con tantos problemas** she was weighed down by all those problems

agobiante, agobiador -dora *adj* ⟨*trabajo/ día*⟩ exhausting; ⟨*calor*⟩ stifling; **es una carga ~ para él** it's/he's/she's a terrible burden on him

agobiar [A1] *vt* «*problemas/responsabilidad*»

to weigh *o* get ... down; «*calor*» to oppress, get ... down; **te agobia con tanta amabilidad** she smothers you with kindness; **este niño me agobia** this child is too much for me

agobio *m*: **una sensación de ~** a sense of oppression

agonía *f* **(a)** (de moribundo) death throes (*pl*) **(b)** (sufrimiento) suffering

agonizar [A4] *vi* «*persona*» to be dying, be in the throes of death; «*imperio/régimen*» to be in its death throes

agosto *m* August; *para ejemplos ver* ENERO; *hacer su* ~ to make a fortune, to make a killing (colloq)

agotado -da *adj* **(a)** [ESTAR] ⟨*recursos*⟩ exhausted; ⟨*edición*⟩ sold out; ⟨*pila*⟩ dead, flat; **S agotadas todas las localidades** sold out **(b)** [ESTAR] ⟨*persona*⟩ exhausted

agotador -dora *adj* exhausting

agotamiento *m* exhaustion

agotar [A1] *vt* **(a)** ⟨*recursos*⟩ to exhaust, use up; ⟨*pila*⟩ to wear out, run down; ⟨*mina/tierra*⟩ to exhaust **(b)** (cansar) ⟨*persona*⟩ to tire ... out, wear ... out
■ **agotarse** *v pron* **(a)** «*existencias/reservas*» to run out, be used up; «*pila*» to run down; «*mina/tierra*» to become exhausted; «*edición*» to sell out; **se me está agotando la paciencia** my patience is running out **(b)** «*persona*» to wear *o* tire oneself out

agraciado -da *adj* ⟨*persona/figura*⟩ attractive; **es muy poco ~** he's not very attractive

agradable *adj* ⟨*persona*⟩ pleasant, nice; ⟨*carácter*⟩ pleasant; ⟨*día/velada*⟩ enjoyable, nice; ⟨*sensación/efecto*⟩ pleasant, pleasing; ⟨*sabor/olor*⟩ pleasant, nice; **~ a la vista** pleasing to the eye

agradar [A1] *vi* (frml): **¿le agrada este, señora?** is this one to your liking, madam? (frml); **la idea no me agrada** the idea doesn't appeal to me; **le agrada verlo contento** it gives her pleasure to see him happy; **me ~ía mucho verlos allí** I would be very pleased to see you there
■ **~** *vt* to please

agradecer [E3] *vt* **(a)** (sentir gratitud por) ⟨*ayuda/ amabilidad*⟩ to appreciate, to be grateful for; **~le algo A algn** to be grateful TO sb for sth; **le ~ía (que) me llamara** (frml) I would appreciate it if you would call me (frml) **(b)** (dar las gracias por) to thank; **~le algo A algn** to thank sb for sth; **¡y así es como me lo agradece!** and this is all the thanks I get!

agradecido -da *adj* ⟨*persona*⟩ grateful; **estar ~** to be grateful; **¡qué poco ~ eres!** you're so ungrateful!

agradecimiento *m* gratitude; **demostrar ~** to show gratitude; **en ~ por todo lo que ha hecho** in appreciation of all you have done

agradezca, agradezcas, etc ▶ AGRADECER

agrado *m* (frml): **espero que sea de su ~** I hope this is to your liking; **con sumo ~** gladly; **tuve el ~ de verla** I had the pleasure of seeing her

agrandar [A1] *vt* **(a)** ⟨*casa*⟩ to extend; ⟨*agujero/pozo*⟩ to make ... larger *o* bigger; ⟨*fotocopia*⟩ to enlarge, blow up; ⟨*vestido*⟩ to let out **(b)** (exagerar) to exaggerate
■ **agrandarse** *v pron* «*agujero/bulto*» to grow larger, get bigger

agrario -ria adj ⟨sector/política⟩ agricultural (before n); ⟨sociedad⟩ agrarian

agravante adj aggravating
■ f or m (Der) aggravating factor o circumstance; **con la ∼ de que estaba borracho** what makes it even worse is that he was drunk

agravar [A1] vt to make … worse, aggravate
■ **agravarse** v pron «problema/situación» to become worse, worsen; «enfermo» to deteriorate, get worse

agredir [I32] vt (frml) to attack, assault

agregar [A3] vt (añadir) to add; **∼ algo A algo** to add sth TO sth

agresión f aggression; **una ∼ brutal** a brutal attack

agresividad f aggressiveness

agresivo -va adj aggressive

agresor -sora adj ⟨ejército⟩ attacking (before n); ⟨país⟩ aggressor (before n)
■ m,f (país, ejército) aggressor; (persona) attacker, assailant (frml)

agreste adj ⟨terreno/camino⟩ rough; ⟨paisaje⟩ rugged; ⟨vegetación/animal⟩ wild

agriarse [A1 or A17] v pron «leche/vino» to turn o go sour; «persona» to become bitter o embittered

agrícola adj ⟨técnicas⟩ agricultural, farming (before n)

agricultor -tora m,f farmer

agricultura f agriculture

agridulce adj bittersweet; (Coc) sweet-and-sour

agrietarse [A1] v pron «tierra/pared» to crack; «piel» to chap, become chapped

agringado -da adj (AmL fam & pey) ⟨persona⟩ Americanized; ⟨acento/costumbres⟩ (norteamericanizado) Americanized; (extranjero) foreign

agrio, agria adj (a) ⟨manzana⟩ sour, tart; ⟨naranja/limón⟩ sour, sharp (b) ⟨tono/persona⟩ sour, sharp; ⟨disputa⟩ bitter

agriparse [A1] v pron (Andes) to get the flu (AmE), to get flu (BrE); **está agripado** he has (the) flu

agronomía f agronomy

agrónomo -ma m,f agronomist

agrupación f **1** (grupo) group; (asociación) association; **∼ coral** choral group, choir
2 (acción) grouping (together)

agrupar [A1] vt (a) (formar grupos) to put … into groups, to group (b) (reunir) ⟨organizaciones/partidos⟩ to bring together
■ **agruparse** v pron (a) (formar un grupo) «niños/policías» to gather; «partidos» to come together (b) (dividirse en grupos) to get into groups

agua f⟩ **1** water; **∼ de lluvia/mar** rainwater; seawater; **∼ corriente/destilada** running/distilled water; **∼ de colonia** eau de cologne; **∼ dulce** fresh water; **∼ mineral** mineral water; **∼ mineral con gas/sin gas** sparkling/still mineral water; **∼ oxigenada** peroxide, hydrogen peroxide (tech); **∼ potable/salada** drinking/salt water; **como ∼ para**

chocolate (Méx fam) furious; **estar con el ∼ al cuello** to be up to one's neck; **estar más claro que el ∼** to be (patently) obvious; **hacérsele ∼ la boca a algn** (AmL): **se me hizo ∼ la boca** my mouth water; **ser ∼ pasada** to be a thing of the past; **∼ que no has de beber déjala correr** if you're not interested, don't spoil things for me/for other people; **nunca digas de esta ∼ no beberé** you never know when the same thing might happen to you
2 (lluvia) rain
3 (AmC, Andes) (infusión) herb tea (AmE), herbal tea (BrE); **∼ de menta** mint tea
4 aguas fpl **(a)** (de mar, río) waters (pl) **(b)** (de balneario, manantial) waters (pl); **tomar las ∼s** to take the waters; **∼s termales** thermal waters (pl)

aguacate m (árbol) avocado; (fruto) avocado (pear)

aguacero m downpour

aguado -da adj **1** ⟨leche/vino⟩ watered-down; ⟨sopa⟩ watery, thin; ⟨café⟩ weak; ⟨salsa⟩ thin
2 (AmC, Méx fam) (aburrido) [ESTAR] ⟨fiesta/película⟩ boring, dull; [SER] ⟨persona⟩ boring, dull

aguafiestas mf (pl ∼) (fam) wet blanket (colloq), party pooper (AmE colloq)

aguafuerte m (grabado) etching

aguaitar [A1] vt (AmS fam) (espiar) to spy on; (vigilar) to keep an eye on
■ **∼** vi (AmS fam) (espiar) to snoop (colloq); (mirar) to have a look

aguanieve f sleet

aguantador -dora adj (AmL) **1** (fam) (resistente) ⟨tela/ropa/zapatos⟩ hard-wearing; ⟨coche⟩ sturdy **2** (fam) **(a)** (paciente, tolerante): **es muy ∼** he puts up with a lot (colloq) **(b)** (del dolor, sufrimiento) tough (colloq)

aguantar [A1] vt **1** ⟨dolor/sufrimiento⟩ to bear, endure; **aguanto bien el calor** I can take the heat; **no tengo por qué ∼ esto** I don't have to put up with this; **este calor no hay quien lo aguante** this heat is unbearable; **no sabes ∼ una broma** you can't take a joke; **no los aguanto** I can't stand them; **no puedo ∼ este dolor de muelas** this toothache's unbearable
2 (a) ⟨peso/carga⟩ to support, bear; ⟨presión⟩ to withstand **(b)** (durar): **estas botas ∼án otro invierno** these boots will last (me/you/him) another winter
3 (sostener) to hold
4 (contener, reprimir) ⟨risa/lágrimas⟩ to hold back; **∼ la respiración** to hold one's breath
■ **∼** vi: **¡ya no aguanto más!** I can't take any more!; **no creo que este clavo aguante** I don't think this nail will hold
■ **aguantarse** v pron **1** (conformarse, resignarse): **me tendré que ∼** I'll just have to put up with it; **si no le gusta, que se aguante** if he doesn't like it, he can lump it (colloq)
2 (euf) (reprimirse, contenerse): **no me pude ∼ y me puse a llorar** I couldn't contain myself and burst into tears; **aguántate un poquito que ya llegamos** just hold o hang on a minute, we'll soon be there

AmC	Central America	Arg	Argentina	Cu	Cuba	Per	Peru
AmL	Latin America	Bol	Bolivia	Ec	Ecuador	RPI	River Plate Area
AmS	South America	Chi	Chile	Esp	Spain	Ur	Uruguay
Andes	Andean Region	CS	Southern Cone	Méx	Mexico	Ven	Venezuela

3 (AmL fam) (esperarse) to hang on (colloq)

aguar [A16] vt (a) ⟨leche/vino⟩ to water down (b) (fam) (estropear) to put a damper on (colloq)
■ **aguarse** v pron (fam) to be spoiled

aguardar [A1] vt ⟨persona⟩ to wait for; ⟨acontecimiento⟩ to await
■ ~ vi «noticia/destino» to await; **les aguardaba una sorpresa** there was a surprise in store for them

aguardiente m eau-de-vie (clear brandy distilled from fermented fruit juice)

aguarrás m turpentine, turps (colloq)

aguayo m (Bol) multicolored cloth

agudeza f **1** (a) (de voz, sonido) high pitch (b) (de dolor — duradero) intensity; (— momentáneo) sharpness **2** (perspicacia) sharpness; (de sentido, instinto) keenness, sharpness **3** (comentario ingenioso) witty comment

agudizar [A4] vt ⟨sensación⟩ to heighten; ⟨crisis/conflicto⟩ to make worse; ⟨instinto⟩ to heighten; ⟨sentido⟩ to sharpen
■ **agudizarse** v pron «sensación» to heighten; «dolor» to get worse; «crisis» to worsen; «instinto» to become heightened; «sentido» to become sharper

agudo -da adj **1** (a) ⟨filo/punta⟩ sharp (b) ⟨ángulo⟩ acute **2** (a) ⟨voz/sonido⟩ high-pitched; ⟨nota⟩ high (b) ⟨dolor⟩ (duradero) intense, acute; (momentáneo) sharp (c) ⟨crisis⟩ severe **3** (a) ⟨aumento/descenso⟩ sharp **3** (a) ⟨perspicaz⟩ ⟨persona⟩ quick-witted, sharp; ⟨comentario⟩ shrewd (b) (gracioso) ⟨comentario/persona⟩ witty (c) ⟨sentido/instinto⟩ sharp

agüero m: **ser de mal/buen ~** (presagio) to be a bad/good omen; (causa) to bring bad/good luck

agüevado -da adj (AmC fam) [ESTAR] upset

aguijón m (a) (vara) goad (b) (Zool) sting

águila f‡ (a) (ave) eagle; **ser un ~** to be very sharp (b) (Méx) (de moneda) ≈heads (pl); **¿~ o sol?** heads or tails?

aguileño -ña adj ⟨nariz⟩ aquiline

aguinaldo m **1** (a) (propina) Christmas bonus (AmE), Christmas box (BrE) (b) (paga extra) extra month's salary paid at Christmas, Christmas bonus (AmE) **2** (Col, Ven) (canción) ≈Christmas carol

aguja f (a) (de coser, tejer) needle; (para inyecciones) needle; (de tocadiscos) stylus, needle; (de instrumento) needle; (de balanza) pointer, needle; (de reloj) hand; **buscar una ~ en un pajar** to look for a needle in a haystack (b) (Inf) pin

agujereado -da adj: **está ~** it has holes in it

agujerear [A1] vt (hacer agujeros en) to make holes in; (atravesar) to pierce

agujero m hole; **hacerse ~s en las orejas** to have one's ears pierced

agujeta f **1** (Méx) (de zapato) (shoe) lace **2 agujetas** fpl (Esp) stiffness; **tengo ~s en las piernas** my legs are stiff

aguzar [A4] vt to sharpen; **aguzó el oído** he pricked up his ears

ah interj (expresando sorpresa, lástima, asentimiento) oh!

ahí adv **1** (a) (en el espacio) there; **~ está/viene** there he is/here he comes; **~ arriba/abajo** up/down there; **~ mismo** or (AmL) **nomás** or (Méx)

mero right o just there (b) **por ahí** somewhere; **debe estar por ~** it must be around somewhere; **fue a dar una vuelta por ~** she went off for a walk; **se fue por ~** she went that way; **yo he estado por ~** I've been around there; **tendrá unos 35 años o por ~** he must be 35 or thereabouts **2 (a)** (refiriéndose a un lugar figurado): **~ está el truco/problema** that's the secret/problem; **de ~ a la drogadicción solo hay un paso** from there it's just a short step to becoming a drug addict; **hasta ~ llego yo** that's as far as I'm prepared to go (b) **de ~** hence; **de ~ mi sorpresa** hence my surprise; **de ~ que hayan fracasado** that is why they failed; **de ~ a que venga es otra cosa** whether or not he actually comes is another matter **3** (en el tiempo) then; **de ~ en adelante** from then on; **~ mismo** there and then

ahijado -da m,f (por bautizo) (m) godson; (f) goddaughter; **mis ~s** my godchildren

ahogado -da adj **1** (en agua): **dos niños resultaron ~s** two children were drowned; **morir ~** (en agua) to drown; (asfixiarse) to suffocate; (atragantarse) to choke to death **2** ⟨llanto/grito⟩ stifled **3** (Méx fam) (borracho) blind o rolling drunk (colloq)

ahogador m (Chi, Méx) (Auto) choke

ahogar [A3] vt **1** (a) ⟨persona/animal⟩ (en agua) to drown; (asfixiar) to suffocate (b) ⟨motor⟩ to flood **2** (a) ⟨palabras/voz⟩ to drown (out); ⟨llanto/grito⟩ to stifle (b) ⟨penas⟩ to drown
■ **ahogarse** v pron (a) «persona/animal» (en agua) to drown; (asfixiarse) to suffocate; (atragantarse) to choke (b) «motor» to flood

ahogo m breathlessness; **tiene ~s** he gets out of breath

ahora adv **1** (a) (en el momento presente) now; **~ que lo pienso** now I come to think of it; **la juventud de ~** young people today; **hasta ~** so far, up to now; **de ~ en adelante** from now on; **por ~** for the time being; **por ~ va todo bien** everything's going all right so far (b) (inmediatamente, pronto): **~ mismo** right now o away; **~ te lo muestro** I'll show it to you in a minute o second o moment; **¡~ voy!** I'm coming!; **¡hasta ~!** (esp Esp) see you soon! (c) (hace un momento) a moment ago **2 ahora bien** (indep) however

ahorcar [A2] vt to hang
■ **ahorcarse** v pron (refl) to hang oneself

ahorita adv (esp AmL fam) (a) (en este momento) just o right now (b) (inmediatamente, pronto): **~ te lo doy** I'll give it to you in a second o moment (c) (hace un momento) a moment ago

ahorrador -dora adj thrifty; **no soy muy ~a** I'm not very good at saving (money)
■ m,f saver, investor

ahorrante mf (Chi) saver, investor

ahorrar [A1] vt **1** ⟨dinero/energía/agua⟩ to save; ⟨tiempo⟩ to save **2** (evitar) ⟨molestia/viaje⟩ (+ me/te/le etc) to save, spare
■ ~ vi to save
■ **ahorrarse** v pron (enf) (a) ⟨dinero⟩ to save (oneself) (b) (evitarse) ⟨molestia/viaje⟩ to save oneself

ahorrista mf (RPl, Ven) saver, investor

ahorro m (a) (acción) saving (b) **ahorros** mpl (cantidad) savings (pl)

ahuecar [A2] vt **(a)** ⟨tronco/calabaza⟩ to hollow out; ⟨mano⟩ to cup **(b)** ⟨almohadón⟩ to plump up; ⟨pelo⟩ to give volume to

ahumado adj **(a)** (Coc) smoked **(b)** ⟨cristal⟩ smoked; ⟨gafas⟩ tinted

ahumar [A23] vt **(a)** ⟨jamón/pescado⟩ to smoke **(b)** ⟨paredes/techo⟩ to blacken

ahuyentar [A1] vt **(a)** (hacer huir) ⟨ladrón/ animal⟩ to frighten off or away **(b)** (mantener a distancia) ⟨fiera/mosquitos⟩ to keep ... away

aimará adj Aymara
■ mf Aymara Indian

airbag /'erbag/ f airbag

aire m **1** air; **sintió que le faltaba el ~** she felt as if she was going to suffocate; **salir a tomar el ~** to go outside for a breath of fresh air; **al ~ libre** outdoors, in the open air; **con ~ acondicionado** air-conditioning; **con ~ acondicionado** air-conditioned; **a mi/tu/su ~: ellos salen en grupo, yo prefiero ir a mi ~** they go out in a group, I prefer doing my own thing (colloq); **quedar en el ~: todo quedó en el ~** everything was left up in the air; **saltar** or **volar por los ~s** to explode, blow up;
2 (viento) wind; (corriente) draft (AmE), draught (BrE)
3 (Rad, TV): **salir al ~** to go on the air
4 (a) (aspecto) air; **tiene un ~ aristocrático** she has an aristocratic air; **la protesta tomó ~s de revuelta** the protest began to look like a revolt; **darse ~s (de grandeza)** to put on o give oneself airs **(b)** (parecido) resemblance; **tienen un ~** they look a bit alike; **~ de familia** family resemblance

airear [A1] vt **(a)** (ventilar) to air **(b)** (hacer público) ⟨asunto⟩ to air **(c)** ⟨masa/tierra⟩ to aerate
■ **airearse** v pron **(a)** «persona» to get some (fresh) air **(b)** «manta/abrigo» to air; **para que se airee el cuarto** to let some air into the room

aislado -da adj **(a)** (alejado) remote, isolated **(b)** (sin comunicación) cut off; **quedar ~** to be cut off; **vive ~ del mundo** he's cut himself off from the world **(c)** ⟨caso⟩ isolated **(d)** (Elec) insulated

aislamiento m **(a)** (en general) isolation **(b)** (Elec) insulation

aislante adj insulating, insulation (before n)
■ m insulator

aislar [A19] vt **(a)** (apartar, separar) ⟨enfermo⟩ to isolate, keep in isolation; ⟨preso⟩ to place ... in solitary confinement; ⟨virus⟩ to isolate **(b)** (dejar sin communicación) ⟨lugar⟩ to cut off **(c)** (Elec) to insulate
■ **aislarse** v pron (refl) to cut oneself off

ajado -da adj ⟨ropa⟩ worn; ⟨manos⟩ wrinkly; ⟨piel⟩ wrinkled

ajedrecista mf chess player

ajedrez m (juego) chess; (tablero y fichas) chess set

ajeno -na adj [SER] **(a)** (que no corresponde, pertenece): **mis ideales le son totalmente ~s** my ideals are completely alien to him; **aquel ambiente me era ~** that environment was alien o foreign to me; **por razones ajenas a nuestra voluntad** for reasons beyond our control **(b)** (que pertenece, corresponde a otro): **conduce un coche ~** he drives someone else's car; **por el bien ~** for the good of others; **las desgracias ajenas** other people's misfortunes

ajetreado -da adj hectic, busy

ajetreo m hustle and bustle; **un día de mucho ~** a hectic day

ají m **(a)** (chile) chili* **(b)** (Andes) (salsa) chili* sauce **(c)** (RPl) (pimiento) pepper

ajo m (Coc) garlic; **un diente de ~** a clove of garlic

ajonjolí m sesame

ajuar m (de novia) trousseau; (de bebé) layette

ajustado -da adj **(a)** (ceñido) tight; **me queda muy ~** it's too tight (for me) **(b)** ⟨presupuesto⟩ tight

ajustar [A1] vt **1 (a)** (apretar) to tighten (up) **(b)** ⟨volumen/temperatura⟩ to adjust; **~ la entrada de agua** to regulate the flow of water **(c)** ⟨retrovisor/asiento/cinturón de seguridad⟩ to adjust **(d)** (encajar) ⟨piezas⟩ to fit **2** (en costura) to take in **3 (a)** ⟨gastos/horarios⟩ ~ **algo A algo** to adapt sth to sth **(b)** ⟨sueldos/precios⟩ to adjust **4** (concertar) to fix, set **5** ⟨cuentas⟩ (sacar el resultado de) to balance; (saldar) to settle
■ **~** vi to fit
■ **ajustarse** v pron **1** (refl) ⟨cinturón de seguridad⟩ to adjust **2** ⟨piezas⟩ to fit

al contraction of A and EL

ala f; **1 (a)** (de ave, de avión) wing; **~ delta** (deporte) hang gliding; (aparato) hang glider; **cortarle las ~s a algn** to clip sb's wings; **darle ~s a algn: si le das ~s, luego no podrás controlarlo** if you let him have his own way, you won't be able to control him later **2** (de sombrero) brim **3 (a)** (de edificio) wing **(b)** (facción) wing **(c)** (flanco) flank, wing **(d)** (Dep) (posición) wing
■ mf; (jugador) wing, winger

alabanza f praise; **digno de ~** praiseworthy

alabar [A1] vt to praise

alacena f larder

alacrán m scorpion

alambrada f (valla) wire fence; (material) wire fencing

alambrado m (AmL) **(a)** (acción) fencing in/off **(b)** (valla) wire fence

alambrar [A1] vt to fence in/off

alambre m (hilo metálico) wire; **~ de púas** barbed wire, barbwire (AmE)

alameda f (avenida) tree-lined avenue; (terreno con álamos) poplar grove

álamo m poplar

alarde m show, display; **hacer ~ de fuerza** to show off strength

alardear [A1] vi **~ DE algo** to boast ABOUT o OF sth; **alardea de tener dinero** she boasts about being well-off

alargado -da adj ⟨forma⟩ elongated; ⟨hoja⟩ elongate

alargador m extension cord (AmE), extension lead (BrE)

alargar [A3] vt **1 (a)** ⟨vestido/pantalón⟩ to let down, lengthen; ⟨manguera/cable⟩ to lengthen, extend; ⟨riendas/paso⟩ to let out; ⟨paso⟩ to lengthen **(b)** ⟨cuento/discurso⟩ to drag out; ⟨vacaciones/plazo⟩ to extend; **puede ~le la vida** it could prolong her life **2 (a)** (extender) ⟨mano/ brazo⟩ to hold out **(b)** (alcanzar) **~le algo A algn** to hand o give o pass sth TO sb

alargarse v pron «cara/sombra» to get longer; «días» to grow longer; «reunión/fiesta» to go on

alarido m (de miedo) shriek; (de dolor) scream

alarma f [1] (ante peligro) alarm; **dar la voz de ~** to sound o raise the alarm [2] (dispositivo) alarm; **~ contra robos/incendios** burglar/fire alarm

alarmante adj alarming

alarmar [A1] vt to alarm

■ **alarmarse** v pron to be alarmed

alba f‡ (del día) dawn, daybreak; **al rayar el ~** (liter) at the break of day (liter); **al** or **con el ~** at the crack of dawn

albacora f (atún) albacore; (pez espada) (Chi) swordfish

albahaca f basil

albanés¹ -nesa adj/m,f Albanian

albanés² m (idioma) Albanian

Albania f Albania

albañil m (constructor) builder; (que coloca ladrillos) bricklayer

albaricoque m (Esp) apricot

albaricoquero m (Esp) apricot tree

albedrío m (free) will; **lo hizo a su ~** he did it of his own free will; **lo dejo a tu libre ~** I leave it entirely up to you

alberca f (a) (embalse) reservoir (b) (Méx) (piscina) swimming pool (c) (Col) (lavadero) sink (for washing clothes) (d) (Bol, Per) (comedero) trough

albergar [A3] vt «personas» to house, accommodate; «biblioteca/exposición» to house

■ **albergarse** v pron (a) (hospedarse) to lodge (b) (refugiarse) to shelter, take refuge

albergue m (a) (alojamiento) lodging, accommodations (pl) (AmE); **darle ~ a algn** to take sb in (b) (hostal) hostel; **~ juvenil** youth hostel (c) (en la montaña) refuge, shelter; (para vagabundos, mendigos) shelter

albino -na adj/m,f albino

albóndiga f meatball

albornoz m bathrobe

alborotado -da adj [1] (a) (nervioso) agitated; (animado, excitado) excited (b) (ruidoso) noisy, rowdy; (amotinado) riotous [2] «mar» rough; «pelo» untidy, disheveled*

alborotador -dora adj rowdy, noisy

■ m,f troublemaker

alborotar [A1] vi to make a racket

■ ~ vt (a) (agitar) to agitate, get ... agitated; (excitar) to get ... excited (b) «muchedumbre» to stir up

■ **alborotarse** v pron (a) (agitarse) to get agitated o upset; (excitarse) to get excited (b) (amotinarse) to riot

alboroto m (a) (agitación, nerviosismo) agitation; (excitación) excitement (b) (ruido) racket (c) (disturbio, jaleo) disturbance, commotion; (motín) riot

álbum m (a) (de fotos, sellos) album; (libro de historietas) comic book (b) (disco) album

alcachofa f (a) (Bot, Coc) artichoke (b) (de ducha) shower head; (de regadera) sprinkler (AmE), rose (BrE)

alcahuete -ta m,f (a) (ant) (mediador) procurer (arch) (b) (CS fam) (chismoso) gossip (colloq); (soplón) tattletale (AmE colloq), telltale (BrE colloq)

alcahuetear [A1] vi (a) (hacer de mediador) to act as a go-between, to procure (b) (Andes fam) (tapar): **les alcahuetea las travesuras** he lets them get away with all kinds of things; **le alcahuetea las mentiras** she covers up for him when he lies (c) (CS fam) (chismear) to gossip (colloq)

■ ~ vt (fam) (delatar) to tell o snitch on (colloq)

alcalde -desa m,f [1] (Gob) mayor

[2] **alcaldesa** f (mujer del alcalde) mayoress

alcance m (a) «de persona» reach; **fuera del ~ de los niños** out of reach of children; **está fuera de mi ~** it is beyond my means (b) (de arma, emisora) range; **misiles de largo ~** long-range missiles (c) (de ley, proyecto) scope; (de declaración, noticia) implications (pl) (d) (en locs) **al alcance de** within reach of; **precios al ~ de su bolsillo** prices to suit your pocket; **un lujo que no está a mi ~** a luxury I can't afford

alcancía f (AmL) (de niño) piggy bank; (para colectas) collection box

alcanfor m camphor

alcantarilla f (cloaca) sewer; (sumidero) drain

alcantarillado m sewer system, drains (pl)

alcanzar [A4] vt [1] (a) «persona» (llegar a la altura de) to catch up with, to catch ... up (BrE); (pillar, agarrar) to catch; **lo alcancé en la curva** I caught up with him on the bend; **¡a que no me alcanzas!** I bet you can't catch me! (colloq) (b) (en tarea, estatura) to catch up with [2] (llegar a) «lugar» to reach, get to; «temperatura/nivel/edad» to reach; **casi no alcanzo el tren** I almost missed the train; **estos árboles alcanzan una gran altura** these trees can reach o grow to a great height; **~ la mayoría de edad** to come of age [3] (conseguir, obtener) «objetivo/éxito» to achieve; «acuerdo» to reach [4] (acercar, pasar) **~le algo A algn** to pass sb sth, to pass sth TO sb

■ ~ vi [1] (llegar con la mano) to reach; **hasta donde alcanzaba la vista** as far as the eye could see; **~ A hacer algo** to manage to do sth [2] (ser suficiente) «comida/provisiones» to be enough; **el sueldo no le alcanza** he can't manage on his salary

alcaparra f caper

alcaucil m (RPI) artichoke

alcázar m (fortaleza) fortress; (palacio) palace

alcista adj «tendencia» upward; «mercado» bull (before n)

alcoba f bedroom, bedchamber (liter)

alcohol m [1] (Quím) alcohol; (Farm) tb **~ de 90 (grados)** rubbing alcohol (AmE), surgical spirit (BrE) [2] (bebida) alcohol, drink

alcoholemia f: **hacerle la prueba de la ~ a algn** to breathalyze sb

alcohólico -ca adj alcoholic; **bebida no alcohólica** nonalcoholic drink

■ m,f alcoholic

alcoholímetro m Breathalyzer®, drunkometer (AmE)

alcoholismo m alcoholism

alcornoque m (a) (árbol) cork oak (b) (fam) (persona) idiot

aldaba f (llamador) doorknocker; (cerrojo) latch

aldea f small village, hamlet

aldeano -na *adj* village (*before n*)
■ *m,f* villager

alebrestarse [A1] *v pron* (a) (Col, Méx)
(alterarse, agitarse) to get worked up, agitated (b)
(Ven fam) (animarse) to get excited; (excesivamente) to
get overexcited

alegación *f* declaration, statement

alegar [A3] *vt* ⟨*motivos/causas*⟩ to cite;
⟨*razones*⟩ to put forward; ⟨*ignorancia/defensa
propia*⟩to plead; ⟨*inmunidad diplomática*⟩ to
claim; **alegó que no lo sabía** she claimed not to
know
■ ~ *vi* (AmL) (a) (discutir) to argue; ~ DE algo to
argue ABOUT sth (b) (protestar) to complain; ~
POR algo to complain ABOUT sth

alegata *f* (Méx) argument

alegato *m* (a) (exposición) statement,
declaration (b) (Der) (escrito) submission (c)
(Andes) (discusión) argument

alegrar [A1] *vt* (a) (hacer feliz) ⟨*persona*⟩ to make
... happy; **me alegra saberlo** I'm glad *o* pleased to
hear it (b) (animar) ⟨*persona*⟩ to cheer up; ⟨*fiesta*⟩
to liven up; ⟨*habitación*⟩ to brighten up; **¡alegra
esa cara!** cheer up!
■ **alegrarse** *v pron* (a) (ponerse feliz, contento): me
alegro mucho por ti I'm really happy for you; se
alegró muchísimo cuando lo vio she was really
happy when she saw him; ¡cuánto me alegro! I'm
so happy *o* pleased!; está mucho mejor — me
alegro she's much better — I'm glad (to hear
that); ~se CON algo to be glad *o* pleased ABOUT
sth; me alegro de verte it's good *o* nice to see
you; me alegro de que todo haya salido bien I'm
glad *o* pleased that everything went well (b)
(animarse) to cheer up (c) (por el alcohol) to get
tipsy (colloq)

alegre *adj* (a) ⟨*persona/carácter*⟩ happy,
cheerful; ⟨*color*⟩ bright; ⟨*fiesta/música*⟩ lively; **su
habitación es muy** ~ her room is nice and bright;
es muy ~ she's very cheerful, she's a very happy
person (b) [ESTAR] (por el alcohol) tipsy (colloq)

alegría *f* (dicha, felicidad) happiness, joy; **¡qué** ~
verte! it's great to see you!; **saltar de** ~ to jump
for joy

alejado -da *adj* (a) ⟨*lugar*⟩ remote (b)
(distanciado) ⟨*persona*⟩: hace tiempo que está ~ de
la política he's been away from *o* out of politics
for some time; está ~ de su familia he's
estranged from his family

alejar [A1] *vt* (a) (poner lejos, más lejos) to move
... (further) away; ~ algo/a algn DE algo/algn to
move sth/sb away FROM sth/sb (b) (distanciar) ~ a
algn DE algn to distance sb FROM sb (c) ⟨*dudas/
temores*⟩ to dispel
■ **alejarse** *v pron* to move away; (caminando) to
walk away; **no se alejen demasiado** don't go too
far; **se alejó de su familia** he drifted apart from
his family; **necesito** ~**me de todo** I need to get
away from everything

aleluya *interj* halleluja!

alemán¹ -mana *adj/m,f* German

alemán² *m* (idioma) German

Alemania *f* Germany

alentador -dora *adj* encouraging

alentar [A5] *vt* (a) ⟨*persona*⟩ to encourage;
⟨*jugador/equipo*⟩ to cheer ... on (b) ⟨*esperanza/
ilusión*⟩ to cherish

alergia *f* allergy; **le produce** ~ she's allergic to
it; ~ A algo allergy TO sth; **tiene** ~ **a la penicilina**
he's allergic to penicillin

alérgico -ca *adj* (a) [SER] ⟨*persona*⟩ allergic;
~ A algo allergic TO sth (b) ⟨*afección/reacción*⟩
allergic

alerta *adj* alert; **estar** ~ (tener cuidado) to be
alert; (estar en guardia) to be on the alert; **mantener
el oído** ~ to keep one's ears open
■ *f*: dar la (voz de) ~ to raise the alarm; **en estado
de** ~ on alert

alertar [A1] *vt* ~ a algn DE algo to alert sb TO
sth

aleta *f* (a) (de pez) fin; (de foca) flipper (b) (para
natación) flipper (c) (de la nariz) wing

aletargado -da *adj* lethargic, drowsy

aletargar [A3] *vt* ⟨*persona*⟩ to make ... feel
lethargic *o* drowsy

aletear [A1] *vi* «*pájaro/gallina*» to flap its
wings; «*mariposa*» to flutter its wings

alfabético -ca *adj* alphabetical

alfabetización *f* teaching of basic literacy;
campaña de ~ literacy campaign

alfabetizar [A4] *vt* (a) (Educ) to teach ... to
read and write (b) ⟨*sistema/fichero*⟩ to put ... in
alphabetical order, to alphabetize (frml)

alfabeto *m* alphabet

alfajor *m*: type of candy or cake varying from
region to region

alfalfa *f* alfalfa, lucerne (BrE)

alfarería *f* pottery

alfarero -ra *m,f* potter

alféizar *m* sill; **el** ~ **de la ventana** the
windowsill

alférez *m* second lieutenant

alfil *m* bishop

alfiler *m* (en costura) pin; (broche) brooch, pin; ~
de corbata tiepin; ~ **de gancho** (CS, Ven) *or* (Col)
de nodriza safety pin

alfombra *f* (a) (suelta) rug; (más grande) carpet
(b) (AmL) (de pared a pared) carpet

alfombrado -da *adj* carpeted

alfombrar [A1] *vt* to carpet

alfombrilla *f* ① (de coche) mat; (de baño) bath
mat; ~ **para ratón** (Inf) mouse mat ② (Med) *type
of measles*

alforja *f* (para caballerías) saddlebag; (sobre el
hombro) knapsack

alga *f* (en el mar) seaweed; (en agua dulce) weed,
waterweed; (nombre genérico) alga

algarroba *f* carob (bean)

algarrobo *m* carob (tree)

álgebra *f* algebra

álgido -da adj ⟨punto/momento⟩ culminating (before n), decisive

algo¹ pron (a) something; (en frases interrogativas, condicionales, etc) anything; (esperando respuesta afirmativa) something; **quiero decirte ∼** I want to tell you something; **si llegara a pasarle ∼** if anything happened to her; **¿quieres ∼ de beber?** do you want something o anything to drink?; **por ∼ será** there must be some o a reason; **le va a dar ∼** he'll have a fit; **o ∼ así** or something like that; **eso ya es ∼** at least that's something; **sé ∼ de francés** I know some French; **¿queda ∼ de pan?** is there any bread left? **(b)** (en aproximaciones): **serán las once y ∼** it must be some time after eleven; **pesa tres kilos y ∼** it weighs three kilos and a bit

algo² adv a little, slightly; **está ∼ nublado** it's a bit cloudy; **es ∼ grande para ti** it's a bit too big for you

algodón m [1] (Bot, Tex) cotton [2] (Farm) **(a)** (material) tb **∼ hidrófilo** cotton (AmE), cotton wool (BrE) **(b)** (trozo) piece of cotton (AmE), piece of cotton wool (BrE); **∼ de azúcar** cotton candy (AmE), candy floss (BrE)

algodonal, algodonar m cotton field

algodonero -ra adj cotton (before n)
■ m,f (agricultor) cotton planter o farmer; (vendedor) cotton dealer

alguacil -cila m,f **(a)** (agente de autoridad) sheriff **(b)** (de tribunal de justicia) bailiff (AmE), constable (BrE)

alguien pron somebody, someone; (en frases interrogativas, condicionales, etc) anybody, anyone; (esperando respuesta afirmativa) somebody, someone; **∼ con experiencia** someone o somebody with experience; **¿ha llamado ∼?** has anybody o anyone called?; **si ∼ preguntara** if anybody o anyone should ask

algún adj: apocopated form of ALGUNO used before masculine singular nouns

alguno¹ -na adj [1] (delante del n) **(a)** (indicando uno indeterminado) some; **algún día** some o one day; **en algún lugar** somewhere **(b)** (en frases interrogativas, condicionales, etc) any; **¿tocas algún instrumento?** do you play any instruments?; **si tienes algún problema** if there's any problem, if you have any problems **(c)** (indicando cantidad indeterminada): **esto tiene alguna importancia** this is of some importance; **hace ∼s años** some years ago, a few years ago; **me quedan tres tazas y algún plato** I have three cups and one or two plates; **escribió algún que otro artículo** he wrote one or two articles
[2] (detrás del n) (con valor negativo): **esto no lo afectará en modo ∼** this won't affect it in the slightest o at all

alguno² -na pron **(a)** (cosa, persona indeterminada) one; **∼ de nosotros** one of us; **siempre hay ∼ que no está conforme** there's always someone who doesn't agree **(b)** (en frases interrogativas, condicionales, etc): **buscaba una guía ¿tiene alguna?** I was looking for a guide, do you have one o any?; **si tuviera ∼** if I had one **(c)** (una cantidad indeterminada — de personas) some (people); (— de cosas) some; **∼s creen que fue así** some (people) believe that was the case; **he visto algunas** I've seen some; **he tenido ∼ que otro** I've had one or two

alhaja f **(a)** (joya) piece of jewelry* **(b)** (persona) gem, treasure

alhajero m, **alhajera** f (AmL) jewel case

alharaca f fuss; **hacer ∼s** to make a fuss

alhelí m wallflower

aliado -da adj allied
■ m,f (Hist, Pol) ally; **los A∼s** the Allies

alianza f **(a)** (pacto, unión) alliance; **la A∼ Atlántica** the Atlantic Alliance **(b)** (anillo) wedding ring

aliarse [A17] v pron to join forces; **∼se CON algn** to form an alliance WITH sb, ally oneself WITH sb

alias adv alias
■ m (pl ∼) alias

alicaído -da adj low, down in the dumps (colloq)

alicate m, **alicates** mpl (Tec) pliers (pl); (para uñas) nail clippers (pl); (para cutícula) cuticle clippers (pl)

aliciente m incentive

aliento m [1] **(a)** (respiración, aire) breath; **sin ∼** out of breath, breathless **(b)** (aire espirado) breath; **mal ∼** bad breath [2] (ánimo, valor): **dar ∼ a algn** to encourage sb

aligerar [A1] vt **(a)** ⟨carga⟩ to lighten; **∼ a algn DE algo** to relieve sb OF sth **(b)** (acelerar): **∼ el paso** to quicken one's pace

alijo m consignment

alimaña f pest; **∼s** vermin

alimentación f **(a)** (nutrición, comida) diet; **la ∼ integral va ganando adeptos** health food o (BrE) wholefood is growing in popularity **(b)** (de máquina, motor) fuel supply

alimentar [A1] vt [1] ⟨persona/animal⟩ to feed [2] **(a)** ⟨ilusión/esperanza⟩ to nurture, cherish; ⟨ego⟩ to boost **(b)** ⟨odio/pasión⟩ to fuel [3] ⟨máquina/motor⟩ to feed; ⟨caldera⟩ to stoke
■ ∼ vi to be nourishing
■ **alimentarse** v pron ⟨persona/animal⟩ to feed oneself; **∼se CON** or **DE algo** to live on sth

alimenticio -cia, alimentario -ria adj ⟨industria⟩ food (before n); **productos ∼s** foodstuffs; **hábitos ∼s** eating habits **(b)** ⟨valor⟩ nutritional; ⟨comida/plato⟩ nutritious, nourishing

alimento m [1] (fml) (comida) food, nourishment; **la leche es un ∼ completo** milk is a complete food; **∼s naturales** health food [2] (valor nutritivo): **no tiene ∼ ninguno** it has no nutritional value; **de mucho ∼** very nutritious

alineación f [1] **(a)** (Dep) (de equipo) lineup; (de jugador) selection **(b)** (puesta en fila) lining up [2] (Pol, Tec) alignment

alinear [A1] vt [1] ⟨equipo/jugador⟩ to select, pick [2] **(a)** (poner en fila, línea) to line up **(b)** (Tec) to align, line up
■ **alinearse** v pron ⟨tropa⟩ to fall in; ⟨niños/presos⟩ to line up

aliñar [A1] vt ⟨ensalada⟩ to dress; ⟨carne/pescado⟩ to season

aliño m (para ensalada) dressing; (para otros alimentos) seasoning

alioli m (mayonesa) garlic mayonnaise; (salsa) garlic and olive oil vinaigrette

alisar [A1] vt ⟨colcha/papel⟩ to smooth out; ⟨pared/superficie⟩ to smooth down ⸱⸱⸱⸺⸱

■ **alisarse** *v pron* (refl) (a) ⟨vestido/falda⟩ to smooth out (b) ⟨pelo⟩ (con la mano) to smooth down; (quitar los rizos) to straighten

alistamiento *m* (acción) enlistment, recruitment; (soldados alistados) call-up, draft (AmE)

alistarse [A1] *v pron* (a) (Mil) to enlist, join up; ~ **en el ejército** to join the army (b) (AmL) (prepararse) to get ready

alivianar *vt* [A1] (AmL) to lighten

aliviar [A1] *vt* ⟨dolor⟩ to relieve, soothe; ⟨síntomas⟩ to relieve; ⟨tristeza/pena⟩ to alleviate; ⟨persona⟩ to make ... feel better

■ **aliviarse** *v pron* (a) ⟨dolor⟩ to let up (b) ⟪persona⟫ to get better

alivio *m* relief; ¡qué ~! what a relief!

aljibe *m* (a) (pozo) well; (depósito de agua) cistern, tank (b) (Per) (cárcel) dungeon

allá *adv* [1] (a) (en el espacio): **ya vamos para ~** we're on our way (over); ~ **en América** over in America; **lo pusiste muy ~** you've put it too far away; ¡~ **voy!** here I come/go! (b) (en locs) **más allá** further away; **más allá de** (más lejos que) beyond; (aparte de) over and above; ~ **tú/él** that's your/his lookout *o* problem (colloq) [2] (en el tiempo): ~ **por los años 40** back in the forties; ~ **para enero** sometime in January

allanamiento *m* (a) (AmL) (con autorización judicial) raid; **orden de ~** search warrant (b) (Esp, Méx) (sin autorización judicial) breaking and entering

allanar [A1] *vt* [1] (a) (AmL) ⟨autoridad/policía⟩ to raid (b) (Esp, Méx) ⟨delincuente⟩ to break into [2] ⟨problemas⟩ to solve, resolve; ⟨obstáculo⟩ to remove, overcome; ⟨terreno⟩ to level out; ~(le) **el terreno a algn** to smooth the way *o* path for sb

allegado -da *adj* close; **mis amigos y parientes más ~s** my close family and friends

■ *m,f* (amigo, pariente): **los ~s del difunto** those closest to the deceased; **un ~ de la familia** a close friend of the family

allí *adv* there; ~ **arriba/dentro** up/in there; ~ **donde estés/vayas** wherever you are/go

alma *f* [1] (espíritu) soul; **tener ~ de niño** to be a child at heart; ~ **mía** *or* **mi ~** (como apelativo) my love; **con toda el** *or* **mi/tu/su ~** with all my/your/his/ heart; **del ~**: **su amigo del ~** his bosom friend; **en el ~**: **lo siento en el ~** I'm really *o* terribly sorry; **te lo agradezco en el ~** I can't tell you how grateful I am; **llegarle a algn al ~**: **aquellas palabras me llegaron al ~** (me conmovieron) I was deeply touched by those words; (me dolieron) I was deeply hurt by those words; **me/le parte el ~** it breaks my/his heart [2] (persona) soul; **ni un ~ viviente** not a living soul; **ser ~s gemelas** to be soul mates; **ser un ~ bendita** *or* **de Dios** to be a kind soul

almacén *m* (a) (depósito) warehouse (b) (CS) (de comestibles) grocery store (AmE), grocer's (shop) (BrE) (c) (AmC, Col, Ven) (de ropa, etc) store (AmE), shop (BrE) (d) (de mayorista) wholesaler's (e) **almacenes** *mpl* department store

almacenamiento *m* storage; ~ **de datos** data storage

almacenar [A1] *vt* ⟨mercancías/datos⟩ to store

almanaque *m* (calendario — de escritorio) almanac, desk calendar; (— de pared) calendar

almeja *f* clam

almendra *f* (a) (fruta) almond (b) (centro) kernel

almendro *m* almond tree

almíbar *m* syrup

almibarar [A1] *vt* ⟨fruta⟩ to preserve ... in syrup; ⟨pastel⟩ to soak ... in syrup

almidón *m* starch

almidonar [A1] *vt* to starch

almirante *m* admiral

almohada *f* pillow; **consultarlo con la ~** to sleep on it

almohadilla *f* [1] (para alfileres) pincushion; (para entintar) ink pad; (para sellos) damper [2] (para sentarse) cushion; (en béisbol) bag

almohadón *m* (cuadrado, redondo) cushion; (cilíndrico) bolster; (en la iglesia) kneeler

almorranas *fpl* (fam) piles (pl)

almorzar [A11] *vi* (a) (a mediodía) to have lunch (b) (en algunas regiones) (a media mañana) to have a mid-morning snack

■ *vt* (a) (a mediodía) to have ... for lunch (b) (en algunas regiones) (a media mañana) to have ... mid-morning

almuerza, almuerzas, etc ▶ ALMORZAR

almuerzo *m* (a) (a mediodía) lunch (b) (en algunas regiones) (a media mañana) mid-morning snack

aló *interj* (AmS excl RPl) (al contestar el teléfono) hello?

alocado -da *adj* (irresponsable, imprudente) crazy, wild; (irreflexivo, impetuoso) rash, impetuous; (despistado) scatterbrained

■ *m,f* (imprudente) crazy *o* reckless fool; (irreflexivo) rash fool; (despistado) scatterbrain

alojado -da *m,f* (Chi) guest; **pieza de ~s** guestroom

alojamiento *m* accommodations (pl) (AmE), accommodation (BrE); **nos dio ~** he put us up

alojar [A1] *vt* [1] (a) (en hotel): **los hemos alojado en el hotel Plaza** we've booked them into the Plaza Hotel; **el hotel en el que estaban alojados** the hotel where they were staying (b) (en casa particular) to put ... up [2] (albergar) ⟨evacuados/refugiados⟩ to house

■ **alojarse** *v pron* (a) (hospedarse) to stay (b) ⟨proyectil/bala⟩ to lodge

alondra *f* lark

alpaca *f* [1] (Zool, Tex) alpaca; **lana de ~** alpaca (wool) [2] (Metal) nickel silver, German silver

alpargata *f* espadrille

Alpes *mpl*: **los ~** the Alps

alpinismo *m* mountaineering, (mountain) climbing

alpinista *mf* mountaineer, (mountain) climber

alpino -na *adj* Alpine

alpiste *m* (semillas) birdseed

alquilar [A1] *vt* [1] (dar en alquiler) ⟨casa/local⟩ to rent (out), let (BrE); ⟨televisor⟩ to rent; ⟨coche/bicicleta⟩ to rent (out) (AmE), to hire out (BrE) [2] (tomar en alquiler) ⟨casa/local/televisor⟩ to rent; ⟨coche/bicicleta/disfraz⟩ to rent (AmE), to hire (BrE)

alquiler *m* (a) (renta — de apartamento) rent; (— de televisor, bicicleta) rental (b) (acción de alquilar — una casa) renting, letting (BrE); (— un televisor) rental; (— un coche, disfraz) rental (AmE), hire (BrE);

se dedica al ~ de coches he's in the car-rental (AmE) o (BrE) car-hire business; **contrato de ~** tenancy agreement; **coches de ~** rental (AmE) o (BrE) hire cars

alquitrán m tar

alrededor adv (a) (en torno) around; **a mi ~** around me (b) **alrededor de** (loc prep) (en torno a) around; (aproximadamente) around, about

alrededores mpl (a) (barrios periféricos, extrarradio de ciudad) outskirts (pl); (otras localidades): surroundings (pl) (b) (de edificio, calle) surrounding area; **en los ~ de la iglesia** in the area around the church

alta f: [1] (Med) discharge; **dar el ~ a** or **dar de ~ a un enfermo** to discharge a patient [2] (Fisco, Servs Socs): **los dieron de ~ en la Seguridad Social** they registered them with Social Security

altanero -ra adj arrogant, haughty

altar m altar

altavoz m (Audio) loudspeaker; (megáfono) megaphone

alteración f (a) (de plan, texto) change, alteration (b) (de hechos, verdad) distortion (c) (del orden, de la paz) disturbance (agitación) agitation ; **~ del orden público** breach of the peace

alterado -da adj [ESTAR] ⟨persona⟩ upset

alterar [A1] vt [1] (a) ⟨plan/texto⟩ to change, alter (b) ⟨hechos/verdad⟩ to distort (c) ⟨alimento⟩ to make ... go off, turn ... bad [2] (perturbar) (a) ⟨paz⟩ to disturb; **~ el orden público** to cause a breach of the peace (b) ⟨persona⟩ to upset
■ **alterarse** v pron [1] «alimentos» to go off, go bad [2] «pulso/respiración» to become irregular; «color» to change [3] «persona» to get upset

altercado m argument

alternar [A1] vt **~ algo CON algo** to alternate sth WITH sth; **alternamos la gimnasia con el tenis** we alternate gymnastics with tennis
■ ~ vi «persona» to socialize; **~ CON algn** to mix WITH sb
■ **alternarse** v pron to take turns

alternativa f (opción) alternative; **la ~ es clara** the choice is clear

alternativo -va adj ⟨medicina/prensa/música⟩ alternative

Alteza mf (tratamiento) Highness; **sí, (su) ~** yes, your Highness

altibajos mpl (a) (cambios bruscos) ups and downs (pl) (b) (del terreno) undulations (pl)

altillo m (desván) attic; (en habitación) (sleeping) loft

altiplanicie f, **altiplano** m high plateau, high plain; **el altiplano boliviano** the Bolivian altiplano

altiro adv (Chi fam) right away, immediately

altitud f altitude

altivo -va adj (arrogante) arrogant, haughty; (noble, orgulloso) proud

alto¹ -ta adj [1] (a) [SER] ⟨persona/edificio/árbol⟩ tall; ⟨pared/montaña⟩ high; **una blusa de cuello ~** a high-necked blouse (b) [ESTAR]: **¡qué ~ estás!** haven't you grown!; **está tan alta como yo** she's as tall as me now [2] (indicando posición, nivel) (a) [SER] high; **los techos eran muy ~s** the rooms had very high ceilings (b) [ESTAR]: **el río está muy ~** the river

is very high; **la marea está alta** it's high tide; **los pisos más ~s** the top floors; **salgan con los brazos en ~** come out with your hands in the air; **con la moral bastante alta** in pretty high spirits; **en lo ~ de la montaña** high up on the mountainside; **en lo ~ del árbol** high up in the tree; **por todo lo ~** in style [3] (en cantidad, calidad) high; **el alto nivel de contaminación** the high level of pollution; **productos de alta calidad** high-quality products; **tirando por lo ~** at the most [4] (a) [ESTAR] (en intensidad) ⟨volumen/televisión⟩ loud; **pon la radio más alta** turn the radio up (b) **en alto** or **en voz alta** aloud, out loud [5] (delante del n) (a) (en importancia, trascendencia) ⟨ejecutivo/funcionario⟩ high-ranking, top; **conversaciones de ~ nivel** high-level talks (b) ⟨ideales/opinión⟩ high; **un ~ sentido del deber** a strong sense of duty (c) (en nombres compuestos) **alta burguesía** f upper-middle classes (pl); **alta costura** f haute couture; **alta fidelidad** f high fidelity, hi-fi; **alta mar** f: **en alta mar** on the high seas; **flota/pesca de alta mar** deep-sea fleet/fishing; **alta sociedad** f high society; **alta tensión** f high tension o voltage; **~ cargo** m (puesto) high-ranking position; (persona) high-ranking official; **~ mando** m high-ranking officer

alto² adv [1] ⟨volar/subir⟩ high [2] ⟨hablar⟩ loud, loudly; **habla más ~** speak up a little

alto³ interj halt!; **¡~ el fuego!** cease fire!

alto⁴ m [1] (a) (altura) de alto high; **tiene tres metros de ~** it's three meters high (b) (en el terreno) high ground; **construido en un ~** built on high ground [2] (a) (parada, interrupción): **hacer un ~** to stop; **~ el fuego** (Esp) (Mil) cease-fire (b) (Méx) (Auto): **pasarse el ~** (un semáforo) to run the red light (AmE), to jump the lights (BrE); (un stop) to go through the stop sign

altoparlante m (AmL) ▶ ALTAVOZ

altruismo m altruism

altruista adj altruistic
■ mf altruist

altura f [1] (de persona, edificio, techo) height; **el muro tiene un metro de ~** the wall is one meter high [2] (indicando posición) height; **ponlos a la misma ~** put them at the same height; **a la ~ de los ojos** at eye level; **estar/ponerse a la ~ de algo/algn**: **para ponernos a la ~ de la competencia** to put ourselves on a par with our competitors; **estar a la ~ de las circunstancias** to rise to the occasion; **no está a la ~ de su predecesor** he doesn't match up to his predecessor [3] (a) (Aviac, Geog) (altitud) altitude; **a 2.240 metros de ~** at an altitude of 2,240 meters (b) **de altura** ⟨pesquero/flota⟩ deep-sea (before n); ⟨remolcador⟩ oceangoing (before n) [4] (en sentido horizontal): **¿a qué ~ de Serrano vive?** how far up Serrano do you live?; **cuando llegamos a la ~ de la plaza** when we reached the square [5] (en sentido temporal): **a estas ~s ya debe haber llegado** he should have arrived by now; **¡a estas ~s me vienes con eso!** you wait till now to bring this to me!; **a estas ~s del año** this late on in the year; **a esas ~s ya no me importaba** by that stage I didn't mind [6] (Mús) pitch

alturado -da adj (Per) calm

alubia f (haricot) bean

alucinación f hallucination

alucinado -da adj (fam): **los dejó a todos** ~s she left everybody stunned

alucinante adj (a) (Med) hallucinatory (b) (Esp, Méx fam) (increíble) amazing (colloq), mind-boggling (colloq)

alucinar [A1] vi to hallucinate

alud m (de nieve) avalanche; (de tierra) landslide, landslip

aludir [I1] vi (a) (sin nombrar) ~ **A algn/algo** to refer TO sb/sth, allude TO sb/sth; **se sintió aludido** he thought we were referring to him; **no se dio por aludido** he didn't take the hint (b) (mencionar) ~ **A algn/algo** to refer TO sb/sth, mention sb/sth

alumbrado m lighting

alumbramiento m (frml) birth

alumbrar [A1] vt (iluminar) to light, illuminate; **está muy mal alumbrado** it's very poorly lit; **alumbra este rincón** shine the light in this corner ■ ~ vi «sol» to be bright; «lámpara/bombilla» to give off light

aluminio m aluminum (AmE), aluminium (BrE)

alumnado m (de colegio) students (pl) (AmE), pupils (pl) (BrE); (de universidad) students (pl)

alumno -na m,f (de colegio) pupil; (de universidad) student; ~ **interno** boarder

alunizar [A4] vi to land on the moon

alusión f ~ (**A algo/algn**) allusion o reference (TO sth/sb); **hacer** ~ **a algo/a algn** to make reference o an allusion to sth/sb

alverjilla f (AmL) sweet pea

alza fↆ rise; **el** ~ **de los precios** the rise in prices; **en** ~ «intereses/precios» rising (before n); **una escritora en** ~ an up-and-coming writer; **estar en** ~ to be on the rise

alzado -da adj (a) (Andes, Ven fam) (levantisco): **la servidumbre anda medio alzada** the servants have been rather uppity lately (colloq); **un chiquillo** ~ a cocky little brat (colloq) (b) (Méx, Ven fam) (altivo) stuck-up (colloq)

alzamiento m uprising

alzar [A4] vt **1** (levantar) (a) ⟨brazo/cabeza/voz⟩ to raise; **alzó al niño para que viera el desfile** she lifted the little boy up so he could see the parade; **alzó la mirada** she looked up (b) (AmL) ⟨bebé⟩ to pick up **2** ⟨edificio/monumento⟩ to erect **3** (Méx) (poner en orden) ⟨juguetes⟩ to pick up; ⟨cuarto/casa⟩ to clean (up) ■ **alzarse** v pron (sublevarse) to rise up; ~**se en armas** to take up arms

ama fↆ (a) (de bebé) tb ~ **de leche** or **de cría** wet nurse (b) (de niño mayor) nanny (c) ~ **de casa/de llaves** housewife/housekeeper; **ver tb** AMO

amabilidad f (a) (cualidad) kindness (b) (gesto): **tuvo la** ~ **de invitarnos** she was kind enough to invite us; **¿tendría la** ~ **de cerrar la puerta?** would you be so kind as to close the door?; **tenga la** ~ **de esperar aquí** would you mind waiting here?

amable adj (a) ⟨persona/gesto⟩ kind; **es muy** ~ **de su parte** that's very kind of you; **¿sería tan** ~ **de ...?** would you be so kind as to ...? (b) (AmS) ⟨rato/velada⟩ pleasant

amablemente adv kindly

amado -da adj dear, beloved ■ m,f love, sweetheart

amadrinar [A1] vt ⟨niño⟩ to be godmother to; ⟨boda⟩ to act as MADRINA at; ⟨barco⟩ to launch, christen

amaestrar [A1] vt ⟨animales⟩ to train

amago m: **tuvo un** ~ **de infarto** he had a mild heart attack; **un** ~ **de revuelta** a threat of revolt; **hacer un** ~ (Dep) to make a feint

amainar [A1] vi «lluvia» to ease up o off, abate; «temporal/viento» to die down, abate

amamantar [A1] vt/vi ⟨mujer⟩ to breastfeed; «animal» to suckle

amanecer¹ [E3] v impers: **¿a qué hora amanece?** what time does it get light?; **amanecía cuando partieron** dawn was breaking when they left ■ ~ vi (+ compl) (a) «persona»: **amaneció con fiebre** he woke up with a temperature; **amanecieron bailando** they were still dancing at dawn (b) (aparecer por la mañana): **amaneció nublado** it was cloudy first thing in the morning; **todo amaneció cubierto de nieve** in the morning everything was covered in snow ■ **amanecerse** v pron (Chi, Méx) to stay up all night

amanecer² m dawn, daybreak; **al** ~ at dawn o at daybreak

amanerado -da adj (afectado) affected, mannered; (afeminado) (fam) mannered, camp (colloq)

amansar [A1] vt ⟨caballo⟩ to break in; ⟨fiera⟩ to tame ■ **amansarse** v pron «fiera» to become tame; «caballo» to quiet (AmE) o (BrE) quieten down

amante mf lover

amañar [A1] vt (fam) ⟨elecciones⟩ to rig; ⟨partido/pelea⟩ to fix; ⟨carnet/documento⟩ to tamper with; ⟨informe⟩ to alter, doctor (pej); ⟨excusa/historia⟩ to dream o cook up, concoct ■ **amañarse** v pron **1** tb **amañárselas** (ingeniarse) to manage **2** (Col, Ven) (acostumbrarse) to settle in

amapola f poppy

amar [A1] vt to love ■ **amarse** v pron (recípr) to love each other

amarga f (Col) beer

amargado -da adj bitter, embittered ■ m,f bitter o embittered person

amargar [A3] vt ⟨ocasión/día⟩ to spoil; ⟨persona⟩ to make ... bitter ■ **amargarse** v pron to become bitter; **no te amargues la existencia** (fam) don't get all uptight about it

amargo -ga adj **1** (a) ⟨fruta/sabor⟩ bitter (b) (sin azúcar) unsweetened, without sugar **2** ⟨experiencia/recuerdo⟩ bitter, painful

23

amargor ···⟩ amigo ···

amargor *m* bitterness

amargura *f* bitterness; **con ∼** bitterly

amarillento -ta *adj* yellowish

amarillista *adj* (Period) (pey): **prensa ∼** sensationalist *o* yellow press

amarillo¹ -lla *adj* **1** ⟨*color/blusa*⟩ yellow; **el semáforo estaba (en) ∼** the light was yellow (AmE), the lights were (on) amber (BrE) **2** (a) ⟨*piel*⟩ (de raza oriental) yellow (b) ⟨*piel/cara*⟩ (por enfermedad) yellow, jaundiced

amarillo² *m* yellow

amarra *f* mooring rope; **∼s** moorings (*pl*); **echar (las) ∼s** to moor

amarradero *m* (a) ⟨poste⟩ bollard; (argolla) mooring ring (b) (lugar) berth, slip (AmE)

amarrado -da *adj* (Col, Méx, Ven fam) stingy (colloq), tightfisted (colloq)

amarrar [A1] *vt* (a) ⟨*embarcación*⟩ to moor; ⟨*animal/persona*⟩ to tie up; **le ∼on las manos** they tied his hands together; **∼ algo/a algn A algo** to tie sth/sb ᴛᴏ sth (b) (AmL exc RPl) ⟨*zapatos/cordones*⟩ to tie; ⟨*paquete*⟩ to tie ... up
■ **amarrarse** *v pron* (AmL exc RPl) ⟨*zapatos/cordones*⟩ to tie up, do up; ⟨*pelo*⟩ to tie up

amarrete -ta *adj* (AmS fam) stingy (colloq), tightfisted (colloq)
■ *m,f* (AmS fam) scrooge (colloq), skinflint (colloq)

amasar [A1] *vt* **1** ⟨*pan*⟩ to knead; ⟨*yeso/argamasa*⟩ to mix **2** ⟨*fortuna/riquezas*⟩ to amass

amateur /amaˈter/ *adj/mf* (*pl* **-teurs**) amateur

amazona *f* (Mit) Amazon; (Equ) horsewoman

Amazonas *m*: **el ∼ the** Amazon

amazónico -ca *adj* Amazonian, Amazon (*before n*)

ámbar *m* (a) ⟨piedra⟩ amber (b) (color) amber

ambición *f* ambition

ambicionar [A1] *vt* to aspire to

ambicioso -sa *adj* ambitious; (codicioso) overambitious

ambidextro -tra *adj* ambidextrous
■ *m,f* ambidextrous person

ambientación *f* (a) (de obra, película) atmosphere (b) (de persona) adjustment

ambientador *m* air freshener

ambiental *adj* environmental

ambientar [A1] *vt* (a) ⟨*obra/película*⟩ to set (b) ⟨*fiesta/local*⟩ to give ... some atmosphere
■ **ambientarse** *v pron* to adjust, adapt

ambiente *m* (a) (entorno físico, social, cultural) environment; **crecí en un ∼ rural** I grew up in a rural environment; **se encuentra realmente en su ∼** he's really in his element; **había una cierta tensión en el ∼** there was a feeling of tension in the air (b) (creado por la decoración, arquitectura, la gente) atmosphere; **un ∼ de camaradería/de fiesta** a friendly/festive atmosphere (c) (animación) life

ambigüedad *f* ambiguity

ambiguo -gua *adj* ambiguous

ámbito *m* (a) (campo, círculo) sphere, field (b) (alcance) scope, range; **el ∼ (de aplicación) de la ley** the scope of the law

ambo *m* (CS) (two-piece) suit

ambos -bas *adj pl* both; **a ∼ lados** on both sides
■ *pron pl* both; **∼ aceptaron la propuesta** they both accepted the proposal; **∼ me gustan** I like both of them

ambulancia *f* ambulance

ambulanciero -ra *m,f* (*m*) ambulance man; (*f*) ambulance woman; **los ∼s** the ambulance crew

ambulante *adj* traveling* (*before n*); **biblioteca ∼** bookmobile (AmE), mobile library (BrE)

ambulatorio¹ -ria *adj* outpatient (*before n*)

ambulatorio² *m* (Esp) outpatients' department

ameba *f* amoeba

amén *m* amen; **∼ de ...** as well as ...

amenaza *f* threat; **no me vengas con ∼s** don't threaten me; **∼ de bomba/muerte** bomb/death threat

amenazador -dora, amenazante *adj* threatening, menacing

amenazar [A4] *vt* ⟨*persona*⟩ to threaten; **nos amenazó con llamar a la policía** he threatened to call the police (b) (dar indicios de): **esas nubes amenazan lluvia** those clouds look threatening
■ ∼ *vi:* **∼ CON hacer algo** to threaten to do sth
■ ∼ *v impers* (Meteo): **amenaza tormenta** there's a storm brewing; **amenaza lluvia** it's threatening to rain

amenizar [A4] *vt* ⟨*conversación/discurso*⟩ to make ... more enjoyable; **la fiesta fue amenizada por un payaso** a clown provided the entertainment for the party

ameno -na *adj* pleasant, enjoyable

América *f* **1** (continente) America; **hacerse la ∼** to make a fortune, get rich; **∼ Central** Central America; **∼ del Norte** *or* **Septentrional** North America; **∼ del Sur** *or* **Meridional** South America; **∼ Latina** Latin America **2** (Esp) (Estados Unidos) America, the States (*pl*)

americana *f* jacket

americanismo *m* Americanism

americano -na *adj/m,f* American

amerindio -dia *adj/m,f* American Indian, Amerindian

ameritado -da *adj* (AmL) meritorious (frml)

ameritar [A1] *vt* (AmL) to deserve

ametralladora *f* machine gun

ametrallar [A1] *vt* to machine-gun

amianto *m* asbestos

amiba *f* amoeba

amigable *adj* ⟨*persona*⟩ friendly; ⟨*trato*⟩ friendly, amicable; **un tono poco ∼** a rather unfriendly manner

amígdalas *fpl* tonsils (*pl*)

amigdalitis *f* tonsillitis

amigo -ga *adj*: **son/se hicieron muy ∼s** they are/they became good friends; **hacerse ∼ de algn** to become friends with sb; **es muy ∼ mío** he's a close friend of mine; **un país ∼** a friendly country; **es muy ∼ de contradecir** he's a great one for contradicting people (colloq); **no es amiga de las fiestas** she's not keen on parties
■ *m,f* friend; **un ∼ mío** a friend of mine; **somos íntimos ∼s** we're very close friends; **¡un momento, ∼!** now, just a minute, pal *o* buddy (AmE) *o* (BrE) mate! (colloq)

amigote *m* (fam) crony (colloq & pej), buddy (AmE colloq), mate (BrE colloq)

amilanar [A1] *vt* to daunt
■ **amilanarse** *v pron* to be daunted

amistad *f* (a) (entre personas, países) friendship; entabló *or* hizo ~ con ella he struck up a friendship with her (b) **amistades** *fpl* (amigos) friends (*pl*)

amistoso -sa *adj* ⟨consejo/palmadita/charla⟩ friendly; ⟨partido⟩ friendly (*before n*)

amnesia *f* amnesia

amnistía *f* amnesty

amnistiado -da *m,f*: person pardoned under an amnesty

amnistiar [A17] *vt* ⟨persona⟩ to grant an amnesty to; ⟨delito⟩ to amnesty

amo, ama *m,f* (de animal, criado) (*m*) master; (*f*) mistress; **son los ~s del pueblo** they own the whole village; *ver tb* AMA

amoblar [A10] *vt* (CS) ▶ AMUEBLAR

amoldable *adj* adaptable

amoldar [A1] *vt* to adjust
■ **amoldarse** *v pron* to adapt; ~se A algo ⟨a un trabajo/una situación⟩ to adjust TO sth; **estos zapatos todavía no se me han amoldado al pie** I haven't broken these shoes in yet

amonestación *f* (reprimenda) warning; (en fútbol) caution, booking

amonestar [A1] *vt* (reprender) to reprimand, admonish (frml); (en fútbol) to caution, book

amoníaco *m* ammonia

amontonar [A1] *vt* (a) (apilar) to pile ... up (b) (juntar) to accumulate
■ **amontonarse** *v pron* «personas» to gather *o* crowd together; «objetos/trabajo» to pile up

amor *m* ⎡1⎤ (a) (sentimiento) love; ~ no correspondido unrequited love; ~ a primera vista love at first sight; ~ al prójimo/a la patria love for one's neighbor/one's country; ~ propio pride, self-esteem; **un gran ~ a la vida/a los animales** a great love of life/animals; **por ~ al arte** (fam) just for the fun of it; **por (el) ~ de Dios** (mendigando) for the love of God; (expresando irritación) for God's sake! (b) (el acto sexual): **hacer el ~ a/con algn** to make love to/with sb (c) (persona, cosa amada) love; ~ mío *or* mi ~ my darling, my love (d) (esmero, dedicación): **hacer algo con ~** to do sth lovingly
⎡2⎤ (fam) (persona encantadora) darling (colloq), dear (colloq)

amoral *adj* amoral

amoratado -da *adj* (de frío) blue; (por un golpe) ⟨piernas/brazos⟩ bruised; **ojo ~** black eye

amordazar [A4] *vt* ⟨persona⟩ to gag; ⟨perro⟩ to muzzle

amorío *m* love affair

amoroso -sa *adj* (a) (AmL) ⟨persona/casa⟩ lovely (b) ⟨vida⟩ love (*before n*); **sus relaciones amorosas** his relationships

amortajar [A1] *vt* to shroud

amortiguador *m* shock absorber

amortiguar [A16] *vt* ⟨golpe⟩ to cushion, absorb; ⟨sonido⟩ to muffle

amortizable *adj* redeemable

amortización *f* (de inversión) recovery; (de préstamo) repayment; (de bonos, hipoteca) redemption

amortizar [A4] *vt* (a) ⟨compra⟩ to recoup the cost of (b) (recuperar) ⟨inversión⟩ to recoup, recover (c) (pagar) ⟨deuda⟩ to repay, amortize (frml); ⟨valores/hipoteca⟩ to redeem

amotinado -da *adj* ⟨soldado/ejército⟩ rebel (*before n*), insurgent (*before n*); ⟨pueblo/ciudadanos⟩ rebellious, insurgent (*before n*)
■ *m,f* insurgent

amotinar [A1] *vt* ⟨tropa⟩ to incite ... to mutiny *o* rebellion; ⟨población/pueblo⟩ to incite ... to rebellion
■ **amotinarse** *v pron* «soldados/oficiales» to mutiny, rebel; «población civil» to rise up

amparar [A1] *vt* (a) (proteger) to protect; **¡que Dios nos ampare!** may the Lord help us! (b) (ofrecer refugio) to shelter, give shelter to
■ **ampararse** *v pron* (a) ~se EN algo ⟨en la ley⟩ to seek protection in sth; **se amparó en su inmunidad diplomática** he used his diplomatic immunity to protect himself (b) (resguardarse) ~se DE *or* CONTRA algo to shelter FROM sth

amparo *m* (a) (protección) protection (b) (refugio) refuge; **dar ~ A algn** to give sb refuge

amperio *m* amp, ampere (frml)

ampliación *f* (a) (de local, carretera) extension; (de negocio) expansion (b) (Com, Fin): **una ~ de capital/de personal** an increase in capital/in the number of staff (c) (de conocimientos, vocabulario) widening (d) (de plazo, período) extension (e) (Fot) enlargement

ampliar [A17] *vt* (a) ⟨local/carretera⟩ to extend; ⟨negocio⟩ to expand (b) ⟨capital/personal⟩ to increase (c) ⟨conocimientos/vocabulario⟩ to increase; ⟨explicación⟩ to expand (on); ⟨campo de acción⟩ to widen, broaden; **para ~ sus estudios** to further her studies (d) ⟨plazo/período⟩ to extend (e) ⟨fotografía⟩ to enlarge, blow up

amplificador *m* amplifier

amplificar [A2] *vt* to amplify

amplio -plia *adj* (a) ⟨calle/valle/margen⟩ wide; ⟨casa⟩ spacious; ⟨vestido/abrigo⟩ loose-fitting; ⟨sonrisa⟩ broad (b) ⟨criterio/sentido⟩ broad; **por amplia mayoría** by a large majority; **una amplia gama de colores** a wide range of colors (c) ⟨garantías/programa⟩ comprehensive

amplitud *f* (a) (de calle, margen) width; (de casa) spaciousness; (de vestido) looseness (b) (de miras, criterios) range; (de facultades, garantías) extent; **la ~ de sus conocimientos** the breadth *o* depth of his knowledge (c) (Fís) amplitude

ampolla *f* ⎡1⎤ (por quemadura, rozamiento) blister ⎡2⎤ (con medicamento) ampoule (frml), vial (AmE), phial (BrE)

ampolleta *f* (Chi) light bulb

amputar [A1] *vt* ⟨brazo/pierna⟩ to amputate

amueblar [A1] *vt* to furnish; **casa amueblada/sin ~** furnished/unfurnished house

amuleto *m* charm, amulet

anacardo *m* cashew (nut)

anaconda *f* anaconda

anacrónico -ca *adj* anachronistic

anacronismo *m* anachronism

ánade *mf* duck

anafe, anafre *m* (Chi, Méx) portable stove

anagrama *m* anagram

anal *adj* anal

anales *mpl* annals (*pl*)

analfabetismo *m* illiteracy

analfabeto -ta *adj* illiterate

■ *m,f* **(a)** (que no sabe leer) illiterate (person) **(b)** (fam & pey) (ignorante) ignoramus (colloq & pej)

analgésico *m* analgesic, painkiller

análisis *m* (*pl* ~) analysis; **hacerse un ~ de sangre** to have a blood test

analista *mf* analyst

analítico -ca *adj* analytic

analizar [A4] *vt* **(a)** (examinar) to analyze*, examine **(b)** (Med, Quím) to analyze* **(c)** (Ling) to parse

■ **analizarse** *v pron* to undergo *o* have analysis

analogía *f* analogy

ananá *m* (*pl* **-nás**) (RPl) pineapple

anaquel *m* shelf

anaranjado -da *adj* orangish (AmE), orangey (BrE)

anarquía *f* anarchy

anárquico -ca *adj* anarchic

anarquismo *m* anarchism

anarquista *adj* anarchist (*before n*)

■ *mf* anarchist

anarquizar [A4] *vt* to cause chaos *o* anarchy in

anatomía *f* anatomy

anatómico -ca *adj* **(a)** (Anat) anatomical **(b)** ⟨asiento/respaldo⟩ anatomically designed

anca *f̱* (de animal) haunch; **~s de rana** frogs' legs; **llevar a algn en ~s** (AmL) to take sb on the crupper

ancestral *adj* ⟨costumbre⟩ ancient; ⟨temor⟩ primitive, ancient

ancestro *m* ancestor

ancho¹ -cha *adj* **1** **(a)** ⟨camino/río/mueble⟩ wide; **a todo lo ~ de la carretera** right across the road; **a lo ~** breadthways *o* (BrE) widthways **(b)** ⟨manos/cara/espalda⟩ broad; **es ~ de espaldas** he's broad-shouldered **(c)** ⟨ropa⟩ loose-fitting, loose; **me queda ~ de cintura** it's too big around the waist for me **2** (cómodo, tranquilo): **allí estaremos más ~s** (Esp) we'll have more room there; **estar/sentirse/ponerse a sus anchas** to be/feel/make oneself at home

ancho² *m* width; **¿cuánto mide de ~?** how wide is it?; **tiene 6 metros de ~** it's 6 meters wide

anchoa *f* anchovy

anchura *f* **(a)** (de camino, río, mueble) width **(b)** (medida): **~ de caderas** hip measurement

ancianato *m* (Col, Ven) old people's home

anciano -na *adj* elderly

■ *m,f* (*m*) elderly man; (*f*) elderly woman

ancla *f̱* anchor; **echar el ~** to drop anchor; **levar ~s** to weigh anchor

anclar [A1] *vt/vi* to anchor

andadera *f* (Méx, Ven) ▶ ANDADOR 1

andador *m* **1** **(a)** (con ruedas) baby walker **(b)** **andadores** *mpl* (amés) baby harness, reins (*pl*) **2** (para ancianos) Zimmer® frame

Andalucía *f* Andalusia

andaluz -luza *adj/m,f* Andalusian

andamio *m*: *tb* **~s** scaffolding

andanzas *fpl* adventures (*pl*)

andar¹ [A24] *vi* **1** **(a)** (esp Esp) (caminar) to walk; **¿has venido andando?** did you come on foot?, did you walk? **(b)** (AmL): **~ a caballo/en bicicleta** to ride (a horse/a bicycle) **(c)** (*en imperativo*) (AmS) (ir): **anda a comprar el periódico** go and buy the newspaper **2** (marchar, funcionar) to work; **el coche anda de maravilla** the car's running *o* (BrE) going like a dream **3** (+ *compl*) **(a)** (estar) to be; **¿cómo andas?** how are you?, how's it going? (colloq); **¿quién anda por ahí?** who's there?; **anda en Londres** he's in London; **anda buscando pelea** he's out for *o* he's looking for a fight; **me anda molestando** (AmL fam) he keeps bothering me **(b)** ~ **CON algn** (juntarse) to mix WITH sb; (salir con) to go out WITH sb; **dime con quién andas y te diré quién eres** a man is known by the company he keeps **(c)** ~ **DETRÁS DE** *or* **TRAS algn/algo** (buscar, perseguir) to be AFTER sb/sth **4** (rondar): **~á por los 60 (años)** he must be around *o* about 60 **5** ~ **CON algo** (esp AmL fam) ⟨con revólver/dinero⟩ to carry sth; ⟨con traje/sombrero⟩ to wear sth **6** (en exclamaciones) **(a)** (expresando sorpresa, incredulidad): **¡anda! ¡qué casualidad!** good heavens! what a coincidence!; **¡anda! ¡mira quién está aquí!** well, well! look who's here! **(b)** (expresando irritación, rechazo): **¡anda! ¡déjame en paz!** oh, leave me alone!; **¡se me ha vuelto a olvidar!** damn! I've forgotten it again! (colloq) **(c)** (instando a hacer algo): **préstamelo, anda** go on, lend it to me!; **¡ándale** (Méx) *or* (Col) **ándele que llegamos tarde!** come on, we'll be late! (colloq)

■ ~ *vt* **1** (caminar) to walk **2** (AmC) (llevar): **no ando dinero** I don't have any money on me; **siempre ando shorts** I always wear shorts

■ **andarse** *v pron* **1** ~**se CON algo: ese no se anda con bromas** he's not one to joke; **ándate con cuidado** take care, be careful **2** (*en imperativo*) (AmL) (irse): **ándate de aquí** get out of here; **ándate luego** get going, get a move on (colloq)

andar² *m*, **andares** *mpl* gait, walk

andarivel *m* **(a)** (AmL) (cable) ferry cable **(b)** (AmS) (en una piscina — carril) lane; (— soga) lane divider

andas *fpl* portable platform (*used in religious processions*); **llevar a algn en ~** (CS) to carry sb on one's shoulders

ándele, ándale *interj*: ▶ ANDAR¹ 6B, C

andén *m* **(a)** (en estación) platform **(b)** (AmC, Col) (acera) sidewalk (AmE), pavement (BrE)

Andes *mpl*: **los ~** the Andes

andinismo *m* (AmL) mountaineering, mountain climbing, climbing

andinista *mf* (AmL) mountaineer, mountain climber, climber

andino -na *adj* Andean

andrajo *m* rag

andrajoso -sa *adj* ragged

anduve, anduviste, etc ▶ ANDAR

anécdota *f* anecdote

anecdótico -ca adj (a) ‹relato› anecdotal (b) ‹interés/valor› incidental

anegar [A3] vt to flood
■ **anegarse** v pron «campo/terreno» to be flooded

anemia f anemia*

anémico -ca adj anemic*
■ m,f anemic person

anestesia f (proceso) anesthesia*; (droga) anesthetic*; **bajo los efectos de la** ~ under (the) anesthetic; **lo operaron con** ~ he was operated on under (an) anesthetic; **sin** ~ without an anesthetic

anestesiar [A1] vt ‹encía/dedo› to anesthetize*; **me** ~**on** they gave me an anesthetic

anestesista mf anesthetist*

anexo¹ -xa adj (a) ‹edificio/local› joined, annexed (b) ‹cláusula› added, appended (frml); ‹documento› (en informe) attached; (en carta) enclosed

anexo² m (a) (edificio) annex* (b) (documento — en informe) appendix; (— en carta) enclosure (c) (Chi) (del teléfono) extension

anfetamina f amphetamine

anfibio¹ -bia adj amphibious; **avión** ~ seaplane

anfibio² m amphibian

anfiteatro m (Arquit) amphitheater*; (Geol) natural amphitheater*; (en la universidad) lecture hall

anfitrión -triona m,f (m) host; (f) hostess

ánfora f‡ (cántaro) amphora

angas (Andes, Méx fam): **por** ~ **o por mangas, nunca estás trabajando** for one reason or another, you're never working; **por** ~ **o por mangas tengo que salir** I have to go out whether I like it or not

ángel m (a) (Relig) angel; ~ **guardián** or **de la guarda** guardian angel; **que sueñes con los angelitos** sweet dreams; **pobre angelito** poor little darling (b) (encanto) charm; **tener** ~ to be charming

angelical adj angelic

angelito m (AmL) dead child; ver tb ÁNGEL

angina f **1** (Arg, Col, Ven) (de la garganta) inflammation of the palate, tonsils and/or pharynx **2** tb ~ **de pecho** angina (pectoris)

anginas fpl (a) (Esp, Méx) (inflamación) throat infection (b) (Méx, Ven) (amígdalas) tonsils (pl)

anglicano -na adj/m,f Episcopalian (in US and Scotland), Anglican (in UK)

anglicismo m Anglicism

angloparlante adj English-speaking

Angola f Angola

angoleño -leña adj/m,f Angolan

angora f angora

angosto -ta adj ‹calle/cama› narrow; ‹falda› tight

anguila f eel

angular adj angular

ángulo m (Mat) angle; (rincón, esquina) corner; (punto de vista) angle; ~ **recto** right angle

anguloso -sa adj angular

angustia f (a) (congoja) anguish, distress; **gritos de** ~ anguished cries (b) (desasosiego) anxiety; **vive con la** ~ **de que…** she's constantly worried that… (c) (Psic) anxiety

angustiado -da adj (a) (acongojado) distressed (b) (preocupado) worried, anxious; **vive angustiada** she lives in a constant state of anxiety

angustiar [A1] vt (a) (acongojar) to distress (b) (preocupar) to worry, make … anxious
■ **angustiarse** v pron (acongojarse) to get distressed, get upset; (preocuparse) to get worried, become anxious

angustioso -sa adj ‹situación› distressing; ‹mirada/grito› anguished

anhelante adj (liter) ‹mirada› longing (before n); **esperaba** ~ **su regreso** she longed o she yearned for his return; **con voz** ~ in a voice full of longing

anhelar [A1] vt (liter) ‹fama/poder› to yearn for, to long for; ~ **hacer algo** to long to do sth, yearn to do sth; **anhelaba que su hijo fuera feliz** his greatest wish was for his son to be happy

anhelo m (liter) wish, desire; **mi mayor** ~ my greatest wish

anhídrido m anhydride; ~ **carbónico** carbon dioxide

anidar [A1] vi «aves» to nest

aniego m (Per) flood

anilla f (a) (de cortina, llavero) ring; (de puro) band; (de lata) ringpull; (de ave) ring (b) **anillas** fpl (Dep) rings (pl)

anillo m **1** (sortija) ring; ~ **de boda/compromiso** wedding/engagement ring; **como** ~ **al dedo** (fam) ‹sentar/quedar› to suit down to the ground; ‹venir› to come in very handy (colloq) **2** (aro, arandela) ring; (de columna) annulet; (en árbol) ring

ánima f‡ (liter) (alma) soul

animación f **1** (bullicio, actividad) activity; **un bar con mucha** ~ a very lively bar **2** (de una velada) entertainment **3** (Cin) animation

animado -da adj **1** (a) ‹fiesta/ambiente› lively; ‹conversación/discusión› lively, animated (b) (optimista, con ánimo) cheerful, in good spirits **2** (impulsado) ~ **DE** or **POR algo** inspired o motivated BY sth

animador -dora m,f (a) (de programa) (m) presenter, host; (f) presenter, hostess (b) **animadora** f (de equipo) cheerleader

animal adj **1** ‹instinto› animal (before n) **2** (fam) (a) (estúpido) stupid (b) (grosero) rude, uncouth
■ m (a) (Zool) animal; ~ **doméstico** (de granja) domestic animal; (mascota) pet (b) (fam) (persona — violenta) brute, animal; (— grosera) lout

animar [A1] vt **1** (a) (alentar) to encourage; (levantar el espíritu) to cheer … up; **tu visita lo animó mucho** your visit cheered him up a lot; ~ **a algn A hacer algo** or **A que haga algo** to

AmC	América Central	Arg	Argentina	Cu	Cuba	Per	Perú
AmL	América Latina	Bol	Bolivia	Ec	Ecuador	RPI	Río de la Plata
AmS	América del Sur	Chi	Chile	Esp	España	Ur	Uruguay
Andes	Región andina	CS	Cono Sur	Méx	México	Ven	Venezuela

encourage sb to do sth **(b)** ⟨*fiesta/reunión*⟩ to liven up; **el vino empezaba a ~los** the wine was beginning to liven them up **(c)** (con luces, colores) to brighten up
2 ⟨*programa*⟩ to present, host
3 (impulsar) to inspire
■ **animarse** *v pron* **(a)** (alegrarse, cobrar vida) «*fiesta/reunión*» to liven up, warm up; «*persona*» to liven up **(b)** (cobrar ánimos) to cheer up; **si me animo a salir te llamo** if I feel like going out, I'll call you **(c)** (atreverse): **¿quién se anima a decírselo?** who's going to be brave enough to tell him?; **no me animo a saltar** I can't bring myself to jump; **al final me animé a confesárselo** I finally plucked up the courage to tell her

anímicamente *adv* emotionally

anímico -ca *adj*: **su estado ~** her state of mind

ánimo *m* **1 (a)** (espíritu): **no estoy con el ~ para bromas** I'm not in the mood for jokes; **tu visita le levantó el ~** your visit cheered her up; **con el ~ por el suelo** in very low spirits, feeling very down-hearted; **apaciguar los ~s** to calm everyone down; **hacerse el ~ de hacer algo** to bring oneself to do sth **(b)** (aliento, coraje) encouragement; **darle ~(s) a algn** (animar) to encourage sb; (con aplausos, gritos) to cheer sb on; **¡~, que ya falta poco para llegar!** come on! it's not far now!; **no tengo ~(s) de** *or* **para nada** I don't feel up to anything
2 (a) (intención, propósito) intention; **lo dije sin ~ de ofender** I meant no offense, no offense intended (colloq) **(b)** (mente, pensamiento) mind

animosidad *f* animosity, hostility; **~ CONTRA algn** animosity *o* hostility TOWARD(S) sb

aniquilar [A1] *vt* ⟨*enemigo/población*⟩ to annihilate, wipe out; ⟨*defensas/instalaciones*⟩ to destroy

anís *m* **(a)** (Bot) (planta) anise; (semilla) aniseed **(b)** (licor) anisette

aniversario *m* anniversary

ano *m* anus

anoche *adv* last night

anochecer¹ [E3] *v impers* to get dark
■ **anochecerse** *v pron* (Chi, Méx) to stay up till really late

anochecer² *m* nightfall; **al ~** at nightfall

anomalía *f* anomaly

anonadado -da *adj* dumbfounded, speechless

anonimato *m* anonymity; **salir del ~** to rise from obscurity

anónimo -ma *adj* anonymous

anorak /ano'rak/ *m* parka (AmE), anorak (BrE)

anorexia *f* anorexia

anoréxico -ca *adj/m,f* anorexic

anormal *adj* abnormal
■ *mf* (fam) idiot

anormalidad *f* abnormality

anotación *f* **(a)** (nota) note **(b)** (AmL) (en fútbol) goal; (en fútbol americano) touchdown; (en básquetbol) point

anotador -dora *m,f* (AmL) (en fútbol) scorer, goalscorer; (en fútbol americano, básquetbol) scorer

anotar [A1] *vt* **1 (a)** (tomar nota de) ⟨*dirección/*

nombre⟩ to make a note of **(b)** ⟨*texto*⟩ to annotate **(c)** (RPI) ▶ APUNTAR *vt* 1B **2** (aml) ⟨*gol/tanto*⟩ to score
■ **anotarse** *v pron* **1** (AmL) ⟨*gol/tanto*⟩ to score **2** (RPI) (inscribirse) ▶ APUNTARSE A

anquilosado -da *adj* **(a)** ⟨*articulación*⟩ (atrofiado) ankylosed; (entumecido) stiff **(b)** ⟨*ideas/economía*⟩ stagnant

anquilosarse [A1] *v pron* **(a)** «*miembro/articulación*» (atrofiarse) to ankylose; (entumecerse) to get stiff **(b)** «*ideas/economía*» to stagnate

ansia *f*: **(a)** (avidez, deseo): **con ~** ⟨*comer/beber*⟩ eagerly; **~ DE algo** ⟨*de paz/libertad*⟩ longing FOR sth, yearning FOR sth; ⟨*de poder*⟩ thirst FOR sth, craving FOR sth; **sentir ~ de hacer algo** to long *o* yearn to do sth; **sus ~s de aprender** her eagerness to learn **(b)** (Psic) anxiety **(c) ansias** *fpl* (Col, Ven fam) (náuseas) nausea

ansiar [A17] *vt* (liter) ⟨*libertad/poder*⟩ to long for, yearn for; **~ hacer algo** to long to do sth

ansiedad *f* **(a)** (preocupación) anxiety; **con ~** anxiously **(b)** (Med, Psic) anxiety

ansioso -sa *adj* **(a)** (deseoso) eager; **está ~ por saberlo** he's eager *o* (colloq) dying to know; **estoy ~ de verlos** I can't wait to see them **(b)** [SER] (fam) (voraz) greedy

antagónico -ca *adj* conflicting

antagonismo *m* antagonism

antagonista *adj* antagonistic
■ *mf* antagonist

antártico -ca *adj* Antarctic

Antártida *f*: **la ~** Antarctica, the Antarctic

ante *prep* **1 (a)** (frml) (delante de) before; **ante el juez** before the judge **(b)** (frente a): **~ la gravedad de la situación** in view of the seriousness of the situation; **iguales ~ la ley** equal in the eyes of the law; **nos hallamos ~ un problema** we are faced with a problem **2 ante todo** (primero) first and foremost; (sobre todo) above all
■ *m* (cuero) suede

anteanoche *adv* the night before last

anteayer *adv* the day before yesterday

antebrazo *m* forearm

antecedente *m* **1 (a)** (precedente) precedent; **no hay ningún ~ de la enfermedad en mi familia** there's no history of the illness in my family **(b)** (causa) cause; **estar/poner a algn en ~s** to be/put sb in the picture **2** (Fil, Ling) antecedent **3 antecedentes** *mpl* (historial) background, record; **~s penales** (criminal) record

anteceder [E1] *vt* to precede, come before; **~ A algo** to come BEFORE sth, precede sth

antecesor -sora *m,f* (predecesor) predecessor; (antepasado) ancestor

antecomedor *m* (Méx) breakfast room

antelación *f*: **con ~** ⟨*reservar/pagar*⟩ in advance; ⟨*avisar/salir*⟩ in plenty of time; **saqué la entrada con un mes de ~** I got the ticket one month in advance; **llegó con dos días de ~** she arrived two days early; **con ~ a su boda** prior to her wedding

antemano: **de ~** (*loc adv*) in advance

antena *f* **1** (de radio, televisión, coche) antenna (AmE), aerial (BrE); **en ~** on the air; **~ colectiva** ⋯✧

communal antenna *o* aerial; ~ **de radar** radar dish; ~ **parabólica** satellite dish; ~ **repetidora** relay mast 2 (Zool) antenna

antenoche *adv* (AmL) the night before last

anteojo *m* (a) (telescopio) telescope (b) **anteojos** *mpl* (esp AmL) ▶ GAFAS

antepasado -da *adj* ⟨*año/semana*⟩ before last ■ *m,f* ancestor

antepenúltimo -ma *adj* (*delante del n*) third from last, antepenultimate (fml) ■ *m,f*: **fue el** ~ **en la carrera** he came third from last on the race; **es el** ~ **en la lista** he's third from bottom on the list

anteponer [E22] *vt* ~ **algo a algo** (*poner delante*) to put sth BEFORE *o* IN FRONT OF sth; (*dar preferencia*) to put sth BEFORE sth

anteproyecto *m* draft; ~ **de ley** bill

anterior *adj* (a) (en el tiempo) previous; **el día** ~ the previous day, the day before; **en épocas** ~**es** in earlier times; ~ **a algo** prior TO sth (b) (en un orden) previous, preceding; **el capítulo** ~ **a este** the previous chapter (c) (en el espacio) front (*before n*); **la parte** ~ the front (part); **las patas** ~**es** the forelegs *o* front legs

anterioridad *f* (fml) anteriority (fml); **con** ~ (antes) before, previously; (con antelación) beforehand, in advance; **con** ~ **a algo** before sth, prior to sth

antes *adv* 1 (a) (con anterioridad) before; **lo compré el día** ~ I bought it the day before; **lo** ~ **posible** as soon as possible (b) (más temprano) earlier; **no pude llegar** ~ I couldn't arrive earlier (c) (*en locs*) **antes de** before; ~ **de Jesucristo** before Christ, BC; **no van a llegar** ~ **de dos horas** they won't be here for two hours; **le daré la respuesta** ~ **de una semana** I will give you my reply within a week; ~ **de lo esperado** earlier than expected; ~ **de hacer algo** before doing sth; ~ **(de) que me olvide** before I forget; **no se lo des** ~ **(de) que yo lo vea** don't give it to him until I've seen it (d) (en el espacio) before 2 (en tiempos pasados) before, in the past; **ya no es el mismo de** ~ he's not the same person any more 3 (a) (indicando orden, prioridad) first; ~ **que nada** first of all; **yo estaba** ~ I was here first (b) (indicando preferencia): **¡**~ **me muero!** I'd rather *o* sooner die!; **cualquier cosa** ~ **que eso** anything but that

antiabortista *mf* antiabortionist

antiaborto *adj inv* antiabortion (*before n*)

antiaéreo -rea *adj* antiaircraft (*before n*)

antialérgico -ca *adj* antiallergenic

antibalas *adj inv* bulletproof

antibiótico *m* antibiotic

anticiclón *m* anticyclone

anticipación *f* (antelación): **con (mucha)** ~ (well) in advance; **con un mes de** ~ a month in advance

anticipado -da *adj* ⟨*pago*⟩ advance (*before n*); ⟨*elecciones*⟩ early; **por** ~ in advance

anticipar [A1] *vt* (a) ⟨*viaje/elecciones*⟩ to move up (AmE), to bring forward (BrE) (b) ⟨*dinero/ sueldo*⟩ to advance; **¿nos podría** ~ **de qué se trata?** could you give us an idea of what it is about? ■ **anticiparse** *v pron* (a) ⟨*verano/lluvias*⟩ to be

o come early (b) (adelantarse): **se anticipó a su tiempo** he was ahead of his time; **no nos anticipemos a los acontecimientos** let's not jump the gun

anticipo *m* (a) (del sueldo, dinero) advance (b) (pago inicial) down payment

anticoncepción *f* contraception, birth control

anticonceptivo¹ -va *adj* contraceptive (*before n*); **métodos** ~**s** methods of contraception

anticonceptivo² *m* contraceptive

anticongelante *adj/m* antifreeze

anticuado -da *adj* old-fashioned ■ *m,f*: **eres un** ~ you're so old-fashioned

anticuario -ria *m,f* (a) (persona) antique dealer (b) **anticuario** *m* (tienda) antique shop

anticucho *m* (Bol, Chi, Per) kebab

anticuerpo *m* antibody

antidemocrático -ca *adj* (poco democrático) undemocratic; (opuesto a la democracia) antidemocratic

antideportivo -va *adj* unsportsmanlike

antideslizante *adj* ⟨*superficie/suela*⟩ nonslip; ⟨*neumático/freno*⟩ antiskid (*before n*)

antidisturbios *adj inv* riot (*before n*)

antídoto *m* antidote

antiestético -ca *adj* unsightly

antifaz *m* mask

antigripal *adj* ⟨*vacuna*⟩ flu (*before n*) ■ *m* flu remedy

antiguamente *adv* in the past, in the old days

antigüedad *f* (a) (de monumento, objeto) age; **esas ruinas tienen varios siglos de** ~ those ruins are several centuries old (b) (en el trabajo) seniority (c) (objeto) antique; **tienda de** ~**es** antique shop (d) (época): **en la** ~ in ancient times

antiguo -gua *adj* 1 (a) (viejo) ⟨*ciudad/libro*⟩ old; ⟨*ruinas/civilización*⟩ ancient; ⟨*mueble/ lámpara*⟩ antique, old; ⟨*coche*⟩ vintage, old; ⟨*costumbre/tradición*⟩ old; **el A**~ **Testamento** the Old Testament (b) (veterano) old, long-standing (c) (*en locs*) **a la antigua** in an old-fashioned way; **chapado a la antigua** old-fashioned; **de** *or* **desde antiguo** from time immemorial 2 (*delante del n*) (de antes) old (*before n*), former (*before n*); **la antigua capital del Brasil** the former capital of Brazil 3 (anticuado) old-fashioned

antiguos *mpl*: **los** ~ the ancients

antihéroe *m* antihero

antihigiénico -ca *adj* unhygienic

antiincendios *adj inv* firefighting (*before n*)

antiinflamatorio *m* anti-inflammatory

antillano -na *adj/m,f* West Indian

Antillas *fpl*: **las** ~ the West Indies

antílope *m* antelope

antimanchas *adj inv* stain-resistant

antimisil *adj* antiballistic (*before n*) ■ *m* antiballistic missile

antimonárquico -ca *adj* antimonarchical, antimonarchist (*before n*) ■ *m,f* antimonarchist

antinatural *adj* unnatural

antioxidante *adj* (Quím) antioxidant (*before n*); ⟨*pintura*⟩ antirust (*before n*)

antipatía f dislike, antipathy; **tomarle ~ a algo/algn** to take a dislike to sth/sb
antipático -ca adj (a) ⟨persona⟩ unpleasant; **¡qué tipo más ~!** what a horrible man! **(b)** (fam) ⟨tarea⟩: **esto de planchar es de lo más ~** ironing is such a drag (colloq)
■ *m,f*: **es un ~** he's really unpleasant
antipatriótico -ca adj unpatriotic
antipedagógico -ca adj pedagogically unsound
antiperspirante m antiperspirant
antípodas fpl: **las ~** the antipodes
antirreglamentario -ria adj (Dep): **una jugada antirreglamentaria** (period) **estaba en posición antirreglamentaria** (period) he was offside
antirrobo m antitheft device
antisemita adj anti-Semitic
■ *mf* anti-Semite
antiséptico m antiseptic
antisocial adj antisocial
■ *mf* (Andes period) delinquent
antiterrorista adj antiterrorist (before n)
antítesis f (pl ~) antithesis
antojarse [A1] v pron (+ me/te/le etc): **se me antojó una cerveza** I felt like (having) a beer; **de embarazada se me antojaban las uvas** when I was pregnant, I had a craving for grapes; **hace lo que se le antoja** he does as he pleases; **porque no se me antoja** because I don't feel like it
antojitos mpl (Méx) typical Mexican snacks, usually bought at street stands
antojo m (a) ⟨capricho⟩ whim; **tiene que hacerlo todo a su ~** she has to do everything her own way; **maneja al marido a su ~** she has her husband twisted around her little finger **(b)** (de embarazada) craving **(c)** (en la piel) birthmark
antología f anthology; **de ~** (muy bueno) excellent, fantastic (colloq); (muy malo) terrible
antorcha f torch
antro m (local sórdido) dive (colloq); **~ de perdición** den of iniquity
antropología f anthropology
antropólogo -ga m,f anthropologist
anual adj (a) ⟨cuota/asamblea⟩ annual, yearly; ⟨interés/dividendo⟩ annual; **cinco mil pesetas ~es** five thousand pesetas a year **(b)** ⟨planta⟩ annual
anualidad f (inversión) annuity; (cuota anual) annual payment (o subscription etc)
anuario m yearbook
anudar [A1] vt ⟨cordón/corbata⟩ to tie
■ **anudarse** v pron (refl) ⟨corbata/pañuelo⟩ to tie
anulación f (de contrato, viaje) cancellation; (de matrimonio) annulment; (de sentencia) quashing, overturning; **protestó la ~ del gol** he protested when the goal was disallowed
anular vt (a) ⟨contrato/viaje⟩ to cancel; ⟨matrimonio⟩ to annul; ⟨fallo/sentencia⟩ to quash, overturn; ⟨resultado⟩ to declare ... null and void; ⟨tanto/gol⟩ to disallow **(b)** ⟨cheque⟩ (destruir) to cancel; (dar orden de no pagar) to stop
■ m finger ring
anunciador -dora m,f, **anunciante** mf advertiser
anunciar [A1] vt (a) ⟨noticia/decisión⟩ to

announce, make ... public; ⟨lluvias/tormentas⟩ to forecast **(b)** (frml) ⟨persona⟩ to announce **(c)** ⟨producto⟩ to advertise, promote
anuncio m (a) (de noticia) announcement; (presagio) sign, omen **(b)** (en periódico) advertisement, ad (colloq); (en televisión) commercial; **~s clasificados** or **por palabras** classified advertisements (pl)
anverso m obverse
anzuelo m hook; **morder** or **tragarse el ~** to swallow o take the bait
añadir [I1] vt to add
añejo -ja adj ⟨vino/queso⟩ mature; ⟨costumbre⟩ old, ancient
añicos mpl: **hacerse ~** to shatter; **tiró el florero y lo hizo ~** he knocked the vase over and smashed it to smithereens
año m **1** (período) year; **los ~s 50** the 50s; **el ~ pasado** last year; **una vez al ~** once a year; **hace ~s que no lo veo** I haven't seen him for o in years; **el ~ de la pera** or **de Maricastaña** (fam): **ese peinado es del ~ de la pera** that hairstyle went out with the ark (colloq), that hairstyle is really old-fashioned; **un disco del ~ de la pera** a record that's really ancient; **~ bisiesto** leap year; **~ fiscal** fiscal year (AmE), tax year (BrE); **~ luz** light year; **A~ Nuevo** New Year
2 (indicando edad): **soltero, de 30 ~s de edad** single, 30 years old o (frml) 30 years of age; **¿cuántos ~s tienes?** how old are you?; **tengo 14 ~s** I'm 14 (years old); **hoy cumple 29 ~s** she's 29 today; **ya debe de tener sus añitos** he must be getting on (a bit); **quitarse ~s: se quita ~s** she's older than she admits o says
3 (curso) year; **~ académico/escolar** academic/school year
añoranza f yearning; **siente ~ de** or **por su país** he yearns for his country
añorar [A1] vt ⟨patria/tranquilidad⟩ to yearn for; ⟨persona⟩ to miss
aorta f aorta
apabullante adj ⟨victoria/éxito⟩ resounding (before n), overwhelming; ⟨rapidez/habilidad⟩ incredible, extraordinary; ⟨personalidad⟩ overpowering
apabullar [A1] vt (vencer) to overwhelm, crush; (dejar confuso) to overwhelm
apache adj Apache (before n)
■ *mf* Apache
apachurrar [A1] vt (AmL fam) to squash
apacible adj ⟨carácter/persona⟩ calm, placid; ⟨vida⟩ quiet, peaceful; ⟨clima⟩ mild; ⟨mar⟩ calm; ⟨viento⟩ gentle
apaciguar [A16] vt ⟨ánimos⟩ to pacify; ⟨persona⟩ to calm ... down, to pacify
■ **apaciguarse** v pron «persona» to calm down; «mar» to become calm; «temporal/viento» to abate, die down
apadrinar [A1] vt ⟨niño⟩ to be godfather/godparent to; ⟨boda⟩ to act as PADRINO at; ⟨artista/novillero⟩ to sponsor, be patron to; ⟨político/idea/candidatura⟩ to support, back; ⟨barco⟩ to launch, christen
apagado -da adj **1** ⟨persona⟩ [SER] spiritless, lifeless; [ESTAR] subdued **2** (a) ⟨sonido⟩ muffled **(b)** ⟨color⟩ muted, dull **3** (a) (no encendido): **la** ⋯⟶

televisión/luz está apagada the TV/light is off; **el horno está** ~ the oven is switched off; **con el motor** ~ with the engine off **(b)** ‹volcán› extinct

apagar [A3] vt ‹luz/televisión/motor› to turn off, switch off; ‹cigarrillo/fuego› to put out; ‹vela/cerilla› to put out; (soplando) to blow out
■ **apagarse** v pron «luz/fuego/vela» to go out

apagón m power cut, blackout

apalabrar [A1] vt: **lo había apalabrado pero no llegué a firmar nada** it was all arranged o fixed but I never actually signed anything; **ya tengo apalabrado a un albañil** (fam) I've already fixed up with a builder

apalancar [A2] vt **(a)** (para levantar) to jack up (AmE), to lever up (BrE) **(b)** (para abrir) to force open

apalear [A1] vt **(a)** ‹persona/alfombra› to beat; ‹árbol› to beat the branches of **(b)** ‹arena/carbón› to shovel

apanar [A1] vt (Andes) ▶ EMPANAR

apantallar [A1] vt **1** (Méx) (impresionar) to impress **2** (RPl) (abanicar) to fan

apañar [A1] vt **1** (fam) ‹elecciones› to fix (colloq), to rig **2** (AmS fam) (encubrir) to cover up for
■ **apañarse** v pron (Esp fam) ▶ ARREGLARSE 4

apapachar [A1] vt (Cu, Méx fam) (abrazar) to cuddle; (acariciar) to stroke, caress

apapacho m (Cu, Méx fam) (abrazo) cuddle; (caricia) caress

aparador m **(a)** (mueble) sideboard **(b)** (AmL exc CS) (vitrina) store window (AmE), shop window (BrE)

aparato m **1** **(a)** (máquina): **uno de esos** ~s **para hacer pasta** one of those pasta machines; ~s **eléctricos** electrical appliances **(b)** (de televisión) set; (de radio) receiver **(c)** (dispositivo) device; ~ **ortopédico** surgical appliance; ~ **auditivo** hearing aid **(d)** (Odont) tb ~s braces ‹pl› **(e)** (teléfono) telephone; **ponerse al** ~ to come to the phone **2** (para gimnasia) piece of apparatus; **los** ~s **the** apparatus, the equipment **3** (frml) (avión) aircraft **4** (estructura, sistema) machine; **el** ~ **del partido** the party machine; ~ **circulatorio/digestivo/respiratorio** circulatory/digestive/respiratory system

aparatoso -sa adj ‹gesto› flamboyant; ‹sombrero› showy, flamboyant; ‹caída/accidente› spectacular, dramatic

aparcamiento m (Esp) **(a)** (acción) parking **(b)** (lugar — en ciudad) parking lot (AmE), car park (BrE); (— en carretera) rest area o stop (AmE), lay-by (BrE)

aparcar [A2] vt/vi (Esp) to park; ~ **en doble fila** to double-park

aparear [A1] vt ‹animales› to mate; ‹objetos› to match, pair up
■ **aparearse** v pron to mate

aparecer [E3] vi **1** **(a)** «síntoma/mancha» to appear **(b)** «objeto perdido» to turn up; **hizo** ~ **un ramo de flores** he produced a bouquet of

flowers **(c)** (en documento) to appear; **mi nombre aparece en la lista** my name appears on the list **(d)** «revista/libro» to come out **2** «persona» **(a)** (fam) (llegar) to appear, turn up **(b)** (fam) (dejarse ver) to appear, show up (colloq) **(c)** (en película, televisión) to appear
■ **aparecerse** v pron **(a)** «fantasma/aparición» ~se A algn to appear TO sb **(b)** (AmL fam) «persona» to turn up; **¡no te vuelvas a** ~ **por aquí!** don't you dare show your face round here again!

aparejar [A1] vt ‹caballos› (para montar) to saddle; (a carro) to harness

aparejo m (de caballo) tack; (de pesca) tackle; (polea) block and tackle

aparentar [A1] vt **(a)** (fingir) ‹indiferencia/interés› to feign; **quiere** ~ **que no le importa** he's trying to make out he's not bothered about it **(b)** (parecer): **no aparentas la edad que tienes** you don't look your age
■ ~ vi **(a)** «persona» to show off; **solo por** ~ just for show **(b)** «regalo/joya» to look impressive

aparente adj **1** (que parece real) ‹timidez/interés› apparent (before n); **la** ~ **victoria se tornó en derrota** what had seemed like victory turned into defeat **2** (obvio, palpable) apparent, obvious

apariencia f appearance; **un hombre de** ~ **fuerte** a strong-looking man; **a juzgar por las** ~s judging by appearances; **guardar las** ~s to keep up appearances; **las** ~s **engañan** appearances can be deceptive

apartado¹ -da adj **(a)** ‹zona/lugar› isolated **(b)** ‹persona›: **se mantuvo** ~ **de la vida pública** he stayed out of public life; **vive** ~ **de la familia** he has little to do with his family

apartado² m **1** (Corresp) tb ~ **de correos** or ~ **postal** post office box, P.O. Box **2** (de artículo, capítulo) section

apartamento m apartment

apartar [A1] vt **1** **(a)** (alejar) to move ... away; **sus amigos lo** ~**on del buen camino** his friends led him astray; **apartó los ojos** he averted his eyes **(b)** ‹obstáculo› to move, move ... out of the way **(c)** (frml) (de un cargo) to remove **(d)** (separar) to separate
2 (guardar, reservar) to set aside; **aparta un poco de comida para él** put a bit of food aside for him
■ **apartarse** v pron (refl) **(a)** (despejar el camino) to stand aside (b) (alejarse, separarse): **apártate de ahí** get/come away from there; **no se aparta de su lado** he never leaves her side; **¡apártate de mi vista!** get out of my sight!; **se apartó de su familia** she drifted away from her family; **nos estamos apartando del tema** we're getting off the subject

aparte adv **1** (a un lado, por separado): **pon las verduras** ~ put the vegetables to o on one side; **¿me lo podría envolver** ~? could you wrap it separately?; **lo llamó** ~ **y lo reprendió** he called him aside and reprimanded him; **bromas** ~ joking aside; ~ **de** (excepto) apart from; (además

de) as well as; ~ **de eso me encuentro bien** apart
from that I'm all right; ~ **de hacerlos, los diseña**
she designs them as well as making them
2 (además) as well; (por otra parte) anyway,
besides

■ *adj inv*: **esto merece un capítulo** ~ this deserves
a separate chapter; **es un caso** ~ he's a special
case

apasionado -da *adj* ⟨*amor/persona*⟩
passionate; ⟨*discurso*⟩ impassioned
■ *m,f* enthusiast

apasionante *adj* ⟨*obra*⟩ exciting, enthralling;
⟨*tema*⟩ fascinating

apasionar [A1] *vi*: **le apasiona la música** she
has a passion for music; **no es un tema que me
apasione** the subject doesn't exactly fascinate me

apatía *f* apathy

apático -ca *adj* apathetic

apátrida *mf* (a) (sin patria) stateless person (b)
(RPI) (que no ama a su país) unpatriotic person

apearse [A1] *v pron* (frml) (bajarse) to get off,
alight (frml); ~ **DE algo** ⟨*de un tren/caballo/una
bicicleta*⟩ to get OFF sth

apechugar [A3] *vi* (fam) to grin and bear it
(colloq), to put up with it (colloq); ~ **con las
consecuencias** to put up with *o* suffer the
consequences

apedrear [A1] *vt* (a) (tirar piedras a) to throw
stones at (b) (matar a pedradas) to stone (to death)

apego *m* ~ **A algo/algn** attachment TO sth/sb;
tenerle ~ **a algn/algo** to be attached to sb/sth; **les
tiene poco** ~ **a las cosas materiales** he attaches
little importance to material things

apelación *f* appeal

apelar [A1] *vi* (a) (Der) to appeal; ~ **ante el
Tribunal Supremo** to appeal to the Supreme Court
(b) (invocar, recurrir a) ~ **A algo/algn** to appeal TO
sth/sb

apelativo *m* (a) (sobrenombre) name (b) (Ling)
form of address; **un** ~ **cariñoso** a term of
endearment

apellido *m* surname, last name (AmE); ~ **de
soltera/de casada** maiden/married name

apelmazarse [A4] *v pron* (a) ⟨*arroz/pasta*⟩
to stick together (b) ⟨*colchón/cojín*⟩ to go
lumpy; ⟨*lana*⟩ to get *o* become matted

apenar [A1] *vt* to sadden
■ **apenarse** *v pron* **1** (entristecerse): **se sintió
apenado por su muerte** he was saddened by her
death; **se apenó mucho cuando lo supo** he was
very upset *o* sad when he learned of it **2** (AmL
exc CS) (sentir vergüenza) to be embarrassed

apenas *adv* (a) (a duras penas) hardly; ~
podíamos oírlo we could hardly hear him; **hace**
~ **dos horas** only two hours ago (b) (no bien): ~
había llegado cuando ... no sooner had he
arrived than ... (c) (Méx, Ven fam) (recién): ~ **el
lunes la podré ir a ver** I won't be able to go and
see her until Monday; ~ **va por la página 10** he's
only on page 10
■ *conj* (esp AmL) (en cuanto) as soon as

apendejarse [A1] *v pron* (AmL exc CS fam)
(volverse estúpido) to go soft in the head (colloq)

apéndice *m* (a) (del intestino) appendix; (de otro
miembro) appendage; **lo operaron del** ~ his
appendix was removed (b) (de texto, documento)
appendix

apendicitis *f* appendicitis

apergaminado -da *adj* ⟨*papel*⟩
parchment-like; ⟨*piel*⟩ leathery; ⟨*cara*⟩ wizened

aperitivo *m* (a) (bebida) aperitif; **nos invitaron a
tomar el** ~ they invited us for drinks before
lunch (*o* dinner *etc*) (b) (comida) snack, appetizer

apersonarse [A1] *v pron* (a) (comparecer) to
appear (b) (Col) (encargarse) ~ **DE algo** to take
charge OF sth, take sth in hand (c) (CS, Ven fam)
(presentarse) to appear in person

apertura *f* **1** (a) (de caja, sobre, cuenta) opening
(b) (inauguración) opening; **la sesión de** ~ the
opening session (c) (de curso, año académico)
beginning, start (d) (Fot) aperture **2** (actitud
abierta) openness; (proceso) opening-up

apestado -da *adj* (a) (con la peste): **gente
apestada** plague victims (b) ⟨*lugar*⟩: ~ **de
turistas** crawling *o* infested with tourists

apestar [A1] *vi* (fam) to stink (colloq); ~ **A algo**
to stink *o* reek OF sth (colloq)
■ ~ *vt* (fam) to stink out (colloq)

apetecer [E3] *vi* (esp Esp): **me apetece un
helado/pasear** I feel like an ice-cream/going for a
walk; **haz lo que te apetezca** do whatever you
like

apetecible *adj* ⟨*manjar*⟩ appetizing,
mouthwatering; ⟨*puesto*⟩ desirable

apetito *m* appetite; **no tengo** ~ I don't feel
hungry, I'm not hungry; **tiene buen** ~ he has a
good appetite; **esta caminata me ha abierto el** ~
this walk has given me an appetite

apetitoso -sa *adj* ⟨*plato/manjar*⟩ appetizing,
mouthwatering

apiadarse [A1] *v pron* ~ **DE algn** to take pity
ON sb

apiario *m* (AmL) apiary

apicultura *f* beekeeping, apiculture (tech)

apilar [A1] *vt* to pile up, put ... into a pile

apiñarse [A1] *v pron* ⟨*gente*⟩ to crowd
together

apio *m* celery

apiolarse [A1] *v pron* (RPI fam) to wise up
(colloq)

apisonadora *f* road roller, steamroller

apisonar [A1] *vt* (con apisonadora) to roll,
steamroll; (con pisón) to tamp

aplacar [A2] *vt* (a) ⟨*ira*⟩ to soothe; **supo** ~ **los
ánimos** she was able to calm people down (b)
⟨*sed*⟩ to quench; ⟨*hambre*⟩ to satisfy; ⟨*dolor*⟩ to
soothe

aplanadora *f* (AmL) road roller, steamroller

aplanar [A1] *vt* (con niveladora) to level; (con
apisonadora) to roll

aplastante *adj* ⟨*mayoría*⟩ overwhelming;
⟨*victoria/derrota*⟩ overwhelming, crushing;
⟨*lógica*⟩ devastating

aplastar [A1] *vt* **1** (a) (algo blando) to squash;
(algo duro) to crush (b) (hacer puré) ⟨*plátanos/
papas*⟩ to mash **2** (a) ⟨*rebelión*⟩ to crush, quash
(b) ⟨*rival*⟩ to crush, overwhelm; (moralmente) to
devastate

aplaudir [I1] *vt* to applaud
■ ~ *vi* to applaud, clap

aplauso *m* (a) (ovación) applause; **un** ~ **para ...** ⋯

a round of applause for ...; **fuertes ~s** loud applause **(b)** (elogio) praise; **ser digno de ~** to be commendable *o* praiseworthy

aplazamiento *m* **(a)** (de reunión — antes de iniciarse) postponement; (— una vez iniciada) adjournment **(b)** (de pago) deferment

aplazar [A4] *vt* **1** (a) ⟨viaje⟩ to postpone, put off **(b)** ⟨juicio/reunión⟩ (antes de iniciarse) to postpone; (una vez iniciado) to adjourn **(c)** ⟨pago⟩ to defer **2** (RPl, Ven) ⟨estudiante⟩ to fail

aplazo *m* (RPl) fail

aplicable *adj* applicable

aplicación *f* **1** (a) (frml) (de crema) application (frml); (de pintura, barniz) coat, application (frml) **(b)** (de sanción) imposition; (de técnica, método) application; (de plan, medida) implementation **2** (uso práctico) application, use **3** (Col, Ven) (solicitud) application **4** (Inf) application

aplicado -da *adj* ⟨ciencias/tecnología⟩ applied (before n); ⟨estudiante⟩ diligent, hard-working

aplicar [A2] *vt* **1** (frml) ⟨pomada/maquillaje/ barniz⟩ to apply (frml) **2** ⟨sanción⟩ to impose; ⟨descuento⟩ to allow; **el acuerdo se aplica solo a los afiliados** the agreement only applies to members **3** ⟨método/sistema⟩ to put into practice
■ **~** *vi* (Col, Ven) to apply; **~ a un puesto/una beca** to apply for a job/a scholarship
■ **aplicarse** *v pron* to apply oneself

aplique, appliqué *m* **(a)** (lámpara) wall light **(b)** (adorno — en mueble) overlay; (— en prenda) appliqué

aplomo *m* composure

apocado -da *adj* **(a)** [SER] (de poco carácter) timid **(b)** [ESTAR] (deprimido) depressed, down (colloq)

apocalipsis *m* apocalypse

apocarse [A2] *v pron*: **se apocó** she lost all her self-confidence; **no se apoca ante** *or* **por nada** nothing intimidates *o* daunts him

apócope *f or m* apocope; (vocablo) apocopated form

apodar [A1] *vt* to nickname, call

apoderado -da *m,f* **(a)** (Der) proxy, representative; **nombrar a algn ~** to give sb power of attorney **(b)** (de deportista) agent, manager

apoderarse [A1] *v pron* **~ DE algo** ⟨de ciudad/ fortaleza⟩ to seize sth, take sth; **se apoderó del control de la empresa** he took control of the company

apodo *m* nickname

apogeo *m* height

apolillado -da *adj* ⟨ropa⟩ moth-eaten; ⟨madera⟩ worm-eaten; ⟨ideas⟩ antiquated, fusty

apolillarse [A1] *v pron* «ropa» to get moth-eaten; «madera» to get infested with woodworm

apolítico -ca *adj* apolitical

apología *f* apologia (frml); **hizo ~ del terrorismo** he made a statement (*o* speech *etc*) justifying terrorism

apoltronarse [A1] *v pron* (en asiento) to settle oneself

aporrear [A1] *vt* ⟨puerta/mesa⟩ to bang *o* hammer on; ⟨persona⟩ (fam) to beat

aportación *f* **(a)** (contribución) contribution **(b)** (de socio) investment

aportar [A1] *vt* **(a)** (contribuir) ⟨dinero/tiempo/ idea⟩ to contribute **(b)** «socio» to invest
■ **~** *vi* (RPl) (a la seguridad social) to pay contributions

aporte *m* **(a)** (esp AmL) ▶ APORTACIÓN **(b)** (RPl) (a la seguridad social) social security contribution, ≈ National Insurance contribution (*in UK*)

aposento *m* (arc *o* hum) (habitación) chamber (dated)

apostar [A10] *vt* to bet; **te apuesto una cerveza** I bet you a beer; **~ algo POR algo/algn** to bet sth ON sth/sb
■ **~** *vi* to bet; **~ a las carreras** to bet on the horses; **te apuesto (a) que gana** I bet (you) he wins
■ **apostarse** *v pron* **(a)** (recípr): **se ~on una comida** they bet a meal on it **(b)** (enf) to bet

apóstol *m* (Relig) apostle

apostolado *m* (Relig) ministry, preaching

apostólico -ca *adj* apostolic

apóstrofo *m* apostrophe

apoteósico -ca *adj* tremendous

apoteosis *f* **(a)** (exaltación) apotheosis; **cuando salió en escena aquello fue la ~** (fam) the audience went wild when she came on stage (colloq) **(b)** (Teatr) finale

apoyabrazos *m* (*pl* **~**) armrest

apoyacabezas *m* (*pl* **~**) headrest

apoyar [A1] *vt* **1** (hacer descansar) **~** ⟨algo EN algo⟩ to rest (sth ON sth); **apóyalo contra la pared** lean it against the wall **2** (a) (respaldar) ⟨propuesta/persona⟩ to back, support **(b)** ⟨teoría⟩ to support, bear out
■ **apoyarse** *v pron* **1** (para sostenerse, descansar) **~se EN algo** to lean on sth **2** (basarse, fundarse) **~se EN algo** to be based ON sth

apoyo *m* support; **~ A algo** support FOR sth

apreciable *adj* ⟨cambio/mejoría⟩ appreciable, substantial; ⟨suma/cantidad⟩ considerable, substantial

apreciación *f* **1** (a) (percepción, enfoque) interpretation **(b)** (juicio) appraisal, assessment **2** (aprecio, valoración) appreciation; **~ musical** musical appreciation

apreciado -da *adj* ⟨amigo⟩ valued; **su piel es muy apreciada** its fur is highly prized

apreciar [A1] *vt* **1** ⟨persona⟩ to be fond of **2** ⟨interés/ayuda/arte⟩ to appreciate **3** (percibir, observar) to see; **para ~ la magnitud de los daños** in order to appreciate the extent of the damage

aprecio *m* (estima) esteem; **siente gran ~ por él** she holds him in great esteem; **goza del ~ de sus compañeros** she is highly regarded by her colleagues

apremiante *adj* ⟨necesidad⟩ pressing, urgent

apremiar [A1] *vt* (presionar): **me están apremiando para que lo termine** they are putting pressure on me to get it finished; **estamos apremiados de tiempo** we are pushed for *o* short of time
■ **~** *vi* to be urgent; **el tiempo apremia** time is getting on *o* is pressing

aprender [E1] *vi/vt* to learn; **~ A hacer algo** to learn to do sth

■ **aprenderse** v pron (enf) ⟨lección/parte⟩ to learn; **me la aprendí de memoria** I learnt it by heart

aprendiz -diza m,f apprentice, trainee; **es ~ de mecánico** he's an apprentice mechanic

aprendizaje m (a) (proceso) learning (b) (período como aprendiz) apprenticeship, training period

aprensión f (a) (preocupación, miedo) apprehension (b) (asco) squeamishness; **me da ~ ver sangre** I get squeamish at the sight of blood

aprensivo -va adj: **es muy ~** he's such a worrier

apresar [A1] vt (a) ⟨nave⟩ to seize, arrest; ⟨delincuente⟩ to capture, catch (b) «animal» ⟨presa⟩ to capture, catch

aprestarse [A1] v pron (refl) ⟨~se PARA algo/A hacer algo⟩ to prepare o get ready FOR sth/to do sth

apresurado -da adj (a) ⟨despedida⟩ quick, hurried, ⟨visita⟩ rushed, hurried (b) ⟨decisión⟩ rushed, hasty; ⟨respuesta/comentario⟩ hasty

apresurar [A1] vt (a) (meter prisa a) to hurry (b) (acelerar) ⟨proceso/cambio⟩ to speed up; ⟨paso⟩ to quicken

■ **apresurarse** v pron: ¡apresúrate! hurry up!; **no nos apresuremos demasiado** let's not be hasty; **se apresuró a defenderla** he hastened o rushed to her defense

apretado -da adj 1 (a) (ajustado) tight; **me queda muy ~** it is too tight for me (b) (sin dinero): **andamos** or **estamos algo ~s** we're a little short of money (colloq) (c) (apretujado) cramped 2 ⟨calendario/programa⟩ tight; ⟨victoria⟩ narrow 3 (fam) (tacaño) tight (colloq), tightfisted (colloq)

apretar [A5] vt 1 (a) ⟨botón⟩ to press, push; ⟨acelerador⟩ to put one's foot on, press; ⟨gatillo⟩ to pull, squeeze (b) ⟨nudo/tapa/tornillo⟩ to tighten; ⟨puño/mandíbulas⟩ to clench; **apreté los dientes** I gritted my teeth 2 (a) (apretujar): **apretó al niño contra su pecho** he clasped o clutched the child to his breast; **me apretó el brazo con fuerza** he squeezed o gripped my arm firmly (b) (presionar) to put pressure on
■ **~** vi 1 «ropa/zapatos» (+ me/te/le etc) to be too tight; **el vestido le aprieta** the dress is too tight for her 2 (hacer presión) to press down (o in etc)

■ **apretarse** v pron to squeeze o squash together

apretón m (abrazo) hug; **se dieron un ~ de manos** they shook hands

apretujado -da adj cramped; **tuvimos que comer todos ~s** we had to eat all squashed together round the table

apretujar [A1] vt (fam): **no me apretujes, que me haces daño** don't squeeze me so hard, you're hurting me; **me ~on mucho en el tren** I got squashed on the train
■ **apretujarse** v pron to squash o squeeze together

aprieta, aprietas, etc ▶ APRETAR
aprieto m ▶ APURO 2
aprisa adv ▶ DEPRISA
aprisionar [A1] vt to trap
aprobación f (de proyecto de ley, moción) passing; (de préstamo, acuerdo, plan) approval, endorsement; (de actuación, conducta) approval

aprobado m (Educ) pass

aprobar [A10] vt 1 ⟨proyecto de ley/moción⟩ to pass; ⟨préstamo/acuerdo/plan⟩ to approve, sanction; ⟨actuación/conducta⟩ to approve of 2 (Educ) to pass
■ **~** vi «estudiante» to pass

aprontarse [A1] v pron (CS) (refl) to get ready

apropiado -da adj suitable; **el discurso fue muy ~ a la ocasión** the speech was very fitting for the occasion; **no era el momento ~** it wasn't the right moment

apropiarse [A1] v pron **~ (de) algo** to take o (frml) appropriate sth

aprovechable adj usable

aprovechado -da adj 1 (oportunista) opportunistic; **no seas ~** don't take advantage (of the situation) 2 ⟨estudiante⟩ hardworking
■ m,f opportunist

aprovechar [A1] vt (a) ⟨tiempo/espacio/talento⟩ to make the most of; **dinero/tiempo bien aprovechado** money/time well spent; **es espacio mal aprovechado** it's a waste of space (b) ⟨oportunidad⟩ to take advantage of; **aprovecho la ocasión para decirles que ...** I would like to take this opportunity to tell you that ... (c) (usar) to use; **no tira nada, todo lo aprovecha** she doesn't throw anything away, she makes use of everything
■ **~** vi: **aproveché para venir a verte** I thought I'd take the opportunity to come and see you; **¡que aproveche!** enjoy your meal, bon appétit; **aprovechen ahora, que son jóvenes** make the most of it now, while you're young
■ **aprovecharse** v pron (a) (abusar) **~se DE algo/algn** to take advantage of sth/sb, to exploit sth/sb (b) (abusar sexualmente) **~se DE algn** ⟨de una mujer⟩ to take advantage OF sb; ⟨de un niño⟩ to abuse sb

aprovisionar [A1] vt ⟨buque/tropas⟩ to provision, to supply ... with provisions
■ **aprovisionarse** v pron **~se DE algo** to stock up WITH sth

aproximado -da adj ⟨cálculo/traducción/idea⟩ rough (before n); ⟨costo/velocidad⟩ estimated (before n)

aproximar [A1] vt (a) (acercar): **aproximó la mesa a la ventana** she moved (o brought etc) the table over to the window (b) ⟨países⟩ to bring ... closer together
■ **aproximarse** v pron (a) (acercarse) «fecha/persona/vehículo» to approach; **se aproximó a mí** she came up to me (b) **~se A algo** ⟨a la realidad/una cifra⟩ to come close to sth

aprueba, apruebas, etc ▶ APROBAR
aptitud f flair; **tener ~ para los idiomas** to have a flair for languages; **carece de ~es para el ballet** she shows no talent for ballet
apto -ta adj [SER] **~ PARA algo** suitable FOR sth; **no es ~ para el cargo** he's not suitable o right for the job; **~ para el servicio militar** fit for military service; **no ~ para el consumo** not fit for consumption

apuesta f bet; **le hice una ~** I had a bet with him

apuesta, apuestas, etc ▶ APOSTAR
apuesto -ta adj (liter) ⟨hombre/figura⟩ handsome

apunamiento *m* (AmS) altitude *o* mountain sickness

apunarse [A1] *v pron* (AmS) to get altitude *o* mountain sickness

apuntalar [A1] *vt* ⟨edificio/túnel⟩ to shore up, brace; ⟨cimientos⟩ to underpin

apuntar [A1] *vt* **1** (a) (tomar nota de) to make a note of, note down **(b)** (para excursión, actividad) to put ... down
2 (señalar, indicar) to point at; **no la apuntes con el dedo** don't point (your finger) at her
■ **~** *vi* (a) (con arma) to aim; **preparen ... apunten ... ¡fuego!** ready ... take aim ... fire!; **le apuntó con una pistola** she pointed/aimed a gun at him **(b)** (indicar, señalar) to point
■ **apuntarse** *v pron* (a) (inscribirse) **~se** A *or* EN **algo** ⟨a curso⟩ to enroll* ON sth; ⟨a clase⟩ to sign up FOR sth; **me apunté para ir a la excursión** I put my name down for the outing; **~se al paro** (Esp) to register as unemployed, to sign on (BrE colloq) **(b)** (obtener) ⟨tanto⟩ to score; ⟨victoria⟩ to chalk up, achieve

apunte *m* **1** (a) (nota) note **(b) apuntes** *mpl* (Educ) notes ⟨pl⟩; (texto preparado) handout; **tomar** *or* (CS) **sacar ~s** to take notes **2** (a) (Art) sketch; (Lit) outline **(b)** (AmL) (Teatr, TV) sketch **3** (Com) entry

apuñalar [A1] *vt* to stab

apurado -da *adj* **1** (avergonzado) embarrassed **2** (AmL) (con prisa) in a hurry; **andaba ~** he was in a hurry; **a las apuradas** (RPl fam) in a rush **3** (en apuros): **se vio muy ~ para contestar las preguntas** he was hard put to answer the questions; **si te encuentras ~, dímelo** if you run into any difficulties, let me know **4** (a) (agobiado) **~ de trabajo** overwhelmed with work **(b)** (escaso) **~** DE **algo** ⟨de dinero/tiempo⟩ short OF sth

apurar [A1] *vt* **1** ⟨copa/botella⟩: **apuró la cerveza y se fue** he finished (off) his beer and left **2** (meter prisa): **nos están apurando para que lo terminemos** they're pushing us to finish it; **no me apures** (AmL) don't hurry *o* rush me
■ **~** *vi* (Chi) (+ *me/te/le etc*) (urgir): **no me apura** I'm not in a hurry for it
■ **apurarse** *v pron* **1** (preocuparse) to worry **2** (AmL) (darse prisa) to hurry; **¡apúrate!** hurry up!

apuro *m* **1** (vergüenza): **¡qué ~!** how embarrassing!; **me daba ~ pedirle dinero** I was too embarrassed to ask him for money **2** (aprieto, dificultad) predicament; **estar/verse en ~s** to be/find oneself in a predicament *o* tight spot; **me sacó del ~** he got me out of trouble; **me puso en un ~** she put me in a real predicament; **pasaron muchos ~s** they had an uphill struggle *o* they went through a lot **3** (AmL) (prisa) rush; **esto tiene ~** this is urgent

aquel, aquella *adj dem* ⟨pl **aquellos, aquellas**⟩ that; ⟨pl⟩ those

aquél, aquélla *pron dem* ⟨pl **aquéllos, aquéllas**⟩ [The written accent may be omitted when there is no risk of confusion with the adjective] **(a)** (refiriéndose a cosa) that one; ⟨pl⟩ those; **ese no, ~** *or* **aquel** not that one, the *o* that other one **(b)** (refiriéndose a persona): **todo ~** *o* **aquel que lo necesite** (frml) anyone *o* (frml) any person needing it; **el cuento de ~** *or* **aquel que ...** the story about the man who ...

aquello *pron dem* (neutro): **¿qué es ~ que se ve allá?** what's that over there?; **~ que te dije el otro día** what I told you the other day

aquí *adv* **1** (en el espacio): **está ~ dentro** it's in here; **~ mismo** right here; **no soy de ~** I'm not from these parts *o* from around here; **pase por ~** come this way; **viven por ~** they live around here; **el agua me llegaba hasta ~** the water came up to here; **dando vueltas de ~ para allá** going to and fro *o* from one place to another **2** (en el tiempo): **de ~ al 2015** from now until 2015; **de ~ en adelante** from now on; **de ~ a un año** a year from now

ara *f* (altar) altar; (piedra consagrada) altar stone

árabe *adj* **(a)** ⟨país/plato⟩ Arab; ⟨escritura/manuscritos⟩ Arabic **(b)** (Hist) (de Arabia) Arabian; (de los moros) Moorish
■ *mf* **(a)** (de país árabe) Arab **(b)** (Hist) (de Arabia) Arabian; (moro) Moor
■ *m* (idioma) Arabic

Arabia Saudí, Arabia Saudita *f* Saudi Arabia

arado *m* plow* (AmE), plough (BrE)

arancel *m* (tarifa) tariff; (impuesto) duty

arancelario -ria *adj* ⟨derecho/tarifa/barrera⟩ customs (before n)

arandela *f* washer

araña *f* (Zool) spider

arañar [A1] *vt/vi* to scratch

arañazo *m* scratch

arar [A1] *vt/vi* to plow (AmE), to plough (BrE)

araucano -na *adj/m,f* Araucanian

arbitraje *m* **(a)** (en fútbol, boxeo) refereeing; (en tenis, béisbol) umpiring **(b)** (Der, Rels Labs) (acción) arbitration; (resolución) decision, judgment

arbitrar [A1] *vt/vi* **(a)** (en fútbol, boxeo) to referee; (en tenis, béisbol) to umpire **(b)** (en conflicto, disputa) to arbitrate

arbitrario -ria *adj* arbitrary

árbitro -tra *m,f* **(a)** (en fútbol, boxeo) referee; (en tenis, béisbol) umpire; **los ~s de la moda** the arbiters of fashion **(b)** (en conflicto) arbitrator

árbol *m* (Bot) tree; **~ de Navidad** *or* (Andes) **de Pascua** Christmas tree; **~ genealógico** family tree; **los ~es no dejan ver el bosque** you can't see the forest (AmE) *o* (BrE) wood for the trees

arbolado -da *adj* ⟨terreno⟩ wooded; ⟨calle⟩ tree-lined (before n)

arboleda *f* grove

arbusto *m* shrub, bush

arca *f* **1** (cofre) chest; **el A~ de Noé** Noah's Ark **2 arcas** *fpl* (de institución) coffers ⟨pl⟩

---

arcada *f* **1** (Med): **tener ∼s** to retch; **me provocó ∼s** it made me retch **2** (Arquit) arcade; (de puente) arch

arcaico -ca *adj* archaic

arcángel *m* archangel

arce *m* maple

arcén *m* shoulder (AmE), hard shoulder (BrE)

archidiócesis *f* (*pl* ∼) archdiocese

archiduque -quesa *m,f* (*m*) archduke; (*f*) archduchess

archipiélago *m* archipelago

archivador *m* (mueble) filing cabinet; (carpeta) ring binder, file

archivar [A1] *vt* ⟨*documentos*⟩ to file; ⟨*investigación/asunto*⟩ (por un tiempo) to shelve; (para siempre) to close the file on

archivo *m* (a) (local) archive; (conjunto de documentos) *tb* ∼s archives (*pl*), archive; **los ∼s de la policía** the police files *o* records (b) (Inf) file

arcilla *f* clay

arco *m* **1** (Arquit) arch; (Anat) arch; (Mat) arc; ∼ **de triunfo** triumphal arch; ∼ **iris** rainbow **2** (AmL) (en fútbol) goal **3** (a) (Arm, Dep) bow (b) (de violín) bow

arcón *m* large chest

arder [E1] *vi* **1** (quemarse) to burn **2** (estar muy caliente) to be boiling (hot); **estar que arde** «*persona*» to be fuming; **la cosa está que arde** things have reached boiling point **3** (escocer) «*herida/ojos*» to sting, smart

ardid *m* trick, ruse

ardiente *adj* ⟨*defensor*⟩ ardent; ⟨*deseo*⟩ ardent, burning; ⟨*amante*⟩ passionate

ardilla *f* squirrel

ardor *m* (dolor) burning; (escozor) smarting; ∼ **de estómago** heartburn

ardoroso -sa *adj* ardent

arduo -dua *adj* arduous

área *f* area; ∼ **chica** *or* **pequeña** goal area; ∼ **de castigo** penalty area; ∼ **de servicio** service area, services (*pl*)

arena *f* **1** (Const, Geol) sand; ∼ **movediza** quicksand **2** (palestra) arena; **en la ∼ política** in the political arena

arenoso -sa *adj* ⟨*playa/terreno*⟩ sandy

arenque *m* herring; ∼ **ahumado** kipper

arepa *f*: cornmeal roll

arete *m* (Col, Méx) earring

argamasa *f* mortar

Argel *m* Algiers

Argelia *f* Algeria

argelino -na *adj/m,f* Algerian

Argentina *f*: *tb* **la ∼** Argentina

argentino -na *adj* ⟨*gobierno/presidente*⟩ Argentine (*before n*); ⟨*escritor/música*⟩ Argentinian
■ *m,f* Argentinian

argolla *f* ring; ∼ **de compromiso/de matrimonio** (AmL) engagement/wedding ring; **tener ∼** (AmC fam) to have contacts (colloq)

argot *m* (*pl* **-gots**) slang

argüendero -ra *m,f* (Méx fam) gossip

argumentación *f* line of argument (frml)

argumentar [A1] *vt* to argue

argumento *m* (a) (razón) argument (b) (Cin, Lit) plot, story line

aria *f* aria

aridez *f* aridity, dryness

árido -da *adj* arid, dry

Aries *m* (signo, constelación) Aries; **es (de)** ∼ she's an Aries *o* an Arian
■ *mf* (*pl* ∼) (persona) *tb* **aries** Aries, person born under (the sign of) Aries

arisco -ca *adj* (a) (huraño) ⟨*persona*⟩ unfriendly, unsociable; ⟨*animal*⟩ unfriendly (b) [ESTAR] (Méx fam) (enojado) upset, angry

arista *f* (Mat) edge; (de viga) arris; (de bóveda) groin; (en montañismo) arête, ridge

aristocracia *f* aristocracy

aristócrata *mf* aristocrat

aristocrático -ca *adj* aristocratic

aritmética *f* arithmetic

aritmético -ca *adj* arithmetic

arma *f* (a) (Arm, Mil) weapon; ∼ **nuclear** nuclear weapon; ∼ **blanca** *any sharp instrument used as a weapon*; ∼ **de fuego** firearm; **deponer las ∼s** to lay down one's arms; **tomar (las) ∼s** to take up arms; **no llevaba ∼s** he wasn't carrying a weapon; **de ∼s tomar** formidable; **ser un ∼ de doble filo** to be a double-edged sword (b) (instrumento, medio) weapon

armada *f* navy

armadillo *m* armadillo

armado -da *adj* ⟨*lucha/persona*⟩ armed; ∼ **DE** *or* **CON algo** armed with sth

armador -dora *m,f* shipowner

armadura *f* **1** (Hist, Mil) armor*; **2** (Const) framework

armamentista *adj* arms (*before n*)

armamento *m* armaments (*pl*)

armar [A1] *vt* **1** (a) (Mil) ⟨*ciudadanos/país*⟩ to arm, supply ... with arms (b) (equipar) ⟨*embarcación*⟩ to fit out, equip **2** (a) ⟨*estantería/reloj*⟩ to assemble; ⟨*tienda/carpa*⟩ to pitch, put up (b) (AmL) ⟨*rompecabezas*⟩ to do, piece together (c) (Col, RPl) ⟨*cigarro*⟩ to roll **3** (fam) ⟨*alboroto/ruido/lío*⟩ to make; ∼ **jaleo** to kick up *o* make a racket (colloq); ∼ **un escándalo** to kick up a fuss; ∼**la** (fam): **¡buena la has armado!** you've really done it now! (colloq); **la que me armó porque llegué tarde** you should have seen the way he went on because I was late
■ **armarse** *v pron* **1** (a) (Mil) to arm oneself (b) ∼**se DE algo** ⟨*de armas/herramientas*⟩ to arm oneself WITH sth; ∼**se de paciencia** to be patient; ∼**se de valor** to pluck up courage **2** (a) (fam) «*pelea/discusión*» to break out; **¡qué jaleo se armó!** there was a real commotion (b) (fam) «*persona*»: **me armé un lío/una confusión** I got into a mess (colloq)

armario *m* (a) (para ropa — mueble) wardrobe; (— empotrado) closet (AmE), wardrobe (BrE) (b) (de cocina) cupboard; (de cuarto de baño) cabinet

armatoste *m* (fam) huge great thing (colloq)

armazón *m or f* **1** (Const) skeleton; (de avión) airframe; (de barco, mueble) frame; (de gafas) frames (*pl*) **2** (de obra literaria) framework, outline

Armenia *f* Armenia

armenio¹ -nia *adj/m,f* Armenian

armenio² *m* (idioma) Armenian

a

armisticio *m* armistice

armonía *f* harmony

armónica *f* harmonica, mouth organ

armónico -ca *adj* (**a**) (Mús) harmonic (**b**) (armonioso) harmonious

armonioso -sa *adj* harmonious

armonizar [A4] *vt* (**a**) (Mús) to harmonize (**b**) ‹*tendencias/opiniones*› to reconcile, harmonize; ‹*diferencias*› to reconcile

■ ~ *vi* «*estilos/colores*» to blend in, harmonize; ~ CON algo «*color/estilo*» to blend (in) WITH sth

arnés *m* (para niño) baby reins (*pl*); (Dep) harness; (arreos) harness

aro *m* (**a**) (Jueg) hoop (**b**) (Arg, Chi) (para el lóbulo) earring; (en forma de aro) hooped earring (**c**) (de servilleta) napkin ring

aroma *m* (de flores) scent, perfume; (del café, de hierbas) aroma; (del vino) bouquet

aromaterapia *f* aromatherapy

aromático -ca *adj* aromatic

arpa *f*; harp

arpegio *m* arpeggio

arpillera *f* sacking, hessian, burlap (AmE)

arpista *mf* harpist

arpón *m* harpoon; ~ **submarino** speargun

arquear [A1] *vt* ‹*espalda*› to arch; ‹*cejas*› to raise, arch; ‹*estante*› to bow, bend

■ **arquearse** *v pron* «*estante*» to sag, bend; «*persona*» to arch one's back

arqueología *f* archaeology

arqueológico -ca *adj* archaeological

arqueólogo -ga *m,f* archaeologist

arquero *m* [1] (Hist, Mil) archer [2] (AmL) (en fútbol) goalkeeper

arquetipo *m* archetype

arquitecto -ta *m,f* architect

arquitectónico -ca *adj* architectural

arquitectura *f* architecture

arrabal *m* poor quarter o area

arraigado -da *adj* ‹*costumbre*› deeply rooted, deep-rooted; ‹*vicio*› deeply entrenched

arraigar [A3] *vi* «*costumbre*» to become rooted, take root; «*vicio*» to become entrenched; «*planta*» to take root

■ **arraigarse** *v pron* «*costumbres/ideas*» to take root; «*persona*» to settle

arrancar [A2] *vt* [1] ‹*hoja de papel*› to tear out; ‹*etiqueta*› to tear off; ‹*botón/venda*› to pull off; ‹*planta*› to pull up; ‹*flor*› to pick; ‹*diente/pelo*› to pull out; **le arrancó el bolso** he snatched her bag [2] ‹*confesión/declaración*› to extract [3] ‹*motor/coche*› to start

■ ~ *vi* ‹*motor/vehículo*› to start

■ **arrancarse** *v pron* [1] (*refl*) ‹*pelo/diente*› to pull out; ‹*piel/botón*› to pull off [2] (Chi fam) (huir) to run away

arranque *m* (**a**) (Auto, Mec) starting mechanism; **tengo problemas con el** ~ I have problems starting the car (**b**) (arrebato) ~ **DE algo** fit OF sth

arrasar [A1] *vi* ~ CON algn ‹*con contrincante*› to demolish sb; ‹*con enemigo*› to destroy sb; **nuestro equipo volvió a** ~ our team swept to victory again; ~ CON algo: **la inundación arrasó**

con las cosechas the flood devastated the crops; ~**on con toda la comida** they polished off all the food (colloq)

■ ~ *vt* ‹*zona*› to devastate; ‹*edificio*› to destroy

arrastrar [A1] *vt* [1] (**a**) (por el suelo) to drag (**b**) ‹*remolque/caravana*› to tow (**c**) (llevar consigo): **arrastró todo a su paso** it swept away everything in its path; **la corriente lo arrastraba mar adentro** the current was carrying him out to sea [2] (**a**) ‹*problema/enfermedad*›: **arrastra esa tos desde el invierno** that cough of hers has been dragging on since the winter; **vienen arrastrando el problema desde hace años** they've been dragging out the problem for years (**b**) (atraer) to draw; **se dejan** ~ **por la moda** they are slaves to fashion

■ ~ *vi* «*mantel/cortina*» to trail along the ground

■ **arrastrarse** *v pron* (**a**) (por el suelo) «*persona*» to crawl; «*culebra*» to slither (**b**) (humillarse) to grovel, crawl

arrastre *m* (**a**) (acción) dragging; **estar para el** ~ (fam) to be done in (colloq) (**b**) (CS fam) (atractivo) appeal

arre *interj* (a un caballo) gee up!, giddy up!

arrear [A1] *vt* (**a**) ‹*ganado*› to drive, herd; ‹*caballerías*› to spur, urge on (**b**) (AmL fam) ‹*gente*› to chivy* (colloq), to hurry … along (**c**) (AmL fam) (llevar) ~ CON algo/algn to cart sth/sb off (colloq)

arrebatador -dora *adj* ‹*belleza*› breathtaking; ‹*sonrisa*› dazzling; ‹*mirada*› captivating

arrebatar [A1] *vt* (quitar) to snatch

arrebato *m* (**a**) (arranque) ~ **DE algo** fit OF sth; **le dio un** ~ he flew into a rage (**b**) (éxtasis) ecstasy, rapture

arrechar [A1] *vt* (**a**) (AmL vulg) (excitar sexualmente) to turn … on (colloq) (**b**) (AmL fam) (enojar) to bug (colloq)

■ **arrecharse** *v pron* (**a**) (AmL vulg) (sexualmente) «*persona*» to get horny (sl); «*animal*» to come in (AmE) o (BrE) on heat (**b**) (AmL fam) (enfurecerse) to get furious

arrecho -cha *adj* [1] (**a**) (AmL vulg) (sexualmente excitado) ‹*persona*› horny (sl), turned-on (colloq); ‹*animal*› in heat (AmE), on heat (BrE) (**b**) (Col, Ven fam) (valiente) gutsy (colloq) [2] (AmL fam) (enojado) furious, mad (AmE colloq) [3] (AmC, Ven fam) (difícil) tough

arrecife *m* reef

arreglado -da *adj* [1] (**a**) (limpio, ordenado) tidy (**b**) (ataviado) smartly turned out, smart [2] (AmL fam) ‹*partido/elecciones*› fixed (colloq)

arreglar [A1] *vt* [1] ‹*aparato/reloj*› to mend, fix; ‹*zapatos*› to mend, repair; ‹*falda/vestido*› to alter; ‹*calle*› to repair; **el dentista me está arreglando la boca** (fam) the dentist is fixing my teeth (colloq); **esto te** ~**á el estómago** (fam) this'll sort your stomach out (colloq) [2] (**a**) ‹*casa/habitación*› (ordenar) to straighten up, to tidy (up) (BrE); (hacer arreglos en) to do up (colloq) (**b**) (preparar, organizar): **ve arreglando a los niños ¿quieres?** can you start getting the children ready?; **tengo todo arreglado para el viaje** I've got everything ready for the trip; **un amigo me está arreglando los papeles** a friend is sorting out the papers for me; ∼ **una entrevista** to arrange an interview **(c)** (disponer) ⟨*flores/muebles*⟩ to arrange

3 (solucionar) ⟨*situación*⟩ to sort out; ⟨*asunto*⟩ to settle, sort out; **lo quiso ∼ diciendo que …** she tried to put things right by saying that …

■ **arreglarse** *v pron* **1** (refl) (ataviarse): **tarda horas en ∼se** she takes hours to get ready; **no te arregles tanto** you don't need to get so dressed up; **sabe ∼se** she knows how to make herself look good

2 ⟨*pelo/manos*⟩ **(a)** (refl) to do **(b)** (caus): **tengo que ir a ∼me el pelo** I must go and have my hair done

3 (solucionarse) «*situación/asunto*» to get sorted out

4 (fam) (amañarse): **ya me ∼é para volver a casa** I'll make my own way home; **la casa es pequeña pero nos arreglamos** it's a small house, but we manage; **arreglárselas** (fam) to manage; **no sé cómo se las arreglan** I don't know how they manage; **arréglatelas como puedas** sort *o* work it out as best you can; **ya me las ∼é** I'll manage, I'll be OK

5 «*día/tiempo*» to get better, clear up

arreglo *m* **1 (a)** (reparación) repair; **hacerle ∼s a algo** to carry out repairs on sth; **la casa necesita algunos ∼s** the house needs some work done on it; **no tiene ∼** «*reloj/máquina*» it's beyond repair; «*persona*» he/she is a hopeless case **(b)** (de ropa) alteration **(c)** (Mús) *tb* ∼ **musical** musical arrangement **2** (acuerdo) arrangement, agreement

arrellanarse [A1] *v pron*: **se arrellanó en el sofá** he settled himself into the sofa

arremangarse [A3] *v pron* ▶ REMANGARSE

arremeter [E1] *vi* (embestir) to charge; (atacar) to attack; ∼ **CONTRA algo/algn** (acometer) to charge AT sth/sb; (atacar, criticar) to attack sth/sb

arremolinarse [A1] *v pron* «*agua/hojas*» to swirl; «*personas/animales*» to mill around

arrendador -dora *m,f* (*m*) landlord, lessor (frml); (*f*) landlady, lessor (frml)

arrendamiento *m* **1 (a)** (de casa) renting, letting (BrE); (de tierras, local) renting, leasing; **contrato de ∼** tenancy agreement **(b)** (de otra cosa — por el propietario) renting (out); (— por el que la recibe) renting **(c)** (precio — de casa, local) rent; (— de otra cosa) rental

arrendar [A5] *vt* **1** (Der) **(a)** (dar en arriendo) ⟨*casa*⟩ to rent (out), let (BrE); ⟨*local/tierras*⟩ to rent (out), lease **(b)** (tomar en arriendo) ⟨*casa*⟩ to rent; ⟨*local/tierras*⟩ to rent, lease **(c)** (contratar) ⟨*servicios*⟩ to hire **2** (Andes) ⟨*coche/bicicleta*⟩ (dar en arriendo) to rent (out) (AmE), to hire out (BrE); (tomar en arriendo) to rent (AmE), to hire (BrE) **❸ se arriendan coches** cars for rent (AmE), car hire (BrE)

arrendatario -ria *m,f* (de propiedad) lessee, tenant; (de contrata) contractor

arrepentido -da *adj* ⟨*pecador*⟩ repentant; **estaba ∼ de lo que había hecho** he was sorry for *o* feeling remorse for what he had done; **estoy ∼ de haberlo dicho** I regret having said it

arrepentimiento *m* remorse, repentance

arrepentirse [I11] *v pron* **(a)** (lamentar) to be

sorry; ∼ **DE algo** to regret sth; ∼ **DE hacer algo** to regret doing sth **(b)** (cambiar de idea) to change one's mind

arrepienta, arrepintió, etc ▶ ARREPENTIRSE

arrestar [A1] *vt* to arrest

arresto *m* (Der, Mil) **(a)** (detención) arrest; **bajo ∼** under arrest **(b)** (prisión) detention

arriar [A17] *vt* ⟨*bandera/vela*⟩ to lower

arriba *adv* **1 (a)** (lugar, parte): **ahí/aquí ∼** up there/here; **en el estante de ∼** (el siguiente) on the shelf above; (el último) on the top shelf; **ponlo un poco más ∼** put it a little higher up; **la parte de ∼** the top (part); ∼ **del ropero** (AmL) on top of the wardrobe; ∼ **de la cocina está el baño** (AmL) the bathroom is above the kitchen; **de ∼ abajo**: **me miró de ∼ abajo** he looked me up and down; **limpiar la casa de ∼ abajo** to clean the house from top to bottom **(b)** (en edificio) upstairs; **los vecinos de ∼** the people upstairs **(c)** (en escala, jerarquía) above; **órdenes de ∼** orders from above; **las puntuaciones de 80 para ∼** scores of 80 or over

2 (expresando dirección, movimiento): **corrió escaleras ∼** he ran upstairs; **calle ∼** up the street; **miró hacia ∼** he looked up

3 (en interjecciones) **(a)** (expresando aprobación): **¡∼ la democracia!** long live democracy! **(b)** (expresando estímulo) come on!; (llamando a levantarse) get up!

arribista *adj* socially ambitious
■ *mf* arriviste, social climber

arriendo *m* (esp Andes) ▶ ARRENDAMIENTO

arriesgado -da *adj* ⟨*acción/empresa*⟩ risky, hazardous; ⟨*persona*⟩ brave, daring

arriesgar [A3] *vt* **(a)** ⟨*vida/dinero*⟩ to risk **(b)** ⟨*opinión*⟩ to venture
■ **arriesgarse** *v pron*: **¿nos arriesgamos?** shall we risk it *o* take a chance?; **∼se A hacer algo** to risk doing sth

arrimar [A1] *vt* (acercar) to move/bring … closer; **arrimó la cama a** *or* **contra la pared** he pushed *o* moved the bed up against the wall
■ **arrimarse** *v pron* **1** (refl) (acercarse): **se arrimó mucho a la orilla** he went too close to the edge; **arrímate al fuego** come (up) closer to the fire; **se arrimó a** *or* **contra la pared** he moved up against the wall; **∼se A algn** to move closer TO sb; (buscando calor, abrigo) to snuggle up TO sb **2** (Méx, Ven fam) (en casa de algn): **se ∼on en mi casa** they came to live *o* stay with me, they dumped themselves on me (pey)

arrinconado -da *adj* **(a)** (bloqueado) blocked in, boxed in **(b)** (acorralado, acosado) cornered **(c)** (arrumbado) lying around

arrinconar [A1] *vt* **(a)** (poner en rincón) to put … in a corner **(b)** (acosar, acorralar) to corner **(c)** (marginar) to exclude **(d)** (arrumbar) to leave, dump (colloq)

arrocero -ra *adj* ⟨*cultivo/producción*⟩ rice (*before n*); ⟨*región*⟩ rice-growing (*before n*)
■ *m,f* rice grower

arrodillarse [A1] *v pron* to kneel (down)

arrogancia *f* arrogance; **con ∼** arrogantly

arrogante *adj* arrogant, haughty

arrojar [A1] *vt* **1 (a)** (tirar) to throw; (AV) ⋯✣

⟨*bomba*⟩ to drop (**b**) ⟨*lava*⟩ to spew (out); ⟨*humo*⟩ to belch out; ⟨*luz*⟩ to shed **2** (vomitar) to bring up, throw up

■ **arrojarse** *v pron* (*refl*) to throw oneself; ~**se SOBRE** algo/algn «*persona*» to throw oneself ONTO sth/sb; «*perro/tigre*» to pounce ON sth/sb

arrollador -dora *adj* (**a**) ⟨*éxito/mayoría/ victoria*⟩ overwhelming (**b**) ⟨*fuerza/ataque*⟩ devastating (**c**) ⟨*personalidad/elocuencia*⟩ overpowering

arrollar [A1] *vt* (**a**) «*vehículo*» to run over; «*muchedumbre/agua/viento*» to sweep *o* carry away (**b**) (derrotar, vencer) to crush, overwhelm

arropar [A1] *vt* ⟨*niño/enfermo*⟩ (abrigar) to wrap … up; (en la cama) to tuck … in

■ **arroparse** *v pron* (abrigarse) to wrap up warm; (en la cama) to pull the covers up

arroyo *m* (**a**) (riachuelo) stream (**b**) (cuneta) gutter (**c**) (AmC) (torrentera) gully (**d**) (Méx) (Auto) slow lane

arroz *m* rice; ~ **a la cubana** *rice with fried egg, plantain and tomato sauce*; ~ **con leche** rice pudding; ~ **integral** brown rice

arrozal *m* ricefield, paddy

arruga *f* (en piel) wrinkle, line; (en tela, papel) crease

arrugado -da *adj* ⟨*persona/manos/piel*⟩ wrinkled; ⟨*ropa*⟩ wrinkled (AmE), creased (BrE); ⟨*papel*⟩ crumpled

arrugar [A3] *vt* ⟨*piel*⟩ to wrinkle; ⟨*tela*⟩ to wrinkle (AmE), to crease (BrE); ⟨*papel*⟩ to crumple; ⟨*ceño*⟩ to knit; ⟨*nariz*⟩ to screw up; arrugó **el entrecejo** he frowned

■ **arrugarse** *v pron* (**a**) «*persona/piel*» to become wrinkled (**b**) (por acción del agua) ⟨*piel/ manos*⟩ to shrivel up, go wrinkled (**c**) «*tela*» to wrinkle *o* get wrinkled (AmE), to crease *o* get creased (BrE); «*papel*» to crumple

arruinar [A1] *vt* to ruin

■ **arruinarse** *v pron* to be ruined

arrullo *m* (de palomas) cooing; (para adormecer) lullaby

arrumbar [A1] *vt* ▸ ARRINCONAR C, D

arsenal *m* (**a**) (Mil) arsenal; un ~ **de datos** a mine of information (**b**) (Esp) (Náut) navy yard (AmE), naval dockyard (BrE)

arsénico *m* arsenic

arte (*gen m en el singular y f en el plural*) **1** (Art) art; el ~; el ~ **por el** ~ art for art's sake; **no trabajo por amor al** ~ (hum) I'm not working for the good of my health (hum); ~**s gráficas** graphic arts; (**como**) **por** ~ **de magia** as if by magic **2** (habilidad, destreza) art; el ~ **de la conversación** the art of conversation; **tiene** ~ **para arreglar flores** she has a flair *o* gift for flower arranging

artefacto *m* (instrumento) artifact; (dispositivo) device; ~**s de baño** (CS) bathroom fixtures (*pl*), sanitary ware (frml); **un raro** ~ a contraption

arteria *f* artery

arterial *adj* arterial

artesa *f* trough

artesanal *adj*: de fabricación ~ ⟨*muebles*⟩ handcrafted; ⟨*queso*⟩ farmhouse; **productos** ~**es** handicrafts, craftwork

artesanía *f* (**a**) (actividad) handicraft; **una** ~ a piece of craftwork; **objetos de** ~ craftwork, handicrafts (**b**) **artesanías** *fpl* (AmL) (productos) crafts (*pl*), craftwork; **mercado de** ~**s** craft market

artesano -na *m,f* (*m*) craftsman, artisan; (*f*) craftswoman, artisan

ártico -ca *adj* Arctic

Ártico *m*: el ~ (región) the Arctic; (océano) the Arctic Ocean

articulación *f* **1** (**a**) (Anat, Mec) joint (**b**) (organización) organization, coordination **2** (Ling) articulation

articulado -da *adj* articulated

articular [A1] *vt* (Tec, Ling) to articulate

articulista *mf* feature writer, columnist

artículo *m* **1** (Com): ~**s del hogar/de consumo** household/consumer goods; ~ **de primera necesidad** essential item, essential; ~**s de escritorio** stationery; ~**s de tocador** toiletries; ~**s de punto** knitwear **2** (**a**) (en periódico, revista) article; ~ **de fondo** editorial, leader (BrE) (**b**) (de ley) article **3** (Ling) article

artífice *mf* (**a**) (responsable, autor): **fue el** ~ **del secuestro** he planned the kidnapping; **el** ~ **de esta victoria** the architect of this victory (**b**) (artista) (*m*) craftsman, artisan; (*f*) craftswoman, artisan

artificial *adj* ⟨*flor/satélite/sonrisa*⟩ artificial; ⟨*fibra*⟩ man-made, artificial

artificio *m* (**a**) (artimaña) trick, artful device (**b**) (afectación) affectation (**c**) (artilugio) device

artillería *f* artillery

artilugio *m* (**a**) (aparato) device, contraption (**b**) **artilugios** *mpl* (de oficio) equipment

artimaña *f* trick

artista *mf* (**a**) (Arte) artist (**b**) (actor) actor; (actriz) actress; (cantante, músico) artist; **una** ~ **de cine** a movie star (AmE) *o* (BrE) film star

artístico -ca *adj* artistic

artritis *f* arthritis

arveja *f* (AmL) pea

arvejilla, arverjilla *f* (RPl) sweet pea

arzobispado *m* archbishopric

arzobispal *adj* ⟨*sede/comisión*⟩ archiepiscopal (frml)

arzobispo *m* archbishop

as *m* ace

asa *f⌇* (asidero) handle

asadera *f* (RPl) roasting pan *o* dish *o* tin

asadero *m* (Coc) griddle

asado¹ -da *adj* **1** (**a**) ⟨*carne/pollo*⟩ (en horno) roast (*before n*); (con espetón) spit-roast (*before n*); (a la parrilla) barbecued, grilled (**b**) ⟨*castaña/papa*⟩ roast (*before n*); ⟨*papa con piel*⟩ baked **2** (fam) [ESTAR] (acalorado) roasting (colloq)

asado² *m* **(a)** (al horno) roast; ~ **de cordero** roast lamb **(b)** (AmL) (a la parrilla) barbecued meat **(c)** (AmL) (reunión) barbecue

asador¹ *m* (espetón) spit; (aparato — de espetones) rotisserie; (— de parrilla) barbecue

asador² **-dora** *m,f* (RPl) cook (*person who cooks the meat at a barbecue*)

asalariado **-da** *adj* wage-earning (*before n*)
■ *m,f* wage *o* salary earner

asaltante *mf* **(a)** (ladrón) robber **(b)** (atacante) attacker; **los** ~**s de la embajada** those who stormed the embassy

asaltar [A1] *vt* **(a)** (atracar) ‹*banco/tienda*› to hold up, rob; ‹*persona*› to rob, mug **(b)** (tomar por asalto) ‹*ciudad/embajada*› to storm **(c)** (atacar) to attack, assault **(d)** «*idea*» to strike; **me asaltó una duda** I was struck *o* seized by a sudden doubt

asalto *m* ☐1 **(a)** (atraco — a banco, tienda) holdup, robbery; (— a persona) mugging; **un** ~ **a mano armada** an armed robbery *o* raid **(b)** (ataque) attack, assault; **tomar algo por** ~ to take sth by storm ☐2 (en boxeo) round; (en esgrima) bout

asamblea *f* **(a)** (reunión) meeting **(b)** (cuerpo) assembly

asar [A1] *vt* **(a)** ‹*carne/pollo*› (en horno) to roast; (a la parrilla) to grill; (con espetón) to spit-roast **(b)** ‹*castaña/papa*› to roast; ‹*papa con piel*› to bake
■ **asarse** *v pron* **(a)** (en horno) to roast **(b)** (fam) (de calor) to roast (colloq)

asbesto *m* asbestos

ascendencia *f* **(a)** (linaje) descent, ancestry; **es de** ~ **francesa** he is of French descent **(b)** (origen) origin(s); **su** ~ **humilde** her humble origins

ascendente *adj* ‹*movimiento/tendencia*› upward; ‹*astro/marea*› rising

ascender [E8] *vi* ☐1 **(a)** (frml) «*temperatura/ precios*» to rise; «*globo*» to rise, ascend (frml); «*escalador/alpinista*» to climb, to ascend (frml) ☐2 (frml) «*gastos/pérdidas*» ~ **A algo** to amount TO sth ☐3 «*empleado/oficial*» to be promoted; **ascendió rápidamente en su carrera** he advanced rapidly in his career; ~ **al trono** to ascend the throne
■ ~ *vt* ‹*empleado/oficial*› to promote

ascendiente *mf* (antepasado) ancestor

Ascensión *f*: **la** ~ the Ascension

ascenso *m* **(a)** (de temperatura, precios) rise **(b)** (a montaña) ascent; **una industria en** ~ a growing industry **(c)** (de empleado, equipo, oficial) promotion

ascensor *m* elevator (AmE), lift (BrE)

ascensorista *mf* elevator operator (AmE), lift attendant (BrE)

asco *m* **(a)** (repugnancia); **¡qué** ~**!** how revolting!, how disgusting!; **me dio** ~ it made me feel sick; **poner cara de** ~ to make *o* (BrE) pull a face; **tanta corrupción da** ~ all this corruption is sickening **(b)** (fam) (cosa repugnante, molesta): **tienen la casa que es un** ~ their house is like a pigsty; **el parque está hecho un** ~ the park is in a real state (colloq); **¡qué** ~ **de tiempo!** what foul *o* lousy weather!

ascua *f‡* ember; **estar en/tener a algn en** ~**s** (fam) to be on/to keep sb on tenterhooks

aseado **-da** *adj* (limpio) clean; (arreglado) neat, tidy

asear [A1] *vt* (limpiar) to clean; (arreglar) to straighten (up), to tidy up (BrE)
■ **asearse** *v pron* (refl) (lavarse) to wash; (arreglarse) to straighten *o* (BrE) tidy oneself up

asediar [A1] *vt* **(a)** (Mil) ‹*ciudad*› to lay siege to, besiege; ‹*ejército*› to surround, besiege **(b)** (acosar) ‹*persona*› to besiege

asegurado **-da** *adj* insured; **tengo el coche** ~ **a todo riesgo** I have fully comprehensive insurance for the car
■ *m,f* (persona que contrata el seguro) policy-holder; (persona asegurada): **el** ~**/la asegurada** the insured

asegurador **-dora** *adj* ‹*compañía*› insurance (*before n*)
■ *mf* **(a)** (persona) insurer **(b)** **aseguradora** *f* (compañía) insurance company

asegurar [A1] *vt* ☐1 **(a)** (prometer) to assure; **te lo aseguro** I assure you; **asegura no haberlo visto** she maintains that she did not see **(b)** (garantizar) ‹*funcionamiento/servicio*› to guarantee ☐2 (Com, Fin) ‹*persona/casa*› to insure; **aseguró el coche a todo riesgo** she took out fully comprehensive insurance for *o* on the car ☐3 **(a)** (sujetar, fijar) ‹*puerta/estante*› to secure **(b)** ‹*edificio/entrada*› to secure, make … secure
■ **asegurarse** *v pron* ☐1 **(a)** (cerciorarse) to make sure **(b)** (garantizarse, procurarse): **con ese gol se** ~**on el triunfo** by scoring that goal they guaranteed themselves victory ☐2 (Com, Fin) to insure oneself

asemejar [A1] *vt* **(a)** (hacer parecido) to make … (look) like **(b)** (comparar) to compare, liken
■ **asemejarse** *v pron* «*personas*» to be *o* look alike; «*objetos*» to be similar; ~**se A algo/algn** to resemble sth/sb, look like sth/sb

asentado **-da** *adj* **(a)** [ESTAR] (situado): **el pueblo está** ~ **a orillas de un río** the village lies *o* is situated on the banks of a river **(b)** [ESTAR] (establecido) ‹*creencia/tradición*› deep-rooted, deeply rooted; ‹*persona*› settled (in) **(c)** [SER] (esp AmL) (maduro, juicioso) mature

asentamiento *m* settlement

asentar [A5] *vt* ☐1 ‹*campamento*› to set up; ‹*damnificados/refugiados*› to place ☐2 **(a)** ‹*objeto*› to place carefully (*o* firmly *etc*) **(b)** ‹*conocimientos/postura*› to consolidate ☐3 (Com, Fin) to enter
■ **asentarse** *v pron* ☐1 «*café/polvo/terreno*» to settle ☐2 (estar situado) «*ciudad/edificio*» to be situated, be built ☐3 **(a)** (establecerse) to settle **(b)** (esp AmL) (adquirir madurez) to settle down

asentir [I11] *vi* to agree, consent; **asintió con la cabeza** she nodded

aseo *m* (limpieza) cleanliness; ~ **personal** personal hygiene; ❾ **aseos** rest room (AmE), toilets (BrE)

asequible *adj* ‹*precio*› affordable, reasonable; ‹*meta*› attainable, achievable; ‹*proyecto*› feasible; ‹*persona*› approachable; ‹*obra/estilo*› accessible

aserradero *m* sawmill

aserrar [A5] *vt* to saw

aserrín *m* (esp AmL) sawdust

aserrío *m* (Col, Ec) sawmill

aserruchar [A1] *vt* (Chi) to saw

asesinar [A1] *vt* to murder; (por razones políticas) to assassinate

a

asesinato *m* murder; (por razones políticas) assassination

asesino -na *adj* ‹*instinto/odio*› murderous, homicidal; ‹*animal*› killer (*before n*)
■ *m,f* murderer; (por razones políticas) assassin; ~ **a sueldo** hired killer; ~ **en serie** serial killer

asesor -sora *adj* ‹*consejo*› advisory; ‹*arquitecto/ingeniero*› consultant (*before n*)
■ *m,f* advisor*, consultant

asesoramiento *m* advice

asesorar [A1] *vt* to advise
■ **asesorarse** *v pron* ~**se CON** algn to consult sb

asesoría *f* consultancy; ~ **fiscal/jurídica** tax/legal consultancy

asestar [A1] *vt*: **me asestó una puñalada/un puñetazo** he stabbed/punched me

asexuado -da *adj* asexual

asfaltado -da *adj* asphalt (*before n*), asphalted

asfaltar [A1] *vt* to asphalt

asfalto *m* asphalt

asfixia *f* **(a)** (Med) asphyxia, suffocation **(b)** (fam) (agobio) suffocation

asfixiante *adj* **(a)** ‹*gas/humo*› asphyxiating (*before n*) **(b)** (fam) ‹*calor*› suffocating, stifling; ‹*ambiente/relación*› oppressive, stifling

asfixiar [A1] *vt* **(a)** (ahogar) to asphyxiate, suffocate; **murió asfixiado** he died of asphyxiation *o* suffocation **(b)** (agobiar) to suffocate, stifle
■ **asfixiarse** *v pron* **(a)** (ahogarse) to be asphyxiated, to suffocate; (por obstrucción de la tráquea) to choke to death; **me asfixiaba de calor** (fam) I was suffocating in the heat **(b)** (fam) (agobiarse) to suffocate, feel stifled

así¹ *adj inv* like that; **no seas** ~ don't be like that; **con gente** ~ **yo no me meto** I don't mix with people like that; **yo soy** ~ that's the way I am; ~ **es la vida** (fr hecha) that's life; **es un tanto** ~ **de hojas** it's about <u>that</u> many pages; **esperamos horas ¿no es** ~? we waited for hours, didn't we?; **tanto es** ~ **que** … so much so that …

así² *adv* ① (de este modo) like this; (de ese modo) like that; **¿por qué me tratas** ~? why are you treating me like this?; **no le hables** ~ don't talk to him like that; **¡**~ **cualquiera!** that's cheating! (colloq & hum); ~ **es como pasó** this is how it happens; **no te pongas** ~ don't get so worked up; ~ **me podré comprar lo que quiera** that way I'll be able to buy whatever I want; ~ **es** that's right; **¿está bien** ~ **o quieres más?** is that enough, or do you want some more?; **y** ~ **sucesivamente** and so on
② **¡**~ **de fácil!** it's as easy as that; ~ **de alto/grueso** <u>this</u> high/thick
③ (en locs) **así así** (fam) so-so; **así como así** just like that; **¡así me gusta!** (fr hecha) that's what I like to see!; **así nomás** (AmL) just like that; **así pues** so; **así que** (por lo tanto) so; **así y todo** even so; **por así decirlo** so to speak

Asia *f*⸽ Asia

asiático -ca *adj/m,f* Asian, Asiatic

asidero *m* **(a)** (asa) handle **(b)** (punto de sujeción) hand (hold); **sin** ~**s en la realidad** with no grip on reality

asiduo -dua *adj* **(a)** (persistente) ‹*estudiante/lector*› assiduous; ‹*admirador*› devoted **(b)** (frecuente) ‹*cliente*› regular, frequent
■ *m,f* regular

asiento *m* ① **(a)** (para sentarse) seat; ~ **anatómico** anatomically designed seat; **por favor, tome** ~ (frml) please take a seat (frml) **(b)** (de bicicleta) saddle **(c)** (de silla) seat **(d)** (base, estabilidad) base ② (en contabilidad) entry

asignación *f* ① **(a)** (de tarea, función) assignment **(b)** (de fondos, renta) allocation, assignment ② (sueldo) wages (*pl*); (paga) allowance ③ (AmC) (Educ) homework

asignar [A1] *vt* **(a)** (dar, adjudicar) ‹*renta/función/tarea*› to assign; ‹*valor*› to ascribe; ‹*fondos/parcela*› to allocate; **me** ~**on la vacante** I was appointed to the post; **le** ~**on una beca** he was awarded a grant **(b)** (destinar) ‹*persona*› to assign; ~ **a algn A algo** to assign sb TO sth

asignatura *f* subject; ~ **pendiente** (Educ) subject which one has to retake; (asunto sin resolver) unresolved matter

asilado -da *m,f* inmate; ~ **político** political refugee (*who has been granted asylum*)

asilar [A1] *vt* **(a)** (acoger) ‹*anciano/huérfano*› to take … into care; ‹*refugiado*› to grant … asylum **(b)** (internar) to put … in a home
■ **asilarse** *v pron* ‹*anciano/huérfano*› to take refuge; ‹*refugiado*› to seek asylum

asilo *m* ① (Servs Socs) home, institution; (para vagabundos, mujeres maltratadas) shelter; ~ **de ancianos** *or* **de la tercera edad** old people's home ② (Pol) asylum; **pedir** ~ **político** to seek political asylum

asimétrico -ca *adj* asymmetric

asimilación *f* assimilation

asimilar [A1] *vt* ① ‹*alimentos/ideas/cultura*› to assimilate ② (en boxeo) ‹*golpes*› to take, soak up (colloq)

asimismo *adv* **(a)** (también) also **(b)** (igualmente) likewise

asir [I10] *vt* (liter) to seize, grasp; ~ **a algn DE** *or* **POR algo: la asió de un brazo** he seized *o* grasped her arm
■ **asirse** *v pron* (liter) ~**se DE** *or* **A algo: se asió a la cuerda** she grabbed (hold of) *o* seized the rope; **caminaban asidos de la mano** they walked hand in hand

asistencia *f* ① (presencia) attendance; ~ **A algo** attendance AT sth ② (frml) (ayuda) assistance; **prestarle** ~ **a algn** to give sb assistance; ~ **en carretera** breakdown service; ~ **médica** (servicio) medical care; (atención médica) medical attention; ~ **pública** (en CS) municipal health service (*esp for emergencies*); ~ **técnica** after-sales service ③ (Dep) assist

asistencial *adj* welfare (*before n*)

asistenta *f* (Esp) cleaning lady *o* woman

asistente *mf* ① (ayudante) assistant; ~ **social** social worker ② (frml) **los** ~**s** (a una reunión) those present; (a un espectáculo) the audience

asistido -da *adj* assisted

asistir [I1] *vi* (estar presente) ~ **A** algn ‹*a reunión/acto/clase*› to attend sth; **asistió a una sola clase** he only came/went to one class; ~ **a misa** to go to *o* attend Mass
■ ~ *vt* (frml) (ayudar): **en el consulado lo** ~**án** you will receive assistance at the consulate (frml); ~ **a los pobres** to care for the poor

asma *f*⸽ asthma

asmático -ca *adj/m,f* asthmatic

asno *m* (Zool) donkey; (tonto) (fam) dimwit (colloq)

asociación *f* association; **∼ de ideas** association of ideas

asociado -da *adj* associate (*before n*)
■ *m,f* (Com) associate; (de club, asociación) member

asociar [A1] *vt* ⟨*ideas/palabras*⟩ to associate; **∼ algo/a algn CON algo/algn** to associate sth/sb WITH sth/sb; **no logro ∼la con nada** I can't place her
■ **asociarse** *v pron* **(a)** «*empresas/comerciantes*» to collaborate; **∼se CON algn** to go into partnership WITH sb **(b)** «*hechos/factores*» to combine **(c)** (a grupo, club) **∼se A algo** to become a member OF sth

asolar [A1 or A10] *vt* «*guerra/huracán/sequía*» to devastate

asoleada *f* (Andes) (de una persona): **pegarse una ∼** (fam) to sunbathe

asoleado -da *adj* sunny

asolear [A1] *vt* (exponer al sol) ⟨*ropa*⟩ to hang ... out in the sun; ⟨*uvas*⟩ to dry ... in the sun
■ **asolearse** *v pron* (AmL) to sunbathe

asomar [A1] *vi* to show; **empiezan a ∼ los primeros brotes** the first shoots begin to show *o* appear
■ ∼ *vt* ⟨*cabeza*⟩: **asomó la cabeza por la ventanilla** she stuck her head out of the window; **abrió la puerta y asomó la cabeza** she opened the door and stuck her head out/in
■ **asomarse** *v pron*: **∼se POR algo** to lean out OF sth; **se asomó a la ventana** she looked out of the window; **se ∼on al balcón** they came out onto the balcony

asombrar [A1] *vt* to amaze, astonish; **me asombró su reacción** I was astonished *o* taken aback by his reaction
■ **asombrarse** *v pron* to be astonished *o* amazed; **se asombró con los resultados** she was amazed *o* astonished at the results; **yo ya no me asombro por nada** nothing surprises me any more

asombro *m* astonishment; **no salía de su ∼** he couldn't get over his surprise

asombroso -sa *adj* amazing, astonishing

asonante *adj* assonant

asorocharse [A1] *v pron* **(a)** (Chi, Per) (por la altura) to get mountain *o* altitude sickness **(b)** (Chi) (por calor, vergüenza) to flush

aspa *f⁺* (de molino) sail; (de ventilador) blade; (cruz) cross

aspaviento *m*: **deja de hacer ∼s** stop getting in such a flap

aspecto *m* **1** **(a)** (de persona, lugar) look, appearance; **un hombre de ∼ distinguido** a distinguished-looking man; **¿qué ∼ tiene?** what does he look like?; **a juzgar por su ∼** judging by the look of her; **tiene mal ∼** ⟨*persona*⟩ she doesn't look well; «*cosa*» it doesn't look nice **(b)** (de problema, asunto): **no me gusta el ∼ que van tomando las cosas** I don't like the way things are going *o* looking **2** (rasgo, faceta) aspect; **en ese ∼ tienes razón** in that respect you're right

aspereza *f* **1** **(a)** (de superficie, piel) roughness **(b)** (de sabor) sharpness; (de voz, clima) harshness **2** (parte áspera): **usar papel de lija para quitar las ∼s** use sandpaper to remove any roughness; **limar ∼s** to smooth things over

áspero -ra *adj* **1** ⟨*superficie/piel*⟩ rough; ⟨*tela*⟩ coarse **2** **(a)** ⟨*sabor*⟩ sharp **(b)** ⟨*voz/sonido/clima*⟩ harsh **3** **(a)** (en el trato) abrupt, surly **(b)** ⟨*discusión*⟩ acrimonious

aspersor *m* sprinkler

aspiración *f* **1** (deseo, ambición) aspiration **2** (Fisiol) inhalation; (Ling) aspiration; (Mús) breath

aspiradora *f*, **aspirador** *m* (electrodoméstico) vacuum cleaner; **pasé la ∼ por la habitación** I vacuumed *o* (BrE) hoovered the bedroom

aspirante *mf*: **las ∼s al título** the contenders for the title; **ocho ∼s al puesto de redactor** eight candidates *o* applicants for the post of editor

aspirar [A1] *vi* **1** (desear, pretender) **∼ A algo/hacer algo** to aspire TO sth/do sth **2** **(a)** «*aparato*» to suck; «*aspiradora*» to pick up **(b)** (Fisiol) to breathe in **(c)** (AmL) (pasar la aspiradora) to vacuum, hoover (BrE)
■ ∼ *vt* **(a)** «*aparato*» to suck up *o* in; «*aspiradora*» to pick up **(b)** (Fisiol) to inhale **(c)** (Ling) to aspirate

aspirina *f* aspirin

asqueante *adj* sickening, nauseating

asquear [A1] *vt* (dar asco a) to sicken; (aburrir, hartar): **está asqueado de todo** he's fed up with everything (colloq)

asqueroso -sa *adj* **1** **(a)** ⟨*libro/película*⟩ digusting, filthy **(b)** ⟨*olor/comida/costumbre*⟩ disgusting, revolting **(c)** (sucio) filthy **2** (lascivo): **¡viejo ∼!** you dirty old man!

asquiento -ta *adj* (AmL) ▶ ASQUEROSO 1

asta *f⁺* **(a)** (de bandera) flagpole; **con la bandera a media ∼** with the flag at half-mast **(b)** (cuerno) horn **(c)** (de lanza, flecha) shaft

astabandera *f* (Méx) flagpole

asterisco *m* asterisk

asteroide *m* asteroid

astigmatismo *m* astigmatism

astilla *f* **(a)** (fragmento) chip; (de madera, hueso) splinter; **se me metió una ∼ en el dedo** I have a splinter in my finger **(b) astillas** *fpl* (para el fuego) kindling

astillarse [A1] *v pron* «*madera/hueso*» to splinter; «*piedra*» to chip

astillero *m* shipyard

astracán *m* astrakhan

astringente *adj* ⟨*loción*⟩ astringent; ⟨*alimento/medicamento*⟩ binding (*before n*)
■ *m* astringent

astro *m* (Astrol, Astron) heavenly body; (Espec) star

astrología *f* astrology

astrólogo -ga *m,f* astrologist

astronauta *mf* astronaut

astronomía *f* astronomy

astronómico -ca *adj* astronomical

astrónomo -ma *m,f* astronomer

astucia *f* **(a)** (cualidad — de sagaz) astuteness, shrewdness; (— de ladino) (pey) craftiness, cunning; **la ∼ del zorro** the slyness of a fox **(b)** (ardid) trick, ploy

astuto -ta *adj* (sagaz) shrewd, astute; (ladino) (pey) crafty, sly, cunning

a

asueto *m* time off; **tomarse un día de ~** to take a day off

asumir [I1] *vt* **1** **(a)** ⟨*cargo/tarea/responsabilidad*⟩ to take on, assume (frml); ⟨*riesgo*⟩ to take **(b)** (adoptar) ⟨*actitud*⟩ to assume (frml) **(c)** (aceptar) to come to terms with **2** (AmL) (suponer) to assume

asunceno -na, asunceño -ña *adj* of/from Asunción
■ *m,f* person from Asunción

Asunción *f* (Geog) Asunción

asunto *m* **(a)** (cuestión, problema) matter; **~s de negocios** business matters; **~s exteriores** (Esp) foreign affairs; **un ~ muy delicado** a very delicate matter *o* issue; **está implicado en un ~ de drogas** he's mixed up in something to do with drugs; **no es ~ mío/tuyo** it's none of my/your business **(b)** (pey) (relación amorosa) affair

asustado -da *adj* (atemorizado) frightened; (preocupado) worried

asustar [A1] *vt* to frighten; **me asustó cuando se puso tan serio** he gave me a fright when he went all serious
■ **asustarse** *v pron* to get frightened; **me asusté cuando vi que no estaba allí** I got a fright *o* I got worried when I saw he wasn't there; **no se asuste, no es nada grave** there's no need to worry, it's nothing serious

atacante *mf* attacker, assailant (frml)

atacar [A2] *vt* to attack

atado *m* **(a)** (de ropa) bundle **(b)** (CS) (de espinacas, zanahorias) bunch; **ser un ~ de nervios** (CS) to be a bundle of nerves **(c)** (RPl) (de cigarrillos) pack (AmE), packet (BrE)

ataduras *fpl* ties (*pl*)

atajada *f* (CS) save

atajador -dora *m,f* (Méx) (*m*) ballboy; (*f*) ballgirl

atajar [A1] *vt* **1** **(a)** (AmL) (agarrar) ⟨*pelota*⟩ to catch **(b)** (Esp) (interceptar) ⟨*pase/pelota*⟩ to intercept **2** **(a)** ⟨*golpe/puñetazo*⟩ to parry, block **(b)** ⟨*persona*⟩ (agarrar) to stop, catch; (interrumpir, detener) to stop **3** ⟨*enfermedad/problema*⟩ to keep ... in check; ⟨*incendio*⟩ to contain; ⟨*rumor*⟩ to quell

atajo *m* short cut

atañer [E7] *vi* (en *3ᵈ pers*) to concern; **por lo que a mí atañe** as far as I'm concerned

ataque *m* **1** **(a)** (Dep, Mil) attack; **~ aéreo** air strike **(b)** (verbal) attack **2** (Med) attack; **~ de asma** asthma attack; **~ al corazón** heart attack; **~ epiléptico** epileptic fit; **me dio un ~ de nervios** I got into a panic; **un ~ de risa** a fit of hysterics

atar [A1] *vt* **1** **(a)** ⟨*caja/paquete*⟩ to tie; **le até el pelo con una cinta** I tied her hair back with a ribbon **(b)** ⟨*persona/caballo*⟩ to tie ... up; ⟨*cabra*⟩ to tether; **lo ~on de pies y manos** they bound him hand and foot; **ató al perro a un poste** she tied the dog to a lamppost **2** «*trabajo/hijos*» to tie ... down

■ **atarse** *v pron* (*refl*) ⟨*zapatos/cordones*⟩ to tie up, do up; ⟨*pelo*⟩ to tie up

atarantado -da *adj* **(a)** (Col, Méx, Per fam) (por golpe) dazed, stunned **(b)** (Méx, Per fam) (confundido) in a spin, dazed **(c)** (Chi fam) (precipitado) harum-scarum (colloq)

atarantar [A1] *vt* (Col, Méx, Per fam): **con tantas preguntas me ~on** they made my head spin with all their questions; **el golpe lo atarantó** the blow left him dazed
■ **atarantarse** *v pron* **(a)** (Col, Méx, Per fam) (aturdirse, confundirse) to get flustered, get in a dither **(b)** (Chi fam) (precipitarse): **no te atarantes** don't rush into it (colloq)

atardecer¹ [E3] *v impers* to get dark

atardecer² *m* dusk; **al ~** at dusk

atareado -da *adj* busy

atascar [A2] *vt* **(a)** ⟨*cañería*⟩ to block **(b)** (Méx) ⟨*motor*⟩ to stall
■ **atascarse** *v pron* **1** **(a)** «*cañería/fregadero*» to block, get blocked **(b)** «*tráfico*» to get snarled up **2** **(a)** «*mecanismo*» to jam, seize up **(b)** (Méx) «*motor*» to stall

atasco *m* **(a)** (de tráfico) traffic jam; (en proceso) holdup, delay **(b)** (en tubería) blockage

ataúd *m* coffin

ateísmo *m* atheism

atemorizar [A4] *vt* (liter) ⟨*persona*⟩ to frighten, intimidate; ⟨*barrio/población*⟩ to terrorize

Atenas *f* Athens

atención¹ *f* **1** **(a)** (concentración) attention; **pon/presta ~ a esto** pay attention to this; **con ~** attentively **(b)** **llamar la ~:** **se viste así para llamar la ~** he dresses like that to attract attention (to himself); **una chica que llama la ~** a very striking girl; **me llamó la ~ que estuviera sola** I was surprised she was alone; **llamarle la ~ a algn** (reprenderlo) to reprimand sb (frml), to give sb a talking to **2** **(a)** (en hotel, tienda) service; **➓ horario de atención al público** (en banco) hours of business; (en oficina pública) opening hours **(b)** (cortesía): **nos colmaron de atenciones** we were showered with attention *o* (BrE) attentions; **no tuvo ninguna ~ con ella a pesar de su hospitalidad** he didn't show the slightest appreciation despite her hospitality

atención² *interj* **(a)** (para que se atienda) attention; **¡~, por favor!** (your) attention, please! **(b)** (para avisar de peligro) look out!, watch out!

atender [E8] *vi* **(a)** (prestar atención) to pay attention; **~ A algo/algn** to pay attention TO sth/sb **(b)** (cumplir con) **~ A algo** ⟨*a compromisos/gastos/obligaciones*⟩ to meet sth **(c)** (prestar un servicio): **el doctor no atiende los martes** the doctor does not see anyone on Tuesdays; **en esa tienda atienden muy mal** the service is very bad in that store
■ **~** *vt* **1** **(a)** ⟨*paciente*⟩: **¿qué médico la atiende?** which doctor usually sees you?; **los atendieron enseguida en el hospital** they were seen immediately at the hospital; **no tiene quien lo**

---

atienda he has no one to look after him **(b)** ‹*cliente*› to attend to, see to; (en tienda) to serve; **¿la están atendiendo?** are you being served? **(c)** ‹*asunto*› to deal with; ‹*llamada*› to answer; ‹*demanda*› to meet
2 ‹*consejo/advertencia*› to listen to
■ **atenderse** *v pron* (AmL): **¿con qué médico se atiende?** which doctor usually sees you?

atenerse [E27] *v pron* **(a)** (ajustarse, someterse) **~ A algo** ‹*a las reglas*› to abide BY *o* comply WITH sth; ‹*a las órdenes*› to obey sth; ‹*a las consecuencias*› to live WITH *o* abide BY sth; **no sé a qué atenerme** I don't know where I stand **(b)** (limitarse): **si nos atenemos a lo que dijeron ellos ...** if we go by what they said ...; **aténgase a los hechos** confine yourself to the facts

atentado *m* **(a)** (ataque): **un ~ terrorista** a terrorist attack; **un ~ contra el presidente** an assassination attempt on the president **(b)** (afrenta) **~ CONTRA** *or* **A algo** ‹*a honor/dignidad*› affront TO sth; **un ~ contra la moral** an offense against decency

atentamente *adv* **(a)** ‹*escuchar/mirar*› attentively, carefully **(b)** (amablemente) thoughtfully, kindly; **lo saluda ~** (Corresp) sincerely (AmE), yours faithfully/sincerely (BrE)

atentar [A1] *vi*: **~on contra su vida** they made an attempt on her life; **~ contra la seguridad del Estado** to threaten national security

atento -ta *adj* **1** **(a)** (que presta atención) ‹*alumno/público*› attentive; **estar ~ (A algo)** to pay attention (TO sth) **(b)** (alerta): **estáte ~ y avísame si viene alguien** stay alert and let me know if anyone comes; **estar ~ A algo** to be on the alert FOR sth **2** **(a)** (amable) ‹*esposo/anfitrión/camarero*› attentive; **ser ~ CON algn** to be kind TO sb **(b)** (cortés) courteous

atenuante *adj* extenuating
■ *m or f* mitigating factor, extenuating circumstance

atenuar [A18] *vt* **(a)** (disminuir, moderar) ‹*luz*› to dim; ‹*color*› to tone down; **deberías ~ el tono de tus críticas** you should tone down your criticism **(b)** (Der) ‹*responsabilidad*› to reduce, lessen

ateo, atea *adj* atheistic
■ *m,f* atheist

aterrador -dora *adj* terrifying

aterrar [A1] *vt* ‹*persona*› to terrify; **le aterra la idea** she's terrified at the thought

aterrizaje *m* landing; **un ~ forzoso** an emergency landing

aterrizar [A4] *vi* to land, touch down

aterrorizado -da *adj* terrified

aterrorizar [A4] *vt* to terrorize

atesorar [A1] *vt* ‹*dinero*› to amass

atestado -da *adj* packed, crammed; **~ DE algo** packed *o* crammed full OF sth; **el salón estaba ~ (de gente)** the hall was packed *o* crammed (with people)

atestiguar [A16] *vt* **(a)** (Der) to testify **(b)** (probar) to bear witness to

atiborrar [A1] *vt* **~ algo/a algn DE algo** to stuff sth/sb WITH sth; **atiborrado de gente** packed *o* jam-packed with people
■ **atiborrarse** *v pron* **~se DE algo** to stuff oneself WITH sth

ático *m* **(a)** (apartamento) top-floor apartment *o* (BrE) flat; (de lujo) penthouse; (de techo bajo) garret (AmE), attic flat (BrE) **(b)** (desván) attic, loft (BrE)

atienda, atiendas, etc ▶ ATENDER

atinado -da *adj* ‹*respuesta/comentario*› pertinent, spot-on *adj*; ‹*decisión/medida*› sensible, wise; ‹*solución*› sensible

atinar [A1] *vi*: **~ en el blanco** to hit the target; **¡atinaste!** you're dead right!; **no atiné a decir nada** I couldn't say a word; **~ CON algo** ‹*con solución/respuesta*› to hit ON *o* UPON sth, come up WITH sth; **atinaste con el regalo** the gift you got him/her was perfect; **no atinaba con la calle** I couldn't find the street

atizador *m* poker

atizar [A4] *vt* ‹*fuego*› to poke

Atlántico *m*: **el (océano) ~** the Atlantic (Ocean)

Atlántida *f*: **la ~** Atlantis

atlas *m* (*pl* **~**) atlas

atleta *mf* athlete

atlético -ca *adj* **(a)** ‹*club/competición*› athletics (*before n*) **(b)** ‹*figura*› athletic

atletismo *m* athletics

atmósfera *f* atmosphere

atmosférico -ca *adj* atmospheric

atole *m* (Méx) hot corn *o* maize drink

atolladero *m* **(a)** (lugar cenagoso) mire **(b)** (aprieto, apuro) predicament, awkward situation

atolondrado -da *adj* **(a)** [SER] (impetuoso) rash, impetuous; (despistado) scatterbrained **(b)** [ESTAR] (por golpe) dazed, stunned
■ *m,f* scatterbrain

atolondrar [A1] *vt* **(a)** (confundir) to fluster **(b)** ‹«*golpe*»› to daze, stun
■ **atolondrarse** *v pron* **(a)** (confundirse) to get flustered **(b)** (precipitarse): **no te atolondres, piénsalo bien** don't rush into it, think it over carefully

atómico -ca *adj* atomic

atomizador *m* spray, atomizer

átomo *m* atom

atónito -ta *adj* astonished, amazed; **se quedó mirándola ~** he stared at her in amazement

atontado -da *adj* (por golpe, asombro) stunned, dazed; (distraído): **contesta, que estás medio ~** answer me, you're in a daze; *ver tb* ATONTAR

atontar [A1] *vt* ‹«*golpe*»› to stun, daze; **estas pastillas me atontan** these pills make me groggy; **la televisión los atonta** television turns them into vegetables *o* zombies

atorar [A1] *vt* **1** (esp AmL) ‹*cañería*› to block (up) **2** (Méx) (sujetar): **atoramos la puerta con una silla** we jammed the door shut/open with a chair; **atóralo con este alambre** secure it with this bit of wire
■ **atorarse** *v pron* (esp AmL) **(a)** (atragantarse) to choke **(b)** ‹«*cañería*»› to get blocked; ‹«*puerta/cajón*»› to jam; (+ *me/te/le etc*): **se me atoró el cierre** my zipper got stuck; **se le atoró el chicle en la garganta** the chewing gum got stuck in her throat

atormentar [A1] *vt* ‹«*persona*»› (físicamente) to torture; (mentalmente) to torment
■ **atormentarse** *v pron* (*refl*) to torment oneself

atornillar [A1] *vt* to screw on (*o* down *etc*)

atorrante adj (a) (Andes, CS fam) (holgazán) lazy; (desaseado) scruffy (b) (Bol, RPl fam) (sinvergüenza) crooked (c) (Col, Per fam) (pesado, cargante): **no seas ~** don't be such a pain in the neck (colloq)
■ mf (a) (Andes, CS fam) (vagabundo) tramp; (holgazán) good-for-nothing, layabout; (desaseado) slob (colloq) (b) (Bol, RPl fam) (sinvergüenza): **es un ~** he's a bit of a crook (colloq) (c) (Col, Per fam) (pesado, cargante) pain in the neck (colloq)

atosigar [A3] vt (importunar) to pester, hassle (colloq); (presionar) to pressure (AmE), to pressurize (BrE)

atrabancado -da adj (Méx fam) (precipitado) rash, reckless

atracador -dora m,f (de banco) bank robber, raider (journ); (de persona) mugger

atracar [A2] vi «barco» to dock, berth
■ ~ vt (asaltar) ⟨banco⟩ to hold up; ⟨persona⟩ to mug

atracción f attraction; **la ~ más concurrida** the most popular attraction; **una ~ turística** a tourist attraction; **las atracciones están en la playa** the funfair is on the beach; **siente una gran ~ por ella** he feels strongly attracted to her

atraco m (a banco) robbery, raid (journ); (a persona) mugging; **~ a mano armada** armed robbery o (journ) raid

atracón m (fam): **se dio un ~ de paella** he stuffed himself with paella (colloq)

atractivo¹ -va adj attractive

atractivo² m (a) (encanto) charm, attractiveness; **tiene mucho ~** she's very charming; **el mayor ~ de la ciudad** the city's main attraction o appeal (b) (interés) appeal; **para mí viajar no tiene ningún ~** travel holds no appeal to me

atraer [E23] vt (a) (Fís) to attract (b) (traer, hacer venir) to attract; **un truco para ~ al público** a gimmick to attract the public (c) (cautivar, gustar): **se siente atraído por ella** he feels attracted to her; **no me atrae la idea** the idea doesn't attract me o appeal to me (d) ⟨atención/miradas⟩ to attract
■ **atraerse** v pron (a) (ganarse) ⟨amistad⟩ to gain; ⟨interés⟩ to attract (b) (recípr) to attract (each other)

atragantarse [A1] v pron (al tragar) to choke; **se le atragantó una espina** he choked on a fish bone

atraiga, atrajo, etc ▶ ATRAER

atrancar [A2] vt ⟨cañería⟩ to block (up); ⟨puerta/ventana⟩ to bar
■ **atrancarse** v pron (a) «cañería» to get blocked (b) (fam) «persona» (en tarea) to get stuck

atrapar [A1] vt to catch

atrás adv ① (en el espacio) (a) (expresando dirección) back; **muévelo para** or **hacia ~** move it back; **da un paso ~** take one step back (b) ¡~! (como interj) get back! (c) (lugar, parte): **está allí ~** it's back there; **me senté ~** (en coche) I sat in the back; (en clase, cine) I sat at the back; **la parte de ~** the back; **me estaba quedando ~** I was getting left behind; **dejamos ~ la ciudad** we left the city behind us; **estar hasta ~** (Méx fam) to be as high as a kite (colloq)

② (en el tiempo): **sucedió tres años ~** it happened three years ago; **había sucedido tres años ~** it had happened three years earlier o before
③ **atrás de** (loc prep) (AmL) behind

atrasado -da adj ① (a) [ESTAR] ⟨reloj⟩ slow (b) (con respecto a lo esperado): **está muy ~ en los estudios** he's really behind in his studies; **el proyecto está ~** the project is behind schedule; **el tren llegó/salió ~** (AmL) the train arrived/left late; **apúrate que voy ~** (AmL) hurry up, I'm late ② (acumulado, pasado): **tengo mucho sueño ~** I have a lot of sleep to catch up on; **tengo trabajo ~** I'm behind with my work; **todas las cuotas atrasadas** all outstanding payments; **un ejemplar ~** a back number o issue
③ (a) (anticuado, desfasado) ⟨ideas/persona⟩ old-fashioned (b) ⟨país/pueblo⟩ backward

atrasar [A1] vt (a) ⟨reloj⟩ to put back (b) ⟨reunión/viaje⟩ to postpone, put back
■ ~ vi «reloj» to lose time
■ **atrasarse** v pron ① (a) «reloj» to lose time; **se me ha atrasado 15 minutos** it's 15 minutes slow (b) (esp AmL) (llegar tarde) «avión/tren» to be late, be delayed; «persona» to be late ② (a) (en estudios, trabajo, pagos) to fall behind, get behind (b) «país/industria» to fall behind

atraso m (a) (de país, ideas) backwardness (b) (esp AmL) (retraso) delay; **perdona el ~** I'm sorry about the delay; **salió con unos minutos de ~** it left a few minutes late; **viene con una hora de ~** it's (running) an hour late

atravesado -da adj (cruzado): **el piano estaba ~ en el pasillo** the piano was stuck (o placed etc) across the corridor; **un árbol/camión ~ en la carretera** a tree lying across/a truck blocking the road

atravesar [A5] vt ① (a) ⟨río/frontera⟩ to cross; **atravesó el río a nado** she swam across the river (b) «bala/espada» to go through; **le atravesó la pierna** it went through his leg (c) ⟨crisis/período⟩ to go through ② (colocar) to put ... across
■ **atravesarse** v pron: **se nos atravesó un camión** a truck crossed right in front of us; **se me atravesó una espina en la garganta** I got a fish bone stuck in my throat

atraviesa, atraviesas, etc ▶ ATRAVESAR

atrayente adj appealing

atreverse [E1] v pron to dare; **¡anda, atrévete!** go on then, I dare you (to); **no me atrevo a decírselo** I daren't tell him; **¿cómo te atreves a pegarle?** how dare you hit him?; **¿a que conmigo no te atreves?** I bet you wouldn't dare take me on

atrevido -da adj (a) (insolente) sassy (AmE colloq), cheeky (BrE colloq) (b) (osado) ⟨escote/persona⟩ daring; ⟨chiste⟩ risqué; ⟨diseño⟩ bold (c) (valiente) brave

atrevimiento m nerve

atribuir [I20] vt (a) **~ algo A algn/algo** to attribute sth TO sb/sth; **le atribuyen algo que no dijo** they attribute words to him which he did not say; **le atribuyen propiedades curativas** it is held o believed to have healing powers (b) ⟨funciones/poder⟩ to confer
■ **atribuirse** v pron (refl) (a) ⟨éxito/autoría⟩ to claim (b) ⟨poderes/responsabilidad⟩ to assume

atributo *m* (cualidad) attribute, quality; (símbolo) insignia

atril *m* (para partituras) music stand; (para libros) lectern

atrincherar [A1] *vt* to entrench
■ **atrincherarse** *v pron* to entrench oneself

atrocidad *f* (cualidad) barbarity; (acto) atrocity; ¡qué ∼! how atrocious! *o* how awful!

atrofiarse [A1] *v pron* to atrophy

atropellado -da *adj*: ¡qué ∼ eres! you always do things in such a rush!

atropellar [A1] *vt* (a) «coche/camión» to knock … down; (pasando por encima) to run … over (b) ⟨libertades/derechos⟩ to violate, ride roughshod over
■ **atropellarse** *v pron* (a) (al hablar, actuar) to rush (b) (recípr) (empujarse): salieron corriendo, atropellándose unos a otros they came running out, pushing and shoving as they went

atropello *m* (abuso) outrage; ∼ DE *or* A algo violation OF sth

atroz *adj* atrocious

atte. (Corresp) (= **atentamente**): lo saluda ∼ sincerely yours (AmE), yours sincerely/faithfully (BrE)

atuendo *m* (frml) outfit

atún *m* tuna (fish)

aturdimiento *m* (perplejidad) bewilderment; (por golpe, noticia) daze

aturdir [I1] *vt* (a) «música/ruido»: la música te aturdía the music was deafening; este ruido me aturde I can't think straight with this noise (b) (dejar perplejo) to bewilder, confuse (c) «golpe/ noticia/suceso» to stun, daze
■ **aturdirse** *v pron* (confundirse) to get confused *o* flustered; (por golpe, noticia) to be stunned *o* dazed

audacia *f* (valor) courage, daring; (osadía) boldness, audacity

audaz *adj* (valiente) brave, courageous; (osado) daring, bold

audición *f* ⓵ (facultad de oír) hearing ⓶ (prueba) audition ⓷ (RPl) (Rad) program*

audiencia *f* ⓵ (cita) audience; pedir ∼ to seek an audience ⓶ (Der) (a) (tribunal) court (b) (sesión) hearing ⓷ (espectadores, oyentes) audience; un programa de mucha ∼ a program with a large audience; horas de máxima/mayor ∼ peak viewing/prime time

audífono *m* (a) (para sordos) hearing aid, deaf-aid (BrE) (b) (de radio) earphone (c) **audífonos** *mpl* (AmL) headphones (*pl*)

audiolibro *m* audiobook

audiomensajería *f* voice mail

audiovisual *adj* audiovisual
■ *m* audiovisual presentation

auditar [A1] *vt* to audit

auditivo -va *adj* (a) ⟨nervio/conducto⟩ auditory (b) ⟨problemas⟩ hearing (before n)

auditor -tora *m,f* (a) (persona) auditor (b) **auditora** *f* (empresa) auditors (*pl*), firm of auditors

auditoría *f* audit

auditorio *m* (público) audience; (sala) auditorium

auge *m* (a) (punto culminante) peak; en el ∼ de su carrera at the peak *o* height of his career (b) (aumento): la comida vegetariana está en ∼ vegetarian food is on the increase; un período de ∼ económico a period of economic growth

augurar [A1] *vt* ⟨futuro⟩ to predict, foretell

augurio *m* (presagio): sus ∼s no se cumplieron his predictions did not come true; es un ∼ de mala suerte it's (a sign of) bad luck *o* a bad omen

aula ⨍ (a) (en escuela) classroom (b) (en universidad) lecture *o* seminar *etc*) room; ∼ magna main lecture theater* *o* hall

aullar [A23] *vi* «lobo/viento» to howl

aullido *m* howl; los ∼s del perro the howling of the dog

aumentar [A1] *vt* (a) (en general) to increase; ⟨precio/sueldo⟩ to increase, raise (b) (Opt) to magnify
■ ∼ *vi* «temperatura/presión» to rise; «velocidad» to increase; «precio/producción/ valor» to increase, rise; ∼á el frío it will become colder; ∼ DE ⟨de volumen/tamaño⟩ to increase IN sth; aumentó de peso he put on *o* gained weight

aumento *m* (a) (incremento) rise, increase; ∼ de peso increase in weight; ∼ de temperatura rise in temperature; ∼ de precio price rise *o* increase; ∼ de sueldo salary increase, pay raise (AmE), pay rise (BrE) (b) (Opt) magnification; lentes de mucho ∼ glasses with very strong lenses

aun *adv* even; ni ∼ trabajando 12 horas al día (not) even if we worked 12 hours a day; ∼ así, creo que … even so, I think …; ni ∼ así me quedaría even then I wouldn't stay

aún *adv* ⓵ (todavía) (a) (en frases afirmativas o interrogativas) still; ∼ tenemos there's still a month to go; ¿∼ estás aquí? are you still here? (b) (en frases negativas) yet; ∼ no ha llamado she hasn't called yet ⓶ (en comparaciones) even

aunar [A23] *vt* ⟨ideas⟩ to combine
■ **aunarse** *v pron* to unite, come together

aunque *conj* ⓵ (a pesar de que) (a) (refiriéndose a hechos) although; ∼ no estaba bien fue a trabajar although he wasn't well he went to work (b) (respondiendo a una objeción) (+ subjuntivo): es millonario, ∼ no lo parezca he's a millionaire though he may not look it; ∼ no lo creas … believe it or not … ⓶ (refiriéndose a posibilidades, hipótesis) (+ subjuntivo) even if; iré ∼ llueva I'll go even if it rains

au pair /oˈper/ *mf* (*pl* **-pairs**) au pair

aura ⨍ (halo) aura

aureola *f* (a) (Relig) halo, aureole (liter) (b) (de gloria, fama) aura (c) (Astron) aureole, corona (d) (CS) (de mancha) ring

auricular *m* (a) (del teléfono) receiver (b) **auriculares** *mpl* (Audio) headphones (*pl*), earphones (*pl*)

aurora *f* dawn

auscultar [A1] *vt* to auscultate (tech); el médico me auscultó the doctor listened to my chest (with a stethoscope)

ausencia *f* (a) (de persona) absence; *brillar por su* ∼ to be conspicuous by one's absence; el orden brilla por su ∼ there's a distinct lack of order (b) (no existencia) lack, absence (c) (frml) (inasistencia) absence

ausentarse [A1] *v pron* (fml) to go away; pidió permiso para ~ un momento he asked to leave the room (*o class etc*)

ausente *adj* [ESTAR] **(a)** (no presente) absent; todos los alumnos ~s all those pupils who are absent **(b)** (distraído) ⟨*persona*⟩ distracted; ⟨*mirada/expresión*⟩ absent (*before n*)

ausentismo *m* absenteeism; ~ escolar absenteeism, truancy

auspiciar [A1] *vt* **(a)** (patrocinar) ⟨*exposición/función*⟩ to back, sponsor **(b)** (propiciar, facilitar) to foster, promote

austeridad *f* austerity

austero -ra *adj* ⟨*vida/costumbres/estilo*⟩ austere; es ~ en el comer he is frugal in his eating habits

austral *adj* southern

Australia *f* Australia

australiano -na *adj/m,f* Australian

Austria *f* Austria

austriaco -ca, austríaco -ca *adj/m,f* Austrian

autenticar [A2] *vt* **(a)** ⟨*firma/documento*⟩ to authenticate **(b)** (RPl) ⟨*fotocopia*⟩ to attest

autenticidad *f* authenticity

auténtico -ca *adj* **(a)** ⟨*cuadro*⟩ genuine, authentic; ⟨*perla/piel*⟩ real; ⟨*documento*⟩ authentic **(b)** ⟨*interés/cariño/persona*⟩ genuine **(c)** ⟨*pesadilla/catástrofe*⟩ ⟨*delante del n*⟩ real (*before n*)

autista *adj* autistic

auto *m* ⟨1⟩ (esp CS) (Auto) car, automobile (AmE); ~ de carrera (CS) racing car; **autitos chocadores** (RPl) bumper cars ⟨2⟩ (Lit, Teatr) play

autoabastecerse [E3] *v pron* to be self-sufficient; ~ DE *or* EN algo to be self-sufficient in sth

autoadhesivo -va *adj* self-adhesive

autobiografía *f* autobiography

autobomba *m* (RPl) fire engine, fire truck (AmE)

autobús *m* bus; ~ de dos pisos double-decker bus; ~ de línea (inter-city) bus

autocar *m* (Esp) bus, coach (BrE)

autocine *m* drive-in

autocross *m* autocross

autóctono -na *adj* ⟨*flora/fauna*⟩ indigenous, native; el elefante es ~ de la India the elephant is indigenous *o* native to India

autodefensa *f* self-defence

autodeterminación *f* self-determination

autodidacta *mf* self-taught person, autodidact (fml)

autodisciplina *f* self-discipline

auto-escuela, autoescuela *f* driving school

autoestop *m* ▶ AUTOSTOP

autoestopista *mf* hitchhiker

autogol *m* own goal

autografiar [A17] *vt* to autograph

autógrafo *m* autograph

autómata *m* automaton

automático¹ -ca *adj* automatic; es ~, se sienta a ver la tele y se queda dormido (fam) it happens every time, he sits down in front of the TV and falls asleep

automático² *m* **(a)** (Fot) self-timer; (Elec) circuit breaker, trip switch **(b)** (cierre) snap fastener (AmE), press stud (BrE)

automatizado -da *adj* automated

automatizar [A4] *vt* to automate

automedicación *f* self-medication

automercado *m* (AmC) supermarket

automotor¹ -triz *or* **-tora** *adj* (fml) ⟨*vehículo/industria*⟩ motor (*before n*)

automotor² *m* (Ferr) railcar (*diesel or electric motor unit*)

automóvil *m* car, automobile (AmE)

automovilismo *m* motoring; ~ deportivo motor racing

automovilista *mf* motorist

automovilístico -ca *adj* ⟨*carrera*⟩ motor (*before n*); ⟨*accidente*⟩ car (*before n*)

autonomía *f* ⟨1⟩ **(a)** (independencia) autonomy; (Pol) autonomy, self-government; obran con ~ they act autonomously **(b)** (en Esp, comunidad autónoma) autonomous *or* self-governing region ⟨2⟩ (Aviac, Náut) range

autonómico -ca *adj* **(a)** (independiente) autonomous **(b)** ⟨*presidente/elecciones*⟩ (en Esp) regional

autónomo -ma *adj* **(a)** ⟨*departamento/entidad*⟩ autonomous **(b)** (Pol) (en Esp) ⟨*región*⟩ autonomous **(c)** ⟨*trabajador*⟩ self-employed; ⟨*fotógrafo/periodista*⟩ freelance ■ *m,f* (trabajador) self-employed worker *o* person; (fotógrafo, periodista) freelancer

autopista *f* expressway (AmE), motorway (BrE); ~ de peaje *or* (Méx) de cuota turnpike (road) (AmE), toll motorway (BrE); la ~ de la información (Inf) the information superhighway

autopsia *f* autopsy, post mortem; hacerle la ~ a algn to perform an autopsy *o* a post mortem on sb

autor -tora *m,f* **(a)** (de libro, poema) author, writer; (de canción) writer; (de obra teatral) playwright **(b)** (de delito) perpetrator (fml); el ~ del gol the goalscorer

autoridad *f* ⟨1⟩ **(a)** (poder, competencia) authority **(b)** (persona, institución): la máxima ~ en el ministerio the top official in the ministry; se entregó a las ~es she gave herself up to the authorities ⟨2⟩ (experto) authority; una ~ en la materia an authority on the subject

autoritario -ria *adj* authoritarian

autorización *f* authorization (fml); los menores necesitan la ~ paterna minors need their parents' consent; no tiene ~ de sus padres he doesn't have his parents' permission

autorizado -da *adj* ⟨fuente/portavoz⟩ official; ⟨distribuidor⟩ authorized, official; ⟨opinión⟩ expert (before n)

autorizar [A4] *vt* **(a)** ⟨manifestación/ documento/firma⟩ to authorize; ⟨aumento/pago/ obra⟩ to authorize, approve **(b)** ⟨persona⟩: ¿quién te autorizó? who gave you permission?; lo autoricé para recibir el pago I authorized him to receive the payment; me autorizó para salir he gave me permission to go out; eso no te autoriza a *or* para hablarme así that doesn't give you the right to talk to me like that

autorretrato *m* self-portrait

autoservicio *m* (tienda) supermarket; (restaurante) self-service restaurant, cafeteria

autostop, auto-stop /auto'(e)stop/ *m* hitchhiking; hacer ∼ to hitchhike

autosuficiencia *f* self-sufficiency

autosuficiente *adj* **(a)** (Econ) self-sufficient **(b)** (presumido) smug, self-satisfied

autovagón *m* (Per) railcar

autovía *f* divided highway (AmE), dual carriageway (BrE)

auxiliar¹ *adj* **(a)** ⟨profesor⟩ assistant (before n); ⟨personal/elementos⟩ auxiliary (before n) **(b)** ⟨servicios⟩ auxiliary **(c)** (Tec) auxiliary **(d)** (Inf) peripheral
▪ *mf* **(a)** (persona) assistant; ∼ de vuelo flight attendant **(b)** auxiliar *f* (RPl) (Auto) spare tire

auxiliar² [A1] *vt* to help

auxilio *m* **(a)** (ayuda) help; pedir ∼ to ask for help; ∼ en carretera breakdown *o* recovery service; acudieron en ∼ de las víctimas they went to the aid of the victims **(b)** (RPl) (grúa) recovery *o* breakdown truck

Av. *f* (= **Avenida**) Ave.

aval *m* (Com, Fin) guarantee; (respaldo) backing, support; (recomendación) reference

avalancha *f* avalanche

avalar [A1] *vt* (Com, Fin) ⟨documento⟩ to guarantee; ⟨persona/préstamo⟩ to guarantee, act as guarantor for

avaluar [A18] *vt* (AmL) to value

avalúo *m* (AmL) valuation

avance *m* **(a)** (adelanto) advance; un ∼ en este campo an advance *o* a step forward in this field **(b)** (movimiento) advance; (Mil) advance; (Dep) move forward

avanzado -da *adj* advanced; de avanzada edad of advanced years, advanced in years; a horas tan avanzadas at such a late hour

avanzar [A4] *vi* **(a)** ⟨persona/tráfico⟩ to advance, move forward **(b)** «ciencia/medicina» to advance **(c)** «cinta/rollo» to wind on **(d)** «persona» (en los estudios, el trabajo) to make progress; «negociaciones/proyecto» to progress **(e)** «tiempo» to draw on
▪ ∼ *vt* **(a)** (adelantarse) to move forward, advance **(b)** (mover) to move ... forward, advance

avaricia *f* avarice; la ∼ rompe el saco if you're too greedy you end up with nothing

avaricioso -sa, avariento -ta *adj* greedy, avaricious
▪ *m,f* greedy *o* avaricious person

avaro -ra *adj* miserly
▪ *m,f* miser

avasallador -dora, avasallante *adj* **(a)** ⟨persona/actitud⟩ domineering, overbearing **(b)** ⟨triunfo⟩ resounding (before n

Avda. *f* (= **Avenida**) Ave.

ave *f* bird; ∼ de corral fowl; ∼ de mal agüero bird of ill omen; ∼ rapaz *or* de rapiña (Zool) bird of prey; (persona) shark

AVE *m* (= **Alta Velocidad Española**) high-speed train

avecinarse [A1] *v pron* to approach

avejentado -da *adj*: está muy ∼ he's aged a lot; un rostro ∼ an old face

avejentar [A1] *vt* to age, make ... look older

avellana *f* hazelnut

avellano *m* hazel

Avemaría *f* (Relig) Hail Mary; (Mús) Ave Maria

avena *f* oats (pl)

avenida *f* **(a)** (calle) avenue, boulevard **(b)** (de río) freshet, flood

avenido -da *adj*: bien ∼ well-matched; es una pareja mal avenida they don't get on well as a couple

avenirse [I31] *v pron* **(a)** (ponerse de acuerdo) ∼se EN algo to agree ON sth **(b)** (llevarse bien) ∼se CON algn to get on WITH sb

aventajado -da *adj* outstanding, excellent

aventajar [A1] *vt* (estar por delante de) to be ahead of; (adelantarse) to overtake, get ahead of

aventar [A5] *vt* **(a)** (Col, Méx, Per) ⟨pelota/ piedra⟩ to throw; le aventé un sopapo (fam) I smacked *o* (BrE) thumped him (colloq) **(b)** (Méx) (empujar) to push
▪ aventarse *v pron* **(a)** (Méx fam) (atreverse) to dare; ∼se A hacer algo to dare to do sth **(b)** (refl) (Col, Méx) (arrojarse, tirarse) to throw oneself; se aventó al agua he dived into the water

aventón *m* (Méx) (fam) lift; darle ∼ a algn to give sb a lift *o* ride; pedir ∼ to hitch *o* thumb a lift; ir de ∼ to go hitching

aventura *f* **(a)** (suceso extraordinario) adventure **(b)** (empresa arriesgada) venture **(c)** (relación amorosa — pasajera) fling; (— ilícita) affair

aventurado -da *adj* risky, hazardous

aventurar [A1] *vt* ⟨opinión⟩ to venture, put forward; ⟨conjetura⟩ to hazard
▪ aventurarse *v pron* to venture; me ∼ía a decir que ... I would go so far as to say that ...

aventurero -ra *adj* adventurous
▪ *m,f* adventurer

avergonzado -da *adj* **(a)** (por algo reprensible) ashamed; ∼ POR *or* DE algo ashamed OF sth **(b)** (en situación embarazosa) embarrassed

avergonzar [A13] *vt* **(a)** (por algo reprensible): ¿no te avergüenza salir así a la calle? aren't you ashamed to go out looking like that? **(b)** (en situación embarazosa) to embarrass; me avergüenza decírselo I'm embarrassed to tell him
▪ avergonzarse *v pron* to be ashamed (of oneself); ∼se DE algo to be ashamed OF sth; se avergonzó de haberle mentido she was ashamed of herself for having lied to him

avergüenza, avergüenzas, etc ▶
AVERGONZAR

avería *f* (Auto, Mec) breakdown

averiado -da *adj* [ESTAR] ⟨coche/máquina⟩ broken down; ⟨ascensor/teléfono⟩ out of order

averiarse [A17] *v pron* to break down

averiguación *f* inquiry

averiguar [A16] *vt* to find out
■ ~ *vi* (Méx) to quarrel, argue; **averiguárselas** (Méx) to manage

aversión *f* aversion

avestruz *m* ostrich

aviación *f* (civil) aviation; (Mil) air force

aviador -dora *m,f* (Aviac, Mil) pilot

avícola *adj* poultry (*before n*)

avicultura *f* poultry farming

avidez *f* eagerness, avidity; **lee con** ~ he reads avidly

ávido -da *adj* ~ DE algo *⟨de noticias/aventuras⟩* eager FOR sth; *⟨de poder⟩* hungry FOR sth

avinagrar [A1] *vt ⟨vino⟩* to make ... taste vinegary; *⟨carácter⟩* to make ... sour *o* bitter
■ **avinagrarse** *v pron* «*vino*» to turn *o* go vinegary; «*persona*» to become bitter *o* sour

avión *m* (Aviac) plane, aircraft (frml), airplane (AmE), aeroplane (BrE); **viajar en** ~ to fly; **❸ por avión** (Corresp) air mail; ~ **a chorro** *or* **a reacción** jet (plane); ~ **de combate/de pasajeros** fighter/passenger plane

avionazo *m* (Méx) plane crash

avioneta *f* light aircraft

avisar [A1] *vt* (a) (notificar): **¿por qué no me avisaste que venías?** why didn't you let me know you were coming?; **nos han avisado que...** they've notified us that... (b) (Esp, Méx) (llamar) to call; ~ **al médico** to call the doctor (c) (advertir) to warn; **quedas** *or* **estás avisado** you've been warned
■ ~ *vi:* **llegó sin** ~ she showed up without any prior warning *o* unexpectedly; **avísame cuando acabes** let me know when you've finished; ~ **a algn** DE **algo** to let sb know ABOUT sth

aviso *m* **1** (a) (notificación) notice; **❸ aviso al público** notice to the public; **dio** ~ **a la policía** he notified *o* informed the police; **sin previo** ~ without prior warning; **último** ~ **para los pasajeros** ... last call for passengers ... (b) (advertencia) warning; **poner sobre** ~ **a algn** to warn sb (c) (Cin, Teatr) bell (d) (Taur) warning **2** (AmL) (anuncio, cartel) advertisement, ad

avispa *f* wasp

avispado -da *adj* (fam) sharp, bright

avispero *m* (nido) wasps' nest

avivar [A1] *vt ⟨fuego⟩* to get ... going; *⟨color⟩* to make ... brighter; *⟨pasión/deseo⟩* to arouse; *⟨dolor⟩* to intensify
■ **avivarse** *v pron* (a) «*fuego*» to revive, flare up; «*debate*» to come alive, liven up (b) (AmL fam) (despabilarse) to wise up (colloq)

axila *f* (Anat) armpit, axilla (tech)

axilar *adj* underarm (*before n*)

ay *interj* (a) (expresando — dolor) ow!, ouch!; (— susto, sobresalto) oh! (b) (expresando aflicción) oh dear! (c) (expresando amenaza): **¡~ del que se atreva!** woe betide anyone who tries it!

ayer *adv* (refiriéndose al día anterior) yesterday; ~ **hizo un mes** a month ago yesterday; ~ **por** *or* (esp AmL) **en la mañana** yesterday morning; **antes de** ~ the day before yesterday; **el periódico de** ~ yesterday's paper

ayuda *f* (asistencia) help; **nadie acudió en su** ~ nobody went to his aid; ~**s para la inversión** incentives for investment; **ha sido de gran** ~ it has been a great help

ayudante *mf* assistant; ~ **de cátedra** assistant professor (AmE), (junior) lecturer (BrE); ~ **de cocina** kitchen assistant

ayudar [A1] *vt* to help; ~ **al prójimo** to help one's neighbor; **¿te ayudo?** do you need any help?; **vino a** ~**me** she came to help me out; **ayúdame a poner la mesa** help me (to) set the table
■ ~ *vi* to help; **¿puedo** ~ **en algo?** can I do anything to help?

ayunar [A1] *vi* to fast

ayunas: en ~ (*loc adv*): **estoy en** ~ I haven't eaten anything; **debe tomarse en** ~ it should be taken on an empty stomach

ayuno *m* fast, fasting

ayuntamiento *m* (corporación) town/city council; (edificio) town/city hall

azabache *m* jet; **negro como el** ~ jet black

azada *f* hoe

azadón *m* mattock

azafata *f* **1** (a) (en avión) flight attendant, air hostess; ~ **de tierra** ground stewardess (b) (en programa, concurso) hostess; ~ **de congresos** conference hostess **2** (Per) (bandeja) tray

azafate *m* (AmS) tray

azafrán *m* saffron

azahar *m* (del naranjo) orange blossom; (del limonero) lemon blossom

azar *m* (a) (casualidad) chance; **dejar algo al** ~ to trust sth to chance; **al** ~ at random (b) **azares** *mpl* (vicisitudes) ups and downs (*pl*), vicissitudes (*pl*)

azaroso -sa *adj ⟨viaje⟩* hazardous; *⟨proyecto⟩* risky; *⟨vida⟩* eventful

Azerbaiyán, Azerbaiján *m* Azerbaijan, Azerbaidzhan

azerbaiyaní *adj/mf* Azerbaijani, Azeri
■ *m* (idioma) Azerbaijani

azorado -da *adj* (a) (turbado) embarrassed (b) (Col, Méx, RPl) (asombrado) amazed, astonished

azorar [A1] *vt* (turbar) to embarrass
■ **azorarse** *v pron* to get embarrassed

azotador *m* (Méx) caterpillar

azotaina *f* (fam) spanking

azotar [A1] *vt* **1** (con látigo) to whip, flog **2** (Méx) *⟨puerta⟩* to slam

azote *m* **1** (a) (látigo) whip, lash; (latigazo) lash (b) (fam) (a un niño): **te voy a dar unos** ~**s** I'm going to spank you **2** (calamidad) scourge

azotea *f* terrace roof, flat roof

azteca *adj/mf* Aztec

azúcar *m or f* sugar; **el nivel de** ~ **en la sangre** the blood-sugar level; **chicle sin** ~ sugar-free gum; ~ **blanca** white sugar; ~ **en terrones** *or* (RPl) **pancitos** sugar lumps *o* cubes (*pl*); ~ **glasé** *or* (Méx) **glas** confectioners sugar (AmE), icing sugar (BrE); ~ **lustre/morena** castor*/brown sugar

azucarar [A1] *vt ⟨café/leche⟩* to add sugar to; *⟨fruta⟩* to sprinkle ... with sugar

azucarera *f* (a) (AmL) (recipiente) sugar bowl (b) (fábrica) sugar refinery

azucarero¹ -ra *adj* ‹*industria*› sugar (*before n*); ‹*zona*› sugar-producing (*before n*)

azucarero² *m* sugar bowl

azucena *f* Madonna lily, Annunciation lily

azufre *m* sulfur*

azul *adj/m* blue; de un ～ **intenso** deep blue; ～ **verdoso (a)** *m* greenish blue **(b)** *adj inv* (*before n*) greenish-blue; ～ **cielo** *or* **celeste (a)** *m* sky

blue **(b)** *adj inv* sky-blue (*before n*); ～ **marino (a)** *m* navy blue **(b)** *adj inv* navy blue, navy-blue (*before n*)

azulado -da *adj* bluish

azulejo *m* (glazed ceramic) tile

azuzar [A4] *vt* **(a)** ‹*perros*› to sic; ～**le los perros a algn** to set the dogs on sb **(b)** ‹*persona*› to egg … on

b

Bb

B, b *f* (*read as* /be ('larva)/) *the letter* B, b

baba *f* **(a)** (de niño) dribble, drool (AmE) **(b)** (de adulto) saliva; **caérsele a algn la ～ por** *or* **con algn** to drool over sb **(c)** (de perro, caballo) slobber; (de caracol) slime

babear [A1] *vi* **(a)** «*persona*» to dribble, drool (AmE) **(b)** «*animal*» to slaver, slobber

babero *m* bib

babor *m* port; **a ～** to port

babosa *f* slug

babosada *f* (AmL fam) drivel; **decir ～s** to talk drivel

baboso -sa *adj* ⓵ (con babas) slimy ⓶ (AmL fam) (estúpido) ‹*persona*› dim (colloq); ‹*libro*/ *espectáculo*› ridiculous ■ *m,f* (AmL fam) (tonto) dimwit (colloq)

babucha *f* (zapatilla) slipper

baca *f* roof-rack, luggage-rack

bacalao *m* cod, codfish (AmE); ～ **seco** salt cod

bacenilla *f* (Col, Ven) chamber pot

bache *m* **(a)** (Auto) pothole **(b)** (Aviac) air pocket **(c)** (mal momento) bad time *o* (BrE) patch

bachillerato *m* **(a)** (educación secundaria) *secondary education and the qualification obtained,* ≈high school diploma (*in US*) **(b)** (Per) (licenciatura) bachelor's degree

bacinica *f* (AmL exc RPl fam) chamber pot, potty (colloq)

bacteria *f* bacterium; ～**s** bacteria (*pl*)

badén *m* **(a)** (vado) ford **(b)** (montículo) road hump **(c)** (depresión) dip

bádminton /'baðminton/ *m* badminton

baffle /'bafle/, **bafle** *m* (altavoz) speaker, loudspeaker

bagaje *m*: ～ **cultural** (de persona) cultural knowledge; (de un pueblo) cultural heritage

bagatela *f* (alhaja) trinket; (adorno) knickknack

bah *interj* (expresando — desprecio) huh!, bah!; (— conformidad) oh well!

bahía *f* bay

bailaor -laora *m,f* flamenco dancer

bailar [A1] *vi* ⓵ (Mús) to dance; **salir a ～** to go out dancing; **la sacó a ～** he asked her to dance ⓶ «*trompo*/*peonza*» to spin ⓷ (fam) (quedar grande) (+ *me*/*te*/*le etc*): **estos zapatos me bailan** these shoes are too big for me (colloq) ■ ～ *vt* to dance; ～ **un tango** to (dance a) tango

bailarín -rina *m,f* dancer; **primer ～** leading dancer; **primera bailarina** prima ballerina

baile *m* **(a)** (acción) dancing; **abrir el ～** to start the dancing **(b)** (arte, composición, fiesta) dance; ～ **de disfraces**/**máscaras** fancy-dress/masked ball

baja *f* ⓵ (descenso) fall, drop; **una ～ en los precios** a fall *o* drop in prices; **la ～ de las tasas de interés** the cut in interest rates; **tendencia a la ～** downward trend ⓶ (Esp) (Rels Labs) (permiso) sick leave; (certificado) medical certificate; **está (dado) de ～** he's off sick *o* on sick leave; ～ **por maternidad** (Esp) maternity leave **(b)** (Dep): **el equipo tiene varias ～s** the team is missing several regulars **(c)** (Mil) (muerte) loss, casualty ⓷ (en entidad): **darse de ～** (en club) to cancel one's membership, leave; (en partido) to resign, leave; (Mil) (cese) discharge; **dar de ～** to discharge

bajada *f* ⓵ (acción) descent; **durante la ～** on the way down; **tuvo una ～ de tensión** his blood pressure dropped; ～ **de bandera** (en taxi) minimum fare ⓶ **(a)** (pendiente) slope; **una ～ muy empinada** a very steep slope **(b)** (camino): **la ～ a la playa es muy empinada** the path (*o* road *etc*) down to the beach is very steep

bajamar *f* low tide

bajar [A1] *vi* ⓵ **(a)** «*ascensor*/*persona*» (alejándose) to go down; (acercándose) to come down; ～ **por las escaleras** to go/come down the stairs; **ya bajo** I'll be right down **(b)** (apearse) ～ **DE algo** ‹*de tren*/*avión*› to get off sth; ‹*de coche*› to get out *o* off sth; ‹*de caballo*/*bicicleta*› to get off sth **(c)** (Dep) «*equipo*» to go down ⓶ **(a)** «*marea*» to go out **(b)** «*fiebre*/*tensión*» to go down, drop; «*hinchazón*» to go down; «*temperatura*» to fall, drop **(c)** «*precio*/*valor*» to fall, drop; «*calidad*» to deteriorate; «*popularidad*» to diminish; ～ **de precio** to go down in price ■ ～ *vt* ⓵ ‹*escalera*/*cuesta*› to go down ⓶ ‹*brazo*/*mano*› to put down, lower ⓷ **(a)** ～ **algo** (DE algo) ‹*de armario*/*estante*› to get sth down (FROM sth); ‹*del piso de arriba*› (traer) to bring sth down (FROM sth); (llevar) to take sth down (TO sth) **(b)** ～ **a algn DE algo** ‹*de mesa*/ *caballo*› to get sb off sth ⓸ **(a)** ‹*persiana*/*telón*› to lower; ‹*ventanilla*› to open **(b)** ‹*cremallera*› to undo ⓹ ‹*precio*› to lower; ‹*fiebre*› to bring down; ‹*volumen*› to turn down; ‹*voz*› to lower

■ **bajarse** v pron ⓵ (apearse) ~**se** DE algo ⟨de tren/autobús⟩ to get off sth; ⟨de coche⟩ to get out OF sth; ⟨de caballo/bicicleta⟩ to get off sth; ⟨de pared/árbol⟩ to get down off sth ⓶ ⟨pantalones⟩ to take down; ⟨falda⟩ to pull down

bajativo m (CS) liqueur, digestif

bajío m (a) (zona poco profunda) shallows (pl); (banco de arena) sandbank (b) (AmL) (terreno bajo) low-lying area

bajista mf bass player, bassist

bajo¹ -ja adj ⓵ [SER] ⟨persona⟩ short ⓶ (a) [SER] ⟨techo⟩ low; ⟨tierras⟩ low-lying (b) [ESTAR] ⟨lámpara/cuadro/nivel⟩ low; **la marea está baja** the tide is out; **están ~s de moral** their morale is low; **está ~ de defensas** his defenses are low ⓷ (a) ⟨calificación/precio/temperatura⟩ low; ~ **en nicotina y alquitrán** low in nicotine and tar; ~ **en calorías** low-calorie; **de baja calidad** poor-quality (b) ⟨volumen/luz⟩ low; **en voz baja** quietly, in a low voice ⓸ (grave) ⟨tono/voz⟩ deep, low ⓹ (vil) ⟨acción/instinto⟩ low, base; **los ~s fondos** the underworld

bajo² adv (a) ⟨volar/pasar⟩ low (b) ⟨hablar/cantar⟩ softly, quietly; **¡habla más ~!** keep your voice down!
■ m ⓵ (a) (planta baja) first (AmE) o (BrE) ground floor (b) **los bajos** (CS) the first (AmE) o (BrE) ground floor ⓶ (contrabajo) (double) bass
■ prep under; ~ **techo** under cover, indoors; **tres grados ~ cero** three degrees below zero; ~ **juramento** under oath

bajón m (fam) (a) (descenso fuerte) sharp drop o fall (b) (de ánimo) depression

bajorrelieve m bas-relief

bala f ⓵ (Arm) (de pistola, rifle) bullet; (de cañón) cannon ball; ~ **de fogueo** blank (round o cartridge); ~ **de goma/plástico** rubber/plastic bullet; **a prueba de ~s** bulletproof; **una ~ perdida** a stray bullet; **como (una)** ~ ⟨salir/entrar⟩ like a shot (colloq) ⓶ (AmL) (Dep) shot; **lanzamiento de ~** shot put

balaca f (Col) (a) (Indum) hair-band (b) (Dep) sweatband, headband

balacera f (AmL) shooting

balada f ballad

balance m ⓵ (a) (resumen, valoración) assessment, evaluation; **hacer ~** DE algo to take stock OF sth, to evaluate sth (b) (resultado) result, outcome ⓶ (Com, Fin) (cálculo, cómputo) balance; (documento) balance sheet; (de cuenta) balance

balancear [A1] vt ⓵ ⟨paquetes/carga⟩ to balance ⓶ ⟨pierna/brazo⟩ to swing; ⟨barco⟩ to rock
■ **balancearse** v pron (a) ⟨árbol/ramas⟩ to sway; ⟨objeto colgante⟩ to swing (b) ⟨barco⟩ to rock

balanceo m (de hamaca) swinging; (de árboles) swaying; (de barco) rocking

balancín m (de niños) seesaw, teeter-totter (AmE)

balanza f scales (pl); (de dos platillos) scales (pl),

balance; ~ **comercial/de pagos** balance of trade/of payments; **poner en la ~** to weigh (AmE), to weigh up (BrE)

balar [A1] vi to bleat, baa

balazo m (Arm) (tiro) shot; (herida) bullet wound; **recibió un ~** he was shot

balboa m balboa (Panamanian unit of currency)

balbucear [A1] vt to stammer
■ ~ vi ⟨adulto⟩ to mutter, mumble; ⟨bebé⟩ to babble

balbuceo m (de adulto) mumbling, muttering; (de bebé) babble

balcón m balcony

balde m ⓵ (cubo) bucket, pail; **caer como un ~ de agua fría** to come as a complete shock ⓶ (en locs) **de balde** ⟨trabajar/viajar⟩ for nothing, for free; **en balde** in vain

baldío¹ -día adj (a) (sin cultivar): **terreno ~** waste land (b) ⟨esfuerzo⟩ vain, useless

baldío² m (a) (terreno sin cultivar) area of waste land (b) (Bol, Méx, RPl) (solar) piece o plot of land, vacant lot (AmE)

baldosa f floor tile; **suelo de ~s** tiled floor

baldosín m tile

balear [A1] vt (AmL) to shoot; **murió baleado** he was shot dead

baleo m (AmL) shooting

balero m (Méx, RPl) (juguete) cup-and-ball toy

balido m bleat, baa

balín m (perdigón) pellet; (bala pequeña) shot

balística f ballistics

baliza f (a) (boya) buoy; (señal fija) marker (b) (Aviac) beacon

ballena f (Zool) whale

ballenato m whale calf

ballenero -ra m,f (a) (persona) whaler (b) **ballenero** m (barco) whaleboat, whaler

ballet /ba'le/ m (pl **-llets**) ballet

balneario m ⓵ (de baños medicinales) spa ⓶ (AmL) (núcleo residencial) seaside resort, (holiday) resort

balompié m soccer, football (BrE)

balón m (a) (Dep) ball (b) (recipiente) cylinder; ~ **de oxígeno** oxygen cylinder

baloncesto m basketball

balonmano m handball

balonvolea m volleyball

balsa f (embarcación) raft; ~ **inflable/salvavidas** inflatable/life raft

bálsamo m (a) (Farm, Med) balsam, balm (b) (Chi) (para el pelo) conditioner

baluarte m bastion

bambalina f (Teatr) drop (curtain); **entre ~s** behind the scenes

bambolearse v pron ⟨persona/árbol/torre⟩ to sway; ⟨objeto colgante⟩ to swing; ⟨barco/tren⟩ to rock; ⟨avión/ascensor⟩ to lurch

bambú m (pl **-búes** or **-bús**) bamboo

banal adj banal

banana f (Per, RPl) banana

bananal, bananar m (AmL) banana plantation

bananero¹ -ra adj (AmL) banana (before n)

bananero² m (AmL) banana tree

banano m (árbol) banana tree; (fruta) (AmC, Col) banana

banca f [1] la ~ (sector) banking; (bancos) the banks [2] (AmL) (a) (asiento) bench; (pupitre) desk **(b)** (Dep) (asiento) bench; (jugadores) substitutes (pl)

bancario -ria adj ⟨interés/préstamo⟩ bank (before n); ⟨sector⟩ banking (before n)

bancarrota f bankruptcy; **en ~** bankrupt; **ir a la ~** to go bankrupt

banco m [1] **(a)** (de parque) bench; (de iglesia) pew; (de barca) thwart; (pupitre) (Chi) desk **(b)** (de carpintero) workbench [2] (Com, Fin) bank; (de órganos, sangre) bank; (de información) bank; **~ de datos** data base o bank; **~ de esperma** or **semen** sperm bank [3] (de peces) shoal; (bajío) bar, bank; **~ de arena** sandbank

banda f [1] (en la cintura, cruzando el pecho) sash; (franja, lista) band; (para pelo) (Méx) hair-band; (en brazo) armband; **~ de frecuencias** frequency band; **~ sonora** (Cin) sound track; **~ transportadora** (Méx) conveyor belt [2] (de barco) side; (en billar) cushion; (en fútbol, rugby) touchline; **saque de ~** (en fútbol) throw-in; (en rugby) put-in [3] **(a)** (de delincuentes) gang; **(b)** (Mús) band

bandada f (de pájaros) flock; (de peces) shoal

bandazo m: **dar ~s** «equipaje» to move about; «coche» to swerve about

bandeja f tray; **servirle algo a algn en ~** to hand sb sth on a platter (AmE) o (BrE) plate

bandera f **(a)** (de nación, club) flag; (de regimiento) colors* (pl); **izar la ~** to run up o raise the flag; **arriar la ~** to lower o strike the flag **(b)** (para señales) flag, pennant; **~ ajedrezada** or **a cuadros** checkered* flag **(c)** (de taxi): **bajar la ~** to start the meter **(d)** (Inf) flag

banderilla f (Taur) banderilla (barbed dart stuck into the bull's neck)

banderillero m banderillero (person who sticks the banderillas into the bull's neck)

banderín m (banderita triangular) pennant; (Dep) flag

banderola f (enseña) banderole

bandido -da m,f (delincuente) bandit; (granuja) crook; (pícaro) rascal

bando m [1] (edicto) edict [2] (facción) side, camp; **están en ~s contrarios** they're on opposing sides

bandolera f (cinturón) Sam Browne (belt); (para cartuchos) bandolier; **en ~** slung across one's shoulder

bandolero -ra m,f bandit

bandoneón m: type of accordion

banjo /'bandʒo/ m banjo

banquero -ra m,f banker

banqueta f **(a)** (taburete) stool; (para los pies) footstool **(b)** (Méx) (acera) sidewalk (AmE), pavement (BrE)

banquete m banquet; **~ de bodas/de gala** wedding/gala reception

banquillo m **(a)** (Der): **el ~** (de los acusados) the dock **(b)** (Dep) bench

banquina f (RPl) (en autopista) shoulder (AmE), hard shoulder (BrE); (cuneta) ditch

bañado -da adj (Bol, RPl) **~ en algo** (en sangre/ sudor) covered WITH sth; (en lágrimas) bathed IN sth; **~ en oro/plata** gold-plated/silver-plated

bañador m (Esp) (de mujer) bathing suit (esp AmE), swimming costume (BrE); (de hombre) swimming trunks

bañar [A1] vt [1] (niño/enfermo) to bath, give ... a bath (pulsera/cubierto) to plate

■ **bañarse** v pron (refl) **(a)** (en bañera) to have o take a bath, to bathe (AmE) **(b)** (en mar, río) to swim, bathe

bañera f bath, bathtub

bañero -ra m,f (RPl) lifeguard

bañista mf bather

baño m

■ **Nota** Con referencia al cuarto de baño de una casa particular, el inglés americano emplea normalmente *bathroom*. El inglés británico emplea *toilet*, *lavatory* o (coloquialmente) *loo*. Cuando se habla de los servicios de un edificio público, el inglés americano utiliza *washroom*, *restroom*, *men's room* o *ladies' room*. El inglés británico emplea *the Gents*, *the ladies*, o *the toilets*. En la calle y en los parques públicos se emplea *public toilets*, o en inglés británico más formal, *public conveniences*.

[1] (en bañera) bath; (en mar, río) swim; **darse un ~** to have a bath/to go for a swim; **~ de sangre** bloodbath; **~s públicos** public baths (pl); **~ turco** Turkish bath [2] **(a)** (bañera) bath **(b)** (esp AmL) (en casa privada) bathroom (AmE), toilet (BrE); (en edificio público) restroom (AmE), toilet (BrE); **~ público** (AmL) public toilet [3] (de metal) plating

baptista adj Baptist (before n)

■ mf Baptist

baqueta f **(a)** (Arm) ramrod **(b)** (Mús) drumstick

baquiano -na m,f (AmL) guide

bar m (local) bar; (mueble) liquor cabinet (AmE), drinks cabinet (BrE)

baraja f deck o (BrE) pack (of cards)

barajar [A1] vt [1] ⟨cartas⟩ to shuffle [2] ⟨nombres/posibilidades⟩ to consider, look at; ⟨cifras⟩ to talk about, mention

baranda, (Esp) barandilla f (de balcón) rail; (de escalera) handrail, banister

barata f [1] (Chi) (cucaracha) cockroach [2] (Méx) (liquidación) sale

baratija f (alhaja) trinket; (adorno) knickknack

barato¹ -ta adj **(a)** ⟨vestido/restaurante/viaje⟩ cheap, low-priced **(b)** (como adv) ⟨costar/comprar⟩ cheap

barato² adv ⟨comer/vivir⟩ cheaply; **se compra más ~ en el mercado** you can get things cheaper in the market

barba f **(a)** (de quien se la afeita) stubble; **una ~ de dos días** two days' growth of stubble **(b)** (de quien se la deja) beard; **dejarse (la) ~** to grow a beard; **un hombre con ~** a man with a beard; **hacerle la ~ a algn** (Méx fam) to suck up to sb (colloq) **(c)** (mentón, barbilla) chin

b

barbacoa *f* (a) (parrilla) barbecue; (carne) barbecued meat (b) (Méx) *meat roasted in an oven dug in the earth*

barbaridad *f* (a) (acto atroz) atrocity (b) (disparate): **pagar tanto es una ~** it's madness to pay that much; **lo que hiciste/dijiste es una ~** what you did/said is outrageous; **es capaz de cualquier ~** he's quite capable of doing something really terrible *o* stupid; **¡qué ~!** good heavens!; **una ~** (fam) ⟨*comer*⟩ like a horse; ⟨*fumar*⟩ like a chimney; ⟨*pagar/costar*⟩ a fortune

barbarie *f* (de tribu, pueblo) barbarism, savagery; (brutalidad) barbarity

barbarismo *m* (extranjerismo) loan word, borrowing; (solecismo) barbarism

bárbaro¹ -ra *adj* **1** (Hist) barbarian **2** (bruto): **el muy ~ la hizo llorar** the brute made her cry; **no seas ~, no se lo digas** don't be crass *o* cruel, don't tell him **3** (fam) (como intensificador) ⟨*casa/coche*⟩ fantastic; **tengo un hambre bárbara** I'm starving

bárbaro² *adv* (fam): **lo pasamos ~** we had a fantastic time (colloq)

bárbaro³ -ra *m,f* **1** (Hist) Barbarian **2** (fam) (bruto) lout, thug

barbecho *m* (estado): **dejar la tierra en ~** to leave the land fallow; **estar en ~** (CS) to be in preparation

barbería *f* barber's (shop)

barbero¹ *m* barber

barbero² -ra *m,f* (Méx fam) toady

barbilampiño *adj*: **un hombre ~** a man with a light beard

barbilla *f* chin

barbitúrico *m* barbiturate

barbudo *m* bearded man, man with a beard

barca *f* boat; **~ de remos** rowboat (AmE), rowing boat (BrE)

barcaza *f* (en canales, ríos) barge; (entre barco y tierra) lighter

barco *m* (Náut) boat; (grande) ship, vessel (frml); **un viaje en ~** a journey by sea (*o* river *etc*); **ir/viajar en ~** to go/travel by boat/ship; **~ de guerra** warship; **~ de vapor** steamboat, steamer; **~ de vela** sailing boat, sailboat (AmE)

barda *f* (Méx) (de cemento) wall; (de madera) fence

barítono -na *adj/m* baritone

barman /'barman/ *m* (*pl* **-mans**) barman, bartender (AmE)

barniz *m* (a) (para madera) varnish (b) (de cultura, educación) veneer; **~ de** *or* **para las uñas** nail polish, nail varnish (esp BrE)

barnizar [A4] *vt* to varnish

barómetro *m* barometer

barón *m* (título nobiliario) baron; (de organización) influential member

baronesa *f* baroness

barquero -ra *m* (m) boatman; (f) boatwoman

barquilla *f* (de globo) basket, carriage; (Náut) log

barquillo *m* (galleta) wafer; (cono) ice-cream cone *o* (BrE) cornet

barra *f* **1** (de armario) rail; (para cortinas) rod, pole; (de bicicleta) crossbar (b) (de oro, jabón, chocolate) bar; (de turrón, helado) block; (de desodorante) stick; (de pan) (Esp, Méx) stick, French loaf; **~ de labios** lipstick **2** (a) (banda, franja) bar (b) (Mús) bar (line) (c) (signo de puntuación) oblique, slash **3** (para ballet, gimnasia) bar; **~ fija** horizontal bar; **~s asimétricas/paralelas** asymmetric/parallel bars (*pl*) **4** (de bar, cafetería) bar **5** (AmL fam) (a) (de hinchas, seguidores) supporters (*pl*) (b) (de amigos) gang (colloq) **6** (Inf): **~ de herramientas** toolbar

barrabasada *f* (fam) prank; **hacer ~s** to play pranks

barraca *f* (a) (puesto) stall; (caseta) booth (b) (Mil) barrack hut (c) (casa) adobe house (*typical of Valencia and Murcia*) (d) (CS) (de materiales de construcción) builders merchant *o* yard

barranca *f*, **barranco** *m* gully; (más profundo) ravine

barrena *f* (punzón) gimlet; (taladro, perforadora) drill

barrenar [A1] *vt* (perforar) to drill; (volar) ⟨*roca*⟩ to blast

barrendero -ra *m,f* road sweeper, street cleaner

barreno *m* (barrena) drill; (para explosivo) shot hole

barrer [E1] *vt* **1** ⟨*suelo/cocina*⟩ to sweep **2** (a) (arrastrar) to sweep away (b) ⟨*rival*⟩ to thrash, trounce
■ ~ *vi* **1** (con escoba) to sweep **2** (arrasar) «*equipo/candidato*» to sweep to victory; **~ con algo** ⟨*con premios/medallas*⟩ to walk off WITH sth; **la inundación barrió con todo** the flood swept everything away; **barrió con todos los premios** she walked off with all the prizes
■ **barrerse** *v pron* (Méx) «*vehículo*» to skid; (en fútbol, béisbol) to slide

barrera *f* barrier; **~ de peaje** toll barrier; **~ generacional** generation gap; **~ idiomática** language barrier

barriada *f* (a) (barrio) area, district (*often poor or working-class*) (b) (AmL) (barrio marginal) slum area, shantytown

barrial *m* (AmL) quagmire

barricada *f* barricade

barriga *f* (fam) (vientre) belly (colloq), tummy (colloq); **dolor de ~** bellyache (colloq), tummy ache (colloq); **echar ~** to develop a paunch *o* (colloq) gut

barrigón -gona *adj* (fam): **se está volviendo barrigona** she's getting a bit of a belly *o* tummy (colloq); **un viejo ~** an old man with a paunch

barril *m* barrel; (de pólvora, cerveza) keg; **ser un ~ sin fondo** (AmL fam) to be a bottomless pit (colloq)

barrio *m* (a) (zona) neighborhood*; **la gente del ~** people in the neighborhood, local people; **el mercado del ~** the local market; **~ alto** (Chi) smart neighborhood; **~ chino** (Esp) red-light district; **~ espontáneo** (AmC) shantytown; **~s bajos** poor neighborhoods (*pl*); **~ de invasión** (Col) shantytown (b) (de las afueras) suburb

barriobajero -ra *adj* (pey) common (pej)

barrizal *m* quagmire, muddy area

barro *m* (lodo) mud; (Art) clay, earthenware (*before n*)

barroco -ca *adj* ⟨*estilo*⟩ baroque; (recargado) overelaborate

barrote *m* (de celda, ventana) bar; (en carpintería) crosspiece

bartola f: **echarse a la ~** (fam) (estar sin trabajar) to laze about

bártulos mpl (fam) gear (colloq), stuff (colloq)

barullo m (alboroto) racket (colloq), ruckus (AmE); (desorden) muddle, mess

basar [A1] vt ‹teoría/idea› **~ algo EN algo** to base sth on sth

■ **basarse** v pron (a) «persona» **~se EN algo**: ¿en qué te basas para decir eso? and what basis o grounds do you have for saying that?; **se basó en esos datos** he based his argument (o theory etc) on that information (b) «teoría/creencia/idea/opinión» **~se EN algo** to be based ON sth

báscula f scales (pl); **~ de baño** bathroom scales

base f **1** (a) (parte inferior) base (b) tb **~ de maquillaje** foundation

2 (a) (fundamento) basis; **la ~ de una buena salud** the basis of good health; **tengo suficiente ~ para asegurar eso** I have sufficient grounds to claim that; **sentar las ~s de algo** to lay the foundations of sth; **tomar algo como ~** to take sth as a starting point (b) (conocimientos básicos): **tiene una sólida ~ científica** he has a sound grounding in science; **llegó al curso sin ninguna ~** he didn't have the basics when he began the course; **~ de datos** database

3 (en locs) **a base de: un régimen a ~ de verdura** a vegetable-based diet; **vive a ~ de pastillas** he lives on pills

4 (centro de operaciones) base; **~ aérea/naval/militar** air/naval/military base

5 **bases** fpl (de concurso) rules (pl)

6 (a) (en béisbol) base (b) **base** mf (en baloncesto) guard

básica f (Esp) primary o elementary education

básico -ca adj (a) (fundamental, esencial) basic; **alimento ~** staple food (b) (requisito) essential, fundamental

basílica f basilica

basket, básquet m basketball

básquetbol, basquetbol m (AmL) basketball

basquetbolista mf (AmL) basketball player

bastante adj (a) (suficiente) enough; **~s vasos/~ vino** enough glasses/wine (b) (cantidad considerable) plenty of, quite a lot of; **había ~ gente/~s coches** there were plenty of people/cars

■ pron **1** (suficiente) enough; **ya tenemos ~s** we already have enough **2** (demasiado): **deja ~ que desear** it leaves rather a lot to be desired

■ adv **1** (suficientemente) enough; **no te has esforzado ~** you haven't tried hard enough **2** (considerablemente) (con verbos) quite a lot; (con adjetivos, adverbios) quite; **le gusta bastante** she likes him quite a lot; **me pareció ~ agradable/aburrido** I thought he was quite pleasant/rather boring

bastar [A1] vi to be enough; **¿basta con esto?** will this be enough?; **basta con marcar el 101** just dial 101; **¡basta ya!** that's enough!; (+ me/te/le etc) **me basta con tu palabra** your word is good enough for me

bastardilla f italic type, italics (pl)

bastardo -da adj (a) (ilegítimo) illegitimate (b) (innoble) base

■ m,f bastard

bastidor m (Teatr) wing; **entre ~es** behind the scenes

basto -ta adj coarse

bastón m (para caminar) walking stick, cane; (en desfiles) baton; (de esquí) ski stick o pole

basura f (a) (recipiente) garbage o trash can (AmE), dustbin (BrE); **echar o tirar algo a la ~** to throw sth in the garbage o trash (can) o dustbin (b) (desechos) garbage (AmE), trash (AmE), rubbish (BrE); (en sitios públicos) litter; **sacar la ~** to take out the garbage o trash o rubbish (c) (fam) (porquería) trash (AmE colloq), rubbish (BrE colloq)

basural m (AmL) ▶ BASURERO B

basurero -ra m,f **1** (persona) garbage collector (AmE), dustman (BrE) **2** (a) **basurero** m (vertedero) garbage dump (AmE), rubbish dump o tip (BrE) (b) (recipiente) (Chi, Méx) trash can (AmE), dustbin (BrE)

bata f (para estar en casa) dressing gown, robe; (de médico) white coat; (de colegio) work coat (AmE), overall (BrE)

batahola f (esp AmL fam) racket, din, ruckus (AmE)

batalla f battle; **librar ~** to do battle; **~ campal** pitched battle; **de ~** (fam) ‹zapatos/abrigo› everyday (before n)

batallar [A1] vi (a) (luchar) to battle; **~ CON algn/algo** (lidiar) to battle WITH sb/sth (b) (Mil) to fight

batallón m (Mil) battalion

batata f sweet potato, yam

bate m (en béisbol, cricket) bat

batea f (a) (bandeja) tray (b) (AmL) (recipiente) shallow pan o tray (for washing)

bateador -dora m,f (en béisbol, softbol) batter; (en cricket) batsman

batear [A1] vi to bat

■ **~** vt to hit

batería f **1** (Auto) battery; **se me descargó la ~** my battery went dead (AmE) o (BrE) flat **2** (a) (Mús) drums (pl), drum kit (b) **batería** mf drummer

baterista mf (AmL) drummer

batido m (de leche) (milk) shake; (para panqueques) (AmL) batter

batidor m (a) (manual) whisk, beater; (eléctrico) mixer, blender (b) **batidora** f (máquina eléctrica) mixer, blender

batir [I1] vt **1** ‹huevos› to beat, whisk; ‹crema/nata› to whip; ‹mantequilla› to churn **2** ‹marca/récord› to break; ‹enemigo/rival› to beat **3** (a) ‹ala› to beat, flap (b) **~ palmas** to clap

■ **batirse** v pron **1** (enfrentarse): **~se a o en duelo** to fight a duel **2** (Méx) (ensuciarse) to get dirty; **llegó todo batido de lodo** he arrived all covered in mud

batracio m batrachian

batuta f baton; **llevar la ~** (fam) to be the boss (colloq)

baúl m (arca) chest; (de viaje) trunk; (del coche, carro) (Col, Ven, RPl) trunk (AmE), boot (BrE)

bautismo m (de bebé) baptism, christening; (de adulto) baptism

bautizar [A4] vt (a) (Relig) ‹bebé› to baptize, ⋯⋮

christen; ⟨*adulto*⟩ to baptize; **la ~ron con el nombre de Ana** she was christened Ana **(b)** ⟨*barco*⟩ to name

bautizo *m* **(a)** (de bebé) christening, baptism; (de adulto) baptism; (fiesta) christening party **(b)** (de barco) naming, launching

bayeta *f* **(a)** (para limpiar) cloth **(b)** (Bol, Col) (tela) baize

bayoneta *f* bayonet

bazar *m* **(a)** (mercado oriental) bazaar **(b)** (tienda) hardware store (*often selling a wide range of electrical goods and toys*)

bazo *m* spleen

bazofia *f* (fam) (comida) crap (colloq); (libro, película) garbage (AmE colloq), rubbish (BrE colloq)

bazooka /baˈsuka, baˈθuka/, **bazuca** *f* bazooka

be *f*: *name of the letter* b, *often called* BE LARGA *or* GRANDE *to distinguish it from* v

beato -ta *adj* (Relig) blessed; (piadoso) pious; (santurrón) (pey) excessively devout

bebe -ba *m,f* (RPl, Per) baby

bebé *m* baby; **~ probeta** test-tube baby

bebedero *m* (paraje) watering hole; (recipiente) trough; (para personas) (CS, Méx) drinking fountain

bebedor -dora *m,f* drinker; **un ~ empedernido** a hardened drinker

beber [E1] *vt/vi* to drink; **¿quieres ~ algo?** do you want something to drink?; **~ a sorbos** to sip; **si bebes no conduzcas** don't drink and drive; **~ a la salud de algn** to drink sb's *o* (BrE) to sb's health; **~ POR algn/algo** to drink TO sb/sth

■ **beberse** *v pron* (*enf*) to drink up; **nos bebimos la botella entera** we drank the whole bottle

bebida *f* (líquido) drink, beverage (frml); (vicio) drink

bebido -da *adj* [ESTAR] (borracho) drunk

beca *f* (ayuda económica) grant; (que se otorga por méritos) scholarship

becado -da *m,f* (AmL) ▶ BECARIO

becar [A2] *vt* (dar ayuda ecónómica) to give *o* (frml) award a grant to; (dar beca por méritos) to give *o* (frml) award a scholarship to

becario -ria *m,f* recipient of a grant; (por méritos) scholarship holder, scholar

becerro -rra *m,f* calf, young bull; (piel) calfskin

bedel *mf* ≈ porter

beduino -na *adj/m,f* bedouin

beige, (Esp) **beis** /beʒ, beis/ *adj inv/m* beige

béisbol, (Méx) **beisbol** *m* baseball

belén *m* nativity scene, crib, crèche (AmE)

Belén *m* Bethlehem

belga *adj/mf* Belgian

Bélgica *f* Belgium

bélico -ca *adj* ⟨*conflicto/material*⟩ military; **preparativos ~s** preparations for war

belicosidad *f* aggressiveness

belicoso -sa *adj* ⟨*pueblo*⟩ warlike; ⟨*persona/ carácter*⟩ bellicose, belligerent

beligerante *adj* belligerent; **los países ~s** the belligerent *o* warring nations

bellaco -ca *m,f* (fam & hum) rogue (colloq & hum)

belleza *f* **(a)** (cualidad) beauty **(b)** (mujer bella) beauty **(c)** (cosa bella): **este paisaje es una ~** this is beautiful countryside

bello -lla *adj* **(a)** ⟨*mujer/paisaje/poema*⟩ (liter) beautiful; **ser una bella persona** to be a good person **(b)** (Art) **bellas artes** fine art

bellota *f* acorn

bemba *f* (AmL fam) thick lips (*pl*)

bemol *adj* flat; **si ~** B flat

bencina *f* **(a)** (Quím) benzine, petroleum ether **(b)** (Andes) (gasolina) gasoline (AmE), petrol (BrE)

bencinera *f* (Andes) filling station, gas station (AmE), petrol station (BrE)

bencinero -ra *m,f* (Andes) filling station attendant

bendecir [I25] *vt* to bless; **¡que Dios te bendiga!** God bless you!; **~ la mesa** to say grace

bendice, etc ▶ BENDECIR

bendición *f* **(a)** (Relig) blessing, benediction **(b)** (aprobación) blessing; (regalo divino) godsend

bendiga, bendijo, etc ▶ BENDECIR

bendito -ta *adj* **(a)** (Relig) blessed; **¡~ sea Dios!** (expresando contrariedad) good God *o* grief!; (expresando alivio) thank God! **(b)** ⟨*agua/pan*⟩ holy ■ *m,f* simple soul

benedictino -na *adj/m,f* Benedictine

benefactor -tora *m,f* benefactor

beneficencia *f* (caridad) charity; **asociación/ obra de ~** charitable organization/work

beneficiar [A1] *vt* (favorecer) to benefit, to be of benefit to; **esto beneficia a ambas partes** this benefits both sides; **salir beneficiado con algo** to be better off with sth

■ **beneficiarse** *v pron* to benefit; **~se CON/DE algo** to benefit FROM sth

beneficiario -ria *m,f* beneficiary; (de cheque) payee

beneficio *m* **(a)** (Com, Fin) profit; **producir** *or* **reportar ~s** to yield *o* bring returns *o* profits **(b)** (ventaja, bien) benefit; **a ~ de** in aid of; **en ~ de todos** in the interests of everyone

beneficioso -sa *adj* beneficial

benéfico -ca *adj* ⟨*influencia*⟩ benign, beneficial; ⟨*espectáculo*⟩ charity (*before n*), benefit (*before n*)

beneplácito *m* approval

benevolencia *f* (indulgencia) leniency, indulgence; (bondad) kindness, benevolence (frml)

benevolente, benévolo -la *adj* (indulgente) lenient, indulgent; (bondadoso) kind, benevolent (frml)

bengala *f* flare

benignidad *f* (del clima) mildness; (de tumor) benignancy

benigno -na *adj* ‹clima/invierno› mild; ‹tumor› benign

benjamín -mina *m,f* *(m)* youngest son, *(f)* youngest daughter

beodo -da *adj* (frml o hum) inebriated (frml or hum)

■ *m,f* (frml o hum) drunkard, toper (liter o hum)

berberecho *m* cockle

berenjena *f* eggplant (AmE), aubergine (BrE)

Berlín *m* Berlin

berlinés -nesa *adj* of/from Berlin

■ *m,f* Berliner

berma *f* (Andes) (de asfalto) shoulder (AmE), hard shoulder (BrE); (de tierra) verge

bermudas *fpl or mpl* Bermuda shorts (*pl*)

Bermudas *fpl*: **las ~** Bermuda; **el triángulo de las ~** the Bermuda Triangle

berrear [A1] *vi* «becerro/ciervo» to bellow

berrido *m* (de becerro, ciervo) bellow

berrinche *m* (fam) tantrum; **le dio un** *or* (Méx) **hizo un ~** he threw *o* had a tantrum

berro *m* watercress

besar [A1] *vt* to kiss

■ **besarse** *v pron* (recípr) to kiss (each other)

beso *m* kiss; **darle un ~ a algn** to give sb a kiss

bestia *adj* (fam) **(a)** (grosero) rude **(b)** (violento, brusco): **¡qué hombre más ~!** ha vuelto a pegarle what a brute *o* an animal! he's hit her again

■ *f* beast; **~ salvaje** *or* **feroz** wild animal

■ *mf* (persona violenta) animal, brute

bestial *adj* (fam) (muy grande): **tengo un hambre ~** I'm starving; **hace un frío ~** it's incredibly cold

best-seller /bes'seler/ *m* (*pl* **-llers**) best-seller

besugo *m* (Coc, Zool) red bream

besuquear [A1] *vt* (fam) to smother ... with kisses

■ **besuquearse** *v pron* (recípr) (fam) to neck (colloq)

betabel *m* (Méx) beet, beetroot (BrE)

betún *m* (para calzado) shoe polish; **dales ~ a esos zapatos** give those shoes a polish

bianual *adj* biannual

biberón *m* (baby's *o* feeding) bottle; **hay que darle el ~** I have to give the baby his bottle *o* feed

biblia *f* bible; **La B~** the Bible

bíblico -ca *adj* biblical

bibliografía *f* (en libro, informe) bibliography; (para curso) booklist

biblioteca *f* **(a)** (institución, lugar) library; **pública/de consulta** public/reference library **(b)** (colección) book collection **(c)** (mueble) bookshelves (*pl*), bookcase

bibliotecario -ria *m,f* librarian

bicameral *adj* bicameral (frml)

bicampeón -peona *m,f* twice champion

bicarbonato *m* bicarbonate

bicentenario *m* bicentenary

bíceps *m* (*pl* **~**) biceps

bicho *m* **1** (fam) **(a)** (insecto) bug (colloq), creepy-crawly (colloq) **(b)** (animal) animal, creature; **me picó** *or* (Esp) **ha picado un ~** I've

been bitten by something **2** (fam) (persona) nasty piece of work (colloq); **~ raro** weirdo (colloq); **todo ~ viviente** everyone

bici *f* (fam) bike (colloq)

bicicleta *f* bicycle; **va en ~ al trabajo** she cycles to work; **¿sabes montar** *or* (AmL) **andar en ~?** can you ride a bicycle?; **~ de carreras/ejercicio/montaña** racing/exercise/mountain bike

bicimoto *m* (Méx) moped

bicolor *adj* two-colored*

bidé, bidet /bi'ðe/ *m* bidet

bidón *m* **(a)** (para gasolina, agua) can; (más grande) jerry can **(b)** (barril) barrel

bien¹ *adj inv* **1** [ESTAR] (de salud, en general) well; **sentirse** *or* **encontrarse ~** to feel well; **¿cómo estás? — muy ~, gracias** how are you? — (I'm) very well, thank you; **¡qué ~ estás!** you look really well!; **¡tú no estás ~ de la cabeza!** you are not right in the head

2 [ESTAR] (cómodo, agradable): **¿vas ~ ahí atrás?** are you all right in the back?; **se está ~ a la sombra** it's nice in the shade; **la casa está muy ~** the house is very nice **(b)** [ESTAR] (correcto, adecuado) right; **la fecha/el reloj está ~** the date/the clock is right; **¿está ~ así?** is this all right?; **si te parece ~** if that's all right with you; **el cuadro no queda ~ ahí** the picture doesn't look right there **(c)** (suficiente): **estar** *or* **andar ~ de algo** to be all right for sth; **¿estamos ~ de aceite?** are we all right for oil?; **ya está ~** that's enough

3 [ESTAR] **(a)** (en calidad) good; **¿lo has leído? está muy ~** have you read it? it's very good **(b)** (fam) (sexualmente atractivo) good-looking, attractive

4 (fam) **(a)** (de buena posición social) ‹familia/gente› well-to-do **(b)** ‹barrio› well-to-do, posh (BrE)

bien² *adv* **1** **(a)** (de manera satisfactoria) ‹dormir/funcionar/cantar› well; **no le fue ~ en Alemania** things didn't work out for her in Germany **(b)** (correctamente) well; **habla muy ~ inglés** she speaks English very well *o* very good English; **¡~ hecho/dicho!** well done/said!; **pórtate ~** behave yourself; **hiciste ~ en decírselo** you were right to tell him; **siéntate ~** sit properly **(c)** (de manera agradable) ‹oler/saber› good

2 **(a)** (a fondo, completamente) well, properly; **~ cocido** well *o* properly cooked; **¿cerraste ~?** did you lock the door properly?; **~ sabes que ...** you know perfectly well that ... **(b)** (con cuidado, atención) ‹escuchar/mirar› carefully

3 **(a)** (como intensificador) (muy) very; **canta ~ mal** he sings really badly; **~ entrada la noche** very late at night; **¿estás ~ seguro?** are you positive? **(b)** (en locs) **más bien** rather; **no bien** as soon as; **si bien** although

■ *interj*: **¡(muy) ~!** well done!, (very) good!; **¡qué ~!** great!

■ *conj*: **~ ... o ...** either ... or ...; **se puede subir ~ a pie o a caballo** you can go up either on foot or on horseback

bien³ *m* **1** (Fil) good; **el ~ y el mal** good and evil; **hacer el ~** to do good deeds; **un hombre de ~** a good man

2 **(a)** (beneficio, bienestar) good; **es por mi/tu ~** it's for my/your own good **(b)** hacer bien (+ *me/te/le etc*): **esto te hará ~** this will do you good

3 (en calificaciones escolares) grade of between 6 and 6.9 on a scale of 1-10   ⋯⟩

4 bienes *mpl* (a) (Com) goods; ~**es de consumo** consumer goods (b) (Der) property; **le dejó todos sus ~es** she left him everything she owned; ~**es inmuebles** *or* **raíces** real estate, property (BrE); ~**es muebles** personal property, goods and chattels; ~**es públicos** public property

bienal *adj* biennial

bienaventurado -da *adj* blessed

bienestar *m* well-being, welfare; **estado de ~** social welfare state; ~ **social** social welfare

bienhablado -da *adj* well-spoken

bienintencionado -da *adj* well-meaning, well-intentioned

bienvenida *f* welcome; **darle la ~ a algn** to welcome sb; **un discurso de ~** a welcoming speech

bienvenido -da *adj* welcome; **ser ~** to be welcome

bies *m*: **al ~** on the cross

bife *m* (CS) (Coc) steak

bifocal *adj* bifocal

bifurcación *f* (en carretera) fork; (en la vía férrea) junction

bifurcarse [A2] *v pron* «*camino*» to fork, diverge (fml); «*vía férrea*» to diverge

bigamia *f* bigamy

bígamo -ma *adj* bigamous
■ *m,f* bigamist

bigote *m* 1 (de persona) *tb* ~**s** mustache* 2 (de gato, ratón) whisker

bigotudo -da, (Méx) **bigotón -tona** *adj* (fam): **un hombre ~** a man with a big mustache*

bigudí *m* (*pl* **-díes -dís**) curler, roller

bikini *m or* (RPl) *f* bikini

bilateral *adj* bilateral

bilingüe *adj* bilingual

bilis *f* (Fisiol) bile

billar *m* (con tres bolas) billiards; (con 16 bolas) pool; (con 22 bolas) snooker

billete *m* 1 (Fin) bill (esp AmE), note (BrE) 2 (de lotería, rifa, de transporte) ticket; **sacar/pagar un ~** to get/pay for a ticket; ~ **de ida y vuelta** (Esp) round-trip ticket (AmE), return (ticket) (BrE); ~ **sencillo** *or* **de ida** (Esp) one-way ticket, single (ticket) (BrE)

billetera *f*, **billetero** *m* wallet, billfold (AmE); (con monedero) change purse (AmE), purse (BrE)

billetero -ra *m,f* (Méx, Ven) lottery ticket vendor

billón *m* trillion

bimensual *adj* (dos veces al mes) twice-monthly, fortnightly (BrE)

bimestral *adj* (cada dos meses) bimonthly; (que dura dos meses) two-month (*before n*)

bimestre *m* (period of) two months; (pago) bimonthly payment

bimotor *m* twin-engined aircraft

binario -ria *adj* binary

bingo *m* (juego) bingo; (sala) bingo hall

binoculares, (Col, Ven) **binóculos** *mpl* binoculars (*pl*)

biodegradable *adj* biodegradable

biografía *f* biography

biográfico -ca *adj* biographical

biógrafo -fa *m,f* biographer

biología *f* biology

biológico -ca *adj* (Biol) biological; ⟨*verduras*⟩ organic

biólogo -ga *m,f* biologist

biombo *m* folding screen

biopsia *f* biopsy

bioquímica *f* biochemistry

bioquímico -ca *adj* biochemical
■ *m,f* biochemist

bióxido *m* dioxide

bip *m* (a) (sonido) pip, beep (b) (Méx) (aparato) pager, beeper, bleeper (BrE)

bipartidismo *m* two-party system

bípedo *m* biped

biplaza *m* two-seater

biquini *m* bikini

birlar [A1] *vt* (fam) to swipe (colloq), to pinch (BrE colloq)

Birmania *f* Burma

birmano¹ -na *adj/m,f* Burmese; **los ~s** the Burmese

birmano² *m* (idioma) Burmese

birome *f* (RPl) ballpoint pen, Biro®

birrete *m* (a) cap (*worn by lawyers, professors, etc*) (b) (birreta) biretta

bis *m* encore

bisabuelo -la *m, f* (*m*) great-grandfather; (*f*) great-grandmother; **mis ~s** my great-grandparents

bisagra *f* hinge

biselar [A1] *vt* to bevel

bisexual *adj/mf* bisexual

bisexualidad *f* bisexuality

bisiesto *adj*: **1992 fue (año) ~** 1992 was a leap year

bisne *m* (AmC fam) hustling (colloq), black marketeering

bisnieto -ta *m, f* (*m*) great-grandson; (*f*) great-granddaughter; **mis ~s** my great-grandchildren

bisonte *m* bison

bisoñé *m* toupee, hairpiece

bisoño -ña *adj* inexperienced; **soldados ~s** raw recruits

bistec /biˈstek/ *m* (*pl* **-tecs**) steak, beefsteak

bisturí *m* scalpel

bisutería *f* costume o imitation jewelry*

bit *m* (*pl* **bits**) (Inf) bit

bividí /biβiˈði/ *m* (Per) undershirt (AmE), vest (BrE)

bizantino -na *adj* (Hist) Byzantine

bizco -ca *adj* cross-eyed
■ *m,f* cross-eyed person

bizcocho *m* (pastel) sponge (cake); (galleta) sponge finger

blanca *f* 1 (Mús) half note (AmE), minim (BrE) 2 (en dominó) blank; (en ajedrez) white piece 3 (Esp fam) (dinero): **estar sin** *or* **no tener ~** to be broke (colloq)

Blancanieves Snow White

blanco¹ -ca *adj* 1 (a) ⟨*color/vestido/pelo*⟩ white; **en ~** ⟨*cheque/página*⟩ blank; **rellenar los espacios en ~** fill in the blanks; **me quedé en ~**

my mind went blank **(b)** (pálido) [**SER**] fair-skinned, pale-skinned; [**ESTAR**] white; **estoy muy** ~ I'm very white *o* pale **2** ⟨*persona/raza*⟩ white **3** ⟨*vino*⟩ white
■ *m,f* white person

blanco² *m* **1** (color) white; **en ~ y negro** black and white **2** (Dep, Jueg) (objeto) target; (centro) bullseye; **tirar al ~** to shoot at the target; **dar en el ~** to hit the target/bullseye **3** (vino) white (wine)

blancura *f* whiteness

blandir [I1] *vt* to brandish, wave

blando -da *adj* **1** **(a)** ⟨*carne*⟩ tender; ⟨*queso/ mantequilla*⟩ soft; **ponerse ~** to go soft **(b)** ⟨*cama/madera/agua*⟩ soft; **un cepillo de cerdas blandas** a soft brush **2** ⟨*carácter*⟩ (débil) weak; (poco severo) soft

blandura *f* **1** (en general) softness; (de la carne) tenderness **2** (falta de severidad) leniency; **trata a sus alumnos con demasiada ~** she's too lenient with *o* too soft on her pupils

blanqueador *m* (para visillos) whitener; (lejía) (Col, Méx) bleach

blanquear [A1] *vt* **(a)** ⟨*ropa*⟩ to bleach; ⟨*pared*⟩ to whitewash **(b)** ⟨*dinero*⟩ to launder

blanqueo *m* **(a)** (de paredes) whitewashing **(b)** (de dinero) laundering

blasfemia *f* blasphemy

blindado -da *adj* ⟨*coche*⟩ armor-plated*, armored*; ⟨*puerta*⟩ reinforced

blindar [A1] *vt* ⟨*barco/coche*⟩ to armor-plate*; ⟨*puerta*⟩ to reinforce

bloc *m* (*pl* **blocs**) (de papel) pad; ~ **de notas** note *o* writing pad

blof *m* (Col, Méx) bluff

blofear [A1] *vi* (Col, Méx) **(a)** (en el juego) to bluff **(b)** (fam) (alardear) to show off

bloque *m* **1** (de piedra, hormigón) block **2** (edificio) block; **un ~ de departamentos** (AmL) *or* (Esp) **pisos** an apartment block, a block of flats (BrE) **3** (Inf) block **4** (fuerza política) bloc; **en ~** (*loc adv*) en bloc, en masse

bloquear [A1] *vt* **1** **(a)** ⟨*camino/entrada/ salida*⟩ to block; **estamos bloqueados por un camión** there's a truck blocking our way **(b)** (Mil) to blockade **2** ⟨*cuenta/fondos*⟩ to freeze, block
■ **bloquearse** *v pron* **1** «*mecanismo*» to jam; «*frenos*» to jam, lock on; «*ruedas*» to lock **2** «*negociaciones*» to reach deadlock

bloqueo *m* (de ciudad) blockade, siege; (de puerto) blockade; (Dep) block

bluff /bluf/ *m* (*pl* **bluffs**) **(a)** (Jueg) bluff **(b)** (fam) (fanfarronería): **es puro ~** he's all talk (colloq)

blusa *f* blouse

blusón *m* loose shirt *o* blouse

blvar. *m* (= **bulevar**) Blvd (*in US*)

Bº = Banco

boa *f* (Zool) boa

bobada *f* (cosa boba) silly thing; **deja de hacer ~s** stop being so stupid *o* silly; **deja de decir ~s** stop talking nonsense

bobina *f* **(a)** (de hilo) reel **(b)** (Auto, Elec) coil

bobo -ba *adj* (fam) silly
■ *m,f* (fam) fool

boca *f* **1** **(a)** (Anat, Zool) mouth **(b)** (en locs) **boca abajo/arriba** ⟨*dormir/echarse*⟩ on one's

stomach/back; **puso los naipes ~ arriba** she laid the cards face up; **en boca de: la pregunta que anda en ~ de todos los niños** the question which is on every child's lips; **el escándalo andaba en ~ de todos** the scandal was common knowledge; **por boca de** from; **lo supe por ~ de su hermana** I heard it from his sister; **a pedir de ~** just fine; **hacerle el ~ a ~ a algn** to give sb the kiss of life; **hacérsele la ~ agua a algn** (Esp): **se le hacía la ~ agua mirando los pasteles** looking at the cakes made her mouth water; **quedarse con la ~ abierta** to be dumbfounded *o* (colloq) flabbergasted **2** (de buzón) slot; (de túnel) mouth, entrance; (de puerto) entrance; (de vasija, botella) rim; ~ **de incendios** fire hydrant, fireplug (AmE); ~ **del estómago** (fam) pit of the stomach; ~ **de metro** *or* (RPl) **subte** subway entrance (AmE), underground *o* tube station entrance (BrE)

bocacalle *f*: *entrance to a street*; **la primera a la derecha** the first turning on the right

bocadillo *m* **1** (Esp) (emparedado) roll **2** (Col, Ven) (dulce) guava jelly

bocado *m* **(a)** (de comida) bite; **de un ~** in one bite; **no ha probado ~** she hasn't had a bite to eat **(b)** (comida ligera) snack

bocajarro: a ~ (*loc adv*) **(a)** ⟨*disparar*⟩ at point-blank range **(b)** ⟨*decir/preguntar*⟩ point-blank

bocamanga *f* cuff

bocanada *f* (de humo, aliento) puff, mouthful; (ráfaga) gust, blast

bocatoma *f* (Andes) water inlet

boceto *m* (dibujo) sketch; (de proyecto) outline

bochar [A1] *vt* **(a)** (RPl fam) ⟨*sugerencia/ propuesta*⟩ to squash (colloq) **(b)** (RPl arg) (en examen) ⟨*estudiante*⟩ to fail, to flunk (AmE colloq)

bochas *fpl* (RPl) (Jueg) bowls

bochinche *m* (esp AmL fam) **(a)** (riña, pelea) fight, brawl **(b)** (barullo, alboroto) racket (colloq), ruckus (AmE colloq), row (BrE colloq) **(c)** (confusión, lío) muddle, mess (colloq)

bochinchear [A1] *vi* (AmL fam) to fight

bochinchero -ra *adj* (AmL fam) rowdy

bochorno *m* **1** (calor) sultry *o* muggy weather **2** (vergüenza) embarrassment; **¡qué ~!** how embarrassing!

bochornoso -sa *adj* **1** ⟨*tiempo*⟩ sultry, muggy; ⟨*calor*⟩ sticky; **hacía un día ~** it was a close *o* muggy day **2** ⟨*espectáculo/situación*⟩ embarrassing

bocina *f* **1** (de coche) horn; (de fábrica) hooter, siren; (de faro) foghorn **2** (AmL) (auricular) receiver **3** (Méx) (Audio) loudspeaker

bocio *m* goiter*

boda *f* wedding; ~**s de oro/plata** (de matrimonio) golden/silver wedding anniversary; (de organización) golden/silver jubilee

bodega *f* **1** **(a)** (Vin) (fábrica) winery; (almacén) wine cellar; (tienda) wine merchant's, wine shop **(b)** (taberna) bar **(c)** (en casa) cellar **2** **(a)** (AmC, Per, Ven) (tienda de comestibles) grocery store (AmE), grocer's (BrE) **(b)** (AmL exc RPl) (depósito) store, warehouse

bodegón *m* **1** (Art) still life **2** (casa de comidas) inn

bodeguero -ra *m,f* **1** (Vin) (productor)

wine-producer **2** (a) (AmC, Per, Ven) (tendero) shopkeeper (b) (AmL exc RPl) (de un depósito) warehouseman

bodrio *m* (fam): **es un ~** it is garbage (AmE) *o* (BrE) rubbish (colloq)

bofetada *f*, **bofetón** *m* slap; **le di** *or* **pegué una ~** I slapped him (in the face)

boga *f*: **estar en ~** to be in fashion *o* in vogue

Bogotá *m* Bogotá

bogotano -na *adj* of/from Bogotá

bohemio -mia *adj* (a) ‹vida/artista› bohemian (b) (de Bohemia) Bohemian
■ *m,f* bohemian

bohío *m* (AmC, Col, Ven) hut

boicot /boj'kot/ *m* (*pl* **-cots**) boycott

boicotear [A1] *vt* to boycott

boina *f* beret

boite /bwat/ *f* night club

bol *m* bowl

bola *f* **1** (cuerpo redondo) ball; (de helado) scoop; (Dep) ball; (de petanca) boule; (canica) (Col, Per) marble; **~ de cristal** crystal ball; **~ de nieve** snowball; **~ de partido/de set** match/set point **2 bolas** *fpl* (fam: en algunas regiones vulg) (testículos) balls (*pl*) (colloq *or* vulg); **estar en ~s** (fam *or* vulg) to be stark naked (colloq); **hacerse ~s con algo** (Méx) to get in a mess over sth **3** (fam) (mentira) lie, fib (colloq); **me metió una ~** he told me a fib; **contar/decir ~s** to fib (colloq), to tell fibs (colloq) **4** (Méx fam) (montón): **una ~ de** loads of (colloq)

bolchevique *adj/mf* Bolshevik

boleador -dora *m,f* **1** (Méx) (lustrabotas) bootblack **2** (en las pampas) *person who uses bolas to catch cattle*

boleadoras *fpl* bolas

bolear [A1] *vi* (Col) to knock up, knock a ball about
■ **~** *vt* (Méx) to polish, shine

bolera *f* bowling alley

bolero¹ *m* **1** (Mús) bolero **2** (Indum) bolero jacket/top

bolero² -ra *m,f* (Méx) bootblack

boleta *f* (AmL) (a) (en rifa) ticket (b) (CS) (de multa) ticket (c) (CS) (recibo) receipt (d) (Col) (entrada) ticket; **~ de calificaciones** (Méx) school report, report card (AmE); **~ de depósito** (RPl) deposit slip (AmE), paying-in slip (BrE); **~ electoral** (Méx, RPl) ballot paper

boletaje *m* (Méx, Per) tickets (*pl*)

boletería *f* (AmL) (de teatro, cine) box office; (de estación, estadio) ticket office

boletín *m* bulletin; **~ de calificaciones** *or* **notas** school report, report card (AmE)

boleto *m* (de lotería, rifa) ticket; (de quinielas) (Esp) coupon; (de tren, autobús) (AmL) ticket; **~ de ida** (AmL) one-way ticket, single (ticket) (BrE); **~ de ida y vuelta** (AmL) round trip (ticket) (AmE), return (ticket) (BrE); **~ de viaje redondo** (Méx) round trip (ticket) (AmE), return (ticket) (BrE)

boli *m* (Esp fam) ballpoint pen, Biro® (BrE)

boliche *m* **1** (a) (en petanca) jack (b) (juguete) cup-and-ball toy (c) (Col) (bolo) tenpin **2** (Méx) (juego) bowling, ten pin bowling (BrE); (lugar) bowling alley **3** (a) (CS) (tienda pequeña) (fam) small store (AmE), small shop (BrE) (b) (Bol, RPl) (taberna) bar

bolígrafo *m* ballpoint pen, Biro®

bolillo *m* (en pasamanería) bobbin; **encaje de ~s** bobbin lace

bolita *f* (AmS) (Jueg) marble; **jugar a las ~s** to play marbles

bolívar *m* bolivar (*Venezuelan unit of currency*)

Bolivia *f* Bolivia

boliviano -na *adj/m,f* Bolivian

bollo *m* (Coc) bun; **ser un ~** (RPl fam) to be a piece of cake (colloq)

bolo *m* (a) (palo) skittle, tenpin (b) **bolos** *mpl* (juego) bowling, ten pin bowling (BrE); **jugar a los ~s** to play skittles, to go bowling

bolsa *f* **1** (a) (en general) bag; **~ de plástico/de la compra** plastic/shopping bag; **~ de (la) basura** garbage *o* trash bag (AmE), rubbish bag *o* bin liner (BrE); **una ~ de patatas fritas** (Esp) a bag of chips (AmE), a packet *o* bag of crisps (BrE); **~ de agua caliente** hot-water bottle (b) (Méx) (bolso) handbag, purse (AmE) **2** (a) (de marsupial) pouch (b) scrotum (c) (Méx) (bolsillo) pocket **3** (de aire, gas, agua) pocket **4** (Econ, Fin) stock exchange, stock market; **jugar a la ~** to play the market; **se cotizará en ~** it will be listed on the stock exchange; **~ de empleo** (Col) employment agency; **~ de trabajo** *job vacancies and place where they are advertised*

bolsear [A1] *vt* (a) (Méx fam) (robar): **me ~on en el camión** I had my pocket picked on the bus (b) (Chi fam) ‹comida/cigarillos› **~le algo A algn** to scrounge sth FROM *o* OFF sb

bolsillo *m* pocket; **de ~** ‹calculadora/diccionario› pocket (*before n*); **meterse a algn en el ~** to get sb eating out of one's hand

bolso *m* (de mujer) (Esp) handbag, purse (AmE); **~ de mano** (de viaje) (overnight) bag; (de mujer) (Esp) handbag, purse (AmE); **~ de viaje** (overnight) bag

boludo -da *adj* (Col, RPl, Ven vulg) (imbécil): **es tan ~** he's such a jerk (colloq) *o* (vulg) prick
■ *m,f* (Col, RPl, Ven vulg) asshole (AmE vulg), dickhead (BrE vulg)

bomba *f* **1** (a) (Arm, Mil) bomb; **lanzar/arrojar ~s** to drop bombs; **poner una ~** to plant a bomb; **~ atómica** atom *o* atomic bomb; **~ de tiempo** time bomb; **~ lacrimógena** tear gas canister; **caer como una ~** ‹noticia› to come as a bombshell (b) (noticón) big news (c) (en fútbol americano) bomb **2** (Tec) pump; **~ de aire** pump; **~ de agua** water pump **3** (Andes, Ven) (gasolinera) gas station (AmE), petrol station (BrE) **4** (Chi) (vehículo) fire engine, fire truck (AmE); (estación) fire station

bombacha *f* **(a)** (CS) (de gaucho) baggy trousers (*pl*) **(b)** (RPl) (de mujer) panties (*pl*), knickers (*pl*) (BrE)

bombardear [A1] *vt* (desde avión) to bomb; (con artillería) to bombard, shell; **me ~on a preguntas** they bombarded me with questions

bombardeo *m* (desde aviones) bombing; (con artillería) bombardment, shelling

bombardero *m* bomber

bombazo *m* **1** (Méx) (explosión) bomb explosion **2** (fam) (noticia) bombshell

bombear [A1] *vt* to pump

bombero *mf*, **bombero -ra** *m,f* (de incendios) (*m*) firefighter, fireman; (*f*) firefighter; **llamar a los ~s** to call the fire department (AmE) *o* (BrE) brigade; **cuerpo de ~s** fire department (AmE) *o* (BrE) brigade

bombilla *f* **1** (Esp) (Elec) light bulb **2** (para el mate) *tube through which mate tea is drunk*

bombillo *m* (AmC, Col, Ven) light bulb

bombín *m* **1** (Indum) derby (AmE), bowler hat (BrE) **2** (para inflar) pump

bombita *f* (RPl) (Elec) light bulb

bombo *m* **1** (Mús) (instrumento) bass drum; (músico) bass drummer; **tengo la cabeza como un ~** my head's about to explode; **con ~s y platillos** *or* (Esp) **a ~ y platillo** with a great fanfare; **darle ~ a algo** to give sth a lot of hype (colloq) **2** (de sorteo) drum

bombón *m* **(a)** (confite) chocolate **(b)** (fam) (persona) stunner (colloq) **(c)** (Méx) (malvavisco) marshmallow

bombona *f* gas cylinder *o* canister

bombonería *f* candy store (AmE), sweet shop (BrE)

bonachón -chona *adj* (fam) (amable) good-natured, kind
■ *m,f* (fam) (persona amable) good-natured *o* kind person

bonaerense *adj*: *of/from the province of Buenos Aires*

bonche *m* **1** (AmC, Col fam) (riña) fight; (contienda) contest **2** (Ven fam) (fiesta) party, rave-up (BrE sl)

bondad *f* **(a)** (afabilidad, generosidad) goodness, kindness; **¿tendría la ~ de cerrar la puerta?** (frml) would you mind closing the door? **(b)** (del clima) mildness

bondadoso -sa *adj* kind, kindhearted, kindly

bongó, bongo *m* bongo

boniato *m* sweet potato

bonificación *f* **(a)** (aumento, beneficio) bonus **(b)** (descuento) discount

bonito¹ -ta *adj* pretty; ⟨canción/apartamento⟩ nice, lovely

bonito² *m* tuna, bonito

bono *m* (vale) voucher; (Econ, Fin) bond

boquera *f* cold sore

boquerón *m* anchovy

boquete *m* hole

boquiabierto -ta *adj*: **quedarse ~** to be speechless *o* dumbfounded

boquilla *f* (de instrumento musical) mouthpiece; (de pipa) stem; (para cigarrillos) cigarette holder

borbotón *m* gush; **a borbotones** ⟨hervir⟩ fiercely; ⟨salir⟩ «sangre/agua» to gush out

borda *f* gunwale, rail; **echar** *or* **tirar algo por la ~** to throw sth overboard

bordado¹ -da *adj* ⟨mantel/sábana⟩ embroidered

bordado² *m* embroidery

bordar [A1] *vt* ⟨sábana/blusa⟩ to embroider; **lo bordó a mano** she embroidered it by hand

borde *m* (de mesa, cama, acantilado) edge; (de moneda, taza, vaso) rim; **llenó el vaso hasta el ~** she filled the glass to the brim; **al ~ de algo** ⟨de la guerra/locura⟩ on the brink of sth; ⟨de las lágrimas/del caos/de la ruina⟩ on the verge of sth; **al ~ de la muerte** on the point of death

bordear [A1] *vt* **(a)** (seguir el borde de) ⟨costa⟩ to go along; ⟨isla⟩ to go around **(b)** (estar a lo largo del borde): **un camino bordeado de álamos** a road lined with poplars

bordillo *m* curb (AmE), kerb (BrE)

bordo *m*: **a ~** on board; **subir a ~** to go aboard *o* on board

borgoña *m* (Vin) Burgundy, burgundy

borra *f* (sedimento — del café) dregs; (— del vino) lees (*pl*), sediment

borrachera *f*: **pegarse** *or* (Esp) **cogerse** *or* (esp AmL) **agarrarse una ~** to get drunk

borracho -cha *adj* **(a)** [ESTAR] drunk **(b)** [SER]: **es muy ~** he is a drunkard *o* a heavy drinker
■ *m,f* drunk; (habitual) drunkard, drunk

borrador *m* **1** (de redacción, carta) rough draft; (de contrato, proyecto) draft; (de dibujo) sketch; **lo hice en ~** I did a rough draft **2** (para la pizarra) eraser (AmE), board rubber (BrE)

borraja *f* borage

borrar [A1] *vt* **(a)** ⟨palabra/dibujo⟩ (con goma) to rub out, erase; (con líquido corrector) to white out, tippex out (BrE); ⟨pizarra⟩ to clean; ⟨huellas digitales⟩ to wipe off **(b)** ⟨cassette/disquete⟩ to erase, wipe **(c)** (Inf) ⟨archivo⟩ delete; ⟨pantalla⟩ to clear **(d)** ⟨recuerdos/imagen⟩ to blot out
■ **borrarse** *v pron* «inscripción/letrero» to fade; **se borró con la lluvia** the rain washed it away *o* off

borrasca *f* **(a)** (área de bajas presiones) area of low pressure **(b)** (tormenta) squall

borrascoso -sa *adj* ⟨viento⟩ squally; ⟨tiempo⟩ stormy, squally

borrego -ga *m,f* (cordero) lamb; (oveja) sheep

borrón *m* (mancha) inkblot; (mancha borroneada) smudge; **~ y cuenta nueva** let's make a fresh start

borronear [A1] *vt* to smudge

borroso -sa *adj* ⟨foto/imagen⟩ blurred; ⟨inscripción⟩ worn; ⟨contorno⟩ indistinct, blurred

boscoso -sa *adj* wooded

bosque *m* wood; (más grande) forest, woods (*pl*); (terreno) woodland; **~ ecuatorial** *or* **pluvial** (equatorial) rainforest

bosquejar [A1] *vt* (Art) to sketch, make a sketch of; ⟨idea/proyecto⟩ to outline, sketch out

bosquejo *m* (Art) sketch; (de novela) outline

bostezar [A4] *vi* to yawn

bostezo *m* yawn

bota *f* **1** (calzado) boot; **~s de caña alta/de** ···⋗

b

media caña knee-high/calf-length boots; ~**s de agua** rubber boots, wellingtons (BrE); ~**s de esquí/montar** ski/riding boots ② (para vino) small wineskin

botadero *m* (Andes) *tb* ~ **de basura** garbage dump (AmE), rubbish dump *o* tip (BrE)

botado -da *adj* [ESTAR] (AmS exc RPI fam) **(a)** (barato) dirt cheap (colloq) **(b)** (fácil) dead easy (colloq)

botadura *f* launching

botana *f* (Méx) snack, appetizer

botánico -ca *adj* botanical

botar [A1] *vt* ① ‹*barco*› to launch
② ‹*pelota*› to bounce
③ (AmL exc RPI) (tirar) to throw ... out; **no lo botes al suelo** don't throw it on the ground; **bótalo a la basura** chuck *o* throw it out (colloq); ~ **el dinero** to throw your money away
④ (AmL exc RPI fam) **(a)** (echar — de lugar) to throw ... out (colloq); (— de trabajo) to fire (colloq), to sack (BrE colloq) **(b)** (abandonar) ‹*novio/novia*› to chuck (colloq), to ditch (colloq); ‹*marido/esposa*› to leave; **el tren nos dejó botados** we missed the train
⑤ (AmL exc RPI fam) (derribar) ‹*puerta/árbol*› to knock down; ‹*botella/taza*› to knock over; **no empujes que me botas** stop pushing, you're going to knock me over
⑥ (AmL exc RPI) (perder) ‹*aceite/gasolina*› to leak
■ ~ *vi* (Esp) ‹*pelota*› to bounce
■ **botarse** *v pron* (AmL exc CS fam) **(a)** (apresurarse) to rush **(b)** (arrojarse) to jump

botarate *mf* (fam) (irresponsable) irresponsible fool **(b)** (AmL exc RPI) (derrochador) spendthrift

bote *m* ① (Náut) boat; ~ **de** *or* **a remos** rowboat (AmE), rowing boat (BrE); ~ **salvavidas** lifeboat ② (recipiente — de lata) tin; (— de vidrio, plástico) storage jar; (— de cerveza) (Esp) can; (— de mermelada) (Esp) jar; **el** ~ **de la basura** (Méx) the trash can (AmE), the rubbish bin (BrE); **de** ~ **en** ~ packed ③ (de pelota) bounce; **dio dos** ~**s** it bounced twice

botella *f* bottle; **una** ~ **de vino** (recipiente) a wine bottle; (con contenido) a bottle of wine; **cerveza de** *or* **en** ~ bottled beer

botica *f* (en algunas regiones ant) (farmacia) pharmacy

botijo *m*: drinking jug with spout

botillería *f* (Chi) liquor store (AmE), off licence (BrE)

botín *m* ① (bota corta) ankle boot; (de bebé) bootee; (de futbolista) (CS) boot ② (de guerra) plunder, booty; (de ladrones) haul, loot

botiquín *m* **(a)** (armario — para medicinas) medicine chest *o* cabinet; (— para colonias, jabón, etc) bathroom cabinet **(b)** (maletín) *tb* ~ **de primeros auxilios** first-aid kit

botón *m* ① (Indum) button; ~ **de presión** (AmL) snap fastener (AmE), press stud (BrE) ② (de mecanismo) button; **el** ~ **del volumen** the volume control ③ (AmL) (insignia) badge, button (AmE) ④ (de flor) bud

botones *mf* (*pl* ~) (de hotel) bellboy; (de oficina) (*m*) office boy; (*f*) office girl

bouquet /bu'ke/ *m* (*pl* -**quets**) **(a)** (del vino) bouquet **(b)** (ramillete) bouquet

boutique /bu'tik/ *f* boutique

bóveda *f* ① (Arquit) vault; ~ **de seguridad** (AmL) bank vault ② (RPI) (sepulcro) tomb

bovino -na *adj* bovine

bowling /'boulin/ *m* **(a)** (deporte) tenpins (AmE), tenpin bowling (BrE) **(b)** (lugar) bowling alley

box /boks/ *m* (AmL) (boxeo) boxing

boxeador -dora *m,f* boxer

boxear [A1] *vi* to box

boxeo *m* boxing

boya *f* (Náut) buoy; (en pesca) float

boyante *adj* ‹*situación/economía*› buoyant

bozal *m* (de perro) muzzle; (de caballo) halter

bozo *m* down (on upper lip)

bracero -ra *m,f* temporary farm worker

bragas *fpl* (Esp) (de mujer) panties (*pl*), knickers (*pl*) (BrE)

braguero *m* truss

bragueta *f* fly, flies (*pl*)

braille /'brajle/ *adj* braille (before n)
■ *m* braille

bramante *m* twine, string

bramar [A1] *vi* ‹*toro/ciervo*› to bellow; ‹*elefante*› to trumpet

bramido *m* (de toro, ciervo) bellowing; (de elefante) trumpeting; **dio un** ~ it bellowed/trumpeted

branquia *f* gill

brasa *f* ember; **carne/pescado a la(s)** ~**(s)** charcoal-grilled meat/fish

brasero *m* (de carbón — para interiores) small brazier; (— para la intemperie) brazier; (eléctrico) electric heater

brasier *m* (Col, Méx, Ven) bra

Brasil *m*: *tb* **el** ~ Brazil

brasileño -ña, (AmL) **brasilero -ra** *adj/m,f* Brazilian

bravío -vía *adj* ‹*toro*› fierce, wild; ‹*potro*› wild, unmanageable

bravo¹ -va *adj* **(a)** [SER] ‹*toro/perro*› fierce; *ver tb* TORO **(b)** [ESTAR] ‹*mar*› rough **(c)** [ESTAR] (AmL fam) (enojado) angry

bravo² *interj* (expresando aprobación) well done!, good job! (AmE); (tras actuación) bravo!

bravucón -cona *adj* (fam) bragging (before n)

bravuconada *f* piece of bravado; ~**s** bravado

braza *f* (Esp) (en natación) breaststroke; **nadar a** ~ to swim (the) breaststroke

brazada *f* (al nadar) stroke

brazalete *m* **(a)** (pulsera — de una pieza) bangle, bracelet; (— de eslabones) bracelet **(b)** (de tela) armband

brazo *m* ① (Anat) arm; (parte superior) upper arm; **llevaba una cesta al** ~ she had a basket on one arm; **caminar/ir del** ~ to walk arm in arm; **llevaba al niño en** ~**s** he was carrying the child in his arms; *cruzado de* ~**s**: **no te quedes ahí cruzado de** ~**s** don't just stand/sit there (doing nothing); *dar el* ~ *a torcer* to give in; **no dio el** *or* **su** ~ **a torcer** he didn't let them/her twist his arm
② (de sillón) arm; (de tocadiscos) arm; (de grúa) jib; (de río) branch, channel; ~ **de gitano** (Coc) jelly roll (AmE), swiss roll (BrE); ~ **de mar** inlet, sound ③ **brazos** *mpl* (trabajadores) hands (*pl*)

brea *f* pitch, tar

brebaje *m* potion; **un** ~ **mágico** a magic potion

brecha *f* (en muro) breach, opening; (en la frente, cabeza) gash; ~ **generacional** generation gap

bretel *m* (CS) strap

bretón¹ -tona *adj/m,f* Breton

bretón² *m* (idioma) Breton

breva *f* (Bot) early fig, black fig

breve *adj* (fml) brief, short; ‹*viaje/distancia*› short; **dentro de ~s momentos** in a few moments; **sea usted ~, por favor** please be brief; **en ~** shortly, soon

brevedad *f* **(a)** (de discurso, texto) brevity **(b)** (fml) (prontitud): **con la mayor ~** *or* **a la ~ posible** as soon as possible *o* (fml) at your earliest convenience

brevete *m* (Per) driver's license (AmE), driving licence (BrE)

bribón -bona *m,f* (fam) rascal (colloq), scamp (colloq)

bricolaje, bricolage *m* do-it-yourself, DIY

brida *f* bridle

briega *f* (Col) hard work, struggle

brigada *f* (Mil) brigade; (de policía) squad; ~ **de explosivos** bomb squad; ~ **antidroga** *or* **de estupefacientes** drug squad; ~ **de salvamento** rescue team

brillante *adj* **(a)** ‹*luz/estrella/color*› bright; ‹*zapatos/metal/pelo*› shiny; ‹*pintura*› gloss (*before* n); ‹*papel*› glossy; ‹*tela*› with a sheen **(b)** ‹*escritor/porvenir*› brilliant; ‹*mente*› great; **su actuación fue ~** she performed brilliantly
■ *m* (diamante) diamond; **un anillo de ~s** a diamond ring

brillar [A1] *vi* **(a)** «*sol/luz*» to shine; «*estrella*» to shine, sparkle; «*zapatos/suelo/metal*» to shine, gleam; «*diamante/ojos*» to sparkle **(b)** (destacarse) «*persona*» to shine
■ ~ *vt* (Col) to polish

brillo *m* **(a)** (en general) shine; (de estrella) brightness, brilliance; (de diamante, ojos) sparkle; (de tela) sheen; **darle ~ al suelo** to polish the floor; **fotos con ~** gloss finish photos; **dale un poco de ~** (TV) turn the brightness up a bit **(b)** (esplendor, lucimiento) splendor*; **sin ~** ‹*discurso/ interpretación*› dull **(c)** (para labios) lip gloss; (para uñas) clear nail polish

brilloso -sa *adj* (AmL) shiny

brincar [A2] *vi* «*niño*» to jump up and down; «*cordero*» to gambol, skip around; «*liebre*» to hop; ~ **de alegría** to jump for joy
■ ~ *vt* (Méx) ‹*valla/obstáculo*› to jump

brinco *m* jump, leap, bound; **pegó** *or* **dio un ~ del susto** (fam) he jumped with fright

brindar [A1] *vi* to drink a toast; ~ **POR algn/ algo** to drink a toast ⊤o sb/sth
■ ~ *vt* (fml) (proporcionar) to give; **le brindó su apoyo** she gave him her support
■ **brindarse** *v pron* (fml) ~**se** ʌ **hacer algo** to offer *o* volunteer to do sth; **se brindó a acompañarme** he offered *o* volunteered to accompany me

brindis *m* (*pl* ~) toast; **hacer un ~ por algn** to drink a toast to sb

brío *m* **(a)** (ánimo, energía) spirit; **luchó con ~** he fought with great spirit *o* determination **(b)** (de caballo) spirit

brioso -sa *adj* ‹*caballo*› spirited

brisa *f* breeze

británico -ca *adj* British
■ *m,f* British person, Briton; **los ~s** the British, British people

brizna *f* (hebra) strand; (de hierba) blade

briznar [A1] *v impers* (Ven) to drizzle

broca *f* (drill) bit

brocado *m* brocade

brocha *f* (de pintor) paintbrush, brush; (de afeitar) shaving brush; (en cosmética) blusher brush

broche *m* **(a)** (joya) brooch **(b)** (de collar, monedero) clasp; ~ **de presión** (AmL) snap fastener (AmE), press stud (BrE) **(c)** (Méx, Ur) (para el pelo) barrette (AmE), hair slide (BrE) **(d)** (Arg) (grapa) staple

brocheta *f* (aguja) brochette, skewer; (plato) kebab

brócoli *m* broccoli

broma *f* joke; **hacerle** *or* **gastarle una ~ a algn** to play a (practical) joke on sb; **déjate de ~s** stop kidding around (colloq); **no estoy para ~s** I'm not in the mood for jokes; **~s aparte** joking apart; **lo dije de** *or* **en ~** I was joking; **ni en ~** no way (colloq)

bromear [A1] *vi* to joke

bromista *adj*: **es muy ~** he's always joking; **¡qué ~ eres!** you're such a joker
■ *mf* joker

bromuro *m* bromide

bronca *f* **1 (a)** (fam) (disputa, lío) row; **armar** *or* **montar una ~** to kick up a fuss (colloq); **buscar ~** to look for trouble *o* a fight **(b)** (alboroto, bullicio) racket (colloq) **2** (esp Esp fam) (regañina) scolding, telling off (colloq); **echarle la ~ a algn** to tell sb off **3** (AmL fam) (rabia): **está con una ~** he's furious; **me da mucha ~** it really gets to *o* bugs me (colloq); **tenerle ~ a algn** to have it in for sb (colloq)

bronce *m* **(a)** (para estatuas, cañones) bronze; **una medalla de ~** a bronze medal **(b)** (AmL) (para llamadores, placas) brass

bronceado¹ -da *adj* tanned, suntanned

bronceado² *m* (de la piel) tan, suntan; (Metal) bronzing

bronceador *m* suntan lotion

broncear [A1] *vt* «*piel*» to tan
■ **broncearse** *v pron* to get a tan *o* a suntan

bronconeumonía *f* bronchopneumonia

bronquio *m* bronchial tube

bronquitis *f* bronchitis

brotar [A1] *vi* **(a)** «*planta*» to sprout, come up; «*hoja*» to appear, sprout; «*flor*» to come out **(b)** «*sarampión/grano*» to appear
■ **brotarse** *v pron* (AmL) to come out in spots

brote *m* **(a)** (Bot) shoot; **echar ~s** to sprout, put out shoots **(b)** (de violencia, enfermedad) outbreak **(c)** (Col) (sarpullido) rash

bruces: **de ~** (loc adv) face down; **se cayó de ~** he fell flat on his face

brujería *f* witchcraft

brujo -ja *adj* ‹*ojos/amor*› bewitching **(b)** (AmC, Méx fam) (sin dinero) broke (colloq)
■ *m,f* (*m*) warlock; (*f*) witch

brújula *f* compass

bruma *f* (marina) (sea) mist; (del alba) mist

brumoso -sa *adj* misty

bruñir [I9] *vt* to polish

brusco -ca *adj* **(a)** ⟨*movimiento/cambio*⟩ abrupt, sudden; ⟨*subida/descenso*⟩ sharp, sudden **(b)** ⟨*carácter/modales*⟩ rough; ⟨*tono/gesto*⟩ brusque, abrupt; ⟨*respuesta*⟩ curt, brusque

Bruselas *f* Brussels

brusquedad *f* **(a)** (en el trato) roughness; **con ~** ⟨*hablar/actuar*⟩ abruptly **(b)** (de movimiento) abruptness, suddenness; **frenó con ~** he braked sharply

brutal *adj* ⟨*crimen*⟩ brutal; ⟨*atentado*⟩ savage

brutalidad *f* brutality, savageness

bruto -ta *adj* ⓵ ⟨*persona*⟩ **(a)** (ignorante) ignorant **(b)** (violento, brusco): **¡qué ~!** what a brute! ⓶ ⟨*peso/sueldo*⟩ gross; **en ~** ⟨*diamante*⟩ uncut; ⟨*mineral*⟩ crude
■ *m,f* **(a)** (ignorante) ignorant person **(b)** (persona violenta) brute, animal

bucal *adj* ⟨*lesión*⟩ mouth (*before n*); ⟨*antiséptico/higiene*⟩ oral (*before n*)

buceador -dora *m,f* diver

bucear [A1] *vi* to swim underwater, to dive

buceo *m* underwater swimming, diving

buchaca *f* (Col) pocket

buche *m* ⓵ **(a)** (de aves) crop **(b)** (de otros animales) maw ⓶ (Med, Odont): **hacer ~s con algo** to rinse one's mouth out with sth

bucle *m* **(a)** (en el pelo) ringlet **(b)** (Inf) loop

bucólico -ca *adj* bucolic, pastoral

budín *m* **(a)** (dulce) pudding **(b)** (salado) pie

budismo *m* Buddhism

budista *adj/mf* Buddhist

buen *adj* ▶ BUENO¹

buenaventura *f* **(a)** (buena suerte) good fortune **(b)** (futuro): **me dijo/leyó la ~** she told my fortune

buen mozo, -na moza *adj* ⟨*hombre*⟩ good-looking, handsome; ⟨*mujer*⟩ attractive, good-looking

bueno¹ -na *adj* [BUEN *is used before masculine singular nouns*]
⓵ [SER] **(a)** ⟨*hotel/producto/trabajo*⟩ good; **ropa buena** good-quality clothes; **la buena mesa** good cooking **(b)** ⟨*remedio/método*⟩ good; **es ~ para la gripe/los dolores de cabeza** it's good for the flu/headaches **(c)** ⟨*médico/alumno*⟩ good; **un buen padre/amigo** he's a good father/friend; **es muy buena en francés** she's very good at French; **es buena para los negocios** she's got a good head for business **(d)** (amable, bondadoso) good, kind; **fueron muy ~s conmigo** they were very good *o* kind to me **(e)** (conveniente, correcto) good; **no es buena hora** it's not a good time; **no es ~ comer tanto** it isn't good to eat so much; **es ~ para la salud** it's good for your health; **su inglés es ~** her English is good
⓶ **(a)** (agradable) nice; **hace muy buen tiempo** the weather is nice **(b)** ⟨*comida*⟩ (en general) **ser ~** to be good, be nice; (en particular) **estar ~** to be good, be nice; **el guacamole es buenísimo** guacamole is

really good; **esta sopa está muy buena** this soup is very good **(c)** (favorable) ⟨*oferta/crítica*⟩ good; **una buena noticia** a piece of good news
⓷ [ESTAR] **(a)** (en buen estado) ⟨*leche/pescado*⟩ fresh; **esta leche no está buena** this milk is off *o* sour **(b)** (fam) (sexualmente atractivo): **está buenísimo** he's really gorgeous
⓸ (saludable, sano) ⟨*costumbre/alimentación*⟩ good; **estar en buena forma** to be in good shape
⓹ **(a)** (en fórmulas, saludos) good; **¡~s días!** good morning; **¡buenas tardes!** (temprano) good afternoon; (más tarde) good evening; **¡buenas noches!** (al llegar) good evening; (al despedirse) good night; **¡buen viaje!** have a good trip!; **¡buen provecho!** enjoy your meal **(b)** ⟨*delante del n*⟩ (uso enfático) ⟨*susto*⟩ terrible; **una buena cantidad** a fair amount; **un buen día** one day **(c)** **¡qué ~!** (AmL) great **(d)** **de buenas a primeras** suddenly; **por las buenas** willingly
■ *m,f* **(a)** (hum *o* leng infantil) (en películas, cuentos) goody (colloq); **los ~s y los malos** the good guys and the bad guys (colloq) **(b)** (bonachón, buenazo): **el ~ de Juan/la buena de Pilar** good old Juan/Pilar

bueno² *interj* ⓵ **(a)** (expresando — duda) well; (— conformidad) OK (colloq), all right; **¿un café? — bueno** coffee? — OK *o* all right **(b)** (expresando resignación): **~, otra vez será** never mind, maybe next time **(c)** (expresando irritación): **~, se acabó ¡a la cama!** right, that's it, bed!; **¡y ~! ¿qué querías que hiciera?** (RPl) well, what did you expect me to do? ⓶ (Méx) (al contestar el teléfono) **¡~!** hello

Buenos Aires *m* Buenos Aires

buey *m* (Agr, Zool) ox
■ *adj* (Méx fam) dumb (colloq)

búfalo¹ -la *adj* (AmC fam) great (colloq), fantastic (colloq)

búfalo² *m* buffalo

bufanda *f* scarf

bufar [A1] *vi* to snort

bufet /buˈfe/, **bufé** *m* ⓵ (Coc) buffet ⓶ (Andes) (aparador) sideboard

bufete *m* (Der) (despacho) lawyer's office; (negocio) legal practice, law firm

bufido *m* snort

bufón *m* (Hist) jester; (gracioso) (fam) clown (colloq)

buhardilla *f* **(a)** (desván) attic **(b)** (apartamento) attic apartment (AmE) *o* (BrE) room **(c)** (ventana) dormer window

búho *m* owl

buitre *m* vulture

bujía *f* **(a)** (Auto) spark plug **(b)** (AmC) (Elec) light bulb

bula *f* (Relig) bull; **~ papal** papal bull

bulbo *m* bulb

bulevar *m* boulevard

Bulgaria *f* Bulgaria

búlgaro¹ -ra *adj/m,f* Bulgarian

búlgaro² *m* (idioma) Bulgarian

bulín *m* ⓵ (RPl fam) **(a)** (de soltero) bachelor pad

(b) (vivienda): **se compraron un bulincito** they bought a little place of their own (colloq) **2** (Per) (burdel) brothel

bulla *f* (ruido) racket (colloq), ruckus (AmE colloq); (actividad) bustle; **armar** *or* **meter** ~ to make a racket, to create a ruckus

bullanguero -ra *adj* (fam) ⟨persona⟩ fun-loving; ⟨música/ambiente⟩ lively

bullicio *m* **(a)** (ruido) noise, racket (colloq) **(b)** (actividad): **el** ~ **de la gran ciudad** the hustle and bustle of the city

bullicioso -sa *adj* noisy

bullir [I9] *vi*: **la calle bullía de gente** the street was teeming *o* swarming with people; **el lugar bullía de actividad** the place was a hive of activity

bulto *m* **1 (a)** (cuerpo, forma) shape; **vi un** ~ **que se movía** I saw a shape moving; **escurrir el** ~ (fam) (en el trabajo) to duck out; (en entrevista) to dodge the issue **(b)** (volumen): **hace mucho/poco** ~ it is/isn't very bulky **2** (Med) lump **3 (a)** (maleta, bolsa) piece of luggage; ~ **de mano** piece *o* item of hand baggage *o* luggage; **cargada de** ~**s** laden with packages (*o* bags *etc*) **(b)** (Col, Méx) (saco) sack

búnker /ˈbuŋker/ *m* (*pl* **-kers**) bunker

buñuelo *m* fritter

BUP /bup/ *m* (en Esp) = **Bachillerato Unificado Polivalente**

buque *m* ship, vessel; ~ **cisterna/de guerra** tanker/warship

burbuja *f* (de gas, aire) bubble; **una bebida con/ sin** ~**s** a fizzy/still drink

burbujear [A1] *vi* **(a)** «champán/agua mineral» to fizz **(b)** (al hervir) to bubble

burdel *m* brothel

burdeos *adj inv* (color) burgundy

burdo -da *adj* **(a)** ⟨persona/modales⟩ coarse **(b)** ⟨mentira⟩ blatant; ⟨imitación⟩ crude; ⟨excusa⟩ flimsy **(c)** ⟨paño/tela⟩ rough, coarse

burgués -guesa *adj* (Hist) bourgeois; (de clase media) middle-class; (pey) bourgeois (pej)
■ *m,f* **(a)** (Hist) bourgeois **(b)** (persona de clase media) member of the middle class; (pey) bourgeois

burguesía *f* (Hist) bourgeoisie; (clase media) middle class, middle classes (*pl*); (pey) bourgeoisie

burla *f* **(a)** (mofa): **hacerle** ~ **a algn** to make fun of sb, to mock sb **(b)** (atropello): **esto es una** ~ **del reglamento** this makes a mockery of the regulations

burladero *m*: *barrier behind which the bullfighter takes refuge*

burlar [A1] *vt* **(a)** ⟨medidas de seguridad⟩ to evade, get around; ~**on la vigilancia de la policía** they slipped past the police **(b)** ⟨enemigo⟩ to outwit
■ **burlarse** *v pron* ~**se DE algo/algn** to make fun *o*f sth/sb

burlesco -ca *adj* ⟨género⟩ burlesque; ⟨espectáculo⟩ comic

burlete *m* draft* excluder

burlón -lona *adj* **(a)** (de mofa) ⟨actitud/tono⟩ mocking; ⟨risa⟩ sardonic, derisive **(b)** (de broma) ⟨actitud⟩ joking, teasing

buró *m* **(a)** (escritorio) writing desk, bureau (BrE) **(b)** (Méx) (mesa de noche) bedside table

burocracia *f* bureaucracy

burócrata *mf* **(a)** (pey) bureaucrat (pej) **(b)** (Méx) (funcionario) civil servant, official

burocrático -ca *adj* **(a)** (pey) ⟨trámite/ proceso⟩ bureaucratic **(b)** (Méx) ⟨empleado/ jerarquía⟩ government (*before n*), state (*before n*)

burrada *f* (fam) (necedad, barbaridad): **decir** ~**s** to talk nonsense *o* drivel; **¿cómo pudiste hacer semejante** ~? how could you do such a stupid thing?

burro¹ -rra *adj* **(a)** (fam) (ignorante) stupid, dumb (AmE colloq), thick (BrE colloq) **(b)** (fam) (obstinado, cabezón) pigheaded (colloq)
■ *m,f* **1** (Zool) (asno) (*m*) donkey; (*f*) female donkey, jenny; **trabajar como un** ~ to slog one's guts out **2** (fam) **(a)** (ignorante) idiot **(b)** (cabezón, obstinado) stubborn mule, obstinate pig (colloq)

burro² *m* **(a)** (en carpintería) sawhorse; (en herrería) workbench **(b)** (Méx) (para planchar) ironing board; (caballete) trestle; (escalera) stepladder

bursátil *adj* stock market *o* exchange (*before n*)

bus *m* (Auto, Transp) bus; (Inf) bus

busca *f* (búsqueda) search; **en** ~ **de algo** in search of sth; **salieron en su** ~ they set out to look for him
■ *m* (Esp fam) pager, beeper (AmE), bleeper (BrE)

buscador¹ -dora *m,f*: ~ **de oro** gold prospector; ~ **de tesoros** treasure hunter

buscador² *m* (Inf) search engine

buscapleitos *mf* (*pl* ~) (fam) troublemaker

buscar [A2] *vt* **1 (a)** (intentar encontrar) to look for; ⟨fama/fortuna⟩ to seek; **te buscan en la portería** someone is asking for you at reception **(b)** (en libro, lista) to look up; **busca el número en la guía** look up the number in the directory **2 (a)** (recoger) to collect, pick up; **fui a** ~**lo al aeropuerto** (para traerlo — en coche) I went to pick him up from the airport; (— en tren, a pie) I went to meet him at the airport; **vengo a** ~ **mis cosas** I've come to collect *o* pick up my things **(b)** (conseguir) to get; **yo le busqué trabajo** I found him a job; **fue a** ~ **un médico/un taxi** he went to get a doctor/a taxi; **¿qué buscas con eso?** what are you trying to achieve by that?
■ ~ *vi* to look; **busca en el cajón** look *o* have a look in the drawer
■ **buscarse** *v pron* **1** (intentar encontrar) to look for **2** ⟨problemas⟩ to ask for; **no quiero** ~**me complicaciones/problemas** I don't want any trouble; **tú te lo has buscado** you've brought it on yourself, it serves you right; **buscársela(s)** (fam): **te la estás buscando** you're asking for it (colloq)

buseta *f* (Col, Ven) small bus

búsqueda *f* ~ (DE algo/algn) search (FOR sth/ sb)

busto *m* bust

butaca *f* **(a)** (con respaldo) (esp Esp) armchair; (sin respaldo) (esp AmL) stool **(b)** (en teatro, cine) seat; ~ **de patio** (Esp) orchestra (AmE) *o* (BrE) stall seat

buzo *m* **1** (Náut) diver **2** (Indum) **(a)** (Chi, Per) (para hacer ejercicio) track suit **(b)** (Col) (suéter de

cuello alto) turtleneck sweater (AmE), polo-neck
jumper (BrE) **(c)** (Arg, Col) (camiseta) sweatshirt **(d)**
(Ur) (jersey) sweater, jumper (BrE)

buzón m (en la calle) postbox, mailbox (AmE),
letter-box (BrE); (en una casa) mailbox (AmE),
letter-box (BrE); **echar una carta al** or **en el** ~ to
mail (AmE) o (BrE) post a letter

byte m /'bait/ byte

Cc

C, c f (read as /se/ or (Esp) /θe/) the letter C, c

c/ (= **calle**) St, Rd

C m (= **centígrado** or **Celsius**) C, Centigrade,
Celsius

cabales mpl: **no está en sus** ~ he's not in his
right mind

cabalgar [A3] vi (liter) «jinete» to ride

cabalgata f (desfile) parade; **la** ~ **de los Reyes
Magos** the Epiphany parade o procession

caballa f mackerel

caballerango m (Méx) groom

caballería f (Mil) cavalry

caballeriza f (edificio) stable; (caballos) stable,
stables (pl)

caballero m **(a)** (en general) gentleman; **es todo
un** ~ he's a perfect gentleman; **sección de** ~**s**
men's department; **¿en qué puedo servirle,** ~?
how can I help you, sir?; **☻ caballeros** Men o
Gentlemen o Gents **(b)** (Hist) knight

caballeroso -sa adj gentlemanly, gallant

caballete m (para mesa) trestle; (para lienzo,
pizarra) easel; (de moto) kickstand; (del tejado) ridge

caballito m **(a)** (juguete — que se mece) rocking
horse; (— con palo) hobbyhorse; ~ **de mar** sea
horse; ver tb CABALLO **(b) caballitos** mpl
(carrusel) carousel, merry-go-round

caballo¹ -lla adj (AmC fam) (estúpido) stupid

caballo² m **1 (a)** (Equ, Zool) horse; **montar** or
(AmL) **andar a** ~ to ride (a horse); **dieron un
paseo a** ~ they went for a ride (on horseback);
~ **de carga/de tiro** packhorse/carthorse; ~ **de
carreras** racehorse; **a** ~ **entre ...** halfway between
...; **llevar a algn a** ~ to give sb a piggyback **(b)**
(en ajedrez) knight; (en naipes) ≈queen (in a
Spanish pack of cards) **(c)** (Méx) (en gimnasia)
horse **2** (Auto, Fís, Mec) tb ~ **de vapor** (metric)
horsepower

cabaña f (choza) cabin, shack

cabaré, cabaret /kaβa'rre/ m (pl **-rets**)
cabaret

cabeceada f **(a)** (AmL) ▶ CABEZADA **(b)** (CS)
(Dep) header

cabecear [A1] vi **(a)** «persona» to nod off **(b)**
«caballo» to toss its head; «barco» to pitch
■ ~ vt «balón» to head

cabecera f **(a)** (de la cama) headboard **(b)** (de
una mesa) head, top **(c)** (de una manifestación) head,
front

cabecero m headboard

cabecilla mf ringleader

cabellera f **(a)** (melena) hair **(b)** (de un cometa)
tail

cabello m hair; ~**s de ángel** (fideos) vermicelli

caber [E15] vi **1 (a)** (en un lugar) to fit; **no cabe
en la caja** it won't fit in the box; **no cabemos los
cuatro** there isn't room for all four of us; **en esta
botella caben diez litros** this bottle holds ten
liters; **no** ~ **en sí de alegría** to be beside oneself
with joy **(b)** (pasar) to fit, go; ~ **POR algo** to go
THROUGH sth **(c)** «falda/zapatos» to fit; **estos
pantalones ya no me caben** these trousers don't
fit me any more
2 (en 3ª pers) (frml) (ser posible): **cabe la
posibilidad de que haya perdido el tren** he may
have missed the train; **no cabe duda de que ...**
there is no doubt that ...; **cabría decir que ...** it
could be said that ...; **es, si cabe, aún mejor** it is
even better, if such a thing is possible; **dentro de
lo que cabe** all things considered
3 (Mat): **17 entre 5 cabe a 3 y sobran 2** 5 into 17
goes 3 times and 2 over

cabestrillo m sling; **llevaba el brazo en** ~ he
had his arm in a sling

cabeza f **1 (a)** (Anat) head; **de la** ~ **a los pies**
from head to toe o foot; **me duele la** ~ I've got a
headache; **marcó de** ~ he scored with a header;
pararse en la or **de** ~ (AmL) to do a handstand; ~
rapada skinhead **(b)** (medida) head; **me saca una**
~ he's a head taller than me **(c)** (pelo) hair; **me
lavé la** ~ I washed my hair **(d)** (inteligencia): **usa la**
~ use your head; **¡qué poca** ~! have you/has he
no sense? **(e)** (mente): **¡que** ~ **la mía!** what a
memory!; **tú estás mal de la** ~ you're out of your
mind; **se me ha ido de la** ~ it's gone right out of
my head; **se le ha metido en la** ~ **que ...** she's got
it into her head that ...; **no se me pasó por la** ~
it didn't cross my mind; ~ **de chorlito** mf (fam)
scatterbrain (colloq); **írsele a algn la** ~ to feel
dizzy; **levantar** ~ (fam) (superar problemas) to get
back on one's feet; **perder la** ~: **no perdamos la**
~ let's not panic o lose our heads; **perdió la** ~
por esa mujer he lost his head over that woman;
quitarle a algn algo de la ~ to get sth out of sb's
head; **romperse la** ~ (fam) (preocuparse) to rack
one's brains; (lastimarse) to break one's neck
(colloq); **subírsele a algn a la** ~ «vino/éxito» to go
to one's head; **tener la** ~ **llena de pájaros** (fam) to
have one's head in the clouds
2 (a) (individuo): **por** ~ each, a head **(b)** (de
ganado) head; **50** ~**s de ganado** 50 head of cattle
3 (primer lugar, delantera): **estamos a la** ~ **del
sector** we are the leading company in this sector;
a la ~ **de la manifestación** at the front o head of
the demonstration; **el equipo va en** ~ **de la
clasificación** the team is at the top of the
division; ~ **de familia** head of the family; ~ **de
serie** seed

4 **(a)** (de alfiler, clavo, fósforo) head **(b)** (de misil) warhead
5 (Audio, Video) head
6 (de plátanos) hand, bunch; **∼ de ajo** bulb of garlic

cabezada *f* (movimiento) nod; **iba dormido, dando ∼s** his head kept nodding in his sleep; **dar** *or* **echar una ∼** (fam) to have a nap (colloq)

cabezal *m* **1** **(a)** (almohada) bolster **(b)** (de sillón) headrest **(c)** (AmL) (de cama) headboard/footboard **2** (AmL) (terminal) terminal **3** (Audio, Video) head

cabezazo *m* **(a)** (golpe): **se dio un ∼ en el estante** he hit *o* banged his head on the shelf **(b)** (Dep) header

cabezón -zona *adj* **(a)** (fam) (terco) pigheaded (colloq) **(b)** (fam) (de cabeza grande): **¡qué ∼ es!** what a big head he has! **(c)** ⟨vino⟩ heady
■ *m,f* (fam): **¡eres un ∼!** you're so pigheaded! (colloq)

cabezota *adj/mf* ▶ CABEZÓN A, B

cabezudo¹ -da *adj* (de cabeza grande): **es ∼** he has a very big head

cabezudo² *m*: *carnival figure with a large head*

cabida *f* (capacidad de recipiente, estadio, teatro) capacity; **solo hay ∼ para diez pasajeros** there's only room *o* space for ten passengers; **el estadio puede dar ∼ a 100.000 personas** the stadium can hold 100,000 people

cabina *f* **1** **(a)** (vestuario) cubicle, stall (AmE) **(b)** (de laboratorio de idiomas, estudio de radio) booth; **∼ telefónica** telephone booth *o* (BrE) box **2** **(a)** (de camión, grúa) cab **(b)** (Aviac) (para pilotos — en avión grande) flight deck; (— en avión pequeño) cockpit; (para pasajeros) cabin

cabizbajo -ja *adj* (alicaído) downcast; **caminaba ∼** he walked along, head bowed

cable *m* (Elec, Telec) cable

cablevisión *f* (esp AmL) cable television

cabo *m* **1** (Geog) cape **2** **(a)** (Mil) corporal **(b)** (en remo) stroke **3** (extremo) end; **al ∼ de** after; **de ∼ a rabo** (fam) from beginning to end; **llevar a ∼** ⟨misión⟩ to carry out; **lleva a ∼ una excelente labor** he does an excellent job

cabra *f* goat; **estar como una ∼** (fam) to be completely nuts (colloq)

cabrá, cabré, etc ▶ CABER

cabreado -da *adj* (fam) furious, mad (colloq)

cabrear [A1] *vt* (fam) (enfadar) to make ... mad (colloq), to piss ... off (sl)
■ **cabrearse** *v pron* (fam) (enojarse) to get mad (colloq)

cabreo *m* (fam) (enojo, irritación): **¡qué ∼ tiene!** he's in a foul *o* a terrible mood! (colloq); **agarrarse un ∼** to get mad (colloq), to hit the roof (colloq)

cabría, etc ▶ CABER

cabriola *f*: **hacer ∼s** ⟨niño⟩ to caper *o* jump around; ⟨caballo⟩ to buck, prance around

cabritas *fpl* (Chi) popcorn

cabrito *m* (Zool) kid

cabro -bra *adj* (Chi fam): **es muy ∼ para eso** he's too young for that
■ *m,f* (Chi fam) (niño) kid (colloq)

cabrón¹ -brona *adj* (Esp, Méx vulg): **el muy ∼/ la muy cabrona** the bastard *o* (AmE) son of a bitch (vulg)/the bitch (vulg)
■ *m,f* (Esp, Méx vulg) (*m*) bastard (vulg), son of a bitch (AmE vulg); (*f*) bitch (vulg)

cabrón² *m* (vulg) (cornudo) cuckold; (proxeneta) (Andes fam *o* vulg) pimp, ponce (BrE)

cabús *m* (Méx) caboose (AmE), guard's van (BrE)

caca *f* (fam *o* leng infantil): **hacer ∼** to go to the bathroom (AmE) *o* (BrE) toilet (euph), to do a poop (AmE) *o* (BrE) pooh (used to *or* by children); **hacerse ∼** to mess oneself; **el niño se hizo ∼** the baby dirtied his diaper (AmE) *o* (BrE) nappy (colloq); **∼ de perro** dog mess; **¡no toques eso! ¡∼!** don't touch that, it's dirty!

cacahuete, cacahuate *m* peanut, monkey nut; **me/te/le importa un (reverendo) ∼** (Méx fam) I/you/he couldn't give a damn (colloq)

cacao *m* **1** **(a)** (Coc) (polvo, bebida) cocoa **(b)** (Bot) (planta) cacao; (semillas) cocoa beans (*pl*) **(c)** (Esp) (para los labios) lipsalve **2** (fam) (jaleo) ruckus (AmE), to-do (BrE); **¡qué ∼ se armó!** all hell broke loose (colloq)

cacarear [A1] *vi* **(a)** ⟨*gallo*⟩ to crow; ⟨*gallina*⟩ to cluck **(b)** (fam) (presumir) to brag

cacatúa *f* (Zool) cockatoo

cacería *f* (de zorro, jabalí) hunt; (de conejo, perdiz) shoot; **ir de ∼** to go hunting/shooting

cacerola *f* saucepan, pan

cachalote *m* sperm whale

cachapa *f* (Ven) *corn-based pancake*

cachar [A1] *vt* **(a)** (AmL fam) ⟨pelota⟩ to catch; ⟨persona⟩: **la caché del brazo** I caught *o* grabbed her by the arm **(b)** (AmL fam) (sorprender, pillar) to catch **(c)** (RPl fam) (gastar una broma) to kid (colloq) **(d)** (Andes fam) (enterarse) to get (colloq)

cacharrería *f* (Col) hardware store, ironmonger's (BrE)

cacharro *m* **(a)** (de cocina) pot **(b)** (fam) (chivachache) thing; (coche viejo) jalopy (AmE), old banger (BrE colloq); (aparato) gadget

cachaza *f* (bebida) *type of rum*

cachear [A1] *vt* **1** (fam) (registrar) to frisk, search **2** (AmL) (Taur) to gore

cachemir *m*, **cachemira** *f* cashmere

cachetada *f* (AmL) slap

cachete *m* **1** (mejilla) (esp AmL) cheek; (nalga) (CS fam) cheek **2** (esp Esp) (bofetada) slap

cachetear [A1] *vt* (AmL) to slap

cachetón -tona *adj* (Andes, Méx fam) (carrilludo) chubby-cheeked

cachimba *f* pipe; **fumar ∼** to smoke a pipe

cachiporra *f* (palo) billy club (AmE), truncheon (BrE)

cachito *m* **1** (Méx) (de lotería) *one twentieth of a lottery ticket*; **ver tb** CACHO 1 **2** (Ven) (Coc) croissant

cachivache *m* (fam) (trasto inútil) piece of junk; **tiró todos los ∼s que tenía** she threw out all her old junk (colloq)

cacho *m* **1** (fam) (pedazo) bit **2** **(a)** (AmS) (cuerno) horn **(b)** (Andes) (juego) poker dice; (cubilete) shaker

cachondearse [A1] *v pron* (Esp fam) **∼ DE algn/algo** to make fun OF sb/sth

cachondeo *m* (Esp fam): **estar de ~** to be joking; **se lo toma a ~** he treats it as a joke

cachondo -da *adj* (fam) **(a)** (Esp) (divertido) funny **(b)** (Esp, Méx) (sexualmente) hot (colloq), horny (sl)

cachorro -rra *m,f* (de perro) puppy, pup; (de león) cub

cachucha *f* (Col, Méx, Ven) (Indum) cap

cacillo *m* (cacerola) small saucepan; (cucharón) ladle

cacique *m* (Hist) chief, cacique; (Pol) local political boss; (hombre poderoso) tyrant

caco *m* (fam) burglar

cactus (*pl* ~), **cacto** *m* cactus

cada *adj inv* **1** **(a)** (con énfasis en el individuo o cosa particular) each; (con énfasis en la totalidad del conjunto) every; **los ganadores de ~ grupo** the winners from each group; **hay un bar en ~ esquina** ther's a bar in every corner; **~ día** every day, each day; **¿~ cuánto viene?** how often does she come?; **hay cinco para ~ uno** there are five each; **cuestan $25 ~ uno** they cost $25 each; **~ uno** *or* **cual sabe qué es lo que más le conviene** everyone *o* each individual knows what's best for him *or* her; **~ vez que viene** every time *o* whenever he comes **(b)** (delante de numeral) every; **~ dos días** every two days, every other day; **siete de ~ diez** seven out of (every) ten **2** (indicando progresión): **~ vez más rápido** faster and faster; **lo hace ~ vez mejor** she's getting better all the time; **~ vez más gente** more and more people; **~ vez menos tiempo** less and less time

cadalso *m* (patíbulo) scaffold; (horca) gallows (*pl*)

cadáver *m* (de persona) corpse; (de animal) carcass

cadavérico -ca *adj* cadaverous, ghastly

caddie, caddy /'kaδi/ *mf* (*pl* **-dies**) caddy

cadena *f* **1** **(a)** (de eslabones) chain; (para la nieve) (snow) chain; **~ antirrobo** bicycle lock; **~ perpetua** life imprisonment **(b)** (del water) chain; **tirar de la ~** to flush the toilet **2** **(a)** (de hechos, fenómenos) chain; **una larga ~ de atentados** a long series of attacks; **~ de fabricación** *or* **producción** production line; **~ de montañas** mountain range *o* chain; **en ~** ‹*transmisión*› simultaneous; **una choque en ~** a pileup **(b)** (de hoteles, supermercados) chain; **~ de radiodifusión** radio network **3** (TV) channel

cadencia *f* cadence

cadeneta *f* (labor) chain stitch; (de papel) paper chain

cadera *f* hip

cadete *m* (Mil, Náut) cadet

caducar [A2] *vi* **(a)** ‹*carné/pasaporte*› to expire; **el plazo caduca el 17 de enero** the closing date (*for enrollment, etc*) is January 17; **estar caducado** to be out of date; ‹*yogurt*› to be past

its sell-by date/use-by date **(b)** ‹*medicamento*› to expire (frml); ❸ **caduca a los tres meses** use within three months

caduco -ca *adj* **(a)** ‹*hoja*› deciduous **(b)** ‹*teoría/costumbres/valores*› outdated

caer [E16] *vi* **1** (de una altura) to fall; (de posición vertical) to fall over; **el coche cayó por un precipicio** the car went over a cliff; **cayó muerto allí mismo** he dropped down dead on the spot; **cayó en el mar** it came down in the sea; **~ parado** (AmL) to land on one's feet; **dejar ~ algo** ‹*objeto*› to drop sth; ‹*indirecta*› to drop sth; **dejó ~ la noticia que ...** she let drop the news that ... **2** **(a)** ‹*chaparrón/nevada*›: **cayó un chaparrón** it poured down; **cayó una fuerte nevada** it snowed heavily; **el rayo cayó cerca** the lightning struck nearby **(b)** «*noche*» to fall; **al ~ la tarde/noche** at sunset *o* dusk/nightfall **3** **(a)** (pender) ‹*cortinas/falda*» to hang **(b)** «*terreno*» to drop; **~ en pendiente** to slope down **4** (en error, trampa): **no caigas en ese error** don't make that mistake; **todos caímos (en la trampa)** we all fell for it; **cayó en la tentación de mirar** she succumbed to the temptation to look; **~ muy bajo** to stoop very low **5** (fam) (entender, darse cuenta): **¡ah, ya caigo!** (ya entiendo) oh, now I get it! (colloq); (ya recuerdo) oh, now I remember; **no caigo** I'm not sure what (*o* who *etc*) you mean; **no caí en que tú no tenías llave** I didn't realize *o* (fam) I didn't click that you didn't have keys **6** (en un estado): **~ en el olvido** to sink into oblivion; **~ enfermo** to fall ill **7** «*gobierno/ciudad*» to fall; «*soldado*» (morir) to fall, die **8** «*precios/temperatura*» to fall, drop **9** **(a)** (sentar): **el pescado me cayó mal** the fish didn't agree with me; **le cayó muy mal que no la invitaran** she was very upset about not being invited **(b)** ‹*persona*»: **tu primo me cae muy bien** I really like your cousin; **me cae muy mal** (fam) I can't stand him (colloq); **¿qué tal te cayó?** what did you think of him? **10** «*cumpleaños/festividad*» to fall on; **¿el 27 en qué (día) cae?** what day's the 27th?

■ **caerse** *v pron* **(a)** (de una altura) to fall; (de posición vertical) to fall, fall over; **me caí por las escaleras** I fell down the stairs; **~se del caballo/de la cama** to fall off one's horse/out of bed; **está que se cae de cansancio** (fam) she's dead on her feet (colloq) **(b)** **caérsele algo ʌ algn**: **oiga, se le cayó un guante** excuse me, you dropped your glove; **no se te vaya a ~** don't drop it; **se me cayó de las manos** it slipped out of my hands; **se me están cayendo las medias** my stockings are falling down **(c)** (desprenderse) «*diente*» to fall out; «*hojas*» to fall off; «*botón*» to come off, fall off; **se le empieza a ~ el pelo** he's started to lose his hair

café *adj* (gen inv) (AmC, Chi, Méx) (marrón) brown; **ojos ~(s)** brown eyes

■ *m* **1** (cultivo, bebida) coffee; **me sirvió un ~** he gave me a cup of coffee, he gave me a coffee

(BrE); ~ **cerrero** (Col) large strong black coffee; ~ **con leche** (bebida) regular coffee (AmE), white coffee (BrE); ~ **cortado** *coffee with a dash of milk*; ~ **expreso** espresso; ~ **instantáneo** *o* **soluble** instant coffee; ~ **natural/torrefacto** light roast/ high roast coffee; ~ **negro** (AmL) *or* (Chi) **puro** *or* (Col) **tinto** *or* (Esp) **solo** black coffee **2** (cafetería) café; ~ **bar** café **3** (AmC, Chi, Méx) (marrón) brown

cafeína *f* caffeine

cafetal *m* coffee plantation

cafetera *f* **(a)** (para hacer café) coffee maker; (para servir café) coffeepot; *estar como una* ~ (fam) to be off one's rocker *o* head (colloq) **(b)** (fam) (coche viejo) old heap (colloq)

cafetería *f* (café) café; (en museo, fábrica) cafeteria

cafetero -ra *adj* ‹*industria/finca*› coffee (*before n*); ‹*país*› coffee-producing (*before n*), coffee-growing (*before n*); **ser muy** ~ to be a real coffee addict
■ *m,f* coffee planter *o* grower

cafeto *m* coffee tree

caficultor -tora *m,f* (Col) coffee grower

cagar [A3] *vi* (vulg) (defecar) to have a shit (vulg)
■ **cagarse** *v pron* (vulg) to shit oneself (vulg)

caída *f* **1** (en general) fall; **sufrir una** ~ «*persona*» to have a fall; ~ **libre** free fall; **la** ~ **del gobierno** the fall of the government; **la** ~ **del cabello** hair loss **2** (de tela, falda): **necesitas una tela con más** ~ you need a heavier material; **tiene buena** ~ it hangs well **3** (descenso) ~ **DE algo** ‹*del dólar/de los precios/de la demanda*› fall IN sth; ‹*de temperatura/voltaje*› drop IN sth; ~ **de agua** waterfall

caído¹ -da *adj* **1** **(a)** (en el suelo) fallen **(b)** ‹*pechos*› drooping, sagging; **tener los hombros** ~**s** to be round-shouldered **(c)** (en la guerra): **soldados** ~**s en combate** soldiers who fell in combat **2** (Col) ‹*vivienda*› dilapidated, run-down

caído² *m*: **los** ~**s** the fallen

caiga, caigas, etc ▶ CAER

caimán *m* (Zool) caiman, cayman, alligator

Cairo *m*: **el** ~ Cairo

caja *f* **1** **(a)** (recipiente) box; **una** ~ **de fósforos** (con fósforos) a box of matches; (vacía) a matchbox; **una** ~ **de vino** a crate of wine; ~ **de cambios** gearbox; ~ **de herramientas** toolbox; ~ **de música** music box; ~ **de resonancia** (Mús) soundbox; ~ **de seguridad** safe-deposit box, safety deposit box; ~ **fuerte** safe, strongbox; ~ **tonta** (fam) goggle box (colloq) **(b)** (de reloj) case, casing **(c)** (Mús) (de violín, guitarra) soundbox; (tambor) drum **(d)** (fam) (ataúd) coffin **2** (Com) **(a)** (lugar — en banco) window; (— en supermercado) checkout; (— en tienda, restaurante) cash desk, till **(b)** (máquina) *tb* ~ **registradora** till, cash register **(c)** (dinero) cash; **hicimos una** ~ **de medio millón** we took half a million pesos (*o* pesetas *etc*); ~ **de ahorros** savings bank; *hacer* (*la*) ~ to cash up

cajero -ra *m,f* (en tienda) cashier; (en banco) teller, cashier; (en supermercado) check out operator; ~ **automático** *or* **permanente** cash dispenser, automated teller machine (AmE), ATM (AmE)

cajeta *f* (Méx) caramel topping/filling

cajetilla *f* pack (AmE), packet (BrE)

cajón *m* **1** **(a)** (en mueble) drawer **(b)** (caja grande) *tb* ~ **de embalaje** crate; (para mudanzas) packing case **(c)** (AmL) (ataúd) coffin, casket (AmE) **2** (Méx) (en un estacionamiento) parking space

cajuela *f* (Méx) trunk (AmE), boot (BrE)

cal *f* lime

cala *f* **(a)** (ensenada) cove **(b)** (Náut) hold

calabacín *m*, (Méx) **calabacita** *f* zucchini (AmE), courgette (BrE)

calabaza *f* (fruto — redondo) pumpkin; (— alargado) squash

calabozo *m* (en comisaría, cárcel) cell; (en cuartel) guardroom; (Hist) dungeon

calada *f* (Esp fam) (de cigarro) drag (sl), puff (colloq)

caladero *m* fishing ground

calado -da *adj* **1** (empapado) [ESTAR] soaked, drenched **2** ‹*jersey/tela*› openwork (*before n*)

calamar *m* squid; ~**es a la romana** squid fried in batter

calambre *m* **(a)** (espasmo) cramp; **me ha dado un** ~ **en el pie** I have a cramp (AmE) *o* (BrE) I've got cramp in my foot **(b)** (sacudida eléctrica) electric shock; **me dio un** ~ I got an electric shock

calamidad *f* **(a)** (desastre, desgracia) disaster, calamity; **¡las** ~**es que ha pasado!** the terrible things he's gone through! **(b)** (persona inútil) disaster (colloq)

calar [A1] *vt* **1** ‹*líquido*› (empapar) to soak; (atravesar) to soak through; **el agua me caló los calcetines** water soaked through my socks **2** (fam) ‹*persona/intenciones*› to rumble (colloq), to suss ... out (BrE colloq) **3** «*barco*» to draw **4** (Esp) ‹*coche/motor*› to stall
■ ~ *vi* **1** «*moda*» to catch on; «*costumbre/ filosofía*» to take root **2** ‹*zapatos/tienda de campaña*› to leak, let water in
■ **calarse** *v pron* **1** (empaparse) to get soaked, get drenched **2** (Esp) «*coche/motor*» to stall

calavera¹ *f* **1** (Anat) skull **2** (Méx) (Auto) taillight

calavera² *m* (fam) rake

calcado -da *adj* **(a)** [SER] (fam): **ser** ~ **a algn** to be the spitting image of sb (colloq); **ser** ~ **a algo** to be exactly the same as sth **(b)** [ESTAR] (fam): **están** ~**s** one is a carbon copy of the other; **está** ~ **del de Serra** it's a straight copy of Serra's

calcar [A2] *vt* **(a)** ‹*dibujo/mapa*› to trace **(b)** (plagiar) to copy

calceta *f* (labor) knitting; **hacer** ~ to knit

calcetín *m* sock

calcinar [A1] *vt* **(a)** (abrasar) «*fuego*» to burn; **cadáveres calcinados** charred bodies **(b)** (Quím) to calcine

calcio *m* calcium

calco *m* (copia) exact replica

calcomanía *f* transfer, decal (AmE)

calculador -dora *adj* calculating

calculadora *f* calculator

calcular [A1] *vt* **1** **(a)** (Mat) to calculate, work out; **calculé mal la distancia** I miscalculated the distance **(b)** (evaluar) ‹*pérdidas/gastos*› to estimate **(c)** (conjeturar) to reckon, to guess (esp AmE); **yo le calculo unos sesenta años** I reckon *o* guess he's ⋯⟶

about sixty **(d)** (imaginar) to imagine **2** (planear) to work out; **lo tenía todo calculado** he had it all worked out

cálculo m **1** (Mat) **(a)** (operación) calculation; **según mis ～s** according to my calculations; **hizo un ～ aproximado** she made a rough estimate; **～ mental** mental arithmetic **(b)** (disciplina) calculus **2** (plan): **eso no entraba en mis ～s** I hadn't allowed for that in my plans o calculations; **le fallaron los ～s** things didn't work out as he had planned; **un error de ～** a miscalculation **3** (Med) stone, calculus (tech)

caldear [A1] vt ⟨habitación/local⟩ to heat, heat … up
■ **caldearse** v pron **(a)** «habitación/local» to warm up, heat up **(b)** (enardecerse): **se estaban empezando a ～ los ánimos** feelings started to run high

caldera f **(a)** (industrial, de calefacción) boiler **(b)** (caldero) caldron*, copper (BrE)

calderilla f change, small o loose change

caldero m caldron*, copper (BrE)

caldo m (Coc) clear soup; (con arroz, etc) soup; (para cocinar) stock; (salsa de asado, etc) juices (pl); **～ de pollo** chicken stock

calé adj gypsy (before n)
■ mf gypsy

calefacción f heating; **～ a gas** gas heating; **～ central** central heating

caleidoscopio m kaleidoscope

calendario m **(a)** (en general) calendar; **～ de taco** tear-off calendar; **～ escolar** school calendar **(b)** (programa) schedule; **tiene un ～ muy apretado** she has a very tight schedule

calentador m **(a)** (para agua) (water) heater; (estufa) heater **(b) calentadores** mpl (Dep, Indum) legwarmers (pl)

calentamiento m **(a)** (Dep) warm-up **(b)** (Fís) warming; **～ global o del planeta** global warming

calentar [A5] vt **1 (a)** ⟨agua/comida⟩ to heat (up); ⟨habitación⟩ to heat **(b)** ⟨motor/coche⟩ to warm up **(c)** (Dep): **～ los músculos** to warm up **2** (AmL fam) (enojar) to make … mad (colloq)
■ **～** vi: **¡cómo calienta hoy el sol!** the sun's really hot today!; **esta estufa casi no calienta** this heater is hardly giving off any heat
■ **calentarse** v pron **1 (a)** «horno/plancha» to heat up; «habitación» to warm up, get warm **(b)** «motor/coche» (al arrancar) to warm up; (en exceso) to overheat **2** (vulg) (excitarse sexualmente) to get turned on (colloq) **3** «debate» to become heated; **los ánimos se ～on** tempers flared **4** (AmL fam) (enojarse) to get mad (colloq)

calentura f **(a)** (fiebre) temperature **(b)** (en la boca) cold sore

calesita f (Per, RPl) merry-go-round, carousel

caleta f (ensenada) cove

calibrar [A1] vt **(a)** ⟨arma/tubo⟩ to calibrate **(b)** ⟨consecuencias/situación⟩ to weigh up

calibre m caliber*; **de ～ 22** 22 caliber; **de grueso ～** ⟨arma/proyectil⟩ large-bore; ⟨error⟩ (AmL) serious

calidad f **1** (de producto, servicio) quality; **un artículo de primera ～** a top-quality product; **productos de mala ～** poor-quality products; **～ de**

vida quality of life **2** (condición): **asistió en ～ de observador** he attended as an observer; **en su ～ de presidente** in his capacity as president

cálido -da adj **(a)** (Meteo) hot **(b)** ⟨acogida/bienvenida⟩ warm **(c)** ⟨color/tono⟩ warm

calidoscopio m kaleidoscope

calienta, etc ▶ CALENTAR

caliente adj **1** ⟨agua/comida/horno⟩ hot; **aquí estaremos más calentitas** we'll be warmer here; **tomó la decisión en ～** she made the decision in the heat of the moment **2** (fam) (sexualmente) hot (colloq), horny (sl)

caliento ▶ CALENTAR

califa m caliph

calificación f **(a)** (Educ) grade (AmE), mark (BrE) **(b)** (descripción) description **(c)** (de película) rating

calificado -da adj (esp AmL) ⟨mano de obra⟩ skilled; ⟨profesional⟩ qualified

calificar [A2] vt **1** ⟨algo/a algn DE algo⟩ (describir) to describe sth/sb AS sth; (categorizar) to label sth/sb AS sth **2** (Educ) **(a)** ⟨examen⟩ to grade (AmE), to mark (BrE); ⟨alumno⟩ to give a grade (AmE) o (BrE) mark to **(b)** (habilitar) «título/diploma» **～ a algn PARA hacer algo** to qualify sb TO do sth **3** (Ling) to qualify

California f California

californiano -na adj/m,f Californian

caligrafía f (arte) calligraphy; (de persona) writing, handwriting

calipso m **(a)** (Mús) calypso **(b)** (de color) **～** deep turquoise

cáliz m **(a)** (Relig) chalice **(b)** (Bot) calyx

caliza f limestone

calizo -za adj ⟨tierra⟩ limy; **piedra caliza** limestone

callado -da adj (estar) (silencioso) quiet; **estuvo ～ durante toda la reunión** he kept quiet throughout the whole meeting; **lo escucharon ～s** they listened to him quietly **(b)** [SER] (poco hablador) quiet

callampa f (Chi) **(a)** (hongo) mushroom **(b)** (vivienda) shanty (dwelling) **(c) callampas** fpl (poblaciones marginales) shantytown

callar [A1] vi to be quiet, shut up (colloq); **no pude hacerlo ～** I couldn't get him to be quiet; **hacer ～ a la oposición** to silence the opposition
■ **～** vt **(a)** ⟨secreto/información⟩ to keep … quiet **(b)** (AmL) ⟨persona⟩ to get … to be quiet, to shut … up (colloq)
■ **callarse** v pron **(a)** (guardar silencio) to be quiet; **¡cállate!** be quiet!, shut up! (colloq); **cuando entró todos se ～on** when he walked in everyone went quiet o stopped talking; **la próxima vez no me ～é** next time I'll say something **(b)** (no decir) ⟨noticia⟩ to keep … quiet, keep … to oneself

calle f **1** (vía) street; **～ ciega** (Andes, Ven) dead end, cul-de-sac (BrE); **～ de dirección única** or (Col) **de una vía** one-way street; **～ peatonal** pedestrian street; **hoy no he salido a la ～** I haven't been out today; **el libro saldrá a la ～ mañana** the book comes out tomorrow; **el hombre de la ～** the man in the street; **el lenguaje de la ～** colloquial language; **echar a algn a la ～** to throw sb out (on the street); **en la ～** ⟨estar/quedar⟩ (en la ruina) penniless; (sin vivienda) homeless; (sin trabajo) out of work

2 (Esp) (en atletismo, natación) lane; (en golf) fairway

callejear [A1] *vi* to hang around the streets (colloq)

callejero¹ -ra *adj* ⟨riña/venta/músico⟩ street (*before n*); ⟨perro⟩ stray (*before n*)

callejero² *m* (Esp) street map *o* plan

callejón *m* alley, narrow street; ~ **sin salida** (calle) dead end, blind alley; (situación) dead end

callejuela *f* narrow street

callista *mf* chiropodist

callo *m* **(a)** (en los dedos del pie) corn; (en la planta del pie, en las manos) callus; (en una fractura) callus **(b) callos** *mpl* (Esp) (Coc) tripe

callosidad *f* callus

calma *f* calm; **con ~** calmly; **mantener la ~** to keep calm; **tómatelo con ~** take it easy; **no hay que perder la ~** the thing is not to lose your cool; **el mar está en ~** the sea is calm; **¡~, por favor!** (en situación peligrosa) please, keep calm! *o* don't panic!; (en discusión acalorada) calm down, please!

calmante *m* (para dolores) painkiller; (para los nervios) tranquilizer

calmar [A1] *vt* **(a)** (tranquilizar) ⟨persona⟩ to calm ... down; ⟨nervios⟩ to calm; **esto calmó los ánimos** this eased the tension **(b)** (aliviar) ⟨dolor⟩ to relieve, ease; ⟨sed⟩ to quench; ⟨hambre⟩ to take the edge off

■ **calmarse** *v pron* **(a)** «persona» to calm down **(b)** «mar» to become calm

calmo -ma *adj* (esp AmL) calm

caló *m* gypsy slang

calor *m* [*Use of the feminine gender, although common in some areas, is generally considered to be archaic or non-standard*] **1 (a)** (Fís, Meteo) heat; **hace ~** it's hot; **hacía un ~ agobiante** the heat was stifling *o* suffocating **(b)** (sensación): **tener ~** to be hot; **pasamos un ~ horrible** it was terribly hot; **entrar en ~** to get warm; **esta chaqueta me da mucho ~** I feel very hot in this jacket; **al ~ del fuego** by the fireside **2** (afecto) warmth **3 calores** *mpl* (de la menopausia) hot flashes (*pl*) (AmE), hot flushes (*pl*) (BrE)

caloría *f* calorie

calumnia *f* (oral) defamation, slander; (escrita) libel; **levantaron ~s contra la institución** they spread slanderous rumors about the institution

calumniar [A1] *vt* (por escrito) to libel; (oralmente) to slander

caluroso -sa *adj* **(a)** ⟨día/clima⟩ hot **(b)** ⟨acogida/aplauso⟩ warm; **recibe un ~ saludo** (Corresp) best wishes

calva *f* (cabeza sin pelo) bald head; (parte sin pelo) bald patch

calvicie *f* baldness

calvo -va *adj* ⟨persona⟩ bald; **quedarse ~** to go bald

■ *m,f* bald person

calza *f* **1 (a)** (cuña) chock **(b)** (Col) (en una muela) filling; **2 calzas** *fpl* (Ind, arc) hose (*pl*), breeches (*pl*)

calzada *f* (camino) road; (de calle) road; (de autopista) side, carriageway

calzado *m* (frml) footwear (frml)

calzador *m* shoehorn

calzar [A4] *vt* **1 (a)** ⟨persona⟩ (proveerla de

calzado) to provide ... with shoes; (ponerle los zapatos): **calzó a los niños** she put the children's shoes on **(b)** (llevar): **calzo (un) 39** I take (a) size 39, I'm a 39; **calzaba zapatillas de deporte** he was wearing training shoes **2** ⟨rueda⟩ to chock, wedge a block under **3** (Col) ⟨muela⟩ to fill

■ **calzarse** *v pron* (refl) **(a)** (ponerse los zapatos) to put one's shoes on **(b)** ⟨zapato⟩ to put on

calzoncillos *mpl*, **calzoncillo** *m* underpants, shorts (*pl*) (AmE), pants (*pl*) (BrE); ~ **largos** long underwear, long johns (*pl*) (colloq)

calzones *mpl*, **calzón** *m* **1 (a)** (antiguos) long underwear, long johns (*pl*) (colloq) **(b)** (AmS) (modernos) panties (*pl*), knickers (*pl*) (BrE) **2** (Esp) (para deporte) shorts (*pl*)

cama *f* (para dormir) bed; **hacer** *or* (AmL) **tender la ~** to make the bed; **¡métete en la ~!** get into bed!; **guardar ~** to stay in bed; **está en ~** she's in bed; ~ **camarote** (AmL) bunk bed; ~ **doble** *or* (AmL) **de matrimonio** *or* (AmL) **de dos plazas** double bed; ~ **individual** *or* (AmL) **de una plaza** single bed; ~ **solar** sunbed; **caer en ~** to fall ill

camada *f* (Zool) litter; (de ladrones, sinvergüenzas) (pey) gang

camaleón *m* chameleon

cámara *f* **1 (a)** (arc) (aposento) chamber (frml) **(b)** (recinto): ~ **acorazada** *or* **blindada** strongroom, vault; ~ **de descompresión** decompression chamber; ~ **de gas** gas chamber; ~ **frigorífica** cold store **2** (Gob, Pol): **C~ de los Diputados** Chamber of Deputies; **C~ de los Comunes/de los Lores** House of Commons/of Lords; **C~ de Representantes** House of Representatives **3** (Com, Fin) association; ~ **de comercio** chamber of commerce **4** (aparato) camera; **en** *or* (Esp) **a ~ lenta** in slow motion; ~ **de cine** film camera; ~ **de video** *or* (Esp) **vídeo** video camera; ~ **fotográfica** camera

camarada *mf* **(a)** (de partido político) comrade **(b)** (de colegio) school friend; (de trabajo) colleague

camaradería *f* camaraderie, comradeship

camarero -ra *m,f* **1** (esp Esp) (en bar, restaurante) (*m*) waiter; (*f*) waitress; (detrás de mostrador) (*m*) barman, bartender (AmE); (*f*) barmaid, bartender (AmE) **2 (a)** (en hotel) (*m*) bellboy; (*f*) maid **(b)** (Transp) (*m*) steward; (*f*) stewardess

camarín *m* (CS) **(a)** (Teatr) dressing room **(b)** (en vestuarios) changing cubicle **(c) camarines** *mpl* (Chi) (Dep) changing rooms (*pl*), locker rooms (*pl*)

camarógrafo -fa *m,f* (*m*) cameraman; (*f*) camerawoman

camarón *m* (crustáceo — pequeño) shrimp; (— más grande) shrimp (AmE), prawn (BrE)

camarote *m* cabin

cambalache *m* **(a)** (fam) (trueque) swap (colloq); **hacer ~s** to swap (colloq) **(b)** (RPl fam & pey) (tienda) thrift store (AmE), junk shop (BrE)

cambiante *adj* ⟨tiempo⟩ changeable, unsettled; ⟨persona/carácter⟩ moody, temperamental

cambiar [A1] *vt* **1 (a)** (alterar, modificar) ⟨horario/imagen/persona⟩ to change **(b)** (de lugar, posición): ~ **los muebles de lugar** to move the furniture around; **cambié las flores de florero** I put the flowers in a different vase **(c)** (reemplazar) ⋯⋗

⟨*pieza/fecha/sábanas*⟩ to change; **le cambió la pila al reloj** she changed the battery in the clock; **∼le el nombre a algo** to change the name of sth **(d)** ⟨*niño/bebé*⟩ to change **(e)** (Fin) to change; **cambié 100 libras a** *or* (Esp) **en dólares** I changed 100 pounds into dollars

2 (canjear) ⟨*sellos/estampas*⟩ to swap, to trade (esp AmE); **∼ algo POR algo** ⟨*sellos/estampas*⟩ to swap *o* (esp AmE) trade sth FOR sth; ⟨*compra*⟩ to exchange *o* change sth FOR sth; **¿quieres que te cambie el lugar?** do you want me to swap *o* change places with you?

■ **∼** *vi* **(a)** «*ciudad/persona*» to change; **∼ para peor** to change for the worse; **le está cambiando la voz** his voice is breaking **(b)** (Auto) to change gear **(c)** (hacer transbordo) to change; **∼ de avión/tren** to change planes/train **(d)** **∼ de algo** ⟨*de tema/canal/color*⟩ to change sth; **∼ de idea** to change one's mind; **∼ de sentido** to make (AmE) *o* (BrE) do a U-turn

■ **cambiarse** *v pron* **(a)** (refl) (de ropa) to change, get changed **(b)** (refl) ⟨*camisa/nombre/peinado*⟩ to change; **∼se DE algo** ⟨*de camisa/zapatos*⟩ to change sth; **me cambié de sitio** I changed places; **∼se de casa** to move house; **cámbiate de camisa** change your shirt **(c)** **∼se POR algn** to change places WITH sb **(d)** (recípr) ⟨*sellos/estampas*⟩ to swap, to trade (esp AmE) **(e)** (CS) (mudarse de casa) to move

cambio *m* **1** **(a)** (alteración) change; **∼ DE algo** ⟨*de planes/domicilio*⟩ change *or* sth; **un ∼ de aire(s)** *or* **ambiente** a change of scene **(b)** (Auto) gearshift (AmE), gear change (BrE); **un coche con cinco ∼s** (AmL) a car with a five-speed gearbox; **∼ de sentido** U-turn **2** **(a)** (canje) exchange; **❸ no se admiten cambios** goods cannot be exchanged **(b)** (en locs) **a cambio (de)** in exchange (for), in return (for); **en cambio: el viaje en autobús es agotador, en ∼ en tren es muy agradable** the bus journey is exhausting; by train however *o* on the other hand is very pleasant **3** **(a)** (Fin) (de moneda extranjera) exchange; **∼ de divisas** foreign exchange; **¿a cómo está el ∼?** what's the exchange rate?; **❸ cambio** bureau de change, change **(b)** (diferencia) change; **me ha dado mal el ∼** he's given me the wrong change **(c)** (dinero suelto) change

cambista *mf* moneychanger

cambur *m* (Ven) (fruta) banana

camelia *f* camellia

camello *m* **1** (Zool) camel **2** **camello** *mf* (arg) (traficante) pusher (sl), dealer (colloq)

camellón *m* (Méx) (en la calle) traffic island

camelo *m* (fam) (timo) con (colloq); (mentira) lie

camerino *m* **(a)** (Teatr) dressing room **(b)** **camerinos** *mpl* (Col) (Dep) changing rooms (*pl*)

camilla *f* (de lona) stretcher; (con ruedas) trolley, gurney (AmE); (en un consultorio) couch

camillero -ra *m,f* stretcher-bearer

caminante *mf* hiker; (liter) traveler*

caminar [A1] *vi* **1** (andar) to walk; **salieron a**

∼ they went out for a walk; podemos ir caminando we can walk, we can go on foot; **∼ HACIA algo** ⟨*hacia meta/fin*⟩ to move TOWARD(s) sth **2** (AmL) «*reloj/motor*» to work; **el asunto va caminando** (fam) things are moving (colloq)

■ **∼** *vt* ⟨*distancia*⟩ to walk

caminata *f* long walk; (en el campo) long walk, hike; **después de darme semejante ∼** after walking *o* (colloq) trekking all that way

camino *m* **1** (en general) road; (de tierra) track; (sendero) path; **∼ vecinal** minor road (*built and maintained by local council*)

2 **(a)** (ruta, dirección) way; **saberse el ∼** to know the way; **me salieron al ∼** «*asaltantes*» they blocked my path *o* way; «*amigos*» they came out to meet me; **este es el mejor ∼ a seguir** this is the best course to follow; **el ∼ a la fama** the road *o* path to fame; **se abrió ∼ entre la espesura** she made her way through the dense thickets; **abrirse ∼ en la vida** to get on in life; **buen/mal ∼: este niño va por mal ∼** this boy's heading for trouble; **ibas por buen ∼ pero te equivocaste** you were on the right track but you made a mistake; **llevar a algn por mal ∼** to lead sb astray **(b)** (trayecto, viaje): **el ∼ de regreso** the return journey; **se pusieron en ∼** they set off; **todavía nos quedan dos horas de ∼** we still have two hours to go **(c)** (en locs) **camino de/a …** on my/his/her way to …; **ir ∼ de algo: una tradición que va ∼ de desaparecer** a tradition which looks set to disappear; **de camino** on the way; **pilla de ∼** it's on the way; **me queda de ∼** I pass it on my way; **de ∼ a la estación** on the way to the station; **en camino** on the way; **deben estar ya en ∼** they must be on their way already; **por el camino** on the way; **a mitad de** *or* **a medio ∼** halfway through

camión *m* **(a)** (de carga) truck, lorry (BrE); (contenido) truckload; **∼ cisterna** tanker; **∼ de la basura** garbage truck (AmE), dustcart (BrE); **∼ de mudanzas** moving van (AmE), removal van (BrE) **(b)** (AmC, Méx) (autobús) bus

camionero -ra *m,f* truck driver, lorry driver (BrE); (conductor de autobús) (AmC, Méx) bus driver

camioneta *f* **(a)** (furgoneta) van; (camión pequeño) light truck, pickup truck (AmL) (coche familiar) station wagon (AmE), estate car (BrE)

camisa *f* shirt; **en mangas de ∼** in shirtsleeves; **∼ de fuerza** straitjacket; **cambiar de ∼** to change sides

camiseta *f* **(a)** (prenda interior) undershirt (AmE), vest (BrE) **(b)** (prenda exterior) T-shirt; (de fútbol) shirt, jersey (AmE); (sin mangas) jersey (AmE), vest (BrE)

camisón *m* nightdress

camomila *f* camomile, chamomile

camorra *f* (fam) (bronca, riña) fight; **armar ∼** to start a fight; **buscar ∼** to look for a fight (colloq)

camorrero -ra *adj/mf* (Col, CS) ▶ CAMORRISTA

camorrista *adj* (fam) (pendenciero): **no seas ∼** stop being a troublemaker

■ *mf* troublemaker (colloq)

camote *m* (Bot) (Andes, Méx) (batata) sweet potato; *hacerse* ~ (Méx fam) to get in a muddle (colloq)

campamento *m* camp; **nos fuimos a Bariloche de** ~ we went camping in Bariloche

campana *f* **(a)** (de iglesia, colegio) bell; **oía las** ~**s** I could hear the bells ringing; **tocar la** ~ to ring the bell; **¿ya ha sonado la** ~**?** has the bell gone yet? **(b)** (de chimenea) hood; (de cocina) extractor hood

campanada *f* **(a)** (de campana) chime, stroke; (de reloj) stroke; **el reloj dio 12** ~**s** the clock struck 12 **(b)** (fam) (sorpresa): **la noticia fue una** ~ the news came like a bolt from the blue (colloq); *dar la* ~ to cause a stir

campanario *m* bell tower, belfry

campanazo *m* (AmL) ▶ CAMPANADA

campanilla *f* **(a)** (campana pequeña) small bell, hand bell **(b)** (Anat) uvula **(c)** (Bot) campanula, bellflower

campante *adj*: **se quedó tan** ~ he didn't bat an eyelash (AmE) *o* (BrE) eyelid; **nosotros muertos de miedo y él tan** ~ we were scared stiff but he was as cool as a cucumber

campaña *f* campaign; ~ **electoral** electoral *o* election campaign; ~ **publicitaria** advertising campaign; **hacer una** ~ to run *o* conduct a campaign

campechano -na *adj* (sin complicaciones) straightforward; (bondadoso) good-natured

campeón -peona *adj* champion (*before n*)
■ *m,f* champion; **el** ~ **del mundo** the world champion

campeonato *m* championship

cámper *f* (Chi, Méx) camper (van)

campera *f* **(a)** (RPl) (chaqueta) jacket **(b) camperas** *fpl* (Esp) (botas) cowboy boots

campero *m* (Col) (Auto) jeep

campesino -na *adj* ⟨vida/costumbre⟩ rural, country (*before n*); ⟨modales/aspecto⟩ peasant-like
■ *m,f* (persona del campo) country person; (con connotaciones de pobreza) peasant; **son** ~**s** they are country people *o* folk; **los obreros y los** ~**s** the manual workers and the agricultural workers

campestre *adj* ⟨escena/vida⟩ rural, country (*before n*); ⟨casa/club⟩ country (*before n*)

camping /'kampin/ *m* (*pl* **-pings**) **(a)** (actividad) camping; **irse de** ~ to go camping **(b)** (lugar) campsite, campground (AmE)

campiña *f* countryside; **la** ~ **inglesa** the English countryside

campista *mf* camper

campo *m* **1** (zona no urbana) country; (paisaje) countryside; **la gente del** ~ the country people; **el** ~ **se ve precioso** the countryside looks beautiful; ~ **a través** *or* **a** ~ **traviesa** ⟨caminar/ir⟩ cross-country **2** (zona agraria) land; (terreno) field; **trabajar el** ~ to work the land; **las faenas del** ~ farm work; **los** ~**s de cebada** the field of barley; ~ **de aterrizaje** landing field; ~ **de batalla** battlefield; ~ **de minas** minefield; ~ **petrolífero** oilfield **3** (Dep) (de fútbol) field, pitch (BrE); (de golf) course; **jugar en** ~ **propio/contrario** to play at home/away; ~ **a través** cross-country running; ~ **de tiro** firing range

4 (ámbito, área de acción) field; **el** ~ **de la informática** the field of computing **5** (campamento) camp; ~ **de concentración/de refugiados** concentration/refugee camp

camposanto *m* (liter) graveyard, cemetery

campus *m* (*pl* ~) campus

camuflaje *m* camouflage

camuflar [A1] *vt* ⟨tanques/contrabando⟩ to camouflage; ⟨intenciones⟩ to disguise
■ **camuflarse** *v pron* «persona» to camouflage oneself; «animal» to camouflage itself

cana¹ *f* **1** (pelo) gray* hair, white hair; *echar una* ~ *al aire* to let one's hair down (colloq) **2** (AmS arg) (cárcel) slammer (sl), nick (BrE colloq) **3** (RPl arg) (cuerpo de policía): **la** ~ the cops (*pl*) (colloq)

cana² *mf* (RPl arg) (agente) cop (colloq)

Canadá *m*: *tb* **el** ~ Canada

canadiense *adj/mf* Canadian

canal *m* **1** (Náut) (cauce artificial) canal; (Agr, Ing) channel; ~ **de la Mancha** English Channel; ~ **de Panamá** Panama Canal; ~ **de San Lorenzo** St Lawrence Seaway **2** **(a)** (Rad, Telec, TV) channel; **cambia de** ~ change *o* switch channels **(b)** (medio) channel
■ *f or m* (canalón) gutter; (ranura) groove

canalizar [A4] *vt* to channel

canalla *mf* (fam) (bribón, granuja) swine (colloq)

canallada *f* (fam): **¡qué** ~**!** what a rotten *o* mean thing to do (colloq)

canalón *m* (Esp) gutter

canapé *m* **1** (Coc) canapé **2** (sofá) couch

Canarias *fpl*: *tb* **las** (**Islas**) ~ the Canaries, the Canary Islands

canario¹ -ria *adj* of/from the Canary Islands
■ *m,f* (de las Canarias) person from the Canary Islands

canario² *m* (Zool) canary

canasta *f* **(a)** (para la compra) basket **(b)** (AmL) (en rifa) hamper **(c)** (en baloncesto) basket; **meter una** ~ to make *o* score a basket **(d)** (Jueg) canasta

canastilla *f* layette

canasto *m* basket (*gen large and with a lid*)

cancel *m* (contrapuerta) inner door; (tabique) (Col, Méx) partition; (biombo) (Méx) folding screen

cancelación *f* **1** (suspensión) cancellation **2** (liquidación) payment

cancelar [A1] *vt* **(a)** ⟨reunión/viaje/pedido⟩ to cancel **(b)** ⟨deuda⟩ to settle, pay off; ⟨cuenta⟩ to pay

cáncer *m* (Med) cancer; **tiene (un)** ~ **de mama** she has breast cancer

Cáncer *m* (signo) Cancer; **es (de)** ~ he's a Cancer *o* Cancerian
■ *mf* (persona) *tb* **cáncer** Cancerian, Cancer

cancha *f* **1** **(a)** (Dep) (de baloncesto, frontón, squash, tenis) court; (de fútbol, rugby) (AmL) field, pitch; (BrE) (de golf) course; (CS) course; (de polo) (AmL) field; (de esquí) (CS) slope **(b)** (Chi) (Aviac) *tb* ~ **de aterrizaje** runway **2** (AmL fam) (desenvoltura): **un político con mucha** ~ a politician with a great deal of experience, a seasoned politician

canchita *f* (Per) popcorn

canciller m (a) (jefe de estado) chancellor (b) (AmS) (ministro) ≈ Secretary of State (*in US*), ≈ Foreign Secretary (*in UK*)

cancillería f (a) (de embajada) chancery, chancellery (b) (AmS) (ministerio) ≈ State Department (*in US*), ≈ Foreign Office (*in UK*)

canción f song; ~ **de cuna** lullaby; ~ **nacional** (Chi) national anthem

candado m (cerradura) padlock; **está cerrada con** ~ it is padlocked

candela f (a) (fuego) fire; **¿tienes** ~? (fam) have you got a light? (b) (vela) candle

candelabro m candelabra

candelero m candlestick; **estar en el** ~ to be in the limelight

candente adj (a) ⟨hierro⟩ red-hot (b) ⟨tema⟩ burning

candidato -ta m,f candidate; ~ **a la presidencia** presidential candidate; **los** ~**s al puesto de ...** the applicants for the post of ...; **presentarse como** ~ **para algo** (Pol) to run (AmE) o (BrE) stand for sth

candidatura f (a) (propuesta) candidacy, candidature (b) (Esp) (lista) list of candidates

cándido -da adj naive

candil m oil lamp

candilejas fpl footlights (*pl*)

candor m innocence, naivety

caneca f (Col) (papelera) wastebasket, waste-paper basket (BrE); (cubo de la basura) garbage o trash can (AmE), dustbin (BrE)

canela f (Bot, Coc) cinnamon; ~ **en polvo/en rama** ground/stick cinnamon

canelón m (a) (Const) gutter (b) **canelones** mpl cannelloni

cangrejo m (de mar) crab; (de río) crayfish

canguro m [1] (Zool) kangaroo [2] (a) (anorak) cagoule (b) (para llevar a un niño) sling [3] (Esp) **canguro** mf babysitter; **hacer de** ~ to babysit

caníbal mf (antropófago) cannibal

canica f marble

caniche mf /ka'nitʃe, ka'niʃ/ poodle

canijo -ja adj [1] (fam) (pequeño) tiny, puny (hum or pej) [2] (Méx fam) (terco) stubborn, pig-headed (colloq)

canilla f (a) (RPl) (grifo) faucet (AmE), tap (BrE); **cerrar la** ~ to turn off the faucet o tap (b) (bobina) bobbin

canillita mf (Bol, CS) newspaper vendor o seller

canino m (Odont) canine (tooth); (Zool) canine

canjear [A1] vt to exchange

cannabis m cannabis

cano -na adj white

canoa f canoe

canódromo m greyhound stadium, dog track (colloq)

canon m [1] (norma) rule, canon (frml) [2] (Mús) canon

canónico -ca adj canonical, canonic

canonizar [A4] vt to canonize

canoso -sa adj ⟨persona⟩ gray-haired*, white-haired*; ⟨pelo/barba⟩ gray*, white

cansado -da adj [1] [ESTAR] (a) (fatigado) tired; ~**s de tanto caminar** tired from so much walking; **tienes cara de** ~ you look tired; **en un tono** ~ in

a weary tone of voice (b) (aburrido) ~ **DE algo/ hacer algo** tired OF sth/doing sth [2] [SER] ⟨viaje/ trabajo⟩ tiring

cansador -dora adj (AmS) tiring

cansancio m tiredness; **me caigo de** ~ I'm absolutely worn out o exhausted

cansar [A1] vt (a) (fatigar) to tire, tire ... out; **le cansa la vista** it makes her eyes tired, it strains her eyes (b) (aburrir) **¿no te cansa oír la misma música?** don't you get tired of listening to the same music?
■ ~ vi (a) (fatigar) to be tiring (b) (aburrir) to get tiresome
■ **cansarse** v pron (a) (fatigarse) to tire oneself out; **se le cansa la vista** her eyes get tired (b) (aburrirse) to get bored; ~**se DE algo/algn** to get tired OF sth/sb, get bored WITH sth/sb, ~**se DE hacer algo** to get tired OF doing sth

cantábrico -ca adj Cantabrian

Cantábrico m: **el (mar)** ~ the Bay of Biscay

cantante adj singing (*before n*)
■ mf singer

cantar [A1] vt ⟨canción⟩ to sing
■ ~ vi [1] (a) (Mús) to sing (b) «pájaro» to sing; «gallo» to crow; «cigarra/grillo» to chirp, chirrup [2] (fam) (confesar) to talk (colloq)
■ m poem (*gen set to music*)

cántara f churn

cantarín -rina, (CS) **cantarino -na** adj ⟨voz/ tono/risa⟩ singsong; ⟨fuente/aguas⟩ (liter) babbling

cántaro m pitcher, jug; **llover a** ~**s** to pour with rain

cantautor -tora m,f singer-songwriter

cante m (Mús) Andalusian folk song; ~ **flamenco** flamenco (singing)

cantera f (de piedra) quarry

cántico m canticle

cantidad f (a) (volumen) quantity, amount (b) (suma de dinero) sum, amount (c) (número) number; **la** ~ **de cartas recibidas** the number of letters received (d) (volumen impresionante): **había** ~ **de turistas** there were lots of tourists; **¡qué** ~ **de gente/de comida había!** there were so many people/there was so much food!; **tenemos** ~ or ~**es** (fam) we have lots o tons (colloq); **cualquier** ~ **de** (AmS) lots of, loads of (colloq)

cantimplora f water bottle, canteen

cantina f [1] (a) (en estación) buffet, cafeteria; (en universidad) refectory; (en fábrica) canteen (b) (AmL exc RPl) (bar) bar (c) (RPl) (restaurante italiano) trattoria [2] (Col) (para la leche) churn

cantinela f: **siempre la misma** ~ always the same old story (o thing etc)

cantinflear [A1] vi (fam) to babble

canto m [1] (Mús) (acción, arte) singing; (canción) chant [2] (de pájaro) song; (del gallo) crowing [3] (Lit) (canción) hymn [4] (borde, filo) edge; **colocó el ladrillo de** ~ he lay the brick on its side [5] (Geol) tb ~ **rodado** (roca) boulder; (guijarro) pebble

cantor -tora adj singing (*before n*)
■ m,f (cantante) singer

canturrear [A1] vi to sing softly to oneself
■ ~ vt to sing ... softly to oneself

canuto m (tubo) document tube

caña f (a) (planta) reed (b) (tallo del bambú, azúcar)

cane; **muebles de** ∼ cane furniture; ∼ **de azúcar** sugar cane **(c)** (de pescar) rod **(d)** (de la bota) leg; **botas de media** ∼ calf-length boots

cañada *f* **(a)** (Geog) gully; (más profunda) ravine **(b)** (AmL) (arroyo) stream

cáñamo *m* (planta) cannabis plant, hemp; (tela) canvas

cañaveral *m* (de juncos) reedbed; (de cañas de azúcar) (Col) sugar-cane plantation

cañería *f* (tubo) pipe; (conjunto de tubos) piping, pipes (*pl*)

cañero -ra *adj* (AmL) (Agr) sugarcane (*before n*)

cañizal *m* reedbed

caño *m* (conducto) pipe; (de una fuente) spout; (grifo) (Per) faucet (AmE), tap (BrE)

cañón *m* **(a)** (Arm) (arma) cannon; (de una escopeta, pistola) barrel **(b)** (valle) canyon; **el Gran C**∼ **del Colorado** the Grand Canyon **(c)** (de pluma) quill

cañonazo *m* (Arm, Mil) cannonshot; **una salva de 21** ∼**s** a 21-gun salute

caoba *f* **(a)** (árbol) mahogany tree (madera) mahogany **(b)** (de) **color** ∼ mahogany

caos *m* chaos; **será un verdadero** ∼ there'll be absolute chaos

caótico -ca *adj* chaotic

capa *f* 1 **(a)** (en general) layer; **una** ∼ **de nieve** a layer *o* carpet of snow; **la** ∼ **de ozono** the ozone layer; **lleva el pelo cortado en** *or* (Esp) **a** ∼**s** she has layered hair **(b)** (de barniz, pintura) coat **(c)** (estrato) stratum; **las** ∼**s de la sociedad** the social strata 2 **(a)** (Indum) cloak, cape; ∼ **de agua** raincape **(b)** (Taur) cape

capacidad *f* 1 **(a)** (competencia) ability **(b)** (potencial) capacity; **su gran** ∼ **de trabajo** her great capacity for work; ∼ DE *or* PARA **hacer algo** ability *o* capacity to do sth **(c)** (Der) capacity 2 (cupo) capacity

capacitado -da *adj* ∼ PARA algo/hacer algo qualified FOR sth/to do sth

capacitar [A1] *vt* (formar) to prepare; (profesionalmente) ∼ **a algn** PARA **algo** to qualify sb FOR sth; ∼ **a algn** PARA **hacer algo** to qualify *o* entitle sb to do sth

■ **capacitarse** *v pron* (formarse) to train; (obtener un título) to qualify, become qualified

capar [A1] *vt* 1 (castrar) to castrate 2 (Col fam) ∼ **clase** to play hooky (esp AmE colloq), to skive off (school) (BrE colloq)

caparazón *m or f* shell

capataz *mf* (*m*) foreman; (*f*) forewoman

capaz *adj* **(a)** (competente) capable, able **(b)** (de una hazaña) capable; **es** ∼ **de grandes logros** he's capable of great things; **¿te sientes** ∼ **de enfrentarte con ella?** do you feel able to face her?; **¿a qué no eres** ∼ **de saltar esto?** I bet you can't jump over this; **es (muy)** ∼ **de irse sin pagar** he's quite capable of leaving without paying

capazo *m* (cesta) basket; (para un niño) portacrib® (AmE), carrycot (BrE)

capea *f: amateur bullfight using young bulls*

capear [A1] *vt* 1 (Taur) to make passes at (*with the cape*) 2 (Chi fam) (*trabajo*) to skip, to skive off (BrE colloq); ∼ **clase** to play hooky (esp AmE colloq), to skive off (school) (BrE colloq)

capellán *m* chaplain

Caperucita Roja Little Red Riding Hood

caperuza *f* **(a)** (Indum) pointed hood **(b)** (de un bolígrafo) top, cap

capicúa *adj* palindromic (frml); **era un número** ∼ the number read the same both ways

capilar *adj* **(a)** ⟨*loción*⟩ hair (*before n*) **(b)** ⟨*vaso/tubo*⟩ capillary (*before n*)
■ *m* capillary

capilla *f* chapel; ∼ **ardiente** funeral chapel

capital *adj* ⟨*importancia*⟩ cardinal, prime; ⟨*influencia*⟩ seminal (frml); ⟨*obra*⟩ key, seminal (frml)
■ *m* **(a)** (Com, Fin) capital **(b)** (recursos, riqueza) resources (*pl*)
■ *f* (de país) capital; (de provincia) provincial capital, ≈ county seat (*in US*), ≈ county town (*in UK*); **Valencia** ∼ the city of Valencia

capitalino -na *adj* (AmL) of/from the capital
■ *m,f* (AmL) inhabitant of the capital

capitalismo *m* capitalism

capitalista *adj* capitalist (*before n*)
■ *mf* capitalist

capitán -tana *m,f* 1 **(a)** (del ejército) captain; (de la Fuerza Aérea) captain (AmE), flight lieutenant (BrE) **(b)** (Náut) (de transatlántico, carguero) captain, master; (de buque de pesca) skipper **(c)** (Aviac) captain 2 (Dep) captain

capitel *m* capital

capítulo *m* (de libro) chapter; (de serie) episode

capó *m* hood (AmE), bonnet (BrE)

capón *adj* castrated
■ *m* (gallo) capon

caporal *m* (Méx) foreman, charge hand (BrE)

capot /ka'po/ *m* hood (AmE), bonnet (BrE)

capota *f* (de automóvil) convertible top; (de cochecito de bebé) canopy, hood

capote *m* 1 (capa) cloak; (de militar, torero) cape 2 (Méx) (Auto) hood (AmE), bonnet (BrE)

capricho *m* 1 (antojo) whim, caprice (liter); **le consienten todos los** ∼**s** they indulge his every whim; **se lo compró por puro** ∼ he bought it on a whim; **entran y salen a** ∼ they come in and go out at will *o* as they please 2 (Mús) capriccio

caprichoso -sa *adj* **(a)** (inconstante) ⟨*carácter/ persona*⟩ capricious; ⟨*tiempo/moda*⟩ changeable **(b)** (difícil, exigente) fussy
■ *m,f*: **es un** ∼ (es inconstante) he's always changing his mind; (es difícil, exigente) he's so fussy

Capricornio *m* (signo, constelación) Capricorn; **es (de)** ∼ she's a Capricorn
■ *mf* (persona) *tb* **capricornio** Capricornean, Capricorn

cápsula *f* **(a)** (Farm, Espac) capsule **(b)** (Audio) cartridge

captar [A1] *vt* **(a)** ⟨*atención/interés*⟩ to capture; ⟨*clientes*⟩ to win, gain; ⟨*partidarios/empleados*⟩ to attract, recruit **(b)** ⟨*sentido/matiz*⟩ to grasp; ⟨*significado/indirecta*⟩ to get **(c)** ⟨*emisora/señal*⟩ to pick up, receive

captura *f* (de delincuente, enemigo, animal) capture; (de un alijo) seizure; (en pesca) catch

capturar [A1] *vt* ⟨*delincuente/enemigo/animal*⟩ to capture; ⟨*alijo*⟩ to seize, confiscate; ⟨*peces*⟩ to catch

capucha *f* hood

capuchón m (de pluma, bolígrafo) top, cap; (Indum) hood

capullo m **(a)** (Bot) bud **(b)** (Zool) cocoon

caqui adj inv/m khaki

cara f **1 (a)** (Anat) face; **dímelo a la ~** say it to my face; **se le rio en la ~** she laughed in his face; **mírame a la ~** look at me **(b)** (en locs) **cara a cara** face to face; **de cara: el sol me da de ~** the sun is in my eyes; **se puso de ~ a la pared** she turned to face the wall, she turned her face to the wall; **dar la ~:** nunca da la ~ he never does his own dirty work; **dar la ~ por algn** to stand up for sb; **echarle algo en ~ a algn** to throw sth back in sb's face; **romperle la ~ a algn** (fam) to smash sb's face in (colloq)

2 (a) (expresión): **no pongas esa ~ que no es para tanto** don't look like that, it's not that bad; **alegra esa ~** cheer up; **le cambió la ~ cuando ...** her face changed when ...; **poner ~ de bueno** to play o act the innocent; **poner ~ de asco** to make o (BrE) pull a face; **andaba con/puso ~ larga** (fam) he had/he pulled a long face **(b)** (aspecto) look; **tiene ~ de cansado** he looks tired; **tienes mala ~** you don't look well; **¡qué buena ~ tiene la comida!** that food looks delicious!

3 (a) (Mat) face **(b)** (de disco, papel) side; **~ o cruz** or (Arg) **ceca** or (Andes, Ven) **sello** heads or tails; **lo echaron a ~ o cruz** they tossed for it **4** (fam) (frescura, descaro) nerve (colloq), cheek (BrE colloq); **¡qué ~ (más dura) tienes!** you have some nerve!

■ mf: tb **~ dura** (fam) (persona) sassy devil (AmE colloq), cheeky swine (BrE colloq)

carabina f **(a)** (Arm) carbine **(b)** (Esp fam) (acompañante): **ir de ~** to play gooseberry (colloq)

carabinero -ra m,f **(a)** (policía) (m) police officer, policeman; (f) police officer, policewoman **(b)** (agente fronterizo) border guard **(c) carabineros** mpl (institución) police (force); (policía fronteriza) border police

Caracas m Caracas

caracol m **(a)** (Zool) (de mar) winkle; (de tierra) snail **(b)** (AmL) (concha) conch

caracola f conch

carácter m (pl **-racteres**) **(a)** (en general) character; **tenemos un ~ muy distinto** we have very different characters; **el restaurante tiene mucho ~** the restaurant has lots of character; **una persona de ~ fuerte** a person of strong character; **una persona de buen ~** a good-natured person; **un ~ abierto** an open nature; **tener mal ~** to have a (bad) temper **(b)** (índole, naturaleza) nature; **una visita de ~ oficial** a visit of an official nature; **heridas de ~ leve** (period) minor wounds **(c)** (Biol) characteristic **(d)** (Col, Méx) (personaje) character

característica f **(a)** (rasgo) feature, characteristic **(b)** (RPl) (Telec) exchange code

característico -ca adj characteristic

caracterizar [A4] vt **1** (distinguir) to

characterize; **con la franqueza que lo caracteriza** with his characteristic frankness **2** (describir) to portray, depict **3** (Teatr) (encarnar) to play, portray

■ **caracterizarse** v pron: **~se POR algo** «enfermedad/región/raza» to be characterized BY sth; «persona» to be noted FOR sth

caradura adj (fam) sassy (AmE colloq), cheeky (BrE colloq)

■ m,f (fam) sassy devil (AmE colloq), cheeky swine (BrE colloq)

■ f (fam) nerve (colloq), cheek (BrE colloq)

carajillo m (café) coffee with brandy or similar

carajito -ta m,f (Ven fam) (niño) kid (colloq)

caramba interj (expresando — sorpresa) good heavens!; (— disgusto) dammit! (colloq)

carámbano m icicle

carambola f **(a)** (en billar) carom (AmE), cannon (BrE) **(b)** (fam) (casualidad): **fue de ~** it was pure chance **(c)** (Méx) (choque múltiple) pileup

caramelo m **(a)** (golosina) candy (AmE), sweet (BrE); **un ~ de menta** a mint **(b)** (azúcar fundida) caramel

carantoña f (Esp fam) caress

caraota f (Ven) bean

caraqueño -ña adj of/from Caracas

carátula f **(a)** (de disco) jacket (AmE), sleeve (BrE); (de video) case **(b)** (Méx) (de reloj) face, dial **(c)** (máscara) mask

caravana f **1 (a)** (de tráfico — retención) backup (AmE) tailback (BrE); (— hilera) convoy; **ir en ~** to drive in (a) convoy **(b)** (remolque) trailer (AmE), caravan (BrE) **2** (Méx) (reverencia) bow

carbohidrato m carbohydrate

carbón m **(a)** (mineral) coal; **negro como el ~** as black as coal **(b)** (vegetal) charcoal

carboncillo m charcoal; **dibujo al ~** charcoal drawing

carbonilla f **(a)** (polvo de carbón) cinders (pl) **(b)** (RPl) (Art) charcoal

carbonizarse [A4] v pron **(a)** «edificio/muebles» to be reduced to ashes; **los cuerpos carbonizados de las víctimas** the victims' charred remains **(b)** (Quím) to carbonize

carbono m carbon

carburador m carburetor*

carburante m fuel

carburar [A1] vi **(a)** «motor» to carburet **(b)** (fam) (funcionar) «electrodoméstico/coche» to work

■ ~ vt (Andes) «motor» to tune

carca adj (fam) old-fashioned, fuddy-duddy (colloq)

■ mf old fogey (colloq)

carcacha f (Andes, Méx fam) (auto viejo) wreck (colloq), old heap (colloq); (otro aparato) contraption (colloq)

carcajada f guffaw; **soltar una ~** to give a guffaw, to burst out laughing; **reírse a ~s** to roar with laughter

carcasa *f* (a) (armazón, estructura) frame; (de aparato) casing; (de barca) hulk (b) (esqueleto de animal) skeleton

cárcel *f* (prisión) prison, jail; **la metieron en la ~** she was put in prison

carcelero -ra *m,f* jailer

carcoma *f* (Zool) woodworm

carcomer [E1] *vt* (a) «*carcoma*» to eat away (at); **el marco está carcomido** the frame is worm-eaten (b) ‹*salud*› to undermine; **la envidia lo carcomía** he was eaten up with envy

cardar [A1] *vt* (a) ‹*lana*› to card (b) ‹*pelo*› to backcomb, tease
■ **cardarse** *v pron* (*refl*) to backcomb

cardenal *m* ⓵ (Relig) cardinal ⓶ (fam) (moretón) bruise

cardíaco, cardiaco -ca *adj* heart (*before n*), cardiac (tech); **enfermos ~s** heart patients

cárdigan *m* (*pl* **-gans**) cardigan

cardiólogo -ga *m,f* cardiologist

cardo *m* (Bot) thistle

carecer [E3] *vi* (frml) **~ DE algo** to lack sth; **carece de interés** it is lacking in interest, it lacks interest; **carece de valor** it has no value, it is worthless

carencia *f* (a) (escasez) lack, shortage; **~ de recursos financieros** lack of financial resources (b) (Med) deficiency; **~ de vitamina A** vitamin A deficiency

carente *adj* (frml): **lugares ~s de interés** places which are of no interest; **niños ~s de cariño** children lacking affection

carero -ra *adj* (fam) ‹*comerciante*› pricey (colloq)

carestía *f* (costo elevado) high cost; **la ~ de la vida** the high cost of living

careta *f* mask

carey *m* (Zool) hawksbill turtle; (material) tortoiseshell

carga *f* ⓵ (a) (de barco, avión) cargo; (de camión) load; (de tren) freight; ⓢ **zona de carga y descarga** loading and unloading only (b) (peso) load; **no lleves tanta ~** don't carry such a heavy load ⓶ (a) (de escopeta, cañón) charge (b) (de bolígrafo, pluma) refill; (de lavadora) load ⓷ (Elec) (de cuerpo) charge; (de circuito) load ⓸ (responsabilidad) burden; **es una ~ para la familia** he is a burden to his family ⓹ (a) (de tropas, policía) charge; **¡a la ~!** charge! (b) (Dep) *tb* **~ defensiva** blitz

cargada *f* (RPl fam) practical joke

cargaderas *fpl* (Col) suspenders (*pl*) (AmE), braces (*pl*) (BrE)

cargado -da *adj* ⓵ (a) (con peso): **iba muy cargada** she had a lot to carry; **~ DE algo** ‹*de regalos*› laden WITH sth; ‹*de paquetes/maletas*› loaded down WITH sth; **~ de deudas** heavily in debt; **un árbol ~ de fruta** a tree laden with fruit; **~ de trabajo** overloaded with work (b) ‹*ambiente/atmósfera*› (bochornoso) heavy, close; (con humo, olores desagradables) stuffy; (tenso) strained, tense (c) ‹*café*› strong ⓶ **~ de hombros** *or* **de espaldas** with bowed shoulders

cargador *m* (a) (Arm) clip, magazine (b) (de pilas, baterías) battery charger

cargamento *m* (de camión) load; (de barco, avión) cargo; (de tren) freight

cargante *adj* (a) (CS fam) (antipático) unpleasant, horrible (colloq) (b) (Esp fam) annoying

cargar [A3] *vt* ⓵ (a) ‹*barco/avión/camión*› to load; **~on la camioneta de cajas** they loaded the van with boxes; **no cargues tanto el coche** don't put so much in the car (b) ‹*pistola/escopeta*› to load; ‹*pluma/encendedor*› to fill; ‹*cámara*› to load, put a film in (c) (Elec) to charge ⓶ (a) ‹*mercancías*› to load (b) ‹*combustible*› to fuel; **tengo que ~ nafta** (RPl) I have to fill up with gasoline (AmE) *o* (BrE) petrol (c) (Inf) to load ⓷ (de obligaciones) **~ a algn DE algo** to burden sb WITH sth; **me ~on la culpa** they put *o* laid the blame on me ⓸ (a) ‹*paquetes/bolsas*› to carry; ‹*niño*› (AmL) to carry (b) (AmL exc RPl) ‹*armas*› to carry (c) (Ven fam) (llevar puesto) to wear; (tener consigo): **cargo las llaves** I have the keys ⓹ (a una cuenta) to charge ⓺ (Méx fam) (matar) to kill
■ **~** *vi* ⓵ **~ CON algo** ‹*con bulto*› to carry sth; **tiene que ~ con todo el peso de la casa** she has to shoulder all the responsibility for the household ⓶ **~ CONTRA algn** «*tropas/policía*» to charge ON *o* AT sb ⓷ «*batería*» to charge ⓸ (fam) (fastidiar): **me cargan los fanfarrones** I can't stand show-offs
■ **cargarse** *v pron* ⓵ (a) «*pilas/flash*» to charge; «*partícula*» to become charged (b) **~se DE algo** ‹*de bolsas/equipaje*› to load oneself down WITH sth; ‹*de responsabilidades*› to take on a lot OF sth; ‹*de deudas*› to saddle oneself WITH sth ⓶ (a) (fam) (matar) to kill (b) (Esp fam) ‹*motor*› to wreck; ‹*jarrón*› to smash

cargo *m* ⓵ (puesto) post, position (frml); (de presidente, ministro) office; **tener un ~ público** to hold public office; **un ~ de responsabilidad** a responsible job *o* post ⓶ (responsabilidad, cuidado): **los niños están a mi ~** the children are in my care; **estar a ~ de algo** to be in charge of sth; **los gastos corren a ~ de la empresa** expenses will be paid *o* met by the company; **hacerse ~ de algo** ‹*de puesto/tarea*› to take charge of sth; ‹*de gastos*› to take care of sth; **me da ~ de conciencia** I feel guilty ⓷ (a) (Com, Fin) charge; **sin ~** free of charge (b) (Der) charge

cargoso -sa *adj* (CS, Per fam) annoying

cargue *m* (Col, Ven) loading; ⓢ **zona de cargue y descargue** loading and unloading only

carguero *m* freighter, cargo ship

Caribe *m*: **el (mar) ~** the Caribbean (Sea)

caribeño -ña *adj* Caribbean
■ *m,f*: person from the Caribbean region

caribú *m* caribou

caricatura *f* (dibujo) caricature

caricaturizar [A4] *vt* to caricature

caricia *f* caress; **hacer ~s** to caress; **le hizo una ~ al perro** she stroked the dog

caridad *f* charity; **vivir de la ~** to live on charity; **por ~** for pity's sake

caries *f* (*pl* **~**) (a) (proceso) tooth decay, caries (*pl*) (tech) (b) (cavidad) cavity

cariño *m* (a) (afecto) affection; **les tengo mucho** ···ᗮ

~ I am very fond of them; **te ha tomado mucho**
~ he's become very fond of you; **~s por tu casa/
a tu mujer** (AmL) (send my) love to your family/
your wife; **~s, Beatriz** (en cartas) (AmL) love,
Beatriz **(b)** (caricia): **le hice un cariñito al niño** I
gave the little boy a cuddle (*o* kiss *etc*) **(c)** (como
apelativo) dear, honey, love (BrE)

cariñoso -sa *adj* ⟨*persona*⟩ affectionate;
⟨*bienvenida*⟩ warm; **un ~ saludo de mi parte**
regards

carioca *adj* of/from Rio de Janeiro

carisma *m* charisma

carismático -ca *adj* charismatic

caritativo -va *adj* charitable; **una
organización con fines ~s** a charitable
organization

cariz *m*: **el ~ que están tomando las cosas** the
way things are going *o* developing; **la situación
está tomando mal ~** the situation is beginning to
look bad

carmín *adj inv* carmine
■ *m* **(a)** (para labios) lipstick **(b)** (color) carmine

carnada *f* bait

carnal *adj* ⟨*amor/deseo*⟩ carnal
■ *m* (Méx arg) pal (colloq), buddy (AmE colloq), mate
(BrE colloq)

carnaval *m* (fiesta) carnival

carne *f* **1 (a)** (de mamífero, ave) meat; (de
pescado) flesh; **~ de cerdo** *or* (Chi, Per) **chancho** *or*
(Ven) **cochino** *or* (Méx) **puerco** pork; **~ de cordero**
lamb; **~ de ternera** veal; **~ de vaca** *or* (AmC, Col,
Méx, Ven) **res** beef; **~ molida** *or* (Esp, RPl) **picada**
ground beef (AmE), mince (BrE) **(b)** (de fruta) flesh
2 (de una persona) flesh; **es ~ de mi ~** he's my
flesh and blood; **tenía la herida en ~ viva** her
wound was raw; **(de) color ~** flesh-colored*; *en
~ y hueso* in the flesh; **me pone la ~ de gallina**
it gives me goose pimples (colloq)

carné *m* identity card; **sacar el ~** to have one's
identity (*o* membership *etc*) card issued; **~ de
conducir** driver's license (AmE), driving licence
(BrE); **~ de estudiante** student card; **~ de
identidad** identity card; **~ de socio** (de club,
mutual) membership card; (de biblioteca) library
card

carnear [A1] *vt* (CS) to slaughter
■ **~** *vi* (CS) to slaughter a cow (*o* lamb *etc*)

carnecería *f* butcher's shop (*o* stall *etc*)

cárneo -nea *adj* (CS) meat (*before n*)

carnero *m* ram

carnet /kar'ne/ *m* (*pl* **-nets**) ▶ CARNÉ

carnicería *f* **(a)** (tienda) butcher's shop (*o* stall
etc) **(b)** (fam) (matanza) slaughter

carnicero -ra *m,f* **(a)** (vendedor) butcher **(b)**
(fam & pey) (cirujano) butcher (colloq & pej)

carnitas *fpl* (Méx) pieces of barbecued pork
(*pl*)

carnívoro¹ -ra *adj* carnivorous, meat-eating

carnívoro² *m* carnivore

caro¹ -ra *adj* **(a)** ⟨*coche/entrada/ciudad*⟩
expensive; **la vida está muy cara** everything costs
so much nowadays **(b)** (como *adv*): **me costó muy
~** I had to pay a lot of money for it; **pagarás ~
tu error** you'll pay dearly for your mistake

caro² *adv*: **vender ~** to charge a lot; *ver tb*
CARO¹ B

carpa *f* **1 (a)** (de circo) big top; (para actuaciones)
marquee **(b)** (AmL) (para acampar) tent **2** (Zool)
carp

carpeta *f* (para documentos, dibujos) folder; **~ de
anillos** *or* (Esp) **anillas** *or* (RPl) **ganchos** ring
binder

carpintería *f* **(a)** (taller) carpenter's workshop;
(actividad) carpentry **(b)** (de construcción, casa)
woodwork; **~ metálica** metalwork

carpintero -ra *m,f* carpenter

carraca *f* **(a)** (matraca) rattle **(b)** (fam) (trasto)
wreck (colloq)

carraspear [A1] *vi* to clear one's throat

carraspera *f*: **tener ~** to have a rough throat

carrasposo -sa *adj* **(a)** ⟨*garganta*⟩ rough **(b)**
(Col) ⟨*superficie*⟩ rough

carrera *f* **1** (Dep) (competición) race; **~ de
caballos** horse race; **la ~ de los 100 metros vallas**
the 100 meters hurdles; **te echo una ~** I'll race
you; **~ de armamentos** arms race; **~ contra reloj**
(Dep) time trial; **~ de fondo** long-distance race;
~ de postas *o* **relevos** relay race
2 (fam) (corrida): **darse** *or* **pegarse una ~** to run
as fast as one can; **me fui de una ~ a su casa** I
raced *o* rushed round to her house (colloq); **a la(s)
~(s)** in a rush
3 (a) (Educ) degree course; **está haciendo la ~
de Derecho** he's doing a degree in law **(b)**
(profesión, trayectoria) career; **un diplomático de ~** a
career diplomat; **~ media/superior** *three-year/
five-year university course*
4 (en la media) run, ladder (BrE); (en el pelo) (Col,
Ven) part (AmE), parting (BrE)

carrerear [A1] *vt* (Méx fam) to push (colloq)

carrerilla *f*: **se lo saben de ~** they know it
(off) by heart; **me lo dijo de ~** he reeled it off
parrot-fashion; **coger ~** (Esp) to take a run-up

carreta *f* (con toldo) wagon; (sin toldo) cart

carrete *m* (de hilo, cinta) spool, reel (BrE); (de
película) film; (de caña de pescar) reel

carretear [A1] *vi* (AmL) (Aviac) to taxi

carretela *f* (Chi) cart

carretera *f* road; **~ de circunvalación** bypass,
beltway (AmE), ring road (BrE); **~ nacional**
≈highway (in US), ≈A-road (in UK)

carretilla *f* **1** (de mano) wheelbarrow **2** (CS)
(quijada) jaw, jawbone

carricoche *m* covered wagon

carril *m* **(a)** (Auto) lane; **~ bus** bus lane; **~ de
adelantamiento** overtaking lane, fast lane; **~ de
bicicletas** cycleway, cycle path **(b)** (Ferr) rail **(c)**
(AmL) (Dep) lane

carrillo *m* cheek

carriola *f* (Méx) baby carriage (AmE), baby
buggy (BrE)

carrito *m* **(a)** (para el equipaje) trolley; (en
supermercado) shopping cart (AmE), trolley (BrE);
(de la compra) shopping trolley *o* (AmE) cart; **~
chocón** (Méx, Ven) bumper car **(b)** (mesita de servir)
trolley

carro *m* **1 (a)** (carreta) cart; **un ~ de tierra** a
cartload of earth; **~ de combate** tank (AmL
exc CS) (Auto) car, automobile (AmE); **~ bomba**
(Col) car bomb; **~ loco** (Andes) bumper car; **~
sport** (AmL exc CS) sports car; **~ de bomberos**
(Andes, Méx) fire engine **(c)** (Chi, Méx) (vagón)

coach, carriage (BrE); ~ **comedor/dormitorio** (Méx) dining/sleeping car **(d)** (Hist) (romano) chariot **2** (de máquina de escribir) carriage

carrocería f (de automóvil) bodywork

carroña f **(a)** (de animal muerto) carrion **(b)** (gente despreciable) riffraff (+ *sing or pl vb*)

carroza f **(a)** (coche de caballos) carriage **(b)** (de carnaval) float **(c)** (Chi, Ur) (coche fúnebre) hearse

carruaje m carriage

carrusel m **(a)** (para diapositivas) carousel, slide tray **(b)** (para niños) merry-go-round, carousel (AmE)

carta f **1** (Corresp) letter; ¿hay ~ **para mí?** are there any letters for me?; **echar una ~ al correo** to mail (*esp AmE*) o (*esp BrE*) post a letter; ~ **adjunta** or **explicatoria** covering letter; ~ **blanca** carte blanche; ~ **certificada** registered letter; ~ **de amor** love letter; ~ **de recomendación** reference, letter of recommendation; ~ **urgente** special-delivery letter
2 (naipe) card; **jugar a las ~s** to play cards; **dar las ~s** to deal the cards; *echarle las ~s a algn* to tell sb's fortune; *poner las ~s sobre la mesa* to put o lay one's cards on the table
3 (en restaurante) menu; **comer a la ~** to eat à la carte; ~ **de vinos** wine list

cartearse [A1] *v pron:* **nos carteamos durante años** we wrote to each other o corresponded for years; ~ **CON algn** to correspond WITH sb

cartel m (de publicidad, propaganda) poster; (letrero) sign; ~ **luminoso** neon sign; **lleva dos meses en ~** «*obra/película*» it has been on for two months; **de ~** ‹*cantante/actor*› famous; ‹*torero*› star (*before n*)

cartelera f **(a)** (Cin, Teatr) publicity board; **la película sigue en ~** the movie is still on o still showing; **la obra estuvo en ~ durante cuatro años** the play ran for four years **(b)** (en el periódico) listings (*pl*); ~ **de espectáculos** entertainment guide **(c)** (AmL) (tablón de anuncios) bulletin board (AmE), notice board (BrE)

cárter m (del cigüeñal) crankcase, sump; (del embrague) housing

cartera f **1** **(a)** (billetera) wallet, billfold (AmE) **(b)** (para documentos) document case, briefcase; (de colegial) satchel; (de cobrador) money bag; (de cartero) sack, bag **(c)** (AmS) (bolso de mujer) purse (AmE), handbag (BrE) **2** (Com, Fin) portfolio

carterear [A1] *vt* (Chi): **me ~on en la micro** my handbag was picked on the bus

carterista *mf* pickpocket

cartero (m) mailman (AmE), postman (BrE); (f) mailwoman (AmE), postwoman (BrE)

cartílago m cartilage

cartilla f **(a)** (para aprender a leer) reader, primer **(b)** (libreta) book; ~ **de ahorros** passbook, savings book; ~ **de racionamiento** ration book

cartón m **(a)** (material) cardboard; ~ **ondulado** corrugated cardboard; ~ **piedra** papier-mâché **(b)** (de cigarrillos, leche) carton; (de huevos) tray

cartoné m: en ~ hardback

cartuchera f **1** **(a)** (estuche — para cartuchos) cartridge clip; (— para pistola) holster **(b)** (cinturón — para cartuchos) cartridge belt; (— para pistola) gun belt **2** (RPl) (de escolar) pencil case

cartucho m cartridge

cartuja f charterhouse, monastery

cartulina f card

casa f **1** **(a)** (vivienda) house; **cambiarse de ~** to move house; **casita del perro** kennel; ~ **adosada** or **pareada** semi-detached o terraced house; **C~ Blanca** White House; ~ **de acogida** refuge; ~ **de huéspedes** boardinghouse; ~ **de socorro** first-aid post; ~ **de vecinos** or (Méx) **de vecindad** tenement house; **C~ Real** Royal Household; ~ **refugio** refuge o hostel for battered women; ~ **rodante** (CS) trailer (AmE), caravan (BrE) **(b)** (hogar) home; **a los 18 años se fue de ~** or (AmL) **de la ~** she left home at 18; **no está nunca en ~** or (AmL) **en la ~** he's never (at) home; **está en casa de Ana** she's (over) at Ana's (house); **¿por qué no pasas por ~** or (AmL) **por la ~?** why don't you drop in?; *de* or *para andar por ~* ‹*vestido*› for wearing around the house; ‹*definición/terminología*› crude, rough; *echar* or *tirar la ~ por la ventana* to push the boat out
2 **(a)** (empresa) company, firm (BrE); **una ~ de discos** a record company; ~ **de cambios** bureau de change **(b)** (bar, restaurante): **especialidad de la ~** house specialty (AmE), speciality of the house (BrE); **invita la ~** it's on the house
3 (Dep): **perdieron en ~** they lost at home

casabe m (Col, Ven) cassava bread

casaca f (chaqueta) jacket; (Equ) riding jacket

casado -da *adj* married; **está ~ con una japonesa** he's married to a Japanese woman
■ *m,f* (m) married man; (f) married woman; **los recién ~s** the newlyweds

casamiento m (unión) marriage; (boda) wedding

casar [A1] *vt* ‹*cura/juez*› to marry
■ ~ *vi* **(a)** (encajar) «*dibujos*» to match up; «*piezas*» to fit together; «*cuentas*» to match, tally **(b)** (armonizar) «*colores/estilos*» to go together; ~ **CON algo** to go well WITH sth
■ **casarse** *v pron* to get married; ~**se por la Iglesia** to get married in church; **se casó con un abogado** she married a lawyer; ~**se en segundas nupcias** to marry again, to remarry

cascabel m **(a)** (campanita) bell **(b)** (Chi) (sonajero) rattle
■ f (Zool) rattlesnake

cascada f (Geog) waterfall, cascade

cascajo m (fam) **1** (trasto viejo) wreck (colloq) **2** (Col) (Const) piece of gravel

cascanueces m (*pl* ~) (a pair of) nutcrackers

cascar [A2] *vt* ‹*nuez/huevo*› to crack; ‹*taza*› to chip
■ **cascarse** *v pron* «*huevo*» to crack; «*taza*» to chip

cáscara f (de huevo, nuez) shell; (del queso) rind; (de naranja, limón) peel, rind; (de plátano, papa) skin; (de manzana) peel

cascarilla f (de cacao) roasted cacao husks (*pl*) (used in infusions); (de cereal) husk

cascarón m (de huevo, nuez) shell

cascarrabias *adj inv* (fam) cantankerous, grumpy
■ *mf* (*pl* ~) grouch (colloq)

casco m **1** **(a)** (para la cabeza) helmet; ~ **protector** (de obrero) safety helmet; (de motorista) crash helmet **(b) cascos** *mpl* (Audio) ···⟩·

headphones (pl) [2] (Equ, Zool) hoof [3] (Náut) hull
[4] **(a)** (de ciudad): ~ **antiguo** old quarter; ~
urbano urban area, built-up area **(b)** (RPl) (de
estancia) farmhouse and surrounding buildings
[5] (Col) (gajo) segment [6] (Esp, Méx) (envase) bottle

cascote m piece of rubble; ~**s** rubble

caserío m (poblado) hamlet; (finca) (Esp)
farmhouse

casero -ra adj **(a)** ⟨vino/flan⟩ homemade;
⟨reparación⟩ amateur; ⟨trabajo⟩ domestic **(b)**
⟨persona⟩ home-loving
■ m,f [1] **(a)** (propietario) (m) landlord; (f) landlady
(b) (cuidador) caretaker [2] (Chi) (cliente) customer;
(vendedor) storekeeper (AmE), stallholder

caseta f **(a)** (en la playa, de guardia etc) hut **(b)**
(en exposición) stand **(c)** (para perro) kennel **(d)** (en
fútbol) dugout

casete m or f (cinta) cassette; ~ **digital** digital
audio tape
■ m (Esp) (grabador) cassette recorder/player

casi adv [1] (cerca de) almost, nearly; ~ **me**
caigo I nearly fell over [2] (en frases negativas): ~
no se le oía you could hardly hear him; ~ **nunca**
hardly ever; **no nos queda** ~ **nada de pan** there's
hardly any bread left; **¿pudiste dormir? —** ~
nada did you manage to sleep? — hardly at all; ~
no vengo I almost didn't come [3] (expresando una
opinión tentativa): ~ **sería mejor venderlo** maybe it
would be better to sell it

casilla f [1] (para cartas, llaves) pigeonhole; ~
postal or **de correo** (CS, Per) post office box, P.O.
Box [2] (en ajedrez, crucigrama) square; (en formulario)
box [3] **(a)** (de guardia, sereno) hut **(b)** (de perro)
kennel **(c)** (Méx) (de votación) polling booth

casillero m **(a)** (mueble) set of pigeonholes;
(compartimento) pigeonhole **(b)** (CS) (en formulario)
box

casino m [1] (de juego) casino [2] (club social) club

casitas fpl (Chi fam & euf) (baño) bathroom
(euph)

caso m [1] (situación, coyuntura) case; **en esos** ~**s**
in cases like that; **yo en tu caso ...** if I were you
...; **en último** ~ if it comes to it, if the worst
comes to the worst; **en el mejor de los** ~**s** at (the
very) best; **en el peor de los** ~**s te multarán** the
worst they can do is fine you; **eso no venía al** ~
that had nothing to do with what we were
talking about; **pongamos por** ~ **que ...** let's
assume that ...; **en** ~ **de incendio** in case of fire;
en ~ **contrario** otherwise; **en cualquier** ~ in any
case; **en tal** ~, in that case, in such a case (frml);
en todo ~ **dijo que llamaría** in any case she said
she'd ring; **llegado el** ~ if it comes to it; **según el**
~ as appropriate; **no hay/hubo caso** (AmL fam) it
is no good o no use/it was no good o no use
[2] (Der, Med) case; **ser un** ~ **perdido** (fam) to be a
hopeless case (colloq)
[3] (atención): **hacerle** ~ A **algn** to pay attention TO
sb, take notice OF sb; **hacer** ~ DE **algo** to pay
attention TO sth, to take notice OF sth; **hacer** ~
omiso de algo to ignore sth

caspa f dandruff

casquillo m **(a)** (de bala, cartucho) case **(b)**
(portalámparas) lampholder, bulbholder; (de
bombilla): ~ **de rosca/bayoneta** screw-in/bayonet
fitting

cassette /ka'set/ m or f ▶ CASETE

casta f caste; **de** ~ ⟨toro⟩ thoroughbred;
⟨torero⟩ top-class

castaña f (fruto) chestnut; ~ **de Indias** horse
chestnut; ~ **de Pará** (RPl) Brazil nut; ~ **pilonga**
dried chestnut

castañetear [A1] vi: **me castañetean los**
dientes my teeth are chattering

castaño¹ -ña adj ⟨pelo⟩ chestnut; ⟨ojos⟩
brown

castaño² m **(a)** (Bot) chestnut tree; ~ **de**
Indias horse chestnut **(b)** (color) chestnut

castañuela f castanet

castellano¹ -na adj (de Castilla) Castilian;
(español) Spanish
■ m,f (persona) Castilian

castellano² m (idioma — de Castilla) Castilian;
(— español) Spanish

castidad f chastity

castigar [A3] vt **(a)** (en general) to punish;
fueron castigados con la pena máxima they
received the maximum sentence **(b)** ⟨niño⟩ (a
quedarse en el colegio) to keep ... in detention; (a
quedarse en casa) to ground; (esp AmE colloq): **lo** ~**on sin postre** as a
punishment he was made to go without dessert

castigo m punishment; ~ **corporal** corporal
punishment; **les impusieron** ~**s severos** they
were severely punished; **levantar un** ~ to lift a
punishment

Castilla f Castile

castillo m castle; ~ **de arena** sandcastle;
construir ~**s en el aire** to build castles in the air

castizo -za adj **(a)** (puro, tradicional) ⟨estilo/
costumbre⟩ traditional **(b)** (típicamente castellano):
un lenguaje muy ~ very pure Castilian/Spanish

casto -ta adj chaste

castor m beaver

castrar [A1] vt ⟨caballo⟩ to geld; ⟨toro/hombre⟩
to castrate; ⟨gato⟩ to neuter

casual adj chance (before n)

casualidad f chance; por (pura) ~ by (sheer)
chance; **si por** ~ **la ves** if you happen to see her;
¿no tendrás su dirección por ~? you wouldn't
(happen to) have her address by any chance?;
¡qué ~! what a coincidence!; **da la** ~ **de que ...**
as it happens ...

cataclismo m natural disaster, cataclysm
(frml)

catacumbas fpl catacombs (pl)

catador -dora m,f taster

catalán¹ -lana adj/m,f Catalan

catalán² m (idioma) Catalan

catalejo m (ant) telescope, spyglass

catalizador m (Auto) catalytic converter

catalogar [A3] *vt* **(a)** (en un catálogo) to catalog (AmE), to catalogue (BrE); (en una lista) to record, list **(b)** (considerar) to class

catálogo *m* (Art, Com) catalog (AmE), catalogue (BrE); **compra por** ~ mail-order shopping

Cataluña *f* Catalonia

catamarán *m* catamaran

cataplasma *f* poultice, cataplasm (tech)

catapulta *f* catapult

catapultar [A1] *vt* to catapult

catar [A1] *vt* ‹*vino*› to taste

catarata *f* **(a)** (Geog) waterfall; **las ~s del Iguazú** Iguaçú Falls **(b)** (Med) cataract

catarro *m* **(a)** (resfriado) cold; **pescarse** *or* (esp Esp) **coger un** ~ to catch a cold **(b)** (inflamación) catarrh

catastro *m* (censo) cadastre, land registry; (impuesto) property tax

catástrofe *f* catastrophe, disaster

catastrófico -ca *adj* catastrophic, disastrous

catear [A1] *vt* **1** (Esp arg) (suspender) to fail **2 (a)** (Chi) (Min) to prospect **(b)** (Méx) (registrar) ‹*persona*› to frisk; ‹*vivienda*› to search

catecismo *m* catechism

cátedra *f* (en universidad) professorship, chair; (en colegio) post of head of department

catedral *f* cathedral

catedrático -ca *m,f* (de universidad) professor; (en colegio) head of department

categoría *f* **(a)** (grupo) category; ~ **gramatical** part of speech; **hotel de primera** ~ first-class hotel **(b)** (calidad): **de** ~ ‹*actor/espectáculo/revista*› first-rate; **un periódico de poca** ~ a second-rate newspaper; **el hotel de más** ~ the finest *o* best hotel **(c)** (estatus): **tiene** ~ **de embajador** he has ambassadorial status; **gente de cierta** ~ people of some standing

categórico -ca *adj* ‹*respuesta*› categorical

cateo *m* (Chi, Méx) (cacheo) body search

catequesis *f*: teaching of the catechism

catire -ra *adj* (Ven) (de piel blanca) fair-skinned; (de pelo rubio) fair, fair-haired
■ *m,f* (Ven) (de piel blanca) fair-skinned person; (de pelo rubio) fair-haired person

catita *f* (CS) budgerigar

catolicismo *m* Catholicism

católico -ca *adj* **(a)** (Relig) Catholic; **es** ~ he's a Catholic **(b)** (ortodoxo) orthodox
■ *m,f* Catholic

catorce *adj inv/m/pron* fourteen; *para ejemplos ver* CINCO

catre *m* **(a)** (cama — plegable) folding bed; (— de campaña) camp bed **(b)** (CS) (armazón) bedstead

catsup *m* ketchup, catsup (AmE)

cauce *m* **(a)** (Geog) bed; **el río se salió de su** ~ the river burst its banks; **desviaron el** ~ **del arroyo** they changed the course of the stream **(b)** (rumbo, vía): **desvió la conversación hacia otros** ~**s** he steered the conversation onto another tack; **seguir los** ~**s establecidos** to go through the normal channels

cauchera *f* (Col) (tirachinas) (fam) slingshot (AmE), catapult (BrE)

caucho *m* **(a)** (sustancia) rubber; (árbol) (Col) rubber tree **(b)** (neumático) (Ven) tire*; (gomita) (Col) rubber band, elastic band (BrE)

caudal *m* **(a)** (de un fluido) volume of flow; **el río tiene muy poco** ~ the water level is very low **(b)** (riqueza) fortune **(c)** (abundancia) wealth; **un** ~ **de conocimientos** a wealth of knowledge

caudaloso -sa *adj* ‹*río*› large

caudillo *m* (líder) leader; **el C~** *title used to refer to General Franco*

causa *f* **1** (motivo) cause; **la** ~ **de todas mis desgracias** the cause of *o* the reason for all my misfortunes; **se enfadó sin** ~ **alguna** she got annoyed for no reason at all *o* for no good reason; **a** *or* **por** ~ **de** because of **2** (ideal) cause; **una** ~ **perdida** a lost cause **3** (Der) (pleito) lawsuit; (proceso) trial

causante *adj*: **los factores** ~**s de la crisis** the factors which caused the crisis
■ *mf* (causa) cause; **la** ~ **de todas mis desgracias** the cause of all my misfortunes

causar [A1] *vt* ‹*daños/problema/sufrimiento*› to cause; ‹*indignación*› to cause, arouse; ‹*alarma*› to cause, provoke; ‹*placer*› to give; **le causó mucha pena** it made him very sad; **me causó muy buena impresión** I was very impressed with her

cautela *f* caution; **con** ~ cautiously

cauteloso -sa *adj* [SER] ‹*persona*› cautious

cautivador -dora *adj* captivating

cautivar [A1] *vt* (atraer) to captivate

cautiverio *m* captivity

cautivo -va *adj/m,f* captive

cauto -ta *adj* careful, cautious

cava *f* cellar
■ *m* cava (*sparkling wine*)

cavar [A1] *vt* **(a)** ‹*fosa/zanja*› to dig; ‹*pozo*› to sink **(b)** ‹*tierra*› to hoe

caverna *f* cave, cavern

cavernícola *adj* (Hist) cave-dwelling; **un hombre** ~ a caveman
■ *mf* (Hist) cave dweller

caviar *m* caviar

cavidad *f* cavity

cavilar [A1] *vi* to ponder, think deeply; **después de mucho** ~ after much thought *o* deliberation

cayena *f* cayenne (pepper)

cayera, cayese, etc ▶ CAER

caza *f* **(a)** (para subsistir) hunting; (como deporte — caza mayor) hunting; (— caza menor) shooting; **ir de** ~ to go hunting/shooting; ~ **del tesoro** treasure hunt; ~ **furtiva** poaching; **salieron a la** ~ **del ladrón** they set off in pursuit of the thief; **dar** ~ **a algn** (perseguir) to pursue *o* chase sb; (alcanzar) to catch sb **(b)** (animales) game
■ *m* fighter

cazabombardero *m* fighter-bomber

cazador -dora *m,f* hunter; ~ **furtivo** poacher

cazadora *f* (Esp) (Indum) jacket

cazamariposas *m* (*pl* ~) butterfly net

cazar [A4] *vt* **(a)** (para subsistir) to hunt; (como deporte—caza mayor) to hunt; (— caza menor) to shoot **(b)** ‹*mariposas*› to catch **(c)** (fam) (conseguir, atrapar): **ha cazado un millonario/buen empleo** she's landed herself a millionaire/good job　⋯⟐

■ **~** *vi* to hunt; (con fusil) to shoot; **salimos a ~** we
went out hunting/shooting

cazo *m* (cacerola) small saucepan; (cucharón) ladle

cazuela *f* casserole

cazurro -rra *adj* (fam) (huraño) sullen, surly;
(obstinado) stubborn, pig-headed (colloq)
■ *m,f* (fam) (huraño) sullen *o* surly person; (obstinado)
stubborn *o* (colloq) pig-headed person

c.c. (= **centímetros cúbicos**) cc

CD *m* (= **compact disc**) CD

CD-ROM *m* (= **compact disc read-only
memory**) CD-ROM

ce *f*: name of the letter c

cebada *f* barley

cebar [A1] *vt* **1** (a) ⟨animal⟩ to fatten ... up
2 ⟨anzuelo/cepo⟩ to bait **3** (CS) ⟨mate⟩ to
prepare (*and serve*)

cebo *m* (a) (en pesca, caza) bait (b) (Arm) primer

cebolla *f* onion

cebolleta *f*, **cebollino** *m* (a) (con tallo verde)
scallion (AmE), spring onion (BrE) (b) (hierba)
chive

cebra *f* zebra

cebú *m* (*pl* **-bús** *or* **-búes**) zebu

cecear [A1] *vi* (a) (Ling) to pronounce the
Spanish [/s/] as [θ] (b) (como defecto) to lisp

ceceo *m* (a) (Ling) pronunciation of the Spanish
[/s/] as [θ] (b) (como defecto) lisp

cedazo *m* sieve

ceder [E1] *vt* **1** (a) ⟨derecho⟩ to transfer,
assign; ⟨territorio⟩ to cede; ⟨puesto/título⟩
(voluntariamente) to hand over; (a la fuerza) to give
up; **~ el poder** to hand over power; **me cedió el
asiento** he let me have his seat; ▶ PASO 1B (b)
⟨balón/pelota⟩ to pass
2 (prestar) ⟨jugador⟩ to loan
■ **~** *vi* **1** (cejar) to give way; **no cedió ni un ápice**
she didn't give *o* yield an inch; **cedió en su
empeño** she gave up the undertaking; **~ A algo**
to give in TO sth
2 «fiebre/lluvia/viento» to ease off; «dolor» to
ease
3 «muro/puente/cuerda» to give way; «zapatos/
muelle» to give

cedro *m* cedar

cédula *f* (Fin) bond, warrant; **~ de identidad**
identity card

cegador -dora *adj* blinding

cegar [A7] *vt* **1** (a) (deslumbrar) to blind (b)
(ofuscar) to blind; **cegado por los celos** blinded by
jealousy **2** ⟨conducto/cañería⟩ to block

ceguera *f* blindness

ceja *f* (a) (Anat) eyebrow; **arquear las ~s** to raise
one's eyebrows (b) (Mús) capo

cejilla *f* capo

celador -dora *m,f* (a) (en museo, biblioteca)
security guard (b) (AmL) (en la cárcel) prison
guard (AmE), prison warder (BrE) (c) (en hospital)
orderly, porter

celda *f* cell

celebración *f* celebration

celebrar [A1] *vt* **1** (a) ⟨éxito/cumpleaños/
festividad⟩ to celebrate (b) (liter) ⟨belleza/valor/
hazaña⟩ to celebrate (liter) (c) ⟨chiste/ocurrencia⟩
to laugh at **2** (frml) (alegrarse) to be delighted at,

be very pleased at; **celebro su éxito** I'm delighted
to hear about your success **3** (a) (frml) ⟨reunión/
elecciones/juicio⟩ to hold; ⟨partido⟩ to play (b)
⟨misa⟩ to say, celebrate; ⟨boda⟩ to perform
■ **~** *vi* «sacerdote» to say *o* celebrate mass

célebre *adj* (a) (famoso) famous, celebrated (b)
(Col) ⟨mujer⟩ elegant

celebridad *f* (fama) fame; (persona) celebrity

celeste *adj* **1** (del cielo) heavenly, celestial
2 ⟨ojos⟩ blue; ⟨pintura/vestido⟩ (claro) light *o* pale
blue; (intenso) sky-blue (*before n*)
■ *m* (claro) light *o* pale blue; (intenso) sky blue

celestial *adj* (a) (Relig) celestial (b) ⟨placer⟩
heavenly

célibe *adj/mf* celibate

celo *m* **1** (esmero, fervor) zeal **2** (Zool) (a) (de los
machos) rut (b) (de las hembras) heat; **estar en ~** to
be in season, to be in heat (AmE) *o* (BrE) on heat
3 **celos** *mpl* jealousy; **tener ~s** DE **algn** to be
jealous *of* sb; **darle ~s a algn** to make sb jealous
4 (Esp) (cinta adhesiva) Scotch® tape (AmE),
Sellotape® (BrE)

celofán *m* cellophane

celoso -sa *adj* (a) ⟨marido/novia⟩ jealous;
estar ~ DE **algn** to be jealous OF sb (b) (diligente,
esmerado) conscientious, zealous

celta *adj* Celtic
■ *mf* (persona) Celt
■ *m* (Ling) Celtic

célula *f* cell

celular *adj* cellular
■ *m* (a) (AmL) (teléfono) mobile phone (b) (Esp)
(furgoneta para presos) patrol wagon (AmE), police
van (BrE)

celulitis *f* (gordura) cellulite; (inflamación)
cellulitis

cementerio *m* cemetery; (junto a una iglesia)
graveyard; **~ de coches** salvage *o* wrecker's yard
(AmE), scrapyard (BrE)

cemento *m* (a) (Const, Odont) cement; **~
armado** reinforced concrete (b) (AmL) (pegamento)
glue, adhesive

cena *f* dinner, supper; (en algunas regiones del
Reino Unido) tea; (formal, fuera de casa) dinner; **¿qué
hay de ~?** what's for dinner *o* supper?; **~ de
gala** banquet

cenagal *m* (barrizal) bog, mire

cenar [A1] *vi* to have dinner *o* supper; (en
algunas regiones del Reino Unido) to have tea; **nos
invitaron a ~** they invited us for *o* to dinner;
salimos a ~ we went out for dinner
■ *vt* ⟨tortilla/pescado⟩ to have ... for dinner *o*
supper

cencerro *m* cowbell

cenefa *f* (en ropa, sábanas) border; (en techos,
muros) frieze

cenicero *m* ashtray

cenicienta *f* drudge; **la C~** Cinderella

cenit *m* zenith

ceniza *f* ash

censo *m* **1** (a) (de población) census (b) (Esp) *tb*
~ electoral electoral roll *o* register **2** (Der, Fin)
charge; (sobre una finca) ground rent

censor -sora *m,f* (a) (Cin, Period) censor (b)
(crítico) critic (c) (Der, Fin) *tb* **~ de cuentas**
auditor

censura f (a) (reprobación) censure (fml), condemnation (b) (de libros, películas) censorship

censurar [A1] vt (a) (reprobar) to censure (fml), to condemn (b) ⟨libro/película⟩ to censor, ⟨escena/párrafo⟩ to cut, censor

centavo m (a) (en AmL) *hundredth part of many currencies;* **estar sin un ~** to be penniless (b) (del dólar) cent

centella f (rayo) flash of lightning; (chispa) spark; **como una ~** like greased lightning

centelleante adj ⟨estrella⟩ twinkling; ⟨luz/joya⟩ sparkling; ⟨ojos⟩ blazing

centellear [A1] vi ⟨luz/joya⟩ to sparkle, ⟨estrella⟩ to twinkle

centena f: **una ~** a hundred; **unidades, decenas y ~s** units, tens and hundreds

centenar m: **un ~ de personas** a hundred or so people; **~es de cartas** hundreds of letters

centenario m centenary, centennial (AmE)

centeno m rye

centésima f hundredth; **en una ~ de segundo** in a fraction of a second

centésimo m (Fís, Mat) hundredth

centígrado -da adj centigrade, Celsius

centigramo m centigram

centímetro m centimeter*

céntimo m: *hundredth part of the Spanish peseta, the Venezuelan bolívar and the Paraguayan guaraní;* **no tener un ~** to be penniless o (colloq) broke; **no vale ni un ~** it's totally worthless

centinela mf (Mil) guard, sentry; (no militar) lookout; **estar de ~** (Mil) to be on sentry duty

centolla f, **centollo** m spider crab

centrado -da adj (equilibrado) stable, well-balanced; (en un trabajo, lugar) settled

central adj central
■ f head office; **~ telefónica** telephone exchange; **~ hidroeléctrica/nuclear** hydroelectric/nuclear power station

centralista adj/mf centralist

centralita f switchboard

centralizar [A4] vt to centralize

centrar [A1] vt (a) ⟨imagen⟩ to center* (b) (Dep) to center* (c) ⟨atención/investigación/esfuerzos⟩ **~ algo en algo** to focus sth on sth
■ **~** vi (Dep) to center*, cross
■ **centrarse** v pron **~se en algo** ⟨investigación/atención/esfuerzos⟩ to focus o center* on sth

céntrico -ca adj ⟨área/calle⟩ central; **un bar ~** a downtown bar (AmE), a bar in the centre of town (BrE)

centrifugado m spin

centrifugar [A3] vt (a) ⟨ropa⟩ to spin (b) (Tec) to centrifuge

centrista adj/mf centrist

centro m (a) (en general) center*; **~ ciudad/urbano** downtown (AmE), city/town centre (BrE); **ser el ~ de atención** to be the center of attention; **se convirtió en el ~ de interés** it became the focus of attention; **~ turístico** tourist resort o center; **~ comercial** shopping mall (AmE), shopping centre (BrE); **~ de planificación familiar** family planning clinic (b) (en fútbol) cross, center*
■ mf (jugador) center*; **~ delantero** center* forward

Centroamérica f Central America

centroamericano -na adj/m,f Central American

centrocampista mf midfield player

ceñido -da adj tight; **me queda muy ~** it's very tight on me

ceñir [I15] vt: **esa falda te ciñe demasiado** that skirt is too tight for you; **el vestido le ceñía el talle** the dress clung to her waist
■ **ceñirse** v pron **~se a algo** ⟨a las reglas⟩ to adhere to o (colloq) stick to sth; **~se al tema** to keep to the subject

ceño m: **arrugó el ~** he frowned; **me miró con el ~ fruncido** she frowned at me

cepa f (Bot) stump; (Vin) stock (of a vine)

cepillar [A1] vt (a) ⟨ropa/dientes/pelo⟩ to brush (b) ⟨madera⟩ to plane
■ **cepillarse** v pron (refl) ⟨ropa⟩ to brush; ⟨dientes⟩ to brush, clean

cepillo m **1** (para ropa, zapatos, pelo) brush; (para suelo) scrubbing brush; **lleva el pelo cortado al ~** he has a crew cut; **~ de dientes/uñas** toothbrush/nailbrush **2** (de carpintería) plane **3** (en la iglesia) collection box (o plate etc)

cepo m (trampa) trap; (Auto) wheel clamp; (Hist) stocks (pl)

cera f (para velas) wax; (para pisos, muebles) wax polish; (de abejas) beeswax; (de los oídos) wax; **le di ~ al suelo** I polished the floor

cerámica f (arte) ceramics, pottery; (pieza) piece of pottery

cerca adv (a) (en el espacio) near, close; **~ de algo/algn** near sth/sb; **¿hay algún banco ~?** is there a bank nearby o close by?; **está por aquí ~** it's near here (somewhere); **mirar algo/a algn de ~** to look at sth/sb close up o close to; **seguir algo de ~** to follow sth closely (b) (en el tiempo) close; **los exámenes estaban ~** the exams were close; **estás tan ~ de lograrlo** you're so close to achieving it; **serán ~ de las dos** it must be nearly 2 o'clock (c) (indicando aproximación): **~ de** almost, nearly
■ f (de alambre, madera) fence; (de piedra) wall

cercado m (a) (de alambre, madera) fence; (de piedra) wall (b) (terreno) enclosure (c) (Per) (distrito) district

cercanía f **1** (en el espacio) closeness, proximity; (en el tiempo) proximity, imminence **2** cercanías fpl: **Madrid y sus ~s** Madrid and its environs; **en las ~s del aeropuerto** in the vicinity of the airport

cercano -na adj **1** (a) (en el espacio) nearby, neighboring*; **~ a algo** near sth, close to sth; **el C~ Oriente** the Near East (b) (en el tiempo) close, near; **en fecha cercana** soon; **~ a algo** close to sth **2** ⟨pariente/amigo⟩ close

cercar [A2] vt (a) ⟨campo/terreno⟩ to enclose, surround; (con valla) to fence in (b) ⟨persona⟩ to surround (c) (Mil) ⟨ciudad⟩ to besiege; ⟨enemigo⟩ to surround

cerciorarse v pron **~se de algo** to make certain of sth

cerco m (a) (asedio) siege (b) (de una mancha) ring (c) (AmL) (valla) fence; (seto) hedge

cerda f (a) (animal) sow (b) (fam) (mujer — sucia) slob (colloq); (— despreciable) bitch (sl) (c) (pelo) bristle

cerdo m (a) (animal) pig, hog (AmE) (b) (carne) pork (c) (fam) (hombre — sucio) slob (colloq); (— despreciable) bastard (sl), swine (colloq)

cereal m cereal

cereales mpl (Esp) (para desayunar) cereal

cerebral adj ⟨actividad/tumor/derrame⟩ brain (before n); ⟨persona⟩ cerebral

cerebro m (a) (Anat) brain; **lavarle el ～ a algn** to brainwash sb (b) (persona) brains; **el ～ de la operación** the brains behind the operation

ceremonia f ceremony; **no andemos con ～s** let's not stand on ceremony

cereza f (fruta) cherry

cerezo m cherry tree

cerilla f ① (esp Esp) (fósforo) match ② (de los oídos) wax

cerillo m (esp AmC, Méx) match

cernícalo m (Zool) kestrel

cero m (a) (Fís, Mat) zero; (en números de teléfono) zero (AmE), oh (BrE); **～ coma cinco** zero point five; **empezar** or **partir de ～** to start from scratch; **ser un ～ a la izquierda** (b) (en fútbol, rugby) zero (AmE), nil (BrE); (en tenis) love; **ganan por tres a ～** they're winning three-zero (AmE) o (BrE) three-nil (c) (Educ) zero, nought (BrE)

cerquillo m (AmL) (flequillo) bangs (pl) (AmE), fringe (BrE)

cerrado -da adj ① (a) ⟨puerta/ventana/ojos/boca⟩ closed, shut; ⟨mejillones/almejas⟩ closed; ⟨sobre/carta⟩ sealed; ⟨puño⟩ clenched; ⟨cortinas⟩ drawn; **estaba ～ con llave** it was locked (b) ⟨válvula⟩ closed, shut off; ⟨grifo/llave⟩ turned off ② ⟨tienda/restaurante/museo⟩ closed, shut ③ ⟨espacio/recinto⟩ enclosed; ⟨curva⟩ sharp ④ ⟨acento/dialecto⟩ broad ⑤ ⟨persona⟩ (poco comunicativo) uncommunicative; **está ～ a todo cambio** his mind is closed to change; **～ a influencias externas** shut off from outside influence

cerradura f lock; ▶ OJO

cerrajería f locksmith's shop

cerrajero -ra m,f locksmith

cerrar [A5] vt ① (a) ⟨puerta/ventana⟩ to close, shut; ⟨ojos/boca⟩ to shut, close; **cierra la puerta con llave** lock the door (b) ⟨botella⟩ to put the top on/cork in; ⟨frasco⟩ to put the lid on; ⟨sobre⟩ to seal (c) ⟨paraguas/abanico/mano⟩ to close; ⟨libro⟩ to close, shut; ⟨puño⟩ to clench (d) ⟨cortinas⟩ to close, draw; ⟨persianas⟩ to lower, pull down; ⟨abrigo⟩ to fasten, button up; ⟨cremallera⟩ to do ... up (e) ⟨grifo/agua/gas⟩ to turn off; ⟨válvula⟩ to close, shut off ② (a) ⟨fábrica/comercio/oficina⟩ (en el quehacer diario) to close; (definitivamente) to close (down) (b) ⟨aeropuerto/carretera/frontera⟩ to close ③ (a) ⟨cuenta bancaria⟩ to close (b) ⟨caso/juicio⟩ to close (c) ⟨acuerdo/negociación⟩ to finalize (d) ⟨acto/debate⟩ to bring ... to an end

■ **～** vi ① (hablando de puerta, ventana): **cierra, que hace frío** close o shut the door (o window etc), it's cold; **¿cerraste con llave?** did you lock up?

② «puerta/ventana/cajón» to close, shut

③ «comercio/oficina» (en el quehacer diario) to close, shut; (definitivamente) to close (down)

■ **cerrarse** v pron ① (a) «puerta/ventana» to shut, close; **la puerta se cerró de golpe** the door slammed shut (b) «ojos» to close; **se le cerraban los ojos** his eyes were closing (c) «flor/almeja» to close up (d) «herida» to heal (up) ② (refl) ⟨abrigo⟩ to fasten, button up; ⟨cremallera⟩ to do ... up ③ «acto/debate/jornada» to end

cerrazón m (terquedad) stubbornness; (mentalidad poco flexible) blinkered attitude

cerro m (Geog) hill

cerrojo m bolt; **echar el ～** to bolt the door

certamen m competition, contest

certero -ra adj (a) ⟨tiro⟩ accurate; ⟨golpe⟩ well-aimed (b) ⟨juicio⟩ sound; ⟨respuesta⟩ good

certeza, certidumbre f certainty; **no lo sé con ～** I'm not sure, I don't know for sure

certificado¹ -da adj ⟨paquete/carta⟩ registered; **mandé la carta certificada** I sent the letter by registered mail

certificado² m certificate

certificar [A2] vt to certify

cervatillo m fawn

cerveza f beer; **～ tirada** o **de barril** draft beer (AmE), draught beer (BrE); **～ rubia** lager; **～ negra** dark beer

cesante adj [ESTAR] (Chi) (sin empleo) unemployed; **quedó ～** he lost his job

■ mf (Chi) (sin empleo) unemployed person

cesantía f (desempleo) (Chi) unemployment; (despido) (RPl frml) dismissal; (pago) (Col) severance pay

cesar [A1] vi ① (parar) to stop; **～ DE hacer algo** to stop doing sth; **sin ～** incessantly ② (frml o period) (dimitir): **cesó en su cargo** she left her post, she resigned

cesárea f cesarean* (section); **le tuvieron que hacer una ～** she had to have a cesarean

cese m (frml o period) (a) (interrupción) cessation (frml); **el ～ de hostilidades** the cessation of hostilities; **～ del fuego** (AmL) ceasefire (b) (renuncia) resignation

césped m (a) (planta) grass; (extensión) lawn, grass; ⊘ **prohibido pisar el césped** keep off the grass (b) (Dep) field, pitch (BrE); (en tenis) (AmL) grass

cesta f (a) (recipiente) basket; **～ de Navidad** Christmas hamper; **～ punta** (deporte) pelota; (canasta) basket (for playing pelota) (b) (esp AmL) (en baloncesto) basket

cesto m (a) (esp Esp) (recipiente) basket; **el ～ de la ropa sucia** the laundry basket (b) (esp AmL) (en baloncesto) basket

cetro m scepter*

CFC m (= clorofluorocarbono) CFC

cg. (= centigramo) cg

Ch, ch *f* (*read as* /ˈtʃe/ *or* /se ˈatʃe/ *or* (Esp) /θe ˈatʃe/) *combination traditionally considered as a separate letter in the Spanish alphabet*

chabacano¹ -na *adj* ⟨ropa/decoración⟩ gaudy, tasteless; ⟨espectáculo/persona⟩ vulgar; ⟨chiste/cuento⟩ coarse, tasteless

chabacano² *m* (Méx) (árbol) apricot tree; (fruta) apricot

chabola *f* (Esp) (a) (en los suburbios) shack, shanty dwelling (b) **chabolas** *fpl* shantytown

chabolismo *m* (Esp): **para resolver la cuestión del ~** in order to find a solution to the shanty town problem

chacal *m* jackal

chacarero -ra *m,f* (CS, Per) farmer (*who works a* CHACRA)

cháchara *f* **1** (fam) (conversación) chatter; **se pasa la mañana de ~** she spends the whole morning chattering **2** (Méx) (objeto de poca importancia) piece of junk; **un cajón lleno de ~s** a drawer's full of junk

chacharear [A1] *vi* (fam) to chatter

Chaco *m*: **el Gran ~** *region of scrub and swamp plains covering parts of Paraguay, Bolivia and Argentina*

chacra *f* (CS, Per) (granja) small farm; (casa) farmhouse

chafar [A1] *vt* (fam) (a) ⟨peinado⟩ to flatten; ⟨plátano/pulpa⟩ to mash; ⟨huevos⟩ to break; ⟨ajo⟩ to crush (b) ⟨vestido/falda⟩ to wrinkle (AmE), to crumple (BrE)
■ **chafarse** *v pron* to get squashed

chal *m* shawl, wrap

chala *f* (a) (RPl) (Bot) corn husk (b) (Chi) (Indum) sandal

chalado -da *adj* (fam) [ESTAR] crazy (colloq), nuts (colloq)
■ *m,f* nutter (colloq)

chale *interj* (Méx fam) you're kidding! (colloq)

chalé *m* ▶ CHALET

chaleca *f* (Chi) cardigan

chaleco *m* (de traje) vest (AmE), waistcoat (BrE); (jersey sin mangas) sleeveless sweater; (acolchado) body warmer; (chaqueta de punto) (CS) cardigan; **~ antibalas** bulletproof vest; **~ de fuerza** straitjacket; **~ salvavidas** lifejacket; **a ~** (Méx) no matter what

chalet /tʃaˈle/ *m* (*pl* **-lets**) (en urbanización) house; (en el campo) cottage; (en la montaña) chalet; (en la playa) villa

chalote *m*, **chalota** *f* shallot, scallion (AmE)

chalupa *f* **1** (barca) skiff; (canoa) (AmL) small canoe **2** (Méx) (Coc) stuffed tortilla

chamaco -ca *m,f* (Méx fam) (muchacho) kid (colloq), youngster (colloq)

chamagoso -sa *adj* (Méx fam) dirty, filthy

chamarra *f* (chaqueta) jacket

chamba *f* **1** (Méx, Per, Ven fam) (trabajo) work; (empleo) job; (lugar) work **2** (Col) (a) (zanja) ditch (b) (herida) wound, gash

chambear [A1] *vi* (Méx, Per fam) to work

chambón -bona *adj* (AmL fam) clumsy, klutzy (AmE colloq)

chambonada *f* (AmL fam) botch (colloq)

chamizo *m* **1** (a) (leña quemada) charred log (b) (Col) (ramas secas) *tb* **~s** brushwood **2** (choza) thatched hut

chamo -ma *m,f* (Ven fam) (niño, muchacho) kid (colloq)

champán *m*, **champaña** *m or f* champagne

champiñón *m* mushroom

champú *m* (*pl* **-pús** *or* **-púes**) shampoo

champurrear [A1] *vt* (CS) ▶ CHAPURREAR

chamuscar [A2] *vt* to scorch, singe; **madera chamuscada** charred wood
■ **chamuscarse** *v pron*: **~se el pelo** to singe one's hair

chamuyar [A1] *vi* (RPl fam) to chatter
■ ~ *vt* (RPl fam) to mutter

chan *m* (AmC) mountain guide

chancaca *f* (a) (Andes) (melaza) brown sugarloaf (b) (Per) (dulce de maíz) maize cake

chancar [A2] *vt* **1** (Andes) (triturar) to crush, grind **2** (Per arg) (estudiar) to cram (colloq)

chance *f or m* (AmL) (oportunidad) chance; **dar ~ a algn** to give sb the chance; **tiene pocas ~s de ganar** he doesn't have *o* stand much chance of winning

chancear [A1] *vi* (Col fam) to joke, kid around (colloq)
■ **chancearse** *v pron* **~se DE algn** to make fun OF sb

chanchada *f* (AmL fam) (a) (porquería, suciedad) mess (b) (acción indigna) dirty trick (colloq); **hacerle una ~ a algn** to play a dirty trick on sb

chanchería *f* (AmL) pork butcher's shop

chanchito *m* (fam) **1** (Andes, CS) (Zool) woodlouse **2** (CS) (alcancía) piggy bank

chancho¹ -cha *adj* (AmL fam) (sucio) filthy, gross (colloq); (miserable, ruin) mean
■ *m,f* (AmL) (a) (Zool) pig (b) (fam) (persona sucia) dirty *o* filthy pig (colloq)

chancho² *m* (Chi, Per) (Coc) *tb* **carne de ~** pork

chanchullero -ra *adj* (fam) shady (colloq), crooked (colloq)
■ *m,f* (fam) racket (colloq)

chanchullo *m* (fam) racket (colloq), fiddle (BrE colloq)

chancla *f* (sandalia) thong (AmE), flip-flop (BrE); (pantufla) (Col) slipper

chancleta *f* (sandalia) thong (AmE), flip-flop (BrE)

chándal *m* (*pl* **-dals**) (Esp) tracksuit

changador *m* (RPl) porter

changarro *m* (Méx) small store

chango -ga *m,f* (Méx) monkey

changuito® *m* (Arg) (para las compras) shopping cart (AmE), shopping trolley (BrE); (para el bebé) stroller (AmE), pushchair (BrE)

chanquetes *mpl* whitebait (*pl*)

chanta *adj* (RPl arg) (informal) unreliable; (mentiroso) deceitful
■ *mf* (RPl arg) (informal) unreliable person; (mentiroso) liar

chantaje *m* blackmail; **le hacen ~** he is being blackmailed

chantajear [A1] *vt* to blackmail

chantajista *mf* blackmailer

chantillí, chantilly /ʃanti'ɣi, tʃanti'ɣi/ m: tb
crema ~ f whipped cream, chantilly

chao interj (fam) bye (colloq), bye-bye (colloq)

chapa f ① (a) (plancha — de metal) sheet; (— de
madera) panel (b) (lámina de madera) veneer (c)
(carrocería) bodywork ② (a) (distintivo) badge; (de
policía) shield (AmE), badge (BrE); (con el nombre)
nameplate; (de perro) identification disc o tag (b)
(RPl) (de matrícula) license plate (AmE),
numberplate (BrE) ③ (de botella) cap, top ④ (AmL)
(cerradura) lock ⑤ **chapas** fpl (AmL fam) (en las
mejillas): **le salieron** ~s (por vergüenza) her cheeks
flushed (red); (por el aire fresco) her cheeks were
red ⑥ (AmC fam) (joya) earring; (dentadura postiza)
false teeth (pl)

chapado -da adj ⟨metal⟩ plated; **un reloj** ~ **en
oro** a gold-plated watch

chaparrastroso -sa adj (Méx fam) scruffy

chaparro -rra adj (AmL fam) short, squat;
quedarse ~ to stop growing
■ m,f (AmL fam) shorty (colloq), titch (colloq)

chaparrón m (Meteo) downpour, cloudburst

chape m (Chi) (trenza) braid (AmE), plait (BrE);
(pelo atado) bunch

chapetes mpl (Méx) ▶ CHAPA 5

chapista mf panel beater

chapopote m (Méx) (alquitrán) tar; (asfalto)
asphalt

chapotear [A1] vi (en agua) splash (around);
(en barro) squelch (around)

chapucero -ra adj ⟨persona⟩ sloppy, slapdash;
⟨trabajo/reparación⟩ botched
■ m,f: **es un** ~ his work is very slapdash

chapulín m (AmC, Méx) (Zool) locust

chapurrear [A1] vt (fam): ~ **el inglés** to speak
broken o poor English

chapuza f (fam) (trabajo mal hecho) botched job
(colloq), botch (colloq)

chapuzón m dip; **darse un** ~ to have a dip

chaquet (pl **-quets**), **chaqué** m morning
coat

chaqueta f ① (Indum) jacket; ~ **de punto**
cardigan ② (Col) (Odont) crown

chaquetón m three-quarter length coat

charanga f brass band; (militar) military band

charango m small five-stringed guitar

charca f pond, pool

charco m (a) puddle, pool (b) **el** ~ (fam) (océano
Atlántico) the Atlantic, the Pond (colloq & hum)

charcutería f delicatessen, charcuterie (AmE)

charla f (a) (conversación) chat; **estábamos de** ~
we were having a chat (b) (conferencia) talk

charlar [A1] vi to chat, talk

charlatán -tana adj (fam) talkative
■ m,f (fam) (a) (parlanchín) chatterbox (colloq) (b)
(vendedor) dishonest hawker; (curandero) charlatan

charlestón m charleston

charme /ʃarm/ m charm

charol m ① (barniz) lacquer; (cuero) patent
leather; **zapatos de** ~ patent leather shoes
② (Col, Per) (bandeja) tray

charola f (Bol, Méx, Per) tray

charqui m (AmS) charqui, jerked beef

charrasquear [A1] vt ① (AmL) ⟨guitarra⟩ to
strum ② (Méx) ⟨persona⟩ to stab

charrería f (Méx) the culture of horsemanship
and rodeo riding

charretera f epaulette

charro -rra adj ① (fam) (de mal gusto) gaudy,
garish ② (en Méx) ⟨tradiciones/música⟩ of/
relating to the CHARRO
■ m,f (en Méx) (jinete) (m) horseman, cowboy; (f)
horsewoman, cowgirl

chárter adj inv charter (before n)
■ m charter (flight)

chasco m (decepción) disappointment, let-down
(colloq); **me llevé un** ~ I felt let down o
disappointed

chasis, chasís m (pl ~) (Auto) chassis; (Fot)
plateholder

chasquear [A1] vt ⟨lengua⟩ to click;
⟨dedos⟩ to click, snap (b) ⟨látigo⟩ to crack

chasquido m (a) (de la lengua) click; (de los
dedos) click, snap (b) (de látigo) crack; (de rama
seca) crack, snap

chasquilla f (Chi) bangs (pl) (AmE), fringe
(BrE)

chatarra adj inv (Méx): **comida** ~ junk food;
productos ~ cheap goods
■ f (Metal) scrap (metal); **el coche es pura** ~ the
car is just a heap of scrap

chatarrero -ra m,f scrap merchant

chatel -tela m,f (AmC fam) (m) little boy; (f)
little girl

chato -ta adj (a) ⟨nariz⟩ snub (before n) (b)
(Per fam) (bajo) short (c) (AmS) ⟨nivel⟩ low; ⟨obra⟩
pedestrian

chaucha f (RPl) (Bot, Coc) French bean

chauvinismo /tʃoβi'nismo/ m chauvinism

chauvinista /tʃoβi'nista/ adj chauvinistic
■ mf chauvinist

chaval -vala m,f (esp Esp fam) (niño) kid (colloq),
youngster

chavalo -la m,f (AmC, Méx) ▶ CHAVAL

chavo -va adj (Méx fam) young
■ m,f (Méx) (a) (fam) (muchacho) guy (colloq);
(muchacha) girl (b) (como apelativo) kid (colloq)

chayote m (planta, fruto) chayote, mirliton

che interj (RPl fam): **no te hagas el bobo,** ~ come
on, don't act the innocent; ~, **Marta, ¿qué tal?**
hey Marta, how are you?; **¡pero** ~! **¡cómo le
dijiste eso!** for Heaven's sake! whatever made
you tell him that?

checar [A2] vt (Méx) (a) (revisar, mirar) to check;
me chequé la presión (Med) I had my blood
pressure checked; **¿por qué no vas a que te
chequen?** why don't you go for a checkup? (b)
(verificar) to check (c) (vigilar) to check up on

checo¹ -ca adj/m,f Czech

checo² m (idioma) Czech

checoslovaco -ca adj/m,f (Hist)
Czechoslovakian, Czechoslovak

Checoslovaquia f (Hist) Czechoslovakia

chef /ʃef, tʃef/ m chef

chele -la adj (AmC) (de piel) light-skinned; (de
pelo) blond-haired

chelín m shilling

chelista mf cellist

chelo m cello

cheque m check (AmE), cheque (BrE); **pagar con**

~ to pay by check; **un ~ a nombre de** ... a check made out to *o* made payable to ...; ~ **bancario** *o* (AmL) **de gerencia** banker's draft; ~ **cruzado/en blanco** crossed/blank check*; ~ **de viaje** *or* **de viajero** traveler's check (AmE), traveller's cheque (BrE); ~ **sin fondos** bad *o* (frml) dishonored* check*

chequear [A1] *vt* **1** (revisar, verificar) to check; ~ **algo con** algo to check sth AGAINST sth **2** (AmL) ⟨*equipaje*⟩ to check in
■ **chequearse** *v pron* **(a)** (Col, Ven) (Aviac) to check in **(b)** (Med) to have a checkup

chequeo *m* **(a)** (Med) checkup; (*para entrar en el ejército, a trabajar*) medical; **someterse a un ~ médico** to have a medical/a checkup **(b)** (control, inspección) check; **mostradores de ~ de tiquetes** (Col) check-in desks

chequera *f* checkbook (AmE), chequebook (BrE)

chévere *adj* (AmL exc CS fam) great (colloq), fantastic (colloq); **¡qué ~!** that's great!

chic /ʃik, tʃik/ *adj inv* chic, fashionable
■ *m* chic; **tiene ~** she's very chic

chica *f* (fam) maid; *ver tb* CHICO

chicanero -ra *adj* (Andes, Méx) tricky, crafty

chicano -na *adj/m,f* Chicano

chicha *f* **1** **(a)** (bebida alcohólica) *alcoholic drink made from fermented maize, also called* CHICHA BRUJA; ~ **andina** *alcoholic drink made with corn flour and pineapple juice* **(b)** ~ **de manzana/uva** *alcoholic drink made from apple/grape juice* **(b)** (bebida sin alcohol) *cold drink made with maize or fruit* **2** (AmC vulg) (teta) tit (sl)

chícharo *m* (esp Méx) pea

chicharra *f* **(a)** (Zool) cicada **(b)** (timbre) buzzer

chicharrón *m* piece of crackling; **chicharrones** cracklings (*pl*), pork scratchings (*pl*) (BrE)

chiche *adj* (AmC fam) dead easy (colloq)
■ *m* **1** (juguete) (CS fam) toy; (adorno) (Chi) trinket **2** (AmC fam) (pecho) tit (sl)

chichi *f* (Méx fam) (de mujer) tit (sl); (de animal) teat

chicho -cha *adj* (Méx fam) **(a)** (bonito) nice, neat (AmE colloq) **(b)** ⟨*persona*⟩: **es muy chicha para los deportes** she's brilliant at sport (colloq)

chichón *m* swelling *o* bump on the head

chicle, chiclé *m* chewing gum

chiclero -ra *m,f* **1** (Méx) (vendedor) street vendor (*selling chewing gum, candy, etc*) **2** (AmC) (Agr) rubber tapper

chico -ca *adj* (esp AmL) **(a)** (joven) young; **cuando éramos ~s** when we were little (colloq) **(b)** (bajo) small **(c)** (pequeño) small
■ *m,f* **1** **(a)** (niño) *m* boy; (*f*) girl **(b)** (hijo) (*m*) son, boy; (*f*) daughter, girl **(c)** (joven) (*m*) guy (colloq), boy (colloq), bloke (BrE colloq); (*f*) girl; **unos ~s** (varones) some boys; (varones y hembras) some boys and girls **(d)** (empleado joven) (*m*) boy; (*f*) girl **(e)** (como apelativo): **¡~! ¿tú por aquí?** well, well! what brings you here? **2** **chico** *m* (AmL) (en billar) frame; (en bolos) game

chicoria *f* chicory

chicotazo *m* (AmL) whipping

chicote *m* (fam) (AmL) (látigo) whip

chicotear [A1] *vt* (AmL) to whip

chifa *m* (Per fam) Chinese (restaurant)

chifla *f* whistling, catcalls (*pl*)

chiflado -da *adj* (fam) crazy (colloq), mad (BrE); **estar ~ POR** algo/algn to be crazy *o* mad ABOUT sth/sb (colloq)
■ *m,f* (fam) nutter (colloq)

chiflar [A1] *vt* ⟨*actor/cantante*⟩ to whistle at (*as sign of disapproval*), ≈ to boo
■ ~ *vi* **1** (silbar) to whistle **2** (fam) (gustar mucho): **le chiflan los coches** he's crazy about cars (colloq)
■ **chiflarse** *v pron* (fam) ~**se POR** algo/algn to be crazy ABOUT sth/sb (colloq)

chihuahua *mf* chihuahua

chilaba *f* djellaba

chilango -ga *adj* (Méx) of/from Mexico City

chilaquiles *mpl* (Méx) *corn tortilla in tomato and chili sauce*

chile *m* **1** (AmC, Méx) (Bot, Coc) chili, hot pepper; ~ **con carne** chili con carne **2** (AmC fam) (chiste) joke

Chile *m* Chile

chilear [A1] *vi* (AmC fam) to tell jokes

chileno -na *adj/m,f* Chilean

chilicote *m* (AmS) cricket

chillar [A1] *vi* **(a)** «*pájaro*» to screech; «*cerdo*» to squeal; «*ratón*» to squeak; «*persona*» to shout, yell (colloq); (de dolor, miedo) to scream; ~**le A** algn to yell *o* shout AT sb **(c)** «*bebé/niño*» (llorar) to scream

chillido *m* **(a)** (de ave) screech; (de cerdo) squeal; (de ratón) squeak **(b)** (grito) shout, yell; (de dolor, miedo) scream, shriek; **dar ~s** *o* **un ~** (fam) to shout, to yell

chillón -llona *adj* (fam) ⟨*voz*⟩ shrill, piercing; ⟨*color*⟩ loud

chilote *m* (AmC) baby sweetcorn

chiltoma *f* (AmC) sweet pepper

chimbo -ba *adj* **(a)** (Col fam) (falsificado) ⟨*perfume*⟩ fake (*before n*); ⟨*whisky/grabación*⟩ bootleg (*before n*); **un cheque ~** a dud check (colloq) **(b)** (Ven arg) lousy (colloq)

chimbomba *f* (AmC) balloon

chimenea *f* **1** **(a)** (de casa) chimney; (de locomotora, fábrica) smokestack (AmE), chimney (BrE) **(b)** (de volcán) vent **2** (hogar) fireplace, hearth

chimpancé *mf* chimpanzee

chimpún *m* (Per) football boot

china *f* **(a)** (piedra) pebble, small stone **(b)** (Esp) (porcelana) porcelain

China *f*: *tb* **la ~ China**

chinamo *m* (AmC fam) (en feria) stall; (bar) small bar

chinchar [A1] *vt* (fam) to pester (colloq)

chinche *adj* (fam) (pesado) irritating; (quisquilloso): **es muy ~** he's a real nit-picker
■ *f or m* **1** (insecto) bedbug **2** (RPl fam) (mal humor) bad mood
■ *mf* **(a)** (fam) (pesado) nuisance, pain in the neck (colloq) **(b)** (fam) (quisquilloso) nit-picker (colloq)
■ *f* (*en algunas regiones m*) (clavito) thumbtack (AmE), drawing pin (BrE)

chincheta *f* (Esp) thumbtack (AmE), drawing pin (BrE)

chinchilla *f* chinchilla

chin-chin *interj* (fam) cheers!

chinchorro *m* (Col, Ven) (hamaca) hammock

chinchulines *mpl* (Bol, RPl) chitterlings (*pl*)

chincol *m* (Chi) (pájaro) crown sparrow

chinela *f* (pantufla) slipper; (chancla) (AmC) thong (AmE), flip-flop (BrE)

chingada *f* (Méx vulg): **está pa' la** ~ he's/she's had it (colloq); **¡vete a la** ~**!** screw you! (vulg); **la casa estaba en la** ~ the house was in the middle of nowhere (colloq); **¡hijo de la** ~**!** you son-of-a-bitch! (sl)

chingadera *f* (Méx vulg) trash (colloq), crap (sl)

chingar [A3] *vi* **(a)** (esp Méx vulg) (copular) to screw (vulg), to fuck (vulg) **(b)** (Méx vulg) (molestar): **te lo dijo para** ~ **nada más** he only said it to annoy you; **¡deja de** ~**!** stop being such a pain in the ass! (vulg); **¡no chingues!** (no digas) you're kidding! (colloq)

■ ~ *vt* **(a)** (AmL vulg) (en sentido sexual) to fuck (vulg), to screw (vulg) **(b)** (Méx vulg) (jorobar) to screw (vulg); ~**la: ¡no la chingues!** (Méx vulg) shit! (vulg)

■ **chingarse** *v pron* [1] **(a)** (*enf*) (AmL vulg) (en sentido sexual) to fuck (vulg), to screw (vulg) **(b)** (esp Méx vulg) (jorobarse): **creyó que ganaría pero se chingó** he thought he'd win but he got a shock; **se chingó el motor** the engine's had it (colloq); **estamos chingados** we're in deep shit (vulg) [2] (Méx vulg) **(a)** (aguantarse): **si no te gusta, te chingas** if you don't like it, tough (colloq) **(b)** (robar) to rip … off (colloq)

chingaste *m* (AmC) coffee grounds (*pl*)

chingo¹ -ga *adj* (AmC fam) (desnudo) stark naked (colloq)

■ *m,f* (Ven fam) snub-nosed person

chingo² *m* (Méx fam o vulg): **un** ~ **de** loads of (colloq); **me costó un** ~ it cost me a bundle *o* (BrE) packet (colloq)

chingón -gona *adj* (Méx vulg) ⟨partido/película⟩ fantastic (colloq); ⟨persona⟩ cool (sl)

chingue *m* (Chi) **(a)** (Zool) skunk **(b)** (fam) (persona hedionda) smelly person

chinguear [A1] *vi/vt* (AmC) ▶ CHINGAR

chinita *f* (Chi) ladybug (AmE), ladybird (BrE)

chino¹ -na *adj* [1] (de la China) Chinese [2] (Méx) ⟨pelo⟩ curly

■ *m,f* [1] (de la China) (*m*) Chinese man; (*f*) Chinese woman; **los** ~**s** the Chinese [2] (Arg, Per) (mestizo) mestizo, person of mixed Amerindian and European parentage **(b)** (Col fam) (joven) kid (colloq)

chino² *m* [1] (idioma) Chinese; **me suena a** ~ it's all Greek to me [2] (Méx) (pelo rizado) curly hair; (para rizar el pelo) curler, roller [3] (Per fam) (tienda) convenience store, corner shop (BrE)

chip *m* (*pl* **chips**) **(a)** (Inf) chip **(b)** (papa frita) potato chip (AmE), crisp (BrE) **(c)** (Arg) (pancito) bridge roll

chipirón *m* small cuttlefish

chipote *m* (Méx fam) bump, lump

Chipre *f* Cyprus

chipriota *adj/mf* Cypriot

chiqueado *adj* (Méx fam) spoilt

chiquear [A1] *vt* (Méx fam) to spoil

chiquero *m* (AmL) (pocilga) pigpen (AmE), pigsty (BrE)

chiquilín -lina *adj* (AmL fam) (infantil) childish; **ser** ~ to be childish, to act like a kid (colloq)

■ *m,f* (fam) (persona infantil) (AmL) big kid (colloq); (niño) (Ur) kid (colloq)

chiquillada *f*: **se pelearon por una** ~ they fought over something really silly

chiquillo -lla *adj*: **no seas** ~ don't be childish

■ *m,f* kid (colloq)

chiquito¹ -ta, chiquitito -ta *adj* (esp AmL fam) small

chiquito² -ta *m,f* (esp AmL fam) (niño) (*m*) little boy; (*f*) little girl

chiribita *f* **(a)** (chispa) spark **(b) chiribitas** *fpl* (en la vista) spots in front of the eyes; **los ojos le hacían** ~**s** his eyes glowed

chirigota *f* (fam) (broma) joke; **estar de** ~ to be kidding around (colloq)

chirimiri *m* fine drizzle

chirimoya *f* custard apple

chiripa *f* [1] (fam) (casualidad) fluke; **de** *or* **por** ~ (fam) by sheer luck, by a fluke [2] (Ven) **(a)** (insecto) cockroach **(b)** (palmera) palm

chirla *f* (Coc, Zool) baby clam

chirona *f* (Esp fam) can (AmE sl), nick (BrE sl)

chiros *mpl* (Col) rags (*pl*)

chirriar [A17] *vi* «puerta/gozne» to squeak, creak; «frenos/neumáticos» to screech

chirrido *m* (de puerta) squeaking, creaking; (de frenos, neumáticos) screech, screeching

chis, chist *interj* shush!, ssh!

chisme *m* **(a)** (chismorreo) piece of gossip; ~**s** gossip, tittle-tattle (colloq); **contar** ~**s** to gossip **(b)** (Esp, Méx fam) (trasto, cacharro) thing, thingamajig (colloq); **un cuarto lleno de** ~**s** a room full of junk *o* stuff (colloq)

chismear, chismorrear [A1] *vi* (fam) to gossip

chismorreo *m* (fam) gossip, tittle-tattle (colloq)

chismoso -sa *adj* gossipy (colloq)

■ *m,f* gossip, scandalmonger (colloq)

chispa *f* [1] **(a)** (del fuego) spark; **está/están que echa/echan** ~**s** (fam) he's/they're hopping mad (colloq) **(b)** (Auto, Elec) spark [2] (fam) (pizca) little bit [3] (gracia, ingenio) wit; **tener** ~ to be witty

■ *adj inv* (Esp fam) tipsy (colloq)

chisparse [A1] *v pron* (Méx) to come loose

chispazo *m* (Elec, Tec) spark

chispeante *adj* **(a)** ⟨leña/fuego⟩ crackling **(b)** ⟨lenguaje/personalidad⟩ witty; ⟨ingenio⟩ lively, sparkling **(c)** ⟨ojos⟩ (de alegría) sparkling; (de ira) flashing

chispear [A1] *vi* **(a)** «leña» to spark **(b)** (Elec) to spark, give off sparks

■ ~ *v impers* (fam) (lloviznar) to spit, spot

chispero *m* (AmC) (encendedor) (fam) lighter; (Auto) spark plug

chisporrotear [A1] *vi* «*leña/fuego*» to spark, crackle; «*aceite*» to spit, splutter; «*carne/pescado*» to sizzle

chistar [A1] *vi*: ¡y sin ∼! and not another word!; **no chistó** he didn't say a word

chiste *m* **(a)** (*cuento gracioso*) joke; **contar** *or* (Col) **echar un** ∼ to tell a joke; ∼ **picante** *or* **verde** *or* (Bol, Méx) **colorado** dirty joke **(b)** (Bol, CS, Méx) (*broma*) joke; **hacerle un** ∼ **a algn** to play a joke *o* trick on sb; **me lo dijo en** ∼ he was joking **(c)** (Col, Méx fam) (*gracia*): **el** ∼ **está en hacerlo rápido** the idea *o* point is to do it quickly; **tener su** ∼ (Méx) to be tricky **(d) chistes** *mpl* (RPl) (*historietas*) comic strips (*pl*), funnies (*pl*) (AmE colloq)

chistera *f* top hat

chistoso -sa *adj* funny, amusing
■ *m,f* comic, joker

chiva *f* [1] (AmL) (*barba*) goatee [2] (Col) (*bus*) rural *o* country bus [3] (Col period) (*primicia*) scoop, exclusive [4] (Chi fam) (*mentira*) cock-and-bull story (colloq); *ver tb* CHIVO [5] **chivas** *fpl* (Méx fam) (*cachivaches*) junk (colloq)

chivarse [A1] *v pron* (Esp fam) to tell; (a la policía) to squeal (sl)

chivatazo *m* (Esp fam) tip-off (colloq); **les dieron el** ∼ they were tipped off

chivato¹ -ta *m,f* (Esp, Ven fam) **(a)** (*informador*) informer, stool pigeon (colloq) **(b)** (*acusetas*) tattletale (AmE colloq), telltale (BrE colloq)

chivato² *m* (Esp fam) (*dispositivo sonoro*) bleeper (colloq); (*luz piloto*) pilot light

chivearse [A1] *v pron* (Méx) (fam) (*turbarse*) to get embarrassed

chivo -va *m,f* [1] **(a)** (*cría de la cabra*) kid **(b)** (Ven) (*cabra*) goat; *ver tb* CHIVA [2] **(a) chivo** *m* (AmL) (*macho cabrío*) billy goat **(b)** ∼ **expiatorio** scapegoat

chocado -da *adj* (AmL fam) smashed up (colloq); (*superficialmente*) dented

chocante *adj* **(a)** (*que causa impresión*): **su reacción me pareció** ∼ I was shocked *o* taken aback by her reaction, his reaction shocked me **(b)** (*en cuestiones morales*) shocking **(c)** (Col, Méx, Ven) (*desagradable*) unpleasant

chocar [A2] *vi* [1] **(a)** (*colisionar*) to crash; (*entre sí*) to collide; ∼ **de frente** to collide *o* crash head-on; ∼ **CON** *or* **CONTRA algo** «*vehículo*» to crash *o* run INTO sth; (*con otro en marcha*) to collide WITH sth; **el balón chocó contra el poste** the ball hit the goalpost; ∼ **CON algn** «*persona*» to run INTO sb; (*con otra en movimiento*) to collide WITH sb **(b)** (*entrar en conflicto*) ∼ **CON algn** to clash with sb **(c)** ∼ **CON algo** «*con problema/obstáculo*» to come up AGAINST sth
[2] **(a)** (*extrañar*): **me chocó que no me lo dijera** I was surprised that he hadn't told me **(b)** (*escandalizar*) to shock; **me chocó su lenguaje** I was shocked by her language
[3] (Col, Méx, Ven fam) (*irritar, molestar*) to annoy, bug (colloq)
■ ∼ *vt* **(a)** «*copas*» to clink; ¡**chócala!** (fam) put it there! (colloq), give me five! (colloq) **(b)** (AmL) «*vehículo*» (*que se conduce*) to crash; (*de otra persona*) to run into
■ **chocarse** *v pron* (Col) [1] (*en vehículo*) to have a crash *o* an accident

[2] (fam) (*molestarse*) to get annoyed

chochada *f* (AmC fam) silly little thing (colloq)

chochear [A1] *vi* (fam) **(a)** «*anciano*» to be gaga (colloq) **(b)** (*sentir adoración*) ∼ **POR algn** to dote ON sb

chocho -cha *adj* (fam) **(a)** «*viejo*» gaga (colloq) **(b)** (*encantado*): **está** ∼ **con su hijita** he dotes on his daughter; **se quedó** ∼ **con el regalo** he was delighted with his present

choclo *m* [1] (Per) (*mazorca*) corn cob; (*granos*) sweet corn; (*cultivo*) corn (AmE), maize (BrE) [2] (Méx fam) (Indum) brogue

chocolate *m* [1] **(a)** (*para comer*) chocolate; ∼ **blanco/con leche** white/milk chocolate; ∼ **negro** plain chocolate, dark chocolate; **(b)** (AmL) chocolate; **sirvieron unos** ∼**s con el café** they gave us chocolates with our coffee **(c)** (*bebida*) hot chocolate [2] (Esp arg) (*hachís*) dope (sl), pot (colloq)

chocolatería *f* (*cafetería*) *café serving hot chocolate as a speciality*

chocolatina *f*, (RPl) **chocolatín** *m* chocolate bar

chocoyo *m* (AmC) parakeet

chofer, (Esp) **chófer** *mf* **(a)** (*asalariado – de coche particular*) chauffeur; (*– de transporte colectivo*) driver **(b)** (*persona que maneja*) driver

cholga *f* (Chi) mussel

chollo *m* (Esp fam) (*trabajo fácil*) cushy job *o* number (colloq); (*ganga*) steal (colloq), bargain

chomba *f* (*sin botones*) (Chi) sweater; (*con botones*) (Arg) polo shirt

chompa *f* (*chaqueta*) (Col, Ec) jacket; (*suéter*) (Bol, Per) sweater

chompipe *m* (AmC, Méx) turkey

choncho -cha *adj* (Méx fam) **(a)** «*problema/situación*» serious **(b)** «*persona*» hefty (colloq), big

chongo *m* (Méx) (*moño*) bun

chopo *m* (Bot) black poplar

choque *m* **(a)** (*de vehículos*) crash, collision; ∼ **múltiple** pile-up; ∼ **frontal** (Auto) head-on collision; (*enfrentamiento*) head-on confrontation **(b)** (*conflicto*) clash **(c)** (*sorpresa, golpe*) shock

chorear [A1] *vt* (AmL) [1] (CS, Per) (*robar*) to swipe (colloq) [2] (Chi) (*aburrir*): **esto me choreó** I'm fed up with this (colloq) **(b)** (*molestar, enojar*) to annoy
■ **chorearse** *v pron* (fam) [1] (CS) (*robarse*) to swipe (colloq) [2] (Chi) **(a)** (fam) (*aburrirse*) to get bored, get fed up **(b)** (*molestarse, enojarse*) to get annoyed

choreto -ta *adj* (Ven fam) crooked

chorito *m* (Chi) baby mussel

chorizar [A4] *vt* (Esp fam) to swipe

chorizo *m* (*embutido curado*) chorizo (*highly-seasoned pork sausage*); (*salchicha*) (RPl) sausage

chorlito *m* plover

choro *m* (Chi, Per) [1] (Coc, Zool) mussel [2] (fam) (*delincuente*) crook (colloq)

chorrada *f* (Esp fam) **(a)** (*estupidez*): **decir** ∼**s** to talk drivel *o* twaddle (colloq) **(b)** (*cosa insignificante*) little thing

chorrear [A1] *vi* to drip; **estaba chorreando** (*muy mojado*) it was dripping wet; **chorreando de sudor** dripping with sweat; **la sangre le chorreaba de la nariz** blood was pouring from his nose ⋯❯

c

■ ~ *vt* **1** (AmL fam) (manchar): **chorreado de café** covered in coffee stains **2** (Col, RPl arg) (robar) to swipe (colloq)

■ **chorrearse** *v pron* (*refl*) (CS, Per fam) (mancharse): **cuidado con ~te** mind you don't get it all over yourself

chorrillo *m* (Méx fam) diarrhea*, the runs (colloq)

chorro *m* **1** (de agua) stream, jet; (de vapor, gas) jet; un chorrito de agua a trickle of water; a ~ ⟨motor/avión⟩ jet (*before n*); **el agua salía a ~s** water gushed out **2** (AmC, Ven) (llave) faucet (AmE), tap (BrE) **3** (Méx fam) (cantidad): **¡qué ~ de gente!** what a lot of people!; **~s de dinero** loads of money (colloq); **me gusta un ~ salir** I really love going out

chotis *m* schottische

chovinismo *m* chauvinism

chovinista *adj/mf* chauvinist

choza *f* hut, shack

christmas /ˈkrismas/ *m* (*pl* ~) (Esp) Christmas card

chubasco *m* heavy shower

chubasquero *m* slicker (AmE), cagoule (BrE)

chuchería *f* **(a)** (alhaja) trinket; (adorno) knickknack **(b)** (dulce) tidbit (AmE), titbit (BrE)

chucho -cha *m,f* **1** (Esp fam) (perro) mongrel **2** **chucho** *m* (RPl fam) (escalofrío) shiver; **tengo ~s de frío** I have the shivers (colloq)

chueca *f* (Chi) (juego) *game similar to hockey, and the stick with which it's played*

chueco¹ -ca *adj* **1** (AmL) (torcido) crooked, askew **(a)** (Chi, Méx fam) (deshonesto) ⟨persona⟩ crooked (colloq); ⟨documento⟩ false; ⟨elecciones⟩ rigged

■ *m,f* (Chi, Méx fam) (deshonesto): **es un ~** he's crooked (colloq)

chueco² *adv* (AmL fam) **(a)** (torcido): **camina/escribe ~** he can't walk/write straight **(b)** ⟨jugar/pelear⟩ dirty (colloq)

chufa *f* tiger nut, earth almond

chuico *m* (Chi) demijohn

chulear [A1] *vt* **1** (Arg fam) (provocar) to needle (colloq) **2** (Méx fam) (piropear) to compliment; ⟨vestido/peinado⟩ to make nice comments about **3** (Col) (con un signo) to check (AmE), to tick (BrE)

chuleta *f* **1** (Coc) chop; **~ de cordero** lamb chop **2** (Esp arg) (para copiar) crib (colloq) **3** (Chi fam) (patilla) sideburn

chulla *mf* (Ec) (quiteño) *person from Quito*

chulo¹ -la *adj* **1** (fam) (bonito) **(a)** (Esp, Méx) ⟨vestido/casa⟩ neat (AmE colloq), lovely (BrE) **(b)** (Méx) ⟨hombre⟩ good-looking, cute (esp AmE); ⟨mujer⟩ pretty, cute (esp AmE) **2** (Esp fam) (bravucón) nervy (AmE colloq), cocky (BrE colloq) **3** (Chi fam) (de mal gusto) tacky (colloq)

■ *m,f* (Esp fam) (bravucón) flashy type

chulo² *m* (Esp fam) **1** (proxeneta) pimp **2** (Col) (Zool) black vulture **3** (Col) (signo) check mark (AmE), tick (BrE)

chumero -ra *m,f* (AmC) apprentice

chunche *m* (AmC) (fam) (cosa) thing, thingamajig (colloq)

chuño *m* (CS) (fécula de papa) potato flour

chupachups® *m* (*pl* ~) (Esp) lollipop

chupada *f* (fam) (de helado) lick; (de cigarrillo) puff; **le dio unas ~s a la pipa** he puffed on his pipe a few times

chupado -da *adj* **1** [ESTAR] (fam) (flaco) skinny **2** [ESTAR] (Esp fam) (fácil) dead easy (colloq) **3** [ESTAR] (AmL fam) (borracho) plastered (colloq) **4** **(a)** [ESTAR] (Chi, Per fam) (inhibido) withdrawn **(b)** [SER] (Chi, Per fam) (tímido) shy

chupalla *f* (Chi) straw hat

chupamedias *mf* (*pl* ~) (CS, Ven fam) bootlicker (colloq)

chupar [A1] *vt* **(a)** (extraer) ⟨sangre/savia⟩ to suck **(b)** ⟨biberón/chupete⟩ to suck (on); ⟨naranja/caramelo⟩ to suck; ⟨pipa/cigarrillo⟩ to puff on **(c)** (AmL fam) (beber) to drink

■ ~ *vi* **(a)** «bebé/cría» to suckle **(b)** (AmL fam) (beber) to booze (colloq)

■ **chuparse** *v pron* ⟨dedo⟩ to suck

chupeta *f* (Col) lollipop

chupete *m* **1** **(a)** (de bebé) pacifier (AmE), dummy (BrE) **(b)** (CS) (del biberón) nipple (AmE), teat (BrE) **2** (Chi, Per) (golosina) lollipop **3** (Chi) (Auto) choke

chupetín *m* (RPl) lollipop

chupón *m* **(a)** (AmL) ▶ CHUPETE 1A **(b)** (Méx) (del biberón) nipple (AmE), teat (BrE) **(c)** (Col) (chupada) lick

churrasquería *f* (AmS) steak house

churro *m* **1** (Coc) *strip of fried dough* **2** (Esp fam) (chapuza) botched job

churrusco *m* (Col) (Zool) caterpillar; (cepillo) bottle brush

chusco -ca *adj* **1** (gracioso) ⟨persona/humor⟩ earthy **2** (Chi, Per fam & pey) **(a)** (ordinario) ⟨persona⟩ common (pej); ⟨perro⟩ mongrel; ⟨barrio/lugar⟩ plebeian (pej) **(b)** ⟨mujer⟩ loose (colloq)

chusma *f* rabble (*pl*), plebs (*pl*) (colloq)

chuspa *f* (Col) (para lápices) pencil case; (para gafas) glasses case

chutar [A1] *vi* (Dep) to shoot

chute *m* (Dep) shot

chutear [A1] *vt/vi* (CS) to shoot

chuza *f* (Méx) (Dep) (jugada) strike; (marca) mark

chuzo *adj* (CS fam) ⟨pelo⟩ dead straight (colloq); ⟨persona⟩ hopeless (colloq)

■ *m*: **llover a ~s** to pour (down with rain)

Cía. *f* (= **Compañía**) Co

cianuro *m* cyanide

ciática *f* sciatica

cibercafé *m* cybercafe

ciberespacio *m* (Inf) cyberspace

cibernética *f* cybernetics

cicatero -ra *adj* (fam) tightfisted (colloq)

■ *m,f* (fam) skinflint (colloq)

cicatriz *f* scar; **la herida le dejó ~** the wound left her with a scar

cicatrizar [A4] *vi*, **cicatrizarse** [A4] *v pron* to heal (up), cicatrize (tech)

cicerone *mf* (liter) guide, cicerone (liter)

ciclismo *m* cycling, biking (colloq)

ciclista *adj* cycle (*before n*)

■ *mf* cyclist

ciclo *m* **(a)** (de fenómenos, sucesos) cycle **(b)** (de películas) season; (de conferencias) series **(c)** (Educ): **el primer ～** primary school

ciclocross *m* cyclo-cross; **bicicleta de ～** mountain bike

ciclomotor *m* moped

ciclón *m* cyclone

ciclovía *f* (Col) cycle path

cicuta *f* hemlock

ciego -ga *adj* **1** **(a)** (invidente) blind; **es ～ de nacimiento** he was born blind; **se quedó ～** he went blind; **anduvimos a ciegas por el pasillo** we groped our way along the corridor **(b)** (ante una realidad) **estar ～ ▲ algo** to be blind to sth **(c)** (ofuscado) blind; **～ de ira** blind with fury **2** ⟨*fe/ obediencia*⟩ blind **3** ⟨*conducto/cañería*⟩ blocked; ■ *m,f* (invidente) (*m*) blind man; (*f*) blind woman; **los ～s** the blind

cielo *m* **1** (firmamento) sky; **～ cubierto** overcast sky; **a ～ abierto** (Min) opencast (*before n*); **este dinero me viene como caído del ～** this money is a godsend **2** (Relig) **(a)** **el ～** (Paraíso) heaven; **ir al ～** to go to heaven; **ganarse el ～** to earn oneself a place in heaven **(b)** (*como interj*): **¡～s!** (good) heavens! **3** (techo) ceiling **～ raso** ceiling **4** **(a)** (aplicado a personas) angel **(b)** (como apelativo) sweetheart, darling; **¡mi ～!** my darling

ciempiés *m* (*pl* **～**) centipede

cien *adj inv/pron* a/one hundred; **～ mil** a/one hundred thousand; **es ～ por ～ algodón** (esp Esp) it's a hundred percent cotton
■ *m*: **el ～** (number) one hundred

ciénaga *f* swamp

ciencia *f* **(a)** (rama del saber) science; (saber, conocimiento) knowledge, learning; **～ ficción** science fiction; **a ～ cierta** for sure, for certain **(b)** **ciencias** *fpl* (Educ) science; **C～s Empresariales/de la Información** Business/Media Studies; **C～s Políticas/de la Educación** Politics/ Education

cieno *m* silt, mud

científico -ca *adj* scientific
■ *m,f* scientist

ciento *adj/pron* (*delante de otro número*) a/one hundred; **～ dos** a/one hundred and two; *para ejemplos ver* QUINIENTOS
■ *m* **(a)** (número): **～s de libros** hundreds of books; **vinieron a ～s** they came in the (AmE) *o* (BrE) in their hundreds **(b) por ciento** percent; **cien por ～** a hundred percent

cierra, cierras, etc ▶ CERRAR

cierre *m* **1** (acción) **(a)** (de fábrica, empresa, hospital) closure **(b)** (de establecimiento) closing **(c)** (de frontera) closing **(d)** (de emisión) end, close **(e)** (Fin) close **2** **(a)** (de bolso, pulsera) clasp, fastener; (de puerta, ventana) lock **(b)** (cremallera) zipper (AmE), zip (BrE); **～ metálico** (en tienda) metal shutter *o* grille; **～ relámpago** (CS, Per) zipper (AmE), zip (BrE)

cierro ▶ CERRAR

cierto -ta *adj* **1** (verdadero) true; **no hay nada de ～ en ello** there is no truth in it; **una cosa es cierta** one thing's certain; **es ～** of course, **parece más joven, ¿no es ～?** he looks younger, doesn't he *o* don't you think?; **estabas en lo ～** you were right; **lo ～ es que ...** the fact is

that ...; **si bien es ～ que ...** while *o* although it's true to say that ...; **por ～** (a propósito) by the way, incidentally
2 (*delante del n*) (que no se especifica, define) certain; **cierta clase de gente** a certain kind of people; **de cierta edad** of a certain age; **en cierta ocasión** on one occasion; **en ～ modo** in some ways; **hasta ～ punto** up to a point; **durante un ～ tiempo** for a while

ciervo -va *m,f* (especie) deer; (macho) stag; (hembra) hind

cifra *f* **1** **(a)** (dígito) figure; **un número de cinco ～s** a five-figure number **(b)** (número, cantidad) number; **la ～ de muertos** the number of dead, the death toll (*period*) **(c)** (de dinero) figure, sum **2** (clave) code, cipher; **en ～** in code

cifrar [A1] *vt* **1** **(a)** ⟨*mensaje/carta*⟩ to write ... in code, encode (*frml*) **(b)** (Inf) to encrypt
2 ⟨*esperanza*⟩ to place, pin

cigala *f* crawfish, crayfish

cigarra *f* cicada

cigarrería *f* (Andes) tobacco shop (AmE), tobacconist's (BrE)

cigarrillo *m* cigarette; **～ con filtro** filter tipped cigarette

cigarro *m* (puro) cigar; (cigarrillo) cigarette

cigüeña *f* stork

cigüeñal *m* crankshaft

cilantro *m* coriander

cilindrada *f*, **cilindraje** *m* cubic capacity

cilíndrico -ca *adj* cylindrical

cilindro *m* cylinder; **un motor de cuatro ～s** a four-cylinder engine

cima *f* (de montaña) top, summit; (de árbol) top; (de profesión) top; (de carrera) peak, height; **está en la ～ de su carrera** she is at the peak of her career

cimarra *f* (Chi): **hacer la ～** to play hooky (esp AmE colloq); to skive off (school) (BrE colloq)

cimentar [A1] *or* [A5] *vt* **(a)** ⟨*edificio*⟩ to lay the foundations of **(b)** (consolidar) to consolidate, strengthen **(c)** (basar) **～ algo EN algo** to base sth ON sth

cimientos *mpl* foundations (*pl*); **poner los ～ de algo** to lay the foundations of sth

cinc *m* ▶ ZINC

cincel *m* (de escultor, albañil) chisel; (de orfebre) graver

cincelar [A1] *vt* ⟨*piedra*⟩ to chisel, carve; ⟨*metal*⟩ to engrave

cinco *adj inv/pron* five; [*nótese que algunas frases requieren el uso del número ordinal 'fifth' en inglés*] **noventa y ～** ninety-five; **quinientos ～** five hundred and five; **la fila ～** row five, the fifth row; **vinimos los ～** the five of us came; **somos ～** there are five of us; **entraron de ～ en ～** they went in five at a time; **tiene ～ años** she's five (years old); **son las ～ de la mañana** it's five (o'clock) in the morning; **las ocho y ～** five after (AmE) *o* (BrE) past eight; **～ para las dos** (AmL exc RPl) five to two; *ver tb* MENOS *prep* 2 B; **hoy estamos a ～** today is the fifth
■ *m* **1** (número) (number) five; **el ～ de corazones** the five of hearts
2 (Per) (momento) moment

cincuenta *adj inv/m/pron* fifty; **los (años) ～** *or* **la década de los ～** the fifties; **tiene unos ～** ⋯⋗

años she's about 50 years old; ~ **y tantos/pico** fifty-odd, fifty something; **la página** ~ page fifty; **el** ~ **aniversario** the fiftieth anniversary
cincuentón -tona *adj* (fam): **es** ~ he's in his fifties
■ *m,f* (fam): **una cincuentona** a woman in her fifties
cine *m* **(a)** (arte, actividad) cinema; **el** ~ **francés** French cinema; **actor de** ~ movie *o* film actor; **hacer** ~ to make movies **(b)** (local) movie house *o* theater (AmE), cinema (BrE); **¿vamos al** ~? shall we go to the movies (AmE) *o* (BrE) cinema?; ~ **de barrio** local movie theater (AmE), local cinema (BrE); ~ **de estreno** *movie theater where new releases are shown*
cineasta *mf* filmmaker, moviemaker (AmE)
cineclub, cine-club *m* film club
cinéfilo -la *m,f* movie buff, cinema buff (BrE)
cinematografía *f* cinematography
cinematográfico -ca *adj* movie (*before n*), film (BrE) (*before n*)
cínico -ca *adj* cynical
■ *m,f* cynic
cinismo *m* cynicism
cinta *f* **(a)** (para adornar, envolver) ribbon; ~ **adhesiva** (en papelería) adhesive tape; (Med) sticking plaster; ~ **durex®** (AmL excl CS) *or* (AmL) **scotch®** *or* (Col) **pegante** Scotch tape® (AmE), Sellotape® (BrE); ~ **métrica** tape measure; ~ **negra** (Méx) *mf* (Dep) black belt; ~ **transportadora** conveyor belt **(b)** (en gimnasia rítmica) ribbon; (en carreras) tape **(c)** (Audio, Video) tape; ~ **virgen** blank tape; ~ **de video** *or* (Esp) **vídeo** videotape
cintura *f* (de persona, prenda) waist; **me tomó de la** ~ he grabbed me round the waist; **me queda grande de** ~ it's too big for me round the waist
cinturilla *f* waistband
cinturón *m* **(a)** (Indum) belt; ~ **de castidad** chastity belt; ~ **de seguridad** seat belt, safety belt; ~ **negro/verde** (Dep) black/green belt **(b)** (de ciudad) belt; **el** ~ **industrial** the industrial belt
ciprés *m* cypress
circo *m* (Espec, Hist) circus
circuito *m* **(a)** (pista) track, circuit; (de circo, exposición) circuit **(b)** (Elec, Electrón) circuit
circulación *f* **(a)** (en general) circulation; **tener mala** ~ to have poor circulation **(b)** (movimiento) movement; (Auto) traffic
circular¹ *adj* circular; **de forma** ~ circular
■ *f* circular
circular² [A1] *vi* **(a)** «*sangre/savia*» to circulate, flow; «*agua/corriente*» to flow **(b)** «*transeúnte/peatón*» to walk; (referido al tráfico): **circulan por la izquierda** they drive on the left **(c)** «*autobús/tren*» (estar de servicio) to run, operate **(d)** «*dinero/billete/sello*» to be in circulation **(e)** «*noticia/rumor/memo*» to circulate, go around
■ ~ *vt* to circulate
circulatorio -ria *adj* circulation (*before n*)
círculo *m* **(a)** (en general) circle; **coloca las mesas en** ~ arrange the tables in a circle; **en**

(los) ~**s teatrales** in theatrical circles; **C**~ **Polar Antártico/Ártico** Antarctic/Arctic Circle; ~ **vicioso** vicious circle **(b)** (asociación) society; ~ **de Bellas Artes** Fine Arts Association *o* Society
circuncisión *f* circumcision
circundante *adj* surrounding (*before n*)
circunferencia *f* **(a)** (Mat) circle; **dibujar una** ~ to draw a circle **(b)** (perímetro) circumference; **tiene 1 km de** ~ it has a circumference of 1 km
circunscripción *f* (distrito) district
circunstancia *f* **1** (particularidad): **si por alguna** ~ **no puede ir** if for any reason you cannot go; **se da la** ~ **de que ...** as it happens ...; **bajo ninguna** ~ under no circumstances
2 circunstancias *fpl* (situación) circumstances (*pl*); **dadas las** ~**s** given the circumstances; **debido a sus** ~**s familiares** due to her family situation
cirio *m* candle
cirrosis *f* cirrhosis
ciruela *f* (Bot, Coc) plum; ~ **pasa** *or* (CS) **seca** prune
ciruelo *m* plum tree
cirugía *f* surgery; **hacerse la** ~ **estética/plástica** to have cosmetic/plastic surgery
cirujano -na *m,f* surgeon; ~ **dentista** dental surgeon
Cisjordania *f* the West Bank
cisma *m* (Rel) schism; (en partido) split
cisne *m* (Zool) swan
cisterna *f* (depósito) tank; (subterránea) cistern; (del retrete) cistern
cistitis *f* cystitis
cita *f* **1** **(a)** (con profesional) appointment; **pedir** ~ to make an appointment; **concertar una** ~ to arrange an appointment **(b)** (con novio, amigo): **tengo una** ~ **con mi novio/con un amigo** I have a date with my boyfriend/I'm going out with a friend; **faltó a la** ~ he didn't show up (colloq); ~**s por computadora** *or* (Esp) **ordenador** computer dating **2** (en texto, discurso) quote; **una** ~ **de Cervantes** a quotation *o* quote from Cervantes
citadino -na *adj* (AmL) urban, city (*before n*)
■ *m,f* **(a)** (AmL) (ciudadano) city dweller **(b)** (Méx) (defeño) inhabitant of México City
citar [A1] *vt* **1** **(a)** (dar una cita) «*doctor/jefe de personal*» to give ... an appointment; **estar citado con algn** to have an appointment with sb **(b)** (convocar): **nos citó a todos a una reunión** she called us all to a meeting **(c)** (Der) to summon; ~ **a algn como testigo** to call sb as a witness **2** **(a)** (mencionar) to mention **(b)** «*escritor/pasaje*» to quote
■ **citarse** *v pron* ~**se con algn** to arrange to meet sb; **se** ~**on en la plaza** (recípr) they arranged to meet in the square
citófono *m* (Andes) internal phone system
citología *f* (análisis) smear test
cítrico¹ -ca *adj* citrus (*before n*)
cítrico² *m* citrus

ciudad f town; (de mayor tamaño) city; **❾ centro ciudad** town o city center; **~ balneario** (AmL) coastal resort; **C~ del Vaticano/de México** Vatican/Mexico City; **~ dormitorio** bedroom community (AmE), dormitory town (BrE); **~ perdida** (Méx) shantytown; **~ satélite** satellite town; **~ universitaria** university campus

ciudadanía f **(a)** (nacionalidad) citizenship **(b)** (conjunto de ciudadanos) citizenry (frml), citizens (pl)

ciudadano -na adj ‹vida› city (before n); **la inseguridad ciudadana** the lack of safety in towns o cities; **es un deber ~** it's the duty of every citizen
■ m,f (habitante) citizen

cívico -ca adj **(a)** ‹deberes/derechos› civic **(b)** ‹acto› public-spirited, civic-minded

civil adj **(a)** ‹derechos/responsabilidades› civil **(b)** (no religioso) civil; **casarse por lo ~** or (Per, RPl, Ven) **sólo por ~** or (Chi, Méx) **por el ~** to be married in a civil ceremony (AmE), to have a registry office wedding (BrE) **(c)** (no militar) civilian (before n); **iba (vestido) de ~** he was in civilian clothes
■ mf **(a)** (persona no militar) civilian **(b)** (Esp) (guardia civil) Civil Guard

civilización f civilization

civilizado -da adj civilized

civilizar [A4] vt ‹país/pueblo› to civilize; ‹persona› to teach … to behave properly
■ **civilizarse** v pron «pueblo» to become civilized; «persona» to learn to behave properly

civismo m public-spiritedness

cizaña f darnel

clamar [A1] vi **~ CONTRA algo** to protest AGAINST sth; **~ POR algo** to clamor* FOR sth, cry out FOR sth
■ **~** vt: **~ venganza** to cry out for vengeance

clamor m clamor*

clamoroso -sa adj ‹acogida› rousing (before n); ‹ovación› rapturous, thunderous; ‹éxito› resounding (before n)

clan m clan

clandestinidad f secrecy, secret nature; **trabajar en la ~** to work underground; **pasar a la ~** to go underground

clandestino -na adj ‹reunión/relación› clandestine, secret; ‹periódico› underground
■ m,f (fam) illegal immigrant

claqué m tap (dancing); **bailar ~** to tap dance

claqueta f clapperboard

clara f **(a)** tb **~ de huevo** (egg) white **(b)** (Esp) (bebida) shandy

claraboya f skylight

clarear [A1] v impers **(a)** (amanecer): **estaba clareando** it was getting light o day was breaking **(b)** (Meteo): **comenzó a ~** the sky/the clouds began to clear
■ **~** vi «pelo» to go gray*/white

clarete m (rosado) rosé; (tinto) claret

claridad f **(a)** (luz) light **(b)** (luminosidad) brightness **(c)** (de explicación, imagen, sonido) clarity; **con ~** clearly

clarificar [A2] vt to clarify

clarín m bugle

clarinete m clarinet

clarinetista mf clarinetist

clarividente adj (que adivina el futuro) clairvoyant; (perspicaz) discerning, clear-sighted
■ mf clairvoyant

claro¹ -ra adj **(a)** (luminoso) ‹cielo/habitación› bright **(b)** (pálido) ‹color/verde/azul› light, pale; ‹piel› fair; **tiene los ojos ~s** she has blue/green/gray eyes **(c)** ‹salsa/sopa› thin **(d)** ‹agua/sonido› clear; ‹ideas/explicación/instrucciones› clear; ‹situación/postura› clear; **tener algo ~** to be clear about sth; **¿está ~?** is that clear?; **quiero dejar (en) ~ que …** I want to make it clear that …; **sacar algo en ~ de algo** to make sense of sth **(e)** (evidente) clear, obvious; **está ~ que …** it is clear o obvious that …; **a no ser, ~ está, que esté mintiendo** unless, of course, he's lying

claro² adv **①** ‹ver› clearly; **voy a hablarte ~** I'm not going to beat around o about the bush; **me lo dijo muy ~** he made it very quite clear (to me) **②** (indep) (en exclamaciones de asentimiento) of course
■ m **(a)** (en bosque) clearing; (en pelo, barba) bald patch **(b)** (Meteo) sunny spell o period

clase f **①** (tipo) kind, sort, type; **distintas ~s de arroz** different kinds of rice
② (Transp, Sociol) class; **viajar en segunda ~** to travel (in) second class; **~ económica** or **turista** economy o tourist class; **~ ejecutiva** or **preferente** business class; **~ alta/baja/media** upper/lower/middle class; **~ dirigente** or **dominante** ruling class; **~ obrera** working class
③ (a) (distinción, elegancia) class; **tiene ~** she has class **(b)** (categoría): **productos de primera ~** top-quality products
④ (Educ) **(a)** (lección) class; **~s de conducir** or **manejar** driving lessons; **dictar ~** (DE algo) (AmL frml) to lecture (IN sth); **dar ~** or (Chi) **hacer ~s** (DE algo) ‹profesor› to teach (sth); **da ~s de piano** (Esp) she has piano lessons; **~ particular** private class o lesson **(b)** (grupo de alumnos) class **(c)** (aula — en escuela) classroom; (— en universidad) lecture hall o room

clásico¹ -ca adj **(a)** ‹lengua/mundo› classical; ‹decoración/estilo/ropa› classical **(b)** ‹método› standard, traditional; ‹error/malentendido/caso› classic

clásico² m **(a)** (obra) classic **(b)** (AmL) (Dep) traditional big game

clasificación f **①** (de documentos, animales, plantas) classification; (de cartas) sorting **②** (de película) certificate **③ (a)** (Dep) (para una etapa posterior) qualification; **partido de ~** qualifying match **(b)** (tabla) placings (pl); (puesto) position, place; **quinto en la ~ final del rally** fifth in the final placings for the rally

clasificador m **(a)** (carpeta) ring binder **(b)** (de una máquina) sorter **(c)** (mueble) filing cabinet

clasificar [A2] vt **(a)** ‹documentos/datos› to sort, put in order; ‹cartas› to sort **(b)** ‹planta/animal/elemento› to classify **(c)** ‹hotel› to class, rank; ‹fruta› to class; ‹persona› to class, rank
■ **clasificarse** v pron (Dep) **(a)** (para etapa posterior) to qualify; **~ para la final** to qualify for the final **(b)** (en tabla, carrera): **se clasificó en sexto lugar** he finished in sixth place

clasista adj ‹actitud/sociedad› classist; ‹persona› class-conscious

claustro *m* (a) (Arquit, Relig) cloister (b) (Educ) (de universidad) senate; (de colegio) staff; (reunión) senate/staff meeting

claustrofobia *f* claustrophobia; **siento ∼ allí dentro** I get claustrophobia in there

cláusula *f* clause

clausura *f* (a) (de congreso, festival) closing ceremony; **de ∼** ⟨ceremonia/discurso⟩ closing (*before n*) (b) (de local) closure

clausurar [A1] *vt* (a) ⟨congreso/sesión⟩ «*acto/discurso*» to bring ... to a close; «*persona*» to close (b) ⟨local/estadio⟩ to close ... down

clavada *f* (Méx) (en natación) dive

clavadista *mf* (Méx) diver

clavado¹ -da *adj* ⨇¹⨈ (a) **∼ EN algo** ⟨puñal/tachuela/espina⟩ stuck IN sth; ⟨estaca⟩ driven INTO sth (b) (fijo): **con la vista clavada en un punto** staring at a point, with his gaze fixed on a point; **se quedó ∼ en el lugar** he was rooted to the spot ⨇²⨈ (fam) (a) (idéntico) **ser ∼ A algn** «*persona*» to be the spitting image of sb (colloq); **ser ∼ A algo** «*objeto*» to be identical TO sth (b) (en punto): **llegó a las cinco clavadas** he arrived on the dot of five (colloq)

clavado² *m* (AmL) dive

clavar [A1] *vt* ⨇¹⨈ (a) **∼ algo EN algo** ⟨clavo⟩ to hammer sth INTO sth; ⟨puñal/cuchillo⟩ to stick sth IN sth; ⟨estaca⟩ to drive sth INTO sth; **me clavó los dientes/las uñas** he sank his teeth/dug his nails into me (b) ⟨cartel/estante⟩ to put up (*with nails, etc*) (c) ⟨ojos/vista⟩ to fix ... on ⨇²⨈ (fam) (a) (cobrar caro) to rip ... off (colloq); **nos ∼on $10,000** they stung us for $10,000 (b) (CS) (engañar) to cheat (c) (Méx) (robar) to swipe (colloq), to filch (colloq)

■ **clavarse** *v pron* ⨇¹⨈ (a) ⟨aguja⟩ to stick ... into one's finger (*o thumb etc*); **me clavé una espina en el dedo** I got a thorn in my finger (b) (*refl*) ⟨cuchillo/puñal⟩: **se clavó el puñal en el pecho** he plunged the dagger into his chest ⨇²⨈ (CS fam) **∼se CON algo** (por no poder venderlo) to get stuck WITH sth (colloq); (por ser mala compra): **se clavó con el auto que compró** the car turned out to be a bad buy ⨇³⨈ (Méx) (Dep) to dive

clave *adj* (*pl ∼ o* **-ves**) key (*before n*); **un factor ∼** a key factor

■ *f* (a) (código) code; **en ∼** in code; **∼ de acceso** (Inf) password (b) (de problema, misterio) key (c) (Mús) clef; **∼ de fa/sol** bass/treble clef

■ *m* harpsichord

clavel *m* carnation

clavicordio *m* clavichord

clavícula *f* collarbone, clavicle (tech)

clavija *f* (a) (Mec) pin (b) (Elec) (enchufe) plug; (de enchufe) pin (c) (de guitarra) tuning peg

clavo *m* (a) (Tec) nail; **dar en el ∼** to hit the nail on the head (b) (Med) pin (c) (en montañismo) piton (d) (Bot, Coc) *tb* **∼ de olor** clove

claxon /'klakson/ *m* (*pl* **-xons**) horn; **tocar el ∼** to sound *o* blow one's horn, to honk

clemencia *f* mercy, clemency (frml)

clementina *f* clementine

cleptómano -na *m,f* kleptomaniac

clérigo -ga *m,f* ⨇¹⨈ (en el clero protestante) (*m*)

clergyman, cleric; (*f*) clergywoman, cleric ⨇²⨈ **clérigo** *m* (en el clero católico) clergyman, priest

clero *m* clergy

clic *m* (*pl* **clics**) click; (al romperse algo) snap; **hacer doble ∼** (Inf) to double-click

cliché *m* (a) (expresión, idea) cliché (b) (de multicopista) stencil; (Impr) plate; (Fot) negative

cliente -ta *m,f* (de tienda, restaurante) customer; (de empresa, abogado) client; (de hotel) guest; (en taxi) fare, customer; **∼ habitual** regular customer (*o* client *etc*)

clientela *f* (de tienda, restaurante) clientele, customers (*pl*); (de hotel) guests (*pl*); (de abogado) clients (*pl*)

clima *m* (a) (Meteo) climate (b) (ambiente) atmosphere; **un ∼ festivo** a festive atmosphere; **el ∼ económico** the economic climate

climatizado -da *adj* ⟨local/casa⟩ air-conditioned; ⟨piscina⟩ heated

climax *m* (*pl* **∼**) climax

clínica *f* private hospital *o* clinic; **∼ dental** dental office (AmE), dental surgery (BrE); **∼ de reposo** convalescent *o* rest home

clínico -ca *adj* ⟨ensayo⟩ clinical (*before n*); ▶ HOSPITAL

■ *m,f* (RPl) general practitioner

clip *m* (*pl* **clips**) ⨇¹⨈ (a) (sujetapapeles) paperclip (b) (para el pelo) bobby pin (AmE), hairgrip (BrE) (c) (cierre) clip; **aretes** *or* **pendientes de ∼** clip-on earrings ⨇²⨈ (Video) (pop) video

cloaca *f* ⨇¹⨈ (alcantarilla) sewer ⨇²⨈ (de ave, reptil) cloaca

clon *m* clone

clonar [A1] *vt* to clone

cloro *m* (Quím) chlorine; (lejía) (AmC, Chi) bleach

clorofila *f* chlorophyll

clorofluorocarbono *m* chlorofluorocarbon, CFC

cloroformo *m* chloroform

clóset *m* (*pl* **-sets**) (AmL exc RPl) (en dormitorio) built-in closet (AmE), fitted *o* built-in wardrobe (BrE)

clotch /'klotʃ/ *m* ▶ CLUTCH

clown /'klaun/ *m* (*pl* **clowns**) clown

club *m* (*pl* **clubs** *or* **-es**) club; **∼ juvenil** youth club; **∼ nocturno** nightclub

clueca *adj* broody

clutch /'klotʃ/ *m* (AmC, Col, Méx, Ven) clutch

cm. (= **centímetro**) cm.

coacción *f* coercion; **bajo ∼** under duress

coaccionar [A1] *vt* to coerce

coagular [A1] *vt* to clot, coagulate

■ **coagularse** *v pron* to clot, coagulate

coágulo *m* clot

coalición *f* coalition; **gobierno de ∼** coalition government

coartada *f* alibi

coartar [A1] *vt* ⟨persona⟩ to inhibit; ⟨libertad/voluntad⟩ to restrict

coba *f* (Ven arg) (mentira, engaño) lie; **darle ∼ a algn** (adular) (Esp, Méx, Ven fam) to suck up to sb (colloq)

cobarde *adj* cowardly

■ *mf* coward

cobardía *f* cowardice; **fue una ∼** it was an act of cowardice

cobaya *f*, **cobayo** *m* guinea pig

cobertizo *m* shed

cobertura *f* (a) (de seguro) cover (b) (Period, Rad, TV) coverage; **∼ informativa** news coverage

cobija *f* (AmL) (a) (manta) blanket (b) **cobijas** *fpl* (ropa de cama) bedclothes (*pl*)

cobijar [A1] *vt* ⟨persona⟩ (proteger) to shelter; (hospedar) to give … shelter, take … in
■ **cobijarse** *v pron* to shelter, take shelter

cobijo *m* shelter; **darle ∼ a algn** to shelter sb

cobra *f* cobra

cobrador -dora *m,f* (a domicilio) collector; (de autobús) bus conductor

cobrar [A1] *vt* **1** (a) ⟨precio/suma/intereses⟩ to charge; **nos cobran 30.000 pesos de alquiler** they charge us 30,000 pesos in rent; **∼ algo POR algo/ hacer algo** to charge sth FOR sth/doing sth; **vino a ∼ el alquiler** she came for the rent *o* to collect the rent; **¿me cobra estas cervezas?** can I pay for these beers, please?; **me cobró el vino dos veces** he charged me twice for the wine (b) ⟨sueldo⟩ to earn; ⟨pensión⟩ to draw; **cobra 200.000 pesetas al mes** he earns/draws 200,000 pesetas a month; **todavía no hemos cobrado junio** we still haven't been paid for June (c) ⟨deuda⟩ to recover; **nunca llegó a ∼ esas facturas** he never received payment for those bills (d) ⟨cheque⟩ to cash **2** (a) (Chi) (pedir): **le cobré los libros que le presté** I asked him to give back the books I'd lent him (b) (Chi) ⟨gol/falta⟩ to give **3** (adquirir) ⟨fuerzas⟩ to gather; **∼ fama/ importancia** become famous/important **4** (period) ⟨vidas/víctimas⟩ to claim
■ *vi* (a) **∼ POR algo/hacer algo** to charge FOR sth/doing sth; **¿me cobra, por favor?** can you take for this, please?, can I pay, please?; **llámame por ∼** (Chi, Méx) call collect (AmE), reverse the charges (BrE) (b) (recibir el sueldo) to be paid
■ **cobrarse** *v pron* (a) (recibir dinero): **tenga, cóbrese** here you are; **cóbrese las cervezas** can you take for the beers, please? (b) (period) ⟨vidas/ víctimas⟩ to claim

cobre *m* (Metal, Quím) copper

cobrizo -za *adj* coppery, copper-colored*

cobro *m* (a) (de cheque) cashing; (de sueldo, pensión): **para el ∼ de la pensión** in order to collect your pension (b) (Telec): **llamó a ∼ revertido** she called collect (AmE), she reversed the charges (BrE)

coca *f* (Bot) coca; (cocaína) (arg) coke (sl)

cocaína *f* cocaine

cocainómano -na *m,f* cocaine addict

cocaví *m* (Chi) things to eat

cocer [E10] *vt* (a) (Coc) (cocinar) to cook; (hervir) to boil; **∼ algo a fuego lento** to simmer sth, cook sth over a low heat (b) ⟨ladrillos/cerámica⟩ to fire
■ **cocerse** *v pron* **1** «verduras/arroz» (hacerse) to cook; (hervir) to boil; **tardan unos 15 minutos en ∼se** they take about 15 minutes to cook **2** (Chi) «bebé» to have a diaper (AmE) *o* (BrE) nappy rash

coche *m* (a) (Auto) car, auto (AmE), automobile (AmE); **nos llevó en ∼ a la estación** he drove us to the station; **∼ bomba** car bomb; **∼ de bomberos** fire engine, fire truck (AmE); **∼ de carreras**

racing car; **∼ de choque** bumper car; **∼ fúnebre** hearse (b) (Ferr) car (AmE), carriage (BrE); **∼ cama** *o* (CS) **dormitorio** sleeper, sleeping car (c) (de bebé) baby carriage (AmE), pram (BrE); (en forma de sillita) stroller (AmE), pushchair (BrE) (d) (carruaje) coach, carriage; **∼ de caballos** carriage

cochera *f* (a) (para autobuses) depot, garage; **las ∼s** the depot (b) (garaje) (Esp, Méx) garage

cochinada *f* (a) (fam) (suciedad) filth (b) (palabra, acción): **¡no digas esas ∼s!** don't use such filthy language!; **eso es una ∼** that's a disgusting thing to do (c) (mala pasada) dirty trick

cochino -na *adj* (a) (fam) (sucio) ⟨persona/ manos⟩ filthy (b) (fam) (indecoroso) ⟨persona⟩ disgusting; ⟨revista/película⟩ dirty (colloq) (c) (Chi) (Dep, Jueg) (violento) dirty (colloq); (tramposo): **es muy ∼** he's a terrible cheat
■ *m,f* (a) (Zool) pig, hog (AmE) (b) (fam) (persona sucia) filthy pig (colloq), slob (colloq)

cocido¹ -da *adj* (a) (hervido) ⟨huevos/verduras⟩ boiled (b) (CS) (no crudo) cooked; **muy/poco ∼** well done/rare (c) ⟨arcilla⟩ fired

cocido² *m* (a) (Esp) stew (*made with meat and chickpeas*) (b) (Col, Ven) stew (*made with meat, plantains and cassava*)

cociente *m* quotient

cocina *f* (a) (habitación) kitchen (b) (aparato) stove, cooker (BrE); **∼ de** *o* **a gas** gas stove *o* (BrE) cooker; **∼ eléctrica** electric stove *o* (BrE) cooker (c) (arte) cookery; (gastronomía) cuisine; **libro de ∼** cookbook, cookery book (BrE); **la ∼ casera** home cooking

cocinar [A1] *vt/vi* to cook; **¿quién cocina en tu casa?** who does the cooking in your house?

cocinero -ra *m,f* cook

cocineta *f* (Méx) (cocina) kitchenette

cocinilla *f* camp stove (AmE), camping stove (BrE)

cocktail /'koktel/ *m* (*pl* **-tails**) ▶ CÓCTEL

coco *m* (a) (Bot, Coc) coconut (b) (fam) (cabeza) head; **está mal del ∼** he's off his head (colloq) (c) (fam) (fantasma, espantajo) boogeyman (AmE), bogeyman (BrE)

cocoa *f* (AmL) cocoa

cocodrilo *m* crocodile

cocol *m* (Méx) (bizcocho) cookie (*covered in sesame seeds*)

cocotero *m* coconut palm

cóctel *m* (*pl* **-teles** *or* **-tels**) (a) (bebida) cocktail; **∼ de frutas** (AmC, Col) fruit salad, fruit cocktail; **∼ de gambas** (Esp) shrimp (AmE) *o* (BrE) prawn cocktail; **∼ Molotov** Molotov cocktail (b) (fiesta) cocktail party

cocuyo *m* (a) (AmL) (insecto) firefly (b) (Col, Ven) (Auto) parking light (AmE), sidelight (BrE)

codazo *m*: **darle un ∼ a algn** (leve) to nudge sb; (fuerte) to elbow sb; **se abrió camino a ∼s** he elbowed his way through

codearse [A1] *v pron* **∼ CON algn** to rub shoulders WITH sb

codera *f* (Indum) elbow patch

codicia *f* (avaricia) greed, avarice

codiciar [A1] *vt* to covet

codicioso -sa *adj* ⟨persona/mirada⟩ covetous, greedy
■ *m,f* covetous *o* greedy person

codificar [A2] *vt* **(a)** ‹leyes/normas› to codify **(b)** (Inf) ‹información› to code **(c)** (Ling) ‹mensaje› to encode

código *m* **(a)** (de signos) code; ~ **barrado** *or* **de barras** bar code; ~ **postal** zipcode (AmE), postcode (BrE) **(b)** (de leyes, normas) code; ~ **de la circulación** Highway Code

codillo *m* **(a)** (Zool) elbow **(b)** (Coc) knuckle

codo¹ -da *adj* (Méx fam) tightfisted (colloq)

codo² *m* elbow; ~ **con** *or* **a** ~ side by side; **empinar el** ~ (fam) to prop up the bar; **hablar (hasta) por los** ~**s** (fam) to talk nineteen to the dozen (colloq)

codorniz *f* quail

coeficiente *m* (Mat) coefficient; ~ **intelectual** *or* **de inteligencia** IQ, intelligence quotient

coexistir [I1] *vi* to coexist

cofia *f* cap

cofradía *f* (Relig) brotherhood

cofre *m* **(a)** (joyero) jewel case, jewelry* box **(b)** (arcón) chest **(c)** (Méx) (capó) hood (AmE), bonnet (BrE)

coger [E6] *vt* **1** **(a)** (tomar) to take; **lo cogió del brazo** she took him by the arm; **coge un folleto** pick up *o* take a leaflet **(b)** (quitar) to take; **siempre me está cogiendo los lápices** she's always taking my pencils **(c)** ‹flores/fruta› to pick **(d)** (levantar) to pick up; **coge esa revista del suelo** pick that magazine up off the floor; **no cogen el teléfono** (Esp) they're not answering the phone
2 (atrapar) (esp Esp) **(a)** ‹ladrón/pelota› to catch **(b)** ‹pescado/liebre› to catch **(c)** (descubrir) to catch; **lo cogieron robando** he was caught stealing **(d)** ‹toro› to gore
3 **(a)** ‹tren/autobús/taxi› to catch, take **(b)** ‹calle/camino› to take
4 (Esp fam) **(a)** (obtener) ‹billete/entrada› to get; ~ **hora para el médico** to make an appointment to see the doctor; ~ **sitio** to save a place **(b)** (aceptar) ‹dinero/trabajo/casa› to take **(c)** (admitir) ‹alumnos/solicitudes› to take
5 (esp Esp) (adquirir) **(a)** ‹enfermedad› to catch; ‹insolación› to get; **vas a** ~ **frío** you'll catch cold **(b)** ‹acento› to pick up; ‹costumbre/vicio› to pick up; **le cogí cariño** I got quite fond of him
6 (esp Esp) (captar) ‹sentido/significado› to get **(b)** ‹emisora› to pick up, get
7 (Méx, RPl, Ven vulg) to screw (vulg), to fuck (vulg)
■ ~ *vi* **1** (esp Esp) ‹planta› to take; ‹tinte/permanente› to take
2 (Méx, RPl, Ven vulg) to screw (vulg), to fuck (vulg)
■ **cogerse** *v pron* (esp Esp) **(a)** (agarrarse, sujetarse) to hold on; **cógete de la barandilla** hold on to the railing **(b)** (recípr): **se cogieron de la mano** they held hands

cogida *f* (Taur) goring; **sufrió una** ~ he was gored

cognac *m* brandy

cogollo *m* (de lechuga, col) heart; (de hinojo) bulb

cogote *m* (fam) (nuca) scruff of the neck; (cuello) (AmL) neck

cohabitar [A1] *vi* (frml) to cohabit (frml), to live together

coherencia *f* **(a)** (congruencia) coherence, logic; **con** ~ coherently *o* logically **(b)** (consecuencia) consistency; **actuar con** ~ to be consistent **(c)** (Fís) coherence

coherente *adj* **(a)** (congruente) ‹discurso/razonamiento› coherent, logical **(b)** (consecuente) ‹actitud› consistent; **una mujer** ~ a woman who acts according to her beliefs

cohesión *f* **(a)** (de ideas, pensamientos) coherence **(b)** (en grupo) cohesion, unity

cohete *m* **1** (Espac, Mil) rocket **2 cohetes** *mpl* fireworks (*pl*)

cohibido -da *adj* (tímido) shy; (inhibido) inhibited; (incómodo) awkward

cohibir [I22] *vt* **(a)** (inhibir) to inhibit; **su presencia me cohíbe** I feel inhibited in front of him **(b)** (hacer sentir incómodo): **hablar en público lo cohíbe** he feels awkward about speaking in public
■ **cohibirse** *v pron* **(a)** (inhibirse) to feel inhibited **(b)** (sentirse incómodo) to feel awkward

coincidencia *f* **(a)** (casualidad) coincidence; **se dio la** ~ **de que él también estaba allá** by coincidence *o* chance he was there too; **¡que** ~! what a coincidence! **(b)** (de opiniones) agreement

coincidir [I1] *vi* **(a)** ‹fechas/sucesos/líneas› to coincide; ‹dibujos› to match up; ‹versiones/resultados› to coincide, match up, tally; ~ **CON algo** to coincide (*o* match up etc) **WITH sth (b)** (en opiniones, gustos): **coinciden en sus gustos** they share the same tastes; **todos coincidieron en que ...** everyone agreed that ...; ~ **CON algn** to agree **WITH sb (c)** (en un lugar): **a veces coincidimos en el supermercado** we sometimes see each other in the supermarket

coito *m* intercourse, coitus (frml)

cojear [A1] *vi* **(a)** (por herida, dolor) to limp; (permanentemente) to be lame; **entró cojeando** he limped *o* hobbled in **(b)** ‹silla/mesa› to wobble **(c)** (fam) ‹explicación/definición› to fall short

cojera *f* limp

cojín *m* cushion

cojo -ja *adj* **(a)** ‹persona/animal› lame; **está** ~ **del pie derecho** he's lame in his right leg; **andar a la pata coja** *or* (Méx) **brincar de cojito** (fam) to hop **(b)** ‹mesa/silla› wobbly **(c)** (fam) ‹razonamiento› shaky, weak
■ *m,f* lame person

cojones *mpl* (vulg) (testículos) balls (*pl*) (sl *o* vulg); **estar hasta los** ~ (vulg) to be pissed off (sl); **tener** ~ (vulg) to have guts (colloq), to have balls (sl)

col *f* (Esp, Méx) cabbage; ~ **de Bruselas** Brussels sprout

cola *f* **1** **(a)** (Zool) tail; ~ **de caballo** (en el pelo) ponytail **(b)** (de vestido) train; (de frac) tails (*pl*) **(c)** (de avión, cometa) tail **(d)** (RPl fam) (nalgas) bottom (colloq)
2 (fila) line (AmE), queue (BrE); **hacer** ~ to line up (AmE), to queue (up) (BrE); **pónganse a la** ~

AmC	Central America	Arg	Argentina	Cu	Cuba	Per	Peru
AmL	Latin America	Bol	Bolivia	Ec	Ecuador	RPl	River Plate Area
AmS	South America	Chi	Chile	Esp	Spain	Ur	Uruguay
Andes	Andean Region	CS	Southern Cone	Méx	Mexico	Ven	Venezuela

por favor please join the (end of the) line *o* queue; **brincarse la ~** (Méx) to jump the line *o* queue; **a la ~ del pelotón** at the tail end of the group

[3] **(a)** (pegamento) glue; **~ de contacto** superglue **(b)** (bebida) Coke®, cola

[4] (Ven) (Auto): **pedir ~** to hitchhike; **darle la ~ a algn** to give sb a lift *o* a ride

colaboración *f* collaboration; **en ~ con algn/algo** in collaboration with sb/sth

colaborador -dora *m,f* (en revista) contributor; (en tarea) collaborator

colaborar [A1] *vi* to collaborate; **~ CON algn** to collaborate WITH sb; **~ con dinero** to contribute some money; **~ EN algo** ⟨*en proyecto/tarea*⟩ to collaborate ON sth; ⟨*en revista*⟩ to contribute TO sth

colada *f* (Esp) (lavado) laundry, washing

coladera *f* **(a)** (Méx) (sumidero) drain **(b)** (Col) ▶ COLADOR

colador *m* (para té) tea strainer; (para pastas, verduras) colander

colapso *m* **(a)** (Med) collapse; **sufrió un ~** he collapsed **(b)** (paralización) standstill

colar [A10] *vt* **(a)** ⟨*verdura/pasta*⟩ to strain, drain; ⟨*caldo/té*⟩ to strain **(b)** ⟨*billete falso*⟩ to pass

■ *vi* (fam) «*cuento/historia*»: **no va a ~** it won't wash (colloq)

■ **colarse** *v pron* (fam) **(a)** (en cola) to jump the line (AmE) *o* (BrE) queue **(b)** (entrar a hurtadillas) to sneak in; (en cine, autobús) to sneak in without paying (colloq); (en fiesta) to gatecrash

colcha *f* bedspread

colchón *m* (de cama) mattress; **~ de muelles** sprung mattress

colchoneta *f* (de playa) air bed, Lilo® (BrE); (de gimnasia) mat; (de cama) (Méx) comforter (AmE), duvet (BrE)

colección *f* collection

coleccionar [A1] *vt* to collect

coleccionista *mf* collector

colecta *f* (de donativos) collection; **hacer una ~** (para comprar un regalo) to have a collection; (con fines caritativos) to collect

colectar [A1] *vt* to collect

colectivero -ra *m,f* (de autobús) (Arg) bus driver

colectividad *f* group, community; **en ~** collectively

colectivo¹ -va *adj* collective

colectivo² *m* **(a)** (periodo) (agrupación) group **(b)** (Andes) (taxi) collective taxi ⟨*with a fixed route and fare*⟩ **(c)** (Arg) (autobús) bus **(d)** (Per, Ur) (para regalo) collection

colega *mf* **(a)** (de profesión) colleague **(b)** (homólogo) counterpart **(c)** (fam) (amigo) buddy (AmE), mate (BrE colloq)

colegiado -da *m,f* (profesional) member (*of a professional association*)

colegial -giala *m,f* (de colegio) (*m*) schoolboy; (*f*) schoolgirl; **los ~es** (the) schoolchildren

colegiatura *f* (Méx) school fees (*pl*)

colegio *m* **(a)** (Educ) school; **los niños están en el ~** the children are at school; **un ~ de monjas** convent school; **un ~ de curas** a Catholic boys'

school; **~ privado** *or* **de pago** fee-paying *o* private school; **~ electoral** electoral college; **~ estatal** *or* **público** public school (AmE), state school (BrE) **(b)** (de profesionales): **C~ de Abogados** ≈ Bar Association; **C~ Oficial de Médicos** ≈ Medical Association

colegir [I8] *vt* to deduce

cólera *m* cholera

■ *f* rage, anger

colérico -ca *adj* **(a)** [ESTAR] (furioso) furious **(b)** [SER] (malhumorado) quick-tempered

colesterol *m* cholesterol

coleta *f* ponytail; (de torero) braid (AmE), ponytail (BrE)

coletazo *m* **(a)** (con la cola) thrash of the tail; **dar ~s** to thrash about **(b)** (Auto): **el coche dio un ~** the rear of the car skidded

coletilla *f* tag

colgado -da *adj*: **dejar a algn ~** (dejarlo en la estacada) to leave sb in the lurch; *ver tb* COLGAR

colgante *adj* hanging; ▶ PUENTE 1

■ *m* pendant

colgar [A8] *vt* **(a)** ⟨*cuadro*⟩ to hang, put up; ⟨*lámpara*⟩ to put up; ⟨*ropa lavada*⟩ to hang (out); **~ algo DE algo** to hang sth ON sth; **el abrigo estaba colgado de un gancho** the coat was hanging on a hook **(b)** (ahorcar) to hang **(c)** ⟨*teléfono/auricular*⟩ to put down; **tienen el teléfono mal colgado** their phone is off the hook

■ **~** *vi* **(a)** (pender) to hang; **colgaba del techo** it was hanging from the ceiling; **el vestido me cuelga de un lado** my dress is hanging down on one side **(b)** (Telec) to hang up; **no cuelgue, por favor** hold the line please, please hold; **me colgó** he hung up on me

■ **colgarse** *v pron* (*refl*) [1] **(a)** (ahorcarse) to hang oneself **(b)** (agarrarse, suspenderse): **no te cuelgues de ahí** don't hang off there; **no te cuelgues de mí** don't cling on to me; **se pasa colgada del teléfono** (fam) she spends her time on the phone

[2] (Chi, Méx) (Elec): **~se del suministro eléctrico** to tap into the electricity supply

colibrí *m* hummingbird

cólico *m* colic

coliflor *f* or (RPI) *m* cauliflower

colilla *f* (de cigarrillo) cigarette end *o* butt

colina *f* hill

colirio *m* eye drops (*pl*)

colisión *f* **(a)** (de trenes, aviones) collision, crash; **~ en cadena** pileup **(b)** (conflicto) conflict, clash

colitis *f* colitis

collado *m* (colina) hill; (entre montañas) pass

collage /koˈlaʒ/ *m* (*pl* **-llages**) collage

collar *m* **(a)** (alhaja) necklace; **~ de perlas** string of pearls **(b)** (para animales) collar **(c)** (plumaje) collar, ruff

colleras *fpl* (Chi) (gemelos) cuff links (*pl*)

colmado -da *adj* ⟨*cucharada*⟩ heaped; *ver tb* COLMAR

colmar [A1] *vt* **(a)** ⟨*vaso/cesta*⟩ to fill ... to the brim **(b)** ⟨*deseos/aspiraciones*⟩ to fulfill* **(c)** ⟨*paciencia*⟩ to stretch ... to the limit; **~ a algn DE algo** ⟨*de atenciones*⟩ to lavish sth on sb; ⟨*de regalos*⟩ to shower sb WITH sth

colmena *f* beehive

colmillo *m* (de persona) eyetooth, canine (tech); (de elefante, jabalí, morsa) tusk; (de perro, lobo) fang, canine

colmo *m*: el ∼ de la vagancia the height of laziness; para ∼ de desgracias to top *o* cap it all; sería el ∼ que … it would be too much if …; ¡esto es el ∼! this is the limit *o* the last straw!

colocación *f* (a) (empleo) job; buscar ∼ to look for a job (b) (acción) positioning, placing; (de losas, alfombra) laying

colocado -da *adj* **1** (en un trabajo): está muy bien ∼ he has a very good job; ya está ∼ he's found a job **2** (Esp) (a) (fam) (borracho) plastered (colloq) (b) (arg) (con drogas) stoned (colloq)

colocar [A2] *vt* **1** (a) (en lugar) to place, put; ⟨losas/alfombra⟩ to lay; ⟨cuadro⟩ to hang; ⟨bomba⟩ to plant (b) (Com, Fin) ⟨acciones⟩ to place; ⟨dinero⟩ to place, invest **2** ⟨persona⟩ (a) (en lugar) to put (b) (en trabajo) to get … a job
■ **colocarse** *v pron* (a) (situarse, ponerse): se colocó a mi lado she stood/sat beside me (b) (en trabajo) to get a job

colocho -cha *m,f* (AmC) (a) (persona) curly-haired person (b) **colocho** *m* (rizo) curl

Colombia *f* Colombia

colombiano -na *adj/m,f* Colombian

colón *m* colon (*Costa Rican and Salvadoran unit of currency*)

Colón (Hist) Columbus; Cristóbal ∼ Christopher Columbus

colonia *f* **1** (a) (Hist, Pol, Zool, Biol) colony (b) (de viviendas) residential development; ∼ militar housing estate (*for service families*); ∼ penal (Per) penal colony (c) (Méx) (barrio) quarter, district (d) (campamento) camp; ∼ de vacaciones holiday camp **2** (perfume) (eau de) cologne

colonial *adj* colonial

colonialismo *m* colonialism

colonización *f* colonization

colonizador -dora *m,f* colonizer

colonizar [A4] *vt* to colonize

colono *m* (a) (inmigrante) colonist (b) (Agr) (en tierras baldías) settler; (en tierras arrendadas) tenant farmer

coloquial *adj* colloquial

coloquio *m* (a) (debate) discussion, talk; (simposio) (AmL) colloquium, symposium; conferencia ∼ talk (*followed by discussion*) (b) (Lit) dialogue

color *m* (a) color*; ¿de qué ∼ es? what color is it?; cambiar de ∼ to change color; un sombrero de un ∼ oscuro/claro a dark/light hat; las de ∼ amarillo the yellow ones; ilustraciones a todo ∼ full color illustrations; cintas de ∼es colored ribbons; fotos en ∼es *or* (Esp) en ∼ color photos; sin distinción de credo ni ∼ regardless of creed or color; una chica de ∼ (euf) a colored girl (dated); tomar ∼ «pollo» to brown; «cebolla frita/pastel» to turn golden-brown; «fruta» to ripen; «piel» to become tanned; ponerse ∼ de hormiga (AmL) to start looking pretty grim; subido de ∼ (chiste) risqué (b) **colores** *mpl* (lápices) colored* pencils (*pl*), crayons (*pl*)

colorado¹ -da *adj* (a) red; ponerse ∼ to blush, turn red, go red (BrE) (b) (Méx fam) ⟨chiste⟩ risqué

colorado² *m* red

colorante *m* coloring*; ☻ no contiene colorantes no artificial colors

colorear [A1] *vt* (Art) to color*; ∼ algo DE algo to color* sth IN sth

colorete *m* blusher, rouge

colorido *m* colors* (*pl*); un desfile de gran ∼ a very colorful parade

colosal *adj* ⟨estatua/obra/fortuna⟩ colossal; ⟨ambiente/idea⟩ (fam) great (colloq)

coloso *m* (estatua) colossus; (gigante) giant

columna *f* (a) (Arquit) column, pillar (b) (Anat) *tb* ∼ VERTEBRAL spine, backbone (c) (Impr, Period, Mil) column

columnista *mf* columnist

columpiar [A1] *vt* to push (*on a swing*)
■ **columpiarse** *v pron* (*refl*) to swing

columpio *m* (Jueg, Ocio) swing (b) (sofá de jardín) couch hammock

colza *f* rape, colza; aceite de ∼ rapeseed oil

coma *m* (Med) coma; entrar en (estado de) ∼ to go into a coma
■ *f* (Ling) comma; ▶ PUNTO 1B (c) (Mat) point

comadre *f*: godmother of one's child or mother of one's godchild

comadreja *f* (mustélido) weasel

comadrona *f* midwife

comal *m* (Méx) ceramic dish or metal hotplate for cooking TORTILLAS 2

comandante *mf* (a) (en el ejército) major; (en las fuerzas aéreas) major (AmE), squadron leader (BrE); ∼ en jefe commander in chief (b) (oficial al mando) commanding officer (c) (Aviac) captain

comando *m* **1** (a) (grupo de combate) commando group; ∼ terrorista terrorist cell *o* squad (b) (AmL) (mando militar) command **2** (Inf) command

comarca *f* region

comarcal *adj* regional

comba *f* (a) (de viga, cable) sag; (de pared) bulge (b) (Esp) (Jueg) jump rope (AmE), skipping rope (BrE); saltar la ∼ to jump rope (AmE), to skip (BrE)

combarse [A1] *v pron* «viga/cable» to sag; «pared» to bulge; «disco» to warp

combate *m* (a) (Mil) combat; zona de ∼ combat zone; avión de ∼ fighter plane (b) (en boxeo) fight

combatiente *mf* combatant (frml); antiguo *or* ex ∼ veteran

combatir [I1] *vi* ⟨soldado/ejército⟩ to fight
■ ∼ *vt* ⟨enemigo/enfermedad/fuego⟩ to fight, to combat (frml); ⟨proyecto/propuesta⟩ to fight; ⟨frío⟩ to fight off

combativo -va *adj* (a) (luchador) spirited, combative; espíritu ∼ fighting spirit (b) (agresivo) combative

combi® *f* (Méx, Per, RPl) VW® van, combi (van) (BrE)

combinación *f* (a) (de colores, sabores) combination (b) (de caja fuerte) combination (c) (Mat) permutation (d) (Indum) slip (e) (Transp) connection

combinado *m* (a) (bebida) cocktail (b) (Andes period) (Dep) team, line-up (*journ*)

combinar [A1] *vt* (a) (en general) to combine

(b) ⟨colores⟩ to put together; ⟨ropa⟩ to coordinate; ~ **el rojo con el violeta** to put red and purple together

■ ~ *vi* ⟨⟨colores/ropa⟩⟩ to go together; ~ **CON algo** to go WITH sth

combustible *adj* combustible

■ *m* (Fís, Quím) combustible; (Transp) (carburante) fuel

combustión *f* combustion

comedero *m* (Agr) (para el ganado) feeding trough

comedia *f* (a) (Teatr) (obra) play; (cómica) comedy; ~ **musical** musical (b) (serie cómica) comedy series (c) (AmL) (telenovela) soap (opera); (radionovela) radio serial

comediante -ta *m,f* (a) (Teatr) (*m*) actor; (*f*) actress (b) (farsante) fraud

comedido -da *adj* (a) (moderado) moderate, restrained (b) (AmL) (atento) obliging, well-meaning

comedor *m* (a) (sala — en casa, hotel) dining room; (— en colegio, universidad) dining hall, refectory; (— en fábrica, empresa) canteen, cafeteria (b) (muebles) dining-room furniture

comedura de coco *f* (Esp fam) (a) (lavado de cerebro): **la tele es una ~ de ~** TV just tries to brainwash you (b) (preocupación): **tener una ~ de ~** to worry nonstop

comentar [A1] *vt* (a) ⟨suceso/película⟩ to talk about, discuss; ⟨obra/poema⟩ to comment on (b) (mencionar) to mention; (hacer una observación) to remark on; **comentó que …** he remarked that … (c) (CS) (Rad, TV) ⟨partido⟩ to commentate on

comentario *m* **1** (a) (observación) comment; **hacer un ~** to make a comment; **fue un ~ de mal gusto** it was a tasteless remark; **sin ~(s)** no comment (b) (mención): **no hagas ningún ~ sobre esto** don't mention this (c) (análisis) commentary; ~ **de texto** textual analysis **2** (Rad, TV) commentary

comentarista *mf* commentator

comenzar [A6] *vt* to begin, commence (frml)

■ ~ *vi* to begin; **al ~ el día** at the beginning of the day; ~ **haciendo algo/POR hacer algo** to begin BY doing sth; ~ **A hacer algo** to start doing *o* to do sth; **~on a disparar** they started firing *o* to fire; ~ **POR algo** to begin WITH sth

comer [E1] *vi* (a) (en general) to eat; **no tengo ganas de ~** I'm not hungry; **este niño no me come nada** (fam) this child won't eat anything (colloq); **dar(le) de ~ a algn (en la boca)** to spoonfeed sb; **darle de ~ al gato/al niño** to feed the cat/the kid; **salir a ~ (fuera)** to go out for a meal, to eat out; **¿qué hay de ~?** (a mediodía) what's for lunch?; (por la noche) what's for dinner *o* supper? (b) (esp Esp, Méx) (almorzar) to have lunch; **nos invitaron a ~** they asked us to lunch (c) (esp AmL) (cenar) to have dinner

■ ~ *vt* (a) ⟨fruta/verdura/carne⟩ to eat; **¿puedo ~ otro?** can I have another one?; **no tienen qué ~** they don't have anything to eat (b) (fam) (hacer desaparecer) ▶ COMERSE 3 (c) (en ajedrez, damas) to take

■ **comerse** *v pron* **1** (a) (al escribir) ⟨acento/ palabra⟩ to leave off; ⟨línea/párrafo⟩ to miss out (b) (al hablar) ⟨letra⟩ to leave off; ⟨palabra⟩ to swallow

2 (enf) ⟨comida⟩ to eat; **cómetelo todo** eat it all up; **~se las uñas** to bite one's nails

3 (fam) (hacer desaparecer) (a) «⟨acido/óxido⟩» to eat away (at); «⟨polilla/ratón⟩» to eat away (at) (b) «⟨inflación/alquiler⟩» ⟨sueldo/ahorros⟩ to eat away at

comercial *adj* (a) ⟨zona/operación/carta⟩ business (before n); **una firma ~** a company; **el déficit ~** the trade deficit; ▶ GALERÍA, CENTRO (b) ⟨película/arte⟩ commercial

■ *m* (a) (anuncio) commercial, advert (BrE) (b) (CS) (Educ) business school

comercializar [A4] *vt* ⟨producto⟩ to market; ⟨lugar/deporte⟩ to commercialize

■ **comercializarse** *v pron* to become commercialized

comerciante *mf* (a) (dueño de tienda) storekeeper (AmE), shopkeeper (BrE); (negociante) dealer, trader (b) (mercenario) money-grubber (colloq)

comerciar [A1] *vi* to trade, do business; ~ **EN algo** to trade *o* deal IN sth

comercio *m* (a) (actividad) trade; **el ~ de armas** the arms trade; **el mundo del ~** the world of commerce (b) (tiendas): **hoy cierra el ~** the stores (AmE) *o* (BrE) shops are closed today (c) (tienda) store (AmE), shop (BrE)

comestible *adj* edible

comestibles *mpl* food; **tienda de ~** grocery store (AmE), grocer's (shop) (BrE)

cometa *m* comet

■ *f* kite; **hacer volar una ~** *or* (RPI) **remontar una ~** to fly a kite

cometer [E1] *vt* ⟨crimen/delito/pecado⟩ to commit; ⟨error/falta⟩ to make

cometido *m* (a) (tarea, deber) task, mission (b) (Chi) (actuación) performance

comezón *f* (Med) itching, itch; **tenía ~ en la espalda** his back was itching

comic /'komik/, **cómic** *m* (*pl* **-mics**) (esp Esp) (tira ilustrada) comic strip; (revista) comic

comicios *mpl* elections (*pl*)

cómico -ca *adj* ⟨actor/género/obra⟩ comedy (before n); ⟨situación/mueca⟩ comical, funny

■ *m,f* (actor) comedy actor, comic actor; (humorista) comedian, comic

comida *f* (a) (en general) food; ~ **para perros** dog food; ~ **basura/rápida** junk/fast food (b) (ocasión en que se come) meal; **la ~ fuerte del día** the main meal of the day; **¿quién hace la ~ en tu casa?** who does the cooking in your house?; **todavía no he hecho la ~** I still haven't cooked the meal (c) (esp Esp, Méx) (almuerzo) lunch (d) (esp AmL) (cena) dinner, supper; (en algunas regiones del Reino Unido) tea

comidilla *f*: **ser la ~ del pueblo** to be the talk of the town

comience, comienza, etc ▶ COMENZAR

comienzo *m* beginning; **al ~** at first, in the beginning; **dar ~** to begin; **dar ~ a algo** «⟨persona⟩» to begin sth; «⟨ceremonia/acto⟩» to mark the beginning of sth; **el proyecto está en sus ~s** the project is still in its early stages

comillas *fpl* quotation marks (*pl*), inverted commas (BrE) (*pl*); **poner algo entre ~** to put sth in quotation marks *o* in inverted commas

comilona *f* (fam) feast (colloq); **nos dimos una ~** we had a blowout

comino m (Bot, Coc) cumin

comisaría f (edificio) tb ~ **de policía** (police) station

comisario m (a) (de policía) captain (AmE), superintendent (BrE) (b) (delegado) commissioner

comisión f (a) (delegación, organismo) committee; C~ **Europea** European Commission (b) (Com) commission; **trabajar a** ~ to work on a commission basis

comisionado -da m,f commissioner

comisionista mf commission agent

comiso m (Col) packed lunch

comisura f (de los labios) corner

comité m (junta) committee; ~ **de redacción** editorial board o committee

comitiva f (a) (séquito) procession; ~ **fúnebre** funeral procession, cortège (b) (grupo) delegation

como prep (a) (en calidad de) as; **quiero hablarte** ~ **amigo** I want to speak to you as a friend (b) (con el nombre de) as; **se la conoce** ~ **'flor de luz'** it's known as 'flor de luz' (c) (en comparaciones, contrastes) like; **uno** ~ **el tuyo** one like yours; **¡no hay nada** ~ **un buen coñac!** there's nothing like a good brandy!; **es** ~ **para echarse a llorar** it's enough to make you want to cry (d) (en locs) **así como** (frml) as well as; **como mucho/poco** at (the) most/at least; **como ser** (CS) such as, for example; **como si** (+ subj) as if, as though

■ conj (a) (de la manera que) as; **tal** ~ **había prometido** just as he had promised; ~ **era de esperar** as was to be expected; **no me gustó** ~ **lo dijo** I didn't like the way she said it; **(tal y)** ~ **están las cosas** as things stand; **hazlo** ~ **quieras/** ~ **mejor puedas** do it any way you like/as best as you can; **no voy —** ~ **quieras** I'm not going — please yourself (b) (puesto que) as, since; ~ **era temprano, fui a dar una vuelta** as it was early, I went for a walk (c) (si) (+ subj) if; ~ **te pille ...** if I catch you ...

■ adv (expresando aproximación) about; **está** ~ **a cincuenta kilómetros** it's about fifty kilometers away; **un sabor** ~ **a almendras** a kind of almondy taste

cómo adv (a) (de qué manera) how; **¿**~ **estás?** how are you?; **¿**~ **es tu novia?** what's your girlfriend like?; **¿**~ **es de grande?** how big is it?; **¿**~ **te llamas?** what's your name? (b) (por qué) why, how come (colloq); **¿**~ **no me lo dijiste antes?** why didn't you tell me before? (c) (al solicitar que se repita algo) sorry?, pardon?; **¿**~ **dijo?** sorry, what did you say? (d) (en exclamaciones) **¡**~ **llueve!** it's really raining!; **¡**~ **comes!** the amount you eat!; **¡**~**!** **¡no te lo han dicho?** what! haven't they told you? (e) (en locs) **¿a cómo ...?: ¿a** ~ **están los tomates?** (fam) how much are the tomatoes?; **¿a** ~ **estamos hoy?** (AmL) what's the date today?; **¡cómo no!** of course!; **¿cómo que ...?: ¿**~ **que no fuiste tú?** what do you mean it wasn't you?; **aquí no está — ¿**~ **que no?** it isn't here — what do you mean it isn't there?

cómoda f chest of drawers

comodidad f **1** (a) (confort) comfort; **la** ~ **del**

hogar the comfort of home (b) (conveniencia) convenience; **por** ~ for the sake of convenience (c) (holgazanería): **no lo hace por** ~ he doesn't do it because he's lazy **2** **comodidades** fpl (aparatos, servicios) comforts (pl)

comodín m (a) (Jueg) (mono) joker; (otra carta) wild card (b) (Inf) wild card

cómodo -da adj (a) (confortable) comfortable, comfy (colloq); **ponte** ~ make yourself comfortable (b) (conveniente, fácil) ⟨horario/sistema⟩ convenient; **esa es una actitud muy cómoda** that's a very easy attitude to take (c) (holgazán) lazy, idle

compact disc /kompak'ðis(k)/ m (pl -**discs**) (disco) compact disc, CD; (aparato) compact disc player, CD player

compacto -ta adj (a) ⟨tejido⟩ close; ⟨estructura/coche⟩ compact (b) ⟨muchedumbre⟩ dense

compadecer [E3] vt to feel sorry for

■ **compadecerse** v pron (apiadarse) ~**se DE algn** to take pity ON sb; ~**se de sí mismo** to feel sorry for oneself

compadre m (a) (padrino) godfather of one's child or father of one's godchild (b) (esp AmL fam) (amigo) buddy (AmE colloq), mate (BrE colloq)

compaginar [A1] vt ⟨actividades/soluciones⟩ to combine; **compagina el trabajo con los estudios** she combines work with studying

■ vi (a) (combinar) to go together (b) (llevarse bien) to get on; ~ **CON algn** to get on well WITH sb

compañerismo m comradeship

compañero -ra m,f (a) (en actividad): **un** ~ **de equipo** a fellow team member; **fuimos** ~**s de universidad** we were at college together; ~ **de clase/de trabajo** classmate/workmate (b) (pareja sentimental, en juegos) partner; (de guante, calcetín) (fam) pair (c) (Pol) comrade

compañía f **1** (acompañamiento) company; **llegó en** ~ **de sus abogados** he arrived accompanied by his lawyers; **hacerle a algn** to keep sb company; **andar en malas** ~**s** to keep bad company **2** (empresa) company, firm; ~ **de seguros** insurance company; ~ **de teatro** theater* company; **✆ Muñoz y Compañía** Muñoz and Co. **3** (Mil) company

comparable adj comparable; ~ **A** or **CON** comparable **TO** o **WITH**

comparación f comparison; **hacer una** ~ to make a comparison; **en** ~ **a** or **con el año pasado** compared to o with last year; **no tienen ni punto de** ~ you cannot even begin to compare them

comparar [A1] vt to compare; ~ **algo/a algn A** or **CON algo/algn** to compare sth/sb **TO** o **WITH** sth/sb; **no puede ni** ~**se al otro** it doesn't even compare at all to o with the other one

■ ~ vi to make a comparison, to compare

comparecer [E3] vi to appear (in court)

compartimento, compartimiento m compartment

compartir [I1] vt to share; ~ **algo CON algn** to share sth WITH sb

compás *m* **1** (Mús) **(a)** (ritmo) time, meter (esp AmE); **marcar/llevar el** ∼ to beat/keep time; **perder el** ∼ to get out of time; **se movía al** ∼ **de la música** she moved in time to the music **(b)** (división) measure (AmE), bar (BrE); ∼ **de dos por cuatro** two-four time; ∼ **mayor/menor** four-four/ two-four time **2** (Mat, Náut) (instrumento) compass

compasión *f* pity, compassion; **lo hace por** ∼ he does it out of compassion

compasivo -va *adj* compassionate

compatible *adj* compatible

compatriota *m,f* (*m*) fellow countryman, compatriot; (*f*) fellow countrywoman, compatriot

compendio *m* (libro) textbook, coursebook; (resumen) summary, compendium (BrE)

compenetrarse [A1] *v pron* ∼ **CON algo** ⟨*con ideas/objetivos*⟩ to identify WITH sth; ∼ **CON algn** to have a good relationship WITH sb; (en trabajo) to work well WITH sb; **se han compenetrado a la perfección** they understand each other perfectly

compensación *f* (contapartida) compensation; **en** ∼ by way of compensation; **en** ∼ **por algo** in compensation for sth

compensar [A1] *vi*: **no compensa hacer un viaje tan largo** it's not worth making such a long journey; **no me compensa** it's not worth my while

■ ∼ *vt* **1** **(a)** (contrarrestar) ⟨*pérdida/deficiencia*⟩ to compensate for, make up for; ⟨*efecto*⟩ to offset; **su entusiasmo compensa su falta de experiencia** his enthusiasm makes up for his lack of experience **(b)** ⟨*persona*⟩ ∼ **a algn POR algo** ⟨*por pérdidas/ retraso*⟩ to compensate sb FOR sth; **lo** ∼**on con $2.000 por los daños** he was awarded $2,000 compensation in damages **2** ⟨*cheque*⟩ to clear

■ **compensarse** *v pron* (*recípr*) to compensate each other, cancel each other out

competencia *f* **1** **(a)** (pugna) competition, rivalry; **hacerse la** ∼ to be rivals *o* in competition; **hacerle la** ∼ **a algn** to compete with sb **(b)** (persona, entidad) competition; **la** ∼ **se nos adelantó** the competition got in first **(c)** (AmL) (certamen) competition **2** **(a)** (de juez, tribunal) competence; **este asunto no es de mi** ∼ I have no authority *o* say in this matter **(b)** (habilidad, aptitud) competence, ability; **falta de** ∼ incompetence

competente *adj* competent

competición *f* (Esp) **(a)** (rivalidad): **espíritu de** ∼ competitive spirit **(b)** (certamen) competition

competidor -dora *m,f* competitor, rival

competir [I14] *vi* **(a)** (pugnar, luchar) to compete; ∼ **CON** *or* **CONTRA algn** (**FOR sth**) to compete WITH *o* AGAINST sb (FOR sth) **(b)** (estar al mismo nivel): **los dos modelos compiten en calidad** the two models rival each other in quality

competitividad *f* competitiveness

competitivo -va *adj* competitive

compilar [A1] *vt* to compile

compinche *m,f* (compañero) (fam) buddy (AmE colloq), mate (BrE colloq); (cómplice en crimen) partner in crime

complacer [E3] *vt* to please

■ **complacerse** *v pron* ∼**se EN algo** to take pleasure IN sth

complaciente *adj* indulgent

complejidad *f* complexity

complejo¹ -ja *adj* complex

complejo² *m* **(a)** (de edificios) complex; ∼ **deportivo/industrial** sports/industrial complex **(b)** (Psic) complex; **tiene** ∼ **porque es bajito** he's got a complex about being short; ∼ **de culpa** *or* **culpabilidad** guilt complex; ∼ **de inferioridad/ superioridad** inferiority/superiority complex

complementar [A1] *vt* to complement

■ **complementarse** *v pron* (*recípr*) to complement each other

complementario -ria *adj* **(a)** ⟨*personalidades/ángulos/colores*⟩ complementary **(b)** (adicional) additional

complemento *m* **(a)** (Ling, Mat) complement; ∼ **directo/indirecto** direct/indirect object **(b)** (acompañamiento) accompaniment **(c)** **complementos** *mpl* (Auto, Indum) accessories (*pl*)

completar [A1] *vt* **(a)** (terminar) to finish, complete **(b)** (AmL) ⟨*cuestionario/impreso*⟩ to complete, fill out *o* in

completo -ta *adj* **1** **(a)** (entero) complete; **las obras completas de Neruda** the complete works of Neruda **(b)** (total, absoluto) complete, total; **lo olvidé por** ∼ I completely forgot about it **(c)** (exhaustivo) ⟨*explicación*⟩ detailed; ⟨*obra/ diccionario*⟩ comprehensive; ⟨*tesis/ensayo*⟩ thorough **(d)** ⟨*deportista/actor*⟩ complete, very versatile **2** (lleno) ⟨*vagón/hotel*⟩ full; **ⓢ completo** (en hostal) no vacancies; (en taquilla) sold out

complexión *f* constitution

complicación *f* **(a)** (contratiempo, dificultad) complication **(b)** (cualidad) complexity **(c)** (esp AmL) (implicación) involvement

complicado -da *adj* ⟨*problema/sistema/ situación*⟩ complicated, complex **(b)** ⟨*carácter*⟩ complex; ⟨*persona*⟩ complicated **(c)** ⟨*diseño/ adorno*⟩ elaborate

complicar [A2] *vt* **(a)** ⟨*situación/problema/ asunto*⟩ to complicate, make ... complicated **(b)** (implicar) ⟨*persona*⟩ to involve, get ... involved

■ **complicarse** *v pron* **(a)** ⟪*situación/problema/ asunto*⟫ to get complicated; ⟪*enfermedad*⟫: **se le complicó con un problema respiratorio** he developed respiratory complications; ▶ VIDA 2 **(b)** (implicarse) ∼**se EN algo** to get involved IN sth

cómplice *mf* accomplice; ∼ **EN algo** accomplice TO sth

complicidad *f* complicity

compló, complot *m* (*pl* **-plots**) plot, conspiracy

compondré, compondría, etc ▶ COMPONER

componente *m* **(a)** (de sustancia) constituent (part), component (part); (de equipo, comisión) member **(b)** (Tec) component

componer [E22] *vt* **(a)** (constituir) ⟨*jurado/ equipo/plantilla*⟩ to make up; **el tren estaba compuesto por ocho vagones** the train was made up of eight cars **(b)** ⟨*sinfonía/canción/verso*⟩ to compose **(c)** (esp AmL) (arreglar) ⟨*reloj/radio/ zapatos*⟩ to repair **(d)** (AmL) ⟨*hueso*⟩ to set

■ ∼ *vi* to compose

■ **componerse** *v pron* **1** (estar formado) ∼**se DE algo** to be made up OF sth, to consist OF sth; **un** ⋯⋮

conjunto compuesto de falda y chaqueta an outfit consisting of a skirt and a jacket 2 (esp AmL fam) «*persona*» to get better

comportamiento *m* **(a)** (conducta) behavior*; **mal ~** bad behavior **(b)** (Mec) performance

comportarse [A1] *v pron* to behave; **~ mal** to behave badly, misbehave

composición *f* composition

compositor -tora *m,f* composer

compostura *f* **(a)** (circunspección) composure; **guardar la ~** to maintain *o* keep one's composure **(b)** (CS) (arreglo) repair

compota *f* compote

compra *f* **(a)** (acción): **ir de ~s** to go shopping; **hacer las ~s** *or* (Esp) **la ~** to do the shopping; **~ por teléfono** teleshopping **(b)** (cosa comprada) buy, purchase (frml); **fue una buena ~** it was a good buy

comprador -dora *m,f* buyer, purchaser (frml)

comprar [A1] *vt* **(a)** «*casa/regalo/comida*» to buy, purchase (frml); **~le algo** (a quien lo vende) to buy sth FROM sb; (a quien lo recibe) to buy sth FOR sb **(b)** (fam) (sobornar) to buy (colloq)

comprender [E1] *vt* 1 **(a)** (entender) to understand, comprehend (frml); **nadie me comprende** nobody understands me **(b)** (darse cuenta) to realize, understand; **comprendió que lo habían engañado** he realized that he had been tricked 2 (abarcar, contener) «*libro*» to cover; «*factura/precio*» to include
■ **~** *vi* (entender) to understand; **hacerse ~** to make oneself understood

comprensible *adj* understandable

comprensión *f* understanding; **capacidad de ~** comprehension; **~ auditiva** listening comprehension

comprensivo -va *adj* understanding

compresa *f* **(a)** (Med) compress **(b)** (Esp) *tb* **~ higiénica** sanitary napkin (AmE) *o* (BrE) towel

comprimido *m* (Farm) pill, tablet

comprimir [I1] *vt* to compress

comprobación *f* **(a)** (acción) verification, checking **(b)** (Col) (examen) test

comprobante *m* proof; **~ de pago** proof of payment

comprobar [A10] *vt* **(a)** (verificar) «*operación/resultado/funcionamiento*» to check **(b)** (demostrar) to prove **(c)** (darse cuenta) to realize **(d)** «*hecho*» (confirmar) to confirm

comprometedor -dora *adj* compromising

comprometer [E1] *vt* **(a)** (poner en un apuro) to compromise **(b)** «*vida/libertad*» to jeopardize, threaten **(c)** (obligar) **~ a algn A algo** to commit sb TO sth; **esto no me compromete a nada** this does not commit me to anything
■ **comprometerse** *v pron* **(a)** (dar su palabra) **~se A hacer algo** to promise to do sth; **me he comprometido para salir esta noche** I've arranged to go out tonight **(b)** «*autor/artista*» to commit oneself politically **(c)** «*novios*» to get engaged; **~se CON algn** to get engaged TO sb

comprometido -da *adj* **(a)** [SER] «*asunto/situación*» awkward, delicate **(b)** [SER] «*cine/escritor*» politically committed **(c)** [ESTAR] (para casarse) engaged; **~ CON algn** engaged TO sb

compromiso *m* **(a)** (moral, financiero)

commitment; **adquirir un ~ con algn** to make a commitment to sb; **sin ~ alguno** without obligation; **los invitó por ~** she felt obliged to invite them; **yo con ellos no tengo ningún ~** I'm under no obligation to them **(b)** (cita) engagement; **~s sociales** social engagements *o* commitments **(c)** (de matrimonio) engagement **(d)** (acuerdo) agreement; (con concesiones recíprocas) compromise; **llegaron a un ~** they came to *o* reached an agreement/a compromise **(e)** (apuro) awkward situation; **me puso en un ~** he put me in an awkward position

compuesto -ta *adj* «*oración/número/flor*» compound (*before n*); *ver tb* COMPONER

compungido -da *adj* (arrepentido) remorseful, contrite; (triste) sad

compuse, compuso, etc ▶ COMPONER

computadora *f*, **computador** *m* (esp AmL) computer; **~ personal/de escritorio** *or* **mesa** personal/desktop computer

computerizar [A4] *vt* to computerize

comulgar [A3] *vi* (Relig) to receive *o* take communion

común *adj* **(a)** «*intereses/características*» common (*before n*); «*amigo*» mutual **(b)** (en locs) **de común acuerdo** by common consent; **de ~ acuerdo con algn** in agreement with sb; **en común** «*esfuerzo/regalo*» joint (*before n*); **no tenemos nada en ~** we have nothing in common **(c)** (corriente, frecuente) common; **es un nombre muy ~** it's a very common name; **un modelo fuera de lo ~** a very unusual model; **~ y corriente** (normal, nada especial) ordinary

comuna *f* **(a)** (de convivencia) commune **(b)** (CS, Per) (municipio) town, municipality (frml)

comunal *adj* **(a)** (de todos) communal **(b)** (CS, Per) (del municipio) town (*before n*), municipal

comunicación *f* **(a)** (enlace) link; **~ vía satélite** satellite link **(b)** (contacto) contact; **ponerse en ~ con algn** to get in contact *o* in touch with sb **(c)** (por teléfono): **se ha cortado la ~** I've/we've been cut off **(d)** (entendimiento, relación) communication **(e)** **comunicaciones** *fpl* (por carretera, teléfono, etc) communications (*pl*)

comunicado *m* communiqué; **~ de prensa** press release

comunicar [A2] *vt* 1 (frml) **(a)** (informar) to inform; **~le algo A algn** to inform sb OF sth **(b)** (AmL) (por teléfono) «*persona*» to put ... through 2 (transmitir) **(a)** «*entusiasmo/miedo*» to convey, communicate **(b)** «*conocimientos*» to impart, pass on; «*información*» to convey, communicate; «*idea*» to put across **(c)** «*fuerza/calor*» to transmit 3 «*habitaciones/ciudades*» to connect, link; **un barrio bien comunicado** an area easily accessible by road/well served by public transport; **~ algo CON algo** to connect sth WITH sth
■ **~** *vi* 1 «*habitaciones*» to be connected 2 (Esp) «*teléfono*» to be busy (AmE) *o* (BrE) engaged; **está comunicando** it's busy *o* engaged
■ **comunicarse** *v pron* 1 **(a)** (recípr) (relacionarse) to communicate; **~ por señas** to communicate using sign language; **~se CON algn** to communicate WITH sb **(b)** (ponerse en contacto) **~se CON algn** to get in touch *o* in contact WITH sb 2 «*habitaciones/ciudades/lagos*» (recípr) to be connected; **~se CON algo** to be connected TO sth

comunicativo -va *adj* communicative

comunidad *f* community; **C~** (Económica) Europea European (Economic) Community

comunión *f* (Relig) communion; **hacer la primera ~** to make one's first Holy Communion

comunismo *m* communism

comunista *adj/mf* communist

comunitario -ria *adj* **(a)** ⟨*bienes*⟩ communal; ⟨*espíritu/trabajo*⟩ community (*before n*) **(b)** (de la CE) EC (*before n*), Community (*before n*)

con *prep* **(a)** (en general) with; **vive ~ su novio** she lives with her boyfriend; **¡~ mucho gusto!** with pleasure!; **córtalo ~ la tijera** cut it with the scissor; **amaneció ~ fiebre** he woke up with a temperature; **hablar ~ algn** to talk to sb; **está casada ~ mi primo** she's married to my cousin; **portarse mal ~ algn** to behave badly toward(s) sb; **tener paciencia ~ algn** to be patient with sb; **pan ~ mantequilla** bread and butter; **¿vas a ir ~ ese vestido?** are you going in that dress? **(b)** (indicando una relación de causa): **¿cómo vamos a ir ~ esta lluvia?** how can we go in this rain?; **ella se lo ofreció, ~ lo que** *or* **lo cual me puso a mí en un aprieto** she offered it to him, which put me in an awkward position; **~ lo tarde que es, ya se debe haber ido** it's really late, he should have gone by now **(c)** **~ + INF: ~ llorar no se arregla nada** crying won't solve anything; **~ llamarlo por teléfono ya cumples** as long as you call him, that should do; **me contento ~ que apruebes** as long as you pass I'll be happy; ▶ **TAL** *adv* 2 **(d)** (AmL) (indicando el agente, destinatario): **me peino ~** Gerardo Gerardo does my hair; **se estuvo quejando ~migo** she was complaining to me

cóncavo -va *adj* concave

concebir [I14] *vt* **1** (Biol) to conceive **2** ⟨*plan/idea*⟩ to conceive **3** (entender, imaginar): **no concibe la vida sin él** she can't conceive of life without him; **yo concibo la amistad de modo distinto** I have a different conception of friendship
■ **~ vi** to conceive

conceder [E1] *vt* **1** **(a)** ⟨*premio/beca*⟩ to give, award; ⟨*descuento/préstamo*⟩ to give; ⟨*privilegio/favor/permiso*⟩ to grant; **nos concedió una entrevista** she agreed to give us an interview; **¿me podría ~ unos minutos?** could you spare me a few minutes? **(b)** ⟨*importancia/valor*⟩ to give **2** (admitir, reconocer) to admit, acknowledge

concejal -jala *m,f* town/city councilor*

concejero -ra *m,f* (AmL) town/city councilor*

concejo *m* council

concentración *f* **(a)** (Psic, Quím) concentration; **falta de ~** lack of concentration **(b)** (acumulación) concentration **(c)** (Pol) rally, mass meeting

concentrado¹ -da *adj* concentrated (*before n*)

concentrado² *m* (de verdura, tomate) concentrate; **~ de carne** meat extract

concentrar [A1] *vt* **(a)** ⟨*solución/caldo*⟩ to make ... more concentrated **(b)** ⟨*esfuerzos*⟩ to concentrate; ⟨*atención*⟩ to focus **(c)** (congregar) ⟨*multitud/tropas*⟩ to assemble, bring ... together
■ **concentrarse** *v pron* **(a)** (Psic) to concentrate; **~se EN algo** to concentrate on sth **(b)** (reunirse) to assemble, gather together

concéntrico -ca *adj* concentric

concepción *f* (Biol) conception

concepto *m* **(a)** (idea): **el ~ de la libertad** the concept of freedom; **tener un ~ equivocado de algo/algn** to have a mistaken idea of sth/sb; **tengo (un) mal ~ de su trabajo** I have a very low opinion of her work; **bajo** *or* **por ningún ~** on no account **(b)** (Com, Fin): **en** *or* **por ~ de** in respect of

conceptuoso -sa *adj* (CS) (amable, elogioso): **una conceptuosa felicitación** warm congratulations

concerniente *adj* **~ A algo** concerning sth; **en lo ~ a este problema** as far as this problem is concerned

concernir [I12] *vi* (*en 3ª pers*) to concern; **~ A algn** to concern sb; **por lo que a mí concierne** as far as I'm concerned; **en lo que concierne a su pedido** with regard to your order

concertar [A5] *vt* ⟨*cita/entrevista*⟩ to arrange, set up; ⟨*plan*⟩ to arrange; ⟨*precio*⟩ to agree (on)

concertista *mf* soloist; **~ de piano** concert pianist

concesión *f* **(a)** (de premios) awarding; (de préstamo) granting **(b)** (en una postura) concession; **hacer concesiones** to make concessions **(c)** (Com) dealership, concession, franchise

concesionario *m* dealer, concessionaire

concha *f* **(a)** (de moluscos) shell; **~ nácar** (Méx) *or* (Chi) **de perla** mother-of-pearl **(b)** (carey) tortoise shell **(c)** (Teatr) prompt box **(d)** (Ven) (cáscara — de verduras, fruta) skin; (— del queso) rind; (— del pan) crust; (— de nueces) shell

cónchale *interj* (Ven fam) good heavens!

concho *m* (Chi) **(a)** (del vino) lees (*pl*); (del café) dregs (*pl*) **(b)** (fam) (parte final) end, last bit **(c)** **conchos** *mpl* (restos) leftovers (*pl*)

conciencia *f* **(a)** (en moral) conscience; **tener la ~ tranquila** to have a clear *o* clean conscience; **tener la ~ sucia** to have a bad *o* guilty conscience; **me remuerde la ~** my conscience is pricking me; **no siente ningún cargo de ~** she feels no remorse; **hacer algo a ~** to do something conscientiously **(b)** (conocimiento) awareness; **tener/tomar ~ de algo** to be/become aware of sth

concienciar [A1] *vt* (Esp) ▶ CONCIENTIZAR

concientizar [A4] *vt* (esp AmL) ⟨*población/sociedad*⟩ to make ... aware; **~ a algn DE algo** to raise sb's consciousness ABOUT *o* awareness OF sth
■ **concientizarse** *v pron* (esp AmL) **~se DE algo** to become aware OF sth

concienzudo -da *adj* ⟨*trabajador/estudiante*⟩ conscientious; ⟨*estudio/repaso/análisis*⟩ thorough, painstaking

concierto *m* (Mús) **(a)** (obra) concerto **(b)** (función) concert, recital

conciliación *f* conciliation

conciliar [A1] *vt* **1** **(a)** ⟨*personas*⟩ to conciliate **(b)** ⟨*ideas*⟩ to reconcile; ⟨*actividades*⟩ to combine **2** ⟨*sueño*⟩: **~ el sueño** to get to sleep

concilio *m* council

conciso -sa *adj* concise

conciudadano -na *m,f* fellow citizen

concluir [I20] *vt* **(a)** (frml) (terminar) ⟨*obras*⟩ to complete, finish; ⟨*trámite*⟩ to complete; ⟨*acuerdo/* ⋯⋯▶

tratado⟩ to conclude **(b)** (frml) (deducir) to conclude, come to the conclusion; ∼ **algo DE algo** to conclude sth FROM sth

■ ∼ *vi* (frml) **(a)** «*congreso/negociaciones*» to end, conclude; **el plazo concluyó el día 17** the time limit expired on the 17th **(b)** «*persona*» ∼ **DE hacer algo** to finish doing sth

conclusión *f* **(a)** (terminación) completion **(b)** (deducción) conclusion; **saqué la** ∼ **de que ...** I came to the conclusion that ...; **tú saca tus propias conclusiones** you can draw your own conclusions; **en** ∼ (en suma) in short; (en consecuencia) so

concluyente *adj* ⟨razón/respuesta/prueba⟩ conclusive; **fue** ∼ **al responder** he answered categorically

concordante *adj* concordant (frml), concurrent

concordar [A10] *vi* **(a)** (Ling) to agree; ∼ **CON algo** to agree WITH sth **(b)** «*cifras*» to tally; «*versiones*» to agree, coincide; ∼ **CON algo** ⟨con documento/versión⟩ to coincide WITH sth; **su comportamiento no concuerda con sus principios** his behavior is not in keeping with his principles

concordato *m* concordat

concretamente *adv* (específicamente) specifically; **vive en Wisconsin,** ∼ **en Madison** he lives in Wisconsin, in Madison to be precise

concretar [A1] *vt* **(a)** (concertar) ⟨fecha/precio⟩ to fix, set **(b)** (precisar, definir) to be specific about; **no concretamos nada** we didn't settle on anything definite

■ ∼ *vi*: **a ver si concretas** try and be more specific; **llámame para** ∼ give me a call to arrange the details

■ **concretarse** *v pron* to become a reality

concreto¹ -ta *adj* **(a)** (específico) ⟨política/solución/acusación⟩ concrete, specific; ⟨motivo/ejemplo/pregunta⟩ specific; ⟨fecha/hora⟩ definite; ⟨caso⟩ particular; ⟨lugar⟩ specific, particular; **en tu caso** ∼ in your particular case; **en** ∼ specifically; **en una zona en** ∼ in a particular *o* specific area; **no sé nada en** ∼ I don't know anything definite **(b)** (no abstracto) concrete

concreto² *m* (AmL) concrete; ∼ **armado** reinforced concrete

concubina *f* concubine

concuñado -da *m,f*: **mi** ∼ my wife's brother-in-law; **mi concuñada** my husband's sister-in-law

concurrido -da *adj* **(a)** [ESTAR] (con mucha gente) ⟨discoteca/local⟩ busy, crowded; ⟨concierto/exposición⟩ well-attended **(b)** [SER] (frecuentado) popular

concursante *mf* (en concurso) competitor, contestant; (para empleo) candidate

concursar [A1] *vi* (en concurso) to take part in; (para puesto) to compete (*through interviews and competitive examinations*)

concurso *m* **(a)** (certamen) competition; **presentarse a un** ∼ to take part in a competition; ∼ **de belleza** beauty contest *o* (esp AmE) pageant; ∼ **hípico** show jumping competition **(b)** (para puestos, vacantes) *selection process involving interviews and competitive examinations* **(c)** (TV) (de preguntas y respuestas) quiz show; (de juegos y pruebas) game show **(d)** (licitación) tender; **sacar algo a** ∼ to put sth out to tender

condado *m* (división territorial) county

conde -desa *m,f* (en Gran Bretaña) (*m*) earl; (*f*) countess; (en otros países) (*m*) count; (*f*) countess

condecoración *f* decoration

condecorar [A1] *vt* to decorate

condena *f* **(a)** (Der) sentence; **está cumpliendo su** ∼ he is serving his sentence **(b)** (reprobación) ∼ **DE** or **A algo** condemnation OF sth

condenado -da *adj* **(a)** (destinado) ∼ **A algo** doomed TO sth **(b)** (obligado) ∼ **A hacer algo** condemned *o* forced to do sth **(c)** (fam) (expresando irritación) wretched (colloq), damn (colloq)

■ *m,f* **(a)** (Der) convicted person; **el** ∼ **a muerte** the condemned man **(b)** (Relig): **los** ∼**s** the damned; **como** (un) ∼ (fam) ⟨correr⟩ like hell (colloq); ⟨work⟩ like mad

condenar [A1] *vt* **(a)** (Der) to sentence, condemn; ∼ **a algn A algo** to sentence sb TO sth; ∼ **a algn a muerte** to sentence sb to death; **lo** ∼**on por robo** he was convicted of *o* found guilty of robbery **(b)** (reprobar, censurar) to condemn

condensación *f* condensation

condensar [A1] *vt* to condense

■ **condensarse** *v pron* to condense

condesa *f* countess

condescendiente *adj* **(a)** ⟨actitud/respuesta⟩ (con aires de superioridad) condescending **(b)** (comprensivo) understanding

condición *f* ❶ (requisito) condition; **sin condiciones** unconditionally; **a** ∼ or **con la** ∼ **de que** on condition (that); **acepto con una** ∼ I accept on one condition; **me puso una** ∼ she made one condition

❷ **(a)** (calidad, situación): **en su** ∼ **de sacerdote** as a priest; **en su** ∼ **de jefe de la delegación** in his capacity as head of the delegation **(b)** (naturaleza) condition; **la** ∼ **humana** the human condition

❸ **condiciones** *fpl* **(a)** (estado, circunstancias) conditions (*pl*); **condiciones de trabajo/de vida** working/living conditions; **estar en perfectas condiciones** ⟨coche/mueble⟩ to be in perfect condition; «*persona*» to be in good shape; **estar en condiciones de hacer algo** (de ayudar,exigir) to be in a position to do sth; (de correr,viajar, jugar) to be fit to do sth **(b)** (aptitudes) talent; **tener condiciones para algo** (para la música, el arte) to have a talent for sth; (para un trabajo) to be suited for sth

condicional *adj* conditional

condicionar [A1] *vt* **(a)** (determinar) to condition, determine **(b)** (supeditar) ∼ **algo A algo** to make sth conditional ON sth

condimentar [A1] *vt* to season

condimento *m*: **el comino es un** ∼ cumin is a

condiment; **le falta** ~ it needs some seasoning; **los ~s usados en la cocina india** the herbs and spices used in Indian cooking

condominio *m* **(a)** (propiedad) joint ownership, joint control **(b)** (Pol) (territorio) condominium **(c)** (AmL) (edificio) condominium (esp AmE), block of flats (BrE)

condón *m* condom

cóndor *m* condor

conducción *f* **(a)** (Elec, Fís) conduction **(b)** (esp Esp) (Auto) driving **(c)** (AmL) (de programa) presentation; **está a cargo de la ~ del programa** he's in charge of presenting the program **(d)** (Arg) (cúpula) leadership

conducir [I6] *vi* **(a)** (llevar) ~ **algo** «*camino/sendero*» to lead to sth; **esa actitud no conduce a nada** that attitude won't achieve anything *o* (colloq) won't get us anywhere; **a qué conduce eso?** what's the point of that? **(b)** (esp Esp) (Auto) to drive; ~ **por la izquierda** to drive on the left
■ ~ *vt* **(a)** (guiar, dirigir) to lead; ~ **a algn A algo** to lead sb TO sth; ~ **a algn ANTE algn** to take sb BEFORE sb **(b)** (AmL) «*programa*» to host, present; «*debate*» to chair **(c)** (esp Esp) «*vehículo*» to drive **(d)** «*electricidad/calor*» to conduct

conducta *f* behavior*, conduct; **mala ~** bad behavior, misconduct (frml)

conducto *m* **(a)** (Anat) duct, tube **(b)** (Tec) (canal, tubo) pipe, tube

conductor¹ -tora *adj* conductive; **materiales ~es de la electricidad** materials which conduct electricity
■ *m,f* **(a)** (de vehículo) driver **(b)** (AmL) (de programa) host

conductor² *m* (Elec, Fís) conductor

conduje, condujiste, etc ▶ CONDUCIR

conduzca, conduzcas, etc ▶ CONDUCIR

conectar [A1] *vt* **(a)** «*cables/aparatos*» to connect (up); «*luz/gas/teléfono*» to connect **(b)** (relacionar) «*hechos/sucesos*» to connect, link **(c)** (AmL) (poner en contacto) ~ **a algn CON algn** to put sb in touch *o* in contact WITH sb
■ ~ *vi* **(a)** (Rad, TV) ~ **CON algn/algo** to go over TO sb/sth **(b)** (empalmar) to connect, link up **(c)** (llevarse bien, entenderse) to get along *o* on well **(d)** (AmL) ~ **algo** «*vuelo/tren*» to connect WITH sth; **conectamos con el vuelo a Lima** we took a connecting flight to Lima

conecte *mf* **(a)** (Méx arg) (traficante) (drug) dealer **(b)** (AmC fam) (contacto) friend on the inside (colloq)

conector *m* connector

conejera *f* (madriguera) burrow; (para crianza) (rabbit) hutch

conejillo de Indias *m* guinea pig

conejo -ja *m,f* (Zool) rabbit

conexión *f* **(a)** (Elec) connection; ~ **a tierra** ground (AmE), earth (BrE); ~ **a la red** connection to the mains **(b)** (relación entre hechos, etc) connection **(c)** (Transp) connection; **perdí la ~ con Roma** I missed my connection to Rome **(d) conexiones** *fpl* (AmL) (amistades) connections (*pl*), contacts (*pl*)

confabularse [A1] *v pron* ~ **(CONTRA algn)** to plot *o* conspire (AGAINST sb)

confección *f* **(a)** (de trajes) tailoring; (de vestidos) dressmaking; **industria de la ~** clothing industry; **de ~** ready-to-wear, off-the-peg **(b)** (de lista) drawing-up

confeccionar [A1] *vt* «*falda/vestido*» to make (up); «*artefactos*» to make; «*lista*» to draw up

confederación *f* confederation

conferencia *f* **(a)** (charla — formal) lecture; (— más informal) talk; **dar una ~ SOBRE algo** to give a lecture/talk ON sth **(b)** (reunión) conference; ~ **de prensa** press conference **(c)** (Esp) (Telec) long distance call; **poner una ~** to make *o* (AmE) place a long-distance call; ~ **a cobro revertido** collect call (AmE), reverse charge call (BrE)

conferenciante, (AmL) **conferencista** *mf* lecturer

conferir [I11] *vt* (frml o liter) **(a)** «*honor/dignidad/responsabilidad*» to confer **(b)** «*prestigio*» to confer; «*encanto*» to lend; **la barba le confería un aire distinguido** the beard lent him an air of distinction

confesar [A5] *vt* **(a)** (Relig) «*pecado*» to confess; **el cura que la confiesa** the priest who hears her confession **(b)** «*sentimiento/ignorancia/delito*» to confess; «*error*» to admit
■ ~ *vi* **(a)** (Relig) to hear confession **(b)** (admitir culpabilidad) to confess, make a confession
■ **confesarse** *v pron* **(a)** (Relig) to go to confession; **~se DE algo** to confess sth; **~se CON algn** (Relig) to go to sb for confession; (hacer confidencias) to open up one's heart to sb **(b)** (declararse) (+ *compl*) to confess to being, admit to being

confesión *f* confession

confesionario *m* confessional

confesor *m* confessor

confeti *m* confetti

confiable *adj* (esp AmL) **(a)** «*estadísticas*» reliable **(b)** «*persona*» (cumplidor) reliable, dependable; (honesto) trustworthy

confiado -da *adj* **(a)** [SER] (crédulo) trusting **(b)** [ESTAR] (seguro): **está muy ~ en que lo van a llevar** he's convinced they're going to take him; **no estés tan ~** don't get over-confident

confianza *f* **(a)** (fe) confidence; **ella me inspira ~** I feel I can trust her; **lo considero digno de toda ~** he has my complete trust; **tiene ~ EN algn/algo** confidence IN sb/sth; **tiene ~ en sí misma** she is self-confident; **había puesto toda mi ~ en él** I had put all my trust *o* faith in him; **de ~** «*persona*» trustworthy, reliable; «*producto*» reliable; «*puesto/posición*» of trust; **nombró a alguien de su ~** he appointed someone he trusted **(b)** (intimidad): **tenemos mucha ~** we are close friends; **no les des tanta(s) ~(s)** don't let them be so familiar with you; **estamos en ~** we're among friends; **te lo digo en ~** I'm telling you in confidence; **tratar a algn con ~** to be friendly with sb

confianzudo -da *adj* (esp AmL fam) forward

confiar [A17] *vi* **(a)** (tener fe) ~ **EN algn/algo** to trust sb/sth; **no confío en ella** I don't trust her; **confiamos en su discreción** we rely *o* depend on your discretion **(b)** (estar seguro) ~ **EN algo** to be confident OF sth; ~ **en la victoria** to be confident of victory; **confiamos en poder llevarlo a cabo** we are confident that we can do it; **confiemos en que venga** let's hope she comes

⸭

■ ~ *vt* ~**le algo** A **algn** ‹*secreto*› to confide sth TO
sb; ‹*trabajo/responsabilidad*› to entrust sb with
sth

■ **confiarse** *v pron* (a) (hacerse ilusiones) to be
overconfident; **no te confíes demasiado** don't get
overconfident *o* too confident (b) (desahogarse,
abrirse) ~**se** A **algn** to confide IN sb

confidencia *f* secret, confidence (frml); **hacer
una** ~ **a algn** to tell sb a secret

confidencial *adj* confidential

confidente *mf* (a) (amigo) (m) confidant; (f)
confidante (b) (de la policía) informer

confinamiento *m* confinement

confinar [A1] *vt* ~ **a algn** A **algo** ‹*a hospital/a
calabozo*› to put sb INTO sth; ‹*a casa*› to confine
sb to sth; ‹*a isla*› to banish sb TO sth; **la parálisis
lo confinó a una silla de ruedas** he was confined
to a wheelchair because of paralysis

confirmación *f* ⌐1⌐ (de noticia, de pasaje)
confirmation ⌐2⌐ (Relig) confirmation; **hacer la** ~
to be confirmed

confirmar [A1] *vt* to confirm; **la excepción que
confirma la regla** the exception that proves the
rule

confiscar [A2] *vt* ‹*contrabando/armas*› to
confiscate, seize (b) (para uso del estado) to
requisition

confitería *f* (a) (tienda) patisserie, cake shop
(*also selling sweets*) (b) (Bol, RPI) (salón de té)
tearoom

confitura *f* preserve, jam

conflictivo -va *adj* (a) (problemático)
‹*situación*› difficult; ‹*época*› troubled; **una zona
conflictiva** a trouble spot (b) (polémico) ‹*tema/
persona*› controversial

conflicto *m* (a) (enfrentamiento) conflict; **estar en**
~ to be in conflict; **entrar en** ~ **con algn/algo** to
come into conflict with sb/sth (b) (Psic) conflict
(c) (apuro) difficult situation

confluir [I20] *vi* (a) «*calles/ríos*» to converge,
meet; «*corrientes/ideologías*» to come together,
merge (b) «*grupos/personas*» to congregate,
come together

conformar [A1] *vt* (a) (contentar) ‹*persona*› to
satisfy (b) ‹*cheque*› to authorize payment of

■ **conformarse** *v pron* (a) (contentarse) ~**se** CON
algo to be satisfied WITH sth; **no se conforma con
nada** he's never satisfied; **tuvo que** ~**se con lo
que tenía** he had to make do with what he had
(b) (esp AmL) (resignarse): **no tienes más remedio
que** ~**te** you'll just have to accept it *o* to resign
yourself to it; **no se puede** ~ she can't get over it

conforme *adj* [ESTAR] (a) (satisfecho) satisfied,
happy; ~ **con algo/algn** satisfied *o* happy WITH
sth/sb (b) (de acuerdo): **¡**~**!** agreed!, fine!; **estoy** ~
en que se haga así I agree that it should be done
like that; ~ A **algo** in accordance WITH sth (frml)
(c) (en regla) in order

■ *conj* as; ~ **se entra, está a mano izquierda** it's on
the left as you go in

conformidad *f* (a) (aprobación) consent,
approval (b) (esp AmL) (resignación) resignation

conformista *adj/mf* conformist

confort /kom'for/ *m* comfort; **apartamento todo**
~ well-appointed *o* fully equipped apartment

confortable *adj* comfortable

confortar [A1] *vt* to reassure, comfort

confrontación *f* (a) (enfrentamiento)
confrontation (b) (de textos) comparison

confrontar [A1] *vt* (a) ‹*textos/versiones*› to
compare (b) ‹*testigos/equipos*› to bring ... face to
face; ‹*ejércitos*› to bring ... into conflict (c)
‹*dificultad/peligro*› to confront, face

■ **confrontarse** *v pron* ~**se** CON **algo** to face up
to sth

confundir [I1] *vt* (a) (por error) ‹*fechas/datos*› to
confuse, get ... mixed *o* muddled up; ‹*personas*›
to confuse, mix up; ~ **algo/a algn** CON **algo/algn**
to mistake sth/sb FOR sth/sb; **me confundió con
mi hermana** he mistook me for my sister (b)
(desconcertar) to confuse (c) (turbar) to embarrass

■ **confundirse** *v pron* (a) (equivocarse) to make
mistakes/a mistake; **me confundí de calle** I got
the wrong street (b) (desconcertarse) to get
confused

confusión *f* (a) (en general) confusion; **para que
no haya confusiones** to avoid any confusion (b)
(turbación) embarrassment, confusion

confuso -sa *adj* (a) ‹*idea/texto/explicación*›
confused; ‹*recuerdo*› confused, hazy; ‹*imagen*›
blurred, hazy; ‹*información*› confused (b)
(turbado) embarrassed, confused

congelado -da *adj* (a) ‹*alimentos*› frozen (b)
(Med) frostbitten; *ver tb* CONGELAR

congelador *m* (en el refrigerador) freezer
compartment; (independiente) freezer, deepfreeze

congelar [A1] *vt* to freeze

■ **congelarse** *v pron* (a) «*agua/lago*» to freeze
(b) (Med): **se le congeló el pie** he got frostbite in
his foot (c) (tener mucho frío) to be freezing; **me
estoy congelando** I'm freezing!

congeniar [A1] *vi* to get along (esp AmE), to get
on (esp BrE); ~ CON **algn** to get along *o* on WITH
sb

congénito -ta *adj* congenital

congestión *f* congestion

congestionado -da *adj* (a) (Med) congested
(b) ‹*cara*› flushed (c) ‹*calle/área*› congested

congestionarse [A1] *v pron* (a) «*cara*» to
become flushed (b) (Med) to become congested *o*
blocked (c) «*calle/área*» to become congested

conglomerado *m* conglomeration

conglomerarse [A1] *v pron* to conglomerate

congratular [A1] *vt* (frml) to congratulate; ~ **a
algn por algo** to congratulate sb ON sth

■ **congratularse** *v pron* ~**se** DE *or* POR **algo**
(alegrarse) to be pleased ABOUT sth, congratulate
oneself ON sth (frml)

congregar [A3] *vt* to bring together

■ **congregarse** *v pron* to assemble, gather

congreso *m* ⌐1⌐ (reunión) conference, congress
⌐2⌐ **Congreso** (Gob, Pol) (a) (asamblea)
Parliament; (in US) Congress; **C**~ **de los
Diputados** (Esp) Chamber of Deputies (*lower
chamber of Spanish Parliament*) (b) (edificio)
Parliament (*o* Congress *etc*) building

congrio *m* (Coc, Zool) conger eel

congruente *adj* (coherente) coherent; **ser** ~
con algo to be consistent with sth

cónico -ca *adj* ‹*pieza/forma*› conical, conic
(tech); ‹*sección*› conic

conífera *f* conifer

conjetura *f* conjecture, speculation; **hacer ∼s** to surmise, conjecture (frml); **son simples ∼s** that's pure conjecture *o* speculation

conjugar [A3] *vt* (Ling) to conjugate

conjunción *f* **(a)** (Ling, Astron) conjunction **(b)** (unión) combination; **en ∼ con** in conjunction with

conjuntivitis *f* conjunctivitis

conjunto¹ -ta *adj* ⟨*esfuerzo/acción*⟩ joint *before n*

conjunto² *m* **(a)** (de objetos, obras) collection; (de personas) group; **en su ∼** (referido a — obra, exposición) as a whole; (— comité, partido) as a group; **∼ residencial** residential complex **(b)** (Mús) *tb* **∼ musical** (de música clásica) ensemble; (de música popular) pop group **(c)** (Indum) (de pulóver y chaqueta) twinset; (de prendas en general) outfit; **un ∼ de chaqueta y pantalón** matching jacket and trousers; **hacer ∼ con algo** to go well with sth **(d)** (Mat) set

conjura, conjuración *f* conspiracy, plot

conjurar [A1] *vi* to conspire, plot

conjuro *m* (fórmula mágica) spell

conllevar [A1] *vt* **(a)** (en 3ᵃ pers) (comportar, implicar) to entail; **conlleva mucha responsabilidad** it entails a great deal of responsibility **(b)** ⟨*desgracia/enfermedad*⟩ to bear
■ **∼** *vi* (Ven) **∼ A algo** to lead TO sth

conmemoración *f* commemoration; **en ∼ de** in commemoration of

conmemorar [A1] *vt* to commemorate

conmemorativo *adj* commemorative; **un monumento ∼** a memorial

conmigo *pron pers* with me; **vino ∼** she came with me; **estoy furiosa ∼ misma** I'm furious with myself; **ha sido muy bueno ∼** he's been very good to me

conmoción *f* **(a)** (Med) *tb* **∼ cerebral** concussion **(b)** (trastorno, agitación): **la noticia produjo una ∼ familiar** the news shocked the whole family **(c)** (Geol) shock

conmocionar [A1] *vt* to shake

conmovedor -dora *adj* moving, touching

conmover [E9] *vt* **(a)** (emocionar) to move **(b)** (inducir a piedad) to move … to pity
■ **conmoverse** *v pron* (enternecerse, emocionarse) to be moved

conmutar [A1] *vt* (Der) ⟨*pena*⟩ to commute

connotación *f* connotation

cono *m* (figura) cone; **el C∼ Sur** the Southern Cone (*Argentina, Chile, Paraguay and Uruguay*)

conocedor -dora *m,f* connoisseur, expert

conocer [E3] *vt* **1** ⟨*persona*⟩ to know; (por primera vez) to meet; ⟨*ciudad/país*⟩ to know; **¿conoces a Juan?** do you know/have you met Juan?; **te conocía de oídas** he'd heard of you; **lo conozco de nombre** I know the name; **∼ a algn de vista** to know sb by sight; **es de todos conocido** he's well known; **quiero que conozcas a mi novio** I want you to meet my boyfriend; **nunca llegué a ∼lo bien** I never really got to know him; **¿conoces Irlanda?** do you know Ireland? *o* have you been to Ireland?; **quiere ∼ mundo** she wants to see the world; **me encantaría ∼ tu país** I'd love to visit your country

2 (estar familiarizado con, dominar) ⟨*tema/autor/obra*⟩ to know, be familiar with; ⟨*lengua*⟩ to speak, know

3 (a) (saber de la existencia de) to know, know of; **conocían sus actividades** they knew *o* about his activities **(b)** ⟨*noticia/resultado*⟩ to announce; ⟨*identidad/intenciones*⟩ to reveal; **darse a ∼** «*persona*» to make oneself known; **intentó no darse a ∼** he tried to keep his identity a secret

4 (reconocer) to recognize*; **te conocí por la voz** I knew it was you by your voice

5 (*impers*) (notar): **se conoce que no están en casa** they don't seem to be in; **se conoce que ya llevaba algún tiempo enfermo** apparently he'd been ill for some time
■ **∼** *vi* (saber) **∼ DE algo** ⟨*de tema/materia*⟩ to know ABOUT sth
■ **conocerse** *v pron* **1** (recípr) (tener cierta relación con) to know each other; (por primera vez) to meet; (aprender cómo se es) to get to know each other
2 (refl) **(a)** (aprender cómo se es) to get to know oneself **(b)** (saber cómo se es) to know oneself

conocido -da *adj* **(a)** (famoso) ⟨*actor/cantante*⟩ famous, well-known **(b)** ⟨*cara/voz*⟩ familiar **(c)** ⟨*hecho/nombre*⟩ well-known; **más ∼ como …** better known as …
■ *m,f* acquaintance

conocimiento *m* **(a)** (saber) knowledge; **tiene algunos ∼s de inglés** he has some knowledge of English; **poner algo en ∼ de algn** to inform sb of sth; **tener ∼ de algo** to be aware of sth **(b)** (sentido) consciousness; **perder/recobrar el ∼** to lose/regain consciousness; **estar sin ∼** to be unconscious

conozca, conozco, etc ▶ CONOCER

conque *conj* so; **∼ ya lo sabes** so now you know

conquista *f* **(a)** (de territorio, pueblo) conquest; **la C∼** (Hist) the Spanish conquest (*of America*) **(b)** (logro) achievement **(c)** (fam) (amorosa) conquest

conquistador -dora *adj* ⟨*ejército*⟩ conquering
■ *m,f* **(a)** (Hist) conqueror; (en la conquista de América) conquistador **(b)** (fam) (en el amor) (*m*) lady-killer; (*f*) femme fatale

conquistar [A1] *vt* **(a)** ⟨*territorio/pueblo/ montaña*⟩ to conquer; ⟨*mercado*⟩ to capture **(b)** ⟨*victoria/título*⟩ to win; ⟨*éxito/fama*⟩ to achieve **(c)** ⟨*simpatía/respeto*⟩ to win; ⟨*persona/público*⟩ to captivate; ⟨*corazón*⟩ to capture; **acabó conquistándola** he won her heart in the end

consagrado -da *adj* **(a)** (Relig) consecrated **(b)** ⟨*artista*⟩ acclaimed **(c)** ⟨*costumbre/ procedimiento*⟩ established

consagrar [A1] *vt* **(a)** (Relig) to consecrate **(b)** **∼ algo A algo/algn** ⟨*monumento/edificio*⟩ to dedicate sth TO sth/sb; ⟨*vida/tiempo/esfuerzo*⟩ to dedicate *o* devote sth TO sth/sb; ⟨*programa/ publicación*⟩ to devote sth TO sth/sb **(c)** (establecer) ⟨*artista/profesional*⟩ to establish; **la película que la consagró como actriz** the movie that established her as an actress
■ **consagrarse** *v pron* (refl) (dedicarse) **∼se A algo/algn** to devote oneself TO sth/sb

consciencia *f* ▶ CONCIENCIA B

consciente *adj* **(a)** [ESTAR] (Med) conscious ⸱⸱⸱⟫

(c) (de problema, hecho) **ser** *or* (Chi, Méx) **estar ∼ DE algo** to be aware *o* conscious OF sth **(c)** [SER] (sensato) sensible; (responsable) responsible

conscripto *m* (AmL) conscript

consecuencia *f* consequence; **atenerse a las ∼s** to accept the consequences; **esto trajo como ∼ su renuncia** this resulted in his resignation; **a ∼ de** as a result of; **en ∼** (frml) (por consiguiente) consequently, as a result; (actuar/obrar) accordingly

consecuente *adj* consistent; **hay que ser ∼** you have to be consistent; **es ∼ con sus ideas** she acts according to her beliefs (o principles etc)

consecutivo -va *adj* consecutive

conseguir [I30] *vt* (objetivo/fin/resultado) to achieve, obtain; (entrada/permiso/empleo) to get; (medalla/título) to win; **si lo intentas, al final lo ∼ás** if you try, you'll succeed in the end; **la película consiguió un gran éxito** the film was a great success; **∼ hacer algo** to manage to do sth; **no consigo entenderlo** I can't work it out; **conseguí que me lo prestara** I got him to lend it to me

consejero -ra *m,f* **(a)** (asesor) adviser **(b)** (Adm, Com) director **(c)** (en embajada) counselor*

consejo *m* **(a)** (recomendación) piece of advice; **te voy a dar un ∼** let me give you some advice *o* a piece of advice; **me pidió ∼** he asked me for advice *o* asked (for) my advice; **sus ∼s son siempre acertados** she always gives good advice **(b)** (organismo) council, board; **∼ de administración** board of directors; **∼ de guerra** court-martial; **∼ de ministros** (grupo) cabinet; (reunión) cabinet meeting; **C∼ de Europa** Council of Europe; **C∼ de Seguridad** Security Council

consenso *m* consensus; **por ∼** by general consent *o* assent

consentido -da *adj* spoiled
■ *m,f*: **es un ∼** he's spoiled

consentimiento *m* (autorización) consent

consentir [I11] *vt* **(a)** (permitir, tolerar) to allow; **¡no te consiento que me hables así!** I won't have you speak to me like that; **se lo consienten todo** he's allowed to do whatever he likes **(b)** (mimar) (niño) to spoil
■ **∼** *vi*: **∼ EN algo** to consent *o* agree TO sth

conserje *mf* **(a)** (de establecimiento público) superintendent (AmE), caretaker (BrE) **(b)** (de colegio) custodian (AmE), caretaker (BrE) **(c)** (de hotel) receptionist

conserjería *f* reception

conserva *f*: **latas de ∼** cans *o* (BrE) tins of food; **piña en ∼** canned *o* (BrE) tinned pineapple; **∼s** canned *o* (BrE) tinned food

conservación *f* **(a)** (de alimentos) preserving **(b)** (Ecol) conservation **(c)** (de monumentos, obras de arte) preservation

conservador -dora *adj* conservative
■ *m,f* **(a)** (Pol) conservative **(b)** (de museo) curator

conservante *m* preservative

conservar [A1] *vt* **(a)** (mantener, preservar) (alimentos) to preserve; (sabor/calor) to retain; (tradiciones/costumbres) to preserve; (amigo/cargo) to keep; (naturaleza) to conserve; **conservo buenos recuerdos suyos** I have good memories of him; **∼ la calma** to keep calm; **∼ la línea** to keep one's figure **(b)** (guardar) (cartas/fotografías) to keep
■ **conservarse** *v pron* **(a)** «alimentos» to keep **(b)** (perdurar) «restos/tradiciones» to survive **(c)** «persona» (+ compl) to keep; **se conserva joven** she keeps herself young; **está muy bien conservada** she's very well preserved

conservatorio *m* conservatory, conservatoire

considerable *adj* considerable

consideración *f* consideration; **tomar algo en ∼** to take sth into consideration *o* account; **por ∼ a su familia** out of consideration for his family; **en ∼ a sus méritos** in recognition of her merits; **la trataron sin ninguna ∼** they treated her most inconsiderately; **¡qué falta de ∼!** how thoughtless!; **de ∼** serious

considerado -da *adj* [SER] considerate; **ser ∼ CON algn** to be considerate TOWARD(s) sb

considerar [A1] *vt* (asunto/posibilidad/oferta) to consider; (ventajas/consecuencias) to weigh up, consider; **considerando que ha estado enfermo** considering (that) he's been ill; **tenemos que ∼ que …** we must take into account that …; **eso se considera de mala educación** that's considered bad manners; **está muy bien considerado** he is very highly regarded
■ **considerarse** *v pron* «persona» (juzgarse) to consider oneself; **se considera afortunado** he considers himself (to be) lucky

consiga, consigas, etc ▶ CONSEGUIR

consigna *f* **(a)** (eslogan) slogan **(b)** (para equipaje) baggage room (AmE), left-luggage (office) (BrE); **∼ automática** (coin-operated *o* automatic) luggage locker (AmE) *o* (BrE) left-luggage locker

consignar [A1] *vt* [1] (depositar) **(a)** (mercancías) to consign **(b)** (equipaje) to check (AmE), to place *o* deposit … in left luggage (BrE) **(c)** (Der) to pay … into court **(d)** (Col) (dinero/cheques) to deposit [2] (frml) (hecho/dato) to record [3] (frml) (enviar) (paquete/carga) to dispatch [4] (frml) (asignar) to allocate [5] (Méx) (Der) (presunto delincuente) to bring … before the authorities

consigo *pron pers* (con él) with him; (con ella) with her; (con uno) with you *o* one; (con usted, ustedes) with you; **no está satisfecho ∼ mismo** he's not happy with himself; **traigan ∼ todo lo necesario** bring everything you'll need with you; **hablaba ∼ misma** she was talking to herself

consigo, consigues, etc ▶ CONSEGUIR

consiguiente *adj* resulting (before n), consequent (before n) (frml); **por ∼** consequently

consistencia *f* **(a)** (de mezcla, masa) consistency; **tomar ∼** to thicken **(b)** (de teoría, argumento) soundness; **un argumento sin ∼** a flimsy argument

AmC	América Central	Arg	Argentina	Cu	Cuba	Per	Perú
AmL	América Latina	Bol	Bolivia	Ec	Ecuador	RPI	Río de la Plata
AmS	América del Sur	Chi	Chile	Esp	España	Ur	Uruguay
Andes	Región andina	CS	Cono Sur	Méx	México	Ven	Venezuela

consistente adj (a) ‹salsa/líquido› thick; ‹masa› solid (b) ‹argumentación/tesis› sound (c) (Andes, Méx) ‹conducta› consistent; ‹persona› ▶ CONSECUENTE

consistir [I1] vi (a) (expresando composición) ~ EN algo to consist OF sth; **el mobiliario consistía en una cama y una silla** the furniture consisted of a bed and a chair (b) (expresando naturaleza): **¿en qué consiste el juego?** what does the game involve?; ~ EN hacer algo to involve o entail doing sth (c) (radicar) ~ EN algo to lie IN sth; **en eso consiste su gracia** that is where its charm lies

consola f (a) (mueble) console table (b) (panel de controles) console

consolar [A10] vt to console, comfort; **si en algo te consuela** if it's any consolation to you

■ **consolarse** v pron (refl): **me consuelo pensando que …** I take comfort o I find some consolation in the thought that …

consolidar [A1] vt (a) ‹situación/posición/acuerdo› to consolidate; ‹amistad› to strengthen (b) ‹deuda/préstamo› to consolidate

■ **consolidarse** v pron «situación/acuerdo» to be consolidated; «amistad/relación» to grow stronger

consomé m consommé

consonante f consonant

conspiración f conspiracy, plot

conspirador -dora m,f conspirator

conspirar [A1] vi to conspire, plot

constancia f **1** (perseverancia) perseverance **2** (prueba) proof; **dejar ~ DE algo** (en registro, acta) to record sth (in writing); (verbalmente) to state sth; (atestiguar) to prove sth

constante adj (a) (continuo) constant (b) (perseverante) ‹persona› persevering

■ f (a) (Mat) constant (b) (característica) constant feature (c) **constantes** fpl (Med) tb **~s vitales** vital signs (pl)

constar [A1] vi (a) (figurar) ~ EN algo ‹en acta/documento› to be stated o recorded in sth; ‹en archivo/catálogo› to be listed in sth; ‹en libro/texto› to appear IN sth (b) (quedar claro): (que) **conste que yo no fui** it certainly wasn't me; **yo nunca dije eso, que conste** just to set the record straight, I never actually said that; **eso me consta** I am sure of that (c) hacer ~ algo (manifestar) to state sth; (por escrito) to register sth, to put sth on record (d) (estar compuesto de) ~ DE algo to consist OF sth

constelación f constellation

consternación f consternation, dismay

consternar [A1] vt to fill … with dismay

constipación f (esp AmL) constipation

constipado¹ -da adj (a) (resfriado) **está muy ~** he has a bad cold (b) (AmL) (estreñido) constipated

constipado² m cold

constiparse [A1] v pron to catch a cold

constitución f (a) (establecimiento) setting-up (b) (Pol) (de país) constitution (c) (complexión) constitution; **un hombre de ~ fuerte** a man with a strong constitution

constitucional adj constitutional

constituir [I20] vt (frml) (a) (componer, formar) to make up, constitute (frml) (b) (ser, representar) to represent, constitute (frml); **esta acción no constituye delito** this action does not constitute a crime (c) (crear) ‹comisión/compañía› to set up, establish

construcción f (a) (acción) construction, building; **en ~** under construction; **obrero de la ~** building o construction worker (b) (edificio, estructura) construction (c) (Ling) construction

constructivo -va adj constructive

constructor -tora m,f (a) (Const) builder, building contractor (b) **constructora** f construction company, building firm

construir [I20] vt (a) ‹edificio/barco/sociedad› to build (b) ‹figura/frases/oraciones› to construct

construya, etc ▶ CONSTRUIR

consuegro -gra m,f (m) father-in-law of one's son or daughter; (f) mother-in-law of one's son or daughter

consuelo m consolation, comfort

cónsul mf consul

consulado m (oficina) consulate; (cargo) consulship

consulta f (a) (pregunta, averiguación): **¿te puedo hacer una ~?** can I ask you something?; **de ~** ‹biblioteca/libro› reference (before n) (b) (Med) (entrevista) consultation; (consultorio) office (AmE), practice (AmE), surgery (BrE); **¿a qué horas tiene ~s el Dr. Sosa?** what are Dr Sosa's office hours (AmE) o (BrE) surgery times?; **~ a domicilio** home o house visit

consultar [A1] vt ‹persona/obra› to consult; ‹dato/duda› to look up; ~ algo CON algn to consult sb ABOUT sth

■ ~ vi: ~ CON algn to consult sb

consultor -tora m,f consultant

consultorio m (a) (de médico, dentista) office (AmE), practice (AmE), surgery (BrE); (de abogado) office (b) (consultoría) consultancy (c) **~ sentimental** (en revista) problem page; (en la radio) phone-in (about personal problems)

consumición f (esp Esp) (bebida) drink; **~ mínima** minimum charge

consumido -da adj [ESTAR] (por enfermedad, hambre) emaciated; ver tb CONSUMIR

consumidor -dora m,f consumer

consumir [I1] vt (a) (frml) ‹comida/bebida› to eat/drink, consume (frml) (b) ‹gasolina/energía/producto› to consume, use; ‹tiempo› to take up (c) ‹salud› to ruin (d) (destruir) ‹fuego/llamas› to consume; «envidia/celos»: **la envidia la consumía** she was consumed by o with envy

■ **consumirse** v pron (a) ‹enfermo/anciano› to waste away; **se consumía de pena** she was being consumed by grief (b) «vela/cigarrillo» to burn down (c) «líquido» to reduce

consumismo m consumerism

consumo m consumption; **~ mínimo** (AmL) minimum charge; **el ~ de drogas** drug-taking

contabilidad f (a) (ciencia) accounting (b) (profesión) accountancy (c) (cuentas) accounts (pl), books (pl); **lleva la ~** she does the accounts o the books

contabilizar [A4] vt (en contabilidad) to enter; (contar) to count

contable mf (Esp) accountant

contactar [A1] *vi* ~ **con algn** to contact sb, get in touch with sb
■ ~ *vt* to contact

contacto *m* **(a)** (entre dos cuerpos) contact; **entrar en** ~ to come into contact; **hacer** ~ to make contact **(b)** (comunicación) contact; **estar/ponerse en** ~ **con algn** to be/get in touch *o* contact with sb **(c)** (entrevista, reunión) encounter **(d)** (persona, conocido) contact **(e)** (Auto) ignition **(f)** (Méx) (Elec) socket, power point

contado¹ -da *adj* few; **en contadas ocasiones** on (a) very few occasions; **salimos con los minutos** ~**s** we left with only a few minutes to spare

contado² *m* **(a) al** ~ *or* (Col) **de** ~ ⟨*pago/precio*⟩ cash (*before n*); ⟨*pagar*⟩ (in) cash; **lo compré al** ~ I paid cash for it, I paid for it in cash **(b)** (Col) (cuota, plazo) installment*

contador¹ *m* **(a)** (de luz, de gas) meter; (taxímetro) meter, taximeter **(b)** (AmL) (ábaco) abacus

contador² -dora *m,f* (AmL) accountant; ~ **público** (AmL) certified public (AmE) *o* (BrE) chartered accountant

contagiar [A1] *vt* ⟨*enfermedad*⟩ to pass on, transmit; (tech) ⟨*persona*⟩ to infect; **me contagió la gripe** she passed her flu on to me; **no te acerques que te voy a** ~ don't come near or I'll give it to you
■ **contagiarse** *v pron* **(a)** «*persona/animal*» to become infected; **se ha contagiado de mí** she has caught it from me **(b)** «*enfermedad*» to be transmitted; «*manía/miedo*» to spread; **se contagia con facilidad** it is very contagious; **se contagió de la enfermedad** she caught the disease

contagioso -sa *adj* **(a)** (por contacto — directo) contagious; (— indirecto) infectious **(b)** ⟨*risa/alegría*⟩ infectious

contaminación *f* (del mar, aire) pollution; (de agua potable, comida) contamination; (por radiactividad) contamination; ~ **acústica** noise pollution

contaminante *m* pollutant, contaminant

contaminar [A1] *vt* ⟨*mar/atmósfera*⟩ to pollute; ⟨*agua potable/comida*⟩ to contaminate; (por radiactividad) to contaminate

contar [A10] *vt* **1** ⟨*dinero/votos/días*⟩ to count; **eran 6 sin** ~ **al conductor** there were 6 of them not counting the driver; **y eso sin** ~ **las horas extras** and that's without including overtime; **lo cuento entre mis amigos** I consider him (to be) one of my friends
2 ⟨*cuento/chiste/secreto*⟩ to tell; **no se lo cuentes a nadie** don't tell anyone; **es muy largo de** ~ it's a long story; **¿qué cuentas (de nuevo)?** (fam) how're things? (colloq)
■ ~ *vi* **1** (en general) to count; ~ **con los dedos** to count on one's fingers; **¿este trabajo cuenta para la nota final?** does this piece of work count toward(s) the final grade?; **ella no cuenta para nada** what she says (*o* thinks *etc*) doesn't count for anything
2 contar con (a) ⟨*persona/ayuda/discreción*⟩ to count on, rely on; **cuento contigo para la fiesta** I'm counting *o* relying on you being at the party; **sin** ~ **con que** ... without taking into account that ... **(b)** (prever) to expect; **no contaba con que hiciera tan mal tiempo** I wasn't expecting the

weather to be so bad **(c)** (frml) (tener) to have; **cuenta con 10 años de experiencia** she has 10 years of experience
■ **contarse** *v pron* **(a)** (frml) (estar incluido): **me cuento entre sus partidarios** I count myself as one of their supporters; **su novela se cuenta entre las mejores** his novel is among the best **(b)** **¿qué te cuentas?** how's it going? (colloq)

contemplación *f* **1** (observación) contemplation **2 contemplaciones** *fpl* (miramientos): **tienes demasiadas contemplaciones con él** you're too soft on him; **lo echaron sin contemplaciones** they threw him out without ceremony

contemplar [A1] *vt* **(a)** ⟨*paisaje/cuadro*⟩ to gaze at, contemplate **(b)** ⟨*posibilidad/idea*⟩ to consider, contemplate

contemporáneo -nea *adj* contemporary; **ser** ~ **de algn** to be a contemporary of sb, to be contemporary with sb
■ *m,f* contemporary

contenedor *m* container; (para basuras) bin, container; (para escombros) Dumpster® (AmE), skip (BrE); ~ **de recogida de vidrio** bottle bank

contener [E27] *vt* **(a)** ⟨*recipiente/producto/libro*⟩ to contain **(b)** (parar, controlar) ⟨*infección/epidemia*⟩ to contain; ⟨*tendencia*⟩ to curb; ⟨*respiración*⟩ to hold; ⟨*risa/lágrimas*⟩ to contain (frml), to hold back; ⟨*invasión/revuelta*⟩ to contain
■ **contenerse** *v pron* (*refl*) to contain oneself; **no se pudo** ~ **más** he could contain himself no longer

contenido *m* (de recipiente, producto, mezcla) contents; (de libro, carta) content

contentar [A1] *vt* to please; **¡qué difícil de** ~ **eres!** you're so hard to please!
■ **contentarse** *v pron* ~**se con algo** to be satisfied with sth; **se contenta con muy poco** he's easy to please

contento -ta *adj* [ESTAR] **(a)** (feliz, alegre) happy; **se puso muy** ~ **al oír que venías** he was very happy to hear you were coming; ~ **con algo/algn** happy with sth/sb **(b)** (satisfecho) pleased; **estamos** ~**s con la nueva secretaria** we're pleased with the new secretary; **no** ~ **con que le prestara el coche** ... not content *o* satisfied with me lending him the car ...

conteo *m* (Andes, Ven) count

contestación *f* (respuesta) answer, reply

contestador -dora *adj* (CS fam) ▶ CONTESTÓN

contestador automático *m* answering machine

contestar [A1] *vt* ⟨*pregunta/teléfono*⟩ to answer; ⟨*carta*⟩ to answer, reply to; **me contestó que no** he said no
■ ~ *vi* **(a)** (a pregunta, al teléfono) to answer; (a carta, a invitación) to answer, reply; **no contesta nadie** (Telec) there's no answer **(b)** (insolentarse) to answer back

contestón -tona *adj* (fam): **es muy** ~ he's always answering back

contexto *m* context

contigo *pron pers* with you; **¿puedo ir** ~**?** can I go with you?; **en paz** ~ **misma** at peace with yourself; **ha sido muy amable** ~ she's been very kind to you

contiguo -gua *adj* adjoining

continental *adj* continental

continente *m* (Geog) continent

continuación *f* **(a)** (acción) continuation **(b)** (de calle) continuation **(c)** (de novela) sequel; (de serie) next part *o* episode **(d)** a continuación next, then; a ~ de after, following

continuamente *adv* (con frecuencia, repetidamente) continually, constantly; (sin interrupción) continuously

continuar [A18] *vt* to continue
■ ~ *vi* «*guerra/espectáculo/vida*» to continue; si las cosas continúan así if things go on *o* continue like this; ❺ continuará to be continued; la película continúa en cartelera the movie is still showing; ~ CON algo to continue with sth; continuó diciendo que ... she went on to say that ...

continuidad *f* continuity

continuo -nua *adj* **(a)** (sin interrupción) «*dolor*» constant; «*movimiento/sonido*» continuous, constant; «*lucha*» continual **(b)** (frecuente) «*llamadas/viajes*» continual, constant

contonearse [A1] *v pron* to swing one's hips

contorno *m* **(a)** (forma) outline **(b)** (de árbol, columna) girth; medir el ~ de cintura to take the waist measurement **(c)** (de ciudad) surrounding area

contorsión *f* contortion; hacer contorsiones to contort one's body

contorsionista *mf* contortionist

contra *prep* against; lo puso ~ la pared he put it against the wall; nos estrellamos ~ un árbol we crashed into a tree; dos ~ uno two against one; yo estoy en ~ I'm against it; 40 votos en ~ 40 votes against; en ~ de (opuesto a) against; (contrariamente a) contrary to
■ *f* **(a)** (esp AmL fam) (dificultad) snag; llevarle la ~ a algn to contradict sb **(b)** (Col) (antídoto) antidote **(c)** (Pol, Hist) (grupo): la ~ the Contras (*pl*)
■ *mf* (individuo) Contra rebel
■ *m* ▶ PRO

contraatacar [A2] *vi* to counterattack

contraataque *m* counterattack

contrabajo *m* (instrumento) double bass; (cantante) basso profundo
■ *mf* double-bass player

contrabandista *mf* smuggler

contrabando *m* **(a)** (actividad) smuggling; ~ de armas gunrunning; pasaba relojes de ~ he smuggled watches **(b)** (mercancías) smuggled goods (*pl*), contraband

contracción *f* contraction

contracorriente *f* crosscurrent; ir a ~ «*barco*» to go against the current; «*nadador*» to swim against the current; «*diseñador/escritor*» to go *o* swim against the tide

contradecir [I24] *vt* «*persona/argumento*» to contradict
■ **contradecirse** *v pron* **(a)** «*persona*» to contradict oneself **(b)** (recípr) «*afirmaciones/órdenes*» to contradict each other, be contradictory; ~se CON algo to conflict with sth, contradict sth

contradicción *f* contradiction; eso está en ~ con lo que predica that is a contradiction of what he advocates

contradictorio -ria *adj* contradictory

contraer [E23] *vt* **①** (frml) **(a)** «*enfermedad*» to contract (frml), to catch **(b)** «*obligación/deudas*» to contract (frml); «*compromiso*» to make; ~ matrimonio con algn to marry sb **②** **(a)** «*músculo*» to contract, tighten; «*facciones/cara*» to contort **(b)** «*metal/material*» to cause ... to contract
■ **contraerse** *v pron* to contract

contrafuerte *m* (Arquit) buttress

contraincendios *adj inv* fire-prevention (*before n*)

contraindicado -da *adj* «*remedio/preparado*» contraindicated (tech)

contralto *m,f* (*f*) (en coro) alto; (solista) contralto; (*m*) countertenor

contraluz *m or f* back light; a ~ against the light

contramano: el coche venía a ~ (en calle de dirección única) the car was coming the wrong way down the street; (por el lado contrario) the car was on the wrong side of the road

contraofensiva *f* counteroffensive

contraparte *f* (Andes) opposing party

contrapartida *f* **(a)** (compensación) compensation; (contraste) contrast; como ~ in contrast **(b)** (Com) balancing entry

contrapelo: cepillar a ~ «*tela*» to brush ... against the nap; «*pelo*» to brush ... the wrong way

contrapesar [A1] *vt* to counterbalance

contrapeso *m* (del ascensor) counterweight; (de equilibrista) balancing pole; siéntate al otro lado para hacer ~ sit on the other side to balance it

contraportada *f* (de libro, revista) back cover; (de periódico) back page

contraposición *f* comparison; en ~ a *or* con algo in comparison to *o* with sth

contraproducente *adj* counterproductive

contrapunto *m* counterpoint

contrariado -da *adj* (disgustado) upset; (enojado) annoyed

contrariar [A17] *vt* (disgustar) to upset; (enojar) to annoy

contrariedad *f* **(a)** (dificultad, problema) setback, hitch; nos surgió una ~ something came up; ¡qué ~! how annoying! **(b)** (disgusto) annoyance, vexation (frml)

contrario -ria *adj* **①** (opuesto) «*opiniones/intereses*» conflicting; «*dirección/lado*» opposite; «*equipo*» opposing; «*bando*» opposite; yo pienso lo ~ I think the opposite; mientras no se demuestre lo ~ until proven otherwise; sería ~ a mis intereses it would be against *o* (frml) contrary to my interests; ▶ SENTIDO² 4
② (en locs) al contrario on the contrary; al ~ de su hermano ... unlike his brother, ...; de lo contrario or else, otherwise; por el contrario on the contrary; en el sur, por el ~, el clima es seco the south, on the other hand, has a dry climate; todo lo contrario quite the opposite; llevarle la contraria a algn to contradict sb
■ *m,f* opponent

contrarreloj *adj* «*carrera/etapa*» timed; a ~ against the clock

contrarrestar [A1] *vt* to counteract

contrasentido *m* contradiction in terms

contraseña f (Mil) watchword, password; (Teatr, Cin) stub; (Inf) password

contrastar [A1] vi ~ CON algo to contrast WITH sth

■ ~ vt ~ algo CON algo to contrast sth WITH sth

contraste m contrast; hacer ~ con algo to contrast with sth; en ~ con algo in contrast to sth

contrata f contract

contratar [A1] vt (a) ⟨empleado/obrero⟩ to hire, take on; ⟨artista/deportista⟩ to sign up; ⟨servicios⟩ to contract (b) (Const) ⟨ejecución de una obra⟩ to put ... out to contract

contratiempo m (problema) setback, hitch; (accidente) mishap; sufrir or tener un ~ to have a setback/a mishap

contratista mf contractor

contrato m contract; ~ de alquiler rental agreement; ~ de compraventa/de trabajo contract of sale and purchase/of employment

contravenir [I31] vt to contravene

contraventana f shutter

contravía (Col): ir en ~ to drive the wrong way down the road; un carro que venía en ~ an oncoming car

contribución f (colaboración, donación) contribution; (Fisco) tax

contribuir [I20] vi (a) (en general) to contribute; contribuyó con 100 pesetas he contributed 100 pesetas; ~ A algo to contribute TO sth (b) (Fisco) to pay taxes

contribuyente mf taxpayer

contrincante mf opponent

control m 1 (en general) control; bajo ~ under control; sin ~ out of control; perdí el ~ I lost control (of myself); hacerse con el ~ de algo to gain control of sth; lleva el ~ de los gastos she keeps a check on the money that is spent; ~ de (la) natalidad birth control; ~ de calidad quality control o check; ~ de pasaportes passport control; ~ remoto remote control 2 (en carretera, rally) checkpoint 3 (a) (Educ) test (b) (Med) check-up; ~ antidoping dope test, drug test

controlador -dora m,f controller; ~ aéreo or de vuelo air traffic controller

controlar [A1] vt 1 ⟨nervios/impulsos/persona⟩ to control; ⟨incendio⟩ to bring ... under control; controlamos la situación we are in control of the situation; pasaron a ~ la empresa they took control of the company 2 ⟨inflación/proceso⟩ to monitor; ⟨persona⟩ to keep a check on; ~ el peso/la línea to watch one's weight/one's waistline; controlé el tiempo que me llevó I timed how long it took me 3 (regular) ⟨presión/inflación⟩ to control

■ **controlarse** v pron (dominarse) to control oneself; (vigilar) ⟨peso/colesterol⟩ to check, monitor

controversia f controversy

controversial adj (Ven) ▶ CONTROVERTIDO

controvertido -da adj [SER] ⟨persona/tema⟩ controversial

contundente adj (a) ⟨objeto/instrumento⟩ blunt; ⟨golpe⟩ severe, heavy (b) ⟨argumento/respuesta⟩ forceful; ⟨prueba⟩ convincing; ⟨fracaso/victoria⟩ resounding (before n); fue ~ en sus declaraciones he was categorical in his statements

conurbano m (Arg): el ~ the suburbs (pl)

convalecencia f convalescence

convaleciente adj convalescent

convalidar [A1] vt ⟨estudios/título⟩ to validate, recognize

convencer [E2] vt (a) (de hecho, idea) to convince; no se dejó ~ she wouldn't be convinced; la convencí de que estaba equivocada I convinced her that she was wrong (b) (para hacer algo) to persuade; no pude ~lo de que or para que me prestara dinero I couldn't persuade him to lend me any money (c) (en frases negativas) (satisfacer): no me convence del todo la idea I'm not absolutely sure about the idea; su explicación no convenció a nadie his explanation wasn't at all convincing

■ **convencerse** v pron to be convinced; ¿te convenciste? are you convinced?; ~se DE algo to accept sth; ¿te convences de que tenía razón? do you believe o accept I was right?

convención f convention

convencional adj conventional

convenenciero -ra m,f (Méx fam) user (colloq)

convenible adj ⟨solución⟩ suitable; ⟨precio⟩ reasonable

conveniencia f (a) (interés, provecho): solo piensa en su propia ~ he only thinks of his own interests; lo hizo por ~ she only did it because it was in her own interest; se casó por ~ it was a marriage of convenience (b) (comodidad) convenience (c) (de proyecto, acción) advisability

conveniente adj (a) (cómodo) convenient (b) (aconsejable, provechoso) advisable; sería ~ que guardaras cama it would be advisable for you to stay in bed

convenio m agreement

convenir [I31] vi 1 (a) (ser aconsejable): no conviene que nos vean juntos we'd better not be seen together; convendría que descansaras it would be a good idea if you rest; no te conviene venderlo it's not worth your while selling it; no le conviene que eso se sepa it's not in his interest for anybody to know that (b) (venir bien): el jueves no me conviene Thursday's no good for me; te convendría tomarte unas vacaciones it would do you good to take a vacation 2 (acordar) ~ EN algo ⟨en fecha/precio⟩ to agree (ON) sth

■ ~ vt ⟨precio/fecha⟩ to agree (on); a la hora convenida at the agreed o (frml) appointed time

conventillo m (CS) tenement; esta oficina es un ~ (fam) this office is a hotbed of gossip

convento m convent

convergente adj convergent

conversación f (a) (charla) conversation;

trabar ~ con algn to strike up a conversation with sb; **no tiene ~** she has no conversation **(b) conversaciones** *fpl* (negociaciones) talks (*pl*)

conversador -dora *adj* chatty
■ *m,f* conversationalist

conversar [A1] *vi* **(a)** (hablar) to talk **(b)** (esp AmL) (charlar) to chat, gab (AmE *colloq*); **conversé largo rato con ella** I had a long talk *o* chat with her

conversión *f* conversion

convertible *m* (AmL) convertible

convertir [I11] *vt* ⒈ **(a)** (transformar) **~ algo/a algn EN algo** to turn sth/sb INTO sth **(b)** (a una religión) to convert; **~ a algn A algo** to convert sb TO sth **(c)** ⟨*medida/peso*⟩ **~ algo A algo** *or* (Esp) **EN algo** to convert sth INTO sth ⒉ (period) (Dep) to score
■ **convertirse** *v pron* **(a)** (transformarse) **~se EN algo** to turn INTO sth **(b)** (a una religión) to convert, be converted; **~se A algo** to convert TO sth

convicción *f* **(a)** (convencimiento) conviction; **tengo la ~ de que lo sabe** I'm certain *o* convinced he knows it **(b)** (persuasión) persuasion; **poder de ~** powers of persuasion **(c) convicciones** *fpl* (ideas, creencias) convictions (*pl*)

convicto -ta *m,f* prisoner, convict

convidado -da *m,f* guest

convidar [A1] *vt* **(a)** (invitar) to invite; **~ a algn A algo** ⟨*a una boda/fiesta*⟩ to invite sb TO sth; **nos ~on a unas copas** they invited us for a few drinks; **~ a algn a cenar** to invite sb to *o* for dinner **(b)** (AmL) (ofrecer) to offer; **~ a algn CON algo** *or* (Chi, Méx) **~ algo A algn** to offer sth TO sb, offer sb sth

convincente *adj* convincing

convivencia *f* (de etnias, sectas) coexistence; (de individuos): **la ~ pone el amor a prueba** living together puts love to the test

convivir [I1] *vi* ⟨*personas*⟩ to live together; ⟨*ideologías/etnias*⟩ to coexist; **~ CON algn** to live WITH sb

convocar [A2] *vt* ⟨*huelga/elecciones*⟩ to call; ⟨*manifestación*⟩ to organize; ⟨*concurso/certamen*⟩ to announce; ⟨*reunión/asamblea*⟩ to call, convene (*frml*); **~ a algn A algo** to summon sb to sth

convocatoria *f* **(a)** (llamamiento a huelga, elecciones) call; **la ~ de huelga** the strike call **(b)** (anuncio — para una reunión) notification; (— de exámenes, concursos) official announcement **(c)** (Esp) (Educ) (período de exámenes): **la ~ de junio** the June exams

convoy *m* (de barcos, camiones) convoy; (Ferr) (period) train

convulsión *f* (Med) convulsion

convulsionar [A1] *vt* to throw … into confusion

conyugal *adj* (frml) marital, conjugal (frml); **problemas ~es** marital problems

cónyuge *mf* (frml) spouse (frml); **los ~s** the married couple

coñac, coñá *m* brandy, cognac

coñazo *m* **(a)** (Esp fam *o* vulg) (persona o cosa pesada) pain (in the neck) (colloq); **dar el ~** (fam) to be a pain (colloq) **(b)** (Col, Ven fam) (golpe) blow

coño *m* (vulg) (de la mujer) cunt (vulg), beaver (AmE sl), fanny (BrE sl)

cooperación *f* cooperation

cooperador -dora *adj* cooperative, helpful

cooperar [A1] *vi* to cooperate; **~ CON algn** to cooperate WITH sb; **~ en la lucha contra el cáncer** to work together in the fight against cancer

cooperativa *f* (asociación) cooperative; (tienda) company store

coordinación *f* coordination

coordinado -da *adj* coordinate

coordinador -dora *m,f* **(a)** (organizador) coordinator **(b) coordinadora** *f* coordinating committee

coordinar [A1] *vt* ⟨*movimientos/actividades/ropa*⟩ to coordinate; **no lograba ~ las ideas** he couldn't speak/think coherently
■ **~** *vi* «colores» to match, go together

copa *f* ⒈ **(a)** (para vino) glass (*with a stem*); (para postres) parfait dish; (para helado) sundae dish; **~ de champán/coñac** champagne/brandy glass; **~ de vino** wineglass **(b)** (contenido) drink; **vamos a tomar una(s) ~(s)** let's go for a drink ⒉ (Dep) cup ⒊ **(a)** (de árbol) top, crown **(b)** (de un sostén) cup **(c)** (de sombrero) crown ⒋ **copas** *fpl* (en naipes) *one of the suits in a Spanish pack of cards*

Copenhague *m* Copenhagen

copeo *m* (fam): **ir/estar de ~** to go/be out drinking; **fuimos de ~ por los pubs del barrio** we went barhopping around the area (AmE), we went on a pub crawl around the area (BrE *colloq*)

copera *f* (AmS) hostess

coperacha *f* (Méx fam) (recaudación) kitty (colloq), collection; (contribución) contribution; **hacer una ~** to get up a collection (AmE *colloq*), to have a whip round (BrE *colloq*)

copetín *m* (RPl) aperitif

copia *f* copy; **saqué dos ~s** I made two copies

copiadora *f* photocopier, copier

copiar [A1] *vt* to copy; **copió el artículo a máquina** he typed out a copy of the article; **le copia todo al hermano** he copies his brother in everything; **le copié la respuesta a Ana** I copied the answer from Ana
■ **~** *vi* to copy

copihue *m* Chile-bells (*national flower of Chile*)

copiloto *mf* (Aviac) copilot; (Auto) co-driver

copión -piona *m,f* (fam) copycat (colloq)

copioso -sa *adj* ⟨*cosecha/comida*⟩ abundant, plentiful; ⟨*nevada/lluvia*⟩ heavy; ⟨*información/ejemplos*⟩ copious; ⟨*llamadas*⟩ numerous

copla *f* **(a)** (Lit) stanza **(b)** (Mús) popular folk song

copo *m* (de nieve) flake, snowflake; (de algodón) ball; **~s de avena** rolled oats (*pl*); **~s de maíz** cornflakes (*pl*)

coproducción *f* coproduction, joint production

copucha *f* (Chi fam) (rumor, chisme) rumor*; (curiosidad) nosiness (colloq)

copuchar [A1] *vi* (Chi fam) (conversar) to chat (colloq); (curiosear) to nose around (colloq)

cópula *f* **(a)** (Biol, Zool) copulation **(b)** (Ling) copula

copular [A1] *vi* to copulate

copulativo -va adj copulative

copyright /kopi'rraj(t)/ m (pl **-rights**) copyright

coqueta f (a) (chica que flirtea) flirt, coquette (liter); (presumida) vain girl/woman; **eres una ~** you are so vain (b) (mueble) dressing table

coquetear [A1] vi to flirt; **~ CON algn** to flirt WITH sb

coqueto -ta adj (a) (en el arreglo personal): **es muy coqueta** she's very concerned about her appearance (b) ⟨casa/dormitorio⟩ cute, sweet (c) ⟨sonrisa/mirada/mujer⟩ flirtatious, coquettish (liter)

coraje m (a) (valor) courage (b) (fam) (desfachatez) nerve; **¡qué ~!** what a lot of nerve! (AmE), what a nerve! (BrE)

coral adj choral
■ m (Zool) coral; **color ~** coral (before n), coral-colored*
■ f (Mús) (coro) choir

Corán m: **el ~ the** Koran

coraza f (a) (armadura) cuirasse (b) (de tortuga) shell

corazón m [1] (a) (en general) heart; **sufre del ~** she has heart trouble; **es un hombre de buen/ gran~** he's very kind-hearted/big-hearted; **no tener ~** to be heartless (colloq); **con todo mi ~** with all my heart; **de (todo) ~** sincerely; **le partió el ~** it broke her heart; **tener un ~ de oro/de piedra** to have a heart of gold/of stone (b) (apelativo cariñoso) (fam) sweetheart (colloq) [2] (a) (de manzana, pera) core; (de alcachofa) heart (b) (de ciudad, área) heart [3] (en naipes) (a) (carta) heart (b) **corazones** mpl (palo) hearts (pl)

corazonada f hunch; **tuve la ~ de que ibas a venir** I had a hunch o feeling you'd come

corbata f (Indum) tie, necktie (AmE); **hay que ir de ~** you have to wear a tie; **~ de lazo** or (AmL) **de moño** or (Chi) **de humita** bow tie

corbatín m bow tie

corchete m (a) (Impr) square bracket (b) (en costura) hook and eye (c) (Chi) (para sujetar papeles) staple

corchetear [A1] vt (Chi) to staple

corchetera f (Chi) stapler

corcho m cork; (para pescar, nadar) float

corcholata f (Méx) bottle top

corcovear [A1] vi to buck

cordel m (a) (fino) cord, string (b) (Chi) (cuerda) rope; **saltar al ~** to jump rope (AmE), to skip (BrE)

cordero m (a) (cría) lamb (b) (carne — de cordero) lamb; (— de oveja) mutton (c) (piel) lambskin (d) (fam) (persona dócil): **ser un corderito** to be as good as gold

corderoy m (AmS) corduroy

cordial adj (frml) (amistoso) cordial, friendly; ⟨ambiente⟩ congenial; **recibe un ~ saludo** (Corresp) (kindest) regards

cordialidad f (frml) cordiality

cordillera f (mountain) range; **la ~ de los Andes** the Andes

cordillerano -na adj (AmL) Andean, mountain (before n)

córdoba m cordoba (Nicaraguan unit of currency)

cordón m [1] (a) (cuerda) cord; **~ umbilical** umbilical cord (b) (de zapatos) shoelace, lace (c) (Elec) cord (d) (de personas) cordon; **~ policial** police cordon [2] (a) (CS) (de cerros) chain (b) (RPI) (de la vereda) curb (AmE), kerb (BrE)

cordura f (Psic) sanity; (sensatez) good sense; **obrar con ~** to act sensibly

Corea f Korea

coreano -na adj/m,f Korean

corear [A1] vt ⟨consignas/insultos⟩ to chant, chorus; ⟨marcha/estrofa⟩ to sing … in unison

coreografía f choreography

coreógrafo -fa m,f choreographer

corista f (en revista musical) chorus girl

cornada f (golpe) thrust (with the horns); (herida) wound (caused by a bull's horn); **darle una ~ a algn** to gore sb

córnea f cornea

córner m (pl **-ners**) corner (kick); **lanzar un ~** to take a corner

corneta f (a) (Mús) (sin llaves) bugle; (con llaves) cornet (b) (Ven) (Auto) horn

cornetista mf (de corneta sin llaves) bugler; (de corneta con llaves) cornet player

cornisa f (Arquit) cornice

corno m (Mús) horn; **~ inglés** English horn (AmE), cor anglais (BrE)

cornudo -da m,f (fam) (m) deceived husband; (f) deceived wife

coro m (a) (conjunto vocal) choir; (en revista musical) chorus line; **a ~** ⟨repetir⟩ together, in unison; ⟨cantar⟩ in chorus, together (b) (composición) chorus (c) (Arquit) choir

corola f corolla

corona f [1] (a) (de soberano) crown (b) (institución): **la ~ the** Crown (c) (de flores) crown, wreath; (para funerales) wreath (d) (Astron) corona [2] (moneda) crown [3] (Odont) crown

coronación f (a) (de soberano) coronation (b) (culminación) culmination

coronar [A1] vt (a) ⟨soberano⟩ to crown; **lo ~on rey** he was crowned king (b) ⟨montaña/ cima⟩ to reach the top of (c) (en damas) to crown

coronel -nela m,f (en el ejército) colonel; (en las fuerzas aéreas) ≈ Colonel (in US), ≈ Group Captain (in UK)

coronilla f crown (of the head); **estar hasta la ~ (de algo/algn)** to be fed up to the back teeth (with sth/sb) (colloq)

coronta f (Chi, Per) tb **~ de choclo** stripped corn cob

coroto m (a) (Col, Ven fam) (trasto) piece of junk (colloq); **recoge tus ~s** get your things o stuff together (b) (Ven) (poder político) (political) power

corpiño m (chaleco) bodice; (del vestido) bodice; (prenda interior) (RPI) brassière

corporación f (Com, Fin) corporation

corporal adj ⟨trabajo⟩ physical; ⟨necesidades⟩ bodily (before n); ⟨castigo⟩ corporal (before n)

corpulento -ta adj ⟨persona/animal⟩ hefty, burly; ⟨árbol⟩ solid, sturdy

corpus m (pl **~**) corpus

Corpus, Corpus Christi Corpus Christi

corral m (a) (en granja) yard, farmyard (b) (para ganado) corral (c) tb **corralito** (para niños) playpen

corralón m (a) (Méx) (de la policía) car pound

(b) (Per) (terreno baldío) piece of waste land (*sometimes with shanty dwellings*) **(c)** (Arg) (Const) lumberyard

correa *f* **(a)** (tira) strap; (cinturón) belt; (de perro) leash; ~ **de reloj** watchband (AmE), watchstrap (BrE) **(b)** (Mec) belt; ~ **del ventilador** fan belt

corrección *f* **1 (a)** (buenos modales): **es un hombre de una gran** ~ he is very well-mannered *o* correct; **vestir con** ~ to dress correctly *o* properly **(b)** (honestidad) correctness **(c)** (propiedad): **habla el francés con** ~ he speaks French well *o* correctly **2** (de exámenes, errores) correction; ~ **de pruebas** proofreading

correccional *f or* (Esp) *m*: *tb* ~ **de menores** reformatory (AmE), detention centre (BrE)

correctamente *adv* **(a)** (sin errores) correctly **(b)** (con cortesía) politely **(c)** (honestamente) honorably

correcto -ta *adj* **(a)** (educado) correct, polite; (honesto) honest **(b)** ⟨respuesta/solución⟩ correct, right **(c)** ⟨funcionamiento/procedimiento⟩ correct

corrector¹ -tora *m,f* (de exámenes) marker; ~ **de pruebas** proofreader

corrector² *m*: ~ **ortográfico** (Inf) spell checker

corredor¹ -dora *m,f* **1** (Dep) runner; (ciclista) cyclist; ~ **de coches** racing driver; ~ **de fondo** long-distance runner **2 (a)** (agente) agent; ~ **de Bolsa** stockbroker; ~ **de bienes raíces** *or* (Esp) **de fincas** real estate agent (AmE), estate agent (BrE) **(b)** (RPl) (viajante) sales representative

corredor² *m* (Arquit, Geog, Pol) corridor

corregir [I8] *vt* (en general) to correct; ⟨modales⟩ to improve, mend; ⟨examen/prueba⟩ to correct; (puntuar) to grade (AmE), to mark (BrE)

■ **corregirse** *v pron* **(a)** (en el comportamiento) to change *o* mend one's ways **(b)** (refl) (al hablar) to correct oneself; **un defecto físico que se corrige solo** a defect which corrects itself

correlación *f* correlation

correntoso -sa *adj* (CS) fast-flowing

correo *m* **(a)** mail, post (BrE); **envíamelo por** ~ mail (AmE) *o* (BrE) post it to me; **echar una carta al** ~ to mail (AmE) *o* (BrE) post a letter; ~ **aéreo** air mail; ~ **certificado** *o* (Col, Ur) **recomendado** registered mail; ~ **electrónico** e-mail, electronic mail; ~ **urgente** special delivery; **de** ~**s** ⟨servicio/huelga⟩ postal (*before n*) **(b)** (tren) mail train **(c)** (oficina) *tb* **C**~**s** (Esp) post office **(d)** (mensajero) messenger

correoso -sa *adj* tough, leathery

correr [E1] *vi* **1 (a)** (en general) to run; **bajó/subió las escaleras corriendo** she ran down/up the stairs; **salieron corriendo del banco** they ran out of the bank; **echó a** ~ he started to run **(b)** (Auto, Dep) ⟨piloto/conductor⟩ to race **2 (a)** (apresurarse): **¡corre, ponte los zapatos!** hurry *o* quick, put your shoes on!; **no corras tanto que te equivocarás** don't go so quickly, you'll only make mistakes ; **corrí a llamarte** I rushed to call you; **me tengo que ir corriendo** I have to rush off **(b)** (fam) ⟨vehículo⟩ to go fast; ⟨conductor⟩ to drive fast **3 (a)** ⟨carretera/río⟩ to run; ⟨agua⟩ to run; ⟨sangre⟩ to flow; **corría una brisa suave** there was a gentle breeze **(b)** ⟨rumor⟩: **corre el rumor/la voz de que ...** there is a rumor going around that ...

4 (pasar, transcurrir): **corría el año 1973 cuando ...** it was 1973 when ...; **con el** ~ **de los años** as time went/goes by; **¡cómo corre el tiempo!** how time flies!

5 (hacerse cargo) ~ **CON algo** ⟨con gastos⟩ to pay sth; ⟨con organización⟩ to be responsible FOR sth

■ ~ *vt* **1 (a)** (Dep) ⟨maratón⟩ to run **(b)** (Auto, Dep) ⟨prueba/gran premio⟩ to race in **2** (exponerse a): **corres el riesgo de perderlo** you run the risk of losing it; **aquí no corres peligro** you're safe here **3 (a)** ⟨botón/ficha/silla⟩ to move; ⟨cortina⟩ (cerrar) to draw, close; (abrir) to open, pull back; **corre el cerrojo** bolt the door **(b)** (Inf) ⟨texto⟩ to scroll

■ **correrse** *v pron* **1 (a)** ⟨silla/cama⟩ to move; ⟨pieza/carga⟩ to shift **(b)** (fam) ⟨persona⟩ to move up *o* over **2 (a)** ⟨tinta⟩ to run; ⟨rímel/maquillaje⟩ to run, smudge; **se me corrió el rímel** my mascara ran **(b)** (AmL) ⟨media⟩ to ladder

correspondencia *f* **(a)** (relación por correo) correspondence; (cartas) mail, post (BrE); **mantener** ~ **con algn** to correspond with sb **(b)** (equivalencia) correspondence

corresponder [E1] *vi* **1 (a)** (en un reparto): **le corresponde la mitad de la herencia** he's entitled to half the inheritance; **la parte que te corresponde** your part *o* share **(b)** (incumbir): **te corresponde a ti preparar el informe** it's your job to prepare the report; **el lugar que le corresponde** his rightful place **(c)** (en 3ª pers) (ser adecuado): **debe disculparse, como corresponde** he must apologize, as is right and proper (frml); **según corresponda** as appropriate **2** (encajar, cuadrar): **su aspecto corresponde a la descripción** his appearance fits *o* matches the description; **el texto no corresponde a la foto** the text doesn't belong with *o* match the photograph **3** ~ **A algo** ⟨a un favor⟩ to return sth; ⟨a amabilidad/generosidad⟩ to repay sth

■ ~ *vt* ⟨favor/atención⟩ to return; **un amor no correspondido** an unrequited love

correspondiente *adj* **(a)** (en general) corresponding (*before n*); **la etiqueta** ~ the corresponding label; **los números** ~**s a cada página** the numbers corresponding to each page **(b)** (propio) own; **viene con su** ~ **caja** it comes with its own box **(c)** (pertinente) relevant; **rellene el impreso** ~ complete the relevant form

corresponsal *mf* (Period, Rad, TV) correspondent; ~ **extranjero/de guerra** foreign/war correspondent

corretear [A1] *vi* (correr) to run around

■ ~ *vt* **1** (esp AmL) (perseguir) to chase, pursue **2** (RPl) (Com) to wholesale

corrida *f* **1** (Taur) bullfight **2** (Chi) (serie) series; (fila) row; (de bebidas) round

corrido *m*: *Mexican folk song*

corriente *adj* **1** (que se da con frecuencia) common; (normal, no extraño) usual, normal; **es un error muy** ~ it's a very common mistake; **lo** ~ **es pagar al contado** the normal thing is to pay cash; **un tipo normal y** ~ an ordinary guy; ~ **y moliente** (fam) ordinary, run-of-the-mill **2 (a)** (en curso) ⟨mes/año⟩ current **(b)** **al corriente: estoy al** ~ **en los pagos** I'm up to date with the payments; **empezó con retraso pero se** ···✧

ha puesto al ∼ she started late but she has caught up; **mantener a algn al** ∼ **de algo** to keep sb informed about sth

■ *f* **(a)** (de agua) current; ∼**s marinas** ocean currents; *dejarse llevar por la* ∼ to go along with the crowd; *seguirle la* ∼ *a algn* to humor* sb **(b)** (de aire) draft (AmE), draught (BrE) **(c)** (Elec) current; **me dio (la)** ∼ I got a shock *o* an electric shock; **se cortó la** ∼ there was a power cut

corro *m* **(a)** (círculo) circle, ring; **hacer un** ∼ to stand/sit in a circle; **se formó un** ∼ **a su alrededor** a circle of people formed around her **(b)** (Jueg) **jugar al** ∼ *to play a singing game standing in a ring*

corroborar [A1] *vt* to corroborate

corroer [E13] *vt* ⟨*metal*⟩ to corrode; ⟨*mármol*⟩ to erode

corromper [E1] *vt* **(a)** ⟨*persona/lengua/ sociedad*⟩ to corrupt **(b)** ⟨*materia orgánica*⟩ to rot
■ **corromperse** *v pron* **(a)** ⟨*costumbres/ persona/lengua*⟩ to become corrupted **(b)** «*materia orgánica*» to rot

corrompido -da *adj* **(a)** ⟨*persona/sociedad*⟩ corrupt **(b)** ⟨*materia orgánica*⟩ rotten

corrosión *f* corrosion

corrosivo -va *adj* ⟨*sustancia/acción*⟩ corrosive

corrupción *f* **(a)** (de moral, persona, lengua) corruption; ∼ **de menores** corruption of minors **(b)** (de materia) decay

corrupto -ta *adj* corrupt

corsé, corset /kor'se/ *m* (*pl* **-sets**) corset

cortacésped *m* lawnmower

cortada *f* **(a)** (Col, Méx) (herida) cut; **hacerse una** ∼ to cut oneself **(b)** (RPI) (calle sin salida) no through road

cortado¹ -da *adj* **1** ⟨*persona*⟩ **(a)** [ESTAR] (Chi, Esp) (turbado, avergonzado) embarrassed **(b)** [ESTAR] (Esp, CS) (aturdido) stunned; **me quedé** ∼ **con su respuesta** I was stunned by her reply **(c)** [SER] (Esp) (tímido) shy **2** [ESTAR] **(a)** ⟨*calle/carretera*⟩ closed, closed off **(b)** ⟨*película*⟩ cut **3** [ESTAR] ⟨*mayonesa/salsa*⟩ separated; **la leche está cortada** the milk is curdled *o* off **(b)** ⟨*café*⟩ with a dash of milk

cortado² *m* expresso with a dash of milk

cortante *adj* **(a)** ⟨*instrumento/objeto*⟩ sharp **(b)** ⟨*viento*⟩ biting **(c)** ⟨*respuesta/tono*⟩ sharp

cortaplumas *m or f* (*pl* ∼) penknife

cortar [A1] *vt* **1** (dividir) ⟨*cuerda/pastel*⟩ to cut, chop; ⟨*asado*⟩ to carve; ⟨*leña/madera*⟩ to chop; ⟨*baraja*⟩ to cut; ∼ **algo por la mitad** to cut sth in half *o* in two; ∼ **algo en rodajas/en cuadritos** to slice/dice sth; ∼ **algo en trozos** to cut sth into pieces
2 (quitar, separar) ⟨*rama/punta/pierna*⟩ to cut off; ⟨*árbol*⟩ to cut down, chop down; ⟨*flores*⟩ (CS) to pick; **me cortó un trozo de melón** she cut me a piece of melon
3 (hacer más corto) ⟨*pelo/uñas*⟩ to cut; ⟨*césped/ pasto*⟩ to mow; ⟨*seto*⟩ to cut; ⟨*rosal*⟩ to cut back; ⟨*texto*⟩ to cut down

4 (en costura) ⟨*falda/vestido*⟩ to cut out
5 (interrumpir) **(a)** ⟨*agua/gas/luz/teléfono*⟩ to cut off; ⟨*película/programa*⟩ to interrupt **(b)** ⟨*calle*⟩ «*policía/obreros*» to close, block off; «*manifestantes*» to block; **me cortó el paso** he stood in my way
6 (censurar, editar) ⟨*película*⟩ to cut; ⟨*escena/ diálogo*⟩ to cut (out)
7 ⟨*frío*⟩: **el frío me cortó los labios** my lips were chapped *o* cracked from the cold weather
■ ∼ *vi* **1** «*cuchillo/tijeras*» to cut
2 (Cin): **¡corten!** cut! **(b)** (CS) (por teléfono) to hang up; **no me cortes** don't hang up on me **(c)** (en naipes) to cut
■ **cortarse** *v pron* **1** (interrumpirse) «*proyección/ película*» to stop; «*llamada/gas*» to get cut off; **se cortó la luz** there was a power cut; **se me cortó la respiración** I could hardly breathe
2 **(a)** (*refl*) (hacerse un corte) to cut oneself; ⟨*brazo/cara*⟩ to cut; **me corté un dedo** I cut my finger **(b)** (*refl*) ⟨*uñas/pelo*⟩ to cut; **se corta el pelo ella misma** she cuts her own hair **(c)** (*caus*) ⟨*pelo*⟩ to have ... cut; **tengo que** ∼**me el pelo** I have to have my hair cut **(d)** «*piel/labios*» to crack, become chapped
3 (cruzarse) «*líneas/calles*» to cross
4 «*leche*» to curdle; «*mayonesa/salsa*» to separate
5 (Chi, Esp) «*persona*» (turbarse, aturdirse) to get embarrassed

cortaúñas *m* (*pl* ∼) nail clippers (*pl*)

corte *m* **1** (en general) cut; **se hizo un** ∼ **en la cabeza** he cut his head; ∼ **de pelo** haircut; ∼ **a (la) navaja** razor cut; **un** ∼ **de luz** a power cut; **tuvimos varios** ∼**s de agua** the water was cut off several times; ∼ **de digestión** stomach cramp; ∼ **publicitario** (RPI) commercial break
2 **(a)** (de tela) length, length of material **(b)** (en costura) cut; **un traje de buen** ∼ a well-made *o* well-cut suit; ∼ **y confección** dressmaking
3 (Esp fam) (vergüenza) embarrassment; **me da** ∼ **ir sola** I'm embarrassed to go by myself; **¡qué** ∼**!** how embarrassing!
4 (RPI fam) (atención): **darle** ∼ **a algn** to take notice of sb
■ *f* **(a)** (del rey) court **(b)** (esp AmL) (Der) Court of Appeal; **C**∼ **Suprema (de Justicia)** (AmL) Supreme Court **(c)** **las Cortes** *fpl* (Pol) (en Esp) Parliament, the legislative assembly

cortejo *m* (de rey) retinue, entourage; (de ministro) entourage; ∼ **fúnebre** funeral procession *o* (frml) cortege

cortés *adj* polite, courteous

cortesía *f* **(a)** (urbanidad, amabilidad) courtesy, politeness; **la trató con** ∼ he was polite to her; **tuvo la** ∼ **de invitarnos** she was kind enough to invite us **(b)** **de cortesía** ⟨*entrada*⟩ complimentary; ⟨*visita*⟩ courtesy (*before n*)

corteza *f* (de árbol) bark; (del pan) crust; (del queso) rind; (de naranja, limón) peel, rind; **la** ∼ **terrestre** the earth's crust

cortijo *m* (en Esp) (finca) country estate; (casa) country house

cortina *f* curtain, drape (AmE); ~ **de ducha** shower curtain; ~ **de humo** smokescreen

cortisona *f* cortisone

corto¹ -ta *adj* **1** (a) (en longitud) ⟨*calle/río*⟩ short; **de manga corta** short-sleeved; **el vestido le quedó** ~ the dress is too short for her now; **iba vestida de** ~ she was wearing a short dress/skirt (b) (en duración) ⟨*película/curso/viaje*⟩ short; ⟨*visita/conversación*⟩ short, brief; *a la corta o a la larga* sooner or later **2** (escaso, insuficiente): **un niño de corta edad** a very young child; ~ **de vista** near-sighted, shortsighted (BrE); **andar** ~ **de tiempo** to be pressed for time **3** (fam) (poco inteligente) stupid; ~ **de entenderas** *or* **alcances** dim, dense (colloq)

corto² *m* (Cin) (a) (cortometraje) short (movie *o* film) (b) **cortos** *mpl* (Col, Méx, Ven) (de película) trailer

cortocircuito *m* short circuit; **hacer** ~ to short-circuit

cortometraje *m* short (movie *o* film)

cosa *f* **1** (en general) thing; **cualquier** ~ anything; **¿alguna otra** ~**?** anything else?; **pon cada** ~ **en su lugar** put everything in its place; **entre una(s)** ~**(s) y otra(s) ...** what with one thing and another ...; **¡qué** ~**s dices!** really, what a thing to say!; **dime una** ~ **...** tell me something ...; **tengo que contarte una** ~ there's something I have to tell you; **fue** ~ **fácil** it was easy; **se enfada por cualquier** ~ he gets angry over the slightest thing; **si por cualquier** ~ **no puedes venir** if you can't come for any reason; **por una** ~ **o por otra** for one reason or another; **esto no es** ~ **de risa/broma** this is no laughing matter/no joke

2 cosas *fpl* (pertenencias) things (*pl*); **mis** ~**s de deporte** my sports things

3 (situación, suceso): **así están las** ~**s** that's how things are *o* stand; **la** ~ **se pone fea** things are starting to get unpleasant; **¿cómo (te) van las** ~**s?** how are things?; **son** ~**s de la vida** that's life!; **¡qué** ~ **más extraña!** how strange *o* funny!

4 (a) (fam) (ocurrencia): **¡tienes cada** ~**!** the things you come up (AmE) *o* (BrE) out with!; **esto es** ~ **de tu padre** this is your father's doing *o* idea (b) (comportamiento típico): **son** ~**s de niños** children are like that; **son** ~**s de Ana** that's one of Ana's little ways

5 (asunto): **no es** ~ **tuya** it's none of your business; **no te preocupes, eso es** ~ **mía** don't worry, I'll handle it

6 (en locs) **cosa de** (AmS fam) so as to; ~ **de terminarlo** so as to finish it; **cosa que** (AmS fam) so that; ~ **que no me olvide** so that I don't forget; **no sea cosa que: llévate el paraguas, no sea** ~ **que llueva** take your umbrella just in case; **átalo, no sea** ~ **que se escape** tie it up so that it doesn't get away; **ser** ~ **de ...** (fam): **es** ~ **de unos minutos** it'll (only) take a couple of minutes; **es** ~ **de intentarlo** you just have to give it a go

cosecha *f* (a) (acción, época) harvest; **un vino de la** ~ **del 70** a 1970 vintage wine (b) (producto) crop

cosechador -dora *m,f* (a) (persona) harvester (b) **cosechadora** *f* (máquina) combine (harvester)

cosechar [A1] *vt* (a) (recoger) ⟨*cereales*⟩ to

harvest; ⟨*legumbres*⟩ to pick (b) (Esp) (cultivar) ⟨*cereales/patatas*⟩ to grow (c) ⟨*aplausos/premios/ honores*⟩ to win; ⟨*éxitos*⟩ to achieve
∎ ~ *vi* to harvest

coser [E1] *vt* (a) ⟨*dobladillo*⟩ to sew; ⟨*botón*⟩ to sew on; ⟨*agujero*⟩ to sew (up); **cóselo a máquina** sew it on the machine (b) ⟨*herida*⟩ to stitch
∎ ~ *vi* to sew

cosmético¹ -ca *adj* cosmetic (*before n*)

cosmético² *m* cosmetic

cósmico -ca *adj* cosmic

cosmopolita *adj/mf* cosmopolitan

cosmos *m* cosmos

cosquillas *fpl*: **hacerle** ~ **a algn** to tickle sb; **tener** ~ to be ticklish

costa *f* **1** (Geog) (del mar — área) coast; (— perfil) coastline; **una** ~ **muy accidentada** a very rugged coastline; **la** ~ **atlántica** the Atlantic coast **2** (en locs) **a costa de: lo terminó a** ~ **de muchos sacrificios** he had to make a lot of sacrifices to finish it; **a** ~ **mía/de los demás** at my/other people's expense; **a toda costa** at all costs **3 costas** *fpl* (Der) costs (*pl*)

costado *m* side; **pasar de** ~ to go through sideways; **duerme de** ~ she sleeps on her side

costal *m* sack, bag

costanera *f* (CS) (de río) riverside path (*o* road etc); (del mar) promenade; (de lago) lakeside path (*o* road etc)

costar [A10] *vt* (a) (en dinero) to cost; **¿cuánto me** ~**á arreglarlo?** how much will it cost to fix it? (b) (en perjuicios): **el atentado que le costó la vida** the attack in which he lost his life; **le costó el puesto** it cost him his job (c) (en esfuerzo): **me costó mucho trabajo** it took me a lot of hard work; **cuesta abrirlo** it's hard to open; **me cuesta trabajo creerlo** I find it hard *o* difficult to believe
∎ ~ *vi* (a) (en dinero) to cost; **el reloj me costó caro** the watch cost a lot (b) (resultar perjudicial): **esto te va a** ~ **caro** you're going to pay dearly for this (c) (resultar difícil): **cuesta un poco acostumbrarse** it's not easy to get used to; **no te cuesta nada intentarlo** it won't do you any harm to give it a try; **la física le cuesta** he finds physics difficult; **me costó dormirme** I had trouble getting to sleep

Costa Rica *f* Costa Rica

costarricense *adj/mf* Costa Rican

costarriqueño -ña *adj/m,f* Costa Rican

coste *m* (Esp) ▶ COSTO

costear [A1] *vt* (financiar) to finance
∎ **costearse** *v pron* (refl) (financiarse): **yo me costeé el viaje** I paid for the trip myself

costeño -ña *adj* coastal
∎ *m,f*: **los** ~**s** people from coastal regions

costero -ra *adj* ⟨*camino/pueblo*⟩ coastal

costilla *f* (a) (Anat) rib (b) (AmS) (chuleta — de vaca) T-bone steak; (— de cerdo, cordero) chop

costipado -da *adj/m* ▶ CONSTIPADO

costo *m* (Com, Econ, Fin) cost; **de bajo** ~ low-cost, budget; **precio de** ~ cost price; **al** ~ at cost price; ~ **de (la) vida** cost of living

costoso -sa *adj* (a) ⟨*casa/coche/joya*⟩ expensive (b) ⟨*error*⟩ costly (c) ⟨*trabajo/tarea*⟩ difficult

costra *f* (a) (de herida) scab (b) (de suciedad) layer, coating

costumbre *f* (a) (de individuo) habit; **tenía (la) ~ de madrugar** he was in the habit of getting up early; **agarró la ~ de …** she got into the habit of …; **hacer algo por ~** to do sth out of habit; **a la hora de ~** at the usual time; **como de ~** as usual; **se quejó menos que de ~** he complained less than he usually does (b) (de país, pueblo) custom

costura *f* (a) (acción) sewing (b) (puntadas) seam

costurera *f* seamstress

costurero *m* (caja, estuche) workbox; (canasta) sewing basket; **~ de viaje** sewing kit

cotejar [A1] *vt* ⟨documentos⟩ to compare; ⟨información/respuesta⟩ to collate; **~ algo CON algo** to check sth AGAINST sth

cotelé *m* (Chi) corduroy

cotidiano -na *adj* daily; ⟨vida⟩ everyday, daily

cotilla *mf* (Esp fam) gossip (colloq)

cotillear [A1] *vi* (Esp fam) to gossip

cotilleo *m* (Esp fam) gossip

cotización *f* (a) (de moneda) value; (de acciones, valores, producto) price; **su ~ llegó a 500 pesos** it reached 500 pesos (b) (Andes) (evaluación) valuation; (presupuesto) estimate

cotizado -da *adj* sought-after

cotizar [A4] *vt* (a) (Fin) ⟨acciones⟩ to quote; **las acciones se cotizan a 525 pesos** the shares are quoted at 525 pesos; **la libra se cotizó a 198 pesetas** the pound stood at 198 pesetas (b) (Andes) ⟨cuadro/joyas⟩ to value; ⟨obra/reparación⟩ to give an estimate for

coto *m* (Dep, Ecol) reserve; **~ de caza/pesca** game/fishing preserve

cotorra *f* (a) (Zool) (loro) parrot (b) (fam) (persona) chatterbox (colloq)

cototo *m* (Chi fam) bump (*on the head*)

cottolengo /koto'leŋgo/ *m* (RPl) (para ancianos) old people's home; (para niños) children's home; (para drogadictos, desamparados, etc) shelter, refuge

cotufas *fpl* (Ven) (maíz tostado) popcorn

COU /kou/ *m* (en Esp) = **Curso de Orientación Universitaria**

courier /ku'rje(r)/ *mf* courier

coya *mf*: indian from the Andean region of Bolivia, Peru and the NW of Argentina

coyote *m* (Zool) coyote

coyuntura *f* (Anat) joint

coz *f* kick; **dar coces** to kick

crac *m* (*pl* **cracs**) (a) (sonido) crack, snap (b) (Fin) crash

crack *m* (*pl* **cracks**) (droga) crack

cráneo *m* skull, cranium (tech)

cráter *m* crater

crawl /krol/ *m*: *tb* **estilo ~** crawl, front crawl

crayón *m* (Méx, RPl) wax crayon

creación *f* (a) (en general) creation (b) (Relig) **la C~** the Creation

creador -dora *adj* creative
■ *m,f* (a) (en general) creator; **~es de moda** fashion designers (b) (Relig) **el C~** the Creator

crear [A1] *vt* to create; ⟨producto⟩ to develop; ⟨institución/comisión/fondo⟩ to set up; ⟨fama/prestigio⟩ to bring; ⟨reputación⟩ to earn; **crea**

muchos problemas it causes *o* creates a lot of problems; **no quiero ~ falsas expectativas** I don't want to raise false hopes
■ **crearse** *v pron* ⟨problema⟩ to create … for oneself; ⟨enemigos⟩ to make

creatividad *f* creativity

creativo -va *adj* creative

crecer [E3] *vi* **1** (a) «ser vivo/pelo/uñas» to grow; **dejarse ~ la barba** to grow a beard (b) (criarse) to grow up; **crecieron en un pueblo** they grew up in a village **2** (a) «río» to rise; «ciudad» to grow; «luna» to wax (b) «sentimiento/interés» to grow; «rumor» to spread (c) «economía» to grow; **el número de desempleados ha crecido** the number of unemployed has risen (d) (en importancia, sabiduría) **~ EN algo** to grow IN sth

creces: **pagar con ~ un error** to pay dearly for a mistake; **superar algo con ~** ⟨nivel/previsiones⟩ to far exceed sth

crecida *f* (a) (subida de nivel): **el río experimentó una fuerte ~** the river level rose sharply (b) (desbordamiento): **las ~s del Paraná** the flooding of the Paraná

creciente *adj* (a) ⟨interés/necesidad⟩ increasing (b) (Astron): **luna ~** waxing moon

crecimiento *m* growth; **una industria en ~** a growth industry; **durante el ~** while they are growing

credibilidad *f* credibility

crédito *m* **1** (a) (en negocio) credit; **tengo ~ aquí** they let me have credit here; **a ~** on credit (b) (cuenta) account *o* (préstamo) loan; **~ hipotecario** mortgage loan **2** (credibilidad): **fuentes dignas de ~** reliable sources; **no di ~ a sus palabras** I doubted his words (frml) **3** (Cin, TV, Educ) credit

credo *m* creed

crédulo -la *adj* credulous, gullible

creencia *f* belief

creer [E13] *vi* (a) (tener fe, aceptar como verdad) to believe; **~ EN algo/algn** to believe IN sth/sb; **¿me crees?** do you believe me? (b) (pensar, juzgar) to think; **¿tú crees?** do you think so?; **no creo** I don't think so; **no creas, es bastante difícil** believe me, it's quite hard
■ **~ ~** (a) (dar por cierto) to believe; **hay que verlo para ~lo** it has to be seen to be believed; **aunque no lo creas** believe it or not; **¡no lo puedo ~!** I don't believe it!; **¡ya lo creo!** of course! (b) (pensar, juzgar) to think; **creo que sí/creo que no** I think so/I don't think so; **creo que va a llover** I think it's going to rain; **no la creo capaz** I do not think she is capable; **se cree que el incendio fue provocado** the fire is thought to have been started deliberately; **no lo creí necesario** I didn't think it necessary; **no creo que pueda ir** I doubt if *o* I don't think I'll be able to go; **creí oír un ruido** I thought I heard a noise; **creo recordar que …** I seem to remember that …
■ **creerse** *v pron* (a) (enf) (con ingenuidad) to believe; **eso nadie se lo cree** no one believes that (b) (con arrogancia) to think; **se cree muy listo** he thinks he's really clever; **¿quién se ~á que es?** who does he think he is? (c) (CS fam) (estimarse superior) to think one is special (*o* great *etc*) (d) (Méx) (fiarse) **~se DE algn** to trust sb

creído -da *adj* [SER] (engreído) conceited

crema *f* **(a)** (plato dulce) *type of custard* **(b)** (esp AmL) (de la leche) cream; ~ **batida** whipped cream; ~ **agria** *or* **ácida** (AmL) sour *o* soured cream; ~ **chantilly** *or* **chantilli** (AmL) whipped cream (*with sugar, vanilla and egg white*); ~ **doble/líquida** (AmL) double/single cream; ~ **pastelera** crème pâtissière, confectioner's custard **(c)** (sopa) cream **(d)** (en cosmética) cream; ~ **bronceadora** suntan lotion *o* cream; ~ **de afeitar** shaving cream; ~ **de calzado** (Esp) shoe cream; ~ **hidratante** moisturizer, moisturizing cream
■ *adj inv* cream; **(de) color** ~ cream, cream-colored

cremallera *f* **(a)** (Indum) zipper (AmE), zip (BrE) **(b)** (Mec, Tec) rack

cremar [A1] *vt* to cremate

crematorio *m* crematorium

cremoso -sa *adj* ‹salsa› creamy; ‹queso› soft, creamy

crep *m* (*pl* **creps**), (Méx) **crepa** *f* crepe

crepe /krep/ *m or f* (Coc) crepe

crepé *m* (Tex) crepe

crepería *f* creperie

crepúsculo *m* (del anochecer) twilight; (del amanecer) dawn light

crespo¹ -pa *adj* (rizado) (AmL) curly; (muy rizado) frizzy

crespo² *m* (AmL) curl

cresta *f* **(a)** (Zool) crest; (de gallo) comb **(b)** (de ola, monte) crest

cretino -na *adj* cretinous
■ *m,f* cretin

creyente *adj*: **es muy** ~ she has a strong faith
■ *mf* believer; **los no** ~**s** the nonbelievers

creyera, creyese, etc ▶ CREER

cría *f* **(a)** (crianza) rearing, raising; (para la reproducción) breeding **(b)** (Zool) (camada) litter; (nidada) brood **(c)** (animal): **una** ~ **de ciervo** a baby deer

criadero *m* farm; ~ **de pollos/de truchas** poultry/trout farm; ~ **de perros** kennel (AmE), kennels (BrE); ~ **de ostras** oyster bed

criado -da *m,f* (*m*) servant; (*f*) servant, maid

criador -dora *m,f* breeder

crianza *f* **1** (Agr) raising, rearing; (para la reproducción) breeding **2** (de niños) upbringing

criar [A17] *vt* **1** (a) (cuidar, educar) to bring up, raise **(b)** (amamantar) to breast-feed; **criado con biberón** bottle-fed **2** (a) ‹ganado› to raise, rear; (para la reproducción) to breed **(b)** ‹pollos/pavos› to breed
■ **criarse** *v pron* to grow up; **me crie en el campo** I grew up in the country; **me crie con mi abuela** I was brought up by my grandmother

criatura *f* **(a)** (niño — pequeño) child; (— recién nacido) baby **(b)** (cosa creada) creature

criba *f* **(a)** (instrumento) sieve **(b)** (proceso de selección): **la primera** ~ the first stage of the selection process; **hicimos una** ~ **de las solicitudes** we went through the applications

cribar [A1] *vt* to sieve, sift

cricket /'krike(t)/ *m* cricket

crimen *m* (delito grave) serious crime; (asesinato) murder; ~ **de guerra** war crime; ~ **pasional** crime of passion; **es un** ~ **tirar esta comida** it's a crime to throw away this food; **¡qué** ~**!** it's wicked *o* criminal

criminal *adj/mf* criminal

criminalidad *f* **(a)** (cualidad) criminality **(b)** (número de crímenes) crime

criminalista *adj* criminal (*before n*)
■ *mf* criminal lawyer

crin *f* **(a)** (del caballo) *tb* ~**es** mane **(b)** (pelo de caballo) horsehair **(c)** (esparto) esparto grass

crío, cría (esp Esp fam) *m,f* kid (colloq)

criollo -lla *adj* **(a)** (Hist) Creole **(b)** (AmL) (por oposición a extranjero) Venezuelan (*o Peruvian etc*); ‹plato/artesanía/cocina› national
■ *m,f* **(a)** (Hist) Creole (*of European descent born in a Spanish American colony*) **(b)** (AmL) (nativo) Venezuelan (*o Peruvian etc*)

cripta *f* crypt

criquet *m* (Dep) cricket

crisantemo *m* chrysanthemum

crisis *f* (*pl* ~) **(a)** (en general) crisis; ~ **nerviosa** nervous breakdown **(b)** (period) (remodelación ministerial) *tb* ~ **de Gobierno** cabinet reshuffle

crismas *m* (*pl* ~) (Esp) Christmas card

crispar [A1] *vt* **(a)** (contraer): **con la expresión crispada por el dolor** his face tensed/contorted with pain **(b)** (exasperar) to infuriate; **me crispa los nervios** it really irritates me *o* gets on my nerves
■ **crisparse** *v pron* ‹rostro/expresión› to tense up; ‹persona› to get irritated

cristal *m* **1** (a) (vidrio fino) crystal; ~ **de roca** rock crystal; ~ **tallado** *or* (AmL) **cortado** cut glass **(b)** (lente) lens **2** (Esp) (vidrio) glass; (trozo) piece of glass; (de ventana) pane; **puerta de** ~ glass door; ~**es rotos** pieces of glass; **limpiar los** ~**s** to clean the windows; ~ **delantero** (Esp) windshield (AmE), windscreen (BrE); ~ **trasero** (Esp) rear windshield (AmE), rear windscreen (BrE)

cristalera *f* (Esp) **(a)** (mueble) display cabinet, dresser **(b)** (escaparate) shop window **(c)** (puertas) French windows (*pl*), French doors (*pl*) (AmE); (ventanas) windows (*pl*)

cristalería *f* (objetos) glassware; (juego) set of glasses

cristalero -ra *m,f* (Esp) (persona que instala) glazier

cristalino -na *adj* crystalline

cristalizar [A4] *vi/vt* to crystallize

cristiandad *f* Christendom

cristianismo *m* Christianity

cristianizar [A4] *vt* to Christianize

cristiano -na *adj/m,f* Christian; **¿eres** ~**?** are you a Christian?

Cristo Christ; **antes/después de** ~ before Christ *o* BC/AD

criterio *m* **(a)** (norma, principio) criterion; **tenemos que unificar** ~**s** we have to agree on our criteria **(b)** (capacidad para juzgar, discernir) discernment (fml); judgment*; **te dejo a tu** ~ I leave that to your discretion *o* judgment; **no tiene** ~ he has no common sense **(c)** (opinión, juicio) opinion

crítica *f* **(a)** (ataque, censura) criticism; **fue objeto de numerosas** ~**s** she was the object of a lot of criticism **(b)** (reseña) review; (ensayo) critique; **la** ···✦

película recibió muy buenas ∼s the movie had very good reviews; **la ∼** (los críticos) the critics (*pl*); **∼ literaria** literary criticism

criticar [A2] *vt* **(a)** (censurar) to criticize **(b)** (Art, Espec, Lit) ⟨*libro/película*⟩ to review
■ ∼ *vi* to gossip, backbite

crítico -ca *adj* critical
■ *m,f* critic

criticón -cona *adj* (fam & pey) critical, hypercritical
■ *m,f* (fam & pey) faultfinder

Croacia *f* Croatia

croar [A1] *vi* to croak

croata *adj* Croatian, Croat
■ *mf* Croat; **los ∼s** the Croats, Croatian people

crochet /kro'tʃe/ *m* crochet; **hacer ∼** to crochet

croissant /krwa'san/ *m* (*pl* **-ssants**) croissant

crol *m* (Dep) crawl

cromo *m* **(a)** (metal) chromium, chrome **(b)** (Esp) (estampa) picture card, sticker

cromosoma *m* chromosome

crónica *f* **(a)** (Period) report, article; (Rad, TV) report; **∼ deportiva/de sociedad** sport(s)/society page (*o* section *etc*) **(b)** (Hist) chronicle

crónico -ca *adj* chronic

cronista *mf* **(a)** (esp AmL) (periodista) journalist, reporter; **∼ de radio** radio broadcaster **(b)** (Hist) chronicler

cronología *f* chronology

cronológico -ca *adj* chronological

cronometrar [A1] *vt* to time

cronómetro *m* (Tec) chronometer; (Dep) stopwatch

croqueta *f* croquette

croquis *m* (*pl* ∼) sketch

cross /kros/ *m* **(a)** (deporte — en atletismo) cross-country running; (— en motociclismo) motocross **(b)** (carrera — a pie) cross country, cross-country race; (— en moto) motocross race

cruce *m* **①** **(a)** (acción) crossing **(b)** (de calles) crossroads; **⊖ cruce peligroso** dangerous junction; **∼ peatonal** *or* **de peatones** pedestrian crossing **(c)** (Telec): **hay un ∼ en las líneas** there's a crossed line **②** (Agr, Biol) cross

cruceiro *m* (unidad monetaria) cruzeiro (*former Brazilian unit of currency*)

crucero *m* **(a)** (viaje) cruise; **hizo un ∼ por el Caribe** he went on a Caribbean cruise **(b)** (barco de guerra) cruiser **(c)** (Méx) (de carreteras) crossroads; (Ferr) grade crossing (AmE), level crossing (BrE)

crucial *adj* crucial

crucificar [A2] *vt* to crucify

crucifijo *m* crucifix

crucigrama *m* crossword, crossword puzzle

cruda *f* (AmC, Méx fam) hangover

crudeza *f* harshness; (del clima) severity, harshness

crudo -da *adj* **①** [ESTAR] ⟨*carne/verduras/pescado*⟩ (sin cocinar) raw; (poco hecho) underdone **②** [SER] **(a)** ⟨*invierno/clima*⟩ severe, harsh **(b)** ⟨*lenguaje/imágenes/realidad*⟩ harsh

cruel *adj* cruel; **ser ∼ con algn** to be cruel to sb

crueldad *f* cruelty; **eso es una ∼** that's cruel; **∼ mental** mental cruelty

crujido *m* **(a)** (de tablas, muelles, ramas) creaking **(b)** (de papel, hojas secas) rustling; (de seda) rustle **(c)** (de los nudillos, las rodillas) cracking **(d)** (de la grava, nieve) crunching **(e)** (de los dientes) grinding

crujiente *adj* ⟨*galletas/tostadas*⟩ crunchy; ⟨*pan*⟩ crusty

crujir [I1] *vi* **(a)** «*tabla/muelles/ramas*» to creak; «*hojas secas*» to rustle **(b)** «*nudillos/rodillas*» to crack **(c)** «*grava/nieve*» to crunch **(d)** «*galletas/tostadas*» to be crunchy **(e)** «*dientes*»: **le crujen los dientes** he grinds his teeth

crustáceo *m* crustacean

cruz *f* **①** **(a)** (figura) cross; **ponte con los brazos en ∼** stand with your arms stretched out to the sides; **la C∼** (Relig) the Cross; **∼ gamada** swastika; **la C∼ Roja** the Red Cross **(b)** (ornamento, condecoración) cross **②** (de moneda) reverse; **cara o ∼** heads or tails

cruzada *f* crusade

cruzado -da *adj* **①** **(a)** (atravesado): **había un árbol ∼ en la carretera** there was a tree lying across the road **(b)** ⟨*abrigo/chaqueta*⟩ double-breasted **②** ⟨*cheque*⟩ crossed; *ver tb* CRUZAR

cruzar [A4] *vt* **①** (atravesar) ⟨*calle/mar/puente*⟩ to cross **②** ⟨*piernas*⟩ to cross; ⟨*brazos*⟩ to cross, fold **③** **(a)** ⟨*cheque*⟩ to cross **(b)** (tachar) to cross out **(c)** ⟨*palabras/saludos*⟩ to exchange **④** (llevar al otro lado) to take (*o* carry *etc*) ... across **⑤** ⟨*animales/plantas*⟩ to cross
■ ∼ *vi* (atravesar) to cross; **∼on por el puente** they went across the bridge
■ **cruzarse** *v pron* **①** (*recípr*) **(a)** «*caminos/líneas*» to intersect, meet **(b)** (en viaje, camino): **nos cruzamos en el camino** we met *o* passed each other on the way; **nuestras cartas se han debido de ∼** our letters must have crossed in the post; **∼se CON algn** to see *o* pass sb **②** (interponerse): **se me cruzó una moto** a motorcycle pulled out in front of him; **se me cruzó otro corredor** another runner cut in front of me

cta. (= **cuenta**) a/c

cuaderno *m* (de ejercicios) exercise book; (de notas) notebook; **∼ (de) borrador** rough notebook; **∼ de espiral** *o* (Chi) **de anillos** spiral-bound notebook

cuadra *f* **(a)** (Equ) stable, stables (*pl*) **(b)** (AmL) (distancia entre dos esquinas) block

cuadrado¹ -da *adj* **①** (de forma) square **(b)** (Mat) ⟨*metro/centímetro*⟩ square (*before n*); **2 m² ∼s** (*read as: dos metros cuadrados*) m² (*léase:*

two square meters) **2** [ESTAR] (fam) (fornido) well-built, big, hefty (colloq) **3** [SER] (AmL fam) (cerrado de mente) inflexible

cuadrado² *m* square; **25 elevado al ∼ 25** squared

cuadrar [A1] *vi* **(a)** «*cuentas*» to tally, balance **(b)** «*declaraciones/testimonías*» to tally; ∼ **CON algo** to fit in WITH sth, tally WITH sth **(c)** (Ven) (*para una cita*) ∼ **CON algn** to arrange to meet sb; ∼ **PARA hacer algo** to arrange to do sth
■ **cuadrarse** *v pron* **(a)** «*soldado*» to stand to attention **(b)** «*caballo/toro*» to stand stock-still **(c)** (Col, Ven fam) (estacionarse) to park

cuadriculado -da *adj* ⟨*papel*⟩ squared; **mapa** ∼ grid map

cuadrilátero *m* **(a)** (Mat) quadrilateral **(b)** (*period*) (de boxeo) ring

cuadrilla *f* **(a)** (Taur) cuadrilla *(team of matador's assistants)* **(b)** (de obreros) team, gang; (de soldados) squad; (de maleantes) gang

cuadro *m* **1** **(a)** (Art) (pintura) painting; (grabado, reproducción) picture **(b)** (Teatr) scene **(c)** (gráfico) table, chart **2** **(a)** (cuadrado) square, check; **tela a** ∼**s** checked material; **zanahorias cortadas en cuadritos** diced carrots **(b)** (tablero) board, panel; ∼ **de mandos** *or* **instrumentos** (Auto) dashboard; (Aviac) instrument panel **(c)** (de bicicleta) frame **3** (en organización): **los** ∼**s directivos del partido** the top party officials; **los** ∼**s superiores de la empresa** the company's senior management; ∼**s de mando** (Mil) commanders (*pl*)

cuadrúpedo -da *adj/m* quadruped (*before n*)

cuádruple, cuádruplo *m*: **esta cifra es el** ∼ **de la que esperábamos** this figure is four times what we expected

cuajada *f* junket, curd

cuajar [A1] *vi* **1** **(a)** «*leche*» to curdle; «*flan/ yogur*» to set **(b)** «*nieve*» to settle **2** **(a)** «*ideología*» to be accepted; «*plan/proyecto*» to come off; «*moda*» to catch on, take off **(b)** «*persona*» to fit in
■ ∼ *vt* ⟨*leche*⟩ to curdle

cuajo *m* **1** (sustancia) rennet **2** (raíz): **arrancar algo de** ∼ ⟨*planta*⟩ to pull sth out by the roots; ⟨*vicio/corrupción*⟩ to root out (completely)

cual *pron* **1** **(a)** **el/la** ∼**/los/las** ∼**es** (hablando de personas) (*sujeto*) who; (*complemento*) who, whom (frml); (hablando de cosas) which; **mis vecinos, a los** ∼**es no conocía** my neighbors who I didn't know *o* (frml) whom I did not know; **el motivo por el** ∼ **lo hizo** the reason why he did it; **según lo** ∼ ... by which ...; **dos de los** ∼**es** two of whom/which **(b)** **lo** ∼ which; **por lo** ∼ as a result, therefore; **con lo** ∼ so **2** (*en locs*) **cada cual** everyone, everybody; **sea cual sea** *or* **fuera** *or* **fuere** whatever

cuál *pron* (uno en particular) which; (uno en general) what; **¿**∼ **quieres?** which (one) do you want?; **¿y** ∼ **es el problema?** so, what's the problem?
■ *adj* (esp AmL): **¿a** ∼ **colegio vas?** what *o* which school do you go to?

cualidad *f* quality

cualificado -da *adj* (Esp) ▶ CALIFICADO

cualificar [A2] *vt* (Esp) ▶ CALIFICAR 2 B

cualquier *adj*: apocopated form of CUALQUIERA used before nouns

cualquiera¹ (*pl* **cualesquiera** or (crit)

cualquiera) *adj* [*see also note under* CUALQUIER] any; **en cualquier momento** (at) any time; **cualquier cosa/persona** anything/anyone; **en cualquier lado** anywhere; **de cualquier forma que se haga** whichever way you do it; **lo voy a hacer de** ∼ **mercenario** he's nothing but a mercenary
■ *pron* (refiriéndose — a dos personas o cosas) either (of them); (— a más de dos personas) anybody, anyone; (— a más de dos cosas) any one; **¿cuál de los dos?** — **cualquiera** which one? — either (of them); **pregúntaselo a** ∼ ask anybody *o* anyone (you like); ∼ **que elijas estará bien** whichever (one) you choose *o* any one you choose will be fine

cualquiera² *mf*: **un** ∼ a nobody; **una** ∼ a floozy *o* (BrE) tart (colloq & pey)

cuando *conj* **(a)** (con valor temporal) when; **ven** ∼ **quieras** come when *o* whenever you like; ∼ **se mejore** when she gets better; **ahora es** ∼ **me viene mejor** now is the best time for me **(b)** (si) if; **será verdad** ∼ **él lo dice** it must be true if he says so **(c)** (*en locs*) **cada cuando** (esp AmL) every so often; **de vez en cuando** from time to time, every so often

cuándo *adv* when; **¿de** ∼ **es esa foto?** when was that photo taken?; **¿desde** ∼ **lo sabes?** how long have you known?; **¿desde** ∼**?** since when?; **¡**∼ **no!** (AmL) as usual!

cuantificar [A2] *vt* ⟨*valor/daños/pérdidas*⟩ to quantify, assess

cuantioso -sa *adj* substantial

cuanto¹ *adv* **(a)** (tanto como) as much as; **grita** ∼ **quieras** shout as much as you like **(b)** (*como conj*): ∼**s más/menos seamos, mejor** the more/ the fewer of us there are the better; ∼ **antes empecemos, más pronto terminaremos** the sooner we begin, the sooner we'll finish **(c)** (*en locs*) **cuanto antes** as soon as possible; **en cuanto** (tan pronto como) as soon as; **en cuanto a** (en lo que concierne) as for, as regards

cuanto² -ta *adj*: **llévate** ∼**s discos quieras** take as many records as you want *o* like; **unos** ∼**s amigos** a few friends; **tiene** ∼ **libro hay sobre el tema** she has every book there is on the subject
■ *pron*: **le di todo** ∼ **tenía** I gave her everything I had; **fuimos solo unos** ∼**s** only a few of us went

cuánto¹ *adv* **(a)** (en preguntas) how much **(b)** (uso indirecto): **si supieras** ∼ **lo quiero/lo siento** if you knew how much I love her/how sorry I am

cuánto² -ta *adj* **(a)** (en preguntas) (*sing*) how much; (*pl*) how many; **¿**∼ **café queda?** how much coffee is there left?; **¿**∼**s alumnos tienes?** how many students do you have?; **¿**∼**s años tienes?** how old are you?; **¿**∼ **tiempo tardarás?** how long will you take? **(b)** (uso indirecto) (*sing*) how much; (*pl*) how many; **no sé** ∼ **dinero/**∼**s libros tengo** I don't know how much money/how many books I have **(c)** (en exclamaciones): **¡**∼ **vino!** what a lot of wine!; **¡**∼ **tiempo sin verte!** I haven't seen you for ages! (colloq)
■ *pron* **1** (en preguntas) **(a)** (*sing*) how much; (*pl*) how many; **¿**∼ **pesas?** how much do you weigh?; **¿**∼ **mides?** how tall are you?; **¿**∼**s quieres?** how many do you want?; **¿a** ∼ **estamos hoy?** what's the date today? **(b)** (referido a tiempo) how long; **¿**∼ **falta para llegar?** how long before we get there? ···⊰·

(c) (referido a precios, dinero) how much; ¿~ cuesta? how much is it?; ¿~ es? how much is that (altogether)?

2 (uso indirecto): pregúntale ~ va a demorar ask her how long she'll be; no sé ~ puede costar/~s tiene I don't know how much it might cost/how many she has

3 (en exclamaciones): ¡~ has tardado! it's taken you a long time!

cuarenta adj inv/pron/m forty; para ejemplos ver CINCUENTA; cantarle las ~ a algn to give sb a piece of one's mind

cuarentena f (aislamiento) quarantine

cuarentón -tona m,f (fam) person in his/her forties

Cuaresma f Lent

cuarta f (Auto) fourth (gear); mete la ~ put it in fourth

cuartel m **(a)** (Mil) barracks (sing o pl); ~ de bomberos (RPl) fire station, fire house (AmE); ~ general headquarters (sing o pl) **(b)** (tregua): no dieron ~ a los rebeldes they showed no mercy to the rebels; una lucha sin ~ a merciless fight

cuartelada f, **cuartelazo** m putsch, military uprising

cuarteto m (Mús) quartet

cuarto¹ -ta adj/pron fourth; la cuarta parte a quarter; para ejemplos ver QUINTO

cuarto² m **1** (habitación) room; (dormitorio) room, bedroom; ~ de baño bathroom; ~ de estar living room, parlor (AmE), sitting room (BrE); ~ de (los) huéspedes guest room, spare room; ~ trastero lumber room, junk room **2 (a)** (cuarta parte) quarter; un ~ de kilo a quarter (of a) kilo; un ~ de pollo a quarter chicken; ~ creciente/menguante first/last quarter; ~s de final quarterfinals (pl) **(b)** (en expresiones de tiempo) quarter; un ~ de hora a quarter of an hour; la una y ~ (a) quarter after (AmE) o (BrE) past one, one fifteen; es un ~ para las dos or (Esp, RPl) son las dos menos ~ it is a quarter to two

cuarzo m quartz

cuate mf (Méx) **(a)** (mellizo) twin **(b)** (fam) (amigo) pal (colloq) **(c)** (fam) (tipo, tipa) (m) guy (colloq); (f) woman

cuatrapearse [A1] v pron (Méx) «aparato» to break; «planes» to fall through

cuatrero -ra m,f rustler

cuatrillizo -za m,f quadruplet, quad

cuatro adj inv/pron four; ¿llueve? — no, solo son ~ gotas is it raining? no, it's just a drop or two; le escribí ~ líneas I wrote him a couple of lines; para más ejemplos ver tb CINCO
■ m **(a)** (número) (number) four; para ejemplos ver CINCO **(b)** (Ven) (guitarra) four-stringed guitar

cuatrocientos -tas adj/pron four hundred; para ejemplos ver QUINIENTOS

cuba f **(a)** (barril) barrel, cask; estar como una ~ (fam) to be plastered (colloq) **(b)** (tina) tub, vat

Cuba f Cuba

cubalibre m (de ron) rum and coke; (de ginebra) gin and coke

cubano -na adj/m,f Cuban

cubertería f cutlery; una ~ de plata a set of silver cutlery

cubeta f **(a)** (Fot, Quím) tray; (de paredes más altas) tank **(b)** (para hielo) ice tray **(c)** (barril) keg, small cask **(d)** (Méx) (balde) bucket

cúbico -ca adj cubic; 2m³ (read as: dos metros cúbicos) 2m³ (léase: two cubic meters)

cubierta f **1 (a)** (funda) cover; (de libro) cover, sleeve **(b)** (Auto) tire* **2** (Náut) (en barco) deck; salir a ~ to go up on deck

cubierto¹ -ta adj ‹cielo› overcast, cloudy; ver tb CUBRIR

cubierto² m **1 (a)** (pieza) piece of cutlery; los ~s de plata the silver cutlery **(b)** (servicio de mesa) place setting; pon otro ~ can you set another place? **2** (en locs) a cubierto: ponerse a ~ de la lluvia to take cover o to shelter from the rain

cubilete m **(a)** (vaso) beaker; (para dados) shaker, cup **(b)** (Col) (sombrero) top hat

cubitera f (bandeja) ice tray; (cubo) ice bucket

cubo m **1** (Esp) bucket; ~ de (la) basura (de la cocina) garbage can (AmE), (kitchen) bin (BrE); (de edificio) garbage can (AmE), rubbish bin (BrE) **2 (a)** (cuerpo geométrico) cube; cubito de hielo ice cube; cubito de caldo stock cube **(b)** (Mat) cube; elevar un número al ~ to cube a number

cubrecama m bedspread

cubrir [I33] vt **(a)** (en general) to cover; ~ algo DE algo to cover sth WITH sth; cubrí al niño con una manta I covered the child with a blanket **(b)** ‹demanda/necesidad› to meet **(c)** ‹plaza/vacante› to fill
■ **cubrirse** v pron **1 (a)** (refl) (taparse) to cover oneself; ‹cara› to cover **(b)** (ponerse el sombrero) to put one's hat on **(c)** (protegerse) to take cover **(d)** (contra riesgo) to cover oneself **2** (llenarse): las calles se habían cubierto de nieve the streets were covered with snow

cucaracha f (Zool) cockroach

cuchara f spoon; ~ de postre dessertspoon; ~ sopera or de sopa soup spoon

cucharada f spoonful; ~ sopera ≈ tablespoonful

cucharadita f teaspoon, teaspoonful

cucharilla, cucharita f (Coc) teaspoon

cucharón m ladle

cucheta f (RPl) trundle bed, truckle bed

cuchichear [A1] vi (fam) to whisper

cuchilla f **(a)** (de segadora, batidora, cuchillo) blade; (de arado) coulter, share **(b)** tb ~ de afeitar (hoja) razor blade; (maquinilla) razor

cuchillada f, **cuchillazo** m **(a)** (golpe) stab; le dio una ~ she stabbed him **(b)** (herida) stab wound

cuchillo m knife; ~ de cocina kitchen knife

cuchitril m hole (colloq), hovel

cucho -cha m,f **1** (Col fam) **(a)** (padre) dad (colloq); (madre) mom (AmE colloq), mum (BrE colloq) **(b)** (profesor) teacher (colloq); (viejecito) (m) old guy (colloq); (f) old girl (colloq) **2** (Chi fam) (gato) puss (colloq)

cuclillas fpl: en ~ squatting, crouching; ponerse en ~ to squat

cuco m **1** (Zool) cuckoo **2** (Esp) (de bebé) Moses basket **3** (CS, Per leng infantil) bogeyman

cucú m cuckoo

cucurucho *m* **(a)** (de papel, cartón) cone; (de barquillo) cone **(b)** (helado) cone, cornet (BrE) **(c)** (capirote) hood, pointed hat

cuece, cuecen, etc ▶ COCER

cuello *m* **(a)** (Anat) neck; **le cortaron el ~** they slit *o* cut his throat **(b)** (de botella) neck; **~ de botella** (Auto) bottleneck **(c)** (de prenda de vestir) collar; **sin ~** collarless **(d)** (escote) neck; **~ alto** *or* **vuelto** *or* (AmL) **tortuga** turtleneck (AmE), polo neck (BrE); **~ de pico** V neck; **~ redondo** round neck

cuenca *f* **(a)** (Geog, Geol) basin **(b)** (del ojo) socket

cuenco *m* (recipiente) bowl

cuenta *f*

> ■ **Nota** Cuando la frase *darse cuenta* va seguida de una oración subordinada introducida por *de que*, en el español latinoamericano existe cierta tendencia a omitir la preposición *de* en el lenguaje coloquial: *se dio cuenta que no iba a convencerla* = he realized (that) he wasn't going to convince her

1 **(a)** (operación, cálculo) calculation, sum; **hacer una ~** to do a calculation *o* sum; **saca la ~** add it up, work it out; **hacer** *or* **sacar ~s** to do some calculations; *a fin de* **~s** after all **(b) cuentas** *fpl* (contabilidad) accounts: **yo llevo las ~s del negocio** I do the accounts for the business, I handle the money side of the business (colloq); **ella se ocupa de las ~s de la casa** she pays all the bills and looks after the money **(c)** (cómputo) count; **llevar/perder la ~** to keep/lose count; **~ atrás** countdown; *más de la* **~** too much

2 **(a)** (factura) bill; **¿nos trae la ~, por favor?** could we have the check (AmE) *o* (BrE) bill, please?; **la ~ del gas** the gas bill; **a cuenta** on account; **entregó $2.000 a ~** she gave me/him/ them $2,000 on account; **este dinero es a ~ de lo que te debo** this money is to go toward(s) what I owe you **(b)** (Com, Fin) (en banco, comercio) account; **abrir/cerrar/liquidar una ~** to open/close/to settle an account; **~ corriente/de ahorro(s)** current/ savings account

3 **cuentas** *fpl* (explicaciones): **no tengo por qué darte ~s** I don't have to explain *o* justify myself to you; **dar** *or* **rendir ~s de algo** to account for sth; *en resumidas cuentas* in short

4 (cargo, responsabilidad): **los gastos corren por ~ de la empresa** the expenses are covered *o* paid by the company; **se instaló por su ~** she set up (in business) on her own; **trabaja por ~ propia** she's self-employed

5 **darse ~ (de algo)** (comprender) to realize (sth); (notar) to notice (sth); **se da ~ de todo** she's aware of everything that's going on (around her); **date ~ de que es imposible** you must realize (that) it's impossible; **tener algo en ~** to bear sth in mind; **ten en ~ que es joven** bear in mind that he's young; **sin tener en ~ los gastos** without taking the expenses into account; **tomar algo en ~** to take sth into consideration

6 (de collar, rosario) bead

cuenta, cuentas, etc ▶ CONTAR

cuentagotas *m* (*pl* **~**) dropper

cuentakilómetros *m* (*pl* **~**) (de distancia recorrida) odometer (AmE), mileometer (BrE); (de velocidad) speedometer

cuentero -ra *adj* (Méx, RPI fam) **(a)** (mentiroso): **ser ~** to be a fibber (colloq) **(b)** (chismoso) gossipy

cuentista *adj* **(a)** (fam) (exagerado): **no seas ~, que no duele tanto** don't exaggerate, it doesn't hurt that much **(b)** (fantasioso): **ser ~** to be a fibber (colloq)

> ■ *mf* **(a)** (Lit) short-story writer **(b)** (fam) (exagerado): **no te fíes de ese ~, es puro teatro** don't fall for his playacting, he's just putting it on **(c)** (fantasioso) fibber (colloq)

cuento *m* **(a)** (narración corta) short story; (para niños) story, tale; **cuéntame un ~** tell me a story; **~ de hadas** fairy story, fairy tale; **venir a ~**: **eso no viene a ~** that doesn't come into it; **sin venir a ~** for no reason at all **(b)** (chiste) joke, story **(c)** (fam) (mentira, excusa) story (colloq); **no me vengas con ~s** I'm not interested in your excuses *o* stories **(d)** (fam) (exageración): **todo ese llanto es puro ~** all that crying is just put on; **eso es un ~ chino** what a load of baloney; **el ~ del tío** a con trick

cuento ▶ CONTAR

cuerda *f* **1** **(a)** (gruesa) rope; (delgada) string; **~ floja** (Espec) tightrope **(b)** (Jueg) jump rope (AmE), skipping rope (BrE); **saltar a la ~** to jump rope (AmE), to skip (BrE) **(c)** (para tender ropa) washing line, clothes line **(d)** (de arco) bowstring **2** (Mús) **(a)** (de guitarra, violín) string **(b) cuerdas** *fpl* (instrumentos) strings (*pl*); **~s vocales** vocal chords (*pl*) **3** (de reloj, juguete): **un juguete de ~** a clockwork toy; **le dio ~ al despertador** she wound up the alarm clock

cuerdo -da *adj* [ESTAR] sane; **no está ~** he is insane

cuerno *m* **(a)** (de toro) horn; (de caracol) feeler; (de ciervo) antler; **irse al ~** (fam) «*plan*» to fall through; «*fiesta*» to be ruined *o* spoiled; **ponerle los ~s a algn** (fam) to be unfaithful to sb **(b)** (Mús) horn

cuero *adj* (Méx fam) gorgeous (colloq)

> ■ *m* (piel) leather; (sin curtir) skin, hide; **chaqueta de ~** leather jacket; **~ de chancho** (AmL) pigskin; **~ de vaca** cowhide; **en ~(s)** (vivos) (fam) (desnudo) stark naked (colloq); **ser un ~** (Chi, Méx fam) «*mujer*» she's a real stunner (colloq); «*hombre*» he's a real hunk (colloq)

cuerpo *m* **1** **(a)** (Anat) body; **el ~ humano** the human body; **retrato/espejo de ~ entero** full-length portrait/mirror; **~ a ~** hand-to-hand **(b)** (cadáver) body, corpse **(c)** (Fís) (objeto) body, object **2** (conjunto de personas, de ideas, normas) body; **~ de bomberos** fire department (AmE), fire brigade (BrE); **~ de policía** police force; **~ diplomático** diplomatic corps **3** (consistencia, densidad) body; **de mucho ~** «*tela*» heavy; «*vino*» full-bodied

cuervo *m* raven; (como nombre genérico) crow

cuesco *m* (Bot) stone

cuesta *f* **(a)** (pendiente) slope; **una ~ muy pronunciada** a very steep slope; **ir ~ arriba** to go uphill; **iba corriendo ~ abajo** I was running downhill **(b) a cuestas**: **llevar algo a ~s** to carry sth on one's shoulders/back; **echarse algo a ~s** «*carga/bulto*» to put sth on one's back; «*problema*» to burden oneself with sth

cuesta, cuestan, etc ▶ COSTAR

cuestión *f* **(a)** (tema, problema) question, matter; **cuestiones de derecho internacional** matters *o* ⋯⋗

questions of international law; **llegar al fondo de
la** ~ to get to the heart of the matter **(b)** *(en locs)*
en cuestión in question; **en cuestión de** in a
matter of; **la cuestión es ...** the thing is ...; **la** ~
es divertirnos the main thing is to enjoy
ourselves; **ser cuestión de** to be a matter of; **todo
es** ~ **de ...** it's just a question of ...

cuestionar [A1] *vt* to question

cuestionario *m* (encuesta) questionnaire;
(Educ) question paper, questions *(pl)*

cuete *m* ⊡ (Méx, RPl fam) (borrachera): **agarrar un**
~ to get plastered (colloq) ⊡ (AmL fam) (petardo)
firecracker ⊡ (Per fam) (pistola) shooter (colloq),
rod (sl) ⊡ (Méx) (Coc) braising steak

cueva *f* cave

cueza, cuezan, etc ▸ COCER

cuidado¹ -da *adj* *(presentación)* meticulous,
careful; *(aspecto)* impeccable; *(dicción)* precise

cuidado² *m* **(a)** (precaución): **tener** ~ to be
careful; **lo envolvió con mucho** ~ she wrapped it
very carefully; **¡**~ **con el escalón!** mind the step!;
~ **con lo que haces** watch *o* be careful what you
do ; **de** ~ (fam) *(problema/herida)* serious **(b)**
(atención) care; **pone mucho** ~ **en su trabajo** he
takes a great deal of care over his work **(c)** (de
niños, enfermos): **no tiene experiencia en el** ~ **de
los niños** he has no experience of looking after
children; **estar al** ~ **de algn/algo** (cuidar) to look
after sb/sth; (ser cuidado por) to be in sb's care **(d)**
cuidados *mpl* (Med) attention, care, treatment;
necesita los ~**s de una enfermera** she needs to be
looked after by a nurse; ~**s intensivos** intensive
care **(e)** (preocupación): **pierde** ~ (AmL) don't
worry; **me tiene sin** ~ it doesn't matter to me in
the slightest
■ *interj* be careful!, watch out!

cuidador -dora *m,f* (de niños) baby sitter
(AmE), childminder (BrE); (de animales) zookeeper

cuidadoso -sa *adj* **(a)** *(persona)* careful; ~
CON algo careful WITH sth **(b)** *(búsqueda/
investigación)* careful, thorough

cuidar [A1] *vt* **(a)** *(juguetes/plantas/casa)* to
look after; *(niño)* to look after, take care of;
(enfermo) to care for, look after **(b)** *(estilo/
apariencia)* to take care over; **debes** ~ **la
ortografía** you must take care over your spelling
■ ~ *vi* ~ **DE algo/algn** to take care OF sth/sb; **~ré
de que no les falte nada** I'll make sure they have
everything they need
■ **cuidarse** *v pron* *(refl)* to take care of oneself,
look after oneself; **¡cuídate!** take care!; **se cuidó
bien de no volver por ahí** he made very sure he
didn't go back there; **cuídate de decir algo que te
comprometa** take care not to say something
which might compromise you

cuije *mf* (Méx) office junior

culantro *m* (fam) coriander

culata *f* (a) (de escopeta, revólver) butt; (de cañón)
breech **(b)** (de motor) cylinder head

culebra *f* (Zool) snake

culebrón *m* (fam) soap opera, soap (colloq)

culinario -ria *adj* culinary (frml)

culminación *f* **(a)** (de carrera, negociaciones)
culmination; (de fiesta) climax **(b)** (realización)
fulfillment*

culminante *adj:* **punto** ~ (de carrera) peak,
high point; (de historia, película) climax; (de
negociaciones) crucial stage

culminar [A1] *vi* (llegar al clímax): **la novela
culmina cuando ...** the novel reaches its climax
when ...; ~ **EN** *or* **CON algo** to culminate IN sth

culo *m* (fam: en algunas regiones vulg) **(a)** (nalgas)
backside (colloq), butt (AmE colloq), bum (BrE colloq),
ass (AmE vulg), arse (BrE vulg); **te voy a pegar en el**
~ I'm going to spank *o* smack you **(b)** (de vaso,
botella) bottom

culpa *f* **(a)** (responsabilidad) fault; **yo no tengo la**
~ it's not my fault; **echarle la** ~ **a algn** (de algo)
to blame sb *o* put the blame on sb (for sth); **llegó
tarde por** ~ **del tráfico** he arrived late because of
the traffic **(b)** (falta, pecado) sin

culpabilidad *f* (Der,Psic) guilt

culpable *adj* [SER] *(persona)* guilty; **sentirse** ~
de algo to feel guilty about sth; **ser** ~ **de algo** to
be to blame for sth; (Der) to be guilty of sth
■ *mf* **(a)** (de delito) culprit **(b)** (de problema, situación):
tú eres el ~ **de todo esto** this is all your fault,
you're to blame for all this

culpar [A1] *vt* to blame; ~ **a algn DE algo** to
blame sb FOR sth, blame sth ON sb

cultivable *adj* cultivable

cultivado -da *adj* cultivated

cultivar [A1] *vt* *(campo/tierras)* to cultivate,
farm; *(plantas)* to grow, cultivate **(b)** *(bacterias/
perlas)* to culture **(c)** *(amistad)* to cultivate;
(inteligencia/memoria) to develop; *(artes/interés)*
to encourage

cultivo *m* **(a)** (de tierra) farming, cultivation; (de
plantas, frutas) growing, cultivation; ~ **intensivo**
intensive farming **(b)** (cosa cultivada) crop; ~**s de
secano** dry-farmed crops **(c)** (Biol, Med) (acción)
culturing; (producto) culture **(d)** (de las artes)
promotion, encouragement

culto¹ -ta *adj* **(a)** *(persona/pueblo)* educated,
cultured **(b)** (Ling) *(palabra)* learned; *(literatura/
música)* highbrow

culto² *m* **(a)** (adoración, creencia) worship; **rendir**
~ **a algo/algn** to worship sth/sb; **libertad de** ~**(s)**
freedom of worship **(b)** (interés obsesivo) cult; **el** ~
del dinero the cult of money

cultura *f* **(a)** (civilización) culture **(b)**
(conocimientos, ilustración): **una persona de gran** ~ a
very well-educated *o* cultured person; ~ **general/
musical** general/musical knowledge; **la** ~ **popular**
popular culture

cultural *adj* cultural; **un acto** ~ a cultural
event; **bajo nivel** ~ low standard of general
education

culturismo *m* bodybuilding

cumbre *f* **(a)** (de montaña) top **(b)** (apogeo)
height; **en la** ~ **del éxito** at the height of his
success **(c)** (Pol) summit (meeting)

cumpleañero -ra m,f (fam) (m) birthday boy (colloq); (f) birthday girl (colloq)

cumpleaños m (pl ∼) (a) (aniversario) birthday; ¡feliz ∼! happy birthday!; ¿qué vas a hacer el día de tu ∼? what are you going to do on your birthday? (b) (fiesta) birthday party

cumplido¹ -da adj [SER] (a) (atento, cortés) polite (b) (considerado) thoughtful (c) (Col) (puntual) punctual; ver tb CUMPLIR

cumplido² m: hacerle un ∼ a algn to pay sb a compliment; una visita de ∼ a duty o courtesy call; la invitó por ∼ he invited her because he felt he ought to

cumplidor -dora adj reliable

cumplimiento m [1] (a) (de ley, norma) performance; falleció en el ∼ del deber he died in the line of duty; en ∼ con lo dispuesto por la legislación vigente in compliance with current legislation; la ley es de obligado ∼ para todas las empresas the law is binding on all companies (frml) (b) (logro): esto favorecerá el ∼ de nuestros objetivos this will help to achieve our objectives [2] (elogio, piropo) ▶ CUMPLIDO²

cumplir [I1] vt [1] (a) (ejecutar) ⟨orden⟩ to carry out; ⟨ley⟩ to obey; la satisfacción del deber cumplido the satisfaction of having done one's duty (b) ⟨promesa/palabra⟩ to keep; ⟨compromiso⟩ to honor*, fulfill*; ⟨obligación/contrato⟩ to fulfill* (c) (alcanzar) ⟨objetivo/ambición⟩ to achieve; ⟨requisitos⟩ fulfill*; ¡misión cumplida! mission accomplished (d) (desempeñar) ⟨papel⟩ to perform, fulfill*
[2] ⟨condena/sentencia⟩ to serve; ⟨servicio militar⟩ to do
[3] ⟨años/meses⟩: mañana cumple 20 años she'll be 20 tomorrow; ¡que cumplas muchos más! many happy returns!; mañana cumplimos 20 años de casados (AmL) tomorrow we'll have been married 20 years

■ ∼ vi (a) ∼ CON algo ⟨con obligación⟩ to fulfill* sth, satisfy sth; ⟨con tarea⟩ to carry out sth; ⟨con trámite⟩ to comply WITH sth; ⟨con requisito/condición⟩ to fulfill* sth; cumple con su deber he does his duty (b) (con una obligación social): nos invitó solo por ∼ she only invited us because she felt she ought to; con los Lara ya hemos cumplido we've done our bit as far as the Laras are concerned (colloq)

■ **cumplirse** v pron (a) «deseo/predicción» to come true; «ambición» to be realized, fulfilled (b) «plazo»: mañana se cumple el plazo para pagar el impuesto tomorrow is the last day for paying the tax; hoy se cumple el primer aniversario de ... today marks the first anniversary of ...

cuna f (a) (tradicional) cradle; (cama con barandas) crib (AmE), cot (BrE); (portabebé) portacrib (AmE), carrycot (BrE) (b) (liter) (lugar de nacimiento) birthplace

cuncho m (Col) (poso — del café) grounds (pl); (— del vino) lees (pl)

cuncuna f (Chi) (Zool) caterpillar

cundir [I1] vi (a) «rumor» to spread; «miedo» to grow; ¡que no cunda el pánico! don't panic!; cundió la alarma there was widespread alarm (b) (rendir) «detergente/lana» to go a long way; hoy no me ha cundido el trabajo I haven't got much work done today

cuneta f (a) (en carretera) ditch (b) (Chi) (de calle) curb (AmE), kerb (BrE)

cuña f [1] (a) (pieza triangular) wedge; en ∼ in a V-formation o wedge formation (b) (Col) (muesca) groove [2] (CS fam) ▶ PALANCA 2

cuñado -da m,f (a) (pariente político) (m) brother-in-law; (f) sister-in-law; mis ∼s (solo varones) my brothers-in-law; (varones y mujeres) my brothers and sisters-in-law (b) (Per fam) (compañero) buddy (AmE colloq), mate (BrE colloq)

cuño m (troquel) die; (sello) stamp; de nuevo ∼ ⟨palabra⟩ newly-coined (before n)

cuota f (a) (de club, asociación) membership fees (pl); (de sindicato) dues (pl); ∼ inicial deposit, down payment (b) (AmL) (plazo) installment*, payment; (parte proporcional) quota; ∼s de producción production quotas (c) (Méx) (Auto) toll

cupe ▶ CABER

Cupido m Cupid

cupiera, cupiese, etc ▶ CABER

cupimos, cupisteis, etc ▶ CABER

cupo m (a) (cantidad establecida) quota (b) (AmL) (capacidad) room; una sala con ∼ para 300 personas a hall with room for 300 people (c) (AmL) (plaza) place

cupo, cupiste, etc ▶ CABER

cupón m (a) (vale) coupon, voucher (b) (Esp) (de lotería) ticket

cúpula f (Arquit) dome, cupola

cura m (sacerdote) priest; se metió de o a ∼ he became a priest
■ f (a) (curación, tratamiento) cure; tener/no tener ∼ to be curable/incurable; ∼ de urgencias first aid (b) (vendaje) dressing; (curita) (Col) Band-Aid® (AmE), (sticking) plaster (BrE)

curable adj curable

curación f (a) (tratamiento) treatment (b) (recuperación—de enfermo) recovery; (— de herida) healing

curado -da adj [1] ⟨jamón/carne⟩ cured; ⟨cuero/piel⟩ tanned [2] (fam) (borracho) plastered (colloq)

curandero -ra m,f (en medicina popular) folk healer; (hechicero) witch doctor; (charlatán) (pey) quack doctor (pej)

curar [A1] vt [1] (a) (poner bien) ⟨enfermo/enfermedad⟩ to cure; ⟨herida⟩ to heal (b) (tratar) ⟨enfermo/enfermedad⟩ to treat; ⟨herida⟩ (desinfectar) to clean; (vendar) to dress [2] ⟨jamón/pescado⟩ to cure; ⟨cuero/piel⟩ to tan
■ **curarse** v pron ⟨enfermo⟩ to recover, get better; «herida» to heal up; ∼se DE algo to get over sth

curda mf (RPl fam) (borracho) soak (colloq)

curiosear [A1] vi (a) (fisgonear) to pry; ∼ en la vida ajena to pry into other people's affairs; estaba curioseando en mis cajones he was going o looking through my drawers (b) (por las tiendas, en una biblioteca) to browse

curiosidad f (cualidad) curiosity; por ∼ out of curiosity; siente mucha ∼ he is very curious; tengo ∼ por saberlo I'm curious to know; están muertos de ∼ they are dying to see him (o to know etc)

curioso -sa adj [1] (interesante, extraño) curious, ⋯⟫

strange, odd **2** **(a)** [SER] (inquisitivo) inquisitive;
(entrometido) (pey) nosy* (colloq) **(b)** [ESTAR]
(interesado) curious
■ *m,f* **(a)** (espectador) onlooker **(b)** (fam) (fisgón)
busybody (colloq)

curita *f* (AmL) Band-Aid® (AmE), (sticking)
plaster (BrE)

currículo *m* (Educ) curriculum

curriculum, currículum *m* (*pl* **-lums**) **(a)**
(antecedentes) *tb* ~ **vitae** curriculum vitae, CV **(b)**
(Educ) curriculum

curry /'kurri/ *m* (*pl* **-rries**) (polvo) curry
powder; (plato) curry; **pollo al** ~ curried chicken

cursar [A1] *vt* (estudiar): **cursa segundo** (año)
she is in her second year; **cursó estudios de
Derecho** she did *o* studied *o* (BrE) read Law

cursi *adj* (fam) (objeto) corny, twee (BrE); (idea)
sentimental, twee (BrE); (decoración) chichi;
(persona) affected;
■ *mf* (fam): **es un** ~ he's so affected *o* (BrE) twee

cursillo *m* **(a)** (curso corto) short course; ~ **de
natación** swimming lessons **(b)** (ciclo de
conferencias) series of lectures

cursiva *f* italics (*pl*)

curso *m* **1** (Educ) **(a)** (año académico) year; **está
en (el) tercer** ~ he's in the third year; **el** ~
escolar/universitario the academic year **(b)** (de
inglés, mecanografía) course; ~ **intensivo** crash *o*
intensive course; **C**~ **de Orientación Universitaria**
(en Esp) pre-university course; ~ **por
correspondencia** correspondence course **2** **(a)**
(transcurso, desarrollo) course; **dejar que algo siga su**

~ **to let sth take its course (b)** (de río) course
3 (circulación): **monedas de** ~ **legal** legal tender,
legal currency

cursor *m* cursor

curtido -da *adj* (rostro/piel) weather-beaten;
(manos) hardened

curul *f* (Col, Méx) (Pol) seat

curva *f* **(a)** (línea) curve **(b)** (en camino, carretera)
curve; (más pronunciada) bend; **una** ~ **cerrada** a
sharp bend **(c)** (Dep) curveball **(c)** **curvas** *fpl*
(de una mujer) curves (*pl*); **con** ~**s** curvaceous

curvo -va *adj* curved

cúspide *f* **(a)** (de montaña) top, summit; (de
pirámide) top, apex **(b)** (de fama, poder) height,
pinnacle **(c)** (de organización) leadership

custodia *f* custody; **le otorgaron la** ~ **de los
hijos** she was granted custody of the children

cusuco *m* (AmC) armadillo

cutáneo -nea *adj* skin (before n), cutaneous
(tech)

cutícula *f* cuticle

cutis *m* (*pl* ~) skin

cuy *m* (AmS) guinea pig

cuye *m* (Chi) guinea pig

cuyo -ya *adj* whose; **un amigo** ~**s hijos van a
ese colegio** a friend whose children go to that
school; **vocablos** ~ **uso es extendido** words
which are in widespread use, **en** ~ **caso** in
which case

C.V. *m* (= **curriculum vitae**) CV

Dd

D, d *f* (read as /de/) the letter D, d

D. = **Don**

dactilar *adj* finger (before n); ▶ HUELLA A

dactilografía *f* typing, typewriting

dactilógrafo -fa *m,f* typist

dado¹ -da *adj* **1** (determinado) given; **en un
momento** ~ at a given moment **2** (como conj)
given; **dadas las circunstancias** given *o* in view of
the circumstances; ~ **que** given that **3** [SER]
(proclive) ~ A **algo/hacer algo** given TO sth/doing
sth

dado² *m* **1** (Juego) dice, die (frml); **jugar a los** ~**s**
to play dice **2** (Arquit) dado

daga *f* dagger

dalia *f* dahlia

daltónico -ca *adj* color-blind*
■ *m,f*: **los** ~**s** people suffering from
color-blindness*

daltonismo *m* color-blindness*

dama *f* **1** (frml) (señora) lady; ~**s y caballeros**
ladies and gentlemen; ~ **de honor** (de novia)
bridesmaid; (de reina) lady-in-waiting **2** (figura —

en damas) king; (— en ajedrez, en naipes) queen
3 **damas** *fpl* (juego) checkers (AmE), draughts
(BrE); **jugar a las** ~**s** to play checkers *o* draughts

damasco *m* **1** (Tex) damask **2** (AmS) (fruta)
apricot; (árbol) apricot tree

Damasco *m* Damascus

damnificado -da *m,f* (frml) victim

danés -nesa *adj* Danish
■ *m,f* **(a)** (persona) (*m*) Dane, Danish man; (*f*)
Dane, Danish woman **(b)** **danés** *m* (idioma)
Danish

danza *f* dance; ~ **moderna** modern dance

danzar [A4] *vi* (frml) (bailar) to dance

danzarín -rina *adj*: **es muy** ~ he loves
dancing
■ *m,f* dancer

dañar [A1] *vt* (en general) to damage; (salud/
organismo) to be bad for
■ **dañarse** *v pron* **1** (en general) to be/get
damaged; (salud) to damage **2** (Col, Ven) **(a)**
«carne/comida» to rot, go bad **(b)** «carro» to
break down; «aparato» to break

dañino -na *adj* [SER] (planta/sustancia)
harmful; ~ PARA **algo** harmful TO sth

daño *m* **(a)** (dolor físico): **hacerse ~** to hurt oneself; **me he hecho ~ en la espalda** I've hurt my back; **hacerle ~ a algn** «*persona*» to hurt sb; **el picante me hace ~** hot, spicy food doesn't agree with me **(b)** (destrozo) damage; **sufrir ~s** to be damaged, to suffer damage **(c)** **~s y perjuicios** damages (*pl*)

dar [A25] *vt*
I **1** **(a)** (entregar) to give; **dale las llaves a Pedro** give the keys to Pedro; **déme un kilo de peras** can I have a kilo of pears?; ▶ CONOCER *vt* 3 B, ENTENDER *vt* **(b)** ‹*cartas/mano*› to give
2 **(a)** (donar, regalar) ‹*sangre/limosna*› to give; **me dio su reloj** she gave me her watch **(b)** (proporcionar) ‹*fuerzas/valor/esperanza*› to give; ‹*información/idea*› to give
3 **(a)** (conferir, aportar) ‹*sabor/color/forma*› to give **(b)** (aplicar) ‹*mano de pintura/barniz*› to give **(c)** ‹*sedante/masaje*› to give
4 (conceder) ‹*prórroga/permiso*› to give; **el dentista me dio hora para el miércoles** I have an appointment with the dentist on Wednesday; **nos dieron un premio** we won *o* got a prize
5 **(a)** (expresar, decir) ‹*parecer/opinón*› to give; **¿le diste las gracias?** did you thank him?, did you say thank you?; **dales saludos** give/send them my regards; **tuve que ~le la noticia** I was the one who had to break the news to him **(b)** (señalar, indicar): **me da ocupado** *or* (Esp) **comunicando** the line's busy *o* (BrE) engaged; **el reloj dio las cinco** the clock struck five
II **1** **(a)** (producir) ‹*fruto/flor*› to bear; ‹*dividendos*› to pay; **un negocio que da mucho dinero** a business which makes a lot of money **(b)** (AmL) (alcanzar hasta): **da 150 kilómetros por hora** it can do *o* go 150 kilometres an hour; **venía a todo lo que daba** it was travelling at full speed; **ponen la radio a todo lo que da** they turn the radio on full blast
2 (causar, provocar) ‹*placer/susto*› to give; ‹*problemas*› to cause; **~ trabajo** to be hard work; **el calor le dio sueño/sed** the heat made him sleepy/thirsty
III **1** (presentar) ‹*concierto*› to give; **¿qué dan esta noche en la tele?** what's on TV tonight? (colloq); **¿dónde están dando esa película?** where's that film showing?
2 **(a)** ‹*fiesta/conferencia*› to give; ‹*baile/banquete*› to hold; ‹*discurso*› (AmL) to make **(b)** (CS) ‹*examen*› to take *o* (BrE) sit; *ver tb* CLASE 4
IV (realizar la acción que se indica) ‹*grito*› to give; **~ un paso atrás** to take a step back; **dame un beso** give me a kiss; *ver tb* GOLPE, PASEO, VUELTA, ETC
V (considerar) **~ algo/a algn POR algo: lo dieron por muerto** they gave him up for dead; **ese tema lo doy por sabido** I'm assuming you've already covered that topic; **¡dalo por hecho!** consider it done!
■ **~** *vi*
I **1** **dar a** «*puerta*» to give onto, open onto; «*ventana/balcón*» to look onto, give onto; «*fachada/frente*» to face
2 (ser suficiente, alcanzar) **~ PARA algo/algn** to be enough FOR sth/sb; **no me dio (el) tiempo** I didn't have time; **~ de sí** ‹*zapatos/jersey*› to stretch
3 (arrojar un resultado): **el análisis le dio positivo** her test was positive; **¿cuánto da la cuenta?** what does it come to?; **a mí me dio 247** I made it (to be) 247

4 (importar): **da lo mismo** it doesn't matter; **¡qué más da!** what does it matter!; **¿qué más da?** what difference does it make?; **me da igual** I don't mind
5 (en naipes) to deal
II **1** **(a)** (pegar, golpear): **~le A algn** to hit sb; (como castigo) to smack sb; **dale al balón** kick the ball; **el balón dio en el poste** the ball hit the post **(b)** (acertar) to hit; **~ en el blanco** to hit the target
2 (accionar, mover) **~le A algo** ‹*a botón/tecla*› to press sth; ‹*a interruptor*› to flick sth; ‹*a manivela/volante*› to turn sth
3 **dar con** (encontrar) ‹*persona*› to find; ‹*solución*› to hit upon, find; ‹*palabra*› to come up with
4 (hablando de manías, ocurrencias) **~le a algn POR hacer algo** ‹*por pintar/cocinar*› to take to doing sth; **le ha dado por decir que …** he's started saying that …
5 «*sol/luz*»: **aquí da el sol toda la mañana** you get the sun all morning here; **la luz le daba de lleno en los ojos** the light was shining right in his eyes
■ **darse** *v pron*
I **1** (producirse) «*fruta/trigo*» to grow
2 (presentarse) «*oportunidad/ocasión*» to arise
3 (resultar) (+ *me/te/le etc*): **se le dan los idiomas** she's good at languages
II **(a)** (*refl*) (realizar lo que se indica) ‹*ducha/banquete*› to have; **dárselas de algo: se las da de valiente/de que sabe mucho** he likes to make out he's brave/he knows a lot; **dárselas de listo** to act smart **(b)** (golpearse, pegarse): **se dio con el martillo en el dedo** he hit his finger with the hammer; **se dieron contra un árbol** they crashed into a tree; **se dio un golpe en la rodilla** he hit his knee
III (considerarse) **~se POR algo: con eso me ~ía por satisfecha** I'd be quite happy with that; *ver tb* ALUDIR A, ENTERADO 1

dardo *m* **(a)** (Jueg) dart; **jugar a los ~s** to play darts **(b)** (arma) small spear

datar [A1] *vi* to date; **data del siglo XII** it dates from the 12th century; **data de hace muchos años** it goes back many years

dátil *m* (Bot) date

dativo *m* (Ling) dative

dato *m* **(a)** (elemento de información) piece of information; **no dispongo de todos los ~s** I don't have all the information; **~s personales** personal details (*pl*) **(b) datos** *mpl* (Inf) data (*pl*), information

d. de C. (= **después de Jesucristo**) AD

de¹ *prep* **1** **(a)** (pertenencia, posesión): **la casa ~ ~ mis padres** my parents' house; **el rey ~ Francia** the king of France; **no es ~ él** it isn't his; **es un amigo ~ mi hijo** he's a friend of my son's; **un estudiante ~ quinto año** a fifth-year student; **la tapa ~ la cacerola** the saucepan lid; **un avión ~ Mexair** a Mexair plane **(b)** (con un nombre en aposición) of; **la ciudad ~ Lima** the city of Lima; **el aeropuerto ~ Barajas** Barajas airport; **el mes ~ enero** the month of January
2 **(a)** (procedencia, origen, tiempo) from; **es ~ Bogotá** she's/she comes from Bogotá; **una carta ~ Julia** a letter from Julia; **un amigo ~ la infancia** a childhood friend; **la literatura ~ ese período** the literature of *o* from that period; **~ aquí a tu casa** from here to your house **(b)** (material, contenido, composición): **son ~ plástico** they're (made of)

⋯⁘

plastic; **una mesa ~ caoba** a mahogany table; **un vaso ~ agua** a glass of water; **un millón ~ dólares** a million dollars **(c)** (causa, modo): **murió ~ viejo** he died of old age; **~ tanto gritar** from shouting so much; **verde ~ envidia** green with envy; **temblando ~ miedo** trembling with fear; **~ memoria** by heart; **lo tumbó ~ un golpe** he knocked him down with one blow **(d)** (en oraciones pasivas) by; **un poema ~ Neruda** a poem by Neruda; **rodeada ~ árboles** surrounded by trees **3 (a)** (cualidades, características): **de gran inteligencia** of great intelligence; **objetos ~ mucho valor** objects of great value; **¿~ qué color lo quiere?** what color do you want it?; **tiene cara ~ aburrido** he looks bored; **una botella ~ un litro** a liter bottle; **la chica ~ azul** the girl in blue **(b)** (al definir, especificar): **el botón ~ abajo** the bottom button; **tiene dos metros ~ ancho** it's two meters wide; **es fácil ~ pronunciar** it's easy to pronounce; **uno ~ los míos** one of mine; **el mayor ~ los Soto** the eldest of the Soto children **4 (a)** (con cifras): **pagan un interés ~l 15%** they pay 15% interest *o* interest at 15% **(b)** (en comparaciones de cantidad) than; **más ~ £100** more than *o* over £100; **pesa menos ~ un kilo** it weighs less than *o* under a kilo; **un número mayor/menor ~ 29** a number over/under 29 **(c)** (con un superlativo): **es el más caro ~ todos** it's the most expensive one; **la ciudad más grande ~l mundo** the biggest city in the world **(d)** (refiriéndose a una parte del día): **~ día/noche** during the day/at night; **~ madrugada** early in the morning **5 (a)** (en calidad de) as; **trabaja ~ secretaria** she works as a secretary; **hace ~ rey en la obra** he plays (the part of) a king in the play **(b)** (en expresiones de estado, actividad): **~ mal humor** in a bad mood; **estamos ~ fiesta** we're having a party **(c)** (indicando uso, destino, finalidad): **el cepillo ~ la ropa** the clothes brush; **copas ~ vino** wine glasses; **ropa ~ cama** bed clothes; **dales algo ~ comer** give them something to eat; **¿qué hay ~ postre?** what's for dessert? **6** (con sentido condicional): **~ haberlo sabido** if I had known, had I known; **~ no ser así** otherwise

de² *f: name of the letter* d

dé ▶ DAR

deambular [A1] *vi* to wander around *o* about

debajo *adv* **1** [*Latin American Spanish also uses* ABAJO *in many of these examples*] underneath; **no hay nada ~** there's nothing underneath; **el que está ~** the one below, the next one down **2 debajo de** (*loc prep*) under, underneath; **~ del coche** under *o* underneath the car; **~ del agua** underwater; **por ~ de la puerta** under the door; **temperaturas por ~ de lo normal** temperatures below average

debate *m* debate; (*más informal*) discussion

debatir [I1] *vt* to debate; (*más informal*) to discuss

debe *m* debit

deber¹ [E1] *vt* ⟨*dinero/favor/explicación*⟩ to owe; **te debo las entradas de ayer** I owe you for the tickets from yesterday
■ **~** *v aux* **1** (expresando obligación): **debemos**

trabajar más we must work harder; **no debes usarlo** you must not use it; **~ías** *or* **debías habérselo dicho** you ought to have *o* you should have told her; **no se debe mentir** you mustn't tell lies; **no ~ías haberlo dejado solo** you shouldn't have left him alone
2 (expresando suposición, probabilidad): **deben (de) ser más de las cinco** it must be after five o'clock; **deben (de) haber salido** they must have gone out; **debe (de) estar enamorado** she/he must be in love; **no deben (de) saber la dirección** they probably don't know the address; **no les debe (de) interesar** they can't be interested

■ **deberse** *v pron* **1** (tener su causa en) **~se A algo** to be due to sth; **se debe a que no estudia** it's due to the fact that she doesn't study; **¿a qué se debe este escándalo?** what's all this racket about?
2 ⟨*persona*⟩ (tener obligaciones hacia) **~se A algn** to have a duty TO sb

deber² *m* **1** (obligación) duty; **cumplió con su ~** he carried out *o* did his duty **2 deberes** *mpl* (tarea escolar) homework, assignment (AmE)

debido -da *adj* **(a)** (apropiado): **a su ~ tiempo** in due course; **tratar a algn con el ~ respeto** to show due respect to sb; **tomó las debidas precauciones** she took the necessary precautions; **como es ~** ⟨*sentarse/comer*⟩ properly; ⟨*comida/regalo*⟩ proper; **más de lo ~** too much **(b)** (en locs) **debido a** owing to, on account of; **debido a que** owing to the fact that

débil *adj* ⟨*persona/economía/gobierno*⟩ weak **(b)** ⟨*sonido/voz*⟩ faint; ⟨*moneda/argumento*⟩ weak; ⟨*excusa*⟩ feeble, lame; ⟨*luz*⟩ dim, faint; ⟨*sílaba/vocal*⟩ unstressed, weak

debilidad *f* weakness; **siento una gran ~** I feel terribly debilitated *o* weak; **se aprovechan de su ~** they take advantage of his weak character; **tener ~ por algn/algo** to have a soft spot for sb/a weakness for sth

debilitar [A1] *vt* to weaken
■ **debilitarse** *v pron* **(a)** ⟨*persona*⟩ to become weak; ⟨*salud*⟩ to deteriorate; ⟨*voluntad*⟩ to weaken **(b)** ⟨*sonido*⟩ to get *o* become faint/fainter **(c)** ⟨*economía*⟩ to grow *o* become weak/weaker

débito *m* debit; **~ bancario** (AmL) direct debit, direct billing (AmE)

debutante *mf* (Dep, Espec) *player or artist making his/her public debut*

debutar [A1] *vi* to make one's debut

década *f* decade; **la ~ de los ochenta** the eighties

decadencia *f* **(a)** (proceso) decline **(b)** (estado) decadence

decadente *adj* ⟨*moral/costumbres*⟩ decadent **(b)** ⟨*salud*⟩ declining

decaer [E16] *vi* **(a)** ⟨*ánimo/fuerzas*⟩ to flag; ⟨*enfermo*⟩ to deteriorate; ⟨*interés/popularidad*⟩ to wane **(b)** ⟨*barrio/restaurante*⟩ to go downhill; ⟨*calidad/prestigio*⟩ to decline **(c)** ⟨*imperio/civilización*⟩ to decay, decline

decaído -da *adj* [ESTAR] low, down (colloq)

decálogo *m* decalogue

decano -na *m,f* (de una facultad) dean; (de una profesión, un grupo) senior member

decapitar [A1] *vt* to behead, decapitate

decatlón *m* decathlon

decena *f*: unidades, ~s y centenas (Mat) units, tens and hundreds; **una ~ de personas** about ten people; **~s de personas lo presenciaron** dozens *o* scores of people witnessed it

decencia *f* decency

decenio *m* decade

decente *adj* (a) (honrado, decoroso) decent, respectable (b) (aceptable) ⟨sueldo/vivienda⟩ decent, reasonable (c) [ESTAR] (de apariencia aceptable) respectable

decepción *f* disappointment, letdown (colloq); **me llevé una gran ~** I was very disappointed

decepcionado -da *adj* disappointed; **estar ~ con algo/de algn** to be disappointed with sth/sb

decepcionante *adj* disappointing

decepcionar [A1] *vt* to disappoint; **la película me decepcionó** I was disappointed with the movie

decidido -da *adj* (a) [SER] ⟨persona/tono⟩ (resuelto, enérgico) decisive, determined (b) [ESTAR] **~ A hacer algo** determined *o* resolved to do sth

decidir [I1] *vt* [1] (a) (tomar una determinación) to decide; **decidí comprarlo** I decided to buy it (b) ⟨persona⟩ to make … decide; **lo que me decidió** what made me decide [2] ⟨asunto⟩ to settle; ⟨resultado⟩ to decide
▪ **~** *vi* to decide; **tiene que ~ entre los dos** she has to choose *o* decide between the two; **~ SOBRE algo** to decide ON sth
▪ **decidirse** *v pron* to decide, to make up one's mind; **~se A hacer algo** to decide to do sth; **~se POR algo** to decide ON sth

décima *f* (de segundo, grado) tenth; **tiene 39 y tres ~s** his temperature is 39.3 (degrees)

decimal *m* (número) decimal (number)

décimo¹ -ma *adj/pron* tenth; *para ejemplos ver* QUINTO; **la décima parte** a tenth

décimo² m (a) (partitivo) tenth (b) (de lotería) *tenth share in a lottery ticket*

decir¹ *m*: **¿cientos de personas? — bueno, es un ~** hundreds of people? — well, figuratively speaking

decir² [I24] *vt* [1] (a) ⟨palabra/frase/poema⟩ to say; ⟨mentira/verdad⟩ to tell; [para ejemplos con complemento indirecto ver división 2] **no digas estupideces** don't talk nonsense!; **¿eso lo dices por mí?** are you referring to me?; **¡no lo dirás en serio!** you can't be serious!; **dijo que sí con la cabeza** he nodded; **no se dice 'ande', se dice 'anduve'** it isn't 'ande', it's 'anduve'; **¡eso no se dice!** you mustn't say that!; **¿cómo se dice 'amor' en ruso?** how do you say 'love' in Russian?; **¿lo encontró? — dice que sí/no did he find it? —** he says he did/he didn't (b) **decir misa** to say mass [2] **~le algo A algn** to tell sb sth; **voy a ~le a papá que …** I'm going to tell Dad …; **¡ya te lo decía yo!** I told you so! [3] (a) (expresando órdenes, deseos, advertencias): **¡porque lo digo yo!** because I say so!; **harás lo que yo diga** you'll do as I say; **dice que llames**

cuando llegues she says (you are) to phone when you get there; **dijo que tuviéramos cuidado** she said to be careful; **diles que empiecen** tell them to start; **le dije que no lo hiciera** I told him not to do it (b) **~(le) adiós (a algn)** to say goodbye (to sb)
[4] (a) (opinar, pensar) to think; **¿y los padres qué dicen?** what do her parents think of it?, how do her parents feel about it?; **¡quién lo hubiera dicho!** who would have thought *o* believed it?; **es muy fácil — si tú lo dices …** it's very easy — if you say so … (b) (sugerir, comunicar): **el tiempo lo dirá** time will tell; **¿te dice algo ese nombre?** does that name mean anything to you?
[5] **querer decir** «palabra/persona» to mean; **¿qué quieres ~ con eso?** what do you mean by that?
[6] (*en locs*) **a decir verdad** to tell you the truth, to be honest; **como quien dice** so to speak; **es decir** that is; **¡he dicho!** that's that *o* final!; **ni que decir tiene que …** it goes without saying that …; **¡no me digas!** no!, you're kidding *o* joking! (colloq); **por así decirlo** so to speak; **¡el qué dirán** (fam) what other people (might) think; *ver tb* DICHO¹
▪ **~** *vi* (a) (invitando a hablar): **papá — dime, hijo** dad — yes, son?; **quería pedirle un favor — usted dirá** I wanted to ask you a favour — certainly, go ahead (b) (Esp) (al contestar el teléfono): **¿diga?** *or* **¿dígame?** hello?
▪ **decirse** *v pron* (a) (*refl*) to say … to oneself (b) (*recípr*) to say … to each other; **se decían secretos al oído** they were whispering secrets to each other

decisión *f* (a) (acción) decision; **tomar una ~** to make a decision; **su ~ de marcharse** her decision to leave (b) (cualidad) decisiveness, decision; **una mujer con ~** a woman of decision (c) (AmL) (en boxeo): **ganó por ~** he won on points *o* by a decision

decisivo -va *adj* ⟨fecha/voto/resultado⟩ crucial, decisive; ⟨prueba⟩ conclusive; ⟨papel⟩ decisive

declaración *f* [1] (a) (afirmación) declaration; **una ~ de amor** a declaration of love (b) (a la prensa, en público) statement; **hacer una ~** to issue a statement (c) (proclamación) declaration; **~ de guerra** declaration of war [2] (Der) statement, testimony; **el policía me tomó ~** the policeman took my statement; **prestar ~ como testigo** to give evidence, to testify; **~ del impuesto sobre la renta** income tax return

declarado -da *adj* declared, professed

declarar [A1] *vt* [1] (a) (manifestar) ⟨apoyo/oposición/intención⟩ to announce, state; **le declaró su amor** he declared his love to her (b) (proclamar) ⟨guerra/independencia⟩ to declare; **el jurado lo declaró inocente** the jury found him not guilty
[2] (a) (en la aduana) to declare (b) (Fisco) ⟨bienes/ingresos⟩ to declare
▪ **~** *vi* to give evidence, testify; **~ como testigo** to give evidence, to testify
▪ **declararse** *v pron* [1] (a) (manifestarse) to declare oneself; **~se en quiebra** to declare oneself bankrupt; **~se culpable/inocente** to plead guilty/not guilty; **~se en huelga** to go on strike (b) (confesar amor): **se le declaró** he declared himself *o* his love to her
[2] «incendio/epidemia» to break out

declinación f (Ling) declension

declinar [A1] vt (a) ‹invitación/oferta/honor› to turn down, decline (frml) (b) (Ling) to decline

declive m (a) (de una superficie) slope, incline (frml); **terreno en ~** sloping ground (b) (decadencia) decline

decolaje m (AmL) take-off

decolar [A1] vi (AmL) to take off

decoración f (a) (de pasteles, platos) decoration; (de habitación) decor; (de árbol de Navidad) (AmL) decoration (b) (interiorismo) tb **~ de interiores** interior decoration

decorado m set

decorador -dora m,f: tb **~ de interiores** interior decorator

decorar [A1] vt to decorate

decorativo -va adj decorative

decoro m (pudor, respeto) decorum

decoroso -sa adj decent, respectable

decrecer [E3] vi (a) ‹afición/interés› to wane, decrease; ‹importancia› to decline (b) ‹número/cantidad› to decline, fall (c) ‹aguas› to drop, fall

decreciente adj decreasing (before n)

decrépito -ta adj decrepit

decretar [A1] vt to order, decree (frml)

decreto m decree

dedal m thimble

dedicación f dedication

dedicar [A2] vt (a) (consagrar) **~ algo A** algo/hacer algo ‹tiempo/esfuerzos› to devote sth TO sth/doing sth; **dedicó su vida a la ciencia/ayudar a los pobres** she devoted her life to science/to helping the poor (b) (ofrendar, ofrecer) ‹obra/canción› to dedicate

■ **dedicarse** v pron (a) (consagrarse) **~se A** algo/hacer algo to devote oneself TO sth/doing sth (b) (tener cierta ocupación, profesión): **¿a qué se dedica tu padre?** what does your father do?; **se dedica a la investigación** she does research; **se dedica a pintar en sus ratos libres** she spends her free time painting

dedicatoria f dedication

dedillo m: **conocer algo al ~** to know sth like the back of one's hand; **sabía la lección al ~** I knew the lesson (off) by heart

dedo m (de mano, guante) finger; (del pie) toe; **señalar con el ~** to point; **~ anular/(del) corazón** ring/middle finger; **~ gordo** (fam) (del pie) big toe; (de la mano) thumb; **~ índice** forefinger, index finger; **~ meñique** little finger; **~ pulgar** thumb; **a ~** (fam): **ir a ~** to hitchhike, hitch (colloq); **recorrió Europa a ~** she hitchhiked around Europe; **hacer ~** (fam) to hitchhike, hitch (colloq); **poner el ~ en la llaga** to hit o touch a raw nerve; **señalar a algn con el ~** (literal) to point at sb; (culpar) to point the finger at sb

deducción f deduction

deducible adj 1 (que se puede inferir) deducible 2 (Com, Fin) deductible

deducir [16] vt 1 (inferir) to deduce; **~ algo DE** algo to deduce sth FROM sth 2 (descontar) to deduct

deduje, deduzca, etc ► DEDUCIR

defecto m (a) (en un sistema) fault, flaw, defect;

~ de fábrica manufacturing fault o defect (b) (de una persona) fault, shortcoming; **~ físico** physical handicap

defectuoso -sa adj faulty, defective

defender [E8] vt to defend; ‹intereses› to protect; **~ a** algo/algn **DE** algo/algn to defend sth/sb AGAINST sth/sb

■ **defenderse** v pron (a) (refl) (contra una agresión) to defend o protect oneself; (Der) to defend oneself; **~se DE** algo/algn to defend oneself AGAINST sth/sb (b) (fam) (arreglárselas) to get by (colloq); **me defiendo bastante bien en francés** I can get by quite well in French

defensa f 1 (a) (protección) defense*; **salir en ~ de** algn to come to sb's defense; **actuó en ~ propia** he acted in self-defense; **~ DE** algo/algn defense* OF sth/sb; **~ personal** self-defense* (b) (Dep) defense* 2 (a) **la Defensa** f the Defense Department (AmE), the Ministry of Defence (BrE) (b) **defensas** fpl (Biol, Med) defenses* ■ (pl) (c)

defensa mf (jugador) defender

defensivo -va adj ‹arma/actitud/táctica› defensive; **estar/ponerse a la defensiva** to be/get on the defensive

defensor -sora adj (a) ‹ejército› defending (before n) (b) (Der) ‹abogado› defense* (before n)

■ m,f (a) (Mil) defender (b) (de una causa) champion (c) (Der) defense counsel (AmE), defence lawyer (BrE)

defeño -ña m,f (Méx) person from the DISTRITO FEDERAL

deferencia f (frml) deference; **por ~ a** algn/algo out of o in deference to sb/sth

deficiencia f (a) (defecto) fault (b) (insuficiencia alimentaria, inmunológica) deficiency

deficiente adj poor, inadequate; ‹salud› poor; **~ EN** algo deficient IN sth

■ mf (persona) tb **~ mental** mentally subnormal person

■ m (calificación) poor

déficit m (pl **~** or **-cits**) (a) (Com, Fin) deficit (b) (en la producción) shortfall; (de lluvias) shortage

defienda, defiendas, etc ► DEFENDER

definición f (de palabra, postura) definition

definido -da adj clearly-defined

definir [I1] vt to define

definitivamente adv ‹resolver/rechazar› once and for all; ‹quedarse/instalarse› permanently, for good

definitivo -va adj ‹texto/solución/respuesta› definitive; ‹cierre› permanent, definitive; **ya es ~ que no viene** he's definitely not coming

deforestación f deforestation

deforestar [A1] vt to deforest

deformación f (a) (en general) distortion (b) (Anat, Med) deformity

deformar [A1] vt (a) (en general) to distort (b) (Anat, Med) to deform

■ **deformarse** v pron (a) (en general) to become distorted (b) (Anat, Med) to become deformed

deforme adj deformed

defraudar [A1] vt (a) (decepcionar) to disappoint (b) (estafar) to defraud; **defraudó al fisco** he evaded his taxes

defunción f (frml) death; **Ⓢ cerrado por defunción** closed owing to bereavement

degenerado -da *adj/m,f* degenerate

degenerar [A1] *vi* to degenerate; **~ EN algo** to degenerate INTO sth

degollar [A12] *vt* ‹persona/animal›: **lo ~on** they slit his/its throat

degradante *adj* degrading

degradar [A1] *vt* **(a)** (Mil) to demote **(b)** (envilecer) to degrade **(c)** (empeorar) ‹calidad/valor› to diminish

■ **degradarse** *v pron* «persona» to demean oneself, degrade oneself

dehesa *f* **(a)** (terreno) meadow, pasture **(b)** (hacienda) farm

dejación *f* (AmC, Chi) ▶ DEJADEZ

dejadez *f* **(a)** (en el aseo personal) slovenliness **(b)** (en tarea, trabajo) laziness, slackness

dejado -da *adj* **(a)** (en aseo personal, aspecto) slovenly **(b)** (en tarea, trabajo) slack, lazy

dejar [A1] *vt*

I **1** **(a)** (en lugar determinado) to leave; **lo dejé en recepción** I left it in reception; **dejó a los niños en el colegio** she dropped the children (off) at school; **~ un recado** to leave a message; **~ propina** to leave a tip; **deja ese cuchillo** put that knife down; **déjala, ella no tuvo la culpa** leave her alone, it wasn't her fault; **~ mucho que desear** to leave a great deal to be desired **(b)** (olvidar) ‹dinero/objeto›to leave; **¡déjalo!** forget it! **(c)** (como herencia) to leave

2 **(a)** ‹mancha/huella/sabor› to leave **(b)** ‹ganancia› to produce; **el negocio dejó pérdidas** the business made a loss

3 (abandonar) ‹novia/marido› to leave; ‹familia› to leave, abandon; ‹trabajo› to give up, leave; ‹lugar› to leave; **quiere ~ el ballet** he wants to give up ballet dancing

4 (+ *compl*) (en cierto estado) to leave; **dejé la ventana abierta** I left the window open; **me dejó esperando afuera** she left me waiting outside; **¡déjame en paz!** leave me alone!; **me lo dejó en 1.000 pesos** he let me have it for 1,000 pesos; ▶ LADO 3

5 **(a)** (posponer) leave; **no lo dejes para después, hazlo ahora** don't put it off *o* leave it until later, do it now **(b)** (reservar, guardar) ‹espacio/margen/comida› to leave

II (permitir) **~a algo/algn hacer algo** to let sth/sb do sth; **déjalo entrar** let it/him in; **deja correr el agua** let the water run; **¿me dejas ir?** will you let me go?; **~ que algo/algn haga algo** to let sb/sth do sth; **déjame que te ayude** let me help you; ▶ CAER 1, PASO 1B

■ **~ vi ~ DE hacer algo** to stop doing sth; **~ de fumar** to give up *o* to stop smoking; **no dejes de escribirme** make sure you write to me

■ **dejarse** *v pron* **1** **(a)** (abandonarse) to let oneself go **(b)** **~se hacer algo: se deja dominar por la envidia** he lets his feelings of envy get the better of him; **se deja influir fácilmente** he's easily influenced; **~se llevar por la música** to let oneself be carried along by the music; **~se estar** (AmL); (descuidarse) to be careless; (abandonarse) to let oneself go

2 ‹barba/bigote› to grow

3 **~se DE hacer algo** to stop doing sth; **déjate de lamentarte** stop complaining

4 (esp Esp fam) (olvidar) to leave

deje *m* ▶ DEJO A

dejo *m* **(a)** (acento) (slight) accent, lilt **(b)** (de una bebida, comida) aftertaste; **~ A algo** slight taste OF sth **(c)** (de arrogancia, ironía) touch, hint **(d)** (impresión, sensación): **me quedó un ~ triste** I was left with a feeling of sadness

del: *contraction of* DE *and* EL

delantal *m* (para cocinar) apron; (de escolar) pinafore

delante *adv* **1** (lugar, parte) [*Latin American Spanish also uses* ADELANTE *in many of these examples*]: **yo voy ~** I'll go ahead *o* in front; **no te pongas ~** don't stand in front of me; **lo tengo aquí ~** I have it right here; **el asiento de ~** the front seat; **la parte de ~** the front; **el pasajero de ~** the passenger in the front **2** **delante de** (*loc prep*) in front of

delantera *f* **(a)** (en general) lead; **llevar/tomar la ~** to be in/to take the lead **(b)** (Dep) (de equipo) forwards (*pl*), forward line

delantero -ra *adj* **(a)** ‹asiento/rueda› front (*before n*) **(b)** (Dep) ‹línea/posición› forward (*before n*), offensive (*before n*) (AmE)

■ *m,f* (Dep) forward; **~ forward** center* forward

delatar [A1] *vt* «persona» (acusar) to denounce, inform on

■ **delatarse** *v pron* (*refl*) to give oneself away

delator -tora *adj* **(a)** ‹prueba/arma› incriminating **(b)** ‹mirada/sonrisa› revealing

■ *m,f* informer

delegación *f* **1** (grupo) delegation **2** (de poderes) delegation **3** **(a)** (Méx) (comisaría) police station **(b)** (Esp) (oficina local) regional *o* local office

delegado *m,f* (representante) delegate; **~ de curso** student representative

delegar [A3] *vt* to delegate; **~ algo EN algn** to delegate sth TO sb

■ **~ vi** to delegate

deleitar [A1] *vt* to delight

■ **deleitarse** *v pron* **~se haciendo algo** to delight IN doing sth, enjoy doing sth

deleite *m* delight

deletrear [A1] *vt* to spell

delfín *m* (Zool) dolphin

delgado -da *adj* **(a)** ‹persona/piernas› (esbelto) slim; (flaco) thin **(b)** ‹tela/lámina/pared› thin; ‹hilo› fine, thin

deliberado -da *adj* deliberate

delicadeza *f* **1** (cuidado, suavidad) gentleness; **con mucha ~** very gently **2** **(a)** (tacto, discreción) tact; **fue una falta de ~** it was tactless of him (*o* you *etc*) **(b)** (gesto amable): **fue una ~ de su parte traerme** it was very kind of him to bring me; **ni siquiera tuvo la ~ de informarme** he didn't even have the courtesy to inform me

delicado -da *adj* **1** (fino) ‹rasgos/manos› delicate; ‹sabor› delicate, subtle; ‹lenguaje/modales› refined **2** **(a)** (que requiere cuidados) ‹cerámica/cristal› fragile; ‹tela› delicate; ‹piel› sensitive **(b)** ‹salud/estómago› delicate; ‹corazón› weak **3** ‹asunto/cuestión/tema› delicate, sensitive; ‹situación› delicate, tricky **4** **(a)** (melindroso) delicate, fussy **(b)** (susceptible) touchy

delicia *f* delight; **ser una ~** to be delicious

delicioso -sa *adj* ‹comida/bebida/sabor› delicious; ‹tiempo› delightful

delimitar [A1] *vt* (a) ⟨*terreno/espacio*⟩ to demarcate (frml), to delimit (frml) (b) ⟨*poderes/ responsabilidades*⟩ to define, specify

delincuencia *f* crime, delinquency (frml); ∼ **juvenil** juvenile delinquency

delincuente *mf* criminal; ∼ **común** common criminal; ∼ **juvenil** juvenile delinquent

delinear [A1] *vt* (a) ⟨*dibujo/plano*⟩ to outline, draft; ⟨*contorno*⟩ to delineate (b) ⟨*programa/ proyecto*⟩ to formulate, draw up

delinquir [I3] *vi* to commit a criminal offense*

delirar [A1] *vi* (Med) to be delirious; **la fiebre lo hacía** ∼ the fever made him delirious

delirio *m* (Med) delirium; ∼**s de grandeza** *mpl* delusions of grandeur (*pl*)

delito *m* crime, offense*; ∼ **ambiental** environmental crime; ∼ **informático** computer crime

delta *m* (Geog) delta
■ *f* (letra griega) delta

demacrado -da *adj* (pálido) haggard, drawn; (delgado) emacieted

demagogia *f* demagogy, demagoguery

demagogo -ga *m,f* demagogue, demagog (AmE)

demanda *f* **1** (Com) demand; **tiene mucha** ∼ it's in great demand **2** (a) (Der) lawsuit; **presentar una** ∼ **contra algn** to bring a lawsuit against sb (b) (petición) request; **accedí a su** ∼ I agreed to his request

demandado -da *m,f* defendant

demandante *mf* plaintiff

demandar [A1] *vt* **1** (Der) to sue **2** (AmL) (requerir) to require

demarcar [A2] to demarcate

demás *adj inv* (delante del *n*): **los** ∼ **estudiantes** the rest of the *o* the remaining students
■ *pron* **1** (a) **lo** ∼ the rest; **todo lo** ∼ everything else (b) (*en locs*) **por lo demás** apart from that, otherwise; **por demás** extremely **2** **los/las** ∼ (referido a cosas) the rest, the others; (referido a personas) the rest, everybody else; **me dio uno y se quedó con los** ∼ he gave me one and kept the rest *o* the others; **los** ∼ **han terminado** the rest (of them) have finished, everybody else has finished

demasía: **en** ∼ ⟨*beber/comer*⟩ to excess; **todo alimento, tomado en** ∼, **es perjudicial** any food, when eaten in excess, can be harmful

demasiado¹ -da *adj* (delante del *n*): ∼ **dinero** too much money; **había** ∼**s coches** there were too many cars; **hace** ∼ **calor** it's too hot
■ *pron*: **es** ∼ it's too much; **somos** ∼**s** there are too many of us; **hizo** ∼**s** she made too many

demasiado² *adv* **1** ⟨*pequeño/caliente/caro*⟩ too; **fue un esfuerzo** ∼ **grande para él** it was too much of an effort for him **2** ⟨*comer/hablar/ preocuparse*⟩ too much; ⟨*trabajar*⟩ too hard

demencia *f* dementia

demente *adj* insane

■ *mf* insane person

democracia *f* democracy

demócrata *mf* democrat

democratacristiano -na *adj/m,f* Christian Democrat

democrático -ca *adj* democratic

demografía *f* demography

demográfico -ca *adj* demographic, population (*before n*)

demoledor -dora *adj* (a) ⟨*máquina*⟩ demolition (*before n*) (b) ⟨*ataque/crítica*⟩ devastating

demoler [E9] *vt* (a) ⟨*edificio*⟩ to demolish, pull down (b) ⟨*mito/teoría*⟩ (fam) to debunk, demolish

demonio *m* **1** (diablo) devil **2** (fam) (uso expletivo): **¡cómo** ∼**s lo hizo!** how on earth did he do it?; **¿qué** ∼ ... **?** what the hell ... ? (colloq); **¡**∼**(s)!** (expresando enfado) damn! (colloq); (expresando sorpresa) goodness!, heavens!

demora *f* **1** (esp AmL) (retraso) delay; **perdón por la** ∼ I'm sorry I'm late; ∼ **EN hacer algo** delay IN doing sth; **sin** ∼ without delay **2** (Náut) bearing

demorar [A1] *vt* (a) (AmL) (tardar): **demoró tres horas en llegar** he took *o* it took him three hours to arrive (b) (AmL) (retrasar) ⟨*viaje/decisión*⟩ to delay
■ *vi* (AmL): **¡no demores!** don't be long!
■ **demorarse** *v pron* (AmL) (a) (tardar cierto tiempo): **¡qué poco te demoraste!** that didn't take you very long; **me demoro 3 horas** it takes me 3 hours (b) (tardar demasiado) to be *o* take too long; ∼**se** **hacer algo** to take a long time *o* **To** do sth

demoroso -sa *adj* (Bol, Chi) ⟨*persona/vehículo*⟩ slow; ⟨*trabajo*⟩ time-consuming

demostración *f* demonstration; (de teorema) proof

demostrar [A10] *vt* **1** ⟨*verdad/teorema*⟩ to prove, demonstrate; ⟨*ignorancia*⟩ to show, prove; **ha demostrado ser muy capaz** he's shown himself to be very able; ∼ **que algo es/no es cierto** to prove sth right/wrong **2** (a) ⟨*interés/ sentimiento*⟩ to show (b) ⟨*funcionamiento/método*⟩ to demonstrate

demostrativo -va *adj* (a) ⟨*ejemplo*⟩ illustrative (b) ⟨*adjetivo/pronombre*⟩ demonstrative (c) (AmL) ⟨*persona/carácter*⟩ demonstrative

denantes *adv* (Chi fam) a moment ago, just now

denegar [A7] *vt* (frml) ⟨*permiso/autorización*⟩ to refuse; ⟨*petición*⟩ to turn down; ⟨*recurso*⟩ (Der) to refuse

dengue *m* (Med) dengue fever

denigrante *adj* degrading, humiliating

denigrar [A1] *vt* (a) (hablar mal de) to denigrate (b) (degradar) to degrade

denominar [A1] *vt* (frml) (a) (dar nombre a) to call; **el denominado efecto invernadero** the so-called greenhouse effect (b) (con carácter oficial) to designate

denotar [A1] *vt* **(a)** (frml) (demostrar, indicar) to show, denote (frml); **sus modales denotan una esmerada educación** her manners are the sign of an impeccable upbringing **(b)** (Ling) to denote

densidad *f* density; (de vegetación, niebla) thickness, denseness

denso -sa *adj* dense

dentado -da *adj* ‹filo› serrated; **una rueda dentada** a gearwheel, a cogwheel

dentadura *f* teeth (*pl*); **~ postiza** false teeth (*pl*), dentures (*pl*)

dental *adj* dental

dentera *f* (sensación): **darle ~ a algn** to set sb's teeth on edge

dentífrico *m* toothpaste

dentista *mf* dentist

dentística *f* (Chi) dentistry, dental surgery

dentro *adv* [1] (lugar, parte) [*Latin American Spanish also uses* ADENTRO *in this sense*] inside; **aquí/ahí ~** in here/there; **el perro duerme ~** the dog sleeps indoors; **por ~** on the inside; **la parte de ~** the inside [2] **dentro de (a)** (en el espacio) in, inside; **~ del edificio** in *o* inside the building **(b)** (en el tiempo) in; **~ de dos semanas** in two weeks' time **(c)** (de límites, posibilidades) within; **~ de nuestras posibilidades** within our means

denuncia *f* [1] (de robo, asesinato) report; **hizo la ~ del robo del coche** he reported the theft of his car; **presentar una ~** to make a formal complaint [2] (crítica pública) denunciation

denunciar [A1] *vt* [1] ‹robo/asesinato/persona› to report [2] (condenar públicamente) to denounce, condemn

Dep., Dept. (= **Departamento**) Dept

departamento *m* [1] **(a)** (de empresa, institución) department **(b)** (provincia, distrito) department [2] (AmL) (apartamento) apartment (esp AmE), flat (BrE)

dependencia *f* [1] (condición) dependence; **~ DE algo** dependence ON sth [2] **dependencias** *fpl* (edificios) buildings (*pl*); (salas) rooms (*pl*)

depender [E1] *vi* **(a)** «resultado/solución» to depend; **~ DE algo/algn** to depend ON sth/sb **(b)** «persona» **~ DE algn/algo** to be dependent ON sb/sth

dependiente -ta *m,f* salesclerk (AmE), shop assistant (BrE)

depilación *f* (con cera) waxing; (con crema) hair-removal, depilation (frml); (de cejas) plucking

depilar [A1] *vt* ‹piernas/axilas› to wax (*o* shave *etc*); ‹cejas› to pluck
■ **depilarse** *v pron*: **~se las piernas** to shave (*o* wax *etc*) one's legs; (*caus*) to have one's legs waxed

deplorable *adj* deplorable

deportar [A1] *vt* to deport

deporte *m* sport; **no practican ningún ~** they don't play *o* do any sport(s); **hace ~ para estar en forma** she does sports (AmE) *o* (BrE) some sport to keep fit; **~ acuático/de invierno** water/winter sport

deportista *adj* sporty; **fue muy ~ en su juventud** he was a keen sportsman in his youth;
■ *mf* (*m*) sportsman (*f*) sportswoman

deportividad *f* sportsmanship

deportivo¹ -va *adj* **(a)** ‹club/centro› sports (*before n*) **(b)** ‹ropa› (para deporte) sports (*before n*); (informal) sporty, casual

deportivo² *m* sports car

depositar [A1] *vt* [1] (frml) **(a)** (colocar) to place, deposit (frml) **(b)** (dejar) to leave, deposit (frml) [2] (Fin) ‹dinero› to deposit; (en cuenta corriente) (AmL) to deposit, pay in (BrE)

depósito *m* [1] **(a)** (almacén) warehouse; **~ de armas** arms depot; **~ de cadáveres** morgue, mortuary (BrE) **(b)** (tanque) tank; **~ de gasolina** gas tank (AmE), petrol tank (BrE) [2] (sedimento) deposit, sediment; (yacimiento) deposit [3] (Fin) **(a)** (AmL) (en una cuenta) deposit **(b)** (garantía) deposit

depravado -da *m,f* degenerate

depreciarse [A1] *v pron* to depreciate, fall in value

depredador¹ -dora *adj* (Zool) ‹animal/ave› predatory

depredador² *m* predator

depresión *f* depression

deprimente *adj* depressing

deprimido -da *adj* depressed

deprimir [I1] *vt* to depress
■ **deprimirse** *v pron* to get/become depressed

deprisa *adv* fast; **trabajar más ~** to work faster; **¡~! escóndelo** quick! hide it

depurado -da *adj* ‹lenguaje/estilo› polished, refined; ‹gusto› refined

depuradora *f* **(a)** (de aguas residuales) sewage treatment plant **(b)** (en piscina) filter system

depurar [A1] *vt* [1] **(a)** ‹agua› to purify, treat; ‹aguas residuales› to treat **(b)** ‹sangre› to cleanse [2] **(a)** ‹organización/partido› to purge **(b)** ‹lenguaje/estilo› to polish, refine

derecha *f* [1] **(a)** (lado derecho) right; **la primera calle a la ~** the first street on the right; **dobla a la ~** turn right; **por la ~** ‹conducir/caminar› on the right; **mantenga su ~** keep to the right **(b)** (mano derecha) right hand [2] (Pol): **la ~** the Right; **un político de ~** *or* (Esp) **~s** a right-wing politician

derecho¹ -cha *adj* [1] ‹mano/ojo/zapato› right; ‹lado› right, right-hand; **el ángulo superior ~** the top right-hand corner; **queda a mano derecha** it's on the right-hand side *o* on the right [2] **(a)** (recto) straight; **ese cuadro no está ~** that picture isn't straight; **siéntate ~** sit up straight **(b)** (fam) (justo, honesto) honest, straight

derecho² *adv* straight; **siga todo ~** go *o* keep straight on

derecho³ *m* [1] **(a)** (facultad, privilegio) right; **~s humanos** human rights (*pl*); **estás en tu ~** you're within your rights; **~ A algo** right TO sth; **el ~ al voto** the right to vote; **tengo ~ a saber** I have a *o* the right to know; **esto da ~ a participar** this entitles you to participate; **¡no hay ~!** (fam) it's not fair! **(b)** (Com, Fin) tax; **~s de aduana** customs duties (*pl*); **~s de autor** royalties; **~ de matrícula** registration fee; **~ de reproducción** copyright [2] (Der) law [3] (de prenda) right side, outside; (de tela) right side, face; **póntelo al ~** put it on properly *o* right side out

deriva *f*: **a la ~** adrift

derivar [A1] *vi* **(a)** (proceder) **~ DE algo** ⋯✣

«*palabra*» to derive FROM sth, come FROM sth; «*problema/situación*» to arise FROM sth **(b)** (traer como consecuencia) ∼ EN algo to result IN sth, lead TO sth

■ ∼ *vt* (Med) (AmL) ∼ **a algn a un especialista** to refer sb to a specialist

■ **derivarse** *v pron* (proceder) ∼se DE algo «*palabra*» to be derived FROM sth, come FROM sth; «*problema/situación*» to arise FROM sth

dermatólogo -ga *m,f* dermatologist

derogar [A3] *vt* to abolish, repeal

derramar [A1] *vt* **(a)** ⟨*agua/leche/azúcar*⟩ to spill; ⟨*cuentas/sangre*⟩ to shed **(b)** ⟨*lentejas/botones*⟩ to spill, scatter

■ **derramarse** *v pron* **(a)** «*tinta/leche*» to spill; «*corriente*» to pour out **(b)** «*cuentas/botones*» to scatter, spread

derrame *m* **(a)** (Med): tengo un ∼ **en el ojo** I have a burst blood vessel in my eye; ∼ **cerebral** brain hemorrhage* **(b)** (de líquido) spillage

derrapar [A1] *vi* «*vehículo*» to skid; «*embrague*» to slip; «*llantas*» to spin

derredor: al/en ∼ (*loc adv*) around

derretir [I14] *vt* ⟨*mantequilla/helado*⟩ to melt; ⟨*hielo/nieve*⟩ to melt, thaw

■ **derretirse** *v pron* «*mantequilla/helado*» to melt; «*nieve/hielo*» to thaw, melt

derribar [A1] *vt* **(a)** ⟨*edificio/muro*⟩ to demolish, knock down; ⟨*puerta*⟩ to break down **(b)** ⟨*avión*⟩ to shoot down, bring down **(c)** ⟨*persona*⟩ to floor, knock … down; ⟨*novillo*⟩ to knock … over **(d)** ⟨*viento*⟩ to bring down **(e)** ⟨*gobierno*⟩ to overthrow, topple

derrocar [A2] *vt* to overthrow, topple

derrochador -dora *adj*: es muy ∼ he's a real spendthrift

■ *m,f* squanderer, spendthrift

derrochar [A1] *vt* (malgastar) ⟨*dinero*⟩ to squander, waste; ⟨*electricidad/agua*⟩ to waste

■ ∼ *vi* to throw money away, to squander money

derroche *m* (de dinero, bienes) waste

derrota *f* (Dep, Mil) defeat

derrotado -da *adj* **(a)** ⟨*ejército*⟩ defeated; ⟨*equipo/contrincante*⟩ defeated, beaten **(b)** (desesperanzado) despondent

derrotar [A1] *vt* ⟨*ejército/partido*⟩ to defeat; ⟨*equipo/contrincante*⟩ to defeat, beat

derrotista *adj/mf* defeatist

derruido -da *adj* ⟨*casa*⟩ ruined; medio ∼ virtually in ruins

derrumbamiento *m* collapse

derrumbar [A1] *vt* ⟨*casa/edificio*⟩ to demolish, pull down

■ **derrumbarse** *v pron* **(a)** «*edificio*» to collapse **(b)** «*persona*» to go to pieces; «*esperanzas/ilusiones*» to be shattered, collapse

desabastecimiento, (Méx) **desabasto** *m* shortage of supplies (o food *etc*)

desabotonarse [A1] *v pron* **(a)** «*prenda*» to come undone **(b)** (*refl*) «*persona*» ⟨*camisa/abrigo*⟩ to unbutton, undo

desabrido -da *adj* (comida) tasteless, bland

desabrigado -da *adj* ⟨*lugar*⟩ exposed; estás muy ∼ you're not wearing warm enough clothes

desabrochar [A1] *vt* ⟨*prenda/zapatos/pulsera*⟩ to undo; ¿me desabrochas? can you undo me? (colloq)

■ **desabrocharse** *v pron* **(a)** «*prenda*» to come undone **(b)** (*refl*) «*persona*» ⟨*camisa/abrigo*⟩ to undo

desaconsejar [A1] *vt* to advise against

desacostumbrarse [A1] *v pron* to get out of the habit; ∼ A hacer algo to get out of the habit OF doing sth; se desacostumbró al tráfico de la ciudad she forgot what city traffic was like

desacreditar [A1] *vt* to discredit

■ **desacreditarse** *v pron* (*refl*) to discredit oneself, damage one's reputation

desactivar [A1] *vt* ⟨*bomba/explosivo*⟩ to defuse, deactivate

desacuerdo *m* disagreement; ∼ CON algo/algn disagreement WITH sth/sb

desadaptado -da *adj*: un niño ∼ a child who has problems settling in *o* adjusting; sentirse ∼ to feel unsettled

desafiante *adj* ⟨*gesto/palabras*⟩ defiant

desafiar [A17] *vt* **(a)** ⟨*persona*⟩ to challenge; ∼ a algn A algo/hacer algo to challenge sb TO sth/do sth **(b)** ⟨*peligro/muerte*⟩ to defy

desafilado -da *adj* blunt

desafinado -da *adj* out of tune

desafinar [A1] *vi* «*instrumento*» to be out of tune; «*músico/cantante*» to be off key *o* out of tune

desafío *m* (reto) challenge; (al peligro, a la muerte) defiance

desaforado -da *m,f*: como un ∼ ⟨*correr*⟩ hell for leather; ⟨*gritar*⟩ at the top of one's voice

desafortunado -da *adj* **(a)** (desdichado) ⟨*persona*⟩ unlucky; ⟨*suceso*⟩ unfortunate **(b)** (desacertado) ⟨*medidas/actuación*⟩ unfortunate

desagradable *adj* unpleasant; ⟨*respuesta/comentario*⟩ unkind

desagradar [A1] *vt*: me desagrada el calor/tener que decírselo I don't like the heat/having to tell her

desagradecido -da *adj* ⟨*persona*⟩ ungrateful; ⟨*trabajo/tarea*⟩ thankless

desagrado *m* displeasure; lo hizo con ∼ she did it reluctantly *o* unwillingly

desagüe *m* **(a)** (de lavabo, lavadora) wastepipe; (de patio, azotea) drain **(b)** (acción) drainage

desahogado -da *adj* ⟨*posición económica/vida*⟩ comfortable; ⟨*casa/habitación*⟩ uncluttered, spacious

desahogar [A3] *vt* ⟨*penas/ira*⟩ to give vent to

■ **desahogarse** *v pron* to let off steam ; se desahogó dándole patadas a la rueda he vented his anger (*o* frustration *etc*) by kicking the wheel; ∼se CON algn to pour one's heart out to sb

desahogo *m* **(a)** (alivio) relief; llorar le servirá de ∼ crying will make him feel better **(b)** con ∼ ⟨*vivir*⟩ to be comfortably off

desahuciar [A1] *vt* **1** ⟨*enfermo*⟩ to declare … terminally ill **2 (a)** ⟨*inquilino*⟩ to evict **(b)** (Chi) ⟨*empleado*⟩ (despedir) to dismiss; (notificar el despido) to give … notice

desaire *m* snub, slight; hacerle un ∼ a algn to snub *o* slight sb

desalentador -dora adj disheartening, discouraging

desalentar [A5] vt to discourage, dishearten

desaliento m dejection, despondency

desaliñado -da adj slovenly

desalojar [A1] vt **(a)** ⟨edificio/recinto⟩ «ocupantes» to vacate; «policía/juez» to clear **(b)** ⟨residentes⟩ to evacuate; ⟨inquilino⟩ (esp AmL) to evict

desamarrar [A1] vt (AmL exc RPl) ⟨embarcación⟩ to cast off; ⟨zapatos/paquete⟩ to undo, untie; ⟨animal/persona⟩ to untie
■ **desamarrarse** v pron (AmL exc RPl)
1 «paquete/zapatos» to come undone; «bultos/barco» to come untied 2 (refl) «persona» to get free; «animal» to get loose o free

desamparado -da adj ⟨niño/anciano⟩ defenseless*; ⟨lugar⟩ bleak, unprotected

desamparo m neglect

desangrarse v pron to bleed to death

desanimado -da adj discouraged, dispirited

desanimar [A1] vt to discourage
■ **desanimarse** v pron to become disheartened o discouraged

desánimo m dejection, despondency

desaparecer [E3] vi «persona/objeto» to disappear; «dolor/síntoma/cicatriz» to disappear, go; «costumbre» to disappear, die out; «mancha» to come out
■ **desaparecerse** v pron (Andes) to disappear

desaparecido -da adj **(a)** (que no se encuentra) missing **(b)** (period) (muerto) late (before n), deceased (frml)
■ m,f **(a)** (en un accidente) missing person **(b)** (Pol): los ~s the disappeared o those who have disappeared

desaparición f disappearance; una especie en vías de ~ an endangered species

desapercibido -da adj: pasar ~ to go unnoticed

desaprovechar [A1] vt ⟨oportunidad⟩ to waste; ⟨tiempo/comida⟩ to waste

desarmable adj ⟨mueble/mecanismo⟩ which can be dismantled o taken apart

desarmado -da adj ⟨policía/criminal⟩ unarmed

desarmador m (Méx) **(a)** (herramienta) screwdriver **(b)** (bebida) screwdriver

desarmar [A1] vt 1 ⟨mueble/mecanismo⟩ to dismantle; ⟨carpa⟩ (AmL) to take down; ⟨rifle/motor⟩ to strip (down); ⟨rompecabezas⟩ to take ... to pieces, break up; ⟨juguete/maqueta⟩ to take ... apart 2 **(a)** (quitar armas) to disarm **(b)** (dejar sin argumentos) to disarm

desarme m disarmament

desarrollado -da adj developed; un niño muy/poco ~a well-developed/an underdeveloped child

desarrollar [A1] vt 1 (en general) to develop 2 **(a)** (exponer) ⟨teoría/tema⟩ to explain **(b)** (llevar a cabo) ⟨actividad/labor⟩ to carry out
■ **desarrollarse** v pron 1 (en general) to develop 2 «acto/entrevista/escena» to take place

desarrollo m development; países en vías de ~ developing countries; según el ~ de los acontecimientos according to how things develop

desastrado -da adj ⟨persona⟩ scruffy, untidy; ⟨habitación/trabajo⟩ untidy

desastre m disaster; como cantante es un ~ he's a hopeless singer; tienes la habitación hecha un ~ your room is a shambles; vas hecha un ~ you look a real mess (colloq)

desastroso -sa adj disastrous

desatado -da adj: estar ~ ⟨perro⟩ to be loose; ⟨cordón/nudo⟩ to be undone

desatar [A1] vt **(a)** ⟨nudo/lazo⟩ to untie, undo **(b)** ⟨persona⟩ to untie; ⟨perro⟩ to let ... loose
■ **desatarse** v pron **(a)** «nudo/cordones» to come undone o untied; «perro/caballo» to get loose **(b)** (refl) «persona» to untie oneself; ⟨cordones/zapatos⟩ to untie, undo

desatascador m (instrumento) plunger; (producto) nitric acid (o caustic soda etc) (used to clear blocked drains)

desatascar [A2] vt ⟨cañería/fregadero⟩ to unblock, clear
■ **desatascarse** v pron «cañería/fregadero» to unblock; ⟨carretera⟩ to clear

desatender [E8] vt **(a)** ⟨trabajo/familia⟩ to neglect **(b)** ⟨tienda/mostrador⟩ to leave ... unattended

desatento -ta adj **(a)** [SER] (desconsiderado) thoughtless, inconsiderate **(b)** [ESTAR] (distraído) inattentive

desatornillador m (AmC, Chi) screwdriver

desatornillar [A1] vt to unscrew

desautorizar [A4] vt **(a)** (restar autoridad a) ⟨persona⟩ to undermine the authority of; ⟨declaraciones⟩ to disavow (frml) **(b)** (retirar la autorización para) ⟨marcha/huelga⟩ to ban

desayunar [A1] vt to have ... for breakfast; ¿qué desayunaste? what did you have for breakfast?
■ ~ vi to have breakfast
■ **desayunarse** v pron (AmL) (tomar el desayuno) to have breakfast; ~se CON algo to have sth FOR breakfast

desayuno m breakfast; tomar el ~ to have breakfast

desbarajuste m (fam) mess; un ~ económico an economic mess o chaos

desbaratar [A1] vt **(a)** ⟨planes⟩ to spoil, ruin; ⟨sistema⟩ to disrupt **(b)** (Méx) ⟨papeles⟩ to jumble (up), muddle (up); ⟨mecanismo⟩ to ruin, destroy
■ **desbaratarse** v pron **(a)** «plan» to be ruined, be spoiled; «sistema» to be disrupted, break down **(b)** (Méx) «papeles» to get jumbled up, get muddled (up); «mecanismo» to break, get broken

desbarrancarse [A2] v pron to go over a sheer drop

desbloquear [A1] vt **(a)** ⟨carretera/entrada⟩ to clear; ⟨mecanismo⟩ to release, free **(b)** ⟨negociaciones/diálogo⟩ to break the deadlock in **(c)** (Com, Fin) ⟨cuenta⟩ to unfreeze

desbocado -da adj **(a)** ⟨caballo⟩ runaway (before n) **(b)** ⟨cuello/escote⟩ loose, wide

desbocarse [A2] v pron «caballo» to bolt

desbordante adj ⟨entusiasmo/júbilo⟩ boundless; está ~ de entusiasmo he's bursting with enthusiasm

desbordarse [A1] *v pron* (a) «*río/canal*» to burst its banks (b) «*vaso/cubo*» to overflow (c) «*multitud*» to get out of hand, get out of control

descabellado -da *adj* crazy, ridiculous

descafeinado -da *adj* decaffeinated

descalabro *m* (a) (desastre) disaster (b) (Mil) defeat

descalificación *f* (Dep) disqualification

descalificar [A2] *vt* ‹*deportista/equipo*› to disqualify

descalzarse [A4] *v pron* to take off one's shoes

descalzo -za *adj* ‹*pie*› bear; ‹*persona*› barefoot

descaminado -da *adj*: andar ~ to be on the wrong track

descampado *m* (a) (terreno) area *o* piece of open ground *o* land (b) al descampado (AmS) ‹*dormir*› in the open (air)

descansado -da *adj* (a) [ESTAR] ‹*persona*› rested, refreshed (b) [SER] ‹*actividad/trabajo*› easy, undemanding; ‹*vida*› quiet, peaceful

descansar [A1] *vi* (a) (de actividad, trabajo) to rest, have a rest; sin ~ without a break; ~ de algo to have a rest *o* break FROM sth (b) (yacer) to lie; que en paz descanse God rest his soul
■ ~ *vt* ~ la vista to rest one's eyes, to give one's eyes a rest; ~ la mente to give one's mind a break *o* rest

descansillo *m* (Esp) landing

descanso *m* ⊡ (a) (reposo) rest (b) (en trabajo, colegio) break; sin ~ without a break (c) (Mil): estar en posición de ~ to be standing at ease ⊡ (intervalo) (Dep) half time; (Teatr) interval ⊡ (alivio, tranquilidad) relief ⊡ (AmL) (rellano) landing

descapotable *adj/m* convertible

descarado -da *adj* ‹*persona/actitud*› brazen, shameless; es muy ~ he has a lot of nerve

descarga *f* ⊡ (de mercancías) unloading ⊡ (Elec) discharge; una ~ eléctrica an electric shock ⊡ (de arma) shot, discharge (frml); (de conjunto de armas) volley

descargar [A3] *vt* ⊡ ‹*vehículo/mercancías*› to unload ⊡ (a) ‹*pistola*› (extraer las balas) to unload; (disparar) to fire, discharge (frml); la pistola está descargada the pistol is not loaded (b) ‹*tiro*› to fire; ‹*golpe*› to deal, land ⊡ ‹*ira/agresividad*› to vent; ‹*preocupaciones/tensiones*› to relieve
■ ~ *v impers* ‹*aguacero*› to pour down; «*temporal*» to break
■ **descargarse** *v pron* ⊡ (Elec) «*pila*» to run down; «*batería*» to go dead *o* flat ⊡ «*tormenta*» to break; «*lluvias*» to come down, fall

descaro *m* audacity, nerve (colloq); ¡qué ~! what a nerve!

descarriado -da *adj*: hoy día la juventud anda descarriada the youth of today has lost its way; ▶ OVEJA

descarrilamiento *m* derailment

descarrilar [A1] *vi* to derail, be derailed

descarrilarse *v pron* (AmL) to derail, be derailed

descartar [A1] *vt* to rule out

descascararse [A1] *vpron* «*pared/pintura*» to peel; «*taza/plato*»to chip

descendencia *f* descendants (*pl*)

descendente *adj* ‹*curva/linea*› downward; ‹*escala*› descending

descender [E8] *vi* ⊡ (a) «*temperatura/ nivel*» to fall, drop (b) (frml) (desde una altura) «*avión*» to descend; «*persona*» to descend (frml), to come/go down ⊡ (en clasificación) to go down ⊡ (proceder) ~ DE algn to be descended FROM sb

descendiente *mf* descendant

descenso *m* ⊡ (a) (de temperatura, nivel) fall, drop; (de precios) fall (b) (desde una altura) descent ⊡ (Dep) relegation

descentrado -da *adj* (a) ‹*eje/rueda*› off-center* (b) ‹*persona*› disoriented, disorientated (BrE)

descentralizar [A4] *vt* to decentralize

descifrar [A1] *vt* (a) ‹*mensaje*› to decode, decipher; ‹*escritura/jeroglífico/código*› to decipher (b) ‹*misterio/enigma*› to work out, figure out

descodificador *m* decoder

descolgar [A8] *vt* (a) ‹*cuadro/cortina*› to take down (b) ‹*teléfono*› to pick up; dejar el teléfono descolgado to leave the phone off the hook
■ **descolgarse** *v pron* ⊡ (por una cuerda) to lower oneself ⊡ (en carrera) to pull away, break away

descollar [A10] *vi* to be outstanding

descolorido -da *adj* ‹*tela/papel*› faded

descomponer [E22] *vt* ⊡ ‹*alimento/cadáver*› to rot, cause ... to decompose *o* rot ⊡ (esp AmL) ‹*máquina/aparato*› to break; ‹*peinado*› to mess up ⊡ ‹*persona*› (a) (producir malestar) «*olor*» to make ... queasy (b) (producir diarrea) to give ... diarrhea*
■ **descomponerse** *v pron* ⊡ «*luz*» to split; «*sustancia*» to break down, separate ⊡ ‹*cadáver/alimento*› to rot, decompose (frml) ⊡ (esp AmL) «*máquina/aparato*» to break down ⊡ «*persona*» (sentir malestar) to feel sick; (del estómago) to have an attack of diarrhea* ⊡ (CS) «*tiempo*» to become unsettled; «*día*» to cloud over

descompuesto -ta *adj* ⊡ ‹*alimento*› rotten, decomposed (frml); ‹*cadáver*› decomposed ⊡ ‹*expresión*› changed, altered ⊡ (esp AmL) [ESTAR] ‹*máquina/aparato*› broken; ‹*teléfono*› out of order ⊡ estar ~ (indispuesto) to feel sick; (del estómago) to have diarrhea*/an upset stomach

descompuse, descompuso, etc ▶ DESCOMPONER

desconcertado -da *adj* disconcerted; quedarse ~ to be taken aback

desconcertante *adj* disconcerting

desconcertar [A5] *vt* to disconcert; su respuesta me desconcertó I was disconcerted by her reply

desconchado *m* (en taza, plato) chip; (en pared) place where plaster or paint has come off

desconcharse [A1] *v pron* «taza/plato» to chip, get chipped; «pared/piel» to peel

desconcierto *m*: su llamada los llenó de ∼ they were disconcerted by his call; **el ∼ reinante** the prevailing atmosphere of uncertainty

desconectar [A1] *vt* ‹alarma/teléfono› to disconnect; ‹calefacción› to switch off, turn off; ∼ **algo** DE **algo** to disconnect sth FROM sth
■ **desconectarse** *v pron* «aparato» to switch o turn off

desconfiado -da *adj* (receloso) distrustful; (suspicaz) suspicious

desconfianza *f* distrust, suspicion

desconfiar [A17] *vi* ∼ **DE algn** to mistrust sb, to distrust sb; ∼ **DE algo** ‹de motivos› to mistrust sth; ‹de honestidad› to doubt sth

descongelante *m* deicer

descongelar [A1] *vt* ‹refrigerador› to defrost; ‹alimentos› to defrost, thaw
■ **descongelarse** *v pron* ‹refrigerador› to defrost; «alimentos» to defrost, thaw

descongestionar [A1] *vt* to clear

desconocer [E3] *vt* (a) (no conocer): **por razones que desconocemos** for reasons unknown to us; **desconocía este hecho** I was unaware of this fact (b) (no reconocer): **te desconocí** I didn't recognize you

desconocido -da *adj* (en general) unknown; **un cantante ∼** an unknown singer; **una persona desconocida** a stranger
■ *m,f* (no conocido) stranger

desconocimiento *m* ignorance

desconsiderado -da *adj* thoughtless, inconsiderate

desconsolado -da *adj* **estar ∼ POR algo** to be heartbroken OVER sth; **lloraba ∼** he cried inconsolably

desconsuelo *m* grief, despair

descontado *adj*: **eso dalo por ∼** you can be sure of that; **doy por ∼ que vendrás a cenar** I'm assuming that you're coming to dinner

descontaminar [A1] *vt* ‹alimentos/cultivos› to decontaminate; ‹atmósfera› to clean up

descontar [A10] *vt* 1 (a) (rebajar): **me descontó el 15%** he gave me a 15% discount (b) (restar) ‹gastos/impuestos› to deduct, take off; ‹horas› to deduct 2 (exceptuar): **si descontamos a Pedro/los domingos** ... if we don't count Pedro/Sundays ... 3 ‹letra/pagaré› to discount

descontento¹ -ta *adj* [ESTAR] dissatisfied; ∼ **CON algo/algn** unhappy o dissatisfied WITH sth/sb

descontento² *m* discontent

descontrolado -da *adj* out of control

descontrolarse [A1] *v pron* to get out of control

desconvocar [A2] *vt* to call off

descorazonar [A1] *vt* to dishearten, discourage

descorchar [A1] *vt* to uncork, open

descorrer [E1] *vt* ‹cortinas› to draw (back); ‹cerrojo› to draw back

descortés *adj* ‹persona› impolite, ill-mannered; ‹comportamiento› rude, impolite

descortesía *f* (a) (acto descortés) discourtesy (b) (cualidad) rudeness, impoliteness

descoserse [E1] *v pron* «prenda/costura» to come unstitched

descosido -da *adj* ‹dobladillo/costura› unstitched

descremado -da *adj* skimmed

describir [I34] *vt* to describe

descripción *f* description

descriptivo -va *adj* descriptive

descrito -ta *pp*: ▶ DESCRIBIR

descuartizar [A4] *vt* (a) ‹res› to quarter (b) «asesino» to chop ... (up) into pieces

descubierto -ta *adj* 1 ‹piscina/terraza› open-air, outdoor (*before n*); ‹carroza› open-top 2 ‹cielos› clear 3 **al descubierto: quedar al ∼** ‹planes/escándalo› to come to light; **han puesto al ∼ sus chanchullos** his shady dealings have been exposed; **girar al** *or* **en ∼** (Com, Fin) to overdraw

descubridor -dora *m,f* discoverer

descubrimiento *m* discovery

descubrir [I33] *vt* 1 ‹tierras/oro/artista› to discover 2 (a) (enterarse de, averiguar) ‹razón/solución› to discover, find out; ‹complot/engaño› to uncover; ‹fraude› to detect (b) ‹persona escondida› to find, track down (c) ‹culpable› find ... out (d) (delatar) to give ... away 3 (a) ‹estatua/placa› to unveil (b) (revelar) ‹planes/intenciones› to reveal

descuento *m* 1 (a) (rebaja) discount; **hacen un ∼ del 15%** they give a 15% discount (b) (del sueldo) deduction 2 (Dep) injury time 3 (de letra, pagaré) discount

descuidado -da *adj* (a) [SER] (negligente) careless; (en el vestir) sloppy (b) [ESTAR] (desatendido) neglected

descuidar [A1] *vt* ‹negocio/jardín› to neglect
■ ∼ *vi*: **descuide, yo me ocuparé de eso** don't worry, I'll see to that
■ **descuidarse** *v pron* (a) (no prestar atención, distraerse): **se descuidó un momento y el perro se le escapó** his attention strayed for a moment and the dog ran off; **si te descuidas, te roban** if you don't watch out, they'll rob you; **como te descuides, te van a quitar el puesto** if you don't look out, they'll take your job from you (b) (en el aspecto físico) to neglect one's appearance

descuido *m* (a) (distracción): **en un ∼ el niño se le escapó** she took her eyes off the child for a moment and he ran off; **basta el más pequeño ∼** the smallest lapse of concentration is enough (b) (error) slip; (omisión) oversight

desde *prep* 1 (en el tiempo) since; ∼ **entonces/∼ que se casó** since then/since he got married; **¿∼ cuándo trabajas aquí?** how long have you been working here?; ∼ **el primer momento** right from the start; **no los veo ∼ hace meses** I haven't seen them for months; ∼ **el 15 hasta el 30** from the 15th to *o* until the 30th 2 (en el espacio) from; ∼ **aquí/allá** from here/there; **¿∼ dónde tengo que leer?** where do I have to read from?; ∼ **la página 12 hasta la 20** from page 12 (up) to page 20 3 (en escalas, jerarquías) from; **blusas ∼ 2.000 ptas.** blouses from 2,000 ptas.

desdén *m* disdain, scorn

desdeñable adj insignificant

desdeñar [A1] vt (a) (menospreciar) to scorn (b) ⟨pretendiente⟩ to spurn

desdeñoso -sa adj disdainful

desdicha f (desgracia) misfortune; (infelicidad) unhappiness

desdichado -da adj (a) (infeliz) unhappy (b) [SER] ⟨día⟩ ill-fated; **ser ~ en amores** to be unlucky in love
■ m,f: **es un pobre ~** he's a poor unfortunate wretch

desdoblar [A1] vt ⟨servilleta/pañuelo⟩ to unfold
■ **desdoblarse** v pron to divide into two, split into two

deseable adj desirable

desear [A1] vt 1 ⟨suerte/éxito/felicidad⟩ to wish; **te deseo un feliz viaje** I hope you have a good trip 2 (querer): **un embarazo no deseado** an unwanted pregnancy; **las tan deseadas vacaciones** the long-awaited holidays; **lo que más deseo es ...** my greatest wish is ...; **si tú lo deseas** if you want to; **~ía una respuesta ahora** I would like a reply now; **está deseando verte** he's really looking forward to seeing you; **¿desea que se lo envuelva?** (frml) would you like me to wrap it for you? 3 ⟨persona⟩ to desire, want

desechable adj disposable

desechar [A1] vt (a) ⟨ayuda/propuesta⟩ to reject; ⟨idea/plan⟩ (rechazar) to reject; (renunciar a) to drop, give up (b) ⟨restos/residuos⟩ to throw away o out; ⟨ropa⟩ to throw out

desecho m waste

desembarcar [A2] vi (de barco, avión) «pasajeros» to disembark; «tropas» to land, disembark
■ **~** vt ⟨mercancías⟩ to unload; ⟨pasajeros⟩ to disembark; (en emergencia) to evacuate

desembocadura f mouth, estuary

desembocar [A2] vi **~ EN algo** ⟨en mar/río⟩ to flow INTO sth; ⟨en calle⟩ to come out ONTO sth; ⟨en plaza⟩ to come out INTO sth

desembolsar [A1] vt to spend, pay out

desembolso m expenditure; (gasto inicial) outlay

desempacar [A2] vt/vi (esp AmL) to unpack

desempaquetar [A1] vt to unwrap

desempatar [A1] vi (a) (Dep) to break the tie (AmE), to break the deadlock (BrE) (b) (en una votación) to break the deadlock

desempate m (a) (Dep): **el ~ se produjo en el minuto 36** the breakthrough came in the 36th minute; **un partido de ~** a decider; **~ a penaltys** penalty shoot-out (b) (en concurso) tiebreak, tiebreaker; (en una votación) run-off

desempeñar [A1] vt (a) (Teatr) ⟨papel⟩ to play (b) ⟨funciones⟩ to carry out, perform; ⟨cargo⟩ to hold
■ **desempeñarse** v pron (AmL): **se desempeña bien en su trabajo** she does her job well; **se desempeñó muy bien** she did o managed very well

desempleado -da m,f: **un ~** someone who is out of work o unemployed; **los ~s** the unemployed

desempleo m (a) (situación) unemployment (b) (subsidio) unemployment benefit

desencadenar [A1] vt (a) ⟨crisis/protesta/reacción⟩ to trigger (b) ⟨perro⟩ to unleash; ⟨preso⟩ to unchain
■ **desencadenarse** v pron ⟨explosión/reacción⟩ to be triggered off; «guerra» to break out; «tempestad» to break

desencajado -da adj (a) ⟨pieza⟩ out of position (b) ⟨mandíbula/rótula⟩ dislocated (c) (alterado) shaken

desencajar [A1] vt (a) (Mec) to knock out of position (b) ⟨mandíbula/rótula⟩ to dislocate
■ **desencajarse** v pron (a) (Mec) to be knocked/come out of position (b) «mandíbula/rótula» to become/get dislocated

desencaminado -da adj (AmL) ▶ DESCAMINADO

desencanto m disillusionment, disenchantment

desenchufar [A1] vt to unplug, disconnect

desenfadado -da adj (a) (seguro de sí mismo) self-assured, confident; (sin inhibiciones) uninhibited (b) ⟨estilo/moda/actitud⟩ free-and-easy, carefree

desenfocado -da adj out of focus

desenganchar [A1] vt ⟨caballos/remolque⟩ to unhitch; ⟨vagones⟩ to uncouple

desengañar [A1] vt (decepcionar) to disillusion; (sacar del engaño, error) to get ... to face the facts
■ **desengañarse** v pron (a) (decepcionarse) **~se DE algo** to become disillusioned WITH o ABOUT sth (b) (salir del engaño, error) to stop fooling oneself

desengaño m disappointment; **llevarse un ~** to be disappointed; **un ~ amoroso** an unhappy love affair

desenlace m (de película, libro) ending; (de aventura) outcome

desenredar [A1] vt ⟨pelo/lana⟩ to untangle, disentangle; ⟨lío⟩ to straighten out, sort out
■ **desenredarse** v pron (refl) ⟨pelo⟩ to get the knots out of

desenrollar [A1] vt ⟨alfombra/póster⟩ to unroll; ⟨persiana⟩ to let down; ⟨ovillo/cuerda⟩ to unwind

desenroscar [A2] vt to unscrew

desentenderse [E8] v pron **~ DE algo** ⟨de un asunto⟩ to wash one's hands of sth; **se desentiende de los hijos** he doesn't take an interest in the children

desenterrar [A5] vt ⟨cadáver⟩ to exhume, dig up; ⟨ruinas/tesoro⟩ to unearth, dig up

desentonar [A1] vi (a) (Mús) to go out of tune o off key (b) «color» to clash (c) «atuendo/comentario» to be out of place

desentrenado -da adj out of condition o training

desenvoltura f self-assurance

desenvolver [E11] vt to unwrap, open
■ **desenvolverse** v pron (a) (manejarse) to get by, manage; **se desenvuelve muy bien en inglés** she gets by very well in English; **se desenvolvió bien en la entrevista** she managed the interview all right (b) (en situaciones difíciles) to cope (c) «hechos/sucesos» to develop

desenvuelto -ta *adj* ⟨persona⟩ self-assured, confident

deseo *m* **(a)** (anhelo) wish; **formular un** ~ to make a wish **(b)** (apetito sexual) desire

desequilibrado -da *adj* ⟨rueda/mecanismo⟩ out of balance; ⟨persona⟩ unbalanced

desequilibrar [A1] *vt* **(a)** ⟨embarcación/vehículo⟩ to unbalance, make ... unbalanced; ⟨persona⟩ (físicamente) to throw ... off balance; (mentalmente) to unbalance **(b)** ⟨fuerzas/poder⟩ to upset the balance of

■ **desequilibrarse** *v pron* ⟨⟨ruedas/mecanismo⟩⟩ to get out of balance

desequilibrio *m* **(a)** (desigualdad) imbalance**(b)** (Psic) unbalanced state of mind

desertar [A1] *vi* (Mil) to desert; (de partido) to defect

desértico -ca *adj* ⟨zona/clima⟩ desert (*before n*)

desertización *f* desertification

desertor -tora *m,f* (Mil) deserter; (de un partido) defector

desesperación *f* **(a)** (angustia) desperation; **con** ~ ⟨luchar/gritar⟩ desperately; ⟨mirar/suplicar⟩ despairingly; ⟨llorar⟩ bitterly; **de** ~ out of desperation **(b)** (desesperanza) despair

desesperado -da *adj* desperate

desesperante *adj* **(a)** (exasperante) exasperating **(b)** (angustioso) distressing

desesperar [A1] *vt* to drive ... to distraction *o* despair

■ ~ *vi* to despair, give up hope

■ **desesperarse** *v pron* to become exasperated

desestabilizar [A4] *vt* to destabilize

desfachatez *f* audacity, nerve (colloq)

desfalco *m* embezzlement

desfallecer [E3] *vi* **(a)** (flaquear) ⟨⟨persona⟩⟩ to become weak; ⟨⟨fuerzas⟩⟩ to fade, fail; ⟨⟨ánimos⟩⟩ to flag; **lucharon sin** ~ they fought tirelessly **(b)** (desmayarse) to faint, pass out

desfasado -da *adj* ⟨ideas/persona⟩ old-fashioned

desfase *m* (falta de correspondencia): **hay un** ~ **entre su madurez física y su desarollo mental** his physical maturity is out of step with his intellectual development; ~ **de horario** jetlag

desfavorable *adj* unfavorable*; **el tiempo nos ha sido** ~ we had unfavorable weather conditions

desfigurado -da *adj* disfigured

desfigurar [A1] *vt* **1** ⟨⟨quemaduras/cicatriz⟩⟩ ⟨persona⟩ to disfigure **2** ⟨hechos⟩ to distort, twist; ⟨realidad⟩ to distort

desfiladero *m* (barranco) ravine, narrow gorge; (puerto) narrow pass

desfilar [A1] *vi* **(a)** ⟨⟨soldados⟩⟩ to parade **(b)** ⟨⟨manifestantes⟩⟩ to march; **la manifestación desfiló por la Gran Vía** the demonstration passed along the Gran Via **(c)** ⟨modelo⟩ to parade up and down the catwalk

desfile *m* (de carrozas) parade, procession; (Mil) parade, march past; ~ **de modelos** fashion show

desgajar [A1] *vt* ~ **algo DE algo** ⟨rama⟩ to break *o* snap sth OFF sth; ⟨páginas⟩ to tear *o* rip sth OUT OF sth

■ **desgajarse** *v pron* ⟨⟨rama⟩⟩ to break off, snap off

desgana *f* **(a)** (inapetencia) lack of appetite **(b)** (falta de entusiasmo): **con** *or* **a** ~ ⟨trabajar⟩ half-heartedly; ⟨obedecer⟩ reluctantly

desganado -da *adj* **(a)** (inapetente): **me siento** ~ I'm not hungry **(b)** (apático) lethargic

desgano *m* (AmL) ▶ DESGANA

desgarbado -da *adj* ⟨persona/aspecto⟩ gangling, gawky; ⟨movimientos/andar⟩ ungainly

desgarrador -dora *adj* heartbreaking, heartrending

desgarrar [A1] *vt* **(a)** ⟨vestido/papel⟩ to tear, rip **(b)** ⟨corazón⟩ to break

■ **desgarrarse** *v pron* **(a)** ⟨⟨vestido/camisa⟩⟩ to tear, rip **(b)** (Med) to tear

desgarro *m* (de ligamento, músculo): **sufrió un** ~ she tore a muscle

desgastar [A1] *vt* **(a)** (gastar) ⟨suelas/ropa⟩ to wear out; ⟨roca⟩ to wear away, erode **(b)** (debilitar) to wear ... down

■ **desgastarse** *v pron* **(a)** (gastarse) ⟨⟨ropa⟩⟩ to wear out; ⟨⟨roca⟩⟩ to wear away; ⟨⟨tacón⟩⟩ to wear down **(b)** ⟨⟨persona⟩⟩ to wear oneself out; ⟨⟨relación⟩⟩ to grow stale

desgaste *m* **(a)** (de ropa, suelas) wear; (de rocas) erosion, wearing away **(b)** (debilitamiento físico) debilitation

desgracia *f* **(a)** (desdicha, infortunio) misfortune; **tiene la** ~ **de ser ciego** he has the misfortune to be blind; **caer en** ~ to fall from favor **(b) por desgracia** (indep) unfortunately

desgraciado -da *adj* **(a)** [SER] (infeliz) unhappy **(b)** [SER] (desafortunado) ⟨viaje⟩ ill-fated **(c)** (desacertado) ⟨elección/coincidencia⟩ unfortunate, unwise

■ *m,f* **1** (desdichado) wretch **2** (persona vil) swine (colloq)

desgravación *f* tax exemption (AmE), tax relief (BrE)

desgravar [A1] *vt* **(a)** ⟨gastos/suma⟩ to claim tax exemption on (AmE), to claim tax relief on (BrE) **(b)** ⟨producto/importación⟩ to eliminate the tax *o* duty on

■ ~ *vi* to be tax-deductible

desguazar [A4] *vt* to scrap

deshabitado -da *adj* ⟨región⟩ uninhabited; ⟨edificio⟩ empty, unoccupied

deshacer [E18] *vt* **1 (a)** ⟨costura/bordado⟩ to unpick **(b)** ⟨nudo/lazo/trenza⟩ to undo; ⟨ovillo⟩ to unwind

2 (a) (desarmar, desmontar) ⟨maqueta/mecanismo⟩ to take ... apart; ⟨paquete⟩ to undo, unwrap **(b)** ⟨cama⟩ (para cambiarla) to strip; (desordenar) to mess up; ⟨maleta⟩ to unpack

3 (a) (derretir) ⟨nieve/helado⟩ to melt **(b)** (desmenuzar) to break up **(c)** (en líquido) to dissolve **4** ⟨acuerdo/trato⟩ to break; ⟨noviazgo⟩ to break off; ⟨planes/compromiso⟩ to cancel

■ **deshacerse** *v pron* **1** ⟨⟨dobladillo/costura⟩⟩ to come undone *o* unstitched; ⟨⟨nudo/trenza/moño⟩⟩ to come undone; ⟨⟨peinado⟩⟩ to get messed up, be ruined

2 (a) (desintegrarse) to disintegrate **(b)** ⟨⟨nieve/helado⟩⟩ to melt **(c)** (en líquido) to dissolve

···⇢

3 ~se EN algo: ~se en llanto to dissolve into tears; me deshice en cumplidos I went out of my way to be complimentary

4 deshacerse de (a) (librarse de) to get rid of (b) (desprenderse de) to part with

deshaga, deshagas, etc ▶ DESHACER

deshecho -cha adj [ESTAR] (a) (cansado, agotado) exhausted (b) (destrozado moralmente) shattered, devastated (c) (estropeado) ruined

deshelar [A5] vt ⟨cañería⟩ to thaw out, unfreeze; ⟨nevera/congelador⟩ to defrost; ⟨parabrisas⟩ to deice
■ **deshelarse** v pron to thaw, melt; «nieves» to thaw, melt; «río/lago» to thaw; «relaciones» to thaw

desheredar [A1] vt to disinherit

deshice, deshiciera, etc ▶ DESHACER

deshidratarse [A1] v pron to become dehydrated

deshielo m (a) (de ríos, nieves) thaw; agua de ~ meltwater (b) (de relaciones) thaw, thawing-out

deshizo ▶ DESHACER

deshojar [A1] vt ⟨flor⟩ to pull the petals off; ⟨cuaderno⟩ to tear o rip the pages out of

deshonesto -ta adj (a) (tramposo, mentiroso) dishonest (b) (indecente) ⟨proposiciones⟩ improper, indecent

deshonor m ▶ DESHONRA A

deshonra f (a) (vergüenza) disgrace; ese chico es una ~ para su familia that boy is a disgrace to his family (b) (pérdida de la honra) dishonor*

deshonrar [A1] vt ⟨familia/patria⟩ to dishonor*, disgrace; ⟨mujer⟩ to dishonor*

deshonroso -sa adj dishonorable*, disgraceful

deshora: a ~(s) off hours (AmE), out of hours (BrE)

deshuesar [A1] vt **1** (a) ⟨aceitunas⟩ to pit (b) ⟨pollo⟩ to bone **2** (Méx) ⟨coche/barco⟩ to scrap

desidia f (a) (apatía) slackness, indolence (fml) (b) (desaseo) slovenliness

desierto¹ -ta adj ⟨lugar⟩ deserted

desierto² m desert

designar [A1] vt **1** (fml) (elegir) (a) ⟨persona⟩ to appoint, designate (fml) (b) ⟨lugar/fecha⟩ to fix, set; (con carácter oficial) to designate **2** (fml) (denominar) to designate (fml)

designio m plan

desigual adj **1** (a) (diferente) uneven; las mangas quedaron ~es one sleeve turned out longer (o wider etc) than the other (b) (desequilibrado) ⟨lucha⟩ unequal; ⟨fuerzas⟩ unevenly-matched **2** (irregular) ⟨terreno/superficie⟩ uneven; ⟨letra⟩ uneven, irregular; ⟨calidad⟩ variable, varying (before n); ⟨rendimiento⟩ inconsistent, erratic

desigualdad f **1** (a) (diferencia) inequality (b) (desequilibrio) inequality, disparity **2** (de superficie) unevenness

desilusión f (decepción) disappointment; se llevó una ~ she was disappointed

desilusionado -da adj (decepcionado) disappointed

desilusionar [A1] vt to disappoint
■ **desilusionarse** v pron (decepcionarse) to be disappointed; (perder las ilusiones) to become disillusioned

desinfectante m disinfectant

desinfectar [A1] vt to disinfect

desinflar [A1] vt ⟨globo/balón/neumático⟩ to let the air out of, to deflate, let down (esp BrE)
■ **desinflarse** v pron «globo/balón/neumático» to deflate, go down

desinformación f disinformation, misleading information

desinformar [A1] vt to misinform

desinhibido -da adj uninhibited

desintegrarse [A1] v pron to disintegrate, break up; «familia» to break up

desinterés m (falta de interés) lack of interest; (altruismo) unselfishness

desinteresado -da adj ⟨consejo/ayuda⟩ disinterested; ⟨persona⟩ selfless

desintoxicación f detoxification

desintoxicarse [A2] v pron to undergo detoxification

desistir [I1] vi to give up; ~ DE algo ⟨de propósito⟩ to give up sth, desist FROM sth (fml); ⟨de demanda/derecho⟩ to relinquish sth; ~ DE hacer algo to give up doing sth, desist FROM doing sth (fml)

desleal adj [SER] disloyal; ~ CON or A algn/algo disloyal TO sb/sth

desligarse [A3] v pron (a) (librarse) ~se algo ⟨de obligaciones⟩ to free oneself OF sth; ⟨de compromiso⟩ to get out of sth (b) (apartarse) ~se DE algo/algn to cut oneself off FROM sth/sb

desliz m (error, falta) slip; (al hablar) gaffe, faux pas

deslizador m (Méx) (ala delta) hang glider

deslizar [A4] vt (hacer resbalar) to slip, slide
■ **deslizarse** v pron (a) «patinador/bailarines» to glide; «esquiador» to ski, slide; «serpiente» to slither, glide; ~se POR algo to slide down sth; se deslizó por la cuerda he slid down the rope (b) «barco/cisne» to glide; ~se SOBRE algo to glide OVER sth (c) ⟨cajón/argollas de cortina⟩ to slide (d) «agua/arroyo» to flow gently (e) (escurrirse, escaparse) to slip away

deslucido -da adj ⟨actuación/desfile⟩ dull, lackluster*; ⟨colores/paredes⟩ faded, drab; ⟨plata⟩ tarnished

deslumbrante, deslumbrador -dora adj ⟨luz⟩ blinding; ⟨belleza⟩ dazzling, stunning

deslumbrar [A1] vt to dazzle

desmadrarse [A1] v pron (fam) «persona» to go wild (colloq)

desmán m (exceso, abuso) outrage, excess

desmanchar [A1] vt (AmL) to get the stains out of

desmandarse [A1] *v pron* «niños/tropas» to get out of control *o* hand

desmano: a ∼ (*loc adv*) ⟨estar/quedar⟩ out of the way; **me pilla a** ∼ it's out of my way

desmantelar [A1] *vt* to dismantle; ⟨coche⟩ to strip

desmarcarse [A2] *v pron* (Dep) to slip the coverage (AmE), to slip one's marker (BrE)

desmayado -da *adj* ⟨persona⟩ unconscious (*from having fainted*)

desmayarse [A1] *v pron* to faint

desmayo *m* (a) (Med) faint; **sufrir un** ∼ to faint (b) **sin** ∼ ⟨luchar/trabajar⟩ resolutely, tirelessly

desmedido -da *adj* excessive; **le han dado una importancia desmedida** they have attributed too much importance to it

desmejorado -da *adj* (a) (de salud): **lo encontré muy** ∼ he didn't look at all well to me (b) (de atractivo): **está desmejorada** she's lost her looks

desmemoriado -da *adj* forgetful, absent-minded

desmentir [I11] *vt* ⟨noticia/rumor⟩ to deny; ⟨acusación⟩ to deny, refute

desmenuzar [A4] *vt* ⟨pescado⟩ to flake; ⟨pollo⟩ to shred; ⟨pan⟩ to crumble

desmigajarse [A1] *v pron* to crumble

desmilitarizar [A4] *vt* to demilitarize

desmontable *adj* (a) (desarmable) ⟨mecanismo/mueble⟩ which can be dismantled *o* taken apart (b) (separable) ⟨forro/pieza⟩ detachable, removable

desmontar [A1] *vt* (a) (desarmar) ⟨mueble/mecanismo⟩ to dismantle, take apart; ⟨tienda de campaña⟩ to take down (b) (separar) ⟨forro/pieza⟩ to detach, remove
■ ∼ *vi* «jinete» to dismount

desmoralizar [A4] *vt* to demoralize, dishearten
■ **desmoralizarse** *v pron* to get demoralized *o* disheartened, to lose heart

desmoronarse [A1] *v pron* (a) «muro/edificio» to collapse; «imperio/sociedad» to crumble, collapse (b) «fe/moral» to crumble; «persona» to go to pieces

desnatado -da *adj* (Esp) skimmed

desnaturalizado -da *adj* (a) ⟨aceite/vino⟩ denatured (b) ⟨madre⟩ unnatural

desnivel *m* **1** (en superficie) (a) (irregularidad) unevenness, irregularity; **es un terreno lleno de** ∼**es** it is a very uneven piece of land; **un** ∼ **entre la cocina y el comedor** a difference in floor level between the kitchen and the dining room (b) (inclinación, pendiente) slope, incline (frml) (c) (depresión) drop (*in the level of the ground*) **2** (diferencia) difference, disparity

desnivelado -da *adj* (a) (irregular) ⟨terreno⟩ uneven (b) (fuera de nivel): **la mesa está desnivelada** the table isn't level

desnucarse [A2] *v pron* to break one's neck

desnuclearizar [A4] *vt* to denuclearize; **zona desnuclearizada** nuclear-free zone

desnudar [A1] *vt* (desvestir) to undress
■ **desnudarse** *v pron* (*refl*) (desvestirse) to undress, take one's clothes off; ∼**se de (la) cintura para arriba** to strip to the waist

desnudez *f* (de persona) nakedness, nudity

desnudo¹ -da *adj* (a) (sin ropa) ⟨persona⟩ naked; **nadar** ∼ to swim in the nude; **totalmente** ∼ stark naked; ∼ **de la cintura para arriba** naked to the waist (b) (descubierto) ⟨hombros/brazos/torso⟩ bare

desnudo² *m* (Art) nude

desnutrido -da *adj* malnourished, undernourished

desobedecer [E3] *vt/vi* to disobey

desobediente *adj* disobedient

desocupado -da *adj* **1** (vacío, libre) ⟨casa/habitación⟩ unoccupied, vacant; ⟨asiento/baño⟩ free **2** (desempleado) unemployed

desodorante *m* deodorant; ∼ **en barra** stick deodorant; ∼ **ambiental** (CS) air freshener

desolado -da *adj* **1** ⟨paisaje/campos⟩ desolate; ⟨ciudad⟩ devastated **2** (afligido) desolated, devastated

desolador -dora *adj* **1** (devastador) ⟨tormenta/epidemia⟩ devastating **2** (triste, penoso) ⟨noticia/espectáculo⟩ distressing

desollar [A10] *vt* ⟨animal⟩ to skin, flay

desorbitado -da *adj* (a) ⟨precios⟩ exorbitant, astronomical (b) **con los ojos** ∼**s** with her/his eyes popping out of her/his head (colloq)

desorden *m* **1** (a) (de persona, cuarto, cajón) untidiness, mess (colloq); **perdona el** ∼ sorry about the mess; **en** ∼ ⟨salir/entrar⟩ in a disorderly fashion; **todo estaba en** ∼ everything was in disorder *o* in a mess (b) (confusión) disorder **2 desórdenes** *mpl* (disturbios) disturbances (*pl*), disorder

desordenado -da *adj* **1** (a) ⟨persona/habitación⟩ untidy, messy (colloq); **tengo la casa toda desordenada** my house is in a mess *o* is very untidy (b) [ESTAR] ⟨naipes/hojas⟩ out of order **2** ⟨vida⟩ disorganized

desordenar [A1] *vt* ⟨mesa/habitación⟩ to make … untidy, mess up (colloq); ⟨naipes/hojas⟩ to get … out of order

desorganización *f* lack of organization

desorganizado -da *adj* disorganized

desorientado -da *adj* disoriented, disorientated (BrE)

desorientar [A1] *vt* to confuse
■ **desorientarse** *v pron* to lose one's bearings, become disoriented

despabilado -da *adj* ▶ ESPABILADO

despabilar [A1] *vt* ▶ ESPABILAR

despachar [A1] *vt* **1** (a) ⟨asunto/tarea/⟩ to take care of, deal with; ⟨correspondencia⟩ to deal with, attend to (b) ⟨carta/paquete⟩ to send; ⟨mercancías⟩ (por barco) to ship; (por avión, tren) to send, dispatch **2** (Com) (en tienda) to serve, deal with
■ ∼ *vi* (Com) «dependiente» to serve

despacho *m* **1** (a) (oficina) office; (estudio) study (b) (mobiliario) office furniture **2** (envío) dispatch, despatch **3** (comunicado) communiqué; (Mil) dispatch; (Period) report

despacio *adv* **1** (lentamente) slowly **2** (CS) (en voz baja) quietly, softly; (sin hacer ruido) quietly

despampanante *adj* (fam) stunning (colloq)

desparpajo *m* (desenvoltura) self-confidence; (desfachatez) audacity, nerve (colloq)

desparramado -da *adj* (esparcido) scattered; (derramado) spilt

desparramar [A1] *vt* ⟨*líquido/azúcar*⟩ to spill; ⟨*botones/monedas*⟩ to spill, scatter; ⟨*papeles/juguetes*⟩ to scatter
■ **desparramarse** *v pron* «*líquido/azúcar*» to spill; «*botones/monedas*» to scatter, spill

despavorido -da *adj* terrified, petrified

despecho *m* spite; **por ~** out of spite

despectivo -va *adj* ⟨*trato/gesto/actitud*⟩ contemptuous; ⟨*tono*⟩ disparaging; ⟨*término*⟩ pejorative, derogatory

despedazar [A4] *vt* **(a)** (cortar en trozos) to cut ... into pieces **(b)** ⟨*presa*⟩ to tear ... to pieces *o* shreds

despedida *f* **(a)** (acción) goodbye, farewell (liter) **(b)** (celebración) farewell party; **regalo de ~** a farewell gift; **~ de soltera/soltero** hen/stag night *o* party

despedir [I14] *vt* **1** (decir adiós): **vinieron a ~me al aeropuerto** they came to see me off at the airport **2** (del trabajo) to dismiss, fire (colloq); (por reducción de personal) to lay off **3** ⟨*olor*⟩ to give off; ⟨*humo/vapor*⟩ to emit, give off; **salir despedido** «*corcho/pelota*» to shoot out; **el conductor salió despedido del asiento** the driver was thrown out of his seat
■ **despedirse** *v pron* (decir adiós) to say goodbye; **~se DE algn** to say goodbye TO sb

despegar [A3] *vt* ⟨*etiqueta/esparadrapo*⟩ to remove, peel off; ⟨*piezas/ensambladura*⟩ to get ... unstuck *o* apart; **no despegó los labios** she didn't say a word
■ **~** *vi* «*avión*» to take off; «*cohete*» to lift off, be launched
■ **despegarse** *v pron* «*sello/etiqueta*» to come unstuck, peel off; «*esparadrapo/empapelado*» to come off

despegue *m* (de avión) takeoff; (de cohete) launch, lift-off

despeinado -da *adj* ⟨*pelo/melena*⟩ unkempt, disheveled*; **estar ~** to have one's hair in a mess

despeinar [A1] *vt*: **~ a algn** to mess up sb's hair
■ **despeinarse** *v pron* to mess one's hair up

despejado -da *adj* **1** (Meteo) ⟨*día/cielo*⟩ clear **2** (libre, vacío) ⟨*carretera/camino*⟩ clear **3** (a) ⟨*persona*⟩ clearheaded; ⟨*mente*⟩ clear **(b)** [ESTAR] (sobrio) sober

despejar [A1] *vt* **1** **(a)** (desocupar, desalojar) to clear **(b)** ⟨*nariz*⟩ to unblock, clear; **el paseo me despejó** the walk cleared my head **2** ⟨*balón*⟩ (en fútbol) to clear; (en fútbol americano) to punt
■ **~** *vi* (en fútbol) to clear; (en fútbol americano) to punt
■ **~** *v impers* (Meteo) to clear up
■ **despejarse** *v pron* (espabilarse) to wake (oneself) up; (desembotarse) to clear one's head; «*borracho*» to sober up

despellejar [A1] *vt* ⟨*animal*⟩ to skin
■ **despellejarse** *v pron* to peel; **se me despellejó la nariz** my nose peeled

despelote *m* (AmL fam) (caos, lío) shambles (colloq)

despenalizar [A4] *vt* to legalize, decriminalize

despensa *f* larder, pantry

despeñadero *m* cliff, precipice

despeñarse [A1] *v pron* to go over a cliff (*o* precipice *etc*)

desperdiciar [A1] *vt* ⟨*comida/papel/tela*⟩ to waste; ⟨*oportunidad*⟩ to miss, waste

desperdicio *m* **(a)** (de comida, papel) waste **(b)** **desperdicios** *mpl* (residuos) scraps (*pl*)

desperdigado -da *adj* scattered

desperezarse [A4] *v pron* to stretch

desperfecto *m* **(a)** (daño) damage **(b)** (defecto) flaw

despertador *m* alarm clock; **poner el ~** to set the alarm

despertar [A5] *vt* **(a)** ⟨*persona*⟩ to wake, wake ... up **(b)** ⟨*sentimientos/pasiones*⟩ to arouse; ⟨*apetito*⟩ to whet; ⟨*recuerdos*⟩ to evoke; ⟨*interés*⟩ to awaken, stir up
■ **~** *vi* (del sueño) to wake (up); (de la anestesia) to come round
■ **despertarse** *v pron* (del sueño) to wake (up)

despiadado -da *adj* ⟨*persona*⟩ ruthless, heartless; ⟨*ataque/crítica*⟩ savage, merciless

despida, despidas, etc ▶ DESPEDIR

despido *m* dismissal; (por falta de trabajo) redundancy, layoff

despierta, despiertas, etc ▶ DESPERTAR

despierto -ta *adj* **(a)** [ESTAR] (del sueño) awake **(b)** [SER] ⟨*persona/mente*⟩ bright, alert

despilfarrar [A1] *vi* to waste *o* squander money
■ **~** *vt* to squander, waste

despilfarro *m* waste

despistado -da *adj* **(a)** [SER] vague, absentminded; **soy muy ~ para los nombres** I never remember names **(b)** **estar ~** to be miles away (colloq) *o* daydreaming; (desorientado, confuso) to be bewildered *o* lost
■ *m,f* scatterbrain (colloq)

despistar [A1] *vt* **(a)** (desorientar, confundir) to confuse **(b)** ⟨*perseguidor*⟩ to shake off; ⟨*sabueso*⟩ to throw ... off the scent
■ **despistarse** *v pron* (confundirse) to get confused *o* muddled; (distraerse) to lose concentration

despiste *m* **(a)** (distracción) absentmindedness; **fue un ~** it was a lapse of concentration **(b)** (equivocación) slip, mistake

desplazamiento *m* **1** (movimiento) movement, displacement **2** (frml) (traslado, viaje) trip; **gastos de ~** traveling expenses

desplazar [A4] *vt* **1** (frml) (mover, correr) to move; (Inf) to scroll **2** (suplantar, relegar) ⟨*persona*⟩ to displace; **~ A algo** to take the place OF sth
■ **desplazarse** *v pron* (frml) (trasladarse, moverse) ⟨*animal*⟩ to move around; «*avión/barco*» to travel, go; «*persona*» to get around

desplegar [A7] *vt* **1** **(a)** ⟨*alas*⟩ to spread; ⟨*mapa*⟩ to open out, spread out; ⟨*velas*⟩ to unfurl **(b)** (demostrar) ⟨*talento/ingenio*⟩ to display; (emplear) ⟨*encantos/poder*⟩ to use **(c)** (llevar a cabo) ⟨*campaña*⟩ to mount; ⟨*esfuerzo*⟩ to make **2** (Mil) ⟨*tropas/misiles*⟩ to deploy
■ **desplegarse** *v pron* (Mil) to deploy

despliegue *m* **1** (de tropas, recursos) deployment **2** (de riqueza, sabiduría) display

desplomarse [A1] *v pron* «*persona/edificio*» to collapse

desplumar [A1] *vt* (a) «*ave*» to pluck (b) (fam) ‹*persona*› to fleece (colloq)

despoblación *f* depopulation; ~ **forestal** (Esp) deforestation

despoblado -da *adj* [1] (sin habitantes) deserted, uninhabited; (subpoblado) underpopulated, sparsely populated [2] ‹*cejas*› thin, sparse

despojar [A1] *vt* (frml) ~ **A** algn **DE** algo ‹*de privilegios/poderes*› to divest sb of sth (frml); ‹*título/posesiones*› to dispossess (frml) *o* strip sb of sth
■ **despojarse** *v pron* (frml *o* liter) ~**se DE** algo ‹*de ropa*› to remove sth; ‹*de bienes*› to relinquish sth

despojos *mpl* (a) (restos) remains (*pl*) (b) (presa, botín) spoils (*pl*), loot (c) (de aves) head, wings, feet and giblets; (de reses) head, feet and offal

desportillado -da *adj* chipped

desposeído -da *m,f*: **los** ~**s** the destitute, the dispossessed

déspota *mf* tyrant, despot

despótico -ca *adj* despotic, tyrannical

despotricar [A2] *vi* (fam) ~ (**CONTRA** algo/ algn) to rant and rave (ABOUT sth/sb)

despreciable *adj* (a) ‹*persona/conducta*› despicable, contemptible (b) no/nada ~ ‹*suma/ número*› not inconsiderable, significant

despreciar [A1] *vt* (a) (menospreciar) ‹*persona*› to look down on; (profundamente) to despise (b) (rechazar) ‹*oferta/ayuda*› to reject

despreciativo -va *adj* disdainful

desprecio *m* (a) (menosprecio) disdain; (más intenso) contempt; **me miró con** ~ she gave me a disdainful *o* scornful look (b) (indiferencia por el peligro, la vida) disregard (c) (desaire) snub, slight; **hacerle un** ~ **a** algn to snub *o* slight sb

desprender [E1] *vt* (soltar, separar) ‹*teja*› to dislodge; ‹*etiqueta*› to detach
■ **desprenderse** *v pron* (a) «*teja*» to come loose; «*botón*» to come off; «*retina*» to become detached; ~**se DE** algo to come away FROM sth [2] (renunciar, entregar) ~**se DE** algo ‹*de posesiones*› to part WITH sth

desprendido -da *adj* [SER] generous, open-handed; *ver tb* DESPRENDER

desprendimiento *m* detachment; ~ **de retina** detachment of the retina; ~ **de tierras** landslide

despreocupado -da *adj* (a) (sin preocupaciones) ‹*vida*› carefree (b) (descuidado) negligent (c) (indiferente) unworried

despreocuparse [A1] *v pron* (a) ▶ DESENTENDERSE (b) (dejar de preocuparse): **despreocúpate de todo** don't worry about anything

desprestigiar [A1] *vt* to discredit
■ **desprestigiarse** *v pron* «*persona/producto/ empresa*» to lose prestige

desprestigio *m* (a) (pérdida de prestigio) loss of prestige; **ir en** ~ **de** algo/algn to bring discredit on *o* upon sth/sb (b) (falta de prestigio) bad reputation

desprevenido -da *adj*: **estar** ~ to be unprepared *o* unready; **pillar a** algn ~ «*pregunta*» to catch sb unawares *o* off guard; «*lluvia*» to catch sb by surprise

desprolijo -ja *adj* (CS) (a) [ESTAR] ‹*trabajo*› untidy, messy (b) [SER] ‹*persona*› careless

desproporción *f* disparity, disproportion

desproporcionado -da *adj* out of proportion

desprovisto -ta *adj* ~ **DE** algo lacking IN sth

después *adv* [1] (a) (más tarde) later; **para** ~ for later (b) (en una serie de sucesos) then, afterward(s); ~ **no lo he vuelto a ver** I haven't seen him since then (c) (*en locs*) **después de** after; ~ **de Cristo** AD; ~ **DE hacer** algo after doing sth; **después de todo** after all; **después (de) que** after; (refiriéndose al futuro) once, when; ~ **(de) que todos se hayan ido** once *o* when everybody has left; **después que** after
[2] (en el espacio): **bájate dos paradas** ~ get off two stops further on; **hay una casa y** ~ **está el colegio** there is a house and then you come to the school; **está justo** ~ **del puente** it's just past the bridge

despuntado -da *adj* blunt

despuntar [A1] *vt* to blunt
■ ~ *vi* (a) «*día*» to break, dawn; **al** ~ **el día** at daybreak (b) «*flor*» to bud; «*plantas*» to sprout (c) «*persona*» ~ **EN** algo to excel AT *o* IN sth

desquiciado -da *adj* ‹*mundo/persona*› crazy; **tengo los nervios** ~**s** my nerves are in tatters

desquiciante *adj* maddening, infuriating

desquicio *m* (RPl fam) chaos

desquitarse [A1] *v pron* to get even; **lo hizo para** ~ **de él** she did it to get even with him; ~ **CON** algn/algo to take it out ON sb/sth

destacado -da *adj* [1] ‹*profesional/artista*› prominent, distinguished; ‹*actuación*› outstanding [2] [ESTAR] ‹*tropas*› stationed

destacar [A2] *vt* [1] (recalcar, subrayar) to emphasize, stress [2] (realzar) ‹*belleza/figura*› to enhance; ‹*color/plano*› to bring out [3] (a) (Mil) ‹*tropas*› to post (b) ‹*periodista/fotógrafo*› to send
■ ~ *vi* to stand out; ~ **EN** algo to excel AT *o* IN sth

destajo *m* (Com, Rels Labs) piecework; **trabajar a** ~ to do piecework

destapado -da *adj* (a) (sin tapa) ‹*olla*› uncovered; **dejó la botella destapada** he left the top off the bottle (b) (en la cama): **siempre duerme** ~ he always sleeps with the covers thrown back

destapador *m* (AmL) bottle opener

destapar [A1] *vt* [1] (a) ‹*botella/caja*› to open, take the top/lid off; ‹*olla*› to uncover, take the lid off (b) (descubrir) ‹*mueble*› to uncover; ‹*escándalo*› to uncover (c) (en la cama) to pull the covers off [2] (AmL) ‹*cañería/inodoro*› to unblock
■ **destaparse** *v pron* (*refl*) [1] (en la cama) to throw the covers *o* bedclothes off [2] «*nariz/ oídos*» to unblock

destaponar [A1] *vt* ‹*cañería*› to unblock

destartalado -da *adj* (fam) ‹*coche*› beat-up (AmE colloq), clapped-out (BrE colloq); ‹*mueble*› shabby; ‹*casa*› ramshackle, rundown

destellar [A1] *vi* «*brillante/joya*» to sparkle, glitter; «*estrella*» to twinkle, sparkle

destello *m* (de estrella) twinkle, sparkle; (de brillante, joya) sparkle, glitter

d

d

destemplado -da adj ①〈persona〉: estoy ∼ (con fiebre) I have a slight fever; (indispuesto) I'm feeling off-color* ② (a) 〈instrumento/voz/tono〉 discordant (b) 〈nervios〉 frayed

destemplar [A1] vt ① 〈guitarra/violín〉 to make ... go out of tune ② 〈ánimos/nervios〉 to fray ③ (AmL) 〈dientes〉 to set ... on edge

desteñir [I15] vi 《prenda/color》 to run; (decolorarse) to fade
■ **desteñirse** v pron to run; (decolorarse) to fade

desternillarse [A1] v pron (fam): ∼ de risa to split one's sides (laughing) (colloq)

desterrado -da m,f exile

desterrar [A5] vt 〈persona〉 to exile, banish (liter)

destiempo: a ∼ 〈marchar〉 out of step; 〈tocar〉 out of time; habló a ∼ she picked the wrong moment to say it

destierro m exile, banishment

destilar [A1] vt (a) 〈alcohol/petróleo〉 to distill*; 〈hulla/madera〉 to char (b) (rezumar) to ooze

destilería f distillery

destinado -da adj ① (a) (predestinado): ∼ a triunfar/al fracaso destined to succeed/to fail (b) (dirigido, asignado): ∼ A algn 〈carta/paquete〉 addressed to sb; (intended) FOR sb; 〈libro/novela〉 aimed AT sb; las cajas destinadas a Montevideo the boxes destined for Montevideo; los aviones ∼s a este fin the planes used for this purpose ② (a) 〈militar〉: ∼ en Ceuta stationed in Ceuta (b) 〈funcionario/diplomático〉: ahora está ∼ en Lima now he's been posted to Lima

destinar [A1] vt ① 〈funcionario/militar〉 to post, send, assign ② (asignar un fin): destinó todos sus ahorros a pagar las deudas she used all her savings to pay her debts; ∼on el dinero a la investigación the money was used for research; ∼on parte de los fondos a este fin they earmarked part of the funds for this purpose

destinatario -ria m,f (de carta, paquete) addressee; (de giro, transferencia) payee

destino m ① (sino) fate ② (a) (de avión, autobús) destination; con ∼ a Roma 〈vuelo/tren〉 to Rome; 〈pasajero〉 traveling to Rome; 〈carga〉 destined for Rome; salieron con ∼ a Lima they set off for Lima (b) (puesto) posting, assignment ③ (uso, fin) use

destituir [I20] vt (frml) (despedir) to dismiss

destornillador m screwdriver

destornillar [A1] vt to unscrew

destreza f skill; con gran ∼ very skillfully

destronar [A1] vt 〈rey〉 to dethrone, depose; 〈líder/campeón〉 to depose, topple

destrozar [A4] vt (a) (romper, deteriorar) 〈zapatos〉 to ruin; 〈cristal/jarrón〉 to smash; 〈juguete〉 to pull ... apart; 〈coche〉 to wreck; 〈libro〉 to pull apart (b) 〈felicidad/matrimonio/vida〉 to wreck, destroy; 〈corazón〉 to break; tiene los nervios destrozados he's a nervous wreck

■ **destrozarse** v pron (a) (romperse) 《zapatos》 to be ruined; 《jarrón/cristal》 to smash (b) 〈estómago/hígado〉 to ruin

destrozo m: tb ∼s damage

destrucción f destruction

destructivo -va adj destructive

destructor m destroyer

destruir [I20] vt (a) 〈documentos/pruebas〉 to destroy; 〈ciudad〉 to destroy; 〈medio ambiente〉 to damage (b) (echar por tierra) 〈reputación〉 to ruin; 〈plan〉 to wreck; 〈esperanzas〉 to dash, shatter

desubicado -da adj (AmS) (a) [ESTAR] (desplazado) out of position (b) [ESTAR] (desorientado) confused, disoriented (c) [SER] (en cuestiones sociales): es tan ∼ he just doesn't have a clue (colloq)

desuso m disuse; caer en ∼ to fall into disuse

desvaído -da adj 〈color〉 faded, washed-out; 〈persona〉 colorless*, insipid

desvalido -da m,f helpless person

desvalijar [A1] vt (a) 〈casa/tienda〉 to strip ... bare (b) 〈persona〉 (robar) to rob; (en juego) (fam) to clean ... out (colloq)

desván m attic, loft

desvanecerse [E3] v pron (a) 《humo/nubes/niebla》 to clear, disperse; 《dudas/temores/sospechas》 to vanish, be dispelled; 《fantasma/visión》 to disappear, vanish (b) 《color》 to fade

desvariar [A17] vi (Med) to be delirious; (decir tonterías) to talk nonsense, rave

desvelado -da adj: estoy ∼ I can't sleep

desvelar [A1] vt ① 〈persona〉 to keep ... awake, stop ... from sleeping ② (Esp) ▶ DEVELAR
■ **desvelarse** v pron (perder el sueño): me desvelé anoche I couldn't sleep last night

desvelo m ① (insomnio) sleeplessness ② **desvelos** mpl (esfuerzos) efforts (pl), pains (pl)

desvencijado -da adj 〈silla/cama〉 rickety; 〈coche〉 dilapidated, beat-up (AmE colloq), clapped-out (BrE colloq)

desventaja f disadvantage; en ∼ at a disadvantage

desvergonzado -da m,f: ser un ∼ (impúdico) to have no shame; (descarado) to be very impertinent

desvestir [I14] vt to undress
■ **desvestirse** v pron to undress, get undressed; ∼se de la cintura para arriba to strip to the waist

desviación f (a) (en general) diversion (b) (Med) curvature (c) (alejamiento) ∼ DE algo deviation FROM sth

desviar [A17] vt 〈tráfico/vuelo/fondos〉 to divert; 〈río〉 to alter the course of; 〈golpe/pelota〉 to deflect, parry; ∼ la conversación to change the subject; desvió la mirada he looked away
■ **desviarse** v pron ① 《carretera》 to branch off; 《vehículo》 to turn off; la conversación se desvió hacia otros temas the conversation turned to other things ② 《persona》 ∼se DE algo 〈de ruta〉 to deviate FROM sth; 〈de tema〉 to get off sth

---

AmC	Central America	Arg	Argentina	Cu	Cuba
AmL	Latin America	Bol	Bolivia	Ec	Ecuador
AmS	South America	Chi	Chile	Esp	Spain
Andes	Andean Region	CS	Southern Cone	Méx	Mexico

Per	Peru
RPI	River Plate Area
Ur	Uruguay
Ven	Venezuela

desvincularse [A1] *v pron* ~se DE algn/algo to dissociate oneself FROM sth/sb; **está desvinculado de la política** he is no longer involved in politics

desvío *m* (a) (por obras) diversion, detour (AmE); **tomar un** ~ to make a detour (b) (Esp) (salida, carretera) exit

desvivirse [I1] *v pron* ~ POR algn to be completely devoted TO sb; ~ POR hacer algo to go out of one's way to do sth

detallado -da *adj* ⟨factura/cuenta⟩ itemized; ⟨estudio/descripción⟩ detailed

detallar [A1] *vt* to detail

detalle *m* ① (a) (pormenor) detail; **entrar en** ~s to go into details; **describir algo con todo** ~ to describe sth in great detail (b) (elemento decorativo) detail ② (a) (pequeño regalo) little gift (b) (Esp, Méx) (atención, gesto) nice (*o* thoughtful *etc*) gesture; **tener un** ~ CON algn to do sth nice FOR sb ③ (Com) **al detalle** retail

detallista *adj* (minucioso) precise, meticulous

detectar [A1] *vt* to detect

detective *mf* detective

detector *m* detector; ~ **de mentiras/metales** lie/metal detector

detención *f* ① (arresto) arrest; (encarcelamiento) detention ② ▶ DETENIMIENTO

detener [E27] *vt* ① (parar) ⟨vehículo/máquina⟩ to stop; ⟨trámite/proceso⟩ to halt; ⟨hemorragia⟩ to stop, staunch ② (arrestar) to arrest; (encarcelar) to detain; **¡queda usted detenido!** you're under arrest!

■ **detenerse** *v pron* (a) (pararse) ⟨vehículo/ persona⟩ to stop; ~se A hacer algo to stop to do sth (b) (tomar mucho tiempo) ~se EN algo: **no nos detengamos demasiado en los detalles** let's not spend too much time discussing the details

detenido -da *adj* (a) ⟨vehículo/tráfico⟩ held up (b) ⟨investigación/estudio⟩ detailed, thorough (c) [ESTAR] ⟨persona⟩ under arrest; (por período más largo) in custody
■ *m,f* person under arrest; (durante un período más largo) detainee, person held in custody

detenimiento *m*: **con** ~ carefully *o* in detail

detergente *m* (a) (para ropa) laundry detergent (AmE), washing powder (BrE) (b) (Bol, CS) (para vajilla) dishwashing liquid (AmE), washing-up liquid (BrE)

deteriorado -da *adj* ⟨mercancías⟩ damaged; ⟨edificio⟩ dilapidated, run down; ⟨mueble/cuadro⟩ in bad condition

deteriorar [A1] *vt* ⟨relaciones/salud/situación⟩ to cause ... to deteriorate
■ **deteriorarse** *v pron* «relaciones/salud/ situación» to deteriorate, worsen; «mercancías» to get damaged

deterioro *m* (a) (de edificio, muebles) deterioration, wear (b) (empeoramiento) deterioration, worsening

determinación *f* (cualidad) determination, resolve; (decisión) decision; **tomar una** ~ to make a decision

determinado -da *adj* ⟨fecha/lugar⟩ certain; **en determinadas circunstancias** in certain circumstances; **una determinada dosis** a particular dosage

determinante *adj* ⟨causa⟩ main (*before n*); ⟨factor⟩ deciding (*before n*)

determinar [A1] *vt* ① (establecer, precisar) (a) «ley/contrato» to state; «persona» to determine (b) (por deducción) to establish, determine ② (motivar) to cause, bring about

detestar [A1] *vt* to hate, detest

detiene, detienes, etc ▶ DETENER

detonación *f* (a) (ruido) explosion; (acción) detonation (b) (Auto) (de motor) backfire

detonador *m* detonator

detonar [A1] *vi* to detonate, explode

detrás *adv* ① (lugar, parte) [*Latin American Spanish also uses* ATRÁS *in this sense*]: **iba corriendo** ~ he ran along behind; **las cajas de** ~ the boxes at the back; **por** ~ ⟨abrocharse⟩ at the back; ⟨atacar⟩ from behind ② **detrás de** (*loc prep*) behind; ~ **de la puerta** behind the door; ~ **de mi/ti** behind me/you; **un cigarrillo** ~ **de otro** one cigarette after another

detuve, detuvo, etc ▶ DETENER

deuda *f* (a) (Com, Fin) debt; **pagar una** ~ to pay (off) a debt; **contraer una** ~ to run up *o* (frml) contract a debt; ~ **pública** public debt (AmE), national debt (BrE) (b) (compromiso moral): **estoy en** ~ **con usted** I am indebted to you

deudor -dora *adj* debtor (*before n*)
■ *m,f* debtor

devaluación *f* devaluation

devaluar [A18] *vt* to devalue
■ **devaluarse** *v pron* «moneda» to fall; «terrenos/propiedad» to depreciate, fall in value

devanar [A1] *vt* ⟨hilo/lana/alambre⟩ to wind

devaneo *m* (a) (amorío) affair; (pasajero) fling (b) (pasatiempo frívolo) idle pursuit

devastador -dora *adj* devastating

devastar [A1] *vt* to devastate

develar [A1] *vt* (AmL) ⟨secreto⟩ to reveal, disclose; ⟨misterio⟩ to uncover; ⟨monumento/ placa⟩ to unveil

devoción *f* devotion; **siente** ~ **por sus hijos** she's devoted to her children

devolución *f* (de artículo) return; (de dinero) refund

devolver [E11] *vt* ① (a) (restituir) ⟨objeto prestado⟩ to return, give back; ⟨dinero⟩ to give back, pay back; ⟨envase⟩ to return; ⟨objeto comprado⟩ to bring/take ... back; **devuélvelo a su lugar** put it back in its place; ~**le algo A algn** to return sth TO sb; ⟨dinero⟩ to give *o* pay sth back TO sb; **me devolvieron los documentos** I got my papers back; **el teléfono me devolvía las monedas** the telephone kept rejecting my coins; **la operación le devolvió la vista** the operation restored his sight (b) ⟨refugiado⟩ to return, send back (c) (Fin) ⟨letra⟩ to return ② (corresponder) ⟨visita/favor⟩ to return ③ (vomitar) to bring up, throw up (colloq)
■ ~ *vi* to bring up; **tengo ganas de** ~ I feel sick
■ **devolverse** *v pron* (AmL exc RPl) (regresar) to go/come/turn back

devorar [A1] *vt* ⟨animal⟩ to devour; «persona» to devour, wolf down (colloq); ~ **a algn con los ojos** *or* **la mirada** to devour sb with one's eyes (colloq); **fue devorado por las llamas** it was consumed by the flames

devoto -ta adj ‹persona› devout; ‹lugar/obra› devotional
■ m,f (a) (Relig) ~ DE algn devotee OF sb (b) (aficionado) ~ DE algo/algn devotee OF sth/admirer of sb

devuelva, devuelvas, etc ▶ DEVOLVER

DF m (en Méx) = **Distrito Federal**

di ▶ DAR, DECIR

día m **1** (a) (en general) day; **todos los** ~**s** every day; ~ **a** ~ day by day; **de** or **durante el** ~ during the day; **el** ~ **anterior** the day before, the previous day; **el** ~ **siguiente** the next o the following day; **trabaja doce horas por** ~ she works twelve hours a day; **un** ~ **sí y otro no** or (AmL) ~ **(de) por medio** every other day, on alternate days; **dentro de quince** ~**s** in two weeks o (BrE) a fortnight; **cada** ~ every day; **buenos** ~**s** or (RPl) **buen** ~ good morning; **al** ~: **una vez al** ~ once a day; **estoy al** ~ **en los pagos** I'm up to date with the payments; **poner algo al** ~ to bring sth up to date; **ponerse al** ~ **con algo** (con noticias) to get up to date with sth; (con trabajo) to catch up on sth; **mantenerse al** ~ to keep up to date; **de un** ~ **para otro** overnight; **hoy en** ~ nowadays, these days (b) (fecha): **¿qué** ~ **es hoy?** what day is it today?; **empieza el** ~ **dos** it starts on the second; **el** ~ **de Año Nuevo** New Year's Day; ~ **de los enamorados** (St) Valentine's Day; ~ **de los inocentes** December 28, ≈ April Fool's Day; ~ **de Reyes** Epiphany; ~ **festivo** or (AmL) **feriado** public holiday; ~ **laborable** working day; ~ **libre** (sin trabajo) day off; (sin compromisos) free day
2 (a) (tiempo indeterminado) day; **algún** ~ one day; **lo haremos otro** ~ we'll do it some other time; **un** ~ **de estos** one of these days; **¡hasta otro** ~! so long!, see you!; **el** ~ **menos pensado** when you least expect it (b) **días** mpl (vida, tiempo) days (pl); **tiene los** ~**s contados** his days are numbered; **hasta nuestros** ~**s** (up) to the present day

diabetes f diabetes

diabético -ca adj/m,f diabetic

diablo m **1** (demonio) devil; **como (el** or **un)** ~ like crazy o mad (colloq); **del** ~ or **de mil** ~**s** (fam) devilish (colloq); **está de un humor de mil** ~**s** she's in a devil of a mood (colloq); **donde el** ~ **perdió el poncho** (AmS fam) (en un lugar — aislado) in the back of beyond; (— lejano) miles away (colloq); **mandar algo/a algn al** ~ (fam) to pack sth in/to tell sb to go to hell (colloq) **2** (fam) (uso expletivo): **¿cómo/dónde/qué/quién** ~**s** ... ? how/where/what/who the hell ... ? (colloq)

diablura f (fam) prank

diabólico -ca adj (del diablo) diabolic, satanic; ‹persona› evil; ‹plan/intenciones› devilish, fiendish

diadema f (para el pelo) hair-band; (corona) crown, diadem; (media corona) tiara

diafragma m (Anat, Fot, Med) diaphragm

diagnosticar [A2] vt to diagnose

diagnóstico m diagnosis

diagonal f (a) (Mat) diagonal (b) (en fútbol americano) endzone

diagrama m diagram

dial m (Rad, Tec) dial; (del teléfono) dial

dialecto m dialect

dialogar [A3] vi to talk; ~ **CON algn** to talk TO sb

diálogo m (a) (conversación) conversation; (Lit) dialogue, dialog (AmE) (b) (Pol, Rels Labs) talks (pl), negotiations (pl)

diamante m (a) (piedra) diamond; **un anillo de** ~**s** a diamond ring (b) (Dep) diamond (c) **diamantes** mpl (en naipes) diamonds (pl)

diámetro m diameter

diana f **1** (Mil) reveille **2** (Dep, Jueg) (objeto) target; (para dardos) dartboard; (centro) bull's-eye

diapasón m (para afinar) tuning fork; (de instrumento de cuerda) fingerboard

diapositiva f slide, transparency

diariero -ra m,f (CS) newspaper vendor

diario -ria adj (a) (de todos los días) ‹tarea/clases› daily; ‹gastos› everyday, day-to-day (b) (por día): **trabaja cuatro horas diarias** she works four hours a day (c) (en locs) **a diario** every day; **de diario** ‹ropa/vajilla› everyday (before n); **para diario** for everyday (use)
■ m **1** (periódico) newspaper; ~ **mural** (Chi) bulletin board (AmE), notice board (BrE) **2** (libro personal) diary, journal (AmE) **3** (Méx, Col, Ven) (gastos cotidianos): **el** ~ day-to-day expenses

diarrea f diarrhea*

dibujante mf (m) draftsman*; (f) draftswoman*; (de cómics) comic book artist, strip cartoonist

dibujar [A1] vt/vi to draw; ~ **a mano alzada** to draw freehand

dibujo m (a) (arte) drawing; **clase de** ~ drawing class; ~ **lineal** line drawing (b) (representación) drawing; **un** ~ **al carboncillo** a charcoal drawing; ~**s animados** cartoons (pl) (c) (estampado) pattern

diccionario m dictionary; ~ **bilingüe** bilingual dictionary; ~ **de sinónimos** dictionary of synonyms, ≈ thesaurus

dice, dices, etc ▶ DECIR

dicha f (a) (felicidad) happiness; **¡qué** ~ **verlos a todos reunidos!** what a joy to see you all together!; **¡qué** ~! **dejó de llover** (AmL fam) fantastic o wonderful! it's stopped raining! (b) (suerte) good luck, good fortune; **nunca es tarde si la** ~ **es buena** better late than never

dicharachero -ra adj (que habla mucho) chatty (colloq), talkative; (gracioso) witty

dicho¹ -cha pp [ver tb DECIR²]: ~ **esto, se fue** having said this, he left; **con eso queda todo** ~ that says it all; ~ **de otro modo** to put it another way, in other words; ~ **sea de paso** incidentally, by the way; **y** ~ **y hecho!** en **diez minutos estaba listo** and, sure enough, ten minutes later there it was
■ adj dem (frml): **en dichas ciudades** ... in these cities ...; **dicha información** that information; ~**s documentos** (en escrito, documento) the above o (frml) said documents

dicho² m saying

dichoso -sa adj **1** (feliz) happy; (afortunado) fortunate, lucky **2** (delante del n) (fam) (maldito) blessed (colloq), damn (sl)

diciembre m December; para ejemplos ver ENERO

diciendo ▶ DECIR

dictado *m* dictation; **nos hizo un ~** she gave us a dictation; **escribir al ~** to take dictation

dictador -dora *m,f* dictator

dictadura *f* dictatorship

dictar [A1] *vt* **(a)** ⟨*carta/texto*⟩ to dictate **(b)** ⟨*leyes/medidas*⟩ to announce; ⟨*sentencia*⟩ to pronounce, pass **(c)** ⟨*acción/tendencia/moda*⟩ to dictate **(d)** (AmL) ⟨*clase/curso/conferencia*⟩ to give ■ **~** *vi* to dictate

didáctico -ca *adj* ⟨*juguete/programa*⟩ educational; ⟨*poema/exposición*⟩ didactic

diecinueve *adj inv/m/pron* nineteen; *para ejemplos ver* CINCO

dieciocho *adj inv/m/pron* eighteen; *para ejemplos ver* CINCO

dieciséis *adj inv/m/pron* sixteen; *para ejemplos ver* CINCO

diecisiete *adj inv/m/pron* seventeen; *para ejemplos ver* CINCO

diente *m* **(a)** (Anat, Zool) tooth; **lavarse** *or* **cepillarse los ~s** to clean *o* brush one's teeth; **~ de leche** milk tooth; **daba ~ con ~** my/his teeth were chattering; **hablar** *or* **murmurar entre ~s** to mutter (under one's breath) **(b)** (de engranaje, sierra) tooth; (de tenedor) prong, tine; **~ de ajo** clove of garlic

diera, dieras, etc ▶ DAR

diéresis *f* (*pl* **~**) diaeresis

diese, dieses, etc ▶ DAR

diestra *f* (liter *o* period) right hand; **a ~ y siniestra** left and right (AmE), left, right and centre (BrE)

diestro¹ -tra *adj* **(a)** (frml) ⟨*mano*⟩ right; ⟨*persona*⟩ right-handed **(b)** (hábil) ⟨*persona/jugada*⟩ skillful*

diestro² *m* matador, bullfighter; **a ~ y siniestro** (Esp) left and right (AmE), left, right and centre (BrE)

dieta *f* **1** (alimentación, régimen) diet; **ponerse a ~** to go on a diet **2** **(a)** (para viajes) allowance **(b)** (de parlamentario) salary

diez *adj inv/m/pron* ten; *para ejemplos ver* CINCO

difamar [A1] *vt* (por escrito) to libel, defame (frml); (oralmente) to slander, defame (frml)

difamatorio -ria *adj* ⟨*palabras/discurso*⟩ slanderous; ⟨*artículo/carta*⟩ libelous*

diferencia *f* **(a)** (disparidad) difference; **la ~ de precio** the difference in price; **a ~ del marido, ella es encantadora** unlike her husband, she's really charming **(b)** (distinción) distinction; **hacer una ~** to make a distinction **(c)** (desacuerdo) difference; **resolver sus** (*or* **mis** *etc*) **~s** to resolve one's differences **(d)** (resto) difference, **yo pagué la ~** I paid the difference

diferenciar [A1] *vt* ⟨*colores/sonidos*⟩ to tell the difference between, differentiate between ■ **diferenciarse** *v pron*: **¿en qué se diferencia esta especie?** what makes this species different?; **no se diferencian en nada** there's no difference between them; **~se DE algo/algn** to differ FROM sth/sb; **solo se diferencia del otro en** *or* **por el precio** the only difference between this one and the other one is the price

diferente *adj* **(a)** (distinto) different; **ser ~ A** *or* **DE algn/algo** to be different FROM sb/sth **(b)** (en *pl, delante del n*) ⟨*motivos/soluciones/maneras*⟩ various; **nos vimos en ~s ocasiones** we've met on several occasions

diferido: **una transmisión en ~** a prerecorded broadcast

difícil *adj* **1** **(a)** ⟨*problema/situación*⟩ difficult; ⟨*examen*⟩ hard, difficult; **me fue muy ~ decírselo** it was very hard *o* difficult for me to tell him; **es ~ de hacer/entender** it's difficult *o* hard to do/understand **(b)** ⟨*persona/carácter*⟩ difficult **2** (poco probable) unlikely; **va a ser ~ que acepte** it's unlikely that he'll accept; **veo ~ que gane** I doubt if she'll win

dificultad *f* difficulty; **respira con ~** he has difficulty breathing; **tiene ~es en hacerse entender** she has difficulty in making herself understood; **me pusieron muchas ~es para entrar** they made it very hard for me to get in; **meterse en ~es** to get into difficulties

dificultar [A1] *vt* to make ... difficult

dificultoso -sa *adj* difficult, problematic

difteria *f* diphtheria

difundir [I1] *vt* ⟨*noticia/rumor*⟩ to spread; ⟨*ideas/doctrina*⟩ to spread, disseminate; ⟨*cultura*⟩ to disseminate; ⟨*comunicado*⟩ to issue; (por radio) to disseminate; **muy difundidas** very widespread

difunto -ta *adj* (frml) late (*before n*), deceased (frml); **su ~ marido** her late husband ■ *m,f* (frml) deceased (frml)

difusión *f* (de noticia, rumor) spreading; (de ideas, doctrina, cultura) spreading, diffusion (frml); **los medios de ~** the media

difuso -sa *adj* ⟨*luz*⟩ dim, diffused; ⟨*idea/conocimientos*⟩ vague

diga, digas, etc ▶ DECIR

digerir [I11] *vt* to digest

digestión *f* digestion; **hacer la ~** to let one's food go down

digestivo -va *adj* ⟨*aparato*⟩ digestive

digital *adj* **(a)** (dactilar) finger (*before n*), digital (frml) **(b)** ⟨*aparato/sonido*⟩ digital

dignarse [A1] *v pron* **~ (A) hacer algo** to condescend *o* deign TO sth

dignatario -ria *m,f* dignitary

dignidad *f* **(a)** (cualidad) dignity **(b)** (título) rank; (cargo) position

digno -na *adj* **1** **(a)** ⟨*persona/actitud*⟩ honorable* **(b)** ⟨*sueldo*⟩ decent, living (*before n*); ⟨*vivienda*⟩ decent **2** (merecedor) **~ DE algo/algn** worthy OF sth/sb; **una persona digna de admiración** a person worthy of admiration; **una medida digna de elogio** a praiseworthy measure; **un espectáculo ~ de verse** a show worth seeing

dije *adj* (Chi fam) **(a)** (agradable) nice, lovely **(b)** (bondadoso) kind ■ *m* charm

dije, dijera, etc ▶ DECIR

dilapidar [A1] *vt* to squander

dilatado -da *adj* ⟨*pupila/conducto*⟩ dilated

dilatarse [A1] *v pron* **1** «*cuerpo/metal*» to expand; «*corazón*» to expand, dilate; «*pupila*» to dilate; «*embarazada*» to dilate **2** **(a)** (prolongarse) to be prolonged **(b)** (diferirse) to be postponed, be put off **3** (Méx, Ven) **▶** DEMORARSE B

dilema *m* (disyuntiva) dilemma

diligencia *f* **(a)** (aplicación) diligence, ⋯⟶

conscientiousness; **con ~ diligently** (b) (gestión): **tengo que hacer unas ~s** I have some business to attend to

diligente *adj* (trabajador) diligent, conscientious

diluir [I20] *vt* ⟨*líquido*⟩ to dilute; ⟨*pintura*⟩ to thin (down); ⟨*sólido*⟩ to dissolve

diluviar [A1] *vi* to pour (with rain)

diluvio *m* (lluvia) heavy rain, deluge; (inundación) flood; **el D~ Universal** the Flood

diluyente *m* thinner

dimensión *f* ⸢1⸣ (a) (Fís, Mat) dimension; **una figura en tres dimensiones** a three-dimensional figure (b) **dimensiones** *fpl* (tamaño) dimensions (*pl*); **de enormes dimensiones** huge, enormous ⸢2⸣ (alcance, magnitud — de problema) magnitude, scale; (— de tragedia) scale

diminutivo *m* diminutive

diminuto -ta *adj* tiny, minute

dimisión *f* resignation

dimitir [I1] *vi* to resign; **~ DE algo** to resign FROM sth

dimos ▸ DAR

Dinamarca *f* Denmark

dinamarqués -quesa *adj/m,f ▸* DANÉS

dinámico -ca *adj* dynamic

dinamita *f* dynamite

dinamitar [A1] *vt* to dynamite

dínamo, dinamo *m or* (Esp) *f* dynamo

dinastía *f* dynasty

dineral *m* fortune, huge amount of money

dinero *m* money; **estar escaso de ~** to be short of money; **gente de ~** well-off *o* wealthy people; **hacer ~** to make money; **~ de bolsillo** pocket money; **~ (en) efectivo** cash; **~ suelto** change; **~ contante y sonante** (fam) hard cash

dinosaurio *m* dinosaur

dio ▸ DAR

diócesis *f* diocese

dioptría *f* diopter*; **¿cuántas ~s tiene?** what's your correction *o* gradation?

dios, diosa *m,f* ⸢1⸣ (Mit) (*m*) god; (*f*) goddess ⸢2⸣ **Dios** *m* (Relig) God; **el D~ de los musulmanes** the Muslim God; **gracias a D~** thank God *o* heaven; **si D~ quiere** God willing; **te lo juro por D~** I swear to God; **¡por (el) amor de D~!** for God's sake *o* for heaven's sake!; **que D~ te bendiga** God bless you; **¡D~ me libre!** God *o* heaven forbid!; **¡sabe D~!** God knows!; **¡vaya por D~!** oh dear!; **¡por D~!** for God's *o* heaven's sake!; **¡D~ mío!** *or* **¡D~ santo!** (expresando angustia) my God!, oh God!; (expresando sorpresa) (good) God!; **como D~ manda: un coche como D~ manda** a real *o* a proper car; **pórtate como D~ manda** behave properly; **hacer algo a la buena de D~** to do sth any which way (AmE) *o* (BrE) any old how

diploma *m* diploma, certificate

diplomacia *f* ⸢1⸣ (Pol) (carrera) diplomacy; (cuerpo) diplomatic corps ⸢2⸣ (tacto) diplomacy, tact

diplomado -da *adj* qualified; **~ en peluquería** qualified hairdresser

diplomarse [A1] *v pron* (a) (AmL) (obtener un título universitario) to graduate; **~ DE/EN algo** to graduate AS/IN sth (b) (obtener otro título) to obtain a diploma (*o* certificate *etc*)

diplomático -ca *adj* ⸢1⸣ (Pol) ⟨*carrera/pasaporte*⟩ diplomatic ⸢2⸣ (en el trato) diplomatic, tactful
■ *m,f* diplomat

diptongo *m* diphthong

diputación *f* (a) (delegación) deputation, delegation (b) (Gob) (en Esp) council

diputado -da *m,f* deputy, ≈ representative (*in US*), ≈ member of parliament (*in UK*)

dique *m* dike*

diré, dirá, etc ▸ DECIR

dirección *f* ⸢1⸣ (señas) address ⸢2⸣ (sentido, rumbo) direction; **ellos venían en ~ contraria** they were coming the other way *o* from the opposite direction; **¿en qué ~ iba?** which way was he heading *o* going?; **señal de ~ prohibida** no-entry sign; **~ obligatoria** one way only ⸢3⸣ (Auto) (mecanismo) steering; **~ asistida** power-assisted steering, power steering ⸢4⸣ (Adm) (a) (cargo — en escuela) principalship (AmE), headship (BrE); (— en empresa) post *o* position of manager (b) (cuerpo directivo — de empresa) management; (— de periódico) editorial board; (— de prisión) authorities (*pl*); (— de partido) leadership (c) (oficina — en escuela) principal's office (AmE), headmaster's/headmistress's office (BrE); (— en empresa) manager's/director's office; (— periódico) editorial office

direccional *f* (Col, Méx) turn signal (AmE), indicator (BrE)

directamente *adv* (derecho) straight; (sin intermediarios) directly

directiva *f* ⸢1⸣ (de empresa) board (of directors); (de partido) executive committee, leadership ⸢2⸣ (directriz) guideline

directo -ta *adj* ⸢1⸣ ⟨*vuelo*⟩ direct, nonstop; ⟨*ruta/acceso*⟩ direct; ⟨*tren*⟩ direct, through (*before n*) ⸢2⸣ (Rad, TV): **en ~** live ⸢3⸣ ⟨*lenguaje/pregunta*⟩ direct; ⟨*respuesta*⟩ straight; ⟨*persona*⟩ direct, straightforward

director -tora *m,f* ⸢1⸣ (a) (de escuela) (*m*) head teacher, principal (AmE), headmaster (BrE); (*f*) head teacher, principal (AmE), headmistress (BrE); (de periódico, revista) editor (in chief); (de hospital) administrator; (de prisión) warden (AmE), governor (BrE) (b) (Com) (gerente) manager; (miembro de junta directiva) director, executive; **~ gerente** managing director (c) (Cin, Teatr) director; **~ de orquesta** conductor

directorio *m* (AmL exc CS) (guía telefónica) telephone directory, directory

directriz *f* (Mat) directrix; (guía) guideline, principle; (instrucción) directive

dirigente *mf* (de partido, país) leader

AmC	América Central	Arg	Argentina	Cu	Cuba
AmL	América Latina	Bol	Bolivia	Ec	Ecuador
AmS	América del Sur	Chi	Chile	Esp	España
Andes	Región andina	CS	Cono Sur	Méx	México

Per	Perú
RPI	Río de la Plata
Ur	Uruguay
Ven	Venezuela

dirigible *m* airship, dirigible

dirigir [I7] *vt* **1** (a) ⟨*empresa*⟩ to manage, run; ⟨*periódico/revista*⟩ to run, edit; ⟨*investigación/tesis*⟩ to supervise; ⟨*debate*⟩ to lead, chair; ⟨*tráfico*⟩ to direct **(b)** ⟨*obra/película*⟩ to direct; ⟨*orquesta*⟩ to conduct

2 (a) ~ algo A algn ⟨*mensaje/carta*⟩ to address sth TO sb; ⟨*críticas*⟩ to direct sth TO sb; **la pregunta iba dirigida a usted** the question was meant for you; **no me dirigió la palabra** he didn't say a word to me **(b)** ~ algo HACIA or A algo/algn ⟨*telescopio*⟩ to point sth TOWARD(s) sth/sb; ⟨*pistola*⟩ to point sth TOWARD(s) sth/sb; ~ **la mirada hacia** *or* **a algo/algn** to look at sth/sb; **dirigió sus pasos hacia la esquina** he walked toward(s) the corner

3 (encaminar) ~ algo A hacer algo ⟨*esfuerzos*⟩ to channel sth INTO doing sth; ⟨*energía/atención*⟩ to direct sth TOWARD(s) doing sth

■ **dirigirse** *v pron* **1** (encaminarse): ~se HACIA algo to head FOR sth

2 ~se A algn (oralmente) to speak *o* talk TO sb; (por escrito) to write to sb

discado *m* (AmL) dialing*; ~ **automático** or **directo** (AmL) direct dialing*

discapacitado -da *m,f* disabled person, handicapped person

discar [A2] *vt/vi* (AmL) to dial

disciplina *f* discipline; **mantener la ~** to keep *o* maintain discipline

discípulo -la *m,f* disciple

disco *m* **1** (a) (Audio) record; **grabar un ~** to make a record; **poner un ~** to put on a record; ~ **compacto** CD, compact disc; ~ **de larga duración** album, LP; ~ **volador** (CS) flying saucer **(b)** (Inf) disk; ~ **duro** hard disk; ~ **flexible** *or* **floppy** floppy disk **2** (a) (Dep) discus **(b)** (Anat) disk*; (Auto, Mec) disk **(c)** (del teléfono) dial **3** (señal de tráfico) (road) sign

disconforme *adj* (a) (no satisfecho) dissatisfied; ~ CON algo/algn dissatisfied WITH sth/sb **(b)** (en desacuerdo): ~ CON algo in disagreement WITH sth

discontinuo -nua *adj* ⟨*línea*⟩ broken; ⟨*sonido*⟩ intermittent

discordante *adj* (Mús) discordant; ⟨*opiniones/versiones*⟩ conflicting

discordia *f* discord

discoteca *f* (a) (local) discotheque **(b)** (colección de discos) record collection **(c)** (AmC) (tienda) record store *o* shop

discreción *f* **1** (a) (tacto, mesura) tact, discretion **(b)** (reserva) discretion **2** a discreción ⟨*comer/beber*⟩ as much as you (*o* we *etc*) like; **esto queda a ~ del juez** this is left to the discretion of the judge

discreto -ta *adj* (a) ⟨*persona/carácter/comportamiento*⟩ discreet **(b)** ⟨*color/vestido*⟩ discreet **(c)** ⟨*cantidad/sueldo/actuación*⟩ modest

discriminación *f* discrimination

discriminar [A1] *vt* (a) ⟨*persona/colectividad*⟩ to discriminate against **(b)** (distinguir) to differentiate, distinguish

disculpa *f* apology; **me debe una ~** she owes me an apology; **un error que no tiene ~** an inexcusable error; **pedir(le) ~s (a algn) por algo** to apologize (to sb) for sth

disculpar [A1] *vt* (a) ⟨*error/falta/comportamiento*⟩ to forgive, excuse; **le disculpó la indiscreción** he forgave her her indiscretion; **disculpa mi tardanza** I am sorry I'm late **(b)** ⟨*persona*⟩ to make excuses for; **su madre siempre lo está disculpando** his mother's always making excuses for him

■ ~ *vi*: **disculpe, no lo volveré a hacer** I'm sorry *o* (frml) I apologize, I won't do it again

■ **disculparse** *v pron* to apologize; ~se CON algn to apologize TO sb

discurso *m* speech; **pronunciar un ~** to give *o* make a speech

discusión *f* (a) (de asunto, tema) discussion **(b)** (altercado, disputa) argument

discutible *adj* debatable

discutido -da *adj* controversial

discutir [I1] *vt* (a) (debatir) ⟨*problema/asunto*⟩ to discuss; ⟨*proyecto de ley*⟩ to debate, discuss **(b)** (cuestionar) ⟨*derecho/afirmación*⟩ to question, challenge

■ ~ *vi* to argue, quarrel; **discutió de política con su padre** he argued with his father about politics; ~ POR algo to argue ABOUT sth; ~le A algn to argue WITH sb

disecar [A2] *vt* (a) ⟨*animal muerto*⟩ (para estudiarlo) to dissect; (para conservarlo) to stuff **(b)** ⟨*planta*⟩ to preserve

disección *f* dissection

diseccionar [A1] *vt* to dissect

diseminado -da *adj* scattered; **los pueblos ~s por la región** the villages scattered throughout the region; **los hoteles están muy ~s** the hotels are very spread out

diseminarse [A1] *v pron* «*personas*» to scatter, disperse; «*ideas/cultura*» to spread

diseñador -dora *m,f* designer; ~ **de moda(s)** fashion designer

diseñar [A1] *vt* ⟨*moda/mueble/máquina*⟩ to design; ⟨*parque/edificio*⟩ to design, plan

diseño *m* design; ~ **de moda** fashion design; **blusas de ~ francés** French-designed blouses; **ropa de ~** designer clothes

disforzarse [A11] *v pron* (Per fam) to clown around

disfraz *m* (a) (Indum) (para jugar, fiestas) costume, fancy dress outfit (BrE); (para engañar) disguise; **una fiesta de disfraces** a costume *o* (BrE) fancy dress party **(b)** (simulación) front

disfrazar [A4] *vt* (a) ~ a algn DE algo (para fiesta) to dress sb up as sth; (para engañar) to disguise sb AS sth **(b)** (disimular, ocultar) ⟨*sentimiento/verdad*⟩ to conceal, hide; ⟨*voz/escritura/intención*⟩ to disguise

■ **disfrazarse** *v pron* (a) (por diversión) to dress up; ~se DE algo/algn to dress up as sth/sb **(b)** (para engañar) to disguise oneself; ~se DE algo/algn to disguise oneself AS sth/sb, dress up AS sth/sb

disfrutar [A1] *vi* (a) (divertirse) to enjoy oneself, have fun; ~ CON/DE algo to enjoy sth; ~ **haciendo algo** to enjoy doing sth **(b)** (tener) ~ DE algo ⟨*de privilegio/derecho/buena salud*⟩ to enjoy, have

■ ~ *vt* ⟨*viaje/espectáculo*⟩ to enjoy; ⟨*beneficio/derecho*⟩ to have, enjoy

disgregarse [A3] *v pron* **(a)** «*grupo/familia*» to break up, split up; «*multitud/manifestantes*» to break up, disperse **(b)** (Tec) to disintegrate

disgustado -da *adj* [ESTAR] upset

disgustar [A1] *vt*: me disgustó mucho que me mintiera I was very upset that he lied to me; me disgusta tener que decírselo I don't like having to tell her

■ **disgustarse** *v pron* to get upset

disgusto *m* ⟦1⟧ (sufrimiento, pesar): tiene un ∼ tremendo he's very upset; me ha dado muchos ∼s he's given me lots of upset *o* heartache; lo hizo a ∼ she did it reluctantly ⟦2⟧ (discusión) argument, quarrel

disidente *mf* (que discrepa) dissident; (escindido) member of a splinter *o* breakaway group

disimulado -da *adj* **(a)** (disfrazado, oculto) disguised; un mal ∼ descontento ill-concealed displeasure **(b)** (discreto) discreet; sé más ∼ be more discreet

■ *m,f*: me vio pero se hizo el ∼ he saw me but he pretended he hadn't

disimular [A1] *vt* **(a)** ⟨alegría/rabia/dolor⟩ to hide, conceal **(b)** ⟨defecto/imperfección⟩ to hide, disguise

disimulo *m*: con ∼ without anyone noticing; sin ∼ openly

disiparse [A1] *v pron* «*nubes/niebla*» to clear; «*temores/sospechas*» to be dispelled; «*ilusiones*» to vanish, disappear

dislexia *f* dyslexia

disléxico -ca *adj/m,f* dyslexic

dislocado -da *adj* ⟨articulación⟩ dislocated

dislocarse [A2] *v pron* ⟨articulación⟩ to dislocate

disminución *f* decrease, fall; (de temperatura) drop; (de tarifa) reduction

disminuido -da *m,f*: ∼ psíquico/físico mentally/physically handicapped person

disminuir [I20] *vi* (menguar) «*número/cantidad*» to decrease, fall; «*precios/temperaturas*» to drop, fall; «*dolor*» to diminish, lessen

■ ∼ *vt* (reducir) ⟨gastos/producción⟩ to cut back on; ⟨impuestos⟩ to cut; ⟨velocidad/número/cantidad⟩ to reduce

disolución *f* **(a)** (de contrato, matrimonio) annulment; (de organización, del parlamento) dissolution **(b)** (de manifestación) breaking up **(c)** (Quím) (acción) dissolving

disolvente *m* solvent; (de pintura) thinner

disolver [E11] *vt* **(a)** ⟨matrimonio/contrato⟩ to annul; ⟨parlamento/organización⟩ to dissolve **(b)** ⟨manifestación/reunión⟩ to break up **(c)** (en líquido) to dissolve **(d)** (Med) to dissolve, break up

■ **disolverse** *v pron* «*manifestación/reunión*» to break up; «*azúcar/aspirina*» to dissolve

disonante *adj* (Mús) dissonant; ⟨voz⟩ discordant; ⟨colores⟩ clashing

dispar *adj* **(a)** (irregular) uneven **(b)** (diferente) different, disparate (frml)

disparada -da *adj* (fam): salir ∼ (irse de prisa) to shoot off (colloq); con el choque salió ∼ del asiento the impact catapulted him from his seat; *ver tb* DISPARAR

disparador *m* (de arma) trigger; (Fot) shutter release; (de reloj) escapement

disparar [A1] *vi* (con arma) to shoot, fire; ∼ al aire to fire *o* shoot into the air; ∼ a matar to shoot to kill; le disparó por la espalda he shot him in the back; ∼ a quemarropa *or* a bocajarro to fire at point-blank range; ∼ CONTRA algn to shoot *o* fire AT sb **(b)** (Dep) to shoot

■ ∼ *vt* ⟦1⟧ **(a)** ⟨arma/flecha⟩ to shoot, fire; ⟨tiro/proyectil⟩ to fire; le ∼on un tiro en la nuca they shot him in the back of the head **(b)** (Dep): disparó el balón a portería he shot at goal ⟦2⟧ (Méx fam) (pagar) to buy

■ **dispararse** *v pron* ⟦1⟧ **(a)** «*arma*» to go off **(b)** (refl): se disparó un tiro en la sien he shot himself in the head ⟦2⟧ (fam) «*precio*» to shoot up, rocket

disparatado -da *adj* ⟨acto/proyecto/idea⟩ crazy, ludicrous; ⟨gasto/precio⟩ outrageous, ridiculous

disparate *m* **(a)** (acción insensata, cosa absurda): hacer ∼s to do stupid things; decir ∼s to make foolish remarks; es un ∼ casarse tan joven it's crazy to get married so young; temo que haga algún ∼ I'm afraid he might do something crazy **(b)** (fam) (cantidad exagerada) ridiculous (*o* crazy *etc*) amount

disparo *m* shot

dispensar [A1] *vt* ⟦1⟧ ⟨honor⟩ to give, accord (frml); ⟨acogida⟩ to give, extend (frml); ⟨ayuda/protección⟩ to give, afford (frml); ⟨asistencia médica⟩ to give; ⟨medicamentos⟩ to dispense; le ∼on un caluroso recibimiento he was given *o* (frml) extended a warm reception ⟦2⟧ **(a)** (eximir): a algn DE algo to exempt sb FROM sth; la ∼on de asistir a misa she was excused from attending mass **(b)** (perdonar) to forgive

■ ∼ *vi* to forgive; dispense, por favor excuse me

dispersar [A1] *vt* **(a)** ⟨manifestantes/multitud/enemigo⟩ to disperse **(b)** ⟨rayos⟩ to scatter, diffuse; ⟨niebla/humo⟩ to clear, disperse

■ **dispersarse** *v pron* **(a)** «*manifestantes/manifestación/multitud*» to disperse **(b)** «*rayos*» to diffuse, scatter; «*niebla/humo*» to disperse, clear

disperso -sa *adj* (diseminado) scattered, dispersed (frml)

displicente *adj* (indiferente) indifferent, blasé; (frío) disdainful

disponer [E22] *vt* ⟦1⟧ (frml) (establecer, ordenar) «*ley*» to provide (frml), to stipulate (frml); «*rey*» to decree; «*general/juez*» to order ⟦2⟧ (frml) (colocar, arreglar) to arrange, set out, lay out

■ ∼ *vi*: ∼ DE algo ⟨de tiempo/ayuda⟩ to have sth; con los recursos de que dispongo with the means available to me *o* at my disposal

■ **disponerse** *v pron* (frml) mientras se disponían a tomar el tren as they were about to catch the train; la tropa se dispuso a atacar the troops prepared to attack

disponible *adj* available; ⟨tiempo⟩ free (*before n*), available; cuando estés ∼ when you're free

disposición *f* ⟦1⟧ (norma) regulation ⟦2⟧ **(a)** (actitud) disposition **(b)** (talento) aptitude **(c)** (inclinación, voluntad) willingness ⟦3⟧ **(a)** (de un bien) disposal **(b)** a ∼ de algn ⟨coche/chofer⟩ at sb's disposal; estoy a tu ∼ para lo que sea I'm here to help if you need anything; **será puesto a ~ del juez** he will appear before the judge; **puso su casa a mi ~** he offered me his house

dispositivo *m* **1** (mecanismo) mechanism; (aparato) device **2** (fml) (destacamento): **un fuerte ~ policial/militar** a large police/military presence

dispuesto -ta *adj* **(a)** (preparado) ready **(b)** (con voluntad) willing; **~ A hacer algo** prepared to do sth

dispuse, dispuso, etc ▶ DISPONER

disputa *f* **(a)** (discusión, pelea) quarrel, argument **(b)** (combate) fight **(c)** (controversia) dispute

disputar [A1] *vt* **(a)** ~le algo A algn ⟨*título*⟩ to challenge sb for sth; **le disputaban su derecho a la herencia** they contested his right to the inheritance **(b)** ⟨*partido*⟩ to play; ⟨*combate*⟩ to fight

■ **disputarse** *v pron*: **se disputan el primer puesto** they are competing for first place

disquete, disquette /dis'kete/ *m* diskette, floppy disk

distancia *f* **(a)** distance; **la ~ que separa dos puntos** the distance between two points; **¿a qué ~ está Londres?** how far is it to London?, **se situó a una ~ de un metro** she stood a meter away; ▶ LLAMADA **(b)** (en locs) **a distancia: se situó a ~ para verlo en conjunto** she stood back to see it as a whole; **se veía a ~** one could see it from a distance; **mantenerse a ~** to keep at a distance; **en la distancia** in the distance; ▶ EDUCACIÓN 1, ENSEÑANZA B

distanciado -da *adj* (afectivamente): **estamos algo distanciadas** we're not as close as we were

distanciar [A1] *vt* **(a)** (espaciar) to space ... out **(b)** (en lo afectivo) «*amigos/familiares*» to make ... drift apart; **~ a algn DE algn** to distance sb FROM sb

■ **distanciarse** *v pron* **(a)** (en el espacio) ~se DE algo to get far FROM sth **(b)** (en lo afectivo) (recípr) to grow o drift apart; (refl) ~se DE algn to distance oneself FROM sb

distante *adj* distant

distar [A1] *vi* (en 3ª pers) (estar a): **el colegio dista unos dos kilómetros de su casa** the school is about two kilometers from her house

diste, etc ▶ DAR

distinción *f* **(a)** (diferencia) distinction; **hacer una ~** to make a distinction; **sin ~ de raza o credo** regardless of race or creed; **no hago distinciones con nadie** I don't give anyone preferential treatment **(b)** (elegancia) distinction, elegance **(c)** (honor, condecoración) award

distinguido -da *adj* ⟨*escritor/actor/aire*⟩ distinguished; ⟨*alumno*⟩ outstanding

distinguir [I2] *vt* **1** **(a)** (diferenciar) to distinguish **(b)** (caracterizar) to characterize **2** (percibir) ⟨*figura/sonido*⟩ to make out **3** (con medalla, honor) to honor*

■ **distinguirse** *v pron* (destacarse): ~se POR algo «*persona*» to distinguish oneself BY sth; «*producto*» to be distinguished BY sth

distintivo¹ -va *adj* ⟨*rasgo/característica*⟩ distinctive

distintivo² *m* (insignia) emblem; (símbolo) sign

distinto -ta *adj* **1** (diferente) different; **ser ~ A** or **DE algo/algn** to be different FROM o TO o (AmE)

THAN sth/sb; **estas/te encuentro ~** you look different **2** (*en pl, delante del n*) (varios) several, various

distorsionar [A1] *vt* to distort

distracción *f* **(a)** (entretenimiento) entertainment **(b)** (descuido): **en un momento de ~se la robaron** she took her eye off it for a moment and someone stole it; **la más mínima ~ puede ser fatal** the slightest lapse of concentration could be fatal **(c)** (de fondos) embezzlement

distraer [E23] *vt* **(a)** ⟨*persona/atención*⟩ to distract; **~ a algn DE** ⟨*de trabajo/estudios*⟩ to distract sb FROM sth ⟨*de preocupaciones*⟩ to take sb's mind OFF sth **(b)** (entretener) ⟨*persona*⟩ to keep ... entertained

■ **distraerse** *v pron* **(a)** (despistarse, descuidarse) to get distracted **(b)** (entretenerse): **se distraen viendo la televisión** they pass the time watching television; **se distrae con cualquier cosa** she doesn't need much to keep amused

distraído -da *adj* **(a)** ⟨*persona*⟩ absentminded, vague **(b)** **estaba/iba ~** he was miles away (colloq)

distribución *f* **(a)** (reparto — de dinero, víveres) distribution; (— de tareas) allocation **(b)** (de producto, película) distribution **(c)** (disposición, división) layout, arrangement **(d)** (Auto) valve-operating gear

distribuidor¹ -dora *m,f* (Com) distributor

distribuidor² *m* (Auto, Mec) distributor

distribuidora *f* (empresa) distributor, distribution company

distribuir [I20] *vt* **(a)** ⟨*dinero/víveres/panfletos*⟩ to hand out, distribute; ⟨*ganancias*⟩ to distribute; ⟨*tareas*⟩ to allocate, assign; ⟨*carga/peso*⟩ to distribute, spread **(b)** ⟨*producto/película*⟩ to distribute **(c)** «*canal/conducto*» ⟨*agua*⟩ to distribute **(d)** (disponer) to lay out **(e)** (dividir) to divide ... up; **los distribuyeron en tres grupos** they divided them (up) into three groups

■ **distribuirse** *v pron* (refl) to divide up

distrito *m* district

Distrito Federal *m* Federal District (*including Mexico City*)

disturbio *m* **(a)** (perturbación del orden) disturbance **(b)** **disturbios** *mpl* (motín) riot, disturbances (journ)

disuadir [I1] *vt* to deter, discourage; **~ A algn DE algo/DE que haga algo** to dissuade sb FROM sth/doing sth

disuasión *f* (Mil, Pol) deterrence

disuasivo -va, disuasorio -ria *adj* ⟨*tono/palabras*⟩ dissuasive, discouraging; ⟨*efecto*⟩ deterrent; ⟨*medida*⟩ designed to act as a deterrent

disuelto -ta *pp*: ▶ DISOLVER

diurético *m* diuretic

diurno -na *adj* day (*before n*); **clases diurnas** daytime classes

diva *f* diva, prima donna; *ver tb* DIVO

divagación *f* digression

divagar [A3] *vi* **(a)** (desviarse del tema) to digress **(b)** (hablar sin sentido) to ramble

diván *m* couch

diversidad *f* diversity

diversificar [A2] *vt* ⟨*actividades/métodos*⟩ to diversify; ⟨*inversión/producción*⟩ to diversify
■ **diversificarse** *v pron* to diversify

diversión *f* (a) (esparcimiento) fun (b) (espectáculo, juego): **aquí hay pocas diversiones** there isn't much to do here

diverso -sa *adj* [1] (variado, diferente): **su obra es muy diversa** his work is very diverse; **seres de diversa naturaleza** various types of creatures; **ha desempeñado las más diversas actividades** she has engaged in a very wide range of activities [2] (*pl*) (varios) various, several

divertido -da *adj* (a) (que interesa, divierte) ⟨*espectáculo/fiesta*⟩ fun, enjoyable; ⟨*momento/ situación*⟩ entertaining; **es un tipo muy ~** he's a really fun guy, he's really fun to be with (b) (gracioso) funny

divertir [I11] *vt* to amuse
■ **divertirse** *v pron* (entretenerse) to amuse oneself; (pasarlo bien) to have fun, enjoy oneself; **¡que te diviertas!** have fun!, enjoy yourself!; **nos divertimos mucho en la fiesta** we had a really good time at the party

dividendo *m* dividend

dividir [I11] *vt* (a) (partir) to divide; **lo dividió en partes iguales** he divided it (up) into equal portions (b) (repartir) to divide, share (out) (c) (enemistar) ⟨*partido/familia*⟩ to divide
■ **~** *vi* (Mat) to divide
■ **dividirse** *v pron* (a) ⟨*célula*⟩ to split; ⟨*grupo/ partido*⟩ to split up; ⟨*camino/río*⟩ to divide (b) **~ EN algo** ⟨*obra/período*⟩ to be divided INTO sth (c) (repartirse) to divide up, share out

divierta, divirtió, etc ▶ DIVERTIR

divinidad *f* (a) (deidad) deity, god (b) (cualidad) divinity (c) (fam) (preciosidad) delight

divinizar [A4] *vt* to deify

divino -na *adj* divine

divisa *f* [1] (Com, Fin) currency; **la fuga de ~s** the flight of capital; **una fuente de ~s** a source of foreign currency [2] (emblema) emblem, insignia

divisar [A1] *vt* ⟨*tierra/barco*⟩ to sight, make out; **a lo lejos se divisaba un poblado** they (*or* he *etc*) could make out a village in the distance

divisible *adj* **~ POR algo** divisible BY sth

división *f* (en general) division; **hacer una ~** (Mat) to do a division

divisor *m* divisor

divisorio -ria *adj* dividing (*before n*)

divo -va *m,f* (estrella) celebrity, star; (con actitud soberbia) prima donna; *ver tb* DIVA

divorciado -da *adj* divorced
■ *m,f* (*m*) divorcé (esp AmE), divorcee (esp BrE); (*f*) divorcée (esp AmE), divorcee (esp BrE)

divorciarse [A1] *v pron* to get divorced; **~se DE algn** to divorce sb, get divorced FROM sb

divorcio *m* (Der) divorce

divulgar [A3] *vt* ⟨*noticia/información*⟩ to spread, circulate; ⟨*secreto/plan*⟩ to divulge; ⟨*cultura*⟩ to spread, disseminate
■ **divulgarse** *v pron* to spread

dizque, diz que *adv* (AmL) (a) (según parece) apparently (b) (expresando escepticismo): **esta ~ democracia** this so-called democracy; **estaban allí, ~ trabajando** they were there, supposedly working

Dn. = **Don**

Dña. = **Doña**

do *m* (nota) C; (en solfeo) do, doh (BrE); **~ de pecho** high C, top C

dobladillo *m* hem

doblar [A1] *vt* [1] ⟨*camisa/papel*⟩ to fold; ⟨*brazo/ vara*⟩ to bend [2] ⟨*esquina*⟩ to turn, go around; ⟨*cabo*⟩ to round [3] (aumentar al doble) ⟨*oferta/ apuesta/capital*⟩ to double; (tener el doble que): **la dobla en edad** he's twice her age [4] ⟨*actor*⟩ (en banda sonora) to dub; (en escena) to double for; ⟨*película*⟩ to dub; **doblada al castellano** dubbed into Spanish
■ **~** *vi* [1] (torcer, girar) «*persona*» to turn; «*camino*» to bend, turn; **dobla a la izquierda** turn left [2] «*campanas*» to toll
■ **doblarse** *v pron* [1] ⟨*rama/alambre*⟩ to bend [2] «*precios/población*» to double

doble¹ *adj* [1] ⟨*whisky/flor/puerta*⟩ double; ⟨*café*⟩ large; ⟨*costura/hilo/consonante*⟩ double; **lo veo todo ~** I'm seeing double; **cerrar con ~ llave** to double-lock; **tiene ~ sentido** it has a double meaning; **calle de ~ sentido** two-way street; **~ crema** *f* (Méx) double cream; **~ fondo** *m* false bottom; **~ ve** *or* **~ u** *f*: name of the letter W; **~ ventana** *f* double glazing [2] (Andes, Ven fam) ⟨*persona*⟩ two-faced

doble² *m* [1] (Mat): **los precios aumentaron el ~** prices doubled; **tardó el ~** she took twice as long; **el ~ de tres es seis** two times six is six; **el ~ QUE algn/algo** twice as much AS sb/sth; **el ~ de largo/ rápido** twice as long/quick [2] (a) (en béisbol) double (b) **dobles** *mpl* (en tenis) doubles [3] **doble** *mf* (actor, actriz) stand-in, double; (en escenas peligrosas) (*m*) stuntman; (*f*) stuntwoman; (persona parecida) (fam) double

doblez *m* [1] (en tela, papel) fold [2] **doblez** *m or f* (falsedad) deceitfulness

doce *adj inv/m/pron* twelve; **son las ~ de la noche** it's twelve o'clock, it's midnight; *para más ejemplos ver tb* CINCO

docena *f* dozen; **una ~ de huevos** a dozen eggs; **media ~** half a dozen

dócil *adj* ⟨*niño/comportamiento*⟩ meek, docile; ⟨*perro/caballo*⟩ docile, well-trained; ⟨*pelo*⟩ manageable

doctor -tora *m,f* doctor; **~ en derecho** Doctor of Law

doctorado *m* doctorate, PhD

doctorarse [A1] *v pron* to earn *o* get one's doctorate, do one's PhD

doctrina *f* (ideología) doctrine; (enseñanza) teaching

documentación *f* [1] (de persona) papers (*pl*); (de vehículo, envío) documents (*pl*), documentation (frml) [2] (información) information, data (*pl*)

documental *adj* (a) (Cin, TV) ‹programa/serie› documentary (*before n*) (b) (Der) ‹prueba› documentary
■ *m* documentary

documentar [A1] *vt* [1] ‹trabajo/hipótesis/solicitud› to document [2] (Méx) ‹equipaje› to check in
■ **documentarse** *v pron* [1] (informarse) to do research [2] (Méx) ‹pasajero› to check in

documento *m* (Adm, Der, Inf) document; ~ adjunto (Corresp) enclosed document; (Inf) attachment

dogma *m* dogma

dogmático -ca *adj* dogmatic

dólar *m* dollar

dolencia *f* ailment, complaint

doler [E9] *vi* (a) ‹inyección/herida/brazo› to hurt; **no duele nada** it doesn't hurt at all; (+ *me/te/le etc*) **le dolió mucho** it hurt a lot; **le duele una muela/la cabeza** she has a toothache/a headache; **me dolía el estómago** I had (a) stomachache; **me duele la garganta** I have a sore throat; **me duelen los pies** my feet ache; **me duele todo (el cuerpo)** I ache all over (b) (apenar) (+ *me/te/le etc*): **me duele tener que decirte esto** I'm sorry to have to tell you this; **me dolió muchísimo lo que me dijo** I was deeply hurt by what he said

dolido -da *adj* hurt; **estar ~ POR algo** to be hurt AT sth

dolor *m* (a) (físico) pain; **sentía mucho ~** he was in a lot of pain; **tener ~ de muelas/cabeza/garganta** to have a toothache/a headache/a sore throat (b) (pena, tristeza) pain, grief

dolorido -da *adj* (a) (físicamente): **estoy toda dolorida** I'm aching all over; **tengo el brazo muy ~** I've got a very sore arm (b) (afligido) hurt

doloroso -sa *adj* (a) ‹tratamiento/enfermedad› painful (b) ‹decisión/momento/recuerdo› painful; ‹separación/espectáculo› distressing, upsetting

domador -dora *m,f* (de fieras) tamer; (de caballos) horsebreaker, broncobuster (AmE)

domar [A1] *vt* (a) ‹fieras› to tame; ‹caballo› to break in (b) (fam) ‹niño› to bring o get ... under control (c) (fam) ‹zapatos› to break in

domesticado -da *adj* tame, domesticated

domesticar [A2] *vt* to domesticate

doméstico -ca *adj* [1] ‹vida/problemas/servicio› domestic; ‹gastos› household; **tareas domésticas** housework [2] ‹vuelo› domestic

domiciliar [A1] *vt* (Esp) ‹pago/letras› to pay ... by direct debit o (AmE) direct billing; ‹sueldo› to have ... paid direct into one's bank account
■ **domiciliarse** *v pron* (frml) (residir) to reside (frml), to be domiciled (frml)

domicilio *m* (frml) address; **en su ~ particular** at his home address; **sin ~ fijo** of no fixed abode (frml); **Pat Lee, con ~ en Londres** Pat Lee currently living in London

dominante *adj* [1] ‹color/tendencia› predominant, dominant; ‹opinión› prevailing (*before n*); ‹cultura› dominant (b) (Biol, Mús, Astrol) dominant [2] ‹persona› domineering

dominar [A1] *vt* (a) (controlar) ‹nación/territorio/persona› to dominate; ‹pasión/cólera› to control; ‹vehículo/caballo› to control; **dominado por la ambición/los celos** ruled by ambition/consumed

by jealousy (b) ‹idioma› to have a good command of; ‹tema/asignatura› to know ... very well (c) (abarcar con la vista): **desde allí se domina toda la bahía** there's a view over the whole bay from there
■ ~ *vi* «color/tendencia» to predominate; «opinión» to prevail; «equipo» to dominate
■ **dominarse** *v pron* «persona» to restrain o control oneself

domingo *m* (día) Sunday; (Relig) Sabbath; **traje de ~** Sunday best; **~ de Pascua** or **de Resurrección** Easter Sunday; **~ de Ramos** Palm Sunday; *para más ejemplos ver* LUNES

dominicano -na *adj/m,f* (Geog) Dominican

dominio *m* [1] (a) (control) control; **perdió el ~ de sí mismo** he lost his self-control (b) (de idioma, tema) command; **ser del ~ público** to be public knowledge [2] (a) (Hist, Pol) dominion (b) **dominios** *mpl* (colonias) dominions (*pl*) [3] (Inf) domain

dominó *m* (*pl* **-nós**) (a) (juego) dominoes; **jugar** or (Esp, RPl) **al ~** to play dominoes (b) (ficha) domino

don *m* [1] (a) (liter) (dádiva) gift (b) (talento) talent, gift; **el ~ de la palabra** the gift of speech; **~ de gentes** ability to get on well with people; **~ de mando** leadership qualities (*pl*) [2] (tratamiento de cortesía) ≈ Mr; **buenos días ~ Miguel** good morning Mr López; **ser un ~ nadie** to be a nobody

dona *f* (Méx) (Coc) doughnut, donut (AmE)

donación *f* donation

donador -dora *m,f*, **donante** *mf* donor

donar [A1] *vt* ‹bienes/dinero› to donate, give; ‹sangre› to give, donate; ‹órganos› to donate

donativo *m* donation

doncella *f* (a) (arc) (virgen) maiden (liter) (b) (ant) (criada) maid

donde *conj* where; **la ciudad ~ se conocieron** the city where they met; **siéntate ~ quieras** sit wherever o where you like; **déjalo ~ sea** leave it anywhere; **de ~ se deduce que ...** from which it can be deduced that ...; **la ventana por ~ había entrado** the window through which he had got in
■ *prep* (esp AmL, en algunas regiones crit): **ve ~ tu hermana y dile que ...** (a su casa) go over to your sister's and tell her ...; (al lugar donde está ella) go and tell your sister ...

dónde *adv* [1] where; **¿~ está?** where is it?; **¿de ~ es?** where is he from?; **¿por ~ quieres ir?** which way do you want to go? [2] (Chi, Méx, Per) (cómo) how; **¡~ íbamos a imaginar que ...!** how were we to imagine that ...!

dondequiera *adv*: **~ QUE** wherever

donjuán *m* (tenorio) womanizer, Don Juan

doña *f* (tratamiento de cortesía) ≈ Mrs/Ms; **~ Cristina Fuentes** Mrs/Ms Cristina Fuentes

dopado -da *adj* [ESTAR] drugged

dopar [A1] *vt* ‹enfermo› to drug, dope (colloq); ‹caballo› to dope
■ **doparse** *v pron* (refl) to take drugs

doping *m* (Equ) doping; (Dep) drug-taking

dorada *f* gilthead (bream)

dorado¹ -da *adj* (a) ‹botón/galones› gold; ‹pintura› gold, gold-colored*; ‹cabello› (liter) golden (b) ‹época› golden

dorado² *m* (acción) gilding; (capa) gilt

dorar [A1] *vt* ⟨*marco/porcelana*⟩ to gild; (Coc) ⟨*cebolla/papas*⟩ to brown

■ **dorarse** *v pron* (Coc) to brown

dormida *f* (AmL) sleep

dormido -da *adj* (a) (durmiendo) asleep; **estar/ quedarse** ~ to be/to fall asleep (b) (sin sensibilidad): **tengo la pierna dormida** my leg's gone to sleep (colloq); *ver tb* DORMIR

dormilón -lona *adj* (fam): **es muy** ~ he's a real sleepyhead (colloq)

■ *m,f* (fam) (persona) sleepyhead (colloq)

dormir [I16] *vi* to sleep; **no dormí nada** I didn't sleep a wink; **dormimos en un hotel** we spent the night in a hotel; **durmió de un tirón** she slept right through (the night); **se fue a** ~ **temprano** he went off to bed early, he had an early night; ~ *a* **pierna suelta** (fam) to sleep the sleep of the dead; ~ *como un lirón* or *tronco* to sleep like a log (colloq)

■ ~ *vt* **(a)** (hacer dormir) ⟨*niño/bebé*⟩ to get ... off to sleep; **sus clases me duermen** his classes send *o* put me to sleep **(b)** (anestesiar) ⟨*persona*⟩ to put to sleep, put out (colloq); **todavía tengo este lado dormido** this side is still numb **(c)** ~ **la siesta** to have a siesta *o* nap

■ **dormirse** *v pron* **(a)** (conciliar el sueño) to fall asleep; (lograr conciliar el sueño) to get to sleep; **casi me duermo en la clase** I almost fell asleep *o* (colloq) dropped off in class **(b)** (no despertarse) to oversleep, sleep in (AmE) **(c)** «*pierna/brazo*» (+ *me/te/le etc*) to go to sleep (colloq); **se me durmió el pie** my foot went to sleep **(d)** (fam) (distraerse, descuidarse): **no te duermas** don't waste any time

dormitar [A1] *vi* to doze, snooze (colloq)

dormitorio *m* (en casa) bedroom; (en colegio, cuartel) dormitory

dorso *m* **(a)** (de un papel) back; **al** ~ ⟨*ver*⟩ overleaf; ⟨*escribir*⟩ on the back **(b)** (de la mano, animal) back

dos *adj inv/m/pron* two; **lo hicimos entre los** ~ we did it between the two of us; **sujétalo con las** ~ **manos** hold it with both hands; **llamó** ~ **veces** he called twice; **caminaban de** ~ **en** ~ they walked in pairs; **entraron de** ~ **en** ~ they came in two at a time *o* two by two; ~ **puntos** colon; **en un** ~ **por tres** in a flash; *para más ejemplos ver* CINCO

doscientos¹ -tas *adj/pron* two hundred; *para ejemplos ver* QUINIENTOS

doscientos² *m* (number) two hundred

dosel *m* (de cama) canopy; (de trono, púlpito) baldachin

dosificar [A2] *vt* ⟨*medicamento*⟩ to dose

dosis *f* (*pl* ~) dose

dotado -da *adj* ⟨*persona*⟩ gifted; **estar** ~ **DE algo** ⟨*persona*⟩ to be blessed WITH sth; «*cocina/ oficina*» to be equipped WITH sth

dotar [A1] *vt* **(a)** (frml) ⟨*institución/organismo*⟩ ~ **(A) algo DE** *or* **CON algo** ⟨*de fondos*⟩ to provide sth WITH sth; ⟨*de técnica/maquinaria*⟩ to equip sth WITH sth; ⟨*de poderes*⟩ to invest sth WITH sth **(b)** «*naturaleza/Dios*» ~ **a algn DE** *or* **CON algo** to endow *o* bless sb WITH sth

dote *f* **1** (de novia) dowry **2 dotes** *fpl*: ~**s para el canto** a talent for singing; ~**s de mando** leadership qualities

doy ▶ DAR

Dr. *m* (= **Doctor**) Dr

Dra. *f* (= **Doctora**) Dr

dracma *m* drachma

dragar [A3] *vt* ⟨*río*⟩ to dredge; ⟨*minas*⟩ to sweep for

dragón *m* (Mit) dragon

drama *m* drama; **hacer un** ~ **de algo** (fam) to make a big deal out of sth

dramático -ca *adj* dramatic; **un autor** ~ a playwright *o* dramatist

dramatismo *m* dramatic quality *o* character

dramatización *f* dramatization

dramaturgo -ga *m,f* dramatist, playwright

drástico -ca *adj* drastic

driblar, driblear [A1] *vt* to dribble past *o* around

drible *m* dribble

droga *f* drug; ~**s duras/blandas** hard/soft drugs

drogadicción *f* (drug) addiction

drogadicto -ta *adj* addicted to drugs

■ *m,f* drug addict

drogar [A3] *vt* to drug

■ **drogarse** *v pron* (*refl*) to take drugs

drogata *mf* (fam) junkie (colloq)

drogodependiente *adj* (frml) drug-dependent

■ *mf* (frml) drug addict

droguería *f* **(a)** (Esp) (tienda) store selling cleaning materials and other household goods **(b)** (Col) (farmacia) drugstore (AmE), chemist's (BrE) **(c)** (RPl) (productos químicos) pharmaceutical wholesaler's

dromedario *m* dromedary

dual *adj/m* dual

Dublín *m* Dublin

dublinés -nesa *m,f* Dubliner

ducado *m* (título) dukedom; (territorio) duchy, dukedom

ducha *f* shower; **darse una** ~ to take *o* (BrE) have a shower

ducharse [A1] *v pron* (*refl*) to take *o* (BrE) have a shower

ducto *m* **(a)** (Méx) (de gas, petróleo) pipeline **(b)** (Ur) (para la basura) garbage chute (AmE), rubbish chute (BrE) **(c)** (Col, Ven) (de ventilación) duct, shaft

duda *f* **1** (interrogante, sospecha) doubt; **expuso sus** ~**s sobre** ... he expressed his reservations about ...; **tengo unas** ~**s para consultar** I have a few points I'd like to check; **me ha surgido una** ~ there's something I'm not sure about; **¿tienen alguna** ~**?** are there any queries *o* questions?; **nunca tuve la menor** ~ **de que tenía razón** I never doubted that he was right; **fuera de (toda)** ~ beyond (all) doubt; **de eso no cabe la menor** ~ there's absolutely no doubt about that; **lo pongo en** ~ I doubt it; **sin** ~ *or* **sin lugar a** ~**s** undoubtedly; **sin** ~ **ya te lo habrás preguntado** no doubt you'll have already asked yourself that question; **para salir de** ~**s** just to be doubly sure **2** (estado de incertidumbre, indecisión): **ahora me has hecho entrar en (la)** ~ now you've made me wonder; **a ver si puedes sacarme de la** ~ do you think you can clear something up for me?; **si estás en (la) ~ no lo compres** if you're not sure don't buy it

dudar [A1] *vt* to doubt; **dudo que lo haya terminado** I doubt if *o* whether he's finished it
■ **~** *vi*: **duda entre comprar y alquilar** she can't make up her mind whether to buy or rent; **~ EN hacer algo** to hesitate to do sth; **~ DE algo/algn** to doubt sth/sb

dudoso -sa *adj* **(a)** (incierto) doubtful; **lo veo ~** I doubt it **(b)** (cuestionable) dubious **(c)** (indeciso) hesitant, undecided

duela *f* (Méx) (del suelo) floorboard

duele, duelen, etc ▸ DOLER

duelo *m* **1** (dolor) sorrow, grief; (luto) mourning; **estar de ~** to be in mourning **2** (desafío) duel; **retar a ~** to challenge … to a duel; **batirse en ~** to fight a duel; **~ a muerte** duel to the death

duende *m* **(a)** (en cuentos) goblin, imp **(b)** (espíritu) spirit (*which inhabits a house or room*)

dueño -ña *adj* **1** [SER] (libre) **~ DE hacer algo** free to do sth, at liberty to do sth (frml) **2** [SER] (indicando control): **ser ~ DE algo** to be in control OF sth; **hacerse ~ DE algo** to gain control OF sth
■ *m,f* **(a)** (de casa, pensión) (*m*) owner, landlord; (*f*) owner, landlady; (de negocio) (*m*) owner, proprietor; (*f*) owner, proprietress; **~ de casa** (AmL) (propietario) householder; (en fiesta) (*m*) host; (*f*) hostess **(b)** (de perro) owner

duerma, duermas, etc ▸ DORMIR

dulce *adj* **(a)** ⟨fruta/vino⟩ sweet; **prefiero lo ~** I prefer sweet things **(b)** ⟨agua⟩ fresh; **pez de agua ~** freshwater fish **(c)** ⟨persona⟩ gentle, kind; ⟨sonrisa/voz⟩ sweet; ⟨música⟩ soft, sweet
■ *m* **(a)** (AmL exc RPl) (golosina) candy (AmE), sweet (BrE) **(b)** (RPl) (mermelada) jam; **~ de leche** caramel spread (*made by boiling down milk and sugar*) **(c)** (AmC) (azúcar) *type of sugarloaf* **(d)** **dulces** *mpl* (cosas dulces) sweet things (*pl*)

dulcificar [A2] *vt* ⟨persona⟩ to mellow; ⟨vejez⟩ to make … more pleasant
■ **dulcificarse** *v pron* ⟨carácter/persona⟩ to mellow, soften

dulzor *m* sweetness, sweet taste

dulzura *f* sweetness; **habló con ~** she spoke kindly *o* gently; **los trata con mucha ~** she's very sweet *o* gentle with them

duna *f* dune

dúo *m* **(a)** (composición) duet, duo **(b)** (de músicos, instrumentos) duo; **a ~** ⟨contestar⟩ in unison; **lo cantaron a ~** they sang it as a duet

duodécimo -ma *adj/pron* twelfth

dúplex *m* (*pl* ~) **(a)** (apartamento) duplex apartment, maisonette (BrE) **(b)** (Méx) (casa) semi-detached house

duplicado¹ -da *adj* duplicated; **por ~** in duplicate

duplicado² *m* copy, duplicate

duplicar [A2] *vt* ⟨documento/llave⟩ to copy, duplicate
■ **duplicarse** *v pron* ⟨número⟩ to double

duplo *m*: **el ~ de dos es cuatro** two times two is four

duque *m* duke

duquesa *f* duchess

duración *f* **(a)** (de película, acto, curso) length, duration **(b)** (de pila, bombilla) life; **pila de larga ~** long-life battery; **▸** DISCO 1A

duradero -ra *adj* ⟨amistad/recuerdo⟩ lasting (*before n*); ⟨ropa/zapatos⟩ hardwearing, longwearing (AmE)

durante *prep* (en el transcurso de) during; (cuando se especifica la duración) for; **~ 1980** during *o* in 1980; **gobernó el país ~ casi dos décadas** she governed the country for almost two decades; **los precios aumentaron un 0,3% ~ el mes de diciembre** prices rose by 0.3% in December; **~ todo el invierno** throughout the winter

durar [A1] *vi* **(a)** ⟨reunión/guerra/relación⟩ to last; **¿cuánto dura la película?** how long is the film? **(b)** ⟨coche/zapatos⟩ to last **(c)** (Col, Ven) **▸** DEMORAR A
■ **durarse** *v pron* (Ven) **▸** DEMORARSE

durazno *m* (esp AmL) (fruto) peach; (árbol) peach tree

durex® *m* (AmL) Scotch tape® (AmE), Sellotape® (BrE)

dureza *f* **1** (en general) hardness; (de la carne) toughness **2** **(a)** (severidad, inflexibilidad) harshness; **nos trataban con ~** they treated us harshly; **fue castigado con ~** he was severely punished **(b)** (en el deporte) roughness

durmiera, durmió, etc ▸ DORMIR

duro¹ -ra *adj* **1** (en general) hard; ⟨carne⟩ tough; ⟨pan⟩ stale; **las peras están duras** the pears aren't ripe **2** ⟨luz/voz⟩ harsh; ⟨facciones⟩ hard, harsh **3** **(a)** (severo, riguroso) harsh; ⟨juego⟩ rough, hard; **fuiste demasiado ~ con él** you were too hard on him; **una postura más dura** a tougher line **(b)** (difícil, penoso) ⟨trabajo/vida⟩ hard, tough; **fue un golpe muy ~** it was a very hard blow

duro² *adv* (esp AmL) ⟨trabajar/estudiar/llover⟩ hard; ⟨hablar⟩ (Col, Ven) loudly

duro³ *m* (en España) five-peseta coin

Ee

E, e *f* (*pl* **es**) (*read as* /e/) *the letter* E, e

e *conj* [*used instead of* Y *before* I- *or* HI-] and

E. (= **Este**) E, East

EAU *mpl* (= **Emiratos Árabes Unidos**) UAE

ebanista *mf* cabinetmaker

ébano *m* ebony

ebrio, ebria *adj* (frml) inebriated (frml), drunk

ebullición *f* **(a)** (Coc, Fís): **entrar en** ~ to come to the boil; **punto de** ~ boiling point **(b)** (agitación) turmoil

eccema *m* eczema

echado -da *adj* (acostado): **está** ~ **en el sofá** he's lying down on the sofa

echador -dora *adj* (Méx fam) boastful
■ *m,f* (Méx fam) boaster (colloq)

echar [A1] *vt*
I **1** **(a)** (lanzar, tirar) to throw; **lo eché a la basura** I threw it out *o* away; **echó la moneda al aire** he tossed the coin; ~**on el ancla/la red** they cast anchor/their net; **echó la cabeza hacia atrás** she threw her head back; ~ **algo a perder** to ruin sth; ~ **de menos algo/a algn** to miss sth/sb **(b)** **echar abajo** ⟨*edificio*⟩ to pull down; ⟨*gobierno*⟩ to bring down; ⟨*proyecto*⟩ to destroy; ⟨*esperanzas*⟩ to dash; ⟨*moral*⟩ to undermine; ⟨*puerta/valla*⟩ to break ... down
2 (expulsar) ⟨*persona*⟩ (de trabajo) to fire (colloq), to sack (BrE colloq); (de bar, casa) to throw ... out; (de colegio) to expel
3 ⟨*carta*⟩ to mail (AmE), to post (BrE)
4 **(a)** (pasar, correr) ⟨*cortinas*⟩ to pull, draw; **échale (la) llave** lock it; **¿echaste el cerrojo?** did you bolt the door? **(b)** (mover): **lo echó para atrás/a un lado** she pushed (*o* moved *etc*) it backward(s)/to one side
5 **(a)** (expeler, despedir) ⟨*olor/humo/chispas*⟩ to give off **(b)** (producir) ⟨*hojas*⟩ to sprout; **ya está echando flores** it's flowering already
II **1** **(a)** (poner) ⟨*leña/carbón*⟩ to put; ⟨*gasolina*⟩ to put in; **¿le echas azúcar al café?** do you take sugar in your coffee? **(b)** (servir, dar) to give; **échame un poco de vino** can you give me a little wine? **(c)** ⟨*trago*⟩ to have
2 **(a)** ⟨*sermón/discurso*⟩ (fam) (+ *me/te/le etc*) to give; **le echó una maldición** she put a curse on him **(b)** (fam) ⟨*condena/multa*⟩ (+ *me/te/le etc*) to give; ~**le la culpa a algn** to put *o* lay the blame on sb
3 (fam) (calcular) (+ *me/te/le etc*): **¿cuántos años me echas?** how old do you think I am?; **de aquí a tu casa échale una hora** it's *o* it takes about an hour from here to your house
4 (Esp fam) (dar, exhibir) ⟨*programa/película*⟩ to show

■ **echarse** *v pron* **1** **(a)** (tirarse, arrojarse) to throw oneself; **me eché al suelo** I threw myself to the ground; ~**se de cabeza al agua** to dive into the water; ~**se a perder** «*comida*» to go bad, go off (BrE); «*cosecha/proyecto/plan*» to be ruined **(b)** (tumbarse, acostarse) to lie down **(c)** (apartarse, moverse) (+ *compl*): **se echó a un lado** she moved to one side; **échate un poco para allá** move over that way a bit; ~**se atrás** to back out
2 **(a)** (ponerse) ⟨*crema/bronceador*⟩ to put on **(b)** ⟨*cigarillo*⟩ to have **(c)** (Esp fam) ⟨*novio/novia*⟩: **se ha echado novia** he's found *o* got himself a girlfriend **(d)** (Méx fam) (beberse) to drink
3 (Méx fam) (romper) to break
4 (Col fam) (tardar) ⟨*horas/días*⟩ to take
5 (empezar) ~**se ᴀ** to start *o* begin to, start *o*

begin; **se echó a correr** he started to run *o* started running; **las palomas se** ~**on a volar** the doves flew off

echarpe *m* shawl, stole

ecléctico -ca *adj/m,f* eclectic

eclesiástico -ca *adj* ecclesiastical, church (*before n*)

eclipse *m* eclipse

eco *m* (Fís) echo; **la cueva tiene** ~ there's an echo in the cave; **hacer** ~ to echo

ecografía *f* ultrasound scan

ecología *f* ecology

ecológico -ca *adj* ⟨*problema/estudio*⟩ ecological; ⟨*daño/desastre*⟩ environmental; ⟨*producto*⟩ eco-friendly, environmentally friendly; ⟨*cultivo/agricultura*⟩ organic

ecologismo *m* environmentalism, conservationism

ecologista *adj* ecology (*before n*), environmentalist (*before n*)
■ *mf* ecologist, environmentalist

economato *m* **(a)** (de empresa) company store **(b)** (Mil) PX (AmE), NAAFI shop (BrE)

economía *f* **(a)** (ciencia) economics **(b)** (de país) economy; ~ **de (libre) mercado** (free) market economy **(c)** (ahorro): **hacer** ~**s** to economize **(d)** (de persona, familia) finances (*pl*)

económico -ca *adj* **1** ⟨*crisis/situación*⟩ economic (*before n*); ⟨*problema/independencia*⟩ financial **2** **(a)** ⟨*piso/comida*⟩ cheap; ⟨*restaurante/hotel*⟩ cheap, inexpensive **(b)** (que gasta poco) ⟨*motor*⟩ economical; ⟨*persona*⟩ thrifty

economista *mf* economist

economizar [A4] *vt* ⟨*tiempo*⟩ to save; ⟨*combustible/recursos*⟩ to economize on, save
■ ~ *vi* to economize, save money

ecosistema *m* ecosystem

ecu, ECU /'eku/ *m* (= **Unidad Monetaria Europea**) ECU

ecuación *f* equation

ecuador *m* **1** (línea) equator **2** **Ecuador** (país) Ecuador

ecuatorial *adj* equatorial

ecuatoriano -na *adj/m,f* Ecuadorean

eczema *m* eczema

edad *f* **1** (de persona, árbol) age; **tienen la misma** ~ they are the same age; **un joven de unos quince años de** ~ a boy of about fifteen; **¿qué** ~ **tiene?** how old is he?; **aún no tiene la** ~ **suficiente** he's still not old enough ...; **de** ~ **madura** *or* **de mediana** ~ middle-aged; **una persona de** ~ an elderly person; **niños en** ~ **escolar** children of school age; **estar en la** ~ **del pavo** to be at that awkward age
2 (Hist) (época) age, period; **la E**~ **de bronce/de hierro/de piedra** the Bronze/Iron/Stone Age; **la E**~ **media** the Middle Ages (*pl*)

edema *m* edema*

Edén *m*: **el** ~ (the Garden of) Eden

edición *f* **1** (Impr, Period) (tirada) edition; (acción)

publication; ~ **de bolsillo** pocket edition;
Ediciones Rivera Rivera Publications **2** (Rad, TV)
program*, edition

edificado -da *adj* built-up

edificar [A2] *vt/vi* to build

edificio *m* building

Edimburgo *m* Edinburgh

editar [A1] *vt* **1** (publicar) ⟨*libro/revista*⟩ to
publish **2** (modificar) ⟨*película/grabación/texto*⟩ to
edit; (Inf) to edit

editor -tora *adj* publishing (*before n*)
▪ *m,f* (que publica) publisher; (que revisa, modifica)
editor

editorial *adj* ⟨*casa/actividad*⟩ publishing
(*before n*); ⟨*puesto/decisión*⟩ editorial
▪ *f* (empresa) publishing company *o* house
▪ *m* (en periódico) editorial, leading article

edredón *m* eiderdown, comforter (AmE); (que se
usa sin mantas) duvet, continental quilt (BrE)

educación *f* **1** (enseñanza) education; (para la
convivencia) upbringing; ~ **a distancia**
correspondence courses (*pl*), distance learning;
~ **física** physical education; ~ **general básica** (en
Esp) primary education; ~ **para adultos** adult
education; ~ **primaria/secundaria/superior**
primary/secondary/higher education; ~
universitaria university education, college
education (AmE); ~ **vocacional** (AmS) careers
guidance **2** (modales) manners (*pl*); **es una falta
de** ~ it's rude, it's bad manners

educado -da *adj* polite, well-mannered

educador -dora *m,f* (frml) teacher, educator
(frml)

educar [A2] *vt* **1** (a) (Educ) to educate, teach
(b) (para la convivencia) ⟨*hijos*⟩ to bring up;
⟨*ciudadanos*⟩ to educate **2** ⟨*oído/voz*⟩ to train
▪ **educarse** *v pron* (hacer los estudios) to be
educated

educativo -va *adj* ⟨*programa/juego*⟩
educational; ⟨*establecimiento*⟩ educational,
teaching (*before n*); ⟨*sistema*⟩ education (*before n*)

edulcorante *m* sweetener

EEUU *or* **EE.UU.** (= **Estados Unidos**) USA

efe *f: name of the letter* f

efectista *adj* theatrical, dramatic

efectividad *f* (eficacia) effectiveness

efectivo¹ -va *adj* ⟨*remedio/medio/castigo*⟩
effective; **hacer** ~ ⟨*cheque*⟩ to cash; ⟨*pago*⟩ to
make

efectivo² *m* (Fin) cash; **pagar en** ~ to pay cash

efecto *m* **1** (a) (resultado, consecuencia) effect;
hacer ~ to take effect; **un calmante de** ~
inmediato a fast-acting painkiller; **mecanismo de**
~ **retardado** delayed-action mechanism; **bajo los**
~**s del alcohol** under the influence of alcohol; ~
dos mil (Inf) millennium bug; ~ **invernadero**
greenhouse effect; ~ **óptico** optical illusion; ~
secundario side effect; ~**s especiales** special
effects; ~**s sonoros** sound effects (b) **en efecto** in
fact; (así es) indeed
2 (impresión): **su conducta causó mal** ~ his
behavior made a bad impression *o* (colloq) didn't
go down well; **no sé qué** ~ **le causaron mis
palabras** I don't know what effect my words had
on him

3 (Dep) (desvío) swerve; (movimiento rotatorio) spin;
le dio a la bola con ~ she put some spin on the
ball

4 ~**s personales** personal effects (*pl*)

efectuar [A18] *vt* (frml) ⟨*maniobra/redada*⟩ to
carry out, execute (frml); ⟨*pago*⟩ to make; ⟨*viaje/
cambio*⟩ to make; ⟨*disparo*⟩ to fire; **el tren** ~**á su
salida a las 10.50** the train will depart at 10:50

efervescente *adj* ⟨*pastilla*⟩ effervescent;
⟨*bebida*⟩ sparkling, fizzy (colloq)

eficacia *f* (a) (de acción, remedio) effectiveness,
efficacy (frml) (b) (eficiencia) efficiency

eficaz *adj* (a) ⟨*fórmula/remedio*⟩ effective,
efficacious (frml) (b) (eficiente) efficient

eficiencia *f* efficiency

eficiente *adj* efficient

efigie *f* (cuadro) image, picture; (estatua) statue,
effigy

efímero -ra *adj* ephemeral

efusivo -va *adj* ⟨*temperamento/recibimiento*⟩
effusive; ⟨*persona*⟩ demonstrative; ⟨*recibimiento*⟩
warm

EGB *f* (en Esp) = **Educación General
Básica**

egipcio -cia *adj/m,f* Egyptian

Egipto *m* Egypt

ego *m* ego

egocéntrico -ca *adj* egocentric,
self-centered*

egoísmo *m* selfishness, egotism

egoísta *adj* selfish, egotistic
▪ *mf* (Psic) egotist; **es una** ~ she is very selfish

egresado -da *adj* (AmL): **los alumnos** ~**s** (de
universidad) the graduates; (de colegio) the high
school graduates (AmE), the school leavers (BrE)
▪ *m,f* (AmL) (de universidad) graduate; (de colegio)
high school graduate (AmE), school leaver (BrE)

egresar [A1] *vi* (AmL) (de universidad) to
graduate; (de colegio) to graduate from high school
(AmE), to leave school *o* college *etc*) (BrE)
▪ ~ *vt* (Andes) (Fin) to withdraw, take out

egreso *m* (AmL) (de universidad) graduation; (de
colegio) graduation (AmE)

eh *interj* (a) (para llamar la atención) hey! (b)
(expresando amenaza, advertencia) eh?, huh?, OK? (c)
(contestando una pregunta) eh?, what?

Ej., ej. (*read as* **por ejemplo**) eg

eje *m* **1** (a) (Astron, Fís, Mat) axis (b) (Auto, Mec)
(barra) axle **2** (de asunto, política) core, central
theme

ejecución *f* **1** (de persona) execution **2** (a)
(de plan) implementation; (de orden) carrying out
(b) (Mús) performance

ejecutar [A1] *vt* **1** ⟨*condenado/reo*⟩ to execute
2 ⟨*plan*⟩ to implement, carry out; ⟨*orden/
trabajo*⟩ to carry out; ⟨*sentencia*⟩ to execute,
enforce; ⟨*ejercicio/salto*⟩ to perform; ⟨*sinfonía/
himno nacional*⟩ to play, perform

ejecutivo¹ -va *adj* ⟨*función/comisión*⟩
executive
▪ *m,f* (Bot, Com) executive

ejecutivo² *m* (Gob) executive

ejemplar *adj* ⟨*conducta/vida/castigo*⟩
exemplary; ⟨*trabajador/padre*⟩ model (*before n*)
▪ *m* (a) (de libro, documento) copy (b) (Bot, Zool)
specimen

ejemplarizador -dora *adj* (Chi, Per) exemplary

ejemplo *m* example; **dar (el)** ∼ to set an example; **pongamos por** ∼ **el caso de Elena** let's take Elena's case as an example; **por ejemplo** for example

ejercer [E2] *vt* ⊡ (a) ⟨*profesión*⟩ to practice*; ∼ **la abogacía** to practice law (b) ⟨*derecho*⟩ to exercise ⊡ ⟨*influencia/poder/presión*⟩ to exert ■ *vi* ⟨*abogado/médico*⟩ to practice*; **es maestra pero no ejerce** she's a teacher but she doesn't practice her profession

ejercicio *m* ⊡ (actividad física) exercise; **hacer** ∼ to exercise ⊡ (Educ) (a) (trabajo de práctica) exercise (b) (prueba, examen) test, exam ⊡ (de profesión) practice ⊡ (Mil) exercise, maneuver*

ejercitar [A1] *vt* ⊡ ⟨*músculo/dedos/memoria*⟩ to exercise ⊡ ⟨*caballos*⟩ to train; ⟨*tropa*⟩ to drill, train; ⟨*alumnos*⟩ to train

ejército *m* army; ∼ **del aire** air force; ∼ **de tierra** army

ejidal *adj* (en Méx) cooperative (*before n*)

ejidatario -ria *m,f* (en Méx) member of a cooperative

ejido *m* (en Méx) (sistema) *system of communal or cooperative farming*; (sociedad) cooperative; (terreno) *land belonging to a cooperative*

ejote *m* (Méx) green bean

el (*pl* **los**), **la** (*pl* **las**) *art* [*the masculine article* EL *is also used before feminine nouns which begin with accented* A *or* HA, *e.g.* EL AGUA PURA, EL HADA MADRINA] ⊡ (a) (en general) the; **la Tierra** the Earth (b) (con sustantivos en sentido genérico): **odio el pescado** I hate fish; **así es la vida** that's life; **(nosotros) los Mexicanos** we Mexicans; **¿ya vas a la escuela?** do you go to school yet? (c) (refiriéndose a algo que se conoce o se está definiendo): **en la calle Solís** in Solís street; **las tuyas** yours; **el último** the last one; **el estúpido del marido** that stupid husband of hers ⊡ (a) **el + DE: la del sombrero** the one with the hat; **el de las nueve** the nine o'clock one; **el de mi hijo** my son's (b) **el + QUE: las que yo vi** the ones I saw; **los que estén cansados**; those who are tired, anyone who's tired; **la que te guste** whichever you like ⊡ (en expresiones de tiempo): **ocurrió el domingo** it happened last Sunday; **mi cumpleaños es el 28 de mayo** my birthday's on May 28; **el mes pasado** last month; **toda la mañana** all morning; **a las ocho** at eight o'clock ⊡ (cada): **$80 el metro/kilo** $80 a meter/a kilo, $80 per kilo/meter ⊡ (con fracciones, porcentajes, números): **la mitad/la cuarta parte del dinero** half the money/a quarter of the money; **el 20% de ...** 20% of ... ⊡ (con partes del cuerpo, prendas de vestir, artículos personales, etc): **tenía las manos en los bolsillos** she had her hands in her pockets; **¡te cortaste el pelo!** you've had your hair cut!; **tiene los ojos azules** he has blue eyes ⊡ (a) (con apellidos acompañados de título, adjetivos, etc): **el señor Ortiz/la doctora Vidal** Mr Ortiz/ Doctor Vidal; **los Ortega** the Ortegas (b) (con algunos nombres geográficos): **en la India** in India; ▶ ÁFRICA, ARGENTINA, ETC

él *pron pers* (a) (como sujeto) he; **¿quién se lo va a decir? — él** who's going to tell her? — he is; **lo**

hizo ∼ **mismo** he did it himself; **fue** ∼ it was him (b) (en comparaciones, con preposiciones) him; (refiriéndose a cosas) it; **llegué antes que** ∼ I arrived before him *o* before he did; **con/para** ∼ with/for him; **son de** ∼ they're his

elaboración *f* (de producto, vino) production, making; (de pan) baking, making

elaborado -da *adj* elaborate

elaborar [A1] *vt* ⊡ ⟨*producto/vino*⟩ to produce, make; ⟨*pan*⟩ to bake, make ⊡ ⟨*plan/teoría*⟩ to devise, draw up; ⟨*informe/estudio*⟩ to prepare, write

elasticidad *f* (de material) elasticity; (de horario) flexibility

elástico¹ -ca *adj* ⟨*membrana/cinta*⟩ elastic; ⟨*medias/venda*⟩ elastic, stretch (*before n*); ⟨*horario*⟩ flexible

elástico² *m* (a) (material) elastic; (cordón) piece of elastic; (en géneros de punto) rib, ribbing (b) (Chi) (goma) rubber band

ele *f*. *name of the letter* l

elección *f* (a) (acción de escoger) choice; **llévate tres, a tu** ∼ take *o* choose any three (b) (Pol) (de candidato) election (c) **elecciones** *fpl* (Pol) election; **convocar elecciones** to call an election

elector -tora *m,f* (Pol) voter, elector

electorado *m* electorate

electoral *adj* ⟨*campaña/discurso*⟩ election (*before n*)

electricidad *f* electricity

electricista *mf* electrician

eléctrico -ca *adj* ⟨*tren/motor/luz*⟩ electric; ⟨*instalación/aparato*⟩ electrical; ⟨*carga*⟩ electrical, electric

electrocardiograma *m* electrocardiogram

electrocutar [A1] *vt* to electrocute ■ **electrocutarse** *v pron* to be electrocuted

electrodoméstico *m* electrical appliance

electrón *m* electron

electrónica *f* electronics

electrónico -ca *adj* electronic

elefante -ta *m,f* elephant

elegancia *f* (a) (en el vestir) smartness, elegance; (garbo, gracilidad) elegance; (de barrio, restaurante) smartness (b) (de estilo) elegance

elegante *adj* ⊡ (a) ⟨*moda/vestido*⟩ elegant, smart; **iba muy** ∼ he was very well *o* very smartly dressed (b) ⟨*barrio/restaurante/fiesta*⟩ smart ⊡ ⟨*estilo/frase*⟩ elegant, polished

elegir [I8] *vt* (a) (escoger) to choose; **me dieron a** ∼ I was given a *o* the choice (b) (por votación) to elect

elemental *adj* (a) (esencial) ⟨*norma/principio*⟩ fundamental (b) (básico) ⟨*curso/nivel/texto*⟩ elementary; ⟨*conocimientos/nociones*⟩ rudimentary, basic

elemento *m* (a) (en general) element; **se siente en su** ∼ he's in his element; **los** ∼**s** (fuerzas naturales) the elements (b) (persona): **un** ∼ **pernicioso** a bad influence; ∼**s subversivos** subversive elements; **es un** ∼ **de cuidado** (Esp fam & pey) he's a nasty piece of work (c) (RPl) (tipo de gente) crowd

elepé *m* album, LP

elevado -da *adj* ⊡ ⟨*terreno/montaña*⟩ high; ⟨*edificio*⟩ tall, high ⊡ (a) ⟨*cantidad*⟩ large;

⟨precio/impuestos⟩ high; ⟨pérdidas⟩ heavy, substantial **(b)** ⟨categoría/calidad/posición⟩ high **(c)** ⟨ideas/pensamientos⟩ noble, elevated; ⟨estilo⟩ lofty, elevated

elevador m (montacargas) hoist; (ascensor) (Méx) elevator (AmE), lift (BrE)

elevar [A1] vt **1** (frml) **(a)** (levantar) ⟨objeto⟩ to raise, lift **(b)** ⟨espíritu/mente⟩ to uplift **(c)** ⟨muro/nivel⟩ to raise, make ... higher **2** (frml) **(a)** (aumentar) ⟨precios/impuestos⟩ to raise, increase; ⟨nivel de vida⟩ to raise **(b)** ⟨voz/tono⟩ to raise
■ **elevarse** v pron **1** (tomar altura) «avión/cometa» to climb, gain height; «globo» to rise, gain height **2** (frml) (aumentar) «temperatura» to rise; ⟨precios/impuestos⟩ to rise, increase; «tono/voz» to rise **3** (frml) (ascender): **la cifra se elevaba ya al 13%** the figure had already reached 13%

elige, elija, etc ▶ ELEGIR

eliminación f elimination; (de residuos) disposal

eliminar [A1] vt **(a)** ⟨obstáculo⟩ to remove; ⟨párrafo⟩ to delete, remove **(b)** ⟨candidato⟩ to eliminate; (Dep) to eliminate, knock out **(c)** (euf) (matar) to eliminate (euph), to get rid of (euph) **(d)** ⟨residuos⟩ to dispose of **(e)** ⟨toxinas/grasas⟩ to eliminate

eliminatoria f (en torneo) qualifying round; (para carrera) heat; (certamen) qualifying competition

eliminatorio -ria adj ⟨examen/fase⟩ qualifying (before n), preliminary (before n)

elite /e'lit/, **élite** /'elite e'lit/ f elite, élite

elitista adj ⟨sociedad/actitud⟩ elitist; ⟨colegio/club⟩ exclusive

elixir m **(a)** (Mit) elixir **(b)** (Esp) (Farm) mouthwash

ella pron pers **(a)** (como sujeto) she; **¿quién lo va a hacer? — ella** who's going to do it? — she is; **lo hizo ~ misma** she did it herself; **fue ~** it was her **(b)** (en comparaciones, con preposiciones) her; (referido a cosas) it; **salí después que ~** I left after her o after she did; **con/para ~** with/for her; **son de ~** they're hers

ello pron pers it; **ya que estamos en ~** while we're at it; **todo ~ exquisitamente presentado** all beautifully presented; **para ello hay que obtener un permiso** (frml) you need a permit for this

ellos, ellas pron pers pl **(a)** (como sujeto) they; **lo hicieron ~ mismos** they did it themselves; **fueron ellas** it was them **(b)** (en comparaciones, con preposiciones) them; **llegué antes que ~** I arrived before them o before they did; **con/para ~/ellas** with/for them; **son de ~** they're theirs, they belong to them

elocuencia f eloquence; **con ~** eloquently

elocuente adj eloquent

elogiar [A1] vt to praise

elogio m praise; **digno de ~** praiseworthy

elote m (mazorca) (AmC, Méx) corncob, ear of corn; (granos) (Méx) corn (AmE), sweetcorn (BrE)

El Salvador m El Salvador

eludir [I1] vt **(a)** ⟨problema/compromiso/pago⟩ to evade, avoid **(b)** ⟨persona⟩ to avoid

emancipación f emancipation

emancipado -da adj emancipated

embadurnar [A1] vt **~ algo DE algo** to smear sth WITH sth
■ **embadurnarse** v pron (refl) **~se DE algo** to plaster o smear oneself WITH sth

embajada f (sede, delegación) embassy; (cargo) ambassadorship

embajador -dora m,f (Adm, Pol) ambassador

embalaje m **1** (acción) packing; (envoltura) packaging, wrapping **2** (Col) (Dep) sprint

embalar [A1] vt to pack

embaldosar [A1] vt to tile

embalsamar [A1] vt to embalm

embalse m (depósito) reservoir

embarazada adj pregnant; **(se) quedó ~** she got o became pregnant; **está ~ de dos meses** she's two months pregnant; **la dejó ~** he got her pregnant
■ f pregnant woman

embarazo m (Med) pregnancy

embarazoso -sa adj embarrassing, awkward

embarcación f (frml) vessel (frml), craft (frml)

embarcadero m (atracadero) jetty; (para mercancías) wharf

embarcar [A2] vi (Aviac) to board; (Náut) to embark, board
■ ~ vt **1** ⟨mercancías/equipaje⟩ to load **2** (Ven) to let ... down
■ **embarcarse** v pron **(a)** «pasajero» (en barco) to board, embark; (en tren, avión) to board, get on; **se ~on para América** they set sail for America **(b)** (en asunto, negocio) **~se EN algo** to embark ON sth

embargar [A3] vt ⟨bienes⟩ to seize, to sequestrate (frml); ⟨vehículo⟩ to impound

embargo m **1** **(a)** (Der) (incautación, decomiso) seizure, sequestration (frml); (Mil, Pol) embargo **2** **sin embargo: sin ~, tiene algunas desventajas** however o nevertheless, it has some disadvantages; **sin ~, ayer no decías eso** you weren't saying that yesterday, though; **tiene de todo y sin embargo se queja** he has everything and yet he still complains

embarrada f (AmS fam) (metida de pata) blunder, boo-boo (colloq)

embarrar [A1] vt to cover ... in mud; **~la** (AmS fam) to mess up (AmE colloq), to mess things up (BrE colloq)
■ **embarrarse** v pron «persona» to get covered in mud; ⟨prenda/ropa⟩ to get...muddy

embaucador -dora adj deceitful
■ m,f trickster

embaucar [A2] vt to trick, con (colloq)

embeber [E1] vt **(a)** (en líquido) ⟨bizcocho/esponja⟩ to soak **(b)** «secante/toalla» ⟨líquido⟩ to soak up **(c)** ⟨tela⟩ to gather in
■ ~ vi to shrink
■ **embeberse** v pron **(a)** (enfrascarse) **~se EN algo** to become wrapped up o absorbed IN sth **(b)** (imbuirse) **~se DE algo** to become imbued WITH sth (frml)

embelesado -da adj spellbound

embelesar [A1] vt to captivate

embellecer [E3] vt ⟨persona⟩ to make ... beautiful; ⟨campiña/ciudad⟩ to beautify, improve the appearance of

embestida f charge

embestir [I14] vi to charge; ~ CONTRA algo/algn to charge AT sth/sb
■ ~ vt «*toro*» to charge (at)

embetunar [A1] vt **1** ⟨*zapatos*⟩ to polish, put polish on **2** (CS) (ensuciar) to get ... dirty

emblema m emblem

embobado -da adj spellbound; la miraban ~s they were watching her open-mouthed; está ~ con ella he's besotted with her

embolador -dora m,f (Col) bootblack

embolar [A1] vt **1** (RPl arg) (fastidiar) to bug (colloq), to piss ... off (sl) **2** (Col) ⟨*zapatos*⟩ to shine, polish
■ **embolarse** v pron (AmC fam) to get plastered (colloq)

embolia f embolism

embolsarse [A1] v pron ⟨*dinero ajeno*⟩ to pocket; ⟨*premio*⟩ to collect, receive; ⟨*ganancia*⟩ to make

embonar [A1] vi (Méx) ⟨*tubos/ventana/piezas*⟩ to fit; ~ CON algo to fit in WITH sth

emborrachar [A1] vt «*bebida*» to make ... drunk; «*persona*» to get ... drunk
■ **emborracharse** v pron to get drunk

emborronar [A1] vt (manchar) to smudge; (con tinta) to make blots on, to blot
■ **emborronarse** v pron to smudge, get smudged

emboscada f ambush

emboscar [A2] vt to ambush

embotado -da adj ⟨*punta/filo*⟩ dull, blunt; estoy totalmente ~ my brain's seized up, I can't take in any more

embotar [A1] vt ⟨*mente/sentidos*⟩ to dull

embotellado -da adj (a) ⟨*agua/vino*⟩ bottled (b) ⟨*calle/tráfico*⟩ jammed solid

embotellamiento m (del tráfico) traffic jam

embotellar [A1] vt to bottle

embragar [A3] vi to engage the clutch

embrague m clutch

embriagado -da adj (frml) (borracho) inebriated (frml)

embriagador -dora adj ⟨*vino*⟩ heady; ⟨*sensación*⟩ (liter) intoxicating (liter)

embriagarse [A3] v pron (frml) (con alcohol) to become intoxicated (frml)

embriaguez f (borrachera) drunkenness

embrión m (Biol) embryo

embrollar [A1] vt (a) ⟨*hilo/madeja*⟩ to tangle (up) (b) (confundir) ⟨*situación*⟩ to complicate; ⟨*persona*⟩ to muddle, confuse (c) (implicar) ~ a algn EN algo to embroil sb IN sth, get sb involved IN sth
■ **embrollarse** v pron «*hilo/madeja*» to get tangled; «*situación*» to get confused o muddled; «*persona*» to get muddled, to get mixed up (colloq)

embrollo m (de hilos, cables) tangle; (de callejuelas,

pasillos) maze; (situación confusa) muddle, mess; el argumento es un ~ the plot is extremely involved o complicated

embromado -da adj **1** [ESTAR] (AmS fam) (enfermo, delicado) in a bad way; tiene un pie ~ she has a bad foot **2** (AmS fam) ⟨*situación*⟩ tricky; ⟨*problema*⟩ thorny

embromar [A1] vt (AmS fam) (a) (molestar) to pester (b) (estropear) ⟨*aparato*⟩ to ruin (colloq); ⟨*plan*⟩ to ruin, spoil (c) (perjudicar): la guerra nos embromó a todos we all suffered because of the war; ¡me embromaste! now you've really landed me in it! (colloq)
■ **embromarse** v pron (AmS fam) (a) (jorobarse): que se embrome por estúpido it serves him right for being so stupid; si no te gusta, te embromas if you don't like it, tough! (b) (hacerse daño) to hurt oneself; ⟨*rodilla/hígado*⟩ to screw up (AmE colloq), to do ... in (BrE colloq) (c) (enfermarse) to get ill (colloq) (d) «*aparato/frenos*» to go wrong

embrujado -da adj [ESTAR] ⟨*persona*⟩ bewitched; ⟨*casa/lugar*⟩ haunted

embrujar [A1] vt (a) (hechizar) to bewitch, put ... under a spell (b) (fascinar, enamorar) to bewitch

embrujo m (a) (hechizo) spell; (maleficio) curse (b) (encanto, atractivo) magic, enchantment

embrutecer [E3] vt «*trabajo*» to stultify; «*televisión*» to make ... mindless

embudo m funnel

embuste m tall story, story (colloq)

embustero -ra adj: ¡qué niño más ~! what a little fibber (colloq)
■ m,f fibber (colloq), liar

embutido m (salchicha) sausage; (fiambre) cold meat

eme f: name of the letter m

emergencia f emergency

emerger [E6] vi (a) «*submarino*» to surface (b) «*persona*» to emerge (c) (sobresalir) to emerge

emigración f (de personas) emigration; (de animales) migration

emigrante adj/mf emigrant

emigrar [A1] vi «*persona*» to emigrate; «*animal*» to migrate

eminencia f (a) (personalidad) expert (b) (frml) (Relig) Eminence (frml)

eminente adj eminent

Emiratos Árabes Unidos mpl United Arab Emirates

emisario -ria m,f emissary

emisión f (a) (Tec) emission (b) (Fin) issue (c) (Rad, TV) (acción) broadcasting; (programa) (frml) program*, broadcast

emisor m (aparato) transmitter

emisora f (Rad) radio station

emitir [I1] vt ⟨*sonido/luz/señal*⟩ to emit, give out; ⟨*acciones/sellos/comunicado*⟩ to issue; ⟨*programa*⟩ to broadcast; ⟨*película*⟩ to show; ⟨*veredicto*⟩ to deliver, announce; ⟨*voto*⟩ to cast

emoción *f* (sentimiento) emotion; (expectación, excitación) excitement; ¡qué ∼! how exciting!

emocionado -da *adj* (conmovido) moved; (entusiasmado) excited

emocional *adj* emotional

emocionante *adj* (conmovedor) moving; (excitante, apasionante) exciting

emocionar [A1] *vt* to move, affect
■ **emocionarse** *v pron* (conmoverse) to be moved; (entusiasmarse) to get excited

emotivo -va *adj* ⟨desarrollo/mundo/persona⟩ emotional; ⟨acto/discurso⟩ moving, emotional

empacar [A2] *vt* **(a)** (empaquetar) to pack **(b)** ⟨algodón/heno⟩ to bale **(c)** (AmL) ⟨maleta⟩ to pack
■ ∼ *vi* to pack

empachar [A1] *vt* (fam) (indigestar) to give ... an upset stomach
■ **empacharse** *v pron* (fam) (indigestarse) ∼se DE algo to get an upset stomach FROM sth

empacho *m* (fam) (indigestión): agarrarse un ∼ to get *o* have an upset stomach

empadronarse [A1] *v pron* to register

empalagar [A3] *vt*: los bombones me empalagan chocolates are too sweet *o* sickly for my taste
■ ∼ *vi* ⟨licor/dulce⟩ to be too sweet *o* sickly; ⟨estilo/sentimentalismo⟩ to be cloying

empalagoso -sa *adj* ⟨tarta/licor⟩ sickly; ⟨persona/sonrisa⟩ sickly sweet, cloying

empalizada *f* palisade

empalmar [A1] *vt* ⟨cuerdas/películas/cintas⟩ to splice; ⟨cables⟩ to connect
■ ∼ *vi* ⟨líneas/carreteras⟩ to converge, meet

empalme *m* (de cables) connection; (de cuerdas) splice; (de carreteras, líneas) junction

empanada *f* **(a)** (AmL) (individual) pasty, pie **(b)** (Esp) (grande) pie

empanadilla *f* (Esp) tuna/meat pasty

empanar [A1], (Méx) **empanizar** [A4] *vt* to coat ... in breadcrumbs

empantanado -da *adj* ⟨camino/campo⟩ swampy

empantanarse [A1] *v pron* ⟨camino/campo⟩ to become swamped; ⟨coche⟩ to get bogged down

empañar [A1] *vt* ⟨vidrio/espejo⟩ to steam *o* mist up
■ **empañarse** *v pron* ⟨vidrio/espejo⟩ to steam *o* mist up

empapar [A1] *vt* **(a)** (embeber) ⟨esponja/toalla/galleta⟩ to soak **(b)** (mojar mucho) ⟨persona⟩ to soak, drench
■ **empaparse** *v pron* (mojarse mucho) ⟨persona/zapatos/ropa⟩ to get soaking wet

empapelar [A1] *vt* ⟨habitación/pared⟩ to wallpaper, paper

empaque *m* **1** (Col, Méx, Ven) (Tec) seal; (de llave de agua) washer **2** (Col) (acción de empaquetar) packing; (de regalo) wrapping

empaquetar [A1] *vt* (embalar) to pack

emparedado *m* sandwich

emparejar [A1] *vt* **1** ⟨personas⟩ to pair ... off; ⟨calcetines/zapatos⟩ to pair up **2** (nivelar) ⟨pelo⟩ to make ... even; ⟨dobladillo⟩ to even up; ⟨pared/suelo⟩ to level, make ... level; ⟨montones/pilas⟩ to make ... the same height

■ **emparejarse** *v pron* **(a)** (formar parejas) to pair off **(b)** (nivelarse) to level off, even up

emparentado -da *adj* [ESTAR] related; ∼ CON algn related TO sb

empastar [A1] *vt* ⟨diente/muela⟩ to fill

empaste *m* (Odont) filling; (Chi) (pasta) filler

empatar [A1] *vi* **1** **(a)** (durante un partido) to draw level, equalize; (como resultado) to tie, draw (BrE); ∼on a dos they tied two-two (AmE), it was a two-all draw (BrE); van empatados they're equal *o* level at the moment **(b)** (en una votación) to tie **2** (Col, Ven) ⟨listones/piezas⟩ to fit together
■ ∼ *vt* **(a)** (Ven) (amarrar) to tie *o* join ... together **(b)** (Col, Per, Ven) ⟨cables/tubos⟩ to connect
■ **empatarse** *v pron* (Ven) **(a)** (unirse) ⟨calles/líneas⟩ to join, meet (up); ⟨huesos⟩ to knit together **(b)** (fam) ⟨pareja⟩ to get together (colloq), to start going out together

empate *m* **1** **(a)** (en partido, certamen) tie (AmE), draw (BrE); terminó con ∼ a cero it finished in a scoreless tie (AmE) *o* (BrE) goalless draw; el gol del ∼ the equalizer *o* (AmE) the tying goal **(b)** (en una votación) tie **2** (Col, Per, Ven) (unión — en carpintería) joint; (— de tubos, cables) connection **3** (Ven fam) (novio) boyfriend; (novia) girlfriend

empecinado -da *adj* (esp AmL) (terco) stubborn; (determinado) determined

empecinarse [A1] *v pron* (obstinarse) to get an idea into one's head; (empeñarse) to persist

empedernido -da *adj* ⟨bebedor/fumador⟩ hardened, inveterate; ⟨jugador⟩ compulsive; ⟨solterón⟩ confirmed

empedrado *m* (de adoquines) paving; (de piedras irregulares) cobbled paving

empedrar [A5] *vt* to pave

empeine *m* instep

empellón *m* shove; se abrió paso a empellones she shoved her way through

empeñado -da *adj* **1** **(a)** (resuelto) determined; está ∼ en hacerlo he's determined to do it **(b)** (obstinado): está ∼ en que nos quedemos he's insistent that we should stay **2** (endeudado) in debt

empeñar [A1] *vt* **(a)** ⟨joyas/pertenencias⟩ to pawn, hock (colloq) **(b)** ⟨palabra⟩ to give
■ **empeñarse** *v pron* **1** (endeudarse) to get *o* go into debt **2** ∼se EN hacer algo (esforzarse) to strive to do sth (frml), to make an effort to do sth; (proponerse) to be determined to do sth; (obstinarse) to insist ON doing sth

empeño *m* **(a)** (afán) determination; (esfuerzo) effort; estudiar con ∼ to study hard; pondré todo mi ∼ I will do my best **(b)** (obstinación) ∼ EN algo insistence ON sth **(c)** (intento, empresa) undertaking, endeavor*

empeñoso -sa *adj* (AmL) hard-working

empeoramiento *m* (de la salud) deterioration, worsening; (del tiempo, de una situación) worsening

empeorar [A1] *vi* ⟨salud⟩ to deteriorate, get worse; ⟨tiempo/situación⟩ to get worse, worsen
■ ∼ *vt* to make ... worse

emperador *m* (soberano) emperor

emperatriz *f* empress

empezar [A6] *vi* **1** «*película/conferencia/invierno*» to begin, start; **empezó a nevar** it started to snow *o* snowing
2 «*persona*» to start; **volver a ∼** to start again; **todo es cuestión de ∼** it'll be fine once we/you get started; **no sé por dónde ∼** I don't know where to begin; **vamos a ∼ por ti** let's start with you; **∼ A hacer algo** to start doing sth, to start to do sth; **empezó diciendo que ...** she started *o* began by saying that ...; **empezó trabajando de mecánico** he started out as a mechanic; **empecemos por estudiar el contexto histórico** let's begin *o* start by looking at the historical context
3 **para empezar** first of all, to start with
■ **∼** *vt* **(a)** ⟨*tarea/actividad*⟩ to start **(b)** ⟨*frasco/mermelada*⟩ to start, open

empiece, empieza *etc* ▶ EMPEZAR
empinado -da *adj* ⟨*calle/pendiente*⟩ steep
empinar [A1] *vt* ⟨*bota/botella/vaso*⟩ to raise
■ **empinarse** *v pron* (de puntillas) to stand on tiptoe

emplasto *m* **(a)** (Farm, Med) dressing **(b)** (fam) (cosa blanda, pegajosa) sticky mess (colloq)
empleada *f* maid; **∼ de planta** (Méx) live-in maid; **∼ doméstica** *or* **de servicio** (frml) maid, domestic servant (frml); *ver tb* EMPLEADO
empleado -da *m,f* **(a)** (trabajador) employee; **una nómina de 300 ∼s** a staff of 300; **∼ público** civil servant **(b)** (en oficina) office *o* clerical worker; (en banco) bank clerk, teller; (en tienda) (AmL) clerk (AmE), shop assistant (BrE)
empleador -dora *m,f* employer
emplear [A1] *vt* **1** **(a)** «*empresa/organización*» to employ **(b)** (colocar) ⟨*hijo/sobrino*⟩ to fix ... up with a job **2** (usar) ⟨*energía/imaginación/material*⟩ to use
■ **emplearse** *v pron* (esp AmL) to get a job
empleo *m* **1** **(a)** (trabajo) employment; **la creación de ∼** job creation **(b)** (puesto) job; **está sin ∼** she's out of work **2** (uso) use; **⊙ modo de empleo** instructions for use
emplomadura *f* (RPl) filling
emplomar [A1] *vt* (RPl) to fill
empobrecer [E3] *vt* ⟨*población/tierra/lenguaje*⟩ to impoverish
■ **empobrecerse** *v pron* «*país/lenguaje/vocabulario*» to become impoverished
empobrecimiento *m* impoverishment
empollar [A1] *vi* **1** «*gallina*» to brood **2** (Esp fam) «*estudiante*» to cram (colloq), to swot (BrE colloq)
■ **∼** *vt* **1** ⟨*huevos*⟩ to hatch, sit on **2** (Esp fam) ⟨*lección*⟩ to cram (colloq), to swot up (on) (BrE colloq)
empollón -llona *m,f* (Esp fam & pey) grind (AmE colloq), swot (BrE colloq & pej)
empolvarse [A1] *v pron* (refl) ⟨*nariz/cara*⟩ to powder
empotrado -da *adj* built-in, fitted (before n)
empotrarse [A1] *v pron*: **el coche se empotró en el muro** the car crashed into the wall
emprendedor -dora *adj* enterprising
emprender [E1] *vt* (viaje) to embark on; ⟨*proyecto/aventura*⟩ to undertake; ⟨*ataque/ofensiva*⟩ to launch; **∼ la marcha** to set out; **∼ el regreso** to begin one's return journey

empresa *f* **1** (compañía) company, firm (BrE); **∼ pública** public sector company **2** (tarea, labor) venture, undertaking
empresario -ria *m,f* **(a)** (Com, Fin) (*m*) businessman; (*f*) businesswoman; **∼ de pompas fúnebres** undertaker **(b)** (Teatr) impresario **(c)** (en boxeo) promoter
empujar [A1] *vt* **(a)** ⟨*coche/columpio*⟩ to push; **¡empújame!** give me a push! **(b)** (incitar, presionar) to spur ... on; (obligar) to force **(c)** (Tec) to drive
■ **∼** *vi* **(a)** (hacer presión) to push **(b)** (dar empellones) to push, shove
empuje *m* (dinamismo) drive
empujón *m* **(a)** (empellón) shove, push; **abrió la puerta de un ∼** he pushed the door open; **abrirse paso a (los) empujones** to shove one's way through **(b)** (fam) (para animar, incitar) prod (colloq); **voy a darle un ∼ al asunto** I'm going to push things along a bit (colloq)
empuñadura *f* (de espada) hilt; (de daga, navaja) handle; (de bastón, paraguas) handle
empuñar [A1] *vt* ⟨*arma/espada*⟩ to take up; ⟨*bastón/palo*⟩ to brandish

en *prep* **1** (en expresiones de lugar) **(a)** (refiriéndose a ciudad, edificio): **viven ∼ París/∼ el número diez/∼ un hotel** they live in Paris/at number ten/in a hotel; **∼ el último piso** on the top floor; **está ∼ la calle Goya** it's on *o* (BrE) in Goya Street; **∼ casa** at home **(b)** (dentro de) in; **∼ una caja** in a box **(c)** (sobre) on; **∼ una silla** on a chair; **se le nota ∼ la cara** you can see it in his face
2 (expresando circunstancias, ambiente) in; **∼ peligro** in danger
3 **(a)** (indicando tema, especialidad): **un experto ∼ la materia** an expert on the subject; **doctor ∼ derecho** Doctor of Law **(b)** (indicando proporción, precio): **∼ un diez por ciento** by ten per cent; **∼ dólares** in dollars
4 **(a)** (indicando estado, manera) in; **∼ malas condiciones** in bad condition; **∼ llamas** in flames, on fire **(b)** (en forma de): **termina ∼ punta** it's pointed; **colóquense ∼ círculo** get into *o* in a circle **(c)** (con medios de transporte) by; **ir ∼ taxi** to go by taxi; **fueron ∼ bicicleta** they cycled, they went on their bikes; **dimos una vuelta ∼ coche** we went for a ride in the car
5 **(a)** (indicando el material): **∼ seda natural** in natural silk; **una escultura ∼ bronce** a bronze (sculpture) **(b)** (indicando el modo de presentación *o* expresión) in; **∼ azul/ruso** in blue/Russian
6 (con expresiones de tiempo): **∼ verano** in (the) summer; **∼ varias ocasiones** on several occasions; **∼ la mañana/noche** (esp AmL) in the morning/at night
7 **(a)** (seguido de construcción verbal): **no hay nada de malo ∼ lo que hacen** there's nothing wrong in what they're doing; **fui el último ∼ salir** I was the last to leave **(b)** (con complementos de persona) in; **no sé qué ve ∼ ella** I don't know what he sees in her

enagua *f*, **enaguas** *fpl* **(a)** (prenda interior) petticoat, underskirt **(b)** (AmC) (falda) skirt
enamorado -da *adj* [ESTAR] in love; **∼ DE algn** in love WITH sb; **están muy ∼s** they are very much in love
■ *m,f* lover; **una pareja de ∼s** two lovers; **vino con su ∼** (Bol, Per) she came with her boyfriend; **es un ∼ de su profesión** he loves his work

enamoramiento *m* infatuation

enamorar [A1] *vt* to make ... fall in love, get ... to fall in love

■ **enamorarse** *v pron* to fall in love; ~**se DE algo/algn** to fall in love WITH sth/sb

enano -na *m,f* (de proporciones normales) midget; (de cabeza más grande) dwarf; (en los cuentos) dwarf
■ *adj* ‹especie/planta› dwarf (*before n*); ‹ración› (fam) minute, tiny

encabezado *m* (Chi, Méx) headline

encabezamiento *m* (a) (en carta — saludo) opening; (— dirección, fecha) heading (b) (en ficha, documento) heading

encabezar [A4] *vt* 1 ‹artículo/escrito› to head 2 (a) ‹liga/clasificación/lista› to head, be at the top of; ‹carrera/movimiento/revolución› to lead (b) ‹delegación/comité› to head, lead

encabritarse [A1] *v pron* «caballo» to rear up

encachado -da *adj* (Chi fam) (a) (bonito) ‹ropa/lugar› lovely, nice; ‹persona› attractive (b) (arreglado) well-dressed (c) (entretenido) ‹historia› entertaining

encadenar [A1] *vt* ‹prisionero/bicicleta› to chain (up)

encajar [A1] *vt* 1 (meter, colocar) to fit 2 (esp AmL fam) (endilgar): **me ~on a mí el trabajito** I got saddled with the job (colloq); **le encaja los hijos a la suegra** she dumps the kids on her mother-in-law (colloq); **les ~on tres goles** they put three goals past them
■ ~ *vi* (a) «pieza/cajón» to fit; **no encaja bien** it doesn't fit properly; **las piezas ~on** the pieces fitted together (b) (corresponder, cuadrar) «hechos/descripción» to fit; **no encaja con la decoración** it doesn't fit in with the decor

encaje *m* (Indum) lace; **pañuelo de ~** lace handkerchief

encajonar [A1] *vt* (en lugar estrecho) ~ **algo/a algn EN algo** to cram *o* pack sth/sb INTO sth; **me ~on el coche** my car *o* I got boxed in

encalar [A1] *vt* to whitewash

encalillarse [A1] *v pron* (Chi fam) to get into debt

encallar [A1] *vi* to run aground

encallecido -da *adj* ‹manos› callused

encamar [A1] *vt* (Méx) to confine ... to bed

encaminado -da *adj*: **el proyecto va bien ~** the project is shaping up well *o* is going well; **iba bien ~** he was on the right track; **medidas encaminadas a reducir ...** measures designed to reduce *o* aimed at reducing ...

encaminar [A1] *vt* (a) ‹intereses/esfuerzos› to direct, channel (b) ‹estudiante/niño› to point ... in the right direction
■ **encaminarse** *v pron* (liter) ~**se HACIA algo** (a) «persona» (dirigirse a) to head FOR/TOWARD(s) sth; (emprender el camino) to set off FOR/TOWARD(s) sth (b) «esfuerzos» to be aimed AT sth, be directed TOWARD(s) sth

encandilar [A1] *vt* (a) «luz» to dazzle (b) (asombrar, pasmar) to dazzle

encanecer [E3] *vi* to (go) gray*

encantado -da *adj* 1 (a) (muy contento) delighted; **estoy ~ de haber venido** I am delighted *o* very glad that I came (b) (en fórmulas de cortesía): ~ **de conocerla** pleased to meet you; **le presento al Señor Ruiz — encantado** let me introduce you to Mr Ruiz — how do you do; ~ **de poder ayudarte** I'm glad to be/to have been of help 2 ‹bosque/castillo› enchanted

encantador -dora *adj* ‹persona/lugar› charming, delightful
■ *m,f* magician; ~ **de serpientes** snake charmer

encantar [A1] *vi* (+ *me/te/le etc*): **me encantó la obra** I loved *o* I really enjoyed the play; **me ~ía que me acompañaras** I'd love you to come with me
■ ~ *vt* to cast *o* put a spell on, bewitch

encanto *m* 1 (a) (atractivo) charm; **sabe utilizar sus ~s** she knows how to use her charms; **su sencillez es su mayor ~** its most appealing feature is its simplicity (b) (fam) (maravilla): **¡qué ~ de hombre!** what a lovely *o* charming man!; **tienen un jardín que es un ~** they have a lovely garden 2 (a) (hechizo) spell; **como por ~** as if by magic (b) (Ven fam) (fantasma) ghost

encapotado -da *adj* overcast, cloudy

encapricharse [A1] *v pron*: **se ha encaprichado con esa moto** he's really taken a liking *o* (BrE) a fancy to that motorbike; ~ **CON** *o* (Esp) **DE algn** to fall for sb (colloq)

encarado -da *adj* (Esp, Méx): **mal ~** (enojado) bad-tempered; (de mal aspecto) nasty-looking

encaramarse [A1] *v pron* ‹a árbol/valla› to climb up; ‹a taburete› to climb on to

encarar [A1] *vt* 1 (enfocar) ‹tarea› to approach; (afrontar) ‹desgracia/problema› to face up to; ‹futuro› to face 2 (AmL) ‹persona› to stand up to
■ **encararse** *v pron* ~**se CON algn** to face up to *o* stand up to sb

encarcelar [A1] *vt* to imprison, jail

encarecer [E3] *vt* (hacer más caro): **el envase encarece el producto** the container makes the product more expensive; ~**á los alquileres** it will push rents up
■ **encarecerse** *v pron* «precios» to increase, rise; «productos/vida» to become more expensive

encargado -da *adj* ~ **DE algo/hacer algo** responsible FOR sth/doing sth, in charge OF sth/doing sth
■ *m,f* (a) (de negocio) manager, person in charge (b) (de tarea): **tú serás el ~ de avisarles** it will be your responsibility to tell them

encargar [A3] *vt* 1 (a) ~**le algo A algn** ‹tarea› to entrust sb WITH sth; **me encargó una botella de whisky escocés** she asked me to buy *o* get her a bottle of Scotch (b) ~ **a algn QUE haga algo** to ask sb to do sth 2 ‹mueble/paella/libro› to order; ‹informe/cuadro› to commission
■ **encargarse** *v pron* ~**se DE algo/algn** to take care OF sth/sb; **me tuve que ~ del asunto** I had to take charge of the matter

encargo *m* (a) (recado, pedido): **¿te puedo hacer unos ~s?** could you buy *o* get a few things for me?; **mi hijo está haciendo un ~** my son is out on *o* is running an errand (b) (Com) order; **los hacemos por ~** we make them to order (c) (cargo, misión) job, assignment

encariñarse [A1] *v pron* ∼ CON algo/algn to grow fond of sth/sb

encarnación *f* incarnation

encarnado -da *adj* **1** ⟨*color/vestido*⟩ red **2** ⟨*uña*⟩ ingrowing

encarnarse [A1] *v pron* (a) (Relig) to become incarnate (b) «*uña*» to become ingrown

encarrilar [A1] *vt* ⟨*trabajo/asunto*⟩ to direct; ⟨*persona*⟩ to guide, give guidance to

encasillar [A1] *vt* to class, categorize, pigeonhole

encauzar [A4] *vt* to channel; ∼ algo HACIA algo to channel sth INTO sth

encefalograma *m* encephalogram

enceguecedor -dora *adj* (AmL) blinding

enceguecer [E3] *vt* (AmL) to blind
■ ∼ *vi* (AmL) (por la luz) to be blinded; (de ira) to become furious

encendedor *m* lighter

encender [E8] *vt* (a) ⟨*cigarrillo/hoguera/vela*⟩ to light; ⟨*fósforo*⟩ to strike, light (b) ⟨*luz/calefacción*⟩ to switch on, turn on; ⟨*motor*⟩ to start; **no dejes el televisor encendido** don't leave the television on
■ ∼ *vi* ⟨*fósforo*⟩ to light; «*leña*» to catch light; «*luz/radio*» to come on
■ **encenderse** *v pron* «*aparato/luz*» to come on; «*fósforo/piloto*» to light; «*leña*» to catch light

encendido *m* ignition

enceradora *f* polisher

encerar [A1] *vt* to polish, wax

encerrado -da *adj*: **está ∼ en su habitación** he's shut away *o* shut up in his room; **se quedó ∼ en el cuarto de baño** he got locked in the bathroom; **siguen ∼s en la universidad** they are still occupying the university; **oler a ∼** (AmL) to be stuffy

encerrar [A5] *vt* **1** ⟨*ganado*⟩ to shut up, pen; ⟨*perro*⟩ to shut ... in; ⟨*persona*⟩ (en cárcel, calabozo) to lock up; **me encerró en mi habitación** he shut me *o* locked me in my room; **me dejaron encerrada en la oficina** I got locked in the office **2** (conllevar) ⟨*peligro/riesgo*⟩ to involve, entail
■ **encerrarse** *v pron* (refl) (en habitación) to shut oneself in; (en fábrica, universidad) «*obreros/estudiantes*» to lock oneself in

encerrona *f* (trampa) trap

encestar [A1] *vi* to score (a basket)

enchapar [A1] *vt* (de metal) to plate; (de madera) to veneer

encharcarse [A2] *v pron* «*terreno/zona*» to become waterlogged *o* flooded; «*agua*» to form a pool/pools

enchastrar [A1] *vt* (RPI fam) ⟨*ropa/cocina*⟩ to make a mess of
■ **enchastrarse** *v pron* (RPI fam) to get dirty

enchastre *m* (RPI fam) mess

enchilada *f* enchilada (*tortilla with a meat or cheese filling, served with a tomato and chili sauce*)

enchilado¹ -da *adj* (Méx) (Coc) seasoned with chili

enchilado² *m* stew (*with chili*)

enchilar [A1] *vt* (Méx) (Coc) to add chili to
■ **enchilarse** *v pron* (Méx) (comiendo): **ya me enchilé** my mouth's burning; **con este plato me enchilo** this dish is too hot for me

enchinar [A1] *vt* (Méx) to perm
■ **enchinarse** *v pron* (Méx): **se me enchina la piel** I come out in goose bumps *o* goose pimples

enchuecar [A2] *vt* (AmL fam) ⟨*metal*⟩ to bend; ⟨*madera/lámina*⟩ to warp; ⟨*cara/boca*⟩ to twist; ⟨*cuadro*⟩ to tilt
■ **enchuecarse** *v pron* (Chi fam) «*metal*» to bend, get bent; «*madera/lámina*» to warp; «*cara/boca*» to become twisted

enchufado -da *adj* (fam): **está ∼** he knows all the right people; **estar ∼ con ...** to be well in with ... (colloq)

enchufar [A1] *vt* **1** (fam) ⟨*radio/televisión*⟩ to plug in **2** (fam) ⟨*persona*⟩: **me enchufó en la empresa** he set me up with a job in the company (colloq)

enchufe *m* **1** (a) (Elec) (macho) plug; (hembra) socket, power point (BrE) (b) (del teléfono) socket, point (BrE) **2** (Esp fam) (influencia): **necesitas algún ∼** you need to have connections; **por ∼** by pulling some strings

encía *f* gum

enciclopedia *f* encyclopedia

encienda, enciendas, etc ▶ ENCENDER

encierra, encierras, etc ▶ ENCERRAR

encierro *m* (a) (en fábrica, universidad) sit-in (b) (reclusión): **salió de su ∼ después de ocho meses** she emerged after being holed up for eight months (c) (Taur) (conducción) *running of bulls through the streets*; (toros) *bulls to be used in a bullfight*

encima *adv* **1** (en el espacio): **le puso una piedra ∼** he put a stone on it; **no llevo dinero ∼** I don't have any money on me; **se tiró el café ∼** she spilled the coffee over herself; **se me vino el armario ∼** the cupboard came down on top of me **2** (además): **¡y ∼ se queja!** and then she goes and complains!; **y ∼ no me lo devolvió** and on top of that, he didn't give it back! **3** (en locs) **encima de:** **∼ de la mesa** on the table; **∼ del armario** on top of the cupboard; **llevaba un chal ∼ de la chaqueta** she wore a shawl over her jacket; **viven ∼ de la tienda** they live over *o* above the shop; **∼ de caro es feo** not only is it expensive, it's also ugly; **por encima** over; **saltó por ∼** he jumped over; **le eché un vistazo por ∼** I just looked over it quickly; **una limpieza por ∼** a quick clean; **por encima de** above; **por ∼ de la media** above average; **por ∼ de todo** above everything; **volaban por ∼ de las nubes/del pueblo** they flew above the clouds/over the town; **está por ∼ del jefe de sección** she's above the head of department; **quitarse algo de ∼** ⟨*problema/tarea*⟩ to get sth out of the way; **quitarse a algn de ∼** to get rid of sb

AmC	América Central	Arg	Argentina	Cu	Cuba
AmL	América Latina	Bol	Bolivia	Ec	Ecuador
AmS	América del Sur	Chi	Chile	Esp	España
Andes	Región andina	CS	Cono Sur	Méx	México

Per	Perú
RPI	Río de la Plata
Ur	Uruguay
Ven	Venezuela

encimar [A1] vt (a) (Col) (regalar): **me encimó dos más** she gave me two extra (b) (Méx, RPl) ⟨cajas/libros⟩ to stack up

encina f holm oak, ilex

encinta adj ▶ EMBARAZADA

enclenque adj (a) ⟨persona⟩ (enfermizo) sickly; (delgado) weak, weedy (colloq) (b) ⟨estructura⟩ rickety

encoger [E6] vi to shrink
■ ~ vt (a) ⟨ropa⟩ to shrink (b) ⟨piernas⟩ to tuck ... in; **encogió el cuerpo de miedo** he shrank back in fear
■ **encogerse** v pron ① ⟨ropa/tela⟩ to shrink ② «persona» (a) (físicamente): **~se de hombros** to shrug one's shoulders; **caminar encogido** to walk with one's shoulders hunched (b) (por la edad) to shrink, get shorter (c) (acobardarse) to be intimidated

encomendería f (Per) grocery store (AmE), grocer's shop (BrE)

encomendero m (Per) (tendero) grocer

encomienda f (AmL) (Corresp) package (AmE), parcel (BrE)

encontrar [A10] vt ① (a) (buscando) ⟨casa/trabajo/persona⟩ to find; **no encontré entradas para el teatro** I couldn't get tickets for the theater; **no le encuentro lógica** I can't see the logic in it (b) (casualmente) ⟨cartera/billete⟩ to find, come across (c) (descubrir) ⟨falta/error⟩ to find, spot; ⟨cáncer/quiste⟩ to find, discover (d) ⟨obstáculo/dificultad⟩ to meet (with), encounter ② (+ compl): **te encuentro muy cambiado** you look very different; **lo encuentro ridículo** I find it ridiculous; **¿cómo encontraste el país?** how did the country seem to you?
■ **encontrarse** v pron ① (por casualidad) **~se con algn** to meet sb, bump INTO sb (colloq) ② (recipr) (a) (reunirse) to meet; (por casualidad) to meet, bump into each other (colloq) (b) ⟨carreteras/líneas⟩ to meet ③ (enf) (inesperadamente) ⟨billete/cartera⟩ to find, come across; **me encontré con que todos se habían ido** I found they had all gone ④ (frml) (estar) to be; **me encuentro mejor** I am feeling better; **el hotel se encuentra cerca de la estación** the hotel is (located) near the station

encorvado -da adj: **anda ~** he walks with a stoop

encorvarse [A1] v pron to develop a stoop

encrespar [A1] vt ⟨pelo⟩ to make ... go curly; ⟨mar⟩ to make ... rough o choppy
■ **encresparse** v pron ⟨pelo⟩ to curl, go curly; «mar» to get rough o choppy

encrucijada f crossroads

encuadernación f (a) (cubierta) binding (b) (acción) book binding

encuadernador -dora m,f bookbinder

encuadernar [A1] vt to bind

encuadrar [A1] vt (a) (clasificar) to class, classify (b) (Cin, Fot, TV) to frame, center*

encubrir [I33] vt (a) ⟨delincuente⟩ to harbor* (b) ⟨delito⟩ to cover up; **siempre lo está encubriendo** she's always covering up for him (c) ⟨temor/verdad/problema⟩ to mask

encuclillarse [A1] v pron to squat (down)

encuentra, encuentras, etc ▶ ENCONTRAR

encuentro m (a) (acción) meeting, encounter; **una secretaria le salió al ~** he was met by a secretary (b) (Dep) (period) game

encuerarse [A1] v pron (refl) (AmL fam) (desnudarse) to strip off (colloq), get undressed; (en el escenario) to strip

encuesta f (a) (sondeo) survey; **~ de opinión** opinion poll (b) (investigación) inquiry

encuestado -da m,f: **el 50% de los ~s** 50% of those polled

encumbrar [A1] vt (Chi) ⟨volantín⟩ to fly

endeble adj weak; ⟨salud⟩ delicate, poor

endemoniado -da adj (a) (inaguantable) ⟨niño/asunto⟩ wretched (before n); ⟨genio/humor⟩ foul, wicked (b) (poseído del demonio) possessed (by the devil)

enderezar [A4] vt (a) (destorcer) ⟨clavo⟩ to straighten (b) (poner vertical) ⟨poste/espalda⟩ to straighten; ⟨planta⟩ to stake; ⟨barco⟩ to right (c) ⟨persona⟩ to straighten ... out
■ **enderezarse** v pron (ponerse derecho) «persona» to stand up straight, straighten up; ⟨árbol⟩ to straighten up

endeudado -da adj in debt; **~ CON algn** indebted TO sb

endeudarse [A1] v pron to get (oneself) into debt; **~ CON algn** to get into debt WITH sb

endiablado -da adj (a) (malo) ⟨carácter/genio⟩ terrible; **¡este ~ niño!** this wretched child! (b) (peligroso) ⟨velocidad⟩ reckless, dangerous

endibia f endive, chicory (BrE)

endilgar [A3] vt (fam): **nos endilgó un sermón** he lectured us; **me ~on el trabajito** I got saddled o landed with the job (colloq); **me endilgó a los niños** she dumped the kids on me (colloq)

endivia f endive, chicory (BrE)

endrogarse [A3] v pron (Méx) to get into debt

endulzar [A4] vt (a) ⟨café⟩ to sweeten (b) ⟨tono/respuesta⟩ to soften; ⟨vida/vejez⟩ to brighten up; ⟨carácter⟩ to mellow

endurecer [E3] vt ① (en general) to harden ② ⟨persona/carácter⟩ (volver insensible) to harden; (fortalecer) to toughen ... up; **ese corte te endurece las facciones** that haircut makes you look harsher
■ **endurecerse** v pron (a) (en general) to harden; «pan» to go stale (b) «persona/carácter» (volverse insensible) to harden; (fortalecerse) to toughen up (c) «facciones» to become harder o harsher

ene f. name of the letter n

eneldo m dill

enemigo -ga adj (a) ⟨tropas/soldados/país⟩ enemy (before n) (b) **ser ~ DE algo** to be against sth; **era enemiga de pegarles a los niños** she was against hitting children
■ m,f enemy

enemistad f enmity

enemistado -da adj: **están ~s** they're at odds (with each other); **quedó ~ con ellos** she fell out with them

enemistar [A1] vt ⟨dos facciones/países⟩ to make enemies of; **~ un país con otro** to turn one country against the other; **ella los enemistó** she turned them against each other ⋯

■ **enemistarse** *v pron* to fall out; ∼**se CON algn**
(POR **algo**) to fall out WITH sb (OVER sth)

energético -ca *adj* ⟨*crisis/política/recursos*⟩
energy (*before n*); ⟨*alimento*⟩ energy-giving, fuel
(*before n*) (AmE)

energía *f* [1] (Fís) energy; ∼ **nuclear/solar**
nuclear/solar power [2] (a) (vigor, empuje) energy;
protestar con ∼ to protest vigorously; **está lleno
de** ∼ he's very energetic (b) (firmeza) firmness

enérgico -ca *adj* (a) (físicamente) energetic (b)
(firme, resuelto) ⟨*carácter*⟩ forceful; ⟨*protesta/
ataque*⟩ vigorous; ⟨*medidas*⟩ firm, strong;
⟨*negativa/rechazo*⟩ flat, firm

enero *m* January; **a principios de** ∼ at the
beginning of January; **a mediados de** ∼ in the
middle of January, in mid-January; **el tres de** ∼
the third of January, January the third, January
third (AmE); **en** (**el mes de**) ∼ in (the month of)
January; **Lima, 8 de** ∼ **de 1987** (Corresp) Lima,
January 8 o January 8th, 1987

enfadado -da *adj* (esp Esp) angry; (en menor
grado) annoyed; **están** ∼**s** they've fallen out; **está**
∼ **contigo** he's angry/annoyed with you

enfadar [A1] *vt* (esp Esp) (enojar) to anger, make
... angry; (en menor grado) to annoy
■ **enfadarse** *v pron* (esp Esp) (a) (enojarse) to get
angry, get mad (esp AmE colloq); (en menor grado) to
get annoyed, get cross (BrE colloq); ∼**se CON algn**
to get angry/annoyed WITH sb (b) «*novios*» to
fall out

enfado *m* (esp Esp) anger; (menos serio)
annoyance

énfasis *m* emphasis; **poner** ∼ **en algo** to stress
o emphasize sth

enfático -ca *adj* emphatic

enfatizar [A4] *vt* to emphasize, stress

enfermar [A1] *vi* to fall ill, get sick (AmE)
■ **enfermarse** *v pron* (a) (esp AmL) (caer enfermo)
to fall ill, get sick (AmE); ∼**se del estómago** to
develop stomach trouble (b) (CS euf) (menstruar) to
get one's period

enfermedad *f* illness; **contraer una** ∼ to
contract an illness/a disease (frml); **después de
una larga** ∼ after a long illness; **está con permiso
por** ∼ he's off sick; ∼**es de la piel** skin diseases;
∼ **mental** mental illness; ∼ **nerviosa** nervous
disorder

enfermería *f* [1] (sala) infirmary, sickbay
[2] (carrera) nursing

enfermero -ra *m,f* nurse; ∼ **jefe** ≈ head nurse
(AmE), ≈ charge nurse (BrE)

enfermizo -za *adj* unhealthy, sickly; **de
aspecto** ∼ unhealthy-looking

enfermo -ma *adj* (a) (Med) ill, sick;
gravemente ∼ seriously ill; **está** ∼ **del corazón**
he has heart trouble; **está enferma de los nervios**
she suffers with her nerves; **se puso** ∼ he fell *o*
got ill, he got sick (AmE); **poner** ∼ **a algn** (fam) to
get on sb's nerves (colloq), to get sb (colloq) (b) (CS
euf) (con la menstruación): **estoy enferma** I've got my
period, it's the time of the month (euph)
■ *m,f* (en hospital) patient; **quiere cuidar** ∼**s** she
wants to care for sick people *o* the sick; ∼**s del
corazón** people with heart trouble; ∼**s de cáncer**
cancer sufferers

enfocar [A2] *vt* [1] ⟨*objeto/persona*⟩ (con cámara,
prismáticos) to focus on; **los** ∼**on con la linterna**

they shone the torch on them [2] (a) (Fot, Ópt)
⟨*telescopio/cámara*⟩ to focus (b) ⟨*tema/asunto*⟩ to
approach, look at

enfoque *m* (a) (Fot, Ópt) (acción) focusing*;
(efecto) focus (b) (de asunto) approach; **todo
depende del** ∼ **que se le dé** everything depends
on the way you look at it; ∼ DE **algo** approach TO
sth

enfrentamiento *m* clash; ∼ **bélico** military
confrontation

enfrentar [A1] *vt* [1] ⟨*problema/peligro/
realidad*⟩ to confront, face up to; ⟨*futuro*⟩ to face
[2] (a) ⟨*contrincantes/opositores*⟩ to bring ... face
to face (b) (enemistar) to bring ... into conflict
■ **enfrentarse** *v pron* (a) (hacer frente a) ∼**se CON
algn** ⟨*con rival/enemigo*⟩ to confront sb; ∼**se A
algo** ⟨*a dificultades/peligros*⟩ to face sth; ⟨*a
realidad/responsabilidad*⟩ to face up to sth (b)
(recípr) ⟨*equipos/atletas*⟩ to meet; «*tropas/
oponentes*» to clash

enfrente *adv* [1] (al otro lado de una calle, etc)
opposite; ∼ **de mi/del parque** opposite me/the
park [2] (delante) in front; ∼ DE **algo** in front of
sth

enfriamiento *m* (a) (catarro) chill (b) (de amor,
entusiasmo, relaciones) cooling (off)

enfriar [A17] *vt* (a) ⟨*alimento*⟩ to cool; (en el
refrigerador) to chill, cool (b) ⟨*entusiasmo/relación*⟩
to cool, cause ... to cool
■ ∼ *vi*: **no dejes** ∼ **el café** don't let your coffee go
o get cold; **deja** ∼ **el motor** let the engine cool
down; **ponla a** ∼ put it in the refrigerator to chill
■ **enfriarse** *v pron* [1] (a) «*comida/bebida*»
(ponerse — demasiado frío) to get cold, go cold; (—
suficientemente frío) to cool down (b) «*manos*» to
get cold (c) «*entusiasmo/relaciones*» to cool (off)
[2] (tomar frío) to catch *o* get cold; (resfriarse) to
catch a cold, catch a chill

enfurecer [E3] *vt* to infuriate, make ... furious
■ **enfurecerse** *v pron* to fly into a rage, get
furious

enfurecido -da *adj* [ESTAR] ⟨*persona*⟩ furious

enfurruñarse [A1] *v pron* (fam) to go into a
sulk (colloq), to get into a huff (colloq)

enganchar [A1] *vt* (a) ⟨*cable/cadena*⟩ to hook
(b) ⟨*remolque*⟩ to hitch up, attach; ⟨*caballos*⟩ to
harness; ⟨*vagón*⟩ to couple, attach (c) ⟨*pez*⟩ to
hook
■ **engancharse** *v pron* (a) (quedar prendido) to get
caught; **se me enganchó la media en el clavo** my
tights got caught on the nail (b) (fam) (hacerse
adicto) ∼**se** (A **algo**) to get hooked (ON sth)

enganche *m* [1] (pieza, mecanismo) (Auto) towing
hook; (Ferr) coupling [2] (Esp) (de la luz, del teléfono)
connection [3] (Méx) (Fin) down payment

engañar [A1] *vt* (a) (hacer errar en el juicio) to
deceive, mislead; **me engañó la vista** my eyes
deceived me; **tú a mí no me engañas** you can't
fool me; **lo engañó haciéndole creer que** ... she
deceived him into thinking that ...; ∼ **a algn
PARA QUE haga algo** to trick sb INTO doing sth
(b) (estafar, timar) to cheat, con (colloq) (c) (ser infiel
a) to be unfaithful to, cheat on
■ **engañarse** *v pron* (refl) (mentirse) to deceive
oneself, kid oneself (colloq)

engaño *m* (a) (mentira) deception (b) (timo,
estafa) swindle, con (colloq) (c) (ardid) ploy, trick

165

engañoso -sa adj ‹palabras› deceitful; ‹apariencias› deceptive

engarce m setting

engarzar [A4] vt ① ‹piedra/brillante› to set ② (Col, Ven) (enganchar) to hook
■ **engarzarse** v pron (Col) (engancharse) to get caught

engatusar [A1] vt to sweet-talk; ~ **a algn PARA QUE haga algo** to sweet-talk sb INTO doing sth

engendrar [A1] vt ‹hijos› to father; ‹odio/ sospecha› to breed, engender (frml)

engendro m (a) (feto) fetus* **(b)** (criatura malformada) malformed creature **(c)** (creación monstruosa) freak, monster

engentado -da adj (Méx) dazed, confused

engomado -da adj ‹etiqueta› gummed, self-adhesive; ‹sobre› gummed, self-sealing

engordar [A1] vt (a) (aumentar) to put on, gain **(b)** (cebar) to fatten (up) **(c)** ‹cifras/estadísticas› to swell
■ ~ vi (a) «persona» to put on o gain weight; «animales» to fatten **(b)** «alimentos» to be fattening

engorroso -sa adj ‹problema› complicated, thorny; ‹situación› awkward, difficult; ‹asunto› trying, tiresome

engranaje m ① (Mec) gear assembly (o mechanism etc), gears (pl); **el ~ del reloj** the cogs of the watch ② (de partido, sociedad) machinery

engrandecer [E3] vt (ennoblecer) to ennoble (frml)

engrapadora f (AmL) stapler

engrapar [A1] vt (AmL) to staple

engrasado m lubrication, greasing

engrasar [A1] vt (a) (Auto, Mec) (con grasa) to grease, lubricate; (con aceite) to oil, lubricate **(b)** (Coc) ‹molde› to grease

engreído -da adj (a) (vanidoso) conceited, bigheaded (colloq) **(b)** (Per) (mimado) spoiled*
■ m,f **(a)** (vanidoso) bighead (colloq) **(b)** (Per) (mimado) spoiled brat

engrupir [I1] vt (CS fam) to fool (colloq)

engullir [I9] vt to bolt (down)

enhebrar [A1] vt ‹aguja› to thread; ‹perlas› to string

enhorabuena f congratulations (pl); **darle la ~ a algn** to congratulate sb
■ interj congratulations!

enigma m enigma, mystery

enigmático -ca adj enigmatic, mysterious

enjabonar [A1] vt to soap
■ **enjabonarse** v pron (refl) to soap oneself; ~**se las manos** to soap one's hands

enjambre m (Zool) swarm

enjaular [A1] vt ‹pájaro/fiera› to cage, put ... in a cage

enjuagar [A3] vt ‹boca/ropa/vajilla› to rinse; ‹palangana/cubo› to swill out
■ **enjuagarse** v pron (refl) to wash off the soap; ~**se el pelo** to rinse one's hair

enjuague m (a) (acción de enjuagar) rinse **(b)** (AmL) (para el pelo) conditioner **(c)** ~ **bucal** mouthwash

enjugar [A3] vt (liter) ‹lágrimas/sudor› to wipe away

■ **enjugarse** v pron (refl) (liter) ‹lágrimas› to wipe away; ‹frente› to mop, wipe

enlace m (a) (conexión, unión) link **(b)** (de vías, carreteras) intersection, junction **(c)** tb ~ **matrimonial** marriage **(d)** (persona) liaison; ~ **sindical** (Esp) shop steward, union rep

enlatado¹ -da adj ‹alimentos› canned, tinned (BrE) **(b)** ‹música/programa› canned **(c)** (Inf) ‹programa› stored

enlatado² m ① (proceso) canning ② (AmL pey) (TV) poor-quality program

enlazar [A4] vt ① (a) ‹ciudades› to link (up); ‹ideas/temas› to link, connect **(b)** ‹cintas› to tie ... together ② (Col, RPl) ‹res/caballo› to lasso, rope (AmE) ③ (Méx frml) (casar) to marry
■ ~ vi ~ **CON algo** ‹tren/vuelo› to connect WITH sth; «carretera» to link up WITH sth

enlistarse [A1] v pron (AmC, Col, Ven) to enlist, join up

enloquecedor -dora adj ‹dolor› excruciating; **el ruido era** ~ the noise was enough to drive you crazy

enloquecer [E3] vt to drive ... crazy o mad
■ ~ vi (perder el juicio) to go crazy o mad; **enloqueció de celos** he was driven crazy o insane with jealousy

enlozado -da adj (AmL) ‹cacerola› enameled*; ‹fuente› glazed

enmarañado -da adj (a) ‹pelo/lana› tangled **(b)** (complicado, confuso) complicated, involved

enmarcar [A2] vt ‹lámina/foto› to frame

enmascarado -da adj masked
■ m,f (m) masked man; (f) masked woman

enmendar [A5] vt ‹conducta› to improve, amend (frml); ‹actitud› to change; ‹error› to amend, rectify
■ **enmendarse** v pron (refl) to mend one's ways

enmienda f amendment

enmohecer [E3] vt ‹ropa› to make ... moldy*; ‹metal› to rust
■ **enmohecerse** v pron «ropa/pan/queso» to become moldy*; «metal» to rust, become rusty

enmoquetar [A1] vt (Esp) to carpet

enmudecer [E3] vi to fall silent

ennegrecer [E3] vt (poner negro) to blacken; (oscurecer) to darken
■ **ennegrecerse** v pron (a) (ponerse negro) to go black **(b)** (ponerse oscuro) «cielo/nubes» to darken, go dark; «plata» to tarnish

enojadizo -za adj (esp AmL) irritable, touchy

enojado -da adj (esp AmL) angry, mad (esp AmE colloq); (en menor grado) annoyed, cross (BrE colloq); **está** ~ **contigo** he's angry/annoyed with you; **están** ~**s** they've fallen out

enojar [A1] vt (esp AmL) to make ... angry; (en menor grado) to annoy
■ **enojarse** v pron (esp AmL) to get angry, get mad (esp AmE colloq); (en menor grado) to get annoyed, get cross (BrE colloq); ~**se CON algn** to get angry/annoyed WITH sb

enojo m (esp AmL) anger; (menos serio) annoyance; **¿ya se te pasó el** ~? are you still angry/annoyed?

enojón -jona adj (Chi, Méx fam) irritable, touchy

enojoso -sa *adj* (esp AmL) (violento) awkward; (aburrido) tedious, tiresome

enorgullecer [E3] *vt*: **mi hijo me enorgullece** I am proud of my son

■ **enorgullecerse** *v pron* to be proud; **no es para ∼se** it's nothing to be proud of; **∼se DE algo** to take pride IN sth

enorme *adj* ⟨edificio/animal/suma⟩ huge, enormous; ⟨zona⟩ vast, huge; **sentí una pena ∼** I felt tremendously sad

enraizado -da *adj* ⟨prejuicio⟩ deep-seated, deep-rooted; ⟨tradición⟩ deeply rooted

enrarecido -da *adj* ⟨atmósfera/aire⟩ rarefied (b) ⟨ambiente/relaciones⟩ strained, tense

enredadera *f* creeper, climbing plant

enredado -da *adj* [1] ⟨lana/cuerda⟩ tangled; ⟨pelo⟩ tangled, knotted; ⟨asunto/idea⟩ complicated [2] (a) (involucrado) **∼ EN algo** mixed up IN sth (b) (fam) (en lío amoroso) **∼ CON algn** involved WITH sb

enredar [A1] *vt* (a) ⟨cuerdas/cables⟩ to get ... tangled up, tangle up (b) (embarullar) ⟨persona⟩ to muddle ... up, confuse; ⟨asunto/situación⟩ to complicate (c) (fam) (involucrar) **∼ a algn EN algo** to get sb mixed up *o* caught up IN sth

■ **∼** *vi* (fam) (a) (intrigar) to make trouble, stir up trouble (b) (Esp) (molestar) to fidget; **∼ CON algo** to fiddle (around) WITH sth

■ **enredarse** *v pron* [1] ⟨lana/cuerda⟩ to get tangled, become entangled; ⟨pelo⟩ to get tangled *o* knotted; ⟨planta⟩ to twist itself around [2] (fam) (a) (en lío amoroso) **∼se CON algn** to get involved WITH sb (b) (involucrarse) **∼se EN algo** to get mixed up *o* involved IN sth (c) (fam) (embarullarse) to get mixed up, get muddled up

enredo *m* (a) (de hilos) tangle; (en el pelo) tangle, knot (b) (embrollo) mess; **tengo un ∼ en las cuentas** ... my accounts are in a terrible mess (c) (fam) (lío amoroso) affair

enrejado *m* (de verja, balcón) railing, railings (*pl*); (rejilla) grating, grille; (para plantas) trellis

enrevesado -da *adj* complicated

enrielar [A1] *vt* ▶ ENCARRILAR

enriquecer [E3] *vt* [1] ⟨país/población⟩ to make ... rich [2] ⟨espíritu/lengua/alimento⟩ to enrich

■ **enriquecerse** *v pron* [1] (hacerse rico) to get rich [2] ⟨cultura/relación/lengua⟩ to be enriched

enrojecer [E3] *vt* ⟨rostro/mejillas⟩ to redden, make ... go red; ⟨pelo⟩ to turn ... red, make ... go red

■ **∼** *vi* (liter) (ruborizarse) to redden, blush; (de ira, rabia) to go red in the face

■ **enrojecerse** *v pron* ⟨rostro/mejillas⟩ to redden, blush; ⟨pelo⟩ to go *o* turn red; ⟨cielo⟩ to turn red

enrolarse [A1] *v pron* to enlist, join up; **∼ en la marina** to enlist in *o* join the navy; **∼ en un partido** to join a party

enrollado -da *adj* [1] (a) ⟨papel⟩ rolled up (b) ⟨cable⟩ coiled (up) [2] (Esp) (fam) **estar ∼ CON algn** to have a thing (going) WITH sb (colloq); **están ∼s** they've got sth going between them (colloq)

(c) **estar ∼ CON algo** ⟨con exámenes/preparativos⟩ wrapped up IN sth (c) (arg) (en la onda) ⟨persona/música/coche⟩ cool (sl) [3] (Ven fam) (preocupado) uptight (colloq), freaked out (sl)

enrollar [A1] *vt* [1] ⟨papel/persiana⟩ to roll up; ⟨cable/manguera⟩ to coil; **∼ el hilo en el carrete** wind the thread onto the spool [2] (Esp arg) ⟨persona⟩ (confundir) to confuse, get ... confused; (en asunto) to involve, get ... involved

■ **enrollarse** *v pron* [1] ⟨papel⟩ to roll up; ⟨cuerda/cable⟩ to coil up; **la cadena se enrolló en la rueda** the chain wound itself around the wheel [2] (Esp fam) (a) (hablar mucho): **no te enrolles** stop jabbering on (colloq); **se ∼on hablando** they got deep into conversation (b) (tener relaciones amorosas): **se ∼on en la discoteca** they made out (AmE colloq) *o* (BrE colloq) they got off together in a disco; **∼se CON algn** to make out WITH sb (AmE colloq), to get off WITH sb (BrE colloq)

enroque *m* (en ajedrez) castling

enroscar [A2] *vt* ⟨tornillo⟩ to screw in; ⟨cable/cuerda⟩ to coil; **∼ algo EN algo** to wind sth AROUND *o* ONTO sth

■ **enroscarse** *v pron* (a) ⟨víbora⟩ to coil up (b) ⟨gato/persona⟩ to curl up

enrular [A1] *vt* (Col, CS) to curl

ensalada *f* (Coc) salad; **∼ de fruta** fruit salad

ensaladera *f* salad bowl

ensalzar [A4] *vt* ⟨virtudes⟩ to extol; ⟨persona⟩ to praise, sing the praises of

ensamblar [A1] *vt* to assemble

ensanchar [A1] *vt* (a) ⟨calle⟩ to widen; ⟨vestido⟩ to let out (b) ⟨horizontes/posibilidades⟩ to expand

■ **ensancharse** *v pron* (a) ⟨calle/acera⟩ to widen, get wider; ⟨jersey⟩ to stretch (b) ⟨horizontes⟩ to expand

ensangrentado -da *adj* bloodstained

ensangrentar [A5] *vt* to stain ... with blood

ensañarse [A1] *v pron*: **se ensañaron con los prisioneros** they showed the prisoners no mercy *o* pity; **no te ensañes con él** don't take it out on him (colloq)

ensartar [A1] *vt* (a) ⟨perlas/cuentas⟩ to string (b) (con pincho) to skewer (c) (enhebrar) to thread (d) (clavar) **∼ algo EN algo** to stick sth IN(TO) sth

ensayar [A1] *vt* (a) ⟨obra/baile⟩ to rehearse (b) ⟨método⟩ to test, try out

■ **∼** *vi* to rehearse

ensayo *m* [1] (a) (Espec) rehearsal; **∼ general** (de obra teatral) dress rehearsal; (de concierto) final rehearsal (b) (prueba) trial, test; (intento) attempt [2] (Lit) essay [3] (en rugby) try

enseguida *adv* at once, immediately, right away; **¡∼ voy!** I'll be right with you; **∼ de almorzar** (esp AmL) right *o* straight after lunch

enseñado -da *adj*: **bien/mal ∼** ⟨niño⟩ well/badly brought up; ⟨animal⟩ well/badly trained

enseñanza *f* (a) (docencia) teaching (b) (educación) education; **∼ a distancia** distance

learning; ∼ **media** or **secundaria** high school
(AmE) o (BrE) secondary education; ∼ **primaria**
elementary (AmE) o (BrE) primary education; ∼
universitaria college (AmE) o (BrE) university
education

enseñar [A1] vt [1] **(a)** ⟨asignatura/niño⟩ to
teach; ⟨animal⟩ to train; ∼**le a algn A hacer algo**
to teach sb to do sth **(b)** (dar escarmiento) to teach
[2] (mostrar) ⟨camino/procedimiento⟩ to show
■ **enseñarse** v pron (Méx fam) ∼**se A hacer algo**
(aprender) to learn to do sth; (acostumbrarse) to get
used TO doing sth

ensillar [A1] vt to saddle (up)

ensimismado -da adj [ESTAR] lost in
thought; ∼ **EN algo** engrossed IN sth, absorbed IN
sth

ensordecedor -dora adj deafening

ensuciar [A1] vt **(a)** ⟨ropa/mantel⟩ to get ...
dirty, dirty; **lo vas a** ∼ **todo de barro** you'll get
mud everywhere **(b)** (liter) ⟨honor/nombre⟩ to
sully, tarnish
■ **ensuciarse** v pron **(a)** (refl) «persona» to get
dirty; **no te ensucies los dedos** don't get your
fingers dirty **(b)** «falda/suelo» to get dirty; **que
no se te ensucie** don't get it dirty; **se me ensució
el vestido de grasa** I got grease on my dress

entablar [A1] vt **(a)** (iniciar) ⟨conversación/
amistad⟩ to strike up; ⟨negociaciones⟩ to enter
into **(b)** ⟨partida⟩ to set up

entablillar [A1] vt to splint, put ... in a splint

entallado -da adj ⟨chaqueta/vestido⟩ waisted;
⟨camisa⟩ tailored, fitted

ente m **(a)** (ser) being, entity **(b)** (organismo,
institución) body

entender [E8] vt to understand; ⟨chiste⟩ to
understand, to get (colloq); **no te entiendo la letra** I
can't read your writing; **no entendí su nombre** I
didn't get his name; **lo entendió todo al revés** he
got it all completely wrong; **tú ya me entiendes**
you know what I mean; **me has entendido mal**
you've misunderstood me; **se hace** ∼ or (AmL) **se
da a** ∼ he makes himself understood; **me dio a** ∼
que ... she gave me to understand that ...; **dar
algo a** ∼ to imply sth
■ ∼ vi **(a)** (comprender) to understand **(b)** (saber) ∼
DE algo to know ABOUT sth
■ **entenderse** v pron [1] **(a)** (comunicarse) to
communicate; **se entienden por señas** they
communicate using sign language; ∼**se CON algn**
to communicate WITH sb; **a ver si nos
entendemos ¿quién te pegó?** let's get this
straight, who hit you? **(b)** (llevarse bien); **lo que
pasa es que no nos entendemos** the thing is we
just don't get on very well; ∼**se CON algn** to get
along o on WITH sb
[2] (refl): **déjame, yo me entiendo** leave me alone,
I know what I'm doing

entendido -da adj [1] [ESTAR] (comprendido)
understood; **según tengo** ∼ as I understand it;
tenía ∼ **que** ... I was under the impression that
...; **eso se da por** ∼ that goes without saying
[2] [SER] (experto): **no soy muy** ∼ **en estos temas**
I'm not very well up on these subjects; **es muy** ∼
en política he's very knowledgeable about politics
■ m,f expert

entendimiento m **(a)** (acuerdo)

understanding **(b)** (capacidad para entender) mind;
todavía no tiene suficiente ∼ he's not old enough
to understand

enterado -da adj [1] (de hecho, suceso): **¿estás**
∼ **de lo ocurrido?** have you heard what's
happened?; **no estoy enterada de nada** I have no
idea what's going on; **darse por** ∼ to get the
message, take the hint [2] (Esp) (que sabe mucho)
knowledgeable, well-informed

enterarse [A1] v pron [1] (de suceso, noticia):
ahora me entero this is the first I've heard of it;
me enteré por tus padres I found out from your
parents; **le robaron el reloj y ni se enteró** they
stole her watch and she didn't even notice o
realize; **me enteré de la noticia por la radio** I
heard the news on the radio; **si papá se entera de
esto** ... if Dad finds out about this ...
[2] (averiguar) to find out; ∼ **DE algo** to find out
ABOUT sth
[3] (esp Esp fam) (entender): **te voy a castigar ¿te
enteras?** I'll punish you, have I made myself
clear?; **¡para que te enteres!** (fam) so there! (colloq)

entereza f (serenidad, fortaleza) fortitude; (rectitud)
integrity; (firmeza) determination, strength of
mind

enternecedor -dora adj moving, touching

enternecer [E3] vt to move, touch
■ **enternecerse** v pron to be moved o touched

entero¹ -ra adj **(a)** (en su totalidad) whole; **una
caja entera de bombones** a whole o an entire box
of chocolates; **en el mundo** ∼ all over the world;
por ∼ completely, entirely **(b)** (intacto) intact **(c)**
⟨número⟩ whole

entero² m **(a)** (Fin) point **(b)** (Mat) whole
number, integer **(c)** (de lotería) (whole) lottery
ticket

enterrador -dora m,f gravedigger

enterrar [A5] vt to bury; **lo entierran mañana**
the funeral is tomorrow

entibiar [A1] vt ⟨líquido⟩ (enfriar) to cool;
(calentar) to warm (up)

entidad f (frml) (organización, institución) entity,
body; ∼ **deportiva** sporting body

entienda, entiendas, etc ▶ ENTENDER

entierro m (acto) burial; (ceremonia) funeral;
(procesión) funeral procession; **ir a un** ∼ to attend
a funeral

entoldado m (marquesina) awning; (carpa)
marquee

entonación f intonation

entonado -da adj [1] (Mús) in tune [2] [ESTAR]
(fam) (por el alcohol) tipsy (colloq), merry (BrE colloq)

entonar [A1] vt [1] ⟨canción⟩ to intone, sing;
⟨voz⟩ to modulate; ⟨nota⟩ to sing, give [2] (animar)
«café/sopa» ⟨persona⟩ to perk ... up
■ ∼ vi (Mús) to sing in tune

entonces adv [1] (en aquel momento) then; **por
or en aquel** ∼ in those days [2] **(a)** (introduciendo
conclusiones) so; **¿**∼ **vienes o te quedas?** so are
you coming with us or staying here? **(b)** (uso
expletivo) well, anyway; ∼**, como te iba diciendo** ...
well o anyway, as I was saying ...

entornado -da adj ⟨puerta⟩ ajar, half-open;
⟨ventana⟩ slightly open; ⟨ojos⟩ half-closed

entorno m **(a)** (situación) environment **(b)** (Lit)
setting **(c)** (Inf) environment

entorpecer [E3] vt **(a)** (dificultar) ‹tráfico› to hold up, slow down; ‹planes/movimiento› to hinder; **estas cajas entorpecen el paso** these boxes are (getting) in the way **(b)** ‹entendimiento/reacciones› to dull

■ **entorpecerse** v pron «entendimiento/reacciones» to become dulled

entrada f **1** (acción) entrance; **la ∼ es gratuita** admission o entrance is free; **vigilaban sus ∼s y salidas** they watched his comings and goings; **Ⓢ prohibida la entrada** no entry; **Ⓢ entrada libre** admission free; **la ∼ de divisas** the inflow of foreign currency; **∼ EN** or (esp AmL) **A algo** entry INTO sth; **forzaron su ∼ en el** or **al edificio** they forced an entry into the building; **de ∼** right from the start

2 (a) (en etapa, estado): **la ∼ en vigor del nuevo impuesto** the coming into effect of the new tax **(b)** (ingreso, incorporación) entry; **la ∼ de Prusia en la alianza** Prussia's entry into the alliance; **esto le facilitó la ∼ a la universidad** that made it easier for him to get into university **(c)** (lugar de acceso) entrance; **espérame en** or **a la ∼** wait for me at the entrance; **repartían folletos a la ∼** they were handing out leaflets at the door **(d)** (vestíbulo) hall

3 (Espec) ticket; **los niños pagan media ∼** it's half-price for children

4 (Com, Fin) **(a)** (Esp) (depósito) deposit **(b)** (ingreso) income; **∼s y salidas** income and expenditure, receipts and outgoings

5 (de comida) starter

6 (Dep) **(a)** (en fútbol) tackle; **hacerle una ∼ a algn** to tackle sb **(b)** (en béisbol) inning

7 (en el pelo): **tiene ∼s** he has a receding hairline

entrado -da adj: **era entrada la noche** it was dark o night-time; **duró hasta bien entrada la tarde** it went on well into the evening

entrador -dora adj (AmL fam) (lanzado) daring, forward

entrante adj **(a)** (próximo): **el año ∼** next year, the coming year **(b)** (nuevo) ‹gobierno/presidente› new, incoming (before n)

entrañable adj **(a)** ‹amistad› close, intimate; ‹amigo› very close, bosom (before n); ‹recuerdo› fond (before n) **(b)** ‹persona› pleasant, likable*

entrañar [A1] vt to entail, involve

entrañas fpl (vísceras) entrails (pl)

entrar [A1] vi **1** (acercándose) to come in; (alejándose) to go in; **déjame ∼** let me in; **hazla ∼** tell her to come in, show her in; **entró corriendo** he ran in, he came running in; **¿se puede ∼ con el coche?** can you drive in?; **había gente entrando y saliendo** there were people coming and going; **¿cómo entró?** how did he get in?; **∼ EN** or (esp AmL) **A algo** ‹a edificio/habitación› to go INTO sth; **entró en el** or **al banco** she went into the bank

2 (en etapa, estado) **∼ EN algo** ‹en periodo/guerra/negociaciones› to enter sth; **∼ en calor** to get warm; **entró en coma** he went into a coma

3 (a) (introducirse, meterse): **cierra la puerta, que entra frío** close the door, you're letting the cold in; **me entró arena en los zapatos** I've got sand in my shoes **(b)** (poderse meter): **¿entrará por la puerta?** will it get through the door?; (+ me/te/le etc): **estos vaqueros no me entran** I can't get into

these jeans; **el zapato no le entra** he can't get his shoe on; **no me entra la segunda** (Auto) I can't get it into second (gear)

4 «hambre» (+ me/te/le etc): **le entró hambre** she felt o got hungry; **me ha entrado la duda** I'm beginning to have my doubts; **me entró sueño** I got o began to feel sleepy

5 (empezar) to start, begin; **entró de aprendiz** he started o began as an apprentice

6 (incorporarse) **∼ EN** or (esp AmL) **A algo** ‹en empresa/ejército/club› to join sth; ‹en convento› to enter sth; **el año que entré en** or **a la universidad** the year I started college I've just joined the association

7 (estar incluido): **el postre no entra en el precio** dessert is not included in the price; **¿cuántas entran en un kilo?** how many do you get in a kilo?

■ **∼** vt (traer) to bring in; (llevar) to take in; **¿cómo van a ∼ el sofá?** how are they going to get the sofa in?

entre prep **1 (a)** (dos personas, cosas) between; **lo decidieron ∼ ellos dos** they decided it between the two of them; **está ∼ las dos casas** it's between the two houses; **∼ paréntesis** in brackets; **cuando hablan ∼ los dos** when they talk to each other **(b)** (más de dos personas, cosas) among; **los alumnos hablaban ∼ ellos** the pupils were talking among themselves; **∼ otras cosas** among other things; **se perdió ∼ la muchedumbre** he disappeared into the crowd; **∼ estas cuatro paredes** within these walls **(c)** (indicando cooperación, distribución): **∼ los tres logramos levantarlo** we managed to lift it between the three of us; **lo hicimos con regalo ∼ todos** we all got together and brought him a present; **repártelos ∼ los niños/∼ todos** share them out among the children/between everybody

2 (en expresiones de tiempo): **abierto ∼ semana** open during the week; **llegaré ∼ las tres y las cuatro** I'll be arriving between three and four; **cualquier semana ∼ julio y agosto** any week in July or August

3 **entre tanto** meanwhile, in the meantime

■ adv (esp AmL): **∼ más come más/menos engorda** the more he eats the more/less he puts on weight

entreabierto -ta adj ‹puerta› ajar, half-open; ‹ventana/ojos/boca› half-open

entreabrir [I33] vt to half-open

entrecejo m space between the eyebrows; **fruncir el ∼** to frown

entrecortado -da adj ‹respiración› difficult, labored*; **con la voz entrecortada por la emoción** in a voice choked with emotion

entrecruzar [A4] vt to intertwine, interweave

entredicho m **1** (duda): **estar en ∼** to be in doubt o question; **poner algo en ∼** «persona» to question sth **2** (CS, Per) (entre dos personas) argument; (entre dos países) dispute

entrega f **1** (de pedido, paquete, carta) delivery; (de premio) presentation; **∼ de premios** prize-giving; **la ∼ de los documentos** the handing over of the documents; **el plazo para la ∼ de solicitudes** the deadline for handing in o (fml) submitting applications; **servicio de ∼ a domicilio** delivery service **2 (a)** (partida) delivery, shipment **(b)** (plazo, cuota) installment*

(c) (de enciclopedia) installment*, fascicle; (de revista) issue **3** (dedicación) dedication, devotion; (abandono) surrender

entregar [A3] *vt* **1** (llevar) ⟨*pedido/paquete/carta*⟩ to deliver
2 (a) (dar) to give; **me entregó un cuestionario** she gave me *o* handed me a questionnaire; **no quiso entregármelo** he refused to hand it over to me **(b)** ⟨*premio/trofeo*⟩ to present; ∼**le algo A algn** to present sb WITH sth **(c)** ⟨*trabajo/deberes/informe*⟩ to hand in, give in; ⟨*solicitud/impreso*⟩ to hand in, submit (fml)
3 (a) ⟨*ciudad/armas*⟩ to surrender; ⟨*poder/control*⟩ to hand over **(b)** ⟨*delincuente/prófugo*⟩ to turn in, hand over; ⟨*rehén*⟩ to hand over **(c)** ⟨*novia*⟩ to give away **(d)** (dedicar) to devote
■ **entregarse** *v pron* **1** (dedicarse) ∼**se A algo/algn** to devote oneself TO sth/sb
2 (a) (rendirse) to surrender, give oneself up; ∼**se A algo/algn** ⟨*al enemigo/a la policía*⟩ to give oneself up *o* surrender TO sth/sb **(b)** (abandonarse) **se entregó a la bebida** he gave himself over to drink

entrelazar [A4] *vt* ⟨*cintas/hilos*⟩ to interweave, intertwine; **con las manos entrelazadas** hand in hand
■ **entrelazarse** *v pron* to intertwine, interweave

entremedias, entremedio *adv* **(a)** (entre dos cosas) in between; **son muy caros o muy baratos, no hay nada** ∼ they're very expensive or very cheap, there's nothing in between; **lo metí** ∼ I put it in between **(b)** (mezclado con) ∼ **DE algo** among; ∼ **de mis papeles/de la gente** among my papers/the people **(c)** (en el tiempo) in between

entremés *m* (Coc) hors d'oeuvre, starter

entremezclar [A1] *vt* to intermingle
■ **entremezclarse** *v pron* «*recuerdos*» to intermingle, become intermingled; «*culturas*» to mix, intermingle

entrenador -dora *m,f* (manager) coach, manager; (preparador físico) trainer

entrenamiento *m* **(a)** (por el entrenador) coaching, training **(b)** (ejercicios) training **(c)** (sesión) training session

entrenar [A1] *vt/vi* to train
■ **entrenarse** *v pron* to train

entrepierna *f* (Anat) crotch; (medida) inside leg measurement

entrepiso *m* (AmL) mezzanine

entreplanta *f* mezzanine

entretanto *adv* meanwhile, in the meantime

entretejer [E1] *vt* ⟨*hilos*⟩ (en tela) to weave; (entrelazar) to interweave

entretelones *mpl* (CS, Per) (de un caso) ins and outs (*pl*)

entretención *f* (AmL) ▶ ENTRETENIMIENTO

entretener [E27] *vt* **1** «*crucigrama/libro*» to keep ... amused; «*obra/payaso*» to entertain; **pintar me entretiene** I enjoy painting **2 (a)** (distraer, apartar de una tarea) to distract **(b)** (retener) to keep, detain; **no te entretengo más** I won't keep *o* detain you any longer
■ **entretenerse** *v pron* **1 (a)** (divertirse) to amuse oneself; **se entretiene con cualquier cosa** «*adulto*» she's easily amused; «*niño*» she's

happy playing with anything **(b)** (pasar el tiempo) to keep (oneself) busy *o* occupied **2** (demorarse) to hang around, dally about

entretenido -da *adj* **1** [SER] ⟨*película/conversación*⟩ entertaining, enjoyable; ⟨*persona*⟩ entertaining **2** [ESTAR] ⟨*persona*⟩ (ocupado) busy

entretenimiento *m* entertainment; **lo hace por** ∼ he does it for pleasure *o* for fun

entretiempo *m* **(a)** (período entre estaciones): **de** ∼ ⟨*abrigo*⟩ lightweight; ⟨*ropa*⟩ spring/autumn (*before n*) **(b)** (Chi) (Dep) halftime

entrever [E29] *vt* **(a)** (ver confusamente) to make out **(b)** ⟨*solución/acuerdo*⟩ to begin to see; **ha dejado** ∼ **que ...** she has hinted *o* suggested that ...

entreverado -da *adj* **(a)** (intercalado) interspersed **(b)** (fam) (desordenado, mezclado) muddled up, mixed up

entrevista *f* **(a)** (para trabajo, en periódico) interview **(b)** (período) (reunión) meeting

entrevistador -dora *m,f* interviewer

entrevistar [A1] *vt* to interview

entristecer [E3] *vt* to sadden
■ **entristecerse** *v pron* to grow sad

entrometerse [E1] *v pron* to meddle

entrometido -da *adj* meddling (*before n*), interfering (*before n*)
■ *m,f* meddler, busybody (colloq)

entronque *m* (AmL) (Ferr) junction

entumecerse [E3] *v pron* (perder la sensibilidad) to go numb; (perder la flexibilidad) to get stiff; **estar entumecido de frío** to be numb with cold

entusiasmado -da *adj* excited, enthusiastic; **está** ∼ **con la idea** he's excited *o* enthusiastic about the idea

entusiasmar [A1] *vt* (apasionar): **lo entusiasma el fútbol** he's crazy about football; **no me entusiasma mucho la idea** I'm not very enthusiastic about the idea
■ **entusiasmarse** *v pron* ∼**se CON algo** to get excited *o* enthusiastic ABOUT sth

entusiasmo *m* enthusiasm

entusiasta *adj* enthusiastic
■ *mf* enthusiast

enumerar [A1] *vt* to list, enumerate (fml)

enunciar [A1] *vt* ⟨*idea/teoría*⟩ to state, enunciate (fml); ⟨*problema/teorema*⟩ to formulate

envainar [A1] *vt* ⟨*espada*⟩ to sheathe

envalentonar [A1] *vt* to make ... bolder, encourage
■ **envalentonarse** *v pron* (ponerse valiente) to become bolder *o* more daring; (insolentarse) to become defiant

envasar [A1] *vt* (en botellas) to bottle; (en latas) to can; (en paquetes, cajas) to pack

envase *m* (en general) container; (botella) bottle; (lata) can, tin (BrE)

envejecer [E3] *vi* **(a)** «*persona*» (hacerse más viejo) to age, grow old; (parecer más viejo) to age **(b)** «*vino/queso*» to mature, age
■ ∼ *vt* **(a)** ⟨*persona*⟩ «*tragedia/experiencia*» to age; «*ropa/peinado*» to make ... look older **(b)** ⟨*madera*⟩ to make ... look old; ⟨*vaqueros*⟩ to give ... a worn look

envejecido -da adj (a) ⟨persona⟩: está tan ~ he's aged so much, he looks so old (b) ⟨cuero/madera⟩ distressed

envenenamiento m poisoning

envenenar [A1] vt to poison

■ **envenenarse** v pron (involuntariamente) to be poisoned; (voluntariamente) to poison oneself

envergadura f (importancia) magnitude (frml), importance; **de cierta** ~ of some importance

enviado -da m,f (Pol) envoy; (Period) reporter, correspondent

enviar [A17] vt (a) ⟨carta/paquete⟩ to send; ⟨pedido/mercancías⟩ to send, dispatch (b) ⟨persona⟩ to send; **me envió por pan** she sent me out for bread

enviciarse [A1] v pron to become addicted, get hooked (colloq); ~ CON algo to become addicted TO sth o (colloq) hooked ON sth

envidia f envy, jealousy; **le da** ~ **que yo vaya** he's envious o jealous because I'm going; **le tienes** ~ you are jealous of him; **me muero de** ~ I'm green with envy; **¡qué** ~! I'm so jealous!

envidiable adj enviable

envidiar [A1] vt to envy; ~**le algo** A **algn** to envy sb sth

envidioso -sa adj envious

envío m **1** (acción): **el** ~ **de los fondos** remittance o sending of the money; **fecha de** ~ date of dispatch, date sent; ~ **contra reembolso** COD, cash on delivery **2** (partida — de mercancías) consignment, shipment; (— de dinero) remittance

enviudar [A1] vi to be widowed

envoltorio m (a) (de paquete, regalo) wrapping; (de caramelo) wrapper (b) (bulto) bundle

envolver [E11] vt **1** ⟨paquete/regalo⟩ to wrap (up); **¿me lo puede** ~ **para regalo?** could you gift wrap it?; ~ **algo/a algn** EN **algo** to wrap sth/sb (up) IN sth **2** (rodear) ⟨membrana/capa⟩ to surround; ⟨humo/tristeza⟩ to envelop **3** (involucrar) to involve

■ **envolverse** v pron (a) (refl) (en manta) to wrap oneself (up) (b) (en delito, asunto) to become involved

envuelto -ta adj **1** ⟨paquete/regalo⟩ wrapped; ~ **para regalo** gift-wrapped **2** (rodeado) ~ EN **algo** ⟨en humo/niebla⟩ enveloped IN sth; ⟨en misterio⟩ cloaked o shrouded IN sth; ⟨en una manta⟩ wrapped (up) IN sth **3** (involucrado) ~ EN **algo** involved IN sth

enyesar [A1] vt (a) (Const) to plaster (b) ⟨brazo/pierna⟩ to put ... in a plaster cast, put ... in plaster (BrE)

enzarzarse [A4] v pron ~ EN **algo** to get involved IN sth

eñe f: name of the letter ñ

épica f (a) (género) epic poetry (b) (poema) epic

epicentro m epicenter*

épico -ca adj epic

epidemia f epidemic

epilepsia f epilepsy

epiléptico -ca adj/m,f epileptic

epílogo m (Lit) epilogue; (de suceso) conclusion

episodio m (Cin, Rad, TV) episode; (suceso) episode, incident

epístola f (frml o hum) epistle (frml or hum)

epitafio m epitaph

época f (a) (período de tiempo) time, period; **en la** ~ **de Franco** in Franco's time; **la** ~ **de los Tudor** the Tudor period; **muebles de** ~ period furniture; **en aquella** ~ in those days o at that time; **esa** ~ **de mi vida** that period of my life; **es música de mi** ~ it's music from my time (b) (parte del año) time of year; **la** ~ **de lluvias** the rainy season

epopeya f (a) (Lit) (poema) epic, epic poem (b) (empresa difícil): **el viaje fue toda una** ~ the journey turned out to be a real ordeal

equilátero -ra adj equilateral

equilibrado -da adj ⟨persona/dieta⟩ well-balanced, balanced; ⟨lucha/partido⟩ close

equilibrar [A1] vt ⟨peso/carga/ruedas⟩ to balance; ~ **las diferencias económicas** to redress economic imbalances

■ **equilibrarse** v pron «fuerzas» to even up; «balanza de pagos» to be restored; «platillos de la balanza» to balance out

equilibrio m (de fuerzas, estabilidad) balance; **perdió el** ~ he lost his balance; **en estado de** ~ in equilibrium

equilibrista mf (Espec) tightrope walker

equinoccio m equinox; ~ **de primavera/de otoño** vernal/autumnal equinox

equipaje m baggage (esp AmE), luggage (BrE); **facturar el** ~ to check in one's baggage o luggage; ~ **de mano** hand baggage o luggage; **viaja con poco** ~ he travels light

equipar [A1] vt (a) ⟨persona⟩ to equip, fit ... out; ~ **a algn** CON o DE **algo** to equip sb WITH sth (b) ⟨casa⟩ to furnish; ⟨local/barco⟩ to fit out; (de víveres) to provision; **una cocina bien equipada** a well-equipped kitchen

equiparable adj comparable

equiparar [A1] vt (a) (poner al mismo nivel) ~ **algo/a algn** A o CON **algo/algn** to put sth/sb on a level WITH sth/sb (b) (comparar) ~ **algo** CON **algo** to compare sth TO o WITH sth

equipo m **1** (de trabajadores, jugadores) team; **el** ~ **local/visitante** the home/visiting team; **trabajo de** ~ team work; **trabajar en** ~ to work as a team; ~ **de filmación** film crew **2** (de materiales, utensilios) equipment; ~ **de pesca** fishing tackle; ~ **de gimnasia** gym kit; ~ **de alta fidelidad** hi-fi system

equis f: name of the letter x

equitación f riding, horseback riding (AmE), horse riding (BrE); **practica (la)** ~ he rides

equitativo -va adj ⟨persona⟩ fair; ⟨reparto⟩ equitable

equivalente adj equivalent; ~ A **algo** equivalent TO sth

■ m equivalent; ~ A or DE **algo** equivalent OF sth

equivaler [E28] vi ~ A **algo** to be equivalent

TO sth; ¿a cuánto equivalen mil pesetas en libras? how much is a thousand pesetas equivalent to o worth in pounds?

equivocación f mistake; **por ~** by mistake, in error (frml)

equivocado -da adj **(a)** ⟨dato/número/respuesta⟩ wrong **(b)** [ESTAR] ⟨persona⟩ mistaken, wrong

equivocar [A2] vt ⟨persona⟩ to make ... make a mistake, to make ... go wrong

■ **equivocarse** v pron (cometer un error) to make a mistake; (estar en un error) to be wrong o mistaken; **me equivoqué con él** I was wrong about him; **me equivoqué de autobús** I took the wrong bus; **no te equivoques de fecha** don't get the date wrong; **se equivocó de camino** he went the wrong way

era f (período, época) era, age

era, éramos, etc ▶ SER

eras ▶ SER

erección f erection

erecto -ta adj erect

eres ▶ SER

erguido -da adj upright

erguir [I26] vt (liter) ⟨cabeza⟩ to raise, lift; ⟨cuello⟩ to straighten

■ **erguirse** v pron (liter) «persona» to stand up; «edificio/torre» to rise

erigir [I7] vt **(a)** (frml) ⟨edificio⟩ to build, erect (frml); ⟨monumento⟩ to erect (frml), to raise (frml) **(b)** (frml) (convertir, elevar) **~ algo/a algn EN algo** to set sth/sb up AS sth

■ **erigirse** v pron (llegar a ser) **~se EN algo** to become sth; (atribuirse funciones de) to set oneself up AS sth

erizado -da adj (de punta): **tenía el pelo ~** her hair was standing on end

erizar [A4] vt ⟨pelo/vello⟩ to make ... stand on end

■ **erizarse** v pron «pelo» to stand on end

erizo m hedgehog; **~ de mar** sea urchin

ermita f chapel

ermitaño -ña m,f (asceta) hermit

erosión f erosion

erosionar [A1] vt to erode

■ **erosionarse** v pron to be/become eroded

erótico -ca adj erotic

erotismo m eroticism

erradicar [A2] vt (frml) to eradicate

errado -da adj **1** (desacertado): **cinco tiros ~s** five misses **2** (esp AmL) **(a)** [ESTAR] ⟨persona⟩ mistaken, wrong; **están muy ~s en estos cálculos** they're way off the mark with these calculations **(b)** [SER] ⟨decisión⟩ wrong; ⟨política⟩ misguided

errante adj **(a)** ⟨persona⟩ wandering (before n), roaming (before n); ⟨pueblo⟩ wandering (before n) **(b)** ⟨mirada⟩ faraway, distant; **una vida ~** a nomadic existence

errar [A26] vt ⟨tiro/golpe⟩ to miss; **erró su vocación** she chose the wrong vocation/career

■ **~** vi «tirador» to miss; **erró en su decisión** he made the wrong decision

errata f (error de imprenta) misprint, printer's error; (error de mecanografía) typing error

erre f: name of the letter r

erróneo -nea adj (frml) ⟨decisión/afirmación⟩ wrong, erroneous (frml)

error m mistake; **cometer un ~** to make a mistake o an error; **~ de ortografía** spelling mistake; **~ de cálculo** miscalculation; **~ de imprenta** misprint, printer's error; **por ~** by mistake, in error (frml)

eructar [A1] vi to belch, burp (colloq)

eructo m belch, burp (colloq)

erudición f erudition (frml), learning

erudito -ta adj ⟨lenguaje/obra⟩ erudite; ⟨persona⟩ learned, knowledgeable; **~ EN algo** learned in sth, knowledgeable ABOUT sth

■ m,f scholar

erupción f **(a)** (de volcán) eruption; **el volcán entró en ~** the volcano erupted **(b)** (en la piel) rash, eruption (frml)

es ▶ SER

esbelto -ta adj slender

esbozar [A4] vt **(a)** ⟨figura⟩ to sketch **(b)** ⟨idea/tema⟩ to outline

esbozo m **(a)** (Art) sketch **(b)** (de proyecto) outline, rough draft

escabeche m pickling brine (made with oil, vinegar, peppercorns and bay leaves)

escabroso -sa adj **(a)** ⟨terreno⟩ rugged, rough **(b)** ⟨asunto/problema/tema⟩ thorny, tricky; ⟨escena/relato⟩ shocking

escabullirse [I9] v pron (escaparse) to slip away; **logró ~ entre la multitud** he managed to slip away into the crowd; **no puedes escabullirte de tus responsabilidades** you can't get away from your responsibilities

escafandra f diving suit

escala f **1** (en general) scale; **~ centígrada/Fahrenheit** centigrade o Celsius/Fahrenheit scale; **~ de valores** set of values; **~ musical** (musical) scale; **la ~ social** the social scale; **hecho a ~** done to scale; **a gran ~** on a large scale **2** (Aviac, Náut) stopover; **hicimos ~ en Roma** we stopped over in Rome

escalada f **1** (Dep) (de montaña) climb, ascent **2** (aumento, subida): **una ~ de la violencia** an escalation of violence; **la ~ de los precios** the increase o escalation in prices

escalador -dora m,f (de montañas) mountaineer, climber; (de rocas) rock-climber; (en ciclismo) climber, mountain rider

escalafón m scale; **subir un puesto en el ~** to go up one step on the promotion ladder

escalar [A1] vt ⟨montaña/pared⟩ to climb, scale; (en jerarquía, clasificación) to climb (up)

■ **~** vi (Dep) to climb, go climbing

escaldar [A1] vt **(a)** ⟨acelgas/tomates⟩ to blanch, scald **(b)** ⟨manos/persona⟩ to scald

■ **escaldarse** v pron **(a)** (con agua, vapor) to scald oneself **(b)** «bebé» to get diaper (AmE) o (BrE) nappy rash

escalera f **1** (de edificio) stairs (pl), staircase; **bajó las ~s** he came downstairs o down the stairs; **el hueco de la ~** the stairwell; **~ (de) caracol** spiral staircase; **~ mecánica** escalator **2** (portátil) tb **~ de mano** ladder; (de tijera) stepladder **3** (en naipes) run; (juego de tablero) snakes and ladders

escalfar [A1] vt to poach

escalinata _f_ staircase, steps (_pl_)

escalofriante _adj_ ⟨crimen/escena⟩ horrifying; ⟨cifra⟩ staggering, incredible

escalofrío _m_ shiver; **me da ∼s** it makes me shiver _o_ shudder; **tiene ∼s** she's shivering

escalón _m_ (peldaño) step; (travesaño) rung

escalonar [A1] _vt_ ⟨pagos/vacaciones⟩ to stagger; ⟨terreno⟩ to terrace

escalope _m_ escalope

escama _f_ (a) (Zool) scale (b) (en la piel) flake

escamotear [A1] _vt_ (a) (ocultar) ⟨naipe⟩ to palm; ⟨informe⟩ to keep … secret; **nos escamoteaban la información** they were keeping the information (secret) from us (b) (robar) to swipe

escampar [A1] _v impers_ to stop raining, to clear up

■ ∼ _vi_ (Col) to shelter

escanciar [A1] _vt_ (frml) ⟨vino⟩ to serve; ⟨sidra⟩ to pour (from a height)

escandalizar [A4] _vt/vi_ to shock

■ **escandalizarse** _v pron_ to be shocked

escándalo _m_ ①(hecho, asunto chocante) scandal; **¡qué ∼!** **¡qué manera de vestir!** what a shocking _o_ an outrageous way to dress! ②(alboroto, jaleo) fuss; **tanto ∼ para nada** all this fuss over nothing; **cuando lo sepa va a armar un ∼** when she finds out she'll kick up a fuss; **no armen tanto ∼** don't make such a racket _o_ row (colloq); **nada de ∼s dentro del local** we don't want any trouble in here

escandaloso -sa _adj_ (a) ⟨conducta⟩ shocking, scandalous; ⟨ropa⟩ outrageous; ⟨película⟩ shocking; ⟨vida⟩ scandalous (b) (ruidoso) ⟨persona/griterío⟩ noisy; ⟨risa⟩ loud, uproarious

Escandinavia _f_ Scandinavia

escandinavo -va _adj/m,f_ Scandinavian

escaño _m_ (Esp) (Pol) (cargo, asiento) seat; (banco) bench

escapada _f_ (a) (huida) breakout, escape (b) (de un peligro) escape (c) (en ciclismo) breakaway

escapar [A1] _vi_ ① to escape; **∼ DE algo** ⟨de cárcel/rutina/peligro⟩ to escape FROM sth; ⟨de castigo/muerte⟩ to escape sth ②**dejar escapar** ⟨carcajada/suspiro⟩ to let out, give; ⟨oportunidad⟩ to pass up; ⟨persona/animal⟩ to let … get away

■ **escaparse** _v pron_ ①«prisionero» to escape; «animal/niño» to run away; **∼se DE algo** ⟨de cárcel/jaula⟩ to escape FROM sth; ⟨de situación/castigo⟩ to escape sth; **∼se DE algn** ⟨de policía/perseguidor⟩ to escape (FROM) sth; **∼se de casa** to run away from home; **se me escapó el perro** the dog got away from me ②(+ me/te/le etc) (a) (involuntariamente): **se le escapó un grito** he cried out, he let out a cry (b) (pasar inadvertido): **no se le escapa nada** he doesn't miss anything; **se me escapó ese detalle** that detail escaped my notice ③«gas/aire/agua» to leak

escaparate _m_ (a) (esp Esp) (de tienda) shop window (b) (Col) (vitrina) display cabinet; (aparador) sideboard (c) (Ven) (armario) wardrobe

escapatoria _f_ (salida, solución) way out

escape _m_ (a) (fuga) escape (b) (de gas, fluido) leak (c) (Auto) exhaust

escapismo _m_ escapism

escarabajo _m_ beetle

escaramuza _f_ (Mil) skirmish; (Dep) scrimmage

escarbadientes _m_ (_pl_ ∼) toothpick

escarbar [A1] _vi_ (a) (en la tierra — haciendo un hoyo) to dig; (— superficialmente) to scrabble _o_ scratch around (b) (buscando algo) **∼ EN algo** ⟨en cajón/armario⟩ to rummage (about _o_ around) IN sth; **perros escarbando en la basura** dogs rummaging through the garbage

■ ∼ _vt_: **∼ la tierra** (hacer un hoyo) to dig a hole; (superficialmente) to scratch around in the soil

■ **escarbarse** _v pron_ (refl) ⟨nariz/dientes⟩ to pick

escarcha _f_ frost

escarchar [A1] _vt_ to crystallize

escarlata _adj inv/m_ scarlet

escarlatina _f_ scarlet fever, scarlatina

escarmentar [A5] _vi_ to learn one's lesson; **¡para que escarmientes!** that'll teach you!; **no escarmienta** she never learns

■ ∼ _vt_ to teach … a lesson

escarmiento _m_ lesson; **habrá que darle un buen ∼** he needs to be taught a good lesson

escarola _f_ escarole, endive (BrE)

escarpado -da _adj_ ⟨montaña/terreno⟩ precipitous; ⟨pared/acantilado⟩ sheer, steep

escarpín _m_ (AmL) (calcetín — de bebé) bootee; (— de adulto) bed sock

escasear [A1] _vi_: **empiezan a ∼ los alimentos** food is running short; **va a ∼ el café** there's going to be a coffee shortage

escasez _f_ shortage; **hubo ∼ de agua** there was a water shortage; **por ∼ de medios** owing to a lack of resources

escaso -sa _adj_ (a) ⟨recursos económicos⟩ limited, scant; ⟨posibilidades⟩ slim, slender; ⟨visibilidad⟩ poor; ⟨conocimientos/experiencia⟩ limited (b) [ESTAR] (falto) **∼ DE algo** ⟨de dinero/tiempo⟩ short of sth

escatimar [A1] _vt_ ⟨comida/tela⟩ to skimp on, be sparing with; **no ∼on esfuerzos** they spared no effort

escayola _f_ (Esp) (material) plaster; (Med) plaster cast

escayolar [A1] _vt_ (Esp) to put … in a (plaster) cast, to put … in plaster (BrE)

escena _f_ ① (a) (de obra) scene; **la ∼ del duelo** the duel scene (b) (sin art) (escenario): **poner en ∼** to stage; **entrar en ∼** to come/go on stage ② **la ∼ del accidente** (period) the scene of the accident; **no me hagas una ∼** there's no need to make a scene

escenario _m_ (Teatr) stage

escenografía _f_ (decorado) scenery; (arte) scenography, set design

escenógrafo -fa _m,f_ scenographer, set designer

escepticismo _m_ skepticism*

escéptico -ca _adj_ skeptical*

■ _m,f_ skeptic*

esclarecer [E3] _vt_ ⟨situación/hechos⟩ to clarify, elucidate (frml); ⟨crimen/misterio⟩ to clear up

esclavitud _f_ slavery

esclavizar [A4] _vt_ to enslave; **está esclavizado por el trabajo** he's a slave to his work

esclavo -va *m,f* slave; **es un ~ del trabajo** he is a slave to his work

esclerosis *f* sclerosis; **~ múltiple** multiple sclerosis

esclusa *f* (de canal) lock; (de presa) floodgate

escoba *f* (para barrer) broom; (de bruja) broomstick

escobilla *f* **(a)** (de motor) brush **(b)** (del limpiaparabrisas) wiper-blade, blade **(c)** (del inodoro) toilet brush

escocedura *f* irritation; (de bebé) diaper rash (AmE), nappy rash (BrE)

escocer [E10] *vi* «*herida/ojos*» to sting, smart

escocés -cesa *adj* «*ciudad/persona*» Scottish; «*dialecto*» Scots **(b)** «*whisky*» Scotch; «*tela/manta*» tartan
■ *m,f* (*m*) Scotsman, Scot; (*f*) Scotswoman, Scot

Escocia *f* Scotland

escocido -da *adj* «*cuello/axila*» sore, chafed; **tiene las nalgas escocidas** he has diaper rash (AmE) *o* (BrE) nappy rash

escoger [E6] *vt* to choose; **escoge que quieras** pick *o* choose whichever (one) you want; **no hay mucho (de) donde ~** there isn't a great deal of choice, there isn't much to choose from

escogido -da *adj* **(a)** (selecto) «*mercancía*» choice; «*clientela*» select **(b)** (Méx fam) (manoseado) picked over

escolar *adj* school (*before n*)
■ *m,f* (*m*) schoolboy, schoolchild; (*f*) schoolgirl, schoolchild

escolaridad *f* education, schooling

escolarizar [A4] *vt* to educate, provide schooling for; **niños sin ~** children without any (formal) education *o* schooling

escoleta *f* (Méx) **(a)** (banda) band (*of amateur musicians*) **(b)** (ensayo) rehearsal

escollo *m* (Náut) reef; (dificultad) obstacle, hurdle

escolta *mf* (persona) escort; (en baloncesto) guard
■ *f* (grupo) escort

escoltar [A1] *vt* to escort

escombros *mpl* rubble

esconder [E1] *vt* to hide, conceal (frml)
■ **esconderse** *v pron* [1] (*refl*) «*persona*» to hide; **~se DE algn** to hide FROM sb [2] (estar oculto) to hide, lie hidden

escondidas *fpl* [1] (AmE) (Jueg): **jugar a las ~** to play hide-and-seek [2] **a escondidas** in secret, secretly; **hacer algo a ~ de algn** to do sth behind sb's back

escondido -da *adj* **(a)** (oculto) hidden **(b)** (lejano) remote

escondite *m* **(a)** (para personas) hideout; (para cosas) hiding place **(b)** (Jueg): **jugar al ~** to play hide-and-seek

escondrijo *m* hidden place, recess (liter)

escopeta *f* shotgun

escoria *f* (de fundición) slag; **la ~ de la sociedad** the dregs of society

Escorpio *m* (signo) Scorpio; **es (de) ~** he's a Scorpio
■ *mf* (*pl* ~ *or* **-pios**) (persona) *tb* **escorpio** Scorpio

escorpión *m* scorpion

escotado -da *adj* **(a)** «*blusa/vestido*» low-cut; **~ por detrás** cut low at the back **(b)** (RPl) «*zapato*» strapless

escote *m* (Indum) neck, neckline; (profundo) low-cut neck *o* neckline; **~ redondo** round neck; (en suéters) crew neck; **~ en pico** V neck; **pagar a ~** (Esp fam) to go Dutch

escotilla *f* hatch, hatchway

escozor *m* **(a)** (Med) stinging, burning sensation **(b)** (resentimiento, amargura) bitterness

escribanía *f* (RPl) (Der) (oficina) notary's office; (profesión): **ejerce la ~** he is a practicing notary (public)

escribano -na *m,f* **(a)** (Hist) (amanuense) scribe **(b)** (RPl) (notario) notary (public)

escribiente *mf* clerk

escribir [I34] *vt* **(a)** (anotar) to write; **escríbelo aquí** write it down here **(b)** (ser autor de) «*libro/canción/carta*» to write
[2] (ortográficamente) to write; **la escribió sin acento** she wrote it without an accent; **no sé cómo se escribe** I don't know how you spell it; **se escribe sin acento** it's written without an accent
■ **~** *vi* to write; **nunca le escribe** she never writes him (AmE) *o* (BrE) writes to him; **~ a máquina** to type

■ **escribirse** *v pron* (*recípr*): **me escribo con ella** we write to each other; **se escribe con un peruano** she has a Peruvian penfriend *o* penpal

escrito¹ -ta *adj* «*examen*» written; **por ~** in writing

escrito² *m* (documento) document

escritor -tora *m,f* writer, author

escritorio *m* **(a)** (mueble) desk **(b)** (AmL) (oficina, despacho) office; (en casa particular) study; **~ público** (en Méx) *office or stall offering letter writing, form-filling or typing services*

escritura *f* [1] (sistema de signos) writing; (letra) writing, handwriting [2] (Der) (documento) deed; **la ~ de la casa** the deeds *o* of the house

escrúpulo *m* scruple

escrupuloso -sa *adj* **(a)** (honrado) honest, scrupulous **(b)** (meticuloso) meticulous **(c)** (Esp) (aprensivo) fastidious

escrutinio *m* **(a)** (Pol) count; **los resultados del ~** the results of the ballot **(b)** (inspección) scrutiny

escuadra *f* [1] (instrumento — triangular) set square; (— de carpintero) square [2] (en el ejército) squad; (en la marina) squadron

escuadrón *m* **(a)** (Aviac) squadron **(b)** (de caballería) squadron; (más pequeño) troop

escuálido -da *adj* «*persona/animal*» skinny, scrawny

escuchar [A1] *vt* **(a)** (prestar atención) «*música/persona*» to listen to **(b)** (esp AmL) (oír) to hear
■ **~** *vi* to listen

escudarse [A1] *v pron*: **quiso ~ en su inmunidad diplomática** he tried to hide behind his diplomatic immunity

escudero *m* (Hist, Mil) squire

escudilla *f* bowl

escudo *m* **(a)** (Hist, Mil) shield **(b)** (emblema) *tb* **~ de armas** coat of arms **(c)** (en la solapa, etc) badge

escudriñar [A1] *vt* **(a)** (liter) (mirar intensamente) ⋯⦂

⟨horizonte⟩ to scan **(b)** (examinar) ⟨persona⟩ to scrutinize, examine; ⟨casa/habitación⟩ to search ... thoroughly

escuela f school; ~ **de conductores** or **choferes** (AmL) driving school; ~ **primaria** primary school; ~ **militar/naval** military/naval academy; ~ **pública** public (AmE) o (BrE) state school; E~ **de Medicina** Medical Faculty o School

escueto -ta adj ⟨explicación⟩ succinct; ⟨lenguaje/estilo⟩ concise, plain; **fue muy** ~ he was very succinct

escuincle -cla m,f (Méx fam) kid (colloq)

esculcar [A2] vt (AmC, Col, Méx, Ven) ⟨cajones/papeles⟩ to go through; ⟨persona/casa⟩ to search

esculpir [I1] vt ⟨estatua/busto⟩ to sculpt, sculpture; ⟨inscripción⟩ to engrave, carve
■ ~ vi to sculpt, sculpture

escultor -tora m,f sculptor

escultura f sculpture; ~ **en madera** wood carving

escupida f (RPl) gob (of spit) (colloq)

escupir [I1] vi to spit; ~**le A algn** to spit AT sb; **le escupió en la cara** he spat in her face
■ ~ vt **(a)** ⟨comida⟩ to spit out; ⟨sangre⟩ to spit, cough up **(b)** ⟨llamas/lava⟩ to belch out

escupitajo m gob (of spit) (colloq)

escupo m (Chi, Ven) gob (of spit) (colloq)

escurreplatos m (pl ~) (mueble) cupboard with built-in plate rack; (rejilla) plate rack

escurridizo -za adj ⟨piel/jabón⟩ slippery; ⟨persona/respuesta⟩ evasive; ⟨idea/concepto⟩ elusive

escurrir [I1] vt ⟨ropa⟩ to wring out, wring; ⟨verduras/pasta⟩ to strain, drain; ⟨líquido⟩ to drain (off)
■ ~ vi to drain; **dejar** ~ ⟨platos⟩ to leave ... to drain; ⟨camisa⟩ to leave ... to drip-dry
■ **escurrirse** v pron **1** **(a)** «líquido»: **cuelga la camisa para que se escurra el agua** hang the shirt out to drip-dry **(b)** «verduras/vajilla» to drain **2** **(a)** (fam) (escaparse, escabullirse) to slip away; ~**se DE algo** to wriggle o get out OF sth **(b)** (resbalarse, deslizarse) to slip

escúter m scooter

esdrújula f word with the stress on the antepenultimate syllable

ese¹ f: name of the letter s

ese², esa adj dem (pl **esos, esas**) that; (pl) those; **en** ~ **país/esos países** in that country/those countries

ése, ésa pron dem (pl **ésos, ésas**) [The written accent may be omitted when there is no confusion with the adjective] **(a)** that one; (pl) those; ~ or **ese es el tuyo** that (one) is yours; **prefiero ésos** or **esos** I prefer those (ones); [usually indicates disapproval when used to refer to a person] **ésa** or **esa no sabe lo que dice** (fam) she doesn't know what she's talking about **(b)** **ésas** (fam) (esas cosas, esos asuntos): **¡conque ésas** or **esas tenemos!** so that's it!; **¡no me vengas con ésas** or **esas!** don't give me that! (colloq)

esencia f essence

esencial adj (fundamental) essential; **coincidimos en lo** ~ we agree on the essentials o on the main points; **lo** ~ **es ...** the main o the most important thing is ...

esfera f **(a)** (Astron, Mat) sphere **(b)** (de reloj) face **(c)** (ámbito) sphere; **en las altas** ~**s de la política** in the highest political circles

esférico -ca adj spherical

esfero m (Col fam) ballpoint pen, biro® (BrE)

esfinge f sphinx

esforzar [A11] vt ⟨voz/vista⟩ to strain
■ **esforzarse** v pron: **se esforzó mucho** he tried very hard, he put in a lot of effort; **tienes que** ~**te más** you'll have to work harder; ~**se POR** o **EN hacer algo** to strive to do sth

esfuerzo m effort; **hizo el** ~ **de ser amable** he made an effort o tried to be friendly

esfumarse [A1] v pron **(a)** «ilusiones/sueños» to evaporate; «temores» to melt away, be dispelled **(b)** (fam) «persona/dinero» to vanish, disappear

esgrima f fencing

esgrimista mf fencer

esguince m sprain; **sufrió un** ~ **en el tobillo** he sprained his ankle

eslabón m link

eslálom (pl **-loms**), **eslalon** m slalom

eslavo -va adj Slavic, Slavonic
■ m,f Slav

eslogan m (pl **-lóganes**) slogan

eslovaco¹ -ca adj Slovakian
■ m,f Slovak

eslovaco² m (idioma) Slovak

Eslovaquia f Slovakia

esmaltar [A1] vt ⟨metal⟩ to enamel; ⟨cerámica⟩ to glaze

esmalte m **(a)** (capa — sobre metales) enamel; (— sobre cerámica) glaze; ~ **de** or **para uñas** nail polish o (BrE) varnish **(b)** (Odont) enamel **(c)** (Art) enamel

esmerado -da adj ⟨persona⟩ conscientious, painstaking; ⟨presentación⟩ careful, painstaking; ⟨trabajo⟩ carefully done

esmeralda f emerald

esmerarse [A1] v pron to go to a lot of trouble; **se esmera en hacerlo bien** she goes to great pains to do it properly

esmero m care

esmirriado -da adj (fam) ⟨persona⟩ skinny (colloq), scrawny (colloq); ⟨animal⟩ scrawny

esmog m smog

esmoquin m (pl **-móquines**) tuxedo (AmE), dinner jacket (BrE)

esnifar [A1] vt ⟨cocaína⟩ (arg) to snort (sl); ⟨pegamento⟩ to sniff (colloq)

esnob adj (pl **-nobs**) snobbish
■ mf (pl **-nobs**) snob

esnobismo m snobbery, snobbishness

AmC	Central America	Arg	Argentina
AmL	Latin America	Bol	Bolivia
AmS	South America	Chi	Chile
Andes	Andean Region	CS	Southern Cone

Cu	Cuba	Per	Peru
Ec	Ecuador	RPl	River Plate Area
Esp	Spain	Ur	Uruguay
Méx	Mexico	Ven	Venezuela

eso *pron dem* **(a)** *(neutro)* that; **no digas ∼** don't say that; **∼ que te contaron** what they told you **(b)** *(en locs)* **a eso de** (at) around *o* about; **en eso: en ∼ llegó su madre** (just) at that moment her mother arrived; **¡eso es!** that's it!; **y eso que ...** even though ...; **por ∼** that's why **(c)** ¡eso! *(interj)* exactly!

esófago *m* esophagus*

esos, esas *pron dem:* ▶ ESE²

ésos, ésas *adj dem:* ▶ ÉSE

espabilado -da *adj* **(a)** *(despierto)* awake **(b)** *(vivo, listo)* bright, smart; **tienes que ser más ∼** you have to keep more on the ball
■ *m,f:* **los ∼s de la clase** the smart ones of the class

espabilar [A1] *vt* **(a)** *(quitar el sueño)* to wake ... up **(b)** *(avivar)* to wise ... up *(colloq)*
■ **∼** *vi* **(a)** *(sacudirse el sueño)* to wake up **(b)** *(darse prisa)* to get a move on *(colloq)* **(c)** *(avivarse)* to wise up *(colloq)*
■ **espabilarse** *v pron* **(a)** *(sacudirse el sueño)* to wake (oneself) up **(b)** *(darse prisa)* to get a move on *(colloq)* **(c)** *(avivarse)* to wise up *(colloq)*

espaciado -da *adj* **(a)** *(en el espacio):* **los árboles están muy ∼s** the trees are too far apart **(b)** *(en el tiempo):* **sus visitas se hicieron más espaciadas** her visits became more infrequent

espacial *adj* **(a)** *(cohete/vuelo)* space *(before n)* **(b)** (Fís, Mat) spatial

espacio *m* **1** **(a)** *(amplitud)* space, room; **ocupan demasiado ∼** they take up too much space *o* room **(b)** *(entre líneas, palabras)* space; *(entre objetos)* space; **rellenar los ∼s en blanco** fill in the blank spaces *o* the blanks **(c)** *(recinto, área)* area **2** (Espac): **el ∼** space; **∼ aéreo** airspace **3** *(de tiempo):* **por ∼ de 24 horas** for 24 hours *o* for a period of 24 hours **4** **(a)** (Rad, TV) *(programa)* program*; **∼ publicitario** advertising slot **(b)** *(en periódico, revista)* space

espacioso -sa *adj* spacious

espada *f* **1** *(arma)* sword **2** **(a)** *(carta)* any card of the ESPADAS suit **(b)** **espadas** *fpl* *(palo)* one of the suits in a Spanish pack of cards

espagetis, espaguettis *mpl* spaghetti

espalda *f* back; **ancho de ∼s** broad-shouldered; **perdona, te estoy dando la ∼** sorry, I've got my back to you; **de ∼s a nosotros** with his/her back to us; **vuélvete de ∼s** turn around *o* (BrE) round; **los 100 metros ∼** the 100 meters backstroke; **tenderse de ∼s** to lie on one's back; **lo atacaron por la ∼** he was attacked from behind; **hacer algo a ∼s de algn** to do sth behind sb's back

espantado -da *adj* **(a)** *(asustado)* frightened, scared; **salieron ∼s** they ran off in fright **(b)** *(horrorizado)* horrified, appalled

espantapájaros *m* *(pl* **∼**) scarecrow

espantar [A1] *vt* **1** **(a)** *(ahuyentar)* ‹peces/pájaros› to frighten away **(b)** *(asustar)* ‹caballo› to frighten, scare **2** *(fam)* *(horrorizar)* to horrify, appall*
■ **∼** *vi* **(a)** *(fam)* *(asustar):* **es tan feo que espanta** he's absolutely hideous *(colloq)* **(b)** (Bol, Col, Ven fam) ‹fantasma›: **en esa casa espantan** that house is haunted

■ **espantarse** *v pron* ‹pájaro/peces› to get frightened away; ‹caballo› to take fright, be startled

espanto *m* **1** **(a)** *(miedo)* fright, horror **(b)** *(uso hiperbólico):* **la noticia nos llenó de ∼** we were horrified *o* appalled at the news; **hace un frío de ∼** *(fam)* it's freezing *o* terribly cold *(colloq)*; **ya está curada de ∼** *(fam)* she's seen/heard it all before **2** (Bol, Col, Ven fam) *(espíritu)* ghost, spook *(colloq)*

espantoso -sa *adj* **(a)** ‹escena/crimen› horrific, appalling **(b)** *(fam)* *(uso hiperbólico)* ‹comida/letra/tiempo› atrocious; ‹vestido/color› hideous; ‹ruido/voz› terrible, awful; **pasé un frío ∼** I was absolutely freezing *(colloq)*

España *f* Spain

español¹ -ñola *adj* Spanish
■ *m,f* **(a)** *(persona)* *(m)* Spaniard, Spanish man; *(f)* Spaniard, Spanish woman; **los ∼es** the Spanish, Spaniards, Spanish people

español² *m* *(idioma)* Spanish

esparadrapo *m* surgical tape

esparcir [I4] *vt* **(a)** ‹libros/juguetes› to scatter **(b)** ‹rumor› to spread **(c)** (Chi) ‹mantequilla› to spread
■ **esparcirse** *v pron* **(a)** ‹líquido› to spread; ‹papeles/semillas› to be scattered **(b)** ‹noticia/rumor› to spread

espárrago *m* asparagus; **mandar a algn a freír ∼s** *(fam)* to tell sb to get lost *(colloq)*

espasmo *m* spasm

espátula *f* **(a)** *(paleta)* spatula; (Art) palette knife **(b)** *(para quitar pintura, papel)* scraper

especia *f* *(condimento)* spice

especial *adj* **(a)** *(en general)* special; **en ∼** especially, particularly; **nadie en ∼** nobody in particular; **un día muy ∼ para mí** a very special day for me **(b)** *(difícil)* ‹persona/carácter› fussy

especialidad *f* **(a)** *(actividad, estudio)* specialty (AmE), speciality (BrE); **hizo dos años de ∼** she did two years' specialization **(b)** *(de restaurante)* specialty (AmE), speciality (BrE)

especialista *adj* specialist *(before n)*
■ *mf* **(a)** *(experto)* specialist, expert **(b)** (Med) specialist; **un ∼ de(l) corazón** a heart specialist **(c)** (Cin, TV) *(m)* stuntman; *(f)* stuntwoman

especialización *f* specialization

especializado -da *adj* **(a)** ‹librería/restaurante› specialty *(before n)* (AmE), specialist *(before n)* (BrE); **∼ EN algo** specializing IN sth **(b)** ‹lenguaje› technical, specialized **(c)** ‹obrero› skilled, specialized *(before n)*

especializarse [A4] *v pron* to specialize

especie *f* **(a)** (Biol, Bot, Zool) species **(b)** *(clase)* kind, sort

especificar [A2] *vt* to specify

específico -ca *adj* specific

espécimen *m* *(pl* **-pecímenes**) *(ejemplar)* specimen; *(muestra)* sample, specimen

espectacular *adj* spectacular

espectáculo *m* **1** *(representación)* show; **un ∼ de variedades** a variety show; **❺ espectáculos** *(en periódicos)* entertainment guide; **el mundo del ∼** showbusiness **2** *(visión, panorama)* sight; **un triste ∼** a sad sight *o* spectacle

espectador -dora *m,f* (Dep) spectator; (Espec) ⋯⋙

member of the audience; **asistieron al estreno dos mil ~es** two thousand people attended the premiere

espectro *m* [1] (gama) spectrum [2] (fantasma) specter*, ghost; (amenaza) specter*

especulación *f* speculation

especulador -dora *m,f* speculator

especular [A1] *vi* to speculate

espejismo *m* (fenómeno óptico) mirage; (ilusión) illusion

espejo *m* mirror; ~ **de cuerpo entero** full-length mirror; ~ **lateral/retrovisor** wing/rear-view mirror; **mirarse al** ~ to look (at oneself) in the mirror; **la obra es** ~ **de esa sociedad** the play mirrors that society

espeleología *f* spelunking, potholing (BrE)

espeluznante *adj* ⟨tragedia/estado/experiencia⟩ horrific, horrifying; ⟨grito⟩ terrifying, blood-curdling

espera *f* [1] (acción, período) wait; **una larga** ~ a long wait; **estoy a la** ~ **de una oferta concreta** I am waiting for a concrete offer; **en su respuesta saluda a Vd. atte.** (frml) I look forward to hearing from you, yours faithfully [2] (Der) respite

esperado -da *adj* **(a)** (aguardado) ⟨acontecimiento/carta⟩ eagerly awaited **(b)** (que es de esperar): **no obtuvo los resultados** ~s he didn't get the results he expected

esperanza *f* hope; **mi única** ~ my only hope; **puso todas sus** ~s **en su hijo** he pinned all his hopes on his son; **hay** ~s **de éxito** there are hopes that he/it/they will succeed; **perdimos toda** ~ **de encontrarlos vivos** we gave up *o* lost hope of finding them alive; **fue con la** ~ **de que ...** he went in the hope that ...; **me dio** ~s **de que el niño mejoraría** he gave me hope that the child would recover; ~ **de vida** life expectancy

esperanzado -da *adj* hopeful

esperanzador -dora *adj* encouraging

esperar [A1] *vt* [1] **(a)** ⟨autobús/persona/acontecimiento⟩ to wait for; **¿qué estás esperando para decírselo?** tell him! what are you waiting for? **(b)** (recibir) to meet; **la fuimos a** ~ **al aeropuerto** we went to meet her at the airport **(c)** ⟨sorpresa⟩ to await; **le espera un futuro difícil** he has a difficult future ahead of him
[2] **(a)** (contar con, prever) to expect; **tal como esperábamos** just as we expected; **cuando uno menos lo espera** when you least expect it; **te espero alrededor de las nueve** I'll expect you around nine; **¿esperabas que te felicitara?** did you expect me to congratulate you?; **era de** ~ **que el proyecto fracasara** the project was bound to fail **(b)** ⟨niño/bebé⟩ to be expecting
[3] (con esperanza) to hope; **eso espero** *or* **espero que sí** I hope so; **espero que no** I hope not; ~ **hacer algo** to hope to do sth; **espero que no llueva** I hope it doesn't rain; **esperemos que no sea nada grave** let's hope it's nothing serious
■ ~ *vi* **(a)** (aguardar) to wait; **no podemos** ~ **más** we can't wait any longer; **espera a estar seguro** wait until you're sure; ~**on (a) que él se fuera para entrar** they waited for him to go before they went in **(b)** ⟨embarazada⟩: **estar esperando** to be expecting

■ **esperarse** *v pron* [1] (fam) (aguardar) to hang on (colloq), to hold on (colloq)
[2] (fam) (prever) to expect; **¡quién se lo iba a** ~**!** who would have thought it!

esperma *m or f* (Biol) sperm
■ *f* **(a)** (sustancia) spermaceti **(b)** (Col) (vela) candle

espesar [A1] *vt/vi* to thicken
■ **espesarse** *v pron* «salsa» to thicken; «vegetación» to become thick, become dense

espeso -sa *adj* **(a)** ⟨salsa⟩ thick; ⟨vegetación/niebla⟩ dense, thick; ⟨nieve⟩ thick, deep; ⟨cabello/barba⟩ bushy, thick **(b)** (Per fam) (cargoso) annoying

espesor *m* thickness

espesura *f* vegetation; **se abrieron paso por entre la** ~ they hacked a path through the vegetation

espía *adj inv* ⟨avión/satélite⟩ spy (before n); ⟨cámara⟩ hidden (before n), secret (before n)
■ *mf* (persona) spy

espiar [A17] *vt* ⟨enemigo/movimientos⟩ to spy on, keep watch on
■ ~ *vi* to spy

espiga *f* (Agr, Bot) (de trigo) ear, spike; (de flores) spike

espigón *m* **(a)** (rompeolas) breakwater **(b)** (Per, RPl) (en aeropuerto) terminal (building)

espina *f* **(a)** (de rosal, zarza) thorn; (de cactus) prickle **(b)** (de pez) bone **(c)** (Anat) spine; ~ **dorsal** spine, backbone; **darle a algn mala** ~ to make sb feel uneasy; **esto me da mala** ~ I don't like the look of this

espinaca *f* spinach

espinazo *m* spine, backbone

espinilla *f* [1] (Anat) shin [2] (en la piel) **(a)** (de cabeza negra) blackhead **(b)** (AmL) (barrito) pimple, spot

espino *m* hawthorn

espinoso -sa *adj* [1] **(a)** ⟨rosal/zarza⟩ thorny; ⟨cactus⟩ prickly **(b)** ⟨pescado⟩ bony [2] ⟨problema/asunto⟩ thorny, knotty

espionaje *m* spying, espionage; **novela de** ~ spy novel

espiral *f* **(a)** (forma, movimiento) spiral; **un cuaderno de** ~(es) a spiral-bound notebook; **escalera de** ~ spiral staircase **(b)** (muelle) hairspring **(c)** (dispositivo intrauterino) coil

espirar [A1] *vi* to breathe out, exhale

espiritismo *m* spiritualism; **sesión de** ~ séance

espiritista *adj/mf* spiritualist

espíritu *m* **(a)** (en general) spirit; **un** ~ **maligno** an evil spirit; **E~ Santo** Holy Ghost *o* Spirit; **con** ~ **de sacrificio** in a spirit of self-sacrifice; **el** ~ **de la ley** the spirit of the law **(b)** (naturaleza, carácter) nature; **tiene un** ~ **rebelde** she has a rebellious nature

espiritual *adj* spiritual
■ *m*: **tb** ~ **negro** (Negro) spiritual

espita *f* spigot (AmE), tap (BrE)

espléndido -da *adj* **(a)** ⟨fiesta/comida⟩ splendid, magnificent; ⟨día/tiempo⟩ splendid, marvelous*; ⟨regalo/joya/abrigo⟩ magnificent **(b)** (generoso) ⟨persona⟩ generous; ⟨regalo⟩ lavish, generous

esplendor *m* **(a)** (magnificencia) splendor*, magnificence **(b)** (apogeo) splendor*

espolear [A1] *vt* ‹caballo› to spur (on)

espoleta *f* (Arm) fuse

espolvorear [A1] *vt* to sprinkle

esponja *f* sponge

esponjoso -sa *adj* ‹masa/bizcocho› spongy, fluffy; ‹tejido› soft; ‹lana› fluffy

espontaneidad *f* spontaneity

espontáneo -nea *adj* ‹persona/gesto/ayuda› spontaneous; ‹actuación› impromptu
■ *m,f: spectator who jumps into the ring to join in the bullfight*

esporádico -ca *adj* ‹sucesos/visitas› sporadic, intermittent

esposado -da *adj* handcuffed, in handcuffs

esposas *fpl* handcuffs (*pl*)

esposo -sa *m,f* (*m*) husband; (*f*) wife

espray *m* (*pl* **-prays**) **(a)** (atomizador) spray **(b)** (pintura) spray paint

esprint *m* (*pl* **-prints**) sprint

espuela *f* spur

espuelear [A1] *vt* (AmL) to spur (on)

espuma *f* [1] **(a)** (del mar) foam; (al romper las olas) surf; (en agua revuelta) foam, froth **(b)** (del jabón) lather; **este jabón no hace ~** this soap doesn't lather; **un baño de ~** a foam *o* bubble bath; **~ de afeitar** shaving foam; **~ seca** carpet shampoo **(c)** (de la cerveza) head, froth **(d)** (Coc) (capa) scum [2] **(a)** (caucho celular) foam rubber **(b)** (tejido elástico) stretch nylon

espumadera *f* skimmer, slotted spoon

espumante *m* sparkling wine

espumillón *m* tinsel

espumoso¹ -sa *adj* ‹ola› foaming; ‹cerveza› frothy; ‹vino› sparkling

espumoso² *m* sparkling wine

espueje *m* (para plantar) cutting; (para injertar) scion

esquela *f* **(a)** (AmL) (carta) note **(b)** (Andes) (papel) stationery set **(c)** (Esp) (aviso fúnebre) *tb* ~ **mortuoria** death notice

esqueleto *m* **(a)** (Anat) skeleton **(b)** (de edificio, novela) framework

esquema *m* [1] (croquis) sketch, diagram; (sinopsis) outline [2] (de ideas): **el ~ liberal** liberal philosophy *o* thinking; **no se sale de sus ~s** she doesn't change her way of thinking

esquemático -ca *adj* schematic; **el libro es algo ~** the book is a little oversimplified

esquematizar [A4] *vt/vi* to schematize

esquí *m* (*pl* **-quís** *o* **-quíes**) (tabla) ski; (deporte) skiing; **pista de ~** ski run, piste; **~ acuático** *or* **náutico** waterskiing; **hacer ~ acuático** to water-ski

esquiador -dora *m,f* skier

esquiar [A17] *vi* to ski

esquilar [A1] *vt* to shear, clip

esquimal *adj/mf* Eskimo

esquina *f* **(a)** (en calle) corner; **en la calle Vidal, ~ (a) Cádiz** on the corner of Vidal (Street) and Cadiz (Street); **doblar la ~** to go round *o* turn the corner; **hace ~ con la plaza** it's on the corner of the square **(b)** (Dep): **sacar de ~** to take a corner (kick)

esquinazo *m* [1] (Esp): **darle (el) ~ a algn** (dejar plantado) to stand sb up; (esquivar) to give sb the slip [2] (Chi) (serenata) *serenade of traditional singing and dancing*

esquirol *mf* (pey) strikebreaker, scab (pej)

esquivar [A1] *vt* ‹persona/dificultad› to avoid; ‹golpe/pregunta› to dodge, evade; ‹responsabilidad› to avoid, evade

esquivo -va *adj* **(a)** ‹persona› (difícil de encontrar) elusive; (huraño) aloof, unsociable; (tímido) shy **(b)** ‹respuesta› elusive, evasive

esquizofrenia *f* schizophrenia

esquizofrénico -ca *adj/m,f* schizophrenic

estabilidad *f* stability

estabilizar [A4] *vt* to stabilize
■ **estabilizarse** *v pron* to stabilize

estable *adj* stable; ‹trabajo› steady

establecer [E3] *vt* [1] **(a)** ‹colonia/dictadura› to establish; ‹campamento› to set up; **estableció su residencia en Mónaco** he took up residence in Monaco **(b)** ‹relaciones/contacto› to establish [2] (dejar sentado) **(a)** ‹criterios/bases› to establish, lay down; ‹precio› to fix, set; ‹precedente› to establish, set **(b)** (frml) ‹ley/reglamento› (disponer) to state, establish **(c)** ‹récord/marca/moda› to set; ‹uso› to establish [3] (determinar) to establish
■ **establecerse** *v pron* ‹colono/emigrante› to settle; ‹comerciante/empresa› to set up

establecimiento *m* establishment

establo *m* stable

estaca *f* **(a)** (poste) stake, post **(b)** (para carpa) tent peg **(c)** (garrote) club, stick **(d)** (clavo de madera) peg

estación *f* [1] (de tren, metro, autobús) station; **~ de bomberos** (Col, Méx, Ven) fire station; **~ de policía** (Col, Ven) police station; **~ de esquí** ski resort; **~ de servicio** service station, gas (AmE) *o* (BrE) petrol station; **~ terminal** *or* **término** terminal, terminus (BrE) [2] (del año) season [3] (AmL) (emisora) radio station

estacionamiento *m* **(a)** (acción de estacionar) parking **(b)** (espacio para estacionar) parking space; (en recinto cerrado) (AmL) parking lot (AmE), car park (BrE)

estacionar [A1] *vt* to park
■ ~ *vi* to park; **❂ prohibido estacionar** no parking; **~ en doble fila** to double-park
■ **estacionarse** *v pron* **(a)** ‹crecimiento› to stop; ‹peso› to stabilize; ‹proceso/enfermedad› to halt **(b)** (Chi, Méx) ‹conductor› to park

estadía *f* (AmL) (en un lugar) stay

estadio *m* stadium

estadista *mf* (*m*) statesman; (*f*) stateswoman

estadística *f* **(a)** (estudio) statistical study **(b)** (cifra) statistic, figure **(c)** (disciplina) statistics

estadístico -ca *adj* statistical

estado *m* [1] **(a)** (en general) state; **~ de ánimo** state of mind; **~ de cuenta** bank statement; **~ de emergencia** *or* **excepción** state of emergency; **la casa está en buen ~** the house is in good condition **(b)** (Med) condition; **estar en ~** (euf) to be expecting (colloq); **quedarse en ~** (euf) to get pregnant **(c)** estado civil marital status [2] (nación, gobierno) state; **la seguridad del E~** national *o* state security; **~ de bienestar** welfare state

Estados Unidos m: tb los ~ ~ mpl the United States (+ *sing or pl vb*)

Estados Unidos Mexicanos mpl (frml) United States of Mexico (frml)

estadounidense adj American, US (*before n*)

■ mf American

estafa f (a) (Der) fraud, criminal deception (b) (fam) (timo) rip-off (colloq), con (colloq)

estafador -dora m,f (a) (Der) fraudster (b) (fam) (timador) swindler (colloq)

estafar [A1] vt (a) (Der) to swindle, defraud; ~le algo A algn to defraud sb OF sth, swindle sb OUT OF sth (b) (fam) (timar) to rip … off (colloq), to con (colloq)

estafeta f: tb ~ de correos mail office (AmE), sub-post office (BrE)

estallar [A1] vi (a) «*bomba*» to explode; «*neumático*» to blow out, burst; «*globo*» to burst; «*vidrio*» to shatter; **hizo ~ el dispositivo** he detonated the device (b) «*guerra/revuelta*» to break out; «*tormenta/escándalo/crisis*» to break (c) «*persona*» (ponerse furioso) to blow one's top (colloq); ~ **EN algo** ‹*en llanto/carcajadas*› to burst INTO sth

estallido m (a) (de bomba) explosion; (de neumático) bursting; (de cristal) shattering (b) (de guerra) outbreak

estamento m (de sociedad) stratum, class

estampado¹ -da adj patterned, printed

estampado² m pattern; **los ~s están de moda** patterned o printed fabrics are in fashion

estampar [A1] vt (imprimir) ‹*tela/diseño*› to print; ‹*metal*› to stamp; (formando relieve) to emboss

estampida f stampede; **salir en or de ~** to stampede out

estampido m (de pistola) bang, report; (de bomba) bang

estampilla f (a) (AmL) (sello — postal) postage (stamp); (— fiscal) tax stamp (b) (sello de goma) rubber stamp

estampillar [A1] vt (AmL) (con sello fiscal o de correos) to stamp

estancado -da adj (a) ‹*agua*› stagnant (b) (detenido): **las negociaciones están estancadas** negotiations are at a standstill (c) (con un problema) stuck, bogged down

estancamiento m stagnation

estancarse [A2] v pron (a) ‹*agua*› to become stagnant, to stagnate (b) «*negociación/ proceso*» to come to a halt o standstill (c) (con un problema) to get bogged down o stuck

estancia f [1] (frml) (habitación) large room [2] (Esp, Méx) (permanencia) stay [3] (en el CS) (Agr) farm; (de ganado) ranch

estanciero -ra m,f (en el CS) (Agr) farmer; (de ganado) rancher

estanco m (tienda) tobacconist's

estándar adj/m standard

estandarte m standard, banner

estanque m pond

estanquillo m (Méx) general store (AmE), grocer's shop (BrE)

estante m shelf

estantería f shelves (*pl*); (para libros) bookcase, bookshelves (*pl*)

estaño m (elemento) tin; (para soldar) solder; (peltre) pewter

estar¹ [A27] *cópula* **1** (a) (seguido de adjetivos) [ESTAR *denotes a changed condition or state as opposed to identity or nature, which is normally expressed by* SER. ESTAR *is also used when the emphasis is on the speaker's perception of things, of their appearance, taste, etc. The examples given below should be contrasted with those to be found in* SER¹ *cópula* 1] to be; **estás más gordo** you've put on weight; **estoy cansada** I'm tired; **está muy simpático conmigo** he's being o he's been so nice to me (recently); **¡todo está tan caro!** things are o have become so expensive! (b) (con BIEN, MAL, MEJOR, PEOR): **están todos bien, gracias** they're all fine, thanks; **¡qué bien estás en esta foto!** you look great in this photo!; **está mal que no se lo perdones** it's wrong of you not to forgive him; *ver tb* BIEN, MAL, MEJOR, PEOR

2 (hablando de estado civil) to be; **está casada con un primo mío** she's married to a cousin of mine

3 (seguido de participios) ~ **sentado** to be sitting; **estaban abrazados** they had their arms around each other; *ver tb v aux* 2

4 (seguido de preposición) to be; (*para más ejemplos ver tb la preposición o el nombre correspondiente*); **estoy a régimen** I'm on a diet; **¿a cómo está la uva?** how much are the grapes?; **está con el sarampión** she has (the) measles; **estoy de cocinera** I'm doing the cooking; **estamos sin electricidad** the electricity is off at the moment; **está sin pintar** it hasn't been painted yet

■ ~ vi **1** (en un lugar) to be; **¿dónde está Chiapas?** where's Chiapas?; **está a 20 kilómetros de aquí** it's 20 kilometers from here; **¿sabes dónde está Pedro?** do you know where Pedro is?; **¿está Rodrigo?** is Rodrigo in?; **solo ~é unos días** I'll only be staying a few days; **¿cuánto tiempo ~ás en Londres?** how long are you going to be in London (for)?

2 (en el tiempo): **¿a qué (día) estamos?** what day is it today?; **¿a cuánto estamos hoy?** what's the date today?; **estamos a 28 de mayo** it's May 28th (AmE) o (BrE) the 28th of May; **estamos en primavera** it's spring

3 (a) (tener como función, cometido): **para eso están los amigos** that's what friends are for; **estamos para ayudarlos** we're here to help them (b) (radicar) to lie; **en eso está el problema** that's where the problem lies

4 (estar listo, terminado): **la carne todavía no está** the meat's not ready yet; **lo atas con un nudo y ya está** you tie a knot in it and that's it o there you are; **enseguida estoy** I'll be right with you

5 (Esp) (quedar) (+ *me/te/le etc*) (+ *compl*): **te está pequeña** it's too small for you; **la 46 te está mejor** the 46 fits you better

■ ~ *v aux* **1** (con gerundio): **está lloviendo** it's raining; **estoy viendo que va a ser imposible** I'm beginning to see that it's going to be impossible **2** (con participio): **ese asiento está ocupado** that seat is taken; **ya está hecho un hombrecito** he's a proper young man now; *ver tb* ESTAR *cópula* 3

■ **estarse** *v pron* (enf) (permanecer) to stay; **¿no te puedes ~ quieto?** can't you stay *o* keep still?; **estese tranquilo** don't worry

estar² *m* (esp AmL) living room

estárter *m* choke

estatal *adj* state (*before n*)

estático -ca *adj* static

estatua *f* statue

estatura *f* height; **mide dos metros de ~** he's two meters (tall); **¿qué ~ tenía?** how tall was she?; **de mediana ~** of medium height

estatus *m* status

estatuto *m* (Der, Pol) statute; (regla) rule **(b) estatutos** *mpl* (de empresa) articles of association (*pl*)

este¹ *adj inv* (región) eastern; **iban en dirección ~** they were heading east *o* eastward(s); **el ala/la costa ~** the east wing/coast
■ *m* **(a)** (parte, sector): **el ~** the east; **al ~ de Lima** to the east of Lima; (punto cardinal) east, East; **vientos del E~** easterly winds; **las ventanas dan al ~** the windows face east **(c) el Este** (Hist, Pol) the East; **los países del E~** the Eastern Bloc countries

este², esta *adj dem* (*pl* **estos, estas**) **(a)** this; (*pl*) these; **este chico** this boy; **estos dólares** these dollars; [*usually indicates a pejorative or emphatic tone when placed after the noun*] **la estúpida esta no me avisó** (fam) this idiot here didn't tell me **(b)** (como muletilla) well, er

éste, ésta *pron dem* (*pl* **éstos, éstas**) [*The written accent may be omitted when there is no confusion with the adjective*] this one; (*pl*) these; **~ *or* este es el mío** this (one) is mine; **un día de éstos *or* estos** one of these days; **~ *or* este es el que yo quería** this is the one I wanted; **prefiero éstos *or* estos** I prefer these (ones); [*sometimes indicates irritation, emphasis or disapproval*] **¡qué niña ésta!** (fam) honestly, this child!; **residente en ésta *or* esta** resident in Seville (*o* Lima *etc*)

estela *f* (de barco) wake; (de avión, cohete) trail

estelar *adj* **(a)** (Espec) star **(b)** (Astron) stellar

estelarizar [A4] *vt* (Méx) to star in

estepa *f* steppe

estera *f* mat

estercolero *m* dunghill, dung heap

estéreo *adj inv/m* stereo

estereofónico -ca *adj* stereophonic

estereotipado -da *adj* (frase) clichéd; (idea/personaje) stereotyped

estereotipo *m* stereotype

estéril *adj* **(a)** (animal/persona) sterile; (terreno) infertile, barren **(b)** (esfuerzo/discusión) futile **(c)** (gasa/jeringa) sterile

esterilidad *f* infertility; (de un hombre) sterility

esterilizar [A4] *vt* to sterilize

esterilla *f* **(a)** (alfombrilla) mat **(b)** (AmS) (mimbre) wicker

esternón *m* sternum, breastbone

estero *m* **(a)** (AmS) (laguna, pantano) marsh **(b)** (Chi) (arroyo) stream

esteroide *m* steroid

estética *f* **(a)** (Art) aesthetics **(b)** (Med) cosmetic surgery

esteticien, esteticista *mf* aesthetician, beautician

estético -ca *adj* aesthetic

estetoscopio *m* stethoscope

estiércol *m* (excremento) dung; (abono) manure

estigma *m* stigma

estilar [A1] *vi* (Chi) (gotear) to drip; (escurrir) to drain
■ **estilarse** *v pron* «moda/peinado» to be fashionable

estilista *mf* **(a)** (Lit) stylist **(b)** (diseñador de modas) designer **(c)** (AmL) (peluquero) hairstylist

estilístico -ca *adj* stylistic

estilizado -da *adj* **(a)** (Art) stylized **(b)** (cuerpo/figura) slender, slim

estilo *m* **(a)** (en general) style; **~ barroco** baroque style; **~ de vida** way of life, lifestyle; **ropa ~ deportivo** casual wear; **vestir con ~** to dress stylishly; **al ~ de mi tierra** the way they do it back home; **por el ~**: **son todos por el ~** they are all the same; **algo por el ~** something like that **(b)** (en natación) stroke, style; **~ libre** freestyle; **~ mariposa** butterfly; **~ pecho *or* (Esp) braza** breaststroke

estilográfica *f* fountain pen

estima *f* esteem; **ganarse la ~ de algn** to raise oneself in sb's esteem; **tener(le) ~ a algn** to think highly of sb; **tiene en gran ~ tu amistad** he values your friendship very highly

estimación *f* **1** (cálculo) estimate **2** (aprecio) esteem

estimado -da *adj* dear

estimar [A1] *vt* **1** **(a)** (persona) (respetar) to respect, hold ... in high esteem (frml); (tener cariño) to be fond of **(b)** (objeto) to value; **su piel es muy estimada** its skin is highly prized **2** (frml) (considerar) (+ *compl*) to consider, deem (frml)

estimulante *adj* stimulating

estimular [A1] *vt* **(a)** (en general) to stimulate **(b)** (alentar) (persona) to encourage

estímulo *m* **(a)** (incentivo) incentive **(b)** (Biol, Fisiol) stimulus

estirado -da *adj* (fam) stuck-up (colloq)

estirar [A1] *vt* **1** **(a)** (goma/elástico/suéter) to stretch; (cable/soga) to pull out, stretch **(b)** (sábanas/mantel) (con las manos) to smooth out; (con la plancha) to run the iron over **2** (brazos/piernas/músculo) to stretch; **estiró el cuello para poder ver** she craned her neck to be able to see **3** (dinero/comida/recursos) to make ... go further
■ **estirarse** *v pron* to stretch

estirón *m*: **dar *or* pegar un ~** (fam) to shoot up (colloq)

estirpe *f* stock, lineage

estítico -ca *adj* (Chi) constipated

estitiquez *f* (Chi) constipation

esto *pron dem* (*neutro*) this; ¿qué es ~? what's this?; ~ es lo que quiero this is what I want

estofado¹ -da *adj* stewed; (con menos líquido) braised

estofado² *m* stew

estoico -ca *adj* stoic, stoical

estomacal *adj* stomach (*before n*)

estómago *m* (Anat) stomach; tengo dolor de ~ I have a stomachache, my stomach hurts; beber con el ~ vacío to drink on an empty stomach; revolverle el ~ a algn to turn sb's stomach

estoperol *m* [1] (Andes) (en carretera) cat's eye [2] (Chi) (Dep) stud

estoque *m* sword (*used for killing bull*)

estorbar [A1] *vi* to be/get in the way
■ ~ *vt* to obstruct; el piano estorbaba el paso the piano was in the way

estorbo *m* (obstáculo) hindrance; (molestia) nuisance

estornudar [A1] *vi* to sneeze

estornudo *m* sneeze

estos -tas *adj dem:* ▶ ESTE²

éstos -tas *pron dem:* ▶ ÉSTE

estoy ▶ ESTAR¹

estrabismo *m* squint, strabismus (tech)

estrado *m* (tarima) platform, dais

estrafalario -ria *adj* 〈persona/ideas/conducta〉 eccentric; 〈vestimenta〉 outlandish, bizarre
■ *m,f* eccentric

estragón *m* tarragon

estragos *mpl*: los ~ de la guerra the ravages of war; causar/hacer ~s «terremoto/inundación» to wreak havoc; la epidemia causó ~ entre la población the epidemic devastated the population

estrambótico -ca *adj* 〈persona/idea/conducta〉 eccentric; 〈vestimenta〉 outlandish, bizarre

estrangulador -dora *m,f* strangler

estrangular [A1] *vt* (a) 〈persona/animal〉 to strangle, throttle (b) 〈vena/conducto〉 to strangulate

estraperlo *m* black market

estratagema *f* stratagem

estrategia *f* strategy

estratégico -ca *adj* strategic

estratosfera *f* stratosphere

estrechar [A1] *vt* [1] (a) 〈falda/pantalones〉 to take ... in; 〈carretera〉 to make ... narrower (b) 〈relaciones/lazos〉 to strengthen [2] (abrazar, apretar): la estrechó entre sus brazos he held her tightly in his arms; me estrechó la mano he shook my hand
■ **estrecharse** *v pron* [1] (a) 〈carretera/acera〉 to narrow, get narrower (b) 〈relaciones/lazos〉 to strengthen [2] (recípr) (apretarse): se ~on en un abrazo they embraced; se ~on la mano they shook hands

estrecho¹ -cha *adj* [1] 〈calle/pasillo〉 narrow; 〈falda〉 tight; íbamos muy ~s it was very cramped [2] 〈amistad/colaboración/vigilancia〉 close [3] (limitado) 〈criterio〉 narrow; es muy ~ de miras he's very narrow-minded

estrecho² *m* (Geog) strait, straits (*pl*); el E~ de Gibraltar the Strait(s) of Gibraltar

estrella *f* (a) (en general) star; ~ de mar starfish; ~ fugaz shooting star; ~ polar Pole Star; un hotel de tres ~s a three-star hotel; una ~ de cine a movie star (b) (asterisco) asterisk

estrellado -da *adj* (lleno de estrellas) starry; (en forma de estrella) star-shaped

estrellar [A1] *vt*: estrelló un plato contra la pared he smashed a plate against the wall; estrelló el coche contra un árbol he smashed his car into a tree
■ **estrellarse** *v pron* (chocar) to crash; se estrelló con la moto he had a motorcycle accident; ~se CONTRA algo «coche» to crash INTO sth; «olas» to crash AGAINST sth; se estrelló contra el vidrio he walked smack into the glass door

estremecedor -dora *adj* 〈escena/noticia〉 horrifying; 〈grito/relato〉 spine-chilling, hair-raising

estremecer [E3] *vt* to make ... shudder
■ ~ *vi* to shudder; hacer ~ a algn to make sb shudder
■ **estremecerse** *v pron* (a) «persona» ~se DE algo 〈de miedo/horror〉 to shudder WITH sth; 〈de frío〉 to shiver o tremble WITH sth; se estremeció solo de pensarlo he shuddered at the mere thought of it (b) «edificio/ventana» to shake

estremecimiento *m* (de miedo) shudder; tenía ~s de frío he was shivering with cold

estrenar [A1] *vt* [1] (Cin, Teatr): la película se estrenó en marzo the movie opened o (journ) had its premiere in March; acaban de ~ la obra en Madrid the play's just started showing o just opened in Madrid [2] (usar por primera vez): voy a ~ corbata I'm going to wear a new tie; todavía no he estrenado la blusa I still haven't worn the blouse; todavía no estrenamos el gimnasio we still haven't tried out the gymnasium

estreno *m* [1] (de película, nueva obra) premiere; (de nueva puesta en escena) opening night [2] (primer uso): ir de ~ to be wearing new clothes; el ~ del local the opening of the new premises

estreñido -da *adj* constipated

estreñimiento *m* constipation

estreñir [I15] *vi* to cause constipation
■ ~ *vt* to make ... constipated, bind (colloq)

estrés *m* stress

estresado -da *adj* under stress

estresante *adj* stressful

estría *f* (a) (de la piel) stretch mark (b) (de columna) groove, stria (tech)

estriado -da *adj* 〈piel〉 stretch-marked (b) 〈columna〉 fluted

estribillo *m* (Lit) refrain; (Mús) chorus

estribo *m* (a) (Equ) stirrup; perder los ~s to fly off the handle, lose one's cool; tomarse la del ~ to have one for the road (colloq) (b) (de vehículo) running board; (de moto) footrest

estribor *m* starboard

estricto -ta *adj* strict

estridente *adj* (a) 〈pitido/chirrido〉 shrill (b) 〈voz〉 (agudo) shrill; (fuerte) strident (c) 〈color〉 garish, loud

estrofa *f* stanza, verse

estropajo *m* scourer

181

estropeado ⋯⋗ evaluación ⋯

estropeado -da adj: estar ~ «zapato/sillón» to be falling apart; «motor/coche» to be broken down; ver tb ESTROPEAR

estropear [A1] vt ① (a) ‹aparato/mecanismo› to damage, break; ‹coche› to damage (b) (malograr) ‹plan/vacaciones› to spoil, ruin ② (deteriorar, dañar) ‹piel› to damage, ruin; ‹juguete› to break; ‹ropa› to ruin; **el calor estropeó la fruta** the heat made the fruit go bad
■ **estropearse** v pron ① (a) (averiarse) «motor/coche» to break down; **la lavadora está estropeada** the washing machine is broken (b) «plan/vacaciones» to go wrong ② (deteriorarse) «fruta» to go bad; «leche/pescado» to go off; «zapatos/chaqueta» to get ruined

estructura f structure

estructurar [A1] vt to structure, to organize

estruendo m (de las olas) roar; (de cascada, tráfico) thunder, roar; (de maquinaria) din

estrujar [A1] vt ① (a) (apretar arrugando) ‹papel› to crumple up, scrunch up; ‹tela› to crumple (up) (b) (para escurrir) to wring (out) (c) ‹uvas› to press ② ‹persona› to squeeze, hold ... tightly

estuche m (de gafas, lápices, violín) case; (de cubiertos) canteen; (de collar, reloj) box, case

estudiante mf (de universidad) student; (de secundaria) (high-school) student (AmE), (secondary school) pupil (BrE)

estudiantil adj student (before n)

estudiar [A1] vt ① (a) ‹asignatura› to study; (en la universidad) to study, read (frml); **¿qué carrera estudió?** what subject did he do at college/university? (b) ‹instrumento› to learn (c) ‹lección/tablas› to learn ② (observar) ‹rostro/comportamiento› to study ③ (considerar, analizar) ‹mercado/situación/proyecto› to study; ‹propuesta› to study, consider; ‹causas› to look into, investigate
■ ~ vi to study; **estudia en un colegio privado** he goes to a private school; **debes ~ más** you must work harder; **dejó de ~ a los 15 años** she left school at 15; **~ PARA algo** to study to be sth
■ **estudiarse** v pron (enf) ‹lección› to study; ‹papel› to learn

estudio m ① (a) (Educ) (actividad): **primero está el ~** studying o your studies o work must come first (b) (investigación, análisis) study; **~ de mercado** market research (c) (de asunto, caso) consideration; **está en ~** it is being considered ② (lugar) (a) (de artista) studio; (de arquitecto) office, studio (b) (Cin, Rad, TV) studio (c) (en casa) study; (apartamento) studio apartment ③ **estudios** mpl (Educ) education; **quiso darle ~s a su hijo** she wanted to give her son an education; **tener ~s superiores** to have a degree; **dejar los ~s** to give up one's studies

estudioso -sa adj studious
■ m,f scholar

estufa f (a) (de calefacción) stove; **~ eléctrica** electric heater (b) (Col, Méx) (cocina) stove; **~ de gas** gas stove o (BrE) cooker

estupefaciente m narcotic (drug); **tráfico de ~s** drug trafficking

estupefacto -ta adj astonished, amazed

estupendo¹ -da adj (a) (excelente) marvelous*, fantastic (colloq), great (colloq); **¡~!** great! (b) (guapo) gorgeous

estupendo² adv ‹cantar› marvelously*; **lo pasé ~** I had a great o wonderful time

estupidez f (a) (cualidad) stupidity, foolishness (b) (dicho): **no digas estupideces** don't talk nonsense (c) (acto): **eso sería una ~** that would be stupid o foolish

estúpido -da adj ‹persona› stupid; ‹argumento› stupid, silly; **¡ay, qué estúpida soy!** oh, how stupid of me!
■ m,f idiot, fool

estupor m astonishment

estuve, estuviste, etc ▶ ESTAR¹

esvástica f swastika

ETA /'eta/ f (= Euzkadi ta Azkatasuna) ETA

etapa f stage; **por ~s** in stages; **la ~ más feliz de mi vida** the best o happiest time of my life

etarra mf: member of ETA

etcétera etcetera, and so on (and so forth)

etéreo -rea adj ethereal

eternidad f eternity

eterno -na adj eternal; ‹amor› everlasting

ética f ethics

ético -ca adj ethical

etimología f etymology

etíope, etiope adj/mf Ethiopian

Etiopía f Ethiopia

etiqueta f ① (a) (adherida) label (b) (atada) tag; (en prenda) label ② (protocolo) etiquette; **baile/traje de ~** formal ball/dress

etiquetar [A1] vt ‹producto› to label; ‹persona› **~ a algn DE** algo to label sb (AS) sth

étnico -ca adj ethnic

eucalipto m eucalyptus

Eucaristía f Eucharist

eufemismo m euphemism

euforia f elation, euphoria

eufórico -ca adj ecstatic, euphoric

euro m euro

eurocheque m eurocheque

eurodiputado -da m,f Euro MP, MEP, Member of the European Parliament

Europa f Europe

europeísta adj pro-European

europeo -pea adj/m,f European

Eurotunnel®, eurotúnel m Channel Tunnel

Euskadi f the Basque Country

euskera, eusquera adj/m Basque

eutanasia f euthanasia

evacuación f (desalojo) evacuation

evacuar [I1] vt or [A1] vt ‹local/zona/población› to evacuate

evadir [I1] vt (a) ‹pregunta/peligro/responsabilidad› to avoid; ‹tema› to dodge, evade (b) ‹impuestos› to evade
■ **evadirse** v pron (a) «preso» to escape (b) **~se DE** algo ‹de responsabilidad/problema› to run away FROM sth; ‹de la realidad› to escape FROM sth

evaluación f (a) (de daños, situación) ⋯⋗

assessment; (de datos, informes) evaluation, assessment **(b)** (Educ) (acción) assessment; (prueba, examen) test

evaluar [A18] *vt* ⟨*pérdidas/situación*⟩ to assess; ⟨*datos*⟩ to evaluate; ⟨*alumno*⟩ to assess

evangélico -ca *adj* **(a)** (del evangelio) evangelical **(b)** (protestante) protestant (*before n*)
■ *m,f* Protestant

evangelio *m* gospel

evaporación *f* evaporation

evaporarse [A1] *v pron* «*líquido*» to evaporate; «*ayuda/dinero*» to evaporate; «*persona*» (fam) to vanish *o* disappear into thin air

evasión *f* escape, breakout; ~ **de impuestos** tax evasion

evasiva *f*: **me contestó con** ~**s** she avoided *o* dodged the issue

evasivo -va *adj* evasive, noncommital

evento *m* **(a)** (period) (suceso) event **(b)** (caso) case; **en este** ~ in such a case

eventual *adj* [1] (posible) ⟨*problema/conflicto*⟩ possible; ⟨*gastos*⟩ incidental; ⟨*riesgos/pasivos*⟩ contingent [2] ⟨*trabajo/trabajador*⟩ casual, temporary; ⟨*cargo*⟩ temporary

evidencia *f* **(a)** (pruebas) evidence, proof; **negar la** ~ to deny the obvious *o* the facts **(b)** (cualidad) obviousness; **dejar** *or* **poner a algn en** ~ to show sb up

evidente *adj* obvious, clear

evidentemente *adv* (*indep*) obviously, clearly

evitar [A1] *vt* **(a)** (eludir, huir de) to avoid; ~ **hacer algo** to avoid doing sth **(b)** (impedir) to avoid, prevent; **para** ~ **que sufran** to avoid *o* prevent them suffering **(c)** (remediar): **me puse a llorar, no lo puede** ~ I started to cry, I couldn't help it **(d)** (ahorrar) ~**le algo A algn** ⟨*molestia/preocupación*⟩ to save *o* spare sb sth
■ **evitarse** *v pron* ⟨*problemas*⟩ to save oneself; **evítese la molestia de ir a la tienda** avoid the inconvenience of going to the store

evolución *f* **(a)** (Biol) evolution **(b)** (de ideas, sociedad, enfermedad) development; (de enfermo) progress

evolucionado -da *adj* ⟨*especie*⟩ highly developed *o* evolved; ⟨*sociedad/ideas*⟩ advanced, highly developed

evolucionar [A1] *vi* **(a)** (Biol) to evolve **(b)** «*ideas/sociedad/ciencia*» to develop, evolve **(c)** «*enfermo*» to progress

exactamente *adv* exactly

exactitud *f* **(a)** (precisión) accuracy, precision; **las órdenes se cumplieron con** ~ the orders were carried out to the letter **(b)** (veracidad, rigor) accuracy

exacto -ta *adj* **(a)** ⟨*medida/cantidad*⟩ exact; **40 kilos** ~**s** exactly 40 kilos; **hay que ser muy** ~ **en los cálculos** you have to be very accurate *o*

precise in your calculations **(b)** ⟨*informe/mapa/descripción*⟩ accurate **(c)** ⟨*copia*⟩ exact; ⟨*reproducción*⟩ accurate

exageración *f* exaggeration

exagerado -da *adj* **(a)** ⟨*persona*⟩: **¡qué** ~ **eres!** you do exaggerate! **(b)** ⟨*historia/relato*⟩ exaggerated **(c)** (excesivo) ⟨*precio*⟩ exorbitant; ⟨*cariño/castigo*⟩ excessive; ⟨*moda*⟩ extravagant, way-out (colloq)

exagerar [A1] *vt* ⟨*suceso/noticia*⟩ to exaggerate
■ ~ *vi* (al hablar) to exaggerate; (al hacer algo) to overdo it, go over the top (colloq)

exaltado -da *adj* **(a)** (vehemente) ⟨*discurso*⟩ impassioned **(b)** (excitado): **los ánimos estaban** ~**s** feelings were running high; **estaba muy** ~ he was really worked up **(c)** [SER] ⟨*persona*⟩ hotheaded
■ *m,f* hothead

exaltar [A1] *vt* [1] **(a)** (excitar) ⟨*personas*⟩ to excite; ⟨*pasiones*⟩ to arouse **(b)** (hacer enojar) to anger [2] (frml) (alabar) to extol (frml)
■ **exaltarse** *v pron* to get worked up

exalumno -na *m,f* (de colegio) ex-pupil; (de universidad) ex-student

examen *m* **(a)** (Educ) exam, examination (frml); ~ **de admisión** entrance examination *o* test; ~ **parcial** modular exam *o* test; **hacer** *or* (CS) **dar un** ~ to take an exam; **presentarse a un** ~ to take *o* (BrE) sit an exam; ~ **de ingreso** entrance examination *o* test **(b)** (estudio, investigación) examination; **someter algo a un** ~ to examine sth; ~ **médico** medical examination, medical

examinador -dora *adj* examining (*before n*)
■ *m,f* examiner

examinar [A1] *vt* to examine; ⟨*situación/caso*⟩ to study, consider
■ **examinarse** *v pron* (Esp) to take an exam

exangüe *adj* (liter) spent (liter), exhausted

exasperante *adj* exasperating

exasperar [A1] *vt* to exasperate
■ **exasperarse** *v pron* to get worked up *o* exasperated

excavación *f* excavation

excavadora *f* excavator

excavar [A1] *vt* **(a)** ⟨*túnel/fosa*⟩ to dig **(b)** (Arqueol) to excavate
■ ~ *vi* to dig, excavate

excedencia *f* (Esp) extended leave of absence

excedente *adj* **(a)** ⟨*producción*⟩ excess (*before n*), surplus (*before n*) **(b)** (con permiso) (Esp) on extended leave of absence
■ *m* surplus

exceder [E1] *vt* ⟨*límite/peso*⟩ to exceed **(b)** (superar, aventajar) ~ A **algo** to be superior TO sth
■ **excederse** *v pron* (al beber, trabajar) to overdo it; **se excedió en sus críticas** she went too far in her criticism

excelencia *f* [1] (cualidad) excellence [2] (frml) (tratamiento): **Su E**~ *(m)* His Excellency; *(f)* Her Excellency

excelente *adj* excellent

excéntrico -ca *adj/m,f* eccentric

excepción *f* exception; **esta norma tiene una ~** there is an exception to this rule; **hacer una ~ (con algn)** to make an exception (for sb); **a excepción de** with the exception of, except for

excepcional *adj* ⟨caso/circunstancia/talento⟩ exceptional; ⟨contribución/labor⟩ outstanding

excepto *prep* except, apart from; **todos ~ yo** everyone but me

exceptuar [A18] *vt* to except (frml); **exceptuando un pequeño incidente** except for *o* with the exception of a minor incident

excesivo *adj* excessive

exceso *m* **(a)** (excedente) excess; **~ de equipaje** excess baggage **(b)** (demasía): **un ~ de ejercicio** too much exercise; **me multaron por ~ de velocidad** I was fined for speeding; **en ~** ⟨beber/fumar/trabajar⟩ too much **(c) excesos** *mpl* (abusos) excesses (*pl*)

excitabilidad *f* excitability

excitación *f* **(a)** (entusiasmo) excitement **(b)** (sexual) arousal, excitement

excitante *adj* ⟨espectáculo/libro⟩ exciting

excitar [A1] *vt* **(a)** (hacer enojar): **la discusión lo excitó mucho** he got very excited *o* worked up during the argument **(b)** (sobreexcitar) to get ... overexcited; **el café me excita** coffee makes me jumpy **(c)** (en sentido sexual) to arouse, excite **(d)** ⟨deseo/odio/curiosidad⟩ to arouse
■ **excitarse** *v pron* **(a)** (enojarse) to get agitated, get worked up **(b)** (sobreexcitarse) to get overexcited **(c)** (sexualmente) to get aroused, get excited

exclamación *f* exclamation

exclamar [A1] *vt* to exclaim

excluir [I20] *vt* to exclude; ⟨posibilidad⟩ to rule out

exclusión *f* exclusion

exclusiva *f* **(a)** (Period) (derechos) exclusive rights (*pl*); (reportaje) exclusive **(b)** (Esp) (Com) exclusive rights (*pl*); **tendrán la ~ de nuestros productos** they will be sole distributors of our products

exclusive *adj inv* (detrás del *n*): **del tres al quince, ambos ~** from the third to the fifteenth not inclusive

exclusividad *f* **(a)** (de club, colegio, diseño) exclusiveness, exclusivity **(b)** (AmL) (Com) exclusive rights (*pl*), sole rights (*pl*)

exclusivo -va *adj* ⟨club/diseño⟩ exclusive; ⟨distribuidor⟩ sole; ⟨derechos⟩ exclusive, sole

excombatiente *mf* (*m*) veteran (AmE), ex-serviceman (esp BrE), (*f*) veteran (AmE), ex-servicewoman (esp BrE)

excomulgar [A3] *vt* to excommunicate

excomunión *f* excommunication

excremento *m* excrement

excursión *f* (viaje organizado) excursion, day trip; (paseo, salida) trip, excursion; **ir de ~ al campo** to go on a trip to the countryside

excursionismo *m* hiking

excursionista *mf* (que hace una excursión) tripper; (que hace excursionismo) hiker

excusa *f* **(a)** (pretexto) excuse **(b) excusas** *fpl* (disculpas) apologies (*pl*)

excusar [A1] *vt* **(a)** (disculpar) ⟨comportamiento⟩ to excuse **(b)** (eximir) **~ a algn DE algo/hacer algo** to excuse sb (FROM) sth/doing sth
■ **excusarse** *v pron* (frml) **(a)** (pedir perdón) to apologize **(b)** (ofrecer excusas) to excuse oneself

exento -ta *adj* (frml) [ESTAR] exempt; **~ DE algo** exempt FROM sth; **~ de impuestos** tax-exempt, tax-free (BrE)

exfoliador *m* (Col) notepad

exhaustivo -va *adj* exhaustive

exhausto -ta *adj* exhausted

exhibición *f* **(a)** (demostración) display **(b)** (de cuadros, artefactos) exhibition, display; **estar en ~** to be on show *o* display

exhibicionista *mf* **(a)** (pervertido) exhibitionist, flasher (colloq) **(b)** (ostentoso) exhibitionist, show-off (colloq)

exhibir [I1] *vt* **(a)** ⟨colección/modelos⟩ to show, display **(b)** ⟨película⟩ to show, screen; ⟨cuadro/ obras de arte⟩ to exhibit **(c)** (con orgullo) ⟨regalos/ trofeos⟩ to show off
■ **~** *vi* (period) (Art) to exhibit
■ **exhibirse** *v pron* (mostrarse en público) to show oneself; (hacerse notar) to draw attention to oneself

exhumar [A1] *vt* to exhume, disinter

exigencia *f* **(a)** (pretensión) demand; **¡no me vengas con ~s!** don't start making demands **(b)** (requisito) requirement

exigente *adj* ⟨persona/prueba⟩ demanding; ⟨clientela/paladar⟩ discerning

exigir [I7] *vt* **(a)** ⟨pago/respuesta/disciplina⟩ to demand; **exigió que se retiraran** he demanded that they leave **(b)** (requerir) ⟨concentración/ paciencia⟩ to call for, demand **(c)** (esperar de algn) (+ *me/te/le etc*): **le exigen demasiado en ese colegio** they ask too much of him at that school

exiliado -da *adj* exiled, in exile
■ *m,f* exile

exiliarse [A1] *v pron* to go into exile

exilio *m* exile

eximir [I1] *vt* (frml) to exempt; **~ a algn DE algo/ hacer algo** to exempt sb FROM sth/doing sth; **esto me exime de toda culpa** this relieves *o* absolves me of all responsibility

existencia *f* **1** **(a)** (hecho de existir) existence **(b)** (vida) life; **amargarle la ~ a algn** to make sb's life a misery **2** (Com) stock

existir [I1] *vi* **(a)** (en 3ª pers) (haber): **siempre ha existido rivalidad entre ellos** there has always been rivalry between them; **no existen pruebas** there is no evidence **(b)** (ser) to exist; **ya no existe** it doesn't exist anymore

éxito *m* success; **con ~** successfully; **tener ~** to be successful; **~ de ventas** best-seller; **~ de taquilla** a box-office hit

exitoso -sa *adj* (AmL) ⟨campaña/gira⟩ successful

éxodo *m* exodus; **el ~ rural** the drift from the land

exorbitante *adj* exorbitant

exorcismo *m* exorcism

exorcizar [A4] *vt* to exorcize

exótico -ca *adj* exotic

expandirse [I1] *v pron* to expand

expansión *f* expansion; **en ~** expanding

expatriado -da *m,f* expatriate

expatriarse [A1] *or* [A17] *v pron* (emigrar) to leave one's country; (exiliarse) to go into exile

expectación *f* sense of expectancy *o* anticipation

expectante *adj* expectant; **esperaba ~** she waited expectantly

expectativa *f* (a) (espera): **estar a la ~ (de algo)** to be waiting (for sth) (b) (esperanza) expectation; **defraudó las ~s de su padre** he failed to live up to his father's expectations (c) **expectativas** *fpl* (perspectivas) prospects (*pl*); **tienen pocas ~s de ganar** they have little hope of winning; **~s de vida** life expectancy

expedición *f* expedition; **~ de salvamento** (misión) rescue mission; (equipo) rescue party

expediente *m* (a) (documentos) file, dossier; **~ académico** student record (b) (investigación) investigation, inquiry (c) (medidas disciplinarias) disciplinary action; **le abrieron ~** disciplinary action was taken against him

expedir [I14] *vt* ⟨*pasaporte/visa*⟩ to issue

expendio *m* (AmL) (tienda) store (AmE), shop (BrE); (venta) sale; **un ~ de licores** a package store (AmE), an off-licence (BrE)

expensas: **a expensas de algo** ⟨*de ideales/ salud*⟩ at the expense of; **vive a ~ de su familia** he lives off his family

experiencia *f* (a) (conocimiento, suceso) experience; **saber algo por ~** to know sth by *o* from experience; **~ piloto** pilot scheme (b) (experimento) experiment

experimentado -da *adj* experienced

experimental *adj* experimental

experimentar [A1] *vi* **~ con algo** to experiment ON *o* WITH sth
■ **~** *vt* (a) ⟨*sensación*⟩ to experience, feel; ⟨*tristeza/alegría*⟩ to feel (b) ⟨*sufrir*⟩ ⟨*cambio*⟩ to undergo; **ha experimentado una leve mejoría** there's been a slight improvement in his condition

experimento *m* experiment

experto -ta *adj*: **es ~ en casos de divorcio** he's an expert on divorce cases; **~ EN hacer algo** very good AT doing sth
■ *m,f* expert

expiar [A17] *vt* to expiate, atone for

explanada *f* (plataforma) raised area, terrace; (delante de un edificio) leveled* area; (al lado del mar) esplanade

explayarse [A1] *v pron* (a) (sobre un tema) to speak at length (b) (desahogarse) to unburden oneself (c) (esparcirse) to relax

explicación *f* explanation

explicar [A2] *vt* to explain; **no sé ~lo** I don't know how to explain it
■ **explicarse** *v pron* (a) (comprender, concebir) to understand; **no me lo explico** I can't understand it *o* (colloq) I just don't get it (b) (hacerse comprender) to express oneself; **explícate** explain what you mean; **¿me explico?** do you understand what I mean?

explícito -ta *adj* explicit

exploración *f* (a) (de territorio) exploration; (de yacimientos) prospecting (b) (Mil) reconnaisance (c) (Med) examination, exploration

explorador -dora *m,f* ⚀ (expedicionario) explorer; (Mil) scout ⚁ **exploradora** *f* (Col) (Auto) fog lamp

explorar [A1] *vt* (a) ⟨*región*⟩ to explore; ⟨*yacimientos*⟩ to prospect for; (Inf) **~ la web** *or* **Red** to surf the Web (b) ⟨*posibilidades*⟩ to explore, investigate; ⟨*situación*⟩ to investigate, examine (c) (Mil) to reconnoiter*, scout; ⟨⟨*radar/ sonar*⟩⟩ to scan

explosión *f* (a) (de bomba) explosion; **la bomba hizo ~** (period) the bomb exploded *o* went off (b) (de cólera, júbilo) outburst (c) (crecimiento brusco) explosion

explosivo¹ -va *adj* explosive; **materiales ~s** explosives

explosivo² *m* explosive

explotación *f* (a) (de tierra, mina) exploitation, working; (de negocio) running, operation (b) (de trabajador) exploitation

explotador -dora *adj* exploitative
■ *m,f* exploiter

explotar [A1] *vt* ⟨*tierra*⟩ to exploit, work; ⟨*mina*⟩ to operate, work; ⟨*negocio*⟩ to run, operate (b) ⟨*idea/debilidad*⟩ to exploit (c) ⟨*trabajador*⟩ to exploit
■ *vi* (a) ⟨⟨*bomba*⟩⟩ to explode, go off; ⟨⟨*caldera/ máquina*⟩⟩ to explode, blow up (b) (fam) ⟨⟨*persona*⟩⟩ to explode, to blow a fuse (colloq)

exponer [E22] *vt* ⚀ (a) (en museo) ⟨*cuadro/ escultura*⟩ to exhibit, show (b) (en vitrina) to display ⚁ ⟨*razones/hechos*⟩ to set out, state; ⟨*ideas/teoría*⟩ to put forward; ⟨*tema*⟩ to present ⚂ (a) (poner en peligro) to put ... at risk (b) (al aire, sol) **~ algo A algo** to expose sth TO sth
■ **~** *vi* to exhibit, exhibit *o* show one's work
■ **exponerse** *v pron* **~se (A algo)** to expose oneself (TO sth); **te expones a que te multen** you're risking a fine

exportación *f* (a) (acción) exportation, export (b) **exportaciones** *fpl* (mercancías) exports (*pl*)

exportador -dora *adj*: **países ~es de petróleo** oil-exporting countries; **una región ~a de cítricos** a region that exports citrus fruit
■ *m,f* exporter

exportar [A1] *vt* to export

exposición *f* ⚀ (a) (acción) exhibition, showing (b) (muestra — de cuadros, esculturas) exhibition; (— de productos, maquinaria) show ⚁ (de hechos, razones) statement; (de tema, teoría) presentation ⚂ (al aire, sol) exposure; (Fot) exposure

expositor -tora *m,f* ⚀ (de cuadros, maquinaria) exhibitor ⚁ (Col, Ven) (conferenciante) speaker

exprés *adj inv* (Esp) ⟨*servicio/envío*⟩ express (*before n*)
■ *m* (Esp) (Ferr) express train, fast train

expresar [A1] *vt* to express
■ **expresarse** *v pron* to express oneself

expresión *f* expression

expresividad *f* expressiveness

expresivo -va *adj* ⟨*persona/rostro/lenguaje*⟩ expressive

expreso¹ -sa *adj* ⚀ (explícito) express (*before n*) ⚁ ⟨*tren*⟩ express (*before n*), fast (*before n*); ⟨*carta/envío*⟩ express (*before n*); **por correo ~** express ⚂ ⟨*café*⟩ espresso

185

expreso ⸱⸱⸱⸦ **extraoficial** ⸱ ⸱ ⸱

expreso² *m* ☐1 (Ferr) express train, fast train ☐2 (café) espresso

exprimidor *m* (manual) reamer (AmE), lemon squeezer (BrE); (eléctrico) juicer

exprimir [I1] *vt* **(a)** ‹naranja/limón› to squeeze; ‹ropa› to wring **(b)** (explotar) ‹trabajadores› to exploit

expropiación *f* (sin indemnización) expropriation; (con indemnización) compulsory purchase

expropiar [A1] *vt* (sin indemnización) to expropriate; (con indemnización) to acquire ... by compulsory purchase

expulsar [A1] *vt* ☐1 **(a)** (de institución) to expel; (de local) to throw ... out, eject (frml) **(b)** (de territorio) to expel, drive out **(c)** (Dep) to send off ☐2 ‹aire/cálculo› to expel

expulsión *f* expulsion; (Dep) sending-off

expurgar [A3] *vt* to expurgate

exquisito -ta *adj* ‹comida› delicious; ‹tela/poema/música› exquisite; ‹persona› refined

éxtasis *m* ecstasy

extático -ca *adj* ecstatic

extender [E8] *vt* ☐1 ‹periódico/mapa› to open ... up o out; ‹mantel/toalla› to spread ... out ☐2 ‹brazos› to stretch out; ‹alas› to spread; **le extendió la mano** he held out his hand to her ☐3 ‹pintura/mantequilla› to spread ☐4 (ampliar) ‹poderes/plazo/permiso› to extend ☐5 (frml) ‹factura/cheque/escritura› to issue; ‹receta› to make out, write
■ **extenderse** *v pron* ☐1 (en el espacio) **(a)** «fuego/epidemia/noticia» to spread **(b)** «territorio/propiedad» to stretch; **se extiende hasta el río** it stretches down to the river **(c)** «influencia/autoridad» to extend; **∼se Λ algo** to extend to sth ☐2 (en el tiempo) **(a)** «época/debate» to last **(b)** «persona»: **se extendió demasiado en ese tema** he spent too much time on that subject; **¿quisiera ∼se sobre ese punto?** would you like to expand on that point?

extendido -da *adj* ‹costumbre/error› widespread **(b)** ‹brazos/alas› outstretched

extensión *f* ☐1 **(a)** (superficie): **una gran ∼ de terreno** a large expanse o stretch of land; **una ∼ de 20 hectáreas** an area of 20 hectares **(b)** (longitud) length; **la ∼ de la novela** the length of the novel; **por ∼** by extension ☐2 (grado, importancia) extent; **en toda la ∼ de la palabra** in every sense of the word ☐3 **(a)** (prolongación) extension; **pidió una ∼ del plazo** he asked for an extension on the deadline **(b)** (de cable) extension cord (AmE), extension lead (BrE); (línea telefónica) extension

extenso -sa *adj* extensive

exterior *adj* ☐1 **(a)** ‹aspecto› external (before n), outward (before n); ‹bolsillo/temperatura/mundo› outside (before n); ‹revestimiento/capa› outer (before n) **(b)** ‹habitación/apartamento› outward-facing ☐2 ‹comercio/política› foreign (before n)
■ *m* ☐1 (fachada) outside, exterior; (espacio circundante) outside; **desde el ∼ de la iglesia** from outside the church ☐2 **el exterior** (países extranjeros): **la influencia del ∼** foreign influence;

las relaciones con el ∼ relations with other countries ☐3 **exteriores** *mpl* (Cin) location shots (*pl*); **rodar en ∼es** to film on location

exteriorizar [A4] *vt* to externalize, exteriorize

exterminar [A1] *vt* to exterminate

exterminio *m* extermination

externar [A1] *vt* (Méx) to display, show

externo -na *adj* **(a)** ‹apariencia/signos› outward (before n), external; ‹influencia› outside, external; ‹superficie› external; ‹ángulo› exterior **(b)** ‹alumno› day (before n)
■ *m,f* day pupil

extinción *f* (de especie, volcán) extinction; **una especie en peligro de ∼** an endangered species

extinguidor *m* (AmL) fire extinguisher

extinguir [I2] *vt* **(a)** ‹especie› to wipe out; ‹violencia/injusticia› to put an end to **(b)** ‹fuego› to extinguish, put out
■ **extinguirse** *v pron* **(a)** ‹especie› to become extinct, die out **(b)** «fuego» to go out; «volcán» to become extinct; «sonido» to die away **(c)** «entusiasmo/amor» to die

extintor *m* (Esp): *tb* **∼ de incendios** fire extinguisher

extirpar [A1] *vt* (Med) to remove

extorsión *f* extortion

extorsionar [A1] *vt* to extort money from

extra *adj* **(a)** (Com) top quality, fancy grade (AmE) **(b)** (adicional) ‹gastos/ración› additional, extra; ‹edición› special
■ *adv* extra
■ *mf* (Cin) extra
■ *m* (gasto) extra expense; (paga) bonus

extracción *f* **(a)** (en general) extraction **(b)** *tb* **∼ social** background, origins (*pl*); **de ∼ humilde** of humble origins

extraconyugal *adj* extramarital

extracto *m* **(a)** (resumen) summary, abstract; **∼ de cuenta** (bank) statement **(b)** (esencia) extract

extractor *m* extractor; **∼ de aire** extractor fan

extradición *f* extradition

extraer [E23] *vt* (en general) to extract; ‹bala› to remove; ‹conclusión› to draw

extraescolar *adj* extramural, out-of-school (before n)

extralimitarse [A1] *v pron* to exceed one's authority

extramatrimonial *adj* extramarital

extranjero -ra *adj* foreign
■ *m,f* **(a)** (persona) foreigner **(b) extranjero** *m*: **al/en el ∼** abroad; **noticias del ∼** foreign news

extrañar [A1] *vt* (esp AmL) ‹amigo/país› to miss
■ **∼** *vi* ☐1 (sorprender) (+ *me/te/le etc*) to surprise; **me extraña que no lo sepas** I'm surprised you didn't know that; **ya me extrañaba a mí que ...** I thought it was strange that ... ☐2 (RPl) (tener nostalgia) to be homesick
■ **extrañarse** *v pron* **∼se DE algo** to be surprised AT sth

extrañeza *f* surprise; **me miró con ∼** she looked at me in surprise

extraño -ña *adj* (raro) strange, odd; **eso no tiene nada de ∼** there's nothing unusual about that
■ *m,f* (desconocido) stranger

extraoficial *adj* unofficial

extraordinario -ria adj (en general) extraordinary; ‹edición› special; ‹contribución› extra, additional; **la película no fue nada** ∼ the movie was nothing special o nothing out of the ordinary

extraplano -na adj ‹reloj/calculadora› slimline; ‹compresa› extra-slim

extrarradio m outlying districts (pl), outskirts (pl)

extrasensorial adj extrasensory

extraterrestre adj/mf alien, extraterrestrial

extravagancia f (acto) outrageous thing (to do); (cualidad) extravagance

extravagante adj ‹comportamiento/ideas› outrageous, extravagant; ‹persona/ropa› flamboyant, outrageous

extraviado -da adj ‹objeto/niño› lost, missing; ‹perro/gato› stray

extraviar [A17] vt (frml) to mislay (frml), to lose
■ **extraviarse** v pron (frml) «persona/animal» to get lost; «documento» to go missing

extremado -da adj extreme

extremar [A1] vt (frml) to maximize (frml)
■ **extremarse** v pron ∼ (**EN hacer algo**) to make a great effort (to do sth)

extremaunción f extreme unction

extremidad f (a) (extremo) end (b) **extremidades** fpl (Anat) extremities

extremista adj (extremo) extreme; (Pol) extremist
■ mf (Pol) extremist

extremo¹ -ma adj extreme; **un caso de extrema gravedad** an extremely serious case; **en caso** ∼ as a last resort; ∼ **derecha/izquierda** (Pol) extreme right/left; ∼ **derecho/izquierdo** (Dep) right/left wing; **E**∼ **Oriente** Far East

extremo² m (a) (de palo, cable) end (b) (postura extrema) extreme; **va de un** ∼ **a otro** she goes from one extreme to the other; **son** ∼**s opuestos** they are complete opposites (c) (límite): **si se llega a ese** ∼ ... if it gets that bad o to that point ...; **en último** ∼ as a last resort

extrovertido -da adj/m,f extrovert

exuberante adj exuberant; ‹mujer› voluptuous

exudar [A1] vt to exude

exultar [A1] vi to exult (frml), to rejoice

eyaculación f ejaculation

eyacular [A1] vi to ejaculate

Ff

F, f f (read as /'efe/) the letter F, f

fa m (nota) F; (en solfeo) fa, fah (BrE)

fábrica f factory; **una** ∼ **de zapatos** a shoe factory; ∼ **de textiles/papel** textile/paper mill; ∼ **de cerveza** brewery; ∼ **de conservas** cannery

fabricación f manufacture; **la** ∼ **de coches** car manufacture; **de** ∼ **japonesa** made in Japan; **de** ∼ **casera** home-made; ∼ **en serie** mass production

fabricante mf manufacturer

fabricar [A2] vt to manufacture; ∼ **en cadena/serie** to mass-produce; ❸ **fabricado en Perú** made in Peru

fábula f (Lit) fable; (mentira) fabrication

fabuloso -sa adj (maravilloso) (fam) fabulous (colloq)

facción f (a) (Pol) faction (b) **facciones** fpl (rasgos) features (pl)

faceta f facet

facha f (fam) (aspecto) look; **no me gustó su** ∼ I didn't like the look of him; **¿vas a salir con esa** ∼? are you going out looking like that?; **estar hecho una** ∼ to be o look a sight (colloq)
■ adj/mf (Chi, Esp fam) fascist

fachada f (a) (de edificio) facade (tech), front (b) (apariencia) facade

fácil adj ① (a) ‹problema/lección/vida› easy; ∼ **de entender** easy to understand (b) (pey) (en lo sexual) easy (pej), loose (pej) ② (probable): **es** ∼ **que se le olvide** he'll probably forget; **no es** ∼ **que me lo den** they are unlikely to let me have it

facilidad f ① (a) (cualidad de fácil) ease; **con** ∼ easily (b) (de una tarea) simplicity ② (aptitud): **tener** ∼ **para los idiomas/los números** to have a gift for languages/to be good at figures; **tiene** ∼ **de palabra** he has a way with words ③ **facilidades** fpl (a) (posibilidades, oportunidades): **se le dieron todas las** ∼**es** they gave her every chance (b) (Fin) tb ∼**es de pago** credit facilities (pl)

facilitar [A1] vt (a) (hacer más fácil) ‹tarea› to make ... easier, facilitate (frml) (b) (frml) (proporcionar) ‹datos/información› to provide

factible adj possible, feasible

factor m factor; **el** ∼ **tiempo** the time factor

factoría f (fábrica) factory; (astillero) shipyard; (fundición) foundry

factura f ① (Com) invoice (frml), bill; **pasarle** ∼ **a algn** (Fin) to invoice sb ② (RPl) (Coc) rolls, croissants, etc

AmC	América Central	Arg	Argentina	Cu	Cuba
AmL	América Latina	Bol	Bolivia	Ec	Ecuador
AmS	América del Sur	Chi	Chile	Esp	España
Andes	Región andina	CS	Cono Sur	Méx	México

Per	Perú
RPl	Río de la Plata
Ur	Uruguay
Ven	Venezuela

facturación f **1** (Com) **(a)** (acción) invoicing **(b)** (volumen) turnover **2** (Ferr) registration; (Aviac) check-in

facturar [A1] vt **1** (Com) **(a)** ⟨mercancías/arreglo⟩ to invoice for, bill for **(b)** (refiriéndose al volumen de ventas) to turn over, have a turnover of **2** (Ferr) to register; (Aviac) to check in ∎ ~ vi (Ferr) to register; (Aviac) to check in

facultad f **1** (capacidad) faculty; **está perdiendo ~es** he's losing his faculties; **~es mentales** (mental) faculties (pl) **2** (Educ) faculty; **F~ de Filosofía y Letras** Faculty of Arts

facultar [A1] vt (frml) **~ a algn PARA hacer algo** «jefe/presidente» to authorize sb to do sth; «carnet/documento» to entitle sb to do sth; «ley» to allow sb to do sth

faena f **1** (tarea) task, job; **es una ~ dura** it's hard work; **~s domésticas** housework; **~s agrícolas** farm work **2** (fam) **(a)** (mala pasada) dirty trick; **hacerle una ~ a algn** to play a dirty trick on sb (colloq) **(b)** (contratiempo) drag (colloq), pain (colloq)

fagot /fa'βo(t)/ m (instrumento) bassoon ∎ mf (músico) bassoonist

faisán m pheasant

faja f **(a)** (prenda interior) girdle **(b)** (cinturón — de traje regional) wide belt; (— de sotana) sash; (— de smoking) cummerbund **(c)** (franja, zona) strip

fajo m (de billetes) wad, roll (AmE); (de papeles) bundle, sheaf

falange f **1** (Anat) phalanx, phalange **2** **(a)** (Mil) phalanx **(b)** (Hist, Pol) phalanx; **la F~ the** Spanish Falangist Movement

falda f **(a)** (Indum) skirt; **~ escocesa** (de mujer) tartan skirt, kilt; (de hombre) kilt; **~ pantalón** split skirt, culottes (pl); **se enemistaron por un asunto de ~s** they fell out over a woman **(b)** (de montaña) side

faldón m, **faldones** mpl **(a)** (de camisa) shirttails; (de frac, chaqué) coattails **(b)** (de bebé) christening robe

falla f **1** **(a)** (de tela, cristal) flaw; **la pieza tenía una ~** the part was defective **(b)** (Geol) fault **2** **(a)** (de motor, máquina, sistema — en la composición) defect, fault; (— en el funcionamiento) failure; **~s en el sistema de seguridad** security failures **(b)** (de persona) mistake; **~ humana** (AmL) human error; **¡qué ~!** what a stupid mistake! **(c)** (Dep) miss **3** (AmL exc CS fam) (lástima) pity, shame **4** **(a)** (figura) model, figure (burned during the FALLAS) **(b)** **las Fallas** fpl (fiesta) the festival of San José in Valencia

fallado -da adj (CS) flawed, defective

fallar [A1] vi **1** «juez/jurado» **~ a or en favor/en contra de algn** to rule in favor*/of/against sb **2** **(a)** «frenos/memoria» to fail; «planes» to go wrong; **le falló el corazón** his heart failed; **le falló la puntería** he missed; **a ti te falla** (AmL) (fam) you've a screw loose (colloq) **(b)** «persona» (+ me/te/le etc) to let ... down ∎ ~ vt (errar) to miss; **fallé el tiro** I missed (the shot)

fallecer [E3] vi (frml o euf) to pass away (frml or euph), to die

fallecimiento m (frml) death, passing (frml or euph)

fallero -ra m,f: person who takes part in the preparation of the FALLAS

fallo m **(a)** (en concurso, certamen) decision; (Der) ruling, judgment **(b)** (Esp) ▶ FALLA 2

falluca f (Méx fam) (comercio ilegal) black market (gen in smuggled goods); (mercancía) smuggled goods (pl)

falsear [A1] vt ⟨hechos/datos⟩ to falsify; ⟨verdad/realidad⟩ to distort

falsedad f **(a)** (de afirmación) falseness; (de persona) insincerity, falseness **(b)** (mentira) lie

falsificador -dora m,f forger

falsificar [A2] vt **(a)** ⟨firma/billete/cheque⟩ to forge **(b)** ⟨documento⟩ (copiar) to forge, counterfeit; (alterar) to falsify

falso -sa adj **(a)** ⟨billete⟩ counterfeit, forged; ⟨cuadro⟩ forged; ⟨documento⟩ false, forged; ⟨diamante/joya⟩ fake; ⟨cajón/techo⟩ false **(b)** (insincero) ⟨persona⟩ insincere, false; ⟨sonrisa/promesa⟩ false **(c)** (no cierto) ⟨dato/nombre/declaración⟩ false; **eso es ~** that is not true o is untrue; **falsa alarma** false alarm; **~ testimonio** m (Der) false testimony, perjury

falta f **1** (carencia, ausencia) **~ DE algo** ⟨de interés/dinero⟩ lack OF sth; **~ de personal** staff shortage; **es la ~ de costumbre** it's because I'm/you're not used to it; **fue una ~ de respeto** it was very rude of you/him/her/them; **eso es una ~ de educación** that's bad manners; **a ~ de más información** in the absence of more information **2** (inasistencia) tb **~ de asistencia** absence; **le pusieron ~** they marked her down as absent **3** **(a)** hacer falta: **no hace ~ que se queden** there's no need for you to stay; **si hace ~ ...** if necessary ...; **hacen ~ dos vasos más** we need two more glasses; **le hace ~ descansar** he/she needs to rest **(b)** **sin falta** without fail **4** (defecto) fault; **a pesar de todas sus ~s** in spite of all his faults; **sacarle** or **encontrarle ~s a algo** to find fault with sth; **~ de ortografía** spelling mistake **5** (Dep) **(a)** (infracción — en fútbol, baloncesto) foul; (— en tenis) fault **(b)** (tiro libre — en fútbol) free kick; (— en balonmano) free throw

faltar [A1] vi **1** **(a)** (no estar) to be missing; **¿quién falta?** who's missing?; (en colegio, reunión) who's absent?; **te falta un botón** you have a button missing; **a esta taza le falta el asa** there's no handle on this cup **(b)** (no haber suficiente): **va a ~ vino** there won't be enough wine; **nos faltó tiempo** we didn't have enough time **(c)** (hacer falta): **le falta alguien que la aconseje** she needs someone to advise her; **les falta cariño** they need affection **2** (quedar): **yo estoy lista ¿a ti te falta mucho?** I'm ready, will you be long?; **nos falta poco para terminar** we're almost finished; **me faltan tres páginas para terminar el libro** I have three pages to go to finish the book; **solo me falta pasarlo a máquina** all I have to do is type it out; **falta poco para Navidad** it's not long until Christmas; **faltan cinco minutos para que empiece** there are five minutes to go before it starts; **¡no faltaba más!** (respuesta — a un agradecimiento) don't mention it!; (— a una petición) of course, certainly; (— a un ofrecimiento) I wouldn't hear of it! **3** **(a)** (no asistir): **te esperamos, no faltes** we're expecting you, make sure you come; **~ A algo** ⟨al ⋯⋙

colegio) to be absent FROM sth; ⟨*a una cita*⟩ to
miss sth; ~ **a clase** to skip lessons; **ha faltado
dos veces al trabajo** she's been off work twice (b)
(no cumplir): **faltó a su promesa** he didn't keep his
promise; **¡no me faltes al respeto!** don't be rude
to me

fama *f* **(a)** (renombre, celebridad) fame; **una marca
de** ~ **mundial** a world-famous brand; **dar** ~ **a
algo/algn** to make sth/sb famous **(b)** (reputación)
reputation; **tener mala** ~ to have a bad
reputation; **tiene** ~ **de ser severo** he has a
reputation for being strict; **tiene** ~ **de bromista**
he's well known as a joker

familia *f* **(a)** (parientes) family; **una** ~ **numerosa**
a large family; **mi** ~ **política** my wife's/husband's
family, my in-laws (colloq); **es de buena** ~ *or* **de**
~ **bien** he's from a good family; **somos como de
la** ~ we're just like family; **le viene de** ~ it runs
in the family **(b)** (hijos) children; **no tienen** ~
they don't have any children

familiar *adj* **(a)** ⟨*vida/vínculo*⟩ family (*before
n*); ⟨*envase/coche*⟩ family (*before n*) **(b)** ⟨*trato/
tono*⟩ familiar, informal; ⟨*lenguaje/expresión*⟩
colloquial **(c)** (conocido) ⟨*cara/lugar*⟩ familiar; **su
voz me resulta** ~ her voice is familiar
■ *mf* relative, relation

familiaridad *f* familiarity

familiarizarse [A4] *v pron* ~ CON algo to
familiarize oneself WITH sth, become familiar
WITH sth

famoso -sa *adj* famous; ~ **POR algo** famous
FOR sth
■ *m,f* celebrity, famous person

fan *mf* (*pl* **fans**) fan

fanático -ca *adj* fanatical
■ *m,f* (en general) fanatic; **es un** ~ **de la gimnasia**
he's a gym fanatic; (de fútbol) (AmS period) fan

fanatismo *m* fanaticism

fanfarrón -rrona *adj* (fam) (al hablar)
loudmouthed (colloq); (al actuar): **no seas** ~ stop
showing off
■ *m,f* (fam) (al hablar) loudmouth (colloq); (al actuar)
show-off (colloq)

fanfarronear [A1] *vi* (fam) **(a)** (al hablar) to
boast, brag **(b)** (al actuar) to show off (colloq)

fango *m* mud

fantasear [A1] *vi* to fantasize

fantasía *f* ⟨1⟩ **(a)** (imaginación) imagination **(b)**
(ficción) fantasy; **vive en un mundo de** ~ he's
living in a fantasy world ⟨2⟩ (bisutería): **joyas de** ~
costume jewelry*; **una pulsera de** ~ an imitation
diamond (o ruby *etc*) bracelet

fantasma *m* **(a)** (aparición) ghost **(b)** (amenaza)
specter*

fantástico -ca *adj* fantastic

fantochear [A1] *vi* (AmL fam) ▶ FANFARRONEAR

faquir *m* fakir

faraón *m* Pharaoh

fardar [A1] *vi* (Esp fam) «*persona*» ▶
FANFARRONEAR

fardo *m* (de algodón, paja) bale; (de ropa) bundle

faringe *f* pharynx

faringitis *f* pharyngitis

farmacéutico -ca *adj* pharmaceutical
■ *m,f* druggist (AmE), chemist (BrE)

farmacia *f* **(a)** (tienda) drugstore (AmE),
chemist's (BrE); ~ **de guardia** *or* **de turno** duty
chemist (b) (disciplina) pharmacy

faro *m* **(a)** (Náut) lighthouse **(b)** (Auto) headlight,
headlamp; ~ **antiniebla** fog light *o* (BrE) lamp

farol *m* (de alumbrado público) streetlight,
streetlamp; (en jardín, portal) lantern, lamp; ~ **de
papel** paper lantern

farola *f* (luz) streetlight, streetlamp; (poste)
lamppost

farolillo *m* (de papel) Chinese lantern

farra *f* (fam) ▶ JUERGA

farrear [A1] *vi* (AmL fam) to go out partying
(colloq), go out on the town (colloq)
■ **farrearse** *v pron* (AmL fam) ⟨*fortuna/dinero*⟩ to
blow (colloq); ⟨*oportunidad*⟩ to throw away

farrero -ra *adj/m,f* (AmL fam) ▶ FARRISTA

farrista *adj* (AmL fam): **estudiantes** ~**s** students
who are always out living it up
■ *mf* (AmL fam): **es un** ~ he's always out living it
up

farsa *f* (Teatr) farce; (engaño) sham, farce

farsante *mf* fraud, fake

fascículo *m* part (*of a serialized publication*),
fascicle (tech)

fascinación *f* fascination

fascinante *adj* fascinating

fascinar [A1] *vi* (fam): **me fascinó ese programa**
I found that program fascinating; **me fascina
viajar** I love travelling
■ ~ *vt* to fascinate, captivate

fascismo *m* fascism

fascista *adj/mf* fascist

fase *f* **(a)** (etapa) stage, phase; **la** ~ **de
clasificación** the preliminary round; **está todavía
en** ~ **de negociación** it is still being negotiated
(b) (Astron, Elec, Fis, Quím) phase

fastidiado -da *adj* (esp Esp fam): **estoy un
poco** ~ I'm not too good *o* too well; **anda** ~ **de
los riñones** he's having trouble with his kidneys

fastidiar [A1] *vt* **(a)** (molestar, irritar) ⟨*persona*⟩ to
bother, pester **(b)** (esp Esp fam) (estropear)
⟨*mecanismo/plan*⟩ to mess up; ⟨*fiesta/excursión*⟩
to spoil; ⟨*estómago*⟩ to upset
■ ~ *vi*: **me fastidia tener que repetir las cosas** it
annoys me to have to repeat things; **¡no fastidies!
¿de veras?** go on! you're kidding! (colloq)
■ **fastidiarse** *v pron* **(a)** (AmL fam) (molestarse) to
get annoyed **(b)** (fam) (jorobarse): **tendré que** ~**me**
I'll have to put up with it (colloq); **¡te fastidias!**
(Esp) tough! (colloq) **(c)** (Esp fam) (estropearse)
«*velada/plan*» to be ruined

fastidio *m* (molestia) annoyance; **¡qué** ~**!** what a
nuisance!

fastidioso -sa *adj* **(a)** (molesto) ⟨*persona*⟩
tiresome, annoying; ⟨*trabajo*⟩ tiresome, irksome
(b) (Méx, Per fam) (quisquilloso) fussy (colloq)

fastuoso -sa *adj* ⟨*salón*⟩ magnificent;
⟨*banquete*⟩ lavish

fatal *adj* ⟨1⟩ ⟨*accidente/enfermedad/
consecuencias*⟩ fatal ⟨2⟩ (fam) (muy malo) terrible,
awful; **fue un fin de semana** ~ it was a terrible
weekend; **me encuentro** ~ I feel awful; **su padre
está** ~ his father's in a really bad way (colloq)
■ *adv* (esp Esp fam): **viste** ~ he dresses really
badly; **me caen** ~ I can't stand them (colloq)

fatiga f (a) (cansancio) tiredness, fatigue (frml)
(b) (ahogo) breathlessness

fatigado -da adj tired, weary

fatigar [A3] vt (físicamente) to tire ... out;
(mentalmente) to tire

■ **fatigarse** v pron (a) (cansarse) to get tired,
wear oneself out (colloq) (b) (ahogarse) to get
breathless

fatigoso -sa adj ‹trabajo› tiring, exhausting

faul m (pl **fauls**) (AmL) foul

faulear [A1] vt (AmL) to foul

fauna f fauna

favor m (a) (ayuda, servicio) favor*; ¿me puedes
hacer un ∼? can you do me a favor?; vengo a
pedirte un ∼ I've come to ask you (for) a favor;
¿me harías el ∼ de copiarme esto? would you
copy this for me, please?; hagan el ∼ de esperar
would you mind waiting, please? (b) (en locs) a
favor in favor*; dos votos a ∼ two votes in favor;
en ∼ de in favour of; estar a ∼ de algo/algn/
hacer algo to be in favor* of sth/sb/doing sth; por
favor please

favorable adj favorable*

favorecedor -dora adj becoming

favorecer [E3] vt (a) (ayudar, beneficiar) to
favor*; una política para ∼ la agricultura a policy
to help agriculture (b) «peinado/color» (sentar
bien) to suit

favoritismo m favoritism*

favorito -ta adj/m,f favorite*

fax m fax; mándaselo por ∼ fax it to him

faxear [A1] vt to fax, send ... by fax

Fdo (= **firmado**) (en correspondencia) signed

fe f (a) (Relig) faith; (creencia, confianza) faith; tener
∼ en algo/algn to have faith in sth/sb; puse toda
mi ∼ en ti I put all my trust in you (b) (intención):
no dudo de su buena ∼ I don't doubt his good
intentions; actuar de buena/mala ∼ to act in
good/bad faith

febrero m February; para ejemplos ver ENERO

fecha f date; ¿qué ∼ es hoy? what's the date
today?, what date is it today?; con ∼ 7 de marzo
(Corresp) dated March 7 o (BrE) 7th March; hasta la
∼ to date; el año pasado por estas ∼s this time
last year; en ∼ próxima soon; ∼ de caducidad or
(AmL) vencimiento (de medicamento) expiration date
(AmE), expiry date (BrE); (de alimento) use-by date;
∼ de consumo preferente best-before date; ∼
límite or tope (para solicitud, suscripción) closing
date; (para proyecto, trabajo) deadline

fechar [A1] vt to date

fechoría f misdeed

fecundación f fertilization; ∼ in vitro in
vitro fertilization

fecundar [A1] vt ‹óvulo› to fertilize; ‹animal›
to inseminate

fecundo -da adj (a) (Biol) ‹mujer› fertile (b)
‹región/tierra› fertile; ‹labor› fruitful

federación f federation

federal adj federal

felicidad f (a) (alegría) happiness (b)
¡**felicidades!** interj (por cumpleaños) Happy
Birthday!; (en Navidad) Merry Christmas!; (por un
logro) congratulations!

felicitación f (a) (escrito — por un logro) letter
of congratulation; (— en Navidad) Christmas card

(or letter wishing sb Merry Christmas) (b)
felicitaciones fpl (deseo — por un logro)
congratulations (pl); (— en Navidad) greetings (pl)
(c) ¡**felicitaciones!** interj (AmL)
congratulations!

felicitar [A1] vt (a) (por un logro) to
congratulate; ¡te felicito! congratulations!; me
felicitó por el premio he congratulated me on
winning the prize (b) (por Navidad) to wish ... (a)
Merry Christmas; (por cumpleaños) to wish ... (a)
Happy Birthday

feligrés -gresa m,f parishioner

feliz adj happy; les deseo que sean muy felices I
wish you every happiness; ¡∼ cumpleaños!
happy birthday!; ¡∼ Navidad! Merry Christmas!;
¡∼ Año Nuevo! Happy New Year!; ¡∼ viaje! have
a good trip!

felpa f (Tex) (para toallas) toweling*; (en tapicería)
plush

felpudo m doormat

femenil adj (Méx) ‹equipo/moda› ladies' (before
n), women's (before n)

femenino -na adj (a) ‹equipo/moda› ladies'
(before n), women's (before n); ‹hormona/sexo›
female (b) ‹vestido/modales/chica› feminine (c)
(Ling) feminine

femineidad, feminidad f femininity

feminismo m feminism

feminista adj/mf feminist

fenomenal adj (fam) great (colloq)
■ adv (fam): lo pasamos ∼ we had a great time
(colloq); me vino ∼ it was exactly o just what I
needed; ¡∼! great! (colloq)

fenómeno¹ -na adj/adv (AmL) ▶ FENOMENAL

fenómeno² m (suceso) phenomenon

feo¹, fea adj (a) ‹persona/edificio› ugly;
‹peinado› unflattering; es fea de cara she has a
very plain face; es un barrio ∼ it's not a very
nice neighborhood (b) ‹asunto/situación›
unpleasant; ‹olor/sabor› (esp AmL) unpleasant;
¡qué ∼ está el día! what an awful day!; la cosa se
está poniendo fea things are getting nasty o ugly;
es or (Esp) está muy ∼ hablar así it's not nice to
talk like that

feo² adv (AmL) ‹oler/saber› bad; me miró ∼ she
gave me a dirty look

féretro m coffin

feria f ① (a) (exposición comercial) fair; ∼ de
muestras trade fair (b) (CS, Per) (mercado) (street)
market ② (a) (fiesta popular) festival (b) (parque de
atracciones) fair ③ (Méx fam) (cambio, suelto) small
change; (dinero) cash (colloq)

feriado m (AmL) (public) holiday

fermentar [A1] vi/vt to ferment

fermento m ferment

feroz adj (a) ‹animal› ferocious, fierce; ‹ataque/
mirada/odio› fierce, vicious; ‹viento/tempestad›
fierce, violent (b) (Col, Méx, Ven fam) (feo)
horrendous (colloq)

ferretería f (tienda) hardware store,
ironmonger's (BrE); (mercancías) hardware,
ironmongery (BrE)

ferrocarril m railroad (AmE), railway (BrE)

ferrocarrilero -ra adj (Chi, Méx) rail (before
n)

ferroviario -ria adj rail (before n)

ferry /'ferri/ *m* (*pl* **-rrys**) ferry

fértil *adj* fertile

fertilización *f* fertilization; ~ **in vitro** in vitro fertilization

fertilizante *m* fertilizer

fertilizar [A4] *vt* to fertilize, put fertilizer on

ferviente *adj* ⟨admiración/creyente⟩ fervent; ⟨deseo⟩ burning; ⟨fe/defensor⟩ passionate

fervor *m* fervor*; **con ~** fervently

festejado -da *m,f* (CS) *person celebrating his/ her birthday* (*o saint's day etc*)

festejar [A1] *vt* (AmL) (celebrar) to celebrate

festejo *m* celebration, festivity

festín *m* feast, banquet

festival *m* festival; ~ **de cine** film festival

festividad *f* **(a)** (fiesta religiosa) feast, festivity **(b) festividades** *fpl* (festejos) festivities (*pl*)

festivo -va *adj* festive; ▶ DÍA 1B

fetidez *f* (cualidad) smelliness; (olor) stench

fétido -da *adj* fetid, foul-smelling

feto *m* fetus*

feúcho -cha *adj* (fam) ⟨mujer⟩ plain, homely (AmE colloq); **es ~** he's not much to look at

feudalismo *m* feudalism

fiable *adj* reliable

fiaca *adj inv* (RPl fam) bone idle (colloq), lazy ■ *f* (Andes, CS fam) (pereza): **me da ~** I can't be bothered

fiador -dora *m,f* (Com, Der, Fin) guarantor

fiambre *m* (Coc): *tb* ~**s** cold cuts (*pl*) (AmE), cold meats (*pl*) (BrE)

fiambrería *f* (AmL) delicatessen

fianza *f* **(a)** (Der) bail; **salió bajo ~** she was released on bail **(b)** (Com) deposit

fiar [A17] *vt* ⟨mercancías⟩ to sell ... on credit ■ ~ *vi* **(a)** (dar crédito) to give credit **(b) ser de ~** «*persona*» (digno de confianza) to be trustworthy; (responsable) to be reliable; «*mecanismo/motor*» to be reliable
■ **fiarse** *v pron*: **no me fío de lo que dice** I don't believe what he says; ~**se** DE **algn** to trust sb

fiasco *m* fiasco

fibra *f* fiber*; ~**s artificiales** man-made fibers; ~ **de vidrio** fiberglass*; ~ **óptica** optical fiber*

ficción *f* fiction

ficha *f* ⏹1 (para datos) card; (de fichero) index card; ~ **médica** medical records (*pl*); ~ **policial** police record ⏹2 **(a)** (de teléfono, estacionamiento) token **(b)** (Jueg) (de dominó) domino; (de damas) checker(AmE), draught (BrE); (de otros juegos de mesa) counter; (de ruleta, póker) chip

fichaje *m* (Dep) (acción) signing (up); (jugador) signing, trade (AmE)

fichar [A1] *vt* **(a)** «*policía*» to open a file on **(b)** «*equipo/club*» to sign (up)
■ ~ *vi* (en fábrica, oficina — a la entrada) to clock in, punch in (AmE); (— a la salida) to clock out *o* (BrE) off, to punch out (AmE)

fichero *m* **(a)** (mueble para carpetas) filing cabinet

(b) (cajón — de carpetas) filing draw; (— para tarjetas) card index draw **(c)** (caja) index card file (AmE), card index box (BrE) **(d)** (conjunto de fichas) file; (Inf) file

ficticio -cia *adj* ⟨personaje/suceso⟩ fictitious

fidelidad *f* **(a)** (de persona, animal) fidelity, faithfulness **(b)** (de reproducción) faithfulness, fidelity; (de instrumento) accuracy, precision

fideo *m* **(a)** (pasta fina) noodle; (muy finos) vermicelli **(b) fideos** *mpl* (RPl) (pasta en general) pasta

fiebre *f* **(a)** (Med) fever; **tener ~** to be feverish, to have a fever (esp AmE), to have a temperature (esp BrE); **le bajó la ~** his fever *o* temperature came down; ~ **del heno** hay fever; ~ **palúdica** malaria **(b)** (furor) obsession; **le dio la ~ de la limpieza** he went crazy and started cleaning the whole house (colloq); ~ **del oro** gold fever

fiel *adj* **(a)** ⟨persona/animal⟩ faithful; **serle ~ a algn** to be faithful to sb; ~ **al rey** loyal to the king **(b)** ⟨traducción/copia⟩ faithful, accurate ■ *mf* (Relig) **los ~es** the faithful

fieltro *m* felt

fiera *f* (animal) wild animal, beast (liter); **ponerse como** *o* **hecho una ~** to go wild (colloq)

fiero -ra *adj* ⟨animal⟩ fierce, ferocious

fierro *m* **(a)** (AmL) (hierro) iron; (fam) (trozo de metal) piece of metal **(b) fierros** *mpl* (Méx fam) (en los dientes) braces (*pl*) (AmE), brace (esp BrE)

fiesta *f* **(a)** (celebración) party; ~ **de cumpleaños** birthday party; **dieron una gran ~** they threw *o* had a big party; **estar de ~** to be having a party; **aguar la ~** to spoil the fun **(b)** (día festivo) (public) holiday; **el lunes es ~** Monday is a holiday; ~ **nacional** (día festivo) public holiday; (Taur) bullfighting; ~ **patria** (AmL) independence day **(c) fiestas** *fpl* (festejos) fiesta, festival; (de fin de año, etc) festive season; **¡felices ~s!** Merry Christmas!; **¿dónde vas a pasar estas ~s?** where are you going to spend the vacation (AmE) *o* (BrE) holidays?

FIFA /'fifa/ *f*: **la ~** FIFA

figura *f* figure; **tiene buena ~** she has a good figure; **una ~ de las letras** an important literary figure; ~ **paterna** father figure

figuración *f* (imaginación) imagining; **son figuraciones tuyas** it's all in your imagination

figurado -da *adj* figurative; **en sentido ~** in a figurative sense

figurar [A1] *vi* (en lista, documento) to appear
■ **figurarse** *v pron* to imagine; **me figuro que sí** I imagine so, I figure she (*o* he *etc*) will (AmE); **me figuro que tardaremos una hora** I reckon *o* (AmE) figure that it'll take us one hour; **¡figúrate, tardamos dos horas!** just imagine! it took us two hours; **ya me lo figuraba yo** I thought as much, so I thought

figurita *f* (de adorno) figurine; (lámina) (RPl) picture card

AmC	Central America	Arg	Argentina	Cu	Cuba	Per	Peru
AmL	Latin America	Bol	Bolivia	Ec	Ecuador	RPl	River Plate Area
AmS	South America	Chi	Chile	Esp	Spain	Ur	Uruguay
Andes	Andean Region	CS	Southern Cone	Méx	Mexico	Ven	Venezuela

fijación *f* (Psic) fixation, obsession; **¡que ~ tienes con ese tema!** you're obsessed with that subject!

fijar [A1] *vt* **1** **(a)** (poner, clavar) ‹poste/ estantería› to fix; ❂ **prohibido fijar carteles** stick no bills; **fijó la mirada en el horizonte** she fixed her gaze on the horizon **(b)** ‹atención/mente› to focus

2 **(a)** ‹residencia› to take up, establish (frml) **(b)** ‹fecha/cifra/precio› to set **(c)** «reglamento/ley» to state

■ **fijarse** *v pron* **(a)** (prestar atención): **fíjate bien en cómo lo hace** watch carefully how she does it; **fíjate en lo que haces** watch *o* pay attention to what you're doing **(b)** (darse cuenta) to notice; **¿te has fijado en que no discuten nunca?** have you noticed that they never quarrel?; **¡fíjate lo que ha crecido!** just look how she's grown!

fijo¹ -ja *adj* **(a)** (no movible) fixed; **una lámpara fija a la pared** a lamp fixed to the wall; **con los ojos ~s en ella** with his eyes fixed on her; **asegúrate de que la escalera está bien fija** make sure the ladder is steady **(b)** ‹sueldo/precios› fixed; ‹trabajo/empleado› permanent; ‹cliente› regular **(c)** (definitivo) ‹fecha› definite, firm

fijo² *adv* (fam): **¿crees que vendrá? — fijo** do you think she'll come? — definitely *o* (colloq) sure; **~ que el domingo llueve** it's bound to rain on Sunday

fila *f* **(a)** (hilera) line; **formen ~ aquí** line up *o* form a line here; **en ~ india** in single file; **estacionado en doble ~** double-parked **(b)** (en teatro, aula) row **(c) filas** *fpl* (Mil) ranks (*pl*); **incorporarse a ~s** to join up; **lo llamaron a ~s** he was drafted

filamento *m* (Elec) filament; (hilo, fibra) thread

filatelia *f* stamp collecting, philately

filete *m* (de pescado) fillet; (de carne — bistec) steak; (— corte entre las costillas y el lomo) (Chi, Méx) fillet

filiación *f* (afiliación) affiliation; **~ política** political affiliation

filial *adj* **(a)** ‹amor› filial **(b)** ‹compañía/ asociación› affiliate (*before n*), subsidiary
■ *f* subsidiary (company)

Filipinas *fpl*: **tb las ~** the Philippines

filipino -na *adj* Philippine, Filipino
■ *m,f* Filipino

film *m* (*pl* **films**) **(a)** (Cin, TV) movie, film (BrE) **(b)** (Coc) **tb ~ transparente** Saran wrap® (AmE), clingfilm (BrE)

filmadora *f* (AmL) movie camera (AmE), cinecamera (BrE)

filmar [A1] *vt* ‹película› to shoot; ‹persona/ suceso› to film

filmina *f* slide

filmoteca *f* film library

filo *m* **(a)** (de cuchillo, espada) cutting edge, blade; **no tiene mucho ~** it isn't very sharp; **le voy a dar ~** I'm going to sharpen it **(b)** (borde) edge; **el ~ de la mesa** the edge of the table; **al ~ de las siete** at seven o'clock sharp

filología *f* philology; **una licenciatura en ~ francesa** a degree in French

filólogo -ga *m,f* philologist; **soy ~** I have a degree in languages

filón *m* **(a)** (Min) seam, vein **(b)** (fam) (negocio) gold mine (colloq)

filoso -sa *adj* (AmL) ‹cuchillo/hoja› sharp

filosofía *f* philosophy

filosófico -ca *adj* philosophical

filósofo -fa *m,f* philosopher

filtración *f* (en general) leak ; (de información) leak; **la ~ de un informe** the leaking of a report

filtrar [A1] *vt* **(a)** ‹líquido/rayos› to filter **(b)** ‹informaciones/noticias› to leak

■ **filtrarse** *v pron* **(a)** «agua» to leak; «humedad» to seep; **la luz se filtraba por entre las persianas** light filtered through the shutters **(b)** «noticia» to leak

filtro *m* filter; **~ solar** sunscreen

fin *m* **1** **(a)** (final) end; **a ~es de junio** at the end of June; **a ~ de mes** at the end of the month; **~ de año** New Year's Eve; **~ de semana** (sábado y domingo) weekend; **puso ~ a la discusión** she put an end to the discussion **(b)** (en locs) **por *o* al fin** at last; **en fin** (expresando resignación) ah well; **en ~ ¡sigamos!** anyway, let's carry on!; **a ~ de cuentas** in the end, at the end of the day; **al ~ y al cabo** after all

2 **(a)** (objetivo, finalidad) purpose; **el ~ de esta visita** the aim *o* purpose of this visit **(b)** (en locs) **a fin de que** (frml) in order to; **con este fin** (frml) with this aim (frml), to this end (frml); **con el fin *o* a fin de** (frml) with the aim *o* purpose of

final *adj* ‹decisión› final; ‹objetivo› ultimate
■ *m* end; **a ~es de junio** at the end of June; **un ~ feliz** a happy ending; **al ~ de la lista** at the bottom of the list; **al ~ tendrá que decidirse** he'll have to make his mind up in the end *o* eventually
■ *f* (Dep) **(a)** (en fútbol, tenis etc) final; **la ~ de copa** the cup final; **pasar a la ~** to go through to *o* make it to the final **(b) finales** *fpl* (en béisbol, baloncesto, fútbol americano) playoffs (*pl*)

finalidad *f* (propósito, utilidad) purpose, aim

finalista *adj*: **los dos equipos ~s** the two teams that reach (*o* reached *etc*) the final
■ *mf* finalist

finalizar [A4] *vt* to finish
■ **~** *vi* to end; **una vez finalizada la reunión** once the meeting is/was over

financiación *f*, **financiamiento** *m* financing

financiar [A1] *vt* **(a)** ‹empresa/proyecto› to finance, fund **(b)** (AmL) (vender a plazos) to give credit facilities for

financiero -ra *adj* financial
■ *m,f* financier

financista *mf* (AmL) financier

finanzas *fpl* finances (*pl*)

finca *f* **(a)** (explotación agrícola) farm **(b)** (casa de campo) country estate **(c)** (Esp) (propiedad urbana) building

fincar [A2] *vt* (Méx) to build

fingido -da *adj* hypocritical, false

fingir [I7] *vt* **(a)** ‹alegría/desinterés› to feign, fake; **fingió no verme** she pretended not to see me **(b)** ‹voz› to imitate
■ **~** *vi* to pretend
■ **fingirse** *v pron*: **se fingió apenado** he pretended to be sorry

finlandés¹ -desa adj Finnish
■ m,f (persona) Finn
finlandés² m (idioma) Finnish
Finlandia f Finland
fino¹ -na adj **1** (en grosor) ⟨papel/capa/hilo⟩ fine, thin; ⟨loncha⟩ thin; ⟨arena/pelo/lluvia⟩ fine; ⟨labios⟩ thin; ⟨cintura/dedos⟩ slender; ⟨punta/lápiz⟩ fine **2** (en calidad) ⟨pastelería/bollería⟩ high quality; ⟨porcelana⟩ fine; ⟨lencería⟩ sheer **3** (en modales) refined **4** (a) ⟨oído/olfato⟩ acute **(b)** ⟨ironía/humor⟩ subtle
fino² m fino, dry sherry
firma f **1** (nombre) signature; (acción) signing **2** (empresa) company, firm (BrE)
firmamento m (liter) firmament (liter)
firmar [A1] vt/vi to sign
firme adj **1** ⟨escalera/silla/mesa⟩ steady; terreno ~ solid ground; con paso/pulso ~ with a firm step/steady hand; una oferta en ~ a firm offer; de ~ ⟨estudiar/trabajar⟩ hard **2** (Mil): ¡~s! attention! **3** (a) ⟨persona⟩ firm; mostrarse ~ con algn to be firm with sb; me mantuve ~ en mi idea I stuck o kept to my idea **(b)** (delante del n) ⟨creencia/convicción⟩ firm
firmeza f (a) (de convicciones, carácter) strength; con ~ firmly **(b)** (del terreno) firmness
fiscal adj fiscal, tax (before n)
■ mf ≈ district attorney (in US), ≈ public prosecutor (in UK)
fiscalizar [A4] vt to supervise, control
fisco m ≈ Treasury (in US), ≈ Exchequer (in UK)
fisgar [A3] vi (fam) to snoop (colloq); andaba fisgando por las oficinas he was snooping around the offices
fisgón -gona adj (fam) nosy (colloq)
■ m,f (fam) busybody (colloq)
fisgonear [A1] vi (fam) to nose around (colloq)
física f physics; ~ nuclear nuclear physics
físico¹ -ca adj physical
■ m,f physicist
físico² m (cuerpo — de hombre, atleta) physique; (— de mujer) figure; (apariencia) appearance
fisionomía, fisonomía f (a) (de persona) features (pl) **(b)** (de objeto, lugar) appearance
fisioterapia f physiotherapy, physical therapy (AmE)
flaccidez f flaccidity
fláccido -da adj flaccid, flabby
flaco -ca adj thin, skinny (colloq)
flagelar [A1] vt to flagellate (frml); (Bib) to scourge
■ **flagelarse** v pron to flagellate oneself (frml), to whip oneself
flagrante adj ⟨mentira⟩ blatant; ⟨injusticia⟩ glaring, flagrant; lo sorprendieron en ~ delito they caught him red-handed
flama f (Méx) flame
flamable adj (Méx) inflammable, flammable
flamante adj (gen delante del n) (nuevo) brand-new; (vistoso) smart (colloq)
flamenco¹ -ca adj **1** ⟨cante/baile⟩ flamenco (before n) **2** (de Flandes) Flemish
■ m,f Fleming; los ~s the Flemish

flamenco² m **1** (Mús) flamenco **2** (idioma) Flemish **3** (Zool) flamingo
flan m (a) (dulce) crème caramel **(b)** (de arroz) mold*; (de pescado, verduras) terrine
flanco m (a) (Mil) flank **(b)** (de animal) flank, side; (de persona) side
Flandes m Flanders
flaquear [A1] vi ⟨persona/fuerzas⟩ to flag; su voluntad empezó a ~ she began to lose heart
flaqueza f weakness
flash /'flas/ m (pl flashes) (Fot) flash
flato m (a) (Esp) (dolor en el costado): tengo ~ I have a stitch **(b)** (Chi fam) (eructo) burp (colloq)
flauta f (Mús) flute; ~ dulce recorder
■ mf flute player, flutist (AmE), flautist (BrE)
flautín m piccolo
■ mf piccolo (player)
flautista mf flute player, flutist (AmE), flautist (BrE)
flecha f arrow
flechazo m (a) (fam) (enamoramiento): fue un ~ it was love at first sight **(b)** (herida) arrow wound
fleco m (Méx) (en el pelo) bangs (pl) (AmE), fringe (BrE)
flecos mpl (a) (adorno) fringe; un chal con ~ a fringed shawl **(b)** (borde deshilachado) frayed edge
flema f phlegm
flemático -ca adj phlegmatic
flemón m boil, abscess; (en la encía) gumboil
flequillo m bangs (pl) (AmE), fringe (BrE)
fletar [A1] vt (Com, Transp) ⟨barco/avión⟩ to charter; ⟨autobús/camión⟩ to hire, rent (AmE)
flete m (a) (contratación — de barco, avión) charter; (— de autobús, camión) hire **(b)** (precio de contratación — de barco, avión) charter fee; (— de autobús, camión) hire charge, rental charge (AmE)
flexibilidad f flexibility
flexible adj flexible
flexión f (Dep) (de brazos) push-up, press-up (BrE); (de piernas) squat; hacer flexiones (de brazos) to do push-ups o press-ups; (de cintura) to touch one's toes
flexionar [A1] vt (Dep) ⟨pierna/rodillas⟩ to bend
flirt /'flirt/ m (pl flirts) (a) (relación) fling **(b)** (hombre) boyfriend; (mujer) girlfriend
flirtear [A1] vi to flirt
flojear [A1] vi (a) (debilitarse) to grow o get weak; me flojean las piernas my legs are getting weak **(b)** (fam) (holgazanear) to laze around
flojera f (a) (fam) (debilidad) lethargy **(b)** (fam) (pereza) laziness; me da ~ I can't be bothered; tengo ~ I feel lazy
flojo -ja adj **1** (a) ⟨nudo/tornillo/vendaje⟩ loose; ⟨cuerda/goma⟩ slack **(b)** (débil) weak **(c)** ⟨vientos⟩ light **(d)** ⟨café/té⟩ weak **2** (mediocre) ⟨trabajo/examen⟩ poor; ⟨película/vino⟩ second-rate; ⟨estudiante⟩ poor; está ~ en física he's weak in (AmE) o (BrE) at physics **3** ⟨persona⟩ (fam) (perezoso) lazy
■ m,f (fam) (perezoso) lazybones (colloq)
floppy /'flopi/ m (pl floppys) floppy disk, diskette
flor f (de planta) flower; (de árbol frutal) blossom; ~es secas dried flowers; un vestido de ~es a

flowery dress; **en** ~ in flower o bloom/in blossom; ~ **de azahar** orange/lemon blossom; *la* ~ **y nata** the cream, la crème de la crème

flora *f* flora

florear [A1] *vi* **(a)** (Chi, Méx) (Bot) to flower, blossom **(b)** (Méx) (halagar): **le** ~**on mucho su vestido** her dress got a lot of compliments

florecer [E3] *vi* **(a)** «*tulipán/rosa*» to flower, bloom; «*árbol*» to flower, blossom **(b)** (prosperar) to flourish, thrive

floreciente *adj* flourishing, thriving

Florencia *f* Florence

florentino -na *adj/m,f* Florentine

florería *f* (AmL) florist's, flower shop

florero *m* vase

florido -da *adj* **(a)** «*campo*» full of flowers **(b)** «*estilo/lenguaje*» flowery

florín *m* (moneda holandesa) guilder

florista *mf* florist

floristería *f* florist's, flower shop

flota *f* ⓵ (de barcos, camiones, aviones) fleet ⓶ (Col) (autobús) bus (AmE), coach (BrE)

flotador *m* (en general) float; (para la cintura) rubber ring; (para los brazos) armband

flotante *adj* floating

flotar [A1] *vi* to float

flote: **a** ~ afloat; **mantenerse a** ~ to stay afloat; **logró mantener el negocio a** ~ he managed to keep the business afloat; **salir a** ~ «*cuerpo sumergido*» to float to the surface; «*país/persona en apuros*» to get back on its/one's feet

flotilla *f* (Náut) flotilla; (Aviac) fleet

fluctuar [A18] *vi* to fluctuate

fluidez *f* **(a)** (de expresión) fluency; **habla griego con** ~ she speaks Greek fluently **(b)** (de tráfico) smooth flow **(c)** (Fís, Quím) fluidity

fluido -da *adj* «*estilo/languaje*» fluent; «*circulación*» free-flowing; «*movimientos*» fluid, fluent ■ *m* fluid

fluir [I20] *vi* to flow

flujo *m* ⓵ (circulación, corriente) flow; ~ **sanguíneo** blood flow ⓶ (Med) (secreción) discharge; ~ **menstrual** menstrual flow ⓷ (Náut) tide; ~ **y reflujo** ebb and flow

fluminense *adj* of/from Río de Janeiro

flúor, fluor *m* (gas) fluorine; (fluoruro) fluoride

fluorescente *adj* fluorescent

fluvial *adj* river (*before n*)

fobia *f* phobia; **tiene** ~ **a los aviones** he has a phobia about flying

foca *f* (animal) seal; (piel) sealskin

focal *adj* focal

foco *m* ⓵ **(a)** (Fís, Fot, Mat) focus **(b)** (centro, núcleo) focus; **fue el** ~ **de todas las miradas** everybody's eyes were focused on him **(c)** (de incendio) seat ⓶ **(a)** (reflector) (Cin, Teatr) spotlight; (en estadio, monumento) floodlight **(b)** (AmL) (Auto) light **(c)** (Ec, Méx, Per) (de lámpara) light bulb **(d)** (AmC) (linterna) flashlight (AmE), torch (BrE)

fogata *f* bonfire

fogón *m* (quemador) burner; (fogata) (AmL) bonfire, campfire; (de caldera) firebox

fogonazo *m* flash, explosion

fogueado -da *adj* (AmS fam) experienced

fogueo *m* (Mil): **un cartucho de** ~ a blank (cartridge)

folio *m* **(a)** (hoja) sheet (of paper); **papel tamaño** ~ A4 paper **(b)** (de un trabajo, una tesis) page

folk /'fo(l)k/ *adj* folk (*before n*) ■ *m* folk (music)

folklore *m* folklore

folklórico -ca *adj* **(a)** «*danza/música/leyenda*» folk (*before n*) **(b)** (fam) (pintoresco) quaint

follaje *m* foliage

folletín *m* (en periódicos, revistas) newspaper serial; (revista mala) rag (colloq); (película, novela mala) melodrama

folleto *m* (hoja) leaflet, flier (AmE); (librito) brochure, pamphlet; ~ **de viaje** travel brochure

follón *m* (Esp fam) **(a)** (trifulca) commotion, ruckus; (ruido) racket (colloq), din (AmE colloq); **armó un buen** ~ (montó una trifulca) he kicked up a hell of a fuss (colloq); (hizo ruido) he made such a racket o din (colloq) **(b)** (situación confusa, desorden) mess **(c)** (problema) trouble; **no te metas en follones** don't get into trouble

fomentar [A1] *vt* «*industria/turismo*» to promote; «*ahorro/inversión*» to encourage, boost; «*disturbio/odio*» to incite, foment (frml); «*interés/afición*» to encourage

fonda *f* **(a)** (esp AmL) (restaurant) cheap restaurant **(b)** (esp Esp) (pensión) boarding house **(c)** (Chi) (puesto) refreshment stand

fondista *mf* (Dep) long-distance runner

fondo *m* ⓵ **(a)** (parte más baja) bottom; **el** ~ **del mar** the bottom of the sea; **llegaré al** ~ **de esta cuestión** I'll get to the bottom of this matter **(b)** (parte de atrás — de pasillo, calle) end; (— de habitación) back; **al** ~ **de la sala** at the back of the room **(c)** (profundidad): **tiene poco** ~ it is not very deep **(d)** (de edificio) depth **(e)** (en cuadro, fotografía) background ⓶ (Lit) (contenido) content ⓷ (Fin) **(a)** (de dinero) fund; **hacer un** ~ **común** to start a joint fund o (colloq) a kitty **(b) fondos** *mpl* (dinero) money, funds (*pl*); **recaudar** ~**s** to raise money; **un cheque sin** ~**s** a dud o (AmE) rubber check (colloq) ⓸ (Dep) (en atletismo): **de** ~ «*corredor/carrera/prueba*» long-distance (*before n*) ⓹ (Méx) (Indum) slip, underskirt ⓺ (en locs) **a fondo** (*loc adj*) «*estudio/investigación*» in-depth (*before n*); «*limpieza*» thorough; (*loc adv*) «*prepararse/entrenar*» thoroughly; **conoce el tema a** ~ she knows the subject really well; **de fondo** «*ruido/música*» background (*before n*); **en el fondo**: **en el** ~ **nos llevamos bien** we get on all right, really; **en el** ~ **no es malo** deep down he's not a bad person

fonética *f* phonetics

fonógrafo *m* phonograph

fontanería *f* (esp Esp) plumbing

fontanero -ra *m,f* (esp Esp) plumber

footing /'futin/ *m* jogging; **hacer** ~ to jog

forajido -da *m,f* fugitive, outlaw

foráneo -nea *adj* foreign, strange

forastero -ra *m,f* stranger, outsider

forcejear [A1] *vi* to struggle

forcejeo *m* struggle

fórceps *m* (*pl* ~) forceps (*pl*)

forense *adj* forensic
■ *mf* forensic scientist

forestal *adj* forest (*before n*)

forjar [A1] *vt* (a) ⟨*utensilio/pieza*⟩ to forge;
⟨*metal*⟩ to work (b) ⟨*porvenir*⟩ to shape, forge;
⟨*plan*⟩ to make; ⟨*ilusiones/esperanzas*⟩ to build up
(c) ⟨*nación/bases*⟩ to create; ⟨*amistad/alianza*⟩ to
forge
■ **forjarse** *v pron* ⟨*porvenir*⟩ to shape, forge;
⟨*ilusiones*⟩ to build up

forma *f* **1** (a) (contorno, apariencia) shape; **en ~
de cruz** in the shape of a cross; **tiene la ~ de un
platillo** it's the shape of a saucer; **dar ~ a algo** (al
barro) to shape sth; (a proyecto) to give shape to sth
(b) (tipo, modalidad) form; **distintas ~s de vida
animal** different forms of animal life; **~ de pago**
form *o* method of payment
2 (Dep, Med): **estar en ~** to be fit; **está en baja ~**
he's not on form; **en plena ~** on top form; **en ~:
nos divertimos en ~** we had a really good time
3 (manera, modo) way; **es su ~ de ser** it's just the
way he is; **¡vaya ~ de conducir!** what a way to
drive!; **~ de vida** way of life; **de ~ distinta**
differently; **de cualquier ~** *or* **de todas ~s**
anyway, in any case
4 formas *fpl* (a) (de mujer) figure (b)
(apariencias) appearances (*pl*); **guardar las ~s** to
keep up appearances
5 (Méx) (formulario) form

formación *f* **1** (en general) formation; **la ~ de
un gobierno** the formation of a government
2 (educación recibida) education; (para trabajo)
training; **~ profesional** *or* (CS) **vocacional**
professional *o* vocational training

formal *adj* **1** (en general) formal; ⟨*promesa/
oferta*⟩ firm **2** ⟨*persona*⟩ (cumplidora) reliable,
dependable; (responsable) responsible

formalidad *f* **1** (de persona) reliability; **no
tiene ~** he's so unreliable **2** (requisito) formality

formalizar [A4] *vt* ⟨*noviazgo/relación*⟩ to make
... official; ⟨*transacción/contrato*⟩ to formalize

formar [A1] *vt* **1** (a) (crear) ⟨*círculo/figura*⟩ to
make, form; ⟨*asociación/gobierno*⟩ to form, set
up; ⟨*barricada*⟩ to set up; **¡formen parejas!** (en
clase) get into pairs *o* twos!; (en baile) take your
partners! (b) (Ling) to form (c) (Mil) ⟨*tropas*⟩ to
have ... fall in
2 (componer) to make up; **un equipo formado por
cinco personas** a team made up of five people; **~
parte de algo** to be part of sth, to belong to sth
3 ⟨*carácter/espíritu*⟩ to form, shape
4 (educar) to bring up; (para trabajo) to train
■ **~** *vi* (Mil) to fall in
■ **formarse** *v pron* **1** (a) (hacerse, crearse)
«*grupo/organismo*» to form; **se formó una cola** a
line (AmE) *o* (BrE) queue formed (b) (desarrollarse)
«*niño/huesos*» to develop (c) ⟨*idea/opinión*⟩ to
form
2 (educarse) to be educated; (para trabajo) to be
trained

formatear [A1] *vt* (Inf) to format

formato *m* **1** (a) (tamaño, forma) format (b)
(Inf) format; **sin ~** unformatted **2** (Méx) (formulario,
solicitud) form

formidable *adj/interj* (fam) fantastic (colloq)

fórmula *f* **1** (a) (Mat, Quím) formula (b)
(manera, sistema) way (c) (frase, expresión) standard
expression, formula; **~s de cortesía** polite
expressions (d) (Col) (receta médica) prescription
2 (Auto) formula; **un coche de F~ 1** a Formula 1
car

formular [A1] *vt* **1** ⟨*queja*⟩ to make, lodge;
⟨*teoría/plan*⟩ to formulate **2** (Col) «*médico*» to
prescribe

formulario *m* form

forrado -da *adj* **1** ⟨*prenda*⟩ lined; ⟨*sillón/
libro*⟩ covered; **un abrigo ~ de seda** a coat lined
with silk **2** [ESTAR] (fam) (de dinero) loaded (colloq)

forrar [A1] *vt* ⟨*prenda*⟩ to line; ⟨*libro/sillón*⟩ to
cover
■ **forrarse** *v pron* (fam) *tb* **~se de dinero** to make
a killing *o* mint (colloq)

forro *m* (de abrigo) lining; (de sillón) cover; (de
libro) cover, jacket

fortalecer [E3] *vt* ⟨*organismo/músculos/
amistad*⟩ to strengthen
■ **fortalecerse** *v pron* «*organismo/músculo*» to
get stronger

fortaleza *f* **1** (física) strength; (moral) fortitude,
strength of spirit **2** (Mil) fortress

fortificar [A2] *vt* (a) (Mil) ⟨*lugar/plaza*⟩ to
fortify (b) (dar fuerza) to strengthen, make ...
stronger

fortín *m* (fuerte pequeño) (small) fort;
(emplazamiento) pillbox, bunker

fortuito -ta *adj* ⟨*encuentro/suceso*⟩ chance
(*before n*), fortuitous

fortuna *f* (a) (riqueza) fortune (b) (azar, suerte)
fortune; **por ~** fortunately; **probar ~** to try one's
luck

forzado -da *adj* forced, unnatural

forzar [A11] *vt* **1** (obligar) to force **2** (a) ⟨*vista*⟩
to strain; **estaba forzando la vista** I was straining
my eyes (b) ⟨*sonrisa*⟩ to force **3** ⟨*puerta/
cerradura*⟩ to force

forzoso -sa *adj* ⟨*aterrizaje/anexión/paro*⟩
forced; ⟨*jubilación/liquidación*⟩ compulsory

fosa *f* (zanja) ditch; (hoyo) pit; (tumba) grave; **~
común** common *o* communal grave

fosfato *m* phosphate

fosforescente *adj* (a) (Fís) phosphorescent
(b) ⟨*color/pintura*⟩ fluorescent

fósforo *m* (a) (Quím) phosphorus (b) (cerilla)
match

fósil *adj* fossilized, fossil (*before n*)
■ *m* fossil

foso *m* (a) (zanja) ditch; (en fortificaciones) moat;
(Equ) water jump (b) (Teatr) pit; **~ de la orquesta**
orchestra pit (c) (Auto) (inspection) pit

foto *f* picture, photo (esp BrE); **me sacó** *or* **tomó
una ~** he took a picture *o* photo of me; **~ de
carné/pasaporte** passport photo

fotocopia *f* photocopy, Xerox®; **hizo** *or* **sacó una ~ de la carta** he made *o* took a photocopy of the letter

fotocopiadora *f* photocopier, Xerox® machine

fotocopiar [A1] *vt* to photocopy, xerox

fotogénico -ca *adj* photogenic

fotografía *f* (técnica, arte) photography; (retrato, imagen) photograph

fotografiar [A17] *vt* to photograph, take a photograph of

fotográfico -ca *adj* photographic

fotógrafo -fa *m,f* photographer

fotomatón *m* photo booth

fotómetro *m* (Fot) exposure *o* light meter; (Fís) photometer

foul /'faul/ *m* (*pl* **fouls**) (AmL) foul

FP (en Esp) = **Formación Profesional**

frac *m* (*pl* **fracs** *or* **fraques**) (chaqueta) tail coat, tails (*pl*); (traje) morning suit

fracasado -da *adj* failed, unsuccessful
■ *m,f* failure

fracasar [A1] *vi* to fail

fracaso *m* failure

fracción *f* fraction

fractura *f* (a) (Med) fracture (b) (Geol) fault

fracturar [A1] *vt* to fracture
■ **fracturarse** *v pron* to fracture

fragancia *f* fragrance, perfume

fragata *f* frigate

frágil *adj* (a) ⟨cristal/fuente⟩ fragile (b) ⟨salud/ constitución⟩ delicate; ⟨persona⟩ frail; ⟨economía⟩ fragile

fragmento *m* (a) (de jarrón) shard; (de hueso) fragment (b) (de conversación) snippet, snatch (c) (extracto de novela, carta) extract, passage

fragua *f* forge

fraguar [A16] *vt* (a) (Metal) to forge (b) ⟨complot⟩ to hatch; ⟨plan⟩ to conceive
■ **~** *vi* «cemento» to set

fraile *m* friar, monk

frailecillo *m* puffin

frambuesa *f* raspberry

francés¹ -cesa *adj* French
■ *m,f* (*m*) Frenchman; (*f*) Frenchwoman; **los franceses** the French, French people

francés² *m* (idioma) French

Francia *f* France

franco¹ -ca *adj* ① (sincero) ⟨persona⟩ frank; ⟨sonrisa⟩ natural; **para serte *o* ...** to be frank *o* honest ...; **una mirada franca** an honest *o* open expression ② (delante del *n*) ⟨patente⟩ ⟨mejoría/ decadencia⟩ marked; **un clima de franca cordialidad** an atmosphere of genuine warmth ③ (Com) free; **~ de porte** carriage free; **paso ~** free passage; **~ de derechos** duty-free ④ [ESTAR] (a) (Mil) off duty (b) (RPl) (libre de trabajo): **el lunes estoy ~** I have Monday off

franco² *m* (unidad monetaria) franc

francotirador -dora *m,f* sniper

franela *f* (a) (Tex) flannel (b) (Ven) (camiseta) T-shirt (c) (Col) (camiseta de interior) undershirt (AmE), vest (BrE)

franja *f* (banda) stripe, band; (cinta, adorno) border, fringe

franquear [A1] *vt* ① ⟨paso/entrada⟩ to clear; ⟨puerta⟩ to go through; ⟨umbral/río⟩ to cross ② ⟨carta⟩ (pagar) to pay the postage on
■ **franquearse** *v pron* **~se CON algn** to confide IN sb

franqueo *m* postage

franqueza *f* frankness, openness; **hablar con (toda) ~** to be (perfectly) frank *o* honest

franquicia *f* ① (exención) exemption; (en seguros) excess; **~ aduanera** (condición) duty-free status; (cantidad) duty-free allowance ② (concesión) franchise

franquismo *m* Franco's regime

frasco *m* bottle; (de mermelada) jar

frase *f* (oración) sentence; (sintagma) phrase; **~ hecha** set phrase

fraternal *adj* brotherly, fraternal

fraude *m* fraud; **~ fiscal** tax evasion

fraudulento -ta *adj* ⟨negocio⟩ fraudulent; ⟨elecciones⟩ rigged

fray *m* (delante de *n* propio) Brother

frazada *f* (AmL) blanket; **~ eléctrica** electric blanket

frecuencia *f* frequency; **con ~** frequently; **~ modulada** frequency modulation, FM

frecuentar [A1] *vt* to frequent

frecuente *adj* ⟨llamada/visita⟩ frequent

freelance /'frilans/ *mf* freelancer; **trabaja de ~** he works freelance

freezer /'friser/ *m* (a) (AmL) (electrodoméstico) freezer, deep freeze (b) (Chi, Ven) (en el refrigerador) freezer (compartment)

fregadero *m* (de la cocina) kitchen sink; (para lavar ropa) (Méx) sink

fregado -da *adj* (AmL exc RPl fam) (a) (molesto) annoying; **¡no seas ~, hombre!** stop being such a pain (colloq) (b) (difícil) ⟨examen/tema⟩ tricky (colloq), tough (colloq); ⟨persona/carácter⟩ difficult (c) [ESTAR] (enfermo, delicado) in a bad way (colloq); (sin dinero) broke (colloq)
■ *m,f* (AmL exc RPl fam) (persona difícil) difficult person

fregar [A7] *vt* ① (lavar, limpiar) to wash; **fregué el suelo** I washed the floor; (con cepillo) I scrubbed the floor; **~ los platos** to wash the dishes, to do the dishes (colloq) ② (AmL exc RPl fam) (a) (molestar) to bug (colloq) (b) ⟨planes/vacaciones⟩ to ruin
■ **~** *vi* ① (lavar los platos) to wash the dishes, to do the dishes (colloq); (limpiar) to clean; (restregar) to scrub ② (AmL exc RPl fam) (molestar): **¡déjate de ~!** stop being such a pest!; **¡no friegues!** (no digas) you're kidding! (colloq)
■ **fregarse** *v pron* ① (AmL fam) (embromarse): **¡te friegas!** tough! (colloq); **¡me fregué!** I've really done it now! (colloq) ② (AmL exc RPl fam) (malograrse): **se ~on nuestros planes** that's ruined *o* messed up our plans (colloq)

fregona *f* (Esp) (utensilio) mop

freidora *f* deep fryer

freír [I35] *vt* to fry
■ **freírse** *v pron* to fry

frenada *f* (esp AmL) ▶ FRENAZO

frenar [A1] *vt* **1** (Transp) to brake **2** ⟨*proceso/ deterioro*⟩ to slow … down; ⟨*alza/inflación*⟩ to curb, check; ⟨*progreso/desarrollo*⟩ to hold … back
■ ~ *vi* to brake, apply the brake(s) (frml)

frenazo *m* (fam): oí el ~ I heard the screeching of brakes; **dio un** ~ she slammed *o* jammed on her brakes

frenético -ca *adj* frenzied, frenetic; **ponerse** ~ (fam) to go crazy *o* wild

frenillos *mpl* (AmL) (para los dientes) braces (*pl*) (AmE), brace (esp BrE)

freno *m* **(a)** (Mec, Transp) brake; ~ **de mano** emergency brake (AmE), handbrake (BrE) **(b)** (Equ) bit **(c)** (contención): **poner** ~ **a algo** ⟨a gastos, importaciones⟩ to curb sth; ⟨a abusos⟩ to put a stop to sth **(d) frenos** *mpl* (Méx) ▶ FRENILLOS

frente *f* forehead, brow (liter); **arrugar la** ~ to frown
■ *m* **1** **(a)** (de edificio) front, facade (frml); *hacer* (*le*) ~ **a algo** (a la realidad, una responsabilidad) to face up to sth; (a gastos, obligaciones) to meet sth; *hacerle* ~ **a algn** (a enemigo, atacante) to face sb **(b)** (*en locs*) **al frente: dar un paso al** ~ to take a step forward; **vive al** ~ (Chi) she lives opposite; **estar al** ~ **de algo** (de una clasificación) to be at the top of sth; (de una empresa) to be in charge of sth; **de frente** ⟨*chocar*⟩ head on; **una foto de** ~ a full-face photo; **de frente a** (AmL) facing; **frente a** opposite; **estamos** ~ **a un grave problema** we are faced with a serious problem
2 (Meteo, Mil, Pol) front

fresa *f* (planta) strawberry plant; (fruta) strawberry

fresco¹ -ca *adj* **1** **(a)** ⟨*viento*⟩ cool, fresh; ⟨*agua*⟩ cold; ⟨*bebida*⟩ cool, cold; **el tiempo está** ~ the weather is a bit chilly **(b)** ⟨*ropa/tela*⟩ cool **2** **(a)** ⟨*pescado/fruta*⟩ fresh; **trae noticias frescas** she has the latest news; ❾ **pintura fresca** wet paint **(b)** ⟨*cutis/belleza*⟩ fresh, young **(c)** (no viciado) ⟨*aire*⟩ fresh **3** ⟨*persona*⟩ **(a)** [SER] (fam) (descarado): **¡qué tipo más** ~**!** that guy sure has some nerve! (colloq) **(b)** [ESTAR] (descansado) refreshed; (no cansado) fresh **(c)** (tranquilo): **él estaba tan** ~ he was as cool as a cucumber
■ *m,f* (fam) (descarado): **¡eres un** ~**!** you have a lot of nerve! (colloq)

fresco² *m* **1** **(a)** (aire) fresh air; **tomar el** ~ to get some fresh air **(b)** (frío moderado): **hace un fresquito que da gusto** it's lovely and cool; **hace** ~ it's chilly **2** (Art) fresco; **pintura al** ~ fresco painting **3** (AmL) (gaseosa) soda (AmE), fizzy drink (BrE); (refresco de frutas) fruit drink

frescura *f* (descaro) nerve (colloq)

fresón *m* (long stem) strawberry

frialdad *f* (en general) coldness; **la** ~ **de su mirada** the coldness in his eyes; **me trató con** ~ he treated me coldly *o* frostily; **la** ~ **del público** the audience's lack of enthusiasm

friega *f* (fricción) rub; **date una(s)** ~**(s) en el pecho** con este rub this on your chest

friega, friegas, etc ▶ FREGAR

frígido -da *adj* frigid

frigorífico *m* **(a)** (Esp) (nevera) refrigerator, fridge **(b)** (en tiendas) cold store **(c)** (AmS) (de carne) meat processing plant

frijol *m* (AmL exc CS) (Bot, Coc) bean; ~ **colorado/ negro** kidney/black bean; **ganarse los** ~**es** to earn a living

frío¹, fría *adj* **1** ⟨*comida/agua/motor/viento*⟩ cold; **tengo los pies** ~**s** my feet are cold; **dejar** ~ **a algn: la noticia lo dejó** ~ (indiferente) he was quite unmoved by the news; (atónito) he was staggered by the news; **el jazz me deja fría** jazz does nothing for me **2** **(a)** ⟨*persona*⟩ cold; ⟨*público*⟩ unresponsive; ⟨*recibimiento*⟩ cool; **estuvo** ~ **conmigo** he was cold towards me **(b)** ⟨*decoración/color*⟩ cold

frío² *m* cold; **no salgas con este** ~ don't go out in this cold; **¡qué** ~ **hace!** it's so cold!; **tener/ pasar** ~ to be cold; **tengo** *or* **tengo los pies** ~ are cold; **tomar** *or* (Esp) **coger** ~ to catch cold

friolento -ta *adj* (AmL): **es muy** ~ he really feels the cold

friolero -ra *adj* (Esp) ▶ FRIOLENTO

friso *m* frieze

fritanga *f* **(a)** (AmC, Andes, Méx) (alimento frito) fried snack **(b)** (pey) (comida frita) greasy fried food

frito -ta *adj* **1** (Coc) fried **2** **(a)** (fam) (harto) fed up (colloq); **me tienes** ~ I'm fed up with you **(b)** (CS, Méx fam) (en apuros) done for (colloq)

frivolidad *f* (cualidad) frivolousness, frivolity; (cosa vana) triviality, frivolous thing

frívolo -la *adj* frivolous

frondoso -sa *adj* ⟨*árbol*⟩ leafy; ⟨*vegetación*⟩ lush; ⟨*bosque*⟩ thick

frontal *adj* ⟨*colisión*⟩ head-on; ⟨*ataque*⟩ direct, frontal (frml); ⟨*oposición*⟩ direct

frontenis *m* pelota (*played with tennis rackets*)

frontera *f* border, frontier (frml)

frontón *m* (juego) pelota; (cancha) pelota court; (pared) fronton

frotar [A1] *vt/vi* to rub
■ **frotarse** *v pron* (refl) ⟨*ojos/rodillas*⟩ to rub; ⟨*manos*⟩ to rub … together

fructífero -ra *adj* fruitful, productive

fruncir [I4] *vt* **(a)** ⟨*tela*⟩ to gather **(b)** ~ **el ceño** *or* **entrecejo** to frown

frustración *f* frustration

frustrado -da *adj* **(a)** ⟨*persona*⟩ frustrated; ⟨*actor/bailarina*⟩ frustrated (*before n*) **(b)** ⟨*atentado/intento*⟩ failed (*before n*)

frustrar [A1] *vt* ⟨*persona*⟩ to frustrate; ⟨*planes*⟩ to thwart; ⟨*esperanzas*⟩ to dash; **me frustra que no entiendan** I find it frustrating that they don't understand
■ **frustrarse** *v pron* «*planes*» to be thwarted, fail; «*esperanzas*» to come to nothing

fruta *f* fruit; **una** ~ a piece of fruit; ~ **confitada** *or* **escarchada** crystallized fruit, candied fruit; ~ **del tiempo** *or* **de (la) estación** seasonal fruit

frutal *adj* fruit (*before n*)
■ *m* fruit tree

frutería *f* fruit store *o* shop, greengrocer's (BrE)

frutero¹ -ra *m,f* (vendedor) fruit seller, greengrocer (BrE)

frutero² *m* (recipiente) fruit bowl

frutilla *f* (Bol, CS) strawberry

fruto *m* **1** (Bot) fruit; ~**s secos** nuts and dried fruit (*pl*) **2** (resultado, producto) fruit; **dar** *or* **rendir** ~**s** to bear fruit; ~ **DE algo** ⟨de inversión⟩ return

ON sth; ‹de trabajo/investigación› fruits OF sth; **todo fue ~ de su imaginación** it was all a figment of his imagination

FTP m (= **protocolo de transferencia de archivo**) FTP

fucsia f fuchsia
■ m/adj inv fuchsia

fue ▶ IR, SER

fuego m **(a)** (en general) fire; **¡~!** fire!; **le prendieron ~ a la casa** they set the house on fire; **abrieron ~ sobre los manifestantes** they opened fire on the demonstrators; **~s artificiales** fireworks (pl) **(b)** (para cigarrillo): **¿me da ~, por favor?** have you got a light, please? **(c)** (Coc): **cocinar a ~ lento** to cook over a low heat; (apenas hirviendo) to simmer; **poner la sartén al ~** put the frying pan on to heat

fuel, fuel-oil m fuel oil

fuelle m bellows (pl)

fuente f 1 **(a)** (manantial) spring; **~ termal** thermal spring **(b)** (origen) source; **la ~ del río** the source of the river; **~ de ingresos** source of income; **información de buena ~** information from reliable sources 2 (construcción) fountain; **~ de soda** (Chi, Méx) soda fountain (AmE), (place where drinks and ice creams are bought and consumed) 3 (plato) dish; **~ de horno** ovenproof dish

fuera adv 1 **(a)** (lugar, parte) [Latin American Spanish also uses AFUERA in this sense] outside; **comeremos ~** (en el jardín) we'll eat outside; (en un restaurante) we'll eat out; **por ~ es rojo** it's red on the outside; **aquí ~ se está muy bien** it's very nice out here; **se pasa el día ~** she's out all day **(b)** (en el extranjero) abroad, out of the country; (del lugar de trabajo, de la ciudad, etc) away 2 **fuera de** (loc prep) **(a)** (en el exterior de, más allá de) out of; **está ~ del país** he's out of the country; **ocurrió ~ del edificio** it happened outside the building; **~ de peligro/lugar** out of danger/place; **¡~ (de aquí)!** get out (of here)! **(b)** (excepto) apart from; **~ de eso, me encuentro bien** apart o (AmE) aside from that, I feel fine 3 (en otras locs): **fuera de combate: lo dejó ~ de combate** (Dep) he knocked him out; **fuera de serie** ‹jugador/cantante› exceptional, outstanding; **fuera de sí: estaba ~ de sí** he was beside himself; **fuera de temporada** out of season

fuera, fuéramos, etc ▶ IR, SER

fueraborda m outboard

fuereño -ña m,f (Méx fam): **un ~** some guy from out of town (colloq)

fuero m **(a)** (jurisdicción) jurisdiction **(b)** (privilegio, derecho) privilege; **en mi/su ~ interno** in my/his heart of hearts, deep down inside

fuerte adj 1 (en general) strong; **un equipo/una cuerda ~** a strong team/rope 2 **(a)** ‹viento› strong; ‹terremoto› severe; ‹lluvia/nevada› heavy **(b)** ‹dolor› intense, bad; ‹golpe› heavy; ‹resfriado› bad; ‹abrazo/beso› big **(c)** ‹ruido/música› loud **(d)** ‹olor/sabor/medicina› strong; ‹comida/dosis› heavy **(e)** ‹acento› strong, thick 3 (violento) ‹discusión› violent, heated; ‹película/escena› shocking
■ adv 1 ‹golpear/empujar› hard; ‹agarrar/apretar› tightly; ‹llover› heavily 2 ‹hablar› loudly; **pon la radio más ~** turn the radio up; **habla más ~** speak up

■ m **(a)** (Mil) fort **(b)** (especialidad) strong point, forte

fuerza f 1 **(a)** (vigor, energía) strength; **tener ~** to be strong; **no me siento con ~s** I don't have the strength; **tiene mucha ~ en los brazos** she has very strong arms; **agárralo con ~** hold on to it tightly; **empuja con ~** push hard; **le fallaron las ~s** his strength failed him; **recuperar ~s** to get one's strength back; **gritó con todas sus ~s** she shouted with all her might; **~ de voluntad** willpower **(b)** (del viento, de olas) strength, force **(c)** (de estructura, material) strength 2 (violencia) force; **recurrir a la ~** to resort to force; **~ bruta** brute force 3 (Mil, Pol, Fís) force; **~s políticas** political forces; **las ~s armadas** the armed forces; **las ~s de orden público** (period) the police; **~ de gravedad** (force of) gravity 4 (en locs) **a la fuerza: a la ~ tuvo que verme** he must have seen me; **lo llevaron a la ~** they dragged him there; **comí a la ~** I forced myself to eat; **entraron a la ~** they forced their way in; **a fuerza de by; aprobó a ~ de estudiar** he managed to pass by studying hard; **por fuerza: por ~ tiene que saberlo** he <u>must</u> know about it; **por la fuerza** by force

fuerza, fuerzas, etc ▶ FORZAR

fuese, fuésemos, etc ▶ IR, SER

fuete m (AmL exc CS) riding crop; (más largo) whip

fuga f 1 (huida) escape; **un intento de ~** an attempted escape; **se dieron a la ~** they fled; **~ de capitales** or **divisas** flight of capital; **~ de cerebros** brain drain 2 (de líquido, gas) leak, escape (frml) 3 (Mús) fugue

fugarse [A3] v pron **(a)** (huir) to flee, run away; «preso» to escape; **~ DE algo** to escape FROM sth **(b)** «enamorados» to run away together

fugaz adj ‹sonrisa/visión/amor› fleeting; ‹visita/tregua› brief

fugitivo -va adj fugitive; **anda ~** he is on the run

fui, fuimos, etc ▶ IR, SER

fuiste, etc ▶ IR, SER

fulano -na m,f (fam) (persona cualquiera) so-and-so; **don ~ de tal** Mr so-and-so
■ m (fam) (tipo) guy (colloq)

fulminante adj ‹enfermedad› sudden and devastating; ‹mirada› withering; **tuvo un efecto ~** it had an immediate and devastating effect

fulminantes mpl (AmL) (Jueg) caps (pl); **pistola de ~** cap gun

fumador -dora m,f smoker; **~ pasivo** passive smoker; **sección de ~es/no ~es** smoking/no-smoking section

fumar [A1] vt 1 ‹cigarrillo/puro› to smoke 2 (Méx fam) (hacer caso) to take notice of
■ ~ vi to smoke; **~ en pipa** to smoke a pipe

fumigar [A3] vt ‹campo/cultivo› to spray, dust; ‹local› to fumigate

función f 1 **(a)** (cometido, propósito) function; **tiene la ~ de ...** it performs the function of ...; **salario en ~ de la experiencia** salary according to experience **(b)** **funciones** mpl duties (pl); **en el ejercicio de sus funciones** in the performance of her duties; **el secretario en funciones** the acting secretary; **entrar en funciones** (AmL) «empleado» ⋯▷

to take up one's post; «*presidente*» to assume office **2** (Fisiol, Mat, Ling) function **3** (de teatro, circo) performance; (de cine) showing, performance; ~ **de noche** late night performance

funcionamiento *m*: **me explicó su** ~ he explained (to me) how it works (*o* worked *etc*); **para el buen** ~ **de la escuela** for the smooth running of the school; **ponerse en** ~ «*hospital/ estación/fábrica*» to become operational; «*central nuclear*» to come into operation; «*mecanismo/ máquina*» to start up; «*servicio/sistema*» to start; **estar en** ~ to be running; **poner en** ~ ‹*central/fábrica*› to bring into operation; ‹*mecanismo/máquina*› to start … up

funcionar [A1] *vi* ‹*aparato/máquina*› to work; «*servicio*» to operate; ❾ **no funciona** out of order; ~ **con pilas/gasolina** to run off batteries/on gasoline

funcionario -ria *m,f* **(a)** (empleado público) *tb* ~ **público** *or* **del Estado** government employee; **un alto** *o* ~ a high-ranking official **(b)** (de organización internacional) member of staff, staff member **(c)** (RPl) (de empresa, banco) employee

funda *f* **(a)** (de libro) dustjacket; (de disco) sleeve **(b)** (de raqueta, cojín, sillón) cover **(c)** *tb* ~ **de almohada** pillowcase, pillowslip **(d)** (Odont) cap

fundación *f* **1** (institución) foundation; **una** ~ **benéfica** a charity **2** (de ciudad, escuela) founding; (de empresa, partido) establishment

fundado -da *adj* ‹*temor/sospecha*› justified, well founded

fundador -dora *m,f* founder

fundamental *adj* fundamental

fundamento *m* **(a)** (base, sustentación) foundation; **los rumores carecen de** ~ the rumors are totally without foundation **(b) fundamentos** *mpl* (nociones básicas) fundamentals (*pl*), basics (*pl*)

fundar [A1] *vt* **(a)** ‹*ciudad/hospital/escuela*› to found; ‹*partido/empresa*› to establish **(b)** (basar) ‹*sospecha/argumento*› ~ **algo EN algo** to base sth ON sth

■ **fundarse** *v pron* ~**se EN algo** «*afirmación/ sospecha*» to be based ON sth; **¿en qué te fundas para decirlo?** what grounds do you have for saying that?

fundir [I1] *vt* **1 (a)** ‹*metal/hierro*› to melt; ‹*mineral*› to smelt **(b)** ‹*estatua/campana*› to cast **2** (Elec) to blow **3** (fusionar) to merge

■ **fundirse** *v pron* **1** «*metal*» to melt; «*nieve/ hielo*» to melt, thaw **2** (Elec): **se ha fundido la bombilla** the bulb has gone (colloq); **se fundieron los fusibles** the fuses blew **3** (fusionarse) «*empresas/partidos*» to merge; ~**se EN algo** to merge sth INTO sth

fundo *m* (Chi) country estate, large farm

fúnebre *adj* ‹*música/ambiente*› funereal; ▶ COCHE A, CORTEJO, ETC

funeral *m*, **funerales** *mpl* (exequias) funeral; (oficio religioso) funeral service

funeraria *f* undertaker's, funeral parlor*

funesto -ta *adj* disastrous, terrible

fungir [I7] *vi* (Méx, Per) ~ **COMO** *or* **DE algo** to act as sth

funicular *m* (tren) funicular (railway); (teleférico) cable car

furgón *m* (Auto) truck, van; (Ferr) boxcar (AmE), goods van (BrE)

furgoneta *f* (para carga) van; (para pasajeros) van, minibus

furia *f* fury; **estar/ponerse hecho una** ~ (fam) to be/to get furious

furioso -sa *adj* furious; **se puso** ~ he was furious, he flew into a rage

furor *m* **(a)** (rabia) fury, rage **(b)** (de las olas, del viento, de una tempestad) fury **(c)** (entusiasmo) enormous enthusiasm; **causar** *or* **hacer** ~ to be all the rage (colloq)

furtivo -va *adj* **(a)** (ilegal): **la caza/pesca furtiva** poaching; **un cazador** ~ a poacher **(b)** ‹*mirada/ caricia*› furtive

furúnculo *m* boil

fusible *m* (Elec) fuse; **saltaron los** ~**s** the fuses blew

fusil *m* **1** (Arm) rifle **2** (Méx fam) (plagio) plagiarism

fusilar [A1] *vt* **1** (Mil) to shoot; **fue fusilado** he was executed by firing squad **2** (fam) (plagiar) to plagiarize, lift (colloq)

fusión *f* **1** (de empresas, partidos) merger **2 (a)** (de un metal) melting; (de metales, piezas) fusion, fusing together **(b)** (Fís) fusion

fusionar [A1] *vt* **(a)** ‹*piezas/metales*› to fuse, fuse together **(b)** ‹*empresas/partidos*› to merge **(c)** (Inf) to merge

■ **fusionarse** *v pron* **(a)** «*piezas/metales*» fuse (together) **(b)** «*empresas/partidos*» to merge; «*ideas*» to fuse

fusta *f* riding crop; (más larga) whip

fustigar [A3] *vt* ‹*caballo*› to whip

futbito *m* (Esp) five-a-side soccer *o* football, ≈indoor soccer (AmE)

fútbol, (AmC, Méx) **futbol** *m* soccer, football (esp BrE); ~ **americano** American football; ~ **sala** five-a-side soccer *o* football, ≈indoor soccer (AmE)

futbolín *m* **(a)** (juego) table football **(b) futbolines** *mpl* (local) amusement arcade

futbolista *mf* soccer *o* football player

futuro¹ -ra *adj* future (*before n*); **las futuras generaciones** future generations; **la futura mamá** the mother-to-be

futuro² ** *m* **1 (porvenir) future; **¿qué nos deparará el** ~? what will the future bring?; **en un** ~ **cercano** *or* **próximo** in the near future; **en el** *or* **en lo** ~ in future; **un empleo con/sin** ~ a job with good prospects/with no prospects; **su relación no tiene** ~ their relationship has no future **2** (Ling) future (tense)

Gg

G, g *f* (*read as* /xe/) *the letter* G, G

gabacho -cha *m,f* **(a)** (Chi, Esp fam & pey) (francés) frog (colloq & pej) **(b)** (Méx fam & pey) (extranjero) foreigner (*of North American or European origin*)

gabán *m* (abrigo — largo) overcoat; (— corto) jacket

gabardina *f* (prenda) raincoat; (tela) gabardine

gabinete *m* ⟨1⟩ (despacho) office; (en una casa) study ⟨2⟩ (conjunto de profesionales) department; (Pol) cabinet ⟨3⟩ (armario —de la cocina) (Méx) kitchen cabinet *o* cupboard; (— del baño) (Col, Ven) bathroom cabinet

gacela *f* gazelle

gacho -cha *adj* **(a)** ⟨orejas⟩ drooping (*before n*); **con la cabeza gacha** with his head bowed **(b)** **a gachas** (agachado) crouching; (a gatas) on all fours

gachupín *m* (Méx pey) Spaniard

gaélico¹ -ca *adj* Gaelic

gaélico² *m* (idioma) Gaelic

gafar [A1] *vt* (Esp fam) to jinx

gafas *fpl* **(a)** (anteojos) glasses (*pl*), spectacles (*pl*, frml); **unas ~s nuevas** a new pair of glasses; **~ de sol** sunglasses; **~ oscuras** dark glasses **(b)** (de protección) goggles (*pl*)

gafe *adj* (Esp fam): **es ~** she has a jinx on her; **no seas ~** don't say that, you'll bring us bad luck

gafo -fa *adj* (Ven fam) (estúpido) dumb (colloq)

gagá *adj inv* ⟨1⟩ (fam) (senil) gaga (colloq) ⟨2⟩ (Per fam) (elegante) smart (colloq)

gaita *f tb* **~ gallega/escocesa** (Galician/Scottish) bagpipes (*pl*)

gaitero -ra *m,f* (Mús) (bag)piper

gajes *mpl*: **son (los) ~ del oficio** it's all part of the job

gajo *m* ⟨1⟩ (de naranja, limón) segment ⟨2⟩ (Col) (de pelo) lock

gala *f* **(a)** (cena) gala; **cena de ~** gala (dinner); (en el teatro) *tb* **función de ~** gala (evening *o* performance); **vestido de ~** formal *o* full dress; **hacer ~ de algo** to display sth **(b)** **galas** *fpl* (ropa) clothes (*pl*); **mis/tus mejores ~s** my/your best clothes *o* Sunday best

galán *m* **(a)** (actor) hero **(b)** (hum) (novio) young man (hum)

galante *adj* ⟨hombre⟩ gallant, attentive

galantería *f* **(a)** (caballerosidad) gallantry **(b)** (piropo) compliment; (gesto cortés) polite gesture, attention

galápago *m* (Zool) (tortuga — gigante) giant turtle; (— europea) terrapin

galaxia *f* galaxy

galera *f* ⟨1⟩ (Hist, Náut) galley ⟨2⟩ (RPl) (sombrero) top hat

galería *f* **(a)** (interior) corridor; (exterior) gallery

(c) (Teatr) gallery **(c)** **~ comercial** shopping mall (AmE), shopping arcade (BrE); **~ de arte** art gallery

Gales *m*: *tb* **el país de ~** Wales

galés¹ -lesa *adj* Welsh
■ *m,f* (persona) (*m*) Welshman; (*f*) Welshwoman; **los galeses** the Welsh, Welsh people

galés² *m* (idioma) Welsh

galgo *mf* greyhound

galgódromo *m* (Méx) dog track

galicismo *m* gallicism

galimatías *m* (*pl* ~) (lenguaje incomprensible) gibberish; (de cosas, ideas) jumble

gallada *f* (Andes fam): **la ~** the crowd

gallego¹ -ga *adj* **(a)** (de Galicia) Galician **(b)** (AmL fam) (español) Spanish
■ *m,f* **(a)** (de Galicia) Galician **(b)** (AmL fam) (español) Spaniard

gallego² *m* (idioma) Galician

galleta *f* (Coc) (dulce) cookie (AmE), biscuit (BrE); (salada) cracker

gallina *f* ⟨1⟩ (Zool) hen; (Coc) chicken; **~ clueca** (empollando) broody hen; (cuidando la pollada) mother hen; **gallinita ciega** blind man's buff ⟨2⟩ **gallina** *mf* (fam) (cobarde) chicken (colloq)

gallinazo *m* (Zool) (de cabeza roja) turkey buzzard *o* vulture; (de cabeza negra) black vulture

gallinero *m* **(a)** (Zool) (corral) henhouse, coop **(b)** (fam) (sitio ruidoso) madhouse (colloq) **(c)** (fam) (en el cine, teatro): **el ~** the gods (colloq)

gallito *m* ⟨1⟩ (fam) (persona) tough guy (colloq) ⟨2⟩ (Col, Méx) (Dep) shuttlecock, birdie (AmE)

gallo¹ *m* ⟨1⟩ (Zool) (ave) cockerel; **~ de pelea** *or* (AmS) **de riña** fighting *o* game cock; (más grande) rooster; **en menos (de lo) que canta un ~** in no time at all; **otro ~ cantaría** *or* **otro ~ me/te/nos cantara** (fam) things would be very different ⟨2⟩ (Méx fam) (bravucón) macho, tough guy (colloq) ⟨3⟩ (fam) **(a)** (de un cantante) false note **(b)** (de adolescente): **soltó un ~** his voice went squeaky ⟨4⟩ (Méx) (serenata) serenade

gallo² -lla *adj* (AmL fam) tough (colloq)
■ *m,f* (Chi fam) (*m*) guy (colloq); (*f*) woman; **hola ~** hi, buddy (AmE) *o* (BrE) mate (colloq)

galón *m* ⟨1⟩ (Mil) stripe ⟨2⟩ (medida) gallon

galopante *adj* ⟨inflación/tuberculosis⟩ galloping (*before n*)

galopar [A1] *vi* (Equ) to gallop

galope *m* gallop; **a** *or* **al ~** at a gallop

galpón *m* (AmL) (cobertizo) shed; (almacén) storehouse

gama *f* **(a)** (de colores, productos) range **(b)** (de notas musicales) scale

gamba *f* (esp Esp) (Coc, Zool) shrimp (AmE), prawn (BrE)

gamberrada *f* (Esp) (grosería) loutish act; (acto violento) act of hooliganism

gamberrismo *m* (Esp) (comportamiento — escandaloso) loutishness; (— violento) hooliganism

gamberro -rra *m,f* (Esp) (grosero) lout; (vándalo) hooligan

gamín -mina *m,f* (Col) street urchin

gamo -ma *m,f* fallow deer

gamulán® *m* (CS) (prenda) sheepskin coat/jacket

gamuza *f* **(a)** (Zool) chamois **(b)** (piel) chamois (leather); (de otros animales) suede

gana *f* (deseo): **¡con qué ~s me comería un helado!** I'd love an ice cream!; **lo hizo sin ~s** he did it very half-heartedly; **siempre hace lo que le da la ~** she always does just as she pleases; **quería ir pero me quedé con las ~s** (fam) I wanted to go, but it wasn't to be; **tener ~s de hacer algo** to feel like doing sth; **(no) tengo ~s de ir** I (don't) feel like going; **tengo ~s de volver a verte** I'm looking forward to seeing you again; **le dieron ~s de reírse** she felt like bursting out laughing; **se me quitaron las ~s de ir** I don't feel like going any more; **tengo ~s de que llegue el verano** I'm looking forward to the summer; **con ~s: llover con ~s** to pour down; **es feo/tonto con ~s** he is so ugly/stupid!; **de buena/mala ~** willingly/reluctantly

ganadería *f* (actividad) ranching, stockbreeding; (ganado) cattle (*pl*), livestock (+ *sing or pl vb*)

ganadero -ra *adj* ranching (*before n*), stockbreeding (*before n*)
■ *m,f* rancher, stockbreeder

ganado *m* cattle (*pl*), livestock (+ *sing or pl vb*); **~ bovino** *or* **vacuno** cattle (*pl*); **~ caballar** *or* **equino** horses (*pl*); **~ en pie** (AmL) cattle on the hoof (*pl*); **~ ovino/porcino** sheep (*pl*)/pigs (*pl*)

ganador -dora *adj* ⟨equipo/caballo⟩ winning (*before n*); **la película ~a del Oscar** the Oscar-winning film
■ *m,f* winner

ganancia *f* (Com, Fin) profit; **~ neta/bruta** net/gross profit; **~ del capital** capital gain

ganar [A1] *vt* **1** **(a)** ⟨sueldo⟩ to earn; **lo único que quiere es ~ dinero** all he's interested in is making money **(b)** ⟨tiempo⟩ to gain; **¿qué ganas con eso?** what do you gain by (doing) that? **(c)** (adquirir) ⟨experiencia⟩ to gain
2 ⟨partido/guerra/premio⟩ to win; **le gané la apuesta** I won my bet with him
■ ~ *vi* **(a)** (vencer) to win; **van ganando 2 a 1** they're winning 2-1; **~le a algn** to beat sb; **nos ~on por cuatro puntos** they beat us by four points **(b)** (aventajar): **le ganas en estatura** you're taller than him; **me gana en todo** he beats me on every count; *salir ganando*: **salió ganando con el trato** he did well out of the deal; **al final salí ganando** in the end I came out of it better off
■ **ganarse** *v pron* **1** (enf) (mediante el trabajo) to earn; **~se la vida** to earn a/one's living
2 (enf) ⟨premio/apuesta⟩ to win
3 ⟨afecto/confianza⟩ to win; **se ganó el respeto de todos** she won *o* earned everyone's respect
4 ⟨descanso⟩ to earn oneself; **te lo has ganado** you've earned it, you deserve it

ganchillo *m* (aguja) crochet hook; (labor) crochet; **hacer ~** to crochet

gancho *m* **1** **(a)** (garfio) hook **(b)** (AmL) (para la ropa) hanger **(c)** (Andes, Ven) (imperdible) safety pin
2 **(a)** (en boxeo) hook **(b)** (en baloncesto) hook shot

gandalla *mf* (Méx fam) (persona deshonesta) crook (colloq); (sinvergüenza) swine (colloq)

gandul -dula *m,f* (fam) lazybones (colloq)

ganga *f* (compra ventajosa) bargain; **a precio de ~** at a bargain *o* giveaway price

ganglio *m* (en los vasos linfáticos) gland; (de células nerviosas) ganglion

gangrena *f* gangrene

ganso -sa *m,f* **1** (Zool) (*m*) goose, gander; (*f*) goose **2** (fam) **(a)** (persona torpe) clumsy oaf (colloq) **(b)** (tonto) idiot, clown (colloq)

ganzúa *f* picklock

garabatear [A1] *vi/vt* (escribir) to scribble, scrawl; (dibujar) to doodle

garabato *m* **1** **(a)** (dibujo) doodle **(b)** **garabatos** *mpl* (escritura) scrawl, scribble **2** (Chi) (palabrota) swearword

garaje /ga'raxe/ *m*, (esp AmL) **garage** /ga'raʒ/ *m* garage

garantía *f* **1** (Com) guarantee, warranty; **estar bajo** *or* **en ~** to be under guarantee *o* warranty **2** **(a)** (Der) (fianza) surety, guarantee **(b)** (seguridad) guarantee **(c)** **~s constitucionales** constitutional rights (*pl*)

garantizar [A4] *vt* **1** (Com) ⟨producto⟩ to guarantee, warrant (AmE) **2** (asegurar) to guarantee

garapiña *f* (Méx) pineapple squash

garbanzo *m* chickpea

garbo *m* (elegancia) poise, grace; (gracia, desenvoltura) jauntiness

garfio *m* hook

gargajo *m* (fam) gob (sl)

garganta *f* **1** **(a)** (Anat) throat; **me dolía la ~** I had a sore throat **(b)** (cuello) neck **2** (desfiladero) gorge, ravine; (entre montañas) narrow pass
■ *mf* (Per fam) scrounger (colloq)

gargantilla *f* choker, necklace

gárgara *f* gargle; **hacer ~s** to gargle

garita *f* (de centinela) sentry box; (de portero) lodge

garito *m* gambling den

garra *f* **1** (de animal) claw; (de águila) talon **2** (arrojo, valor) fighting spirit; (personalidad) personality **3** **garras** *fpl* (poder, dominio) clutches (*pl*)

garrafa *f* **(a)** (para vino) demijohn **(b)** (RPl) (para gas) cylinder

garrafal *adj* terrible; ⟨error⟩ monumental

garrapata *f* tick

garrapiñada *f* (esp AmL) caramel-coated peanuts/almonds (*pl*)

garrobo *m* (AmC) iguana

garrocha *f* **1** (Taur) lance, goad **2** (AmL) (Dep) pole

garrochista *mf* (AmL) pole-vaulter

garrotazo *m* (golpe) blow (*with a club*)

garrote *m* (palo) club, stick; (método de ejecución) garrotte

garúa *f* (AmL) drizzle

garuar [A18] *v impers* (AmL) to drizzle

garza *f* (Zool) heron

garzón -zona *m,f* (Chi) (*m*) waiter; (*f*) waitress

gas *m* [1] (Fís, Quím) gas; **~es tóxicos** toxic fumes; **~ ciudad** town gas; **~ lacrimógeno/licuado** tear/liquified gas [2] **gases** *mpl* (Fisiol) wind, gas (AmE)

gasa *f* (Med, Tex) gauze

gaseosa *f* **(a)** (bebida efervescente) soda (AmE), fizzy drink (BrE) **(b)** (CS) (cualquier refresco) soft drink

gaseoso -sa *adj* **(a)** ‹cuerpo/estado› gaseous **(b)** ‹bebida› carbonated, fizzy (BrE)

gásfiter *mf* (*pl* **-ters**) (Chi) plumber

gasfitería *f* (Chi, Per) plumbing

gasfitero -ra *m,f* (Per) plumber

gasoducto *m* gas pipeline

gas-oil, gasóleo *m* (para calefacción) (gas) oil; (para motores) diesel (fuel *o* oil)

gasolina *f* gasoline (AmE), gas (AmE), petrol (BrE); **~ normal** regular gasoline (AmE), two-star petrol (BrE); **~ sin plomo** unleaded gasoline (AmE) *o* (BrE) petrol; **~ super** premium gasoline (AmE), four-star petrol (BrE)

gasolinera *f* gas station (AmE), petrol station (BrE)

gastado -da *adj* ‹ropa/zapatos› worn-out; ‹político/cantante› washed-up (colloq)

gastador -dora *adj/m,f* spendthrift

gastar [A1] *vt* [1] (consumir) **(a)** ‹dinero› to spend; **~ algo EN algo** to spend sth on sth **(b)** ‹gasolina/electricidad› to use [2] (desperdiciar, malgastar) ‹dinero/tiempo/energía› to waste [3] (desgastar) ‹ropa/zapatos› to wear out; ‹tacones› to wear down [4] (fam) (llevar, usar) ‹ropa/gafas› to wear; **gasto el 37** I'm a size 37 [5] ‹broma› to play; **le ~on una broma** they played a joke *o* trick on him
■ **gastarse** *v pron* [1] (enf) ‹dinero› to spend [2] ‹pilas/batería› to run down; **se me gastó la tinta** I ran out of ink [3] ‹ropa/zapatos› (desgastarse) to wear out [4] (enf) (fam) (tener) to have; **se gasta un genio ...** he has a terrible temper!

gasto *m* expense; **un ~ innecesario** an unnecessary expense; **este mes he tenido muchos ~s** this has been an expensive month for me; **el ~ público** public expenditure; **~s de correo** postage; **~s de envío** postage and handling (AmE) *o* (BrE) packing

gastritis *f* gastritis

gastronomía *f* gastronomy

gata *f* [1] (Chi, Per) (Auto) jack; *ver tb* GATO¹ [2] **a gatas** (*loc adv*) (a cuatro patas): **ir** *o* **andar a ~s** to crawl; **tuve que entrar a ~s** I had to go in on all fours

gatear [A1] *vi* (andar a gatas) to crawl

gatera *f* cathole (AmE), cat flap (BrE)

gatillero *m* (Méx) gunman

gatillo *m* trigger; **apretar el ~** to pull the trigger

gatito -ta *m,f* kitten

gato¹ -ta *m,f* (Zool) cat; **~ montés** wild cat; **aquí hay ~ encerrado** there's something fishy going

gato² *m* [1] (Auto) jack [2] (Chi, Méx) (Jueg) ticktacktoe (AmE), noughts and crosses (BrE) [3] (Méx) (signo) hash sign

gauchada *f* (Bol, CS fam) favor*, good turn

gaucho *m* gaucho

gaveta *f* drawer

gavilán *m* sparrowhawk

gavilla *f* (de cereales) sheaf

gaviota *f* seagull, gull

gay /gai, gei/ *adj* (*pl* **~** *or* **gays**) gay
■ *mf* (*m*) gay man, gay; (*f*) gay woman, lesbian

gazmoño -ña *adj* (pudoroso) prudish; (mojigato) sanctimonious

gaznate *m* (garganta) (fam) throat, gullet; **refrescar el ~** (fam) to have a drink

gazpacho *m*: *tb* **~ andaluz** gazpacho (*cold soup made from tomatoes, peppers, etc*)

ge *f*. name of the letter G

gel *m* gel

gelatina *f* **(a)** (sustancia) gelatin* **(b)** (postre) Jell-O® (AmE), jelly (BrE)

gelatinoso -sa *adj* gelatinous

gema *f* gem

gemelo¹ -la *adj* twin (*before n*)
■ *m,f* twin

gemelo² *m* **(a)** (de camisa) cuff link **(b) gemelos** *mpl* (Ópt) binoculars (*pl*)

gemido *m* **(a)** (de dolor, pena) groan, moan **(b)** (de animal) whine

Géminis *m* (signo, constelación) Gemini; **es (de) ~** she's (a) Gemini, she's a Geminian
■ *mf* (*pl* **~**) (persona) *tb* **géminis** Geminian, Gemini

gemir [I14] *vi* **(a)** «persona» to moan, groan **(b)** «animal» to whine

gen *m* gene

gendarme *mf* gendarme

gendarmería *f* gendarmerie

genealógico -ca *adj* genealogical

generación *f* generation

generacional *adj* generation (*before n*), generational

generador *m* generator

general *adj* **(a)** (no específico, global) general; **de interés ~** of general interest; **hablando en líneas ~es** broadly speaking; **un panorama ~ de la situación** an overall view of the situation **(b)** (*en locs*) **en general** on the whole, in general; **el público en ~** the general public; **por lo general** as a (general) rule
■ *mf* (Mil) general

generalidad *f* (vaguedad) general comment, generality; (mayoría) majority

generalizado -da *adj* widespread

generalizar [A4] *vi* to generalize, make generalizations
■ **generalizarse** *v pron* to spread

generalmente *adv* generally

generar [A1] *vt* to generate

género *m* [1] **(a)** (clase, tipo) kind, type; **el ~** ⋯‣

humano the human race, mankind **(b)** (Biol)
genus **(c)** (Lit, Teatr) genre; **el ~ dramático** drama
(d) (Ling) gender **2** (tela) cloth, material

generosidad *f* generosity

generoso -sa *adj* generous

genética *f* genetics

genéticamente *adv* genetically; **~
modificado** genetically modified, GM

genético -ca *adj* genetic

genial *adj* **(a)** ⟨idea/escritor/pintor⟩ brilliant **(b)**
(fam) (estupendo) great (colloq), fantastic (colloq);
(fam) (ocurrente, gracioso) witty, funny

genialidad *f* (cualidad) genius; (ocurrencia)
brilliant idea, stroke of genius

geniecillo *m* elf

genio *m* **(a)** (carácter) temper; **tener buen/mal ~**
to be even-tempered/bad-tempered **(b)** (lumbrera)
genius **(d)** (ser fantástico) genie

genitales *mpl* genitals (*pl*), genital organs (*pl*)

genocidio *m* genocide

Génova *f* Genoa

gente *f*

■ Nota Nótese que en español, cuando el nombre
gente significa *personas*, se traduce al inglés por
people con verbo en plural - *allí la gente es muy
amable* = people are very nice there. Cuando tiene el
sentido de *familia* se traduce al inglés por *family* con
el verbo en singular o plural - *mi gente está de
vacaciones* = my family is o are on holiday

(a) (personas) people (*pl*); **la gente está asustada**
people are frightened; **había muy poca/tanta ~**
there were very few/so many people; **~ bien** (de
respeto) respectable people; (adinerada) well-to-do
people; **la ~ de a pie** the man in the street; **ser
buena ~** to be nice (o kind *etc*); **ser ~** (AmS) to
behave (properly) **(b)** (Méx) (persona) person
■ *adj* (AmL) (de buenas maneras) respectable; (amable)
kind, good
■ *adv* (Chi, Méx): **se portó muy ~ conmigo** she was
very good o kind to me

gentil *adj* (amable) kind

gentileza *f* (cualidad) kindness; (atención, gesto):
tuvo la ~ de cederme el asiento she was kind
enough to let me have her seat; **ni siquiera tuvo
la ~ de avisarnos** he didn't even have the
courtesy to inform us

gentilicio *m*: name given to the people from a
particular region or country

gentío *m* crowd

gentuza *f* (pey) riffraff (pej), rabble (pej)

genuflexión *f* genuflection

genuino -na *adj* genuine

geografía *f* geography

geográfico -ca *adj* geographical

geología *f* geology

geólogo -ga *m,f* geologist

geometría *f* geometry

geométrico -ca *adj* geometric

geranio *m* geranium

gerencia *f* **(a)** (cargo) post o position of
manager **(b)** (personas) management **(c)** (oficina)
manager's office

gerenciar [A1] *vt* (AmL) to manage

gerente *mf* manager; **~ comercial** business
manager

geriatría *f* geriatrics

geriátrico -ca *adj* geriatric

germen *m* **1** (microbio) germ **2** **(a)** (embrión)
germ **(b)** (origen) seeds (*pl*)

germicida *m* germicide

germinar [A1] *vi* to germinate

gerundio *m* gerund

gestación *f* gestation

gesticular [A1] *vi* to gesticulate

gestión *f* **(a)** (trámite) step; **la única ~ que había
hecho** the only step he had taken; **hizo gestiones
para adoptar un niño** he went through the
procedure for adopting a child; **su apoyo a las
gestiones de paz** their support for the peace
process **(b) gestiones** *fpl* (negociaciones)
negotiations (*pl*)

gestionar [A1] *vt* ⟨compra/préstamo⟩ to
negotiate; **le están gestionando el permiso de
trabajo** they are getting his work permit sorted
out o arranged

gesto *m* **1** (en general) gesture; **un ~ grosero** a
rude gesture; **le hizo un ~ para que se callara** she
gestured to him to be quiet **2** (expresión)
expression; **hacer ~s** to make faces

gestoría *f* agency (which obtains official
documents on clients' behalf)

ghetto /'geto/ *m* ghetto

Gibraltar *m* Gibraltar

gibraltareño -ña *adj/m,f* Gibraltarian

gigabyte /xiva'βaɪt/ *m* gigabyte

gigante¹ *adj* giant (before n)

gigante² -ta *m,f* (en cuentos) (*m*) giant; (*f*)
giantess; (persona alta) giant

gigantesco -ca *adj* huge, gigantic

gil *mf* (RPI fam o vulg) jerk (sl)

gilipollas *adj inv* (Esp fam o vulg): **¡qué ~ es
ese tío!** that guy's such a jerk! (sl & pej)
■ *mf* (*pl* **~**) (Esp fam o vulg) jerk (sl & pej)

gilipollez *f* (Esp fam o vulg): **decir gilipolleces** to
talk garbage (AmE) o (BrE) rubbish; **no discutáis
por esa ~** don't argue over a stupid o silly thing
like that; **pagar tanto es una ~** it's stupid paying
that much

gimnasia *f* gymnastics; (como asignatura) gym,
PE (BrE); **hago ~ todos los días** I do exercises
every day; **~ de mantenimiento** keep-fit

gimnasio *m* gymnasium, gym

gimnasta *mf* gymnast

gimotear [A1] *vi* to whine, whimper

ginebra *f* gin

Ginebra *f* Geneva

ginecólogo -ga *m,f* gynecologist*

gira *f* tour; **de ~** on tour

---

girar [A1] *vi* **1** **(a)** «*rueda*» to turn, go around; «*disco*» to revolve, go around; «*trompo*» to spin; ∼ **ALREDEDOR DE algo/algn** to revolve AROUND sth/sb **(b)** (darse la vuelta) to turn **2** (torcer, desviarse) to turn; ∼**on a la derecha** they turned right
■ ∼ *vt* **1** (*manivela/volante*) to turn **2** (Com, Fin) (*cheque/letra de cambio*) to draw

girasol *m* sunflower

giratorio -ria *adj* revolving (*before n*)

giro *m* **1** (en general) turn; **hizo un** ∼ **a la derecha** she made a right turn; **un** ∼ **de 180 grados** a volte-face, an about-turn; **el** ∼ **que estaba tomando la conversación** the direction the conversation was taking **2** (Fin): **enviar un** ∼ (a través de un banco) to transfer money; (por correo) to send a money order; ∼ **bancario** (cheque) bank *o* banker's draft; (transferencia) credit transfer; ∼ **postal** money order

gis *m* (Méx) chalk

gitano -na *adj* gypsy (*before n*)
■ *m,f* gypsy

glacial *adj* **(a)** (*zona/período*) glacial **(b)** (*viento/temperatura*) icy

glaciar *m* glacier

gladiador *m* gladiator

gladiolo *m* gladiolus

glamoroso -sa *adj* glamorous

glándula *f* gland

glandular *adj* glandular

glicerina *f* glycerin

global *adj* global; (*informe*) full, comprehensive; (*resultado*) overall; (*precio/cantidad*) total

globo *m* **1** **(a)** (Aviac, Jueg, Meteo) balloon; ∼ **aerostático/sonda** hot-air/observation balloon **(b)** (de chicle) bubble **(c)** (de lámpara) globe **(d)** ∼ **ocular** eyeball **2** (mundo) world; *tb* ∼**terráqueo** globe

glóbulo *m* (cuerpo esférico) globule; (corpúsculo) corpuscle; ∼ **blanco/rojo** white/red corpuscle

gloria *f* **1** **(a)** (Relig) glory; **estar/sentirse en la** ∼ to be in seventh heaven **(b)** (fama, honor) glory; **cubrirse de** ∼ to win glory **2** (personalidad) figure; **es una de las** ∼**s del deporte** he is one of the great sporting figures *o* heroes

glorieta *f* **(a)** (plaza) square; (Auto) traffic circle (AmE), roundabout (BrE) **(b)** (en el jardín) arbor*

glorioso -sa *adj* (*hecho*) glorious; (*personaje*) great

glotón -tona *adj* gluttonous, greedy
■ *m,f* glutton

glotonería *f* gluttony

glúteo *m* gluteus

gnomo /'nomo/ *m* gnome

gobelino *m* Gobelin

gobernador -dora *m,f* governor

gobernante *adj* (*partido/organismo*) ruling (*before n*), governing (*before n*)
■ *mf* leader, ruler

gobernar [A5] *vt* (*país*) to govern, rule; (*barco*) to steer
■ ∼ *vi* (Gob, Pol) to govern; (Náut) to steer

gobierna, gobiernas ▶ GOBERNAR

gobierno *m* government

goce *m* **(a)** (de derecho, título) enjoyment; **en pleno** ∼ **de sus facultades** in full possession of her faculties **(b)** (placer) pleasure

gol *m* goal; **marcar** *or* **meter un** ∼ to score a goal

goleada *f* heavy defeat

goleador -dora *adj* high-scoring
■ *m,f* scorer, goal-scorer

golear [A1] *vt*: **el Madrid goleó al Osasuna** Real Madrid thrashed Osasuna

golero -ra *m,f* (CS) goalkeeper

golf *m* golf

golfa *f* (fam) (prostituta) whore (colloq)

golfillo -lla *m,f* street urchin

golfista *mf* golfer

golfito *m* (AmL) mini-golf, miniature golf

golfo¹ -fa *m,f* **(a)** (holgazán) good-for-nothing, layabout **(b)** (fam) (niño travieso) rascal (colloq), little devil (colloq)

golfo² *m* (Geog, Náut) gulf; **G**∼ **de México** Gulf of Mexico; **G**∼ **de Vizcaya** Bay of Biscay

golilla *f* **1** (Indum) (cuello fruncido) ruff **2** (RPl) (pañuelo) neckerchief **2** (arandela) washer

gollete *m* neck (*of a bottle*); **estar hasta el** ∼ (fam) to be fed up to the back teeth (colloq); **no tiene** ∼ (RPl fam) it's the limit

golondrina *f* (Zool) swallow

golosa *f* (Col) hopscotch

golosina *f* (dulce) candy (AmE), sweet (BrE)

goloso -sa *adj* (amante de lo dulce): **es muy** ∼ he has a really sweet tooth

golpe *m* **1** (choque, impacto) knock; **me di un** ∼ **en la cabeza** I got a knock on the head, I hit *o* banged my head; **darse un** ∼ **contra algo** to bang *o* knock into sth; **dio unos** ∼**s en la mesa** he tapped on the table; (más fuerte) he knocked on the table; (aún más fuerte) he banged on the table; **a** ∼ **de** (Ven) around; **de** ∼ **(y porrazo)** suddenly; **se abrió/cerró de** ∼ it flew open/slammed shut; **de un** ∼ (de una vez) all at once; (de un trago) in one go *o* gulp
2 **(a)** (al pegarle a algn) blow; **lo derribó de un** ∼ he knocked him down with one blow; **casi lo matan a** ∼**s** they almost beat him to death; **siempre andan a** ∼**s** they're always fighting **(b)** (marca) bruise, mark
3 (Dep) stroke
4 **(a)** (desgracia) blow **(b)** ∼ **de suerte** stroke of luck
5 (fam) (atraco, timo) job (colloq); **dar el** ∼ to do the job
6 (Pol) *tb* ∼ **de estado** coup (d'état)

golpear [A1] *vt* **1** (*objeto/superficie*) to bang; (repetidamente) to beat; **no golpees la puerta al salir** don't slam *o* bang the door as you go out; **la lluvia golpeaba los cristales** the rain beat against the window panes; **golpeó la mesa con el puño** he banged his fist on the table
2 (pegar) to hit; **algo me golpeó en la cara** something hit me in the face; **su marido la golpea** her husband hits her
■ ∼ *vi* **(a)** (dar, pegar) ∼ **CONTRA algo** to beat AGAINST sth **(b)** (AmS) (llamar a la puerta) to knock **(c)** (en fútbol americano) to scrimmage
■ **golpearse** *v pron* **(a)** (refl) (*cabeza/codo*) to bang, hit **(b)** (AmL) «*puerta*» to bang

golpetazo *m* (fam) hard blow

golpeteo *m* (tamborileo) drumming, tapping; (de la lluvia) patter, pitter-patter; (de una puerta) banging

golpismo *m* pro-coup tendency

golpista *adj* ⟨minoría/tendencia⟩ in favor of a coup; **los militares ∼s** the soldiers who took part in the coup

golpiza *f* (AmL) beating

goma *f* **1** **(a)** (caucho) rubber; **suelas de ∼** rubber soles **(b)** (pegamento) glue, gum; **∼ de mascar** chewing gum **2** **(a)** (para sujetar) rubber band, elastic band (BrE) **(b)** (de borrar) eraser **(c)** (RPl) (neumático) tire* **3** (AmC fam) (resaca) hangover; **ando de ∼** I've got a hangover

gomina *f* hair gel

gomita *f* **1** (RPl) (para sujetar) rubber band, elastic band (BrE) **2** (Chi, Méx, Ven) (dulce) gumdrop, gum (BrE)

góndola *f* gondola

gondolero *m* gondolier

gordo¹ -da *adj* **1** ⟨persona/piernas⟩ fat; **siempre ha sido ∼** he's always been overweight *o* fat; **estás ∼** you've put on weight; **es más bien gordita** she's quite plump **2** (grueso) ⟨libro/lana/suéter⟩ thick **3** ⟨carne/tocino⟩ fatty
■ *m,f* **(a)** (persona) (*m*) fat man; (*f*) fat woman **(b)** (fam) (como apelativo ofensivo) fatso (colloq), fatty (colloq)

gordo² *m* (Jueg) (premio mayor) jackpot (*in the state lottery*)

gordura *f* **(a)** (grasa) fat **(b)** (exceso de peso) fatness; **me preocupa su ∼** I'm worried about how fat he is

gorgorito *m* trill

gorgotear [A1] *vi* (en cañería) to gurgle; (al hervir) to bubble

gorila *m* **1** (Zool) gorilla **2** (fam) **(a)** (matón) thug **(b)** (guardaespaldas) heavy (colloq) **(c)** (reaccionario) fascist **(d)** (Esp) (en un club) bouncer

gorjear [A1] *vi* «pájaro» to trill, warble; «niño» to gurgle

gorra *f* cap; (con visera) peaked cap; (de bebé) bonnet

gorrear [A1] *vt* **1** (fam) (pedir) to scrounge (colloq); **me gorreó $20** he scrounged $20 off me **2** (Chi fam) ⟨cónyuge⟩ to cheat on (colloq)

gorrero -ra *m,f* (AmL fam) (aprovechado) scrounger (colloq)

gorrión *m* sparrow

gorro *m* cap; **∼ de baño** (para nadar) bathing cap; (para la ducha) shower cap; **estar hasta el ∼** (fam) to be fed up to the back teeth (colloq)

gorrón -rrona *m,f* (Esp, Méx fam) scrounger (colloq)

gorronear [A1] *vt/vi* (Esp, Méx fam) to scrounge (colloq)

gota *f* **1** (de líquido) drop; **∼s de sudor** beads of sweat; **la ∼ que colma** *o* **rebasa el vaso** the last straw; **parecerse/ser como dos ∼s de agua** to be as like as two peas in a pod **2** (enfermedad) gout

gotear [A1] *vi* «líquido/grifo/vela» to drip; «cañería» to leak
■ **∼** *v impers* (lloviznar) to spit, drizzle

goteo *m* dripping

gotera *f* **(a)** (filtración) leak **(b)** (mancha) damp stain

gótico -ca *adj* Gothic

gourde *m* gourde (*Haitian unit of currency*)

gozador -dora *adj* (AmL) fun-loving

gozar [A4] *vi*: **∼ DE algo** to enjoy sth; **∼ de la vida** to enjoy life; **goza viéndolos jugar** she enjoys watching them play; **∼ CON algo** to enjoy sth; **goza de perfecta salud** he enjoys perfect health; **goza de una buena posición** he has a good position

gozne *m* hinge

gozo *m* **1** **(a)** (alegría) joy; **no caber en sí de ∼** to be beside oneself with joy **(b)** (placer) pleasure, enjoyment **2** **gozos** *mpl* (Relig) verses (*pl*)

gozque *mf* (Col) mongrel

grabación *f* recording; **∼ en video** video recording

grabado *m* engraving

grabador -dora *m,f* **1** (Art) engraver **2** **grabadora** *f* **(a)** (casa discográfica) record company **(b)** (magnetófono) tape recorder

grabar [A1] *vt/vi* **(a)** (Audio, TV) to record, tape **(b)** (Art) to engrave
■ **grabarse** *v pron*: **sus palabras se me ∼on en la memoria** her words are etched on my memory; **su cara se me quedó grabada** I'll never forget her face

gracia *f*
I **1** (comicidad): **yo no le veo la ∼** I don't think it's funny; **tener ∼** «chiste/broma» to be funny; **me hace ∼ que digas eso** it's funny you should say that; **no me hace ninguna ∼ tener que ir** I don't relish the idea of having to go **2** **(a)** (chiste) joke; (broma) joke, trick **(b)** (de niño) party piece **3** (encanto, elegancia) grace; **con ∼** «moverse/bailar» gracefully; **un vestido sin ∼** a very plain dress; **tiene mucha ∼ para arreglar flores** she has a real flair for flower arranging
II **gracias** *fpl* **(a)** (expresión de agradecimiento): **darle las ∼s a algn** to thank sb; **no dieron ni las ∼s** they didn't even say thank you **(b)** (como interj) thank you, thanks (colloq); **muchas ∼s** thank you very much, thanks a lot (colloq); **un millón de ∼s por ayudarme/tu ayuda** thank you very much for helping me/your help **(c) gracias a** thanks to; **∼s a Dios** thank God

gracioso -sa *adj* **1** (divertido) «chiste/persona» funny; **¡qué ∼!** how funny!; **hacerse el ∼** to play the fool **2** (atractivo) «cara/figura» attractive; **las pecas le dan un aspecto muy ∼** those freckles make her look really cute *o* sweet

grada *f* **(a)** (peldaño) step **(b) gradas** *fpl* (Dep) stand, grandstand

gradería *f*, (Esp) **graderío** *m* stands (*pl*)

gradiente *f* (AmL) (pendiente) slope, gradient

grado *m* **1** (en general) degree; **estamos a tres ∼s bajo cero** it's three degrees below zero; **∼ centígrado** *or* **Celsius/Fahrenheit** degree centigrade *o* Celsius/Fahrenheit; **el ∼ de confusión reinante** the degree of confusion that prevails; **en ∼ sumo** extremely **2** (de escalafón) grade; (Mil) rank **3** (disposición): **de buen/mal ∼** willingly/unwillingly **4** **(a)** (esp AmL) (Educ) (curso, año) year **(b)** (título): **tiene el ∼ de licenciado** he has a college (AmE) *o* (BrE) university degree

graduable *adj* adjustable

graduación f **(a)** (acción de regular) adjustment **(b)** (de bebida alcohólica) alcohol content **(c)** (Mil) rank **(d)** (Educ) graduation

graduado -da adj **(a)** ‹gafas/lentes› prescription (before n) **(b)** ‹termómetro› graduated
■ m,f (Educ) graduate

gradual adj gradual

graduar [A18] vt **(a)** (regular) to adjust **(b)** (marcar) ‹instrumento/termómetro› to calibrate
■ **graduarse** v pron **(a)** (Educ) to graduate **(b)** (Mil) to take a commission

graffiti /gra'fiti/ mpl graffiti

gráfico¹ -ca adj graphic; ‹gesto› expressive

gráfico² m **(a)** (Mat) graph **(b)** (Inf) graphic

grafología f graphology

gragea f **(a)** (Farm) tablet **(b)** (Coc) small candy (AmE) o (BrE) sweet

Gral. m (= **General**) Gen.

grama f (AmC, Ven) (césped) lawn

gramática f **(disciplina)** grammar; (libro) grammar (book)

gramatical adj grammatical

gramo m gram

gran adj: ▶ GRANDE

granada f **1** (Bot) pomegranate **2** (Arm, Mil) grenade; ~ de mano hand grenade

Granada f (en España) Granada; (en el Caribe) Grenada

granadilla f (fruta — redonda, oscura) passion fruit; (— más grande, amarilla) granadilla

granate adj inv maroon (before n)
■ m (color) maroon

Gran Bretaña f Great Britain

grande adj [GRAN is used before singular nouns] **1 (a)** (en dimensiones) ‹casa/área/nariz› big, large; **un tipo ~** a big guy; **unos ~ almacenes** a department store **(b)** (en demasía) too big; **me queda ~** it's too big for me **(c)** (en número) ‹familia› large, big; ‹clase›big; **la gran parte** or **mayoría** the great majority **2 (a)** (alto) tall; **¡qué ~ está Andrés!** isn't Andrés tall! **(b)** (en edad): **cuando sea ~** when I grow up; **ya son ~s** they are all grown up now **3** (Geog): **el G~ Santiago** Greater Santiago **4** (delante del n) **(a)** (notable, excelente) great; **un gran hombre** a great man **(b)** (poderoso) big; **los ~s bancos** the big banks; **a lo ~** in style **5 (a)** (en intensidad, grado) ‹pena/honor/ventaja› great; ‹explosión› powerful; **¡me llevé un susto más ~ ...** ! I got such a fright!; **una temporada de gran éxito** a very o a highly successful season; **son ~s amigos** they're great friends; **eso es una gran verdad** that is absolutely true; **¡qué mentira más ~!** that's a complete lie! **(b)** (elevado): **a gran velocidad** at high o great speed; **volar a gran altura** to fly at a great height; **un gran número de personas** a large number of people; **objetos de gran valor** objects of great value; **en ~:** lo **pasamos en ~** we had a great time (colloq)
■ m,f **(a)** (mayor): **la grande ya está casada** their eldest (daughter) is already married **(b)** (adulto): **los ~s** the grown-ups

grandeza f **1** (excelencia, nobleza) nobility; ~ **de alma** (liter) magnanimity; ~ **de ánimo** (liter)

valor* (liter) **2 (a)** (dignidad de Grande) rank of grandee **(b)** (conjunto de Grandes): **la ~** the (Spanish) nobility o grandees

grandilocuencia f grandiloquence

grandiosidad f grandeur

grandioso -sa adj **(a)** ‹espectáculo/obra› impressive, magnificent **(b)** (rimbombante) ‹gesto/ palabras› grandiose

granel: **a ~ (a)** (loc adj) (en abundancia) ‹comida/ bebida› stacks of **(b)** (loc adv) **comprar/vender a ~** ‹vino/aceite› to buy/sell ... by the liter (o pint etc); ‹galletas/nueces› to buy/sell ... loose; (en grandes cantidades) to buy/sell ... in bulk

granero m granary, barn

granito m (roca) granite

granizado m (bebida) drink served on crushed ice

granizar [A4] v impers to hail

granizo m (grano, bola) hailstone; (conjunto) hail

granja f (Agr) farm; ~ **avícola** poultry farm

granjearse [A1] v pron to earn, win

granjero -ra m,f farmer

grano m **1** (de arena, azúcar, trigo, arroz) grain; (de café) bean; (de mostaza) seed; **~s de pimienta** peppercorns; **ir al ~** (fam) to get (straight) to the point **2** (Med) spot, pimple (esp AmE) **3 (a)** (de la piedra, la madera) grain **(b)** (Fot) grain

granuja mf rascal

grapa f **1 (a)** (para papeles) staple; (para cables) cable clip **(b)** (Arquit) cramp iron **2** (CS) (aguardiente) grappa

grapadora f stapler

grapar [A1] vt to staple

grasa f **(a)** (Biol, Coc) fat; **la comida tenía mucha ~** the food was very greasy **(b)** (suciedad) grease; **está lleno de ~** it's all greasy **(c)** (Mec) grease **(2)** (Méx) (betún) shoe polish

grasiento -ta adj greasy

grasitud f (AmL) greasiness

graso -sa adj **(a)** ‹pelo/cutis› greasy **(b)** (Coc) greasy, oily, fatty; **queso ~** full fat cheese

grasoso -sa adj (AmL) greasy

gratificación f **(a)** (bonificación) bonus; (recompensa) reward **(b)** (satisfacción) gratification

gratificador -dora adj (AmL) rewarding, gratifying (frml)

gratificante adj rewarding, gratifying (frml)

gratificar [A2] vt **(a)** ‹persona› to give ... a bonus **(b)** (recompensar) to give ... a reward; **Ⓢ se gratificará** reward offered

gratinado -da adj au gratin

gratinador m grill

gratis adj/adv free; **es ~** it is free (of charge); **entramos ~** we got in free o for nothing

gratitud f gratitude

grato -ta adj pleasant

gratuito -ta adj **(a)** (gratis) free **(b)** (infundado) ‹afirmaciones› unwarranted; ‹insulto› gratuitous

grava f gravel

gravamen m (impuesto) tax; (carga) burden; (sobre finca, casa) encumbrance

gravar [A1] vt (con impuesto) ‹ingresos/productos› to tax

grave adj **1 (a)** [ESTAR] ‹enfermo› seriously ill ····⟩

(a) [SER] ⟨*herida/enfermedad*⟩ serious
2 ⟨*situación/asunto/error*⟩ serious **3 (a)** ⟨*tono/expresión/gesto*⟩ grave, solemn **(b)** ⟨*voz*⟩ deep **(c)** ⟨*sonido/nota*⟩ low **4** (Ling) ⟨*acento*⟩ grave; ⟨*palabra*⟩ paroxytone

gravedad *f* **1** (en general) seriousness; **está herido de** ~ he is seriously injured; **es un asunto de mucha** ~ it is a very serious matter **2** (Fís) gravity

gravilla *f* gravel

graznar [A1] *vi* «*cuervo*» to caw; «*ganso*» to honk; «*pato*» to quack

graznido *m* (del cuervo) caw; (del ganso) honk; (del pato) quack

Grecia *f* Greece

greda *f* (para cerámica) clay

grei *m* (Col) grapefruit

greifrú *mf* (*pl* **-frús**) (AmC, Ven fam) grapefruit

gremial *adj* **(a)** (profesional) ⟨*asociación*⟩ professional **(b)** (AmL) (sindical) union (*before n*)

gremialista *mf* (AmL) trade unionist

gremio *m* **(a)** (de oficio, profesión) trade **(b)** (CS, Per) (sindicato) union

greña *f* **(a)** (enredo) tangle **(b) en greña** (Méx) ⟨*trigo*⟩ unthreshed; ⟨*plata/azúcar*⟩ unrefined; ⟨*tabaco*⟩ leaf (*before n*) **(c) greñas** *fpl* untidy hair

gresca *f* (fam) (jaleo) rumpus (colloq); (riña) fight

griego¹ -ga *adj/m,f* Greek

griego² *m* (idioma) Greek

grieta *f* (en una pared) crack; (en la tierra) crack, crevice; (en la piel) crack

grifo¹ *m* **1** (Esp) (de lavabo, bañera) faucet (AmE), tap (BrE); **abrir/cerrar el** ~ to turn the faucet *o* tap on/off **2** (Per) (gasolinera) filling station **3** (Chi) (de incendios) fire hydrant, fireplug (AmE)

grifo² -fa *m,f* (Méx fam) pothead (sl), dopehead (sl)

grillo *m* **1** (Zool) cricket **2 grillos** *mpl* (de los presos) fetters (*pl*), shackles (*pl*)

grima *f* (Esp fam): **darle** ~ **a algn** (repulsión) to make sb's flesh crawl; (dentera) to set sb's teeth on edge

gringo -ga *adj* **(a)** (AmL fam & pey) gringo, foreign (*of o relating to a person from a non-Spanish speaking country*) **(b)** (Andes fam) (rubio) fair-haired
■ *m,f* **(a)** (AmL fam & pey) (extranjero) gringo, foreigner (*from a non-Spanish speaking country*); (norteamericano) Yank (colloq & pej), Yankee (colloq & pej) **(b)** (Andes fam) (rubio) (*m*) fair-haired boy/man; (*f*) fair-haired girl/woman

Gringolandia *f* (Andes fam & pey) Yankeeland (colloq & pej)

gripa *f* (Col, Méx) ▶ GRIPE

gripe *f* flu; **estar con/tener** ~ to have (the) flu

gris *adj/m* gray*

gritar [A1] *vi* to shout; **no hace falta que grites** there's no need to shout *o* yell; ~ **de dolor** to

scream with pain; ~ **de alegría** to shout for joy; ~ **pidiendo ayuda** to shout for help; ~**le** **A algn** to shout AT sb; (para llamarlo) to shout (out) TO sb
■ ~ *vt* to shout

griterío *m* shouting, clamor*

grito *m* **(a)** (de dolor, alegría) shout, cry; (de terror) scream; **un** ~ **de socorro** a cry for help; ~**s de protesta** shouts *o* cries of protest; **hablar a** ~**s** to talk at the top of one's voice; **ser el último** ~ to be the last word in fashion **(b)** (de pájaro, animal) call, cry

groenlandés -desa *adj* of/from Greenland

Groenlandia *f* Greenland

grosella *f* redcurrant

grosería *f* **(a)** (acción): **fue una** ~ **de su parte** it was very rude of him **(b)** (comentario) rude comment; **¡qué** ~**!** how rude!; **decir** ~**s** to swear

grosero -ra *adj* **(a)** (descortés) ⟨*persona/lenguaje*⟩ rude **(b)** (vulgar) crude, vulgar
■ *m,f*: **es un** ~ (vulgar) he's so vulgar *o* crude!; (descortés) he's so rude!

grosor *m* thickness

grotesco -ca *adj* ⟨*personaje/mueca*⟩ grotesque; ⟨*espectáculo*⟩ hideous, grotesque

grúa *f* **(a)** (Const) crane **(b)** (Auto) (de taller) wrecker (AmE), breakdown van (BrE); (de la policía) tow truck; **se lo llevó la** ~ it was towed (away)

grueso -sa *adj* thick

grulla *f* crane

grumete *m* cabin boy

grumo *m* lump

grumoso -sa *adj* lumpy

gruñido *m* grunt; (del perro) growl

gruñir [I9] *vi* **(a)** «*cerdo*» to grunt; «*perro*» to growl **(b)** (fam) «*persona*» to grumble

gruñón -ñona *adj* (fam) grumpy (colloq)

grupa *f* rump, hindquarters (*pl*)

grupo *m* **(a)** (de personas, empresas, países) group; (de árboles) clump; ~ **sanguíneo** blood group; ~**s sociales** social groups; **de** ~ ⟨*terapia/trabajo*⟩ group (*before n*); **en** ~ ⟨*salir/trabajar*⟩ in a group/in groups **(b)** (Mús) *tb* ~ **musical** group, band

gruta *f* (natural) cave; (artificial) grotto

guaca *f* (Andes) pre-Columbian tomb

guacal *m* **(a)** (Col, Méx, Ven) (caja) wooden crate **(b)** (Ven) (medida) crate, crateload **(c)** (AmC) (calabaza) large gourd (*used for storing tortillas*)

guacamaya *f* (Méx) **1** (ave) macaw **2** (fam) (persona) loudmouth (colloq)

guacamayo *m* macaw

guacamole *m* guacamole

guachimán *m* (AmS fam) watchman

guachinango *m* (Méx) red snapper

guacho¹ -cha *adj* (Andes, RPI) **(a)** (fam) ⟨*niño*⟩ orphaned; ⟨*perro*⟩ stray **(b)** (fam & pey) ⟨*hijo*⟩ bastard (*before n*) (pej) **2** (Chi, Per fam) ⟨*calcetín/guante*⟩ odd
■ *m,f* (Andes, RPI) **(a)** (fam) (niño abandonado) orphan,

AmC	Central America	Arg	Argentina	Cu	Cuba
AmL	Latin America	Bol	Bolivia	Ec	Ecuador
AmS	South America	Chi	Chile	Esp	Spain
Andes	Andean Region	CS	Southern Cone	Méx	Mexico

Per	Peru
RPI	River Plate Area
Ur	Uruguay
Ven	Venezuela

waif; (perro) stray **(b)** (fam & pey) (hijo ilegítimo) bastard (vulg) **(c)** (insulto — a un hombre) bastard (pej); (— a una mujer) bitch (sl & pej)

guacho² *m* (Per) (de la lotería) *tenth share in a lottery ticket*

guaco *m* (Andes) pot (*found in pre-Columbian tomb*)

guadaña *f* scythe

guagua *f* (fam) **1** (Andes) (bebé) baby **2** (Cu) (autobús) bus

guaje -ja *m,f* **1** (Méx fam) sucker (colloq); *hacerle ~ a algn* (serle infiel) to cheat on sb (colloq); (engañarlo) to rip sb off (colloq); *hacerse ~* to act dumb (colloq) **2** **guaje** *m* (Méx) **(a)** (planta, fruto) bottle gourd **(b)** (vasija) gourd **(c)** (instrumento) maraca (*made from a bottle gourd*)

guajiro -ra *m,f* **(a)** (en Cuba) peasant **(b)** (en Col, Ven) *native of the Guajira peninsula*

guajolote -ta *m,f* (Méx) turkey

guanábana *f* (fruto) soursop; (árbol) soursop tree

guanaco *m* **1** (Zool) guanaco **2** (Chi fam) (de la policía) water cannon

guanera *f* guano deposit

guanero -ra *adj* guano (*before n*)

guano *m* guano

guante *m* glove; *~s de lana/boxeo* woollen/ boxing gloves; *echarle el ~ a algn* (fam) to nab sb (colloq)

guantera *f* glove compartment

guapetón -tona *adj* (fam) ⟨chico⟩ handsome; ⟨chica⟩ pretty

guapo -pa *adj* **1** ⟨hombre⟩ handsome, good-looking; ⟨mujer⟩ attractive, good-looking; ⟨bebé⟩ beautiful; *estás muy ~ con ese traje* you look very nice in that suit **2** **(a)** (fam) (bravucón): *ponerse ~* to get cocky (colloq) **(b)** (AmS fam) (valiente) gutsy (colloq)

guarangada *f* (RPl, Ven fam) ▶ GROSERÍA B

guarango -ga *adj* (CS, Ven fam) (grosero) rude, loutish
■ *m,f* (CS, Ven fam) (grosero) lout (colloq)

guaraní *adj/m,f* Guarani
■ *m* (idioma) Guarani

guarapear [A1] *vi* (Per fam) to get plastered (colloq)

guarda *mf* (de museo, parque) keeper; (de edificio público) *tb ~ jurado* security guard

guardabarros *m* (*pl ~*) **(a)** (Auto) fender (AmE), mudguard (BrE) **(b)** (de bicicleta) mudguard

guardabosque *mf* (en parque nacional) forest ranger

guardacostas *mf* (*pl ~*) **(a)** (persona) coastguard **(b)** **guardacostas** *m* (buque) coastguard vessel

guardaespaldas *mf* (*pl ~*) bodyguard

guardalíneas *mf* (*pl ~*) (Chi) (*m*) linesman; (*f*) lineswoman

guardameta *mf* goalkeeper

guardapelo *m* locket

guardapolvo *m* (bata — de niño) overall; (— de profesor, tendero) workcoat (AmE), overall (BrE)

guardar [A1] *vt* **1** (reservar) to save, keep; *guarda algo para después* save *o* keep sth for later

2 **(a)** (poner en un lugar) ⟨juguetes/libros⟩ to put ... away; *ya guardé toda la ropa de invierno* I've already put away all my winter clothes **(b)** (conservar, mantener) to keep; *lo guardó durante años* she kept it for years; *~ las apariencias* to keep up appearances **(c)** ⟨secreto⟩ to keep; ⟨rencor⟩ to bear, harbor*; *guardo muy buenos recuerdos de él* I have very good memories of him
■ **guardarse** *v pron* **1** **(a)** (quedarse con) to keep **(b)** (reservar) to save, keep
2 (poner en un lugar): *se guardó el cheque en el bolsillo* he put the check (away) in his pocket

guardarropa *m* **(a)** (en restaurantes, teatros) cloakroom **(b)** (ropa) wardrobe **(c)** (armario) dressing room

guardavallas *mf* (*pl ~*) (AmL) goalkeeper

guardería *f; tb ~* infantil nursery

guardia *f* **1** **(a)** (vigilancia): *estar de ~* «soldado» to be on guard duty; «médico» to be on duty *o* call; «empleado» to be on duty; «marino» to be on watch; *montar ~* to stand guard; *poner en ~ a algn* to warn sb **(b)** (en esgrima): *en ~* on guard **2** (cuerpo militar) guard; *cambio de ~* changing of the guard; *G~ Civil* Civil Guard; *~ municipal or urbana* police (mainly involved in traffic duties) **3** **guardia** *mf* (*m*) policeman; (*f*) policewoman

guardiamarina *mf* midshipman

guardián -diana *m,f* **(a)** (de un edificio) security guard, guard **(b)** (protector, defensor) guardian

guarecer [E3] *vt* to shelter, protect
■ **guarecerse** *v pron* (*refl*) to shelter, take shelter

guarén *m* water rat

guargüero *m* (AmL fam) (garganta) throat

guarida *f* (de animales) den, lair; (de personas) hideout

guarnecer [E3] *vt* (Coc) to garnish

guarrada *f* (Esp fam) **(a)** (porquería, suciedad) mess (colloq) **(b)** (mala pasada) dirty trick (colloq) **(c)** (indecencia, vulgaridad): *no digas ~s* don't be filthy; *esa película es una ~* that's a filthy movie

guarro -rra *m,f* (Esp fam) **(a)** (persona sucia) filthy pig (colloq) **(b)** (indecente, vulgar): *es un ~* he's really disgusting

guarura *m* (Méx) bodyguard

guasa *f* (fam) (broma, burla) joke; *de ~* as a joke; *no te lo tomes a ~* it's no joke, it's no laughing matter

guasca *f* (Chi, Per) (ramal de cuero) strap

guasón -sona *m,f* (fam) (bromista) joker

guata *f* **1** (Esp) (algodón) wadding **2** (Andes fam) (barriga) paunch; *echar ~* to get a paunch; *me duele la ~* I've got a tummy ache (colloq)

Guatemala *f* Guatemala

guatemalteco -ca *adj/m,f* Guatemalan

guateque *m* (Esp, Méx fam) (fiesta) bash (colloq), party

guatitas *fpl* (Chi) tripe

guatón -tona *adj* (Chi, Per fam): *está muy ~* he has a real paunch (colloq)
■ *m,f* (Chi, Per fam) fatty (colloq)

guau *interj* (del perro) woof!, bow-wow!

guayaba *f* (fruta) guava

guayabera *f: loose lightweight shirt*
guayabo *m* ⊡ (Bot) guava tree ⊡ (Col fam) (resaca) hangover
Guayana *f: tb* la ~ **Francesa** French Guiana
gubernatura *f* (Méx) government
güero -ra *adj* (Méx fam) (rubio) blond, fair-haired; (amarillo) yellow
■ *m,f* (Méx fam) (*m*) blond *o* fair-haired man; (*f*) blonde *o* fair-haired woman
guerra *f* ⊡ (Mil, Pol) war; **nos declararon la ~** they declared war on us; **estar en ~** to be at war; **hacerle la ~ a algn** to wage war on *o* against sb; **~ bacteriológica** *or* **biológica** germ *o* biological warfare; **~ civil** civil war; **~ fría** cold war; **~ mundial** world war; **~ nuclear** nuclear war; **~ química** chemical warfare ⊡ (fam) (problemas) trouble, hassle (colloq); **estos niños me dan mucha ~** these kids give me a lot of hassle
guerrera *f* army jacket
guerrero -ra *adj* ⟨pueblo/espíritu⟩ warlike; **canto ~** war cry
■ *m,f* warrior
guerrilla *f* (a) (grupo) guerrillas (*pl*) (b) (lucha) guerrilla warfare
guerrillero -ra *m,f* guerrilla
guía *f* ⊡ (libro, folleto) guide (book); (de calles) map; **~ turística/de hoteles** tourist/hotel guide; **~ telefónica** *or* **de teléfonos** telephone directory, phone book ⊡ **guía** *mf* (persona) guide; **~ de turismo** tourist guide
guiar [A17] *vt* to guide
■ **guiarse** *v pron* ~**se por algo** ⟨por mapa/consejo⟩ to follow sth; ~**se por las apariencias** to be led by appearances; ~**se por el instinto** to follow one's instincts
guijarro *m* pebble
guillotina *f* guillotine
guillotinar [A1] *vt* to guillotine
guinda *f* morello cherry; (confitada) glacé cherry
guindar [A1] *vt* ⊡ (Esp arg) (robar) ⟨novia/trabajo⟩ to steal ⊡ (a) (Col, Méx, Ven fam) ⟨ropa⟩ to hang up (b) (Col fam) ⟨hamaca⟩ to hang
■ **guindarse** *v pron* (Col, Méx, Ven) (colgarse) to hang
guindilla *f* chili
guindo *m* morello cherry tree
guiñar [A1] *vt* to wink; ~**le el ojo** *or* **un ojo a algn** to wink at sb
guiño *m* wink; **hacerle un ~ a algn** to give sb a wink
guion *m* ⊡ (a) (Cin, TV) script; ~ **cinematográfico** screenplay ⊡ (Impr) (en diálogo) dash; (en palabras compuestas) hyphen; **lleva ~** it's hyphenated
guionista *mf* scriptwriter, screenwriter
güirila *f* (AmC) maize pancake

guirnalda *f* garland
guisante *m* (Esp) pea
guisar [A1] *vi* (Esp) to cook; **guisa muy bien** he's a very good cook
■ ~ *vt* (con bastante líquido) to stew; (con poco líquido) to braise
guiso *m* stew, casserole
guita *f* (arg) cash (colloq), dough (sl)
guitarra *f* guitar; ~ **eléctrica/española/clásica** electric/Spanish/classical guitar
guitarrear [A1] *vi* (Mús) to play the guitar
guitarrista *mf* guitarist
gula *f* greed, gluttony
gusano *m* ⊡ (a) (como nombre genérico) worm; (lombriz de tierra) earthworm, worm (b) (larva — de mariposa) caterpillar; (— de mosca) maggot; ~ **de luz** glowworm; ~ **de seda** silkworm ⊡ (pey) (persona despreciable) worm (pej)
gustar [A1] *vi* ⊡ (+ *me/te/le etc*): **¿te gustó el libro?** did you like *o* enjoy the book?; **me gusta su compañía** I enjoy her company; **los helados no me/te/nos gustan** I/you/we don't like ice cream; **le gusta mucho la música** he likes music very much; **a Juan le gusta María** Juan likes María; **le gusta tocar la guitarra** she likes to play the guitar (AmE), she likes playing the guitar (BrE); **le gusta mucho viajar** she's very fond of traveling (colloq); **nos gusta dar un paseo después de comer** we like to have a walk after lunch; **¿te ~ía visitar el castillo?** would you like to visit the castle?; **me ~ía que vinieras temprano** I'd like you to come early
⊡ (en frases de cortesía) to wish (frml); **como guste** as you wish; **cuando usted guste** whenever it is convenient for you
■ ~ *vt* (AmL) (querer) to like; **¿gustan tomar algo?** would you like something to drink?
gusto *m* ⊡ (a) (sentido, sabor) taste; **resulta amargo al ~** it has a bitter taste; **tiene un ~ medio raro** it has a funny taste to it; **tiene ~ a fresa** it tastes of strawberry; **deja un ~ a menta** it has a minty aftertaste (b) (sentido estético) taste; **tiene muy buen ~ para vestirse** she has very good taste in clothes; **una broma de mal ~** a tasteless joke; **para todos los ~s** to suit all tastes ⊡ (a) (placer, agrado) pleasure; **tendré mucho ~ en acompañarlos** (frml) it will be a pleasure for me to accompany you (frml); **da ~ estar aquí** it's so nice (being) here; **me dio mucho ~ volverlo a ver** it was lovely to see him again; **por ~** for fun, for pleasure; **un lugar donde se está a ~** a place where you feel comfortable *o* at ease (b) (en fórmulas de cortesía): **mucho ~ (en conocerla)** pleased *o* nice to meet you; **el ~ es mío** the pleasure is mine
gustoso -sa *adj* willingly
gutural *adj* guttural

Hh

H, h *f* (*read as* /'atʃe/) *the letter* H, h (*ver tb* HACHE)

h. (= **hora**) hr

ha *interj* ah!, ha!

Ha. (= **hectárea**) ha., hectare

haba *f* (Bot) (broad) bean

Habana *f*: **La ~** Havana

habanero -ra *adj/m,f* Havanan

habano *m* (cigarro) Havana cigar

haber¹ [E17] *v aux* (en tiempos compuestos) to have; **no habían llegado** they hadn't arrived; **de ~lo sabido** had I known, if I'd known; **¡deberías ~lo dicho!** you should have said so!
■ **~** *v impers*
I (existir, estar, darse): **hay una carta/varias cartas para ti** there's a letter/there are several letters for you; **¿hay un banco por aquí?** is there a bank near here?; **hubo dos accidentes** there were two accidents; **¿hay helado?** do you have any ice cream?; **no hay como un buen descanso** there's nothing like a good rest; **hubo varios heridos** several people were injured; **las hay rojas y verdes** there are red ones and green ones; **gracias — no hay de qué** thank you — don't mention it *o* not at all *o* you're welcome; **no hay de qué preocuparse** there's nothing to worry about; **¿qué hay de nuevo?** (fam) what's new?; **hola ¿qué hay?** (fam) hello, how are things?; **¿qué hubo?** (Andes, Méx, Ven fam) how are you?
II (ser necesario) ~ QUE + INF: **hay que estudiar** you/we/they must study; **hubo que romperlo** we/ they had to break it; **no hay que lavarlo** (no es necesario) you don't need *o* have to wash it; (no se debe) you mustn't wash it

haber² *m* (a) (bienes) assets (*pl*) (b) (en contabilidad) credit side (c) **haberes** *mpl* (frml) (ingresos) income, earnings (*pl*)

habichuela *f* (a) (semilla) bean (b) (Col) (con vaina) green bean, French bean (BrE)

hábil *adj* ① (a) (diestro) ⟨carpintero⟩ skilled, adept; ⟨conductor⟩ good, skillful*; ⟨juego/táctica⟩ skillful* (b) (astuto, inteligente) clever, able ② ⟨horas/días⟩ working (*before n*) ③ (Der) competent

habilidad *f* ① (a) (para actividad manual, física) skill; **tiene ~ para la carpintería** he is good at carpentry (b) (astucia, inteligencia) skill, cleverness; **con ~** cleverly, skillfully ② (Der) competence

habilidoso -sa *adj* [SER] good with one's hands, handy

habilitación *f* ① (de lugar) fitting out ② (autorización) authorization ③ (Col) (Educ): **exámenes de ~** retakes

habilitar [A1] *vt* ① ⟨lugar⟩ to fit out ② ⟨persona/institución⟩ to authorize; ⟨título⟩ to qualify, authorize; ⟨documento⟩ to authorize, empower ③ (Col) (Educ) to retake, to make up (AmE)

habiloso -sa *adj* (Chi fam) (inteligente) bright, smart (colloq)

habitable *adj* habitable

habitación *f* (cuarto) room; (dormitorio) bedroom; **~ individual** single room

habitacional *adj* (CS) housing (*before n*)

habitante *mf* (Geog, Sociol) inhabitant; (de barrio) resident

habitar [A1] *vt* ⟨vivienda⟩ to live in; ⟨isla/ planeta⟩ to inhabit
■ **~** *vi* (frml) to dwell (frml)

hábitat /'aβita(t)/ *m* (*pl* **-tats**) (Ecol, Zool) habitat; (Geog, Sociol) environment

hábito *m* ① (costumbre) habit; **adquirir/tener el ~ de hacer algo** to get into/have the habit OF doing sth ② (de religioso) habit

habitual *adj* ⟨sitio/hora⟩ usual; ⟨cliente/lector⟩ regular

habituar [A18] *vt* **~ a algn** A **algo** to get sb used TO sth
■ **habituarse** *v pron* **~se** A **algo** to get used TO sth, get *o* become accustomed TO sth

habla *f* ① (facultad) speech; **perder el ~** to lose one's powers of speech; **al verla me quedé sin ~** when I saw her I was speechless ② (a) (idioma): **países de ~ hispana** Spanish-speaking countries (b) (manera de hablar): **el ~ de esta región** the local way of speaking ③ **al habla** (en el teléfono) speaking; **estamos al ~ con nuestro corresponsal** we have our correspondent on the line

hablado -da *adj* (a) ⟨lenguaje⟩ spoken (b) **bien/mal ~** ⟨persona⟩ well-spoken/foul-mouthed

hablador -dora *adj* (a) (charlatán) talkative, chatty (colloq) (b) (chismoso) gossipy (c) (Méx fam) (mentiroso): **es tan ~** he's such a fibber (colloq);
■ *m,f* (a) (charlatán) chatterbox (colloq) (b) (chismoso) gossip (colloq) (c) (Méx fam) (mentiroso) storyteller, fibber (colloq)

habladurías *fpl* idle gossip *o* talk

hablar [A1] *vi* ① (a) (articular palabras) to speak; **habla más alto** speak up; **habla más bajo** keep your voice down (b) (expresarse) to speak; **~ claro** (claramente) to speak clearly; (francamente) to speak frankly; **~ por señas** to use sign language; **un político que habla muy bien** a politician who is a very good speaker; **~ por ~** to talk for the sake of it
② (a) (conversar) to talk; **habla mucho** he talks a lot; **tenemos que ~** we must (have a) talk; **~ CON algn** to speak *o* talk TO sb; **tengo que ~ que or que ~ contigo** I need to speak to you *o* have a word with you; **está hablando por teléfono** he's on the phone; **¡ni ~!** no way! (colloq), no chance! (colloq) (b) (bajo coacción) to talk (c) (murmurar) to talk, gossip; **dar que ~** to start people talking (d) (rumorear): **se habla ya de miles de víctimas** there is already talk of thousands of casualties; **se habla de que va a renunciar** it is said *o* rumored that she's going to resign (e) (al teléfono): **¿con quién hablo?** who am I speaking with (AmE) *o* (BrE) speaking to?
③ (a) (tratar, referirse a) **~ DE algo/algn** to talk ···▷

ABOUT sth/sb⟩; ~ **de negocios** to talk (about) o discuss business; **siempre habla mal de ella** he never has a good word to say about her; **hablan muy bien de él** people speak very highly of him; **me ha hablado mucho de ti** she's told me a lot about you; **en tren sale caro, y no hablemos ya del avión** going by train is expensive, and as for flying …; **háblame de tus planes** tell me about your plans; ~ SOBRE OR ACERCA DE **algo** to talk ABOUT sth **(b)** (dirigirse a) to speak; **no me hables así** don't speak to me like that; **háblale de tú** use the 'tú' form with him **(c)** (anunciar propósito) ~ DE **hacer algo** to talk OF doing sth; **habla de jubilarse** he's talking of retiring

4 (Méx) (por teléfono) to call, phone

■ ~ *vt* **1** ⟨*idioma*⟩ to speak

2 (tratar): **tenemos que** ~ **las cosas** we must talk things over; **ya lo** ~**emos más adelante** we'll talk about o discuss that later

■ **hablarse** *v pron*: **llevan meses sin** ~**se** they haven't spoken to each other for months; **no se habla con ella** he's not speaking o talking to her, he's not on speaking terms with her

habrá, habría, etc ▶ HABER¹

hacendado -da *adj* landowning (*before n*)
■ *m,f* landowner, owner of a ranch (*o* farm *etc*)

hacendoso -sa *adj* hardworking (*esp referring to housework*)

hacer [E18] *vt*
I **1 (a)** (crear) ⟨*mueble/vestido*⟩ to make; ⟨*casa/carretera*⟩ to build; ⟨*nido*⟩ to build, make; ⟨*túnel*⟩ to make, dig; ⟨*dibujo/plano*⟩ to do, draw; ⟨*lista*⟩ to make, draw up; ⟨*resumen*⟩ to do, make; ⟨*película*⟩ to make; ⟨*nudo/lazo*⟩ to tie; ⟨*pan/pastel*⟩ to make, bake; ⟨*vino/café/tortilla*⟩ to make; ⟨*cerveza*⟩ to make, brew; **me hizo un lugar en la mesa** he made room for me at the table; **hacen buena pareja** they make a lovely couple **(b)** (producir, causar) ⟨*ruido*⟩ to make; **los chistes no me hacen gracia** I don't find jokes funny; **estos zapatos me hacen daño** these shoes hurt my feet

2 (a) (efectuar, llevar a cabo) ⟨*sacrificio*⟩ to make; ⟨*milagro*⟩ to work, perform; ⟨*deberes/ejercicios/limpieza*⟩ to do; ⟨*mandado*⟩ to run; ⟨*transacción/investigación*⟩ to carry out; ⟨*experimento*⟩ to do, perform; ⟨*entrevista*⟩ to conduct; ⟨*gira/viaje*⟩ to do; ⟨*regalo*⟩ to give; ⟨*favor*⟩ to do; ⟨*trato*⟩ to make; **me hicieron una visita** they paid me a visit; **aún queda mucho por** ~ there is still a lot (left) to do; **dar que** ~ to make a lot of work **(b)** ⟨*cheque/factura*⟩ to make out, write out **3** (formular, expresar) ⟨*declaración/promesa/oferta*⟩ to make; ⟨*proyecto/plan*⟩ to make, draw up; ⟨*crítica/comentario*⟩ to make, voice; ⟨*pregunta*⟩ to ask; **nadie hizo ninguna objeción** nobody raised any objections

4 (a) (refiriéndose a necesidades fisiológicas): ~ **caca** (fam) to do a poop (AmE) *o* (BrE) a pooh (colloq); ~ **pis** *or* **pipí** (fam) to have a pee (colloq); ~ **sus necesidades** (euf) to go to the bathroom *o* toilet (euph) **(b)** (refiriéndose a sonidos onomatopéyicos) to go; **las vacas hacen 'mu'** cows go 'moo'

5 (adquirir) ⟨*dinero/fortuna*⟩ to make; ⟨*amigo*⟩ to make

6 (preparar, arreglar) ⟨*cama*⟩ to make; ⟨*maleta*⟩ to pack; **hice el pescado al horno** I did *o* cooked the fish in the oven; **tengo que** ~ **la comida** I must make lunch; *ver tb* COMIDA B

7 (recorrer) ⟨*trayecto/distancia*⟩ to do, cover

8 (en cálculos, enumeraciones): **son 180 … y 320 hacen 500** that's 180 … and 320 is *o* makes 500

II **1 (a)** (ocuparse en actividad) to do; ~ **la(s) compra(s)** to do the shopping; **¿hacemos algo esta noche?** shall we do something tonight?; ~ **ejercicio** to do (some) exercise; **¿hace algún deporte?** do you play *o* do any sports?; ▶ AMOR 1B **(b)** (como profesión, ocupación) to do; **¿qué hace tu padre?** what does your father do? **(c)** (estudiar) to do

2 (realizar cierta acción, actuar de cierta manera) to do; **¡eso no se hace!** you shouldn't do that!; **¡qué le vamos a** ~**!** what can you *o* (frml) one do?; **toca bien el piano** — **antes lo hacía mejor** she plays the piano well — she used to play better; ~**la buena** (fam): **¡ahora sí que la hice!** now I've really done it!; ▶ TONTO *m,f*

III **1** (transformar en, volver) to make; **ella lo hizo posible** she made it possible; **hizo pedazos la carta** she tore the letter into tiny pieces; **ese vestido te hace más delgada** that dress makes you look thinner; ~ **algo** DE **algo** to turn sth INTO sth; **quiero** ~ **de ti un gran actor** I want to make a great actor of you

2 (a) (obligar a, ser causa de que) ~ **a algn hacer algo** to make sb do sth; **me hizo abrirla** he made me open it; **me hizo llorar** it made me cry; **hágalo pasar** tell him to come in; **me hizo esperar tres horas** she kept me waiting for three hours; ~ **que algo/algn haga algo** to make sth/sb do sth **(b)** ⟨*hacer hacer algo*⟩ to have *o* get sth done/made; **hice acortar las cortinas** I had *o* got the curtains shortened

■ ~ *vi*
I **1** (obrar, actuar): **déjame** ~ **a mí** just let me handle this *o* take care of this; **¿cómo se hace para que te den la beca?** what do you have to do to get the scholarship?; **hiciste bien en decírmelo** you did *o* were right to tell me; **haces mal en mentir** it's wrong of you to lie

2 (fingir, simular): **hice como que no oía** I pretended not to hear; **haz como si no lo conocieras** act as if *o* pretend you don't know him

3 (servir): **esta sábana hará de toldo** this sheet will do for *o* as an awning; **la escuela hizo de hospital** the school served as *o* was used as a hospital

4 (interpretar personaje) ~ DE **algo/algn** to play (the part of) sth/sb

II (+ *compl*) (sentar): **tanto sol hace mal** (AmL) too much sun is not good for you; (+ *me/te/le etc*) **el descanso le hizo bien** the rest did him good; **la trucha me hizo mal** (AmL) the trout didn't agree with me

■ ~ *v impers* **1** (refiriéndose al tiempo atmosférico):

---

hace frío/sol it's cold/sunny; hace tres grados it's three degrees; (nos) hizo un tiempo espantoso the weather was terrible
2 (expresando tiempo transcurrido): hace dos años que murió he's been dead for two years; hace mucho que lo conozco I've known him for a long time; hacía años que no lo veía I hadn't seen him for o in years; ¿cuánto hace que se fue? how long ago did she leave?; hace poco/un año a short time/a year ago; hasta hace poco until recently

■ **hacerse** v pron
I 1 (producirse) (+ me/te/le etc): se me hizo un nudo en el hilo I got a knot in the thread; se le hizo una ampolla she got a blister; hacérsele algo a algn (Méx): por fin se le hizo ganar el premio she finally got to win the award
2 (a) (refl) (hacer para sí) «café/falda» to make oneself; se hicieron una casita they built themselves a little house (b) (caus) (hacer que otro haga): se hicieron una casita they had a little house built; se hizo la cirugía estética she had plastic surgery
3 (causarse): ¿qué te hiciste en el brazo? what did you do to your arm?; ¿te hiciste daño? did you hurt yourself?
4 (refiriéndose a necesidades fisiológicas): todavía se hace pis/caca (fam) she still wets/messes herself
5 (refl) (adquirir) to make; ~se un nombre to make a name for oneself
II 1 (a) (volverse, convertirse en) to become; se hicieron amigos they became friends; se están haciendo viejos they are getting o growing old (b) (resultar): se hace muy pesado it gets very boring; (+ me/te/le etc) se me hizo interminable it seemed interminable; se me hace difícil creerlo I find it very hard to believe (impers): se hace de noche muy pronto it gets dark very early; se está haciendo tarde it's getting late (d) (cocinarse) «pescado/guiso» to cook (e) (AmL) (pasarle a): ¿qué se habrá hecho María? what can have happened to María?
2 (acostumbrarse) ~se A algo to get used TO sth
3 (fingirse): no te hagas el inocente don't act the innocent; ¿es bobo o se (lo) hace? (fam) is he stupid or just a good actor? (colloq); ~se pasar por algn (por periodista, doctor) to pass oneself off as sb
4 (moverse) (+ compl) to move; ~se a un lado to move to one side
5 **hacerse de** (AmL) (de fortuna, dinero) to get; (de amigos) to make

hacha f⚥ (herramienta) ax (AmE), axe (BrE)

hache f: the name of the letter h

hachís m hashish, hash (colloq)

hacia prep (a) (dirección) toward (esp AmE), towards (esp BrE): ~ el sur southward(s), toward(s) the south; ~ adelante forward(s); ~ adentro/arriba inward(s)/upward(s); el centro queda ~ allá the center is (over) that way; ¿~ dónde tenemos que ir? which way do we have to go? (b) (aproximación) toward(s); llegaremos ~ las dos we'll arrive toward(s) o at around two (c) (con respecto a) toward(s); su actitud ~ mí his attitude toward(s) o to me

hacienda f 1 (a) (esp AmL) (finca) estate; (dedicada a ganadería) ranch (b) (bienes) possessions (pl), property 2 **Hacienda** (a) (ministerio) ≈ the Treasury Department (in US), ≈ the Treasury (in

UK) (b) (oficina) tax office; el dinero que debo a H~ the money I owe the IRS (AmE) o (BrE) the Inland Revenue

hada f⚥ fairy; el ~ madrina the fairy godmother

haga, etc ▶ HACER

hago ▶ HACER

Haití m Haiti

haitiano -na adj/m,f Haitian

hala interj (Esp) (a) (para animar) come on! (b) (expresando sorpresa) wow!

halagador -dora adj flattering

halagar [A3] vt to flatter; me halaga que me lo ofrezcas a mí I am flattered that you're offering it to me; le ~on el vestido they complimented her on her dress

halago m praise; ~s praise, flattery

halagüeño -ña adj «palabras/frases» flattering, complimentary; «situación» promising, encouraging; «noticia» encouraging; «futuro» promising

halcón m (Zool) falcon

hall /'xol/ m (pl **halls**) (de casa) hall, hallway; (de teatro, cine) foyer

hallaca f (Ven) cornmeal, meat and vegetables wrapped in banana leaves

hallar [A1] vt 1 (frml) (encontrar) to find; halló la puerta abierta she found the door open 2 (esp AmL) (a) (en frases negativas) (saber): no halla cómo sentarse she can't find a comfortable position to sit in; no hallo cómo decírselo I don't know how to tell her (b) (opinar, creer) to find
■ **hallarse** v pron (a) (frml) (estar, encontrarse) (+ compl) to be (b) (sentirse) (+ compl) to feel

hallazgo m find

hallulla f 1 (Chi) (pan) slightly leavened white bread 2 (Chi) (sombrero) straw boater

halo m (a) (aureola) halo (b) (de inocencia, santidad) aura

halógeno -na adj halogen (before n)

halterofilia f weightlifting

hamaca f (a) (para colgar) hammock (b) (RPl) (mecedora) rocking chair; (columpio) swing (c) (Esp) (asiento plegable) deckchair

hamacar [A2] vt (columpiar) (RPl) to swing; (mecer) (CS) to rock
■ **hamacarse** v pron (columpiarse) to swing; (mecerse) to rock (oneself)

hambre f⚥ (a) (sensación) hunger; tengo ~ I'm hungry; pasar ~ to go hungry; morirse de ~ to starve to death; me muero de ~ (fam) I'm starving (colloq) (b) (como problema) el ~ hunger

hambreado -da adj (Andes, Méx, RPl) hungry, starving

hambriento -ta adj [ESTAR] hungry, starving (colloq); ~ DE algo hungry FOR sth
■ m,f: los ~s hungry people

hamburguesa f (bistec) hamburger, beefburger (BrE); (sandwich) hamburger, burger

hampa f⚥: el ~ criminals (pl), the underworld

hámster /'xamster/ m (pl **-ters**) hamster

handicap /'xandikap/ m (pl **-caps**) handicap

hangar m hangar

haragán -gana adj lazy, idle
■ m,f shirker, layabout

harapiento -ta adj ragged

harapo m rag

haré, etc ▶ HACER

harén m harem

haría, etc ▶ HACER

harina f flour; ∼ de avena/maíz oatmeal/cornmeal

harinoso -sa adj floury

hartar [A1] vt ⃞1 (cansar, fastidiar): me hartó con sus quejas I got tired of his complaints
⃞2 (fam) (llenar): nos hartaban a or de sopa they fed us on nothing but soup; lo ∼on a palos they gave him a real beating
■ **hartarse** v pron ⃞1 (cansarse, aburrirse) to get fed up; ∼se DE algo/algn to get tired o sick of sth/sb, get fed up WITH sth/sb; ∼se DE hacer algo to get tired o sick of doing sth, get fed up WITH doing sth
⃞2 (llenarse): ∼se (DE algo) to gorge oneself (ON sth), to stuff oneself (WITH sth) (colloq)

harto¹ -ta adj ⃞1 (a) (cansado, aburrido) fed up; ∼ DE algo/algn fed up WITH sth/sb, tired OF sth/sb; ∼ DE hacer algo tired OF doing sth, fed up WITH doing sth; estaba harta de que le dijeran eso she was tired of o fed up with them telling her that (b) (de comida) full
⃞2 (delante de n) (mucho) (AmL exc RPl): te llamé hartas veces I phoned you lots of times; tiene hartas ganas de verte he really wants to see you
■ pron (AmL exc RPl): tenía ∼ que hacer I had an awful lot to do; ¿tienes amigos allí? — ¡sí, ∼s! do you have friends there? — yes, lots

harto² adv (a) (AmL exc RPl) (modificando un adjetivo) very; es ∼ mejor que el hermano he's much o a lot better than his brother (b) (modificando un verbo): me gustó ∼ I really liked it; bailamos ∼ we danced a lot

hasta prep ⃞1 (en el tiempo) (a) until; no descansó ∼ terminar she didn't rest until she'd finished; ∼ el momento so far, up to now (b) hasta que until, till; espera ∼ que pare de llover wait until o till it stops raining (c) hasta tanto until such time as (d) (AmC, Col, Méx) (con valor negativo): cierran ∼ las nueve they don't close until o till nine (e) (en saludos): ∼ mañana see you tomorrow; ∼ luego/pronto see you (colloq), see you soon
⃞2 (en el espacio) to; el agua me llegaba ∼ los hombros the water came up to my shoulders; el pelo le llega ∼ la cintura her hair goes down to her waist; ¿∼ dónde llega? how far does it go?
⃞3 (en cantidades) up to; ∼ cierto punto up to a point
■ adv even

hastiante adj boring, sickening

hastiarse [A17] v pron ∼se DE algo to grow tired o weary OF sth; hastiado de la vida tired o weary of life

Hawai m Hawaii

hawaiano -na adj/m,f Hawaiian

hay ▶ HABER

haya f (árbol, madera) beech

haya, hayas, etc ▶ HABER

hayaca f (Ven) ▶ HALLACA

haz m (de leña, paja) bundle; (de trigo) sheaf; (de luz) beam

haz ▶ HACER

hazaña f (acción — heróica) great o heroic deed, exploit; (— de mucho esfuerzo) feat, achievement

hazmerreír m (fam) laughing stock

he ▶ HABER

hebilla f (de zapato) buckle; (de cinturón) clasp, buckle

hebra f (a) (Tex) thread, strand (b) (fibra vegetal, animal) fiber*; (c) (del gusano de seda) thread (d) (de la madera) grain

hebreo¹ -brea adj/m,f Hebrew

hebreo² m (idioma) Hebrew

heces f pl: ▶ HEZ

hechicero -ra adj (persona) enchanting, captivating; (ojos/sonrisa) captivating
■ m,f (brujo) (m) sorcerer, wizard; (f) sorceress, witch (b) (de tribu) witch doctor

hechizar [A4] vt (a) «brujo» to cast a spell on, bewitch (b) (cautivar) to captivate

hechizo¹ -za adj (Chi, Méx) home-made

hechizo² m (a) (maleficio) spell (b) (atractivo, encanto) charm

hecho¹ -cha pp [ver tb HACER]
⃞1 (manufacturado) made; ∼ a mano handmade; un traje ∼ a (la) medida a made-to-measure suit; bien/mal ∼ well/badly made
⃞2 (refiriéndose a acción): ¡bien ∼! well done!; no le avisé — pues mal ∼ I didn't let him know — well you should have (done); lo ∼, ∼ o está what's done is done
⃞3 (convertido en): estaba ∼ una fiera he was furious; tú estás ∼ un vago you've become o turned into a lazy devil
■ adj (a) (ropa) ready-to-wear (b) (terminado) (trabajo) done (c) (esp Esp) (carne) done; un filete muy/poco ∼ a well-done/rare steak

hecho² m ⃞1 (a) (acto, acción): yo quiero ∼s I want action, I want something done; demuéstramelo con ∼s prove it to me by doing something about it (b) (suceso, acontecimiento) event; el lugar de los ∼s the scene of the crime
⃞2 (realidad, verdad) fact; de hecho in fact

hechura f (a) (de traje, vestido): no cobran por la ∼ they don't charge for making it up (b) (modelo, estilo) style; la falda tiene una ∼ muy simple the skirt is cut very simply (c) (forma) shape, form

hectárea f hectare

hediondez f stench, stink

hediondo -da adj (fétido) foul-smelling, stinking

hegemonía f hegemony, dominance

helada f frost

heladera f (para hacer helados) ice-cream maker; (nevera) (RPl) refrigerator, fridge; (para picnic) (Arg, Col) cool o cold box

heladería f ice-cream parlor*

heladero -ra m,f (esp AmL) ice-cream vendor o seller

helado¹ -da adj ⃞1 (a) (persona/manos) freezing (colloq), frozen (colloq); (casa/habitación) freezing (colloq); quedarse ∼ (de asombro) to be stunned (b) (comida) stone-cold; (líquido/bebida) (muy frío) freezing; (que se ha enfriado) stone-cold; servir el vino bien ∼ (AmL) serve the wine well chilled ⃞2 (agua/estanque) frozen

helado² *m* ice cream; ~ **de agua** (Andes) water ice, sherbet (AmE); (con palo) Popsicle® (AmE), ice lolly (BrE)

helar [A5] *vt/vi* to freeze
■ ~ *v impers:* **anoche heló** it went below freezing last night (AmE), there was a frost last night (BrE)
■ **helarse** *v pron* [1] «río/charco» to freeze (over); «agua/plantas/cosecha» to freeze [2] (fam) **(a)** «persona» to freeze **(b)** «comida/café» to get o go cold

helecho *m* (como nombre genérico) fern; (más específico) bracken

hélice *f* (de barco) propeller, screw; (de avión) propeller

helicóptero *m* helicopter

hematoma *m* (tumor) hematoma*; (moretón) bruise

hembra *adj inv* female
■ *f* **(a)** (Zool) female; **la ~ del faisán** the hen pheasant **(b)** (mujer) female, woman **(c)** (de enchufe, corchete) female (part)

hemisferio *m* **(a)** (Geog, Mat) hemisphere; **el ~ norte** the northern hemisphere **(b)** (Anat) cerebral hemisphere

hemofilia *f* hemophilia*

hemofílico -ca *adj/m,f* hemophiliac*

hemorragia *f* hemorrhage*

hemorroides *fpl* piles, hemorrhoids (tech)

hendidura *f* (en madera) crack; (en roca) fissure, crack

heno *m* hay

hepatitis *f* hepatitis

heráldica *f* heraldry

heraldo *m* herald

herbáceo -cea *adj* herbaceous

herbicida *m* herbicide, weedkiller

herbívoro -ra *adj* herbivorous
■ *m,f* herbivore

herboristería *f* herbalist's

heredar [A1] *vt* «bienes/título/tradiciones» to inherit; «trono» to succeed to; **heredó los ojos de su madre** he has his mother's eyes

heredero -ra *m,f* (*m*) heir; (*f*) heir, heiress; **príncipe ~** crown prince; **~ DE algo** heir TO sth

hereditario -ria *adj* hereditary

herejía *f* heresy

herencia *f* **(a)** (Der) inheritance; **le dejó en ~ la finca** he bequeathed o left her the farm **(b)** (patrimonio cultural, nacional) heritage **(c)** (Biol) heredity

herida *f* (en el cuerpo): **sufrir ~s de carácter grave** to suffer serious injuries; **se hizo una ~ en la rodilla** he cut his knee; **curar una ~** to clean/dress a wound **(b)** (pena, sufrimiento) wound

herido -da *adj* **(a)** (físicamente) injured; **está gravemente ~** (por accidente) he is seriously injured; (por agresión) he has been seriously wounded; **~ de muerte** fatally wounded **(b)** (en sentimiento) «persona» hurt
■ *m,f:* **los ~s** the injured/wounded

herir [I11] *vt* **(a)** (físicamente) to wound **(b)** «orgullo» to hurt **(c)** «vista» to hurt

hermanar [A1] *vt* **(a)** (en sentimiento, propósito) to unite **(b)** «ciudades» to twin **(c)** «calcetines» to match up, put … in pairs; «fichas/naipes» to match up

hermanastro -tra *m,f* **(a)** (con vínculo sanguíneo) (*m*) half brother; (*f*) half sister **(b)** (sin vínculo sanguíneo) (*m*) stepbrother; (*f*) stepsister

hermandad *f* **(a)** (de hombres) brotherhood, fraternity; (de mujeres) sisterhood **(b)** (asociación) association

hermano -na
■ *m,f* [1] (pariente) (*m*) brother; (*f*) sister; **mis ~s** (solo varones) my brothers; (varones y mujeres) my brothers and sisters; **~ gemelo/hermana gemela** twin brother/twin sister; **~ político/hermana política** brother-in-law/sister-in-law [2] (como apelativo) (Col, Per, Ven fam) buddy (AmE colloq), mate (BrE colloq) [3] **(a)** (religioso) (*m*) brother; (*f*) sister **(b)** (prójimo) (*m*) brother; (*f*) sister [4] (de guante, calcetín) pair
■ *adj* «buque» sister (before n); «ciudades» twin (before n)

hermético -ca *adj* «envase/cierre» airtight, hermetic (tech) **(b)** «persona/rostro» inscrutable, secretive

hermoso -sa *adj* **(a)** (bello) beautiful, lovely **(b)** (magnífico) splendid **(c)** (lozano, corpulento) big and healthy, bonny (BrE) **(d)** (noble) noble

hermosura *f* **(a)** (cualidad) beauty, loveliness **(b)** (persona, cosa hermosa): **¡qué ~ de niño/paisaje!** what a beautiful child/landscape!

hernia *f* hernia, rupture; **~ discal** slipped disk*

herniarse [A1] *v pron* to get a hernia, rupture oneself

héroe *m* hero

heroico -ca *adj* heroic

heroína *f* [1] (persona) heroine [2] (droga) heroin

heroinómano -na *m,f* heroin addict

heroísmo *m* heroism

herpes *m* (*pl* ~) (en boca, genitales) herpes; (en cintura) shingles

herradura *f* horseshoe

herramienta *f* tool

herrería *f* blacksmith's, smithy

herrero -ra *m,f* blacksmith

herrumbre *f* rust

hervidero *m* (de moscas) swarm; (de chismes, delincuencia) hotbed; **un ~ de gente** a seething mass of people; **la casa era un ~** the house was buzzing

hervidor *m* (de agua) kettle; (de leche) milk pan

hervir [I11] *vi/vt* to boil; **el café está hirviendo** the coffee is boiling

heterosexual *adj/mf* heterosexual

hez *f* **(a)** (escoria) dregs (*pl*) **(b)** (Vin) *tb* **heces** sediment, lees (*pl*) **(c)** **heces** *fpl* (excrementos) feces* (*pl*)

hibernar [A1] *vi* to hibernate

híbrido¹ -da *adj* hybrid (before n)

híbrido² *m* hybrid

hice, hiciera, etc ▶ HACER

hidalgo *m* gentleman, nobleman (*from the lower ranks of the nobility*)

hidratante *adj* moisturizing (before n)

hidratar [A1] *vt* «verduras» to hydrate; «piel» to moisturize

hidrato *m* hydrate; **~s de carbono** carbohydrates

hidráulico -ca *adj* hydraulic

hidroavión *m* seaplane

hidroeléctrico -ca *adj* hydroelectric

hidrofobia *f* hydrophobia (tech), rabies

hidrógeno *m* hydrogen

hiedra *f* ivy

hiel *f* bile

hiela, hielas, etc ▶ HELAR

hielo *m* ice; **romper el ~** to break the ice

hiena *f* hyena

hierba *f* [1] (césped) grass; **~ mala nunca muere** the Devil looks after his own [2] **(a)** (Bot, Coc, Med) herb; **malas ~s** weeds **(b)** (arg) (marihuana) grass (colloq)

hierbabuena *f* mint

hierbajo *m* (esp Esp) weed

hierro *m* **(a)** (Metal) iron; **~ forjado** wrought iron; **~ fundido** cast iron; **de ~** iron (before n) **(b)** (de lanza, flecha) head, tip **(c)** (en golf) iron; **un ~ cuatro** a four iron

hígado *m* liver

higiene *f* hygiene

higiénico -ca *adj* hygienic

higo *m* (de la higuera) fig; **~ chumbo** (Esp) prickly pear

higuera *f* fig tree

hijastro -tra *m,f* (*m*) stepson; (*f*) stepdaughter; **mis ~s** (varones y mujeres) my stepchildren

hijo -ja *m,f* [1] (pariente) (*m*) son; (*f*) daughter; **mis ~s** (solo varones) my sons; (varones y mujeres) my children; **espera un ~** she's expecting a baby; **no tienen ~s** they don't have any children; **~ adoptivo/hija adoptiva** adopted son/daughter; **~/hija natural** illegitimate son/daughter; **~ político/hija política** son-in-law/daughter-in-law; **~ único/hija única** only child; **M. Pérez, ~** M. Pérez Junior; **~ de tigre sale pintado** (AmL fam) he's just like his father/mother [2] (apelativo): **¡~, por Dios!** (hablándole a un niño) for heaven's sake, child!; (hablándole a un adulto) for heaven's sake, Pedro (o Luis *etc*)!

híjole *interj* (Méx) jeez! (AmE colloq), gosh (colloq)

hilacha *f* loose thread

hilar [A1] *vi* to spin; **~ fino** to split hairs ■ **~** *vt* **(a)** (algodón/lana) to spin; «araña» to spin **(b)** (ideas/hechos) to string together

hilera *f* **(a)** (fila) row, line **(b)** (Mil) file (frml *o* liter) **(c)** (de ladrillos) course (de semillas) row, drill

hilo *m* [1] **(a)** (en costura) thread; **~ dental** dental floss **(b)** (lino) linen **(c)** (de araña) thread **(d)** (fam) (de las judías) string [2] (Elec) wire; **~ musical** (Esp) piped music [3] (de relato, conversación) thread [4] (de sangre, agua) trickle

hilvanar [A1] *vt* [1] (coser) to baste (AmE), to tack (BrE) [2] (frases/ideas) to put together

himen *m* hymen

himno *m* **(a)** (religioso) hymn; (de colegio) school song *o* anthem; **~ nacional** national anthem **(b)** (Lit) ode

hincada *f* (Col, Per) sharp pain

hincapié *m*: **hacer ~ en algo** to stress *o* emphasize sth

hincar [A2] *vt* (clavar) **~ algo EN algo** (estaca) to drive *o* thrust sth INTO sth; **me hincó los dientes en la mano** it buried its teeth in *o* sunk its teeth into my hand
■ **hincarse** *v pron* tb **~se de rodillas** to kneel

hincha *mf* (fam) (Dep) fan (colloq), supporter

hinchado -da *adj* (vientre/pierna) swollen; (estilo/lenguaje) overblown

hinchar [A1] *vt* (Esp) (globo) to inflate (frml), to blow up; (rueda) to inflate, pump up; (suceso/noticia) (fam) to blow ... up (colloq)
■ **~** *vi* (CS fam) (fastidiar) «persona» to be a pain in the ass (AmE vulg) *o* (BrE vulg) arse; (+ me/te/le etc) **me hincha su actitud** his attitude really pisses me off (sl)
■ **hincharse** *v pron* **(a)** «vientre/pierna» (+ me/te/le etc) to swell up **(b)** (fam) (enorgullecerse) to swell with pride **(c)** (Esp fam) (hartarse) **~se DE algo** (de pasteles/ostras) to stuff oneself WITH sth

hinchazón *f* swelling

hindú *adj/mf* **(a)** (Relig) Hindu **(b)** (crit) (de la India) Indian

hinduismo *m* Hinduism

hinojo *m* (Bot, Coc) fennel

hiperactivo -va *adj* hyperactive

hipermercado *m* large supermarket, hypermarket (BrE)

hipertensión *f* high blood pressure, hypertension

hípica *f* equestrian sports (*pl*); (carreras) horse racing

hípico -ca *adj* (deportes/centro) equestrian (before n)

hipnosis *f* hypnosis

hipnotismo *m* hypnotism

hipnotizador -dora *adj* (mirada) hypnotic ■ *m,f* hypnotist

hipnotizar [A4] *vt* (Psic) to hypnotize; (fascinar) to mesmerize

hipo *m* hiccups (*pl*), hiccoughs (*pl*)

hipocondríaco -ca *m,f* hypochondriac

hipocresía *f* hypocrisy

hipócrita *adj* hypocritical ■ *mf* hypocrite

hipodérmico -ca *adj* hypodermic

hipódromo *m* (Equ, Ocio) racecourse, racetrack (AmE); (Hist) hippodrome

hipopótamo *m* hippopotamus

hipoteca *f* mortgage

hipotecar [A2] *vt* to mortgage

hipotecario -ria *adj* mortgage (before n)

hipótesis *f* hypothesis

hipotético -ca *adj* hypothetical

AmC	Central America	Arg	Argentina
AmL	Latin America	Bol	Bolivia
AmS	South America	Chi	Chile
Andes	Andean Region	CS	Southern Cone

Cu	Cuba	Per	Peru
Ec	Ecuador	RPl	River Plate Area
Esp	Spain	Ur	Uruguay
Méx	Mexico	Ven	Venezuela

hippy, hippie /'xipi/ adj (pl **hippies**) hippy (before n), hippie (before n)
■ mf hippy, hippie

hiriente adj hurtful, wounding (before n)

hirviendo ▶ HERVIR

hisopo m (a) (bastoncillo) cotton swab (AmE), cotton bud (BrE) (b) (Chi) (de afeitar) shaving brush

hispánico -ca adj (a) (de los países de habla hispana) Hispanic (b) (relativo a España) Spanish

hispanismo m (giro propio del español de España) word/expression peculiar to Spain; (palabra derivada del español) hispanicism; (estudio) Hispanic studies

hispano -na adj (a) (español) Spanish, Hispanic (frml); **países de habla hispana** Spanish-speaking countries (b) (hispanoamericano) Spanish American, Latin American; (en EE UU) Hispanic
■ m,f (a) (liter) (español) Spaniard (b) (hispanoamericano) Spanish American, Latin American; (en EE UU) Hispanic

Hispanoamérica f Spanish America

hispanoamericano -na adj/m,f Spanish American

hispanohablante, hispanoparlante mf Spanish speaker

histeria f hysteria; ~ **colectiva** mass hysteria

histérico -ca adj (Med, Psic) hysterical; (exaltado): **ponerse** ~ to have hysterics o a fit; **me pones** ~ you drive me mad
■ m,f (Med, Psic) hysteric; (exaltado): **es un** ~ he gets quite hysterical about things

historia f [1] (Hist) history; ~ **antigua** ancient history; ~ **clínica** medical history; **pasar a la** ~ (por ser importante) to go down in history; (perder actualidad) (fam): **aquello ya pasó a la** ~ that's ancient history now (colloq) [2] (relato) story; **la** ~ **de su vida** the story of his life [3] (fam) (cuento, asunto): **me vino con la** ~ **de que ...** he came up with this story o tale about ...; **déjate de** ~**s** stop making excuses; **se quejó de no sé qué** ~**s** he complained about something or other (colloq)

historiador -dora m,f historian

historial m record; ~ **clínico** or **médico** medical history; ~ **personal** resumé (AmE), curriculum vitae (BrE)

histórico -ca adj (real) historical; (importante) historic

historieta f comic strip, cartoon story

hit /'xit/ m (pl **hits**) hit

hito m (hecho trascendental) landmark, milestone

hizo ▶ HACER

Hnos. (= **hermanos**) Bros.

hobby /'xoβi/ m (pl **-bbies**) hobby

hocico m (de cerdo) snout; (de perro, lobo) snout, muzzle

hocicón -cona m,f (CS, Méx fam & pey) bigmouth (colloq & pej), blabbermouth (colloq & pej)

hockey /'(x)oki/ m hockey; ~ **sobre hielo** ice hockey

hogar m home; **formar un** ~ to set up home; **artículos para el** ~ household goods; **las labores del** ~ housework; **quedarse sin** ~ to be left homeless; ~ **de ancianos** residential home for the elderly, old people's home (colloq)

hogareño -ña adj ⟨persona⟩ home-loving; ⟨vida/escena⟩ domestic (before n)

hoguera f bonfire; **murió en la** ~ he was burned at the stake

hoja f [1] (Bot) leaf [2] (a) (folio) sheet; ~ **de vida** (Col, Ven) resumé (AmE), curriculum vitae (BrE) (b) (de libro) page, leaf; **pasar las** ~**s** to turn the pages (c) (formulario) form, sheet; ~ **electrónica** spreadsheet program [3] (a) (de puerta, mesa) leaf (b) (de madera, metal) sheet (c) (de cuchillo) blade; ~ **de afeitar** razor blade

hojalata f tinplate

hojalatería f (Méx) body work (AmE), panel-beating (BrE)

hojalatero -ra m,f (Auto) (Méx) body shop worker (AmE), panel beater (BrE)

hojaldre m puff pastry, puff paste (AmE)

hojear [A1] vt to leaf o glance through

hojilla f (Ven) razor blade

hojuela f (AmL exc CS) flake

hola interj (saludo) hello, hi! (colloq)

holá interj (RPl) (por teléfono) hello?

holán m (Méx) flounce, frill

Holanda f Holland

holandés[1] -desa adj Dutch
■ m,f (m) Dutchman; (f) Dutchwoman; **los holandeses** the Dutch, Dutch people

holandés[2] m (idioma) Dutch

holgado -da adj (a) ⟨prenda⟩ loose-fitting, baggy (b) ⟨posición⟩ comfortable; **viven** ~**s** they're comfortably off (c) ⟨victoria/mayoría⟩ comfortable (d) (de espacio): **así iremos más** ~**s** we'll be more comfortable like that

holgar [A8] vi (en 3ª pers) (frml) (estar de más): **huelga decir que ...** it goes without saying that ...; **huelgan los comentarios** what can one say? ~ **man**

holgazán -zana adj lazy
■ m,f idler, lazybones (colloq)

holgazanear [A1] vi to idle, laze o loaf around

holgura f (a) (bienestar económico, comodidad): **vivir con** ~ to live comfortably (b) (de prenda) fullness, looseness

hollejo m skin

hollín m soot

hombre m (a) (varón) man; ~**s, mujeres y niños** men, women and children; **no es lo bastante** ~ **para ...** he's not man enough to ...; **¡**~ **al agua!** man overboard!; **este** ~ **no sabe lo que dice** this guy doesn't know what he's talking about; ~ **de confianza** right-hand man; ~ **del tiempo** weatherman; ~ **de negocios** businessman; ~ **lobo** werewolf; ~ **medio** man in the street; ~ **rana** frogman, diver; ~ **precavido vale por dos** forewarned is forearmed (b) (especie humana): **el** ~ **man**
■ interj: **¡**~! **¡qué sorpresa!** well! what a nice surprise!; **¿te gustaría venir?** — **¡**~! **I would you like to come?** — you bet! what do you think?; ~, **no es lo mismo** come off it, it's not the same thing at all (colloq)

hombrera f (almohadilla) shoulder pad; (Mil) (de uniformes) epaulet

hombría f manliness

hombrillo m (Ven) shoulder (AmE), hard shoulder (BrE)

hombro m shoulder; **encogerse de** ~**s** to shrug (one's shoulders); **lo llevaron a** ~**s** they ⋯▷

h

carried him on their shoulders o shoulder high;
arrimar el ~ to pull one's weight, put one's
shoulder to the wheel; **mirar a algn por encima
del** ~ to look down on sb

hombruno -na *adj* (*pey*) ⟨*mujer*⟩ mannish,
butch (colloq & pej); ⟨*gestos/modales*⟩ masculine,
mannish

homenaje *m* **(a)** (tributo) tribute; **rendir(le)** ~ **a
algn** to pay tribute o homage to sb; **en** ~ **a** in
honor of **(b)** (acto): **le ofrecieron un** ~ they held a
party (o reception, *etc*) in his honor

homeópata *mf* homeopath

homeopatía *f* homeopathy

homeopático -ca *adj* (Med) homeopathic

homicida *adj* (frml) ⟨*instinto*⟩ homicidal;
⟨*arma*⟩ murder (*before n*)
■ *mf* (frml) murderer, homicide (frml)

homicidio *m* (frml) homicide

homogéneo -nea *adj* ⟨*grupo*⟩ homogeneous;
⟨*masa/mezcla*⟩ smooth

homologación *f* ⓵ **(a)** (de un producto —
recomendación) endorsement; (— autorización)
authorization **(b)** (Dep) (de un récord) ratification
⓶ (equiparación) ~ **con algo: han pedido su** ~ **con
los técnicos** they have asked for their with the
technicians; **la** ~ **de los títulos australianos con
los europeos** the recognition of Australian
qualifications as equivalent to European ones

homologar [A3] *vt* **(a)** ⟨*producto*⟩ (recomendar)
to approve, endorse; (autorizar) to authorize,
approve **(b)** (Dep) ⟨*récord*⟩ to ratify, recognize **(c)**
⟨*convenio*⟩ to recognize

homólogo -ga *adj* equivalent
■ *m,f* (period) counterpart

homosexual *adj/mf* homosexual

honda *f* (de cuero) sling; (con elástico) slingshot
(AmE), catapult (BrE)

hondo¹ -da *adj* **(a)** ⟨*piscina/río*⟩ deep; **en lo
más** ~ **de mi corazón** in my heart of hearts, deep
down; **en lo** ~ **del valle** at the bottom of the
valley **(b)** (*gen delante del n*) (frml) ⟨*pena/pesar*⟩
profound (frml), deep

hondo² *adv:* **respirar** ~ to breathe deeply

hondonada *f* hollow

Honduras *f* Honduras

hondureño -ña *adj/m,f* Honduran

honestidad *f* integrity, honesty

honesto -ta *adj* (íntegro) honest, honorable*

hongo *m* **(a)** (Bot, Med) fungus **(b)** (AmL) (Coc)
mushroom **(c)** *tb* **sombrero de** ~ derby (AmE),
bowler hat (BrE) **(d)** ~ **atómico** mushroom cloud

honor *m* **(a)** honor*; **tengo el** ~ **de ... it is my
honor** o I have the honor to ...; **me hizo el** ~ **de
recibirme** he did me the honor of receiving me;
en ~ **a la verdad** to be truthful; **hacer** ~ **a su
nombre** to live up to one's reputation **(b)**
honores *mpl* (homenaje) honors* (*pl*); **le
rindieron los** ~**es correspondientes a su rango** he
was accorded the honors befitting his rank (frml)

honorable *adj* honorable*

honorario -ria *adj* honorary

honorarios *mpl* fees (*pl*)

honorífico -ca *adj* honorary

honra *f* **(a)** (en general) honor*; **¡y a mucha** ~**!**
and proud of it! **(b)** ~**s fúnebres** *fpl* funeral rites
(*pl*)

honradez *f* (honestidad) honesty; (decencia)
decency

honrado -da *adj* **(a)** (honesto) honest,
honorable* **(b)** ⟨*mujer*⟩ respectable

honrar [A1] *vt* ⓵ «*comportamiento/actitud*» to
do ... credit o honor*; **nos honra hoy con su
presencia** she is honoring us with her presence
here today ⓶ (respetar) to honor*
■ **honrarse** *v pron* to be honored*

hora *f* ⓵ (período de tiempo) hour; **media** ~ half
an hour, a half hour (AmE); **las** ~**s de mayor
afluencia** the busiest time; **cobrar por** ~**s** to be
paid by the hour; **8.000 pesetas por** ~ 8,000
pesetas an hour; ~ **libre** free period; ~ **pico**
(AmL) *or* (Esp) **punta** rush hour; ~**s extra(s)** *o*
extraordinaria(s) overtime
⓶ **(a)** (momento puntual) time; **¿tiene** ~**, por favor?**
have you got the time, please?; **¿qué** ~ **es?**
what's the time?, what time is it?; **pon el reloj en**
~ put the clock right; **todavía no es la** ~ it's not
time yet; **nunca llegan a la** ~ they never arrive
on time; **el avión llegó antes de (su)** ~ the plane
arrived early **(b)** (momento sin especificar) time; **es**
~ **de irse a la cama** it's bedtime o time for bed; **a
la** ~ **de almorzar** at lunchtime; **ya es** ~ **de irnos**
it's time for us to go; **¡ya era** ~ **de que llamases!**
it's about time you called; **a primera** ~ **de la
mañana** first thing in the morning; **a última** ~ at
the last moment; **a la** ~ **de:** **a la** ~ **de traducirlo**
when it comes to translating it; **a la** ~ **de la
verdad** when it comes down to it; **entre** ~**s**
between meals; **hacer** ~ (Chi) to kill time
⓷ (cita) appointment; **pedir** ~ to make an
appointment

horadar [A1] *vt* ⟨*roca*⟩ to bore through; ⟨*pared*⟩
to drill a hole in

horario *m* ⓵ (de trenes, aviones) schedule (AmE),
timetable (BrE); (de clases) timetable; **tiene un** ~
muy flexible his hours are very flexible; **la
empresa ofrece** ~ **flexible** the company offers
flextime *or* (BrE) flexitime; ~ **continuo** *or* (AmL)
corrido *or* (Esp) **intensivo** *continuous working day
(usually from eight to three) with no break for
lunch*; ~ **de visitas** visiting hours (*pl*); ~ **partido**
working day with a long break for lunch ⓶ (de
reloj) hour hand

horca *f* ⓵ (patíbulo) gallows (*pl*); (juego): **la** ~
hangman ⓶ (Agr) pitchfork, hayfork

horcajadas: a ~ (*loc adv*) astride

horchata *f* (de chufas) horchata (*cold drink
made from tiger nuts*); (en Méx) *drink made from
ground melon seeds*

horda *f* horde

horizontal *adj/f* horizontal

horizonte *m* **(a)** (línea) horizon **(b)**
horizontes *mpl* (perspectivas) horizons (*pl*)

horma *f* (para hacer zapatos) last; (para conservar su
forma) shoetree

hormiga *f* ant

hormigón *m* concrete

hormigueo *m* pins and needles (*pl*), tingling

hormiguero *m* **(a)** (Zool) (nido) ant's nest;
(montículo) anthill **(b)** (de personas): **era un** ~ **de
gente** it was swarming with people

hormona *f* hormone

hornada *f* (de pan, pasteles) batch

hornalla *f* (RPl) ▶ HORNILLO 1

hornilla f (a) (AmL exc CS) ▶ HORNILLO 1 (b) (Chi) ▶ HORNILLO 2

hornillo m 1 (Esp) (a) (de gas) burner (b) (de una cocina eléctrica — espiral) ring; (— placa) hotplate 2 (cocinilla portátil) portable electric stove

horno m (a) (de cocina) oven; **resistente al ~** ovenproof; **pollo al ~** roast chicken; **pescado al ~** baked fish; (b) (Metal, Tec) furnace (c) (para cerámica) kiln

horóscopo m horoscope

horqueta f (Chi) (de jardinero) fork; (de campesino) pitchfork

horquilla f (a) (para pelo) hairpin (b) (Agr) pitchfork (c) (en bicicleta) fork

horrendo -da adj ▶ HORROROSO

horrible adj (a) ⟨accidente/muerte⟩ horrible, horrific (b) (feo) ⟨persona⟩ hideous, ugly; ⟨camisa/adorno⟩ horrible, hideous (c) ⟨tiempo⟩ terrible, awful (d) (inaguantable) unbearable

horripilante adj terrifying, horrifying

horror m 1 (a) (miedo, angustia) horror; **me causa ~ verlo** it horrifies me to see it; **les tengo ~ a los hospitales** I'm terrified of hospitals (b) (fam) (uso hiperbólico): **¡qué ~!** how awful o terrible! 2 **horrores** mpl (cosas terribles) horrors (pl); **los ~s de la guerra** the horrors of war

horrorizar [A4] vt to horrify, appall
■ **horrorizarse** v pron to be horrified, be appalled; **~se DE algo** to be horrified by o AT sth

horroroso -sa adj ⟨crimen⟩ horrific, horrifying; ⟨película/novela⟩ terrible, awful; ⟨persona/vestido⟩ awful, horrific (colloq); **tengo un hambre horrorosa** I'm absolutely starving (colloq)

hortaliza f vegetable

hortelano -na m,f truck farmer (AmE), market gardener (BrE)

hortensia f hydrangea

hortera adj (Esp fam) ⟨vestido/canción⟩ tacky (colloq); **es muy ~** he has very tacky taste

horticultor -ra m,f horticulturalist, gardener

horticultura f horticulture, gardening

hosco -ca adj ⟨persona/semblante⟩ surly, sullen

hospedaje m accommodations (AmE), accommodation (BrE)

hospedar [A1] vt to provide ... with accommodations (AmE) o (BrE) accommodation
■ **hospedarse** v pron to stay, put up (AmE colloq)

hospedería f (posada) inn; (Rel) hospice

hospicio m (para niños huérfanos) orphanage

hospital m hospital; **~ clínico** teaching hospital

hospitalario -ria adj (a) ⟨pueblo/persona⟩ hospitable, welcoming (b) (Med) hospital (before n)

hospitalidad f hospitality

hospitalizar [A4] vt to hospitalize
■ **hospitalizarse** v pron (AmL) to go into the hospital (AmE) o (BrE) into hospital

hostal m cheap hotel; **~ residencia** guesthouse, boarding house

hostelería f (Esp) ▶ HOTELERÍA

hostia f 1 (Relig) host 2 (Esp vulg o fam) (golpe) slap, smack in the face (o mouth etc); **se pegó una ~ con el coche** he smashed his car up badly (colloq) 3 (uso expletivo) (Esp vulg o fam) **¡~(s)!** jeez!

(AmE colloq), bloody hell! (BrE sl); **hace un frío de la ~** (BrE) bloody freezing! (sl); **¡qué ~s ...!** what the hell ...! (sl)

hostigar [A3] vt 1 (a) (acosar) to bother, pester (b) (Mil) to harass (c) ⟨caballo⟩ to whip 2 (Andes fam) ⟨comida/bebida⟩ to pall on

hostigoso -sa adj (Andes) ⟨comida/bebida⟩ sickly, sickly-sweet; ⟨persona⟩ annoying, irritating

hostil adj [SER] ⟨medio/clima⟩ hostile; ⟨gente/ actitud⟩ hostile, unfriendly

hostilidad f (a) (del clima) hostility; (de actitud) hostility, unfriendliness (b) **hostilidades** fpl hostilities (pl)

hotel m hotel; **~ residencia** guesthouse, boarding house

hotelería f (AmL) (negocio, industria) hotel and catering trade o business; (profesión) hotel management

hotelero -ra adj hotel (before n)
■ m,f hotel manager, hotelier

hoy adv 1 (este día) today; **~ hace un año** a year ago today; **¿a cuánto estamos ~?** what's the date today? 2 (a) (actualmente) today, nowadays (b) (en locs) **hoy** (en día) nowadays, these days; **hoy por hoy** at this precise moment, at this moment in time

hoyo m (agujero) hole; (depresión) hollow; (fosa) pit; (en golf) hole; (sepultura) (fam) grave

hoyuelo m dimple

hoz f sickle

huacal m (Col, Méx, Ven) (caja) wooden crate

huachafo -fa adj (Per fam) (a) ⟨persona⟩ pretentious, affected (b) ⟨vestido/adorno⟩ tacky (colloq)

huachinango m (Méx) red snapper

huacho -cha adj/m,f ▶ GUACHO

huarache m (Méx) (Indum) sandal

huasca f (Chi, Per) ▶ GUASCA

huaso -sa m,f (Chi) (a) (campesino) peasant (b) (fam) (persona — rústica) hick (AmE colloq), country bumpkin (colloq); (—sin modales) uncouth yob (colloq)

hube, hubo, etc ▶ HABER

hucha f (Esp) moneybox, piggybank

hueco¹ -ca adj (a) [ESTAR] ⟨árbol/bola⟩ hollow; ⟨nuez⟩ empty, hollow; **tienes la cabeza hueca** (fam & hum) you've got a head full of sawdust (colloq & hum) (b) [SER] (vacío) ⟨palabras⟩ empty; ⟨estilo⟩ superficial; ⟨persona⟩ shallow, superficial (c) (esponjoso) ⟨lana⟩ soft; ⟨colchón⟩ soft, spongy (d) ⟨sonido/tos⟩ hollow; ⟨voz⟩ resonant

hueco² m (a) (cavidad en árbol, roca) hollow; (de ascensor) shaft; **suena a ~** it sounds hollow; **el ~ de la escalera** the stairwell (b) (espacio) space; (entre dos dientes) gap; **un ~ para aparcar** a parking space; **hazme un ~** make room for me; **llenar un ~ en el mercado** to fill a gap in the market (c) (concavidad) hollow

huela, huele, etc ▶ OLER

huelga f strike; **hacer ~** to (go on) strike; **estar en ~** to be on strike

huelga, huelgan, etc ▶ HOLGAR

huelguista mf striker

huella f (a) (pisada — de persona) footprint, ⸺⸽⸽⸽⸽

footstep; (— de rueda) track; **las ~s del animal** the animal's tracks *o* pawprints (*o* hoofmarks *etc*); **~s dactilares** fingerprints **(b)** (vestigio) mark; **sin dejar ~** without (a) trace

huelo ▶ OLER

huemul *m* deer (*native to the Southern Andes*)

huérfano -na *adj*: **un niño ~** an orphan; **quedó ~** he was orphaned; **es ~ de padre** he doesn't have a father
■ *m,f* orphan

huerta *f* **(a)** (huerto grande) (vegetable) garden; (con frutales) orchard **(b)** (explotación agrícola) truck farm (AmE), market garden (BrE)

huerto *m* (para verduras) vegetable garden; (con frutales) orchard

hueso *m* **1 (a)** (Anat) bone; **en los ~s** (fam) nothing but skin and bone(s) (colloq) **(b)** (de color ~** off-white, bone-colored **2** (de fruta) pit (AmE), stone (BrE)

huésped *mf* (en casa, hotel) guest

huesudo -da *adj* bony

hueva *f* **1** *tb* **~s** (Coc) roe; (Zool) spawn **2** (Andes vulg) (testículo): **~s** balls (vulg), bollocks (BrE vulg)

huevada *f* (Andes vulg) (estupidez): **¿dónde compraste esa ~?** where did you buy that crap (sl) *o* (vulg) that shit?; **¡no digas ~s!** don't talk crap! (sl); **déjate de ~s y ponte a trabajar** stop screwing around (AmE) *o* (BrE) pissing about and get on with some work (vulg)

huevear [A1] *vi* (Chi, Per vulg) (perder el tiempo) to goof off (AmE colloq), to piss around (BrE sl)
■ ~ *vt* (Chi vulg) (*persona*) (molestar) to bug (colloq), to hassle (colloq); (tomar el pelo a) to kid

hueveo *m* (Chi vulg) (tomadura de pelo) pisstake (vulg); **agarrar a algn para el ~** to make fun of sb, to take the piss out of sb (BrE sl)

huevera *f* **1** (para guardar huevos) egg box; (para servir huevos) eggcup **2** (Per) (huevas) roe

huevo *m* **1** (Biol, Coc, Zool) egg; **~ a la copa** (Chi) boiled egg; **~ de Pascua** Easter egg; **~ duro** *or* (Ven) **sancochado** hard-boiled egg; **~ escalfado** *or* (Méx, RPl) **poché** poached egg; **~ estrellado** (frito) fried egg; **~ pasado por agua** *or* (Col, Méx) **tibio** soft boiled egg; **~s revueltos** *or* (Col) **pericos** scrambled eggs (*pl*); **a ~: tuve que leer el libro a ~** (Méx vulg) I had no damn *o* (BrE) bloody choice but to read the book (vulg); **comprar/vender a ~** (Andes fam) to buy/sell for peanuts (colloq); **mirar a ~** (Chi fam) to look down on
2 (vulg) (testículo) ball (vulg); *para modismos ver* COJONES 1

huevón -vona *adj* **(a)** (Andes, Ven fam *o* vulg) (tonto, estúpido) (fam) dumb (colloq); **es tan ~** he's so fucking stupid (vulg) **(b)** (Méx vulg) (holgazán) lazy (colloq)
■ *m,f* **(a)** (Andes, Ven vulg) (imbécil) dickhead (vulg), asshole (AmE vulg) **(b)** (Méx vulg) (holgazán) lazy bum (colloq)

huida *f* (fuga) flight; **emprender la ~** to take flight (frml)

huidizo -za *adj* ⟨*mirada*⟩ evasive, shy; ⟨*carácter/persona*⟩ elusive; ⟨*animal*⟩ timid

huila *f* (Chi) rag

huincha *f* **(a)** (Andes) (cinta) ribbon; (en carrera) tape **(b)** (Andes) (para pelo) hair-band **(c)** (Bol, Chi, Per) (para medir) tape measure

huipil *m* (en AmC, Méx) huipil (*traditional embroidered dress worn by Indian women*)

huir [I20] *vi* **(a)** (escapar) to flee (liter *or* journ), escape; **huyó de la cárcel** he escaped from prison; **~ del país** to flee the country **(b)** (tratar de evitar) **~ DE algo** to avoid sth; **~le A algn** to avoid sb

huira *f* (Per) rope

huiro *m* (Chi, Per) seaweed

hule *m* **1** (para mantel) oilcloth; (para ropa impermeable) oilskin **2** (Méx) (goma) rubber

hule-espuma *m* (Méx) foam rubber

hulera *f* (AmC) slingshot (AmE), catapult (BrE)

hulla *f* coal

humanidad *f* **(a)** (los humanos): **la ~** the human race, humanity, mankind **(b)** (piedad, benevolencia) humanity **(c) humanidades** *fpl* (estudios de letras) humanities (*pl*); (enseñanza secundaria) (Chi) secondary education

humanista *mf* humanist

humanitario -ria *adj* humanitarian

humano¹ -na *adj* **(a)** ⟨*naturaleza*⟩ human (*before n*) **(b)** (benevolente) humane

humano² *m* human being; **los ~s** humans

humareda *f* cloud of smoke

humeante *adj* ⟨*leño/lava*⟩ smoking; ⟨*sopa/café*⟩ steaming (hot), piping hot

humear [A1] *vi* «*chimenea/hoguera*» to smoke; «*sopa/café*» to steam

humectante *m* moisturizer

humedad *f* **(a)** (Meteo) dampness; (con calor) humidity **(b)** (en paredes, suelo) damp

humedecer [E3] *vt* to moisten, dampen
■ **humedecerse** *v pron* «*paredes/ropa*» to get damp

húmedo -da *adj* **(a)** (Meteo) damp; (con calor) humid **(b)** ⟨*suelo/casa/ropa*⟩ damp **(c)** ⟨*labios*⟩ moist

humildad *f* **(a)** (sumisión) humility; **con ~** humbly **(b)** (pobreza) humbleness, lowliness

humilde *adj* ⟨*carácter/tono*⟩ meek; ⟨*vivienda/ropa*⟩ humble, lowly

humillación *f* humiliation

humillante *adj* humiliating

humillar [A1] *vt* to humiliate
■ **humillarse** *v pron*: **no se humilla ante nadie** she doesn't kowtow to anyone; **no me voy a ~ a pedirle que vuelva** I'm not going to demean myself by begging him to come back

humita *f* **1** (CS) (Coc) *flavored corn paste wrapped in corn leaves* **2** (Chi) (Indum) bow tie

humo *m* **1** (de tabaco, incendio) smoke; (gases) fumes (*pl*); **echaba ~** smoke was pouring out of it; **hacerse ~** (AmL fam) to make oneself scarce (colloq) **2 humos** *mpl* (aires) airs (*pl*); **¡qué ~s se da!** she really gives herself airs (colloq); **bajarle los ~s a algn** to take sb down a peg or two

humor *m* **(a)** (estado de ánimo) mood; **estar de buen ~** to be in a good mood; **no estoy de ~ para salir** I'm not in the mood to go out **(b)** (gracia) humor*

humorada *f* **(a)** (extravagancia): **hacer una ~** to do something crazy **(b)** (broma) little joke, witticism

humorista *mf* (autor) humorist, comic writer; (dibujante) cartoonist; (cómico) comic, comedian

humorístico -ca *adj* humorous

hundido -da *adj* **(a)** (barco) sunken **(b)** (ojos) deep-set; (por enfermedad) sunken

hundimiento *m* **(a)** (de barco) sinking **(b)** (de negocio) collapse **(c)** (de edificio — bajada de nivel) subsidence; (— derrumbe) collapse

hundir [I1] *vt* (barco) to sink; (persona) to destroy; (negocio/empresa) to drive ... under
■ **hundirse** *v pron* **(a)** «barco» to sink **(b)** (en barro, nieve) to sink **(c)** «empresa/negocio» to fold **(d)** «edificio» (bajar de nivel) to sink, subside; (derrumbarse) to collapse

húngaro¹ -ra *adj/m,f* Hungarian

húngaro² *m* (idioma) Hungarian

Hungría *f* Hungary

huracán *m* hurricane

huraño -ña *adj* (persona) unsociable; (animal) timid

hurgar [A3] *vi* **~ EN algo** (en basura) to rummage o rake THROUGH sth; **~ en el pasado** to delve into the past
■ **hurgarse** *v pron* (refl): **~se la nariz** to pick one's nose

hurguetear [A1] *vi* (CS) **~ EN algo** (en papeles) to nose THROUGH sth; (en cartera) to ferret around in sth
■ **~** *vt* (cajón/cartera) to rummage around in, rummage through
■ **hurguetearse** *v pron* (refl) (esp AmL) ▶ HURGARSE

hurra, hurrah *interj* hurrah!, hooray!

hurtadillas *fpl*: **entrar/salir a ~** to sneak in/out

hurtar [A1] *vt* (frml) to purloin (frml), to steal

hurto *m* (frml) (robo) robbery, theft; (en las tiendas) shoplifting

husmear [A1] *vt* to sniff
■ **~** *vi* **(a)** «perro» to sniff around **(b)** (fam) (fisgonear) to snoop, sniff (around) (colloq)

huso *m* spindle

huy *interj* (fam) (para expresar— dolor) ouch!, ow!; (— asombro) wow!; (— alivio) phew!

huya, huyas, etc ▶ HUIR

I i

I, i *f* (*pl* **íes**) (read as /i/) *tb* **i latina** the letter I, i; **i griega** the letter Y

iba, íbamos, etc ▶ IR

Iberia *f* Iberia

ibérico -ca *adj* Iberian

Iberoamérica *f* Latin America

iberoamericano -na *adj/m,f* Latin American

icaco *m* (Col, Méx, Ven) coco plum

iceberg /'aisβer, 'iθe'βer/ *m* (*pl* **-bergs**) iceberg

icono, ícono *m* icon

ictericia *f* jaundice

ida *f* **(a)** (viaje) outward journey; **a la ~** on the way out; **¿cuánto cuesta la ~?** how much does it cost one way?; **¿saco de ~ y vuelta?** shall I buy a round-trip ticket (AmE) o (BrE) return ticket? **(b)** (partida) departure

idea *f* idea; **la ~ de libertad** the idea o concept of freedom; **es de ~s fijas** he has very set ideas about things; **no tiene ~ de cómo funciona** he has no idea how it works; **no tengo ~** I don't have a clue; **hacerse una ~ de la situación** to get an idea of the situation; **se me ocurre una ~** I've got an idea; **cambió de ~** she changed her mind; **hacerse (a) la ~ de algo** to get used to the idea of sth

ideal *adj* ideal

■ *m* **(a)** (prototipo) ideal **(b)** (aspiración) dream **(c) ideales** *mpl* (valores, principios) ideals (*pl*)

idealismo *m* idealism

idealista *adj* idealistic
■ *mf* idealist

idealizar [A4] *vt* to idealize

ídem *adv* ditto, idem (frml)

idéntico -ca *adj* identical; **es ~ al padre** (físicamente) he looks just like his father, he's the spitting image of his father (colloq); (en el carácter) he's exactly like his father; **~ A algo** identical TO sth

identidad *f* identity

identificar [A2] *vt* to identify
■ **identificarse** *v pron* **(a)** (compenetrarse, solidarizarse) **~se CON algo/algn** to identify WITH sth/sb **(b)** (demostrar la identidad) to identify oneself

ideología *f* ideology

ideológico -ca *adj* ideological

idílico -ca *adj* idyllic

idilio *m* **(a)** (Lit) idyll **(b)** (romance) romance

idioma *m* language

idiota *adj* (fam) (tonto) stupid, idiotic; **¡no seas ~!** don't be such an idiot!
■ *mf* (tonto) (fam) idiot, stupid fool (colloq)

idiotez *f* (fam) (cosa estúpida): **decir idioteces** to talk nonsense; **fue una ~ hacer eso** that was a stupid thing to do

ido, ida adj (distraído) ⟨mirada⟩ faraway (before n); **estás como ~** you seem miles away

ídolo m idol

idóneo -nea adj suitable; **es la persona idónea para el cargo** he's suitable for the job, he's the right person for the job

iglesia f church; **no van a la ~** they don't go to church; **casarse por la ~** or (Bol, Per, RPI) **por ~** to have a church wedding

iglú m igloo

ignorancia f ignorance; **por ~** out of o through ignorance

ignorante adj (a) (sin instrucción) ignorant (b) (sin información): **estar ~ de algo** to be unaware of sth
■ mf ignoramus, ignorant fool (colloq)

ignorar [A1] vt (a) (desconocer): **lo ignoro** I've no idea; **ignoran las causas del accidente** they do not know what caused the accident; **ignora los peligros que le acechan** he's unaware of the dangers which await him (b) (no hacer caso de) to ignore

igual adj 1 (a) (idéntico): **de ~ peso** of equal o the same weight; **son ~es** they are the same o alike; **de forma son ~es** they're the same shape; **~ A** or **QUE algo/algn** the same AS sth/sb; **es ~ita a** or **que su madre** (físicamente) she looks just like her mother; (en personalidad) she's exactly the same as o just like her mother; **es ~ a x** (Mat) it equals x; **me/nos es** or **da ~** I/we don't mind, it makes no difference to me/to us (b) (en una jerarquía) equal; **~es ante la ley** equal in the eyes of the law
2 (en tenis): **quince ~es** fifteen all; **van ~es** they're even
■ adv 1 (a) (de la misma manera): **los trato a todos ~** I treat them all the same (b) (en locs) **al igual que** (frml) as, like; **igual que: tiene pecas, ~ que su hermano** she has freckles, (just) like her brother; **se llama ~ que su padre** he's named after his father; **me aburrí — ~ que yo** I got bored — so did I o me too; **opino ~ que tú** I agree with you; **por igual** equally
2 (de todos modos) anyway
3 (expresando posibilidad): **~ llueve y no podemos salir** it might rain and then we won't be able to go out; **~ llamaron y no estábamos** they may have called and we weren't in
■ mf (par) equal; **le habló de ~ a ~** he spoke to him on equal terms; **me trató de ~ a ~** she treated me as an equal; **sin ~** ⟨belleza/talento⟩ unequaled*, matchless (frml); **es un compositor sin ~** he's unrivaled as a composer
■ m (signo) equals sign

igualado -da adj 1 (a) (Dep): **van muy ~s** they're very close, they're neck and neck; **quedaron ~s** they drew; **iban ~s a tres** they were level at three-three (b) ⟨superficie⟩ even, level 2 (Méx fam) (irrespetuoso) sassy (AmE colloq), cheeky (BrE colloq)

igualar [A1] vt 1 (a) ⟨superficie/terreno⟩ to level, level off; ⟨flequillo/dobladillo⟩ to even up, make ... straight (b) ⟨salarios⟩ to make ... equal o the same; **~ algo CON** or **A algo** to make sth the same AS sth 2 ⟨éxito/récord⟩ to equal, match
■ **igualarse** v pron: **nada se le iguala** it has no equal, there's nothing like it; **~se A** or **CON algo** to match o equal sth

igualdad f equality; **~ de oportunidades** equal opportunities; **en ~ de condiciones** on equal terms

igualmente adv (a) (en fórmulas de cortesía): **que lo pases muy bien — igualmente** have a great time — you too o and you (b) ⟨bueno/malo⟩ equally (c) (frml) (también) likewise

iguana f (Zool) iguana

ilegal adj illegal; **de manera ~** illegally

ilegible adj illegible, unreadable

ilegítimo -ma adj ⟨hijo⟩ illegitimate

ileso -sa adj unhurt, unharmed

ilícito -ta adj illicit

ilimitado -da adj unlimited

ilógico -ca adj illogical

iluminación f (de habitación) lighting; (de monumento) illumination; (Teatr) lighting

iluminar [A1] vt (a) ⟨calles⟩ to light, illuminate; ⟨monumento⟩ to illuminate; ⟨escenario⟩ to light (b) (con focos muy potentes) ⟨estadio⟩ to floodlight (c) ⟨rostro/ojos⟩ (liter) to light up

ilusión f 1 (a) (esperanza) hope; **no te hagas ilusiones** don't build your hopes up; **no me hago muchas ilusiones** I'm not very hopeful; **su mayor ~ es ...** her dearest o fondest wish is ... (b) (esp Esp) (alegría, satisfacción): **me hizo mucha ~** I was thrilled; **le hace ~ el viaje** he's looking forward to the trip; **¡qué ~!** isn't it wonderful! 2 (noción falsa) illusion

ilusionar [A1] vt: **me ilusiona mucho** I'm very excited about it; **no la ilusiones** don't raise her hopes
■ **ilusionarse** v pron (a) (hacerse ilusiones) to build one's hopes up (b) (entusiasmarse) **~se CON algo** to get excited ABOUT sth

iluso -sa adj naive
■ m,f dreamer

ilustración f illustration

ilustrado -da adj (a) ⟨revista/libro⟩ illustrated (b) (frml) ⟨persona⟩ erudite, learned

ilustrar [A1] vt to illustrate

ilustre adj illustrious, distinguished

imagen f 1 (a) (Fís, Ópt) image; (TV) picture, image (b) (foto) picture (c) (en espejo) reflection; **ser la viva ~ de algn** to be the image of sb (d) (en la mente) picture 2 (de político, cantante, país) image

imaginación f imagination; **¡ni (se) me pasó por la ~!** it never even crossed my mind!; **son imaginaciones tuyas** you're imagining things

imaginar [A1] vt (a) (suponer, figurarse) ▶ IMAGINARSE (b) (idear) ⟨plan/método⟩ to think up, come up with
■ **imaginarse** v pron to imagine; **me imagino que no querrá ir** I don't imagine o suppose he feels like going; **no te puedes ~ lo mal que nos trató** you've no idea how badly she treated us; **¿quedó contento? — ¡imagínate!** was he pleased? — what do you think!; **me imagino que sí** I suppose so; **me lo imaginaba más alto** I imagined he'd be taller

imaginario -ria adj imaginary

imaginativo -va adj imaginative

imán m magnet

imbécil adj (a) (fam) (tonto) stupid (b) (Med) imbecilic

■ *mf* **(a)** (fam) (tonto) stupid idiot, moron (colloq & pej) **(b)** (Med) imbecile

imberbe *adj*: un joven ∼ (sin barba) a beardless youth; (sin experiencia) a callow youth, a fresh-faced youth

imborrable *adj* lasting (*before n*), indelible

imitación *f* **(a)** (acción) imitation **(b)** (parodia) impression **(c)** (copia) imitation; bolso ∼ cuero imitation-leather bag

imitador -dora *m,f* (Teatr) impressionist, impersonator; (plagiario) imitator

imitar [A1] *vt* **(a)** (persona) (copiar) to copy, imitate; (para hacer reír) to do an impression of, mimic; se sentó y todos lo ∼on he sat down and everyone followed suit **(b)** (voz/gesto/estilo) to imitate; (para hacer reír) to imitate, mimic **(c)** (tener el aspecto de) to simulate

impaciencia *f* impatience

impacientarse [A1] *v pron* (por retraso) to get impatient; (exasperarse) to lose (one's) patience, get exasperated

impaciente *adj* **(a)** [SER] impatient **(b)** [ESTAR]: estaba ∼ he was (getting) impatient; ∼ POR hacer algo impatient to do sth

impactante *adj* (noticia) shocking; (libro/imagen) powerful; (espectáculo/efecto) stunning, impressive

impactar [A1] *vt* **(a)** (golpear) to hit **(b)** (impresionar) to have a profound impact on ■ ∼ *vi* **(a)** (impresionar) to shock **(b)** (chocar) to hit, strike

impacto *m* **(a)** (choque) impact; recibió un ∼ de bala she was shot **(b)** (huella, señal) hole, mark; el cadáver tiene varios ∼s de bala there are several bullet wounds in the body **(c)** (en el ánimo, público) impact **(d)** (Inf) hit

impago -ga *adj* (AmL) (persona) unpaid; (deuda/impuesto) unpaid, outstanding

impalpable *adj* impalpable

impar *adj* (número) odd ■ *m* odd number

imparcial *adj* impartial, unbiased

imparcialidad *f* impartiality

impasible *adj* impassive

impecable *adj* impeccable; va siempre ∼ she is always impeccably dressed

impedido -da *adj* disabled ■ *m,f* disabled person

impedimento *m* obstacle, impediment; si no surge ningún ∼ if there are no hitches; ∼ físico physical handicap

impedir [I14] *vt* **(a)** (imposibilitar) to prevent; nadie te lo impide nobody's stopping you; ∼le a algn hacer algo to prevent sb FROM doing sth; quiso ∼ que nos viéramos he tried to stop us seeing each other **(b)** (paso/entrada) to block **(c)** (dificultar) to hamper, hinder

impenetrable *adj* (bosque) impenetrable; (fortaleza) impregnable **(b)** (persona/expresión) inscrutable; (misterio/secreto) unfathomable

impensable *adj* unthinkable, inconceivable

imperante *adj* (moda/tendencia/condiciones) prevailing (*before n*); (dinastía/régimen) ruling (*before n*)

imperativo¹ -va *adj* **(a)** (Ling) imperative **(b)** (voz/tono) commanding, authoritative

imperativo² *m* imperative

imperdible *m* safety pin

imperdonable *adj* (error/comportamiento) unforgivable, inexcusable

imperfección *f* **(a)** (en tela) flaw; (en mecanismo) defect **(b)** (cualidad) imperfection

imperfecto¹ -ta *adj* **1** (trabajo/tela/facciones) flawed **2** (Ling) imperfect

imperfecto² *m* imperfect (tense)

imperial *adj* (dinastía/corona) imperial

imperialismo *m* imperialism

imperialista *adj/mf* imperialist

imperio *m* empire

impermeable *adj* (material/tela) waterproof, impermeable (tech) ■ *m* (Indum) raincoat

impersonal *adj* impersonal

impersonar [A1] *vt* (Méx) to impersonate

impertinencia *f* **(a)** (cualidad) impertinence **(b)** (hecho, dicho): me dijo que me callara — ¡qué ∼! he told me to shut up — how impertinent!; me contestó con una ∼ she gave me a very cheeky reply

impertinente *adj* (persona/pregunta/tono) impertinent; (comentario) uncalled-for ■ *mf* (persona): eres una ∼ you're extremely impertinent

imperturbable *adj* **(a)** [SER] (sereno) imperturbable **(b)** [ESTAR] (ante un peligro) unperturbed **(c)** (rostro/sonrisa) impassive

ímpetu *m* **(a)** (Fís, Mec) impetus, momentum **(b)** (energía, ardor) vigor*, energy **(c)** (violencia) force

impetuoso -sa *adj* impetuous, impulsive

impida, impidas, etc ▶ IMPEDIR

implacable *adj* **(a)** (odio/furia) implacable; (avance/lucha) relentless; (sol) relentless **(b)** (juez/crítico) implacable **(c)** (enemigo/contrincante) ruthless

implantar [A1] *vt* **1** (método/norma/moda) to introduce; (régimen político) to establish; (estado de excepción) to impose **2** (embrión/cabello) to implant

implante *m* implant

implementar [A1] *vt* **1** (medidas/plan) to implement **2** (Ven) (instalar) to install*, set up

implicación *f* **1** (participación) involvement **2** implicaciones *fpl* (consecuencias) implications (*pl*)

implicancia *f* (AmL) (consecuencia) implication

implicar [A2] *vt* **1** (significar, conllevar) to entail, involve **2** (envolver, enredar) to involve; estuvo implicado en un delito (participó) he was involved in a crime; (estuvo bajo sospecha) he was implicated in a crime ■ **implicarse** *v pron* to get involved

implícito -ta *adj* implicit

implorar [A1] *vt* (perdón/ayuda) to beg for; ∼le algo A algn to beg sth OF sb; ∼ a algn QUE haga algo to implore o beg sb TO do sth

imponente *adj* (belleza) impressive; (edificio/paisaje) imposing, impressive

imponer [E22] *vt* (frml) **(a)** to impose (frml); le impusieron una pena de un año de cárcel he was ⋯⟡

sentenced to one year in prison **(b)** ‹*respeto*› to command; ‹*temor*› to inspire, instill* **(c)** ‹*moda*› to set

■ **imponerse** *v pron* **1** **(a)** (*refl*) ‹*horario/meta*› to set oneself **(b)** ‹*idea*› to become established **(c)** ‹*color/estilo*› to come into fashion **2** (hacerse respetar) to assert oneself *o* one's authority **3** (*frml*) (vencer) to win; **se impondrá el sentido común** common sense will prevail

importación *f* **(a)** (acción) importation; **de ~** ‹*artículos/mercancías*› imported; ‹*permiso*› import (*before n*) **(b) importaciones** *fpl* (mercancías) imports (*pl*)

importado -da *adj* imported

importador -dora *adj*: **países ~es de petróleo** oil-importing countries

■ *m,f* importer

importancia *f* importance; **darle ~ a algo** to attach importance to sth; **quitarle ~ a algo** to play down the importance of sth; **detalles sin ~** minor *o* insignificant details; **no tiene ~** it doesn't matter; **darse ~** to give oneself airs

importante *adj* **(a)** ‹*noticia/persona*› important; ‹*acontecimiento/cambio*› important, significant; **dárselas de** *or* **hacerse el ~** to give oneself airs **(b)** ‹*pérdidas*› serious, considerable; ‹*daños*› severe, considerable; ‹*cantidad*› considerable, significant

importar [A1] *vi* **(a)** (tener importancia, interés) to matter; **no importa quién lo haga** it doesn't matter *o* it makes no difference who does it; **lo que importa es que te recuperes** the important thing is for you to get better; **no me importa lo que piense** I don't care what he thinks; **¿a mí qué me importa?** what do I care?; **¿a ti qué te importa?** what business is it of yours?; **yo no le importo** I don't mean a thing to him; *me importa un bledo or un comino or un pepino or un rábano* (fam) I couldn't care less, I don't give a damn (colloq); *meterse en lo que no le importa* (fam) to poke one's nose into other people's business (colloq); **no te metas en lo que no te importa** mind your own business! **(b)** (molestar): **no me ~ía venir el sábado** I wouldn't mind coming on Saturday; **no me importa que me llame a casa** I don't mind him calling me at home

■ **~** *vt* (Com, Fin) ‹*productos*› to import

importe *m* **(a)** (de factura, letra) amount; **el ~ total** the full *o* total amount; **el ~ de la compra** the purchase price **(b)** (costo) cost

importunar [A1] *vt* (frml) to inconvenience, disturb

■ **~** *vi*: **espero no ~** I hope it's not inconvenient, I hope I'm not disturbing you

importuno -na *adj* inopportune

imposibilitado -da *adj* [ESTAR] (Med) disabled

imposibilitar [A1] *vt* **(a)** (hacer imposible) to make ... impossible **(b)** (impedir) to prevent

imposible *adj* **1** [SER] ‹*sueño/amor*› impossible; **me es ~ acompañarte** I won't be able to go with you; **es ~ que lo sepan** they can't

possibly know; **hicieron lo ~** they did everything they could **2** (inaguantable) ‹*persona*› impossible; **está ~ hoy** he's (being) impossible today

impositivo -va *adj* ‹*sistema/reforma*› tax (*before n*)

impostor -tora *m,f* impostor

impotencia *f* (falta de poder) powerlessness, helplessness; (Med) impotence

impotente *adj* (incapaz, sin poder) powerless, helpless; (Med) impotent

impreciso -sa *adj* vague, imprecise; **un número ~ de personas** an indeterminate number of people

impredecible *adj* unpredictable

imprenta *f* (taller) printer's; (aparato) (printing) press

imprescindible *adj* ‹*requisito/herramienta/factor*› essential, indispensable; **lleva lo ~** take the bare essentials; **es ~ hacerlo** it is essential to do it; **es ~ que nos acompañe** it is essential that you come with us

impresión *f* **(a)** (idea, sensación) impression; **nos causó** *or* **nos hizo muy buena ~** he made a very good impression on us; **da la ~ de ser demasiado ancho** it looks too wide; **me da/tengo la ~ de que me está mintiendo** I have a feeling he's lying to me; **cambiar impresiones** to exchange ideas **(b)** (sensación desagradable): **el accidente me produjo mucha ~** the accident really shocked me

impresionable *adj* squeamish, easily affected

impresionante *adj* ‹*éxito/cantidad/paisaje*› amazing, incredible; ‹*accidente*› horrific

impresionar [A1] *vt* **1** **(a)** (causar buena impresión): **París me impresionó** I was really taken with Paris **(b)** (afectar) to affect; **verlo llorar me impresionó mucho** seeing him cry really affected *o* moved me **(c)** (alarmar) to shock; **me impresionó verla tan delgada** it shocked me to see her looking so thin **(d)** (sorprender) to strike **2** (Fot) ‹*película*› to expose

■ **~** *vi* to impress

impresionismo *m* impressionism

impresionista *adj* ‹*movimiento/pintor*› Impressionist; ‹*estilo/descripción*› impressionistic

impreso¹ -sa *pp*: ▶ IMPRIMIR

impreso² *m* (formulario) form; **~ de solicitud** application form

impresora *f* (Inf) printer; **~ láser** *or* **de láser** laser printer

imprevisible *adj* ‹*hecho/factor*› unforeseeable; ‹*persona*› unpredictable

imprevisión *f* lack of foresight

imprevisto¹ -ta *adj* unforeseen, unexpected; **de modo ~** unexpectedly

imprevisto² *m* unforeseen event (*o* factor *etc*); **si no surge ningún ~** if nothing unexpected happens

imprimir [I36] *vt* (Impr) to print; **impreso en Perú** printed in Peru

AmC	Central America	Arg	Argentina	Cu	Cuba	Per	Peru
AmL	Latin America	Bol	Bolivia	Ec	Ecuador	RPI	River Plate Area
AmS	South America	Chi	Chile	Esp	Spain	Ur	Uruguay
Andes	Andean Region	CS	Southern Cone	Méx	Mexico	Ven	Venezuela

223

improbable *adj* unlikely, improbable

impropio -pia *adj* **(a)** ⟨*actitud/respuesta*⟩ inappropriate; **un comportamiento ~ de una persona educada** behavior unbecoming to an educated person (frml) **(b)** (incorrecto) incorrect

improvisación *f* (acción) improvisation; (actuación) impromptu performance

improvisar [A1] *vt* to improvise; **~ una comida** to rustle up a meal
■ *vi* «*actor/músico*» to improvise

improviso: **de ~** (loc adv) ⟨*llegar/aparecer*⟩ unexpectedly, out of the blue

imprudencia *f* imprudence; **no cometas esa ~** don't be so rash *o* reckless; **su ~ al conducir** his reckless driving

imprudente *adj* (que actúa sin cuidado) imprudent, careless; (temerario) reckless; **fuiste muy ~ al decírselo** it was very rash *o* imprudent of you to tell him

impúdico -ca *adj* (frml *o* hum) **(a)** (obsceno) indecent **(b)** (desvergonzado) shameless

impuesto *m* tax; **libre de ~s** tax-free, duty-free; **~ a *or* sobre la renta** income tax; **~ de circulación** road tax

impugnar [A1] *vt* ⟨*decisión/fallo*⟩ to contest, challenge

impulsar [A1] *vt* **(a)** ⟨*motor/vehículo*⟩ to propel, drive **(b)** ⟨*persona*⟩ to drive **(c)** ⟨*comercio, producción*⟩ to boost, give a boost to; ⟨*cultura/ relaciones*⟩ to promote

impulsivo -va *adj* impulsive

impulso *m* **(a)** (empuje): **un fuerte ~ para el comercio** a major boost for trade; **dar ~ a algo** (a comercio) to give a boost to sth; (a iniciativa) to give impetus to sth; **tomar** *or* **darse ~** to gather momentum, to get up speed **(b)** (reacción, deseo) impulse; **mi primer ~ fue ...** my first instinct was ... **(c)** (Fís) impulse

impuntualidad *f* unpunctuality

impureza *f* impurity

impuro -ra *adj* impure

impuse, impuso, etc ▶ IMPONER

in *adj inv* ⟨*discoteca*⟩ trendy (colloq); **lo que está muy ~** the in thing (colloq), the trendy thing (colloq)

inaccesible *adj* **(a)** ⟨*montaña/persona/ concepto*⟩ inaccessible **(b)** (crit) ⟨*precios*⟩ prohibitive; ⟨*objetivo*⟩ unattainable

inaceptable *adj* unacceptable

inactividad *f* inactivity

inactivo -va *adj* inactive

inadaptación *f* failure to adapt

inadaptado -da *adj* maladjusted

inadecuado -da *adj* ⟨*color/traje*⟩ inappropriate, unsuitable; ⟨*norma/sistema*⟩ inadequate

inadmisible *adj* **(a)** ⟨*comportamiento/ pretensiones*⟩ unacceptable, inadmissible **(b)** (Der) inadmissible

inadvertido -da *adj* (no notado): **pasar ~** to go unnoticed

inagotable *adj* ⟨*fuente/reservas*⟩ inexhaustible, endless

inaguantable *adj* unbearable

inalámbrico -ca *adj* ⟨*teléfono*⟩ cordless; ⟨*comunicaciones*⟩ wireless

inalcanzable *adj* unattainable, unachievable

inanimado -da *adj* inanimate

inapetente *adj* lacking in appetite

inapreciable *adj* **1** (muy valioso) ⟨*ayuda/ amistad*⟩ invaluable; **un cuadro de un valor ~** a priceless painting **2** (insignificante) negligible

inapropiado -da *adj* inappropriate

inaudible *adj* inaudible

inaudito -ta *adj* ⟨*decisión/suceso*⟩ unprecedented

inauguración *f* opening, inauguration (frml)

inaugurar [A1] *vt* ⟨*teatro/hospital*⟩ to open, inaugurate (frml); ⟨*monumento*⟩ to unveil; ⟨*exposición/sesión*⟩ to open

inca *mf* Inca

incaico -ca *adj* Inca, Incaic

incalculable *adj* inestimable, incalculable

incandescente *adj* incandescent

incansable *adj* tireless

incapacidad *f* **1** (física) disability, physical handicap; (mental) mental handicap; (Der) incapacity; **~ laboral** invalidity **2** (ineptitud) incompetence; (falta de capacidad) inability **3** (Col) (baja) sick leave

incapacitado -da *adj* (físicamente) disabled, physically handicapped; (mentalmente) mentally handicapped

incapacitar [A1] *vt* «*enfermedad*» to incapacitate; **la lesión lo incapacita para su trabajo** the injury has made him unfit for work

incapaz *adj* [SER] (de un logro, una hazaña): **no lo conseguirá nunca, es ~** he'll never do it, he simply isn't capable; **es ~ de una cosa así** he's incapable of doing something like that; **es ~ de llamarme** he can't even be bothered to phone me
■ *mf* (inútil, inepto) incompetent (fool)

incendiar [A1] *vt* **(a)** (prender fuego a) to set fire to **(b)** (quemar) ⟨*edificio*⟩ to burn down; ⟨*coche*⟩ to burn; ⟨*pueblo/bosque*⟩ to burn ... to the ground
■ **incendiarse** *v pron* **(a)** (empezar a arder) to catch fire **(b)** (destruirse) ⟨*edificio*⟩ to be burned down; **los bosques que se ~on** the forests that were destroyed by fire

incendiario -ria *m,f* arsonist

incendio *m* fire; **~ provocado** arson attack

incentivo *m* incentive

incertidumbre *f* uncertainty

incesante *adj* incessant

incesto *m* incest

incestuoso -sa *adj* incestuous

incidente *m* incident

incienso *m* incense; (Bib) frankincense

incierto -ta *adj* (dudoso, inseguro) uncertain

incineración *f* **(a)** (de basura) incineration **(b)** (de cadáveres) cremation

incinerador *m* incinerator

incinerar [A1] *vt* ⟨*basura*⟩ to incinerate, burn; ⟨*cadáver*⟩ to cremate

incitar [A1] *vt* **~ a algn A algo** to incite sb TO sth; **~ a algn CONTRA algn** to incite sb AGAINST sb

incivilizado -da *adj* uncivilized

inclinación *f* **1 (a)** (pendiente) slope **(b)** (ángulo) inclination **2** (movimiento del cuerpo) bow; ⋯⫶

asintió con una ∼ de la cabeza he nodded (his head) in agreement **3** (interés, tendencia): **tener ∼ por** *or* **hacia la música** to have a musical bent *o* musical inclinations; **inclinaciones políticas/ sexuales** political/sexual leanings

inclinado -da *adj* **1** ‹*tejado/terreno*› sloping; ‹*torre*› leaning (*before n*); ‹*cuadro*› crooked; **una pendiente muy inclinada** a very steep slope *o* incline **2** (predispuesto): **sentirse ∼ a hacer algo** to feel inclined to do sth

inclinar [A1] *vt* **1** ‹*botella/sombrilla/plato*› to tilt; **inclinó la cabeza a un lado** she tilted her head to one side; **inclinó la cabeza en señal de asentimiento** he nodded (his head) in agreement; **∼ el cuerpo** to bend over; (en señal de respeto) to bow; **el viento inclinaba los árboles** the wind bent the trees

2 (inducir, predisponer) ‹*persona*›: **ello me inclina a pensar que ...** this inclines me to think that ... (frml)

■ **inclinarse** *v pron* **1** (tender) **∼se a hacer algo** to be inclined to do sth; **me inclino por su candidato** I'm inclined to go for your candidate; **me ∼ía por esta opción** I would tend to favor this option

2 (doblarse) to bend; (en señal de respeto) to bow; **∼se ante algn** to bow to sb; **se inclinó sobre la cuna** she leaned over the cradle; **∼se hacia adelante/atrás** to lean forward/back

incluir [I20] *vt* **1** (comprender) **(a)** ‹*impuestos/ gastos*› to include; **$500 todo incluido** $500 all inclusive *o* all in **(b)** ‹*tema/sección*› to include, contain **2** (poner, agregar) **(a)** (en un grupo) to include **(b)** (en una carta) to enclose

inclusive *adj inv* inclusive; **del 10 al 18, ambos ∼** from 10 to 18 inclusive; **domingos ∼** including Sundays

incluso *adv* even

incógnita *f* **(a)** (Mat) unknown (factor *o* quantity) **(b)** (misterio) mystery

incógnito: de ∼ (loc adv) incognito

incoherente *adj* incoherent, illogical

incoloro -ra *adj* colorless*

incomible *adj* inedible, uneatable

incómodo -da *adj* **(a)** (en general) uncomfortable; **¿no estás ∼ en esa silla?** aren't you uncomfortable in that chair?; **se siente muy ∼ en las fiestas** he feels ill at ease *o* uncomfortable at parties **(b)** (inconveniente) inconvenient; **es muy ∼ vivir tan lejos** it's very inconvenient living so far away

incompatibilidad *f* mutual incompatibility; **∼ de caracteres** incompatibility

incompatible *adj* ‹*personas/caracteres*› incompatible; **el horario de clases es ∼ con el de mi trabajo** the times of the classes clash with my work hours

incompetente *adj/mf* incompetent

incompleto -ta *adj* incomplete

incomprensible *adj* incomprehensible

incomprensión *f* lack of understanding

incomunicado -da *adj* ‹*prisionero*› in solitary confinement; **hay varios pueblos ∼s** several villages have been cut off

inconcebible *adj* inconceivable

inconcluso -sa *adj* unfinished

incondicional *adj* **(a)** ‹*apoyo*› unconditional, wholehearted; ‹*obediencia*› absolute; ‹*aliado/ admirador*› staunch; ‹*amigo*› true, loyal **(b)** ‹*rendición*› unconditional

inconexo -xa *adj* unconnected

inconfesable *adj* unmentionable

inconformista *adj/mf* nonconformist

inconfundible *adj* unmistakable

incongruente *adj* ‹*imágenes*› unconnected; **decía palabras ∼s** his words didn't make sense

inconsciencia *f* **(a)** (Med) unconsciousness **(b)** (insensatez) irresponsibility

inconsciente *adj* **1** [ESTAR] (Med) unconscious **2** [SER] (insensato) irresponsible **3** [SER] (no voluntario) ‹*movimiento/gesto*› unwitting, unconscious; **de una manera ∼** unconsciously

■ *mf* irresponsible person; **son unos ∼s** they are very irresponsible

inconsecuente *adj*: **ser ∼ con uno mismo** to be inconsistent with one's principles

inconsistente *adj* **(a)** ‹*material*› flimsy, weak **(b)** ‹*argumento*› (falto de solidez) weak, flimsy; (falto de coherencia) inconsistent, flawed

inconsolable *adj* inconsolable

inconstante *adj* **(a)** (falto de perseverancia) lacking in perseverance **(b)** (voluble) fickle

inconstitucional *adj* unconstitutional

incontable *adj* countless, innumerable

incontrolado -da *adj* **(a)** ‹*furia/pasión/ira*› uncontrolled, unbridled (liter) **(b)** ‹*llanto/risa*› uncontrollable

inconveniencia *f* **(a)** (cualidad) inconvenience **(b)** (comentario inoportuno) tactless remark

inconveniente *adj* (incómodo) ‹*hora/fecha*› inconvenient

■ *m* **(a)** (problema) problem; **si no surge ningún ∼** if everything goes according to plan, if there are no problems; **¿habría algún ∼ en que nos quedemos?** would it be alright if we stayed? **(b)** (desventaja) drawback; **tiene sus ∼s** it has its disadvantages *o* drawbacks **(c)** (objeción) objection; **no tengo ∼** I have no objection; **no tengo ∼ en decírselo** I don't mind telling him; **no veo ningún ∼ en que venga** I see no reason why he shouldn't come

incordiar [A1] *vt* (Esp fam) to annoy, to pester (colloq)

■ *vi* (Esp): **¡no incordies!** don't be such a nuisance!

incordio *m* (Esp fam) nuisance, pain in the neck (colloq)

incorporación *f* incorporation

incorporado -da *adj* integral, built-in

incorporar [A1] *vt* (frml) **1 (a)** (agregar) to add; **∼ algo a algo** to add sth TO sth **(b)** (integrar) to incorporate **2** ‹*enfermo/niño*› to sit ... up

■ **incorporarse** *v pron* (frml) **1** (a equipo, puesto) to join; **∼se a algo** to join sth **2** (levantarse) to sit up

incorrecto -ta *adj* **(a)** ‹*respuesta/ interpretación*› incorrect, wrong **(b)** ‹*comportamiento*› impolite, discourteous (frml)

incorregible *adj* ‹*mentiroso/idealista*› incorrigible; ‹*defecto*› irremediable, irreparable

incredulidad *f* skepticism*

incrédulo -la *adj* skeptical*
■ *m,f* skeptic*

increíble *adj* incredible, unbelievable

incrementar [A1] *vt* (frml) to increase

incremento *m* (frml) increase

incriminar [A1] *vt* (frml) **(a)** «*pruebas*» to incriminate **(b)** (acusar, inculpar) to charge

incrustación *f* **(a)** (de madera, metal) inlay **(b)** (Col) (Odont) filling

incrustar [A1] *vt* ⟨*piedra preciosa*⟩ ~ algo EN algo to set sth in sth
■ **incrustarse** *v pron* ~se EN algo «*bala*» to embed itself IN sth; «*suciedad*» to get embedded IN sth

incubadora *f* incubator

incubar [A1] *vt* to incubate

inculcar [A2] *vt* to instill*, inculcate (frml); **las ideas que les inculcan** the ideas they fill their heads with

inculto -ta *adj* (sin cultura) uncultured, uneducated; (ignorante) ignorant
■ *m,f* **(a)** (persona sin cultura): **es un** ~ he's uneducated **(b)** (persona ignorante) ignorant person

incumplido -da *adj* (AmL exc CS) unreliable

incumplidor -dora *adj* (CS) unreliable

incumplir [I1] *vt* ⟨*ley/promesa*⟩ to break; ⟨*contrato*⟩ to breach
■ ~ *vi* (AmL exc CS): **no me vayas a** ~ don't let me down; **incumplió a la cita** she didn't show *o* turn up

incurable *adj* incurable

indagación *f* (frml) investigation; **hacer indagaciones** to make inquiries, to investigate

indagar [A3] (frml) *vi* to investigate; ~ SOBRE algo to investigate sth

indecencia *f* **(a)** (cualidad) indecency **(b)** (cosa, hecho): **presentarse así en público es una** ~ it's indecent to appear in public like that

indecente *adj* ⟨*persona/vestido*⟩ indecent; ⟨*película/lenguaje*⟩ obscene
■ *mf* rude *o* shameless person

indecisión *f* indecision

indeciso -sa *adj* ⟨*persona*⟩ **(a)** [SER] indecisive **(b)** [ESTAR] undecided
■ *m,f* **(a)** (en general) indecisive person **(b)** (sobre un tema): **hay un gran número de** ~s there are a lot of people who are as yet undecided

indecoroso -sa *adj* unseemly, indecorous (frml)

indefenso -sa *adj* ⟨*niño/animal*⟩ defenseless*; ⟨*fortaleza*⟩ undefended

indefinido -da *adj* **(a)** ⟨*forma*⟩ undefined, vague; **un color** ~ a difficult color to describe **(b)** (ilimitado) indefinite, unlimited; **por tiempo** ~ for an indefinite *o* unlimited period

indemnización *f* **(a)** (por pérdidas sufridas) compensation, indemnity (frml); (por posibles pérdidas) indemnity (frml); ~ **por daños y perjuicios** damages (*pl*) **(b)** (por despido) severance pay

indemnizar [A4] *vt* **(a)** (por pérdidas sufridas) to compensate, indemnify (frml); (por posibles pérdidas) to indemnify (frml); **fue indemnizado con dos**

millones de pesetas he was given two million pesetas (in) compensation **(b)** (por despido) to pay severance pay to

independencia *f* independence

independentista *adj* ⟨*político/ideas*⟩ pro-independence (*before n*)
■ *mf* supporter of the independence movement

independiente *adj/mf* independent

independizarse [A4] *v pron* to become independent, gain independence; ~ DE algn to become independent OF sb

indescriptible *adj* indescribable

indestructible *adj* indestructible

indeterminado -da *adj* **(a)** (indefinido) indefinite; **por tiempo** ~ indefinitely **(b)** (no establecido) undetermined **(c)** (vago, impreciso) ⟨*contorno/forma*⟩ indeterminate **(d)** (Ling) indefinite

India *f*: **la** ~ India

indicación *f* **(a)** (instrucción) instruction; **me dio indicaciones de cómo llegar** he gave me directions as to how to get there **(b)** (muestra) indication; **no dio ninguna** ~ **de sus intenciones** she gave no indication of her intentions

indicado -da *adj* **(a)** (adecuado) suitable; **es el menos** ~ **para hacerlo** he's the last person who should do it; **lo más** ~ **sería** ... the best thing to do would be ... **(b)** (señalado) ⟨*hora/fecha*⟩ specified

indicador *m* (Auto) indicator **(b)** (señal de tráfico) sign **(c)** (del aceite, gasolina) gauge; ~ **de velocidad** speedometer

indicar [A2] *vt* to indicate, show; **hay una flecha que indica el camino** there's an arrow indicating the way; **¿me podría** ~ **cómo llegar allí?** could you tell me how to get there?; **me indicó el lugar en el mapa** he showed me *o* pointed out the place on the map; **todo parece** ~ **que** ... there is every indication that ...; **el asterisco indica que** ... the asterisk indicates *o* shows that ...

indicativo *m* (Ling) indicative; **presente de** ~ present indicative

índice *m* **1** (de una publicación) index; (catálogo) catalog* **2** (Anat) index finger, forefinger **3** (tasa, coeficiente) rate; ~ **de natalidad** birth rate

indicio *m* **(a)** (señal, huella) sign, indication **(b)** (vestigio) trace, sign; ~**s de potasio** traces of potassium

Índico *adj*: **el** (Océano) ~ the Indian Ocean

indiferencia *f* indifference

indiferente *adj* **(a)** (poco importante, de poco interés): **es** ~ **que venga hoy o mañana** it doesn't matter *o* it makes no difference whether he comes today *o* tomorrow; **me es** ~ **su amistad** I'm not concerned *o* (colloq) bothered about his friendship **(b)** (poco interesado) indifferent; ~ A algo indifferent TO sth

indígena *adj* indigenous, native (*before n*)
■ *mf* native

indigestión *f* indigestion

indignación *f* indignation, anger; (más fuerte) outrage; **sentí una gran** ~ I was outraged

indignado -da *adj* indignant, angry; (más fuerte) outraged, incensed

indignante *adj* outrageous

indignar [A1] *vt* to make ... angry *o* indignant; (más fuerte) to outrage
■ **indignarse** *v pron* to get angry, become indignant; (más fuerte) to be outraged *o* incensed

indigno -na *adj* (a) (impropio) unworthy; ~ **DE algn** unworthy OF sb (b) (no merecedor) unworthy (c) (humillante) degrading, humiliating (d) (vergonzoso) shameful, disgraceful

indio -dia *adj* (a) (de América) (American) Indian, Amerindian (b) (de la India) Indian, of/from India
■ *m,f* (a) (de América) (American) Indian, Amerindian (b) (de la India) Indian

indirecta *f* hint; **lanzar** *or* **soltar una** ~ to drop a hint

indirecto -ta *adj* indirect

indisciplinado -da *adj* ⟨alumno⟩ undisciplined, unruly; ⟨soldado⟩ insubordinate

indiscreción *f* (a) (dicho, declaración — que molesta) indiscreet *o* tactless remark; (— que revela un secreto) indiscreet *o* unguarded remark; ¿**su edad, si no es** ~? how old are you, if you don't mind my asking?; **cometió la** ~ **de preguntárselo** he was indiscreet *o* tactless enough to ask her (b) (cualidad) lack of discretion

indiscreto -ta *adj* (a) (falto de tacto) indiscreet, tactless (b) (que revela un secreto) indiscreet

indiscutible *adj* (a) ⟨pruebas/hecho/verdad⟩ indisputable (b) ⟨líder/campeón⟩ undisputed

indispensable *adj* ⟨persona⟩ indispensable; ⟨objeto⟩ indispensable, essential; **lleva lo** ~ take the bare essentials

indispuesto -ta *adj* (a) (enfermo) unwell, indisposed (frml) (b) (CS euf) ⟨mujer⟩: **está indispuesta** it's the time of the month (euph)

individual *adj* (a) ⟨características/libertades⟩ individual (b) ⟨cama/habitación⟩ single (before *n*); **mantel** ~ place mat (c) ⟨caso⟩ one-off (before *n*), isolated (d) (Dep) ⟨prueba/final⟩ singles (before *n*)
■ *m* (Dep) singles (*pl*); ~ **femenino** women's singles

individualismo *m* individualism

individualista *adj* individualistic
■ *mf* individualist

individuo *m* (a) (persona indeterminada): **un** ~ **alto** a tall man (b) (pey) (tipo) character (colloq), individual (colloq); **ese** ~ **que iba contigo** (fam) that guy you were with (colloq)

indivisible *adj* indivisible

Indochina *f* Indo-China

índole *f* (a) (tipo, clase) kind, nature; **un problema de** ~ **afectiva** a problem of an emotional nature (b) (manera de ser) nature; **ser de buena/mala** ~ to be good-natured/ill-natured

indolente *adj* lazy, slack, indolent

indoloro -ra *adj* painless

indomable *adj* (a) ⟨animal salvaje⟩ untamable*; ⟨caballo⟩ unbreakable (b) ⟨pueblo/

tribu⟩ indomitable, unconquerable; ⟨persona⟩ indomitable (c) (fam) ⟨pelo/remolino⟩ unruly, unmanageable

Indonesia *f* Indonesia

indonesio -sia *adj/m,f* Indonesian

indudable *adj* unquestionable; **es** ~ **que ...** there is no doubt that ...

indulgente *adj* (tolerante) indulgent; (para perdonar castigos) lenient; ~ **CON algn** indulgent WITH/lenient TOWARD(S) sb

indultar [A1] *vt* (Der) to pardon; (la pena de muerte) to reprieve

indulto *m* (Der) pardon; (de la pena de muerte) reprieve

indumentaria *f* clothing, clothes (*pl*), attire (frml)

industria *f* (Com, Econ) industry; ~ **del turismo** tourist industry; ~ **pesquera** fishing industry

industrial *adj* industrial
■ *mf* industrialist

industrialización *f* industrialization

industrializarse [A4] *v pron* to become industrialized

inédito -ta *adj* (a) ⟨obra/autor⟩ unpublished (b) (nuevo, sin precedente) unprecedented; **una técnica inédita en nuestro país** a technique unknown in our country

ineficacia *f* (de medida) ineffectiveness; (de método, persona) inefficiency

ineficaz *adj* (a) ⟨remedio/medida⟩ ineffectual, ineffective (b) ⟨método/sistema/persona⟩ inefficient

ineficiencia *f* inefficiency

ineficiente *adj* inefficient

inepto -ta *adj* inept, incompetent
■ *m,f* incompetent

inercia *f* (a) (Fís) inertia (b) **por** ~ (por rutina) out of habit; (por apatía) out of inertia *o* apathy

inescrutable *adj* inscrutable

inesperado -da *adj* unexpected; **de manera inesperada** unexpectedly

inestabilidad *f* instability

inestable *adj* (a) (en general) unstable (b) ⟨tiempo⟩ changeable, unsettled

inestimable *adj* ⟨ayuda⟩ invaluable

inevitable *adj* (ineludible) inevitable; ⟨cambio/conflicto/controversia⟩ unavoidable; **era** ~ **que empeorase la situación** the situation was bound to get worse

inexcusable *adj* ⟨comportamiento/error⟩ inexcusable, unforgivable; ⟨deber⟩ inescapable, unavoidable

inexistente *adj* nonexistent

inexperiencia *f* inexperience

inexperto -ta *adj* (falto de experiencia) inexperienced; (falto de habilidad) inexpert, unskilled

inexplicable *adj* inexplicable

inexpresivo -va *adj* expressionless, inexpressive

infalibilidad *f* infallibility

infalible *adj* ⟨persona/método⟩ infallible; ⟨puntería⟩ unerring

infancia *f* (período) childhood

infante -ta *m,f* (hijo del Rey) (*m*) prince, infante; (*f*) princess, infanta

infantería *f* infantry; ~ **de marina** marines (*pl*), Marine Corps

infantil *adj* **(a)** ⟨enfermedad⟩ children's (before n), childhood (before n); ⟨literatura/programa/moda⟩ children's (before n); ⟨rasgos/sonrisa⟩ childlike; ⟨población⟩ child (before n) **(b)** (pey) ⟨persona/actitud/reacción⟩ childish (pej), infantile (pej)

infarto *m* heart attack

infección *f* infection

infeccioso -sa *adj* infectious

infectar [A1] *vt* to infect
■ **infectarse** *v pron* to become infected

infelicidad *f* unhappiness

infeliz *adj* **(a)** ⟨persona/vida⟩ unhappy **(b)** ⟨intervención/tentativa⟩ unfortunate
■ *mf* poor wretch, poor devil

inferior *adj* **1** (en el espacio) ⟨piso/planta⟩ lower **2** (en jerarquía) ⟨especie/rango⟩ inferior **3** (en comparaciones) lower; **temperaturas ~es a los 10°** temperatures lower than o below 10°; **un número ~ al 20** a number below twenty

inferioridad *f* inferiority

infernal *adj* ⟨ruido⟩ infernal, hideous; ⟨música⟩ diabolical; **hacía un calor ~** it was baking hot (colloq)

infértil *adj* infertile

infertilidad *f* infertility

infestado -da *adj* ~ **DE algo** ⟨de insectos, parásitos⟩ infested WITH sth; ~ **de turistas** crawling with tourists

infestar [A1] *vt* to infest

infidelidad *f* infidelity, unfaithfulness

infiel *adj* **(a)** (desleal) unfaithful; **ser ~ A algn/algo** to be unfaithful TO sb/sth **(b)** (Relig) unbelieving (before n), infidel (before n) (dated)

infiernillo *m* (Esp) kerosene stove, primus® stove (BrE)

infierno *m* **(a)** (en general) hell; **¡vete al ~!** (fam) go to hell! (sl); **su vida es un ~** her life is hell **(b)** (fam) (lugar — ruidoso) madhouse (colloq), bedlam (colloq); (— horrendo) hellhole (colloq)

infilder *mf* (Col, Ven) infielder

infiltración *f* infiltration

infiltrado -da *m,f* infiltrator

infiltrar [A1] *vt* to infiltrate; ~ **a algn EN algo** to infiltrate sb INTO sth
■ **infiltrarse** *v pron* to infiltrate; ~**se EN algo** ⟨en partido/organización⟩ to infiltrate sth

infinidad *f* (gran cantidad): **en ~ de ocasiones** on countless occasions; ~ **de veces** innumerable o countless times

infinitivo *m* infinitive

infinito¹ -ta *adj* **(a)** (Fil, Mat) infinite **(b)** ⟨bondad/sabiduría⟩ infinite; ⟨amor⟩ boundless **(c)** (delante del n, en pl) (innumerables) innumerable, countless

infinito² *m* **(a) el ~** (Fil) the infinite; **mirar al ~** to look into the distance **(b)** (Mat) infinity

inflación *f* inflation

inflador *m* (Bol, Per, RPl) bicycle pump

inflamable *adj* flammable, inflammable

inflamación *f* (Med) inflammation; (Quím) ignition

inflamar [A1] *vt* **(a)** (Med) to inflame **(b)** (Quím) to ignite, set ... on fire
■ **inflamarse** *v pron* **(a)** (Med) to become inflamed **(b)** (Quím) to ignite

inflar [A1] *vt* **(a)** ⟨balón/rueda⟩ to inflate; ⟨globo⟩ to blow up **(b)** ⟨noticia/acontecimiento⟩ to exaggerate
■ **inflarse** *v pron* «velas» to swell, fill

inflexible *adj* inflexible; **se mostró ~** he refused to give in

inflexión *f* inflection

influencia *f* **1** (influjo) influence; **bajo la ~ del alcohol** under the influence of alcohol; ~ **EN** o **SOBRE algo** influence ON o UPON sth; ~ **SOBRE algn** influence ON sb **2 influencias** *fpl* (contactos) contacts (*pl*)

influenciable *adj* easily influenced

influenciar [A1] *vt* to influence

influir [I20] *vi* ~ **EN algo/algn** to influence sth/sb, have an influence ON sth/sb
■ ~ *vt* to influence

influyente *adj* influential

infografía *f* computer graphics

información *f* **1** **(a)** (datos, detalles) information; **el mostrador de ~** the information desk **(b)** (Telec) information (AmE), directory enquiries (BrE) **2** (Period, Rad, TV) news; **la ~ internacional** the foreign news **3** (Inf) data (*pl*)

informado -da *adj* (sobre tema, noticia) informed; **está usted muy mal informada** you have been misinformed o wrongly informed; **fuentes bien informadas** reliable sources

informal *adj* **1** **(a)** ⟨persona⟩ unreliable **(b)** ⟨ropa/estilo⟩ informal, casual; ⟨cena/ambiente⟩ informal **(c)** (no oficial) ⟨reunión⟩ informal **2** (AmL) ⟨economía/sector⟩ black (before n), informal (before n)

informar [A1] *vt* ⟨persona/prensa⟩ to inform; **te han informado mal** you've been misinformed; **¿podría ~me sobre los cursos de idiomas?** could you give me some information about language courses?
■ *vi* (dar noticias, información) to report; ~ **SOBRE algo** to report ON sth, give a report ON sth; ~ **DE algo** to announce sth
■ **informarse** *v pron* to get information; ~**se SOBRE algo** to find out o inquire ABOUT sth

informática *f* computer science, computing

informático -ca *adj* computer (before n)

informativo -va *adj* ⟨servicios/campaña⟩ information (before n); **programa ~** news program* **(b)** (instructivo) informative

informatizar [A4] *vt* to computerize

informe *m* **1** (exposición, dictamen) report; ~ **médico** medical report **2 informes** *mpl* **(a)** (datos) information, particulars (*pl*) **(b)** (de empleado) reference, references (*pl*); **pedir ~s** to ask for a reference/for references

infovía *f* information highway

infracción f offense*, infraction (frml); ~ de tráfico traffic violation (AmE), driving offence (BrE)

infractor -tora m,f offender

infraestructura f infrastructure

in fraganti loc adv red-handed

infrarrojo -ja adj infrared

infringir [I7] vt to infringe, break

ínfulas fpl: darse or tener muchas ~ to put on o give oneself airs

infundado -da adj unfounded, groundless

infundir [I1] vt ⟨confianza/respeto⟩ to inspire; ⟨sospechas⟩ to arouse; **les infundía miedo** it filled them with fear; **para ~les ánimo** to give them encouragement

infusión f infusion; ~ **de manzanilla** chamomile tea

ingeniar [A1] vt ⟨método/sistema⟩ to devise, think up; **ingeniárselas** (fam): **se las ingenió para arreglarlo** he managed to fix it

ingeniería f engineering; ~ **civil** civil engineering

ingeniero -ra m,f engineer; ~ **agrónomo** agriculturist; ~ **civil/industrial** civil/industrial engineer; ~ **técnico** engineer (qualified after a three-year university course)

ingenio m **1** (a) (talento) ingenuity, inventiveness; **aguzar el** ~ to rack one's brains **(b)** (chispa, agudeza) wit **2** (aparato) device **3** (AmL) (refinería) tb ~ **azucarero** sugar refinery

ingenioso -sa adj (a) (lúcido) ⟨persona/idea⟩ clever, ingenious **(b)** (con chispa, agudeza) ⟨persona/dicho/chiste⟩ witty **(c)** ⟨aparato/invención⟩ ingenious

ingenuidad f naivety, ingenuousness

ingenuo -nua adj naive, ingenuous
■ m,f: **es un** ~ he's so naive

Inglaterra f England

ingle f groin

inglés¹ -glesa adj (a) (de Inglaterra) English **(b)** (crit) (británico) British, English (crit)
■ m,f (a) (de Inglaterra) (m) Englishman; (f) Englishwoman; **los ingleses** the English, English people **(b)** (crit) ▶ **BRITÁNICO**

inglés² m (idioma) English

ingratitud f ingratitude

ingrato -ta adj (a) (desagradecido) ⟨persona⟩ ungrateful; ~ **con ella** ungrateful to her **(b)** (desagradable, difícil) ⟨vida⟩ hard; ⟨trabajo/tarea⟩ unrewarding
■ m,f ungrateful wretch (o swine etc) (colloq), ingrate (liter)

ingrediente m ingredient

ingresar [A1] vi **1** «persona» (en organización, club) to join; (en colegio) to enter; (en el ejército) to join; **después de** ~ **en el hospital** after being admitted to (the) hospital; **ingresó cadáver** (Esp) he was dead on arrival **2** «dinero» to come in
■ ~ vt **1** ⟨persona⟩ (en hospital): **el médico decidió** ~**lo** the doctor decided to send him to hospital; **hubo que** ~**lo de urgencia** he had to be admitted as a matter of urgency; **fueron ingresados en esta prisión** they were taken to this prison **2** (Esp) (Fin) ⟨dinero/cheque⟩ to pay in; ~ **una**

cantidad en una cuenta «persona» to pay a sum into an account; «banco» to credit an account with a sum

ingreso m **1** (a) (en organización): **el año de mi** ~ **a** or **en la universidad/el ejército/la compañía** the year I started o entered university/joined the army/joined the company; **examen de** ~ entrance examination **(b)** (en hospital) admission **2** (Fin) **(a)** (Esp) (depósito) deposit **(b) ingresos** mpl (ganancias) income; ~**s brutos/netos** gross/net income

íngrimo -ma adj (Col, Méx, Ven fam) **(a)** (sin compañía) all alone, all by oneself **(b)** ⟨lugar⟩ lonely, deserted

inhábil adj **(a)** (torpe) unskillful*, clumsy **(b)** (no apto) ~ **PARA algo** unsuited TO sth

inhabitado -da adj uninhabited

inhalación f inhalation; **hacer inhalaciones** to inhale; ~ **de pegamento** or (Méx) **cemento** glue sniffing

inhalador m inhaler

inhalar [A1] vt to inhale; ⟨pegamento⟩ to sniff

inhibición f inhibition

inhibir [I1] vt to inhibit
■ **inhibirse** v pron to become inhibited

inhóspito -ta adj inhospitable

inhumano -na adj **(a)** (falto de compasión) inhumane **(b)** (cruel) inhuman

iniciación f **(a)** (frml) (comienzo) beginning, start **(b)** (introducción) introduction; **curso de** ~ introductory course **(c)** (a secta) initiation

inicial adj initial
■ f **(a)** (letra) initial **(b)** (en béisbol) first base

iniciar [A1] vt (a) (frml) ⟨curso/viaje⟩ to begin, commence (frml); ⟨negociaciones/diligencias⟩ to initiate, commence (frml) **(b)** ~ **a algn EN algo** ⟨en secta⟩ to initiate sb INTO sth; ⟨en un arte⟩ to introduce sb TO sth
■ **iniciarse** v pron **1** «ceremonia/negociaciones» to begin, commence (frml) **2** «persona» ~**se EN algo** ⟨en secta⟩ to be initiated INTO sth; ⟨en un arte⟩ to take one's first steps in sth

iniciativa f initiative; **tomó la** ~ he took the initiative

inicio m beginning, start

inigualable adj ⟨belleza⟩ matchless, incomparable; ⟨precios/oferta⟩ unbeatable

ininteligible adj unintelligible, incomprehensible

ininterrumpido -da adj ⟨lluvias/trabajo⟩ continuous, uninterrupted; ⟨sueño⟩ uninterrupted; ⟨línea⟩ continuous

injertar [A1] vt to graft

injerto m (a) (Agr) (acción) grafting; (tallo) graft, scion **(b)** (Med) graft

injusticia f (a) (acto injusto) injustice, act of injustice; **es una** ~ **que te hayan dicho eso** it's unfair of them to have said that to you **(b)** (cualidad) unfairness, injustice

injustificable adj unjustifiable

injustificado -da adj unwarranted, unjustified; **despido** ~ unfair dismissal

injusto -ta adj unfair; **ser** ~ **CON algn** to be unfair TO o ON sb

inmaculado -da *adj* **(a)** ⟨*presentación/vestido/ superficie*⟩ immaculate **(b)** ⟨*fama*⟩ impeccable

inmadurez *f* immaturity, lack of maturity

inmaduro -ra *adj* ⟨*persona/animal*⟩ immature; ⟨*fruta*⟩ unripe

inmediaciones *fpl* vicinity, surrounding area; **el hotel está en las ∼ del aeropuerto** the hotel is in the vicinity of the airport; **en las ∼ de la capital** in the area around the capital

inmediatamente *adv* immediately

inmediato -ta *adj* **(a)** ⟨*efecto/respuesta*⟩ immediate; **de ∼** immediately, right away, straightaway (BrE) ⟨*lugar/ pueblo*⟩ **∼ A algo** close TO sth

inmejorable *adj* ⟨*resultados/posición*⟩ excellent, unbeatable; **está en una situación ∼** it is superbly located

inmenso -sa *adj* ⟨*fortuna/cantidad*⟩ immense, vast, huge; ⟨*casa/camión*⟩ huge, enormous; ⟨*alegría/pena*⟩ great, immense; **¡es ∼!** it's absolutely huge!

inmerecido -da *adj* undeserved, unmerited

inmerso -sa *adj* ⟨*submarino/buzo*⟩ submerged; ⟨*objeto*⟩ immersed

inmigración *f* immigration

inmigrante *mf* immigrant

inmigrar [A1] *vi* to immigrate

inmiscuirse [I20] *v pron* **∼ EN algo** to interfere IN sth, meddle IN sth

inmobiliaria *f* **(a)** (agency) real estate agency (AmE), estate agent's (BrE) **(b)** (empresa propietaria) real estate company (AmE), property company (BrE) **(c)** (empresa constructora) property developer

inmoral *adj* immoral
■ *mf*: **eres un ∼** you have no morals

inmoralidad *f* immorality

inmortal *adj/mf* immortal

inmortalidad *f* immortality

inmortalizar [A4] *vt* to immortalize
■ **inmortalizarse** *v pron* to achieve immortality, be immortalized

inmovible *adj* immovable

inmóvil *adj* still

inmovilismo *m* resistance to change, immobilism (frml)

inmovilizar [A4] *vt* 1 ⟨*persona/país/vehículo*⟩ to immobilize 2 ⟨Com, Fin⟩ ⟨*capital*⟩ to tie up

inmundo -da *adj* **(a)** ⟨*lugar*⟩ filthy **(b)** ⟨*sabor/ comida*⟩ foul, disgusting **(c)** (repulsivo) ⟨*escena/ película*⟩ filthy, disgusting

inmune *adj* immune; **∼ A algo** immune TO sth

inmunidad *f* immunity

inmunizar [A4] *vt* to immunize; **∼ a algn CONTRA algo** to immunize sb AGAINST sth

inmunodeficiencia *f* immunodeficiency

inmunológico -ca *adj* ⟨*tolerancia*⟩ immunological; ⟨*sistema/reacción*⟩ immune (before n)

inmutarse [A1] *v pron* «*persona*»: **cuando se lo dije ni se inmutó** she didn't bat an eyelash *o* (BrE) eyelid when I told her (colloq); **lo escuchó sin ∼se** she listened to him unperturbed

innato -ta *adj* innate, inborn

innavegable *adj* ⟨*río*⟩ unnavigable; ⟨*embarcación*⟩ unseaworthy

innecesario -ria *adj* unnecessary

innegable *adj* undeniable

innovación *f* innovation

innovador -dora *adj* innovative
■ *m,f* innovator

innovar [A1] *vi* to innovate

innumerable *adj* innumerable

inocencia *f* innocence

inocentada *f* ≈ April Fools' joke (*played on 28 December*); **gastarle** *or* **hacerle ∼s a algn** to play practical jokes on sb

inocente *adj* **(a)** (sin culpa) innocent; (Der) innocent, not guilty; **lo declararon ∼** he was found not guilty **(b)** ⟨*broma*⟩ harmless **(c)** (ingenuo) naive, gullible
■ *mf* innocent; **no te hagas el ∼** don't play the innocent

inodoro *m* **(a)** (wáter) toilet, lavatory **(b)** (taza) bowl, pan

inofensivo -va *adj* harmless, inoffensive

inolvidable *adj* unforgettable

inoportuno -na *adj* **(a)** ⟨*visita/llamada*⟩ untimely, inopportune; **llamó en un momento ∼** he phoned at a bad moment **(b)** ⟨*comentario/ crítica*⟩ ill-timed, inopportune

inquebrantable *adj* ⟨*fe*⟩ unshakable, unyielding; ⟨*lealtad*⟩ unswerving; ⟨*voluntad/ salud*⟩ iron (before n)

inquietante *adj* ⟨*noticia/cifras*⟩ disturbing, worrying; ⟨*síntoma*⟩ worrying

inquietarse [A1] *v pron* to worry; **∼ POR algo/algn** to worry ABOUT sth/sb

inquieto -ta *adj* **(a)** [ESTAR] (preocupado) worried **(b)** [SER] (emprendedor) enterprising; (vivo) lively, inquiring (before n) **(c)** (que se mueve mucho) restless

inquietud *f* **(a)** (preocupación) worry; **∼ POR algo** concern ABOUT sth **(b)** (interés): **es una persona sin ∼es** she has no interest in anything; **su ∼ filosófica** his philosophical preoccupations

inquilino -na *m,f* (arrendatario) tenant

Inquisición *f* (Hist): **la ∼** the Inquisition

inquisidor *m* inquisitor

insaciable *adj* insatiable; ⟨*sed*⟩ unquenchable

insalubre *adj* unhealthy

insalvable *adj* insurmountable, insuperable

insatisfacción *f* dissatisfaction

insatisfactorio -ria *adj* unsatisfactory

insatisfecho -cha *adj* **(a)** (descontento) dissatisfied; **∼ CON algo/algn** dissatisfied WITH sth/sb **(b)** ⟨*hambre/deseo*⟩ unsatisfied

inscribir [I34] *vt* (en registro) to register; (en curso, escuela) to register, enroll*
■ **inscribirse** *v pron* «*persona*» (en curso, colegio) to enroll*, register; (en concurso) to enter; (en congreso) to register

inscripción *f* **(a)** (para curso) enrollment*, registration; (para concurso) entry; (en congreso) registration; **la ∼ se cierra el ... día** the last day for enrollment is ... **(b)** (de un nacimiento) registration **(c)** (leyenda, lema) inscription

inscrito -ta, (RPI) **inscripto -ta** *pp*: ▶ INSCRIBIR

insecticida *m* insecticide

insecto *m* insect

inseguridad f (a) (falta de confianza) insecurity (b) (falta de firmeza, estabilidad) unsteadiness (c) (falta de garantías) insecurity, lack of security (d) (en ciudad, barrio): la ~ ciudadana the lack of safety on our streets

inseguro -ra adj (a) (falto de confianza) insecure (b) (falto de firmeza, estabilidad) unsteady (c) ⟨situación/futuro⟩ insecure (d) ⟨ciudad/barrio⟩ unsafe, dangerous

inseminación f insemination; ~ artificial artificial insemination

insensatez f (a) (cualidad) foolishness, senselessness (b) (dicho, hecho): lo que has dicho/hecho es una ~ that was a stupid thing to say/do

insensato -ta adj foolish
■ m,f fool

insensible adj insensitive; ~ al frío insensitive to the cold

inseparable adj inseparable

insertar [A1] vt to insert

inservible adj (inútil) useless; (inutilizable) unusable

insignia f (a) (distintivo, emblema) insignia, emblem; (prendedor) badge, button (AmE) (b) (bandera) flag; (estandarte) standard, banner

insignificante adj ⟨asunto/detalle/suma⟩ insignificant, trivial; ⟨objeto/regalo⟩ small; ⟨persona⟩ insignificant

insinuación f hint; (que ofende) insinuation; hacerle insinuaciones (amorosas) a algn ▶ INSINUARSE

insinuante adj ⟨mirada/voz⟩ suggestive; ⟨escote⟩ provocative

insinuar [A18] vt to imply, hint at; (algo ofensivo) to insinuate
■ **insinuarse** v pron: insinuársele a algn to make advances to sb, to make a pass at sb

insípido -da adj insipid, bland

insistencia f insistence; con ~ insistently

insistente adj ⟨persona⟩ insistent; ⟨recomendaciones/pedidos⟩ repeated (before n), persistent; ⟨timbrazos⟩ insistent, repeated (before n)

insistir [I1] vi to insist; ya que insistes if you insist; es inútil que insistas there's no point going on about it; ~ EN hacer algo to insist ON doing sth; insiste en que lo hagamos he insists (that) we do it; insiste en que es suyo she is adamant that it's hers; ~ SOBRE or EN algo to stress sth

insociable adj unsociable

insolación f (Med) sunstroke; agarrar una ~ to get sunstroke

insolencia f (a) (cualidad) insolence (b) (dicho): no pienso tolerar sus ~s I don't intend putting up with his insolence o his insolent behavior; contestarle así fue una ~ it was very rude of you to answer him like that

insolente adj rude, insolent
■ mf: es una ~ she's so rude o insolent

insólito -ta adj unusual

insolvencia f insolvency

insolvente adj insolvent

insomnio m insomnia

insonorizado -da adj soundproof

insoportable adj unbearable, intolerable

insostenible adj (a) ⟨situación/gasto⟩ unsustainable (b) ⟨posición/tesis⟩ untenable

inspección f inspection

inspeccionar [A1] vt to inspect

inspector -tora m,f inspector; ~ de Hacienda revenue agent (AmE), tax inspector (BrE); ~ de policía (police) inspector

inspiración f (Art, Lit, Mús) inspiration

inspirado -da adj inspired

inspirar [A1] vt [1] ⟨confianza⟩ to inspire; ⟨compasión⟩ to arouse, inspire; sabe ~les confianza she knows how to inspire confidence in them [2] ⟨obra/canción/persona⟩ to inspire
■ **inspirarse** v pron ~se EN algo «persona/obra/ley» to be inspired BY sth

instalación f (a) (colocación) installation (b) (equipo, dispositivo) system; la ~ sanitaria the plumbing (c) **instalaciones** fpl (dependencias) installations (pl); instalaciones deportivas sports facilities

instalar [A1] vt (a) (colocar y conectar) ⟨teléfono/lavaplatos⟩ to install; ⟨antena⟩ to erect, put up; (Inf) ⟨programa⟩ to install (b) (colocar) ⟨archivador/piano⟩ to put (c) ⟨oficina/consultorio⟩ to open, set up
■ **instalarse** v pron to settle, install oneself

instantánea f snapshot

instantáneo -nea adj (a) ⟨resultado/crédito⟩ instant (before n); ⟨reacción⟩ instantaneous, immediate (b) ⟨café⟩ instant (before n)

instante m moment; un ~, por favor just a second o moment, please; me llama a cada ~ he calls me all the time; al ~ right away, straightaway (BrE)

instigar [A3] vt ~ a algn A algo/hacer algo to incite sb TO sth/do sth

instintivo -va adj instinctive

instinto m instinct; por ~ instinctively; ~ de conservación survival instinct

institución f institution

instituto m institute; ~ nacional de bachillerato (Esp) high school (AmE), secondary school (BrE)

institutriz f governess

instrucción f [1] (educación) education; (práctica) training; ~ militar military training [2] **instrucciones** fpl (a) (de aparato, juego) instructions (pl); (para llegar a un lugar) directions (pl) (b) (órdenes) instructions

instructor -tora m,f instructor

instruir [I20] vt (adiestrar, educar) ~ a algn EN algo to instruct o train sb IN sth
■ **instruirse** v pron (refl) to broaden one's mind, improve oneself

instrumental adj (Mús) instrumental

■ *m* (Med) equipment, set of instruments

instrumentar *vt* [A1] (Mús) to orchestrate

instrumento *m* **1** (en general) instrument; ~ de cuerda string instrument; ~s de precisión precision instruments **2** (medio) means

insubordinación *f* insubordination

insubordinarse [A1] *v pron* ~ (CONTRA algn) (desobedecer) to be insubordinate (TO sb); (sublevarse) to rebel (AGAINST sb)

insuficiencia *f* (escasez): ~ de medios lack of resources; ~ de personal staff shortage

insuficiente *adj* **(a)** ⟨medios/cantidad⟩ inadequate, insufficient **(b)** (Educ) ⟨trabajo⟩ poor, unsatisfactory
■ *m* (Esp) fail

insular *adj* insular

insulina *f* insulin

insulso -sa *adj* **(a)** ⟨comida⟩ insipid, tasteless **(b)** ⟨persona⟩ insipid, dull; ⟨conversación/libro⟩ dull

insultante *adj* insulting

insultar [A1] *vt* **(a)** ⟨proferir insultos⟩ to insult **(b)** (ofender) to insult, offend

insulto *m* insult

insumiso -sa *m,f*: person refusing to do military service

insumos *mpl* (esp AmL) consumables (*pl*)

insuperable *adj* **(a)** (insalvable) ⟨problema/dificultad⟩ insurmountable, insuperable **(b)** (inmejorable) ⟨calidad/precio⟩ unbeatable

insurgente *mf* (frml) rebel, insurgent (frml)

insurrección *f* (frml) uprising, insurrection (frml)

intachable *adj* impeccable, irreproachable

intacto -ta *adj* (íntegro, no dañado) intact

integración *f* integration

integrado -da *adj* integrated

integral *adj* **(a)** (completo, total) comprehensive **(b)** (incorporado) built-in

integrante *mf* member

integrar [A1] *vt* **1** (formar) ⟨grupo/organización⟩ to make up **2** (incorporar) ⟨idea/plan⟩ to incorporate **3** (Mat, Sociol) to integrate **4** (CS) ⟨suma/cantidad⟩ to pay
■ **integrarse** *v pron* **(a)** (asimilarse) to integrate, fit in; ~se A *or* EN algo to integrate INTO sth, fit INTO sth **(b)** (unirse) ~se A *or* EN algo to join sth

integridad *f* integrity

íntegro -gra *adj* **1** ⟨texto⟩ unabridged; se proyectó en versión íntegra they screened the full-length version **2** ⟨persona⟩ upright

intelecto *m* intellect

intelectual *adj/mf* intellectual

inteligencia *f* **1** **(a)** (facultad, ser inteligente) intelligence **(b)** (comprensión) understanding **2** (Mil, Pol) intelligence

inteligente *adj* intelligent; ⟨persona⟩ intelligent, clever

inteligible *adj* intelligible

intemperie *f*: pasar la noche a la ~ to spend the night out in the open; gente sin hogar que duerme a la ~ people who sleep rough

intención *f* intention; no fue mi ~ ofenderte I didn't mean to offend you; tiene buenas/malas intenciones she's well-intentioned/up to no good;

lo dijo con segunda *or* doble ~ she had an ulterior motive for saying it; con la mejor ~ with the best of intentions; lo que cuenta es la ~ it's the thought that counts; vine con (la) ~ de ayudarte I came to help you; tiene (la) ~ de abrir un bar she plans *o* intends to open a bar; no tengo la menor ~ de venderlo I have no intention whatsoever of selling it

intencionado -da *adj* (hecho a propósito) deliberate, intentional; mal ~ malicious, hostile; bien ~ well-intentioned

intendencia *f* **(a)** (Andes) (división territorial) administrative division **(b)** (RPl) (gobierno municipal) town/city council; (edificio) town/city hall

intendente *mf* **(a)** (Andes) governor **(b)** (RPl) mayor

intensidad *f* **(a)** (de terremoto) intensity, strength; (del viento) strength; (de dolor, sentimiento) intensity **(b)** (Elec, Fís) intensity

intensivo -va *adj* intensive

intenso -sa *adj* **(a)** ⟨frío/luz/color⟩ intense **(b)** ⟨emoción/mirada⟩ intense; ⟨dolor/sentimiento⟩ intense, acute **(c)** ⟨esfuerzo⟩ strenuous; ⟨negociaciones⟩ intensive

intentar [A1] *vt* to try; ¡inténtalo otra vez! try again!; ~ un aterrizaje de emergencia to attempt an emergency landing; ~ hacer algo to try to do sth; ¿has intentado que te lo arreglen? have you tried getting *o* to get it fixed?

intento *m* **(a)** (tentativa) attempt **(b)** (Méx) (propósito) intention, aim

intercalar [A1] *vt* ~ algo EN algo ⟨en texto⟩ to insert sth INTO sth; intercaló algunas citas en su discurso she interspersed her speech with some quotations; intercala uno rojo cada dos azules put a red one between every two blue ones

intercambiable *adj* interchangeable

intercambiar [A1] *vt* ⟨impresiones/ideas⟩ to exchange; ⟨sellos/revistas⟩ to swap

intercambio *m* **(a)** (de ideas, información, bienes) exchange **(b)** (de sellos, revistas) swap; (de estudiantes, prisioneros) exchange

interceder [E1] *vi* (frml) to intercede; intercedió por ellos ante el rey he interceded for them with the king

interceptar [A1] *vt* **(a)** ⟨correspondencia/mensaje⟩ to intercept **(b)** ⟨teléfono⟩ to tap **(c)** (Dep) ⟨balón/pase⟩ to intercept; ⟨golpe⟩ to block **(d)** ⟨calzada/carretera⟩ to block; ~ el paso to block the way

intercomunicar [A2] *vt* to link (up)

interés *m* **1** (en general) interest; de ~ turístico of interest to tourists; pon más ~ en tus estudios take more interest in your schoolwork; tengo especial ~ en que ... I am particularly concerned *o* keen that ...; tienen gran ~ en verlo they are very interested in seeing it; por tu propio ~ in your own interest, for your own good; actúa solo por ~ he acts purely in his own interest *o* out of self-interest; conflicto de intereses conflict of interests **2** (Fin) interest; a *or* con un ~ del 12% at 12% interest *o* at an interest rate of 12%; ganar intereses to earn interest; tipo de ~ rate of interest

interesado -da *adj* **(a)** [ESTAR] (que muestra ⋯⋗

interés) interested; **~ EN** algo interested IN sth **(b)** [SER] (egoísta) selfish; **actuó de manera interesada** he acted selfishly **(c)** (parcial) biased, biassed
■ *m,f* **(a)** (que tiene interés) interested party (frml); **los ~s deberán** ... all those interested *o* (frml) all interested parties should ... **(b)** (que busca su provecho): **es un ~** he always acts in his own interest *o* out of self-interest

interesante *adj* interesting; **hacerse el ~** (fam) to try to draw attention to oneself

interesar [A1] *vi* **(a)** (suscitar interés): (+ *me/te/le etc*) **no me interesa la política** I'm not interested in politics; **esto a ti no te interesa** this doesn't concern you, this is no concern of yours **(b)** (convenir): **~ía comprobar los datos** it would be useful/advisable to check the data; **me interesa este tipo de préstamo** this sort of loan would suit me
■ ~ *vt* **~ a algn EN algo** to interest sb IN sth, get sb interested IN sth
■ **interesarse** *v pron* **(a)** (tener interés) to take interest; **~se EN** *or* **POR algo** to take an interest IN sth **(b)** (preguntar) **~se POR algo/algn** to ask *o* inquire ABOUT sth/sb

interferencia *f* interference

interferir [I11] *vt* **(a)** (obstaculizar) to interfere in **(b)** (emisión) to jam
■ ~ *vi* to interfere, meddle; **~ EN algo** (en asunto) to interfere *o* meddle in sth
■ **interferirse** *v pron* **~se EN algo** to interfere *o* meddle IN sth

interfono *m* **(a)** (portero automático) intercom (AmE), entryphone (BrE); (intercomunicador) intercom **(b)** (para bebés) baby alarm

interinato *m* (esp AmL) (cargo) temporary post *o* position

interino -na *adj* (secretario/director) acting (*before n*); (profesor) substitute (AmE) (*before n*), supply (BrE) (*before n*); (gobierno) interim (*before n*); **médico ~** locum
■ *m,f* (funcionario) temporary clerk (*o* accountant *etc*); (profesor) substitute teacher (AmE), supply teacher (BrE); (médico) locum

interior *adj* **(a)** (patio/escalera) interior, internal, inside (*before n*); (habitación/piso) with windows facing onto a central staircase or patio **(b)** (bolsillo/revestimiento) inside (*before n*); **en la parte ~** inside *o* on the inside **(c)** (vida/mundo) inner **(d)** (política/comercio) domestic, internal
■ *m* **1** **(a)** (de cajón, maleta, coche) inside; (de edificio) interior, inside; (de un país) interior; **en el ~ de la habitación** inside the room **(b)** (Méx, RPl, Ven) (provincias) provinces (*pl*) **(c)** (de una persona): **en su ~ estaba muy intranquilo** inside he was very worried; **allá en su ~ la amaba** deep down he really loved her
  2 Interior *m* (period) (Ministerio del Interior) Ministry of the Interior, ≈ Department of the Interior (*in US*), ≈ Home Office (*in UK*)
  3 interiores *mpl* (Col, Ven) (Indum) underwear

interjección *f* interjection

intermediario -ria *adj* intermediary
■ *m,f* **(a)** (Com) middleman, intermediary **(b)** (mediador) intermediary, mediator, go-between

intermedio¹ -dia *adj* **(a)** (punto/etapa) intermediate; **alumnos de nivel ~** students at

intermediate level **(b)** (calidad/tamaño) medium (*before n*); **un color ~ entre el gris y el verde** a color halfway between gray and green

intermedio² *m* (Espec) intermission, interval

interminable *adj* (serie/discusión/espera) interminable, never-ending; (cola/fila) endless, never-ending

intermitente *adj* **(a)** (lluvia) intermittent, sporadic **(b)** (luz) flashing; (señal) intermittent **(c)** (fiebre) intermittent
■ *m* turn signal (AmE), indicator (BrE)

internacional *adj* international; (noticia) foreign (*before n*), international (*before n*); (política) foreign (*before n*); **de fama ~** internationally famous; **🅢 salidas internacionales** international departures

internado¹ -da *adj* (AmL): **está ~** he's been admitted to (the) hospital, he's been hospitalized

internado² *m* **(a)** (Educ) boarding school **(b)** (Med) position or term as an intern or a houseman at a hospital, internship (AmE)

internar [A1] *vt*: **la ~on en un manicomio** she was put in an asylum; **lo ~on en el hospital** he was admitted to (the) hospital; **tuvimos que ~lo** we had to take him to (the) hospital
■ **internarse** *v pron* **(a)** (adentrarse) **~se EN algo** (en bosque/espesura) to penetrate INTO sth, to go deep INTO sth **(b)** (AmL) (en hospital) to go into hospital

internauta *mf* Internet user

Internet /inter'ne/ *m* (*a veces f*): **(el) ~** the Internet

interno¹ -na *adj* **1** (en general) internal **2** **(a)** (Educ): **está ~ en un colegio inglés** he is a boarder at an English school **(b)** (Med): **médico ~** ≈ intern (*in US*), ≈ houseman (*in UK*)
■ *m,f* **(a)** (Educ) boarder **(b)** (en cárcel) inmate **(c)** (médico) ≈ intern (*in US*), ≈ houseman (*in UK*)

interno² *m* (RPl) (Telec) (extensión) extension

interponerse [E22] *v pron*: **se interpuso y paró la pelea** he stepped in and stopped the fight; **nada se interpone en su camino** nothing stands in her way

interpretación *f* **(a)** (de un texto) interpretation **(b)** (Cin, Mús, Teat) interpretation **(c)** (traducción oral) interpreting; **~ simultánea** simultaneous interpreting

interpretar [A1] *vt* **1** (texto/comentario/sueño) to interpret; **interpretó mal tus palabras** she misinterpreted what you said **2** **(a)** (papel/personaje) to play **(b)** (pieza/sinfonía) to play, perform; (canción) to sing

intérprete *mf* **1** (traductor oral) interpreter; **~ jurado** sworn interpreter **2** (Mús) performer; (cantante) singer

interpuesto -ta *pp*: ▶ INTERPONERSE

interrogación *f* **(a)** (de un sospechoso) interrogation **(b)** (Chi) (Educ) test

interrogar [A3] *vt* (testigo/acusado) to question, examine; (detenido/sospechoso) to interrogate, question; (examinando) to examine

interrogatorio *m* (de acusado, testigo) questioning, examination; (de detenido) interrogation, questioning

interrumpir [I1] *vt* **1** (temporalmente) **(a)** (persona/reunión) to interrupt **(b)** (suministro) to cut off; (servicio) to suspend; (tráfico) to hold up;

las obras no ~ **án el paso** the work will not block the road **2** **(a)** (acortar) ⟨viaje/vacaciones/reunión⟩ to cut short **(b)** ⟨embarazo⟩ to terminate ∎ ~ *vi* to interrupt

interrupción *f* interruption; ~ **(voluntaria) del embarazo** termination of pregnancy

interruptor *m* switch

intersección *f* **(a)** (en geometría) intersection **(b)** (frml) (Transp) intersection, junction

intertanto *m*: **en el** ~ (AmL) in the meantime

interurbano -na *adj* ⟨transporte/autobús/llamada⟩ long-distance; ⟨tren⟩ intercity

intervalo *m* **(a)** (de tiempo) interval; (entre clases) recess (AmE), break (BrE) **(b)** (Mús) interval **(c)** (Teatr) (intermedio) intermission (AmE), interval (BrE) **(d)** (en el espacio) gap

intervención *f* **(a)** (en general) intervention; **se probó su** ~ **en el atraco** his involvement in the robbery was proved; **una política de no** ~ **a** policy of nonintervention; ~ **quirúrgica** operation **(b)** (de droga, armas) seizure, confiscation

intervenir [I31] *vi* **(a)** (en debate, operación) to take part; (en espectáculo) to appear, perform **(b)** (mediar) to intervene, intercede (frml); **en mi decisión intervinieron muchos factores** there were many factors involved in my decision; ~ **en una pelea** to intervene *o* step in to stop a fight; (involucrarse) to get involved in a fight ∎ ~ *vt* **1** **(a)** ⟨teléfono⟩ to tap **(b)** (tomar control de) ⟨empresa⟩ to place ... in administration **(c)** (inspeccionar) ⟨cuentas⟩ to audit, inspect **(d)** ⟨armas/droga⟩ to seize, confiscate **2** (operar) to operate on; **fue intervenido en una clínica privada** he underwent surgery in a private clinic

interviú *f* interview

intestinal *adj* intestinal

intestino *m* intestine, gut

inti *m* inti (*former Peruvian unit of currency*)

intimar [A1] *vi* ~ **con algn** to get close TO sb

intimidación *f* intimidation

intimidad *f* **1** **(a)** (ambiente privado) privacy; **en la** ~ **del hogar** in the privacy of one's home **(b)** (relación estrecha) intimacy **2** **intimidades** *fpl* **(a)** (cosas íntimas) private life, personal *o* private affairs (*pl*) **(b)** (euf) (partes pudendas) private parts (*pl*) (euph), privates (*pl*) (colloq)

intimidante *adj* intimidating

intimidar [A1] *vt* **(a)** (atemorizar) to intimidate **(b)** (amenazar) to threaten

íntimo -ma *adj* **(a)** ⟨vida/diario/ceremonia⟩ private; ⟨secreto⟩ intimate; ⟨ambiente⟩ intimate; **una cena íntima** a small dinner (with a few friends/members of the family); (en pareja) a candlelit *o* romantic dinner **(b)** ⟨amistad⟩ close; ⟨amigo⟩ close, intimate (*before n*)

intocable *adj* **(a)** (sagrado) sacred, sacrosanct **(b)** ⟨tema⟩ taboo **(c)** ⟨casta⟩ untouchable

intolerable *adj* intolerable

intolerancia *f* intolerance

intolerante *adj* intolerant

intoxicación *f* (Med) intoxication, poisoning; ~ **alimenticia** food poisoning; ~ **etílica** (Med) alcohol poisoning

intoxicar [A2] *vt* to poison ∎ **intoxicarse** *v pron* to get food poisoning

intranquilizar [A4] *vt* to worry

intranquilo -la *adj* **(a)** [ESTAR] (preocupado) worried, anxious **(b)** (agitado) restless

intranscendente *adj* ▶ INTRASCENDENTE

intransferible *adj* not transferable, untransferable

intransigente *adj* intransigent

intransitivo -va *adj* intransitive

intrascendente *adj* ⟨episodio/detalle⟩ insignificant, unimportant; ⟨comentario⟩ trivial

intravenoso -sa *adj* intravenous

intriga *f* intrigue; **novela/película de** ~ thriller

intrigante *mf* schemer, intriguer (AmE)

intrigar [A3] *vt* to intrigue ∎ ~ *vi* to scheme

intrincado -da *adj* **(a)** ⟨problema/asunto⟩ intricate, complex; ⟨laberinto/sistema⟩ complicated **(b)** ⟨nudo⟩ tangled

introducción *f* introduction; ~ **A algo** introduction TO sth

introducir [I6] *vt* **1** (en general) to put ... in; ⟨moneda⟩ to insert; ~ **algo EN algo** to put sth INTO sth; ⟨moneda⟩ to insert sth IN sth **2** **(a)** ⟨cambios/medidas/ley⟩ to introduce, bring in; ⟨producto⟩ to introduce **(b)** ⟨contrabando/drogas⟩ to bring in, smuggle in **3** (presentar) ⟨acto/cantante⟩ to introduce ∎ **introducirse** *v pron* **(a)** (meterse) «ladrón» to gain access; **la moneda se introdujo por una grieta** the coin fell down a crack **(b)** (entrar en uso) «moda» to come in; «costumbre» to be introduced **(c)** (hacerse conocido) «escritor/actor» to become known

introductorio -ria *adj* introductory

introvertido -da *adj* introverted ∎ *m,f* introvert

intruso -sa *m,f* intruder; (Inf) cracker (colloq)

intuición *f* intuition; **hacer algo por** ~ to do sth intuitively; **tuve la** ~ **de que ...** I had a feeling that ...

intuir [I20] *vt* to sense; **intuía que me iba a llamar** I had a feeling he was going to ring me

intuitivo -va *adj* intuitive

inundación *f* (en área limitada, casa) flood; (en zona más amplia) floods (*pl*), flooding

inundar [A1] *vt* **(a)** «riada/aguas» to flood, inundate (frml); «turistas/manifestantes» to inundate, crowd **(b)** «persona» (con agua) to flood; (con productos) to flood, swamp; ~ **algo . DE** *or* **CON algo** to flood sth with sth ∎ **inundarse** *v pron* (de agua) to be flooded

inusitado -da *adj* unusual, rare

inusual *adj* unusual

inútil *adj* useless; **es** ~ **que insistas** there's no point (in) insisting ∎ *mf*: **es un** ~ he's useless

invadir [I1] *vt* **(a)** «ejército/fuerzas» to invade **(b)** «espacio aéreo/aguas» to enter, encroach upon **(c)** «tristeza/alegría» to overcome, overwhelm

invalidez *f* (Med) disability, disablement

inválido -da *adj* (Med) ⟨persona⟩ disabled, handicapped ∎ *m,f* invalid, disabled person

invariable *adj* **(a)** ⟨precio/estado⟩ constant, stable **(b)** (Ling) invariable

invasión *f* ① (de zona, país) invasion ② (Col) (chabolas) shantytown

invasor -sora *m,f* invader

invencible *adj* (a) ‹luchador/equipo› unbeatable, invincible (b) ‹miedo/timidez› insuperable, insurmountable

invención *f* (a) (en general) invention (b) (mentira) fabrication

inventar [A1] *vt* (a) ‹aparato/sistema› to invent (b) ‹juego/palabra› to make up, invent; ‹cuento/excusa/mentira› to make up

inventario *m* (de negocio) inventory, stock list; (de casa) inventory

inventiva *f* inventiveness; **tiene mucha ~** she's very inventive

invento *m* invention

inventor -tora *m,f* inventor

invernadero *m* greenhouse

invernal *adj* ‹lluvias› winter (before n); ‹frío› wintry

inverosímil *adj* implausible

inversión *f* ① (de dinero, tiempo, esfuerzos) investment ② (de posiciones, términos) reversal; (de una imagen) inversion; **~ térmica** thermal inversion

inversionista *mf* investor

inverso -sa *adj* ‹sentido/orden› reverse; **puedes ordenarlo así o a la inversa** you can arrange it like this or the other way around

inversor -sora *m,f* investor

invertido -da *adj* ‹posición/orden› reversed; ‹imagen/figura› inverted, reversed

invertir [I11] *vt* ① ‹dinero/capital› to invest; ‹tiempo› to invest, devote ② ‹orden/papeles/términos› to reverse; ‹imagen/figura› to invert, reverse
■ ~ *vi* to invest; **~ EN algo** to invest IN sth
■ **invertirse** *v pron* «papeles/funciones» to be reversed

investigación *f* (a) (de caso, delito) investigation; (por comisión especial) inquiry (b) (Educ, Med, Tec) research; **~ científica** scientific research; **~ de mercados** market research

investigador -dora *m,f* (a) (que indaga) investigator (b) (Educ, Med, Tec) researcher

investigar [A3] *vt* (a) ‹delito/caso› to investigate (b) (Educ, Med, Tec) ‹persona› to research, do research into
■ ~ *vi* (a) «policía» to investigate (b) (Educ, Med, Tec) **~ SOBRE algo** to research o do research INTO sth

invierno *m* winter; (en la zona tropical) rainy season; **en ~** in winter, in wintertime; **ropa de ~** winter clothes

invierta, inviertas, etc ▸ INVERTIR

invirtiera, invirtió, etc ▸ INVERTIR

invisible *adj* invisible

invitación *f* invitation

invitado -da *m,f* guest; **tenemos ~s a cenar** we have people coming to dinner; **los ~s a la boda** the wedding guests

invitar [A1] *vt* to invite; **~ a algn A algo** to invite sb TO sth; **te invito a una copa** I'll buy o get you a drink; **~ a algn A hacer algo** o **A QUE haga algo** to invite sb to do sth; **me invitó a cenar** (en casa) she invited me (round) to dinner; (en restaurante) she invited me out to dinner
■ ~ *vi* «persona»: **invito yo** it's on me, I'm buying; **invita la casa** it's on the house

invocar [A2] *f* (a) ‹divinidad/santos› to invoke (frml), to call on (b) ‹auxilio/protección› to appeal for

involucrar [A1] *vt* (a) (implicar) to involve; **~ a algn EN algo** ‹en asunto/crimen› to involve sb IN sth (b) (AmL) (conllevar) to involve
■ **involucrarse** *v pron* «persona» to get involved

involuntario -ria *adj* ‹error/movimiento/gesto› involuntary; ‹testigo/cómplice› unwitting

inyección *f* (Med) injection; (dosis) injection, shot (colloq); **le puso una ~** she gave him an injection

inyectado -da *adj*: **ojos ~s en sangre** bloodshot eyes

inyectar [A1] *vt* to inject; **le ~on morfina** they gave him morphine injections/a shot of morphine
■ **inyectarse** *v pron* (refl) «persona» to give oneself an injection, inject oneself; **se inyectó heroína** he injected himself with heroin

ion *m* ion

ir [I27] *vi*
I ① (a) (trasladarse, desplazarse) to go; **~ en taxi** to go by taxi; **iban a caballo/a pie** they were on horseback/on foot; **~ por mar** to go by sea; **¡Fernando! — ¡voy!** Fernando! — (just) coming! o I'll be right there!; **el ~ y venir de los invitados** the coming and going of the guests; **vamos a casa** let's go home; **¿adónde va este tren?** where's this train going (to)?; **~ de compras/de caza** to go shopping/hunting; **ya vamos para allá** we're on our way; **¿por dónde se va a ...?** how do you get to ...?; **~ por** o **(Esp) a por algo/algn** to go to get sth/sb; **voy (a) por pan** I'm going to get some bread (b) (asistir) to go to; **voy a clases nocturnas** I go to evening classes; **ya va al colegio** she's already at school
② (expresando propósito) **~ A + INF: ¿has ido a verla?** have you been to see her?; **ve a ayudarla** go and help her; **ver tb** ▸ V AUX 1
③ (al arrojar algo, arrojarse): **tírame la llave — ¡allá va!** throw me the key — here you are o there you go!; **tírate del trampolín — ¡allá voy!** jump off the board! — here I go/come!
④ «comentario»: **no iba con mala intención** it wasn't meant unkindly; **eso va por ti también** that goes for you too, and the same goes for you
II ① (+ compl) (sin énfasis en el movimiento): **iban cantando por el camino** they sang as they went along; **¿van cómodos?** are you comfortable?;

íbamos sentados we were sitting down; **vas muy cargada** you have a lot to carry; **yo iba a la cabeza** I was in the lead

2 (refiriéndose al atuendo): **iban de largo** they wore long dresses; **voy a ~ de Drácula** I'm going to go as Dracula; **iba de verde** she was dressed in green **3** (en calidad de) ~ DE algo to go (along) AS sth; **yo fui de intérprete** I went along as interpreter

III 1 «*camino/sendero*» (llevar) ~ A algo to lead TO sth, to go TO sth

2 (extenderse, abarcar): **la autopista va desde Madrid hasta Valencia** the highway goes from Madrid to Valencia; **el período que va desde … hasta …** the period from … to …

IV 1 (marchar, desarrollarse): **¿cómo va el nuevo trabajo?** how's the new job going?; **va de mal en peor** it's going from bad to worse; **¿cómo te va?** how's it going?, how are things? (colloq), what's up? (AmE colloq); **¿cómo les fue en Italia?** how was Italy?, how did you get on in Italy?; **me fue mal/bien en el examen** I did badly/well in the exam; **¡que te vaya bien!** all the best!, take care!; **¡que te vaya bien (en) el examen!** good luck in the exam

2 (en competiciones): **¿cómo van? — 3-1** what's the score? — 3-1; **voy ganando yo** I'm ahead, I'm winning

3 (en el desarrollo de algo): **¿por dónde van en historia?** where have you got (up) to in history?; **¿todavía vas por la página 20?** are you still on page 20?

4 (estar en camino): **¡vamos para viejos!** we're getting on o old!; **va para los cincuenta** she's going on fifty; **ya va para dos años que …** it's getting on for two years since …

5 (sumar, hacer): **ya van tres veces que te lo digo** this is the third time I've told you; **con este van seis** six, counting this one

6 (haber transcurrido): **en lo que va del** or (Esp) **de año/mes** so far this year/month

V 1 (deber colocarse) to go; **¿dónde van las toallas?** where do the towels go?; **¡qué va!** (fam): **¿has terminado? — ¡qué va!** have you finished? — you must be joking!; **¿se disgustó? — ¡qué va!** did she get upset? — not at all!; **¡vamos a perder el avión — ¡qué va!** we're going to miss the plane — no way!

2 (a) (combinar) ~ CON algo to go WITH sth **(b)** (sentar bien, convenir) (+ *me/te/le etc*): **el negro no te va bien** black doesn't suit you; **te ~á bien un descanso** a rest will do you good

3 (Méx) (tomar partido por, apoyar) ~le A algo/algn to support sth/sb; **le va al equipo peruano** he supports the Peruvian team

VI 1 vamos (a) (expresando incredulidad, fastidio): **¡vamos! ¿eso quién se lo va a creer?** come off it o come on! who do you think's going to believe that? **(b)** (intentando tranquilizar, animar, dar prisa): **vamos, mujer, dile algo** go on, say something to him; **¡vamos, date prisa!** come on, hurry up! **(c)** (al aclarar, resumir): **eso sería un disparate, vamos, digo yo** that would be a stupid thing to do, well, that's what I think anyway; **vamos, que no es una persona de fiar** basically, he's not very trustworthy; **es mejor que el otro, vamos** it's better than the other one, anyway

2 vaya (a) (expresando sorpresa, contrariedad): **¡vaya! ¡tú por aquí!** what a surprise! what are you

doing here?; **¡vaya! ¡se ha vuelto a caer!** oh no o (colloq) damn! it's fallen over again! **(b)** (Esp) (para enfatizar): **¡vaya cochazo!** what a car!

■ ~ *v aux* ~ A + INF: **1 (a)** (para expresar tiempo futuro, propósito) to be going to + INF; **voy a estudiar medicina** I'm going to study medicine; **va a hacer dos años que …** it's getting on for two years since … **(b)** (en propuestas, sugerencias): **vamos a ver** let's see; **¿cómo dices que te llamas?** now then, what did you say your name was?; **bueno, vamos a trabajar** all right, let's get to work

2 (al prevenir, hacer recomendaciones): **que no se te vaya a caer** make sure you don't drop it; **cuidado, no te vayas a caer** mind you don't fall (colloq); **lleva el paraguas, no vaya a ser que llueva** take the umbrella, in case it rains

3 (expresando un proceso paulatino): **poco a poco irá aprendiendo** she'll learn little by little; **ya puedes ~ haciéndote a la idea** you'd better get used to the idea; **la situación ha ido empeorando** the situation has been getting worse and worse

■ **irse** *v pron* **1** (marcharse) to leave; **¿por qué te vas tan temprano?** why are you leaving o going so soon?; **¡vámonos** let's go; **bueno, me voy** right then, I'm taking off (AmE) o (BrE) I'm off; **no te vayas** don't go; **vete a la cama** go to bed; **se fue de casa/de la empresa** she left home/the company; **vete de aquí** get out of here; **se han ido de viaje** they're away, they've gone away

2 (consumirse, gastarse): **¡cómo se va el dinero!** I don't know where the money goes!; **se me va medio sueldo en el alquiler** half my salary goes on the rent

3 (desaparecer) «*mancha/dolor*» to go; **se ha ido la luz** the electricity's gone off; (+ *me/te/le etc*) **¿se te ha ido el dolor de cabeza?** has your headache gone?

4 (salirse, escaparse) «*líquido/gas*» to escape; **se le está yendo el aire al globo** the balloon's losing air o going down

5 (caerse, perder el equilibrio) (+ *compl*): ~**se de boca/espaldas** to fall flat on one's face/back; **me iba para atrás** I was falling backwards; **frenó y nos fuimos todos para adelante** he braked and we all went flying forwards

ira *f* rage, anger

Irak, Iraq *m* Iraq

Irán *m* Iran

iraní *adj/mf* Iranian

iraquí *adj/mf* Iraqi

irguieron, irguió, etc ▶ ERGUIR

iris *m* (*pl* ~) iris

Irlanda *f* Ireland; ~ **del Norte** Northern Ireland

irlandés¹ -desa *adj* Irish
■ *m,f* (persona) (*m*) Irishman; (*f*) Irishwoman; **los irlandeses** the Irish, Irish people

irlandés² *m* (idioma) Irish (Gaelic)

ironía *f* irony

irónico -ca *adj* **(a)** ⟨*situación*⟩ ironic **(b)** ⟨*persona/comentario/tono*⟩ sarcastic; **en tono ~** sarcastically

irracional *adj* irrational

irradiar [A1] *vt* **(a)** ⟨*calor/luz*⟩ to radiate **(b)** ⟨*simpatía/felicidad*⟩ to radiate, irradiate

irrazonable *adj* unreasonable

irreal *adj* unreal

irrealizable ···> jai alai

irrealizable *adj* ‹proyecto› unfeasible; ‹deseo› unattainable, unrealizable
irreconocible *adj* unrecognizable
irrecuperable *adj* unrecoverable, irretrievable
irreemplazable *adj* irreplaceable
irregular *adj* (en general) irregular; ‹letra/superficie› irregular, uneven
irregularidad *f* irregularity
irrelevante *adj* irrelevant
irremediable *adj* irreparable
irrepetible *adj* unrepeatable; **una actuación ~** a once-in-a-lifetime performance
irreprochable *adj* irreproachable
irresistible *adj* (a) ‹sonrisa/mujer/hombre› irresistible; ‹deseo/tentación› irresistible (b) ‹dolor› unbearable
irrespetar [A1] *vt* (Col, Ven) ‹persona› to be disrespectful o rude to; ‹lugar sagrado› to desecrate
irrespetuoso -sa *adj* disrespectful
irrespirable *adj* unbreathable
irresponsabilidad *f* irresponsibility
irresponsable *adj* irresponsible
■ *mf*: **es un ~** he's irresponsible, he's an irresponsible person
irreversible *adj* irreversible
irritable *adj* irritable
irritación *f* (a) (Med) irritation, inflammation (b) (enfado) irritation, annoyance
irritante *adj* ‹situación/actitud› irritating, annoying
irritar [A1] *vt* (a) ‹piel/garganta› to irritate; **tiene la garganta irritada** his throat is sore o inflamed (b) ‹persona› to annoy, irritate
■ **irritarse** *v pron* (a) «piel/ojos» to become irritated (b) «persona» to get annoyed, get irritated
irrompible *adj* unbreakable
isla *f* (a) (Geog) island, isle (liter) (b) (Ven) (en

autopistas) median strip (AmE), central reservation (BrE); **~ peatonal** safety island (AmE), traffic island (BrE)
Isla de Pascua *f*: **la ~ de ~** Easter Island
Islam *m*: **el ~** Islam
islámico -ca *adj* Islamic
islandés¹ -desa *adj* Icelandic
■ *m,f* (persona) Icelander
islandés² *m* (idioma) Icelandic
Islandia *f* Iceland
Islas Británicas *fpl* British Isles (*pl*)
Islas Canarias *fpl* Canary Islands (*pl*), Canaries (*pl*)
Islas Malvinas *fpl* Falkland Islands (*pl*)
isleño -ña *adj* ‹población/productos› island (*before n*)
■ *m,f* (habitante de una isla) islander
islote *m* small island, islet
ISP *m* (= proveedor de servicios Internet) ISP
Israel *m* Israel
israelí *adj/mf* Israeli
itacate *m* (Méx) pack, bundle
Italia *f* Italy
italiano¹ -na *adj/m,f* Italian
italiano² *m* (idioma) Italian
ítem *m* (*pl* **items**) item
itinerario *m* itinerary, route
IVA /'iβa/ *m* (= Impuesto al Valor Agregado *or* sobre el Valor Añadido) VAT
izar [A4] *vt* ‹vela/bandera› to hoist, raise, run up
izquierda *f* [1] (a) (mano izquierda): **la ~** the left hand (b) (lado) left; **la puerta de la ~** the door on the left, the left-hand door; **torció a la ~** he turned left; **ahí enfrente a la ~** over there on the left; **conducen por la ~** they drive on the left [2] (Pol) left; **de ~** *or* (Esp) **de ~s** left-wing
izquierdo -da *adj* left (*before n*)

Jj

J, j *f* (*read as* /'xota/) the letter J, j
ja *interj* ha!
jabalí *m* (*pl* **-líes**) wild boar
jabalina *f* (a) (Arm, Dep) javelin (b) (Zool) wild sow
jabón *m* (producto) soap; **una barra** *or* **pastilla de ~** a bar o cake of soap; **~ de afeitar** shaving soap
jabonada *f* (con jabón): **dale una buena ~** wash it well in soapy water
jabonar [A1] *vt* ▶ ENJABONAR
jabonera *f* soap dish
jabonoso -sa *adj* soapy
jacal *m* (Méx) hut, small house (*made of adobe or reeds*)
jacarandá *m or f* jacaranda

jacinto *m* (Bot) hyacinth
jactarse [A1] *v pron* to boast, brag; **~ DE algo** to boast o brag ABOUT sth
Jacuzzi® /dʒə'kuzi/ *m* Jacuzzi®
jade *m* jade
jadeante *adj*: **venía ~ por la cuesta** he came up the hill (puffing and) panting; **con voz ~** in a breathless voice
jadear [A1] *vi* to pant
jadeo *m* panting
jaguar *m* jaguar
jagüey, jagüel *m* (AmL) pool
jai *f* (AmS fam) (alta sociedad) high society
jai alai *m* jai alai, pelota

jaiba *f* (AmL) crab; (de río) freshwater crab

jaibol *m* (Méx) highball (AmE), whisky and soda (BrE)

jalada *f* (Méx fam) [1] (tirón) pull, tug [2] (tontería, exageración): **esas son puras ∼s** that's a load of garbage (AmE) *o* (BrE) rubbish (colloq)

jalado¹ -da *adj* [1] (AmC, Col, Méx fam) (borracho) tight (colloq) [2] (Méx fam) (descabellado) crazy (colloq) [3] (Per fam) ⟨ojos⟩ slanting
■ *m,f* (Per fam) oriental-looking person

jalado² *m* (Per arg) (Educ) fail

jalador -dora *adj* [1] (Méx fam) (a) (trabajador) hard-working (b) (animoso) willing (c) (que atrae) ⟨oferta⟩ attractive; ⟨cantante/actor⟩ popular [2] (Per arg) ⟨profesor⟩ tough (colloq)

jalapeño *m* (Méx) jalapeño pepper

jalar [A1] *vt* [1] (a) (AmL exc CS) (tirar de) to pull; **me jaló la manga** he pulled *o* tugged at my sleeve (b) (Méx) (agarrar y acercar) ⟨periódico/libro⟩ to pick up, take; ⟨silla⟩ to draw up [2] (Per arg) ⟨alumno⟩ to fail, flunk (esp AmE colloq) [3] (Per fam) (en automóvil, moto) to give ... a lift *o* ride
■ ∼ *vi* [1] (AmL exc CS) (tirar) to pull; **∼ DE algo** to pull sth; **∼ con algn** (Méx fam) (llevarse bien) to get on *o* along well with sb [2] (a) (Méx fam) (apresurarse) to hurry up, get a move on (colloq); **¡jálale!** hurry up! (b) (Col, Méx fam) (ir) to go; **jálale por el pan** go and get the bread [3] (Méx fam) «motor/aparato» to work; **mi coche no jalaba en la mañana** my car wouldn't start this morning; **¿cómo van los negocios? — jalando, jalando** how's business? — oh, not so bad (colloq) [4] (AmC fam) «pareja» to date, go out; **«persona» ∼ CON algn** to date sb, go out WITH sb
■ **jalarse** *v pron* [1] (Méx) ⟨enf⟩ ▶ JALAR *vt* 1B [2] (Méx) ⟨enf⟩ (a) (irse) to go (b) (venir) to come [3] (Col, Méx fam) (emborracharse) to get tight (colloq)

jalea *f* jelly; **∼ real** royal jelly

jaleo *m* (fam) (a) (alboroto, ruido) racket (colloq), row (colloq) (b) (confusión) muddle, mess; (desorden) mess; (problemas) hassle (colloq) (c) (actividad intensa): **hemos tenido mucho ∼ en casa** everything's been very hectic at home; **con todo el ∼ de la mudanza** with all the upheaval of the move (d) (riña) brawl

jallán *m* (AmC, Col) lout

jalón *m* (a) (AmL exc CS fam) (tirón) pull, yank; **de un ∼** in one go (b) (Méx) (tramo) stretch

jalonazo *m* (AmL exc CS fam) tug, yank; **el carro iba a ∼s** the car jerked *o* lurched along

jalonear [A1] *vt* (Méx, Per fam) to tug (at)
■ ∼ *vi* (a) (AmL exc CS fam) (dar tirones) to pull, tug (b) (AmC fam) (regatear) to haggle

jamaica *f* (Bot) hibiscus

Jamaica *f* Jamaica

jamaicano -na *adj/m,f* Jamaican

jamás *adv* never; **∼ volverá a suceder** it will never happen again; **nunca ∼** never ever; **por** *or* **para siempre ∼** for ever and ever

jamón *m* (Coc) ham; **∼ serrano** ≈ Parma ham

jaña *f* (AmC fam) (compañera) girlfriend; (chica) girl

Japón *m*: *tb* **el ∼** Japan

japonés¹ -nesa *adj/m,f* Japanese

japonés² *m* (idioma) Japanese

jaque *m* check; **∼ mate** checkmate

jaqueca *f* migraine, severe headache

jarabe *m* [1] (Coc, Farm, Med) syrup; **∼ para la tos** cough mixture *o* syrup [2] (Mús) *Mexican folk dance and music*

jarana *f* [1] (fam) (a) (bromas): **basta de ∼** that's enough fun and games *o* fooling around (colloq) (b) (juerga): **salir de ∼** to go out on the town *o* out partying (colloq) [2] (a) (baile) *folk dance from south-east Mexico* (b) (Per) (fiesta) party (*with folk music*)

jaranero -ra *adj* (fam): **es muy ∼** he's always out on the town *o* out partying (colloq)

jardín *m* [1] (con plantas) garden; **∼ botánico** botanical garden; **∼ zoológico** zoological garden, zoo; **∼ de infancia** *or* **de niños** nursery school, kindergarten [2] **los jardines** *mpl* (en béisbol) the outfield; **∼ central** center* field

jardinear [A1] *vi* [1] (en béisbol) to field [2] (Chi) (en el jardín) to do the gardening

jardinera *f* (para la ventana) window box; (con pedestal) jardinière

jardinería *f* gardening

jardinero -ra *m,f* [1] (persona) gardener [2] (Dep) outfielder

jareta *f* (a) (para pasar una cinta) casing; (de adorno) tuck (b) (AmC) (bragueta) fly

jaripeo *m*: *Mexican rodeo*

jarra *f* [1] (a) (para servir) pitcher (AmE), jug (BrE) (b) (para beber) stein (AmE), tankard (BrE); **en ∼s**: **con los brazos en ∼s** (with) arms akimbo, hands on hips [2] (Méx fam) (borracho) bender (colloq); **irse de ∼** to go on a bender

jarro *m* (a) (para servir) pitcher (AmE), jug (BrE) (b) (AmS) (tazón) mug; (para cerveza) beer mug

jarrón *m* vase

jaspe *m* (piedra) jasper; (mármol) veined marble

jaspeado -da *adj* ⟨mármol⟩ veined; ⟨tela/lana⟩ flecked; ⟨plumaje/huevos⟩ speckled

jauja *f* (fam): **piensan que la universidad es ∼** they think that university is a bed of roses; **¡esto es ∼!** this is the life!

jaula *f* cage

jauría *f* (de perros) pack (of hounds)

jayán -yana *adj* (AmC fam) foul (colloq); **no seas ∼** don't be a jerk *o* creep (colloq)

jazmín *m* jasmine

jazz /(d)ʒas/ *m* jazz

jebo -ba *m,f* (Ven arg) (a) (novio) (*m*) boyfriend; (*f*) girlfriend (b) **jeba** *f* (muchacha) chick (AmE colloq), bird (BrE colloq)

Jeep® /(d)ʒip/ *m* (*pl* **Jeeps**) Jeep®

jefatura *f* [1] (sede) headquarters (*sing o pl*) [2] (de partido) leadership

jefe -fa *m,f*, **jefe** *mf* (a) (superior) boss; **∼ de estudios** director of studies; **∼ de personal/ventas** personnel/sales manager; **∼ de redacción** editor-in-chief (b) (de empresa) manager; (de sección) head; (de tribu) chief (c) (Pol) leader; **∼ de Estado/gobierno** head of state/government

jején *m*: *small mosquito*

jengibre *m* ginger

jeque *m* sheik, sheikh

jerarca *mf* leader

jerarquía f **(a)** (organización) hierarchy **(b)** (categoría, rango) rank

jerez m sherry

jerga f [1] **(a)** (de gremio, profesión) jargon; (de los adolescentes) slang **(b)** (galimatías) mumbo jumbo (colloq) [2] (Méx) (trapo) floorcloth

jergón m straw mattress

jeringa f (Med) syringe

jeringuilla f syringe

jeroglífico m (escritura) hieroglyphic, hieroglyph; (acertijo) rebus

jersey m (pl **-seys**) **(a)** /'ʒersi/ (AmL) (tela) jersey **(b)** /ˈxerˈsei/ (Esp) (prenda) sweater

Jerusalén m Jerusalem

Jesucristo m Jesus Christ

jesuita adj/m Jesuit

Jesús (a) (Relig) Jesus **(b)** (como interj) ¡~! (expresando — dolor, fatiga) heavens!; (— susto, sorpresa) good heavens!, good grief!; (cuando alguien estornuda) (Esp) bless you!

jet /'(d)ʒet/ m (pl **jets**) (Aviac) jet

jeta f (fam) **(a)** (cara) face, mug (colloq) **(b)** (AmL fam) (boca) trap (sl)

jet lag /'(d)ʒetlav/ m jet lag

jet set /'(d)ʒetset/ m or (Esp) f jet set

jíbaro -ra adj/m,f Jivaro

jibia f cuttlefish

jícama f yam bean

jícara f [1] (Méx) (Bot) calabash [2] **(a)** (Méx) (taza) (drinking) bowl **(b)** (Col, Méx) (vasija — de calabaza) gourd, calabash; (— de otro material) pot

jicote m (Méx) wasp

jicotera f **(a)** (Méx) (nido) wasp's nest **(b)** (ruido) row (colloq)

jilguero m goldfinch

jinete mf (Equ) (m) horseman, rider; (f) horsewoman, rider

jinetear [A1] vt [1] (Equ) (Chi) (montar) to ride [2] (Méx fam) ‹dinero› to speculate with

jirafa f (Zool) giraffe

jirón m [1] (de tela) shred; **hecho jirones** in tatters o shreds [2] (Per) (avenida) avenue, street

jitomate m (Méx) tomato

jo interj (Esp fam) (expresando — sorpresa) wow! (colloq); (— enfado, disgusto) damn it! (colloq)

jockey /'(d)ʒoki/ mf (pl **-ckeys**) jockey

jocoso -sa adj humorous, jocular

joda f (AmL fam)**(a)** (molestia) pain (colloq), drag (colloq) **(b)** (broma): **en ~** as a joke

joder¹ [E1] vi [1] (vulg) (copular) to screw (vulg), fuck (vulg)
[2] (fam: en algunas regiones vulg) (molestar) to annoy (sl); **lo hace solo por ~** he only does it to annoy
■ ~ vt [1] (vulg) (copular con) to screw (vulg), fuck (vulg)
[2] (fam: en algunas regiones vulg) **(a)** (molestar) to bug (colloq) **(b)** (engañar) to rip ... off (colloq)
[3] (fam: en algunas regiones vulg) ‹televisor/reloj› to

bust (colloq), to fuck up (vulg); ‹planes› to mess up (colloq), to screw up (vulg); **~la** (fam) to screw up (vulg)
■ **joderse** v pron (fam: en algunas regiones vulg) **(a)** (jorobarse): **y si no te gusta, te jodes** and if you don't like it, that's tough! (colloq) **(b)** ‹espalda› to do ... in (colloq); ‹hígado/estómago› to mess up (colloq) **(c)** «planes» to get screwed up (vulg), fucked up (vulg); **se ha jodido el motor** the engine's had it (colloq)

joder² interj (esp Esp fam: en algunas regiones vulg) (expresando — fastidio) for heaven's sake! (colloq), for fuck's sake! (vulg); (— asombro) good grief!, holy shit! (vulg)

jodido -da adj [1] (fam: en algunas regiones vulg) **(a)** [SER] (difícil) ‹trabajo› tricky, tough (colloq); ‹persona› difficult, pain in the neck (colloq) **(b)** (delante del n) (maldito) damn (colloq), fucking (vulg) **(c)** [SER] (AmL) (exigente) demanding, tough (colloq) [2] [ESTAR] (fam: en algunas regiones vulg) **(a)** (estropeado) ‹ascensor/radio› bust (colloq), fucked (vulg) **(b)** (enfermo) in a bad way (colloq) **(c)** (deprimido) down (colloq) [3] [SER] (Col fam) (astuto) sharp

jogging /'(d)ʒovin/ m **(a)** (Dep, Ocio) jogging; **hacer ~** to jog, go jogging **(b)** (RPl) (Indum) jogging suit

jojoto m (Ven) corn (AmE), maize (BrE)

jolgorio m revelry, merrymaking; **irse de ~** (fam) to go out on the town o out partying (colloq)

jonrón m (AmL) home run

Jordania f Jordan

jordano -na adj/m,f Jordanian

jornada f [1] **(a)** (period) (día) day **(b)** (Rels Labs) tb ~ **laboral** working day; **trabajar ~ completa/ media ~** to work full-time/part-time; **~ continuada** or **intensiva** or (Chi) **única** working day with no break for lunch so as to finish earlier; **~ partida** split shift (working day with long break for lunch) [2] (esp Col) (viaje) journey

jornal m day's wages (pl), day's pay; **trabajar a ~** to be paid on a daily basis

jornalero -ra m,f day laborer*

joroba f **(a)** (de persona, camello) hump **(b)** (fam) (molestia) drag (colloq), pain in the neck (colloq)

jorobado -da adj [1] (giboso) hunchbacked [2] (fam) **(a)** (enfermo, delicado): **todavía anda algo jorobada** she's still a bit low (colloq); **está ~ del estómago** his stomach's been playing (him) up (colloq) **(b)** (sin dinero) broke (colloq) **(c)** ‹asunto› tricky
■ m,f hunchback

jorobar [A1] vt (fam) **(a)** (molestar) to bug (colloq) **(b)** (malograr) to ruin, spoil
■ ~ vi (fam) (molestar) to annoy; **lo que más me joroba es ...** what really bugs o gets me is ... (colloq)
■ **jorobarse** v pron (fam) **(a)** (aguantarse): **y si no te gusta, te jorobas** and if you don't like it, that's tough (colloq) **(b)** (dañarse) ‹hígado/estómago› to

AmC	Central America	Arg	Argentina	Cu	Cuba
AmL	Latin America	Bol	Bolivia	Ec	Ecuador
AmS	South America	Chi	Chile	Esp	Spain
Andes	Andean Region	CS	Southern Cone	Méx	Mexico

Per	Peru
RPI	River Plate Area
Ur	Uruguay
Ven	Venezuela

mess up (colloq); ⟨*espalda*⟩ to do ... in (colloq) **(c)**
«*plan*» to be scuppered (colloq); «*fiesta*» to be
ruined

jorongo *m* (Méx) poncho

joropo *m*: Colombian/Venezuelan folk dance

jota *f* **(a)** (letra) *name of the letter* j; **ni ~** (fam): **no
entiendo/no veo ni ~** I don't understand/I can't
see a thing; **no sabe ni ~** he doesn't have a clue
(colloq) **(b)** (Mús) jota (*Aragonese folk song/dance*)
(c) (en naipes) jack

joven *adj* young
■ *mf* (*m*) young person, young man; (*f*) young
person, young woman; **de aspecto ~** youthful
looking; **los jóvenes de hoy** ... young people
today ...

jovencito -ta (*m*) young man; (*f*) young lady,
young woman; **moda para jovencitas** teenage
fashions (*for girls*)

jovial *adj* jovial, cheerful

joya *f* **(a)** (alhaja) piece of jewelry*; **~s** jewelry *o*
jewels; **~ de fantasía** piece *o* item of costume
jewelry **(b)** (persona) gem, treasure; (cosa): **este
coche es una ~** this is a real gem of a car

joyería *f* (tienda) jeweler's*

joyero -ra *m,f* **(a)** (persona) jeweler* **(b)**
joyero *m* (estuche) jewelry* box, jewel case

joystick /'(d)ʒoiʃstik/ *m* joystick

jr (en Perú) (= *jirón*) street

Jr. (= **Júnior**) Jr

juanete *m* (Med) bunion

jubilación *f* (retiro) retirement; (pensión)
pension; **~ anticipada/forzosa** early/compulsory
retirement

jubilado -da *adj* retired
■ *m,f* pensioner, retired person (*o* worker *etc*)

jubilar [A1] *vi* (Andes) to retire
■ **jubilarse** *v pron* (del trabajo) to retire

júbilo *m* jubilation

jubiloso -sa *adj* (liter) jubilant

judaísmo *m* Judaism

judía *f* (Esp) bean; **~ verde** green bean

judicial *adj* judicial
■ *m* (Méx) policeman

judío -día *adj* **1** (Relig, Sociol) Jewish **2** (fam &
pey) (tacaño) miserly, tightfisted (colloq)
■ *m,f* Jewish person, Jew

judo /'(d)ʒuðo/ *m* judo

juega, juegas, etc ▶ JUGAR

juego *m* **1** **(a)** (en general) play; **entrar en ~**
«*jugador*» to come on; «*factores/elementos*» to
come into play; **estar en ~** to be at stake; **~
limpio/sucio** fair/foul play; **seguirle el ~ a algn** to
go *o* play along with sb **(b)** (por dinero): **el ~**
gambling **(c)** (fam) (maniobras, estratagemas) game
(colloq) **(d)** (en naipes) hand, cards (*pl*)
2 **(a)** (de mesa, de niños, etc) game; **~ de azar**
game of chance; **~ de manos** conjuring trick; **~
de palabras** pun, play on words; **~s malabares**
juggling; **J~s Olímpicos** Olympic Games (*pl*),
Olympics (*pl*) **(b)** (AmL) (en la feria) fairground
attraction, ride **(c)** (en tenis) game **(d) juegos**
mpl (columpios, etc) swings, slide, etc (*in a
children's playground*)
3 (conjunto) set; **un ~ de cuchillos/llaves** a set of
knives/keys; **un ~ de platos** a dinner service; **~**

de café/té coffee/tea set; **~ de escritorio** desk set;
hacer **~** «*colores/cortinas*» to go together; **te
hace ~ con los zapatos** it goes with your shoes

juerga *f* (fam): **ir de ~** to go out on the town *o*
out partying (colloq); **organizar una ~** to have *o*
throw a party

juerguista *mf* (fam) reveller

jueves *m* (*pl* **~**) Thursday; *para ejemplos ver*
LUNES; **J~ Santo** Maundy Thursday

juez *mf*, **juez -za** *m,f* **(a)** (Der) judge **(b)** (Dep)
referee; **~ de banda** *or* **línea** (en fútbol, tenis) (*m*)
linesman; (*f*) lineswoman; (en fútbol americano,
rugby) line judge; **~ de silla** umpire

jugada *f* **(a)** (con pelota – individual) move; (–
entre varios) play **(b)** (en ajedrez, damas, etc) move;
hacerle una (mala) ~ a algn to play a (dirty) trick
on sb

jugado -da *adj* (Col, Méx) experienced

jugador -dora *m,f* (Dep) player; (en naipes,
juegos de mesa) player; (que juega habitualmente por
dinero) gambler

jugar [A15] *vi* **1** **(a)** (en general) to play; **~ A
algo** to play sth; **~ a la pelota** to play ball; **~ al
fútbol** (Esp, RPl) to play football; **~ a las muñecas**
to play with dolls; **~ limpio/sucio** to play fair/
dirty **(b)** (en ajedrez, damas) to move; (en naipes) to
play; (en otros juegos) to play; **me tocaba ~ a mí** it
was my turn/move/go **(c)** (apostar fuerte) to gamble
2 jugar con (a) ⟨*persona/sentimientos*⟩ to play
with, toy with **(b)** (manejar) ⟨*colores/luz/palabras*⟩
to play with
■ *vt* **1** **(a)** ⟨*partido/carta*⟩ to play **(b)** (AmL exc
RPl) ⟨*tenis/fútbol/ajedrez*⟩ to play
2 (apostar) **~ algo A algo** to bet sth ON sth
3 ⟨*rol/papel*⟩ to play
■ **jugarse** *v pron* **(a)** (gastarse en el juego) ⟨*sueldo*⟩
to gamble (away) **(b)** (arriesgar) ⟨*reputación/vida*⟩
to risk, put ... at risk; **~se el pellejo** (fam) to risk
one's neck (colloq) **(c)** (apostarse) (recipr): **nos
jugamos una comida** we bet a meal on it

jugarreta *f* (fam) dirty trick (colloq); **hacerle una
~ a algn** to play a dirty trick on sb

juglar *m* minstrel, jongleur

jugo *m* (líquido) juice; **~ de tomate** tomato juice

jugoso -sa *adj* **(a)** ⟨*fruta/carne*⟩ juicy **(b)**
⟨*historia/anécdota*⟩ colorful*; ⟨*chisme*⟩ juicy **(c)**
⟨*artículo/guion*⟩ meaty **(d)** ⟨*negocio*⟩ lucrative,
profitable

juguera *f* (CS) (para hacer jugos) juicer

juguete *m* toy; **un tren de ~** a toy train

juguetear [A1] *vi* to play

juguetería *f* (tienda) toy store; (ramo) toy trade
o business

juguetón -tona *adj* playful

juicio *m* **1** (facultad) judgment; **no está en su
sano ~** he's not in his right mind; **perder el ~** to
go out of one's mind **2** (prudencia, sensatez) sense
3 (opinión) opinion; **a mi ~** in my opinion, to my
mind; **lo dejo a tu ~** I'll leave it up to you; **~ de
valor** value judgment **4** (Der) trial; **llevar a ~ a
algn** to take sb to court ; **ir a ~** to go to court; **~
civil/criminal** civil/criminal proceedings (*pl*); **el
J~ Final** (Relig) the Final Judgment

juicioso -sa *adj* sensible

jul. (= **julio**) Jul

julepe m ① (Jueg) card game similar to whist ② (AmS fam) (susto) fright; **le da ~ la oscuridad** she's terrified of the dark

julia f (Méx fam) Black Maria (colloq)

julio m (mes) July; *para ejemplos ver* ENERO

jumbo /'(d)ʒumbo/ m jumbo jet

jun. (= **junio**) Jun

junco m ① (planta) rush, reed ② (Náut) *tb* **~ chino** junk

jungla f jungle

junio m June; *para ejemplos ver* ENERO

júnior /'(d)ʒunjo(r)/ *adj inv* ‹equipo/categoría› junior (*before n*), youth (*before n*) (BrE)
■ *mf* (*pl* **~s**) (a) (Dep): **los ~s** the juniors (b) (el más joven, el hijo) Junior
■ *m* (a) (Chi) (en oficina) office junior (b) (Méx) (hijo de papá) rich kid (colloq)

junta f ① (a) (comité, comisión) board, committee; (de empresa) board; (reunión) meeting; **~ directiva** board of directors (b) (de militares) junta (c) (gobierno regional) autonomous government in some regions of Spain ② (Mec) (acoplamiento) joint; (para cerrar herméticamente) gasket

juntar [A1] *vt* (a) (unir) ‹pies/manos/camas› to put ... together (b) (reunir) ‹fichas/piezas› to collect up, gather together; ‹dinero› to save (up); **~ sellos** (esp AmL) to collect stamps (c) (cerrar) ‹puerta› to push ... to
■ **juntarse** *v pron* ① «personas» (a) (acercarse) to move o get closer together (b) (reunirse) to get together; **~se con algn** to join sb, meet up with sb (c) (como pareja) to live together; **se volvieron a ~** they got back together again ② (a) «desgracias/sucesos» to come together (b) «carreteras/conductos» to meet, join

junto -ta *adj* ① (a) (unido, reunido) together; **nunca había visto tanto dinero ~/tanta gente junta** I'd never seen so much money/so many people in one place (b) (*pl*) (cercanos, contiguos) together; **están demasiado ~s** they're too close together; **bailaban muy ~s** they were dancing very close ② (como adv) (a) ‹estudiar/trabajar/vivir› together (b) ‹llegar/saltar› at the same time; **¡ahora todos ~s!** all together now! ③ (en locs) **junto a** next to; **junto con** (together) with

juntura f join, joint

Júpiter m Jupiter

jurado m (cuerpo) (Der) jury; (de concurso) panel of judges, jury
■ *mf* (persona) (Der) juror, member of a jury; (de concurso) judge, member of the jury

juramento m oath; **prestar ~** to take an oath; **tomarle ~ a algn** (Der) to swear sb in; **bajo ~** under o on oath

jurar [A1] *vt* to swear; **juró su cargo el 22 de julio** he was sworn in on July 22; **~on (la) bandera** or (AmL) **a la bandera** they swore allegiance to the flag; **juró vengarse** he swore to get his revenge; **no lo entiendo, te lo juro** I honestly don't understand

■ **~** *vi* (a) (maldecir) to curse, swear (b) (prometer): **~ en falso** or **vano** to commit perjury

jurídico -ca *adj* legal (*before n*)

jurisdicción f jurisdiction

justicia f (a) (equidad) justice; **pedir ~** to call for justice; **en ~** in all fairness, to be fair; **la ~ de su decisión** the fairness of her decision; **nunca se le ha hecho ~ como escritor** he has never received due recognition as a writer (b) (sistema, leyes): **la ~** the law; **huir de la ~** to flee from justice o the law; **tomarse la ~ por su mano** to take the law into one's own hands

justificable *adj* justifiable

justificación f (disculpa, razón) justification; (Der) (prueba) proof

justificante m receipt; **~ de pago** receipt, proof of payment; **~ de asistencia** certificate of attendance; **~ de ausencia** note explaining reasons for one's absence

justificar [A2] *vt* (a) (en general) to justify; **eso no justifica su actitud** that does not justify her attitude; **sus sospechas no estaban justificadas** his suspicions were not justified; **trabajar por tan poco no se justifica** it isn't worth working for so little (b) (disculpar) ‹persona› to find o make excuses for
■ **justificarse** *v pron* to justify oneself, excuse oneself

justo¹ -ta *adj* ① ‹persona/castigo/sociedad› just, fair; ‹causa› just ② (a) (exacto) ‹medida/peso/cantidad› exact; **me dio el dinero ~** he gave me the right money; **son 5.000 pesetas justas** that's 5,000 pesetas exactly; **buscaba la palabra justa** he was searching for exactly o just the right word (b) (apenas suficiente): **tener lo ~ para vivir** to have just enough to live on; **andan muy ~s de dinero** they're very short of money; **teníamos las sillas justas** we had just enough chairs for everybody (c) (ajustado): **estos zapatos me quedan demasiado ~s** these shoes are too tight (for me)

justo² *adv* (a) (exactamente) just; **~ a tiempo** just in time; **es ~ lo que quería** it's just o exactly what I wanted; **vive ~ al lado** he lives just o right next door; **y ~ hoy que pensaba salir** and today of all days, when I was planning to go out (b) (ajustado): **con el sueldo que gana vive muy ~** he only just manages to scrape by on what he earns; **me cupo todo, pero muy ~** I managed to get everything in, but only just

juvenil *adj* ‹moda› young; ‹aspecto› youthful; ‹categoría/competición› junior (*before n*), youth (*before n*) (BrE)
■ *mf* junior; **los ~es** the juniors

juventud f (edad) youth; (gente joven) youth; **¡esta ~ de hoy!** young people today!

juzgado m court

juzgar [A3] *vt* (a) (Der) ‹acusado› to try; ‹caso› to try, judge (b) ‹conducta/persona› to judge; **~ mal a algn** to misjudge sb (c) (considerar) to consider; **a ~ por las apariencias** judging by appearances

Kk

K, k *f (read as* /ka/) *the letter* K, k
ka *f: name of the letter* k
kaleidoscopio *m* kaleidoscope
karate, kárate *m* karate
kárdex *m* (archivo) file; (mueble) filing cabinet
kart *m (pl* **karts**) kart
Kenia, Kenya *f* Kenya
kermesse /ker'mes/ *f* (CS, Méx) charity fair, kermess (AmE), fête (BrE)
ketchup /'katʃup 'katsup/ *m* ketchup, catsup (AmE)
Kg. (= **kilogramo**) kg
kilo *m* kilogram, kilo
kilogramo *m* kilogram
kilometraje *m* ≈ mileage
kilométrico -ca *adj (fam)* ⟨pasillo⟩ endless; **una cola kilométrica** a line (AmE) *o* (BrE) queue a mile long
kilómetro *m* kilometer*
kilovatio *m* kilowatt
kimono *m* kimono

kindergarten *m (pl* ~ *or* **-tens**) kindergarten
kiosco, kiosko *m* **(a)** (de periódicos) newsstand, newspaper kiosk; (de refrescos) drinks stand; (de helados) ice-cream stand; (de caramelos, tabaco) kiosk **(b)** (para orquesta) bandstand
kiwi /'kiwi/ *m* **(a)** (Bot) kiwifruit, Chinese gooseberry **(b)** (Zool) kiwi
klaxon *m* ▶ CLAXON
Kleenex®, **kleenex** /'klineks/ *m (pl* ~) tissue
Km. (= **kilómetro**) km
K.O. /'nokau(t)/ *or* (Esp) /'kao/ *m* KO; **lo dejó** ~ he knocked him out
koala *m* koala (bear)
kuchen /'kuxen/ *m* (Chi) (Coc) tart
Kurdistán *m* Kurdistan
kurdo -da *adj* Kurdish
■ *m,f* Kurd
Kuwait *m* Kuwait
Kuwaití *adj/mf* Kuwaiti

Ll

L, l *f (read as* /'ele/) *the letter* L, l
l. (= **litro**) l, liter*
la *art: ver* **el**
■ *pron pers* **(a)** (referido — a ella) her; (— a usted) you; (— a cosa) it; **no** ~ **conozco** I don't know her; **¿**~ **atienden?** can I help you?; **yo se** ~ **llevo** I'll take it to him **(b)** *(impers)* you, one *(frml)*
■ *m* (nota) A; (en solfeo) la
laberinto *m* (de caminos, pasillos) maze, labyrinth; (en jardín, parque) maze
labia *f (fam)* gift of the gab (colloq)
labio *m* lip; **leer los** ~**s** to lip-read; **sin despegar los** ~**s** without uttering a single word
labor *f* **(a)** (trabajo) work; **una** ~ **de equipo** teamwork; ~**es domésticas** housework; ~**es agrícolas** *or* **del campo** farm work **(b)** (de coser, bordar) needlework; (de punto) knitting
laborable *adj* **(a)** ⟨día⟩ working *(before n)* **(b)** ⟨tierra⟩ arable
laboral *adj* ⟨problemas/conflictos⟩ labor* *(before n)*, work *(before n)*; ▶ ACCIDENTE
laboratorio *m* laboratory
laborioso -sa *adj* ⟨persona⟩ hardworking, industrious; ⟨abejas⟩ industrious; ⟨tarea⟩ laborious
laborista *adj* Labour *(before n)*
■ *mf* member of the Labour Party

labrador -dora *m,f* (Agr) (propietario) farmer; (trabajador) farmworker
labrar [A1] *vt* **1** (Agr) ⟨tierra⟩ to work **2** ⟨madera⟩ to carve; ⟨piedra⟩ to cut; ⟨cuero⟩ to tool, work; ⟨metales⟩ to work
■ **labrarse** *v pron* (forjarse): ~**se un porvenir** to carve out a future for oneself
labriego -ga *m,f* farmworker
laburar [A1] *vi* (CS fam) to work
laca *f* (resina) lac, shellac; (barniz) lacquer; (para el pelo) hairspray
lacear [A1] *vt* (CS) ⟨ganado⟩ to lasso
lacio -cia *adj* ⟨pelo⟩ straight; ⟨cuerpo⟩ limp, weak
lacónico -ca *adj* laconic
lacrar [A1] *vt* (con cera) to seal
lacre *adj* (AmL) bright-red; (Chi) red
■ *m* sealing wax
lacrimógeno -na *adj* (fam) ⟨película⟩ weepy (colloq), tear-jerking *(before n)* (colloq); ▶ GAS
lactancia *f* (secreción de leche) lactation; **durante el período de** ~ while breastfeeding
lácteo -tea *adj* dairy *(before n)*, milk *(before n)*
ladeado -da *adj:* **el cuadro está** ~ the picture ···❖

is on a slant *o* is askew; **llevaba el sombrero ~** he wore his hat at an angle; **con la cabeza ladeada** with his head tilted to one side
ladear [A1] *vt* ⟨*cabeza*⟩ to tilt ... to one side; ⟨*objeto*⟩ to tilt
■ **ladearse** *v pron* (inclinarse) to lean to one side
ladera *f* hillside, mountainside; **la ~ norte** the northern slope *o* side
ladino -na *adj* [1] (taimado) sly, cunning [2] (AmC, Méx) **(a)** (mestizo) of mixed race **(b)** (hispanohablante) Spanish-speaking (*often used to refer to Indians who adopt Spanish ways*) [3] (Méx fam) (agudo) high-pitched, piercing
■ *m,f* (AmC, Méx) **(a)** (mestizo) mestizo, person of mixed race **(b)** (hispanohablante) Spanish-speaking Indian
lado *m* [1] **(a)** (en general) side; **está en el ~ derecho** it is on the right-hand side; **a este/al otro ~ del río** on this/on the other side of the river; **hacerse a un ~** to move to one side; **echarse a un ~** ⟨*coche*⟩ to swerve; ⟨*persona*⟩ to move over; **ponlas a un ~** set them aside; **¿de qué ~ estás?** whose side are you on?; **cambiar de ~** (Dep) to change sides (AmE) *o* (BrE) ends; **ver el ~ positivo de las cosas** to look on the bright side of things; **por el ~ de mi padre** on my father's side (of the family) ⟨*de papel, moneda, tela*⟩ side [2] (sitio, lugar): **a/en/por todos ~s** everywhere; **en algún ~** somewhere; **en cualquier ~** anywhere; **ir de un ~ para otro** to run around [3] (*en locs*) **al lado: viven en la casa de al ~** they live next door; **los vecinos de al ~** the next-door neighbors; **al lado de algn/algo** (contiguo a) next to sb/sth; beside sb/sth; (en comparación con) compared to sb/sth; **de lado** ⟨*meter/colocar*⟩ sideways; ⟨*tumbarse/dormir*⟩ on one's side; **de ~ a ~** ⟨*extenderse/cruzar*⟩ from one side to the other; **por otro lado** (en cambio) on the other hand; (además) apart from anything else; **por un ~ ..., pero por otro ~ ...** on the one hand ..., but on the other hand ...; **dejar algo de ~** to leave sth aside *o* to one side; **ir cada uno por su ~:** **cada uno se fue por su ~** they went their separate ways
ladrar [A1] *vi* **(a)** ⟨*perro*⟩ to bark **(b)** (fam) ⟨*persona*⟩ to yell (colloq), to bark (colloq)
ladrido *m* bark; **~s** barking
ladrillo *m* brick; **(de) color ~** brick-red
ladrón -drona *m,f* [1] (de bolsos, coches) thief; (de bancos) bank robber; (de casas) burglar [2] **ladrón** *m* (Elec) adaptor
ladronzuelo -la *m,f* petty thief
lagartija *f* wall lizard
lagarto *m* [1] (Zool) lizard [2] (Col fam) (persona) crawler (colloq)
lago *m* lake
lágrima *f* (Fisiol) tear; **le caían las ~s** tears were running down her face; **se le saltaron las ~s** it brought tears to his eyes; **~s de cocodrilo** crocodile tears (*pl*); **llorar a ~ viva** to cry one's eyes *o* heart out
lagrimal *m* **(a)** (extremo del ojo) corner of the eye **(b)** *tb* **conducto ~** tear duct

laguna *f* [1] (de agua dulce) lake, pool; (de agua salada) lagoon [2] **(a)** (en estudio, artículo) gap **(b)** (en la memoria) memory lapse
laico -ca *adj* secular, lay (*before n*)
■ *m,f* (*m*) layman, layperson; (*f*) laywoman, layperson
laísmo *m*: use of LA/LAS instead of LE/LES (*as in* LA/LAS DIJE QUE NO), *common in certain regions of Spain but not acceptable to most speakers*
laja *f* (AmS) slab
lama *m* lama
■ *f* (AmL) (musgo) moss; (verdín) green slime; (moho) mold*
lambetear [A1] *vt* (Col, Méx, Ven) to lick
lambiscón -cona *m,f* (Méx fam) bootlicker (colloq)
lambisquear [A1] *vt* **(a)** (Col) (lamer) to lick **(b)** (Méx fam) (lisonjear) to suck up to (colloq)
lamentable *adj* **(a)** ⟨*conducta/error/suceso*⟩ deplorable, terrible **(b)** ⟨*pérdida*⟩ sad; ⟨*estado/aspecto*⟩ pitiful; ⟨*error*⟩ regrettable
lamentación *f* lamentation (liter); **estoy harta de oír tus lamentaciones** (fam) I'm fed up with your complaining *o* grumbling
lamentar [A1] *vt* to regret; **lamento molestarlo** I'm sorry to disturb you; **lamentamos tener que comunicarle que ...** (frml) we regret to have to inform you that ...; **lo lamento mucho** I am very sorry
■ **lamentarse** *v pron* to complain, to grumble (colloq)
lamento *m* **(a)** (quejido — por un dolor físico) groan; (— por tristeza) wail **(b)** (elegía) lament
lamer [E1] *vt* ⟨*persona/animal*⟩ to lick
lámina *f* [1] (hoja, plancha) sheet [2] (Impr) **(a)** (plancha, ilustración) plate; (estampa) picture card **(b)** (Educ) wall chart
laminar [A1] *vt* to laminate
lámpara *f* lamp; **~ de pie/mesa** standard/table lamp
lamparín *m* (Per) kerosene lamp
lamparita *f* (RPl) (light) bulb
lampiño -ña *adj* (sin barba) smooth-faced; (con poco vello) with little body hair
lana *f* [1] (material) wool; (vellón, pelambre) fleece; **~ virgen** new wool; **una bufanda de ~** a wool *o* woolen scarf [2] (AmL fam) (dinero) dough (sl); **tienen mucha ~** they're loaded (colloq)
lanceta *f* **(a)** (Med) lancet **(b)** (Andes, Méx) (aguijón) sting
lancha *f* (barca grande) launch, cutter; (bote) motorboat; **~ fuera borda** (outboard) launch; **~ neumática** inflatable (dinghy); **~ salvavidas** lifeboat
langosta *f* (crustáceo) lobster; (insecto) locust
langostino *m* (grande) king prawn; (pequeño) prawn; **~ de río** crayfish, crawfish (esp AmE)
langüetear [A1] *vt* (Chi) to lick
languidecer [E3] *vi* ⟨*persona*⟩ to languish (liter); ⟨*entusiasmo/conversación*⟩ to flag

---

lánguido -da *adj* **(a)** (débil) listless, weak **(b)** ⟨*mirada/aspecto*⟩ languid

lanolina *f* lanolin

lanudo -da *adj* long-haired, shaggy

lanza *f* (arma — en las lides) lance; (— arrojadiza) spear

■ *m* (Chi) (delincuente) pickpocket, thief

lanzacohetes *m* (*pl* ~) rocket launcher

lanzado -da *adj* **1** [SER] (fam) (precipitado) impulsive, impetuous; (decidido, atrevido) forward **2** (fam) (rápido): **ir** ~ to shoot along (colloq); **pasar** ~ to shoot past

lanzador -dora *m,f* (Dep) (de disco, jabalina) thrower; (en béisbol) pitcher; ~ **de bala** *or* (Esp) **de peso** shot-putter

lanzamiento *m* **1** **(a)** (de objetos, pelota) throwing; (de misil, torpedo) launch; (de bomba) dropping **(b)** (de cohete, satélite) launch **(c)** (Dep) (de disco, jabalina) throw; (de bala) put; (en béisbol) pitch; ~ **de bala** *or* (Esp) **de peso** shot put; ~ **de disco/jabalina** discus/javelin throwing **2** (de producto, libro) launch, launching **3** (CS) (Der) *tb* **orden de** ~ eviction order

lanzamisiles *adj inv* missile-launching (*before n*)

■ *m* (*pl* ~) missile launcher

lanzar [A4] *vt* **1** **(a)** ⟨*pelota/objetos/jabalina*⟩ to throw; (en béisbol) to pitch **(b)** ⟨*misil/satélite*⟩ to launch; ⟨*bomba*⟩ to drop **2** ⟨*producto/libro*⟩ to launch **3** **(a)** ⟨*ofensiva/ataque/crítica*⟩ to launch **(b)** ⟨*mirada*⟩ to shoot, give; ⟨*indirecta*⟩ to drop; ⟨*grito*⟩ to give; **lanzó un grito de dolor** he cried out in pain

■ ~ *vi* (en béisbol) to pitch

■ **lanzarse** *v pron* **(a)** (*refl*) (arrojarse) to throw oneself; ~**se al agua/al vacío** to leap into the water/the void; ~**se en paracaídas** to parachute; (en una emergencia) to bale out **(b)** (abalanzarse, precipitarse): ~**se sobre algo/algn** to pounce on sth/sb; ~**se al ataque** to attack

lapa *f* **(a)** (molusco) limpet **(b)** (Ven) (mamífero) paca **(c)** (AmC) (ave) macaw

lapicera *f* (CS) pen; ~ **fuente** *or* **estilográfica** fountain pen

lapicero *m* **(a)** (portaminas) automatic pencil (AmE), propelling pencil (BrE) **(b)** (Esp) (lápiz) pencil **(c)** (AmC, Per) (bolígrafo) ballpoint pen

lápida *f* (en tumba) tombstone, gravestone; (losa conmemorativa) stone plaque

lapislázuli *m* lapis lazuli

lápiz *m* (de madera) pencil; (portaminas) automatic pencil (AmE), propelling pencil (BrE); **con** *or* **a** ~ in pencil; **lápices de colores** crayons (*pl*); ~ **de labios** lipstick; ~ **de ojos** eye pencil; ~ **de pasta** (Chi) ballpoint pen

lapso *m* **(a)** (de tiempo) space **(b)** (error, olvido) ▶ LAPSUS

lapsus *m* (*pl* ~) (error) slip, blunder; (olvido): **tuve un pequeño** ~ it slipped my mind

laptop *m* laptop (computer)

larga *f* **(a)** (largo plazo): **a la** ~ in the long run; **darle** ~**s a algn/algo** to put sb/sth off **(b)** (Auto) high beam (AmE), full *o* main beam (BrE)

largar [A3] *vt* **1** **(a)** (Náut) ⟨*amarras/cabo*⟩ to let out, pay out **(b)** (RPl) (soltar, dejar caer) to let ... go **2** ⟨*discurso/sermón*⟩ to give; ⟨*palabrota/insulto*⟩ to let fly **3** (fam) (despedir) to fire, to give ... the boot (colloq); ⟨*novio*⟩ to ditch **4** (CS, Méx) (Dep) ⟨*pelota*⟩ to throw; ⟨*carrera*⟩ to start

■ **largarse** *v pron* **(a)** (fam) (irse) to beat it (colloq); **¡yo me largo!** I'm taking off! (AmE), I'm off! (BrE) (colloq) **(b)** (CS fam) (empezar) to start, get going (colloq); ~**se** A **hacer algo** to start to do sth, to start doing sth

largavistas *m* (*pl* ~) (CS) binoculars (*pl*)

largo¹ -ga *adj* **(a)** (en general) long; **me queda largo** it's too long (for me); **es muy** ~ **de contar** it's a long story; **un tren de** ~ **recorrido** a long-distance train **(b)** (*en locs*) **a lo largo** ⟨*cortar/partir*⟩ lengthways; **a lo largo de** (de camino, río) along; (de jornada, novela) throughout; (de una semana, vida) in the course of; **de largo** ⟨*vestirse*⟩ to wear a long skirt/dress; *ver tb* PASAR I 1A; **va para** ~ (fam) it's going to be a while

largo² *m* **(a)** (longitud) length; **¿cuánto mide de** ~? how long is it? **(b)** (en natación) lap (AmE), length (BrE)

■ *interj* (fam) *tb* **¡**~ **de aquí!** get out of here!

largometraje *m* feature film, full-length film

larguero *m* **(a)** (Arquit, Const) (viga) crossbeam; (de puerta) jamb **(b)** (de cama) side **(c)** (Dep) crossbar

larguirucho -cha *adj* (fam) gangling (*before n*)

laringe *f* larynx

laringitis *f* laryngitis

larva *f* larva, grub

lasaña *f* lasagna, lasagne

lascivo -va *adj* lascivious, lustful

láser *m* laser

lástima *f* **(a)** (pena) shame, pity; **¡qué** ~! what a shame *o* pity!; **me da** ~ **tirarlo** it seems a pity *o* shame to throw it out **(b)** (compasión): **sentir** ~ **por algn** to feel sorry for sb; **digno de** ~ worthy of compassion

lastimadura *f* (AmL) graze

lastimar [A1] *vt* to hurt

■ **lastimarse** *v pron* (*refl*) (esp AmL) to hurt oneself; ⟨*dedo/rodillas*⟩ to hurt

lastimero -ra *adj* pitiful

lastre *m* **(a)** (de buque, globo) ballast **(b)** (carga, estorbo) burden

lata *f* **1** **(a)** (hojalata) tin **(b)** (envase) can, tin (BrE); **sardinas en** ~ canned *o* tinned sardines **(c)** (para galletas, etc) tin **2** (fam) (pesadez) nuisance, pain (colloq); **¡qué** ~! what a nuisance!; **dar (la)** ~ (fam) to be a nuisance; **¡deja ya de darme** ~! stop bugging *o* pestering me! (colloq)

latente *adj* latent

lateral *adj* ⟨*puerta/salida/calle*⟩ side (*before n*); ⟨*línea/sucesión*⟩ indirect, lateral

■ *m* (Dep) (poste) goalpost

■ *m or f* (Auto) (calle perpendicular) side street; (calle paralela) service road, frontage road (AmE)

■ *mf* (Dep) (alero) wing, winger; (defensa) left/right back

latido *m* (del corazón) heartbeat; (en la sien, una herida) throbbing

latifundio *m* large estate

latigazo *m* **(a)** (golpe) lash **(b)** (chasquido) crack of the whip

látigo *m* whip

latín *m* Latin

latino -na *adj* **(a)** ⟨literatura/gramática/pueblo⟩ Latin **(b)** (fam) (latinoamericano) Latin American ■ *m,f* **(a)** (español, italiano, etc) Latin **(b)** (fam) (latinoamericano) Latin American

Latinoamérica *f* Latin America

latinoamericano -na *adj/m,f* Latin American

latir [I1] *vi* **1** «corazón» to beat; «vena» to pulsate; «herida/sien» to throb **2** **(a)** (Chi, Méx fam) (parecer) (+ me/te/le etc): **me late que no vendrá** I have a feeling o something tells me he isn't going to come **(b)** (Méx fam) (parecer bien, gustar) (+ me/te/le etc): **¿te late ir al cine?** do you feel like going to the movies?

latitud *f* (Astron, Geog) latitude; **la flora de otras ~es** the flora of other parts of the world

latón *m* **(a)** (Metal) brass **(b)** (RPl) (palangana) metal bowl

latonería *f* (Col) body shop

latoso -sa *adj* **(a)** (fam) (molesto) annoying, tiresome; **no seas ~** don't be such a pain (colloq) **(b)** (Andes fam) (aburrido) dull, boring ■ *m,f* **(a)** (fam) (pesado) pain (in the neck) (colloq) **(b)** (Andes fam) (aburrido) bore

laucha *f* (CS) mouse

laúd *m* lute

laurel *m* (árbol) laurel; (Coc) bay leaf

lava *f* lava

lavable *adj* washable

lavabo *m* **(a)** (pila) sink (AmE), washbasin (BrE) **(b)** (retrete) toilet, bathroom; Ⓢ **lavabos** rest rooms (in US), toilets (in UK)

lavadero *m* **(a)** (habitación) utility room, laundry room; (pila) sink; (al aire libre) washing place **(b)** (RPl) (lavandería) laundry **(c)** (Col) (tina de lavar) washtub

lavado¹ -da *adj* **(a)** ⟨ropa/manos⟩ washed **(b)** (RPl fam) ⟨color⟩ (descolorido) washed-out; (muy claro) light; ⟨persona⟩ pale

lavado² *m* **1** **(a)** (de ropa) wash, washing; (de coche) wash; **~ en seco** dry cleaning; **hacerle un ~ de cerebro a algn** to brainwash sb; **le hicieron un ~ de estómago** they pumped his stomach out **(b)** (ropa, tanda) wash **2** (AmL) (de dinero) laundering

lavadora *f* washing machine

lavamanos *m* sink (AmE), washbasin (BrE)

lavanda *f* lavender ■ *m* lavender

lavandería *f* laundry; **~ automática** Laundromat® (AmE), launderette (BrE)

lavaplatos *mf* (*pl* ~) (persona) dishwasher ■ *m* (*pl* ~) **(a)** (máquina) dishwasher **(b)** (Andes) (fregadero) sink

lavar [A1] *vt* **1** ⟨ropa/coche⟩ to wash; ⟨suelo⟩ to mop; ⟨fruta/verdura⟩ to wash; **hay que ~lo en seco/a mano** it has to be dry-cleaned/hand-washed **2** (AmL) ⟨dinero⟩ to launder ■ ~ *vi* (lavar ropa) to do the laundry o (BrE) washing **(b)** (en peluquería): **~ y marcar** to shampoo and set ■ **lavarse** *v pron* **(a)** (refl) to have a wash; ⟨cara/manos⟩ to wash; ⟨dientes⟩ to clean, brush; **~se el pelo** *or* **la cabeza** to wash one's hair **(b)** (Col fam) (empaparse) to get soaked

lavarropas *m* (*pl* ~) (RPl) washing machine

lavatorio *m* **(a)** (CS) (lavamanos) sink (AmE), washbasin (BrE) **(b)** (Chi, Per) (palangana) washbowl (AmE), washbasin (BrE)

lavavajillas *m* (*pl* ~) (detergente) dishwashing liquid (AmE), washing-up liquid (BrE); (máquina) dishwasher

laxante *adj* laxative (before n) ■ *m* laxative

lazar [A4] *vt* (Méx) to rope, lasso

lazo *m* **1** **(a)** (cinta) ribbon; (nudo decorativo) bow; **¿te hago un ~?** shall I tie it in a bow? **(b)** (Méx) (del matrimonio) cord with which the couple are symbolically united during the wedding ceremony **2** **(a)** (Agr) lasso **(b)** (cuerda) (Col, Méx) rope; (para saltar) (Col) ▶ CUERDA 1B **(c)** (para cazar) snare, trap **3** ▶ (vínculo) bond, tie

le *pron pers* **1** (como objeto indirecto): **~ dije la verdad** (a él) I told him the truth; (a ella) I told her the truth; (a usted) I told you the truth; **~ di otra mano de barniz** I gave it another coat of varnish; **~ robaron el dinero** they stole the money from him; **a este libro ~ faltan páginas** there are some pages missing from this book **2** (como objeto directo) (esp Esp) (referido — a él) him; (— a usted) you; **¿le conoces?** do you know him?; **hoy no ~ puedo recibir** I can't see him/you today

leal *adj* loyal, trusty; ⟨tropas⟩ loyal

lealtad *f* loyalty

leasing /'lisin/ *m* (contrato) lease; (sistema) leasing

lección *f* lesson; **no me supe la ~** I hadn't learned the lesson; **eso te servirá de ~** let that be a lesson to you

lechal *adj* suckling

leche *f* **1** (de madre, de vaca) milk; **~ descremada** *or* (Esp) **desnatada** skim milk (AmE), skimmed milk (BrE); **~ en polvo** powdered milk; **~ entera** whole milk, full-cream milk **2** (en cosmética) milk, lotion **3** (Esp vulg) (mal humor): **tiene una ~ ...** he's got a foul temper; **hacer algo con mala ~** to do sth deliberately o to be nasty; **tener mala ~** to be bad-tempered **4** (Andes fam) (suerte) luck; **estar con** *or* **de ~** to be lucky

lechera *f* (para transportar) churn; (para servir) milk jug

lechería *f* dairy, creamery

lechero -ra *adj* **1** **(a)** ⟨industria/vaca⟩ dairy (before n) **(b)** ⟨producción⟩ milk (before n) **2** (Col, Per fam) (afortunado) lucky ■ *m,f* (vendedor) (*m*) milkman; (*f*) milkwoman

lecho *m* **1** (liter) (cama) bed; **en su ~ de muerte** on her deathbed **2** (de río) bed; (capa, estrato) layer

lechón *m* (Coc) (cochinillo) suckling o sucking pig

lechosa *f* (AmC, Col, Ven) papaya

lechoso -sa *adj* ⟨líquido⟩ milky; ⟨piel⟩ pale

lechuga *f* lettuce

lechuza *f* owl

lectivo -va *adj* ⟨día⟩ school (before n); ⟨año⟩ academic (before n)

lector -tora *m,f* **(a)** (de libros, revistas) reader **(b)** (Esp) (Educ) foreign language assistant

lectura *f* **(a)** (acción) reading; **la ~ es su**

pasatiempo preferido reading is her favorite pastime **(b)** (texto) reading matter; ~s para niños reading material for children

leer [E13] vt **(a)** ⟨libro/texto⟩ to read; ~ los labios to lip-read; ~le el pensamiento a algn to read sb's mind **(b)** (Educ) ⟨tesis doctoral⟩ to defend **(c)** (Inf) to scan
■ ~ vi to read

legado m (Der) bequest, legacy

legal adj [1] (Der) **(a)** ⟨trámite/documentos⟩ legal **(b)** (lícito, permitido) lawful; lo haré si es ~ I'll do it as long as it's within the law [2] (Col, Per arg) (estupendo) great (colloq)

legalización f (Der) (de droga, aborto) legalization; (de documento) authentication

legalizar [A4] vt (Der) ⟨droga/aborto⟩ to legalize; ⟨documento⟩ to authenticate

legaña f sleep; tienes ~s en los ojos you have (some) sleep in your eyes

legar [A3] vt (en testamento) to bequeath, leave

legendario -ria adj legendary

legible adj legible

legión f (Hist, Mil) legion; (multitud) crowd

legionario¹ -ria adj legionary

legionario² m (romano) legionary; (de otras asociaciones) legionnaire

legislación f legislation

legislar [A1] vi to legislate

legislatura f **(a)** (mandato) term (of office); (año parlamentario) session **(b)** (AmL) (cuerpo) legislature, legislative body

legítimo -ma adj [1] ⟨hijo⟩ legitimate; ⟨esposa⟩ lawful (before n); ⟨heredero⟩ rightful (before n); ⟨derechos/reclamación/representante⟩ legitimate; en legítima defensa in self-defense [2] ⟨cuero⟩ genuine, real; ⟨oro⟩ real

lego -ga adj [1] (seglar) lay (before n) [2] (ignorante): soy ~ en la materia I know nothing at all about the subject
■ m,f **(a)** (fiel laico) layperson **(b)** (religioso) (m) lay brother; (f) lay sister **(c)** (Col) (curandero) quack

legua f league

legumbre f (garbanzo, lenteja, etc) pulse, legume; (hortaliza) vegetable

leído -da adj: ser muy ~ to be well-read

leísmo m: use of LE/LES instead of LO/LOS/LA/LAS (as in ESTE LIBRO NO TE LE PRESTO), common in certain regions of Spain but not acceptable to most speakers

lejanía f remoteness; en la ~ in the distance

lejano -na adj **(a)** ⟨época/futuro⟩ distant; ⟨lugar⟩ remote, far-off; el L~ Oriente the Far East **(b)** ⟨pariente⟩ distant

lejía f bleach

lejísimos adv ⟨quedar/estar⟩ very far (away); vive ~ she lives miles away

lejos adv [1] (en el espacio) far; no está muy ~ it isn't very far; queda ~ del centro it's a long way from the center; estaba ~ de imaginarme la verdad I was far from guessing the truth **(b)** (en locs) a lo lejos in the distance; de lejos from a distance; ir demasiado ~ to go too far; sin ir más ~ for example, for instance **(c)** (fam) (con mucho): es ~ (CS) o (Col, Méx) de ~ by far [2] (en el futuro) a long way off; las vacaciones aún están ~s the holidays are still a long way off

lelo -la adj (fam) (tonto) slow on the uptake; (pasmado) speechless

lema m (de insignia, de persona) motto; (de partido, anuncio publicitario) slogan

lempira m lempira (Honduran unit of currency)

lencería f lingerie

lengua f [1] **(a)** (Anat) tongue; se me traba la ~ I get tongue-tied (colloq); irse de la ~ or írsele la ~ a algn (fam): no debía haberlo dicho pero se me fue la ~ I shouldn't have said it but it just slipped out; no te vayas a ir de la ~ make sure you don't tell anybody; ▶ MALO 2 **(b)** (Coc) tongue **(c)** (de tierra) spit, tongue; (de fuego) tongue [2] (Ling) language; ~ materna mother tongue

lenguado m sole

lenguaje m language

lengüeta f (de zapato) tongue; (Mús) reed

lente m [en algunas regiones f] lens; ~ de contacto contact lens; ver tb LENTES

lenteja f lentil

lentejuela f sequin

lentes mpl (esp AmL) ▶ GAFAS A

lentilla f (Esp) contact lens

lentitud f slowness; con ~ slowly

lento¹ -ta adj slow

lento² adv slowly

leña f wood, firewood

leñador -dora m,f woodcutter

leño m log

Leo m (signo) Leo; es (de) ~ he's (a) Leo;
■ mf (pl ~) (persona) tb leo Leo

león -ona m,f (de África) (m) lion; (f) lioness

leonera f **(a)** (de león) lion's den **(b)** (Esp fam) (lugar desordenado) tip (colloq)

leopardo m leopard; ~ hembra leopardess

leotardo m: tb ~s (woolen) tights (pl)

lépero -ra adj (Méx) coarse

lepra f leprosy

leproso -sa adj leprous
■ m,f leper

lerdo -da adj (fam) (torpe) clumsy; (tonto) slow

les pron pers [1] (como objeto indirecto): ~ quiero mostrar algo (a ellos, ellas) I want to show them something; (a ustedes) I want to show you something; ~ puse fundas a los muebles I put covers on the furniture [2] (como objeto directo) (esp Esp) (referido — a ellos) them; (— a ustedes) you; no ~ reconocí I didn't recognize them/you; ¿~ atienden? can I help you?

lesbiana f lesbian

lesear [A1] vi (Chi fam) (tontear) to clown o fool around (colloq); (bromear) to joke (colloq); (flirtear) to flirt; (perder el tiempo) to laze around

lesera f (Chi fam) nonsense, tripe (colloq)

lesión f injury; sufrió una ~ cerebral he suffered brain damage

lesionado -da adj injured

lesionar [A1] vt ⟨persona⟩ to injure; le ~on la pierna en el partido his leg was hurt o injured in the game
■ **lesionarse** v pron «persona» to injure oneself; ⟨pierna/rodilla⟩ to injure

leso -sa adj (Chi fam) dumb (colloq); hacer ~ a algn (fam) to make a monkey out of sb (colloq)

letárgico -ca adj lethargic
letargo m lethargy
letra f ⓵ (a) (Impr, Ling) letter; ~ **bastardilla** or **cursiva** italic script, italics (pl); ~ **de imprenta** print; ~ **negrita** boldface, bold type; ~ **pequeña** or (AmS) **chica** small print (b) (caligrafía) writing, handwriting; **no entiendo tu** ~ I can't read your writing (c) **letras** fpl (carta breve): **solo unas** ~s **para decirte que ...** just a few lines to let you know that ...
⓶ (Mús) (de canción) words (pl), lyrics (pl)
⓷ (Fin) tb ~ **de cambio** bill of exchange, draft; **me quedan tres** ~s **por pagar** I still have three payments to make
⓸ **letras** fpl (Educ) arts (pl), liberal arts (pl) (AmE)
letrado -da adj learned
■ m,f (frml) lawyer
letrero m sign, notice; ~ **luminoso** neon sign
letrina f latrine
leucemia f leukemia
levadura f yeast; **pan sin** ~ unleavened bread; ~ **de cerveza** brewer's yeast; ~ **en polvo** (Esp) baking powder
levantado -da adj: **estar** ~ to be up
levantador -dora m,f (Dep) tb ~ **de pesas** weightlifter
levantamiento m (a) (sublevación) uprising (b) (de embargo, sanción) lifting; ~ **de pesas** weightlifting
levantar [A1] vt ⓵ (a) (del suelo) ⟨bulto/peso⟩ to lift, pick up (b) ⟨tapadera/mantel⟩ to lift (up); ⟨cabeza/mano/copa⟩ to raise; ⟨alfombra⟩ to lift up (c) ⟨persiana⟩ to pull up, raise (d) (elevar) ⟨voz⟩ to raise; **sin** ~ **la vista del libro** without looking up from her book (e) ⟨polvo⟩ to raise (f) (Jueg) ⟨carta⟩ to pick up
⓶ (a) ⟨ánimo⟩ to boost; ⟨moral⟩ to raise, boost (b) ⟨industria/economía⟩ to help ... to pick up
⓷ ⟨estatua/muro/edificio⟩ to erect, put up
⓸ ⟨embargo/sanción⟩ to lift; **le levantó el castigo** he let him off; **se levanta la sesión** the meeting is adjourned
⓹ ⟨rumor/protestas⟩ to spark (off); ⟨polémica⟩ to cause; ~ **sospechas** to arouse suspicion
⓺ ⟨campamento⟩ to strike; ~ **la mesa** (AmL) to clear the table
⓻ (en brazos) ⟨persona⟩ to pick up; (de la cama) to get ... out of bed; (poner de pie) to get ... up
⓼ (AmS) ⟨mujer⟩ to pick up (colloq)
■ **levantarse** v pron ⓵ (a) (de la cama) to get up (b) (ponerse en pie) to stand up, to rise (frml); **¿me puedo** ~ **de la mesa?** may I leave the table?
⓶ «polvareda» to rise; «temporal» to brew; «viento» to begin to blow, rise
⓷ (sublevarse) to rise (up)
⓸ (refl) ⟨solapas/cuello⟩ to turn up
⓹ (AmS fam) ⟨mujer⟩ to pick up (colloq)
levante m ⓵ (a) (Geog) (este) east (b) (viento) east wind ⓶ (AmS fam) (conquista) pick up
levar [A1] vt: ~ **anclas** to weigh anchor
leve adj (a) ⟨perfume/gasa⟩ delicate (b)

⟨sospecha/duda⟩ slight; ⟨sonrisa⟩ slight; ⟨brisa⟩ gentle, slight; ⟨golpe⟩ gentle, light; ⟨enfermedad⟩ mild; ⟨herida/lesión⟩ slight; ⟨pecado⟩ venial; ⟨castigo/sanción⟩ light; ⟨infracción⟩ minor
levita f (Indum) frock coat
léxico¹ -ca adj lexical
léxico² m (vocabulario) vocabulary, lexis (tech); (diccionario) lexicon; (glosario) glossary, lexicon
ley f ⓵ (en general) law; **violar la** ~ to break the law; **iguales ante la** ~ equal in the eyes of the law; ~ **de la oferta y la demanda** law of supply and demand; **la** ~ **del más fuerte** the survival of the fittest; ~ **pareja no es dura** (CS) a rule isn't unfair if it applies to everyone ⓶ (de oro, plata) assay value
leyenda f (a) (Lit) (narración) legend (b) (de moneda, escudo) legend; (de ilustración) caption, legend
leyeron, leyó, etc ▶ LEER
liado -da adj (fam) (a) (ocupado) tied up (b) (relacionado) ~ **CON algn** involved **WITH** sb
liana f liana
liar [A17] vt ⓵ (a) ⟨cigarrillo⟩ to roll (b) (atar) to tie (up); (envolver) to wrap (up); (en un fardo, manojo) to bundle (up) ⓶ (fam) (a) ⟨situación/asunto⟩ to complicate (b) (confundir) ⟨persona⟩ to confuse, get ... in a muddle (c) (en un asunto) ⟨persona⟩ to involve
■ **liarse** v pron ⓵ (fam) (a) «asunto» to get complicated (b) «persona» to get confused ⓶ (Esp fam) (a) (entretenerse): **nos liamos a hablar y ... we** got talking and ... (b) (emprenderla): **se** ~**on a golpes** they started throwing punches at each other
libanés -nesa adj/m,f Lebanese
Líbano m: tb **el** ~ Lebanon
libélula f dragonfly
liberación f (de preso, rehén) release, freeing; (de pueblo, país) liberation; **la** ~ **de la mujer** Women's Liberation, Women's Lib
liberado -da adj ⟨mujer⟩ liberated
liberal adj liberal
■ mf Liberal
liberalismo m liberalism
liberalizar [A4] vt ⟨comercio/importaciones⟩ to relax the restrictions on
liberar [A1] vt (a) ⟨prisionero/rehén⟩ to release, free; ⟨pueblo/país⟩ to liberate (b) (de una obligación) ~ **a algn DE algo** to free sb **FROM** sth
■ **liberarse** v pron ~**se DE algo** ⟨de ataduras/deudas⟩ to free oneself **FROM** sth
libertad f ⓵ (para actuar) freedom; **queda usted en** ~ you are free to go; **poner a algn en** ~ to release sb; ~ **bajo fianza** bail; ~ **condicional** parole; ~ **de expresión/de prensa** freedom of speech/of the press ⓶ (confianza): **pídelo con toda** ~ feel free to ask; **habla con toda** ~ speak freely; **tomarse la** ~ **de hacer algo** to take the liberty of doing sth
libertador -dora m,f liberator
libertinaje m licentiousness

libertino -na *adj* dissolute, licentious
■ *m,f* libertine

Libia *f* Libya

libidinoso -sa *adj* lustful

libido, líbido *f* libido

libio -bia *adj/m,f* Libyan

libra *f* pound; **∼ esterlina** pound sterling

Libra *m* (signo) Libra; **es (de) ∼** she's (a) Libra, she's a Libran
■ *mf* (*pl* **∼** *or* **-bras**) (persona) *tb* **libra** Libran, Libra

libramiento *m* (Méx) (Transp) beltway (AmE), relief road (BrE)

librar [A1] *vt* **1** (liberar) **∼ a algn** DE **algo** ⟨*de peligro*⟩ to save sb FROM sth; ⟨*de obligación/responsabilidad*⟩ to free sb FROM sth; **¡Dios nos libre!** God forbid! **2** ⟨*batalla/combate*⟩ to fight
■ **librarse** *v pron*: **se libró por poco** he had a lucky escape; **∼se** DE **algo** ⟨*de tarea/obligación*⟩ to get out of sth; **∼se de un castigo** to escape punishment; **se libró de tener que ayudarlo** she got out of having to help him; **se ∼on de morir asfixiados** they escaped being suffocated; **∼se** DE **algn** to get rid OF sb

libre *adj* **1** ⟨*país/pueblo*⟩ free; **lo dejaron ∼** they set him free; **eres ∼ de ir donde quieras** you're free to go wherever you want; **∼ albedrío** free will; **∼ cambio** *or* **comercio** free trade; **∼ mercado** free market **2** ⟨*traducción/adaptación*⟩ free; **los 200 metros ∼s** the 200 meters freestyle **3** (no ocupado) ⟨*persona/tiempo/asiento*⟩ free; **¿tienes un rato ∼?** do you have a free moment?; **en sus ratos ∼s** in her spare *o* free time; **tengo el día ∼** I have the day off **4** (exento): **artículos ∼s de impuestos** duty-free goods

librecambista *adj* free-trade (*before n*)

librería *f* **1** (tienda) bookstore (AmE), bookshop (BrE); **∼ de ocasión** second-hand bookstore **2** (Esp) (mueble) bookcase

librero -ra *m,f* **(a)** (Com) bookseller **(b) librero** *m* (Chi, Méx) (mueble) bookcase

libreta *f* notebook; **∼ de ahorro** passbook, bankbook; **∼ de calificaciones** (AmL) school report

libretearse [A1] *v pron* (AmC fam) to play hooky (esp AmE colloq), to skive off (school) (BrE colloq)

libreto *m* **1** **(a)** (de ópera) libretto **(b)** (AmL) (guion) script **2** (Chi) *tb* **∼ de cheques** checkbook*

libro *m* (Impr) book; **un ∼ de cocina** a cookbook; **llevar los ∼s** (Fin) to do the bookkeeping; **∼ de bolsillo** paperback; **∼ de consulta** reference book; **∼ de escolaridad** school record; **∼ de familia** *booklet recording details of one's marriage, children's birthdates, etc*; **∼ de texto** textbook

liceal *mf* (Ur) high school student (AmE), secondary school pupil (BrE)

liceano -na *m,f* (Chi) ▶ LICEAL

liceísta *mf* (Ven) ▶ LICEAL

licencia *f* **1** (documento) license*; **∼ de caza** hunting permit; **∼ de conducir** *or* (AmC, Méx, Ven) **de manejar** driver's license (AmE), driving licence (BrE) **2** **(a)** (Mil) leave; **con ∼** on leave **(b)** (AmL) (de un trabajo) leave; **estar de ∼** to be on leave

licenciado -da *m,f* **(a)** (Educ) graduate; **∼ en Filosofía y Letras** ≈ arts *o* (AmE) liberal arts graduate **(b)** (AmC, Méx) (abogado) lawyer

licenciar [A1] *vt* ⟨*soldado*⟩ to discharge
■ **licenciarse** *v pron* «*estudiante*» to graduate

licenciatura *f* degree

licencioso -sa *adj* dissolute

liceo *m* (CS, Ven) high school (AmE), secondary school (BrE)

licitación *f* (esp AmL) tender; **se llamará a ∼ para la construcción del puente** the construction of the bridge will be put out to tender

licitar [A1] *vt* (esp AmL) (llamar a concurso para) to invite tenders for; (presentar una propuesta para) to put in a tender for

lícito -ta *adj* **(a)** (dentro de la ley) ⟨*acto/conducta*⟩ legal, lawful; ⟨*jugada*⟩ legal **(b)** (admisible) justifiable, reasonable

licor *m* (bebida dulce) liqueur; (alcohol) liquor, spirits (*pl*)

licuado *m* (AmL) (con leche) (milk) shake; (de frutas) fruit drink

licuadora *f* blender, liquidizer (BrE)

licuar [A18] *vt* **(a)** (Coc) ⟨*frutas/verduras*⟩ to blend, liquidize **(b)** (Fís, Quím) to liquefy

líder¹ *mf* **(a)** (Com, Dep, Pol) leader **(b)** (como adj) ⟨*equipo/marca/empresa*⟩ leading (*before n*)

líder², **lideresa** *m,f* (Méx) (Dep, Pol) leader

liderazgo, liderato *m* leadership

lidiar [A1] *vt* ⟨*toro*⟩ to fight
■ ∼ *vi*: **∼** CON **algn/algo** to battle WITH sb/sth

liebre *f* **1** (Zool) hare **2** (Chi) (Transp) small bus

liendre *f* nit

lienzo *m* **1** **(a)** (Art) canvas **(b)** (Tex) cloth **2** (Arquit) (pared) wall

lifting /'liftin/ *m* facelift

liga *f* **1** (asociación) league; (Dep) league, conference (esp AmE) **2** **(a)** (Indum) garter **(b)** (AmL) (gomita) rubber *o* (BrE) elastic band

ligado *adj* [ESTAR] (conectado) connected, linked; (apegado) **∼ A algn** attached TO sb; **se siente muy ∼ a su país** he feels a strong bond with his country

ligadura *f* **(a)** (Med) ligature **(b) ligaduras** *fpl* (ataduras) bonds (*pl*), ties (*pl*)

ligamento *m* ligament

ligar [A3] *vt* **(a)** (unir) to bind; **los ligaba una gran amistad** they were bound together by a strong friendship **(b)** (atar): **le ∼on las manos** they tied his hands together; **un fajo de billetes ligados con una goma elástica** a bundle of bills held together with a rubber band **(c)** ⟨*metales*⟩ to alloy; ⟨*salsa*⟩ to bind
■ ∼ *vi* (fam) (con el sexo opuesto): **salieron a ∼** they went out on the make *o* (BrE) pull (colloq); **∼** CON **algn** to make out WITH sb (AmE), to get off WITH sb (BrE)
■ **ligarse** *v pron* (fam) (conquistar) to make out with (AmE colloq), to get off with (colloq BrE)

ligazón *f* connection, link

ligereza *f* **1** (de objeto) lightness **2** **(a)** (de carácter) flippancy; con **∼** ⟨*actuar/hablar*⟩ flippantly **(b)** (acto, dicho irreflexivo): **cometió la ∼ de mencionarlo** he thoughtlessly mentioned it **3** (agilidad) agility, nimbleness; (rapidez) speed

ligero¹ -ra *adj* **1** (liviano) **(a)** ⟨*paquete/gas/* ⋯⫶

metal⟩ light; ⟨*tela*⟩ light, thin; ∼ **de ropa** lightly
dressed; **viajar ∼ de equipaje** to travel light **(b)**
⟨*comida/masa*⟩ light **2** ⟨*leve*⟩ **(a)** ⟨*dolor/sabor/
olor*⟩ slight; ⟨*inconveniente*⟩ slight, minor; ⟨*golpe*⟩
gentle, slight; **tener el sueño ∼** to be a light
sleeper **(b)** ⟨*sensación/sospecha*⟩ slight **3** ⟨*no
serio*⟩ ⟨*conversación*⟩ lighthearted; ⟨*película/
lectura*⟩ lightweight; **a la ligera** ⟨*actuar*⟩ without
thinking, hastily; **todo se lo toma a la ligera** he
doesn't take anything seriously **4** ⟨*ágil*⟩
⟨*movimiento*⟩ agile, nimble; ⟨*rápido*⟩ ⟨*persona/
animal/vehículo*⟩ fast

ligero² *adv* quickly, fast

light /lajt/ *adj inv* ⟨*cigarrillos*⟩ low-tar;
⟨*alimentos*⟩ low-calorie; ⟨*refresco*⟩ diet (*before n*)

ligue *m* (Esp, Méx fam) **(a)** ⟨*persona*⟩: **el nuevo ∼
de Ana** Ana's new man (colloq) **(b)** ⟨*acción*⟩: **ir de
∼** to go out on the make *o* (BrE) pull

liguero *m* garter belt (AmE), suspender belt
(BrE)

lija *f* **(a)** ⟨*para madera, metales*⟩ *tb* **papel de ∼**
sandpaper **(b)** (Ven) ▶ LIMA 1B

lijar [A1] *vt* to sand (down)

lila *f* (Bot) lilac
■ *adj* ⟨*gen inv*⟩ ⟨*color*⟩ lilac
■ *m* ⟨*color*⟩ lilac

lima *f* **1** **(a)** ⟨*herramienta*⟩ file **(b)** ⟨*para uñas — de
metal*⟩ nail file; ⟨*—de papel*⟩ emery board **2** (Bot)
⟨*fruto*⟩ lime; ⟨*árbol*⟩ lime (tree)

Lima *f* Lima

limar [A1] *vt* ⟨*uñas/metal*⟩ to file
■ **limarse** *v pron* ⟨*uñas*⟩ to file

limeño -ña *adj* of/from Lima
■ *m,f* person from Lima

limitación *f* **(a)** ⟨*restricción*⟩ restriction,
limitation **(b)** ⟨*carencia*⟩ limitation; ⟨*defecto*⟩
shortcoming

limitado -da *adj* ⟨*poder/número/edición*⟩
limited; **estar ∼ A/POR algo** to be restricted TO/BY
sth

limitar [A1] *vt* ⟨*funciones/derechos*⟩ to limit,
restrict
■ ∼ *vi* ∼ **CON algo** «*país/finca*» to border ON sth
■ **limitarse** *v pron*: **el problema no se limita a las
ciudades** the problem is not confined *o* limited to
cities; **me limité a repetir lo dicho** I just repeated
what was said

límite *m* **1** (Geog, Pol) boundary **2** ⟨*tope*⟩ limit;
el ∼ de velocidad the speed limit; **su ambición no
tiene ∼s** his ambition knows no limits; **sin ∼s**
unlimited; **¡todo tiene un ∼!** enough is enough!
3 (*como adj inv*): **tiempo ∼** time limit; **situación
∼** extreme situation; **fecha ∼** deadline

limítrofe *adj* ⟨*país/provincia*⟩ neighboring*
(*before n*); ⟨*conflicto*⟩ border (*before n*)

limo *m* **1** ⟨*barro*⟩ mud, slime **2** (Col) (Bot) lime
(tree)

limón *m* **(a)** ⟨*fruto amarillo*⟩ lemon **(b)** (AmL) ⟨*árbol*⟩
lemon tree **(c)** (Méx, Ven) ⟨*fruto verde*⟩ lime

limonada *f* lemonade

limonero *m* lemon tree

limosna *f* alms (*pl*) (arch); **pedir ∼** to beg; **dar
∼** to give money to beggars

limosnear [A1] *vi* (AmL) to beg

limosnero -ra *m,f* (AmL) beggar

limpiabotas *mf* (*pl* ∼) bootblack; ⟨*niño*⟩
shoeshine boy

limpiacristales *m* (*pl* ∼) (Esp) ⟨*líquido*⟩
window cleaner
■ *mf* ⟨*persona*⟩ window cleaner

limpiador¹ -dora *m,f* ⟨*persona*⟩ cleaner

limpiador² *m* (Méx) (Auto) ▶ LIMPIAPARABRISAS

limpiamuebles *m* (*pl* ∼) furniture polish

limpiaparabrisas *m* (*pl* ∼) windshield
wipers (*pl*) (AmE), windscreen wipers (*pl*) (BrE)

limpiar [A1] *vt* **1** **(a)** ⟨*casa/mueble/zapatos*⟩ to
clean; ⟨*arroz/lentejas*⟩ to wash; ⟨*pescado*⟩ to
clean; ⟨*aire/atmósfera*⟩ to clear; **lo limpió con un
trapo** he wiped it with a cloth; **∼ algo en seco** to
dry-clean sth **(b)** ⟨*nombre*⟩ to clear; ⟨*honor*⟩ to
restore **2** ⟨*dejar libre*⟩ ∼ **algo DE algo** to clear sth
OR sth **3** (fam) **(a)** (en el juego) ⟨*persona*⟩ to clean
... out (colloq) **(b)** «*ladrones*» ⟨*casa*⟩ to clean ...
out (colloq)
■ ∼ *vi* to clean
■ **limpiarse** *v pron* (refl) ⟨*boca/nariz*⟩ to wipe; **se
∼on los zapatos al entrar** they wiped their shoes
as they came in

limpiavidrios *mf* (*pl* ∼) (esp AmL) ⟨*persona*⟩
window cleaner
■ *m* ⟨*líquido*⟩ window cleaner

limpieza *f* **1** ⟨*estado, cualidad*⟩ cleanliness
2 ⟨*acción*⟩ cleaning; **la señora de la ∼** the
cleaning lady; **∼ de cutis** skin cleansing; **∼ en
seco** drycleaning; **∼ general** spring-cleaning
(AmE), spring-clean (BrE); **∼ étnica** ethnic
cleansing **3** ⟨*por la policía*⟩ clean-up operation;
(Pol) purge

limpio¹ -pia *adj* **1** **(a)** [ESTAR] ⟨*casa/vestido/
vaso*⟩ clean **(b)** ⟨*aire*⟩ clean; ⟨*cielo*⟩ clear **(c)**
pasar algo en *or* (Esp) **a ∼** to make a clean (AmE)
o (BrE) fair copy of sth
2 [SER] **(a)** ⟨*persona*⟩ clean **(b)** ⟨*dinero/
campaña*⟩ clean; ⟨*elecciones/juego*⟩ fair, clean; **un
asunto poco ∼** an underhand business **(c)** ⟨*libre*⟩
∼ DE algo ⟨*de impurezas/polvo*⟩ free OF sth
3 ⟨*neto*⟩: **saca unos $70 ∼s por mes** she makes
$70 a month after deductions; **sacar en ∼: no
sacó nada en ∼ de todo lo que dijo** he didn't
make sense of anything he said; **lo único que
saqué en ∼ es que ...** the only thing that I got
clear was that ...

limpio² *adv* ⟨*jugar/pelear*⟩ fairly, clean

linaje *m* descent, lineage (frml)

linaza *f* linseed

lince *m* (Zool) lynx; ⟨*persona*⟩: **es un ∼ para los
negocios** he's a very shrewd businessman

linchar [A1] *vt* to lynch

lindar [A1] *vi* ∼ **CON algo** (limitar) to adjoin sth;
(aproximarse a) to border ON sth, verge ON sth

lindo¹ -da *adj* **1** ⟨*bonito*⟩ ⟨*bebé*⟩ cute, sweet;
⟨*casa/canción*⟩ lovely; ⟨*cara*⟩ pretty **2** (esp AmL)
⟨*agradable*⟩ ⟨*gesto/detalle*⟩ nice; ⟨*fiesta/viaje*⟩
wonderful; ⟨*ceremonia*⟩ beautiful; **¡es una
persona tan linda!** she's such a lovely person; **de
lo ∼** (fam): **nos divertimos de lo ∼** we had a great
time

lindo² *adv* (AmL) ⟨*cantar/bailar*⟩ beautifully; **se
siente ∼** (Méx) it feels wonderful

lindura *f* (AmL) delight; **me pareció una ∼** I
thought it was lovely

línea *f* **1** ⟨*en general*⟩ line; **la ∼ de puntos** the

liso -sa adj [1] ⟨piel/superficie⟩ smooth; ⟨pelo⟩ straight; ⟨terreno⟩ flat [2] (sin dibujos) plain [3] (Per fam) (insolente) fresh (AmE colloq), cheeky (BrE colloq)

lisonjero -ra adj ⟨palabras⟩ flattering; **es un hombre muy ~** he's a terrible flatterer

lista f (a) (de nombres, números) list; **pasar ~** (Educ) to take roll call, to take the register (BrE); **~ de boda** wedding list; **~ de espera** waiting list; **~ de éxitos** (Mús) charts (pl); (Lit) best-seller list (b) (raya) stripe; **a ~s** striped

listado m (Inf) printout; (lista) list; **~ electoral** (RPI) electoral roll o register

listar [A1] vt to list

listín m (Esp) tb **~ de teléfonos** telephone directory

listo -ta adj [1] [SER] ⟨persona⟩ clever, bright, smart (colloq); **se pasó de ~** he tried to be too clever; **estar ~** (fam): **ahora sí que estamos ~s** we're in real trouble now (colloq); **está lista si cree eso** if that's what she thinks, she's got another think coming (colloq) [2] (a) [ESTAR] (preparado) ready; **~ PARA algo/ hacer algo** ready FOR sth/to do sth (b) [ESTAR] (terminado) finished; **lo doblas así y ~** you fold it like this and that's it (finished) (c) (Andes fam) (manifestando acuerdo) okay (colloq)

■ m,f (esp Esp) (a) (inteligente) clever one; **el ~ de la clase** (pey) the class know-it-all (colloq & pej) (b) (vivo, astuto) tricky customer (colloq)

listón m (a) (de madera) strip; (en salto de altura) bar (b) (Méx) (cinta) ribbon

lisura f (Per) (a) (fam) (grosería) four-letter word (colloq) (b) (gracia) gracefulness

litera f (en dormitorio) bunk; (en barco) bunk, berth; (en tren) berth, couchette (BrE)

literal adj literal

literalmente adv ⟨traducir⟩ literally; ⟨repetir⟩ word for word

literario -ria adj literary

literato -ta m,f (m) man of letters; (f) woman of letters

literatura f literature; **~ infantil** juvenile books (AmE), children's books (BrE)

litigar [A3] vi to be at law o in litigation (frml), to be in dispute

litigio m (a) (Der) lawsuit (b) (disputa) dispute

litografía f (sistema) lithography; (grabado) lithograph

litoral adj coastal
■ m coast; **un largo ~** a long coastline

litro m liter*

Lituania f Lithuania

lituano¹ -na adj/m,f Lithuanian

lituano² m (idioma) Lithuanian

liturgia f liturgy

liviano -na adj (esp AmL) (a) ⟨paquete/tela⟩ light (b) ⟨comida⟩ light; **tiene un sueño muy ~** she's a very light sleeper (c) ⟨obra/película⟩ lightweight

lívido -da adj (pálido) pallid; (morado) livid

living /'liβiŋ/ m (pl **-vings**) (esp AmS) living room

Ll, ll f (read as /'eʎe/) combination traditionally considered as a separate letter in the Spanish alphabet

llaga f (Med) sore, ulcer; (Bib) wound

---

lineal adj linear

lingo m (Per) leapfrog

lingote m ingot

lingüística f linguistics

lingüístico -ca adj ⟨fenómeno/aptitud⟩ linguistic; ⟨barrera⟩ language (before n)

lino m (planta) flax; (tela) linen

linóleo m lino, linoleum

linterna f (fanal) lantern; (de pilas) flashlight (AmE), torch (BrE)

lío m [1] (a) (fam) (embrollo, confusión) mess; **armarse/hacerse un ~ (con algo)** to get into a mess (with sth) (colloq) (b) (fam) (problema, complicación) trouble; **meterse en un ~** to get oneself into trouble; **tiene ~s con la policía** he's in trouble with the police (colloq); **¡qué ~ se va a armar!** there's going to be hell to pay! (colloq) (c) (fam) (amorío) affair [2] (fardo) bundle

lioso -sa adj (fam) confusing, muddling

liquidación f [1] (en tienda) sale; **~ total** clearance sale [2] (de negocio, activo) liquidation [3] (a) (de cuenta, deuda) settlement (b) (Méx) (compensación por despido) severance pay

liquidar [A1] vt [1] ⟨existencias⟩ to sell off [2] ⟨negocio⟩ to wind up; ⟨activo⟩ to liquidate [3] (a) ⟨deuda/cuenta⟩ to settle; ⟨sueldo/pago⟩ to pay (b) (Méx) ⟨trabajador⟩ to pay ... off [4] (fam) ⟨persona⟩ (matar) to do away with (colloq); (destruir) (AmL) to destroy (colloq)

liquidez f liquidity

líquido¹ -da adj [1] ⟨sustancia⟩ liquid [2] ⟨sueldo/renta⟩ net

líquido² m [1] (sustancia) liquid; **~ de frenos** brake fluid [2] (dinero) cash

lira f (a) (Mús) lyre (b) (Fin) lira

lírica f poetry

lírico -ca adj (a) (Lit, Mús) lyric (b) (Per, RPI fam) ⟨persona⟩ dreamy, starry-eyed (colloq)

lirio m iris

lirón m dormouse; ▶ DORMIR vi

lis f lily

lisiado -da adj crippled
■ m,f cripple; **un ~ de guerra** a disabled veteran

lisiarse [A1] v pron (refl): **se lisió la columna vertebral** he damaged his spine

llama f [1] (de fuego) flame; **la casa ardía en ~s** the house was in flames; **~ piloto** pilot light [2] (Zool) llama

llamada f call; **hacer una ~** to make a phone call; **~ a cobro revertido** or (Chi, Méx) **por cobrar** collect call (AmE), reverse-charge call (BrE); **~ de larga distancia** long-distance call; **~ local** or **urbana** local call; **~ al orden** call to order

llamado¹ -da adj [1] (por un nombre) called; **un lugar ~ La Dehesa** a place called La Dehesa; **el 747, también ~ 'jumbo'** the 747, also known as the jumbo jet; **el ~ 'boom' de los sesenta** the so-called 'boom' of the sixties [2] (a la fama, éxito) ▶ DESTINADO 1A

llamado² m (a) (AmL) (al público) ▶ LLAMAMIENTO (b) (Arg) (Telec) ▶ LLAMADA

llamamiento m call; **hacer un ~ a la calma** to appeal for calm

llamar [A1] vt [1] ‹bomberos/policía› to call; ‹médico› to call (out); ‹camarero/criada/ascensor› to call; ‹súbditos/servidores› to summon; ‹taxi› (por teléfono) to call; (en la calle) to hail; **lo llamó por señas** she beckoned to him; **el sindicato los llamó a la huelga** the union called them out on strike [2] (por teléfono) to phone, to call; **te llamó Eva** Eva phoned (for you) [3] (a) (dar el nombre de) to call, name; (dar el título, apodo de) to call (b) (considerar) to call; **eso es lo que yo llamo un amigo** that's what I call a friend ■ ~ vi [1] (con los nudillos) to knock; (tocar el timbre) to ring (the doorbell); **llaman a la puerta** there's someone at the door [2] (Telec) ‹persona› to telephone, phone, call; ‹teléfono› to ring; **¿quién llama?** who's calling?; ver tb COBRO B ■ **llamarse** v pron to be called; **su padre se llama Pedro** his father is called Pedro, his father's name is Pedro; **¿cómo te llamas?** what's your name?

llamarada f (de fuego) sudden blaze, flare-up

llamativo -va adj ‹color› bright; ‹mujer/vestido› striking

llanamente adv: **lisa** or **simple y ~** ‹explicar/hablar› in straightforward terms; **lisa y ~, hay que despedirlos** they should be fired, it's as simple as that

llanero -ra m,f (a) (habitante del llano) (m) plainsman; (f) plainswoman (b) (vaquero) cattle herder, cowboy (of the Colombian/Venezuelan LLANOS)

llaneza f simplicity

llano¹ -na adj (a) ‹terreno/superficie› (horizontal) flat; (sin desniveles) even; **los 100 metros ~s** (RPI) the 100 meters dash o sprint (b) ‹persona› straightforward; ‹trato› natural; ‹lenguaje› plain

llano² m (a) (Geog) (llanura) plain (b) (extensión de terreno) area of flat ground

llanta f (a) (de metal) rim (b) (AmL) (neumático) tire*; **~ de repuesto** or (Méx) **de refacción** spare tire*

llanto m (de niño) crying; (de adulto) crying, weeping (liter)

llanura f (Geog) plain, prairie

llapa f ▶ YAPA

llave f [1] (en general) key; **cierra la puerta con ~** lock the door; **~ del éxito** the key to success; **~ de contacto** ignition key; **~ maestra** master key, passkey [2] (Mec) (herramienta) wrench (AmE), spanner (BrE); **~ inglesa** monkey wrench [3] (a) (interruptor) switch; (en tubería) valve; **la ~ del gas** the gas jet (AmE) o (BrE) tap; **cerrar la ~ de paso** to turn the water/gas off at the main valve (AmE) o (BrE) at the mains (b) (AmL) (de lavabo, bañera) faucet (AmE), tap (BrE) [4] (en un texto) brace [5] (en lucha, judo) hold; **lo inmovilizó con una ~ (de brazo)** he got him in an armlock

llavero m key ring

llegada f (a) (de un viaje) arrival; (b) (Dep) (meta) finishing line, wire (AmE); (Equ) winning post

llegar [A3] vi [1] «persona/tren/carta» to arrive; **tienen que estar por** or **al ~** they'll be arriving any minute now; **~on cansadísimos** they were exhausted when they arrived; **¿falta mucho para ~?** is it much further (to go)?; **siempre llega tarde** he's always late; **no me llegó el telegrama** I didn't get the telegram; **~ A algo** ‹a país/ciudad› to arrive IN sth; ‹a edificio› to arrive AT sth; **~ a casa** to arrive o get home; **el rumor llegó a oídos del alcalde** the rumor reached the mayor [2] «camino/ruta/tren» (ir) **~ A** or **HASTA** to go all the way to, to go as far as; **solo llega al tercer piso** it only goes (up) to the third floor [3] «día/invierno» (venir) to come, arrive; **ha llegado el momento de ...** the time has come to ... [4] (a) (alcanzar) to reach; **~ A algo** ‹a acuerdo/conclusión› to reach sth, come to sth; ‹a estante/techo› to reach; **llegué a la conclusión de que...** I reached o came to the conclusion that ...; **los pies no le llegan al suelo** her feet don't touch the floor; **la falda le llegaba a los tobillos** her skirt came down to her ankles; **el agua le llegaba al cuello** the water came up to her neck; **las cosas ~on a tal punto que ...** things reached such a point that ... (b) (expresando logro): **~á lejos** she'll go far o a long way; **así no vas a ~ a ningún lado** you'll never get anywhere like that; **llegó a (ser) director** he became director; **~ a viejo** to live to old age; **llegué a conocerlo mejor** I got to know him better [5] **~ A + INF** (a) (al extremo de): **llegó a amenazarme** she even threatened me; **no llegó a pegarme** he didn't actually hit me (b) (en oraciones condicionales): **si lo llega a saber, no vengo** if I'd known, I wouldn't have come; **si llego a enterarme de algo, te aviso** if I happen to hear anything, I'll let you know

llenado m filling, filling up

llenador -dora adj (CS) ‹comida› filling

llenar [A1] *vt* **1** (a) ⟨*vaso/plato/cajón*⟩ to fill; ⟨*tanque*⟩ to fill (up); ⟨*maleta*⟩ to fill, pack; **no me llenes el vaso** don't fill my glass right up; **~ algo DE/CON algo** to fill sth WITH sth (b) ⟨*formulario*⟩ to fill out, to fill in (esp BrE)
2 (a) (cubrir) **~ algo DE algo** to cover sth WITH sth (b) ⟨*vacante*⟩ to fill
3 (colmar) ⟨*persona*⟩: **la noticia nos llenó de alegría** we were overjoyed by the news; **nos llenó de atenciones** he made a real fuss of us
4 (hacer sentirse realizado) ⟨*persona*⟩: **su carrera no la llena** she doesn't find her career fulfilling
~ *vi* «*comida*» to be filling
■ **llenarse** *v pron* **1** (a) «*recipiente/estadio*» to fill (up); **el teatro solo se llenó a la mitad** the theater only filled to half capacity *o* was only half full; **~se DE algo** to fill with sth (b) (cubrirse) **~se DE algo** ⟨*de polvo/pelos*⟩ to be covered IN sth
2 ⟨*bolsillo/boca*⟩ to fill; **~se algo DE algo** to fill sth WITH sth
3 (colmarse): **su corazón se llenó de alegría** she filled with joy; **se ~on de deudas** they got heavily into debt
4 «*persona*» (de comida): **con un plato de ensalada ya se llena** one plate of salad and she's full; **me llené** (colloq) I'm full (up) (colloq)

lleno¹ -na *adj* **1** (a) ⟨*estadio/autobús/copa*⟩ full; **~ DE algo** full OF sth (b) ⟨*cubierto*⟩ **~ DE algo** ⟨*de granos/manchas/polvo*⟩ covered IN sth (c) (después de comer) full (up) (colloq) **2 de lleno** ⟨*consagrarse/dedicarse*⟩ fully; **el sol nos daba de ~** the sun was shining down on us

lleno² *m* sellout

llevadero -ra *adj* bearable

llevar [A1] *vt*
I **1** (a) (de un lugar a otro) to take; **le llevé unas flores** I took her some flowers; **te lo ~é cuando vaya** I'll bring it when I come; **¿qué llevas en la bolsa?** what have you got in your bag?; **comida para ~** take out (AmE) *o* (BrE) takeaway meals (b) (transportar) ⟨*carga*⟩ to carry; **la ayudé a ~ las bolsas** I helped her carry her bags (c) ⟨*persona*⟩ to take; **nos llevó a cenar** he took us out to dinner; **me llevó (en su coche) hasta la estación** she gave me a lift to the station; **lo llevaba en brazos/de la mano** she was carrying him in her arms/holding her hand (d) (tener consigo) ⟨*llaves/dinero/documentación*⟩ to have
2 (a) (guiar, conducir) to take; **la llevaba de la mano** I/he was holding her hand; **esto no nos ~á a ninguna parte** this won't get us anywhere (b) (impulsar, inducir) to lead; **esto me lleva a pensar que …** this leads me to believe that …
3 (a) ⟨*ropa/perfume/reloj*⟩ to wear (b) (tener) ⟨*barba/bigote*⟩ to have; **llevaba el pelo corto** she had short hair
II **1** (tener a su cargo) ⟨*negocio/tienda*⟩ to run; ⟨*caso*⟩ to handle; ⟨*contabilidad*⟩ to do
2 (esp Esp) (conducir) ⟨*vehículo*⟩ to drive; ⟨*moto*⟩ to ride
3 ⟨*vida*⟩ to lead; **~ una vida tranquila** to lead a quiet; **¿cómo llevas el informe?** how are you getting on with the report?
4 (seguir, mantener): **~ el ritmo** *or* **el compás** to keep time; **¿llevas la cuenta de lo que te debo?** are you keeping track of what I owe you?; **¿qué dirección llevaban?** which direction were they going in?
III **1** (a) (requerir) ⟨*tiempo*⟩ to take; **le llevó**

horas aprendérselo it took her hours to learn it (b) (aventajar) (+ *me/te/le* etc): **me lleva un año** he's a year older than me; **nos llevan un día de ventaja** they have a one-day lead over us
2 (Esp) (cobrar) to charge
■ **~** *v aux*: **llevo una hora esperando** I've been waiting for an hour; **lleva tres días sin comer** he hasn't eaten for three days; **el tren lleva una hora de retraso** the train's an hour late; **llevo revisada la mitad** I've already checked half of it
■ **~** *vi* ⟨*camino/carretera*⟩ to go, lead
■ **llevarse** *v pron* **1** (a) (a otro lugar) to take; **la policía se llevó al sospechoso** the police took the suspect away; **¿quién se llevó mi paraguas?** who took my umbrella?; **el agua se llevó las casas** the water swept away the houses (b) ⟨*premio/dinero*⟩ to win (c) (quedarse con, comprar) to take; **me llevo este** I'll take this one (d) (Mat) to carry; **9 y 9 son 18, me llevo una** 9 plus 9 is 18, carry one (e) (Arg) ⟨*asignatura*⟩ to carry over
2 ⟨*susto/regañina*⟩ to get; **me llevé una decepción** I was disappointed; **se llevó un buen recuerdo** he left here with pleasant memories
3 **~se bien con algn** to get along with sb
4 (hablando de modas) to be in fashion; **vuelven a ~se las faldas cortas** short skirts are back in fashion

llorar [A1] *vi* (derramar lágrimas) (a) «*persona*» to cry; **estaba a punto de ~** she was on the verge of tears; **~ DE algo** ⟨*de risa/rabia*⟩ to cry WITH sb; ⟨*de emoción*⟩ to weep WITH sth; **~ POR algo/algn** to cry over sth/sb (b) «*ojos*» (+ *me/te/le* etc) to water

lloriquear [A1] *vi* (fam) to whine (colloq)

lloro *m* crying, weeping (liter)

llorón -rona *adj* (fam): **es muy ~** he cries a lot; **no seas tan ~** don't be such a crybaby (colloq)
■ *m,f* (a) (fam) (que llora mucho) crybaby (colloq) (b) (Col, RPI, Ven fam) (quejón) whiner (colloq)

llover [E9] *v impers* to rain; **aquí llueve mucho** it rains a lot here; **llueve a cántaros** *or* **a mares** *or* **a chuzos** it's pouring (with rain)

llovizna *f* drizzle

llovizar [A1] *v impers* to drizzle

llueva, llueve ▶ LLOVER

lluvia *f* (a) (Meteo) rain; **un día de ~** a rainy day; **zonas de mucha ~** areas of heavy rainfall; **~ radiactiva** nuclear fallout (b) (de balas) hail; (de críticas) barrage

lluvioso -sa *adj* ⟨*tiempo/día/época*⟩ rainy; ⟨*región*⟩ wet

lo *art* **1**: **prefiero ~ dulce** I prefer sweet things; **~ interesante del caso es …** the interesting about the case is …; **¿estoy en ~ cierto?** am I right?; **en ~ alto de la sierra** high up in the mountains; **ser ~ más objetivo posible** to be as objective as possible; **me dijo ~ de siempre** he came out with the same old story; **se ha enterado de ~ nuestro/de ~ de Pablo** she's found out about us/about Pablo; **voy a ~ de Eva** (RPI) I'm going to Eva's (place)
2 (a) **lo cual** which; **~ cual fue desmentido por el gobierno** which was denied by the Government (b) **lo que** what; **no entiendo ~ que dices** I don't understand what you're saying; **pide ~ que quieras** ask for whatever you want; **límpialo con un trapo o ~ que sea** clean it with a cloth or whatever; **¡~ que debe haber sufrido!** how she

must have suffered!; **¡no te imaginas ~ que fue
aquello!** you can't imagine what it was like!; **¡~
que es saber idiomas!** it sure is something (AmE)
o (BrE) what it is to be able speak languages
■ *pron pers* **1** **(a)** (referido — a él) him; (— a usted)
you; (— a cosa, etc) it; **¿~ conozco?** do I know
you?; **~ compré hoy** I bought it today; **ya ~ sé** I
know **(b)** (*impers*): **duele que a uno ~ traten así**
it hurts when people treat you like that
2 (*con estar, ser*): **¿que si estoy harta? pues sí,
~ estoy** am I fed up? well, yes, I am; **si ella es
capaz, yo también ~ soy** if she can, so can I

loable *adj* commendable, praiseworthy

lobezno -na *m,f* wolf cub

lobo -ba *m,f* (Zool) wolf; **~ marino** seal

lóbrego -ga *adj* gloomy

lóbulo *m* lobe

locación *f* (Méx) (lugar): **visite el museo Rivera,
~: Calle Altavista** visit the Rivera Museum on
Altavista Street; **¿en qué ~?** whereabouts?

local *adj* local; **el equipo ~** the home team
■ *m* premises (*pl*)

localidad *f* **1** (población) town, locality (frml)
2 (Espec) seat, ticket

localizar [A4] *vt* **(a)** ⟨*persona/lugar/tumor*⟩ to
locate; **estoy intentando ~la** I am trying to get
hold of her **(b)** ⟨*incendio/epidemia*⟩ to localize

loción *f* lotion

loco¹ -ca *adj* **(a)** (Med, Psic) mad, insane **(b)**
(chiflado) crazy (colloq), nuts (colloq); **este tipo está
medio ~** (fam) the guy's not all there (colloq); **eso
no lo hago (pero) ni ~** there's no way I'd do that;
hacer algo a lo ~ to do sth any which way (AmE)
o (BrE) any old how (colloq); **estar ~ de remate**
(fam) to be completely nuts (colloq); **tener** *or* (Esp)
traer ~ a algn to be driving sb crazy (colloq);
volver ~ a algn to drive sb crazy (colloq); **volverse
~** to go mad **(c)** (entusiasmado): **está loca por él**
she's crazy about him (colloq); **está ~ por volver**
he's dying to come back (colloq) **(d)** (fam)
(ajetreado): **anda (como) ~ con los preparativos**
the preparations are driving him mad (colloq) **(e)**
(indicando gran cantidad): **tengo unas ganas locas de
verla** I'm dying to see her (colloq); **tuvo una suerte
loca** she was incredibly lucky **(f)** **estar ~ DE**
algo ⟨*de entusiasmo/furia/celos*⟩ to be wild WITH
sth; ⟨*de dolor/remordimiento*⟩ to be racked WITH
sth; **estaba loca de alegría** she was blissfully
happy
■ *m,f* (enfermo mental) (*m*) madman; (*f*) madwoman;
se puso como un ~ he went crazy *o* mad;
corrimos como ~s (fam) we ran like crazy *o* mad
(colloq); **hacerse el ~** to act dumb (colloq)

loco² *m* (Chi) (Zool) abalone

locomoción *f* **(a)** (acción) locomotion **(b)** (Chi)
(Transp) *tb* **~ colectiva** public transport

locomotora *f* (Ferr) locomotive, engine

locuaz *adj* talkative, loquacious (frml)

locución *f* phrase

locura *f* **(a)** (demencia) madness, insanity; **lo que
hizo/dijo fue una ~** what he did/said was sheer
madness **(b)** (inclinación exagerada): **siente ~ por la
pequeña** she's absolutely besotted with the little
one; **la quiero con ~** I'm crazy about her (colloq)

locutor -tora *m,f* (en general) broadcaster

(informativo) newscaster (AmE), newsreader (BrE);
(deportivo) sports commentator; (de continuidad)
commentator, announcer (BrE)

lodo *m* mud; *para modismos ver* BARRO

logia *f* **(a)** (de los masones) lodge **(b)** (Arquit)
loggia

lógica *f* logic

lógico¹ -ca *adj* **(a)** (normal, natural) natural,
logical; **como es ~** naturally, obviously; **es ~
que así sea** it's (only) natural that it should be
so; **lo ~ sería …** the logical thing would be … **(b)**
⟨*conclusión/consecuencia*⟩ logical

lógico² *adv* (*indep*) (fam) of course

logotipo *m* logo, logotype

logrado -da *adj* (satisfactorio) successful;
(verosímil) ⟨*retrato/personaje*⟩ lifelike

lograr [A1] *vt* ⟨*objetivo*⟩ to attain, achieve;
⟨*éxito*⟩ to achieve; **logró el quinto puesto** she
managed fifth place; **~ hacer algo** to manage to
do sth

logro *m* (de un objetivo) achievement; (éxito)
success

loísmo *m*: use of LO/LOS instead of LE/LES (as in
LO/LOS DIJE QUE NO), common in certain regions of
Spain but not acceptable to most speakers

lolo -la *m,f* (Chi fam) teenager

loma *f* hill; (más pequeño) hillock

lombriz *f* (de tierra) worm, earthworm; (en el
intestino) (fam) worm (colloq)

lomo *m* **(a)** (de animal) back; **~ de burro** (RPl) *or*
(Chi) **de toro** (Auto) speed bump **(b)** (Coc) (de cerdo)
loin; (de vaca) (AmL) fillet steak **(c)** (de libro) spine;
(de cuchillo) back

lona *f* canvas

loncha *f* slice

lonche *m* (Per) (merienda) tea

lonchera *f* (AmL) lunch box

londinense *adj* ⟨*público/teatro/periódico*⟩
London (*before n*); **es ~** she's from London, she's
a Londoner
■ *mf* Londoner

Londres *m* London

longaniza *f*: spicy pork sausage

longitud *f* **(a)** (largo) length; **de 30 metros de ~**
30 meters long **(b)** (Astron, Geog) longitude; **~ de
onda** (Fís, Rad) wavelength

lonja *f* **1** **(a)** (loncha) slice **(b)** (RPl) (de cuero)
strip **2** **(a)** (Esp) (mercado de pescado) fish market
(b) (institución mercantil) guild; **~ de propiedad raíz**
(Col) association of realtors (AmE) *o* (BrE) estate
agents

loro¹ -ra *m,f* (Zool) parrot

loro² *m* (fam) (charlatán) chatterbox (colloq), gasbag
(colloq)

los, las *art*; *ver* el
■ *pron pers* **1** (referido — a ellos, ellas, cosas, etc)
them; (— a ustedes) you; **¿las atienden?** can I help
you? **2** (*con el verbo* haber): **las hay de muchos
tamaños** they come in many different sizes;
también ~ hay de chocolate we have chocolate
ones too

losa *f* (de sepulcro) tombstone; (de suelo) flagstone

lote *m* **(a)** (de un producto) batch; (en subastas) lot
(b) (terreno) plot (of land)

lotería f lottery; **me tocó** or **me gané la ~** I won the lottery

loto m lotus

loza f **(a)** (material) china **(b)** (vajilla) crockery; (de mejor calidad) china

lozano -na adj ⟨persona⟩ healthy-looking; ⟨cutis⟩ fresh; ⟨verduras⟩ fresh

Ltda (= **Limitada**) Ltd, Limited

lubina f sea bass

lubricante adj lubricating
■ m lubricant

lubricar [A2] vt to lubricate

lucero m bright star; **~ del alba** morning star

luces fpl ▶ LUZ

lucha f **(a)** (combate, pelea) fight; (para conseguir algo) struggle; **~ de clases** class struggle; **la ~ contra el cáncer** the fight against cancer **(b)** (Dep) wrestling; **~ libre** all-in wrestling

luchador -dora m,f **(a)** (persona esforzada) fighter **(b)** (Dep) wrestler

luchar [A1] vi **(a)** (combatir, pelear) to fight **(b)** (para conseguir algo) to struggle, fight; **~ para salir adelante** struggle hard to get on in life; **~ por la paz** to fight for peace **(c)** (batallar) **~ CON algo** ⟨con problema⟩ to wrestle WITH sth **(d)** (Dep) to wrestle

luche m (Chi) (Jueg) hopscotch

lucidez f lucidity

lucido -da adj ⟨fiesta⟩ magnificent, splendid; **su actuación no fue muy lucida** her performance wasn't particularly brilliant

lúcido -da adj **(a)** [SER] ⟨mente/análisis⟩ lucid, clear; ⟨persona⟩ clear-thinking **(b)** [ESTAR] ⟨enfermo⟩ lucid

luciente adj bright, shining

luciérnaga f glowworm; (insecto volador) firefly

lucir [I5] vi (aparentar) to look good, look special; **gasta mucho en ropa pero no le luce** she spends a fortune on clothes but it doesn't do much for her
■ **~** vt **(a)** (period) ⟨vestido/modelo⟩ to wear, sport (journ); ⟨peinado/collar⟩ to sport (journ) **(b)** ⟨figura/piernas⟩ to show off, flaunt
■ **lucirse** v pron **(a)** (destacarse) to excel oneself **(b)** (presumir) to show off

lucrativo -va adj lucrative, profitable; **una entidad sin fines ~s** a nonprofit (AmE) o (BrE) non-profit-making organization

lucro m profit, gain; **sin ánimo de ~** with no profit motive in mind

lúcuma f eggfruit

lúdico -ca adj ⟨fantasías/diversiones⟩ playful, ludic (before n) (liter)

luego adv **1** **(a)** (más tarde) later (on); (después de otro suceso — en el futuro) afterwards; (— en el pasado) then, next; **¡hasta ~!** goodbye!, see you!; **~ DE hacer algo** after doing sth **(b)** (Chi, Méx) (pronto) soon, quickly; **~ ~** (Méx) immediately **2** **(a)** (en el espacio): **hay una tienda y ~ está el banco** you come to a shop and the bank is next **(b)** (Méx) (cerca) nearby; **aquí ~** just here **(c)** (indicando orden, prioridad) then; **primero está él y ~ nosotros** he's first and then we're next **3** **desde luego** of course; **desde ~ que no** of course not
■ conj (frml) therefore

lugar m **1** **(a)** (en general) place; **este es el ~** this is

the place; **en cualquier otro ~** anywhere else; **en algún ~** somewhere; **cambiar los muebles de ~** to move the furniture around; **el ~ del suceso** the scene of the incident; **yo en tu ~ ...** if I were you ...; **ponte en mi ~** put yourself in my place; **se clasificó en primer ~** she finished in first place
2 (localidad, región): **los habitantes del ~** the local people; **~ y fecha de nacimiento** place and date of birth
3 **(a)** (espacio libre) room; **hacer ~ para algn/algo** to make room o space for sb/sth; **me hizo un ~** he made me some room **(b)** (asiento) seat
4 **dar lugar a** (a disputa, comentarios) to provoke, give rise to
5 (en locs) **en lugar de** instead of; **ella firmó en mi ~** she signed on my behalf; **en primer lugar** (antes que nada) first of all, firstly; **en último lugar** (finalmente) finally, lastly; **sin ~ a dudas** without doubt, undoubtedly; **tener ~** to take place

lugareño -ña adj/mf local

lugarteniente mf deputy

lúgubre adj gloomy

lujo m luxury; **no puedo permitirme el ~ de llegar tarde** I can't afford to be late; **nos dimos el ~ de viajar en primera** we treated ourselves and traveled first class; **a todo ~** in style; **de ~** luxury (before n); **con ~ de detalles** with a wealth of detail

lujoso -sa adj luxurious

lujuria f (liter) lust, lechery

lumbago m lumbago

lumbre f (de hoguera, chimenea) fire; (de la cocina): **puso el cazo en la ~** she put the saucepan on the stove

lumbrera f (fam) (persona brillante) genius, whiz* (colloq)

luminoso -sa adj **(a)** ⟨habitación⟩ bright, light; ⟨fuente⟩ luminous; ⟨letrero⟩ illuminated **(b)** ⟨idea⟩ bright, brilliant

luna f **1** (Astron) moon; **a la luz de la ~** in the moonlight; **hay ~** the moon's out; **~ creciente/menguante/llena/nueva** waxing/waning/full/new moon; **~ de miel** honeymoon; **estar en la ~** (fam) to have one's head in the clouds **2** (espejo) mirror; (de puerta, ventana) glass; (escaparate) window; (parabrisas) windshield (AmE), windscreen (BrE) **3** (de la uña) half-moon, lunule (tech)

lunar adj lunar
■ m **(a)** (en la piel) mole; (pintado) beauty spot **(b)** (en el pelo) gray* patch **(c)** (en un diseño) polka-dot

lunático -ca adj lunatic (before n)
■ m,f lunatic

lunes m (pl **~**) Monday; **el ~ por la mañana/noche** on Monday morning/night; **todos los ~** every Monday; **el próximo ~** next Monday; **el ~ pasado** last Monday; **el ~ es fiesta** Monday is a holiday; **nos vemos el ~** I'll see you on Monday; **los ~ voy a nadar** on Mondays I go swimming

luneta f **1** (Auto) window **2** (Col, Méx) (Teatr) orchestra seats (pl) (AmE), front stalls (pl) (BrE)

lunfardo m Buenos Aires slang

lupa f magnifying glass

lustrabotas mf (pl **~**) ▶ LUSTRADOR

lustrada f (AmS) polish, shine

lustrador -dora *m,f* (AmS) bootblack; (niño)
shoeshine boy

lustrar [A1] *vt* (esp AmL) ⟨zapatos/muebles⟩ to
polish

■ **lustrarse** *v pron* **1** (esp AmL) ⟨zapatos⟩ to
polish **2** (AmC) (en una actividad) to excel

lustre *m* **(a)** (brillo) shine, luster*; **darle** *or*
sacarle ~ a algo to polish sth **(b)** (distinción) glory,
distinction

lustrín *m* (AmS) (cajón) bootblack's box; (puesto)
shoeshine stand

lustro *m* period of five years

luterano -na *adj/m,f* Lutheran

luto *m* mourning; **estar de ~** to be in mourning;
~ riguroso deep mourning; **ir de ~** to wear
mourning (clothes); **ponerse de ~** to go into
mourning

Luxemburgo *m* Luxembourg

luxemburgués -guesa *adj* of/from
Luxembourg

luz *f* **1** (en general) light; **la ~ del sol** the
sunlight; **me da la ~ en los ojos** the light's in my
eyes; **a plena ~ del día** in broad daylight; **este
reflector da mucha ~** this spotlight is very
bright; **leer con poca ~** to read in poor light; **a la
~ de los últimos acontecimientos** in the light of
recent events; **a todas luces**: whichever way you
look at it; **dar a ~** to give birth; **sacar algo a la ~**
⟨secreto/escándalo⟩ to bring sth to light;
⟨publicación⟩ to bring out; **salir a la ~** «secreto/
escándalo» to come to light; «publicación» to
come out
2 (a) (fam) (electricidad) electricity; **les cortaron la
~** their electricity was cut off; **se fue la ~** (en una
casa) the electricity went off; (en una zona) there
was a power cut **(b)** (dispositivo) light; **encender** *or*
(AmL) **prender** *or* (Esp) **dar la ~** to turn on *o*
switch on the light; **apagar la ~** to turn off *o*
switch off the light; **cruzar con la luz roja** to cross
when the lights are red; **luces de estacionamiento**
or (Esp) **de situación** parking lights (*pl*) (AmE),
sidelights (*pl*) (BrE); **luces de cruce** *or* **cortas** *or*
(AmL) **bajas** dipped headlights (*pl*); **poner las
luces largas** *or* **altas** to put the headlights on
high (AmE) *o* (BrE) full beam; **~ de frenado**
stoplight, brake light (BrE); **~ de giro** (Arg)
indicator

luzca, luzcan, etc ▶ LUCIR

M m

M, m *f* (read as /'eme/) the letter M, m

m (= **metro**) m, meter*

macabro -bra *adj* macabre

macaco -ca *m,f* (Zool) macaque

macana *f* **1** (AmL) (de policía) billy club (AmE),
truncheon (BrE) **2 (a)** (CS fam) (tontería, disparate):
decir ~s to talk nonsense; **no hagas la ~ de
renunciar** don't be so stupid as to resign (colloq)
(b) (CS fam) (problema) trouble, snag; **¡qué ~ que
no puedas venir!** what a shame *o* (colloq) drag you
can't come! **(c)** (RPI fam) (mentira) lie

macanear [A1] *vt* (Méx) (golpear) to beat
■ **~** *vi* (RPI fam) (mentir) to lie; (decir tonterías) to talk
garbage (AmE) *o* (BrE) rubbish (colloq)

macanudo -da *adj* (CS, Per fam) great (colloq)

macarrón *m* **(a)** (pasta) piece of macaroni;
macarrones macaroni **(b)** (galleta) macaroon

macedonia *f* (de frutas) fruit salad, macedoine;
(de verduras) mixed vegetables (*pl*), macedoine

macerar [A1] *vt* ⟨fruta⟩ to soak, macerate;
⟨carne⟩ to marinate, marinade

maceta *f* flowerpot

macetero *m* **(a)** (para tiestos) flowerpot holder
(b) (AmS) (tiesto) large flowerpot; (jardinera)
window box

machacar [A2] *vt* **(a)** ⟨ajo⟩ to crush;
⟨almendras⟩ to grind, crush; ⟨piedra⟩ to crush,
pound **(b)** (fam) ⟨contrincante⟩ to thrash (colloq)
■ **~** *vi* **(a)** (insistir): **~ con** *or* **sobre algo** to go
on *o* harp on about sth (colloq) **(b)** (fam) (para un
examen) to cram (colloq)

machacón -cona *adj* (insistente) insistent;
(pesado) tiresome

machamartillo: a ~ (loc adj) ⟨monárquico/
feminista⟩ ardent, staunch; (loc adv) firmly

machete *m* (cuchillo) machete
■ *adj inv* (Ven fam) great (colloq)

machetero -ra *m,f* (cañero) cane cutter
■ *adj* (Méx fam) persevering

machismo *m* (actitud, ideología) sexism, male
chauvinism

machista *adj* sexist, chauvinist
■ *mf* sexist, male chauvinist

macho *m* **1** (Biol, Zool) male; **~ cabrío** billy
goat **2** (fam) (hombre fuerte) tough guy (colloq);
(pey) macho man (colloq & pej) **3** (Mec, Tec) pin;
(Elec) male (plug); (de un corchete) hook; (en
carpintería) peg, pin
■ *adj* **1** ⟨animal/planta⟩ male; **ballena/elefante ~**
bull whale/elephant; **gato ~** tomcat **2** (fam)
(valiente, fuerte) tough, brave; (pey) macho (pej)
3 ⟨pieza⟩ male

machote -ta *m,f* **(a)** (fam) (hombre) tough guy (colloq); (pey) macho man (colloq & pej) **(b)** (fam & pey) (mujer) butch woman (colloq & pej)

machucar [A2] *vt* **(a)** ⟨*fruta*⟩ to bruise **(b)** (fam) ⟨*dedo*⟩ to crush **(c)** (Méx) ⟨*ajo*⟩ to crush

machucón *m* (Méx fam) (moretón) bruise

macilento -ta *adj* **(a)** ⟨*persona/cara*⟩ gaunt, haggard **(b)** ⟨*luz*⟩ wan (liter)

macillo *m* hammer

macizo¹ -za *adj* **(a)** [SER] ⟨*sólido*⟩ solid **(b)** [ESTAR] (fam) ⟨*persona*⟩ (robusto) strapping (colloq)

macizo² *m* (de montañas) massif; (de flores, arbustos) clump

maco *m* (Col) monkey

macramé *m* macramé

macrobiótico -ca *adj* macrobiotic

macroeconomía *f* macroeconomics

macuco -ca *adj* (Chi, Per fam) cute (AmE colloq), sharp (BrE colloq)

macuto *m* back pack, rucksack (BrE)

madalena *f* ≈cupcake (AmE), ≈fairycake (BrE)

madeja *f* (de lana, hilo) hank, skein

madera *f* (material) wood; (para construcción, carpintería) lumber (esp AmE), timber (BrE); ~ **blanda/dura** softwood/hardwood; **es de ~** it's made of wood, it's wooden; **mesa de ~** wooden table; **~ de pino** pine (wood); **tener ~ de algo** to have the makings of sth; **tocar ~** to knock (on) wood (AmE), touch wood (BrE)

maderero -ra *adj* timber (*before n*); lumber (*before n*) (esp AmE)
■ *m,f* timber merchant

madero *m* (piece of) timber

madrastra *f* stepmother

madrazo *m* (Méx fam) blow; **darle un ~ a algn** to give sb a beating; **películas de ~** violent movies

madre *f* mother; **ser ~** to be a mother; **~ de familia** mother; **~ política** mother-in-law; **~ soltera** single *o* unmarried mother; **~ superiora** Mother Superior; **¡~ mía!** *o* **¡mi ~!** (my) goodness!, (good) heavens!; **me vale ~s** (Méx vulg) I don't give a damn (colloq) *o* (vulg) shit; **salirse de ~** ⟨*río*⟩ to burst its banks; ⟨*situación*⟩ to get out of hand

madreperla *f* mother-of-pearl

madreselva *f* honeysuckle

Madrid *m* Madrid

madriguera *f* **(a)** (de conejos) warren, burrow; (de zorros) earth; (de tejones) set **(b)** (de maleantes) den, lair

madrileño -ña *adj* of/from Madrid
■ *m,f* person from Madrid

madrina

■ **Nota** En inglés *godmother* no se usa como apelativo

f [1] **(a)** (en bautizo) godmother; (en boda) ≈matron of honor* **(b)** (de barco) *woman who launches a ship* [2] (Méx fam) paddy wagon (AmE sl), police van (BrE)

madroño *m* (Bot) tree strawberry

madrugada *f* **(a)** (amanecer, alba) dawn, daybreak; **se levantó de ~** (muy temprano) she got up very early (in the morning); (al amanecer) she got up at dawn *o* daybreak **(b)** (después de

medianoche) (early) morning; **las tres de la ~** three o'clock in the morning; **llegó de ~** he arrived in the early hours of the morning *o* in the small hours

madrugador -dora *adj*: **ser ~** to be an early riser

madrugar [A3] *vi* to get up early

maduración *f* **(a)** (de fruta) ripening (process) **(b)** (de persona) maturing (process) **(c)** (de idea) development, maturing

madurar [A1] *vi* **(a)** «*fruta*» to ripen **(b)** «*persona*» to mature **(c)** «*ideas*» to mature, come to fruition
■ **~** *vt* **(a)** ⟨*fruta*⟩ to ripen **(b)** ⟨*plan*⟩ to develop, bring to fruition

madurez *f* **(a)** (de fruta) ripeness **(b)** (de persona) maturity

maduro -ra *adj* [1] [ESTAR] ⟨*fruta*⟩ ripe [2] **(a)** [SER] (entrado en años) mature, of mature years **(b)** [SER] (sensato) mature; **es joven pero muy ~** he's young but very mature for his age

maestría *f* [1] (liter) (habilidad) skill, mastery [2] (esp AmL) (Educ) (postgrado) master's degree, master's

maestro -tra *m,f* [1] **(a)** (Educ) teacher, schoolteacher; **maestra jardinera** (Arg, Col) kindergarten teacher, nursery school teacher (BrE) **(b)** (en un arte): **es un ~ de la danza española** he is a master of Spanish dance; **un ~ de las letras españolas** a leading authority *o* an expert on Spanish literature **(c)** (en un oficio) master (*before n*); **~ carpintero** master carpenter **(d)** (Chi) (obrero) builder [2] (Mús) maestro [3] (en ajedrez) master

mafia *f* mafia

mafioso -sa *adj* mafia (*before n*)
■ *m,f* (criminal) gangster, racketeer; (de la Mafia siciliana) mafioso

magdalena *f* (Esp) ≈cupcake (AmE), ≈fairycake (BrE)

magia *f* magic; **hacer ~** to do magic (tricks)

mágico -ca *adj* **(a)** ⟨*poderes/número*⟩ magic (*before n*) **(b)** ⟨*belleza/ambiente*⟩ magical

magisterio *m* (enseñanza) teaching; (carrera) teacher training; **estudia ~** he's training to be a teacher

magistrado -da *m,f* judge

magistral *adj* ⟨*actuación/libro*⟩ masterly; ⟨*tono/actitud*⟩ magisterial (frml)

magnánimo -ma *adj* magnanimous

magnate *mf* magnate, tycoon; **los ~s de la prensa** the press barons

magnesia *f* magnesia

magnesio *m* magnesium

magnético -ca *adj* magnetic

magnetismo *m* magnetism

magnetófono, magnetofón *m* (reel-to-reel) tape recorder

magnífico -ca *adj* **(a)** (estupendo) ⟨*edificio/ panorama*⟩ magnificent, superb; ⟨*espectáculo/ escritor/oportunidad*⟩ marvelous*, wonderful; **¡~!** excellent! **(b)** (suntuoso) magnificent, splendid

magnitud *f* magnitude; **la ~ de la tragedia** the extent *o* magnitude of the tragedy

magnolia *f* magnolia

m

mago -ga *m,f* **(a)** (prestidigitador) conjurer, magician **(b)** (en cuentos) wizard, magician **(c)** (persona habilidosa) wizard

magro -gra *adj* lean

magulladura *f* bruise

magullar [A1] *vt* to bruise
■ **magullarse** *v pron* to bruise

mahometano -na *adj* Islamic
■ *m,f* follower of Islam

mahonesa *f* mayonnaise

maicena® *f* cornstarch (AmE), cornflour (BrE)

maillot /maˈyo(t)/ *m* **(a)** (traje de baño) swimsuit **(b)** (de ciclista) jersey

maíz *m* (planta) maize, corn (AmE); (Coc) corn (AmE), sweet corn (esp BrE); ~ **tostado** *or* **pira** *or* **tote** (Col) popcorn

maizal *m* cornfield (AmE), maize field (BrE)

maizena® *f* cornstarch (AmE), cornflour (BrE)

majadería *f* (a) (cualidad) stupidity **(b)** (dicho, acto): **no dice más que ~s** he talks a lot of rubbish *o* nonsense (colloq); **fue una ~** it was a stupid thing to do

majadero -ra *adj* (fam) (insensato) stupid
■ *m,f* clown (colloq)

majar [A1] *vt* to crush

maje *mf* **1** (AmC arg) (individuo) (*m*) guy (colloq), bloke (BrE colloq); (*f*) girl **2** (Méx fam) (persona crédula) sucker (colloq)

majestad *f* **1** (aspecto grandioso) majesty **2** **su Majestad** (al referirse — al rey) His Majesty; (— a la reina) Her Majesty; (al dirigirse al rey, a la reina) Your Majesty; **sus M~es los Reyes** Their Majesties the King and Queen

majestuosidad *f* majesty

majestuoso -sa *adj* majestic

majo -ja *adj* (Esp fam) **(a)** (simpático) nice **(b)** (guapo) ⟨*hombre*⟩ handsome, good-looking; ⟨*mujer*⟩ good-looking, pretty **(c)** ⟨*casa/vestido*⟩ lovely, nice

mal *adj*: ▶ MALO
■ *adj inv* **1** [ESTAR] (enfermo) ill; (anímicamente) in a bad way (colloq); (incómodo) uncomfortable; **andar ~ del estómago** to have trouble with one's stomach; **¡este está ~ de la cabeza!** he's not right in the head; **esas cosas me ponen ~** things like that really upset me
2 (fam) (*en frases negativas*) (refiriéndose al aspecto): **no está nada ~** she's/he's/it's not at all bad (colloq)
3 (insatisfactorio): **estoy** *or* **salí muy ~ en esta foto** I look awful in this photograph; **le queda ~ ese color** that color doesn't suit her
4 [ESTAR] (incorrecto) wrong
5 (indicando escasez) **estar** *or* **ir ~ DE algo** ⟨*de dinero/tiempo*⟩ to be short *or* sth
■ *adv* **1** (de manera no satisfactoria) ⟨*vestir/cantar/jugar*⟩ badly; **le fue ~ en los exámenes** his exams went badly; **te oigo muy ~** I can hardly hear you; **el negocio marcha ~** the business isn't doing well; **de ~ en peor** from bad to worse
2 (desfavorablemente) badly, ill; **hablar ~ de algn** to speak badly *o* ill of sb
3 (a) (de manera errónea) wrong, wrongly; **te han informado ~** you've been badly *o* wrongly informed; **te entendí ~** I misunderstood you **(b)** (de manera reprensible) ⟨*obrar/partarse*⟩ badly;

haces ~ en no ir a verla it's wrong of you not to go and see her; **me contestó muy ~** she answered me very rudely
4 (desagradable) ⟨*oler/saber*⟩ bad; **aquí huele ~** there's a horrible smell *o* it smells in here
5 (*en locs*) **hacer mal** (AmL) (a la salud): **esto hace ~ al hígado** this is bad for the liver; **el pescado me hizo ~** the fish didn't agree with me; **menos mal: ¡menos ~!** thank goodness!; **¡menos ~ que le avisaron a tiempo!** it's just as well they told him in time!; **tomarse algo a ~** to take sth to heart
■ *m* **1** (Fil) evil; **el bien y el ~** good and evil, right and wrong
2 (daño, perjuicio): **el divorcio de sus padres le hizo mucho ~** her parents' divorce did her a lot of harm
3 (cosa dañina) ill, evil; **los ~es sociales** the social ills; **no hay ~ que por bien no venga** every cloud has a silver lining
4 (Med) (liter) (enfermedad) illness; **tiene ~ de amores** (fam) he's lovesick; **~ de (las) altura(s)** altitude sickness, mountain sickness
5 (pena) trouble

malabarismo *m* juggling; **hacer ~s** «*malabarista*» to juggle; (en situación difícil) to do a juggling *o* balancing act

malabarista *mf* juggler

malacostumbrado -da *adj* spoiled*, pampered

malacostumbrar [A1] *vt* to spoil
■ **malacostumbrarse** *v pron* to become spoilt

malacrianza *f* (AmL) rudeness

malaria *f* malaria

Malasia *f* Malaysia

malasio -sia *adj/m,f* Malaysian

malayo¹ -ya *adj/m,f* Malay

malayo² *m* (idioma) Malay

malcriado -da *adj* (mimado) spoiled*; (travieso) bad-mannered, badly brought up

malcriar [A17] *vt* to spoil, bring ... up badly

maldad *f* **(a)** (cualidad) evilness, wickedness **(b)** (acto) evil deed, wicked thing

maldecir [I25] *vt* to curse
■ ~ *vi* **(a)** (renegar) to curse; ~ **DE algo/algn** to speak ill of sth/sb **(b)** (blasfemar) to swear, curse (AmE)

maldición *f* **(a)** (imprecación) curse; **nos echó una ~** she put a curse on us **(b)** (palabrota) swearword; **soltó una ~** he swore

maldiga, maldijo, etc ▶ MALDECIR

maldito -ta *adj* (fam) (expresando irritación) damn (*before n*) (colloq), wretched (*before n*) (colloq); **¡este ~ ruido!** this damn *o* wretched noise!; **¡maldita/~ sea!** damn (it)! (colloq)

maldoso -sa *adj* (Méx) mischievous

malecón *m* **(a)** (rompeolas) breakwater; (embarcadero) jetty **(b)** (AmL) (paseo marítimo) seafront

maleducado -da *adj* rude, bad-mannered

maléfico -ca *adj* ⟨*poderes/espíritus*⟩ evil; ⟨*influencia*⟩ harmful

malenseñado -da *adj* (CS) (maleducado) rude, bad-mannered; (mimado) spoiled

malenseñar [A1] *vt* (CS) to spoil

malentender [E8] *vt* to misunderstand

malentendido *m* misunderstanding

malestar *m* **(a)** (Med) discomfort **(b)** (desazón, inquietud) unease

maleta *f* **1** (valija) suitcase, case; **hacer la ~** to pack (one's case) **2** (Chi, Per) ▶ MALETERA

maletera *f* (Chi, Per) trunk (AmE), boot (BrE)

maletero *m* **(a)** (Auto) trunk (AmE), boot (BrE) **(b)** (mozo de estación) porter

maletín *m* (para documentos) briefcase; (maleta pequeña) overnight bag, small case; (de médico) bag

malévolo -la *adj* malevolent, malicious

maleza *f* **1** (espesura) undergrowth; (malas hierbas) weeds (*pl*) **2** (AmL) (mala hierba) weed

malformación *f* malformation

malgastador -dora *adj* wasteful, spendthrift ∎ *m,f* squanderer, spendthrift

malgastar [A1] *vt* ⟨tiempo/esfuerzo⟩ to waste; ⟨dinero/herencia⟩ to squander

malhablado -da *adj* foul-mouthed

malhechor -chora *m,f* criminal, delinquent

malhumorado -da *adj* **(a)** [SER] ⟨persona/gesto⟩ bad-tempered **(b)** [ESTAR] ⟨persona⟩ in a bad mood

malicia *f* **(a)** (intención malévola) malice, malevolence **(b)** (picardía) mischief

malicioso -sa *adj* **(a)** (malintencionado) malicious, spiteful **(b)** (pícaro) mischievous

maligno -na *adj* **(a)** ⟨tumor⟩ malignant **(b)** ⟨persona/intención⟩ evil; ⟨influencia⟩ harmful, evil

malinchista *adj* (Méx) *preferring foreign things*

malinformar [A1] *vt* (CS frml) to misinform (frml)

malintencionado -da *adj* ⟨persona/palabras⟩ malicious, spiteful; ⟨golpe⟩ malicious

malinterpretar [A1] *vt* to misinterpret

malla *f* **1** (red) mesh; **una ~ para los insectos** a screen *o* mesh to stop insects **2** **(a)** (para gimnasia) leotard; **~ de baño** (RPl) bathing suit, swimsuit **(b)** **mallas** *fpl* (medias) tights (*pl*); (sin pie) leggings (*pl*)

Mallorca *f* Majorca

mallorquín¹ -quina *adj/m,f* Majorcan

mallorquín² *m* (idioma) Majorcan

mallugar [A3] *vt* (Méx, Ven) to bruise

malnutrición *f* malnutrition

malnutrido -da *adj* malnourished

malo -la *adj* [*The form* MAL *is used before masculine singular nouns*] **1** **(a)** [SER] (en general) bad; **una novela mala** a bad novel; **un mal amigo** a bad friend; **una mala caída** a bad fall; **soy muy ~ para los números** I'm very bad with figures; **¡qué mala suerte** *o* (fam) **pata!** what bad luck!, how unlucky!; **lo ~ es que ...** the thing *o* trouble is that ...; **las malas compañías** bad company; **mala hierba** weed; **~s tratos** ill-treatment; **es ~ tomar tanto sol** it's not good to sunbathe so much; **tienes mala cara** *or* **mal aspecto** you don't look well **(b)** ⟨calidad/visibilidad⟩ poor; **tiene mala ortografía** her spelling is poor; **estar de malas** (de mal humor) (fam) to be in a bad mood; (con mala suerte) (esp AmL) to be unlucky; **más vale ~ conocido que bueno por conocer** better the devil you know (than the devil you don't)

2 [SER] ⟨persona⟩ (en sentido ético) nasty; (travieso) naughty; **¡qué ~ eres con tu hermano!** you're really horrible *o* nasty to your brother; **no seas mala, préstamelo** don't be mean *o* rotten, lend it to me (colloq); **una mala mujer** a loose woman; **una mujer mala** a wicked *o* an evil woman; **lo hizo a** *or* **con mala idea** he did it deliberately *o* to be nasty; **mala palabra** (esp AmL) rude *o* dirty word; **dicen las malas lenguas que ...** (fam) there's a rumor going around that ..., people are saying that ... **hacerse mala sangre** to get upset *ver tb* LECHE 3

3 [ESTAR] **(a)** (en mal estado) ⟨alimento⟩: **el pescado/queso está ~** the fish/cheese has gone bad, that fish/cheese is off (BrE) **(b)** (Esp, Méx fam) (enfermo) sick (AmE), ill (BrE); **el pobre está malito** the poor thing's not very well (colloq); ∎ *m,f* (leng infantil *o* hum) baddy (colloq)

malograr [A1] *vt* ⟨oportunidad⟩ to waste; ⟨trabajo⟩ to ruin, spoil ∎ **malograrse** *v pron* **1** «proyecto/cosecha» to fail **2** **(a)** «persona» (morir joven) to die young *o* before one's time **(b)** (Per) «reloj» to stop working; «lavadora» to break down

maloliente *adj* stinking, smelly

malparado -da *adj*: **salir ~** to come off badly

malpensado -da *adj*: **no seas ~** why do you always think the worst of people?

malsano -na *adj* ⟨clima/lugar⟩ unhealthy; ⟨influencia⟩ bad, unhealthy

malsonante *adj* rude

malta *f* **(a)** (cereal) malt **(b)** (Chi) (cerveza) stout

malteada *f* (AmL) milk shake

maltratar [A1] *vt* **(a)** ⟨persona/animal⟩ to maltreat, ill-treat, mistreat; (pegar) ⟨niño/mujer⟩ to batter **(b)** ⟨juguete/coche⟩ to mistreat, treat ... very roughly

maltrecho -cha *adj*: **lo dejaron muy ~** they left him in a bad way

malucho -cha *adj* (fam) (algo enfermo): **estar ~** to be *o* feel under the weather (colloq)

malva *adj inv/m* mauve ∎ *f* mallow; **~ real** hollyhock, rose mallow (AmE)

malvado -da *adj* wicked, evil

malvavisco *m* marshmallow

malvender [E1] *vt* to sell ... off cheap, sell ... at a loss

malversación *f*: *tb* **~ de fondos** embezzlement (of funds)

malversar [A1] *vt* to embezzle, misappropriate

Malvinas *fpl*: **las ~** the Falkland Islands, the Falklands

malvón *m* (RPl, Méx) geranium

mama *f* (Anat) breast; (Zool) mammary gland

mamá *f* (*pl* **-más**) (fam) mom (AmE colloq), mum (BrE colloq); (usado por niños) mommy (AmE colloq), mummy (BrE colloq)

mamadera *f* (CS, Per) (biberón) (feeding) bottle, baby bottle

mamado -da *adj* **(a)** (fam) (borracho) tight(colloq), sloshed (colloq) **(b)** (Col, Ven fam) (cansado) dead beat (colloq), shattered (colloq); (aburrido) bored

mamar [A1] *vi* **1** **(a)** «bebé» to feed; **dar de ~** to breastfeed **(b)** «gato/cordero» to suckle **2** (fam) (beber alcohol) to booze (colloq)

mameluco m (AmL) **(a)** (de niño, bebé) rompers (pl), romper suit (BrE) **(b)** (pantalón con peto) overalls (pl) (AmE), dungarees (pl) (BrE); (de trabajo) coveralls (pl) (AmE), overalls (pl) (BrE)

mamífero adj mammalian
■ m mammal

mamila f (Méx) (biberón) (feeding) bottle; (tetilla) nipple (AmE), teat (BrE)

mampara f **(a)** (biombo, tabique) screen, partition **(b)** (Chi, Per) (puerta) inner door

mampostería f masonry

manada f **(a)** (Zool) (de elefantes) herd; (de leones) pride; (de lobos) pack **(b)** (fam) (de gente) herd

Managua f Managua

managüense adj of/from Managua

manantial m (de agua) spring

manar [A1] vi to pour

manatí m manatee

mancha f **1** **(a)** (de suciedad) spot, mark; (difícil de quitar) stain; **una ~ de grasa** a grease stain; **~s de humedad** damp patches; **~ de petróleo** oil slick **(b)** (borrón) blot **2** **(a)** (en la piel) mark **(b)** (en el pelaje, las plumas) patch; (del leopardo) spot **3** (liter) (imperfección, mácula) stain; **sin ~** ⟨alma⟩ pure; ⟨reputación⟩ spotless **4** (Per fam) (pandilla) gang

manchado -da adj ⟨mantel/vestido⟩ stained; **está ~ de vino** it has wine stains on it; **~ de sangre** blood-stained

manchar [A1] vt **1** (ensuciar) to mark, get ... dirty; (de algo difícil de quitar) to stain **2** ⟨reputación/honra/memoria⟩ to tarnish
■ ~ vi to stain
■ **mancharse** v pron **(a)** «ropa/mantel» to get dirty; (de algo difícil de quitar) to get stained; **~se DE** or **CON algo** to get stained WITH sth **(b)** (refl) «persona» to get dirty; **me manché la blusa de aceite** I got oil stains on my blouse

manchego -ga adj of/from La Mancha

manco -ca adj: **es ~ de un brazo/una mano** he only has one arm/hand

mancomunidad f community, association; **M~ Británica de Naciones** British Commonwealth

mancorna f (Col) cufflink

mancuernilla f (Méx) cufflink

manda f (Chi, Méx) offering, promise

mandadero -ra m,f (esp AmL) (m) office boy; (f) office girl

mandado¹ -da adj (Méx fam): **es muy ~** he's a real opportunist; **no seas mandada, solo te ofrecí uno** don't be so greedy, I only offered you one (colloq)
■ m,f (esp Esp) (subordinado) minion (hum or pej); **no soy más que un ~** I'm just following orders

mandado² m (a) (esp AmL) (compra): **hacer los ~s** or (Méx) **ir al ~** to do the shopping **(b)** (Méx) (cosa comprada): **¿me trajiste el ~?** did you get the shopping o the things I asked you for? **(c)** (diligencia) errand

mandamiento m **1** (Relig) commandment **2** (orden) order; (Der) warrant, order

mandar [A1] vt **1** **(a)** (ordenar): **a mí nadie me manda** nobody tells me what to do, nobody orders me about; **haz lo que te mandan** do as you're told; **la mandó callar** he told o ordered her to be quiet; **mandó que sirvieran la comida** she ordered lunch to be served **(b)** (recetar) to prescribe; **el médico le mandó descansar** the doctor advised him to rest **2** (enviar) to send; **la mandé por el pan** I sent her out to buy the bread **3** (AmL) (tratándose de encargos): **mis padres me ~on llamar** my parents sent for me; **mandó decir que ...** she sent a message to say that ...; **~ algo a arreglar** to get o have sth mended **4** (AmL fam) (arrojar, lanzar): **mandó la pelota fuera de la cancha** he kicked/sent/hit the ball out of play
■ ~ vi (ser el jefe) to be in charge, be the boss (colloq); **¿mande?** (Méx) (I'm) sorry?, pardon?; **¡María! — ¿mande?** (Méx) María! — yes?

mandarina f (Bot, Coc) mandarin (orange), tangerine

mandatario -ria m,f (Pol) tb **primer ~/primera mandataria** head of state

mandato m **1** **(a)** (período) term of office **(b)** (orden) mandate **2** (Der) mandate

mandíbula f jaw

mandil m (delantal) leather apron

mandioca f (planta) cassava; (fécula) tapioca

mando m **1** (en general) command; **entregarle el ~ a algn** to hand over command to sb; **dotes de ~** leadership qualities; **estar al ~ (de algo)** to be in charge (of sth) **2** (Auto, Elec) control; **~ a distancia** remote control

mandolina f mandolin

mandón -dona adj bossy

mandonear [A1] vt (fam) to boss ... around (colloq)

mandril m (Zool) mandrill

manearse [A1] v pron (Chi fam) to get in a tangle (colloq), to be all fingers and thumbs (colloq)

manecilla f hand; **la ~ grande/pequeña** the minute/hour hand

manejable adj **1** ⟨coche⟩ maneuverable*; ⟨máquina⟩ easy-to-use; ⟨pelo⟩ manageable **2** ⟨persona⟩ easily led, easily manipulated

manejar [A1] vt **1** (usar) ⟨herramienta/arma/diccionario⟩ to use; ⟨máquina⟩ to use, operate **2** (dirigir, llevar) ⟨negocio/empresa⟩ to manage; ⟨asuntos⟩ to manage, handle **3** (manipular) to manipulate **4** (AmL) ⟨auto⟩ to drive
■ ~ vi (AmL) to drive
■ **manejarse** v pron **1** (desenvolverse) to get by, manage **2** (Col) (comportarse) to behave

manejo m **1** (uso): **el ~ de la máquina es muy sencillo** the machine is easy to use o operate; **su ~ de la lengua** his use of the language **2** (de asunto, negocio) management **3** (AmL) (Auto) driving

manera f **1** (modo, forma) way; **yo lo hago a mi ~** I do it my way; **a ~ de** by way of; **de todas ~s**

anyway; **su ∼ de ser** the way she is; **se puede ir vestido de cualquier ∼** you can dress however you want; **no lo pongas así, de cualquier ∼** don't just put it in any which way (AmE) o (BrE) any old how; **de ninguna ∼ lo voy a permitir** there's no way I'm going to allow it; **de alguna ∼ tendré que conseguirlo** I'll have to get it somehow (or other); **no hay/hubo ∼** it is/it was impossible; **de ∼ que** so; **de mala ∼** ‹*contestar*› rudely; ‹*tratar*› badly

[2] **maneras** *fpl* (modales) manners (*pl*)

manga *f* [1] (a) (de abrigo, blusa) sleeve; **sin ∼s** sleeveless; **de ∼ corta/larga** short-sleeved/long-sleeved; **en ∼s de camisa** in shirtsleeves; **tener (la) ∼ ancha** to be tolerant o lenient **(b)** (capa de jerga) (AmC) poncho [2] (Coc) (filtro) strainer; (para repostería) *tb* **∼ pastelera** pastry bag [3] (Dep) round [4] (manguera) hose; **∼ de incendio** fire hose; **∼ de riego** hosepipe [5] (AmL) (de langostas) swarm

manglar *m* mangrove swamp

mangle *m* mangrove

mango *m* [1] (de cuchillo, paraguas) handle [2] (Bot) (árbol) mango (tree); (fruta) mango [3] (Méx fam & hum) (persona atractiva): **es un ∼** «*mujer*» she's a real stunner (colloq); «*hombre*» he's a real hunk (colloq)

mangonear [A1] *vi* (fam) **(a)** (mandonear) to order o (colloq) boss people around **(b)** (entrometerse) to meddle
■ **∼** *vt* (fam) to boss … around (colloq)

mangosta *f* mongoose

manguera *f* (para regar) hose, hosepipe; (de bombero) hose

maní *m* (*pl* **-níes** *or* (crit) **-níses**) (AmC, AmS) peanut

manía *f* [1] (obsesión, capricho): **tiene sus ∼s** he has his funny little ways; **tiene la ∼ de la limpieza** she has a mania for cleanliness o (colloq) a thing about cleaning; **le ha dado la ∼ de vestirse de negro** she has this fad o craze of dressing in black; **∼ persecutoria** *or* de **persecución** persecution complex o mania [2] (antipatía): **tenerle ∼ a algn** to have it in for sb (colloq)

maniaco -ca, maníaco -ca *m,f* **(a)** (Psic) manic **(b)** (fam) (loco) maniac; **∼ sexual** sex maniac

maniatar [A1] *vt* **(a)** ‹*persona*›: **los ladrones lo ∼on** the burglars tied his hands **(b)** ‹*animal*› to hobble

maniático -ca *adj* **(a)** (delicado, difícil) finicky, fussy **(b)** (obsesionado) obsessive

manicero -ra *m,f* (AmC, AmS) peanut seller

manicomio *m* mental hospital, lunatic asylum

manicura *f* manicure; **hacerse la ∼** (*refl*) to do one's nails; (*caus*) to have a manicure

manido -da *adj* ‹*frase*› hackneyed; ‹*tema*› stale

manifestación *f* [1] (Pol) demonstration [2] (expresión, indicio) sign; **las manifestaciones artísticas culturales de la época** the artistic cultural expression of the era

manifestante *mf* demonstrator

manifestar [A5] *vt* **(a)** (expresar) ‹*desaprobación/agradecimiento*› to express; **∼on**

su apoyo a esta propuesta they expressed their support for the proposal **(b)** (demostrar) ‹*emociones*› to show
■ **manifestarse** *v pron* [1] (hacerse evidente) to become apparent o evident; (ser evidente) to be apparent o evident [2] (Pol) to demonstrate, take part in a demonstration [3] (dar opinión): **∼se en contra/a favor de algo** to express one's opposition to/support for sth

manifiesta, manifiestas, etc ▶
MANIFESTAR

manifiesto¹ -ta *adj* (frml) manifest (frml), evident (frml); **poner algo de ∼** to highlight sth; **quedar de ∼** to become plain o obvious o evident

manifiesto² *m* (Pol) manifesto

manija *f* (esp AmL) handle

manilla *f* **(a)** (de reloj) hand **(b)** (de cajón) handle **(c)** (Col) (guante) baseball glove

manillar *m* (esp Esp) handlebars (*pl*)

maniobra *f* maneuver*; **estar de ∼s** (Mil) to be on maneuvers

maniobrar [A1] *vi/vt* to maneuver*

manipulador -dora *adj* manipulative
■ *m,f* (aprovechado) manipulator

manipular [A1] *vt* [1] **(a)** ‹*mercancías*› to handle **(b)** ‹*aparato/máquina*› to operate, use [2] ‹*persona/información/datos*› to manipulate; **∼ los resultados** to fix o rig the results

maniquí *mf* **(a)** (persona) model **(b)** **maniquí** *m* (de sastre, escaparate) mannequin, dummy

manirroto -ta *adj* **(a)** (fam) extravagant **(b)** (generoso) generous, open-handed
■ *m,f* (fam) spendthrift

manitas *mf* (Esp, Méx fam) handyman (colloq)

manito -ta *m,f*: ▶ MANO²

manivela *f* crank, handle

manjar *m* delicacy; **∼ blanco** (Andes) ▶ DULCE DE LECHE

mano¹ *f* [1] **(a)** (Anat) hand; **tengo las ∼s sucias** my hands are dirty; **levantar la ∼** to raise one's hands, put one's hand up; **¡∼s arriba!** *or* **¡arriba las ∼s!** hands up!; **con la ∼ en el corazón** hand on heart; **le hizo adiós con la ∼** he waved goodbye to her; **su carta pasó de ∼ en ∼** her letter was passed around; **darle la ∼ a algn** (para saludar) to shake hands with sb, to shake sb's hand; (para ayudar, ser ayudado) to give sb one's hand; **dame la ∼** hold my hand; **me tendió la ∼** he held out his hand to me; **me tomó de la ∼** she took me by the hand; **ir (tomados) de la ∼** to walk hand in hand; **∼ de obra** labor **(b)** (Zool) (de oso, perro) paw; (de mono) hand; (Equ) forefoot, front foot
[2] (control, posesión) *gen* **∼s** hands (*pl*); **ha cambiado de ∼s** it has changed hands; **cayó en ∼s del enemigo** it fell into the hands of the enemy; **haré todo lo que esté en mis ∼s** I will do everything in my power; **la oportunidad se nos fue de las ∼s** we let the opportunity slip through our fingers; **se tomó la justicia por su propia ∼** he took the law into his own hands
[3] (en fútbol) handball
[4] (del mortero) pestle
[5] (de pintura, barniz) coat
[6] (Jueg) (vuelta, juego) hand; (conjunto de cartas) hand; (jugador): **soy/eres ∼** it's my/your lead
[7] (en locs) **a mano** (no a máquina) by hand; **hecho** ···⫶

a ~ handmade; **escrito a** ~ handwritten; **tejido a** ~ handwoven; **las tiendas me quedan muy a** ~ the shops are very close by o near; **siempre tengo un diccionario a** ~ I always keep a dictionary by me; **a la mano** (AmL) close at hand; **de mano** hand (*before n*); **en mano** ⟨*lápiz/copa*⟩ in hand; *agarrar* or (esp Esp) **coger a algn con las** ~**s en la masa** to catch sb red-handed; *agarrarle* or *tomarle la* ~ *a algo* (CS fam) to get the hang of sth (colloq); *bajo* ~ on the quiet, on the sly (colloq); *con las* ~**s vacías** empty-handed; *darse la* ~ (para saludar) to shake hands; (para cruzar, jugar, etc) to hold hands; *de segunda* ~ secondhand; *echar* or *dar una* ~ to give o lend a hand; *echar* ~ *a algo* (fam) to grab sth; *estar/quedar a* ~ (AmL fam) to be even o quits (colloq); *lavarse las* ~**s** to wash one's hands; *levantarle la* ~ *a algn* to raise one's hand to sb; *llegar* or *pasar a las* ~**s** to come to blows; *pedir la* ~ *de algn* to ask for sb's hand in marriage; *ser la* ~ *derecha de algn* to be sb's right-hand man/woman; *tenderle una* ~ *a algn* to offer sb a (helping) hand; *tener* ~ *dura* to have a firm hand; *tener* ~ *para algo* to be good at sth; *traerse algo entre* ~**s** to be up to sth (colloq)

⑧ (a) (lado) side; **queda de esta** ~ it's on this side of the street; **a** ~ **derecha** on the right (b) (Auto) side of the road

mano² **-na** *m,f* (AmL fam) (apelativo) buddy (AmE colloq), mate (BrE colloq)

manojo *m* bunch; **ser un** ~ **de nervios** to be a bundle of nerves

manoseado -da *adj* ⟨*libro*⟩ well-thumbed; **fruta manoseada** fruit that has been handled by lots of people (b) ⟨*tema*⟩ hackneyed, well-worn

manosear [A1] *vt* (a) ⟨*objeto*⟩ to handle (b) (fam) ⟨*persona*⟩ to grope (colloq)

manotada *f* (Col) handful

manotazo *m* swipe

mansalva: **a** ~ (*loc adv*) ⟨*disparar*⟩ at close range

mansión *f* mansion; ~ **señorial** stately home

manso -sa *adj* (a) ⟨*caballo*⟩ tame; ⟨*toro*⟩ docile; ⟨*perro*⟩ friendly (b) (liter) ⟨*río*⟩ gently-flowing (liter)

manta *f* ① (de cama) blanket ② (Chi) (poncho) poncho ③ (Méx) (tela) *a coarse muslin-like cloth*, calico (BrE)

manteca *f* (a) (grasa) fat; (de cerdo) lard (b) (mantequilla) (RPI) butter; ~ **de cacao** cocoa butter; ~ **de maní** (RPI) peanut butter

mantecoso -sa *adj* greasy

mantel *m* (de mesa) tablecloth; (del altar) altar cloth; ~ **individual** place mat

mantelería *f* table linen

mantención *f* (CS) maintenance

mantener [E27] *vt* ① (económicamente) ⟨*familia/persona*⟩ to support, maintain; ⟨*amante*⟩ to keep ② (conservar, preservar) to keep; ~ **la calma** to keep calm; ~ **el equilibrio** to keep one's balance; ~ **algo en equilibrio** to balance sth; **para** ~ **su peso actual** to maintain his present weight ③ (a) ⟨*conversaciones*⟩ to have; ⟨*contactos*⟩ to maintain, keep up; ⟨*correspondencia*⟩ to keep up; ⟨*relaciones*⟩ to maintain (b) (cumplir) ⟨*promesa/palabra*⟩ to keep ④ (afirmar, sostener) to maintain

■ **mantenerse** *v pron* ① (sustentarse económicamente) to support oneself

② (en cierto estado, cierta situación) to keep; ~**se en forma** to keep fit; **la torre aún se mantiene en pie** the tower is still standing; ~**se en contacto (con algn)** to keep in touch (with sb) ③ (alimentarse): ~**se a base de latas** to live off tinned food

mantenimiento *m* maintenance; **ejercicios de** ~ keep-fit exercises

mantequilla *f* butter; ~ **de cacao** (Chi, Per) cocoa butter

mantequillera *f* butter dish

mantiene, mantienes, etc ▶ MANTENER

mantilla *f* (a) (de mujer) mantilla (b) (de bebé) terry diaper (AmE), terry nappy (BrE)

manto *m* (Indum) cloak

mantón *m* shawl

mantuve, mantuvo, etc ▶ MANTENER

manual *adj* ⟨*trabajo/destreza*⟩ manual; **tener habilidad** ~ to be good with one's hands
■ *m* manual, handbook

manualidades *fpl* handicrafts (*pl*)

manubrio *m* (a) (manivela) crank, handle (b) (AmL) (de bicicleta) handlebars (*pl*) (c) (Chi, Par) (de auto) steering wheel

manufacturar [A1] *vt* to manufacture

manuscrito¹ -ta *adj* hand-written, manuscript (frml)

manuscrito² *m* manuscript

manutención *f* maintenance

manzana *f* ① (Bot) apple ② (de edificios) block; **dar una vuelta a la** ~ to go round the block ③ (AmL) (Anat) *tb* ~ **de Adán** Adam's apple

manzanar *m* apple orchard

manzanilla *f* (planta) camomile; (infusión) camomile tea
■ *m* manzanilla (*dry sherry*)

manzano *m* apple tree

maña *f* ① (habilidad) skill, knack (colloq); **tener** or **darse** ~ **para algo** to be good at sth; **más vale** ~ **que fuerza** brain is better than brawn ② **mañas** *fpl* (artimañas) wiles (*pl*), guile ③ (capricho) bad habit; (manía) (AmL fam): **tiene** ~**s de viejo** he's like an old man with all his funny little ways (colloq); **tiene la** ~ **de morderse las uñas** he has the annoying habit of biting his nails

mañana *adv* tomorrow; **pasado** ~ the day after tomorrow; ~ **por la** ~ tomorrow morning; **adiós, hasta** ~ goodbye, see you tomorrow; **el día de** ~ tomorrow
■ *m* future
■ *f* morning; **a la** ~ **siguiente** (the) next o the following morning; **a media** ~ **nos reunimos** we met mid-morning; **a las nueve de la** ~ at nine (o'clock) in the morning; **en** or (esp Esp) **por** or (RPI) **a la(s)** ~**(s)** in the morning; **muy de** ~ very early in the morning; **el tren de la** ~ the morning train

mañanero -ra *adj* (fam): **soy muy** ~ I'm a very early riser

mañanitas *fpl* (en Méx) song often sung on birthdays

mañosear [A1] *vi* (Chi fam) to play o act up (colloq)

mañoso -sa *adj* ① (habilidoso) good with one's hands ② (AmL) (caprichoso) difficult

261

mapa ⸱⸱⸱⟡ marchar ⸱⸱⸱

mapa *m* map; ∼ **de carreteras** road map; **cambios en el** ∼ **político** changes in the political scene *o* landscape; *desaparecer del* ∼ to disappear off the face of the earth

mapache *m* racoon

mapamundi *m* map of the world, world map

mapurite *m* (AmC, Ven) skunk

maqueta *f* (de edificio) model, mock-up

maquiladora *f* (Méx) (cross-border) assembly plant

maquillador -dora *m,f* makeup artist

maquillaje *m* makeup; ∼ **de fondo** foundation

maquillar [A1] *vt* to make up
■ **maquillarse** *v pron* to put one's makeup on, to make up

máquina *f* ⊞ (a) (aparato) machine; *¿se puede lavar a* ∼?* can it be machine-washed?; **escribir a** ∼ to type; ∼ **de afeitar** safety razor; (eléctrica) electric razor, shaver; ∼ **de coser/lavar** sewing/ washing machine; ∼ **de escribir** typewriter; ∼ **expendedora** vending machine; ∼ **tragamonedas** *or* (Esp) **tragaperras** slot machine, fruit machine (b) (Jueg) fruit machine; (Fot) camera ⊡ (a) (Ferr, Náut) engine (b) (Ven fam) (auto) car

maquinación *f* plot, scheme

maquinar [A1] *vt* to plot, scheme

maquinaria *f* (a) (conjunto) machinery (b) (mecanismo) mechanism; **la** ∼ **del estado** the state machinery

maquinilla *f* ⊞ *tb* ∼ **de afeitar** safety razor; (éléctrica) electric razor, shaver ⊡ (AmC) (máquina de escribir) typewriter

maquinista *mf* ⊞ (operador de una máquina) machine operator ⊡ (Ferr) engine driver, engineer (AmE); (Náut) engineer

mar *m* (*sometimes f in literary language and in set idiomatic expressions*) ⊞ (Geog) sea; **a orillas del** ∼ by the sea; **el fondo del** ∼ the seabed, the bottom of the sea; ∼ **abierto** open sea; **la corriente llevó la barca** ∼ **adentro** the boat was swept out to sea by the current; **hacerse a la** ∼ (liter) to set sail; **por** ∼ by sea; ∼ **Cantábrico** Bay of Biscay; ∼ **de las Antillas** Caribbean Sea; ∼ **Mediterráneo** Mediterranean Sea; ∼ **gruesa** rough *o* heavy sea ⊡ (costa): **prefiero el** ∼ **a la montaña** I prefer the seaside to the mountains

maraca *f* maraca

maracuyá *m* passion fruit

maraña *f* tangle; **la** ∼ **burocrática** the tangle of bureaucracy

maratón *m or f* marathon

maravilla *f* ⊞ (portento, prodigio) wonder; **las** ∼**s de la tecnología moderna** the wonders of modern technology; **mi secretaria es una verdadera** ∼ my secretary is absolutely wonderful; *a las mil* ∼**s** marvelously; *de* ∼ wonderfully; *hacer* ∼**s** to work wonders ⊡ (Bot) marigold

maravillar [A1] *vt* to amaze, astonish
■ **maravillarse** *v pron* to be amazed *o* astonished; ∼**se DE algo/algn** to marvel AT sth/sb

maravilloso -sa *adj* marvelous*, wonderful

marca *f* ⊞ (a) (señal, huella) mark (b) (en el ganado) brand ⊡ (Com) (de coches, cámaras) make; (de productos alimenticios, cosméticos, etc) brand; **comprar artículos de** ∼ to buy brand products *o* brand names; **ropa de** ∼ designer clothes; ∼

patentada *or* **registrada** registered trademark ⊟ (Dep) record; **superar** *or* **batir una** ∼ to break a record

marcado¹ -da *adj* marked; **un** ∼ **acento escocés** a marked *o* pronounced Scottish accent

marcado² *m* (a) (del pelo) set (b) (de reses) branding

marcador *m* ⊞ (Dep) scoreboard; *¿cómo va el* ∼? what's the score? ⊡ (a) (para libros) bookmark (b) (AmL) (rotulador) felt-tip pen, fiber-tip* pen

marcaje *m* (Dep) coverage, cover

marcapasos *m* (*pl* ∼) pacemaker

marcar [A2] *vt* ⊞ (a) (con señal) ⟨ropa/página/ baraja⟩ to mark; ⟨ganado⟩ to brand (b) ⟨experiencia/suceso⟩ (dejar huella) to mark ⊡ (a) (indicar, señalar) to mark; **el precio va marcado en la tapa** the price is marked on the lid; **el reloj marca las doce en punto** the time is exactly twelve o'clock (b) (hacer resaltar) ⟨cintura/ busto⟩ to accentuate (c) (Mús): ∼ **el compás/el ritmo** to beat time/the rhythm ⊟ ⟨pelo⟩ to set ⊞ (Telec) to dial ⊟ (Dep) (a) ⟨gol/tanto⟩ to score (b) ⟨jugador⟩ to mark
■ ∼ *vi* ⊞ (Dep) to score ⊡ (Telec) to dial
■ **marcarse** *v pron*: ∼**se el pelo** (refl) to set one's hair; (caus) to have one's hair set

marcha *f* ⊞ (a) (Mil) march; (manifestación) march; (caminata) hike, walk; **ir de** ∼ to go walking *o* hiking; **recojan todo y ¡en** ∼! pick up your things and off you/we go!; **ponerse en** ∼ to set off (b) (en atletismo) *tb* ∼ **atlética** walk ⊡ (paso, velocidad) speed; **el vehículo disminuyó la** ∼ the car reduced speed *o* slowed down; **acelerar la** ∼ to speed up; *a toda* ∼ at full *o* top speed, flat out ⊟ (Auto) gear; **cambiar de** ∼ to change gear; **meter la** ∼ **atrás** to put the car into reverse; *dar or hacer* ∼ *atrás* (Auto) to go into reverse; (arrepentirse, retroceder) to pull out, back out ⊞ (funcionamiento) running; **estar en** ∼ «motor» to be running; «proyecto» to be up and running, to be under way; «gestiones» to be under way; **poner en** ∼ ⟨coche/motor⟩ to start; ⟨plan/sistema⟩ to set … in motion; **ponerse en** ∼ «tren» to move off ⊟ (curso, desarrollo) course; **la** ∼ **de los acontecimientos** the course of events; **sobre la** ∼: **hago correciones sobre la** ∼ I make corrections as I go along; **lo decidiremos sobre la** ∼ we'll play it by ear ⊟ (partida) departure ⊟ (Mús) march; ∼ **nupcial** wedding march ⊟ (Esp fam) (animación, ambiente): **una ciudad con mucha** ∼ a very lively city; **¡qué** ∼ **tiene!** he's so full of energy

marchante -ta *m,f* ⊞ (de obras de arte) art dealer ⊡ (Méx) (en mercado — vendedor) stallholder; (— comprador) customer

marchar [A1] *vi* ⊞ (a) «coche» to go, run; «reloj/ máquina» to work; «negocio/relación/empresa» to work; **su matrimonio no marcha muy bien** his marriage isn't going *o* working very well ⊡ (a) (Mil) to march (b) (caminar) to walk

■ **marcharse** *v pron* (esp Esp) to leave; **se marcha a Roma** he's leaving for *o* going off to Rome

marchitarse [A1] *v pron* **(a)** «*flores*» to wither **(b)** (liter) «*belleza/juventud*» to fade

marchito -ta *adj* ‹*flores*› withered **(b)** (liter) ‹*belleza/juventud*› faded

marchoso -sa *adj* (Esp fam) ‹*ambiente/ciudad*› lively; **es un tío ~** he's really into the night life (colloq), he's really into having a good time (colloq)

marcial *adj* martial

marciano -na *adj/m,f* Martian

marco *m* ⒈ **(a)** (de cuadro) frame; (de puerta) doorframe **(b)** (Dep) goalposts (*pl*), goal **(c)** (Andes) (de bicicleta) frame ⒉ (contexto) framework; **dentro del ~ de la ley** within the framework of the law ⒊ (Fin) mark

marea *f* tide; **cuando baja/sube la ~** when the tide goes out/comes in; **~ creciente** rising tide, flood tide; **~ menguante** falling tide, ebb tide; **~ negra** oil slick

mareado -da *adj* **(a)** (Med): **está ~** (con náuseas) he's feeling sick *o* queasy; (con pérdida del equilibrio, etc) he's feeling dizzy *o* giddy; (a punto de desmayarse) he's feeling faint **(b)** (confundido): **me tienes ~ con tanta cháchara** all your chatter is making my head spin

marear [A1] *vt* **(a)** (Med) (con náuseas) to make ... feel sick *o* queasy; (con pérdida de equilibrio) to make ... dizzy **(b)** (confundir) to confuse, get ... confused *o* muddled; **me mareas con tantas preguntas** you're confusing me with all these questions

■ **marearse** *v pron* **(a)** (al viajar — en coche) to get carsick; (— en barco) to get seasick; (— en avión) to get airsick; (perder el equilibrio) to feel dizzy; (con alcohol) to get tipsy **(b)** (confundirse) to get muddled *o* confused

marejada *f* heavy sea, swell

maremoto *m* **(a)** (sismo) seaquake **(b)** (ola) tidal wave

mareo *m* **(a)** (del estómago) sickness, nausea; (producido por movimiento) motion sickness; (en coche) carsickness; (en avión) airsickness; (en barco) seasickness; (pérdida de equilibrio, etc) dizziness, giddiness; **me dio un ~** I felt dizzy **(b)** (confusión) muddle, mess

marfil *m* ivory

margarina *f* margarine

margarita *f* (Bot) (pequeña) daisy; (grande) marguerite

margen *f* (*a veces m*) (de río) bank; (de carretera) side

■ *m* ⒈ (en general) margin; **~ de beneficio** *or* **ganancias** profit margin; **~ de error** margin of error; **ver nota al ~** see margin note; **al margen de** apart from: **al ~ de la ley** on the fringes of the law; **mantenerse al ~ de algo** to keep out of sth; **dejar a algn al ~** to leave sb out; **~ de acción/tiempo** leeway ⒉ **márgenes** *mpl* (límites, parámetros) limits (*pl*); **dentro de ciertos márgenes** within certain limits

marginación *f* (Sociol) marginalization

marginado -da *adj* **(a)** (Sociol) marginalized **(b)** (excluido) excluded

■ *m,f* social outcast

marginal *adj* ⒈ (Sociol): **en los barrios ~es** in the poor, outlying areas of the city ⒉ (secundario) ‹*posición*› peripheral; ‹*asunto*› marginal, peripheral ⒊ (Impr): **una nota ~** a note in the margin, a marginal note

marginar [A1] *vt* (en la sociedad) to marginalize; (en un grupo) to ostracize

mariachi *m* mariachi musician

marialuisa *f* (Méx) mount, passe-partout

maricón¹ -cona *adj* (fam & pey) **(a)** (homosexual) queer (colloq & pej), bent (sl & pej) **(b)** (como insulto): **el muy ~** the bastard *o* (AmE) son of a bitch (vulg); **la muy maricona** the bitch (vulg) **(c)** (AmL) (cobarde) wimpy (colloq), wimpish (colloq)

maricón² *m* (fam & pey) fag (AmE colloq & pej), poof (BrE colloq & pej)

mariconera *f* (fam & hum) (men's) handbag

marido *m* husband

marihuana *f* marijuana

marihuanero -ra *m,f* (fam) dope fiend (colloq)

marimacho *m or f* (fam & pey) **(a)** (niña) tomboy (colloq) **(b)** (mujer hombruna) butch woman (colloq)

marimba *f* marimba (*type of xylophone*)

marina *f* ⒈ (organización) navy; (barcos) fleet; **~ de guerra** navy ⒉ (Art) seascape

marinar [A1] *vt* to marinate, marinade

marinera *f* ⒈ (blusa) sailor top; (chaqueta) (Col) sailor jacket ⒉ (baile) *Andean folk dance*

marinero *m* sailor

marino¹ -na *adj* ‹*brisa/corriente*› sea (*before n*); ‹*fauna/biología*› marine (*before n*)

marino² *m* (marinero) sailor; (oficial) naval officer; **~ mercante** merchant seaman

marioneta *f* puppet, marionette

mariposa *f* butterfly; **~ nocturna** moth; **estilo ~** butterfly; **nadar** *or* (Esp) **a** *or* (Méx) **de ~** to swim butterfly

mariquita *f* (Zool) ladybug (AmE), ladybird (BrE)
■ *m* (fam & pey) fag (AmE colloq & pej), poof (BrE colloq & pej)

mariscal *m* (Hist, Mil) marshal; **~ de campo** (Mil) field marshal; (en fútbol americano) quarterback

marisco *m* shellfish (*pl*), seafood

marisma *f* marsh

marisquería *f* seafood *o* shellfish restaurant/bar/shop

marital *adj* ‹*relaciones*› marital (*before n*); ‹*vida*› married (*before n*)

marítimo -ma *adj* ‹*comercio*› maritime; ‹*ruta/agente*› shipping (*before n*); ‹*transporte*› sea (*before n*); ‹*ciudad*› coastal, maritime; **un puerto ~** a seaport

marketing /'marketin/ *m* marketing

mármol *m* marble

AmC Central America	Arg Argentina	Cu Cuba	Per Peru
AmL Latin America	Bol Bolivia	Ec Ecuador	RPI River Plate Area
AmS South America	Chi Chile	Esp Spain	Ur Uruguay
Andes Andean Region	CS Southern Cone	Méx Mexico	Ven Venezuela

marmota f (a) (Zool) marmot (b) (fam) (persona dormilona) sleepyhead (colloq)

maroma f [1] rope [2] (a) (Andes) (acrobacia, malabarismo) trick, stunt; **las ~s del payaso** the clown's antics (b) (Méx) (voltereta) somersault, tumble; **dar una ~** to do a somersault

marqués -quesa m,f [1] (persona) (m) marquis, marquess (BrE); (f) marquise, marchioness (BrE) [2] **marquesa** f (Chi) (catre) bed

marquesina f (en parada, andén) shelter; (de teatro, hotel) marquee (AmE), canopy (BrE); (en estadio) roof

marquetería f marquetry

marranada f (fam) (faena) dirty trick

marrano -na adj filthy
■ m,f (fam) (a) (animal) (m) pig, hog; (f) pig, sow (b) (Col) (carne) pork (c) (persona grosera) dirty swine (colloq)

marraqueta f (Chi) bread roll

marrón adj/m brown; **zapatos ~ oscuro** dark brown shoes

marroquí adj/mf Moroccan

marroquinería f (a) (artículos de cuero) leather goods (pl) (b) (tienda) leather goods shop

marrueco m (Chi) fly, flies (pl)

Marruecos m Morocco

marsupial adj/m marsupial

marta f (pine) marten; **~ cibelina** sable

Marte m Mars

martes m (pl ~) Tuesday; **~ (y) trece** ≈ Friday the thirteenth; **~ de carnaval** Shrove Tuesday, Mardi Gras; para ejemplos ver LUNES

martillar, martillear [A1] vt/vi to hammer

martilleo m hammering; **un ~ terrible en las sienes** a terrible pounding in the temples

martillero -ra m,f (CS, Per) auctioneer

martillo m hammer; **~ neumático** jackhammer, pneumatic drill

martín pescador m kingfisher

mártir mf martyr

martirio m (a) (muerte) martyrdom (b) (sufrimiento) torment, ordeal

martirizar [A4] vt (a) (matar) to martyr (b) (atormentar) to torment

marxismo m Marxism

marxista adj/mf Marxist

marzo m March; para ejemplos ver ENERO

mas conj (liter) but

más adv [1] (a) (comparativo): **¿tiene algo ~ barato/moderno?** do you have anything cheaper/more modern; **duran ~** they last longer; **me gusta ~ sin azúcar** I prefer it without sugar; **ahora la vemos ~** we see more of her now; **tendrás que estudiar ~** you'll have to study harder; **~ lejos/atrás** further away/back; **el ~ allá** the other world; **~ que nunca** more than ever; **me gusta ~ el vino seco que el dulce** I prefer dry wine to sweet, I like dry wine better than sweet; **pesa ~ de lo que parece** it's heavier than it looks; **es ~ complicado de lo que tú crees** it's more complicated than you think; **eran ~ de las cinco** it was after five o'clock; **~ de 30** more than 30, over 30 (b) (especialmente) particularly, especially

[2] (superlativo): **la ~ bonita/la ~ inteligente** the prettiest/the most intelligent; **el que ~ sabe** the one who knows most; **el que ~ me gusta** the one I like best; **estuvo de lo ~ divertido** it was great fun

[3] (en frases negativas): **no tiene ~ que tres meses** she's only three months old; **nadie ~ que ella** nobody but her; **no tengo ~ que esto** this is all I have; **no tuve ~ remedio** I had no alternative; **no juego ~** I'm not playing any more; **nunca ~** never again

[4] (con valor ponderativo): **¡cantó ~ bien...!** she sang so well!; **¡qué cosa ~ rara!** how strange!
■ adj inv [1] (comparativo) more; **~ dinero** more money; **una vez ~** once more; **ni un minuto ~** not a minute longer; **hoy hace ~ calor** it's warmer today; **son ~ que nosotros** there are more of them than us

[2] (superlativo) most; **el equipo que ganó ~ partidos** the team that won most games; **las ~ de las veces** more often than not

[3] (con valor ponderativo): **¡me da ~ rabia ...!** it makes me so mad!; **¡tiene ~ amigos ...!** he has so many friends!

[4] **¿qué ~?** what else?; **nada/nadie ~** nothing/nobody else; **algo/alguien ~** something/somebody else; **¿quién ~ vino?** who else came?; **¿algo ~?** — **nada ~ gracias** anything else? — no, that's all, thank you
■ pron [1] more; **¿te sirvo ~?** would you like some more?

[2] (en locs) **a lo ~** at the most; **a más no poder: corrimos a ~ no poder** we ran as fast o hard as we could; **a más tardar** at the latest; **cuanto más** at the most; **de más: ¿tienes un lápiz de ~?** do you have a spare pencil?; **me dio cinco dólares de ~** he gave me five dollars too much; **no está de ~ repetirlo** there's no harm in repeating it; **es más** in fact; **más bien** (un poco) rather; **más o menos** (aproximadamente) more or less; (no muy bien) so-so; **ni más ni menos** no less; **de más** ▶ NOMÁS; **por más: por ~ que llores** however much you cry; **por ~ que trataba** however hard he tried; **¿qué más da?** what does it matter?; **sin más (ni más)** just like that
■ prep (a) (Mat) (en sumas) plus; **8+7 =15** (read as: **ocho más siete (es) igual (a) quince**) eight plus seven equals fifteen (b) (además de) plus; **mil pesos, ~ los gastos** a thousand pesos, plus expenses
■ m plus sign

masa f [1] (Coc) (a) (para pan, pasta) dough; (para empanadas, tartas) pastry; (para bizcocho) mixture; (para crepes) batter; **~ de hojaldre** puff pastry (b) (RPI) (pastelito) pastry, cake [2] (Pol, Sociol, Fís) mass; **educar a las ~s** to educate the masses [3] **en masa** (a) (loc adj) ⟨fabricación/despidos⟩ mass (before n) (b) (loc adv) ⟨acudir⟩ en masse

masacrar [A1] vt to massacre

masacre f massacre

masaje m massage; **darle ~s** or **un ~ a algn** to give sb a massage

masajear [A1] vt to massage

masajista mf [1] (que da masajes) (m) masseur; (f) masseuse [2] (en fútbol) coach, trainer

mascada f (a) (Chi) (mordisco) bite (b) (Méx) (pañuelo grande) scarf

mascar [A2] vt to chew

máscara f mask; ~ **antigás** gas mask; ~ **de oxígeno** oxygen mask; ~ **facial** face pack

mascarilla f mask; (en cosmética) face pack

mascota f (talismán) mascot; (animal doméstico) pet

masculino¹ -na adj (a) ⟨actitud/hormona⟩ male; ⟨mujer/aspecto⟩ masculine, manly (b) (Ling) masculine

masculino² m masculine

mascullar [A1] vt to mumble, mutter

masía f (granja) farm; (casa) country house

masificación f overcrowding

masificado -da adj ⟨universidad⟩ overcrowded

masilla f (para cristales) putty; (para rellenar grietas) mastic, filler

masivo -va adj (a) ⟨ejecución/migración⟩ mass (before n); ⟨protesta⟩ large-scale (before n), mass (before n); ⟨concurrencia⟩ massive (b) ⟨dosis⟩ massive, huge

masón adj Masonic
■ m Freemason, Mason

masonería f Freemasonry

masoquismo m masochism

masoquista adj masochistic
■ mf masochist

máster /'master/ m (pl **-ters**) [1] (Audio, Vídeo) master [2] (Educ) master's degree

masticar [A2] vt/vi to chew

mástil m (a) (Náut) mast; (para una bandera) flagpole, flagstaff (b) (de guitarra, violín) neck (c) (de carpa) centerpole*

mastín m mastiff

mastodonte m (a) (animal prehistórico) mastodon (b) (fam) (persona grande) giant

mastuerzo m (planta) (garden) cress

masturbación f masturbation

masturbarse [A1] v pron to masturbate

mata f [1] (arbusto) bush, shrub; (planta) (AmL) plant [2] (ramita) sprig; (de hierba) tuft [3] (fam) (de pelo) mane (colloq), mop (colloq)

matadero m slaughterhouse, abattoir

matado -da m,f (Méx fam & pey) grind (AmE colloq), swot (BrE colloq)

matador m matador

matamoscas m (pl ~) (a) (paleta) flyswatter (b) (spray) fly spray, fly killer

matanza f (acción de matar) killing, slaughter; (de res, cerdo) slaughter; **la ~ de gente inocente** the mass killing of innocent people

matapolillas m (pl ~) moth killer

matar [A1] vt [1] (a) ⟨persona⟩ to kill (b) (sacrificar) ⟨perro/caballo⟩ to put down, destroy; ⟨reses⟩ to slaughter; **lo mató un coche** he was run over and killed by a car (c) (en sentido hiperbólico): **la vas a ~ a disgustos** you'll be the death of her; **es para ~los** I could murder o kill them (colloq); **nos mataban de hambre** they used to starve us; **estos zapatos me están matando** these shoes are killing me!
[2] (fam) ⟨sed⟩ to quench; ⟨tiempo⟩ to kill; **compraron fruta para ~ el hambre** they bought some fruit to keep them going
■ ~ vi to kill
■ **matarse** v pron [1] (a) (morir violentamente) to be

killed; **casi me mato** I almost got killed (b) (refl) (suicidarse) to kill oneself; **se mató de un tiro** she shot herself
[2] (fam) (a) (esforzarse): **me maté estudiando** or (Esp) **a estudiar** I studied like crazy o mad (colloq)
(b) (Méx fam) (para un examen) to cram (colloq), to swot (BrE colloq)

matarife m (en matadero) slaughterman

matarratas m (pl ~) (veneno) rat poison

matasellos m (pl ~) (a) (marca) postmark (b) (instrumento) datestamp, stamp

matazón f (Col, Méx, Ven fam) massacre, slaughter

mate adj or adj inv ⟨pintura/maquillaje⟩ matt; **fotos** ~ photos with a matt finish
■ m [1] (en ajedrez) tb **jaque** ~ checkmate, mate [2] (a) (infusión) maté; **cebar** ~ to brew maté (b) (AmL) (calabaza) gourd

matear [A1] vi (CS fam) to drink maté
■ **matearse** v pron (Chi fam) to cram (colloq), to swot (Br colloq)

matemáticas fpl mathematics, math (AmE), maths (BrE)

matemático -ca adj mathematical
■ m,f mathematician

mateo -tea m,f (Chi fam) grind (AmE colloq), swot (BrE colloq)

materia f [1] (sustancia) matter; ~ **gris** gray* matter; ~ **prima** (Econ, Tec) raw material; (Fin) commodity [2] (a) (tema, asunto) subject; **en** ~ **de** as regards, with regard to (b) (asignatura) subject

material adj (a) ⟨necesidades/ayuda/valor⟩ material; **daños** ~**es** damage to property, material damage (b) ⟨autor/causante⟩ actual
■ m [1] (en general) material; ~**es para la construcción** building materials [2] (útiles) materials (pl); ~ **de oficina** office stationery; ~ **didáctico/escolar** teaching/school materials (pl)

materialismo m materialism

materialista adj materialistic
■ mf [1] (persona) materialist [2] (Méx) (constructor) building contractor; (camionero) truck driver, lorry driver (BrE)

maternal adj ⟨instinto⟩ maternal; ⟨amor⟩ motherly, maternal

maternidad f (a) (estado) motherhood, maternity (b) (hospital) maternity hospital; (sala) maternity ward

materno -na adj ⟨amor⟩ motherly; ⟨pariente⟩ maternal; ⟨lengua⟩ mother

matinal adj morning (before n)

matinée, matiné f (a) (AmS) (de tarde) matinée (b) (Méx) (de mañana) morning performance

matiz m (a) (de color) shade, hue (b) (de palabra, frase) nuance, shade of meaning; **tiene cierto** ~ **peyorativo** it has a slightly pejorative nuance (c) (de ironía) touch, hint

matizar [A4] vt [1] ⟨colores⟩ to blend [2] (concretar, puntualizar) to qualify, clarify

matón m (del barrio) thug; (en la escuela) bully; (criminal) thug, heavy (colloq)

matorral m (a) (conjunto de matas) thicket, bushes (pl) (b) (terreno) scrubland

matraca f [1] (juguete) rattle [2] (Méx fam) (coche) rattletrap (colloq)

matrero -ra adj ⒈ (Col fam) (basto) shoddy ⒉ (RPl) (fugitivo): **un gaucho ∼** a gaucho on the run from the law ⒊ (Col) (traicionero) sly, crafty

matriarcado m matriarchy

matriarcal adj matriarchal

matrícula f ⒈ (Educ) (inscripción) registration, enrollment*; (derechos or tasas de ∼) registration fees; **∼ de honor** (Esp) ≈distinction, ≈magna cum laude ⒉ (Transp) (número) registration number; (placa) license* plate, number plate (BrE)

matricular [A1] vt **(a)** ⟨persona⟩ to register, enroll* **(b)** ⟨coche/barco⟩ to register
■ **matricularse** v pron (refl) to register, enroll*; **∼se EN algo** to enroll on sth

matrimonial adj marital

matrimonio m **(a)** (institución) marriage, matrimony (frml); **contraer ∼** (frml) to marry **(b)** (pareja) (married) couple; **el ∼ Garrido** Mr and Mrs Garrido, the Garridos **(c)** (AmS exc RPl) (boda) wedding; **∼ civil/religioso** civil/church wedding

matriz f **(a)** (útero) womb, uterus **(b)** (molde) mold* **(c)** (de talonario) stub

matrona f (comadrona) midwife

matutino¹ -na adj morning (before n)

matutino² m morning paper

maullar [A23] vi to miaow

maullido m miaow

mausoleo m mausoleum

maxilar m jawbone, maxilla (tech)

máxima f maxim

máxime adv especially

máximo¹ -ma adj ⟨temperatura/velocidad⟩ top (before n), maximum (before n); ⟨carga/altura⟩ maximum (before n); ⟨punto⟩ highest; ⟨esfuerzo/ambición⟩ greatest (before n); **el ∼ dirigente francés** the French leader

máximo² m maximum; **como ∼** at the most; **aprovechar algo al ∼** to make the most of sth; **se esforzó al ∼** she did her utmost; **rendir al ∼** «persona» to give a hundred percent; «máquina» to work to its full capacity

maya adj Mayan
■ mf Maya, Mayan; **los ∼s** the Maya o Mayas

mayo m May; **el primero de ∼** May Day; para ejemplos ver ENERO

mayonesa f mayonnaise, mayo (AmE) (colloq)

mayor adj ⒈ **(a)** (comparativo de GRANDE) ⟨número/porcentaje⟩ greater, higher; ⟨beneficio⟩ greater; **vuelan a ∼ altura** they fly at a greater height; **a ∼ escala** on a larger scale; **un número ∼ que 40** a number greater than 40 **(b)** (superlativo de GRANDE): **el ∼ número de accidentes** the greatest o highest number of accidents; **su ∼ preocupación** her greatest o biggest worry; **a la ∼ brevedad posible** as soon as possible; **la ∼ parte de los estudiantes** most students, the majority of students
⒉ (en edad) **(a)** (comparativo) older; **∼ QUE algn** older THAN sb **(b)** (superlativo): **es la ∼ de las dos** she is the older o elder of the two; **mi hijo ∼** my eldest o oldest son **(c)** (anciano) elderly **(d)** (adulto): **las personas ∼es** adults, grown-ups (colloq); **cuando sea ∼** when I grow up; **ser ∼ de edad** (Der) to be of age; **soy ∼ de edad y haré lo que quiera** I'm over 18 (o 21 etc) and I'll do as I please

⒊ (en nombres) (principal) main; **Calle M∼** Main Street (in US), High Street (in UK) ⒋ (Mús) major ⒌ (Com): **(al) por ∼** wholesale
■ mf (adulto) adult, grown-up (colloq); **solo para ∼es** adults only; **mis/tus ∼es** my/your elders; **∼ de edad** person who is legally of age

mayoral m (capataz) foreman; (de finca) farm manager, steward

mayordomo m (criado principal) butler, majordomo; (capataz) (CS) foreman; (portero) (Chi) superintendent (AmE), caretaker (BrE)

mayoría f majority; **la gran ∼ de ...** the great majority of ...; **ser ∼ or estar en ∼** to be in the majority; **gobierno de la ∼** majority rule; **∼ absoluta/relativa** absolute/simple majority; **llegar a la ∼ de edad** to come of age

mayorista adj wholesale
■ mf wholesaler

mayoritario -ria adj **(a)** ⟨apoyo/decisión/partido⟩ majority (before n) **(b)** (Fin) ⟨socio/accionista⟩ principal

mayúscula f capital (letter), uppercase letter (tech); **se escribe con ∼** it is written with a capital letter; **rellenar en or con ∼s** write in block capitals o in capital letters

mayúsculo -la adj **(a)** ⟨letra⟩ capital (before n), upper-case (tech) **(b)** ⟨susto/error⟩ terrible

maza f **(a)** (Const) drop hammer **(b)** (de bombo) drumstick **(c)** (arma) mace

mazacote m **(a)** (fam) (Coc): **un ∼** a lumpy mess **(b)** (fam) (obra tosca) eyesore

mazamorra f **(a)** (AmS) milky pudding made with maize **(b)** (Per) pudding made with corn starch, sugar and honey **(c)** (Col) maize soup

mazapán m marzipan

mazmorra f dungeon

mazo m ⒈ **(a)** (herramienta) mallet; (del mortero) pestle; (para la carne) meat tenderizer; (porra) club **(b)** (en croquet, polo) mallet ⒉ (esp AmL) (manojo) bunch; (de naipes) deck (of cards) (AmE), pack (of cards) (BrE)

mazorca f (Bot, Coc) cob; **∼ de maíz** corncob

mazurca f mazurka

me pron pers me; **¿∼ lo prestas?** will you lend it to me o lend me it?; **∼ arregló el televisor** he fixed the television for me; **∼ lo quitó** he took it off me o away from me; **∼ robaron el reloj** my watch was stolen; **∼ miré en el espejo** (refl) I looked at myself in the mirror; **∼ corté el pelo** (refl) I cut my hair; (caus) I had my hair cut; **∼ equivoqué** I made a mistake; **∼ alegro mucho** I'm very pleased; **se ∼ murió el gato** my cat died

mear [A1] vi (vulg) to (have a) piss (vulg)
■ **mearse** v pron (fam) to wet oneself; **me estoy meando** I'm dying for a pee (colloq)

mecánica f mechanics

mecánico -ca adj mechanical
■ m,f (de vehículos) mechanic; (de maquinaria industrial) fitter; (de fotocopiadoras, lavadoras) engineer

mecanismo m mechanism; **∼ de defensa** defense* mechanism

mecanizado -da adj mechanized

mecanizar [A4] vt to mechanize

mecanografía f typing

mecanografiar [A17] vt to type

m

mecanógrafo -fa *m,f* typist
mecate *m* (AmC, Méx, Ven) string, cord; (más grueso) rope
mecedora *f* rocking chair
mecenas *mf* (*pl* ~) patron, sponsor
mecer [E2] *vt* ‹*bebé/cuna*› to rock; ‹*niño*› (en columpio) to push
■ **mecerse** *v pron* (a) (en mecedora) to rock; (en columpio) to swing (b) (bambolearse) to sway
mecha *f* **1** (de vela) wick; (de armas, explosivos) fuse **2 mechas** *fpl* (en peluquería) highlights (*pl*)
mechero *m* (a) (Esp) (encendedor) lighter (b) (Col) (candil) oil lamp
mechón¹ *m* (a) (de pelo) lock (b) (de lana) tuft (c) **mechones** *mpl* (Col) (en peluquería) highlights (*pl*)
mechón² -chona *m,f* (Chi) (estudiante) freshman, fresher (BrE)
medalla *f* (Dep, Mil) medal; (Relig) medallion (*with religious engraving on it*)
medallón *m* medallion
media *f* **1** (Indum) (a) (hasta el muslo) stocking; ~s con/sin costura seamed/seamless stockings (b) **medias** *fpl* (hasta la cintura) panty hose (*pl*) (AmE), tights (*pl*) (BrE); ~s bombacha(s) (RPI) *or* (Col, Ven) pantalón panty hose (*pl*) (AmE), tights (BrE) (*pl*) (c) (AmL) (calcetín) sock **2** (Mat) average; la ~ de velocidad the average speed **3** a medias (*loc adv*) (a) (incompleto): dejó el trabajo a ~s he left the work half-finished; me dijo la verdad a ~s she didn't tell me the whole truth *o* story (b) (entre dos): pagar a ~s to pay half each, go halves; lo hicimos a ~s we did half (of it) each
mediación *f* mediation; por ~ de through
mediador -dora *m,f* mediator
mediados: a ~ de mes halfway through the month, in the middle of the month; a ~ de los años 30 in the mid thirties
mediagua *f* (Andes) hut, shack
medialuna *f* (a) (esp RPI) (Coc) croissant (*often with ham and cheese*) (b) (Chi) (corral) ring
mediana *f* (Auto) median strip (AmE), central reservation (BrE)
medianero -ra *adj* dividing (*before n*)
mediano -na *adj* (a) ‹*tamaño/porción*› medium; ‹*coche*› medium-sized; de mediana estatura/inteligencia of average height/intelligence; de mediana edad middle-aged (b) (mediocre) average, mediocre
medianoche *f* midnight; a ~ at midnight
mediante *prep* through, by means of
mediar [A1] *vi* (a) (intervenir) to mediate; ~ EN algo ‹*en conflicto/negociaciones*› to mediate IN sth, to act as mediator IN sth (b) (interceder) ~ POR algn to intercede FOR sb; ~ ANTE algn to intercede *o* intervene WITH sb
mediasnueves *fpl* (Col) mid-morning snack, elevenses (BrE colloq)

medicamento *m* (frml) medicine, medicament (frml)
medicatura *f* (Ven) first aid post, clinic
medicina *f* medicine
medicinal *adj* ‹*aguas/planta*› medicinal; ‹*champú/jabón*› medicated
medición *f* (a) (acción) measuring (b) (frml) (medida) measurement
médico¹ -ca *adj* medical; un reconocimiento ~ a medical (examination)
médico² -ca *mf* doctor; ~ de cabecera family doctor *o* (AmE) physician, general practitioner, GP; ~ de medicina general general practitioner, GP
medida *f* **1** (Mat) (dimensión) measurement; tomarle las ~s a algn to take sb's measurements; tomar las ~s de algo to measure something **2** (*en locs*) a (la) medida ‹*traje/zapato*› custom-made (AmE), made-to-measure (BrE); a medida que as; a ~ que fue creciendo as he grew up **3** (utensilio) measure; (contenido) measure **4** (grado, proporción): en gran/cierta ~ to a large/certain extent; en la ~ de lo posible as far as possible **5** (disposición) measure; tomar ~s to take steps *o* measures
medido -da *adj* (CS) ‹*persona/comportamiento*› restrained; es muy ~ con la bebida he's a very moderate drinker
medidor *m* (AmL) meter
medieval *adj* medieval
medio¹ -dia *adj* **1** (*delante del n*) (la mitad de): ~ kilo half a kilo; media manzana half an apple; pagar ~ pasaje to pay half fare *o* half price; media hora half an hour, a half hour (AmE); dos horas y media two and a half hours; a las cinco y media at half past five; a media mañana/tarde in the middle of the morning/afternoon; a ~ camino halfway; media pensión (en hoteles) half board; (se) dio ~ vuelta y se fue she turned on her heel and left; un jugador de ~ campo a midfield player; ~ tiempo (AmL) half-time; mi media naranja (fam & hum) my better half (colloq & hum) **2** (mediano, promedio) average; el ciudadano ~ the average citizen; a ~ y largo plazo in the medium and long term
medio² *adv* half; está ~ loca she's half crazy; todo lo deja a ~ terminar he leaves everything half finished
■ *m* **1** (Mat) (mitad) half **2** (centro) middle; en (el) ~ de la habitación in the middle *o* center of the room; quitarse de en *or* del ~ to get out of the way **3** (a) (recurso, manera) means (*pl*); como ~ de coacción as a means of coercion; los ~s de comunicación the media; ~ de transporte means of transport (b) **medios** *mpl* (recursos económicos) *tb* ~s económicos means (*pl*), resources (*pl*) **4** (*en locs*) en medio de: en ~ de tanta gente (in) among so many people; en ~ de la confusión in *o* amid all the confusion; por medio (CS, Per): día/semana por ~ every other day/week; dos casas

por ~ every two houses; **por medio de** (de proceso/técnica) by means of; **por ~ de tu primo** from o through your cousin

5 (a) (círculo, ámbito): **en ~s literarios/políticos** in literary/political circles; **no está en su ~** he's out of his element **(b)** (Biol) environment; **la adaptación al ~** adaptation to one's environment; **~ ambiente** environment; **que no da daña el ~ ambiente** eco-friendly, environmentally friendly

mediocampista *mf* midfield player

mediocre *adj* mediocre

mediocridad *f* mediocrity

mediodía *m* **(a)** (las doce de la mañana) midday, noon; **a ~** or **al ~** at midday **(b)** (hora de comer) lunch time

Medio Oriente *m* Middle East, Mid-East (AmE)

medir [I14] *vt* **1** ⟨*habitación/distancia/velocidad*⟩ to measure **2** (tener ciertas dimensiones) to be, measure; **mido 60 cm de cintura** I measure o I'm 60 cm round the waist; **¿cuánto mide de alto/largo?** how tall/long is it?; **mide casi 1,90 m** he's almost 1.90 m (tall) **3** (calcular, considerar) to consider, weigh up; **~ los pros y contras de algo** to weigh up the pros and cons of sth

■ **medirse** *v pron* **1** (*refl*) to measure oneself; ⟨*caderas/pecho*⟩ to measure **2** (Col, Méx, Ven) (probarse) to try on

meditación *f* meditation

meditar [A1] *vi* to meditate; **~ sobre algo** to reflect o meditate on sth

■ **~** *vt* (considerar) to think about; (durante más tiempo) to ponder, meditate on; **una decisión muy meditada** a very carefully thought-out decision

mediterráneo -nea *adj* Mediterranean

Mediterráneo *m*: *tb* **el (mar) ~** the Mediterranean (sea)

médula *f* (Anat) marrow, medulla (tech); **~ ósea** bone marrow; **británico hasta la ~** British through and through

medusa *f* jellyfish, medusa

megafonía *f* PA system

megáfono *m* megaphone

mejicano -na *adj/m,f* Mexican

Méjico *m* ▶ MEXICO

mejilla *f* cheek; **poner la otra ~** to turn the other cheek

mejillón *m* mussel

mejor *adj* **1 (a)** (comparativo de BUENO) ⟨*producto/profesor*⟩ better; ⟨*calidad*⟩ better, higher, superior; **tanto ~** so much the better; **cuanto más grande ~** the bigger the better **(b)** (comparativo de BIEN) better; **está ~ así** it's better like this

2 (a) (superlativo de BUENO) (entre dos) better; (entre varios) best; **mi ~ amiga** my best friend; **productos de la ~ calidad** products of the highest quality; **lo ~ es se lo digas** the best thing (to do) is to tell her; **le deseo lo ~** I wish you the very best o all the best **(b)** (superlativo de BIEN): **la que está ~ de dinero** the one who has the most money

■ *adv* **1** (comparativo) better; **luego lo pensé ~** then I thought better of it; **pintas cada vez ~** your painting is getting better and better; **me lleva dos años, ~ dicho, dos y medio** she's two years older than me, or rather, two and a half

2 (superlativo) best; **este es el lugar desde donde se ve ~** this is where you can see best (from); **la versión ~ ambientada de la obra** the best-staged production of the play; **lo hice lo ~ que pude** I did it as best I could o (frml) to the best of my ability; **a lo ~** maybe, perhaps; **a lo ~ vamos a Italia** we may o might go to Italy

3 (esp AmL) (en sugerencias): **~ lo dejamos para otro día** why don't we leave it for another day?; **~ me callo** I think I'd better shut up

■ *mf*: **el/la ~** (de dos) the better; (de varios) the best; **es la ~ de la clase** she's the best in the class

mejora *f* improvement

mejorana *f* marjoram

mejorar [A1] *vt* ⟨*condiciones/situación/oferta*⟩ to improve; ⟨*marca*⟩ to improve on, beat; **el tratamiento la mejoró** the treatment made her a lot better

■ **~** *vi* ⟨*tiempo/calidad/situación*⟩ to improve, get better; ⟨*persona*⟩ (Med) to get better; **ha mejorado de aspecto** he looks a lot better

■ **mejorarse** *v pron* ⟨*enfermo*⟩ to get better; **que te mejores** get well soon, I hope you get better soon

mejoría *f* improvement; **le deseamos una pronta ~** we wish you a speedy recovery

melancolía *f* melancholy, sadness

melancólico -ca *adj* melancholy

■ *m,f* melancholic

melaza *f* molasses

melé *f* (Dep) (libre) ruck, maul; (organizada) scrum

melena *f* **(a)** (pelo suelto) long hair **(b)** (estilo de corte) bob **(c)** (del león) mane

melenudo -da *adj* (fam) long-haired

melindroso -sa *adj* **(a)** (remilgado) affected **(b)** (Méx) (delicado) choosy, finicky **(c)** (mojigato) prudish

mellado -da *adj* ⟨*diente/taza*⟩ chipped; ⟨*cuchillo/borde*⟩ jagged

mellar [A1] *vt* **(a)** ⟨*cuchillo/hoja*⟩ to notch, nick; ⟨*diente/porcelana*⟩ to chip **(b)** (esp AmL) ⟨*honor/fama*⟩ to damage

mellizo -za *adj* twin (*before n*)

■ *m,f* (*m*) twin (brother); (*f*) twin (sister); **tuvo ~s** she had twins

melocotón *m* **(a)** (esp Esp) (fruta redonda) peach **(b)** (AmC) (fruta en forma de estrella) star fruit

melodía *f* melody, tune

melódico -ca *adj* melodic

melodioso -sa *adj* melodious, tuneful

melodrama *m* melodrama

melodramático -ca *adj* melodramatic

melómano -na *m,f* music lover

melón *m* (Bot) melon

meloso -sa *adj* ⟨*persona/voz*⟩ sickly-sweet; ⟨*música/canción*⟩ schmaltzy, slushy

membrana *f* membrane

membresía *f* (AmL frml) membership

membrete *m* letterhead; **papel con ~** headed paper

membrillo *m* (árbol) quince (tree); (fruta) quince; **dulce de ~** quince jelly

memorable *adj* memorable

memorándum *m* (*pl* **-dums**), **memorando** *m* (nota) memorandum, memo

m

memoria *f* **1** (en general) memory; **tener
buena/mala ∼** to have a good/poor memory; **si la
∼ no me falla** *or* **engaña** if my memory serves me
right; **desde que tengo ∼** for as long as I can
remember; **aprender/saber algo de ∼** to learn/
know sth by heart; **respetar la ∼ de algn** to
respect the memory of sb; **a la** *or* **en ∼ de algn** in
memory of sb **2 memorias** *fpl* (Lit) memoirs
(*pl*) **3 (a)** (Adm, Com) report; **∼ anual** annual
report **(b)** (Educ) written paper

memorial *m* memorial

memorizar [A4] *vt* to memorize

menaje *m*: **artículos de ∼** household items;
sección de ∼ del hogar household department

mención *f* mention; **hacer ∼ de algo** to
mention sth

mencionar [A1] *vt* to mention; **no quiero oír
∼ ese nombre** I don't want to hear that name
mentioned

mendicidad *f* begging

mendigar [A3] *vi* to beg

▪ **∼** *vt* «*mendigo*» to beg for

mendigo -ga *m,f* beggar

mendrugo *m*: *tb* **∼ de pan** piece of stale bread

menear [A1] *vt* ‹*rabo*› to wag; ‹*cabeza*› to
shake; ‹*caderas*› to wiggle

▪ **menearse** *v pron* **(a)** (con inquietud) to fidget **(b)**
(provocativamente) to wiggle one's hips

menester *m* **1** **ser ∼** (frml) (ser necesario) to be
necessary; **es ∼ que lo hagamos sin demora** we
must do it without delay **2** (frml) (tarea)
occupation; **se ganaba la vida en los ∼es más
diversos** he earned his living from some very
diverse activities

menestra *f* vegetable stew

menguar [A16] *vi* **1** (frml) «*temperatura/
nivel*» to fall, drop; «*cantidad/número/reservas*»
to diminish **2** (al tejer) to decrease

▪ **∼** *vt* **1** (frml) ‹*responsabilidad/influencia*› to
diminish; ‹*reputación*› to damage **2** ‹*puntos*› (en
tejido) to decrease

meningitis *f* meningitis

menisco *m* cartilage, meniscus (tech)

menopausia *f* menopause

menopáusico -ca *adj* menopausal

menor *adj* **1** **(a)** (comparativo de PEQUEÑO)
‹*número/porcentaje*› lower, smaller; **en ∼
medida/grado** to a lesser extent *o* degree; **∼ QUE**
algo lower THAN sth; **un ingreso ∼ que el mío** an
income lower than mine **(b)** (superlativo de
PEQUEÑO): **el país con el ∼ número de parados**
the country with the lowest unemployment
figures; **haciendo el ∼ ruido posible** making as
little noise as possible; **el de ∼ tamaño** the
smallest one

2 (en edad) **(a)** (comparativo) younger; **∼ QUE** algn
younger THAN sb **(b)** (superlativo): **¿cuál es el ∼ de
los hermanos?** who's the youngest of the
brothers?; **el ∼ de los dos niños** the younger of
the two boys

3 (secundario) ‹*escritor/obra*› minor; **lesiones de
∼ importancia** minor injuries

4 (Mús) minor

5 (Com): **(al) por ∼** retail

▪ *mf*: *tb* **∼ de edad** minor; **ser ∼ de edad** to be a
minor, to be under age; **película no apta para
menores** film not suitable for under-18s

menorista *mf* (Col, Méx, Ven) retailer

menos *adv* **1** (comparativo) less; **cada vez
estudia ∼** she's studying less and less; **ya me
duele ∼** it hurts less now; **ahora lo vemos ∼** we
don't see him so often now, we don't see so much
of him now; **pesa ∼ de 50 kilos** it weighs less
than *o* under 50 kilos; **éramos ∼ de diez** there
were fewer than ten of us; **los niños de ∼ de 7
años** children under seven

2 (superlativo) least; **es la ∼ complicada** it is the
least complicated one; **el que ∼ me gusta** the one
I like (the) least; **se esfuerza lo ∼ posible** he
makes as little effort as possible; **cuando ∼ lo
esperaba** when I was least expecting it

▪ *adj inv* **1** (comparativo) (en cantidad) less; (en
número) fewer; **alimentos con ∼ fibra/calorías** food
with less fiber/fewer calories; **hay ∼ errores**
there are fewer mistakes; **mide medio metro ∼**
it's half a meter shorter; **∼ estudiantes que el
año pasado** fewer students than last year; **tengo
∼ tiempo que tú** I haven't as *o* so much time as
you

2 (superlativo) (en cantidad) least; (en número)
fewest; **donde hay ∼ luz** where there's least light;
el que obtuvo ∼ votos the one who got (the)
fewest votes

▪ *pron* **1** (en cantidad) less; (en número) fewer;
sírveme ∼ give me less; **ya falta ∼** it won't be
long now

2 (en locs) **al menos** at least; **a menos que**
unless; **cuando menos** at least; **de menos: me dió
100 pesos de ∼** he gave me 100 pesos too little;
me cobró de ∼ he undercharged me; **lo menos**
the least; **menos mal** just as well, thank
goodness; **por lo menos** at least; **eso es lo de ∼**
that's the least of my (*o* our *etc*) problems

▪ *prep* **1** (excepto): **todos ∼ Alonso** everybody
except *o* but Alonso; **∼ estos dos, ...** apart from
o with the exception of these two, ...; **tres latas
de pintura, ∼ la que usé para la puerta** three cans
of paint, less what I used on the door

2 (a) (Mat) (en restas, números negativos) minus **(b)**
(Esp, RPl) (en la hora): **son las cinco ∼ diez/cuarto**
it's ten to five/(a) quarter to five; **son ∼ veinte**
it's twenty to

menoscabar [A1] *vt* ‹*autoridad/fortuna*› to
diminish, reduce; ‹*derechos*› to impinge upon,
infringe; ‹*honor/fama/salud*› to damage, harm

menospreciar [A1] *vt* **(a)** (despreciar)
‹*persona/obra*› to despise, look down on **(b)**
(subestimar) to underestimate

menosprecio *m* contempt, scorn

mensaje *m* (en general) message; (nota) note

mensajero -ra *adj* messenger (*before n*)

▪ *m,f* (en general) messenger; (Com) messenger,
courier (BrE)

menso -sa *adj* (AmL fam) stupid

▪ *m,f* (AmL fam) fool

menstruación *f* menstruation; **estar con la
∼** to have one's period

menstruar [A3] *vi* to menstruate

mensual *adj* ‹*publicación/sueldo*› monthly;
9.000 pesos ∼es 9,000 pesos a month

mensualidad (a) *f* (sueldo) monthly salary **(b)**
(cuota) monthly payment *o* installment*

menta *f* mint; **licor de ∼** crème de menthe;
caramelos de ∼ mints, peppermints

mentada *f* (Col, Méx, Ven euf) *tb* ∼ **de madre**
insult (*usually about a person's mother*)
mental *adj* mental
mentalidad *f* mentality; **tener una** ∼ **muy**
cerrada a very closed mind
mentalizar [A4] *vt* ∼ **a algn DE algo** to make
sb aware OF sth
■ **mentalizarse** *v pron* (a) (*prepararse*
mentalmente) to prepare oneself (mentally), get into
the right frame of mind (b) (*tomar conciencia*): **tuve**
que ∼**me de que mi carrera se había acabado** I
had to come to terms with the fact that my
career was over
mentar [A5] *vt* to mention
mente *f* mind; **tenía la** ∼ **en blanco** my mind
was a blank; **de repente me vino a la** ∼ it
suddenly came to me; **tener algo en** ∼ to have
sth in mind
mentecato -ta *m,f* fool
mentir [I11] *vi* to lie; **me mintió** he lied to me
mentira *f* lie; **eso es** ∼ that's a lie; **¡**∼**! yo no**
le pegué that's a lie, I didn't hit him!; **¡parece** ∼**!**
¡cómo pasa el tiempo! isn't it incredible! doesn't
time fly!; ∼ **piadosa** white lie; **una araña de** ∼ *or*
(Méx) **de** ∼**s** (leng infantil) a toy spider; **una** ∼ **como**
una casa *or* **un templo** (fam) a whopping great lie
(colloq), a whopper (colloq)
mentiroso -sa *adj*: **es muy** ∼ he's an awful *o*
terrible liar; (*dicho sin ánimo de ofender*) he's a real
fibber (colloq)
■ *m,f* liar; (*dicho sin ánimo de ofender*) fibber (colloq)
mentolado -da *adj* menthol (*before n*)
mentón *m* chin
menú *m* (*pl* **-nús**) menu; ∼ **del día** set menu
menudencia *f* **1** (*cosa insignificante*): **eso es**
una ∼ that's not important **2** **menudencias**
fpl (AmL) (Coc) giblets (*pl*)
menudeo *m* (Col, Méx) retail trade; **ventas al** ∼
retail sales
menudillos *mpl* giblets (*pl*)
menudo¹ -da *adj* **1** (a) (*persona*) slight (b)
(*letra/pie*) small **2** (Esp) (en exclamaciones)
(*delante del n*): **¡**∼ **lío!** what a mess!; **¡**∼ **cochazo!**
that's some car! **3** **a menudo** often
menudo² *m* (Col, Ven) (*dinero suelto*) loose change
meñique *m* little finger
meollo *m* (a) (Anat) marrow (b) (de un tema)
heart
mercadería *f* (esp AmS) merchandise
mercadillo *m* street market
mercado *m* market; **ir al** ∼ *or* (Col, Méx) **hacer**
el ∼ to go to market; ∼ **de abastos** market
(*selling fresh food*); ∼ **de (las) pulgas** flea market;
∼ **persa** (CS) bazaar, street market; **el** ∼ **del**
petróleo the oil market; **salir al** ∼ to come onto
the market; **el M**∼ **Común** the Common Market;
∼ **de divisas** foreign exchange market; ∼ **de**
trabajo job market; ∼ **negro** black market; ∼
paralelo parallel market
mercancía *f*, **mercancías** *fpl* (Com) goods
(*pl*), merchandise
mercante *adj* merchant (*before n*)
mercantil *adj* (*ley/operación*) commercial,
mercantile
merced *f* (arc) (*favor*) favor*; **conceder una** ∼ to
grant a favor; **a (la)** ∼ **de** at the mercy of

mercenario -ria *adj/m,f* (Mil) mercenary
mercería *f* (tienda de hilos, botones) notions store
(AmE), haberdashery (BrE); (ferretería) (Chi)
hardware store
Mercosur *m*: *economic community comprising*
Argentina, Brazil, Paraguay and Uruguay
mercurio *m* mercury
Mercurio *m* Mercury
merecedor -dora *adj* ∼ **DE algo** worthy OF
sth, deserving OF sth (frml)
merecer [E3] *vt* (*premio/castigo*) to deserve;
merece que le den el puesto she deserves to get
the job
■ **merecerse** *v pron* (*enf*) (*premio/castigo*) to
deserve; **te lo tienes bien merecido** it serves you
right; **se merece que la asciendan** she deserves to
be promoted
merecido *m*: **recibió** *or* **se llevó su** ∼ he got
what he deserved
merendar [A5] *vi* to have a snack in the
afternoon, have tea; **merendamos en el campo** we
had a picnic (tea) in the country
■ ∼ *vt* to have … as an afternoon snack
merendero *m* (bar) outdoor bar; (instalaciones
para picnics) picnic area
merengada *f* (Ven) milkshake
merengue *m* **1** (pastel) meringue **2** (baile)
merengue
meridiano *m* meridian; ∼ **cero** *or* **de**
Greenwich /'grɪntʃ/ Greenwich Meridian
meridional *adj* southern
■ *mf* southerner
merienda *f* afternoon snack, tea; (para la
escuela) (RPl) snack; **ir de** ∼ **al campo** to go for a
picnic (tea) in the country
mérito *m* merit, worth; **no le veo ningún** ∼ **a**
eso I can't see any merit in that; **una persona de**
∼ a worthy person; **tener** ∼ to be praiseworthy;
quitarle ∼**s a algn** to take the credit away from
sb; **atribuirse el** ∼ **de algo** to take the credit for
sth
meritorio -ria *adj* [SER] (frml) commendable,
praiseworthy (frml); ∼ **DE algo** worthy OF sth
■ *m,f* unpaid trainee
merluza *f* (Coc, Zool) hake
mermar [A1] *vi* (frml) (*viento/frío*) to abate
(frml); «*luz*» to fade
■ ∼ *vt* (frml) to reduce
mermelada *f* (de cítricos) marmalade; (de otras
frutas) jam
mero¹ -ra *adj* (*delante del n*) **1** (solo, simple)
mere; **el** ∼ **hecho de** … the mere *o* simple fact of
…; **es un** ∼ **juego** it's only *o* just a game **2** (AmC,
Méx fam) (uso enfático): **¿cuántas quedaron? — una**
mera how many were left? — just one; **el** ∼ **día**
de su boda the very day of her wedding; **el** ∼
patrón the boss himself; **en la mera esquina** right
on the corner
mero² *m* grouper; **el** ∼ ∼ (Méx fam) the boss
■ *adv* (Méx fam) (a) (casi) nearly, almost (b) (uso
enfático): **así** ∼ **me gustan los tacos** this is just
how I like tacos; **ya** ∼ right now; **aquí merito**
right here
merodear [A1] *vi* to prowl
mersa *adj* (RPl fam & pey) (*ropa/lugar*) tacky
(colloq); (*persona*) common (pej)
⋯⊱

■ *mf* (RPI fam & pey) **(a)** 〈persona〉: **es un ~** he's so common (pej) **(b) la mersa** *f* the plebs (pl) (colloq & pej), the riffraff (hum or pej)

mes *m* month; **el ~ pasado/que viene** last/next month; **una vez al ~** once a month; **tiene siete ~es** he's seven months old; **nos deben dos ~es** they owe us two months' rent (o pay *etc*)

mesa *f* [1] (mueble) table; **poner/recoger la ~** to lay/clear the table; **bendecir la ~** to say grace; **sentarse a la ~** to sit at the table; **se levantó de la ~** he got up from o left the table; **reservar ~** to reserve a table; **~ de centro** coffee table; **~ de noche** or (RPI) **de luz** bedside table [2] (conjunto de personas) committee; **~ redonda/de negociaciones** round/negotiating table

mesada *f* (AmL) (dinero) monthly allowance; (para niños) pocket money

mesero -ra *m,f* (AmL) (*m*) waiter; (*f*) waitress

meseta *f* (Geog) plateau

Mesías *m* Messiah

Mesoamérica *f* Middle America (*most of Mexico and Central America*)

mesón *m* [1] (bar) *old-style bar/restaurant* [2] (Chi) (en tienda) counter; (de bar) bar, counter; **~ de información** information desk

mesonero -ra *m,f* **(a)** (de bar) (*m*) landlord; (*f*) landlady **(b)** (Ven) (camarero) (*m*) waiter; (*f*) waitress

mestizo -za *adj* **(a)** 〈persona〉 of mixed race (*particularly of Indian and white parentage*); **de sangre mestiza** of mixed blood **(b)** 〈animal〉 crossbred

■ *m,f* mestizo, person of mixed race

meta *f* [1] **(a)** (en atletismo) finishing line; (en ciclismo, automovilismo) finish; (en carreras de caballos) winning post **(b)** (en fútbol) goal [2] **(a)** (propósito) aim; **su única ~ es ganar dinero** his only aim o ambition is to earn money **(b)** (objetivo) goal; **trazarse ~s** to set oneself targets o goals

metabolismo *m* metabolism

metafísico -ca *adj* metaphysical

metáfora *f* metaphor

metal *m* **(a)** (material, elemento) metal; **~ noble** or **precioso** precious metal **(b)** *tb* **metales** (Mús) brass (section)

metálico¹ -ca *adj* **(a)** (de metal) metallic, metal (*before n*) **(b)** 〈sonido/brillo/color〉 metallic

metálico² *m*: **pagar en ~** to pay (in) cash; **un premio en ~** a cash prize

metalurgia *f* metallurgy

metalúrgico -ca *adj* metallurgical

■ *m,f* metalworker

metamorfosis, metamórfosis *f* (pl **~**) metamorphosis

metate *m* (AmC, Méx) *flat stone used for grinding corn*

metedura de pata *f* (esp Esp fam) blunder, gaffe

metegol *m* (Arg) table football

meteorito *m* meteorite

meteoro *m* meteor

meteorología *f* meteorology

meteorológico -ca *adj* meteorological, weather (*before n*)

meteorólogo -ga *m,f* meteorologist

meter [E1] *vt* [1] **(a)** (introducir, poner) to put; **~ algo EN algo** to put sth IN(TO) sth; **~ la llave en la cerradura** to put the key into the lock; **logró ~ todo en la maleta** he managed to fit everything into the suitcase **(b)** (hacer entrar): **~ a algn en la cárcel** to put sb in prison; **consiguió ~lo en la empresa** she managed to get him a job in the company **(c)** (involucrar): **~ a algn EN algo** to involve sb IN sth, get sb involved IN sth [2] **(a)** (invertir) 〈ahorros/dinero〉 to put **(b)** 〈tanto/gol〉 to score **(c)** (en costura) 〈dobladillo〉 to turn up **(d)** (Auto): **mete (la) tercera** put it into third (gear); **~ la marcha atrás** to get into reverse [3] (provocar, crear): **~le prisa a algn** to rush sb; **~le miedo a algn** to frighten o scare sb; **no metas ruido** keep the noise down

■ **meterse** *v pron* [1] **(a)** (entrar): **me metí en el agua** (en la playa) I went into the water; (en la piscina) I got into the water; **nos metimos en un museo** we went into a museum; **~se en la cama/la ducha** to get into bed/the shower; **¿dónde se habrá metido el perro?** where can the dog have got to?; **se me metió algo en el ojo** I got something in my eye **(b)** (introducirse): **me metí el dedo en el ojo** I stuck my finger in my eye; **se metió el dinero en el bolsillo** he put the money in(to) his pocket [2] **(a)** (en trabajo): **se metió de secretaria** she got a job as a secretary; **~se de** or **a cura/monja** to become a priest/nun **(b)** (involucrarse) **~se EN algo** to get involved IN sth; **te has metido en un buen lío** you've got yourself into a fine mess; **no te metas en lo que no te importa** mind your own business; **~se con algn** (fam) to pick on sb; **~se por medio** to interfere

metiche *adj* (AmL fam) nosy (colloq)

■ *mf* busybody (colloq)

meticuloso -sa *adj* 〈trabajo/investigación〉 meticulous, thorough; 〈persona〉 meticulous

metida de pata *f* (AmL fam) blunder, gaffe

metódico -ca *adj* methodical

metodista *adj/mf* Methodist

método *m* method; **con ~** methodically

metodología *f* methodology

metomentodo *mf* (pl **~**) (fam) busybody (colloq)

metralla *f* (trozos) shrapnel; (munición) grapeshot

metralleta *f* submachine gun

métrico -ca *adj* metric, metrical

metro *m* [1] **(a)** (medida) meter*; **~ cuadrado/cúbico** square/cubic meter; **vender algo por ~(s)** to sell sth by the meter; **los 100 ~s valla** the 100-meter hurdles **(b)** (cinta métrica) tape measure [2] (Transp) subway (AmE), tube (BrE) [3] (en poesía) meter*

metrónomo *m* metronome

AmC	Central America	Arg	Argentina	Cu	Cuba
AmL	Latin America	Bol	Bolivia	Ec	Ecuador
AmS	South America	Chi	Chile	Esp	Spain
Andes	Andean Region	CS	Southern Cone	Méx	Mexico

Per	Peru
RPI	River Plate Area
Ur	Uruguay
Ven	Venezuela

metrópolis (*pl* ~), **metrópoli** *f* metropolis
metropolitano¹ -na *adj* metropolitan
metropolitano² *m* subway (AmE), underground (BrE)
mexicanismo *m* Mexicanism
mexicano -na *adj/m,f* Mexican
México *m* Mexico; (*capital*) Mexico City
mexiquense *adj* (Méx) of/from Mexico City
mezcal *m* mescal
mezcla *f* 1 (proceso) (a) (en general) mixing (b) (de vinos, tabacos, cafés) blending 2 (combinación) (a) (de cosas diversas) mixture; (de vinos, tabacos, cafés) blend; (de tejidos) mix; **una ~ de harina y azúcar** a mixture of flour and sugar (b) (de razas, culturas) mix (c) (Audio) mix
mezclador -dora *m,f* (persona) *tb* ~ **de sonido** *or* **audio** sound mixer
mezcladora *f* (Const) mixer
mezclar [A1] *vt* 1 (a) (combinar) to mix; ~ **algo CON algo** to mix sth WITH sth (b) ‹café/vino/tabaco› to blend 2 ‹documentos/ropa› to mix up, get ... mixed up; ~ **algo CON algo** to get sth mixed up WITH sth 3 (involucrar) ~ **a algn EN algo** to get sb mixed up *o* involved IN sth
■ **mezclarse** *v pron* 1 (a) (involucrarse) ~**se EN algo** to get mixed up *o* involved IN sth (b) (tener trato con) ~**se CON algn** to mix WITH sb 2 ‹razas/culturas› to mix
mezclilla *f* (a) (tela de mezcla) cloth of mixed fibers (b) (Chi, Méx) (tela de jeans) denim
mezcolanza *f* (pey) hodgepodge (esp AmE), hotchpotch (BrE)
mezquindad *f* (a) (cualidad — de tacaño) meanness, stinginess (colloq); (— de vil): smallmindedness, pettiness (b) (acción egoísta) mean thing to do
mezquino¹ -na *adj* (a) (tacaño) mean, stingy (colloq); (vil) mean, small-minded (b) (escaso) ‹sueldo/ración› paltry, miserable
mezquino² *m* (Col, Méx) wart
mezquita *f* mosque
mezzo-soprano *f* mezzo soprano
mg. (= miligramo) mg
mi *adj* (delante del n) my; ~**s libros** my books; **sí, ~ vida** yes, darling; **sí, ~ capitán** yes, sir
■ *m* (nota) E; (en solfeo) mi
mí *pron pers* me; **¿es para ~?** is it for me?; **por ~ no hay problema** as far as I'm concerned that's fine, that's fine by me; **¿y a ~ qué?** so what?, what do I care?; **a ~ no me importa** I couldn't care less; ~ **mismo/misma** (refl) myself
miau *m* miaow; **hacer ~** to miaow
mica *f* 1 (a) (Min) mica (b) (AmL) (de un reloj) crystal 2 (Col) (de niño) potty (colloq)
mico -ca *m,f* (Zool) long-tailed monkey; (como término genérico) monkey
micrero -ra *m,f* (Chi) bus driver
micro *m* 1 (fam) (microbús) small bus; (autobús) (Arg) bus, coach (BrE) 2 (fam) (micrófono) mike (colloq)
■ *f* (Chi) bus
microbio *m* microbe
microbiología *f* microbiology
microbús *m* small bus

microchip /mikro'tʃip/ *m* (*pl* -**chips**) microchip
microcomputadora *f* (esp AmL) microcomputer, micro
microcosmos (*pl* ~), **microcosmo** *m* microcosm
microfilm (*pl* -**films**), **microfilme** *m* microfilm
micrófono *m* microphone; **hablar por el ~** to speak over the microphone
microondas *m* (*pl* ~) microwave (oven)
microordenador *m* (Esp) microcomputer, micro
microorganismo *m* microorganism
microscópico -ca *adj* microscopic
microscopio *m* microscope; **mirar algo al** *or* **por el ~** to look at sth under the microscope
mida, midas, etc ▶ MEDIR
miedo *m* fear; **¡qué ~ pasamos!** we were so frightened *o* scared!; **temblaba de ~** he was trembling with fear; **me da ~ salir de noche** I'm afraid to go *o* of going out at night; ~ **A algo/algn** fear OF sth/sb; **el ~ a lo desconocido** fear of the unknown; **le tiene ~ a su padre** he's scared *o* afraid of his father; ~ **a salir a escena** stage fright; **agarrarle** *or* (esp Esp) **cogerle ~ a algo/algn** to become frightened *o* scared of sth/sb; **por ~ a** for fear of; **tener ~** to be afraid *o* frightened *o* scared; **tiene ~ de caerse** he's afraid he might fall; **tengo ~ de que se ofenda** I'm afraid he will take offense
miedoso -sa *adj*: **¡no seas ~!** no te va a hacer daño don't be frightened *o* scared! it won't hurt you; **¡qué ~ es!** he's such a coward!
■ *m,f* coward, scaredy cat (colloq)
miel *f* honey; ~ **de palma** palm syrup
miembro *m* 1 (a) (de organización, asociación) member (b) (como adj) ‹estado/países› member (before n) 2 (Anat) limb; ~**s anteriores/posteriores** fore/back limbs
mienta, mientas, etc ▶ MENTIR
mientras *adv* 1 (al mismo tiempo) *tb* ~ **tanto** in the meantime, meanwhile 2 (esp AmL) (cuanto): ~ **más se le da, más pide** the more you give him, the more he wants; ~ **menos coma, mejor** the less I eat the better
■ *conj* 1 (indicando simultaneidad) while; ~ **dormíamos** while we were asleep 2 (con idea de futuro, condición, etc) as long as; ~ **viva/él no se entere** as long as I live/he doesn't find out 3 **mientras que** (con valor adversativo) whereas, while
miércoles *m* (*pl* ~) Wednesday; ~ **de ceniza** Ash Wednesday; *para ejemplos ver* LUNES
mierda *f* 1 (vulg) (excremento) shit (vulg) 2 (vulg) (a) (cosa despreciable): **una ~ de empleo** a crappy *o* lousy job (colloq); **la película es una ~** the movie is (a load of) crap (sl) (b) (mugre) filth, crap (sl); **¡a la ~ con ... !** to hell with ... ! (colloq); **irse a la ~** (vulg) ‹proyecto/empresa› to go to the dogs, go to pot (colloq); **mandar a algn a la ~** (vulg) to tell sb to go to hell (colloq) *o* (vulg) to screw himself/herself; **¡vete a la ~!** (vulg) go to hell! (colloq), fuck off! (vulg)
mies *f* ripe grain; ~**es** cornfields
miga *f* 1 (de pan) crumb; **hacer buenas/malas ~s (con algn)** to get on well/badly (with sb)

2 migas *fpl* (Coc) breadcrumbs fried with
garlic, etc **3** (contenido, sustancia) substance;
(dificultad) difficulties (*pl*); **el asunto tiene su ~** it
has its difficulties *o* it's quite tricky

migajas *fpl* (de pan) breadcrumbs (*pl*); (sobras)
leftovers (*pl*), scraps (*pl*)

migración *f* migration

migraña *f* migraine

mijo[1] *m* millet

mijo[2] **-ja** *pron* (apelativo) (AmL fam) dear; **¿qué le
pasa, mijita?** what's the matter, darling? (colloq)

mil *adj inv/pron* thousand; **~ quinientos pesos**
fifteen hundred pesos, one thousand five hundred
pesos; **20 ~ millones** 20 billion (AmE), 20
thousand million (BrE); **tengo ~ cosas que hacer**
I have a thousand and one things to do
■ *m* (number) one thousand

milagro *m* miracle; **alcancé el tren de ~** by a
miracle I caught the train; **escaparon de ~** they
had a miraculous escape; **hacer ~s** to work
wonders

milagroso -sa *adj* miraculous

milanesa *f*: thin breaded cutlet of meat/chicken

milano *m* kite

milenio *m* millennium

milésima *f* thousandth

milésimo -ma *adj/pron* thousandth; **la
milésima parte** a thousandth

milhojas *f* (*pl* ~) (Coc) millefeuille

mili *f* (Esp fam) military service; **hacer la ~** to do
one's military service

milicia *f* militia

miliciano -na *m,f* militiaman

milico *m* (AmL fam & pey) soldier; **los ~s** the
military

miligramo *m* milligram

mililitro *m* milliliter*

milímetro *m* millimeter*

militancia *f* (filiación) political affiliation;
(militantes) members (*pl*)

militante *adj* politically active
■ *mf* activist

militar[1] *adj* military
■ *mf* soldier, military man; **los ~es** the military

militar[2] [A1] *vi* to be politically active; **~ en un
partido político** to be an active member of a
political party

milla *f* mile

millar *m* thousand; **un ~ de seguidores** about a
thousand supporters

millón *m* million; **15 mil millones** 15 billion
(AmE), 15 thousand million (BrE); **un ~ de gracias**
thank you very much

millonario -ria *adj*: **es ~** he's a millionaire
■ *m,f* millionaire

milonga *f* **1** (Mús) *a type of dance and music
from the River Plate region* **2** (RPl arg) **(a)** (fiesta)
party, bash (colloq) **(b)** (mujer fácil) slut (colloq & pej)

milonguero -ra *m,f* (RPl arg) reveler, raver
(BrE colloq)

milpa *f* (AmC, Méx) (campo) field (*used mainly for
the cultivation of maize*); (cultivo) crop

mimado -da *adj* spoiled, pampered
■ *m,f* spoiled child; **este niño es un ~** this child is
spoiled *o* (pej) is a spoiled brat

mimar [A1] *vt* to spoil, pamper

mimbre *m* (material) wicker; **silla de ~** wicker *o*
basket chair

mimbrera *f* (arbusto) osier; (sauce) willow

mímica *f* (Teatr) mime; (gestos, señas) sign
language, mime

mimo *m* **(a)** (caricia) cuddle; **hacerle ~s a algn** to
cuddle sb **(b)** (trato indulgente) pampering; **lo
criaron con mucho ~** he had a very pampered
upbringing
■ *mf* mime

mimosa *f* mimosa

min (= **minuto**) min

mina *f* **1** (yacimiento, excavación) mine; **~ de
carbón** coalmine; **~ a cielo abierto** *or* (Andes) **a
tajo abierto** strip mine (AmE), opencast mine
(BrE); **es una ~ de información** he's a mine of
information **2** (Mil, Náut) mine; **un campo de ~s**
a minefield **3** (de lápiz) lead **4** (CS arg) (mujer)
broad (AmE sl), bird (BrE sl)

minar [A1] *vt* **(a)** (campo/mar) to mine **(b)**
(debilitar) (salud) to damage; (autoridad/moral) to
undermine

minarete *m* minaret

mineral *adj* mineral
■ *m* **(a)** (sustancia) mineral **(b)** (de un metal) ore

minería *f* mining industry

minero -ra *adj* mining (*before n*)
■ *m,f* miner

mini *f* (fam) miniskirt, mini (colloq)

miniatura *f* (Art) miniature; **¡qué ~ de pie!**
(fam) what a tiny little foot!

minicomputadora *f* (esp AmL)
minicomputer

minifalda *f* miniskirt

minifundio *m* (propiedad) smallholding

mini-golf *m* miniature golf

mínima *f* minimum temperature

minimizar [A4] *vt* (reducir al mínimo) to
minimize; (quitar importancia) to make light of, play
down

mínimo[1] **-ma** *adj* **(a)** (temperatura/peso)
minimum (*before n*); **no le importa lo más ~** he
couldn't care less; **el trabajo no le interesa en lo
más ~** he is not in the slightest (bit) interested
in his work; **no tengo la más mínima idea** I
haven't the faintest idea **(b)** (insignificante) (detalle)
minor; (diferencia/beneficios) minimal

mínimo[2] *m* minimum; **reducir los gastos al ~**
to keep costs to a minimum; **como ~** at least

miniordenador *m* (Esp) minicomputer

ministerial *adj* (reunión) cabinet (*before n*);
(orden) ministerial

ministerio *m* **1** (Pol) ministry, department
(AmE); **M~ de Hacienda** ≈ Treasury Department
(*in US*), ≈ Treasury (*in UK*); **M~ del Interior**
≈ Department of the Interior (*in US*), ≈ Home
Office (*in UK*); **M~ de Relaciones** *or* **Asuntos
Exteriores** ≈ State Department (*in US*), ≈ Foreign
Office (*in UK*) **2** (Relig) ministry

ministro -tra *m,f* minister, government
minister; **M~ de Hacienda** ≈ Secretary of the
Treasury (*in US*), ≈ Chancellor of the Exchequer
(*in UK*); **M~ del Interior** ≈ Secretary of the

Interior (*in US*), ≈ Home Secretary (*in UK*); **M∼ de Relaciones** *or* **Asuntos Exteriores** ≈ Secretary of State (*in US*), ≈ Foreign Secretary (*in UK*)

minoría *f* minority; **estar en ∼** to be in a/the minority; **∼ de edad** minority

minorista *adj* retail (*before n*)
■ *mf* retailer

minoritario -ria *adj* minority (*before n*)

mintiera, mintió, etc ▶ MENTIR

minucia *f* **(a)** (detalle pequeño) minor detail **(b)** (cualidad) detail; **explicar algo con ∼** to explain sth in detail *o* thoroughly

minuciosidad *f* attention to detail

minucioso -sa *adj* ⟨*búsqueda/investigación/ persona*⟩ meticulous, thorough; ⟨*informe*⟩ detailed

minúscula *f* lower case letter, minuscule (tech)

minúsculo -la *adj* **(a)** (diminuto) minute, tiny **(b)** ⟨*letra*⟩ lower case

minusvalía *f* **1** (física) physical handicap *o* disability; (psíquica) mental handicap **2** (Econ) drop *o* fall in value

minusválido -da *adj* (físico) physically handicapped, disabled; (psíquico) mentally handicapped
■ *m,f* (físico) disabled person, physically handicapped person; (psíquico) mentally handicapped person; **coches para ∼s** cars for the disabled

minuta *f* **1** (de abogado, notario) bill **2** (plato rápido) (RPl) quick meal

minutero *m* minute hand

minuto *m* minute; **a tres ∼s de su casa** three minutes (away) from his house

mío, mía *adj* (*detrás del n*) mine; **un primo ∼** a cousin of mine; **eso es asunto ∼** that's my business; **Muy señor ∼** (Corresp) (frml) Dear Sir
■ *pron*: **el ∼/la mía, etc** mine; **sus hijos y los ∼s** their children and mine; **los idiomas no son lo ∼** languages are not my thing; **los ∼s** my family and friends

miope *adj* **(a)** (Med, Ópt) myopic (tech), nearsighted (AmE), short-sighted (BrE) **(b)** (falto de perspicacia) short-sighted
■ *mf* myopic person (tech), nearsighted person (AmE), short-sighted person (BrE)

miopía *f* **(a)** (Med, Ópt) myopia (tech), nearsightedness (AmE), short-sightedness (BrE) **(b)** (falta de perspicacia) shortsightedness

mira *f* **(a)** (Arm, Ópt) sight; **(b)** (intención, objetivo): **con ∼s a reducir los gastos** with a view to reducing costs; **con la ∼ puesta en el porvenir** with one's sight set on the future; **es muy estrecho de ∼s** he's very narrow-minded

mirada *f* **(a)** (modo de mirar) look; **una ∼ reprobatoria** a disapproving look; **su ∼ era triste** he had a sad look in his eyes; **lo fulminó con la ∼** she looked daggers at him **(b)** (vistazo, ojeada) glance; **echarle una ∼ por encima a algo** to take a quick glance at sth; **échales una ∼ a los niños** have a look at the children **(c)** (vista): **tenía la ∼ fija en el suelo** she had her eyes fixed on the ground; **recorrió la habitación con la ∼** she cast her eyes over the room; **bajar/levantar la ∼** to look down/up

miradero *m* (Col) viewpoint

mirado -da *adj* (considerado): **eso no está bien ∼**

that's not approved of, that's looked down on; **está muy mal ∼ en el barrio** he is not at all well thought of *o* well regarded in the neighborhood; *ver tb* MIRAR *vt*

mirador *m* viewpoint

miramiento *m*: **tratar a algn sin ningún ∼** to treat sb with a total lack of consideration

mirar [A1] *vt* **1 (a)** (observar, contemplar) to look at; **∼ un cuadro** to look at a picture; **no me mires así** don't look at me like that; **∼ a algn a los ojos** to look sb in the eye; **se me quedó mirando** he just stared at me; **miraba distraída por la ventana** he was gazing absent-mindedly out of the window; **miraba cómo lo hacía** he was watching how she did it; **ir a ∼ escaparates** *or* (AmL) **vidrieras** to go window shopping **(b)** ⟨*programa/ partido/televisión*⟩ to watch

2 (fijarse) to look; **¡mira lo que has hecho!** look what you've done!; **mira bien que esté apagado** make sure *o* check it's off; **miré a ver si estaba listo** I had a look to see if he was ready

3 (considerar): **míralo desde otro punto de vista** look at it from another point of view; **lo mires por donde lo mires** whatever *o* whichever way you look at it; **mirándolo bien** (pensándolo detenidamente) all things considered; (pensándolo mejor) on second thoughts; **∼ a algn en menos** to look down on sb; **∼ mal a algn** to disapprove of sb

4 (expresando incredulidad, irritación, etc): **¡mira que poner un plato de plástico en el horno …!** honestly *o* really! imagine putting a plastic dish in the oven …! (colloq); **¡mira que eres tacaño!** boy, you're mean! (colloq); **¡mira las veces que te lo habré dicho …!** the times I've told you!
■ *vi* **1** (en general) to look; **he mirado por todas partes** I've looked everywhere; **∼ por la ventana** to look out of the window; **¿miraste bien?** did you have a good look?, did you look properly?; **∼ atrás** to look back

2 (estar orientado) **∼ A/HACIA algo** ⟨*fachada*⟩ to face sth; ⟨*terraza/habitación*⟩ to look out over sth, overlook sth; **ponte mirando hacia la ventana** stand (*o* sit *etc*) facing the window

3 mirar por (a) (preocuparse por) to think of **(b)** (Col) (cuidar) to look after
■ **mirarse** *v pron* **(a)** (refl) to look at oneself; **∼se en el espejo** to look at oneself in the mirror **(b)** (recípr) to look at each other

mirilla *f* peephole, spyhole

mirlo *m* blackbird

mirto *m* myrtle

misa *f* mass; **están en ∼** they're at mass; **ir a ∼** to go to mass; **decir ∼** ⟨*sacerdote*⟩ to say *o* celebrate mass; **∼ de cuerpo presente** funeral mass; **∼ de difuntos** Requiem (mass); **∼ de** *or* **del gallo** midnight mass (on Christmas Eve)

miscelánea *f* **(a)** (variedad) miscellany **(b)** (Méx) (tienda) small general store, corner shop (BrE)

misceláneo -nea *adj* miscellaneous

miserable *adj* **(a)** (pobre) ⟨*vivienda*⟩ miserable, wretched; ⟨*sueldo*⟩ paltry, miserable **(b)** (avaro) mean, stingy (colloq) **(c)** (malvado) malicious, nasty
■ *mf* wretch, scoundrel

miseria *f* **1** (pobreza) poverty, destitution **2** (cantidad insignificante) miserable amount, paltry ···⫶⟩

amount; **gana una** ~ she earns a pittance
3 (desgracia) misfortune; **las ~s de la guerra** the miseries of war

misericordia *f* mercy, compassion

misericordioso -sa *adj* merciful

mísero -ra *adj* miserable

misil *m* missile; ~ **antiaéreo/balístico** antiaircraft/ballistic missile

misión *f* **1** (tarea) mission **2** (delegación): **una ~ científica** a team of scientists; **una ~ diplomática** a diplomatic delegation

misionero -ra *adj* missionary (*before n*)
■ *m,f* missionary

Misisipí *m* (río): **el (río) ~** the Mississippi (River); (estado) Mississippi

mismo¹ -ma *adj* **1** **(a)** (*delante del n*) (expresando identidad) same; **hacer dos cosas al ~ tiempo** to do two things at once *o* at the same time **(b)** (*como pron*) same; **Roma ya no es la misma** Rome isn't the same any more; **el ~ que vimos ayer** the same one we saw yesterday **2** (uso enfático) **(a)** (refiriéndose a lugares, momentos, cosas): **en el ~ centro de Lima** right in the center of Lima; **en este ~ instante** this very minute; **eso ~ pienso yo** that's exactly what I think **(b)** (refiriéndose a personas): **el mismísimo presidente** the president himself; **te perjudicas a ti ~** you're only hurting yourself; **ella misma lo trajo** she brought it herself **3** **lo mismo: siempre dice lo ~** he always says the same thing; **lo ~ para mí** the same for me, please; **nuestra empresa, lo ~ que tantas otras** our company, like so many others; **los niños pueden ir lo ~ que los adultos** children can go as well as adults; **o lo que es lo ~** in other words; **da lo ~** it doesn't matter; **me/le da lo ~** I don't care/he/she doesn't care

mismo² *adv* (uso enfático): **aquí/ahora ~** right here/now; **hoy ~ te mando el cheque** I'll send you the check today; **ayer ~ hablé con él** I spoke to him only yesterday

miss /mis/ *f* beauty queen; **M~ Universo** Miss Universe

misterio *m* mystery

misterioso -sa *adj* mysterious

misticismo *m* mysticism

místico -ca *adj* (*experiencia*) mystic, mystical; (*escritor*) mystic (*before n*)
■ *m,f* mystic

mitad *f* **1** (parte) half; **la ~ de la población** half (of) the population; **sólo quiero la ~** I only want half; **a ~ de precio** half price; **lo hizo en la ~ del tiempo** she did it in half the time; **~ y ~** half and half **2** (medio, centro): **cortar algo por la ~** to cut sth in half; **dividir algo por la ~** to halve sth; **a or en (la) ~ de la reunión** in the middle of the meeting; **a ~ de camino** halfway; **en la ~ de la película/del libro** halfway through the movie/the book

mítico -ca *adj* mythical

mitigar [A3] *vt* (*dolor*) to relieve, ease; (*pena/sufrimiento*) to alleviate, mitigate (frml); (*sed*) to quench

mitin, mitín *m* (Pol) political meeting, rally

mito *m* **(a)** (leyenda) legend **(b)** (invención, mentira) myth

mitología *f* mythology

mitológico -ca *adj* mythological

mixto¹ -ta *adj* mixed; **educación mixta** coeducation

mixto² *m* toasted sandwich (*with two different fillings*)

ml. (= **mililitro**) ml

mm. (= **milímetro**) mm

moaré *m* moiré

mobiliario *m* furniture, furnishings (*pl*); **renovar el ~ del comedor** to refurnish the dining room; **~ de baño** bathroom furnishings (*pl*); **~ de cocina** kitchen fittings *o* units (*pl*)

moca *m*: *tb* **café ~** mocha; **tarta de ~** coffee cake

mocasín *m* moccasin

mochila *f* (de excursionista, soldado) backpack; (de escolar) satchel

mochilear [A1] *vi* (CS) to backpack

mochilero -ra *m,f* (CS) backpacker

moción *f* motion; **presentar una ~** to propose *o* (BrE) table a motion; **~ de censura** vote of censure *o* no confidence

moco *m* **(a)** (líquido) snot (colloq); **límpiate los ~s** wipe *o* blow your nose; **le colgaban los ~s** he had a runny nose (colloq) *o* (sl) snotty nose **(b)** (seco) booger (AmE colloq), bogey (BrE colloq)

mocoso -sa *m,f* (fam) squirt (colloq), pipsqueak (colloq)

moda *f* fashion; **la ~ joven** *or* **juvenil** young fashion; **la ~ de los 30** 30's fashion; **ir a la ~** to be trendy; **estar de ~** to be in fashion, be in (colloq); **ponerse/pasar de ~** to come into/go out of fashion; **seguir la ~** to follow fashion

modal *adj* modal

modales *mpl* manners (*pl*); **tener buenos/malos ~** to be well-mannered/bad-mannered

modalidad *f*: **varias ~es de pago** several methods *o* modes of payment; **la medalla de oro en la ~ de esquí alpino** the gold medal for downhill skiing

modelaje *m* (Andes, Ven) modeling*; **hacer ~** to model

modelar [A1] *vt* (Art) (*arcilla*) to model; (*estatua/figura*) to model, sculpt; (*carácter*) to mold*
■ *vi* **1** (Art) to model **2** (Andes) (para fotos, desfiles) to model

modelo *adj inv* **(a)** (*niño/estudiante*) model (*before n*); (*comportamiento/carácter*) exemplary **(b)** (de muestra): **visité la casa ~** I visited the model home (AmE) *o* (BrE) the showhouse
■ *m* **1** (en general) model; **tomar/utilizar algo como ~** to take/use sth as a model; **tomó a su padre**

como ~ he followed his father's example; ~ **en** or **a escala** scale model **2** (Indum) design; **un ~ de Franelli** a Franelli (design); **llegó con un nuevo modelito** (fam) she arrived wearing a new little number

■ *mf* model; **desfile de ~s** fashion show

módem *m* (*pl* **-dems**) modem

moderación *f* moderation; **beber con ~** to drink in moderation

moderado -da *adj* (a) ⟨persona/comportamiento⟩ restrained (b) ⟨temperatura⟩ moderate; ⟨precio⟩ reasonable; ⟨ideología/facción⟩ moderate

■ *m,f* moderate

moderador -dora *m,f* (en debate) moderator, chair; (Rad, TV) presenter

moderar [A1] *vt* **1** (a) ⟨impulsos/aspiraciones⟩ to curb, moderate; **por favor modera tu vocabulario** please mind your language (b) ⟨gasto/consumo⟩ to curb; ⟨velocidad⟩ to reduce **2** ⟨debate/coloquio⟩ to moderate, chair

■ **moderarse** *v pron*: **modérate, estás comiendo mucho** restrain yourself *o* (colloq) go easy, you're eating too much; **~se en los gastos** to cut down on spending

modernismo *m* (Arquit, Art, Lit) modernism; (cualidad) modernness, modernity

modernista *adj/mf* modernist

modernizar [A4] *vt* ⟨fábrica/técnica/sociedad⟩ to modernize; ⟨costumbres⟩ to update; ⟨vestido/abrigo⟩ to do up

■ **modernizarse** *v pron*: **debes ~te** you have to keep up with the times

moderno -na *adj* (a) (actual) modern; **el hombre ~** modern man; **una edición más ~** a more up-to-date edition (b) (a la moda) ⟨vestido/peinado⟩ fashionable, trendy (c) ⟨edad/historia⟩ modern

modestia *f* modesty

modesto -ta *adj* (a) (falto de pretensión) modest (b) (humilde) ⟨familia⟩ humble; ⟨posición social⟩ modest, humble (c) ⟨sueldo/ingresos⟩ modest

módico -ca *adj* reasonable

modificar [A2] *vt* (a) ⟨aparato⟩ to modify; ⟨plan⟩ to change; ⟨horario/ley⟩ to change, alter (b) (Ling) to modify; **modifica al verbo** it modifies the verb

■ **modificarse** *v pron* to change, alter

modismo *m* idiom

modista *mf* (que diseña) couturier, designer; (que confecciona) dressmaker

modistería *f* (Col) (actividad) dressmaking; (establecimiento) dressmaker's shop/workshop

modisto *m* couturier, designer

modo *m* **1** (a) (manera, forma) way, manner (frml); **el ~ de hacerlo** the way of doing it; **del siguiente ~** in the following manner; **a mi ~ de ver** to my way of thinking, in my opinion; **no lo digas de ese ~** don't say it like that; **de un ~ u otro** one way or another; **su ~ de ser** the way he is; **❺ modo de empleo** instructions for use, directions; **me lo pidió de muy mal ~** (AmL) she asked me (for it) very rudely (b) (en locs) **a mi/tu/su modo** (in) my/your/his (own) way; **de cualquier modo** (de todas formas) (indep) in any case, anyway; (sin cuidado) anyhow; **del mismo** *or* **de igual modo que** just as, in the same way

(that); **de modo que** (así que) so; (para que) so that; **de ningún modo** no way; **de ningún ~ puedo aceptar** there's no way I can accept; **de todos modos** anyway, anyhow; **en cierto modo** in a way; **ni modo** (AmL exc CS fam) no way; **traté de persuadirlo pero ni ~** I tried to persuade him but it was no good; **ni ~ que te quedes aquí** there's no way you're staying here (colloq)

2 modos *mpl* (modales) manners (*pl*); **con buenos/malos ~s** politely/rudely *o* impolitely

modulación *f* modulation; **~ de amplitud/frecuencia** amplitude/frequency modulation

modular [A1] *vt/vi* to modulate

módulo *m* (a) (de mueble) unit, module (b) (de prisión) unit (c) (Espac, Educ) module

mofarse [A1] *v pron* ~ **DE algo/algn** to make fun of sth/sb

mofle *m* (AmC, Méx) muffler (AmE), silencer (BrE)

moflete *m* (fam) chubby cheek

mofletudo -da *adj* (fam) chubby-cheeked

mogolla *f* (Col) bread roll

mohair /mo'er/ *m* mohair

mohín *m* face; **hacer un ~** to make *o* (BrE) pull an angry face

mohíno -na *adj* (a) (enfurruñado): **está ~ porque lo regañaron** he's sulking because he's been told off (b) (alicaído) depressed

moho *m* (a) (en fruta, pan) mold*, mildew; **criar ~** ⟨fruta/queso⟩ to go moldy* (b) (en cobre) patina, verdigris; (en hierro) rust

moisés *m* (cuna) cradle, Moses basket; (portátil) portacrib (AmE), carrycot (BrE)

mojado -da *adj* wet

■ *m,f* (Méx fam) wetback (colloq & pej)

mojar [A1] *vt* (a) ⟨suelo/papel/pelo⟩ (accidentalmente) to get *o* make ... wet; (a propósito) to wet; **pasó un coche y me mojó** a car went by and splashed me; **~ la cama** (euf) to wet the bed (b) (sumergiendo) ⟨galleta/bizcocho⟩ to dip, dunk (colloq)

■ **mojarse** *v pron* (a) «persona/ropa/suelo» to get wet; **se me ~on los zapatos** my shoes got wet; **me mojé toda** I got soaked (b) ⟨pelo/pies⟩ (a propósito) to wet; (accidentalmente) to get ... wet

mojigatería *f* prudishness

mojigato -ta *adj* prudish

■ *m,f* prude

mojón *m* (señal) marker, boundary stone; (hito) landmark; (Auto) *tb* ~ **kilométrico** ≈ milestone

molar *m* molar, back tooth

molcajete *m* (Méx) mortar

molde *m* (a) (para hornear) baking pan (AmE), baking tin (BrE); (para flanes, gelatina) mold*; **~ de pan** loaf pan (AmE) *o* (BrE) tin (b) (Tec) cast; **un ~ de yeso** (Art) a plaster cast (c) (AmL) (para coser) pattern

moldeable *adj* (a) ⟨barro⟩ moldable*, malleable (b) ⟨persona/carácter⟩ malleable

moldear [A1] *vt* (a) (en bronce) to cast; (en barro) to mold*, model (b) ⟨persona/carácter⟩ to mold*, shape; ⟨pelo⟩ to style

moldura *f* molding*

mole *f* mass; **una ~ de hormigón** a huge mass of concrete

■ m (Méx) (salsa) chili sauce (with chocolate and peanuts); (plato) turkey, chicken or pork with MOLE sauce

molécula f molecule

moler [E9] vt ‹especias/café› to grind; ‹trigo› to grind, mill; ‹aceitunas› to crush; ‹carne› to grind (AmE), to mince (BrE); ‹plátano› (Chi, Méx) to mash; **café molido** ground coffee

molestar [A1] vt **1** (a) (importunar) to bother; **perdone que lo moleste** sorry to trouble o bother you (b) (interrumpir) to disturb
2 (ofender, disgustar) to upset
■ ~ vi **1** (importunar): **¿le molesta si fumo?** do you mind if I smoke?; **me molesta su arrogancia** her arrogance irritates o annoys me; **no me duele, pero me molesta** it doesn't hurt but it's uncomfortable
2 (fastidiar) to be a nuisance; **no quiero ~** I don't want to be a nuisance o to cause any trouble
■ **molestarse** v pron **1** (disgustarse) to get upset; **~se POR algo** to get upset ABOUT sth; **~se CON algn** to get annoyed WITH sb
2 (tomarse el trabajo) to bother, trouble oneself (frml); **ni se molestó en llamarme** he didn't even bother to call me; **se molestó en venir hasta aquí a avisarnos** she took the trouble to come all this way to tell us

molestia f **1** (a) (incomodidad, trastorno): **ser una ~** to be a nuisance; **siento causarte tantas ~s** I'm sorry to cause you so much trouble; **perdona la ~, pero ...** sorry to bother you, but ... (b) (trabajo) trouble; **se tomó la ~ de escribirnos** she took the trouble to write to us; **¿para qué te tomaste la ~?** why did you bother to do that?; **no es ninguna ~** it's no trouble o bother
2 (malestar): **~s estomacales** stomach problems o upsets; **no es un dolor, solo una ~** it's not a pain, just a feeling of discomfort

molesto -ta adj **1** [SER] (a) (fastidioso) ‹ruido/tos› annoying, irritating; ‹sensación/síntoma› unpleasant (b) (violento, embarazoso) awkward, embarrassing **2** [ESTAR] (ofendido) upset; (irritado) annoyed; **está muy ~ por lo que hiciste** he's very upset/annoyed about what you did

molestoso -sa adj (AmL fam) annoying

molido -da adj (a) (fam) (agotado) bushed (AmE colloq), shattered (BrE colloq) (Andes fam) (dolorido) stiff

molinero -ra m,f miller

molinillo m (a) (de café, especias) grinder, mill; **~ de carne** grinder (AmE), mincer (BrE) (b) (juguete) pinwheel (AmE), windmill (BrE) (c) (Col, Méx) (para batir) whisk

molino m (a) (máquina — para el trigo) mill; (— para la carne) grinder (AmE), mincer (BrE) (b) (fábrica) mill; **~ de agua** waterwheel; **~ de viento** windmill; **~ de papel** paper mill

molleja f (de res) sweetbread; (de ave) gizzard

mollera f (fam) head; **está mal de la ~** he's off his head o rocker (colloq); **cerrado o duro de ~** pigheaded (colloq)

molo m (Chi) tb **~ de abrigo** breakwater, mole

molusco m mollusk*

momentáneo -nea adj (a) (breve) momentary (b) (pasajero) temporary

momento m **1** (a) (instante puntual) moment; **justo en ese ~** just at that moment; **a partir de ese ~** from that moment on; **en todo ~** at all times (b) (lapso breve) minute, moment; **dentro de un ~** in a minute o moment; **¡un momentito!** (por teléfono) just a moment, just a minute; **eso te lo arreglo en un ~** I'll fix that for you in no time at all (c) (época, período) time, period; **atravesamos ~s difíciles** we're going through a difficult time o period; **está en su mejor ~** he is at his peak (d) (ocasión) time; **llegas en buen/mal ~** you've arrived at the right time/at a bad time; **en ningún ~** at no time
2 (en locs) **al momento** at once; **de momento** (ahora mismo) right now; (mientras tanto) for the time being; (por ahora) for the moment; **de un momento a otro** (dentro de muy poco) any minute now; **en cualquier momento** at any time; **en el momento** immediately; **en el momento menos pensado** when they (o you etc) least expect it; **por el momento** for the time being
3 (Fís, Mec) momentum

momia f mummy

mona f **1** (fam) (borrachera): **agarrar una ~** to get plastered (colloq); **dormir la ~** to sleep it off
2 (a) (en naipes) old maid (b) (Col) (para un álbum) picture card; **como la ~** (CS fam) terrible

monada f (fam) (a) (cosa bonita): **¡qué ~ de vestido!** what a lovely dress! (b) (persona bonita): **su novia es una ~** his girlfriend's really pretty; **¡qué ~ de niño!** what a lovely o (colloq) cute kid (c) (RPl) (persona encantadora) angel (colloq)

monaguillo m altar boy, acolyte, server

monarca mf monarch

monarquía f monarchy

monárquico -ca adj ‹régimen› monarchical; ‹persona/ideas› monarchist (before n)
■ m,f monarchist, royalist

monasterio m monastery

monástico -ca adj monastic

mondadientes m (pl ~) toothpick

mondar [A1] vt (Esp) ‹fruta/patatas› to peel
■ **mondarse** v pron (refl): **se mondaba los dientes** she was picking her teeth; **~se de risa** (Esp fam) to die laughing

moneda f **1** (a) (pieza) coin; **una ~ de cinco pesos** a five-peso coin o piece (b) (de país) currency; **acuñar ~** to mint money **2** **la Moneda** (en Chi) Presidential Palace

monedero m change purse (AmE), purse (BrE)

monerías fpl (fam): **hacer ~** (tontear) to mess around (colloq); (hacer payasadas) to monkey o clown around (colloq)

mongólico -ca adj (a) (ant o crit) (Med) ‹rasgos› mongoloid (dated or crit); **niños ~s** Down's syndrome children (b) (fam & pey) (tonto) moronic (colloq & pej)

mongolismo m (ant o crit) Down's syndrome

monigote m (muñeco) rag doll; (de papel) paper doll; (dibujo) doodle

monitor -tora m,f **1** (a) (CS) (Dep): **~ de esquí/natación** ski/swimming instructor; **~ de tenis** tennis coach (b) (Educ) (en la escuela) (RPl) monitor; (en la universidad) (Col) student who acts as an assistant teacher **2** **monitor** m (Inf, Med, Tec) monitor

monja f nun; **meterse a** or **de ~** to become a nun

monje m monk

mono¹ -na *adj* **1** (fam) ⟨*mujer*⟩ pretty,
lovely-looking (colloq); ⟨*niño*⟩ lovely, cute (colloq);
⟨*vestido/piso*⟩ gorgeous, lovely **2** (Col) ⟨*rubio*⟩
⟨*hombre/niño*⟩ blond; ⟨*mujer/niña*⟩ blonde
3 (Audio) mono
■ *m,f* **1** (Zool) monkey; **ser el último** ~ (fam) to be
the lowest of the low **2** *m* **(a)** (de mecánico)
coveralls (*pl*) (AmE), overalls (*pl*) (BrE) **(b)** (de
moda — de cuerpo entero) jumpsuit; (— con peto)
overalls (*pl*) (AmE), dungarees (*pl*) (BrE) **(c)** (Méx)
(malla de bailarina) leotard

mono² *m* (monigote) **1** doodle; (dibujo de
monitos (Andes, Méx) a comic; ~ **animado** (Chi)
cartoon; ~ **de nieve** (Chi) snowman **2 (a)** (de
mecánico) coveralls (*pl*) (AmE), overalls (*pl*) (BrE),
boiler suit (BrE) **(b)** (de moda — de cuerpo entero)
jumpsuit; (— con peto) overalls (*pl*) (AmE),
dungarees (*pl*) (BrE) **(c)** (Méx) (malla de bailarina)
leotard **3** (arg) (síndrome de abstinencia) cold turkey
(sl); **está con el** ~ he's gone cold turkey (sl)

monocarril *m* monorail

monocolor *adj* one-color* (*before n*)

monóculo *m* monocle

monogamia *f* monogamy

monógamo -ma *adj* monogamous
■ *m,f* monogamist

monografía *f* monograph

monográfico -ca *adj* monographic

monolingüe *adj* monolingual

monolítico -ca *adj* monolithic

monolito *m* monolith

monólogo *m* monologue

monoparental *adj*: **las familias** ~**es**
one-parent families

monopatín *m* (con manillar) (CS) scooter; (sin
manillar) (Esp) skateboard

monopolio *m* monopoly

monopolizar [A4] *vt* to monopolize

monorriel *m* (AmL) monorail

monosílabo *m* monosyllable

monoteísmo *m* monotheism

monotonía *f* (de tarea) monotony; (de sonido)
monotone

monótono -na *adj* monotonous

monóxido *m* monoxide; ~ **de carbono** carbon
monoxide

monseñor *m* Monsignor

monstruo *m* **(a)** (en general) monster **(b)**
(fenómeno) phenomenon; **un** ~ **de la música pop** a
pop phenomenon

monstruosidad *f* **(a)** (cosa fea, grande)
monstrosity **(b)** (atrocidad) atrocity **(c)** (cualidad)
monstrous nature, monstrousness

monstruoso -sa *adj* **(a)** ⟨*crimen/*
comportamiento⟩ monstrous, atrocious **(b)** ⟨*ser/*
facciones⟩ hideous, grotesque

monta *f* (monto) total (value); **de poca** ~
⟨*asunto*⟩ of little importance *o* note; ⟨*escritor*⟩
third-rate; ⟨*daños*⟩ slight, minor

montacargas *m* (*pl* ~) freight *o* service
elevator (AmE), service *o* goods lift (BrE)

montado -da *adj* ⟨*policía*⟩ mounted; **iba** ~ **a**
caballo he was riding a horse; **estaba montada en**
su bicicleta she was sitting on her bicycle; *ver tb*
MONTAR

montador -dora *m,f* (Mec, Tec) fitter; (Cin, TV)
film editor

montaje *m* **(a)** (de máquina, mueble) assembly **(b)**
(de obra) staging; (de película) editing; **seguro que**
todo es un ~ I bet it's all a big con *o* a set-up
(colloq)

montallantas *m* (*pl* ~) (Col) (taller) *workshop*
where tires* are retreaded; (mecánico) *person who*
retreads tires*

montaña *f* **1** (Geog) mountain; **tienen un**
chalet en la ~ they have a chalet in the
mountains; ~ **rusa** roller coaster **2** (montón) pile

montañero -ra *m,f* mountaineer, mountain
climber

montañés -ñesa *adj* mountain (*before n*),
highland (*before n*)
■ *m,f* highlander

montañismo *m* mountaineering, mountain
climbing

montañoso -sa *adj* ⟨*cadena*⟩ mountain
(*before n*); ⟨*terreno/país*⟩ mountainous

montar [A1] *vt* **1 (a)** ⟨*caballo*⟩ (subirse a) to
mount, get on; (ir sobre) to ride **(b)** (subir, colocar):
montó al niño en el poni he lifted the boy up onto
the pony
2 ⟨*vaca/yegua*⟩ to mount
3 (a) (poner, establecer) ⟨*feria/exposición*⟩ to set
up; ⟨*negocio*⟩ to start up, set up **(b)** ⟨*máquina/*
mueble⟩ to assemble; ⟨*estantería*⟩ to put up;
⟨*tienda de campaña*⟩ to put up, pitch **(c)** ⟨*piedra*
preciosa⟩ to set; ⟨*diapositiva*⟩ to mount **(d)**
(organizar) ⟨*obra/producción*⟩ to stage
4 (Esp) ⟨*nata*⟩ to whip; ⟨*claras*⟩ to whisk
■ ~ *vi* **1 (a)** (ir): ~ **a caballo/en bicicleta** to ride
a horse/bicycle **(b)** (Equ) to mount
2 (cubrir parcialmente) ~ **sobre algo** to overlap sth
■ **montarse** *v pron* (en coche) to get in; (en tren,
autobús, bicicleta) to get on; (en caballo) to mount, get
on; **¿me dejas** ~**me en tu bicicleta?** can I have a
ride on your bicycle?

monte *m* (Geog) **(a)** (montaña) mountain **(b)**
(terreno — cubierto de maleza) scrubland, scrub; (—
cubierto de árboles) woodland

montera *f* (gorra) cap; (de torero) bullfighter's
hat

montés *adj* ⟨*animal/planta*⟩ wild

montevideano -na *adj* of/from Montevideo

Montevideo *m* Montevideo

montgomery *m* (CS) duffle coat

montículo *m* mound

montón *m* **(a)** (pila) pile; **del** ~ (fam) ordinary,
average **(b)** (fam) (gran cantidad): **un** ~ **de gente**
loads of people (colloq); **me gusta un** ~ I like her/
him/it a lot

montonero -ra *m,f* (guerrillero) guerrilla

montura *f* **1** (Equ) (silla) saddle; (animal) mount
2 (a) (de anteojos) frame **(b)** (engarce) setting,
mount

monumental *adj* (fam) **(a)** ⟨*cocina/jardín*⟩
huge, massive **(b)** ⟨*error/esfuerzo*⟩ monumental

monumento *m* **1** (obra conmemorativa)
monument; ~ **histórico/nacional** historical/
national monument; ~ **a los caídos** war
memorial; ~ **funerario** commemorative stone
2 (obra excepcional) masterpiece, classic **3** (fam)
(mujer atractiva) stunner (colloq)

m

monzón *m* monsoon

moña *f* (Taur) ribbon; (lazo) (RPl) bow

moño *m* (a) (peinado) bun; **se hizo un** ~ she put her hair up in a bun; **estar hasta el** ~ to be fed up (to the back teeth) (colloq) (b) (AmL) (lazo) bow

moñona *f* (Col fam) strike; **hacer** ~ to get a strike

moqueta *f* (Esp) wall-to-wall carpet, fitted carpet (BrE)

moquillento -ta *adj* (Andes fam) (a) (resfriado) coldy (colloq) (b) (con mocos) ⟨*nariz*⟩ runny, snotty (colloq); ⟨*niño*⟩ runny-nosed, snotty-nosed (colloq)

moquillo *m* distemper

mora *f* (de zarzamora) blackberry; (de moral) mulberry; (de morera) white mulberry

morada *f* (frml o liter) dwelling (frml), abode (frml or liter)

morado¹ -da *adj* ⟨*color*⟩ purple; ~ **del frío** blue with cold; **ponerle a algn un ojo** ~ to give sb a black eye

morado² *m* (Esp, Ven) bruise

moral *adj* moral
■ *f* [1] (Fil, Relig) (a) (doctrina) moral doctrine (b) (moralidad) morality, morals (*pl*) [2] (estado de ánimo) morale; **levantarle la** ~ **a algn** to raise sb's morale, lift sb's spirits; **estar bajo de** ~ to be feeling low; **tener la** ~ **alta** to be in good spirits
■ *m* mulberry (tree)

moraleja *f* moral

moralidad *f* morality, ethics (*pl*)

morar [A1] *vi* (liter) to dwell (liter)

moratón *m* bruise

morboso -sa *adj* ⟨*escena/película*⟩ gruesome; ⟨*persona/mente*⟩ ghoulish; (truculento, retorcido) morbid
■ *m,f* (fam) ghoul

morcilla *f* blood sausage (AmE), black pudding (BrE)

mordaz *adj* ⟨*estilo/lenguaje*⟩ scathing, caustic; ⟨*crítica*⟩ sharp, scathing

mordaza *f* (a) (en la boca) gag (b) (Tec) clamp

mordedura *f* bite

morder [E9] *vt* [1] (con los dientes) to bite; **el perro le mordió la mano** the dog bit her hand [2] (Méx fam) ⟨*policía/funcionario*⟩ to extract a bribe from
■ ~ *vi* to bite
■ **morderse** *v pron* (refl) to bite oneself; ~**se las uñas** to bite one's nails

mordida *f* [1] (CS) (en general) bite; (huella) toothmarks (*pl*) [2] (Méx fam) (soborno) bribe, backhander (BrE colloq)

mordisco *m* bite; **le dio un** ~ **en el brazo** it bit her (on the) arm

mordisquear [A1] *vt* to nibble

moreno -na *adj* (a) [SER] ⟨*persona*⟩ (de pelo oscuro) dark, dark-haired; (de tez oscura) dark; (de raza negra) (euf) dark-skinned (euph) (b) [ESTAR] (bronceado) brown, tanned (c) ⟨*piel*⟩ brown, dark
■ *m,f* (a) (de pelo oscuro) (*m*) dark-haired man (o boy *etc*); (*f*) dark-haired woman (o girl *etc*), brunet* (b) (de tez oscura) dark person (o man *etc*); (de raza negra) (euf) dark-skinned person (o man *etc*) (euph), coloured man (o woman *etc*) (BrE euph)

morera *f* white mulberry tree

moretón *m* bruise

morfar [A1] *vi* (RPl arg) to eat

morfina *f* morphine

morgue *f* (AmL) morgue, mortuary

moribundo -da *adj* dying, moribund (frml)
■ *m,f* dying man (o woman *etc*)

morir [I37] *vi* (a) «*persona/animal*» to die; ~ **ahogado** to drown; **murió asesinada** she was murdered; ~ **DE algo** ⟨*de vejez/cáncer*⟩ to die OF sth; **murió de hambre** she starved to death; **¡y allí muere!** (AmC fam) and that's all there is to it! (b) (liter) «*civilización/costumbre*» to die out
■ **morirse** *v pron* «*persona/animal/planta*» to die; **se les murió la madre** their mother died; **se me murió la perra** my dog died; **no te vas a** ~ **por ayudarlo** (fam) it won't kill you to help him (colloq); **como se entere me muero** (fam) I'll die if she finds out (colloq); ~**se DE algo** ⟨*de un infarto/de cáncer*⟩ to die OF sth; **se moría de miedo/aburrimiento** he was scared stiff/bored stiff; **me muero de frío** I'm freezing; **me estoy muriendo de hambre** I'm starving (colloq); **me muero por una cerveza** I'm dying for a beer (colloq); **se muere por verla** he's dying to see her (colloq)

morisco -ca *adj* Moorish, Morisco

morisqueta *f* (CS): **hacer** ~**s** to make o (BrE) pull faces

mormado -da *adj* (Méx) ⟨*nariz*⟩ blocked; **estoy** ~ I'm all stuffed up (colloq)

mormón -mona *adj/m,f* Mormon

moro -ra *adj* [1] (Hist) Moorish [2] (Esp) (de África del Norte) (fam & pey) North African; (referido a un hombre machista) (fam) chauvinistic, sexist
■ *m,f* [1] (a) (Hist) Moor (b) (mahometano) Muslim [2] (Esp) (de África del Norte) (fam & pey) North African; (hombre machista)
■ *m* (fam) sexist, male chauvinist pig

morocho -cha *adj* (AmS fam) (de pelo oscuro) dark, dark-haired; (de piel oscura) dark
■ *m,f* (de pelo oscuro) dark-haired person (o man *etc*); (de piel oscura) dark person (o man *etc*)

morral *m* (a) (al hombro) rucksack, haversack; (a la espalda) backpack, rucksack (b) (para el pienso) nosebag

morralla *f* [1] (cosas sin valor) junk [2] (chusma) riffraff, rabble [3] (Méx) (dinero suelto) loose change

morriña *f* (fam) homesickness; **tener** ~ to feel o be homesick

morro *m* [1] (a) (hocico) snout (b) (Esp fam) (boca) *tb* ~**s** mouth, chops (*pl*) (BrE colloq); **estar de** ~**s** (con algn) (Esp fam) to be in a bad mood (with sb) (c) (Esp fam) (descaro) nerve (colloq) (d) (Esp fam) (de coche, avión) nose [2] (cerro) hill

morrón *m* (CS) (pimiento) red pepper

morsa *f* walrus

mortadela *f* mortadella

mortaja *f* **1** (sábana) shroud **2** (Tec) mortise

mortal *adj* **1** (a) ⟨*ser*⟩ mortal (b) ⟨*herida*⟩ fatal, mortal; ⟨*dosis*⟩ fatal, lethal; ⟨*enfermedad/veneno*⟩ deadly; **un golpe ~** a death blow **2** ⟨*odio/enemigo*⟩ mortal
■ *mf* mortal

mortalidad *f* mortality; **la ~ infantil** infant mortality

mortecino -na *adj* ⟨*luz*⟩ weak; ⟨*color*⟩ pale

mortero *m* mortar

mortífero -ra *adj* deadly, lethal

mortificar [A2] *vt* (a) (atormentar) to torment; **los celos lo mortifican** he's tortured *o* tormented by jealousy (b) (Relig) to mortify
■ **mortificarse** *v pron* (*refl*) to fret, distress oneself; (Relig) to mortify the flesh

mortuorio -ria *adj* funeral (*before n*)

mosaico *m* (a) (Art) mosaic (b) (Méx, RPl) (baldosa) floor tile; **piso de ~** tiled floor (c) (Col) (foto) school/college photograph

mosca *f* fly; **no se oía ni una ~** you could have heard a pin drop (colloq); **por si las ~s** (fam) just in case (colloq)

moscardón *m* botfly

moscatel *adj* muscat (*before n*)
■ *m* muscatel

moscovita *adj/mf* Muscovite

Moscú *m* Moscow

mosqueado -da *adj* (esp Esp fam) (a) (molesto, disgustado) annoyed, sore (AmE colloq), cross (BrE colloq) (b) (desconfiado, suspicaz) suspicious, wary

mosquearse [A1] *v pron* (esp Esp fam) (a) (sospechar, desconfiar) to get suspicious, smell a rat (colloq) (b) (disgustarse) to get annoyed, get sore (AmE colloq), to get cross (BrE colloq)

mosquetero *m* musketeer

mosquitero *m*, **mosquitera** *f* (de ventana) mosquito netting; (de tela) mosquito net

mosquito *m* mosquito

mostaza *f* mustard; (color) : **(de) color ~** mustard, mustard-colored*

mosto *m* grape juice, must

mostrador *m* (en tienda) counter; (en bar) bar; (en aeropuerto) check-in desk

mostrar [A10] *vt* to show; **muéstrame cómo funciona** show me how it works
■ **mostrarse** *v pron* (+ *compl*): **se mostró muy atento con nosotros** he was very obliging (to us); **se ~on partidarios de la propuesta** they expressed support for the proposal

mota *f* **1** (partícula) tiny bit, dot; **una ~ de polvo** a speck of dust **2** (Tex): **una tela a ~s** a spotted fabric; **una lana azul con ~s de colores** blue wool with flecks of colors **3** (AmC, Méx arg) (marihuana) grass (colloq), weed (sl) **4** (a) (para empolvarse) powder puff (b) (Méx) (borla) pom-pom

mote *m* **1** (apodo) nickname; **le pusieron como ~ 'el Oso'** they nicknamed him 'the Bear' **2** (Andes) (trigo) boiled wheat; (maíz) boiled corn (AmE) *o* (BrE) maize

moteado -da *adj* ⟨*tela*⟩ (jaspeado) flecked; (a lunares) dotted, spotted; ⟨*piel*⟩ mottled

motel *m* motel

motín *m* (de tropas, tripulación) mutiny; (de prisioneros) riot, rebellion

motivación *f* (incentivo) motivation; (motivo) motive

motivar [A1] *vt* **1** (en general) to motivate; **motivado por la venganza** motivated by revenge; **¿qué te motivó a hacerlo?** what made you do it? **2** (causar) to bring about, cause

motivo *m* **1** (a) (razón, causa) reason, cause; **el ~ de su viaje** the reason for her trip; **por este ~ nos hallamos aquí** that's (the reason) why we're here; **con ~ de algo** on the occasion of sth; **no des ~s para que te critiquen** don't give them cause to criticize you; **hay ~s para preocuparse** there is cause for concern; **el adulterio es ~ suficiente de divorcio** adultery is sufficient grounds for divorce; **sin ningún ~** for no reason at all; **¡que sea un ~!** (Col fam) let's drink to that! (colloq) (b) (propósito, finalidad) purpose; **el ~ de esta carta es ...** the purpose of this letter is ... **2** (Art, Lit, Mús) motif; **~s decorativos** decorative motifs

moto *f* (motocicleta) motorcycle, motorbike (BrE); (motoneta, escúter) (motor) scooter; **fue en ~** he went on his motorcycle

motocicleta *f* motorcycle

motociclismo *m* motorcycling

motociclista *mf* motorcyclist

motocross, moto-cross *m* motocross

motoneta *f* (AmL) (motor) scooter

motor¹ -triz, motor -tora *adj* motor (*before n*)

motor² *m* **1** (Tec) engine; **~ fuera (de) borda** outboard motor **2** (impulsor) driving force

motora *f* small motorboat, powerboat

motorismo *m* motorcycling

motorista *mf* (a) (que va en moto) motorcyclist (b) (Col) (automovilista) motorist (frml), driver

motorizado -da *adj* ⟨*ejército*⟩ motorized
■ *m,f* (Ven) motorcycle messenger *o* (BrE) courier

motudo -da *adj* (CS fam) frizzy

mousse /mus/ *f o m* mousse

mouton /mu'ton/ *m* sheepskin

movedizo -za *adj* ⟨*niño*⟩ restless, fidgety

mover [E9] *vt* **1** (a) (trasladar, desplazar) to move (b) (Jueg) ⟨*ficha/pieza*⟩ to move (c) (agitar): **no muevas la cámara** keep the camera still; **el viento movía los árboles** the wind shook the trees; **movió la cabeza** (asintiendo) he nodded (his head); (negando) she shook her head; **mueve la cola** it wags its tail (d) (accionar) to drive **2** (inducir): **~ a algn a hacer algo** to move sb to do sth
■ **~** *vi* (Jueg) to move
■ **moverse** *v pron* (a) (en general) to move; **no te muevas de ahí** don't move; **la lámpara se movía con el viento** the lamp was moving *o* swaying in the wind (b) (apresurarse) to hurry up, get a move on (colloq)

movida *f* **1** (Jueg) move **2** (Esp) (fam) (a) (asunto, rollo): **no me interesa la ~ ecológica** I'm not into this ecology thing (colloq); **anda en ~s chuecas** (Méx) he's into some shady deals (colloq) (b) (actividad cultural): **la ~ madrileña** the Madrid scene; **donde está la ~** where it's all going on

movido -da *adj* (a) (Fot) blurred (b) (agitado) ⟨*mar*⟩ rough, choppy; ⟨*día/año*⟩ hectic, busy; ⟨*fiesta*⟩ lively

móvil *adj* mobile
■ *m* [1] (frml) (impulso) motive [2] (adorno) mobile
movilidad *f* mobility
movilización *f* [1] (a) (Mil) mobilization (b)
(Rels Labs) (manifestación) demonstration; **un
calendario de movilizaciones** a program of
industrial action [2] (Chi) (Transp) public
transportation (AmE), public transport (BrE)
movilizar [A4] *vt* ‹tropas/población› to
mobilize
■ **movilizarse** *v pron* [1] (Mil, Rels Labs) to
mobilize [2] (CS) (desplazarse) to move *o* get
around
movimiento *m* [1] (a) (en general) movement;
el menor ~ de la mano the slightest movement
of the hand; **el ~ surrealista** the surrealist
movement; **~ pictórico** school of painting; **~
sísmico** earth tremor (b) (Fís, Tec) motion,
movement; **poner algo en ~** to set sth in motion;
se puso en ~ it started moving (c) (agitación,
actividad) activity; **una calle de mucho ~** a very
busy street [2] (Mús) (parte de obra) movement;
(compás) tempo [3] (Jueg) move
mozárabe *adj* Mozarabic
■ *mf* Mozarab
mozo -za *adj*: **en mis años ~s** in my youth; **sus
hijos ya son ~s** her children are quite grown-up
now
■ *m,f* (a) (ant) (joven) (*m*) young boy; (*f*) young
girl; **los ~s del pueblo** the young people in the
village (b) (AmS) (camarero) (*m*) waiter; (*f*)
waitress (c) (Ferr) *tb* **~ de equipajes** *or* **de
estación** porter
muaré *m* moiré
mucamo -ma (AmL) (*m*) servant; (*f*) maid,
servant; **mucama de hotel** chambermaid
muchacha *f*: *tb* **~ de servicio** maid; *ver tb*
MUCHACHO
muchacho -cha *m,f* (*m*) kid (colloq), boy, guy
(colloq); (*f*) girl
muchedumbre *f* crowd
mucho¹ *adv* (a) ‹salir/ayudar› a lot; ‹trabajar›
hard; **no salen ~** they don't go out much *o* a lot;
me gusta muchísimo I like it very much *o* a lot;
~ mejor a lot better; **por ~ que insistas** no
matter how much you insist; **después de ~
discutir** after much discussion (b) (en respuestas):
¿estás preocupado? — mucho are you worried?
— (yes, I am,) very; **¿te gusta? — sí, ~** do you
like it? — yes, very much
mucho² -cha *adj* (a) (*sing*) a lot of; (en
oraciones negativas, interrogativas) much, a lot of; **~
vino** a lot of wine; **no gano ~ dinero** I don't earn
much *o* a lot of money; **¿ves mucha televisión?**
do you watch much *o* a lot of television; **tiene
mucha hambre** he's very hungry (b) (*pl*) many, a
lot of; **había ~s extranjeros/muchas personas allí**
there were many *o* a lot of foreigners/people
there; **hace ~s años** many years ago
■ *pron* [1] (referido a cantidad) (a) (*sing*) a lot; (en
oraciones negativas) much; **~ de lo dicho** a lot of
what was said; **tengo ~ que hacer** I have a lot to
do; **eso no es ~** that's not much; **no queda
mucha** there isn't much left (b) (*pl*) many; **~s
creen que ...** many (people) believe that ...; **~s
de nosotros** many of us
[2] **mucho (a)** (referido a tiempo): **hace ~ que no
la veo** I haven't seen her for a long time; **¿te falta**

~ para terminar? will it take you long to finish?;
~ antes long before; **¿tuviste que esperar ~?** did
you have to wait long? (b) (en locs) **como mucho**
at (the) most; **con mucho** by far, easily; **ni mucho
menos** far from it; **por mucho que ...** however
much ...
mucosidad *f* mucus, mucosity
muda *f* (de ropa) change of clothes; (de la piel)
shedding, sloughing off
mudanza *f* move, removal (BrE); **camión de ~s**
moving (AmE) *o* (BrE) removal van; **estoy de ~**
I'm in the process of moving (house)
mudar [A1] *vi* [1] (cambiar): **las serpientes mudan
de piel** snakes slough off *o* shed their skin;
cuando mudó de voz when his voice broke
[2] (Méx) (cambiar los dientes) to lose one's milk
teeth
■ **~** *vt* [1] ‹bebé/sábanas› to change [2] (Zool) ‹piel/
plumas› to molt, shed
■ **mudarse** *v pron* (a) (de casa) to move (house);
se ~on a una casa más grande they moved to a
bigger house (b) (de ropa) to get changed, change
(one's) clothes
mudéjar *adj/mf* Mudejar
mudo -da *adj* (a) (Med) dumb, mute; **es ~ de
nacimiento** he was born mute; **se quedó ~ de
asombro** he was dumbfounded (b) ‹letra› silent,
mute
■ *m,f* mute
mueble *m* piece of furniture; **los ~s del
dormitorio** the bedroom furniture; **~ bar** drinks
cabinet, cocktail cabinet; **~ cama** foldaway bed
mueca *f*: **hacerle ~s a algn** to make *o* (BrE) pull
faces at sb; **sus graciosísimas ~s** her funny
faces; **una ~ burlona** a sneer
muela *f* [1] (Odont) molar, back tooth; (como
término genérico) tooth; **me sacaron una ~** I had a
tooth taken out; **tengo dolor de ~s** I have (a)
toothache; **~ del juicio** wisdom tooth [2] (de
molino) millstone; (para afilar) whetstone [3] (Col) (en
calle) parking bay; (en carretera) rest stop (AmE),
lay-by (BrE)
muelle *m* [1] (Náut) (saliente) pier, mole; (rústico,
más pequeño) jetty; (sobre la costa) quay, wharf
[2] (resorte) spring
muera, mueras, etc ▶ MORIR
muérdago *m* mistletoe
muerte *f* death; **condenado a ~** sentenced to
death; **a la ~ de su padre** on her father's death;
~ de cuna crib death (AmE), cot death (BrE); **me
dio un susto de ~** (fam) she scared me to death
(colloq); **dar ~ a algn** (frml) to kill sb; **de mala ~**
(fam) ‹pueblo/hotel› grotty (colloq); **ser la ~** (fam)
(ser atroz) to be hell *o* murder (colloq); (ser
estupendo) to be fantastic (colloq)
muerto -ta *adj* [1] [ESTAR] (a) ‹persona/
animal/planta› dead; **lo dieron por ~** he was
given up for dead; **resultaron ~s 30 mineros** 30
miners died *o* were killed; **caer ~** to drop dead
(b) (fam) (cansado) dead beat (colloq) (c) (fam)
(pasando, padeciendo): **estar ~ de hambre/frío/
sueño** to be starving/freezing/dead-tired (colloq);
estaba ~ de miedo he was scared stiff (colloq);
de (la) risa (fam): **estaba ~ de risa** he was
laughing his head off
[2] (a) ‹pueblo/zona› dead, lifeless (b) (inerte)
limp

■ *m,f* [1] (persona muerta): **hubo dos** ∼**s** two people
died *o* were killed; **hacerse el** ∼ to pretend to be
dead; *cargar con el* ∼ (fam) (con un trabajo pesado)
to do the dirty work; *cargarle el* ∼ *a algn* (fam)
(responsabilizar) to pin the blame on sb; (endilgarle la
tarea) to give sb the dirty work (colloq); *hacer el* ∼
to float on one's back
　[2] **muerto** *m* (en naipes) dummy

muesca *f* **(a)** (hendidura) nick, notch **(b)** (para
encajar) slot, groove

muesli /'musli/ *m* muesli

muestra *f* [1] **(a)** (de mercancía) sample **(b)** (de
sangre, orina) specimen, sample **(c)** (en estadísticas)
sample [2] (prueba, señal) sign; **una** ∼ **de
cansancio/falta de madurez** a sign of tiredness/
immaturity; **como** *or* **en** ∼ **de mi gratitud** as a
token of my gratitude [3] (exposición) exhibition,
exhibit (AmE); (de teatro, cine) festival

mueva, muevas, etc ▶ MOVER

mufa *f* (RPl fam) **(a)** (mal humor) bad mood **(b)**
(moho) mold*

mugido *m* moo; **los** ∼**s de las vacas** the
mooing of the cows

mugir [I7] *vi* «*vaca*» to moo; «*toro*» to bellow

mugre *f* (suciedad) dirt, filth; (grasa) grime,
grease

mugriento -ta *adj* filthy

mugroso -sa *adj* (Chi, Méx fam) filthy

mujer *f* **(a)** woman; **ser** ∼ to be a woman; ∼ **de
la limpieza** cleaning lady, cleaner; ∼ **de mala vida**
or **de mal vivir** prostitute; ∼ **de negocios**
businesswoman; **hacerse** ∼ (euf) to reach
puberty, become a woman (euph) **(b)** (esposa) wife

mujeriego *m* womanizer

mújol *m* gray* mullet

mula *f* mule; ∼ **de carga** pack mule; *terco/
tozudo como una* ∼ as stubborn as a mule (colloq)
■ *adj* (Méx fam) stubborn

mulato -ta *adj* of mixed race (*black and white*),
mulatto (dated *or* pej)
■ *m,f* person of mixed race (*of a black and a white
parent*), mulatto (dated *or* pej)

muleta *f* [1] (bastón) crutch; (apoyo) crutch, prop
[2] (Taur) red cape (*attached to a stick*)

muletilla *f* tag, filler (tech)

mulita *f* (Per) (de pisco) glass, shot

mullido -da *adj* ⟨colchón/sofá⟩ soft; ⟨hierba⟩
springy

mulo *m* (male) mule

multa *f* fine; **le pusieron una** ∼ she was fined

multar [A1] *vt* to fine

multicine *m* multiscreen movie complex
(AmE), multiscreen cinema (BrE)

multicolor *adj* multicolored*

multicultural *adj* multicultural

multimillonario -ria *adj*: **es** ∼ he is a
multimillionaire; **un contrato** ∼ a multi-million
dollar (*o* pound *etc*) contract
■ *m,f* multimillionaire

multinacional *adj/f* multinational

múltiple *adj* [1] ⟨aplicaciones/causas⟩ many,
numerous [2] ⟨flor/imagen/fractura⟩ multiple

multiplicación *f* [1] (Biol, Mat) multiplication
[2] (incremento) increase

multiplicar [A2] *vt* to multiply; ∼ **algo POR
algo** to multiply sth BY sth
■ ∼ *vi* to multiply
■ **multiplicarse** *v pron* [1] «*especie*» to
multiply, reproduce [2] (aumentar) to increase
several times over

múltiplo *m* multiple

multitud *f* [1] (muchedumbre) crowd [2] ∼ **DE
algo** (muchos): **tengo (una)** ∼ **de cosas que hacer** I
have dozens of things to do (colloq); **una** ∼ **de
usos** an enormous variety of uses

multitudinario -ria *adj* ⟨manifestación/
movilizaciones⟩ mass (*before n*); ⟨concierto⟩ with
mass audiences

mundano -na *adj* **(a)** ⟨problemas/placeres⟩
worldly **(b)** ⟨fiesta⟩ society (*before n*)

mundial *adj* ⟨historia/mercado⟩ world (*before
n*); **la marca** ∼ the world record; **de fama** ∼
world-famous; **es un problema** ∼ it's a global *o*
worldwide problem
■ *m*: *tb* ∼**es** *mpl* World Championship(s); **el** ∼ **de
fútbol** the World Cup

mundialmente *adv*: **es** ∼ **famoso** he is
world famous; **un producto conocido** ∼ a product
well-known throughout the world

mundo *m* [1] (en general) world; **artistas venidos
de todo el** ∼ artists from all over the world; **el
mejor del** ∼ the best in the world; **me parece lo
más normal del** ∼ it seems perfectly normal to
me; **es conocido en todo el** ∼ he is known
worldwide; **el** ∼ **árabe** the Arab world; **el** ∼ **de la
droga** the drugs world; **el** ∼ **del espectáculo**
showbusiness; **todo el** ∼ **lo sabe** everybody
knows it; *el* ∼ *es un pañuelo* it's a small world;
por nada del or *en el* ∼: **yo no me lo pierdo por
nada del** ∼ I wouldn't miss it for the world; **no lo
vendería por nada en el** ∼ I wouldn't sell it for
anything in the world *o* (colloq) for all the tea in
China; *traer a algn*/*venir al* ∼ to bring sb/come
into the world; *ver* ∼ to see the world
　[2] (planeta, universo) planet, world; **él vive en otro**
∼ he's on another planet *o* in another world

munición *f* (carga) *tb* **municiones** ammunition,
munitions (*pl*)

municipal *adj* ⟨impuesto⟩ local; ⟨elecciones/
piscina/mercado⟩ municipal

municipalidad *f* ▶ MUNICIPIO

municipio *m* (territorio) municipality; (entidad)
town council; (edificio) town hall

muñeca *f* [1] **(a)** (Jueg) doll; ∼ **de trapo** rag
doll; **jugar a las** ∼**s** to play with dolls; *ser* or
parecer una ∼ to be a little doll **(b)** (fam) (como
apelativo) darling, honey (colloq) [2] (Anat) wrist

muñeco *m* [1] **(a)** (con forma humana) doll; (con
forma de animal) toy animal; ∼ **de peluche** stuffed
animal (AmE), soft toy (BrE); ∼ **de nieve** snowman
(b) (de ventrílocuo, sastre, etc) dummy **(c)** (dibujo)
figure [2] **muñecos** *mpl* (Per fam): **estar con los**
∼**s** to be very nervous

muñequera *f* (Dep) wristband; (Med) wrist
bandage

muñón *m* (de un miembro) stump

mural *adj* wall (*before n*), mural (*before n*)
■ *m* mural

muralista *adj/mf* muralist

muralla *f* (a) (de ciudad) walls (*pl*), city wall; (de convento) walls; **la M~ China** the Great Wall of China (b) (Chi) (pared) wall

murciélago *m* bat

muriera, murió, etc ▶ MORIR

murmullo *m* (de voces) murmur

murmuraciones *fpl* gossip

murmurador -dora *adj* gossipy
■ *m,f* gossip

murmurar [A1] *vt* (a) (hablar bajo) to murmur; **le murmuró algo al oído** he whispered something in her ear (b) (con enojo) to mutter; **— no pienso hacerlo — murmuró** I won't do it, she muttered (c) (en son de crítica): **cosas que se murmuran en la oficina** rumors that go around the office
■ *vi* (criticar) to gossip (*maliciously*); **~ DE algn** to gossip ABOUT sb

muro *m* wall; **M~ de las Lamentaciones** *or* **los Lamentos** Wailing Wall

mus *m: a Spanish card game*

musa *f* (Mit) Muse; (inspiración) muse

muscular *adj* muscular

musculatura *f* muscles (*pl*), musculature (tech)

músculo *m* muscle; **sacar ~** to flex one's muscles

musculoso -sa *adj* muscular

muselina *f* muslin

museo *m* museum; **~ de cera** wax museum, waxworks (*pl*); **~ de ciencias naturales** natural science museum

musgo *m* moss

música *f* music; **pon algo de ~** put some music on; **~ ambiental** background music; (en tienda, fábrica) piped *o* canned music

musical *adj/m* musical

músico -ca *m,f* (compositor) composer; (instrumentista) musician; **~ callejero** street musician, busker (BrE)

musitar [A1] *vt* to whisper, murmur

muslera *f* thighband

muslo *m* (Anat) thigh (Coc); **~s de pollo** chicken legs

mustio -tia *adj* ① ⟨flor/planta⟩ withered ② (Méx fam) (hipócrita) two-faced (colloq)

musulmán -mana *adj/m,f* Muslim, Moslem

mutable *adj* changeable, mutable (frml)

mutación *f* mutation

mutilado -da *m,f* disabled person; **un ~ de guerra** a disabled serviceman

mutilar [A1] *vt* (a) ⟨persona/pierna⟩ to mutilate; **quedó mutilado en el accidente** he was maimed as a result of the accident (b) ⟨árbol/estatua⟩ to vandalize

mutua *f* benefit society (AmE), friendly society (BrE)

mutual *f* (CS) (de asistencia económica) benefit society (AmE), friendly society (BrE)

mutuo -tua *adj* mutual; **de ~ acuerdo** by mutual *o* joint agreement; **redundará en beneficio ~** it will be to our mutual benefit

muy *adv* (a) very; **~ poca gente** very few people; **son ~ amigos** they're great friends; **~ admirado** much admired; **~ respetado** highly respected; **~ bien, sigamos adelante** OK *o* fine, let's go on; **por ~ cansado que estés** however *o* no matter how tired you are (b) (demasiado) too; **quedó ~ dulce** it's rather *o* too sweet

N n

N, n *f* (*read as* /'ene/) *the letter* N, n

N. (= **norte**) North, N

nabo *m* turnip

nácar *m* mother-of-pearl, nacre

nacer [E3] *vi* ① (a) ⟨niño/animal⟩ to be born; **¿dónde naciste?** where were you born?; **al ~** at birth; **nació para (ser) músico** he was born to be a musician (b) ⟨pollito/insecto⟩ to hatch (c) ⟨hoja/rama⟩ to sprout (d) ⟨río⟩ to have its source; ⟨carretera⟩ to start (e) ⟨pelo/plumas⟩ to grow ② (surgir) ⟨amistad/relación⟩ to spring up; **~ DE algo** ⟨problema/situación⟩ to arise *o* spring FROM sth; **nació de ella invitarlo** it was her idea to invite him

nacido -da *adj* born; **un niño recién ~** a newborn baby

naciente *adj* ⟨sol⟩ rising (*before n*); **el ~ interés por la ecología** the new interest in ecology

nacimiento *m* ① (de niño, animal) birth; **es argentino de ~** he's Argentinian by birth; **es sorda de ~** she was born deaf ② (de idea, movimiento) birth; **el ~ de una amistad duradera** the start *o* beginning of a lasting friendship ③ (belén) crib

nación *f* nation; **las Naciones Unidas** the United Nations (*pl*)

nacional *adj* (a) (de la nación) ⟨deuda/reservas/industria⟩ national; **en todo el territorio ~**

throughout the country; **un programa de difusión** ~ a program broadcast nationwide **(b)** ⟨*vuelo*⟩ domestic
■ *mf* (frml) (ciudadano) national

nacionalidad *f* (ciudadanía) nationality

nacionalismo *m* nationalism

nacionalista *adj* nationalist (*before n*)
■ *mf* nationalist

nacionalización *f* (de industria) nationalization; (naturalización) naturalization

nacionalizar [A4] *vt* ⟨*industria*⟩ to nationalize; ⟨*persona*⟩ to naturalize
■ **nacionalizarse** *v pron* «*persona*» to become naturalized

naco -ca *adj* (Méx fam & pey) plebby (colloq & pej)
■ *m, f* pleb (colloq & pej)

nada *pron* ① **(a)** nothing; **es mejor que** ~ it's better than nothing; **de** ~ **sirve que le compres libros** there's no point in buying him books; **antes que** *o* **de** ~ first of all; **no quiere** ~ he doesn't want anything; **¡no sirves para** ~**!** you're useless; **sin decir** ~ without a word **(b)** (*en locs*) **de nada** you're welcome; **nada de nada** (fam) not a thing; **nada más: no hay** ~ **más** there's nothing else; **¿algo más?** — ~ **más** anything else? — no, that's it *o* that's all; ~ **más fui yo** (Méx) I was the only one who went; **salí** ~ **más comer** I went out right *o* straight after lunch; **sacó** ⟨~ **más ni**⟩ ~ **menos que el primer puesto** she came first no less; **para nada: no me gustó para** ~ I didn't like it at all; **por nada: la compraron por** ~ they bought it for next to nothing; **discuten por** ~ they argue over nothing; **llora por** ~ she cries at the slightest little thing
② (Esp) (en tenis) love; **quince-**~ fifteen-love
■ *adv* : **no está** ~ **preocupado** he isn't at all *o* the least bit worried; **esto no me gusta** ~ I don't like this at all *o* (colloq) one bit

nadador -dora *m,f* swimmer

nadar [A1] *vi* **(a)** «*persona/pez*» to swim; **¿sabes** ~**?** can you swim?; ~ **(estilo) mariposa/ pecho** to do (the) butterfly/breaststroke; ~ **de espalda** *or* (Méx) **de dorso** to do (the) back stroke **(b)** «*ramas/hojas*» (flotar) to float **(c) nadar en** (tener mucho): ~ **en dinero** to be rolling in money (colloq); **el pollo nadaba en grasa** the chicken was swimming in grease
■ ~ *vt* to swim

nadie *pron* nobody, no one; **no me ayudó** ~ nobody helped me; **no vi a** ~ I didn't see anybody; **sin que** ~ **se diera cuenta** without anyone noticing

nado *m* **(a) a nado: cruzó el río a** ~ he swam across the river **(b)** (Méx, Ven) (natación) swimming

nafta *f* **(a)** (Quím) naphtha **(b)** (RPl) (gasolina) gas (AmE), petrol (BrE)

naftalina *f* (Quím) naphthalene; (para ropa) mothballs (*pl*)

naguas *fpl* (Méx fam) petticoat

náhuatl¹ *adj/mf* (*pl* **nahuas**) Nahuatl

náhuatl² *m* (idioma) Nahuatl

nailon *m* nylon

naipe *m* (playing) card; **juegos de** ~**s** card games

nalga *f* (Anat) buttock; **una inyección en la** ~ an injection in the buttock *o* bottom

nalgada *f* (Méx) smack on the bottom

nana *f* **(a)** (canción de cuna) lullaby **(b)** (fam) (abuela) grandma (colloq), granny (colloq) **(c)** (Andes, Ven) (niñera) nanny

naranja *f* (fruta) orange; ~ **amarga** Seville orange
■ *m* (color) orange
■ *adj* (*gen inv*) orange

naranjada *f* orangeade

naranjal *m* orange grove

naranjo *m* orange tree

narciso *m* **(a)** (Bot) daffodil; (género) narcissus **(b)** (persona) narcissist

narcótico *m* narcotic

narcotraficante *mf* drug-trafficker

narcotráfico *m* drug trafficking

nardo *m* spikenard, nard

nariz *f* **(a)** (Anat) nose; **sonarse la** ~ to blow one's nose; **no te metas los dedos en la** ~ don't pick your nose; **en mis/sus propias narices** (fam) right under my/his nose; **estar hasta las narices de algo/algn** (fam) to be fed up (to the back teeth) with sth/sb (colloq); **meter las narices** *or* **la** ~ **en algo** (fam) to poke one's nose into sth (colloq) **(b)** (de avión) nose

narizota *f* (fam) schnozzle (AmE colloq), conk (BrE colloq)

narración *f* (relato) story; (acción de contar) account

narrador -dora *m,f* narrator

narrar [A1] *vt* (frml) **(a)** «*película/libro*» ⟨*hazañas/experiencias*⟩ to tell of (frml), to relate; ⟨*historia*⟩ to tell, relate **(b)** «*persona*» ⟨*historia*⟩ to tell, narrate (frml)

narrativa *f* (género) fiction; (narración) narrative

narrativo -va *adj* narrative

nasal *adj* nasal

nata *f* **(a)** (sobre leche hervida) skin **(b)** (Esp) ▶ CREMA B

natación *f* swimming

natal *adj* **(a)** ⟨*país*⟩ native (*before n*); ⟨*ciudad*⟩ home (*before n*) **(b)** (Méx) (originario): **es** ~ **de Chiapas** she was born in Chiapas

natalidad *f* birthrate

natillas *fpl* custard

natividad *f* **(a) la** ~ (nacimiento de Cristo) the Nativity **(b) la N**~ (navidad) Christmas

nativo -va *adj* **(a)** ⟨*tierra/país/lengua*⟩ native **(b)** ⟨*flora/fauna*⟩ native; ~ **DE algo** native TO sth
■ *m,f* (aborigen) native; (hablante) native speaker

nato -⟨ta⟩ *adj* ⟨*artista/deportista*⟩ born (*before n*)

natural *adj* ① **(a)** ⟨*fenómeno/ingrediente*⟩ natural; ⟨*fruta*⟩ fresh; **al** ~ ⟨*mejillones*⟩ in brine **(b)** (a temperatura ambiente) ⟨*cerveza/gaseosa*⟩ unchilled **(c)** (Mús) natural ② **(a)** (espontáneo) ⟨*gesto/persona*⟩ natural **(b)** (inherente) natural, innate **(c)** (normal) natural; **me parece lo más** ~ **del mundo** it seems perfectly natural to me ③ (frml) (nativo) **ser** ~ **DE** to be a native OF, to come FROM
■ *m* **(a)** (carácter) nature **(b)** (nativo) native; **los** ~**es del lugar** people from the area

naturaleza *f* **(a)** (Ecol): **la** ~ nature; ~ **muerta** still life **(b)** (índole) nature

naturalidad *f*: su ~ her natural manner; con la mayor ~ del mundo as if it were the most natural thing in the world

naturalización *f* naturalization

naturalizarse [A4] *v pron* to become naturalized

naturismo *m* (estilo de vida) natural lifestyle

naturista *adj* ‹médico/tratamiento› natural

naufragar [A3] *vi* (a) «barco» to be wrecked; «persona» to be shipwrecked (b) «plan/negocio» to go under

naufragio *m* (a) (Náut) shipwreck (b) (fracaso) failure

náufrago -ga *adj* shipwrecked
■ *m,f* (Náut) shipwrecked person

náuseas *fpl* nausea, sickness; **sentir** *or* **tener ~** to feel sick *o* nauseous; **me da ~** it makes me sick

náutico -ca *adj* nautical

navaja *f* (de bolsillo) penknife; (para afeitar) razor

navajazo *m* (herida) knife wound

naval *adj* naval

nave *f* [1] (Náut) (arc o liter) ship; **~ espacial** spacecraft, spaceship [2] (de iglesia) nave

navegabilidad *f* (de río) navigability; (de embarcación) seaworthiness

navegable *adj* ‹río› navigable; ‹barco› seaworthy

navegación *f* (acción de navegar) navigation; (tráfico) shipping; **~ aérea** aerial navigation; **~ fluvial** river navigation

navegador *m* (Inf) browser

navegante *mf* (a) (arc) (marino) mariner (arch) (b) (que determina el rumbo) navigator

navegar [A3] *vi* (a) «nave» to sail (b) «persona» (a vela) to sail (c) (determinar el rumbo) to navigate (d) (Inf): **~ en la web** *or* **Red** to surf the Web
■ **~** *vt* (liter) to sail

Navidad *f* Christmas; **el día de ~** Christmas Day; **¡feliz ~!** happy Christmas!; **en ~** at Christmas (time)

navideño -ña *adj* Christmas (before n)

navío *m* ship

nazi *adj/mf* Nazi

nazismo *m* Nazism

NE (= **nordeste**) NE

neblina *f* mist

nebuloso -sa *adj* (a) (Meteo) misty (b) ‹idea/imagen› hazy, nebulous

necedad *f* (a) (cualidad) crassness (b) (dicho, acto): **decir ~es** to talk nonsense; **es una ~** it's sheer stupidity

necesario -ria *adj* (imprescindible) necessary; **haré lo que sea ~** I'll do whatever's necessary; **si es ~** if necessary, if need be; **no es ~** there's no need, it isn't necessary; **me sentía ~** I felt needed

neceser *m* (estuche) toilet kit (AmE), toilet bag (BrE); (maleta pequeña) overnight bag

necesidad *f* [1] (a) (urgencia, falta) need; **no hay ~ de que se entere** there's no need for her to know; **en caso de ~** if necessary, if need be (b) (cosa necesaria) necessity, essential (c) (pobreza) poverty, need [2] **necesidades** *fpl* (a) (requerimientos) needs (pl), requirements (pl) (b)

(privaciones) hardship; **pasar ~es** to suffer hardship (c) **hacer sus ~es** (euf) to relieve oneself (euph)

necesitado -da *adj* (a) (falto) **~ DE algo** ‹de dinero› short of sth; ‹de afecto› in need of sth (b) (pobre) in need, needy
■ *m,f* needy person; **los ~s** the needy

necesitar [A1] *vt* to need; **☺ se necesita vendedora** saleswoman required; **necesito verte hoy** I need to see you today
■ **~** *vi* (frml) **~ DE algo** to need sth

necio -cia *adj* (a) (tonto) stupid (b) (AmC, Col, Ven fam) (travieso) naughty

néctar *m* nectar

nectarina *f* nectarine

nefasto -ta *adj* ‹consecuencias› disastrous; ‹influencia› harmful; ‹tiempo/fiesta› (fam) awful (colloq)

negación *f* (acción) denial, negation; (antítesis) antithesis; (Ling) negative

negado -da *adj*: **ser ~ para algo** to be useless *o* hopeless at sth

negar [A7] *vt* (a) ‹acusación/rumor› to deny; **no puedo ~lo** I can't deny it; **niega habértelo dicho** she denies having told you (b) (no conceder) ‹permiso/favor› to refuse; **les ~on la entrada** they were refused entry
■ **~** *vi*: **~ con la cabeza** to shake one's head
■ **negarse** *v pron* (rehusar) to refuse; **~se A hacer algo** to refuse to do sth; **se negó a que llamáramos a un médico** he refused to let us call a doctor

negativa *f* (ante acusación) denial; (a propuesta) refusal

negativo¹ -va *adj* negative

negativo² *m* (Fot) negative

negligé /nevli'ʒe/ *m* negligee

negligencia *f* negligence

negociable *adj* negotiable

negociación *f* [1] (Pol, Rels Labs) negotiation [2] (Méx) (empresa) business

negociado *m* [1] (departamento) department [2] (AmS fam) (negocio sucio) shady deal (colloq)

negociador -dora *adj* negotiating (before n)
■ *m,f* negotiator

negociante *mf* (a) (Com, Fin) (m) businessman; (f) businesswoman (b) (pey) (mercenario) money-grubber (colloq & pej)

negociar [A1] *vt/vi* to negotiate

negocio *m* (a) (Com) business; **montar** *or* **poner un ~** to set up a business; **dedicarse a los ~s** to be in business; **hablar de ~s** to talk business; **en el mundo de los ~s** in the business world (b) (transacción) deal; **un buen ~** a good deal (c) (CS) (tienda) store (AmE), shop (BrE) (d) (fam) (asunto) business (colloq)

negra *f* (a) (Mús) crotchet (b) (en ajedrez): **las ~s** the black pieces

negrita *f* boldface, bold type; **en ~(s)** in boldface, in bold (type)

negro¹ -gra *adj* (a) ‹pelo/hombre/raza› black; ‹ojos› dark (b) (fam) (por el sol) tanned (c) (sombrío) black, gloomy; **lo ve todo tan ~** she's always so pessimistic; **pasarlas negras** (fam) to have a rough time of it (colloq)
■ *m,f* (persona de raza negra) black person

negro² m (color) black

negrura f blackness

nene -na m,f (Esp, RPl fam) **(a)** (niño pequeño) (m) little boy; (f) little girl; **los ~s** the kids (colloq) **(b)** (apelativo cariñoso) darling, honey **(c) nena** f (arg) (mujer) chick (AmE colloq), bird (BrE colloq)

nené mf (Ven fam) (m) little boy; (f) little girl

neocelandés -desa adj of/from New Zealand
■ m,f New Zealander

neologismo m neologism

neonazi adj/mf neonazi

neoyorquino -na adj of/from New York
■ m,f New Yorker

nepotismo m nepotism

Neptuno m Neptune

nervio m ⟨1⟩ **(a)** (Anat) nerve **(b)** (en la carne) sinew; **carne con ~s** gristly meat ⟨2⟩ **nervios** mpl nerves (pl); **tiene los ~s destrozados** his nerves are in shreds; **está enfermo de los ~s** he suffers with his nerves; **tengo unos ~s ...** I'm o I feel so nervous; **me muero de ~s** I'm a nervous wreck (colloq); **ponerle a algn los ~s de punta** to get on sb's nerves

nerviosismo m nervousness; **el ~ que producen los exámenes** the feeling of nervousness o nerves that exams produce

nervioso -sa adj ⟨1⟩ ⟨persona/animal⟩ **(a)** [SER] (excitable) nervous **(b)** [ESTAR] (preocupado, tenso) nervous; **estoy muy ~ por lo de los exámenes** I'm very nervous about the exams **(c)** [ESTAR] (agitado) agitated; **últimamente se le nota ~** he's been on edge o (colloq) uptight lately; **ese ruido me pone muy nerviosa** that noise is getting on my nerves; **me pongo ~ cada vez que la veo** I get flustered every time I see her ⟨2⟩ ⟨trastorno⟩ nervous; ⟨célula⟩ nerve (before n)

nervudo -da adj sinewy

neto -ta adj **(a)** ⟨sueldo/precio⟩ net **(b)** (claro) ⟨silueta/perfil⟩ distinct, clear

neumático m tire (AmE), tyre (BrE)

neumonía f pneumonia

neura adj (fam): **eso me pone ~** that drives me crazy o (BrE) mad (colloq); **es tan ~** he's so neurotic
■ m,f (fam) ⟨1⟩ (persona): **es un ~** he's a complete neurotic (colloq) ⟨2⟩ **neura** f: **está con la ~** she's in a real state (colloq)

neurasténico -ca adj/m,f **(a)** (Med) neurasthenic **(b)** (fam) ▶ NEURA

neurólogo -ga m,f neurologist

neurosis f neurosis

neurótico -ca adj/m,f neurotic

neutral adj neutral

neutralizar [A4] vt to neutralize

neutro¹ -tra adj **(a)** (Elec, Fís) neutral **(b)** (Biol, Ling) neuter

neutro² m **(a)** (Ling) neuter **(b)** (AmL) (Auto) neutral

nevada f snowfall

nevado -da adj ⟨cumbres/picos⟩ snowcapped, snow-covered; ⟨campos/techos⟩ covered with snow

nevar [A5] v impers to snow

nevasca f, (CS) **nevazón** f blizzard, snowstorm

nevera f **(a)** (refrigerador) refrigerator, fridge, icebox (AmE); **~ congelador** fridge-freezer **(b)** (para picnic) cooler (AmE), cool bag/box (BrE)

nevoso -sa adj snowy

nexo m (enlace, vínculo) link

ni conj **(a)** (con otro negativo): **no vino él ~ su mujer** neither he nor his wife came; **yo no pienso ir — ~ yo (tampoco)** I don't intend going — neither do I; **~ fumo ~ bebo** I don't smoke or drink, I neither smoke nor drink; **no nos avisó ~ a él ~ a mí** he didn't tell him or me (either); **~ siquiera nos avisó** not even; **¿~ siquiera piensas llamarlo?** aren't you even going to call him?; **no vendieron ~ un libro** they didn't sell a single book **(b)** (expresando rechazo, enfado): **¡~ hablar!** out of the question!; **~ aunque me lo ruegue** not even if he gets down on his knees

Nicaragua f Nicaragua

nicaragüense adj/mf Nicaraguan

nicho m (Arquit) niche; (en cementerio) deep recess in a wall used as a tomb

nicotina f nicotine

nidada f (de huevos) clutch; (de crías) clutch, brood

nido m nest; **un ~ de ladrones** a den of thieves; **un ~ de amor** a love nest

niebla f fog; **había ~** it was foggy

niega, niegas, etc ▶ NEGAR

nieto -ta m,f (m) grandson, grandchild; (f) granddaughter, grandchild; **mis ~s** my grandchildren

nieva ▶ NEVAR

nieve f **(a)** (Meteo) snow **(b)** (Coc): **batir las claras a (punto de) ~** whisk the egg whites until stiff **(c)** (Méx) (helado) sorbet, water ice

nimiedad f triviality

nimio -mia adj trivial, petty

ningún adj: apocopated form of NINGUNO used before masculine singular nouns

ninguncar [A1] vt (Méx fam) to treat ... like dirt (colloq)

ninguno -na adj (see note under NINGÚN) **(a)** (delante del n): **no prestó ninguna atención** he didn't pay any attention; **en ningún momento** never; **no lo encuentro por ningún lado** I can't find it anywhere **(b)** (detrás del n): **no hay problema ~** there's absolutely no problem
■ pron **(a)** (refiriéndose — a dos personas o cosas) neither; (— a más de dos) none; **~ de los dos vino** neither of them came; **no trajo ~ de los dos** she didn't bring either of them; **~ de nosotros la conoce** none of us know her **(b)** (nadie) nobody, no-one

niña f pupil; ver tb NIÑO m,f

niñera f nanny, nursemaid (AmE)

niñería f (pey): **déjate de ~s** stop being so childish

niñez f childhood

niño -ña adj (joven) young; (infantil, inmaduro) immature, childish
■ m,f **(a)** (m) boy, child; (f) girl, child; (bebé) baby; **¿te gustan los ~s?** do you like children?; **de ~** as a child; **~ bien** rich kid (colloq); **~ de pecho** small o young baby; **el ~ mimado de la maestra** the teacher's favorite* o pet; **~ prodigio** ⋯▷

child prodigy **(b)** (con respecto a los padres) (*m*)
son, child; (*f*) daughter, child; **tengo que llevar al
~ al dentista** I have to take my son to the dentist
nipón -pona *adj/m,f* Japanese
níquel *m* nickel
níspero *m* loquat
nitidez *f* (de imagen, del día) clarity; (de recuerdo)
vividness
nítido -da *adj* ‹foto/imagen› clear
nitrógeno *m* nitrogen
nivel *m* **(a)** (altura) level **(b)** (en escala, jerarquía)
level; **conversaciones de alto ~** high-level talks;
~ de vida standard of living; **no está al ~ de los
demás** he's not up to the same standard as the
others; **el ~ de las universidades mexicanas** the
standard of Mexican universities
nivelar [A1] *vt* **(a)** (Const) ‹suelo/terreno› to
level; ‹estante› to get ... level **(b)** ‹presupuesto› to
balance
no *adv* **(a)** (como respuesta) no; (modificando
adverbios, oraciones, verbos) not [*la negación de la
mayoría de los verbos ingleses requiere el uso del
auxiliar 'do'*] **¿te gustó? — no** did you like it? —
no, I didn't; **¿vienes o ~?** are you coming or
not?; **~ te preocupes** don't worry; **¿por qué ~
quieres ir? — porque ~** why don't you want to
go? — I just don't **(b)** (con otro negativo): **~ veo
nada** I can't see a thing o anything; **~ viene
nunca** she never comes **(c)** (en coletillas
interrogativas): **está mejor ¿~?** she's better, isn't
she?; **ha dimitido ¿~?** he has resigned, hasn't he?
(d) (expresando incredulidad): **se ganó la lotería —
¡no!** he won the lottery — he didn't! o no! **(e)**
(sustituyendo a una cláusula): **creo que ~** I don't
think so; **¿te gustó? a mí ~** did you like it? I
didn't **(f)** (*delante de n, adj, pp*): **los ~ fumadores**
nonsmokers; **la ~ violencia** non-violence; **un hijo
~ deseado** an unwanted child
■ *m* (*pl* **noes**) no
NO (= **noroeste**) NW
Nobel *m* **(a)** *tb* **Premio ~ Nobel Prize (b)**
(ganador) Nobel prizewinner
noble *adj* **(a)** (en general) noble; **un caballero de
~ linaje** (liter) a knight of noble lineage (liter) **(b)**
‹madera› fine
■ *mf* (*m*) nobleman; (*f*) noblewoman; **los ~** the
nobles, the nobility
nobleza *f* nobility
nocaut *adj* (AmL): **lo dejó ~** he/it knocked him
out; **está ~** he's out for the count
■ *m* (*pl* **-cauts**) (AmL) knockout
noche *f* **(a)** night; **la ~ anterior** the night
before, the previous evening; **esta ~** tonight, this
evening; **¡buenas ~s!** (al saludar) good evening!; (al
despedirse) goodnight **(b)** (*en locs*) **de noche**
‹trabajar/conducir› at night; ‹vestido/función›
evening (*before n*); **hacerse de ~** to get dark; **en
la** *or* (*esp Esp*) **por la** *or* (RPl) **a la noche: en la ~
fuimos al teatro** in the evening we went to the
theater; **el lunes en la ~** on Monday evening/
night; **de la ~ a la mañana** overnight
Nochebuena *f* Christmas Eve

Nochevieja *f* New Year's Eve (*in the evening*)
noción *f* **(a)** (idea, concepto) notion, idea; **no
tiene la menor ~ del tema** he doesn't know the
first thing about the subject **(b)** **nociones** *fpl*
(conocimientos): **tengo nociones de ruso** I have a
smattering of Russian; **las nociones de
electrónica** the basics o rudiments of electronics
nocivo -va *adj* ‹sustancia› harmful;
‹influencia› damaging
noctámbulo -la *adj*: **siempre ha sido ~** he's
always been a night bird o (AmE) nighthawk
(colloq)
nocturno -na *adj* **(a)** ‹vuelo/tren/vida› night
(*before n*); ‹clases› evening (*before n*) **(b)**
‹animal/planta› nocturnal
nodriza *f* (ama de cría) wet nurse; (niñera) (ant)
nursemaid
nogal *m* (árbol) walnut tree; (madera) walnut
nómada *adj* nomadic
■ *mf* nomad
nomás *adv* **(a)** (AmL): **pase ~** come on in; **no lo
vas a convencer así ~** you're not going to
convince him as easily as that; **déjelo aquí ~** just
leave it here; **lo dijo por molestar ~** she only said
it to be difficult **(b)** **nomás (que)** (Col, Méx fam) as
soon as; **~ (que) tenga dinero** as soon as I have
some money
nombramiento *m* (designación) appointment;
(documento) letter of appointment
nombrar [A1] *vt* **(a)** (citar, mencionar) to mention;
no lo volvió a ~ she never mentioned his name o
him again **(b)** (designar) to appoint
nombre *m* **(a)** (de cosa, persona, animal) name; **~
y apellidos** full name, name in full; **~ artístico**
stage name; **~ de pila** first name, christian
name; **~ de soltera** maiden name; **¿qué ~ le
pusieron?** what did they call him?; **lo conozco de
~** I know him by name; **en ~ de** (en representación
de) on behalf of; (apelando a) in the name of; **a ~
de** ‹paquete/carta› made payable to, made out to;
lo que ha hecho no tiene ~ what she has done is
unspeakable **(b)** (Ling) noun; **~ compuesto**
compound noun **(c)** (fama): **un científico de ~** a
renowned scientist; **hacerse un ~ en la vida** to
make a name for oneself
nómina *f* (lista de empleados) payroll; (hoja de
pago) payslip; (suma de dinero) salary, wages (*pl*)
nominación *f* nomination
nominar [A1] *vt* to nominate
nominativo *adj* (Fin): **un cheque ~ a favor de
...** a check made out to o payable to ...
nomo *m* gnome
non *adj* odd
■ *m* odd number; **pares y ~es** odds and evens
noqueada *f* knockout
noquear [A1] *vt* to knock out
noratlántico -ca *adj* north-Atlantic (*before
n*)
nordeste, noreste *adj inv* ‹región›
northeastern; **iban en dirección ~** they were
heading northeast

AmC	Central America	Arg	Argentina	Cu	Cuba	Per	Peru
AmL	Latin America	Bol	Bolivia	Ec	Ecuador	RPl	River Plate Area
AmS	South America	Chi	Chile	Esp	Spain	Ur	Uruguay
Andes	Andean Region	CS	Southern Cone	Méx	Mexico	Ven	Venezuela

■ *m* (punto cardinal) northeast, Northeast; **vientos del ~** northeasterly winds

nórdico -ca *adj* ‹país/pueblo› Nordic (*esp Scandinavian*)

noria *f* **(a)** (para sacar agua) waterwheel **(b)** (Ocio) Ferris wheel (AmE), big wheel (BrE)

norma *f* **(a)** (regla) rule, regulation; **~s de conducta** rules of conduct; **~s de seguridad** safety regulations; **tengo por ~ ...** I make it a rule ... **(b)** (manera común de hacer algo): **la ~ es que acudan los directivos** it is standard practice for the directors to attend

normal *adj* normal; **es ~ que reaccionen así** it's normal for them to react like that; **hoy en día es muy ~** it's very common nowadays; **no es ~ que haga tanto frío** it's unusual *o* it isn't normal for it to be so cold; **superior a lo ~** above-average; **~ y corriente** ordinary
■ *f* **(a)** (escuela): **la N ~** teacher training college **(b)** (gasolina) regular gas (AmE), two-star petrol (BrE)

normalidad *f* **(a)** (cualidad): **con ~** normally **(b)** (situación) normality, normalcy (AmE); **el país volvió a la ~** the country returned to normal

normalización *f* **(a)** (de situación) normalization **(b)** (estandarización) standardization

normalizar [A4] *vt* **(a)** ‹situación/relaciones› to normalize **(b)** (estandarizar) to standardize
■ **normalizarse** *v pron* «‹situación/relaciones›» to return to normal **(b)** (estandarizarse) to become standardized

normalmente *adv* normally, usually

noroeste *adj inv* ‹región› northwestern; **iban en dirección ~** they were heading northwest
■ *m* (punto cardinal) northwest, Northwest; **vientos del ~** northwesterly winds

norte *adj inv* ‹región› northern; ‹costa/ala› north (*before n*); **iban en dirección ~** they were heading north *o* northward(s)
■ *m* north, North; **al ~ de Matagalpa** to the north of Matagalpa; **vientos del N~** northerly winds; **caminaron hacia el N~** they walked north *o* northward(s); **la casa da al ~** the house faces north

Norteamérica *f* (América del Norte) North America; (EEUU) America, the States (colloq)

norteamericano -na *adj/m,f* (de América del Norte) North American; (estadounidense) American

norteño -ña, (Chi, Per) **nortino -na** *adj* northern
■ *m,f* northerner

Noruega *f* Norway

noruego[1] -ga *adj/m,f* Norwegian

noruego[2] *m* (idioma) Norwegian

nos *pron pers* **(a)** (como complemento directo, indirecto) us; **~ ayudaron mucho** they helped us a lot; **escúchanos** listen to us; **~ han robado el coche** our car's been stolen **(b)** (*refl*) ourselves; **~ hicimos daño** we hurt ourselves; **sentémonos** let's sit down **(c)** (*recípr*): **~ conocemos desde hace años** we have known each other for years

nosotros -tras *pron pers pl* **(a)** we; **¿quién lo trajo? — nosotros** who brought it? — we did; **ábrenos, somos nosotros** open the door, it's us; **~ mismos lo arreglamos** we fixed it ourselves **(b)** (en comparaciones, con preposiciones) us; **antes/después que ~** before/after us; **ven con ~** come with us

nostalgia *f* nostalgia; **siente ~ por su país** he feels homesick

nostálgico -ca *adj* nostalgic

nota *f* **1** (apunte, mensaje) note; **tomar ~ de algo** (apuntar) to make a note of sth; (fijarse) to take note of sth; **tomar ~s** to take notes; **~ a pie de página** footnote **2 (a)** (Educ) (calificación) grade (AmE), mark (BrE); **sacar buenas ~s** to get good grades *o* marks **(b)** (Mús) note **3** (detalle) touch; **una ~ de humor** a touch of humor

notable *adj* ‹diferencia/mejoría› notable; **una actuación ~** an outstanding performance; **posee una ~ inteligencia** she is remarkably *o* extremely intelligent
■ *m* **(a)** (Educ) *grade between 7 and 8.5 on a scale from 1 to 10* **(b)** (persona importante) dignitary

notar [A1] *vt* **(a)** (advertir) to notice; **no noté nada extraño** I didn't notice anything strange; **hacer(le) ~ algo (a algn)** to point sth out (to sb); **te noto muy triste** you look very sad; **se le notaba indeciso** he seemed hesitant **(b)** (*impers*): **se nota que es novato** you can tell *o* see he's a beginner; **se te nota en la cara** it's written all over your face
■ **notarse** *v pron* (+ *compl*) to feel; **me noto rara con este vestido** I feel funny in this dress

notaría *f* **(a)** (profesión) *profession of notary*; (oficina) notary's office **(b)** (Col) (registro civil) registry office

notarial *adj* notarial

notario -ria *m,f* notary, notary public

noticia *f* **1** (información): **una ~** a piece *o* an item of news; **buenas/malas ~s** good/bad news; **la última ~ del programa** the final item on the news; **una ~ de última hora** a late *o* last-minute news item **2 noticias** *fpl* **(a)** (referencias) news; **no hemos tenido ~s suyas** (provenientes de él) we haven't heard from him; (provenientes de otra persona) we haven't had (any) news of him **(b)** (Rad, TV) news

noticiario *m*, (AmL) **noticiero** *m* (Rad, TV) news; (Cin) newsreel

notificación *f* (frml) notification (frml)

notificar [A2] *vt* (frml) to notify

notorio -ria *adj* **(a)** (evidente) evident, obvious **(b)** (conocido) well-known **(c)** (notable) ‹descenso/mejora› marked

nov. (= **noviembre**) Nov

novato -ta *adj* inexperienced, new
■ *m,f* novice, beginner

novecientos -tas *adj/pron* nine hundred; *para ejemplos ver* QUINIENTOS

novedad *f* **1 (a)** (innovación) innovation; **la última ~ en el campo de la informática** the latest innovation in the field of computing **(b)** (cualidad, cosa nueva) novelty; **eran una ~ en aquel entonces** they were a novelty then **2** (noticia): **¿alguna ~?** any news?; **eso no es ninguna ~** everybody knows that; **sin ~** ‹llegar› safely; **¿cómo sigue? — sin ~** how is he? — much the same

novedoso -sa *adj* ‹idea/enfoque› novel, original

novela *f* (Lit) novel; (TV) soap opera; **~ policíaca** detective novel *o* story; **~ rosa** (pey) novelette (pej), romantic novel

novelesco -ca *adj* ⟨*vida*/*historia*⟩ like
something out of a novel; ⟨*viajes*/*andanzas*⟩
fabulous

novelista *mf* novelist

noveno¹ -na *adj*/*pron* ninth; **la novena parte**
a ninth; *para ejemplos ver* QUINTO

**noveno² ** *m* ninth

noventa *adj inv*/*pron*/*m* ninety; *para ejemplos*
ver CINCUENTA

noviar [A1] *vi* (AmL fam) to go out together, to
date (AmE); **~ CON algn** to go out WITH sb, to date
sb (AmE)

noviazgo *m*: **el ~ duró un año** they went out
(together) for one year; **~s a larga distancia**
long-distance relationships

novicio -cia *m,f* novice

noviembre *m* November; *para ejemplos ver*
ENERO

novillo -lla *m,f* (*m*) young bull; (*f*) heifer;
hacer ~s (fam) to play hooky (esp AmE colloq), to
skive off (school) (BrE colloq)

novio -via *m,f* (a) (no formal) (*m*) boyfriend; (*f*)
girlfriend; (después del compromiso) (*m*) fiancé; (*f*)
fiancée (b) (el día de la boda) (*m*) groom; (*f*) bride;
los ~s the bride and groom

nubarrón *m* storm cloud

nube *f* (Meteo) cloud; (de polvo, humo) cloud; (de
insectos) cloud, swarm; **un cielo cubierto de ~s** an
overcast o a cloudy sky; **~ atómica** mushroom
cloud; **estar** or **andar en las ~s** (fam) to have
one's head in the clouds

nublado -da *adj* ⟨*cielo*/*día*⟩ cloudy, overcast

nublar [A1] *vt* (a) ⟨*vista*⟩ to cloud (b) (liter)
⟨*felicidad*⟩ to cloud (liter)
■ **nublarse** *v pron* (a) «*cielo*» to cloud over (b)
«*vista*» to cloud over

nubosidad *f*: **la ~ irá en aumento** it will
become increasingly cloudy; **un día con mucha ~**
a day with a lot of cloud about

nuboso -sa *adj* cloudy

nuca *f* back o nape of the neck

nuclear *adj* nuclear

núcleo *m* (a) (Biol, Fís) nucleus (b) (Elec) core

nudillo *m* knuckle

nudismo *m* nudism

nudista *adj*/*mf* nudist

nudo *m* (a) (en general) knot; **se hizo un ~ en el**
hilo the thread got into a knot; **¿me haces el ~**
de la corbata? can you do my tie for me?; **tenía**
un ~ en la garganta I had a lump in my throat
(b) (de carreteras, vías férreas) junction

nuera *f* daughter-in-law

nuestro -tra *adj* our; **~ coche** our car; **un**
amigo ~ a friend of ours
■ *pron*: **el ~, la nuestra** *etc* ours; **es de los ~s** he's
one of us; **nosotros a lo ~** let's just get on with
our own business; **sabe lo ~** he knows about us

Nueva York *f* New York

Nueva Zelandia, Nueva Zelanda *f* New
Zealand

nueve *adj inv*/*pron*/*m* nine; *para ejemplos ver*
CINCO

nuevo -va *adj* (a) [SER] ⟨*estilo*/*coche*/*novio*⟩
new; **soy ~ en la oficina** I'm new in the office; **de**
~ again; **¿qué hay de ~?** what's new? (colloq); **~**
rico nouveau riche (b) (delante del n) ⟨*intento*/
cambio⟩ further; **ha surgido un ~ problema**
another o a further problem has arisen; **N~**
Testamento New Testament (c) [ESTAR] (no
desgastado) as good as new

Nuevo México *m* New Mexico

nuez *f* 1 (a) (del nogal) walnut (b) (Méx) (pacana)
pecan (nut) (c) **~ moscada** nutmeg 2 (Anat)
Adam's apple

nulidad *f* 1 (Der) nullity 2 (fam) (calamidad)
dead loss (colloq); **soy una ~ para los idiomas** I'm
useless at languages

nulo -la *adj* (a) (Der) ⟨*testamento*/*votación*⟩ null
and void; ⟨*voto*⟩ void (b) ⟨*persona*⟩ useless
(colloq), hopeless (colloq) (c) (inexistente): **mis**
conocimientos del tema son ~s my knowledge of
the subject is virtually nil

Núm., núm. (= **número**) no.

numerable *adj* countable

numeración *f* (acción) numbering; (números)
numbers (*pl*); (sistema) numerals (*pl*)

numeral *adj*/*m* numeral

numerar [A1] *vt* to number

número *m* 1 (a) (Mat) number; **~ de**
identificación personal PIN number, Personal
Identification Number; **~ de matrícula** license
number (AmE), registration number (BrE); **~ de**
serie serial number; **~ de teléfono/fax** phone/fax
number; **una suma de seis ~s** a six figure sum;
problemas sin ~ innumerable o countless
problems (b) (de zapatos) size; **¿qué ~ calzas?**
what size shoe do you take? (c) (billete de lotería)
lottery ticket 2 (a) (Espec) act (b) (de publicación)
issue

numeroso -sa *adj* ⟨*clase*/*grupo*⟩ large;
⟨*ocasiones*/*ejemplos*⟩ numerous, many

nunca *adv* never; **como ~** like never before;
casi ~ hardly ever; **más que ~** more than ever
(before); **~ más** never again

nuncio *m* (Relig) *tb* **~ apostólico** papal nuncio

nupcial *adj* ⟨*festejos*⟩ (liter) nuptial (liter);
⟨*ceremonia*⟩ wedding (*before n*)

nupcias *fpl* (liter) nuptials (*pl*) (liter), wedding;
en 1970 se casó en segundas ~ con doña Inés
Díaz in 1970 he married his second wife, Inés
Díaz

nutria *f* otter

nutrición *f* nutrition

nutrido -da *adj*: **mal ~** undernourished,
malnourished; **bien ~** well-nourished

nutrir [I1] *vt* ⟨*organismo*⟩ to nourish; ⟨*niño*/
planta⟩ to nourish, feed

nutritivo -va *adj* ⟨*alimento*⟩ nutritious; ⟨*valor*⟩
nutritional

nylon /ˈnajlon, niˈlon/ *m* nylon

Ññ

Ñ, ñ *f* (*read as* /'eɲe/) *the letter* Ñ, ñ
ñandú *m* rhea
ñandutí *m* nanduti (*fine Paraguayan lace*)
ñango -ga *adj* (Méx fam) wimpish (colloq)
ñapa *f* (AmL fam) *small amount of extra goods given free*, lagniappe (AmE); **dar algo de ~** to throw sth in (for free) (colloq); **me dio dos de ~** she threw in a couple extra

ñato -ta *adj* (AmS fam) ⟨*persona*⟩ snub-nosed; ⟨*animal*⟩ pug-nosed
ñauca (Chi), (RPl) **ñaupa** *f* (fam): **es del año de ~** it's really ancient (colloq); **ropa del año de ~** clothes that went out with the ark (colloq)
ñoquis *mpl* (Coc) gnocchi (*pl*)
ñorbo *m* (Ec, Per) passionflower
ñu *m* gnu, wildebeest

Oo

O, o *f* (*read as* /o/) *the letter* O, o
o *conj* or; **¿vienes o no?** are you coming or not?; **o ... o ...** either ... or ...; **o mañana o el jueves** either tomorrow or Thursday; [*between two digits* o *is written with an accent*: **unas 100 ó 120** about 100 or 120]; **o sea ▶** SER *vi* II
O. (= **oeste**) W, West
oasis *m* (*pl* ~) oasis
obcecarse [A2] *v pron* to become obsessed; **está obcecado con la idea** he's obsessed with the idea
obedecer [E3] *vt* (a) ⟨*orden/norma*⟩ to obey, comply with (b) ⟨*persona*⟩ to obey; **obedece a tu madre** do as your mother tells you
■ **~** *vi* (a) «*persona*» to obey; **para que aprendas a ~** to teach you to do as you're told (b) «*mecanismo*» to respond (c) (frml) (a un motivo, causa) **~ A algo** to be due TO sth
obediente *adj* obedient
obelisco *m* obelisk
obertura *f* overture
obesidad *f* obesity
obeso -sa *adj* obese
obispo *m* bishop
objeción *f* objection; **nadie puso objeciones** nobody objected *o* made any objection; **~ de conciencia** conscientious objection
objetar [A1] *vt* to object; **¿tienes algo que ~?** do you have any objection?
■ **~** *vi* (Esp fam) to declare oneself a conscientious objector
objetividad *f* objectivity; **con ~** objectively
objetivo¹ -va *adj* objective
objetivo² ** *m* **1 (finalidad) objective, aim; (Mil) objective **2** (Fot, Ópt) lens
objeto *m* **1** (cosa) object; **~s de valor** valuables; **~s de uso personal** items *o* articles for personal use; **~s perdidos** lost and found (AmE), lost property (BrE); **~ volador no identificado** unidentified flying object, UFO
2 (a) (finalidad) aim, object; **con el ~ de hacer**

algo in order to do sth, with the aim of doing sth; **con el ~ de que se conozcan** so that they can get to know each other; **ser ~ de algo** (de admiración/críticas) to be the object of sth; (de investigación/estudio) to be the subject of sth; **ser ~ de malos tratos** to be ill-treated (b) (Ling) object
objetor -tora *m,f* objector; **~ de conciencia** conscientious objector
oblicuo -cua *adj* ⟨*línea*⟩ oblique
obligación *f* (deber) obligation; **cumplió con sus obligaciones** he fulfilled his obligations; **tiene (la) ~ de ...** it is his duty to ..., he has an obligation to ...; **es mi ~ decírtelo** it is my duty to tell you; **lo hace por ~** she does it out of obligation; **si sus obligaciones se lo permiten** if her commitments permit
obligado -da *adj* [ESTAR] ⟨*persona*⟩ obliged; **~ A hacer algo** obliged to do sth; **se vio ~ a acompañarla** he felt obliged to accompany her
obligar [A3] *vt* (a) **~ a algn A hacer algo** to force sb to do sth, to make sb do sth; **no lo obligues a comer** don't force him to eat; **nos obligan a llevar uniforme** we are required to wear uniform; **~ a algn A QUE haga algo** to make sb do sth (b) «*ley/disposición*» to bind
obligatorio -ria *adj* compulsory, obligatory; **no es ~ firmarlo** it doesn't have to be signed
oboe *m* (instrumento) oboe
■ *mf* (músico) oboist
obra *f* **1** (creación artística) work; **sus primeras ~s** her earliest works; **una ~ de artesanía** a piece of craftsmanship; **sus ~s de teatro** her plays; **~ de arte** work of art; **~ maestra** masterpiece **2** (acción): **mi buena ~ del día** my good deed for the day; **~ benéfica** (acto) act of charity; (organización) charity, charitable organization **3** (Arquit, Const) (a) (construcción) building work; **estamos de ~s** we're having some building work done (b) (sitio) building *o* construction site
obrar [A1] *vi* (actuar) to act; **~ de buena fe** to act in good faith   ⋯·

■ ~ *vt* ‹*milagros*› to work

obrera *f* (hormiga) worker (ant); (abeja) worker (bee); *ver tb* OBRERO *m, f*

obrero -ra *adj* ‹*barrio*› working-class; **el movimiento ~** the workers' movement; **la clase obrera** the working class

■ *m,f* (de fábrica, industria) worker; **los ~s dejaron la arena en el jardín** the workmen left the sand in the garden

obsceno -na *adj* obscene

obscuro, etc ▶ OSCURO, ETC

obsequio *m* (frml) gift

observación *f* **1** (examen, vigilancia) observation; **tener a algn en ~** (Med) to keep sb under observation; **tener mucha capacidad de ~** to be very observant **2** (comentario) observation, remark; (en texto) note

observador -dora *m,f* observer

observar [A1] *vt* **(a)** (en general) to observe; **alguien la observaba** someone was watching *o* (frml) observing her **(b)** (notar) to observe (frml); **¿has observado algún cambio?** have you noticed *o* observed any changes?

observatorio *m* observatory

obsesión *f* obsession

obsesionar [A1] *vt* to obsess; **estaba obsesionado con la idea** he was obsessed with the idea

■ **obsesionarse** *v pron* to become obsessed

obsesivo -va *adj* obsessive

obsidiana *f* obsidian

obsoleto -ta *adj* obsolete

obstaculizar [A4] *vt* ‹*progreso/trabajo*› to hinder, hamper; ‹*tráfico*› to hold up; **no obstaculice el paso** don't stand in the way

obstáculo *m* obstacle

obstante: **no obstante** (sin embargo) nevertheless, nonetheless; (a pesar de) despite, in spite of

obstinado -da *adj* **(a)** (tozudo) obstinate, stubborn **(b)** (tenaz) tenacious, dogged

obstinarse [A1] *v pron* **~ EN hacer algo** to (obstinately) insist ON doing sth; **se obstinó en no ir** he obstinately refused to go; **se ha obstinado en que hay que terminarlo hoy** he is bent on finishing it today

obstrucción *f* obstruction

obstruir [I20] *vt* **1** (bloquear) ‹*conducto*› to block; ‹*salida*› to block, obstruct **2** (entorpecer) ‹*plan/proceso*› to obstruct; ‹*tráfico*› to obstruct, hold up; ‹*progreso*› to impede **3** (Dep) to obstruct

■ **obstruirse** *v pron* to get blocked (up)

obtener [E27] *vt* ‹*premio*› to win, receive; ‹*resultado/autorización*› to obtain; ‹*calificación*› to obtain, set

obturador *m* (Fot) shutter

obtuve, obtuvo, etc ▶ OBTENER

obvio -via *adj* obvious

oca *f* (Zool) goose

ocasión *f* **1** **(a)** (vez, circunstancia) occasion;

con ~ de on the occasion of; **en alguna ~** occasionally **(b)** (momento oportuno) opportunity; **no tuve ~ de hablarle** I didn't have an opportunity *o* a chance to talk to him **2** (ganga) bargain; **de ~** ‹*precios*› bargain (*before n*); ‹*muebles*› (usados) secondhand; (baratos) cut-rate *o* (BrE) cut-price; ‹*coches*› secondhand

ocasional *adj* ‹*encuentro*› chance (*before n*); ‹*trabajo*› temporary

ocasionar [A1] *vt* to cause

occidental *adj* ‹*zona*› western; ‹*cultura/países*› Western; **África O~** West Africa

■ *mf* westerner

occidentalizarse [A4] *v pron* to become westernized

occidente *m* west

Oceanía *f* Oceania

océano *m* ocean

ochenta *adj inv/pron/m* eighty; *para ejemplos ver* CINCUENTA

ocho *adj inv/pron/m* eight; *para ejemplos ver* CINCO

ochocientos -tas *adj/pron* eight hundred; *para ejemplos ver* QUINIENTOS

ocio *m* **(a)** (tiempo libre) spare time, leisure time **(b)** (inactividad, holgazanería) inactivity, idleness

ociosidad *f* inactivity, idleness

ocioso -sa *adj* (inactivo) idle

ocre *m* : **(de) color ~** ocher-colored*

oct. (= octubre) Oct

octavilla *f* pamphlet

octavo¹ -va *adj/pron* eighth; **la octava parte** an eighth; *para ejemplos ver* QUINTO

octavo² *m* eighth; **~s de final** *round before the quarter-finals*

octubre *m* October; *para ejemplos ver* ENERO

oculista *mf* ophthalmologist

ocultar [A1] *vt* (en general) to conceal, hide; ‹*persona*› to hide; **~le algo A algn** to conceal *o* hide sth FROM sb

■ **ocultarse** *v pron* ‹*persona*› to hide; (estar oculto) to hide, lie hidden **(c)** ‹*sol*› to disappear

ocultismo *m* occult, occultism

oculto -ta *adj* **(a)** [ESTAR] (escondido) hidden **(b)** [SER] (misterioso) ‹*razón/designio*› mysterious, secret

ocupación *f* (empleo) occupation; (actividad) activity

ocupado -da *adj* **(a)** (atareado) busy **(b)** ‹*línea telefónica*› busy, engaged (BrE); **¿este asiento está ~?** is this seat taken? **(c)** ‹*territorio*› occupied

ocupante *mf* occupant; **~ ilegal** squatter

ocupar [A1] *vt* **1** ‹*espacio/tiempo*› to take up; **me ocupó toda la mañana** it took up my whole morning; **¿en qué ocupas tu tiempo libre?** how do you spend your spare time? **2** ‹*persona*› **(a)** (situarse en) ‹*asiento*› to take; **volvió a ~ su asiento** she returned to her seat, she took her seat again; **ocupaban (todo) un lado**

de la sala they took up one (whole) side of the
room **(b)** (estar en) ‹*vivienda*› to live in, occupy;
‹*habitación*› to be in; ‹*asiento*› to be (sitting) in
(c) (en clasificación): **¿qué lugar ocupan en la liga?**
what position are they in the division? **(d)**
‹*cargo*› to hold, occupy (frml); ‹*vacante*› to fill
3 ‹*fábrica/territorio*› to occupy
4 (AmC, Chi, Méx) (usar) to use
■ **ocuparse** *v pron* ∼**se DE algo/algn** ‹*de tarea/
trabajo*› to take care OF sth; ‹*de problema/asunto*›
to deal WITH sth; **yo me ∼é de eso** I'll see to that;
∼**se DE algn** ‹*de niño/enfermo*› to take care OF sb,
to look after sb

ocurrencia *f* (comentario gracioso) witty *o* funny
remark, witticism; (idea disparatada) crazy idea

ocurrente *adj* (gracioso) witty; (ingenioso) clever

ocurrir [I1] *vi* (en *3ª pers*) to happen; **ocurra lo
que ocurra** whatever happens; **lo que ocurre es
que ...** the trouble is (that) ...; **lamento lo
ocurrido** I'm sorry about what happened
■ **ocurrirse** *v pron* (en *3ª pers*): **se me ha
ocurrido una idea** I've had an idea; **no se les
ocurría nada** they couldn't think of anything; **di
lo primero que se te ocurra** say the first thing
that comes into your head; **¿cómo se te ocurrió
comprarlo?** whatever made you buy it?

odiar [A1] *vt* to hate; **odio planchar** I hate
ironing

odio *m* hate, hatred; **tenerle ∼ a algn** to hate sb

odioso -sa *adj* ‹*trabajo/tema*› horrible, hateful;
‹*persona*› horrible, odious

oeste *adj inv* ‹*región*› western; **conducían en
dirección ∼** they were driving west *o*
westward(s); **la costa ∼** the west coast
■ *m* **1** **(a)** (parte, sector): **el ∼** the west; **en el ∼
de la provincia** in the west of the province; **al ∼
de Oaxaca** to the west of Oaxaca **(b)** (punto
cardinal) west, West; **vientos del O∼** westerly
winds; **caminaron hacia el O∼** they walked west
o westward(s) **2** **el Oeste** (de los Estados Unidos)
the West; **una película del O∼** a Western

ofender [E1] *vt* to offend
■ **ofenderse** *v pron* to take offense*

ofensa *f* (agravio) insult

ofensiva *f* offensive

ofensivo -va *adj* offensive

oferta *f* **1** **(a)** (proposición) offer **(b)** (Econ, Fin)
supply **2** (Com) offer; **están de** *or* **en ∼** they are
on special offer

oficial *adj* official
■ *mf* (de policía) police officer (*above the rank of
sergeant*); (Mil) officer

oficialismo *m* (AmL): **representantes del ∼**
representatives of the ruling *o* governing party

oficialista *adj* (AmL) ‹*candidato*› pro-government;
‹*candidato*› fielded by the party
in power

oficina *f* (despacho) office; **en horas de ∼** during
office hours; **∼ de empleo/turismo**
unemployment/tourist office

oficinista *mf* office worker

oficio *m* **1** (trabajo) trade; **carpintero de ∼**
carpenter by trade **2** (Der) **de ∼** court-appointed
(*before n*) **3** (Relig) service, office

ofimática *f* office automation

ofrecer [E3] *vt* **1** **(a)** ‹*ayuda/cigarrillo/empleo*›

to offer **(b)** ‹*dinero*› to offer; (en una subasta) to
bid **(c)** ‹*fiesta*› to give; ‹*recepción*› to lay on **(d)**
‹*sacrificio/víctima*› to offer (up)
2 **(a)** ‹*oportunidad/posibilidad*› to give, provide;
‹*dificultad*› to present **(b)** «*persona*»
‹*resistencia*› to put up, offer
■ **ofrecerse** *v pron* **1** «*persona*» to offer,
volunteer; ∼**se A** *or* **PARA hacer algo** to offer *o*
volunteer ᴛᴏ do sth
2 (frml) (querer, necesitar) (*gen neg o interrog*):
¿qué se le ofrece, señora? what would you like,
madam? (frml); **si no se le ofrece nada más** if
there's nothing else I can do for you

ofrecimiento *m* offer

ofrenda *f* offering

ofuscarse [A2] *v pron* to get worked up

OGM *m* (= **organismo genéticamente
modificado**) GMO

ogro *m* ogre

oídas: de ∼ (*loc adv*) **lo conozco de ∼** I've
heard of him, I know of him

oído *m* **(a)** (Anat) ear; **me lo susurró al ∼** she
whispered it in my ear **(b)** (sentido) hearing; (para
la música, los idiomas) ear; **es duro de ∼** he's hard
of hearing; **aguzar el ∼** to prick up one's ears; **no
tiene ∼** she's tone-deaf, she has no ear for music;
tocar de ∼ (Mús) to play by ear

oiga, oigas, etc ▶ oɪʀ

oír [I28] *vt* **1** (percibir sonidos) to hear; **no oigo
nada** I can't hear anything *o* a thing; **se oyeron
pasos** I (*or you etc*) heard footsteps; **he oído
hablar de él** I've heard of him **2** (escuchar)
‹*música/radio*› to listen to **3** **oír misa** to go to
mass **4** **oiga/oye** (para llamar la atención) excuse
me; **¡oiga! se le cayó la cartera** excuse me, you've
dropped your wallet; **oye, si ves a Gustavo dile
que me llame** listen, if you see Gustavo tell him
to call me
■ ∼ *vi* to hear

ojal *m* buttonhole

ojalá *interj*: **seguro que apruebas — ¡∼!** I'm
sure you'll pass — I hope so!; **¡∼ que todo salga
bien!** let's hope things turn out all right!; **∼
fuera rico!** if only I were rich!, I wish I was rich!

ojeada *f* glance; **echar una ∼ a algo** to have a
quick glance *o* look at sth

ojear [A1] *vt* to (have a) look at

ojeras *fpl* rings under the eyes (*pl*)

ojeriza *f* grudge; **tenerle ∼ a algn** to have a
grudge against sb

ojeroso -sa *adj*: **estar ∼** to have rings under
one's eyes

ojo *m* **1** **(a)** (en general) eye; **un niño de ∼s
negros** a boy with dark eyes; **mirar fijamente a
los ∼s** to stare straight into sb's eyes; **no me
quita los ∼s de encima** he won't take his eyes off
me; **a los ∼s de la sociedad** in the eyes of
society; **∼ de la cerradura** keyhole; **∼ de buey**
porthole; **∼ de vidrio** *or* (Esp) **cristal** glass eye; **∼
mágico** (AmL) spyhole, peephole; **∼ morado** *or*
(Méx) **moro** *or* (CS fam) **en tinta** black eye; *costar
un ∼ de la cara* (fam) to cost an arm and a leg
(colloq); *cuatro ∼s ven más que dos* two heads are
better than one; *en un abrir y cerrar de ∼s* in the
twinkling of an eye; *∼ por ∼* an eye for an eye
(b) (vista): **bajó los ∼s avergonzada** she lowered
her eyes in shame; **sin levantar los ∼s del libro** ···⟶

without looking up from her book; **a ~** (**de buen cubero**) or (AmS) **al ~** at a guess; **echar un ~ a algo/algn** (fam) to have o take a (quick) look at sth/sb; **tener ~ de lince** or **de águila** to have eyes like a hawk

2 (perspicacia): ¡**vaya ~ que tiene!** he's pretty sharp o on the ball!; **tener ~ para los negocios** to have a good eye for business

3 (fam) (cuidado, atención): **hay que andar** or **ir con mucho ~** you have to keep your eyes open; ¡**~!** **que viene un coche** watch out! o be careful! there's a car coming

ojota f (CS) (para playa, piscina) thong (AmE), flip-flop (BrE); (calzado rústico) sandal

okey interj (esp AmL) OK!, okay!

okupa mf (Esp fam) squatter

ola f wave; **~ de calor** heat wave; **~ de frío** cold spell

olán m (Méx) flounce, frill

olé, ole interj olé!, bravo!

oleada f wave

oleaje m swell

óleo m (sustancia) oil; (cuadro) oil painting; **pintura al ~** oil painting

oleoducto m (oil) pipeline

oler [E12] vi **1** (percibir olores) **~ A algo** to smell sth; ¿**no hueles a humo?** can't you smell smoke? **2** (despedir olores) «**comida/perfume**» to smell; ¡**qué bien/mal huele!** it smells good/awful!; **le huelen los pies** his feet smell; **~ A algo** ‹a rosas/ ajo› to smell OF sth **3** (fam) (expresando sospecha) (+ me/te/le etc): **esto me huele mal** it sounds fishy to me; **me huele que fue ella** I have a feeling it was her

■ **~** vt «**persona**» to smell; «**animal**» to sniff, smell

■ **olerse** v pron (fam) to suspect; **ya me lo olía** I thought so

olfatear [A1] vt **(a)** (oler con insistencia) to sniff **(b)** ‹rastro/presa› to scent, follow

olfato m (sentido) smell; (perspicacia, intuición) nose

oligarquía f oligarchy

olimpiada, olimpíada f: tb **~s** Olympic Games (pl), Olympics (pl)

olímpico -ca adj **(a)** ‹campeón/récord› Olympic (before n) **(b)** (AmL fam) ‹pase/gol› fantastic (colloq), sensational (colloq)

olisquear [A1] vt to sniff

oliva f olive

olivar m olive grove

olivo m olive (tree)

olla f pot; **~ a presión** pressure cooker

olmo m elm (tree)

olor m smell; **tiene un ~ raro** it has a funny smell; **tomarle el ~ a algo** (AmL) to smell sth; **~ A algo** smell OF sth

oloroso -sa adj **(a)** ‹jabón/flor› scented, fragrant **(b)** ‹queso/pies› smelly

olote m (AmC, Méx) cob, corncob

olvidadizo -za adj forgetful

olvidar [A1] vt **1** ‹pasado/nombre› to forget; **había olvidado que ...** I had forgotten that ...; **~ hacer algo** to forget to do sth **2** (dejar en un lugar) to forget, leave ... behind; **olvidó el pasaporte en casa** she left her passport at home

■ **olvidarse** v pron **1** (en general) to forget; **~se**

DE algo to forget sth; **~se DE hacer algo** to forget to do sth; (+ me/te/le etc) ¡**ah! se me olvidaba** ah! I almost forgot; **se me olvidó decírtelo** I forgot to tell you **2** (dejar en un lugar) to forget, leave ... behind

olvido m **(a)** (abandono, indiferencia) obscurity; **caer en el ~** to fall o sink into obscurity o oblivion **(b)** (descuido) oversight; **fue un ~** it was an oversight, I forgot

ombligo m navel, belly button (colloq)

omisión f omission

omitir [I1] vt ‹frase/nombre› to omit, leave out; **omitió mencionar que ...** he omitted o failed to mention that ...

ómnibus m (pl **~** or **-buses**) (autobús — urbano) (Per, Ur) bus; (— de larga distancia) (Arg) bus, coach (BrE)

omnipotente adj omnipotent

omoplato, omóplato m shoulder blade, scapula (tech)

once adj inv/pron/m eleven; para ejemplos ver CINCO

onces fpl (Andes) tea

onda f (en general) wave; **~ corta/larga** short/ long wave; **~ expansiva** blast, shock wave; **longitud de ~** wavelength; **agarrarle la ~ a algo** (AmL fam) to get the hang of sth (colloq); **estar en la ~** (fam) (a la moda) to be trendy (colloq); (al tanto) to be bang up to date (colloq); ¡**qué buena/mala ~!** (AmL fam) that's great/terrible! (colloq); ¿**qué ~?** (AmL fam) what's up? (colloq)

ondear [A1] vi «bandera» to fly

ondulado -da adj ‹pelo› wavy; ‹terreno› undulating, rolling

ondulante adj ‹movimiento› undulatory; ‹terreno› undulating, rolling

ondularse [A1] v pron to go wavy

onix m onyx

onomatopeya f onomatopoeia

onomatopéyico -ca adj onomatopoeic

ONU /'onu/ f (= Organización de las Naciones Unidas): **la ~** the UN, the United Nations

onza f **1** (peso) ounce **2** (de chocolate) square

opaco -ca adj (no transparente) opaque; (sin brillo) dull

ópalo m opal

opción f option; **no tenía ~** I had no option o choice; **con ~ a compra** with option to buy

opcional adj optional

open m open championship o tournament

ópera f (obra musical) opera; (edificio) opera house

operación f **(a)** (Mat) operation **(b)** (Med) operation; **una ~ a corazón abierto** open-heart surgery **(c)** (Fin) transaction **(d)** (misión) operation; **~ de rescate** rescue operation

operador -dora m,f **(a)** (Inf, Tec, Telec) operator **(b)** (Cin, TV) (de cámara) (m) cameraman; (f) camerawoman; (de proyección) projectionist **(c)** (Chi, Méx) (obrero) ▶ OPERARIO **(d)** **~ turístico** tour operator

operar [A1] vt **1** (Med) to operate on; **me van a ~ de la vesícula** I'm having a gallbladder operation; **lo ~on de apendicitis** he had his

appendix taken out **2** (fml) ⟨cambio/
transformación⟩ to produce, bring about **3** (Chi,
Méx) ⟨máquina⟩ to operate
■ ~ vi **(a)** (Med) to operate **(b)** (fml) «servicio/
vuelo» to operate
■ **operarse** v pron **1** (Med) (caus) to have an
operation; ~se **del corazón** to have a heart
operation **2** (fml) «cambio/transformación» to
take place
operario -ria m,f (fml) operator; **el ~ de la
máquina** the machine operator
opinar [A1] vi to express an opinion; **prefiero no
~ I** would prefer not to comment
■ ~ vt **(a)** (pensar) to think; **¿qué opinas del
aborto?** what do you think about abortion?; **¿qué
opinas de ella?** what do you think of her?; **no
opino lo mismo** I do not share that view o
opinion; **opino que debería renunciar** in my
opinion he should resign **(b)** (expresar un juicio):
opinó que deberían aplazarlo he expressed the
view that it should be postponed
opinión f opinion; **en mi ~** in my opinion;
cambió de ~ he changed his mind; **la ~ pública**
public opinion
opio m (Bot, Farm) opium
oponente mf opponent
oponer [E22] vt ⟨resistencia⟩ to offer, put up;
⟨objeción⟩ to raise
■ **oponerse** v pron (ser contrario) to object; ~se **a
algo** to oppose sth; **nuestros caracteres se oponen**
(recípr) we are opposites
oporto m (vino) port
oportunidad f **1** (momento oportuno, posibilidad)
chance, opportunity; **a la primera ~** at the
earliest opportunity; **tuve ~ (la) de conocerla** I
got to meet her; **igualdad de ~es** equal
opportunities **2** (AmL) (vez, circunstancia) occasion;
en aquella ~ that time o on that occasion
oportunismo m opportunism
oportunista mf opportunist
oportuno -na adj **(a)** ⟨visita/lluvia⟩ timely,
opportune; **llegó en el momento ~** he arrived at
just the right moment **(b)** ⟨medida/respuesta⟩
appropriate; **sería ~ avisarle** we ought to inform
her; **estuvo muy ~** what he said was very much
to the point
oposición f **1** (en general) opposition **2** (Esp,
Ven) (concurso) (public) competitive examination;
hacer oposiciones to take o (BrE) sit a
competitive examination
opresión f (de un pueblo) oppression; (en el
pecho) tightness
opresivo -va adj oppressive
oprimido -da adj ⟨pueblo⟩ oppressed
oprimir [I1] vt **(a)** (fml) (apretar, presionar) to
press **(b)** (tiranizar) to oppress
optar [A1] vi **1** (decidirse) ~ **POR algo** to choose
sth, opt **POR** sth; ~ **POR hacer algo** to choose o
opt to do sth **2** ~ **A algo** ⟨a plaza/puesto⟩ to
apply **FOR** sth
optativo -va adj optional
óptica f (Fís, Ópt) optics; (tienda) optician's
óptico -ca adj optical
■ m,f optician
optimismo m optimism
optimista adj optimistic

■ mf optimist
óptimo -ma adj ⟨posición⟩ ideal, optimum; **en
condiciones óptimas** ⟨persona⟩ in peak condition;
⟨coche⟩ in perfect condition; ⟨alimento⟩ fresh
opuesto -ta adj ⟨versiones/opiniones⟩
conflicting; ⟨extremo/polo/lado⟩ opposite; **tienen
caracteres ~s** they have very different
personalities; **venía en dirección opuesta** he was
coming from the opposite direction
opulento -ta adj opulent, affluent
oración f **(a)** (Relig) prayer **(b)** (Ling) sentence
orador -dora m,f speaker
oral adj oral
órale interj (Méx fam) (expresando acuerdo) right!,
OK!; (para animar) come on!
orangután m orangutan
orar [A1] vi (fml) (Relig) to pray
oratorio m (Relig) oratory, chapel; (Mús)
oratorio
órbita f **1** (Astron) orbit; **poner en ~** to put into
orbit **2** (Anat) (eye) socket, orbit (tech)
orca f killer whale
orden¹ f **1** (mandato) order; **deja de darme
órdenes** stop ordering me about; **hasta nueva ~**
until further notice; **estamos a la ~ para lo que
necesite** (AmL) just let us know if there's
anything we can do for you; **¡a la ~!** (Mil) yes,
sir!; (fórmula de cortesía) (Andes, Méx, Ven) you're
welcome, not at all; ~ **de arresto** or **de busca y
captura** arrest warrant; ~ **de registro** or (Chi, Méx)
de cateo search warrant; ~ **judicial** court order
2 (Fin) order; ~ **bancaria** banker's order **3** (Hist,
Mil, Relig) order **4** (AmL) (pedido) order
orden² m **1** (en general) order; **en** or **por ~
alfabético** in alphabetical order; **por ~ de
estatura** according to height; **vayamos por ~** let's
begin at the beginning; **poner algo en ~**
⟨habitación/armario/juguetes⟩ to straighten sth (up)
(esp AmE), to tidy sth up (esp BrE); ⟨asuntos/
papeles⟩ to sort sth up; ⟨fichas⟩ to put sth in
order; **mantener el ~ en la clase** to keep order in
the classroom; ~ **del día** agenda; ~ **público**
public order; **alterar el ~ público** to cause a
breach of the peace
2 (a) (fml) (carácter, índole) nature; **problemas de
~ económico** problems of an economic nature
(b) (cantidad): **del ~ de** (fml) on the order of
(AmE), in o of the order of (BrE)
ordenado -da adj **(a)** [ESTAR] (en orden) tidy
(b) [SER] ⟨persona⟩ (metódico) organized, orderly;
(para la limpieza) tidy
ordenador m (Esp) ▶ COMPUTADORA
ordenanza m (en oficinas) porter; (Mil) orderly,
batman (BrE)
ordenar [A1] vt **1** ⟨habitación/armario/
juguetes⟩ to straighten (up) (esp AmE), to tidy (up)
(BrE); ⟨fichas⟩ to put in order; **ordené los libros
por materias** I arranged the books according to
subject **2 (a)** (dar una orden) to order; **le ordenó
salir de la oficina** she ordered him to leave the
office **(b)** (AmL) (pedir) ⟨taxi/bebida/postre⟩ to
order **3** ⟨sacerdote⟩ to ordain
■ **ordenarse** v pron to be ordained
ordeñar [A1] vt to milk
ordinal m ordinal (number)
ordinariez f **(a)** (falta de refinamiento) vulgarity; ⋯✧

(grosería) rudeness, bad manners (*pl*); (en la manera de hablar) vulgarity, coarseness **(b)** (comentario — poco refinado) vulgar comment; (— grosero) rude comment

ordinario -ria *adj* **1** (poco refinado) vulgar, common (*pej*); (grosero) rude, bad-mannered; (en el hablar) vulgar, coarse **2** (de mala calidad) poor *o* bad quality **3** (no especial) ordinary; **correo ~** regular (AmE) *o* (BrE) normal delivery **4 de ordinario** usually, normally; **hay menos gente que de ~** there are fewer people than usual *o* normal
■ *m,f* (persona — poco refinada) vulgar *o* (*pej*) common person; (— grosera) rude *o* bad-mannered person

orégano *m* oregano

oreja *f* (Anat) ear; **el perro puso las ~s tiesas** the dog pricked up its ears; **tirarle a algn de las ~s** *or* (AmL) **tirarle las ~s a algn** to pull sb's ears
■ *mf* (Méx *fam*) (soplón — de la policía) stool pigeon (*colloq*), grass (BrE *colloq*); (que escucha a escondidas) eavesdropper

orfanato, (Méx) **orfanatorio** *m* orphanage

orfelinato *m* orphanage

orgánico -ca *adj* organic

organismo *m* (Biol) organism; (Adm, Pol) organization

organización *f* organization

organizado -da *adj* organized

organizador -dora *m,f* organizer

organizar [A4] *vt* to organize, arrange
■ **organizarse** *v pron* to organize oneself

órgano *m* organ

orgasmo *m* orgasm

orgía *f* orgy

orgullo *m* pride; **con ~** proudly

orgulloso -sa *adj* **(a)** [ESTAR] (satisfecho) proud; **~ DE algn/algo** proud OF sb/sth **(b)** [SER] (soberbio) proud

orientación *f* **(a)** (de habitación, edificio) aspect (*frml*); **¿cuál es la ~ de la casa?** which way does the house face?; **la ~ de la antena** the way the antenna (AmE) *o* (BrE) aerial is pointing **(b)** (enfoque, dirección) orientation **(c)** (guía) guidance, direction; (acción de guiar) orientation; **~ profesional** (para estudiantes) vocational guidance, careers advice; (para desempleados) career guidance *o* advice **(d)** (en un lugar) bearings (*pl*)

oriental *adj* (del este) eastern; (del Lejano Oriente) oriental; (uruguayo) (AmL) Uruguayan
■ *mf* (del Lejano Oriente) oriental; (uruguayo) (AmL) Uruguayan

orientar [A1] *vt* **1 (a)** ⟨reflector/antena⟩ to position; **la casa está orientada al sur** the house faces south (*frml*) **(b)** (Náut) ⟨velas⟩ to trim **2** (encaminar) ⟨esfuerzos/política⟩ to direct **3** ⟨persona⟩ **(a)** ⟨faro/estrellas⟩ to guide **(b)** (aconsejar) to advise; (mostrar el camino): **una mujer nos orientó** a woman told us the way
■ **orientarse** *v pron* (ubicarse) to get one's bearings, orient oneself; **~se por las estrellas** (Náut) to steer by the stars

oriente *m* (punto cardinal) east; (viento) east wind; **O~ Medio/Próximo** Middle/Near East

orificio *m* (*frml*) (de bala) hole; **los ~s de la nariz** the nostrils

origen *m* origin; **en su ~** originally, in the beginning; **dar ~ a algo** to give rise to sth; **país de ~** country of origin; **de ~ humilde** of humble origin(s)

original *adj/m* original

originalidad *f* (cualidad) originality; (comentario) clever remark

originar [A1] *vt* to start, give rise to
■ **originarse** *v pron* ⟨idea/costumbre⟩ to originate; «*movimiento*» to start, come into being, originate; «*incendio/disputa*» to start

originario -ria *adj* (de un lugar) native; **ser ~ de algo** ⟨*persona*⟩ to come from sth; «*especie*» to be native to sth

orilla *f* **(a)** (del mar, de lago) shore; (de río) bank; **viven a la ~ del mar** they live by the sea; **un paseo a la ~ del mar** a walk along the seashore **(b)** (de mesa, plato) edge **(c)** (dobladillo) hem

orillar [A1] *vt* **1 (a)** ⟨muro/costa/zona⟩ to skirt (around) **(b)** (Col, Méx, Ven) (hacer a un lado): **orilló el coche** he pulled over **2** (Méx) (obligar) **~ a algn A algo** to drive sb TO sth
■ **orillarse** *v pron* (Col, Méx, Ven) to move over

orina *f* urine

orinal *m* (de dormitorio) chamber pot; (para niños) pot, potty (*colloq*); (para enfermos) bedpan

orinar [A1] *vi* to urinate
■ *~ vt*: **~ sangre** to pass blood
■ **orinarse** *v pron* to wet oneself; **se orina en la cama** he wets the bed

Orinoco *m*: **el (río) ~** the Orinoco (River)

oriundo -da *adj* ▶ ORIGINARIO

ornamentación *f* ornamentation

oro *adj inv* gold
■ *m* **1** (metal) gold; **~ (de) 18 quilates** 18-carat gold; **bañado en ~** gold-plated; **~ negro** black gold; **ni por todo el ~ del mundo** not for all the tea in China (*colloq*) **2** (en naipes) **(a)** (carta) *any card of the* OROS *suit* **(b) oros** *mpl* (palo) *one of the suits in a Spanish pack of cards*

orquesta *f* orchestra; **~ de jazz** jazz band

orquídea *f* orchid

ortiga *f* (stinging) nettle

ortodoxo -xa *adj* orthodox

ortografía *f* spelling, orthography (*frml*)

ortopédico -ca *adj* orthopedic*; ⟨pierna⟩ artificial

oruga *f* (Zool) caterpillar; (Auto) caterpillar *o* crawler track

orzuela *f* (Méx): **tengo ~** I've got split ends

orzuelo *m* sty*

os *pron pers* (Esp) **(a)** (complemento directo, indirecto) you; **~ veo mañana** I'll see you tomorrow; **~ lo prometió** she promised it to you **(b)** (*refl*)

---

yourselves; **no ~ engañéis** don't kid yourselves **(c)** (*recípr*): **creía que ~ conocíais** I thought you knew each other

osar [A1] *vi* (liter) **~ + INF** to dare to + INF; **no osó decirles la verdad** he dared not tell them the truth (liter)

oscar /'oskar/ *m* (*pl* **~** *or* **-cars**) Oscar

oscilación *f* (movimiento) oscillation; (fluctuación) fluctuation

oscilar [A1] *vi* 1 «*péndulo*» to swing, oscillate (tech); «*aguja*» to oscillate; «*torre/ columna*» to sway 2 (fluctuar) «*cotización/ valores*» to fluctuate; **sus edades oscilaban entre** … their ages ranged between …

oscuras: a ~ (*loc adv*) in darkness

oscurecer [E3] *v impers* to get dark
■ ~ *vt* ⟨*habitación/color*⟩ to darken, make … darker
■ **oscurecerse** *v pron* to get darker

oscuridad *f* (de la noche, de lugar) darkness, dark; **¡qué ~!** it's so dark in here!

oscuro -ra *adj* 1 **(a)** ⟨*calle/habitación*⟩ dark; **a las seis ya está ~** at six it's already dark **(b)** ⟨*color/ojos/pelo*⟩ dark; **vestía de ~** she was wearing dark clothes 2 **(a)** (dudoso) ⟨*intenciones*⟩ dark; ⟨*asunto*⟩ dubious **(b)** (poco claro) ⟨*significado/asunto*⟩ obscure **(c)** (poco conocido) ⟨*escritor/orígenes*⟩ obscure

oso, osa *m,f* bear; **~ de felpa** *or* **peluche** teddy bear; **~ hormiguero** anteater, ant bear (AmE); **~ panda** panda; **~ polar** polar bear

ostensible *adj* obvious, evident

ostentación *f* ostentation

ostentar [A1] *vt* 1 (frml) (tener) ⟨*cargo/título*⟩ to hold 2 (exhibir) ⟨*alhajas/dinero*⟩ to flaunt
■ ~ *vi* to show off

ostentoso -sa *adj* ostentatious

ostión *m* **(a)** (CS) scallop **(b)** (Méx) oyster

ostra *f* oyster; **aburrirse como una ~** (fam) to get bored stiff *o* to death (colloq)

ostracismo *m* ostracism

OTAN /'otan/ *f* (= **Organización del Tratado del Atlántico Norte**) NATO

otitis *f* inflammation of the ear, otitis (tech)

otoñal *adj* ⟨*colores/paisaje*⟩ autumnal, fall (*before n*) (AmE), autumn (*before n*) (BrE)

otoño *m* fall (AmE), autumn (BrE); **en ~** in the fall, in (the) autumn

otorgar [A3] *vt* (frml) ⟨*premio*⟩ to award; ⟨*favor/ préstamo*⟩ to grant; ⟨*poderes*⟩ to bestow (frml), to give

otro, otra *adj* 1 (con carácter adicional) (*sing*) another; (*pl*) other; (con numerales) another;

¿puedo comer ~ trozo? can I have another piece?; **prueba otra vez** try again; **una y otra vez** time and time again; ▶ TANTO² *pron* 2
2 (diferente) (*sing*) another; (*pl*) other; **otra manera de hacerlo** another way of doing it; **¿no sabes ninguna otra canción?** don't you know any other songs?; **en ~ sitio** somewhere else; **en ~ momento** some other time
3 (estableciendo un contraste) other; **queda del ~ lado de la calle** it's on the other side of the street
4 (siguiente, contiguo) next; *ver tb* DÍA
■ *pron* 1 (con carácter adicional) (*sing*) another (one); **¿quieres ~?** would you like another (one)?
2 (diferente): **parece otra** she looks like a different person; **no voy a aceptar ningún ~** I won't accept any other; **lo cambié por ~** I changed it for another one; **¿no tiene ~s?** have you any other ones?; **~s piensan que no es así** others feel that this is not so
3 (estableciendo un contraste): **los ~s no están listos** (hablando — de personas) the others aren't ready; (— de cosas) the others *o* the other ones aren't ready
4 (siguiente, contiguo): **la semana que viene no, la otra** not next week, the week after; **uno detrás del ~** one after the other

ovación *f* (frml) ovation

ovalado -da *adj* oval

óvalo *m* oval

ovario *m* ovary

oveja *f* (nombre genérico) sheep; (hembra) ewe; **un rebaño de ~s** a flock of sheep; **la ~ negra** the black sheep; **la ~ descarriada** (Bib) the lost sheep

overol *m* (AmL) (pantalón con peto) overalls (*pl*) (AmE), dungarees (*pl*) (BrE); (con mangas) coveralls (*pl*) (AmE), overalls (*pl*) (BrE)

ovillo *m* ball (*of yarn*); **hacerse un ~** to curl up (in a ball)

ovni, OVNI /'oβni/ *m* (= **objeto volador** *or* **volante no identificado**) UFO

ovulación *f* ovulation

ovular [A1] *vi* to ovulate

óvulo *m* (Biol) ovule; (Farm) pessary

oxidado -da *adj* rusty

oxidarse [A1] *v pron* «*hierro*» to rust, go rusty, oxidize (tech); «*cobre*» to oxidize, form a patina

óxido *m* (herrumbre) rust; (Quím) oxide

oxígeno *m* oxygen

oye, etc ▶ OÍR

oyente *mf* **(a)** (Educ) occasional student, auditor (AmE) **(b)** (Rad) listener

oyera, oyese, etc ▶ OÍR

ozono *m* ozone; **la capa de ~** the ozone layer

Pp

P, p *f* (*read as* /pe/) *the letter* P, p

pabellón *m* 1 **(a)** (en hospital, cuartel) block,

building; (en feria, exposición) pavilion; (de palacio) pavilion; (en jardín) summerhouse **(b)** (de instrumento de viento) bell 2 (frml) (bandera) flag

paceño -ña *adj* of/from La Paz
■ *m,f* person from La Paz

pacer [E3] *vi* to graze

pacha *f* (AmC) baby's bottle

pachanga *f* (esp AmL fam) ▶ JARANA

pachanguero -ra *adj* (esp AmL fam) ▶ JARANERO

pachón -chona *adj* (Méx) ⟨suéter⟩ chunky; ⟨perro⟩ wooly*

pachucho -cha *adj* [ESTAR] (Esp fam) ⟨persona⟩ poorly (colloq); ⟨fruta⟩ overripe

pachuco -ca *m,f* (Méx) young Mexican influenced by US culture

paciencia *f* patience; perder la ∼ to lose patience; ten ∼ be patient, have a little patience

paciente *adj* ⟨tolerante⟩ patient
■ *mf* patient

pacificador -dora *adj* peace (before n)
■ *m,f* peacemaker

pacificar [A2] *vt* (Mil) to pacify (frml); (calmar) to pacify, appease; ∼ los ánimos to calm people down

pacífico -ca *adj* (a) ⟨manifestación/medios⟩ peaceful, pacific (frml) (b) ⟨carácter/persona⟩ peace-loving, peaceable; ⟨animal⟩ peaceful

Pacífico *m*: el (océano) ∼ the Pacific (Ocean)

pacifista *adj/mf* pacifist

paco -ca *m,f* (Andes fam) cop (colloq)

pacotilla *f* trash; de ∼ ⟨escritor/novela⟩ second-rate; ⟨reloj⟩ cheap, shoddy

pactar [A1] *vt* ⟨paz/tregua⟩ to negotiate, agree terms for; ⟨plazo/indemnización⟩ to agree on
■ ∼ *vi* to make a pact, negotiate an agreement

pacto *m* pact, agreement; cumplir/romper un ∼ to abide by the terms of/to break an agreement; P∼ de Varsovia Warsaw Pact

padecer [E3] *vt* ⟨enfermedad/hambre⟩ to suffer from; ⟨desgracias/injusticias/privaciones⟩ to suffer, undergo
■ ∼ *vi* to suffer; ∼ DE algo to suffer FROM sth; padece del corazón he has heart trouble

padrastro *m* [1] (pariente) stepfather [2] (Anat) hangnail

padre *m* [1] (pariente) father; mis ∼s my parents; ∼ de familia father, family man [2] (Relig) (sacerdote) father
■ *adj* (a) (Méx) (grande) terrible (colloq) (b) [ESTAR] (Méx fam) ⟨coche/persona⟩ great (colloq), fantastic

padrenuestro *m* Lord's Prayer

padrino *m*

■ **Nota** En inglés *godfather* no se usa como apelativo.Nótese también que cuando el plural *padrinos* se refiere al padrino y a la madrina se traduce por *godparents*.

(a) (en bautizo) godfather; (de boda) *man who gives away the bride, usually her father* (b) (en duelo) second (c) (protector) sponsor, patron

padrón *m* (a) (Gob, Pol) register; ∼ electoral (AmL) electoral roll o register (b) (Chi) (Auto) registration documents (*pl*)

paella *f* paella

pág. *f* (= página) p.; **760 págs.** 760 pp.

paga *f* (a) (acción de pagar) payment (b) (sueldo)

pay; ∼ de Navidad *extra month's salary paid at Christmas*; ∼ extra *or* extraordinaria *extra month's salary gen paid twice a year*

paganismo *m* paganism

pagano -na *adj/m,f* pagan; (pey) heathen

pagar [A3] *vt* (a) (abonar) ⟨cuenta/alquiler⟩ to pay; ⟨deuda⟩ to pay (off), repay; ⟨comida/entradas/mercancías⟩ to pay for; ¿cuánto pagas de alquiler? how much rent do you pay?; le pagan los estudios they are paying for his education; no puedo ∼ tanto I can't afford (to pay) that much; ∼ algo POR algo to pay sth FOR sth (b) ⟨favor/desvelos⟩ to repay (c) (expiar) ⟨delito/atrevimiento⟩ to pay for; ∼ algo CON algo to pay FOR sth WITH sth; ¡me las vas a ∼! you'll pay for this!
■ ∼ *vi* (Com, Fin) to pay; ∼le a algn to pay sb

pagaré *m* promissory note, IOU

página *f* page; ∼s amarillas yellow pages; ∼ web (Inf) Web page; ∼ inicial *or* frontal *or* principal (Inf) home page

pago *m* (a) (Com, Fin) payment; ∼ adelantado *or* anticipado payment in advance; ∼ inicial down payment; ∼ al contado/a plazos/en especie payment in cash/by installments/in kind (b) (recompensa) reward; en ∼ a algo as a reward for sth

pagoda *f* pagoda

pai *m* (AmC, Méx) pie

país *m* (a) (unidad política) country; ∼ de origen (de persona) home country, native land; (de producto) country of origin; los P∼es Bajos the Netherlands; el P∼ de Gales Wales; el P∼ Vasco the Basque Country (b) (ciudadanos) nation (c) (en ficción) land

paisaje *m* (a) (panorama) landscape, scenery (b) (Art) landscape

paisanaje *m* civilians (*pl*); civil population

paisano -na *m,f* [1] (a) (compatriota) (*m*) fellow countryman, compatriot; (*f*) fellow countrywoman, compatriot (b) (de la misma zona, ciudad): es un ∼ mío he's from the same area/place as I am [2] (Indum): vestir de ∼ «soldado» to wear civilian clothes *o* (colloq) civvies; «policía» to be in/to wear plain clothes; «sacerdote» to be in/to wear secular dress [3] (a) (Per) mountain-dweller of Indian origin (b) (RPI) peasant

paja *f* [1] (a) (Agr, Bot) straw; sombrero de ∼ straw hat; techo de ∼ thatched roof (b) (para beber) (drinking) straw [2] (a) (fam) (en texto, discurso) padding, waffle (BrE colloq) (b) (Col fam): hablar *or* echar ∼ (decir mentiras) to tell lies; (charlar) to chat, gab (colloq) [3] (AmC) (grifo) faucet (AmE), tap (BrE)

pajar *m* (granero) barn; (desván) hayloft

pajarita *f* (a) *tb* ∼ de papel origami bird (b) (Esp) (Indum) bow tie

pajarito *m* (cría) baby bird; (pájaro) (fam) little bird, birdie (colloq)

pájaro *m* [1] (Zool) bird; ∼ carpintero woodpecker; más vale ∼ en mano que cien *or* ciento volando a bird in the hand is worth two in the bush [2] (fam) (granuja) nasty piece of work (colloq)

pajarraco *m* (fam) (a) (Zool) big, ugly bird (b) (granuja) rogue

paje *m* (a) (Hist) page (b) (en boda) page (boy)

pajita, pajilla *f* (drinking) straw

pajizo -za *adj* straw-colored*

pajuerano -na *m,f* (RPl fam) country bumpkin, hick (AmE colloq)

Pakistán *m* Pakistan

pakistaní *adj/mf* Pakistani

pala *f* ⟦1⟧ (para cavar, de niño) spade; (para mover arena, carbón) shovel; (para recoger la basura) dustpan ⟦2⟧ (Coc) (para servir — pescado) slotted spatula (AmE), fish slice (BrE); (— tarta) cake slice ⟦3⟧ (de remo, hélice) blade; (de frontenis) racket; (de ping-pong) paddle, bat (BrE); (en piragüismo) paddle

palabra *f* ⟦1⟧ (vocablo) word; **una ~ de seis letras** a six-letter word; **no son más que ~s** it's all talk; **en pocas ~s, es un cobarde** in a word, he's a coward; **~ por ~** word for word; **yo no sabía ni una ~ del asunto** I didn't know a thing o anything about it; **no entendí (ni) una ~** I didn't understand a (single) word; **sin decir (una) ~** without a word; **~ compuesta** compound word; **tener la última ~** to have the final say ⟦2⟧ (promesa) word; **~ de honor** word of honor*; **una mujer de ~** a woman of her word; **cumplió con su ~** she kept her word; **nunca falta a su ~** he never breaks o goes back on his word ⟦3⟧ (a) (habla) speech; **el don de la ~** the gift of speech; **un acuerdo de ~** a verbal agreement; **no me dirigió la ~** she didn't speak to me; **dejar a algn con la ~ en la boca** to cut sb off in mid-sentence (b) (frml) (en ceremonia, asamblea): **pedir la ~** to ask for permission to speak; **tener/tomar la ~** to have/to take the floor (frml)

palabrería *f*, **palabrerío** *m* talk; **no dice más que ~s** he's full of hot air (colloq)

palabrota *f* (fam) swearword; **decir ~s** to swear

palacio *m* (a) (residencia) palace; **el personal de ~** the Royal Household; **P~ Episcopal** Bishop's Palace; **P~ Real** Royal Palace (b) (edificio público) *large public building*; **P~ de Justicia** lawcourts (*pl*)

paladar *m* palate

paladear [A1] *vt* to savor*

palanca *f* ⟦1⟧ (en general) lever; (para forzar, abrir algo) crowbar; **lo levanté haciendo ~** I lifted it using a lever; **~ de cambios** gearshift (AmE), gear lever o stick (BrE); **~ de mando** joystick ⟦2⟧ (AmL fam) (influencia) influence; (persona influyente) contact

palangana *f* (a) (para fregar) bowl (b) (jofaina) washbowl (AmE), washbasin (BrE)

palanquear [A1] *vt* ⟦1⟧ (AmL) ▶ APALANCAR ⟦2⟧ (AmL fam) (usando influencias): **le ~on un puesto** they pulled some strings to get him a job (colloq) ■ ~ *vi* (AmL fam) to pull strings (colloq)

palapa *f* (Méx) palm shelter

palco *m* box

palenque *m* ⟦1⟧ (RPl) (poste) tethering post ⟦2⟧ (Méx) (a) (fiesta popular) festival (*with cockfights, music, etc*) (b) (para gallos) cockpit

Palestina *f* Palestine

palestino -na *adj/m,f* Palestinian

paleta *f* ⟦1⟧ (a) (de pintor) palette; (de cocina) spatula; (de ventilador) blade; (de albañil) trowel (b) (Dep) (de ping-pong) paddle, bat (BrE); (Jueg) (AmL) beach tennis ⟦2⟧ (fam) (diente) front tooth ⟦3⟧ (Coc)

shoulder; (Anat, Zool) (Andes) shoulder blade ⟦4⟧ (a) (Andes, Méx) (helado) Popsicle® (AmE), ice lolly (BrE) (b) (Méx) (dulce) lollipop

paletilla *f* (a) (Anat, Zool) shoulder blade (b) (Coc) shoulder

paleto -ta *m,f* (Esp fam & pey) country bumpkin, hick (AmE colloq & pej)

paliacate *m* (Méx) brightly colored* scarf

palidecer [E3] *vi* ⟪*persona*⟫ to turn o go pale

palidez *f* paleness

pálido -da *adj* ⟪*persona/luz/color*⟫ pale; **estás ~** you're very pale; **se puso ~** he went pale

paliducho -cha *adj* (fam) pale, peaky (colloq)

palillo *m* (a) (mondadientes) *tb* **~ de dientes** toothpick (b) (para comida oriental) chopstick; (de tambor) drumstick; (para tejer) (Chi) knitting needle (c) (fam) (persona flaca): **es un ~** he's as thin as a rake

palio *m* (a) (dosel) canopy (b) (prenda) pallium

paliza *f* ⟦1⟧ (a) (zurra) hiding, beating; **su padre le dio una buena ~** his father gave him a good hiding; **los matones le pegaron una ~** the thugs beat him up (b) (fam) (derrota) thrashing (colloq) ⟦2⟧ (fam) (a) (esfuerzo): **fue una ~ de viaje** the journey was a real killer; **darse la ~** (fam) (trabajando, estudiando) to work one's butt off (AmE colloq), to slog one's guts out (BrE colloq) (b) (aburrimiento) drag (colloq)

palizada *f* (valla) palisade; (terreno) fenced enclosure

pallar *m* (Per) (Bot, Coc) butter bean

palma *f* ⟦1⟧ (de la mano) palm; *conocer algo como la ~ de la mano* to know sth like the back of one's hand ⟦2⟧ (a) (Bot) (planta) palm; (hoja) palm leaf; **~ de coco** (Col) coconut palm (b) (gloria, triunfo) distinction ⟦3⟧ **palmas** *fpl* (a) (aplaudir) to clap (one's hands), applaud; **tocar las ~s** (marcando el ritmo) to clap in time

palmada *f* (a) (golpecito amistoso) pat; **le dio una ~ en la espalda** he gave him a pat on the back; **me dio unas palmaditas en la mejilla** he patted me on the cheek (b) (para llamar la atención) clap; **dio unas ~s para pedir silencio** he clapped his hands for silence (c) (AmL) (golpe, azote) smack, slap

palmado *adj* (a) (AmC fam) (sin dinero) broke (colloq) (b) (Arg fam) (cansado) worn out (colloq)

palmatoria *f* candlestick

palmera *f* (a) (Bot) palm tree (b) (Coc) palmier

palmito *m* (planta) European fan palm; (tallo) palm heart

palmo *m* span, handspan; **casi un ~** several inches; *conocer algo ~ a ~* to know sth like the back of one's hand

palo *m* ⟦1⟧ (a) (trozo de madera) stick; (de valla, portería) post; (de herramienta) handle; (de tienda, carpa) tent pole; **~ de escoba** broomstick, broomhandle; *de tal ~, tal astilla* a chip off the old block, like father like son (o like mother like daughter *etc*) (b) (AmC, Col fam) (árbol) tree (c) (Dep) (de golf) (golf) club; (de hockey) hockey stick (d) (Náut) mast; **~ mayor** mainmast ⟦2⟧ (madera) wood; **cuchara de ~** wooden spoon ⟦3⟧ (fam) (golpe) blow (with a stick); **lo molieron a ~s** they beat him till he was black and blue ⟦4⟧ (en naipes) suit

paloma *f* (Zool) pigeon; (blanca) dove; (como ⋯⋗

símbolo) dove; ~ **de la paz** dove of peace; ~
mensajera carrier pigeon; ~ **torcaz** *or* **torcaza**
ringdove, wood pigeon (BrE)
palomar *m* dovecot, pigeon loft
palomilla *f* 1 (mariposa nocturna) moth; (crisálida)
chrysalis 2 (tuerca) wing nut, butterfly nut;
(soporte) wall bracket 3 (Méx fam) (pandilla, grupo)
gang
■ *mf* (Andes fam) (muchacho — callejero) street kid
(colloq); (— travieso) little monkey (colloq), little
devil (colloq)
palomita *f* 1 (Méx fam) (marca) check (AmE),
tick (BrE) 2 **palomitas** *fpl: tb* ~**s de maíz**
popcorn
palomo *m* (ave) cock pigeon
palote *m* 1 (en caligrafía) line, stroke 2 (RPl)
(de amasar) rolling pin
palpable *adj* (claro, evidente) palpable (frml),
obvious; (al tacto) palpable, tangible
palpar [A1] *vt* (Med) to palpate; (tantear) to touch,
feel
■ **palparse** *v pron* ‹bolsillo› to feel
palpitación *f* palpitation
palpitar [A1] *vi* (a) ‹corazón› to beat (b)
‹vena/sien› to throb
pálpito *m* (AmS fam) feeling (colloq); **me dio el** *or*
tuve un ~ I had a feeling *o* a hunch
palta *f* (Bol, CS, Per) (Bot, Coc) avocado (pear)
palto *m* (Bol, CS, Per) avocado tree
paludismo *m* malaria
palurdo -da *m,f* (fam) yokel (pej & hum), hick
(AmE colloq & pej)
pamela *f* picture hat
pampa *f* pampa, pampas (*pl*); **la** ~ **argentina**
the Argentinian Pampas; **la** ~ **salitrera** *region of
nitrate deposits in northern Chile*
pampeano -na *adj* pampas (*before n*)
pamplinas *fpl* (fam) (a) (zalamerías) sweet talk
(colloq); **no me vengas con** ~ don't try to
sweet-talk me (colloq) (b) (tonterías) nonsense
pan *m* (Coc) bread; (pieza) loaf; (panecillo) roll;
¿**quieres** ~? would you like some bread?; **una
rebanada de** ~ a slice of bread; ~ **blanco/de
centeno/integral** white/rye/whole wheat bread; ~
de molde *bread/loaf baked gen in a rectangular
tin*, tin *o* pan loaf (BrE); ~ **de Pascua** (Chi)
panettone; ~ **dulce** (con pasas) (RPl) panettone;
(bollo) (AmC, Méx) bun, pastry; ~ **rallado**
breadcrumbs (*pl*); ~ **tostado** toast; **un** ~ **tostado**
(Chi, Méx) a piece of toast; **ganarse el** ~ to earn
one's daily bread; **ser** ~ **comido** (fam) to be a
piece of cake (colloq)
pana1 *f* 1 (tela) corduroy; **panatalones de** ~
corduroy trousers 2 (Chi) (avería) breakdown
pana2 *mf* (Ven fam) pal (Colloq), buddy (AmE
colloq), mate (BrE colloq)
panacea *f* panacea
panadería *f* (tienda) bakery, baker's (shop);
(fábrica) bakery
panadero -ra *m,f* baker

panal *m* honeycomb
panamá *m* panama hat
Panamá *m* (a) (país) Panama; **el Canal de** ~
the Panama Canal (b) (capital) *tb* **ciudad de** ~
Panama (City)
panameño -ña *adj/m,f* Panamanian
Panamericana *f*: **la** ~ the Pan-American
Highway
pancarta *f* banner, placard
panceta *f* (a) (Esp) (sin curar) belly pork (b)
(RPl) (curada) streaky bacon
pancho1 -cha *adj* (tranquilo) calm; **quedarse tan**
~ (fam): **se lo dije y se quedó tan** ~ he didn't bat
an eyelash *o* (BrE) eyelid when I told him
pancho2 *m* (RPl) hot dog
pancito *m* (AmL) (bread) roll
páncreas *m* (*pl* ~) pancreas
panda *mf* panda
■ *f* (Esp fam) gang
pandemónium *m* pandemonium
pandereta *f* (Mús) tambourine
pandero *m* 1 (Mús) tambourine 2 (Per) (Fin)
cooperative savings scheme
pandilla *f* (fam) gang
panecillo *m* (Esp) bread roll
panecito *m* (AmL) bread roll
panel *m* 1 (a) (de puerta, pared) panel (b) (tablero
— de anuncios) noticeboard; (— en exposición)
exhibition panel; (— en estación) arrivals/
departures board (c) (Chi) (de auto) dashboard (d)
~ **de instrumentos** instrument panel *o* console
2 (de personas) panel
panela *f* (Col, Ven) *brown sugarloaf*
panera *f* (para servir pan) bread basket; (para
guardar pan) bread box (AmE), bread bin (BrE)
pánfilo -la *adj* (fam) dimwitted (colloq)
■ *m,f* (fam) dimwit (colloq)
panfleto *m* pamphlet
pánico *m* panic; **tenerle** ~ **a algo** to be terrified
of sth; **sembrar el** ~ to spread panic
panocha *f* 1 (de maíz, trigo) ear 2 (Méx)
(melaza) *candy made from molasses*
panorama *m* (a) (vista, paisaje) view, panorama
(b) (perspectiva) outlook, prospect
panorámica *f* (Cin, TV) pan; (perspectiva)
outlook
panorámico -ca *adj* panoramic
panque *m* (Méx) sponge cake
panqueque *m* (AmL) pancake, crepe
pantaletas *fpl* (AmC, Ven) panties (*pl*),
knickers (*pl*) (BrE)
pantalla *f* 1 (Cin, Inf, TV) screen; ~ **de radar**
radar screen; **la** ~ **chica** (AmL) the small screen
2 (a) (de lámpara) shade (b) (de chimenea)
fireguard (c) (cobertura) front
pantalones *mpl*, **pantalón** *m* pants (*pl*)
(AmE), trousers (*pl*) (BrE); **unos** ~ a pair of pants

o trousers; ∼ **cortos** shorts (*pl*); ∼ **de peto** overalls (*pl*) (AmE), dungarees (*pl*) (BrE); ∼ **tejanos** *or* **vaqueros** jeans (*pl*)

pantano *m* ⏹1 (natural) marsh, swamp; (artificial) reservoir ⏹2 (dificultad) mess, predicament

pantanoso -sa *adj* ⏹1 ⟨terreno⟩ marshy, swampy ⏹2 ⟨asunto/negocio⟩ difficult, tricky (colloq)

panteón *m* (a) (monumento) pantheon, mausoleum; ∼ **familiar** *or* **de familia** family vault (b) (AmL) (cementerio) cemetery

pantera *f* panther

panti *m* (*pl* **-tis**), (Méx) **pantimedia** *f* ▶ PANTY

pantomima *f* pantomime

pantorrilla *f* calf

pants *mpl* (Méx) tracksuit, sweat suit (AmE)

pantufla *f* slipper

panty *m* (*pl* **-tys**) panty hose (*pl*) (AmE), tights (*pl*) (BrE)

panza *f* (a) (fam) (barriga) belly, paunch (colloq); **tener** ∼ to have a belly *o* paunch (b) (de cántaro) belly (c) (de rumiante) rumen

panzada *f* (fam) ⏹1 (en el agua) belly flop (colloq); **se dio una** ∼ he did a belly flop ⏹2 (comilona): **darse una** ∼ **de algo** to pig out on sth (colloq)

panzón -zona *adj* (fam) potbellied (colloq)

pañal *m* diaper (AmE), nappy (BrE)

pañito *m* doily

paño *m* (a) (Tex) woollen cloth; **abrigo de** ∼ wool coat; **en** ∼**s menores** (fam & hum) in my/his undies (colloq & hum) (b) (para limpiar) cloth; ∼ **de cocina** (para limpiar) dishcloth; (para secar) teatowel; ∼ **higiénico** sanitary napkin (AmE), sanitary towel (BrE) (c) (de adorno) antimacassar

pañolenci *m* (CS) baize, felt

pañoleta *f* (de mujer) shawl; (de torero) neckerchief

pañuelo *m* (para la nariz) handkerchief; (para la cabeza) headscarf, scarf; (para el cuello) scarf, neckerchief

papa[1] *m* pope; **el P**∼ the Pope

papa[2] *f* (esp AmL) (Bot) potato; ∼ **caliente** hot potato; ∼ **dulce** (AmL) sweet potato; ∼**s fritas** (esp AmL) (de paquete) potato chips (AmE) *o* (BrE) crisps (*pl*); (de cocina) French fries (*pl*) (AmE), chips (*pl*) (BrE); **ni** ∼ (fam) not a thing; **no sé ni** ∼ **de coches** I haven't a clue about cars (colloq)

papá *m* (*pl* **-pás**) (fam) daddy (colloq), pop (AmE colloq); **mis** ∼**s** (AmL) my parents, my mom and dad (AmE), my mum and dad (BrE colloq); **P**∼ **Noel** Santa Claus, Father Christmas

papada *f* (de persona) double chin, jowl

papagayo *m* ⏹1 (ave) parrot; *recitar algo como* **un** ∼ to recite sth parrot-fashion ⏹2 (Ven) (juguete) kite

papalote *m* (AmC, Méx) (juguete) kite; (ala delta) hang glider

Papanicolau *m* (AmL) smear test

papaya *f* papaya, pawpaw

papel *m* ⏹1 (material) paper; **un** ∼ a piece of paper; **toalla de** ∼ paper towel; ∼ **carbón** carbon paper; ∼ **cuadriculado/rayado** squared/lined paper; ∼ **de aluminio** tinfoil, aluminum* foil; ∼ **de embalar/de envolver/de regalo** wrapping paper; ∼ **higiénico** *or* **de water** toilet paper; ∼ **picado** (RPl) confetti

⏹2 (documento) document, paper; **no tenía los** ∼**es en regla** her papers were not in order

⏹3 (a) (Cin, Teatr) role, part; **hace el** ∼ **de monja** she plays the part of a nun (b) (actuación) performance; **hizo un lamentable** ∼ **en el congreso** his performance at the conference was abysmal (c) (función) role; **juega un** ∼ **importante en …** it plays an important role in …

papeleo *m* (fam) red tape, paperwork

papelera *f* (a) (de oficina) wastepaper basket; (en la calle) litter basket (AmE), litter bin (BrE) (b) (fábrica) paper mill

papelería *f* (tienda) stationery store (AmE), stationer's (BrE); **artículos de** ∼ stationery

papelero -ra *adj* paper (*before n*)
■ *m,f* ⏹1 (fabricante) paper manufacturer; (vendedor) stationer ⏹2 **papelero** *m* (CS) ▶ PAPELERA A

papeleta *f* (a) (de votación) ballot (paper); ∼ **en blanco** blank ballot (paper) (b) (de rifa) raffle ticket (c) (de calificación) grade slip (d) (de empeño) pawn ticket

papelillo *m* cigarette paper

papelitos *mpl* (Ur) confetti

papelón *m* (fam) (cosa vergonzosa): **hacer un** ∼ to make a fool of oneself; **¡qué** ∼! how embarrassing!

paperas *fpl* mumps

papi *m* (fam) ▶ PAPÁ

papilla *f* (para bebés) baby food, formula (AmE); (para enfermos) puree, pap; **estar hecho** ∼ ⟨persona⟩ to be absolutely shattered (colloq)

papiro *m* papyrus

paprika *f* paprika

paquete[1] **-ta** *adj* (RPl fam) smart, chic

paquete[2] *m* ⏹1 (a) (bulto envuelto) package, parcel; **hacer un** ∼ to wrap up a parcel; ∼ **bomba** parcel bomb; ∼ **postal** parcel (*sent by mail*) (b) (de galletas, cigarrillos) pack (AmE), packet (BrE); **un** ∼ **de papas fritas** (AmL) a bag of chips (AmE), a packet of crisps (BrE) ⏹2 (conjunto) package; (Inf) package ⏹3 (Méx fam) (problema) headache (colloq)

Paquistán *m* Pakistan

paquistaní *adj/mf* Pakistani

par *adj* ⟨número⟩ even; **jugarse algo a** ∼**es o nones** *to decide sth by guessing whether the number of objects held is odd or even*
■ *m* ⏹1 (a) (de guantes, zapatos) pair; **un** ∼ **de preguntas/de veces** a couple of questions/of times; **a** ∼**es** two at a time (b) (comparación) equal; **sin** ∼ (liter) incomparable, matchless (liter) ⏹2 (Arquit) rafter; ⟨abierto⟩ **de** ∼ **en** ∼ wide open ⏹3 (en golf) par; **sobre/bajo** ∼ over/under par
■ *f* par; **a la** ∼ (Fin) at par (value); **sabroso a la** ∼ **que sano** both tasty and healthy; **baila a la** ∼ **que canta** he dances and sings at the same time

para *prep*
⏹1 ⏹1 (destino, finalidad, intención) for; **una carta para él** a letter for him; **¿**∼ **qué sirve esto?** what's this (used) for?; **champú** ∼ **bebés** baby shampoo; ∼ **eso no voy** I might as well not go; ∼ **+ INF**: **ahorra** ∼ **comprarse un coche** he's saving up to buy a car; **tomé un taxi** ∼ **no llegar tarde** I took a taxi so I wouldn't be late; **está listo** ∼ **pintar** it's ready to be painted *o* for painting; ∼ **aprobar** (in order) to pass; **entró en puntillas para no despertarla** he went in on tiptoe so as not to ⋯∻

wake her; **lo dice ~ que yo me preocupe** he (only) says it to worry me; **cierra ~ que no nos oigan** close the door so (that) they don't hear us **2 (a)** (suficiencia) for; **no hay ~ todos** there isn't enough for everybody; **no es ~ tanto** it's not that bad; **soy lo bastante viejo (como) ~ recordarlo** I'm old enough to remember it **(b)** (en comparaciones, contrastes): **hace demasiado frío ~ salir** it's too cold to go out; **son altos ~ su edad** they're tall for their age; **~ lo que come, no está gordo** considering how much he eats, he's not fat; **¿quién es él ~ hablarte así?** who does he think he is, speaking to you like that?; **es mucho ~ que lo haga sola** it's too much for you to do it on your own

II 1 (dirección): **salieron ~ el aeropuerto** they left for the airport; **empuja ~ arriba** push up o upward(s); **¿vas ~ el centro?** are you going to o toward(s) the center?

2 (tiempo) **(a)** (señalando una fecha, un plazo): **estará listo ~ el día 15** it'll be ready by o for the 15th; **deberes ~ el lunes** homework for Monday; **faltan cinco minutos ~ que termine** there are five minutes to go before the end; **me lo prometió ~ después de Pascua** he promised me it for after Easter; **¿cuánto te falta ~ terminar?** how much have you got left to do?; **~ entonces estaré en Madrid** I'll be in Madrid (by) then; **tengo hora ~ mañana** I have an appointment (for) tomorrow **(b)** (AmL exc RPl) (al decir la hora) to; **son cinco ~ las diez** it's five to ten **(c)** (duración): **~ siempre** forever; **tengo ~ rato** (fam) I'm going to be a while (yet)

parábola f **(a)** (Relig) parable **(b)** (Mat) parabola

parabrisas m (pl ~) windshield (AmE), windscreen (BrE)

paracaídas m (pl ~) (Aviac) parachute; **tirarse** or **lanzarse en ~** to parachute

paracaidismo m parachuting

paracaidista adj parachute (before n)
■ mf **(a)** (Mil) paratrooper; (Dep) parachutist **(b)** (AmL fam) (en fiesta) gatecrasher; **llegar de ~ to** come/go uninvited (to a party)

parachoques m (pl ~) (Auto) bumper

parada f **1** (Transp) **(a)** (acción) stop **(b)** (lugar) tb **~ de autobús** (or **de ómnibus** etc) bus stop; **me bajo en la próxima ~** I'm getting off at the next stop; **~ de taxi** taxi stand, taxi rank (BrE) **2** (Dep) (en fútbol) save, stop **3** (desfile) parade **4** (Per) (mercado) street market

paradero m **(a)** (frml) (de persona) whereabouts (pl) **(b)** (AmL exc RPl) ▶ PARADA 1B

parado -da adj **1** (detenido): **un coche ~ en medio de la calle** a car sitting o stopped in the middle of the street; **no te quedes ahí ~, ven a ayudarme** don't just stand there, come and help me **2** (AmL) (de pie): **estar ~** to stand, be standing **(b)** (erguido): **tengo el pelo todo ~** my hair's standing on end; **ver tb ▶ PARAR** vt 2B **3** (Esp) (desempleado) unemployed **4** **salir (de algo) bien/mal parado** (de pelea, discusión) to come off well/badly (in sth); **es el que mejor ~ ha salido** he's the one who's come off best
■ m,f (Esp) unemployed person; **los ~s the** unemployed

paradoja f paradox

paradójico -ca adj paradoxical

parador m **(a)** (mesón) roadside bar/hotel **(b)** (en Esp) parador, state-owned hotel

parafina f **(a)** (sólida) paraffin (wax); **~ líquida** mineral oil (AmE), liquid paraffin (BrE) **(b)** (AmL) (combustible) kerosene

paragolpes m (pl ~) (RPl) bumper

paraguas m (pl ~) umbrella

Paraguay m: tb **el ~** Paraguay

paraguayo -ya adj/m,f Paraguayan

paragüero m umbrella stand

paraíso m (Relig) **el ~** paradise, heaven; **~ fiscal** tax haven

paraje m spot, place

paralela f **1** (línea) parallel (line) **2** **paralelas** fpl (Dep) parallel bars (pl)

paralelismo m parallelism, parallel

paralelo¹ -la adj **(a)** ‹líneas/planos› parallel; **~ A algo** parallel TO sth **(b)** (como adv) ‹marchar/crecer› parallel

paralelo² m parallel

paralelogramo m parallelogram

parálisis f paralysis; **~ cerebral** cerebral palsy; **~ infantil** poliomyelitis, infantile paralysis

paralítico -ca adj paralytic (before n); **se quedó ~** he was paralyzed
■ m,f paralytic

paralizar [A4] vt **(a)** (Med) to paralyze; **se quedó paralizada de un lado** she was paralyzed down one side **(b)** ‹industria/economía› to paralyze; ‹circulación/producción› to bring ... to a halt o standstill

paramilitar adj paramilitary

páramo m high plateau, bleak upland o moor

paramuno -na m,f (Col) person from the high plateau

paraninfo m main hall o auditorium

paranoia f paranoia

paranoico -ca adj/m,f paranoid

paranormal adj paranormal

parapente m paragliding

parapetarse [A1] v pron to take cover

parapeto m (Arquit) parapet; (barricada) barricade

paraplejía, paraplejia f paraplegia

parapléjico -ca adj/m,f paraplegic

parapsicología f parapsychology

parar [A1] vi **1** (detenerse) to stop; **paró en seco** she stopped dead; **ir/venir a ~** to end up; **fue a ~ a la cárcel** he ended up in prison; **¿a dónde habrá ido a ~ aquella foto?** what can have happened to that photo?; **¡a dónde iremos a ~!** I don't know what the world's coming to
2 (cesar) to stop; **para un momento** hang on a minute; **ha estado lloviendo sin ~** it hasn't stopped raining; **no para quieto ni un momento** he can't keep still for a minute; **no para en casa** she's never at home; **~ DE + INF** to stop -ING; **paró de llover** it stopped raining
3 (AmL) «obreros/empleados» to go on strike
■ ~ vt **1 (a)** ‹coche/tráfico/persona› to stop; ‹motor/máquina› to stop, switch off **(b)** ‹hemorragia› to stanch (AmE), to staunch (BrE) **(c)** ‹balón/tiro› to save, stop; ‹golpe› to block, ward off

2 (AmL) (a) ‹poner de pie› to stand (b) ‹poner vertical› ‹vaso/libro› to stand ... up; **el perro paró las orejas** the dog pricked up its ears
■ **pararse** v pron 1 (detenerse) (a) «persona» to stop (b) «reloj/máquina» to stop; «coche/motor» to stall; **se me paró el reloj** my watch stopped 2 (a) (AmL) (ponerse de pie) to stand up; **párate derecho** stand up straight; **se paró en una silla** she stood on a chair; **¿te puedes ~ de cabeza/de manos?** can you do headstands/handstands? (b) (AmL) «pelo» (hacia arriba) to stick up; (en los lados) to stick out (c) (Méx, Ven) (levantarse de la cama) to get up

pararrayos m (pl ~) (en edificio) lightning rod (AmE), lightning conductor (BrE)

parasailing /'pærəseɪlɪŋ/ m parasailing

parásito m parasite

parasol m (sombrilla) parasol, sunshade

parcela f plot (of land), lot (AmE)

parchar [A1] vt (AmL) (arreglar) to repair; (con parche) to patch (up)

parche m patch; **~ de nicotina** nicotine patch

parchís m (Esp, Méx) Parcheesi® (AmE), ludo (BrE)

parcial adj 1 ‹solución/victoria› partial 2 (no equitativo) biased, partial
■ m (examen) assessment examination (taken during the year and counting towards the final grade)

parcialidad f (a) (cualidad) partiality, bias (b) (seguidores) supporters (pl)

parco -ca adj (a) (lacónico) laconic (b) (sobrio, moderado) frugal; **ser ~ en palabras** to be sparing with words

pardo -da adj ‹color› dun, brownish-gray*

parecer¹ [E3] vi 1 (aparentar ser): **parece fácil** it looks easy; **no pareces tú en esta foto** this picture doesn't look like you (at all); **parecía de cuero** it looked like leather; **parece ser muy inteligente** she seems to be very clever 2 (expresando opinión) (+ me/te/le etc): **todo le parece mal** he's never happy with anything; **¿qué te parecieron?** what did you think of them?; **vamos a la playa ¿te parece?** what do you think, shall we go to the beach?; **si te parece bien** if that's alright with you; **me parece que sí** I think so; **¿a ti qué te parece?** what do you think?; **me parece importante** I think it's important; **me pareció que no era necesario** I didn't think it necessary; **hazlo como mejor te parezca** do it however o as you think best; **me parece mal que vaya sola** I don't think it's right that she should go on her own 3 (dar la impresión) (en 3ᵃpers): **así parece** or **parece que sí** it looks like it; **aunque no lo parezca, está limpio** it may not look like it, but it's clean; **parece que va a llover** it looks like (it's going to) rain; **parece que fue ayer** it seems like only yesterday; **parece mentira que tenga 20 años** it's hard to believe o I can't believe that he's 20; **parece que fuera más joven** you'd think she was much younger
■ **parecerse** v pron (a) (asemejarse) **~se a** algn/algo (en lo físico) to look o to be like sb/sth; (en el carácter) to be like sb/sth (b) (recípr) to be alike; **no se parecen en nada** they're not/they don't look in the least bit alike; **se parecen mucho** they are very similar

parecer² m (opinión) opinion; **a mi ~** in my opinion; **son del mismo ~** they're of the same opinion

parecido¹ -da adj [SER] ‹personas› alike; ‹cosas› similar; **son muy parecidas de cara** they have very similar features; **una especie de capa o algo ~** a cape or something like that; **~ A algo** similar TO sth; **eres muy ~ a tu padre** you're a lot like your father

parecido² m resemblance, similarity; **tiene cierto ~ con su hermano** he bears some o a certain resemblance to his brother; **hay un ~ en sus estilos** there is a resemblance o similarity in their styles

pared f 1 (a) (Arquit, Const) wall; **viven ~ por medio** they live next door; **las ~ oyen** walls have ears (b) (de recipiente) side (c) (de montaña) face 2 (en fútbol) one-two

paredón m (a) (de roca) rock face, wall of rock (b) (pared gruesa) thick wall (c) (de fusilamiento) wall

pareja f 1 (a) (equipo, conjunto) pair; **salieron por ~s** they came out in pairs; **formar ~s** to get into pairs (b) (en una relación) couple; **hacen buena ~** they make a good couple (c) (en naipes) pair 2 (a) (compañero) partner (b) (de guante, zapato) pair; **no encuentro la ~ de este guante** I can't find the pair for this glove; **un calcetín sin ~** an odd sock

parejo -ja adj 1 (a) (esp AmL) (sin desniveles) even; **los dos ciclistas van muy ~s** the two cyclists are neck and neck; **el nivel en la clase es muy ~** the class are all at the same level (b) (afín, semejante) similar (c) (CS, Méx) (equitativo) ‹trato› equal; ‹ley› fair, impartial 2 (Méx fam) **al ~ (a la par)**: **trabajan al ~** they all do the same amount of work; **al ~ de los mejores del mundo** on a par with the world's best

parentela f (fam) clan (colloq), tribe (colloq)

parentesco m relationship; **tener ~ con algn** to be related to sb

paréntesis m (pl ~) (a) (signo) parenthesis, bracket (BrE); **cerrar el ~** close parentheses o brackets; **entre ~** (literal) in parentheses, in brackets; (a propósito) by the way (b) (digresión) digression, parenthesis

parezca, parezcas, etc ▶ PARECER¹

paria mf pariah

pariente mf, **pariente -ta** m,f (familiar) relative, relation; **~ lejano** distant relative o relation; **~ político** in-law

parir [I1] vi «mujer» to give birth; «vaca» to calve; «yegua/burra» to foal; «oveja» to lamb
■ **~** vt (a) «mujer» to give birth to, have (b) «mamíferos» to have, bear (frml)

París m Paris

parisiense adj/mf Parisian

parisino -na adj/m,f Parisian

parking /'parkin/ m (esp Esp) parking lot (AmE), car park (BrE)

parlamentar [A1] vi **~ (CON algn)** to talk (TO sb)

parlamentario -ria m,f member of parliament, parliamentarian

parlamento m (asamblea) parliament; (Lit, Teatr) speech

parlanchín -china adj (fam) chatty (colloq)
■ m,f (fam) chatterbox (colloq)

parlante m (AmL) (en lugar público) loudspeaker;
(de equipo de música) speaker

paro m [1] (esp AmL) (huelga) strike; **hacer un ~
de 24 horas** to go on a 24-hour strike; **están en** or
de ~ (AmL) they're on strike; **~ cívico** (Col)
community protest; **~ general** (esp AmL) general
strike [2] (Esp) **(a)** (desempleo) unemployment;
está en ~ he's unemployed **(b)** (subsidio)
unemployment benefit; **cobrar el ~** to claim
unemployment benefit [3] **~ cardíaco** or **cardiaco**
cardiac arrest

parodia f parody, send-up (colloq)

parpadear [A1] vi **(a)** «persona/ojo» to blink
(b) «luz» to flicker; «estrellas» to twinkle

párpado m eyelid

parque m [1] (terreno) park; **~ de atracciones** or
(Col, RPl) **de diversiones** or (Chi) **de entretenciones**
amusement park, funfair; **~ de bomberos** (Esp)
fire station; **~ natural** nature reserve; **~
zoológico** zoo [2] (para niños) playpen

parqué m (suelo) parquet (flooring)

parqueadero m (Col) parking lot (AmE), car
park (BrE)

parquear [A1] vt (Col) to park
■ **parquearse** v pron (Col) to park

parquet m (pl -quets) ▶ PARQUÉ

parquímetro m parking meter

parra f vine

párrafo m paragraph; **~ aparte** new paragraph

parral m (en un jardín) vine arbor*; (viñedo)
vineyard

parranda f (fam): **estar/irse de ~** to be/go out
on the town o out partying (colloq)

parrilla f [1] **(a)** (Coc) grill, broiler (AmE);
pescado a la ~ grilled o (AmE) broiled fish **(b)**
(restaurante) grillroom, grill bar **(c)** (de la chimenea)
grate [2] (AmL) (para el equipaje) luggage rack, roof
rack

parrillada f **(a)** (comida) grill, barbecue **(b)**
(RPl) (restaurante) grillroom, grill bar

párroco m parish priest

parroquia f (iglesia) parish church; (área)
parish; (feligreses) parishioners (pl)

parroquiano -na m,f **(a)** (Relig) parishioner
(b) (cliente) regular customer o (fml) patron

parsimonia f **(a)** (calma) calm **(b)** (frugalidad)
parsimony

parsimonioso -sa adj **(a)** (tranquilo)
phlegmatic, unhurried **(b)** (frugal) parsimonious

parte m [1] (informe, comunicación) report; **dar ~
de un incidente** «(particular)» to report an
incident; «autoridad» to file a report about an
incident; **dar ~ de enfermo** to call in sick; **~
meteorológico** weather report [2] (Andes) (multa) ticket (colloq), fine
■ f [1] **(a)** (porción, fracción) part; **tres ~s iguales**
three equal parts; **pasa la mayor ~ del tiempo al
teléfono** she spends most of her o the time on the
phone; **la mayor ~ de los participantes** the

majority of o most of the participants **(b)** (en una
distribución) share; **su ~ de la herencia** his share of
the inheritance **(c)** (de lugar) part; **¿de qué ~ de
México eres?** what part of Mexico are you from?;
en la ~ de atrás at the back
[2] (en locs) **en parte** partly; **en gran ~** to a large
extent, largely; **en su mayor ~** for the most part;
de un tiempo a esta parte for some time now; **de
parte de algn** on behalf of sb; **llamo de ~ de
María** I'm ringing on behalf of María; **dale
recuerdos de mi ~** give him my regards; **vengo
de ~ del señor Díaz** Mr Díaz sent me; **¿de ~ de
quién?** (por teléfono) who's calling?, who shall I
say is calling? (fml); **formar parte de algo** «pieza/
sección» to be part of sth; «persona/país» to
belong to sth; **entrar a formar ~ de algo** to join
sth; **por mi/tu/su parte** as far as I'm/you're/he's
concerned; **por partes**: **revisémoslo por ~s** let's
go over it section by section; **vayamos por ~s**
let's take it step by step; **por otra parte** (además)
anyway, in any case; (por otro lado) however, on
the other hand; **por una parte ..., por la otra ...** on
the one hand ..., on the other ...
[3] (participación) part; **tomar ~** to take part
[4] (lugar): **vámonos a otra ~** let's go somewhere
else o (AmE) someplace else; **esto no nos lleva a
ninguna ~** this isn't getting o leading us
anywhere; **¿adónde vas? — a ninguna ~** where
are you going? — nowhere; **en cualquier ~**
anywhere; **a/en/por todas ~s** everywhere; **en
alguna ~** somewhere
[5] (en negociación, contrato, juicio) party
[6] (Teatr) part, role
[7] (Méx) (repuesto) part, spare (part)

participación f [1] (intervención) participation;
la ~ del público audience participation; **~ EN
algo** «en debate/clase/huelga» participation IN
sth; «en robo/fraude» involvement IN sth; «en
obra/película» role IN sth [2] **(a)** (en ganancias)
share **(b)** (en empresa) stockholding, interest **(c)**
(de lotería) share (in a lottery ticket)

participante adj participating (before n)
■ mf (en debate) participant; (en concurso)
contestant; (en carrera) competitor

participar [A1] vi **(a)** (tomar parte) **~ (EN algo)**
to take part (IN sth), participate (IN sth) (fml) **(b)**
~ EN algo (en ganancias) to have a share IN sth;
(en empresas) to have a stockholding IN sth

participio m participle; **~ pasado** or **pasivo**
past participle

partícula f particle

particular adj **(a)** (privado) «clases/profesor»
private; «teléfono» home (before n) **(b)** (específico)
«caso/aspecto» particular; **en ~** in particular,
particularly **(c)** (especial) «estilo/gusto» individual,
personal; **es un tipo muy ~** (fam) he's a very
peculiar guy; **no tiene nada de ~ que vaya**
there's nothing unusual o strange in her going; **la
casa no tiene nada de ~** there's nothing special
about the house
■ m **(a)** (fml) (asunto) matter, point; **sin otro ~
saluda a usted atentamente** sincerely yours

(AmE), yours faithfully (BrE) **(b)** (persona)
(private) individual; **viajar como ~ to travel on
private o personal business**

partida f [1] (Jueg) game; **una ~ de ajedrez/
cartas** a game of chess/cards; **echar una ~ to
have a game** [2] (en registro, contabilidad) entry; (en
presupuesto) item [3] (certificado) certificate; **~ de
defunción/nacimiento** death/birth certificate
[4] (frml) (salida) departure, leaving

partidario -ria adj (a favor) **~ DE algo/hacer
algo** in favor* oF sth/doing sth
■ m,f supporter; **los ~s de Gaztelu** Gaztelu's
supporters; **los ~s de la violencia** those who
favor o advocate the use of violence

partido¹ -da adj [1] ‹labios› chapped;
‹barbilla› cleft [2] (Mat): **siete ~ por diez** seven
over ten; **nueve ~ por tres da ...** nine divided by
three gives ...

partido² m [1] **(a)** (de fútbol) game, match (BrE);
(de tenis) match; **echar un ~ to have a game; un
~ de béisbol** a baseball game; **~ amistoso**
friendly game o match; **~ de desempate** deciding
game, decider; **~ en casa/fuera de casa** home/
away match **(b)** (AmL) (Pol) party; game; **un ~ de
ajedrez** a game of chess [2] (Pol) party; **~ de la
oposición** opposition party; **tomar ~ to take sides**
[3] (provecho): **sacar ~ de algo** to benefit from sth;
sacarle ~ a algo to make the most of sth [4] (para
casarse): **un buen ~** a good catch

partir [I1] vt **(a)** (con cuchillo) ‹tarta/melón› to
cut; **lo partió por la mitad** he cut it in half **(b)**
(romper) ‹piedra/coco› to break, smash; ‹nuez/
avellana› to crack; ‹rama/palo› to break **(c)** (con
golpe) ‹labio› to split (open); ‹cabeza› to split open
(d) «frío» ‹labios› to chap
■ ~ vi [1] **(a)** (frml) (marcharse) to leave, depart
(frml) **(b)** ‹auto› (Chi) to start
[2] **(a)** **~ DE algo** ‹de una premisa/un supuesto›
to start FROM sth **(b)** **a partir de** from; **a ~ de
ahora/ese momento** from now on/that moment
on; **a ~ de hoy** (as o starting) from today
■ **partirse** v pron **(a)** «mármol/roca» to split,
smash **(b)** (refl) ‹labio› to split; ‹diente› to break,
chip

partitura f (de obra orquestada) score

parto m (Med) labor*; **estar de ~** to be in labor;
fue un ~ difícil it was a difficult birth; **provocar
el ~** to induce labor; **~ sin dolor** pain-free labor*

parvulario m kindergarten, nursery school
(BrE)

pasa f raisin

pasable adj (tolerable) passable

pasabordo m (Col) boarding pass

pasada f **(a)** (con un trapo) wipe; (de barniz, cera)
coat **(b)** (paso): **trató el tema de ~** he dealt with
the subject in passing; **hacerle** or **jugarle una
mala ~ a algn** to play a dirty trick on sb

pasadizo m passageway, passage

pasado¹ -da adj [1] (en expresiones de tiempo): **el
año/sábado ~** last year/Saturday; **~s dos días**
after two days; **son las cinco pasadas** it's after o
past five o'clock; **~ mañana** the day after
tomorrow [2] (anticuado) tb **~ de moda**
old-fashioned [3] ‹fruta› overripe; ‹arroz/pastas›
overcooked; ‹leche› sour; **el pescado está ~** the
fish is bad; **el filete muy ~, por favor** I'd like my
steak well done

pasado² m **(a)** (época pasada) past **(b)** (Ling)
past (tense)

pasador m **(a)** (de pelo — decorativo) barrette
(AmE), hair slide (BrE); (— en forma de horquilla)
(Méx) bobby pin (AmE), hair clip (BrE) **(b)** (de
corbata) tiepin **(c)** (Per) (cordón) shoelace

pasaje m [1] (esp AmL) (Transp) ticket; **un ~ de
ida/de ida y vuelta** a one-way/round-trip ticket
(AmE), a single/return ticket (BrE) [2] (callejón)
passage, narrow street; (galería comercial) arcade,
mall [3] (Lit, Mús) passage

pasajero -ra adj ‹capricho/moda› passing
(before n); ‹amor› fleeting (before n); ‹molestia/
dolor› temporary
■ m,f passenger

pasamanos m (pl ~) banister

pasamontañas m (pl ~) balaclava

pasapalo m (Ven fam) nibble (colloq)

pasaporte m passport; **sacar el ~** to get a
passport

pasapurés m (pl ~) (con manivela) food mill;
(para aplastar) potato masher

pasar [A1] vi
I [1] **(a)** (ir por un lugar) to come/go past; **no ha
pasado ni un taxi** not one taxi has come/gone
past; **los otros coches no podían ~** the other
cars weren't able to get past; **no dejan ~ a nadie**
they're not letting anyone through; **~ de largo** to
go right o straight past; **~ por la aduana** to go
through customs; **es un vuelo directo, no pasa
por Miami** it's a direct flight, it doesn't go via
Miami; **¿este autobús pasa por el museo?** does
this bus go past the museum?; **pasamos por
delante de su casa** we went past her house;
pasaba por aquí y ... I was just passing by o I
was in the area and ... **(b)** (deteniéndose en un
lugar): **¿podríamos ~ por el banco?** can we stop
off at the bank?; **pasa un día por casa** why don't
you drop o come by the house sometime?; **puede
~ a recogerlo mañana** you can come and pick it
up tomorrow **(c)** (atravesar) to cross; **~ de un lado
a otro** «persona/barco» to go o cross from one
side to the other; «humedad» to go through
from one side to the other **(d)** (caber): **no ~á por
la puerta** it won't go through the door
[2] (entrar — acercándose al hablante) to come in; (—
alejándose del hablante) to go in; **pase, por favor**
please, do come in; **¡que pase el siguiente!** next,
please!; **haga ~ al Sr Díaz** show Mr Díaz in please
[3] **(a)** (transmitirse, transferirse) «corona/título» to
pass; **pasó de mano en mano** it was passed
around (to everyone) **(b)** (comunicar): **te paso con
Javier** (en el mismo teléfono) I'll hand o pass you
over to Javier; (en otro teléfono) I'll put you
through to Javier
[4] **(a)** (Educ) to pass; **~ de curso** to get through
o pass one's end-of-year exams **(b)** (ser aceptable):
no está perfecto, pero puede ~ it's not perfect,
but it'll do; **por esta vez, (que) pase** I'll let it pass
o go this time
[5] **pasar por (a)** (ser tenido por): **podrían ~ por
hermanas** they could pass for sisters; **ver tb**
HACERSE II 3 **(b)** (experimentar) to go through; **~
por una crisis** to go through a crisis
II (suceder) to happen; **cuéntame lo que pasó** tell
me what happened; **lo que pasa es que...** the
thing o the problem is ...; **pase lo que pase**
whatever happens, come what may; **siempre pasa** ⋯➔

igual *or* lo mismo it's always the same; **¿qué pasa?** what's the matter?, what's up? (colloq); **¿qué te pasa?** what's the matter with you?; **¿qué te pasó en el ojo?** what happened to your eye?; **¿qué le pasa a la tele?** what's wrong with the TV?; **eso le pasa a cualquiera** that can happen to anybody; **no le pasó nada** nothing happened to him

III 1 (transcurrir) «*tiempo/años*» to pass, go by; ∼**on muchos años** many years went by *o* passed; **ya han pasado dos horas** it's been two hours now; **un año pasa muy rápido** a year goes very quickly; **¡cómo pasa el tiempo!** doesn't time fly!

2 (cesar) «*crisis/mal momento*» to be over; «*efecto*» to wear off; «*dolor*» to go away

3 (arreglárselas) ∼ **SIN algo** to manage WITHOUT sth

■ ∼ *vt*

I 1 (a) (cruzar, atravesar) ⟨*frontera*⟩ to cross; ⟨*pueblo/ciudad*⟩ to go through (b) (dejar atrás) ⟨*edificio/calle*⟩ to go past (c) (adelantar, sobrepasar) to overtake

2 (a) (hacer atravesar) ∼ **algo POR algo** to put sth THROUGH sth; ∼ **la salsa por un tamiz** to put the sauce through a sieve (b) (por la aduana — legalmente) to take through; (— ilegalmente) to smuggle

3 (hacer recorrer): ∼ **la aspiradora** to vacuum, to hoover (BrE); **pásale un trapo al piso** give the floor a quick wipe; **hay que** ∼**le una plancha** it needs a quick iron

4 (exhibir, mostrar) ⟨*película/anuncio*⟩ to show

5 ⟨*examen/prueba*⟩ to pass

6 ⟨*página/hoja*⟩ to turn; ∼ **por alto** ⟨*falta/error*⟩ to overlook; ⟨*tema/punto*⟩ to leave out, omit

II 1 (entregar, hacer llegar): **pásaselo a Miguel** pass it on to Miguel; **¿me pasas el martillo?** can you pass me the hammer?

2 (contagiar) to give, to pass on

III 1 (a) ⟨*tiempo*⟩ to spend; **pasamos las Navidades en casa** we spent Christmas at home; **fuimos a Toledo a** ∼ **el día** we went to Toledo for the day (b) (con idea de continuidad): **pasé toda la noche en vela** I was awake all night; **pasa todo el día al teléfono** she spends all day on the phone (c) **pasarlo** *or* **pasarla bien** to have a good time; **¿qué tal lo pasaste en la fiesta?** did you have a good time at the party?, did you enjoy the party?; **lo pasé mal** I didn't enjoy myself

2 (sufrir, padecer) ⟨*penalidades/desgracias*⟩ to go through, to suffer; **pasé mucho miedo/frío** I was very frightened/cold

■ **pasarse** *v pron*

I 1 (cambiarse): ∼**se al enemigo** to go over to the enemy

2 (a) (ir demasiado lejos) to go too far; **nos pasamos de estación** we went past our station; **esta vez te has pasado** (fam) you've gone too far this time (b) (*enf*) (fam) (ir): **pásate por casa** come round; **¿podrías** ∼**te por el mercado?** could you go down to the market?

3 (a) «*peras/tomates*» to go bad, to get overripe; «*carne/pescado*» to go off, go bad; «*leche*» to go off, go sour (b) (recocerse) «*arroz/pasta*» to get overcooked

II 1 (a) (desaparecer) «*efecto*» to wear off; «*dolor*» to go away; (+ *me/te/le etc*) **ya se me pasó el dolor** the pain's gone *o* eased now; **espera**

a que se le pase el enojo wait until he's calmed *o* cooled down (b) (transcurrir): **el año se ha pasado muy rápido** this year has gone very quickly; *ver tb* PASAR *vt* III 1A, B

2 (+ *me/te/le etc*) (a) (olvidarse): **se me pasó su cumpleaños** I forgot his birthday (b) (dejar escapar): **se me pasó la oportunidad** I missed the opportunity

pasarela *f* (a) (en desfiles de modelos) runway (AmE), catwalk (BrE) (b) (Náut) gangway

pasatiempo *m* (a) (entretenimiento) hobby, pastime (b) **pasatiempos** *mpl* (en periódico) puzzles (*pl*)

Pascua *f* (a) (fiesta de Resurrección) Easter (b) (Navidad) Christmas (c) (fiesta judía) Passover

pase *m* 1 (a) (permiso) pass; ∼ **de abordar** (Méx) boarding pass; ∼ **de periodista** press pass (b) (para espectáculo) *tb* ∼ **de favor** complimentary ticket (c) (Col) (licencia de conducción) license*

2 (a) (Dep) (en fútbol, baloncesto, rugby) pass; (en esgrima) feint (b) (Taur) pass (c) (en magia) sleight of hand

pasear [A1] *vi* (a) (a pie) to go for a walk *o* stroll; **salir a** ∼ to go out for a walk *o* stroll (b) (en bicicleta) to go for a (bike) ride; (en coche) to go for a drive

■ ∼ *vt* ⟨*perro*⟩ to walk

paseo *m* 1 (a) (caminata) walk; **dar un** ∼ to go for a walk *o* (colloq) stroll; **mandar a algn a** ∼ (fam) to tell sb to get lost (colloq) (b) (en bicicleta) ride; (en coche) drive; **fuimos a dar un** ∼ **en coche** we went for a drive (c) (AmL) (excursión) trip, outing; **no vivo aquí, estoy de** ∼ I don't live here, I'm just visiting 2 (en nombres de calles) walk, avenue; ∼ **marítimo** esplanade, seafront

pasillo *m* (corredor) corridor; (en avión) aisle

pasión *f* passion; **tiene** ∼ **por el fútbol** he has a passion for football

pasional *adj*: **un crimen** ∼ a crime of passion

pasito *adv* (Col, Ven) ⟨*hablar*⟩ quietly, softly; **poner** ∼ **la música** to turn the music down

pasivo¹ -va *adj* passive

pasivo² *m* (en negocio) liabilities (*pl*); (en cuenta) debit side

pasmado -da *adj* (fam) ⟨*persona*⟩: **la noticia me dejó pasmada** I was stunned by the news (colloq)

pasmar [A1] *vt* (fam) to amaze, stun

paso *m* 1 (a) (acción): **el** ∼ **del tren** the passing of the train; **el** ∼ **del tiempo** the passage of time; **el** ∼ **de la dictadura a la democracia** the transition from dictatorship to democracy; **de** ∼: **están de** ∼ they're just visiting *o* just passing through; **me pilla de** ∼ it's on my way; **y dicho sea de** ∼ ... and incidentally ... (b) (camino, posibilidad de pasar) way; **abrir/dejar** ∼ (**a algn/algo**) to make way (for sth/sb); **me cerró el** ∼ she blocked my way; **dejen el** ∼ **libre** leave the way clear; **🅢 ceda el paso** yield (*in US*), give way (*in UK*); **🅢 prohibido el paso** no entry; ∼ **de cebra** zebra crossing; ∼ **de peatones** crosswalk (AmE), pedestrian crossing (BrE); ∼**a nivel** grade (AmE) *o* (BrE) level crossing; ∼ **elevado** *or* (Méx) **a desnivel** overpass (AmE), flyover (BrE); ∼ **subterráneo** (*para peatones*) underpass, subway (BrE); (*para vehículos*) underpass; **abrirse** ∼ to make one's way; (a codazos) to elbow one's way; **salir al** ∼ **de algn** (abordar) to waylay sb; (detener) to stop sb

pasodoble ⋯∻ patilla ⋯

2 (Geog) (en montaña) pass; **salir del ~** to get out of a (tight) spot *o* (AmE) crack (colloq)

3 **(a)** (al andar, bailar) step; **dio un ~ para atrás** he took a step backward(s); **oyó ~s** she heard footsteps; **entró con ~ firme** he came in purposefully; **~ a ~** step by step; **seguirle los ~s a algn** to tail sb; **seguir los ~s de algn** to follow in sb's footsteps **(b)** (distancia corta): **vive a dos ~s de mi casa** he lives a stone's throw (away) from my house; **está a un ~ de aquí** it's just around the corner/down the road from here **(c)** (avance) step forward; **eso ya es un ~ (adelante)** that's a step forward in itself **(d)** (de gestión) step

4 (ritmo, velocidad): **apretó/aminoró el ~** he quickened his pace/he slowed down; **a este ~ ...** at this rate ...; **a ~ de hormiga** *or* **tortuga** at a snail's pace; **marcar el ~** to mark time

5 (en contador) unit

pasodoble *m* paso doble

pasota *mf* (Esp fam): **ese tío es un ~** that guy couldn't give a damn about anything (colloq)

pasparse [A1] *v pron* (RPl) «*cara/labios*» to get chapped

pasta *f* **1** (Coc) **(a)** (fideos, macarrones, etc) pasta **(b)** (Esp) (masa de harina) pastry; (galleta) *tb* **~ de té** cookie **(c)** (de tomates, anchoas, etc) paste **2** **(a)** (materia moldeable) paste; **~ dentífrica** *or* **de dientes** toothpaste; **un libro en ~** a book in boards; **libros de ~ blanda** (Méx) paperback books **(b)** (Chi) (betún) polish **3** (Esp fam) (dinero) money, dough (sl)

pastar [A1] *vi* to graze

pastel *m* **1** **(a)** (dulce) cake; **~ de boda/cumpleaños** wedding/birthday cake **(b)** (cubierto de masa) pie; **~ de papas** (CS) shepherd's pie, cottage pie **2** (Art) pastel; **al ~ pastel** (*before n*)
■ *adj inv* pastel

pastelería *f* (tienda) cake shop, patisserie (BrE); (actividad) (cake) baking

pastelero -ra *m,f* (fabricante) patissier, pastry cook; (vendedor) cake seller

pasteurizado -da, pasterizado -da *adj* pasteurized

pastilla *f* **1** **(a)** (Farm, Med) (para tragar) pill, tablet; (para chupar) pastille, lozenge; **~s para dormir** sleeping tablets *o* pills; **~s para los nervios** tranquilizers **(b)** (caramelo) candy (AmE), sweet (BrE); **~ de menta** mint **2** (de jabón) bar; (de chocolate) bar; (de caldo) cube **3** (Electrón) chip, microchip

pasto *m* **(a)** (Agr) pasture **(b)** (AmL) (hierba) grass; (extensión) lawn, grass

pastor -tora *m,f* **1** (Agr) (*m*) shepherd; (*f*) shepherdess; **~ alemán** German shepherd, Alsatian **2** (Relig) minister

pastoso -sa *adj* **(a)** ‹*sustancia/masa*› doughy **(b)** ‹*boca/lengua*› furry **(c)** ‹*voz/tono*› rich, mellow

pata *f* **1** (Zool) **(a)** (pierna — de animal, ave) leg; **las ~s delanteras/traseras** the front/hind legs **(b)** (pie — de perro, gato) paw; (— de ave) foot **2** (de persona) (fam & hum) (pierna) leg; (pie) (AmL) foot; **~ de palo** wooden leg; **a ~** (fam & hum) on foot; **estirar la ~** (fam) to kick the bucket (colloq); **meter la ~** (fam) to put one's foot in it (colloq); **~s**

(*para*) *arriba* (fam) upside down; **saltar a (la) ~ coja** to hop; **tener ~** (AmL fam) to have contacts; ▶ MALO 1A

3 (de mueble) leg
■ *m* (Per fam) **(a)** (tipo) guy (colloq), bloke (BrE colloq) **(b)** (amigo) buddy (AmE colloq), mate (BrE colloq)

patada *f* **1** (puntapié) kick; **le dio una ~ al balón** he kicked the ball, he gave the ball a kick; **tiró la puerta abajo de una ~** he kicked the door down; **dio una ~ en el suelo** he stamped his foot; **los echaron a ~s** they were kicked out **2** (AmL) **(a)** (de arma) kick **(b)** (fam) (producida por la electricidad) shock (colloq); **me dio tremenda ~** I got a real shock

Patagonia *f*: **la ~** Patagonia

patagónico -ca *adj* Patagonian

patalear [A1] *vi* **(a)** (con enfado) to stamp (one's feet) **(b)** (en el aire, agua) to kick (one's legs in the air/water) **(c)** (fam) (protestar) to kick up a fuss (colloq)

pataleta *f* (fam) (de niño pequeño) tantrum; **le dio una ~ «*niño*»** he threw a tantrum; «*adulto*» he had a fit (colloq)

patán *adj* (fam) loutish, uncouth; **no seas ~** don't be such a lout *o* so uncouth
■ *m* **1** (fam) (grosero) lout, yob (BrE colloq) **2** (Chi) (holgazán) good-for-nothing

patata *f* (Esp) potato; **~ frita** (Esp) (de sartén) French fry, chip (BrE); (de bolsita) (potato) chip (AmE), (potato) crisp (BrE)

patatús *m* (fam) fit (colloq)

paté, pâté *m* pâté; **~ de hígado** liver pâté

patear [A1] *vt* **(a)** «*persona*» to kick, boot (colloq) **(b)** (AmL) «*animal*» to kick
■ *vi* **(a)** (dar patadas en el suelo) to stamp (one's feet) **(b)** (AmL) «*animal*» to kick

patentado -da ‹*invento*› patented; ‹*marca*› registered

patentar [A1] *vt* **1** ‹*marca*› to register; ‹*invento*› to patent **2** (CS) ‹*coche*› to register

patente *adj* clear, evident; **dejó ~ cuál era su objetivo** he made his aim quite clear
■ *f* **1** (de invento) patent **2** (Auto) **(a)** (CS) (impuesto) road tax; (placa) license* plate, numberplate (BrE); **el número de la ~** the registration number, the license number (AmE) **(b)** (Col) (carnet de conducir) driving license*

paternal *adj* paternal

paternalismo *m* paternalism

paternalista *adj* paternalistic

paternidad *f* **1** (del padre) **(a)** (Der) paternity (frml) **(b)** (circunstancia) fatherhood; **la ~ lo ha cambiado** fatherhood *o* being a father has changed him **2** (de los padres) parenthood

paterno -na *adj* (a) ‹*abuelo*› paternal (*before n*) **(b)** ‹*autoridad/herencia*› paternal; ‹*cariño*› paternal, fatherly; **su domicilio ~** her parents' home

patético -ca *adj* pathetic, moving

patetismo *m* pathos (liter); **imágenes de (un) gran ~** very moving images

patíbulo *m* **(a)** (tablado) scaffold **(b)** (horca) gallows

patilla *f* **1** **(a)** (barba) sideburn, sideboard (BrE) **(b)** (de las gafas) sidepiece, arm **2** (fruta) (Col, Ven) watermelon; (esqueje) (Chi) cutting

patín *m* (a) (con ruedas) (roller) skate; (para el hielo) (ice) skate; **le regalé unos patines** I gave him a pair of skates; ~ **en línea** Rollerblade® (b) (tabla) skateboard (c) (Esp) (bote) pedalo, pedal boat

pátina *f* patina

patinador -dora *m,f* (Dep) (sobre ruedas) (roller) skater; (sobre hielo) (ice) skater

patinaje *m* (sobre ruedas) roller skating; (sobre hielo) ice skating; ~ **artístico/de velocidad** figure/ speed skating

patinar [A1] *vi* **1** (a) (Dep) (con ruedas) to skate, roller-skate; (sobre hielo) to skate, ice-skate (b) (resbalar) «*persona*» to slip, slide; «*vehículo*» to skid; «*embrague*» to slip **2** (fam) (equivocarse) to slip up

patinazo *m* **1** (de vehículo) skid; **el coche pegó un** ~ the car skidded **2** (fam) (equivocación) blunder, slip-up (colloq)

patineta *f* (a) (con manillar) scooter (b) (CS, Méx, Ven) (sin manillar) skateboard

patinete *m* scooter

patio *m* **1** (en una casa) courtyard, patio; (de escuela) playground, schoolyard **2** (Esp) (Cin, Teatr) *tb* ~ **de butacas** (Esp) orchestra (AmE), stalls (*pl*) (BrE)

patizambo -ba *adj* (con las piernas arqueadas — hacia adentro) knock-kneed; (— hacia afuera) bowlegged

pato¹ -ta *m,f* (Zool) duck

pato² **m* **1 (Esp fam) (persona) clodhopper (colloq) **2** (Andes, Méx) (Med) bedpan

patochada *f* (fam) piece of nonsense; **decir** ~**s** talk nonsense

patología *f* pathology

patológico -ca *adj* pathological

patón -tona *adj* (AmL fam) ▶ PATUDO 1

patoso -sa *adj* (Esp fam) clumsy
■ *m,f* (Esp fam) clumsy idiot (colloq)

patota *f* (AmL fam) mob, gang

patraña *f* tall story

patria *f* homeland, motherland, fatherland; **luchar por la** ~ to fight for one's country

patriarca *m* patriarch

patrimonio *m* patrimony; ~ **personal** personal assets (*pl*); **el** ~ **nacional** national wealth; ~ **histórico** heritage; ~ **artístico/cultural** artistic/cultural heritage

patriota *adj* patriotic
■ *mf* patriot

patriotero -ra *adj* jingoistic, chauvinistic
■ *m,f* jingoist, chauvinist

patriótico -ca *adj* patriotic

patriotismo *m* patriotism

patrocinador -dora *m,f* (de acto, proyecto) sponsor; (Art) patron

patrocinar [A1] *vt* **1** «*acto/proyecto*» to sponsor **2** (Chi, Méx) «*abogado*» to represent

patrón -trona *m,f* **1** (a) (Rels Labs) employer (frml), boss (b) (Esp) (de casa de huéspedes) (*m*)

landlord; (*f*) landlady **2** (Relig) patron saint **3** (CS fam) (como apelativo) (*m*) sir; (*f*) madam **4** **patrón** *m* (a) (en costura) pattern (b) (para mediciones) standard

patrono -na *m,f* (a) (esp AmL) (Relig) patron saint (b) (Rels Labs) employer

patrulla *f* patrol; **están de** ~ they are on patrol; **la** ~ **costera** the coastguard (patrol)
■ *m or f* (coche) patrol *o* squad car

patrullar [A1] *vi/vt* to patrol

patrullera *f* (lancha) patrol boat

patrullero *m* (barco) patrol boat; (avión) patrol plane; (coche — militar) patrol car; (— policial) (CS, Per) patrol *o* squad car

patudo -da *adj* **1** (AmL fam) (de pies grandes) with big feet;**¡qué niño tan** ~**!** what big feet he has! **2** (Chi fam) (descarado) nervy (AmE colloq), cheeky (BrE colloq)

paulatino -na *adj* gradual

paulista *adj* of/from São Paulo

pausa *f* (a) (interrupción) pause; (Rad, TV) break; **hacer una** ~ to pause/have a break (b) (Mús) rest

pauta *f* **1** (guía) guideline; ~**s de comportamiento** rules *o* norms of behavior **2** (de un papel) lines (*pl*)

pava *f* **1** (para calentar agua) kettle **2** (Col fam) (de cigarrillo) butt; *ver tb* PAVO

pavada *f* (RPl fam) (a) (dicho, acción) silly thing to say/do (b) (cosa insignificante) little thing

pavimentar [A1] *vt* (con asfalto) to surface, asphalt; (con cemento, adoquines) to pave

pavimento *m* (de asfalto) road surface; (de cemento, adoquines) paving

pavo -va *m,f* (a) (Coc, Zool) turkey; ~ **real** peacock; **de** ~ (Chi, Per fam) *‹viajar/entrar›* without paying
■ *adj* (a) (fam) (tonto, bobo) silly, dumb (AmE colloq) (b) (Chi fam) (ingenuo) naive (colloq)

pavonearse [A1] *v pron* (fam) to show off; ~ **DE algo** to brag *o* crow ABOUT sth (colloq)

pavor *m* terror; **me da** ~ it terrifies me; **les tiene** ~ **a los perros** (fam) she's terrified of dogs

pavoroso -sa *adj* terrifying, horrific

paya (Chi), **payada** (RPl) *f*: improvised musical dialogue

payador *m* (CS) singer (*who performs* PAYADAS)

payasada *f* **1** (bufonada): **deja de hacer** ~**s** stop clowning around *o* acting the clown (colloq) **2** (fam) (a) (ridiculez) ridiculous thing to say/do (b) (Chi) (tontería) stupid thing to say/do; **son puras** ~**s** that's utter nonsense (c) (Chi) (cosa) thingamajig (colloq)

payasear [A1] *vi* (AmL fam) to clown around (colloq)

payaso -sa *m,f* (a) (Espec) clown; **hacer (se) el** ~ to clown around (colloq) (b) (persona — cómica) clown, comedian; (— poco seria) joker (colloq & pej)

payo -ya *m,f* (Esp) *word used by gypsies to refer to a non-gypsy*

paz *f* (a) (Mil, Pol) peace; **firmar la** ~ to sign a peace agreement *o* treaty; **en época de** ~ in

peacetime; *hacer las paces* to make (it) up **(b)**
(calma) peace; **no me dejan vivir en ~** they don't
give me a moment's peace; **dejar algo/a algn en
~** to leave sth/sb alone; **descanse en ~** (frml) rest
in peace (frml)

PC *m or f* personal computer, PC

P.D. (= *post data*) PS

pe *f: name of the letter* P

peaje *m* (dinero) toll; (lugar) toll barrier; **carretera
de ~** toll road

pearse [A1] *v pron* (AmL fam) to fart (sl)

peatón *m* pedestrian

peatonal *adj* pedestrian (*before n*)

pebete -ta *m,f* (RPI fam) kid (colloq)

pebre *m: sauce made with onion, chili,
coriander, parsley and tomato*

peca *f* freckle

pecado *m* **(a)** (Relig) sin; **~ capital** deadly sin;
~ mortal mortal sin **(b)** (lástima) crime, sin

pecador -dora *m,f* sinner

pecaminoso -sa *adj* sinful

pecar [A2] *vi* (Relig) to sin

pecera *f* (redonda) goldfish bowl; (rectangular) fish
tank

pechera *f* (de camisa, vestido) front

pecho *m* (tórax) chest; (mama) breast; **dar (el) ~
a un niño** to breast-feed *o* suckle a child; *tomarse
algo a ~* (crítica) to take sth to heart;
(responsabilidad) to take sth seriously

pechuga *f* (de pollo) breast

pechugona *f* (fam & hum) big-breasted woman

pecoso -sa *adj* freckly

pectoral *adj* **1** (músculos) pectoral (*before n*)
2 (Med): **jarabe ~** cough mixture *o* syrup

peculiar *adj* **1** (característico) particular; **un
rasgo ~** a particular trait; **con su ~ buen humor**
with his characteristic good humor **2** (poco
común, raro) (sensación) peculiar, unusual

peculiaridad *f* peculiarity

pedagogía *f* pedagogy, teaching

pedagógico -ca *adj* pedagogical, teaching
(*before n*)

pedagogo -ga *m,f* (estudioso) educationalist;
(educador) educator, teacher, pedagogue (frml)

pedal *m* pedal; **~ de embrague/de freno** clutch/
brake pedal; **~ de arranque** kickstart

pedalear [A1] *vi* to pedal

pedante *adj* pedantic
■ *mf* pedant

pedantería *f* pedantry

pedazo *m* **1** (trozo) piece; **un ~ de pan** a piece
of bread; **se hizo ~s** it smashed (to pieces); **el
coche saltó** *or* **voló en ~s** the car was blown to
pieces; **lo hice ~s** I smashed it; *caerse a ~s* to
fall to pieces **2** (fam) (en insultos): **¡~ de idiota!**
you idiot! (colloq)

pederasta *m* (homosexual) homosexual;
(pedófilo) pederast

pedernal *m* flint

pedestal *m* pedestal

pedestre *adj* prosaic

pediatra *mf* pediatrician*

pediatría *f* pediatrics*

pediátrico -ca *adj* pediatric*

pedicuro -ra *m,f* chiropodist

pedido *m* **1** (Com) order; **hacer un ~** to place
an order **2** (AmL) (solicitud) request; **a ~ de** at the
request of

pedigree /peði'vri/, **pedigrí** *m* pedigree; **un
perro de** *or* **con ~** a pedigree dog

pedinche *mf* (Méx fam) scrounger (colloq)

pedir [I14] *vt* **1 (a)** (dinero/ayuda) to ask for;
pidieron un préstamo al banco they asked for
a loan; **pidió permiso para salir** she
asked permission to leave; **pide limosna** he begs
(for money); **~le algo a algn** to ask sb for sth; **le
pidió ayuda** he asked her for help; **me pidió
disculpas** *or* **perdón** he apologized (to me); **~
hora** to make an appointment; **~ la palabra** to
ask for permission to speak; **me pidió que le
enseñara** he asked me to teach him; ▸ PRESTADO
(b) (en bar, restaurante) (plato/bebida) to order;
(cuenta) to ask for
2 (Com) **(a)** (como precio) **~ algo POR algo** to ask
sth FOR sth; **¿cuánto pide por la casa?** how much
is she asking for the house? **(b)** (mercancías) to
order
■ ~ *vi* **(a)** (en bar, restaurante) to order **(b)** (mendigar)
to beg

pedo *m* **1** (ventosidad) fart (sl); **tirarse un ~**
to fart (sl), to let off (BrE colloq); **al ~** (RPI fam) for
nothing **2** (arg) (borrachera): **agarró un buen ~** he
got really plastered (colloq); **tenía un ~ que no
veía** he was blind drunk (colloq) **3** (Méx fam)
(problema, lío) hassle (colloq); *hacérsela de ~ a algn*
(Méx vulg) to give sb hell (colloq)

pedofilia *f* pedophilia*

pedófilo *m* pedophile*

pedorreta *f* (fam) raspberry (colloq)

pedrada *f* **1** (golpe): **me dio una ~ en la
cabeza** she hit me on the head with a stone
2 (Méx fam) (indirecta) hint

pedrisco *m* hail

pega *f* **1** (Col fam) (broma) trick; **de ~** (Esp fam)
(araña/culebra) joke (*before n*), trick (*before n*);
(revólver) dummy (*before n*) **2** (Esp fam) (dificultad,
inconveniente) problem, snag (colloq); **te ponen
muchas ~s** they make it really difficult for you
3 (Andes fam) **(a)** (trabajo) work; (empleo) work;
está sin ~ he's out of work **(b)** (lugar) work

pegadizo -za *adj* catchy

pegado -da *adj* [ESTAR] **(a)** (junto) **~ A algo**: **su
casa está pegada a la mía** her house is right next
to mine; **iba muy ~ al coche de delante** he was
too close to the car in front; **pon la cama pegada
a la pared** put the bed right up against the wall
(b) (adherido) stuck; (con cola, goma) glued; **está ~
al suelo** it's stuck to the floor; **las piezas están
pegadas** the pieces are glued together

pegajoso -sa *adj* **(a)** (superficie/sustancia)
sticky **(b)** (calor) sticky **(c)** (fam) (persona)
clinging (colloq) **(d)** (AmL fam) (canción/música)
catchy

pegamento *m* glue, adhesive

pegar [A3] *vt* **1 (a)** (bofetada/patada) to give;
le pegó una paliza terrible he gave him a terrible
beating; **le ~on un tiro** they shot her **(b)** (grito/
chillido) to let out; **~ un salto de alegría** to jump
for joy; **~le un susto a algn** to give sb a fright ⋯⟶

2 (a) (adherir) to stick; (con cola) to glue, stick **(b)** (coser) ⟨mangas/botones⟩ to sew on **(c)** (arrimar) to move ... closer

3 (fam) (contagiar) ⟨enfermedad⟩ to give; **me pegó la gripe** he gave me the flu

■ ∼ vi **1** (a) (golpear): ∼**le** A **algn** to hit sb; (a un niño, como castigo) to smack sb; **le pega a su mujer** he beats his wife; **la pelota pegó en el poste** the ball hit the goalpost **(b)** (fam) (hacerse popular) ⟨producto/moda⟩ to take off; ⟨artista⟩ to be very popular

2 (a) (adherir) to stick **(b)** (armonizar) to go together; ∼ **CON algo** to go WITH sth; **no pega con el vestido** it doesn't go (very well) with the dress

■ **pegarse** v pron **1** (a) (golpearse): **me pegué con la mesa** I knocked o hit myself on the table; **me pegué en la cabeza** I banged o knocked my head **(b)** (recípr) (darse golpes) to hit each other **2** ⟨susto⟩ to get; ∼**se un tiro** to shoot oneself **3** (contagiarse) ⟨enfermedad⟩ to be infectious; **eso se pega** you can easily catch it; **se te va a** ∼ **mi catarro** you'll catch my cold; **se le ha pegado el acento mexicano** he's picked up a Mexican accent

pegatina f (Esp) sticker

pegoste mf (Méx fam) hanger-on (colloq)

peinado¹ -da adj: **no estaba peinada** she hadn't combed her hair; **siempre va muy bien peinada** her hair always looks very nice

peinado² m (arreglo del pelo) hairstyle; **lavado y** ∼ shampoo and set

peinador -dora m,f (Méx, RPl) (persona) hairdresser, stylist

peinar [A1] vt **1** (a) ⟨melena/flequillo⟩ (con peine) to comb; (con cepillo) to brush **(b)** ⟨peluquero⟩: **¿quién te peina?** who does your hair? **2** ⟨lana⟩ to card **3** (peinar) ⟨área/zona⟩ to comb

■ **peinarse** v pron (a) (refl) (con peine) to comb one's hair; (con cepillo) to brush one's hair **(b)** (caus) to have one's hair done; **me peino en esta peluquería** I have my hair done at this salon

peine m comb

peineta f (a) (para sujetar, adornar) ornamental comb **(b)** (Chi) (peine) comb

p. ej. (= por ejemplo) eg, for example

Pekín m Peking, Beijing

pekinés -nesa m,f Pekinese

pela f (Esp fam) (peseta) peseta

peladez f (Méx) rude word

pelado -da adj **1** (a) (con el pelo corto): **lo dejaron** ∼ or **con la cabeza pelada** (al rape) they cropped his hair very short **(b)** (CS) (calvo) bald **2** (a) ⟨manzana⟩ peeled; ⟨hueso⟩ clean; ⟨almendras⟩ blanched **(b)** ⟨nariz/espalda⟩: **tengo la nariz/espalda pelada** my nose/back is peeling **3** (Chi fam) ⟨pies/trasero⟩ bare; **ir a pie** ∼ to go barefoot **4** (Méx fam) (grosero) foulmouthed

■ m,f (CS fam) (calvo) baldy (colloq)

peladura f (a) (de fruta) peel; ∼**s de papa** potato peelings **(b)** (Andes) (en la piel) graze

pelaje m (de animal) coat, fur

pelar [A1] vt **1** (a) ⟨fruta/zanahoria⟩ to peel; ⟨habas/marisco⟩ to shell; ⟨caramelo⟩ to unwrap **(b)** ⟨ave⟩ to pluck **2** (rapar): **lo** ∼**on al cero** or **al rape** they cropped his hair very short **3** (fam) (en

el juego) to clean ... out (colloq) **4** (Chi fam) ⟨persona⟩ to badmouth (AmE colloq), to slag off (BrE colloq)

■ **pelarse** v pron (a causa del sol) ⟨persona⟩ to peel; ⟨cara/hombros⟩ (+ me/te/le etc) to peel; **se te está pelando la nariz** your nose is peeling

peldaño m (escalón) step, stair; (travesaño) rung

pelea f (a) (discusión) quarrel, fight (colloq), argument; **buscar** ∼ to try to pick a quarrel o fight; **tuvimos una** ∼ we quarreled o had an argument **(b)** (en sentido físico) fight; ∼ **de gallos** cockfight

peleado -da adj (a) (enfadado): **están** ∼**s** they've fallen out; **estar** ∼ **con algn** to have fallen out with sb **(b)** ⟨partido/carrera/elecciones⟩ keenly-contested

peleador -dora adj (fam) (que discute) argumentative; (que pelea): **es muy** ∼ he's always fighting

pelear [A1] vi (a) (discutir) to quarrel; ∼**on por una tontería** they quarreled o (colloq) had a fight over a silly little thing **(b)** ⟨novios⟩ (discutir) to quarrel, argue; (terminar) to break up, split up **(c)** (en sentido físico) to fight; ∼ **POR algo** to fight OVER sth

■ **pelearse** v pron (a) (discutir) to quarrel; (pegarse) to fight; ∼**se POR algo** to quarrel/fight OVER sth **(b)** ⟨novios⟩ (discutir) to quarrel; (terminar) to break up, split up

pelele m (a) (de trapo) rag doll; (de paja) straw doll **(b)** (persona — manipulada) puppet; (— débil) (fam) wimp (colloq)

peletería f (oficio) fur trade; (tienda) furrier's, fur shop; (género) furs (pl)

peliagudo -da adj ⟨problema⟩ difficult, tricky; ⟨asunto⟩ thorny

pelícano m pelican

película f **1** (a) (Cin, TV) movie, film (BrE); **hoy dan** or (Esp) **echan** or **ponen una** ∼ there's a movie o film on today, they're showing a movie o film today; ∼ **de dibujos animados** cartoon; ∼ **del Oeste** or **de vaqueros** Western; ∼ **de miedo** or **de terror** horror movie o film; ∼ **de suspenso** or (Esp) **suspense** suspense thriller; ∼ **muda** silent movie o film **(b)** (Fot) film **2** (capa fina — de aceite) film; (— de polvo) thin layer

peligrar [A1] vi to be at risk; **hacer** ∼ **algo** to put sth at risk

peligro m danger; **estar en** or **correr** ∼ ⟨persona⟩ to be in danger; ⟨vida⟩ to be in danger o at risk; **un** ∼ **para la salud** a health risk; **poner algo/a algn en** ∼ to put sth/sb at risk; **corren el** ∼ **de perder la final** they're in danger of losing the final; **corres el** ∼ **de que te despidan** you run the risk of being fired; **estar fuera de** ∼ to be out of danger; **Ⓢ peligro de incendio** fire hazard

peligrosidad f dangerousness

peligroso -sa adj dangerous

pelillo m small hair

pelirrojo -ja adj red-haired, ginger-haired ■ m,f redhead

pellejerías fpl (Andes fam) hard times (pl)

pellejo m (a) (piel — de animal) skin, hide; (— de persona) (fam) skin (colloq); **ponerse en el** ∼ **de**

algn (fam) to put oneself in sb's shoes **(b)** (fam) (vida) neck (colloq); **jugarse** *or* **arriesgar el ~** to risk one's neck (colloq) **(c)** (odre) wineskin

pellizcar [A2] *vt* ⟨*persona/brazo*⟩ to pinch

pellizco *m* **(a)** (en la piel) pinch; **me dio un ~ en la pierna** she pinched my leg **(b)** (fam) (cantidad pequeña) little bit; **un ~ de sal** a pinch of salt

pelmazo -a *adj* (fam) boring
■ *m,f* (fam) bore

pelo *m* **1** (de personas) hair; **~ rizado/liso** *or* **lacio** curly/straight hair; **tiene mucho/poco ~** he has really thick/thin hair; **llevar el ~ suelto** to wear one's hair down *o* loose; **se le está cayendo el ~** he's losing his hair; **con ~s y señales** (fam) down to the last detail; **no tiene ~s en la lengua** (fam) he doesn't mince his words; **se me/le ponen los ~s de punta** (fam) it sends shivers down my/his spine, it makes my/his hair stand on end; **tomarle el ~ a algn** (fam) (bromeando) to pull sb's leg (colloq); (burlándose) to mess around with sb (AmE), to mess sb around (BrE) **2** (Zool) (filamento) hair; (pelaje — de perro, gato) hair, fur; (— de conejo, oso) fur; **~ de camello** camelhair **3** (de alfombra) pile

pelón -lona *adj* (fam) (sin pelo) bald
■ *m,f* **1** (fam) (sin pelo) baldy (colloq) **2** **pelón** *m* (RPl) (duranzo) nectarine

pelota *f* **1** (Dep, Jueg) ball; **una ~ de fútbol** (esp AmL) a football; **jugar a la ~** to play ball; **~ vasca** jai alai, pelota; **darle ~ a algn** (CS fam) to take notice of sb; **hacerle la ~ a algn** (Esp fam) to suck up to sb (colloq) **2** **pelotas** *fpl* (vulg) (testículos) balls (*pl*) (colloq *o* vulg); **en ~s** (vulg) (sin ropa) stark naked; (sin dinero) flat broke (colloq)
■ *mf* **1** (AmS vulg) (imbécil) jerk (sl) **2** (Esp fam) (adulador) creep (colloq)

pelotari *mf* jai alai *o* pelota player

pelotazo *m* (golpe): **me dio un ~** he hit me with the ball

pelotera *f* (fam) **(a)** (lío, jaleo) ruckus (AmE colloq), rumpus (BrE colloq) **(b)** (riña) argument, row (colloq)

pelotero -ra *m,f* **(a)** (AmL) (jugador — de béisbol) baseball player; (— de fútbol) soccer *o* football player, footballer **(b)** (Chi) (recogepelotas) (*m*) ballboy; (*f*) ballgirl

pelotón *m* **(a)** (Mil) squad; **~ de ejecución** *or* **fusilamiento** firing squad **(b)** (en ciclismo) bunch, pack; (en atletismo) pack **(c)** (fam) (de gente) gang (colloq)

pelotudo -da *adj* (AmS vulg): **¡qué ~!** what a jerk! (sl)
■ *m,f* (AmS vulg) jerk (sl)

peluca *f* wig

peluche *m* felt, plush; **un juguete de ~** a cuddly toy; ▶ **oso**

pelucón -cona *adj* (Chi, Per fam) (con mucho pelo) hairy; (de pelo largo) long-haired

peludo -da *adj* ⟨*hombre/brazo*⟩ hairy; ⟨*barba*⟩ bushy; ⟨*animal*⟩ hairy, furry; ⟨*cola*⟩ bushy; ⟨*lana/jersey*⟩ hairy

peluquería *f* **(a)** (establecimiento) hairdresser's, hairdressing salon **(b)** (oficio) hairdressing, hairstyling

peluquero -ra *m,f* hairdresser, hairstylist

peluquín *m* toupee, hairpiece

pelusa¹, pelusilla *f* **1** (en la cara) down, fuzz; (de fruta) down; (en jersey) ball of fluff *o* fuzz; (de suciedad) ball of fluff **2** (Esp fam) (celos) jealousy; **tener ~** to be jealous

pelusa² *mf* (Chi fam) (niño — callejero) street kid (colloq); (— travieso) little rascal (colloq)

pelvis *f* (*pl* ~) pelvis

pena *f* **1** **(a)** (tristeza): **tenía/sentía mucha ~** he was *o* felt very sad; **me da ~ verlo** it upsets me *o* it makes me sad to see it; **a mí la que me da ~ es su mujer** it's his wife I feel sorry for; **está que da ~** she's in a terrible state **(b)** (lástima) pity, shame; **¡qué ~!** what a pity *o* shame!; **es una ~ que ...** it's a pity (that) ...; **vale** *or* **merece la ~** it's worth it; **vale la ~ leerlo/visitarlo** it's worth reading/a visit **2** **penas** *fpl* **(a)** (problemas) sorrows (*pl*); **ahogar las ~s** to drown one's sorrows; **me contó sus ~s** he told me his troubles; **a duras ~s** (apenas) hardly; (con dificultad) with difficulty **(b)** (penalidades) hardship **3** (Der) sentence; **la ~ máxima** the maximum sentence; **~ capital** *or* **de muerte** death penalty **4** (AmL exc CS) (vergüenza) embarrassment; **¡qué ~!** how embarrassing!; **me da mucha ~ pedírselo** I'm too embarrassed to ask him

penal *adj* criminal (*before n*)
■ *m* **1** (cárcel) prison, penitentiary (AmE) **2** (AmL period) (Dep) penalty

pénal *m* (Andes) penalty

penalidades *fpl* hardship, suffering

penalizar [A4] *vt* (Der) to penalize

penalty /'penalti, pe'nalti/ *m* (*pl* **-tys**) penalty; **pitar** *or* **señalar un ~** to award *o* give a penalty

penca *f* **(a)** (de hoja) main rib **(b)** (del nopal) stalk **(c)** (Méx) (de bananas) bunch

pendejada *f* **(a)** (AmL exc CS fam) (estupidez) stupid thing to say/do **(b)** (Per vulg) (mala jugada) dirty trick

pendejear [A1] *vi* (Méx fam) to clown around (colloq)

pendejez *f* (Méx vulg) stupidity

pendejo -ja *adj* **(a)** (AmL exc CS fam) (estúpido) dumb (AmE colloq), thick (BrE colloq) **(b)** (Per fam) (listo) sly, sharp (colloq)
■ *m,f* **(a)** (AmL exc CS fam) (estúpido) dummy (colloq), nerd (colloq); **hacerse el ~** (AmL) (hacerse el tonto) to act dumb (colloq); (no hacer nada) to loaf around (colloq) **(b)** (Per fam) (persona lista) sly devil

pendenciero -ra *adj* quarrelsome
■ *m,f* troublemaker

pendiente *adj* **1** ⟨*asunto/problema*⟩ unresolved; ⟨*cuenta*⟩ outstanding **2** ⟨*atento*⟩: **está ~ del niño a todas horas** she devotes every minute of the day to the child; **estoy ~ de que me llamen** I'm waiting for them to call me
■ *m* (Esp) earring
■ *f* (de terreno) slope, incline; (de tejado) slope; **una ~ muy pronunciada** a very steep slope *o* incline; **tiene mucha ~** it slopes steeply

péndulo *m* pendulum

pene *m* penis

penetración *f* penetration

penetrante *adj* **1** **(a)** ⟨*mirada/voz*⟩ penetrating, piercing; ⟨*olor*⟩ pungent, penetrating; ⟨*sonido*⟩ piercing **(b)** ⟨*viento/frío*⟩ bitter, biting **2** ⟨*inteligencia/mente/ironía*⟩ sharp

penetrar [A1] *vi* (entrar) ~ **POR** algo «*agua/
humedad*» to seep THROUGH sth; «*luz*» to shine
THROUGH sth; «*ladrón*» to enter THROUGH sth; ~
EN algo to penetrate sth
■ ~ *vt* to penetrate; **la bala le penetró el pulmón**
the bullet penetrated *o* entered his lung

penicilina *f* penicillin

península *f* peninsula

peninsular *adj* peninsular
■ *mf*: **los** ~**es** people from mainland Spain

penique *m* penny

penitencia *f* [1] (Relig) penance; **en** ~ **as** (a)
penance [2] (a) (Andes) (en juegos) forfeit; **(b)** (RPI
fam) (castigo) punishment; **el maestro me puso en**
~ the teacher punished me

penitenciaría *f* penitentiary

penitente *mf* penitent

penoso -sa *adj* [1] (lamentable) terrible, awful
[2] (a) (triste) sad **(b)** «*viaje*» grueling*; «*trabajo*»
laborious, difficult [3] (AmL exc CS fam) (a)
«*persona*» shy **(b)** (embarazoso) embarrassing

pensamiento *m* [1] (a) (facultad) thought **(b)**
(cosa pensada) thought **(c)** (doctrina) thinking **(d)**
(máxima) thought [2] (Bot) pansy

pensar [A5] *vi* to think; **después de mucho** ~
... after much thought ...; **actuó sin** ~ he did it
without thinking; **pensé para mí** *or* **para mis
adentros** I thought to myself; ~ **EN** algo/algn to
think ABOUT sth/sb; **cuando menos se piensa** ...
just when you least expect it ...; ~ **mal/bien de
algn** to think ill *o* badly/well of sb; *dar que or
hacer* ~ *a algn* to make sb think
■ ~ *vt* [1] (a) (creer, opinar) to think; **pienso que no**
I don't think so; **¿qué piensas del divorcio/del
jefe?** what do you think about divorce/the boss?
(b) (considerar) to think about; **lo** ~**é** I'll think
about it; **piénsalo bien antes de decidir** think it
over before you decide; **pensándolo bien,** ... on
second thought(s) *o* thinking about it, ...; **¡y** ~
que ...! (and) to think that ...!; **¡ni** ~**lo!** no way!
(colloq), not on your life! (colloq) **(c)** (Col) «*persona*»
to think about
[2] (tener la intención de): ~ **hacer algo** to think of
doing sth; **pensamos ir al teatro** we're thinking of
going to the theater; **no pienso ir** I'm not going
■ **pensarse** *v pron* (enf) (fam) «*decisión/
respuesta*» to think about; *ver tb* PENSAR *vt* 1B

pensativo -va *adj* pensive, thoughtful

pensión *f* [1] (Servs Socs) pension; **cobrar la** ~
to draw one's pension; ~ **alimenticia**
maintenance; ~ **de invalidez** disability
(allowance) (AmE), invalidity benefit (BrE) [2] (a)
(casa — de huéspedes) guesthouse, rooming house
(AmE), boarding house (BrE); **(— para estudiantes)**
student hostel; ~ **completa** full board ▶ MEDIO¹ 1
(b) (alojamiento) accommodations (*pl*) (ame),
lodging, accommodation (BrE) [3] (Col)
(mensualidad) tuition (AmE), school fees (*pl*) (BrE

pensionado -da *m,f* [1] (Servs Socs) pensioner
[2] **pensionado** *m* (a) (Esp) (internado) boarding
school **(b)** (CS) (pensión para estudiantes) student
hostel

pensionarse [A1] *v pron* (Col) to retire

pensionista *mf* [1] (Servs Socs) pensioner
[2] (en casa de huéspedes) resident, lodger

pentágono *m* (a) (Mat) pentagon **(b) el
Pentágono** the Pentagon

pentagrama *m* (Mús) stave, staff

pentatlón *m* pentathlon

penúltimo -ma *adj* penultimate
■ *m,f*: **ser el** ~ to be second to last

penumbra *f* (media luz) half-light, semidarkness

penuria *f* (a) (escasez) shortage, dearth; **pasar**
~**s** to suffer hardship **(b)** (pobreza) poverty

peña *f* [1] (roca) crag, rock [2] (a) (grupo) circle,
group; ~ **taurina** bullfighting club **(b)** (AmL) *tb* ~
folklórica folk club

peñasco *m* crag, rocky outcrop

peón *m* [1] (Const) laborer*; (Agr) (esp AmL)
agricultural laborer*, farm worker; ~ **albañil**
(building) laborer*; ~ **caminero** road worker
[2] (en ajedrez) pawn; (en damas) piece, checker
(AmE), draughtsman (BrE)

peonza *f* spinning top

peor *adj/adv* [1] (uso comparativo) worse; **va a ser**
~ **para él como no estudie** if he doesn't study so
much the worse for him; **y si vienen los dos,
tanto** ~ and it'll be even worse if the two of them
come; **cada vez** ~ worse and worse; **su situación
es** ~ **que la mía** his situation is worse than mine;
está ~ **que nunca** it's worse than ever
[2] (uso superlativo) worst; **el** ~ **alumno de la clase**
the worst pupil in the class; **lo** ~ **que puede
pasar** the worst (thing) that can happen; **en el** ~
de los casos if the worst comes to the worst; **el
lugar donde** ~ **se come** the worst place to eat in
■ *mf*: **el/la** ~ (de dos) the worse; (de varios) the
worst

pepa *f* (AmS) (semilla — de uva, naranja) pip; (— de
durazno, aguacate) stone, pit

Pepe: *diminutive of José*

pepenador -dora *m,f* (Méx) scavenger (*on
garbage dumps*)

pepenar [A1] *vt* (Méx fam) (en la basura) to
scavenge

pepinillo *m* gherkin

pepino *m* cucumber

pepita *f* (a) (de uva) pip; (de tomate) seed; (de
calabaza) (Méx) dried pumpkin seed **(b)** (de oro)
nugget

pepona *f* large doll

pequeño -ña *adj* (a) (de tamaño) small; **me
queda** ~ it's too small for me; **en** ~ in miniature
(b) (de edad) young, small; **mi hermano** ~ my
younger *o* little brother; **cuando era** ~ when I
was small *o* little **(c)** (de poca importancia)
«*distancia*» short; «*retraso*» short, slight;
«*cantidad*» small; «*esfuerzo*» slight; «*problema/
diferencia*» slight, small
■ *m,f*: **el** ~**/la pequeña** the little one (colloq); (edad
— de dos) **/la** ~ the younger; (— de muchos) the youngest

pera *f* [1] (Bot) pear; ~ **de agua** dessert pear;
pedirle ~**s** *al olmo* to ask the impossible [2] (de

AmC	Central America	Arg	Argentina	Cu	Cuba	Per	Peru
AmL	Latin America	Bol	Bolivia	Ec	Ecuador	RPI	River Plate Area
AmS	South America	Chi	Chile	Esp	Spain	Ur	Uruguay
Andes	Andean Region	CS	Southern Cone	Méx	Mexico	Ven	Venezuela

goma) bulb **3** (en boxeo) punching ball (AmE), punchball (BrE) **4** (CS fam) (mentón) chin; (barba) goatee

peral *m* pear tree

percal *m* percale

percance *m* (contratiempo) mishap; (accidente) minor accident

percatarse [A1] *v pron* to notice; **∼ DE algo** to notice sth

percebe *m* (molusco) goose barnacle

percepción *f* (por los sentidos) perception; **∼ extrasensorial** extrasensory perception, ESP

perceptible *adj* (por los sentidos) perceptible, noticeable

percha *f* (a) (para el armario) (coat) hanger (b) (gancho) coat hook; (perchero) coat stand

perchero *m* (de pared) coat rack; (de pie) coat stand

percibir [I1] *vt* **1** (sonido/olor) to perceive; (peligro) to sense **2** (frml) (sueldo/cantidad) to receive

percusión *f* percussion

perdedor -dora *adj* losing (before n)
■ *m,f* loser; **es un mal ∼** he's a bad loser

perder [E8] *vt* **1** (en general) to lose; **perdí el pasaporte** I lost my passport; **quiere ∼ peso** he wants to lose weight; **con preguntar no se pierde nada** we've/you've nothing to lose by asking; **∼ la vida** to lose one's life, to perish; ▶ CABEZA 1E, VISTA 3; **yo no pierdo las esperanzas** I'm not giving up hope; **∼ la práctica** to get out of practice; **∼ el equilibrio** to lose one's balance; **∼ el conocimiento** to lose consciousness, to pass out; **∼ el ritmo** (Mús) to lose the beat; (en trabajo) to get out of the rhythm **2** (a) (autobús/tren/avión) to miss (b) (ocasión/oportunidad) to miss; **sin ∼ detalle** without missing any detail (c) (tiempo) to waste; **¡no me hagas ∼ (el) tiempo!** don't waste my time!; **no hay tiempo que ∼** there's no time to lose **3** (a) (guerra/pleito/partido) to lose (b) (curso/año) to fail; (examen) (Ur) to fail **4** (agua/aceite/aire) to lose
■ ∼ *vi* **1** (ser derrotado) to lose; **perdieron 3 a 1** they lost 3-1; **no sabes ∼** you're a bad loser; **llevar las de ∼** to be onto a loser; **la que sale perdiendo soy yo** I'm the one who loses out *o* comes off worst **2** «cafetera/tanque» to leak **3** echar(se) a perder ▶ ECHAR I 1A, ECHARSE 1A
■ **perderse** *v pron* **1** «persona/objeto» to get lost; **siempre me pierdo en esta ciudad** I always get lost in this town; **se le perdió el dinero** he's lost the money; **cuando se ponen a hablar rápido me pierdo** when they start talking quickly I get lost **2** (fiesta/película/espectáculo) to miss

perdición *f* ruin

pérdida *f* (a) (en general) loss; **∼ de calor/energía** heat/energy loss; **tuvo una ∼ de conocimiento** he lost consciousness, he passed out; **no tiene ∼** (Esp) you can't miss it (b) (Fin) loss; **la compañía sufrió grandes ∼s** the company made a huge loss; **∼s materiales** damage; **∼s y ganancias** profit and loss (c) (desperdicio) waste; **fue una ∼ de tiempo** it was a waste of time (d) (escape de gas, agua) leak

perdido -da *adj* **1** [ESTAR] (a) (objeto/persona) lost; **dar algo por ∼** to give sth up for lost; **de ∼** (Méx fam) at least (b) (confundido, desorientado) lost, confused (c) (bala/perro) stray (before n) **2** [ESTAR] (en un apuro): **si se enteran, estás ∼** if they find out, you've had it *o* you're done for (colloq) **3** (aislado) (lugar) remote, isolated; (momento) idle, spare **4** (idiota) complete and utter (before n), total (before n); (loco) raving (before n); (borracho) out and out (before n)
■ *m,f* degenerate

perdidoso -sa *m, f* (Méx) loser

perdigón *m* (Arm) pellet

perdiz *f* partridge

perdón *m* (Der) pardon; (Relig) forgiveness; **me pidió ∼ por su comportamiento** he apologized to me for his behavior, he said he was sorry about his behavior; **con ∼** if you'll pardon the expression
■ *interj* (expresando disculpas) I beg your pardon (frml), excuse me (AmE), sorry; (para atraer la atención) excuse me, pardon me (AmE); (al pedir que se repita algo) sorry?, pardon me?

perdonar [A1] *vt* (a) (persona/falta/pecado) to forgive; **te perdono** I forgive you; **perdona mi curiosidad, pero …** forgive my asking but …; **perdone que lo moleste, pero …** sorry to bother you *o* (AmE) pardon me for bothering you, but … (b) (Der) to pardon (c) (deuda) to write off; **le perdonó el castigo** she let him off the punishment
■ ∼ *vi*: **perdone ¿me puede decir la hora?** excuse me *o* (AmE) pardon me, can you tell me the time?; **perdone ¿cómo ha dicho?** sorry? what did you say?, excuse *o* pardon me? what did you say? (AmE); **perdona, pero yo no dije eso** I'm sorry but that's not what I said

perdurar [A1] *vi* «duda/sentimiento/recuerdo» to remain, last; «crisis/situación/relación» to last

perecear [A1] *vi* (Col) to laze around

perecedero -ra *adj* (producto) perishable

perecer [E3] *vi* (frml) to die, perish (journ or liter)

peregrinación *f*, **peregrinaje** *m* pilgrimage

peregrino -na *adj* **1** (idea/respuesta) outlandish, peculiar **2** (a) (ave) migratory (b) (monje) wandering (before n)
■ *m,f* pilgrim

perejil *m* (Bot, Coc) parsley

perenne *adj* perennial; **árbol de hoja ∼** evergreen tree

pereza *f* laziness; **me da ∼ ir** I can't be bothered to go; **tengo una ∼ horrible** I feel terribly lazy; **¡qué ∼ tener que ir!** what a bind *o* drag having to go! (colloq)

perezosa *f* (Col, Per) deck chair

perezoso -sa *adj* lazy, idle
■ *m,f* **1** (holgazán) lazybones (colloq) **2** **perezoso** *m* (Zool) sloth

perfección *f* perfection; **habla francés a la ∼** she speaks perfect French

perfeccionar [A1] *vt* (mejorar) to improve; (hacer perfecto) to perfect

perfeccionista *mf* perfectionist

perfecto¹ -ta *adj* (a) (ideal, excelente) perfect ⋯⊹

(b) (*delante del n*) (absoluto): **un ~ caballero** a perfect gentleman; **es un ~ desconocido** he is completely unknown

perfecto² *interj* fine!

perfil *m* **(a)** (del cuerpo, la cara) profile; **una foto de ~** a profile photograph; **visto de ~** seen from the side **(b)** (contorno, silueta) profile, silhouette

perfilar [A1] *vt* ⟨*plan/estrategia*⟩ to shape

■ **perfilarse** *v pron* **(a)** «*silueta/contorno*» to be outlined **(b)** (tomar forma) «*posición/actitud*» to become clear

perforación *f* **(a)** (en general) drilling, boring; (pozo) borehole **(b)** (Med) perforation **(c)** (en papeles, sellos) perforation

perforadora *f* **1** (Min, Tec) drill **2** (de papeles) hole puncher; (de sellos) perforator

perforar [A1] *vt* **1** **(a)** ⟨*pozo*⟩ to sink, drill, bore **(b)** ⟨*madera*⟩ to drill o bore holes/a hole in **(c)** ⟨*ácido*⟩ to perforate; ⟨*bala*⟩ to pierce **2** ⟨*papel/tarjeta*⟩ to perforate

■ **perforarse** *v pron* «*úlcera/intestino*» to become perforated

perfumar [A1] *vt* to perfume

■ **perfumarse** *v pron* (*refl*) to put perfume o scent on

perfume *m* perfume, scent

perfumería *f* perfumery

pergamino *m* (material) parchment; (documento) scroll

pérgola *f* pergola

pericia *f* (destreza) skill

periferia *f* **(a)** (de círculo) periphery, circumference **(b)** (de ciudad) outskirts (*pl*) **(c)** (Inf) peripherals (*pl*)

periférico¹ -ca *adj* ⟨*barrio/zona*⟩ outlying (*before n*)

periférico² *m* **1** (Inf) peripheral **2** (AmC, Méx) (carretera) beltway (AmE), ring road (BrE)

perilla *f* (barba) goatee; **venir de ~(s)** (fam) to come in very handy (colloq)

perímetro *m* perimeter

periódico¹ -ca *adj* periodic

periódico² *m* newspaper, paper

periodiquero -ra *m,f* (Méx) news o newspaper vendor

periodismo *m* journalism

periodista *mf* journalist, reporter; **~ gráfico** press photographer

período, periodo *m* period

peripecia *f* **(a)** (incidente): **un viaje lleno de ~s** an eventful journey; **sus ~s en el extranjero** her adventures abroad **(b)** (problema) vicissitude

periquito *m* (americano) parakeet; (australiano) budgerigar, budgie (colloq)

periscopio *m* periscope

peritaje *m* **(a)** (informe) expert's report; (de casa) survey (report) **(b)** (Educ) technical studies (*pl*)

perito -ta *m,f* (experto) expert; **~ agrónomo** agricultural technician; **~ industrial** engineer; **~ mercantil** qualified accountant

peritonitis *f* (*pl* **~**) peritonitis

perjudicado -da *adj*: **el que resultó ~** the one who lost out o who was worst hit; **los más ~s** the worst hit, the worst affected

■ *m,f*: **el ~ fui yo** I was the one who lost out

perjudicar [A2] *vt* (dañar) to be detrimental to (frml), damage; **el tabaco perjudica la salud** smoking is detrimental to o damages your health; **estas medidas perjudican a los jóvenes** these measures are detrimental to o harm young people

perjudicial *adj* [SER] damaging, harmful, detrimental (frml); **~ PARA algo/algn** damaging o harmful to sth/sb

perjuicio *m* (daño) damage; **no sufrió ningún ~** it did him no harm o damage; **le causó un gran ~** it was very damaging to him; **redunda o va en ~ de todos** it works against o (frml) is detrimental to everyone; **sin ~ para su salud** without detriment to his health (frml); **sin ~ de que cambiemos de opinión** even though we may change our minds later

perjurio *m* perjury

perla *f* (joya) pearl; **~ cultivada** *or* **de cultivo** cultured pearl

permanecer [E3] *vi* (frml) **(a)** (en lugar) to stay, remain (frml) **(b)** (en actitud, estado) to remain; **permaneció en silencio** he was o remained silent

permanencia *f* (en lugar) stay; (en organización, cargo) continuance (frml)

permanente *adj* permanent

■ *f* **1** (en el pelo) perm; **hacerse la ~** to have one's hair permed, to have a perm **2** (Col) (juzgado) emergency court (*for cases of violent crime*)

permisible *adj* permissible

permisionario -ria *m,f* (Méx) concessionaire, official agent

permisivo -va *adj* permissive

permiso *m* **1** (autorización) permission; (documento) permit, license*; **me dio ~** she gave me permission; (con) **permiso** (al abrirse paso) excuse me; (al entrar) may I come in?; **~ de conducir** driver's license (AmE), driving licence (BrE); **~ de residencia** residence permit, green card (AmE); **~ de trabajo** work permit **2** (días libres) leave; **de ~** on leave

permitir [I1] *vt* **(a)** (autorizar) to allow, permit (frml); **no le permitieron verla** he was not allowed to see her; **no van a ~les la entrada** they're not going to let them in; **¿me permite?** (frml) may I? **(b)** (tolerar, consentir): **no te permito que me hables así** I won't have you speak o I won't tolerate you speaking to me like that; **si se me permite la expresión** if you'll pardon the expression **(c)** (hacer posible) to enable, to make ... possible; **esto ~á mejores comunicaciones** this will enable better communications; **si el tiempo lo permite** weather permitting

■ **permitirse** *v pron* (*refl*) to allow oneself; (económicamente): **puedo/no puedo ~me ese lujo** I can't/can't afford that luxury

permutación *f* permutation

pernera *f* (del pantalón) leg

pero *conj* but; **ella fue, ~ yo no** she went, but I didn't; **¡~ si queda lejísimos!** but it's miles (away)!; **¿~ tú estás loca?** are you crazy?

■ *m* **(a)** (defecto) defect, bad point; (dificultad, problema) drawback; **ponerle ~s a algo/algn** to find fault with sth/sb **(b)** (excusa) objection; **¡no hay ~ que valga!** I don't want any excuses (o arguments *etc*)

perogrullada *f* (fam) platitude, truism

Perogrullo m: **ser de** ∼ to be patently obvious

perol m (pequeño) saucepan; (grande) pot

peroné m fibula

perorata f (fam) lecture (colloq)

perpendicular adj/f perpendicular

perpetrar [A1] vt to perpetrate (frml), to carry out

perpetuar [A18] vt to perpetuate

perpetuo -tua adj perpetual

perplejidad f perplexity, puzzlement

perplejo -ja adj perplexed, puzzled; **estar** ∼ **by algo** to be puzzled o perplexed con sth

perra f ①(Zool) dog, bitch [BITCH solo se emplea cuando se quiere hacer referencia al sexo del animal] ver tb PERRO ② (Esp fam) **(a)** (rabieta) tantrum; **coger una** ∼ to have o throw a tantrum **(b)** (manía) obsession; **le ha logido la** ∼ **de tener uno** he's obsessed with having one

perrada f (AmL fam) dirty trick

perrera f **(a)** (lugar) dog pound, dog's home **(b)** (vehículo) dog catcher's van

perrería f (fam) terrible thing (colloq)

perrero -ra m,f dog catcher, dog warden (BrE)

perrito m ① (Zool) little dog; ver tb PERRO ② (AmL) (Bot) snapdragon

perro -rra m,f (Zool) dog; ∼ **callejero** stray (dog); ∼ **de compañía** pet dog; ∼ **guardián** guard dog; ∼ **guía** or **lazarillo** guide dog; ∼ **pastor** sheepdog; **perrito caliente** (Coc) hot dog; **perrito faldero** lapdog; ∼ **policía** German shepherd, Alsatian (BrE); ∼ **rastreador** (para seguir una huella) tracker dog; (para buscar drogas) sniffer dog; ∼ **salchicha** dachshund, sausage dog (colloq); **de** ∼**s** (fam) foul; **hace un tiempo de** ∼**s** the weather's foul o horrible; **está de un humor de** ∼**s** he's in a foul mood; **llevarse como** (el) ∼ **y** (el) **gato** to fight like cats and dogs (AmE) o (BrE) cat and dog ■ adj (fam) **(a)** ⟨vida/suerte⟩ rotten (colloq), lousy (colloq) **(b)** ⟨persona⟩ nasty

persa adj/mf Persian
■ m (idioma) Persian

persecución f **(a)** (en sentido físico) pursuit; **salir en** ∼ **de algn** to set off in pursuit of sb **(b)** (por la ideología) persecution; **sufrir persecuciones** to be subjected to persecution, to be persecuted

perseguir [I30] vt ① **(a)** ⟨fugitivo/delincuente/ presa⟩ to pursue, chase **(b)** (por la ideología) to persecute ② ⟨objetivo/fin⟩ to pursue; ∼ **la fama** to be in pursuit of fame; **me persigue la mala suerte** I'm dogged by bad luck

perseverante adj persevering, persistent

perseverar [A1] vi to persevere

Persia f Persia

persiana f **(a)** (que se enrolla o levanta) blind; ∼ **veneciana** or **de lamas** Venetian blind **(b)** (AmL) (contraventana, postigo) shutter

persignarse [A1] v pron to cross oneself

persistencia f persistence

persistente adj persistent

persistir [I1] vi: **persiste el temporal** there is still a storm blowing; ∼ **EN algo** to persist IN sth

persona f **(a)** (ser humano) person; **una** ∼ **muy educada** a very polite person; **dos o más** ∼**s** two or more people; **las** ∼**s interesadas ...** all those interested ... **(b)** (en locs) **en persona** ⟨ir/ presentarse⟩ in person; **no lo conozco en** ∼ I

don't know him personally; **por persona** per person; **solo se venden dos entradas por** ∼ you can only get two tickets per person; **la comida costó 20 dólares por** ∼ the meal cost 20 dollars per o a head **(c)** (Ling) person

personaje m **(a)** (Cin, Lit) character **(b)** (persona importante) important figure, personage (frml); **un** ∼ **de la política** an important political figure; **es todo un** ∼ **en el pueblo** he's something of a local celebrity

personal adj personal; **objetos de uso** ∼ personal effects
■ m (de fábrica, empresa) personnel (pl), staff (sing or pl); **estamos escasos de** ∼ we're short-staffed

personalidad f **(a)** (Psic) personality **(b)** (persona importante) ▶ PERSONAJE B

personalizar [A4] vi: **no quiero** ∼ I don't want to name names o mention any names
■ ∼ vt to personalize

personería f (Col, RPl) legal capacity

personero -ra m,f (AmL) (representante) representative; (portavoz) (m) spokesman, spokesperson; (f) spokeswoman, spokesperson

personificar [A2] vt to personify; **es la bondad personificada** she is kindness itself

perspectiva f **(a)** (Arquit, Art) perspective; **en** ∼ in perspective **(b)** (vista, paisaje) view, perspective (frml) **(c)** (punto de vista) perspective **(d)** (posibilidad) prospect; **las** ∼**s son buenas** the prospects are good; **no tengo ningún plan en** ∼ I've no plans for the immediate future

perspicacia f shrewdness, insight

perspicaz adj shrewd, perceptive

persuadir [I1] vt to persuade; ∼ **a algn** DE QUE or PARA QUE **haga algo** to persuade sb to do sth

persuasión f persuasion

persuasivo -va adj persuasive

pertenecer [E3] vi **(a)** (ser propiedad) ∼ A **algn/ algo** to belong to sb/sth **(b)** (formar parte) ∼ A **algo** to belong TO sth, be a member OF sth

perteneciente adj: **los países** ∼**s al grupo** the countries belonging to o which are members of the group

pertenencia f **(a)** (a grupo, organización) membership **(b)** (frml) (propiedad): **los objetos de su** ∼ his belongings **(c) pertenencias** fpl belongings (pl), possessions (pl)

pértiga f **(a)** (vara) pole **(b)** (Esp) (Dep) pole; **salto con** ∼ pole vault

pertinente adj **(a)** (oportuno, adecuado) ⟨medida⟩ appropriate **(b)** (relevante) ⟨observación/ comentario⟩ relevant, pertinent

perturbación f (alteración) disruption; (Psic) disturbance

perturbado -da adj disturbed
■ m,f: tb ∼ **mental** mentally disturbed person

perturbar [A1] vt to disturb

Perú m: tb **el** ∼ Peru

peruanismo m Peruvianism, Peruvian word/ expression

peruano -na adj/m,f Peruvian

perversión f **(a)** (maldad) evil, wickedness **(b)** (corrupción) perversion

perverso -sa adj evil
■ m,f evil o wicked person

pervertido -da m,f pervert

pervertir [I11] *vt* to corrupt, pervert
■ **pervertirse** *v pron* to become corrupted
pesa *f* **(a)** (de balanza, reloj) weight **(b)** (Dep)
(grande) weight; (pequeña) dumbbell; **levantamiento
de** ∼**s** weightlifting; *hacer* ∼**s** to do weight
training **(c)** (balanza) scales (*pl*)
pesadez *f* **1** (sensación de cansancio) heaviness
2 (fam) **(a)** (aburrimiento, molestia) drag (colloq); ¡**qué**
∼ **de conversación!** what a boring conversation!
(b) (Andes) (broma) tiresome joke; (comentario)
nasty remark
pesadilla *f* **(a)** (sueño) nightmare, bad dream
(b) (situación) nightmare; **de** ∼ 〈*viaje/visión*〉
nightmare (*before n*)
pesado -da *adj* **1** (en general) heavy;
〈*estómago*〉 bloated; 〈*sueño*〉 deep **2** **(a)** (fam)
(fastidioso, aburrido) 〈*libro/película*〉 tedious;
〈*persona*〉: ¡**qué** ∼ **es!** he's such a pain in the
neck! (colloq); **no te pongas** ∼ don't be so
annoying *o* (colloq) such a pest! **(b)** (AmL) (difícil,
duro) 〈*trabajo/tarea*〉 heavy, hard **3** (Andes fam)
(antipático) unpleasant; ¡**qué tipo tan** ∼**!** what a
jerk! (colloq)
■ *m,f* **(a)** (latoso) pain (colloq), pest (colloq) **(b)**
(Andes fam) (antipático) jerk (colloq)
pesadumbre *f* grief, sorrow
pésame *m* condolences (*pl*); **darle el** ∼ **a algn**
to offer sb one's condolences; **mi más sentido** ∼
(fr hecha) my deepest sympathies
pesar¹ *m* **1** **(a)** (pena, tristeza) sorrow; **a** ∼ **mío**
or **muy a mi** ∼ much to my regret
(b) (remordimiento) regret, remorse **2** **a pesar de**
despite, in spite of; **a** ∼ **de todo** in spite of *o*
despite everything; **a** ∼ **de que** even though
pesar² [A1] *vi* **1** «*paquete/maleta*» to be
heavy; **estas gafas no pesan** these glasses don't
weigh much; **no me pesa** it's not heavy
2 (causar arrepentimiento) (+ *me/te/le etc*): **ahora me
pesa mucho** now I deeply regret it; **me pesa
haberlo ofendido** I'm very sorry I offended him
3 **pese a** despite, in spite of; **pese a que** even
though; **mal que me/le pese** whether I like/he
likes it or not
■ ∼ *vt* **(a)** 〈*niño/maleta*〉 to weigh; 〈*manzanas*〉 to
weigh (out) **(b)** (tener cierto peso) to weigh; **pesa 80
kilos** he weighs 80 kilos
■ **pesarse** *v pron* (*refl*) to weigh oneself
pesca *f* **(a)** (en general) fishing; **ir** *or* **salir de** ∼
to go fishing; ∼ **con caña** angling; ∼ **con red** net
fishing; ∼ **submarina** underwater fishing **(b)**
(peces) fish (*pl*); **aquí hay mucha** ∼ there are a
lot of fish here **(c)** (lo pescado) catch
pescada *f* hake
pescadería *f* fish shop, fishmonger's (BrE)
pescadero -ra *m,f* fish dealer (AmE),
fishmonger (BrE)
pescadilla *f* whiting, young hake
pescado *m* (Coc) fish; (pez) (AmL) fish; ∼ **azul/
blanco** blue/white fish
pescador -dora (*m*) fisherman;
(*f*) fisherwoman
pescar [A2] *vt* **1** 〈*trucha/corvina*〉 to catch;

fuimos a ∼ **trucha(s)** we went trout-fishing, we
went fishing for trout **2** (fam) **(a)** 〈*catarro/gripe*〉
to catch **(b)** 〈*novio/marido*〉 to get, hook (colloq &
hum) **(c)** 〈*chiste/broma*〉 to get (colloq) **(d)** (pillar) to
catch; **lo** ∼**on robando** they caught him
red-handed (as he was stealing something)
■ ∼ *vi* to fish; ∼ **a mosca** to fly-fish
pescuezo *m* (fam) neck
pese a *loc prep* ▶ PESAR² 3
pesebre *m* (en establo) manger, trough; (de
Navidad) crib
pesebrera *f* (Col) stable
pesero *m* (Méx) minibus
peseta *f* peseta (*Spanish unit of currency*)
pesimismo *m* pessimism
pesimista *adj* pessimistic
■ *mf* pessimist
pésimo -ma *adj* dreadful, terrible, abysmal
peso *m* **1** **(a)** (Fís, Tec) weight; **ganar/perder** ∼
to gain *o* put on/lose weight; ∼ **bruto/neto** gross/
net weight **(b)** **al peso** by weight
2 **(a)** (carga, responsabilidad) weight, burden;
quitarle un ∼ **de encima a algn** to take a load *o* a
weight off sb's mind **(b)** (influencia) weight; **todo el**
∼ **de la ley** the full weight of the law **(c)** de peso
〈*argumento*〉 strong, weighty; 〈*razón*〉 forceful
3 (Dep) **(a)** (Esp) (en atletismo) shot; **lanzamiento
de** ∼ shot-put, shot-putting **(b)** (Esp) (en halterofilia)
weight; **levantamiento de** ∼**s** weightlifting **(c)** (en
boxeo) weight; ∼ **ligero/mosca/pesado/pluma**
lightweight/flyweight/heavyweight/featherweight
4 (báscula) scales (*pl*)
5 (Fin) peso (*unit of currency in many Latin
American countries*); **no tiene un** ∼ he doesn't
have a cent *o* penny
pespunte *m* backstitch
pesquero -ra *adj* fishing (*before n*)
pesquisa *f* investigation, inquiry
pestaña *f* (Anat) eyelash
pestañear [A1] *vi* to blink; **sin** ∼ (literal)
without blinking; (sin inmutarse) without batting
an eyelash (AmE) *o* (BrE) eyelid
peste *f* **(a)** (Med, Vet) plague, epidemic; ∼ **cristal**
(Chi) chickenpox; ∼ **negra** Black Death **(b)** (AmL
fam) (enfermedad contagiosa) bug (colloq); (resfriado)
cold **(c)** (fam) (mal olor) stink
pesticida *m* pesticide
pestilente *adj* 〈*olor*〉 foul
pestillo *m* (cerrojo) bolt; (de cerradura) latch,
catch; **echó** *or* **corrió el** ∼ she put the bolt across
petaca *f* **(a)** (cigarrera) cigarette case; (para
tabaco — de cuero) tobacco pouch; (— de metal)
tobacco tin **(b)** (para bebidas alcohólicas) hipflask
pétalo *m* petal
petanca *f* petanque
petardo *m* firecracker, banger (BrE)
petate *m* **1** (Mil) (para dormir) bedroll; (bolsa)
knapsack **2** (Col, Méx) (estera) matting
3 **petates** *mpl* (CS fam) (pertenencias) gear
(colloq)

AmC	América Central	Arg	Argentina	Cu	Cuba	Per	Perú
AmL	América Latina	Bol	Bolivia	Ec	Ecuador	RPI	Río de la Plata
AmS	América del Sur	Chi	Chile	Esp	España	Ur	Uruguay
Andes	Región andina	CS	Cono Sur	Méx	México	Ven	Venezuela

petición f (a) (acción) request; **a ~ del público**
by popular request o demand; **a ~ fiscal** at the
prosecutor's request **(b)** (escrito) petition; **~ de
divorcio** petition for divorce; **~ de extradición**
application for extradition

petirrojo m robin

petiso -sa m,f [1] (AmS fam) (de baja estatura)
shorty (colloq) [2] **petiso** m (CS) (Equ) small
horse, pony

peto m (a) (de pantalón, delantal) bib; **pantalones
de ~** (Esp) overalls (pl) (AmE), dungarees (pl)
(BrE) **(b)** (de armadura) breastplate **(c)** (Taur)
protective covering (for picador's horse) **(d)** (en
béisbol) chest protector

petrificado -da adj ⟨madera⟩ petrified;
⟨animal⟩ fossilized; **al oírlo se quedó ~** he was
thunderstruck when he heard

petrificar [A2] vt to petrify
■ **petrificarse** v pron to become petrified, turn
to stone

petrodólar m petrodollar

petróleo m (a) (Min) oil, petroleum; **~ crudo**
crude oil **(b)** (combustible) kerosene, paraffin (BrE)

petrolero¹ -ra adj oil (before n)

petrolero² m oil tanker

petrolífero -ra adj oil (before n);
▶ YACIMIENTO

petulante adj smug, self-satisfied
■ mf smug o self-satisfied fool

petunia f petunia

peyorativo -va adj pejorative

pez m fish; **~ de río** freshwater fish; **~ de
colores** goldfish; **~ espada** swordfish; **~ gordo**
(fam) (persona importante) bigwig (colloq); (en delito)
big shot (colloq); **~ volador** flying fish; **estar** or
sentirse como ~ en el agua to be in one's
element
■ f (sustancia) pitch, tar

pezón m (Anat) nipple; (Zool) teat

pezuña f (Zool) hoof

piadoso -sa adj ⟨personas⟩ devout, pious;
⟨obra⟩ kind

pianista mf pianist

piano m piano; **~ de cola/de media cola** grand
piano/baby grand; **~ vertical** upright piano

pianola f Pianola®, player piano

piar [A17] vi to chirp, tweet

PIB m (Esp) (= **Producto Interior Bruto**)
GDP

pibe -ba m,f (RPl fam) kid (colloq)

pica f [1] (Arm) pike; (Taur) lance, goad; (para
cavar) pick, pickax* [2] (Jueg) **(a)** (carta) spade **(b)
picas** fpl (palo) spades

picada f [1] (AmL) (descenso pronunciado): **caer en
~** ⟨avión⟩ to nose-dive; ⟨pájaro⟩ to plunge, to
dive; ⟨acciones/valores⟩ to plummet [2] (AmL)
(aperitivo) nibbles (pl)

picadero m (para caballos) exercise ring;
(escuela) riding school

picado¹ -da adj **(a)** ⟨diente/muela⟩ decayed,
bad; ⟨manguera/llanta⟩ perished **(b)** ⟨ajo/perejil⟩
chopped; ⟨carne⟩ (Esp, RPl) ground (AmE), minced
(BrE) **(c)** ⟨manzana⟩ rotten; ⟨vino⟩ sour **(d)** (fam)
(enfadado, ofendido) put out (colloq), miffed (colloq)
(e) ⟨mar⟩ choppy

picado² m (Esp) ▶ PICADA 1

picador m **(a)** (Taur) picador **(b)** (en mina) face
worker

picadura f [1] (de mosquito, serpiente) bite; (de
abeja) sting; (de polilla) hole [2] (en diente, muela)
cavity

picaflor m (AmL) (Zool) hummingbird; (donjuán)
(fam) womanizer

picana f (AmL) **(a)** (para bueyes) prod, goad **(b)**
tb **~ eléctrica** cattle prod

picante adj **(a)** (Coc) ⟨comida⟩ hot **(b)** ⟨chiste/
libro⟩ risqué; ⟨comedia⟩ racy

picaporte m (manivela) door handle; (mecanismo)
latch

picar [A2] vt [1] **(a)** ⟨mosquito/víbora⟩ to bite;
⟨abeja/avispa⟩ to sting; **me ~on los mosquitos** I
got bitten by mosquitoes; **una manta picada por
las polillas** a moth-eaten blanket **(b)** ⟨ave⟩
⟨comida⟩ to peck at; ⟨enemigo⟩ to peck **(c)**
⟨anzuelo⟩ to bite **(d)** (fam) (comer) to eat; **solo
quiero ~ algo** I just want a snack o a bite to eat
(e) ⟨billete/boleto⟩ to punch **(f)** (Taur) to jab
[2] **(a)** (Coc) ⟨carne⟩ (Esp, RPl) to grind (AmE), to
mince (BrE); ⟨cebolla/perejil⟩ to chop (up) **(b)**
⟨hielo⟩ to crush; ⟨pared⟩ to chip; ⟨piedra⟩ to
break up, smash
[3] ⟨dientes/muelas⟩ to rot, decay
■ **~** vi [1] **(a)** (morder el anzuelo) to bite, take the
bait **(b)** (comer) to nibble
[2] **(a)** (ser picante) to be hot **(b)** (producir comezón)
⟨lana/suéter⟩ to itch, be itchy; **me pica la
espalda** my back itches o is itchy; **me pican los
ojos** my eyes sting
[3] (AmL) ⟨pelota⟩ to bounce
[4] (RPl arg) (irse, largarse) to split (sl); **~le** (Méx fam)
to get a move on (colloq)
■ **picarse** v pron [1] **(a)** ⟨muelas⟩ to decay, rot;
⟨manguera/llanta⟩ to perish; ⟨cacerola/pava⟩
to rust; ⟨ropa⟩ to get moth-eaten **(b)**
⟨manzana⟩ to go rotten; ⟨vino⟩ to go sour
[2] ⟨mar⟩ to get choppy
[3] (fam) (enfadarse) to get annoyed; (ofenderse) to
take offense

picardía f **(a)** (astucia) craftiness, cunning **(b)**
(malicia) mischief **(c)** (travesura) prank

picaresco -ca adj picaresque

pícaro -ra adj **(a)** (ladino) crafty, cunning **(b)**
(malicioso) ⟨persona⟩ naughty, wicked (colloq);
⟨chiste/comentario⟩ naughty, racy; ⟨mirada/
sonrisa⟩ mischievous, cheeky (BrE)
■ m,f **(a)** (Lit) rogue, villain **(b)** (astuto) cunning o
crafty devil (colloq)

picatoste m (para sopa) crouton

picazón f irritation, itch

pichanga f (Chi) (partido — improvisado)
kickabout, friendly game; (— malo) bad game

pichi m (Esp) jumper (AmE), pinafore (BrE)

pichí m (CS fam) wee-wee (used to or by children)

pichicatearse [A1] v pron (CS, Per fam) to
take drugs

pichincha f (RPl fam) (ganga) bargain, steal
(colloq)

pichirre mf (Ven fam) skinflint (colloq)

pichón -chona m,f (de paloma) young pigeon;
(de otros pájaros) chick

picnic m (pl **-nics**) picnic

pico m [1] **(a)** (de pájaro) beak **(b)** (fam) (boca)
mouth; **¡cierra el ~!** shut up (colloq), keep your ⋯⋗

trap shut! (colloq) **2** **(a)** (cima, montaña) peak **(b)** (en gráfico) peak **(c)** (en diseños, costura) point; **cuello de ∼** V neck **(d)** (de jarra, tetera) spout **3** (fam) (algo): **tiene 50 y ∼ de años** she's fifty odd o fifty something (colloq); **son las dos y ∼** it's past o gone two; **tres metros y ∼** (just) over three meters **4** **picos** mpl (Méx) (zapatillas) spikes (pl) **5** (arg) shot

picor m irritation, itch

picoso adj (Méx) hot, spicy

picotazo m peck

picotear [A1] vt to peck
■ **∼** vi (fam) (entre comidas) to nibble, snack

picudo -da adj **(a)** ‹nariz› pointed, sharp **(b)** ‹ave› long-beaked

pida, pidas, etc ▷ PEDIR

pie¹ m **1** **(a)** (Anat) foot; **un dedo del ∼** a toe; **tiene (los) ∼s planos** she has flat feet; **∼ de atleta** athlete's foot **(b)** (en locs) **a pie** on foot; **ir a ∼** to go on foot, walk; **hoy ando a ∼** (AmL) I'm without wheels today; **de pie** standing; **ponte de ∼** stand up; **en pie:** **estoy en ∼ desde las siete** I've been up since seven o'clock; **no puedo tenerme en ∼** I can hardly walk/stand; **solo la iglesia quedó en ∼** only the church remained standing; **mi oferta sigue en ∼** my offer still stands; **a ∼ pelado** (Chi) barefoot, in one's bare feet; **de a ∼** common, ordinary; **de la cabeza a los ∼s o de ∼s a cabeza** from head to foot o toe, from top to bottom (colloq); **en ∼ de guerra** on a war footing; **en (un) ∼ de igualdad** on an equal footing; **por mí/tu/su (propio) ∼** unaided, without any help **2** **(a)** (de calcetín, media) foot **(b)** (de lámpara, columna) base; (de copa — base) base; (— parte vertical) stem; (de montaña) foot **(c)** (de página, escrito) foot, bottom; **una nota a ∼ o al ∼ de página** a footnote; **∼ de fotografía** caption; **al ∼ de la letra** ‹copiar/repetir› word by word, exactly **(d)** (de cama) tb **∼s** foot
3 **(a)** (medida) foot **(b)** (Lit) foot

pie² /pai/ m (AmL) pie

piedad f **(a)** (compasión) mercy; **ten ∼ de nosotros** have mercy on us; **es un hombre sin ∼** he's merciless; **¡por ∼!** for pity's sake! **(b)** (devoción) devotion

piedra f **1** (material) stone; (trozo) stone, rock (esp AmE); **casas de ∼** stone houses; **me tiró una ∼** he threw a stone o rock at me; **∼ caliza** or **de cal** limestone; **∼ de molino** millstone; **∼ pómez** pumice stone; **∼ preciosa** precious stone; **dejar a algn de ∼** (fam) to stun sb; **‹duro› como una ∼** ‹pan/asado› rock hard; **tiene el corazón duro como una ∼** he has a heart of stone **2** **(a)** (de mechero) flint **(b)** (cálculo) stone; **tiene ∼s en el riñón/la vesícula** she has kidney stones/gallstones

piel f **1** (Anat, Zool) skin; **∼ grasa/seca** oily o greasy/dry skin; **∼ roja** nf (fam & pey) redskin (colloq & pej), Red Indian; **se me/te pone la ∼ de gallina** I/you get gooseflesh o goose pimples **2** (Indum) **(a)** (Esp, Méx) (cuero) leather; **guantes de ∼** leather gloves; **∼ de cocodrilo** crocodile skin; **∼ de serpiente** snakeskin; **∼ sintética** (cuero sintético) (Esp, Méx) synthetic leather; (imitación

nutria, visón, etc) synthetic fur **(b)** (de visón, zorro, astracán) fur; **abrigo de ∼(es)** fur coat **(c)** (sin tratar) pelt
3 (Bot) (de cítricos, papa) peel; (de manzana) peel, skin; (de otras frutas) skin

pienso m (comida) fodder, feed

pierda, pierdas, etc ▷ PERDER

pierna f **(a)** (Anat) leg; **con las ∼s cruzadas** cross-legged; **abrirse de ∼s** (en gimnasia) to do the splits **(b)** (Coc) leg; **∼ de cordero** leg of lamb

pieza f **1** **(a)** (elemento, parte) piece **(b)** (de motor, reloj) part; **∼ de recambio** or **de repuesto** spare part; **quedarse de una ∼** to be dumbfounded; **ser de una sola ∼** (AmL) to be as straight as a die **(c)** (en ajedrez) piece; (unidad, objeto) piece; **ser una ∼ de museo** (fam) to be a museum piece **(d)** (en caza) piece, specimen **2** (Mús, Teatr) piece **3** (esp AmL) (dormitorio) bedroom; (en hotel) room

pifia f **1** **(a)** (fam) (error) boob (colloq) **(b)** (en billar) miscue **(c)** (Chi) (defecto) fault **2** (Chi, Per) (del público) booing and hissing

pifiar [A1] vt **1** (fam) (fallar) to fluff (colloq); **∼la** (fam) to blow it (colloq) **2** (Chi, Per) «público» to boo

pigmentación f pigmentation

pigmento m pigment

pigmeo -mea adj/m,f pygmy

pijama m pajamas (pl) (AmE), pyjamas (pl) (BrE)

pije adj/mf (Chi) ▷ PIJO

pijo -ja adj (Esp fam & pey) ‹persona/moda/lugar› posh (colloq & pej)
■ m,f (Esp fam & pey) rich kid (colloq & pej)

pila f **1** (Elec, Fís) battery; **funciona a ∼(s)** or **con ∼s** it runs on batteries, it's battery-operated **2** (fregadero) sink; (de una fuente) basin, bowl; **∼ bautismal** baptismal font **3** (fam) (de libros, platos) pile, stack

pilar m **1** (Arquit) pillar, column; (de puente) pier
■ mf (en rugby) prop (forward)

pilchas fpl (CS fam) clothes (pl), gear (colloq)

píldora f **(a)** (pastilla) pill, tablet **(b)** tb **∼ anticonceptiva** (contraceptive) pill; **tomar la ∼** to be on the pill; **∼ del día siguiente** morning-after pill

pileta f **(a)** (RPl) (fregadero) kitchen sink; (del baño) washbowl (AmE), washbasin (BrE) **(b)** (RPl) (piscina) swimming pool **(c)** (Chi) (estanque) pond; (bebedero) drinking fountain

pillaje m pillage

pillar [A1] vt **1** (fam) **(a)** (atrapar) to catch; **le pilló un dedo** it caught o trapped her finger; **¡te pillé!** caught o got you! **(b)** ‹catarro/resfriado› to catch **2** (Esp fam) «coche» to hit
■ **pillarse** v pron (fam) ‹dedos/manga› to catch

pillo -lla adj (fam) (travieso) naughty, wicked (colloq); (astuto) crafty, cunning
■ m,f (fam) (travieso) rascal (colloq); (astuto) crafty o cunning devil (colloq)

pilón m **1** **(a)** (de fuente) basin **(b)** (Arquit) pillar; (de puente) pylon **2** (Méx fam) (en la compra) small amount of extra goods given free; **me dio tres manzanas de ∼** he threw in three extra apples (for free)

pilotar [A1] *vt* **(a)** ⟨*avión*⟩ to pilot, fly; ⟨*barco*⟩ to pilot, steer; ⟨*coche*⟩ to drive; ⟨*moto*⟩ to ride **(b)** ⟨*empresa/país*⟩ to guide, steer

pilotear [A1] *vt* (AmL) ▶ PILOTAR

piloto *mf* **1** (Aviac, Náut) pilot; (de coche) driver; (de moto) rider; ~ **de carreras** racing driver; ~ **de pruebas** (de avión) test pilot; (de coche) test driver; (de moto) test rider **2 piloto** *m* **(a)** (de aparato eléctrico, a gas) pilot light **(b)** (CS) (impermeable) raincoat **3** (*como adj inv*) ⟨*programa/producto*⟩ pilot (*before n*)

piltrafa *f* **(a)** (de comida) scrap **(b)** (cosa inservible) useless thing

pimentón *m* **(a)** (dulce) paprika; (picante) cayenne pepper **(b)** (AmS exc RPI) (fruto) pepper, capsicum

pimienta *f* pepper

pimiento *m* pepper, capsicum; ~ **rojo/verde** red/green pepper

pimpón *m* Ping-Pong®, table tennis

pin *m* (broche) pin

PIN *m* PIN

pináculo *m* (Arquit) pinnacle; (apogeo) pinnacle, peak

pinar *m* pine forest

pincel *m* (Art) paintbrush; (para maquillarse) brush

pincelada *f* brushstroke

pinchadiscos *mf* (*pl* ~) (Esp fam) disc jockey, DJ (colloq)

pinchar [A1] *vt* **1 (a)** ⟨*globo/balón*⟩ to burst; ⟨*rueda*⟩ to puncture **(b)** (con alfiler, espina) to prick **(c)** (para recoger) to spear **2** (fam) (poner una inyección) to give ... a shot (colloq) **3** ⟨*teléfono*⟩ to tap, bug **4** (Esp fam) ⟨*discos*⟩ to play
■ ~ *vi* **1** «*planta*» to be prickly **2** (Auto) to get a flat (tire*), get a puncture **3** (Chi fam) (con el sexo opuesto) ▶ LIGAR *vi*
■ **pincharse** *v pron* **1** (*refl*) «*persona*» (accidentalmente) to prick oneself; (inyectarse) (fam) to shoot up (sl), to jack up (sl) **2** «*rueda*» to puncture; «*globo/balón*» to burst; **se me pinchó un neumático** I got a flat (tire*) *o* a puncture

pinchazo *m* **(a)** (herida) prick; (inyección) shot (colloq) **(b)** (en una rueda) flat, puncture **(c)** (dolor agudo) sharp pain **(d)** (fam) (de droga) fix (colloq)

pinche *adj* **(a)** (AmL exc CS fam) (*delante del n*) (maldito): ¡~ **vida!** what a (lousy *o* rotten) life!; **por unos** ~**s pesos** for a few measly pesos (colloq); **vámonos de este** ~ **lugar** let's get out of this damn place! **(b)** (Méx fam) (de poca calidad) lousy (colloq); (despreciable) horrible **(c)** (AmC fam) (tacaño) tightfisted (colloq)
■ *mf* (Coc) kitchen assistant

pincho *m* **1** (de rosa, zarza) thorn, prickle (colloq); (de cactus) spine, prickle (colloq) **2** (Esp) (de aperitivo) bar snack

pingo -ga *m,f* (Méx fam) little scamp *o* rascal (colloq)

Ping-Pong® *m* Ping-Pong®, table tennis

pingüino *m* penguin

pino *m* **1** (Bot) (árbol) pine (tree); (madera) pine **2** (Esp) (en gimnasia): **hacer el** ~ to do a handstand **3** (Méx) (en bolos) pin

pinolillo *m* (AmC) (maíz) cornstarch (AmE), maize flour (BrE); (bebida) *drink made with cornstarch and water*

pinta *f* **1** (fam) (aspecto) look; **eso le da** ~ **de intelectual** it gives him an intellectual look; **tiene** ~ **de extranjero** he looks foreign; ¿**dónde vas con esa(s)** ~(**s)?** where are you going looking like that?; **echar** *or* **tirar** (Andes) *or* (RPI) **hacer** ~ (fam) to impress **2** (en tela, animal) spot **3** (medida) pint **4** (Méx fam) (de la escuela): **irse de** ~ to play hooky* (esp AmE colloq), to skive off (school) (BrE colloq)

pintada *f* piece of graffiti; (Pol) slogan

pintado -da *adj* ⟨*vaca*⟩ spotted; ⟨*caballo*⟩ dappled, pied

pintalabios *m* (*pl* ~) (fam) lipstick

pintar [A1] *vt* **(a)** (en general) to paint; **pintó la puerta de rojo** she painted the door red; ~ **algo al óleo** to paint sth in oils **(b)** (fam) (dibujar) to draw
■ ~ *vi* **1 (a)** (con pintura) to paint **(b)** (fam) (dibujar) to draw **2** (en naipes) to be trumps
■ **pintarse** *v pron* (*refl*) (maquillarse) to put on one's makeup; ~**se los labios** to put on some lipstick; ~**se los ojos** to put on eye makeup; ~**se las uñas** to paint one's nails

pintarrajear [A1] *vt* to daub

pintor -tora *m,f* (de cuadros) painter, artist; (de paredes) (house) painter; ~ **de brocha gorda** (de casas, barcos) painter

pintoresco -ca *adj* picturesque

pintura *f* **(a)** (arte, cuadro) painting; ~ **a la acuarela/al óleo** watercolor*/oil painting **(b)** (material) paint; (en cosmética) makeup

pinza *f* **1 (a)** (para la ropa) clothespin (AmE), clothes peg (BrE) **(b)** (para el pelo) bobby pin (AmE), hairgrip (BrE) **(c)** (de un cangrejo) pincer **(d)** (en costura) dart; **un pantalón con** ~**s** pleated pants (AmE) *o* (BrE) trousers **2** *tb* ~**s (a)** (para depilar) tweezers (*pl*); (de cirujano) forceps (*pl*); (de cocina, chimenea) tongs (*pl*) **(b)** (alicates) pliers (*pl*)

piña *f* (Bot) (fruta) pineapple; (del pino) pine cone

piñata *f*: *container hung up during festivities and hit with a stick to release candy inside*

piñón *m* **1** (Bot) pine kernel *o* nut **2** (Mec) pinion; (de bicicleta) sprocket wheel

pío¹, pía *adj* devout, pious

pío² *m* peep, tweet; **no decir ni** ~ (fam) not to say a word

piojo *m* louse; ~**s** lice

piojoso -sa *adj* **(a)** (con piojos) lousy, lice-ridden **(b)** (fam) (sucio) filthy

piola *adj inv* (RPI fam) **(a)** (divertido) fun (*before n*) (colloq) **(b)** (astuto) crafty (colloq) **(c)** ⟨*ropa*⟩ trendy (colloq)
■ *f* (AmL) cord

piolet /pjo'le(t)/ *m* (*pl* **-lets**) ice ax*

pionero -ra *adj* pioneering (*before n*)
■ *m,f* pioneer

pipa *f* **1** (para fumar) pipe; **fumar** (en) ~ to smoke a pipe **2** (tonel) cask, barrel **3** (Esp) (de sandía, mandarina) pip; (de girasol, calabaza) seed; **pasarlo** ~ (fam) to have a great time **4** (Méx) (camión) tanker

pipí *m* (fam) pee (colloq), wee (BrE colloq); **hacer** ~ to have a pee *o* (BrE) wee

pique *m* **1 a pique: una caída a** *or* (Méx) **en** ~ ···>

hasta el mar a vertical *o* sheer drop to the sea below; **a pique de** on the point of, about to; *irse a* ~ «*barco*» to sink; «*negocio*» to go under **2** (fam) **(a)** (enfado, resentimiento): **tener un ~ con algn** to be at odds with sb **(b)** (rivalidad) rivalry, needle **3** **(a)** (carta) spade **(b)** **piques** *fpl* (palo) spades (*pl*)

piqueta *f* pick, pickax*

piquete *m* **1** (de huelguistas) picket; (de soldados) squad, picket (arch) **2** (Méx fam) **(a)** (herida) prick; (inyección) shot (colloq), jab (colloq) **(b)** (de insecto) sting, bite

pira *f* pyre

piragua *f* (Dep) canoe

piragüismo *m* canoeing

pirámide *f* pyramid

piraña *f* (Zool) piranha

pirarse [A1] *v pron* (Esp fam) to make oneself scarce (colloq)

pirata *adj* **(a)** ‹barco› pirate (*before n*) **(b)** (clandestino) ‹casete/copia› pirate (*before n*), bootleg (*before n*) (colloq)
■ *mf* **(a)** (Náut) pirate; ~ **aéreo** hijacker **(b)** (de casetes, videos) pirate

piratear [A1] *vt* ‹videos/casetes› to pirate; ‹sistema› to hack into

piratería *f* piracy; ~ **informática** hacking (colloq)

Pirineos *mpl*, **Pirineo** *m*: **los ~** *or* **el Pirineo** the Pyrenees (*pl*)

pirinola *mf* (Andes, Méx) (peonza) spinning top

pirómano -na *m,f* pyromaniac

piropear [A1] *vt* to make flirtatious/flattering comments to

piropo *m* flirtatious/flattering comment

pirueta *f* (en danza) pirouette; (de un caballo) pesade

pis *m* ▶ PIPÍ

pisada *f* (acción) footstep; (huella) footprint

pisapapeles *m* (*pl* ~) paperweight

pisar [A1] *vt* **1** **(a)** (con el pie) ‹mina/clavo› to step on; ‹charco› to step in, tread in (esp BrE); **la pisó sin querer** he accidentally stepped *o* (esp BrE) trod on her foot; 🌐 **prohibido pisar el césped** keep off the grass **(b)** (humillar) to trample on, walk all over **2** (RPI, Ven) **(a)** (Coc) to mash **(b)** (fam) (atropellar) to run over
■ ~ *vi* to tread; **pisó mal y se cayó** she lost her footing and fell

pisca *f* (Méx) harvest

piscina *f* swimming pool; ~ **cubierta/climatizada** covered/heated swimming pool

Piscis *m* (signo, constelación) Pisces; **es (de) ~** he's (a) Pisces, he's a Piscean
■ *mf* (*pl* ~) (persona) *tb* **piscis** Piscean, Pisces

pisco *m* (aguardiente) ≈ grappa

piso *m* **1** **(a)** (de edificio) floor, story*; (de autobús) deck; **una casa de seis ~s** a six-story building; **un autobús de dos ~s** a double-decker bus **(b)** (de pastel) layer **2** (AmL) **(a)** (suelo) floor

(b) (de carretera) road surface **3** (Esp) (apartamento) apartment (esp AmE), flat (BrE); ~ **piloto** (Esp) show apartment *o* (BrE) flat **4** (Chi) (taburete) stool; (alfombrita) rug; (felpudo) doormat

pisotear [A1] *vt* **(a)** (con los pies) to trample, stamp on **(b)** ‹persona/derecho› to ride roughshod over

pisotón *m* stamp; **darle un ~ a algn** (intencional) to stamp on sb's foot *o* toes; (sin querer) to tread *o* step on sb's foot *o* toes

pista *f* **1** **(a)** (rastro) trail, track; **seguirle la ~ a algn** to be/get on sb's trail **(b)** (indicio) clue **2** **(a)** (carretera) road, track **(b)** (Chi) (carril) lane **(c)** (Audio) track **3** **(a)** (en el circo) ring; (en el picadero) ring; (en el hipódromo) track (AmE), course (BrE); ~ **de aterrizaje** runway, landing strip; ~ **de baile** dance floor; ~ **de esquí** ski slope, piste; ~ **de hielo/de patinaje** ice/skating rink **(b)** (Esp) (de tenis) court

pistacho *m* pistachio (nut)

pistola *f* **(a)** (Arm) pistol; **a punta de ~** at gunpoint **(b)** (para pintar) spray gun

pistolero *m* gunman

pistón *m* **(a)** (émbolo) piston **(b)** (de arma) percussion cap **(c)** (de instrumento) key

pitada *f* **1** **(a)** (pitido) beep **(b)** (en espectáculo) ≈ booing and hissing, whistling (*as sign of disapproval*) **2** (AmL) (de cigarrillo) puff, drag (colloq)

pitar [A1] *vi* **(a)** «guardia/árbitro» to blow one's whistle **(b)** «vehículo» to blow the horn, to hoot **(c)** «público» (como protesta) to boo and hiss
■ ~ *vt* ‹falta› to blow for, award, call (AmE)

pítcher *mf* pitcher

pitido *m* (sonido agudo) whistle, whistling; (de claxon) beep, hoot, honk

pitillera *f* cigarette case

pitillo *m* **1** (fam) (cigarrillo) smoke (colloq), fag (BrE colloq) **2** (Col) (para beber) straw

pito *m* **1** **(a)** (silbato) whistle; **tocar el ~** to blow the whistle; **tener voz de ~** (fam) to have a squeaky voice **(b)** (fam) (de coche) horn, hooter; (de tren) whistle; **tocar el ~** to hoot, honk **2** (Chi fam) (de marihuana) joint (colloq), spliff (sl) **3** (fam) (pene) weenie (AmE colloq), willy (BrE colloq)

pitón *f or m* python

pitonisa *f* fortuneteller

pitorrearse [A1] *v pron* (Esp fam) ~ **DE algn** to make fun OF sb

pituco -ca *adj* (CS, Per fam) **(a)** (elegante) posh (colloq) **(b)** (engreído) stuck-up (colloq)
■ *m,f* (CS, Per fam) **es un ~** he's stuck-up (colloq)

pituto *m* (Chi fam) (para conseguir algo) contact

pívot *mf* (*pl* **-vots**) (Dep) center*, pivot

piyama *m or f* (AmL) pajamas (*pl*) (AmE), pyjamas (*pl*) (BrE)

pizarra *f* **(a)** (Min) slate **(b)** (en el aula) blackboard, chalkboard; (del alumno) slate **(c)** (Cin) clapperboard **(d)** (en béisbol) scoreboard

pizarrón *m* (AmL) blackboard, chalkboard

pizca *f* **1** (cantidad pequeña): **una ∼ de algo** (de sal, azúcar) a pinch of sth; (de vino, agua) a drop of sth; **no tiene ni ∼ de gracia** it's not the slightest bit funny **2** (Méx) (cosecha) harvest

pizcar [A2] *vt* (Méx) ⟨*maíz*⟩ to harvest; ⟨*algodón*⟩ to pick
■ ∼ *vi* (Méx) to take in the harvest

pizza /'pitsa, 'pisa/ *f* pizza

pizzería /pitse'ria, pise'ria/ *f* pizzeria

Pl. (= **Plaza**) Sq, Square

placa *f* **1** (lámina, plancha) sheet **2** (a) (con inscripción) plaque; **una ∼ con el nombre** a nameplate; **∼ de matrícula** license (AmE) *o* (BrE) number plate **(b)** (de policía) badge **3** (Chi) (dentadura) dentures (*pl*), dental plate

placaje *m* (en fútbol americano) block; (en rugby) tackle

placar [A2] *vt* (en fútbol americano) to block; (en rugby) to tackle

placard /pla'kar/ *m* (RPl) built-in closet (AmE), fitted wardrobe (BrE)

placenta *f* placenta, afterbirth

placentero -ra *adj* pleasant, agreeable

placer [E4] *vi* (*en 3ª pers*) (+ *me/te/le etc*): **haz lo que te plazca** do as you please; **me place informarle que ...** (fml) it is my pleasure to inform you that ... (fml)
■ *m* (gusto, satisfacción) pleasure; **ha sido un ∼ conocerla** (fml) it has been a pleasure to meet you; **un viaje de ∼** a pleasure trip

placero *m* (Per) street vendor

placidez *f* placidity, placidness, calmness

plácido -da *adj* placid, calm

plaga *f* **(a)** (de insectos, ratas) plague; **las ardillas son consideradas una ∼** squirrels are considered to be a pest **(b)** (calamidad, azote) plague

plagado -da *adj*: **[ESTAR] ∼ DE algo** ⟨*de faltas/errores*⟩ riddled WITH sth; ⟨*de turistas/insectos*⟩ swarming WITH sth

plagiar [A1] *vt* ⟨*idea/libro*⟩ to plagiarize

plagio *m* (copia) plagiarism

plan *m* **1** (proyecto, programa) plan; **hacer ∼es** to make plans; **∼ de estudios** syllabus **2** (fam) (cita, compromiso): **si no tienes otros ∼es** if you're not doing anything else; **¿tienes algún ∼ para esta noche?** do you have any plans for tonight? **3** (fam) (actitud): **vienen en ∼ de diversión** they're here to have fun; **lo dijo en ∼ de broma** he was only kidding (colloq); **en ∼ económico** cheaply, on the cheap (colloq)

plana *f* **1** (de periódico) page; **aparece en primera ∼** it's on the front page **2** (Educ) (ejercicio) handwriting exercise **3 la ∼ mayor** (Mil) the staff officers (*pl*); (jefes) (fam) the top brass (colloq)

plancha *f* **1 (a)** (electrodoméstico) iron **(b)** (acto) ironing; (ropa para planchar) ironing **2 (a)** (Const, Tec) sheet **(b)** (Impr) plate **3** (utensilio de cocina) griddle; **filete a la ∼** a grilled steak **4 (a)** (fam) (metedura de pata) boo-boo (colloq), boob (colloq) **(b)** (Chi fam) (vergüenza) embarrassment

planchar [A1] *vt* ⟨*sábana/mantel*⟩ to iron; ⟨*pantalones*⟩ to press, iron; ⟨*traje*⟩ to press
■ ∼ *vi* (con la plancha) to do the ironing

plancton *m* plankton

planeación *f* (Méx) planning

planeador *m* glider

planear [A1] *vt* to plan
■ ∼ *vi* (Aviac) to glide; ⟨*águila*⟩ to soar; (Náut) to plane

planeta *m* planet

planetario *m* planetarium

planificación *f* planning; **∼ familiar** family planning

planificar [A2] *vt* to plan, draw up a plan for

planilla *f* **1 (a)** (tabla) table, chart; (lista) list **(b)** (AmL) (nómina) payroll; **estar en ∼** to be on the payroll **(c)** (AmL) (personal) staff **2 (a)** (Méx) (en elección) list of candidates **(b)** (Col) (censo electoral) electoral register

plano¹ -na *adj* **1** ⟨*superficie/terreno/zapato*⟩ flat; **los 100 metros ∼s** the hundred meters dash *o* sprint **2** ⟨*figura/ángulo*⟩ plane

plano² *m* **1** (de edificio) plan; (de ciudad) street plan, map **2** (Mat) plane **3 (a)** (nivel) level; **en el ∼ afectivo** on an emotional level **(b)** (Cin, Fot) shot **4 de plano** ⟨*rechazar/rehusar*⟩ flatly

planta *f* **1** (Bot) plant; **∼ de interior** houseplant, indoor plant **2** (Arquit) **(a)** (plano) plan **(b)** (piso) floor; **una casa de dos ∼s** a two-story house; **∼ baja** first floor (AmE), ground floor (BrE) **3** (Tec) (instalación) plant **4** (del pie) sole

plantación *f* **(a)** (terreno plantado) field; (de árboles) plantation **(b)** (explotación agrícola) plantation **(c)** (acción) planting

plantado -da *adj* **∼ DE algo** planted WITH sth; **dejar ∼ a algn** ▶ PLANTAR 2B

plantar [A1] *vt* **1 (a)** ⟨*árboles/cebollas*⟩ to plant **(b)** ⟨*postes*⟩ to put in; ⟨*tienda*⟩ to pitch, put up **2** (fam) **(a)** (abandonar) ⟨*novio*⟩ to ditch (colloq), to dump (colloq); ⟨*estudios*⟩ to give up, to quit (AmE) **(b)** (dejar plantado) ⟨*persona*⟩ (en cita) to stand ... up; (el día de la boda) to jilt
■ **plantarse** *v pron* **1** (fam) (quedarse, pararse) to plant oneself (colloq) **2** (Jueg) (en cartas, apuesta) to stick

planteamiento *m* **(a)** (enfoque) approach **(b)** (exposición): **no les sabe dar el ∼ adecuado a sus ideas** he doesn't know how to set his ideas out; **ese no es el ∼ que me hicieron** that's not the way they explained the situation to me

plantear [A1] *vt* **1 (a)** ⟨*teoría/razones*⟩ to set out **(b)** (exponer) ⟨*tema/pregunta*⟩ to raise; **me lo planteó de la siguiente manera** he explained it to me in the following way; **∼le algo a algn** to raise sth with sb; **le ∼é la cuestión a mi jefe** I'll raise the matter with my boss; **nos ∼on dos opciones** they presented us with *o* gave us two options; **planteé la posibilidad de ir a Grecia** I suggested going to Greece **2** ⟨*problemas/dificultades*⟩ to pose
■ **plantearse** *v pron* **1** (considerar) ⟨*problema/posibilidad*⟩ to think about, consider **2** (presentarse) ⟨⟨*problema/posibilidad*⟩⟩ to arise

plantel *m* **1** (cuerpo) staff **2** (Agr) nursery **3** (AmL fml) (escuela) educational establishment (fml)

plantilla *f* **1** (de zapato) insole **2** (Esp) (personal) staff; (nómina) payroll; **estar en ∼** to be on the staff *o* payroll **3** (para marcar, cortar) template; (para corregir exámenes) mask

plantón *m* **(a)** (fam) (espera) long wait; *darle el ∼ a algn* ▶ PLANTAR 2B **(b)** (Méx) (para protestar) sit-in

plasma *m* (Biol, Fís) plasma

plasta *f* (fam) (masa — blanda) soft lump; (— aplastada) flat *o* shapeless lump

plasticina® *f* (CS) Plasticine®

plástico¹ -ca *adj* plastic

plástico² *m* **(a)** (material) plastic **(b)** (explosivo) plastic explosive, plastique **(c)** (fam) (tarjetas de crédito) credit cards (*pl*), plastic (colloq)

plastificar [A2] *vt* ⟨tela⟩ to plasticize; ⟨carné/documento⟩ to laminate

plata *f* ① **(a)** (metal) silver; ∼ *de ley* hallmarked silver **(b)** (vajilla) silver, silverware ② (AmS fam) (dinero) money; *tiene mucha ∼* she has a lot of money

plataforma *f* platform; ∼ *de lanzamiento* launchpad

platal *m* (AmS fam) fortune (colloq)

platanal, platanar *m* banana plantation

platanera *f* (empresa) banana company

platanero *m* (árbol) banana tree

plátano *m* ① (árbol) *tb* ∼ *oriental* plane tree ② **(a)** (fruto que se come crudo) banana; (árbol) banana tree **(b)** (fruto para cocinar) plantain; (árbol) plantain

platea *f* **(a)** (patio de butacas) orchestra (AmE), stalls (*pl*) (BrE) **(b)** (localidad) seat (*in the orchestra/stalls*)

plateado -da *adj* **(a)** (del color de la plata) silver **(b)** (con baño de plata) silver-plated

platería *f* **(a)** (arte) silverwork **(b)** (objetos) silver(ware) **(c)** (tienda) silversmith's

plática *f* **(a)** (conferencia) talk **(b)** (esp AmL) (conversación) [*this noun is widely used in Mexico and Central America but is formal in other areas*] talk; *estar de ∼* to talk, to chat (colloq)

platicar [A2] *vi* (esp AmL) [*this verb is widely used in Mexico and Central America but is literary in other areas*] to talk, chat (colloq) ■ ∼ *vt* (Méx) (contar) to tell

platillo *m* ① **(a)** (plato pequeño) saucer; (de balanza) pan; (para limosnas) collection plate *o* bowl; ∼ *volador or* (Esp) *volante* flying saucer **(b)** (Mús) cymbal **(c)** (Dep) clay pigeon ② (Méx) (en una comida) course

platino *m* ① (metal) platinum ② **platinos** *mpl* (Auto, Mec) (contact breaker) points (*pl*)

plato *m* ① **(a)** (utensilio) plate; *lavar or fregar los ∼s* to wash *o* do the dishes; ∼ *de postre* dessert plate; ∼ *hondo or sopero* soup dish; ∼ *llano or* (RPl) *playo or* (Chi) *bajo or* (Méx) *extendido* (dinner) plate **(b)** (para taza) *tb* **platito** saucer ② (contenido) plate, plateful ③ **(a)** (receta) dish; ∼ *típico* typical dish **(b)** (en una comida) course; ∼ *central* (Ven) main course; ∼ *combinado* (Esp) *meal served on one plate, eg burger, eggs and fries*; ∼ *del día* dish of the day; ∼ *fuerte or principal* (Coc) main course ④ **(a)** (de balanza) (scale) pan **(b)** (de tocadiscos) turntable **(c)** (Dep) clay pigeon **(d)** (en béisbol) home plate

plató *m* set

platónico -ca *adj* platonic

platudo -da *adj* (AmS fam) well-heeled (colloq)

playa *f* **(a)** (extensión de arena) beach; (lugar de veraneo) seaside **(b)** ∼ *de estacionamiento* (CS, Per) parking lot (AmE), car park (BrE)

playera *f* (zapatilla) canvas shoe, beach shoe; (camiseta) (Méx) T-shirt

plaza *f* ① (espacio abierto) square; ∼ *de armas* (Mil) parade ground; (lugar público) (Andes) main square; ∼ *de toros* bullring; ∼ *mayor* main square ② **(a)** (esp AmL) (bolsa) market **(b)** (Esp) (mercado) market (place) ③ **(a)** (puesto de trabajo) post, position; (en una clase, universidad) place; *hay varias ∼s vacantes* there are several vacancies **(b)** (asiento) seat

plazo *m* ① (de tiempo) period; *dentro de un ∼ de dos meses* within a two-month period; *el ∼ vence el próximo lunes* (para proyecto, trabajo) the deadline is next Monday; (para entrega de solicitudes) next Monday is the closing date; *tenemos un mes de ∼ para pagar* we have one month to pay; *un objetivo a corto/largo ∼* a short-term/long-term objective ② (mensualidad, cuota) installment*; *pagar a ∼s* to pay in installments; *comprar a ∼s* to buy on installments

plazoleta, plazuela *f* small square

plebe *f* **(a)** (Hist) *la ∼* the masses (*pl*), the populace **(b)** (pey) (chusma) rabble (pej), plebs (*pl*) (colloq & pej)

plebeyo -ya *adj/m,f* plebeian

plebiscito *m* plebiscite

plegable *adj* folding (*before n*)

plegar [A7] *vt* ⟨papel⟩ to fold; ⟨silla⟩ to fold up ■ **plegarse** *v pron* ① (ceder) to yield, submit; ∼*se a algo* to yield TO sth, submit to sth ② (AmS) (unirse) to join in; ∼*se A algo* to join sth

plegaria *f* prayer

pleitear [A1] *vi* (AmL fam) (discutir) to argue

pleito *m* ① (Der) action, lawsuit ② (AmL) **(a)** (disputa, discusión) argument, fight (colloq) **(b)** (de boxeo) fight, boxing match

plenario -ria *adj* plenary, full

plenitud *f*: *en la ∼ de algo* (de la vida) in the prime of sth; (de la carrera) at the height *o* peak of sth; *vivir la vida con ∼* to live life to the full

pleno¹ -na *adj* **(a)** (completo, total) full; *en ∼ uso de sus facultades* in full possession of his faculties **(b)** (uso enfático): *en ∼ verano* in the middle of summer; *le dio una bofetada en plena cara* he slapped her right across the face; *a plena luz del día* in broad daylight; *a ∼ sol* in the full sun

pleno² *m* ① (reunión) plenary *o* full meeting/session ② (Jueg) (en bolos) strike; (en lotería, bingo) full house; (en las quinielas) correct forecast *o* prediction

pliego *m* **(a)** (hoja de papel) sheet of paper **(b)** (Impr) section, signature **(c)** (documento) document

pliegue *m* **(a)** (en papel) fold, crease; (en la piel) fold; (en tela) pleat **(b)** (Geol) fold

plinto *m* (en gimnasia) box

plomería *f* (AmL) plumbing

plomero -ra *m,f* (AmL) plumber

plomizo -za *adj* ⟨cielo⟩ gray*, leaden (liter)

plomo *m* ① **(a)** (metal) lead; *soldado de ∼* tin

soldier **(b)** (arg) (balas) lead (sl) **2** (fam) (persona aburrida): **este profesor es un ~** this teacher is deadly boring (colloq) **3** (Esp) (fusible) fuse

pluma f **1** (de aves) feather; (antigua para escribir) quill; (como adorno) plume, feather; **mudar la ~ to molt*** **2** (para escribir) pen; **~ atómica** (Méx) ballpoint pen; **~ estilográfica** or (AmL) **fuente** fountain pen

plumaje m (de ave) plumage; (en un casco) plume, crest

plumero m **(a)** (para limpiar) feather duster **(b)** (estuche) pencil case; (recipiente) pen holder

plumilla f **1** (para escribir) nib **2** **(a)** (del limpiaparabrisas) blade **(b)** (Mús) brush **(c)** (Dep) shuttlecock

plumón m **1** **(a)** (pluma suave) down **(b)** (edredón) down-filled quilt o (BrE) duvet **2** (Chi) (rotulador) felt-tip pen

plural adj/m plural; **tercera persona del ~** third person plural; **en ~** in the plural

pluralizar [A4] vi to generalize

pluscuamperfecto m pluperfect, past perfect

Plutón m Pluto

plutonio m plutonium

pluviosidad f rainfall

población f **1** (habitantes) population; (Zool) population, colony; **~ activa/pasiva** working/non-working population **2** (ciudad) town, city; (aldea) town, village; **~ callampa** (Chi) shantytown **3** (acción) settlement

poblado¹ -da adj **1** (habitado) populated; **poco ~** sparsely populated **2** (barba/cejas) bushy, thick; (pestañas) thick

poblado² m village

poblador -dora m,f **(a)** (settler **(b)** (Chi) inhabitant of a shantytown

poblar [A10] vt **1** (territorio/región) **(a)** «colonos/inmigrantes» (ir a ocupar) to settle, populate **(b)** (habitar) to inhabit **2** **~ algo DE algo** (bosque) to plant sth WITH sth; (río/colmena) to stock sth WITH sth
■ **poblarse** v pron «tierra/colonia» to be settled

pobre adj **1** **(a)** (persona/barrio/nación) poor; (vestimenta) poor, shabby **(b)** (escaso) (vocabulario) poor, limited; **aguas ~s en minerales** water with a low mineral content **(c)** (mediocre) (examen/trabajo/actuación) poor; (salud) poor, bad; (argumento) weak **(d)** (tierra) poor **2** (delante del n) (digno de compasión) poor; **~ animal** poor animal; **~, tiene hambre** poor thing, he's hungry; **¡~ de mí!** poor (old) me!
■ mf (necesitado) poor person, pauper (arch); **los ~s** the poor

pobreza f **(a)** (económica) poverty; **extrema ~** abject poverty **(b)** (mediocridad) poverty, poorness **(c)** (de la tierra) poorness, poor quality

poceta f (Ven) toilet bowl o pan

pocho -cha adj **1** (Esp fam) [ESTAR] (persona) off-color, peaked (AmE colloq) **(b)** (fruta) overripe; (flor) withered

pocilga f pigsty

pócima f (Farm) potion; (bebida) (fam) concoction (colloq)

poción f potion

poco¹ adv: **habla ~** he doesn't say much o a lot;

es muy **~ agradecido** he is very ungrateful; **un autor muy ~ conocido** a very little-known author; **viene muy ~ por aquí** he hardly ever comes around; **para locs ver POCO² 4**

poco² -ca adj (con sustantivos no numerables) little; (en plural) few; **muy ~ vino** very little wine; **muy ~s niños** very few children; **había poquísimos coches** there were hardly any cars
■ pron **1** (poca cantidad, poca cosa): **había ~ que hacer** there was little to do; **por ~ que gane …** no matter how little o however little she earns …; **se conforma con ~** he's easily satisfied; **todo le parece ~** she is never satisfied; **~s quisieron ayudar** few were willing to help; **~s pueden permitirse ese lujo** not many people can afford to do that
2 **poco** (refiriéndose a tiempo): **lo vi hace ~** I saw him recently o not long ago; **hace muy ~ que lo conoce** she hasn't known him for very long; **tardó ~ en hacerlo** it didn't take him long to do it; **falta ~ para las navidades** it's not long till Christmas; **a ~ de venir él** soon o shortly after he came; **dentro de ~** soon; **~ antes de que … a** short while o shortly before …
3 **un poco (a)** (refiriéndose a cantidades) a little; (refiriéndose a tiempo) a while; **dame un ~** I'll have some o a little; **espera un ~** wait a while **(b)** **un poco de** a little, a bit of **(c)** **un poco + ADJ/ADV**: **un ~ caro/tarde** a bit o a while expensive/late
4 (en locs) **a poco** (Méx): **¡a ~ no está fabuloso Acapulco!** isn't Acapulco just fantastic!; **¡a ~ ganaron!** don't tell me they won!; **de a poco** (AmL) gradually, little by little; **poco a poco** gradually; **poco más o menos** approximately, roughly; **por poco** nearly

poda f (acción) pruning; (temporada) pruning season

podar [A1] vt (árbol) to prune

poder¹ [E21] v aux
I **1** (tener la capacidad o posibilidad de): **puedo ir ahora o mañana** I can go now or tomorrow; **no puedo pagar tanto** I can't pay that much; **no podía dormir** I couldn't sleep; **no va a ~ venir** he won't be able to come; **no pudo asistir** he was unable to o he couldn't attend; **¿pudiste hacerlo sola?** were you able to do it on your own?
2 **(a)** (expresando idea de permiso): **¿puedo servirme otro?** can o may I have another one?; **¿podría irme más temprano hoy?** could I leave earlier today?; **puedes hacer lo que quieras** you can do whatever you like; **no puede comer sal** he isn't allowed to eat salt; **¿se puede? — ¡adelante!** may I? — come in; **aquí no se puede fumar** smoking is not allowed here **(b)** (solicitando un favor): **¿puedes bajar un momento?** can you come down for a moment?; **¿podrías hacerme un favor?** could you do me a favor?
3 (expresando derecho moral): **no podemos hacerle eso** we can't do that to her
4 (en quejas, reproches): **podías** or **podrías haberme avisado** you could o might have warned me!
II (con idea de esfuerzo) **1** **~ CON algo/algn**: **¿puedes con todo eso?** can you manage all that?; **no puedo con este niño** I can't cope with this child; **estoy que no puedo más** (cansado) I'm exhausted; (lleno) I can't eat anything else; **ya no puedo más** I can't go on like this
2 (con idea de eventualidad, posibilidad): **te podrías** or ···✧

podías haber matado you could have killed yourself!; **no podía haber estado más amable** she couldn't have been kinder; **podría volver a ocurrir** it could happen again; **no pudo ser** it wasn't possible; **puede (ser) que tengas razón** you may *o* could be right; **puede que sí, puede que no** maybe, maybe not

3 (Méx) (doler): **nos pudo mucho la muerte de Julio** we were terribly upset by Julio's death

poder² *m* **1** **(a)** (control, influencia) power; **tiene mucho ~** he has a great deal of power; **estamos en su ~** we are in her power; **podría volver a ocurrir** (Pol) **el ~** power; **estar en el ~** to be in power; **tomar el ~** to take *o* seize power

2 (posesión): **la carta está en ~ de …** the letter is in the hands of …

3 **(a)** (derecho, atribución) power; **tener amplios ~es para hacer algo** to have wide-ranging powers to do sth **(b)** (Der) (documento) letter of authorization; (hecho ante notario) power of attorney; **casarse por ~** (AmL) *or* (Esp) **por ~es** to get married by proxy

4 **(a)** (capacidad, facultad) power; **su ~ de convicción** her power of persuasion; **~ adquisitivo** purchasing power **(b)** (de motor, aparato) power

poderío *m* power

poderoso -sa *adj* powerful

poderosos *mpl*: **los ~s** (los ricos) the wealthy; (los que tienen poder) the powerful

podio *m*, **pódium** *m* (*pl* **-diums**) (Dep) podium; (Mús) podium, rostrum

podólogo -ga *m,f* chiropodist, podiatrist (AmE)

podré, etc ▶ PODER¹

podría, etc ▶ PODER¹

podrido -da *adj* **1** **(a)** (descompuesto) rotten; **huele a** *or* (AmL) **hay olor a ~** there's a smell of something rotting *o* rotten **(b)** (corrompido) rotten, corrupt; **estar ~ de dinero** *or* (AmS) **estar ~ en plata/oro** (fam) to be stinking *o* filthy rich (colloq) **2** (RPI fam) (harto, aburrido) fed up (colloq)

podrir [I38] *vt* ▶ PUDRIR

poema *m* poem

poesía *f* (género) poetry; (poema) poem

poeta -tisa *m,f*, **poeta** *mf* poet

poético -ca *adj* poetic

póker *m* ▶ PÓQUER

polaco -ca *adj* Polish
■ *m,f* **1** (persona) Pole **2** **polaco** *m* (idioma) Polish

polar *adj* polar

polarizar [A4] *vt* **(a)** (Fot, Ópt) to polarize **(b)** ⟨atención⟩ to focus **(c)** ⟨nación/opiniones⟩ to polarize

polea *f* (Tec) pulley; (Náut) tackle

polémica *f* controversy, polemic (frml)

polémico -ca *adj* controversial, polemic (frml)

polemizar [A4] *vi* to argue

polen *m* pollen

poleo *m* pennyroyal

polera *f* (suéter) (RPI) polo neck; (Chi) (camiseta) T-shirt

polichinela *m* (títere) string puppet

policía *f* **1** (cuerpo) police; **la ~ está investigando el caso** the police are investigating the case; **~ antidisturbios** riot police; **~ de tráfico** *or* (AmL) **de tránsito** traffic police, highway patrol (AmE); **~ municipal** local *o* city police; **~ nacional** (state) police **2** **policía** (agente) (*m*) policeman, police officer; (*f*) policewoman, police officer

policíaco -ca, policiaco -ca *adj* ⟨novela/serie⟩ crime (before *n*), detective (before *n*)

policial *adj* police (before *n*)

polideportivo *m* sports center*

poliéster *m* polyester

poliestireno *m*: *tb* **~ expandible** polystyrene

polietileno *m* polyethylene (AmE), polythene (BrE)

polifacético -ca *adj* versatile, multifaceted

poligamia *f* polygamy

polígamo -ma *m,f* polygamist

políglota *mf* polyglot

polígono *m* **1** (Mat) polygon **2** (Esp) (zona) area, zone; (urbanización) development, housing estate; **~ industrial** (Esp) industrial area *o* zone

polilla *f* (Zool) moth; **~ de la madera** woodworm

Polinesia *f* Polynesia

polinesio¹ -sia *adj/m,f* Polynesian

polinesio² *m* (idioma) Polynesian

polinización *f* pollination

polio *f* polio

poliomielitis *f* poliomyelitis

politécnico -ca *adj* ⟨universidad⟩ specializing in technical or practical subjects; **escuela politécnica** technical college

politeísmo *m* polytheism

política *f* **1** (Pol) politics **2** (postura) policy; **~ interior/exterior** domestic/foreign policy

político -ca *adj* **1** (Pol) political **2** (diplomático) diplomatic, tactful **3** (en relaciones de parentesco): **la familia política** the in-laws
■ *m,f* politician

politizarse [A4] *v pron* to become politicized

póliza *f* **1** (de seguros) policy **2** (esp Esp) (sello) fiscal stamp

polizón *mf* stowaway; **viajar de ~** to stow away

polla *f* **1** (Esp vulg) (pene) cock (vulg), prick (vulg) **2** **(a)** (AmL) (apuesta) bet **(b)** (Per) (quiniela) ≈ sports lottery (in US), ≈ pools (in UK) **(c)** (Chi) (lotería) lottery; *ver tb* POLLO

pollera *f* (CS) (Indum) skirt

pollería *f* poultry store, poulterer's store

pollito -ta *m,f* chick

pollo -lla *m,f* (Zool) **(a)** (cría) chick **(b)** (adulto) chicken **(c)** (Coc) chicken; **~ asado** roast chicken

polluelo *m* chick

polo *m* **1** **(a)** (Geog) pole; **P~ Norte/Sur** North/South Pole **(b)** (Elec, Fís) pole; **~ negativo**

negative pole; **ser ~s opuestos** (fam) to be poles apart **2** (centro) center*, focus **3** (a) (Dep) polo (b) (Indum) polo shirt **4** (Esp) (helado) Popsicle® (AmE), ice lolly (BrE)

pololear [A1] *vi* (Chi) to have a boyfriend/girlfriend; **~ con** algn to go out **with** sb

pololo -la *m,f* (Chi fam) (*m*) boyfriend; (*f*) girlfriend

Polonia *f* Poland

poltrona *f* armchair, easy chair

polución *f* pollution; **la ~ atmosférica** atmospheric pollution

polvareda *f* dust cloud

polvera *f* powder compact

polvo *m* (a) (suciedad) dust; **limpiar** *or* **quitar el ~** to do the dusting, to dust; *estar hecho ~* (agotado) to be all in (fam); (deprimido) to be devastated; (destruido) to be a wreck (b) (Coc, Quím) powder (c) **polvos** *mpl* (en cosmética) face powder; **~s de talco** talcum powder, talc (colloq)

pólvora *f* (a) (explosivo) gunpowder (b) (fuegos artificiales) fireworks (*pl*)

polvoriento -ta *adj* dusty

polvorín *m* (a) (almacén de explosivos) magazine (b) (lugar, país peligroso) powder keg

pomada *f* (Farm) ointment, cream; **~ de zapatos** (RPl) shoe polish

pomelo *m* (fruto) grapefruit; (árbol) grapefruit tree

pomo *m* (de puerta, mueble) handle, knob; (de espada) pommel

pompa *f* **1** *tb* **~ de jabón** bubble **2** (esplendor) pomp, splendor*; **~s fúnebres** *fpl* (ceremonia) funeral ceremony; (funeraria) funeral parlor*, funeral director's

pomposo -sa *adj* (a) ⟨boda/fiesta⟩ magnificent, splendid; ⟨lenguaje/estilo⟩ pompous, high-sounding (b) (ostentoso) pompous, ostentatious

pómulo *m* (hueso) cheekbone; (mejilla) cheek

pon ▶ **PONER**

ponchadura *f* (Méx) flat, puncture

ponchar [A1] *vt* (Méx) ⟨llanta/balón⟩ to puncture
■ **poncharse** *v pron* **1** (Méx) ⟨balón⟩ to puncture; **se nos ponchó una llanta** we had a flat tire *o* a puncture **2** (Col, Ven) (en béisbol) to fan (colloq), to strike out

ponche *m* (bebida) punch

poncho *m* poncho

ponderar [A1] *vt* (a) ⟨cálculo/índice⟩ to weight, adjust (b) (considerar) to weigh up, consider, ponder (c) (alabar) to praise, speak highly of

pondré, pondría, etc ▶ **PONER**

ponedora *f* layer, laying hen

poner [E22] *vt*
I **1** (a) (colocar) to put; **ponlo en el suelo** put it on the floor; **ponle el collar al perro** put the dog's collar on; **~ una bomba** to plant a bomb (b) ⟨anuncio/aviso⟩ to place, put (c) ⟨ropa⟩ (+ *me/te/le etc*): **le puse el sombrero** I put his hat on (for him)
2 (agregar) to put
3 ⟨inyección/supositorio⟩ to give
4 **poner la mesa** to lay *o* set the table

5 (instalar, montar) (a) ⟨oficina/restaurante⟩ to open (b) ⟨cocina/teléfono/calefacción⟩ to install (c) ⟨cerradura/armario⟩ to fit
6 ⟨ave⟩ ⟨huevo⟩ to lay
7 (Esp) (servir, dar): **póngame un café, por favor** I'll have a coffee, please; **¿cuántos le pongo?** how many would you like?
II **1** ⟨dinero⟩ (contribuir) to put in; **pusimos 500 pesos cada uno** we put in 500 pesos each
2 ⟨atención⟩ to pay; ⟨cuidado/interés⟩ to take; **pon más cuidado en la presentación** take more care over the presentation
3 (a) (imponer) ⟨deberes⟩ to give, set; ⟨examen/problema⟩ to set; **le pusieron una multa** he was fined (b) (oponer) ⟨inconvenientes⟩ to raise; **me pusieron problemas para entrar** they made it difficult for me to get in (c) (adjudicar) ⟨nota⟩ to give
4 (dar) ⟨nombre/apodo⟩ to give; ⟨ejemplo⟩ to give; **le pusieron Eva** they called her Eva
5 (enviar) ⟨telegrama⟩ to send
6 (escribir) ⟨dedicatoria/líneas⟩ to write
7 (Esp) (exhibir, dar) ⟨película⟩ to show; **¿ponen algo interesante en la tele?** is there anything interesting on TV?; **¿qué ponen en el Royal?** what's on *o* what's showing at the Royal?
III **1** (a) (conectar, encender) ⟨televisión/calefacción⟩ to turn on, switch on, put on; ⟨programa/canal⟩ to put on; ⟨cinta/disco/música⟩ to put on; **puso el motor en marcha** she switched on *o* started the engine (b) (ajustar, graduar) ⟨despertador⟩ to set; **pon la música más alta** turn the music up; **puso el reloj en hora** she put the clock right
2 (Esp) (al teléfono): **~ a** algn **con** algo/algn to put sb **through to** sth/sb
IV (en estado, situación) (+ *compl*): **~ a** algn **nervioso** to make sb nervous; **~ a** algn **en un aprieto** to put sb in an awkward position
■ *vi* ⟨ave⟩ to lay
■ **ponerse** *v pron*
I **1** (*refl*) (colocarse): **pongámonos ahí** let's stand (*o* sit *etc*) there; **~se de pie** to stand (up); **~se de rodillas** to kneel (down), get down on one's knees
2 ⟨sol⟩ to set
3 (*refl*) ⟨calzado/maquillaje/alhaja⟩ to put on; **no tengo nada que ~me** I don't have a thing to wear
II **1** (en estado, situación) (+ *compl*): **~se enfermo** to get sick; **se puso triste** she became sad; **cuando lo vio se puso muy contenta** she was so happy when she saw it; **se puso como loco** he went mad; **~se cómodo** to make oneself comfortable
2 (empezar) **~se a + INF** to start -ING, to start + INF; **se puso a llover** it started raining, it started to rain
III (Esp): **~se al teléfono** to come to the phone

ponga, pongas, etc ▶ **PONER**

poni *m* ▶ **PONY**

poniente *m* (occidente) west; (viento) west wind

pontífice *m* pontiff, pope

pony /'poni/ *m* (*pl* **-nies** *or* **-nys**) pony

pop *m* **1** (Mús) pop (music) **2** (Ur) (Coc) popcorn

popa *f* stern

popis, popoff *adj inv* (Méx fam) posh

popote *m* (Méx) straw

popular *adj* **1** (a) ⟨cultura/tradiciones⟩

⋯⟶

popular (*before n*); ‹*canción/baile/costumbres*›
traditional **(b)** (Pol) ‹*movimiento/rebelión*›
popular (*before n*) **2** (que gusta) ‹*actor/programa/
deporte*› popular

popularidad *f* popularity

popularizar [A4] *vt* to popularize, make ...
popular

■ **popularizarse** *v pron* to become popular

popurrí *m* (de cosas, colores) potpourri

póquer *m* (juego — de naipes) poker; (— de dados)
poker dice; **un ~ de ases** four aces

poquísimo *adj* ▸ POCO

por *prep*

I **1** (causa) because of; **~ falta de dinero** because
of *o* owing to lack of money; **~ naturaleza** by
nature; **~ necesidad** out of necessity; **~ eso no
dije nada** that's why I didn't say anything; **fue ~
eso que no te llamé** that was why I didn't call
you; **si no fuera ~ mi hijo** ... if it wasn't for my
son ...; **me pidió perdón ~ haberme mentido** he
apologized for lying *o* for having lied to me
2 (*en locs*) **por qué** why; **no dijo ~ qué** he didn't
say why; **¿por qué no vienes conmigo?** why don't
you come with me?; **por si** in case; **~ si no
entiende** in case he doesn't understand; ▸ ACASO
2, MOSCA
3 (en expresiones concesivas): **~ más que me
esfuerzo** however hard *o* no matter how hard I
try; **~ (muy) fácil que sea** however easy *o* no
matter how easy it is
4 **(a)** (modo): **colócalos ~ orden de tamaño** put
them in order of size; **~ adelantado** in advance;
~ escrito in writing **(b)** (medio): **se lo
comunicaron ~ teléfono** they told him over the
phone; **lo dijeron ~ la radio** they said it on the
radio; **~ avión** by air; **la conocí ~ la voz** I
recognized her by her voice; **me enteré ~ un
amigo** I heard from *o* through a friend
5 **(a)** (proporción): **cobra $30 ~ clase** he charges
$30 a *o* per class; **120 kilómetros ~ hora** 120
kilometers an *o* per hour; **~ metro/docena** by the
meter/dozen; **tú comes ~ tres** you eat enough for
three people; **tiene tres metros de largo ~ uno de
ancho** it's three meters long by one meter wide;
uno ~ uno one by one; ▸ CIENTO *m* B **(b)** (en
multiplicaciones): **tres ~ cuatro (son) doce** three
times four is twelve, three fours are twelve
6 **(a)** (sustitución) for; **su secretaria firmó ~ él** his
secretary signed for him *o* on his behalf; **pasa ~
inglesa** she passes for an Englishwoman **(b)**
(como): **~ ejemplo** for example
7 (introduciendo el agente) by; **compuesto ~ Mozart**
composed by Mozart

II **1** (finalidad, objetivo): **pelearse ~ algo** to fight
over sth; **lo hace ~ el dinero** he does it for the
money; **no entré ~ no molestarlo** I didn't go in
because I didn't want to disturb him; **~ QUE +
SUBJ** (*here* POR QUE *can also be written* PORQUE):
estaba ansioso ~ que lo escucharan he was
eager for them to listen to him
2 (indicando inclinación, elección): **su amor ~ la
música** her love of music; **no siento nada ~ él** I
don't feel anything for him; **votó ~ ella** he voted
for her
3 (en busca de): **salió/fue ~** *or* (Esp) **a ~ pan** he
went (out) for some bread, he went (out) to get
some bread
4 (en lo que respecta a): **~ mí que haga lo que quiera**
as far as I'm concerned, he can do what he likes

5 (esp AmL) **estar ~ + INF** (estar a punto de) to be
about to + INF; **está ~ terminar** he's about to
finish; **deben (de) estar ~ llegar** they should be
arriving any minute

III **1** **(a)** (lugar): **entró ~ la ventana** he came in
through the window; **sal ~ aquí** go out this way;
se cayó ~ la escalera he fell down the stairs; **¿el
121 va ~ (la) Avenida Rosas?** does the 121 go
along Rosas Avenue?; **¿~ dónde has venido?**
which way did you come?; **está ~ ahí** he's over
there somewhere; **¿~ dónde está el hotel?**
whereabouts is the hotel?; **viven ~ mi barrio** they
live around my area; **voy ~ la página 15** I'm up to
o I'm on page 15; **empieza ~ el principio** start at
the beginning; **agárralo ~ el mango** hold it by the
handle **(b)** (indicando extensión): **~ todos lados** *or* **~
todas partes** everywhere; **viajamos ~ el norte de
Francia** we traveled around *o* in the North of
France; *ver tb* DENTRO, FUERA, ENCIMA, ETC
2 (tiempo) for; **~ un mes** for a month; **~ el
momento** *or* **~ ahora** for the time being, for now;
ver tb MAÑANA, TARDE, NOCHE
3 (Esp) (ocasión) for; **me lo regaló ~ mi
cumpleaños** she gave it to me for my birthday

porcelana *f* **(a)** (material) china; (de mejor
calidad) porcelain **(b)** (objeto) piece of china/
porcelain

porcentaje *m* percentage

porche *m* (de casa) porch; (soportal) arcade

porción *f* (de un todo) portion; (en reparto) share;
(de comida) portion, helping, serving

pordiosero -ra *m,f* beggar

porfiado -da *adj* stubborn, pig-headed (colloq)
■ *m,f* (persona) stubborn creature (colloq)

porfiar [A17] *vi* (insistir) to insist; **no me porfíes,
ya te dije que no** don't keep on *o* go on about it, I
said no

pormenor *m* detail; **los ~es del incidente** the
details of the incident; **entrar en ~es** to go into
detail

pornografía *f* pornography

pornográfico -ca *adj* pornographic

poro *m* **1** (Anat, Biol) pore **2** (Méx) (puerro) leek

pororó *m* (RPl) popcorn

poroso -sa *adj* porous

poroto *m* (CS) bean; **~ verde** (Chi) green bean

porque *conj* **(a)** (indicando causa) because; **¿por
qué no vas a ir?** **— ~ no** why don't you go? —
because I don't want to **(b)** (indicando finalidad) ▸
POR II 1

porqué *m* reason; **quiero saber el ~** I want to
know the reason

porquería *f* **1** **(a)** (suciedad) dirt **(b)**
(cochinada): **no hagas ~s** don't do disgusting *o*
filthy things like that; **la casa está hecha una ~**
(fam) the house is in such a state (colloq) **2** (cosa
de mala calidad): **el libro es una ~** the book's a
piece of junk; **la comida es una ~** the food is
dreadful *o* terrible

porra *f* **1** (de guardia, policía) nightstick (AmE),
truncheon (BrE) **2** (fam) (expresando disgusto, enojo):
mandar a algn a la ~ (colloq) to tell sb to get lost
(colloq); **¡vete** *or* **ándate a la ~!** go to hell! (colloq),
get lost! (colloq); **mandar algo a la ~** (colloq)
‹*trabajo*› to chuck sth in (colloq) **3** (Jueg) draw,
lottery **4** (Col, Méx fam) **(a)** (seguidores, hinchas)
fans (*pl*) **(b)** (canto, grito): **¡una ~ para Villalva!**

three cheers for Villalva!; **la ~ de la universidad** the college chant; *echarle* **~s a algn** (Méx fam) *‹a equipo/corredor›* to cheer sb (on)

porrista *mf* (a) (Col, Méx) (seguidor) fan (b) **porrista** *f* (Col, Méx) (animadora) cheerleader

porro *m* (Esp arg) (de hachís) joint (colloq), spliff (sl)

porrón *m* 1 (a) (de vino) wine bottle *(with a long spout for drinking from)* (b) (Arg) (de cerveza) bottle of beer 2 (CS) (pimiento) green pepper; (puerro) leek

portabebés *m* (*pl* ~) portacrib® (AmE), carrycot (BrE)

portada *f* 1 (de libro) title page; (de periódico) front page; (de revista) cover 2 (de iglesia) front, facade

portadocumentos *m* (*pl* ~) (AmL) (grande) briefcase, attaché case; (pequeño) document wallet

portador -dora *m,f* 1 (Med) (de virus, germen) carrier 2 (Com, Fin) bearer; **páguese al ~** pay the bearer

portaequipajes *m* (*pl* ~) (a) (Auto) (para el techo) roofrack; (maletero) trunk (AmE), boot (BrE) (b) (en tren, autobús) luggage rack

portafolios *m* (*pl* ~) (maletín) briefcase

portal *m* (a) (de casa — entrada) doorway; (— vestíbulo) hall (b) (de iglesia, palacio) portal (c) (en muralla) gate

portar [A1] *vt* (frml) *‹arma/bandera›* to carry, bear (frml)
■ **portarse** *v pron* (a) (comportarse): **~se bien** to behave (oneself); **~se mal** to behave badly; **~se bien/mal con** algn to treat sb well/badly(b) (cumplir): **el Zaragoza se portó en la final** Zaragoza delivered the goods in the final; **hoy te portaste** you've really excelled today

portátil *adj* portable

portaviones *m* (*pl* ~) aircraft carrier

portavoz *mf* (*m*) spokesperson, spokesman; (*f*) spokesperson, spokeswoman

portazo *m* slam, bang; **dar un ~** to slam the door

porte *m* 1 (tamaño) size; **es de este ~** (AmL) it's about this big 2 (acción de portar) carrying; (costo) carriage; **~s pagados** freight/postage paid

porteño -ña *adj* of/from the city of Buenos Aires

portería *f* 1 (a) (de edificio) *desk/area from where the super/caretaker supervises the building* (b) (vivienda) super's *o* superintendent's apartment (AmE), caretaker's flat (*o* house *etc*) (BrE) 2 (Dep) goal

portero -ra *m,f* 1 (que abre la puerta) doorman, porter; (que cuida el edificio) super (AmE), superintendent (AmE), caretaker (BrE); **~ eléctrico** *or* (Esp) **automático** *m* entryphone 2 (Dep) goalkeeper

portezuela *f* door

pórtico *m* (entrada) portico, porch; (galería) arcade

portón *m* (puerta grande) large door; (puerta principal) front door; (en cerca) gate

portorriqueño -ña *adj/m,f* Puerto Rican

Portugal *m* Portugal

portugués[1] **-guesa** *adj/m,f* Portuguese

portugués[2] *m* (idioma) Portuguese

porvenir *m* future; **un joven sin ~** a young man with no future *o* no prospects

posada *f* (a) (arc) (taberna) inn (arch) (b) (cobijo) hospitality

posaderas *fpl* (fam) backside (colloq), butt (AmE colloq), bum (BrE colloq)

posar [A1] *vi* to pose
■ **posarse** *v pron* «*pájaro/insecto*» to alight, land; «*avión/helicóptero*» to land

posavasos *m* (*pl* ~) coaster; (de cartón) beermat

pose *f* (a) (para foto) pose (b) (pey) (afectación) pose

poseedor -dora *m,f* (frml) (de título, récord, billete) holder

poseer [E13] *vt* (a) *‹tierras/fortuna›* to own (b) *‹conocimientos›* to have (c) *‹récord/título›* to hold

posesión *f* possession; **tomar ~ de algo** (de casa) to take possession of sth; (de cargo) to take up sth; **está en ~ de todas sus facultades** he is in full possession of his faculties

posesivo -va *adj* possessive

posguerra *f* postwar period

posibilidad *f* 1 (circunstancia) possibility; **tener la ~ de hacer algo** to have the chance of doing sth; **tiene muchas ~es de salir elegido** he has a good chance of being elected; **existe la ~ de que estés equivocado** you might just be wrong 2 **posibilidades** *fpl* (a) (medios económicos) means (*pl*); **vivo de acuerdo a mis ~es** I live within my means; **la casa está por encima de mis ~es** I can't afford the house (b) (potencial) potential; **un cantante con muchas ~es** a singer of great potential

posibilitar [A1] *vt* to make ... possible

posible *adj* possible; **es ~** it's possible; **a ser ~** *or* **si es ~** if possible; **hicieron todo lo ~** they did everything possible *o* everything they could; **prometió ayudarlo dentro de lo ~** *or* **en lo ~** she promised to do what she could to help (him); **¡no es ~!** that can't be true! (colloq); **en cuanto te sea ~** as soon as you can; **no creo que me sea ~** I don't think I'll be able to; **es ~ hacerlo más rápido** it's possible to do it more quickly; **no me fue ~ terminarlo** I wasn't able to finish it; **es ~ que sea cierto** it might *o* may *o* could be true
■ *adv*: **lo más pronto ~** as soon as possible; **lo mejor ~** the best you can

posición *f* (a) (en general) position; **en ~ vertical** in an upright position (b) (en la sociedad) social standing; **gente de buena ~** people of high social standing (c) (actitud) position, stance; **adoptar una ~ intransigente** to take a tough stand *o* stance

positivo -va *adj* positive

poso *m* (del vino) sediment, lees (*pl*), dregs (*pl*); (del café) dregs (*pl*), grounds (*pl*)

posponer [E22] *vt* (aplazar) to postpone, put off

posta *f* 1 (AmL) (Dep) relay (race) 2 (AmC) (Mil) sentry post 3 (Esp) **a posta** on purpose, deliberately 4 (Chi) (centro médico) accident and emergency center*

postal *adj* *‹distrito/servicio›* postal
■ *f* postcard

postdata *f* postscript

poste ⋯⊹ precalentamiento

326

poste *m* (a) (de alambrado) (fence) post; (de teléfono, telégrafo) pole (b) (Dep) post, upright

postemilla *f* (AmL) gumboil, abscess

póster *m* (*pl* **-ters**) poster

postergar [A3] *vt* 1 (esp AmL) (aplazar) ⟨juicio/reunión⟩ to postpone, put back 2 (relegar) ⟨empleado⟩ to pass over

posteridad *f* posterity

posterior *adj* 1 (a) (en el tiempo) later, subsequent; **en años ~es** in later *o* subsequent years; **ese incidente fue ~ a su llegada** that incident happened after his arrival (b) (en orden) subsequent 2 (trasero) ⟨patas⟩ back (*before n*), rear (*before n*); **la parte ~** the back *o* rear

posterioridad *f*: **con ~** subsequently, later

postgrado *m* postgraduate course

postgraduado -da *adj/m,f* postgraduate

postguerra *f* postwar period

postigo *m* shutter

postizo¹ -za *adj* (a) ⟨pestañas⟩ false; **dentadura postiza** dentures, false teeth (b) ⟨manga/cuello⟩ detachable

postizo² *m* hairpiece

postor *m* bidder

postrarse [A1] *v pron* (frml) (arrodillarse) to kneel

postre *m* dessert, pudding (BrE)
■ *f*: **a la ~** (*loc adv*) (frml) in the end

postulante -ta *m,f* (a) (Pol) (candidato) candidate (b) (CS) (para puesto) applicant

postular [A1] *vt* (AmL) (Pol) ⟨candidato⟩ to nominate, propose
■ *vi* **~ PARA algo** (CS) (para puesto) to apply FOR sth
■ **postularse** *v pron* (AmL) to stand, run

póstumo -ma *adj* posthumous

postura *f* 1 (del cuerpo) position 2 (a) (actitud) stance, stand; **adoptar una ~ firme con respecto a algo** to take a tough stance *o* stand on sth (b) (opinión) opinion; **tomar ~** to take a stand 3 (AmL) (de ropa, zapatos): **se le rompieron a la primera ~** they broke the first time she wore them; **~ de argollas** (Chi) (acción) exchange of rings (*to seal one's engagement*); (fiesta) engagement party

potable *adj* ⟨agua⟩ drinkable, potable (frml); ⑤ **agua no potable** not drinking water

potaje *m* (Coc) vegetable stew/soup (*gen with pulses*)

potasio *m* potassium

pote *m* (olla) pot; (de crema, maquillaje) (CS) pot, jar

potencia *f* power; **~ militar/nuclear** military/nuclear power; **este niño es un artista en ~** this child has the makings of an artist

potencial *adj* (posible) potential; (Ling) conditional
■ *m* (capacidad, posibilidades) potential

potenciar [A1] *vt* (period) (a) ⟨desarrollo/investigación/exportaciones⟩ to boost; ⟨relaciones/unidad/talento⟩ to foster; ⟨cultura⟩ to promote (b) (mejorar) ⟨seguridad⟩ to improve

potentado -da *m,f* tycoon

potente *adj* (a) (en general) powerful (b) ⟨hombre⟩ virile

potestad *f* legal authority

potingue *m* (fam) cream, lotion

poto *m* (Andes fam) (de persona) butt (AmE colloq), bum (BrE colloq); (de botella) bottom

potpourri /popu'rri/ *m* medley

potrero *m* (AmL) (terreno cercado) field; (para pastar) pasture

potrillo -lla *m,f* (Zool) foal

potro -tra *m,f* 1 (caballo joven) (*m*) colt; (*f*) filly 2 **potro** *m* (instrumento de tortura) rack; (cepo) stocks (*pl*); (en gimnasia) vaulting horse, buck

pozo *m* (a) (de agua) well; **~ ciego** *or* **negro** *or* **séptico** septic tank, cesspool, cesspit; **~ de petróleo** oil well (b) (en mina) shaft (c) (en río) deep pool

práctica *f* 1 (a) (en actividad) practice; (en trabajo) experience; **perder la ~** to be out of practice (b) (de profesión) practicing* 2 (aplicación) practice; **en la ~** in practice; **poner algo en ~** *or* **llevar algo a la ~** to put sth into practice 3 **prácticas** *fpl* (de Anatomía, Química) practicals (*pl*); (de maestro) teaching practice; **~s de tiro** target practice 4 (costumbre) practice

practicante *adj* (Rel) practicing* (*before n*)
■ *mf* (Med) nurse (*specializing in giving injections, dressing wounds, etc*)

practicar [A2] *vt* 1 (a) ⟨idioma/pieza musical⟩ to practice*; ⟨tenis⟩ to play; **~ la natación** to swim; **no practica ningún deporte** he doesn't play *o* do any sport(s) (b) ⟨profesión⟩ to practice* 2 (frml) (llevar a cabo, realizar) ⟨corte/incisión⟩ to make; ⟨autopsia/operación⟩ to perform, do; ⟨redada/actividad⟩ to carry out; ⟨detenciones⟩ to make
■ *vi* (repetir) to practice*; (ejercer) to practice*

práctico -ca *adj* 1 ⟨envase/cuchillo⟩ useful, handy; ⟨falda/diseño⟩ practical; **es muy ~ tener el coche para hacer la compra** it's very handy *o* convenient having the car to do the shopping 2 (no teórico) practical 3 ⟨persona⟩ [SER] (desenvuelto) practical

pradera *f* meadow; **las ~s de los Estados Unidos** the prairies of the United States

prado *m* (a) (Agr) meadow, field (b) (lugar de paseo) park (*with lawns*) (c) (Col) (jardín) garden, yard (AmE)

Praga *f* Prague

pragmático -ca *adj* pragmatic
■ *m,f* pragmatist

pragmatismo *m* pragmatism

preámbulo *m* (a) (de obra) introduction; (de constitución) preamble (b) (rodeo): **sin más ~s** without further ado; **dímelo sin tanto ~** stop beating about the bush and tell me (c) (de curso, negociaciones) preliminary

preaviso *m* notice

precalentamiento *m* (a) (Dep) warm-up (b) (del horno) preheating (c) (de motor) warming up

AmC	Central America	Arg	Argentina	Cu	Cuba	Per	Peru
AmL	Latin America	Bol	Bolivia	Ec	Ecuador	RPI	River Plate Area
AmS	South America	Chí	Chile	Esp	Spain	Ur	Uruguay
Andes	Andean Region	CS	Southern Cone	Méx	Mexico	Ven	Venezuela

precalentar [A5] *vt* ⟨*horno*⟩ to preheat; ⟨*motor*⟩ to warm up

precario -ria *adj* ⟨*vivienda*⟩ poor; ⟨*medios*⟩ scarce, meager*; ⟨*salud/situación*⟩ precarious, unstable; ⟨*gobierno/puesto*⟩ unstable

precaución *f* **1** (medida) precaution **2** (prudencia): **medida de** ~ precautionary measure; **actuar con** ~ to act with caution

precaverse [E1] *v pron* to take precautions

precavido -da *adj* cautious, prudent

precedencia *f* precedence, priority

precedente *adj* previous
■ *m* precedent; **sentar (un)** ~ to set a precedent

preceder [E1] *vt* to precede

precepto *m* rule, precept (fml)

preciado -da *adj* ⟨*bien/objeto*⟩ prized, valued; ⟨*don*⟩ valuable

preciarse [A1] *v pron* (a) (estimarse): **un abogado que se precie no haría eso** no self-respecting lawyer would do that (b) (jactarse) ~ **DE algo** to pride oneself **ON** sth

precintar [A1] *vt* (a) ⟨*paquete/botella*⟩ to seal (b) ⟨*local*⟩ (tras crimen) to seal; (clausurar) to close down (*often on health or safety grounds*)

precinto *m* seal

precio *m* **1** (de producto) price; ~ **al contado/a plazos** cash/credit price; **¿qué** ~ **tiene este vestido?** how much is this dress?; ~ **de costo** *or* (Esp) **coste** cost price; ~ **de venta al público** (de alimento, medicamento) recommended retail price; (de libro) published price; *no tener* ~ to be priceless **2** (sacrificio, costo) price, cost; **a cualquier** ~ at any price, whatever the cost

preciosidad *f*: **ser una** ~ to be absolutely beautiful

precioso -sa *adj* (hermoso) beautiful, gorgeous, lovely; (de gran valor) precious, valuable

preciosura *f* (AmL) ▶ PRECIOSIDAD

precipicio *m* (despeñadero) precipice

precipitación *f* **1** (prisa) rush, hurry; **lo hizo con mucha** ~ she did it in a rush *o* hurry **2** (Meteo) rainfall; **la** ~ **mensual** the monthly rainfall; **habrá precipitaciones débiles** there will be some light rain

precipitado -da *adj* ⟨*decisión/actuación*⟩ hasty; ⟨*juicio*⟩ snap (*before n*)

precipitarse [A1] *v pron* **1** (en decisión, juicio) to be hasty; **te precipitaste juzgándolo así** you were rash to judge him like that **2** (apresurarse) to rush; ~**se A hacer algo** to rush to do sth **3** (a) (caer) to plunge (b) (*refl*) (arrojarse) to throw oneself

precisado -da *adj* (AmL fml): **verse** ~ **a hacer algo** to be forced *o* obliged to do sth

precisar [A1] *vt* **1** (determinar con exactitud) to specify **2** (necesitar) to need

precisión *f* (a) (exactitud) precision; **no puedo decírtelo con** ~ I can't tell you exactly; **de** ~ ⟨*instrumento/máquina*⟩ precision (*before n*) (b) (claridad, concisión) precision

preciso -sa *adj* **1** (a) (exacto, claro) precise (b) (*delante del n*) (como intensificador) very; **en este** ~ **momento** this very minute, right now; **en el** ~ **momento en que salía** just as he was going out; **en este** ~ **lugar** in this very spot **2** (necesario) necessary; **si es** ~ if necessary, if need be; **ser** ~

hacer algo to be necessary to do sth; **es** ~ **que la veas** you must see her; **no es** ~ **que vayamos todos** there's no need for all of us to go

preconcebido -da *adj* preconceived

precoz *adj* ⟨*niño/desarrollo*⟩ precocious; ⟨*diagnóstico/fruto/helada*⟩ early

precursor -sora *m,f* precursor, forerunner

predecesor -sora *m,f* predecessor

predecir [I25] *vt* to predict, foretell (fml)

predestinación *f* predestination

predestinar [A1] *vt* to predestine; **estar** ~ **a algo/hacer algo** to be predestined to sth/to do sth

predeterminar [A1] *vt* to predetermine

predicado *m* predicate

predicador -dora *m,f* preacher

predicamento *m* (AmL) (situación difícil) predicament

predicar [A2] *vt/vi* to preach

predicativo -va *adj* predicative

predicción *f* prediction, forecast

predecible *adj* (Andes) predictable

predilección *f* predilection; **tiene/siente** ~ **por su hijo** she's especially fond of her son

predilecto -ta *adj/m,f* favorite*

predisponer [E22] *vt* **1** (Med) to predispose **2** (influir en) to prejudice; **lo predispusieron en contra mía** they prejudiced him against me

predisposición *f* **1** (Med) predisposition **2** (inclinación): **tener** ~ **contra algn** to be prejudiced against sb

predispuesto -ta *adj* (a) [SER] (propenso) ~ **A algo** prone **TO** sth (b) [ESTAR] (prejuiciado) ~ **A FAVOR/EN CONTRA DE algo/algn** biased **TOWARDS**/ **AGAINST** sth/sb

predominante *adj* predominant

predominar [A1] *vi* ⟨*actitud/opinión*⟩ to prevail; ~ **EN algo** to dominate sth; **el tema predominó en el congreso** the subject dominated the conference; ~ **SOBRE algo** to be predominant **OVER** sth

predominio *m* predominance

preescolar *adj* ⟨*edad/educación*⟩ preschool (*before n*); **centro de educación** ~ kindergarten, nursery school (BrE)

preestreno *m* preview

prefabricado -da *adj* prefabricated

prefacio *m* preface

prefecto *m* (a) (Relig) prefect (b) (Gob) (en Francia) prefect (c) (Per) (gobernador) civil governor (d) (Col) (Educ) *teacher responsible for discipline*

preferencia *f* (a) (prioridad) priority, precedence; (Auto) right of way, priority (BrE) (b) (predilección) preference; **tiene** ~ **por el más pequeño** the youngest one is her favorite (c) (Espec) (localidad) grandstand

preferente *adj* (especial) special

preferible *adj* preferable, better; **es** ~ **quedarse callado** it's better to stay quiet; **es** ~ **a uno de plástico** it's better than *o* preferable to a plastic one; **es** ~ **que no vayas** you'd better not go

preferido -da *adj/m,f* favorite*

preferir [I11] *vt* to prefer; **prefiero esperar aquí** ┄┈▷

I'd rather wait here, I'd prefer to wait here; ~ algo A algo to prefer sth TO sth; **prefiero que te quedes** I'd rather you stayed, I prefer you to stay

prefiera, prefieras, etc ▶ PREFERIR

prefijo *m* (Ling) prefix; (de teléfono) (dialing*) code

prefiriera, prefirió, etc ▶ PREFERIR

pregonar [A1] *vt* **(a)** ⟨noticia/secreto⟩ to make ... public **(b)** ⟨virtudes/méritos⟩ to extol **(c)** ⟨mercancía⟩ to hawk, cry

pregunta *f* question; **hacer/contestar una ~** to ask/answer a question

preguntar [A1] *vt* to ask; **eso no se pregunta** you shouldn't ask things like that; **la maestra me preguntó la lección** the teacher tested me on the lesson
■ ~ *vi* to ask; **le preguntó sobre** *or* **acerca de lo ocurrido** he asked her (about) what had happened; **~ POR algo/algn** to ask ABOUT sth/sb; **preguntaban por un tal Mario** they were looking for *o* asking for someone called Mario
■ **preguntarse** *v pron* (refl) to wonder

prehistoria *f* prehistory

prehistórico -ca *adj* prehistoric

prejuiciado -da *adj* (AmL) prejudiced

prejuicio *m* prejudice; **tener ~s raciales** to be racially prejudiced

prejuzgar [A3] *vt/vi* to prejudge

prelavado *m* prewash

preliminar *adj* preliminary

preludio *m* prelude

premamá *adj inv* (Esp fam) maternity (before n)

prematrimonial *adj* ⟨relaciones⟩ premarital

prematuro -ra *adj* premature

premeditación *f* premeditation

premeditado -da *adj* premeditated

premeditar [A1] *vt* to premeditate

premenstrual *adj* premenstrual

premiación *f* (AmL) (acción) awarding of prizes; (ceremonia) awards ceremony, prize-giving (BrE)

premiado -da *adj* ⟨número/boleto⟩ winning; ⟨novela/película/escritor⟩ prizewinning (before n); *ver tb* PREMIAR

premiar [A1] *vt* **(a)** ⟨actor/escritor⟩ to award a/ the prize to, award ... a/the prize **(b)** ⟨generosidad/sacrificio⟩ to reward

premio *m* **(a)** (en general) prize; **conceder** *or* **dar un ~** to award *o* give a prize; **ganar** *or* **llevarse un ~** to win a prize; **el ~ a la mejor película** the award *o* prize for the best movie; **~ de consolación** *or* (CS) **(de) consuelo** consolation prize; **~ gordo** jackpot; **P~ Nobel** (galardón) Nobel Prize; (galardonado) Nobel Prize winner **(b)** (a esfuerzos, sacrificios) reward; **como ~ a su dedicación** as a reward for your dedication

premisa *f* premise

premonición *f* premonition

prenatal *adj* prenatal (AmE), antenatal (BrE)

prenda *f* **1** (de vestir) garment; **~ íntima** undergarment, item of underwear **2** (señal, garantía) security, surety **3** (Jueg) forfeit

prendarse [A1] *v pron* (liter) **~ DE algn** to fall in love WITH sb

prender [E1] *vt* **1** ⟨persona⟩ to catch, seize **2** (sujetar) to pin; ⟨bajo/dobladillo⟩ to pin up

3 (a) ⟨cigarrillo/cerilla⟩ to light; **~(le) fuego a algo** to set fire to sth **(b)** (AmL) ⟨gas⟩ to light; ⟨estufa/horno⟩ to turn on; ⟨radio/luz/televisión⟩ to turn on, switch on
■ ~ *vi* **1** «rama/planta» to take **2 (a)** «fósforo/ piloto» to light; «leña» to catch (light) **(b)** (AmL) «luz/radio/televisión» to come on; **la televisión no prende** the TV won't come on **3** «idea/ moda» to catch on
■ **prenderse** *v pron* **(a)** (con fuego) to catch fire **(b)** (AmL) «luz/radio/televisión» to come on

prensa *f* **(a)** (Impr, Period, Tec) press; **la ~ oral** radio and television; **estar en ~** to be in *o* at the press **(b)** (periodistas) **la ~** the press; **~ amarilla** gutter press, yellow press; **~ del corazón** gossip magazines (*pl*); **~ roja** (CS) sensationalist press (specializing in crime stories)

preñado -da *adj* ⟨animal⟩ pregnant

preocupación *f* **(a)** (problema) worry; **les causa muchas preocupaciones** she causes them a lot of worry *o* problems **(b)** (inquietud) concern

preocupado -da *adj* worried; **~ POR algo** worried ABOUT sth

preocupante *adj* worrying

preocupar [A1] *vt* to worry; **no quiero ~lo** I don't want to worry him; **le preocupa el futuro** she's worried *o* concerned about her future; **me preocupa que no haya llamado** it worries me that she hasn't phoned; **no me preocupa** it doesn't bother *o* worry me
■ **preocuparse** *v pron* **1** (inquietarse) to worry; **~se POR algo/algn** to worry ABOUT sth/sb **2** (ocuparse) **~se DE algo: me preocupé de que no faltara nada** I made sure *o* I saw to it that we had everything; **no se preocupó más del asunto** he gave the matter no further thought

preparación *f* **1** (de examen, discurso) preparation **2 (a)** (conocimientos, educación) education; (para trabajo) training **(b)** (de deportista) training; **su ~ física es muy buena** he's in peak condition **3** (Farm, Med) preparation

preparado -da *adj* **1** [ESTAR] (listo, dispuesto) ready; **~ PARA algo** ready FOR sth; **¡~s, listos, ya!** get ready, get set, go! (AmE), on your marks, get set, go! (BrE) **2** [SER] (instruido, culto) educated; **un profesional muy bien ~** a highly-trained professional

preparar [A1] *vt* **1** ⟨plato⟩ to make, prepare; ⟨comida⟩ to prepare, get ... ready; ⟨medicamento⟩ to prepare, make up; ⟨habitación⟩ to prepare, get ... ready; ⟨cuenta⟩ to draw up (AmE), make up (BrE) **2** ⟨examen/prueba⟩ to prepare **3** ⟨persona⟩ (para examen) to tutor, coach (BrE); (para partido) to train, coach, prepare; (para tarea, reto) to prepare
■ **prepararse** *v pron* **1** (refl) (disponerse): **~se PARA algo** to get ready FOR sth **2** (refl) (formarse) to prepare; **~se PARA algo** ⟨para examen/ competición⟩ to prepare FOR sth

preparativos *mpl* preparations (*pl*)

preparatoria *f* (Méx) *three-year pre-university course and college where this is taught*

preparatorio -ria *adj* ⟨curso⟩ preparatory; ⟨ejercicios⟩ warm-up (before n)

preponderante *adj* predominant, preponderant (frml)

preposición *f* preposition

prepotencia *f* arrogance

prepotente *adj* ⟨*persona*⟩ arrogant, overbearing; ⟨*actitud*⟩ high-handed

prepucio *m* foreskin, prepuce (tech)

presa *f* **1** (en caza) prey; **ser ~ de algo** (de terror, pánico) to be seized with sth **2** (dique) dam; (embalse) reservoir, lake **3** (AmS) (de pollo) piece

presagio *m* **(a)** (señal) omen **(b)** (premonición) premonition

prescindir [I1] *vi* **1** (arreglárselas sin) **~ DE algo/algn** to do WITHOUT sth/sb **2** (omitir) **~ DE algo** ⟨*de detalles/formalidades*⟩ to dispense WITH sth

prescribir [I34] *vt* to prescribe

prescripción *f* prescription; **por ~ facultativa** *or* **médica** on doctor's orders

prescrito -ta, prescripto -ta *pp* ▶ PRESCRIBIR

preselección *f*: **hacer una ~ de los candidatos** to draw up a shortlist of candidates; **una vez terminada la ~** once the initial selection process is/was complete

preseleccionar [A1] *vt* ⟨*candidatos/solicitantes*⟩ to shortlist

presencia *f* **(a)** (en lugar, acto) presence; **su ~ me cohíbe** I feel awkward in his presence; **en ~ de algn** in the presence of sb **(b)** (euf) (aspecto físico) appearance; **se requiere buena ~** good *o* (BrE) smart appearance required **(c) ~ de ánimo** (serenidad) presence of mind; (valor) courage, strength

presenciar [A1] *vt* ⟨*suceso/asesinato*⟩ to witness; ⟨*acto/espectáculo*⟩ to be present at, to attend

presentable *adj* presentable

presentación *f* (en general) presentation; (de personas) introduction

presentador -dora *m,f* presenter

presentar [A1] *vt* **1 (a)** (mostrar) to present **(b)** (exponer por primera vez) ⟨*libro/disco*⟩ to launch; ⟨*obra de arte*⟩ to present; ⟨*colección de moda*⟩ to present, exhibit **(c)** (entregar) ⟨*informe/solicitud*⟩ to submit; ⟨*trabajo*⟩ to hand in; ⟨*renuncia*⟩ to hand in, submit **(d)** (enseñar) ⟨*carnet/pasaporte*⟩ to show **(e)** ⟨*disculpas/excusas*⟩ to make; ⟨*queja*⟩ to file, make; ⟨*cargos*⟩ to bring; **~on una denuncia** they reported the matter (to the police), they made an official complaint; **~ pruebas** to present evidence **(f)** (Mil): **~ armas** to present arms

2 (TV) ⟨*programa*⟩ to present, introduce

3 ⟨*persona*⟩ to introduce; **te presento a mi hermana** I'd like you to meet my sister, this is my sister

4 ⟨*novedad/ventaja*⟩ to offer; ⟨*síntoma*⟩ to show

■ **presentarse** *v pron* **1 (a)** (en lugar) to turn up, appear; **~se (como) voluntario** to volunteer **(b) ~se A algo** ⟨*a examen*⟩ to take sth; ⟨*a concurso*⟩ to enter sth; ⟨*a elecciones*⟩ to take part IN sth; **se presenta como candidato independiente** he's running (AmE) *o* (BrE) he's standing as an independent; **~se para un cargo** to apply for a post

2 «*dificultad/problema*» to arise, come up; «*oportunidad*» to arise

3 (darse a conocer) to introduce oneself

presente *adj* **1** (en un lugar) [ESTAR] present; **⑤ Presente** (CS) (Corresp) ≈ by hand; **tener algo**

~ **to bear sth in mind 2** (actual) present; **hasta el momento ~** up to the present time; **el día 15 del ~ mes** the 15th of this month; **en su atenta carta del 3 ~** (Méx frml) (Corresp) in your letter of the 3rd of this month *o* (frml) of the 3rd inst.

■ *m* **1 (a)** (en el tiempo) **el ~** the present **(b)** (Ling) present (tense) **2 los presentes** *mpl* (asistentes) those present

presentimiento *m* premonition; **tengo el ~ de que ...** I have a feeling that ...

presentir [I11] *vt* ⟨*desgracia*⟩ to have a premonition of; **presiento que ...** I have a feeling that ...

preservar [A1] *vt* **(a)** (proteger) to preserve **(b)** (AmL) (conservar, mantener) to maintain

preservativo *m* **1** (condón) condom **2** (Andes) (conservante) preservative

presidencia *f* **(a)** (Gob, Pol) (cargo) presidency; **~ municipal** (Méx) town hall **(b)** (de compañía, banco) presidency (esp AmE), chairmanship (BrE); (de reunión, comité) chairmanship, chair

presidente -ta *m,f* **(a)** (Gob, Pol) president; **el ~ del gobierno** the premier, the prime minister **(b)** (de compañía, banco) president (AmE), chairman (BrE) **(c)** (de reunión, comité, acto) chairperson, chair **(d)** (Der) (de tribunal) presiding judge/magistrate **(e)** (de jurado) chairman/chairwoman

presidiario -ria *m,f* convict, inmate, prisoner

presidio *m* (lugar) prison; (pena) prison sentence; **condenado a cinco años de ~** sentenced to five years imprisonment

presidir [I1] *vt* ⟨*país*⟩ to be president of; ⟨*reunión*⟩ to chair, preside at *o* over; ⟨*comité*⟩ to chair; ⟨*tribunal/cortes/jurado*⟩ to preside over; ⟨*compañía*⟩ to be president of (AmE), to be chairman of (BrE)

presilla *f* (para abrochar) eye; (lazo) loop

presión *f* **(a)** (Fís, Med, Meteo) pressure; **~ arterial** *or* **sanguínea** blood pressure **(b)** (coacción) pressure; **bajo ~** under pressure

presionar [A1] *vt* **(a)** (coaccionar) to put pressure on, to pressure (esp AmE), to pressurize (esp BrE) **(b)** ⟨*botón/timbre*⟩ to press

■ **~** *vi* (Dep) to put on the pressure

preso -sa *adj*: **estuvo ~ diez años** he was in prison for ten years; **llevarse a algn ~** to take sb prisoner

■ *m,f* prisoner

prestaciones *fpl* (Servs Socs) benefits (*pl*), assistance

prestado -da *adj*: **el libro está ~** the book is on loan *o* (colloq) is already out; **esta chaqueta es prestada** this jacket is borrowed; **pedir algo ~** to borrow sth; **me pidió el coche ~** she asked if she could borrow my car; **pídeselo ~** ask (him) if you can borrow it

prestamista *mf* moneylender

préstamo *m* (Econ, Fin) (acción — de prestar) lending; (— de tomar prestado) borrowing; (cosa prestada) loan

prestar [A1] *vt* **1** ⟨*dinero/libro*⟩ to lend; **¿me prestas el coche?** will you lend me your car?, can I borrow your car? **2 (a)** ⟨*ayuda*⟩ to give; ⟨*servicio*⟩ to render; ⟨*servicio militar*⟩ to do **(b)** ⟨*atención*⟩ to pay **3** ⟨*juramento*⟩ to swear

■ **prestarse** *v pron* **1** (dar ocasión) **~se A algo** ⟨*a críticas/malentendidos/abusos*⟩ to be open TO sth ····⟫

2 (ser apto, idóneo) ~se PARA algo to be suitable FOR sth **3** *(refl)* **(a)** (ofrecerse) ~se a hacer algo to offer to do dth **(b)** (en frases negativas): **no me presto a negocios sucios** I won't take part in anything underhand

prestidigitador -dora *m,f* conjurer

prestigio *m* prestige; **de ~** prestigious

prestigioso -sa *adj* famous, prestigious

presumido -da *adj* **(a)** (engreído) conceited, full of oneself; (arrogante) arrogant **(b)** (coqueto) vain

presumir [I1] *vi* to show off; ~ **DE algo** *(de dinero)* (hablando) to boast *o* brag ABOUT sth; (enseñándolo) to flash sth around; **presume de guapo** he thinks he's good-looking
■ **~** *vt*: **se presume una reacción violenta** there is likely to be a violent reaction; **era de ~ lo que ocurriría** it was quite predictable what would happen

presunto -ta *adj* (delante del n) (frml) *(asesino/ terrorista)* alleged *(before n)*

presuntuoso -sa *adj* conceited, vain

presuponer [E22] *vt* to presuppose (frml), assume

presupuesto *m* **1** **(a)** (Fin) budget **(b)** (precio estimado) estimate; **hacer un ~** to give an estimate **2** (supuesto) assumption, supposition

pretencioso -sa *adj* *(casa/película)* pretentious

pretender [E1] *vt*: **¿qué pretendes con esa actitud?** what do you hope to gain with that attitude?; **pretendía entrar sin pagar** he was trying to get in without paying; **no pretendo saberlo todo** I don't claim to know everything; **lo único que pretendía era ayudar** I was only trying to help; **¿pretendes que te crea?** do you expect me to believe you?

pretendido -da *adj* (delante del n) *(interés/ amabilidad)* feigned; **el ~ duque** the so-called duke; **con ~ interés** with false interest

pretendiente *mf* **1** (al trono) pretender; (a un puesto) applicant **2 pretendiente** *m* (de una mujer) suitor

pretensión *f* **1** (a trono, herencia) claim **2 pretensiones** *fpl* (infulas): **tener pretensiones** to be pretentious; **una película sin pretensiones** an unpretentious film

pretensioso -sa *adj* (AmL) vain

pretérito *m* preterit*; **~ indefinido** simple past, preterit*; **~ perfecto/pluscuamperfecto** present/past perfect

pretexto *m* pretext; **volvió con el ~ de recoger el paraguas** he went back on the pretext of getting his umbrella; **siempre sale con algún ~** she always comes out with some excuse; **bajo ningún ~** under no circumstances

prevalecer [E3] *vi* to prevail

prevención *f* **(a)** (de un mal, problema) prevention **(b)** (medida) precaution; **tomar prevenciones** to take precautionary measures

prevenido -da *adj* **(a)** [SER] (precavido)

well-prepared, well-organized; **es muy prevenida** she likes to be prepared *o* ready for all eventualities **(b)** [ESTAR] (advertido) forewarned; **ahora ya estás ~** you've been warned

prevenir [I31] *vt* **(a)** *(enfermedad/accidente)* to prevent **(b)** (advertir, alertar) to warn
■ **prevenirse** *v pron* ~SE CONTRA algo to take preventive *o* preventative measures AGAINST sth, take precautions AGAINST sth

preventiva *f* (Méx) yellow (AmE) *o* (BrE) amber light

preventivo -va *adj* preventive, preventative

prever [E29] *vt* **(a)** (anticipar) *(acontecimiento/ consecuencias)* to foresee, anticipate; *(tiempo)* to forecast; **se prevé un aumento de precios** a rise in prices has been predicted **(b)** (proyectar, planear): **medidas previstas por el gobierno** measures planned by the government; **tiene prevista su llegada a las 11 horas** it is due *o* scheduled to arrive at 11 o'clock; **todo salió tal como estaba previsto** everything turned out just as planned **(c)** *(ley)* to envisage
■ **~** *vi*: **como era de ~** as was to be expected

previo -via *adj* **(a)** (anterior) *(experiencia/ conocimientos)* previous; **sin ~ aviso** without (prior) warning **(b)** *(reunión/asunto)* preliminary

previsible *adj* foreseeable

previsión *f* **(a)** (precaución) precaution; **en ~ de ...** as a precaution against ...; **por falta de ~** owing to a lack of foresight **(b)** (predicción) forecast

previsor -sora *adj* (con visión de futuro) farsighted; (precavido) well-prepared

prieta *f* (Chi) blood sausage, black pudding (BrE)

prieto -ta *adj* (Méx fam) (oscuro) dark; (de piel oscura) dark-skinned

prima *f* **(a)** (de seguro) premium **(b)** (pago extra) bonus; **~ de** *or* **por peligrosidad** danger money

primar [A1] *vi*: **debería ~ el interés público** the public interest should be (a) top priority; **~ SOBRE algo** to take precedence *o* priority OVER sth

primaria *f* **1** (Educ) elementary *o* (BrE) primary education **2** (Pol) (en EEUU) primary

primario -ria *adj* **(a)** (básico) *(necesidades/ objetivo)* primary, basic **(b)** (primitivo) *(instintos)* primitive

primavera *f* **1** (estación) spring; **en ~** in spring, in springtime **2** (Bot) primrose

primaveral *adj* *(tiempo/moda)* spring *(before n)*; *(ambiente)* spring-like

primer ▶ PRIMERO

primera *f* **(a)** (Auto) first (gear) **(b)** (Transp) (clase) first class; **viajar en ~** to travel first class; *ver tb* PRIMERO

primerizo -za *m,f* **(a)** novice, beginner **(b) primeriza** *f* first-time mother

primero -ra *adj/pron* [PRIMER is used before masculine singular nouns] **1** (en el espacio, el tiempo) first; **el primer piso** the second (AmE) *o* (BrE) first floor; **en primer lugar ...** first (of all), ..., firstly, ...; **1º de julio** (read as: *primero de julio*)

AmC	América Central	Arg	Argentina	Cu	Cuba	Per	Perú
AmL	América Latina	Bol	Bolivia	Ec	Ecuador	RPI	Río de la Plata
AmS	América del Sur	Chi	Chile	Esp	España	Ur	Uruguay
Andes	Región andina	CS	Cono Sur	Méx	México	Ven	Venezuela

1st July, July 1st (*léase: July the first*); **Olaf I**
(*read as: Olaf primero*) Olaf I (*léase: Olaf the
First*); **a primeras horas de la madrugada** in the
early hours of the morning; **primera plana** front
page; **∼s auxilios** *mpl* first aid; **primer plano** (Fot)
close-up (shot)
2 (en calidad, jerarquía): **un artículo de primera
calidad** a top-quality product; **de primera
(categoría)** first-class, first-rate; **es el ∼ de la
clase** he is top of the class; **primer ministro** Prime
Minister
3 (básico, fundamental): **nuestro primer objetivo** our
primary objective; **artículos de primera necesidad**
basic necessities; **lo ∼ es** ... the most important
thing is ...
■ *adv* **1** (en el tiempo) first
2 (en importancia): **estar ∼** to come first
primicia *f* (Period): **conseguimos la ∼ del
reportaje** we were the first to carry the report;
una ∼ informativa a scoop
primitivo -va *adj* primitive
primo -ma *adj* ⟨*número*⟩ prime; ⟨*materia*⟩ raw;
■ *m,f* **(a)** (pariente) cousin; **∼ hermano** first cousin
(b) (Esp fam) (bobo) sucker (AmE colloq), mug (BrE
colloq); *hacer el ∼* (Esp fam) to be taken for a ride
primogénito -ta *m,f* first *o* firstborn child
primordial *adj* ⟨*objetivo*⟩ fundamental, prime
(*before n*); ⟨*interés/importancia*⟩ paramount
prímula *f* primula; (amarilla) primrose
princesa *f* princess
principal *adj* main; ⟨*papel*⟩ leading (*before n*);
lo ∼ es que... the main thing is that...
príncipe *m* prince; **∼ heredero** crown prince
principiante *mf* beginner; **un error de ∼** a
basic mistake
principio *m* **1** (comienzo): **a ∼s de
temporada** at the beginning of the season;
empieza por el ∼ start at the beginning; **eso es
un buen ∼** that's a good start; **en** *o* **al ∼** at
first, in the beginning **2 (a)** (postulado, norma
moral) principle; **es una mujer de ∼s** she's a
woman of principle; **por ∼** on principle
pringar [A3] *vt* (fam) (ensuciar) to get ... dirty
(with grease, oil etc)
■ **pringarse** *v pron* (fam) (ensuciarse) **∼se DE algo**
⟨*de grasa/mermelada*⟩ to get covered IN sth
pringoso -sa *adj* greasy
prioridad *f* priority
prisa *f* **1** (rapidez, urgencia) rush, hurry; **¿a qué
viene tanta ∼?** what's the rush *o* hurry?; **con las
∼s olvidé decírselo** in the rush I forgot to tell
her; **tenía ∼ por llegar a casa** he was in a rush to
get home; **no me metas ∼** don't rush *o* hurry me;
tengo ∼ (Esp, Méx) I'm in a rush *o* a hurry; **darse
∼** to hurry (up) **2** (*en locs*) **a** *o* **de prisa ▶**
DEPRISA; **a toda prisa** as fast as possible; **correr
prisa: estos no (me) corren ∼** there's no rush for
these
prisco *m* (CS) *type of peach*
prisión *f* **1** (edificio) prison, jail, penitentiary
(AmE) **2** (pena) prison sentence; **seis años de ∼**
six years' imprisonment
prisionero -ra *m,f* prisoner; **lo hicieron ∼** he
was taken prisoner *o* captured
prisma *m* (Fís, Ópt) prism; (perspectiva)
perspective

prismáticos *mpl* binoculars (*pl*), field-glasses
(*pl*); **unos ∼** a pair of binoculars
privacidad *f* privacy
privación *f* **(a)** (acción) deprivation; **la ∼ de
libertad** deprivation of liberty **(b)** (falta, carencia)
privation, deprivation; **pasar privaciones** to
suffer privations *o* deprivations
privada *f* (Méx) private road (*with security
control*)
privado -da *adj* **(a)** ⟨*reunión/vida*⟩ private; **en
∼** in private **(b)** (Col, Méx) (desmayado)
unconscious **(c)** (Méx) ⟨*teléfono/número*⟩ unlisted
(AmE), ex-directory (BrE)
privar [A1] *vt* **1 ∼ a algn DE algo** ⟨*de derecho/
libertad*⟩ to deprive sb *o* sth **2** (Col, Méx) (dejar
inconsciente) to knock ... unconscious
■ **privarse** *v pron* **1 ∼se DE algo** ⟨*de lujos/
placeres*⟩ to deprive oneself OF sth **2** (Col, Méx)
(desmayarse) to lose consciousness, pass out
privatización *f* privatization
privatizar [A4] *vt* to privatize
privilegiado -da *adj* **(a)** ⟨*persona/clase*⟩
privileged **(b)** (excelente) ⟨*posición*⟩ privileged;
⟨*clima/inteligencia/memoria*⟩ exceptional
■ *m,f*: **unos pocos ∼s** a privileged few
privilegio *m* privilege
pro *m* (ventaja) advantage; **sopesar los ∼s y los
contras de algo** to weigh up the pros and cons of
sth
■ *prep*: **los sectores ∼ amnistía** the sectors in
favor of an amnesty
proa *f* bow, prow
probabilidad *f* (Mat) probability; **con toda ∼**
in all probability *o* likelihood; **¿qué ∼es tiene de
ganar?** what are her chances of winning?
probable *adj* (posible) probable; **es ∼** probably;
es ∼ que llegue hoy he will probably arrive
today
probado -da *adj* (delante del *n*) proven
probador *m* fitting room, changing room (BrE)
probar [A10] *vt* **1** (demostrar) ⟨*teoría/inocencia*⟩
to prove **2 (a)** ⟨*vino/sopa*⟩ to taste; (por primera
vez) to try **(b)** ⟨*método*⟩ to try; ⟨*coche/mecanismo*⟩
to try out **(c)** ⟨*ropa*⟩ to try on; **∼le algo A algn** to
try sth ON sb **(d)** (poner a prueba) ⟨*empleado/
honradez*⟩ to test; ⟨*arma/vehículo*⟩ to test (out)
■ **∼** *vi* (intentar) to try; **∼ A hacer algo** to try doing
sth
■ **probarse** *v pron* ⟨*ropa/zapatos*⟩ to try on
probeta *f* test tube
■ *adj inv* ⟨*gemelos/hijos*⟩ test-tube (*before n*)
problema *m* problem; **resolver/solucionar un
∼** to solve a problem; **los coches viejos dan
muchos ∼s** old cars give a lot of trouble; **no te
hagas ∼** (AmL) don't worry about it
problemático -ca *adj* problematic, difficult
procaz *adj* ⟨*comentario/chiste*⟩ indecent, lewd;
⟨*lenguaje*⟩ obscene
procedencia *f* **(a)** (origen) origin **(b)** (de barco)
port of origin
procedente *adj*: **el vuelo/tren ∼ de París** the
flight/train from Paris
proceder [E1] *vi* **1** (provenir) **∼ DE algo** to
come FROM sth **2** (actuar) to act, to proceed (frml);
procedió con mucha corrección he behaved very
correctly; **∼ contra algn** (Der) to iniciate ┅╌➔

proceedings against sb **3** (frml) (iniciar) ∼ A algo to proceed TO sth **4** (ser conveniente): **procede actuar rápidamente** it would be wise to act swiftly; **rellenar lo que proceda** complete as appropriate

procedimiento m **1** (método) procedure; (Tec) process **2** (Der) proceedings (pl)

prócer m national hero (esp of a struggle for independence)

procesado -da m,f (Der) accused, defendant

procesador m processor; ∼ **de textos** word processor

procesamiento m **1** (Der) prosecution, trial **2** (Tec, Inf) processing; ∼ **de textos** word processing

procesar [A1] vt **1** (Der) to try, prosecute **2** (materia prima/datos/solicitud) to process

procesión f procession

proceso m **1** (serie de acciones, sucesos) process **2** (Der) trial **3** (Inf) processing; ∼ **de datos/ textos** data/word processing **4** (transcurso) course

proclamación f proclamation, declaration

proclamar [A1] vt to proclaim
■ **proclamarse** v pron to proclaim oneself

procrear [A1] vi to procreate, breed

procurador -dora m,f (Der) (abogado) attorney, lawyer; (asistente) ≈ paralegal (in US), ≈ clerk (in UK)

procurar [A1] vt (intentar) ∼ **hacer algo** to try to do sth; **procura que no te vea** try not to let him see you

prodigio m (a) (maravilla) wonder (b) (milagro) miracle

prodigioso -sa adj prodigious, phenomenal; (éxito/jugador/músico) phenomenal

producción f **1** (Com, Econ) (proceso, acción) production; (cantidad) output, production; ∼ **en cadena** or **serie** mass production **2** (Cin, Teatr, TV) production

producir [I6] vt **1** (a) (en general) to produce (b) (sonido) to cause, generate **2** (causar) (conmoción/reacción/explosión) to cause; **le produjo una gran alegría** it made her very happy
■ **producirse** v pron **1** (frml) (tener lugar) «accidente/explosión» to occur (frml), to take place; «cambio» to occur (frml), to happen; **se produjeron 85 muertes** there were 85 deaths, 85 people died o were killed **2** (refl) (frml) (heridas) to inflict ... on oneself (frml)

productividad f (cualidad) productivity; (rendimiento) productivity, output

productivo -va adj productive; (empresa/ negocio) lucrative

producto m (a) (artículo producido) product; ∼s **agrícolas/de granja** agricultural/farm produce; ∼ **alimenticio** foodstuff; ∼ **lácteo** dairy product (b) (resultado) result, product

productor -tora adj producing (before n)
■ m,f (a) (en general) producer (b) **productora** f (empresa) production company

produje, produzca, etc ▶ PRODUCIR

proeza f (logro) feat, exploit; (Mil) heroic deed o exploit

profanar [A1] vt (templo/sepultura) to desecrate, defile

profano -na adj **1** (a) (no sagrado) (escritor/

música) secular, profane (frml); (fiesta) secular (b) (antirreligioso) profane (frml), irreverent **2** (no especializado): **soy ∼ en la materia** I'm not an expert on the subject
■ m,f **1** (Relig) (m) layman; (f) laywoman **2** (no especialista) non-specialist

profecía f prophecy

proferir [I11] vt (palabras/amenazas) to utter; (insultos) to hurl

profesar [A1] vt (a) (declarar) (religión/doctrina) to profess (b) (sentir) (cariño) to feel; (respeto) to have

profesión f (ocupación) profession; (en formularios) occupation; ∼ **liberal** profession

profesional adj (fotógrafo/deportista) professional (before n)
■ mf professional

profesionalidad f professionalism

profesionista mf (Méx) professional

profesor -sora m,f (de escuela secundaria) teacher, schoolteacher; (de universidad) professor (AmE), lecturer (BrE); **tiene un ∼ particular** he has a private tutor

profesorado m (cuerpo) faculty (AmE), teaching staff (BrE); (actividad) teaching profession

profeta m prophet

profetizar [A4] vt to prophesy

prófugo -ga m,f (Der) fugitive; (Mil) deserter

profundidad f (a) (de pozo, río, mar) depth; **tiene 20 metros de ∼** it's 20 meters deep (b) (de conocimientos, ideas) depth; **en ∼** (analizar) in depth; (reformar) radically

profundizar [A4] vi ∼ **EN algo** (en tema) to go into sth in depth

profundo -da adj (a) (herida/pozo/raíz) deep; **un río poco ∼** a shallow river (b) (pensamiento) profound, deep; (respeto/desprecio) profound; (lazos) strong; (desengaño) grave, terrible (c) (misterio) profound; (silencio) deep, profound (d) (voz/suspiro) deep (e) (sueño) deep, sound

progenitor -tora m,f (a) (antepasado) ancestor (b) (frml) (m) (padre) father; (f) (madre) mother

programa m **1** (a) (Rad, TV) program*; ∼ **concurso** quiz show; ∼ **de entrevistas** chat show (b) (folleto) program* **2** (programación, plan) program* **3** (a) (político) program*; **su ∼ electoral** their election manifesto (b) (Educ) (de asignatura) syllabus; (de curso) curriculum, syllabus **4** (Inf, Elec) program*

programación f **1** (a) (Rad, TV) programs* (pl) (b) (de festejos, visitas — lista) program*; (— organización) organization, planning **2** (Inf) programming

programador -dora m,f programmer

programar [A1] vt **1** (a) (Rad, TV) to schedule (b) (actividades/eventos) to plan, draw up a program* for; (horario/fecha) to schedule, program*; (viaje) to organize (c) (Transp) (llegadas/salidas) to schedule, timetable (BrE) **2** (Inf) to program

progresar [A1] vi «persona» to make progress, to progress; «negociaciones/proyecto» to progress

progresión f (Mat, Mús) progression

progresista adj/mf progressive

progresivo -va adj progressive

progreso m (a) (adelanto): supuso un gran ~ it was a great step forward; **hacer ~s** to make progress (b) (evolución, desarrollo) progress

prohibición f (acción) prohibition, banning; (orden) ban

prohibir [I22] vt (a) ⟨acto/venta⟩ to ban, prohibit (frml); **iba en dirección prohibida** I was going the wrong way up a one-way street; ➒ **prohibido el paso** o **prohibida la entrada** no entry; ➒ **prohibido fumar** no smoking; ➒ **se prohíbe la entrada a menores de 16 años** over 16s only, no admission to persons under 16 years of age (b) **~le algo a algn** to ban sb FROM sth; **~le a algn hacer algo** to forbid sb to do sth, prohibit sb FROM doing sth (frml); **~ a algn QUE haga algo** to forbid sb to do sth

prohibitivo -va adj prohibitive

prójimo m (semejante) fellow man; **amar al ~** to love one's neighbor

prole f kids (pl) (colloq), offspring (hum)

proletario -ria adj/m,f proletarian

proliferar [A1] vi to proliferate, spread

prolífico -ca adj prolific

prolijo -ja adj ① (extenso) protracted, long-winded; (minucioso) detailed ② (RPl) (ordenado, aseado) ⟨persona/casa⟩ tidy; ⟨cuaderno⟩ neat

prólogo m (de libro) preface, foreword; (de acto) prelude

prolongación f extension

prolongado -da adj prolonged, lengthy

prolongar [A3] vt (a) ⟨contrato/plazo⟩ to extend; ⟨vacaciones/visita⟩ to prolong, extend; **~le la vida a algn** to prolong sb's life (b) ⟨línea/calle⟩ to extend
■ **prolongarse** v pron (a) (en el tiempo) «debate/fiesta» to go on, carry on (b) (en el espacio) «carretera/línea» to extend

promedio m (a) (Mat) average; **el ~ de mis ingresos** my average earnings; **como ~** on average (b) (nota media) average grade o (BrE) mark (c) (punto medio) mid-point

promesa f (a) (palabra) promise; **cumplí (con) mi ~** I kept my promise o word; **romper una ~** to break a promise (b) (persona) hope

prometedor -dora adj promising

prometer [E1] vt (a) (dar su palabra) to promise; **te lo prometo** I promise (b) (augurar) to promise
■ **~** vi «persona/negocio» to show o have promise
■ **prometerse** v pron (a) (en matrimonio) to get engaged (b) (refl) ⟨viaje/descanso⟩ to promise oneself

prometido -da adj (a) (para casarse) engaged (b) ⟨aumento/regalo⟩ promised; **cumplir con lo ~** to keep one's promise o word
■ m, f (m) fiancé; (f) fiancée

prominente adj prominent

promiscuidad f promiscuity

promiscuo -cua adj promiscuous

promoción f ① (a) (de actividad, producto) promotion; **hacer la ~ de un producto** to promote a product (b) (ascenso) promotion ② (Educ): **somos de la misma ~** we graduated at the same time

promocionar [A1] vt to promote

promontorio m (en tierra) hill, rise; (en el mar) promontory, headland

promotor -tora m,f (persona) (a) (Const) developer (b) (Espec) promoter (c) (de rebelión, huelga) instigator

promover [E9] vt ⟨ahorro/turismo⟩ to promote; ⟨conflicto/enfrentamientos⟩ to provoke; ⟨querella/pleito⟩ to bring

promulgar [A3] vt to enact, to promulgate (frml)

pronombre m pronoun

pronosticar [A2] vt ⟨tiempo/resultado⟩ to forecast; ⟨victoria/muerte⟩ to predict

pronóstico m (a) (predicción) forecast, prediction; **el ~ del tiempo** the weather forecast (b) (Med) prognosis (c) (en carreras de caballos) tip

prontitud f promptness

pronto¹ -ta adj (a) (rápido) ⟨entrega/respuesta⟩ prompt (b) (RPl) (preparado) ready

pronto² adv ① (a) (en poco tiempo) soon; **¡hasta ~!** see you soon!; **lo más ~ posible** as soon as possible (b) (Esp) (temprano) early ② (en locs) **de pronto** (repentinamente) suddenly; **por lo pronto** o **por de pronto** for the moment, for now; **tan pronto como** as soon as

pronunciación f pronunciation

pronunciado -da adj (a) ⟨curva⟩ sharp, pronounced; ⟨pendiente⟩ steep, pronounced (b) ⟨facciones/rasgos⟩ pronounced, marked (c) ⟨tendencia⟩ marked, noticeable

pronunciamiento m rebellion, military uprising

pronunciar [A1] vt ① (a) (Ling) to pronounce (b) ⟨discurso⟩ to deliver, give ② (resaltar) to accentuate
■ **pronunciarse** v pron ① (dar una opinión) **~se A FAVOR/EN CONTRA DE algo** to declare oneself to be IN FAVOR OF/AGAINST sth ② (acentuarse) to become more marked, become more pronounced

propaganda f (a) (Pol) propaganda (b) (Com, Marketing) advertising; **hacer ~ de un producto** to advertise a product (c) (material publicitario) advertisements (pl); **no trae más que ~** it has nothing but advertisements in it; **repartir ~** to hand out advertising leaflets

propagar [A3] vt (a) ⟨doctrina/rumores/enfermedad⟩ to spread, propagate (b) ⟨especie⟩ to propagate
■ **propagarse** v pron to spread; «especie/sonido/luz» to propagate

propasarse [A1] v pron (a) (excederse) to go too far, overstep the mark (b) (en sentido sexual) **~ CON algn** to make a pass AT sb

propenso -sa adj **~ A algo** prone TO sth

propiamente adv exactly; **no vive en Londres ~ dicho** he doesn't live in London proper

propiciar [A1] vt (favorecer) to favor*; (causar) to bring about

propicio -cia adj ⟨momento⟩ opportune, propitious (frml); ⟨condiciones⟩ favorable*, propitious (frml)

propiedad f ① (a) (pertenencia) property; **son ~ del museo** they are the property of the museum; **la casa es ~ de mi hijo** the house belongs to my son (b) (lo poseído) property; **~ intelectual** copyright; **~ privada/pública** private/public property ② (cualidad) property; (corrección): **con ~** ⟨hablar⟩ correctly; ⟨comportarse⟩ with decorum

p

propietario -ria *m,f* **(a)** (de comercio) owner, proprietor **(b)** (de casa) owner **(c)** (de tierras) landowner

propina *f* **(a)** (a camarero, empleado) tip, gratuity (fml); **dejó 25 pesos de ~** she left a 25 peso tip; **darle ~ a algn** to tip sb **(b)** (Per) (de niño) pocket money

propio -pia *adj* ⓵ **(a)** (indicando posesión) own; **¿es ~ o alquilado?** is it your own or is it rented?; **tienen piscina propia** they have their own swimming pool **(b)** (de uno mismo) own; **por tu ~ bien** for your own good; **todo lo hace en beneficio ~** everything he does is for his own gain; **lo vi con mis ~s ojos** I saw it with my own two eyes *o* with my (very) own eyes ⓶ (característico, típico): **esa actitud es muy propia de él** that kind of attitude is very typical of him; **una enfermedad propia de la vejez** an illness common among old people; **no es un comportamiento ~ de una señorita** it's not ladylike behaviour ⓷ *(delante del n)* (mismo): **fue el ~ presidente** it was the president himself; **debe ser el ~ interesado quien lo pida** it must be the person concerned who makes the request

proponer [E22] *vt* **(a)** ⟨*idea*⟩ to propose, suggest; ⟨*brindis*⟩ to propose; **nos propuso ir al campo** he suggested we go to the countryside; **te voy a ~ un trato** I'm going to make you a proposition **(b)** ⟨*persona*⟩ (para cargo) to put forward, nominate; (para premio) to nominate **(c)** ⟨*moción*⟩ to propose **(d)** ⟨*teoría*⟩ to propound
■ **proponerse** *v pron*: **~se hacer algo** to set out to do sth; **me lo propuse como meta** I set myself that goal; **me propuse decírselo** I made up my mind *o* I decided to tell her

proporción *f* ⓵ (relación) proportion; **en ~ a los ingresos** in proportion to income ⓶ **proporciones** *fpl* (dimensiones) proportions (*pl*)

proporcionado -da *adj*: **~ a la figura humana** in proportion to the human body; **mal ~** ⟨*dibujo*⟩ poorly proportioned; **es bajo pero bien ~** he's short but he's well-proportioned

proporcional *adj* proportional, proportionate

proporcionar [A1] *vt* ⟨*materiales/ información/comida*⟩ to provide; **~ algo A algn** to provide sb WITH sth

proposición *f* proposal, proposition; **~ de matrimonio** proposal of marriage

propósito *m* **(a)** (intención) intention, purpose; **con el ~ de verla** with the intention *o* purpose of seeing her; **tiene el firme ~ de dejar de fumar** she's determined to give up smoking; **buenos ~s** good intentions **(b)** a propósito (adrede) deliberately, on purpose; (por cierto) by the way

propuesta *f* **(a)** (sugerencia) proposal **(b)** (oferta) offer

propulsar [A1] *vt* ⟨*desarrollo/actividad*⟩ to promote, stimulate; ⟨*avión/cohete*⟩ to propel; ⟨*vehículo*⟩ to drive, propel

propulsión *f* propulsion; **~ a chorro** jet propulsion

propulsor -sora *adj* ⟨*mecanismo*⟩ driving (*before n*), propulsion (*before n*); ⟨*cohete*⟩ propulsion (*before n*)
■ *m,f* (de actividad, idea) promoter
(b) propulsor *m* (Tec) propellant

propuse, propuso, etc ▶ PROPONER

prórroga *f* **(a)** (extensión) extension; (Dep) overtime (AmE), extra time (BrE) **(b)** (aplazamiento) deferral, deferment

prorrogar [A3] *vt* **(a)** (alargar) to extend **(b)** (aplazar) ⟨*fecha*⟩ to postpone, put back

prosa *f* prose

prosaico -ca *adj* ⟨*existencia/vida*⟩ mundane, prosaic

proseguir [I30] *vi/vt* (fml) to continue

prospecto *m* **(a)** (de fármaco) directions for use (*pl*), patient information leaflet **(b)** (de propaganda) pamphlet, leaflet

prosperar [A1] *vi* **(a)** ⟨⟨*negocio/país*⟩⟩ to prosper, thrive; ⟨⟨*persona*⟩⟩ to do well, make good **(b)** ⟨⟨*iniciativa/proyecto*⟩⟩ (aceptarse) to be accepted, prosper

prosperidad *f* prosperity

próspero -ra *adj* prosperous

próstata *f* prostate (gland)

prostíbulo *m* brothel

prostitución *f* prostitution

prostituir [I20] *vt* to prostitute
■ **prostituirse** *v pron* to prostitute oneself

prostituto -ta *m,f* (*m*) male prostitute; (*f*) prostitute

protagonista *mf* **(a)** (personaje principal) main character **(b)** (actor) **el ~ de la nueva serie** the actor who is playing the leading role in the new series; **los principales ~s de nuestra historia** the major figures of our history

protagonizar [A4] *vt* **(a)** (Cin, Teatr) to star in, play the lead *o* leading role in **(b)** ⟨*tiroteo*⟩ to be involved in; ⟨*debate*⟩ to take part in; ⟨*disturbios*⟩ to be responsible for

protección *f* protection

proteccionismo *m* protectionism

proteccionista *adj/mf* protectionist

protector -tora *adj* protective; **sociedad ~a de animales** society for the prevention of cruelty to animals
■ *m,f* (defensor) protector; (benefactor) patron

protectorado *m* protectorate

proteger [E6] *vt* **(a)** (en general) to protect; **~ algo/a algn DE** *or* **CONTRA algo/algn** to protect sth/sb FROM *o* AGAINST sth/sb **(b)** ⟨*artes*⟩ to champion, patronize; ⟨*pintor/poeta*⟩ to act as patron to
■ **protegerse** *v pron* (refl) **~se DE** *or* **CONTRA algo** to protect oneself FROM *o* AGAINST sth; **~se de la lluvia** to shelter from the rain

protegido -da *adj* **(a)** ⟨*especie*⟩ protected **(b)** ⟨*vivienda*⟩ subsidized **(c)** (Inf) write-protected

AmC	Central America	Arg	Argentina	Cu	Cuba	Per	Peru
AmL	Latin America	Bol	Bolivia	Ec	Ecuador	RPI	River Plate Area
AmS	South America	Chi	Chile	Esp	Spain	Ur	Uruguay
Andes	Andean Region	CS	Southern Cone	Méx	Mexico	Ven	Venezuela

■ *m,f* (*m*) protegé; (*f*) protegée

proteína *f* protein

prótesis *f* prosthesis

protesta *f* **1** (a) (queja) protest; **en señal de** ~ in protest (b) (manifestación) demonstration, protest march (*o* rally *etc*) **2** (Méx) (a) (promesa) promise; **cumplieron con su** ~ they kept their promise *o* word (b) ▶ JURAMENTO

protestante *adj/mf* Protestant

protestantismo *m* Protestantism

protestar [A1] *vi* (mostrar desacuerdo) to protest; ~ CONTRA algo to protest AGAINST *o* ABOUT sth (b) (quejarse) to complain; ~ POR *or* DE algo to complain ABOUT sth

protocolo *m* (a) (ceremonial, etiqueta) protocol; (b) (Inf) protocol

prototipo *m* (a) (de especie) archetype, prototype (b) (Tec) prototype

protuberancia *f* bulge, protuberance (frml)

provecho *m* (a) (beneficio, utilidad) benefit; **no sacó mucho** ~ **de la experiencia** she didn't benefit much from the experience; **le sacó mucho** ~ **a su estancia** she got a lot out of her stay; **solo piensa en su propio** ~ he's only out for himself (colloq); **de** ~ ⟨*estudiante*⟩ hardworking; ⟨*experiencia/visita*⟩ worthwhile (b) (en la mesa): **¡buen** ~**!** (dicho por uno mismo) bon appetit!; (dicho por camarero) enjoy your meal!

provechoso -sa *adj* profitable, fruitful

proveedor -dora *m,f* supplier, purveyor (frml); ~ **de servicios Internet** Internet service provider

proveer [E14] *vt* (suministrar) to provide; ~ **a algn DE algo** to provide sb WITH sth; **iban provistos de botes salvavidas** they were equipped with *o* they carried lifeboats

■ **proveerse** *v pron* (*refl*): ~**se DE algo** ⟨*de herramientas/armas*⟩ to equip oneself WITH sth; ⟨*de comida*⟩ to get sth

provenir [I31] *vi* ~ **DE algo/algn** to come FROM sth/sb

proverbio *m* proverb

providencia *f* (Relig): **la (divina) P**~ (divine) Providence

providencial *adj* (a) (oportuno) fortunate, lucky, providential (frml); **fue** ~ **que** … it was fortunate that … (b) (Relig) providential

provincia *f* **1** (Gob, Relig) province **2 provincias** *fpl* (por oposición a la capital) provinces (*pl*); **la vida de** ~**s** provincial life

provinciano -na *adj* (a) (de provincias) provincial (b) (pey) (estrecho de miras) provincial, parochial

■ *m,f* (a) (de provincias): **los** ~**s** people from the provinces (b) (pey) (de mentalidad estrecha) provincial (c) (paleto) country bumpkin, hick (AmE colloq)

provisional *adj* provisional

provisiones *fpl* (víveres) provisions (*pl*)

provisto -ta *pp* ▶ PROVEER

provocación *f* provocation

provocador -dora *adj* provocative

■ *m,f* agitator

provocar [A2] *vt* **1** (a) ⟨*explosión*⟩ to cause; ⟨*incendio*⟩ to start; ⟨*polémica*⟩ to spark off,

prompt; ⟨*reacción*⟩ to cause (b) (Med) ⟨*parto*⟩ to induce **2** ⟨*persona*⟩ (al enfado) to provoke; (sexualmente) to lead … on

■ ~ *vi* (Andes) (apetecer): **¿le provoca un traguito?** do you want a drink?, do you fancy a drink? (BrE colloq)

provocativo -va *adj* **1** (insinuante) provocative **2** (Col, Ven) (apetecible) tempting, mouthwatering

proxeneta *mf* (*m*) procurer (frml), pimp (colloq); (*f*) procuress (frml), pimp (colloq)

proximidad *f* (a) (en el tiempo, espacio) closeness, proximity (frml) (b) **proximidades** *fpl* (cercanías) vicinity

próximo -ma *adj* **1** (a) (siguiente) next; **el** ~ **jueves** next Thursday (b) (*como pron*): **esto lo dejamos para la próxima** we'll leave this for next time; **tome la próxima a la derecha** take the next (on the) right **2** [ESTAR] (cercano) (a) (en el tiempo) close; **la fecha ya está próxima** the day is close; **en fecha próxima** in the near future (b) (en el espacio) near, close; ~ **A algo** close *o* near to sth

proyección *f* (a) (Cin) showing (b) (de sombra) casting; (de luz) throwing

proyectar [A1] *vt* **1** (planear) to plan; ~ **hacer algo** to plan to do sth **2** (a) ⟨*película*⟩ to show, screen; ⟨*diapositivas*⟩ to project, show (b) ⟨*sombra*⟩ to cast; ⟨*luz*⟩ to throw, project

proyectil *m* projectile, missile

proyecto *m* (a) (plan) plan; **¿qué** ~**s tienes para el próximo año?** what are your plans for next year?; **tiene un viaje en** ~ she's planning a trip; ~ **de ley** bill (b) (trabajo) project (c) (Arquit, Ing) plans and costing

proyector *m* **1** (Cin, Fot) projector **2** (Teatr) spotlight; (para monumentos) floodlight; (Mil) searchlight

prudencia *f* (cuidado) caution; (sabiduría) wisdom, prudence; **conduce con** ~ drive carefully

prudente *adj* (sensato. responsable) prudent, sensible; (cauto, precavido) cautious, prudent

prueba *f* **1** (a) (demostración, testimonio) proof; **no hay** ~**s de que eso sea verdad** there's no proof that that's true; **eso es** ~ **de que le caes bien** that proves he likes you; **en** *or* **como** ~ **de mi agradecimiento** as a token of my gratitude (b) (Der) piece of evidence **2** (Educ) test; (Cin) screen test, audition; (Teatr) audition **3** (a) (ensayo, experimento) test; **vamos a hacer la** ~ let's try; ~ **de la alcoholemia** Breathalyzer® test, sobriety test (AmE), drunkometer test (AmE); ~ **del embarazo** pregnancy test (b) (*en locs*) **a prueba: tomar a algn a** ~ to take sb on for a trial period; **tener algo a** ~ to have sth on trial; **poner algo a** ~ to put sth to the test; **a** ~ **de golpes/de balas** shockproof/bulletproof (c) (en costura) fitting **4** (Fot, Impr) proof; **corregir** ~**s** to proofread **5** (Dep): **en las** ~**s de clasificación** in the qualifying heats; **la** ~ **de los 1.500 metros** the 1,500 meters (event *o* race)

prueba, pruebas, etc ▶ PROBAR

PSI *m* (= **provedor de sevicios Internet**) ISP

psicoanálisis *m* psychoanalysis

psicoanalista *mf* psychoanalyst

psicodélico -ca *adj* psychedelic

psicología *f* psychology

psicológico -ca *adj* psychological

psicólogo -ga *m,f* psychologist

psicópata *mf* psychopath

psicosis *f* (*pl* ∼) psychosis

psicosomático -ca *adj* psychosomatic

psicoterapia *f* psychotherapy

psiquiatra *mf* psychiatrist

psiquiatría *f* psychiatry

psiquiátrico¹ -ca *adj* psychiatric (*before n*)

psiquiátrico² *m* psychiatric hospital, mental hospital

psíquico -ca *adj* psychic

ptas, pts = **pesetas**

púa *f* **1** (a) (de erizo) spine, quill; (de alambre) barb; (de peine) tooth (b) (Chi, Ven) (en zapatos de atletismo) spike **2** (para guitarra) plectrum, pick; (de tocadiscos) (RPl) needle

pub /puβ, pʌβ/ *m* (*pl* **pubs** or **pubes**) bar (*gen with music, open late at night*)

pubertad *f* puberty

pubis *m* (*pl* ∼) pubis

publicación *f* publication

publicar [A2] *vt* (a) ⟨artículo/noticia⟩ to publish (b) (divulgar) to divulge, disclose

publicidad *f* (a) (de tema, suceso) publicity (b) (Com, Marketing) advertising; **hacer ∼ de algo** to advertise sth

publicista *mf* (a) (AmL) (Com) advertising executive *o* agent, publicist (b) (Period) publicist

publicitario -ria *adj* ⟨campaña/espacio⟩ advertising (*before n*); ⟨truco/montaje⟩ publicity (*before n*)

público¹ -ca *adj* public; **hacer ∼ algo** to announce sth; **es un peligro ∼** he's a danger to the public

público² *m* (en teatro) audience, public; (Dep) spectators (*pl*); **☉ horario de atención al público** (en oficinas públicas) opening hours; (en bancos) hours of business; **película apta para todo(s) (los) ∼(s)** 'G' movie (AmE), 'U' film (BrE); **el ∼ en general** the general public; **en ∼** ⟨hablar⟩ in public; ⟨cantar/bailar⟩ in front of an audience; **salir al ∼** (Andes) ⟨periódico/revista⟩ to come out, appear; ⟨noticia/información⟩ to be published

pucherazo *m* (fam) electoral rigging; **hubo ∼** the election was fixed *o* rigged

puchero *m* **1** (Coc) (recipiente) pot, stewpot; (cocido) stew **2** (mueca) pout; **hacer ∼s** to pout

pucho *m* (AmS fam) (a) (cigarrillo — de tabaco) smoke (colloq), fag (BrE colloq); (— de marihuana) joint (colloq) (b) (resto — de cigarrillo) butt, fag end (BrE colloq); (— de comida) scrap; (— de bebida) drop

pude ▶ PODER

púdico -ca *adj* ⟨ropa⟩ modest; ⟨comportamiento/beso⟩ chaste

pudiera, pudiese, etc ▶ PODER

pudín *m* ▶ BUDÍN

pudiste, etc ▶ PODER

pudor *m* (a) (recato sexual) modesty; **no se desnudó por ∼** she was too embarrassed *o* shy to take her clothes off; **es una falta de ∼** it shows a lack of (a sense of) decency (b) (reserva) reserve; **nos habló sin ∼** he talked to us very openly

pudoroso -sa *adj* ▶ PÚDICO

pudrir [I38] *vt* (descomponer) ⟨carne/fruta/madera⟩ to rot, decay

■ **pudrirse** *v pron* **1** (descomponerse) «fruta/carne» to rot, decay; «madera/tela» to rot; «cadáver» to decompose, rot **2** (fam) (por el abandono): **∼se en la cárcel** to rot in jail

pueblerino -na *adj* ⟨aire⟩ provincial; **¡qué ∼ eres!** you're such a country bumpkin *o* (AmE colloq) hick!

pueblo *m* **1** (poblado) village; (más grande) small town; **∼ joven** (Per) shantytown **2** (a) (comunidad) people; **un ∼ nómada** a nomadic people (b) (ciudadanos, nación) people; **el ∼ vasco** the Basque people

pueda, puedas, etc ▶ PODER

puente *m* **1** (Ing) bridge; **∼ colgante/giratorio** suspension/swing bridge; **∼ levadizo** (en castillo) drawbridge; (en carretera) lifting bridge; **∼ aéreo** (servicio frecuente) shuttle (service); (Mil) airlift **2** (Mús, Odont) bridge; (de anteojos) bridge **3** (Elec) bridge (circuit) **4** (vacación) ≈ long weekend (*linked to a public holiday by an extra day's holiday in between*) **5** (Náut) **tb ∼ de mando** bridge

puerco -ca *adj* (fam & pey) (sucio) dirty; (despreciable) low-down (colloq)

■ *m,f* **1** (a) (animal) (*m*) pig, hog, boar; (*f*) pig, hog, sow; **∼ espín** porcupine (b) (Méx) (carne) pork **2** (fam) (persona — sucia) pig (colloq); (— despreciable) swine (colloq)

puericultor -tora *m,f*: nurse or doctor who specializes in babycare/childcare

puericultura *f* babycare, childcare

pueril *adj* (a) (infantil) childish, puerile (frml) (b) (ingenuo) naive

puerro *m* leek

puerta *f* (de casa, coche, horno) door; (en jardín, valla) gate; **llamar a la ∼** to ring the doorbell/knock on the door; **te espero en la ∼ del teatro** I'll meet you at the entrance of the theater; **te acompaño a la ∼** I'll see *o* show you out; **servicio ∼ a ∼** door-to-door service; **un coche de dos ∼s** a two-door car; **∼ de embarque** gate; **∼ principal** *or* **de la calle** (de casa) front door; (de edificio público) main door *or* entrance; **∼ trasera** back door

puerto *m* **1** (Náut) port, harbor*; **entrar a ∼** to enter port *o* harbor; **∼ deportivo** marina; **∼ franco** *or* **libre** free port; **∼ pesquero** fishing port **2** (Geog) **tb ∼ de montaña** (mountain) pass

Puerto Príncipe *m* Port-au-Prince

Puerto Rico *m* Puerto Rico

pues *conj* (a) (en general) well (b) (indicando consecuencia) then; **∼ si te gusta tanto, cómpralo** if you like it that much, then buy it

puesta *f* **1** (acción de poner): **hasta la ∼ en servicio de los autobuses** until the buses come into service; **la ∼ en libertad de los prisioneros** the freeing *o* release of the prisoners; **∼ a punto** (de vehículo) tune-up; (de máquina) adjustment; **∼ de sol** sunset; **∼ en escena** production; **∼ en marcha** (de vehículo, motor) starting (up); **∼ al día** updating **2** (de huevos) lay

puestero -ra *m,f* (AmL) **(a)** (vendedor) stallholder, market vendor **(b)** (en una estancia) farmer (*responsible for the running of part of a large ranch*)

puesto¹ -ta *adj*: ¿qué haces con el abrigo ∼? what are you doing with your coat on?; **tenía las botas puestas** she was wearing her boots; **la mesa estaba puesta** the table was laid; *ver tb* PONER

puesto² m ⓵ **(a)** (lugar, sitio) place; **se sentó en mi** ∼ he sat in my place **(b)** (en una clasificación) place, position; **sacó el primer** ∼ **de la clase** she came top *o* (AmE) came out top of the class ⓶ (empleo) position, job; ∼ **de trabajo** (empleo) job; (Inf) workstation ⓷ **(a)** (Com) (en mercado) stall; (quiosco) kiosk; (tienda) stand, stall **(b)** (de la policía, del ejército) post; ∼ **de socorro** first-aid post/ station ⓸ **puesto que** (*conj*) (frml) since

puf *m* (*pl* **pufs**) hassock (AmE), pouffe (BrE) ■ *interj* (expresando — repugnancia) ugh! (colloq), pee-yoo! (AmE); (— cansancio, sofoco) whew!, oof!

púgil *m* (period) boxer, pugilist (frml)

pugna *f* **(a)** (lucha) struggle **(b)** (conflicto): **tendencias/intereses en** ∼ conflicting trends/ interests; **entrar en** ∼ **con algo/algn** to clash *o* come into conflict **with** sth/sb

pugnar [A1] *vi* (liter) (luchar) ∼ **POR + INF** to strive to + INF (frml)

pujante *adj* booming (*before n*)

pujanza *f* vigor*, strength

pujar [A1] *vi* ⓵ (luchar) ∼ **POR algo/hacer algo** to struggle **POR** sth/to do sth ⓶ (Esp) (en subasta) to bid ⓷ (Méx fam) (gemir) to moan, whimper

pulcro -cra *adj* ⟨persona/aspecto⟩ immaculate, neat and tidy; ⟨informe/trabajo⟩ meticulous

pulga *f* (Zool) flea; **tener malas** ∼**s** (fam) to be bad-tempered

pulgada *f* inch

pulgar *m* (de la mano) thumb; (del pie) big toe

pulgón *m* aphid, plant louse

pulido -da *adj* ⟨estilo/trabajo/lenguaje⟩ polished; ⟨modales⟩ refined

pulir [I1] *vt* ⓵ **(a)** ⟨metal/piedra/vidrio⟩ to polish **(b)** ⟨madera⟩ to sand **(c)** (lustrar) to polish ⓶ (refinar) ⟨estilo/trabajo⟩ to polish up; ⟨persona⟩ to make ... more refined; ⟨idioma⟩ to brush up

pulla *f* gibe

pulmón *m* lung; ∼ **de acero** iron lung

pulmonía *f* pneumonia; ∼ **doble** double pneumonia

pulóver *m* (*pl* **-vers**) (suéter) pullover, sweater, jumper (BrE)

pulpa *f* (de fruta, vegetal) pulp; (de madera) (wood) pulp

pulpería *f* (AmL) local store

pulpero -ra *m,f* (AmL) local storekeeper

púlpito *m* pulpit

pulpo *m* (Zool) octopus

pulque *m* pulque (*drink made from fermented cactus sap*)

pulquería *f* (Méx) bar, restaurant (*serving pulque*)

pulquero -ra *m,f* (Méx) *owner of a* PULQUERÍA

pulsación *f* ⓵ (latido) beat ⓶ (en mecanografía)

keystroke; **¿cuántas pulsaciones piden por minuto?** ≈ how many words a minute do they want?

pulsar [A1] *vt* ⓵ **(a)** (Mús) ⟨cuerda⟩ to pluck; ⟨tecla⟩ to press **(b)** ⟨botón⟩ to push, press; ⟨timbre⟩ press, ring ⓶ ⟨opinión/situación⟩ to gauge, assess

pulsera *f* bracelet; ∼ **de tobillo** ankle bracelet, anklet

pulso *m* **(a)** (Med) pulse; **tomarle el** ∼ **a algn** to take sb's pulse; **tomarle el** ∼ **a algo** to gauge sth **(b)** (firmeza en la mano): **tengo muy mal** ∼ I have a very unsteady hand; **me temblaba el** ∼ my hand was shaking; **a** ∼ ⟨levantar⟩ with one's bare hands; ⟨dibujar⟩ freehand

pulular [A1] *vi* **(a)** (bullir) «muchedumbre» to mill around **(b)** (abundar): **aquí pululan los mosquitos** there are swarms of mosquitos here

pulverizador *m* (de perfume) atomizer, spray; (de pintura) spray gun; (del carburador) jet

pulverizar [A4] *vt* ⟨líquido⟩ to atomize, spray; ⟨sólido⟩ to pulverize, crush

puma *m* (animal) cougar, mountain lion, puma

puna *f* **(a)** (páramo) high Andean plateau **(b)** (Andes) (soroche) mountain *o* altitude sickness

punki /'puŋki, 'paŋki/ *adj/mf* (fam) punk

punta *f* ⓵ **(a)** (de lengua, dedos) tip; (de nariz) end, tip; (de pan) end; (de pincel) tip; **vivo en la otra** ∼ **de la ciudad** I live on the other side *o* at the other end of town; **con la** ∼ **del pie** with the print of one's foot; **la** ∼ **del iceberg** the tip of the iceberg; **tener algo en la** ∼ **de la lengua** to have sth on the tip of one's tongue **(b) puntas** *fpl* (del pelo) ends (*pl*) ⓶ **(a)** (de aguja, clavo, cuchillo, lápiz) point; (de flecha, lanza) tip; ∼ **de lanza** spearhead; **sácale** ∼ **al lápiz** sharpen the pencil; **de** ∼ point first; **es** ∼ pointed; **por un extremo acaba en** ∼ it's pointed at one end **(b) a punta de** (AmL fam): **a** ∼ **de repetírselo mil veces** by telling him it a thousand times; **a** ∼ **de palos lo hicieron obedecer** they beat him until he did as he was told ⓷ (de pañuelo) corner ■ *adj inv*: **la hora** ∼ the rush hour

puntabola *f* (Bol) ballpoint pen, Biro® (BrE)

puntada *f* ⓵ (en costura) stitch ⓶ (CS) (de dolor) stab of pain, sharp pain ⓷ (Méx fam) (comentario ingenioso) quip, witticism

puntaje *m* (AmL) (en competencia, prueba) score; (Educ) grades (*pl*) (AmE), marks (BrE)

puntal *m* (Const) prop **(b)** (sostén, apoyo) mainstay

puntapié *m* kick; **darle** *or* **pegarle un** ∼ **a algo/ algn** to kick sth/sb, to give sth/sb a kick; *para modismos ver* PATADA

puntear [A1] *vt* ⓵ (Mús) to pluck ⓶ (AmL) (Dep) to lead

punteo *m* plucking

puntería *f* aim; **tener buena/mala** ∼ to have a good/poor aim; **afinar la** ∼ to take careful aim; **¡qué** ∼! what a shot!

puntero *m* ⓵ (para señalar) pointer; (Inf) cursor; (de reloj) (Andes) hand ⓶ (Dep) **(a)** (equipo) leader, leaders (*pl*) **(b)** (Andes, RPI) (en fútbol) winger

puntiagudo -da *adj* (acabado en punta) pointed; (afilado) sharp

p

puntilla f **1** (Taur) dagger (*used to administer the coup de grâce in a bullfight*); **dar la ~** (Taur) to administer the coup de grâce **2** (punta del pie): **de ~s** *or* (AmL) **en ~s** on tiptoe; **entró de ~s** she tiptoed into the room **3** (encaje) lace edging

puntilloso -sa adj particular, punctilious

punto m **1** (a) (señal, marca) dot (b) (Ling) (sobre la 'i', la 'j') dot; (signo de puntuación) period (AmE), full stop (BrE); **~ decimal** decimal point ; **~ final** period (AmE), full stop (BrE); **~s suspensivos** ellipsis (tech), suspension points (*pl*) (AmE), dot, dot, dot; **~ y aparte** period (AmE) *o* (BrE) full stop, new paragraph; **~ y coma** semicolon; **~ com** (Com, Inf) dot com; **a ~ fijo** exactly, for certain; **... y punto ...** and that's that, ... period (AmE); ▶ DOS

2 (a) (momento, lugar) point; **en ese ~ de la conversación** at that point in the conversation; **el ~ donde ocurrió el accidente** the spot *o* place where the accident happened; **~ cardinal** cardinal point ; **~ ciego** blind spot; **~ de apoyo** (de palanca) fulcrum; **no hay ningún ~ de apoyo para la escalera** there is nowhere to lean the ladder; **~ de vista** (perspectiva) viewpoint, point of view; (opinión) views; **~ flaco/fuerte** weak/strong point; **~ muerto** (Auto) neutral; (en negociaciones) deadlock (b) (en geometría) point

3 (grado) point, extent; **hasta cierto ~ tiene razón** she's right, up to a point; **hasta tal ~ que ...** so much so that ...

4 (asunto, aspecto) point; **analizar algo ~ por ~** to analyze sth point by point; **los ~s a tratar en la reunión** the matters *o* items on the agenda for the meeting

5 (*en locs*) **a punto** (a tiempo) just in time; **estábamos a ~ de cenar** we were about to have dinner; **estuvo a ~ de caerse** he almost fell over; **batir las claras a ~ de nieve** beat the egg whites until they form stiff peaks; **en su punto** just right; **en punto: a las 12 en ~** at 12 o'clock sharp; **son las tres en ~** it's exactly three o'clock; **llegaron en ~** they arrived exactly on time

6 (a) (en costura, labores) stitch; **artículos de ~** knitwear; **hacer ~** (Esp) to knit; **~ (de) cruz** cross-stitch (b) (en cirugía) *tb* **~ de sutura** stitch

7 (unidad) (a) (Dep, Jueg) point; **~ para partido/set** (Méx) match/set point (b) (Educ) point, mark; (Fin) point

puntuación f **1** (Impr, Ling) punctuation **2** (a) (acción) (Educ) grading (AmE), marking (BrE); (Dep) scoring (b) (esp Esp) (Educ) grade (AmE), mark (BrE); (Dep) score

puntual adj **1** (a) ⟨persona⟩ punctual (b) (como adv) ⟨llegar⟩ punctually, on time **2** (detallado) detailed; (exacto) precise

puntualidad f punctuality

puntualizar [A4] vt (a) (especificar) to state (b) (señalar) to point out

puntuar [A18] vt **1** ⟨examen/prueba⟩ to grade (AmE), to mark (BrE) **2** ⟨texto⟩ to punctuate ■ **~** vi (a) «partido/prueba» to **PARA** algo to count TOWARD(s) sth (b) «deportista» to score (points)

puntudo -da adj (Andes, RPl) ▶ PUNTIAGUDO

punzada f sharp pain, stab of pain; **me dio una ~ en el costado** I felt a sharp pain *o* a stab of pain in my side

punzante adj ⟨objeto⟩ sharp; ⟨dolor⟩ sharp, stabbing (*before n*); ⟨palabras/comentario⟩ biting, incisive; ⟨estilo⟩ caustic

punzón m (para hacer agujeros) bradawl, awl; (para hacer ojetes) hole punch; (de grabador, escultor) burin

puñado m handful

puñal m dagger

puñalada f (a) (navajazo) stab; **lo mató a ~s** she stabbed him to death (b) (herida) stab wound

puñeta f (Esp fam): **hacerle la ~ a algn** to mess things up for sb; **mandar a algn a hacer ~s** to tell sb to go to hell; **¡vete a hacer ~s!** go to hell! (colloq)

puñetazo m punch; **darle** *or* **pegarle un ~ a algn** to punch sb; **pegó un ~ en la mesa** he thumped the table with his fist; **le rompió la cara de un ~** he smashed his face in (colloq)

puñetero -ra adj (Esp fam) (a) ⟨delante del n⟩ (uso enfático) damn, blasted (b) [SER] ⟨persona⟩: **no seas ~** don't be a swine (colloq), don't be a jerk (colloq)

puño m **1** (Anat) fist; **apretar los ~s** to clench one's fists **2** (de camisa) cuff **3** (de espada) hilt; (de bastón) handle, haft; (de moto) grip

pupa f (a) (fam) (en los labios) cold sore (b) (Esp leng infantil) (dolor, daño): **mamá, (tengo) ~** mummy, it hurts; **¿te has hecho ~?** have you hurt yourself?

pupila f pupil

pupilo -la m,f (a) (de maestro) pupil; (de tutor) ward, charge (b) (RPl) (alumno interno) boarder

pupitre m desk

purasangre mf thoroughbred

puré m: **~ de verduras** puréed vegetables; **~ de tomates** tomato purée *o* paste; **~ de papas** *or* (Esp) **patatas** mashed *o* creamed potatoes

pureza f purity

purgante adj/m purgative, laxative

purgatorio m purgatory

purificador m purifier; **~ de ambientes** (Col) air freshener

purificadora f *tb* **~ de agua** water treatment plant, waterworks (*sing or pl*)

purificar [A2] vt to purify

puritanismo m puritanism

puritano -na adj (Relig) Puritanical, Puritan (*before n*); (mojigato) puritanical
■ m,f (Relig) Puritan; (mojigato) puritan

puro¹ -ra adj **1** (sin mezcla) pure; (limpio) ⟨aire⟩ fresh, clean (b) (casto, inocente) ⟨mujer⟩ chaste, pure; ⟨niño⟩ innocent; ⟨mirada/amor⟩ innocent, pure **2** ⟨delante del n⟩ (a) (mero, simple) ⟨verdad⟩ plain, honest (colloq); ⟨casualidad/coincidencia⟩ pure, sheer; **lo hizo por ~ capricho** she did it purely on a whim; **de ~ cansancio**

AmC	América Central	Arg	Argentina	Cu	Cuba	Per	Perú
AmL	América Latina	Bol	Bolivia	Ec	Ecuador	RPl	Río de la Plata
AmS	América del Sur	Chi	Chile	Esp	España	Ur	Uruguay
Andes	Región andina	CS	Cono Sur	Méx	México	Ven	Venezuela

from sheer exhaustion **(b)** (AmL fam) (sólo): **a ese bar van ∼s viejos** only old men go to that bar; **son puras mentiras** it's just a pack of lies (colloq)

puro² *adv* (fam) (muy, tan): **se murió de ∼ vieja** she just died of old age; **lo hizo de ∼ egoísta** he did it out of sheer selfishness
■ *m* cigar

púrpura *f* (de) color ∼ purple

purpurina *f* (en pinturas) metallic powder; (para adornar) glitter

pus *m* pus

puse, pusiera, etc ▶ PONER

pusilánime *adj* fainthearted, pusillanimous (frml)

pusiste, etc ▶ PONER

puso ▶ PONER

puta *f* (vulg & pey) (prostituta) whore (colloq & pej), hooker (colloq); **hijo (de) ∼** son of a bitch (vulg), bastard (vulg)

putada *f* (vulg): **hacerle una ∼ a algn** to play a dirty trick on sb (colloq)

putrefacción *f* putrefaction

putrefacto -ta, pútrido -da *adj* putrid

puya *f* **(a)** (Taur) point (*of the picador's lance*) **(b)** (comentario irónico) gibe; **lanzar** *or* **echar una ∼** to make a gibe

puzzle /'pusle, 'puele/ *m* (rompecabezas) (jigsaw) puzzle

Pza. *f* (= **Plaza**) Sq

Qq

Q, q *f* (*read as* /ku/) *the letter* Q, q

que *conj* ... (details omitted)

rama» to snap; «*vaso/plato»* (romperse) to break;
(rajarse) to crack **(b)** ‹*pierna/brazo*› to break;
‹*diente*› to chip **2** (Col) (arruinarse) to go bankrupt

quechua *adj* Quechua
■ *mf* (persona) Quechuan
■ *m* (idioma) Quechua

quedar [A1] *vi*
I 1 (en un estado, una situación): ~ **viudo/huérfano**
to be widowed/orphaned; **quedó paralítico** he was
left paralyzed; **el coche quedó como nuevo** the
car is as good as new (now); **y que esto quede
bien claro** and I want to make this quite clear;
¿quién quedó en primer lugar? who was *o* came
first?
2 (en la opinión de los demás): **si no voy ~é mal
con ellos** it won't go down very well *o* it'll look
bad if I don't turn up; **lo hice para ~ bien con el
jefe** I did it to get in the boss's good books; **quedé
muy bien con el regalo** I made a very good
impression with my present; **me hiciste ~ muy
mal diciendo eso** you really showed me up
saying that; **nos hizo ~ mal a todos** he
embarrassed us all; **quedó en ridículo** (por culpa
propia) he made a fool of himself; (por culpa ajena)
he was made to look a fool
3 (permanecer): **¿queda alguien adentro?** is there
anyone left inside?; **le quedó la cicatriz** she was
left with a scar; **esto no puede ~ así** we can't
leave things like this; **nuestros planes ~on en
nada** our plans came to nothing; **~ atrás**
«*persona*» to fall behind; «*rencillas/problemas*»
to be in the past
4 (+ *me/te/le etc*) **(a)** «*tamaño/talla*»: **me queda
largo** it's too long for me; **la talla 12 le queda bien**
the size 12 fits (you/him) fine **(b)** (sentar): **el azul
le queda bien/mal** blue suits her/doesn't suit her
II (a) (acordar, convenir): **¿en qué ~on?** what did
you decide?; **¿entonces en qué quedamos?** so,
what's happening, then?; **~on en** *or* (AmL) **de no
decirle nada** they agreed *o* decided not to tell him
anything; **quedó en** *or* (AmL) **de venir a las nueve**
she said she would come at nine **(b)** (citarse): **¿a
qué hora quedamos?** what time shall we meet?;
quedé con unos amigos para cenar I arranged to
meet some friends for dinner
III (estar situado) to be; **queda justo entrente de la
estación** it's right opposite the station; **me queda
muy lejos** it's very far from where I live (*o* work
etc)
IV (en *3ª pers*) **1 (a)** (haber todavía) to be left;
¿te queda algo de dinero? do you have any
money left?; **¿queda café?** is there any coffee
left?; **solo quedan las ruinas** only the ruins
remain; **no nos queda más remedio que ir** we
have no choice but to go **(b)** (sobrar) «*comida/
vino*» to be left (over)
2 (faltar): **queda poco para que acabe la clase**
it's not long till the end of the class; **¿cuántos
kilómetros quedan?** how many kilometers are
there to go?; **todavía le quedan dos años** he
still has two years to go *o* do; **queda mucho por
ver** there is still a lot to see; **aún me queda
todo esto por hacer** I still have all this to do;
no me/le queda otra (fam) I have/he has no
choice
■ **quedarse** *v pron*
I 1 (a) (en un lugar, país) to stay; **~se en la cama**
to stay in bed **(b)** (en un estado, una situación)

(+ *compl*): te estás quedando calvo you're going
bald; **~se dormido** to fall asleep; **~se sin trabajo**
to lose one's job
2 (+ *me/te/le etc*) **(a)** (permanecer): **~se soltera** to
stay single; **no me gusta ~me sola en casa** I
don't like being alone in the house; **¡no te quedes
ahí parado!** don't just stand there!; **nos quedamos
charlando hasta tarde** we went on chatting until
late in the evening; **se me quedó mirando** he sat/
stood there staring at me; **de repente el motor se
quedó** (AmL) the engine suddenly died on me **(b)**
(Andes) (olvidarse): **se me quedó el paraguas** I left
my umbrella behind **(c)** (Esp) (llegar a ser): **la casa
se les está quedando pequeña** the house is
getting (to be) too small for them
II ‹*cambio/lápiz*› to keep; **se quedó con mi libro**
she kept my book; **me quedo con este** I'll take
this one

quehacer *m* (actividad, tarea) work; **~es
domésticos** housework, household chores; **el ~
diario** the daily routine

queja *f* (protesta) complaint; **presentar una ~** to
make a complaint

quejarse [A1] *v pron* **(a)** (protestar) to complain;
(refunfuñar) to grumble; **~ DE algo/algn** to
complain ABOUT sth/sb **(b)** (de una afección, un
dolor) **~ DE algo** to complain OF sth **(c)** (gemir)
to moan, groan

quejica *adj/mf* (Esp fam) ▶ QUEJÓN

quejido *m* groan, moan; (más agudo) whine; **un
~ de dolor** a cry of pain

quejón -jona *adj* (fam) whining (*before n*)
(colloq)
■ *m,f* (fam) crybaby (colloq)

quemada *f* **(a)** (Andes, Ven fam) (del sol): **pegarse
una ~** to get sunburned **(b)** (Méx) ▶ QUEMADURA

quemado -da *adj* **1** [ESTAR] **(a)** ‹*comida/
tostada*› burnt; **esto sabe a ~** this tastes burnt;
huele a ~ I can smell burning **(b)** (rojo) ‹*cara/
espalda*› burnt **(c)** (AmL) (bronceado) tanned,
brown **2** [ESTAR] (desgastado, agotado) burned-out

quemador *m* burner

quemadura *f* **(a)** (herida causada — por fuego,
ácido) burn; (— por líquido caliente) scald; **~ de sol**
sunburn **(b)** (en prenda — de cigarrillo) cigarette
burn; (— al planchar) scorch mark; (en mueble) burn
mark

quemar [A1] *vt* **1 (a)** ‹*basura/documentos/
leña*› to burn **(b)** ‹*herejes/brujas*› to burn ... at
the stake
2 ‹*calorías*› to burn up; ‹*grasa*› to burn off
3 (a) ‹*comida/mesa/mantel*› to burn; (con la
plancha) to scorch **(b)** ‹*líquido/vapor*› to scald
(c) ‹*ácido*› ‹*ropa/piel*› to burn **(d)** ‹*motor*› to
burn ... out; ‹*fusible*› to blow **(e)** ‹*sol*› ‹*plantas*›
to scorch; ‹*piel*› to burn; (broncear) (AmL) to tan
■ **~** *vi* **(a)** «*plato/sartén*» to be very hot; «*café/
sopa*» to be boiling (hot) (colloq) **(b)** ‹*sol*› to
burn
■ **quemarse** *v pron* **1 (a)** (refl) (con fuego, calor)
to burn oneself; (con líquido, vapor) to scald oneself;
‹*mano/lengua*› to burn; ‹*pelo/cejas*› to singe **(b)**
(al sol — ponerse rojo) to get burned; (— broncearse)
(AmL) to tan
2 (a) (destruirse) «*papeles*» to get burned;
«*edificio*» to burn down **(b)** (sufrir daños)
«*alfombra/vestido*» to get burned; «*comida*» to
burn; **se me ~on las tostadas** I burned the toast

quemarropa ⋯⋗ quinientos ⋯

3 «*persona*» (desgastarse) to burn oneself out

quemarropa: a ~ (*loc adv*) ⟨*disparar*⟩ at point-blank range; ⟨*preguntar*⟩ point-blank

quemazón *f* (sensación de ardor) burning

quena *f* reed flute (*used in Andean music*)

quepa, etc ▶ CABER

quepo ▶ CABER

querella *f* **(a)** (Der) private prosecution; **presentar ~ contra algn** to bring a private prosecution against sb **(b)** (disputa) dispute

querendón -dona *adj* (AmL fam) (cariñoso) affectionate; (enamoradizo) flighty

querer [E24] *vt*
I (amar) to love; **te querré siempre** I'll always love you; **sus alumnos lo quieren mucho** his pupils are very fond of him; **¡por lo que más quieras!** for pity's sake!, for God's sake!

II **1** **(a)** (expresando deseo, intención, voluntad): **no sabe lo que quiere** she doesn't know what she wants; **quisiera una habitación doble** I'd like a double room; **¿qué más quieres?** what more do you want?; **hazlo cuando/como quieras** do it whenever/however you like; **iba a hacerlo pero él no quiso** I was going to do it but he didn't want me to; **tráemelo mañana ¿quieres?** bring it tomorrow, will you?; **no quiero** I don't want to; **quiero ir** I want to go; **quisiera reservar una mesa** I'd like to book a table; **quisiera poder ayudarte** I wish I could help you; **no quiso comer nada** she wouldn't eat anything; **quiero que estudies más** I want you to study harder; **¡qué quieres que te diga ...!** quite honestly *o* frankly ...; **el destino así lo quiso** it was destined to be; **~ es poder** where there's a will there's a way **(b)** (al ofrecer algo): **¿quieres un café?** would you like a coffee?; (menos formal) do you want a coffee? **(c)** (introduciendo un pedido): **¿querrías hacerme un favor?** could you do me a favor?; **¿te quieres callar?** be quiet, will you?

2 (*en locs*) **cuando quiera que** whenever; **donde quiera que** wherever; **queriendo** (adrede) on purpose, deliberately; **sin querer** accidentally; **fue sin ~** it was an accident; **querer decir** to mean; **¿qué quieres decir con eso?** what do you mean by that?

3 (como precio): **¿cuánto quieres por el coche?** how much do you want *o* are you asking for the car?

■ **quererse** *v pron* (*recípr*): **se quieren mucho** they love each other very much

querido -da *adj* **(a)** (amado) ⟨*patria*⟩ beloved; **mis recuerdos más ~s** my fondest memories; **seres ~s** loved ones; **un profesor muy ~ por todos** a well-liked teacher **(b)** (Corresp) Dear **(c)** (Col fam) (simpático) nice
■ *m,f* **(a)** (como apelativo) darling, dear, sweetheart **(b)** (amante) (*m*) fancy man; (*f*) fancy woman

querré, querría, etc ▶ QUERER

querubín *m* cherub

quesadilla *f* **(a)** (Méx) (tortilla): *tortilla filled with a savory mixture and topped with melted cheese* **(b)** (Ven) (panecillo) small roll (*flavored with cheese*)

quesera *f* cheese dish

queso *m* (Coc) cheese; **~ crema** (AmL) cream cheese; **~ fundido** processed cheese; **~ para untar** cheese spread

quetzal *m* (Fin) quetzal (*Guatemalan unit of currency*)

quicio *m* doorjamb; **sacar de ~ a algn** to drive sb crazy (colloq)

quid *m*: **el ~ de la cuestión** the crux of the matter

quiebra *f* (Com, Fin) (de empresa, individuo) bankruptcy; **declarse en ~** to go into liquidation

quiebra, quiebras, etc ▶ QUEBRAR

quien *pron* **1** **(a)** (*sujeto*) who, that; (*complemento*) who, that, whom (frml); **tienes que ser tú misma ~ lo decida** you are the one who *o* that has to decide; **es a él a ~ debemos agradecérselo** he's the one (who) we must thank; **la chica con ~ salía** the girl (who) I was going out with **(b)** (frml *o* liter) (en frases explicativas) who, whom (frml); **su hermano, a ~ no había visto, ...** her brother, who *o* whom she had not seen, ...

2 (la persona que): **~es hayan terminado** those who have finished; **~ la haya encontrado** the person who found it; **~ se lo haya dicho** whoever told him

quién *pron* who; **¿~es eran?** who were they?; **¿~ de ustedes se atrevería?** which of you would dare?; **¿con ~es fuiste?** who did you go with?; **¿de ~ es esto?** whose is this?; **llegó una postal — ¿de ~?** there's a postcard — who's it from?

quienquiera *pron* (*pl* **quienesquiera**) whoever

quiera, quieras, etc ▶ QUERER

quieto -ta *adj* still; **¡estte ~!** keep still!

quietud *f* (ausencia de movimiento) stillness; (tranquilidad, sosiego) calm, peace

quihubo *interj* (Chi, Méx fam) hi! (colloq), how's it going? (colloq)

quihúbole *interj* (Méx fam) ▶ QUIHUBO

quijada *f* jaw (bone)

Quijote *m*: **Don ~** Don Quixote

quilate *m* karat (AmE), carat (BrE); **oro de 18 ~s** 18-karat gold

quilla *f* keel

quilombo *m* (Bol, RPI arg) (lío, jaleo) mess

quiltro -tra *m,f* (Chi fam) mongrel

quimera *f* (ilusión) illusion, chimera (liter)

química *f* chemistry

químico -ca *adj* chemical
■ *m,f* chemist

quimioterapia *f* chemotherapy

quince *adj inv/pron/m* fifteen; **dentro de ~ días** in two weeks' time, in a fortnight's time (BrE); *para ejemplos ver tb* CINCO

quinceañero -ra *m,f* (de quince años) fifteen-year-old; (menos específico) teenager

quincena *f* (dos semanas) two weeks (*pl*), fortnight (BrE); **la primera ~ de marzo** the first two weeks in March

quincenal *adj* bimonthly (AmE), fortnightly (BrE)

quiniela *f* (Esp) (boleto) sports lottery ticket (AmE), pools coupon (BrE); (juego): **las ~s** the sports lottery (AmE), the football pools (BrE)

quinientos -tas *adj/pron* five hundred; **~ cinco** five hundred and five; **~ y pico** five hundred odd; **el ~ aniversario** the five hundredth anniversary

q

quinqué *m* oil lamp

quinquenal *adj* ‹revisión/censo› five-yearly, quinquennial (frml); **un plan ~** a five-year plan

quinta *f* 1 (a) (casa) *house in its own grounds, usually in the country* (b) (Agr) estate, farm 2 (Esp) (Mil) draft, call up

quintaesencia *f* quintessence (frml)

quinteto *m* quintet

quintillizo -za *m,f* quintuplet

quinto1 **-ta** *adj/pron* fifth; **llegó en ~ lugar** he came fifth; **Carlos V** (*read as: Carlos quinto*) Charles V (*read as: Charles the fifth*); **vive en el ~ (piso)** she lives on the sixth (AmE) *o* (BrE) fifth floor; **la quinta parte** a fifth

quinto2 *m* 1 (a) (partitivo) fifth; **tres ~s** three-fifths (b) (en Méx) (moneda) five centavo coin; **estar sin un ~** (Méx fam) to be broke (colloq) 2 (Esp) (Mil) conscript

quíntuple *m* quintuple
■ *mf* (Chi, Ven) quintuplet

quíntuplo1 **-pla** *adj* quintuple, fivefold

quíntuplo2 *m* quintuple

quiosco *m* ▶ KIOSCO

quirófano *m* operating room (AmE), operating theatre (BrE)

quiromancia *f* palmistry, chiromancy (frml)

quirúrgico -ca *adj* surgical; **fue sometido a una intervención quirúrgica** (frml) he underwent surgery (frml)

quise, quisiera, etc ▶ QUERER

quisquilloso -sa *adj* (meticuloso, exigente) fussy, picky (colloq); (susceptible) touchy

quiste *m* cyst

quitaesmalte *m* nail polish remover

quitamanchas *m* (*pl* **~**) stain remover

quitar [A1] *vt* 1 (apartar, retirar): **¡quítalo de aquí!** get it out of here!; **quité la silla de en medio** I got the chair out of the way; **quita tus cosas de mi escritorio** take your things off my desk; **~ la mesa** (Esp) to clear the table; **¡quítame las manos**

de encima! take your hands off me!; **no le puedo ~ la tapa** I can't get the top off; **le quitó los zapatos** she took his shoes off
2 (+ *me/te/le etc*) (a) (de las manos): **le quitó la pistola al ladrón** he got *o* took the gun off the thief; **le quité el cuchillo** I took the knife (away) from her (b) (privar de) ‹pasaporte/carnet de conducir› to take away (c) ‹cartera/dinero› to take, steal; ‹asiento/lugar› to take
3 (restar) (+ *me/te/le etc*): **me quita mucho tiempo** it takes up a lot of my time; **~le años a algn** to take years off sb; **~le importancia a algo** to play sth down; **le quita valor** it detracts from its value
4 (hacer desaparecer) ‹mancha› to remove, get ... out; ‹dolor› to relieve, get rid of; ‹sed› to quench; ‹apetito› to take away; (+ *me/te/le etc*) **eso te ~á el hambre** that will stop you feeling hungry; **hay que ~le esa idea de la cabeza** we must get that idea out of his head
5 **quitando** (*ger*) (fam) except for
■ *~ vi* 1 (Esp fam): **¡quita (de ahí)!** get out of the way!
2 (*en locs*) **de quita y pon** ‹funda/etiqueta› removable; **eso no quita que ...** that doesn't mean that ...
■ **quitarse** *v pron* 1 (desaparecer) «mancha» to come out; «dolor» to go (away); **ya se me ~on las ganas** I don't feel like it any more
2 (apartarse, retirarse) to get out of the way; **¡quítate de mi vista!** get out of my sight!
3 (*refl*) (a) ‹prenda/alhaja/maquillaje› to take off (b) ‹dolor/resfriado› to get rid of; ‹miedo› to overcome, get over; **se quita la edad** she lies about her age; **~se algo/a algn de encima** to get rid of sth/sb

quitasol *m* sunshade

quiteño -ña *adj* of/from Quito

Quito *m* Quito

quiubo *interj* (Chi, Méx fam) ▶ QUIHUBO

quizá, quizás *adv* maybe, perhaps

quórum /'kworum/ *m* (*pl* **-rums**) quorum

Rr

R, r *f* (*read as* /'ere/) *the letter* R

rábano *m* radish; ▶ IMPORTAR

rabia *f* 1 (enfermedad) rabies 2 (a) (expresando fastidio): **no sabes la ~ que me da** you've no idea how much it annoys *o* irritates me; **¡qué ~!** how annoying! (b) (furor, ira) anger, fury; **tener ~** to be angry; **con ~** angrily, in a rage (c) (antipatía, manía): **tenerle ~ a algn** to have it in for sb (colloq)

rabiar [A1] *vi* (de furor, envidia): **el jefe está que rabia contigo** the boss is furious with you; **no lo hagas ~** don't annoy him

rabieta *f* tantrum; **le dio una ~** he threw a tantrum

rabino -na *m,f* rabbi

rabioso -sa *adj* 1 (Med, Vet) rabid 2 (furioso) furious

rabo *m* (a) (Zool) tail (b) (de letra) tail (c) (Bot) stem, stalk

AmC	Central America	Arg	Argentina	Cu	Cuba	Per	Peru
AmL	Latin America	Bol	Bolivia	Ec	Ecuador	RPI	River Plate Area
AmS	South America	Chi	Chile	Esp	Spain	Ur	Uruguay
Andes	Andean Region	CS	Southern Cone	Méx	Mexico	Ven	Venezuela

racha *f* **(a)** (secuencia) una ~ DE algo ⟨*de buena/ mala suerte*⟩ a run *o* spell OF sth; ⟨*de enfermedades/éxitos*⟩ a string OF sth; **pasar una mala** ~ to go through bad times *o* (BrE) a bad patch; **tengo una buena** ~ **, voy a seguir jugando** I'm on a winning streak so I'm going to carry on playing; **va/viene por** ~**s** it goes/comes in phases **(b)** (Meteo) gust of wind

racial *adj* racial; ⟨*disturbio*⟩ race (*before n*)

racimo *m* bunch

raciocinio *m* (facultad) reason; (argumento) reasoning

ración *f* **(a)** (parte) share **(b)** (porción de comida) portion, helping; **una** ~ **de calamares** a portion *o* plate of squid **(c)** (Mil) ration

racional *adj* rational

racionalizar [A4] *vt* to rationalize

racionamiento *m* rationing

racionar [A1] *vt* to ration

racismo *m* racism

racista *adj/mf* racist

radar *m* radar

radiación *f* radiation

radiactividad *f* radioactivity

radiactivo -va *adj* radioactive

radiador *m* radiator

radiante *adj* **(a)** (brillante) brilliant; **hace un sol** ~ it's brilliantly *o* beautifully sunny; **un día** ~ a bright, sunny day **(b)** [ESTAR] ⟨*persona*⟩ radiant; ~ **de alegría** radiant with happiness

radical *adj/mf* radical

radicar [A2] *vi* «*problema/dificultad*» to lie ▪ **radicarse** *v pron* to settle

radio *m* **(a)** (Mat) radius **(b)** (distancia) range, radius; **en un** ~ **de diez kilómetros** within a ten kilometer radius **(c)** (de rueda) spoke; ~ **de acción** (de avión, barco) operational range; (de organización) area of operations ▪ *f or* (AmL exc CS) *m* **(a)** (medio de comunicación) radio; **por (la)** ~ on the radio; **escuchar la** ~ to listen to the radio **(b)** (aparato) radio **(c)** (emisora) radio station

radioactividad *f* radioactivity

radioactivo -va *adj* radioactive

radioaficionado -da *m,f* radio ham

radiocassette /rraðiokaˈset/, **radiocasete** *m* radio cassette player

radiodifusión *f* broadcasting

radiodifusora *f* (AmL frml) radio station

radiofónico -ca *adj* radio (*before n*)

radiografía *f* X-ray; **hacerse una** ~ to have an X-ray taken

radiólogo -ga *m,f* radiologist

radionovela *f* radio serial

radiooperador -dora *m,f* (AmL) radio operator

radiopatrulla *m* radio patrol car

radioterapia *f* radiotherapy

radioyente *mf* listener

raer [E16] *vt* ⟨*superficie*⟩ to scrape; ⟨*barniz/ pintura*⟩ to scrape off

ráfaga *f* (de viento) gust; (de ametralladora) burst

raid *m* (AmC) (en carro) ride; **pedir** ~ to hitch a ride *o* lift

raído -da *adj* worn-out, threadbare

raíz *f* (en general) root; **arrancar de** ~ ⟨*planta*⟩ to uproot; ⟨*vello*⟩ to remove … at the roots; ~ **cuadrada** (Mat) square root; **a** ~ **de** as a result of; **echar raíces** «*planta/costumbre/ideología*» to take root; «*persona*» to put down roots

raja *f* **(a)** (en pared, cerámica) crack **(b)** (rotura — en costura) split; (— en tela) tear, rip **(c)** (abertura — en falda) slit; (— en chaqueta) vent **(d)** (de melón, salami) slice

rajar [A1] *vt* 1 **(a)** (agrietar) to crack, cause … to crack **(b)** (con cuchillo, navaja) to slash 2 **(a)** (CS fam) (criticar) to run … down **(b)** (Andes) (en examen) (fam) to fail, flunk (AmE colloq) ▪ **rajarse** *v pron* 1 «*pared/cerámica*» to crack; «*tela*» to split, tear, rip 2 (fam) (acobardarse) to back off

rajatabla: **a** ~ (loc adv) to the letter

rallador *m* grater

ralladura *f*: ~ **de limón** grated lemon rind

rallar [A1] *vt* to grate

ralo -la *adj* ⟨*bosque*⟩ sparse; ⟨*monte*⟩ bare; ⟨*pelo/ barba*⟩ thin, sparse

rama *f* branch; **una ramita de perejil** a sprig of parsley; **andarse/irse por las** ~**s** to beat about the bush

ramada *f* **(a)** (AmS) (cobertizo) shelter (*made from branches*) **(b)** (Chi) (pérgola) arbor, arbour (BrE)

ramal *m* (Ferr) branch line; (Geog) branch; (cuerda) strap

rambla *f* **(a)** (RPl) (paseo marítimo) esplanade, promenade **(b)** (avenida) boulevard

ramera *f* prostitute

ramificación *f* ramification

ramificarse [A2] *v pron* **(a)** ⟨*árbol/plantas/ nervios*⟩ to branch **(b)** «*carretera/ciencia*» to branch **(c)** «*problema*» to ramify (frml), to become complex

ramillete *m* **(a)** (de flores) posy **(b)** (iró) (grupo selecto) bunch (colloq)

ramo *m* 1 (de flores) bunch; (para novia, dignatario) bouquet 2 **(a)** (en industria) industry **(b)** (Chi) (Educ) subject

rampa *f* (pendiente) ramp; ~ **de lanzamiento** launch pad

rana *f* (Zool) frog

ranchera *f* (Mús) *Mexican folk song*

ranchería *f* **(a)** (Col) ▶ RANCHERÍO **(b)** (Méx) dairy

rancherío *m* (CS) (poblado) settlement; (en suburbios) shantytown

ranchero -ra *adj* (Méx fam) shy ▪ *m,f* (Méx) rancher

rancho *m* 1 (comida) food (*for a group of soldiers, workers, etc*) 2 **(a)** (AmL) (choza) hut; (casucha) hovel; (chabola) shack, shanty **(b)** (Méx) (hacienda) ranch

rancio -cia *adj* 1 ⟨*mantequilla/tocino*⟩ rancid 2 **(a)** ⟨*vino*⟩ mellow **(b)** (delante del n) ⟨*abolengo/tradición*⟩ ancient, long-established

rango *m* 1 **(a)** (Mil) rank **(b)** (categoría, nivel) level 2 (Chi) (lujo, pompa) luxury; (de persona) high social status

rangoso -sa *adj* (Chi) ⟨*fiesta/casa*⟩ lavish; ⟨*persona*⟩ of high social status

ranura *f* (a) (para monedas, tarjetas, cartas) slot; **por la ∼ de la puerta** through the chink *o* gap in the door (b) (en ensambladura, tornillo) groove

rapapolvo *m* (Esp) telling-off (colloq), talking-to (colloq)

rapar [A1] *vt* ⟨*cabeza*⟩ to shave; ⟨*pelo*⟩ to crop

rapaz *adj* (Zool) predatory; **ave ∼** bird of prey

rape *m* (a) (Coc, Zool) monkfish, goosefish (AmE) (b) **al rape: tiene el pelo cortado al ∼** he has closely-cropped hair

rápidamente *adv* quickly

rapidez *f* speed; **con ∼** quickly; **¡qué ∼!** that was quick!

rápido¹ *adv* ⟨*hablar/trabajar*⟩ quickly, fast; ⟨*conducir/ir*⟩ fast; **tráemelo ¡∼!** bring it to me, quick!

rápido² -da *adj* ⟨*aumento*⟩ rapid; ⟨*cambio*⟩ quick, rapid, swift; ⟨*desarrollo*⟩ rapid, swift; **a paso ∼** quickly, swiftly; **comida rápida** fast food
■ *m* (Ferr) express train, fast train
■ *m* ① (Ferr) fast train ② **rápidos** *mpl* (Geog) rapids (*pl*)

rapiña *f* robbery, pillage

raptar [A1] *vt* (secuestrar) to kidnap, abduct (frml)

rapto *m* (secuestro) kidnapping, abduction (frml)

raptor -tora *m,f* kidnapper

raqueta *f* (de tenis, squash) racket; (para nieve) snowshoe

raquítico -ca *adj* ⟨*niño/animal*⟩ rickety, rachitic (tech); ⟨*árbol*⟩ stunted

rareza *f* (a) (de persona) peculiarity, quirk (b) (cosa poco común) rarity (c) (cualidad) rareness

raro -ra *adj* (a) (extraño) strange, odd, funny (colloq); **es ∼ que …** it's strange *o* odd *o* funny that …; **¡qué ∼!** how odd *o* strange!; **te noto muy ∼ hoy** you're acting very strangely today (b) (poco frecuente) rare; **salvo raras excepciones** with a few rare exceptions; **aquí es ∼ que nieve** it's very unusual *o* rare for it to snow here

ras: a ras de (*loc prep*): **llega a ∼ del suelo** it reaches down to the floor; **volar a ∼ de tierra** to fly very low

rasca *adj* (CS fam) (a) ⟨*persona*⟩ vulgar, common (pej); ⟨*lugar/canción*⟩ tacky (colloq) (b) (de mala calidad) trashy (colloq)

rascacielos *m* (*pl* ∼) skyscraper

rascar [A2] *vt* (a) (con las uñas) to scratch (b) (con cuchillo) ⟨*superficie*⟩ to scrape; ⟨*pintura*⟩ to scrape off
■ **rascarse** *v pron* (*refl*) to scratch (oneself)

rasgado -da *adj* ⟨*ojos*⟩ almond (*before n*), almond-shaped

rasgar [A3] *vt* to tear, rip
■ **rasgarse** *v pron* to tear, rip

rasgo *m* ① (a) (característica) characteristic, feature (b) (gesto) gesture (c) (de la pluma) stroke; (en pintura) brushstroke; **a grandes ∼s** in outline, broadly speaking ② **rasgos** *mpl* (facciones) features (*pl*)

rasguear [A1] *vt* to strum

rasguñar [A1] *vt* to scratch
■ **rasguñarse** *v pron* (*refl*) (con uña, púa) to scratch oneself; (con algo áspero) to graze oneself; **me rasguñé la rodilla** I grazed my knee

rasguño *m* scratch

rasmillarse [A1] *v pron* (Chi fam) to graze oneself

raso¹ -sa *adj* ① ⟨*taza/cucharada*⟩ level (*before n*) ② (exterior) open country; **dormir al ∼** to sleep out in the open

raso² *m* satin

raspado *m* (Col, Méx) ▶ GRANIZADO

raspadura *f* (arañazo) scratch; (ralladura de metal, chocolate) shavings (*pl*)

raspar [A1] *vt* (a) (con espátula) ⟨*superficie*⟩ to scrape; ⟨*pintura*⟩ to scrape off (b) (limar) to file, rasp (c) ⟨*piel*⟩ to scrape, graze
■ *vi* (a) «*toalla/manos*» to be rough; «*barba*» to scratch, be scratchy (b) «*garganta*» (+ *me/te/le etc*) to feel rough
■ **rasparse** *v pron* ⟨*rodillas/codos*⟩ (con algo puntiagudo) to scratch; (con algo áspero) to scrape, graze

raspón *m* (AmL) (por algo puntiagudo) scratch; (por algo áspero) graze, scrape; **hay un ∼ en la puerta** the door is scratched

rastra: **a rastras** (*loc adv*): **llevar algo/a algn a ∼s** to drag sth/sb; **fue a ∼s hasta la puerta** she dragged herself to the door

rastreador -dora *m,f* tracker

rastrear [A1] *vt* (a) ⟨*zona*⟩ to comb (b) ⟨*persona/satélite*⟩ to track (c) ⟨*río/lago*⟩ «*pescadores*» to trawl; «*policías*» to drag, dredge

rastrero -ra *adj* (a) (despreciable) despicable, contemptible (b) ⟨*tallo*⟩ creeping (*before n*); ⟨*animal*⟩ crawling (*before n*)

rastrillo *m* ① (Agr) rake ② (Méx) (para afeitarse) safety razor

rastro *m* ① (pista, huella) trail; (señal, vestigio) trace, sign; **sin dejar ∼** without (a) trace ② (mercado) flea market

rasurador *m*, **rasuradora** *f* (AmC, Méx) electric razor *o* shaver

rasurar [A1] *vt* (AmL) to shave
■ **rasurarse** *v pron* (AmL) to shave

rata *f* ① (Zool) rat; **hacerse la ∼** (RPl fam) to play hooky (esp AmE colloq), to skive off (school) (BrE colloq) ② (Col) (Econ, Mat) (tasa) rate; (razón) ratio; (porcentaje) percentage
■ *mf* (fam) (tacaño) miser, stingy devil (colloq), tightwad (AmE colloq)

ratán *m* rattan

ratero -ra *m,f* (fam) (carterista) pickpocket; (ladrón) petty thief

ratificar [A2] *vt* ⟨*tratado/contrato*⟩ to ratify; ⟨*persona*⟩ (en un puesto) to confirm; ⟨*noticia*⟩ to confirm

rato *m* (a) (tiempo breve) while; **hace un ∼ a** while ago; **espera un ratito** wait a minute (colloq); **en mis ∼s libres** in my spare time; **pasé un mal ∼** it was terrible; **iré dentro de un ∼** I'll go shortly (b) (*en locs*) **a cada rato** (AmL): **me interrumpe a cada ∼** he keeps interrupting me; **al (poco) rato** shortly afterwards; **al poco ∼ de irte tú** shortly *o* just after you left; **a ratos** from time to time; **para ∼** (fam): **tengo para ∼** I'll be a while, I'll be some time; **todavía hay para ∼** there's still a long way to go; **pasar el ∼** to while away the time

ratón¹ -tona *m,f* (Zool) mouse; **∼ de biblioteca** (fam) bookworm

ratón² *m* **1** (Inf) mouse; **~ de bola** trackball **2** (AmC) **(a)** (Coc) *sinewy cut of meat* **(b)** (fam) (biceps) biceps **3** (Ven fam) (resaca) hangover

ratonera *f* (trampa) mousetrap; (madriguera) mousehole

raudal *m* (de agua) torrent; **el agua entraba a ~es** the water poured out in torrents

ravioles, raviolis *mpl* ravioli

raya *f* **1** **(a)** (línea) line; (lista) stripe; **a** *or* **de ~s** ⟨tela/vestido⟩ striped; **pasarse de la ~** to overstep the mark, to go too far; **tener a algn a ~** to keep a tight rein on sb **(b)** (del pantalón) crease **(c)** (del pelo) part (AmE), parting (BrE); **hacerse la ~** to part one's hair **(d)** (Impr) dash **2** (Zool) ray, skate

rayado -da *adj* **1** ⟨papel⟩ lined, ruled (frml); ⟨tela/vestido⟩ striped; (loco) screwy (colloq) **2** [ESTAR] (AmS fam) (loco) screwy (colloq), nutty (colloq)

rayar [A1] *vt* **(a)** ⟨pintura/mesa⟩ to scratch **(b)** (garabatear) to scrawl
■ **~** *vi* **1** (dejar marca) to scratch **2** (aproximarse) **~ EN algo** to border ON sth, verge ON sth **3** (Méx) «obreros» to get one's wages, get paid
■ **rayarse** *v pron* **1** «superficie» to get scratched **2** (AmS fam) (volverse loco) to crack up (colloq)

rayo *m* **1** (en general) ray; **un ~ de luz** a ray *o* beam (of light); **un ~ de luna** a moonbeam; **~ láser** laser beam; **~s ultravioleta** ultraviolet rays (*pl*); **~s X** X-rays (*pl*) **2** (Meteo) bolt (of lightning); **como un ~** (fam) ⟨salir⟩ like greased lightning (colloq) **3** (AmL) (de rueda) spoke

rayuela *f* **(a)** ⟨juego de adultos⟩ *game similar to pitch-and-toss* **(b)** (RPl) ⟨juego de niños⟩ hopscotch

raza *f* (etnia) race; (Agr, Zool) breed; **un perro de ~** a pedigree dog

razón *f* **1** (motivo, causa) reason; **la ~ por la que te lo digo** the reason (that) I'm telling you; **se enojó** *o* **con ~** she got angry and rightly so; **con ~ o sin ella** rightly or wrongly; **se quejan sin ~/ con ~** they're complaining for no good reason/ they have good reason to complain; **¡con ~ no contestaban!** no wonder they didn't answer!; **~ de más para ...** all the more reason to ... **2** (verdad, acierto): **tener** *or* **llevar ~** to be right; **tuve que darle la ~** I had to admit she was right; **tienes toda la ~** (fam) you're absolutely right **3** (habilidad para razonar) reason; **actuó guiado por la ~** he was guided by reason; **desde que tengo uso de ~** for as long as I can remember; **entrar en ~** to see reason *o* sense; **perder la ~** to go out of one's mind; (en sentido hiperbólico) to take leave of one's senses

razonable *adj* reasonable

razonamiento *m* reasoning

razonar [A1] *vi* to reason

re *m* (nota) D; (en solfeo) re, ray

reacción *f* **1** (en general) reaction **2** (Pol) (AmL) right wing

reaccionar [A1] *vi* to react; **~ A** *or* **FRENTE A** *or* **ANTE algo** to react TO sth

reaccionario -ria *adj/m,f* reactionary

reacio -cia *adj* reluctant

reactor *m* **(a)** (Fís) reactor; **~ nuclear** nuclear reactor **(b)** (Aviac) (motor) jet engine; (avión) jet (plane)

readmitir [I1] *vt* ⟨trabajador⟩ to reemploy; ⟨alumno⟩ to readmit

reafirmar [A1] *vt* to reaffirm, reassert

reajuste *m* adjustment; **~ ministerial** cabinet reshuffle; **~ salarial** wage settlement

real *adj* **(a)** (verdadero, no ficticio): **un hecho ~** a true story; **en la vida ~** in real life; **historias de la vida ~** real-life *o* true-life stories **(b)** (de la realeza) royal; **porque me da la ~ gana** (fam) because I damn well want to (colloq)
■ *m* **(a)** (Hist) real (*old Spanish coin*); **no valer un ~** (fam) to be worth nothing **(b)** (Fin) real (*Brazilian unit of currency*) **(c)** **reales** *mpl* (AmC fam) (dinero) cash (colloq)

realce *m*: **dar ~ A algo** ⟨a belleza/figura⟩ to enhance sth; ⟨a ocasión⟩ to add luster TO sth

realeza *f* royalty; **la ~** (personas) the royal family

realidad *f* reality; **la ~ paraguaya** the reality of life *o* of the situation in Paraguay; **esa es la dura ~** those are the harsh facts; **en ~** in reality, actually

realismo *m* realism

realista *adj* (pragmático) realistic; (Art, Lit, Fil) realist
■ *mf* realist

realizable *adj* feasible, practicable

realización *f* **1** (de tarea) carrying out, execution (frml); (de sueños, deseos) fulfillment*, realization **2** (Cin, TV) production

realizado -da *adj* fulfilled*

realizador -dora *m,f* producer

realizar [A4] *vt* **(a)** ⟨tarea⟩ to carry out, execute (frml); ⟨viaje/visita⟩ to make; ⟨entrevista/ pruebas⟩ to conduct; ⟨encuesta/investigación⟩ to carry out; ⟨experimento⟩ to perform, do; ⟨compra/ inversión⟩ to make; **realizó una magnífica labor** she did a magnificent job **(b)** ⟨ambiciones/ ilusiones⟩ to fulfill*, realize
■ **realizarse** *v pron* «sueños/ilusiones» to come true, be realized; «persona» to fulfill* oneself

realmente *adv* really, in fact

realzar [A4] *vt* ⟨belleza/figura⟩ to enhance, set off; ⟨color⟩ to highlight, bring out

reanimar [A1] *vt* to revive
■ **reanimarse** *v pron* (recobrar fuerzas) to revive; (recobrar el conocimiento) to come to *o* around

reanudar [A1] *vt* (frml) ⟨conversaciones/ negociaciones/viaje⟩ to resume; ⟨hostilidades⟩ to renew, resume; ⟨amistad/relación⟩ to renew, revive
■ **reanudarse** *v pron* to resume

reaparición *f* (de publicación, persona) reappearance; (de artista) comeback

reapertura *f* reopening

rearme *m* rearmament

reata *f* **(a)** (Méx) (cuerda) rope; (Agr) lasso **(b)** (Col) (correa) cartridge belt

reavivar [A1] *vt* to revive
■ **reavivarse** *v pron* to be revived

rebaja *f* **(a)** (descuento) discount, reduction; **nos hicieron una ~ del 10%** they gave us a 10% discount *o* reduction; **de ~** reduced **(b)** **rebajas** *fpl* (saldos) sale, sales (*pl*); **están de ~s** there's a sale on, they're having a sale

rebajar [A1] *vt* **1** ⟨precio⟩ to lower, bring ... down; ⟨artículo⟩ to reduce; **me rebajó $200** he took $200 off **2** ⟨peso/kilos⟩ to lose

■ ~ *vi* (humillar) to degrade, be degrading

■ **rebajarse** *v pron* ~se A hacer algo to lower oneself TO doing sth; ~se ANTE algn to humble oneself BEFORE sb

rebalsarse [A1] *v pron* (CS) «*agua/cauce/vaso*» to overflow; **se rebalsó el río** the river burst its banks

rebanada *f* slice

rebanar [A1] *vt* to slice, cut

rebaño *m* (de ovejas) flock; (de cabras) herd

rebasar [A1] *vt* **(a)** (sobrepasar) ⟨*límite de velocidad*⟩ to exceed, go over; ⟨*cifras previstas*⟩ to exceed; ⟨*punto*⟩ to go beyond; **el agua ha rebasado el límite** the water has risen above the limit **(b)** (Méx) (Auto) to pass, overtake

■ ~ *vi* (Méx) to pass, overtake (BrE)

rebatir [I1] *vt* to refute

rebeca *f* (Esp) cardigan

rebelarse [A1] *v pron* to rebel

rebelde *adj* **(a)** ⟨*tropas/ejército*⟩ rebel (*before n*) **(b)** ⟨*niño/carácter*⟩ unruly, rebellious **(c)** ⟨*tos*⟩ persistent; ⟨*mancha*⟩ stubborn

■ *mf* (Mil, Pol) rebel

rebeldía *f* (cualidad) rebelliousness

rebelión *f* rebellion, uprising

reblandecer [E3] *vt* to soften

■ **reblandecerse** *v pron* to become *o* go soft

rebobinar [A1] *vt* to rewind

rebosante *adj* ~ DE algo ⟨*de alegría/optimismo*⟩ brimming WITH sth; ⟨*de vino/agua*⟩ filled to the brim WITH sth

rebosar [A1] *vi* **(a)** ~ DE algo ⟨*de felicidad/entusiasmo*⟩ to be brimming *o* bubbling over WITH sth; ⟨*de salud*⟩ to be bursting *o* brimming WITH sth **(b)** «*agua/embalse*» to overflow

■ ~ *vt* ⟨*alegría/felicidad*⟩: **rebosaba felicidad** she was radiant with happiness

rebotar [A1] *vi* «*pelota/piedra*» to bounce; «*bala*» to ricochet

rebote *m* **(a)** (al golpear algo): **la pelota dio un** ~ **en el poste** the ball bounced off the post; **de** ~ «*pelota*» ⟨*pegar/entrar*⟩ on the rebound; **la bala le dio de** ~ he was hit by a ricochet **(b)** (en baloncesto) rebound

rebozar [A4] *vt* to coat ... in batter (*o* in egg and breadcrumbs *etc*)

rebozo *m* (AmL) (Indum) shawl, wrap

rebuscado -da *adj* ⟨*explicación*⟩ over-elaborate, overcomplicated; ⟨*ejemplo/argumento*⟩ far-fetched; ⟨*estilo*⟩ affected

rebuscar [A2] *vi*: **rebuscó entre los papeles** he searched through the papers; **rebuscaba en la basura** he was rummaging about in the garbage

rebuznar [A1] *vi* to bray

recadero -ra *m, f* messenger, runner

recado *m* **(a)** (mensaje) message; **le mandó** ~ **de que volviera** she sent word that he should return **(b)** (Esp) (encargo, diligencia) errand; **hacer un** ~ to run an errand

recaer [E16] *vi* [1] «*enfermo*» to have *o* suffer a relapse [2] **(a)** «*sospechas/responsabilidad*» ~ SOBRE algn to fall ON sb **(b)** «*premio/nombramiento*» ~ EN algn to go TO sb

recaída *f* relapse

recalcar [A2] *vt* to stress, emphasize

recalentamiento *m* overheating; ~ **global** global warming

recalentar [A5] *vt* **(a)** ⟨*motor*⟩ to cause ... to overheat **(b)** ⟨*comida*⟩ to heat up, warm up; **me dio un guiso recalentado** he gave me some reheated stew

■ **recalentarse** *v pron* to overheat, become overheated

recámara *f* (Méx) (dormitorio) bedroom; (muebles) bedroom furniture

recamarera *f* (Méx) chambermaid

recambio *m* **(a)** (Auto, Mec) spare (part); **rueda de** ~ spare wheel **(b)** (de bolígrafo) refill

recapacitar [A1] *vi* to reconsider, think again; ~ SOBRE algo to reconsider sth

recargable *adj* ⟨*batería/pila*⟩ rechargeable; ⟨*encendedor/pluma*⟩ refillable

recargado -da *adj* ⟨*decoración*⟩ overelaborate; ⟨*texto*⟩ overwritten

recargar [A3] *vt* ⟨*batería*⟩ to recharge; ⟨*encendedor/estilográfica*⟩ to refill; ⟨*arma/programa*⟩ to reload

■ **recargarse** *v pron* (Col, Méx, Ven) (apoyarse) ~se CONTRA algo to lean AGAINST sth

recargo *m* surcharge; **sin** ~ at no extra charge

recatado -da *adj* (pudoroso) demure, modest

recato *m* (pudor) modesty

recauchar, (Esp) **recauchutar** [A1] *vt* to retread, remold*

recaudación *f* **(a)** (acción) collection **(b)** (ganancia — en tienda) takings (*pl*); (— en cine) box office receipts (*pl*); (— en estadio) gate

recaudador -dora *m,f*: *tb* ~ **de impuestos** tax collector

recaudar [A1] *vt* to collect

recelo *m* suspicion, distrust; **con** ~ distrustfully

recepción *f* (en general) reception; (de mercancías) receipt (frml)

recepcionista *mf* receptionist

receptivo -va *adj* receptive

receptor -tora *m,f* [1] (Med, Ling) recipient [2] (Dep) (en fútbol americano) receiver; (en béisbol) catcher [3] **receptor** *m* (Rad) radio, receiver; (TV) television (receiver *o* set)

recesión *f* recession

receso *m* (AmL) recess

receta *f* (Coc) recipe; (Med) prescription

recetar [A1] *vt* to prescribe

rechazar [A4] *vt* **(a)** ⟨*invitación/propuesta/individuo*⟩ to reject; ⟨*moción/enmienda*⟩ to defeat; ⟨*oferta/trabajo*⟩ to turn down **(b)** ⟨*ataque/enemigo*⟩ to repel, repulse **(c)** (Med) ⟨*órgano*⟩ to reject

rechazo *m* (de invitación, individuo, órgano) rejection; (de moción, enmienda) defeat

rechifla *f* whistling (*as a sign of disapproval*), ≈booing

rechinar [A1] *vi* «*polea/bisagra*» to creak, squeak; **le rechinan los dientes** he grinds his teeth

rechinón *m* (Méx) screech

rechistar [A1] *vi* ▶ CHISTAR

rechoncho -cha *adj* (fam) dumpy (colloq), short and fat

rechupete (fam): **de rechupete** (*loc adj*) «*comida*» delicious, scrumptious (colloq)

recibidor *m* entrance hall

recibimiento *m* reception

recibir [I1] *vt* (en general) to receive; **recibió muchos regalos** she got lots of gifts; **reciba un atento saludo de ...** (Corresp) sincerely yours (AmE), yours faithfully/sincerely (BrE); **~ a algn con los brazos abiertos** to welcome sb with open arms; **van a ir a ~lo** they are going to meet him; **el encargado la ~á enseguida** the manager will see you right away

■ **recibirse** *v pron* (AmL) (Educ) to graduate; **~se DE algo** to qualify AS sth

recibo *m* (en general) receipt; (de luz, teléfono) bill

reciclado, reciclaje *m* **(a)** (de papel, vidrio) recycling **(b)** (de persona) retraining

reciclar [A1] *vt* «*papel/vidrio*» to recycle

recién *adv* 1 (con participio): **pan ~ hecho** freshly baked bread; **está ~ pintado** it's just been painted; **tiene un año ~ cumplido** he's just one; **los ~ casados** the newlyweds; **un ~ nacido** a newborn baby 2 (AmL) **(a)** (hace poco tiempo) just; **~ llegaron** they have just arrived **(b)** (solo ahora) only just; **~ me entero** I've only just found out **(c)** (sólo) only; **~ voy por la página 20** I'm only on page 20; **~ el lunes iré** the first day I'll be able to go is Monday

reciente *adj* «*acontecimiento/foto*» recent; «*huella*» fresh; **en fecha ~** recently

recinto *m* enclosure; **el público abandonó el ~** the public left the premises/building; **~ ferial** (de muestras) showground, exhibition site; (de atracciones) fairground

recio -cia *adj* «*hombre/aspecto*» robust, sturdy

recipiente *m* (utensilio) container, receptacle (frml)

recíproco -ca *adj* reciprocal

recital *m* recital

recitar [A1] *vt* to recite

reclamación *f* **(a)** (petición, demanda) claim **(b)** (queja) complaint

reclamar [A1] *vt* **(a)** «*persona*» «*derecho/indemnización*» to claim; (con insistencia) to demand **(b)** «*situación/problema*» to require, demand

■ **~** *vi* to complain; **reclamó ante los tribunales** she took the matter to court

réclame *m or f* (AmL) commercial, advertisement; **~ publicitario** advertising

reclamo *m* **(a)** (de pájaro) call **(b)** (esp AmL) (para atraer la atención, provocar interés) lure **(c)** (AmL) (queja) complaint

reclinable *adj* reclining (*before n*)

reclinar [A1] *vt* to rest, lean

■ **reclinarse** *v pron* to lean back; **reclinado contra la pared** leaning against the wall

recluir [I20] *vt* (en prisión) to imprison; (en hospital psiquiátrico), to intern (frml)

reclusión *f* imprisonment; **~ perpetua** life imprisonment

recluso -sa *m,f* prisoner, inmate

recluta *mf* (Mil) recruit; (en servicio militar) conscript, recruit

reclutar [A1] *vt* to recruit

recobrar [A1] *vt* **(a)** «*confianza/conocimiento*» to regain; «*salud/vista*» to recover; **~ las fuerzas** to recover one's strength **(b)** «*dinero/botín/joyas*» to recover, retrieve **(c)** «*ciudad/plaza fuerte*» to recapture

■ **recobrarse** *v pron* **~se DE algo** (de enfermedad/susto) to recover FROM sth, get over sth; (de pérdidas económicas) to recoup sth

recogedor *m* dustpan

recogepelotas *mf* (*pl* **~**) (*m*) ball boy; (*f*) ball girl

recoger [E6] *vt* 1 **(a)** (levantar) «*objeto/papeles*» to pick up; **recogí el agua con un trapo** I mopped the water up **(b)** «*casa/habitación*» to straighten (up) (AmE), to tidy (up) (BrE); «*platos*» to clear away; **~ la mesa** to clear the table 2 **(a)** «*dinero/firmas*» to collect **(b)** «*deberes/cuadernos*» to collect, take in **(c)** «*trigo/maíz*» to harvest, gather in; «*fruta*» to pick; «*flores/hongos*» to pick, gather **(d)** «*tienda de campaña/vela*» to take down **(e)** «*pelo*» to tie ... back; **le recogió el pelo en una cola** he tied her hair back in a ponytail 3 (ir a buscar) «*persona*» to pick up, fetch, collect; «*paquete*» to collect, pick up; «*basura*» to collect; «*equipaje*» to reclaim

■ **~** *vi* (guardar) to clear up, to straighten up (AmE), to tidy up (BrE)

■ **recogerse** *v pron* «*pelo*» to tie up; «*falda*» to gather up

recogida *f* **(a)** (de basura, correo) collection **(b)** (Agr) harvest

recolección *f* **(a)** (Agr) harvest **(b)** (de fondos, dinero) collection

recolectar [A1] *vt* **(a)** «*trigo*» to harvest, gather in; «*fruta*» to pick, harvest **(b)** «*dinero*» to collect

recomendación *f* **(a)** (consejo) advice **(b)** (para empleo) reference, recommendation

recomendado -da 1 **(a)** «*método/producto*» recommended **(b)** (apropiado) suitable; **no recomendada para menores de 15 años** not suitable for under-15s 2 (Col, Ur) «*carta*» registered

recomendar [A5] *vt* **(a)** «*libro/restaurante/persona*» to recommend **(b)** (aconsejar) to advise; **no te lo recomiendo** I wouldn't advise it

recomienda, recomiendas, etc ▶ RECOMENDAR

recompensa *f* reward

recompensar [A1] *vt* to reward

reconciliación *f* reconciliation

reconciliar [A1] *vt* to reconcile

■ **reconciliarse** *v pron* **(a)** **~se (CON algn)** to make (it) up (WITH sb) **(b)** **~se CON algo** «*con idea/postura*» to reconcile oneself TO sth

r

reconfortante adj ‹palabras/pensamientos› comforting; ‹baño› relaxing

reconfortar [A1] vt to comfort

reconocer [E3] vt 1 (a) ‹hecho/error› to admit; ‹verdad/autoridad› to acknowledge (b) ‹hijo/gobierno/derecho› to recognize 2 (identificar) ‹persona/letra/voz› to recognize 3 ‹terreno› to reconnoiter*

reconocimiento m (a) (en general) recognition (b) (Med) tb ~ médico medical (examination) (c) (de territorio) reconnaissance

reconquista f reconquest; la R~ the Reconquest

reconquistar [A1] vt ‹territorio› to reconquer, regain; ‹cariño/afecto› to win back

reconstituyente m tonic, restorative

reconstruir [I20] vt to reconstruct

reconversión f (a) (reestructuración) restructuring, rationalization (b) (de un trabajador) tb ~ profesional retraining

reconvertir [I11] vt (a) ‹industria› to rationalize, restructure (b) ‹profesional› to retrain
■ **reconvertirse** v pron (a) «industria» to be rationalized o restructured (b) «profesional» to retrain

recopilación f compilation, collection

recopilar [A1] vt to compile, gather together

récord, record adj inv record (before n)
■ m (pl -cords) record; batir un ~ to break a record; posee el ~ mundial she is the world record holder

recordar [A10] vt 1 (a) ‹nombre/fecha› to remember, recall; recuerdo que lo puse ahí I remember o recall putting it there (b) (rememorar) ‹niñez/pasado› to remember 2 (a) (traer a la memoria) ~le A algn algo/QUE haga algo to remind sb ABOUT sth/to do sth; les recuerdo que ... I would like to remind you that ... (b) (por asociación, parecido) to remind; me recuerdas a tu hermano you remind me of your brother
■ ~ vi (acordarse) to remember; si mal no recuerdo if I remember right

recorrer [E1] vt (a) (viajar por): recorrí toda España I traveled o went all over Spain; (como turista) I toured all over Spain; ~ mundo to travel all around the world; recorrimos toda la costa we traveled the whole length of the coast (b) ‹distancia/trayecto› to cover, do (c) (con la mirada): recorrió la sala con la mirada he looked around the hall

recorrido m (a) (viaje): un ~ por Perú a trip around Peru; (turístico) a tour around Peru (b) (trayecto) route; cubrir el ~ to cover the route (c) (de proyectil) trajectory; (de balón) path (d) (en golf) round; (en esquí) run

recortable adj cutout (before n)

recortar [A1] vt 1 (a) ‹figura/artículo/anuncio› to cut out (b) ‹pelo/puntas› to trim 2 ‹gastos/plantilla› to reduce

recorte m 1 (de periódico, revista) cutting, clipping 2 (Fin) (acción) cutting; (efecto) cut, reduction

recostar [A10] vt (apoyar) to lean
■ **recostarse** v pron (a) (acostarse) to lie down; recuéstate en el almohadón lie back on the pillow

(b) (apoyarse) to lean; recostados en el escritorio leaning on the desk; estaba recostado en un sillón he was sitting back in an armchair

recoveco m: un camino lleno de ~s a road full of twists and turns; en todos los ~s de la casa in every nook and cranny of the house

recreativo -va adj recreational

recreo m (a) (diversión): nos servía de ~ it served as entertainment; viaje de ~ pleasure trip (b) (en el colegio) recess (AmE), break (BrE)

recriminar [A1] vt to reproach

recta f (Mat) straight line; (Dep) straight; ~ final (Dep) home stretch

rectángulo m rectangle

rectificar [A2] vt to correct
■ ~ vi (corregirse) to correct oneself

rectitud f rectitude (frml), honesty

recto¹ -ta adj (a) ‹línea/nariz/falda› straight (b) (honrado) honest, upright

recto² m (Anat) rectum
■ adv straight; todo ~ straight on

rector -tora m,f (de universidad) rector (AmE), vice-chancellor (BrE)

recuadro m box

recubrir [I33] vt ~ algo DE or CON algo to cover sth WITH sth

recuento m (de votos) recount

recuerdo m 1 (a) (reminiscencia) memory (b) (souvenir) souvenir; (regalo) memento, keepsake; un ~ de familia a family heirloom 2 recuerdos mpl regards (pl), best wishes (pl); dale ~s give him my regards

recuperación f (a) (en general) recovery (b) (Esp) (Educ) tb examen de ~ retake, makeup (exam) (AmE)

recuperar [A1] vt (a) ‹dinero/joyas/botín› to recover, get back; ‹pérdidas› to recoup (b) ‹vista/salud› to recover; ‹confianza› to regain; ~ fuerzas to get one's strength back (c) (compensar) ‹tiempo perdido› to make up for; tienes que ~ esas tres horas you have to make up those three hours (d) ‹examen/asignatura› to retake, make up (AmE)
■ **recuperarse** v pron ~se DE algo ‹de enfermedad› to recover FROM sth, recuperate FROM sth (frml); ‹de sorpresa/desgracia› to get over sth, recover FROM sth

recurrir [I1] vi (frente a problema) ~ A algn to turn TO sb; ~ A algo to resort TO sth

recursivo adj (Col) resourceful

recurso m 1 (medio): agoté todos los ~s I exhausted all the options; como último ~ as a last resort; un hombre de ~s a resourceful man 2 recursos mpl (medios económicos — de país) resources (pl); (— de persona) means (pl); ~s energéticos energy resources (pl); ~s humanos human resources (pl); ~s naturales natural resources (pl)

red f 1 (a) (para pescar) net (b) (Dep) net (c) (para pelo) hairnet (d) (en tren) (luggage) rack 2 (de comunicaciones, emisoras, transportes) network; (de comercios, empresas) chain, network; (de espionaje, contrabando) ring 3 (de electricidad) power supply, mains; (de gas) mains 4 la Red (Inf) the Net

redacción f 1 (a) (de carta) writing; (de

borrador) drafting; (de tratado) drawing-up, drafting **(b)** (lenguaje, estilo) wording, phrasing **2** (Educ) composition, essay **3** (Period) **(a)** (acción) writing **(b)** (equipo) editorial staff o team **(c)** (oficina) editorial department o office

redactar [A1] vt ‹informe/artículo/composición› to write; ‹acuerdo/tratado› to draw up
■ ~ vi: **redacta muy bien** she writes very well

redactor -tora m,f editor; ~ **jefe** editor in chief

redada f raid

redentor -tora adj redeeming
■ m,f redeemer

redimir [I1] vt to redeem

redoblar [A1] vt (aumentar) ‹esfuerzos/críticas› to redouble; ‹vigilancia› to step up, tighten
■ ~ vi «tambor» to roll

redoble m drumroll

redoma f (Ven) (Auto) traffic circle (AmE), roundabout (BrE)

redomado -da adj utter, out-and-out

redonda f **1** (Mús) semibreve **2** **a la redonda**: **en diez metros a la** ~ within a ten meter radius; **se oyó a varios kilómetros a la** ~ it could be heard for miles around

redondear [A1] vt **(a)** (dar forma curva) to round (off) **(b)** ‹cifra/número› to round off; (por lo alto) to round up; (por lo bajo) to round down
■ ~ vi: **digamos 200, para** ~ let's make it a round 200

redondel m (figura circular) ring

redondela f (Andes) ▶ REDONDEL

redondo -da adj **1** ‹cara/espejo› round; **caer (se)** ~ (desplomarse) to collapse; **en** ~ ‹girar› (right) around **2** ‹cifra/número› round **3** (perfecto): **un negocio** ~ a great o excellent deal; **nos salió todo** ~ everything turned out perfectly for us **4** (Méx) ‹boleto/pasaje› return (before n), round-trip (before n) (AmE)

reducción f reduction; ~ **de impuestos** tax cuts, reduction in taxes; **una** ~ **de personal** a reduction o cutback in the workforce

reducido -da adj **(a)** (pequeño) ‹espacio/ presupuesto› limited; ‹tamaño› small **(b)** (rebajado, achicado) ‹precio/fotografía› reduced; **un número** ~ **de personas** a small number of people; **trabaja jornada reducida** she is on short-time (working)

reducidor -dora m,f (AmS) (de objetos robados) receiver, fence (colloq)

reducir [I6] vt **1** **(a)** ‹gastos/costos› to cut, reduce; ‹velocidad/producción/consumo› to reduce; **debería** ~ **el consumo de sal** you should cut down on salt; ~ **algo a algo** to reduce sth TO sth; ~ **algo EN algo** to reduce sth BY sth **(b)** ‹fotocopia/fotografía› to reduce **2** **(a)** (transformar): ~ **los gramos a miligramos** to convert the grams to milligrams; **quedaron reducidos a cenizas** they were reduced to ashes **(b)** (AmS) ‹objeto robado› to receive, fence (colloq) **3** (dominar) ‹enemigo/rebeldes› to subdue; ‹ladrón› to overpower
■ **reducirse** v pron: **todo se reduce a tener tacto** it all comes down to being tactful

redundancia f (Ling) tautology, redundancy; **valga la** ~ if you'll forgive the repetition

redundante adj redundant

reedición f reissue, reprint

reeditar [A1] vt to reprint, reissue

reelegir [I8] vt to reelect

reembolsar [A1] vt ‹gastos› to refund, reimburse (frml); ‹depósito› to refund; ‹préstamo› to repay

reembolso m (de gastos) refund, reimbursement (frml); (de depósito) refund; (de préstamo) repayment; **contra** ~ cash on delivery, COD

reemplazar [A4] vt ‹persona› (durante período limitado) to substitute for, stand in for; (durante más tiempo) to replace; ‹aparato/pieza› to replace; ~ **algo/a algn POR** or **CON algo/algn** to replace sth/ sb WITH o BY sth/sb

reemplazo m (durante período limitado) substitution; (durante más tiempo) replacement; **entró en** ~ **del jugador lesionado** he came on as a substitute for the injured player

reencarnación f reincarnation

reencarnarse [A1] v pron to be reincarnated; ~ **EN algn/algo** to be reincarnated AS sb/sth

reencuentro m reunion

reestreno m (de película) rerelease; (de obra teatral) revival

reestructurar [A1] vt to restructure

refacción f **1** (AmS) (para ampliar, mejorar) refurbishment **2** (Méx) (pieza de repuesto) spare part; **llanta de** ~ spare tire

refaccionar [A1] vt (AmS) to refurbish

refaccionaria f (Méx) (tienda) auto spares store; (taller) garage

referencia f reference; **hacer** ~ **a algo** to refer to o mention sth; **con** ~ **a ...** with reference to ...; **número de** ~ reference number; **tener buenas** ~s to have good references

referéndum m (pl -dums) referendum; **someter algo a** ~ to hold a referendum on sth

referente adj: **las noticias** ~s **al accidente** the news about the accident; **en lo** ~ **a ...** regarding ...

réferi, referí mf (AmL) referee

referirse [I11] v pron **(a)** (aludir) ~**se A algo/ algn** to refer TO sth/sb **(b)** (estar relacionado con): **por lo que se refiere a este asunto ...** with regard to this matter ..., as far as this matter is concerned ...

refilón: **de refilón** (loc adv): **lo miré de** ~ I gave him a sidelong glance; **la vi solo de** ~ I just caught a glimpse of her

refinado -da adj ‹persona/modales› refined; ‹ironía› subtle

refinar [A1] vt to refine; ‹estilo› to polish

refinería f refinery

reflector m **(a)** (pantalla reflectante) reflector **(b)** (foco) (Teat) spotlight; (Dep) floodlight; (Mil) searchlight; (en monumento) floodlight

reflejar [A1] vt to reflect
■ **reflejarse** v pron **(a)** «imagen» to be reflected **(b)** «emoción/cansancio/duda» to show

reflejo¹ -ja adj reflex (before n)

reflejo² m **1** **(a)** (en general) reflection; (luz reflejada) reflected light **(b)** **reflejos** mpl (en peluquería) highlights (pl) **2** (Fisiol) reflex

reflexionar [A1] vi to reflect (frml); **¿has** ····⟩

reflexionado bien? have you thought it over *o* through carefully?; ~ **SOBRE** algo to think ABOUT sth, reflect on sth (frml)
reflexivo -va *adj* (a) (Ling, Mat) reflexive (b) ⟨*persona*⟩ thoughtful, reflective
reflujo *m* (de marea) ebb (tide)
reforestación *f* reforestation
reforestar [A1] *vt* to reforest
reforma *f* (a) (en general) reform; **la R~** (Relig) the Reformation (b) (en edificio, traje) alteration
reformar [A1] *vt* (a) (en general) to reform (b) ⟨*casa/edificio*⟩ to make alterations to
■ **reformarse** *v pron* to mend one's ways
reformatorio *m* reformatory
reforzar [A11] *vt* ⟨*puerta/costura*⟩ to reinforce; ⟨*guardia*⟩ to increase, strengthen; ⟨*relaciones*⟩ to reinforce; ⟨*medidas de seguridad*⟩ to step up, tighten
refrán *m* saying, proverb; **como dice el ~** as the saying goes
refregar [A7] *vt* ⟨*puños/cuello*⟩ to scrub
refrendar [A1] *vt* (Col, Méx) ⟨*pasaporte*⟩ to renew
refrescante *adj* refreshing
refrescar [A2] *vt* (a) ⟨*bebida*⟩ to cool; ⟨*ambiente*⟩ to make ... fresher *o* cooler (b) ⟨*conocimientos*⟩ to brush up (on)
■ ~ *v impers* to turn cooler
refresco *m* soft drink, soda (AmE)
refrigerador *m* (a) (nevera) refrigerator, fridge (b) (del aire acondicionado) cooling unit
refrigeradora *f* (Col, Per) refrigerator, fridge
refrigerar [A1] *vt* (a) ⟨*alimentos/bebidas*⟩ to refrigerate (b) ⟨*motor*⟩ to cool; ⟨*cine/bar*⟩ to air-condition; **ⓢ** local **refrigerado** air-conditioned premises
refrito *m* (Coc): **un ~** de tomate y cebolla fried onions and tomato
refuerzo *m* (a) (para puerta, pared, costura) reinforcement (b) (de vacuna) booster (c) **refuerzos** *mpl* (Mil) reinforcements (*pl*)
refugiado -da *adj* refugee (*before n*)
■ *m,f* refugee
refugiar [A1] *vt* to give ... refuge
■ **refugiarse** *v pron* to take refuge; **~se DE** algo ⟨*de bombardeo/ataque*⟩ to take refuge FROM sth; ⟨*de lluvia/tormenta*⟩ to take shelter FROM sth
refugio *m* (a) (de la lluvia, bombardeo) shelter; (en montaña) refuge, shelter (b) (de un ataque, perseguidores) refuge; **buscar ~** to seek refuge (c) (en calzada) traffic island
refunfuñar [A1] *vi* (fam) to grumble, grouch (colloq)
refunfuñón -ñona *adj* (fam) grouchy (colloq), grumpy (colloq)
regadera *f* (a) (para jardín) watering can (b) (Col, Méx, Ven) (de ducha) rose, shower head (AmE); (ducha) shower
regadío *m* (sistema) irrigation; **tierras de ~** irrigated land

regalado -da *adj* (a) (fam) (muy barato): **precios ~s** giveaway prices (colloq); **esos zapatos están ~s** those shoes are dirt cheap *o* are a steal (colloq) (b) (Chi, Méx, Ven fam) (muy fácil) easy
regalar [A1] *vt* (a) (obsequiar): **¿qué te ~on para tu cumpleaños?** what did you get for your birthday?; **le ~on un reloj de oro** he was given a gold watch (b) (vender muy barato) to sell ... at bargain prices
regaliz *m* licorice (AmE), liquorice (BrE)
regalo *m* (a) (obsequio) gift, present (b) (cosa barata) steal (colloq) (c) (deleite, festín) treat
regalón -lona *adj* (CS fam) spoiled
■ *m,f* (CS fam) spoilt brat (colloq)
regalonear [A1] *vt* (CS fam) to spoil
■ *vi* (CS fam): **le encanta ~ con su abuela** she loves being made a fuss of by her grandmother
regañadientes: **a regañadientes** (*loc adv*) reluctantly, unwillingly
regañar [A1] *vt* (esp AmL) to scold, to tell ... off (colloq)
■ ~ *vi* (Esp) (pelearse) to quarrel
regañina, (Méx) **regañiza** *f* (fam) scolding, talking-to (colloq), telling-off (colloq)
regaño *m* (AmL fam) scolding, telling-off (colloq)
regar [A7] *vt* (a) ⟨*planta/jardín*⟩ to water; ⟨*tierra/campo*⟩ to irrigate; ⟨*calle*⟩ to hose down (b) ⟨*río*⟩ to water (c) (AmC, Ven) ⟨*noticia/versión*⟩ to spread
regata *f* (carrera) yacht race; (serie de carreras) regatta
regate *m* (Esp) (en fútbol) feint
regatear [A1] *vi* (Com) to bargain, haggle
■ ~ *vt* ① (escatimar): **no han regateado esfuerzos para ...** no efforts have been spared to ...; **sin ~ medios** whatever it takes ② (Esp) (Dep) to get past, swerve past
regencia *f* (en lugar del soberano) regency
regenerar [A1] *vt* to regenerate
■ **regenerarse** *v pron* (a) (Biol, Tec) to be regenerated (b) ⟨*persona*⟩ to be reformed
regente *mf* regent
régimen *m* ① (dieta) diet; **hacer ~** to be on a diet; **ponerse a ~** to go on a diet ② (Pol) regime
regimiento *m* (Mil) regiment
regio -gia *adj* (a) (majestuoso) regal (b) (Col, CS fam) (estupendo) great (colloq); **te queda ~** it looks fantastic on you (colloq); **me viene ~** it suits me fine
región *f* region
regional *adj* regional
regir [I8] *vt* to govern
■ ~ *vi* ⟨*ley/disposición*⟩ to be in force, be valid; **ese horario ya no rige** that timetable is no longer valid
■ **regirse** *v pron* **~se POR** algo ⟨*sociedad*⟩ to be governed BY sth; ⟨*economía/mercado*⟩ to be controlled BY sth *o* subject to sth
registrar [A1] *vt* ① (a) ⟨*nacimiento/defunción/patente*⟩ to register (b) ⟨*sonido/temperatura*⟩ to record; ⟨*temblor*⟩ to register ② ⟨*equipaje/lugar/*

· ·

AmC	Central America	Arg	Argentina	Cu	Cuba
AmL	Latin America	Bol	Bolivia	Ec	Ecuador
AmS	South America	Chi	Chile	Esp	Spain
Andes	Andean Region	CS	Southern Cone	Méx	Mexico

Per	Peru
RPI	River Plate Area
Ur	Uruguay
Ven	Venezuela

persona⟩ to search; **estaba registrando mis cajones** (fam) he was going through my drawers **3** (Méx) *⟨carta⟩* to register
■ **registrarse** *v pron* (inscribirse) to register; (en hotel) to register, check in

registro *m* **1** (libro) register; (acción de anotar) registration; (cosa anotada) record, entry; ~ **civil** (oficina) registry, registry office (BrE) **2** (por la policía) search; **orden de** ~ search warrant

regla *f* (a) (utensilio) ruler (b) (norma) rule; **todo está en** ~ everything is in order; **por** ~ **general** as a (general) rule (c) (menstruación) period; **tengo la** ~ I have my period

reglamentario -ria *adj* ⟨*horario*⟩ set (*before n*); ⟨*uniforme/arma*⟩ regulation (*before n*)

reglamento *m* rules (*pl*), regulations (*pl*)

regocijarse [A1] *v pron* to rejoice; ~ **DE** *or* **POR algo** (por buena noticia) to rejoice AT sth; (por mal ajeno) to take delight IN sth, delight IN sth

regocijo *m* (a) (júbilo, alborozo) rejoicing; (alegría) joy, delight; **sintió gran** ~ **al verla** he was delighted to see her (b) (ante el mal ajeno) pleasure

regodearse [A1] *v pron* (a) (complacerse) to delight in, take great delight in; **se regodea haciéndome sufrir** he delights in making me suffer; ~ **EN** *or* **CON algo** to delight IN sth, gloat OVER sth (b) (Chi) (al elegir) to hesitate

regordete -ta *adj* (fam) chubby

regresar [A1] *vi* to return, come/go back; **no sé cuándo va a** ~ I don't know when he'll be back
■ ~ *vt* (AmL exc CS) (a) ⟨*libro/llaves*⟩ to return, give back (b) ⟨*persona*⟩ to send ... back
■ **regresarse** *v pron* (AmL exc RPl) to return, go/come back; **ya se regresó** she's back now

regreso *m* (a) (vuelta) return; **emprendió el** ~ she set off on the return journey *o* trip; **de** ~ **paramos en León** on the way back we stopped in León (b) (AmL) (devolución) return

reguero *m* (rastro) trail

regulable *adj* adjustable

regulador *m* regulator

regular¹ *adj* **1** (en general) regular **2** (a) (no muy bien): **¿qué tal te va? — regular** how's it going? — so-so; **¿qué tal la película? — regular** how was the movie? — nothing special (b) (de tamaño) medium-sized, middling
■ *m* (calificación) fair

regular² [A1] *vt* **1** (a) ⟨*espejo/asiento*⟩ to adjust (b) ⟨*caudal/temperatura/velocidad*⟩ to regulate, control **2** ⟨*ley/norma*⟩ to regulate

regularidad *f* regularity; **con** ~ regularly

regusto *m* aftertaste

rehabilitación *f* (a) (de enfermo, delincuente) rehabilitation (b) (en cargo) reinstatement (c) (de vivienda) renovation, restoration

rehabilitar [A1] *vt* (a) ⟨*paciente/delincuente*⟩ to rehabilitate (b) (en cargo) to reinstate (c) ⟨*vivienda/local*⟩ to renovate, restore

rehacer [E18] *vt* (volver a hacer) to redo; **trató de** ~ **su vida** she tried to rebuild her life
■ **rehacerse** *v pron* ~**se DE algo** to get over sth

rehén *m* hostage

rehogar [A3] *vt* to fry ... lightly

rehuir [I21] *vt* to shy away from

rehusar [A23] *vt/vi* to refuse

■ **rehusarse** *v pron* (esp AmL) to refuse

reilón -lona *adj* (Per, Ven fam) smiley (colloq)

reimpresión *f* (a) (acción) reprinting (b) (obra) reprint

reimprimir [I36] *vt* to reprint

reina *f* queen; ~ **de belleza** beauty queen

reinado *m* reign

reinante *adj* (a) ⟨*casa/dinastía*⟩ reigning (b) ⟨*frío/lluvias*⟩ prevailing; **el malestar** ~ **en el partido** the unease prevailing in the party

reinar [A1] *vi* (a) ⟨*monarca/dinastía*⟩ to reign (b) «*silencio/paz*» to reign; «*terror/buen tiempo*» to prevail

reincidente *mf* reoffender

reincidir [I1] *vi* (Der) to reoffend

reincorporarse [A1] *v pron* to return; ~ **a filas** to rejoin the army

reiniciar [A1] *vt* to resume; (Inf) to reboot

reino *m* kingdom; ~ **animal** animal kingdom; **el** ~ **de la fantasía** the realm of fantasy

Reino Unido *m*: **el** ~~ the United Kingdom

reinserción *f*: *tb* ~ **social** social rehabilitation, reintegration into society

reintegrar [A1] *vt* **1** ⟨*persona*⟩ (a cargo) to reinstate; (a la comunidad) to reintegrate; ~ **a algn A** *or* **EN algo** ⟨*a cargo*⟩ to reinstate sb IN sth; ⟨*a la comunidad*⟩ to reintegrate sb INTO sth **2** (frml) ⟨*depósito*⟩ to refund, return; ⟨*gastos*⟩ to reimburse; ⟨*préstamo*⟩ to repay
■ **reintegrarse** *v pron* to return; ~**se A algo** ⟨*a trabajo/equipo*⟩ to return TO sth; ~**se en la comunidad** to reintegrate into the community

reintegro *m* (a) (en banco) withdrawal; (de depósito) refund; (de gastos) reimbursement; (de préstamo) repayment (b) (en lotería) refund (*of the ticket price*)

reír [I18] *vi* to laugh; **se echaron a** ~ they burst out laughing
■ ~ *vt* ⟨*gracia/chiste*⟩ to laugh at
■ **reírse** *v pron* to laugh; ~**se a carcajadas** to guffaw; ~**se DE algo/algn** to laugh AT sth/sb

reivindicación *f* (a) (demanda) demand, claim (b) (reconocimiento) recognition (c) (rehabilitación): **luchó por la** ~ **de su buen nombre** she fought to vindicate her good name (d) (de atentado): **la** ~ **del atentado** the claiming of responsibility for the attack

reivindicar [A2] *vt* (a) ⟨*derecho*⟩ to demand; ⟨*tierras*⟩ to claim (b) (rehabilitar) ⟨*imagen/reputación*⟩ to restore (c) ⟨*atentado*⟩ to claim responsibility for

reja *f* (a) (de ventana) grille (b) (para cercar) railing

rejego *adj* (Méx fam) ⟨*persona*⟩ mouthy (AmE), cheeky (BrE)

rejilla *f* (a) (de ventilación) grille; (Auto) grille; (del confesionario) screen; (del desagüe) grating (b) (para equipajes) luggage rack; (de horno) rack; (base de chimenea) grate

rejuntar [A1] *vt* (Méx fam) ⟨*reses*⟩ to round up; ⟨*borregos*⟩ to gather

rejuvenecer [E3] *vt* to rejuvenate
■ **rejuvenecerse** *v pron* to be rejuvenated

relación *f* **1** (a) (conexión) connection; **con** ~ **a** *or* **en** ~ **con** (con respecto a) in connection with; (en comparación con) relative to; **en** ~ **con su carta** ⋯⟶

... with regard to o regarding your letter ... **(b)**
(correspondencia): **en una ~ de diez a uno** (Mat) in a
ratio of ten to one; **una ~ causa-efecto** a
relationship of cause and effect
2 (a) (entre personas) relationship; **las relaciones
entre padres e hijos** the relationship between
parents and their children; **estoy en buenas
relaciones con él** I'm on good terms with him **(b)
relaciones** *fpl* (influencias) contacts (*pl*),
connections (*pl*); (trato comercial, diplomático)
relations (*pl*); (trato carnal) sex; **relaciones
exteriores** foreign affairs; **relaciones
prematrimoniales** premarital sex; **relaciones
públicas** (actividad) public relations (*pl*); (persona)
public relations officer; (de cantante, artista) PR;
relaciones sexuales sexual relations
3 (a) (exposición) account **(b)** (lista) list

relacionado -da *adj* **(a)** [ESTAR] ⟨temas/
ideas/hechos⟩ related, connected **(b)** ⟨persona⟩:
está muy bien ~ he is very well connected; **estar
~ CON algn/algo** to be connected WITH sb/sth

relacionar [A1] *vt* (conectar) to relate, connect;
~ algo A o CON algo to relate o connect sth TO
sth
■ **relacionarse** *v pron* **(a)** ~se CON algo ⟨con
tema/asunto⟩ to be related TO sth **(b)** ⟪persona⟫
~se CON algn to mix with sb

relajación *f* (de músculos, mente) relaxation

relajado -da *adj* **(a)** (tranquilo) relaxed **(b)**
⟨costumbres⟩ dissolute, lax

relajante *adj* **1** ⟨música/baño⟩ relaxing
2 (CS fam) (empalagoso) sickly-sweet (pej)

relajar [A1] *vt* ⟨músculo/persona/mente⟩ to relax
■ **~** *vi* ⟨ejercicio/música⟩ to be relaxing
■ **relajarse** *v pron* **1 (a)** (físicamente, mentalmente)
to relax; (tras período de tensión, mucho trabajo) to
relax, unwind **(b)** ⟪tensión⟫ to ease;
⟪ambiente⟫ to become more relaxed
2 (degenerar) ⟪costumbres/moral⟫ to decline

relajo *m* **1** (de la moral) decline **2** (esp Esp fam)
(relax): **¡qué ~!** how relaxing! **3 (a)** (Méx fam)
(persona divertida) laugh (colloq) **(b)** (persona
problemática) troublemaker

relamerse [E1] *v pron* (por algo sabroso) to lick
one's lips; (de satisfacción) to smack one's lips

relámpago *m* (Meteo) bolt o flash of lightning;
como un ~ ⟨salir/pasar⟩ like greased lightning

relatar [A1] *vt* ⟨historia/aventura⟩ to recount,
relate

relativo -va *adj* **1** (no absoluto) relative; **eso es
muy ~** that depends; **una enfermedad de relativa
gravedad** a relatively serious illness
2 (concerniente) **~ A algo** relating TO sth; **todo lo
~ a la política** anything to do with o related to
politics; **en lo ~ a este problema** with regard to
this problem

relato *m* **(a)** (historia, cuento) story, tale **(b)**
(relación) account

relax *m* relaxation

relegar [A3] *vt*: **se siente relegado** he feels left
out; **el problema quedó relegado a un segundo
plano** the matter was pushed into the
background; **relegado al olvido** consigned to
oblivion

relevante *adj* notable, outstanding

relevar [A1] *vt* **(a)** (sustituir) ⟨guarda/enfermera⟩

to relieve; ⟨jugador⟩ to replace, take over from;
~ la guardia (Mil) to change the guard **(b)**
(destituir) to remove
■ **relevarse** *v pron* to take turns, take it in
turn(s)

relevo *m* **(a)** de ~ ⟨conductor/equipo⟩ relief
(*before n*) **(b)** (Dep) *tb* **~s** relay (race)

relieve *m* **1 (a)** (Art, Geog) relief; **la costa tiene
un ~ muy accidentado** the coast is very rugged;
letras en ~ embossed letters **(b)** (parte que
sobresale): **el marco tiene un centímetro de ~** the
frame protrudes by a centimeter **2** (importancia)
prominence; **personas de ~** prominent people;
dar ~ a algo to lend (special) importance to sth;
poner de ~ to highlight

religión *f* religion

religiosidad *f* religiousness, religiosity

religioso -sa *adj* religious
■ *m,f* member of a religious order

relinchar [A1] *vi* to neigh, whinny

reliquia *f* relic; **una ~ de familia** a family
heirloom

rellano *m* (de escalera) landing; (de ladera,
montaña) shelf

rellenar [A1] *vt* **1 (a)** ⟨pavo/pimientos/cojín⟩
to stuff; ⟨pastel⟩ to fill; **~ algo DE o CON algo** to
stuff/fill sth WITH sth **(b)** ⟨agujero/grieta⟩ to fill
2 (volver a llenar) to refill **3** ⟨impreso/formulario⟩
to fill out o in; ⟨examen/discurso⟩ to pad out

relleno¹ -na *adj* ⟨pavo/pimientos⟩ stuffed;
caramelos ~s de chocolate candies with a
chocolate filling

relleno² *m* (para pasteles, tortas) filling; (para
pavo, pimientos, cojín) stuffing; (de ropa interior)
padding; (para agujeros, grietas) filler

reloj *m* (de pared, mesa) clock; (de pulsera, bolsillo)
watch; **funciona como un ~** it's going like
clockwork; **contra ~** against the clock; **~ de
arena** hourglass; **~ de pie** grandfather clock;
~ de sol sundial; **~ despertador** alarm clock

relojería *f* (tienda, taller) clockmaker's,
watchmaker's; (actividad) watchmaking

relojero -ra *m,f* (de relojes — de pulsera)
watchmaker; (— de pared, mesa) clockmaker

reluciente *adj* ⟨dientes/coche⟩ gleaming;
⟨metal/suelo⟩ shiny, shining; **una mañana ~** a
bright, sunny morning

relucir [I5] *vi* ⟪sol⟫ to shine; ⟪estrellas⟫ to
twinkle, glitter; ⟪plata/zapatos⟫ to shine, gleam;
salir/sacar a ~ to come to the surface/to bring up

relumbrante *adj* brilliant, dazzling

relumbrar [A1] *vi* to shine brightly

remachar [A1] *vt* **(a)** ⟨clavo⟩ to clinch; ⟨perno/
chapas⟩ to rivet **(b)** (recalcar) to repeat, reiterate;
(finalizar) to round off, finish off
■ **~** *vi* (en tenis) to smash; (en vóleibol) to spike

remache *m* **1** (perno) rivet **2** (en tenis) smash;
(en vóleibol) spike

remangarse [A3] *v pron* (refl) ⟨pantalones/
manga⟩ to roll up; **se remangó para lavar los
platos** he rolled up his sleeves to wash the dishes

remanso *m* pool; **un ~ de paz** a haven of
peace (liter)

remar [A1] *vi* (en bote) to row; (en canoa) to
paddle

remarcar [A2] *vt* (hacer notar) to stress, emphasize

rematado -da *adj* complete, absolute; **es un loco ~** he's a raving lunatic

rematar [A1] *vt* ⃞1 **(a)** ⟨*actuación/intervención*⟩ to round off, finish off; ⟨*negocio*⟩ to conclude, close; ⟨*torre/bastón*⟩ to top, crown; **y para ~la** (fam) and to crown *o* cap it all (colloq) **(b)** ⟨*costura*⟩ to finish off **(c)** ⟨*animal/persona*⟩ to finish off
⃞2 (en tenis) to smash; (en vóleibol) to spike; (en fútbol): **remató el centro a la portería** he hit the cross straight into the goal
⃞3 (AmL) **(a)** (en subasta — vender) to auction; (— comprar) to buy ... at an auction **(b)** (liquidar) to sell ... off cheaply
■ **~** *vi* ⃞1 (terminar) **~ EN algo** to end IN sth
⃞2 (en tenis) to smash; (en vóleibol) to spike; (en fútbol) to shoot; **~ de cabeza** to head the ball

remate *m* ⃞1 **(a)** (de activades, esfuerzos) culmination; **y como ~** (fam) and to crown *o* cap it all (colloq) **(b)** (en costura) double stitch (*to finish off*) ⃞2 (en tenis) smash; (en vóleibol) spike; (en fútbol) shot; **~ de cabeza** header ⃞3 (AmL) (subasta) auction

remedar [A1] *vt* to mimic, ape

remediar [A1] *vt* ⃞1 ⟨*situación/problema*⟩ to remedy; ⟨*daño*⟩ to repair; **¿qué piensas hacer para ~lo?** what are you going to do to put things right?; **con llorar no remedias nada** crying won't solve anything ⃞2 (evitar): **no lo puedo/pude ~** I can't/couldn't help it

remedio *m* ⃞1 **(a)** (Med) (cura) remedy, cure **(b)** (esp AmL) (Farm) medicine ⃞2 (solución) solution; **ya no tiene ~** there's nothing we (*or* you *etc*) can do now; **su matrimonio no tiene ~** her marriage is beyond hope; **un caso sin ~** a hopeless case ⃞3 (alternativa, recurso) option; **no queda más ~ que ...** we have no alternative *o* choice but ...; **iré si no hay otro ~** I'll go if I really have to *o* if I must

remendar [A5] *vt* to mend

remera *f* (RPl) (camiseta) T-shirt

remero -ra *m,f* (*m*) rower, oarsman; (*f*) rower, oarswoman

remesa *f* (de mercancías) consignment, shipment; (de dinero) remittance

remezón *m* (Andes) (temblor) earth tremor; (sacudida brusca) shake; (suceso inesperado) shake-up

remiendo *m* (pedazo de tela, cuero) patch; **le hizo un ~** she mended *o* patched it

remilgado -da *adj* fussy

remilgón -gona, remilgoso -sa *adj* (delicado) (Andes, Méx) fussy; (difícil) (Méx) difficult

remisión *f* ⃞1 (en texto) reference; **~ A algo** reference TO sth ⃞2 (de enfermedad) remission ⃞3 (Relig, Der) remission

remite *m* (persona) sender; (dirección) return address

remitente *mf* sender

remitir [I1] *vt* ⃞1 **(a)** (frml) (mandar) to send **(b)** ⟨*lector/estudiante*⟩ **~ A algn A algo** to refer sb TO sth
■ **~** *vi* «*fiebre*» to drop, go down; «*tormenta*» to abate, subside
■ **remitirse** *v pron* **~se A algo** ⟨*a obra*⟩ to refer TO sth

remo *m* (con soporte) oar; (sin soporte) paddle

remodelación *f* (Arquit) remodeling*, redesigning; (de organización) reorganization, restructuring; (del gabinete) (Pol) reshuffle

remodelar [A1] *vt* ⟨*plaza/barrio*⟩ to remodel, redesign; ⟨*organización*⟩ to reorganize; ⟨*gabinete*⟩ to reshuffle

remojar [A1] *vt* ⟨*ropa/lentejas*⟩ to soak

remojo *m* (en agua): **poner algo a** *or* **en ~** to put sth to soak; **dejar algo en ~** to leave sth to soak

remojón *m* ⃞1 (fam) (en agua) soaking, drenching; **¿quién quiere darse un ~?** who's for a dip? (colloq) ⃞2 (Méx fam) (de algo nuevo): **nos dio el ~** (en el coche) he took us for a spin in his new car; (en la casa) he had us over for a housewarming party

remolacha *f* beet (AmE), beetroot (BrE); **~ azucarera** sugar beet

remolcador *m* (Náut) tug; (Auto) tow truck (AmE), breakdown van (BrE)

remolcar [A2] *vt* ⟨*barco*⟩ to tug; ⟨*coche*⟩ to tow

remolino *m* **(a)** (de viento) eddy, whirl **(b)** (de agua) eddy; (más violento) whirlpool **(c)** (en el pelo) cowlick

remolón -lona *adj* (fam) idle, lazy
■ *m,f* (fam) slacker (colloq)

remolque *m* **(a)** (vehículo) trailer **(b)** (acción) towing; **ir a ~** (Auto) to be in tow **(c)** (AmS) (grúa) tow truck (AmE), breakdown van (BrE)

remontar [A1] *vt* ⃞1 ⟨*dificultad/problema*⟩ to overcome, surmount (frml) ⃞2 **(a)** **~ el vuelo** «*avión*» to gain height; «*pájaro*» to fly *o* soar up **(b)** **~ el río** to go upriver **(c)** (RPl) ⟨*barrilete*⟩ to fly
■ **remontarse** *v pron* ⃞1 «*avión*» to gain height; «*pájaro*» to soar up ⃞2 (en el tiempo) to go back

remorder [E9] *vi* (+ *me/te/le etc*): **me remuerde haberlo dicho** I feel guilty for having said it; **¿no te remuerde la conciencia?** don't you feel guilty?

remordimiento *m* remorse; **sentir** *or* **tener ~s de conciencia** to suffer pangs of conscience

remoto -ta *adj* **(a)** ⟨*tiempo/época*⟩ distant, far-off (*before n*) **(b)** ⟨*lugar/mares/tierras*⟩ remote, far-off **(c)** ⟨*posibilidad*⟩ remote, slim; ⟨*esperanza*⟩ faint; **no tengo (ni) la más remota idea** I haven't the remotest *o* faintest idea

remover [E9] *vt* ⃞1 **(a)** ⟨*líquido/salsa*⟩ to stir; ⟨*ensalada*⟩ to toss; ⟨*tierra/piedras*⟩ to turn over; ⟨*escombros*⟩ to dig about in; ⟨*brasas*⟩ to poke, stir **(b)** ⟨*asunto*⟩ to bring ... up again; ⟨*pasado*⟩ to revive, stir up ⃞2 (frml) **(a)** ⟨*impedimento/obstáculo*⟩ to remove **(b)** (esp AmL) (destituir) **~ A algn DE algo** to remove sb FROM sth

remunerar [A1] *vt* to pay, remunerate (frml)

renacentista *adj* Renaissance (*before n*)

renacer [E3] *vi* to be reborn; **sentí ~ la esperanza** I felt renewed hope

renacimiento *m* **(a)** (acción) revival, rebirth **(b)** (Art, Hist) **el R~** the Renaissance

renacuajo *m* (Zool) tadpole; (niño, persona baja) (fam) shrimp (colloq)

rencilla *f* quarrel, row

rencor *m* resentment; **con el corazón lleno de** ⋯

~ with his heart full of resentment; **no te guardo**
~ I don't bear you any grudge; **siento ~ por lo
que me hizo** I feel bitter about what he did to me
rencoroso -sa *adj* [SER] resentful
rendición *f* surrender
rendido -da *adj* [ESTAR] (exhausto) exhausted;
cayó ~ (de cansancio) he collapsed from
exhaustion; *ver tb* RENDIR
rendidor -dora *adj* (AmL) ⟨*tierra*⟩ productive;
un detergente ~ a detergent that goes a long way
rendija *f* (grieta) crack, crevice; (hueco) gap
rendimiento *m* **(a)** (de persona, coche)
performance **(b)** (de máquina, factoría) output;
funciona a pleno ~ it is working at full capacity
(c) (de terreno) yield **(d)** (Fin) yield, return
rendir [I14] *vt* **1** ⟨*homenaje/tributo*⟩ to pay; **~le
culto a algn** to worship sb
2 (Fin) to yield; (producir) to produce
3 ⟨*persona*⟩: **me rindió el sueño** I was overcome
by sleep; **tanto trabajo rinde a cualquiera** working
that hard is enough to exhaust anyone
4 (CS) (Educ) ⟨*examen*⟩ to take, sit (BrE)
■ **~** *vi* **(a)** (cundir) (+ *me/te/le etc*): **me rindió mucho
la mañana** I had a lot done this morning; **trabaja
mucho pero no le rinde** he works hard but he
doesn't make much headway **(b)** «*alumno/
obrero/empleado*» to perform well **(c)** «*tela/
arroz/jabón*» to go a long way
■ **rendirse** *v pron* (en pelea, guerra) to surrender;
(en tarea, adivinanza) to give up
renegado -da *m,f* renegade
renegar [A7] *vi* **(a)** (Relig) to apostatize; **~ DE
algo** ⟨*de creencias/principios*⟩ to renounce sth **(b)**
(maldecir) to swear, curse; (blasfemar) to blaspheme
(c) (refunfuñar) to grumble; **~ DE algo** to grumble
ABOUT sth **(d)** (AmL) (enojarse) to get annoyed
RENFE /'rrenfe/ *f* = **Red Nacional de los
Ferrocarriles Españoles**
renglón *m* (línea) line
rengo -ga *adj* (AmL) lame
■ *m,f* (AmL) lame person, cripple (pej)
renguear [A1] *vi* (AmL) to limp
renguera *f* (AmL) limp
reno *m* reindeer
renombrado -da *adj* well-known, renowned
renombre *m* renown; **de ~** renowned
renovación *f* **(a)** (de pasaporte, contrato) renewal
(b) (del mobiliario) complete change; (de edificio,
barrio) renovation **(c)** (de organización, sistema)
updating **(d)** (reanudación) renewal
renovar [A10] *vt* **(a)** ⟨*pasaporte/contrato*⟩ to
renew **(b)** ⟨*mobiliario*⟩ to change; ⟨*edificio/
barrio*⟩ to renovate **(c)** ⟨*organización/sistema*⟩ to
update, bring up to date **(d)** ⟨*ataque/esperanza/
promesa*⟩ to renew
■ **renovarse** *v pron* **(a)** «*sospechas/dolor/
interés*» to be renewed **(b)** «*persona*» to be
revitalized
renta *f* **(a)** (beneficio) income; **inversiones de ~**

fija fixed interest investments; **vivir de las ~s** (de
dinero) to live off the interest; (de propiedades) to
live off the rent **(b)** (esp Méx) (alquiler) rent
rentabilidad *f* profitability
rentable *adj* ⟨*inversión/negocio*⟩ profitable
rentar [A1] *vt* (Méx) **(a)** ⟨*departamento*⟩
«*propietario*» to rent out, let (BrE); «*usuario*» to
rent **(b)** ⟨*coche*⟩ to rent, hire (BrE)
renuncia *f* **1** (dimisión) resignation; **presentar
la ~** to resign, tender one's resignation (frml)
2 (abandono) **~ A algo** renunciation OF sth
3 (abnegación) self-sacrifice
renunciar [A1] *vi* (dimitir) to resign; **~ A algo** ⟨*a
puesto*⟩ to resign sth; ⟨*a derecho*⟩ to relinquish
sth, renounce sth (frml); ⟨*a título*⟩ to give up sth,
relinquish sth; ⟨*a trono*⟩ to renounce sth
reñido -da *adj* **1** ⟨*partido/batalla*⟩
hard-fought, tough **2** [ESTAR] **(a)** (peleado): **está
~ con su novia** he has fallen out with his
girlfriend (colloq) **(b)** (en contradicción) **~ CON algo**
⟨*con principios*⟩ against sth
reñir [I15] *vi* (esp Esp) **(a)** (discutir) to argue,
quarrel **(b)** **~ con algn** (pelearse) to quarrel o
have a row WITH sb; (enemistarse) to fall out WITH
sb
■ **~** *vt* (Esp) (regañar) to scold, tell ... off (colloq)
reo *mf* (en lo penal — acusado) accused, defendant;
(— condenado) convicted offender; (en lo civil) (Méx)
defendant
reojo: **de reojo** (*loc adv*): **mirar a algn de ~** to
look at sb out of the corner of one's eye
reorganizar [A4] *vt* to reorganize
reparación *f* **(a)** (arreglo) repair; **taller de
reparaciones** repair shop **(b)** (de daño, ofensa)
redress, reparation
reparador -dora *adj* ⟨*sueño/descanso*⟩
refreshing
reparar [A1] *vt* **(a)** ⟨*coche*⟩ to repair, fix;
⟨*gotera/avería*⟩ to mend, fix **(b)** ⟨*error*⟩ to correct,
put right; ⟨*ofensa/agravio*⟩ to make amends for,
make up for; ⟨*daño/perjuicio*⟩ to make good,
compensate for
■ **~** *vi* **1** **~ EN algo** (darse cuenta) to notice sth;
(considerar): **no repara en gastos** she spares no
expense **2** (Méx) «*caballo/toro*» to rear, shy
reparo *m* **(a)** (inconveniente, objeción): **pone ~s a
todo** she finds fault with everything; **no tengo
ningún ~ en decírselo** I have no qualms about
telling him **(b)** (duda) reservation
repartición *f* **(a)** (división) distribution,
share-out **(b)** (CS) (departamento, sección)
department; (del ejército) division
repartidor -dora *m,f* (*m*) delivery man; (*f*)
delivery woman; (de periódicos) newspaper man (*o*
boy *etc*)
repartir [I1] *vt* **(a)** ⟨*ganancias/trabajo*⟩ to
distribute, share out **(b)** ⟨*panfletos/propaganda*⟩
to hand out, give out; ⟨*periódicos/correo*⟩ to
deliver; ⟨*naipes/fichas*⟩ to deal **(c)** (esparcir) to
spread, distribute
■ **~** *vi* (Jueg) to deal

355

reparto ···⟩ representación ··· ·

reparto *m* [1] **(a)** (distribución) distribution; (entre socios, herederos) share-out; ~ **de premios** prize-giving **(b)** (servicio de entrega) delivery; ~ **a domicilio** delivery service [2] (Cin, Teatr) cast

repasador *m* (RPl) dish towel (AmE), tea towel (BrE)

repasar [A1] *vt* ‹lección/tema› to review (AmE), to revise (BrE); ‹lista/cuenta/carta› to go over, check
■ ~ *vi* to review (AmE), to revise (BrE)

repaso *m* (revisión — para aprender algo) review (AmE), revision (BrE); (— para detectar errores) check; **dio un** ~ **a sus apuntes** she went *o* looked over her notes

repatriado -da *m,f* repatriate

repatriar [A1 *or* A17] *vt* to repatriate

repelar [A1] *vi* (Méx fam) to grumble, to moan (BrE colloq)

repelente *adj* ‹persona› repulsive, repellent; ‹niño› obnoxious
■ *m* insect repellent

repeler [E1] *vt* ‹ataque/agresión› to repel, repulse (frml)
■ ~ *vi* (+ *me/te/le etc*): **las serpientes me repelen** I find snakes repellent *o* repulsive

repente: **de repente** (*loc adv*) **(a)** (de pronto) suddenly **(b)** (RPl, Per) (quizás) maybe, perhaps

repentino -na *adj* sudden

repentizar [A4] *vt/vi* to sight-read

repercusión *f* (consecuencia) repercussion

repercutir [I1] *vi* **(a)** ‹sonido› to reverberate **(b)** (afectar) ~ **EN algo** to have an effect *o* an impact ON sth

repertorio *m* repertoire

repetición *f* **(a)** (de experimento, palabra) repetition; (de un sueño, fenómeno) recurrence **(b)** (de programa) repeat, rerun

repetido *adj* **(a)** ‹sello/disco›: **este lo tengo** ~ I have two of these **(b)** (*delante del n*) ‹casos/avisos/intentos› repeated (*before n*)

repetir [I14] *vt* **(a)** ‹pregunta/explicación› to repeat; **¿me lo puedes** ~**?** could you repeat it, please?; **¡que no te lo tenga que volver a** ~**!** don't let me have to tell you again! **(b)** ‹tarea› to do … again; ‹programa› to repeat, rerun; ‹experimento/curso/asignatura› to repeat **(c)** ‹plato› to have a second helping of, to have seconds of (colloq)
■ ~ *vi* [1] (volver a comer) to have a second helping, to have seconds (colloq)
[2] «pimientos/pepinos» to repeat; **el ajo me repite** garlic repeats on me
[3] (Educ) to repeat a year/course
■ **repetirse** *v pron* **(a)** «fenómeno/incidente/sueño» to recur, happen again; «persona» to repeat oneself **(b)** (Chi) (volver a comer) to have a second helping, have seconds (colloq)

repetitivo -va *adj* repetitive

repicar [A2] *vi* to ring out, peal

repiquetear [A1] *vi* **(a)** «campanas» to peal, ring out **(b)** (golpear) «lluvia» to patter; ~ **con los dedos en la mesa** to drum *o* tap one's fingers on the table

repiqueteo *m* **(a)** (de campanas) ringing, pealing **(b)** (de lluvia) pattering, pitter-patter (colloq); (con los dedos) drumming, tapping

repisa *f* (estante) shelf; (de chimenea) mantelpiece

repita, repitas, etc ▶ REPETIR

repleto -ta *adj* **(a)** ‹calle/vehículo/sala› ~ DE **algo** full OF sth, packed WITH sth; **el tren iba** ~ the train was packed *o* (colloq) jam-packed **(b)** ‹persona› replete (frml *or* hum), full

réplica *f* **(a)** (copia) replica **(b)** (Chi, Méx) (de terremoto) aftershock

replicar [A2] *vt* (frml) to retort, reply
■ ~ *vi* [1] (argumentar) to argue [2] (Der) to reply

repoblar [A10] *vt* **(a)** ‹río/lago› to restock **(b)** (de árboles) to reforest **(c)** (de personas) to repopulate, resettle

repollo *m* cabbage

reponer [E22] *vt* **(a)** (reemplazar) ‹existencias› to replace; ‹dinero› to put back, repay; ~ **fuerzas** to get one's strength back **(b)** ‹funcionario/trabajador› to reinstate **(c)** ‹obra› to put … on again, revive; ‹serie› to repeat, rerun; ‹película› to show … again
■ **reponerse** *v pron* to recover

reportaje *m* (en periódico, revista) article, feature; (en televisión) report, item; (entrevista) (AmL) interview

reportar [A1] *vt* [1] ‹beneficios/pérdidas› to produce, yield; **solo me reportó disgustos** it brought *o* caused me nothing but trouble [2] (AmL) (denunciar, dar cuenta de) to report [3] (Méx) ▶ REPORTEAR
■ **reportarse** *v pron* (AmL) (presentarse) to report

reporte *m* (Méx) (informe) report; (queja) complaint

reportear [A1] *vt* (Andes) to cover, report on
■ ~ *vi* (Andes) to report

reportero -ra *m,f* reporter; ~ **gráfico** press photographer

reposacabezas *m* (*pl* ~) headrest

reposado -da *adj* [SER] ‹persona/temperamento› calm; ‹ademanes/habla› unhurried

reposar [A1] *vi* **(a)** (descansar) «persona» to rest; «restos mortales» to lie **(b)** «líquido/solución» to settle; **dejar** ~ **la masa** let the dough stand

reposición *f* **(a)** (reemplazo) replacement **(b)** (de serie) repeat, rerun; (de obra) revival; (de película) reshowing

reposo *m* **(a)** (descanso) rest **(b)** (Coc): **dejar en** ~ leave to stand

repostar [A1] *vt* ‹gasolina› to fill up with; ‹provisiones› to stock up with
■ ~ *vi* (Auto) to fill up, to get some gas (AmE) *o* (BrE) petrol; (Aviac, Náut) to refuel

repostería *f* confectionery, baking (*of pastries, desserts*)

repostero -ra *m,f* (persona) confectioner, pastrycook

reprender [E1] *vt* to scold, tell … off (colloq)

represa *f* **(a)** (en río — dique) dam; (— embalse) reservoir **(b)** (de molino) millpond

represalia *f* reprisal; **como** ~ **por** … in retaliation for …

representación *f* [1] (acción) representation; ~ **legal** legal representation; **asistió en** ~ **del Rey** she attended as the King's representative; **en** ~ ···⟩

de mis **compañeros** on behalf of my companions
2 (delegación) delegation 3 (Teatr) performance,
production 4 (símbolo) representation

representante *mf* representative; (de artista,
cantante) agent; **es ~ de una editorial** she
represents a publishing house

representar [A1] *vt* 1 ⟨persona/
organización/país⟩ to represent 2 ⟨obra⟩ to
perform, put on; ⟨papel⟩ to play 3 (aparentar) to
look; **no representa su edad** he doesn't look his
age 4 (simbolizar) to represent, symbolize
5 (reproducir) «dibujo/fotografía/escena» to show,
depict; «obra/novela» to portray, depict
6 (equivaler a, significar) to represent; **esto
representa un aumento del 5%** this represents a
5% increase; **eso ~ía tres días de trabajo** that
would mean *o* involve three days' work

representativo -va *adj* representative

represión *f* repression

reprimenda *f* reprimand

reprimido -da *adj* repressed
■ *m,f:* **es un ~** he's repressed

reprimir [I1] *vt* (a) ⟨rebelión⟩ to suppress,
crush (b) ⟨risa/llanto/bostezo⟩ to suppress, stifle
(c) (Psic) to repress
■ **reprimirse** *v pron* (refl) to control oneself

reprobar [A10] *vt* (a) ⟨actitud/conducta⟩ to
condemn (b) (AmL) ⟨estudiante/materia/curso⟩ to
fail; **me ~on en física** I failed physics

reprochar [A1] *vt* to reproach; **~le algo a algn**
to reproach sb for sth

reproche *m* reproach; **hacerle ~s a algn** to
reproach sb

reproducción *f* reproduction

reproducir [I6] *vt* to reproduce
■ **reproducirse** *v pron* (a) (Biol, Bot) to
reproduce, breed (b) «fenómeno» to recur,
happen again

reproductor -tora *adj* ⟨animal⟩ breeding
(before n); ⟨órgano⟩ reproductive

reptar [A1] *vi* «serpiente» to slither;
«cocodrilo» to crawl, slide

reptil *m* reptile

república *f* republic

República Dominicana *f* Dominican
Republic

republicano -na *adj/m,f* republican

República Oriental del Uruguay *f*
(frml) official name of Uruguay

repudiar [A1] *vt* 1 ⟨atentado/violencia⟩ to
condemn 2 (Der) ⟨mujer⟩ to disown, repudiate
(frml); ⟨herencia⟩ to repudiate

repuesto *m* (pieza) (spare) part; **de ~** spare
(before n)

repugnancia *f:* **me causa ~** I find him
repulsive *o* repugnant; **siento ~ hacia las
culebras** I find snakes repulsive

repugnante *adj* ⟨olor⟩ disgusting, revolting;
⟨crimen⟩ abhorrent, repugnant; ⟨persona⟩
(físicamente) repulsive, revolting; (moralmente)
repugnant

repugnar [A1] *vi:* **me repugna beber de un
vaso sucio** I find having to drink out of a dirty
glass disgusting; **me repugna su comportamiento**
I find his behavior disgusting *o* repulsive

repulsa *f* (condena) condemnation; (rechazo)
rejection

repulsivo -va *adj* ⟨persona⟩ (físicamente)
repulsive, revolting; (moralmente) repugnant; ⟨olor⟩
disgusting, revolting

reputación *f* reputation; **~ de algo** reputation
as sth

requerir [I11] *vt* (a) (necesitar) to require (b)
⟨documento⟩ to require; ⟨persona⟩ to summon

requesón *m* curd (cheese)

requisar [A1] *vt* (a) (expropiar) ⟨vehículo/
suministros⟩ to requisition; (confiscar) ⟨drogas/
objetos robados⟩ to seize (b) (Col, Ven) (registrar) to
search

requisito *m* requirement; **reunir los ~s** to
fulfill *o* meet the requirements; **~ previo**
prerequisite

res *f* (a) (animal) animal (b) (Col, Méx, Ven) (Coc) *tb*
carne de ~ beef

resaca *f* 1 (de las olas) undertow 2 (después de
beber) hangover

resaltador *m* (Col) highlighter

resaltante *adj* (AmL) outstanding

resaltar [A1] *vi* (sobresalir, destacarse) to stand
out; **hacer ~** ⟨color⟩ to bring out; ⟨importancia/
necesidad⟩ to highlight, stress
■ **~** *vt* ⟨cualidad/importancia/necesidad⟩ to
highlight

resarcir [I4] *vt* **~ a algn DE algo** ⟨de daños/
inconvenientes⟩ to compensate sb FOR sth; ⟨de
gastos⟩ to reimburse sb FOR sth
■ **resarcirse** *v pron* **~se DE algo** (desquitarse) to
get one's own back FOR sth; (compensar) to make
up FOR sth

resbalada *f* (AmL) slip

resbaladilla *f* (Méx) slide, chute

resbaladizo -za *adj* (a) ⟨superficie/carretera⟩
slippery (b) ⟨asunto/tema⟩ delicate, tricky (colloq)

resbalar [A1] *vi* 1 (caerse) to slip; **las lágrimas
le resbalaban por las mejillas** the tears ran *o*
trickled down his cheeks 2 (fam) (ser indiferente):
todo lo que le digas le resbala anything you say
to him is just like water off a duck's back (colloq);
todo le resbala he couldn't care less about
anything (colloq)
■ **resbalarse** *v pron* (caerse) to slip

resbalín *m* (Chi) slide, chute

resbalón *m* slip

resbaloso -sa *adj* (AmL) ⟨superficie⟩ slippery

rescatar [A1] *vt* (a) (salvar) to rescue (b)
⟨dinero/pulsera⟩ to recover, get back

rescate *m* (a) (salvamento) rescue; **equipo de ~**
rescue team (b) (precio) ransom (c) (de dinero, joya)
recovery

rescoldo *m* embers (pl)

resecar [A2] *vt* ⟨piel/ambiente⟩ to make ... very
dry
■ **resecarse** *v pron* to dry up, get very dry

reseco -ca *adj* ⟨planta⟩ dried-up; ⟨pan⟩ dry;
⟨tierra/garganta⟩ parched

resentido -da *adj* (a) (dolorido) painful (b)
(disgustado) upset, hurt; (con rencor) resentful
■ *m,f:* **es un ~** he has a chip on his shoulder

resentimiento *m* resentment, bitterness

resentirse [I11] *v pron* (a) (sentir dolor): **aún se
resiente de la lesión** he is still suffering the

effects of the injury; **aún se resienten de la derrota** they're still smarting from the defeat **(b)** (sufrir las consecuencias) «*salud/trabajo*» to suffer **(c)** (ofenderse, molestarse) to get upset

reseña *f* **(a)** (de congreso, reunión) summary, report; (de libro) review; **una ~ biográfica** a biographical outline **(b)** (descripción) description; (sobre escritor, deportista) profile

reserva *f* **1** (de habitación, pasaje) reservation; (de mesa) booking, reservation; **¿tiene ~?** do you have a reservation?, have you booked? **2** (cantidad guardada) reserve; **tengo otro par de ~** I have a spare pair **3** **(a)** (Dep) (equipo) reserves (*pl*), reserve team; (conjunto de suplentes) substitutes (*pl*) **(b)** (de indígenas) reservation; (de animales) reserve; **~ natural** nature reserve **4** (secreto, discreción): **en la más absoluta ~** in the strictest confidence **5** **reservas** *fpl* **(a)** (dudas) reservations (*pl*) **(b)** (reparos): **habló sin ~s** he talked openly *o* freely **6** (Méx): **a ~ de que (no) llueva** as long as *o* provided (that) it doesn't rain
■ *mf* (Dep) reserve

reservación *f* (AmL) ▶ RESERVA 1

reservado -da *adj* ⟨*persona/actitud*⟩ reserved; ⟨*asunto/tema*⟩ confidential; *ver tb* RESERVAR

reservar [A1] *vt* **1** ⟨*asiento/habitación/mesa*⟩ to reserve, book; ⟨*pasaje/billete*⟩ to book **2** (guardar) ⟨*porción de comida/dinero*⟩ to set aside; **nos reservaba una sorpresa** he had a surprise in store for us; **reservó lo mejor para el final** she kept the best till last
■ **reservarse** *v pron* **(a)** (para sí mismo) ⟨*porción/ porcentaje*⟩ to keep ... for oneself; **~se la opinión** to reserve judgment **(b)** (*refl*) (para otra tarea) to save oneself

resfriado¹ -da *adj*: **estoy (algo) ~** I have a (slight) cold

resfriado² *m* cold

resfriarse [A17] *v pron* to catch a cold

resfrío *m* (esp AmS) cold

resguardar [A1] *vt* **~ algo/a algn DE algo** ⟨*de peligro/frío*⟩ to protect sth/sb FROM sth
■ **resguardarse** *v pron* (de peligro) to protect oneself; (de la lluvia, el frío) to shelter, take shelter

resguardo *m* **1** (Esp) (de depósito) deposit slip; (en tintorería, zapatería) slip, ticket **2** (Col) (reserva) reservation, reserve **3** (Méx) (control, vigilancia) control

residencia *f* **1** **(a)** (en país, ciudad) residence; **fijar ~** to take up residence **(b)** (documento) *tb* **permiso de ~** residence permit **2** **(a)** (casa) residence **(b)** (de estudiantes) dormitory (AmE), hall of residence (BrE); (de enfermeras) hostel, home; **~ de ancianos** old people's home **(c)** (hostal, fonda) boarding house, guest house (*not providing meals*) **3** (AmL) (Med) residency (AmE), time spent as a houseman (BrE)

residencial *adj* residential
■ *f* (CS) guest house, boarding house

residente *adj* resident
■ *m,f* **(a)** (en país) resident **(b)** (médico) resident (AmE), houseman (BrE)

residir [I1] *vi* **(a)** ⟨*persona*⟩ to live, reside (frml) **(b)** ⟨*encanto/interés*⟩ (radicar) **~ EN algo** to lie IN sth

residuo *m* **(a)** (Mat) remainder; (Quím) residue **(b)** **residuos** *mpl* (desperdicios) waste, waste materials *o* products (*pl*); **~s radiactivos** radioactive waste

resignación *f* resignation

resignado -da *adj* resigned; **~ A algo** resigned TO sth

resignarse [A1] *v pron* to resign oneself; **~ a hacer algo** to resign oneself to doing sth

resina *f* resin

resistencia *f* **1** **(a)** (en general) resistance **(b)** (aguante físico) stamina; **prueba de ~** endurance test **2** (componente de circuito) resistor; (de secador, calentador) element

resistente *adj* ⟨*material/metal*⟩ resistant, tough; ⟨*tela*⟩ tough, hard-wearing; ⟨*persona/ animal/planta*⟩ tough, hardy; **~ al calor** heat-resistant

resistir [I1] *vt* **(a)** (aguantar) ⟨*dolor/calor/ presión*⟩ to withstand, take; **no la resisto** (Col, Per fam) I can't stand her **(b)** ⟨*tentación/impulso*⟩ to resist **(c)** ⟨*ataque/enemigo*⟩ to resist
■ **~** *vi* **(a)** (aguantar) «*cuerda/puerta*» to hold; **ya no resisto más** I can't take (it) any more **(b)** «*ejército*» to hold out, resist
■ **resistirse** *v pron* **(a)** (oponer resistencia) to resist **(b)** (tener reticencia): **se resiste a aceptarlo** she's unwilling *o* reluctant to agree to it; **me resisto a creerlo** I find it hard to believe

resolución *f* **1** (de problema) solution; (de conflicto) settlement, resolution **2** (decisión) decision; **tomar una ~** to make a decision; **tomaron la ~ de emigrar** they decided to emigrate **3** (determinación) determination, resolve

resolver [E11] *vt* **(a)** ⟨*crimen/problema/ misterio*⟩ to solve, clear up; ⟨*asunto/conflicto*⟩ to resolve, settle; ⟨*duda*⟩ to clear up; **tiene resuelto su futuro** his future is sorted out **(b)** (decidir) to decide

resonancia *f* (Mús, Fís) resonance; (eco) echo; (de noticia, suceso) impact

resonante *adj* ⟨*sonido*⟩ resonant; ⟨*éxito*⟩ resounding, tremendous

resonar [A10] *vi* **(a)** (hacer eco) to echo, resound **(b)** «*gritos/risas*» to ring (out)

resoplar [A1] *vi* (por cansancio) to puff; (por enfado) to snort

resoplido *m* **(a)** (de enfado) snort **(b)** (de cansancio): **dando ~s** puffing and panting **(c)** (de caballo) snort

resorte *m* **(a)** (muelle) spring **(b)** (AmC, Col, Méx) (elástico) elastic

resortera *f* (Méx) slingshot (AmE), catapult (BrE)

respaldar [A1] *vt* ⟨*persona*⟩ (apoyar) to support, back; (en discusión) to back up; ⟨*propuesta/plan*⟩ to support, back; ⟨*versión/teoría*⟩ to support, back up

respaldo *m* **(a)** (de asiento) back **(b)** (apoyo) support, backing; **en ~ de** in support of **(c)** (Fin) backing

respectar [A1] *vi* (en 3ª pers): **en or por lo que a mí respecta** as far as I'm concerned

respectivo -va *adj* (correspondiente) respective

respecto *m*: **a este ~** on this respect, in this regard (frml); **(con) ~ a algo** regarding sth, with regard to sth

r

respetable *adj* ⟨digno de respeto⟩ respectable; ⟨considerable⟩ considerable

respetar [A1] *vt* **(a)** ⟨*persona*⟩ to respect; **se hizo ~ por todos** he won *o* gained everyone's respect **(b)** ⟨*opinión/tradiciones*⟩ to respect; ⟨*señal/luz roja*⟩ to obey; ⟨*ley/norma*⟩ to observe

respeto *m* **(a)** ⟨consideración, deferencia⟩ respect; **con ~** respectfully, with respect; **por *o* a algn/ algo** out of consideration *o* respect for sb/sth; **faltarle al** *or* (CS) **~ a algn** to be rude *o* disrespectful to sb; **presentaron sus ~s a ...** they paid their repects to ... (frml) **(b)** (temor): **su presencia impone ~** her presence commands (a feeling of) respect; **les tengo mucho ~ a los perros** I have a healthy respect for dogs

respetuoso -sa *adj* ⟨*persona/silencio*⟩ respectful

respingado -da *adj* (AmL) ⟨*nariz*⟩ turned-up

respingo *m* start; **dio un ~** he gave a start

respingón -gona *adj* **(a)** ⟨*nariz*⟩ turned-up **(b)** (Méx fam) ⟨*persona*⟩ touchy

respiración *f* (Fisiol) breathing, respiration (frml); **me quedé sin ~** I was out of breath; **contener la ~** to hold one's breath; **~ boca a boca** mouth-to-mouth resuscitation, kiss of life

respirar [A1] *vi* to breathe; **respire hondo** take a deep breath
■ **~** *vt* **(a)** ⟨*aire*⟩ to breathe; ⟨*humo/gases*⟩ to breathe in **(b)** ⟨*tranquilidad*⟩: **la paz que se respira aquí** the feeling of peace that you get here

respiratorio -ria *adj* respiratory

respiro *m* ⟨descanso⟩ break; **tomarse un ~** to take a break *o* (colloq) have a breather

resplandecer [E3] *vi* «*sol*» to shine; «*luna/ metal/cristal*» to gleam; «*hoguera*» to blaze

resplandeciente *adj* **(a)** ⟨*luna/metal/ cristal*⟩ gleaming; ⟨*sol*⟩ dazzling **(b)** (limpio) ⟨*cocina/coche*⟩ sparkling clean

resplandor *m* ⟨del sol⟩ glare, brightness; ⟨de luna, metal, cristal⟩ gleam; ⟨de relámpago, explosión⟩ flash

responder [E1] *vi* **1 (a)** (contestar) to reply, answer, respond (frml); **respondió con una evasiva** he gave an evasive reply **(b)** (replicar) to answer back
2 (reaccionar) to respond; **~ A algo** ⟨*a amenaza/ estímulo*⟩ to respond TO sth
3 (corresponder): **no responden a la descripción** they do not answer the description; **las cifras no responden a la realidad** the figures do not reflect the true situation
4 (responsabilizarse): **si ocurre algo, yo no respondo** if anything happens I will not be held responsible; **~ ante la justicia** to answer for one's acts in a court of law; **yo respondo de su integridad** I will vouch for his integrity; **no respondo de lo que hizo** I am not responsible for what he did; **~ POR algn** to vouch FOR sb
■ **~** *vt* **(a)** (contestar) to reply, answer **(b)** ⟨*pregunta*⟩ to answer **(c)** ⟨*llamada/carta*⟩ to answer, reply to

respondón -dona *adj* (fam) ⟨*niño*⟩ mouthy (AmE colloq), cheeky (BrE colloq)
■ *m,f* (fam): **es un ~** he's always answering back

responsabilidad *f* responsibility; **un puesto de mucha ~** a post which involves a great deal of responsibility; **tener sentido de la ~** to have a sense of responsibility; **cargó con toda la ~** she took full responsibility

responsabilizar [A4] *vt* **~ a algn** DE **algo** to hold sb responsible *o* accountable FOR sth
■ **responsabilizarse** *v pron* to take responsibility; **~se** DE **algo** ⟨*de tarea/error/ accidente*⟩ to take responsibility FOR sth; ⟨*de atentado*⟩ to claim responsibility FOR sth; ⟨*de delito*⟩ to admit responsibility FOR sth

responsable *adj* [SER] (concienzudo) responsible; **~** DE **algo** ⟨*de tarea/error*⟩ responsible FOR sth; (culpable) responsible FOR sth; ⟨*de accidente/delito*⟩ liable FOR sth; **nadie se ha hecho ~ del atentado** no one has claimed responsibility for the attack
■ *mf*: **el ~ de ventas** the person responsible for sales; **los ~s serán castigados** those responsible will be punished

respuesta *f* **(a)** ⟨a carta, mensaje⟩ reply, answer, response (frml) **(b)** (reacción) response **(c)** (solución) answer, solution

resquebrajar [A1] *vt* ⟨*loza/roca*⟩ to crack; ⟨*madera*⟩ to split
■ **resquebrajarse** *v pron* ⟨*loza/roca*⟩ to crack; «*madera*» to split

resquicio *m* **1** (grieta) crack; (abertura) gap **2** (huella, resto) trace

resta *f* subtraction

restablecer [E3] *vt* ⟨*relaciones/ comunicaciones*⟩ to re-establish; ⟨*orden/ democracia/normalidad*⟩ to restore
■ **restablecerse** *v pron* to recover

restablecimiento *m* ⟨de relaciones, comunicaciones⟩ re-establishment; ⟨de orden, paz⟩ restoration; ⟨de enfermo⟩ recovery

restante *adj* remaining

restantes *mpl/fpl*: **los ~s** the rest, the remainder

restar [A1] *vt* **(a)** (Mat) ⟨*número*⟩ to subtract, take away; **~ algo** DE **algo** to take (away) *o* subtract sth FROM sth **(b)** ⟨*gastos/cantidad*⟩ to deduct, take away **(c)** (quitar): **~le importancia a algo** to minimize *o* play down the importance of sth
■ **~** *vi* **1** (Mat) to subtract, take away **2** (Esp) (Dep) to return (service)

restauración *f* restoration

restaurante *m* restaurant

restaurar [A1] *vt* to restore

resto *m* **1 (a)** (lo demás, lo que queda) **el ~** the rest **(b)** (Mat) remainder **2 restos** *mpl* (humanos, arqueológicos) remains (*pl*); ⟨de avión, barco siniestrado⟩ wreckage; ⟨de comida⟩ leftovers (*pl*) **3** (Esp) (Dep) return (of service)

AmC	Central America	Arg	Argentina	Cu	Cuba	Per	Peru
AmL	Latin America	Bol	Bolivia	Ec	Ecuador	RPI	River Plate Area
AmS	South America	Chi	Chile	Esp	Spain	Ur	Uruguay
Andes	Andean Region	CS	Southern Cone	Méx	Mexico	Ven	Venezuela

restregar [A7] *vt* ‹*suelo*› to scrub; ‹*ropa*› to rub, scrub
■ **restregarse** *v pron* (*refl*) ‹*ojos/mejilla*› to rub
restricción *f* restriction
restringido -da *adj* ‹*libertad*› restricted, limited; ‹*posibilidades/cantidad*› limited
restringir [I7] *vt* to restrict
resucitar [A1] *vt* **(a)** (Relig) to raise … from the dead, to bring … back to life **(b)** (Med) to resuscitate, revive **(c)** ‹*costumbres/rencores*› to revive, resurrect
■ ~ *vi* «*persona*» to rise (from the dead); «*costumbre/grupo*» to take on a new lease of life
resuelto -ta *adj* **(a)** [SER] ‹*persona*› decisive; **en tono** ~ decisively **(b)** [ESTAR] (decidido) determined, resolved (frml); *ver tb* RESOLVER
resultado *m* result; **como** ~ **de** as a result of; **mi idea dio** ~ my idea worked; **intentó convencerlo, pero sin** ~ she tried to persuade him, but without success *o* to no avail; ~ **final** (Dep) final score
resultar [A1] *vi* **1** (dar resultado) to work; **su idea no resultó** his idea didn't work (out) **2** (+ *compl*): **resulta más barato así** it works out cheaper this way; **me resulta simpático** I think he's very nice; **resultó ser un malentendido** it turned out to be *o* proved to be a misunderstanding; **resultó tal como lo planeamos** it turned out *o* worked out just as we planned **3** (*en 3ª pers*): **ahora resulta que era periodista** now it turns out that he was a journalist **4** (derivar) ~ **EN algo** to result IN sth, lead TO sth
resumen *m* summary; **hacer un** ~ **de un texto** to summarize a text; **en** ~ in short
resumidero *m* (AmL) drain
resumir [I1] *vt* **(a)** (condensar) ‹*texto/libro*› to summarize **(b)** (recapitular) ‹*discurso/argumento*› to sum up
■ ~ *vi*: **resumiendo** … in short …, to sum up …
resurgir [I7] *vi* to reemerge
resurrección *f* resurrection
retachar [A1] *vt* (Méx fam) **(a)** ‹*carta/trabajo*› to reject, refuse to accept **(b)** (no dejar entrar): **nos** ~**on** they turned us away
■ ~ *vi* (Méx) «*bala*» to ricochet
retador -dora *m,f* (AmL) challenger
retaguardia *f* (Mil) rearguard
retahíla *f* string
retaliación *f* (AmL) retaliation
retar [A1] *vt* **(a)** (desafiar) to challenge **(b)** (CS) (regañar) to tell … off (colloq), to scold
retardado -da *adj* **1** (Tec) delayed; **de apertura retardada** with time-delay lock **2** ‹*persona*› mentally handicapped *o* retarded
retardar [A1] *vt* (frenar) to delay, hold up, retard (tech); (posponer) to postpone
retén *m* **(a)** (patrulla) patrol; (pelotón) squad; (puesto de policía) police post **(b)** (Ven) (correccional) reformatory (AmE), remand home (BrE)
retener [E27] *vt* **1** **(a)** ‹*datos/información*› to keep back, withhold **(b)** ‹*pasaporte/tarjeta*› to retain **(c)** (Fin, Fisco) ‹*dinero/cuota*› to deduct, withhold **2** **(a)** «*policía*» ‹*persona*› to detain, hold **(b)** (hacer permanecer): **no te retendré mucho** I

won't keep you long **3** ‹*calor/carga/líquidos*› to retain **4** ‹*atención/interés*› to keep, retain **5** (recordar) to retain, keep … in one's head
reticencia *f* **(a)** (renuencia) reluctance; **con** ~ reluctantly **(b)** (reserva) reticence
reticente *adj* **(a)** (reacio) reluctant **(b)** (reservado) reticent
retina *f* retina
retintín *m* (fam) (tonillo sarcástico) sarcastic tone of voice; **con** ~ sarcastically
retirada *f* **(a)** (en general) withdrawal **(b)** (Mil) retreat; **batirse en** ~ to retreat **(c)** (de actividad profesional) retirement **(d)** (de competición — antes de iniciarse) withdrawal; (— una vez iniciada) retirement
retirado -da *adj* **1** **(a)** ‹*lugar/casa*› remote, out-of-the-way; **una casa retirada de la calle** a house set back from the road; **un barrio** ~ **del centro** an outlying district **(b)** ‹*vida*› secluded, quiet **2** (jubilado) retired
retirar [A1] *vt* **1** **(a)** (quitar) to remove, take away; (apartar) to move away; **retiró la cacerola del fuego** he removed the saucepan from the heat; ~ **de la circulación** to withdraw from circulation **(b)** ‹*cabeza/mano*› to pull … back **(c)** ‹*embajador/tropas*› to withdraw, pull out **(d)** (+ *me/te/le etc*) ‹*apoyo*› to withdraw; ‹*pasaporte/carnet*› to withdraw, take away **2** ‹*afirmaciones/propuesta*› to withdraw; **retiro lo dicho** I take back what I said **3** (de cuenta) ‹*dinero*› to withdraw
■ **retirarse** *v pron* **1** **(a)** (apartarse) to move back *o* away; (irse) to leave, withdraw **(b)** «*ejército/tropas*» to withdraw, pull out **(c)** (irse a dormir) to go to bed, retire (frml) **2** (jubilarse) to retire; (de competición — antes de iniciarse) to withdraw, pull out; (— una vez iniciada) to pull out
retiro *m* **(a)** (jubilación) retirement; (pensión) (retirement) pension **(b)** (AmL) (de fuerzas, empleados) withdrawal; (de apoyo, fondos) withdrawal
reto *m* **(a)** (desafío) challenge **(b)** (CS) (regañina) telling-off (colloq), scolding
retobar [A1] *vi* (Méx fam) to answer back
retocar [A2] *vt* ‹*fotografía/maquillaje*› to touch up, retouch
retoño *m* (Bot) shoot
retoque *m*: **dar los últimos** ~**s a algo** to put the final *o* the finishing touches to sth
retorcer [E10] *vt* to twist
■ **retorcerse** *v pron* **1** **(a)** (enrollarse) to become tangled (up) **(b)** «*serpiente*» to writhe **(c)** «*persona*»: ~**se de dolor** to writhe in agony; ▶ RISA **2** (*refl*) ‹*manos*› to wring
retorcido -da *adj* ‹*persona/mente*› twisted, devious; ‹*estilo/argumento*› convoluted, involved
retorcijón *m* (AmL) sharp pain (*in the stomach or gut*); **retorcijones de tripas** stomach cramps
retórico -ca *adj* rhetorical
retornable *adj* returnable; **no** ~ non-returnable
retornar [A1] *vi/vt* (frml *o* liter) to return
retorno *m* (frml *o* liter) (regreso, devolución) return; (viaje de regreso) return journey
retortijón *m* (Esp, Méx) ▶ RETORCIJÓN
retraído -da *adj* withdrawn, retiring (*before n*)

retransmisión *f* (a) (transmisión) transmission; ∼ **en directo** live broadcast *o* transmission (b) (repetición) repeat

retransmitir [I1] *vt* (a) (repetir) to repeat, rebroadcast (frml) (b) (Esp period) (Rad, TV) to broadcast

retrasado -da *adj* (a) [SER] (Med, Psic) mentally handicapped (b) [ESTAR] (en tarea, actividad): **está muy ∼ con respecto a los demás** he lags a long way behind the others; **están ∼s en los pagos** they are behind in their payments; **tengo trabajo ∼** I have work to catch up on (c) ⟨país/sociedad⟩ backward (d) ⟨reloj⟩ slow
■ *m,f: tb* ∼ **mental** mentally handicapped person, (mentally) retarded person

retrasar [A1] *vt* (a) ⟨persona⟩ to make ... late; **el tráfico nos retrasó** we got held up in the traffic (b) ⟨producción/proceso⟩ to delay, hold up; **la niebla retrasó la salida del avión** the departure (of the plane) was delayed by fog (c) ⟨partida/fecha⟩ to postpone (d) ⟨reloj⟩ to put back
■ **retrasarse** *v pron* (a) (llegar tarde) to be late (b) «producción/trámite» to be delayed, be held up (c) (en trabajo, estudios, pagos) to fall behind; **se retrasó en presentarlo** she was late (in) submitting it (d) ⟨reloj⟩ to run slow

retraso *m* (a) (demora) delay; **viene con media hora de ∼** it's (running) half an hour late; **llevamos un ∼ de dos meses sobre lo previsto** we're two months behind schedule (b) (de país) backwardness

retratar [A1] *vt* (a) (pintar) to paint a portrait of; (fotografiar) to photograph (b) ⟨realidad/costumbres⟩ to portray, depict

retrato *m* (a) (Art, Fot) portrait; **ser el vivo ∼ de algn** to be the (spitting) image of sb (colloq) (b) (descripción) depiction, portrayal

retreta *f* [1] (Mil) (toque) retreat [2] (AmL) (concierto) open-air concert

retribuir [I20] *vt* (a) ⟨esfuerzos/trabajo⟩ to pay (b) (recompensar) to reward (c) (AmL) ⟨favor⟩ to return

retroactivo -va *adj* retrospective, retroactive; **un aumento con efecto ∼ desde enero** an increase backdated to January

retroceder [E1] *vi* (a) «persona/coche» to go back, move back; «ejército» to withdraw, retreat (b) (volverse atrás) to back down

retroceso *m* (a) (movimiento hacia atrás) backward movement; (en plan, desarrollo) backward step (b) (de ejército) withdrawal, retreat (c) (Arm) recoil (d) (Ven) (Auto) reverse

retrógrado -da *adj* ⟨persona/actitud⟩ reactionary; ⟨planteamiento/idea⟩ retrograde
■ *m,f* reactionary

retroproyector *m* overhead projector

retrospectiva *f* retrospective

retrospectivo -va *adj* retrospective

retrovisor *m* (interior) (rear-view) mirror; (lateral) (wing) mirror

retumbar [A1] *vi* «voz/explosión» to boom; «eco» to resound; «paso» to echo; «trueno» to roll, boom; «habitación» to resound

reubicar [A2] *vt* (AmL) ⟨trabajadores⟩ to relocate, redeploy; ⟨empresas⟩ to relocate;

⟨pobladores/damnificados⟩ to resettle (b) (cambiar de lugar) to put ... in a different place, change the position of

reuma, reúma *m or f* rheumatism

reumático -ca *adj* rheumatic

reunido -da *adj*: **estuvieron ∼s tres horas** the meeting lasted three hours; **está reunida** (Esp) she's in a meeting; *ver tb* REUNIR

reunificar [A2] *vt* ⟨nación⟩ to reunify; ⟨familia⟩ to reunite, bring together

reunión *f* (a) (para discutir algo) meeting; (de carácter social) gathering; (reencuentro) reunion (b) (de datos, información) gathering, collecting

reunir [I23] *vt* [1] ⟨cualidades/características⟩ to have; ⟨requisitos⟩ to satisfy, meet; ⟨condiciones⟩ to fulfill, satisfy [2] ⟨datos⟩ to gather; ⟨dinero/fondos⟩ to raise; ⟨información⟩ to gather together, collect [3] ⟨amigos/familia⟩ to get ... together; **reunió a los jefes de sección** he called a meeting of the heads of department
■ **reunirse** *v pron* «consejo/junta» to meet; «amigos/parientes» to get together; ∼**se CON algn** (encontrarse) to meet up with sb; (tener una reunión) to have a meeting with sb, meet with sb (AmE)

reutilizable *adj* reusable

reutilización *f* reuse, recycling

reutilizar [A4] *vt* to reuse

reválida *f* (RPl) validation

revalidación *f* (a) (Chi, Méx) (convalidación) validation (b) (Col, Ven) (del pasaporte) renewal

revalidar [A1] *vt* [1] ⟨campeonato/título⟩ to defend, win ... again; ⟨victoria⟩ to repeat [2] (a) (Chi, Méx) (convalidar) to validate (b) (Col, Ven) ⟨pasaporte⟩ to renew

revalorización *f* (a) (de una divisa) revaluation; (de una pensión) increase, adjustment (b) (de un activo) appreciation (frml), increase in value

revalorizar [A4] *vt* (a) ⟨moneda⟩ to revalue; ⟨pensiones⟩ to increase, adjust (b) ⟨sistema/situación⟩ to reassess
■ **revalorizarse** *v pron* «acciones/propiedad» to appreciate; «moneda» to gain in value

revancha *f* (a) (Dep, Jueg) return game (b) (desquite): **¡me tomaré la ∼!** I'll get my own back! (colloq)

revelación *f* [1] (de secreto, noticia) revelation, disclosure [2] (éxito, figura) revelation

revelado *m* developing

revelador -dora *adj* revealing

revelar [A1] *vt* (a) ⟨secreto/verdad⟩ to reveal (b) (Cin, Fot) to develop

revendedor -dora *m,f* (de entradas) scalper (AmE), ticket tout (BrE)

revender [E1] *vt* ⟨alimentos/artículos⟩ to resell; ⟨entradas⟩ to scalp (AmE), to tout (BrE); ⟨acciones⟩ to sell off

reventa *f* (de alimentos, artículos) resale; (de entradas) scalping (AmE), touting (BrE)

reventar [A5] *vi* [1] «globo» to burst, pop; «neumático» to blow out, burst; «ampolla/tubería» to burst; «ola» to break [2] (a) «persona» (uso hiperbólico): **si sigue comiendo así,**

va a ~ if he carries on eating like that, he'll burst! **(b)** (fam) (irritar) to rile (colloq), to make ... mad (colloq); **me revienta cocinar** I hate cooking
■ ~ *vt* ⟨*globo/neumático*⟩ to burst

■ **reventarse** *v pron* **(a)** «*globo/tubería*» ▶ REVENTAR *vi* 1 **(b)** (*refl*) ⟨*grano*⟩ to squeeze; ⟨*ampolla*⟩ to burst

reventón *m* ⟨1⟩ (de neumático) blowout; (de tubería) burst ⟨2⟩ (Méx fam) (fiesta) party

reverencia *f* (de hombre, niño) bow; (de mujer, niña) curtsy; **hacer una** ~ «*hombre*» to bow; «*mujer*» to curtsy

reverendo -da *adj* **(a)** (Relig) reverend (*before n*) **(b)** (esp AmL fam) (como intensificador) (*delante del n*) ▶ SOBERANO 2

reversa *f* (Col, Méx) reverse; **meter** ~ to put the car into reverse

reversible *adj* reversible

reverso *m* **(a)** (de papel, cuadro) back **(b)** (de moneda, medalla) reverse

revés *m* ⟨1⟩ **(a)** **el** ~ (de prenda) the inside; (de tela) the back, the wrong side; (de papel, documento) the back **(b)** **al revés** (*loc adv*) (con lo de adelante atrás) back to front; (con lo de arriba abajo) upside down; (con lo de dentro fuera) inside out; **así no, va al** ~ not that way, it goes the other way around *o* (BrE) round; **se puso los zapatos al** ~ he put his shoes on the wrong feet; **todo lo entiende al** ~ she's always getting the wrong end of the stick; **todo me sale al** ~ nothing goes right for me; **saberse algo al** ~ **y al derecho** to know sth (off) by heart
⟨2⟩ (Dep) backhand
⟨3⟩ (contratiempo) setback

revestir [I14] *vt* (cubrir) ⟨*pared/suelo*⟩ to cover; ⟨*cable*⟩ to sheathe, cover; ⟨*tubería*⟩ (con material aislante) to lag; **paredes revestidas de madera** wood-paneled walls

revienta, revientas, etc ▶ REVENTAR

revisación *f* (RPl) (Med, Odont) examination; (periódica) checkup

revisar [A1] *vt* **(a)** ⟨*documento*⟩ to go through, look through; ⟨*traducción/cuenta*⟩ to check, go through **(b)** ⟨*criterio/doctrina/edición*⟩ to revise **(c)** ⟨*máquina/instalación/frenos*⟩ to check; ⟨*coche*⟩ (hacer revisión periódica) (Esp) to service **(d)** (AmL) ⟨*equipaje/bolsillos*⟩ to search, go through **(e)** (AmL) ⟨*paciente*⟩ to examine; ⟨*dentadura*⟩ to check; **se hizo** ~ **la dentadura** he had a dental checkup

revisión *f* **(a)** (de trabajo, documento) checking, check **(b)** (de criterio, doctrina) revision **(c)** (de instalación) inspection; (de frenos) check; (de coche) (Esp) service **(d)** (AmL) (de equipaje) inspection **(e)** (Med, Odont) checkup; ~ **médica** (Esp) (periódica) checkup; (para trabajo) medical examination

revisor -sora *m,f* (Esp) ticket inspector

revista *f* **(a)** (publicación ilustrada) magazine; (de profesión) journal; ~ **del corazón** real-life *o* true-romance magazine **(b)** (Espec, Teatr) revue; **teatro de** ~ variety theater **(c)** (inspección) review; **pasar** ~ **a las tropas** to inspect *o* review the troops

revistero *m* magazine rack

revitalizar [A4] *vt* to revitalize

revivir [I1] *vi* to revive
■ ~ *vt* to relive

revocar [A2] *vt* ⟨1⟩ (Der) ⟨*consentimiento/ testamento*⟩ to revoke; ⟨*fallo*⟩ to reverse, revoke ⟨2⟩ (Const) ⟨*pared interior*⟩ to plaster; ⟨*pared exterior*⟩ to render

revolcar [A9] *vt*: **lo** ~**on por el suelo** they knocked him to the ground and pushed him around
■ **revolcarse** *v pron* to roll around; (en lodo) to wallow, roll around

revolcón *m* (caída) tumble; (vuelta) roll

revolotear [A1] *vi* «*mariposa*» to flutter; «*polilla*» to flit; «*pájaro*» to flutter around; «*papeles/hojas*» to fly *o* swirl around

revoltijo, revoltillo *m* (fam) **(a)** (desorden) mess, jumble **(b)** (comida, bebida) mixture, concoction

revoltoso -sa *adj* ⟨*niño*⟩ naughty; ⟨*soldados/ estudiantes*⟩ rebellious

revolución *f* revolution

revolucionar [A1] *vt* **(a)** ⟨*costumbres/ industria*⟩ to revolutionize **(b)** ⟨*niños*⟩ to get ... excited; ⟨*estudiantes/obreros*⟩ to stir up

revolucionario -ria *adj,m,f* revolutionary

revolver [E11] *vt* **(a)** ⟨*salsa/guiso*⟩ to stir; **me revuelve el estómago** it turns my stomach **(b)** (AmL) ⟨*dados*⟩ to shake **(c)** ⟨*cajones/papeles*⟩ to rummage through, go through; «*ladrones*» ⟨*casa*⟩ to turn ... upside down
■ ~ *vi*: **revolvió en mis cosas** he rummaged through my things

revólver *m* revolver

revuelo *m* (conmoción) stir

revuelta *f* **(a)** (de civiles) uprising; (de tropas) uprising, revolt; (de estudiantes, presos) riot **(b)** (jaleo) commotion, row (colloq)

revuelto¹ -ta *adj* **(a)** (desordenado) in a mess; ⟨*pelo*⟩ disheveled*; **tener el estómago** ~ to feel sick *o* nauseous **(b)** ⟨*mar*⟩ rough; ⟨*tiempo*⟩ unsettled

revuelto² *m* vegetables sautéed with egg

rey *m* ⟨1⟩ **(a)** (monarca) king; **los R**~**es de Suecia** the King and Queen of Sweden; **los R**~**es y sus hijos** the royal couple and their children **(b)** (en ajedrez, naipes) king **(c)** (como apelativo) pet (colloq), precious (colloq) ⟨2⟩ **Reyes** Epiphany, January 6th; **Los R**~**es Magos** the Three Wise Men, The Three Kings

rezagado -da *adj*: **quedar(se)** ~ to fall *o* drop behind; **iban** ~**s** they were lagging behind; **los alumnos más** ~**s** the slower students

rezar [A4] *vi* (Relig) to pray; ~ **POR algn/algo** to pray FOR sb/sth; **reza por que todo salga bien** pray that everything turns out all right
■ ~ *vt* ⟨*oración/rosario*⟩ to say

rezo *m* prayer

rezongar [A3] *vi* to grumble
■ ~ *vt* (AmC, Ur fam) (regañar) to tell ... off (colloq)

rezumar [A1] *vt/vi* to ooze

RFA *f* (= **República Federal de Alemania**) FRG

ría *f* ria (*long, narrow, tidal inlet*)

ría, rías, etc ▶ REÍR

riachuelo *m* stream, brook

riada *f* flood; (en área más extensa) flooding

ribera *f* **(a)** (orilla — de río) bank; (— de lago, mar) shore **(b)** (vega) strand, riverside

ribete *m* (adorno) trimming, edging

rico -ca *adj* ① (a) ⟨persona/país⟩ rich, wealthy
(b) ⟨tierra⟩ rich; ⟨vegetación⟩ lush; ⟨lenguaje/
historia⟩ rich; ~ **EN algo** rich in sth ② (a)
⟨comida⟩ good, nice; **¡esto está riquísimo!** this is
delicious! (b) (esp CS) ⟨perfume⟩ nice, lovely; **¡qué
~ olor tiene!** what a lovely smell! (c) (fam) (mono)
⟨niño/chica⟩ lovely, cute (d) (AmL exc RPl)
(agradable) lovely, wonderful
■ *m,f* (a) (*m*) rich *o* wealthy man; (*f*) rich *o*
wealthy woman; **los ~s** rich people, the rich (b)
(como apelativo) (fam & iró) sweetie (colloq & iro),
honey (colloq & iro)

ricura *f* (fam): **tiene un bebé que es una ~** she
has the cutest little baby (colloq); **ven, ~** come
here, darling (colloq)

ridiculez *f* (a) (tontería, insignificancia): **lo que dijo
fue una ~** what he said was ridiculous; **¡qué ~!**
that's ridiculous!; **pagué una ~ por esto** I paid
next to nothing for this (b) (cualidad)
ridiculousness

ridiculizar [A4] *vt* to ridicule

ridículo¹ -la *adj* (a) ⟨persona/comentario/
vestimenta⟩ ridiculous; **lo ~ de la situación era
que ...** the ridiculous thing about the situation
was that ...; **eso es ~** it's absurd *o* ridiculous (b)
⟨cantidad/precios⟩ ridiculous, ludicrous; ⟨sueldo⟩
ridiculous, laughable

ridículo² *m*: **sentido del ~** sense of the
ridiculous *o* absurd; **dejar** *or* **poner a algn en ~**
to make a fool of sb; **hacer el ~** to make a fool of
oneself

ríe, etc ▶ REÍR

riega, riegas, etc ▶ REGAR

riego *m* (a) (Agr) irrigation (b) **falta de ~
sanguíneo** insufficient blood supply

riel *m* rail

rienda *f* rein; **aflojar las ~s** to slacken the
reins; **llevar las ~s** to be in charge *o* control;
tomar las ~s to take charge

riesgo *m* risk; **un ~ para la salud** a health
hazard; **a ~ de perder su amistad** at the risk of
losing his friendship; **~s que hay que correr**
risks you have to take; **corres el ~ de perderlo**
you run the risk of losing it; **un seguro a** *or*
contra todo ~ an all-risks *o* a comprehensive
insurance policy

riesgoso -sa *adj* (AmL) risky

rifa *f* (sorteo) raffle, draw

rifar [A1] *vt* to raffle

rifle *m* rifle

rigidez *f* (a) (de material) stiffness, rigidity; (de
un miembro) stiffness (b) (de ley, doctrina, horario)
inflexibility; (de educación, dieta) strictness

rígido -da *adj* (a) ⟨material⟩ rigid, stiff (b)
⟨educación/dieta⟩ strict; ⟨regla/horario/carácter⟩
inflexible; ⟨actitud⟩ rigid, inflexible; ⟨moral/
principios⟩ strict

rigor *m* (en general) rigor*; (de medidas, castigo)
harshness, severity; **con todo el ~ de la ley** with

the full rigor of the law; **el ~ del invierno** the
rigors of winter; **con ~** rigorously, strictly; **los
saludos de ~** the usual greetings

riguroso -sa *adj* (a) ⟨método⟩ rigorous; ⟨dieta/
control/orden⟩ strict; ⟨examen⟩ thorough;
rigurosas medidas de seguridad tight security (b)
⟨juez⟩ harsh; ⟨maestro⟩ strict; ⟨castigo⟩ severe,
harsh (c) ⟨invierno⟩ hard; ⟨clima⟩ harsh

rima *f* (de sonidos) rhyme

rimar [A1] *vi* to rhyme

rimbombante *adj* ⟨estilo⟩ grandiose,
overblown; ⟨palabras⟩ high-flown; ⟨boda/fiesta⟩
ostentatious, showy

rímel *m* mascara

rin *m* ① (Col, Méx) (rueda) wheel; (llanta) rim
② (Per) (teléfono) public telephone; (ficha)
(telephone) token

rincón *m* ① (de habitación, armario) corner
② (lugar) spot, place; **bellos rincones de Perú**
beautiful places *o* spots in Peru; **registraron hasta
el último ~ de la casa** they searched every nook
and cranny of the house

ring /rrin/ *m* (*pl* **rings**) (Dep) ring

rinoceronte *m* rhinoceros

riña *f* (a) (pelea) fight; **~ de gallos** (AmS)
cockfight (b) (discusión) quarrel, argument, row
(colloq)

riñón *m* (a) (Anat) kidney (b) (Coc) kidney (c)
riñones *mpl* (fam) (espalda baja) lower part of the
back, kidneys (*pl*)

río *m* river; **~ abajo/arriba** downstream/
upstream; **el R~ de la Plata** the River Plate

río, rio, etc ▶ REÍR

Río de Janeiro *m* Rio de Janeiro

rioplatense *adj* of/from the River Plate

riqueza *f* (a) (bienes) wealth; **las ~s del museo**
the treasures of the museum (b) (recursos): **las ~s
del suelo** the earth's riches; **las ~s naturales de
un país** a country's natural resources (c)
(variedad, abundancia) richness

risa *f* laugh; **una risita nerviosa** a nervous giggle
o laugh; **¡qué ~!** what a laugh!, how funny!; **entre
las ~s del público** amid laughter from the
audience; **me entró la ~** I got the giggles; **da ~
oírla hablar** it's very funny hearing her talk;
morirse de (la) ~ (fam) to die laughing (colloq);
estábamos muertos de (la) ~ we were killing
ourselves laughing (colloq); **retorcerse de la ~** to
double up with laughter; **tomarse algo a ~** (fam)
to treat sth as a joke

risotada *f* guffaw

risueño -ña *adj* ⟨cara/expresión⟩ smiling;
⟨persona⟩ cheerful; ⟨porvenir/perspectivas⟩ bright

rítmico -ca *adj* rhythmic, rhythmical

ritmo *m* (a) (compás) rhythm; **al ~ de la música**
to the rhythm of the music, in time to the music;
llevaba el ~ con los pies he kept time with his
feet; **seguir el ~** to keep in time, follow the beat
(b) (velocidad) pace, speed; **llevan un buen ~ de**

trabajo they work at a steady pace *o* speed; **a este ∼ no terminaremos nunca** at this rate we'll never finish; **el ∼ de crecimiento** the rate of growth

rito *m* (Relig) rite; (costumbre) ritual

ritual *adj/m* ritual

rival *adj* rival (*before n*)
■ *mf* rival; **sin ∼** unrivaled

rivalidad *f* rivalry

rizado -da *adj* ⟨pelo⟩ curly; ⟨mar⟩ slightly choppy

rizar [A4] *vt* ⟨pelo/melena⟩ to curl, perm
■ **rizarse** *v pron* (a) ⟨pelo⟩ (con la humedad) to frizz, go frizzy (b) (*refl*) ⟨pelo⟩ to curl

rizo *m* (a) (de pelo) curl (b) (Tex) bouclé (c) (Aviac) loop

róbalo *m* sea bass

robar [A1] *vt* 1 (a) ⟨dinero/bolso⟩ to steal; ⟨banco⟩ to rob; **∼le algo a algn** to steal sth FROM sb; **le robó dinero a su jefe** he stole some money from his boss; **le robaron el bolso** she had her bag stolen (b) (raptar) ⟨niño⟩ to abduct, kidnap 2 (estafar) to cheat, rip off (colloq) 3 (Jueg) (en naipes, dominó) to draw, pick up (colloq)
■ ∼ *vi* to steal; **∼on en la casa de al lado** the house next door was broken into; **¡me han robado!** I've been robbed!

roble *m* (árbol) oak (tree); (madera) oak

robo *m* (a) (en banco, museo) robbery; (hurto de dinero, objeto) theft; **∼ a mano armada** armed robbery (b) (en vivienda) burglary; (forzando la entrada) break-in (c) (fam) (estafa) rip-off (colloq)

robot *m* (*pl* **-bots**) robot

robustecer [E3] *vt* to strengthen
■ **robustecerse** *v pron* to become *o* grow stronger

robustez *f* robustness, sturdiness

robusto -ta *adj* ⟨árbol⟩ robust, strong; ⟨persona⟩ robust, sturdy; ⟨construcción⟩ sturdy

roca *f* rock

roce *m* (a) (contacto) rubbing; (fricción) friction; **no soporta el ∼ de la sábana** he can't bear the sheet rubbing against his skin; **el ∼ de su mejilla** the brush of her cheek; **tiene los puños gastados por el ∼** his cuffs are worn (b) (trato frecuente) regular contact (c) (desacuerdo): **∼s dentro del partido** friction within the party; **tener un ∼ con algn** to have a brush with sb

rociar [A17] *vt* (con pulverizador) to spray; **lo ∼on de keroseno** they doused it with kerosene; **rocíelo con limón** sprinkle with lemon

rocío *m* dew; **una gota de ∼** a dewdrop

rock *adj inv* rock (*before n*)
■ *m* rock music; **∼ duro** *or* (AmL) **pesado** hard rock

rockero -ra *adj* ⟨grupo/ambiente⟩ rock (*before n*)
■ *m,f* rock artist *o* musician, rocker (colloq)

rocola *f* (AmL) jukebox

rocoso -sa *adj* rocky

rocote, rocoto *m* (AmS) hot pepper

rodaballo *m* turbot

rodachina *f* (Col) caster, roller

rodaja *f* slice; **en ∼s** sliced

rodaje *m* (a) (Cin) filming, shooting (b) (Auto) breaking-in (AmE), running-in (BrE); **estar en ∼ to** be breaking in (AmE) *o* (BrE) running in

rodapié *m* baseboard (AmE), skirting board (BrE)

rodar [A10] *vi* 1 «moneda/pelota» to roll; «rueda» to go round, turn; **la moneda rodó por la mesa** the coin rolled across the table; **rodó escaleras abajo** she went tumbling down the stairs 2 (Cin) to film, shoot; **¡se rueda!** action!
■ ∼ *vt* (Cin) to shoot, film

rodeado -da *adj* **∼ de algo** surrounded BY sth

rodear [A1] *vt* (a) ⟨edificio/persona⟩ to surround; **∼ algo DE algo** to surround sth WITH sth; **las circunstancias que ∼on su muerte** the circumstances surrounding his death; **le rodeó la cintura con los brazos** he put his arms around her waist (b) (AmL) ⟨ganado⟩ to round up 2 (estar alrededor de) to surround; **todos los que lo rodean** everyone who works with him/knows him
■ **rodearse** *v pron* **∼se DE algo/algn** to surround oneself WITH sth/sb

rodeo *m* (a) (desvío) detour; **dar un ∼** to make a detour; **andarse con ∼s** to beat about the bush (b) (Espec) rodeo

rodilla *f* knee; **ponerse de ∼s** to kneel down, to get down on one's knees

rodillera *f* (a) (Dep) kneepad; (Med) knee bandage (b) (parche) knee patch

rodillo *m* (de cocina) rolling pin; (para pintar) paint roller; (de máquina de escribir) roller, platen

roedor -dora *m,f* rodent

roer [E13] *vt* ⟨hueso/cable⟩ to gnaw (at)

rogar [A8] *vt*: **te lo ruego** I beg you; **se ruega no fumar** you are kindly requested not to smoke; **te ruego que me perdones** please forgive me; **le rogó que tuviera misericordia** she begged him to have mercy
■ ∼ *vi* (Relig) to pray; **roguemos al Señor** let us pray; **hacerse (de)** *or* (Méx) **(del)** ∼ to play hard to get; **aceptó sin hacerse (de)** ∼ he accepted immediately, without any persuading

rojizo -za *adj* reddish

rojo¹ -ja *adj* 1 (a) ⟨color/vestido⟩ red; **ponerse ∼** «persona» to blush, turn red; «semáforo» to turn red, go red (BrE); **ponerse ∼ de ira** to turn *o* (BrE) go red with anger (b) ⟨piel⟩ (por el sol) sunburnt, red 2 (pey *o* hum) (Pol) (a) (de izquierda) red (pej *or* hum), commie (pej *or* hum) (b) (en la Guerra Civil española) Republican
■ *m,f* (pey *o* hum) (a) (izquierdista) red (pej *or* hum), commie (pej *or* hum) (b) (en la Guerra Civil española) Republican

rojo² *m* red; **al ∼ vivo** ⟨metal⟩ red-hot

rol *m* (a) (lista) roll, list (b) (papel) role

rolar [A1] *vi* (Méx fam) (dar vueltas) to wander about
■ ∼ *vt* (Méx fam) ⟨persona⟩ to move
■ **rolarse** *v pron* (recipr) (Méx fam) (turnarse) to take turns; **tenemos que ∼nos el libro** we have to take turns with the book *o* pass the book around

rollizo -za *adj* chubby

rollo *m* 1 (a) (de papel, tela, película) roll (b) (de cable, cuerda) reel (c) (fam) (de gordura) roll of fat 2 (a) (Esp fam) (cosa aburrida) bore; **¡qué ∼ de conferencia!** what a boring lecture! (b) (Esp, Méx fam) (lata) nuisance, pain (colloq); **¡qué ∼!** what a nuisance *o* pain! 3 (fam) (a) (perorata) speech (colloq), lecture (colloq); **siempre nos suelta el mismo ~** he always gives us the same speech; **bueno, corta el ~ ya** OK, can it, will you? (AmE colloq), OK, put a sock in it, will you? (BrE colloq) **(b)** (mentira) story **4** (Esp, Méx fam) (asunto) business

■ *adj inv* (Esp fam) boring; **¡qué tío más ~!** that guy's such a pain o bore! (colloq)

Roma *f* Rome

romance *m* romance

románico -ca *adj* ⟨arquitectura/columna⟩ Romanesque; ⟨lengua⟩ Romance (*before n*)

romano -na *adj* (Hist) Roman; (de la ciudad) of/from Rome, Roman

■ *m,f* (Hist) Roman; (de la ciudad) person from Rome

romanticismo *m* (Art, Lit, Mús) Romanticism; (sentimentalismo) romanticism

romántico -ca *adj/m,f* (Art, Lit, Mús) Romantic; (sentimental) romantic

rombo *m* **(a)** (Mat) rhombus **(b)** (carta) diamond **(c) rombos** *mpl* (palo) diamonds (*pl*)

romería *f* **(a)** (Relig) procession (*to a local shrine, gen followed by festivities*) **(b)** (AmL fam) (multitud) mass, crowd

romero *m* (Bot, Coc) rosemary

rompecabezas *m* (*pl ~*) puzzle

rompehielos *m* (*pl ~*) icebreaker

rompeolas *m* (*pl ~*) breakwater

romper [E30] *vt* **1** **(a)** ⟨loza/mueble⟩ to break; ⟨ventana⟩ to break, smash; ⟨lápiz/cuerda⟩ to break, snap **(b)** ⟨hoja/póster⟩ (rasgar) to tear; (en varios pedazos) to tear up **(c)** ⟨camisa⟩ to tear, split **2** **(a)** ⟨silencio/monotonía⟩ to break; ⟨tranquilidad⟩ to disturb **(b)** ⟨promesa/pacto⟩ to break; ⟨relaciones/compromiso⟩ to break off

■ ~ *vi* **1** **(a)** «olas» to break **(b)** (liter) «alba» to break; **al ~ el día** at daybreak, at the crack of dawn **(c)** (empezar): **rompió a llorar/reír** she burst into tears/burst out laughing

2 «novios» to break up, split up; **~ CON algn** ⟨con novio⟩ to split o break up WITH sb; **~ CON algo** ⟨con el pasado⟩ to break WITH sth; ⟨con tradición⟩ to break away FROM sth

■ **romperse** *v pron* **(a)** «vaso/plato» to break, smash, get broken o smashed; «papel» to tear, rip, get torn o ripped; «televisor/ascensor» (RPl) to break down **(b)** «pantalones/zapatos» to wear out **(c)** (refl) ⟨brazo/pierna⟩ to break

rompevientos *m* (*pl ~*) (Méx, RPl) (pulóver) sweater; (anorak) windbreaker (AmE), windcheater (BrE)

ron *m* **(a)** (bebida) rum **(b)** (Per) (combustible) methanol

roncar [A2] *vi* (al dormir) to snore; (dormir) (fam) to sleep

roncha *f* (Med) (por picadura de insecto) bump; **se llenó de ~s** she came out in a rash

ronco -ca *adj* **(a)** ⟨persona⟩ hoarse; **se quedó ~ de tanto gritar** he shouted himself hoarse **(b)** ⟨voz⟩ husky

ronda *f* **1** (de soldado, guarda) patrol; (de enfermera) round; (de policía) patrol, beat; **hacer la ~** «policía» to patrol one's beat; «soldado/guarda» to be on patrol; «repartidor» to do one's round **2** (vuelta, etapa) round; (de bebidas) round **3** (CS, Per) (de niños): **formaron una ~**

tomándose de la mano they held hands in a circle; **danzaban en ~** they were dancing around in a circle **4** (Esp, Méx) (serenata) serenade

rondar [A1] *vt* **(a)** «vigilante/patrulla» to patrol **(b)** «pensamiento»: **hace días que me ronda esa idea** that idea has been going round and round in my head for days **(c)** ⟨lugar⟩ to hang around **(d)** (acercarse a): **debe estar rondando los 60** she must be getting on for 60

■ ~ *vi* (merodear) to hang around

ronquido *m* snore

ronronear [A1] *vi* to purr

roña *f* **1** **(a)** (mugre) dirt, grime; **lleno de ~** covered in dirt o grime **(b)** (en metal) rust **(c)** (Vet) mange **2** (Méx) (juego) tag; **jugar a la ~** to play tag

roñoso -sa *adj* **1** [ESTAR] **(a)** (mugriento) grubby **(b)** (oxidado) rusty **(c)** (Vet) mangy **2** [SER] (fam) (tacaño) tight-fisted (colloq), stingy (colloq)

■ *m,f* (fam) scrooge (colloq), skinflint (colloq)

ropa *f* clothes (*pl*); **cambiarse de ~** to get changed, to change (one's clothes); **la ~ sucia** the dirty laundry; **tengo un montón de ~ para planchar** I've got a stack of ironing to do; **~ interior** underwear, underclothes (*pl*)

ropero *m* wardrobe

roquero -ra *adj/m,f* ▶ ROCKERO

rosa *f* **(a)** (flor) rose **(b)** (rosal) rosebush **(c)** (Chi) (nudo) bow

■ *adj* (gen inv) pink; **un vestido (de color) ~** a pink dress; **verlo todo de color ~** to see things through rose-colored glasses o (BrE) rose-tinted spectacles

■ *m* pink

rosado -da *adj* **(a)** ⟨color/vestido⟩ pink **(b)** ⟨mejillas⟩ rosy; ⟨vino⟩ rosé

■ *m* **(a)** (color) pink **(b)** (vino) rosé

rosal *m* (árbol) rosetree; (arbusto) rosebush

rosario *m* **(a)** (Relig) (rezo) rosary; (cuentas) rosary (beads) **(b)** (serie, sarta) string

rosca *f* **(a)** (de tornillo, tuerca) thread; **tapón de ~** screw top; **pasarse de ~: el tornillo se pasó de ~** the screw isn't biting; **te has pasado de ~** (fam) you've gone too far **(b)** (Bol, Col) (círculo, grupo) clique, clan

rosedal *m* (CS, Méx) rose garden

roseta *f* (Arquit) rose, rosette; (de ducha) showerhead; (de regadera) spinkler (AmE), rose (BrE)

rosetón *m* (ventana) rose window, rosette; (en el techo) ceiling rose

rosquilla *f.* type of doughnut

rosticería *f* (Méx) ▶ ROTISERÍA

rostizar [A4] *vt* (Méx) to roast; **pollo rostizado** roast chicken

rostro *m* **(a)** (cara) face **(b)** (Esp fam) (desfachatez) nerve (colloq), cheek (BrE colloq)

rotación *f* rotation

rotar [A1] *vt/vi* to rotate

■ **rotarse** *v pron* (en trabajo) to work on a rota system; **~se para hacer algo** to take it in turns to do sth

rotativo *m* **(a)** (period) (diario) newspaper **(b)** (Chi) (Cin) movie theater (AmE), cinema (BrE) (*showing a continuous performance*)

rotería f (Chi) (fam) (hecho): **fue una ∼ no invitarlo** it was incredibly rude not to invite him; **me hizo una ∼** he was rude to me

rotisería f (CS) delicatessen selling spit-roast chickens

roto¹ -ta adj [1] (a) ‹camisa› torn, ripped; ‹zapato› worn-out (b) ‹vaso/plato/brazo› broken (c) ‹papel› torn; **me devolvió el libro ∼** the book was falling apart when he gave it back to me (d) (RPl) ‹televisor/heladera› broken; ‹coche› broken down [2] (Chi fam & pey) (a) ‹barrio/gente› lower-class (pej), plebby (colloq & pej) (b) (mal educado) rude
■ m,f [1] (Chi) (a) (fam & pey) (de clase baja) pleb (colloq & pej) (b) (fam & pey) (mal educado): **es una rota, nunca saluda** she's so rude, she doesn't even say hello [2] (Per fam) (chileno) Chilean

roto² m (Esp) (agujero) hole

rotonda f (glorieta) traffic circle (AmE), roundabout (BrE)

rotoso -sa adj (a) (CS, Per fam) ‹persona/ropa› scruffy (b) (Chi fam & pey) ‹barrio/gente› lower-class (pej)

rótula f (Anat) kneecap

rotulador m (Esp) felt-tip pen

rótulo m (a) (Impr) (título) title; (encabezamiento) heading (b) (etiqueta) label (c) (letrero) sign

rotundo -da adj (a) ‹respuesta› categorical, emphatic; ‹negativa› categorical, outright (before n); **me contestó con un 'no' ∼** his answer was an emphatic 'no' (b) ‹éxito/fracaso› resounding

rotura f: **hay una ∼ en la cañería** there's a burst in the pipe; **sufrió ∼ de cadera** she fractured her hip; **tiene ∼ de ligamentos** she has torn ligaments; **tiene una ∼ en la manga** (CS) it has a rip in the sleeve

round /rraun/ m (Dep) round

rozado -da adj (gastado) worn; (sucio) grubby

rozadura f scratch; **le hizo una ∼ al coche** he scratched the car; **los zapatos nuevos le hicieron una ∼** her new shoes rubbed

rozagante adj (AmL) healthy

rozamiento m friction

rozar [A4] vt (tocar ligeramente): **el gato me rozó la pierna** the cat brushed against my leg; **sus labios ∼on mi frente** her lips brushed my forehead; **las sillas rozan la pared** the chairs rub o scrape against the wall; **la bala le rozó el brazo** the bullet grazed his arm; **me roza el zapato** my shoe's rubbing
■ **rozarse** v pron (a) (recípr) «cables/piezas» to chafe; «manos/labios» to touch (b) (refl) ‹brazo/rodillas› to graze (c) «cuello/puños» to wear (d) (Méx) «bebé» to get diaper rash (AmE), get nappy rash (BrE); **el bebé está rozado** the baby has diaper (AmE) o (BrE) nappy rash

Rte. (= **remite** or **remitente**) sender

ruana f ruana (Colombian, Venezuelan poncho)

rubeola f German measles

rubí m (a) (Min) ruby (b) (de reloj) jewel (c) (color) : **de color ∼** ruby red

rubio -bia adj ‹pelo› fair, blonde; ‹hombre› fair-haired, blond; ‹mujer› fair-haired, blonde
■ m,f (m) blond o fair-haired man; (f) blonde o fair-haired woman, blonde (colloq)

rublo m ruble*

rubor m (a) (liter) (sonrojo) flush; **el ∼ de sus mejillas la delató** her flushed cheeks betrayed her (b) (Méx, RPl) (cosmética) rouge, blusher

ruborizarse [A4] v pron to blush, to turn red (in the face), to flush

rúbrica f (de firma) flourish; (firma) signing

rubro m (esp AmL) (a) (área) area; **nuestro ∼ de peletería** our line in furs; **trabaja en el ∼ de la computación** he works in computers (b) (en contabilidad — apartado) heading; (— renglón) item

rucio -cia adj (a) ‹caballo› gray* (b) (Chi fam) ‹pelo› fair, blonde; ‹hombre› fair-haired, blond; ‹mujer› fair-haired, blonde

ruco -ca adj (Méx fam) old

rudimentario -ria adj rudimentary

rudimento m rudiment

rudo -da adj (tosco) rough, rude (arch)

rueca f distaff

rueda f (a) (de vehículo, mecanismo) wheel; **∼ de molino** millstone; **∼ dentada** gear wheel, cogwheel; **∼ de recambio** or **repuesto** or (RPl) **de auxilio** spare wheel; **patinar sobre ∼s** to roller-skate; **ir sobre ∼s** to go o run smoothly (b) (neumático) tire*; **se me pinchó una ∼** I got a flat tire o a puncture (c) (de mueble) caster, roller (d) (corro) ring, circle; **∼ de prensa** press conference (e) (en gimnasia) cartwheel

ruedo m (a) (Taur) bullring (b) (esp AmL) (de falda, pantalón) hem

ruego m (a) (súplica) plea; **de nada te servirán tus ∼s** your pleading will get you nowhere (b) (petición) request; **en respuesta a un ∼ de sus oyentes** in response to a request from his listeners

rufián m (granuja) rogue, scoundrel (dated); (chulo) pimp

rugby /'rruɣbi/ m rugby

rugido m roar

rugir [I7] vi ‹león/mar/viento› to roar

rugoso -sa adj rough, bumpy

ruibarbo m rhubarb

ruido m noise; **sin hacer ∼** quietly; **no hagas tanto ∼** don't make so much noise

ruidoso -sa adj ‹calle/máquina/persona› noisy

ruin adj (mezquino, vil) despicable, contemptible; (avaro) miserly, mean (BrE)

ruina f (a) (bancarrota) ruin; **dejar a algn en la ∼** to ruin sb; **estar en la ∼** «empresario» to be ruined; «país» to be in financial ruin; **la compañía está en la ∼** the company has collapsed (b) (perdición) downfall; **el juego fue su ∼** gambling was his downfall (c) (hundimiento) collapse; **la casa amenaza ∼** the house is on the point of collapse (d) **ruinas** fpl (de edificio, ciudad) ruins (pl); **en ∼s** in ruins

ruiseñor m nightingale

rulero m (Per, RPl) curler

ruleta f roulette

ruletero -ra m,f (Méx fam) cab o taxi driver, cabbie (colloq)

rulo m (para el pelo) curler, roller; (rizo) (CS, Per) curl

rulot f (Esp) trailer (AmE), caravan (BrE)

ruma f (Chi) pile, heap

Rumania, Rumanía f Romania

rumano[1] **-na** *adj/m,f* Romanian, Rumanian

rumano[2] *m* (idioma) Romanian, Rumanian

rumba *f* rumba

rumbo *m* (dirección) direction, course; (Náut) course; **caminar sin ~ fijo** to wander aimlessly; **partió (con) ~ a Toluca** he set off for Toluca; **navegar con ~ norte** to sail a northerly course; **los acontecimientos tomaron un ~ trágico** events took a tragic turn

rumiante *m* ruminant

rumiar [A1] *vi* «*vaca*» to chew the cud, ruminate

rumor *m* **(a)** (murmuración) rumor*; **circulan ~es de que ...** rumors are circulating that ..., rumor has it that ... **(b)** (sonido) murmur

rumorear [A1] *vt*: **se rumorea que ...** rumor has it that ...

rupestre *adj* ⟨*pintura/dibujo*⟩ cave (*before n*); ⟨*planta*⟩ rock (*before n*)

rupia *f* rupee

ruptura *f* **(a)** (de relaciones, negaciones) breaking-off; (de contrato) breach, breaking; (de matrimonio) breakup; (con pasado, tradición) break; **esa fue la causa de la ~ de las negociaciones** that was what caused the negotiations to be broken off **(b)** (Dep) (en tenis) service break

rural *adj* rural

Rusia *f* Russia

ruso[1] **-sa** *adj/m,f* Russian

ruso[2] *m* (idioma) Russian

rústica (esp Esp): **en rústica** (*loc adj*) ⟨*edición*⟩ paperback (*before n*); **un libro en ~** a paperback

rústico -ca *adj* (del campo) rustic; (basto) coarse

ruta *f* **(a)** (itinerario) route **(b)** (RPl) (carretera) road

rutina *f* routine; **inspección de ~** routine inspection; **por pura ~** out of habit

rutinario -ria *adj* **(a)** ⟨*trabajo/vida*⟩ monotonous **(b)** ⟨*inspección/procedimiento*⟩ routine (*before n*)

Ss

S, s *f* (*read as* /'ese/) *the letter* S, s

S. *m* (= **siglo**) C; **s.XX** C20

S (= **sur**) S, South

S. (= **santo**) St

S.A. (= **Sociedad Anónima**) ≈Inc (*in US*), ≈Ltd (*in UK*), ≈PLC (*in UK*)

sábado *m* Saturday; (Relig) Sabbath; **S~ de Gloria** *or* **Santo** Easter Saturday; **~ inglés** (CS) non-working Saturday

sabana *f* (Geog) savanna*, grassland

sábana *f* sheet; **~ ajustable** *or* (Méx) **de cajón** fitted sheet; **~ bajera/encimera** bottom/top sheet

sabandija *f* **1** (insecto) creepy-crawly (colloq), bug; (reptil) creepy-crawly (colloq) **2** **sabandija** *mf* (AmL fam) (pícaro) rascal (colloq)

sabañón *m* chilblain

sabático -ca *adj* sabbatical

sabelotodo *mf* (fam) know-it-all (AmE colloq), know-all (BrE colloq)

saber[1] *m* knowledge; **una persona de gran ~** a person of great learning

saber[2] [E25] *vt* **1** **(a)** ⟨*nombre/dirección/canción*⟩ to know; **ya lo sé** I know; **no lo sé** I don't know; **no sé cómo se llama** I don't know his name; **¡yo qué sé!** how (on earth) should I know! (colloq); **que yo sepa** as far as I know; **~ algo DE algo** to know sth ABOUT sth; **sé muy poco de ese tema** I know very little about the subject; **no sabe lo que dice** he doesn't know what he's talking about **(b)** (enterarse) to find out; **lo supe**

por mi hermana I found out about it through my sister; **sin que lo supiéramos** without our knowing; **¡si yo lo hubiera sabido antes!** if I had only known before!; **¡cómo iba yo a ~ que ...!** how was I to know that ...!

2 (ser capaz de): **~ hacer algo** to know how to do sth; **¿sabes nadar?** can you swim?, do you know how to swim?; **sabe escuchar** she's a good listener; **sabe hablar varios idiomas** she can speak several languages

■ **~** *vi*

I (a) (tener conocimiento) to know; **¿quién sabe?** who knows?; **~ DE algo/algn** to know of sth/sb; **yo sé de un lugar donde te lo pueden arreglar** I know of a place where you can get it fixed **(b)** (tener noticias, enterarse): **no sé nada de ella desde hace más de un mes** I haven't heard from her for over a month; **yo supe del accidente por la radio** I heard about the accident on the radio

II (a) (tener sabor) (+ *compl*) to taste; **sabe dulce/bien** it tastes sweet/nice; **~ A algo** to taste OF sth; **no sabe a nada** it doesn't taste of anything; **sabe a podrido** it tastes rotten **(b)** (causar cierta impresión): **me sabe mal** *or* **no me sabe bien tener que decírselo** I don't like having to tell him

■ **saberse** *v pron* (*enf*) ⟨*lección/poema*⟩ to know

sabido -da *adj* [SER] well-known; **como es ~** as everybody knows

sabiduría *f* wisdom

sabiendas: **a sabiendas** (*loc adv*): **lo hizo a ~ de que me molestaba** he did it knowing full well *o* perfectly well that I found it annoying

sabihondo -da *m,f* (fam) know-it-all (AmE colloq), know-all (BrE colloq)

sabio -bia *adj* (con grandes conocimientos) learned, wise; (sensato) ⟨*persona/medida*⟩ wise; ⟨*consejo*⟩ sound, wise
■ *m,f* (*m*) wise man, sage (liter); (*f*) wise woman

sable *m* [1] (Arm) saber*; (Náut) batten [2] (en heráldica) sable

sabor *m* (a) (de comida, bebida, etc) taste, flavor*; con ∼ a menta mint-flavoured; viene en tres ∼es it comes in three flavors; no tiene ∼ it has no taste to it (b) (carácter) flavor*

saborear [A1] *vt* to savor*; ⟨*éxito/triunfo*⟩ to relish

sabotaje *m* sabotage

saboteador -dora *m,f* saboteur

sabotear [A1] *vt* to sabotage

sabré, sabría, etc ▶ SABER

sabroso -sa *adj* [1] ⟨*comida*⟩ tasty, delicious; ⟨*chisme/historia*⟩ spicy (colloq), juicy (colloq) [2] (AmL fam) (agradable) ⟨*música/ritmo*⟩ pleasant, nice; ⟨*clima/agua*⟩ beautiful

sabrosón -sona *adj* (a) (AmL fam) ⟨*guiso*⟩ tasty, delicious; ⟨*fruta*⟩ delicious (b) (AmL fam) ⟨*clima*⟩ mild (c) (Col, Méx, Ven fam) ⟨*música*⟩ pleasant

sabueso *m* (Zool) bloodhound

sacacorchos *m* (*pl* ∼) corkscrew

sacapuntas *m* (*pl* ∼) pencil sharpener

sacar [A2] *vt*
I [1] (extraer) (a) ⟨*billetera/lápiz*⟩ to take out, get out; ⟨*pistola/espada*⟩ to draw; ∼ algo DE algo to take *o* get sth OUT OF sth; lo saqué del cajón I took *o* it out of the drawer (b) ⟨*muela*⟩ to pull out, take out; ⟨*riñón/cálculo*⟩ to remove; me ∼on sangre they took some blood (c) ⟨*diamantes/ cobre/petróleo*⟩ to extract (d) ⟨*carta/ficha*⟩ to draw

[2] (poner, llevar fuera) (a) ⟨*maceta/mesa/basura*⟩ to take out; sácalo aquí al sol bring it out here into the sun; tuvimos que ∼lo por la ventana we had to get it out through the window; ∼ el perro a pasear to take the dog out for a walk; ∼ el coche del garaje to get the car out of the garage (b) (invitar): el marido no la saca nunca her husband never takes her out; ∼ a algn a bailar to ask sb to dance (c) ⟨*parte del cuerpo*⟩ to put out; me sacó la lengua he stuck *o* put his tongue out at me

[3] (retirar) to take out; ∼ dinero del banco to take out *o* withdraw money from the bank

[4] (de una situación difícil) ∼ a algn DE algo ⟨*de apuro/atolladero*⟩ to get sb OUT OF sth

[5] (Esp) ⟨*dobladillo*⟩ to let down; ⟨*pantalón/falda*⟩ (alargar) to let down; (ensanchar) to let out

II (obtener) [1] ⟨*pasaporte/permiso*⟩ to get; ⟨*entrada/billete*⟩ to get, buy

[2] (a) ⟨*votos/puntos/calificación*⟩ to get (b) ⟨*premio*⟩ to get, win (c) ⟨*conclusión*⟩ to draw (d) ⟨*suma/cuenta*⟩ to do, work out

[3] ⟨*beneficio*⟩ to get; ⟨*ganancia*⟩ to make; ¿qué sacas con eso? what do you gain by doing that?; no sacó ningún provecho del curso she didn't get anything out of the course

[4] ∼ algo DE algo ⟨*idea/información*⟩ to get sth FROM sth; ⟨*porciones/unidades*⟩ to get sth OUT OF sth; ∼le algo A algn ⟨*dinero/información*⟩ to get sth OUT OF sb

[5] ⟨*brillo*⟩ to bring out; ∼le brillo a algo to polish sth to a shine

III [1] (a) ⟨*libro*⟩ to publish, bring out; ⟨*disco*⟩ to bring out, release; ⟨*modelo/producto*⟩ to bring out (b) ⟨*tema*⟩ to bring up (c) ⟨*foto*⟩ to take; ⟨*copia*⟩ to make, take; ⟨*apuntes*⟩ to make, take; ∼le una foto a algn to take a photo of sb (d) (Esp) ⟨*defecto/falta*⟩ (+ me/te/le etc) to find; a todo le tiene que ∼ faltas he always has to find fault with everything

[2] sacar adelante ⟨*proyecto*⟩ (poner en marcha) to get sth off the ground; (salvar de la crisis) to keep sth going; luché tanto para ∼ adelante a mis hijos I fought so hard to give my children a good start in life

[3] (Dep) ⟨*tiro libre/falta*⟩ to take

IV (quitar) [1] (esp AmL) ∼le algo A algn ⟨*botas/gorro*⟩ to take sth OFF sb (b) ∼le algo A algo ⟨*tapa/cubierta*⟩ to take sth OFF sth (c) (retirar): saca esto de aquí take this away; saquen los libros de la mesa take the books off the table (d) (hacer desaparecer) ⟨*mancha*⟩ to remove, get ... out
■ ∼ *vi* (Dep) (en tenis, vóleibol) to serve; (en fútbol) to kick off

■ **sacarse** *v pron* (refl) [1] (extraer) ⟨*astilla/púa*⟩ to take ... out; ⟨*ojo*⟩ to poke ... out; me tengo que ∼ una muela (caus) I have to have a tooth out; ∼se algo de algo to take sth OUT OF sth; sácate las manos de los bolsillos take your hands out of your pockets

[2] (AmL) (quitarse) ⟨*ropa/zapatos*⟩ to take off; ⟨*maquillaje*⟩ to remove, take off

[3] (a) (caus) ⟨*foto*⟩: tengo que ∼me una foto I have to have my photo taken (b) (AmL) ⟨*calificación/nota*⟩ to get

sacarina *f* saccharin

sacerdote *m* priest

sacerdotisa *f* priestess

saciar [A1] *vt* ⟨*hambre*⟩ to satisfy; ⟨*sed*⟩ to quench; ⟨*deseo*⟩ (liter) to satiate (liter); ⟨*ambición*⟩ to fulfill*, realize
■ **saciarse** *v pron*: comer/beber hasta ∼se to eat/drink one's fill

saco *m* [1] (continente) sack; (contenido) sack, sackful; ∼ de dormir sleeping bag [2] (AmL) (de tela) jacket; ∼ sport (AmL) sports coat (AmE), sports jacket (BrE)

sacramento *m* sacrament; los últimos ∼s the last rites

sacrificado -da *adj* ⟨*persona*⟩ selfless, self-sacrificing

sacrificar [A2] *vt* (a) (Relig) ⟨*cordero/víctimas*⟩ to sacrifice (b) ⟨*res/ganado*⟩ to slaughter; ⟨*perro/ gato*⟩ (euf) to put ... to sleep (euph) (c) ⟨*carrera/ juventud*⟩ to sacrifice
■ **sacrificarse** *v pron* to make sacrifices

sacrificio *m* (a) (privación, renuncia) sacrifice (b) (inmolación) sacrifice (c) (de res) slaughter

sacrilegio *m* sacrilege

sacrílego -ga *adj* sacrilegious

sacristán *m* sacristan, verger

sacristía *f* vestry, sacristy

sacudida *f* (a) (agitando) shake, shaking; (golpeando) beating (b) (de terremoto) tremor; (de explosión) blast; (de tren, coche) jerk, jolt (c) (fam) (descarga) electric shock

S

sacudir [I1] *vt* **1** **(a)** (agitar) ⟨toalla/alfombra⟩ to shake; (golpear) ⟨alfombra/colchón⟩ to beat; **sacudió la arena de la toalla** he shook the sand out of the towel **(b)** (fam) ⟨niño⟩ to clobber (colloq); **∼ la cabeza** (para negar) to shake one's head; (para afirmar) to nod (one's head) **(c)** (hacer temblar) to shake **(d)** (CS, Méx) (limpiar) to dust, do the dusting **2** (conmover, afectar) to shake
■ ∼ *vi* (CS, Méx) to dust
■ **sacudirse** *v pron* (refl) (quitarse) ⟨arena/polvo⟩ to shake off

sádico -ca *adj* sadistic
■ *m,f* sadist

sadismo *m* sadism

sadomasoquismo *m* sadomasochism

sadomasoquista *mf* sadomasochist

safari *m* **(a)** (gira, viaje) safari; **ir de ∼** to go on safari **(b)** (zoológico) safari park

sagaz *adj* shrewd, astute

Sagitario *m* (signo, constelación) Sagittarius; **es (de) ∼** she's (a) Sagittarian
■ *mf* (*pl* ∼ *or* **-rios**) (persona) *tb* **sagitario** Sagittarian, Sagittarius

sagrado -da *adj* **1** (Relig) ⟨altar⟩ holy; ⟨lugar⟩ holy, sacred **2** (fundamental, intocable) sacred

Sahara /sa'ara/ *m*: **el (desierto del) ∼** the Sahara (Desert)

sajón -jona *adj/m,f* Saxon

sal *f* **1** (Coc) salt; **mantequilla sin ∼** unsalted butter; **echarle la ∼ a algn** (Méx fam) to put a jinx on sb **2** (Quím) salt; **∼ de fruta** liver salts (*pl*); **∼es de baño** bath salts (*pl*)

sal ▶ SALIR

sala *f* **(a)** (de casa) *tb* **∼ de estar** living room, lounge (BrE) **(b)** (de hotel) lounge; (en hospital) ward; (para reuniones, conferencias) hall; (Teatr) theater*; (Cin) movie theater (AmE), cinema (BrE); **∼ cuna** (Chi) day nursery, creche; **∼ de clases** (CS frml) classroom; **∼ de conciertos** concert hall; **∼ de embarque** departure lounge; **∼ de espera** waiting room; **∼ de exposiciones** gallery, exhibition hall; **∼ de fiestas** night club (*usually featuring dancing and cabaret*); **∼ de profesores** staff room **(c)** (sede de tribunal) courtroom, court

salado -da *adj* **1** (Coc) **(a)** (con sal) ⟨almendras/bacalao⟩ salted; ⟨gusto⟩ salty; **está demasiado ∼** it's too salty **(b)** [SER] (no dulce) ⟨plato/comida⟩ savory* **2** **(a)** (fam) ⟨persona⟩ (gracioso) funny, witty **(b)** (fam) ⟨chiste⟩ risqué; ⟨anécdota⟩ spicy **3** (Méx fam) (que trae mala suerte) jinxed (colloq)

salamandra *f* (Zool) salamander; (estufa) salamander stove

salame *m* **(a)** (CS) (Coc) salami **(b)** (RPl fam) (tonto) idiot

salar¹ [A1] *vt* **(a)** (para conservar) ⟨carne/pescado⟩ to salt (down); ⟨pieles⟩ to salt **(b)** (para condimentar) to salt, add salt to
■ **salarse** *v pron* (Méx fam) (echarse a perder) «planes» to fall through; «negocio» to go bust

salar² *m* (Chi) salt pan, salt flat

salario *m* (frml) wage, salary

salchicha *f* sausage

salchichón *m: spiced sausage similar to salami*

salchichonería *f* (Méx) delicatessen

saldar [A1] *vt* **(a)** ⟨cuenta⟩ to settle; ⟨deuda⟩ to settle, pay (off) **(b)** ⟨mercancías/productos⟩ to sell off

saldo *m* **1** (de cuenta) balance; **∼ a su/nuestro favor** credit/debit balance **2** **(a)** (artículo): **los ∼s no se cambian** sale goods cannot be exchanged; **precios de ∼** sale prices; **🅢 venta de saldos** clearance sale **(b)** **saldos** *mpl* (rebajas) sales (*pl*)

saldré, saldría, etc ▶ SALIR

salero *m* **1** (recipiente) salt shaker (AmE), saltcellar (BrE) **2** (fam) (gracia): **tener ∼** (contando chistes) to be funny; (bailando) to be stylish

salga, salgas, etc ▶ SALIR

salida *f*
I (hacia el exterior) **1** **(a)** (lugar, puerta) exit; **∼ de emergencia/incendios** emergency/fire exit; **todas las ∼s de Bilbao** all the roads out of Bilbao; **es una calle sin ∼** it's a dead end **(b)** (de tubería) outlet, outflow; (de circuito) outlet **2** **(a)** (acción): **me encontré a la ∼** I met him on my way out; **nos encontramos a la ∼ del concierto** we met at the door after the concert; **una ∼ al campo** an outing *o* a trip to the country **(b)** (de líquido, gas, electricidad) output **(c)** **la ∼ del sol** sunrise
II (partida) **1** (de tren, avión) departure; **el tren efectuará su ∼ por la vía cinco** the train will leave from track five; **🅢 salidas nacionales/internacionales** domestic/international departures **2** (Dep) (en una carrera) start
III **1** **1** (solución): **no le veo ninguna ∼ a esta situación** I can see no way out of this situation; **no nos queda otra ∼** we have no other option **2** (Com, Fin) (gasto) payment

salido -da *adj* ⟨ojos/dientes⟩ protruding; ⟨frente/mentón⟩ prominent

saliente *adj* ⟨pómulo/hueso⟩ prominent; ⟨cornisa/balcón⟩ projecting
■ *f or* (Esp) *m* (de edificio, muro) projection; (de precipicio) ledge

salir [I29] *vi*
I **1** (partir) to leave; **¿a qué hora sale el tren?** what time does the train leave?; **el jefe había salido de viaje** the boss was away; **salió corriendo** (fam) she was off like a shot (colloq); **∼ DE algo** to leave FROM sth; **¿de qué andén sale el tren?** what platform does the train leave from?; **salgo de casa a las siete** I leave home at seven; **∼ PARA algo** to leave FOR sth
2 (al exterior — acercándose al hablante) to come out; (— alejándose del hablante) to go out; **no salgas sin abrigo** don't go out without a coat; **no puedo ∼, me he quedado encerrado** I can't get out, I'm trapped in here; **∼ DE algo** to come out/get out OF sth; **¡sal de ahí/de aquí!** come out of there/get out of here!; **¿de dónde salió este dinero?** where did this money come from?; **nunca ha salido de España** he's never been out of Spain; **∼ por la ventana/por la puerta** to get out through the window/leave by the door; **salieron al balcón/al jardín** they went out onto the balcony/into the garden; **¿por aquí se sale a la carretera?** can I get on to the road this way?; **salió a hacer las compras** she's gone out (to do the) shopping
3 (habiendo terminado algo) to leave; **¿a qué hora sales de clase?** what time do you get out of class *o* finish your class?; **¿cuándo sale del hospital?** when is he coming out of (the) hospital?

4 **(a)** (como entretenimiento) to go out; ~ **a cenar** to go out for dinner **(b)** (tener una relación) to go out; ~ **CON algn** to go out WITH sb

5 «*clavo/tapón/mancha*» to come out; «*anillo*» to come off

II **1** (aparecer, manifestarse) **(a)** «*cana/sarpullido*» to appear; (+ *me/te/le etc*) **me empiezan a ~ canas** I'm starting to go gray; **le están saliendo los dientes** she's teething; **me salió una ampolla** I've got a blister; **le salió un sarpullido** he came out in a rash; **me salieron granos** I broke out *o* (BrE) came out in spots; **me sale sangre de la nariz** my nose is bleeding; **a la planta le están saliendo hojas nuevas** the plant's putting out new leaves **(b)** «*sol*» (por la mañana) to rise, come up; (de detrás de una nube) to come out **(c)** (surgir) «*tema/idea*» to come up **(d)** «*carta*» (en naipes) to come up

2 **(a)** «*revista/novela*» to come out; «*disco*» to come out, be released; ~ **al mercado** to come on to the market **(b)** (en televisión, en el periódico) to appear **(c)** (en una foto) to appear; (+ *compl*) **saliste muy bien en la foto** you came out very well in the photo

III **1** (expresando logro) (+ *me/te/le etc*): **no me sale esta ecuación** I can't do this equation; **ahora mismo no me sale su nombre** (fam) I can't think of her name right now; **no le salían las palabras** he couldn't get his words out

2 **(a)** (costar) to work out; **sale más barato/caro** it works out less/more expensive **(b)** (resultar): **todo salió bien** everything turned out *o* worked out well; **salió tal como lo planeamos** it turned out just as we planned; **no salió ninguna de las fotos** none of the photographs came out; **¿qué número salió premiado?** what was the winning number?; ~ **bien/mal en un examen** (Chi fam) to pass/fail an exam; (+ *me/te/le etc*) **el postre no me salió bien** the dessert didn't come out right

3 (de situación, estado) ~ **DE algo** «*de apuro*» to get out of sth; «*de depresión*» to get over sth; **salieron ilesos del accidente** they were not hurt in the accident; ~ **adelante** «*negocio*» to stay afloat, survive; «*propuesta*» to prosper; **lograron ~ adelante** they managed to get through it

4 (con preposición) **(a) salir a** (parecerse a) to take after **(b) salir con** (Col) (combinar con) to go with

■ **salirse** *v pron* **1** **(a)** (de borde, límite) «*agua*» to overflow; «*leche*» to boil over; ~**se DE algo** «*de carretera*» to come/go off sth; «*de tema*» to get off sth; **el río se salió de su cauce** the river overflowed its banks; **procura no ~te del presupuesto** try to keep within the budget **(b)** (por orificio, grieta) «*agua/tinta*» to leak (out), come out; «*gas*» to escape, come out

2 (soltarse) «*pedazo/pieza*» to come off; (+ *me/te/le etc*) **estos zapatos se me salen** these shoes are too big for me

3 (irse) to leave; ~**se DE algo** «*de asociación*» to leave sth; ~**se con la suya** to get one's (own) way

saliva *f* saliva, spit (colloq)

salivar [A1] *vi* to salivate

salmo *m* psalm

salmón *m* salmon
■ *adj inv* salmon-pink, salmon, salmon-colored*

salmonete *m* red mullet, surmullet (AmE)

salmuera *f* brine

salón *m* **(a)** (en casa particular) living room,

sitting room (BrE), lounge (BrE) **(b)** (en hotel) reception room, function room **(c)** (en palacio) hall **(d)** (de clases) classroom; ~ **de actos** auditorium (AmE), assembly hall (BrE); ~ **de baile** ballroom; ~ **de belleza** beauty salon, beauty parlor; ~ **de fiestas** (AmL) function room, reception room; ~ **náutico/del automóvil** boat/motor show

salpicadera *f* (Méx) (de coche, bicicleta) fender (AmE), mudguard (BrE)

salpicadero *m* (Esp) dashboard

salpicadura *f* splash

salpicar [A2] *vt* (de agua) to splash; (de barro, aceite) to splash, spatter

salpicón *m* (de pescado, ave) *chopped seafood or meat with onion, tomato and peppers*

salsa *f* **1** (Coc) sauce; (de jugo de carne) gravy; ~ **bechamel** *or* **blanca** bechamel (sauce); ~ **de tomate** (sofrito) tomato sauce; (catsup) (Col) ketchup, catsup (AmE) **2** (Mús) salsa

saltamontes *m* (*pl* ~) grasshopper

saltar [A1] *vi* **1** **(a)** (brincar) to jump; (más alto, más lejos) to leap; ~ **a la cuerda** *or* (Esp) **comba** to jump rope (AmE), to skip (BrE); ~ **de alegría** to jump for joy; ~ **con** *or* **en una pierna** to hop; ~ **de la cama/silla** to jump out of bed/one's chair **(b)** (en atletismo) to jump **(c)** «*pelota*» to bounce **(d)** (lanzarse) to jump; ~ **al agua** to jump into the water; ~ **en paracaídas** to parachute; **¿sabes ~ del trampolín?** can you dive off the springboard?; **saltó al vacío** he leapt into space; ~ **SOBRE algo/algn** to jump ON sth/sb

2 (pasar) ~ **DE algo A algo** to jump FROM sth TO sth; **saltaba de una idea a otra** she kept jumping from one idea to the next

3 «*botón*» to come off, pop off; «*chispas*» to fly; «*aceite*» to spit; «*corcho*» to pop out; «*fusibles*» to blow; **la bomba hizo ~ el coche por los aires** the bomb blew the car into the air

■ ~ *vt* «*obstáculo/valla/zanja*» to jump (over); (apoyándose) to vault (over)

■ **saltarse** *v pron* **1** **(a)** (omitir) «*línea/página/nombre*» to skip, miss out; «*comida*» to miss, skip **(b)** «*semáforo/stop*» to jump

2 «*botón*» to come off, pop off; «*pintura*» to chip; **se le ~on las lágrimas** her eyes filled with tears

3 (Chi) «*diente/loza*» to chip

salteado -da *adj*: **¿se pueden contestar las preguntas salteadas?** can we answer the questions in any order?; **leí unos capítulos ~s** I read a few odd chapters

saltear [A1] *vt* (Coc) to sauté

saltimbanqui *m* (Espec, Hist) tumbler, acrobat

salto *m* **1** **(a)** (brinco) jump; **se levantó de un ~** (de la cama) he leapt *o* sprang out of bed; (del suelo) he leapt *o* jumped up from the floor; **se puso en pie de un ~** she leapt *o* sprang to her feet; **los pájaros se acercaban dando saltitos** the birds were hopping closer to me/us; **dar** *or* **pegar un ~** (dar un brinco) to jump; (de susto) to start, jump; **daban ~s de alegría** they were jumping for joy **(b)** (Dep) (en atletismo, esquí, paracaidismo) jump; (en natación) dive; ~ **con pértiga** *or* (AmL) **garrocha** pole vault; ~ **de altura/longitud** high/long jump; ~ **(en) alto/(en) largo** (AmL) high/long jump; ~ **mortal** somersault

2 (Geog) *tb* ~ **de agua** waterfall

saltón -tona *adj* «*ojos*» bulging

salud f **1** (Med) health; **estar bien de** ∼ to be in good health; **gozar de buena** ∼ to enjoy good health **2** ¡∼! (al brindar) cheers!; (cuando alguien estornuda) (AmL) bless you!

saludable adj ⟨clima/alimentación⟩ healthy; ⟨experiencia⟩ salutary

saludar [A1] vt (a) ⟨persona⟩ to greet, say hello to; **saluda a tu hermano de mi parte** give my regards to your brother; **lo saluda atentamente** (Corresp) Sincerely (yours) (AmE), Yours sincerely (BrE); **los saludó con la mano** she waved at them (b) (Mil) to salute
■ ∼ vi (a) (de palabra) to say hello (o good morning etc) (b) (con la mano) to wave (c) (Mil) to salute
■ **saludarse** v pron (recípr) to say hello to o greet each other

saludo m (a) greeting; **te mandan** ∼s they send (you) their regards o best wishes; ∼s (Corresp) best wishes; **le hice un** ∼ **con la mano** I gave him a wave, I waved to him (b) (Mil) salute

salva f: **una** ∼ **de 21 cañonazos** a 21-gun salute o salvo; **una** ∼ **de aplausos** a burst o round of applause

salvación f salvation

salvado m bran

salvador -dora m,f savior*

Salvador ▶ El Salvador

salvadoreño -ña adj/m,f Salvadoran, Salvadorean

salvaguardar [A1] vt to safeguard

salvaguardia f safeguard, defense*

salvaje adj **1** (a) ⟨animal⟩ wild (b) (primitivo) ⟨tribu⟩ savage (c) ⟨vegetación/terreno⟩ wild **2** (cruel) ⟨persona/tortura⟩ brutal; ⟨ataque/matanza⟩ savage
■ mf (primitivo) savage; (bruto) (pey) animal, savage

salvamanteles m (pl ∼) (para platos, fuentes) tablemat; (para vasos) coaster

salvamento m rescue; **equipo de** ∼ rescue team

salvar [A1] vt **1** (en general) to save; ∼ **algo/a algn DE algo** to save sth/sb FROM sth **2** (a) ⟨dificultad/obstáculo⟩ to overcome (b) ⟨distancia⟩ to cover (c) (Per, Ur) ⟨examen⟩ to pass
■ **salvarse** v pron to survive; **¡sálvese quien pueda!** every man for himself!; ∼**se DE algo** ⟨de accidente/incendio⟩ to survive sth; **se** ∼**on de una muerte segura** they escaped certain death

salvavidas mf (pl ∼) (a) (persona) lifeguard (b) **salvavidas** m (flotador) life jacket, life preserver (frml)

salvia f sage

salvo: **a salvo** (loc adv) **poner algo a** ∼ to put sth in a safe place; **los niños están a** ∼ the children are safe o unharmed; **ponerse a** ∼ to reach safety; **a** ∼ **de** safe from
■ prep (excepto) except, apart from; ∼ **que** unless

salvoconducto m safe-conduct

samba m or f samba

San adj (apócope de SANTO usado delante de nombres de varón excepto Domingo, Tomás y Tomé) St, Saint

sanar [A1] vi «enfermo» to get well, recover; «herida» to heal; ∼ **DE algo** to recover FROM sth

sanatorio m (a) (para convalecientes) nursing home, sanitarium (AmE), sanatorium (BrE) (b) (hospital) clinic, hospital (usually private) (c) (Col, Ven) (hospital psiquiátrico) psychiatric hospital

sanción f **1** (castigo a empleado, obrero) disciplinary measure; (Der) sanction, penalty; **una** ∼ **de tres partidos** a three-game ban o suspension; ∼ **económica** (multa) fine; **sanciones económicas** (a país) economic sanctions **2** (de ley) sanction; (de costumbre) sanction (frml), authorization

sancionar [A1] vt **1** (multar) to fine; (castigar) ⟨empleado/obrero⟩ to discipline; ⟨jugador⟩ to penalize **2** ⟨ley/disposición/acuerdo/huelga⟩ to sanction; ⟨costumbre⟩ to approve, sanction

sancochar [A1] vt (AmL) (cocer a medias) to parboil

sandalia f sandal

sándalo m sandalwood

sandez f (fam) silly o stupid thing to say; **¡no digas sandeces!** don't talk nonsense!

sandía f watermelon

sándwich /'saŋgwitʃ/ m, **sándwiche** /'saŋgwitʃe/ m (esp AmL) (de pan de molde) sandwich; (de pancito) (filled) roll

sanfermines mpl: festival in Pamplona in which bulls are run through the streets

sangrar [A1] vi «persona/herida/nariz» to bleed

sangre f **1** (Biol) blood; **una transfusión de** ∼ a blood transfusion; **no me salió** ∼ it didn't bleed; **te sale** ∼ **or por la nariz** your nose is bleeding; **los ojos inyectados en** ∼ bloodshot eyes; **animales de** ∼ **fría/caliente** cold-blooded/warm-blooded animals; ∼ **fría** calmness and courage; **a** ∼ **fría** ⟨matar⟩ in cold blood; ▶ MALO 2 **2** (linaje) blood; **era de** ∼ **noble** he was of noble blood o birth; **es de** ∼ **mestiza** he is of mixed race; **no son de la misma** ∼ they are not from the same family; ∼ **azul** blue blood

sangría f **1** (bebida) sangria (type of red wine punch) **2** (a) (Med) bleeding (b) (de capital, recursos) outflow, drain **3** (Impr) indentation

sangriento -ta adj bloody

sangrón -grona adj (Méx fam) annoying
■ m,f (Méx fam) nuisance

sanguijuela f (a) (Zool) leech (b) (fam) (persona) leech, bloodsucker

sanguinario -ria adj ⟨persona⟩ cruel, bloodthirsty; ⟨animal⟩ vicious, ferocious

sanidad f **1** (calidad de sano) health, healthiness **2** (a) (salud pública) public health (b) **Sanidad** (sin art) (departamento) Department of Health

sanitario¹ -ria adj ⟨medidas⟩ public health

(*before n*); ‹*condiciones*› sanitary (*before n*);
servicios ~s sanitation; **asistencia sanitaria**
health-care

sanitario² *m* (a) (retrete) toilet, lavatory (b)
sanitarios *mpl* (para cuarto de baño) bathroom
fittings (*pl*)

sano -na *adj* ⓵ ‹*persona/planta/cabello*›
healthy; ‹*clima/vida*› healthy; ‹*alimentación*›
healthy, wholesome; **~ y salvo** safe and sound
⓶ (en sentido moral) ‹*lecturas/ideas*› wholesome;
‹*ambiente*› healthy; ‹*persona*› good

San Salvador *m* San Salvador

sánscrito *m* Sanskrit

Santa Sede *f*: **la ~ ~** the Vatican, the Holy
See (frml)

Santiago (de Chile) *m* Santiago

Santiago (de Compostela) *m* Santiago
(de Compostela)

santiaguino -na *adj* of/from Santiago (*Chile*)

santiamén *m*: **en un ~** (fam) in no time at all

santiguarse [A16] *v pron* (refl) to cross
oneself, make the sign of the cross

santo -ta *adj* ⓵ (Relig) (a) ‹*lugar/mujer/vida*›
holy (b) (con nombre propio) St, Saint; **Santa Teresa**
Saint Theresa; *ver tb* SAN ⓶ (fam) (uso enfático)
blessed; **llovió todo el ~ día** it rained the whole
blessed day (colloq)
■ *m,f* ⓵ (persona) saint; **una paciencia de ~** the
patience of a saint; **no te hagas el ~** don't come
over all virtuous; **~ y seña** password ⓶ **santo**
m (festividad) name day, saint's day; (cumpleaños)
(esp AmL) birthday

Santo Domingo *m* (Geog) Santo Domingo;
(Relig) Saint Dominic

santuario *m* (Relig) sanctuary, shrine; (refugio)
sanctuary

saña *f* viciousness, brutality; **con ~** brutally,
viciously

São Paulo *m* São Paulo

sapo *m* (Zool) toad

saque *m* (a) (en tenis, vóleibol) serve, service (b)
(en fútbol) kickoff; **~ de banda** (en fútbol) throw-in;
(en rugby) line-out; **~ de esquina** corner (kick); **~
de puerta** *or* (CS) **valla** goal kick; **~ inicial** kickoff

saquear [A1] *vt* ‹*ciudad/población*› to sack,
plunder; ‹*tienda/establecimiento*› to loot

sarampión *m* measles

sarape *m* (Méx) ▶ ZARAPE

sarcasmo *m* (a) (cualidad) sarcasm; **con ~**
sarcastically (b) (comentario) sarcastic remark

sarcástico -ca *adj* sarcastic

sarcófago *m* sarcophagus

sardina *f* sardine

sardinel *m* (Col) (a) (de la acera) curb (AmE),
kerb (BrE) (b) (de ventana) windowsill

sargento *mf* (Mil) (en el ejército) sergeant; (en las
fuerzas aéreas) ≈ staff sergeant (*in US*), ≈ sergeant
(*in UK*)

sari *m* sari

sarita *f* (Per) straw hat

sarna *f* (Med) scabies; (Vet) mange

sarpullido *m* rash, hives (*pl*)

sarro *m* (en los dientes) plaque, tartar; (en la
lengua) fur; (en tetera eléctrica, cañería) scale

sarta *f* string

sartén *f*, (AmL) *m or f* frying pan, fry pan (AmE),
skillet

sastre *mf* (persona) tailor

sastrería *f* tailor's shop

Satanás, Satán *m* Satan

satánico -ca *adj* (del diablo) satanic; (malvado)
evil, satanic

satélite *m* satellite; **~ artificial** artificial
satellite

satén, (AmL) **satín** *m* satin

sátira *f* satire

satírico -ca *adj* satirical

satirizar [A4] *vt* to satirize

satisfacción *f* satisfaction; **la ~ del deber
cumplido** the satisfaction of a job well done; **es
una ~ para mí estar aquí** it is a pleasure to be
here

satisfacer [E20] *vt* to satisfy; **su respuesta no
me satisface** I am not satisfied *o* happy with your
reply
■ **satisfacerse** *v pron* (a) (contentarse) to be
satisfied (b) (de agravio) to obtain satisfaction

satisfactorio -ria *adj* satisfactory

satisfaga, satisfará, etc ▶ SATISFACER

satisfecho -cha *adj* ⓵ [ESTAR] (complacido,
contento) satisfied, pleased ⓶ [ESTAR] (saciado,
lleno): **estoy ~** I've had plenty; **no queda nunca ~**
he never seems to be full

saturado -da *adj* (en general) saturated; ‹*líneas
telefónicas*› busy, engaged (BrE)

saturar [A1] *vt* to saturate

Saturno *m* Saturn

sauce *m* willow; **~ llorón** weeping willow

saudí, saudita *adj/mf* (Saudi) Arabian

sauna *f or* (AmL) *m* sauna

savia *f* (Bot) sap

sávila *f* (Méx) aloe vera

saxo *m* (fam) (a) (instrumento) sax (colloq)
(b) **saxo** *mf* (persona) sax player (colloq)

saxofón, saxófono *m* saxophone

saxofonista *mf* saxophonist

sazón *f* ⓵ (a) (condimento) seasoning; (sabor)
flavor*; (b) (de la fruta) ripeness; **estar en ~** to be
ripe ⓶ **a la sazón** (liter) at that time

sazonar [A1] *vt* to season

schop /ʃop/ *m* (Chi) (vaso) beer mug; (cerveza)
keg beer

Scotch® /(e)s'kotʃ/ *m* (Andes) Scotch® tape
(AmE), Sellotape® (BrE)

scout /(e)s'kau(t)/ *mf* scout

se *pron pers* ⓵ [*seguido de otro pronombre:
sustituyendo a* LE, LES]: **ya ~ lo he dicho** (a él)
I've already told him; (a ella) I've already told
her; (a usted, ustedes) I've already told you; (a ellos)
I've already told them; **el vestido tenía cuello
pero ~ lo quité** the dress had a collar but I took
it off
⓶ (*en verbos pronominales*): **¿no ~ arrepienten?**
«*ellos/ellas*» aren't they sorry?; «*ustedes*» aren't
you sorry?; **el barco ~ hundió** the ship sank; **~
secó/secaron** (refl) he dried himself/they dried
themselves; **~ secó el pelo** (refl) she dried her
hair; **~ hizo un vestido** (refl) she made herself a
dress; (*caus*) she had a dress made; **no ~ hablan** ⋯⟶

S

(*recípr*) they're not on speaking terms, they're not speaking to each other; ~ **lo comió todo** (*enf*) he ate it all

3 (a) (*voz pasiva*): ~ **oyeron unos gritos** there were shouts, I (*o we etc*) heard some shouts; ~ **publicó el año pasado** it was published last year (b) (*impersonal*): **aquí** ~ **está muy bien** it's very nice here; ~ **castigará a los culpables** those responsible will be punished (c) (*en normas, instrucciones*): **¿cómo** ~ **escribe tu nombre?** how is your name spelled?, how do you spell your name?; ~ **pica la cebolla bien menuda** chop the onion finely

sé ▶ SABER, SER

sea, seas, etc ▶ SER

sebo *m* (grasa) grease, fat; (para jabón, velas) tallow; (Coc) suet

secador *m* **1** *tb* ~ **de pelo** hairdryer **2** (Per) (paño) dishtowel (AmE), tea towel (BrE); (toalla) towel

secadora *f* (de ropa, tabaco) dryer; (para el pelo) (Méx) hairdryer

secano *m*: **de secano** ‹campo/tierra› dry, unirrigated

secar [A2] *vt* (a) ‹ropa/pelo/platos› to dry; ‹pintura/arcilla› to dry (b) ‹tierra/plantas/hierba› to dry up; ‹piel› to make ... dry
■ ~ *vi* to dry

■ **secarse** *v pron* **1** (a) «ropa/pintura/pelo» to dry; «piel» to get dry; **se me seca mucho la piel** my skin gets very dry (b) «herida» to heal (up) (c) «tierra/planta/hierba» to dry up (d) «río/pozo/fuente» to dry up (e) «arroz/guiso» to go dry **2** (*refl*) «persona» to dry oneself; ‹manos/pelo› to dry; ‹lágrimas› to dry, wipe away

sección *f* **1** (corte) section **2** (a) (división, área — en general) section; (— de empresa, en grandes almacenes) department (b) (de periódico, orquesta) section **3** (Mil) platoon

seccionar [A1] *vt* (cortar) to cut off; (dividir en secciones) to section

seco -ca *adj* **1** (a) [ESTAR] ‹ropa/platos/pintura› dry; ‹boca/garganta› dry (b) [ESTAR] ‹planta/río/comida› dry (c) [SER] ‹clima/región› dry **2** ‹higos/flores› dried; **bacalao** ~ stockfish, dried salt cod **3** [SER] (no graso) ‹piel/pelo› dry **4** [SER] (no dulce) ‹vino/licor/vermut› dry **5** ‹golpe/sonido› sharp; ‹tos› dry **6** ‹respuesta/carácter› dry; **estuvo muy** ~ **conmigo** he was very short with me **7** (*en locs*) **en seco** ‹frenar/parar› sharply, suddenly; **limpieza en** ~ dry cleaning

secreción *f* (de glándula) secretion; (de herida) discharge

secretaría *f* **1** (a) (cargo) office of secretary (b) (oficina) secretary's office (c) (departamento administrativo) secretariat **2** (Méx) (ministerio) department, ministry (BrE)

secretariado *m* secretarial work; **estudia** ~ she's doing a secretarial course

secretario -ria *m,f* **1** (a) (trabajador administrativo) secretary (b) (de asociación, sociedad) secretary; ~ **de dirección** secretary to the director; ~ **general** secretary general **2** (Méx) (Gob, Pol) secretary of state, minister; **S**~ **de Gobernación** (en Méx) Minister of the Interior, ≈ Home Secretary (*in UK*)

secretear [A1] *vi* (AmL fam) to whisper
■ **secretearse** *v pron* (AmL fam) to whisper

secreter *m* writing desk

secreto¹ -ta *adj* secret

secreto² *m* (a) (información confidencial) secret; **los preparamos en** ~ we prepared them secretly *o* in secret; ~ **a voces** open secret (b) (truco) secret; **el** ~ **está en ...** the secret is in ...

secta *f* sect

sectario -ria *adj* sectarian

sector *m* (a) (grupo) sector, group (b) (Mat) sector (c) (de ciudad) area (d) (Com, Econ) sector

secuela *f* consequence

secuencia *f* sequence, series

secuestrador -dora *m,f* (de persona) kidnapper; (de avión) hijacker

secuestrar [A1] *vt* ‹persona› to kidnap; ‹avión› to hijack

secuestro *m* (de persona) kidnapping; (de avión) hijack(ing)

secundaria *f* (a) (enseñanza media) secondary education, high school (AmE) (b) (Méx) (instituto) middle school

secundario -ria *adj* ‹factor/problema› secondary; ‹actor/actriz› supporting (*before n*)

sed *f* thirst; **el agua le quitó la** ~ the water quenched his thirst; **tengo** ~ I'm thirsty; **me da** ~ it makes me (feel) thirsty; **su** ~ **de venganza/riqueza** her thirst for vengeance/riches

seda *f* (Tex) silk; (Odont) ~ **dental** dental floss

sedal *m* fishing line

sedante *adj/m* (Med) sedative

sede *f* (a) (del gobierno) seat (b) (Relig) see (c) (de organización internacional) headquarters (*sing or pl*); (de compañía) headquarters (*sing or pl*); **head office** (d) (de congreso, feria) venue; **la** ~ **de los Juegos Olímpicos** the venue for the Olympic Games

sedentario -ria *adj* sedentary

sediento -ta *adj* thirsty

sedimento *m* sediment, deposit

sedoso -sa *adj* silky

seducción *f* seduction

seducir [I6] *vt* (a) (en sentido sexual) to seduce (b) (fascinar, cautivar) to captivate (c) ‹idea/proposición» (atraer) to attract, tempt; **no me seduce la idea** the idea doesn't appeal to me at all

seductor -tora *adj* (a) (en sentido sexual) seductive (b) (que cautiva, fascina) enchanting, charming (c) ‹idea/proposición› attractive, tempting
■ *m,f* (*m*) seducer; (*f*) seducer, seductress

seg. *m* (= **segundo/segundos**) sec.

segar [A7] *vt* ‹mies› to reap (liter), to cut

seglar *adj* lay (*before n*)
■ *mf* (*m*) layman; (*f*) laywoman

segmento *m* (Mat) segment; (Zool) segment; (Com) sector

segregación *f* segregation; ~ **racial** racial segregation

segregar [A3] *vt* ‹personas/grupos› to segregate

seguida: **en seguida** (*loc adv*) immediately,

right *o* (BrE) straight away; **vinieron en ~** they came at once *o* right away; **en ~ voy/vuelvo** I'll be right there/back

seguido¹ -da *adj* consecutive, in a row; **faltó tres días ~s** she was absent three days running *o* in a row; **pasaron tres autobuses ~s** three buses went by one after the other; **~ DE algo/algn** followed BY sth/sb

seguido² ** *adv* 1 (recto, sin desviarse) straight on; **vaya todo ~ go straight on 2 (AmL) (a menudo) often

seguidor -dora *m,f* (de teoría, filósofo) follower; (Dep) supporter, fan

seguir [I30] *vt* 1 ⟨*persona/vehículo/presa*⟩ to follow; **camina muy rápido, no la puedo ~** she walks very fast, I can't keep up with her 2 ⟨*camino/ruta*⟩ to follow, go along; **siga esta carretera hasta llegar al puente** go along *o* follow this road as far as the bridge; **la saludé y seguí mi camino** I said hello to her and went on (my way); **la enfermedad sigue su curso normal** the illness is running its normal course 3 (a) ⟨*instrucciones/consejo/flecha*⟩ to follow (b) ⟨*autor/método/tradición/moda*⟩ to follow; **~ los pasos de algn** to follow in sb's footsteps 4 (a) ⟨*trámite/procedimiento*⟩ to follow; ⟨*tratamiento*⟩ to undergo (b) (Educ) ⟨*curso*⟩ to do, take 5 ⟨*explicaciones/profesor*⟩ to follow; **dicta demasiado rápido, no la puedo ~** she dictates too quickly, I can't keep up

■ **~ ** *vi* 1 (a) (por un camino) to go on; **siga derecho** *or* **todo recto** keep *o* go straight on; **sigue por esta calle** go on down this street; **~ de largo** (AmL) to go straight past (b) seguir adelante to carry on; **resolvieron ~ adelante con los planes** they decided to go ahead with their plans (c) (Col, Ven) (entrar): **siga por favor** come in, please 2 (en lugar, estado): **¿tus padres siguen en Ginebra?** are your parents still in Geneva?; **espero que sigan todos bien** I hope you're all keeping well; **sigue soltera** she's still single; **si las cosas siguen así ...** if things carry on like this ... 3 «*tareas/buen tiempo/lluvia*» to continue; «*rumores*» to persist; **sigo pensando que deberíamos haber ido** I still think we ought to have gone; **~é haciéndolo a mi manera** I'll go on *o* carry on doing it my way 4 (a) (venir después): **lee lo que sigue** read what comes next; **el capítulo que sigue** the next chapter (b) «*historia/poema*» to continue, go on

según *prep* 1 (de acuerdo con) according to; **~ Elena** according to Elena; **~ parece** apparently 2 (dependiendo de): **~ cómo lo hagas** depending (on) how you do it; **¿me llevas a casa? — ~ dónde vivas** will you take me home? — (it) depends where you live
■ *adv* it depends; **puede resultar o no, ~** it may or may not work, it depends
■ *conj* (a medida que) as; **~ van entrando** as they come in

segunda *f* 1 (a) (Auto) (marcha) second (gear); **mete (la) ~** put it in second (gear) (b) (Transp) (clase) second class; **viajar en ~** to travel second class 2 **segundas** *fpl*: **todo lo dice con ~s** there's a hidden meaning to everything he says

segundero *m* second hand

segundo¹ -da *adj/pron* (a) (ordinal) second; **relegar a algn a un ~ plano** to push sb into the background; *para ejemplos ver* QUINTO (b) ⟨*categoría/clase*⟩ second
■ *m,f* deputy, second-in-command

segundo² ** *m* second; **un ~, ahora te atiendo just a second, I'll be right with you

seguridad *f* 1 (ausencia de peligro) safety; (protección contra robos, atentados) security; **medidas de ~** (contra accidentes, incendios) safety measures; (contra robos, atentados) security measures; **una prisión de alta ~** a high security prison; **~ ciudadana** public safety 2 (estabilidad, garantía) security; **~ social** social security 3 (a) (certeza) certainty; **podemos decir con ~ que ... we** can say for sure *o* with certainty that ... (b) (confianza, aplomo) confidence, self-confidence

seguro¹ -ra *adj* 1 (a) (exento de riesgo) safe; **en un lugar ~** in a safe place (b) (estable) secure; **un trabajo ~** a secure job; **esa escalera no está segura** that ladder isn't safe *o* steady (c) [SER] (fiable) ⟨*test/método*⟩ reliable; ⟨*anticonceptivo*⟩ safe; **el cierre de la pulsera es muy ~** the fastener on the bracelet is very secure (d) [ESTAR] (a salvo) safe 2 (a) [ESTAR] (convencido) sure; **no estoy ~** I'm not sure; **~ DE algo** sure *o* certain of sth (b) [SER] (que no admite duda) ⟨*muerte/victoria*⟩ certain; ⟨*fecha*⟩ definite; **todavía no es ~** it's not definite yet; **no te preocupes, ~ que no es nada** don't worry, I'm sure it's nothing; **~ que se le olvida** he's sure *o* bound to forget (c) (con confianza en sí mismo) self-assured, self-confident

seguro² ** *m* 1 (a) (mecanismo — de armas) safety catch; (— de pulsera, collar) clasp, fastener; **echó el ~ antes de acostarse he locked the door before going to bed (b) (Méx) (imperdible) safety pin 2 (a) (contrato) insurance; **~ contra** *or* **a todo riesgo** comprehensive insurance, all-risks insurance; **~ contra** *or* **de incendios** fire insurance; **~ de desempleo** unemployment benefit; **~ de viaje** travel insurance; **~ de vida** life assurance, life insurance (b) (Seguridad Social): **el ~** *or* **el S~** the state health care system, ≈ Medicaid (*in US*), ≈ the National Health Service (*in UK*)
■ *adv*: **dijo que llegaría mañana ~** she said she'd definitely be arriving tomorrow; **no lo sabe ~** she doesn't know for sure *o* certain; **~ que sospecha lo nuestro** I'm sure he suspects we're up to something

seis *adj inv/pron/m* six; *para ejemplos ver* CINCO

seiscientos -tas *adj/pron* six hundred

seísmo *m* (Esp) (temblor) tremor; (terremoto) earthquake

selección *f* selection; **hizo una ~ de los mejores** she selected the best ones; **la ~ mexicana** (Dep) the Mexican national team

seleccionador -dora *m,f* (Dep) (a) (entrenador) coach (AmE), manager (BrE) (b) (miembro de una junta) selector

seleccionar [A1] *vt* to select, choose

selectividad *f* (a) (cualidad) selectivity (b) (Educ) (en Esp) *university entrance examination*

selectivo -va *adj* selective

selecto -ta adj ⟨fruta/vino⟩ select, choice; ⟨ambiente/club⟩ select, exclusive

sellar [A1] vt ① (a) ⟨pasaporte⟩ to stamp (b) ⟨plata/oro⟩ to hallmark ② (cerrar) to seal

sello m ① (de correos) (postage) stamp; (útil de oficina) rubber stamp; (marca) stamp ② (a) (en el oro, la plata) hallmark (b) (AmL) (de una moneda) reverse; ¿cara o ∼? (Andes, Ven) heads or tails? (c) (anillo) signet ring, seal ring (d) (distintivo) hallmark (e) (Mús) tb ∼ **discográfico** record label ③ (precinto) seal

selva f (bosque) forest; (de vegetación tropical) jungle; **S**∼ **Negra** Black Forest; ∼ **tropical** tropical rainforest, selva

semáforo m (a) (Auto) traffic lights (pl); **se pasó un** ∼ **en rojo** she went through o (AmE) ran a red light (b) (Ferr) stop signal (c) (Náut) semaphore

semana f ① (periodo) week; ∼ **laboral** workweek (AmE), working week (BrE); **S**∼ **Santa** Easter ② (Col) (dinero) allowance, pocket money

semanal adj weekly

semanario m (Period) weekly magazine (o newspaper etc), weekly

semántico -ca adj semantic

sembrado¹ m sown field

sembrado² **-da** m,f (Méx) (Dep) seed

sembrar [A5] vt ⟨terreno/campo⟩ to sow; ⟨trigo/hortalizas⟩ to sow, plant; ∼ **algo DE algo** to plant sth WITH sth

semejante adj (a) (similar) similar; ∼ **A algo** similar TO sth (b) (delante del n) (para énfasis): **¡cómo puedes decir** ∼ **cosa!** how can you say such a thing!; **nunca había oído** ∼ **estupidez** I'd never heard such nonsense o anything so stupid ■ m: **nuestros** ∼**s** our fellow men

semejanza f similarity; **a** ∼ **de sus antepasados** like his ancestors

semen m semen

semental m (caballo) stud horse; (toro) stud bull

semestral adj (a) (en frecuencia) ⟨exámenes/reuniones⟩ half-yearly, six-monthly (b) (en duración) ⟨curso⟩ six-month (before n)

semestre m (a) (seis meses): **cada curso dura un** ∼ each course lasts six months (b) (Educ) (en algunos países latinoamericanos) tb ∼ **lectivo** semester (AmE), term (BrE)

semicírculo m semicircle

semicorchea f sixteenth note (AmE), semiquaver (BrE)

semidesnatado -da adj (Esp) semi-skimmed, half-cream (before n)

semifinal f semifinal

semifinalista mf semifinalist

semilla f seed

semillero m (a) (Agr, Bot) seedbed (b) (de discordias) source; (de delincuencia) hotbed, breeding ground

seminario m (a) (Relig) seminary (b) (Educ) seminar

seminarista m seminarian

semita adj Semitic
■ mf Semite

sémola f semolina; ∼ **de arroz** ground rice

Sena m: **el** ∼ the Seine

senado m senate

senador -dora m,f senator

sencillez f simplicity; **con** ∼ ⟨vestir⟩ simply; ⟨comportarse⟩ with modesty; **habla con** ∼ she uses plain language

sencillo¹ **-lla** adj ① (a) ⟨ejercicio/problema⟩ simple, straightforward; **no fue** ∼ **hacerlos entrar** it wasn't easy getting them in (b) ⟨persona⟩ modest, unassuming; ⟨vestido/estilo⟩ simple, plain; ⟨casa/comida⟩ simple, modest ② (Esp, Méx) (Transp) one-way (AmE), single (BrE)

sencillo² m ① (disco) single ② (AmL) (dinero suelto) change ③ (Esp, Méx) (Transp) one-way ticket (AmE), single (ticket) (BrE)

senda f (a) (camino) path (b) (Ur) (de carretera) lane

sendero m path, track

sendos -das adj pl (cada uno): **llevaban sendas pistolas** each of them was carrying o they were each carrying a gun; **con sendas fiestas en Madrid y Barcelona** with parties in both Madrid and Barcelona

Senegal m Senegal

senilidad f senility

seno m (a) (mama) breast; (pecho) bosom; **los** ∼**s** the breasts; **dar el** ∼ (Ven) to breastfeed (b) (de organización, empresa) heart

sensación f ① (percepción, impresión) feeling; **una** ∼ **de tristeza/impotencia** a feeling of sadness/impotence; **una vaga** ∼ **de placer** a vague sensation of pleasure; **una** ∼ **de pérdida/espacio** a sense of loss/space; **tengo** o **me da la** ∼ **de que no vamos a ganar** I have a feeling we're not going to win ② (furor, éxito) sensation; **ser una** ∼ to be a sensation

sensacional adj sensational

sensacionalismo m sensationalism

sensacionalista adj ⟨prensa⟩ sensationalist (before n); ⟨artículo/foto⟩ sensationalistic

sensatez f sense; **tuvo la** ∼ **de ...** she had the (good) sense to ...; **obró con** ∼ she acted sensibly

sensato -ta adj sensible

sensibilidad f (a) (en general) sensitivity (b) (en brazo, pierna) feeling

sensibilizar [A4] vt to raise ... awareness

sensible adj ① (en general) sensitive; ∼ **A algo** sensitive TO sth ② (gen delante del n) (frml) (ostensible) ⟨cambio/diferencia⟩ appreciable; ⟨mejoría⟩ noticeable; ⟨aumento/pérdida⟩ considerable

sensiblero -ra adj (pey) mawkish

sensitivo -va adj sensory

sensorial adj sensory

sensual adj ⟨boca/cuerpo⟩ sensual, sensuous; ⟨placeres/gesto⟩ sensual; ⟨descripción⟩ sensuous

AmC	Central America	Arg	Argentina	Cu	Cuba	Per	Peru
AmL	Latin America	Bol	Bolivia	Ec	Ecuador	RPI	River Plate Area
AmS	South America	Chi	Chile	Esp	Spain	Ur	Uruguay
Andes	Andean Region	CS	Southern Cone	Méx	Mexico	Ven	Venezuela

sensualidad *f* (de boca, gesto) sensuality; (de descripción) sensuousness

sentada *f* (a) (protesta) sit-in, sit-down protest (b) de *or* en una sentada in one go

sentado -da *adj* sitting, seated (frml); **estaban ~s a la mesa** they were (sitting) at the table; *dar algo por ~* to assume sth

sentador -dora *adj* (AmL) flattering, fetching

sentar [A5] *vi* (+ *me/te/le etc*) **(a)** «*ropa/color*» (+ *compl*): **ese vestido le sienta de maravilla** that dress really suits her **(b)** «*comida/bebida/clima*» (+ *compl*): **el café no le sienta bien** coffee doesn't agree with her; **me sentó bien el descanso** the rest did me a lot of good **(c)** «*actitud/comentario*» (+ *compl*): **me sentó mal que no me invitaran** I was rather put out that they didn't ask me (colloq)
■ **~** *vt* [1] «*niño/muñeca*» to sit; «*invitado*» to seat, sit
[2] (establecer) to establish
■ **sentarse** *v pron* to sit; **~se a la mesa** to sit at (the) table; **siéntese, por favor** please (do) sit down

sentencia *f* (Der) judgment, ruling

sentenciar [A1] *vt* to sentence; **la ~on a muerte** (Der) she was sentenced to death

sentido¹ -da *adj* [1] «*palabras/carta*» heartfelt; «*anhelo/dolor*» deep; **mi más ~ pésame** my deepest sympathy [2] [ESTAR] (AmL) (ofendido) hurt, offended

sentido² *m* [1] **(a)** (Fisiol) sense **(b)** (noción, idea) **~ DE algo** sense OF sth; **su ~ del deber** her sense of duty; **~ común** common sense; **~ del humor** sense of humor*
[2] (conocimiento) consciousness; **perder el ~** to lose consciousness; **el golpe lo dejó sin ~** he was knocked unconscious by the blow
[3] (significado) sense; **en el buen ~ de la palabra** in the nicest sense of the word; **en ~ literal** in a literal sense; **lo dijo con doble ~** he was intentionally ambiguous; **el ~ de la vida** the meaning of life; **en cierto ~ ...** in a sense ...; **no le encuentro ~ a lo que haces** I can't see any sense *o* point in what you're doing; **esa política ya no tiene ~** that policy doesn't make sense anymore *o* is meaningless now; **palabras sin ~** meaningless words
[4] (dirección) direction; **gírese en ~ contrario al de las agujas del reloj** turn (round) in a counterclockwise (AmE) *o* (BrE) an anticlockwise direction; **venían en ~ contrario al nuestro** they were coming in the opposite direction to us; **calle de ~ único** *or* (Méx) **de un solo ~** one-way street

sentimental *adj* **(a)** (relativo a los sentimientos) sentimental **(b)** «*persona/canción/novela*» sentimental; **ponerse ~** to get sentimental **(c)** «*aventura/vida*» love (*before n*)

sentimentalismo *m* sentimentalism

sentimiento *m* [1] **(a)** (emoción) feeling; **ser de buenos ~s** to be a caring person; **no se deja llevar por los ~s** she doesn't let herself get carried away by her emotions **(b)** (pesar): **les acompaño en el ~** my commiserations
[2] **sentimientos** *mpl* feelings (*pl*); **herir los ~s de algn** to hurt sb's feelings

sentir [I11] *vt* [1] **(a)** «*dolor/pinchazo*» to feel; **~**

hambre/frío/sed to feel hungry/cold/thirsty **(b)** «*emoción*» to feel; **sentimos una gran alegría** we were overjoyed; **~ celos** to feel jealous
[2] **(a)** (oír) «*ruido/disparo*» to hear **(b)** (esp AmL) (percibir): **siento olor a gas** I can smell gas; **le siento gusto a vainilla** I can taste vanilla
[3] (lamentar): **lo siento mucho** I'm really sorry; **sentí mucho no poder ayudarla** I was very sorry not to be able to help her; **ha sentido mucho la pérdida de su madre** she has been very affected by her mother's death
■ **sentirse** *v pron* [1] (+ *compl*) to feel; **me siento mal** I don't feel well, I'm not feeling well; **no me siento con ánimos** I don't feel up to it
[2] (Chi, Méx) (ofenderse) to be offended *o* hurt; **~se CON algn** to be offended *o* upset WITH sb

seña *f* [1] (gesto) sign; **hacer una ~** to make a sign, to signal; **les hice ~s de que se callaran** I gestured *o* motioned to them to keep quiet
[2] **señas** *fpl* (dirección) address [3] **señas** *fpl* (indicios): **dar ~s DE algo** to show signs OF sth
[4] (RPl) ▶ SEÑAL 5

señal *f* [1] **(a)** (aviso, letrero) sign; **~es de tráfico** traffic signs; **S~ de la Cruz** sign of the cross **(b)** (signo) signal; **nos hacía ~es para que nos acercáramos** she was signaling *o* gesturing for us to come nearer; **~ de auxilio** *or* **socorro** distress signal **(c)** (Ferr) signal
[2] (marca, huella): **pon una ~ en la página** mark the page; **~es de violencia** signs of violence
[3] **(a)** (Rad, TV) signal **(b)** (Telec): **la ~ para marcar** the dial (AmE) *o* (BrE) dialling tone; **la ~ de ocupado** *or* (Esp) **comunicando** the busy signal (AmE), the engaged tone (BrE)
[4] (indicio) sign; **eso es mala ~** that's a bad sign; **no daba ~es de vida** he showed no signs of life; **en ~ de respeto/amor** as a token of respect/love
[5] (Esp) (Com) (depósito) deposit, down payment

señalar [A1] *vt* [1] (indicar) «*ruta/camino*» to show; **el reloj señalaba las doce** the clock showed twelve; **me señaló con el dedo** he pointed at me (with his finger); **~le algo A algn** to show sb sth, point sth out TO sb; **me señaló con el dedo qué pasteles quería** he pointed out (to me) which cakes he wanted
[2] (marcar con lápiz, rotulador) to mark
[3] (afirmar) to point out; **señaló que ...** she pointed out that ...
[4] (fijar) «*fecha*» to fix, set; **en el lugar señalado** in the appointed *o* agreed place
[5] (anunciar) to mark
■ **~** *vi* to point

señalización *f* **(a)** (en carretera, calle) signposting; (en edificio, centro comercial) signs (*pl*) **(b)** (Ferr) signaling*

señalizar [A4] *vt* **(a)** «*carretera/calle/ciudad*» to signpost; «*edificio/centro comercial*» to put up directions on/in **(b)** (Ferr) «*tramo/vía*» to install signals on

señor -ñora *m,f* [1] **(a)** (persona adulta) (*m*) man, gentleman; (*f*) lady; **peluquería de ~as** ladies' hairdresser's **(b)** (persona distinguida) (*m*) gentleman; (*f*) lady; **es todo un ~** he's a real gentleman
[2] (dueño, amo): **el ~/la ~a de la casa** the gentleman/the lady of the house (frml)
[3] (Relig) **(a)** **Señor** *m* Lord **(b)** **Señora** *f*: **Nuestra S~a de Montserrat** Our Lady of Montserrat

 ⋯⁑

4 señora *f* (esposa) wife
5 (tratamiento de cortesía) **(a)** (con apellidos) (*m*) Mr;
(*f*) Mrs; **los ~es de Paz** Mr and Mrs Paz **(b)** (frml)
(con otros sustantivos): **la ~a directora está ocupada**
the director is busy; **S~** Director (Corresp) Dear
Sir, Sir (frml) **(c)** (frml) (sin mencionar el nombre):
perdón, ~ ¿tiene hora? excuse me, could you tell
me the time?; **muy ~ mío/~es míos** (Corresp)
Dear Sir/Sirs; **Teresa Chaves — ¿~a o ~ita?**
Teresa Chaves — Miss, Mrs or Ms?; **los ~es han
salido** Mr and Mrs Paz (*o* López *etc*) are not at
home

señorial *adj* ⟨casa⟩ stately; ⟨ciudad⟩ noble

señorita *f* **1 (a)** (mujer joven) young lady **(b)**
(joven distinguida) young lady **(c)** (maestra) teacher
2 (tratamiento de cortesía) **(a)** (con apellidos) Miss **(b)**
(con nombres de pila): **~ Teresa ¿puede atender a la
señora?** Teresa/Miss Chaves (*o* López *etc*), could
you serve this lady please? **(c)** (maestra) Miss **(d)**
(sin mencionar el nombre) (frml) Miss

señorito *m* (pey) rich young man, rich kid
(colloq)

señuelo *m* (persona) bait; (para aves) decoy

sepa, sepas, etc ▶ SABER

separación *f* **1 (a)** (división) separation; **la ~
de la Iglesia y del Estado** the separation of the
Church and the State **(b)** (espacio) gap, separation
2 (del matrimonio) separation

separado -da *adj* **1** ⟨persona⟩ separated
2 (a) ⟨camas⟩ separate **(b) por separado**
separately
■ *m,f*: **es hijo de ~s** his parents are separated

separador *m* **1** (de carpeta) divider **2** (Col)
(Auto) median strip (AmE), central reservation (BrE)

separar [A1] *vt* **1 (a)** (apartar, alejar) to
separate; **~ los machos de las hembras** to
separate the males from the females; **separa la
cama de la pared** move the bed away from the
wall **(b)** (dividir un todo) to divide **(c)** (guardar,
reservar) to put *o* set aside
2 (a) (actuar de división) «valla/línea» to
separate; **los Andes separan a Chile de Argentina**
the Andes separate Chile from Argentina **(b)**
(despegar): **no puedo ~ estas dos fotos** I can't get
these two photographs apart
■ **separarse** *v pron* **(a)** «matrimonio» to
separate; **~se DE algn** to separate FROM sb **(b)**
(seguir direcciones distintas) to split up; **a mitad de
camino nos separamos** we split up half way **(c)**
(apartarse, alejarse): **no se separen, que los
pequeños se pueden perder** please stay together
in case the children get lost; **no me he separado
nunca de mis hijos** I've never been away *o* apart
from my children

separatismo *m* separatism

separatista *mf* separatist

separo *m* (Méx) cell

sepia *f* **(a)** (Coc, Zool) cuttlefish, sepia (tech) **(b)**
(en pintura) sepia
■ *m* (color) sepia

septentrional *adj* northern

septiembre *m* September; *para ejemplos ver*
ENERO

séptimo¹ -ma *adj/pron* seventh; **la séptima
parte** a seventh; **el ~ arte** the movies (*pl*) (AmE),
the cinema (BrE); *para ejemplos ver* QUINTO

séptimo² *m* seventh

sepulcral *adj* (liter) ⟨silencio⟩ deathly

sepulcro *m* tomb, sepulcher* (liter)

sepultar [A1] *vt* **(a)** (frml) ⟨muerto⟩ to inter
(frml), to bury **(b)** (period) (cubrir): **fue sepultado
por un alud de nieve** he was buried by an
avalanche

sepultura *f* **(a)** (acción) burial **(b)** (tumba) tomb,
grave

sepulturero -ra *m,f* gravedigger

sequedad *f* **(a)** (de terreno, región, piel) dryness
(b) (de respuesta, tono) curtness

sequía *f* drought

séquito *m* (de rey) retinue, entourage

ser [E26] *cópula* **1** (seguido de adjetivos) to be [SER
expresses identity or nature as opposed to condition
or state, which is normally conveyed by ESTAR. The
examples given below should be contrasted with
those to be found in ESTAR¹ cópula 1] **es bajo/muy
callado** he's short/very quiet; **es sorda de
nacimiento** she was born deaf; **es inglés/católico**
he's English/(a) Catholic; **era cierto** it was true; **sé
bueno, estate quieto** be a good boy and keep still;
que seas muy feliz I hope you'll be very happy;
(+ *me/te/le etc*) **siempre le he sido fiel** I've always
been faithful to her; *ver tb* IMPOSIBLE, DIFÍCIL *etc*
2 (hablando de estado civil) to be; **el mayor es
casado** the oldest is married; **es viuda** she's a
widow; *ver tb* ESTAR¹ cópula 2
3 (seguido de nombre, pronombre) to be; **soy
abogada** I'm a lawyer; **ábreme, soy yo** open the
door, it's me
4 (con predicado introducido por 'de'): **esos zapatos
son de plástico** those shoes are (made of) plastic;
soy de Córdoba I'm from Cordoba; **es de los
vecinos** it belongs to the neighbors, it's the
neighbors'; **no soy de aquí** I'm not from around
here
5 (hipótesis, futuro): **será un error** it must be a
mistake; **¿será cierto?** can it be true?
■ **~** *vi*
I **1 (a)** (existir) to be **(b)** (liter) (en cuentos): **érase
una vez ...** once upon a time there was ...
2 (a) (tener lugar, ocurrir): **la fiesta va a ~ en su
casa** the party is going to be (held) at her house;
¿dónde fue el accidente? where did the accident
happen? **(b)** (en preguntas): **¿qué habrá sido de él?**
I wonder what happened to *o* what became of
him; **¿qué es de Marisa?** (fam) what's Marisa up
to (these days)? (colloq); **¿qué va a ser de
nosotros?** what will become of us?
3 (sumar): **¿cuánto es (todo)?** how much is that
(altogether)?; **son 3.000 pesos** that'll be *o* that's
3,000 pesos; **somos diez en total** there are ten of
us altogether
4 (indicando finalidad, adecuación) **~ PARA algo** to be
FOR sth; **este agua es para beber** this water is for
drinking
II (en locs) **a no ser que** (+ *subj*) unless; **¿cómo
es eso?** why is that?, how come? (colloq); **como/
cuando/donde sea: tengo que conseguir ese
trabajo como sea** I have to get that job no matter
what; **hazlo como sea, pero hazlo** do it any way *o*
however you want but get it done; **el lunes o
cuando sea** next Monday or whenever; **puedo
dormir en el sillón o donde sea** I can sleep in the
armchair or wherever you like *o* anywhere you
like; **de ser así** (frml) should this be so *o* the case
(frml); **¡eso es!** that's it!, that's right!; **es que ...**:

¿es que no lo saben? do you mean to say they don't know?; **es que no sé nadar** the thing is I can't swim; **lo que sea:** cómete una manzana, o lo que sea have an apple or something; **estoy dispuesta a hacer lo que sea** I'm prepared to do whatever it takes; **o sea: en febrero, o sea hace un mes** in February, that is to say a month ago; **o sea que no te interesa** in other words, you're not interested; **o sea que nunca lo descubriste** so you never found out; **(ya) sea ..., (ya) sea ...** either ..., or ...; **sea como sea** at all costs; **sea cuando sea** whenever it is; **sea donde sea** no matter where; **sea quien sea** whoever it is; **si no fuera/hubiera sido por ...** if it wasn't o weren't/ hadn't been for ...

III (en el tiempo) to be; **¿qué fecha es hoy?** what's the date today?, what's today's date; **serían las cuatro cuando llegó** it must have been (about) four (o'clock) when she arrived; *ver tb v impers*

■ ~ *v impers* to be; **era primavera** it was spring(time)

■ ~ *v aux* (en la voz pasiva) to be; **fue construido en 1900** it was built in 1900

■ *m* [1] (a) (ente) being; ~ **humano/vivo** human/ living being (b) (individuo, persona): **un ~ querido** a loved one

[2] (naturaleza): **desde lo más profundo de mi ~** from the bottom of my heart

Serbia *f* Serbia

serbio¹ -bia *adj/m,f* Serbian

serbio² *m* (idioma) Serbian

serbocroata *adj/mf* Serbo-Croat, Serbo-Croatian

■ *m* (idioma) Serbo-Croat

seré, seremos, etc ▶ SER

serenarse [A1] *v pron* (calmarse) to calm down

serenata *f* serenade; **dar una** *or* (Méx) **llevar ~** to serenade

serenidad *f* calmness, serenity; **no pierdas la ~** keep calm

sereno¹ -na *adj* (a) ⟨*rostro/expresión/belleza*⟩ serene; ⟨*persona*⟩ serene, calm (b) ⟨*cielo*⟩ cloudless, clear; ⟨*tarde*⟩ still; ⟨*mar*⟩ calm, tranquil (frml)

sereno² *m* (vigilante nocturno) night watchman

sería, etc ▶ SER

serial *m*, (CS) *f* ▶ SERIE 2

serie *f* [1] (a) (sucesión) series; **una ~ de pueblos** a series of villages (b) (clase) series; **coches de ~** production cars; **fabricación en ~** mass production; **producir/fabricar en ~** to mass produce; **fuera de ~** (fam) out of this world (colloq) (c) (Dep) heat [2] (Rad, TV) series; (historia continua) serial

seriedad *f* (a) (en general) seriousness (b) (sensatez, responsabilidad): **se comportó con mucha ~** she behaved very sensibly o responsibly; **¡un poco de ~!** come on, let's be serious now!

serio -ria *adj* [1] (poco sonriente) serious [2] ⟨*empleado*⟩ responsible, reliable; ⟨*empresa*⟩ reputable [3] (a) ⟨*cine/tema*⟩ serious (b) (grave) ⟨*enfermedad/problema*⟩ serious; **tengo serias dudas acerca de él** I have serious doubts about him (c) **en serio** ⟨*hablar*⟩ seriously, in earnest; **¿lo dices en ~?** are you (being) serious?, do you really mean it?; **tomarse algo en ~** to take sth seriously

sermón *m* sermon; **me echó un ~** (fam) he gave me a lecture

seropositivo -va *adj* (en general) seropositive; (con el VIH) HIV positive

serpentear [A1] *vi* ⟨*río*⟩ to meander, wind; ⟨*camino*⟩ to wind, twist

serpentina *f* streamer

serpiente *f* snake, serpent; ~ **(de) cascabel** rattlesnake; ~ **pitón** python

serrar [A5] *vt* to saw (up)

serrín *m* sawdust

serruchar [A1] *vt* (AmL) to saw

serrucho *m* handsaw

servicentro *m* (Andes) service station

servicial *adj* helpful, obliging

servicio *m* [1] (a) (acción de servir) service; **estamos a su ~** we are at your service; **estar de ~** ⟨*policía/bombero*⟩ to be on duty; ~ **público** public service; ~**s informativos** broadcasting services (*pl*) (b) (favor) favor*, service (c) **servicios** *mpl* (asistencia) services (*pl*); **me ofreció sus ~s** he offered me his services [2] (funcionamiento) service, use; **está fuera de ~** it's out of service; **han puesto en ~ el nuevo andén** the new platform is now in use o is now open [3] (en hospital) department; ~ **de urgencias** casualty department [4] (en restaurante, hotel) (a) (atención al cliente) service (b) (propina) service (charge) [5] (servidumbre): **entrada de ~** tradesman's entrance; **cuarto de ~** servant's quarters (frml), maid's room; ~ **doméstico** (actividad) domestic service; (personas) servants (*pl*), domestic staff [6] (Mil) service; ~ **militar** military service [7] (retrete) restroom (AmE), bathroom (esp AmE), toilet (esp BrE) [8] (en tenis) service, serve [9] (Relig) service [10] (AmL) (Auto) service

servidor -dora *m,f* [1] (a) (sirviente) servant (b) (frml) (Corresp): **su (atento y) seguro ~** your humble servant (frml) [2] **servidor** *m* (Inf) server

servidumbre *f* [1] (esclavitud) servitude [2] (conjunto de criados) domestic staff, servants (*pl*)

servil *adj* (a) ⟨*persona/actitud*⟩ servile, obsequious (frml) (b) ⟨*trabajo*⟩ menial

servilleta *f* napkin, serviette (esp BrE)

servilletero *m* napkin ring, serviette ring (BrE)

servir [I14] *vi* [1] (ser útil): **esta caja no sirve** this box won't do o is no good; **ya no me sirve** it's (of) no use to me anymore; **¿para qué sirve este aparato?** what's this device for?; **no lo tires, puede ~ para algo** don't throw it away, it might come in useful for something; **este cuchillo no sirve para cortar pan** this knife is no good for cutting bread; **no sirves para nada** you're useless; **no creo que sirva para este trabajo** I don't think he's right o suitable for this job; ~ **DE algo: de nada sirve llorar** it's no use o good crying; **¿de qué sirve?** what's the point o the use?; **puede ~ de mesa** you can use this as a table [2] (a) (en la mesa) to serve (b) (trabajar de criado) to be in (domestic) service (c) (Mil) to serve (frml) [3] (Dep) (en tenis) to serve

■ ~ *vt* **1** ‹*comida*› to serve; ‹*bebida*› to serve, pour

2 (estar al servicio de) ‹*persona/a la patria*› to serve; **¿en qué puedo ~la?** (frml) how can I help you?

■ **servirse** *v pron* (*refl*) ‹*comida*› to help oneself to; ‹*bebida*› to pour oneself, help oneself to

sésamo *m* sesame

sesear [A1] *vi: to pronounce the Spanish* [θ] *as* [s], *eg* /ser'βesa/ *instead of* /θer'βeθa/ *for* CERVEZA

sesenta *adj inv/m/pron* sixty; *para ejemplos ver* CINCUENTA

seseo *m: pronunciation of the Spanish* /θ/ *as* /s/, *eg* /ser'βesa/ *instead of* /θer'βeθa/ *for* CERVEZA

sesión *f* **(a)** (reunión) session; **~ de clausura** closing session **(b)** (de tratamiento, actividad) session; (de fotografía, pintura) sitting **(c)** (de cine) showing, performance; (de teatro) show, performance; **~ de noche** late evening performance

sesionar [A1] *vi* (AmL) to be in session

seso *m* **(a)** (Anat, Zool) brain **(b) sesos** *mpl* (Coc) brains (*pl*)

set *m* (*pl* **sets**) set

seta *f* (comestible) mushroom; (venenosa) toadstool

setecientos -tas *adj/pron* seven hundred; *para ejemplos ver* QUINIENTOS

setenta *adj inv/m/pron* seventy; *para ejemplos ver* CINCUENTA

setiembre *m* ▶ SEPTIEMBRE

seto *m* hedge

seudónimo *m* pseudonym; (de escritor) pen name, pseudonym

severidad *f* (de castigo, pena) severity, harshness; (de padre, educador) strictness; (de clima) harshness

severo -ra *adj* ‹*padre/profesor*› strict; ‹*castigo*› severe, harsh; ‹*invierno*› hard, severe; ‹*dieta/ régimen*› strict

Sevilla *f* Seville

sexismo *m* sexism

sexista *adj/mf* sexist

sexo *m* sex; **el ~ débil** the weaker sex; **~ seguro** safe sex

sexto¹ -ta *adj/pron* sixth; *para ejemplos ver* QUINTO; **la sexta parte** a sixth; **~ sentido** sixth sense

sexto² *m* sixth

sexual *adj* ‹*relaciones/órganos/comportamiento*› sexual; ‹*educación/vida*› sex (*before n*)

sexualidad *f* sexuality

sexy /'seksi, 'sesi/ *adj* (fam) sexy

sh, shh *interj* shush!, ssh!, hush!

sha, shah *m* shah

sheriff /'ʃerif/ *mf* sheriff

shock /ʃok/ *m* **(a)** (Med) shock; **en estado de ~** in (a state of) shock **(b)** (sorpresa desagradable) shock

show /ʃou, tʃou/ *m* (*pl* **shows**) show

si *conj* **1** **(a)** (en general) if; **~ pudiera** if I could;

~ lo hubiera *or* **hubiese sabido ...** if I'd known ..., had I known ...; **empezó a decir que ~ esto, que ~ lo otro** he said this, that and the other **(b)** (en frases que expresan deseo) if only; **¡~ yo lo supiera!** if only I knew! **(c)** (en frases que expresan protesta, indignación, sorpresa): **¡pero ~ te avisé ...!** but I warned you ...! **(d)** (planteando eventualidades, sugerencias): **y ~ no quiere hacerlo ¿qué?** and if she doesn't want to do it, what then?; **¿y ~ lo probáramos?** why don't we give it a try? **(e)** (en locs) **si no** otherwise

2 (en interrogativas indirectas) whether; **no sé ~ marcharme o quedarme** I don't know whether to go or to stay

■ *m* (nota) B; (en solfeo) ti, te (BrE); **~ bemol/ sostenido** B flat/sharp

sí *adv* **1** (respuesta afirmativa) yes; **¿has terminado? — sí** have you finished? — yes (I have); **decir que ~ con la cabeza** to nod

2 (uso enfático): **ahora ~ que lo has hecho bien** now you've really done it! (colloq); **tú ~ que sabes vivir** you certainly know how to live!; **eso ~ que es caro** that *is* expensive; **no puedo — ¡~ que puedes!** I can't — yes, you can! *o* of course, you can!; **que ~ cabe** it does fit; **es de muy buena calidad — eso ~** it's very good quality — (yes,) that's true

3 (sustituyendo a una cláusula): **creo que ~** I think so; **me temo que ~** I'm afraid so; **¿lloverá? — puede que ~** do you think it will rain? — it might; **un día ~ y otro no** every other day; **no puedo ir pero ella ~** I can't go but she can

■ *m* yes

■ *pron pers* **1** **(a)** (*refl*) (él) himself; (ella) herself; (ellos, ellas) themselves; **solo piensa en ~ (mismo)** he only thinks of himself; **parece muy segura de ~ (misma)** she seems very sure of herself; **fueron para convencerse a ~ mismos/mismas** they went to convince themselves **(b)** (*refl*) (usted) yourself; (ustedes) yourselves; **describase a ~ mismo** describe yourself; **léanlo para ~ (mismos)** read it (to) yourselves **(c)** (*impers*): **hay cosas que uno tiene que ver por ~ mismo** there are some things you have to see for yourself

2 (en locs) **entre sí** (entre dos) between themselves; (entre varios) among themselves; **lo discutieron entre ~** they discussed it between/ among themselves; **no se respetan entre ~** they don't respect each other; **de por sí: es de por ~ nervioso** he is nervous by nature; **el sistema es de por ~ complicado** the system is in itself complicated; **en sí (mismo): el hecho en ~ (mismo)** no tenía demasiada importancia this in itself was not so important

siamés -mesa *adj* Siamese
■ *m,f* (gemelo) Siamese twins

sibarita *mf* (amante de los lujos) lover of luxury, sybarite (frml); (en cuestiones de comida) gourmet, epicure (frml)

Siberia *f* Siberia

Sicilia *f* Sicily

siciliano -na *adj/m,f* Sicilian

379

sida *m* (= **Síndrome de Inmunodeficiencia Adquirida**) AIDS

sidecar /siðe'kar, 'saikar/ *m* (*pl* **-cares** *or* **-cars**) sidecar

sideral *adj* (Astron) sidereal

siderurgia *f* iron and steel industry

sidra *f* hard cider (AmE), cider (BrE)

siempre *adv* [1] always; ~ **se sale con la suya** he always gets his own way; **como** ~ as usual; **lo de** ~ the usual thing; **a la hora de** ~ at the usual time; **los conozco desde** ~ I've known them for as long as I can remember; **para** ~ (definitivamente) ⟨*regresar/quedarse*⟩ for good; (eternamente) ⟨*durar/vivir*⟩ for ever [2] (en todo caso) always; ~ **podemos modificarlo después** we can always modify it later [3] (AmL) (todavía) still; **¿**~ **viven en Malvín?** do they still live in Malvín? [4] (*en locs*) **siempre que** (cada vez que) whenever; (a condición de que) (+ *subj*) provided (that), providing (that) [5] (Méx) (en definitiva) after all; ~ **no se va** he's not leaving after all

sien *f* temple

sienta, sientas, etc ▶ SENTAR, SENTIR

sierra *f* [1] (Tec) saw; ~ **de mano** handsaw; ~ **mecánica** power saw [2] (Geog) (cordillera) mountain range; (zona montañosa): **fuimos a la** ~ we went to the mountains

Sierra Leona *f* Sierra Leone

sierraleonés -nesa *adj* of/from Sierra Leone

siervo -va *m,f* serf, slave

siesta *f* siesta, nap; **dormir la** ~ *or* **echar una** ~ to have a siesta *o* nap

siete *adj inv/pron* seven; *para ejemplos ver* CINCO
■ *m* (a) (cardinal) (number) seven; *para ejemplos ver* CINCO (b) (rotura) tear (*L-shaped*)

sietemesino -na *m,f* premature baby (*esp when born two months early*)

sífilis *f* syphilis

sifilítico -ca *m,f* person with *o* suffering from syphilis, syphilitic

sifón *m* [1] (a) (botella) siphon* (b) (Esp fam) (soda) soda (water) (c) (Col) (cerveza) draft* beer [2] (para trasvasar líquidos) siphon; (en fontanería) U-bend, trap

siga, sigas, etc ▶ SEGUIR

sigilo *m* stealth; **con** ~ stealthily

sigiloso -sa *adj* stealthy

sigla *f* abbreviation; (pronunciado como una palabra) acronym

siglo *m* (período) century; **hace** ~**s** *or* **un** ~ **que no le escribo** (fam) I haven't written to her for ages (colloq)

significación *f* (importancia) significance, importance

significado *m* [1] (de palabra) meaning; (de símbolo) meaning, significance [2] (importancia) ▶ SIGNIFICACIÓN

significar [A2] *vt* (a) (querer decir) to mean (b) (suponer, representar) ⟨*mejora/ruina*⟩ to represent; ⟨*esfuerzo/riesgo*⟩ to involve (c) (valer, importar) to mean

significativo -va *adj* [1] ⟨*cambio/detalle*⟩ significant [2] ⟨*gesto/sonrisa*⟩ meaningful

signo *m* [1] (en general) sign; ~ **de admiración** exclamation point (AmE), exclamation mark (BrE); ~ **de interrogación** question mark; ~ **de la victoria** V-sign; ~ **de puntuación** punctuation mark [2] (Astrol) *tb* ~ **del zodiaco** sign; **¿de qué** ~ **eres?** what sign are you?

sigo, sigue, etc ▶ SEGUIR

siguiente *adj* [1] (a) (en el tiempo) following (*before n*); **al día** ~ the next *o* the following day (b) (en secuencia) next; **en el capítulo** ~ in the next *o* following chapter (c) (*como n*): **serán los** ~**s en entrar** they'll be the next to go; **¡(que pase) el** ~**!** next please! [2] (que se va a nombrar) following (*before n*); **la carta decía lo** ~ ... the letter said the following ...

sílaba *f* syllable

silbar [A1] *vt* (a) ⟨*melodía*⟩ to whistle (b) ⟨*cantante/obra*⟩ (en señal de desaprobación) to whistle at, catcall
■ *vi* (a) (Mús) to whistle (b) «*viento*» to whistle (c) «*oídos*»: **me silban los oídos** I've got a ringing *o* whistling in my ears

silbato *m* (a) (pito) whistle; **tocar el** ~ to blow the whistle (b) (Col period) (árbitro) referee

silbido *m* (a) (con la boca, un silbato) whistle; **dio un** ~ he whistled (b) (del viento, balas) whistling; (de respiración) wheezing (c) (en los oídos) ringing, whistling (d) **silbidos** *mpl* (en señal de desaprobacion) catcalls (*pl*)

silenciador *m* (a) (Auto) muffler (AmE), silencer (BrE) (b) (de arma) silencer

silencio *m* [1] (en general) silence; **deben guardar** ~ you must remain silent; **en el** ~ **más absoluto** in dead *o* total silence [2] (Mús) rest

silenciosamente *adv* silently, quietly

silencioso -sa *adj* [1] ⟨*máquina/motor*⟩ quiet, silent, noiseless; ⟨*persona*⟩ silent, quiet [2] ⟨*calle/barrio*⟩ quiet

silicona *f* silicone

silicosis *f* silicosis

silla *f* (a) (mueble) chair; ~ **de ruedas** wheelchair; ~ **eléctrica** electric chair; ~ **plegable** *or* **de tijera** folding chair (b) (Equ) *tb* ~ **de montar** saddle

sillín *m* (de bicicleta) saddle

sillón *m* armchair, easy chair

silogismo *m* syllogism

silueta *f* (a) (cuerpo) figure (b) (contorno) silhouette

silvestre *adj* wild

simbólico -ca *adj* symbolic

simbolizar [A4] *vt* to symbolize, represent

símbolo *m* symbol

simetría *f* symmetry

simétrico -ca *adj* symmetric, symmetrical

símil *m* (a) (comparación) comparison (b) (Lit) simile

similar *adj* similar; ~ **A algo** similar TO sth

similitud *f* similarity, resemblance

simio *m* ape, simian (tech)

simpatía *f* (a) (de una persona) friendliness (b)

sida ⋯⟡ simpatía

(sentimiento): **se ganó la(s) ~(s) de todos** everyone came to like him; **no le tengo mucha ~** I don't really like him

simpático -ca *adj* **(a)** ⟨*persona*⟩ nice; **me cae** *or* **me resulta muy ~** I really like him **(b)** ⟨*gesto/ detalle*⟩ nice, lovely **(c)** ⟨*ambiente*⟩ pleasant, congenial; ⟨*paseo*⟩ pleasant, nice

simpatizante *mf* (de partido) sympathizer, supporter

simpatizar [A4] *vi* **(a)** (caerse bien) **~ (CON algn)** to get on well (WITH sb); **~on desde el primer momento** they took to each other right from the start **(b)** (Pol) **~ CON algo** to be sympathetic TO sth, to sympathize WITH sth

simple *adj* **1** (sencillo, fácil) simple; ▶ LLANAMENTE **2** (delante del n) (mero) simple; **el ~ hecho de ...** the simple fact of ...; **es un ~ resfriado** it's just a common cold; **un ~ soldado** an ordinary soldier **3** (tonto) simple, simple-minded
■ *mf* simpleton

simpleza *f* **(a)** (falta de inteligencia) simpleness; (ingenuidad) gullibility **(b)** (tontería): **deja de hacer/ decir ~s** stop being silly; **discutieron por una ~** they argued over a trifling matter

simplicidad *f* simplicity

simplificar [A2] *vt* to simplify

simplista *adj* simplistic

simposio, simposium *m* symposium

simulacro *m* **(a)** (cosa fingida): **no era de verdad, solo fue un ~** it wasn't for real, they (*o* he *etc*) just pretending **(b)** (farsa) sham; **~ de ataque** mock attack; **~ de incendio** fire drill, fire practice

simular [A1] *vt* ⟨*sentimiento*⟩ to feign; ⟨*accidente*⟩ to fake; ⟨*efecto/sonido*⟩ to simulate

simultánea *f* (en ajedrez) simultaneous match

simultáneo -nea *adj* simultaneous

sin *prep* **1** without; **~ azúcar** without sugar; **seguimos ~ noticias** we still haven't had any news; **agua mineral ~ gas** still mineral water; **cerveza ~ alcohol** non-alcoholic beer, alcohol-free beer; **me quedé ~ pan** I ran out of bread **2** **(a)** (con significado activo) without; **se fue ~ pagar** he left without paying; **estuvo una semana ~ hablarme** she didn't speak to me for a week; **sigo ~ entender** I still don't understand; **la pisé ~ querer** I accidentally trod on her foot **(b)** (con significado pasivo): **preguntas ~ contestar** unanswered questions; **esto está aún ~ terminar** it still isn't finished **3** **~ QUE + SUBJ:** **no voy a ir ~ que me inviten** I'm not going if I haven't been invited; **quítaselo ~ que se dé cuenta** get it off him without his *o* without him noticing; ▶ EMBARGO 2

sinagoga *f* synagogue

sinceridad *f* sincerity; **te voy a contestar con toda ~** I'm going to be quite honest *o* frank with you

sincero -ra *adj* sincere

sincronía *f* synchrony

sincronizar [A4] *vt* **(a)** ⟨*frecuencias/relojes*⟩ to synchronize; **~ algo CON algo** to synchronize sth WITH sth **(b)** (Col) ⟨*carro*⟩ to tune

sindical *adj* union (*before n*), labor union (*before n*) (AmE), trade union (*before n*) (BrE)

sindicalismo *m* **(a)** (movimiento) labor union movement (AmE), trade union movement (BrE) **(b)** (sistema, ideología) unionism, trade unionism (BrE)

sindicalista *mf* **(a)** (Rels Labs) member of the unions, trade unionist (BrE) **(b)** (Pol) syndicalist

sindicalizarse [A4] *v pron* (formar un sindicato) to unionize, form a union; (afiliarse a un sindicato) to join a union

sindicato *m* (Rels Labs) union, labor union (AmE), trade union (BrE)

síndrome *m* syndrome; **~ de abstinencia** withdrawal symptoms (*pl*); **~ de inmunodeficiencia adquirida** Acquired Immune Deficiency Syndrome, AIDS; **el ~ premenstrual** premenstrual syndrome *o* (BrE) tension, PMS, PMT (BrE); **~ de Down** Down's syndrome

sinfín *m*: **un ~ de** a great many

sinfonía *f* symphony

sinfónico -ca *adj* ⟨*música*⟩ symphonic; ⟨*orquesta*⟩ symphony (*before n*)

Singapur *m* Singapore

single /'singel/ *m* **1** (Mús) single **2** (en tenis) **(a)** (CS) (partido) singles (match) **(b)** **singles** *mpl* (AmL) (partido) singles (match)

singular *adj* singular
■ *m* singular; **en ~** (Ling) in the singular

siniestro¹ -tra *adj* ⟨*mirada/aspecto*⟩ sinister; ⟨*intenciones*⟩ sinister, evil

siniestro² *m* (frml) (accidente) accident; (causado por una fuerza natural) disaster, catastrophe

sinnúmero *m* ▶ SINFÍN

sino *conj* but; **se comió no uno, ~ tres** he ate not one, but three; **no hace ~ criticar a los demás** he does nothing but criticize everybody else; **no vino, ~ que llamó** he didn't come, he telephoned; **no solo ... ~ que ...** not only ... but ...
■ *m* (liter) fate

sínodo *m* synod

sinónimo¹ -ma *adj* synonymous; **~ DE algo** synonymous WITH sth

sinónimo² *m* synonym; **~ DE algo** synonym FOR sth

sinsabores *mpl* (problemas) troubles (*pl*); (experiencias tristes) heartaches (*pl*)

sintáctico -ca *adj* syntactic

sintagma *m* syntagm, syntagma

sintaxis *f* syntax

síntesis *f* (*pl* ~) **(a)** (resumen) summary **(b)** (deducción) synthesis; (combinación) synthesis, combination

sintético -ca *adj* ⟨*fibra*⟩ synthetic, man-made; ⟨*suelas*⟩ man-made

sintetizador *m* synthesizer

sintetizar [A4] *vt* **(a)** (resumir) to summarize **(b)** (combinar) to synthesize, combine

sintiera, sintió, etc ▶ SENTIR

síntoma *m* (Med) symptom; (señal) sign, indication

sintonía *f* **(a)** (Rad, TV): **están ustedes en la ~ de Radio Victoria** you are listening to Radio Victoria; **para una mejor ~** for better reception **(b)** (armonía): **en ~ con el pueblo** in tune with the people

sintonizador *m* tuner

sintonizar [A4] *vt* ⟨*emisora*⟩ to tune (in) to

■ ~ *vi* (Rad, TV) to tune in

sinvergüenza *adj* **(a)** (canalla): ¡qué tipo más ~! what a swine! (colloq) **(b)** (hum) (pícaro) naughty

■ *mf* **(a)** (canalla) swine (colloq); (estafador, ladrón) crook (colloq) **(b)** (hum) (pícaro) rascal (hum)

síper *m* (Méx) zipper (AmE), zip (BrE)

siquiera *adv* ⓵ (por lo menos) at least; **dile ~ adiós** at least say goodbye to her; **¡si (tan) ~ me hubiera avisado ...!** if only you'd warned me ...! ⓶ (en frases negativas) even; **ni ~ nos saludó** he didn't even say hello to us

sirena *f* ⓵ (Mit) mermaid; (en mitología clásica) siren ⓶ (de fábrica, ambulancia, alarma) siren ⓷ (Col) (en pirotecnia) rocket

Siria *f* Syria

sirope *m* syrup

sirviente -ta *m,f* (*m*) servant; (*f*) maid, servant

sísmico -ca *adj* seismic

sismo *m* (terremoto) earthquake; (temblor) earth tremor

sismógrafo *m* seismograph

sistema *m* ⓵ (método) system; **trabajar con ~** to work systematically *o* methodically ⓶ (conjunto organizado) system; **~ nervioso** nervous system; **~ solar** solar system; **S~ Monetario Europeo** European Monetary System ⓷ (Inf) system; **entrar en el/salir del ~** to log on/off

sistemático -ca *adj* ⟨persona⟩ systematic, methodical; ⟨método⟩ systematic

sistematizar [A4] *vt* to systematize

sitiar [A1] *vt* **(a)** (Mil) to besiege; **estamos sitiados** we are under siege **(b)** (acorralar) to corner

sitio *m* ⓵ **(a)** (lugar) place; **pon ese libro en su ~** put that book back in its place; **cambié la tele de ~** I moved the TV; **déjalo en cualquier ~** leave it anywhere; **tiene que estar en algún ~** it must be around somewhere **(b)** (espacio) room, space; **¿hay ~ para todos?** is there (enough) room for everyone?; **hacer ~** to make room **(c)** (plaza, asiento): **guárdame el ~** keep my seat *o* place; **le cambié el ~** I changed places with him **(d)** (Inf); *tb* **~ web** Web site **(e)** (Méx) (parada de taxis) taxi stand *o* rank **(f)** (Chi) (terreno urbano) vacant lot

⓶ (Mil) siege

situación *f* ⓵ **(a)** (coyuntura) situation **(b)** (en la sociedad) position, standing ⓶ (emplazamiento) position, situation (frml), location (frml)

situado -da *adj* **(a)** (ubicado) situated **(b)** ⟨persona⟩: **estar bien ~** to have a good position in society

situar [A18] *vt* **(a)** (colocar, ubicar) ⟨fábrica/aeropuerto⟩ to site, to locate (frml) **(b)** (Lit) ⟨obra/acción⟩ to set **(c)** ⟨soldados⟩ to post, station

■ **situarse** *v pron* **(a)** (colocarse, ubicarse): **con esta victoria se sitúan en primer lugar** this victory puts them in first place; **se situó entre los cinco mejores** she got a place among the top five **(b)** (socialmente): **se ha situado muy bien** he has done very well for himself

siútico -ca *adj/m,f* (Chi) ▶ CURSI

skai®, **skay**® /(e)s'kai/ *m* imitation leather

S.L. *f* = **Sociedad Limitada**

slalom /(e)s'lalom/ *m* (*pl* **-loms**) slalom

slip /(e)s'lip/ (*pl* **slips**) *m* ⓵ (prenda interior) **(a)** (de hombre) underpants (*pl*), pants (*pl*) (BrE) **(b)** (de mujer) panties (*pl*), knickers (*pl*) (BrE) ⓶ (bañador) swimming trunks (*pl*)

SME *m* (= **Sistema Monetario Europeo**) EMS

smog /(e)s'moy/ *m* (AmL) smog

snowboard /es'nobor(d)/ *m* snowboard

sobaco *m* armpit

sobado -da *adj* ⟨tapizado/cortinas/prenda⟩ worn, shabby; ⟨libro⟩ dog-eared, well-thumbed

sobajear [A1] *vt* (AmL fam) ▶ SOBAR 1A, B

sobar [A1] *vt* ⓵ **(a)** (manosear) ⟨tela/ropa/tapizado⟩ to handle, finger **(b)** (hum) ⟨chica⟩ to feel up (colloq), to grope (esp BrE colloq) **(c)** (Méx, Per fam) (adular) to suck up to (colloq) ⓶ (Col, Ven) (dar masajes) to massage

soberanía *f* sovereignty

soberano -na *adj* ⓵ ⟨estado/pueblo/poder⟩ sovereign ⓶ (fam) (enorme) tremendous; **eso es una soberana estupidez** that's an absolutely ridiculous thing to say/do

■ *m,f* (Gob, Pol) sovereign

soberbia *f* (orgullo) pride; (altivez) arrogance, haughtiness

soberbio -bia *adj* ⓵ ⟨persona/carácter⟩ (orgulloso) proud; (altivo) arrogant, haughty ⓶ (magnífico) superb, magnificent

sobornar [A1] *vt* to bribe, suborn (frml)

soborno *m* (acción) bribery; (dinero, regalo) bribe

sobra *f* ⓵ de sobra **(a)** (mucho): **hay comida de ~** there's plenty of food **(b)** (de más): **tengo una entrada de ~** I have a spare *o* an extra ticket; **tú aquí estás de ~** you're not wanted/needed here **(c)** (muy bien): **saber de ~ que ...** to know full well *o* perfectly well that ... ⓶ **sobras** *fpl* (de comida) leftovers (*pl*)

sobrado -da *adj* ⓵ **(a)** ⟨experiencia⟩ ample, more than enough; **tengo ~s motivos para sospechar** I have every reason to be suspicious **(b)** ⟨persona⟩: **estar ~ de algo** to have plenty of sth; **no ando muy ~ de tiempo** I'm a bit short of time ⓶ (Andes fam) (engreído) full of oneself (colloq)

sobrar [A1] *vi* **(a)** (quedar, restar): **sobró mucha comida** there was a lot of food left over; **¿te ha sobrado dinero?** do you have any money left? **(b)** (estar de más): **ya veo que sobro aquí** I can see I'm not wanted/needed here; **a mí no me sobra el dinero** I don't have money to throw around (colloq); **sobra un cubierto** there's an extra place

sobre *m* ⓵ (Corresp) envelope ⓶ (AmL) (cartera) clutch bag

■ *prep* ⓵ (indicando posición) **(a)** (encima de) on; **lo dejé ~ la mesa** I left it on the table; **los puso uno ~ otro** she placed them one on top of the other; **estamos ~ su pista** we're on their trail **(b)** (por encima de) over; **volamos ~ Lima** we flew over Lima; **en el techo, justo ~ la mesa** on the ceiling right above *o* over the table; **4.000 metros ~ el nivel del mar** 4,000 meters above sea level **(c)** (alrededor de) on; **gira ~ su eje** it spins on its axis ⓶ (en relaciones de jerarquía): **amar a Dios ~ todas las cosas** to love God above all else ⓷ (acerca de) on; **hay muchos libros ~ el tema** there are many books on *o* about the subject ····❖

4 (Esp) (con cantidades, fechas, horas) around, about (BrE); ~ **unos 70 kilos** around o about 70 kilos **5** **sobre todo** above all

sobrecama f or m (AmL exc CS) bedspread, counterpane

sobrecarga f **(a)** (en vehículo) excess load o weight **(b)** (de circuito, motor) overload; (de batería) overcharging

sobrecargar [A3] vt **(a)** ⟨vehículo/animal⟩ to overload **(b)** ⟨circuito/motor⟩ to overload; ⟨batería⟩ to overcharge **(c)** ⟨persona⟩ ~ **a algn DE algo** ⟨de trabajo/responsabilidad⟩ to overburden sb WITH sth

sobrecargo mf **(a)** (Aviac) (supervisor) purser, chief flight attendant; (auxiliar de vuelo) flight attendant **(b)** (Náut) purser

sobrecogedor -dora adj shocking, horrific

sobrecoger [E6] vt **(a)** (conmover) to move **(b)** (asustar) to strike fear into

sobredosis f (pl ~) overdose

sobregirado -da adj (esp AmL) overdrawn

sobregirar [A1] vt (esp AmL) to overdraw (on) ■ **sobregirarse** v pron to overdraw

sobregiro m (esp AmL) overdraft

sobrehumano -na adj superhuman

sobrellevar [A1] vt ⟨dolor/enfermedad⟩ to endure, bear; ⟨tragedia⟩ to bear; ⟨soledad⟩ to endure

sobremesa f (conversación) after-lunch/after-dinner conversation; **estuvimos de** ~ we sat around the table chatting

sobrenatural adj supernatural

sobrenombre m nickname

sobrepasar [A1] vt **(a)** ⟨nivel/cantidad⟩ to exceed, go above; ~ **el límite de velocidad** to exceed o go over the speed limit **(b)** ⟨persona⟩ (en capacidad) to outstrip; (en altura) to overtake

sobrepeso m (AmL) (exceso — de equipaje) excess (baggage); (— de carga) excess load o weight

sobreponerse [E22] v pron (recuperarse) to pull oneself together; ~**se A algo** to get over sth, recover FROM sth

sobrepuesto pp ▶ SOBREPONER

sobresaliente adj ⟨actuación⟩ outstanding; ⟨noticia/hecho⟩ most significant o important ■ m (Educ) grade between 8.5 and 10 on a scale of 10

sobresalir [I29] vi **(a)** «alero/viga» to project, overhang; «borde» to protrude **(b)** (destacarse, resaltar) to stand out; **sobresale entre los demás** it/she stands out from the rest; ~ **EN algo** ⟨en deportes/idiomas⟩ to excel o shine AT sth

sobresaltar [A1] vt to startle, make ... jump ■ **sobresaltarse** v pron to jump, be startled

sobresalto m fright

sobretiempo m (Chi, Per) **(a)** (horas extra, pago) overtime **(b)** (Dep) overtime (AmE), extra time (BrE)

sobretodo m overcoat

sobrevenir [I31] vi «desgracia/accidente» to strike

sobrevivencia f survival

sobreviviente adj/mf ▶ SUPERVIVIENTE

sobrevivir [I1] vi to survive; ~ **A algo** to survive sth

sobrevolar [A10] vt to fly over

sobrino -na m,f (m) nephew; (f) niece; **mis** ~**s** (solo varones) my nephews; (varones y mujeres) my nephews and nieces

sobrio -bria adj **1** [SER] **(a)** ⟨persona⟩ sober, restrained; ⟨hábitos⟩ frugal **(b)** ⟨decoración/estilo/color⟩ sober **2** [ESTAR] (no borracho) sober

sobros mpl (AmC) leftovers (pl)

socarrón -rrona adj (sarcástico) sarcastic, snide; (taimado) sly, crafty

socavón m (hoyo) hole; (excavación) shaft, tunnel; (cueva) cave

sociable adj sociable

social adj social

socialdemocracia f social democracy

socialdemócrata adj social democratic ■ mf social democrat

socialismo m socialism

socialista adj/mf socialist

socializar [A4] vt to socialize

sociedad f **1** (Sociol) society; ~ **de consumo** consumer society **2** (asociación, club) society **3** (Der, Fin) company; ~ **anónima** ≈ public corporation (in US), ≈ public limited company (in UK); ~ **de responsabilidad limitada** limited corporation (in US), (private) limited company (in UK); ~ **inmobiliaria** (Esp) (que construye) construction company; (que administra) real estate (AmE) o (BrE) property management company; ~ **mercantil** trading company **4** (clase alta) (high) society

socio -cia m,f **1** (miembro) member; **hacerse** ~ **de un club** to join a club **2** (Der, Fin) partner; ~ **accionista** shareholder **3** (fam) (camarada) buddy (AmE colloq), mate (BrE colloq)

sociología f sociology

sociológico -ca adj sociological

sociólogo -ga m,f sociologist

socorrer [E1] vt to help, come to the aid of

socorrido -da adj ⟨excusa/recurso⟩ handy, useful

socorrismo m (en el agua) lifesaving; (en la montaña) mountain rescue; (primeros auxilios) first aid

socorrista mf (en el agua) lifeguard, lifesaver; (en la montaña) mountain rescue worker; (de primeros auxilios) first-aider

socorro m help; **pedir** ~ to ask for help; ¡~! help!; **un grito de** ~ a cry for help

soda f **(a)** (bebida) soda water, soda (AmE) **(b)** (AmC) (cafetería) coffee bar

sodio m sodium

sofá m sofa, settee, couch

sofá-cama m sofa bed

sofisticado -da *adj* sophisticated

sofocante *adj* stifling

sofocar [A2] *vt* ⟨fuego⟩ to smother, put out; ⟨motín/revolución⟩ to stifle, put down
■ **sofocarse** *v pron* (acalorarse) to get upset *o* (colloq) worked up

sofoco *m* **(a)** (fam) (disgusto): **estaba con un ~ terrible** I was so upset **(b)** (por el calor) suffocation; (en la menopausia) hot flash (AmE), hot flush (BrE)

sofreír [I35] *vt* to sauté, fry lightly

sofrito *m*: lightly fried tomatoes, onion, garlic, etc

software /'sofwer/ *m* software

soga *f* (cuerda) rope

sois ▶ SER

soja *f* (Esp) soy (AmE), soya (BrE)

sol *m* **1** (Astron, Meteo) sun; **brillaba el ~** the sun was shining; **al salir/ponerse el ~** at sunrise/ sunset; **ayer hizo** *or* **hubo ~** it was sunny yesterday; **un día de ~** a sunny day; **en esa habitación no da el ~** that room doesn't get any sunlight *o* sun; **ayer hubo siete horas de ~** we had seven hours of sunshine yesterday; **tomar el ~** *or* (CS) **tomar ~** to sunbathe
2 (fam) (persona encantadora): **es un ~** she's an angel (colloq)
3 (Mús) (nota) G; (en solfeo) so*, sol; **~ bemol/ sostenido** G flat/sharp
4 (moneda) sol (Peruvian unit of currency)

solamente *adv* ▶ SÓLO

solapa *f* (de chaqueta) lapel; (de bolsillo, libro, sobre) flap

solapado -da *adj* ⟨persona⟩ sly, underhand (BrE); ⟨maniobra⟩ surreptitious, sly

solar *adj* ⟨energía/año/placa⟩ solar; **los rayos ~es** the sun's rays
■ *m* **1** (terreno) piece of land, site **2 (a)** (casa solariega) ancestral home **(b)** (linaje) lineage
3 (Per) (casa de vecindad) tenement building

solario, solárium *m* solarium

soldado *mf* soldier; **~ de caballería** cavalryman; **~ de infantería** infantryman; ; **~ raso** private; **~** *or* **soldadito de plomo** tin soldier

soldar [A10] *vt* (con estaño) to solder; (sin estaño) to weld

soleado -da *adj* sunny

soledad *f*: **en la ~ de su cuarto** in the solitude of his room; **bebe para olvidar su ~** she drinks to forget her loneliness; **no soporta la ~** he can't stand being alone; **pasó sus últimos años en ~** she spent her last years alone

solemne *adj* **1** (en general) solemn **2** (delante del n) (fam) ⟨mentira⟩ complete, downright

solemnidad *f* solemnity

soler [E9] *vi*: **suele venir una vez a la semana** she usually comes once a week; **no suele retrasarse** he's not usually late; **solía correr todos los días** he used to go for a run every day

solera *f* **1** (tradición, calidad): **una familia con ~ a** family with a long pedigree, a long-established family **2** (CS) (Indum) sundress

solfear [A1] *vt* to sol-fa

solfeo *m* (asignatura) music theory, sol-fa

solicitado -da *adj* ⟨persona⟩ in demand; ⟨canción⟩ popular

solicitante *mf* applicant

solicitar [A1] *vt* ⟨empleo/plaza⟩ to apply for; ⟨permiso/entrevista/información, servicios/apoyo/ cooperación⟩ to request, ask for

solícito -ta *adj* (dispuesto a ayudar) attentive; (amable) thoughtful, kind

solicitud *f* **(a)** (para trabajo) application; (para licencia) application, request; (para información, ayuda) request **(b)** (formulario) application form

solidaridad *f* solidarity; **en** *or* **por ~ con algn** in solidarity with *o* in sympathy with sb

solidario -ria *adj* (fraterno) supportive; **un gesto ~** a gesture of solidarity

solidarizar [A4] *vi* **~ CON algn** to support sb
■ **solidarizarse** *v pron* **~se CON algn** to support sb; **~se CON algo** to support sth, to back sth

solidez *f* (de muro, edificio) solidity; (de argumento, empresa) soundness; (de relación) strength

sólido¹ -da *adj* **1** (en sentido físico) solid **2 (a)** ⟨argumento/razonamiento⟩ solid, sound; ⟨preparación/principios⟩ sound **(b)** ⟨empresa⟩ sound; ⟨relación⟩ steady, strong

sólido² *m* **(a)** (Fís, Mat) solid **(b)** **sólidos** *mpl* (Med) solids (*pl*)

solista *mf* soloist

solitaria *f* tapeworm

solitario -ria *adj* **(a)** ⟨persona/animal⟩ solitary; ⟨vejez/niñez⟩ solitary; **(b)** ⟨calles⟩ empty, deserted; ⟨paraje/lugar⟩ lonely, solitary
■ *m,f* **1** (persona) loner **2 solitario** *m* solitaire (AmE), patience (BrE)

sollozar [A4] *vi* to sob

sollozo *m* sob

solo¹ -la *adj* **(a)** (sin compañía): **estar/sentirse ~** to be/feel lonely; **lo dejaron ~** (sin compañía) they left him on his own *o* by himself; (para no molestar) they left him alone; **el niño ya camina ~** the baby's walking on his own now; **hacen los deberes ~s** they do their homework by themselves; **hablar ~** to talk to oneself; **a solas** alone, by oneself **(b)** ⟨café/té⟩ black; ⟨whisky⟩ straight, neat; ⟨pan⟩ dry **(c)** (delante del n) (único): **lo haré con una sola condición** I'll do it on one condition; **hay un ~ problema** there's just one problem

solo² *m* (Mús) solo

sólo *adv* [The written accent may be omitted if there is no confusion with the adjective] only; **~** *or* **solo quería ayudarte** I only wanted to help, I was only *o* just trying to help; **~** *or* **solo de pensarlo me dan escalofríos** just *o* merely thinking about it makes me shudder; **canto ~ porque me gusta** I sing just for pleasure

solomillo *m* fillet/tenderloin/sirloin steak

solsticio *m* solstice

soltar [A10] *vt* **1** (dejar ir) ⟨persona⟩ to release, to let ... go; **soltó al perro** he let the dog off the leash
2 (dejar de tener agarrado) to let go of; **no lo sueltes** don't let go of it; **soltó el dinero y huyó** he dropped/let go of the money and ran; **¡suelta la pistola!** drop the gun!
3 (a) (desatar) ⟨cuerda/cable⟩ to undo, untie; **~ amarras** to cast off **(b)** (aflojar): **suelta la cuerda poco a poco** let *o* pay out the rope gradually **(c)** ···⟫

S

⟨*freno*⟩ to release; ⟨*embrague*⟩ to let out **(d)** (desatascar) ⟨*cable/cuerda*⟩ to free; ⟨*tuerca*⟩ to undo, get ... undone

4 (desprender) ⟨*calor/vapor*⟩ to give off; ⟨*pelo*⟩ to shed

5 ⟨*carcajada*⟩ to let out; ⟨*palabrotas/disparates*⟩ to come out with; ⟨*grito*⟩ to let out

■ **soltarse** *v pron* **1** (*refl*) «*perro*» to get loose; **no te sueltes de la mano** don't let go of my hand **2** (desatarse) «*nudo*» to come undone, come loose; (aflojarse) «*nudo*» to loosen, come loose; «*tornillo*» to come loose

soltería *f*: the fact or state of being unmarried; (en hombre) bachelorhood (frml); (en mujer) spinsterhood (frml)

soltero -ra *adj* single; **soy** *or* (esp Esp) **estoy soltera** I'm single, I'm not married
■ *m,f* (*m*) single man, bachelor; (*f*) single woman, spinster (dated *or* pej)

solterón -rona *m,f* (pey) (*m*) old *o* confirmed bachelor; (*f*) old maid (pej)

soltura *f*: **habla dos idiomas con ~** he speaks two languages fluently; **se desenvuelve con ~ en cualquier situación** she is at ease in any situation

soluble *adj* **1** (Quím) soluble; **~ en agua** water-soluble **2** ⟨*problema*⟩ soluble, solvable

solución *f* solution; **encontrar una ~ a algo** to find a solution to sth

solucionar [A1] *vt* ⟨*problema*⟩ to solve; ⟨*asunto/conflicto*⟩ to settle, resolve
■ **solucionarse** *v pron* «*problema*» to be resolved; **al final todo se solucionó** everything worked out in the end

somalí *adj/mf* Somali

Somalia *f* Somalia

sombra *f* (lugar sin sol) shade; (proyección) shadow; **las ~s de los árboles** the shadows of the trees; **sentarse a** *or* **en la ~** to sit in the shade; **este árbol casi no da ~** this tree gives hardly any shade; **~ de** *or* **para ojos** eyeshadow

sombrero *m* hat; **~ de copa** top hat; **~ de jipijapa** Panama (hat); **~ hongo** derby (AmE), bowler (hat) (BrE); **~ mexicano** sombrero

sombrilla *f* **(a)** (de mano) parasol; (de playa) sunshade **(b)** (Col, Ven) (paraguas) lady's umbrella

sombrío -bría *adj* (liter) ⟨*lugar*⟩ (umbrío) dark **(b)** (lúgubre) cheerless, dismal; ⟨*persona*⟩ gloomy

someter [E1] *vt* **1** (dominar) ⟨*país*⟩ to subjugate; **fue necesario usar la fuerza para ~lo** they had to use force to subdue him **2** (a torturas, presiones, prueba) to subject; **lo sometieron a un interrogatorio** they subjected him to an interrogation; **~ algo a votación** to put sth to the vote
■ **someterse** *v pron* **(a)** (a autoridad) to submit to, yield to; (a capricho) to give in to; (a ley) to comply with **(b)** (a prueba, examen, operación) to undergo

somier /so'mje(r)/ *m* (*pl* **-miers** *or* **-mieres**) sprung bed base

somnífero *m* sleeping pill, soporific (frml)

somnolencia *f* drowsiness, sleepiness

somnoliento -ta *adj* sleepy, drowsy

somos ▶ SER

son *m* **1 (a)** (sonido) sound; **al ~ del violín** to the strains *o* to the sound of the violin **(b)** **en son de:** **lo dijo en ~ de burla** she said it

mockingly; **venimos en ~ de paz** we come in peace **2** (canción latinoamericana) *song with a lively, danceable beat*

son ▶ SER

sonado -da *adj* **1** ⟨*boda/suceso/noticia*⟩ much-talked-about **2 (a)** ⟨*boxeador*⟩ punch-drunk **(b)** (fam) (torpe) stupid (colloq) **3** (AmL fam) (en dificultades) [ESTAR] in a mess (colloq), in trouble (colloq)

sonaja *f* (Méx) rattle

sonajero *m* rattle

sonámbulo -la *adj* somnambulistic (frml); **es ~** he sleepwalks, he walks in his sleep
■ *m,f* sleepwalker, somnambulist (frml)

sonar [A10] *vi* **1** «*teléfono/timbre*» to ring; «*disparo*» to ring out; **el despertador sonó a las cinco** the alarm went off at five o'clock; **~on las doce en el reloj** the clock struck twelve; **me suenan las tripas** (fam) my tummy's rumbling (colloq) **2** (+ *compl*) **(a)** «*motor/instrumento*» to sound; «*persona*» to sound; **suena raro** it sounds funny; **sonaba preocupada** she sounded worried; **suena a hueco** it sounds hollow **(b)** «*palabra/expresión*» to sound **3 (a)** (resultar conocido) (+ *me/te/le etc*): **me suena tu cara** your face is *o* looks familiar; **¿te suena este refrán?** does this proverb ring a bell (with you) *o* sound familiar to you? **(b)** (parecer) **~ A algo** to sound like sth **4** (AmL fam) (fracasar): **soné en el examen** I blew it in the exam (colloq); **sonamos** we've blown it now (colloq)
■ **~** *vt* **1 (a)** (+ *me/te/le etc*) ⟨*nariz*⟩ to wipe **(b)** ⟨*trompeta*⟩ to play **2** (Méx fam) **(a)** (pegar) ⟨*persona*⟩ to thump (colloq), to clobber (colloq) **(b)** (en competición) to beat, thrash (colloq)
■ **sonarse** *v pron*: *tb* **~se la nariz** to blow one's nose

sonata *f* sonata

sonda *f* **(a)** (Med) catheter **(b)** (para perforar) drill **(c)** (Náut) sounding line, lead line **(d)** (Espac, Meteo) probe

sondeo *m* **1** (encuesta) poll, survey **2** (perforación) test drilling; (Náut) sounding; (Espac, Meteo) exploration

soneto *m* sonnet

sonido *m* sound

sonoro -ra *adj* ⟨*golpe*⟩ resounding (*before n*), loud; ⟨*voz/lenguaje*⟩ sonorous, resonant; (Ling) voiced

sonreír [I18] *vi* **(a)** «*persona*» to smile; **~(le) A algn** to smile AT sb **(b)** «*vida/fortuna*» (+ *me/te/le etc*) to smile on

sonriente *adj* ⟨*ojos/expresión*⟩ smiling (*before n*); ⟨*persona*⟩ cheerful

sonrisa *f* smile

sonrojarse [A1] *v pron* to blush

sonsacar [A2] *vt*: **me costó trabajo ~le la verdad** I had a hard time getting the truth out of her

soñado -da *adj* (AmL fam) divine (colloq), heavenly (colloq); *ver tb* SOÑAR

soñador -dora *adj* ⟨*mirada*⟩ dreamy, faraway; **soy muy ~** I'm a real dreamer
■ *m,f* dreamer

soñar [A10] *vt* **(a)** (durmiendo) to dream **(b)** (fantasear) to dream; **la casa soñada** her/his/their dream house
■ ~ *vi* **(a)** (durmiendo) to dream; ~ CON algo/algn to dream ABOUT sth/sb; **que sueñes con los angelitos** (fr hecha) sweet dreams **(b)** (fantasear) to dream; ~ **despierto** to daydream; ~ CON algo to dream OF sth

sopa *f* (caldo) soup; ~ **de sobre** packaged soup (AmE), packet soup (BrE)

sopapo *m* (fam) (bofetón) slap, smack (colloq)

sope *m* (Méx) *fried tortilla topped with refried beans, onion and hot sauce*

sopera *f* soup tureen

sopesar [A1] *vt* ‹situación/ventajas› to weigh up; ‹palabras› to weigh

soplar [A1] *vi* **(a)** (con la boca) to blow **(b)** «*viento*» to blow **2** (fam) (en examen) to whisper (*answers in an exam*)
■ ~ *vt* **1** **(a)** ‹vela› to blow out; ‹fuego/brasas› to blow on **(b)** ‹vidrio› to blow **2** (fam) ‹respuesta› (en examen) to whisper **3** (fam) (robar) to swipe (colloq), to pinch (BrE colloq); (cobrar) to sting (colloq)
■ **soplarse** *v pron* (Méx, Per fam) (aguantar) ‹persona› to put up with; ‹discurso/película› to sit through, suffer

soplete *m* (para soldar) gas welding torch; (para quitar pintura) blowtorch

soplido *m* puff

soplo *m* **1** **(a)** (soplido) puff; **de un ~** with one puff, in one go **(b)** (de aire) puff; (más fuerte) blast **(c)** (de viento) puff; (más fuerte) gust **2** (fam) (chivatazo): **alguien dio el ~ a la policía** someone tipped off the police (colloq) **3** (Med) heart murmur

soplón -plona *m,f* **(a)** (fam) (en colegio) tattletale (AmE colloq), telltale (BrE colloq) **(b)** (fam) (a la policía) informer, stoolie (AmE colloq), grass (BrE colloq)

soponcio *m* (fam) **(a)** (desmayo): **le dio un ~** she fainted **(b)** (ataque de nervios) fit (colloq)

sopor *m* **(a)** (somnolencia) drowsiness, sleepiness **(b)** (letargo) torpor

soporífero -ra *adj* ‹efecto/discurso/clase› soporific

soportable *adj* bearable

soportal *m* **(a)** (de casa) porch **(b) soportales** *mpl* (de calle) arcade, colonnade

soportar [A1] *vt* **1** **(a)** ‹situación/frío/dolor› to put up with, bear, endure (frml); ‹persona› to put up with; **no soporto este calor/la gente así** I can't stand this heat/people like that **2** ‹peso/carga› to support, withstand; ‹presión› to withstand

soporte *m* **(a)** (de estante) bracket; (de viga) support; (de maceta, portarretratos) stand **(b)** (Inf) medium

soprano *mf* soprano

soquete *m* **1** (CS) (Indum) ankle sock **2** (Chi) (Elec) lampholder, socket **3** (Col, Méx, RPl fam) (tonto) fool, idiot

sor *f* (Relig) sister

sorber [E1] *vt* **(a)** (beber) to suck in *o* up; (tomar poco a poco) to sip **(b)** «*esponja*» to absorb, soak up

sorbete *m* sherbet (AmE), sorbet (esp BrE)

sorbo *m* **(a)** (cantidad pequeña) sip; **bébetelo a sorbitos** sip it **(b)** (trago grande) gulp; **de un ~** in one gulp

sordera *f* deafness

sórdido -da *adj* ‹lugar/ambiente› squalid; ‹asunto/libro› sordid

sordina *f* (de trompeta, violín) mute; (de piano) damper

sordo -da *adj* **1** (Med) deaf; **se quedó ~** he went deaf; **es ~ de nacimiento** he was born deaf **2** ‹ruido/golpe› dull, muffled; ‹dolor› dull; (Ling) voiceless
■ *m,f* deaf person; **hacerse el ~** to pretend not to hear

sordomudo -da *adj* deaf-mute (before n), deaf and dumb (BrE)
■ *m,f* deaf-mute

soroche *m* (Andes) (en la montaña) mountain sickness, altitude sickness

sorprendente *adj* surprising

sorprender [E1] *vi* to surprise; **me sorprende que no lo sepas** I'm surprised you don't know
■ ~ *vt* (coger desprevenido) to surprise, catch ... unawares; **nos sorprendió la lluvia** we got caught in the rain
■ **sorprenderse** *v pron* to be surprised

sorprendido -da *adj* surprised; **me miró ~** he looked at me in surprise; *ver tb* SORPRENDER

sorpresa *f* **(a)** (emoción) surprise; **se va a llevar una ~** she's going to be surprised, she's in for a surprise (colloq); **tomar** *or* (esp Esp) **coger a algn de ~** to take sb by surprise **(b)** (regalo) surprise
■ *adj inv* ‹fiesta/ataque› surprise (before n)

sorpresivo -va *adj* (AmL) surprise (before n), unexpected

sortear [A1] *vt* **1** ‹premio/puesto› to draw lots for; **se ~á un coche** there will be a prize draw for a car **2** **(a)** ‹bache/obstáculo› to avoid, negotiate **(b)** ‹problema/dificultad› to get around

sorteo *m* draw; **por ~** by drawing lots

sortija *f* **(a)** (anillo) ring **(b)** (en el pelo) ringlet

sortilegio *m* (embrujo) spell, charm; (brujería) sorcery; (adivinación) fortune-telling

sos: *equivalent of 'eres' in Central America and the River Plate area*

SOS *m* SOS, distress call

sosa *f* soda

soslayo: **de soslayo** ‹mirada› sidelong (before n), sideways; ‹mirar› sideways

soso -sa *adj* **(a)** ‹comida› (sin sabor) bland, tasteless; **está ~** (sin sabor) it's bland *o* tasteless; (sin sal) it needs more salt **(b)** ‹persona/película› boring, dull; ‹estilo› flat, drab

sospecha *f* suspicion; **tengo la ~ de que ...** I suspect *o* I have a feeling that ...

sospechar [A1] *vt* to suspect
■ ~ *vi* ~ DE algn to suspect sb, have one's suspicions ABOUT sb

sospechoso -sa *adj* ‹movimiento/comportamiento› suspicious; ‹paquete› suspicious, suspect; **tres hombres de aspecto ~** three suspicious-looking men
■ *m,f* suspect

sostén *m* **(a)** (físico) support; (económico) means of support **(b)** (Indum) bra, brassiere

sostener [E27] *vt* **1** (apoyar) **(a)** ⟨*estructura/ techo*⟩ to hold up, support; ⟨*carga/peso*⟩ to bear **(b)** (sustentar) ⟨*familia*⟩ to support, maintain **2** (sujetar, tener cogido) ⟨*paquete*⟩ to hold; **no tengas miedo, yo te sostengo** don't be afraid, I've got you *o* I'm holding you **3** ⟨*conversación/relación/reunión*⟩ to have **4** **(a)** (opinar) to hold **(b)** ⟨*argumento/afirmación*⟩ to support, back up **5** **(a)** ⟨*lucha/ritmo/resistencia*⟩ to keep up, sustain; **ella sostuvo mi mirada** she held my gaze **(b)** (Mús) ⟨*nota*⟩ to hold, sustain ■ **sostenerse** *v pron* **(a)** (no caerse): **la estructura se sostiene sola** the structure stays up without support; **apenas se sostenía en pie** he could hardly stand **(b)** (en un estado) to remain; **se sostuvo en el poder** she managed to remain in power

sostenido -da *adj* sharp; **re** ∼ **D** sharp

sostuve, sostuvo, etc ▶ SOSTENER

sota *f* jack (*in Spanish pack of cards*)

sotana *f* cassock, soutane

sótano *m* (habitable) basement; (para almacenamiento) cellar, basement

souvenir /suβe'nir/ *m* (*pl* **-nirs**) souvenir

soviético -ca *adj/m,f* (Hist) Soviet

soy ▶ SER

soya *f* (AmL) soy (AmE), soya (BrE)

sport /(e)s'por/ *m*: **ropa (de)** ∼ leisure wear, casual clothes (*pl*); **vestido de** ∼ casually dressed

spot /(e)s'pot/ *m* (*pl* **spots**) *tb* ∼ **publicitario** (espacio) slot; (anuncio) commercial, advertisement (BrE)

spray /(e)s'prai/ *m* (*pl* **sprays**) spray

Sr. *m* (= **señor**) Mr

Sra. *f* (= **señora**) Mrs

Sres. *mpl* = **señores**

Srta. *f* (= **señorita**) Miss

SS.MM. = **Sus Majestades**

Sta. (= **Santa**) St

status /(e)s'tatus/ *m* (*pl* ∼) status

Sto. (= **Santo**) St

stop /(e)s'top/ *m* (disco) stop sign

su *adj* (delante del *n*) (de él) his; (de ella) her; (de usted, ustedes) your; (de ellos, ellas) their; (de animal, cosa) its

suave *adj* **1** ⟨*piel/cutis*⟩ smooth, soft; ⟨*pelo*⟩ soft; ⟨*superficie/pasta*⟩ smooth **2** **(a)** ⟨*tono*⟩ gentle; ⟨*acento/música*⟩ soft **(b)** ⟨*color*⟩ soft, pale **(c)** ⟨*sabor*⟩ (no fuerte) delicate, mild; (sin acidez) smooth **3** **(a)** ⟨*movimiento/gesto*⟩ gentle, slight **(b)** ⟨*temperatura/clima*⟩ mild; ⟨*brisa*⟩ gentle **(c)** ⟨*modales/carácter/reprimenda*⟩ mild, gentle **(d)** ⟨*cuesta/curva*⟩ gentle, gradual **(e)** ⟨*jabón/ champú*⟩ gentle, mild **(f)** ⟨*laxante/sedante*⟩ mild **4** (Méx fam) (fantástico): **¡qué** ∼**!** great! (colloq), fantastic! (colloq)

suavidad *f* (de la piel) smoothness, softness; (de jabón, champú, clima) mildness; (de tono, acento)

gentleness, softness; (de color) softness, paleness; (de movimiento) gentleness; (de carácter) mildness, gentleness

suavizante *m* (para el pelo) (Esp) conditioner; (para la ropa) (fabric) softener *o* conditioner

suavizar [A4] *vt* ⟨*piel*⟩ to leave ... smooth/soft; ⟨*color*⟩ to soften, tone down; ⟨*sabor*⟩ to tone down; ⟨*carácter*⟩ to mellow, make ... gentler; ⟨*dureza/severidad*⟩ to soften, temper; ⟨*situación*⟩ to calm, ease ■ **suavizarse** *v pron* «*piel*» to become smoother/softer; «*carácter*» to mellow, become gentler; «*situación*» to calm down, ease

subalterno -na *m,f* **(a)** (en jerarquía) subordinate **(b)** (Taur) *member of a matador's support team*

subarrendar [A5] *vt* to sublease, sublet

subasta *f* **(a)** (venta) auction; **sacar algo a** ∼ to put sth up for auction **(b)** (de obras) invitation to tender

subastar [A1] *vt* ⟨*cuadro*⟩ to auction, sell ... at auction; ⟨*contrato/obra pública*⟩ to put ... out to tender

subcampeón -peona *m,f* (en liga) runner-up; (en torneo eliminatorio) losing finalist

subcomisión *f* subcommittee

subcomité *m* subcommittee

subconsciente *adj/m* subconscious

subcontratar [A1] *vt* to subcontract

subdesarrollado -da *adj* underdeveloped

subdesarrollo *m* underdevelopment

subdirector -ra *m,f* (de organización) deputy director; (de comercio) assistant manager, deputy manager

súbdito -ta *m,f* subject

subdividir [I1] *vt* to subdivide

subestimar [A1] *vt* to underestimate

subida *f* **(a)** (pendiente) rise, slope **(b)** (a montaña) ascent, climb; (al poder) rise **(c)** (de temperatura, precios, salarios) rise, increase

subir [I1] *vi* **1** **(a)** «*ascensor/persona/coche*» (ir arriba) to go up; (venir arriba) to come up; **hay que** ∼ **a pie** you have to walk up; **ahora subo** I'll be right up; **el camino sube hasta la cima** the path goes up to the top of the hill **(b)** ∼ **A algo** ⟨*a autobús/tren/avión*⟩ to get ON *o* ONTO sth; ⟨*a coche*⟩ to get IN *o* INTO sth; ⟨*a caballo/bicicleta*⟩ to get ON *o* ONTO sth, to mount sth (frml); ∼ **a bordo** to go *o* get on board **(c)** (de categoría) to go up; (en el escalafón) to be promoted **2** **(a)** «*marea*» to come in; «*aguas/río*» to rise **(b)** «*fiebre/tensión*» to go up, rise; «*temperatura*» to rise **3** «*precio/valor/cotización/salario*» to rise, go up ■ ∼ *vt* **1** ⟨*montaña*⟩ to climb; ⟨*escaleras/cuesta*⟩ to go up, climb **2** **(a)** ⟨*objeto/niño*⟩ (traer arriba) to bring up; (llevar arriba) to take up; **tengo que** ∼ **unas cajas al desván** I have to put some boxes up in the attic

(b) (poner más alto) ‹objeto› to put up … (higher); ‹cuello de prenda› to turn up: **sube al niño al caballo** lift the child onto the horse **(c)** ‹persiana/telón/ventanilla› to raise; ‹pantalones› to pull up; **¿me subes la cremallera?** will you zip me up?, will you fasten my zipper (AmE) o (BrE) zip? **(d)** ‹dobladillo› to take up; ‹falda› to take o turn up
3 (a) ‹precios/salarios› to raise, put up **(b)** ‹volumen/radio/calefacción› to turn up

■ **subirse** v pron **1 (a)** (a coche, autobús, etc) ▶
∼ vi 1B **(b)** (trepar) to climb; **se subió al árbol/al muro** she climbed up the tree/(up) onto the wall; **estaba subido a un árbol** he was up a tree **(c)** (a la cabeza) (+ me/te/le etc): **el éxito se le subió a la cabeza** the success went to his head
2 (refl) ‹calcetines/pantalones› to pull up; ‹cuello› to turn up

súbitamente adv suddenly

súbito -ta adj **(a)** (repentino) sudden; **de** ∼ suddenly, all of a sudden **(b)** (precipitado) hasty

subjetivo -va adj subjective

subjuntivo m subjunctive

sublevarse [A1] v pron to revolt, rise up, rebel

sublime adj ‹acción/sacrificio› noble; ‹cuadro/música› sublime

submarinismo m scuba diving

submarinista mf (buzo) scuba diver; (tripulante de submarino) submariner

submarino¹ -na adj underwater (before n), submarine (before n)

submarino² m submarine

subnormal adj **(a)** (Psic) mentally handicapped, subnormal **(b)** (fam & pey) (como insulto) moronic (colloq & pej)
■ mf **(a)** (Psic) mentally handicapped person **(b)** (fam & pey) (cretino) moron (colloq & pej), cretin (colloq & pej)

subordinado -da adj/mf subordinate

subordinar [A1] vt to subordinate; ∼ **algo A algo** to subordinate sth TO sth

subrayar [A1] vt **(a)** ‹texto› to underline, underscore **(b)** (poner énfasis en) to underline, emphasize, stress

subsanar [A1] vt ‹error› to rectify, correct; ‹carencia› to make up for; ‹obstáculo/dificultad› to overcome

subscribirse etc ▶ SUSCRIBIRSE, ETC

subsidio m subsidy; ∼ **de enfermedad** sickness benefit; ∼ **de desempleo** unemployment compensation (AmE), unemployment benefit (BrE)

subsistencia f subsistence, survival

subsistir [I1] vi «persona/planta» to survive, subsist (fml); «creencia/tradición» to persist, survive

subte m (RPl fam) subway (AmE), tube (BrE colloq)

subterráneo¹ -nea adj underground, subterranean

subterráneo² m **(a)** (pasaje) subway, tunnel **(b)** (RPl) (Transp) subway (AmE), underground (BrE)

subtitular [A1] vt to subtitle; **versión original subtitulada** original version with subtitles

subtítulo m subtitle

suburbano -na adj suburban

suburbio m (extrarradio) suburb; (barrio pobre) depressed area (on the outskirts of town)

subvención f subsidy, subvention (fml)

subvencionar [A1] vt to subsidize

subversivo -va adj subversive

subyacer [E5] vi ∼ (EN algo) to underlie (sth)

succionar [A1] vt to suck (up)

sucedáneo m substitute

suceder [E1] vi **1** (ocurrir) to happen; **¿le ha sucedido algo?** has something happened to him?; **le expliqué lo sucedido** I explained to him what had happened; **por lo que pueda** ∼ just in case
2 (en el tiempo) «hecho/época» ∼ A **algo** to follow sth
■ ∼ vt (en trono, cargo) to succeed

sucesión f **1 (a)** (al trono, en un cargo) succession **(b)** (herederos) heirs (pl), issue (fml) **(c)** (Der) (herencia) estate, inheritance **2** (serie) succession, series

sucesivo -va adj consecutive; ∼**s gobiernos lo han intentado** successive governments have tried it; **en lo** ∼ from now on, in future

suceso m **(a)** (acontecimiento) event **(b)** (accidente, crimen): **el lugar del** ∼ the scene of the incident/crime/accident; **sección de** ∼**s** accident and crime reports

sucesor -sora m,f (al trono, en un puesto) successor; (heredero) heir, successor (fml)

suciedad f **(a)** (mugre) dirt **(b)** (estado) dirtiness

sucio -cia adj **1 (a)** [ESTAR] ‹ropa/casa/vaso› dirty; **hacer algo en** ∼ to do a rough draft of sth (AmE), do sth in rough (BrE) **(b)** ‹lengua› furred, coated **2** [SER] **(a)** ‹trabajo› dirty; ‹dinero/negocio/juego› dirty **(b)** ‹lenguaje› filthy; ‹mente› dirty; **una jugada sucia** a dirty trick

sucre m sucre (Ecuadorean unit of currency)

sucursal f (de banco, comercio) branch; (de empresa) office

sudadera f (Dep, Indum) (suéter) sweatshirt; (conjunto) (Col, Ven) tracksuit

Sudáfrica f South Africa

sudafricano -na adj/m,f South African

Sudamérica f South America

sudamericano -na adj/m,f South American

Sudán m: tb **el** ∼ (the) Sudan

sudanés -nesa adj/m,f Sudanese

sudar [A1] vi to sweat, perspire (fml)

sudario m shroud

sudeste adj inv ‹región› southeastern; **iban en dirección** ∼ they were heading southeast
■ m **(a)** (parte, sector): **el** ∼ the southeast, the Southeast **(b)** (punto cardinal) southeast, Southeast

sudoeste adj inv ‹región› southwestern; **iban en dirección** ∼ they were heading southwest
■ m **(a)** (parte, sector): **el** ∼ the southwest, the Southwest **(b)** (punto cardinal) southwest, Southwest

sudor m sweat, perspiration (fml)

sudoroso -sa adj sweaty

Suecia f Sweden

sueco¹ -ca adj Swedish
■ m,f (persona) Swede

S

sueco² m (idioma) Swedish; **me hice/se hizo el ~** (fam) I/he pretended not to have heard (o seen etc)

suegro -gra m,f (m) father-in-law; (f) mother-in-law; **mis ~s** my in-laws, my mother-and father-in-law

suela f sole

sueldo m (de funcionario, oficinista) salary; (de obrero) wage; **~ base** base salary (AmE), basic salary (BrE)

suelo m (a) (tierra) ground; **se cayó al ~** she fell over (b) (en casa) floor (c) (en calle, carretera) road (surface) (d) (Agr) land (e) (territorio) soil; **el ~ patrio** one's native soil o land

suelta, sueltas, etc ► SOLTAR

suelto¹ -ta adj ① (a) ⟨tornillo/tabla/hoja⟩ loose; ⟨cordones⟩ loose, untied (b) (libre): **el perro está ~ en el jardín** the dog's loose in the garden; **el asesino anda ~** the murderer is on the loose (c) ⟨vestido/abrigo⟩ loose; **déjate el pelo ~** leave your hair loose o down (d) (separado): **ejemplares ~s** individual o single issues; **no los vendemos ~s** ⟨yogures/sobres⟩ we don't sell them individually o separately; ⟨caramelos/tornillos⟩ we don't sell them loose ② (a) (fraccionado): **dinero ~** loose change; **mil pesetas sueltas** a thousand pesetas in change (b) ⟨lenguaje/estilo⟩ fluent; ⟨movimientos⟩ fluid (c) (euf) ⟨vientre⟩ loose

suelto² m (Esp, Méx) (monedas) (small) change

suena, suenan, etc ► SONAR

sueño m ① (a) (estado) sleep; **oyó un ruido entre ~s** she heard a noise in her sleep; **tener el ~ ligero/pesado** to be a light/heavy sleeper; **perder el ~ (por algo)** to lose sleep (over sth) (b) (ganas de dormir): **¿tienes ~?** are you tired/sleepy?; **el vino me dio ~** the wine made me sleepy; **me empezó a entrar ~** I started feeling sleepy; **se me quitó el ~** I don't feel sleepy any more ② (a) (cosa soñada) dream; **un mal ~** a bad dream (b) (ilusión) dream; **la mujer de sus ~s** the woman of his dreams; **su ~ dorado es llegar a ser actriz** her (greatest) dream is to become an actress

suero m (a) (Med) (para alimentar) saline solution; (para inmunizar) serum (b) (de la sangre) blood serum (c) (de la leche) whey

suerte f (a) (fortuna) luck; **buena/mala ~** good/ bad luck; **ha sido una ~ que vinieras** it was lucky you came; **¡qué mala ~!** how unlucky!; **¡qué ~ tienes!** you're so lucky!; **no tengo ~** I'm not a lucky person; **hombre de ~** lucky man; **por ~ no estaba sola** luckily o fortunately I wasn't alone; **¡(que tengas) buena ~!** good luck!; **probar ~** to try one's luck; **traer** or **dar mala ~** to bring bad luck (b) (azar) chance; **echar algo a ~s** (con monedas) to toss for sth; (con pajitas) to draw straws for sth (c) (destino) fate

suertero -tera m,f (Per) lottery ticket seller

suéter m sweater, pullover, jersey (BrE), jumper (BrE)

suficiencia f (a) (aptitud) aptitude (b) (presunción) self-satisfaction, smugness; **aire de ~** air of self-satisfaction

suficiente adj (a) (bastante) enough; **con esto hay más que ~** there's more than enough here (b) ⟨persona⟩ self-satisfied, smug

■ m pass (equivalent to a grade of 5 on a scale from 0-10)

sufijo m suffix

suflé m soufflé

sufragio m (sistema) suffrage; (voto) (frml) vote

sufrido -da adj ⟨persona⟩ long-suffering, uncomplaining; ⟨ropa/tejido⟩ hard-wearing; **un color ~** a color that doesn't show the dirt

sufrimiento m suffering; **pasar ~s** to suffer

sufrir [I1] vt (a) ⟨dolores/molestias⟩ to suffer; **sufre lesiones de gravedad** he has serious injuries (b) ⟨derrota/persecución/consecuencias⟩ to suffer; ⟨cambio⟩ to undergo; ⟨accidente⟩ to have; **sufrió un atentado** there was an attempt on his life; **el coche sufrió una avería** the car broke down
■ ~ vi to suffer; **~ DE algo** to suffer FROM sth

sugerencia f suggestion

sugerente adj ⟨mirada/pose⟩ suggestive; ⟨vestido/blusa⟩ sexy

sugerir [I11] vt to suggest; **me sugirió que lo probara** he suggested that I (should) try it; **¿qué te sugiere este cuadro?** what does this picture make you think of?

sugestión f (convencimiento): **es pura ~** it's all in your (o his etc) mind; **tiene gran poder de ~** he is very persuasive

sugestionarse [A1] v pron to get ideas into one's head

sugestivo -va adj ⟨mirada⟩ suggestive; ⟨escote⟩ sexy; ⟨libro/idea⟩ stimulating

suicida adj suicidal
■ mf suicide victim

suicidarse [A1] v pron to commit suicide

suicidio m suicide

suite /swit/ f (Mús) suite

Suiza f Switzerland

suizo -za adj/m,f Swiss

sujetador m (Esp) bra, brassiere

sujetar [A1] vt ① (a) (mantener sujeto) to hold; **sujétalo bien, que no se escape** hold it tight, don't let it go; **tuvimos que ~los para que no se pegaran** we had to hold them back to stop them hitting each other (b) (sostener) to hold; **sujétame los paquetes** hold on to the packages for me (c) (fijar, trabar — con clip) to fasten ... together; (— con alfileres) to pin ... together ② (dominar) to subdue, conquer
■ **sujetarse** v pron ① (a) (agarrarse) **~se A algo** to hold on TO sth (b) (trabar, sostener): **se sujetaba los pantalones con la mano** he held his trousers up with his hand; **se sujetó la falda con un imperdible** she fastened her skirt with a safety pin ② (someterse) **~se A algo** ⟨a ley/reglas⟩ to abide BY sth

sujeto¹ -ta adj ① (sometido) **~ A algo** ⟨a cambios/revisión⟩ subject TO sth ② (fijo) secure

sujeto² m ① (individuo) character, individual ② (Fil, Ling) subject

sultán m sultan

suma f ① (cantidad) sum ② (Mat) addition; **hacer ~s** to do addition, to do sums (BrE)

sumamente adv extremely, exceedingly (frml)

sumar [A1] *vt* **(a)** ‹*cantidades*› to add (up) **(b)** (totalizar) to add up to; **8 y 5 suman 13** 8 and 5 add up to *o* make 13
■ ~ *vi* to add up
■ **sumarse** *v pron* **(a)** (agregarse) **~se A algo: esto se suma a los problemas ya existentes** this comes on top of *o* is in addition to any already existing problems **(b)** (adherirse) **~se A algo** ‹*a protesta/celebración*› to join sth

sumario *m* **1** (Der) **(a)** (en lo penal) indictment **(b)** (juicio administrativo) disciplinary action **2** (índice) (table of) contents

sumergible *adj* ‹*reloj*› waterproof; ‹*nave*› submersible

sumergido -da *adj* ‹*submarino*› submerged; ‹*ciudad*› submerged, sunken

sumergir [I7] *vt* (en líquido) to immerse, submerge
■ **sumergirse** *v pron* **(a)** «*submarino/buzo*» to dive, submerge **(b)** (en ambiente) to immerse oneself

sumidero *m* drain

suministrar [A1] *vt* (frml) to supply; **~ algo A algn** to supply sb WITH sth

suministro *m* supply; **el ~ de gas** the gas supply

sumir [I1] *vt* **1** (sumergir) **~ algo/a algn EN algo** ‹*en tristeza/desesperación*› to plunge sth/sb INTO sth **2** (Col, Méx) (abollar) to dent, make a dent in
■ **sumirse** *v pron* **1** (hundirse) **~se EN algo** ‹*en tristeza*› to plunge INTO sth; ‹*en pensamientos*› to become lost IN sth **2** (Col, Méx) (abollarse) to get dented

sumisión *f* (acción) submission; (actitud dócil) submissiveness

sumiso -sa *adj* submissive

sumo -ma *adj* utmost (before n); **de suma importancia** of the utmost importance; **con ~ cuidado** with great *o* the utmost care; **a lo ~** at the most

suntuoso -sa *adj* sumptuous; ‹*palacio*› magnificent

supe ▶ SABER

súper *adv* (fam): **lo pasamos ~ bien** we had a great *o* fantastic time (colloq); **es ~ bueno** it's great *o* fantastic (colloq); **lo hizo ~ rápido** he did it incredibly quickly
■ *f* ≈ premium grade gasoline (*in US*), ≈ four-star petrol (*in UK*)

superación *f* (de problema) surmounting, overcoming; (de récord) breaking, beating; (de teoría) superseding

superar [A1] *vt* **1** **(a)** (ser superior a) to exceed; **superó todas las expectativas** she exceeded all expectations; **nadie lo supera en experiencia** no one has more experience than him; **supera en estatura a su hermano** he's taller than his brother **(b)** (mejorar) ‹*marca*› to beat **2** **(a)** (vencer, sobreponerse a) ‹*timidez/dificultad/etapa*› to overcome; ‹*trauma*› to get over **(b)** (frml) ‹*examen/prueba*› to pass
■ **superarse** *v pron* to better oneself

superbloque *m* (Ven) large apartment building

superdotado -da *adj* highly gifted
■ *m,f* highly-gifted person

superficial *adj* **1** ‹*persona*›

superficial, shallow; ‹*charla/comentario*› superficial **2** ‹*herida*› superficial; ‹*marca/grieta*› surface (before n)

superficie *f* **1** (parte expuesta, aparente) surface; **salir a la ~** to surface, come to the surface **2** (Mat) (área) area

superfluo -flua *adj* superfluous, unnecessary; ‹*gastos*› unnecessary

superior¹ *adj* **1** (en posición) ‹*parte/piso*› top (before n), upper (before n); ‹*nivel*› higher; ‹*labio/mandíbula*› upper (before n) **2** **(a)** (en calidad) superior; **~ A algo/algn** superior TO sth/sb; **se siente ~ a los demás** he thinks he's better than everyone else; **una inteligencia ~ a la media** above-average intelligence **(b)** (en jerarquía) ‹*oficial*› superior; ‹*clase social*› higher **(c)** (en cantidad, número): **los atacantes eran ~es en número** the attackers were greater *o* more in number; **~ A algo** above sth; **un número ~ a 9** a number greater than *o* higher than *o* above 9

superior² -riora *m,f* **(a)** (Relig) *(m)* Superior; *(f)* Mother Superior **(b) superior** *m* (en rango) superior

superioridad *f* superiority

superlativo *m* superlative

supermercado *m* supermarket

superpoblación *f* (de una región) overpopulation; (de una ciudad) overcrowding

superpoblado -da *adj* ‹*mundo/país*› overpopulated; ‹*barrio/ciudad*› overcrowded

superpotencia *f* superpower

superstición *f* superstition

supersticioso -sa *adj* superstitious

supervisar [A1] *vt* to supervise

supervisor -sora *m,f* supervisor

supervivencia *f* survival

superviviente *adj* surviving (before n)
■ *mf* survivor

supiera, supiste, etc ▶ SABER

suplantar [A1] *vt* ‹*persona*› to impersonate, pass oneself off as

suplementario -ria *adj* ‹*información/ingresos*› additional, supplementary; ‹*trabajo*› extra

suplemento *m* supplement

suplencia *f* **(a)** (sustitución): **hacer una ~** «*profesor*» to do substitute (AmE) *o* (BrE) supply teaching **(b)** (trabajo) temporary job

suplente *mf* **(a)** (de médico) covering doctor (AmE), locum (BrE) **(b)** (de actor) understudy **(c)** (Dep) substitute **(d)** (de profesor) substitute (teacher) (AmE), supply teacher (BrE)

supletorio -ria *adj* ‹*cama*› extra, additional; **teléfono ~** extension

súplica *f* (ruego) entreaty, plea; (Der) petition

suplicante *adj* imploring (before n)

suplicar [A2] *vt* (rogar) to beg; **~le a algn que haga algo** to beg *o* implore *o* (liter) beseech sb to do sth

suplicio *m* **(a)** (tortura) torture **(b)** (castigo) punishment

suplir [I1] *vt* **1** (compensar) ‹*falta/deficiencia*› to make up for **2** (reemplazar) ‹*profesor/médico*› to stand in for, substitute for; ‹*jugador*› to replace, substitute **3** (Chi, Col, Ven) (suministrar) to provide, supply

suponer [E22] *vt* ⟦1⟧ **(a)** (tomar como hipótesis) to suppose, assume; **supongamos que lo que dice es cierto** let's suppose *o* assume what he says is true; **suponiendo que todo salga bien** assuming everything goes OK **(b)** (imaginar): **supongo que tienes razón** I suppose you're right; **¿va a venir hoy? — supongo que sí** is she coming today? — I should think so *o* I suppose so; **es de ~ que se lo habrán dicho** presumably *o* I should think he's been told; **se supone que empieza a las nueve** it's supposed to start at nine ⟦2⟧ (significar, implicar) to mean; **eso supondría tener que repetirlo** that would mean having to do it again

suposición *f* supposition

supositorio *m* suppository

supremacía *f* supremacy

supremo -ma *adj* supreme

suprimir [I1] *vt* **(a)** ⟨impuesto/ley/costumbre⟩ to abolish; ⟨restricción⟩ to lift; ⟨servicio⟩ to withdraw; ⟨gasto/ruido/alcohol⟩ to cut out **(b)** (Impr) ⟨párrafo/capítulo⟩ to delete **(c)** ⟨noticia/detalles⟩ to suppress

supuesto¹ -ta *adj* **(a)** (falso) false; **un nombre ~** a false name; **el ~ mendigo** the supposed beggar **(b)** (que se rumorea) ⟨milagro⟩ alleged (*before n*) **(c) por supuesto** of course; **dar algo por ~** to take sth for granted

supuesto² *m* supposition

supurar [A1] *vi* to weep, ooze, suppurate (tech)

supuse, supuso, etc ▶ SUPONER

sur *adj inv* ⟨región⟩ southern; **conducían en dirección ~** they were driving south *o* southward(s); **la costa ~** the south coast ■ *m* **(a)** (parte, sector): **el ~** the south; **al ~ de Cartagena** to the south of Cartagena **(b)** (punto cardinal) south, South; **vientos del ~** southerly winds; **viajábamos hacia el ~** we were travelling south *o* southward(s)

Suráfrica *f* South Africa

surafricano -na *adj/m,f* South African

Suramérica *f* South America

suramericano -na *adj/m,f* South American

surco *m* ⟦1⟧ **(a)** (en la tierra) furrow **(b)** (en el agua) wake, track **(c)** (en disco) groove; (en superficie) groove, line; (marca de rueda) ruts, track ⟦2⟧ (Col) (de flores) flowerbed

sureño -ña *adj* southern ■ *m,f* southerner

sureste *adj inv/m* ▶ SUDESTE

surf /'surf/, **surfing** /'surfin/ *m* surfing

surfista *mf* surfer

surgir [I7] *vi* «manantial» to rise; «problema/dificultad» to arise, come up, emerge; «interés/sentimiento» to develop, emerge; «idea» to emerge, come up; «tema» to come up, crop up; «movimiento/partido» to come into being, arise

suroeste *adj inv/m* ▶ SUDOESTE

surrealismo *m* surrealism

surrealista *adj* ⟨artista/exposición⟩ surrealist (*before n*); ⟨estilo/efecto⟩ surrealistic

surtido¹ -da *adj* **(a)** ⟨bombones/galletas⟩ assorted **(b)** (provisto) stocked; **una tienda bien/mal surtida** a well-stocked/poorly-stocked shop

surtido² *m* (de bombones, galletas) assortment; (de herramientas, ropa) range, selection, assortment

surtidor *m* (aparato) gas pump (AmE), petrol pump (BrE); (estación de servicio) gas station (AmE), petrol station (BrE)

surtir [I1] *vt* **(a)** (proveer) **~ a algn DE algo** to supply sb WITH sth **(b) surtir efecto** to take effect ■ **surtirse** *v pron* **~se DE algo** ⟨de provisiones⟩ to stock up WITH sth

susceptibilidad *f* sensitivity, touchiness

susceptible *adj* ⟨persona⟩ sensitive, touchy; **~ A algo** sensitive TO sth

suscribirse [I34] *v pron* (refl) **~ A algo** to take out a subscription TO sth

suscripción *f* (a una publicación) subscription

suscriptor -tora *m,f* subscriber

suspender [E1] *vt* ⟦1⟧ **(a)** ⟨pagos⟩ to suspend; ⟨garantía/derecho⟩ to suspend, withdraw; ⟨sesión⟩ to adjourn; ⟨vuelo⟩ (cancelar) to cancel; (aplazar) to postpone; ⟨viaje/reunión⟩ (cancelar) to call off; (aplazar) to put off; ⟨tratamiento⟩ to stop, suspend; ⟨servicio⟩ to suspend, discontinue; ⟨programa⟩ to cancel **(b)** ⟨empleado/jugador⟩ to suspend; ⟨alumno⟩ (AmL) to suspend ⟦2⟧ (colgar) **~ algo DE algo** to hang sth FROM sth ⟦3⟧ (Esp) ⟨asignatura/examen/alumno⟩ to fail ■ **~** *vi* (Esp) to fail

suspense *m* (Esp) ▶ SUSPENSO 1

suspensión *f* suspension

suspenso *m* ⟦1⟧ (AmL) (Cin, Lit) suspense; **película/novela de ~** thriller ⟦2⟧ (Esp) (Educ) fail, failure; **no he tenido ningún ~** I haven't failed anything

suspensores *mpl* (Chi) (tirantes) suspenders (*pl*) (AmE), braces (*pl*) (BrE)

suspicacia *f* suspicion

suspicaz *adj* suspicious

suspirar [A1] *vi* **(a)** (de pena, alivio) to sigh **(b)** (anhelar) **~ POR algo** to yearn *o* long FOR sth

suspiro *m* sigh; **un ~ de alivio** a sigh of relief

sustancia *f* substance

sustantivo *m* noun, substantive (frml)

sustentar [A1] *vt* **(a)** ⟨peso⟩ to support **(b)** ⟨persona/familia⟩ to support, maintain

sustento *m* **(a)** (apoyo) means of support **(b)** (alimento) sustenance

sustitución *f* **(a)** (permanente) replacement **(b)** (transitoria) substitution

sustituir [I20] *vt* **(a)** (permanentemente) to replace; **~ A algo** to replace sth; **~ algo/a algn POR algo/algn** to replace sth/sb WITH sth/sb **(b)** (transitoriamente) ⟨trabajador/profesor⟩ to stand in for; ⟨deportista⟩ to come on as a substitute for

sustituto -ta *m,f* **(a)** (permanente) replacement **(b)** (transitorio) substitute; (de médico) covering

s

doctor (AmE), locum (BrE); (de actor) understudy; **el ~ de la profesora de alemán** the substitute (AmE) *o* (BrE) stand-in for the German teacher

susto *m* (impresión momentánea) fright; **darle un ~ a algn** to give sb a fright; **darse** *or* **llevarse un ~** to get a fright (colloq)

susurrar [A1] *vi* **(a)** «*persona*» to whisper **(b)** (liter) «*agua*» to murmur; «*viento*» to sigh; «*hojas*» to rustle
■ ~ *vt* to whisper; **le susurró algo al oído** she whispered something in his ear

susurro *m* **(a)** (murmullo) whisper **(b)** (liter) (del agua) murmuring; (del viento) sighing; (de las hojas) rustling

sutil *adj* **(a)** ⟨*diferencia*⟩ subtle, fine; ⟨*ironía*⟩ subtle; ⟨*mente/inteligencia*⟩ keen, sharp **(b)** ⟨*gasa/velo*⟩ fine; ⟨*fragancia*⟩ subtle, delicate

sutileza *f* subtlety

suyo -ya *adj* (de él) his; (de ella) hers; (de usted, ustedes) yours; (de ellos, ellas) theirs; **Marta y un amigo ~** Marta and a friend of hers
■ *pron* **el ~, la suya**, *etc* (de él) his; (de ella) hers; (de usted, ustedes) yours; (de ellos, ellas) theirs; **él me prestó el ~** he lent me his

svástica *f* swastika

switch /'(e)switʃ/ *m* **(a)** (Col, Ven, Méx) (interruptor) light switch **(b)** (Méx) (Auto) ignition switch

···················

Tt

···················

T, t *f* (read as /te/) the letter T, t

tabaco *m* **(a)** (planta, producto) tobacco; **~ de hebra/de pipa** loose/pipe tobacco; **~ negro/rubio** dark/Virginia tobacco **(b)** (Esp) (cigarrillos) cigarettes (*pl*) **(c)** (Col) (puro) cigar

tábano *m* horsefly

tabaquismo *m* nicotine poisoning; **~ pasivo** passive smoking

tabasco *m* Tabasco® (sauce)

taberna *f* bar, tavern (arch), pub (BrE)

tabernáculo *m* tabernacle

tabernero -ra *m,f* (propietario) (*m*) bar owner, landlord (BrE); (*f*) bar owner, landlady (BrE); (camarero) (*m*) bartender; (*f*) barmaid

tabique *m* **(a)** (pared) partition **(b)** (Méx) (ladrillo) brick

tabla *f* **1** (de madera) plank; **las ~s del suelo** the floorboards; **~ de picar/planchar** chopping/ironing board; **tener ~s** «*actor/cantante*» (fam) to be an old hand *o* an expert **2** (de surfing) surfboard; (de windsurf) sailboard, windsurfer; (para natación) float **3** (gráfico, listado) table; (Mat) *tb* **~ de multiplicar** multiplication table **4** (de falda) pleat; **una falda de ~s** a pleated skirt **5** **tablas** *fpl* (en ajedrez): **acabar** *or* **quedar en ~s** to end in a draw; **estar ~s** (Méx fam) to be even *o* quits (colloq)

tablado *m* (para discursos) platform; (para espectáculos) stage

tablao *m*: *tb* **~ flamenco** *bar or club where flamenco is performed*

tablero *m* **(a)** (en estación, aeropuerto) board; (para anuncios) bulletin board (AmE), noticeboard (BrE); **~ de dibujo** drawing board; **~ de instrumentos** *or* **de mandos** instrument panel **(b)** (Jueg) board; **un ~ de ajedrez** a chessboard; **un ~ de damas** a checkerboard (AmE), a draughtboard (BrE) **(c)** (pizarra) blackboard **(d)** (de mesa) top

tableta *f* **(a)** (Farm) tablet, pill **(b)** (de chocolate) bar

tablilla *f* (Méx) (de chocolate) bar

tablón *m* **(a)** (de madera) plank **(b)** *tb* **~ de anuncios** (Esp) bulletin board (AmE), noticeboard (BrE)

tabú *adj inv* taboo
■ *m* (*pl* **-búes** *or* **-bús**) taboo

tabulador *m* tabulator, tab

taburete *m* stool

tacañería *f* stinginess, meanness (colloq)

tacaño -ña *adj* stingy, mean
■ *m,f* miser, tightwad (AmE colloq)

tacha *f* stain, blemish; **sin ~** ⟨*reputación*⟩ unblemished, spotless; ⟨*conducta*⟩ irreproachable

tachadura *f* crossing out, correction

tachar [A1] *vt* **1** (en escrito) to cross out **2** (tildar) **~ a algn DE algo** to brand *o* label sb AS sth

tacho *m* **(a)** (CS) (recipiente) (metal) container **(b)** (CS, Per) (papelero) wastebasket (AmE), wastepaper basket (BrE); **~ de la basura** (en la cocina) garbage can (AmE), rubbish bin (BrE); (en la calle) garbage *o* trash can (AmE), dustbin (BrE)

tachón *m* (en escrito) crossing out

tachuela *f* (clavo) tack; (en cinturón) stud

tácito -ta *adj* ⟨*acuerdo*⟩ tacit, unspoken

taciturno -na *adj* **(a)** [SER] (callado, silencioso) taciturn, uncommunicative **(b)** [ESTAR] (triste) glum, gloomy

taco *m* **1** **(a)** (de madera) plug; (para tornillo) Rawl® (AmE), Rawlplug® (BrE) **(b)** (de billetes) book; (de folletos) wad; (de queso, jamón) (Esp) cube **2** **(a)** (en billar) cue **(b)** (Col) (de golf) tee **3** **(a)** (de botas de deporte) cleat (AmE), stud (BrE) **(b)** (CS, Per) (tacón) heel; **zapatos de ~ alto/bajo** high-heeled/low-heeled *o* flat shoes **4** **(a)** (Coc) taco **(b)** (Méx) (comida ligera) snack, bite to eat (colloq) **5** (Esp fam) (palabrota) swearword; **soltar ~s** to swear **6** (Chi) (embotellamiento) traffic jam

tacón *m* heel; **zapatos de ~ alto/bajo** high-heeled/low-heeled *o* flat shoes; **~ de aguja** spike heel

táctica *f* tactic, strategy

táctico -ca *adj* tactical

táctil *adj* tactile

tacto *m* ☐1☐ (a) (sentido) sense of touch (b) (acción) touch; **áspero al** ~ rough to the touch (c) (cualidad) feel ☐2☐ (delicadeza) tact; **¡qué falta de** ~**!** how tactless!; **tiene mucho** ~ he's very tactful

Tahití *m* Tahiti

tailandés¹ -desa *adj/m,f* Thai

tailandés² *m* (idioma) Thai

Tailandia *f* Thailand

taimado -da *adj* ☐1☐ (astuto) crafty, cunning ☐2☐ (Chi) (malhumorado) sulky, huffy

taimarse [A1] *v pron* (Chi fam) (a) «*persona*» to get into a huff (colloq) (b) «*mula*» to balk

tajada *f* (a) (de melón, queso) slice (b) (Ven) (de plátano frito) slice of fried plantain

tajante *adj* «*respuesta*» categorical, unequivocal; «*tono*» sharp; **un 'no'** ~ an emphatic *o* categorical 'no'

tajear [A1] *vt* (AmL) to slash

tajo *m* ☐1☐ (corte) cut ☐2☐ (a) (Geol) gorge, ravine (b) (Min) face

tal *adj* ☐1☐ (dicho) such; **en** ~**es casos** in such cases; **nunca dije** ~ **cosa** I never said anything of the kind *o* such a thing ☐2☐ (seguido de consecuencia): **se llevó** ~ **disgusto que ...** she was so upset (that) ...; **había** ~ **cantidad de gente que ...** there were so many people that ... ☐3☐ (con valor indeterminado) such-and-such; ~ **día, en** ~ **lugar** such-and-such a day, at such-and-such a place; **llamó un** ~ **Méndez** a Mr Méndez phoned
■ *pron:* **eres un adulto, compórtate como** ~ you're an adult, behave like one; **que si** ~ **y que si cual** and so on and so forth; **son** ~ **para cual** they're as bad as each other
■ *adv* ☐1☐ (fam) (en preguntas): **hola ¿qué** ~**?** hello, how are you?; **¿qué** ~ **es Marisa?** what's Marisa like?; **¿qué** ~ **lo pasaron?** how did it go? ☐2☐ (*en locs*) **con tal de: hace cualquier cosa con** ~ **de llamar la atención** he'll do anything to get attention; **con** ~ **de no tener que volver** as long as I don't have to come back; **tal (y) como:** ~ **(y) como están las cosas** the way things are; **hazlo** ~ **(y) como te indicó** do it exactly as she told you; **tal cual: lo dejé todo** ~ **cual** I left everything exactly as it was; **tal vez** maybe

talacha *f* (a) (Méx) (reparación de llantas) flat *o* puncture repair (b) (Méx fam) (trabajo manual) work

taladradora *f* pneumatic drill

taladrar [A1] *vt* «*pared/madera*» to drill (through)

taladro *m* (a) (mecánico) hand drill; (eléctrico) electric *o* power drill (b) (agujero) drill hole

talante *m* (humor) mood; **estar de buen** ~ to be in a good mood

talar [A1] *vt* «*árbol*» to fell, cut down

talco *m* talc; **polvos de** ~ talcum powder

talento *m* (a) (aptitud) talent; **tiene** ~ **para la música** he has a talent *o* gift for music; **un joven de** ~ a talented young man (b) (persona) talented person

talentoso -sa *adj* talented, gifted

TALGO /'talɣo/ *m* (= **Tren Articulado Ligero Goicoechea Oriol**) air-conditioned express train

talismán *m* talisman, lucky charm

talla *f* (a) (Indum) size; **¿cuál es su** ~**?** what size are you?; **de** *o* **en todas las** ~**s** in all sizes (b) (estatura) size, height; **de** ~ **mediana** of medium height

tallado *m* (de madera) carving; (de piedras preciosas) cutting

tallar [A1] *vt* ☐1☐ «*madera*» to carve; «*escultura/mármol*» to sculpt; «*piedras preciosas*» to cut ☐2☐ (Méx) (a) (para limpiar) to scrub (b) (para aliviar) to rub
■ ~ *vi* (Col) «*zapatos*» to be too tight
■ **tallarse** *v pron* (Méx) (a) (para limpiarse) to scrub oneself (para aliviar) to rub oneself; «*ojos*» to rub

tallarín *m* noodle

talle *m* (a) (cintura) waist (b) (figura) figure (c) (en costura) trunk measurement; **es corta de** ~ she's short-waisted

taller *m* ☐1☐ (a) (Auto) *tb* ~ **mecánico** garage, repair shop (AmE) (b) (de carpintero, técnico) workshop ☐2☐ (Educ) workshop

tallo *m* stem, stalk

talón *m* ☐1☐ (a) (del pie, zapato, calcetín) heel; ~ **de Aquiles** Achilles' heel (b) (de zapato, calcetín) heel ☐2☐ (a) (AmL) (matriz) stub, counterfoil (b) (Esp) (cheque) check (AmE), cheque (BrE); (vale) chit; ~ **de compra** receipt

talonario *m* (de cheques) checkbook (AmE), chequebook (BrE); (de recibos) receipt book; (de volantes) book of vouchers

talonear [A1] *vt* (AmL) «*caballo*» to spur (on)

tamal *m* tamale

tamaño *m* size; **pañuelos de todos los** ~**s** handkerchiefs in all sizes; **de** ~ **bolsillo** pocket-size; **un busto** ~ **natural** a life-size bust

tamarindo *m* (a) (Bot) tamarind (b) (Méx fam) (agente) traffic cop (colloq)

tambache *m* (Méx fam) (bulto) bundle; (montón) pile

tambalearse [A1] *v pron vi* «*silla/botella*» to wobble; «*persona*» to stagger; **caminaba tambaleándose** he was staggering; **todo empezó a** ~ everything began to shake

también *adv* too, as well ~ **habla ruso** she speaks Russian too *o* as well; **que te diviertas —** **tú** ~ have fun! — you too *o* and you; **Pilar fuma — yo** ~ Pilar smokes — so do I *o* (colloq) me too

tambo *m* ☐1☐ (Méx) (a) (recipiente) can (AmE), bin (BrE) (b) (fam) (cárcel) slammer (sl), can (AmE sl) ☐2☐ (Per) (tienda) wayside stall

tambor *m* ☐1☐ (a) (instrumento) drum; **un redoble de** ~**es** a drum roll (b) (persona) drummer ☐2☐ (a) (del freno) drum (b) (AmL) (barril) drum

tamborilear [A1] *vi* to drum, tap

Támesis *m:* **el** ~ the (River) Thames

tamiz *m* sieve; **pasar algo por el** ~ «*harina*» to sift sth; «*salsa*» to sieve sth

tamizar [A4] *vt* «*harina*» to sift; «*salsa*» to sieve

tampoco *adv* not ... either; **yo** ~ **entendí** I didn't understand either; **él no va, ni yo** ~ he isn't going and neither am I; **no he estado en Roma ni** ~ **en París** I've never been to Rome or Paris

tampón *m* (a) (para entintar) ink pad (b) (Farm, Med) tampon

tan *adv: apocopated form of* TANTO *used before adjectives (except some comparatives), adverbs, and adjetival or adverbial phrases*

tanda *f* ⓵ (grupo) batch, lot; **cada dos minutos hay una ∼ de avisos** (AmL) every couple of minutes there's another lot of commercials; **los horneamos en dos ∼s** we baked them in two batches ⓶ (AmC, Méx fam) (función — de teatro) performance; (∼ de cine) showing, performance ⓷ (Col, Méx) (ronda) round (of drinks)

tándem *m* (bicicleta) tandem

tanga *f or m* tanga

tangente *f* tangent; *irse or salirse por la* ∼ to go off at a tangent

tangerina *f* tangerine

tango *m* tango; **bailar el ∼** to tango

tano -na *adj/m,f* (RPl fam & pey) Italian

tanque *m* ⓵ (Arm) (carro) tank ⓶ (de agua, gasolina) tank; (de gas, oxígeno) cylinder, bottle

tantear [A1] *vt* **(a)** (con el tacto) to feel **(b)** ⟨situación⟩ to weigh up, size up; ⟨persona⟩ to sound out **(c)** (calcular aproximadamente) to estimate
■ ∼ *vi* to feel one's way

tanteo *m* (Dep) score

tantito *adv* (Méx fam) a bit; **espérame ∼, ya voy** just wait a bit, I'm coming

tanto[1] *adv* ⓵ [*see note under* TAN] (aplicado a adjetivo o adverbio) so; (aplicado a verbo) so much; **es tan bonito** it's so beautiful; **¡es una chica tan amable!** she's such a nice girl!; **∼ mejor** so much the better; **tan solo** only; **∼ es así que ...** so much so that ...; **ya no salimos ∼** we don't go out so often *o* so much now; **llegó tan tarde que ...** he arrived so late (that) ...; **no es tan tímida como parece** she's not as shy as she looks; **sale ∼ como tú** he goes out as much as you do; **tan pronto como puedas** as soon as you can; **∼ Suárez como Vargas votaron en contra** both Suárez and Vargas voted against
⓶ (AmL exc RPl) **qué tanto/qué tan**: **¿qué ∼ te duele?** how much does it hurt?; **¿qué tan alto es?** how tall is he?
■ *m* ⓵ (cantidad): **un ∼ por ciento** a percentage; **hay que dejar un ∼ de depósito** you have to put down a certain amount as a deposit
⓶ (punto — en fútbol) goal; (— en fútbol americano, tenis, juegos) point
⓷ (*en locs*) **al tanto: me puso al ∼** she put me in the picture; **mantenerse al ∼ de algo** to keep up to date with sth; **estar al ∼** (pendiente, alerta) to be on the ball (colloq); **está al ∼ de lo ocurrido** he knows what's happened; **un tanto** somewhat, rather; **un ∼ triste** somewhat sad

tanto[2] **-ta** *adj* **(a)** (*sing*) so much; (*pl*) so many; **había ∼ espacio/∼s niños** there was so much space/there were so many children; **¡∼ tiempo sin verte!** it's been so long!; **∼ dinero/∼s turistas como ...** as much money/as many tourists as ... **(b)** (fam) (expresando cantidades indeterminadas): **tenía setenta y ∼s años** he was seventy something, he was seventy-odd (colloq)
■ *pron* ⓵ **(a)** (*sing*) so much; (*pl*) so many; **¡tengo ∼ que hacer!** I've so much to do!; **vinieron ∼s que ...** so many people came (that) ...; **¿de verdad gana ∼?** does he really earn that much?; **no ser para ∼** (fam): **duele, pero no es para ∼** it hurts, but it's not *that* bad **(b)** (fam) (expresando cantidades indeterminadas): **hasta las tantas de la**

madrugada until the early hours of the morning; **treinta y tantas** thirty or so **(c)** (refiriéndose a tiempo): **hace ∼ que no me llama** it's been so long since she called me; **aún faltan dos horas — ¿tanto?** there's still two hours to go — what? that long?
⓶ (*en locs*) **en tanto** while; **entre tanto** meanwhile, in the meantime; **otro tanto** as much again; **me queda otro ∼ por hacer** I have as much again still to do; **por (lo) tanto** therefore

tañer [E7] *vt* (liter) ⟨arpa⟩ to strum
■ ∼ *vi* ⟨campana⟩ to peal, ring out

tapa *f* ⓵ **(a)** (de caja, cacerola) lid; (de botella, frasco) top; **∼ de rosca** screw top **(b)** (de lente, bolígrafo) cap; **la ∼ del tanque de gasolina** the gas (AmE) *o* (BrE) petrol cap ⓶ **(a)** (de libro, revista) cover; (de disco) sleeve **(b)** (de tacón) heelpiece **(c)** (de bolsillo) flap **(d)** (Auto) head ⓷ (Esp) (para acompañar la bebida) tapa, bar snack

tapabarros *m* (*pl* ∼) (Chi, Per) (de coche) fender (AmE), wing (BrE); (de bicicleta) splashguard (AmE), mudguard (BrE)

tapadera *f* **(a)** (de cazo) lid **(b)** (de fraude, engaño) cover, front **(c)** (Méx) (de botella) cap, top

tapado *m* ⓵ (RPl, Ven) (abrigo) (winter) coat ⓶ (Méx) (Pol) potential candidate (*with official support*)

tapadura *f* (Andes, Méx) filling

tapar [A1] *vt* ⓵ (cubrir) ⟨caja⟩ to put the lid on; ⟨botella/frasco⟩ to put the top on; ⟨olla⟩ to cover, put the lid on; ⟨bebé/enfermo/cara⟩ to cover ⓶ **(a)** ⟨agujero/hueco⟩ to fill in; ⟨puerta/ventana⟩ to block up **(b)** (Andes, Méx) ⟨muela⟩ to fill; **me ∼on dos muelas** I had two fillings **(c)** ⟨defecto/error⟩ to cover up ⓷ **(a)** ⟨vista/luz⟩ to block **(b)** ⟨salida/entrada⟩ to block; ⟨excusado/cañería⟩ (AmL) to block
■ **taparse** *v pron* ⓵ (*refl*) (cubrirse) to cover oneself up; ⟨cara⟩ to cover ⓶ **(a)** ⟨oídos/nariz⟩ to get *o* become blocked; **tengo la nariz tapada** my nose is blocked **(b)** (AmL) ⟨cañería/excusado⟩ to get blocked

taparrabos *m* (*pl* ∼) loincloth

tapatío -tía *adj* of/from Guadalajara (*in Mexico*)

tapeo *m* (Esp fam): **ir de ∼** to go for a drink and a few tapas *o* bar snacks; **bares de ∼** tapas bars

tapete *m* ⓵ (para mesa) decorative table cloth; (para sofá) antimacassar ⓶ (Col, Méx, Ven) (alfombra) rug

tapia *f* (muro) wall; (cerca) fence; **ser/estar más sordo que una ∼** (fam) to be as deaf as a post (colloq)

tapiar [A1] *vt* **(a)** ⟨espacio⟩ to wall in **(b)** ⟨puerta/ventana⟩ to brick up

tapicería *f* **(a)** (de coches, muebles) upholstery **(b)** (arte) tapestry making; (tapiz) tapestry

tapicero -ra *m,f* (de muebles) upholsterer

tapilla *f* (Chi) heelpiece

tapir *m* tapir

tapiz *m* (para pared) tapestry; (para suelo) carpet

tapizado *m* upholstery

tapizar [A4] *vt* ⟨sillón⟩ to upholster; ⟨pared⟩ to line

tapón *m* ⓵ **(a)** (de vidrio, goma) stopper; (de corcho) cork; (del lavabo) plug; (de botella) (Esp) top

(b) (para los oídos) earplug; (de cerumen) plug **2** **(a)** (fam) (atasco) traffic jam, tailback (BrE) **(b)** (en baloncesto) block **3** (CS) (Elec) fuse

taponar [A1] *vt* ⟨*agujero*⟩ to block
■ **taponarse** *v pron* **(a)** «*oídos/nariz*» to get blocked **(b)** «*cañería*» to get blocked **(c)** (Col, RPI) «*ciudad/zona*» to block

taquigrafía *f* shorthand, stenography (AmE)

taquilla *f* **(a)** (de cine) box office; (en estación, estadio) ticket office **(b)** (cantidad recaudada) takings (*pl*) **(c)** (casillero) rack, pigeonholes (*pl*)

taquillero -ra *m,f* box-office clerk

tara *f* **1** (peso) tare **2** (defecto) defect

tarántula *f* tarantula

tararear [A1] *vt* to la-la-la

tardado -da *adj* (Méx) ⟨*proceso/tarea*⟩ time-consuming; ⟨*persona*⟩ slow

tardanza *f* delay; **sin ~** without delay; **perdona la ~ en contestar** forgive my delay in replying; **me preocupa su ~** I'm worried that he's so late; **su ~ se debió a ...** his lateness was due to ...

tardar [A1] *vt* (emplear cierto tiempo): **está tardando mucho** she's taking a long time; **tarda una hora en hacerse** it takes about an hour to cook; **tardó un mes en contestar** it took him a month to reply; **no tardo ni un minuto** I won't be a minute; **¿cuánto se tarda en coche?** how long does it take by car?
■ **~** *vi* (retrasarse) to be late; (emplear demasiado tiempo) to take a long time; **empieza a las seis, no tardes** it starts at six, don't be late; **parece que tarda** he seems to be taking a long time; **¡no tardo!** I won't be long!; **aún ~á en llegar** it'll be a while yet before he gets here; **no ~on en detenerlo** it didn't take them long to arrest him
■ **tardarse** *v pron* (Méx, Ven) ▶ TARDAR *vt, vi*

tarde *adv* late; **llegar ~** to be late; **se está haciendo ~** it's getting late; **~ o temprano** sooner or later
■ *f* (temprano) afternoon; (hacia el anochecer) evening; **a las seis de la ~** at six in the evening; **¡buenas ~s!** (temprano) good afternoon!; (hacia el anochecer) good evening!; **en la** *or* (esp Esp) **por la** *or* (RPI) **a la ~** in the afternoon/evening

tardón -dona *adj* (fam) slow
■ *m,f* (fam) slowpoke (AmE colloq), slowcoach (BrE colloq)

tarea *f* **(a)** (trabajo) task, job; **las ~s de la casa** the housework **(b)** (deberes escolares) homework

tarifa *f* **(a)** (baremo, escala) rate; **~s postales** postal rates **(b)** (Transp) fare **(c)** (lista de precios) price list **(d)** (arancel) tariff

tarima *f* (plataforma) dais

tarjar [A1] *vt* (Andes) to cross out, delete (frml)

tarjeta *f* card; **marcar** (AmL) *or* (Méx) **checar ~** to clock in/out, punch in/out (AmE); **~ amarilla/roja** yellow/red card; **~ de crédito** credit card; **~ de embarque** boarding pass *o* card; **~ de Navidad** Christmas card; **~ de visita** *or* (Méx) **de**

presentación (personal) visiting card; (de negocios) business card; **~ postal/telefónica** postcard/phonecard

tarro *m* **1** (recipiente— de vidrio) jar; (— de cerámica) pot; (— de metal) (Chi) can, tin (BrE) **2** (Méx, Ven) (taza) mug

tarta *f* (Esp) cake; (de hojaldre — descubierta) tart; (— cubierta) pie

tartamudear [A1] *vi* to stutter, stammer

tartamudo -da *adj* stuttering (*before n*), stammering (*before n*); **es ~** he has a stutter *o* stammer
■ *m,f*: **hay un ~ en mi clase** one of the boys in my class has a stutter *o* stammer

tartera *f* (para cocinar) cake tin

tarumba *adj* crazy (colloq); **me vuelve ~** he drives me crazy (colloq)

tasa *f* **(a)** (valoración) valuation **(b)** (impuesto) tax **(c)** (índice) rate; **~ de desempleo** rate of unemployment; **~ de mortalidad/natalidad** mortality rate/birthrate

tasación *f* valuation

tasajear [A1] *vt* (Méx, Per) to slash

tasar [A1] *vt* ⟨*objeto/coche*⟩ to value

tasca *f* (taberna) bar, tavern

tata *m* (AmL fam) **(a)** (padre) dad (colloq), pop (AmE colloq) **(b)** (abuelo) grandpa (colloq)

tatarabuelo -la *m,f* (*m*) great-great-grandfather; (*f*) great-great-grandmother; **mis ~s** my great-great-grandparents

tataranieto -ta *m,f* (*m*) great-great-grandson; (*f*) great-great-granddaughter; **sus ~s** his great-great-grandchildren

ta-te-ti *m* (RPI) tic-tac-toe (AmE), noughts and crosses (BrE)

tatuaje *m* (acción) tattooing; (dibujo) tattoo

tatuar [A18] *vt* to tattoo

taurino -na *adj* ⟨*temporada/afición*⟩ bullfighting (*before n*), taurine (fml)

Tauro *m* (signo, constelación) Taurus; **es (de) ~** he's (a) Taurus, he's a Taurean
■ *mf* (*pl* **-ros**) (persona) *tb* **tauro** Taurean, Taurus

taxi *m* taxi, cab; **~ colectivo** (Col) minibus

taxímetro *m* taximeter

taxista *mf* taxi driver, cabdriver

taza *f* **(a)** (recipiente) cup; **~ de café/té** coffee cup/teacup **(b)** (contenido) cupful; **una ~ de azúcar** a cupful of sugar; **tomar una ~ de té** to have a cup of tea **(c)** (del retrete) (toilet) bowl **(d)** (de fuente) basin

tazón *m* bowl

te *pron pers* **(a)** you; **no ~ lo quiero prestar** I don't want to lend it to you; **¿~ lo paso a máquina?** shall I type it for you?; **voy a serte sincera** I'll be frank with you; **cuídate** (*refl*) look after yourself; **¿~ has cortado el pelo?** (*caus*) have you had your hair cut?; **¿~ sientes bien?**

are you feeling all right?; **no ~ muevas** don't move **(b)** (*impers*): **cuando ~ pasa eso** ... when that happens ...

■ *f. name of the letter* t

té *m* **(a)** (infusión, planta) tea; **¿quieres un ~?** do you want a cup of tea? **(b)** (AmL) (reunión) tea party

tea *f* torch

teatral *adj* **(a)** (Teatr) ⟨grupo/temporada⟩ theater* (*before n*); **una obra ~** a play; **un autor ~** a playwright **(b)** ⟨persona/gesto/tono⟩ theatrical

teatro *m* ⏢1⏢ (Teatr) **(a)** (arte, actividad) theater*; **una obra de ~** a play; **actor de ~** stage actor; **~ de guiñol** puppet theater*; **~ de variedades** vaudeville (AmE), music hall (BrE) **(b)** (local) theater*; **un ~ al aire libre** an open-air theater ⏢2⏢ (fam) (exageración): **es puro ~** it's all an act

tebeo *m* (Esp) comic (*for children*)

techo *m* **(a)** (cielo raso) ceiling **(b)** (AmL) (tejado, cubierta) roof; **~ corredizo** sunroof **(c)** (hogar, casa) house; **sin ~** homeless; **bajo el mismo ~** under the same roof

techumbre *f* roof

tecla *f* key

teclado *m* keyboard; **~ numérico** numeric keypad

teclear [A1] *vt* ⟨palabra/texto⟩ to key in, type in

■ **~** *vi* (en máquina de escribir) to type; (en ordenador) to key

técnica *f* ⏢1⏢ **(a)** (método) technique **(b)** (destreza) skill ⏢2⏢ (tecnología) technology ⏢3⏢ (en baloncesto) technical foul

tecnicismo *m* (cualidad) technical nature; (palabra) technical term

técnico -ca *adj* technical

■ *m,f* **(a)** (en fábrica) technician **(b)** (de lavadoras, etc) repairman (AmE), engineer (BrE) **(c)** (Dep) trainer, coach (AmE), manager (BrE)

tecnicolor *m* Technicolor®

tecnología *f* technology; **~ punta** state-of-the-art technology

tecnológico -ca *adj* technological

tecolote *m* (Méx) (Zool) owl

tedio *m* boredom, tedium

teja *f* tile; **~s de pizarra** slates

tejado *m* (esp Esp) roof

tejano -na *adj/m,f* Texan

Tejas *m* Texas

tejaván *m* (Méx) shed

tejedor -dora *m,f* **(a)** (con telar) weaver **(b)** (con agujas, máquina) knitter

tejer [E1] *vt* **(a)** (en telar) to weave; **tejido a mano** hand-woven **(b)** (con agujas, a máquina) to knit; (con ganchillo) to crochet; **máquina de ~** knitting machine **(c)** «araña» to spin

■ **~** *vi* (en telar) to weave; (con agujas, a máquina) to knit; (con ganchillo) to crochet

tejido *m* ⏢1⏢ **(a)** (tela) fabric; **~s sintéticos** synthetic fabrics **(b)** (AmL) (con agujas, máquina) knitting; (con ganchillo) crochet ⏢2⏢ (Anat) tissue

tejo *m* **(a)** (disco) disc **(b)** (juego — de niños) hopscotch; (— de adultos) *game similar to pitch-and-toss*

tejolote *m* (Méx) pestle

tejón *m* badger

tela *f* ⏢1⏢ (Tex) (material) material, fabric; **~ de lana** wool (fabric); **~ de araña** ▶ TELARAÑA; **~ metálica** wire mesh ⏢2⏢ (Art) (cuadro) canvas, painting ⏢3⏢ (membrana) skin, film

telar *m* **(a)** (máquina) loom **(b)** **telares** *mpl* (fábrica) textile mill

telaraña *f* spiderweb (AmE), spider's web (BrE); (polvorienta) cobweb; **~ mundial** (Inf) World Wide Web

tele *f* (fam) TV (colloq), telly (BrE colloq)

telebanca *f* telebanking

telebanco *m* cash dispenser

telecomunicación *f* telecommunication

teleculebra *f* (Ven fam) soap opera (colloq)

telediario *m* (Esp) (television) news

teledirigido -da *adj* ⟨coche⟩ radio-controlled, remote-controlled; **misiles ~s** guided missiles

teleférico *m* cable railway

telefonazo *m* (fam) buzz (colloq); **darle** *or* (Méx) **echarle un ~ a algn** to give sb a buzz (colloq)

telefonear [A1] *vt* to telephone, phone, call; **¿puedo ~ a Londres?** can I make a (telephone) call to London?

■ **~** *vi* to telephone, phone

telefónico -ca *adj* telephone (*before n*)

telefonista *mf* telephone operator

teléfono *m* ⏢1⏢ (Telec) telephone, phone; **número de ~** phone number; **contestar el ~** to answer *o* (colloq) get the phone; **me colgó el ~** she hung up on me; **hablé por ~ con ella** I spoke to her on the phone; **está hablando por ~** he's on the phone; **llamar a algn por ~** to call sb (up), phone sb; **~ celular** *or* (Esp) **móvil** mobile telephone; **~ rojo** hotline ⏢2⏢ (de la ducha) shower head

telegrafiar [A17] *vi/vt* to telegraph

telégrafo *m* telegraph

telegrama *m* telegram

telemarketing /teleˈmarketin/ *m* telemarketing

telenovela *f* soap opera

telepatía *f* telepathy

telescopio *m* telescope

telespectador -dora *m,f* viewer

telesquí *m* ski lift

teletexto, teletex *m* teletext, videotex

televentas *fpl* telesales

televidente *mf* viewer

televisar [A1] *vt* to televise

televisión *f* **(a)** (sistema) television; **¿qué hay en (la) ~?** what's on television?; **lo transmitieron por ~** it was broadcast on television; **~ a** *or* **en color(es)** color* television; **~ de alta definición** high definition television, HDTV; **~ en blanco y negro** black and white television; **~ en circuito cerrado** closed circuit television; **~ por cable/por satélite** cable/satellite television; **~ matinal** breakfast television **(b)** (programación) television; **ver (la) ~** to watch television **(c)** (televisor) television (set)

televisor *m* television (set)

télex *m* (*pl* **~**) telex

telón *m* curtain; **~ de fondo** (Teatr) backdrop

tema *m* **(a)** (asunto, cuestión) matter; (de conferencia, composición) topic; (de examen) subject; ⋯▷

(Art, Cin, Lit) subject; **es un ~ delicado** it's a delicate matter; **~ de conversación** topic of conversation; **cambiar de ~** to change the subject **(b)** (Mús) (motivo) theme

temario *m* **(a)** (*para examen*) syllabus, list of topics **(b)** (en congreso) agenda

temblar [A5] *vi* **(a)** «*persona*» (de frío) to shiver; (*por nervios, miedo*) to shake, tremble; (+ *me/te/le etc*) «*párpado*» to twitch; «*mano*» to shake; «*voz*» to tremble; **la voz le temblaba de emoción** her voice was trembling with emotion **(b)** 〈*edificio/tierra*〉 to shake
■ **~** *v impers:* **¡está temblando!** (AmL) it's an earthquake!; **tembló ayer** there was an (earth) tremor yesterday

temblor *m* **(a)** (de frío, fiebre) shivering; (de miedo, nervios) trembling, shaking; **con un ligero ~ en la voz** in a tremulous voice **(b)** *tb* **~ de tierra** (earth) tremor

tembloroso -sa *adj* **(a)** 〈*manos*〉 trembling, shaking; 〈*voz*〉 trembling, tremulous; **~ de frío** shivering with cold **(b)** 〈*llama/luz*〉 flickering, quivering

temer [E1] *vt* 〈*castigo/reacción*〉 to fear, dread; 〈*persona*〉 to be afraid of; **sus hijos le temen** her children are afraid of her; **temo ofenderlo** I'm afraid of offending him
■ **~** *vi* to be afraid; **no temas** don't be afraid
■ **temerse** *v pron* **(a)** (sospechar) to fear; **ya me lo temía** I knew this would happen; **me temo que tenía razón** I fear that he was right **(b)** (en fórmulas de cortesía) to be afraid; **me temo que no ha llegado** I'm afraid he hasn't arrived

temeridad *f* **(a)** (acción): **eso fue una ~ that** was a very rash *o* bold thing to do **(b)** (cualidad) temerity; **conduce con ~** she drives recklessly

temible *adj* fearsome, fearful

temor *m* fear; **no dije nada por ~ a ofenderlo** I didn't say anything for fear of offending him

témpano *m* ice floe

témpera *f* tempera

temperamental *adj* (irascible, cambiable) temperamental; (de mucho carácter) spirited

temperamento *m* **(a)** (manera de ser) temperament; **son de ~s muy diferentes** they have very different temperaments **(b)** (vigor de carácter): **un chico con mucho ~** a boy with a lot of spirit

temperatura *f* temperature; **tomarle la ~ a algn** to take sb's temperature; **tiene ~** (CS) she has a fever (AmE) *o* (BrE) a temperature; **~ ambiente** room temperature

tempestad *f* storm, tempest (liter); **~ de arena** sandstorm

tempestuoso -sa *adj* stormy, tempestuous

templado -da *adj* **(a)** 〈*clima*〉 mild, temperate; 〈*zona*〉 temperate; 〈*día*〉 warm **(b)** 〈*agua/comida*〉 lukewarm

templo *m* temple

temporada *f* **(a)** (época establecida) season; **verduras de ~** seasonal vegetables; **fuera de/en ~** out of/in season; **~ alta/baja** high/low season **(b)** (periodo de tiempo) spell; **una ~ de mucho trabajo** a very busy spell *o* period

temporal *adj* **1** (transitorio) temporary **2** (relativo al tiempo) temporal
■ *m* (Meteo) storm; **~ de nieve** snowstorm, blizzard

temporalero -ra *m,f* (Méx) seasonal worker

temporario -ria *adj* (AmL) temporary

temprano *adv* early; **levantarse ~** to get up early; **por la mañana ~** in the morning

ten ▶ TENER

tenacidad *f* (perseverancia) tenacity

tenacillas *fpl* hair crimper

tenaz *adj* **(a)** 〈*persona*〉 tenacious **(b)** 〈*dolor*〉 persistent; 〈*mancha*〉 stubborn

tenaza *f*, **tenazas** *fpl* **(a)** (Mec, Tec) pliers (*pl*) **(b)** (de chimenea, cocina) tongs (*pl*) **(c)** (del cangrejo) pincer **(d)** (Méx) (de pelo) curling iron (AmE), hair crimper (BrE)

tendajón *m* (Méx) shack (serving as a store or stall)

tendal *m* (AmL) (para el café) drying area

tendedero *m* (cuerda) clothes-line; (caballete) clotheshorse

tendencia *f* tendency; **~s homosexuales** homosexual tendencies *o* leanings; **~ A algo** trend TOWARD(s) sth; **tiene ~ a exagerar** she has a tendency to exaggerate; **existe una ~ a la centralización** there is a trend toward centralization

tender [E8] *vt* **1** 〈*ropa*〉 (afuera) to hang out; (dentro de la casa) to hang (up); **tengo ropa tendida** I have some washing on the line
2 (a) (extender) 〈*manta*〉 to spread out, lay out; 〈*mantel*〉 to spread; **le tendió la mano** he held out his hand to him **(b)** (AmL) 〈*cama*〉 to make; 〈*mesa*〉 to lay, set **(c)** 〈*persona*〉 to lay
3 (a) 〈*cable*〉 (sobre superficie) to lay; (suspendido) to hang **(b)** (vía férrea) to lay
4 〈*emboscada*〉 to lay, set; 〈*trampa*〉 to set
■ **~** *vi* (inclinarse) **~ A hacer algo** to tend to do sth; **tiende a encoger** it tends to shrink
■ **tenderse** *v pron* (tumbarse) to lie down

tendero -ra *m,f* storekeeper (esp AmE), shopkeeper (esp BrE)

tendido *m* **1** (Elec) (cables) cables (*pl*), wires (*pl*) **2** (Col, Ven) (ropa de cama) bedclothes (*pl*)

tendón *m* tendon

tendré, tendría, etc ▶ TENER

tenebroso -sa *adj* 〈*lugar*〉 dark, gloomy; 〈*asunto/maquinaciones*〉 sinister; 〈*porvenir*〉 dismal, gloomy

tenedor *m* (cubierto) fork

tenencia *f* (Méx) (Auto) road tax

tener [E27] *vt* [*El uso de* **got** *en frases como* '*I've got a new dress*' *está mucho más extendido en el inglés británico que en el americano. Este prefiere la forma* '*I have a new dress*'] **1 (a)** (poseer, disponer de) 〈*dinero/trabajo/tiempo*〉 to have; **¿tienen hijos?** do they have any children?, have they got any children?; **no tenemos pan** we don't have any bread, we haven't got any bread; **tiene el pelo largo** she has *o* she's got long hair **(b)** (llevar encima) 〈*lápiz/cambio*〉 to have; **¿tiene hora?** have you got the time? **(c)** (hablando de actividades, obligaciones) to have; **tengo invitados a cenar** I have *o* I've got some people coming to dinner; **tengo cosas que hacer** I have *o* I've got things to do **(d)** (dar a luz) 〈*bebé/gemelos*〉 to have
2 (a) (señalando características, tamaño) to be; **la casa tiene mucha luz** the house is very light; **tiene un metro de largo** it is one meter long; **le lleva 15 años — ¿y eso qué tiene?** (AmL fam) she's

15 years older than he is — so what does that matter? **(b)** (señalando edad) to be; **¿cuántos años tienes?** how old are you?; **tengo veinte años** I'm twenty (years old)

3 **(a)** (sujetar, sostener) to hold; **tenlo derecho** hold it upright **(b)** (tomar): **ten la llave** take o here's the key

4 **(a)** (sentir): **tengo hambre/frío** I'm hungry/cold; **le tengo mucho cariño** I'm very fond of him; **tengo el placer de …** it gives me great pleasure to … **(b)** (refiriéndose a enfermedades) ‹gripe/cáncer› to have; **tengo dolor de cabeza** I have o I've got a headache **(c)** (refiriéndose a experiencias) ‹discusión/accidente› to have; **que tengas buen viaje** have a good trip

5 (refiriéndose a actitudes): **ten más respeto** have a little more respect; **ten paciencia/cuidado** be patient/careful; **tiene mucho tacto** he's very tactful

6 (indicando estado, situación): **la mesa tiene una pata rota** one of the table legs is broken; **tengo las manos sucias** my hands are dirty; **tienes el cinturón desabrochado** your belt's undone; **me tiene muy preocupada** I'm very worried about it

■ ~ v aux 1 + QUE hacer algo **(a)** (expresando obligación, necesidad) to have (got) to do sth; **tengo que estudiar hoy** I have to o I must study today; **tienes que comer más** you ought to eat more **(b)** (expresando propósito, recomendación): **tenemos que ir a ver esa película** we must go and see that movie; **tendrías que llamarlo** you should ring him **(c)** (expresando certeza): **tiene que estar en este cajón** it must be in this drawer; **¡tú tenías que ser!** it had to be you!

2 (con participio pasado): **tengo entendido que sí viene** I understand he is coming; **te tengo dicho que …** I've told you before (that) …; **teníamos pensado irnos hoy** we intended leaving today

3 (AmL) (en expresiones de tiempo): **tienen tres años de casados** they've been married for three years; **tenía un año sin verlo** she hadn't seen him for a year

■ **tenerse** v pron (sostenerse): **no podía ~se en pie** he couldn't stand; **no ~se de sueño** to be dead on one's feet

tenga, tengas, etc ▶ TENER

tenia f (Med) tapeworm, taenia (tech)

tenida f (Chi) outfit

teniente mf **(a)** (en ejército) lieutenant **(b)** (en fuerzas aéreas) ≈ first lieutenant (in US), ≈ flying officer (in UK)

tenis m (pl ~) tennis; **~ de mesa** table tennis

tenista mf tennis player

tenor m (Mús) tenor

tensar [A1] vt ‹músculo› to tense; ‹cuerda/cable› to tighten; ‹arco› to draw; ‹relaciones/lazos› to strain

tensión f 1 **(a)** (de cuerda, músculo) tension **(b)** tb ~ **arterial** blood pressure; **tomarle la ~ a algn** to take sb's blood pressure; ~ **nerviosa** nervous tension 2 (estrés) strain, stress; (en relaciones, situación) tension 3 (Elec) voltage

tenso -sa adj 1 ‹cuerda/cable› taut, tight; ‹músculo› tense 2 ‹persona/situación› tense; ‹relación› strained, tense

tentación f **(a)** (impulso) temptation; **no resistió la ~ de comérselo** he couldn't resist the

temptation to eat it **(b)** (cosa, persona): **los bombones son mi ~** I can't resist chocolates (colloq)

tentáculo m tentacle

tentador -dora adj tempting

tentar [A5] vt **(a)** (atraer, seducir) «plan/idea» to tempt; «persona» to tempt; **me tienta tu propuesta** I am very tempted by your proposal; **estuve tentado de decírselo** I was tempted to tell him; ~ **a algn A hacer algo** to tempt sb to do sth 2 (probar) **(a)** ‹cuerda/tabla› to test **(b)** (palpar) to feel

tentativa f attempt

tentempié m (bocado) snack

tenue adj **(a)** ‹luz› faint, weak; ‹voz/sonido/sonrisa› faint; ‹neblina/llovizna› light; ‹línea› faint, fine **(b)** ‹color› subdued, pale

teñir [I15] vt **(a)** ‹ropa/zapatos/pelo› to dye **(b)** (manchar) to stain; **la tinta le tiñó los dedos de rojo** the ink stained his fingers red

■ **teñirse** v pron (refl) ‹pelo/zapatos› to dye

teología f theology

teoría f theory; **en ~** in theory

teórico -ca adj ‹existencia/valor/curso› theoretical; **examen ~** theory (exam)

tequila m tequila

terapeuta mf therapist

terapéutico -ca adj therapeutic

terapia f therapy; ~ **de pareja** marriage counseling*; ~ **intensiva** (Méx, RPl) intensive care

tercer ▶ TERCERO[1]

tercera f (Auto) third (gear); **mete (la) ~** put it into third (gear)

tercermundista adj third-world (before n)

tercero[1] -ra adj/pron [TERCER is used before masculine singular nouns] third; **en el tercer piso** on the third floor; **el Tercer Mundo** the Third World; **personas de la tercera edad** senior citizens; **la tercera parte** a third; para ejemplos ver QUINTO

tercero[2] m third party; **seguro contra ~s** third party insurance

tercio m **(a)** (tercera parte) third **(b)** (Taur) each of the three main stages of a bullfight

terciopelo m velvet

terco -ca adj stubborn, obstinate

tergiversar [A1] vt to distort, twist

termas fpl (baños) hot o thermal baths (pl); (manantial) hot o thermal springs (pl)

térmico -ca adj thermal

terminación f **(a)** (finalización) termination (frml) **(b)** (acabado) finish **(c)** (Ling) ending

terminal adj ‹enfermedad/caso› terminal; **los enfermos ~es** the terminally ill
■ m (Elec, Inf) terminal
■ f (de autobuses) terminus, bus station; (Aviac, Inf) terminal

terminante adj ‹respuesta› categorical; ‹orden› strict

terminar [A1] vt ‹trabajo/estudio› to finish; ‹casa/obras› to finish, complete; ‹discusión/conflicto› to put an end to; **termina esa sopa** finish up that soup; ~ **la comida con un café** to end the meal with a cup of coffee
■ ~ vi 1 «persona» **(a)** (de hacer algo) to finish; ⋯⃗

~ **DE hacer algo** to finish doing sth; **déjame ~ de hablar** let me finish (speaking) **(b)** (en estado, situación) to end up; **terminé muy cansada** I ended up feeling very tired; **va a ~ mal** he's going to come to a bad end; **terminó marchándose** or **por marcharse** he ended up leaving
2 (a) «*reunión/situación*» to end, come to an end; **al ~ la clase** when the class ended; **esto va a ~ mal** this is going to turn out o end badly **(b)** (rematar) ~ **EN algo** to end IN sth; **termina en consonante** it ends in a consonant **(c)** (llegar a): **no termina de convencerme** I'm not totally convinced; **no terminaba de gustarle** she wasn't totally happy about it
3 terminar con (a) (acabar) ~ **CON algo** «*con libro/tarea*» to finish WITH sth; «*con problema/abuso*» to put an end to sth **(b)** ~ **CON algn** (pelearse) to finish WITH sb; (matar) to kill sb
■ **terminarse** v pron **1** «*azúcar/pan*» to run out; **se me terminó la lana** I've run out of wool **2** «*curso/reunión*» to come to an end, be over **3** (*enf*) «*libro/comida*» to finish, polish off

término m **1** (posición, instancia): **en primer ~** first, first of all; ~ **medio** happy medium; **por ~ medio** on average **2** (Ling) term; **en ~s reales** in real terms **3 términos** mpl (condiciones, especificaciones) terms (*pl*) **4** (Col, Méx, Ven) (Coc): **¿qué ~ quiere la carne?** how would you like your meat (done)?

termita f termite

termo® m (recipiente) Thermos®, vacuum flask

termómetro m thermometer

termostato m thermostat

ternera f veal

ternero -ra m,f calf

terno m (AmS) suit (*in some countries specifically a three-piece suit*)

ternura f tenderness; **con ~** tenderly

terquedad f obstinacy, stubbornness

terracería f (Méx) (camino) rough dirt track

terracota f terra-cotta

terrateniente mf landowner

terraza f **(a)** (balcón) balcony **(b)** (azotea) terrace **(c)** (de bar) *area outside a bar or café where tables are placed*; **sentémonos en la ~** let's sit outside **(d)** (Agr) terrace

terregal m (Méx) loose topsoil

terremoto m earthquake

terrenal adj worldly, earthly

terreno¹ -na adj (Relig) earthly

terreno² m **1 (a)** (lote, parcela) plot of land, lot (AmE); **heredó unos ~s en Sonora** she inherited some land in Sonora; **un ~ plantado de viñas** a field planted with vines; ~ **de juego** field, pitch **(b)** (extensión de tierra) land; **una casa con mucho ~** a house with a lot of land **2** (Geog) (refiriéndose al relieve) terrain; (refiriéndose a la composición) land, soil; **un ~ fértil** fertile land **3** (esfera, campo de acción) sphere, field; **en el ~ político** within the field of politics

terrestre adj **(a)** «*transportes/comunicaciones*»

land (*before n*), terrestrial (frml); **por vía ~** overland, by land; **fuerzas ~s** ground o land forces; **la superficie ~** the earth's surface **(b)** (Relig) «*vida*» earthly

terrible adj **(a)** «*tortura/experiencia*» terrible, horrific **(b)** (uso hiperbólico) terrible; **tengo un sueño ~** I'm terribly tired

territorial adj territorial

territorio m territory

terrón m (de azúcar) lump; (de tierra) clod, lump

terror m **(a)** (miedo) terror; **le tengo ~** it terrifies me, I find it terrifying; **de ~** «*novela/relato*» horror (*before n*) **(b)** (persona) terror

terrorífico -ca adj horrific

terrorismo m terrorism

terrorista adj/mf terrorist

terso -sa adj smooth

tertulia f (reunión) gathering (*to discuss philosophy, politics, art, etc*)

tertuliano -na m,f participant in a TERTULIA

tesina f dissertation (*submitted as part of a first degree*)

tesis f (*pl* ~) **(a)** (Educ, Fil) thesis; ~ **doctoral** doctoral thesis **(b)** (opinión): **los dos sostienen la misma ~** they are both of the same opinion; **esto confirma la ~ inicial** this confirms the initial theory

tesón m tenacity, determination

tesorería f (oficina) treasury; (cargo) post of treasurer

tesorero -ra m,f treasurer

tesoro m **(a)** (cosa valiosa) treasure **(b)** (persona) treasure, gem (colloq); **¿qué te pasa, ~?** what's the matter, darling?

test m (*pl* **tests**) test; **un examen tipo ~** a multiple-choice exam

testamento m will, testament (frml); **hacer ~** to make one's will

testarudo -da adj stubborn, pigheaded

testículo m testicle

testificar [A2] vt/vi to testify, give evidence

testigo mf witness; **ser ~ de algo** to witness sth, be a witness to sth

testimonio m **(a)** (Der) (declaración) testimony, statement **(b)** (prueba) proof, testimony (frml); **dar ~ de algo** to bear witness to sth

tétanos, tétano m tetanus

tetera f **(a)** (para servir té) teapot **(b)** (Andes, Méx) (para hervir agua) kettle **(c)** (Méx) (biberón) baby's bottle

tetero m (Col, Ven) baby's bottle

tetilla f **(a)** (Anat) nipple; (Zool) teat **(b)** (del biberón) teat

tetina f teat

tétrico -ca adj dismal, gloomy

textil adj textile (*before n*)

texto m text

textual adj «*traducción*» literal; «*palabras*» exact; «*cita*» direct

textura *f* texture

tez *f* complexion

ti *pron pers* **(a)** you; **para** ~ for you; **delante de** ~ in front of you; **a mí me gusta ¿y a** ~? I like it, do you? **(b)** *(refl)*: ~ **mismo/misma** yourself; **piensa un poco en** ~ **mismo** just think of yourself a little **(c)** *(impers)* you; **si a** ~ **te cuentan que ...** if someone tells you that ...

tianguis *m* (Méx) street market

tibio -bia *adj* **(a)** *⟨agua/baño⟩* lukewarm, tepid **(b)** *⟨atmósfera/ambiente⟩* warm **(c)** *⟨relación⟩* lukewarm; *⟨acogida⟩* unenthusiastic, cool

tiburón *m* **(a)** (Zool) shark **(b)** (fam) (persona) shark **(c)** (Fin) raider

tic *m* $\boxed{1}$ (movimiento) *tb* ~ **nervioso** nervous tic $\boxed{2}$ (marca en escrito) tick

tico -ca *adj/m,f* (AmL fam) Costa Rican

tiempo *m* $\boxed{1}$ **(a)** (en general) time; **¡cómo pasa el** ~! how time flies!; **te acostumbrarás con el** ~ you'll get used to it in time; **perder el** ~ to waste time; **¡no hay** ~ **que perder!** there's no time to lose!; **para ganar** ~ (in order) to gain time; ~ **libre** spare time, free time; **¿cuánto** ~ **hace que no lo ves?** how long is it since you last saw him?; **hace** ~ **que no sé de él** I haven't heard from him for a long time; **ya hace** ~ **que se marchó** she left quite some time ago; **¡cuánto** ~ **sin verte!** I haven't seen you for ages; **la mayor parte del** ~ most of the time; **me llevó mucho** ~ it took me a long time; **no pude quedarme más** ~ I couldn't stay any longer; **poco** ~ **después** a short time after; **de un** ~ **a esta parte** for some time (now); **a** ~ **completo/parcial** full time/part time; **no vamos a llegar a** ~ we won't get there in time; **al mismo** ~ at the same time; **avísame con** ~ let me know in good time; **¡qué** ~**s aquellos!** those were the days!; **en aquellos** ~**s at** that time, in those days **(b)** (temporada) season; **fruta del** ~ fruits in season **(c)** (momento propio, oportuno): **a su** **(debido)** ~ in due course; **cada cosa a su** ~ everything in (its own) good time **(d)** (edad de bebé): **¿cuánto** ~ **tiene?** how old is he?

$\boxed{2}$ (Dep) (en partido) half; **primer** ~ first half $\boxed{3}$ (Mús) (compás) tempo, time; (de sinfonía) movement $\boxed{4}$ (Ling) tense $\boxed{5}$ (Meteo) weather; **hace buen/mal** ~ the weather's good/bad; **del** *or* (Méx) **al** ~ *⟨bebida⟩* at room temperature

tienda *f* $\boxed{1}$ (Com) (en general) store (esp AmE), shop (esp BrE); **ir de** ~**s** to go shopping; ~ **de comestibles** *or* (AmC, Andes, Méx) **abarrotes** grocery store (AmE), grocer's (shop) (BrE) $\boxed{2}$ (Dep, Mil, Ocio) *tb* ~ **de campaña** tent; **poner** *or* **montar una** ~ to put up *o* pitch a tent; **desmontar una** ~ to take down a tent

tiene, tienes, etc ▶ TENER

tienta *f*: **a tientas** *(loc adv)*: **andar** *or* **ir a** ~**s** to feel one's way; **buscó el timbre a** ~**s** he fumbled *o* felt around for the bell

tierno -na *adj* $\boxed{1}$ *⟨carne⟩* tender; *⟨pan⟩* fresh; *⟨brote/planta⟩* young, tender $\boxed{2}$ *⟨persona⟩* affectionate, loving; *⟨mirada/corazón⟩* tender

tierra *f* $\boxed{1}$ (campo, terreno) land; ~**s fértiles** fertile land; ~ **de cultivo** arable land $\boxed{2}$ (suelo, superficie) ground; (materia, arena) earth; **cavar la** ~ to dig the ground; **un camión de** ~ a

truckload of soil *o* earth; **no juegues con** ~ don't play in the dirt; **un camino de** ~ a dirt road *o* track; **echar algo por** ~ *⟨planes⟩* to wreck, ruin; *⟨argumentos⟩* to demolish, destroy; *⟨esperanzas⟩* to dash

$\boxed{3}$ (AmL) (polvo) dust $\boxed{4}$ (Elec) ground (AmE), earth (BrE); **estar conectado a** ~ *or* (AmL) **hacer** ~ to be grounded *o* earthed

$\boxed{5}$ (por oposición al mar, al aire) land; **viajar por** ~ to travel overland *o* by land; ~ **firme** solid ground; **tomar** ~ to land, touch down $\boxed{6}$ (país, lugar): **su** ~ **(natal)** his homeland, his native land; **costumbres de aquellas** ~**s** customs in those places *o* countries; **la T**~ **Santa** the Holy Land

$\boxed{7}$ (planeta) **la T**~ (the) Earth

tieso -sa *adj* $\boxed{1}$ **(a)** (rígido) stiff; **con las orejas tiesas** with ears pricked up **(b)** (Col, Ven) (duro) *⟨pan⟩* hard; *⟨carne⟩* tough $\boxed{2}$ *⟨persona⟩* (erguido) upright, erect; (orgulloso) stiff; **quedarse** ~ (fam) (helarse) to get frozen stiff (colloq)

tiesto *m* **(a)** (para plantas) flowerpot **(b)** (Chi) (palangana) basin

tifón *m* typhoon

tifus *m* **(a)** (transmitido por parásitos) typhus (fever) **(b)** (fiebre tifoidea) typhoid

tigre -gresa *m,f* (animal asiático) *(m)* tiger; *(f)* tigress

tijeras *fpl*, **tijera** *f* (para cortar papel, tela) scissors *(pl)*; (para uñas) nail scissors *(pl)*; (para césped) shears *(pl)*; **unas** ~**s** a pair of scissors; ~ **de podar** pruning shears *(pl)*; **de** ~ *⟨silla/cama⟩* folding (*before n*); **escalera de** ~ stepladder

tila *f* (infusión) lime (blossom) tea

tilde *f* (acento) accent; (sobre la ñ) tilde, swung dash

tiliches *mpl* (Méx fam) stuff (colloq)

tilo *m* **(a)** (árbol) lime (tree) **(b)** (Chi) ▶ TILA

timador -dora *m,f* swindler, cheat

timar [A1] *vt* to swindle, cheat

timbal *m* (Mús) kettledrum; **los** ~**es** the timpani, the timps (colloq)

timbrar [A1] *vt* *⟨documento⟩* to stamp; *⟨carta⟩* to frank

■ ~ *vi* (Col, Méx) to ring the bell

timbre *m* $\boxed{1}$ (para llamar) (door)bell; **tocar el** ~ to ring the bell; ~ **de alarma** alarm bell $\boxed{2}$ (de sonido, voz) tone, timbre $\boxed{3}$ **(a)** (sello) fiscal stamp **(b)** (Méx) (sello postal) (postage) stamp

timidez *f* (retraimiento) shyness; (falta de decisión, coraje) timidity

tímido -da *adj* (retraído) shy; (falto de decisión, coraje) timid

timo *m* (fam) con (colloq), scam (colloq)

timón *m* **(a)** (Aviac, Náut) rudder **(b)** (Col, Per) (volante) steering wheel; **ir al** ~ to be at the wheel

timonel *mf* *(m)* helmsman; *(f)* helmswoman

tímpano *m* (Anat) eardrum

tinaco *m* (Méx) water tank

tinaja *f* large earthenware jar

tinca *f* (Andes) (fam) (empeño) effort

tincada *f* (Andes fam) feeling, hunch (colloq)

tincar [A2] *vi* (Andes fam) **(a)** (parecer): **me tinca que ya no viene** I get the feeling she's not coming ┈┈⟶

(b) (parecer bien, gustar): **ese pescado me tinca** I like the look of that fish; **¿te tinca ir al cine?** do you feel like going to the movies?

tiniebla *fpl* darkness

tino *m* **(a)** (sentido común) sound judgment, good sense **(b)** (tacto) tact, sensitivity

tinta *f* ink; ∼ **China** India ink; **escribir con** ∼ to write in ink (AmE), Indian ink (BrE); *saber algo de buena* ∼ to have sth on good authority

tinte *m* **1** (acción) dyeing; (sustancia) dye **2** (Esp) (establecimiento) dry cleaner's

tintero *m* inkwell

tintín *m* (de campanilla) tinkling, jingling; (de copa) clinking

tinto¹ -ta *adj* ⟨vino/uva⟩ red

tinto² *m* **1** (Vin) red wine **2** (Col) (café) black coffee

tintorería *f* dry cleaner's

tiña *f* (Med) ringworm

tiñoso -sa *adj* (Med) scabby, mangy

tío, tía *m,f* **1** (pariente) (*m*) uncle; (*f*) aunt; **mis** ∼**s** (varones) my uncles; (varones y mujeres) my aunts and uncles **2** (Esp) (individuo) (fam) ▶ TIPO¹

tiovivo *m* (Esp) merry-go-round, carousel (AmE)

tipear [A1] *vt* (AmS) to type

típico -ca *adj* typical; ⟨plato/traje⟩ typical, traditional; **¡eso es** ∼ **de él!** that's typical of him!

tipo¹ -pa *m,f* (fam) (*m*) guy (colloq), bloke (BrE colloq); (*f*) woman

tipo² *m* **1** (clase) kind, type, sort; **todo** ∼ **de plantas** all kinds of plants; **no es mi** ∼ he's not my type **2** (figura — de mujer) figure; (— de hombre) physique **3** (como adv) (CS fam) around, about; **vénganse** ∼ **cuatro** come around about four o'clock

tique, tíquet (*pl* ∼**ts**) *m* **(a)** (de tren, bus) ticket **(b)** (recibo) receipt, sales slip (AmE)

tiquete *m* (Col) ▶ TIQUE

tira *f* (de papel, tela) strip; (de zapato) strap; ∼ **cómica** comic strip, strip cartoon

■ *mf* **(a)** (Chi, Méx fam) (agente) cop (colloq) **(b)** (Per, RPI arg) (detective infiltrado) police plant (colloq), undercover cop (colloq) **(c) la tira** *f* (Méx fam) (cuerpo) the cops (colloq)

tirabuzón *m* **1** (sacacorchos) corkscrew **2** (rizo, bucle) ringlet **3** (en béisbol) screwball

tirada *f* **1** (Juego) (en juegos de mesa) throw **2** (Impr) print run; **con una** ∼ **de 300.000 ejemplares diarios** a newspaper with a daily circulation of 300,000 copies

tiradero *m* (Méx) (basurero) garbage (AmE) o (BrE) rubbish dump; (casa, habitación) mess, pigsty

tirado -da *adj* **1** (en desorden): **lo dejan todo** ∼ they leave everything lying around **2** (fam) **[ESTAR] (a)** (muy fácil) dead easy (colloq) **(b)** (muy barato) dirt cheap (colloq)

tirador¹ *m* **(a)** (de cajón, puerta) knob, handle **(b)** (tirachinas) slingshot (AmE), catapult (BrE) **(c) tiradores** *mpl* (Arg, Bol) (de pantalón) suspenders (*pl*) (AmE), braces (*pl*) (BrE)

tirador² -dora *m,f* (*m*) marksman; (*f*) markswoman; **es un buen** ∼ he's a good shot

tiraje *m* **(a)** (AmL) (Impr) ▶ TIRADA 2 **(b)** (CS) (de la chimenea) damper

tiranía *f* tyranny

tirano -na *adj* tyrannical

■ *m,f* tyrant

tirantas *fpl* (Col) suspenders (*pl*) (AmE), braces (*pl*) (BrE)

tirante *adj* **(a)** ⟨piel/costura/cuerda⟩ taut **(b)** ⟨situación⟩ tense; ⟨relaciones⟩ tense, strained

■ *m* **1** (Const) strut, brace **2** (Indum) **(a)** (de prenda) strap, shoulder strap; **pantalones de** ∼**s** overalls (*pl*) (AmE), dungarees (*pl*) (BrE) **(b) tirantes** *mpl* (Esp, Méx, Ven) (de pantalón) suspenders (*pl*) (AmE), braces (*pl*) (BrE)

tirar [A1] *vt* **1 (a)** (lanzar) to throw; **tiró la pelota al aire** he threw the ball up in the air; ∼**le algo A algn** (para que lo agarre) to throw sb sth; (con agresividad) to throw sth AT sb **(b)** (desechar) to throw out *o* away **(c)** (desperdiciar) to waste; **¡qué manera de** ∼ **el dinero!** what a waste of money! **2 (a)** (hacer caer) ⟨jarrón/silla⟩ to knock over; **el perro me tiró al suelo** the dog knocked me over **(b)** (derribar) ⟨pared/puerta⟩ to knock down **3 (a)** ⟨bomba⟩ to drop; ⟨cohete⟩ to fire, launch; ⟨flecha⟩ to shoot **(b)** ⟨foto⟩ to take **4** (AmL) (atrayendo hacia sí) to pull; **tiró la cadena** he pulled the chain

■ ∼ *vi* **1** (atrayendo hacia sí) to pull; ∼ DE **algo** to pull sth; **no le tires del pelo** don't pull her hair **2 (a)** (disparar) to shoot; ∼ **a matar** to shoot to kill **(b)** (Dep) to shoot; ∼ **al arco** (AmL) *or* (Esp) **a puerta** to shoot at goal **(c)** (Jueg) (descartarse) to throw away; (en juegos de dados) to throw; (en dardos) to throw; (en bolos) to bowl **3 (a)** «chimenea/cigarro» to draw **(b)** «coche/ motor» to pull **4 tirando** *ger* (fam): **gano poco pero vamos tirando** I don't earn much but we're managing; **¿qué tal andas? — tirando** how are things? — not too bad **5 tirar a** (tender a): **tira más bien a azul** it's more of a bluish color; **ella tira más a la madre** she takes after her mother more

■ **tirarse** *v pron* **1 (a)** (lanzarse, arrojarse) to throw oneself; **se tiró por la ventana** he threw himself out of the window; ∼**se en paracaídas** to parachute; (en emergencia) to bale out; ∼**se al agua** to jump into the water; ∼**se a** dive in, to jump in headfirst **(b)** (AmL) (tumbarse) to lie down **2** (fam) ⟨horas/días⟩ to spend; **se tiró dos años escribiéndolo** he spent two years writing it **3** (fam) (expulsar): ∼**se un pedo** to fart (sl)

tirita *f* (Esp) Band-Aid® (AmE), sticking plaster (BrE)

tiritar [A1] *vi* to shiver, tremble; ∼ **de frío** to shiver with cold

tiro *m* **1** (disparo) shot; **le dispararon un** ∼ they shot him; **lo mató de un** ∼ she shot him dead; **al** ∼ (Chi fam) right away, straightaway (BrE); **errar el** ∼ (literal) to miss; (equivocarse) to get it wrong **2** (en fútbol, baloncesto) shot; (deporte) shooting; ∼ **al arco** (deporte) archery; (en fútbol) (AmL) shot at goal; ∼ **al blanco** (deporte) target shooting; (lugar) shooting gallery; ∼ **al plato** skeet shooting (AmE), clay-pigeon shooting (BrE); ∼ **de esquina** (AmL) corner (kick); (en fútbol) free kick; (en baloncesto) free shot *o* throw **3** (de chimenea) flue; **tiene muy buen** ∼ it draws well **4 animal/caballo de** ∼ draught animal/horse

tirón *m* **(a)** (movimiento) tug, pull; **me dio un ~ de pelo** he pulled my hair; **dale un ~ de orejas** tweak his ears for him (colloq); **el autobús avanzaba a tirones** the bus jerked along; *de un ~*: **me arrancó la cadena de un ~** he ripped the chain from my neck; **lo leyó/bebió de un ~** (fam) she read/downed it in one go **(b)** (de músculo): **sufrió un ~ en la pierna** he pulled a muscle in his leg **(c)** (forma de robo): **le dieron un** *or* **el ~** they snatched her bag

tironear [A1] *vi* (AmL fam) to tug, pull
■ ~ *vt* (AmL fam) to tug (at)

tiroteo *m* (tiros) shooting; (intercambio de tiros) shoot-out

tirria *f* (fam) grudge; **tenerle ~ a algn** to have a grudge against sb

tisú *m* (*pl* **-sús** *or* **-súes**) (pañuelo) tissue; (tela) lamé

titánico -ca *adj* huge, colossal (*before n*)

títere *m* **(a)** (marioneta, persona) puppet **(b) títeres** *mpl* (función) puppet show

titiritar [A1] *vi* to shiver, tremble

titiritero -ra *m,f* (de marionetas) puppeteer; (acróbata) acrobat

titubeante *adj* (voz/respuesta) faltering, halting; (actitud) hesitant

titubear [A1] *vi* **(a)** (dudar, vacilar) to hesitate; **sin ~** without hesitation **(b)** (balbucear) to stutter

titubeo *m* (duda, vacilación) hesitancy, hesitation

titulación *f* qualifications (*pl*); **personas con ~ universitaria** university graduates, college graduates (AmE)

titulado -da *adj* qualified
■ *m,f* graduate; **~ medio** *graduate with a qualification obtained after a three-year degree course as opposed to a five-year course*; **~ superior** *or* **universitario** university graduate, college graduate (AmE)

titular¹ *adj* (médico/profesor) permanent
■ *mf* (de pasaporte, cuenta, cargo) holder
■ *m* **(a)** (en periódico) headline **(b)** (Rad, TV) main story; **los ~es** the main stories, the news headlines

titular² [A1] *vt* (obra): **su novela titulada 'Julia'** his novel called *o* (frml) entitled 'Julia'
■ **titularse** *v pron* [1] «obra/película» to be called, be entitled (frml) [2] (Educ) to graduate, get one's degree; **~se EN/DE algo** to graduate IN/AS sth

título *m* [1] (en general) title; **un poema que lleva por ~ ...** a poem called *o* (frml) entitled ...; **el ~ de campeón juvenil** the junior title; **nobiliario** title; *a ~ de*: **a ~ de introducción** by way of introduction; **asiste a ~ de observador** he's attending as an observer [2] (Educ) degree; (diploma) certificate; **~ académico** academic qualification; **~ universitario** university degree, college degree (AmE)

tiza *f* (material) chalk; (barra) (piece of) chalk; (en billar) chalk

tizón *m* (leño) charred stick/log

toalla *f* **(a)** (tejido) toweling* **(b)** (para secarse) towel; **~ higiénica** sanitary napkin (AmE), sanitary towel (BrE); *tirar* **or** *arrojar la* **~** to throw in the towel

toallero *m* (barra) towel rail; (aro) towel ring

tobillera *f* **(a)** (Med) ankle support **(b)** (de ciclista) cycle clip

tobillo *m* ankle

tobogán *m* **(a)** (en parque) slide; (en piscina) water chute **(b)** (Aviac) escape chute **(c)** (trineo) toboggan

toca *f* (de religiosa) wimple; (de tocado) circlet

tocadiscos *m* (*pl* **~**) record player

tocador *m* (mueble) dressing table

tocar [A2] *vt* [1] **(a)** (en general) to touch; (palpar) to feel; (manosear) to handle; **¡no vayas a ~ ese cable!** don't touch that cable!; **mis ahorros no los quiero ~** I don't want to touch my savings; **la planta ya toca el techo** the plant is already touching the ceiling **(b)** (hacer sonar) (timbre/ campana) to ring; (claxon) to blow, sound **(c)** (Mús) (instrumento/pieza) to play
[2] (tema) (tratar) to touch on, refer to; (sacar) to bring up
[3] (atañer, concernir) to affect; **un problema que nos toca de cerca** a problem which affects us directly
■ ~ *vi* [1] **(a)** (AmL) (llamar) «persona» to knock at the door; **alguien está tocando (a la puerta)** there's somebody at the door **(b)** «campana/ timbre» to ring; **las campanas tocaban a misa** the bells were ringing for mass **(c)** (Mús) to play
[2] **(a)** (corresponder en reparto, concurso, sorteo): **a ella le toca la mitad de la herencia** she gets half of the inheritance; **le tocó el primer premio** she won the first prize; **me tocó la maestra más antipática del colegio** I got the most horrible teacher in the school **(b)** (ser el turno): **te toca a ti** it's your turn; **¿a quién le toca cocinar?** whose turn is it to do the cooking?
■ **tocarse** *v pron* **(a)** (refl) (herida/grano) to touch; (barba) to play with **(b)** (recípr) «personas» to touch each other; «cables» to touch

tocayo -ya *m,f* namesake

tocino *m* (para guisar) pork fat; (con vetas de carne) fatty salt pork; (para freír) bacon

tocología *f* obstetrics

tocólogo -ga *m,f* obstetrician

todavía *adv* [1] **(a)** (aún) still; **¿~ estás aquí?** are you still here? **(b)** (en frases negativas) yet; **~ no está lista** she isn't ready yet [2] (en comparaciones) even, still; **sus primos son ~ más ricos** her cousins are even richer *o* richer still [3] (fam) (encima) still; **¡y ~ se queja!** and he still complains!

todo¹ -da *adj* [1] (la totalidad de) all; **nos comimos ~ el pan** we ate all the bread; **toda la mañana** all morning, the whole morning; **invitó a toda la clase** she invited the whole class; **por ~s lados** all over the place; **~s ustedes lo sabían** you all knew; ▶ MUNDO 1
[2] (cualquier, cada): **~ artículo importado** all imported items, any imported item; **~ aquel que quiera** anyone who wishes to; **~s los días** every day
[3] (uso enfático): **a toda velocidad** at top speed; **con toda inocencia** in all innocence; **le dieron ~ tipo de facilidades** they gave him all kind of facilities; *a* **~** *esto* (mientras tanto) meanwhile, in the meantime; (a propósito) incidentally, by the way
■ *pron* [1] **(a)** (sin excluir nada) everything; **lo perdieron ~** they lost everything; **~ le parece** ····❖

poco he's never satisfied; **come ~ lo que quieras** eat as much as you like; **~ o nada** all or nothing **(b)** **~s/todas** (referido a — cosas) all; (— a personas) all, everybody; **los compró ~s** she bought all of them; **vinieron ~s** they all came, everybody came; **buena suerte a ~s** good luck to everybody; **es el más alto de ~s** he's the tallest of the lot *o* of them all; **¿están ~s?** is everyone *o* everybody here?; **~s y cada uno** each and every one **2** (*en locs*) **con todo (y eso)** (*fam*) (aun así) all the same, even so; **de todo: come de ~** she'll eat anything; **venden de ~** they sell everything *o* all sorts of things; **hace de ~ un poco** he does a bit of everything; **del todo** totally **3** (*como adv*) **(a)** (completamente) all; **está ~ mojado** it's all wet **(b)** (en frases ponderativas) quite; **fue ~ un espectáculo** it was quite a show!

todo² *m*: **el/un ~** the/a whole; **jugarse el ~ por el ~** to risk *o* gamble everything on one throw

todopoderoso -sa *adj* all-powerful

Todopoderoso *m*: **el ~** the Almighty

todoterreno *m* (Auto) four-wheel-drive vehicle, 4 x 4 (*léase: four by four*)

Tokio *m* Tokyo

toldo *m* **(a)** (de terraza) canopy; (de tienda) awning; (en la playa) awning; (en camión) tarpaulin **(b)** (para fiestas) tent (AmE), marquee (BrE) **(c)** (RPl) (de los indios) hut

tolerable *adj* tolerable

tolerancia *f* tolerance

tolerante *adj* tolerant

tolerar [A1] *vt* to tolerate; **¡eso no se puede ~!** that's intolerable!; **⊕ tolerada** (**para menores de 14 años**) (Esp) ≈PG; **le toleras demasiado** you're too lenient with him

toma *f* **1** **(a)** (Mil) capture, taking **(b)** (de universidad, fábrica) occupation; (de tierras) seizure **2** (Cin, Fot — imagen) shot; (— acción de filmar) take **3** (de medicamento) dose **4** (de datos) gathering; (de muestras) taking; **la ~ de decisiones** the decision-making **5** (AmL) (acequia) irrigation channel **6 (a)** **~ de tierra** (Elec) ground (wire) (AmE), earth (wire) (BrE) **(b)** (Aviac) landing, touchdown

tomado -da *adj* **1** (*voz*): **tengo la voz tomada** I'm hoarse **2** (AmL fam) (*persona*) drunk

tomadura de pelo *f* **(a)** (broma, chiste) joke **(b)** (burla): **esto es una ~ de ~** they're just messing around with us (AmE) *o* (BrE) messing us around

tomar [A1] *vt* **1** (en general) to take; **tomé un libro de la estantería** I took a book from the shelf; **la tomé de la mano** I took her by the hand; **toma lo que te debo** here's what I owe you; **¿lo puedo ~ prestado?** can I borrow it?; **tomó el asunto en sus manos** she took charge of the matter; **~ precauciones/el tren/una foto** to take precautions/the train/a picture; **~le la temperatura a algn** to take sb's temperature; **~ algo por escrito** to write sth down; **~ algo/a algn POR algo/algn** to take sth/sb FOR sth/sb; **¿por quién me has tomado?** who *o* what do you take

me for?; **lo tomó a mal/a broma** he took it the wrong way/as a joke; **eso toma demasiado tiempo** that takes up too much time **2** **(a)** (beber) to drink; **el niño toma (el) pecho** the baby's being breast-fed **(b)** (servirse, consumir) to have; **¿qué vas a ~?** what are you going to have? **3** (esp AmL) (contratar) to take on **(b)** «*profesor*» «*alumnos/clases*» to take on **(c)** «*colegio*» «*niño*» to take **4** (apoderarse de) «*fortaleza/tierras*» to seize; «*universidad/fábrica*» to occupy **5** (adquirir) «*forma*» to take; «*aspecto*» to take on; «*velocidad/altura*» to gain; «*costumbre*» to get into **6** (cobrar): **le he tomado cariño a esta casa/a la niña** I've become quite attached to this house/quite fond of the girl **7** (exponerse a): **~ el aire** to get some (fresh) air; **~ (el) sol** to sunbathe; **vas a ~ frío** (CS) you'll get *o* catch cold

■ **~** *vi* **1** (asir): **toma, aquí tienes tus tijeras** here are your scissors; **tome, yo no lo necesito** take it, I don't need it **2** (esp AmL) (beber alcohol) to drink **3** (AmL) (ir) to go; **~on para el norte** they went north; **~ a la derecha** to turn *o* go right **4** «*injerto*» to take

■ **tomarse** *v pron* **1** «*vacaciones/tiempo*» to take; **se tomó el día libre** he took the day off **2** «*molestia/libertad*» to take; **~se la molestia/libertad de hacer algo** to take the trouble to do sth/the liberty of doing sth **3** (enf) **(a)** «*café/vino*» to drink **(b)** «*medicamento/vitaminas*» to take **(c)** «*desayuno/merienda/sopa*» to eat, have; «*helado/yogur*» to have **4** «*autobús/tren/taxi*» to take **5** (Med) **(a)** (refl) to take; **se tomó la temperatura** she took her temperature **(b)** (caus): **~se la tensión** to have one's blood pressure taken **6** (caus) (esp AmL) «*foto*» to have ... taken **7** (enf) (reaccionar frente a) «*comentario/noticia*» to take; **no te lo tomes a mal** don't take it the wrong way **8** (Chi) «*universidad/fábrica*» to occupy

tomate *m* tomato; **estar/ponerse (colorado) como un ~** (de vergüenza) to be/turn as red as a beet (AmE), to be/go as red as a beetroot (BrE); (por el sol) to be/turn as red as a lobster

tomavistas *m* (*pl* **~**) movie camera

toma y daca *m* give-and-take

tómbola *f* tombola

tomillo *m* thyme

tomo *m* volume

ton *m*: **hacer algo sin ~ ni son** to do sth for no reason

tonada *f* **(a)** (melodía) tune; (canción) ballad, song **(b)** (AmL) (acento) accent

tonel *m* barrel

tonelada *f* ton

tongo *m* (fam) (en partido, pelea) fix (colloq); **hubo ~** it was fixed (colloq)

tónica f ① (bebida) tonic (water) ② (tendencia, tono) trend, tendency

tónico¹ -ca adj ① (Med) tonic (before n) ② (a) ‹sílaba/vocal› tonic (before n), stressed (b) (Mús) tonic

tónico² m (Med) tonic; (en cosmética) toner

tono m ① (a) (en general) tone; **en ~ cariñoso** in an affectionate tone of voice; **en ~ de reproche** reproachfully; **el ~ en que lo dijo** the way he said it; **el ~ general de la conversación** the general tone of the conversation (b) (Rad, Telec, TV) tone; **este teléfono no da** or **tiene ~** I can't get a dial tone (AmE) o (BrE) dialling tone on this phone; **~ de marcar** or (AmL) **de discado** or (AmS) **de discar** dial tone (AmE), dialling tone (BrE); **~ de ocupado** busy signal (AmE), engaged tone (BrE); **no venir a ~** to be out of place ② (de color) shade; **subido de ~** risqué ③ (Mús) key

tontear [A1] vi (a) (hacer el tonto) to play the fool; (decir tonterías) to talk nonsense (b) (flirtear) to fool around (colloq)

tontería f (a) (cosa tonta) silly o stupid thing; (dicho tonto) silly remark; **¡déjate de ~s!** stop fooling around; **¡~s!** nonsense! (b) (cosa insignificante) silly thing, small thing; **se enoja por cualquier ~** she gets angry over the slightest little thing (c) (cualidad) stupidity

tonto -ta adj ① (a) [SER] (falto de inteligencia) stupid, dumb (colloq); (ingenuo) silly (b) [ESTAR] (intratable) difficult, silly; (disgustado) upset ② ‹excusa/error/historia› silly
■ m,f (falto de inteligencia) idiot, dummy (colloq); (ingenuo) idiot, fool; **hacer el ~** (hacer payasadas) to play o act the fool; (actuar con necedad) to make a fool of oneself; **hacerse el ~** to act dumb

topacio m topaz

toparse [A1] v pron **~se CON algn** (tropezarse) to bump INTO sb; (encontrarse) to bump o run INTO sb; **~se CON algo** (tropezarse) to bump INTO sth; (encontrarse) to come across sth

tope m ① (a) (límite) limit; **han establecido un ~ máximo** an upper limit has been set (b) (como adj inv) ‹edad/precio› maximum (before n); **fecha ~** deadline ② (a) (para las puertas) doorstop; (Ferr) buffer (b) (Méx) (Auto) speed bump ③ (Andes) (cima) top ④ (a) (Andes) (golpe, choque) bump (b) (Méx fam) (cabezazo): **me di un ~** I bumped my head

tópico¹ -ca adj ① ‹comentario/afirmación› trite ② (Farm) ❺ **uso tópico** for external use only

tópico² m (a) (tema, asunto) topic, subject (b) (tema trillado) hackneyed subject; (expresión) cliché

top-less, topless /'toples/ m: **el ~ es habitual aquí** it is quite normal for people to go topless here

topo m (a) (Zool) mole (b) (Col) (pendiente) earring

topografía f topography, surveying

toque m ① (a) (de timbre) ring; (de campana) stroke, chime; **al ~ de las doce** on the stroke of twelve; **~ de queda** curfew (b) (Esp fam) (llamada) call, ring (BrE colloq) ② (en béisbol) bunt ③ (detalle) touch; **falta darle los últimos ~s** we have to put the finishing touches to it ④ (Méx fam) (descarga) electric shock

toquetear [A1] vt (fam) to touch; (sexualmente) to touch up

toquilla f shawl

tórax m thorax

torbellino m (a) (de viento) whirlwind; (de polvo) dust storm (b) (de actividad) whirl (c) (persona inquieta) bundle of energy

torcedura f sprain

torcer [E10] vt ① ‹cuerpo› to twist; ‹cabeza› to turn; **me torció el brazo** she twisted my arm ② ‹esquina› to turn ③ ‹curso/rumbo› to change
■ **~** vi (girar) «persona/vehículo» to turn; «camino» to bend, curve
■ **torcerse** v pron ① ‹tobillo/muñeca› to sprain ② «madera/viga» to warp

torcido -da adj ① [ESTAR] (a) (con respecto a otra cosa) crooked; **tiene la nariz torcida** he has a crooked nose; **llevas la falda torcida** your skirt's twisted (b) (curvo) bent; **una rama torcida** a bent branch; **tiene las piernas torcidas** (para adentro) he is knock-kneed; (para afuera) he is bowlegged ② ‹intenciones› devious, crooked

torcijón m stomach cramp

tordo -da m,f (a) (caballo) dapple, dapple-gray* (b) (pájaro) thrush

torear [A1] vi to fight; **quiere ~** he wants to be a bullfighter
■ **~** vt ① ‹toro/novillo› to fight ② (fam) (a) ‹perseguidor/pregunta› to dodge (b) (AmL) (provocar) to torment, needle

toreo m bullfighting

torero -ra m,f bullfighter, matador

tormenta f ① (Meteo) storm; **~ de nieve** snowstorm; (con viento) blizzard; **hacer frente a la ~** to weather the storm ② (de pasiones) storm; (de celos) frenzy

tormentoso -sa adj stormy

tornado m tornado

tornamesa f or m (Col, Méx) (plato giratorio) turntable

tornar [A1] vi (liter) (a) (regresar) to return; **tornó a nevar** it snowed again (b) (volver, hacer) to make, render
■ **tornarse** v pron (liter) to become; **~se EN algo** to turn INTO sth

torneo m tournament

tornero -ra m,f lathe operator

tornillo m (Tec) screw; **te/le falta un ~** you have/he has a screw loose (colloq)

torniquete m (Med) tourniquet

torno m ① (a) (de carpintero) lathe; **~ de alfarero** potter's wheel (b) (Odont) drill (c) (para alzar pesos) winch ② **en torno a** around

toro m (animal) bull; **~ bravo** or **de lidia** fighting bull; **los ~s** (el espectáculo) bullfighting; **ir a los ~s** to go to a bullfight

toronja f (AmL) grapefruit

torpe adj (a) (en las acciones) clumsy (b) (de entendimiento) slow (colloq) (c) (sin tacto) ‹persona/comentario› clumsy; **de manera ~** clumsily

torpedo m ① (Arm) torpedo ② (Chi fam) (de estudiante) crib (note) (colloq)

torpeza f ① (cualidad) (a) (en las acciones) clumsiness (b) (falta de inteligencia) stupidity; **perdona mi ~, pero no entiendo** I'm sorry to be ···⊱

so stupid *o* dim, but I don't understand **(c)** (falta de tacto) clumsiness ⊡ (dicho desacertado) gaffe; (acción desacertada) blunder

torrar [A1] *vt* to roast

torre *f* **(a)** (de castillo, iglesia) tower; (en punta) steeple, spire **(b)** (de cables de alta tensión) pylon; (de pozo de petróleo) derrick **(c)** (en ajedrez) rook, castle **(d)** (edificio alto) apartment block (AmE), tower block (BrE)

torreja *f* ⊡ (AmL) (pan frito) ▶ TORRIJA ⊡ (Chi) (rodaja) slice

torrencial *adj* torrential

torrente *m* (Geog) torrent

torrentoso -sa *adj* (AmL) fast-flowing

torreón *m* tower

torrija *f* piece *o* slice of French toast; **~s** French toast

torsión *f* torsion

torso *m* (Anat) torso, trunk; (Art) bust

torta *f* ⊡ (CS, Ven) (de cumpleaños, etc) cake; (decorada, con crema, etc) gateau ⊡ (Méx) (bocadillo) sandwich ⊡ (fam) (golpe): **darle una ~ a algn** to hit *o* wallop sb (colloq); **pegarse una ~** to bang one's head (*o* arm *etc*) (colloq); **liarse a ~s** to come to blows

tortazo *m* (fam) ▶ TORTA 3

tortícolis *f* stiff neck, torticollis (tech)

tortilla *f* ⊡ (de huevos) omelet*; **~ de papas** *or* (Esp) **de patatas** Spanish omelet* (*made with potatoes and sometimes onion*) ⊡ (de maíz) tortilla

tortillero -ra *m,f* tortilla seller

tórtola *f* turtledove

tortuga *f* (Zool) (de tierra) tortoise, turtle (AmE); (de mar) turtle

tortuoso -sa *adj* **(a)** ⟨sendero⟩ tortuous, winding **(b)** ⟨maquinaciones/conducta⟩ devious; ⟨mente⟩ devious, twisted

tortura *f* torture

torturar [A1] *vt* (con violencia física) to torture; (angustiar) to torment, torture

tos *f* cough; **tener ~** to have a cough; **~ convulsa** *or* **convulsiva** whooping cough

tosco -ca *adj* **(a)** ⟨utensilio/mueble/construcción⟩ crude, basic; ⟨tela⟩ coarse, rough **(b)** ⟨persona/manos⟩ rough; ⟨lenguaje⟩ unrefined; ⟨modales⟩ coarse; ⟨facciones⟩ coarse

toser [E1] *vi* to cough

tostada *f* **(a)** (de pan) piece *o* slice of toast; **desayuno café con ~s** I have coffee and toast for breakfast **(b)** (Méx) (de tortilla) tostada (*fried maize tortilla*)

tostado -da *adj* ⟨pan/almendras⟩ toasted; ⟨café⟩ roasted; ⟨piel⟩ tanned

tostadora *f*, **tostador** *m* (para pan) toaster; (para café) roaster

tostar [A10] *vt* **(a)** ⟨pan/almendras⟩ to toast; ⟨café⟩ to roast **(b)** ⟨piel/persona⟩ to tan
■ **tostarse** *v pron* (broncearse) to tan

tostón *m* ⊡ **(a)** (Esp) (pan frito) crouton **(b)** (Ven) (plátano frito) fried plantain ⊡ (Esp fam) (cosa fastidiosa) drag (colloq); **darle el ~ a algn** (Esp fam) to pester somebody ⊡ (Méx fam) (moneda) fifty-cent coin

total *adj* **(a)** (absoluto) ⟨desastre/destrucción⟩ total; ⟨éxito⟩ resounding (*before n*), total; ⟨cambio⟩ complete **(b)** (global) ⟨costo/importe⟩ total
■ *m* total; **en ~** altogether
■ *adv* (*indep*) (fam) (al resumir una narración) so, in the end; **~, que me di por vencida** so in the end I gave up

totalidad *f*: **la ~ de la población** the whole *o* entire population; **fue destruido en su ~** it was totally destroyed; **se pagó en su ~** it was paid in full

totalitario -ria *adj* totalitarian

totalitarismo *m* totalitarianism

totogol *m* (Col) sports lottery (AmE), football pools (*pl*) (BrE)

totopo *m* (Méx) tortilla chip

totora *f* reed mace, bulrush

tóxico¹ -ca *adj* toxic

tóxico² -ca *m* poison, toxin

toxicómano -na *m,f* drug addict

tozudo -da *adj* obstinate, stubborn
■ *m,f*: **es un ~** he's extremely stubborn *o* obstinate

traba *f* ⊡ (en ventana) catch; (de cinturón) belt loop ⊡ (dificultad, impedimento) obstacle; **me puso muchas ~s** he made things really difficult for me

trabajado -da *adj* ⟨diseño/bordado/plan⟩ elaborate

trabajador -dora *adj* (que trabaja mucho) hard-working
■ *m,f* worker; **un ~ no calificado** (AmL) *or* (Esp) **cualificado** an unskilled worker *o* laborer; **~ autónomo** self-employed worker *o* person; **~ de medio tiempo** (AmL) *or* (Esp) **a tiempo parcial** part-time worker; **~a social** (Méx) social worker

trabajar [A1] *vi* ⊡ (en general) to work; **~ por cuenta propia** to be self-employed; **~ jornada completa** *or* **a tiempo completo** to work full-time; **~ media jornada** to work part-time; **~ mucho** to work hard; **¿en qué trabajas?** what do you do (for a living)?; **estoy trabajando en una novela** I'm working on a novel; **~ DE** *or* **COMO algo** to work AS sth ⊡ (actuar) to act, perform; **¿quién trabaja en la película** who's in the movie?
■ *vt* ⊡ **(a)** ⟨campo/tierra/madera⟩ to work **(b)** ⟨masa⟩ (con las manos) to knead, work ⊡ (perfeccionar, pulir) to work on

trabajo *m* ⊡ **(a)** (empleo) job; **buscar ~** to look for work *o* for a job; **quedarse sin ~** to lose one's job; **un ~ fijo** a steady job; **un ~ de media jornada** a part-time job; **un ~ de jornada completa** *or* **a tiempo completo** a full-time job **(b)** (lugar) work; **está en el ~** she's at work; **ir al ~** to go to work
⊡ (actividad, labor) work; **~ en equipo** teamwork; **el ~ de la casa** housework; **los niños dan mucho ~** children are hard work; **¡buen ~!** well done!; **~ de campo** fieldwork; **~s forzados** hard labor*; **~s manuales** handicrafts (*pl*); **~ voluntario** voluntary *o* (AmE) volunteer work
⊡ **(a)** (tarea) job; **limpiar el horno es un ~ que odio** cleaning the oven is a job I hate **(b)** (obra escrita) piece of work; (en universidad, escuela) essay
⊡ (esfuerzo): **con mucho ~ consiguió levantarse** with great effort she managed to get up; **me cuesta ~ creerlo** I find it hard to believe

trabajoso -sa *adj* ‹subida› arduous; ‹tarea› laborious

trabalenguas *m* (*pl* ~) tongue twister

trabar [A1] *vt* **1 (a)** ‹puerta/ventana› (para que no se abra) to hold ... shut; (para que no se cierre) to hold ... back *o* open **(b)** ‹caballo› to hobble **2 (a)** ‹conversación/amistad/relación› to strike up **(b)** ‹historia› to weave together **3** ‹proceso/ negociaciones› to hamper the progress of

■ **trabarse** *v pron* «cajón/cierre» to get jammed *o* stuck; **se le traba la lengua** he gets tongue-tied

trabilla *f* (de pantalón) stirrup; (para cinturón) belt loop

trácala *m* (Méx, Ven fam) cheat
■ *f* (Méx, Ven fam) trick, swindle; **se la pasa haciendo ~** he's always cheating people

tracalada *f* (Andes fam) bunch (colloq)

tracalear [A1] *vt* (Méx, Ven fam) to cheat, swindle

tracalero -ra *adj* (Méx, Ven fam) dishonest

tracción *f* (Auto, Mec) traction, drive; **un vehículo con** *or* **de ~ a cuatro ruedas** a four-wheel-drive vehicle

tractor *m* tractor

tradición *f* (costumbre) tradition

tradicional *adj* traditional

tradicionalista *adj/mf* traditionalist

traducción *f* translation; **~ del inglés al español** translation from English into Spanish

traducir [I6] *vt* ‹texto/escritor› to translate; **~ DE algo A algo** to translate FROM sth INTO sth

traductor -tora *m,f* translator

traer [E23] *vt* **1** (de un lugar a otro) to bring; **me trajo en la moto** he brought me on his motorbike; **¿qué te trae por aquí?** what brings you here? **2** (ocasionar, causar) ‹problemas/dificultades› to cause; **~ buena suerte** to bring good luck **3** «libro/artículo» ‹artículo/capítulo› to have; **este diccionario no lo trae** it's not in this dictionary **4 (a)** ‹ropa/sombrero› to wear **(b)** (tener consigo) to bring; **traje poco dinero** I didn't bring much money (with me)

■ **traerse** *v pron* **1** (enf) (a un sitio) to bring (along); **lo invité a él y se trajo a toda la familia** I invited him and he brought the whole family along **2** (fam) (tramar) to be up to (colloq); **¿qué se ~án esas dos?** what are those two up to?

traficante *mf* dealer, trafficker; **~ de drogas** drug dealer *o* trafficker; **~ de esclavos** slave trader

traficar [A2] *vi* **~ EN** *or* **CON algo** to deal IN sth

tráfico *m* **1** (de vehículos) traffic; **accidente de ~** road accident **2** (de mercancías) trade; **~ de armas** arms trade; **~ de drogas** drug dealing *o* trafficking

tragaluz *m* (en el techo) skylight; (en una puerta, ventana) fanlight

traganíqueles *m* (*pl* ~) (AmC) slot machine

tragaperras *m or f* (*pl* ~) (Esp fam) slot machine

tragar [A3] *vt* **1** ‹comida/agua/medicina› to swallow **2** (fam) (aguantar): **no lo trago** I can't stand him

■ **~** *vi* **1** (Fisiol) to swallow **2** (RPl fam) (estudiar) to cram

■ **tragarse** *v pron* **1** (enf) **(a)** ‹comida› to swallow; **~se el humo** to inhale **(b)** ‹lágrimas› to choke back; ‹orgullo› to swallow **(c)** «máquina» ‹dinero/tarjeta› to swallow up **2** (fam) **(a)** (soportar) ‹obra/recital› to sit through **(b)** (creerse) ‹excusa/cuento› to swallow, fall for (colloq)

tragedia *f* tragedy

trágico -ca *adj* **(a)** ‹actriz/obra› tragic (*before n*) **(b)** ‹vida/final/consecuencia› tragic; **no te pongas ~** don't be so melodramatic

tragicomedia *f* tragicomedy

trago *m* **1 (a)** (de líquido) drink, swig; **un ~ de agua** a drink of water; **de un ~** in one gulp **(b)** (esp AmL fam) (bebida alcohólica) drink; **¿vamos a tomar un ~?** shall we go for a drink? **2** (experiencia): **pasar un ~ amargo** to have a rough time

traición *f* **(a)** (delito) treason **(b)** (acto desleal) treachery, betrayal; **lo mataron a ~** they killed him by treachery

traicionar [A1] *vt* **(a)** ‹patria/amigo› to betray **(b)** (delatar) «mirada/nerviosismo» to give ... away

traicionero -ra *adj* **(a)** ‹persona/acción› treacherous **(b)** ‹mar/carretera› treacherous, dangerous

traidor -dora *adj* traitorous, treacherous
■ *m,f* traitor; **~ A algo** traitor TO sth

traiga, traigas, etc ▶ TRAER

trailer /'trailer/ *m* (*pl* **~s**) **1 (a)** (AmL) (casa rodante) trailer (AmE), caravan (BrE) **(b)** (para caballos) horsebox **2** (Méx) (camión) semitrailer (AmE), articulated lorry (BrE)

tráiler *m* (*pl* **~s**) **1** (Esp) (Cin) trailer **2** ▶ TRAILER

trailero -ra *m,f* (Méx) truck driver

traje *m* (de dos, tres piezas) suit; (vestido de mujer) dress; (Teatr) costume; (de país, región) dress; **~ de baño** (de hombre) swimming trunks (*pl*); (de mujer) bathing suit, swimsuit; **~ de etiqueta/gala** formal/evening dress; **~ largo** evening dress

traje, etc ▶ TRAER

trajera, trajese, etc ▶ TRAER

trajimos, trajiste, etc ▶ TRAER

trajín *m*: **un día de mucho ~** a very hectic day; **con todo este ~ ...** with all this coming and going...; **el ~ de las grandes ciudades** the hustle and bustle of big cities

trajinar [A1] *vi* (fam) to rush about (colloq)

trajiste, etc ▶ TRAER

trama *f* **1** (de tejido) weave, weft **2** (de película, novela) plot

tramar [A1] *vt* ‹engaño› to devise; ‹venganza› to plot; ‹complot› to hatch, lay; **¿qué andan tramando?** what are they up to? (colloq)

tramitación *f* processing; **la ~ del divorcio tardó años** the divorce proceedings took years

tramitar [A1] *vt* ‹préstamo› «funcionario» to deal with; «interesado» to arrange; **están tramitando el divorcio** ‹cónyuges› they have started divorce proceedings; **~ un permiso de trabajo** «organismo» to deal with a work permit application; «interesado» to apply for one's work permit

trámite *m* (proceso) procedure; (etapa) step, stage; **simplificar los ∼s aduaneros** to simplify customs procedures; **el préstamo está en ∼ the** loan application is being processed; **tengo que hacer unos ∼s en el centro** I have some business to attend to in the centre

tramo *m* (de carretera, vía) stretch; (de escalera) flight

tramoyista *mf* (Teatr) sceneshifter, stagehand

trampa *f* (a) (para animales) trap; (de lazo) snare (b) (ardid) trap; **le tendieron una ∼** they laid *o* set a trap for him (c) (en el juego): **hacer ∼(s)** to cheat; **eso es ∼** that's cheating

trampilla *f* trapdoor

trampolín *m* (en natación — flexible) springboard; (— rígido) diving board; (en gimnasia) trampoline; (en esquí) ski jump

tramposo -sa *adj*: **ser ∼** to be a cheat ■ *m,f* cheat

tranca *f* ①(a) (de puerta, ventana) bar (b) (palo) cudgel, club ②(esp AmL fam) (borrachera) bender (colloq); **agarrarse una ∼** to get plastered *o* smashed (colloq) ③(Ven fam) (Auto) holdup, tailback

trancar [A1] *vt* ⟨puerta/ventana⟩ to bar

trance *m* (Psic, Relig) trance; **estar en ∼** to be in a trance

tranque *m* (CS) reservoir

tranquilidad *f* (a) (calma) peace; **ni un minuto de ∼** not a moment's peace; **con ∼** (sin prisas) at my (*o* your *etc*) leisure; (sin nerviosismo) calmly (b) (falta de preocupación): **llámame a la hora que sea, con toda ∼** feel free to call me at any time; **lo hice para mi propia ∼** I did it for my own peace of mind

tranquilizante *adj* (a) ⟨noticia⟩ reassuring; ⟨música⟩ soothing (b) (Med) tranquilizing* ■ *m* tranquilizer*

tranquilizar [A4] *vt* (a) (apaciguar) to calm ... down; **intenté ∼lo** I tried to calm him down; **sus palabras la ∼on** his words reassured her (b) (atenuar la preocupación): **eso me tranquiliza mucho** that makes me feel a lot better ■ **tranquilizarse** *v pron* (calmarse) to calm down; (dejar de preocuparse): **al oír su voz me tranquilicé** when I heard his voice I felt reassured

tranquilo¹ -la *adj* ①(a) [SER] ⟨persona⟩ (pacífico) calm (b) ⟨mar/ambiente⟩ calm; ⟨lugar⟩ quiet, peaceful, tranquil ②[ESTAR] (a) (libre de preocupacion) ⟨conciencia⟩ clear; ⟨persona⟩: **ahora que trabaja estoy más ∼** I feel better now that he's found a job; **¡tranquilo!** relax!; **tú, ∼, de eso me encargo yo** there's no need for you to worry, I'll take care of that; **lo hice para quedarme ∼** I did it for my own peace of mind; **déjalo ∼** leave him alone (b) (sin inmutarse): **su hermano en el hospital y él tan ∼** his brother's in hospital and he doesn't seem at all bothered; **...y se quedó tan tranquila** ...and she didn't bat an eyelash (AmE) *o* (BrE) eyelid

tranquilo² *adv* (Méx fam): **te cuesta ∼ unas 2,000 libras** it costs 2,000 pounds easily (colloq)

tranquiza *f* (Méx fam) hiding (colloq)

transa *adj/mf* (Méx fam) ▶ TRANZA

transacción *f* (Com, Fin) transaction, deal

transandino¹ -na *adj* trans-Andean

transandino² *m* trans-Andean railroad *o* railway

transar [A1] *vi* (AmL) (a) (hacer concesiones) ▶ TRANSIGIR A (b) (llegar a un acuerdo) to reach an agreement *o* a compromise; **∼ EN algo** to settle FOR sth

transatlántico¹ -ca *adj* transatlantic

transatlántico² *m* ocean liner

transbordador *m* ferry

transbordar [A1] *vt* ⟨mercancías/equipajes⟩ to transfer ■ *vi* ⟨pasajeros⟩ to change

transbordo *m* (a) (de viajeros) change; **hacer ∼** to change (b) (de equipaje, mercancías) transfer

transcribir [I34] *vt* to transcribe

transcurrir [I1] *vi* (a) ⟨tiempo/años⟩ to pass, go by (b) ⟨acontecimiento/acto⟩ to take place

transcurso *m* course; **en el ∼ del año** during the course of the year; **con el ∼ del tiempo** as time goes/went by

transeúnte *mf* (peatón) passer-by; (no residente) non-resident

transexual *adj/mf* transsexual

transferencia *f* transfer; **∼ bancaria** credit *o* bank transfer

transferir [I11] *vt* to transfer

transformación *f* (a) (cambio) transformation, change (b) (en rugby) conversion (c) (Ling) transformation

transformador *m* transformer

transformar [A1] *vt* (a) (convertir) to convert; **∼ algo EN algo** to convert sth INTO sth (b) (cambiar radicalmente) ⟨persona/situación/país⟩ to transform, change *o* alter ... radically (c) (en rugby) to convert ■ **transformarse** *v pron* (a) (convertirse) **∼se EN algo** to turn INTO sth (b) (cambiar radicalmente) ⟨persona/país⟩ to change completely, be transformed

transfusión *f* transfusion; **le hicieron una ∼ de sangre** they gave him a blood transfusion

transgénico¹ -ca *adj* genetically modified

transgénico² *m* genetically modified organism (*o* product *etc*)

transgredir [I1] *vt* (frml) to transgress (frml)

transgresión *f* (frml) transgression (frml)

transgresor -sora *m,f* transgressor

transición *f* transition; **∼ DE algo A algo** transition FROM sth TO sth

transigente *adj* accommodating

transigir [I7] *vi* (a) (hacer concesiones) to compromise, give way; **∼ EN algo** to compromise ON sth (b) (tolerar) **∼ CON algo** to tolerate sth, put up WITH sth

transistor *m* transistor

transitar [A1] *vi* «*vehículo*» to travel; «*peatón*» to walk

transitivo -va *adj* transitive

tránsito *m* **1** (tráfico) traffic; ~ **rodado** vehicular traffic; **una calle de mucho** ~ a very busy road; **un accidente de** ~ (AmL) a road accident; **infracción de** ~ (AmL) traffic violation (AmE), motoring offense (BrE) **2** (paso) movement; **el** ~ **de turistas en los meses de verano** the movement of tourists during the summer months; **pasajeros en** ~ passengers in transit

transitorio -ria *adj* **(a)** ‹*medida*› provisional; ‹*situación*› temporary; ‹*período*› transitional **(b)** (efímero) transitory, fleeting

transmisión *f* **(a)** (acción) transmission **(b)** (Rad, TV) (señal) transmission; (programa) broadcast; **una** ~ **en directo/en diferido** a live/ prerecorded broadcast; ~ **de pensamiento** thought transference

transmisor *m* transmitter

transmitir [I1] *vt* **1** (Rad, TV) ‹*señal*› to transmit; ‹*programa*› to broadcast **2 (a)** ‹*sonido/movimiento*› to transmit **(b)** ‹*enfermedad/ lengua/costumbres*› to transmit, pass on; ‹*conocimientos*› to pass on **(c)** ‹*saludos/ felicidades*› to pass on
■ ~ *vi* (Rad, TV) to transmit

transparentarse [A1] *v pron* **(a)** «*blusa/ falda*»: **una blusa que se transparenta** a see-through blouse; **con ese vestido se le transparenta la enagua** her petticoat shows through that dress **(b)** «*intenciones*» to be evident, be apparent

transparente *adj* **(a)** ‹*cristal/agua*› transparent, clear; ‹*aire*› clear **(b)** ‹*tela/papel*› transparent; ‹*blusa*› see-through **(c)** ‹*persona/ carácter*› transparent; ‹*intenciones*› clear, plain

transpirar [A1] *vi* (Fisiol) to perspire, sweat; (Bot) to transpire

transportador *m* (Mec) conveyor

transportar [A1] *vt* **(a)** ‹*personas/mercancías*› to transport; ~ **algo por aire** to ship sth by air **(b)** ‹*energía/sonido*› to transmit

transporte *m* **1** (de pasajeros, mercancías) transportation (esp AmE), transport (esp BrE); ~ **aéreo** airfreight; ~ **público** public transportation (AmE), public transport (BrE) **2** (medio, vehículo) means of transport **3** (gastos de viaje) traveling expenses

transportista *mf* haulage contractor

transversal *adj* ‹*eje/línea*› transverse; **una calle** ~ **al Paseo de Recoletos** a street which crosses the Paseo de Recoletos; **un corte** ~ a cross section
■ *f* (Mat) transversal

tranvía *m* **(a)** (vehículo urbano) streetcar (AmE), tram (BrE) **(b)** (Esp) (Ferr) local train

tranza *adj* (Méx fam) crooked
■ *mf* (Méx fam) (persona) con artist (colloq), shark (colloq)
■ *f* (Méx fam) (engaño, fraude) scam (colloq)

tranzar [A4] *vt* (Méx fam) ‹*persona*› to con (colloq)

trapear [A1] *vt* (AmL) to mop

trapecio *m* **(a)** (Mat) trapezoid (AmE), trapezium (BrE) **(b)** (Espec) trapeze

trapecista *mf* trapeze artist

trapero -ra *m,f* **1** (ropavejero) junkman (AmE), rag and bone man (BrE) **2 trapero** *m* (AmL) (para el suelo) floorcloth

trapo *m* (para limpiar) cloth; **pásale un** ~ **a la mesa** wipe the table; ~ **de cocina** dishtowel (AmE), tea towel (BrE); ~ **de sacudir** dust cloth (AmE), duster (BrE)

tráquea *f* windpipe, trachea

traquetear [A1] *vi* «*tren/carreta*» (hacer ruido) to clatter; (moverse) to jolt

traqueteo *m* (de tren, carreta — movimiento) jolting; (— ruido) clatter, clattering

tras *prep* **1 (a)** (frml) (después de) after; ~ **interrogarlo lo pusieron en libertad** after questioning him they released him **(b)** (indicando repetición) after; **día** ~ **día** day after day **2 (a)** (detrás de) behind; **la puerta se cerró** ~ **él** the door closed behind him; **la policía anda** ~ **él** the police are after him **(b)** (más allá de) beyond

trascendental *adj* **(a)** (importante) ‹*noticia/ ocasión*› momentous; (de gran alcance) ‹*decisión/ cambio/efecto*› far-reaching **(b)** (Fil) transcendental

trascendente *adj* **(a)** (importante) ‹*hecho/ suceso*› significant, important **(b)** (Fil) transcendent

trascender [E8] *vi* (ir más allá) ~ **DE algo** to transcend sth (frml), to go beyond sth
■ ~ *vt* to go beyond, transcend (frml)

trasero¹ -ra *adj* ‹*puerta/habitación/asiento*› back (*before n*); ‹*rueda/pata/asiento*› rear (*before n*), back (*before n*); ‹*motor*› rear-mounted

trasero² *m* (fam) (de persona) bottom, backside (colloq); (de animal) hindquarters (*pl*)

trasladar [A1] *vt* **1** (cambiar de sitio) ‹*objeto/ oficina/tienda*› to move; ‹*preso/enfermo*› to move, transfer; ‹*información*› to transfer; **los heridos fueron trasladados al hospital** the injured were taken to hospital **2** (cambiar de destino) ‹*empleado/ funcionario*› to transfer
■ **trasladarse** *v pron* (mudarse) to move

traslado *m* (de prisioneros) transferal; (de oficina) removal; (de empleados) transfer; (de objeto): **el** ~ **del cuadro se llevó a cabo ayer** the picture was moved yesterday; **gastos de** ~ relocation expenses

traslúcido -da *adj* translucent

trasluz *m*: **al** ~ against the light

trasmano: **a trasmano** (*loc adv*) out of the way; **vive muy a** ~ she lives in a very out-of-the-way place

trasnochar [A1] *vi* (no acostarse) to be up all night; (acostarse de madrugada) to stay up late
■ **trasnocharse** *v pron* (Col, Per, Ven) ▶ TRASNOCHAR

traspasar [A1] *vt* **1 (a)** «*bala/espada*» to pierce, go through; «*líquido*» to go through, soak through **(b)** (sobrepasar) to go beyond **2** ‹*bar/farmacia*› (vender) to sell; (arrendar) to let, lease **3** ‹*poderes/fondos/negocio*› to transfer **4** (Dep) ‹*jugador*› to transfer, trade (AmE)

traspaso *m* **1 (a)** (de bar, farmacia — venta) sale; (— arrendamiento) leasing, letting **(b)** (suma) premium **2** (de poderes, fondos, negocio) transfer **3** (Dep) **(a)** (de jugador) transfer, trade (AmE) **(b)** (suma) transfer fee

traspié m (tropezón) stumble; **dar un ~** to stumble

trasplantar [A1] vt (Bot, Med) to transplant

trasplante m (Bot, Med) transplant

trasquilar [A1] vt **(a)** ⟨ovejas⟩ to shear, clip **(b)** (fam) ⟨pelo⟩ to hack … about (colloq); ⟨persona⟩ to scalp (colloq)

trastada f **(a)** (fam) (mala pasada) dirty trick; **hacerle una ~ a algn** to play a dirty trick on sb **(b)** (travesura) prank

traste m **1** (Mús) fret **2** (fam) (trasero) backside (colloq) **3** (AmC, Méx) (utensilio) utensil; **lavar los ~s** to do the dishes o (BrE) the washing-up

trastero m junk room, lumber room (AmE)

trastienda f back room (of a shop)

trasto m (fam) (cosa inservible) piece of junk (colloq); **el cuarto de los ~s** the junk room

trastornado -da adj ⟨persona/mente⟩ disturbed; **su muerte lo dejó ~** he was deeply disturbed o traumatized by his death

trastornar [A1] vt **1** (Psic) to disturb; **la muerte de su hijo la trastornó** her son's death left her deeply disturbed; **esa chica lo ha trastornado** (fam) he's lost his head over that girl (colloq) **2** (alterar la normalidad) to upset, disrupt
■ **trastornarse** v pron (Psic) to become disturbed

trastorno m **1** (Med, Psic) disorder **2** (alteración de la normalidad) disruption; **los ~s provocados por la huelga** the disruption caused by the strike; **me ocasionó muchos ~s** it caused me a great deal of inconvenience

trastrocar [A9] vt to alter, change; **~ algo EN algo** to transform o change sth INTO sth

trasvasar [A1] vt **(a)** ⟨vino/aceite⟩ to decant **(b)** (Inf) to download

tratado m **1** (Der, Pol) treaty; **~ de paz** peace treaty **2** (libro) treatise

tratamiento m **1 (a)** (en general) treatment; **estoy en ~ médico** I am undergoing medical treatment; **no me quejo del ~ que recibí** I can't complain about the treatment I received **(b)** (Inf) (de información, datos) processing; **~ de textos** word processing **2** (título de cortesía) form of address

tratar [A1] vi **1** (intentar) to try; **traten de llegar temprano** try to arrive early; **~é de que no vuelva a suceder** I'll try to make sure it doesn't happen again
2 «obra/libro/película» **~ DE algo** to be ABOUT sth; **~ SOBRE algo** to deal WITH sth; **la conferencia ~á sobre medicina alternativa** the lecture will deal with alternative medicine
3 (tener contacto, relaciones) **~ CON algn** to deal WITH sb; **en mi trabajo trato con gente de todo tipo** in my job I deal with all kinds of people
■ **~** vt **1** ⟨persona/animal/instrumento⟩ to treat; **me tratan muy bien** they treat me very well **2** (frecuentar): **lo trataba cuando era joven** I saw quite a lot of him when I was young **3** ⟨tema/asunto⟩ to discuss, to deal with **4 (a)** (Med) to treat **(b)** ⟨sustancia/metal⟩ to treat
■ **tratarse** v pron **1 ~se CON algn** (ser amigo de) to be friendly WITH sb; (alternar) to socialize o mix WITH sb; **no nos tratamos mucho** (recíp) we don't have much to do with each other

2 (+ compl) (recípr): **se tratan sin ningún respeto** they show no respect for each other **3** (Med) to have o undergo treatment **4 tratarse de** (en 3ª pers) **(a)** (ser acerca de) to be about; **¿de qué se trata?** what's it about? **(b)** (ser cuestión de) to be a question of; **se trata de participar, no de ganar** it's a question of taking part, not of winning; **solo porque se trata de ti** just because it's you

trato m **1 (a)** (acuerdo) deal; **cerrar un ~** to finalize a deal; **¡~ hecho!** it's a deal! **(b) tratos** mpl (negociaciones): **estamos en ~s con otra compañía** we are talking to o negotiating with another company **2 (a)** (relación): **no tiene ~ con los vecinos** he doesn't have much to do with his neighbors; **tengo poco ~ con ella** I don't really have much contact with her o much to do with her **(b)** (manera de tratar) treatment; **le dan un ~ preferente** they give him preferential treatment

trauma m trauma

traumatizado -da adj traumatized

traumatizar [A4] vt to traumatize
■ **traumatizarse** v pron (fam) to be traumatized

través (a) a través de (loc prep) (de lado a lado) across; (por medio de) through; **pusieron barricadas a ~ de la calle** they erected barricades across the street; **se enteró a ~ de un amigo** she heard about it through a friend **(b) al** or (Méx) **de través** (loc adv) diagonally

travesaño m **(a)** (Const) crossbeam **(b)** (Dep) crossbar

travesía f **1** (viaje) crossing **2** (Esp) (callejuela) alleyway, side street

travesti, travestí m transvestite

travesura f prank; **hacer ~s** to play pranks

travieso -sa adj naughty, mischievous

trayecto m **(a)** (viaje) journey; **charlamos todo el ~** we chatted the whole journey **(b)** (ruta) route; **¿qué ~ hace este autobús?** which route does this bus take? **(c)** (trayectoria) trajectory, path

trayectoria f **(a)** (de proyectil, pelota) trajectory, path **(b)** (de persona, institución): **una brillante ~ profesional** a brilliant career; **una larga ~ democrática** a long democratic tradition

trayendo ▶ TRAER

trazar [A4] vt **1** ⟨línea⟩ to trace, draw; ⟨plano⟩ to draw; **~on la ruta a seguir** they traced out the route to be followed; **~ el contorno de algo** to outline sth **(b)** (Arquit) ⟨puente/edificio⟩ to design **2** ⟨plan/proyecto/estrategia⟩ to draw up, devise

trazo m stroke

trébol m **1** (Bot) clover **2** (Jueg) **(a)** (carta) club **(b) tréboles** mpl (palo) clubs (pl)

trece adj inv/m/pron thirteen; para ejemplos ver CINCO; **mantenerse** or **seguir en sus ~** to stand one's ground

trecho m **(a)** (tramo) stretch **(b)** (distancia) distance; **aún nos queda un buen ~** we still have a good distance o a fair way to go

tregua f **(a)** (Mil) truce; **acordar una ~** to agree to a truce **(b)** (interrupción): **sin ~** relentlessly

treinta adj inv/m/pron thirty; para ejemplos ver CINCO, CINCUENTA

tremendo -da adj **1 (a)** (muy grande, extraordinario) ⟨diferencia/cambio⟩ tremendous, enormous; ⟨*velocidad*/*éxito*⟩ tremendous; ⟨*chichón*⟩ huge; **hace un frío** ∼ it's incredibly cold! (colloq); **me dio (una) tremenda patada** he kicked me really hard **(b)** (terrible) ⟨*ruido*/*dolor*/*situación*⟩ terrible; **la película tiene unas escenas tremendas** (AmL) the film has some horrific scenes 2 (fam) ⟨*persona*⟩ terrible

trémulo -la *adj* (liter) ⟨*manos*⟩ trembling; ⟨*voz*⟩ tremulous; ⟨*llama*/*luz*⟩ flickering; **trémula de gozo** (liter) trembling with pleasure

tren *m* 1 (Ferr) train; **tomar** *or* (esp Esp) **coger el** ∼ to take *o* catch the train; **ir en** ∼ to go by train; **cambiar de** ∼ to change trains; ∼ **correo** *or* **postal** mail train; ∼ **de alta velocidad** high-speed train; ∼ **de cercanías** local *o* suburban train; ∼ **directo** through train; ∼ **expreso** *or* **rápido** express train 2 (fam) ⟨*ritmo*⟩ rate; **a este** ∼ at this rate (colloq); ∼ **de vida** lifestyle

trenazo *m* (Méx) train crash

trenca *f* (Esp) duffle *o* duffel coat

trenza *f* (de cintas, fibras) plait; (de pelo) braid (AmE), plait (BrE)

trepador -dora *m,f* 1 (Col, CS, Ven) social climber 2 **trepadora** *f* (Bot) climber

trepar [A1] *vi* to climb; ∼ **a un árbol** to climb (up) a tree

tres *adj inv*/*m*/*pron* three; ∼ **en raya** tic-tac-toe (AmE), noughts and crosses (BrE); *para ejemplos ver* CINCO

trescientos -tas *adj*/*pron* three hundred; *para ejemplos ver* QUINIENTOS

tresillo *m* (Esp) (sofá) three-seater sofa; (juego de muebles) suite

treta *f* **(a)** (ardid) trick, ruse **(b)** (en esgrima) feint

trial *m* motocross

triangular *adj* triangular

triángulo *m* 1 (Mat) triangle; ∼ **rectángulo** right-angled triangle 2 **(a)** (en relaciones amorosas) (love) triangle **(b)** (Mús) triangle **(c)** (Auto) *tb* ∼ **reflectante** advance-warning triangle

tribu *f* tribe

tribuna *f* **(a)** (para orador) platform, rostrum **(b)** (para autoridades) platform; (para espectadores) grandstand, stand; **la** ∼ **de la prensa** the press box **(c)** (de iglesia) gallery

tribunal *m* 1 (Der) **(a)** (lugar) court; (jueces) judges (*pl*); ∼ **militar** court martial, military court; ∼ **supremo** ≈ supreme court (*in US*), ≈ high court (*in UK*); ∼ **(tutelar) de menores** juvenile court **(b) tribunales** *mpl* (justicia): **acudir a los** ∼**es** to go to court 2 (*in examen*) examining board; (en concurso) panel of judges

tributar [A1] *vt* **(a)** (Fisco) to pay **(b)** (rendir, ofrecer): ∼ **un homenaje a algn** to pay tribute to sb

tributo *m* **(a)** (Fisco) tax **(b)** (ofrenda, homenaje) tribute; **rendirle** ∼ **a algn**/**algo** to pay tribute to sb/sth

triciclo *m* tricycle

tricotar [A1] *vt* (Esp) to knit

tridimensional *adj* three-dimensional

trifulca *f* (fam) rumpus, commotion

trigal *m* wheat field

trigo *m* wheat

trigueño -ña *adj* ⟨*pelo*⟩ light brown; ⟨*persona*⟩ dark; **una niña de tez trigueña** an olive-skinned girl

trillar [A1] *vt* to thresh

trillizo -za *m,f* triplet

trilogía *f* trilogy

trimestral *adj* ⟨*publicación*/*pago*⟩ quarterly; **examen** ∼ end-of-semester examination (AmE), end-of-term examination (BrE)

trimestre *m* **(a)** quarter, three-month period; **pago por** ∼**s** I pay quarterly **(b)** (Educ) term, ≈ semester (*in US*)

trinar [A1] *vi* «*pájaro*» to sing

trinchar [A1] *vt* to carve

trinchera *f* **(a)** (Mil) trench **(b)** (Indum) trench coat

trineo *m* **(a)** (Dep, Jueg) sled (AmE), sledge (BrE) **(b)** (tirado por perros, caballos) sleigh

trinidad *f* trinity; **La (Santísima) T**∼ (Relig) the Trinity

trino *m* trill

trío *m* trio

tripa *f* 1 **(a)** *tb* **tripas** *fpl* (intestino) intestine, gut; (vísceras) (fam) innards (*pl*) (colloq); **se me revuelven las** ∼**s de solo verlo** just looking at it turns my stomach **(b)** (material) gut 2 (Esp fam) (barriga) belly (colloq)

triple *adj* triple

■ *m* 1 (Mat): **el precio aumentó al** ∼ the price tripled *o* trebled; **tardó el** ∼ it took him three times as long; **el** ∼ **de tres es nueve** three times three equals nine 2 (Elec) three-way adapter *o* adaptor

triplicado: **por triplicado** (*loc adv*) in triplicate

triplicar [A2] *vt* ⟨*capacidad*/*precio*/*ventas*⟩ to treble; ⟨*longitud*/*cifra*⟩ to triple

■ **triplicarse** *v pron* to treble, triple

trípode *m* tripod

tripulación *f* crew

tripulante *mf* crew member; **los** ∼**s** the crew

tripular [A1] *vt* to crew, man

triquiñuela *f* (fam) trick, dodge (colloq)

trisílabo -ba *adj* trisyllabic

triste *adj* 1 **(a)** [ESTAR] ⟨*persona*⟩ sad; **esa música me pone** ∼ that music makes me sad **(b)** ⟨*expresión*/*mirada*⟩ sad, sorrowful **(c)** [SER] (que causa tristeza) ⟨*historia*/*película*/*noticia*⟩ sad; ⟨*paisaje*/*color*⟩ dismal, gloomy; ⟨*lugar*/*ambiente*⟩ gloomy 2 (*delante del n*) (miserable, insignificante) miserable; **por cuatro** ∼**s pesetas** for a few miserable pesetas; **es la** ∼ **realidad** it's the sad truth

tristeza *f* (de mirada, persona) sadness, sorrow; (de lugar, ambiente) gloominess

triturador *m*: ∼ **de basura** garbage disposal unit (AmE), waste disposal unit (BrE); ∼ **de ajos** garlic press

trituradora *f* crushing machine, crusher

triturar [A1] *vt* ⟨*almendras*/*ajo*⟩ to crush; ⟨*minerales*⟩ to grind, crush

triunfador -dora *adj* ⟨*ejército*⟩ triumphant; ⟨*equipo*⟩ winning (*before n*), triumphant

■ *m,f* winner

triunfal *adj* ⟨*marcha*/*arco*⟩ triumphal; ⟨*gesto*/*sonrisa*/*entrada*⟩ triumphant

triunfalismo *m* triumphalism

triunfar [A1] *vi* **(a)** (ganar) ~ SOBRE algo/algn to triumph OVER sth/sb; **triunfó en el concurso** she won the competition **(b)** (tener éxito) to succeed, be successful **(c)** «*justicia/verdad/razón*» (prevalecer) to prevail, win out (AmE) *o* (BrE) through

triunfo *m* **1** **(a)** (victoria) victory; **el ~ del equipo irlandés** the Irish team's victory **(b)** (logro) triumph; **uno de los ~s de la ciencia** one of the triumphs of science **(c)** (éxito) success **2** (en naipes) trump; **palo del ~** trumps (*pl*)

trivial *adj* trivial

trivialidad *f* **(a)** (cualidad) triviality **(b)** (dicho) trivial *o* trite remark; (cosa) triviality

trivializar [A4] *vt* «*asunto*» to trivialize; «*éxito*» to play down

trizarse [A4] *v pron* (Chi) (rajarse) «*anteojos/vaso*» to crack; «*diente*» to chip

trizas *fpl*: **hacer ~ algo** «*tela/carta*» to tear sth to shreds; **el jarrón se cayó y se hizo ~** the vase fell and smashed (to bits *o* smithereens); **tengo los nervios hechos ~** my nerves are in shreds *o* tatters

trofeo *m* (premio) trophy

troglodita *mf* **(a)** (cavernícola) troglodyte **(b)** (fam) (bruto) lout

trolebús *m* trolleybus

tromba *f* (terrestre) whirlwind, tornado; (marina) waterspout; **~ de agua** downpour

trombón *m* **1** (instrumento) trombone **2** **trombón** *mf* (músico) trombonist

trombonista *mf* trombonist

trombosis *f* thrombosis

trompa *f* **1** (de elefante) trunk; (de insecto) proboscis **2** (boca) (AmL fam) lips (*pl*), mouth **3** (instrumento) horn **4** (Esp fam) (borrachera): **coger una ~** to get plastered (colloq) **5** **trompa** *mf* (músico) horn-player

trompada *f* (AmS fam) (puñetazo) punch; **darle** *or* **pegarle una ~ a algn** to punch sb

trompazo *m* (fam): **me di un ~ con la puerta** I walked (*o* ran *etc*) smack into the door (colloq)

trompear [A1] *vt* (AmL fam) to thump (colloq), to punch

trompeta *f* **1** (instrumento) trumpet **2** **trompeta** *mf* (persona) trumpet player; (Mil) trumpeter

trompetista *mf* trumpet player

trompicón *m*: **iba dando trompicones** he was staggering; **a trompicones** in fits and starts

trompo *m* **(a)** (Jueg) (spinning) top **(b)** (Auto) spin

trona *f* (Esp) high chair

tronar [A10] *v impers* to thunder
■ **~** *vi* **1** «*cañones/voz*» to thunder **2** (Méx fam) **(a)** (en relación) to split up (colloq) **(b)** (fracasar) to flop (colloq); (en examen) to fail
■ **~** *vt* **1** (AmC, Méx fam) (fusilar) to shoot **2** (Méx fam) «*examen/alumno*» to fail, flunk (AmE colloq)

tronchar [A1] *vt* «*tallo/rama*» to snap
■ **troncharse** *v pron* «*tallo/rama*» to break *o* snap off; **~se de (la) risa** (Esp fam) to die laughing (colloq)

tronco *m* **1** (Bot) trunk; (leño) log **2** (en genealogía) stock **3** (Anat) trunk, torso

tronera *f* (en billar) pocket

trono *m* throne; **subir al ~** to come to the throne

tropa *f* **(a)** (soldados rasos): **la ~** the troops (*pl*) **(b)** **tropas** *fpl* (ejército, soldados) troops

tropel *m* (de personas) mob; **entraron al estadio en ~** they poured into the stadium

tropezar [A6] *vi* **(a)** (al caminar, correr) to stumble, trip; **~ CON algo** «*con piedra/escalón*» to trip OVER sth; «*con árbol/muro*» to walk (*o* run *etc*) INTO sth **(b)** (encontrarse) **~ CON algo** «*con dificultad/problema*» to come up AGAINST sth; **~ CON algn** to run *o* bump INTO sb (colloq)
■ **tropezarse** *v pron* (encontrarse) **~se CON algn** to run *o* bump INTO sb (colloq)

tropezón *m* **(a)** (acción de tropezar) stumble; **dio un ~ y cayó** he stumbled and fell; **a tropezones** (fam) in fits and starts **(b)** (equivocación) mistake, slip

tropical *adj* tropical

trópico *m* tropic

tropiece, tropieces, etc ▶ TROPEZAR

tropieza, tropiezas, etc ▶ TROPEZAR

tropiezo *m* (contratiempo) setback, hitch; (equivocación) mistake, slip

trotar [A1] *vi* **(a)** «*caballo/jinete*» to trot **(b)** (fam) (ir de un lado a otro) to rush around **(c)** (CS, Méx) (como ejercicio) to jog

trote *m* **1** (Equ) trot; **al ~** at a trot **2** (fam) (ajetreo): **¡qué ~ he tenido hoy!** it's been so hectic today (colloq); **ya no estoy para esos ~s** I'm not up to that sort of thing any more

trovador *m* troubadour, minstrel

trozar [A4] *vt* (AmL) to cut ... into pieces, cut up

trozo *m* **(a)** (de pan, pastel) piece, bit, slice; (de madera, papel, tela) piece, bit; (de vidrio, cerámica) piece, fragment; **cortar la zanahoria en trocitos** dice the carrot **(b)** (Lit, Mús) passage

trucar [A2] *vt* **(a)** «*dados/juego/elecciones*» to fix, rig **(b)** «*fotografía*» to touch up

trucha *f* (Coc, Zool) trout

truco *m* trick; **el ~ está en...** the trick *o* secret is...; **pillarle el ~ a algo** to get the hang of sth

trueno *m* **(a)** (Meteo) thunderclap, clap of thunder; **~s** thunder **(b)** (de cañones) thunder

trueque *m* (cambio) barter

trufa *f* truffle

truncar [A2] *vt* **(a)** «*frase/discurso/texto*» to cut short **(b)** «*vida*» to cut short; «*planes*» to frustrate, thwart; «*ilusiones*» to shatter

tu *adj* (delante del *n*) your; **~s amigos** your friends

tú *pron pers* [*familiar form of address*] **1** (como sujeto, en comparaciones, con preposición) you; **¿quién**

lo va a hacer? — tú who's going to do it? — you are; **llegó después que** ~ he arrived after you (did); **entre** ~ **y yo** between you and me; **tratar de** ~ **a algn** to address sb using the familiar TÚ form ② (uno) you; **te dan varias opciones y** ~ **eliges una** you're given several options and you choose one

tuba f tuba

tubérculo m (Bot) tuber

tuberculosis f tuberculosis

tuberculoso -sa m,f tuberculosis sufferer (o patient etc)

tubería f (cañería) pipe; (conjunto de tubos) piping, pipes (pl)

tubo m ① (a) (cilindro hueco) tube; ~ **de escape** exhaust (pipe) (b) (del órgano) pipe (c) (Chi, Méx) (para el pelo) roller, curler ② (RPl) (del teléfono) receiver

tuco m (Per, RPl) (Coc) tomato sauce

tuerca f nut

tuerce, tuerces, etc ▶ TORCER

tuerto -ta adj one-eyed; **es** ~ (sin un ojo) he only has one eye; (ciego de un ojo) he's blind in one eye
■ m,f: person blind in one eye or with only one eye

tuerza, tuerzas, etc ▶ TORCER

tuétano m marrow

tufo m (fam) (olor — a sucio, podrido) stink (colloq); (— a cerrado): **aquí dentro hay un** ~ **horrible** it smells really stuffy in here

tugurio m (vivienda) hovel; (bar) dive

tul m tulle

tulipa f lampshade

tulipán m tulip

tullido -da adj crippled
■ m,f cripple

tumba f (excavada) grave; (construida) tomb

tumbar [A1] vt (a) (hacer caer) to knock down; **lo tumbó en el primer asalto** he knocked him down in the first round; **un olor que te tumbaba** a smell that knocked you backward(s) (b) (AmL) ⟨árbol⟩ to fell, cut down; ⟨muro/casa⟩ to demolish, knock down
■ **tumbarse** v pron to lie down

tumbo m ① (vaivén): **salió del bar dando** ~**s** he staggered out of the bar; **la carreta iba dando** ~**s por el camino** the cart jolted along the path ② (Bol) (fruta) passion fruit

tumbona f (Esp) sun lounger, deck chair

tumor m tumor*

tumulto m (multitud) crowd; (alboroto) commotion, tumult

tumultuoso -sa adj tumultuous

tuna f ① (Bot, Coc) (planta, fruto) prickly pear ② (Mús) tuna (musical group made up of university students)

tundra f tundra

túnel m tunnel; ~ **de lavado** car wash

túnica f (Hist) tunic; (Relig) robe

tuntún m (fam): **al** ~ ⟨elegir⟩ at random; **contestó al** ~ he just said the first thing that came into his head

tupé m ① (fam) (descaro) nerve ② (Esp) (peluquín) toupee; (mechón de pelo) forelock

tupido¹ -da adj ⟨follaje/vegetación⟩ dense; ⟨tela⟩ closely-woven; ⟨cejas⟩ bushy; ⟨niebla⟩ thick

tupido² adv (Méx) intensely

turbante m turban

turbar [A1] vt ① (liter o period) ⟨orden/silencio⟩ to disturb ② (liter o period) (a) (aturdir, confundir): **sus insistentes miradas la** ~**on** the way he kept looking at her embarrassed and confused her; **su presencia lo turbó** her presence made him uncomfortable
■ **turbarse** v pron (liter o period) (a) (aturdirse, confundirse): **la besó en la mejilla y se turbó** he kissed her on the cheek and she was covered with confusion (liter); **se turbó ante tantos elogios** such praise confused and embarrassed him

turbina f turbine

turbio -bia adj (a) ⟨agua⟩ cloudy; ⟨río⟩ muddy (b) ⟨visión/ojos⟩ blurred, misty (c) ⟨asunto/negocio⟩ shady, murky

turbo adj inv turbocharged
■ m (turbocompresor) turbocharger; (automóvil) turbo

turbulencia f turbulence

turbulento -ta adj turbulent

turco¹ -ca adj (Geog) Turkish
■ m,f (a) (Geog) (persona) Turk (b) (AmL) (árabe) term used (often pejoratively) to refer to someone of Middle Eastern origin

turco² m (idioma) Turkish

turismo m (Com, Ocio) tourism; **los ingresos del** ~ income from tourism o from the tourist industry; **dependen del** ~ **alemán** they rely on German tourists; **oficina de** ~ tourist office; **hacer** ~ to travel (around)

turista adj tourist (before n); **clase** ~ tourist o economy class
■ mf tourist

turistear [A1] vi (Andes, Méx) (en país) to tour around; (en ciudad) to do some sightseeing

turístico -ca adj ⟨información/folleto⟩ tourist (before n); ⟨viaje⟩ sightseeing (before n); ⟨empresa⟩ travel (before n); ⟨atracción/actividad/lugar⟩ tourist (before n)

turnarse [A1] v pron to take turns

turnio -nia adj (Chi fam) ⟨persona⟩ cross-eyed; ⟨ojos⟩ squint

turno m (a) (horario de trabajo): **hacer el** ~ **de noche** to work the night shift; **estar de** ~ to be on duty (b) (personas) shift (c) (en un orden): **cuando te toque el** ~ when your turn comes; **cuidémoslo por** ~**s** let's take turns looking after him; **pedir** ~ (Esp) to ask who is last in the line (AmE) o (BrE) queue

turquesa f (Min) turquoise
■ m/adj inv turquoise

Turquía f Turkey

turrón m: type of candy traditionally eaten at Christmas

tute m: card game in which the object is to win all the kings or queens

tutear [A1] vt: to address sb using the familiar TÚ form
■ **tutearse** v pron: to address each other using the familiar TÚ form

tutela f (a) (Der) guardianship, tutelage (b) (protección) protection

tuteo m: use of the familiar TÚ form

tutor -tora *m,f* **1** (Educ) (encargado de curso) course tutor, class teacher; (en la universidad) tutor **2** (Der) guardian

tutoría *f* **1** (Educ) tutorship **2** (Der) guardianship, tutelage

tutú *m* (Indum) tutu

tuve, tuviera, etc ▶ TENER

tuyo -ya *adj* yours; **esto es ~** this is yours; **¿es amigo ~?** is he a friend of yours?; **fue idea tuya** it was your idea

■ *pron*: **el ~, la tuya etc** yours; **la música no es lo ~** music isn't your strong point *o* your forte; **los ~s** (tu familia) your family and friends

twist /twis(t)/ *m* twist

U u

U, u *f* (*pl* **úes**) (*read as* /u/) *the letter* U, u

u *conj* [*used instead of* o *before* o- *or* HO-] or; **siete u ocho** seven or eight

ubicación *f* **(a)** (esp AmL) (situación, posición) location **(b)** (AmL) (localización): **se hizo difícil la ~ del avión** locating the airplane was very difficult

ubicar [A2] *vt* (AmL) **(a)** (colocar, situar): **me ~on a su lado** they placed me next to him; **~on las sillas para la reunión** they arranged the chairs for the meeting **(b)** (localizar) ⟨persona/lugar⟩ to find, locate **(c)** (identificar): **la ubico solo de nombre** I only know her by name; **lo ubiqué por el color** I recognized it by the color; **me suena el nombre, pero no lo ubico** the name rings a bell, but I can't quite place him

■ **ubicarse** *v pron* **1** (AmL) **(a)** (colocarse, situarse): **se ubicó en la primera fila** he sat in the front row **(b)** (en empleo) to get oneself a good job **(c)** (orientarse) to find one's way around; **¿te ubicas?** have you got your bearings? **2** (esp AmL) (estar situado) to be, be situated *o* located

ud. = **usted**

uds. = **ustedes**

UE *f* (= **Unión Europea**) EU

uf *interj* (expresando — cansancio, sofocación) whew! (colloq); (— repugnancia) yuck (colloq)

ufano -na *adj* **(a)** (satisfecho, orgulloso) proud **(b)** (engreído) self-satisfied, smug

ujier *m* uniformed doorman; (en tribunales) usher

úlcera *f* ulcer

ulpo *m* (Chi) *cold drink made with roasted flour and sugar*

ultimar [A1] *vt* **1** ⟨preparativos⟩ to complete; ⟨detalles⟩ to finalize **2** (AmL frml) (matar) to kill, murder

ultimátum *m* (*pl* **~** *or* **-tums**) ultimatum

último -ma *adj* (delante del n) **1** (en el tiempo) last; **a última hora** at the last minute *o* moment; **su ~ libro** his latest book; **en los ~s tiempos** recently; **¿cuándo fue la última vez que lo usaste?** when did you last use it? **2 (a)** (en una serie) last; **estar en ~ lugar** to be last; **por última vez** for the last time; **como ~ recurso** as a last resort; **última voluntad** last wishes (*pl*) **(b)** (como adv) (CS) ⟨salir/terminar⟩ last **3** (en el espacio): **el ~ piso** the top floor; **la última fila** the back row **4** (definitivo): **es mi última oferta** it's my final offer

■ *m,f* last one; **era el ~ que me quedaba** it was my last one; **es el ~ de la clase** he's bottom of the class; **a ~s de** (Esp) toward(s) the end of; **por ~** finally, lastly

ultra *mf* (Esp) right-wing extremist

ultraderecha *f*: **la ~** the far *o* extreme right

ultraderechista *adj* extreme right-wing

■ *mf* right-wing extremist

ultrafino -na *adj* ultrafine, superfine

ultrajar [A1] *vt* (fml) ⟨persona⟩ to outrage, offend ... deeply; ⟨bandera⟩ to insult; ⟨honor⟩ to offend against

ultraje *m* outrage, insult

ultramarinos *mpl* (comestibles) groceries; **tienda de ~** grocery store (AmE), grocer's shop (BrE)

ultrasónico -ca *adj* ultrasonic

ultravioleta *adj* (*pl* **~** *or* **-tas**) ultraviolet

umbilical *adj* umbilical

umbral *m* **(a)** (de puerta) threshold **(b)** (borde, frontera) *tb* **~es** threshold; **en los ~es de la muerte** at death's door; **en los ~es de la civilización** at the dawn of civilization

un (*pl* **unos**), **una** (*pl* **unas**) *art* [*the masculine article* UN *is also used before feminine nouns which begin with stressed* A *or* HA *e.g.* UN ARMA PODEROSA, UN HAMBRE FEROZ] **1** (*sing*) a; (delante de sonido vocálico) an; (*pl*) some; **una nueva droga** a new drug; **un asunto importante** an important matter; **hay unas cartas para ti** there are some letters for you; **tiene unos ojos preciosos** he has lovely eyes **2** (con valor ponderativo): **tú haces unas preguntas ...** you do ask some questions! **3** (con nombres propios) a; **es un Miró** it's a Miró **4** (*pl*) (expresando aproximación) about; **tiene unos 30 años** she's about 30

una *pron* (*ver tb* UN, UNO): **a la ~, a las dos, ¡a las tres!** ready, steady, go!

unánime *adj* unanimous

unanimidad *f* unanimity; **por ~** unanimously

undécimo -ma *adj/pron* eleventh; *para ejemplos ver* QUINTO

UNED /u'neð/ *f* (en Esp) = **Universidad Nacional de Educación a Distancia**

UNESCO /u'nesko/ *f*: **la ~** UNESCO

ungüento *m* ointment

únicamente *adv* only

UNICEF /uni'sef, uni'θef/ *f*: **la ~** UNICEF

único -ca *adj* [1] (a) (solo) only; **soy hijo ~** I'm an only child; **¡es lo ~ que faltaba!** that's all we needed! (b) ⟨*mercado/moneda*⟩ single; **tarifa única** flat rate; **talla única** one size [2] (extraordinario) extraordinary
∎ *m,f*: **el ~/las únicas que tengo** the only one/ones I have

unicornio *m* unicorn

unidad *f* [1] (Com, Mat) unit; **costo por ~** unit cost; **~ de peso** unit of weight; **~ de cuidados intensivos** *or* (Esp) **de vigilancia** *or* (Arg, Méx) **terapia intensiva** *or* (Chi) **de tratamiento intensivo** intensive care unit [2] (unión, armonía) unity [3] (Inf): **~ de disco** (Inf) disk drive

unido -da *adj* (a) ⟨*familia/amigos*⟩ close (b) (sobre un tema) united

unificación *f* unification

unificar [A2] *vt* ⟨*país*⟩ to unify; ⟨*precios*⟩ to standardize

uniforme *adj* ⟨*velocidad/temperatura*⟩ constant, uniform; ⟨*superficie*⟩ even, uniform; ⟨*terreno*⟩ even, level; ⟨*paisaje/estilo*⟩ uniform; ⟨*criterios/precios*⟩ standard, uniform
∎ *m* uniform

unilateral *adj* ⟨*desarme/decisión*⟩ unilateral; ⟨*criterio/opinión*⟩ one-sided

unión *f* [1] (a) (acción): **la ~ de las dos empresas** the merger of the two companies; **la ~ de estos factores** the combination of these factors (b) (agrupación) association (c) **la U~ Americana** (Méx) (Period) the United States [2] (relación) union, relationship; (matrimonio) union, marriage [3] (juntura) joint

Unión Europea *f*: **la ~ ~** the European Union

Unión Soviética *f* (Hist): **la ~ ~** the Soviet Union

unir [I1] *vt* [1] (a) ⟨*cables*⟩ to join; (con cola, pegamento) to stick … together; ⟨*esfuerzos*⟩ to combine (b) «*sentimientos/intereses*» to unite (c) ⟨*características/cualidades/estilos*⟩ to combine; **~ algo A algo** to combine sth WITH sth [2] (comunicar) ⟨*lugares*⟩ to link [3] (fusionar) ⟨*empresas/organizaciones*⟩ to merge
∎ **unirse** *v pron* [1] (aliarse) «*personas/colectividades*» to join together; **se unió a nuestra causa** he joined our cause [2] (juntarse) «*caminos*» to converge, meet [3] (fusionarse) «*empresas/organizaciones*» to merge

universal *adj* universal

universalidad *f* universality

universidad *f* university; **~ a distancia** *or* (Méx) **abierta** open university; **~ laboral** ≈ technical college (*school with emphasis on vocational training*)

universitario -ria *adj* university (*before n*)
∎ *m,f* (estudiante) undergraduate, (university) student; (licenciado) (university) graduate

universo *m* universe

uno¹, una *adj* [UNO *becomes* UN *before a masculine noun or noun phrase*] one; **no había ni un asiento libre** there wasn't one empty seat *o* a single empty seat; **treinta y un pasajeros** thirty-one passengers; **el capítulo uno** chapter one

uno *pron* [1] (numeral) one; **uno a** *or* **por uno** one by one; **es la una** it's one o'clock; **más de uno/una** (fam) quite a few
[2] (personal) (*sing*) one; (*pl*) some; **uno es mío, el otro no** one's mine, the other isn't; **¿te gustaron? — unos sí, otros no** did you like them? — some I did, others I didn't; **se ayudan los unos a los otros** they help one another
[3] (fam) (alguien) (*m*) some guy (colloq); (*f*) some woman (colloq); **les pregunté a unos que estaban allí** I asked some people who were there
[4] (uso impersonal) one; **uno no sabe qué decir** you don't *o* (frml) one doesn't know what to say; **nunca le dicen nada a uno** they don't tell you anything

uno² *m* (number) one; **para ejemplos ver** CINCO

untar [A1] *vt* (a) (cubrir): **~ las galletas con miel** spread honey on the cookies; **se unta el molde con mantequilla** grease the cake tin (with butter) (b) (empapar) **~ algo EN algo** to dip sth IN sth
∎ **untarse** *v pron* (a) (ensuciarse): **se untó las manos de pintura** he got paint all over his hands (b) (ponerse): **se untó los hombros con bronceador** she rubbed suntan lotion on her shoulders

uña *f* (a) (Anat) (de la mano) nail, fingernail; (del pie) nail, toenail; **arreglarse** *or* **hacerse las ~s** (*refl*) to do one's nails; (*caus*) to have one's nails done (b) (de oso, gato) claw; (de caballo, oveja) hoof

uralita® *f* asbestos

uranio *m* uranium

Urano *m* Uranus

urbanidad *f* courtesy, urbanity (frml)

urbanismo *m* city (AmE) *o* (BrE) town planning

urbanización *f* (acción) urbanization, development; (núcleo residencial) (Esp) (housing) development

urbanizado -da *adj* built-up; **esta zona está muy urbanizada** this area is heavily developed

urbanizar [A4] *vt* ⟨*zona/terreno*⟩ to develop, urbanize; **una zona sin ~** an undeveloped area

urbano -na *adj* ⟨*núcleo/transporte*⟩ urban, city (*before n*); ⟨*población*⟩ urban

urdir [I1] *vt* (a) (en telar) to warp; ⟨*puntos*⟩ to cast on (b) ⟨*plan*⟩ to devise, hatch

urgencia *f* (a) (cualidad) urgency; **con ~** urgently (b) (Med) emergency; **☉ urgencias** accident and emergency; **lo operaron de ~** he had an emergency operation

urgente *adj* ⟨*asunto*⟩ pressing, urgent; ⟨*mensaje*⟩ urgent; ⟨*caso/enfermo*⟩ emergency (*before n*); ⟨*carta*⟩ express (*before n*)

urgido -da *adj* (AmL): **estaban ~s de dinero** they were in urgent need of money; **estamos ~s de tiempo** we are pressed for time

urgir [I7] *vi* (en *3ª pers*): **urge la finalización del proyecto** the project must be finished as soon as possible; **me urge estar allí el martes** I absolutely must be there on/by Tuesday; **le urge el préstamo** he needs the loan urgently

urinario *m* urinal

urna *f* [1] (vasija) urn; (de exposición) display case; (para votar) ballot box; **~ cineraria** funerary urn [2] (Chi, Ven) (ataúd) coffin, wooden box (euph)

urólogo -ga *m,f* urologist

urraca *f* magpie

URSS /urs/ *f* (Hist) (= **Unión de Repúblicas Socialistas Soviéticas**) USSR

urubú *m* black vulture

Uruguay *m* **(a)** (país) *tb* el ~ Uruguay **(b)** (río): el (río) ~ the Uruguay River

uruguayismo *m* Uruguayan word (*o* phrase *etc*)

uruguayo -ya *adj/m,f* Uruguayan

USA /'usa/ (fam) USA

usado -da *adj* **(a)** [SER] (de segunda mano) secondhand **(b)** [ESTAR] (gastado, viejo) worn

usar [A1] *vt* **(a)** (utilizar) to use; ¿qué champú usas? what shampoo do you use?; ~ algo/a algn DE *or* COMO algo to use sth/sb AS sth **(b)** (llevar) ⟨alhajas/ropa/perfume⟩ to wear; **estos zapatos están sin ~** these shoes are unworn, these shoes have never been worn

■ **usarse** *v pron* (en *3ᵃ pers*) (esp AmL) (estar de moda) «*color/ropa*» to be in fashion, to be popular; **ya no se usa hacer fiestas de compromiso** people don't tend to have engagement parties any more

usina *f* (AmS) (fábrica) large factory; (industria) industry

uso *m* **(a)** (de producto, medicamento, máquina) use; **instrucciones para su ~** instructions for use; **hacer ~ de algo** to use sth **(b)** (de facultad, derecho): **en pleno ~ de sus facultades mentales** in full possession of his mental faculties; **hacer ~ de un derecho** to exercise a right; **desde que tengo ~ de razón** ever since I can remember; **hacer ~ de la palabra** (fml) to speak **(c)** (de prenda): **ropa de ~ diario** everyday clothes; **los zapatos ceden con el ~** shoes give with wear

usted *pron pers* [*Polite form of address but also used in some areas, eg Colombia and Chile, instead of the familiar* TÚ *form*] **1** (como sujeto, en comparaciones, con preposición) you; ¿quién lo va a hacer? — usted who's going to do it? — you (are); **tratar a algn de ~** to address sb using the USTED form; **muchas gracias — a ~** thank you very much — thank you; **son de ~** they're yours **2** (uso impersonal) you, one (fml); **le dicen eso y ~ no sabe qué contestar** when they say that you just don't know what to say in reply

ustedes *pron pers pl* [*Polite plural form of address also used in Latin American countries as the familiar plural form*] you; ¿quién lo va a hacer? — ustedes who's going to do it? — you (are); ~ mismos lo dijeron you said so yourselves; **son de ~** they're yours

usual *adj* usual, normal

usuario -ria *m,f* user

usurero -ra *m,f* usurer

usurpador -dora *m,f* usurper

usurpar [A1] *vt* (fml) ⟨propiedad/título⟩ to misappropriate; ⟨territorio⟩ to seize; ⟨poder⟩ to usurp

utensilio *m* (instrumento) utensil; (herramienta) tool; ~s de cocina kitchen *o* cooking utensils; ~s de laboratorio laboratory apparatus; ~s de pesca fishing tackle

útero *m* womb, uterus (tech)

útil *adj* useful

utilería *f* (esp AmL) (Cin, Teatr) props (*pl*)

utilero -ra *m,f* (esp AmL) (Cin, Teatr) props manager

útiles *mpl* **(a)** (herramientas, instrumentos) tools (*pl*), implements (*pl*); ~ de pesca fishing tackle; ~ de jardinería gardening tools **(b)** (AmL) (artículos escolares) *tb* ~ escolares pencils, pens, rulers, etc *for school*

utilidad *f* **(a)** (de aparato) usefulness; **un coche me sería de mucha ~** a car would be of great use to me **(b) utilidades** *fpl* (AmL) (ganancia, beneficio) profits (*pl*)

utilitario *m* small (economical) car

utilización *f* use, utilization (fml)

utilizar [A4] *vt* to use, utilize (fml)

utopía *f* Utopia

utópico -ca *adj* Utopian

uva *f* grape; ~ blanca/negra white/black grape

uve *f* (Esp) *name of the letter* v; ~ doble (Esp) *name of the letter* w

uy *interj* (expresando — asombro) ooh! (colloq); (— malestar, disgusto) oh!; (— emoción súbita) ah!, oh!; (— dolor) ow!, ouch!

Vv

V, v *f* (*read as* /be/, /be 'korta/, /be 'tʃika/, /be pe'keɲa/ *or* (Esp) /'uβe/) *the letter* V, v

va, vas, etc ▶ IR

vaca *f* **(a)** (Zool) cow; **estar como una ~** (fam) to be very fat; **hacer una ~** (AmL fam) to make a collection **(b)** (Coc): (**carne de**) ~ beef; **filete de ~** fillet steak

vacacionar [A1] *vi* (Méx) to spend one's vacation(s) *o* holidays

vacaciones *fpl* vacation(s) (esp AmE), holiday(s) (esp BrE); ~ de verano summer vacation *o* holidays; **irse de ~** to go away on vacation *o* on holiday; **estamos de ~** we're on vacation o holiday; **tomarse unas** ~ to take a vacation o holiday

vacacionista *mf* (Méx) vacationer (AmE), holidaymaker (BrE)

vacante *adj* ⟨*puesto/plaza*⟩ vacant; ⟨*piso/asiento*⟩ empty, unoccupied
■ *f* vacancy; **cubrir una** ~ to fill a vacancy

vaciar [A17] *vt* ☐ **(a)** ⟨*vaso/botella*⟩ to empty; ⟨*radiador*⟩ to drain; ⟨*bolsillo/cajón*⟩ to empty; ⟨*armario/habitación*⟩ to clean out **(b)** ⟨*contenido*⟩ to empty (out) ☐ (ahuecar) to hollow out
■ **vaciarse** *v pron* to empty

vacilación *f* hesitation, vacillation (frml); **tras un momento de** ~ after a moment's hesitation

vacilante *adj* **(a)** (oscilante) unsteady, shaky; **con paso** ~ unsteadily **(b)** (dubitativo) ⟨*expresión*⟩ doubtful; ⟨*voz*⟩ hesitant **(c)** ⟨*luz*⟩ flickering

vacilar [A1] *vi* ☐ **(a)** (dudar) to hesitate; **sin** ~ without hesitating; **no vaciló en aceptar** he did not hesitate to accept, he accepted without hesitation **(b)** «*fe/determinación*» to waver **(c)** «*luz*» to flicker ☐ (oscilar) «*persona*» to stagger, totter ☐ (AmL exc CS fam) (divertirse) to have fun

vacile *m* (fam) (tomadura de pelo) joke; **basta de** ~ that's enough kidding (colloq)

vacilón *m* (AmL fam) **(a)** (diversión): **le encanta el** ~ he loves having a good time; **la fiesta fue un** ~ the party was great fun **(b)** (tomadura de pelo) joke; **es puro** ~ it's just a joke

vacío¹ -cía *adj* **(a)** ⟨*botella/caja*⟩ empty; ⟨*calle/ciudad*⟩ empty, deserted; ⟨*casa*⟩ empty, unoccupied; ⟨*palabras/retórica*⟩ empty; **con el estómago** ~ on an empty stomach **(b)** (frívolo) ⟨*persona*⟩ shallow; ⟨*vida/frase*⟩ empty, meaningless

vacío² *m* **(a)** (Fís) vacuum; **envasado al** ~ vacuum-packed **(b)** (espacio vacío) space; **mirar al** ~ to gaze into space **(c)** (falta, hueco) gap; **dejó un** ~ **en su vida** she left a gap o a void in his life; **una sensación de** ~ a feeling of emptiness

vacuna *f* vaccine; **me tengo que poner la** ~ I have to have my vaccination

vacunación *f* vaccination

vacunar [A1] *vt* to vaccinate; ~ **a algn CONTRA algo** to vaccinate sb AGAINST sth
■ **vacunarse** *v pron* to get vaccinated; ~**se CONTRA algo** to get vaccinated AGAINST sth

vacuno -na *adj* bovine; **ganado** ~ cattle (*pl*)

vado *m* (de río) ford; Ⓢ **vado permanente** no parking

vagabundear [A1] *vi* to drift (around)

vagabundo -da *adj* ⟨*perro*⟩ stray; **niños** ~**s** street urchins
■ *m,f* tramp, vagrant

vagar [A3] *vi* to wander, roam

vagina *f* vagina

vago -ga *adj* ☐ (fam) ⟨*persona*⟩ lazy, idle ☐ ⟨*recuerdo/idea*⟩ vague, hazy; ⟨*contorno/forma*⟩ vague, indistinct; ⟨*explicación/parecido*⟩ vague
■ *m,f* (fam) layabout, slacker (colloq); **deja ya de hacer el** ~ stop lazing around (colloq)

vagón *m* (de pasajeros) coach, car (AmE), carriage (BrE); ~ **restaurante** dining o (BrE) restaurant car

vagoneta *f* (Méx) (para pasajeros) van, minibus

vaguedad *f* **(a)** (de palabras, ideas) vagueness

(b) (expresión imprecisa) vague remark; **¡déjate de** ~**es y ve al grano!** stop being so vague o stop beating about the bush and get to the point

vaho *m* **(a)** (aliento) breath **(b)** (vapor) steam, vapor*; **(c)** (inhalación): **hacer** ~**s** to inhale

vaina *f* ☐ (de espada) scabbard; (de navaja) sheath ☐ (Bot) (de habas, etc) pod ☐ (Col, Per, Ven fam) **(a)** (problema, contrariedad): **¡qué** ~**!** what a drag o pain (colloq); **la** ~ **es que no sé cómo the thing** o problem is that I don't know how; **estoy metida en una** ~ I'm in a spot of trouble (colloq) **(b)** (cosa, asunto) thing, thingamajig (colloq) **(c)** (comportamiento sospechoso): **tenían una** ~ they were up to something funny; **¿qué** ~ **te traes tú?** what are you up to?

vainilla *f* (Bot, Coc) vanilla

vais ▸ IR

vaivén *m* (de columpio, péndulo) swinging; (de tren) rocking; (de barco) rolling; (de mecedora) rocking; (de gente) toing and froing

vajilla *f* (en general) dishes (*pl*); (juego) dinner service o set

valdré, valdría, etc ▸ VALER

vale *m* **(a)** (para adquirir algo) voucher; (por devolución) credit note o slip; **un** ~ **de descuento** a money-off coupon **(b)** (pagaré) IOU
■ *interj ▸* VALER IV 4

valenciana *f* (Méx) cuff (AmE), turn-up (BrE)

valenciano¹ -na *adj/m,f* Valencian

valenciano² *m* (Ling) Valencian

valentía *f* bravery, courage; **con** ~ courageously

valer [E28] *vt* ☐ (tener un valor de) to be worth; (costar) to cost; **¿cuánto valen?** how much are they?, what do they cost?
☐ (+ *me/te/le etc*) (ganar): **esta obra le valió un premio** this play earned o won her a prize
■ ~ *vi* ☐ (+ *compl*) (tener cierto valor) to be worth; (costar) to cost; **vale más, pero es mejor** it costs more but it's better; **cada cupón vale por un regalo** each voucher is worth a gift
☐ (tener valor no material): **ha demostrado que vale** he has shown his worth; **como profesor no vale (nada)** as a teacher he's useless; **vales tanto como él** you're as good as he is; *hacerse* ~ to assert oneself; **hacer** ~ **algo** ⟨*derecho*⟩ to assert o enforce sth
☐ (servir): **esta no vale, es muy ancha** this one's no good, it's too wide; **no le valió de nada protestar** protesting got him nowhere; **no** ~ **PARA algo** to be useless o no good AT sth
☐ **vale** (Esp fam) **(a)** (expresando acuerdo) OK; **¿a las ocho? — ¡vale!** at eight o'clock? — sure o fine o OK?; **¿vale?** OK?, all right? **(b)** (basta): **¿** ~ **así?** is that OK o enough?
☐ **más vale: más vale así** it's better that way; **más te vale ir** you'd better go
☐ **(a)** (ser válido) «*entrada/pasaporte*» to be valid; «*jugada/partido*» to count **(b)** (estar permitido): **eso no vale, estás haciendo trampa** that's not fair, you're cheating; **no vale mirar** you're not allowed to look
☐ (Méx fam) **(a)** (no importar): **a mí eso me vale** I don't give a damn about that (colloq) **(b)** (no tener valor) to be useless o no good (colloq) **(c)** (estropearse): **mi coche ya valió** my car's had it (colloq)

 ···⫶

■ **valerse** v pron ❘1❘ (servirse) ~**se DE** algo/algn to use sth/sb

❘2❘ «anciano/enfermo»: ~**se por sí mismo** to look after oneself

❘3❘ (estar permitido, ser correcto): **no se vale golpear por debajo del cinturón** hitting below the belt is not allowed; **¡no se vale!** that's not fair!

valeroso -sa adj brave, courageous, valiant (liter)

valga, valgas, etc ▶ VALER

validar [A1] vt to validate

validez f validity

válido -da adj valid

valiente adj «persona» brave, courageous

valija f (RPl) suitcase; ~ **diplomática** diplomatic bag

valioso -sa adj «joya/consejo/experiencia» valuable; **un hombre** ~ a man of great worth

valla f (a) (cerca) fence (b) (Dep) (en atletismo) hurdle; (en fútbol) goal; ~ **publicitaria** billboard (AmE), hoarding (BrE)

valle m valley

valor m ❘1❘ (a) (Com, Fin) value; **libros por** ~ **de $150** books to the value of $150; **objetos de** ~ valuables; ~ **adquisitivo** purchasing power (b) (importancia, mérito) value; ~ **sentimental** sentimental value (c) (validez) validity; **sin la firma no tiene ningún** ~ it's not valid without the signature ❘2❘ (a) (coraje, valentía) courage; **me faltó** ~ I didn't have the courage; **armarse de** ~ to pluck up courage (b) (fam) (descaro, desvergüenza) nerve (colloq); **¡encima tiene el** ~ **de protestar!** and then she has the nerve to complain! ❘3❘ **valores** mpl (a) (principios morales) values (b) (Fin) securities, stocks, shares

valoración f (a) (de bienes, joyas) valuation; (de pérdidas, daños) assessment (b) (frml) (de suceso, trabajo) assessment, appraisal (frml)

valorar [A1] vt (a) «joya/cuadro» to value; «pérdida/daño» to assess; ~ **algo EN algo** to value/assess sth AT sth; **eso no se puede** ~ **en dinero** you cannot put a value on it (b) (frml) «trabajo/actuación» to assess (c) «amistad/lealtad» to value

valorización f (a) (tasación) ▶ VALORACIÓN A (b) (AmL) (aumento de valor) appreciation

vals m waltz; **bailar un** ~ to waltz

valuar vt [A18] (AmL) to value

válvula f valve

vamos ▶ IR

vampiresa f femme fatale, vamp (dated)

vampiro m (a) (en historias de horror) vampire; (explotador) vampire, bloodsucker (b) (Zool) vampire (bat)

van ▶ IR

vanagloriarse [A1] v pron ~ **DE** algo to boast o brag ABOUT sth

vandalismo m vandalism, hooliganism

vándalo -la m,f (gamberro) vandal, hooligan

vanguardia f (Mil) vanguard; (Art, Lit) avant-garde; **teatro de** ~ avant-garde theater; **ir** or **estar a la** ~ **(de algo)** to be in the vanguard (of sth)

vanguardista adj avant-garde

vanidad f vanity

vanidoso -sa adj (presumido) vain, conceited; (en cuanto al aspecto físico) vain

■ m,f: **es un** ~ he's so vain o conceited

vano -na adj (a) (ineficaz) «discusión/intento» vain, futile; «esfuerzo» futile; **en** ~ in vain (b) (falto de realidad) vain; **ilusiones vanas** wishful thinking (c) «palabra/promesa» empty

vapor m (a) (Fís, Quím) vapor*, steam (b) (Coc): **al** ~ steamed (c) (Náut) steamer, steamship

vaquero¹ -ra adj (a) «falda/cazadora» denim; **un pantalón** ~ a pair of jeans o denims (b) «estilo» cowboy (before n)

■ m,f (Agr) (m) cowboy, cowhand; (f) cowgirl, cowhand

vaquero² m (Indum) tb ~**s: unos** ~**s** a pair of jeans o denims

vaquilla f heifer

vara f ❘1❘ (palo) stick, pole ❘2❘ (Per fam) (influencia) connections (pl) (colloq)

varado -da adj ❘1❘ (a) (Náut) «barco» aground (b) (AmL) (detenido): **miles de turistas se quedaron** ~**s** thousands of tourists were left stranded; **me quedé** ~ **con el trabajo** I got stuck with my work ❘2❘ (a) (Col, Méx fam) (sin dinero) broke (colloq) (b) (Andes) (sin empleo) out of work

variable adj «carácter/humor» changeable; **tiempo** ~ unsettled o changeable weather

variación f variation

variado -da adj (a) «programa/vida/trabajo» varied (b) (diverso): **ropa de colores** ~**s** clothes in a variety of colors

variante f ❘1❘ (de palabra) variant ❘2❘ (carretera) turnoff

variar [A17] vi «precio/temperatura» to vary; **las temperaturas varían entre 20°C y 25°C** temperatures range o vary between 20°C and 25°C; **para** ~ (iró) (just) for a change (iro)

■ ~ vt ❘1❘ (hacer variado) «menú» to vary; «producción» to vary, diversify ❘2❘ (cambiar) «decoración/rumbo» to change, alter

varicela f chicken pox

várices, (Esp) **varices** fpl ▶ VARIZ

varicoso -sa adj varicose

variedad f (a) (en general) variety (b) **variedades** fpl (Espec) vaudeville (AmE), variety (BrE)

varilla f (en general) rod; (de abanico, paraguas) rib; (de jaula) bar; (de rueda de bicicleta) spoke; (para medir el aceite) dipstick

vario -ria adj ❘1❘ ~**s/varias** (más de dos) several; **hace** ~**s años** several years ago ❘2❘ (variado, diverso) various; **asuntos** ~**s** various matters

varios -rias pron several; **lo compraron entre** ~**s** several of them got together to buy it

varita f wand; ~ **mágica** magic wand

variz (pl **várices** or (Esp) **varices**) f varicose vein

varón adj «heredero/descendiente» male; **un hijo** ~ a son

■ m (niño) boy; (hombre) man, male

varonil adj (a) (viril) manly, masculine; **voz** ~ masculine voice (b) «mujer» (hombruna) mannish, masculine

vas ▶ IR

vasallo m vassal

vasco¹ -ca adj/m,f Basque

vasco² *m* (idioma) Basque

vasectomía *f* vasectomy

vaselina *f* Vaseline®, petroleum jelly

vasija *f* (Arqueol) vessel (frml)

vaso *m* **1** (recipiente, contenido) glass; **un ∼ de vino** (con vino) a glass of wine; (para vino) a wine glass; **∼ de papel** paper cup **2** (Anat) vessel; **∼ sanguíneo** blood vessel

vasto -ta *adj* (*gen delante del n*) ⟨*mar/llanura*⟩ vast, immense; ⟨*conocimientos/experiencia*⟩ vast, enormous

váter *m* (Esp fam) (inodoro) toilet, lavatory; (cuarto) bathroom (esp AmE), toilet (BrE), loo (BrE colloq)

Vaticano *m*: **el ∼** the Vatican

vatio *m* watt

vaya, vayas, etc ▶ IR

Vd. = **usted**

ve *f* (AmL) *tb* **∼ corta** *or* **chica** *or* **pequeña** *name of the letter* v

ve ▶ IR, VER²

vea, veas, etc ▶ VER²

vecindad *f* **1** (lugar, barrio) neighborhood*, area; (vecinos) residents (*pl*) **2** (Méx) (edificio) tenement house

vecindario ▶ VECINDAD 1

vecino -na *adj* (a) (contiguo) neighboring*; **los países ∼s** the neighboring countries; **∼ A algo** bordering ON sth, adjoining sth (b) (cercano) neighboring*, nearby

■ *m,f* (a) (persona que vive cerca) neighbor*; **mi ∼ de al lado** my next-door neighbor (b) (habitante — de población, municipio) inhabitant; (— de barrio, edificio) resident

veda *f* (en caza y pesca) closed (AmE) *o* (BrE) close season; **la perdiz está en ∼** it is the closed *o* close season for partridge

vedar [A1] *vt* (a) ⟨*caza/pesca*⟩ to prohibit, ban (*during the closed season*) (b) (prohibir) to ban

vedette /beˈðet/ *f* cabaret star

vegetación *f* (a) (Bot) vegetation (b) (Med) **vegetaciones** *fpl* adenoids (*pl*)

vegetal *adj* ⟨*vida*⟩ plant (*before n*); ⟨*aceite/reino*⟩ vegetable (*before n*)

■ *m* plant, vegetable

vegetar [A1] *vi* (a) (Bot) to grow (b) (fam) «*persona*» to vegetate (colloq & pej)

vegetariano -na *adj/m,f* vegetarian

vehemente *adj* vehement

vehículo *m* vehicle

veía, veíamos, etc ▶ VER

veinte *adj inv/m/pron* twenty; *para ejemplos ver* CINCO, CINCUENTA

veintitantos -tas *adj/pron* twenty-odd

veintiuno¹ -na *adj/pron* [VEINTIÚN *is used before masculine nouns and before feminine nouns which begin with accented* A *or* HA] twenty-one; **veintiún años** twenty-one years; *para ejemplos ver tb* CINCO

veintiuno² *m* (number) twenty-one

vejestorio *m* (a) (fam) (persona): **la profesora es un ∼** the teacher is ancient (colloq) (b) (AmL fam) (cosa) old relic (colloq), piece of old junk (colloq)

vejez *f* old age

vejiga *f* (Anat) bladder

vela *f* **1** (para alumbrar) candle **2** (vigilia): **pasé la noche en ∼** (por preocupación, dolor) I couldn't get to sleep all night; (cuidando a un enfermo) I was up all night **3** (a) (de barco) sail (b) (deporte) sailing; **hacer ∼** to go sailing

velado -da *adj* ⟨*película*⟩ fogged; ⟨*amenaza/referencia*⟩ veiled; ⟨*sonido*⟩ muffled

velador¹ *m* (a) (mesa) pedestal table (b) (AmS) (mesilla de noche) bedside table, night stand (AmE)

velador² -dora *m,f* **1** (Méx) (de fábrica) watchman, guard **2** **veladora** *f* (Méx) (vela) candle

velar [A1] *vt* **1** (a) ⟨*difunto*⟩ to hold a wake over (b) ⟨*enfermo*⟩ to watch over **2** ⟨*película*⟩ to fog, expose

■ **∼** *vi* **1** (permanecer despierto) to stay up *o* awake **2** (cuidar) **∼ POR algo/algn** to watch OVER sth/sb

■ **velarse** *v pron* «*película*» to get fogged *o* exposed

velatorio *m* (a) (reunión) wake, vigil (frml) (b) (establecimiento) funeral parlor*; (sala) chapel of rest

velero *m* (a) (Náut) (grande) sailing ship; (pequeño) sailboat (AmE), sailing boat (BrE) (b) (Aviac) glider

veleta *f* **1** (para el viento) weather vane, weathercock **2** **veleta** *mf* (fam) (persona inconstante) fickle person

vello *m* **1** (pelusa) down; (en las piernas, etc) hair **2** (Bot) bloom

velo *m* veil

velocidad *f* **1** (en general) speed; **cobrar ∼** to pick up *o* gather speed; **¿a qué ∼ iba?** how fast was he going?; **disminuir la ∼** to slow down; **a toda ∼** at top speed; **la ∼ con que lo hizo** the speed with which he did it **2** (Auto, Mec) gear; **un modelo de cinco ∼es** a five-gear model

velocímetro *m* speedometer

velódromo *m* cycle track, velodrome

veloz *adj* ⟨*corredor*⟩ fast; ⟨*movimiento*⟩ swift, quick

ven ▶ VENIR, VER

vena *f* **1** (Anat) vein; **cortarse las ∼s** to slash *o* cut one's wrists **2** (Geol, Min) vein, seam **3** (de madera) grain; (de piedra) vein, stripe

venado *m* (a) (Zool) deer; **pintar ∼** (Méx fam) to play hooky (esp AmE colloq), skive off (school) (BrE colloq) (b) (Coc) venison

vencedor -dora *adj* ⟨*ejército/país*⟩ victorious; ⟨*equipo/jugador*⟩ winning (*before n*)

■ *m,f* (en guerra) victor; (en competición) winner

vencer [E2] *vt* (a) ⟨*enemigo*⟩ to defeat, vanquish (liter); ⟨*rival/competidor*⟩ to defeat, beat; **no te dejes ∼** don't give in (b) ⟨*miedo/pesimismo/obstáculo*⟩ to overcome (c) (dominar): **me venció el sueño** I was overcome by sleep

■ **∼** *vi* **1** ⟨*ejército/equipo*⟩ to win, be victorious; **¡∼emos!** we shall overcome! **2** (a) ⟨*pasaporte/garantía*⟩ to expire; **el lunes vence el plazo** Monday is the deadline (b) «*letra*» to be due for payment

■ **vencerse** *v pron* (AmL) ⟨*pasaporte/garantía*⟩ to expire; **se me venció el carnet** my card expired *o* ran out

vencido -da *adj* **1** ⟨*ejército/país*⟩ defeated, vanquished (liter); ⟨*equipo/jugador*⟩ losing (*before n*), ···⟶

V

beaten; **darse por** ~ to give up *o* in ② **(a)** ‹*visa/ pasaporte*› expired, out-of-date (*before n*); **estos antibióticos están** ~**s** (AmL) these antibiotics are past their expiration (AmE) *o* (BrE) expiry date **(b)** ‹*boleto/cheque*› out-of-date (*before n*) **(c)** ‹*letra/ intereses*› due for payment
■ *m,f*: **los** ~**s** the defeated, the vanquished (liter)

vencimiento *m* (de letra, pago) due date; (de carnet, licencia) expiration (AmE) *o* (BrE) expiry date

venda *f* bandage; ~ **elástica** elastic bandage

vendaje *m* dressing; **poner un** ~ to put on a dressing

vendar [A1] *vt* to bandage

vendaval *m* gale, strong wind

vendedor -dora *m,f* **(a)** (en mercado) stallholder, stallkeeper (AmE); (en tienda) salesclerk (AmE), shop assistant (BrE); (viajante, representante) sales representative; ~ **a domicilio** door-to-door sales agent; ~ **ambulante** peddler, hawker; ~ **de periódicos** newspaper vendor *o* seller **(b)** (Der) (propietario que vende) vendor

vender [E1] *vt* ‹*mercancías/casa*› to sell; **le vendí el reloj** I sold him the watch; **vendió la casa muy bien** she got a very good price for her house; Ⓢ **se vende** for sale; **lo venden a $500 el kilo** they sell it at $500 a kilo; **vendí el cuadro en** *or* **por $20.000** I sold the painting for $20,000; **se vende por kilo(s)/unidades** it's sold by the kilo/unit
■ ~ *vi* ‹*producto*› to sell
■ **venderse** *v pron* (dejarse sobornar) to sell out

vendimia *f* grape harvest, wine harvest

vendimiar [A1] *vt* to pick, harvest

vendré, vendría, etc ▶ VENIR

venduta *f* (Col) public sale (*of household goods*)

Venecia *f* Venice

veneno *m* **(a)** (sustancia tóxica) poison; (de culebra) venom **(b)** (malevolencia) venom

venenoso -sa *adj* ‹*sustancia/planta*› poisonous; ‹*araña/serpiente*› poisonous, venomous; ‹*palabras/mirada*› venomous

venerable *adj/m,f* venerable

venerar [A1] *vt* (adorar) to revere, worship; (Relig) to venerate

venéreo -rea *adj* venereal

venezolanismo *m* Venezuelan word (*o* phrase *etc*), Venezuelanism

venezolano -na *adj/m,f* Venezuelan

Venezuela *f* Venezuela

venga *interj* (Esp fam) **(a)** (para animar) come on **(b)** (expresando insistencia): **y** ~ **a protestar** and they just kept *o* went on (and on) complaining

vengáis, vengamos, etc ▶ VENIR

venganza *f* revenge, vengeance (liter)

vengar [A3] *vt* ‹*insulto/derrota*› to take revenge for, to avenge; ‹*persona*› to avenge
■ **vengarse** *v pron* to take revenge; ~**se DE** *or* **POR algo** to take revenge FOR sth; ~**se DE/EN algn** to take (one's) revenge ON sb

vengativo -va *adj* vindictive, vengeful (liter)

vengo ▶ VENIR

venia *f* (AmS) (inclinación de cabeza) bow

venial *adj* venial

venida *f* **(a)** (llegada) arrival **(b)** (AmL) (vuelta): **a la** *or* **de** ~ on the way back

venidero -ra *adj* future (*before n*)

venir [I31] *vi* ① **(a)** (a un lugar) to come; **vine en tren** I came by train; **¿a qué vino?** what did he come by *o* around for?; **vine dormida todo el tiempo** I slept (for) the whole journey; ~ **POR** *or* (Esp) **A algo/algn** to come FOR sb/sth, come to pick sb/sth up; **la vino a buscar su madre** her mother came to pick her up; **ven a ver esto** come and see this **(b)** (volver) to come back; **ahora vengo** I'll be back in a moment; **no vengas tarde** don't be late home *o* back **(c)** (salir): **me vino con un cuento** he came up with some excuse; **no me vengas con exigencias** don't start making demands

② **(a)** (tener lugar): **ahora viene esa escena que te conté** that scene I told you about is coming up now; **¿qué viene después de las noticias?** what's on after the news?; **ya vendrán tiempos mejores** things will get better **(b)** (indicando procedencia) ~ **DE algo** to come FROM sth; **viene de la India** it comes from India; **le viene de familia** it runs in his family; **¿a qué viene eso?** why do you say that? **(c)** (indicando presentación) to come; **viene en tres tamaños** it comes in three sizes **(d)** (estar incluido): **viene en primera página** it's on the front page; **no viene nada sobre la huelga** there's nothing about the strike

③ (convenir): **estas cajas me vendrían muy bien** these boxes would come in handy; **el jueves no me viene bien** Thursday's no good for me; **me vendría bien un descanso** I could do with a rest

④ (*como aux*): **esto viene a confirmar mis sospechas** this confirms my suspicions; **hace mucho que lo venía diciendo** I'd been saying so all along
■ **venirse** *v pron* (*enf*) **(a)** (a un lugar) to come; **se vinieron a pie** they came on foot; ~**se abajo** ‹*persona*› to go to pieces; ‹*techo*› to fall in, collapse; ‹*estante*› to collapse; ‹*ilusiones*› to go up in smoke; ‹*proyectos*› to fall through **(b)** (volver) to come back

venta *f* (Com) sale; ~ **al contado** cash sale; ~ **al por mayor/menor** wholesale/retail; ~ **a plazos** installment plan (AmE), hire purchase (BrE); ~ **por catálogo** *or* **correo** mail order; **pronto saldrá a la** ~ it will be on sale soon; **estar en** *or* **a la** ~ ‹*coche/bicicleta*› to be for sale; ‹*casa*› to be for (up) for sale

ventaja *f* **(a)** (beneficio) advantage; **tiene la** ~ **de que está cerca** it has the advantage of being near; **tienes** ~ **por tu experiencia** you have an advantage because of your experience **(b)** (en carrera): **lleva una** ~ **de diez segundos** she has a ten-second lead; **jugar con** ~ to be at an advantage

ventajero -ra *m,f* (RPI) opportunist

ventajoso -sa *adj* **(a)** ‹*negocio*› profitable; ‹*acuerdo/situación*› favorable*, advantageous **(b)** (Col) ‹*persona*› opportunistic

AmC	América Central	Arg	Argentina	Cu	Cuba	Per	Perú
AmL	América Latina	Bol	Bolivia	Ec	Ecuador	RPI	Río de la Plata
AmS	América del Sur	Chi	Chile	Esp	España	Ur	Uruguay
Andes	Región andina	CS	Cono Sur	Méx	México	Ven	Venezuela

ventana f **1** (Arquit, Const, Inf) window **2** (de la nariz) nostril

ventanilla f **(a)** (de coche, tren) window **(b)** (en oficinas) window; (en cines, teatros) box office; **horario de ~** opening hours **(c)** (Inf) window

ventilación f **(a)** (posibilidad de ventilarse) ventilation **(b)** (acción de ventilar) airing

ventilador m (aparato) fan; (abertura) ventilator, air vent

ventilar [A1] vt ‹habitación› to air, ventilate; ‹ropa/colchón› to air

■ **ventilarse** v pron **1** «habitación/ropa» to air **2** (fam) (tomar el aire) to get a breath of fresh air, get some air

ventisca f snowstorm; (con más viento) blizzard

ventolera f gust of wind

ventosa f **(a)** (de goma, plástico) suction pad **(b)** (Zool) sucker

ventosidad f wind, flatulence

ventoso -sa adj windy

ventrículo m ventricle

ventrílocuo -cua m,f ventriloquist

ventura f **1** (liter) (suerte) fortune; **tiene la ~ de ...** he has the good fortune to ...; **echarle la buena ~ a algn** to tell sb's fortune **2** (en locs) **a la ventura: viven a la ~** they take each day as it comes; **salieron a la ~** they set out with no fixed plan

Venus m (Astron) Venus
■ f (Art, Mit) Venus

veo ▶ VER 2

ver¹ m **1** (aspecto): **ser de buen ~** to be good-looking o attractive **2** (opinión): **a mi/su ~** in my/his view

ver² [E29] vt **1 (a)** (percibir con la vista) to see; **¿ves algo?** can you see anything?; **no se ve nada aquí** you can't see a thing in here; **lo vi hablando con ella** I saw him talking to her **(b)** (mirar) ‹programa/partido› to watch; **~ (la) televisión** to watch television; **esa película ya la he visto** I've seen that movie before; **no poder (ni) ~ a algn**: **no la puede ~** he can't stand her
2 (entender, notar) to see; **¿no ves lo que está pasando?** don't o can't you see what's happening?; **se la ve preocupada** she looks worried; **hacerse ~** (RPI) to show off
3 (a) (constatar, comprobar) to see; **ve a ~ quién es** go and see who it is; **¡ya ~ás lo que pasa!** you'll see what happens; **¡ya se ~á!** we'll see **(b)** (ser testigo de) to see; **¡nunca he visto cosa igual!** I've never seen anything like it!; **¡si vieras lo mal que lo pasé!** you can't imagine how awful it was!; **¡hubieras visto cómo se asustaron!** (AmL) you should have seen the fright they got!
4 a ver (vamos) **a ~ ¿de qué se trata?** OK o all right, now, what's the problem?; **está aquí, en el periódico — ¿a ~?** it's here in the newspaper — let's see; **apriétalo a ~ qué pasa** press it and see what happens; **a ~ si escribes pronto** make sure you write soon
5 (a) (estudiar): **esto mejor que lo veas tú** you'd better have a look at this; **tengo que ~ cómo lo arreglo** I have to work out how I can fix it; **ya ~é qué hago** I'll decide what to do later **(b)** «médico» (examinar) to see; **¿la ha visto un médico?** has she been seen by a doctor yet?
6 (a) (juzgar, considerar): **yo eso no lo veo bien** I

don't think that's right; **a mi modo or manera de ~** the way I see it **(b)** (encontrar) to see; **no le veo salida a esto** I can't see any way out of this; **no le veo la gracia** I don't think it's funny
7 (visitar, entrevistarse con) ‹amigo/pariente› to see, visit; ‹médico/jefe› to see; **¡cuánto tiempo sin ~te!** I haven't seen you for ages!
8 tener ... que ver: **¿y eso qué tiene que ~?** and what does that have to do with it?; **no tengo nada que ~ con él** I have nothing to do with him; **¿qué tiene que ~ que sea sábado?** what difference does it make that it's Saturday?

■ **~** vi **1** (percibir con la vista) to see; **así no veo** I can't see like this; **no veo bien de lejos/de cerca** I'm shortsighted/longsighted
2 (constatar): **¿hay cerveza? — no sé, voy a ~** is there any beer? — I don't know, I'll have a look; **pues ~ás, todo empezó cuando ...** well you see, the whole thing began when ...
3 (pensar) to see; **ya ~é** I'll see; **estar/seguir en ~emos** (AmL fam): **todavía está en ~emos** it isn't certain yet; **seguimos en ~emos** we still don't know anything

■ **verse** v pron **1** (refl) (percibirse, imaginarse) to see oneself
2 (hallarse) (+ compl) to find oneself; **me vi en un aprieto** I found myself in a tight spot; **me vi obligado a despedirlo** I had no choice but to dismiss him
3 (esp AmL) (parecer): **se ve bien con esa falda** she looks good in that skirt; **no se ve bien con ese peinado** that hairdo doesn't suit her
4 (recípr) **(a)** (encontrarse) to meet; **nos vemos a las siete** I'll meet o see you at seven; **¡nos vemos!** (esp AmL) see you! **(b)** (visitarse, encontrarse) to see each other; **nos vemos a menudo** we see each other often; **~se CON algn** to see sb

veraneante m,f vacationer (AmE), holidaymaker (BrE)

veranear [A1] vi: **solía ~ en un pueblo** she used to spend her summer vacation (AmE) o (BrE) holidays in a small town

veraneo m: **fuimos de ~ al campo** we spent our summer vacation (AmE) o (BrE) holidays in the country; **lugar de ~** summer resort

veraniego -ga adj summer (before n)

verano m summer; (en la zona tropical) dry season; **ropa de ~** summer clothes

veras: **de veras** (loc adv) really; **lo siento de ~** I really am sorry; **¡no lo dirás de ~!** you can't be serious!

verbal adj verbal

verbena f **1** (Bot) verbena **2** (fiesta popular) festival; (baile) open-air dance

verbo m (Ling) verb

verdad f **(a)** (en general) truth; **dime la ~** tell me the truth; **es la pura ~** it's the gospel truth; **a decir ~ ...** to tell you the truth ...; **la ~, no lo sé** I don't honestly know; **¡no es ~!** that's not true!; **eso es una gran ~** that is so true! **(b)** de verdad (loc adv) really; (loc adj) real; **¡de ~ que me gusta!** I really do like it!; **una pistola de ~** a real gun **(c)** (buscando corroboración): **es guapa ¿~?** she's beautiful, isn't she?; **¿~ que tú me entiendes?** you understand me, don't you?

verdadero -ra adj **1** (a) ‹premisa/historia› true; ‹caso/nombre› real **(b)** ‹pieles/joyas› real ⋯▶

2 *(delante del n)* (uso enfático) real; **se portó como un ~ imbécil** he behaved like a real *o* (colloq) proper idiot

verde *adj* **1** *‹color/ojos/vestido›* green; **zapatos ~ oliva** olive-green shoes; **ojos ~ azulado** bluish *o* (BrE) bluey green eyes **2** *‹fruta›* green, unripe; *‹leña›* green; **estar ~** (fam) (no tener experiencia) to be green (colloq); (en una asignatura): **está ~ en historia** he doesn't know much about history (colloq) **3** (Pol) Green **4** (fam) *‹chiste›* dirty, blue (colloq)
■ *m* (color) green; (Bot) greenery
■ *mf* (Pol) Green; **los ~s** the Greens

verdín *m* **(a)** (musgo) moss **(b)** (moho) mold*; (en el agua) slime; (en metal) verdigris

verdor *m* greenness

verdoso -sa *adj* greenish

verdugo *m* **1** **(a)** (en ejecuciones) executioner; (en la horca) hangman **(b)** (persona cruel) tyrant **2** (Indum) balaclava; (para el esquí) ski mask

verdulería *f* fruit and vegetable store, greengrocer's (BrE)

verdulero -ra *m,f* (persona) greengrocer

verdura *f* (Bot, Coc) vegetable; **sopa de ~(s)** vegetable soup

vereda *f* **(a)** (senda) path **(b)** (CS, Per) (acera) sidewalk (AmE), pavement (BrE) **(c)** (Col) (distrito) district

veredicto *m* (Der) verdict; (dictamen) opinion, verdict

vergonzoso -sa *adj* **1** (tímido) shy, bashful **2** *‹asunto/comportamiento›* disgraceful, shameful

vergüenza *f* **1** (turbación) embarrassment; **no lo hagas pasar ~** don't embarrass him; **me da ~ pedírselo otra vez** I'm embarrassed to ask him again; **sentí ~ ajena** I felt embarrassed for him (*o* her *etc*) **2** (sentido del decoro) (sense of) shame; **no tiene ~** he has no (sense of) shame **3** (escándalo, motivo de oprobio) disgrace; **ser una ~ para algo/algn** to be a disgrace to sth/sb; **estos precios son una ~** these prices are outrageous

verídico -ca *adj* true

verificar [A2] *vt ‹hechos›* to establish, verify; *‹resultado›* to check; *‹pagos/cuentas›* to check, audit; *‹máquina/instrumento›* to check, test

verja *f* (cerca) railings (*pl*); (puerta) wrought-iron gate; (de ventana) (wrought-iron) grille

vermut /berˈmu(t)/ *m* (*pl* **-muts**) vermouth
■ *f* (CS) early evening performance

verosímil *adj* *‹excusa/versión›* plausible; *‹argumento/historia›* realistic

verruga *f* **(a)** (Med) (en la mano, cara) wart; (en los pies) verruca **(b)** (Bot) wart

versículo *m* verse

versión *f* **(a)** (de obra, suceso) version; **~ original** movie in its original language **(b)** (traducción) translation **(c)** (modelo) model

verso *m* (Lit) (línea) line, verse; (poema) poem; (género) verse; **en ~** in verse

vértebra *f* vertebra

vertebrado¹ -da *adj* vertebrate

vertebrado² *m* vertebrate; **los ~s** the vertebrates

vertedero *m* **1** (para basura) dump; **un ~ de residuos nucleares** a dumping site for nuclear waste **2** (desagüe) outlet

verter [E31] *or* [E8] *vt* **(a)** (en un recipiente) *‹agua/vino/trigo›* to pour **(b)** (derramar) *‹líquido›* to spill; *‹lágrimas/sangre›* (liter) to shed (liter) **(c)** *‹residuos radiactivos›* to dump

vertical *adj* **1** **(a)** *‹línea/madero›* vertical; **en posición ~** in a vertical position **(b)** (en crucigramas): **el tres ~** three down **2** (Pol, Rels Labs) vertical
■ *f* (Mat, Tec) vertical line, vertical (tech) **(b)** (Dep) handstand

vértice *m* (de ángulo, figura) vertex, apex; (coronilla) crown

vertiente *f* **(a)** (de montaña, tejado) slope **(b)** (faceta, aspecto) aspect **(c)** (CS) (manantial) spring

vertiginoso -sa *adj* *‹velocidad›* dizzy, giddy, vertiginous (frml)

vértigo *m* vertigo; **tener ~** to have vertigo; **me produce ~** it makes me dizzy *o* giddy

ves ▶ VER²

vesícula *f* vesicle; **~ biliar** gallbladder

vespa® *f* Vespa®, scooter

vespertino -na *adj* evening (*before n*); **diario ~** evening newspaper

vespino® *m* moped

vestíbulo *m* (de casa particular) hall; (de edificio público) lobby; (de teatro, cine) foyer

vestido¹ -da *adj* dressed; **bien ~** well/badly dressed; **¿cómo iba ~?** what was he wearing?; **iba vestida de azul** she was wearing blue; **~ de uniforme** in uniform; **¿de qué vas a ir ~?** what are you going to go as?

vestido² *m* **(a)** (de mujer) dress; **~ de baño** (Col) swimsuit; **~ de noche** evening dress; **~ de novia** wedding dress *o* gown **(b)** (Col) (de hombre) suit

vestidor *m* (en casa) dressing room; (en club, gimnasio) (Chi, Méx) locker room (AmE), changing room (BrE)

vestier *m* (Col) (en tienda) fitting room; (en club, gimnasio) locker room (AmE), changing room (BrE)

vestigio *m* trace; **no quedan ~s de aquella civilización** no trace remains of that civilization; **~s históricos** historical remains

vestir [I14] *vt* **1** **(a)** *‹niño/muñeca›* to dress **(b)** (proporcionar ropa a) to clothe (frml) **(c)** (confeccionar ropa a) *‹‹modisto›› to dress **2** (liter *o* period) (llevar puesto) to wear
■ ~ *vi* **1** *‹‹persona›› to dress; **~ bien** to dress well; **~ DE algo** *‹de uniforme/azul›* to wear sth; **~ de etiqueta** to wear formal dress **2** (ser elegante): **no sabe ~** he has no dress sense; **de ~** *‹traje/zapatos›* smart
■ **vestirse** *v pron* (*refl*) **1** (ponerse ropa) to dress, get dressed; **date prisa, vístete** hurry up, get dressed **(b)** (de cierta manera): **se viste mal** he dresses badly; **se viste a la última moda** she wears the latest styles; **siempre se viste de verde** she always wears green **(c)** (disfrazarse) **~se DE algo** to dress up AS sth

vestón *m* (CS) jacket

vestuario *m* **1** (conjunto de ropa) wardrobe; (Cin, Teatr) wardrobe **2** (en club, gimnasio) locker room (AmE), changing room (BrE)

veta *f* ⟦1⟧ **(a)** (en madera) streak **(b)** (en la carne) streak **(c)** (en roca, mármol) vein ⟦2⟧ (inclinación) bent, leanings (*pl*)

vetar [A1] *vt* to veto

veteranía *f* (experiencia) experience; (antigüedad) seniority

veterano -na *adj/m,f* veteran

veterinaria *f* (ciencia) veterinary science *o* medicine; (clínica) veterinary surgery

veterinario -ria *adj* ⟨clínica⟩ veterinary (*before n*); **médico** ~ vet, veterinarian (AmE), veterinary surgeon (BrE)

■ *m,f* vet, veterinarian (AmE), veterinary surgeon (BrE)

veto *m* veto; **poner el** ~ **a algo** to veto sth

vez *f* ⟦1⟧ (ocasión) time; **una** ~/**dos veces** once/ twice; **una** ~ **por semana** once a week; **me acuerdo de una/aquella** ~ **cuando …** I remember once/that time when …; **la última** ~ **que lo vi** the last time I saw him; **mil veces** *or* **miles de veces** a thousand times, thousands of times; **algunas veces** sometimes; **¿te has arrepentido alguna** ~? have you ever regretted it?; **érase una** ~ (liter) once upon a time (liter); **por primera** ~ for the first time; **otra** ~ again; **déjalo para otra** ~ leave it for another time *o* day; **otra** ~ **será** maybe next time; **una** ~ **más** once again

⟦2⟧ (*en locs*) **a la vez** at the same time; **a veces** sometimes; **cada vez** every *o* each time; **cada** ~ **más** more and more; **lo encuentro cada** ~ **más viejo** he looks older every time I see him; **cada** ~ **menos** less and less; **de una vez** (expresando impaciencia) once for all; (simultáneamente) in one go; **de vez en cuando** from time to time, every now and then; **en vez de** instead of; **rara vez** seldom, hardly ever; **una vez** once; **una** ~ **que hayas terminado** once *o* when you have finished

⟦3⟧ (Esp) (turno en una cola): **¿quién tiene** *or* **me da la** ~? who's last?; **pedir la** ~ to ask who's last

vi ▶ VER²

vía *f* ⟦1⟧ **(a)** (ruta, camino): **la** ~ **rápida** the fast route; **una** ~ **al diálogo** a channel *o* an avenue for dialogue; **¡dejen** ~ **libre!** clear the way!; ~ **de comunicación** road (*o* rail *etc*) link; **V~ Láctea** Milky Way; ~ **marítima** sea route, seaway **(b)** (medio de transporte): **por** ~ **aérea/marítima/terrestre** by air/by sea/by land; **❺ vía aérea** airmail **(c)** (medio, procedimiento) channels (*pl*); **por la** ~ **diplomática/política** through diplomatic/political channels

⟦2⟧ **en vías de: está en** ~**s de solucionarse** it's in the process of being resolved; **países en** ~**s de desarrollo** developing countries; **una especie en** ~**s de extinción** an endangered species

⟦3⟧ (Ferr) track; **saldrá por la** ~ **dos** it will depart from track (AmE) *o* (BrE) platform two

⟦4⟧ (Anat, Med): **por** ~ **oral/venosa** orally/ intravenously; ~**s respiratorias/urinarias** respiratory/urinary tract

■ *prep* via; ~ **Miami** via Miami

viable *adj* ⟨proyecto/plan⟩ viable, feasible; ⟨bebé⟩ viable

viaducto *m* viaduct

viajante *mf* traveling* salesman/saleswoman

viajar [A1] *vi* to travel; ~ **en avión** to travel by plane; ~ **en primera clase** to travel *o* go first class

viaje *m* trip, journey; **hacer un** ~ to go on a trip *o* journey; **un** ~ **en tren** a train journey; **hizo el** ~ **en coche** he drove; **estar de** ~ to be away; **salir de** ~ to go on a trip; **en el** ~ **de vuelta** on the way back; **¡buen** ~! have a good trip!; **hicimos un** ~ **por todo Chile** we traveled all around Chile; ~ **de negocios** business trip; ~ **de novios** honeymoon; ~ **organizado** package tour; **hice varios** ~**s para llevarlas todas** I made several trips to take them all

viajero -ra *m,f* traveler*; (pasajero) passenger

vial *adj* road (*before n*)

viáticos *mpl* (esp AmL) travel allowance

víbora *f* **(a)** (Zool) viper; ~ **de cascabel** (Méx) rattlesnake **(b)** (fam & pey) (persona): **es una** ~ he has a vicious tongue

vibración *f* vibration

vibrante *adj* ⟨voz⟩ vibrant, resonant; ⟨discurso⟩ vibrant

vibrar [A1] *vi* ⟨cuerdas/cristales⟩ to vibrate

vicaría *f* vicariate

vicario -ria *m,f* (párroco) vicar

vicecampeón -peona *m,f* runner-up

vicepresidencia *f* (Gob, Pol) vice presidency; (de empresa) vice presidency (AmE), deputy chairmanship (BrE)

vicepresidente -ta *m,f*, **vicepresidente** *mf* (Gob, Pol) vice president; (de empresa) vice president (AmE), deputy chairman/chairwoman (BrE)

vice versa *adv* vice versa

vichar [A1] *vi* (RPl fam) to peep (colloq)

■ *vt* to peep at

viciado -da *adj* ⟦1⟧ ⟨atmósfera⟩ stuffy; **aquí dentro el aire está** ~ it's very stuffy in here

⟦2⟧ ⟨estilo/dicción⟩ marred

viciar [A1] *vt* ⟨persona⟩ to get … into a bad habit; ⟨estilo/lenguaje⟩ to mar

■ **viciarse** *v pron* **(a)** «persona»: ~**se CON algo** to become addicted TO sth **(b)** «estilo/lenguaje» to deteriorate

vicio *m* ⟦1⟧ (corrupción) vice; **darse al** ~ to give oneself over to vice ⟦2⟧ (hábito): **el único** ~ **que tengo** my only vice *o* bad habit; **el juego se convirtió en** ~ **para él** his gambling became an addiction; **se queja de** ~ (fam) she complains for the sake of it

vicioso -sa *adj* ⟨persona⟩ depraved, debauched

■ *m,f* dissolute person

víctima *f* victim; ~ **DE algo** victim OF sth; **fue** ~ **de una emboscada** he was the victim of an ambush; ~**s del cáncer** cancer victims

victoria *f* victory; (Dep) win; **no cantes** ~ **antes de tiempo** don't count your chickens before they're hatched

victorioso -sa *adj* victorious

vicuña *f* vicuna

vid *f* vine

vida *f* ⟦1⟧ **(a)** (Biol) life; **la** ~ **marina** marine life; **una cuestión de** ~ **o muerte** a matter of life and death; **quitarse la** ~ to take one's (own) life (frml); **salir con** ~ to escape alive **(b)** (viveza, vitalidad) life; **lleno de** ~ full of life; **le falta** ~ it's/she's/ he's not very lively

⟦2⟧ (extensión de tiempo, existencia) life; **a lo largo de su** ~ throughout his life; **toda una** ~ a lifetime; ⋯⋗

la ~ **de un coche** the life-span of a car; **un amigo de toda la** ~ a lifelong friend; *amargarle la* ~ *a algn* to make sb's life a misery; *complicarse la* ~ to make life difficult for oneself; *de por* ~ for life; *hacerle la* ~ *imposible a algn* to make sb's life impossible

3 (manera de vivir, actividades) life; **lleva una** ~ **muy ajetreada** she leads a very busy life; **¿qué es de tu** ~? what have you been up to?; **hace** *or* **vive su** ~ he lives his own life; **¡esto sí que es** ~! this is the life!; **¡(así) es la** ~! that's life, such is life; ~ **privada** private life; **su** ~ **sentimental** his love life; **una mujer de** ~ **alegre** a woman of easy virtue; **¡qué** ~ **de perros!** it's a dog's life; **hacer** ~ **social** to socialize; *estar encantado de la* ~ to be thrilled, to be over the moon (colloq)

4 (necesidades materiales): **la** ~ **está carísima** the cost of living is very high; **ganarse la** ~ to earn one's *o* a living; **tiene la** ~ **resuelta** he's set up for life

5 (como apelativo) darling; **¡mi** ~! (my) darling!

vidente *mf* (que ve) sighted person; (que adivina) clairvoyant

video, vídeo (Esp) **vídeo** *m* **(a)** (medio, sistema) video; **en** ~ on video **(b)** (cinta) videocassette, videotape, video (colloq); (grabación) video **(c)** (aparato) video (cassette recorder), VCR

videocámara *f* video camera, camcorder

videoclip *m* video

videoclub *m* (*pl* **-clubs** *or* **-clubes**) videoclub

videodisco *m* video disk

videojuego *m* video game

videoteca *f* video library

videotex *m* videotex(t), teletext

vidriado -da *adj* glazed

vidriera *f* **(a)** (puerta) glazed door; (ventana) window; (en iglesia) *tb* ~ **de colores** stained glass window **(b)** (AmL) (escaparate) shop window; **mirar** ~**s** to window-shop

vidrierista *mf* (AmL) window dresser

vidriero *m* glazier

vidrio *m* **(a)** (material) glass; **una botella de** ~ a glass bottle; **fábrica de** ~ glassworks **(b)** (esp AmL) (objeto): **limpiar los** ~**s** to clean the windows; **cambié uno de los** ~**s** I replaced one of the panes *o* windowpanes; **me corté con un** ~ I cut myself on a piece of glass; **hay** ~**s rotos en la calle** there is broken glass in the street; *pagar los* ~*s rotos* to take the responsibility *o* the blame **(c)** (de reloj) crystal, glass

vieira *f* (molusco) scallop; (concha) scallop shell

vieja *f* (Col, Méx, Ven fam) (mujer) broad (AmE sl), bird (BrE sl); *ver tb* VIEJO *m,f*

viejo -ja *adj* **1** [SER] ⟨*persona/animal*⟩ old; ⟨*coche/ropa/casa*⟩ old; **hacerse** ~ to get old **2** **(a)** [ESTAR] ⟨*persona/animal*⟩ (envejecido) old; **ya está** ~ he's got(ten) old; **¡qué vieja estoy!** I look so old! **(b)** [ESTAR] ⟨*zapatos/pantalones*⟩ (desgastado) old

3 (*delante del n*) (antiguo) ⟨*costumbre/amigo*⟩ old; **los** ~**s tiempos** the old days; **V**~ **Testamento** Old Testament

■ *m,f* **1** (*m*) old man; (*f*) old woman; **los** ~**s** old people, the elderly; **llegar a** ~ to reach old age; **se casó de** ~ he was an old man when he got married; **se murió de** ~ he died of old age; **V**~ **Pascuero** (Chi) ▶ PAPÁ NOEL; ~ **verde** *or* (Méx) ~ **rabo verde** (fam) dirty old man

2 (fam) (refiriéndose a los padres): **mi** ~/**mi vieja** my old man/lady (colloq); **tus** ~**s** your folks, your Mom and Dad

3 (AmL) (hablándole a un niño, al cónyuge etc) darling (colloq), love (colloq); (a un amigo) buddy (AmE), mate (BrE)

4 (Méx fam) (esposo) (*m*) old man (colloq); (*f*) old woman *o* lady (colloq)

Viena *f* Vienna

viendo ▶ VER²

viene, vienes, etc ▶ VENIR

vienés -nesa *adj,m,f* Viennese

viento *m* **1** (en general) wind; **correr** *or* **hacer** ~ to be windy; **un** ~ **helado** an icy wind; ~ **en contra/a favor** *or* **de cola** head/tail wind; **instrumento de** ~ wind instrument **2** (de tienda de campaña) guy (rope)

vientre *m* **(a)** (cavidad) abdomen; **el bajo** ~ the lower abdomen; **hacer de** ~ to have a bowel movement **(b)** (región exterior) stomach, belly (colloq) **(c)** (de mujer embarazada) womb, belly (colloq)

viera, vieras, etc ▶ VER²

viernes *m* (*pl* ~) Friday; **V**~ **Santo** Good Friday; *para ejemplos ver* LUNES

viese, vieses, etc ▶ VER²

viga *f* (de madera) joist, beam; (de metal) beam, girder

vigencia *f* validity; **entrar en** ~ «*ley*» to come into force *o* effect

vigente *adj* ⟨*pasaporte/contrato*⟩ valid; ⟨*legislación/precio*⟩ current (*before n*); **estar** ~ «*ley*» to be in force

vigésimo -ma *adj/pron* twentieth; ~ **primero** twenty-first; **el** ~ **aniversario** the twentieth anniversary; **la vigésima parte** a twentieth

vigía *mf* (persona) lookout

vigilancia *f* (atención, cuidado) vigilance; (por guardias, la policía) surveillance; **estar bajo** ~ to be under surveillance; **servicio de** ~ security patrol

vigilante *adj* vigilant, on the alert; **en actitud** ~ on the alert
■ *mf* (en tienda) store detective; (en banco, edificio público) security guard; ~ **jurado/nocturno** security guard/night watchman

vigilar [A1] *vt* **(a)** (cuidar, atender) to watch, keep an eye on **(b)** ⟨*preso/local*⟩ to guard, keep watch on; ⟨*frontera/zona*⟩ to guard, patrol; ⟨*examen*⟩ to proctor (AmE), to invigilate at (BrE) **(c)** (fam) (espiar) to watch
■ ~ *vi* to keep watch

AmC	Central America	Arg	Argentina
AmL	Latin America	Bol	Bolivia
AmS	South America	Chi	Chile
Andes	Andean Region	CS	Southern Cone

Cu	Cuba	Per	Peru
Ec	Ecuador	RPI	River Plate Area
Esp	Spain	Ur	Uruguay
Méx	Mexico	Ven	Venezuela

vigilia f ⓵ (vela) wakefulness; **de** ∼ awake ⓶ (Relig) (víspera) vigil; (abstinencia) abstinence; (tiempo de abstinencia) day/period of abstinence

vigor m (a) (fuerza, energía) vigor*, energy; **con** ∼ vigorously (b) **en vigor** ‹estar› in force; **entrar en** ∼ to come into effect o force

vigoroso -sa adj ‹persona/movimiento› vigorous, energetic; ‹esfuerzo› strenuous

VIH m (= **virus de inmunodeficiencia humana**) HIV

vil adj (liter) ‹acto/persona› vile, despicable

villa f ⓵ (Hist) (población) town; ∼ **miseria** (Arg) shantytown ⓶ (casa) villa

villancico m (Christmas) carol

villano -na m,f (persona ruin) rogue, scoundrel

vilo: **en vilo** (loc adv): **la levantó en** ∼ he lifted her up; **permanecen en** ∼ **esperando el resultado** they're on tenterhooks awaiting the result

vinagre m vinegar

vinagrera f (a) (para vinagre) vinegar bottle (b) **vinagreras** fpl (para aceite y vinagre) cruet set o stand

vinagreta f vinaigrette

vinatero -ra adj wine (before n)
■ m,f vintner (AmE), wine merchant (BrE)

vincha f (AmS) (elástica, rígida) hair-band; (hebilla del pelo) barrette (AmE), hair slide (BrE)

vinculación f (relación) links (pl), connections (pl); ∼ **CON** or **A algo/algn** links o connections **WITH** sth/sb

vincular [A1] vt (a) (conectar, relacionar) ∼ **algo/a algn A** or **CON algo/algn** to link sth/sb **TO** o **WITH** sth/sb; **están vinculados por lazos de amistad** they are linked by bonds o ties of friendship; **grupos estrechamente vinculados** closely linked groups (b) (comprometer) to bind, be binding on

vínculo m (unión, relación) tie, bond; ∼**s familiares** family ties

vine ▶ VENIR

vinería f (AmL) wineshop, liquor store (specializing in wines)

vinero -ra adj (Chi, Per) wine (before n)

vinícola adj ‹industria/producción› wine (before n); ‹región› wine-producing, wine-growing

vinicultor -tora m,f wine producer, winegrower

viniera, viniese, etc ▶ VENIR

viniste, etc ▶ VENIR

vino m (bebida) wine; ∼ **dulce/seco** sweet/dry wine; ∼ **blanco/rosado/tinto** white/rosé/red wine; ∼ **de la casa** house wine

vino ▶ VENIR

viña f vineyard

viñatero -ra adj (AmL) wine (before n), wine-growing (before n)
■ m,f (AmL) (a) (propietario) winegrower (b) (trabajador) vineyard worker

viñedo m vineyard

viola f (a) (instrumento) viola (b) **viola** mf (persona) viola player, violist (AmE)

violáceo -cea adj purplish

violación f (a) (de persona) rape (b) (de ley, acuerdo, derecho) violation; (de templo) violation

violador -dora m,f (a) (de persona) rapist (b) (de ley, acuerdo) violator

violar [A1] vt (a) ‹persona› to rape (b) ‹ley› to violate, break; ‹tratado/derecho› to violate; ‹templo› to violate

violencia f violence; **recurrir a la** ∼ to resort to violence

violentar [A1] vt (a) (forzar) ‹cerradura/puerta› to force; ‹persona› to rape (b) (poner en situación embarazosa) to make ... feel awkward
■ **violentarse** v pron to get embarrassed

violento -ta adj ⓵ (en general) violent; **utilizar medios** ∼**s** to use violent means ⓶ (incómodo) ‹situación› embarrassing, awkward; **le resulta** ∼ **hablar del tema** she finds it embarrassing to talk about it; **estaba muy** ∼ I felt very awkward

violeta f violet
■ m/adj violet

violín (a) m (instrumento) violin (b) **violín** mf (persona) violinist

violinista mf violinist

violón (a) m (instrumento) double bass (b) **violón** mf (persona) double bass player

violonchelista mf cellist

violonchelo m cello, violoncello

viral adj viral

virar [A1] vi (a) (Náut) to tack, go about (b) «vehículo/conductor» to turn; **viró bruscamente** she swerved (c) «política/partido» to veer

virgen adj (a) ‹persona›: **una mujer/un hombre** ∼ a virgin; **ser** ∼ to be a virgin (b) ‹cinta› blank; ‹película› unexposed (c) ‹selva› virgin
■ f virgin; **la V**∼ (Relig) the Virgin

virginidad f virginity

Virgo m (signo) Virgo; **es (de)** ∼ she's (a) Virgo, she's a Virgoan
■ mf (pl ∼ or **-gos**) (persona) tb **virgo** Virgo, Virgoan

viril adj ‹cualidades› virile, manly

virilidad f virility

virreinato m viceroyalty

virtual adj (a) (potencial) virtual (b) (tácito) implicit

virtud f (a) (cualidad) virtue (b) (capacidad) power; **con** ∼**es curativas** with healing powers

virtuoso -sa adj virtuous
■ m,f virtuoso

viruela f (enfermedad) smallpox; (marca) pockmark

virus m (pl ∼) virus

viruta f shaving

visa f, (Esp) **visado** m visa

visar [A1] vt ‹documento› to endorse; ‹pasaporte› to visa

visceral adj (a) (Anat) visceral (b) ‹odio/impresión› visceral, deep; **un sentimiento** ∼ a gut feeling

vísceras fpl entrails (pl), viscera (pl)

visconde -desa m (m) viscount; (f) viscountess

viscosa f viscose

viscoso -sa adj viscous

visera f (de casco) visor; (de gorra) peak; (de jugador) eyeshade

visibilidad f visibility

visible adj (a) [SER] visible (b) (fam) [ESTAR] (presentable) presentable, decent

V

visillo *m* net curtain, lace curtain

visión *f* [1] (a) (vista) vision, sight; **perdió la ∼ de un ojo** she lost the sight of one eye (b) (aparición) vision; **ver visiones** to be seeing things [2] (enfoque, punto de vista) view; **una ∼ romántica de la vida** a romantic view of life; **tener ∼ de futuro** to be forward-looking

visionario -ria *adj/m,f* visionary

visir *m* vizier

visita *f* (a) (acción) visit; **hacer(le) una ∼ (a algn)** to pay (sb) a visit; **ir de ∼** to go visiting; **horario de ∼** visiting hours *o* times; **∼ a domicilio** house call; **∼ de cortesía** courtesy call, duty visit; **∼ guiada** (AmL) guided tour (b) (visitante) visitor; (invitado) guest; **espera una ∼ importante** he's expecting an important visitor; **tener ∼** to have visitors/guests

visitador social -dora social *m,f* (AmL) social worker

visitante *adj* visiting (*before n*)
■ *mf* visitor

visitar [A1] *vt* (a) ⟨persona⟩ to visit, visit with (AmE) (b) ⟨lugar⟩ to visit
■ **visitarse** *v pron* (recípr) to visit each other

vislumbrar [A1] *vt* (en la distancia) to make out, discern (frml); (entre los árboles, las nubes) to glimpse; **a lo lejos se vislumbraba una iglesia** a church could just be made out in the distance

viso *m* (Indum) petticoat, underskirt

visón *m* mink

visor *m* (a) (en cámara) viewfinder; (para diapositivas) slide viewer (b) (Arm) sight

víspera *f* (a) (día anterior): **la ∼** the day before (b) (tiempo anterior): **∼s de fiesta** days prior to public holidays; **en ∼s de un viaje** just before a journey

vista *f* [1] (a) (sentido) sight, eyesight; **tener buena ∼** to have good eyesight; **ser corto de ∼** to be near-sighted; **perdió la ∼** he lost his sight; **∼ cansada** eyestrain (b) (ojos) eyes; **le hace daño a la ∼** it hurts his eyes; **lo operaron de la ∼** he had an eye operation [2] (mirada): **alzar/bajar la ∼** to look up/down [3] (en locs) **a la vista: ponlo bien a la ∼** put it where it can be seen easily; **estar/no estar a la ∼** to be within/out of sight; **a la ∼ de todos** in full view of everyone; **¿tienes algún proyecto a la ∼?** do you have any projects in view?; **a primera** *or* **a simple vista** at first sight *o* glance; **con vistas a** with a view to; **en vista de** in view of; **en ∼ de que ...** in view of the fact that ...; **¡hasta la vista!** see you!, so long! (colloq); **perder algo/a algn de ∼** to lose sight of sth/sb; **perderse de ∼** to disappear from view [4] (panorama) view; **con ∼ al mar** with a sea view; **∼ aérea** aerial view [5] (Der) hearing

vistazo *m* look; **darle** *or* **echarle un ∼ a algo** to have a look at sth

viste, visteis ▶ VER²

viste, vistieron, etc ▶ VESTIR

visto¹ -ta *adj* [1] (a) (claro, evidente) obvious, clear; **está/estaba ∼ que ...** it is/was clear *o* obvious that ... (b) **por lo visto** (loc adv) apparently [2] [ESTAR] (común, trillado): **un truco que está muy ∼** an old trick; **eso ya está muy ∼** that's not very original [3] (considerado): **en ciertos**

círculos eso no está bien ∼ in some circles that is not considered correct; **estaba mal ∼ que las mujeres fumaran** it was not the done thing *o* it was frowned upon for women to smoke

visto² *m* (a) (Esp) check (AmE), tick (BrE) (b) **visto bueno** approval; **tiene que dar el ∼ bueno** she has to give her approval

visto ▶ VESTIR, VER²

vistoso -sa *adj* bright and colorful*

visual *adj* visual; **campo ∼** field of vision

vital *adj* [1] (fundamental) vital; **de ∼ importancia** of vital importance [2] (a) (Biol, Med) ⟨órgano⟩ vital (*before n*) (b) ⟨persona⟩ dynamic, full of life

vitalicio -cia *adj* ⟨miembro/presidente⟩ life (*before n*); **cargo ∼** post held for life

vitalidad *f* vitality

vitamina *f* vitamin

viticultor -tora *m,f* vine-grower

viticultura *f* vine-growing

vitorear [A1] *vt* to cheer

vitral *m* stained-glass window

vitrina *f* (a) (mueble — en tienda) showcase; (— en casa) glass cabinet, display cabinet (b) (AmL) (escaparate) shop window

vitrinear [A1] *vi* (Andes fam) to window-shop

viudez *f* (de mujer) widowhood; (de hombre) widowerhood

viudo -da *adj*: **su madre es** *or* (Esp) **está viuda** her mother is a widow; **(se) quedó ∼ a los 40 años** he lost his wife *o* he was widowed when he was 40
■ *m,f* (*m*) widower; (*f*) widow

viva *m*: **dar ∼s** to cheer; **fuera se oían ∼s** cheering could be heard outside

vivacidad *f* (de persona) liveliness, vivacity; (de ojos) brightness

vivaracho -cha *adj* (a) ⟨ojos⟩ sparkling; ⟨niño⟩ lively (b) (AmL) (espabilado) crafty

vivaz *adj* ⟨persona⟩ lively, vivacious; ⟨ojos⟩ bright; ⟨imaginación⟩ vivid, lively

vivencia *f* experience

víveres *mpl* provisions (*pl*), supplies (*pl*)

vivero *m* (de plantas) nursery; (de peces) hatchery; (de moluscos) bed

viveza *f* (a) (rapidez, agilidad) liveliness; **∼ de ingenio** readiness *o* sharpness of wit (b) (de recuerdo) vividness; **lo describió con gran ∼** she described it very vividly (c) (de color) brightness; (de ojos, mirada) liveliness, brightness; (de emoción, deseo) strength, intensity

vividor -dora *m,f* pleasure seeker

vivienda *f*: **el problema de la ∼** the housing *o* accommodation problem; **un bloque de ∼s** an apartment building, a block of flats (BrE); **la construcción de 50 ∼s** the construction of 50 homes *o* (frml) dwellings

vivir [I1] *vi* [1] (en general) to live; **vive solo** he lives alone *o* on his own; **∼ para algo/algn** to live for sth/sb; **∼ en paz** to live in peace; **la pintura no da para ∼** you can't make a living from painting; **el sueldo no le alcanza para ∼** his salary isn't enough (for him) to live on; **∼ DE algo** ⟨de la caridad⟩ to live ON sth; ⟨del arte/de la pesca⟩ to make a living FROM sth; ▶ *ver tb* RENTA [2] (estar vivo) to be alive

3 (como interj): ¡viva el Rey! long live the King!; ¡vivan los novios! three cheers for the bride and groom!; ¡viva! hurray!

■ ~ *vt* (a) (pasar por): ~ momentos difíciles to live in difficult times; los que vivimos la guerra those of us who lived through the war (b) ‹personaje/ música› to live (c) ‹vida› to live

vivisección *f* vivisection

vivo -va *adj* **1** (a) (con vida) alive; no quedó nadie ~ no one was left alive; en ~ ‹actuación/ transmisión› live (b) ‹lengua› living (before n) **2** (a) ‹persona› (despierto, animado) vivacious, bubbly; ‹descripción› vivid, graphic; ‹relato/ imaginación› lively (b) ‹color› bright, vivid; ‹llama/fuego› bright; ‹ojos/mirada› lively, bright (c) ‹sentimiento/deseo› intense, strong **3** (avispado, astuto) sharp; no seas tan ~ don't try to be clever

■ *m,f* (oportunista) sharp *o* smooth operator (colloq); (aprovechado) freeloader

vizconde -desa *m,f* (*m*) viscount; (*f*) viscountess

vocablo *m* (frml) word

vocabulario *m* vocabulary; ¡qué ~! what language!

vocación *f* vocation; tiene ~ de músico he has a vocation for music

vocacional *adj* vocational

vocal *adj* vocal

■ *f* **1** (Ling) vowel **2** *vocal mf* (de consejo, tribunal) member

vocalista *mf* vocalist, singer

vocalizar [A4] *vi* to vocalize

voceador *m* (Col, Méx) (de periódicos) newspaper vendor

vocear [A1] *vt* (a) ‹mercancías› to cry (dated); ‹noticias› to shout out (b) (hacer público) to spread (c) (corear) to shout (d) (Méx) ‹persona› to page

vocerío *m* clamor*, shouting

vocero -ra *m, f* (AmL) (*m*) spokesman, spokesperson; (*f*) spokeswoman, spokesperson

vociferar [A1] *vi* to shout, vociferate (frml)

vodevil *m* vaudeville (AmE), variety (BrE)

vodka *m or f* /'bo(ð)ka/ vodka

volado *m* (a) (Méx fam) (con moneda): te lo juego a un ~ I'll toss you for it; echar un ~ to toss *o* flip a coin (b) (RPl, Ven) (en costura) flounce

volador¹ -dora *adj* flying (before n)

volador² *m* (en pirotecnia) rocket

volanta *f* (RPl) horse-drawn carriage

volantazo *m* (Esp, Méx) swerve; dar un ~ to swerve

volante *m* **1** (Auto) steering wheel; ir/ponerse al ~ to be at/to take the wheel **2** (a) (AmL) (de propaganda) leaflet, flier (b) (Esp) (para el médico) referral note *o* slip **3** (en costura) flounce **4** (Dep) shuttlecock

volantín *m* **1** (Chi) (cometa) kite; encumbrar un ~ to fly a kite **2** (Per) (en gimnasia) somersault

volar [A10] *vi* **1** ‹pájaro/avión› to fly **2** (a) ‹tiempo› to fly; ¡cómo vuela el tiempo! doesn't time fly!; las malas noticias vuelan bad news travels fast (b) **volando** *ger* ‹comer/ cambiarse› in a rush, in a hurry; se fue volando he/she rushed off; sus clases se me pasan volando her classes seem to go so quickly

3 (a) (con el viento) ‹sombrero› to blow off; ~on todos los papeles my papers blew all over the place (b) (fam) (desaparecer) ‹dinero/pasteles› to vanish, disappear

■ ~ *vt* **1** ‹puente/edificio› to blow up; ‹caja fuerte› to blow **2** (Méx, Ven fam) (robar) to swipe (colloq), to nick (BrE colloq)

■ **volarse** *v pron* **1** (a) (Col fam) ‹preso› to escape (b) (Col, Méx fam) ‹alumno› to play hooky (esp AmE colloq), to skive off (school) (BrE colloq) **2** (a) (Méx fam) (coquetear) to flirt (b) (Méx, Ven fam) (robar) to swipe (colloq), nick (BrE colloq)

volcán *m* volcano

volcánico -ca *adj* volcanic

volcar [A9] *vt* **1** (a) (tumbar) to knock over (b) ‹carga› to tip, dump (c) (vaciar) to empty (out) (d) (Inf) to dump

■ ~ *vi* ‹automóvil/camión› to overturn, turn over; ‹embarcación› to capsize

■ **volcarse** *v pron* **1** (a) ‹vaso/botella› to get knocked *o* tipped over (b) ▸ VOLCAR *vi* **2** (entregarse, dedicarse) ~se A algo ‹a tarea› to throw oneself INTO sth **3** (desvivirse) ~se PARA *o* POR hacer algo to go out of one's way to do sth; ~se CON algn: se ~on conmigo they bent over backwards to make me feel welcome

volea *f* volley

volear [A1] *vt/vi* (Dep) to volley

vóleibol, voleibol *m* volleyball

voleo *m*: a *or* al ~ (al azar) at random; contesté al ~ I said the first thing that came into my head

volibol *m* (Col, Méx, Ven) volleyball

voltaje *m* voltage

volteado -da *adj* (Col, Méx fam & pey) bent (pej), queer (pej)

voltear [A1] *vt* **1** (a) ‹mies› to winnow; ‹tierra› to turn (over) (b) (por el aire) ‹toro› to toss; ‹caballo› to throw **2** (AmL exc CS) (a) ‹tortilla/disco› to turn over; ‹cuadro› to turn ... around; ‹copa/jarrón› (poner — boca arriba) to turn ... the right way up; (— boca abajo) to turn ... upside down (b) ‹calcetín/ manga› (poner — del revés) to turn ... inside out; (— del derecho) to turn ... the right way round; ~ la página to turn the page **3** (AmL exc CS) (dar la vuelta): me volteó la espalda she turned her back on me; al oír su voz volteó la cara when she heard his voice she turned her head **4** (CS) (tumbar, echar abajo) ‹bolos/botella› to knock over; ‹puerta› to knock down

■ **voltearse** *v pron* (a) (AmL exc CS) (volverse, darse la vuelta) to turn around; (cambiar de ideas) to change one's ideas (b) (Méx) ‹vehículo› to overturn, turn over

voltereta *f* somersault

voltio *m* volt

voluble *adj* (inconstante) changeable, fickle

volumen *m* **1** (en general) volume; ~ de ventas volume of sales, turnover; bajar/subir el ~ to turn the volume down/up; a todo ~ on full volume, at full blast (colloq) **2** (tomo) volume

voluminoso -sa *adj* ‹paquete› sizeable, bulky

voluntad *f* **1** (a) (facultad) will (b) (deseo) wish; por expresa ~ de los familiares by express wish of the family; lo hizo por (su) propia ~ he ⋯⁝⟩

did it of his own free will; **manifestó su ~ de
renunciar** he expressed his wish to resign; **por
causas ajenas a su ~** for reasons beyond his
control **2** (firmeza de intención) *tb* **fuerza de ~**
willpower **3** (disposición, intención): **con la mejor ~**
with the best of intentions; **agradezco tu buena
~ I** appreciate your willingness to help; **mostrar
buena ~ hacia algn** to show goodwill to *o*
toward(s) sb

voluntario -ria *adj* **(a)** ‹*acto/donación*›
voluntary; **fue una elección voluntaria** I/he did it
of my/his own free will **(b)** (*como adv*)
voluntarily
■ *m,f* volunteer

voluptuoso -sa *adj* voluptuous

volver [E11] *vi* **1** (regresar — al lugar donde se
está) to come back; (— a otro lugar) to go back; **no
sé a qué hora ~é** I don't know what time I'll be
back; **¿cómo vas a ~?** how are you getting
back?; **ha vuelto con su familia** she's gone back to
her family; **~ A algo** ‹*a un lugar*› to go back TO
sth; ‹*a una situación/actividad*› to return TO sth;
mañana volvemos a clases tomorrow we go back
to school; **quiere ~ al mundo del espectáculo** he
wants to return to show business; **volviendo a lo
que decía ...** to get *o* go back to what I was
saying ...; **¿cuándo volviste de las vacaciones?**
when did you get back from your vacation?; **ha
vuelto de París** she's back from Paris
2 «*calma/paz*» to return; **~ A algo** to return TO
sth
3 **volver en sí** to come to *o* round
■ ~ *v aux*: **~ a empezar** to start again *o* (AmE)
over; **no ~á a ocurrir** it won't happen again; **lo
tuve que ~ a llevar al taller** I had to take it back
to the workshop
■ ~ *vt* **1** (dar la vuelta) **(a)** ‹*colchón/tortilla*› to
turn (over); ‹*tierra*› to turn *o* dig over; ‹*calcetín/
chaqueta*› (poner — del revés) to turn ... inside out;
(— del derecho) to turn ... the right way round;
‹*cuello*› to turn; **~ la página** to turn the page **(b)**
‹*cabeza*› to turn; **volvió la mirada hacia mí** he
turned his gaze toward(s) me **(c)** ‹*esquina*› to
turn
2 (convertir en, poner): **la ha vuelto muy egoísta** it
has made her very selfish; **me está volviendo loca**
it's/he's/she's driving me mad
3 (Méx) **~ el estómago** to be sick
■ **volverse** *v pron* **1** (girar) to turn (around); **se
volvió hacia él** she turned to face him; **no te
vuelvas, que nos están siguiendo** don't look back,
we're being followed; **se volvió de espaldas** he
turned his back on me (*o* her *etc*); **~se boca
arriba/abajo** to turn over onto one's back/
stomach
2 (convertirse en, ponerse): **se ha vuelto muy
antipático** he's become very unpleasant; **se vuelve
agrio** it turns *o* goes sour; **se volvió loca** she went
mad

vomitar [A1] *vi* to vomit, be sick; **tengo ganas
de ~** I think I'm going to vomit *o* be sick, I feel
sick
■ ~ *vt* ‹*comida*› to bring up; ‹*sangre*› to cough up

■ **vomitarse** *v pron* (Col, Méx, Ven) to vomit, be
sick
vómito *m* **(a)** (acción) vomiting; **¿ha tenido ~s?**
have you been vomiting *o* (BrE) sick? **(b)** (cosa
vomitada) vomit

voraz *adj* ‹*persona/animal/apetito*› voracious;
‹*incendio/fuego*› fierce

vos *pron pers* [*Familiar form of address which is
widely used instead of* TÚ *mainly in the River
Plate area and parts of Central America*] **1** (como
sujeto, en comparaciones, con preposición) you; **¿quién
lo va a hacer? — vos** who's going to do it? — you
(are); **che, ~** hey, you; **~ misma lo dijiste** you
said so yourself; **menos que ~** less than you;
para/sin ~ for/without you **2** (uso impersonal)
you; **dan tres opciones y ~ elegís** you're given
three options and you choose one

vosear [A1] *vt* to address sb using the vos form
voseo *m* use of the vos form instead of TÚ

vosotros -tras *pron pers pl* [*Familiar form of
address not normally used in Latin America or in
certain parts of Spain, where* USTEDES *is used
instead*] you; **¿quién lo va a hacer? — vosotros**
who's going to do it? — you (are); **lo podéis hacer
~ mismos** you can do it yourselves; **más que ~**
more than you; **para ~** for you

votación *f* (acción) voting; (método) vote; **decidir
por ~** to decide by ballot; **fue elegida por ~** she
was elected *o* voted in; **hagamos una ~** let's vote
on it; **una ~ a mano alzada** a vote by a show of
hands

votante *mf* voter

votar [A1] *vi* to vote; **~ POR algo/algn** to vote
FOR sth/sb; **~ A FAVOR DE/EN CONTRA DE algo** to
vote FOR/AGAINST sth
■ ~ *vt* ‹*candidato*› to vote for; ‹*reforma/aumento*›
to approve, vote to approve

voto *m* **1** (en general) vote; **~ secreto** secret
ballot *o* vote; **por ~ a mano alzada** by a show of
hands; **~ de confianza/censura** vote of
confidence/no confidence; **~ en blanco** blank
ballot paper; **~ por correo** postal vote, absentee
ballot (AmE) **2** (Relig) vow; **hacer los ~s
solemnes** to take solemn vows

voy ▶ IR

voyeurista /bwaje'rista, bojer'ista/ *mf* voyeur

voz *f* **1** (en general) voice; **levantar la ~** to raise
one's voice; **tener la ~ tomada** to be hoarse;
hablar en ~ baja to speak quietly; **en ~ alta**
‹*hablar*› loudly; ‹*leer*› aloud, out loud; **quedarse
sin ~** to lose one's voice; **una pieza a cuatro
voces** (Mús) a piece for four voices, a four-part
piece; **~ activa/pasiva** (Ling) active/passive voice
2 voces *fpl* (gritos) shouting, shouts (*pl*); **hablar
a voces** to talk in loud voices

vozarrón *m* booming voice

vudú *m* voodoo

vuela, vuelan, etc ▶ VOLAR

vuelco *m* **1** (sobre sí mismo): **dar un ~** ‹*coche*›
to overturn, turn over; ‹*embarcación*› to capsize
2 (cambio radical): **las cosas pueden dar un ~**

AmC	América Central	Arg	Argentina	Cu	Cuba	Per	Perú
AmL	América Latina	Bol	Bolivia	Ec	Ecuador	RPI	Río de la Plata
AmS	América del Sur	Chi	Chile	Esp	España	Ur	Uruguay
Andes	Región andina	CS	Cono Sur	Méx	México	Ven	Venezuela

things could change *o* alter drastically; **el mercado dio un ~ favorable** the market registered a favorable upturn ⓷ (Inf) dump

vuelo *m* ⓵ **(a)** (acción): **el ~ de las gaviotas** the seagulls' flight; **remontar el ~** to soar up; *alzar or levantar el ~* «*pájaro*» to fly away *o* off; «*avión*» to take off; «*persona*» to fly *o* leave the nest; **a ~ de pájaro** (AmL): **un cálculo a ~ de pájaro** a rough estimate; **lo leí a ~ de pájaro** I just skimmed through it **(b)** (Aviac) flight; **son dos horas de ~** it is a two-hour flight; **~ charter/ regular** charter/schedule flight; **~ internacional/ nacional** international/domestic *o* internal flight; **~ sin motor** gliding, soaring (AmE)
⓶ (en costura) (amplitud): **la falda tiene mucho ~** it is a very full skirt

vuelo ▶ VOLAR

vuelta *f*

I ⓵ **(a)** (circunvolución): **dar ~s alrededor de algo** to go around sth; **da ~s alrededor de su eje** it spins *o* turns on its axis; **dar la ~ al mundo** to go around the world; **todo/la cabeza me da ~s** everything's/my head's spinning; **dar una ~ a la manzana** to go around the block; **dar toda la ~** to go all the way around **(b)** (Dep) (en golf) round; (en carreras) lap; **~ al ruedo** (Taur) lap of honor; **~ ciclista** cycle race, tour (C) (en carretera) bend; **el camino da muchas ~s** the road winds about a lot; **el autobús da muchas ~s** the bus takes a very roundabout route
⓶ (giro): **darle ~ a algo** «*a llave/manivela*» to turn sth; **dale otra ~** give it another turn; **el coche dio una ~ de campana** the car turned (right) over; **~ (de) carnero** (CS) somersault; **~ en redondo** (vuelta completa) 360 degree turn, complete turn; (cambio radical) U-turn
⓷ **(a)** darle la ~ a algo «*a disco/colchón*» to turn … (over); «*a calcetín*» (ponerlo — del derecho) to turn … the right way out; (— del revés) to turn … inside out; «*a copa*» (ponerla — boca arriba) to turn … the right way up; (— boca abajo) to turn … upside down; **dar la ~ a la página** to turn the page, turn over **(b)** (para cambiar de dirección, posición): **dar la ~** (Auto) to turn (around); **darse la ~** to turn (around)

⓸ (CS) **dar vuelta algo** «*disco/colchón*» to turn sth over; «*calcetín*» (ponerlo — del derecho) to turn the right way out; (— del revés) to turn sth inside out; «*copa*» (ponerla — boca arriba) to turn sth the right way up; (— boca abajo) to turn sth upside down; **dar ~ la página** to turn the page, turn over; **dio ~ la cara** she looked away; **¿damos ~ aquí?** (Auto) shall we turn (around) here?; **darse ~** «*persona*» to turn (around); «*vehículo*» to overturn; «*embarcación*» to capsize
⓹ (paseo): **dar una ~** (a pie) to go for a walk; (en coche) to go for a drive; (en bicicleta) to go for a ride
⓺ **(a) a la vuelta (de la esquina)** (just) around the corner **(b) vuelta y vuelta** (Coc) rare
⓻ **(a)** (regreso) return; (viaje de regreso) return journey; **a la ~ paramos para almorzar** on the way back we stopped for lunch; **a la ~ se encontró con una sorpresa** when he got back he found a surprise; **¡hasta la ~!** see you when you get back! **(b)** (a un estado anterior) **~ A algo** return to sth
⓼ **(a)** (Esp) (cambio) change; **quédese con la ~** keep the change **(b) vueltas** (Col) (cambio, dinero suelto) change
⓽ **(a)** (en elecciones) round **(b)** (de bebidas) round
⓾ (Per, RPl fam) (vez) time; **de ~** (de nuevo) again
⓫ (de collar) strand; (en labores de punto) row; (de pantalones) cuff (AmE), turn-up (BrE)

vuelto -ta *pp* ▶ VOLVER

vuelto *m* (AmL) change; **quédese con el ~** keep the change

vuelva, vuelvas, etc ▶ VOLVER

vuestro -tra *adj* **(a)** (Esp) (de vosotros) your; **~s libros** your books; **un amigo ~** a friend of yours **(b)** (frml) your; **Vuestra Majestad** Your Majesty
■ *pron* (Esp): **el ~, la vuestra,** *etc* yours; **sabe lo ~** he knows about the two of you

vulcanizadora *f* (Chi, Méx) tire* repairshop

vulgar *adj* **(a)** (corriente, común) common; **un ~ resfriado** a common cold **(b)** (poco refinado) vulgar, coarse **(c)** (no técnico) common, popular

vulgaridad *f* (cualidad) vulgarity, coarseness

vulnerable *adj* vulnerable

Ww

W, w *f* (*read as* /'doβle βe/, /'doβle u/ *or* (Esp) /'doβle 'uβe/, /'uβe 'ðoβle/) *the letter* W, w
w. (= watio) w, watt
walkie-talkie /'wo(l)ki 'to(l)ki/ *m* (*pl* **-kies**) walkie-talkie
walkman® /'wo(l)kman/ *m* (*pl* **-mans**) Walkman®
wáter /'(g)water *or* (Esp) 'bater/ *m* **(a)** (inodoro) toilet **(b)** (cuarto) bathroom (esp AmE), toilet (BrE)
waterpolo /'(g)waterpolo/ *m* water polo
WC /'be θe, 'uβe 'ðoβle θe/ *m* WC
web /(g)web/ *f or m*: **la** *or* **el web** the Web
weekend /'wiken/ *m* weekend

western *m* (*pl* **~** *or* **-terns**) western
whisky /'(g)wiski/ *m* (*pl* **-kies** *or* **-kys**) whiskey*; **~ americano** bourbon
windsurf /'winsurf/ *m* (deporte) windsurfing; (tabla) windsurfer, sailboard
windsurfing /'winsurfin/ *m* windsurfing
windsurfista /winsur'fista/ *mf* windsurfer
WWW *m* WWW

Xx

X, x *f* (*read as* /i 'ekis/) *the letter* X, x
xenofobia *f* xenophobia
xenófobo -ba *adj* xenophobic
■ *m,f* xenophobe

xilofón, xilófono *m* xylophone

Yy

Y, y *f* (*read as* /i 'ʏɾjeʏa/, /je/ *or* (RPl) /ʒe/) *the letter* Y, y

y *conj* **1** (en general) and; **habla inglés y alemán** he speaks English and German; **¡yo gano el dinero y él lo gasta!** I earn the money and he spends it! **2** (a) (en preguntas): **¿y tu padre? ¿qué tal está?** and how's your father?; **yo no oigo nada ¿y tú?** I can't hear anything, can you? **(b)** (fam) (expresando indiferencia) so (colloq); **¿y qué?** so what?; **¿y a mí qué?** so, what's it to me? **3** (esp RPl fam) (encabezando respuestas) well; **¿fuiste? — y sí, no tuve más remedio** did you go? — well yes, I had no choice; **y bueno** oh well **4** (en números, la hora): **cuarenta y cinco** forty-five; **doscientos treinta y tres** two hundred and thirty-three; **la una y diez** ten after (AmE) *o* (BrE) past one

ya *adv* [*Both the simple past* YA TERMINÉ *and the present perfect* YA HE TERMINADO *are used to refer to the recent indefinite past. The former is the preferred form in Latin America while in Spain there is a tendency to use the latter*] **1** (a) (en frases afirmativas o interrogativas) already; **¿~ te has gastado todo el dinero?** have you spent all the money already?; **~ terminé** I've (already) finished; **¿~ ha llegado Ernesto?** has Ernesto arrived yet?, did Ernesto arrive yet? (AmE); **aprietas este botón ¡y ~ está!** you press this button, and that's it! **(b)** (expresando que se ha comprendido) yes, sure (colloq) **2** (a) (en frases negativas) any more; **ese color ~ no se lleva** nobody wears that color any more **(b)** **no ya ... sino** not (just) ... but **3** (enseguida, ahora) right now; **desde ~ te digo que no puede ser** (esp AmL) I can tell you right now that it's not possible; **~ mismo** (esp AmL) right away, straightaway (BrE); **¡~ voy!** coming!; **preparados listos ¡~!** on your mark(s), get set, go! **4** (con verbo en futuro): **~ te contaré** I'll tell you all about it; **~ lo entenderás** you'll understand one day **5** (uso enfático): **¡~ quisiera yo!** I should be so lucky!; **~ era hora** about time (too)!; **¡~ me tienes harta!** I'm (just about) fed up with you! **6** **ya que** since, as; **~ que estás aquí** since *o* as you're here

■ *conj*: **se puede solicitar ~ sea en persona o por teléfono** it can be ordered either in person or by telephone

yacer [E5] *vi* (frml) to lie (frml)

yacimiento *m* (a) (de mineral) deposit; **~ petrolífero** oilfield **(b)** (Arqueol) site

yámper *m* (Per) jumper (AmE), pinafore dress (BrE)

yanqui *adj* (*pl* **-quis**) (fam) Yankee (colloq)
■ *mf* Yank (colloq), Yankee (colloq)

yapa *f* (CS, Per fam) *small amount of extra goods given free*, lagniappe (AmE); **dar algo de ~** to throw sth in (for free) (colloq)

yate *m* yacht

yayo -ya *m,f* (fam) (*m*) grandpa (colloq), granddad (colloq); (*f*) granny (colloq), grandma (colloq)

yedra *f* ivy

yegua *f* (Zool) mare

yelmo *m* helmet

yema *f* (a) (de huevo) yolk **(b)** (dulce) *sweet made with egg yolk and sugar* **(c)** (del dedo) fingertip **(d)** (Bot) leaf bud

yen *m* yen

yendo ▶ IR

yerba *f* (a) *tb* **~ mate** maté **(b)** (Andes, Méx, Ven fam) (marihuana) grass (sl) **(c)** (césped) grass

yerbatero -ra *adj* maté (*before n*)
■ *m,f* (Andes) (curandero) witch doctor; (que vende hierbas medicinales) herbalist

yerga, yergue ▶ ERGUIR

yerno *m* son-in-law

yerra, yerras, etc ▶ ERRAR

yeso *m* (a) (Art, Const) plaster **(b)** (AmL) (Med) (plaster) cast; **me quitaron el ~** I had my cast taken off

yesquero *m* (Col, RPl, Ven) cigarette lighter

yo *pron pers* (a) (como sujeto) I; **~ que tú** if I were you; **¿quién quiere más? — ¡yo!** who wants some more? — me! *o* I do!; **soy ~** it's me; **¿quién, ~?** who, me?; **~ misma** myself; **estoy cansada — ~ también** I'm tired — so am I *o* me too **(b)** (en

comparaciones, con ciertas preposiciones) me; **come
más que ~** he eats more than me *o* more than I
do; **llegó después que ~** she arrived after me
yodo *m* iodine
yoga *m* yoga
yogui *m* yogi
yogurt (*pl* **-gurts, yogur**) *m* yogurt, yoghurt
yonqui *mf* (*pl* **-quis**) (fam) junkie (colloq)
yo-yo *m* (*pl* **-yos**) yo-yo
yuca *f* (tubérculo comestible) cassava, manioc;
(planta ornamental) yucca
yudo *m* judo
yudoca *mf* judoka, judoist

yugo *m* yoke
Yugoslavia, Yugoeslavia *f* (Hist)
Yugoslavia
yugoslavo -va, yugoeslavo -va *adj/m,f*
(Hist) Yugoslavian
yugular *adj/f* jugular
yunque *m* anvil
yunta *f* (de bueyes) yoke
yute *m* jute
yuyo *m* **(a)** (Per, RPl) (hierba) herb; **té de ~s**
herbal tea **(b)** (RPl) (mala hierba) weed **(c)** (Per)
(alga) seaweed

Zz

Z, z *f* (*read as* /'seta/ *or* (Esp) /'θeta/) *the letter* Z, z
zacate *m* (AmC, Méx) **(a)** (hierba) grass; (heno)
hay **(b)** (estropajo) scourer
zafar [A1] *vt* **(a)** (Chi, Méx) ‹brazo/dedo› to
dislocate **(b)** (Col, Ven) ‹nudo› to untie; ‹tuerca› to
unscrew; ‹persona/animal› to let ... loose
■ **zafarse** *v pron* **(a)** (de compromiso) **~se DE algo**
to get *o* wriggle OUT OF sth **(b)** (soltarse)
«persona/animal» to get loose, get away **(c)**
(*refl*) (Chi, Méx) (dislocarse): **~se la muñeca** to
dislocate one's wrist
zafiro *m* sapphire
zaga *f* **(a)** (Dep) defense* **(b) a la zaga** ‹ir/
quedarse› in the rear, behind
zaguán *m* hallway
zalamería *f*: *tb* **~s** sweet talk, flattery; **hacerle
~s a algn** to sweet-talk sb
zalamero -ra *adj* ‹palabras› flattering; **¡qué ~
estás!** you're being very nice (to me)! (iro)
zamarra *f* (chaqueta) leather/sheepskin jacket;
(chaleco) leather/sheepskin jerkin
zamba *f* zamba (*South American folk dance*)
zambo -ba *adj* bowlegged
■ *m,f* (AmL) person of mixed black and Amerindian
origin
zambomba *f* (Mús) traditional drum-like
instrument
zambullida *f* (salto) dive, plunge; (baño) dip
zambullirse [I9] *v pron* (lanzarse) to dive (in);
(sumergirse) to duck *o* dive underwater
zamuro *m* (Ven) turkey vulture
zanahoria *adj* **(a)** (RPl fam) (tonto) stupid **(b)**
(Ven fam) (anticuado) square (colloq)
■ *mf* **(a)** (RPl fam) (tonto) idiot, nerd (colloq) **(b)** (Ven
fam) (mojigato) straitlaced person; (anticuado) old
fogey (colloq)
■ *f* (Bot, Coc) carrot
zanca *f* leg
zancada *f* stride; **bajaba la cuesta a ~s** he
came striding down the hill
zancadilla *f* trip; **me hizo** *or* (Esp) **puso una ~**
he tripped me (up)

zancos *mpl* stilts (*pl*)
zancuda *f* wader, wading bird
zancudo¹ -da *adj* ‹ave› wading (*before n*)
(b) (fam) ‹persona› long-legged
zancudo² *m* (típula) crane fly, daddy longlegs;
(mosquito) (AmL) mosquito
zángano -na *m,f* ⊡ (fam) (persona) lazybones
(colloq) ⊡ **zángano** *m* (abeja) drone
zanja *f* (para desagüe) ditch; (para cimientos,
tuberías) trench; (acequia) irrigation channel
zanjar [A1] *vt* ‹polémica/diferencias› to settle,
resolve; ‹deuda› to settle, pay off
zapallito *m* (CS): *tb* **~ largo** *or* **italiano**
zucchini (AmE), courgette (BrE)
zapallo *m* (CS, Per) pumpkin
zapata *f* (Auto, Mec) brake shoe
zapateado *m* **(a)** (en general) ▶ ZAPATEO **(b)**
(baile) zapateado (*type of Flamenco dance*)
zapatear [A1] *vi* **(a)** (en danza) to tap one's feet;
(más fuerte) to stamp (*in time to the music*) **(b)**
(para protestar, vitorear) to stamp (one's feet)
zapateo *m* tapping; (más fuerte) stamping
zapatería *f* **(a)** (tienda) shoe store (AmE), shoe
shop (BrE) **(b)** (taller — de fabricación) shoemaker's,
cobbler's; (— de reparación) shoe repairer's,
cobbler's
zapatero -ra *m,f* shoemaker, cobbler
zapatilla *f* **(a)** (de lona) canvas shoe; (para
deportes) sneaker (AmE), trainer (BrE); (alpargata)
espadrille; (para ballet) ballet shoe; (pantufla)
slipper **(b)** (Méx) (zapato de mujer) lady's shoe; **~
de piso** flat shoe
zapato *m* shoe; **~s bajos/de tacón** low-heeled/
high-heeled shoes; **~ de cordón** lace-up shoe; **~
de goma** (Ven) sneaker (AmE), trainer (BrE)
zaperoco *m* (Ven fam) riot
zar *m* tsar, czar
Zaragoza *f* Saragossa
zarandear [A1] *vt* (de un lado a otro) to shake;
(para arriba y para abajo) to shake *o* jog up and down
■ **zarandearse** *v pron* (esp AmL) «tren» to ···⟩

shake around; «*barco*» to toss about; **nos
zarandeamos mucho durante el vuelo** we got
shaken around *o* buffeted a lot during the flight

zarape *m* (en AmC, Méx) serape (*colorful
blanket-like shawl worn esp by men*)

zarcillo *m* ⨯1⨯ (arete) earring ⨯2⨯ (Bot) tendril

zarina *f* czarina

zarpa *f* (a) (Zool) paw (b) (fam) (mano) paw (colloq)

zarpar [A1] *vi* to set sail, weigh anchor

zarpazo *m* (de gato, león) swipe; **me dio un** ~ it
took a swipe at me (with its paw)

zarza *f* bramble, blackberry bush

zarzamora *f* (fruto) blackberry; (arbusto)
bramble, blackberry bush

zarzo *m* (Col) loft, attic

zarzuela *f* (Espec, Mús) *traditional Spanish
operetta*

zenit *m* zenith

zeppelin /sepeˈlin, θepeˈlin/, **zepelín** *m*
zeppelin, airship

zeta *f: name of the letter z*

zigzag *m* (*pl* **-zags** *or* **-zagues**) zigzag

zigzaguear [A1] *vi* to zigzag

zinc *m* zinc; **techo de chapa de** ~ corrugated
iron roof

zíper *m* (AmC, Méx, Ven) zipper (AmE), zip (BrE)

zócalo *m* ⨯1⨯ (rodapié) baseboard (AmE), skirting
board (BrE) ⨯2⨯ (Méx) (plaza) main square

zodíaco, zodiaco *m* zodiac

zombi *mf* zombie

zona *f* ⨯1⨯ (área, región) area; **fue declarada** ~
neutral it was declared a neutral zone; **❺ zona de
carga y descarga** loading and unloading only; ~
comercial commercial district; ~ **de castigo**
penalty area; ~ **industrial** industrial park; ~
peatonal pedestrian precinct; ~ **roja** (AmL) (zona
de prostitución) red-light district; ~ **verde** park,
green space ⨯2⨯ (en baloncesto) free-throw lane,
three-second area

zonzo -za *m,f* (AmL fam) idiot, fool

zoo *m* zoo

zoología *f* zoology

zoológico *m* zoo, zoological garden (frml)

zoólogo -ga *m,f* zoologist

zoom /sum, θum/ *m* zoom (lens)

zopenco -ca *adj* (fam) stupid, idiotic
■ *m,f* (fam) blockhead (colloq)

zopilote *m* (AmC, Méx) turkey vulture

zoquete *adj* (fam) dim, dense (colloq)
■ *mf* (fam) (persona) dimwit (colloq), blockhead
■ *m* (CS) (Indum) sock, ankle sock

zorra *f* (fam & pey) (prostituta) whore (colloq & pej),
tart (colloq & pej); *ver tb* ZORRO 1A, 2

zorrillo *m* (AmL) (mofeta) skunk

zorro -rra *m,f* ⨯1⨯ (a) (Zool) (*m*) fox; (*f*) vixen
(b) (AmC, Méx fam) (oposum) opossum ⨯2⨯ (fam)
(persona astuta) sly *o* crafty person ⨯3⨯ **zorro** *m*
(piel) fox (fur); *ver tb* ZORRA

zorzal *m* thrush

zozobrar [A1] *vi* ⨯1⨯ «*barco*» (hundirse) to
founder; (volcar) to capsize ⨯2⨯ «*proyecto/negocio*»
to founder

zueco *m* clog

zumbar [A1] *vi* «*insecto*» to buzz; «*motor*» to
hum, whirr; **pasar zumbando** «*bala/coche*» to
whizz by; **me zumbaban los oídos** my ears were
buzzing *o* ringing
■ ~ *vt* ⨯1⨯ (fam) (persona) to give … a good hiding
(colloq) ⨯2⨯ (Ven fam) (tirar) to chuck (colloq), to throw

zumbido *m* (de insecto) buzzing, droning; (de
motor) humming, whirring

zumo *m* (esp Esp) juice

zurcir [I4] *vt* to darn, mend

zurdo -da *adj* left-handed; ⟨futbolista⟩ left-footed;
⟨boxeador/lanzador⟩ southpaw (*before n*)
■ *m,f* left-handed person; (tenista) left-hander;
(boxeador) southpaw

zurra *f* (fam) (good) hiding (colloq)

zurrar [A1] *vt* (fam) to wallop (colloq), to give … a
(good) thrashing *o* hiding (colloq)

zurrón *m* (de pastor) leather bag; (de cazador)
hunter's pouch

Z

Calendario / Calendar
The Spanish-speaking world
Vida y cultura
Letters / Cartas

Calendario de días festivos, fiestas y tradiciones en Gran Bretaña y EEUU / Calendar of traditions, festivals, and holidays in Spanish-speaking countries

January

1 8 15 22 29
2 9 16 23 30
3 10 17 24 31
4 11 18 25
5 12 19 26
6 13 20 27
7 14 21 28

February

1 8 15 22
2 9 16 23
3 10 17 24
4 11 18 25
5 12 19 26
6 13 20 27
7 14 21 28

March

1 8 15 22 29
2 9 16 23 30
3 10 17 24 31
4 11 18 25
5 12 19 26
6 13 20 27
7 14 21 28

April

1 8 15 22 29
2 9 16 23 30
3 10 17 24
4 11 18 25
5 12 19 26
6 13 20 27
7 14 21 28

May

1 8 15 22 29
2 9 16 23 30
3 10 17 24 31
4 11 18 25
5 12 19 26
6 13 20 27
7 14 21 28

June

1 8 15 22 29
2 9 16 23 30
3 10 17 24
4 11 18 25
5 12 19 26
6 13 20 27
7 14 21 28

July

1 8 15 22 29
2 9 16 23 30
3 10 17 24 31
4 11 18 25
5 12 19 26
6 13 20 27
7 14 21 28

August

1 8 15 22 29
2 9 16 23 30
3 10 17 24 31
4 11 18 25
5 12 19 26
6 13 20 27
7 14 21 28

September

1 8 15 22 29
2 9 16 23 30
3 10 17 24
4 11 18 25
5 12 19 26
6 13 20 27
7 14 21 28

October

1 8 15 22 29
2 9 16 23 30
3 10 17 24 31
4 11 18 25
5 12 19 26
6 13 20 27
7 14 21 28

November

1 8 15 22 29
2 9 16 23 30
3 10 17 24
4 11 18 25
5 12 19 26
6 13 20 27
7 14 21 28

December

1 8 15 22 29
2 9 16 23 30
3 10 17 24 31
4 11 18 25
5 12 19 26
6 13 20 27
7 14 21 28

☐ Celebrated in Spanish and English-speaking countries / Celebrado en países de habla española e inglesa

◇ Celebrated in Spanish-speaking countries / Celebrado en países de habla española

○ Celebrated in English-speaking countries / Celebrado en países de habla inglesa

1 January Año Nuevo (New Year's Day). A public holiday in all Spanish-speaking countries.

5 January (Mexico) **Día de la Constitución** (Constitution Day). A public holiday.

6 January **Día de Reyes** (Epiphany/Twelfth Night). In many Spanish-speaking countries, this is when presents are given, rather than on Christmas Day.

20 January San Sebastián (Saint Sebastian's Day). Celebrated in Spain with parades, sporting events, and bullfights, it is also a day of celebration and dancing for the people of the Basque city that bears the name of the saint.

2 February La Candelaria (Candlemas). An occasion for celebrations and parades in many Spanish-speaking countries.

3 February Fiesta de San Blas (patron saint of Paraguay). A public holiday.

21 February (Mexico) **Anniversary of the birth of Benito Juárez**, a famous nineteenth-century statesman, who was twice president. A public holiday.

26 February Aberri Eguna - Basque national day and a public holiday in the Basque country of Spain.

12 - 19 March Las Fallas are one of the best known *fiestas* in Spain. They are held in Valencia in eastern Spain. The high point of the celebration is on the last night, when the *cabezudos* (carnival figures with large heads), which have been carefully prepared by the *falleros*, are paraded through the streets and then burned, all this to the accompaniment of an enormous fireworks display.

14 April (Paraguay) **Día de la Independencia**. A public holiday.

23 April San Jordi The feast day of Catalonia's patron saint. According to custom, women give men books and men give women roses on this Catalan version of St Valentine's Day.

1 May **Día del Trabajo** (Labor Day). A public holiday in all Spanish-speaking countries.

5 May (Mexico) The anniversary of the victory of the state of Puebla against the French invasion of 1862. A public holiday.

25 May (Argentina) The anniversary of the May revolution of 1810.

20 June (Argentina) **Día de la Bandera** (Argentinian National Day). A public holiday. (Colombia) **Día de la Independencia**. A public holiday.

24 June San Juan (Feast of St John). Traditionally fires are lit on the night of San Juan in order to keep away the cold of winter. In some places, people jump over the fires and in others the faithful will try to walk through them barefoot. The custom is slowly dying out, but continues in many parts of the Spanish-speaking world.

5 July (Venezuela) **Día de la Independencia**. A public holiday.

6 - 14 July Sanfermines. The festival of *el encierro* (the 'running of the bulls'), takes place in Pamplona in northern Spain. The animals are released into the barricaded streets and people run in front of them, in honor of the town's patron saint, San Fermín, who was put to death by being dragged by bulls.

9 July (Argentina) **Día de la Independencia**. A public holiday.

25 July Fiesta de Santiago (Feast of St James). The famous *Camino de Santiago*, the pilgrimage of thousands of people from all over Spain and many other parts of Europe to the holy city of Santiago de Compostela, takes place in the week leading up to St James' Day, 25 July. The city also has its *fiestas* around this time. The streets are full of musicians and performers for two weeks of celebrations culminating in the *Festival del Apóstol*.

28 July (Peru) **Día de la Independencia**. A public holiday.

6 August (Bolivia) **Día de la Independencia**. A public holiday.

10 August (Ecuador) **Primer Grito de Independencia**. A public holiday commemorating the first cry of independence in 1809.

17 August (Argentina) A public holiday to celebrate the anniversary of the death of the San Martín who liberated Argentina from Spanish rule in 1816.

25 August (Uruguay) **Día de la Independencia**. A public holiday.

11 September **Día Nacional de Cataluña**. Catalonian National Day and a public holiday in Catalonia.

Calendario / Calendar

13 September (Mexico) Commemoration of the *Niños Héroes* (child heroes) who fell while defending the castle of Chapultepec against European invaders in 1847.

15 September (Mexico) **Conmemoración de la Proclamación de la Independencia**. Throughout the country, at 11 o'clock at night, there is a communal shout, *El Grito*, in memory of Padre Hidalgo's cry of independence from the Spanish in the town of Dolores.

18 September (Chile) **Día de la Independencia**. A public holiday.

12 October **Día de la Hispanidad**. A public holiday, this is also **Columbus Day**, which is celebrated in all Spanish-speaking countries, as well as the US, in commemoration of the discovery of the Americas by Christopher Columbus in 1492. In Spanish-speaking countries of the Americas, it is also called the **Día de la Raza** (literally, Day of the Race) in celebration of the *mestizaje*, the mingling of races, which gave birth to the populations of today.

31 October **Todos los Santos** (All Saints). People all over the Spanish-speaking world flock to the cemeteries on this and the following day *el día de los Difuntos/Muertos* to put flowers on the graves of relatives and friends and to remember the dead. In Mexico this is an important festival in which Catholic traditions are mixed with those of pre-Hispanic religions.

10 November (Argentina) **Fiesta de la Tradición**. This festival takes place throughout the country but is especially important in the town of San Antonio de Areco, near Buenos Aires. The capital also holds a festival in November, the **Semana de Buenos Aires**, in honor of its patron saint San Martín de Tours.

20 November (Mexico) **Día de la Revolución de 1910**. A public holiday to celebrate the revolution of 1910.

2 December (Mexico) **Virgen de Guadalupe**. Celebrations are held in honor of the patron saint of the country, with music and dancers, in particular the *concheros*, who dance, wearing bells around their ankles, to the sound of stringed instruments and conches.

25 December **Navidad** (Christmas Day). A time of great religious celebration in all Spanish-speaking countries. In many places, re-enactments of the nativity are held, with a variety of traditions, parades, and costumes.

28 December **Día de los Inocentes.** This is the equivalent to April Fool's Day. In most Spanish-speaking countries it is a day for playing tricks on people. And if you trick someone into lending you money for that day, you keep it and tell them *que te lo paguen los Santos Inocentes* (let the Holy Innocents pay you back).

31 December **La noche de Fin de Año.** This is often the occasion for parties, and at midnight the New Year is welcomed with much noise and merrymaking. In Spain and in many other Spanish-speaking countries, the families gather together twelve seconds before midnight *para tomar las uvas* (to see the New Year in by eating one grape on each chime of the clock) for good luck.

Movable feasts and holidays

Martes de Carnaval. (Shrove Tuesday). The last Tuesday before the beginning of *Cuaresma* (Lent). *Carnaval* is celebrated in many Spanish-speaking countries just before this date. In many places, there are masked balls and parades. The biggest in Spain are those of Cádiz, on the south coast, and Madrid, where a strange ceremony called *el entierro de la sardina* (literally the burial of the sardine) takes place. In Mexico, the best-known are in Veracruz and Mazatlán.

Pascua (Easter) - **Semana Santa** (Holy Week). The week leading up to Easter Sunday is the most important time of religious celebration throughout the Spanish-speaking world. In many places, there are processions in which statues of Christ or the Virgin Mary, often covered in jewels and flowers, are carried to the church.

Seville's famous **Feria de abril** (April festival) takes place in the week following Easter. The site of the *feria* is decked out with hundreds of *casetas* or small marquees, hired by companies or private individuals, in which people entertain, eat *tapas*, drink *manzanilla* (a pale dry sherry), play music, and dance *sevillanas*, the popular dances of Andalucía. Many people dress up in colorful traditional costumes, some of them on horseback or in horse-drawn carriages.

Corpus Christi - 9 weeks after Easter is celebrated in most Spanish-speaking countries with religious parades.

1 de enero
New Year's Day (día de Año Nuevo).
El primero de enero es festivo y normalmente
es un día tranquilo en el que la gente se
recupera de los festejos de la
noche anterior.

2 de enero
Día festivo en Escocia.

6 de enero
Epiphany o Twelfth night (Día de Reyes).
No hay ninguna costumbre en especial
relacionada con este día, pero
tradicionalmente se guarda el árbol de
Navidad junto con el resto de los adornos
navideños.

25 de enero
Burns Night. Es el aniversario del
nacimiento del poeta escocés Robert Burns en
el siglo XVIII. Los escoceses preparan una
cena llamada *Burns Supper*, cuyo plato
principal se llama *haggis* (estómago de oveja
relleno con una mezcla de avena, hígado y
otras vísceras, cebollas y especias) y que es
acompañado a la mesa por un gaitero (*piper*)
que toca la gaita escocesa.

2 de febrero
Groundhog Day. Según la tradición
estadounidense, la pequeña marmota
(*groundhog*) sale de su madriguera en este día,
luego de su hibernación. Si está soleado y ve
su sombra, regresa a su madriguera, y habrá
otras seis semanas de tiempo invernal. Si no
ve su sombra, la primavera comenzará
temprano.

14 de febrero
St Valentine's Day. En el día de San Valentín
los enamorados se intercambian flores
y regalos.También es tradicional mandarle
una tarjeta anónima a alguien que le guste
a uno.

1 de marzo
St David's Day. San David es el santo patrono
de Gales.

17 de marzo
St Patrick's Day. San Patricio es el santo
patrono de Irlanda, es día festivo y se celebra
por todos los irlandeses con música y bebida
en cantidad.

1 de abril
April Fools' Day (día de los Inocentes).
Se gastan muchas bromas en este día, los
que son objeto de ellas, se llaman *April Fools*.

23 de abril
St George's Day. San Jorge es el santo
patrono de Inglaterra.

4 de julio
Independence Day. Día festivo en los Estados
Unidos para celebrar el Día de la
Independencia con desfiles, fuegos artificiales
y banderas. La gente se reúne haciendo
comidas al aire libre y parrilladas o asados.

12 de octubre
Columbus Day. Día festivo en los Estados
Unidos, en el que se conmemora el
descubrimiento de América por Cristóbal
Colón en 1492.

31 de octubre
Halloween (víspera de Todos Santos).
Ocasión en la que se mezcla la religión con
antiguas creencias paganas. Los niños se
disfrazan de fantasmas y brujas y visitan
casas de la vecindad jugando a la "broma
o golosina" (*trick or treat*). Si los vecinos no les
dan dinero o golosinas, los niños les gastan
una broma. En los Estados Unidos, las
familias suelen hacer una fiesta de disfraces.

5 de noviembre
Bonfire Night/Guy Fawkes. Se conmemora
en Gran Bretaña el intento frustrado por parte
de Guy Fawkes de hacer volar el Parlamento
en 1605. Se tiran fuegos artificiales y se hacen
enormes fogatas en las que se quema una
efigie llamada '*guy*'.

11 de noviembre
Remembrance Day, en Estados Unidos,
Veterans' Day. El día en que se conmemora el
armisticio de 1918, y se recuerdan los caídos en
las dos guerras mundiales y otros conflictos
más recientes. También se lo conoce en Gran
Bretaña como el día de la amapola (*Poppy
Day*), ya que la gente lleva prendida una
amapola roja de papel como signo
recordatorio.

30 de noviembre
St Andrew's Day. San Andrés es el santo
patrono de Escocia.

25 de diciembre
Christmas Day (el día de Navidad). Es
día festivo. Se intercambian regalos alrededor
del árbol de Navidad, y en muchas casas los
niños, al despertar, encuentran en su cama
una media llena de regalitos y golosinas que,
según la tradición, deja *Father Christmas*,
también conocido como *Santa Claus*.

26 de diciembre
Boxing Day en Gran Bretaña, **St Stephen's
Day** en Irlanda. Día festivo en ambos países.

31 de diciembre
New Year's Eve (la noche de Fin de Año)
llamada **Hogmanay** en Escocia, país donde se
acostumbra ir a visitar a amigos y vecinos

a medianoche, para comer y beber hasta las primeras horas de la mañana. Antiguamente era tradicional llevar un pedazo de carbón como símbolo de buena suerte.

Fiestas móviles

El tercer lunes de febrero, es el día de los Presidentes (**Presidents' Day**) en Estados Unidos. Es día festivo en el que se celebran los nacimientos de George Washington y Abraham Lincoln.

Shrove Tuesday (martes de Carnaval) es el último día de carnaval antes del comienzo de la Cuaresma el miércoles de Ceniza. Tradicionalmente se comen creps o panqueques.

El cuarto domingo de la Cuaresma en Gran Bretaña y el segundo domingo de mayo en Estados Unidos, es el día de la Madre (**Mother's Day** o **Mothering Sunday**). Las madres suelen recibir tarjetas y pequeños regalos de sus hijos.

El tercer domingo de junio es el día del Padre (**Fathers' Day**) en el que los padres suelen recibir tarjetas y pequeños regalos de sus hijos.

Good Friday el Viernes Santo. Se celebra en la iglesia, es día festivo.

Easter Sunday (el Domingo de Pascua). La gente religiosa va a la iglesia. A los niños se les dan huevos de Pascua.

Easter Monday. El lunes siguiente al Domingo de Pascua es día festivo en Gran Bretaña e Irlanda.

El primer lunes de mayo (**Early May Bank Holiday**) es día festivo en Gran Bretaña e Irlanda

Whitsun o **Pentecost.** El domingo de Pentecostés es el séptimo después de la Pascua de Resurrección (**Easter Sunday**). Se celebra solamente en la iglesia.

El lunes siguiente solía ser día festivo en Gran Bretaña, pero ha sido reemplazado por el último lunes del mes de mayo (**Spring Bank Holiday**).

El último lunes de agosto (**Late Summer Bank Holiday**) es día festivo en Inglaterra, Gales e Irlanda del Norte.

El primer lunes de septiembre es el día del Trabajo (**Labor Day**) en Estados Unidos. Es día festivo y se celebra con desfiles.

Thanksgiving (el día de Acción de Gracias) en Estados Unidos, es el cuarto jueves de noviembre. Es un día de festejos tanto religiosos como familiares, que culmina con una gran comida consistente en un pavo acompañado con batatas y salsa de arándano, seguido de un pastel de calabaza.

Advent El período que incluye los cuatro domingos previos a la Navidad. Por tradición, los niños tienen calendarios de Adviento (*Advent Calendars*), con pequeñas 'ventanitas' de papel que contienen ilustraciones navideñas y algunas veces golosinas.

A-Z of the Spanish-speaking countries of the world

Argentina

Official Name: The Argentine Republic
Capital: Buenos Aires
Currency: peso
Area: 1,073,809 square miles
(2,780,092 square kilometers)
Population: 35,672,000 (1997 estimate)

The second largest country in South America, Argentina is one of the continent's leading agricultural and industrial nations. Its main exports are meat and grain, and, more recently, minerals.

Colonized by Spain in the sixteenth century, Argentina declared independence in 1816. It has a history of political and economic instability, with periods under military rule. In 1982, Argentina's claim to the Falkland Islands/Malvinas led to an unsuccessful war with Britain. The governing military dictatorship was subsequently ousted, and a democratic government elected in 1983.

Argentina has a directly elected president who can hold office for a maximum of two four-year terms. The legislature (Congreso) consists of a Chamber of Deputies with 257 members who are elected by universal adult suffrage for a period of four years, and a Senate whose members are chosen by legislative elections. Under the amended Constitution of 1994, the Senate will eventually have 72 members who will hold office for 6 years. The country is divided into 22 provinces, the Federal District of Buenos Aires, and the National Territory of Tierra del Fuego. There is an elected governor and legislature for each of these.

The Argentine population is mostly of European origin. A wide number of European languages are spoken in addition to Spanish, including Italian, French, German, and English.

Bolivia

Official Name: Republic of Bolivia
Administrative capital: La Paz
Judicial and legal capital: Sucre
Currency: boliviano
Area: 424,162 square miles
(1,098,580 square kilometers)
Population: 7,767,000 (1997 estimate)

A landlocked country in South America, Bolivia's main topographical feature is the *altiplano*, a plateau between the east and west chains of the Andes. This has a clear atmosphere, and is suited to growing cereals and potatoes, and rearing livestock. Bolivia's major products are petroleum, zinc, tin, silver, gold, and lead; the main cash crops are soya beans, sugar, chestnuts, and coffee. Considerable amounts of coca are also grown illegally.

Bolivia was part of the Inca empire before coming under Spanish rule. It was freed from Spain in 1825, and named after the great Latin American liberator Simón Bolívar.

After independence, Bolivia lost land, including its coastline, to surrounding countries. Since then, it has been plagued by poverty and political instability. Bolivia's President and Congress are elected by universal adult suffrage. The President holds office for five years whilst the 130 members of the Chamber of Deputies, and the 27 members of the Senate, who together comprise the Congress, are elected for a four-year term. The President holds executive power and appoints the Cabinet. Each of the country's nine administrative departments is governed by a prefect appointed by the President.

Bolivia has a very large indigenous population. Aymara and Quechua are spoken in addition to Spanish.

The Spanish-speaking world

Chile

Official Name: The Republic of Chile
Capital: Santiago
Currency: peso
Area: 292,132 square miles
(756,622 square kilometers)
Population: 14,622,000 (1997 estimate)

Chile occupies a long strip down the Pacific coast of South America. Mines in the desert north produce copper, iron ore, and nitrate of soda, while the central region, where most of the country's population lives, is also the main agricultural area, producing grain, fruit, and vegetables. The south is rich in forest and grazing land.

Most of Chile belonged to the Inca empire, becoming part of the Viceroyalty of Peru under Spanish rule. Chilean independence was proclaimed in 1810 by Bernardo O'Higgins, and finally achieved in 1818. The country expanded northward in the War of the Pacific (1879-1883), gaining land from Bolivia and Peru.

In 1973 the government of the Marxist democrat Salvador Allende was overthrown. Chile was then ruled by a military dictatorship until March 1990, when a democratically elected president took office.

Chile's President and Congress are elected by universal adult suffrage. The President holds office for six years. The legislature (Congreso Nacional) consists of a Chamber of Deputies with 120 members and a Senate with 47 members. The President holds executive power and appoints the Cabinet. The country is divided into 12 regions and a metropolitan area.

Colombia

Official Name: The Republic of Colombia
Capital: Bogotá
Currency: peso
Area: 440,365 square miles
(1,140,105 square kilometers)
Population: 40,214,723 (1997 estimate)

Situated in the extreme north-west of South America, Colombia has Pacific and Atlantic coastlines, plus islands in the Pacific and Caribbean. Its chief products are minerals, particularly petroleum, coal, and natural gas, as well as coffee and tobacco. Illegal trading in cocaine is also widespread.

Colombia was conquered by Spain in the early sixteenth century, and became independent in the early nineteenth century, as part of the Republic of Gran Colombia. In 1830 Venezuela, then Ecuador, broke away; the remaining state, New Granada, changed its name to Colombia in 1863.

With a constitution dating from 1886, Colombia is the second oldest democracy in the western hemisphere. However, it suffered civil war between 1949 and 1968, and since then there has been open conflict between its government and drug traffickers who monopolize the world trade in narcotics.

Colombia's President and Congress are elected for four years by universal adult suffrage. The legislature (Congreso) consists of a House of Representatives with 161 members, and a Senate with 102 members. The President holds executive power and appoints the Cabinet.

The country is divided into 32 Departments and a Capital District.

Costa Rica

Official Name: The Republic of Costa Rica
Capital: San José
Currency: colón
Area: 19,707 square miles
(51,022 square kilometers)
Population: 3,464,000 (1997 estimate)

Costa Rica, on the Isthmus of Panama, is a heavily forested, mainly agricultural country, whose exports include bananas, coffee, cocoa beans, sugar, and beef. Its coastal regions have a tropical climate, while the central, highland region is more temperate. The population is mostly of European origin.

Colonized by Spain in the early sixteenth century, Costa Rica became independent in 1823, within the Federation of Central America. It emerged as a separate country in 1838. Since then it has been one of Central America's most stable and prosperous states.

Costa Rica's President and Legislative Assembly are elected by universal adult suffrage for four years. The successful presidential candidate must obtain at least 40% of the vote. The unicameral Legislative Assembly has 57 members. The President has executive power and appoints the Cabinet.

Costa Rica has civil and rural guards, but abolished the army in 1948.

Cuba

Official Name: The Republic of Cuba
Capital: Havana/La Habana
Currency: peso
Area: 42,820 square miles
(110,860 square kilometers)
Population: 11,059,000 (1997 estimate)

Cuba is the largest island in the West Indies. It has a tropical climate and a landscape ranging from rolling plains to 2,000-meter high mountains. Its main export is sugar.

One of Spain's first colonies, Cuba became independent in 1898, but was under heavy North American influence. In 1959, after years of political instability including several dictatorships, Communist rebels, led by Fidel Castro, seized power.

The politics of Castro's government, coupled with Cuba's proximity to the USA, antagonized the USA, which made various attempts to oust Castro, and blockaded the island. This made Cuba heavily reliant on the USSR until the break-up of the Soviet Union in 1991.

The Communist party is Cuba's only authorized political party. The sole legislative authority is the National Assembly of People's Power, consisting of 601 Deputies elected by direct vote for five years. It in turn elects 31 of its members to form the Council of State, whose President is both Head of State and Head of Government. The National Assembly also appoints, on the proposal of the head of State, the executive and administrative authority, the Council of Ministers. There are also municipal, regional, and provincial assemblies.

Dominican Republic/República Dominicana

Capital: Santo Domingo
Currency: peso
Area: 18,704 square miles
(48,442 square kilometers)
Population: 8,190,000 (1997 estimate)

The Dominican Republic forms the eastern part of the Caribbean island of Hispaniola. It is a mountainous country with a tropical climate. Its main exports are sugar, coffee, cocoa beans, tobacco, meat, ferronickel, gold, and silver. Columbus discovered Hispaniola in 1492, and it became a Spanish colony. In 1697 the island was split when Spain ceded its western third (now Haiti) to France. The eastern part was re-named Santo Domingo. The Dominican Republic was proclaimed in 1844.

The Republic has had a turbulent history, including a 31-year dictatorship from 1930 to 1961. This was followed by civil war and US military intervention, until a new, democratic constitution was introduced in 1966.

The Republic's President and Congress are elected by universal adult suffrage for four years. The legislature (Congreso Nacional) consists of a Chamber of Deputies with 149 members and a Senate with 30 members. The President holds executive power and appoints the Cabinet. The country is divided into 26 provinces, each with its own appointed Governor, and a Distrito Nacional, which contains the capital.

Ecuador

Official Name: The Republic of Ecuador
Capital: Quito
Currency: sucre
Area: 109,484 square miles
(270,670 square kilometers)
Population: 12,174,628 (1998 estimate)

Ecuador, on the Pacific coast of South America, is a largely agricultural country, dependent on exports of coffee, bananas, and shrimp. Its coastal plain, in the west, is separated from the tropical jungles of the Amazon by ranges and plateaux of the Andes.

Originally part of the Inca empire,

Ecuador was conquered by Spain in 1534, finally gaining independence in 1822, as part of the Republic of Gran Colombia. In 1830 it became a separate state. It has since lost territory in border disputes with neighbouring Peru and Colombia. In 1832, the Galapagos Islands were added to its territory.

Constitutionally, Ecuador's President and Congress are elected by universal adult suffrage. The President holds office for one four-year term only.

The legislature is the unicameral Congress, 12 members of which are elected nationally for four years, the remaining 65 being elected provincially for one two-year term. The President holds executive power and appoints the Governors of the 21 provinces.

El Salvador

Official Name: The Republic of El Salvador
Capital: San Salvador
Currency: colón
Area: 8,260 square miles (21,393 square kilometers)
Population: 5,118,599 (1992)

El Salvador, on the Pacific coast of Central America, is dominated by volcanic mountain ranges running from east to west. Most of its population lives in the subtropical valleys of the central region. Its economy is mainly agricultural, the chief crops being coffee, cotton, and sugar cane. It also exports shrimp and honey.

Conquered by Spain in 1524, El Salvador became independent in 1821, and joined the Federation of Central America in 1824, emerging as a separate republic in 1839.

For many years El Salvador was ruled by a small number of wealthy landowners; a peasant rebellion in 1932 was brutally suppressed. In 1972, following a military coup, the country dissolved into a vicious civil war, marked by killings by right-wing death squads, and left-wing guerrilla resistance. A peace accord was finally agreed in 1992.

El Salvador's President and National Assembly are elected by universal adult suffrage. The President holds office for five years. The legislature is the unicameral National Assembly whose 84 members are elected for 3 years. The President holds executive power and appoints the Council of Ministers.

Guatemala

Official Name: The Republic of Guatemala
Capital: Guatemala City/Ciudad de Guatemala
Currency: quetzal
Area: 42,056 square miles (108,889 square kilometers)
Population: 10,928,000 (1996 estimate)

Situated in the north of Central America, Guatemala consists of a narrow coastal plain, separating the Pacific from a heavily-populated highland region, and a short Caribbean coastline. The north is densely forested. The main exports are coffee, sugar, bananas, meat, shrimp, and petroleum.

Guatemala has one of the highest indigenous populations in Latin America.

A former center of Mayan civilization, Guatemala was conquered by Spain in 1523-24. After independence it formed the core of the Federation of Central America before becoming a republic in its own right in 1839.

Guatemala's history since then has often been marked by dictatorship and revolution, with conflict since the 1960s between the military and rural guerrilla movements. After a succession of military governments, an elected president took office in 1985.

The President and Congress are elected for four years by universal adult suffrage. The legislature is the unicameral National Congress consisting of 80 members, 16 of whom are elected nationally and the remaining 64 departmentally. The President holds executive power and appoints the Cabinet. The country is divided into 22 Departments.

Honduras

Official Name: The Republic of Honduras
Capital: Tegucigalpa
Currency: lempira
Area: 43,294 square miles
(112,088 square kilometers)
Population: 5,294,000 (1994 estimate)

The landscape of Honduras combines
tropical lowlands with more temperate
regions in the mountain ranges that cross
the country's interior from north to south.
Its main exports are bananas, coffee,
sugar, fruit, grain, shrimp, and beef.
Discovered by Columbus in 1502,
Honduras was governed by Spain from
1524 until it became independent in 1821.
Since then it has suffered from years of
instability, making it one of the most
poorly developed countries in Latin
America.
Under the 1982 Constitution the President
and National Assembly are elected by
universal adult suffrage.
The President holds office for a single
four-year term. The legislature is the
unicameral National Assembly
consisting of 128 members.
The President holds executive power.
If the amended Constitution of 1997 is
adopted, the National Assembly will be
reduced to 80 members. The country is
divided into 18 Departments.

Mexico/México

Official Name: The United Mexican States
Capital: Mexico City/México
Currency: peso
Area: 756,200 square miles
(1,958,200 square kilometers)
Population: 94,400,000 (1997 provisional
estimate)

Bordering the USA, Mexico is by far the
largest country in Central America.
Its topography ranges from low desert
plains and tropical lowlands to high
plateaux. The climate varies with
altitude, the coastal lowlands and the
tropical southern region being hot and
wet and the highlands of the central
plateau temperate.
Mexico has large reserves of petroleum
and many other minerals including zinc,
silver, and copper, and fluorite. A large
part of its export earnings comes from

these; it also exports cotton, coffee, sugar,
shrimp, fruit, and vegetables. Tourism is
a principal source of foreign exchange
with an estimated 10.1 million people
visiting Mexico in 1998.
The center of Aztec and Mayan
civilization, Mexico was conquered by
the Spanish in the early sixteenth
century. It became independent in 1821. In
1836 Texas rebelled and broke away;
Mexico's remaining territory north of
the Río Grande was lost to the USA in the
Mexican War of 1846-48. Half a century of
political instability followed until the
presidency of Porfirio Díaz, which began
in 1876, and, with a brief interruption,
went on until 1911. Civil war broke out in
1910 leading to partial political reform.
Mexican politics since 1946 have been
dominated by the PRI (Partido
Revolucionario Institucional).
Mexico is a federal republic made up of
31 federal states and a Federal District,
which contains the capital.
The President is elected by universal
adult suffrage for six years.
The legislature is the Congress which
consists of the Chamber of Deputies and
the Senate. The Chamber of Deputies has
500 members, directly elected for three
years, whilst the Senate has 128 members,
directly elected for six years at the same
time as the President.
The President has executive power and
appoints the Cabinet. Each state has its
own constitution, its own governor,
elected for six years, and an elected
chamber of deputies.
Education, which is free in state schools,
is officially compulsory between the ages
of six and twelve. Numbers of children
enrolled in secondary schools are
increasing steadily.

Nicaragua

Official Name: The Republic of
Nicaragua
Capital: Managua
Currency: córdoba
Area: 46,448 square miles
(120,254 square kilometers)
Population: 4,357,099 (1995)

Nicaragua in Central America extends
over a central mountan range, from the
Atlantic to the Pacific coastlines. It has a

tropical climate and its chief exports are coffee, cotton, bananas, sugar, meat, and shellfish.

Sighted by Columbus in 1502, and colonized by Spain in the early sixteenth century, Nicaragua gained independence in 1821, becoming a separate republic in 1838 after brief membership of the Federation of Central America.

Since then the country's history has been marked by border disputes, internal disturbances, and resistance to political and economic domination by the USA. In 1979, the left-wing Sandinistas overthrew the dictatorship of Anastasio Somoza, an event that led to a US-sponsored counter-revolutionary campaign.

The Sandinistas were defeated in democratic elections in 1990.

Nicaragua's President is elected by popular vote for five years.

The legislature is the unicameral National Assembly whose members are elected by universal adult suffrage, also for five years. The President holds executive power and appoints the Cabinet.

Panama/Panamá

Official Name: The Republic of Panama
Capital: Panama City/Ciudad de Panamá
Currency: balboa
Area: 29,773 square miles
(77,082 square kilometers)
Population: 2,719,000 (1997 estimate)

Situated on the isthmus connecting North and South America, Panama is mostly agricultural, its chief exports being bananas, coffee, fish, sugar, and clothing. It has tropical lowlands on the coasts, separated by an interior mountain range. The population is mostly of mixed Spanish and Indian stock, with West Indian and indigenous Indian minorities. Colonized by Spain in the early sixteenth century, Panama became independent in 1821 and joined the Republic of Gran Colombia, then became a province of Colombia. It gained full independence in 1903.

Construction of the Panama Canal was completed by the USA in 1914. The surrounding territory, the Canal Zone, was leased to the US until 1977, splitting Panama in two. The Canal was owned and operated by the United States until the Panama treaties, which went into effect in 1979, provided for its operation by the Panama Commission, a US government agency, until 31 December 1999, when the United States transferred ownership of the Canal to Panama.

Panama's President and Legislative Assembly are elected for five years by universal adult suffrage. The unicameral Legislative Assembly has 72 members. The President holds executive power, is assisted by two elected Vice-Presidents, and appoints the Council of Ministers and the Governors of the provinces. The country is divided into nine provinces and three autonomous Indian Reservations.

Paraguay

Official Name: The Republic of Paraguay
Capital: Asunción
Currency: guaraní
Area: 157,108 square miles
(406,752 square kilometers)
Population: 5,085,000 (1997 estimate)

Paraguay is an inland country in South America. The north-west of Paraguay is part of the flat, desolate and sparsely-populated Chaco region, while the south-east is cooler, wetter, and more developed, with farming communities and huge cattle ranches. Its main exports are soy bean seeds, cotton, timber, and meat.

Paraguay achieved independence from Spain in 1811. Between 1865 and 1870, it lost over half its population in the war against Brazil, Argentina, and Uruguay. It gained territory from Bolivia in the Chaco War of 1932-35 but the country has remained largely undeveloped, with a low standard of living.

In 1954, General Alfredo Stroessner seized power in a military dictatorship that lasted until 1989, when he was overthrown by a military coup. Since then, Paraguay has had a turbulent history, marked by struggles for power within the democratic system.

Under the 1992 Constitution, the President and Congress are elected by universal adult suffrage. The President holds office for five years as do the 80 members of the Chamber of Deputies, and the 45 members of the Senate, who together comprise Congress, the legislature. The President holds executive power and appoints the Council of Ministers. The country is divided into 17 departments, each with its own elected governor.

Peru/Perú

Official Name: The Republic of Peru
Capital: Lima
Currency: sol
Area: 496,414 square miles (1,285,216 square kilometers)
Population: 24,371,000 (1997 estimate)

Peru, on the Pacific coast of South America, has a narrow coastal plain with a dry desert climate, separated from the tropical lowlands of the Amazon by the Andes. Sheep, cattle, llamas, and alpacas are bred in mountain districts. Its main exports are fish meal, lead, zinc, copper, iron ore, and silver.

Peru was the center of the Inca empire, and still has a large indigenous population, with Quechua as well as Spanish being an official language. It was conquered for Spain by Pizarro in 1532, liberated between 1820 and 1824, and established as a democratic republic. The War of the Pacific (1879-83) resulted in the loss of territory to Chile.

In recent years, Peru's stability has been threatened by the activities of guerrilla groups, notably Sendero Luminoso (Shining Path). Cultivation of the coca plant in the valleys of the Andes has also led to problems related to the narcotics trade.

Peru's President and two Vice-Presidents are elected by universal adult suffrage. The President holds office for five years. The legislature is the unicameral Congreso, consisting of 120 members, elected for five years by a single national list system. The President holds executive power and appoints the Council of Ministers. The country is divided into 25 departments.

Puerto Rico

Capital: San Juan
Currency: US dollar
Area: 3,460 square miles (8,959 square kilometers)
Population: 3,833,000 (1998 estimate)

Puerto Rico is a mountainous island in the West Indies, partly of volcanic origin and partly formed of limestone. Its main exports are chemicals, electronic goods, clothing, fish, rum, and tobacco products. Visited by Columbus in 1493, Puerto Rico was one of the earliest Spanish settlements. In 1898, after the Spanish-American War, it was ceded to the USA. In 1952 it was established as a commonwealth in voluntary association with the USA, with full powers of local government. Since then there has been a great deal of political wrangling, both with the USA and within Puerto Rico, with a number of moves being made towards the island's transition to full statehood within the USA.

Industrialization and progress in social welfare have given Puerto Rico one of the highest standards of living in Latin America. Nevertheless many Puerto Ricans have emigrated to the United States. Spanish and English are the official languages.

According to the present self-governing commonwealth status, the Governor, the Legislative Assembly, and the Resident Commissioner are elected by universal adult suffrage for four years.

The legislature is the Legislative Assembly consisting of the House of Representatives, which has 54 members, and the Senate, which has 28 members. The Resident Commissioner represents Puerto Rico in the US House of Representatives but is allowed to vote only in committees.

Puerto Ricans have American citizenship, but only those resident in the USA can participate in presidential elections.

The Spanish-speaking world

Spain/España

Official Name: The Kingdom of Spain
Capital: Madrid
Currency: peseta
Area: 194,959 square miles
(505,750 square kilometers)
Population: 39,371,147 (1998 estimate)

Mainland Spain comprises the greater part of the Iberian Peninsula in south-west Europe. It is bounded by France to the north and by Portugal to the west. The kingdom also includes the Canary Islands in the Atlantic, the Balearic Islands in the Mediterranean, and Ceuta and Melilla in North Africa. Much of the interior consists of a high plateau (*meseta*). There are also mountain ranges in the north and south. Summers are hot throughout most of the country and particularly in the south. Winters are cold in the mountains and on the central plateau. The principal language is Castilian Spanish, but Catalan is widely spoken in the north-east, Basque in the north, and Galician in the north-west. There is no official state religion, but the vast majority of the population is Catholic.

Spain has industrialized rapidly in recent years and is now one of the world's largest car exporters.

Other important industries are steel, chemicals, shipbuilding, textiles, and footwear. However, the country is still predominantly agricultural, producing grain, citrus fruits, vegetables, olives, and wine. The Spanish fishing fleet is one of the largest in the world.

Conquered successively by the Carthaginians, Romans, Visigoths, and Moors, Spain was reunited as an independent country at the end of the fifteenth century. It emerged as a European and world power in the sixteenth century, but declined thereafter, losing most of its empire in the early nineteenth century.

The Moorish occupation, which lasted for over 700 years, left behind it a rich architectural heritage, particularly to be seen in Andalusia, in the very south of the country, in such celebrated buildings as the Alhambra in Granada, the Alcázar in Seville, and the great *mezquita* (mosque) of Córdoba.

Political instability in the nineteenth and early twentieth century finally led to the Civil War of 1936-39, resulting in the dictatorship of General Francisco Franco.

Democracy followed Franco's death in 1975 and the succession of King Juan Carlos as Head of State. The first democratic elections after the Franco era were held in 1977, and a constitutional hereditary monarchy re-established. Liberalization and decentralization of the state followed. In 1986, Spain joined the European Economic Community. Since then the country has modernized increasingly rapidly. Transportation systems are fast and efficient, and the big cities, notably Barcelona, have seen programmes of architectural redevelopment which are widely regarded as being amongst the most innovative in Europe.

The Franco era, during which the Basque, Catalan, and Galician languages were banned, saw the rise of increasingly vociferous separatist movements. The process of regional self-government was initiated in 1967, but the first autonomous parliaments, in the Basque Country and Catalonia, were not established until 1980. The Galician parliament was elected in October 1981 and the Andalusian parliament in 1982. The process of devolution was completed in 1983 with the election of the remaining 13 parliaments. However, extreme separatist movements are still active, notably in the Basque country and, to a much lesser extent, in Catalonia. These have the support of only a small minority of the local populations, but ETA, the Basque separatist organization, has frequently resorted to violence in its attempt to gain complete independence from Spain.

Under the 1978 Constitution, the King is Head of State and appoints the Prime Minister and, on the latter's recommendation, the other members of the Council of Ministers. The legislature is the Cortes Generales, consisting of the Congress of Deputies, which has 350 members, and the Senate, which has 208 members. In both cases, election is by direct universal adult suffrage for four years. The Senate has in addition 48 regional representatives, elected by the autonomous regional parliaments. These regional parliaments have varying degrees of autonomy, and each is elected by direct universal adult suffrage for four years.

Spain has a comprehensive system of social welfare and National Insurance is compulsory for all employed or self-employed citizens. Education is compulsory between the ages of six and sixteen, with around 30% of children attending private schools, the vast majority of which are administered by the Roman Catholic Church. In some autonomous regions, for example Catalonia, teaching of the regional language is compulsory in all schools.

Uruguay

Official Name: The Oriental Republic of Uruguay
Capital: Montevideo
Currency: peso
Area: 68,063 square miles
(176,215 square kilometers)
Population: 3,221,000 (1997 estimate)

Uruguay, on the Atlantic coast of South America, comprises an extensive range of well-watered grassy plains and low hills. This, together with a temperate climate, makes most of the country suitable for raising livestock. Its chief exports are live animals, meat, hide, wool, and fish. Although Uruguay was not permanently settled by Europeans until the seventeenth century, the Uruguayan population is now predominantly of European origin. Its proximity to Brazil made it a focus of Spanish-Portuguese rivalry. It was liberated from Spain in 1825. It remained relatively backward in the nineteenth century, but emerged in the early twentieth century as South America's first welfare state. Civil unrest beginning in the 1960s, and particularly fighting against the Marxist Tupamaro guerrillas, led to a period of military rule, but civilian government was restored in 1985.

Uruguay's President and Congress are elected by universal adult suffrage. The President holds office for five years, as do the 99 Deputies of the Chamber of Representatives and the 31 members of the Senate, who together comprise the Congress. The President holds executive power and appoints the Council of Ministers. The country is divided into 19 departments.

Venezuela

Official Name: The Republic of Venezuela
Capital: Caracas
Currency: bolivar
Area: 352,279 square miles
(912,050 square kilometers)
Population: 22,777,000 (1997 estimate)

Venezuela is in northern South America, with a Caribbean coastline. It has mountains in the north-west (Cordillera de Mérida) and south-east (the Guyana Highlands), between which lie the extensive plains (*llanos*) of the interior. Its chief exports are oil, iron ore, aluminum, steel, coffee, and cocoa. Visited by Columbus in 1498, Venezuela was given its name, meaning 'little Venice', by early Italian explorers when they saw Amerindian houses built on stilts over water, and were reminded of Venice. It was settled by the Spanish in the sixteenth century, becoming independent in 1821 as part of the Republic of Gran Colombia. It emerged as a separate nation in 1830.

Since then, Venezuela's political history has been characterized by instability, civil war, and dictatorships. It is however now a functioning democracy, with a well-developed social welfare system. Venezuela is a federal republic made up of 22 states, a Federal District which contains the capital, and 72 Federal Dependencies. The President and the Congress are elected for five years by universal adult suffrage. The legislature is the Congress, consisting of the Chamber of Deputies and the Senate. The President has executive power and appoints the Council of Ministers. Each state has a directly elected governor and an elected legislature.

The Spanish-speaking world

La vida y cultura británicas y estadounidenses desde la 'A' a la 'Z'

ABC - American Broadcasting Company
Una de las principales cadenas de televisión norteamericanas, actualmente propiedad de la compañía Walt Disney.

ACT - American College Test
Una prueba que los estudiantes de la mayor parte de los estados que forman Estados Unidos tienen que aprobar para ser admitidos en la universidad. Normalmente tiene lugar al final de la **HIGH SCHOOL** y cubre un número de materias principales, que incluye inglés y matemáticas.

African-American
Este es el término de más amplia aceptación hoy en día en Estados Unidos para referirse a americanos de origen africano.

Afro-Caribbean
Este es el término de más amplia aceptación hoy en día, tanto en Gran Bretaña como en Estados Unidos, para referirse a gente con antepasados africanos que procede del Caribe o que vive allí.

A level - Advanced level
Un examen sobre una asignatura en particular que tiene lugar en Inglaterra y Gales, en el último año de la enseñanza secundaria (*secondary school*), cuando el estudiante tiene alrededor de 18 años. Los alumnos que aspiran a avanzar hacia la educación terciaria (*higher education*), se presentan normalmente a 3 ó 4 *A levels*. La nota final (*grade*) se da independientemente para cada materia. Las universidades u otras instituciones seleccionan a los alumnos en razón de las notas que hayan obtenido, especialmente en aquellas materias que tienen relación directa con el área de estudio terciario que se ha elegido.

Alliance Party
Un partido político de Irlanda del Norte que reúne a personas de opiniones moderadas y cuyo objetivo es conseguir la resolución del conflicto existente entre grupos religiosos extremistas.

American Indian ▶ NATIVE AMERICAN.

AS level - Advanced Supplementary level
Un examen sobre una materia particular que muchos estudiantes de Inglaterra y Gales hacen, normalmente a los 18 años, en el último año del colegio secundario (*secondary school*). Este examen se sitúa entre el nivel del **GCSE** y del **A LEVEL**. Vale la mitad de un *A level* a la hora de solicitar una vacante en la universidad.

Asian-American
Este es el término de más amplia aceptación hoy en día para referirse a norteamericanos de origen asiático, especialmente del Extremo Oriente.

BBC - British Broadcasting Corporation
Una de las principales cadenas de televisión y radiodifusión británicas. Se creó por cédula real en 1927. No se financia a través de la publicidad, sino que con los ingresos provenientes del pago de una licencia anual que se debe obtener para poder utilizar un receptor de televisión. Tiene la obligación de informar de un modo imparcial.

. . . .

bed and breakfast

También puede verse anunciado como *Bed & Breakfast* o *B&B* y se encuentran por toda Gran Bretaña. Es un sistema de alojamiento en casas privadas o pequeños hoteles por el cual se paga un precio, normalmente razonable, por una habitación por persona y por noche, más un desayuno de jugo, cereales, huevos fritos con panceta y tostadas con mermelada de naranja. A veces, también, suele referirse al establecimiento donde se otorga este servicio.

Big Issue - The Big Issue

Una revista que la gente sin hogar vende en las calles de muchas ciudades de Gran Bretaña. Los artículos cubren normalmente temas de carácter social y a menudo son de alta calidad. Los vendedores compran la revista a uno de los centros de la organización que edita la revista, y luego la venden a un precio superior acordado previamente. Se les permite conservar este margen de ganancia para que de esta forma puedan mantenerse sin tener que mendigar.

Booker Prize

Un premio que se otorga, normalmente en octubre, a la mejor novela, escrita por un autor británico o de un país miembro de la *Commonwealth*, que se haya publicado en el año. La selección de una lista de candidatos y la elección final del ganador son objeto de considerable atención y discusión por parte de los medios de comunicación.

broadsheet

Es cualquier periódico de formato grande que se publica en Gran Bretaña, a diferencia de un **TABLOID** cuyas páginas son de un formato más pequeño. El formato grande está generalmente asociado a un periódico serio, mientras que el más pequeño es utilizado por periódicos de temática popular.

BT

La compañía telefónica más grande de Gran Bretaña. El servicio telefónico británico fue el primer servicio público que se privatizó (en 1984). Inicialmente conocida como *British Telecom*, cambió su nombre a *BT* en 1991. Actualmente hay varias compañías telefónicas privadas operando en Gran Bretaña.

busking

Es una palabra del inglés coloquial para referirse a la práctica de cantar o tocar un instrumento en la calle y otros lugares públicos como una forma de conseguir dinero. Las personas que lo hacen se llaman *buskers* y es frecuente encontrar a algunos de ellos en las grandes ciudades de Gran Bretaña.

Cabinet

El gabinete (ministerial) del gobierno británico es un cuerpo formado por unos 20 ministros (*ministers*) nombrados por el Primer Ministro (*Prime Minister*) y que se reúne regularmente para discutir asuntos administrativos y de política gubernamental. Cada uno de los ministros es responsable de un área en particular, mientras que a la totalidad del gabinete le atañe decidir acerca de la política a seguir por el gobierno. El líder del principal partido de la oposición también nombra un gabinete, llamado a veces gabinete en la sombra (**SHADOW CABINET**), con el objeto de que pueda gobernar en caso de que el gobierno sea derrotado, normalmente como resultado de unas eleciones generales.

Capitol

La sede del Congreso de Estados Unidos, situada en *Capitol Hill*, en Washington DC.

CBS - Columbia Broadcasting System

Una de las tres primeras compañías de radio y televisión nacionales norteamericanas. Las otras dos son **ABC** y **NBC**.

Channel Five

Un canal de televisión comercial británico que emite programas de entretenimiento de contenido ligero y popular.

Vida y cultura

Channel Four
Un canal de televisión comercial británico que emite una amplia variedad de programas de interés social y cultural. Su buen prestigio proviene del hecho de que produce documentales de gran calidad y da cobertura a acontecimientos artísticos y culturales.

City - The City
Es el área que se encuentra dentro de los límites de la antigua ciudad de Londres. Hoy en día es el centro financiero y de negocios de la capital, y es el lugar donde tienen sus oficinas centrales muchos bancos e instituciones financieras. A menudo, cuando se habla de *The City*, se está refiriendo a estas instituciones y no a la zona propiamente dicha.

City Technology College (CTC)
Un tipo de colegio británico de educación secundaria (*secondary education*) que ha sido el resultado de una asociación entre el gobierno y diversas compañías. Están situados en zonas urbanas, normalmente en el centro de ciudades, y dan especial importancia a la enseñanza de ciencias y tecnología.

CNN - Cable News Network
Una compañía de televisión norteamericana que emite programas de noticias e información vía satélite, las veinticuatro horas del día.

college of further education (CFE)
Un tipo de colegio universitario (*college*) de Gran Bretaña que ofrece cursos a tiempo completo y a tiempo parcial para estudiantes de más de 16 años. Su programa incluye cursos de preparación para los **GCSE**s y **A LEVEL**s así como clases diurnas y nocturnas en una amplia variedad de materias.

community college
Una clase de universidad norteamericana que ofrece una variedad de cursos de tipo práctico, especialmente orientados a la población local.

community service
Trabajo organizado y no remunerado que se realiza en beneficio de la comunidad. Puede consistir en proporcionar ayuda a los ancianos, a las personas discapacitadas o en llevar a cabo reparaciones en edificios comunitarios u otras instalaciones. En el caso de delitos menores, este tipo de trabajo se suele dar a delincuentes, en lugar de enviarlos a la cárcel.

comprehensive school
Un colegio británico de educación secundaria con gran número de alumnos de todo nivel, cuyas edades fluctúan entre 11 y 18 años.

Congress
El Congreso es el organismo nacional legislativo de Estados Unidos. Se reúne en el **CAPITOL** y está compuesto por dos cámaras, el Senado (**SENATE**) y la Cámara de Representantes (**HOUSE OF REPRESENTATIVES**). La función del Congreso es elaborar leyes. Toda nueva ley debe ser aprobada primero por las dos cámaras y posteriormente por el Presidente (**PRESIDENT**).

Conservative Party
El Partido Conservador es uno de los principales partidos políticos británicos. Se sitúa a la derecha del espectro político que apoya el sistema capitalista, la libre empresa y la privatización de la industria y los servicios públicos. Surgió alrededor de 1830 como resultado de la evolución del *Tory Party* y a menudo se le denomina aún por este nombre.

council
El ayuntamiento (*council*) es un organismo, elegido por todos los ciudadanos, responsable del gobierno local en áreas tales como un condado (**COUNTY**), parte de un condado, una ciudad pequeña o parte de una ciudad grande del Reino Unido. Debe mantener en buen

• •

estado los caminos y las instalaciones de uso comunitario, así como el mantenimiento de un amplio número de servicios.

council tax
Impuesto que los habitantes de un inmueble deben pagar, en Gran Bretaña, a la municipalidad local. La cantidad que debe pagarse se calcula tomando como base el valor estimado de la vivienda, y el número de personas que viven en ella.

county
Una región administrativa de Gran Bretaña que agrupa un número de distritos (*districts*). Los condados son las principales unidades administrativas de Gran Bretaña y muchos tienen demarcaciones que se remontan a muchos años atrás. Sin embargo, en las últimas décadas, estas se han cambiado mucho como también sus nombres, y el término '*county*' a menudo ya no se usa.

Democratic Party
El Partido Demócrata es uno de los dos principales partidos políticos de Estados Unidos. El otro es el Partido Republicano (**REPUBLICAN PARTY**). El Partido Demócrata está considerado como el propulsor de políticas más liberales, especialmente referidas a temas que afectan a la sociedad. Por esta razón, consigue el apoyo de sindicatos y grupos minoritarios.

Downing Street
Es el nombre de una calle del barrio de Westminster, en el centro de Londres. El número 10 de Downing Street es la residencia oficial del Primer Ministro y el número 11 la del *Chancellor of the Exchequer* (equivalente al cargo del Ministro de Economía y Hacienda). Los periodistas utilizan a menudo las expresiones *Downing Street* o *Number 10* para referirse al despacho del Primer Ministro.

DUP – Democratic Unionist Party ▶ ULSTER DEMOCRATIC UNIONIST PARTY.

elementary school
En los Estados Unidos, un colegio que imparte una educación formal en los primeros niveles de enseñanza. Es el equivalente a un colegio de enseñanza primaria. Estos colegios están dirigidos a niños de edades comprendidas entre seis y doce o trece años. Este nivel de enseñanza se denomina también *grade school*.

football pools
Juego de apuestas muy popular en Gran Bretaña, similar a las quinielas en España y al prode en Argentina. Consiste en intentar acertar los resultados de los partidos de fútbol, llenando unos cupones (*pools coupons*). El premio, que se junta con el dinero que se paga por cada apuesta, se reparte entre aquellos que más se han acercado al resultado. Puede suceder que una sola persona se lleve todo el premio.

further education
En Gran Bretaña, el término *further education* se utiliza normalmente para referirse cualquier tipo de enseñanza dirigida a personas de edad superior a los 16 años, edad mínima en que se puede dejar la escolaridad obligatoria, y que no están en la universidad, en cuyo caso se habla de *higher education*. Sin embargo, en los Estados Unidos, el término *further education* también se utiliza para referirse a la educación universitaria.

Gaelic
Es la lengua de origen celta que hablan algunas personas en Escocia (e Irlanda). El gaélico escocés solo lo hablan unas 40.000 personas que viven en las *Highlands* y en las islas del oeste de Escocia.

GCSE - General Certificate of Secondary Education
Un examen sobre una materia en particular que tiene lugar, en Inglaterra y Gales, en el

• •

quinto año de la enseñanza secundaria (*secondary school*), cuando el estudiante tiene alrededor de 16 años. Todos los alumnos, sea cual sea su nivel de habildad, pueden presentarse a este examen y la mayoría lo hace en varias asignaturas. Las nota final (*grade*) se da en forma independiente para cada materia. Los que deseen seguir estudiando para presentarse más tarde a los exámenes de **A LEVEL**, necesitan tener un cierto número de *GCSE*s. También se pueden presentar a una mezcla de *GCSE*s y de **GNVQ.**

GNVQ - General National Vocational Qualification
Un examen sobre una materia en particular que tiene lugar en Inglaterra y Gales, en el quinto año de la enseñanza secundaria (*secondary school*), cuando el estudiante tiene alrededor de 16 años. Estos exámenes fueron introducidos en 1992, como una alternativa a los del **GCSE,** en un número de materias de orientación más práctica o vocacional. Tiene como objeto preparar a los alumnos para el mundo laboral. Muchos estudiantes se presentan a una mezcla de *GNVQ*s y *GCSE*s.

GP - General Practitioner
Es un médico de medicina general (también llamado a menudo *family doctor*), que trata a todo tipo de pacientes dentro de una localidad de Gran Bretaña. Es el equivalente al médico de cabecera. En un consultorio (*surgery*) suelen atender varios médicos (*group practice*), y los pacientes que están registrados en ese consultorio pueden ser atendidos por el médico de su elección. Los pacientes de la Seguridad Social (**NATIONAL HEALTH SERVICE**) tienen atención gratuita. Cada consultorio tiene financiación directa o indirecta del gobierno. Cuando es necesario, un médico puede remitir a un paciente a un especialista o arreglar su hospitalización.

grade school ▶ ELEMENTARY SCHOOL

graduate school
Especialmente en Estados Unidos, departamento de una universidad que ofrece cursos avanzados para los que quieren seguir estudiando y/o investigando una vez que han obtenido un título, normalmente después de realizar 3 ó 4 años de estudios universitarios.

grammar school
En áreas de Inglaterra y Gales, un tipo de colegio de enseñanza secundaria (*secondary school*) que admite a alumnos de 11 ó 12 años que han aprobado una prueba de aptitud. Desde 1965, estos colegios han sido reeplazados en su mayor parte por los **COMPREHENSIVE SCHOOL**s.

green card
Un documento oficial que autoriza a una persona que no es ciudadana americana a residir y trabajar en Estados Unidos. Este permiso es obligatorio para cualquiera que desee ir a ese país a residir de forma permanente y trabajar.

Greyhound bus
Vehículo que pertenece a la mayor compañía de autobuses de los Estados Unidos (*The Greyhound Lines Company*). Circulan entre ciudades y grandes poblaciones a través de toda la geografía estadounidense y son muy usados por la gente joven y los turistas, quienes a menudo recorren grandes distancias en ellos.

Guardian Angels
Una organización formada por jóvenes en Estados Unidos, creada para proteger a la población de la delincuencia. Sus miembros llevan gorras rojas y camisas que tienen el eslogan *Dare to Care* (que viene a expresar la idea de 'Atrévete a preocuparte por los demás'). Trabajan en colaboración con la policía y no van armados.

high school
El último ciclo del colegio secundario en Estados Unidos, generalmente para alumnos cuyas edades fluctúan entre los 14 y 18 años. En Gran Bretaña, algunos colegios secundarios también se llaman *high schools*.

• •

House of Commons

La Cámara de los Comunes es la cámara baja del Parlamento británico o **HOUSES OF PARLIAMENT**. Los parlamentarios (*Members of Parliament*), que son elegidos por el pueblo, se reúnen aquí para debatir temas de política internacional y nacional de actualidad y para votar a favor o en contra de la nueva legislación.

House of Lords

La Cámara de los Lores es la cámara alta del Parlamento británico o **HOUSES OF PARLIAMENT**. Sus miembros no son elegidos por el pueblo, sino que son nombrados por los partidos políticos. Hasta 1999 un número de los cargos eran hereditarios. Su función es discutir y posteriormente aprobar o sugerir cambios a la legislación que ha sido aprobada en la Cámara de los Comunes (**HOUSE OF COMMONS**). Es también el último tribunal de apelación.

House of Representatives

La Cámara de Representantes es la cámara baja del Congreso (**CONGRESS**) de Estados Unidos. Está formada por 435 representantes (**REPRESENTATIVE**s) que son elegidos cada dos años. Cada estado de la unión tiene un número de representantes proporcional a su población. Esta cámara es la encargada de introducir nueva legislación, por lo que toda nueva ley debe ser aprobada por ella.

Houses of Parliament

Son las dos cámaras del Parlamento británico, la Cámara de los Comunes (**HOUSE OF COMMONS**) y la Cámara de los Lores (**HOUSE OF LORDS**). El Palacio de Westminster (*Palace of Westminster*), que es el grupo de edificios situados en el centro de Londres donde se reúnen los miembros de las dos cámaras, también se conoce con este nombre.

independent school

Un colegio de Gran Bretaña que no recibe dinero alguno del estado y se autofinancia mediante el pago de cuotas por parte de los padres. Los **PUBLIC SCHOOL**s y los **PREPARATORY SCHOOL**s están dentro de esta categoría.

infant school

Un colegio de Gran Bretaña que ofrece los tres primeros años de educación formal. A menudo forma parte de un **PRIMARY SCHOOL**, que junto al **JUNIOR SCHOOL** cubren la educación del niño hasta los 11 años. En Gran Bretaña los niños deben empezar la educación a los cinco años.

International Herald Tribune - The International Herald Tribune

Un periódico estadounidense de difusión internacional. Su equipo editorial está basado en París y se publica en 180 países. Tiene una gran reputación por la seriedad y profundidad con la que cubre la información. Es un periódico de formato grande (**BROADSHEET**).

Internet

Algunos sitios Web en inglés :
CNN Interactive http://www.cnn.com; **BBC** http://www.bbc.co.uk; **New York Times** http://www.nytimes.com; **The Times** http://www.the-times.co.uk; **Museum of Modern Art** http://www.moma.org

interstate (highway)

En Estados Unidos, una ruta nacional de larga distancia que cruza de un estado a otro. Están señalizadas con un símbolo rojo y azul que lleva la letra 'I' seguida del número de la ruta. Las que van de norte a sur tienen números impares y las que van de este a oeste tienen números pares. Cada calzada tiene cuatro carriles.

IRA – Irish Republican Army

El IRA (Ejército Republicano Irlandés) es la rama militar del **SINN FEIN**. Su objetivo es la unión de la República de Irlanda e Irlanda del Norte. Declaró el alto el fuego en 1994 y luego en 1997.

Vida y cultura

ITV - Independent Television
Un grupo de compañías de televisión que emiten en el Canal 3 de la televisión británica. Ofrecen quince programaciones diferentes para quince regiones distintas del Reino Unido. Cada programación incluye sus propios programas y noticias, aunque también efectúan muchas transmisiones en común.

Jobcentre
Es una oficina que proporciona diversos servicios a aquellas personas que están buscando trabajo, servicios tales como anunciar las vacantes de empleo que se producen en un área determinada y concertar entrevistas con los que ofrecen trabajo. Estas oficinas se pueden encontrar en la mayor parte de las poblaciones británicas y están dirigidas por el gobierno a través del *Employment Service*.

junior high school
En Estados Unidos, un colegio que cubre la educación entre el **ELEMENTARY SCHOOL** y el **HIGH SCHOOL** y que tiene normalmente conexiones con este último.

junior school
Un colegio estatal de Gran Bretaña para niños de entre 7 y 11 años.

Labour Party
El Partido Laborista es uno de los tres principales partidos políticos de Gran Bretaña. Accedió por primera vez al poder en 1924 y tiene como objetivo representar los intereses de los trabajadores y sindicatos. En los últimos 20 años, el partido ha abandonado su postura de izquierda en puntos tales como la propiedad pública de la industria y los servicios, por lo que, hoy en día, se le denomina con frecuencia **New Labour**.

L-driver - learner driver
Es el término con el que en Gran Bretaña se denomina a los que están aprendiendo a conducir un coche u otro vehículo. Estas personas cuando están al volante, siempre deben ir acompañadas de otra que tenga una licencia de conducción (*driving license*) en vigencia. También deben llevar una placa de L o de prácticas (*L-plates*), en las partes delantera y trasera del vehículo que conducen, hasta que hayan aprobado su examen de conducir (*driving test*). La placa L es un cuadrado blanco de plástico con una letra 'L' roja.

Liberal Democratic Party
Al Partido Demócrata Liberal también se le conoce informalmente como los **Lib Dems**. Es el tercer partido en importancia en Gran Bretaña. Se formó en 1988 mediante la unión del Partido Liberal (*Liberal Party*) y el Partido Socialdemócrata (*Social Democratic Party*).

Los Angeles Times - The Los Angeles Times
Un diario que se publica en Los Angeles y que está considerado como uno de los mejores periódicos de Estados Unidos. Distribuye sus artículos por todo el mundo y ha ganado más de veinte **PULITZER PRIZE**s.

Medicaid
Un seguro de enfermedad administrado por el gobierno de Estados Unidos para ciudadanos de menos de 65 años y con bajos ingresos.

Medicare
Un seguro de enfermedad administrado por el gobierno de Estados Unidos para ciudadanos de más de 65 años.

motorway
Gran Bretaña tiene un amplio sistema de autopistas (*motorways*) que normalmente tienen tres carriles por calzada. Están señalizadas con la letra 'M' seguida de un número y tienen un límite de velocidad de 70 millas por hora (112 kms/h). En las autopistas británicas no hay que pagar peaje.

MP - Member of Parliament

Un miembro de la Cámara de los Comunes (**HOUSE OF COMMONS**) que representa a una de las 659 circunscripciones electorales de Inglaterra, Escocia, Gales e Irlanda del Norte.

National Book Award

Cualquiera de los varios premios otorgados anualmente, por la *Association of American Publishers*, a un libro nuevo que se haya publicado en Estados Unidos. Los premios corresponden a una serie de categorías tales como ficción, ensayo, y poesía.

National Health Service (NHS)

En Gran Bretaña, es el servicio público que proporciona asistencia médica a toda la población. Está financiado en gran parte por el gobierno y la asistencia, por lo general, es gratuita. Se deben pagar la atención dental y las medicinas que el médico haya recetado. Sin embargo, las personas que pertenecen a ciertos grupos, tales como los niños, jóvenes hasta los 18 años de edad y los jubilados, no pagan por estos servicios.

National Insurance (NI)

En Gran Bretaña, sistema de pagos obligatorios, *National Insurance Contributions* (cotizaciones o contribuciones a la Seguridad Social), que los empleados y empleadores deben realizar a fin de que el gobierno pueda financiar los diferentes beneficios sociales que proporciona, tales como **JOBSEEKEERS' ALLOWANCE** y las jubilaciones, así como el **NATIONAL HEALTH SERVICE**. Todo adulto debe tener un número de la seguridad social (*National Insurance Number*).

National Lottery

Una lotería que se sortea en Gran Bretaña, mediante la cual se recauda dinero tanto para una amplia variedad de proyectos culturales o deportivos como para obras benéficas y la conservación del patrimonio nacional.

National Trust

En Gran Bretaña, una fundación que tiene como objetivo la conservación de lugares de interés histórico o de belleza natural. Se financia mediante legados y subvenciones privadas y es la mayor propietaria de tierras en Gran Bretaña. A lo largo del tiempo ha obtenido, mediante compra o cesión, enormes extensiones de tierras, así como pueblos y casas, muchas de las cuales están abiertas al público en ciertas épocas del año.

Native American

Es actualmente el término cuyo uso se acepta para referirse a cualquiera de los pueblos indígenas de América del Norte, América del Sur y el Caribe. Este término se prefiere al de *American Indian*, especialmente en contextos oficiales. Se considera más preciso y positivo ya que el término *Indian* (indio) deriva del hecho de que Cristóbal Colón, cuando llegó a América, creyó que se encontraba en la India. Con todo, *American Indian* todavía se usa ampliamente y los propios indígenas no lo consideran ofensivo.

NBC - National Broadcasting Company

La primera compañía de radiodifusión que se fundó en Estados Unidos (1926). El primer canal de televisión de la NBC empezó a transmitir en 1940.

Newsweek

Una revista estadounidense que se publica semanalmente en Nueva York. Cubre una gran variedad de temas políticos, sociales, culturales y científicos.

New Yorker - The New Yorker

Una revista muy conocida y respetada que se publica semanalmente en Nueva York. Se especializa en artículos largos que analizan, en profundidad, una gran variedad de temas. Ofrece información sobre novelas de ficción y poesía de reciente publicación, artículos y dibujos humorísticos.

Vida y cultura

• •

NVQ - National Vocational Qualification
Un título que se obtiene en Gran Bretaña mediante planes de educación y formación que se llevan a cabo en el lugar de trabajo o en ciertas universidades y colegios. Las materias guardan una relación directa con el trabajo y se imparten en varios niveles.

pantomime
Un tipo de representación teatral que tiene lugar tradicionalmente, en teatros de toda Gran Bretaña, durante las semanas previas y posteriores a la Navidad. Generalmente está dirigida a los niños. El argumento, a menudo, es una adaptación cómica de un cuento tradicional y cuenta con un número de personajes de características exageradas e increíbles. También requiere de un gran nivel de participación por parte del público. De acuerdo con la tradición, el papel del héroe (*principal boy*) es interpretado por una actriz y el de la *dame*, un personaje femenino grotesco, es interpretado por un actor.

Parliament
El Parlamento británico es el más alto organismo legislativo de Gran Bretaña y está formado por el soberano (el rey o la reina), la Cámara de los Lores (**HOUSE OF LORDS**) y la Cámara de los Comunes (**HOUSE OF COMMONS**).

PBS - Public Broadcasting Service
Un servicio de radiodifusión estadounidense, financiado por el gobierno, famoso por la calidad de sus programas. Consiste en una asociación de emisoras locales que trasmiten sin fines de lucro y sin publicidad.

Pentagon - The Pentagon
Es el edificio de forma pentagonal, situado en Wahington, donde se encuentra la oficina central del Ministerio de Defensa y de las fuerzas armadas de Estados Unidos. A menudo se utiliza el término *'The Pentagon'* para referirse al Estado Mayor, es decir a los generales y jefes militares que trabajan allí.

Plaid Cymru
El partido nacionalista galés. Su objetivo fundamental es conseguir la independencia de Gales del resto del Reino Unido. Gran parte de su esfuerzo se ha visto dirigido a la recuperación de la lengua galesa (**WELSH**) y a la conservación de la cultura de Gales.

preparatory school
En Gran Bretaña, un colegio privado, llamado también *prep school*, para alumnos de edades comprendidas entre siete y trece años. Algunos tienen el régimen de internado y otros no, pero la mayoría son una mezcla de ambos. Normalmente es un colegio no mixto. Los padres pagan por la educación de sus hijos y otros servicios y gran parte de los alumnos pasa, a continuación, a un colegio privado (**PUBLIC SCHOOL**). Los *preparatory schools* y los *public schools* actualmente se llaman a menudo **INDEPENDENT SCHOOL**s.

President
En Estados Unidos el Presidente es la cabeza del Estado, es responsable de la política exterior y es comandante en jefe de las fuerzas armadas. El Presidente puede nombrar a jueces federales y a ministros. A solicitud del Congreso (**CONGRESS**) aprueba las nuevas leyes. Puede gobernar un máximo de dos legislaturas (*terms*) de cuatro años cada una.

primary school
En Gran Bretaña, un colegio estatal para niños cuyas edades fluctúan entre 5 y 11 años.

public school
En Inglaterra y Gales, un colegio privado para alumnos de edades comprendidas entre trece y dieciocho años. La mayor parte de los alumnos que va a estos colegios ha estudiado anteriormente en un **PREPARATORY SCHOOL**. La mayoría de los *public schools* son internados y normalmente no son mixtos. Los padres pagan por la educación de sus hijos y otros servicios. En Escocia y Estados Unidos el término *public school* se utiliza para referirse a un colegio estatal.

Pulitzer Prize

Es un premio de gran prestigio que se otorga anualmente por los éxitos más destacados en el mundo del periodismo, la literatura y la música norteamericanos.

Queen's Speech

Un discurso preparado por los miembros de gobierno británico para que sea leído por la reina en la Cámara de los Lores (**HOUSE OF LORDS**) en la ceremonia de apertura del Parlamento, que tiene lugar todos los años en otoño. Es una ocasión importante, ya que el discurso esboza los planes del gobierno para el año siguiente.

region

Es la unidad administrativa más grande de Escocia. Existen nueve y cada una tiene su propio ayuntamiento (**COUNCIL**).

Representative

Un miembro de la Cámara de Representantes (**HOUSE OF REPRESENTATIVE**s) de Estados Unidos.

Republican Party

El Partido Republicano es uno de los dos principales partidos políticos de Estados Unidos. El otro es el Partido Demócrata (**DEMOCRATIC PARTY**). Está considerado como más conservador que este último.

SAT

1 - **Scholastic Aptitude Test.** Una prueba de aptitud, que se hace normalmente en el último año del **HIGH SCHOOL** y que los estudiantes deben aprobar para entrar a la mayor parte de las universidades estadounidenses.
2 - **Standard Assessment Test.** Una prueba que se hace a los alumnos de todos los colegios de Inglaterra y Gales, a los 7, 11, y 14 años a fin de evaluar su progreso.

Scottish Certificate of Education

El certificado más importante que se obtiene al terminar el colegio en Escocia, que cuenta con su propio sistema educativo dentro de Gran Bretaña. El examen de nivel inferior (*Standard*) se hace a los 16 años y es el equivalente al **GCSE** de Inglaterra. El de nivel superior (*Higher*) se hace a los 17 años y es el equivalente al **A-LEVEL** de Inglaterra.

Scottish National Party (SNP)

El Partido Nacionalista Escocés tiene como objetivo conseguir un gobierno completamente independiente para Escocia.

Scottish Parliament

El Parlamento escocés, cuyos miembros se reúnen en *Holyrood House*, en Edimburgo, la capital de Escocia. Se inauguró en 1999 después de la celebración de elecciones y da al país un mayor grado de autonomía que el que tenía anteriormente con respecto al Parlamento británico de Londres.

SDLP - Social Democratic and Labour Party

Partido de Irlanda del Norte cuyo objetivo es conseguir la igualdad de derechos para los católicos y la unificación de Irlanda del Norte y de la República de Irlanda. Sin embargo, no aprueba el uso de la violencia como medio para conseguirlo.

Senate

El Senado es la cámara alta del Congreso (**CONGRESS**) de Estados Unidos. Está formado por 100 senadores (**SENATOR**s), dos por cada estado y son elegidos por periodos de seis meses. Toda nueva ley debe ser aprobada por el Senado y la Cámara de Representantes (**HOUSE OF REPRESENTATIVE**s), pero el Senado tiene responsabilidad especial en asuntos relacionados con la política exterior y tiene poder para 'asesorar y aprobar' los nombramientos hechos por el Presidente (**PRESIDENT**).

Vida y cultura

Senator
Un miembro del Senado (**SENATE**) de Estados Unidos.

Shadow Cabinet ▶ CABINET

Silicon Valley
Es el nombre utilizado para referirse al Valle de Santa Clara, en California, donde se concentra un gran número de compañías de electrónica e informática. El nombre deriva del uso del silicio *(silicon)* en la electrónica.

Sinn Fein
Partido político cuyo objetivo es una Irlanda republicana unida. Desde los años 20 empezó a funcionar como la rama política del **IRA**.

soap opera
Nombre con el que se designa, de forma humorística, un tipo de serie televisiva extremadamente popular en Gran Bretaña y Estados Unidos. Trata normalmente de la vida diaria de gente corriente perteneciente a una comunidad particular. Algunas de las series británicas más populares son *Coronation Street*, la más antigua ya que empezó emitirse en 1960, y *Eastenders*. En Estados Unidos las más conocidas son *Dallas* y *Dynasty*, que ya han dejado de filmarse pero cuyos capítulos se repiten a veces en la televisión por satélite. Las primeras *soap operas* (literalmente significa óperas de jabón) que se emitieron en Estados Unidos estaban financiadas por compañías de jabón, y de ahí su nombre.

Stars and Stripes
La bandera de Estados Unidos.

Star-Spangled Banner
El himno de Estados Unidos.

state school
En Gran Bretaña, un colegio que está financiado directa o indirectamente por el gobierno, y que ofrece educación gratuita. La mayor parte de los niños británicos va a este tipo de colegios.

tabloid
En Gran Bretaña, un periódico que se imprime en páginas de formato pequeño, a diferencia de los periódicos de formato grande (**BROADSHEET**s), que se imprimen en páginas de un tamaño dos veces mayor. El formato *tabloid* está normalmente asociado con la prensa popular, representada por periódicos como *The Sun* y *The Mirror*, mientras que el formato grande es el utilizado por la mayor parte de los periódicos de calidad, como por ejemplo *The Guardian* y *The Times*.

The City, The Washington Post, The White House, etc. ▶ CITY, WASHINGTON POST, WHITE HOUSE, etc.

Time
Una revista americana que es famosa en todo el mundo por su cobertura de noticias y sucesos internacionales.

TOEFL – Test of English as a Foreign Language
Un examen que, a la hora de solicitar el ingreso a una universidad americana, evalúa el dominio del inglés de aquellos estudiantes cuya lengua materna no es este idioma.

Tory ▶ CONSERVATIVE PARTY

Ulster Democratic Unionist Party
Partido político de Irlanda del Norte apoyado en su mayor parte por protestantes y que sostiene que Irlanda del Norte debe seguir siendo parte del Reino Unido.

Ulster Unionist Party
Partido político de Irlanda del Norte, que sostiene que Irlanda del Norte debe seguir siendo parte del Reino Unido. Está considerado como más moderado que el **ULSTER DEMOCRATIC UNIONIST PARTY**.

Union Jack
Es el nombre que se le da a la bandera del Reino Unido. Está formada por la cruz de San Jorge representando a Inglaterra, la cruz de San Andrés representando a Escocia, y la cruz de San Patricio representando a Irlanda del Norte.

Wall Street
Es una calle en Manhattan, Nueva York, donde se encuentran la Bolsa de Nueva York y las oficinas centrales de muchas instituciones financieras. A menudo, cuando se habla de *Wall Street,* se estás refiriendo a esta instituciones y no a la calle propiamente dicha.

Washington Post - The Washington Post
Un periódico americano que se publica diariamente en Washington. Es famoso por la amplia cobertura de su información, por el alto nivel de calidad de su periodismo de investigación y por sus opiniones liberales.

Welsh
El galés, de origen céltico, es la lengua oficial de Gales, conjuntamente con el inglés. Para más del 20% de la población sigue siendo la lengua materna y como muchas otras lenguas minoritarias, ha experimentado un resurgimiento durante los últimos cuarenta años. Actualmente se estudia como materia obligatoria en todos los colegios de Gales, los letreros y otras señales de las ciudades aparecen normalmente en inglés y galés.

Welsh Assembly
El parlamento galés, cuyos miembros se reúnen en la capital de Gales, Cardiff. Se inauguró en 1999 después de la celebración de elecciones y da al país un mayor grado de autonomía que el que tenía anteriormente con respecto al Parlamento británico de Londres.

Westminster
Un barrio del centro de Londres en el que se encuentran muchos de los principales edificios del gobierno. Entre estos, los más importantes son el Palacio de Westminster (*Palace of Westminster*), también llamado el Parlamento (**HOUSES OF PARLIAMENT**), donde se reúnen las dos cámaras. En el mismo barrio se encuentra la Abadía de Westminster (*Westminster Abbey*), donde han sido coronados todos los monarcas ingleses, a partir de Guillermo el Conquistador en 1066.

Whitehall
Una calle del centro de Londres donde están situadas una gran parte de las oficinas del gobierno. Los periodistas utilizan a menudo el término para referirse al gobierno y la administración.

White House – The White House
La residencia y el despacho oficial del presidente de Estados Unidos, situada en Washington. Los periodistas utilizan a menudo el término '*the White House*' para referirse al Presidente y a sus consejeros.

Vida y cultura

Letter-writing / Redacción de cartas

Holiday postcard

■ *Beginning (quite informal): this formula is used
among young people, very close friends, and,
generally speaking, when addressee and sender
address each other using the familiar form tú.*
Querido Juan *can also be used, or* Querida Ana *if
the addressee is a woman. If addressed to two or
more people, males and females or only males,
the masculine plural* Queridos *is always used:*
Queridos Juan y Ana, Queridos amigos, Queridos
Juan y Pedro. Queridas *is used if the card or
letter is addressed to more than one female:*
Queridas chicas, Queridas Ana y Conchita

■ *Address: Note that the title (Sr., Sra.,
Srta.) is always followed by a full stop
and stands next to the name.*

*The house number (sometimes also
N° ...) comes after the street name. In
addresses of apartments in Spain, this
is often followed by a floor number and
sometimes the apartment's position on
the landing: c/ Hermosilla 98, 6° Dcha.*

The zip code comes before the place

Hola Juan

*¿Qué tal? Hemos llegado a esta maravilla de ciudad hace
dos días y estamos disfrutando muchísimo de todo lo que
vemos, ¡a pesar del tiempo! Ya sabes tú como es el clima
por aquí.*

*Hemos visitado los baños romanos (por supuesto), la
catedral y sus alrededores. Hicimos un paseo por el río en
barca y hemos recorrido la ciudad a pie. Es la mejor forma
de apreciar la increíble arquitectura de este lugar.*

*¡Ah! También tomamos un té inglés como es debido, con
sándwichs de pepino incluidos, en la elegante "Pump
Room". Mañana regresamos a Londres y luego de vuelta a
la dura realidad.*

*Esperamos que todo te haya ido bien con el cambio de
trabajo. Ya nos contarás.*

Hasta pronto.

Ana y Eduardo

Bath, 8 de octubre 1999 ①

Sr. Juan Elizalde

P° Pintor Rosales 101

28008 Madrid

Spain

■ *Endings (informal):* Un fuerte
abrazo, Muchos saludos,
Muchos besos y abrazos. *Also in
Latin America:* Cariños *(NB not
between men),* Hasta pronto
(See you soon).

① *Not only on postcards, but on most
personal letters, Spanish speakers do
not put the address at the top, but just
the name of the place and the date.
The sender's address is recorded on
the back of the envelope.*

Postal desde un lugar de vacaciones

- Por tratarse de una postal, el encabezamiento es muy simple, siempre Dear, seguido del primer nombre del destinatario.

- En la dirección, el título (Mr, Mrs, Miss, Ms) precede al nombre del destinatario en la primera línea. Las abreviaturas Mr, Mrs y Ms no van seguidas de punto. En Gran Bretaña muchas casas suelen tener un nombre, el que aparece encima del de la calle. Tanto en Norteamérica como en Gran Bretaña, el número de la casa se coloca antes del nombre de la calle. Debajo le siguen, en Gran Bretaña, el barrio, la ciudad o el condado y el código postal (postcode) cada uno en una línea. En Norteamérica debajo del número de la casa y el nombre de la calle, se incluyen la ciudad, las iniciales del Estado y el código postal (zip code), todo en una línea:

Mr John Spaline Jr
100 Irving Palace
New York, NY 10001
USA

Dear John

6. 8. 2000 ①

Greetings from Mexico City! Got here a couple of days ago, but already in love with the place (in spite of the traffic and smog). Everything is so different and the food sometimes a bit too hot for us. Delicious though. We have visited the Archaeological Museum (out of this world). The Zócalo, the Cathedral, an Aztec temple and other places. Last night we went to Plaza Garibaldi to see the mariachis sing. Very atmospheric. Tomorrow we're visiting Tehotihuacán and the pyramids, and then on Thursday we head home. Hope ② your mother is fully recovered by now.

See you soon,

Mark and Juliet.

Mr J. Roberts

The Willows

49 North Terrace

Kings Barton

Nottinghamshire

NG8 42l

England

- Fórmula de despedida informal empleada cuando el destinatario es un amigo íntimo o un pariente cercano. Otras alternativas pueden ser: All the best, With love from, o simplemente Love (from).

① No sólo en postales sino también en la mayoría de las cartas de tipo personal, tanto los norteamericanos como los ingleses colocan la fecha en el ángulo superior derecho.

② Estilo telegrama, típico de una postal, en el que se suprime el pronombre: Got here ... y Hope you're ... en lugar de We got here ... y We hope you're ... respectivamente.

. . . .

Christmas and New Year Wishes

On a card:

Feliz Navidad ① y Próspero Año Nuevo ②

Feliz Navidad ① y los mejores *deseos* para el Año
Nuevo ③

① *Or:* Felices Pascuas,
   Felices Navidades.

② *Or:* Próspero Año 2001.

③ *Or:* para el Año 2001.

In a letter:

■ *Beginning: the name on the first line is usually followed by a colon.*

④ *This is a letter to friends who are addressed as* vosotros, *the plural of the
familiar form* tú. *However, Latin American Spanish uses the formal plural*
ustedes *instead of this form, so would replace the words marked * in the
letter as follows:* vosotros *by* ustedes, vuestro *and* vuestra *by* su *or* de
ustedes, os *by* les *or* los. *The verbs, marked **, should be replaced by the
formal plural form, e.g.* estéis *by* estén.

⑤ *Or (if the children are older):* para vosotros y los chicos *(or* y las chicas *if
there are only females),* para vosotros y para toda la familia.

⑥ *Or:* todos muy bien.

Barcelona, 18 de diciembre de 1999

Queridos Juan y Elsa:

④ Antes que nada, os* deseamos a vosotros* y a los niños ⑤ unas muy felices
Navidades y os* enviamos nuestros mejores deseos para el año 2000. Esperamos
que estéis** todos estupendamente ⑥. No sabéis** cómo nos alegramos con el
anuncio de vuestro* viaje para enero. Ya tenemos pensado todo lo que podemos
hacer durante vuestra* estancia aquí. Os* esperamos.

Conchita hizo los exámenes del último año de su carrera y sacó muy buenas notas.
Ahora tiene que hacer su trabajo de práctica. Elena está bien y muy contenta en el
colegio. Tiene muchísimos amigos y es muy buena chica. Luis y yo estamos bien
también y sumamente felices con la reciente noticia del próximo ascenso de Luis. En
definitiva, 1999 ha sido un buen año y no nos podemos quejar. Confiamos en que el
próximo será aún mejor.

Decidnos** con antelación la fecha de vuestro* viaje para que podamos ir a
esperaros* al aeropuerto.

Recibid** todo nuestro cariño y un fuerte abrazo.

Luis y Ana.

. . . .

Saludos de Navidad y Año Nuevo

En una tarjeta:

[Best wishes for a] Happy ① Christmas and
a Prosperous New Year

Best wishes for Christmas and the New Year

Wishing you every happiness this Christmas
and in the New Year

① O: Merry.

En una carta:

44 Louis Gardens
London NW6 4GM

December 20th 1999

Dear Peter and Claire,

First of all, a very happy Christmas and all the best for the New Year to you
and the children. ② We hope you're all well ③ and that we'll see you again.
It seems ages since we last met up.

We've had a very eventful year. Last summer Gavin came off his bike and
broke his arm and collarbone. Kathy scraped through her A Levels and is
now at Sussex doing European Studies. Poor Tony was made redundant in
October and is still looking for a job.

Do come and see us next time you are over this way. Just give us a ring a
couple of days before so we can fix something.

All best wishes

Tony and Ann

Letters / Cartas

② O (si los hijos son mayores): to you and your family.

③ O (coloquial): flourishing.

Letter-writing / Redacción de cartas

Invitation (informal)

> Madrid, 22 de abril del 2000
>
> Querido James:
>
> Te escribo para preguntarte si te apetecería ① pasar las vacaciones de verano con nosotros. A Tito y a Pilar les haría mucha ilusión (y también a Juan y a mí, por supuesto). Pensamos ir al noreste del país a finales de julio o a principios de agosto. Es una región realmente hermosa y nos encantaría que tú también vinieras. Es muy probable que llevemos tiendas de campaña ¡espero que no te importe dormir en el suelo!
>
> Te agradecería que me avisaras lo más pronto posible si puedes venir.
>
> Un cariñoso saludo,
>
> Ana de Salas

① Or (in Latin America and also in Spain): si te gustaría.

Invitation (formal)

Invitations to parties are usually by word of mouth, while for weddings announcements are usually sent out.

> Carmen S. de Pérez y Ramón Pérez Arrate, Lucía N. de Salas y Mario Salas Moro Participan a Ud. de la boda de sus hijos
>
> Consuelo y Hernán
>
> Y le invitan a la ceremonia religiosa que se efectuará en la Capilla del Sagrado Corazón, de Mirasierra, Madrid, el sábado 25 de julio del 2001 a las 7 p.m.
>
> Y luego a una recepción en la Sala de Banquetes del Restaurante Galán en C/Los Santos 10 de Majadahonda, Madrid.
> S.R.C. ②

■ In Latin America invitations to the reception are sent to relatives and close friends in a separate smaller card enclosed with the announcement.

■ In Spanish-speaking countries, the answer is not usually given in writing.

② In Latin America: R.S.V.P.

Invitación (informal)

- La fecha también se puede escribir de la siguiente manera: April 10, 10 April, 10th April.

- La dirección del remitente va en el ángulo superior derecho de la carta y la fecha va inmediatamente debajo.

> 35 Winchester Drive
> Stoke Gifford
> Bristol
> BS34 8PD
>
> April 22nd 2000
>
> Dear Luis,
>
> Is there any chance of your coming to stay with us in the summer holidays? Roy and Debbie would be delighted if you could (as well as David and me, of course). We hope to go to North Wales at the end of July/beginning of August, and you'd be very welcome to come too. It's really beautiful up there. We'll probably take tents - I hope that's OK by you.
>
> Let me know as soon as possible if you can manage it.
>
> All best wishes
>
> Rachel Hemmings

Invitación (formal)

Invitación a una boda con recepción:

> Mr and Mrs Peter Thompson
> request the pleasure of your company
> at the marriage of their daughter
> Hannah Louise
> to
> Steven David Warner
> at St Mary's Church, Little Bourton
> on Saturday 22nd July 2001 at 2 p.m.
> And afterwards at the Golden Cross Hotel, Billing
>
> R.S.V.P
>
> 23 Santers Lane
> Little Bourton
> Northampton
> NN6 1A2

Letters / Cartas

Accepting an invitation

Winchester, 2 de mayo del 2000

Estimada Sra. de Salas:

Muchísimas gracias por su amable carta y su invitación ①.

No tengo nada planeado para las vacaciones de verano, así es que me encantaría acompañarles ② *al norte. Desgraciadamente, no podré quedarme más de cinco o seis días debido a que mi madre no se encuentra muy bien y no me gustaría estar mucho tiempo fuera de casa.*

Por favor dígame lo que tengo que llevar. ¿Hace mucho calor en la región adonde vamos? ¿Hay mar o río donde se pueda nadar? En cuanto a hacer camping, no tengo ningún problema. Nosostros siempre llevamos nuestras tiendas de campaña a todas partes.

Esperando verles ③ *pronto otra vez.*

Un afectuoso saludo,

James

① *Since this is a letter from a younger person writing to the mother of a friend, he uses the formal usted form and the possessive su, and writes to her as* Sra. de Salas *and* Estimada, *which is normally used to begin a letter when the relationship is not too close.* Querida ... *could also be used (*Estimado Sr. ... *or* Querido Sr. ... *if the addressee is a man). On the other hand it was quite natural for* Sra. de Salas *to use the informal tú form to him.*

② *In Latin America:* acompañarlos.

③ *In Latin America:* verlos.

■ *Ending: This is normally used when the relationship is not too close, generally when the person is known to you but the usted form would be used.* Un saludo muy afectuoso *is also possible.*

Letter-writing / Redacción de cartas

· ·

Aceptación de una invitación (informal)

> *Luis Villegas*
> *Las Acacias 30*
> *28020 Madrid*
>
> *2 May 2000*
>
> *Dear Mrs Hemmings ①,*
>
> *Many thanks for your letter and kind invitation. Since I don't have anything fixed yet for the summer holidays, I'd be delighted to come. However I mustn't be away for more than four or five days since my mother hasn't been very well.*
>
> *You must let me know what I should bring. How warm is it in North Wales? Can you swim in the sea? Camping is fine as far as I'm concerned, we take our tents everywhere.*
>
> *Looking forward to seeing you soon,*
>
> *Yours ②,*
>
> *Luis*

① Este es un encabezamiento relativamente formal, puesto que esta es una carta de una persona joven dirigida a la madre de un amigo.

② Otras alternativas para este tipo de carta: With best wishes, Yours sincerely, Kind/Kindest regards.

Respuesta a una invitación (formal)

> *Aceptando: Richard Willis has great pleasure in accepting Mr and Mrs Peter Thompson's kind invitation to the marriage of their daughter Hannah Louise to Steven Warner at St Mary's Church, Little Bourton, on Saturday 22nd July.*
>
> *No aceptando: Richard Willis regrets that he is unable to accept Mr and Mrs Peter Thompson's kind invitation to ....*

■ Se repiten los datos de la invitación, pero no en forma detallada.

■ Si no se acepta la invitación, es de mejor educación enviar una carta a los padres de la novia, si se conocen personalmente.

Letters / Cartas

Replying to a job advertisement

■ *In Spain when the full address is given it is usually written in the top left-hand corner and in Latin America in the bottom left-hand corner, beneath the signature.*

■ *This is the most commonly used opening for a formal or business letter, or when the addressee is not personally known to you. Alternatively* Estimado Sr. *and, in Latin America,* De mi mayor consideración, *can also be used.*

■ *When the full address is given, the name of the town or city is not repeated in the date.*

David Baker
67 Whiteley Avenue
St George
Bristol
BS5 6TW

26 de septiembre de 1999

Gerente del Personal
Renos Software S.A.
Alcalá 52
28014 Madrid

Muy señor mío:

Con referencia al puesto de programador anunciado recientemente en El País del 12 de septiembre del presente, les agradecería me enviaran información más detallada acerca de la plaza vacante (1) .

Actualmente estoy trabajando para una empresa de Bristol, pero mi contrato termina a finales de este mes y querría aprovechar esta oportunidad para (2) trabajar en Madrid. Como se desprende del currículum vitae que adjunto, viví durante algún tiempo en España, tengo perfecto dominio del idioma español y también las cualificaciones (3) y experiencia requeridas.

Estaré disponible para asistir a una entrevista, en cualquier momento desde el 6 de octubre, fecha a partir de la cual se me puede contactar en la siguiente dirección en Madrid:

C/ Sevilla 25
28020 Madrid
Teléf. 91 429-96-67

Sin otro particular, quedo a la espera de su respuesta, (4)

Atentamente, (5)

(1) *Or if you have enough details and want to apply for the job right away:* quisiera solicitar la plaza vacante.

(2) *Or if you are unemployed:* Actualmente estoy buscando trabajo y quisiera ...

(3) *In Latin America:* calificaciones.

(4) *Or:* Agradeciendo de antemano su atención *or* En espera de su respuesta.

(5) *Or:* Le *(Lo in Latin America)* saluda atentamente. Me despido de usted atentamente, Muy atentamente, *or* Esperando su respuesta, se despide atentamente *are also possible.*

Respuesta a un anuncio de trabajo

C/Islas Baleares 18. 2º B
FUENCARRAL
28080 Madrid
Spain

13th February 2000

The Personnel Manager ①
Patterson Software plc
Milton State
Bath BA6 8YZ

Dear Sir o Madam ①,

I am interested in the post of programmer advertised in The Guardian of 12 February and would be very grateful if you could send me further particulars. ②

I am currently working for the Sempo Corporation, but my contract finishes at the end of the month, and I would like ③ to come and work in Spain. As you can see from my CV (enclosed), I have an excellent command of Spanish and also the required qualifications and experience.

I will be available for interview any time after 6th October, from which date I can be contacted at the following address in the UK:

c/o Lewis
51 Dexter Road
London N7 6BW
Tel. 0181 607 5512

I look forward to hearing from you. ④

Yours sincerely

María Luisa Márquez Blanco

Encl.

① *Otra alternativa puede ser* Ms Angela Summers, ..., *si en el anuncio aparece* Reply to Angela Summers *o* Dear Ms Summers, Dear Mrs Wright, *si en el anuncio sólo se indica el apellido.*

② O and would like to apply for this position, *si en el anuncio se incluye suficiente información acerca del puesto.*

③ *O si se encuentra desempleado:* I am currently looking for work and I would like ...

④ *También:* Thanking you in anticipation/advance.

Curriculum Vitae (CV), (*AmE*) Resumé

CURRÍCULUM VITAE

Nombre y apellidos	David Baker
Fecha de nacimiento	30/6/71
Lugar	Londres
Estado civil	Soltero ①
Domicilio actual	67 Whiteley Avenue
	St George
	Bristol
	BS5 6TW
	Gran Bretaña
Teléfono	+43 (0)117 945 3421

DATOS ACADÉMICOS

1986-88 GCSE (equivalente a la ESO en España) en 7 asignaturas.

1988-90 A Levels (equivalente al Curso de Orientación Universitaria en España) en Matemáticas, Informática y Español, Croydon Sixth Form College.

1990-91 Trabajos temporales de oficina en España y estudios de Español para los negocios en clases nocturnas.

1991-95 Universidad de Aston, Birmingham, BSc en Informática (equivalente a Licenciatura en Ciencias de la Información).

EXPERIENCIA PROFESIONAL

1995-1996 Trabajo de práctica como programador de software para IBM, desarrollo de programas para la industria, con especialidad en infografía.

1996-al presente Programador para Wondersoft plc, Bristol.

IDIOMAS

Inglés   Lengua materna.

Español   Dominio total, hablado y escrito.

Francés   Bueno.

AFICIONES

Leer, viajar, esquí, tenis.

① Or: Casado (sin hijos *or* con un hijo/dos/tres *etc*, hijos), Divorciado (sin hijos *or* con un hijo/dos/tres *etc*, hijos).

. . . .

Currículum Vitae

CURRICULUM VITAE ①

Name:	María Luisa Márquez Blanco
Address:	C/Islas Baleares 18. 2°B
	FUENCARRAL
	28080 Madrid
	Spain
Telephone:	(+34) 91. 243 53 94
Nationality:	Spanish
Date of Birth:	11/3/73

EDUCATION:

1990-95	Degree Course in Information Technology and English at Universidad Complutense of Madrid.
1987- 1991	BUP (secondary education)/COU (equivalent to A levels) at the Instituto de Enseñanza Media in Fuencarral.

EMPLOYMENT:

1996-present	Program development engineer with Sempo Informática, Madrid, specializing in computer graphics.
1995-1996	Trainee programmer with Oregón-España, Madrid.

FURTHER SKILLS:

Languages:	Spanish (mother tongue),
	English (fluent, spoken and written),
	French (good).
Interests:	Travel, fashion, tennis.

---

① O: Resumé (AmE).

Inquiry to a tourist office

■ *This is a standard formula for starting a business letter addressed to a firm or organization, and not to a particular person. Alternatively,* Estimados señores *and, also in Latin America,* De nuestra mayor consideración, *could be used.*

■ *A simple business-style letter. The sender's address is on the top left-hand corner, the date is on the right, and the recipient's address is on the left, beneath the sender's address.*

Sally McGregor
16 Victoria Road
Brixton
London SW2 5HU

4 de mayo del 2000

Oficina de Información y Turismo
Princesa 5
Oviedo

Muy señores míos:

Les agradecería me remitieran a la mayor brevedad una lista de hoteles y pensiones, de precio medio, en Oviedo y los pueblos de la provincia.

También me interesaría obtener información acerca de excursiones en autocar ① a los lugares de interés de la zona durante la segunda mitad de agosto.

Agradeciendo de antemano su atención, les saluda atentamente,

Sally McGregor

■ Les (Los *in Latin America*) saluda atentamente *is the standard ending for a formal or business letter. Other possibilities are:* Me despido de ustedes atentamente *or* Reciban un atento saludo de ...

① *In Latin America:* autobús.

Carta a una oficina de turismo

■ *Encabezamiento típico de una carta de negocios cuando no se sabe si el destinatario es hombre o mujer. Otra alternativa sería* Dear Sirs, *si el destinatario fuese una empresa u organización (como por ejemplo si, en este caso, la carta estuviese dirigida a* The Regional Tourist Office *en lugar de a* The Manager).

C/Antonio Cedaceros 9
05002 Ávila
Spain

4th May 2000

The Manager
Regional Tourist Office
3 Virgin Road
Canterbury
CT1 3AA

Dear Sir or Madam,

Please send me a list of hotels and guesthouses in Canterbury in the medium price range.

I would also like details of coach trips to local sights in the second half of August.

Yours faithfully

Antonio López A.

■ *Fórmula típica de despedida de cartas formales dirigidas a un destinatario a quien no se conoce personalmente. Es la fórmula que debe emplearse cuando el encabezamiento de la carta es* Dear Sir or Madam, Dear Sirs, Dear Sir *o* Dear Madam.

Booking a hotel room

Luis Granados
C/Felipe V 32
Segovia

23 de abril del 2000

Sr. Director
Hotel Los Palomos
C/Piedrabuena 40
Cádiz

Apreciado señor: ①

Su hotel aparece en un folleto turístico sobre la zona para el año 2000 y me ha causado muy buena impresión. Por ello le escribo para reservar una habitación doble con baño y una habitación individual ② para nuestro hijo, desde el 2 hasta 11 de agosto (nueve noches). Preferiblemente ambas habitaciones con vista al mar.

Si tiene disponibilidad para esas fechas, le rogaría que me comunicara el precio y si se requiere depósito.

Sin otro particular le saluda ③ atentamente,

Luis Granados

① *Also:* Estimado Sr.

② *Or:* una habitación doble y una individual para nuestro hijo, ambas con baño.

③ *In Latin America:* lo saluda ...

Booking a campsite

Urbanización El Molino
Chalet 88
Villanueva de la Cañada
Madrid

25 de abril del 2000

Camping Loredo
Sr. Roberto Loredo
Nájera
La Rioja

Muy señor mío:

Un amigo que suele acampar en la zona me ha recomendado su camping ① , por lo que quisiera reservar una plaza para una tienda ② , preferiblemente en un lugar abrigado ③ . Dos amigos y yo queremos pasar una semana allí, desde el 18 al 25 de julio inclusive.

Le agradecería que me confirmara la reserva lo antes posible y que me dijera si se requiere depósito. También le estaría muy agradecido si me enviara indicaciones para llegar al camping desde la carretera.

A la espera de su confirmación, le saluda ④ atentamente.

Pedro Salguedo

① *Or:* Su camping aparece anunciado en la revista Guía del Buen Campista.

② *Other possibility:* para una caravana.

③ *Alternatively:* en un lugar sombreado/ cerca de la playa.

④ *In Latin America:* lo saluda ...

. . . .

Reserva de habitación en un hotel

The Manager
Torbay Hotel
Dawlish
Devon
EX37 2LR

35 Prince Edward Road
Oxford OX7 3AA

Tel. 01865 322435

23rd April 2000

Dear Sir or Madam,

I saw your hotel listed in the Inns of Devon guide for last year,
and wish to reserve a double (or twin-bedded) room with
shower ① in a quiet position from August 2nd-11th (nine
nights), also a single room for my son.

If you have anything suitable for this period please let me know
the price and whether you require a deposit.

Yours faithfully,

Charles Fairhurst

① *Otra alternativa:*
with bath/with
ensuite.

Reserva de camping

22 Daniel Avenue
Caldwood
Leeds LS8 7RR

Tel. 01132 998767

25th April 2000

Mr Joseph Vale
Lakeside Park
Rydal
Cumbria
LA22 9RZ

Dear Mr Vale,

Your campsite was recommended to me by James Dallas, who
knows it from several visits ① . I and two friends would like to
come for a week from July 18th to 25th. Could you please reserve
us a pitch for one tent ② , preferably close to the shore ③ .

Please confirm the booking and let me know if you require a
deposit. Would you also be good enough to send me instructions on
how to reach you from the motorway.

Yours sincerely,

Frances Good

① *O si se ha
obtenido
información de
otra fuente:* I
found your site in
the Tourist
Board's list/the
Good Camper's
Guide *etc.*

② *Otra alternativa:*
a pitch for one
caravan.

③ *Otra posición:*
in a shady/
sheltered spot.

Letter-writing / Redacción de cartas

Canceling a reservation

Sra. Rosario de Barros
Av. Colonial
San Isidro
Lima

20 de julio de 1999

Estimada señora (de Barros):

Debido a circunstancias ajenas a nuestra voluntad ①, nos hemos visto obligados a cambiar nuestros planes para las vacaciones, por lo que le rogaría cancelara la reserva ② hecha a mi nombre para la semana del 7 al 14 de agosto.

Lamento muchísimo tener que hacer esta cancelación (tan a último momento) y espero que esto no le cause muchos inconvenientes.

La saluda atentamente,

Paul Roberts
2633 Higland Avenue
Urbandale, IA 51019
EEUU

① Or: Debido al repentino fallecimiento de mi marido/a la hospitalización de mi hijo/a la enfermedad de mi marido etc.

② Also in Latin America: reservación.

■ In Latin America if the full address is given, it is usually written in the bottom left-hand corner, beneath the signature.

Cancelación de una reserva

Sagasta 45
Santander
Spain

July 20th
1999

Mrs J. Warrington
Downlands
Steyning
West Sussex
BN44 6LZ

Dear Mrs Warrington,

Unfortunately I have to cancel my/our reservation for the week of August 7th ①. Due to unforeseen circumstances ②, I/we have had to abandon my/our holiday plans.

I very much regret having to cancel (at such a late stage) and hope it does not cause you undue inconvenience.

Yours sincerely,

Carlos Rubio García

① Otra alternativa: for the period from August 7th to 14th.

② Otro motivo: Owing to my father's sudden death/my wife's illness/son's hospitalization etc.

Letters / Cartas

Sending an e-mail

The illustration shows a typical interface for sending e-mail.

Para enviar correo electrónico

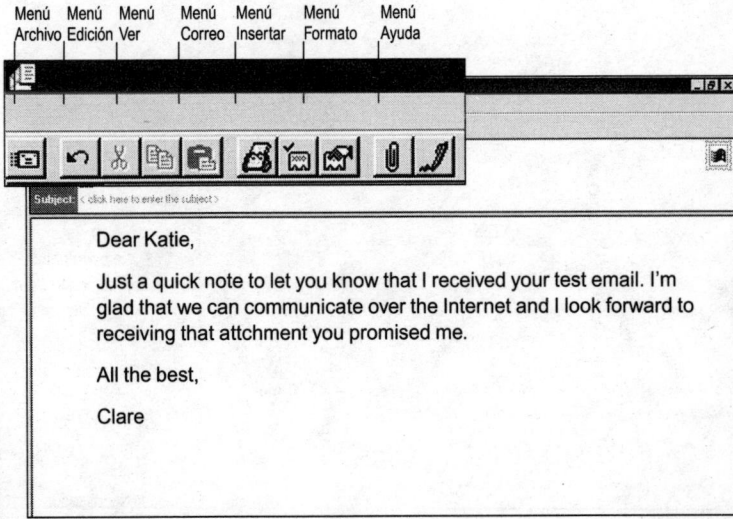

A, a /eɪ/ n (a) (letter) A, a f (b) (Mus) la m

a /ə, stressed form eɪ/ (before vowel **an**) indef art un, una; **a Mrs Smith called** llamó una tal señora Smith; **have you got a car?** ¿tienes coche?; **he didn't say a word** no dijo ni una palabra; **she's a dentist** es dentista; **what a shock!** ¡qué susto!; **it costs 2 dollars a pound** cuesta 2 dólares la libra

AA n [1] (no art) = **Alcoholics Anonymous** [2] (in US) = **Associate in Arts** [3] (in UK) = **Automobile Association**

AAA n = **American Automobile Association**

aback /ə'bæk/ adv ▶ TAKE ABACK

abacus /'æbəkəs/ n (pl -**cuses** or -**ci** /-saɪ/) ábaco m

abandon[1] /ə'bændən/ vt ‹home/family› abandonar; ‹project/idea/search› renunciar a; ‹hope› perder*; **to ~ ship** abandonar el barco

abandon[2] n: **they were dancing with gay ~** bailaban desenfrenadamente

abandoned /ə'bændənd/ adj ‹vehicle/cottage/wife› abandonado

abase /ə'beɪs/ v refl **to ~ oneself** humillarse

abashed /ə'bæʃt/ adj (pred) avergonzado

abate /ə'beɪt/ vi (fml) «storm/wind» amainar; «anger» aplacarse*; «noise/violence» disminuir*; «pain» calmarse

abattoir /'æbətwɑːr ‖'æbətwɑː(r)/ n matadero m

abbey /'æbi/ n (pl **abbeys**) abadía f

abbot /'æbət/ n abad m

abbreviate /ə'briːvieɪt/ vt abreviar

abbreviation /əˌbriːvi'eɪʃən/ n abreviatura f

ABC n [1] (alphabet, rudiments) abecé m [2] (in US) (no art) (= **American Broadcasting Company**) la ABC

abdicate /'æbdɪkeɪt/ vt/i abdicar*

abdication /ˌæbdɪ'keɪʃən/ n abdicación f

abdomen /'æbdəmən/ n abdomen m

abduct /æb'dʌkt ‖əb'dʌkt/ vt (fml) raptar, secuestrar

abduction /æb'dʌkʃən ‖əb'dʌkʃən/ n (fml) rapto m, secuestro m

abet /ə'bet/ vt -**tt-** ▶ AID[2]

abeyance /ə'beɪəns/ n: **to be in ~** estar* suspendido

abhor /əb'hɔːr ‖əb'hɔː(r)/ vt -**rr-** (fml) detestar

abide /ə'baɪd/ vt tolerar, soportar

■ **abide by** [v + prep + o] ‹verdict/rules› acatar

ability /ə'bɪləti/ n (pl -**ties**) capacidad f; **to the best of one's ~** lo mejor que uno pueda

abject /'æbdʒekt/ adj (fml) (before n) ‹slave/flattery› abyecto; **in ~ poverty** en la mayor miseria

ablaze /ə'bleɪz/ adj (pred): **to be ~** arder

able /'eɪbəl/ adj [1] (pred) **to be ~ to** + INF poder* + INF; (referring to particular skills) saber* +

INF; **to be ~ to see/hear** poder* ver/oír [2] **abler** /'eɪblər ‖'eɪblə(r)/, **ablest** /'eɪbləst ‖'eɪblɪst/ (proficient) hábil

able-bodied /'eɪbəl'bɑːdid ‖ˌeɪbəl'bɒdid/ adj sano, no discapacitado

abnormal /æb'nɔːrməl ‖æb'nɔːməl/ adj anómalo, anormal

abnormality /ˌæbnər'mæləti ‖ˌæbnɔː'mæləti/ n (pl -**ties**) anomalía f, anormalidad f

aboard[1] /ə'bɔːrd ‖ə'bɔːd/ adv (on ship, plane) a bordo

aboard[2] prep a bordo de; **~ the bus/train** en el autobús/tren

abode /ə'bəʊd/ n (liter or hum) morada f (liter o hum); **of no fixed ~** (Law) sin domicilio fijo

abolish /ə'bɑːlɪʃ ‖ə'bɒlɪʃ/ vt abolir*

abolition /ˌæbə'lɪʃən/ n abolición f

abominable /ə'bɑːmənəbəl ‖ə'bɒmɪnəbəl/ adj (a) (horrible) ‹deed› abominable (b) (awful) (colloq) ‹weather/food› espantoso

abomination /əˌbɑːmə'neɪʃən ‖əˌbɒmɪ'neɪʃən/ n abominación f

aboriginal[1] /ˌæbə'rɪdʒənl/ adj aborigen

aboriginal[2] n (a) (indigenous inhabitant) aborigen mf (b) ▶ ABORIGINE

Aborigine /ˌæbə'rɪdʒəni/ n aborigen australiano, -na m,f

abortion /ə'bɔːrʃən ‖ə'bɔːʃən/ n aborto m (provocado); **to have an ~** hacerse* un aborto, abortar

abortive /ə'bɔːrtɪv ‖ə'bɔːtɪv/ adj frustrado

abound /ə'baʊnd/ vi abundar; **to ~ IN** o **WITH sth** abundar EN algo

about[1] /ə'baʊt/ adv [1] (approximately) más o menos, aproximadamente; **she must be ~** 60 debe (de) tener unos 60 años; **at ~ six o'clock** alrededor de or a eso de las seis; **~ a month ago** hace cosa de un mes [2] **to be about to** + INF estar* a punto de + INF [3] (movement): **she can't get ~ very easily** le cuesta desplazarse; **he was waving a knife ~** blandía un cuchillo [4] (in the vicinity, in circulation) (esp BrE): **is Teresa ~?** ¿Teresa anda por aquí?; **there's a lot of flu ~** hay mucha gente con gripe

about[2] prep [1] (a) (concerning) sobre, acerca de; **what's the play ~?** ¿de qué se trata la obra?; **he wants to see you about something** quiere verte acerca de or por algo; **she won — how ~ that!** ganó — ¡pues qué te parece! or ¡pues mira tú! (b) (pertaining to): **there's something ~ him that I don't like** tiene un no sé qué que no me gusta [2] (engaged in): **while you're ~ it, could you fetch my book?** ¿ya que estás me traes el libro?

aboutface /ə'baʊt'feɪs/, (BrE also) **about-turn** /-'tɜːrn ‖-'tɜːn/ n cambio m radical de postura

above[1] /ə'bʌv/ prep [1] (a) (on top of, over) encima de; **~ sea level** sobre el nivel del mar (b) (upstream of) más allá or más arriba de [2] (superior ⋯▸

to) por encima de; **to get ~ oneself** (pej) subirse a
la parra **3** (more than): **~ average** por encima de
la media; **~ and beyond** más allá de
above² adv **1** (on top, higher up) arriba **2** (in
text): **as shown ~** como se demostró
anteriormente or más arriba; **see ~, page 43**
véase página 43
above³ adj (frml) (before n): **for the ~ reasons**
por dichas razones, por lo antedicho
above: ~board /əˈbʌvˈbɔːrd ‖əˌbʌvˈbɔːd/ adj
(pred) legítimo; **open and ~board** sin tapujos;
~mentioned /əˈbʌvˈmentʃənd
‖əˌbʌvˈmenʃənd/ adj antedicho (frml)
abrasive /əˈbreɪsɪv/ adj ⟨powder⟩ abrasivo;
⟨surface⟩ áspero; ⟨tone/manner⟩ áspero
abreast /əˈbrest/ adv **(a)** (side by side): **to march
four ~** marchar en columna de cuatro en fondo
(b) (up to date): **to keep ~ of sth** mantenerse* al
día en or al corriente de algo
abridge /əˈbrɪdʒ/ vt ⟨book⟩ compendiar; **~d
edition** edición f condensada
abroad /əˈbrɔːd/ adv ⟨live/work⟩ en el
extranjero or en el exterior; ⟨go⟩ al extranjero, al
exterior; **I've never been ~** nunca he salido del
país
abrupt /əˈbrʌpt/ adj ⟨departure/conclusion⟩
repentino; ⟨rise/decline⟩ abrupto; ⟨manner⟩
brusco
abruptly /əˈbrʌptli/ adv ⟨end/stop⟩
repentinamente; ⟨rise/fall⟩ bruscamente; ⟨speak/
act⟩ abruptamente
abscess /ˈæbses/ n absceso m
abscond /æbˈskɑːnd ‖əbˈskɒnd/ vi (frml)
fugarse*
absence /ˈæbsəns/ n **(a)** (of person) ausencia f
(b) (lack) **~ of sth** falta f de algo
absent /ˈæbsənt/ adj ausente; **to be ~ FROM
sth** faltar A algo
absentee /ˌæbsənˈtiː/ n (pl -**tees**) ausente mf
absenteeism /ˌæbsənˈtiːɪzəm/ n ausentismo
m or (Esp) absentismo m
absentminded /ˈæbsəntˈmaɪndəd
‖ˌæbsəntˈmaɪndɪd/ adj (temporarily) distraído;
(habitually) despistado
absolute /ˈæbsəluːt/ adj **1** (complete) ⟨trust/
confidence⟩ absoluto; **it was an ~ disaster** fue un
absoluto desastre or un desastre total **2** ⟨right⟩
incuestionable; ⟨pardon/freedom⟩ incondicional;
⟨guarantee/monarchy/rule⟩ absoluto
absolutely /ˈæbsəˈluːtli/ adv ⟨deny/reject⟩
rotundamente; ⟨impossible⟩ absolutamente; **I'm ~
certain** estoy segurísima or absolutamente
segura; **you're ~ right!** ¡tienes toda la razón!
absolution /ˌæbsəˈluːʃən/ n absolución f
absolve /əbˈzɑːlv ‖əbˈzɒlv/ vt **to ~ sb OF sth**
absolver* a algn DE algo; **to ~ sb FROM sth**
eximir a algn DE algo
absorb /əbˈsɔːrb ‖əbˈzɔːb/ vt ⟨light/energy⟩
absorber; ⟨impact/shock⟩ amortiguar*;
⟨information⟩ asimilar; **to be ~ed IN sth** estar*
absorto EN algo

absorbent /əbˈsɔːrbənt ‖əbˈzɔːbənt/ adj
absorbente
absorbent cotton n (AmE) algodón m
(hidrófilo)
absorption /əbˈsɔːrpʃən ‖əbˈzɔːpʃən/ n
absorción f
abstain /əbˈsteɪn/ vi **1** (in vote) abstenerse*
2 (refrain) **to ~ FROM sth/-ING** abstenerse* DE
algo/+ INF
abstract /ˈæbstrækt/ adj abstracto
absurd /əbˈsɜːrd ‖əbˈsɜːd/ adj absurdo
absurdity /əbˈsɜːrdəti ‖əbˈsɜːdəti/ n (pl -**ties**)
lo absurdo
abundance /əˈbʌndəns/ n abundancia f
abundant /əˈbʌndənt/ adj ⟨resources⟩
abundante; ⟨enthusiasm⟩ desbordante
abuse¹ /əˈbjuːs/ n **1** (insulting language) insultos
mpl; **a term of ~** un insulto **2** (misuse) abuso m;
sexual ~ abusos mpl deshonestos; **child ~** malos
tratos mpl a la infancia; (sexual) abusos mpl
deshonestos (a un niño); **drug ~** consumo m de
drogas
abuse² /əˈbjuːz/ vt **1 (a)** (use wrongly) ⟨power/
hospitality⟩ abusar de **(b)** ⟨child/woman⟩
maltratar; (sexually) abusar de **2** (insult) insultar
abusive /əˈbjuːsɪv/ adj insultante
abysmal /əˈbɪzməl/ adj pésimo
abyss /əˈbɪs/ n (liter) abismo m
a/c (= **account**) cta.
AC /ˈeɪˈsiː/ **(a)** (= **alternating current**) CA **(b)**
(esp AmE) = **air conditioning**
A/C = **air conditioning**
academic¹ /ˌækəˈdemɪk/ adj **1 (a)** ⟨career/
record⟩ académico **(b)** ⟨child/student⟩
intelectualmente capaz **2** (abstract) ⟨question/
debate⟩ puramente teórico
academic² n académico, -ca m,f
academy /əˈkædəmi/ n (pl -**mies**) academia
f; (before n) **A~ Award** Oscar m
accede /əkˈsiːd/ vi (frml) **to ~ TO sth** (grant)
acceder A algo
accelerate /əkˈseləreɪt/ vi ⟨vehicle⟩ acelerar;
⟨person⟩ acelerar; (Auto) apretar* el acelerador;
⟨process/growth⟩ acelerarse
■ **~** vt acelerar
accelerator /əkˈseləreɪtər ‖əkˈseləreɪtə(r)/ n
acelerador m
accent /ˈæksent ‖ˈæksent, ˈæksənt/ n **(a)** (Ling,
Mus) acento m **(b)** (emphasis) énfasis m
accentuate /əkˈsentʃueɪt/ vt **(a)** ⟨difference⟩
hacer* resaltar; ⟨fact/necessity⟩ subrayar; ⟨eyes/
features⟩ realzar*, hacer* resaltar **(b)** ⟨syllable/
word⟩ acentuar*
accept /əkˈsept/ vt aceptar; **do you ~ that you
were wrong?** ¿reconoces que estabas equivocado?
acceptable /əkˈseptəbəl/ adj (satisfactory)
aceptable; (tolerable) admisible
acceptance /əkˈseptəns/ n **1** (of offer,
responsibility) aceptación f **2** (approval) aprobación f

access¹ /'ækses/ n acceso m; (before n) ~ road carretera f de acceso

access² vt (Comput) obtener* acceso a, entrar a

accessible /ək'sesəbəl/ adj accesible

accession /ək'seʃən, æk'seʃən/ n (frml) **(a)** (to throne, power) acceso m **(b)** (acquisition) adquisición f

accessory /ək'sesəri/ n (pl **-ries**) ⓵ **(a)** (extra) accesorio m **(b) accessories** pl (Clothing) accesorios mpl ⓶ (Law) ~ (TO sth) cómplice mf (EN algo)

accident /'æksədənt ‖'æksɪdənt/ n **(a)** (mishap) accidente m **(b)** (chance) casualidad f; by ~ (by chance) por casualidad; (unintentionally) sin querer

accidental /'æksə'dentl ‖,æksɪ'dentl/ adj ⟨discovery/meeting⟩ fortuito; ⟨blow⟩ accidental; ~ death muerte f por caso fortuito

accidentally /'æksə'dentli ‖,æksɪ'dentəli/ adv **(a)** (unintentionally) sin querer **(b)** (by chance) por casualidad, de manera fortuita

accident-prone /'æksədəntprəʊn ‖'æksɪdəntprəʊn/ adj propenso a los accidentes

acclaim¹ /ə'kleɪm/ vt aclamar

acclaim² n aclamación f

acclimate /'ækləmeɪt/ vt (AmE) ▶ ACCLIMATIZE

acclimatize /ə'klaɪmətaɪz/ vt aclimatar; to become ~d TO sth aclimatarse A algo

accolade /'ækəleɪd/ n (praise) elogio m; (honor) honor m; (award) galardón m

accommodate /ə'kɑːmədeɪt ‖ə'kɒmədeɪt/ vt ⓵ **(a)** (provide lodging for) ⟨guests⟩ alojar **(b)** (have room for) tener* cabida para ⓶ (cater to) ⟨wish/need⟩ tener* en cuenta

accommodating /ə'kɑːmədeɪtɪŋ ‖ə'kɒmədeɪtɪŋ/ adj complaciente

accommodation /ə'kɑːmə'deɪʃən ‖ə,kɒmə'deɪʃən/ n ⓵ **(a)** (AmE also) **accommodations** (lodgings) alojamiento m **(b)** (seat, berth) (AmE) plaza f ⓶ (agreement, compromise) acuerdo m

accompaniment /ə'kʌmpənimənt/ n acompañamiento m

accompanist /ə'kʌmpənəst ‖ə'kʌmpənɪst/ n acompañante mf

accompany /ə'kʌmpəni/ vt **-nies, -nying, -nied (a)** (go with) acompañar **(b)** (Mus) acompañar

accomplice /ə'kɑːmpləs ‖ə'kʌmplɪs/ n cómplice mf

accomplish /ə'kɑːmplɪʃ ‖ə'kʌmplɪʃ/ vt ⟨task⟩ llevar a cabo; ⟨goal⟩ lograr

accomplished /ə'kɑːmplɪʃt ‖ə'kʌmplɪʃt/ adj ⟨performer/liar/thief⟩ consumado; ⟨performance⟩ logrado

accomplishment /ə'kɑːmplɪʃmənt ‖ə'kʌmplɪʃmənt/ n **(a)** (of aim) logro m **(b)** (success) logro m **(c)** (skill) habilidad f

accord /ə'kɔːrd ‖ə'kɔːd/ n acuerdo m; of one's own ~ (de) motu proprio

accordance /ə'kɔːrdns ‖ə'kɔːdns/ n: in ~ with de acuerdo con or a, según

according /ə'kɔːrdɪŋ ‖ə'kɔːdɪŋ/ **according to** prep según

accordion /ə'kɔːrdiən ‖ə'kɔːdiən/ n acordeón m

accost /ə'kɔːst ‖ə'kɒst/ vt abordar

account /ə'kaʊnt/ n
Ⅰ ⓵ (explanation) explicación f; (version) versión f; (report) informe m; by all ~s a decir de todos ⓶ (consideration): to take sth into ~ tener* algo en cuenta ⓷ (in phrases) on account of (as prep) debido a; on no account de ningún modo, de ninguna manera; on sb's account por algn
Ⅱ ⓵ (with bank, at shop) cuenta f ⓶ **accounts** (Busn, Fin) (+ pl vb) contabilidad f
■ **account for** [v + prep + o] ⓵ **(a)** (provide record of, justify) ⟨expenditure/time⟩ dar* cuentas de **(b)** (explain) explicar*; there's no ~ing for taste sobre gustos no hay nada escrito ⓶ (add up to): wages ~ for 70% of the total los sueldos representan un or el 70% del total

accountable /ə'kaʊntəbəl/ adj (pred) responsable; to be ~ TO sb (FOR sth) ser* responsable ANTE algn (DE algo)

accountancy /ə'kaʊntnsi/ n contabilidad f

accountant /ə'kaʊntnt/ n contador, -dora m,f (AmL); contable mf (Esp)

accredit /ə'kredət ‖ə'kredɪt/ vt (usu pass) acreditar

accrue /ə'kruː/ vi acumularse
■ ~ vt acumular

accumulate /ə'kjuːmjəleɪt ‖ə'kjuːmjʊleɪt/ vt ⟨wealth/interest⟩ acumular; ⟨information/evidence⟩ reunir*
■ ~ vi acumularse

accuracy /'ækjərəsi/ n (of measurement, instrument, description, translation) exactitud f; (of weapon) precisión f; (of aim, blow) lo certero

accurate /'ækjərət/ adj ⟨measurement/instrument/description/translation⟩ exacto; ⟨weapon/aim/blow⟩ certero

accusation /'ækjə'zeɪʃən ‖,ækju:'zeɪʃən/ n acusación f

accuse /ə'kjuːz/ vt acusar

accused /ə'kjuːzd/ n (pl ~) (Law) the ~ el acusado, la acusada; (pl) los acusados, las acusadas

accusing /ə'kjuːzɪŋ/ adj acusador

accustom /ə'kʌstəm/ vt to ~ sb TO sth/-ING acostumbrar a algn A algo/+INF

accustomed /ə'kʌstəmd/ adj (pred) to be ~ TO sth/-ING estar* acostumbrado A algo/+ INF; to become ~ TO sth/-ING acostumbrarse A algo/+ INF

AC/DC /'eɪsiː'diːsiː/ adj (Elec) CA/CC

ace /eɪs/ n **(a)** (in cards, dice) as m **(b)** (expert, champion) as m

ache¹ /eɪk/ vi **(a)** «tooth/ear/leg» doler*; my back ~s me duele la espalda **(b) aching** pres p ⟨shoulders/muscles⟩ dolorido

ache² n dolor m (sordo y continuo); ~s and pains achaques mpl

achieve /ə'tʃiːv/ vt **(a)** (accomplish) lograr **(b)** (attain) ⟨success/victory⟩ conseguir*, obtener*; ⟨aim⟩ lograr, conseguir*; ⟨ambition⟩ hacer* realidad

achievement /ə'tʃiːvmənt/ n **(a)** (feat) logro m **(b)** (success) éxito m; a sense of ~ la satisfacción de haber logrado algo

Achilles heel /ə'kɪliːz/ n talón m de Aquiles

acid¹ /'æsəd ‖'æsɪd/ n ácido m

acid², acidic /əˈsɪdɪk/ adj ácido

acid rain n lluvia f ácida

acknowledge /əkˈnɑːlɪdʒ ‖əkˈnɒlɪdʒ/ vt
1 (a) (admit) ⟨mistake/failure⟩ admitir (b)
(recognize) ⟨skill/authority/right⟩ reconocer*;
⟨quotations/sources⟩ hacer* mención de (c)
(express appreciation of) agradecer* **2** ⟨letter/order⟩
acusar recibo de; ⟨greeting⟩ responder a; ⟨person⟩
saludar

acknowledgment, acknowledgement
/əkˈnɑːlɪdʒmənt ‖əkˈnɒlɪdʒmənt/ n (a) (recognition)
reconocimiento m (b) (confirmation, response): **I've
had no ~ of my letter** no han acusado recibo de
mi carta (c) **acknowledgments** pl (in book)
lista f de menciones

acne /ˈækni/ n acné m or f, acne f‡

acorn /ˈeɪkɔːrn ‖ˈeɪkɔːn/ n bellota f

acoustic /əˈkuːstɪk/ adj acústico

acoustics /əˈkuːstɪks/ n (of room) (+ pl vb)
acústica f

acquaintance /əˈkweɪntns/ n (a) (person)
conocido, -da m,f (b) (with person) relación f; **to
make sb's ~** conocer* a algn (c) (knowledge) ~
WITH sth conocimiento m DE algo

acquainted /əˈkweɪntəd ‖əˈkweɪntɪd/ adj
(pred) (a) **to be ~ WITH sb** conocer* a algn (b)
to be ~ WITH sth (be informed of) estar* al
corriente DE algo; (be familiar with) estar*
familiarizado CON algo

acquiesce /ˌækwiˈes/ vi **to ~** (IN sth/-ING)
consentir* (algo/EN + INF)

acquire /əˈkwaɪr ‖əˈkwaɪə(r)/ vt ⟨collection/
skill⟩ adquirir*; ⟨reputation⟩ hacerse*

acquired /əˈkwaɪrd ‖əˈkwaɪəd/ adj
⟨characteristic⟩ adquirido; **it's an ~ taste** es algo
a lo que se le va tomando el gusto con el tiempo

acquisition /ˈækwəˈzɪʃən ‖ˌækwɪˈzɪʃən/ n
adquisición f

acquit /əˈkwɪt/ vt **-tt-** **to ~ sb** (OF sth)
absolver* a algn (DE algo)

acre /ˈeɪkər ‖ˈeɪkə(r)/ n acre m (0,405 hectáreas)

acrid /ˈækrəd ‖ˈækrɪd/ adj acre

acrobat /ˈækrəbæt/ n acróbata mf

acrobatic /ˌækrəˈbætɪk/ adj acrobático

across¹ /əˈkrɔːs ‖əˈkrɒs/ adv (a) (indicating
movement): **the boatman ferried them ~** el
barquero los cruzó (b) (indicating position) del otro
lado; **she sat ~ from me** estaba sentada frente a
mí (c) (in width, diameter): **it is 20m ~** tiene or mide
20m de ancho

across² prep (a) (from one side to other): **they ran
~ the road** cruzaron la calle corriendo (b) (on the
other side of): **they live just ~ the road** viven justo
enfrente; **it's ~ the river** está al otro lado del río

acrylic /əˈkrɪlɪk/ n acrílico m; (before n)
acrílico

act¹ /ækt/ vi **1** (a) (take action, do sth) actuar*
(b) «drug/chemical» hacer* efecto (c) (serve) to
~ AS sth servir* DE algo; **she will ~ as interpreter**
hará de intérprete (d) **acting** pres p ⟨chairman/
director⟩ interino
2 (behave) comportarse; **don't ~ dumb** ¡no te
hagas el tonto!
3 (perform) actuar*; (as profession) ser* actor/
actriz

■ **~ vt** (a) (perform) ⟨role/part⟩ interpretar (b)
(behave like, play role of) hacerse*

■ **act for** [v + prep + o] (represent) representar

■ **act on** [v + prep + o] (a) (follow) ⟨advice⟩
seguir*; ⟨orders⟩ cumplir (b) (affect) «drug/
chemical» actuar* sobre

■ **act out** [v + o + adv, v + adv + o] representar

act² n **1** (deed) acto m; **to catch sb in the ~**
agarrar or (esp Esp) coger* a algn con las manos
en la masa **2** (Govt) ley f **3** (a) (division of play)
acto m (b) (routine) número m; **to get one's ~
together** organizarse* **4** (pretense): **it was all a
big ~** era puro cuento (fam)

acting /ˈæktɪŋ/ n (performance) interpretación f;
have you done any ~ before? ¿has hecho teatro/
cine alguna vez?

action /ˈækʃən/ n **1** (a) (practical measures):
prompt ~ by the police saved several lives la
rápida actuación de la policía salvó varias vidas;
to take ~ (against sb/sth) tomar medidas (contra
algn/algo); **~!** (Cin) ¡acción! (b) (in phrases) **to
put sth into ~** poner* algo en práctica; **to be out
of ~** «car» estar* averiado; «person» estar*
fuera de circulación
2 (deed) acto m
3 (Mil) acción f (de guerra)
4 (a) (plot of play, movie) acción f (b) (exciting
activity) animación f
5 (a) (movement) movimiento m (b) (operation)
funcionamiento m (c) (of drug, chemical) acción f

action: **~-packed** adj lleno de acción; **~
replay** n (BrE) repetición f de la jugada

active /ˈæktɪv/ adj **1** ⟨person/life⟩ activo;
⟨volcano⟩ en actividad **2** (Ling) activo

activist /ˈæktəvəst ‖ˈæktɪvɪst/ n activista mf

activity /ækˈtɪvəti/ n (pl **-ties**) actividad f

actor /ˈæktər ‖ˈæktə(r)/ n actor, actriz m,f

actress /ˈæktrəs/ n actriz f

actual /ˈæktʃuəl/ adj (before n) (a) (real) real; **in
~ fact** en realidad (b) (precise, very) mismo; **on
the ~ day of the election** el mismo día de las
elecciones

actually /ˈæktʃuəli/ adv en realidad; **~, I'd
rather not go** la verdad es que preferiría no ir

acumen /əˈkjuːmən ‖ˈækjuːmən/ n sagacidad
f, perspicacia f; **business ~** visión f para los
negocios

acupuncture /ˈækjʊˌpʌŋktʃər
‖ˈækjʊˌpʌŋktʃə(r)/ n acupuntura f

acute /əˈkjuːt/ adj **1** ⟨condition/pain⟩ agudo;
⟨crisis/shortage⟩ grave; ⟨anxiety⟩ profundo; ⟨sense
of smell⟩ fino; ⟨sight/hearing⟩ agudo **2** (Ling)
⟨accent⟩ agudo

ad /æd/ n (colloq) ▶ ADVERTISEMENT

AD (= **Anno Domini**) después de Cristo; (written
form) d. de C., d. de J.C.

Adam /ˈædəm/ n Adán; **~'s apple** nuez f (de
Adán)

adamant /ˈædəmənt/ adj ⟨refusal⟩ firme; **she
was ~ that she wouldn't go** se mantuvo firme en
su decisión de no ir

adapt /əˈdæpt/ vt adaptar
■ **~ vi** **to ~** (TO sth/-ING) adaptarse (A algo/+ INF)

adaptable /əˈdæptəbəl/ adj adaptable

adaptation /ˌædæpˈteɪʃən/ n adaptación f

adapter, adaptor /ə'dæptər ‖ə'dæptə(r)/ *n*
(plug — with several sockets) enchufe *m* múltiple; (—
for different sockets) adaptador *m*

add /æd/ *vt* ⒈ (put in in addition) añadir; **at least I
think so, she ~ed** —al menos eso creo —añadió
⒉ (Math) sumar; **~ the numbers together** suma
los números
⒊ **added** *past p* ⟨*bonus/incentive*⟩ adicional;
with ~ed vitamins con vitaminas
■ **add to** [*v* + *prep* + *o*] ⟨*building*⟩ ampliar*;
⟨*confusion/difficulties*⟩ aumentar
■ **add up** ⒈ [*v* + *adv*] **(a)** (Math) cuadrar **(b)**
(make sense) (colloq) «*story/facts*» cuadrar; **it just
doesn't ~ up** no tiene sentido
⒉ [*v* + *o* + *adv, v* + *adv* + *o*] (Math) ⟨*figures*⟩
sumar; ⟨*bill*⟩ hacer*, preparar
■ **add up to** [*v* + *adv* + *prep* + *o*] «*figures*»
sumar en total; «*total*» ascender* a

adder /'ædər ‖'ædə(r)/ *n* víbora *f*

addict /'ædɪkt/ *n* adicto, -ta *m,f*; **drug ~**
drogadicto, -ta *m,f*

addicted /ə'dɪktəd ‖ə'dɪktɪd/ *adj* **to be ~** (TO
sth) ser* adicto (A algo)

addiction /ə'dɪkʃən/ *n* adicción *f*

addictive /ə'dɪktɪv/ *adj* ⟨*drug*⟩ que crea
adicción; ⟨*activity*⟩ que crea hábito

addition /ə'dɪʃən/ *n* ⒈ **(a)** (Math) suma *f*,
adición *f* (frml) **(b)** (adding) adición *f* **(c)** (*in
phrases*) **in addition** además; **in addition to**
además de ⒉ (extra thing): **the latest ~s to our
library** las últimas adquisiciones de nuestra
biblioteca

additional /ə'dɪʃŋəl ‖ə'dɪʃənl̩/ *adj* ⟨*cost/
weight*⟩ extra, adicional

additive /'ædətɪv ‖'ædɪtɪv/ *n* aditivo *m*

address¹ /'ædres ‖ə'dres/ *n* ⒈ **(a)** (of house,
offices etc) dirección *f*, señas *fpl*; Ⓢ **address** (on
form) domicilio; (*before n*) **~ book** libreta *f* de
direcciones **(b)** (Comput) dirección *f* ⒉ (speech)
discurso *m* ⒊ **form of ~** tratamiento *m*

address² /ə'dres/ *vt* ⒈ (AmE also) /'ædres/
⟨*mail*⟩ ponerle* la dirección a ⒉ **(a)** (speak to)
⟨*person*⟩ dirigirse* a; ⟨*assembly*⟩ pronunciar un
discurso ante **(b)** (direct) (frml) ⟨*question/remark*⟩
dirigir* ⒊ (deal with, confront) ⟨*problem/issue*⟩
tratar
■ *v refl* **(a)** (speak to) **to ~ oneself** TO sb dirigirse*
A algn **(b)** (turn one's attention to) (frml) **to ~ oneself**
TO sth dedicarse* A algo

addressee /,ædre'siː/ *n* destinatario, -ria *m,f*

adept /ə'dept/ *adj* experto

adequate /'ædɪkwət/ *adj* ⟨*help/funding*⟩
suficiente; ⟨*standard/explanation*⟩ adecuado

adhere /æd'hɪr ‖əd'hɪə(r)/ *vi* (frml) **(a)** (stick) to
~ (TO sth) adherirse* (A algo) **(b)** to **~** TO sth ⟨*to
principles/cause*⟩ adherirse* A algo; ⟨*to
regulations*⟩ observar algo

adhesive¹ /æd'hiːsɪv ‖əd'hiːsɪv/ *adj* adhesivo

adhesive² *n* adhesivo *m*

ad hoc /'æd'hɑːk ‖,æd'hɒk/ *adj* ⟨*arrangement/
measure*⟩ ad hoc; **~ ~ committee** comisión *f*
especial *or* ad hoc

adjacent /ə'dʒeɪsn̩t/ *adj* ⟨*fields*⟩ adyacente;
⟨*rooms*⟩ contiguo; **~ to** sth «*field*» adyacente A
algo; «*room*» contiguo A algo

adjective /'ædʒɪktɪv/ *n* adjetivo *m*

adjoin /ə'dʒɔɪn/ *vt* (frml) **(a)** (be adjacent to) lindar
con **(b) adjoining** *pres p* ⟨*houses*⟩ contiguo; **the
~ing room** el cuarto de al lado

adjourn /ə'dʒɜːrn ‖ə'dʒɜːn/ *vt* ⟨*talks/trial*⟩
suspender; **the meeting was ~ed** se levantó la
sesión
■ **~** *vi*: **the court ~ed** el tribunal levantó la sesión

adjournment /ə'dʒɜːrnmənt ‖ə'dʒɜːnmənt/ *n*
suspensión *f*

adjudicate /ə'dʒuːdɪkeɪt/ *vi* (give judgment)
arbitrar
■ **~** *vt* (frml) ⟨*competition*⟩ juzgar*; ⟨*claim*⟩ decidir
sobre

adjust /ə'dʒʌst/ *vt* ⟨*instrument/prices/wages*⟩
ajustar; ⟨*volume/temperature/speed*⟩ regular; **he
~ed his tie** se arregló la corbata
■ **~** *vi* to **~** (TO sth/-ING) adaptarse (A algo/+ INF)

adjustable /ə'dʒʌstəbəl/ *adj* ⟨*focus/
temperature*⟩ regulable

adjustment /ə'dʒʌstmənt/ *n* ⒈ (to machine,
instrument, figures) ajuste *m*; (to clothes) arreglo *m*;
(to plan, system) cambio *m* ⒉ (act, process) **(a)** (of
machine, instrument) ajuste *m* **(b)** (of person)
adaptación *f*

ad-lib /'æd'lɪb/ *vt/i* **-bb-** improvisar

administer /əd'mɪnəstər ‖əd'mɪnɪstə(r)/ *vt* **(a)**
(manage) administrar **(b)** (frml) ⟨*punishment/drug*⟩
administrar

administration /əd'mɪnə'streɪʃən
‖əd,mɪnɪ'streɪʃən/ *n* **(a)** (of institution, business,
estate) administración *f* **(b)** (managing body)
administración *f*; (Pol) gobierno *m*,
administración *f*; **(c)** (of school, medicine)
administración *f*

administrative /əd'mɪnəstreɪtɪv
‖əd'mɪnɪstrətɪv/ *adj* administrativo

administrator /əd'mɪnəstreɪtər
‖əd'mɪnɪstreɪtə(r)/ *n* administrador, -dora *m,f*

admirable /'ædmərəbəl/ *adj* ⟨*honesty/work*⟩
digno de admiración; ⟨*plan*⟩ excelente

admiral /'ædmərəl/ *n* almirante *mf*

admiration /'ædmə'reɪʃən/ *n* admiración *f*

admire /əd'maɪr ‖əd'maɪə(r)/ *vt* admirar

admirer /əd'maɪrər ‖əd'maɪərə(r)/ *n*
admirador, -dora *m,f*

admission /əd'mɪʃən/ *n* ⒈ **(a)** (to building,
exhibition) entrada *f*; (price) (precio *m* de) entrada *f*;
(into college, society) ingreso *m* **(b)** (into hospital)
ingreso *m* ⒉ (confession) admisión *f*; **he was, by
his own ~, a poor father** él mismo admitía que
no era un buen padre

admit /əd'mɪt/ **-tt-** *vt* ⒈ **(a)** (allow entry) dejar
entrar; ⟨*light/air*⟩ permitir entrar; Ⓢ **admit one**
entrada individual **(b)** ⟨*patient*⟩ ingresar,
internar (CS, Méx) ⒉ (confess) ⟨*crime/mistake*⟩
admitir; **to ~ sth** TO sb confesarle* algo A algn
■ **admit to** [*v* + *prep* + *o*] (confess) ⟨*error*⟩
admitir; ⟨*crime*⟩ declararse culpable de

admittance /əd'mɪtn̩s/ *n* (frml) **~** (TO sth)
acceso *m* (A algo); Ⓢ **no admittance** prohibida la
entrada

admittedly /əd'mɪtədli ‖əd'mɪtɪdli/ *adv*
(indep): **~, it wasn't an easy task, but ...** hay que
reconocer que no era una ¦area fácil pero ...

admonish /æd'mɑːnɪʃ ‖əd'mɒnɪʃ/ *vt* (frml) **to
~ sb** (FOR sth) amonestar a algn (POR algo)

ado /ə'duː/ n: without further o more ~ sin más (preámbulos)

adolescence /'ædə'lesn̩s/ n adolescencia f

adolescent¹ /'ædə'lesn̩t/ n adolescente mf

adolescent² adj adolescente

adopt /ə'dɑːpt ‖ə'dɒpt/ vt (a) ‹child› adoptar (b) ‹idea/custom/title› adoptar (c) ‹recommendation› aprobar*

adopted /ə'dɑːptəd ‖ə'dɒptɪd/ adj ‹son/ country› adoptivo; she's ~ es adoptada

adoption /ə'dɑːpʃən ‖ə'dɒpʃən/ n (a) (of child) adopción f (b) (of approach, custom, title) adopción f (c) (of report, motion) aprobación f

adoptive /ə'dɑːptɪv ‖ə'dɒptɪv/ adj (before n) adoptivo

adorable /ə'dɔːrəbəl/ adj ‹house/hat› divino; ‹child› adorable

adoration /'ædə'reɪʃən/ n adoración f

adore /ə'dɔːr ‖ə'dɔː(r)/ vt (a) (love, worship) adorar (b) **adoring** pres p ‹gaze› lleno de adoración; ‹mother› amantísimo (c) (like, enjoy): I ~ figs me encantan los higos

adorn /ə'dɔːrn ‖ə'dɔːn/ vt (frml or liter) adornar

adornment /ə'dɔːrnmənt ‖ə'dɔːnmənt/ n adorno m

adrenaline /ə'drenlən ‖ə'drenəlɪn/ n adrenalina f

Adriatic /'eɪdri'ætɪk/ n the ~ (Sea) el (mar) Adriático

adrift /ə'drɪft/ adj (pred) (Naut) a la deriva; to come o go ~ ‹plans› fallar

adroit /ə'drɔɪt/ adj (a) ‹answer/speaker› hábil (b) ‹movement› ágil; ‹player› diestro

adulation /'ædʒə'leɪʃən ‖ˌædjʊ'leɪʃən/ n adulación f

adult¹ /ə'dʌlt, 'ædʌlt/ n adulto, -ta m,f

adult² adj (a) (physically mature) adulto (b) (mature) ‹behavior/approach› maduro, adulto (c) (suitable for adults) para mayores or adultos

adult education n educación f para adultos; (before n) ‹class› para adultos

adultery /ə'dʌltəri/ n adulterio m

adulthood /ə'dʌlthʊd , 'ædʌlthʊd/ n edad f adulta, adultez f

advance¹ /əd'væns ‖əd'vɑːns/ vi «person/ vehicle» avanzar*; «science/society» avanzar*, progresar
■ ~ vt [1] (a) (move forward) ‹troops› avanzar* (b) (further) ‹knowledge› fomentar; ‹interests/cause› promover* [2] (a) ‹date/meeting› adelantar (b) ‹money/wages› anticipar

advance² n [1] (of person, army, vehicle) avance m; (of civilization, science) avance m, progreso m [2] **advances** pl (overtures) insinuaciones fpl [3] (a) (early payment) anticipo m (b) (loan) préstamo m [4] **in advance**: to pay in ~ pagar* por adelantado; it was planned well in ~ se planeó con mucha antelación

advance³ adj (before n): ~ booking is essential es imprescindible hacer la reserva por anticipado

advanced /əd'vænst ‖əd'vɑːnst/ adj ‹civilization/course/student› avanzado

advantage /əd'væntɪdʒ ‖əd'vɑːntɪdʒ/ n (a) (superior factor) ventaja f (b) (gain): to take ~ of sth aprovechar algo; (pej) aprovecharse de algo; to take ~ of sb (exploit) aprovecharse de algn; to turn sth to one's ~ sacar* provecho de algo (c) (in tennis) (no pl) ventaja f

advantageous /ˌædvæn'teɪdʒəs ‖ˌædvən'teɪdʒəs/ adj ‹arrangement› ventajoso; ‹position/situation› de ventaja

advent /'ædvent/ n (a) (arrival) llegada f (b) **Advent** (Relig) Adviento m

adventure /əd'ventʃər ‖əd'ventʃə(r)/ n aventura f; (before n) ‹story/film› de aventuras

adventurous /əd'ventʃərəs/ adj ‹traveler› intrépido; ‹spirit/person› aventurero

adverb /'ædvɜːrb ‖'ædvɜːb/ n adverbio m

adversary /'ædvərseri ‖'ædvəsəri/ n (pl -ries) (frml) adversario, -ria m,f

adverse /'ædvɜːrs, æd'vɜːrs ‖'ædvɜːs/ adj adverso

adversity /æd'vɜːrsəti ‖əd'vɜːsəti/ n (pl -ties) adversidad f

advert /'ædvɜːrt ‖'ædvɜːt/ n (BrE colloq) ▶ ADVERTISEMENT

advertise /'ædvərtaɪz ‖'ædvətaɪz/ vt ‹product› hacerle* publicidad a, hacerle* réclame a (AmL); I saw it ~d on TV lo vi anunciado en la tele
■ ~ vi hacer* publicidad

advertisement /'ædvər'taɪzmənt ‖əd'vɜːtɪsmənt/ n anuncio m, aviso m (AmL)

advertiser /'ædvərtaɪzər ‖'ædvətaɪzə(r)/ n anunciante mf

advertising /'ædvərtaɪzɪŋ ‖'ædvətaɪzɪŋ/ n (a) (action, business) publicidad f; (before n) ‹campaign/slot› publicitario; ~ agency agencia f de publicidad (b) (advertisements) propaganda f

advice /əd'vaɪs/ n (counsel) consejos mpl; (professional) asesoramiento m; a piece of ~ un consejo; to give sb ~ aconsejar a algn; to take sb's ~ seguir* los consejos de algn

advisable /əd'vaɪzəbəl/ adj aconsejable

advise /əd'vaɪz/ vt [1] (a) (recommend) aconsejar; to ~ sb to + INF aconsejar(le) A algn QUE (+ subj); they ~d him against marrying so young le aconsejaron que no se casara tan joven (b) (give advice to) aconsejar; (professionally) asesorar [2] (inform) (frml) informar; (in writing) notificar* (frml)
■ ~ vi aconsejar; (professionally) asesorar; to ~ AGAINST sth/-ING desaconsejar algo/+ INF

adviser, advisor /əd'vaɪzər ‖əd'vaɪzə(r)/ n consejero, -ra m,f; (professional) asesor, -sora m,f

advisory /əd'vaɪzəri/ adj ‹body/service› consultivo; in an ~ capacity en calidad de asesor

advocate¹ /ˈædvəkət/ n **(a)** (supporter, defender) ~ **(OF sth)** defensor, -sora m,f (DE algo) **(b)** (in a court of law) abogado, -da m,f

advocate² /ˈædvəkeɪt/ vt recomendar*, abogar* por

Aegean /ɪˈdʒiːən/ n the ~ (Sea) el (mar) Egeo

aerial¹ /ˈeriəl ‖ˈeəriəl/ adj (before n) aéreo; ~ photograph aerofoto f

aerial² n (esp BrE) antena f

aerobics /eˈrəʊbɪks, ə- ‖eəˈrəʊbɪks/ n (+ sing or pl vb) aerobic(s) m, aerobismo m (CS)

aerodynamic /ˌerəʊdaɪˈnæmɪk ‖ˌeərəʊdaɪˈnæmɪk/ adj aerodinámico

aeroplane /ˈerəpleɪn ‖ˈeərəpleɪn/ n (BrE) avión m

aerosol /ˈerəsɑːl ‖ˈeərəsɒl/ n aerosol m, spray m

aerospace /ˈerəʊspeɪs ‖ˈeərəʊspeɪs/ adj (before n) ⟨research/industry⟩ aeroespacial

aesthetic, (AmE also) **esthetic** /esˈθetɪk ‖iːsˈθetɪk/ adj estético

afar /əˈfɑːr ‖əˈfɑː(r)/ adv (liter) lejos

affable /ˈæfəbəl/ adj afable

affair /əˈfer ‖əˈfeə(r)/ n **1** **(a)** (case) caso m **(b)** (event): the wedding was a small, family ~ la boda se celebró en la intimidad; it was a very formal ~ fue una ocasión muy ceremoniosa **(c)** (business, concern) asunto m **(d)** **affairs** pl (matters) asuntos mpl **2** (liaison) affaire m

affect /əˈfekt/ vt (have effect on) afectar a; ⟨organ/nervous system⟩ comprometer

affected /əˈfektəd ‖əˈfektɪd/ adj afectado

affection /əˈfekʃən/ n cariño m

affectionate /əˈfekʃnət/ adj cariñoso

affiliate /əˈfɪlieɪt/ vt (often pass) afiliar

affiliation /əˌfɪliˈeɪʃən/ n afiliación f; her political ~s su filiación política

affinity /əˈfɪnəti/ n (pl **-ties**) afinidad f

affirm /əˈfɜːrm ‖əˈfɜːm/ vt declarar

affirmative /əˈfɜːrmətɪv ‖əˈfɜːmətɪv/ adj afirmativo

affix /əˈfɪks/ vt (fml) ⟨stamp/seal⟩ poner*; ⟨notice⟩ fijar

afflict /əˈflɪkt/ vt ⟨disease/problem⟩⟩ aquejar

affliction /əˈflɪkʃən/ n **(a)** (suffering) aflicción f **(b)** (cause of suffering) desgracia f, (ailment) mal m

affluence /ˈæfluəns/ n prosperidad f

affluent /ˈæfluənt/ adj ⟨suburb/country⟩ próspero; ⟨person⟩ acomodado

afford /əˈfɔːrd ‖əˈfɔːd/ vt: I can't ~ a new car no me alcanza el dinero para comprarme un coche nuevo; you can't ~ to miss this opportunity no puedes perderte esta oportunidad

affordable /əˈfɔːrdəbəl ‖əˈfɔːdəbəl/ adj asequible

affront /əˈfrʌnt/ n (fml) afrenta f

Afghan¹ /ˈæfɡæn/ adj afgano

Afghan² n afgano, -na m,f

Afghanistan /æfˈɡænəstæn ‖æfˈɡænɪstɑːn/ n Afganistán m

afield /əˈfiːld/ adv: she travels as far ~ as China viaja a lugares tan distantes como la China; we had to look further ~ for help tuvimos que buscar ayuda en otra parte

afloat /əˈfləʊt/ adj (pred) a flote; to stay ~ mantenerse* a flote

afoot /əˈfʊt/ adj (pred): plans are ~ to create ... hay planes de crear ...; what's ~? ¿qué se está tramando?

aforementioned /əˈfɔːrˈmenʃənd ‖əˈfɔːˈmenʃənd/ adj (fml) (before n) ⟨clause/ statement⟩ anteriormente mencionado, antedicho (frml); the ~ person el susodicho, la susodicha (frml o hum)

afraid /əˈfreɪd/ adj (pred) **1** (scared): to be ~ OF sb/sth tenerle* miedo A algn/A algo; there's nothing to be ~ of no tienes nada que temer **2** (sorry): she's not in, I'm ~ lo siento pero no está; I'm ~ not me temo que no

afresh /əˈfreʃ/ adv: to start ~ empezar* de nuevo, volver* a empezar

Africa /ˈæfrɪkə/ n África f‡

African¹ /ˈæfrɪkən/ adj africano

African² n africano, -na m,f

African-American¹ /ˈæfrɪkənəˈmerɪkən/adj norteamericano de origen africano

African-American² n norteamericano, -na m,f de origen africano

Afro-American¹ /ˈæfrəʊəˈmerɪkən/ adj afroamericano

Afro-American² n afroamericano, -na m,f

Afro-Caribbean /ˌæfrəʊˌkærɪˈbiːən/ adj (BrE) afroantillano, afrocaribeño

after¹ /ˈæftər ‖ˈɑːftə(r)/ prep **1** (following in time) después de; I'll be at home ~ eight o'clock estaré en casa después de or a partir de las ocho; it's just ~ midnight son las doce pasadas; it's a quarter ~ two (AmE) son las dos y cuarto; the day ~ the party al día siguiente de la fiesta **2** (in sequence, rank) tras; day ~ day día tras día; do go in — ~ you! pase — ¡primero usted! **3** **(a)** (behind): shut the door ~ you cierra la puerta al salir **(b)** (in pursuit of) tras; he ran ~ them corrió tras ellos; he's ~ her money anda a la caza de su dinero (fam); see also ASK AFTER **4** after all después de todo

after² conj: it happened ~ you left ocurrió después de que tú te fuiste; ~ examining it después de examinarlo

after³ adv **(a)** (afterward, following) después; the day ~ al día siguiente **(b)** (behind) detrás

aftereffect /ˈæftərɪˌfekt ‖ˈɑːftərɪˌfekt/ n (of drug) efecto m secundario; (of problem) secuela f

aftermath /ˈæftərmæθ ‖ˈɑːftəmæθ, ˈɑːftəmɑːθ/ n **(a)** (subsequent period): in the ~ of the riots tras los disturbios **(b)** (consequences) repercusiones fpl

afternoon /ˈæftərˈnuːn ‖ˌɑːftəˈnuːn/ n **1** (time of day) tarde f; on Friday ~ el viernes por or (AmL) en la tarde; he came in the ~ vino por la tarde, vino en la tarde (AmL); good ~! ¡buenas tardes! **2** **afternoons** (as adv) por las tardes, en las tardes (AmL)

after-: ~shave (lotion) n loción f para después de afeitarse, aftershave m; ~thought n: it occurred to me as an ~thought that ... después se me ocurrió qué ...; it was added on as an ~thought fue una idea de último momento

afterward /ˈæftərwərd ‖ˈɑːftəwəd/, (BrE also) **afterwards** /-z/ adv después

again /əˈgen, əˈgeɪn/ *adv* otra vez, de nuevo; **to do sth ~** volver* a hacer algo, hacer* algo otra vez *or* de nuevo; **never ~!** ¡nunca más!

against /əˈgenst, əˈgeɪnst/ *prep* contra; **I've nothing ~ her** no tengo nada contra ella *or* en contra suya *or* en contra de ella; **I'm ~ capital punishment** estoy en contra de la pena de muerte; **he put a cross ~ my name** puso una cruz al lado de mi nombre

age¹ /eɪdʒ/ *n* **1** (of person, animal, thing) edad *f*; **he is six years of ~** tiene seis años; **to be under ~** ser* menor de edad; (*before n*) **~ group** grupo *m* etario (frml) **2** **(a)** (epoch, period) era *f*; **through the ~s** a través de los tiempos **(b)** (long time) (colloq): **I haven't seen her for ~s** hace siglos que no la veo (fam)

age² (*pres p* **aging** *or* **ageing**; *past p* **aged** /eɪdʒd/) *vi* «*person*» envejecer*; «*cheese*» madurar
■ ~ *vt* ‹*person*› hacer* envejecer; ‹*wine*› añejar

aged *adj* **1** /ˈeɪdʒəd/ ‖ /ˈeɪdʒɪd/ (elderly) anciano **2** /eɪdʒd/ (*pred*): **he was ~ 20** tenía 20 años de edad

ageing *adj/n* ▶ AGING

ageism /ˈeɪdʒɪzəm/ *n* discriminación *f* por razones de edad

ageist /ˈeɪdʒəst ‖ ˈeɪdʒɪst/ *adj* que discrimina a las personas en razón de su edad

agency /ˈeɪdʒənsi/ *n* (*pl* **-cies**) **(a)** (office) agencia *f* **(b)** (branch) sucursal *f* **(c)** (department) organismo *m*

agenda /əˈdʒendə/ *n* orden *m* del día, agenda *f*

agent /ˈeɪdʒənt/ *n* **1** (person) agente *mf* **2** (substance) agente *m*

aggravate /ˈægrəveɪt/ *vt* **(a)** (make worse) agravar **(b)** (annoy) (colloq) exasperar

aggression /əˈgreʃən/ *n* **(a)** (feeling, attitude) agresividad *f* **(b)** (unprovoked attack) agresión *f*

aggressive /əˈgresɪv/ *adj* ‹*person/country*› agresivo; ‹*tactics/strategy*› de agresión

aghast /əˈgæst ‖ əˈgɑːst/ *adj* (*pred*) aterrado

agile /ˈædʒəl ‖ ˈædʒaɪl/ *adj* ágil

agility /əˈdʒɪləti/ *n* agilidad *f*

aging¹ /ˈeɪdʒɪŋ/ *adj* (*before n*) ‹*person*› envejecido

aging² *n* envejecimiento *m*

agitate /ˈædʒəteɪt ‖ ˈædʒɪteɪt/ *vt* **(a)** (disturb) ‹*surface/liquid*› agitar **(b)** (upset) inquietar
■ ~ *vi* **to ~ FOR/AGAINST sth** hacer* campaña A FAVOR DE/EN CONTRA DE algo

agitated /ˈædʒəteɪtəd ‖ ˈædʒɪteɪtɪd/ *adj* ‹*movements/gestures*› nervioso; **to become/get ~** ponerse* nervioso

agitation /ˈædʒəteɪʃən ‖ ˌædʒɪteɪʃən/ *n* agitación *f*

AGM *n* (BrE) = **annual general meeting**

agnostic /ægˈnɒstɪk ‖ ægˈnɒstɪk/ *n* agnóstico, -ca *m,f*

ago /əˈgəʊ/ *adv*: **five days ~** hace cinco días; **a long time ~** hace mucho (tiempo)

agog /əˈgɒg ‖ əˈgɒg/ *adj* (*pred*): **I was all ~** estaba que me moría de curiosidad

agonize /ˈægənaɪz/ *vi*: **stop agonizing, just do it** no le des más vueltas al asunto y hazlo; **he ~d over the decision** le costó muchísimo decidirse

agonizing /ˈægənaɪzɪŋ/ *adj* ‹*experience*› angustioso; ‹*pain*› atroz; ‹*decision*› muy difícil

agony /ˈægəni/ *n* (*pl* **-nies**): **he was in ~** estaba desesperado de dolor; **she's going through agonies of doubt** las dudas la están atormentando; **to prolong the ~** alargar* el martirio

agoraphobia /ˌægərəˈfəʊbiə/ *n* agorafobia *f*

agree /əˈgriː/ *vt* **1** **(a)** (be in agreement over) **to ~ (THAT)** estar* de acuerdo (EN QUE); **yes, it must feel odd, he ~d** —sí, debe resultar extraño — asintió **(b)** (reach agreement over) decidir; **it was ~d that he should go on his own** se decidió que fuera él solo; **to ~ WHEN/WHAT/HOW** *etc* ponerse* de acuerdo EN CUÁNDO/EN QUÉ/EN CÓMO *etc*; **to ~ to + INF** quedar EN + INF; **(c)** (decide on) ‹*price*› acordar*
2 **(a)** (consent) **to ~ to + INF** aceptar + INF **(b)** (admit) **to ~ (THAT)** reconocer* (QUE)
■ ~ *vi* **1** (be of same opinion) estar* de acuerdo; **to ~ ABOUT sth** estar* de acuerdo EN algo **2** **(a)** (get on well) congeniar **(b)** (tally) «*statements/figures*» concordar*
■ **agree on** [*v + prep + o*] ‹*date/details*› acordar*; **we ~ on the color** estamos de acuerdo en el color
■ **agree to** [*v + prep + o*] ‹*terms/conditions*› aceptar
■ **agree with** [*v + prep + o*] **(a)** (approve of) estar* de acuerdo con **(b)** **to ~ with sb** «‹*food/heat/climate*›» sentarle* bien a algn

agreeable /əˈgriːəbəl/ *adj* **1** (pleasant) agradable **2** (willing) (*pred*): **bring her along, if she's ~** tráela, si quiere venir; **he seemed quite ~ to coming** parecía dispuesto a venir

agreed /əˈgriːd/ *adj* **(a)** (in agreement) (*pred*) de acuerdo **(b)** (prearranged): **we met at ten, as ~** nos encontramos a las diez como habíamos quedado; (*before n*) ‹*price/terms*› acordado

agreement /əˈgriːmənt/ *n* **1** **(a)** (shared opinion) acuerdo *m*; **to be in ~ (with sb)** estar* de acuerdo (con algn) **(b)** (written arrangement) acuerdo *m*; (Busn) contrato *m* **2** (consent) consentimiento *m*

agricultural /ˌægrɪˈkʌltʃərəl/ *adj* agrícola

agriculture /ˈægrɪkʌltʃər ‖ ˈægrɪkʌltʃə(r)/ *n* agricultura *f*

aground /əˈgraʊnd/ *adv*: **to go** *o* **run ~ (ON sth)** encallar (EN algo)

ahead /əˈhed/ *adv* **1** **(a)** (indicating movement): **go straight ~** siga todo recto; **I'll go on ~** yo iré delante **(b)** (indicating position): **the post office is straight ~** la oficina de correos está siguiendo recto **(c)** (in race, competition): **our team was ~** nuestro equipo llevaba la delantera **(d)** (in time): **the months ~** los meses venideros, los próximos meses
2 **ahead of** **(a)** (in front of) delante de **(b)** (in race, competition) por delante de; **the Japanese are way ~ of us in this field** los japoneses nos llevan mucha ventaja en este campo **(c)** (before): **she got there an hour ~ of him** llegó una hora antes que él

aid¹ /eɪd/ *n* **(a)** (assistance, support) ayuda *f*; **to come/go to sb's ~** venir*/ir* en ayuda de algn **(b)** (monetary) ayuda *f*, asistencia *f*; **a concert in ~ of ...** un concierto a beneficio de ...

aid² *vt* ayudar; **to ~ and abet sb** (Law) instigar* *or* secundar a algn (*en la comisión de un delito*)

aide /eɪd/ *n* asesor, -sora *m,f*

AIDS /eɪdz/ *n* (= **acquired immune deficiency syndrome**) sida *m*, SIDA *m*

ailing /'eɪlɪŋ/ *adj* ‹*person*› enfermo; ‹*economy*› renqueante

ailment /'eɪlmənt/ *n* enfermedad *f*, dolencia *f* (frml)

aim¹ /eɪm/ *vt*: he ∼ed the gun at her le apuntó con la pistola; she ∼ed a blow at his head intentó darle en la cabeza; the movie is ∼ed at a young audience la película está dirigida a un público joven
■ ∼ *vi* **(a)** (point weapon) apuntar; **to** ∼ **AT** sth/sb apuntar(le) A algo/algn **(b)** (intend) **to** ∼ **to** + INF querer* + INF

aim² *n* **(a)** (goal, object) objetivo *m* **(b)** (with weapon) puntería *f*; **to take** ∼ hacer* puntería, apuntar

aimless /'eɪmləs ‖'eɪmlɪs/ *adj* ‹*wandering*› sin rumbo (fijo); ‹*existence*› sin norte

ain't /eɪnt/ (colloq & dial) **(a)** = **am not (b)** = **is not (c)** = **are not (d)** = **has not (e)** = **have not**

air¹ /er ‖eə(r)/ *n* **1** aire *m*; **to go by** ∼ ir* en avión; **to be up in the** ∼ «*plans*» estar* en el aire; **to vanish into thin** ∼ esfumarse; ‹*before n*› ‹*route/attack*› aéreo; ‹*pollution*› de la atmósfera; ∼ **pressure** presión *f* atmosférica **2** (Rad, TV): **to be on the** ∼ estar* en el aire; **to come** *o* **go on the** ∼ salir* al aire **3 (a)** (manner, look, atmosphere) aire *m* **(b) airs** *pl* (affectations) aires *mpl*

air² *vt* **1 (a)** ‹*clothes/linen*› airear, orear; ‹*bed/room*› ventilar, airear **(b)** ‹*opinion/grievance*› manifestar*; ‹*knowledge*› hacer* alarde de **2** (broadcast) (AmE) ‹*program*› transmitir, emitir

air: ∼ **bag** *n* (Auto) bolsa *f* de aire; ∼ **base** *n* base *f* aérea; ∼ **bed** *n* (BrE) colchón *m* inflable; ∼**borne** *adj* **(a)** ‹*seeds/dust*› transportado por el aire; ‹*troops/units*› aerotransportado **(b)** (off the ground): **the plane is now** ∼**borne** el avión ha despegado; ∼**conditioned** /'erkən'dɪʃənd ‖'eəkəndɪʃənd/ *adj* con aire acondicionado, climatizado; ∼ **conditioning** *n* aire *m* acondicionado

aircraft /'erkræft ‖'eəkrɑːft/ *n* (*pl* ∼) avión *m*

aircraft carrier *n* portaaviones *m*

air: ∼**fare** *n* precio *m* del pasaje *or* (Esp tb) del billete de avión; ∼**fares are set to rise** van a subir las tarifas aéreas; ∼**field** *n* aeródromo *m*; ∼ **force** *n* (of nation) fuerza *f* aérea; ∼ **freshener** /'freʃnər ‖'freʃnə(r)/ *n* ambientador *m*, desodorante *m* ambiental *or* de ambientes (CS); ∼ **gun** *n* (revolver) pistola *f* de aire comprimido; (rifle) escopeta *f* or rifle *m* de aire comprimido; ∼ **hostess** *n* azafata *f*, aeromoza *f* (AmL); ∼ **letter** *n* aerograma *m*; ∼**lift** *n* puente *m* aéreo; ∼**line** *n* línea *f* aérea, aerolínea *f*; ∼**mail** *n* correo *m* aéreo; **to send sth** (by) ∼**mail** mandar algo por avión *or* por vía aérea; ‹*before n*› ‹*paper/envelope*› de avión; ∼**plane** *n* (AmE) avión *m*; ∼**port** *n* aeropuerto *m*; ∼ **raid** *n* ataque *m* aéreo; ‹*before n*› ∼**raid shelter** refugio *m* antiaéreo; ∼**ship** *n* dirigible *m*, zepelín *m*; ∼**sick** *adj*: **to be** ∼**sick** estar* mareado (en un avión); **to get** ∼**sick** marearse (al viajar en avión); ∼**sickness** *n* mareo *m* (al viajar en avión); ∼ **strike** *n* ataque *m* aéreo; ∼**strip** *n*

pista *f* de aterrizaje; ∼**tight** *adj* ‹*room/box*› hermético; ‹*alibi/argument*› a toda prueba; ∼ **traffic control** *n* control *m* del tráfico aéreo; ∼ **traffic controller** *n* controlador aéreo, controladora aérea *m,f*; ∼**worthy** *adj*: **to be** ∼**worthy** estar* en condiciones de vuelo

airy /'eri ‖'eəri/ *adj* **airier, airiest (a)** ‹*room/house*› espacioso y aireado **(b)** ‹*manner/reply*› displicente

aisle /aɪl/ *n* (gangway) pasillo *m*; (Archit) nave *f* lateral

ajar /ə'dʒɑːr ‖ə'dʒɑː(r)/ *adj* ‹*pred*› entreabierto

AK = Alaska

akin /ə'kɪn/ *adj* ‹*pred*› **to be** ∼ (**TO** sth) ser* similar (A algo)

AL = Alabama

Ala = Alabama

à la carte /'ɑːlə'kɑːrt ‖,ɑːlɑː'kɑːt/ *adj/adv* a la carta

alarm¹ /ə'lɑːrm ‖ə'lɑːm/ *n* **1** (apprehension) gran preocupación *f* **2** (warning, device) alarma *f*

alarm² *vt* (worry) alarmar; (scare) asustar

alarm clock *n* (reloj *m*) despertador *m*

alarmed /ə'lɑːrmd ‖ə'lɑːmd/ *adj* (apprehensive): **don't be** ∼ no te asustes; **I began to be** ∼ empecé a alarmarme

alarming /ə'lɑːrmɪŋ ‖ə'lɑːmɪŋ/ *adj* alarmante

alas /ə'læs/ *interj* (liter or frml) ¡ay! (liter)

Albania /æl'beɪniə/ *n* Albania *f*

Albanian¹ /æl'beɪniən/ *adj* albanés

Albanian² *n* **(a)** (person) albanés, -nesa *m,f* **(b)** (language) albanés *m*

albeit /ɔːl'biːɪt/ *conj* (frml) aunque

albino /æl'baɪnəʊ ‖æl'biːnəʊ/ *n* (*pl* **-nos**) albino, -na *m,f*; ‹*before n*› albino

album /'ælbəm/ *n* **(a)** (book) álbum *m*; **photograph** ∼ álbum de fotos **(b)** (Audio) álbum *m*

alchemist /'ælkəməst ‖'ælkəmɪst/ *n* alquimista *mf*

alcohol /'ælkəhɔːl ‖'ælkəhɒl/ *n* alcohol *m*

alcoholic¹ /'ælkə'hɔːlɪk ‖,ælkə'hɒlɪk/ *adj* alcohólico

alcoholic² *n* alcohólico, -ca *m,f*

alcoholism /'ælkəhɔːlɪzəm ‖'ælkəhɒlɪzəm/ *n* alcoholismo *m*

alcove /'ælkəʊv/ *n* (recess) hueco *m*; (niche) hornacina *f*

alderman /'ɔːldərmən ‖'ɔːldəmən/ *n* (*pl* **-men** /-mən/) **(a)** (in UK) regidor, -dora *m,f* **(b)** (in US) concejal *m*

alderwoman /'ɔːldər,wʊmən ‖'ɔːldə,wʊmən/ *n* (*pl* **-women**) (in US) concejala *f*

ale /eɪl/ *n* cerveza *f*

alert¹ /ə'lɜːrt ‖ə'lɜːt/ *adj* alerta *adj inv*; **to be** ∼ (vigilant) estar* alerta; (lively-minded) estar* despierto

alert² *n* alerta *f*; **to be on the** ∼ estar* alerta

alert³ *vt* **to** ∼ sb (**TO** sth) alertar a algn (DE algo)

A level *n* (in UK) estudios de una asignatura a nivel de bachillerato superior

alga /'ælgə/ *n* (*pl* **algae** /'ældʒiː, 'ælgiː/) alga *f*‡

algebra /'ældʒəbrə ‖'ældʒɪbrə/ *n* álgebra *f*‡

Algeria /æl'dʒɪriə ‖æl'dʒɪəriə/ *n* Argelia *f*

Algerian /æl'dʒɪriən ‖æl'dʒɪəriən/ *adj* argelino

alias /'eɪliəs/ *adv* alias

alibi /'æləbaɪ ‖'ælɪbaɪ/ *n* coartada *f*

alien[1] /'eɪliən/ *n* **(a)** (foreigner) extranjero, -ra *m,f* **(b)** (in science fiction) extraterrestre *mf*

alien[2] *adj* **(a)** (strange, foreign) extraño; **to be ~ TO sb/sth** serle* ajeno A algn/algo **(b)** (in science fiction) (*before n*) extraterrestre

alienate /'eɪliəneɪt/ *vt* (Pol, Psych) alienar; (estrange): **he has ~d all his friends** ha hecho que todos sus amigos se alejen *or* se distancien de él

alight[1] /ə'laɪt/ *adj* (*pred*) **to be ~** estar* ardiendo; **to set sth ~** prender(le) fuego a algo

alight[2] *vi* (fml) «*passenger*» apearse (fml); (land) «*bird/insect*» posarse

align /ə'laɪn/ *vt* alinear

alignment /ə'laɪnmənt/ *n* **(a)** (Tech) alineación *f* **(b)** (Pol) alineamiento *m*

alike[1] /ə'laɪk/ *adj* (*pred*) parecido

alike[2] *adv* ‹*think/act*› igual; **popular with young and old ~** popular tanto entre los jóvenes como entre los mayores

alimony /'æləməʊni ‖'ælɪməni/ *n* pensión *f* alimenticia

alive /ə'laɪv/ *adj* (*pred*) vivo; **is he still ~?** ¿todavía vive?; **to stay ~** sobrevivir; **she's ~ and well** está sana y salva; **the place was ~ with insects** el lugar estaba plagado de insectos

alkaline /'ælkəlaɪn/ *adj* alcalino

all[1] /ɔːl/ *adj* (*before n*) todo, -da; (*pl*) todos, -das; **~ four of us went** fuimos los cuatro; **~ morning** toda la mañana; **of ~ the stupid things to do!** ¡qué estupidez!; *see also* ALL[3] 3D

all[2] *pron* [1] (everything) (+ *sing vb*) todo; **will that be ~, madam?** ¿algo más señora?; **when ~ is said and done** a fin de cuentas; **for ~ I care** por lo que a mí me importa

[2] **all of:** **~ of the children go to school** todos los niños van al colegio; **~ of the cheese** todo el queso

[3] (*after n, pron*) todo, -da; (*pl*) todos, -das; **it was ~ gone** no quedaba nada

[4] (*in phrases*) **(a)** **all in all** en general **(b)** **all told** en total **(c)** **and all** y todo; **he ate it, skin and ~** se lo comió con la cáscara y todo **(d)** **at all: they don't like him at ~** no les gusta nada; **thank you — not at ~** gracias — de nada *or* no hay de qué; **it's not at ~ bad** no está nada mal **(e)** **in all** en total

all[3] *adv* [1] (completely): **you've gone ~ red** te has puesto todo colorado/toda colorada; **she was ~ alone** estaba completamente sola

[2] (each, apiece) (Sport): **the score was one ~** iban (empatados) uno a uno; **30 ~** 30 iguales

[3] (*in phrases*) **(a)** **all along** desde el primer momento **(b)** **all but** casi; **the game had ~ but finished** ya casi había terminado el partido **(c)** **all that** (particularly) (*usu neg*): **I don't know her ~ that well** no la conozco tan bien; **I don't care ~ that much** no me importa demasiado **(d)** **all the**

(+ *comp*): **~ the more reason to fire them!** ¡más razón para echarlos!; **~ the more so because ...** tanto más cuanto que ...

Allah /'ælə/ *n* Alá

all: **~-American** /'ɔːlə'merəkən ‖,ɔːlə'merɪkən/ *adj* ‹*boy/girl*› típicamente americano; **~-around** /'ɔːlə'raʊnd/ *adj* (AmE) (*before n*) **(a)** (versatile) ‹*athlete/scholar*› completo **(b)** ‹*experience/visibility*› amplio

allay /ə'leɪ/ *vt* ‹*doubt/fear*› disipar

all-clear /'ɔːl'klɪr ‖'ɔːl'klɪə(r)/ *n*: **to give sb/sth the ~ dar*** luz verde a algn/algo

allegation /ælɪ'geɪʃən/ *n* acusación *f*

allege /ə'ledʒ/ *vt* afirmar; **she is ~d to have accepted bribes** se dice que aceptó sobornos

alleged /ə'ledʒd/ *adj* (*before n*) ‹*thief/violation*› presunto

allegedly /ə'ledʒədli ‖ə'ledʒɪdli/ *adv* (*indep*) supuestamente

allegiance /ə'liːdʒəns/ *n* lealtad *f*; (political) filiación *f*

allergic /ə'lɜːrdʒɪk ‖ə'lɜːdʒɪk/ *adj* alérgico; **to be ~ TO sth** ser alérgico A algo

allergy /'ælərdʒi ‖'ælədʒi/ *n* (*pl* **-gies**) alergia *f*

alleviate /ə'liːvieɪt/ *vt* ‹*pain*› aliviar; ‹*problem*› paliar

alley /'æli/ *n* (*pl* **alleys**) callejón *m*

alleyway /'æliweɪ/ *n* callejón *m*

alliance /ə'laɪəns/ *n* alianza *f*

allied /'ælaɪd/ *adj* **(a)** (combined) (*pred*) **~ WITH** *o* **TO sth** unido A algo **(b)** ‹*nations/groups*› aliado **(c)** (related) ‹*subjects/industries*› relacionado

alligator /'æləgeɪtər ‖'ælɪgeɪtə(r)/ *n* aligátor *m*

all: **~-important** /'ɔːlɪm'pɔːrtnt ‖,ɔːlɪm'pɔːtnt/ *adj* de suma importancia; **~-night** /'ɔːl'naɪt/ *adj* ‹*party/show*› que dura toda la noche; ‹*café/store*› que está abierto toda la noche

allocate /'æləkeɪt/ *vt* asignar; (distribute) repartir; **$3 million has been ~d for research** se han destinado tres millones de dólares a la investigación

allot /ə'lɑːt ‖ə'lɒt/ *vt* **-tt-** (distribute) repartir; (assign) asignar

all: **~-out** /'ɔːl'aʊt/ *adj* ‹*attack*› con todo; ‹*opposition*› acérrimo; ‹*strike*› general; ‹*war*› total; **~ over** *adv* ‹*search*› por todas partes; **people came from ~ over** vino gente de todas partes

allow /ə'laʊ/ *vt* [1] **(a)** (permit) permitir; **☉ no dogs allowed** no se admiten perros **(b)** (give, grant) dar*; **they are ~ed an hour for lunch** les dan una hora para comer; **within the time ~ed** dentro del plazo concedido [2] (plan for): **~ a good two hours to reach the coast** calculen que les va a llevar por lo menos dos horas llegar a la costa; **I normally ~ about £50 for spending money** normalmente calculo unas 50 libras para gastos [3] (Sport) ‹*referee*› ‹*goal*› dar* por bueno

■ **allow for** [*v + prep + o*] ‹*contingency*› tener* en cuenta

---

allowance /ə'lavəns/ n ⓵ (from employer) complemento m; (from state) prestación f; (private) asignación f; (from parents) mensualidad f, mesada f (AmL) ⓶ **to make ~(s) for sb** ser* indulgente con algn; **we've made ~(s) for delays** hemos tenido en cuenta posibles retrasos

alloy /'ælɔɪ/ n aleación f

all-powerful /'ɔːl'paʊərfəl ‖,ɔːl'paʊəfəl/ adj todopoderoso

all right¹ adj (pred): **are you ~ ~?** ¿estás bien?; **the hotel looks ~ ~** el hotel no parece estar mal; **do I look ~ ~ in this dress?** ¿estoy bien con este vestido?; **I'll pay you back tomorrow: is that ~ ~?** mañana te devuelvo el dinero ¿okey? or (Esp) ¿vale?; **I'm sorry — that's ~ ~** lo siento — no tiene importancia; **it's ~ ~: I'm not going to hurt you** tranquilo, que no te voy a hacer daño

all right² adv bien

all right³ interj (colloq): **I won't be home till late, ~ ~?** volveré tarde ¿okey? or (Esp) ¿vale? (fam); **can I come too? — all right** ¿puedo ir yo también? — bueno

all: **~-round** /'ɔːl'raʊnd/ adj (esp BrE) ▶ ALL-AROUND; **A~ Saints' Day** n día m de Todos los Santos; **~-time** adj ‹record› sin precedentes; ‹favorite› de todos los tiempos

allude /ə'luːd/ vi **to ~ TO sth/sb** aludir A algo/ algn

alluring /ə'lʊrɪŋ ‖ə'lʊərɪŋ/ adj seductor

allusion /ə'luːʒən/ n alusión f

ally¹ /'ælaɪ/ n (pl **allies**) aliado, -da m,f

ally² v refl **allies, allying, allied: to ~ oneself** WITH **sb** aliarse CON algn; see also ALLIED

almanac /'ɔːlmənæk/ n (yearbook) anuario m; (calendar) almanaque m

almighty /ɔːl'maɪti/ adj todopoderoso

almond /'ɑːmənd/ n almendra f

almost /'ɔːlməʊst/ adv casi

■ **Note** Where *almost* is used with a verb in the past tense, it is translated by *casi* or *por poco*, and the verb is usually in the present tense: *I almost fell* casi me caigo; *we almost missed the train* casi or por poco perdemos el tren.In some Latin American countries the preterite tense is often used: *we almost missed the train* casi or por poco perdimos el tren.

alms /ɑːmz/ pl n limosnas fpl

aloft /ə'lɒft ‖ə'lɒft/ adv en el aire; **he held the cup ~** levantó la copa en alto

alone¹ /ə'ləʊn/ adj (a) (without others) solo; **I want to be ~ with you** quiero estar a solas contigo; **leave me ~** ¡déjame en paz! (b) **let alone: I can't afford beer, let ~ champagne** no puedo comprar ni cerveza, para qué hablar de champán; **she can't sew a button on, let ~ make a dress** no sabe ni pegar un botón menos aún hacer un vestido

alone² adv solo

along¹ /ə'lɒŋ ‖ə'lɒŋ/ adv (a) (forward): **a bit further ~ on the right** un poco más adelante, a mano derecha; **I was walking ~** iba caminando; see also COME, GET, MOVE etc ALONG (b) (with one): **why don't you come ~?** ¿por qué no vienes conmigo/con nosotros?; **she brought her brother ~** trajo a su hermano; see also SING ALONG (c) **along with** (junto) con

along² prep: **we walked ~ the shore** caminamos por la playa; **a bit further ~ the road** un poco más adelante

alongside¹ /ə'lɔːŋsaɪd ‖ə'lɒŋsaɪd/ prep al lado de

alongside² adv al costado

aloof /ə'luːf/ adj distante

aloud /ə'laʊd/ adv en alto, en voz alta

alphabet /'ælfəbet/ n alfabeto m

alphabetical /'ælfə'betɪkəl/ adj alfabético; **in ~ order** en or por orden alfabético

alpine /'ælpaɪn/ adj **(a)** (of high mountains) alpino **(b) Alpine** ‹scenery/people› de los Alpes, alpino

Alps /ælps/ pl n **the ~** los Alpes

already /ɔːl'redi/ adv ya; **I've ~ been there** ya he estado allí, ya estuve allí (AmL)

alright /ɔːl'raɪt/ adj/adv/interj ▶ ALL RIGHT

Alsatian /æl'seɪʃən/ n (esp BrE) ▶ GERMAN SHEPHERD (DOG)

also /'ɔːlsəʊ/ adv **(a)** (as well) también **(b)** (moreover) (as linker) además

altar /'ɔːltər ‖'ɔːltə(r)/ n altar m

alter /'ɔːltər ‖'ɔːltə(r)/ vt ‹text/situation› cambiar; ‹garment› arreglar
■ **~** vi cambiar

alteration /'ɔːltə'reɪʃən/ n (to text) cambio m; (to building) reforma f, (to garment) arreglo m

alternate¹ /'ɔːltərnət ‖ɔːl'tɜːnət/ adj (before n) **(a)** (every second): **she works ~ Tuesdays** trabaja un martes sí y otro no; **write on ~ lines** escriba dejando un renglón por medio **(b)** (happening by turns) alterno **(c)** (AmE) ▶ ALTERNATIVE¹ A

alternate² /'ɔːltərneɪt ‖'ɔːltəneɪt/ vt/i alternar

alternately /'ɔːltərnətli ‖ɔːl'tɜːnətli/ adv: **he and she take the class ~** se turnan para dar la clase

alternating /'ɔːltərneɪtɪŋ ‖'ɔːltəneɪtɪŋ/ adj alterno

alternating current n corriente f alterna

alternative¹ /ɔːl'tɜːrnətɪv ‖ɔːl'tɜːnətɪv/ adj (before n) **(a)** (other) ‹plan/method› diferente **(b)** (progressive) ‹lifestyle/medicine› alternativo

alternative² n alternativa f

alternatively /ɔːl'tɜːrnətɪvli ‖ɔːl'tɜːnətɪvli/ adv (indep): **~, you could stay with us** si no, te podrías quedar con nosotros

although /ɔːl'θəʊ/ conj aunque

altitude /'æltɪtuːd ‖'æltɪtjuːd/ n altitud f

alto¹ /'æltəʊ/ n (pl **altos**) contralto f

alto² adj alto

altogether /'ɔːltə'geðər ‖,ɔːltə'geðə(r)/ adv **(a)** (completely) totalmente; **the decision wasn't ~ wise** la decisión no fue del todo acertada **(b)** (in total) en total **(c)** (on the whole) (indep) en general

aluminum /ə'luːmɪnəm/, (BrE) **aluminium** /'æljə'mɪniəm/ n aluminio m

always /'ɔːlweɪz/ adv siempre

am¹ /æm, weak form əm/ 1st pers sing of BE

am² /'eɪem/ (before midday) a.m.; **at 7 ~** a las 7 de la mañana or 7 a.m.

amalgamate /ə'mælgəmeɪt/ vt ‹collections/indexes› unir, amalgamar; ‹companies/departments› fusionar
■ **~** vi «companies» fusionarse

amass /əˈmæs/ vt ⟨fortune⟩ amasar; ⟨arms/ information/debts⟩ acumular

amateur¹ /ˈæmətər ‖ˈæmətə(r)/ n amateur mf

amateur² adj ⟨athlete/musician⟩ amateur; ⟨sport/competition⟩ para amateurs; **an** ~ photographer un aficionado a la fotografía

amaze /əˈmeɪz/ vt asombrar

amazed /əˈmeɪzd/ adj ⟨expression⟩ de asombro; **to be** ~ estar* asombrado

amazement /əˈmeɪzmənt/ n asombro m

amazing /əˈmeɪzɪŋ/ adj increíble

Amazon /ˈæməzɑːn ‖ˈæməzən/ n **(a)** (Myth) amazona f **(b)** (Geog) **the** ~ el Amazonas; ⟨before n⟩ ⟨rain forest⟩ amazónico

ambassador /æmˈbæsədər ‖æmˈbæsədə(r)/ n embajador, -dora m,f

amber /ˈæmbər ‖ˈæmbə(r)/ n **(a)** (substance, color) ámbar m **(b)** (BrE Aut) amarillo

ambidextrous /ˈæmbrˈdekstrəs/ adj ambidiestro, ambidextro

ambiguity /ˈæmbəˈɡjuːəti ‖ˌæmbrˈɡjuːəti/ n (pl **-ties**) ambigüedad f

ambiguous /æmˈbɪɡjuəs/ adj ambiguo

ambition /æmˈbɪʃən/ n ambición f

ambitious /æmˈbɪʃəs/ adj **(a)** ⟨person/plan⟩ ambicioso **(b)** (overadventurous) ⟨pred⟩: **aren't you being a bit** ~? ¿no estás pretendiendo hacer demasiado?

ambivalent /æmˈbɪvələnt/ adj ambivalente

amble /ˈæmbəl/ vi: **to** ~ **along** ir* tranquilamente

ambulance /ˈæmbjələns ‖ˈæmbjʊləns/ n ambulancia f

ambulanceman /ˈæmbjələnsmən ‖ˈæmbjʊlənsmən/ n (pl **-men** /-mən/) (BrE) ambulanciero m

ambush¹ /ˈæmbʊʃ/ vt tenderle* una emboscada a

ambush² n emboscada f

ameba /əˈmiːbə/ (AmE) ▶ AMOEBA

amen /ˈɑːmen, ˈeɪmen/ interj amén

amenable /əˈmiːnəbəl/ adj ⟨temperament⟩ dócil; **they proved quite** ~ **to the idea** se mostraron bien dispuestos frente a la idea

amend /əˈmend/ vt **(a)** ⟨text⟩ corregir* **(b)** (Law) enmendar*

amendment /əˈmendmənt/ n **(a)** (alteration) corrección f **(b)** (Law) enmienda f

amends /əˈmendz/ pl n: **to make** ~ **to sb** desagraviar a algn; **to make** ~ reparar el daño

amenity /əˈmiːnəti/ n (pl **-ties**) servicio m

America /əˈmerəkə ‖əˈmerɪkə/ n (USA) Norteamérica f, Estados mpl Unidos, América f; (continent) América f

American¹ /əˈmerəkən ‖əˈmerɪkən/ adj (of USA) estadounidense, norteamericano, americano

American² n (from USA) estadounidense mf, norteamericano, -na m,f, americano, -na m,f

amethyst /ˈæməθəst ‖ˈæməθɪst/ n amatista f

amiable /ˈeɪmiəbəl/ adj afable

amicable /ˈæmɪkəbəl/ adj ⟨person⟩ amigable; ⟨relations⟩ cordial

amid /əˈmɪd/, **amidst** /əˈmɪdst/ prep en medio de, entre

amiss /əˈmɪs/ adj ⟨pred⟩: **there was nothing** ~ no había ningún problema; **there's something** ~ pasa algo

ammunition /ˈæmjəˈnɪʃən ‖ˌæmjʊˈnɪʃən/ n munición f

amnesia /æmˈniːʒə ‖æmˈniːziə/ n amnesia f

amnesty /ˈæmnəsti/ n (pl **-ties**) amnistía f

amoeba, (AmE also) **ameba** /əˈmiːbə/ n ameba f, amiba f

amok /əˈmʌk ‖əˈmɒk/ adv **to run** ~ ⟨⟨person⟩⟩ tener* un ataque de locura

among /əˈmʌŋ/, **amongst** /əˈmʌŋst/ prep entre

amount /əˈmaʊnt/ n cantidad f

■ **amount to** [v + prep + o] **(a)** (add up to) ⟨⟨debt/ assets⟩⟩ ascender* a **(b)** (be equivalent to) equivaler* a; **it** ~**s to the same thing** viene a ser lo mismo

amp /æmp/ n **(a)** (Elec) amperio m **(b)** (amplifier) (colloq) amplificador m

amphetamine /æmˈfetəmiːn/ n anfetamina f

amphibian /æmˈfɪbiən/ n (Zool) anfibio m

amphibious /æmˈfɪbiəs/ adj anfibio

amphitheater, (BrE) **amphitheatre** /ˈæmfɪˌθiːətər ‖ˈæmfɪˌθɪətə(r)/ n anfiteatro m

ample /ˈæmpəl/ adj **(a)** ⟨space⟩ amplio; ⟨funds/ resources⟩ abundante; ⟨helping⟩ generoso **(b)** (plenty) ⟨pred⟩ más que suficiente

amplifier /ˈæmpləfaɪər ‖ˈæmplɪfaɪə(r)/ n amplificador m

amplify /ˈæmpləfaɪ ‖ˈæmplɪfaɪ/ vt **-fies, -fying, -fied** amplificar*

amputate /ˈæmpjəteɪt ‖ˈæmpjʊteɪt/ vt amputar

Amtrak /ˈæmtræk/ n (in US) Ferrocarriles mpl de los EEUU

amuse /əˈmjuːz/ vt **(a)** (entertain) entretener* **(b)** (make laugh) divertir*

■ v refl **to** ~ **oneself** (entertain oneself) entretenerse*; (have fun) divertirse*

amused /əˈmjuːzd/ adj ⟨expression⟩ divertido; **she was** ~ **at the look on his face** le hizo gracia la cara que puso

amusement /əˈmjuːzmənt/ n **(a)** (entertainment) distracción f, entretención f (AmL) **(b)** (mirth) diversión f; **much to our** ~ para nuestro gran regocijo; ⟨before n⟩ ~ **arcade** sala f de juegos recreativos; ~ **park** parque m de diversiones or (Esp) atracciones

amusing /əˈmjuːzɪŋ/ adj divertido

an /æn, weak form ən/ indef art before vowel ▶ A

anachronism /əˈnækrənɪzəm/ n anacronismo m

anaemia etc (BrE) ▶ ANEMIA etc

anaesthetic n (BrE) ▶ ANESTHETIC

anagram /ˈænəɡræm/ n anagrama m

analogy /əˈnælədʒi/ n (pl **-gies**) analogía f

analyse vt (BrE) ▶ ANALYZE

analysis /əˈnæləsəs ‖əˈnælɪsɪs/ n (pl **-lyses** /-lɪsiːz/) **(a)** (examination) análisis m **(b)** (Psych) psicoanálisis m, análisis m

analyst /ˈænləst ‖ˈænəlɪst/ n **(a)** (of data) analista mf **(b)** (Psych) psicoanalista mf, analista mf

analytical /ˌænəˈlɪtɪkəl/ adj analítico

analyze, (BrE) **analyse** /'ænəlaɪz/ vt **(a)** ⟨data⟩ analizar* **(b)** (Psych) psicoanalizar*, analizar*

anarchist /'ænərkəst ‖'ænəkɪst/ n anarquista mf

anarchy /'ænərki ‖'ænəki/ n anarquía f

anatomy /ə'nætəmi/ n anatomía f

ancestor /'ænsestər ‖'ænsestə(r)/ n antepasado, -da m,f

ancestry /'ænsestri/ n ascendencia f

anchor¹ /'æŋkər ‖'æŋkə(r)/ n (Naut) ancla f↟

anchor² vt ⟨ship⟩ anclar; ⟨rope/tent⟩ sujetar

anchor: ~man /'æŋkərmæn ‖'æŋkəmæn/ n (pl **-men** /-men/) (TV) presentador m; **~woman** n (TV) presentadora f

anchovy /'æntʃəʊvi ‖'æntʃəvi/ n (pl **-vies** or **-vy**) anchoa f

ancient /'eɪnʃənt/ adj **(a)** ⟨civilizations/ruin⟩ antiguo; **A~ Greek** griego m clásico **(b)** (colloq) (old) ⟨car⟩ del año de la pera (fam)

and /ænd, weak form ənd/ conj

■ Note The usual translation of and, y, becomes e when it precedes a word beginning with i, hi, or y.

(a) y; **bread ~ butter** pan con mantequilla **(b)** (in numbers): **one ~ a half** uno y medio; **two hundred ~ twenty** doscientos veinte **(c)** (showing continuation, repetition): **faster ~ faster** cada vez más rápido **(d)** (with inf): **try ~ finish this today** trata de terminar esto hoy

Andalusia /ændə'luːʒə ‖ændə'luːsiə/ n Andalucía f

Andalusian¹ /ˌændə'luːʒən ‖ændə'luːsiən/ adj andaluz

Andalusian² n andaluz, -luza m,f

Andes /'ændiːz/ pl in the **~** los Andes

Andorra /æn'dɔːrə ‖ n Andorra f

anecdote /'ænɪkdəʊt/ n anécdota f

anemia, (BrE) **anaemia** /ə'niːmiə/ n anemia f

anemic, (BrE) **anaemic** /ə'niːmɪk/ adj anémico

anemone /ə'neməni/ n (Bot) anémona f

anesthetic, (BrE) **anaesthetic** /'ænəs'θetɪk ‖ænɪs'θetɪk/ n anestésico m; **to be under ~** estar* bajo los efectos de la anestesia

anesthetize, (BrE) **anaesthetize** /ə'nesθetaɪz ‖ə'niːsθətaɪz/ vt anestesiar

anew /ə'nuː ‖ə'njuː/ adv (liter) de nuevo, otra vez

angel /'eɪndʒəl/ n ángel m

angelic /æn'dʒelɪk/ adj angelical

anger /'æŋgər ‖'æŋgə(r)/ n ira f, enojo m (esp AmL), enfado m (esp Esp)

angina /æn'dʒaɪnə/ n angina f (de pecho)

angle /'æŋgəl/ n ⑴ ángulo m; **she wore her hat at an ~** llevaba el sombrero ladeado ⑵ (point of view) perspectiva f

angler /'æŋglər ‖'æŋglə(r)/ n pescador, -dora m,f (de caña)

Anglican¹ /'æŋglɪkən/ n anglicano, -na m,f

Anglican² adj anglicano

angling /'æŋglɪŋ/ n pesca f (con caña)

Anglo-Saxon¹ /'æŋgləʊ'sæksən/ adj anglosajón

Anglo-Saxon² n **(a)** (person) anglosajón, -jona m,f **(b)** (language) anglosajón m

Angola /æŋ'gəʊlə/ n Angola f

Angolan /æŋ'gəʊlən/ adj angoleño

angrily /'æŋgrəli ‖'æŋgrɪli/ adv con ira

angry /'æŋgri/ adj **angrier, angriest** ⟨person⟩ enojado (esp AmL), enfadado (esp Esp); **to get ~** enojarse (esp AmL), enfadarse (esp Esp)

anguish /'æŋgwɪʃ/ n angustia f

angular /'æŋgjələr ‖'æŋgjʊlə(r)/ adj ⟨shape⟩ angular; ⟨features⟩ anguloso

animal /'ænəməl ‖'ænɪməl/ n animal m

animate /'ænəmeɪt ‖'ænɪmeɪt/ vt animar

animated /'ænəmeɪtəd ‖'ænɪmeɪtɪd/ adj animado

animation /'ænə'meɪʃən ‖ˌænɪ'meɪʃən/ n animación f

animator /'ænəmeɪtər ‖'ænɪmeɪtə(r)/ n animador, -dora m,f

animosity /'ænə'mɑːsəti ‖ˌænɪ'mɒsəti/ n (pl **-ties**) animosidad f

aniseed /'ænəsiːd ‖'ænɪsiːd/ n anís m

ankle /'æŋkəl/ n tobillo m; (before n) **~ boot** botín m; **~ sock** calcetín m corto, soquete m (CS)

annex¹ /ə'neks/ vt ⟨territory⟩ anexar

annex², (BrE) **annexe** /'æneks/ n anexo m, anejo m

annihilate /ə'naɪəleɪt/ vt ⟨army/city⟩ aniquilar

anniversary /'ænə'vɜːrsəri ‖ˌænɪ'vɜːsəri/ n (pl **-ries**) aniversario m; **(wedding) ~** aniversario m de boda de casados

announce /ə'naʊns/ vt **(a)** ⟨flight/guest/marriage⟩ anunciar **(b)** (declare) anunciar **(c)** (AmE Rad, TV) ⟨game/race⟩ comentar

announcement /ə'naʊnsmənt/ n anuncio m

announcer /ə'naʊnsər ‖ə'naʊnsə(r)/ n (Rad, TV) **(a)** (commentator) (AmE) comentarista mf **(b)** (between programs) (BrE) locutor, -tora m,f de continuidad

annoy /ə'nɔɪ/ vt molestar, irritar

annoyance /ə'nɔɪəns/ n **(a)** (irritation) irritación f; (anger) enojo m (esp AmL), enfado m (esp Esp) **(b)** (cause of irritation) molestia f

annoyed /ə'nɔɪd/ adj enojado (esp AmL), enfadado (esp Esp)

annoying /ə'nɔɪɪŋ/ adj ⟨person⟩ pesado; ⟨noise/habit⟩ molesto; **how ~!** ¡qué rabia!

annual¹ /'ænjuəl/ adj (before n) anual

annual² n ⑴ (plant) planta f anual ⑵ (publication) anuario m

annually /'ænjuəli/ adv anualmente

annul /ə'nʌl/ vt **-ll-** anular

annulment /ə'nʌlmənt/ n anulación f

anoint /ə'nɔɪnt/ vt ungir*

anonymity /ˌænə'nɪməti/ n anonimato m

anonymous /ə'nɑːnəməs ‖ə'nɒnɪməs/ adj anónimo; **to remain ~** permanecer* en el anonimato; **~ letter** anónimo m

anorak /'ænəræk/ n (BrE) anorak m

anorexia (nervosa) /'ænə'reksiə (nər'vəʊsə) ‖ˌænə'reksiə (nɜː'vəʊsə)/ n anorexia f (nerviosa)

another¹ /ə'nʌðər ‖ə'nʌðə(r)/ adj otro, otra; (pl) otros, otras

another² pron otro, otra

answer¹ /'ænsər ‖'ɑ:nsə(r)/ n **1** (a) (reply)
respuesta f, contestación f; in ~ to your question
para contestar tu pregunta (b) (response): her ~
to his rudeness was to ignore it respondió a su
grosería ignorándola; Britain's ~ to Elvis Presley
el Elvis Presley británico **2** (a) (in exam, test,
quiz) respuesta f (b) (solution) solución f; ~ TO sth
solución DE algo

answer² vt **1** (a) (reply to) ⟨person/letter⟩
contestar (b) ⟨telephone⟩ contestar, atender*
(AmL), coger* (Esp); will you ~ the door? ¿vas tú
(a abrir)? (c) ⟨critic/criticism⟩ responder a **2** (fit):
to ~ (to) a description responder a una
descripción
■ ~ vi contestar, responder
■ **answer back 1** [v + adv] (rudely) contestar
2 [v + o + adv] to ~ sb back contestarle mal or
de mala manera a algn
■ **answer for** [v + prep + o] (accept responsibility
for) ⟨conduct/consequences⟩ responder de; his
parents have a lot to ~ for sus padres tienen
mucha culpa

answerable /'ænsərəbəl ‖'ɑ:nsərəbəl/ adj:
she said she was not ~ for his behavior dijo que
ella no era responsable de lo que él hiciera; I'm
~ to no one no tengo que rendirle cuentas a
nadie

answering machine /'ænsərɪŋ ‖'ɑ:nsərɪŋ/
n contestador m (automático)

answerphone /'ænsərfəʊn ‖'ɑ:nsəfəʊn/ n
contestador m (automático)

ant /ænt/ n hormiga f

antagonize /æn'tægənaɪz/ vt suscitar el
antagonismo de

Antarctic¹ /ænt'ɑ:rktɪk ‖æn'tɑ:ktɪk/ adj
antártico; the ~ Ocean el Océano Antártico; the
~ Circle el círculo polar antártico

Antarctic² n the ~ la región antártica

Antarctica /ænt'ɑ:rktɪkə ‖æn'tɑ:ktɪkə/ n la
Antártida

anteater /'ænt,i:tər ‖'ænt,i:tə(r)/ n oso m
hormiguero

antecedent /,æntə'si:dṇt ‖,æntɪ'si:dənt/ n
antecedente m

antelope /'æntələʊp ‖'æntɪləʊp/ n (pl ~s or
~) antílope m

antenatal /'ænti'neɪtḷ/ adj prenatal; ~ clinic
consulta médica para mujeres embarazadas

antenna /æn'tenə/ n (a) (pl -nae /-ni:/) (Zool)
antena f (b) (pl -nas) (Rad, TV) antena f

anthem /'ænθəm/ n himno m; national ~
himno nacional

anthology /æn'θɑ:lədʒi ‖æn'θʊlədʒi/ n (pl
-gies) antología f

anthropologist /'ænθrə'pɑ:lədʒəst
‖,ænθrə'pʊlədʒɪst/ n antropólogo, -ga m,f

anthropology /'ænθrə'pɑ:lədʒi
‖,ænθrə'pʊlədʒi/ n antropología f

anti- /'æntaɪ, 'ænti ‖'ænti/ pref anti-

antiaircraft /'æntar'erkræft ‖,ænti'eəkrɑ:ft/
adj antiaéreo

antibiotic /'æntibar'ɑ:tɪk ‖,æntibar'ʊtɪk/ n
antibiótico m

antibody /'ænti,bɑ:di ‖'ænti,bʊdi/ n (pl
-dies) anticuerpo m

anticipate /æn'tɪsəpeɪt ‖æn'tɪsɪpeɪt/ vt **1** (a)
(expect) ⟨consequences⟩ prever*; I don't ~ any
problems no creo que vaya a haber ningún
problema (b) (look forward to) esperar **2** (a)
(foresee and act accordingly) ⟨movements/objections/
needs⟩ prever* (b) (pre-empt) anticiparse a

anticipation /æn'tɪsə'peɪʃən ‖æn,tɪsɪ'peɪʃən/
n (a) (foresight) previsión f; thanking you in ~
agradeciéndole de antemano su atención (b)
(expectation) expectativa f

anticlimax /'æntaɪ'klaɪmæks
‖,æntɪ'klaɪmæks/ n suceso caracterizado por un
descenso de la tensión; (disappointment) decepción f

anticlockwise /'æntɪ'klɑ:kwaɪz
‖,ænti'klɒkwaɪz/ adj/adv (BrE) en sentido
contrario a las agujas del reloj

antics /'æntɪks/ pl n (clowning) payasadas fpl; (of
naughty children) travesuras fpl

antidote /'æntɪdəʊt/ n ~ (TO sth) antídoto m
(CONTRA algo)

antifreeze /'æntɪfri:z/ n anticongelante m

antihero /'ænti,hi:rəʊ ‖'ænti,hɪərəʊ/ n (pl
-roes) antihéroe m

antipathy /æn'tɪpəθi/ n (pl -thies) antipatía f

antiperspirant /'æntɪ'pɜ:rspərənt
‖,ænti'pɜ:spɪrənt/ n antitranspirante m

antique¹ /æn'ti:k/ n antigüedad f; (before n) ~
shop tienda f de antigüedades

antique² adj antiguo

antiquity /æn'tɪkwəti/ n (pl -ties) **1** (ancient
times, age) antigüedad f **2** **antiquities** pl
antigüedades fpl

anti-Semitic /'æntɪsə'mɪtɪk ‖,æntɪsɪ'mɪtɪk/
adj antisemita

anti-Semitism /,æntɪ'semətɪzəm
‖,ænti'semɪtɪzəm/ n antisemitismo m

antiseptic¹ /'æntɪ'septɪk/ n antiséptico m

antiseptic² adj (Pharm) antiséptico

antisocial /'æntɪ'səʊʃəl/ adj (a) (offensive to
society) antisocial (b) (unsociable) poco sociable

antithesis /æn'tɪθəsəs ‖æn'tɪθəsɪs/ n (pl
-eses /-əsi:z/) antítesis f

antler /'æntlər ‖'æntlə(r)/ n cuerno m, asta f‡;
the animal's ~s la cornamenta del animal

anus /'eɪnəs/ n ano m

anvil /'ænvəl ‖'ænvɪl/ n yunque m

anxiety /æŋ'zaɪəti/ n (pl -ties) (a) (distress,
concern) preocupación f (b) (problem, worry)
preocupación f (c) (Med, Psych) ansiedad f

anxious /'æŋkʃəs/ adj (a) (worried) preocupado
(b) (worrying) ⟨time/moment⟩ (lleno) de
preocupación (c) (eager) deseoso; he's very ~ to
please tiene mucho afán de agradar

anxiously /'æŋkʃəsli/ adv (a) (worriedly) con
preocupación (b) (eagerly) ansiosamente

any¹ /'eni/ adj

I **1** (*in questions*) **(a)** (+ *pl n*): **are there ~ questions?** ¿alguien tiene alguna pregunta?; **does she have ~ children?** ¿tiene hijos? **(b)** (+ *uncount n*): **do you need ~ help?** ¿necesitas ayuda?; **do you want ~ more coffee?** ¿quieres más café? **(c)** (+ *sing count n: as indef art*) algún, -guna; **is there ~ chance they'll come?** ¿existe alguna posibilidad de que vengan?
2 (*in 'if' clauses and suppositions*) **(a)** (+ *pl n*): **call me if there are ~ changes** llámame si hay algún cambio; **if you see ~ flowers, buy some** si ves flores, compra algunas **(b)** (+ *uncount n*): **let me know if you have ~ pain** avíseme si siente dolor; **take ~ money you need** toma el dinero que necesites **(c)** (+ *sing count n*): **~ upset could kill him** cualquier disgusto podría matarlo; **~ act of disobedience will be punished** toda desobediencia será castigada
3 (*with neg and implied neg*) **(a)** (+ *pl n*): **don't buy ~ more eggs** no compres más huevos; **aren't there ~ apples left?** ¿no queda ninguna manzana? **(b)** (+ *uncount n*): **don't make ~ noise** no hagas ruido; **it doesn't make ~ sense** no tiene ningún sentido
II **1** **(a)** (*no matter which*): **take ~ book you want** llévate cualquier libro; **~ day now** cualquier día de estos **(b)** (*every, all*): **in ~ large school, you'll find that ...** en cualquier *or* todo colegio grande, verás que ...
2 (*countless, a lot*): **~ number/amount of sth** cualquier cantidad de algo

any² *pron* **1** (*in questions*) **(a)** (*referring to pl n*) alguno, -na; **those chocolates were nice, are there ~ left?** ¡qué ricos esos bombones! ¿queda alguno? **(b)** (*referring to uncount n*): **we need sugar; did you buy ~?** nos hace falta azúcar ¿compraste?; **is there ~ of that cake left?** ¿queda algo de ese pastel?
2 (*in 'if' clauses and suppositions*) **(a)** (*referring to pl n*): **buy some red ones if you can find ~** compra algunas rojas si encuentras; **if ~ of my friends calls, take a message** si llama alguno de mis amigos, toma el recado **(b)** (*referring to uncount n*): **help yourself to cake if you want ~** sírvete pastel si quieres
3 (*with neg and implied neg*) **(a)** (*referring to pl n*): **some children were here — I didn't see ~** aquí había algunos niños — yo no vi (a) ninguno *or* no los vi; **you'll have to go without cigarettes; I forgot to buy ~** te vas a tener que arreglar sin cigarrillos porque me olvidé de comprar **(b)** (*referring to uncount n*): **she offered me some wine, but I didn't want ~** me ofreció vino, pero no quise; **I didn't understand ~ of that lecture** no entendí nada de esa conferencia

any³ *adv* **1** (*with comparative*): **do you feel ~ better now?** ¿te sientes (algo) mejor ahora?; **they don't live here ~ more** ya no viven aquí **2** (*at all*) (AmE): **have you thought about it ~ since then?** ¿has pensado en ello desde entonces?; **it doesn't seem to have affected him ~** no parece haberlo afectado en absoluto

anybody /'eni,bɑːdi ‖ 'eni,bɒdi/ *pron* **1** **(a)** (*somebody*) (*in interrog, conditional sentences*) alguien; **will ~ be seeing Emma today?** ¿alguno de ustedes va a ver a Emma hoy? **(b)** (*with neg*) nadie; **don't tell ~!** ¡no se lo digas a nadie! **2** **(a)** (*whoever, everybody*): **give it to ~ you like** dáselo a quien quieras; **~ who's been to Paris knows ...** cualquier persona que haya estado en París sabe ...; **before ~ could stop her** antes de que nadie pudiera detenerla **(b)** (*no matter who*) cualquiera; **~ could do it** cualquiera podría hacerlo

anyhow /'enihaʊ/ *adv* **1** ▶ ANYWAY **2** (*haphazardly*) de cualquier manera

anyone /'eniwʌn/ *pron* ▶ ANYBODY

anyplace /'enipleɪs/ *adv* (AmE) ▶ ANYWHERE¹ 1

anything /'eniθɪŋ/ *pron* **1** **(a)** (*something*) (*in interrog, conditional sentences*) algo; **have you ever heard ~ so ridiculous?** ¡habráse oído semejante ridiculez! **(b)** (*a single thing*) (*with neg*) nada; **don't say ~!** ¡no digas nada! **2** **(a)** (*whatever*): **~ you say!** ¡lo que tú digas!; **we'll do ~ we can to help** haremos todo lo que podamos para ayudar **(b)** (*no matter what*): **~ is possible** todo es posible; **~ could happen** podría pasar cualquier cosa **3** (*used for emphasis*): **was it interesting? — ~ but!** ¿fue interesante? — ¡qué va!; **the portrait doesn't look ~ like her** el retrato no se parece en nada a ella

anyway /'eniweɪ/ *adv* **1** (*in any case*) de todos modos **2** (*changing the subject, moving conversation on*) (*as linker*) bueno; **~, to cut a long story short, ...** bueno, en resumidas cuentas ...

anywhere¹ /'enihwer ‖ 'eniweə(r)/ *adv* **1** **(a)** (*no matter where*) en cualquier sitio *or* lugar; **you can sit ~ you like** te puedes sentar donde quieras **(b)** (*in, to any unspecified place*): **have you seen my book ~?** ¿has visto mi libro por alguna parte *or* por algún lado?; **we never go ~ together** nunca vamos juntos a ningún lado **2** **anywhere near: is it ~ near Portland?** ¿queda cerca de Portland?; **we aren't ~ near ready yet** todavía no estamos listos ni mucho menos

anywhere² *pron*: **is there ~ that sells oysters?** ¿hay algún sitio donde vendan ostras?; **she hasn't ~ to stay** no tiene donde quedarse

apace /ə'peɪs/ *adv* (liter *or* journ) a paso *or* ritmo acelerado

apart /ə'pɑːrt ‖ ə'pɑːt/ *adv* **1** **(a)** (*separated*): **they've lived ~ for some years** ya hace algunos años que viven separados; **keep them ~** manténgalos separados **(b)** (*into pieces*): ▶ COME, FALL, PULL, TAKE *etc* APART
2 (*distant*): **in places as far ~ as Tokyo and Paris** en lugares tan alejados el uno del otro como Tokio y París
3 (*excluded*) (*after n*): **these faults ~ ...** aparte de estos defectos ...; **joking ~ ...** bromas aparte ...
4 **apart from** (*as prep*) **(a)** (*except for*) excepto, aparte de **(b)** (*separated from*): **she always sits ~ from the rest of the group** siempre se sienta apartada del resto del grupo

apartheid /ə'pɑːrteɪt ‖ ə'pɑːteɪt/ *n* apartheid *m*

apartment /ə'pɑːrtmənt ‖ ə'pɑːtmənt/ *n* (set of rooms) apartamento *m*, departamento *m* (AmL), piso *m* (Esp); (*before n*): **~ building** edificio *m* de apartamentos *or* (AmL tb) de departamentos

apathetic /'æpə'θetɪk/ *adj* apático

apathy /'æpəθi/ *n* apatía *f*

ape¹ /eɪp/ *n* simio *m*, mono *m*

ape² *vt* remedar, imitar

aperitif /ə'perə'tiːf ‖ ə'perətif/ *n* aperitivo *m*

aperture /'æpərtʃər ‖'æpətʃə(r)/ n (a) (Opt, Phot) apertura f (b) (hole, opening) (frml) orificio m; (long and narrow) rendija f

apex /'eɪpeks/ n (pl **apexes** or **apices**) (a) (Math) vértice m (b) (pinnacle) cúspide f (c) (pointed end, tip) ápice m

APEX /'eɪpeks/ adj (= **advance purchase excursion**) (before n) ‹ticket/booking› Apex adj inv

aphid /'eɪfəd ‖'eɪfɪd/ n afídido m, áfido m

aphrodisiac /ˌæfrə'dɪziæk/ n afrodisíaco m

apices /'eɪpəsiːz ‖'eɪpɪsiːz/ pl of APEX

apiece /ə'piːs/ adv cada uno

apocalypse /ə'pɑːkəlɪps ‖ə'pɒkəlɪps/ n apocalipsis m

apologetic /əˌpɑːlə'dʒetɪk ‖ə,pɒlə'dʒetɪk/ adj ‹letter/look› de disculpa; **she was very ~ se deshizo en disculpas**

apologize /ə'pɑːlədʒaɪz ‖ə'pɒlədʒaɪz/ vi pedir* perdón, disculparse; **we ~ for the delay rogamos disculpen el retraso; you must ~ to her for being so rude tienes que pedirle perdón por haber sido tan grosero**

apology /ə'pɑːlədʒi ‖ə'pɒlədʒi/ n (pl **-gies**) (often pl) disculpa f; **please accept my apologies le ruego me disculpe**

apostle /ə'pɑːsəl ‖ə'pɒsəl/ n apóstol m

apostrophe /ə'pɑːstrəfi ‖ə'pɒstrəfi/ n apóstrofo m

appall, (BrE) **appal** /ə'pɔːl/ vt (BrE) **-ll-** horrorizar*

appalling /ə'pɔːlɪŋ/ adj ‹conditions› atroz; **the play is absolutely ~ la obra es pésima**

apparatus /ˌæpə'rætəs ‖ˌæpə'reɪtəs/ n (pl **~**) (a) (equipment) aparatos mpl; **a piece of ~ un aparato** (b) (Pol) aparato m

apparel /ə'pærəl/ n (a) (finery) (liter) atavío m (liter) (b) (AmE Busn) ropa f

apparent /ə'pærənt/ adj (a) (evident): **for no ~ reason sin motivo aparente; it was ~ that ... estaba claro que ..., era evidente que ...** (b) (seeming) ‹interest/concern› aparente

apparently /ə'pærəntli/ adv (a) (indep) al parecer, por lo visto, según parece (b) (seemingly) ‹intelligent/happy› aparentemente

apparition /ˌæpə'rɪʃən/ n aparición f

appeal¹ /ə'piːl/ n [1] (call) llamamiento m, llamado m (AmL); (request) solicitud f, pedido m (AmL); (plea) ruego m [2] (Law) apelación f [3] (fund, organization) campaña para recaudar fondos [4] (attraction) atractivo m

appeal² vi [1] (call) **to ~ FOR sth ‹for funds› pedir* algo; the police ~ed to witnesses to come forward la policía hizo un llamamiento or (AmL tb) un llamado para que se presentaran testigos del hecho** [2] (Law) apelar [3] (be attractive) **to ~ TO sb atraerle*A algn**
■ **~ vt** (AmE) ‹decision/verdict› apelar contra or de

appealing /ə'piːlɪŋ/ adj atractivo

appear /ə'pɪr ‖ə'pɪə(r)/ vi [1] (a) (come into view) aparecer* (b) (be published): **to ~ (in print) publicarse*** (c) (Law) comparecer*; **to ~ in court comparecer*** [2] (seem) parecer*; **so it ~s eso parece; to ~ to + INF parecer* + INF; we ~ to be lost parece que nos hemos perdido**

appearance /ə'pɪrəns ‖ə'pɪərəns/ n [1] (a) (coming into view) aparición f (b) (Law) comparecencia f (c) (of book) publicación f [2] (a) (look) aspecto m; apariencias fpl; **to keep up ~s guardar las apariencias**

appease /ə'piːz/ vt ‹person› apaciguar*; ‹anger› aplacar*

appendices /ə'pendəsiːz ‖ə'pendɪsiːz/ pl of APPENDIX

appendicitis /əˌpendə'saɪtəs ‖ə,pendɪ'saɪtɪs/ n apendicitis f

appendix /ə'pendɪks/ n (pl **-dixes** or **-dices**) apéndice m

appetite /'æpətaɪt ‖'æpɪtaɪt/ n apetito m

appetizer /'æpətaɪzər ‖'æpɪtaɪzə(r)/ n (a) (drink) aperitivo m (b) (snack) aperitivo m, tapa f (Esp), botana f (Méx)

appetizing /'æpətaɪzɪŋ ‖'æpɪtaɪzɪŋ/ adj apetitoso

applaud /ə'plɔːd/ vt/i aplaudir

applause /ə'plɔːz/ n aplausos mpl

apple /'æpəl/ n manzana f; (before n) **~ pie pastel m de manzana, pay m de manzana (Méx); ~ tree manzano m**

appliance /ə'plaɪəns/ n aparato m; **electrical ~s electrodomésticos mpl**

applicable /'æplɪkəbəl, ə'plɪkəbəl/ adj (frml): **these regulations are only ~ to foreigners estas normas se refieren únicamente a los extranjeros; delete as ~ tache lo que no corresponda**

applicant /'æpləkənt ‖'æplɪkənt/ n (for job) candidato, -ta m,f, postulante mf (CS), aplicante mf (Ven)

application /ˌæplə'keɪʃən ‖ˌæplɪ'keɪʃən/ n [1] (request) solicitud f; **~ FOR sth ‹for loan/grant/visa› solicitud DE algo; (before n) ~ form (impreso m de) solicitud f** [2] (a) (of method, skills, theory) aplicación f (b) (of paint, ointment) aplicación f

applied /ə'plaɪd/ adj aplicado

apply /ə'plaɪ/ **applies, applying, applied** vt (a) (put on) aplicar* (b) ‹method/theory/rules› aplicar*; **to ~ the brakes frenar; she applied herself to her work se puso a trabajar con diligencia**
■ **~ vi** (a) (make application): **please ~ in writing to ... diríjase por escrito a ...; to ~ FOR sth ‹for loan/permission› solicitar algo; to ~ for a job solicitar un trabajo, aplicar* a un trabajo (Ven), postular para un trabajo (CS)** (b) (be applicable) «regulation/criterion» aplicarse*

appoint /ə'pɔɪnt/ vt [1] (name, choose) nombrar [2] (frml) ‹date› designar (frml)

appointment /ə'pɔɪntmənt/ n [1] (arrangement to meet) cita f, (with doctor, hairdresser) hora f, cita f; **to make an ~ pedir* hora or una cita** [2] (a) (act of appointing) nombramiento m (b) (post) (frml) puesto m

appraisal /ə'preɪzəl/ n (of situation, employee) evaluación f; (of work, novel) valoración f; (of property) tasación f

appraise /ə'preɪz/ vt ‹situation/employee› evaluar*; ‹novel/painting› valorar; ‹property› tasar, avaluar* (AmL)

appreciable /ə'priːʃəbəl/ adj ‹change/difference› apreciable; ‹loss/sum› importante

appreciate /ə'priːʃɪeɪt/ vt (a) (value) ⟨food/ novel⟩ apreciar (b) (be grateful for) agradecer* (c) (understand) ⟨danger/difficulties⟩ darse* cuenta de; I ∼ that, but … lo comprendo, pero …
■ ∼ vi «shares/property» (re)valorizarse*

appreciation /əˌpriːʃi'eɪʃən/ n (a) (gratitude) agradecimiento m (b) (discriminating enjoyment): he showed a genuine ∼ of music demostró saber apreciar la música

appreciative /ə'priːʃətɪv/ adj (a) (grateful) ⟨smile/gesture⟩ de agradecimiento (b) (of art, good food) apreciativo

apprehend /ˌæprɪ'hend/ vt (frml) apresar, detener*

apprehension /ˌæprɪ'hentʃən ‖ˌæprɪ'henʃən/ n aprensión f

apprehensive /ˌæprɪ'hensɪv/ adj ⟨look⟩ aprensivo, de aprensión; I'm rather ∼ about the consequences estoy algo inquieto por lo que pueda pasar

apprentice¹ /ə'prentəs ‖ə'prentɪs/ n aprendiz, -diza m,f

apprentice² vt: to be ∼d TO sb estar* de aprendiz CON algn

apprenticeship /ə'prentəsʃɪp ‖ə'prentɪsʃɪp/ n aprendizaje m (de un oficio); to serve an ∼ in sth hacer* el aprendizaje de algo

approach¹ /ə'prəʊtʃ/ vi acercarse*, aproximarse
■ ∼ vt (a) (draw near to) aproximarse or acercarse* a (b) (talk to): have you ∼ed her about it? ¿ya se lo ha planteado?, ¿ya ha hablado con ella del asunto?; he ∼ed me for a loan se dirigió a mí para pedirme un préstamo (c) (tackle) ⟨problem/ question⟩ enfocar*

approach² n ① (method, outlook) enfoque m ② (overture — offering sth) propuesta f; (— requesting sth) solicitud f, petición f, pedido m (AmL) ③ (drawing near): at the ∼ of winter al acercarse el invierno ④ (means of entering) acceso m

approachable /ə'prəʊtʃəbəl/ adj ⟨person/ place⟩ accesible

appropriate¹ /ə'prəʊprɪət/ adj apropiado

appropriate² /ə'prəʊprɪeɪt/ vt ⟨possessions⟩ apropiarse de; ⟨money⟩ destinar

approval /ə'pruːvəl/ n aprobación f; on ∼ a prueba

approve /ə'pruːv/ vi to ∼ (OF sth/sb): they don't ∼ of my smoking les parece mal que fume; mother seems to ∼ of him a mamá parece gustarle; I don't ∼ of his methods no estoy de acuerdo con sus métodos
■ ∼ vt ⟨decision/plan⟩ aprobar*

approving /ə'pruːvɪŋ/ adj ⟨smile/look⟩ de aprobación

approximate /ə'prɒksəmət ‖ə'prɒksɪmət/ adj aproximado

approximately /ə'prɒksəmətli ‖ə'prɒksɪmətli/ adv aproximadamente

approximation /əˌprɒksə'meɪʃən ‖əˌprɒksɪ'meɪʃən/ n aproximación f

apricot /'æprəkɒt ‖'eɪprɪkɒt/ n albaricoque m or (Méx) chabacano m or (AmS) damasco m

April /'eɪprəl ‖'eɪprɪl/ n abril m; (before n) ∼ Fools' Day ≈ el día de los (Santos) Inocentes (en EEUU y GB se celebra el 1° de abril)

apron /'eɪprən/ n delantal m, mandil m (Esp)

apt /æpt/ adj (a) (fitting, suitable) acertado (b) (likely) to be ∼ to + INF ser* propenso A + INF

aptitude /'æptətuːd ‖'æptɪtjuːd/ n ∼ (FOR sth) aptitud f (PARA algo)

aquarium /ə'kweəriəm/ n (pl -riums or -ria /-riə/) acuario m

Aquarius /ə'kweəriəs ‖ə'kweəriəs/ n (a) (sign) (no art) Acuario (b) (person) Acuario or acuario mf, acuariano, -na m,f

aquatic /ə'kwætɪk, ə'kwɑːtɪk ‖ə'kwætɪk/ adj acuático

AR = Arkansas

Arab¹ /'ærəb/ adj árabe

Arab² n árabe mf

Arabian /ə'reɪbiən/ adj árabe; the ∼ Sea el Mar de Omán

Arabic¹ /'ærəbɪk/ adj árabe; a∼ numerals números mpl arábigos

Arabic² n árabe m

arable /'ærəbəl/ adj arable; ∼ land tierras fpl de cultivo

arbiter /'ɑːrbətər ‖'ɑːbɪtə(r)/ n árbitro, -tra m,f

arbitrary /'ɑːrbəˌtreri ‖'ɑːbɪtrəri/ adj arbitrario

arbitrate /'ɑːrbətreɪt ‖'ɑːbɪtreɪt/ vt ⟨dispute⟩ arbitrar (en)
■ ∼ vi arbitrar

arbitration /ˌɑːrbə'treɪʃən ‖ˌɑːbɪ'treɪʃən/ n arbitraje m

arc /ɑːrk ‖ɑːk/ n arco m

arcade /ɑːr'keɪd ‖ɑː'keɪd/ n (a) (Archit) arcada f; (around square, along street) soportales mpl, recova f (Arg) (b) (of shops) galería f comercial

arch¹ /ɑːrtʃ ‖ɑːtʃ/ n arco m

arch² vt ⟨eyebrows/back⟩ arquear
■ ∼ vi formar un arco

archaeologist etc (BrE) ▶ ARCHEOLOGIST etc

archaic /ɑːr'keɪɪk ‖ɑː'keɪɪk/ adj arcaico

archangel /'ɑːrkˌeɪndʒəl ‖'ɑːkˌeɪndʒəl/ n arcángel m

archbishop /ˈɑːrtʃ'bɪʃəp ‖ˌɑːtʃ'bɪʃəp/ n arzobispo m

archenemy /'ɑːrtʃ'enəmi ‖ˌɑːtʃ'enəmi/ n (pl -mies) archienemigo, -ga m,f

archeologist, (BrE) **archaeologist** /'ɑːrki'ɑːlədʒəst ‖ˌɑːki'ɒlədʒɪst/ n arqueólogo, -ga m,f

archeology, (BrE) **archaeology** /'ɑːrki'ɑːlədʒi ‖ˌɑːki'ɒlədʒi/ n arqueología f

archer /'ɑːrtʃər ‖'ɑːtʃə(r)/ n arquero, -ra m,f

archery /'ɑːrtʃəri ‖'ɑːtʃəri/ n tiro m con or al arco

architect /'ɑːrkətekt ‖'ɑːkɪtekt/ n arquitecto, -ta m,f

architecture /'ɑːrkətektʃər ‖'ɑːkɪtektʃə(r)/ n arquitectura f

archive /'ɑːrkaɪv ‖'ɑːkaɪv/ n (often pl) archivo m

Arctic¹ /'ɑːrktɪk ‖'ɑːktɪk/ adj ártico; the ∼ Ocean el Océano (Glacial) Ártico, el Ártico; the ∼ Circle el círculo polar ártico

Arctic² n the ∼ la región ártica, el Ártico

ardent /'ɑːrdnt ‖'ɑːdnt/ adj ⟨supporter⟩ apasionado; ⟨plea/desire⟩ ferviente

ardor, (BrE) **ardour** /'ɑːrdər ‖'ɑːdə(r)/ n (liter) (zeal) fervor m, ardor m; (love) pasión f

arduous /'ɑːrdʒuəs ‖'ɑːdjuːəs/ adj ‹task› arduo; ‹training/conditions› duro; ‹march/climb› difícil

are /ɑːr ‖ɑː(r), weak form ər/ 2nd pers sing, 1st, 2nd & 3rd pers pl pres of BE

area /'eriə ‖'eəriə/ n [1] (geographical) zona f, área f‡, región f; (neighborhood) barrio m; (urban) zona f [2] (part of room, building) zona f; **play ~** zona de recreo [3] (expanse, patch): **the shaded ~ represents ...** el área sombreada representa ...; **the wreckage was scattered over a wide ~** los restos del siniestro quedaron esparcidos sobre una extensa zona [4] (Math) superficie f, área f‡; (of room, land) superficie f [5] (field, sphere) terreno m; (of knowledge) campo m

area code n (AmE) código m de la zona (AmL), prefijo m (local) (Esp)

arena /ə'riːnə/ n **(a)** (of stadium) arena f **(b)** (scene of activity) ruedo m; **the political ~** el ruedo político

aren't /ɑːrnt ‖ɑːnt/ = **are not**

Argentina /'ɑːrdʒən'tiːnə ‖,ɑːdʒən'tiːnə/ n Argentina f

Argentine /'ɑːrdʒəntaɪn ‖'ɑːdʒəntaɪn/ adj argentino

Argentinian¹ /'ɑːrdʒən'tɪniən ‖,ɑːdʒən'tɪniən/ adj argentino

Argentinian² n argentino, -na m,f

arguably /'ɑːrgjuəbli ‖'ɑːgjuəbli/ adv (indep): **this is ~ his best novel** podría decirse que esta es su mejor novela

argue /'ɑːrgjuː ‖'ɑːgjuː/ vi [1] (quarrel) discutir; (more heatedly) pelear(se), reñir* (esp Esp); **don't ~ with me!** ¡no me discutas! [2] (reason): **she ~s convincingly** sabe expresar su punto de vista de manera muy convincente; **he ~s against changing the law** da razones en contra de que se cambie la ley

■ **~** vt **(a)** (put forward) ‹case› exponer* **(b)** (present as argument) argüir*, sostener*; **supporters of the bill ~ that ...** los partidarios del proyecto arguyen or sostienen que ...

argument /'ɑːrgjəmənt ‖'ɑːgjumənt/ n [1] (quarrel) discusión f; (more heated) pelea f, riña f (esp Esp); **to have an ~ with sb** tener* una discusión con algn; (more heatedly) pelearse or (esp Esp) reñir* con algn [2] (debate) polémica f [3] **(a)** (case) ~ (FOR/AGAINST) sth razones fpl or argumentos mpl (A FAVOR/EN CONTRA DE) algo **(b)** (line of reasoning) razonamiento m

argumentative /'ɑːrgjə'mentətɪv ‖,ɑːgjuː'mentətɪv/ adj discutidor

arid /'ærəd ‖'ærɪd/ adj árido

Aries /'eriːz ‖'eəriːz/ n **(a)** (sign) (no art) Aries **(b)** (person) Aries or aries mf, ariano, -na m,f

arise /ə'raɪz/ vi (past **arose**; past p **arisen** /ə'rɪzən/) ‹difficulty/opportunity» surgir*; **if the need ~s** si fuera necesario

aristocracy /'ærə'stɑːkrəsi ‖,ærɪ'stɒkrəsi/ n (pl **-cies**) aristocracia f

aristocrat /ə'rɪstəkræt ‖'ærɪstəkræt/ n aristócrata mf

aristocratic /ə'rɪstə'krætɪk ‖,ærɪstə'krætɪk/ adj aristocrático

arithmetic /ə'rɪθmətɪk/ n aritmética f

Ariz = Arizona

Ark¹ = Arkansas

Ark² /ɑːrk ‖ɑːk/ n arca f‡; **Noah's ~** el arca de Noé

arm¹ /ɑːrm ‖ɑːm/ n [1] (Anat) brazo m; **they walked along ~ in ~** iban del brazo [2] **(a)** (of chair, crane) brazo m **(b)** (of garment) manga f [3] **arms** pl (weapons) armas fpl

arm² vt armar; see also ARMED

armament /'ɑːrməmənt ‖'ɑːməmənt/ n armamento m

arm: **~band** n (to denote rank, mourning etc) brazalete m; (for swimming) flotador m (que se coloca en el brazo), alita f (AmS); **~chair** n sillón m, butaca f

armed /ɑːrmd ‖ɑːmd/ adj ‹resistance/struggle› armado; **the ~ forces** las fuerzas armadas; **~ robbery** robo m a mano armada

Armenia /ɑːr'miːniə ‖ɑː'miːniə/ n Armenia f

Armenian /ɑːr'miːniən ‖ɑː'miːniən/ adj armenio

armistice /'ɑːrməstəs ‖'ɑːmɪstɪs/ n armisticio m

armor, (BrE) **armour** /'ɑːrmər ‖'ɑːmə(r)/ n armadura f; **suit of ~** armadura f

armored, (BrE) **armoured** /'ɑːrmərd ‖'ɑːməd/ adj blindado

armor-plated, (BrE) **armour-plated** /'ɑːrmər'pleɪtəd ‖,ɑːmə'pleɪtɪd/ adj blindado

armory, (BrE) **armoury** /'ɑːrməri ‖'ɑːməri/ n (pl **-ries**) **(a)** (storehouse) arsenal m **(b)** (factory) (AmE) fábrica f de armas

arm: **~pit** n axila f, sobaco m; **~rest** n (of chair, sofa) brazo m; (of car, airplane seat) apoyabrazos m

arms race n carrera f armamentista

army /'ɑːrmi ‖'ɑːmi/ n (pl **armies**) ejército m

aroma /ə'rəumə/ n aroma m

aromatic /'ærə'mætɪk/ adj aromático

arose /ə'rəuz/ past of ARISE

around¹ /ə'raund/ adv [1] **(a)** (in a circle): **~ and ~ they drove** estuvieron dando vueltas y vueltas con el coche **(b)** (so as to face in different direction): **she glanced ~** echó un vistazo a su alrededor; see also TURN etc AROUND **(c)** (on all sides): **there's nothing for miles ~** no hay nada en millas a la redonda; **everyone crowded ~** todo el mundo se apiñó alrededor [2] (in the vicinity): **is John ~?** ¿anda or está John por ahí?; **there's no one ~** aquí no hay nadie [3] (from one place to another): **he keeps following me ~** me sigue a todas partes; **he knows his way ~** conoce la ciudad (or la zona etc)

4 (approximately) más o menos; **he must be ∼ 35** debe (de) tener unos 35; **at ∼ five thirty** alrededor de *or* a eso de las cinco y media, sobre las cinco y media (Esp); **∼ 1660** alrededor de 1660

around² *prep* **1** (encircling) alrededor de; **he put his arm ∼ her** la rodeó con el brazo; **they sailed ∼ the world** dieron la vuelta al mundo en un velero **2** **(a)** (in the vicinity of) alrededor de; **do you live ∼ here?** ¿vives por aquí? **(b)** (within, through): **they traveled ∼ Europe** viajaron por Europa; **she took them ∼ the house** les mostró la casa

arouse /əˈraʊz/ *vt* ⟨*interest/suspicion*⟩ despertar*; (sexually) excitar

arrange /əˈreɪndʒ/ *vt* **1** **(a)** (put in certain order, position) ⟨*furniture/flowers*⟩ arreglar **(b)** (put in order) arreglar **2** (fix up in advance) ⟨*meeting/party*⟩ organizar*; ⟨*date/fee*⟩ fijar; ⟨*deal/appointment*⟩ concertar*; ⟨*loan*⟩ tramitar; **she had ∼d to meet them for lunch** había quedado en encontrarse con ellos para comer, había quedado con ellos para comer (Esp)

■ **∼** *vi*: **could you ∼ for the carpets to be cleaned?** ¿podría encargarse de que alguien venga a limpiar las alfombras?; **we've ∼d for you to see the specialist** le hemos pedido hora *or* una cita con el especialista

arrangement /əˈreɪndʒmənt/ *n* **1** (of furniture) disposición *f*; **a flower ∼** un arreglo floral **2** (agreement): **we made an ∼ to meet the next day** quedamos en encontrarnos al día siguiente; **I have an ∼ with the bank** tengo un acuerdo con el banco **3** **arrangements** *pl* (plans) planes *mpl*; (for a funeral) preparativos *mpl*; **what are the sleeping ∼s?** ¿cómo vamos (*or* van *etc*) a dormir? **4** (Mus) arreglo *m*

array /əˈreɪ/ *n* selección *f*

arrears /əˈrɪrz ‖əˈrɪəz/ *pl n* atrasos *mpl*; **to be in ∼ with the rent** estar* atrasado en el pago del alquiler; **salaries are paid monthly in ∼** los sueldos se pagan mensualmente, una vez cumplido cada mes de trabajo

arrest¹ /əˈrest/ *n* detención *f*, arresto *m*; **to be under ∼** estar* detenido *or* arrestado

arrest² *vt* **1** (detain) detener*, arrestar **2** ⟨*progress/growth*⟩ (hinder) dificultar; (halt) detener*; ⟨*decline*⟩ atajar

arrival /əˈraɪvəl/ *n* llegada *f*, arribo *m* (esp AmL frml); **on ∼** al llegar

arrive /əˈraɪv/ *vi* llegar*; **to ∼ AT** llegar* A

arrogance /ˈærəgəns/ *n* arrogancia *f*

arrogant /ˈærəgənt/ *adj* arrogante

arrow /ˈærəʊ/ *n* flecha *f*

arse /ɑːrs ‖ɑːs/ *n* (BrE vulg) culo *m* (fam: en algunas regiones vulg)

arsenal /ˈɑːrsnəl ‖ˈɑːsənl/ *n* arsenal *m*

arson /ˈɑːrsn ‖ˈɑːsn/ *n* incendiarismo *m*

arsonist /ˈɑːrsnəst ‖ˈɑːsənɪst/ *n* incendiario, -ria *m,f*, pirómano, -na *m,f*

art /ɑːrt ‖ɑːt/ *n* **1** **(a)** arte *m*; **she's studying ∼** estudia Bellas Artes; (*before n*) ⟨*class*⟩ de arte; (in school) de dibujo; **∼ gallery** (museum) museo *m* de arte; (commercial) galería *f* de arte; **∼ school** *o* **college** escuela *f* de Bellas Artes **(b)** (artwork) trabajos *mpl* artísticos; **∼s and crafts** artesanía **2** **arts** *pl* **(a)** **the ∼s** la cultura y las artes **(b)** (BrE Educ) letras *fpl*

artefact /ˈɑːrtɪfækt ‖ˈɑːtɪfækt/ *n* (BrE) artefacto *m*

artery /ˈɑːrtəri ‖ˈɑːtəri/ *n* (*pl* **-ries**) arteria *f*

arthritis /ɑːrˈθraɪtəs ‖ɑːˈθraɪtɪs/ *n* artritis *f*

artichoke /ˈɑːrtətʃəʊk ‖ˈɑːtɪtʃəʊk/ *n* **(a)** (globe **∼**) alcachofa *f*, alcaucil *m* (RPl) **(b)** (Jerusalem **∼**) aguaturma *f*, pataca *f*

article /ˈɑːrtɪkəl ‖ˈɑːtɪkəl/ *n* **1** (thing, item) artículo *m*; **an ∼ of clothing** una prenda (de vestir) **2** (in newspaper, encyclopedia) artículo *m* **3** (Ling) artículo *m*

articulate¹ /ɑːrˈtɪkjələrt ‖ɑːˈtɪkjʊleɪt/ *vt* **(a)** ⟨*idea/feeling*⟩ expresar **(b)** ⟨*word/sound*⟩ articular

articulate² /ɑːrˈtɪkjələt ‖ɑːˈtɪkjʊlət/ *adj* ⟨*utterance*⟩ articulado; **he's very ∼** se expresa muy bien

articulated lorry /ɑːrˈtɪkjʊleɪtəd ‖ɑːˈtɪkjələɪtɪd/ *n* (BrE) camión *m* articulado

artifact /ˈɑːrtɪfækt/, (BrE) **artefact** *n* artefacto *m*

artificial /ˌɑːrtəˈfɪʃəl ‖ˌɑːtɪˈfɪʃəl/ *adj* artificial; ⟨*leather*⟩ sintético; ⟨*arm/leg*⟩ ortopédico; **∼ respiration** respiración *f* artificial

artillery /ɑːrˈtɪləri ‖ɑːˈtɪləri/ *n* artillería *f*

artisan /ˈɑːrtəzən ‖ˌɑːtɪˈzæn/ *n* artesano, -na *m,f*

artist /ˈɑːrtəst ‖ˈɑːtɪst/ *n* **(a)** (writer, musician, painter, sculptor) artista *mf* **(b)** (performer) (Mus) intérprete *mf*; (Theat) actor, -triz *m,f*, artista *mf*

artistic /ɑːrˈtɪstɪk ‖ɑːˈtɪstɪk/ *adj* artístico

as¹ /æz, *weak form* əz/ *conj* **1** **(a)** (when, while) cuando; **∼ she was eating breakfast ...** cuando *or* mientras tomaba el desayuno ... **(b)** (indicating progression) a medida que; **∼ the date drew closer, ...** a medida que se acercaba la fecha, ... **2** (because, since) como **3** (though): **try ∼ he might, he could not open it** por más que trató, no pudo abrirlo; **strange ∼ it may seem** por extraño que parezca **4** (in accordance with) como; **∼ I was saying** como iba diciendo **5** **(a)** (in the way that) como; **do ∼ I say** haz lo que te digo; **I'm only interested ∼ the changes ∼ they affect me** solo me interesan los cambios en la medida en que me afectan a mí **(b)** (in phrases) **as it is: we've got too much work ∼ it is** ya tenemos demasiado trabajo; **as it were** por así decirlo **6** (in comparisons of equal degree) **as ... as** tan ... como; **there weren't ∼ many people ∼ last time** no había tanta gente como la última vez **7** **as if/as though** como si (+ *subj*)

as² *adv* **1** (equally): **it's not ∼ cold today** hoy no hace tanto frío; **I can't run ∼ quickly now** no puedo correr tan rápido ahora **2** **as ... as: ∼ many ∼ 400 people** hasta 400 personas; **∼ long ago ∼ 1960** ya en 1960

as³ *prep* **1** (in the condition, role of): **∼ a child she adored dancing** de pequeña le encantaba bailar; **∼ a teacher ...** como maestro ...; **he works ∼ a clerk** trabaja de oficinista **2** (in phrases) **as for** en cuanto a; **as of** *o* (BrE) **as from** desde, a partir de

asbestos /æsˈbestəs/ *n* asbesto *m*, amianto *m*

ascend /əˈsend/ *vi* (frml) **(a)** «*person/rocket*» ascender* (frml) **(b)** **ascending** *pres p* ⟨*slope/spiral/scale*⟩ ascendente   ⋯⟩

a

■ ~ *vt* (frml) ⟨steps⟩ subir; ⟨mountain⟩ escalar

ascension /əˈsentʃən ‖əˈsenʃən/ *n* the A~ (Relig) la Ascensión

ascent /əˈsent/ *n* (a) (of mountain) escalada *f* (b) (rise) ascenso *m* (c) (slope) subida *f*

ascertain /ˌæsərˈteɪn/, ˌæsəˈteɪn/ *vt* establecer*

ASCII /ˈæski/ (*no art*) (= **American standard code for information interchange**) ASCII *m*

ascribe /əˈskraɪb/ *vt* to ~ sth TO sth/sb atribuirle* algo A algo/algn

aseptic /eɪˈseptɪk/ *adj* aséptico

ash /æʃ/ *n* [1] (a) (often *pl*) ceniza *f* (b) **ashes** *pl* (cremated remains) cenizas *fpl* [2] ~ (**tree**) fresno *m*

ashamed /əˈʃeɪmd/ *adj* (*pred*) avergonzado, apenado (AmL exc CS); **she was** ~ **of what she'd done** estaba avergonzada de *or* (AmL exc CS) apenada por lo que había hecho; **to be** ~ **OF sb** avergonzarse* DE algn; **he's** ~ **to ask** le da vergüenza *or* (AmL exc CS) pena preguntar

ashcan /ˈæʃkæn/ *n* (AmE) ▶ GARBAGE CAN

ashore /əˈʃɔːr/ *adv* en tierra; **to go** ~ desembarcar*; **we swam** ~ nadamos hasta la orilla

ash: ~**tray** *n* cenicero *m*; **A**~ **Wednesday** *n* miércoles *m* de Ceniza

Asia /ˈeɪʒə, ˈeɪʃə ‖ˈeɪʃə/ *n* Asia *f*‡

Asian[1] /ˈeɪʒən, ˈeɪʃən ‖ˈeɪʃən/ *adj* (a) (of Asia) asiático (b) (from the Indian subcontinent) (BrE) *de India, Pakistán etc*

Asian[2] *n* (a) (from Asia) asiático, -ca *m,f* (b) (from the Indian subcontinent) (BrE) *persona proveniente de India, Pakistán etc*

aside[1] /əˈsaɪd/ *adv* [1] a un lado; *see also* PUT ASIDE, SET ASIDE, STAND* 2A, STEP ASIDE, TAKE ASIDE [2] **aside from** (*as prep*) (esp AmE) (a) (except for) aparte de (b) (as well as) aparte de, además de

aside[2] *n* aparte *m*

ask /æsk ‖ɑːsk/ *vt* [1] (inquire) preguntar; (inquire of) preguntarle a; **to** ~ **sb sth** preguntarle algo A algn; **have you** ~**ed him about his trip?** ¿le has preguntado por el viaje? [2] (request) ⟨approval/advice/favor⟩ pedir*; **to** ~ **sb FOR sth** pedirle* algo A algn; **to** ~ **sb to** + INF pedirle* A algn QUE (+ *subj*); **I** ~**ed to see the manager** pedí hablar con el director [3] (invite) invitar; **to** ~ **sb** (**to sth**) invitar A algn (A algo); **to** ~ **sb out** invitar a algn a salir ■ ~ *vi* [1] (inquire) preguntar [2] (request): **there's no harm in** ~**ing** con preguntar no se pierde nada; **to** ~ **FOR sth** pedir* algo; **to** ~ **FOR sb** preguntar POR algn ■ **ask after** [*v* + *prep* + *o*] preguntar por

askance /əˈskæns/ *adv*: **to look** ~ **at sb** mirar a algn con recelo

askew /əˈskjuː/ *adv* torcido

asleep /əˈsliːp/ *adj* (*pred*): **to be** ~ estar* dormido; **to fall** ~ dormirse*

asparagus /əˈspærəgəs/ *n* espárrago *m*

ASPCA *n* = **American Society for the Prevention of Cruelty to Animals**

aspect /ˈæspekt/ *n* [1] (feature, facet) aspecto *m* [2] (frml) (orientation) orientación *f*

aspersions /əˈspɜːrʒənz ‖əˈspɜːʃənz/ *pl n* (sometimes *sing*): **to cast** ~ **on sth/sb** poner* algo/a algn en entredicho

asphalt /ˈæsfɔːlt ‖ˈæsfælt/ *n* asfalto *m*

asphyxiate /æsˈfɪksieɪt/ *vt* asfixiar

aspiration /ˌæspəˈreɪʃən ‖ˌæspɪˈreɪʃən/ *n* aspiración *f*

aspire /əˈspaɪr ‖əˈspaɪə(r)/ *vi* (a) **to** ~ **TO sth** aspirar A algo (b) **aspiring** *pres p*: **aspiring writers** personas que aspiran a ser escritores

aspirin /ˈæsprən ‖ˈæsprɪn/ *n* (*pl* ~ *or* **-rins**) aspirina *f*

ass /æs/ *n* [1] (a) (donkey) (liter) asno *m*, jumento *m* (liter) (b) (idiot) (colloq) imbécil *mf* [2] (part of body) (AmE vulg) culo *m* (fam: en algunas regiones vulg)

assailant /əˈseɪlənt/ *n* (fml) agresor, -sora *m,f*

assassin /əˈsæsn̩ ‖əˈsæsɪn/ *n* asesino, -na *m,f* (de un personaje importante)

assassinate /əˈsæsn̩eɪt ‖əˈsæsɪneɪt/ *vt* asesinar (a un personaje importante)

assassination /əˌsæsəˈneɪʃən ‖əˌsæsɪˈneɪʃən/ *n* asesinato *m* (de un personaje importante)

assault[1] /əˈsɔːlt/ *n* [1] (Law) (violence) agresión *f*; (molestation) agresión *f* sexual [2] (a) (Mil) asalto *m* (b) (onslaught) ~ (**on sth**) ataque *m* (A algo)

assault[2] *vt* (use violence against) agredir*; (sexually) agredir* sexualmente

assemble /əˈsembəl/ *vt* (a) (construct) montar; ⟨model⟩ armar (b) (get together) reunir* (c) (gather) ⟨facts⟩ recopilar; ⟨collection⟩ reunir* ■ ~ *vi* (gather) reunirse*

assembly /əˈsembli/ *n* (*pl* **-blies**) [1] (a) (coming together) reunión *f* (b) (group) concurrencia *f* (c) (Govt) asamblea *f* (d) (Educ) (*no art*) reunión de profesores y alumnos, al iniciarse la jornada escolar [2] (Tech)(process) montaje *m*; (*before n*) ~ **line** cadena *f* de montaje

assent[1] /əˈsent/ *n* asentimiento *m*; **to give one's** ~ **to sth** dar* su (*or* mi *etc*) conformidad a algo

assent[2] *vi* asentir*; **to** ~ **TO sth** acceder A algo

assert /əˈsɜːrt ‖əˈsɜːt/ *vt* (a) (declare) afirmar (b) (demonstrate, enforce) ⟨superiority⟩ reafirmar; ⟨rights/claims⟩ hacer* valer ■ *v refl* **to** ~ **oneself** hacerse* valer

assertion /əˈsɜːrʃən ‖əˈsɜːʃən/ *n* (a) (declaration) afirmación *f* (b) (demonstration) reafirmación *f*

assertive /əˈsɜːrtɪv ‖əˈsɜːtɪv/ *adj* ⟨tone⟩ autoritario; **to be** ~ ser* firme y enérgico

assess /əˈses/ *vt* ⟨value/amount⟩ calcular; ⟨student/performance⟩ evaluar*; ⟨situation⟩ aquilatar

assessment /əˈsesmənt/ *n* (of performance, results) evaluación *f*; (of amount) cálculo *m*

asset /ˈæset/ *n* (a) (valuable quality): **her intelligence is her greatest** ~ su inteligencia es su gran baza; **she's an** ~ **to the company** es una empleada muy valiosa para la compañía (b) **assets** *pl* (Fin) activo *m*

asset stripping /ˈstrɪpɪŋ/ *n* vaciamiento *m*

assiduous /əˈsɪdjuəs ‖əˈsɪdjuəs/ *adj* (fml) ⟨student⟩ diligente

assign /əˈsaɪn/ *vt* (a) (appoint) **to** ~ **sb TO sth** nombrar a algn PARA algo (b) (allocate) asignar

assignment ·····⟫ **ATM** · · ·

assignment /əˈsaɪnmənt/ n **1 (a)** (mission) misión f **(b)** (task) función f **(c)** (schoolwork) tarea f **2 (a)** (posting) nombramiento m **(b)** (allocation) asignación f

assimilate /əˈsɪməleɪt ‖əˈsɪmɪleɪt/ vt asimilar

assimilation /əˌsɪməˈleɪʃən ‖əˌsɪmɪˈleɪʃən/ n asimilación f

assist /əˈsɪst/ vt ayudar

assistance /əˈsɪstəns/ n ayuda f

assistant¹ /əˈsɪstənt/ n **(a)** (in shop) dependiente, -ta m,f, empleado, -da m,f (AmL) **(b)** (subordinate, helper) ayudante mf; **clerical ~** auxiliar administrativo, -va m,f **(c)** (language **~**) (BrE) (in university) ayudante mf or (Esp) lector, -tora m,f, (in school) auxiliar mf de lengua

assistant² adj (before n): **~ manager** subdirector, -tora m,f

associate¹ /əˈsəʊʃieɪt, -sieɪt/ vt **(a)** (involve, connect) (usu pass) vincular **(b)** (link in mind) asociar

■ **~** vi to **~** (**with** sb) relacionarse (**con** algn)

associate² /əˈsəʊʃiət, -siət/ n **(a)** (in business, profession) colega mf **(b)** (member of professional body) colegiado, -da m,f

associate³ /əˈsəʊʃiət, -siət/ adj (before n) ⟨member⟩ no numerario; ⟨editor/professor⟩ (AmE) adjunto

association /əˌsəʊʃiˈeɪʃən, -siˈeɪʃən/ n asociación f, **in ~ with** (as prep) en asociación con

assorted /əˈsɔːrtəd ‖əˈsɔːtɪd/ adj (before n) surtido

assortment /əˈsɔːrtmənt ‖əˈsɔːtmənt/ n surtido m

assuage /əˈsweɪdʒ/ vt (liter) **(a)** (satisfy) ⟨hunger/desire⟩ saciar (liter) **(b)** (ease) ⟨pain/grief⟩ aliviar **(c)** (calm) ⟨anxiety⟩ calmar; ⟨fear⟩ disipar

assume /əˈsuːm ‖əˈsjuːm/ vt **1** (suppose) suponer* **2** (frml) ⟨duties/command/responsibility⟩ asumir; **~d name** nombre m ficticio

assumption /əˈsʌmpʃən/ n **1** (supposition): **the ~ was that ...** se suponía que ...; **his reasoning is based on the ~ that ...** su razonamiento se basa en el supuesto de que ... **2** (frml) (of duties, leadership, responsibility) asunción f

assurance /əˈʃʊərəns ‖əˈʃʊərəns/ n **1** (guarantee): **she gave me her ~ that ...** me aseguró que ... **2** (self-confidence) seguridad f en sí mismo **3** (insurance) (BrE) seguro m

assure /əˈʃʊr ‖əˈʃʊə(r), əˈʃɔː(r)/ vt **1 (a)** (guarantee) asegurar **(b)** (convince) convencer* **2** (make certain) **to ~ sb** (**of**) **sth**: **this work will ~ me** (**of**) **a regular income** este trabajo me asegurará una entrada fija **3** (insure) (BrE) ⟨life⟩ asegurar

asterisk /ˈæstərɪsk/ n asterisco m

asteroid /ˈæstərɔɪd/ n asteroide m

asthma /ˈæzmə ‖ˈæsmə/ n asma f‡

asthmatic /æzˈmætɪk ‖æsˈmætɪk/ adj asmático

astonish /əˈstɑːnɪʃ ‖əˈstɒnɪʃ/ vt asombrar; (more intensely) dejar pasmado

astonished /əˈstɑːnɪʃt ‖əˈstɒnɪʃt/ adj asombrado; **the ~ look on their faces** la cara de asombro que pusieron; **I'm ~ (that) he got so far** me asombra que haya llegado tan lejos

astonishing /əˈstɑːnɪʃɪŋ ‖əˈstɒnɪʃɪŋ/ adj asombroso; (more intensely) pasmoso

astonishment /əˈstɑːnɪʃmənt ‖əˈstɒnɪʃmənt/ n asombro m; (more intense) estupefacción f

astound /əˈstaʊnd/ vt dejar estupefacto

astounded /əˈstaʊndəd ‖əˈstaʊndɪd/ adj atónito

astounding /əˈstaʊndɪŋ/ adj increíble

astray /əˈstreɪ/ adv: **to go ~** (get lost) extraviarse*; (do wrong) (euph or hum) descarriarse*; **to lead sb ~** (euph or hum) llevar a algn por mal camino

astride /əˈstraɪd/ prep: **he sat ~ the fence/horse** estaba sentado en la valla/montado en el caballo a horcajadas

astringent /əˈstrɪndʒənt/ adj astringente

astrologer /əˈstrɑːlədʒər ‖əˈstrɒlədʒə(r)/ n astrólogo, -ga m,f

astrology /əˈstrɑːlədʒi ‖əˈstrɒlədʒi/ n astrología f

astronaut /ˈæstrənɔːt/ n astronauta mf

astronomer /əˈstrɑːnəmər ‖əˈstrɒnəmə(r)/ n astrónomo, -ma m,f

astronomical /ˈæstrəˈnɑːmɪkəl ‖ˌæstrəˈnɒmɪkəl/ adj astronómico

astronomy /əˈstrɑːnəmi ‖əˈstrɒnəmi/ n astronomía f

astute /əˈstuːt ‖əˈstjuːt/ adj ⟨person⟩ sagaz; ⟨decision⟩ inteligente

asylum /əˈsaɪləm/ n **(a)** (refuge) asilo m **(b)** (lunatic **~**) manicomio m

at /æt, weak form ət/ prep **1** (location) en; **she's ~ the office** está en la oficina; **he's ~ the bank** ha ido al banco
2 (direction): **to point ~ sth/sb** señalar algo/a algn; **he smiled ~ me** me sonrió
3 (time): **~ 6 o'clock** a las seis; **~ Christmas** en Navidad, por Navidades (Esp); **~ night** por la noche, de noche
4 (a) (indicating state): **~ a disadvantage** en desventaja; **~ war/peace** en guerra/paz **(b)** (occupied with): **people ~ work** gente trabajando; **children ~ play** niños jugando
5 (with measurements, numbers, rates etc): **they sell them ~ around $80** las venden a alrededor de $80
6 (because of): **he was surprised ~ the decision** le sorprendió la decisión

ate /eɪt/ past of EAT

atheism /ˈeɪθiɪzəm/ n ateísmo m

atheist /ˈeɪθiəst ‖ˈeɪθiɪst/ n ateo, atea m,f

Athens /ˈæθənz/ n Atenas f

athlete /ˈæθliːt/ n atleta mf

athlete's foot n pie m de atleta

athletic /æθˈletɪk/ adj atlético

athletics /æθˈletɪks/ n (+ sing or pl vb) **(a)** (active sports) (AmE) deportes mpl **(b)** (track and field) (esp BrE) atletismo m

Atlantic¹ /ətˈlæntɪk/ adj atlántico

Atlantic² n the **~** (Ocean) el (océano) Atlántico

atlas /ˈætləs/ n atlas m

ATM n (AmE) (= **automated** or **automatic teller machine**) cajero m automático or permanente

atmosphere /'ætməsfɪr ‖'ætməsfɪə(r)/ *n* **(a)** (of planet) atmósfera *f* **(b)** (feeling, mood) ambiente *m*

atmospheric /'ætməs'ferɪk/ *adj* atmosférico

atom /'ætəm/ *n* átomo *m*

atomic /ə'tɑːmɪk ‖ə'tɒmɪk/ *adj* ‹warfare/energy› atómico; ~ **bomb** bomba *f* atómica

atone /ə'təʊn/ *vi* (frml) **to** ~ **FOR sth** ‹for sins› expiar* algo; ‹for crime/harm› reparar algo

atrocious /ə'trəʊʃəs/ *adj* **(a)** (very bad) (colloq) ‹spelling/manners› espantoso (fam) **(b)** (horrifying) ‹injuries/conditions› atroz

atrocity /ə'trɑːsəti ‖ə'trɒsəti/ *n* (*pl* **-ties**) atrocidad *f*

attach /ə'tætʃ/ *vt* (fasten) sujetar; (tie) atar, amarrar (AmL exc RPI); (stick) pegar*; (to letter, document) adjuntar; **it is** ~**ed to the wall with screws** está sujeto a la pared con tornillos; **the** ~**ed form** el formulario adjunto; **to** ~ **importance to sth** dar(le) importancia a algo

attaché /ˌætæ'ʃeɪ ‖ə'tæʃeɪ/ *n* agregado, -da *m,f*

attaché case *n* maletín *m*

attached /ə'tætʃt/ *adj* (*pred*) (fond) **to be** ~ **TO sb/sth** tenerle* mucho cariño ᴀ algn/algo

attachment /ə'tætʃmənt/ *n* **1** **(a)** (part) accesorio *m* **(b)** (Comput) documento *m* adjunto **2** (fondness) ~ (**TO sb/sth**) cariño *m* (ᴘᴏʀ algn/algo)

attack¹ /ə'tæk/ *n* **(a)** (physical, verbal) ataque *m*; **terrorist** ~**s** atentados *mpl* terroristas **(b)** (Med) ataque *m*; **heart** ~ infarto *m*

attack² *vt* **1** (physically, verbally) atacar* **2** ‹task› acometer; ‹problem› combatir ▪ ~ *vi* (Mil, Sport) atacar*

attacker /ə'tækər ‖ə'tækə(r)/ *n* agresor, -sora *m,f*

attain /ə'teɪn/ *vt* (frml) ‹position/goal› alcanzar*, lograr; ‹ambition› realizar*

attempt¹ /ə'tempt/ *vt* **(a)** (try) **to** ~ **to +** ɪɴꜰ/-ɪɴɢ tratar ᴅᴇ *or* intentar + ɪɴꜰ **(b)** (have a try at) ‹‹student›› ‹exam question› intentar responder a (frml) **(c)** **attempted** *past p*: ~**ed suicide/murder** intento *m* de suicidio/tentativa *f* de asesinato

attempt² *n* intento *m*; **I made an** ~ **at conversation** traté de *or* intenté entablar conversación; **to make an** ~ **on sb's life** atentar contra la vida de algn

attend /ə'tend/ *vt* **1** (frml) **(a)** (be present at) asistir a (frml) **(b)** (go to regularly) ‹church/school/classes› ir* ᴀ **2** ‹patient› atender* ▪ ~ *vi* **1** (be present) asistir **2** (pay attention) **to** ~ (**TO sth**) atender* (ᴀ algo), poner* atención (ᴀ algo) (AmL) ▪ **attend to** [*v + prep + o*] ‹patient/customer› atender*; ‹correspondence/filing› ocuparse de

attendance /ə'tendəns/ *n* **(a)** (presence) asistencia *f*; **to be in** ~ estar* presente **(b)** (people present): **what was the** ~? ¿cuántos asistentes hubo?; **to take** ~ (AmE) pasar lista

attendant /ə'tendənt/ *n* (in museum, parking lot) guarda *m*; (in pool, toilets) encargado, -da *m,f*

attention /ə'tenʃən ‖ə'tenʃən/ *n* **1** **(a)** (concentration) atención *f*; **to pay** ~ **to sth/sb** prestarle atención a algo/algn **(b)** (notice) atención *f*; **to catch sb's** ~ atraer* la atención de algn; **it has been brought to my** ~ *o* **it has come to my** ~ **that ...** me han informado que ... **(c)** (care) atención *f* **2** (Mil): **to stand to** ~ ponerse* en posición de firme(s)

attentive /ə'tentɪv/ *adj* atento

attenuate /ə'tenjueɪt/ *vt* atenuar*; **attenuating circumstances** circunstancias *fpl* atenuantes

attic /'ætɪk/ *n* desván *m*, ático *m*, altillo *m* (esp AmL)

attire /ə'taɪr ‖ə'taɪə(r)/ *n* (liter) atuendo *m* (frml), atavío *m* (liter)

attitude /'ætətuːd ‖'ætɪtjuːd/ *n* actitud *f*

attorney /ə'tɜːrni ‖ə'tɜːni/ *n* (*pl* **-neys**) (AmE) abogado, -da *m,f*; *see also* ᴘᴏᴡᴇʀ ᴏꜰ ᴀᴛᴛᴏʀɴᴇʏ

Attorney General *n* (*pl* ~ **s** *or* ~**s** ~) (in US — at national level) ≈ Ministro, -tra *m,f* de Justicia; (— at state level) ≈ Fiscal *mf* General

attract /ə'trækt/ *vt* atraer*

attraction /ə'trækʃən/ *n* **(a)** (Phys) atracción *f* **(b)** (interest): **I still feel a great** ~ **toward the place** todavía me atrae mucho el lugar; **what's the** ~? ¿qué atractivo tiene? **(c)** (attractive feature) atractivo *m*; **tourist** ~ atracción *f* turística

attractive /ə'træktɪv/ *adj* atractivo

attribute¹ /ə'trɪbjuːt/ *vt* **to** ~ **sth ᴛᴏ sth/sb** atribuirle* algo ᴀ algo/algn

attribute² /'ætrəbjuːt ‖'ætrɪbjuːt/ *n* atributo *m*

attrition /ə'trɪʃən/ *n* **1** (destruction) desgaste *m*; **war of** ~ guerra *f* de desgaste **2** (AmE Lab Rel) bajas *fpl* vegetativas

aubergine /'əʊbərʒiːn ‖'əʊbəʒiːn/ *n* (BrE) berenjena *f*

auburn /'ɔːbərn ‖'ɔːbən/ *adj* castaño rojizo *adj inv*

auction¹ /'ɔːkʃən/ *n* subasta *f*, remate *m* (AmL)

auction² *vt* subastar, rematar (AmL)

auctioneer /ˌɔːkʃə'nɪr ‖ˌɔːkʃə'nɪə(r)/ *n* subastador, -dora *m,f*, rematador, -dora *m,f* (AmL)

audacious /ɔː'deɪʃəs/ *adj* **(a)** (daring) ‹act/plan› audaz **(b)** (impudent) ‹behavior/person› atrevido

audacity /ɔː'dæsəti/ *n* (daring) audacia *f*; (impudence) atrevimiento *m*

audible /'ɔːdəbəl/ *adj* audible

audience /'ɔːdiəns/ *n* **1** (at play, film) público *m*; (at concert, lecture) auditorio *m*; (TV) audiencia *f* **2** (interview) audiencia *f*

audio- /'ɔːdiəʊ/ *pref* audio-

audio-: ~**book** *n* audiolibro *m*; ~**visual** *adj* audiovisual

audit¹ /'ɔːdət ‖'ɔːdɪt/ *vt* **(a)** (Busn, Fin) ‹accounts› auditar **(b)** (AmE Educ) ‹classes/course› asistir como oyente a

audit² *n* (Busn, Fin) **(a)** (inspection) auditoría *f* **(b)** (report) (AmE) informe *m* de auditoría

audition¹ /ɔːˈdɪʃən/ *vi*: **to ~** (FOR sth) dar* una audición (PARA algo)

audition² *n* audición *f*

auditor /ˈɔːdətər ‖ˈɔːdɪtə(r)/ *n* **(a)** (Busn, Fin) auditor, -tora *m,f* **(b)** (AmE Educ) oyente *mf*

auditorium /ˌɔːdəˈtɔːriəm ‖ˌɔːdɪˈtɔːriəm/ *n* (*pl* **-riums** *or* **-ria** /-riə/) auditorio *m*

augment /ɔːgˈment/ *vt* (fml) aumentar, incrementar (fml)

augur /ˈɔːgər ‖ˈɔːgə(r)/ *vi*: **to ~ well/ill** ser* de buen/mal agüero

august /ɔːˈgʌst/ *adj* augusto

August /ˈɔːgəst/ *n* agosto *m*

aunt /ænt ‖ɑːnt/ *n* tía *f*

auntie, aunty /ˈænti ‖ˈɑːnti/ *n* (colloq) tía *f*, tiíta *f* (fam)

au pair /əʊˈper ‖ˌəʊˈpeə(r)/ *n* au pair *mf*

aura /ˈɔːrə/ *n* halo *m*, aura *m*

aural /ˈɔːrəl/ *adj* auditivo

auspices /ˈɔːspəsəz ‖ˈɔːspɪsɪz/ *pl n* (fml): **under the ~ of sb/sth** bajo los auspicios de algn/algo

auspicious /ɔːˈspɪʃəs/ *adj* (fml) prometedor, auspicioso (CS)

austere /ɔːˈstɪr ‖ɒˈstɪə(r), ɔːˈstɪə(r)/ *adj* austero

austerity /ɔːˈsterəti ‖ɒˈsterəti, ɔːˈsterəti/ *n* austeridad *f*

Australasia /ˌɔːstrəˈleɪʒə, -ˈleɪʃə ‖ˌɒstrəˈleɪʒiə, -ˈleɪʃə/ *n* Australasia *f*

Australia /ɔːˈstreɪliə ‖ɒˈstreɪliə/ *n* Australia *f*

Australian¹ /ɔːˈstreɪliən ‖ɒˈstreɪliən/ *adj* australiano

Australian² *n* australiano, -na *m,f*

Austria /ˈɔːstriə ‖ˈɒstriə/ *n* Austria *f*

Austrian¹ /ˈɔːstriən ‖ˈɒstriən/ *adj* austriaco, austríaco

Austrian² *n* austriaco, -ca *m,f*, austríaco, -ca *m,f*

authentic /əˈθentɪk ‖ɔːˈθentɪk/ *adj* **(a)** (genuine) auténtico **(b)** (realistic) ‹atmosphere› realista

authenticate /əˈθentɪkeɪt ‖ɔːˈθentɪkeɪt/ *vt* **(a)** (declare genuine) autenticar* **(b)** (prove, confirm) probar*

authenticity /ˌɔːθenˈtɪsəti/ *n* (of manuscript, painting) autenticidad *f*

author /ˈɔːθər ‖ˈɔːθə(r)/ *n* (writer) escritor, -ra *m,f*; (in relation to her/his works) autor, -tora *m,f*

authoritarian /ɔːˌθɒːrəˈteriən ‖ɔːˌθɒrɪˈteəriən/ *adj* autoritario

authoritative /əˈθɒːrəteɪtɪv ‖ɔːˈθɒrətətɪv/ *adj* **1** ‹manner/tone› de autoridad **2** (reliable, respected) ‹source› fidedigno; ‹work/study› autorizado

authority /əˈθɒːrəti ‖ɔːˈθɒrəti/ *n* (*pl* **-ties**) **1** **(a)** (power) autoridad *f* **(b)** (authorization) ~ **to +** **INF** autorización *f* PARA **+** INF **2** (person, body) autoridad *f*; **she was detained by the Belgian authorities** fue detenida por las autoridades belgas **3** **(a)** (expert) ~ **(on sth)** autoridad *f* (EN algo) **(b)** (source) autoridad *f*; **to have sth on good ~** saber* algo de buena fuente

authorize /ˈɔːθəraɪz/ *vt* **(a)** ‹publication/

transaction› autorizar*; ‹funds› aprobar* **(b)** (empower) **to ~ sb to +** INF autorizar* a algn PARA **+** INF

autistic /ɔːˈtɪstɪk/ *adj* autista

autobiographical /ˌɔːtəˌbaɪəˈgræfɪkəl/ *adj* autobiográfico

autobiography /ˌɔːtəbaɪˈɑːgrəfi ‖ˌɔːtəbaɪˈɒgrəfi/ *n* (*pl* **-phies**) autobiografía *f*

autocratic /ˌɔːtəˈkrætɪk/ *adj* autocrático

autograph¹ /ˈɔːtəgræf ‖ˈɔːtəgrɑːf/ *n* autógrafo *m*

autograph² *vt* autografiar*

automata /ɔːˈtɑːmətə ‖ɔːˈtɒmətə/ *pl of* AUTOMATON

automate /ˈɔːtəmeɪt/ *vt* automatizar*

automatic¹ /ˌɔːtəˈmætɪk/ *adj* automático

automatic² *n* (car) coche *m* automático; (pistol) automática *f*

automatically /ˌɔːtəˈmætɪkli/ *adv* automáticamente

automation /ˌɔːtəˈmeɪʃən/ *n* automatización *f*

automaton /ɔːˈtɑːmətən ‖ɔːˈtɒmətən/ *n* (*pl* **automata** *or* **-tons**) autómata *m*

automobile /ˈɔːtəməbiːl/ *n* (esp AmE) coche *m*, carro *m* (AmL exc CS), auto *m* (esp CS), automóvil *m* (fml)

autonomous /ɔːˈtɑːnəməs ‖ɔːˈtɒnəməs/ *adj* autónomo

autonomy /ɔːˈtɑːnəmi ‖ɔːˈtɒnəmi/ *n* autonomía *f*

autopsy /ˈɔːtɑːpsi ‖ˈɔːtɒpsi/ *n* (*pl* **-sies**) autopsia *f*

autumn /ˈɔːtəm/ *n* (esp BrE) otoño *m*; (before n) ‹day/weather› de otoño, otoñal

auxiliary¹ /ɔːgˈzɪljəri/ *adj* auxiliar

auxiliary² *n* (*pl* **-ries**) auxiliar *mf*; **nursing ~** enfermero, -ra *m,f* auxiliar

avail¹ /əˈveɪl/ *v refl* (fml) **to ~ oneself OF sth** aprovechar algo

avail² *n* (liter): **to no ~** en vano

available /əˈveɪləbəl/ *adj* **(a)** (obtainable) (*pred*): **to be readily ~** ser* fácil de conseguir; **brochures are ~ on request** hay folletos a disposición de quien los solicite **(b)** (at sb's disposal) ‹resources/ manpower› disponible; **to make sth ~ to sb** poner* algo a disposición de algn **(c)** (free, contactable) (*pred*) libre; (for work, job) disponible

avalanche /ˈævəlænt∫ ‖ˈævəlɑːn∫/ *n* alud *m*, avalancha *f*

avant-garde /ˌɑːvɑːnˈgɑːrd ‖ˌævɒnˈgɑːd/ *adj* vanguardista, de vanguardia

avarice /ˈævərəs ‖ˈævərɪs/ *n* (liter) codicia *f* (liter)

avaricious /ˌævəˈrɪʃəs/ *adj* (liter) codicioso

Ave (= **Avenue**) Avda., Av.

avenge /əˈvendʒ/ *vt* vengar*

avenue /ˈævənu: ‖ˈævənju:/ *n* **1** **(a)** (tree-lined walk) paseo *m* ‹arbolado› **(b)** (broad street) avenida *f* **2** (means, method) vía *f*

average¹ /ˈævrɪdʒ , ˈævərɪdʒ/ *n* (Math) promedio *m*, media *f*

average² *adj* **(a)** (Math) ‹time/age› medio, promedio *adj inv*; **he is of ~ height** es de

estatura mediana **(b)** (typical): **the** ~ **family** la
familia tipo **(c)** (ordinary): **how was the movie?** —
average ¿qué tal la película? — normal
■ **average out** [*v* + *adv*]: **our speed** ~**d out at
about 60mph** hicimos una media *or* un promedio
de 60 millas por hora

averse /ə'vɜːrs ‖ə'vɜːs/ *adj* (*pred*) **to be** ~ **TO
sth** ⟨*to an idea*⟩ ser* reacio A algo

aversion /ə'vɜːrʒən, -ʃən ‖ə'vɜːʃən/ *n* (*no pl*)
aversión *f*

avert /ə'vɜːrt ‖ə'vɜːt/ *vt* **(a)** ⟨*eyes/gaze*⟩ apartar
(b) ⟨*danger/suspicion*⟩ evitar; ⟨*accident/strike*⟩
impedir*

aviary /'eɪvieri ‖'eɪvɪəri/ *n* (*pl* **-ries**) pajarera
f

aviation /'eɪvi'eɪʃən/ *n* aviación *f*

avid /'ævəd ‖'ævɪd/ *adj* ⟨*reader/interest*⟩ ávido;
⟨*fan/follower*⟩ ferviente

avocado /'ævə'kɑːdəʊ/ *n* (*pl* **-dos**) ~ (**pear**)
aguacate *m or* (Bol, CS, Per) palta *f*

avoid /ə'vɔɪd/ *vt* ⟨*obstacle/place/topic*⟩ evitar;
⟨*blow*⟩ esquivar; **why are you** ~**ing me?** ¿por qué
me rehúyes?

avoidable /ə'vɔɪdəbəl/ *adj* evitable

avowed /ə'vaʊd/ *adj* (*before n*) declarado

await /ə'weɪt/ *vt* esperar

awake[1] /ə'weɪk/ *adj* (*pred*) **to be** ~ estar*
despierto

awake[2] (*past* **awoke**; *past p* **awoken**),
awaken /ə'weɪkən/ *vt/i* despertar*

awakening /ə'weɪkənɪŋ/ *n* despertar *m*

award[1] /ə'wɔːrd ‖ə'wɔːd/ *vt* **(a)** ⟨*prize/medal/
pay increase*⟩ conceder; ⟨*honor*⟩ conferir* **(b)**
(Sport) ⟨*penalty/free kick*⟩ conceder

award[2] *n* **(a)** (prize) galardón *m*; (medal)
condecoración *f* **(b)** (sum of money) asignación *f*

award-winning /ə'wɔːrd'wɪnɪŋ
‖ə'wɔːd,wɪnɪŋ/ *adj* (*before n*) galardonado

aware /ə'wer ‖ə'weə(r)/ *adj* (conscious) (*pred*) **to
be** ~ **OF sth** ser* *or* (Chi, Méx) estar* consciente DE
algo; **is your father** ~ **that you drink?** ¿sabe tu
padre que bebes?

awareness /ə'wernəs ‖ə'weənɪs/ *n*
conciencia *f*

awash /ə'wɔːʃ ‖ə'wɒʃ/ *adj* (*pred*) **to be** ~
(**WITH sth**) estar* inundado (DE algo)

away /ə'weɪ/ *adv* **1** (from place, person): **I looked**
~ aparté la vista; **he limped** ~ se alejó cojeando
2 **(a)** (in the distance): **it isn't far** ~ no queda lejos;
it's 20 miles ~ queda a 20 millas; **Easter is a long
way** ~ falta mucho para Pascua **(b)** (absent): **she's**

~ **in Canada** está en Canadá; **I'll be** ~ **all next
week** toda la semana que viene no voy a estar **(c)**
(esp BrE Sport): **to play** ~ jugar* fuera (de casa)
3 (continuously): **he's been painting** ~ **all morning**
se ha pasado toda la mañana pintando; **I could
hear him singing** ~ lo oía cantar
4 **away from** (*as prep*) **(a)** (in opposite direction to):
she pulled him ~ **from the cliff edge** lo apartó del
borde del acantilado **(b)** (at a distance, separated
from) lejos de; **to get** ~ **from it all** alejarse del
mundanal ruido

awe /ɔː/ *n* sobrecogimiento *m*; **to be in** ~ **of sb**
sentirse* intimidado por algn

awe-inspiring /'ɔːrɪn'spaɪrɪŋ ‖'ɔːrɪn,spaɪərɪŋ/
adj impresionante

awesome /'ɔːsəm/ *adj* imponente

awestruck /'ɔːstrʌk/ *adj* atemorizado

awful /'ɔːfəl/ *adj* (colloq) ⟨*journey/weather/day*⟩
horrible; ⟨*clothes*⟩ horroroso; ⟨*joke/movie*⟩
malísimo; **I felt** ~ me sentía fatal

awkward /'ɔːkwərd ‖'ɔːkwəd/ *adj* **1** (clumsy)
⟨*movement/person*⟩ torpe; ⟨*phrase*⟩ poco elegante
2 **(a)** (difficult, inconvenient) ⟨*shape/angle*⟩
incómodo; **at a rather** ~ **moment** en mal
momento; **she could make things very** ~ **for you**
te podría hacer la vida imposible **(b)** (difficult to
deal with) difícil **3** **(a)** (embarrassing) ⟨*decision/
subject*⟩ delicado; **you've put me in a very** ~
position me has puesto en una situación muy
violenta **(b)** (embarrassed) ⟨*silence*⟩ incómodo; **I felt
very** ~ me sentí muy incómodo

awning /'ɔːnɪŋ/ *n* toldo *m*

awoke /ə'wəʊk/ *past of* AWAKE[2]

awoken /ə'wəʊkən/ *past p of* AWAKE[2]

awry /ə'raɪ/ *adj* (*pred*) torcido; **to go** ~ salir* mal

ax[1], (BrE) **axe** /æks/ *n* hacha *f*; **to have an** ~
to grind tener* un interés personal

ax[2], (BrE) **axe** *vt* (journ) ⟨*project/services/jobs*⟩
suprimir; ⟨*employee*⟩ despedir*

axis /'æksəs ‖'æksɪs/ *n* (*pl* **axes** /'æksiːz/) eje *m*

axle /'æksəl/ *n* eje *m*

AZ = **Arizona**

Azerbaijan /'æzərbaɪ'dʒɑːn ‖,æzəbaɪ'dʒɑːn/ *n*
Azerbaiyán *m*, Azerbaiján *m*

Azerbaijani /'æzərbaɪ'dʒɑːni ‖,æzəbaɪ'dʒɑːni/
adj azerbaiyaní

Aztec[1] /'æztek/ *adj* azteca

Aztec[2] *n* azteca *mf*

azure /'æʒər ‖'æʒə(r), 'æʒʊə(r)/ *adj* (liter) azur
(liter)

Bb

B, b /biː/ *n* (a) (letter) B, b *f* (b) (Mus) si *m*

b (= **born**) n.

BA *n* = **Bachelor of Arts**

babble /'bæbəl/ *vi* (talk foolishly) parlotear (fam); (talk unintelligibly) farfullar; «*baby*» balbucear; **a babbling brook** (liter) un arroyo rumoroso (liter)

baby /'beɪbi/ *n* (*pl* **babies**) (a) (infant) bebé *m*, niño, -ña *m,f*, bebe, -ba *m,f* (Per, RPl), guagua *f* (Andes); **to have a ~** tener* un hijo *or* un niño (b) (animal) cría *f* (c) (youngest member) benjamín, -mina *m,f*

baby: ~ buggy, ~ carriage *n* (AmE) cochecito *m* de bebé, carriola *f* (Méx); **~-sit** *vi* (*pres p* **-sitting**; *past & past p* **-sat**) cuidar niños, hacer* de canguro (Esp); **~-sitter** /'beɪbi,sɪtər ‖'beɪbi,sɪtə(r)/ *n* baby sitter *mf*, canguro *mf* (Esp)

bachelor /'bætʃələr ‖'bætʃələ(r)/ *n* [1] (single man) soltero *m* [2] (Educ) licenciado, -da *m,f*; **B~ of Arts/Science** (degree) licenciatura *f* en Filosofía y Letras/en Ciencias

back¹ /bæk/ *n* [1] (Anat) (of human) espalda *f*; (of animal) lomo *m*; **they laugh at him behind his ~** se ríen de él a sus espaldas; **to turn one's ~ on sb** volverle* la espalda a algn
[2] (a) (of chair) respaldo *m*; (of dress, jacket) espalda *f*; (of electrical appliance, watch) tapa *f* (b) (reverse side — of envelope, photo) dorso *m*; (— of head) parte *f* posterior; (— of hand) dorso *m*; **your sweater is on ~ to front** te has puesto el suéter al revés; ▶ HAND¹ 2
[3] (rear part): **the ~ of the house** la parte de atrás de la casa; **at the ~ of the drawer** en el fondo del cajón; **we sat at the ~** nos sentamos al fondo; **I'll sit in the ~** (of car) yo me siento detrás *or* (en el asiento de) atrás; **in the ~ of beyond** quién sabe dónde, donde el diablo perdió el poncho (AmS fam), en el quinto pino (Esp fam)
[4] (Sport) defensa *mf*, zaguero, -ra *m,f*

back² *adj* (*before n, no comp*) [1] ⟨*door*⟩ trasero; ⟨*garden*⟩ de atrás [2] (of an earlier date): **~ number** *o* **issue** número *m* atrasado; **~ pay** atrasos *mpl*

back³ *adv* [1] (indicating return, repetition): **the journey ~** el viaje de vuelta; **he's ~ from Paris** ha vuelto de París; **long hair is ~** (in fashion) vuelve (a estar de moda) el pelo largo; **to run/fly ~** volver* corriendo/en avión; **he asked for the ring ~** pidió que le devolviera el anillo; *see also* GO, TAKE *etc* BACK
[2] (in reply, reprisal): **he slapped her and she slapped him ~** él la abofeteó y ella le devolvió la bofetada
[3] (backward): **take two steps ~** da dos pasos atrás
[4] (in the past): **~ in 1972** (ya) en 1972
[5] **back and forth** = **backward(s) and forward(s)**: ▶ BACKWARD² A

back⁴ *vt* [1] (a) ⟨*person/decision*⟩ respaldar (b) (bet money on) ⟨*horse/winner*⟩ apostar* por

[2] (reverse): **he ~ed the car out of the garage** sacó el coche del garaje dando marcha atrás *or* (Col, Méx) en reversa
[3] (Mus) acompañar
■ ~ *vi* «*vehicle/driver*» dar* marcha atrás, meter reversa (Col, Méx); **he ~ed into a lamppost** se dio contra una farola al dar marcha atrás *or* al meter reversa
■ **back away** [*v + adv*] echarse atrás
■ **back down** [*v + adv*] volverse* atrás
■ **back out** [*v + adv*] volverse* atrás; **they ~ed out of the deal** no cumplieron el trato
■ **back up** [1] [*v + o + adv, v + adv + o*] (a) (support) respaldar, apoyar (b) (Comput) ⟨*file*⟩ hacer* una copia de seguridad de
[2] [*v + adv*] (reverse) dar* marcha atrás, meter reversa (Col, Méx)

back: ~ache *n* dolor *m* de espalda; **~bencher** /'bæk'bentʃər ‖,bæk'bentʃə(r)/, **~ bench MP** *n* (in UK) diputado, -da *m,f* (*sin cargo específico en el gobierno o la oposición*); **~bone** *n* (Anat) columna *f* (vertebral); (main strength) columna *f* vertebral, eje *m*; **~date** /'bæk'deɪt/ *vt* ⟨*wage increase*⟩ pagar* con retroactividad; ⟨*check*⟩ ponerle* una fecha anterior a; **~drop** *n* telón *m* de fondo

backer /'bækər ‖'bækə(r)/ *n* patrocinador, -dora *m,f*

backfire /'bækfaɪr ‖'bæk'faɪə(r)/ *vi* (a) «*car*» producir* detonaciones en el escape (b) (fail) fracasar

background¹ /'bækɡraʊnd/ *n* (a) (of picture, scene) fondo *m*; **she prefers to stay in the ~** prefiere permanecer en un segundo plano (b) (of events) ~ (TO sth) antecedentes *mpl* (DE algo) (c) (of person — origin) origen *m*; (— education) formación *f*; (— previous activities) experiencia *f*

background² *adj* (*before n*) ⟨*noise/music*⟩ de fondo; **~ reading** lecturas *fpl* preparatorias (*acerca del momento histórico, antecedentes etc*)

backhand /'bækhænd/ *n* revés *m*

backing /'bækɪŋ/ *n* (a) (support) respaldo *m* (b) (Mus) acompañamiento *m*

backlash /'bæklæʃ/ *n* reacción *f* violenta; (Mech Eng) contragolpe *m*

backless /'bækləs ‖'bæklɪs/ *adj* sin espalda

back: ~log *n* atraso *m*; **a ~log of work** trabajo atrasado; **~pack** *n* mochila *f*; **~ seat** *n* asiento *m* trasero *or* de atrás; **~side** /'bæk'saɪd/ *n* (colloq) trasero *m* (fam); **~stage** /'bæk'steɪdʒ/ *adj/adv* entre bastidores; (*before n*) ⟨*abortion*⟩ clandestino; **~street** *n* callejuela *f*; (*before n*) ⟨*abortion*⟩ clandestino; estilo *m* espalda; **~track** *vi* (a) (retrace one's steps) retroceder (b) (reverse opinion, plan) dar* marcha atrás; **~up** *n* (a) (support) respaldo *m*, apoyo *m*; (*before n*) ⟨*team/equipment*⟩ de refuerzo (b) (Comput) copia *f* de seguridad; (*before n*) ⟨*disk/file*⟩ de reserva, de seguridad

backward¹ /'bækwərd ‖'bækwəd/ *adj*   ⋯∴

1 *(before n)* *‹movement›* hacia atrás; **a ~ glance** una mirada atrás **2** *‹child›* retrasado; *‹nation›* atrasado

backward², *(esp BrE)* **backwards** /'bækwərdz ‖'bækwədz/ *adv* **(a)** (toward rear) hacia atrás; **~ and forward(s)** para atrás y para adelante; ▶ KNOW¹ *vt* 1A **(b)** (back to front, in reverse order) al revés

back yard *n* (paved) patio *m* trasero; (grassed) (AmE) jardín *m* trasero, fondo *m* (RPl)

bacon /'beɪkən/ *n* tocino *m or* (Esp) bacon *m or* (RPl) panceta *f*

bacteria /bæk'tɪriə ‖bæk'tɪəriə/ *pl n* bacterias *mpl*

bad¹ /bæd/ *adj*

■ **Note** The usual translation of *bad, malo,* becomes *mal* when it is used before a masculine singular noun.

(comp **worse;** *superl* **worst) 1** (not good) malo; **to be ~ AT** sth/-ING ser* malo PARA algo/+ INF; **to go from ~ to worse** ir* de mal en peor; **too much food is ~ for you** comer demasiado es malo; **she's got a ~ knee** tiene problemas con la rodilla; **I feel ~ about not having written to her** me da no sé qué no haberle escrito; **to be in a ~ way** (colloq) estar* fatal (fam) **2** (serious) *‹mistake/injury›* grave; *‹headache›* fuerte **3** (rotten) *‹egg/fruit›* podrido; **to go ~** echarse a perder

bad² *n:* **all the ~ that he's done** todo el mal que ha hecho; **there's good and ~ in everybody** todos tenemos cosas buenas y malas

bad³ *adv* (esp AmE colloq): **to need sth real ~** necesitar algo desesperadamente

bade /bæd, beɪd/ *past of* BID¹ *vt* 2

badge /bædʒ/ *n* (pin-on) chapa *f*, botón *m* (AmL); (sew-on) insignia *f*

badger¹ /'bædʒər ‖'bædʒə(r)/ *n* tejón *m*

badger² *vt* fastidiar

badly /'bædli/ *adv (comp* **worse;** *superl* **worst) 1** (poorly) *‹play/sing›* mal **2** (improperly) *‹behave/treat›* mal **3** *(as intensifier) ‹fail›* miserablemente; **~ injured** gravemente herido

badly off *adj (comp* **worse off;** *superl* **worst off)** *(pred)* mal de dinero

badminton /'bædmɪntn̩/ *n* bádminton *m*

bad-tempered /'bæd'tempərd ‖,bæd'tempəd/ *adj ‹reply/tone›* malhumorado; *‹person›* (as permanent characteristic) de mal genio; (in a bad mood) de mal humor

baffle /'bæfəl/ *vt* **(a)** (perplex) desconcertar* **(b)** (frustrate) *‹efforts›* frustrar

baffled /'bæfəld/ *adj* perplejo; *‹expression›* de perplejidad

bag /bæg/ *n* **1** **(a)** (container, bagful) bolsa *f*; **a paper ~** una bolsa de papel; (hand~) (esp BrE) cartera *f or* (Esp) bolso *m or* (Méx) bolsa *f* **(b)** (piece of luggage) maleta *f*, valija *f* (RPl), petaca *f* (Méx); **to pack one's ~s** hacer* la maleta *(or*

valija *etc)* **2** (of skin) bolsa *f*; **to have ~s under one's eyes** (of skin) tener* bolsas en los ojos; (dark rings) tener* ojeras

baggage /'bægɪdʒ/ *n* equipaje *m; (before n)* **~ room** (AmE) consigna *f*

baggy /'bægi/ *adj* **-gier, -giest** ancho, guango (Méx)

bagpipes /'bægpaɪps/ *pl n* gaita *f*

Bahamas /bə'hɑːməz/ *pl n* **the ~** las Bahamas

bail /beɪl/ *n* (Law) fianza *f*; **he was released on ~** fue puesto en libertad bajo fianza

■ **bail out 1** *[v + o + adv, v + adv + o]* **(a)** (Law): **to ~ sb out** pagarle* la fianza a algn **(b)** (Naut) *‹water›* achicar* **2** *[v + o + adv, v + adv + o]* (rescue) sacar* de apuros **3** *[v + adv]* (Aviat) tirarse en paracaídas

bailiff /'beɪləf ‖'beɪlɪf/ *n* (Law) **(a)** (in UK) alguacil *mf* **(b)** (in US) *funcionario que custodia al acusado en el juzgado*

bait¹ /beɪt/ *n* cebo *m*

bait² *vt* **1** *‹hook/trap›* cebar **2** (persecute) acosar

bake /beɪk/ *vt:* **~ in a hot oven** hornear en horno caliente; **she ~s her own bread** hace el pan en casa; **~d potato** papa *f or* (Esp) patata *f* asada

■ **~** *vi* hacer* pasteles *(or* pan *etc)*

baked beans /beɪkt/ *pl n* **(a)** (in can) frijoles *mpl or* (Esp) judias *fpl or* (CS) porotos *mpl* en salsa de tomate **(b)** (dish) (AmE) *el mismo plato preparado con cerdo*

baker /'beɪkər ‖'beɪkə(r)/ *n* panadero, -ra *m,f*; **~'s** (shop) panadería *f*

bakery /'beɪkəri/ *n (pl* **-ries)** panadería *f*

baking /'beɪkɪŋ/ *n:* **we do a lot of ~** hacemos muchos pasteles *(or* pan *etc); (before n)* **~ dish** fuente *f* para el horno; **~ powder** polvo *m* de hornear, Royal® *m*, levadura *f* en polvo (Esp); **~ tin** molde *m;* **~ tray** bandeja *f* (de horno)

balance¹ /'bæləns/ *n* **1** (apparatus) balanza *f* **2** (equilibrium) equilibrio *m;* **to lose one's ~** perder* el equilibrio **3** **(a)** (in accounting) balance *m* **(b)** (bank ~) saldo *m* **(c)** (difference, remainder) resto *m;* (of sum of money) saldo *m*

balance² *vt* **1** *‹load›* equilibrar; *‹object›* mantener* en equilibrio **2** (Fin) *‹account›* hacer* el balance de

balanced /'bælənst/ *adj* equilibrado

balance of payments *n* balanza *f* de pagos

balcony /'bælkəni/ *n (pl* **-nies) (a)** (Archit) balcón *m;* (large) terraza *f* **(b)** (Theat) (in US) platea *f* alta; (in UK) galería *f*

bald /bɔːld/ *adj* **-er, -est (a)** *‹man›* calvo, pelón (AmC, Méx), pelado (CS); **to go ~** quedarse calvo *(or* pelón *etc)* **(b)** (worn) *‹tire›* gastado

bale /beɪl/ *n* paca *f*

■ **bale out** (BrE) ▶ BAIL OUT

Balearic Islands /ˌbæli'ærɪk/ *pl n* **the ~ ~** las (Islas) Baleares

baleful /'beɪlfəl/ *adj* torvo

AmC	Central America	Arg	Argentina	Cu	Cuba
AmL	Latin America	Bol	Bolivia	Ec	Ecuador
AmS	South America	Chi	Chile	Esp	Spain
Andes	Andean Region	CS	Southern Cone	Méx	Mexico

Per	Peru
RPl	River Plate Area
Ur	Uruguay
Ven	Venezuela

Balkan /'bɔːlkən/ adj balcánico

Balkans /'bɔːlkənz/ pl n the ~ los países balcánicos

ball /bɔːl/ n 1 (in baseball, golf) pelota f, bola f; (in basketball, football) pelota f (esp AmL), balón m (esp Esp); (in billiards) bola f; **to be on the** ~ (colloq) ser* muy espabilado 2 (a) **to play** ~ **(with sb)** (lit: play game) jugar* a la pelota (con algn); (cooperate) (colloq) cooperar (con algn) (b) (base~) (AmE) béisbol m 3 (a) (round mass) bola f; (of string, wool) ovillo m (b) (Anat): **the** ~ **of the foot** la parte anterior de la planta del pie 4 (dance) baile m

ballad /'bæləd/ n (narrative poem, song) romance m; (sentimental song) balada f

ballast /'bæləst/ n (Aviat, Naut) lastre m

ballerina /ˌbælə'riːnə/ n bailarina f (de ballet)

ballet /'bæleɪ/ n ballet m; (before n) ~ **dancer** bailarín, -rina m,f de ballet

ball game n juego m de pelota; (baseball game) (AmE) partido m de béisbol; (US football game) (AmE) partido m de fútbol or (AmC, Méx) futbol americano

ballistics /bə'lɪstɪks/ n (+ sing vb) balística f

balloon /bə'luːn/ n (a) (toy) globo m, bomba f (Col), chimbomba f (AmC) (b) (Aviat) globo m

ballot /'bælət/ n votación f; (before n) ~ **box** urna f; ~ **(paper)** papeleta f, boleta f electoral (Méx, RPl)

ball: ~**park** n (AmE Sport) estadio m or (Méx) parque m de béisbol; (before n) **a** ~**park figure** una cifra aproximada; ~**player** n (AmE) (in baseball) jugador, -dora m,f de béisbol, beisbolista mf; (in US football) jugador, -dora m,f de fútbol or (AmC, Méx) de futbol americano; (in basketball) jugador, -dora m,f de baloncesto, baloncestista mf, basquetbolista mf (AmL); ~**point (pen)** n bolígrafo m, esfero(gráfico) m (Col), pluma f atómica (Méx), birome f (RPl), lápiz m de pasta (Chi); ~**room** n sala f or salón m de baile; ~**room dancing** n baile m de salón

balm /bɑːm/ n bálsamo m

Baltic /'bɔːltɪk/ n the ~ (Sea) el (mar) Báltico

bamboo /ˌbæm'buː; ‖bæm'buː/ n (pl **-boos**) bambú m

ban¹ /bæn/ vt **-nn-** ⟨book/smoking⟩ prohibir*; ⟨organization⟩ proscribir*; **he was** ~ned **from the club** le prohibieron la entrada al club

ban² n prohibición f

banal /bə'næl, 'beɪnəl ‖bə'nɑːl/ adj banal

banana /bə'nænə ‖bə'nɑːnə/ n plátano m, banana f (Per, RPl), banano m (AmC, Col), cambur m (Ven)

band /bænd/ n 1 (a) (group) grupo m; (of thieves, youths) pandilla f (b) (Mus) (jazz ~) grupo m or conjunto m de jazz; (rock ~) grupo m de rock 2 (a) (ribbon) cinta f; (strip — of cloth) banda f; (— for hat) cinta f (b) (stripe) franja f
■ **band together** [v + adv] unirse

bandage¹ /'bændɪdʒ/ n venda f

bandage² vt vendar

Band-Aid® /'bændeɪd/ n (AmE) curita® f, tirita® f (Esp)

B & B /ˌbiːən'biː/ n = **bed and breakfast**

bandit /'bændət ‖'bændɪt/ n bandido, -da m,f, bandolero, -ra m,f

band: ~**stand** n quiosco m de música; ~**wagon** n: **to jump on the** ~**wagon** subirse al carro

bandy¹ /'bændi/ adj **-dier, -diest** arqueado, torcido

bandy² **-dies, -dying, -died** vt ⟨remarks/jokes⟩ intercambiar

bane /beɪn/ n: **to be the** ~ **of sb's life** ser* la cruz de algn

bang¹ /bæŋ/ n 1 (loud noise) estrépito m; (explosion) explosión f 2 (blow) golpe m, trancazo m 3 **bangs** pl (AmE) (fringe) flequillo m, cerquillo m (AmL), chasquilla f (Chi), capul f (Col), fleco m (Méx), pollina f (Ven)

bang² vt (a) (strike) golpear (b) (slam): **he** ~ed **the door** dio un portazo (fam)
■ ~ vi (a) (strike) **to** ~ **on sth** golpear algo; **to** ~ **INTO sth** darse* CONTRA algo (b) (slam) «door» cerrarse* de un golpe

bang³ adv 1: **to go** ~ «gun» dispararse 2 (as intensifier) (esp BrE colloq): ~ **on time** a la hora justa

banger /'bæŋər ‖'bæŋə(r)/ n (BrE colloq) (a) (sausage) salchicha f (b) (firework) petardo m (c) (car) (old ~) cacharro m (fam)

Bangkok /'bæŋkɑːk ‖bæŋ'kɒk/ n Bangkok m

Bangladesh /'bɑːŋglədeʃ ‖ˌbæŋglə'deʃ/ n Bangladesh m

Bangladeshi /'bɑːŋglə'deʃi ‖ˌbæŋglə'deʃi/ adj bangladesí

bangle /'bæŋgəl/ n pulsera f, brazalete m; (thin, of gold or silver) esclava f, aro m

banish /'bænɪʃ/ vt (a) (exile) desterrar*; ⟨fear/doubts⟩ hacer* olvidar (b) (prohibit) prohibir*

banister /'bænəstər ‖'bænɪstə(r)/ n pasamanos m

bank¹ /bæŋk/ n 1 (a) (Fin) banco m; (before n) ~ **balance** saldo m (b) (store, supply) banco m; **blood** ~ banco de sangre 2 (edge of river) orilla f, ribera f 3 ~ **of earth/snow** montículo m de tierra/nieve

bank² vt depositar or (esp Esp) ingresar (en el banco)
■ ~ vi 1 (Fin): **I** ~ **with the National** tengo la cuenta en el National 2 (Aviat) ladearse
■ **bank on** [v + prep + o] ⟨victory/help⟩ contar* con; **I wouldn't** ~ **on it** yo no me confiaría demasiado

bank: ~ **account** n cuenta f bancaria; ~**book** n libreta f de ahorros; ~**card** n (AmE) tarjeta f de crédito (expedida por un banco); (BrE) tarjeta f bancaria

banker /'bæŋkər ‖'bæŋkə(r)/ n (a) (Fin) banquero, -ra m,f (b) (in gambling) banca f

bank holiday n (BrE) día m festivo, feriado m (esp AmL)

banking /'bæŋkɪŋ/ n banca f

bank: ~ **note** n (a) (promissory note) (AmE) pagaré m (b) (paper money) (BrE) billete m de banco; ~ **rate** n tasa f or (esp Esp) tipo m de interés

bankrupt¹ /'bæŋkrʌpt/ adj en quiebra, en bancarrota; **to be** ~ estar* en quiebra or en bancarrota; **to go** ~ quebrar*, ir* a la bancarrota

bankrupt² n fallido, -da m,f

bankrupt³ *vt* llevar a la quiebra *or* a la bancarrota

bankruptcy /'bæŋkrʌptsi/ *n* (*pl* **-cies**) quiebra *f*, bancarrota *f*

banner /'bænər ‖'bænə(r)/ *n* (flag) estandarte *m*; (in demonstration) pancarta *f*

bannister *n* ▶ BANISTER

banns /bænz/ *pl n* amonestaciones *fpl*

banquet /'bæŋkwət ‖'bæŋkwɪt/ *n* banquete *m*

banter /'bæntər ‖'bæntə(r)/ *n* bromas *fpl*

baptism /'bæptɪzəm/ *n* bautismo *m*

Baptist /'bæptəst ‖'bæptɪst/ *n* baptista *mf*, bautista *mf*

baptize /bæp'taɪz/ *vt* bautizar*

bar¹ /baːr ‖baː(r)/ *n* **1** (rod, rail) barra *f*; (— on cage, window) barrote *m* **2** (Sport) (cross~) (in soccer) larguero *m*; (in rugby) travesaño *m*; (in high jump) barra *f or* (Esp) listón *m*; (horizontal ~) barra *f* (fija) **3** (block) barra *f*; ~ **of chocolate** barra *f* de chocolate; **gold** ~ lingote *m* de oro; ~ **of soap** pastilla *f or* (CS) barra *f* de jabón **4** (establishment) bar *m*; (counter) barra *f*, mostrador *m* **5** (Law) **the Bar** (legal profession) (AmE) la abogacía; (barristers) (BrE) *el conjunto de* BARRISTERS **6** (Mus) compás *m*

bar² *vt* **-rr-** **1** (secure) ⟨*door/window*⟩ atrancar* **2** (block) ⟨*path/entrance*⟩ bloquear **3** (prohibit) ⟨*smoking/jeans*⟩ prohibir*; ⟨*person/group*⟩ excluir*

bar³ *prep* salvo, excepto, a *or* con excepción de

barb /baːrb ‖baːb/ *n* (of fishhook, arrow) lengüeta *f*

Barbados /baːr'beɪdəʊs ‖baː'beɪdɒs/ *n* Barbados *m*

barbarian /baːr'beriən ‖baː'beəriən/ *n* bárbaro, -ra *m,f*

barbaric /baːr'bærɪk ‖baː'bærɪk/ *adj* (primitive) primitivo; (brutal) brutal

barbarity /baːr'bærəti ‖baː'bærəti/ *n* (*pl* **-ties**) brutalidad *f*

barbecue /'baːrbɪkjuː ‖'baːbɪkjuː/ *n* **1** (grid and fireplace) barbacoa *f*, parrilla *f*, asador *m* (AmL) **2** (social occasion) barbacoa *f*, parrillada *f*, asado *m* (AmL)

barbed wire /baːrbd ‖baːbd/ *n* alambre *m* de púas *or* (Esp tb) de espino

barber /'baːrbər ‖'baːbə(r)/ *n* peluquero *m*, barbero *m* (ant); **the** ~**('s)** la peluquería

barbwire /'baːrb'waɪr ‖,baːb'waɪə(r)/ *n* (AmE)
▶ BARBED WIRE

bar code *n* código *m* de barras

bare¹ /ber ‖beə(r)/ *adj* **barer** /'berər ‖'beərə(r)/, **barest** /'berəst ‖'beərɪst/ (uncovered) ⟨*blade/flesh/walls*⟩ desnudo; ⟨*head*⟩ descubierto; ⟨*foot*⟩ descalzo; ⟨*floorboards*⟩ sin alfombrar; ⟨*tree*⟩ pelado; ⟨*wire*⟩ pelado *or* (Esp) desnudo; ⟨*room*⟩ con pocos muebles; **the** ~ **essentials** lo estrictamente esencial; **he gave me the** ~ **facts** se ciñó a los hechos; **to lay sth** ~ poner* *or* dejar algo al descubierto

bare² *vt*: **to** ~ **one's head** descubrirse* (la cabeza); **the dog** ~**d its teeth** el perro enseñó *or* mostró los dientes

bareback /'berbæk ‖'beəbæk/ *adv* ⟨*ride*⟩ a pelo

barefoot¹ /'berfʊt ‖'beəfʊt/ *adj* descalzo

barefoot² *adv*: **she ran** ~ corrió descalza

barely /'berli ‖'beəli/ *adv* (hardly) apenas

bargain¹ /'baːrgən ‖'baːgən/ *n* **1** (cheap purchase) ganga *f*; (*before¹ n*) ⟨*price*⟩ de ganga *or* oferta **2** (deal, agreement) trato *m*, acuerdo *m*; **to strike a** ~ llegar a un acuerdo; **into** *o* (AmE also) **in the** ~ encima, por si fuera poco

bargain² *vi* **(a)** (haggle) regatear **(b)** (negotiate) negociar

■ **bargain for** [*v + prep + o*]: **we hadn't** ~**ed for such an eventuality** no habíamos tenido en cuenta esa posibilidad; **I got more than I had** ~**ed for** no me esperaba algo así

bargaining /'baːrgənɪŋ ‖'baːgənɪŋ/ *n* **(a)** (haggling) regateo *m* **(b)** (negotiating) negociaciones *fpl*; (*before n*) ⟨*strategy/position*⟩ negociador

barge¹ /baːrdʒ ‖baːdʒ/ *n* barcaza *f*

barge² *vi* (+ *adv compl*): **he** ~**d past (me)** me dio un empujón para pasar; **he always** ~**s in when we're trying to talk** siempre se entromete cuando queremos hablar

baritone /'bærətəʊn ‖'bærɪtəʊn/ *n* barítono *m*

bark¹ /baːrk ‖baːk/ *n* **1** (on tree) corteza *f* **2** (of dog) ladrido *m*

bark² *vi* ladrar;
■ ~ *vt* (shout) espetar; **to** ~ (**out**) **an order** gritar una orden

barkeep /'baːrkiːp ‖'baːkiːp/, **barkeeper** /-,kiːpər ‖-,kiːpə(r)/ *n* (AmE) (male) barman *m*, camarero *m* (Esp, Ven); (female) mesera *f or* (Esp, Ven) camarera *f or* (AmS) moza *f*

barley /'baːrli ‖'baːli/ *n* cebada *f*

bar: ~**maid** *n* mesera *f or* (Esp, Ven) camarera *f or* (AmS) moza *f*; ~**man** /'baːrmən ‖'baːmən/ *n* (*pl* **-men** /-mən/) (BrE) barman *m*, camarero *m* (Esp, Ven)

barn /baːrn ‖baːn/ *n* **(a)** (for crops) granero *m*; (for livestock) establo *m* **(b)** (for vehicles) (AmE) cochera *f*

barometer /bə'raːmətər ‖bə'rɒmɪtə(r)/ *n* barómetro *m*

baron /'bærən/ *n* **(a)** (nobleman) barón *m* **(b)** (magnate) magnate *m*

baroness /'bærə'nes, 'bærənəs/ *n* baronesa *f*

barracks /'bærəks/ *n* (*pl* ~) (+ *sing or pl vb*) cuartel *m*

barrage /bə'raːʒ ‖'bæraːʒ/ *n* (Mil) (action) descarga *f*; (fire) cortina *f* de fuego

barrel /'bærəl/ *n* **1** (container) barril *m*, tonel *m* **2** (of handgun) cañón *m*; (of cannon) tubo *m*

barren /'bærən/ *adj* **-er**, **-est** ⟨*land/soil*⟩ estéril; ⟨*tree/plant/animal*⟩ (*no comp*) estéril; ⟨*woman*⟩ (dated or liter) infecunda

barrette /baː'ret ‖bə'ret/ *n* (AmE) pasador *m*, broche *m* (Méx, Ur), hebilla *f* (Arg)

barricade¹ /'bærəkeɪd ‖,bærɪ'keɪd/ *n* barricada *f*

barricade² *vt* cerrar* con barricadas; **they** ~**d themselves into the building** se atrincheraron en el edificio

barrier /'bæriər ‖'bæriə(r)/ *n* barrera *f*; **language** ~ barrera idiomática

Barrier Reef *n* **the Great** ~ ~ el Gran Arrecife Coralino, la Gran Barrera Coral

barrister /'bærəstər ‖'bærɪstə(r)/ *n* (BrE) abogado, -da *m,f* (*habilitado para alegar ante un tribunal superior*)

barrow ⋯⋰ bawdy ⋯

505

barrow /'bærəʊ/ n (wheel∼) carretilla f

bar: ∼stool n taburete m; **∼tender** n (esp AmE) (male) barman m, camarero m (Esp, Ven); (female) mesera f or (Esp, Ven) camarera f or (AmS) moza f

barter /'bɑːrtər ‖ 'bɑːtə(r)/ vt cambiar, trocar*
■ ∼ vi hacer* trueques

base¹ /beɪs/ n [1] (of column, wall) base f; (of mountain, tree) pie m; (of spine, skull) base f; (of lamp) pie m [2] (foundation, basis) base f [3] (of patrol, for excursion) base f; (of organization) sede f [4] (in baseball) base f

base² vt [1] (found) to ∼ sth ON sth ‹opinion/conclusion› basar algo EN algo; **the movie is ∼d on a real event** la película se basa en una historia real [2] (locate) basar; **the company is ∼d in Madrid** la compañía tiene su base en Madrid

base³ adj **baser, basest** ‹conduct/motive› abyecto

baseball /'beɪsbɔːl/ n (a) (game) béisbol m; (before n) ∼ **bat** bate m de béisbol (b) (ball) pelota f de béisbol

basement /'beɪsmənt/ n sótano m

base pay n (AmE) sueldo m base or básico

bases¹ /'beɪsiːz/ pl of BASIS

bases² /'beɪsəz ‖ 'beɪsɪz/ pl of BASE¹

bash¹ /bæʃ/ n (colloq) [1] (blow) golpe m, madrazo m (Méx fam) [2] (party) juerga f (fam)

bash² vt (colloq) pegarle* a

bashful /'bæʃfəl/ adj tímido, penoso (AmL exc CS)

basic /'beɪsɪk/ adj [1] (fundamental) fundamental [2] (simple, rudimentary) ‹knowledge/need› básico; ‹hotel/food› sencillo [3] (Econ) ‹pay› básico

basically /'beɪsɪkli/ adv fundamentalmente

basics /'beɪsɪks/ pl n lo básico

basil /'beɪzəl ‖ 'bæzəl/ n albahaca f

basin /'beɪsn/ n (a) (for liquid, food) cuenco m, bol m, tazón m (b) (hand ∼) (BrE) lavamanos m, lavabo m, pileta f (RPl) (c) (Geog, Geol) cuenca f

basis /'beɪsəs ‖ 'beɪsɪs/ n (pl **bases** /'beɪsiːz/) [1] (foundation, grounds) base f [2] (system, level) (no pl): **employed on a daily ∼** contratado por día; **on a regional ∼** a nivel regional

bask /bæsk ‖ bɑːsk/ vi: **to ∼ in the sun** disfrutar (del calor) del sol; **she ∼ed in their adulation** se deleitaba or se regodeaba con su adulación

basket /'bæskət ‖ 'bɑːskɪt/ n [1] (for shopping) canasta f (esp AmL), cesta f (esp Esp) [2] (in basketball) (a) (goal) canasta f, cesto m (b) (score) canasta f, enceste m

basketball /'bæskətbɔːl ‖ 'bɑːskɪtbɔːl/ n (a) (game) baloncesto m, básquetbol m (AmL) (b) (ball) pelota f de básquetbol or (Esp) balón m de baloncesto

Basque¹ /bæsk ‖ bæsk, bɑːsk/ adj vasco; **the ∼ Country** el País Vasco, Euskadi m

Basque² n (a) (person) vasco, -ca m,f (b) (language) euskera m, vasco m, vascuence m

bass¹ n /beɪs/ (pl ∼**es**) (Mus) (a) (voice, singer) bajo m (b) (double bass or bass guitar) (contra)bajo m (c) (Audio) graves mpl

bass² adj ‹voice› de bajo

bass clef clave f de fa

bassoon /bə'suːn/ n fagot m

bastard /'bæstərd ‖ 'bɑːstəd/ n [1] (illegitimate child) bastardo, -da m,f [2] (colloq or vulg) cabrón m (fam o vulg), hijo m de puta (vulg)

baste /beɪst/ vt (a) (Culin) rociar con su jugo o con mantequilla etc durante la cocción (b) (sew loosely) hilvanar

bastion /'bæstʃən ‖ 'bæstiən/ n (a) (Archit) bastión m (b) (stronghold) baluarte m, bastión m

bat¹ /bæt/ n [1] (in baseball, cricket) bate m; (in table tennis) (BrE) paleta f, raqueta f [2] (Zool) murciélago m

bat² vi **-tt-** (Sport) batear

batch /bætʃ/ n (of cakes) hornada f; (of goods) (Busn) lote m; (of trainees, candidates) grupo m; (of mail, paperwork) pila f; (Comput) lote m

bated /'beɪtəd ‖ 'beɪtɪd/ adj: **with ∼ breath** con ansiedad

bath¹ /bæθ ‖ bɑːθ/ n (pl **baths** /bæðz ‖ bɑːðz/) [1] (a) (wash) baño m; **to have o** (AmE also) **take a ∼** bañarse, darse* un baño (b) (tub) bañera f, tina f (AmL) [2] **baths** pl (swimming ∼s) (BrE) piscina f, alberca f (Méx), pileta f (RPl)

bath² (BrE) vt bañar

bathe /beɪð/ vt (wash) ‹wound/eyes› lavar; ‹baby/dog› (AmE) bañar
■ ∼ vi (a) (take bath) (AmE) bañarse (b) (go swimming) (BrE) bañarse

bathing suit, (BrE also) **bathing costume** /'beɪðɪŋ/ n traje m de baño, bañador m (Esp), malla f (de baño) (RPl), vestido m de baño (Col)

bath: ∼mat n alfombrilla f or tapete m or (Chi) piso m de baño; **∼robe** n bata f de baño, albornoz m (Esp); **∼room** n (room with bath) (cuarto m de) baño m (b) (toilet) (esp AmE) baño m, servicio m; **∼tub** n bañera f, tina f (AmL), bañadera f (Arg)

baton /bə'tɑːn ‖ 'bætən/ n (a) (Mus) batuta f (b) (truncheon) (BrE) bastón m (c) (in relay race) testigo m

battalion /bə'tæljən/ n batallón m

batter¹ /'bætər ‖ 'bætə(r)/ vt [1] (beat) ‹victim/opponent› apalear; ‹child/wife› maltratar [2] (cover with batter) rebozar*

batter² n [1] (for fried fish, etc) rebozado m; (for pancakes) masa f; (for cake) (AmE) masa f [2] (in baseball) bateador, -dora m,f

battered /'bætərd ‖ 'bætəd/ adj ‹car› abollado; ‹hat/suitcase› estropeado; ‹reputation/image› maltrecho; ‹baby/wife› maltratado

battering ram /'bætərɪŋ/ n ariete m

battery /'bætəri/ n (pl **-ries**) [1] (in radio, lamp) pila f; (in car, motorcycle) batería f [2] (artillery) batería f [3] (Agr) batería f ‹conjunto de jaulas instaladas para la explotación avícola intensiva›; (before n) ‹eggs/hens› de criadero, de batería; ∼ **farming** cría f intensiva

battle¹ /'bætl/ n batalla f; **to fight a losing ∼** luchar por una causa perdida

battle² vi luchar

battle: ∼field n campo m de batalla; **∼ground** n campo m de batalla

battlements /'bætlmənts/ pl n almenas fpl

battleship /'bætlʃɪp/ n acorazado m

baud /bɔːd/ n (Comput) baudio m

bawdy /'bɔːdi/ adj **-dier, -diest** subido de tono

bawl /bɔːl/ vi (a) (shout) vociferar (b) (cry noisily) berrear

bay¹ /beɪ/ n 1 (Geog) bahía f 2 (a) (loading ∼) muelle m or plataforma f de carga (b) (area, recess) espacio m 3: **at ∼** acorralado; **to keep o hold sth/sb at ∼** mantener* algo/a algn a raya 4 **∼ (tree)** laurel m

bay² vi «hounds» aullar*

bayleaf /'beɪliːf/ n (pl **-leaves**) hoja f de laurel

bayonet /'beɪənət/ n bayoneta f

bay window n ventana f en saliente

bazaar /bə'zɑːr ‖ bə'zɑː(r)/ n (a) (oriental market) bazar m (b) (charity sale) venta f benéfica

BBC n (= **British Broadcasting Corporation**) the ∼ la BBC

BC (= **before Christ**) antes de Cristo; (written form) aC, a. de C., a. de J.C.

be /biː, weak form bi/ (pres **am, are, is**; past **was, were**; past p **been**) vi [See notes at SER and ESTAR]
I 1 (followed by an adjective): **she's French** es francesa; **he's worried** está preocupado; **how are you?** ¿cómo estás?; **I'm much better** estoy or me encuentro mucho mejor; **she's pregnant/tired/ill** está embarazada/cansada/enferma; **I'm cold/hot/hungry/thirsty** tengo frío/calor/hambre/sed; **he's dead** está muerto; **he's blind** es or (Esp tb) está ciego; **he's short** es bajo; **Tony is married/divorced** Tony está or (esp AmL) es casado/divorciado; **these shoes are new** estos zapatos son nuevos; **she was very rude to me** estuvo or fue muy grosera conmigo; **she's very rude** es muy grosera; **∼ good** sé bueno
2 (followed by a noun) ser*; **if I were you, I'd stay** yo que tú me quedaría
3 (a) (talking about age) tener*; **how old are you?** ¿cuántos años tienes?; **I'm 31** tengo 31 años; **Paul was four last Monday** Paul cumplió cuatro años el lunes pasado; **our house is over 100 years old** nuestra casa tiene más de 100 años (b) (giving cost, measurement, weight): **they are $15 each** cuestan or valen 15 dólares cada una; **two plus two is four** dos más dos son cuatro; **how tall is he?** ¿cuánto mide?; **Jim's over six feet tall** Jim mide más de seis pies
II 1 (a) (exist, live): **to let sth/sb ∼** dejar tranquilo algo/a algn (b) (in expressions of time): **I'm drying my hair, I won't ∼ long** me estoy secando el pelo, enseguida estoy; **the party is tomorrow** la fiesta es mañana
2 (be situated, present) estar*; **where is the library?** ¿dónde está la biblioteca?
3 (only in perfect tenses) (visit) estar*; **I've never been to India** nunca he estado en la India
■ ∼ v impers 1 (a) (talking about physical conditions, circumstances): **it's cold/hot** hace frío/calor; **it's so noisy in here!** ¡qué ruido hay aquí!; (b) (in expressions of time) ser*; **it's three o'clock** son las tres; **it's Wednesday today** hoy es miércoles (c) (talking about distance) estar*; **it's 500 miles from here to Detroit** Detroit queda a 500 millas de aquí

2 (introducing person, object) ser*; **it's me/Daniel** soy yo/es Daniel
■ ∼ v aux 1 **to ∼ -ING** estar* + GER; **I'm working** estoy trabajando; **how long have you been waiting?** ¿cuánto (tiempo) hace que esperas?; **when are you seeing her?** ¿cuándo la vas a ver?
2 (in the passive voice) ser* [The passive voice, however, is less common in Spanish than it is in English] **it was built in 1903** fue construido en 1903, se construyó en 1903, lo construyeron en 1903; **it is known that …** se sabe que …
3 **to ∼ to + INF** (a) (with future reference): **the dessert is (still) to come** todavía falta el postre (b) (expressing possibility): **what are we to do?** ¿qué podemos hacer?; **it was nowhere to ∼ found** no se lo pudo encontrar por ninguna parte
4 (a) (in tag questions): **she's right, isn't she?** tiene razón, ¿no? or ¿verdad? (b) (in elliptical uses): **are you disappointed? — yes, I am/no, I'm not** ¿estás desilusionado? — sí (, lo estoy)/no (, no lo estoy); **she was told the news, and so was he/but I wasn't** a ella le dieron la noticia, y también a él/pero a mí no

beach /biːtʃ/ n playa f

beacon /'biːkən/ n (light) faro m; (fire) almenara f

bead /biːd/ n cuenta f, abalorio m; (drop) gota f; **∼s of sweat** gotas fpl de sudor

beady /'biːdi/ adj: **∼ eyes** ojos redondos y brillantes

beak /biːk/ n pico m

beaker /'biːkər ‖ 'biːkə(r)/ n (a) (Chem) vaso m de precipitados (b) (cup) (BrE) taza f (gen alta y sin asa)

be-all and end-all /'biːɔːlən'endɔːl/ n: **it is the ∼ ∼ ∼ of his life** es su razón de ser; **work isn't the ∼ ∼ ∼ ∼** el trabajo no lo es todo

beam¹ /biːm/ n 1 (in building) viga f, (in ship) bao m 2 (ray) rayo m; (broad) haz m de luz; **keep the headlights on high o** (BrE) **full o main ∼** (Auto) deja (las luces) largas or (Chi) altas

beam² vi (shine) brillar (b) (smile) sonreír* (abiertamente)
■ ∼ vt (broadcast) transmitir

bean /biːn/ n (a) (fresh, in pod) ▶ GREEN BEAN (b) (dried) frijol m or (Esp) alubia f or judía f or (CS) poroto m or (Ven) caraota f; **to be full of ∼s** (colloq) estar* lleno de vida

bean: ∼ curd n tofu m, queso m de soya (AmL) or (Esp) soja; **∼shoot, ∼ sprout** n frijol m germinado or (Esp) judía f germinada or (CS) poroto m germinado; (of soy bean) brote m or germinado m de soya (AmL) or (Esp) soja

bear¹ /ber ‖ beə(r)/ (past **bore**; past p **borne**) vt 1 (a) (support) ⟨weight⟩ aguantar; ⟨cost⟩ correr con; ⟨responsibility⟩ cargar* con (b) (endure) ⟨pain/uncertainty⟩ soportar (c) (put up with, stand) (colloq) (with can) ⟨person⟩ aguantar (fam); ⟨noise⟩ aguantar (d) (stand up to): **her argument doesn't ∼ close scrutiny** su razonamiento no resiste un análisis cuidadoso; **it doesn't ∼ thinking about** da miedo solo de pensarlo

---

AmC	América Central	Arg	Argentina	Cu	Cuba	Per	Perú
AmL	América Latina	Bol	Bolivia	Ec	Ecuador	RPI	Río de la Plata
AmS	América del Sur	Chi	Chile	Esp	España	Ur	Uruguay
Andes	Región andina	CS	Cono Sur	Méx	México	Ven	Venezuela

2 (a) (carry) (liter) ⟨*banner/coffin*⟩ llevar, portar (liter) (b) (harbor): **she's not one to ～ a grudge** no es rencorosa; **to ～ sb malice** guardarle rencor a algn

3 (have, show) ⟨*title/signature*⟩ llevar; ⟨*scars*⟩ tener*; ⟨*resemblance*⟩ tener*

4 (a) (produce) ⟨*fruit/crop*⟩ dar*; ⟨*interest*⟩ devengar* (b) (give birth to) ⟨*child*⟩ dar* a luz; *see also* BORN¹

■ ～ *vi* (turn) torcer*; ～ **left** tuerza a la izquierda

■ **bear out** [*v + o + adv, v + adv + o*] ⟨*theory*⟩ confirmar

■ **bear up** [*v + adv*]: **she bore up well under the strain** sobrellevó muy bien la situación

■ **bear with** [*v + prep + o*] ⟨*person/mood*⟩ tener* paciencia con; **if you'll just ～ with me for a moment, …** (asking to wait) si tienen la bondad de esperar un momento, …; (asking for patience) si puedo poner a prueba su paciencia, …

bear² *n* oso, osa *m,f*

bearable /'berəbəl ‖'beərəbəl/ *adj* soportable

beard /bɪrd ‖bɪəd/ *n* barba *f*

bearded /'bɪrdəd ‖'bɪədɪd/ *adj* con *or* de barba

bearer /'berər ‖'beərə(r)/ *n* (a) (of news) portador, -dora *m,f* (b) (carrier, porter) portador, -dora *m,f*, porteador, -dora *m,f* (c) (holder — of check) portador, -dora *m,f*; (— of passport) titular *mf*

bearing /'berɪŋ ‖'beərɪŋ/ *n* **1** (a) (Aviat, Naut) demora *f*; **to get/lose one's ～s** orientarse/desorientarse (b) (relevance): **that has no ～ on the subject** eso no tiene ninguna relación con el tema **2** (way of standing) porte *m*

beast /biːst/ *n* bestia *f*

beat¹ /biːt/ (*past* **beat**; *past p* **beaten** /'biːtn̩/) *vt* **1** (a) (hit) golpear*; ⟨*carpet*⟩ sacudir*; ⟨*wings*⟩ batir*; ⟨*child/wife*⟩ maltratar (b) (hammer) ⟨*metal*⟩ batir* (c) (Culin) batir

2 ⟨*opponent*⟩ ganarle a; ⟨*record*⟩ batir*; **our prices can't be ～en** nuestros precios son imbatibles **3** (arrive before, anticipate): **I ～ him to the telephone** llegué antes que él al teléfono; **to ～ sb to it** adelantársele a algn

3 (Mus) ⟨*time*⟩ marcar*

■ ～ *vi* (strike): **he could hear them ～ing on the door** los oía golpear la puerta; **the waves were ～ing against the cliff** las olas golpeaban contra el acantilado (b) (pulsate) «*heart*» latir, palpitar; «*drum*» redoblar; «*wings*» batir

■ **beat down** **1** [*v + o + adv, v + adv + o*] ⟨*door*⟩ tirar abajo; ⟨*crop*⟩ aplastar

2 [*v + adv*] «*sun*» caer* de lleno; «*rain*» llover* con fuerza

■ **beat up** [*v + o + adv, v + adv + o*] (colloq) darle* una paliza a (fam)

■ **beat up on** [*v + adv + prep + o*] (AmE colloq) darle* una paliza a

beat² *n* **1** (of heart) latido *m*; (of drum) golpe *m* **2** (Mus) (rhythmic accent) tiempo *m*; (rhythm) ritmo *m* **3** (of policeman) ronda *f*

beat³ *adj* (colloq) (*pred*): **to be (dead) ～** estar* reventado (fam)

beaten /'biːtn̩/ *past p of* BEAT¹

beating /'biːtɪŋ/ *n* (a) (thrashing) paliza *f* (b) (defeat) paliza *f* (fam) (c) (surpassing): **her time will take some ～** va a ser difícil superar su marca

beautiful /'bjuːtəfəl ‖'bjuːtɪfl/ *adj* (a) (in

---

appearance) precioso, hermoso, bello (liter) (b) (very good) (colloq) ⟨*meal/weather*⟩ estupendo (c) (kind) (esp AmE) ⟨*person*⟩ encantador

beautifully /'bjuːtəfli ‖'bjuːtɪfəli/ *adv* (excellently, very well) ⟨*sing/dance*⟩ maravillosamente (bien); **she was ～ dressed** iba elegantísima

beauty /'bjuːti/ *n* (*pl* **-ties**) **1** (quality) belleza *f*, hermosura *f*; (*before n*) ～ **contest** *o* (esp AmE) **pageant** concurso *m* de belleza; ～ **queen** reina *f* de la belleza **2** (woman) belleza *f*

beauty: ～ **salon** *n* salón *m* de belleza; ～ **shop** *n* (AmE) salón *m* de belleza; ～ **spot** *n* **1** (place) lugar *m* pintoresco; **2** (on face) lunar *m*

beaver /'biːvər ‖'biːvə(r)/ *n* castor *m*

became /bɪ'keɪm/ *past of* BECOME

because /bə'kɔːz, bɪ'kɒz/ *conj* **1** porque **2** **because of** (*as prep*) por, a *or* por causa de (frml)

beck /bek/ *n*: **to be at sb's ～ and call** estar* siempre a entera disposición de algn

beckon /'bekn̩/ *vt*: **to ～ sb over** hacerle* señas a algn para que se acerque

■ ～ *vi* hacer* una seña; **she ～ed to him to follow** le hizo señas para que la siguiera

become /bɪ'kʌm/ (*past* **became**; *past p* **become**) *vi*: **to ～ famous** hacerse* famoso; **to ～ accustomed to sth** acostumbrarse a algo; **she soon became bored** pronto se aburrió; **the heat became unbearable** el calor se hizo insoportable; **they became friends** se hicieron amigos

■ ～ *vt* (a) (befit) (frml) (*often neg*) ser* apropiado para (b) (suit) favorecer*

■ **become of** (*usu interrog*) ser* de; **what's to ～ of me?** ¿qué va a ser de mí?

becoming /bɪ'kʌmɪŋ/ *adj* (a) (fitting) (frml) apropiado (b) ⟨*outfit/hat*⟩ favorecedor, sentador (AmE)

bed /bed/ *n* **1** (for sleeping) cama *f*; **to make the ～** hacer* *or* (AmE tb) tender* la cama; **to get into/out of ～** acostarse*/levantarse; **to go to ～** acostarse*; **he's in ～ with measles** está en cama con sarampión; **we put the children to ～ early** acostamos a los niños temprano **2** (for plants) arriate *m*, cantero *m* (RPl) **3** (of river) lecho *m*, cauce *m*; (of sea) fondo *m* **4** (base, support) base *f*

bed: ～ **and breakfast** /'bednˌbrekfəst/ *n* (a) (service): **they do ～ and breakfast** dan alojamiento y desayuno (b) (establishment) ≈ pensión *f*; ～**clothes** *pl n* ropa *f* de cama

bedding /'bedɪŋ/ *n* (a) ► BEDCLOTHES (b) (for animals) cama *f*

bedlam /'bedləm/ *n* (colloq): **there was ～ when he announced the news** se armó la de San Quintín cuando anunció la noticia (fam)

bedpan /'bedpæn/ *n* (Med) cuña *f*

bedraggled /bɪ'drægəld/ *adj* desaliñado; ⟨*hair*⟩ despeinado

bed: ～**ridden** *adj* postrado en cama; ～**room** *n* dormitorio *m*, cuarto *m*, pieza *f* (esp AmL), recámara *f* (esp Méx); ～**side** *n*: **they sat at his ～side throughout the night** pasaron toda la noche junto a su cabecera; (*before n*) ～**side table** mesita *f* de noche, velador *m* (AmS), mesa *f* de luz (RPl); ～**sit**, ～**sitter** /'bed.sɪtər ‖,bed'sɪtə(r)/ *n* (BrE colloq) habitación *f* amueblada (*cuyo alquiler suele incluir el uso de baño y cocina comunes*); ～**sore** ⋯⟶

n escara *f*, úlcera *f* de decúbito (frml) (*llaga que se produce por estar mucho tiempo en cama*); **~spread** *n* cubrecama *m*, colcha *f*; **~time** *n* hora *f* de acostarse

bee /biː/ *n* **1** (Zool) abeja *f* **2** (social gathering) (esp AmE) círculo *m*

beech /biːtʃ/ *n* ~ **(tree)** haya *f*

beef /biːf/ *n* carne *f* de vaca *or* (AmC, Méx) de res, ternera *f* (Esp)

beefburger /'biːfˌbɜːrɡər ‖ 'biːfˌbɜːɡə(r)/ *n* (esp BrE) hamburguesa *f*

bee: **~hive** *n* colmena *f*; **~line** *n*: **to make a ~line for sb/sth** (colloq) irse* derechito a algn/ algo (fam)

been /bɪn ‖ biːn/ **(a)** *past p of* BE **(b)** *past p of* GO¹ *vi* I 2

beep¹ /biːp/ *n* (colloq) pitido *m*

beep² *vt/i* (colloq) pitar

beer /bɪr ‖ bɪə(r)/ *n* cerveza *f*

beer: ~ **garden** *n*: *jardín o patio abierto de un bar*; ~ **mat** *n* posavasos *m* (*de cartón*)

beeswax /'biːzwæks/ *n* cera *f* de abeja

beet /biːt/ *n* (*pl* **~s**) (AmE) remolacha *f or* (Méx) betabel *m or* (Chi) betarraga *f*

beetle /'biːtl/ *n* escarabajo *m*

beetroot /'biːtruːt/ *n* (BrE) ▶ BEET

befall /bɪ'fɔːl/ *vt* (*past* **befell** /bɪ'fel/ *past p* **befallen** /bɪ'fɔːlən/) (liter) sucederle *or* ocurrirle a

before¹ /bɪ'fɔːr ‖ bɪ'fɔː(r)/ *prep* **1** (preceding in time) antes de; ~ **long** dentro de poco; ~ **going in** antes de entrar **2** **(a)** (in front of) delante de, ante (frml) **(b)** (in rank, priority): **she puts her work ~ her family** antepone el trabajo a su familia

before² *conj* **(a)** (earlier than) antes de que (+ *subj*), antes de (+ *inf*) **(b)** (rather than) antes que

before³ *adv* (preceding) antes; **the day ~** el día anterior; **have you been to Canada ~?** ¿ya has estado en el Canadá?

beforehand /bɪ'fɔːrhænd ‖ bɪ'fɔːhænd/ *adv* (earlier) antes; (in advance) de antemano

befriend /bɪ'frend/ *vt* hacerse* amigo de

beg /beɡ/ **-gg-** *vt* **1** (*money/food*) pedir*, mendigar* **2** (frml) **(a)** (entreat) ⟨*person*⟩ suplicarle* a, rogarle* a **(b)** (ask for) ⟨*forgiveness*⟩ suplicar*, rogar*

■ ~ *vi* «*beggar*» pedir*, mendigar*; **to ~ for mercy** pedir* *or* suplicar* clemencia

began /bɪ'ɡæn/ *past of* BEGIN

beget /bɪ'ɡet/ *vt* (*pres p* **begetting**; *past* **begot** *or* (arch) **begat** /bɪ'ɡæt/; *past p* **begotten**) (liter) engendrar

beggar /'beɡər ‖ 'beɡə(r)/ *n* mendigo, -ga *m,f*

begin /bɪ'ɡɪn/ (*pres p* **beginning**; *past* **began**; *past p* **begun**) *vt* empezar*, comenzar*; **to ~ -ING/to + INF** empezar* *or* comenzar* A + INF

■ ~ *vi* empezar*, comenzar*; «*custom*» originarse; **to ~ with** para empezar

beginner /bɪ'ɡɪnər ‖ bɪ'ɡɪnə(r)/ *n* principiante *mf*

beginning /bɪ'ɡɪnɪŋ/ *n* **(a)** (in time, place) principio *m*; **at the ~ of the year/of June** a principios del año/de junio; **I'll start again from the ~** volveré a empezar desde el principio; **from**

~ **to end** de principio a fin **(b)** (origin, early stage) (*often pl*) comienzo *m* **(c)** (start, debut) (*no pl*) comienzo *m*

begot /bɪ'ɡɑːt ‖ bɪ'ɡɒt/ *past of* BEGET

begotten /bɪ'ɡɑːtn ‖ bɪ'ɡɒtn/ *past p of* BEGET

begrudge /bɪ'ɡrʌdʒ/ *vt*: **I ~ paying so much** me da rabia pagar tanto; **I don't ~ you your success** no te envidio el éxito que tienes

beguile /bɪ'ɡaɪl/ *vt* (charm) cautivar, seducir*

beguiling /bɪ'ɡaɪlɪŋ/ *adj* cautivador, seductor

begun /bɪ'ɡʌn/ *past p of* BEGIN

behalf /bɪ'hæf ‖ bɪ'hɑːf/ *n*: **on ~ of sb, on ~ of sb, on** *o* (AmE also) **in sb's ~ 1** (as representative of): **I'd like to thank you on ~ of the team** quisiera darle las gracias en nombre de *or* de parte de todo el equipo; **he accepted the award on her ~** aceptó el premio en su nombre **2** (in the interest of): **he argued on her ~ that ...** alegó en su defensa *or* en su favor que ...

behave /bɪ'heɪv/ *vi* **(a)** (act) comportarse; (esp of children) portarse **(b)** (be good) «*child/animal*» portarse bien, comportarse

■ *v refl* **to ~ oneself** portarse bien, comportarse

behavior, (BrE**) behaviour** /bɪ'heɪvjər ‖ bɪ'heɪvjə(r)/ *n* conducta *f*, comportamiento *m*

behead /bɪ'hed/ *vt* decapitar

beheld /bɪ'held/ *past and past p of* BEHOLD

behind¹ /bɪ'haɪnd/ *prep* **1** **(a)** (to the rear of) detrás de, atrás de ~; **we're ten years ~ the Japanese in microelectronics** en microelectrónica llevamos un retraso de diez años respecto a los japoneses **(b)** (on the other side of) detrás de, atrás de (AmL) **2** (responsible for) detrás de; **the motives ~ his decision** los motivos que lo llevaron a esa decisión **3** (in time): **all that is ~ us now** todo eso ha quedado atrás; **I'm ~ schedule** voy retrasado (con el trabajo *or* los preparativos *etc*)

behind² *adv* **(a)** (to the rear, following): **he ran along ~** iba corriendo detrás *or* (AmL tb) atrás; **I was attacked from ~** me atacaron por la espalda; **keep an eye on the car ~** no pierdas de vista al coche de atrás **(b)** (in race, competition): **England were two goals ~** Inglaterra iba perdiendo por dos goles **(c)** (in arrears): **I'm ~ with my work/ payments** estoy atrasada con el trabajo/en los pagos

behind³ *n* (colloq & euph) trasero *m* (fam)

behold /bɪ'həʊld/ (*past and past p* **beheld**) *vt* (liter) contemplar (liter)

beige /beɪʒ/ *adj* beige *adj inv*, beis *adj inv* (Esp)

Beijing /'beɪ'dʒɪŋ/ *n* Beijing *m*

being /'biːɪŋ/ *n* ser *m*

Belarus /'belə'ruːs/ *n* Bielorrusia *f*

belated /bɪ'leɪtəd ‖ bɪ'leɪtɪd/ *adj* tardío

belch /beltʃ/ *vi/t* **(a)** «*person*» eructar; **flames ~ed from the cannon** la boca del cañón escupía llamas

Belgian¹ /'beldʒən/ *adj* belga

Belgian² *n* belga *mf*

Belgium /'beldʒəm/ *n* Bélgica *f*

belie /bɪ'laɪ/ *vt* **belies, belying, belied** **(a)** (disguise) no dejar traslucir **(b)** (show to be false): **this ~s the notion that ...** esto demuestra que no es cierto que ...

belief /bə'li:f ‖bɪ'li:f/ *n* **(a)** (conviction, opinion) creencia *f* **(b)** (confidence) ~ **IN** *sb/sth* confianza *f or* fe *f* EN algn/algo **(c)** (Relig) fe *f*

believable /bə'li:vəbəl ‖bɪ'li:vəbəl/ *adj* ⟨story/ account⟩ verosímil

believe /bə'li:v ‖bɪ'li:v/ *vt* ⟨statement/story⟩ creer*; ⟨person⟩ creerle* a; **I don't ~ it!** ¡no puedo creerlo!; **to make ~ (that)** hacer* de cuenta que **(b)** (think) creer*
■ ~ *vi* creer*; **to ~ IN** *sth/sb* creer* EN algo/algn

believer /bə'li:vər ‖bɪ'li:və(r)/ *n* creyente *mf*

belittle /bɪ'lɪtl/ *vt* ⟨achievements⟩ menospreciar; ⟨person⟩ denigrar

bell /bel/ *n* (of church, clock) campana *f*; (on cat, toy) cascabel *m*; (on door, bicycle) timbre *m*; (of telephone, timer) timbre *m*; **to ring a ~:** the name rings a ~ me suena el nombre; (*before n*) ~ **tower** campanario *m*

belligerent /bə'lɪdʒərənt/ *adj* agresivo

bellow /'beləʊ/ *vi* bramar; (shout) gritar

bellows /'beləʊz/ *n* (*pl* ~) (for fire) fuelle *m*

bell pepper *n* (AmE) ▶ CAPSICUM

belly /'beli/ *n* (*pl* **-lies**) **(a)** (of person) vientre *m*, barriga *f* (fam); (of animal) panza *f*, vientre *m*; (*before n*) ~ **button** (colloq) ombligo *m*; **to do a ~ flop** darse* un planchazo *or* (Andes) un guatazo (fam)

belong /bɪ'lɔːŋ ‖bɪ'lɒŋ/ *vi* **1 (a)** (be property) **to ~ TO** *sb* ser* DE algn, pertenecerle* A algn **(b)** (be member) **to ~ TO** *sth* ⟨to a club⟩ ser* socio DE algo; ⟨to a union/political party⟩ estar* afiliado A algo **2** (have as usual place) ir*; **put them back where they ~** vuélvelos a poner en su lugar

belongings /bɪ'lɔːŋɪŋz ‖bɪ'lɒŋɪŋz/ *pl n* pertenencias *fpl*

beloved /bɪ'lʌvəd ‖bɪ'lʌvɪd/ *adj* (*before n*) querido

below[1] /bɪ'ləʊ/ *prep* **1** (under) debajo de, abajo de (AmL) **2** (inferior, junior to) por debajo de **3** (less than) por debajo de; ~ **zero** bajo cero

below[2] *adv* **1** (underneath) abajo; **put it on the shelf ~** ponlo en el estante de abajo **2** (in text) más abajo **3** (of temperature): **20 (degrees)** ~ 20 (grados) bajo cero

belt[1] /belt/ *n* **1** (Clothing) cinturón *m* **2** (Mech Eng) correa *f*

belt[2] *vt* (colloq) darle* una paliza a

beltway /'beltweɪ/ *n* (AmE) carretera *f* de circunvalación

bemoan /bɪ'məʊn/ *vt* lamentarse de

bemused /bɪ'mju:zd/ *adj* de desconcierto

bench /bentʃ/ *n* **1 (a)** (seat) banco *m* **(b)** (work~) mesa *f* de trabajo **2** (Law) **the bench** *or* **the Bench** (judges collectively) la judicatura; (tribunal) el tribunal

bend[1] /bend/ *n* **(a)** (in road, river) curva *f* **(b) bends** *pl* **the ~s** la enfermedad del buzo

bend[2] (*past and past p* **bent**) *vt* ⟨wire/branch⟩ torcer*, curvar; ⟨back/leg⟩ doblar; **⊗ do not bend** no doblar
■ ~ *vi* **(a)** «pipe/wire» torcerse* **(b)** «person» ▶ BEND DOWN **(c)** ⟨road/river⟩ hacer* una curva
■ **bend down** [*v + adv*] agacharse
■ **bend over** [*v + adv*] inclinarse

beneath[1] /bɪ'ni:θ/ *prep* **1** (under) bajo **2 (a)**
(inferior to): **she married ~ her** no se casó bien **(b)** (unworthy of): **it's ~ her** es indigno de ella; **you're ~ contempt** no mereces ni desprecio

beneath[2] *adv*: **the floor ~** el piso de abajo; **I wondered what lay ~** me preguntaba qué habría debajo *or* abajo

benefactor /'benəfæktər ‖'benɪfæktə(r)/ *n* benefactor, -tora *m,f*

beneficial /ˌbenə'fɪʃəl ‖ˌbenɪ'fɪʃəl/ *adj* beneficioso

beneficiary /ˌbenə'fɪʃieri ‖ˌbenɪ'fɪʃəri/ *n* (*pl* **-ries**) beneficiario, -ria *m,f*

benefit[1] /'benəfɪt ‖'benɪfɪt/ *n* **1** (good) beneficio *m*, bien *m*; (advantage) provecho *m*; **to give sb the ~ of the doubt** darle* a algn el beneficio de la duda **2** (Soc Adm) prestación *f*; *see also* UNEMPLOYMENT **3** (concert, performance) beneficio *m*; (*before n*) con fines benéficos

benefit[2] **-t-** *or* (AmE also) **-tt-** *vt* beneficiar
■ ~ *vi* beneficiarse; **to ~ FROM** *sth* beneficiarse CON algo

benevolent /bə'nevələnt/ *adj* ⟨person/smile⟩ benévolo; ⟨gesture⟩ de benevolencia

benign /bɪ'naɪn/ *adj* **(a)** ⟨person/attitude⟩ benévolo **(b)** (Med) benigno

bent[1] /bent/ *past and past p of* BEND[2]

bent[2] *adj* **1** ⟨pipe⟩ curvado, torcido **2** (determined) **to be ~ ON** doing *sth* estar* empeñado EN hacer algo

bequeath /bɪ'kwi:ð, -'kwi:θ/ *vt* **to ~** *sth* **TO** *sb* legarle* algo A algn

bequest /bɪ'kwest/ *n* legado *m*

berate /bɪ'reɪt/ *vt* (frml) **to ~** *sb* (FOR *sth*) reprender a algn (POR algo)

bereaved /bɪ'ri:vd/ *adj* desconsolado (*por la muerte de un ser querido*)

bereavement /bɪ'ri:vmənt/ *n* dolor *m* (*por la muerte de un ser querido*)

beret /bə'reɪ ‖'bereɪ/ *n* boina *f*

Berlin /'bɜːr'lɪn ‖bɜː'lɪn/ *n* Berlín *m*

Bermuda /bər'mju:də ‖bə'mju:də/ *n* las (islas) Bermudas

berry /'beri/ *n* (*pl* **-ries**) (Bot) baya *f*, (Culin) *fresas, frambuesas, moras etc*

berserk /bər'sɜːrk ‖bə'sɜːk/ *adj*: **to go ~** ponerse* como una fiera

berth[1] /bɜːrθ ‖bɜːθ/ *n* **(a)** (bunk) litera *f*, cucheta *f* (RPl); (cabin) camarote *m* **(b)** (mooring) atracadero *m*; **to give sb a wide ~** eludir a algn

berth[2] *vt/i* atracar*

beseech /bɪ'si:tʃ/ *vt* (*past & past p* **beseeched** *or* **besought**) (liter) suplicar*, rogar*

beset /bɪ'set/ *vt* (*pres p* **besetting**; *past & past p* **beset**) «anxieties/fears» acuciar; **he was ~ by doubts** lo acosaban las dudas

beside[1] /bɪ'saɪd/ *prep* (at the side of) al lado de; **to be ~ oneself**: **he was ~ himself with rage** estaba fuera de sí (de la rabia); **she's ~ herself with happiness** está que no cabe en sí de la alegría **(b)** (compared with) comparado con **(c)** (extraneous to): **that's ~ the point** eso no tiene nada que ver **(d)** ▶ BESIDES[1]

beside[2] *adv* **(a)** (alongside) al lado **(b)** ▶ BESIDES[2]

b

besides¹ /brˈsaɪdz/ *prep* (a) (in addition to) además de (b) (apart from) excepto, aparte de

besides² *adv* además

besiege /brˈsiːdʒ/ *vt* sitiar, asediar; **the village was ~d by reporters** el pueblo se vio asediado por periodistas

besotted /brˈsɑːtəd ‖ brˈsɒtɪd/ *adj* (*usu pred*): **he's totally ~ with her** está perdidamente enamorado de ella

besought /brˈsɔːt/ *past & past p of* BESEECH

bespectacled /brˈspektɪkəld/ *adj* de anteojos *or* lentes (AmL), con gafas (esp Esp)

best¹ /best/ *adj* (*superl of* GOOD¹) mejor; **for the ~ part of an hour/a month** durante casi una hora/un mes; **she's not very tolerant at the ~ of times** la tolerancia no es precisamente una de sus características

best² *adv* (*superl of* WELL¹,²) mejor; **I did it as ~ I could** lo hice lo mejor que pude; **it's ~ forgotten** más vale olvidarlo

best³ *n* **1** **the ~** (a) (+ *sing vb*) lo mejor; **to do one's ~** hacer* todo lo posible; **we'll just have to make the ~ of what we've got** tendremos que arreglarnos con lo que tenemos; (b) (+ *pl vb*): **they're (the) ~ of friends** son de lo más amigos; **she can ski with the ~ of them** (colloq) esquía tan bien como el mejor
2 (a) **at best: at ~, we'll just manage to cover costs** como mucho, podremos cubrir los gastos (b) **at/past one's best: at his ~, his singing rivals that of Caruso** en sus mejores momentos puede compararse a Caruso; **the roses were past their ~** las rosas ya no estaban en su mejor momento
3 (a) (in greetings): **all the ~!** ¡buena suerte! (b) (Sport) récord *m*; **a personal ~ for Flynn** un récord para Flynn

best man *n*: amigo que acompaña al novio el día de la boda, ≈padrino *m*, testigo *m*

bestow /brˈstəʊ/ *vt* (frml *or* liter) **to ~ sth ON** *o* **UPON sb** ⟨*title/award*⟩ conferirle* algo A algn (frml)

best-seller /ˈbestˈselər ‖ ˌbestˈselə(r)/ *n* (book) bestseller *m*; (product) superventas *m*; (author) autor, -tora *m,f* de bestsellers

bet¹ /bet/ *n* apuesta *f*; **I had a ~ with Charlie that Brazil would win** le aposté a Charlie que ganaría Brasil; **your best ~ is to stay here** lo mejor que puedes hacer es quedarte aquí

bet² (*pres p* **betting**; *past & past p* **bet**) *vt* apostar*
■ **~** *vi* jugar*; **to ~ ON sth/sb** apostar* A algo/algn; **I wouldn't ~ on it if I were you** yo no estaría tan seguro, yo no me fiaría

betray /brˈtreɪ/ *vt* ⟨*ally*⟩ traicionar; **he ~ed us to the enemy** nos vendió al enemigo; **her voice ~ed her nervousness** su voz revelaba el miedo que sentía

betrayal /brˈtreɪəl/ *n* traición *f*

betrothal /brˈtrəʊðəl/ *n* (frml) esponsales *mpl* (frml)

better¹ /ˈbetər ‖ ˈbetə(r)/ *adj* **1** (*comp of*

GOOD¹) mejor; **to get ~** mejorar; **if they can both come, so much the ~** si pueden venir los dos, mucho *or* tanto mejor **2** (*pred*) (recovered from illness): **to be ~** estar* mejor; **to get ~** recuperarse

better² *adv* **1** (*comp of* WELL¹,²) mejor **2** **had better** (ought): **I'd ~ leave before it gets dark** va a ser mejor que me vaya antes de que oscurezca; **well, I'd ~ be off** bueno, me tengo que ir

better³ *n* (a) (superior of two): **the ~ of the two** el mejor de los/las dos; **for the ~** para bien; **to get the ~ of sb/sth** ganarle la batalla a algn/algo (b) **betters** *pl* (superiors) superiores *mpl*; **his elders and ~s** sus mayores

better⁴ *vt* mejorar; **to ~ oneself** superarse

better-off /ˌbetərˈɔːf ‖ ˌbetərˈɒf/ *adj* (*pred* **better off**) (a) (financially) de mejor posición económica (b) (emotionally, physically) (*pred*) mejor

betting shop /ˈbetɪŋ/ *n* (BrE) agencia *f* de apuestas

between¹ /brˈtwiːn/ *prep* entre

between² *adv*: **the one ~** el/la de en medio

beverage /ˈbevərɪdʒ/ *n* bebida *f*

beware /brˈwer ‖ brˈweə(r)/ *vi* (*only in inf and imperative*): **~!** ¡(ten) cuidado!; ⑨ **beware of the dog** cuidado con el perro

bewildered /brˈwɪldərd ‖ brˈwɪldəd/ *adj* desconcertado; (overwhelmed) apabullado

bewildering /brˈwɪldərɪŋ/ *adj* desconcertante; (overwhelming) apabullante

bewitch /brˈwɪtʃ/ *vt* (cast spell on) embrujar; (entrance, delight) cautivar

beyond¹ /brˈɑːnd ‖ brˈjɒnd/ *prep* **1** (on other side of): **I live just ~ the station** vivo justo pasando la estación; **~ this point** de aquí en adelante
2 (a) (further than): **try to think ~ the immediate future** trata de pensar más allá del futuro inmediato (b) (more than, apart from): **I can't tell you anything ~ that** no te puedo decir nada más que eso
3 (past): **it's ~ repair** ya no tiene arreglo; **circumstances ~ our control** circunstancias ajenas a nuestra voluntad; **it's ~ me what she sees in him** (colloq) no puedo entender qué es lo que ve en él; **to live ~ one's means** vivir por encima de sus (*or* mis *etc*) posibilidades

beyond² *adv* (a) (in space) más allá (b) (in time): **we're planning for the year 2000 and ~** estamos haciendo planes para el 2000 y más allá del 2000

bias /ˈbaɪəs/ *n* parcialidad *f*; **the course has a scientific ~** el curso tiene un enfoque científico

biased, biassed /ˈbaɪəst/ *adj* ⟨*report/criticism*⟩ tendencioso; ⟨*judge*⟩ parcial; **to be ~ AGAINST/TOWARD(S) sth/sb** estar* predispuesto EN CONTRA DE/A FAVOR DE algo/algn

bib /brb/ *n* (a) (for baby) babero *m* (b) (on dungarees) peto *m*

Bible /ˈbaɪbəl/ *n* Biblia *f*

biblical /ˈbɪblɪkəl/ *adj* bíblico

bibliography /ˌbɪbliˈɑːɡrəfi ‖ ˌbɪbliˈɒɡrəfi/ *n* (*pl* **-phies**) bibliografía *f*

bicarbonate of soda /baɪˈkɑːrbəneɪt ‖baɪˈkɑːbəneɪt/ n bicarbonato m de sodio or de soda or (Esp) de sosa

biceps /ˈbaɪseps/ n (pl ~) bíceps m

bicker /ˈbɪkər ‖ˈbɪkə(r)/ vi pelear, discutir

bicycle /ˈbaɪsɪkəl/ n bicicleta f

bid¹ /bɪd/ vt [1] (pres p **bidding**; past & past p **bid**) (at auction) ofrecer* [2] (pres p **bidding**; past **bade** or **bid**; past p **bidden** or **bid**) (liter) (a) (wish, say): to ~ **sb farewell** despedirse* de algn (b) (request) to ~ **sb** (to) + INF pedirle* a algn QUE + SUBJ

■ ~ vi (pres p **bidding**; past & past p **bid**) (at auction) hacer* ofertas, pujar; to ~ FOR sth pujar POR algo

bid² n [1] (at auction) oferta f, puja f [2] (attempt) intento m, tentativa f; (unsuccessful) intentona f, intento m; ~ **to** + INF intento m DE + INF

bidden /ˈbɪdn̩/ past p of BID¹ vt 2

bidder /ˈbɪdər ‖ˈbɪdə(r)/ n postor, -tora m,f

bidding /ˈbɪdɪŋ/ n [1] (at auction): the ~ **opened at $100** la subasta abrió con una oferta de $100 [2] (wishes): **they had servants to do their ~** tenían criados para lo que se les antojara; **at his father's ~** a petición de su padre

bide /baɪd/ vt: to ~ **one's time** esperar el momento oportuno

bidet /bɪˈdeɪ ‖ˈbiːdeɪ/ n bidet m, bidé m

biennial /baɪˈeniəl/ adj bienal

bier /bɪr ‖bɪə(r)/ n andas fpl

bifocals /ˈbaɪfəʊkəlz/ pl n anteojos mpl or (esp Esp) gafas fpl bifocales

big /bɪg/ adj

■ Note The usual translation of big, grande, becomes gran when it is used before a singular noun.

-gg- grande; **a ~ garden** un jardín grande, un gran jardín; **how ~ is the table?** ¿cómo es de grande la mesa?; **a ~ hug/kiss** un abrazote/ besote (fam); **a ~ decision** una gran decisión; **our ~gest customer** nuestro cliente más importante; **she's really ~ in Europe** es muy conocida en Europa; **my ~ brother** mi hermano mayor

bigamist /ˈbɪgəməst ‖ˈbɪgəmɪst/ n bígamo, -ma m,f

bigamy /ˈbɪgəmi/ n bigamia f

big: ~ business n el gran capital; **to be ~ business ser*** un gran negocio; **~-headed** /ˈbɪgˈhedəd ‖ˌbɪgˈhedɪd/ adj (colloq) creído (fam); **~ league** n (in US) (Sport) liga f mayor; (top rank) los grandes; **~mouth** n (colloq) (boaster) fanfarrón, -rrona m,f; (gossip) chismoso, -sa m,f, cotilla mf (Esp fam), hocicón, -cona m,f (Chi, Méx fam)

bigot /ˈbɪgət/ n intolerante mf

bigotry /ˈbɪgətri/ n intolerancia f

big: ~ shot n (colloq) pez m gordo (fam); **~ top** n carpa f de circo

bike /baɪk/ n (colloq) (bicycle) bici f (fam); (motorcycle) moto f

bikini /bɪˈkiːni/ n bikini m or (RPl) f

bilateral /baɪˈlætərəl/ adj bilateral

bilberry /ˈbɪlˌberi ‖ˈbɪlbəri/ n (pl **-ries**) arándano m

bilingual /baɪˈlɪŋgwəl/ adj bilingüe

bilious /ˈbɪliəs/ adj: **to feel ~** sentirse* descompuesto; **~ attack** ataque m al or de hígado

bill¹ /bɪl/ n [1] (a) (invoice) factura f, cuenta f; **the telephone ~** la cuenta or (Esp tb) el recibo del teléfono (b) (in restaurant) (esp BrE) cuenta f, adición f (RPl) [2] (AmE Fin) (banknote) billete m [3] (Govt) proyecto m de ley [4] (program) programa m; **to top the ~** encabezar* el reparto [5] (certificate): **~ of sale** contrato m de venta; **a clean ~ of health** (favorable report) el visto bueno [6] (beak) pico m

bill² vt [1] (invoice, charge) pasarle la cuenta or la factura a [2] (advertise) ⟨play/performer⟩ anunciar

billboard /ˈbɪlbɔːrd ‖ˈbɪlbɔːd/ n (esp AmE) cartelera f

billet /ˈbɪlət ‖ˈbɪlɪt/ vt alojar

billfold /ˈbɪlfəʊld/ n (AmE) billetera f, cartera f

billiards /ˈbɪljərdz ‖ˈbɪljədz/ n (+ sing vb) billar m

billion /ˈbɪljən/ n mil millones mpl, millar m de millones

billow /ˈbɪləʊ/ vi (a) ~ (**out**) ⟨sail/parachute⟩ hincharse (b) ⟨smoke⟩: **smoke ~ed from the window** nubes de humo salían de or por la ventana

billy /ˈbɪli/ n (pl **-lies**) ~ (**goat**) macho m cabrío

bin /bɪn/ n (for kitchen refuse etc) (BrE) cubo m or (CS) tacho m or (Méx) bote m or (Col) caneca f or (Ven) tobo m de la basura; (wastepaper basket) (BrE) papelera f, papelero m, caneca f (Col); (litter ~) papelera f, basurero m (Chi, Méx), caneca f (Col)

binary /ˈbaɪnəri/ adj binario

bind¹ /baɪnd/ vt (past & past p **bound**) [1] (tie, fasten) ⟨person⟩ atar, amarrar; ► BOUND⁴ 1A [2] (a) (wrap) envolver* (b) ~ (**up**) ⟨wound⟩ vendar [3] (Law) obligar* [4] ⟨book⟩ encuadernar [5] (Culin) ligar*

bind² n (colloq) (difficult situation) aprieto m, apuro m; (nuisance) (BrE) lata f (fam), rollo m (Esp fam)

binder /ˈbaɪndər ‖ˈbaɪndə(r)/ n (file, folder) carpeta f

binding¹ /ˈbaɪndɪŋ/ n (a) (book cover) tapa f, cubierta f (b) (tape) ribete m

binding² adj ⟨promise/commitment⟩ que hay que cumplir; (Law) vinculante

binge /bɪndʒ/ n (colloq): **to go on a ~** irse* de juerga (fam)

bingo /ˈbɪŋgəʊ/ n bingo m

binliner /ˈbɪnˌlaɪnər ‖ˈbɪnˌlaɪnə(r)/ n (BrE) bolsa f de (la) basura

binoculars /bəˈnɑːkjələrz ‖bɪˈnɒkjʊləz/ pl n gemelos mpl, prismáticos mpl, anteojos fpl de larga vista (esp AmL)

biochemistry /ˈbaɪəʊˈkeməstri ‖ˌbaɪəʊˈkemɪstri/ n bioquímica f

biodegradable /ˈbaɪəʊdɪˈgreɪdəbəl/ adj biodegradable

biographer /baɪˈɑːgrəfər ‖baɪˈɒgrəfə(r)/ n biógrafo, -fa m,f

biographical /ˌbaɪəˈgræfɪkəl/ adj biográfico

biography /baɪˈɑːgrəfi ‖baɪˈɒgrəfi/ n (pl **-phies**) biografía f

biological /ˈbaɪəˈlɑːdʒɪkəl ‖ˌbaɪəˈlɒdʒɪkəl/ adj biológico

biologist /baɪˈɑːlədʒəst ‖ baɪˈɒlədʒɪst/ n
biólogo, -ga m,f

biology /baɪˈɑːlədʒi ‖ baɪˈɒlədʒi/ n biología f

biopsy /ˈbaɪɑːpsi ‖ ˈbaɪɒpsi/ n (pl **-sies**)
biopsia f

birch /bɜːrtʃ ‖ bɜːtʃ/ n ~ **(tree)** abedul m

bird /bɜːrd ‖ bɜːd/ n (small) pájaro m; (large) ave
f‡; **to kill two ~s with one stone** matar dos
pájaros de un tiro

bird: ~**cage** n jaula f de pájaros; (large)
pajarera f; ~ **of prey** n (pl **~s of prey**) ave f‡
rapaz or de rapiña or de presa; ~**'s-eye view**
n vista f aérea; ~**watcher** /ˈbɜːrdˌwɑːtʃər
‖ ˈbɜːdˌwɒtʃə(r)/ n observador, -dora m,f de aves;
~**watching** /ˈbɜːrdˌwɑːtʃɪŋ ‖ ˈbɜːdˌwɒtʃɪŋ/ n
observación f de las aves (como hobby)

Biro®**, biro** /ˈbaɪrəʊ ‖ ˈbaɪərəʊ/ n (pl **biros**)
(BrE) bolígrafo m, birome f (RPl), esfero m (Col),
lápiz m de pasta (Chi), boli m (Esp fam)

birth /bɜːrθ ‖ bɜːθ/ n nacimiento m; (childbirth)
parto m; **at ~** al nacer; **date of ~** fecha f de
nacimiento; **to give ~** dar* a luz, parir

birth: ~ **certificate** n partida f or certificado
m or (Méx) acta f de nacimiento; ~ **control** n
control m de la natalidad

birthday /ˈbɜːrθdeɪ ‖ ˈbɜːθdeɪ/ n cumpleaños m;
(of institution) aniversario m; **it'll be his fifth** ~
cumple cinco años; **happy** ~**!** ¡feliz cumpleaños!;
(before n) ⟨cake/card/party⟩ de cumpleaños

birth: ~**mark** n mancha f or marca f de
nacimiento, antojo m; ~**place** n (of person) lugar
m de nacimiento; (of movement, fashion, idea) cuna f

biscuit /ˈbɪskɪt/ n (Culin) (a) (AmE) bollo m,
panecillo m, bisquet m (Méx) (b) (cookie, cracker)
(BrE) galleta f, galletita f (RPl)

bisect /baɪˈsekt/ vt bisecar*

bisexual /ˌbaɪˈsekʃuəl/ adj bisexual

bishop /ˈbɪʃəp/ (a) n (Relig) obispo m (b) (in
chess) alfil m

bison /ˈbaɪsn/ n (pl ~) bisonte m

bit¹ /bɪt/ past of BITE¹

bit² n 1 (fragment, scrap) pedazo m, trozo m; **to
smash sth to ~s** hacer* pedazos algo; ~**s and
pieces** (assorted items) cosas fpl; (belongings) cosas
fpl; (broken fragments) pedazos mpl
2 (section, piece) parte f
3 **a bit of** (+ uncount noun) un poco de; **they
have quite a ~ of work to do** tienen bastante
trabajo que hacer
4 **a bit** (as adv) (a) (somewhat) un poco; **the
town's changed a** ~ la ciudad ha cambiado algo
or un poco; **she hasn't changed a** ~ no ha
cambiado (para) nada (b) (a while) un momento
or rato
5 (in adv phrases) (a) **bit by bit** poco a poco, de
a poco (AmL) (b) **every bit: I'm every** ~ **as
disappointed as you** estoy absolutamente tan
decepcionado como tú
6 (Comput) bit m
7 (of bridle) freno m, bocado m

bitch /bɪtʃ/ n 1 (female dog) perra f 2 (spiteful
woman) (AmE vulg, BrE sl) bruja f (fam), arpía f
(fam), cabrona f (Esp, Méx vulg)

bite¹ /baɪt/ (past **bit**; past p **bitten**) vt
«person/dog» morder*; «bug» picar*; **to ~ off**

more than one can chew tratar de abarcar más
de lo que se puede; **once bitten, twice shy** el gato
escaldado del agua fría huye
■ ~ vi 1 (a) «person/dog» morder*;
«mosquito» picar*; «wind/frost» cortar; **to ~
INTO sth** darle* un mordisco a algo (b) (take bait)
«fish» picar* 2 «law/recession» hacerse*
sentir

bite² n 1 (act) mordisco m; (fierce) tarascada f
2 (wound — from insect) picadura f; (— from dog,
snake) mordedura f 3 (snack) (colloq) (no pl)
bocado m; **to have a** ~ **(to eat)** comer un bocado,
comer algo

biting /ˈbaɪtɪŋ/ adj ⟨wind⟩ cortante; ⟨sarcasm/
criticism⟩ mordaz

bit part n papel m pequeño

bitten /ˈbɪtn/ past p of BITE¹

bitter¹ /ˈbɪtər ‖ ˈbɪtə(r)/ adj 1 (a) (in taste)
amargo (b) (very cold) ⟨weather⟩ glacial; ⟨wind/
frost⟩ cortante 2 (a) (painful, hard)
⟨disappointment⟩ amargo; **they fought on to the** ~
end lucharon valientemente hasta el final (b)
⟨person⟩ resentido, amargado (c) ⟨enemies/
hatred⟩ implacable; ⟨struggle⟩ enconado

bitter² n (BrE) tipo de cerveza ligeramente
amarga

bitterly /ˈbɪtərli ‖ ˈbɪtəli/ adv 1 ⟨cold⟩: **it was**
~ **cold** hacía un frío glacial 2 (a)
⟨disappointed⟩ tremendamente; ⟨weep/complain/
say⟩ amargamente (b) (implacably)
implacablemente

bitterness /ˈbɪtərnəs ‖ ˈbɪtənɪs/ n 1 (of taste)
amargor m 2 (of person, disappointment) amargura f

bittersweet /ˈbɪtərswiːt ‖ ˌbɪtəˈswiːt/ adj
agridulce; ⟨chocolate⟩ (AmE) amargo

bizarre /bɪˈzɑːr ‖ bɪˈzɑː(r)/ adj ⟨story/
coincidence⟩ extraño; ⟨appearance/behavior⟩
estrambótico

black¹ /blæk/ adj **-er**, **-est** 1 ⟨dress/hair/
ink⟩ negro; ⟨sky⟩ oscuro; ⟨coffee⟩ negro (AmL),
solo (Esp), tinto (Col), puro (Chi); ⟨tea⟩ solo, sin
leche, puro (Chi); ~ **cloud** nubarrón m 2 also
Black ⟨person/community⟩ negro 3 (sad,
hopeless) negro

black² n 1 (color) negro m 2 also **Black**
(person) negro, -gra m,f 3 (freedom from debt): **to
be in the** ~ no estar* en números rojos

■ **black out** 1 [v + adv] (lose consciousness)
perder* el conocimiento 2 [v + o + adv, v + adv
+ o] (in wartime) ⟨windows⟩ tapar; ⟨lights⟩ apagar*;
(by accident) ⟨town/district⟩ dejar sin luz

black: ~ **and white** n (Cin, Phot, TV) blanco y
negro m; **she sees things in** ~ **and white** para
ella no hay términos medios; ~**-and-white**
/ˈblækənˈhwaɪt ‖ ˈblækənˈwaɪt/ adj (pred ~ **and
white**) en blanco y negro; ~ **belt** n cinturón m
negro, cinta f negra (Méx); (person) cinturón mf
negro, cinta mf negra (Méx); ~**berry**
/ˈblækˌberi ‖ ˈblækbəri/ n mora f; ~**bird** n
(European) mirlo m; (North American) totí m;
~**board** n pizarra f, pizarrón m (AmL), tablero
m (Col); ~ **box** n (Aviat) caja f negra; ~**currant**
/ˈblækˈkɜːrənt ‖ ˈblækˈkʌrənt/ n grosella f negra

blacken /ˈblækən/ vt (a) (make black)
ennegrecer* (b) (defame) ⟨person⟩ deshonrar;
⟨reputation⟩ manchar

black: ~ **eye** n ojo m morado, ojo m a la

funerala (Esp fam), ojo *m* en compota (CS fam), ojo *m* en tinta (Chi fam); ∼**head** *n* espinilla *f*; ∼ **hole** *n* agujero *m* negro; ∼ **ice** *n* capa fina de hielo en las carreteras

blacklist¹ /'blæklɪst/ *n* lista *f* negra

blacklist² *vt* poner* en la lista negra

blackmail¹ /'blækmeɪl/ *n* chantaje *m*

blackmail² *vt* chantajear, hacerle* chantaje a

black: ∼ **mark** *n* punto *m* en contra; ∼ **market** *n* mercado *m* negro; ∼**out** /'blækaʊt/ *n* ①(loss of consciousness) desvanecimiento *m*, desmayo *m*; ②(in wartime) oscurecimiento de la ciudad para que esta no sea visible desde los aviones enemigos; B∼ **Sea** *n* the B∼ Sea el Mar Negro; ∼ **sheep** *n* oveja *f* negra; ∼**smith** *n* herrero *m*

bladder /'blædər ‖'blædə(r)/ *n* (Anat) vejiga *f*

blade /bleɪd/ *n* ①(of knife, razor) hoja *f* ②(of propeller) pala *f*, paleta *f* ③(Bot) (of grass) brizna *f*

blame¹ /bleɪm/ *vt* echarle la culpa a, culpar; to ∼ **sb** FOR **sth** culpar a algn DE algo, echarle la culpa DE algo A algn; to be to ∼ **for sth** tener* la culpa de algo; to ∼ **sth** ON **sb/sth** echarle la culpa DE algo A algn/algo

blame² *n* culpa *f*, it's always me that gets the ∼ siempre me echan la culpa a mí

bland /blænd/ *adj* **-er, -est (a)** ⟨colors/music⟩ soso; ⟨food/taste⟩ insípido; ⟨statement/reply⟩ anodino; ⟨smile/manner⟩ insulso **(b)** (mild) ⟨food⟩ suave

blank¹ /blæŋk/ *adj* **(a)** (empty) ⟨page/space⟩ en blanco; ⟨tape⟩ virgen; my mind went ∼ me quedé en blanco; a ∼ expression un rostro carente de expresión **(b)** (uncompromising) ⟨refusal/rejection⟩ rotundo **(c)** (Mil) ⟨ammunition⟩ de fogueo

blank² *n* **(a)** (empty space) espacio *m* en blanco; to draw a ∼ no obtener* ningún resultado **(b)** (Mil) cartucho *m* de fogueo

blank check, (BrE) **cheque** *n* cheque *m* en blanco

blanket¹ /'blæŋkət ‖'blæŋkɪt/ *n* manta *f*, cobija *f* (AmL), frazada *f* (AmL)

blanket² *adj* (before *n*, no comp) ⟨measure⟩ global

blare /bler ‖bleə(r)/*vi* atronar*

■ **blare out** [*v + adv + o*]: the radio was blaring out music el radio emitía música retumbante

blasphemous /'blæsfəməs/ *adj* blasfemo

blasphemy /'blæsfəmi/ *n* (*pl* **-mies**) blasfemia *f*

blast¹ /blæst ‖blɑːst/ *n* ①(of air, wind) ráfaga *f*; (of water) chorro *m* ②(explosion) (journ) explosión *f* ③(of sound) toque *m*; he had the TV on full ∼ tenía la tele a todo lo que daba (fam)

blast² *vt* **(a)** (blow) ⟨rock⟩ volar*; they used dynamite to ∼ the safe open usaron dinamita para volar la caja fuerte **(b)** (attack) (journ) atacar*
■ **blast off** [*v + adv*] despegar*

blast-off /'blæstɔf ‖'blɑːstɒf/ *n* despegue *m*

blatant /'bleɪtn̩t/ *adj* ⟨prejudice/disrespect⟩ descarado; ⟨lie⟩ flagrante; ⟨incompetence⟩ patente

blatantly /'bleɪtn̩tli/ *adv* descaradamente; it's ∼ obvious that ... está clarísimo que ...

blaze¹ /bleɪz/ *n* ①(in grate) fuego *m*; (bonfire) fogata *f*; (flames) llamaradas *fpl*; (dangerous fire) (journ) incendio *m* ②(dazzling display) (no *pl*): a ∼ of color un derroche de color; in a ∼ of glory cubierto de gloria

blaze² *vi* ⟨⟨fire⟩⟩ arder; ⟨⟨lights⟩⟩ brillar; ⟨⟨eyes⟩⟩ centellear

blazer /'bleɪzər ‖'bleɪzə(r)/ *n* blazer *m*

bleach¹ /bliːtʃ/ *n* lejía *f*, blanqueador *m* (Col, Méx), lavandina *f* (Arg), agua *f*‡ Jane® (Ur), cloro *m* (AmC, Chi)

bleach² *vt* ⟨cloth⟩ (in the sun) blanquear; (with bleach) poner* en lejía (or blanqueador *etc*)

bleachers /'bliːtʃərz ‖'bliːtʃəz/ *pl n* (AmE) tribuna *f* descubierta

bleak /bliːk/ *adj* **-er, -est (a)** ⟨landscape⟩ inhóspito; ⟨room⟩ lóbrego **(b)** ⟨winter⟩ crudo; ⟨day⟩ gris y deprimente **(c)** (miserable, cheerless) ⟨prospects/news⟩ sombrío

bleary-eyed /'blɪriˌaɪd ‖'blɪəriˌaɪd/ *adj* con cara de sueño

bleat /bliːt/ *vi* balar

bleed /bliːd/ (*past & past p* **bled** /bled/) *vi* sangrar; he bled to death murió desangrado
■ ∼ *vt* **(a)** (Med) sangrar; to ∼ **sb dry** chuparle la sangre a algn (fam) **(b)** ⟨brakes/radiator⟩ purgar*

bleeding /'bliːdɪŋ/ *n* hemorragia *f*

bleep¹ /bliːp/ *n* pitido *m*

bleep² *vi* (BrE) emitir un pitido

blemish /'blemɪʃ/ *n* (on skin) imperfección *f*; (on reputation) mancha *f*

blend¹ /blend/ *n* combinación *f*, mezcla *f*

blend² *vt* mezclar, combinar; (in blender) licuar*
■ ∼ *vi* ⟨flavors/colors⟩ armonizar*
■ **blend in** ①[*v + o + adv, v + adv + o*] ⟨ingredients⟩ añadir y mezclar ②[*v + adv*] (merge, harmonize) armonizar*

blender /'blendər ‖'blendə(r)/ *n* licuadora *f*

bless /bles/ *vt* (*past* **blessed**; *past p* **blessed** *or* (arch) **blest**) **(a)** (Relig) bendecir* **(b)** (in interj phrases) ∼ **you!** (to sb who sneezes) ¡salud! *or* (Esp) ¡Jesús!; ∼ **my soul!** (colloq) ¡válgame Dios!

blessed /'blesəd ‖'blesɪd/ *adj* bienaventurado

blessing /'blesɪŋ/ *n* ① **(a)** (Relig — benediction) bendición *f*; (— of bread, wine) consagración *f* **(b)** (approval) aprobación *f* ②(fortunate thing) bendición *f* (del cielo); to be a mixed ∼ tener* sus pros y sus contras

blest /blest/ (arch) *past & past pt of* BLESS

blew /bluː/ *past of* BLOW¹

blight¹ /blaɪt/ *n* (Agr, Hort) añublo *m*; (loosely) peste *f*; (curse) plaga *f*

blight² *vt* ⟨crop/career/health⟩ arruinar; ⟨region⟩ asolar*; ⟨hopes⟩ malograr

blind¹ /blaɪnd/ *adj* ①**(a)** (Med) ciego; to go ∼ quedarse ciego; to be ∼ TO **sth** no ver* algo **(b)** (Auto) ⟨corner⟩ de poca visibilidad ②⟨faith/fury⟩ ciego

blind² *vt* **(a)** (permanently) dejar ciego **(b)** ⟨ambition/passion⟩ cegar*, enceguecer* (AmL); ⟨⟨light/wealth⟩⟩ deslumbrar

blind³ *n* ①(outside window) persiana *f*; (roller ∼) persiana *f* (de enrollar), estor *m* (Esp); (venetian ∼) persiana *f* veneciana ②(blind people) (+ *pl vb*) the ∼ los ciegos

blind date *n* cita *f* con un desconocido/una desconocida

b

blinders /'blaɪndərz ‖ 'blaɪndəz/ n pl (AmE) (on horse) anteojeras fpl

blindfold¹ /'blaɪndfəʊld/ vt vendarle los ojos a

blindfold² n venda f (para tapar los ojos)

blindfold³ adv con los ojos vendados

blindly /'blaɪndli/ adv (a) (without seeing) ⟨grope⟩ a ciegas (b) (without reasoning) ⟨follow⟩ ciegamente

blindness /'blaɪndnəs ‖ 'blaɪndnɪs/ n ceguera f

blind spot n (a) (weak point) punto m flaco (b) (Auto) punto m ciego

blink¹ /blɪŋk/ n parpadeo m, pestañeo m; to be on the ~ (colloq) no marchar, no andar* bien (AmL)

blink² vi ⟨eye/person⟩ pestañear, parpadear; ⟨light⟩ parpadear

blinker /'blɪŋkər ‖ 'blɪŋkə(r)/ n **1** (a) (Auto colloq) intermitente m, direccional f (Col, Méx), señalizador m (de viraje) (Chi) (b) (AmE Transp) señal f intermitente **2** **blinkers** pl (on horse) anteojeras fpl

blinkered /'blɪŋkərd ‖ 'blɪŋkəd/ adj ⟨attitude⟩ de miras estrechas; ⟨view/outlook⟩ estrecho

blip /blɪp/ n (a) (sound) bip m, pitidito m (b) (irregularity) accidente m; (problem) problema m pasajero

bliss /blɪs/ n dicha f

blissful /'blɪsfəl/ adj ⟨smile⟩ de gozo

blissfully /'blɪsfəli/ adv ⟨smile/sigh⟩ con gran felicidad

blister¹ /'blɪstər ‖ 'blɪstə(r)/ n (a) (Med) ampolla f (b) (on paintwork) ampolla f, burbuja f

blister² vi ampollarse

blithely /'blaɪðli/ adv alegremente

blitz /blɪts/ n (a) (Aviat, Mil) bombardeo m aéreo (b) (intense attack): this weekend we're going to have a ~ on the garden (colloq) este fin de semana vamos a atacar el jardín

blizzard /'blɪzərd ‖ 'blɪzəd/ n ventisca f

bloated /'bləʊtəd ‖ 'bləʊtɪd/ adj hinchado

blob /blɑːb ‖ blɒb/ n (a) (drip) gota f (b) (indistinct shape) mancha f

bloc /blɑːk ‖ blɒk/ n (Pol) bloque m

block¹ /blɑːk ‖ blɒk/ n **1** (of stone, wood) bloque m; (starting ~) (Sport) taco m de salida; (of paper) bloc m
2 (a) (space enclosed by streets) manzana f; (distance between two streets): it's eight ~s from here (AmE) está a ocho cuadras or (Esp) calles de aquí (b) (building): a ~ of flats (BrE) un edificio de apartamentos or de departamentos (AmL), una casa de pisos (Esp); an office ~ un edificio de oficinas
3 (section of text) sección f, bloque m
4 (Comput) bloque m
5 (blockage) obstrucción f, bloqueo m; I have a mental ~ about physics tengo un bloqueo mental con la física
6 (Sport) bloqueo m

block² vt **1** (a) (obstruct) ⟨road/entrance⟩ bloquear; you're ~ing my way me estás

impidiendo el paso; that fat man is ~ing my view ese gordo no me deja ver (b) ⟨drain/sink⟩ atascar*, tapar (AmL); my nose is ~ed tengo la nariz tapada
2 (a) (prevent) ⟨progress⟩ obstaculizar*; ⟨funds/sale⟩ congelar (b) (Sport) bloquear
■ ~ vi (Sport) bloquear
■ **block in** [v + o + adv, v + adv + o] cerrarle* el paso a
■ **block off** [v + o + adv, v + adv + o] ⟨street⟩ cortar
■ **block out** [v + o + adv, v + adv + o] (a) (shut out) ⟨thought⟩ ahuyentar (b) (obstruct) ⟨light⟩ tapar
■ **block up** [v + o + adv, v + adv + o] (a) (seal) ⟨entrance/window⟩ tapiar (b) (cause obstruction in) ⟨drain/sink⟩ atascar*, tapar (AmL); my nose is ~ed up tengo la nariz tapada

blockade¹ /blɑːˈkeɪd ‖ blɒˈkeɪd/ n bloqueo m

blockade² vt bloquear

blockage /'blɑːkɪdʒ ‖ 'blɒkɪdʒ/ n (in pipe, road) obstrucción f; (Med) oclusión f

block capitals, block letters pl n (letras fpl) mayúsculas fpl de imprenta

bloke /bləʊk/ n (BrE colloq) tipo m (fam), tío m (Esp fam)

blond /blɑːnd ‖ blɒnd/ adj (f **blonde**) rubio or (Méx) güero or (Col) mono or (Ven) catire

blood /blʌd/ n sangre f; in cold ~ a sangre fría; (before in) ~ donor donante mf de sangre; ~ group grupo m sanguíneo; ~ test análisis m de sangre; ~ transfusion transfusión f de sangre

blood: ~ **bath** n masacre f, ~**curdling** /'blʌd,kɜːrdlɪŋ ‖ 'blʌd,kɜːdlɪŋ/ adj espeluznante, aterrador

bloodless /'blʌdləs ‖ 'blʌdlɪs/ adj ⟨coup⟩ sin derramamiento de sangre

blood: ~ **pressure** n tensión f or presión f (arterial); ~**shed** n derramamiento m de sangre; ~**shot** adj rojo, inyectado de sangre; ~ **sport** n deporte m sangriento; ~**stain** n mancha f de sangre; ~**stained** /'blʌdsteɪnd/ adj manchado de sangre; ~**stream** n the ~stream el torrente sanguíneo; ~**thirsty** adj (a) (cruel) sanguinario (b) ⟨story/description⟩ sangriento; ~ **vessel** n vaso m sanguíneo

bloody¹ /'blʌdi/ adj -dier, -diest **1** (a) ⟨hands/clothes⟩ ensangrentado; ⟨wound⟩ que sangra, sangrante (b) ⟨battle⟩ sangriento **2** (esp BrE vulg or colloq) (no comp) (expressing annoyance, surprise, shock etc): where's that ~ dog? ¿dónde está ese maldito or (Méx) pinche perro? (fam); ~ hell! ¡coño! (vulg), ¡chingado! (Méx vulg), ¡hostias! (Esp vulg)

bloody² adv (BrE vulg or colloq) (as intensifier): the weather was ~ awful! ¡hizo un tiempo de mierda! (vulg)

bloom¹ /bluːm/ n **1** (a) (flower) flor f (b) to be in ~ estar* en flor; to be in full ~ estar* en plena floración **2** (on fruits, leaves) vello m

bloom² vi ⟨plant/garden⟩ florecer*; ⟨flower⟩ abrirse*

blossom¹ /'blɑːsəm ‖ 'blɒsəm/ n (a) (mass of flowers) flores fpl (b) (by single bloom) flor f

blossom² vi (a) (flower) «tree» florecer* (b) (flourish) «arts» florecer*; «person/relationship» alcanzar* su plenitud

blot¹ /blɑːt ‖ blɒt/ n (a) (of ink) borrón m (b) (blemish): **the factory is a ~ on the landscape** la fábrica afea el paisaje

blot² -tt- vt (a) (stain, smear) ‹page/word› emborronar (b) (dry) ‹ink› secar* ‹con papel secante›
■ **blot out** [v + o + adv, v + adv + o] ‹word› tachar; ‹view› tapar; ‹memory› borrar

blotchy /'blɑːtʃi ‖ 'blɒtʃi/ adj **blotchier, blotchiest** ‹skin› lleno de manchas

blotting paper /'blɑːtɪŋ ‖ 'blɒtɪŋ/ n papel m secante

blouse /blaʊs ‖ blaʊz/ n blusa f

blow¹ /bləʊ/ n golpe m; **to come to ~s** llegar* a las manos; **his death came as a ~ to us** su muerte fue un duro golpe para nosotros

blow² (past **blew**; past p **blown**) vt
1 (propel): **stop ~ing smoke in my face!** ¡no me eches el humo a la cara!; **a gust of wind blew the door shut** una ráfaga de viento cerró la puerta de golpe; **the plane was ~n off course** el viento sacó el avión de su curso
2 (a) (make by blowing): **to ~ bubbles** hacer* pompas de jabón (b) (clear): **to ~ one's nose** sonarse* la nariz (c) (play) ‹note› tocar*; ‹signal› dar*; **the referee blew the whistle** el árbitro tocó el silbato or pito
3 (a) (smash) ‹bridge/safe› volar* (b) (burn out) ‹fuse› hacer* saltar, quemar (c) (burst) ‹gasket› reventar*
4 (colloq) (a) (squander) ‹money› despilfarrar (b) (spoil): **I blew it** la pifié (fam); **I blew the oral test** la pifié en el oral (fam), la regué en el oral (Méx fam)
■ ~ vi 1 (a) ‹wind› soplar (b) ‹person›
soplar; **she came up the stairs, puffing and ~ing** subió las escaleras bufando y resoplando
2 (be driven by wind): **litter was ~ing everywhere** volaba basura por todas partes; **his hat blew off** se le voló el sombrero; **the door blew open** la puerta se abrió con el viento
3 (produce sound) «whistle» sonar*
4 (burn out) «fuse» saltar, quemarse
■ **blow down** 1 [v + o + adv, v + adv + o] tirar (abajo)
2 [v + adv] caerse* (con el viento)
■ **blow out** 1 [v + o + adv, v + adv + o] ‹match/flame› apagar* ‹soplando›; **to ~ sb's brains out** (colloq) saltarle la tapa de los sesos a algn (fam)
2 [v + adv] «candle» apagarse*
■ **blow over** [v + adv] «trouble» caer* en el olvido; «storm» pasar
■ **blow up** 1 [v + adv] (a) (explode) «bomb» estallar; «car» saltar por los aires (b) (begin) «wind/storm» levantarse; «conflict» estallar; **the affair blew up into a major scandal** el caso terminó en un gran escándalo
2 [v + o + adv, v + adv + o] (a) ‹mine/car› volar* (b) ‹balloon› inflar (c) (colloq) ‹incident› exagerar (d) ‹photo› ampliar*

blow: ~-**by-**~ /'bləʊbaɪ'bləʊ/ adj ‹before n› ‹account› con pelos y señales (fam); ~-**dry** vt

-**dries,** -**drying,** -**dries:** to ~-**dry one's hair** hacerse* un brushing (secarse el pelo con secador de mano y cepillo); ~-**gun** n (AmE) cerbatana f

blown /bləʊn/ past p of BLOW²

blow: ~-**out** n (a) (feast) (colloq) comilona f (fam) (b) (burst tire) reventón m; ~-**pipe** n cerbatana f; ~-**torch** n soplete m

blubber¹ /'blʌbər ‖ 'blʌbə(r)/ n grasa f de ballena

blubber² vi (colloq & pej) lloriquear

bludgeon /'blʌdʒən/ vt aporrear

blue¹ /bluː/ adj **bluer, bluest** 1 ‹dress/sea/sky› azul 2 (pornographic) (colloq) verde, porno adj inv, colorado (Méx) 3 (unhappy) (esp AmE) triste, deprimido

blue² n azul m; **out of the ~** ‹call/arrive› cuando menos se (or me etc) lo esperaba

blue: ~-**bell** n jacinto m silvestre; ~-**berry** /'bluːˌberi ‖ 'bluːbəri/ n arándano m; ~-**blooded** /'bluːˈblʌdəd ‖ ˌbluːˈblʌdɪd/ adj de sangre azul; ~-**bottle** n mosca f azul; ~-**collar** /'bluːˈkɑːlər ‖ ˌbluːˈkɒlə(r)/ adj ‹union› obrero; ‹job› manual; ~-**collar workers** los obreros; ~-**print** n (of technical drawing) plano m; (plan of action) programa m

blues /bluːz/ pl n 1 (depression) (colloq): **the ~** la depre (fam) 2 (Mus) blues m

bluff¹ /blʌf/ vi hacer* un bluff or (Col, Méx) blof
■ ~ vt: **he managed to ~ his way out of it** logró salir del apuro embaucándolos

bluff² n (pretense) bluff m, blof m (Col, Méx); **to call sb's ~** poner* a algn en evidencia

blunder¹ /'blʌndər ‖ 'blʌndə(r)/ vi 1 (move clumsily, stumble): **he ~ed into the table** se topó con el jefe en el pasillo; **he ~ed around in the dark** andaba dando tumbos en la oscuridad 2 (make mistake) cometer un error garrafal

blunder² n (mistake) error m garrafal; (faux pas) metedura f or (AmL tb) metida f de pata (fam)

blunt¹ /blʌnt/ adj **-er, -est** (a) (not sharp) ‹pencil› desafilado, mocho (esp AmL); ‹tip/edge› romo; **a ~ instrument** un objeto contundente (b) (straightforward) ‹person/manner› directo, franco; ‹refusal› rotundo

blunt² vt (a) ‹pencil› despuntar; ‹knife/scissors› desafilar (b) (make dull) ‹senses/intellect› embotar

bluntly /'blʌntli/ adv ‹say› sin rodeos; ‹refuse› rotundamente

blur /blɜːr ‖ blɜː(r)/ -**rr-** vt ‹outline› desdibujar; ‹distinction› hacer* menos claro; ‹memory› hacer* borroso
■ ~ vi ‹outline› desdibujarse

blurred /blɜːrd ‖ blɜːd/ adj ‹outline/vision› borroso

blurt out /blɜːrt ‖ blɜːt/ [v + o + adv, v + adv + o] espetar

blush /blʌʃ/ vi ruborizarse*, ponerse* colorado

blusher /'blʌʃər ‖ 'blʌʃə(r)/ n colorete m, rubor m (Méx, RPl)

bluster¹ /'blʌstər ‖ 'blʌstə(r)/ vi bravuconear

bluster² n bravatas fpl, bravuconería f

B-movie /'biːˌmuːvi/ n película f de serie B or de bajo presupuesto

boa /'bəʊə/ n (Zool) boa f; **a ~ constrictor** una boa constrictor

b

boar /bɔːr ‖bɔː(r)/ *n* (*pl* ∼**s** *or* ∼) **(a)** (male pig) cerdo *m* macho, verraco *m* **(b)** (wild ∼) jabalí *m*

board¹ /bɔːrd ‖bɔːd/ *n* **1** (plank) tabla *f*, tablón *m*

2 **(a)** (diving ∼) trampolín *m* **(b)** (for surfing, windsurfing) tabla *f* (de surf) **(c)** (Games) tablero *m*
3 **(a)** (notice∼) tablero *m or* (Esp) tablón *m* de anuncios, cartelera *f* (AmL), diario *m* mural (Chi) **(b)** (sign) letrero *m*, cartel *m* **(c)** (score∼) marcador *m* **(d)** (blackboard) pizarra *f*, pizarrón *m* (AmL), tablero *m* (Col)
4 **(a)** (committee) junta *f*, consejo *m* **(b)** (administrative body): **the Water/Gas B∼** la compañía del agua/gas **(c)** ∼ **(of directors)** (Busn) junta *f* directiva, consejo *m* de administración **(d)** (of examiners) tribunal *m*
5 (provision of meals): ∼ **and lodging** comida y alojamiento; **full/half** ∼ pensión *f* completa/media pensión *f*
6 (*in phrases*) **across the board: they have promised to reduce taxation across the** ∼ han prometido una reducción general de impuestos; **on board** a bordo; **on** ∼ **the ship/plane** a bordo del barco/avión

board² *vt* **1** (go aboard): **to** ∼ **a ship** embarcar(se)*, abordar (Méx) **2** (accommodate) hospedar
■ ∼ *vi* **1** (go aboard) embarcar(se)*, abordar (Col, Méx) **2** (be accommodated) **to** ∼ **WITH sb** alojarse *or* hospedarse en casa de algún
■ **board up** [*v + o + adv, v + adv + o*] cerrar* con tablas

boarder /bɔːrdər ‖bɔːdə(r)/ *n* **(a)** (lodger) huésped *mf* **(b)** (at boarding school) (esp BrE) interno, -na *m,f*

board game *n* juego *m* de mesa

boarding /bɔːrdɪŋ ‖bɔːdɪŋ/**:** ∼ **card** ▶ ∼ PASS; ∼ **house** *n* pensión *f*; ∼ **pass** *n* tarjeta *f* de embarque, pase *m* de abordar (Chi, Méx); ∼ **school** *n* internado *m*

board: ∼**room** *n* sala *f or* salón *m* de juntas; ∼**walk** *n* (AmE) paseo marítimo entarimado

boast¹ /bəʊst/ *vi* presumir, fanfarronear (fam); **to** ∼ **ABOUT sth** alardear *or* jactarse *or* vanagloriarse DE algo
■ ∼ *vt* **(a)** (brag): **I won, he** ∼**ed** —gané yo —dijo vanagloriándose **(b)** (possess) contar* con

boast² *n* alarde *m*

boastful /bəʊstfəl/ *adj* jactancioso

boat /bəʊt/ *n* barco *m*; (small, open) bote *m*, barca *f*; **by** ∼ en barco

boating /bəʊtɪŋ/ *n*: **to go** ∼ ir* a dar un paseo en bote *or* barca

boat: ∼**man** *n* cobertizo *m* (*para botes*); ∼**man** /bəʊtmən/ *n* (*pl* -**men** /-mən/) barquero *m*; ∼ **race** *n* regata *f*, ∼**swain** /bəʊsṇ/ *n* contramaestre *m*

bob¹ /bɑːb ‖bɒb/ *n* **1** **(a)** (movement of head) inclinación *f* **(b)** (curtsy) reverencia *f* **2** (haircut) melena *f*

bob² *vi* -**bb**- (move abruptly): **the cork** ∼**bed up and down on the water** el corcho cabeceaba en el agua

bobbin /bɑːbən ‖bɒbɪn/ *n* bobina *f*

bobby /bɑːbi ‖bɒbi/L**:** ∼ **pin** *n* (AmE)

horquilla *f*, pasador *m* (Méx), pinche *m* (Chi); ∼ **socks,** (AmE also) ∼ **sox** /sɑːks ‖sɒks/ *pl n* calcetines *mpl* cortos

bode /bəʊd/ *vi* (liter): **to** ∼ **well/ill** ser* buena/mala señal

bodice /bɑːdəs ‖bɒdɪs/ *n* (of dress) canesú *m*; (undergarment) corpiño *m*

bodily¹ /bɑːdḷi ‖bɒdɪli/ *adj* (*before n*) corporal; ∼ **functions** funciones *fpl* fisiológicas

bodily² *adv*: **they dragged him** ∼ **into the car** lo agarraron y lo metieron en el coche a la fuerza

body /bɑːdi ‖bɒdi/ *n* (*pl* **bodies**) **1** **(a)** (of human, animal) cuerpo *m*; (*before n*) ∼ **language** lenguaje *m* corporal **(b)** (trunk) cuerpo *m* **(c)** (dead) cadáver *m*; **over my dead** ∼*!* ¡tendrán (*or* tendrá *etc*) que pasar por encima de mi cadáver!
2 (main part — of plane) fuselaje *m*; (— of ship) casco *m*; (Auto) carrocería *f*
3 **(a)** (organization) organismo *m* **(b)** (unit) (*no pl*): **they walked out in a** ∼ salieron en masa **(c)** (collection): **a** ∼ **of evidence** un conjunto de pruebas; **a growing** ∼ **of opinion** una creciente corriente de opinión **(d)** (of water) masa *f*
4 (object) cuerpo *m*; **heavenly** ∼ (poet) cuerpo *m* celeste
5 (density — of wine) cuerpo *m*; (— of hair) volumen *m*, cuerpo *m*

body: ∼ **builder** *n* fisiculturista *mf*; ∼ **building** *n* fisiculturismo *m*; ∼**guard** *n* guardaespaldas *mf*; (group) escolta *f*; ∼ **stocking** *n* body *m*; ∼**work** *n* carrocería *f*

bog /bɔːɡ, bɑːɡ ‖bɒɡ/ *n* ciénaga *f*; (peat ∼) tremedal *m*
■ **bog down** -**gg**- [*v + o + adv*] (*usu pass*): **to be** ∼**ged down with work** estar* inundado de trabajo; **don't get** ∼**ged down in too much detail** no te enredes con demasiados detalles

boggle /bɑːɡəl ‖bɒɡəl/ *vi*: **the mind** ∼**s** (hum) uno se queda helado, uno alucina (Esp, Méx fam)

bogus /bəʊɡəs/ *adj* ⟨*claim/name*⟩ falso; ⟨*argument*⟩ falaz

Bohemian /bəʊhiːmiən/ *adj also* **bohemian** (unconventional) bohemio

boil¹ /bɔɪl/ *n* **1** (Med) furúnculo *m* **2** (boiling point): **the vegetables are on the** ∼ las verduras se están haciendo; **bring the water to the** ∼ dejar que el agua rompa el hervor

boil² *vi* ⟨⟨*water/vegetables*⟩⟩ hervir*; **the rice has** ∼**ed dry** el arroz se ha quedado sin agua
■ ∼ *vt* **1** (bring to boiling point) hervir*; (keep at boiling point) hervir*, dejar hervir; (cook in boiling water) cocer*, hervir* **2** **boiled** *past p* ⟨*potatoes/rice*⟩ hervido; ⟨*ham*⟩ cocido; ⟨*egg*⟩ (soft) pasado por agua; (hard) duro
■ **boil down to** [*v + adv + prep + o*] reducirse* a
■ **boil over** [*v + adv*] ⟨*milk*⟩ irse* por el fuego; ⟨⟨*pan*⟩⟩ desbordarse; ⟨⟨*person*⟩⟩ perder* el control

boiler /bɔɪlər ‖bɔɪlə(r)/ *n* caldera *f*

boiler suit *n* (BrE) overol *m* (AmL), mono *m* (Esp, Méx)

boiling /bɔɪlɪŋ/ *adj* (colloq): **this coffee is** ∼ este café está hirviendo; **I'm** ∼ estoy asado (fam); **it's** ∼ **hot today/in here** (*as adv*) hace un calor espantoso hoy/aquí

boiling point *n* punto *m* de ebullición

boisterous /bɔɪstərəs/ *adj* bullicioso

bold /bəʊld/ adj **-er, -est** [1] (daring) audaz [2] (impudent) ⟨smile/advances⟩ descarado [3] ⟨pattern⟩ llamativo; ⟨color⟩ fuerte

boldly /'bəʊldli/ adv [1] (daringly) con audacia, audazmente [2] (impudently) descaradamente

Bolivia /bə'lɪvɪə/ n Bolivia f

Bolivian[1] /bə'lɪvɪən/ adj boliviano

Bolivian[2] n boliviano, -na m,f

bollard /'bɑːlərd ‖'bɒlɑːd/ n **(a)** (on quay) noray m, bolardo m **(b)** (by road) (BrE) baliza f

bolster[1] /'bəʊlstər ‖'bəʊlstə(r)/ vt to ~ (up) ⟨popularity/economy⟩ reforzar*; ⟨argument⟩ reafirmar; ⟨morale⟩ levantar

bolster[2] n cabezal m (almohada de forma cilíndrica)

bolt[1] /bəʊlt/ n [1] (Tech) tornillo m, perno m [2] **(a)** (on door) pestillo m, pasador m, cerrojo m **(b)** (on firearm) cerrojo m

bolt[2] vt [1] (fasten with bolt) atornillar, sujetar con un tornillo or perno [2] ⟨door⟩ echarle el pestillo or el pasador or el cerrojo a [3] ~ (down) ⟨food/ meal⟩ engullir* ■ ~ vi «horse» desbocarse*; «person» salir* disparado

bolt[3] adv: ~ upright muy erguido; **he sat ~ upright in bed** se irguió en la cama

bomb[1] /bɑːm ‖bɒm/ n bomba f; (before n) **disposal** desactivación f de explosivas; **~ scare** amenaza f de bomba; **~ squad** (colloq) brigada f antiexplosivos

bomb[2] vt (from air) bombardear; (plant bomb in) colocar* una bomba en

bombard /bɑːm'bɑːrd ‖bɒm'bɑːd/ vt (Mil) bombardear; **she was ~ed with questions** la acribillaron a preguntas

bomber /'bɑːmər ‖'bɒmə(r)/ n **(a)** (aircraft) bombardero m **(b)** (terrorist) terrorista mf (que perpetra atentados colocando bombas)

bomber jacket n chaqueta f or (Esp) cazadora f or (Méx) chamarra f or (RPl) campera f de aviador

bombing /'bɑːmɪŋ ‖'bɒmɪŋ/ n **(a)** (from aircraft) bombardeo m **(b)** (by terrorists) atentado m (terrorista)

bombshell /'bɑːmʃel ‖'bɒmʃel/ n (shocking news) bomba f

bona fide /'bəʊnəfaɪd ‖ˌbəʊnə'faɪdi/ adj genuino, auténtico

bonanza /bə'nænzə/ n **(a)** (piece of luck) filón m **(b)** (plentiful supply) superabundancia f

bond[1] /bɑːnd ‖bɒnd/ n [1] **(a)** (link) vínculo m **(b) bonds** pl (fetters) cadenas fpl [2] (adhesion) adherencia f

bond[2] vi (stick) adherirse* **(b)** (form relationship) establecer* vínculos afectivos ■ ~ vt (stick) **to ~ sth to sth** adherir* or pegar* algo A algo

bondage /'bɑːndɪdʒ ‖'bɒndɪdʒ/ n (enslavement) (liter) cautiverio m (liter)

bone[1] /bəʊn/ n **(a)** (Anat) hueso m; **to have a ~ to pick with sb** tener* que ajustar cuentas con algn **(b)** (of fish) espina f

bone[2] vt ⟨meat⟩ deshuesar; ⟨fish⟩ quitarle las espinas a

bone: ~ **china** n porcelana f fina; ~**-dry** /'bəʊn'draɪ/ (pred ~ **dry**) adj completamente seco

bonfire /'bɑːnfaɪr ‖'bɒnfaɪə(r)/ n hoguera f

bonnet /'bɑːnət ‖'bɒnɪt/ n [1] (Clothing) sombrero m; (for baby) gorrito m [2] (BrE Auto) capó m, capote m (Méx)

bonus /'bəʊnəs/ n [1] (payment to employee) plus m, prima f [2] (added advantage): (added) ~ ventaja f

bony /'bəʊni/ adj **bonier, boniest (a)** ⟨knee⟩ huesudo **(b)** (made of bone) óseo

boo[1] /buː/ interj ¡bu!

boo[2] n ≈ silba f

boo[3], boos, booing, booed vt/i abuchear

booby /buːbi/: ~ **prize** n premio m al peor; ~ **trap** n (Mil) trampa f; (bomb) bomba f trampa; ~**-trap** vt **-pp-** (Mil): **his car was ~-trapped** le pusieron una bomba en el coche

book[1] /bʊk/ n [1] (printed work) libro m; **to go by the** ~ ceñirse* (estrictamente) a las normas or reglas; **to throw the** ~ **at sb** castigar* duramente a algn [2] **(a)** (exercise ~) cuaderno m **(b)** (note~) libreta f or cuaderno m (de apuntes) [3] (set — of samples) muestrario m; (— of matches, stamps) librito m [4] **books** pl (Busn, Fin): **the ~s** los libros

book[2] vt (esp BrE) [1] **(a)** ⟨room/seat/flight⟩ reservar; ⟨appointment⟩ concertar*; **the hotel/ flight is fully ~ed** el hotel/vuelo está completo; **I'm ~ed (up) all this week** tengo toda la semana ocupada [2] ⟨performer⟩ contratar [2] (record) ⟨order⟩ asentar* [3] **(a)** (record charge against) multar **(b)** (in soccer) (BrE) amonestar ■ ~ vi (esp BrE) hacer* una reserva

■ **book in** [v + o + adv, v + adv + o] (reserve room for): **she'd ~ed us in at the Hilton** nos había reservado habitación en el Hilton

■ **book up** [v + o + adv, v + adv + o] (reserve) (often pass): **the hotels are all ~ed up** los hoteles están todos completos; **tonight's performance is ~ed up** no quedan localidades para la función de esta noche

book: ~**case** n biblioteca f, librería f (Esp), librero m (Méx); ~**end** n sujetalibros m

booking /'bʊkɪŋ/ n (esp BrE) **(a)** (reservation) reserva f, reservación f (AmL) **(b)** (engagement) compromiso m

booking office n (BrE Theat) taquilla f, boletería f (AmL)

bookkeeping /'bʊkˌkiːpɪŋ/ n contabilidad f, teneduría f de libros

booklet /'bʊklət ‖'bʊklɪt/ n folleto m

bookmaker n /'bʊkˌmeɪkər ‖'bʊkˌmeɪkə(r)/ corredor, -dora m,f de apuestas

bookmark[1] /'bʊkmɑːrk ‖'bʊkmɑːk/ n **(a)** (for book) señalador m, marcador m **(b)** (Comput) marcador m

bookmark[2] vt marcar

book: ~**seller** n librero, -ra m,f; ~**shelf** n **(a)** (shelf) estante m, balda f (Esp) (para libros) **(b)** ~**shelves** ▶ BOOKCASE; ~**shop** n librería f; ~**store** n (AmE) librería f; ~ **token** n (BrE) cheque m regalo, vale m (canjeable por libros)

boom[1] /buːm/ n [1] (Econ, Fin) boom m [2] (sound of guns, explosion) estruendo m

boom² vi [1] «guns» tronar*; «voice/thunder» retumbar [2] (usu in -ing form) «market/industry» vivir un boom

boomerang /'buːməræŋ/ n bumerang m

booming /'buːmɪŋ/ adj (a) «sound» retumbante (b) «industry» en auge

boon /buːn/ n gran ayuda f

boost¹ /buːst/ n (uplift): to give a ~ to sth dar* empuje a algo; it was a tremendous ~ to her confidence le dio mucha más confianza en sí misma

boost² vt «economy/production» estimular; «sales» aumentar; «morale» levantar

booster /'buːstər ‖ 'buːstə(r)/ n (a) (Rad, Telec, TV) repetidor m (b) (Med) ~ (shot) (vacuna f de) refuerzo m

booster cable n (AmE) cable m de arranque

boot¹ /buːt/ n [1] (Clothing) bota f; (short) botín m [2] (kick) (colloq) (no pl) patada f, puntapié m [3] (BrE Auto) maletero m, portamaletas m, cajuela f (Méx), baúl m (Col, CS, Ven), maleta f (Chi), maletera f (Per) [4] to boot (as linker) para rematarla

boot² vt (a) (kick) (colloq) darle* un puntapié a (b) (Comput) ~ (up) cargar*

booth /buːθ ‖ buːð, buːθ/ n (a) (cabin) cabina f; photo ~ fotomatón m (b) (polling ~) cabina f de votación (c) (telephone ~) cabina f (de teléfono) (d) (stall — at fair) barraca f, caseta f; (— at exhibition) stand m

bootleg /'buːtleg/ adj (before n) «liquor» de contrabando; «tape» pirata adj inv

booty /'buːti/ n botín m

booze¹ /buːz/ n (colloq) bebida f, trago m (esp AmL fam)

booze² vi (colloq) beber, tomar (esp AmL)

border¹ /'bɔːrdər ‖ 'bɔːdə(r)/ n [1] (Pol) frontera f; (before n) «dispute/town» fronterizo [2] (a) (edge) borde m (b) (edging — on fabric, plate) cenefa f

border² vt «country/state» limitar con; «fields/lands» lindar con (b) (edge — with ribbon, binding) ribetear

■ **border on** [v + prep + o] (a) «country» limitar con (b) (verge on) rayar en, lindar con

borderline /'bɔːrdərlaɪn ‖ 'bɔːdəlaɪn/ adj «case/score» dudoso; «candidate» en el límite entre el aprobado y el reprobado or (Esp) el suspenso

bore¹ /bɔːr ‖ bɔː(r)/ past of BEAR¹

bore² vt [1] «shaft/tunnel» hacer*, abrir* [2] (weary) aburrir

bore³ n [1] (person) pesado, -da m,f (fam); (thing) aburrimiento m, lata f (fam) [2] (of cylinder, gun barrel) calibre m

bored /bɔːrd ‖ bɔːd/ adj aburrido; to be ~ WITH sth estar* aburrido DE algo; to get ~ aburrirse

boredom /'bɔːrdəm ‖ 'bɔːdəm/ n aburrimiento m

boring /'bɔːrɪŋ/ adj aburrido, aburridor (AmL)

born¹ /bɔːrn ‖ bɔːn/ (past p of BEAR¹): to be ~ nacer*

born² adj (before n) «teacher/leader» nato; he's a ~ loser siempre ha sido y será un perdedor

born-again /'bɔːrnə'gen ‖ ˌbɔːnə'gen/ adj (before n): ~ Christian cristiano convertido, especialmente a una secta evangélica

borne /bɔːrn ‖ bɔːn/ past p of BEAR¹

borough /'bɜːrəʊ ‖ 'bʌrə/ n (a) (in US) distrito m municipal (b) (in UK) municipio m

borrow /'bɑːrəʊ ‖ 'bɒrəʊ/ vt [1] (a) (have on loan): may I ~ your pencil? ¿me prestas or (Esp tb) me dejas el lápiz?; to ~ sth FROM sb pedirle* prestado algo A algn; I ~ed $5,000 from the bank pedí un préstamo de 5.000 dólares al banco (b) (from library) sacar* [2] «idea» sacar*; «word» tomar

borrower /'bɑːrəʊər ‖ 'bɒrəʊə(r)/ n (a) (Fin) prestatario, -ria m,f (b) (from library) usuario, -ria m,f

borrowing /'bɑːrəʊɪŋ ‖ 'bɒrəʊɪŋ/ n (Fin) préstamos mpl

Bosnia Herzegovina /'bɑːzniəˌhertsəgəʊ'viːnə ‖ ˌbɒzniəˌhɜːtsəgəʊ'viːnə/ n Bosnia Herzegovina f

Bosnian /'bɑːzniən ‖ 'bɒzniən/ adj bosnio

bosom /'bʊzəm/ n (a) (breast, chest) (liter) pecho m; (before n) «friend» del alma (b) (of woman — bust) pecho m, busto m; (— breast) pecho m, seno m (c) (heart, center) (liter) seno m

boss /bɑːs ‖ bɒs/ n (colloq) (a) (superior) jefe, -fa m,f; (employer, factory owner) patrón, -trona m,f (b) (leader) dirigente m,f

■ **boss around**, (BrE also) **boss about** [v + o + adv] (colloq) mandonear (fam)

bossy /'bɑːsi ‖ 'bɒsi/ adj **bossier, bossiest** (colloq) mandón (fam)

bosun /'bəʊsən/ n ▶ BOATSWAIN

botanic /bə'tænɪk/, **-ical** /-ɪkəl/ adj botánico

botanist /'bɑːtənəst ‖ 'bɒtənɪst/ n botánico, -ca m,f

botany /'bɑːtəni ‖ 'bɒtəni/ n botánica f

botch /bɑːtʃ ‖ bɒtʃ/ vt (colloq) ~ (up) «repair» hacer* una chapuza de (fam); «plan» estropear

both¹ /bəʊθ/ adj ambos, -bas, los dos, las dos

both² pron ambos, -bas, los dos, las dos; we ~ like chess a los dos nos gusta el ajedrez; the coats are ~ too big los dos abrigos son demasiado grandes

both³ conj both ... and ...: ~ Paul and John are in Italy tanto Paul como John están en Italia, Paul y John están los dos en Italia; she ~ wrote and played the music compuso y tocó la música ella misma

bother¹ /'bɑːðər ‖ 'bɒðə(r)/ vt (a) (irritate, pester) molestar; sorry to ~ you perdone (que lo moleste) (b) (trouble) preocupar; she's very quiet, but don't let it ~ you es muy callada, no te inquietes por ello (c) (make effort) not to ~ + ~ -ING: don't ~ writing a long letter no hace falta que escribas una carta larga; to ~ to + INF tomarse la molestia DE + INF

AmC	Central America	Arg	Argentina	Cu	Cuba	Per	Peru
AmL	Latin America	Bol	Bolivia	Ec	Ecuador	RPI	River Plate Area
AmS	South America	Chi	Chile	Esp	Spain	Ur	Uruguay
Andes	Andean Region	CS	Southern Cone	Méx	Mexico	Ven	Venezuela

■ ~ *vi* (a) (make effort) molestarse (b) (worry) **to ~ ABOUT sth/sb** preocuparse POR algo/algn

bother² *n* molestia *f*; (work) trabajo *m*; (problems) problemas *mpl*

bothered /'bɑːðərd ‖ 'bʊðəd/ *adj* (pred): **I can't be ~ to** go me da pereza ir; **she yelled at him, but he wasn't a bit ~** le pegó un berrido, pero él ni se inmutó

bottle¹ /'bɑːtl ‖ 'bɒtl/ *n* (container, contents) botella *f*; (of perfume) frasco *m*; **baby's ~** biberón *m*, mamila *f* (Méx), mamadera *f* (CS, Per), tetero *m* (Col); (*before n*) **~ opener** abrebotellas *m*, destapador *m* (AmL)

bottle² *vt* (a) ⟨*wine/milk*⟩ embotellar; **~d milk** leche *f* en *or* de botella; **~d water** agua *f*‡ embotellada (b) (BrE) ⟨*fruit/vegetables*⟩ poner* en conserva

■ **bottle up** [*v + o + adv, v + adv + o*] (colloq) ⟨*emotion*⟩ reprimir

bottle: **~ bank** *n* contenedor *m* de recogida de vidrio; **~feed** *vt* (*past & past p* **-fed**) alimentar con biberón *or* (Méx) con mamila *or* (CS, Per) con mamadera *or* (Col) con tetero; **~neck** *n* (narrow stretch of road) cuello *m* de botella; (hold-up) embotellamiento *m*

bottom¹ /'bɑːtəm ‖ 'bɒtəm/ *n* **1** (a) (of box, bottle, drawer) fondo *m*; (of hill, stairs) pie *m*; (of page) final *m*, pie *m*; (of pile) parte *f* de abajo; **to get to the ~ of** sth llegar* al fondo de algo (b) (underneath — of box) parte *f* de abajo; (— of ship) fondo *m* (c) (of bed) pies *mpl*; (of garden) fondo *m*; (of road) final *m* (d) (of sea, river, lake) fondo *m* **2** (of hierarchy): **he is at the ~ of the class** es el último de la clase; **she started out at the ~** empezó desde abajo **3** (a) (of person) trasero *m* (fam), traste *m* (CS fam) (b) (of pyjamas, tracksuit) pantalón *m*, pantalones *mpl*; (of bikini) parte *f* de abajo

bottom² *adj* (*before n*) ⟨*shelf/layer*⟩ de más abajo; ⟨*grade*⟩ más bajo; ⟨*part/edge/lip*⟩ inferior

bottomless /'bɑːtəmləs ‖ 'bɒtəmlɪs/ *adj* ⟨*well/ shaft*⟩ sin fondo

bough /baʊ/ *n* rama *f*

bought /bɔːt/ *past & past p of* BUY¹

boulder /'bəʊldər ‖ 'bəʊldə(r)/ *n* roca *f* (grande, alisada por la erosión)

boulevard /'bʊləvɑːrd ‖ 'buːləvɑːd/ *n* bulevar *m*

bounce¹ /baʊns/ *vi* (a) ⟨*ball/object*⟩ rebotar, picar* (AmL), botar (Esp, Méx); **the child was bouncing up and down on the sofa** el niño saltaba en el sofá (b) ⟨*check*⟩ (colloq) ser* devuelto, rebotar (fam)

■ ~ *vt* (a) ⟨*ball/object*⟩ hacer* rebotar, hacer* picar (AmL), (hacer*) botar (Esp, Méx) (b) ⟨*check*⟩ (colloq) devolver*

■ **bounce back** [*v + adv*] (colloq) levantarse

bounce² *n* (a) (action) rebote *m*, pique *m* (AmL) (b) (springiness, vitality): **this shampoo puts the ~ back into your hair** este champú les da nueva vida a sus cabellos; **she's full of ~** es una persona llena de vida

bouncer /'baʊnsər ‖ 'baʊnsə(r)/ *n* (colloq) gorila *m* (fam), sacabullas *m* (Méx fam)

bound¹ /baʊnd/ *n* **1** **bounds** *pl* (limits) límites *mpl*; **within the ~s of possibility** dentro de lo

posible; **the shop is out of ~s to schoolchildren** los niños tienen prohibido entrar en la tienda **2** (jump) salto *m*, brinco *m*

bound² *vi* saltar; **to ~ in/out** entrar/salir* dando saltos

bound³ *past & past p of* BIND¹

bound⁴ *adj* **1** (a) (tied up) atado, amarrado (AmL exc RPl) (b) (obliged): **they are ~ by law to supply the goods** están obligados por ley a suministrar los artículos; **I'm duty ~ to tell you the truth** es mi deber decirte la verdad **2** (pred) (certain): **it was ~ to happen sooner or later** tarde o temprano tenía que suceder; **it was ~ to go wrong** no cabía duda de que iba a salir mal **3** (headed) (pred): **the truck was ~ for Italy** el camión iba rumbo a Italia; **they are Moscow ~** van camino a Moscú

boundary /'baʊndri, -dəri/ *n* (pl **-ries**) límite *m*

bountiful /'baʊntɪfəl/ *adj* ⟨*king/nature*⟩ munificente (liter); ⟨*harvest/gifts*⟩ copioso

bounty /'baʊnti/ *n* (pl **-ties**) **1** (liter) (generosity) munificencia *f* (liter) **2** (reward) recompensa *f*; (*before n*) **~ hunter** cazador, -dora *m,f* de recompensas

bouquet /bəʊˈkeɪ, buːˈkeɪ ‖ bʊˈkeɪ, bəʊˈkeɪ/ *n* **1** (of flowers) ramo *m*; (small) ramillete *m* **2** (of wine) bouquet *m*

bourbon /'bɜːrbən ‖ 'bɜːbən/ *n* bourbon *m*

bourgeois /'bʊrʒwɑː ‖ 'bɔːʒwɑː, ˈbʊəʒ-/ *adj* burgués

bout /baʊt/ *n* **1** (period, spell): **I had a ~ of flu** tuve una gripe *or* (Col, Méx) una gripa muy mala; **a drinking ~** una borrachera **2** (in boxing, wrestling) combate *m*, encuentro *m*

boutique /buːˈtiːk/ *n* boutique *f*

bow¹ /baʊ/ *n* **1** (movement) reverencia *f* **2** (of ship) (*often pl*) proa *f*

bow² /baʊ/ *vi* hacer* una reverencia; **they ~ed to government pressure** cedieron ante la presión del gobierno

■ ~ *vt* ⟨*head*⟩ inclinar

■ **bow out** [*v + adv*] retirarse

bow³ /bəʊ/ *n* **1** (knot) lazo *m*, moño *m* (esp AmL) **2** (weapon) arco *m* **3** (Mus) arco *m*

bow⁴ /bəʊ/ *vi* «*branch/plank*» arquearse, pandearse (esp AmL)

bowel /'baʊəl/ *n* (Anat) intestino *m* grueso; **in the ~s of the earth** (liter) en las entrañas de la tierra

bowl¹ /bəʊl/ *n* **1** (a) (container) (Culin) bol *m*, tazón *m*, cuenco *m*; (for washing etc) palangana *f*, barreño *m*; **fruit ~** frutero *m*, frutera *f* (CS); **soup ~** sopero *m* (b) (contents) bol *m*, tazón *m* (c) (of toilet) taza *f* **2** (in game of bowls) bola *f*, bocha *f*; *see also* BOWLS

bowl² *vt/i* lanzar*

■ **bowl over** [*v + o + adv, v + adv + o*] derribar; **we were ~ed over by the beauty of the island** la belleza de la isla nos dejó pasmados

bowlegged /'bəʊˈlegd/ *adj* patizambo

bowler /'bəʊlər ‖ 'bəʊlə(r)/ *n* **1** (in cricket) lanzador, -dora *m,f*; (in bowling, bowls) jugador, -dora *m,f* **2** ~ **(hat)** bombín *m*, sombrero *m* de hongo

bowling /'bəʊlɪŋ/ n **(a)** (in bowling alley) bolos
mpl **(b)** (on grass) ▶ BOWLS

bowling: ~ alley n bolera f, bowling m; **~
green** n: pista donde se juega a los BOWLS

bowls /bəʊlz/ n (+ *sing vb*) juego semejante a la
petanca que se juega sobre césped

bow tie /bəʊ/ n corbata f de moño (AmL),
pajarita f (Esp)

box¹ /bɑːks ‖ bɒks/ n **1** (container, contents) caja
f; (large) cajón m; (for watch, pen) estuche m (on
form) casilla f **3** **(a)** (in theater) palco m **(b)** (booth)
cabina f

box² vi boxear

■ ~ vt poner* en una caja, embalar

■ **box in** [v + o + adv, v + adv + o] **(a)** (restrict,
surround) cerrarle* el paso a **(b)** (enclose) ⟨pipes⟩
esconder (tapando con una tabla etc)

boxer /'bɑːksər ‖ 'bɒksə(r)/ n **(a)** (person)
boxeador, -dora m,f **(b)** (dog) bóxer mf

boxer shorts pl n calzoncillos mpl, calzones
mpl (Méx), interiores mpl (Col, Ven)

boxing /'bɑːksɪŋ ‖ 'bɒksɪŋ/ n boxeo m; (before
n) ~ **ring** ring m, cuadrilátero m

Boxing Day /'bɑːksɪŋ ‖ 'bɒksɪŋ/ n: el 26 de
diciembre, día festivo en Gran Bretaña

box: ~ number n (at post office) apartado m (de
correos), apartado m postal (Méx), casilla f postal
or de correo (CS); **~ office** n taquilla f,
boletería f (AmL)

boy /bɔɪ/ n **(a)** (baby, child) niño m, chico m **(b)**
(son) hijo m, chico m **(c)** (young man) (colloq)
muchacho m, chico m

boycott¹ /'bɔɪkɑːt ‖ 'bɔɪkɒt/ n boicot m

boycott² vt boicotear

boyfriend /'bɔɪfrend/ n novio m, pololo m (Chi
fam)

boyish /'bɔɪʃ/ adj ⟨enthusiasm/smile⟩ de chico,
de niño; (used of woman) de muchacho, de chico

boy scout n boy scout m, explorador m

bra /brɑː/ n sostén m, sujetador m (Esp), brasier
m (Col, Méx), corpiño m (RPl), soutien m (Ur)

brace¹ /breɪs/ n **1** (support) abrazadera f
2 (Dent) ▶ **4B** **3** (drill) berbiquí m **4** **braces** pl
(a) (BrE Clothing) tirantes mpl, cargaderas fpl (Col),
tiradores mpl (RPl), suspensores mpl (Chi) **(b)** (esp
AmE Dent) aparato(s) m(pl), frenos mpl (Méx),
fierros mpl (Méx, Per), frenillos mpl (Chi) **5** (pl
~) (pair) (BrE) par m

brace² vt (support) apuntalar

■ v refl to ~ oneself for sth prepararse para algo

bracelet /'breɪslət ‖ 'breɪslɪt/ n pulsera f,
brazalete m

bracing /'breɪsɪŋ/ adj vigorizante

bracken /'brækən/ n helechos mpl

bracket¹ /'brækət ‖ 'brækɪt/ n **1** **(a)** (Print)
(square bracket) corchete m **(b)** (parenthesis) (BrE)
paréntesis m **2** (category): income ~ nivel m de
ingresos; the 25-30 age ~ el grupo etario de
entre 25 y 30 años **3** (support) soporte m; (for
shelves) escuadra f

bracket² vt **(a)** ⟨word/phrase⟩ poner* entre
corchetes; (in parentheses) (BrE) poner* entre
paréntesis **(b)** (categorize) catalogar*

brag /bræg/ vi/t -gg- fanfarronear (fam)

braid¹ /breɪd/ n **(a)** (of hair) (esp AmE) trenza f
(b) (Tex) galón m

braid² vt trenzar*

braille, Braille /breɪl/ n braille m, Braille m

brain /breɪn/ n cerebro m; (before n) ~ **damage**
lesión f cerebral; ~ **tumor** tumor m cerebral

brain: ~child n creación m; **~-dead** adj
clínicamente muerto

brains /breɪnz/ n **1** (+ pl vb) **(a)** (substance)
sesos mpl; (Culin) sesos mpl **(b)** (intelligence)
inteligencia f **2** (+ sing vb) (mastermind) cerebro
m, autor, -tora m,f intelectual (AmL); **he's the ~
of the family** es la lumbrera de la familia

brain: ~wash vt hacerle* un lavado de
cerebro a; **~wave** n (colloq) idea f genial,
lamparazo m (Col fam)

braise /breɪz/ vt estofar

brake¹ /breɪk/ n (on vehicle) freno m; (before n)
~ **lights** luces fpl de freno

brake² vi/t frenar

bramble /'bræmbəl/ n zarza f

bran /bræn/ n salvado m, afrecho m

branch¹ /brɑːntʃ ‖ brɑːntʃ/ n (of tree) rama f;
(of river, road, railway) ramal m; (of family, field of study)
rama f; (of company, bank) sucursal f

branch² vi ⟨river/family⟩ ramificarse*;
⟨road⟩ bifurcarse*; **a path ~es (off) to the right**
un sendero sale a la derecha

■ **branch out** [v + adv] **(a)** (take on new activity)
diversificar* sus (or nuestras etc) actividades; **the
company has ~ed out into publishing** la
compañía ha diversificado sus actividades
lanzándose al campo editorial **(b)** (become
independent): **he has ~ed out on his own** ⟨business
partner⟩ se ha establecido por su cuenta

brand¹ /brænd/ n **1** **(a)** (Busn) marca f **(b)**
(type) tipo m; (style) estilo m **2** (identification mark)
marca f (hecha a fuego)

brand² vt **(a)** (mark) ⟨cattle⟩ marcar* (con hierro
candente) **(b)** (label) **to ~ sb AS sth** tachar a algn
DE algo

brandish /'brændɪʃ/ vt blandir

brand: ~ name n marca f; **~-new**
/'brænd'nuː ‖ ˌbrænd'njuː/ adj nuevo

brandy /'brændi/ n (pl -dies) coñac m, brandy
m

brash /bræʃ/ adj -er, -est excesivamente
desenvuelto

brass /bræs ‖ brɑːs/ n **(a)** (Metall) latón m;
(before n) ⟨button⟩ dorado **(b)** (Mus) (+ sing or pl
vb) bronces mpl, metales mpl

brass band n banda f de música, tambora f
(Méx)

brassiere /brə'zɪr ‖ 'bræziə(r)/ n ▶ BRA

brass knuckles pl n (AmE) nudilleras fpl de
metal, manoplas fpl (AmL)

brat /bræt/ n (pej) mocoso, -sa m,f (pey)

bravado /brə'vɑːdəʊ/ n bravuconadas fpl

brave¹ /breɪv/ adj -ver, -vest valiente

brave² vt ⟨peril⟩ afrontar; **to ~ the weather**
hacerle frente al mal tiempo

brave³ /breɪv/ n **1** (North American Indian) guerrero m
piel roja **2** (liter) (+ pl vb) **the ~** los valientes

bravely /'breɪvli/ adv valientemente

bravery /'breɪvəri/ n valentía f, valor m

bravo /'brɑːvəʊ ‖ brɑː'vəʊ/ interj ¡bravo!

brawl¹ /brɔːl/ n pelea f

brawl² *vi* pelearse

brawny /'brɔːni/ *adj* **-nier, -niest** musculoso

bray /breɪ/ *vi* ⟨*donkey*⟩ rebuznar; ⟨*person*⟩ cacarear

brazen /'breɪzn̩ ‖'breɪzən/ *adj* descarado

brazier /'breɪʒər, 'breɪziər ‖'breɪziə(r)/ *n* brasero *m*

Brazil /brə'zɪl/ *n* Brasil *m*

Brazilian /brə'zɪliən/ *adj* brasileño

brazil nut /brə'zɪl/ *n* coquito *m* del Brasil, castaña *f* de Pará (RPl)

breach¹ /briːtʃ/ *n* [1] (of law) infracción *f*; ~ **of contract** incumplimiento *m* de contrato; **she was arrested for ~ of the peace** la detuvieron por alterar el orden público [2] (gap, opening) (frml) brecha *f* [3] (break) (frml) ruptura *f*

breach² *vt* (a) ⟨*rule*⟩ infringir*, violar; ⟨*security*⟩ poner* en peligro (b) (frml) ⟨*defenses*⟩ abrir* una brecha en

bread /bred/ *n* pan *m*; ~ **and butter** pan con mantequilla *or* (RPl) manteca

bread: ~bin *n* (BrE) ▶ ~BOX; **~board** *n* tabla *f* de cortar el pan; **~box** *n* (AmE) panera *f* (*para guardar el pan*); **~crumb** *n* miga *f* (de pan); **~crumbs** (Culin) pan *m* rallado *or* (Méx) molido; **~line** *n*: **they're on the ~line** (colloq) apenas tienen para vivir

breadth /bredθ/ *n* (a) (width) anchura *f*, ancho *m* (b) (extent) amplitud *f*; ~ **of vision** amplitud de miras

breadwinner /'bred,wɪnər ‖'bred,wɪnə(r)/ *n*: **she's the ~ of the family** es la que mantiene a la familia

break¹ /breɪk/ (*past* **broke**; *past p* **broken**) *vt* [1] ⟨*window/plate*⟩ romper*; ⟨*stick*⟩ partir, quebrar* (AmL); **he broke his wrist** se rompió la muñeca [2] (render useless) ⟨*machine*⟩ romper*, descomponer* (AmL) [3] (violate) ⟨*rule*⟩ infringir*; ⟨*promise*⟩ no cumplir; ⟨*contract*⟩ incumplir; ⟨*strike*⟩ romper*; ▶ LAW B [4] (end) ⟨*strike*⟩ poner* fin a; ⟨*drug ring*⟩ desarticular; ⟨*impasse*⟩ salir* de; ⟨*habit*⟩ dejar [5] (a) (ruin) ⟨*person/company*⟩ arruinar a (b) (crush) ⟨*person*⟩ destrozar* [6] (impart): **Sue broke the news to him** Sue le dio la noticia; **they broke it to her gently** se lo dijeron con mucho tacto [7] (exceed) ⟨*record*⟩ batir [8] (disrupt) ⟨*pattern/monotony*⟩ romper* [9] (decipher) ⟨*code*⟩ descifrar

■ ~ *vi* [1] ⟨*window/plate*⟩ romperse*; ⟨*stick*⟩ partirse, quebrarse* (AmL) [2] (give in) ⟨*resistance*⟩ desmoronarse; **she broke under constant interrogation** no resistió el constante interrogatorio [3] (a) (begin) ⟨*storm*⟩ estallar; ⟨*day*⟩ romper* (b) (change) ⟨*weather*⟩ cambiar; **his voice is ~ing** le está cambiando la voz; **his voice broke** (with emotion) se le entrecortó la voz [4] ⟨*wave/surf*⟩ romper*

■ **break away** [*v* + *adv*] **to ~ away** (FROM sth) ⟨*piece*⟩ desprenderse (DE algo); ⟨*faction/region*⟩ escindirse (DE algo)

■ **break down**
  I [*v* + *adv*] [1] ⟨*vehicle/machine*⟩ estropearse,

averiarse*, descomponerse* (AmL), quedarse en pana (Chi), quedarse varado (Col); ⟨*system*⟩ fallar; ⟨*talks*⟩ fracasar [2] (lose composure) perder* el control
  II [*v* + *o* + *adv*, *v* + *adv* + *o*] [1] ⟨*door/barrier*⟩ echar abajo [2] (divide up) ⟨*expenditure*⟩ desglosar; ⟨*sentence*⟩ descomponer*; **the process can be broken down into three steps** el proceso puede dividirse en tres pasos

■ **break in** [1] [*v* + *adv*] ⟨*intruder*⟩ entrar (*para robar etc*) [2] [*v* + *o* + *adv*, *v* + *adv* + *o*] ⟨*horse*⟩ domar

■ **break into** [*v* + *prep* + *o*] ⟨*building*⟩ entrar en (*para robar etc*)

■ **break off** [1] [*v* + *o* + *adv*, *v* + *adv* + *o*] (a) (detach) partir (b) ⟨*engagement/diplomatic relations*⟩ romper* [2] [*v* + *adv*] (snap off, come free) ⟨*piece of ice*⟩ desprenderse; **the handle broke off** se le rompió el asa

■ **break out** [*v* + *adv*] [1] (start) ⟨*war/epidemic/rioting*⟩ estallar [2] (escape) ⟨*prisoner*⟩ escaparse, fugarse*

■ **break through** [1] [*v* + *adv*] (penetrate) (Mil) penetrar en las defensas enemigas; ⟨*sun*⟩ salir* [2] [*v* + *prep* + *o*] ⟨*barrier*⟩ atravesar*, romper*; **they broke through our defenses** penetraron en nuestras defensas

■ **break up**
  I [*v* + *o* + *adv*, *v* + *adv* + *o*] [1] (divide) ⟨*land*⟩ dividir; ⟨*ship*⟩ desaguazar*; ⟨*sentence*⟩ descomponer* [2] (a) ⟨*demonstration*⟩ disolver* (b) (wreck, ruin) ⟨*home*⟩ deshacer*
  II [*v* + *adv*] (a) ⟨*lovers/band*⟩ separarse; **their marriage broke up** su matrimonio fracasó; **to ~ up WITH sb** romper* CON algn (b) ⟨*meeting*⟩ terminar; ⟨*crowd*⟩ dispersarse

break² *n* [1] (a) (Rad, TV) pausa *f* (comercial); (Theat) entreacto *m*, intermedio *m* (b) (rest period) descanso *m*; (at school) (BrE) recreo *m* (c) (short vacation) vacaciones *fpl* (d) (change, respite) cambio *m*; **I need a ~ from all this** necesito descansar de todo esto; (a holiday) vacaciones *fpl* [2] (gap) interrupción *f* [3] (fracture) fractura *f*, rotura *f*; **to make a clean ~** cortar por lo sano

breakable /'breɪkəbəl/ *adj* frágil

breakage /'breɪkɪdʒ/ *n* (a) (action) rotura *f* (b) **breakages** *pl* (objects broken) roturas *fpl*

break: ~away *n* (separation) ruptura *f*, escisión *f*; (*before n*) ⟨*faction*⟩ disidente, escindido; **~down** *n* [1] (a) (failure — of car, machine) avería *f*, descompostura *f* (Méx), varada *f* (Col), pana *f* (Chi); (— of service, communications) interrupción *f*; (— of negotiations) fracaso *m*; (*before n*) **~down truck** grúa *f* (b) (nervous **~down**) crisis *f* nerviosa; [2] (analysis): **a ~down of expenditure** un desglose de los gastos

breaker /'breɪkər ‖'breɪkə(r)/ *n* gran ola *f*

breakfast /'brekfəst/ *n* desayuno *m*; **to have ~** desayunar, tomar el desayuno; (*before n*) ~ **television** televisión *f* matinal

break-in /'breɪkɪn/ *n* robo *m* (con escalamiento)

breaking /'breɪkɪŋ/**: ~ and entering** /'breɪkɪŋənd'entərɪŋ/ *n* allanamiento *m* de morada; ~ **point** *n* límite *m*

break: ~through *n* gran avance *m*; **~up** *n*   ···⊱

(of structure, family) desintegración f; (of empire, company) desmembramiento m; (of political party) disolución f; (of talks) fracaso m; **the ~up of their marriage** su separación; **~water** n rompeolas m

breast /brest/ n **(a)** (of woman) pecho m, seno m; (before n) **~ cancer** cáncer m de mama or de pecho **(b)** (chest) (liter) pecho m **(c)** (Culin) (of chicken, turkey) pechuga f

breast: **~feed** (past & past p **-fed**) vt darle* el pecho a, darle* de mamar a ■ ~ vi dar* el pecho, dar* de mamar; **~stroke** n (estilo) pecho m (AmL), braza f (Esp)

breath /breθ/ n aliento m; **to have bad ~** tener* mal aliento; **to take a ~** aspirar, inspirar; **take a deep ~** respire hondo; **out of ~** sin aliento; **to hold one's ~** contener* la respiración; **to take sb's ~ away** dejar a algn sin habla

Breathalyzer®, Breathalyser® /'breθəlaɪzər ‖ 'breθəlaɪzə(r)/ n alcohómetro m, alcoholímetro m; (before n) **~ test** prueba f del alcohol or de la alcoholemia

breathe /briːð/ vi respirar
■ ~ vt ⟨air/fumes⟩ aspirar, respirar
■ **breathe in** ⓵ [v + adv] aspirar ⓶ [v + o + adv, v + adv + o] ⟨air/fumes⟩ aspirar, respirar
■ **breathe out** ⓵ [v + adv] espirar ⓶ [v + o + adv, v + adv + o] ⟨smoke⟩ expeler; ⟨air⟩ exhalar

breathing /'briːðɪŋ/ n respiración f

breathing space n respiro m

breathless /'breθləs ‖ 'breθlɪs/ adj: **the blow left me ~** el golpe me dejó sin aliento; **he arrived ~** llegó jadeando

breathtaking /'breθˌteɪkɪŋ/ adj impresionante

bred /bred/ past & past p of BREED²

breeches /'brɪtʃəz ‖ 'brɪtʃɪz/ pl n (knee ~) (pantalones mpl) bombachos mpl; (riding ~) pantalones mpl de montar

breed¹ /briːd/ n (of animals) raza f; (of plants) variedad f

breed² (past & past p **bred**) vt ⟨animals⟩ criar*; ⟨violence⟩ engendrar
■ ~ vi reproducirse*

breeder /'briːdər ‖ 'briːdə(r)/ n (of animals) criador, -dora m,f; (of plants) cultivador, -dora m,f

breeding /'briːdɪŋ/ n **(a)** (reproduction) reproducción f **(b)** (raising — of animals) cría f; (— of plants) cultivo m **(c)** (upbringing): **politeness is a sign of good ~** la cortesía es señal de buena educación

breeze¹ /briːz/ n brisa f

breeze² vi (colloq): **to ~ in/out** entrar/salir* tan campante (fam)

breezy /'briːzi/ adj **-zier, -ziest** ⓵ (windy) ⟨spot⟩ ventoso; **it's a bit ~ today** hace un poco de vientecito hoy ⓶ (lively) (colloq) ⟨person⟩ dinámico

brethren /'breðrən/ pl n (arch or liter) hermanos mpl

brevity /'brevəti/ n brevedad f

brew /bruː/ vt **(a)** ⟨beer⟩ fabricar* **(b)** ⟨tea⟩ preparar **(c)** ⟨mischief⟩ tramar

■ ~ vi **(a)** (make beer) fabricar* cerveza **(b)** ⟨tea⟩: **the tea is ~ing** el té se está haciendo **(c)** ⟨storm⟩ avecinarse; ⟨trouble⟩ gestarse

brewer /'bruːər ‖ 'bruːə(r)/ n cervecero, -ra m,f

brewery /'bruːəri/ n (pl **-ries**) fábrica f de cerveza, cervecería f

bribe¹ /braɪb/ n soborno m

bribe² vt sobornar

bribery /'braɪbəri/ n soborno m

bric-a-brac /'brɪkəbræk/ n baratijas fpl

brick /brɪk/ n ladrillo m

bricklayer /'brɪkˌleɪər ‖ 'brɪkˌleɪə(r)/ n albañil m

bridal /'braɪdl/ adj ⟨procession⟩ nupcial; ⟨shop⟩ para novias

bride /braɪd/ n novia f; **the ~ and groom** los novios; (after ceremony) los recién casados

bride: **~groom** n novio m; **~smaid** n dama f de honor; (child) niña que acompaña a la novia

bridge¹ /brɪdʒ/ n ⓵ **(a)** puente m **(b)** (on ship) puente m (de mando) **(c)** (of nose) caballete m ⓶ (Dent) puente m ⓷ (card game) bridge m

bridge² vt ⟨river⟩ tender* un puente sobre; ⟨differences⟩ salvar

bridle /'braɪdl/ n brida f

brief¹ /briːf/ adj breve; **in ~** en resumen

brief² n **(a)** (Law) expediente entregado por el abogado al BARRISTER **(b)** (instructions) instrucciones fpl **(c)** (area of responsibility) competencia f

brief³ vt ⟨lawyer⟩ instruir*; ⟨pilot/spy⟩ darle* instrucciones a; ⟨committee⟩ informar

briefcase /'briːfkeɪs/ n maletín m, portafolio(s) m (esp AmL)

briefing /'briːfɪŋ/ n **(a)** (~ session) sesión f para dar instrucciones **(b)** (press ~) reunión f informativa (para la prensa)

briefly /'briːfli/ adv **(a)** ⟨visit/rule⟩ por poco tiempo **(b)** ⟨reply/speak⟩ brevemente **(c)** (indep) en resumen

briefs /briːfs/ pl n (man's) calzoncillos mpl, slip m; (woman's) calzones mpl (esp AmL), bragas fpl (Esp), bombachas fpl (RPl), pantaletas fpl (AmC, Ven)

brigade /brɪ'geɪd/ n brigada f

bright /braɪt/ adj **-er, -est** ⓵ **(a)** ⟨star/light⟩ brillante; ⟨room⟩ con mucha luz **(b)** ⟨color⟩ fuerte ⓶ **(a)** (cheerful) ⟨eyes⟩ lleno de vida **(b)** (hopeful) ⟨future⟩ prometedor; **to look on the ~ side of sth** mirar el lado bueno de algo ⓷ (intelligent) ⟨person⟩ inteligente; **whose ~ idea was it to ...?** (iro) ¿quién tuvo la brillante idea de ...? (iró)

brighten /'braɪtn/ vi **(a)** (become brighter) ⟨light⟩ hacerse* más brillante **(b)** ~ **(up)** (become cheerful, hopeful) ⟨person⟩ animarse; ⟨situation/prospects⟩ mejorar
■ ~ vt **(a)** (make brighter) iluminar **(b)** ~ **(up)** ⟨room⟩ alegrar; ⟨occasion/party⟩ animar

brightly /'braɪtli/ adv **(a)** ⟨shine⟩ intensamente **(b)** ⟨say/smile⟩ alegremente

AmC	América Central	Arg	Argentina	Cu	Cuba
AmL	América Latina	Bol	Bolivia	Ec	Ecuador
AmS	América del Sur	Chi	Chile	Esp	España
Andes	Región andina	CS	Cono Sur	Méx	México

Per	Perú		
RPl	Río de la Plata		
Ur	Uruguay		
Ven	Venezuela		

b

brights /braɪts/ *pl n* (Auto) (AmE colloq) (luces *fpl*) largas *or* (Andes, Méx) altas *fpl*

brilliance /'brɪljəns/ *n* **(a)** (brightness) resplandor *m* **(b)** (skill, intelligence) brillantez *f*

brilliant /'brɪljənt/ *adj* **(a)** ⟨*light*⟩ brillante; ⟨*sunshine*⟩ radiante; ⟨*red/green*⟩ brillante **(b)** ⟨*student/performance*⟩ brillante

brilliantly /'brɪljəntli/ *adv* **(a)** ⟨*shine*⟩ intensamente **(b)** ⟨*write*⟩ con brillantez

brim¹ /brɪm/ *n* ⓵ (of hat) ala *f*‡ ⓶ (of vessel) borde *m*

brim² *vi* **-mm-:** her eyes were ∼ming with tears tenía los ojos llenos de lágrimas; **to** ∼ **with confidence** rebosar seguridad

brine /braɪn/ *n* **(a)** (saltwater) salmuera *f* **(b)** (seawater) agua *f*‡ salada *or* de mar

bring /brɪŋ/ (*past & past p* **brought**) *vt* traer*; **I couldn't** ∼ **myself to do it** no pude hacerlo; **it brought tears to my eyes** hizo que se me llenaran los ojos de lágrimas; **to** ∼ **sth to bear: to** ∼ **pressure to bear on sb** ejercer* presión sobre algn

■ **bring about** [*v + o + adv, v + adv + o*] dar* lugar a

■ **bring along** [*v + o + adv, v + adv + o*] traer*

■ **bring back** [*v + o + adv, v + adv + o*] **(a)** (return): **I'll** ∼ **your book back tomorrow** te devolveré *or* (AmL exc CS) te regresaré el libro mañana; **to** ∼ **sb back to life** devolverle* la vida a algn **(b)** ⟨*gift/souvenir*⟩ traer* **(c)** (reintroduce) ⟨*custom*⟩ volver* a introducir **(d)** (recall) recordar*; **it brought back memories** me (*or* le *etc*) trajo recuerdos

■ **bring down** [*v + o + adv, v + adv + o*] **(a)** (lower) ⟨*price*⟩ reducir*; ⟨*temperature*⟩ hacer* bajar **(b)** (cause to fall) ⟨*tree/wall*⟩ tirar; ⟨*player/opponent/plane*⟩ derribar; ⟨*government*⟩ derrocar*

■ **bring forward** [*v + o + adv, v + adv + o*] **(a)** (present) ⟨*witness*⟩ hacer* comparecer; ⟨*evidence/idea*⟩ presentar **(b)** (to earlier time) ⟨*meeting/appointment*⟩ adelantar

■ **bring home** [*v + o + adv, v + adv + o*]: **her letter brought home to me the seriousness of the situation** su carta me hizo dar cuenta cabal de la gravedad de la situación

■ **bring off** [*v + o + adv, v + adv + o*] ⟨*feat/victory*⟩ conseguir*, lograr*; ⟨*plan*⟩ llevar a cabo; ⟨*deal*⟩ conseguir*

■ **bring on** [*v + o + adv, v + adv + o*] ⟨*attack/breakdown*⟩ provocar*; **what brought this on?** ¿esto a qué se debe?
⓶ [*v + o + prep + o*] (cause to befall): **he brought it all on himself** él (mismo) se lo buscó

■ **bring out** [*v + o + adv, v + adv + o*] **(a)** ⟨*product/model*⟩ sacar* (al mercado); ⟨*edition/book*⟩ publicar* **(b)** (accentuate): **children** ∼ **out the best in her** el trato con niños hace resaltar sus mejores cualidades

■ **bring together** [*v + o + adv, v + adv + o*]: **the conference will** ∼ **together scientists from all over the world** el congreso reunirá a científicos de todo el mundo; **a tragedy like this can** ∼ **a family together** una tragedia así puede unir a una familia

■ **bring up** [*v + o + adv, v + adv + o*] **(a)** (rear) ⟨*child*⟩ criar* **(b)** (mention) ⟨*subject*⟩ sacar* **(c)** (vomit) vomitar, devolver*

brink /brɪŋk/ *n* borde *m*; **to be on the** ∼ **of** -ING estar* a punto de +INF

brisk /brɪsk/ *adj* **(a)** (lively, quick) ⟨*pace*⟩ rápido y enérgico; ⟨*walk*⟩ a paso ligero; **ice-cream sellers did a** ∼ **trade** los vendedores de helados vendieron muchísimo **(b)** (efficient) ⟨*person/manner*⟩ enérgico *or* dinámico y eficiente

bristle¹ /'brɪsəl/ *n* (on animal) cerda *f*; (on person): **his face was covered in** ∼(s) tenía la barba crecida

bristle² *vi* **(a)** (stand up) «*hair*» erizarse*, ponerse* de punta **(b)** (show annoyance) erizarse*

Britain /'brɪtn̩ ‖'brɪtən/ *n* Gran Bretaña *f*

British¹ /'brɪtɪʃ/ *adj* británico

British² *pl n* **the** ∼ los británicos

Britisher /'brɪtɪʃər ‖'brɪtɪʃə(r)/ *n* (AmE) británico, -ca *m,f*

British: ∼ **Isles** *pl n* **the** ∼ **Isles** las Islas Británicas; ∼ **Summer Time** *n* hora de verano en Gran Bretaña, adelantada en una hora con respecto a la hora de Greenwich

Briton /'brɪtn̩ ‖'brɪtən/ *n* ciudadano británico, ciudadana británica *m,f*; **the ancient** ∼s los antiguos britanos

Brittany /'brɪtni ‖'brɪtəni/ *n* Bretaña *f*

brittle /'brɪtl/ *adj* quebradizo

broach /brəʊtʃ/ *vt* ⟨*subject*⟩ mencionar

broad¹ /brɔːd/ *adj* ⓵ ⟨*avenue*⟩ ancho; ⟨*valley*⟩ grande; ⟨*forehead*⟩ despejado; ⟨*grin*⟩ de oreja a oreja ⓶ **(a)** (extensive) ⟨*syllabus*⟩ amplio; ⟨*interests*⟩ numeroso; **in its** ∼**est sense** en su sentido más amplio **(b)** (general) ⟨*guidelines/conclusions*⟩ general ⓷ **(a)** **a** ∼ **hint** una indirecta muy clara **(b)** ⟨*accent*⟩ cerrado

broad² *n* (woman) (AmE sl) tipa *f* (fam), vieja *f* (Col, Méx, Ven fam)

broad bean *n* haba *f*

broadcast¹ /'brɔːdkæst ‖'brɔːdkɑːst/ *vt/i* (*past & past p* **broadcast**) transmitir, emitir

broadcast² *n* programa *m*, emisión *f* (frml)

broadcaster /'brɔːdkæstər ‖'brɔːdkɑːstə(r)/ *n*: presentador, locutor *etc* de radio o televisión

broadcasting /'brɔːdkæstɪŋ ‖'brɔːdkɑːstɪŋ/ *n* (Rad) radiodifusión *f*, (TV) televisión *f*

broaden /'brɔːdn̩/ *vt* ⟨*scope/horizons/interests*⟩ ampliar*

broadly /'brɔːdli/ *adv*: **the two systems are** ∼ **similar** en líneas generales, los dos sistemas son similares; ∼ **speaking** en líneas generales

broad: ∼**minded** /'brɔːd'maɪndəd ‖,brɔːd'maɪndɪd/ *adj* de criterio amplio; ∼**sheet** *n*: periódico de formato grande

brocade /brə'keɪd ‖brə'keɪd/ *n* brocado *m*

broccoli /'brɑːkəli ‖'brɒkəli/ *n* brócoli *m*, brécol *m*

brochure /brəʊ'ʃʊr ‖'brəʊʃə(r)/ *n* folleto *m*

brogue /brəʊg/ *n* ⓵ (shoe) zapato bajo de cuero ⓶ (Irish accent) (*no pl*) acento *m* irlandés

broil /brɔɪl/ *vt* (esp AmE) asar a la parrilla *or* al grill

broiler /'brɔɪlər ‖'brɔɪlə(r)/ *n* (AmE) parrilla *f*, grill *m*

broke¹ /brəʊk/ *past of* BREAK¹

broke² adj (colloq) (pred): **to be ~** estar* pelado; **to be flat ~** estar* pelado or (Esp) sin un duro or (Col) en la olla

broken¹ /ˈbrəʊkən/ past p of BREAK¹

broken² adj ⚀ (a) ⟨window/vase/chair/glass⟩ roto; ⟨bone⟩ roto, quebrado (AmL) (b) (not working) roto ⚁ ⟨voice⟩ quebrado; **to die of a ~ heart** morirse* de pena; **he's a ~ man** está destrozado ⚂ ⟨home/marriage⟩ deshecho ⚃ (imperfect): **in ~ English** en inglés chapurreado

broken-down /ˈbrəʊkənˈdaʊn/ adj ⟨car/ machine⟩ averiado, descompuesto (AmL), en pana (Chi), varado (Col); ⟨shed/gate⟩ destartalado

broker /ˈbrəʊkər ‖ˈbrəʊkə(r)/ n (a) (agent) agente mf; **insurance ~** agente mf de seguros (b) (stock~) corredor, -dora m,f de bolsa

bronchitis /brɑːˈkaɪtəs ‖brɒŋˈkaɪtɪs/ n bronquitis f

bronze /brɑːnz ‖brɒnz/ n (Metall) bronce m

brooch /brəʊtʃ/ n prendedor m, broche m

brood¹ /bruːd/ n (of birds) nidada f; (of mammals) camada f; (of children) (hum) prole f (fam & hum)

brood² vi (reflect): **she sat ~ing on the unfairness of life** rumiaba lo injusta que era la vida; **stop ~ing over it** deja de darle vueltas al asunto

brook /brʊk/ n arroyo m

broom /bruːm/ n ⚀ (brush) escoba f ⚁ (plant) retama f, hiniesta f

broomstick /ˈbruːmstɪk/ n palo m de escoba; (of a witch) escoba f

broth /brɔːθ ‖brɒθ/ n caldo m

brothel /ˈbrɑːθəl ‖ˈbrɒθəl/ n burdel m

brother /ˈbrʌðər ‖ˈbrʌðə(r)/ n hermano m; **do you have any ~s and sisters?** ¿tienes hermanos?

brotherhood /ˈbrʌðərhʊd ‖ˈbrʌðəhʊd/ n (a) (fellowship) fraternidad f (b) (association) hermandad f; (Relig) cofradía f

brother-in-law /ˈbrʌðərɪnˌlɔː/ n (pl **brothers-in-law**) cuñado m

brotherly /ˈbrʌðərli ‖ˈbrʌðəli/ adj fraternal

brought /brɔːt/ past & past p of BRING

brow /braʊ/ n (a) (forehead) (liter) frente f (b) (eye~) ceja f (c) (of hill) cima f

browbeat /ˈbraʊbiːt/ vt (past **browbeat**; past p **browbeaten** /ˈbraʊˌbiːtn̩/) intimidar

brown¹ /braʊn/ adj **-er, -est** ⟨shoe/dress/eyes⟩ marrón, café adj inv (AmC, Chi, Méx), carmelito (Col); ⟨hair⟩ castaño; ⟨skin/person⟩ (naturally) moreno; (suntanned) bronceado; **to get ~** broncearse

brown² n marrón m, café m (AmC, Chi, Méx), carmelito m (Col)

brown³ vt (a) (Culin) dorar (b) (tan) broncear

brown bread n pan m negro or (Esp) moreno

brownie /ˈbraʊni/ n ⚀ (cake) bizcocho de chocolate y nueces ⚁ **Brownie**, (BrE) **Brownie** (**Guide**) alita f

brown: ~ paper n papel m de estraza; **~ rice** n arroz m integral; **~ sugar** n azúcar m moreno, azúcar f morena

browse /braʊz/ vi (look) mirar (en una tienda, catálogo etc); **she was browsing through a magazine** estaba hojeando una revista

browser /ˈbraʊzər ‖ˈbraʊzə(r)/ n (Comput) navegador m

bruise¹ /bruːz/ n moretón m, cardenal m, morado m (Esp, Ven)

bruise² vt ⟨body/arm⟩ contusionar (frml); ⟨fruit⟩ magullar, mallugar* (Méx, Ven)

brunch /brʌntʃ/ n (colloq) brunch m (combinación de desayuno y almuerzo)

brunette /bruːˈnet/ n morena f, morocha f (CS)

brunt /brʌnt/ n: **to bear** o **take the ~ of sth** sufrir algo

brush¹ /brʌʃ/ n ⚀ (for cleaning) cepillo m; (for hair) cepillo m; (paint~) pincel m; (large) brocha f ⚁ (of fox) cola f ⚂ (act): **I gave my hair a ~** me cepillé el pelo (b) (faint touch) roce m (c) (encounter) **~ WITH sth/sb** ⟨with the law/the police⟩ roce m con algo/algn ⚃ (scrub) maleza f

brush² vt (a) (clean, groom) ⟨jacket/hair⟩ cepillar; **to ~ one's teeth** lavarse los dientes (b) (sweep): **he ~ed the crumbs off the table** quitó las migas de la mesa (c) (touch lightly) rozar*
■ ~ vi **to ~ AGAINST sth/sb** rozar* algo/a algn
■ **brush off** [v + o + adv, v + adv + o] (a) ⟨mud/ hair⟩ quitar (cepillando) (b) ⟨advances/ suggestions⟩ no hacer* caso de
■ **brush up** (a) [v + o + adv, v + adv + o] (colloq) darle* un repaso a (b) [v + adv] **to ~ up ON sth** darle* un repaso A algo

brusque /brʌsk ‖brʊsk/ adj brusco

Brussels /ˈbrʌsəlz/ n Bruselas f

brussels sprout, Brussels Sprout n col f or (AmS) repollito m de Bruselas

brutal /ˈbruːtl̩/ adj brutal

brutality /bruːˈtæləti/ n (pl **-ties**) brutalidad f

brutally /ˈbruːtli/ adv (a) (cruelly) ⟨attack/treat⟩ brutalmente (b) (mercilessly) ⟨frank⟩ crudamente

brute¹ /bruːt/ n (colloq) (a) (person) animal mf (fam) (b) (animal) bestia f (fam)

brute² adj (before n) **~ force** fuerza f bruta

BS n (AmE), **BSc** n (BrE) = **Bachelor of Science**

BST = **British Summer Time**

bubble¹ /ˈbʌbəl/ n (of air, gas) burbuja f; (of soap) pompa f

bubble² vi ⚀ (form bubbles) «lava» bullir*; «champagne» burbujear ⚁ ⟨person⟩: **she ~s with enthusiasm** rebosa (de) entusiasmo

bubble: ~ bath n baño m de burbujas or espuma; **~ gum** n chicle m (de globos), chicle m de bomba (Col, Ven), chicle m globero (Ur); **~-wrapped** adj envuelto en plástico con burbujas

bubbly /ˈbʌbli/ adj **-lier, -liest** (a) ⟨person⟩ lleno de vida; ⟨personality⟩ efervescente (b) (full of bubbles) burbujeante

Bucharest /ˈbuːkərest ‖ˌbuːkəˈrest/ n Bucarest m

buck¹ /bʌk/ n ⚀ (male deer) ciervo m (macho); (male rabbit) conejo m (macho) ⚁ (dollar) (esp AmE colloq) dólar m, verde m (AmL fam) ⚂ (responsibility): **to pass the ~** (colloq) pasar la pelota (fam); **the ~ stops here** la responsabilidad es mía (or nuestra etc)

buck² vi «horse» corcovear
■ ~ vt ⟨trend⟩ resistirse a

■ **buck up** (colloq) **1** [*v* + *adv*] (become cheerful) levantar el ánimo **2** [*v* + *o* + *adv*, *v* + *adv* + *o*] (cheer up) ⟨*person*⟩ levantarle el ánimo a

bucket /'bʌkət ‖'bʌkɪt/ *n* balde *m or* (Esp) cubo *m or* (Méx) cubeta *f or* (Ven) tobo *m*; **to kick the ~** (colloq & hum) estirar la pata (fam & hum)

buckle¹ /'bʌkəl/ *n* hebilla *f*

buckle² *vt* abrochar

■ **~** *vi* (bend, crumple) «*wheel/metal*» torcerse*; **his knees ~d beneath him** se le doblaron las rodillas

bud /bʌd/ *n* brote *m*, yema *f*; (of flower) capullo *m*

Budapest /'bu:dəpest ‖,bu:də'pest/ *n* Budapest *m*

Buddha /'budə ‖'bʊdə/ *n* Buda *m*

Buddhism /'budɪzəm ‖'bʊdɪzəm/ *n* budismo *m*

Buddhist¹ /'budəst ‖'bʊdɪst/ *n* budista *mf*

Buddhist² *adj* budista

budding /'bʌdɪŋ/ *adj* (before *n*) ⟨*artist/genius*⟩ en ciernes

buddy /'bʌdi/ *n* (*pl* **-dies**) (AmE colloq) amigo *m*, compinche *m* (fam), cuate *m* (Méx fam)

budge /bʌdʒ/ *vi* (*usu with neg*) **(a)** (move) moverse* **(b)** (change opinion) cambiar de opinión

■ **~** *vt* **(a)** (move) correr **(b)** (persuade) convencer*

budgerigar /'bʌdʒəriga:r ‖'bʌdʒəriga:(r)/ *n* periquito *m*

budget¹ /'bʌdʒət ‖'bʌdʒɪt/ *n* presupuesto *m*

budget² *vi* administrarse; **to learn to ~** aprender a administrar el dinero; **I hadn't ~ed for staying in a hotel** no había contado con gastos de hotel

budgie /'bʌdʒi/ *n* (BrE colloq) periquito *m*

buff¹ /bʌf/ *n* (colloq) aficionado, -da *m*,*f*; **film ~** cinéfilo, -la *m*,*f*

buff² *vt* ⟨*metal*⟩ pulir; ⟨*shoes*⟩ sacar* brillo a

buffalo /'bʌfələʊ/ *n* (*pl* **-loes** *or* **-los**) **(a)** (wild ox) búfalo *m*; (water **~**) búfalo *m* de agua, carabao *m* **(b)** (bison) (AmE) bisonte *m*

buffer /'bʌfər ‖'bʌfə(r)/ *n* **1** **(a)** (AmE Auto) parachoques *m*, paragolpes *m* (RPl) **(b)** (BrE Rail) (on train) tope *m*; (in station) parachoques *m*; (before *n*) **~ state** estado *m* tapón **2** (Comput) memoria *f* intermedia

buffet¹ /bə'feɪ ‖'bʊfeɪ, 'bʌfeɪ/ *n* **1** (meal) buffet *m* **2** (BrE) **(a)** (in train) bar *m*; (before *n*) **~ car** (*also* AmE) coche *m* restaurante, coche *m* comedor **(b)** (cafeteria) bar *m* (*en una estación*)

buffet² /'bʌfət ‖'bʌfɪt/ *vt* zarandear, sacudir

bug¹ /bʌg/ *n* **1** (biting insect) chinche *f or m*; (any insect) (esp AmE) bicho *m* **2** (germ, disease) (colloq): **he picked up a stomach ~** se agarró algo al estómago; **she got the travel ~** le entró la fiebre de los viajes **3** (listening device) (colloq) micrófono *m* oculto

bug² *vt* **-gg-** (colloq) **1** ⟨*room/telephone*⟩ colocar* micrófonos ocultos en **2** (bother, irritate) fastidiar

bugger /'bʌgər ‖'bʌgə(r)/ *n* (BrE vulg) hijo, -ja *m*,*f* de puta (vulg)

buggy /'bʌgi/ *n* (*pl* **-gies**) **1** (horse-drawn vehicle) calesa *f* **2** (baby **~**) (baby carriage) (AmE) cochecito *m*; (pushchair) (BrE) sillita *f* de paseo (*plegable*)

bugle /'bju:gəl/ *n* clarín *m*

build¹ /bɪld/ (*past & past p* **built**) *vt* ⟨*house/ road/ship/wall*⟩ construir*; ⟨*fire/nest*⟩ hacer*

■ **build up** **1** [*v* + *o* + *adv*, *v* + *adv* + *o*] **(a)** (make

bigger, stronger) fortalecer* **(b)** (accumulate) ⟨*supplies/experience*⟩ acumular; ⟨*reserves*⟩ acrecentar* **(c)** (develop) ⟨*reputation*⟩ forjarse; **to ~ up one's hopes** hacerse* ilusiones; **he built the firm up from nothing** levantó la empresa de la nada **2** [*v* + *adv*] (increase) «*pressure/noise*» ir* en aumento; **the tension ~s up to a climax** la tensión va en aumento hasta llegar a un punto culminante

build² *n* complexión *f*

builder /'bɪldər ‖'bɪldə(r)/ *n* albañil *mf*; (contractor) contratista *mf*

building /'bɪldɪŋ/ *n* **(a)** (edifice) edificio *m* **(b)** (construction) construcción *f*; (before *n*) **~ contractor** contratista *mf* (de obras); **~ site** obra *f*

building society *n* (in UK) sociedad *f* de crédito hipotecario

buildup /'bɪldʌp/ *n* **(a)** (accumulation) acumulación *f*; (of tension, pressure) aumento *m* **(b)** (of troops) concentración *f* **(c)** (publicity) propaganda *f*

built /bɪlt/ *past & past p of* BUILD¹

built: ~-in /'bɪlt'ɪn/ *adj* (before *n*) ⟨*bookcase/ desk*⟩ empotrado; ⟨*equipment*⟩ fijo; ⟨*mechanism/ feature*⟩ incorporado; **~-up** /'bɪlt'ʌp/ *adj* (before *n*) ⟨*area*⟩ urbanizado

bulb /bʌlb/ *n* **1** (Bot, Hort) (of flower) bulbo *m*, papa *f* (Chi); (of garlic) cabeza *f* **2** (light **~**) bombilla *f or* (Méx) foco *m or* (Col, Ven) bombillo *m or* (RPl) bombita *f or* lamparita *f or* (Chi) ampolleta *f or* (AmC) bujía *f*

bulbous /'bʌlbəs/ *adj* ⟨*growth*⟩ bulboso; ⟨*nose*⟩ protuberante

Bulgaria /bʌl'geriə ‖bʌl'geəriə/ *n* Bulgaria *f*

Bulgarian¹ /bʌl'geriən ‖bʌl'geəriən/ *adj* búlgaro

Bulgarian² *n* **(a)** (person) búlgaro, -ra *m*,*f* **(b)** (language) búlgaro *m*

bulge¹ /bʌldʒ/ *n* bulto *m*

bulge² *vi* **(a)** (protrude) sobresalir*; **the bag was bulging with books** la bolsa estaba repleta de libros **(b) bulging** *pres p* ⟨*pocket/bag*⟩ repleto; ⟨*eyes*⟩ saltón

bulimia (nervosa) /bju:'li:miə(nɜ:r'vəusə) ‖bju:'lɪmiə(nɜ:'vəusə)/ *n* bulimia *f* (nerviosa)

bulk /bʌlk/ *n* **1** **(a)** (Busn) (large quantity): **in ~** en grandes cantidades **(b)** (large mass) mole *f* **2** (largest part): **the ~ of sth** la mayor parte de algo

bulky /'bʌlki/ *adj* **-kier, -kiest** ⟨*package*⟩ voluminoso; ⟨*person*⟩ corpulento; ⟨*sweater*⟩ (AmE) grueso

bull /bʊl/ *n* toro *m*

bull: ~dog *n* bul(l)dog *m*; **~doze** *vt* demoler*; **~dozer** /'bʊldəʊzər ‖'bʊldəʊzə(r)/ *n* bulldozer *m*, topadora *f* (Arg)

bullet /'bʊlət ‖'bʊlɪt/ *n* bala *f*

bulletin /'bʊlətn ‖'bʊlətɪn/ *n* (notice) anuncio *m*; (newsletter) boletín *m*; (report) (Journ) boletín *m* (informativo)

bulletin board *n* (AmE) tablero *m or* (Esp) tablón *m* de anuncios, cartelera *f* (AmL), diario *m* mural (Chi)

bulletproof /'bʊlətpru:f ‖'bʊlɪtpru:f/ *adj* ⟨*vest*⟩ antibalas *adj inv*; ⟨*vehicle*⟩ blindado

bull: ∼**fight** n corrida f de toros; ∼**fighter** n torero, -ra m,f; ∼**fighting** n (deporte m de) los toros; (art) tauromaquia f; ∼**frog** n rana f toro

bullion /'bʊljən ‖'bʊliən/ n: **gold/silver** ∼ oro/ plata en lingotes

bullock /'bʊlək/ n **(a)** (castrated bull) buey m **(b)** (young bull) (esp AmE) novillo m

bull: ∼**ring** n plaza f de toros; ∼**seye** n diana f; ∼**shit** /'bʊlʃɪt/ n (vulg) sandeces fpl (fam), pendejadas (AmL exc CS vulg), gilipolleces fpl (Esp arg), huevadas fpl (Andes, Ven vulg), boludeces fpl (Col, RPl vulg), mamadas fpl (Méx vulg)

bully¹ /'bʊli/ n (pl **-lies**) matón, -tona m,f

bully² vt **-lies, -lying, -lied** intimidar

bum /bʌm/ n (colloq) [1] **(a)** (worthless person) vago, -ga m,f (fam) **(b)** (vagrant) (AmE) vagabundo, -da m,f [2] **(a)** (buttocks) (BrE) trasero m (fam), culo m (fam o vulg), traste m (CS fam), poto m (Chi, Per fam)

bumblebee /'bʌmbəl,biː/ n abejorro m

bumbling /'bʌmblɪŋ/ adj torpe

bump¹ /bʌmp/ n [1] (blow) golpe m; (jolt) sacudida f; (collision) topetazo m [2] (lump — in surface) bulto m; (— on head) chichón m; (— on road) bache m

bump² vt: **I** ∼**ed my elbow on** o **against the door** me di en el codo con or contra la puerta; **I** ∼**ed the post as I was reversing** choqué con or contra el poste al dar marcha atrás
  ▪ ∼ vi (hit, knock) **to** ∼ (AGAINST sth) darse* or chocar* (CONTRA or con algo)
  ▪ **bump into** [v + prep + o] **(a)** (collide with) darse* or chocar* contra **(b)** (meet by chance) (colloq) toparse or tropezarse* con

bumper¹ /'bʌmpər ‖'bʌmpə(r)/ n (Auto) parachoques m, paragolpes m (AmL)

bumper² adj (before n) ⟨crop/year⟩ récord adj inv; ⟨edition⟩ extra; ⟨pack⟩ gigante

bumper car n coche m de choque, autito m chocador (RPl), carro m loco (Andes), carrito m chocón (Méx, Ven)

bumpkin /'bʌmpkɪn/ n: **(country)** ∼ pueblerino, -na m,f, paleto, -ta m,f (Esp fam), pajuerano, -na m,f (RPl fam)

bumpy /'bʌmpi/ adj **-pier, -piest** ⟨surface⟩ desigual; ⟨road⟩ lleno de baches; **we had a** ∼ **flight** el avión se movió mucho

bun /bʌn/ n [1] **(a)** (sweetened) bollo m **(b)** (bread roll) panecillo m, pancito m (CS), bolillo m (Méx) [2] (hairstyle) moño m, rodete m (RPl), chongo m (Méx) [3] **buns** pl (AmE colloq) trasero m (fam), culo m (fam o vulg), traste m (CS fam), poto m (Chi, Per fam)

bunch /bʌntʃ/ n **(a)** (of flowers) ramo m, bonche m (Méx); (small) ramillete m; (of bananas) racimo m, penca f (Méx), cacho m (RPl); (of grapes) racimo m; (of keys) manojo m **(b)** (group) grupo m; **they're an odd** ∼ son gente de lo más rara

bundle¹ /'bʌndl/ n (of clothes) lío m, fardo m, atado m (AmL); (of newspapers, letters) paquete m; (of money) fajo m; (of sticks) haz m, atado m (AmL)

bundle² vt **(a)** (make into a bundle) liar*, atar **(b)** (push) (+ adv compl): **she** ∼**d them off to school** los despachó al colegio; **they** ∼**d him into the car** lo metieron a empujones en el coche

bung /bʌŋ/ n tapón m

bungalow /'bʌŋɡələʊ/ n casa f de una planta

bungle /'bʌŋɡəl/ vt echar a perder; **a** ∼**d attempt** un intento fallido

bungling /'bʌŋɡlɪŋ/ adj (before n, no comp) torpe

bunion /'bʌnjən/ n juanete m

bunk /bʌŋk/ n litera f
  ▪ **bunk off** ▶ SKIVE OFF

bunk bed n litera f

bunny (pl **-nies**), **bunny rabbit** /'bʌni/ n (used to or by children) conejito m (fam)

bunting /'bʌntɪŋ/ n (esp AmE) tela usada para la confección de banderas

buoy /bɔɪ, 'buːi/ n boya f
  ▪ **buoy up** [v + o + adv, v + adv + o] **(a)** ⟨boat/ person⟩ mantener* a flote **(b)** (keep cheerful) animar

buoyant /'bɔɪənt/ adj **(a)** (able to float) flotante **(b)** ⟨mood/spirits⟩ optimista **(c)** (Fin) ⟨currency⟩ fuerte; ⟨market⟩ alcista

burble /'bɜːrbəl ‖'bɜːbəl/ vi **(a)** «stream/ spring» borbotar, borbotear **(b)** (talk meaninglessly) parlotear (fam), cotorrear (fam); (talk excitedly) hablar atropelladamente

burden¹ /'bɜːrdn ‖'bɜːdn/ n carga f

burden² vt cargar*; **I don't want to** ∼ **you with my problems** no te quiero preocupar con mis problemas

bureau /'bjʊrəʊ ‖'bjʊərəʊ/ n (pl **bureaus** or **bureaux** /-z/) [1] **(a)** (agency) agencia f **(b)** (government department) (AmE) departamento m [2] **(a)** (chest of drawers) (AmE) cómoda f **(b)** (desk) (BrE) buró m, escritorio m

bureaucracy /bjʊ'rɑːkrəsi ‖bjʊə'rɒkrəsi/ n (pl **-cies**) burocracia f

bureaucrat /'bjʊrəkræt ‖'bjʊərəkræt/ n burócrata mf

bureaucratic /'bjʊrə'krætɪk ‖,bjʊərə'krætɪk/ adj burocrático

bureau de change /'bjʊrəʊdə'ʃɑːnʒ ‖'bjʊərəʊdə'ʃɑ̃ʒ/ n (pl **bureaux de change**) (casa f de) cambio m

burgeon /'bɜːrdʒən ‖'bɜːdʒən/ vi (liter) florecer*

burglar /'bɜːrɡlər ‖'bɜːɡlə(r)/ n ladrón, -drona m,f; (before n) ∼ **alarm** alarma f antirrobo

burglarize /'bɜːrɡləraɪz ‖'bɜːɡləraɪz/ vt (AmE) robar

burglary /'bɜːrɡləri ‖'bɜːɡləri/ n (pl **-ries**) robo m (con allanamiento de morada o escalamiento)

burgle /'bɜːrɡəl ‖'bɜːɡəl/ vt robar

burial /'beriəl/ n entierro m

Burkina Faso /bɜːr'kiːnə'fæsəʊ ‖,bɜːkiːnə'fæsəʊ/ n Burkina Faso m

burlesque /bɜːr'lesk ‖bɜː'lesk/ n obra f burlesca

· ·

AmC	Central America	Arg	Argentina	Cu	Cuba	Per	Peru
AmL	Latin America	Bol	Bolivia	Ec	Ecuador	RPl	River Plate Area
AmS	South America	Chi	Chile	Esp	Spain	Ur	Uruguay
Andes	Andean Region	CS	Southern Cone	Méx	Mexico	Ven	Venezuela

burly /'bɜːrli ‖'bɜːli/ *adj* **-lier, -liest** fornido

Burma /'bɜːrmə ‖'bɜːmə/ *n* Birmania *f*

Burmese¹ /'bɜːr'miːz ‖bɜː'miːz/ *adj* birmano

Burmese² *n* (*pl* ~) **(a)** (person) birmano, -na *m,f* **(b)** (language) birmano *m*

burn¹ /'bɜːrn ‖bɜːn/ (*past & past p* **burned** *or* **burnt**) *vi* ⃞1 **(a)** «*fire/building/wood/coal*» arder; «*food*» quemarse **(b)** (in sun) «*skin*» quemarse ⃞2 (sting) «*eyes/wound*» escocer*, arder (esp AmL); **a ~ing sensation** un escozor, un ardor (esp AmL)
■ ~ *vt* **(a)** «*letter/rubbish/food*» quemar; «*building/ town*» incendiar; **I ~ed a hole in my sleeve** me quemé la manga (*con un cigarrillo etc*) **(b)** (injure) quemar
■ **burn down** ⃞1 [*v + o + adv, v + adv + o*] incendiar ⃞2 [*v + adv*] incendiarse

burn² *n* quemadura *f*

burner /'bɜːrnər ‖'bɜːnə(r)/ *n* quemador *m*

burning /'bɜːrnɪŋ ‖'bɜːnɪŋ/ *adj* (*before n*) **(a)** (hot) «*sand*» ardiente; «*sun*» abrasador **(b)** (intense) «*desire*» ardiente; «*hatred*» violento

burnt /bɜːrnt ‖bɜːnt/ *past & past p of* BURN¹

burp *v* eructar

burrow¹ /'bərəʊ ‖'bʌrəʊ/ *n* madriguera *f*; (of rabbits) conejera *f*

burrow² *vi* cavar

bursar /'bɜːrsər ‖'bɜːsə(r)/ *n* administrador, -dora *m,f*

burst¹ /bɜːrst ‖bɜːst/ (*past & past p* **burst**) *vi* ⃞1 «*balloon/tire*» reventarse*; «*pipe*» reventar*, romperse*; «*dam*» romperse*; **to ~ open** abrirse* de golpe ⃞2 (move suddenly) (+ *adv compl*): **he ~ into the room** entró de sopetón en la habitación; **they ~ through the police cordon** rompieron el cordón policial
■ ~ *vt* «*balloon/bubble*» reventar*; **the river ~ its banks** el río se desbordó
■ **burst into** [*v + prep + o*]: **to ~ into tears** echarse a llorar; **to ~ into song** romper* a cantar; **to ~ into flames** estallar en llamas

burst² *n* ⃞1 (of applause) salva *f*; (of activity) arrebato *m*; (of gunfire) ráfaga *f* ⃞2 (of pipe) rotura *f*

bursting /'bɜːrstɪŋ ‖'bɜːstɪŋ/ *adj* (pred, no comp) **to be ~** (WITH sth) estar* repleto (DE algo); **he was ~ with energy** rebosaba (de) energía

bury /'beri/ **buries, burying, buried** *vt* (inter) enterrar*; **the village was buried by the avalanche** el pueblo fue sepultado por la avalancha; **he buried his head in his hands** ocultó la cabeza entre las manos
■ *v refl* **to ~ oneself IN sth** «*in one's work/one's books*» enfrascarse* EN algo

bus /bʌs/ *n* (*pl* **buses** *or* (AmE also) **busses**) (Transp) **(a)** (local) autobús *m*, bus *m* (AmL), camión *m* (AmC, Méx), colectivo *m* (Arg), ómnibus *m* (Per, Ur), micro *f* (Chi), guagua *f* (Cu); (*before n*) **~ conductor** cobrador, -dora *m,f*, guarda *mf* (RPl) de autobuses; **~ driver** conductor, -tora *m,f or* chofer *mf or* (Esp) chófer *mf* de autobús, camionero, -ra *m,f* (AmC, Méx), colectivero, -ra *m,f* (Arg), microbusero, -ra *m,f* (Chi); **~ stop** parada *f or* (AmL exc RPl) paradero *m* de autobús (*or* bus *etc*) **(b)** (long-distance) autobús *m*, autocar *m* (Esp), pullman *m* (CS)

bush /bʊʃ/ *n* ⃞1 (shrub) arbusto *m*; **to beat about the ~** andarse* con rodeos ⃞2 (wild country) **the ~** el monte

bushy /'bʊʃi/ *adj* **bushier, bushiest** «*beard*» poblado; «*eyebrows*» tupido; «*undergrowth*» espeso

busily /'bɪzəli ‖'bɪzɪli/ *adv* «*work*» afanosamente

business /'bɪznəs ‖'bɪznɪs/ *n* ⃞1 (Busn) **(a)** (world of commerce, finance) negocios *mpl*; (*before n*) **~ studies** (ciencias *fpl*) empresariales *fpl* **(b)** (commercial activity, trading) comercio *m*; **the firm has been in ~ for 50 years** la empresa tiene 50 años de actividad comercial; **they went into ~ together** montaron un negocio juntos; **she's away on ~** está de viaje por negocios; **to go out of ~** cerrar*; **to get down to ~** ir* al grano; **to mean ~** decir* algo muy en serio; (*before n*) «*appointment/lunch*» de trabajo, de negocios; **~ hours** horas *fpl* de oficina; **~ letter** carta *f* comercial; **~ trip** viaje *m* de negocios **(c)** (custom, clients): **to lose ~** perder* clientes *or* clientela ⃞2 **(a)** (firm) negocio *m*, empresa *f* **(b)** (branch of commerce): **I'm in the antiques ~** trabajo en la compra y venta de antigüedades; **the music ~** la industria de la música ⃞3 (rightful occupation, concern) asunto *m*; **mind your own ~!** ¡no te metas en lo que no te importa!; **that's none of your ~** eso no es asunto tuyo ⃞4 (affair, situation, activity) (colloq) (*no pl*) asunto *m*; **what's all this ~ about you leaving?** ¿qué es eso de que te vas?

business: ~like *adj* «*person/manner*» (serious) formal; (efficient) eficiente; «*discussion*» serio; **~man** /'bɪznəsmæn ‖'bɪznɪsmən/ *n* (*pl* **-men** /-men ‖-mən/) empresario *m*, hombre *m* de negocios; **~woman** *n* empresaria *f*, mujer *f* de negocios

busker /'bʌskər ‖'bʌskə(r)/ *n* (BrE) músico *m* callejero

bust¹ /bʌst/ *vt* **(a)** (*past & past p* **busted** *or* (BrE also) **bust**) (break) (colloq) romper* **(b)** (*past & past p* **busted**) (raid) (sl) «*person*» agarrar (fam), trincar* (Esp fam); «*premises*» hacer* una redada en

bust² *n* **(a)** (sculpture) busto *m* **(b)** (bosom) busto *m*, pecho *m*

bust³ *adj* (bankrupt) (colloq): **to go ~** quebrar*, ir(se)* a la bancarrota, fundirse (Per, RPl fam)

bustle¹ /'bʌsəl/ *vi* **(a)** (move busily): **to ~ around** ir* de aquí para allá **(b)** (be crowded, lively) «*street/ store*» **to ~** (WITH sth) bullir* (DE algo)

bustle² *n* ajetreo *m*

bustling /'bʌslɪŋ/ *adj* «*street/shop*» animado

bust-up /'bʌstʌp/ *n* **(a)** (breakup) ruptura *f* **(b)** (quarrel) (BrE colloq) pelea *f*, bronca *f* (fam)

busy¹ /'bɪzi/ *adj* **busier, busiest** ⃞1 «*person*» ocupado; **the children keep me very ~** los niños me tienen muy atareada ⃞2 «*street/market*» concurrido; **I've had a ~ day** he tenido un día de mucho trabajo; **a ~ road** una carretera con mucho tráfico ⃞3 (AmE Telec) ocupado (AmL), comunicando (Esp); **the ~ signal** la señal de ocupado *or* (Esp) de comunicando

busy² *v refl* **busies, busying, busied**: **to ~ oneself WITH sth** entretenerse* CON algo

busybody /'bɪzi,bɑːdi ‖'bɪzi,bɒdi/ *n* (*pl* **-dies**) (colloq) entrometido, -da *m,f*, metomentodo *mf* (fam)

but[1] /bʌt, *weak form* bət/ *conj* pero; **not ... ∼ ...** no ... sino ...; **∼ then you never were very ambitious, were you?** pero la verdad es que tú nunca fuiste muy ambicioso ¿no?; **not only did she hit him, ∼ she also ...** no solo le pegó, sino que también ...

but[2] *prep*: **everyone ∼ me** todos menos *or* excepto yo; **the last street ∼ one** la penúltima calle; **∼ for them, we'd have lost everything** de no haber sido por ellos, habríamos perdido todo

but[3] *adv* (frml): **we can ∼ try** con intentarlo no se pierde nada

butane /'bjuːteɪn/ *n* butano *m*

butcher[1] /'bʊtʃər ‖ 'bʊtʃə(r)/ *n* (a) (meat dealer) carnicero, -ra *m,f*; **∼'s (shop)** carnicería *f* (b) (murderer) asesino, -na *m,f*

butcher[2] *vt* (a) ⟨*cattle/pig*⟩ matar, carnear (CS) (b) ⟨*people*⟩ masacrar

butler /'bʌtlər ‖ 'bʌtlə(r)/ *n* mayordomo *m*

butt[1] /bʌt/ *n* [1] (a) (of rifle) culata *f* (b) ∼ (end) (blunt end) extremo *m* (c) (of cigarette) colilla *f*, bacha *f* (Méx fam) [2] (target of jokes or criticism) blanco *m* [3] (from goat) topetazo *m* (b) (head ∼) cabezazo *m* [4] (buttocks) (AmE colloq) trasero *m* (fam), culo *m* (fam o vulg), traste *m* (CS fam), poto *m* (Chi, Per fam)

butt[2] *vt* ⟨*goat*⟩ topetar

■ **butt in** [*v* + *adv*] interrumpir

butter[1] /'bʌtər ‖ 'bʌtə(r)/ *n* mantequilla *f*, manteca *f* (RPl)

butter[2] *vt* ⟨*bread*⟩ untar con mantequilla *or* (RPl) manteca

butter: **∼ bean** *n* (a) (dried bean) *tipo de frijol blanco*, poroto *m* de manteca (RPl) (b) (wax bean) (AmE) *tipo de frijol fresco con vaina amarilla*; **∼cup** *n* ranúnculo *m*; **∼fly** *n* (a) (Zool) mariposa *f*; **to have ∼flies (in one's stomach)** ponerse*/estar* nervioso (b) (swimming stroke) estilo *m* mariposa

buttock /'bʌtək/ *n* nalga *f*

button[1] /'bʌtn̩/ *n* botón *m*

button[2] *vt* abotonar

■ ∼ *vi* abotonarse

■ **button up** [*v* + *o* + *adv*, *v* + *adv* + *o*] abotonar

buttonhole /'bʌtn̩həʊl/ *n* (a) (Clothing) ojal *m* (b) (flower) (BrE) *flor que se lleva en el ojal*

buttress /'bʌtrəs ‖ 'bʌtrɪs/ *n* (Archit) contrafuerte *m*; **flying ∼** arbotante *m*

buxom /'bʌksəm/ *adj* con mucho busto *or* pecho

buy[1] /baɪ/ (*past & past p* **bought**) *vt* comprar; **to ∼ sb sth** comprarle algo a algn; **to ∼ sth FROM sb** comprarle algo A algn; **to ∼ sth FOR sb** comprar algo PARA algn

■ ∼ *vi* comprar; **to ∼ FROM sb** comprarle A algn

■ **buy off** [*v* + *o* + *adv*, *v* + *adv* + *o*] sobornar

■ **buy out** [*v* + *o* + *adv*, *v* + *adv* + *o*] ⟨*partner/shareholder*⟩ comprarle su parte a

■ **buy up** [*v* + *adv* + *o*] comprarse todas las existencias de

buy[2] *n* compra *f*

buyer /'baɪər ‖ 'baɪə(r)/ *n* (a) (customer) comprador, -dora *m,f* (b) (buying agent) encargado, -da *m,f* de compras

buzz[1] /bʌz/ *n* (of insect) zumbido *m*; (of voices) rumor *m*; (as signal) zumbido *m*

buzz[2] *vi* ⟨*insect*⟩ zumbar; ⟨*telephone/alarm clock*⟩ sonar*; **my ears were ∼ing** me zumbaban los oídos

buzzard /'bʌzərd ‖ 'bʌzəd/ *n* (a) (hawk) (esp BrE) águila *f*‡ ratonera (b) (vulture) (AmE) aura *f*‡, gallinazo *m*, zopilote *m* (AmC, Méx)

buzzer /'bʌzər ‖ 'bʌzə(r)/ *n* timbre *m*

by[1] /baɪ/ *prep* [1] (indicating agent, cause) (*with passive verbs*) por [*The passive voice is, however, less common in Spanish than it is in English*] **she was brought up ∼ her grandmother** la crio su abuela; **a play ∼ Shakespeare** una obra de Shakespeare

[2] (a) (indicating means, method): **made ∼ hand** hecho a mano; **to travel ∼ car/train/plane** viajar en coche/tren/avión; **to pay ∼ credit card** pagar* con tarjeta de crédito; **I'll begin ∼ introducing myself** empezaré por presentarme (b) (owing to, from): **∼ chance** por casualidad; **they have lost public support ∼ being too extreme** han perdido apoyo popular por ser demasiado extremistas

[3] (a) (at the side of, near to) al lado de; **it's right ∼ the door** está justo al lado de la puerta (b) (to hand) (AmE): **I always keep some money ∼ me** siempre llevo algo de dinero encima

[4] (a) (past): **I said hello, but he walked right ∼ me** lo saludé pero él pasó de largo (b) (via, through) por; **∼ land/sea/air** por tierra/mar/avión

[5] (a) (indicating rate) por; **we are paid ∼ the hour** nos pagan por hora(s) (b) (indicating extent of difference): **she broke the record ∼ several seconds** batió el récord en *or* por varios segundos (c) (indicating gradual progression): **one ∼ one** uno por uno

[6] (a) (not later than): **he told her to be home ∼ 11** le dijo que volviera antes de las 11; **they should be there ∼ now** ya deberían estar allí; **∼ the time he arrived, Ann had left** cuando llegó, Ann se había ido (b) (during, at) **∼ day/night** de día/noche

[7] (according to): **∼ that clock it's almost half past** según ese reloj son casi y media; **that's fine ∼ me** por mí no hay problema

[8] (Math) por; **multiply two ∼ three** multiplica dos por tres; **a room 20ft ∼ 12ft** una habitación de 20 pies por 12

[9] **by oneself** (alone, without assistance) solo

by[2] *adv* (a) (past): **she rushed ∼ without seeing me** pasó corriendo y no me vio; **they watched the parade march ∼** vieron pasar el desfile (b) (to sb's residence): **call** *o* **stop ∼ on your way to work** pasa por casa de camino al trabajo (c) (in phrases) **by and by: ∼ and ∼ they came to the clearing** al poco rato llegaron al claro; **by and large** por lo general, en general

bye, (AmE) **'bye** /baɪ/ *interj* (colloq) ¡adiós!, ¡chao *or* chau! (esp AmL fam)

bye-bye /'baɪ'baɪ/ *interj* (colloq) ¡adiós!, ¡chaucito! (AmL fam), ¡chaíto! (Chi fam)

by: **∼gone** *adj* (liter) (*before n*) ⟨*age/days*⟩ de antaño (liter); **to let ∼gones be ∼gones** olvidar el pasado; **∼law** *n* (BrE) ordenanza *f* municipal

bypass[1] /'baɪpæs ‖ 'baɪpɑːs/ *n* (a) (road) (BrE) carretera *f* de circunvalación (b) (Med) bypass *m*

bypass[2] *vt* (a) (circumvent) ⟨*person/difficulty*⟩ eludir (b) (Transp) ⟨*road*⟩ circunvalar; ⟨*driver*⟩ evitar entrar en

by: **∼-product** *n* (in manufacture) subproducto *m*; (consequence) consecuencia *f*; **∼road** *n* carretera

f secundaria; **~stander** /'baɪˌstændər
‖'baɪˌstændə(r)/ *n*: **they opened fire, killing
innocent ~standers** abrieron fuego y mataron a
varias personas inocentes *or* a varios transeúntes

byte /baɪt/ *n* byte *m*, octeto *m*

by: ~way *n* camino *m* (*apartado*); **~word** *n*:
to be a ~word FOR sth ser* sinónimo DE algo;
~-your-leave /'baɪjər'liːv ‖ˌbaɪjɔː'liːv/ *n*:
without so much as a ~-your-leave sin (ni)
siquiera pedir permiso

Cc

C, c /siː/ *n* **(a)** (letter) C, c *f* **(b)** (Mus) re *m*
c (a) (Corresp) = **copy to (b)** (in US) (= **cent(s)**)
centavo(s) *m* (*pl*) **(c)** = **circa**

C (= **Celsius** *or* **centigrade**) C

ca = **circa**

CA, Ca = **California**

cab /kæb/ *n* ⒈ (taxi) taxi *m*; (*before n*) **~ driver**
taxista *mf* ⒉ (driver's compartment) cabina *f*

cabaret /ˌkæbə'reɪ ‖'kæbəreɪ/ *n* cabaret *m*

cabbage /'kæbɪdʒ/ *n* repollo *m*, col *f*

cabin /'kæbən ‖kæbɪn/ *n* **(a)** (hut) cabaña *f* **(b)**
(Naut) camarote *m* **(c)** (Aerosp, Auto, Aviat) cabina *f*

cabinet /'kæbənət ‖'kæbɪnɪt/ *n* ⒈ (cupboard)
armario *m*; (with glass front) vitrina *f* ⒉ *also*
Cabinet (Govt) gabinete *m* (ministerial)

cable /'keɪbəl/ *n* **(a)** (Elec, Naut) cable *m* **(b)**
(Telec) cable *m* **(c)** ▶ CABLE TELEVISION

cable: ~ car *n* (suspended) teleférico *m*;
(funicular) funicular *m*; (streetcar) (AmE) tranvía *m*;
~ television *n* televisión *f* por cable,
cablevisión *f* (esp AmL)

caboose /kə'buːs/ *n* (AmE Rail) furgón *m* de
cola

cache /kæʃ/ *n* alijo *m*

cackle /'kækəl/ *vi* «*hen*» cacarear; «*person*»
reírse* socarronamente

cactus /'kæktəs/ *n* (*pl* **-ti** /-taɪ/ *or* **-tuses**)
cactus *m*

caddie, caddy (*pl* **-dies**) /'kædi/ *n* caddie *mf*

cadet /kə'det/ *n* cadete *mf*

cadge /kædʒ/ (colloq) *vt* **to ~ sth FROM** *o* **OFF sb**
gorronearle *or* gorrearle *or* (RPl) garronearle *or*
(Chi) bolsearle algo A algn (fam)

Caesarean (section) /sɪ'zæriən
‖sɪ'zeəriən/ *n* ▶ CESAREAN (SECTION)

café, cafe /kæ'feɪ ‖'kæfeɪ/ *n* (coffee bar) café *m*,
cafetería *f*; (restaurant) *restaurante económico*

cafeteria /ˌkæfə'tɪriə ‖ˌkæfə'tɪəriə/ *n* (in
hospital, college) cantina *f*, cafetería *f*; (restaurant)
restaurante *m* autoservicio, self-service *m*

caffeine /kæ'fiːn ‖'kæfiːn/ *n* cafeína *f*

cage¹ /keɪdʒ/ *n* jaula *f*; (in basketball) canasta *f*,
cesta *f*; (in ice hockey) portería *f*, meta *f*, arco *m*
(Col, CS)

cage² *vt* (*usu pass*) enjaular

Cairo /'kaɪroʊ ‖'kaɪərəʊ/ *n* El Cairo

cajole /kə'dʒoʊl/ *vt* convencer* con zalamerías

cake¹ /keɪk/ *n*(Culin) (large) pastel *m*, tarta *f*

(Esp), torta *f* (esp CS); (small, individual) pastel *m*,
masa *f* (RPl); **to be a piece of ~** (colloq) ser* pan
comido (fam)

cake² *vt* (*usu pass*): **our shoes were ~d with
mud** teníamos los zapatos cubiertos de barro
endurecido

cake tin *n* (BrE) (for baking) molde *m* (para
pastel); (for storage) lata *f* (*para guardar pasteles*)

Cal = **California**

calamity /kə'læməti/ *n* (*pl* **-ties**) calamidad *f*

calcium /'kælsiəm/ *n* calcio *m*

calculate /'kælkjələt ‖'kælkjʊleɪt/ *vt* calcular

calculating /'kælkjəleɪtɪŋ ‖'kælkjʊleɪtɪŋ/ *adj*
calculador

calculation /ˌkælkjə'leɪʃən ‖ˌkælkjʊ'leɪʃən/ *n*
cálculo *m*

calculator /'kælkjəleɪtər ‖'kælkjʊleɪtə(r)/ *n*
calculadora *f*

calendar /'kæləndər ‖'kælɪndə(r)/ *n*
calendario *m*, almanaque *m*; (*before n*) **~ month**
mes *m* (del calendario)

calf /kæf ‖kɑːf/ *n* (*pl* **calves**) ⒈ (Zool) **(a)**
(animal) ternero, -ra *m*,*f*, becerro, -rra *m*,*f* **(b)**
(leather) (piel *f* *or* cuero *m* de) becerro *m* ⒉ (Anat)
pantorrilla *f*

caliber, (BrE) **calibre** /'kæləbər ‖'kælɪbə(r)/ *n*
calibre *m*

Calif = **California**

calipers, (BrE) **callipers** /'kæləpərz
‖'kælɪpəz/ *pl n* **(a)** (for measuring) calibrador *m*
(b) (Med) aparato *m* ortopédico (*para la pierna*)

call¹ /kɔːl/ *n* ⒈ (by telephone) llamada *f*; **to give
sb a ~** llamar a algn (por teléfono)
⒉ **(a)** (of person — cry) llamada *f*, llamado *m*
(AmL); (— shout) grito *m* **(b)** (of animal) grito *m*; (of
bird) reclamo *m*
⒊ (summons): **to be on ~** estar* de guardia;
beyond the ~ of duty más de lo que el deber
exigía (*or* exige *etc*) (frml)
⒋ (demand) llamamiento *m*, llamado *m* (AmL);
there were ~s for his resignation pidieron su
dimisión
⒌ (*usu with neg*) **(a)** (reason) motivo *m* **(b)**
(demand) demanda *f*; **there's not much ~ for this
product** no hay mucha demanda para este
producto
⒍ (visit) visita *f*
⒎ (Sport) decisión *f*, cobro *m* (Chi)

call² *vt* **(a)** (shout) llamar; **to ~ the roll** *o* **register**
(Educ) pasar lista **(b)** ⟨*police/taxi/doctor*⟩ llamar;
⟨*strike*⟩ llamar a, convocar* **(c)** (by telephone)
llamar **(d)** (name, describe as) llamar; **we ~ her** ⋯⟫

Betty la llamamos *or* (esp AmL) le decimos Betty;
what are you going to ~ the baby? ¿qué nombre
le van a poner al bebé?; what's this ~ed in
Italian? ¿cómo se llama esto en italiano?
■ ~ *vi* **(a)** «*person*» llamar **(b)** (by telephone)
llamar; who's ~ing, please? ¿de parte de quién,
por favor? **(c)** (visit) pasar
■ **call around** [*v + adv*] **(a)** (Telec) llamar (*a
varias personas*) **(b)** (visit) pasar (por casa)
■ **call at** [*v + prep + o*]: «*train*» parar en; I ~ed
at your place yesterday ayer pasé por tu casa
■ **call back** ⟦1⟧ (Telec) [*v + o + adv*] llamar más
tarde
⟦2⟧ [*v + adv*] (Telec) volver* a llamar
■ **call for** [*v + prep + o*] **(a)** (require) requerir*,
exigir* «*skill/courage*» **(b)** (demand) pedir* **(c)**
(collect) pasar a buscar *or* a recoger
■ **call in** ⟦1⟧ [*v + o + adv, v + adv + o*] **(a)** «*expert/doctor*» llamar **(b)** «*coin/note*» retirar de
circulación
⟦2⟧ [*v + adv*] (Telec) to ~ in (on sb) pasar a ver a algn
■ **call off** [*v + o + adv, v + adv + o*] **(a)** (cancel)
suspender **(b)** «*dog*» llamar
■ **call on** [*v + prep + o*] **(a)** (visit) pasar a ver a
(b) ▶ CALL UPON
■ **call out** [*v + o + adv, v + adv + o*] **(a)** «*fire
brigade/doctor*» llamar **(b)** (utter): he ~ed out her
name la llamó
■ **call round** [*v + adv*] (BrE) ▶ CALL AROUND
■ **call up** [*v + o + adv, v + adv + o*] **(a)** «*spirits*»
invocar* **(b)** (telephone) (esp AmE) llamar **(c)** (Mil)
(*often pass*) llamar (a filas)
■ **call upon** [*v + prep + o*] **(a)** (invite): to ~ upon
sb to speak dar* la palabra a algn **(b)** (appeal to)
apelar a
call:~ box *n* (BrE) cabina *f* telefónica; ~
center, (BrE) ~ **centre** *n* (Telec) centro *m* de
llamadas
caller /'kɔːlər ‖'kɔːlə(r)/ *n*: we didn't have many
~s no vino mucha gente; (Telec) no tuvimos *or* no
hubo muchas llamadas; **the ~ didn't leave her
name** la persona que llamó no dejó su nombre
callipers *n* (BrE) ▶ CALIPERS
callous /'kæləs/ *adj* insensible, cruel
callus /'kæləs/ *n* (*pl* **-luses**) (Med) callo *m*
calm¹ /kɑːm/ *adj* **-er, -est** «*sea*» en calma,
calmo (esp AmL); «*person/voice*» calmo
(esp AmL)
calm² *vt* tranquilizar*, calmar
■ **calm down (a)** [*v + o + adv, v + adv + o*]
tranquilizar*, calmar **(b)** [*v + adv*]
tranquilizarse*; ~ **down!** ¡tranquilízate!,
¡tranquilo!
calm³ *n* calma *f*
calmly /'kɑːmli/ *adv* con calma
Calor Gas® /'kælər ‖'kælə(r)/ *n* (BrE) (gas *m*)
butano *m*, supergás® *m* (RPl)
calorie /'kæləri/ *n* (Culin) (kilo)caloría *f*
calves /kævz ‖kɑːvz/ *pl of* CALF
camcorder /'kæm,kɔːrdər ‖'kæm,kɔːdə(r)/ *n*
videocámara *f*, camcórder *m*
came /keɪm/ *past of* COME

camel /'kæməl/ *n* camello *m*
cameo /'kæmiəʊ/ *n* ⟦1⟧ (jewelry) camafeo *m*
⟦2⟧ (Cin, TV) actuación *f* especial
camera /'kæmərə/ *n* cámara *f* (fotográfica),
máquina *f* fotográfica *or* de fotos
camera: ~**man** /'kæmərəmæn/ *n* (*pl* **-men**
/-men/) camarógrafo, -fa *m,f*, cameraman *mf* (esp
AmL), cámara *mf* (Esp); ~**work** *n* fotografía *f*
Cameroon /'kæmə'ruːn/ *n* Camerún *m*
camomile /'kæməmaɪl/ *n* ▶ CHAMOMILE
camouflage¹ /'kæməflɑːʒ/ *n* camuflaje *m*
camouflage² *vt* camuflar, camuflajear (AmL)
camp¹ /kæmp/ *n* (collection of tents, huts)
campamento *m*; (summer) (in US) campamento
m de verano, colonia *f* de vacaciones *or* verano
camp² *vi* acampar; to go ~ing ir* de camping
camp³ *adj* **(a)** (effeminate) amanerado,
afeminado **(b)** «*performance*» afectado, exagerado
campaign¹ /kæm'peɪn/ *n* campaña *f*
campaign² *vi* (Pol, Sociol) to ~ FOR/AGAINST
sth hacer* una campaña A FAVOR DE/EN CONTRA
DE algo
campaigner /kæm'peɪnər ‖kæm'peɪnə(r)/ *n*
(Pol, Sociol) defensor, -sora *m,f*
camper /'kæmpər ‖'kæmpə(r)/ *n* **(a)** (person)
campista *mf* **(b)** (Transp) cámper *f*
campground /'kæmpgraʊnd/ (AmE),
campsite /'kæmpsaɪt/ *n* camping *m*
camping /'kæmpɪŋ/ *n*: I like ~ me gusta ir de
camping
campus /'kæmpəs/ *n* (*pl* **-puses**) campus *m*
can¹ /kæn/ *n* **(a)** (container) lata *f*, bote *m* (Esp),
tarro *m* (Chi); (before *n*) ~ **opener** abrelatas *m* **(b)**
(for petrol, water) bidón *m*; (for garbage) (AmE) cubo
m or (CS) tacho *m or* (Col) caneca *f*, bote *m* (Méx),
tobo *m* de la basura (Ven)
can² *vt* **-nn-** (put in cans) enlatar; (bottle) (AmE)
«*fruit*» preparar conservas de
can³ /kæn, *weak form* kən/ *v mod*
■ **Note** When can means *to be capable of* or *to be
allowed to*, it is translated by *poder*: he can't eat no
puede comer; can you come out tonight? ¿puedes
salir esta noche? When can means *to know how to*, it
is translated by *saber*: can you swim? ¿sabes nadar?;
she can already read and write ya sabe leer y
escribir.When can is used with a verb of perception
such as *see, hear,* or *feel,* it is often not translated:
can you see her from here? ¿la ves desde aquí?; she
couldn't feel anything no sentía nada.

(past **could**) ⟦1⟧ (indicating ability) poder*; (referring
to particular skills) saber*; **she couldn't answer the
question** no pudo contestar la pregunta; ~ **you
swim?** ¿sabes nadar?
⟦2⟧ **(a)** (with verbs of perception): I ~'t see very well
no veo muy bien; ~ **you hear me?** ¿me oyes? **(b)**
(with verbs of mental activity): I ~'t understand it no
lo entiendo; ~'t you tell he's lying? ¿no te das
cuenta de que está mintiendo?
⟦3⟧ **(a)** (indicating, asking etc permission) poder*; ~ I
come with you? ¿puedo ir contigo? **(b)** (in requests)

poder*; ~ you turn that music down, please?
¿puedes bajar esa música, por favor? **(c)** (in
offers): ~ **I help you?** ¿me permite?; (in shop) ¿lo/la
atienden?, ¿qué desea?; ~ **I carry that for you?**
¿quieres que (te) lleve eso? **(d)** (in suggestions,
advice): ~**'t you give it another try?** ¿por qué no lo
vuelves a intentar?

4 (indicating possibility) poder*; it ~**'t be true!** ¡no
puede ser!, ¡no es posible!

Canada /'kænədə/ n (el) Canadá m

Canadian¹ /kə'neɪdɪən/ adj canadiense

Canadian² n canadiense mf

canal /kə'næl/ n canal m

Canaries /kə'neriz ‖kə'neəriz/ pl n **the ~** (las)
Canarias

canary /kə'neri ‖kə'neəri/ n (pl **-ries**) canario
m

Canary Islands pl n **the ~ ~** las Islas
Canarias

cancel /'kænsəl/, (BrE) **-ll-** vt cancelar; ‹check›
anular

■ **cancel out** [v + o + adv, v + adv + o] ‹deficit/
loss› compensar; ‹debt› cancelar

cancellation /ˌkænsə'leɪʃən/ n cancelación f;
(Theat) devolución f

cancer /'kænsər ‖'kænsə(r)/ n 1 (disease)
cáncer m 2 **Cancer** (Astrol) **(a)** (sign) (no art)
Cáncer **(b)** (person) Cáncer or cáncer mf,
canceriano, -na m,f

candid /'kændəd ‖'kændɪd/ adj franco

candidate /'kændədeɪt ‖'kændɪdət/ n
candidato, -ta m,f

candle /'kændl/ n (for domestic use) vela f; (for
altar) cirio m

candle: ~**light** n: **by** ~**light** a la luz de una
vela/de las velas; ~**stick** n candelero m; (flat)
palmatoria f

candy /'kændi/ n (pl **-dies**) (AmE) **(a)**
(confectionery) golosinas fpl, dulces mpl (AmL exc
RPl) **(b)** (individual piece) caramelo m, dulce m (AmL
exc RPl)

cane¹ /keɪn/ n 1 (for wickerwork) mimbre m
2 (walking stick) bastón m; (for punishment) palmeta
f; (for supporting plants) rodrigón m

cane² vt castigar* con la palmeta

canine¹ /'keɪnaɪn/ n 1 (Zool) canino m, cánido
m 2 ~ **(tooth)** (diente m) canino m, colmillo m

canine² adj canino

canister /'kænəstər ‖'kænɪstə(r)/ n **(a)** (for tea,
coffee) lata f, bote m (Esp) **(b)** (Mil) bote m (de
humo, metralla etc)

cannabis /'kænəbəs ‖'kænəbɪs/ n hachís m,
cannabis m

canned /kænd/ adj **(a)** ‹food› enlatado, en or
de lata, en conserva **(b)** (pre-recorded) (colloq)
‹music› enlatado (fam); ‹laughter› grabado

cannibal /'kænəbəl ‖'kænɪbəl/ n caníbal mf,
antropófago, -ga m,f

cannon /'kænən/ n (pl also ~) cañón m

cannonball /'kænənbɔːl/ n (Mil) bala f de
cañón

cannot /'kænɑːt ‖'kænʊt/ = **can not**

canoe¹ /kə'nuː/ n canoa f, piragua f

canoe² vi **-noes, -noeing, -noed** ir* en
canoa or piragua

canoeing /kə'nuːɪŋ/ n piragüismo m, canotaje
m

canopy /'kænəpi/ n (pl **-pies**) (over bed, throne)
dosel m, baldaquín m, baldaquino m; (over person)
palio m, dosel m

can't /kænt ‖kɑːnt/ = **can not**

canteen /kæn'tiːn/ n 1 (dining hall) (BrE)
cantina f, comedor m, casino m (Chi) (en un lugar
de trabajo, colegio etc) 2 (water bottle) cantimplora
f

canter /'kæntər ‖'kæntə(r)/ vi ir* a medio
galope

canvas /'kænvəs/ n 1 (cloth) lona f 2 (Art) (for
painting) lienzo m, tela f

canvass /'kænvəs/ vt 1 (Pol): **to ~ voters in
an area** hacer* campaña entre los votantes de
una zona 2 (scrutinize) (AmE): **to ~ the votes**
hacer* el escrutinio de los votos
■ ~ vi (Pol) **to ~ (FOR sb)** hacer* campaña (A or
EN FAVOR DE algn)

canyon /'kænjən/ n cañón m

cap¹ /kæp/ n 1 (hat) gorra f; **swimming ~**
gorro m or (esp AmL) gorra f de baño; **baseball/
golf ~** gorra de béisbol/golf 2 (of bottle) tapa f,
tapón m; (metal) chapa f, tapa f; (of pen) capuchón
m, tapa f 3 (upper limit) tope m

cap² vt **-pp-** 1 ‹bottle/tube› tapar 2 (crown): **to
~ it all off** o (BrE) **to ~ it all ...** para colmo (de
desgracias or de males) ..., para rematarla ...
(fam) 3 ‹expenditure› poner* un tope a
4 (Dentistry): **to have a tooth ~ped** ponerse* una
funda or una corona

CAP n (= **Common Agricultural Policy**)
PAC f

capability /ˌkeɪpə'bɪləti/ n (pl **-ties**) **(a)**
(ability) capacidad f **(b) capabilities** pl
aptitudes fpl

capable /'keɪpəbəl/ adj **(a)** (competent) capaz
(b) (pred) (able) **to be ~ OF + ING** ser* capaz DE +
INF

capacity /kə'pæsəti/ n (pl **-ties**) 1 1
(maximum content) capacidad f; (before n) **a ~
crowd** un lleno completo **(b)** (output) capacidad f
2 (ability) capacidad f; ~ **FOR sth** capacidad de
algo; ~ **to + INF** capacidad PARA + INF; **the job
was beyond her** ~ el trabajo estaba por encima
de su capacidad 3 (role) calidad f; **in his ~ as
union delegate** en su calidad de delegado del
sindicato

cape /keɪp/ n 1 (Clothing) capa f 2 (Geog) cabo
m

caper¹ /'keɪpər ‖'keɪpə(r)/ n 1 (jump) salto m
2 (prank) travesura f 3 (Bot, Culin) alcaparra f

caper² vi correr y brincar*, dar* saltos or
brincos

capital¹ /'kæpətl ‖'kæpɪtl/ n **(a)** (city) capital f
(b) (letter) mayúscula f **(c)** (Fin) capital m

capital² adj **(a)** (Law): ~ **punishment** pena f
capital **(b)** (Geog, Pol): ~ **city** capital f **(c)** (Print)
‹letter› mayúscula

capitalism /'kæpətlɪzəm ‖'kæpɪtəlɪzəm/ n
capitalismo m

capitalist¹ /'kæpətləst ‖'kæpɪtəlɪst/ n
capitalista mf

capitalist² adj capitalista

capitulate /kə'pɪtʃəleɪt ‖kə'pɪtʃʊleɪt/ *vi* capitular

Capricorn /'kæprɪkɔːrn ‖'kæprɪkɔːn/ *n* **(a)** (sign) (*no art*) Capricornio **(b)** (person) Capricornio *or* capricornio *mf*, capricorniano, -na *m,f*

caps = **capital letters**

capsicum /'kæpsɪkəm/ *n* pimiento *m*, pimentón *m* (AmS exc RPl), ají *m* (RPl)

capsize /'kæpsaɪz ‖kæp'saɪz/ *vi* volcarse*

capsule /'kæpsəl ‖'kæpsjuːl/ *n* cápsula *f*

captain¹ /'kæptən ‖'kæptɪn/ *n* **(a)** (rank) capitán *m* **(b)** (person in command) capitán, -tana *m,f*, (of airline plane) comandante *mf*

captain² *vt* (Naut, Sport) capitanear

caption /'kæpʃən/ *n* (under picture) leyenda *f*, pie *m* de foto (*or* ilustración *etc*); (headline) título *m*

captivate /'kæptɪveɪt ‖'kæptɪveɪt/ *vt* cautivar

captive¹ /'kæptɪv/ *n* (liter) cautivo, -va *m,f*

captive² *adj*: **to take/hold sb** ~ tomar prisionero/mantener* cautivo a algn; **to have a** ~ **audience** tener* un público que no tiene más remedio que escuchar

captivity /kæp'tɪvəti/ *n* cautiverio *m*, cautividad *f*

captor /'kæptər ‖'kæptə(r)/ *n* captor, -tora *m,f*

capture¹ /'kæptʃər ‖'kæptʃə(r)/ *vt* **1** ⟨person/animal⟩ capturar; ⟨city⟩ tomar **2** **(a)** ⟨attention/interest⟩ captar, atraer* **(b)** ⟨mood/atmosphere⟩ captar, reproducir*

capture² *n* (of person, animal) captura *f*; (of city) conquista *f*, toma *f*

car /kɑːr ‖kɑː(r)/ *n* **(a)** (Auto) coche *m*, automóvil *m* (frml), carro *m* (AmL exc CS), auto *m* (esp CS) **(b)** (Rail, Transp) vagón *m*, coche *m*

caramel /'kɑːməl ‖'kærəməl, -məl/ *n* caramelo *m*

carat /'kærət/ *n* **(a)** (for gold) (AmE also **karat**) quilate *m*; (*before n*) **18-**~ **gold** oro *m* de 18 quilates **(b)** (for precious stones) quilate *m*

caravan /'kærəvæn/ *n* **(a)** (group) caravana *f* **(b)** (vehicle) (BrE) caravana *f*, rulot *f* (Esp), casa *f* rodante (CS), tráiler *m* (Andes, Méx); (*before n*) ~ **park** *o* **site** camping *m* para caravanas

carbohydrate /ˌkɑːrbəʊ'haɪdreɪt ‖ˌkɑːbə'haɪdreɪt/ *n* hidrato *m* de carbono

car bomb *n* coche *m* bomba

carbon /'kɑːrbən ‖'kɑːbən/ *n* carbono *m*

carbon: ~ **copy** *n* copia *f* (hecha con papel carbón); ~ **dioxide** /daɪ'ɑːksaɪd ‖daɪ'ɒksaɪd/ *n* anhídrido *m* carbónico; ~ **monoxide** /məˈnɑːksaɪd ‖məˈnɒksaɪd/ *n* monóxido *m* de carbono

carburetor, (BrE) **carburettor** /ˌkɑːrbə'reɪtər ‖ˌkɑːbə'retə(r)/ *n* carburador *m*

carcass, (BrE also) **carcase** /'kɑːrkəs ‖'kɑːkəs/ *n* (dead animal) cuerpo *m* de animal muerto; (for meat) res *f* (muerta)

card /kɑːrd ‖kɑːd/ *n* **1** **(a)** (for identification, access) tarjeta *f*; (business ~) tarjeta (de visita); (credit ~) tarjeta (de crédito) **(b)** (greeting ~) tarjeta *f* (de felicitación) **(c)** (index ~) ficha *f*; (*before n*) ~ **index** fichero *m* **(d)** (post~) (tarjeta *f*) postal *f* **2** (thin cardboard) cartulina *f* **3** (playing card) carta *f*, naipe *m*, baraja *f* (AmC, Col, Méx, RPl); **to play** ~**s** jugar* a las cartas *or* (Col) jugar* cartas

cardamom /'kɑːrdəməm ‖'kɑːdəməm/ *n* cardamomo *m*

cardboard /'kɑːrdbɔːrd ‖'kɑːdbɔːd/ *n* (stiff) cartón *m*; (thin) cartulina *f*; (*before n*) ~ **box** caja *f* de cartón

cardiac /'kɑːrdiæk ‖'kɑːdiæk/ *adj* cardíaco; ~ **arrest** paro *m* cardíaco

cardigan /'kɑːrdɪgən ‖'kɑːdɪgən/ *n* cárdigan *m*, chaqueta *f* de punto, rebeca *f* (esp Esp), saco *m* (tejido) (RPl), chaleca *f* (Chi)

cardinal /'kɑːrdnəl ‖'kɑːdɪnl/ *n* **1** (Relig) cardenal *m* **2** ~ **(number)** número *m* cardinal

care¹ /ker ‖keə(r)/ *n* **1** (attention, carefulness) cuidado *m*, atención *f*; **to take** ~ tener* cuidado; **take** ~! (saying goodbye) ¡cuídate!; (as a warning) ¡ten cuidado! **2** (of people): **medical** ~ asistencia *f* médica; (of animals, things) cuidado *m*; **in** ~ of (AmE), ~ **of** (BrE) (on letters) en casa de **3** **to take** ~ **of sb/sth (a)** (look after) ⟨of patient⟩ atender* a algn, cuidar de algn; ⟨of children⟩ cuidar a *or* de algn, ocuparse de algn; ⟨of pet/plant/machine⟩ cuidar algo; **I can take** ~ **of myself** yo sé cuidarme **(b)** (deal with) ocuparse *or* encargarse* de algn/algo **4** (worry) preocupación *f*

care² *vi* **to** ~ (ABOUT sth/sb) preocuparse (POR algo/algn); **I don't** ~ no me importa
■ ~ *vt* **(a)** (feel concern) (*usu neg, interrog*): **I couldn't** ~ **less** what he does me tiene sin cuidado lo que haga **(b)** (wish) (frml) **to** ~ **to** + INF: **would you** ~ **to join us for dinner?** ¿le gustaría cenar con nosotros?
■ **care for** [*v + prep + o*] **(a)** (look after) ⟨patient⟩ cuidar (de), atender* **(b)** (be fond of) querer*, sentir* afecto *or* cariño por

career¹ /kə'rɪr ‖kə'rɪə(r)/ *n* carrera *f*

career² *vi* ir* a toda velocidad

carefree /'kerfriː ‖'keəfriː/ *adj* despreocupado

careful /'kerfəl ‖'keəfəl/ *adj* **1** (cautious) cuidadoso, prudente; **(be)** ~ (ten) cuidado; **to be** ~ **of/with sth** tener* cuidado con algo **2** (painstaking) ⟨planning⟩ cuidadoso; ⟨work⟩ cuidado, esmerado; ⟨worker⟩ meticuloso

carefully /'kerfli ‖'keəfəli/ *adv* ⟨handle/drive⟩ con cuidado; ⟨plan/examine⟩ cuidadosamente; ⟨designed/chosen⟩ con esmero

careless /'kerləs ‖'keəlɪs/ *adj* ⟨person⟩ descuidado; ⟨work⟩ poco cuidado; ⟨driving⟩ negligente; **you made some** ~ **mistakes** cometiste errores por descuido

carelessly /'kerləsli ‖'keəlɪsli/ *adv* sin cuidado, sin la debida atención

carelessness /'kerləsnəs ‖'keəlɪsnɪs/ *n* falta *f* de atención *or* de cuidado

carer /'kerər ‖'keərə(r)/ *n*: persona que tiene a su cuidado a un incapacitado sin recibir por ello remuneración

caress¹ /kə'res/ *n* caricia *f*

caress² *vt* acariciar

caretaker /'ker,teɪkər ‖'keə,teɪkə(r)/ *n* conserje *mf*

cargo /'kɑːrgəʊ ‖'kɑːgəʊ/ *n* (*pl* **-goes** *or* **-gos**) **(a)** (load) cargamento *m* **(b)** (goods) carga *f*

Caribbean¹ /ˌkærəˈbiːən, kəˈrɪbiən ‖ˌkærˈbiːən/ *adj* caribeño, del Caribe

Caribbean² *n* the ~ **(Sea)** el (mar) Caribe; **the ~ (region)** el Caribe, las Antillas

caricature /ˈkærɪkətʃʊr ‖ˈkærɪkətʃʊə(r)/ *n* caricatura *f*

caring /ˈkerɪŋ ‖ˈkeərɪŋ/ *adj* ⟨society/approach⟩ humanitario; ⟨person⟩ (kindly) bondadoso; (sympathetic) comprensivo

carnage /ˈkɑːrnɪdʒ ‖ˈkɑːnɪdʒ/ *n* carnicería *f*

carnation /kɑːrˈneɪʃən ‖kɑːˈneɪʃən/ *n* clavel *m*

carnival /ˈkɑːrnəvəl ‖ˈkɑːnɪvəl/ *n* carnaval *m*

carnivorous /kɑːrˈnɪvərəs ‖kɑːˈnɪvərəs/ *adj* carnívoro

carol /ˈkærəl/ *n* villancico *m*

carousel /ˌkærəˈsel/ *n* **(a)** (esp AmE) ▶ MERRY-GO-ROUND **(b)** (for baggage) cinta *f* or correa *f* transportadora **(c)** (in shops) (AmE) expositor *m* giratorio

car park *n* (BrE) (open space) ▶ PARKING LOT; (building) ▶ PARKING GARAGE

carpenter /ˈkɑːrpəntər ‖ˈkɑːpəntə(r)/ *n* carpintero, -ra *m,f*

carpentry /ˈkɑːrpəntri ‖ˈkɑːpəntri/ *n* carpintería *f*

carpet /ˈkɑːrpət ‖ˈkɑːpɪt/ *n* **(a)** (rug) alfombra *f*, tapete *m* (Col, Méx, Ven); ▶ SWEEP² *vt* 1B **(b)** (wall-to-wall) alfombra *f*, moqueta *f* (Esp), moquette *f* (RPl) **(c)** (of flowers, leaves, moss) (liter) alfombra *f* (liter)

carphone /ˈkɑːrfəʊn ‖ˈkɑːfəʊn/ *n* teléfono *m* de automóvil

carriage /ˈkærɪdʒ/ *n* **1 (a)** (horse-drawn) carruaje *m*, coche *m* **(b)** (BrE Rail) vagón *m* **(c)** (baby ~) (AmE) cochecito *m*, carriola *f* (Méx) **2** (transport) transporte *m* **3** (bearing) (frml) porte *m*

carrier /ˈkæriər ‖ˈkæriə(r)/ *n* **1** (company) compañía *f* or empresa *f* de transportes; (Aviat) línea *f* aérea **2** (of disease, gene) portador, -dora *m,f*

carrier bag *n* (BrE) bolsa *f* (de plástico *or* papel)

carrion /ˈkæriən/ *n* carroña *f*

carrot /ˈkærət/ *n* zanahoria *f*

carry /ˈkæri/ **-ries, -rying, -ried** *vt* **1 (a)** (bear, take) llevar; **I can't ~ this, it's too heavy** no puedo cargar con esto, pesa demasiado **(b)** (have with one) llevar encima **(c)** (be provided with) ⟨guarantee⟩ tener* **(d)** (be pregnant with) estar* embarazada *or* encinta de **2 (a)** (convey) ⟨goods/passengers⟩ llevar, transportar; **she was carried along by the crowd** fue arrastrada por la multitud **(b)** (channel, transmit) ⟨oil/water/sewage⟩ llevar **(c)** ⟨disease⟩ ser* portador de **3** (support) ⟨weight⟩ soportar **4** (involve, entail) ⟨responsibility⟩ conllevar **5** (gain support for) ⟨bill/motion⟩ aprobar* **6** (stock) ⟨model⟩ tener*, vender

■ ~ *vi*: **sound carries further in the mountains** en la montaña los sonidos llegan más lejos; **her voice carries well** su voz tiene mucha proyección

■ **carry away** [v + o + adv, v + adv + o] (usu pass): **I got carried away and painted the window**

as well me entusiasmé y pinté la ventana también; **there's no need to get carried away** no te pases

■ **carry off** [v + o + adv, v + adv + o] **1** (abduct) ⟨victim/hostage⟩ llevarse **2 (a)** (win) ⟨trophy/cup⟩ llevarse **(b)** (succeed with): **she tried to appear disinterested but failed to ~ it off** intentó aparentar desinterés pero no lo logró

■ **carry on 1 (a)** [v + o + adv, v + adv + o] ⟨practice⟩ seguir* *or* continuar* con **(b)** [v + adv + o] ⟨conversation/correspondence⟩ mantener* **2** [v + adv] **(a)** (continue) seguir*, continuar* **(b)** (make a fuss) (colloq): **what a way to ~ on!** ¡qué manera de hacer escándalo, por favor!

■ **carry out** [v + o + adv, v + adv + o] ⟨work/repairs/investigation⟩ llevar a cabo; ⟨order⟩ cumplir; ⟨duty⟩ cumplir con

carry: ~**all** *n* (AmE) bolso *m* de viaje, bolsón *m* (RPl); ~**cot** *n* (BrE) cuna *f* portátil; ~**on** *adj* (AmE) (before *n*) ⟨bag/baggage⟩ de mano; ~**out** *n* (esp AmE) comida preparada o bebida que se vende para consumir fuera del lugar de venta

car: ~ **seat** *n* asiento *m* del coche; (for infant) asiento *m* de bebé (*para el coche*); ~**sick** *adj* mareado (*por viajar en coche*)

cart¹ /kɑːrt ‖kɑːt/ *n* **(a)** (waggon) carro *m*, carreta *f* **(b)** (in supermarket, airport) (AmE) carrito *m*

cart² *vt* (colloq): **I had to ~ the books around all day** tuve que cargar con los libros todo el día

cartel /kɑːrˈtel ‖kɑːˈtel/ *n* cártel *m*

carthorse /ˈkɑːrthɔːrs ‖ˈkɑːthɔːs/ *n* caballo *m* de tiro

cartilage /ˈkɑːrtlɪdʒ ‖ˈkɑːtɪlɪdʒ/ *n* cartílago *m*

carton /ˈkɑːrtn ‖ˈkɑːtn/ *n* (of cigarettes) cartón *m*; **a ~ of milk** una leche en cartón

cartoon /kɑːrˈtuːn ‖kɑːˈtuːn/ *n* **(a)** (humorous drawing) chiste *m* (gráfico), viñeta *f* (Esp), mono *m* (Chi) **(b)** (Cin) dibujos *mpl* animados

cartridge /ˈkɑːrtrɪdʒ ‖ˈkɑːtrɪdʒ/ *n* (for gun, pen) cartucho *m*

cartwheel /ˈkɑːrthwiːl ‖ˈkɑːtwiːl/ *n* voltereta *f* lateral, rueda *f*, rueda *f* de carro (Méx, RPl)

carve /kɑːrv ‖kɑːv/ *vt* **1** (Art) ⟨wood/stone⟩ tallar; ⟨figure/bust⟩ esculpir, tallar; ⟨initials⟩ grabar **2** (Culin) ⟨meat⟩ cortar, trinchar

■ **carve out** [v + o + adv, v + adv + o] ⟨reputation⟩ forjarse; ⟨name⟩ hacerse*

carving /ˈkɑːrvɪŋ ‖ˈkɑːvɪŋ/ *n* talla *f*, escultura *f*

carving knife *n* trinchante *m*, cuchillo *m* de trinchar

car wash *n* túnel *m* or tren *m* de lavado

cascade¹ /kæsˈkeɪd/ *n* cascada *f*

cascade² *vi* caer* en cascada

case /keɪs/ *n* **1** (matter) caso *m*; **to lose/win a ~** (Law) perder*/ganar un pleito *or* juicio **2 (a)** (Med, Soc Adm) caso *m* **(b)** (eccentric) (colloq) caso *m* (fam) **3** (instance, situation) caso *m*; **if that's the ~** si es así; **in that ~, I'm not interested** en ese caso, no me interesa **4** (in phrases) **in any case** de todas maneras *or* formas; **in case** (as *conj*): **make a note in ~ you forget** apúntalo por si te olvidas; **just in case** por si acaso

5 (argument): **she has a good** ~ sus argumentos son buenos; **there is a** ~ **for doing nothing** hay razones para no hacer nada

6 (a) (suit~) maleta *f*, valija *f* (RPl) **(b)** (attaché ~) maletín *m* **(c)** (crate) caja *f*, cajón *m*, jaba *f* (Chi, Per); (of wine, liquor) *caja de 12 botellas* **(d)** (hard container — for small objects) estuche *f*; (— for large objects) caja *f*; (soft container) funda *f*

case: ~ **history** *n* (Med) historial *m* clínico, historia *f* clínica (AmL); ~ **study** *n* estudio *m*

cash¹ /kæʃ/ *n* **(a)** (notes and coins) dinero *m* (en) efectivo; **(in)** ~ en efectivo; ~ **on delivery** entrega *f* contra reembolso; ⟨*before n*⟩ ⟨*payment*⟩ en efectivo; ⟨*refund*⟩ al contado **(b)** (funds) (colloq) dinero *m*, lana *f* (AmL fam), plata *f* (AmS fam), tela *f* (Esp fam)

cash² *vt* ⟨*check*⟩ cobrar

■ **cash in** **1** [*v + o + adv, v + adv + o*] (exchange for money) canjear **2** [*v + adv*] (profit) **to** ~ **in** (**on** sth) aprovecharse (DE algo)

cash: ~ **and carry** *n*: tienda de venta al por mayor; ~ **crop** *n* cultivo *m* industrial *or* comercial; ~ **desk** *n* (BrE) caja *f*; ~ **dispenser** *n* (BrE) cajero *m* automático *or* permanente

cashew (nut) /ˈkæʃuː/ *n* anacardo *m*, castaña *f* de cajú (CS, Ven), nuez *f* de la India (Méx)

cash flow *n* flujo *m* de caja, cash-flow *m*

cashier /kæˈʃɪr ‖ kæˈʃɪə(r)/ *n* cajero, -ra *m,f*

cashier's check *n* (AmE) cheque *m* bancario *or* de caja *or* de gerencia

cashmere /ˈkæʒmɪr ‖ ˌkæʃˈmɪə(r)/ *n* cachemir *m*, cachemira *f*

cash: ~**point** *n* (BrE) cajero *m* automático *or* permanente; ~ **register** *n* caja *f* registradora

casing /ˈkeɪsɪŋ/ *n* **(a)** (cover) cubierta *f*; (case) caja *f*

casino /kəˈsiːnəʊ/ *n* (*pl* **-nos**) casino *m*

cask /kæsk ‖ kɑːsk/ *n* barril *m*, tonel *m*

casket /ˈkæskət ‖ ˈkɑːskɪt/ *n* **(a)** (for jewels) cofre *m* **(b)** (coffin) (AmE) ataúd *m*, féretro *m*, cajón (AmL)

casserole /ˈkæsərəʊl/ *n* **(a)** (dish) cazuela *f* **(b)** (food) guiso *m*, guisado *m* (Méx)

cassette /kəˈset/ *n* (Audio) cassette *f or m*; (*before n*) ~ **player** pasacintas *m*, cassette *m* (Esp), pasacassettes *m* (RPl), tocacassettes *m* (Chi)

cast¹ /kæst ‖ kɑːst/ *n* **1 (a)** (molded object) (Art) vaciado *m*; (Metall) pieza *f* fundida **(b)** (mold) molde *m* **2** (Cin, Theat) (+ *sing or pl vb*) reparto *m*, elenco *m* (esp AmL)

cast² (*past & past p* **cast**) *vt* **1 (a)** ⟨*stone*⟩ arrojar, lanzar*, tirar*; ⟨*line*⟩ lanzar*; ⟨*net*⟩ echar **(b)** ⟨*shadow/light*⟩ proyectar; **to** ~ **doubt on** sth poner* algo en duda **(c)** ⟨*vote*⟩ emitir **2** «*snake*» ⟨*skin*⟩ mudar de, mudar **3** (Cin, Theat) ⟨*role*⟩ asignar; **she was** ~ **as the princess** le dieron el papel de la princesa

■ ~ *vi* (in angling) lanzar*

■ **cast away** [*v + o + adv*]: **they were** ~ **away on a desert island** llegaron a una isla desierta tras naufragar

■ **cast off** [*v + adv*] **1 (a)** (in knitting) cerrar* **(b)** (Naut) soltar* amarras

2 [*v + o + adv, v + adv + o*] **(a)** (in knitting) ⟨*stitch*⟩ cerrar* **(b)** (abandon) ⟨*friend/lover*⟩ dejar

■ **cast on** **1** [*v + adv*] (in knitting) poner* *or* montar los puntos

2 [*v + o + adv, v + adv + o*] ⟨*stitch*⟩ montar, poner*

■ **cast out** [*v + o + adv, v + adv + o*] (liter) expulsar

castanets /ˈkæstəˈnets/ *pl n* castañuelas *fpl*

castaway /ˈkæstəweɪ ‖ ˈkɑːstəweɪ/ *n* náufrago, -ga *m,f*

caste /kæst ‖ kɑːst/ *n* casta *f*

caster /ˈkæstər ‖ ˈkɑːstə(r)/ *n* ruedecita *f*, ruedita *f* (esp AmL)

caster sugar *n* (BrE) azúcar *m* blanca de granulado muy fino

Castile /kæsˈtiːl ‖ kæˈstiːl/ *n* Castilla *f*

Castilian¹ /kæsˈtɪljən ‖ kəˈstɪlɪən/ *adj* castellano

Castilian² *n* **(a)** (person) castellano, -na *m,f* **(b)** (language) castellano *m*

cast: ~ **iron** *n* hierro *m* fundido *or* colado; ~**-iron** *adj* ⟨*before n*⟩ ⟨*guarantee*⟩ sólido; ⟨*alibi*⟩ a toda prueba

castle /ˈkæsəl ‖ ˈkɑːsəl/ *n* **(a)** (Archit) castillo *m* **(b)** (in chess) torre *f*

castoff /ˈkæstɔːf ‖ ˈkɑːstɒf/ *n*: **she gave me her** ~**s** me dio la ropa que ya no quería

castrate /ˈkæstreɪt ‖ kæˈstreɪt/ *vt* castrar

casual /ˈkæʒuəl/ *adj* **1 (a)** (superficial) ⟨*before n*⟩ ⟨*inspection*⟩ superficial; **a** ~ **acquaintance** un conocido, una conocida; ~ **sex** relaciones *fpl* sexuales promiscuas **(b)** (chance) ⟨*before n*⟩ ⟨*visit/reader*⟩ ocasional **(c)** (informal) ⟨*chat*⟩ informal; ⟨*clothes*⟩ de sport, informal **2** (unconcerned) ⟨*attitude/tone*⟩ despreocupado; ⟨*remark*⟩ hecho al pasar **3** (not regular) ⟨*employment/labor*⟩ eventual, ocasional

casually /ˈkæʒuəli/ *adv* **(a)** (informally) ⟨*dressed*⟩ de manera informal; ⟨*chat*⟩ informalmente **(b)** (with indifference) con indiferencia

casualty /ˈkæʒuəlti/ *n* (*pl* **-ties**) **1** (injured person) herido, -da *m,f*; (dead person) víctima *f*; (Mil) baja *f* **2** (hospital department) (BrE) (*no art*) urgencias *fpl*

cat /kæt/ *n* gato, -ta *m,f*; **to let the** ~ **out of the bag** descubrir* el pastel, levantar la liebre *or* (RPl) la perdiz; **to rain** ~**s and dogs** llover* a cántaros

Catalan¹ /ˈkætlæn ‖ ˈkætələn/ *adj* catalán

Catalan² *n* **(a)** (person) catalán, -lana *m,f* **(b)** (language) catalán *m*

catalog¹, catalogue /ˈkætlɔːg ‖ ˈkætəlɒg/ *n* catálogo *m*

catalog², catalogue *vt* catalogar*

Catalonia /ˈkætlˈəʊniə ‖ ˌkætəˈləʊniə/ *n* Cataluña *f*

catalyst /ˈkætləst ‖ ˈkætəlɪst/ *n* catalizador *m*

AmC Central America	Arg Argentina	Cu Cuba	Per Peru
AmL Latin America	Bol Bolivia	Ec Ecuador	RPl River Plate Area
AmS South America	Chi Chile	Esp Spain	Ur Uruguay
Andes Andean Region	CS Southern Cone	Méx Mexico	Ven Venezuela

catalytic converter /ˌkætlˈɪtɪk kənˈvɜːrtər ‖ˌkætəˈlɪtɪk kənˈvɜːtə(r)/ n catalizador m

catapult¹ /ˈkætəpʊlt ‖ˈkætəpʌlt/ n (Aviat, Mil) catapulta f

catapult² vt catapultar

cataract /ˈkætərækt/ n [1] (over a precipice) catarata f, (in a river) rápido m [2] (Med) catarata f

catarrh /kəˈtɑːr ‖kəˈtɑː(r)/ n catarro m

catastrophe /kəˈtæstrəfi/ n catástrofe f

catch¹ /kætʃ/ (past & past p **caught**) vt
[1] ⟨ball/object⟩ agarrar, coger* (esp Esp)
[2] (capture) ⟨mouse/lion⟩ atrapar, coger* (esp Esp); ⟨fish⟩ pescar*, coger* (esp Esp); ⟨thief⟩ atrapar
[3] (a) (take by surprise) agarrar, pillar (fam), pescar* (fam); **we got caught in the rain** nos sorprendió la lluvia **(b)** (intercept) ⟨person⟩ alcanzar*; **∼ you later** (colloq) nos vemos
[4] (a) ⟨train/plane⟩ (take) tomar, coger* (esp Esp); (be in time for) alcanzar* **(b)** (manage to see, hear): **we'll just ∼ the end of the game** todavía podemos pescar el final del partido (fam); **we could ∼ a movie before dinner** (AmE) podríamos ir al cine antes de cenar
[5] (entangle, trap): **I caught my skirt on a nail** se me enganchó or (Méx tb) se me atoró or (Chi) se me pescó la falda en un clavo; **I caught my finger in the drawer** me pillé or (AmL tb) me agarré el dedo en el cajón
[6] (hear or understand clearly): **did you ∼ what she said?** ¿oíste lo que dijo?
[7] ⟨disease⟩ contagiarse de; **to ∼ a cold** resfriarse*, agarrar or (esp Esp) coger* un resfriado
[8] (hit): **he caught his head on the beam** se dio en la cabeza con la viga
■ ∼ vi [1] (a) (grasp) agarrar, coger* (esp Esp), cachar (Méx) **(b)** (become hooked) engancharse [2] (ignite) ⟨fire⟩ prender, agarrar (AmL)
■ **catch on** [v + adv] (colloq) (a) (become popular) «fashion/idea» imponerse*; «game/style» ponerse* de moda **(b)** (understand) caer* (fam)
■ **catch out** [v + o + adv, v + adv + o] (a) **to ∼ sb out** pillar or agarrar a algn desprevenido **(b)** (trick) pillar (fam), agarrar (CS fam)
■ **catch up** [1] [v + adv] (with work, studies) ponerse* al día; **to ∼ up WITH sb/sth** (physically) alcanzar* a algn/algo; **she had to ∼ up with the rest of the class** tuvo que ponerse al nivel del resto de la clase [2] [v + o + adv] (draw level with) (BrE) alcanzar* [3] (trap, involve) **to be/get caught up in sth** ⟨in barbed wire/thorns⟩ estar*/quedar enganchado/ atrapado en algo; ⟨in scandal/dispute⟩ verse* envuelto en algo; ⟨in excitement/enthusiasm⟩ contagiarse de algo; **I got caught up in the traffic** me agarró or (esp Esp) me cogió el tráfico

catch² n [1] (a) (Sport) atrapada f, atajada f (CS) **(b)** (of fish) pesca f [2] (on door) pestillo m, pasador m (AmL); (on window, box, necklace) cierre m [3] (hidden drawback) trampa f; **I knew there'd be a ∼ in it somewhere** ya sabía yo que tenía que haber gato encerrado; **it's a C∼-22 situation** es una situación sin salida

catcher /ˈkætʃər ‖ˈkætʃə(r)/ n (in baseball) receptor, -tora m,f, catcher mf

catching /ˈkætʃɪŋ/ adj ⟨pred⟩ contagioso

catchment area /ˈkætʃmənt/ n zona f de captación (distrito que corresponde a un hospital, colegio etc)

catch: **∼phrase** n (of person) latiguillo m; (of political party) eslogan m; **∼word** n (a) (slogan) eslogan m **(b)** ▶ ∼PHRASE

catchy /ˈkætʃi/ adj **catchier, catchiest** pegadizo, pegajoso (AmL exc RPl)

categorical /ˌkætəˈɡɔːrɪkəl ‖ˌkætəˈɡɒrɪkəl/ adj categórico; ⟨refusal⟩ rotundo

categorize /ˈkætəɡəraɪz/ vt ⟨things⟩ clasificar*; ⟨people⟩ catalogar*

category /ˈkætəɡɔːri ‖ˈkætəɡəri/ n (pl **-ries**) categoría f

cater /ˈkeɪtər ‖ˈkeɪtə(r)/ vt (AmE) encargarse* del buffet de
■ **cater to,** (BrE) **cater for** [v + prep + o]: **to ∼ to o for people of all ages** ofrecer* servicios para gente de todas las edades; **we try to ∼ to o for all needs** tratamos de satisfacer todas las necesidades

caterer /ˈkeɪtərər ‖ˈkeɪtərə(r)/ n: persona o firma que se encarga del servicio de comida y bebida para fiestas, cafeterías etc

catering /ˈkeɪtərɪŋ/ n (a) (provision of food): **to do the ∼** encargarse* del servicio de comida y bebida (or del buffet etc) **(b)** (trade, department) restauración f

caterpillar /ˈkætərpɪlər ‖ˈkætəpɪlə(r)/ n oruga f, azotador m (Méx), cuncuna f (Chi)

cathedral /kəˈθiːdrəl/ n catedral f

Catholic¹ /ˈkæθəlɪk/ n católico, -ca m,f

Catholic² adj [1] (Relig) católico; **the Roman ∼ Church** la iglesia católica (apostólica romana) [2] **catholic** ⟨tastes/interests⟩ variado

Catholicism /kəˈθɑːləsɪzəm ‖kəˈθɒlɪsɪzəm/ n catolicismo m

cat: **∼nap** n siestecita f; **C∼'s-eye**® n (Transp) catafaros m, ojo m de gato (CS), esterol m (Col)

catsup /ˈkætsəp/ n (AmE) ▶ KETCHUP

cattle /ˈkætl/ pl n ganado m, reses fpl; (before n) **∼ breeder** ganadero, -ra m,f

catwalk /ˈkætwɔːk/ n pasarela f

Caucasian /kɔːˈkeɪʒən/ n (Anthrop) caucásico, -ca m,f; **the suspect is a male ∼** el sospechoso es un hombre de raza blanca

caught /kɔːt/ past & past p of CATCH¹

cauliflower /ˈkɑːlɪflaʊər ‖ˈkɒlɪflaʊə(r)/ n coliflor f

cause¹ /kɔːz/ n [1] (a) (of accident, event, death) causa f **(b)** (reason, grounds) motivo m, razón f; **there's no ∼ for concern** no hay por qué preocuparse [2] (ideal, movement) causa f

cause² vt causar; **to ∼ sb problems** causarle problemas a algn; **to ∼ sb/sth TO + INF** hacer* que algn/algo (+ subj)

causeway /ˈkɔːzweɪ/ n (path) paso m elevado; (road) carretera f elevada

caustic /ˈkɔːstɪk/ adj cáustico

caution¹ /ˈkɔːʃən/ n (a) (care, prudence) cautela f, prudencia f **(b)** (warning) advertencia f, aviso m; (Law, Sport) amonestación f

caution² vt (a) (warn) advertir* **(b)** (inform of rights) informar de sus derechos

cautious /ˈkɔːʃəs/ adj cauteloso, cauto

cautiously /ˈkɔːʃəsli/ adv cautelosamente

cavalry /'kævəlri/ n caballería f

cave /keɪv/ n cueva f; (before n) ~ **painting** pintura f rupestre
■ **cave in** [v + adv] derrumbarse

caveman /'keɪvmæn/ n (pl **-men** /-men/) hombre m de las cavernas

cavern /'kævərn ‖'kævən/ n caverna f

caviar, caviare /'kæviɑːr ‖'kævɑː(r)/ n caviar m

cavity /'kævəti/ n (pl **-ties**) cavidad f; (Dent) caries f

caw /kɔː/ vi graznar

CBS n (in US) (no art) (= **Columbia Broadcasting System**) la CBS

cc (= **cubic centimeter** o (BrE) **centimetre**) c.c.

CCTV n = **closed-circuit television**

CD n (= **compact disc** or (AmE also) **disk**) CD m

CD-ROM n (= **compact disc read-only memory**) CD-ROM m

cease /siːs/ vt (a) to ~ to + INF/ to ~ -ING dejar DE + INF (b) ⟨production/publication⟩ interrumpir, suspender
■ ~ vi «noise» cesar; «production» interrumpirse; «work» detenerse*

cease-fire /'siːs'faɪr ‖'siːsfaɪə(r)/ n alto m el fuego, cese m del fuego (AmL)

ceaseless /'siːsləs ‖'siːslɪs/ adj incesante

cedar /'siːdər ‖'siːdə(r)/ n cedro m

cede /siːd/ vt to ~ sth (TO sb) ceder(le) algo (A algn)

ceiling /'siːlɪŋ/ n (Const) techo m, cielo m raso; (upper limit) límite m, tope m

celebrate /'seləbreɪt ‖'selɪbreɪt/ vt celebrar
■ ~ vi: we won: let's ~! ¡ganamos, vamos a celebrarlo!

celebration /'selə'breɪʃən ‖,selɪ'breɪʃən/ n (event) fiesta f; he attended the ~s asistió a los festejos

celebrity /sə'lebriti ‖sɪ'lebrəti/ n (pl **-ties**) famoso, -sa m,f, celebridad mf

celery /'seləri/ n apio m, celeri m (Ven)

celibate /'seləbət ‖'selɪbət/ adj célibe

cell /sel/ n [1] (in prison) celda f [2] (Biol, Elec) célula f

cellar /'selar ‖'selə(r)/ n sótano m; (for coal) carbonera f; (for wine) bodega f

cello /'tʃeləʊ/ n (pl **-los**) violoncelo m, violonchelo m, chelo m

cellophane, (BrE) **Cellophane**® /'seləfeɪn/ n celofán m

cellphone /'selfəʊn/ n teléfono m celular

cellulite /'seljəlaɪt ‖'seljʊlaɪt/ n celulitis f

celluloid /'seljəlɔɪd ‖'seljʊlɔɪd/ n celuloide m

cellulose /'seljələʊs ‖'seljʊləʊs/ n celulosa f

Celsius /'selsɪəs/ adj: **20 degrees** ~ 20 grados centígrados or Celsio(s)

Celt /kelt/ n celta mf

Celtic /'keltɪk/ adj celta

cement¹ /sɪ'ment/ n cemento m

cement² vt (a) (Const) unir con cemento (b) ⟨friendship/alliance⟩ consolidar, fortalecer*

cement mixer n hormigonera f

cemetery /'seməteri ‖'semətri/ n (pl **-ries**) cementerio m

censor¹ /'sensər ‖'sensə(r)/ n censor, -sora m,f

censor² vt censurar

censorship /'sensərʃɪp ‖'sensəʃɪp/ n censura f

censure /'sentʃər ‖'sensjə(r)/ vt censurar

census /'sensəs/ n (pl **-suses**) censo m

cent /sent/ n centavo m

centenary /sen'tenəri ‖sen'tiːnəri/ n (pl **-ries**) centenario m

centennial /sen'teniəl/ n (esp AmE) centenario m

center¹, (BrE) **centre** /'sentər ‖'sentə(r)/ n
[1] (middle point, area) centro m [2] (site of activity) centro m [3] (Sport) (in US football, rugby) centro mf; (in basketball) pivot mf, pivote mf (AmL)

center², (BrE) **centre** vt centrar
■ ~ vi (a) (focus on) to ~ ON o UPON sth/sb centrarse EN algo/algn (b) (revolve around) to ~ ON o AROUND sth/sb girar ALREDEDOR DE algo/algn

center: ~ **forward** n delantero mf centro; ~ **half** (pl **halfs** or **halves**) n medio mf centro; ~**piece** n (decoration) centro m (de mesa); (main feature) eje m

centigrade /'sentɪɡreɪd/ adj centígrado

centimeter, (BrE) **centimetre** /'sentəˌmiːtər ‖'sentɪˌmiːtə(r)/ n centímetro m

centipede /'sentəpiːd ‖'sentɪpiːd/ n ciempiés m

central /'sentrəl/ adj (a) (main) central; ⟨problem⟩ fundamental (b) (in the center) ⟨area/street⟩ céntrico; in ~ Chicago en el centro de Chicago

central: C~ America n Centroamérica f, América f Central; **C~ American** adj centroamericano, de (la) América Central; **C~ Europe** n Europa f Central; ~ **heating** n calefacción f central

centralize /'sentrəlaɪz/ vt centralizar*

central reservation n (BrE) mediana f, bandejón m (central) (Chi), camellón m (Méx)

centre etc (BrE) ▶ CENTER etc

century /'sentʃəri/ n (pl **-ries**) siglo m; in the 19th ~ en el siglo XIX

ceramic /sə'ræmɪk ‖sɪ'ræmɪk/ adj ⟨pot⟩ de cerámica; ~ **tile** (for walls) azulejo m; (for floors) baldosa f (de cerámica)

ceramics /sə'ræmɪks ‖sɪ'ræmɪks/ n (+ pl vb) objetos mpl de cerámica, cerámicas fpl

cereal /'sɪriəl ‖'sɪəriəl/ n (a) (plant, grain) cereal m (b) (breakfast ~) cereales mpl

cerebral palsy /sə'riːbrəl 'pɔːlzi ‖'serɪbrəl 'pɔːlzi/ n parálisis f

ceremonial /ˌserə'məʊniəl ‖,serɪ'məʊniəl/ adj ⟨robes⟩ ceremonial; ⟨occasion⟩ solemne

ceremony /'serəməʊni ‖'serɪməni/ n (pl **-nies**) ceremonia f

certain /'sɜːrtn ‖'sɜːtn/ adj [1] (a) (definite) seguro; to make ~ OF sth asegurarse or cerciorarse DE algo; for ~ con certeza (b) (convinced) (pred) to be ~ (OF sth) estar* seguro (DE algo); I checked the list to make ~ (that) ... revisé la lista para asegurarme de que ...

2 (*particular*) (*before n*) cierto; **he has a ~ something** tiene un no sé qué *or* (un) algo especial

certainly /'sɜːrtn̩li ‖'sɜːtn̩li/ *adv* **(a)** (definitely): **we're almost ~ going to win** es casi seguro que vamos a ganar; **do you see what I mean? — certainly** ¿te das cuenta de lo que quiero decir? — desde luego **(b)** (emphatic): **I ~ won't be buying anything there again!** por cierto que no voy a volver a comprar nada allí; **may I use your phone? — certainly!** ¿puedo llamar por teléfono? — pues claro ¡(no) faltaría más!; **~ not!** ¡de ninguna manera!

certainty /'sɜːrtn̩ti ‖'sɜːtn̩ti/ *n* (*pl* **-ties**) certeza *f*, seguridad *f*; **defeat is now a ~** la derrota es algo seguro

certificate /sər'tɪfɪkət ‖sə'tɪfɪkət/ *n* certificado *m*

certify /'sɜːrtəfaɪ ‖'sɜːtɪfaɪ/ *vt* **-fies, -fying, -fied** **(a)** ⟨*facts/claim/death*⟩ certificar*; **this is to ~ that ...** por la presente certifico que ... **(b)** (declare insane) (*usu pass*) declarar demente **(c)** (license) (AmE): **he isn't certified to teach in this state** no está habilitado para ejercer la docencia en este estado **(d) certified** *past p* (AmE) certificado; **certified public accountant** contador público, contadora pública *m,f* (AmL), censor jurado, censora jurada *m,f* de cuentas (Esp)

cervical /'sɜːrvɪkəl ‖'sɜːvɪkəl, sɜː'vaɪkəl/ *adj* del cuello del útero; **~ smear** (BrE) citología *f*, Papanicolau *m* (AmL)

cervix /'sɜːrvɪks ‖'sɜːvɪks/ *n* (*pl* **-vixes** *or* **-vices** /-vəsɪːz/) cuello *m* del útero

Cesarean (section), Cesarian (section) /sɪ'zæriən ‖sɪ'zeəriən/ *n* (AmE) cesárea *f*

cesspit /'sespɪt/ *n* pozo *m* negro *or* séptico *or* ciego

cf (compare) cf.

CFC *n* = **chlorofluorocarbon**

ch *n* (*pl* **chs**) (= **chapter**) c.

chafe /tʃeɪf/ *vt/i* rozar*

chaff /tʃæf ‖tʃɑːf/ *n* barcia *f*

chagrin /'ʃə'ɡrɪn ‖'ʃæɡrɪn/ *n* (liter) disgusto *m*; **to his ~** para su disgusto

chain¹ /tʃeɪn/ *n* cadena *f*; **a ~ of events** una cadena de acontecimientos

chain² *vt* **to ~ sth/sb TO sth** encadenar algo/a algn A algo

chain: ~ reaction *n* reacción *f* en cadena; **~smoke** *vi* fumar un cigarrillo tras otro; **~ store** *n* tienda *f* de una cadena

chair¹ /tʃer ‖tʃeə(r)/ *n* 1 (seat) silla *f*; (arm~) sillón *m*, butaca *f* (esp Esp) 2 (a) (at university) cátedra *f* (b) (in meeting) presidencia *f*; **to take the ~** presidir

chair² *vt* ⟨*meeting*⟩ presidir

chair: ~lift *n* telesilla *f or* (Esp) telesquí *m*; **~man** /'tʃermən ‖'tʃeəmən/ *n* (*pl* **-men** /-mən/) presidente, -ta *m,f*; **~woman** *n* presidenta *f*

chalet /'ʃæleɪ/ *n* **(a)** (cabin) chalet *m* (*de montaña*) **(b)** (in motel) (BrE) bungalow *m*

chalk /tʃɔːk/ *n* 1 (Geol) creta *f*, caliza *f* 2 (for writing) tiza *f*, gis *m* (Méx)

challenge¹ /'tʃæləndʒ ‖'tʃælɪndʒ/ *vt* 1 (a) (summon) desafiar*, retar; **to ~ sb to + INF**

desafiar* a algn A QUE (+ *subj*) **(b)** (question) ⟨*authority/findings*⟩ cuestionar 2 (stop) (Mil) darle* el alto a

challenge² *n* desafío *m*, reto *m*

challenger /'tʃæləndʒər ‖'tʃælɪndʒə(r)/ *n* contendiente *mf*, rival *mf*

chamber /'tʃeɪmbər ‖'tʃeɪmbə(r)/ *n* 1 (room) (arch) cámara *f* (arc) 2 (of gun) recámara *f*

chamber: ~maid *n* camarera *f* (*en un hotel*); **~ music** *n* música *f* de cámara; **~ of commerce** *n* cámara *f* de comercio; **~ pot** *n* orinal *m or* (AmL exc RPl) bacinilla *f or* (CS) escupidera *f*

chameleon /kə'miːliən/ *n* camaleón *m*

chamois (leather) /'ʃæmi/ *n* gamuza *f*

chamomile /'kæməmaɪl/ *n* manzanilla *f*, camomila *f*; **~ tea** manzanilla *f*

champagne /ʃæm'peɪn/ *n* champán *m*, champaña *f or m*

champion¹ /'tʃæmpiən/ *n* **(a)** (Sport) campeón, -peona *m,f* **(b)** (of cause) defensor, -sora *m,f*

champion² *vt* abogar* por, defender*

championship /'tʃæmpiənʃɪp/ *n* (Sport) (*often pl*) campeonato *m*

chance¹ /tʃæns ‖tʃɑːns/ *n* 1 (fate) casualidad *f*, azar *m*; **by ~** por *or* de casualidad; (*before n*) ⟨*meeting*⟩ fortuito 2 (risk) riesgo *m*; **don't take any ~s** no te arriesgues 3 (opportunity) oportunidad *f* 4 (likelihood) posibilidad *f*, chance *f or m* (esp AmL); **(the) ~s are (that) ...** (colloq) lo más probable es que ...

chance² *vt*: **to ~ it** arriesgarse*

chancellor /'tʃænsələr ‖'tʃɑːnsələ(r)/ *n* **(a) Chancellor (of the Exchequer)** (in UK) ≈ ministro, -tra *m,f* de Economía/Hacienda **(b)** (premier) canciller *mf* **(c)** (of university) rector, -tora *m,f*

chandelier /'ʃændə'lɪr ‖ˌʃændə'lɪə(r)/ *n* araña *f* (*de luces*)

change¹ /tʃeɪndʒ/ *n* 1 (a) cambio *m*; **a ~ in temperature** un cambio de temperatura; **for a ~** para variar **(b)** (of clothes) muda *f* 2 (a) (coins) cambio *m*, monedas *fpl*, sencillo *m* (AmL), menudo *m* (Col), dinero *m* suelto, plata *f* suelta (AmS) **(b)** (money returned) cambio *m*, vuelto *m* (AmL), vuelta *f* (Esp), vueltas *fpl* (Col)

change² *vt* cambiar; **the witch ~d her into a stone** la bruja la convirtió en una piedra; **to ~ one's clothes** cambiarse de ropa; **to ~ color** cambiar de color; **let's ~ the subject** cambiemos de tema; **I wouldn't want to ~ places with her** no quisiera estar en su lugar; **to change train(s)** hacer* transbordo, cambiar (de tren); **to ~ dollars into pesos** cambiar dólares a *or* (Esp tb) en pesos
■ ~ *vi* 1 (a) (become different) cambiar; **to ~ INTO sth** convertirse* EN algo **(b) changing** *pres p* ⟨*needs/role/moods*⟩ cambiante 2 (a) (put on different clothes) cambiarse; **she ~d into a black dress** se cambió y se puso un vestido negro; **to get ~d** cambiarse **(b)** (Transp) cambiar, hacer* transbordo
■ **change over** [*v* + *adv*] cambiar

changeable /'tʃeɪndʒəbəl/ *adj* cambiante

change: ~over *n* (transition) ~over (FROM sth) (TO sth) cambio *m* (DE algo) (A algo); **~ purse** *n* (AmE) monedero *m*, portamonedas *m*

changing room /'tʃeɪndʒɪŋ/ n (BrE) **(a)** (Sport) vestuario m, vestidor m (Chi, Méx) **(b)** (in shop) probador m

channel[1] /'tʃænl/ n [1] (strait) canal m; (course of river) cauce m; (navigable course) canal m; **the (English) C~** el Canal de la Mancha [2] (for irrigation) canal m, acequia f [3] (system, method) vía f; **you must go through the official ~s** tiene que hacer el trámite por los conductos oficiales [4] (Comput, TV) canal m

channel[2] vt, (BrE) **-ll-** ‹water/proposals/complaints› canalizar*; ‹efforts/energies› encauzar*

channel: C~ Islands pl n **the C~ Islands** las Islas Anglonormandas, las islas del Canal de la Mancha; **C~ Tunnel** n **the C~ Tunnel** el Eurotúnel, el túnel del Canal de la Mancha

chant[1] /tʃænt ‖tʃɑːnt/ n (of demonstrators) consigna f; (of sports fans) alirón m, canción f

chant[2] vt/i (Mus, Relig) salmodiar; «crowd» gritar

chaos /'keɪɑːs ‖'keɪɒs/ n caos m

chaotic /keɪ'ɑːtɪk ‖keɪ'ɒtɪk/ adj caótico

chap /tʃæp/ n (colloq) tipo m (fam)

chap. n (pl **chaps**) (= **chapter**) c., cap.

chapel /'tʃæpəl/ n capilla f

chaperon, chaperone /'ʃæpərəʊn/ n (of young lady) acompañante f, chaperona f; (for young people) (AmE) acompañante mf

chaplain /'tʃæplən ‖'tʃæplɪn/ n capellán m

chapped /tʃæpt/ adj ‹lips› agrietado

chapter /'tʃæptər ‖'tʃæptə(r)/ n capítulo m

char /tʃɑːr ‖tʃɑː(r)/ vt **-rr-** carbonizar*

character /'kærəktər ‖'kærəktə(r)/ n [1] (of person, thing) carácter m; **to be in/out of ~** ser*/no ser* típico; **her face is full of ~** tiene una cara con mucha personalidad [2] **(a)** (in novel, play, movie) personaje m **(b)** (person) tipo m (fam) **(c)** (eccentric person) caso m [3] (symbol) carácter m

characteristic[1] /'kærəktə'rɪstɪk/ n característica f

characteristic[2] adj característico

characterize /'kærəktəraɪz/ vt caracterizar*

charade /ʃə'reɪd ‖ʃə'rɑːd/ n farsa f; **~s** (+ sing vb) (game) charada f

charcoal /'tʃɑːrkəʊl ‖'tʃɑːkəʊl/ n carbón m (vegetal); (Art) carboncillo m, carbonilla f (RPl)

charge[1] /tʃɑːrdʒ ‖tʃɑːdʒ/ n [1] (Law) cargo m, acusación f; **to bring** o **press ~s against sb** formular cargos contra algn [2] (price) precio m; (fee) honorario m; **free of ~** gratuitamente, gratis [3] (responsibility): **the person in ~** la persona responsable; **to be in ~ of sth/sb** ‹department/child› estar* a cargo de sth/algn, encargarse* de algn, ocuparse de [4] (Elec, Phys) carga f [5] (of explosive) carga f [6] (attack) carga f

charge[2] vt [1] (accuse) **to ~ sb WITH sth/-ING** acusar a algn DE algo/+ INF [2] (ask payment) cobrar [3] (obtain on credit): **to ~ sth TO sb** cargar*

algo a la cuenta de algn [4] **(a)** (entrust) **to ~ sb WITH sth/-ING** encomendarle* A algn algo/QUE (+ subj) **(b)** (allege) (AmE) aducir* [5] (attack) (Mil) cargar* contra; «animal» embestir* or arremeter contra [6] (Elec) ‹battery› cargar*
■ **~** vi **to ~ (AT sth/sb)** (Mil) cargar* (CONTRA algo/algn); «animal» arremeter or embestir* (CONTRA algo/algn)

charge: ~ account n cuenta f de crédito; **~ card** n tarjeta f de pago

charger /'tʃɑːrdʒər ‖'tʃɑːdʒə(r)/ n (battery ~) cargador m de pilas; (Auto) cargador m de baterías

chariot /'tʃæriət/ n carro m (de guerra)

charisma /kə'rɪzmə/ n carisma m

charismatic /'kærəz'mætɪk ‖,kærɪz'mætɪk/ adj carismático

charitable /'tʃærətəbəl ‖'tʃærɪtəbəl/ adj **(a)** (generous, giving) caritativo **(b)** (kind) ‹person› bueno; ‹interpretation› benévolo, generoso

charity /'tʃærəti/ n (pl **-ties**) [1] **(a)** (organization) organización f benéfica or de beneficencia **(b)** (relief) obras fpl de beneficencia; **to raise money for ~** recaudar dinero para un fin benéfico; (before n) ‹work› de beneficencia, benéfico [2] (generosity, kindness) caridad f

charm[1] /tʃɑːrm ‖tʃɑːm/ n [1] **(a)** (attractiveness) encanto m **(b)** (attractive quality, feature) encanto m [2] (spell) hechizo m [3] (amulet) amuleto m, fetiche m; (on bracelet) dije m

charm[2] vt cautivar

charming /'tʃɑːrmɪŋ ‖'tʃɑːmɪŋ/ adj ‹person› encantador; ‹room/house› precioso

chart[1] /tʃɑːrt ‖tʃɑːt/ n [1] (Aviat, Naut) carta f de navegación; (diagram, graph) gráfico m; (table) tabla f [2] **charts** pl (best-selling records) **the ~s** la lista de éxitos

chart[2] vt ‹course› trazar*; ‹progress/changes› (follow closely) seguir* atentamente; (record) registrar gráficamente

charter[1] /'tʃɑːrtər ‖'tʃɑːtə(r)/ n [1] **(a)** (constitution) carta f **(b)** (guarantee of rights) fuero m, privilegio m [2] (Transp) (before n) ‹flight/plane› chárter adj inv

charter[2] vt [1] ‹plane/ship/bus› fletar, alquilar [2] (BrE) **chartered** past p ‹engineer/surveyor› colegiado; **~ed accountant** contador público, contadora pública m,f (AmL), censor jurado, censora jurada m,f de cuentas (Esp)

chase[1] /tʃeɪs/ n persecución f

chase[2] vt perseguir*
■ **~** vi: **we ~d after the thief** fuimos tras el ladrón; **to ~ after girls** ir* detrás de las chicas
■ **chase up** [v + o + adv, v + adv + o] (colloq): **~ up this order for me, please** averíguame qué pasó con este pedido, por favor; **I'll have to ~ him up about the report** voy a tener que recordarle lo del informe

chasm /'kæzəm/ n sima f, abismo m

chassis /'tʃæsi ‖'ʃæsi/ n (pl **chassis** /'tʃæsiz ‖'ʃæ-/) (Auto) chasis m, bastidor m (Esp)

chastise /tʃæsˈtaɪz/ vt (fml) (verbally) reprender; (physically) castigar*

chastity /ˈtʃæstəti/ n castidad f

chat¹ /tʃæt/ n charla f, conversación f (esp AmL), plática f (AmC, Méx)

chat² vi -tt- **to ~** (TO o WITH sb) charlar or (esp AmL) conversar or (AmC, Méx) platicar* (CON algn)

chat: **~ line** n chat m; **~ show** n (BrE) programa m de entrevistas

chatter /ˈtʃætər ‖ˈtʃætə(r)/ vi «person» charlar; «monkeys» parlotear; «birds» cotorrear; **his teeth are ~ing** le castañetean los dientes

chatterbox /ˈtʃætərbɑːks ‖ˈtʃætəbɒks/ n charlatán, -tana m,f

chatty /ˈtʃæti/ adj -tier, -tiest «person» conversador; «letter» simpático y lleno de noticias

chauffeur /ˈʃəʊfər ‖ˈʃəʊfə(r)/ n chofer mf or (Esp) chófer mf

chauvinism /ˈʃəʊvənɪzəm ‖ˈʃəʊvɪnɪzəm/ n chovinismo m; **male ~** machismo m

chauvinist /ˈʃəʊvənəst ‖ˈʃəʊvɪnɪst/ n chovinista mf; **(male) ~** machista m

cheap /tʃiːp/ adj -er, -est [1] (a) (inexpensive) barato; «restaurant/hotel» económico (b) (shoddy) «merchandise/jewelry» ordinario, de baratillo; «mechanic/electrician» (AmE) chapucero [2] (a) (vulgar, contemptible) «joke/gimmick» de mal gusto; «trick/tactics» bajo; «liar/crook» vil (b) (worthless) «flattery/promises» fácil

cheapen /ˈtʃiːpən/ vt quitarle valor a, degradar

cheaply /ˈtʃiːpli/ adv «buy/sell/get» barato; «dress/eat/live» con poco dinero

cheat¹ /tʃiːt/ vt estafar, engañar
■ **~** vi (a) (act deceitfully) hacer* trampas (b) (be unfaithful) **to ~ on sb** engañar a algn

cheat² n (swindler) estafador, -dora m,f; (at cards, in exam) tramposo, -sa m,f

check¹ /tʃek/ n [1] (stop, restraint) control m [2] (inspection — of passport, documents) control m; (— of work) examen m, revisión f; (— of machine, product) inspección f; **to keep a ~ on sth** controlar algo [3] (before n) «jacket/shirt» a or de cuadros [4] (in chess) jaque m [5] (Fin), (BrE) **cheque** cheque m, talón m (Esp); **to pay by ~** pagar* con cheque or (Esp) con talón [6] (restaurant bill) (AmE) cuenta f, adición f (RPI) [7] (tick) (AmE) signo m, tic m, visto m (Esp), palomita f (Méx fam)

check² vt (restrain) «anger/impulse» contener* [2] (a) (inspect) «passport/ticket» revisar, checar* (Méx); «machine/product» inspeccionar; «quality» controlar; «temperature/pressure/volume» comprobar*, checar* (Méx) (b) (verify) «facts/information» comprobar*, verificar*, checar* (Méx); «accounts/bill» revisar [3] (AmE) (a) (in cloakroom) dejar en el guardarropa; (in baggage office) dejar or (firm) depositar en consigna (b) (Aviat) «baggage» facturar, chequear (AmL) [4] (tick) (AmE) marcar*, hacer* un tic or (Méx fam) una palomita en, poner* un visto en (Esp)
■ **~** vi comprobar*, verificar*, checar* (Méx)
■ **check in** [1] [v + adv] (at airport) facturar or (AmL tb) chequear el equipaje; (at hotel) registrarse [2] [v + o + adv, v + adv + o] (Aviat) «luggage» facturar, chequear (AmL)

■ **check out** [1] [v + adv] dejar el hotel (or pensión etc) (habiendo pagado la factura etc) [2] [v + adv] (tally) (AmE) «story» cuadrar [3] [v + o + adv, v + adv + o] (a) «facts/story» verificar*, comprobar*, checar* (Méx) (b) (esp AmE) «shopping» «customer» pagar*; «cashier» cobrar
■ **check up** [v + adv]: **we ~ed up and found out he was lying** hicimos averiguaciones y comprobamos que mentía; **can you ~ up on that?** ¿puedes comprobarlo?

checkbook, (BrE) **chequebook** /ˈtʃekbʊk/ n chequera f, talonario m de cheques (esp Esp)

checked /tʃekt/ adj (no comp) a or de cuadros

checker /ˈtʃekər ‖ˈtʃekə(r)/ n (AmE) (cashier) cajero, -ra m,f

checkered, (BrE) **chequered** /ˈtʃekərd ‖ˈtʃekəd/ adj «career/history» accidentado

checkers /ˈtʃekərz ‖ˈtʃekəz/ n (AmE) (+ sing vb) damas fpl

check-in /ˈtʃekɪn/ n facturación f de equipajes

checking account /ˈtʃekɪŋ/ n (AmE) cuenta f corriente

check: **~list** n lista f de control; **~mate** n (jaque m) mate m; **~out** n caja f; **~point** n control m; **~room** n (AmE) guardarropa m; **~up** n (Med) chequeo m, revisión f

cheek /tʃiːk/ n [1] (of the face) mejilla f, cachete m (AmL fam) [2] (colloq) (impudence) descaro m, cara f (fam)

cheekbone /ˈtʃiːkbəʊn/ n pómulo m

cheeky /ˈtʃiːki/ adj -kier, -kiest (esp BrE) «boy/girl» fresco, descarado; «grin» pícaro

cheep /tʃiːp/ vi piar*

cheer¹ /tʃɪr ‖tʃɪə(r)/ n [1] (of encouragement, approval) ovación f, aclamación f; **three ~s for Fred!** ¡viva Fred! [2] **cheers** pl (as interj) (drinking toast) ¡salud!

cheer² vt (a) (shout in approval) aclamar, vitorear (b) **~ (on)** (shout encouragement at) animar
■ **~** vi aplaudir
■ **cheer up** [1] [v + adv] animarse [2] [v + o + adv, v + adv + o] «person» animar

cheerful /ˈtʃɪrfəl ‖ˈtʃɪəfəl/ adj alegre; «news/prospect» alentador

cheerleader /ˈtʃɪrˌliːdər ‖ˈtʃɪəˌliːdə(r)/ n animador, -dora m,f (en encuentros deportivos, mítines políticos), porrista mf (Col, Méx)

cheese /tʃiːz/ n queso m

cheese: **~board** n tabla f de quesos; **~cake** n tarta f de queso; **~burger** n hamburguesa f con queso; **~cloth** n estopilla f, bambula f

cheetah /ˈtʃiːtə/ n guepardo m, chita f

chef /ʃef/ n chef m, jefe -fa m,f de cocina

chemical¹ /ˈkemɪkəl/ n sustancia f química, producto m químico

chemical² adj químico

chemist /ˈkeməst ‖ˈkemɪst/ n (a) (scientist) químico, -ca m,f (b) (pharmacist) (BrE) farmacéutico, -ca m,f; **the ~'s** la farmacia

chemistry /ˈkeməstri ‖ˈkemɪstri/ n química f

chemotherapy /ˈkiːməʊˈθerəpi/ n quimioterapia f

cheque /tʃek/ n (BrE) ▶ CHECK¹ 5

chequebook /ˈtʃekbʊk/ n (BrE) ▶ CHECKBOOK

chequered /'tʃekərd ‖'tʃekəd/ adj (BrE) ▶ CHECKERED

cherish /'tʃerɪʃ/ vt (a) (care for, value) apreciar (b) (cling to) ⟨memory/hope⟩ conservar

cherry /'tʃeri/ n (pl **-ries**) cereza f; (before n) ~ **tree** cerezo m

chess /tʃes/ n ajedrez m

chessboard /'tʃesbɔːrd ‖'tʃesbɔːd/ n tablero m de ajedrez

chest /tʃest/ n 1 (Anat) pecho m; **to get sth off one's** ~ desahogarse* contando/confesando algo 2 (box) arcón m 3 (AmE) (treasury) tesorería f; (funds) fondos mpl

chestnut¹ /'tʃesnʌt/ n castaña f; (before n) ~ **tree** castaño m

chestnut² adj castaño

chest of drawers n (pl ~**s** ~ ~) cómoda f

chew /tʃuː/ vt ⟨food⟩ mascar*, masticar*; ⟨gum⟩ mascar*

chewing gum /'tʃuːɪŋ/ n chicle m

chick /tʃɪk/ n (young bird) polluelo, -la m,f; (young chicken) pollito, -ta m,f

chicken /'tʃɪkən ‖'tʃɪkɪn/ n (a) (hen) gallina f; (as generic term) pollo m (b) (Culin) pollo m

■ **chicken out** [v + adv] (colloq) acobardarse, achicarse* (fam), rajarse (fam)

chickenpox /'tʃɪkənpɑːks ‖'tʃɪkɪnpɒks/ n varicela f, peste f cristal (Chi)

chickpea /'tʃɪkpiː/ n garbanzo m

chicory /'tʃɪkəri/ n (Bot) endivia f; (in coffee) achicoria f

chief¹ /tʃiːf/ n jefe, -fa m,f, líder mf; ~ **of police** jefe de policía

chief² adj (before n, no comp) principal

chief: ~ **constable** n jefe, -fa m,f de policía; ~ **justice** n (in US) presidente, -ta m,f del tribunal

chilblain /'tʃɪlbleɪn/ n sabañón m

child /tʃaɪld/ n (pl **children** /'tʃɪldrən/) (a) (boy) niño m; (girl) niña f (b) (son) hijo m; (daughter) hija f

childbirth /'tʃaɪldbɜːrθ ‖'tʃaɪldbɜːθ/ n parto m

childhood /'tʃaɪldhʊd/ n niñez f, infancia f

childish /'tʃaɪldɪʃ/ adj infantil

childlike /'tʃaɪldlaɪk/ adj ingenuo, de niño

children /'tʃɪldrən/ pl of CHILD

Chile /'tʃɪli/ n Chile m

Chilean¹ /'tʃɪliən/ adj chileno

Chilean² n chileno, -na m,f

chili, chilli /'tʃɪli/ n (pl **-lies**) ají m, chile m

chill¹ /tʃɪl/ n (a) (coldness — of weather) frío m, fresco m (b) (Med) enfriamiento m, resfriado m

chill² vt enfriar*; ⟨wine/food⟩ poner* a enfriar

chilli n (pl **-lies**) ▶ CHILI

chilly /'tʃɪli/ adj **-lier, -liest** frío

chime¹ /tʃaɪm/ n (of bells, clock) campanada f; (of doorbell) campanilla f

chime² vi ⟨bell⟩ sonar*; ⟨clock⟩ dar* la hora

chimney /'tʃɪmni/ n chimenea f

chimney sweep n deshollinador, -dora m,f

chimpanzee /'tʃɪmpænziː ‖,tʃɪmpən'ziː/ n chimpancé m

chin /tʃɪn/ n barbilla f, mentón m

china /'tʃaɪnə/ n loza f; (fine) porcelana f

China /'tʃaɪnə/ n China f

Chinese¹ /tʃaɪ'niːz/ adj chino

Chinese² n (pl ~) (a) (person) chino, -na m,f (b) (language) chino m

chink /tʃɪŋk/ n grieta f, abertura f

chip¹ /tʃɪp/ n 1 (a) (of wood) astilla f; (of stone) esquirla f; (of stone) esquirla f (b) (in cup) desportilladura f 2 (Culin) (a) (in packet) (AmE) papa f or (Esp) patata f frita, papa f chip (Ur) (BrE) (French fry) (BrE) patata f or (Esp) patata f frita 3 (Games) ficha f 4 (Comput, Electron) chip m

chip² **-pp-** vt ⟨crockery⟩ desportillar, cascar* (RPl), saltar (Chi); ⟨tooth⟩ romper* un trocito de ■ ~ vi «china/cup» desportillarse, cascarse* (RPl), saltarse (Chi); «paint/varnish» saltarse, descharcharse

chipboard /'tʃɪpbɔːrd ‖'tʃɪpbɔːd/ n (a) (of wood) madera f prensada or aglomerada, aglomerado m (b) (of paper) (AmE) cartón m prensado

chipmunk /'tʃɪpmʌŋk/ n ardilla f listada

chiropodist /kə'rɑːpədəst ‖kɪ'rɒpədɪst/ n pedicuro, -ra m,f, podólogo, -ga m,f, callista mf

chirp /tʃɜːrp ‖tʃɜːp/ vi piar*

chisel¹ /'tʃɪzəl/ n (for stone) cincel m; (for wood) formón m, escoplo m

chisel² vt, (BrE) **-ll-** ⟨stone⟩ cincelar; ⟨wood⟩ labrar

chivalry /'ʃɪvəlri/ n caballerosidad f, cortesía f

chives /tʃaɪvz/ pl n cebollinos mpl, cebolletas fpl

chlorine /'klɔːriːn/ n cloro m

chlorofluorocarbon /'klɔːrəʊˌflʊərəʊ'kɑːrbən ‖,klɔːrəʊˌflʊərəʊ'kɑːbən, -flɔːrə-/ n clorofluorocarbono m

chloroform /'klɔːrəfɔːrm ‖'klɒrəfɔːm/ n cloroformo m

chocolate /'tʃɑːklət ‖'tʃɒklət/ n (a) chocolate m; (candy, sweet) bombón m (b) (drinking ~) chocolate m en polvo; **a cup of hot** ~ una taza de chocolate

choice¹ /tʃɔɪs/ n (a) (act, option) elección f; **I don't work here out of** ~ no es por (mi) gusto que trabajo aquí (b) (person, thing chosen): **she's a possible** ~ **for the job** es una de las candidatas posibles para el puesto; **it was an unfortunate** ~ **of words** no fue la mejor manera de decirlo (c) (variety) (no pl) surtido m, selección f

choice² adj **choicer, choicest** ⟨fruit/wine⟩ selecto; ⟨beef/veal⟩ (in US) de primera

choir /kwaɪr ‖'kwaɪə(r)/ n coro m

choke¹ /tʃəʊk/ vt estrangular, ahogar*, asfixiar ■ ~ vi ahogarse*, asfixiarse; **to** ~ **ON sth** atragantarse or (AmL tb) atorarse CON algo

choke² n (Auto) choke m, estárter m, cebador m (RPl), ahogador m (Chi, Méx)

cholera /'kɑːlərə ‖'kɒlərə/ n cólera m

cholesterol /kə'lestərəʊl ‖kə'lestərɒl/ n colesterol m

choose /tʃuːz/ (past **chose**; past p **chosen**) vt (a) (select) elegir*, escoger*; ⟨candidate⟩ elegir* (b) (decide) **to** ~ **to** + INF decidir + INF, optar POR + INF ■ ~ vi elegir*, escoger*

541 choosy ⋯⟡ circular ⋯

choosy /'tʃuːzi/ *adj* **-sier, -siest** (colloq) exigente

chop¹ /tʃɑːp ‖tʃɒp/ *n* **1** (with ax, cleaver) hachazo *m*; (with hand) manotazo *m*; (in karate) golpe *m* **2** (Culin) chuleta *f*, costilla *f* (AmS)

chop² **-pp-** *vt* **(a)** (cut) ‹wood› cortar; ‹meat/ apple› cortar (*en trozos pequeños*); ‹parsley/onion› picar* **(b) chopped** *past p* ‹onions/herbs› picado; ‹meat› (AmE) molido *or* (Esp, RPl) picado
■ **chop down** [v + o + adv, v + adv + o] cortar
■ **chop off** [v + o + adv, v + adv + o] ‹branch› cortar
■ **chop up** [v + o + adv, v + adv + o] ▶ CHOP² A

chopper /'tʃɑːpər ‖'tʃɒpə(r)/ *n* **(a)** (hatchet) hacha *f*; pequeña **(b)** (helicopter) (colloq) helicóptero *m*

chopping board /'tʃɑːpɪŋ ‖'tʃɒpɪŋ/ *n* tabla *f* de picar

choppy /'tʃɑːpi ‖'tʃɒpi/ *adj* **-pier, -piest** ‹sea› picado

chopstick /'tʃɑːpstɪk ‖'tʃɒpstɪk/ *n* palillo *m* (*para comer comida oriental*)

chord /kɔːrd ‖kɔːd/ *n* (Mus) acorde *m*

chore /tʃɔːr ‖tʃɔː(r)/ *n* (routine task) tarea *f*; (tedious task) lata *f* (fam)

choreographer /ˌkɔːriˈɑːgrəfər ‖ˌkɒriˈɒgrəfə(r)/ *n* coreógrafo, -fa *m,f*

choreography /ˌkɔːriˈɑːgrəfi ‖ˌkɒriˈɒgrəfi/ *n* coreografía *f*

chortle /'tʃɔːrtl ‖'tʃɔːtl/ *vi* reírse* (*con satisfacción*)

chorus /'kɔːrəs/ *n* **1** (+ *sing o pl vb*) (in musical, opera) coro *m* **2** (refrain) estribillo *m*; (choral piece) coral *m*

chose /tʃəʊz/ *past of* CHOOSE

chosen /'tʃəʊzən/ *past p of* CHOOSE

Christ /kraɪst/ *n* **(a)** (Relig) Cristo **(b)** (*as interj*) (colloq) ¡Jesús! (fam); **for ~'s sake!** ¡por amor de Dios!

christen /'krɪsn/ *vt* bautizar*

christening /'krɪsnɪŋ/ *n* bautismo *m*, bautizo *m*

Christian¹ /'krɪstʃən/ *n* cristiano, -na *m,f*
Christian² *adj* cristiano

Christianity /ˌkrɪstiˈænəti, ˌkrɪstʃi- ‖ˌkrɪstiˈænəti/ *n* (faith) cristianismo *m*; (believers) los cristianos

Christian name *n* nombre *m* de pila

Christmas /'krɪsməs/ *n* Navidad *f*, Pascua *f* (Chi, Per); (~time) las Navidades, la Navidad, la Pascua (Chi, Per); **merry** *o* (BrE also) **happy ~!** ¡Feliz Navidad!, ¡Felices Pascuas!; (*before n*) ~ **cake** pastel *m* de Navidad (*pastel de frutas cubierto de mazapán y azúcar glaseado*); ~ **card** tarjeta *f* de Navidad, tarjeta *f* de Pascua (Chi, Per), crismas *m* (Esp); ~ **Day** día *m* de Navidad *or* (Chi, Per tb) de Pascua; ~ **Eve** (day) la víspera de Navidad; (evening) Nochebuena *f*; ~ **tree** árbol *m* de Navidad *or* (Chi, Per tb) de Pascua

chrome /krəʊm/ *n* cromo *m*

chromium /'krəʊmiəm/ *n* cromo *m*

chromosome /'krəʊməsəʊm/ *n* cromosoma *m*

chronic /'krɑːnɪk ‖'krɒnɪk/ *adj* (Med) crónico; ‹unemployment/shortages› crónico; ‹smoker/liar› empedernido

chronicle /'krɑːnɪkəl ‖'krɒnɪkəl/ *n* crónica *f*

chronological /ˌkrɑːnəˈlɑːdʒɪkəl ‖ˌkrɒnəˈlɒdʒɪkəl/ *adj* cronológico

chrysalis /'krɪsələs ‖'krɪsəlɪs/ *n* crisálida *f*

chubby /'tʃʌbi/ *adj* **-bier, -biest** (colloq) ‹legs/ cheeks/face› regordete (fam); ‹person› gordinflón (fam)

chuck /tʃʌk/ *vt* (colloq) **(a)** (throw) tirar, aventar* (Méx) **(b)** (throw away) tirar, botar (AmL exc RPl) **(c)** (give up) (colloq) ‹job› dejar, plantar (fam); ‹boyfriend/girlfriend› plantar (fam), botar (AmC, Chi fam), largar* (RPl fam)

chuckle /'tʃʌkəl/ *vi* reírse*

chum /tʃʌm/ *n* (colloq) amigo, -ga *m,f*, compinche *mf* (fam), cuate *m* (Méx fam), pata *m* (Per fam), pana *mf* (Ven fam)

chunk /tʃʌŋk/ *n* pedazo *m*, trozo *m*

chunky /'tʃʌŋki/ *adj* **-kier, -kiest** ‹person› fornido; ‹sweater› grueso

church /tʃɜːrtʃ ‖tʃɜːtʃ/ *n* iglesia *f*

churchgoer /'tʃɜːrtʃˌgəʊər ‖'tʃɜːtʃˌgəʊə(r)/ *n* practicante *mf*

churn¹ /tʃɜːrn ‖tʃɜːn/ *n* mantequera *f*

churn² *vt* ‹milk› batir; ‹butter› hacer*
■ **churn out** [v + o + adv, v + adv + o] (colloq) producir* como salchichas (fam)
■ **churn up** [v + o + adv, v + adv + o] revolver*

chute /ʃuːt/ *n* tolva *f*, vertedor *m*; (in swimming pool, amusement park) tobogán *m*, rodadero *m* (Col)

CIA *n* (= **Central Intelligence Agency**) CIA *f*

cider /'saɪdər ‖'saɪdə(r)/ *n* **(a)** (alcoholic) sidra *f*; **hard ~** (AmE) sidra *f* fermentada **(b)** (non-alcoholic) (AmE): (sweet) ~ jugo *m or* (Esp) zumo *m* de manzana

cigar /sɪˈgɑːr ‖sɪˈgɑː(r)/ *n* cigarro *m*, puro *m*, tabaco *m* (Col)

cigarette /ˌsɪgəˈret/ *n* cigarrillo *m*; (*before n*) ~ **end** colilla *f*; ~ **holder** boquilla *f*; ~ **lighter** encendedor *m*, mechero *m* (Esp)

cinch /sɪntʃ/ *n* (colloq) (*no pl*) (easy task): **it's a ~** es pan comido (fam), es tirado (Esp fam), es una papa *or* un bollo (RPl fam), es botado (Chi fam)

cinder /'sɪndər ‖'sɪndə(r)/ *n* **(a)** (ember) carbonilla *f*, carboncillo *m*; **the dinner was burnt to a ~** la cena estaba carbonizada **(b) cinders** *pl* (ashes) ceniza *f*, rescoldo *m*

cinecamera /'sɪniˌkæmərə/ *n* (BrE) filmadora *f* (AmL), tomavistas *m* (Esp); (large, professional) cámara *f* cinematográfica

cinema /'sɪnəmə ‖'sɪnəmɑː/ *n* cine *m*

cinnamon /'sɪnəmən/ *n* canela *f*

cipher /'saɪfər ‖'saɪfə(r)/ *n* clave *f*, cifra *f*

circa /'sɜːrkə ‖'sɜːkə/ *prep* alrededor de, hacia

circle¹ /'sɜːrkəl ‖'sɜːkəl/ *n* círculo *m*; **their ~ of friends** su círculo de amigos; **to come/go full ~** volver* al punto de partida

circle² *vt* **1** (move around) dar* vueltas alrededor de; (be around) rodear, cercar* **2** (draw circle around) trazar* un círculo alrededor de
■ **~** *vi* dar* vueltas; ‹aircraft/bird› volar* en círculos

circuit /'sɜːrkət ‖'sɜːkɪt/ *n* **1** (passage around) recorrido *m*, vuelta *f* **2** (Elec) circuito *m*

circular¹ /'sɜːrkjələr ‖'sɜːkjʊlə(r)/ *adj* circular

circular² *n* circular *f*

circulate /'sɜːrkjəleɪt ‖'sɜːkjʊleɪt/ *vi* circular
■ ~ *vt* ⟨*report/news*⟩ hacer* circular, divulgar*

circulation /ˌsɜːrkjə'leɪʃən ‖ˌsɜːkjʊ'leɪʃən/ *n*
circulación *f*

circumcise /'sɜːrkəmsaɪz ‖'sɜːkəmsaɪz/ *vt*
circuncidar

circumference /sər'kʌmfərəns
‖sə'kʌmfərəns/ *n* circunferencia *f*

circumflex (accent) /'sɜːrkəmfleks
‖'sɜːkəmfleks/ *n* (acento *m*) circunflejo *m*

circumstance /'sɜːrkəmstæns
‖'sɜːkəmstəns/ *n* **1** (condition, fact) circunstancia
f; dadas las circunstancias;
under no ~s bajo ningún concepto, bajo ninguna
circunstancia **2 circumstances** *pl* (financial
position): **a person in my ~s** una persona en mi
situación económica

circumstantial /ˌsɜːrkəm'stænʃəl
‖ˌsɜːkəm'stænʃəl/ *adj* ⟨*evidence*⟩ circunstancial

circus /'sɜːrkəs ‖'sɜːkəs/ *n* circo *m*

cirrhosis /sə'rəʊsəs ‖sɪ'rəʊsɪs/ *n* cirrosis *f*

CIS *n* (= **Commonwealth of Independent
States**) CEI *f*

cistern /'sɪstərn ‖'sɪstən/ *n* cisterna *f*

cite /saɪt/ *vt* citar

citizen /'sɪtəzən ‖'sɪtɪzən/ *n* ciudadano, -na *m,f*

citizenship /'sɪtəzənʃɪp ‖'sɪtɪzənʃɪp/ *n*
ciudadanía *f*

citrus /'sɪtrəs/ *adj* (before *n*) cítrico

city /'sɪti/ *n* (*pl* **cities**) ciudad *f*; (before *n*) ~
center centro *m* de la ciudad

city: ~ **hall** *n* (AmE) ayuntamiento *m*,
municipio *m*; ~ **planner** *n* (AmE) urbanista *mf*;
~ **planning** *n* (AmE) urbanismo *m*

civic /'sɪvɪk/ *adj* ⟨*authorities*⟩ civil; ⟨*leader*⟩ de
la ciudad; ⟨*duty/virtues*⟩ cívico; ~ **center** edificios
mpl municipales

civil /'sɪvəl ‖'sɪvl/ *adj* **(a)** (of society, citizens) civil
(b) (polite) cortés

civilian /sə'vɪljən ‖sɪ'vɪljən/ *n* civil *mf*

civilization /ˌsɪvələ'zeɪʃən ‖ˌsɪvəlar'zeɪʃən/ *n*
civilización *f*

civilized /'sɪvəlaɪzd/ *adj* ⟨*society*⟩ civilizado;
⟨*person*⟩ educado

civil: ~ **liberties** *pl n* derechos *mpl* civiles; ~
rights *pl n* derechos *mpl* civiles; ~ **servant** *n*
funcionario, -ria *m,f* (del Estado); ~ **service** *n*
the ~ **service** la administración pública;
(employees) el funcionariado (del Estado); ~ **war**
n guerra *f* civil; **the C~ War** (in US) la guerra de
Secesión

claim¹ /kleɪm/ *n* **1** (demand): **wage** *o* **pay** ~
reivindicación *f* salarial; **insurance** ~
reclamación *f* al seguro; **a** ~ **for expenses** una
solicitud de reembolso de gastos **2** (to right, title)
~ **(to sth)** derecho *m* (a *algo*) **3** (allegation)
afirmación *f*

claim² *vt* **1 (a)** ⟨*throne/inheritance/land*⟩
reclamar; ⟨*right*⟩ reivindicar*; ⟨*diplomatic*

immunity⟩ alegar* **(b)** ⟨*lost property*⟩ reclamar
(c) ⟨*social security/benefits*⟩ (apply for) solicitar;
(receive) cobrar; **you can ~ your expenses back**
puedes pedir que te reembolsen los gastos
2 (allege, profess): **no one has ~ed responsibility
for the attack** nadie ha reivindicado el atentado;
he ~ed (that) he knew nothing about it aseguraba
or afirmaba no saber nada de ello

claimant /'kleɪmənt/ *n* **(a)** (Soc Adm)
solicitante *mf* **(b)** (to throne) pretendiente, -ta *m,f*

clairvoyant /kler'vɔɪənt ‖kleə'vɔɪənt/ *n*
clarividente *mf*

clam /klæm/ *n* almeja *f*
■ **clam up: -mm-** [*v + adv*] (colloq) ponerse* muy
poco comunicativo

clamber /'klæmbər ‖'klæmbə(r)/ *vi* trepar;
they ~ed over the wall treparon al muro y
saltaron

clammy /'klæmi/ *adj* **-mier, -miest**
⟨*handshake*⟩ húmedo; ⟨*weather*⟩ bochornoso

clamor, (BrE) **clamour** /'klæmər ‖'klæmə(r)/
vi gritar; **to** ~ **FOR sth** ⟨*for war/resignation*⟩
pedir* algo a gritos

clamp¹ /klæmp/ *n* **(a)** (Const) abrazadera *f*; (in
carpentry) tornillo *m* de banco **(b)** (wheel ~) (BrE)
cepo *m*

clamp² *vt* **(a)** (join, fasten) sujetar con
abrazaderas **(b)** (BrE Auto) (colloq) ⟨*car*⟩ ponerle* el
cepo a
■ **clamp down** [*v + adv*] **to** ~ **down ON sth/sb**
tomar medidas drásticas CONTRA algo/algn

clampdown /'klæmpdaʊn/ *n* (colloq): **a** ~ **on**
illegal immigrants medidas *fpl* drásticas contra
los inmigrantes ilegales; **there's been a** ~ **on**
loans se ha restringido severamente la concesión
de créditos

clan /klæn/ *n* clan *m*

clandestine /klæn'destən ‖klæn'destɪn/ *adj*
clandestino

clang /klæŋ/ *vi* «*bells*» sonar*

clank /klæŋk/ *vi* hacer* ruido

clap¹ /klæp/ *n* **(a)** (applause): **to give sb a** ~
aplaudir a algn **(b)** **a** ~ **of thunder** un trueno

clap² **-pp-** *vt* (applaud) aplaudir; **to** ~ **one's**
hands to the music dar* palmadas al compás de
la música
■ ~ *vi* (applaud) aplaudir; (to music etc) dar* una
palmada

clapping /'klæpɪŋ/ *n* aplausos *mpl*

clarify /'klærəfaɪ ‖'klærɪfaɪ/ **-fies, -fying,**
-fied *vt* **(a)** (explain, make clear) aclarar **(b)** (purify)
⟨*butter/wine*⟩ clarificar*

clarinet /ˌklærə'net/ *n* clarinete *m*

clarity /'klærəti/ *n* claridad *f*

clash¹ /klæʃ/ *n* **1** (of interests) conflicto *m*; (of
cultures, personalities) choque *m*; (of opinions, views)
disparidad *f* **2** (between armies, factions)
enfrentamiento *m*, choque *m* **3** (noise): **the** ~ **of**
the cymbals el sonido de los platillos

clash² *vi* **(a)** «*personalities*» chocar*; «*colors/*

patterns» desentonar **(b)** «*armies/factions/ leaders*» chocar* **(c)** «*dates*» coincidir **(d)** «*cymbals/swords*» sonar* (*al entrechocarse*)

clasp¹ /klæsp ‖klɑːsp/ n broche m, cierre m

clasp² vt: she ~ed her bag firmly sujetó firmemente el bolso; he ~ed her in his arms la estrechó entre sus brazos

class¹ /klæs ‖klɑːs/ n **1** (social stratum) clase f **2** (group of students) clase f; (lesson) clase f; the ~ of '86 la promoción del 86 **3** (group, type) clase f **4** (a) (Transp) clase f **(b)** (in UK) (Post): **send the letter first/second ~** manda la carta por correo preferente/normal **5** (style) (colloq) clase f

class² vt catalogar*

classic¹ /'klæsɪk/ adj clásico; ⟨scene/line⟩ memorable

classic² n clásico m; see also CLASSICS

classical /'klæsɪkəl/ adj (of Greece, Rome) clásico; ~ **music** música f clásica

classics /'klæsɪks/ n (+ sing vb) clásicas fpl

classification /ˌklæsəfə'keɪʃən ‖ˌklæsɪfɪ'keɪʃən/ n clasificación f

classified /'klæsɪfaɪd ‖'klæsɪfaɪd/ adj **(a)** (categorized) clasificado; ~ **advertising** anuncios mpl por palabras, avisos mpl clasificados (AmL) **(b)** (secret) ⟨information⟩ secreto

classify /'klæsəfaɪ ‖'klæsɪfaɪ/ vt **-fies, -fying, -fied** ⟨books/data⟩ clasificar*

class: ~mate n compañero, -ra m,f de clase; **~room** n aula f‡, clase f

clatter¹ /'klætər ‖'klætə(r)/ vi «pans» hacer* ruido; «typewriter» repiquetear

clatter² n (of trains) traqueteo m; (of typewriters) repiqueteo m; (of hooves) chacoloteo m

clause /klɔːz/ n **(a)** (in contract) cláusula f **(b)** (Ling) oración f, cláusula f

claustrophobia /ˌklɔːstrə'fəʊbiə ‖ˌklɒstrə'fəʊbiə/ n claustrofobia f

claustrophobic /ˌklɔːstrə'fəʊbɪk ‖ˌklɒstrə'fəʊbɪk/ adj claustrofóbico

claw /klɔː/ n (of tiger, lion) zarpa f, garra f; (of eagle) garra f; (of crab, lobster) pinza f

clay /kleɪ/ n arcilla f; (for children) (AmE) plastilina® f, plasticina® f (CS)

clean¹ /kliːn/ adj **-er, -est** limpio; ⟨joke⟩ inocente; ⟨game/player⟩ limpio; ⟨driver's license⟩ donde no constan infracciones; ⟨stroke/features⟩ bien definido, nítido; **she made a ~ break with the past** cortó radicalmente con el pasado

clean² adv (colloq) **(a)** (completely): **I ~ forgot about it** se me olvidó por completo **(b)** (fairly) ⟨fight/play⟩ limpio, limpiamente

clean³ vt **(a)** limpiar; ⟨blackboard⟩ borrar; to ~ **one's teeth** lavarse los dientes; **you can ~ it off with a sponge** lo puedes quitar con una esponja **(b)** (dry-clean) limpiar en seco

■ **clean out** [v + o + adv, v + adv + o] (clean thoroughly) vaciar* y limpiar (a fondo)

■ **clean up** **1** [v + o + adv, v + adv + o] (physically, morally) limpiar **2** [v + adv] (do cleaning) limpiar

clean-cut /'kliːn'kʌt/ adj ⟨outline⟩ bien definido; ⟨appearance⟩ muy cuidado

cleaner /'kliːnər ‖'kliːnə(r)/ n **(a)** (person) limpiador, -dora m,f **(b)** (substance) producto m de limpieza

cleaning /'kliːnɪŋ/ n limpieza f; (before n) ~ **fluid** líquido m limpiador; **the ~ lady** la señora de la limpieza

cleanliness /'klenlinəs ‖'klenlinɪs/ n limpieza f; **personal ~** el aseo personal

cleanse /klenz/ vt limpiar

cleanser /'klenzər ‖'klenzə(r)/ n (for household use) producto m de limpieza; (for skin) leche f (or crema f etc) limpiadora or de limpieza

clean-shaven /'kliːn'ʃeɪvən/ adj ⟨face⟩ bien afeitado or (esp Méx) rasurado

cleansing /'klenzɪŋ/ adj limpiador; ~ **lotion** loción f limpiadora or de limpieza

clear¹ /klɪr ‖klɪə(r)/ adj **-er, -est** **1** ⟨sky⟩ despejado; **she has very ~ skin** tiene muy buen cutis; **to keep a ~ head** mantener* la mente despejada **2** (distinct) ⟨outline/picture⟩ nítido, claro; ⟨voice⟩ claro **3** (a) (plain, evident): **it's a ~ case of suicide** es un caso evidente de suicidio; **it became ~ that ...** se hizo evidente que ... **(b)** ⟨explanation/instructions⟩ claro **4** (free, unobstructed) ⟨space/road⟩ despejado

clear² adv: **stand ~ of the doors** manténganse alejados de las puertas; **the curtains should hang ~ of the radiators** las cortinas no deben tocar los radiadores; **to keep/stay ~ of (sth)** mantenerse* alejado (de algo), no acercarse* a (algo)

clear³ vt **1** (make free, unobstructed) ⟨room⟩ vaciar*; ⟨surface⟩ despejar; ⟨drain/pipe⟩ desatascar*, destapar (AmL); ⟨building⟩ desalojar; ⟨land⟩ despoblar de árboles, desmontar; **to ~ the table** levantar or (Esp tb) quitar la mesa; **to ~ one's throat** carraspear **2** ⟨fence/ditch⟩ salvar; **to ~ customs** pasar por la aduana **3** (free from suspicion) ⟨name⟩ limpiar; **he was ~ed of all charges** lo absolvieron de todos los cargos **4** (authorize) autorizar* **5** ⟨debt/account⟩ liquidar, saldar

■ ~ vi **1** «sky/weather/traffic» despejarse; «water» aclararse; «fog/smoke» levantarse **2** (Fin) «check» ser* compensado

■ **clear off** [v + adv] (colloq) largarse* (fam)

■ **clear out** [v + o + adv, v + adv + o] ⟨cupboard/ drawer⟩ vaciar* y ordenar

■ **clear up** **1** [v + o + adv, v + adv + o] **(a)** ⟨crime⟩ esclarecer*; ⟨misunderstanding/doubts⟩ aclarar **(b)** ⟨rubbish/toys⟩ recoger* **2** [v + adv] **(a)** (tidy) ordenar **(b)** «weather» despejar; «cough/cold» mejorarse; **the rash has ~ed up** se le (or me etc) ha ido el sarpullido

clearance /'klɪrəns ‖'klɪərəns/ n **1** (authorization) autorización f; (from customs) despacho m de aduana **2** (of building land) desmonte m, despeje m **3** (of stock) liquidación f

clear-cut /'klɪr'kʌt ‖'klɪə'kʌt/ adj claro, bien definido

clearing /'klɪrɪŋ ‖'klɪərɪŋ/ n (in forest) claro m

clearly /'klɪrli ‖'klɪəli/ adv ⟨visible/marked⟩ claramente; ⟨speak/write/think⟩ con claridad, claramente; **it's ~ impossible** es a todas luces imposible, está claro que es imposible

cleavage /'kliːvɪdʒ/ n escote m

cleaver /'kliːvər ‖'kliːvə(r)/ n cuchilla f de carnicero

clef /klef/ n clave f

cleft¹ /kleft/ adj ⟨chin⟩ partido; ~ **palate** paladar m hendido, fisura f del paladar

cleft² n hendidura f, grieta f

clench /klentʃ/ vt ⟨fist/jaw⟩ apretar* **(b)** (grip) apretar*, agarrar

clergy /'klɜːrdʒi ‖'klɜːdʒi/ n (+ sing or pl vb) clero m

clerical /'klerɪkəl/ adj 1 (Relig) clerical 2 ⟨job/work⟩ de oficina; ~ **assistant** oficinista mf

clerk /klɜːrk ‖klɑːk/ n (in office) empleado (administrativo), empleada (administrativa) m,f, oficinista mf; (in bank) empleado, -da m,f, bancario, -ria m,f (CS); (sales ~) (AmE) vendedor, -dora m,f, dependiente, -ta m,f; (desk ~) (AmE) recepcionista mf

clever /'klevər ‖'klevə(r)/ adj **-verer, -verest (a)** (intelligent) inteligente, listo **(b)** (artful) (pej) listo **(c)** (skillful, adept) ⟨player/politician⟩ hábil; ⟨invention/solution⟩ ingenioso

cliché /kliː'ʃeɪ ‖'kliːʃeɪ/ n lugar m común, cliché m

click¹ /klɪk/ vt ⟨fingers⟩ chasquear, tronar* (Méx); ⟨tongue⟩ chasquear
■ ~ vi hacer* un ruidito seco

click² n (of fingers, tongue) chasquido m; (of camera, switch) clic m

client /'klaɪənt/ n cliente, -ta m,f

clientele /ˌklaɪən'tel ‖ˌkliːɒn'tel, ˌkliːən'tel/ n (+ sing or pl vb) clientela f

cliff /klɪf/ n acantilado m; (not by sea) precipicio m

cliffhanger /'klɪfˌhæŋər ‖'klɪfˌhæŋə(r)/ n situación f de suspenso or (Esp) de suspense

climate /'klaɪmət ‖'klaɪmɪt/ n clima m

climax /'klaɪmæks/ n (pl **-maxes**) clímax m; (orgasm) orgasmo m

climb¹ /klaɪm/ vt ⟨mountain⟩ escalar, subir a; ⟨tree⟩ trepar a, subirse a, treparse a (esp AmL); ⟨stairs⟩ subir
■ ~ vi **(a)** (clamber) trepar, treparse; **she ~ed onto the table** se subió a la mesa, trepó or se trepó a la mesa **(b)** (rise) subir
■ **climb down** 1 [v + prep + o] ⟨rope⟩ bajarse por; ⟨tree⟩ bajarse de 2 [v + adv] (concede) (colloq) ceder

climb² n **(a)** (ascent) subida f **(b)** (Aviat) ascenso m

climber /'klaɪmər ‖'klaɪmə(r)/ n **(a)** (rock ~) escalador, -dora m,f; (mountaineer) alpinista mf, andinista mf (AmL) **(b)** (Hort) enredadera f, trepadora f

climbing /'klaɪmɪŋ/ n (Sport) alpinismo m, andinismo m (AmL)

clinch /klɪntʃ/ vt ⟨deal⟩ cerrar*; ⟨title⟩ ganar; ⟨argument⟩ resolver* de forma contundente

cling /klɪŋ/ vi (past & past p **clung**) 1 **(a)** (hold fast) **to ~ TO sth/sb** estar* aferrado A algo/ algn **(b)** (be dependent) (pej) **to ~ (TO sb)** pegársele* A algn 2 (stick) **to ~ (TO sth)** pegarse* (A algo)

clingfilm /'klɪŋfɪlm/ n (BrE) film m transparente (para envolver alimentos)

clinic /'klɪnɪk/ n (treatment center) centro m médico; (in state hospital) consultorio m; (private hospital) clínica f

clinical /'klɪnɪkəl/ adj **(a)** (Med) (before n) clínico **(b)** (unemotional) ⟨manner/detachment⟩ frío

clink /klɪŋk/ vt hacer* tintinear
■ ~ vi tintinear

clip¹ /klɪp/ n 1 (device) clip m, gancho m 2 (from film) fragmento m, clip m

clip² vt **-pp-** 1 **(a)** (cut) ⟨hair/nails/grass/ hedge⟩ cortar; ⟨sheep⟩ trasquilar; ⟨dog⟩ recortarle el pelo a **(b)** (punch) ⟨ticket⟩ picar*, perforar 2 (cut out) (AmE) recortar 3 (attach) sujetar (con un clip)

clip-on /'klɪpɑːn ‖'klɪpɒn/ adj (before n) ⟨sunglasses⟩ que se engancha; ⟨earrings⟩ de clip

clippers /'klɪpərz ‖'klɪpəz/ pl n (for nails) cortaúñas m; (for hair) maquinilla f (para cortar el pelo); (for hedge, lawn) podadera f, tijeras fpl de podar

clipping /'klɪpɪŋ/ n (from newspaper) recorte m

clique /kliːk/ n camarilla f

cloak¹ /kləʊk/ n capa f; (disguise) tapadera f

cloak² vt ⟨purpose/activities⟩ encubrir*; ~**ed in secrecy** rodeado de un velo de misterio

cloakroom /'kləʊkruːm, -rʊm/ n guardarropa m

clock /klɑːk ‖klɒk/ **(a)** n (timepiece) reloj m; **to work around o round the ~** trabajar las veinticuatro horas del día **(b)** (Auto) (mileometer) cuentakilómetros m; (speedometer) velocímetro m
■ **clock in,** (BrE) **clock on** [v + adv] fichar, marcar* or (Méx) checar* tarjeta (al entrar del trabajo)
■ **clock out,** (BrE) **clock off** [v + adv] fichar, marcar* or (Méx) checar* tarjeta (al salir del trabajo)

clockwise¹ /'klɑːkwaɪz ‖'klɒkwaɪz/ adj ⟨direction⟩ de las agujas del reloj

clockwise² adv en el sentido de las agujas del reloj

clockwork /'klɑːkwɜːrk ‖'klɒkwɜːk/ n mecanismo m de relojería; **like/regular as ~** como un reloj; (before n) ~ **toy** (esp BrE) juguete m de cuerda

clog¹ /klɑːg ‖klɒg/ n zueco m

clog² **-gg-** ~ (**up**) vt ⟨pipe/filter⟩ obstruir*, atascar*
■ ~ vi «pipe/filter» obstruirse*, atascarse*

cloister /'klɔɪstər ‖'klɔɪstə(r)/ n claustro m

clone /kləʊn/ vt clonar

close¹ /kləʊs/ adj **closer, closest** 1 **(a)** (near) próximo, cercano **(b)** ⟨shave⟩ al ras, apurado; **that was a ~ shave** (colloq) se salvó (or me salvé etc) por un pelo or por los pelos (fam) 2 ⟨link/connection⟩ estrecho; ⟨contact⟩ directo; ⟨relative⟩ cercano; **they are ~ friends** son muy amigos 3 (in similarity): **he bears a ~ resemblance to his brother** tiene un gran parecido a or con su hermano 4 ⟨fit⟩ ajustado 5 (careful) ⟨examination⟩ detenido; **to keep a ~ watch on sth/sb** vigilar algo/a algn de cerca 6 ⟨contest/ finish⟩ reñido 7 ⟨weather/atmosphere⟩ pesado, bochornoso

close² /kləʊs/ adv **closer, closest** 1 (in position) cerca; **to draw/get/come ~** acercarse*; ~ **TO sth/sb** cerca DE algo/algn 2 (in intimacy): **the tragedy brought them ~r together** la tragedia los acercó más 3 (in approximation): **the temperature is ~ to …** la temperatura es de casi …; **he was ~ to**

tears estaba a punto de llorar [4] ⟨*in phrases*⟩ **close by** cerca; **close together** (physically) juntos; close up de cerca

close³ /kləʊz/ *n* fin *m*; **to come/draw to a ~** llegar*/acercarse* a su fin

close⁴ /kləʊz/ *vt* cerrar*
■ ~ *vi* [1] ⟨*door/window*⟩ cerrar(se)*; ⟨*gap/ wound*⟩ cerrarse*
[2] ⟨*shop/library/museum*⟩ cerrar*
[3] **(a)** (finish, end) ⟨*lecture/book*⟩ terminar, concluir* **(b) closing** *pres p* ⟨*minutes*⟩ último; ⟨*speech*⟩ de clausura
■ **close down** [1] [*v* + *o* + *adv*, *v* + *adv* + *o*] ⟨*shop/factory*⟩ cerrar*
[2] [*v* + *adv*] ⟨*shop/factory*⟩ cerrar*
■ **close in** [*v* + *adv*] **(a)** ⟨*pursuers/enemy*⟩ acercarse*; **to ~ in on** sth/sb cercar* algo/a algn **(b)** ⟨*winter*⟩ acercarse* **(c)** (get shorter) ⟨*day*⟩ acortarse
■ **close off** [*v* + *o* + *adv*, *v* + *adv* + *o*] clausurar
■ **close out** [*v* + *o* + *adv*, *v* + *adv* + *o*] (AmE) liquidar
■ **close up** [1] [*v* + *adv*] ⟨*shop/museum*⟩ cerrar*; ⟨*wound/gash*⟩ cerrarse*
[2] [*v* + *o* + *adv*, *v* + *adv* + *o*] ⟨*shop/museum*⟩ cerrar*

closed /kləʊzd/ *adj* cerrado

closed circuit *n* circuito *m* cerrado; ⟨*before n*⟩ **closed-circuit television** televisión *f* en circuito cerrado

close /kləʊs/: **~-fitting** *adj* ajustado, ceñido; **~-knit** *adj* unido

closely /ˈkləʊsli/ *adv* [1] ⟨*connected/associated*⟩ estrechamente; **they worked ~ with the French** trabajaron en estrecha colaboración con los franceses [2] **(a)** (at a short distance) ⟨*follow/mark*⟩ de cerca **(b)** (carefully) ⟨*study/examine*⟩ detenidamente; ⟨*watch*⟩ de cerca; ⟨*question*⟩ a fondo; **a ~ guarded secret** un secreto muy bien guardado [3] (in approximation): **somebody who resembled her ~** alguien que se le parecía mucho

closet /ˈklɑːzət ‖ ˈklɒzɪt/ *n* (AmE) (cupboard) armario *m*, placard *m* (RPl); (for clothes) armario *m*, closet *m* (AmL exc RPl), placard *m* (RPl)

close-up /ˈkləʊsʌp/ *n* primer plano *m*

closing /ˈkləʊzɪŋ/: **~ date** *n* fecha *f* límite, fecha *f* tope; **~ time** *n* hora *f* de cierre

closure /ˈkləʊʒər ‖ ˈkləʊʒə(r)/ *n* cierre *m*

clot¹ /klɑːt ‖ klɒt/ *n* (blood ~) coágulo *m*

clot² *vi* **-tt-** ⟨*blood*⟩ coagularse

cloth /klɔːθ ‖ klɒθ/ *n* **(a)** (fabric) tela *f*, género *m*; (thick, woolen) paño *m* **(b)** (for cleaning) trapo *m*

clothe /kləʊð/ *vt* vestir*

clothes /kləʊðz/ *pl n* ropa *f*; **he had no ~ on** estaba desnudo; ⟨*before n*⟩ **~ brush** cepillo *m* para *or* de la ropa, escobilla *f* de ropa (Chi); **~ horse** tendedero *m* (*plegable*); **~ line** cuerda *f* de tender; **~ shop** tienda *f* or casa *f* de modas

clothespin /ˈkləʊðzpɪn/ (AmE), **clothes-peg** /ˈkləʊðzpeg/ (BrE) *n* pinza *f* or (Arg) broche *m* or (Chi) perrito *m* or (Ur) palillo *m* (de tender la ropa)

clothing /ˈkləʊðɪŋ/ *n* ropa *f*

cloud¹ /klaʊd/ *n* **(a)** (Meteo) (single) nube *f*; (mass) nubes *fpl*, nubosidad *f* **(b)** (of smoke, dust) nube *f*; (of suspicion) halo *m*, nube *f*

cloud² *vt* ⟨*view/vision*⟩ nublar

■ **cloud over** [*v* + *adv*] nublarse

cloudiness /ˈklaʊdinəs ‖ ˈklaʊdɪnɪs/ *n* (of sky) lo nublado; (of liquid) lo turbio

cloudless /ˈklaʊdləs ‖ ˈklaʊdlɪs/ *adj* totalmente despejado, sin una nube

cloudy /ˈklaʊdi/ *adj* **-dier, -diest** ⟨*day/sky*⟩ nublado; ⟨*liquid*⟩ turbio; **it's ~** está nublado

clout¹ /klaʊt/ *n* (colloq) [1] (blow) tortazo *m* (fam) [2] (power, influence) peso *m*, influencia *f*

clout² *vt* (colloq) darle* un tortazo a (fam)

clove /kləʊv/ *n* **(a)** (spice) clavo *m* (de olor) **(b)** (of garlic) diente *m*

clover /ˈkləʊvər ‖ ˈkləʊvə(r)/ *n* trébol *m*

clown¹ /klaʊn/ *n* payaso, -sa *m,f*

clown² *vi* **~ (around** *o* **about)** hacer* payasadas, payasear (AmL fam), hacer* el payaso (Esp)

cloying /ˈklɔɪɪŋ/ *adj* empalagoso

club¹ /klʌb/ *n* [1] **(a)** (cudgel) garrote *m*, cachiporra *f* **(b)** (golf ~) palo *m* de golf [2] (society, association) club *m* [3] (Games) **clubs** *pl* (suit) (+ *sing* or *pl* *vb*) tréboles *mpl*, (in Spanish pack) bastos *mpl*

club² **-bb-** *vt* aporrear
■ ~ *vi* (visit nightclubs): **to go ~bing** ir* de nightclubs

cluck /klʌk/ *vi* ⟨*hen*⟩ cloquear

clue /kluː/ *n* pista *f*; (in crosswords) clave *f*; **not to have a ~** (colloq) no tener* ni (la más mínima *or* la menor) idea (fam)

clump /klʌmp/ *n* **(a)** (of trees) grupo *m*; (of flowers) macizo *m* **(b)** (of earth) terrón *m*

clumsily /ˈklʌmzəli ‖ ˈklʌmzɪli/ *adv* ⟨*handle/ apologize*⟩ torpemente

clumsy /ˈklʌmzi/ *adj* **-sier, -siest** ⟨*person/ movement*⟩ torpe; ⟨*tool/shape*⟩ tosco; ⟨*translation*⟩ burdo

clung /klʌŋ/ *past & past p* of CLING

cluster¹ /ˈklʌstər ‖ ˈklʌstə(r)/ *n* (of people, buildings, stars) grupo *m*; (of berries, bananas) racimo *m*

cluster² *vi* apiñarse, agruparse

clutch¹ /klʌtʃ/ *n* [1] **clutches** *pl* garras *fpl*; **to be in/fall into sb's ~es** estar*/caer* en las garras de algn [2] (Auto) embrague *m*, clutch *m* (AmC, Col, Méx) [3] (of eggs) nidada *f*

clutch² *vt* tener* firmemente agarrado
■ ~ *vi* **to ~ AT** sth tratar de agarrarse DE algo

clutter /ˈklʌtər ‖ ˈklʌtə(r)/ *vt* ~ (**up**) abarrotar

cluttered /ˈklʌtərd ‖ ˈklʌtəd/ *adj* abarrotado de cosas

cm (= **centimeter(s)** *or* (BrE) **centimetre(s)**) cm.

c/o (= **in care of** *or* (BrE) **care of**): John Smith, **c/o** Ana Mas John Smith, en casa de Ana Mas

Co (a) /kəʊ/ (= **company**) Cía. **(b)** (Geog) = County

CO [1] (Geog) = **Colorado** [2] (Mil) = **Commanding Officer**

coach¹ /kəʊtʃ/ *n* [1] **(a)** (horse-drawn carriage) coche *m* (de caballos), carruaje *m* **(b)** (long-distance bus) (BrE) autobús *m*, autocar *m* (Esp), pullman *m* (CS) [2] (Rail) **(a)** (AmE) vagón *m* de tercera (clase) **(b)** (BrE) vagón *m* [3] **(a)** (tutor) profesor, -sora ⸱⸱⸱⸱

3100

m,f particular **(b)** (team manager) entrenador, -dora *m,f*, director técnico, directora técnica *mf* (AmL)

coach² *vt* ⟨team/player⟩ entrenar; ⟨pupil/student/singer⟩ preparar

coal /kəʊl/ *n* carbón *m*; (before n) ~ **fire** fuego *m* de *or* a carbón

coalition /ˌkəʊəˈlɪʃən/ *n* coalición *f*

coal: ~**man** /ˈkəʊlmæn/ *n* (pl -**men** /-men/) carbonero *m*; ~**mine** *n* mina *f* de carbón; ~**miner** *n* minero, -ra *m,f* de carbón

coarse /kɔːrs ‖ kɔːs/ *adj* **coarser, coarsest** **(a)** ⟨sand/filter⟩ grueso; ⟨cloth⟩ basto, ordinario, burdo; ⟨features⟩ tosco **(b)** ⟨person/manners/language⟩ ordinario, basto

coast¹ /kəʊst/ *n* **(a)** (shoreline) costa *f*; **the ~ is clear** no hay moros en la costa **(b)** (region) costa *f*, litoral *m*

coast² *vi* «car» deslizarse* (sin llevar el motor en marcha)

coastal /ˈkəʊstl/ *adj* (before n) costero

coaster /ˈkəʊstər ‖ ˈkəʊstə(r)/ *n* **(a)** (ship) barco *m* de cabotaje **(b)** (drink mat) posavasos *m*

coast: ~**guard** *n* guardacostas *mf*; ~**line** *n* costa *f*, litoral *m*; ~ **to** ~ *adv* (AmE) a lo largo y ancho del país; ~**-to-~** /ˈkəʊsttəˈkəʊst/ *adj* (AmE) de costa a costa

coat¹ /kəʊt/ *n* **1** (Clothing) (over~) (for men) abrigo *m or* (RPl) sobretodo *m*; (for women) abrigo *m or* (RPl) tapado *m*; (jacket) chaqueta *f*; (heavier) chaquetón *m*; (before n) ~ **hanger** percha *f*, ~ **stand** perchero *m* **2** (of animals) pelaje *m* **3** (layer) capa *f*; (of paint) capa *f*, mano *f*

coat² *vt* cubrir*

coating /ˈkəʊtɪŋ/ *n* capa *f*

coat of arms *n* (pl ~**s** ~ ~) escudo *m* de armas

coax /kəʊks/ *vt*: **I ~ed the animal into the cage** con paciencia logré que el animal se metiera en la jaula; **I managed to ~ the information out of her** logré sonsacarle la información

cobbled /ˈkɑːbəld ‖ ˈkɒbəld/ *adj* adoquinado

cobbler /ˈkɑːblər ‖ ˈkɒblə(r)/ *n* zapatero *m* (remendón)

cobblestone /ˈkɑːbəlstəʊn ‖ ˈkɒbəlstəʊn/ *n* adoquín *m*

cobra /ˈkəʊbrə/ *n* cobra *f*

cobweb /ˈkɑːbweb ‖ ˈkɒbweb/ *n* telaraña *f*

cocaine /kəʊˈkeɪn/ *n* cocaína *f*

cock¹ /kɑːk ‖ kɒk/ *n* (male fowl) gallo *m*; (male bird) macho *m*

cock² *vt* **1** ⟨gun⟩ montar **2** ⟨head⟩ ladear; ⟨ears⟩ levantar, parar (AmE)

cockerel /ˈkɑːkrəl ‖ ˈkɒkərəl/ *n* gallito *m*

cockeyed /ˈkɑːkaɪd ‖ ˈkɒkaɪd/ *adj* **(a)** (ridiculous) disparatado **(b)** (askew) torcido, chueco (AmL)

cockle /ˈkɑːkəl ‖ ˈkɒkəl/ *n* berberecho *m*

Cockney, cockney /ˈkɑːkni ‖ ˈkɒkni/ *n* (pl **-neys**) cockney *mf* (persona nacida en el East End de Londres, tradicionalmente de clase obrera)

cockpit /ˈkɑːkpɪt ‖ ˈkɒkpɪt/ *n* (Aviat) cabina *f* de mando

cockroach /ˈkɑːkrəʊtʃ ‖ ˈkɒkrəʊtʃ/ *n* cucaracha *f*

cocktail /ˈkɑːkteɪl ‖ ˈkɒkteɪl/ *n* **(a)** (drink) cóctel *m*, coctel *m*, combinado *m*; (before n) ~ **bar** bar *m*, coctelería *f*; ~ **cabinet** mueble-bar *m*; ~ **party** cóctel *m*, coctel *m*; ~ **stick** palillo *m*, mondadientes *m* **(b)** (food): shrimp *o* (BrE) prawn ~ cóctel *m* de camarones *or* (Esp) de gambas *or* (CS) de langostinos, langostinos *mpl* con salsa golf (RPl)

cocky /ˈkɑːki ‖ ˈkɒki/ *adj* **cockier, cockiest** (colloq) gallito (fam), chulo (Esp fam)

cocoa /ˈkəʊkəʊ/ *n* (powder) cacao *m*, cocoa *f* (AmL); (drink) chocolate *m*, cocoa *f* (AmL)

coconut /ˈkəʊkənʌt/ *n* coco *m*

cocoon /kəˈkuːn/ *n* capullo *m*

cod /kɑːd ‖ kɒd/ *n* (pl ~ *or* ~**s**) bacalao *m*

COD *adv* (= **cash** *or* (AmE also) **collect on delivery**) contra reembolso

code¹ /kəʊd/ *n* **(a)** (cipher) clave *f*, código *m*; **in ~** en clave, cifrado **(b)** (for identification) código *m* **(c)** (Comput) código *m* **(d)** (Telec) código *m*, prefijo *m* **2** (social, moral) código *m*

code² *vt* **(a)** (encipher) cifrar, poner* en clave **(b)** (give identifying number, mark) codificar*

coerce /kəʊˈɜːrs ‖ kəʊˈɜːs/ *vt* **to ~ sb (INTO -ING)** coaccionar a algn (PARA QUE (+ subj))

coexist /ˌkəʊɪɡˈzɪst/ *vi* **to ~ (WITH sb/sth)** coexistir (CON algn/algo)

coffee /ˈkɔːfi ‖ ˈkɒfi/ *n* (beans, granules, drink) café *m*; **black** ~ café negro *or* (Esp) solo *or* (Chi) puro *or* (Col) tinto; **white** ~ (BrE) café con leche; (before n) ~ **bean** grano *m* de café; ~ **break** pausa *f* del café; ~ **maker** cafetera *f*; ~ **mill** *o* **grinder** molinillo *m* de café

coffee: ~ **klatsch** /klætʃ, klɑːtʃ/ *n* (AmE) tertulia *f*; ~**pot** *n* cafetera *f*; ~ **table** *n* mesa *f* de centro, mesa *f* ratona (RPl)

coffin /ˈkɔːfən ‖ ˈkɒfɪn/ *n* ataúd *m*, féretro *m*, cajón *m* (AmL)

cog /kɑːɡ ‖ kɒɡ/ *n* **(a)** (tooth) diente *m* **(b)** (wheel) piñón *m*, rueda *f* dentada

cognac /ˈkɑːnjæk ‖ ˈkɒnjæk/ *n* coñac *m*, coñá *m*

cohabit /kəʊˈhæbət ‖ kəʊˈhæbɪt/ *vi* (frml) cohabitar (frml)

coherent /kəʊˈhɪrənt ‖ kəʊˈhɪərənt/ *adj* coherente

coil¹ /kɔɪl/ *n* **1** **(a)** (series of loops — of rope, wire) rollo *m*; (— of smoke) espiral *f*, volutas *fpl* **(b)** (single loop) lazada *f*, vuelta *f* **2** (contraceptive) (BrE) espiral *f*

coil² *vt* enrollar

coin¹ /kɔɪn/ *n* moneda *f*

coin² vt ‹word/expression› acuñar; **to ∼ a phrase** (set phrase) como se suele decir

coin box n depósito m de monedas

coincide /ˈkəʊənˈsaɪd ‖ˌkəʊɪnˈsaɪd/ vi **to ∼ (with sth)** coincidir (con algo)

coincidence /kəʊˈɪnsədəns ‖kəʊˈɪnsɪdəns/ n casualidad f, coincidencia f

coincidental /kəʊˌɪnsəˈdent ‖kəʊˈɪnsɪdentl/ adj casual, fortuito

coin-operated /ˈkɔɪnˈɑːpəreɪtəd ‖ˈkɔɪnˌɒpəreɪtɪd/ adj que funciona con monedas

coke /kəʊk/ n **1** (fuel) (carbón m de) coque m **2** (cocaine) (colloq) coca f (fam) **3 Coke**® (colloq) Coca-Cola® f

colander /ˈkʌləndər ‖ˈkʌləndə(r)/ n colador m, escurridor m (de pasta, verduras)

cold¹ /kəʊld/ adj frío; **I'm ∼** tengo frío; **my feet are ∼** tengo los pies fríos, tengo frío en los pies; **it's ∼ today** hoy hace frío; **your dinner's getting ∼** se te está enfriando la comida; **I got a very ∼ reception** me recibieron con mucha frialdad; **I came to the job ∼** empecé el trabajo sin ninguna preparación

cold² n **1** (low temperature) frío m; **come in out of the ∼** entra, que hace frío; **to feel the ∼** ser* friolento or (Esp) friolero, sentir* el frío **2** (Med) resfriado m, constipado m (Esp), resfrío m (CS); **to have a ∼** estar* resfriado

cold: **∼-blooded** /ˈkəʊldˈblʌdəd ‖ˌkəʊldˈblʌdɪd/ adj **(a)** ‹murder› a sangre fría; ‹killer› despiadado, cruel **(b)** (Zool) de sangre fría; **∼ cream** n crema f limpiadora or de limpieza, cold cream f; **∼ cuts** pl n (AmE) fiambres mpl; **∼-hearted** /ˈkəʊldˈhɑːrtəd ‖ˌkəʊldˈhɑːtɪd/ adj frío, insensible

coldly /ˈkəʊldli/ adv con frialdad, fríamente

cold: **∼ sore** n herpes m (labial), fuego m (AmL), pupa f (Esp fam); **∼ storage** n almacenamiento m en cámaras frigoríficas; **∼ war** n guerra f fría

coleslaw /ˈkəʊlslɔː/ n ensalada de repollo, zanahoria y cebolla con mayonesa

collaborate /kəˈlæbəreɪt/ vi colaborar

collaboration /kəˈlæbəˈreɪʃən/ n (cooperation) colaboración f, (with enemy) colaboracionismo m

collaborator /kəˈlæbəreɪtər ‖kəˈlæbəreɪtə(r)/ n (partner) colaborador, -dora m,f; (with enemy) colaboracionista mf

collapse¹ /kəˈlæps/ vi **1** ‹building› derrumbarse, desmoronarse **2** ‹person› desplomarse; (Med) sufrir un colapso **3** (fail) fracasar **4** (fold up) ‹table/chair› plegarse*

collapse² n **(a)** (of building) derrumbe m, desmoronamiento m **(b)** (Med) colapso m **(c)** (of company) quiebra f

collapsible /kəˈlæpsəbəl/ adj plegable

collar /ˈkɑːlər ‖ˈkɒlə(r)/ n **(a)** (Clothing) cuello m **(b)** (for animal) collar m

collarbone /ˈkɑːlərbəʊn ‖ˈkɒləbəʊn/ n clavícula f

colleague /ˈkɑːliːg ‖ˈkɒliːg/ n colega mf

collect¹ /kəˈlekt/ vt **1** ‹information/evidence/data› reunir*; ‹dust› acumular **2** (as hobby) coleccionar, juntar (esp AmL) **3** (fetch, pick up)

recoger* **4** (obtain payment) ‹rent› cobrar; ‹taxes› recaudar **5** (put in order): **give me some time to ∼ my thoughts** déjame pensar un momento
■ ∼ vi **1** **(a)** (gather, assemble) «people» reunirse* **(b)** (accumulate) «dust/water» acumularse **2** (for charity etc) recaudar dinero

collect² adj (AmE) ‹call› a cobro revertido, por cobrar (Chi, Méx)

collect³ adv (AmE) ‹call› a cobro revertido, por cobrar (Chi, Méx)

collection /kəˈlekʃən/ n **1** **(a)** (of evidence) recopilación f; (of rent, debts) cobro m; (of taxes) recaudación f **(b)** (act of fetching): **the goods are ready for ∼** puede recoger or pasar a buscar las mercancías **(c)** (of mail, refuse) recogida f **2** (of money) colecta f **3** (group of objects) colección f

collective /kəˈlektɪv/ adj (usu before n) colectivo

collector /kəˈlektər ‖kəˈlektə(r)/ n **(a)** coleccionista mf; **a ∼'s item** una pieza de colección **(b)** (official) cobrador, -dora m,f

college /ˈkɑːlɪdʒ ‖ˈkɒlɪdʒ/ n **(a)** (university) (esp AmE) universidad f **(b)** (for vocational training) escuela f, instituto m; see also TEACHERS COLLEGE **(c)** (department of university) facultad f, departamento m; (in Britain) colegio m universitario

collegiate /kəˈliːdʒət, -dʒiət/ adj (esp AmE) universitario

collide /kəˈlaɪd/ vi «vehicle» chocar*, colisionar (frml); **to ∼ with sth/sb** chocar* con algo/algn; **we ∼ed in the corridor** nos chocamos en el pasillo

collie /ˈkɑːli ‖ˈkɒli/ n collie mf, pastor escocés, pastora escocesa m,f

collision /kəˈlɪʒən/ n (of cars, trains) choque m, colisión f (frml); (of boats) abordaje m, colisión f (frml)

colloquial /kəˈləʊkwiəl/ adj coloquial

collusion /kəˈluːʒən/ n colusión f

Colo = **Colorado**

cologne /kəˈləʊn/ n (eau de ∼) colonia f

Colombia /kəˈlʌmbiə/ n Colombia f

Colombian /kəˈlʌmbiən/ adj colombiano

colon /ˈkəʊlən/ n **(a)** (Anat) colon m **(b)** (in punctuation) dos puntos mpl

colonel /ˈkɜːrnl ‖ˈkɜːnl/ n coronel, -nela m,f

colonial /kəˈləʊniəl/ adj colonial

colonize /ˈkɑːlənaɪz ‖ˈkɒlənaɪz/ vt colonizar*

colony /ˈkɑːləni ‖ˈkɒləni/ n (pl **-nies**) colonia f

color¹, (BrE) **colour** /ˈkʌlər ‖ˈkʌlə(r)/ n **1** color m; **what ∼ is the ball?** ¿de qué color es la pelota?; (before n) ‹photograph› en colores or (Esp) en color; ‹television› a color(es) or en colores or (Esp) en color **2 colors** pl **(a)** (flag) bandera f; **with flying ∼s:** **he passed his exams with flying ∼s** le fue estupendamente en los exámenes **(b)** (BrE Sport): **the team ∼s** los colores del equipo

color², (BrE) **colour** vt **(a)** (Art) pintar, colorear; **to ∼ sth blue** colorear algo de azul **(b)** (dye) teñir* **(c)** (influence, bias) ‹atmosphere› empañar; **you shouldn't let that ∼ your judgment** no deberías dejar que eso influya en tu opinión ⋯⫶

■ ~ *vi* (flush) ruborizarse*, sonrojarse, ponerse* colorado

color: ~-blind *adj* daltónico, daltoniano; **~-coded** /'kʌlər'kəʊdəd ‖ˌkʌlə'kəʊdɪd/ *adj* codificado con colores

colored, (BrE) **coloured** /'kʌlərd ‖'kʌləd/ *adj* ⟨*walls/blouse*⟩ de color

-colored, (BrE) **-coloured** /ˌkʌlərd ‖'kʌləd/ *suff*: slate~/coral~ de color pizarra/coral

colorful, (BrE) **colourful** /'kʌlərfəl ‖'kʌləfəl/ *adj* ⟨*clothes/plumage*⟩ de colores muy vivos; ⟨*parade/description*⟩ lleno de color

coloring, (BrE) **colouring** /'kʌlərɪŋ/ *n* **1** (of skin) color *m*, tono *m*; (of fur, plumage) colorido *m* **2** (food ~) colorante *m*

colorless, (BrE) **colourless** /'kʌlərləs ‖'kʌlələs/ *adj* incoloro, sin color; ⟨*person/life*⟩ anodino, gris

color: ~ scheme *n* (combinación *f* de) colores *mpl*; **~ supplement** *n* suplemento *m* a todo color *or* en color

colossal /kə'lɑːsəl ‖kə'lɒsəl/ *adj* (colloq) colosal

colour *etc* (BrE) ▶ COLOR *etc*

colt /kəʊlt/ *n* potro *m*

column /'kɑːləm ‖'kɒləm/ *n* columna *f*

columnist /'kɑːləmnəst, 'kɑːləməst ‖'kɒləmnɪst, 'kɒləmɪst/ *n* columnista *mf*

coma /'kəʊmə/ *n* (*pl* ~s) (Med) coma *m*

comb¹ /kəʊm/ *n* (for hair) peine *m*, peinilla *f* (AmL), peineta *f* (Chi)

comb² *vt* (a) (pass a comb through): **to ~ one's hair** peinarse (b) (search) ⟨*area/field*⟩ peinar

combat¹ /kəm'bæt ‖'kɒmbæt/ *vt*, (BrE) **-tt-** combatir

combat² /'kɑːmbæt ‖'kɒmbæt/ *n* combate *m*

combination /'kɑːmbə'neɪʃən ‖ˌkɒmbɪ'neɪʃən/ *n* combinación *f*

combine /kəm'baɪn/ *vt* ⟨*elements*⟩ combinar; ⟨*ingredients*⟩ (Culin) mezclar; ⟨*efforts*⟩ aunar*
■ ~ *vi* ⟨*elements*⟩ combinarse; ⟨*ingredients*⟩ mezclarse; ⟨*teams/forces*⟩ unirse

combined /kəm'baɪnd/ *adj* conjunto; **our ~ efforts led to success** la suma de nuestros esfuerzos nos condujo al éxito

combine harvester /'kɑːmbaɪn 'hɑːrvəstər ‖'kɒmbaɪn 'hɑːvɪstə(r)/ *n* cosechadora *f*

combustion /kəm'bʌstʃən/ *n* combustión *f*; (*before n*) **~ engine** motor *m* de combustión

come /kʌm/ (*past* **came**; *past p* **come**) *vi*
1 (a) (advance, approach, travel) venir*; **~ here** ven (aquí); **we've ~ a long way since ...** (made much progress) hemos avanzado mucho desde que ...; **can I ~ with you?** ¿puedo ir contigo?, ¿te puedo acompañar?; **after a while, you'll ~ to a crossroads** al cabo de un rato, llegarás a un cruce; **I'm coming, I won't be a moment** enseguida voy (b) (originate): **where do you ~ from?** ¿de dónde eres?; **it ~s from Italy** viene de Italia (c) (to come and go) ir* y venir*; **three o'clock came and went and he still hadn't arrived** pasaron las tres y no llegaba
2 (a) (occur in time, context): **Christmas is coming** ya llega la Navidad; **it came as a complete surprise** fue una sorpresa total; **to take life as it ~s** aceptar la vida tal (y) como se presenta; **~ what may** pase lo que pase (b) (*as prep*) para; **I'll**

be tired out **~ Friday** estaré agotado para el viernes (c) **coming** *pres p*: **this coming Friday** este viernes que viene (d) **to come** (in the future) (*as adv*): **in years to ~** en años venideros; **a taste of things to ~** una muestra de lo que nos espera
3 (reach) (+ *adv compl*) llegar*; **the water came up to our knees** el agua nos llegaba a las rodillas
4 (be gained): **it'll ~, just keep practicing** ya te va a salir; sigue practicando; **driving didn't ~ easily to me** aprender a manejar *or* (Esp) conducir no me fue fácil
5 (be available, obtainable) (+ *adv compl*) venir*; **sugar ~s in half-pound bags** el azúcar viene en paquetes de media libra; **the car ~s with the job** el coche te lo dan con el trabajo
6 (+ *adv compl*) (a) (in sequence, list, structure): **Cancer ~s between Gemini and Leo** Cáncer está entre Géminis y Leo (b) (in race, competition) llegar*; **to ~ first** (in a race) llegar* el primero; (in an exam) quedar *or* salir* el primero (c) (be ranked) estar*; **my children ~ first** primero están mis hijos
7 (a) (become) (+ *adj compl*): **my dream has ~ true** mi sueño se ha hecho realidad (b) (reach certain state) **to ~ to + INF** llegar* a + INF; **~ to think of it ...** ahora que lo pienso ...
8 (*in phrases*) **come, come!** ¡vamos, vamos!, ¡dale! (CS fam); **how come?** (colloq) ¿cómo?
■ **come across 1** [*v + prep + o*] (find) encontrar(se)*; (meet) ⟨*person*⟩ encontrarse* con
2 [*v + adv*] (communicate, be communicated) ⟨*meaning*⟩ ser* comprendido; ⟨*feelings*⟩ transmitirse; **he came across very well in the interview** hizo muy buena impresión en la entrevista
■ **come along** [*v + adv*] **1** (*in imperative*) (a) (hurry up): **~ along, children** ¡vamos, niños!, ¡apúrense, niños! (AmL), ¡órale, niños! (Méx fam) (b) (as encouragement, rebuke) **~ along!** ¡vamos!
2 (accompany): **can I ~ along?** ¿puedo ir (yo) también?; **~ along with me** ven conmigo, acompáñame
3 (progress) ir*, marchar
■ **come apart** [*v + adv*] (a) (fall apart) deshacerse* (b) (have detachable parts) desmontarse
■ **come around**, (BrE also) **come round 1** [*v + prep + o*] (turn) ⟨*bend*⟩ tomar; ⟨*corner*⟩ doblar
2 [*v + adv*] (a) (visit) (esp BrE) venir* (a casa) (b) (recover consciousness) volver* en sí (c) (change mind): **he'll ~ around eventually** ya se va a convencer
■ **come away** [*v + adv*] **1** (leave, depart) **to ~ away** (FROM sth) ⟨*from meeting/stadium*⟩ salir* (DE algo)
2 (become detached) ⟨*handle*⟩ salirse*
■ **come back** [*v + adv*] (a) (return) volver* (b) (be remembered): **it's all coming back (to me)** estoy volviendo a recordarlo todo
■ **come down** [*v + adv*] **1** (a) (descend) bajar (b) (reach) llegar* (c) (collapse) ⟨*ceiling/wall*⟩ caerse* (d) ⟨*plane*⟩ aterrizar*; (in accident) caer*
2 (decrease) ⟨*price*⟩ bajar
■ **come down to** [*v + adv + prep + o*] (*impers*) ser* cuestión de
■ **come forward** [*v + adv*] ⟨*witness*⟩ presentarse*; ⟨*volunteer*⟩ ofrecerse*; ⟨*culprit*⟩ darse* a conocer
■ **come in** [*v + adv*] **1** (enter) entrar; **~ in!** ¡adelante!

2 (a) «*boat*» llegar* (b) «*tide*» subir

3 (be received) «*applications/reports/donations*» llegar*

4 (play useful role): **where do I ∼ in?** ¿cuál es mi papel?; **that's where these boxes ∼ in** para eso están las cajas

■ **come in for** [*v + adv + prep + o*] ‹*criticism*› ser* objeto de

■ **come into** [*v + prep + o*] (a) (enter into) entrar en, entrar a (AmL) (b) (inherit) heredar (c) (be, become relevant): **principles don't ∼ into it** no es cuestión de principios

■ **come off** 1 (a) [*v + adv*] (detach itself) «*handle*» soltarse*; «*button*» desprenderse; «*wallpaper*» despegarse*; «*dirt/grease*» quitarse (b) [*v + prep + o*] (fall off) ‹*horse/ motorcycle*› caerse* de

2 [*v + adv*] (fare, acquit oneself): **he always ∼s off worst** siempre sale perdiendo

3 [*v + prep + o*] (a) (stop taking) ‹*drug*› dejar de tomar (b) (be serious): **∼ off it!** (colloq) ¡anda! ¡no digas tonterías! (fam)

■ **come on** [*v + adv*] 1 (urging sb) (*only in imperative*): **∼ on!** ¡vamos! ¡date prisa! *or* (AmL tb) ¡apúrate!, ¡órale! (Méx fam)

2 (a) (begin) «*night/winter*» entrar (b) (begin to operate) «*heating/appliance*» encenderse*, ponerse* en funcionamiento; «*light*» encenderse*

■ **come out**

I [*v + adv* (+ *prep + o*)] 1 (from inside) salir*

2 «*tooth/hair*» caerse*; «*stain*» salir*

II [*v + adv*] 1 (appear) «*sun/stars*» salir*; «*flowers*» florecer*, salir*

2 (be said, spoken) salir*; (be revealed, emphasized) «*secret/truth*» revelarse, salir* a la luz

3 (a) (declare oneself) declararse; **to ∼ out on strike** declararse en huelga (b) (as being gay) destaparse (fam), declararse abiertamente homosexual

4 «*newspaper/record/product*» salir*

■ **come over** 1 [*v + adv*] (to sb's home) venir* (a casa)

2 [*v + prep + o*] (affect, afflict): **I don't know what came over me** no sé qué me pasó

■ **come round** (BrE) ▶ COME AROUND

■ **come through** 1 «*message/news/supplies*» llegar*; **you're coming through loud and clear** te recibimos muy bien

2 [*v + prep + o*] ‹*ordeal/illness*› salir* de; ‹*war*› sobrevivir a

■ **come to**

I [*v + prep + o*] 1 (a) (reach) llegar* a; **what's the world coming to!** ¡hasta dónde vamos a llegar! (b) (occur) «*idea/answer/name*» ocurrirse; **it came to me in a flash** se me ocurrió de repente (c) (be a question of): **when it ∼s to …** cuando se trata de …

2 (amount to) «*total*» ascender* a (frml); **it ∼s to $15 exactly** son 15 dólares justos; **the plan never came to anything** el plan nunca llegó a nada

II [*v + adv*] (recover consciousness) volver* en sí

■ **come up** [*v + adv*] 1 (a) (ascend, rise) «*person*» subir; «*sun/moon*» salir* (b) (approach) acercarse*; **to ∼ up TO sb** acercársele* A algn

2 (a) (occur, arise) «*problem*» surgir*; **something important has just ∼ up** acaba de surgir algo importante (b) (be raised, mentioned) «*subject/point*» surgir*; «*name*» ser* mencionado

■ **come up against** [*v + adv + prep + o*] ‹*opposition/prejudice*› enfrentarse a

■ **come up for** [*v + adv + prep + o*]: **the car is coming up for its annual service** dentro de poco hay que hacerle la revisión anual al coche; **I should ∼ up for promotion next year** me deberían considerar para un ascenso el año que viene

■ **come up to** [*v + adv + prep + o*] (a) (reach as far as) llegar* a *or* hasta (b) (attain) ‹*standard*› alcanzar*, llegar* a

■ **come up with** [*v + adv + prep + o*] ‹*plan/ scheme*› idear; ‹*proposal*› presentar; ‹*money*› conseguir*; **if you can ∼ up with a better idea** si a ti se te ocurre algo mejor

comeback /'kʌmbæk/ *n* 1 (return, revival) vuelta *f*, retorno *m*; **to make a ∼** volver* a la escena (*or* a la política *etc*) 2 (redress) (*no pl*): **the trouble is that you have no ∼ at all** el problema es que no puedes hacer ninguna reclamación

comedian /kə'mi:diən/ *n* humorista *mf*, cómico, -ca *m,f*

comedy /'kɑ:mədi ǁ'kɒmədi/ *n* (*pl* **-dies**) (a) (play, film) comedia *f* (b) (comic entertainment) humorismo *m*; (*before n*) ‹*show/program*› humorístico

comet /'kɑ:mət ǁ'kɒmɪt/ *n* cometa *m*

comfort¹ /'kʌmfərt ǁ'kʌmfət/ *n* 1 (a) (physical, material) comodidad *f*, confort *m* (b) (sth pleasant, luxury) comodidad *f* 2 (mental) consuelo *m*; **to take ∼ from sth** consolarse* con algo

comfort² *vt* ‹*child/bereaved person*› consolar*

comfortable /'kʌmftərbəl ǁ'kʌmftəbəl/ *adj* 1 ‹*chair/clothes*› cómodo; **a ∼ lifestyle** una vida desahogada 2 ‹*margin/majority*› amplio, holgado

comfortably /'kʌmftərbli ǁ'kʌmftəbli/ *adv* ‹*lie/sit*› cómodamente; ‹*live/win*› holgadamente

comforter /'kʌmfərtər ǁ'kʌmfətə(r)/ *n* (a) (bedcover) (AmE) edredón *m* (b) (for baby) (BrE) ▶ PACIFIER

comforting /'kʌmfərtɪŋ ǁ'kʌmfətɪŋ/ *adj* ‹*words*› de consuelo; **it's a ∼ thought** es reconfortante pensarlo

comic¹ /'kɑ:mɪk ǁ'kɒmɪk/ *adj* ‹*actor/scene*› cómico; ‹*writer*› humorístico

comic² *n* 1 (comedian) cómico, -ca *m,f*, humorista *mf* 2 (a) (BrE) (book) comic *m*, libro *m* de historietas; (magazine) ▶ COMIC BOOK (b) **comics** *pl* (comic strips) (AmE) tiras *fpl* cómicas, historietas *fpl*, monitos *mpl* (Andes, Méx)

comical /'kɑ:mɪkəl ǁ'kɒmɪkəl/ *adj* cómico

comic: ∼ book *n* (AmE) revista *f* de historietas, tebeo *m* (Esp), revista *f* de chistes (RPl); (for adults) comic *m*; **∼ strip** *n* tira *f* cómica, historieta *f*

coming /'kʌmɪŋ/ *adj* (*before n*) ‹*week/year*› próximo; **this ∼ Monday** este lunes, el lunes que viene

comma /'kɑ:mə ǁ'kɒmə/ *n* coma *f*

command¹ /kə'mænd ǁkə'mɑ:nd/ *vt* 1 (a) (order) **to ∼ sb to + INF** ordenarle a algn QUE (+ *subj*) (b) ‹*army/ship*› estar* al mando de 2 ‹*wealth/resources*› contar* con 3 ‹*respect*› imponer*; ‹*fee*› exigir*; ‹*price*› alcanzar*

command² *n* 1 (a) (order) orden *f* (b)   ⋯⫶

c

(authority) mando *m*; **under sb's ~** bajo las órdenes *or* el mando de algn **2** (mastery) dominio *m* **3** (Comput) orden *f*, comando *m*

commandant /'kɑːməndænt ‖'kɒməndænt/ *n* comandante *mf*

commandeer /'kɑːmən'dɪr ‖,kɒmən'dɪə(r)/ *vt* (Mil) requisar

commander /kə'mændər ‖kə'mɑːndə(r)/ *n* **(a)** (officer in command) comandante *mf* **(b)** (navy rank) ≈ capitán *m* de fragata

commanding /kə'mændɪŋ ‖kə'mɑːndɪŋ/ *adj* **(a)** ⟨position⟩ de superioridad; ⟨lead⟩ considerable **(b)** ⟨presence⟩ que impone; ⟨tone⟩ autoritario

commanding officer *n* oficial *mf* al mando

commandment /kə'mændmənt ‖kə'mɑːndmənt/ *n* precepto *m*; **the Ten C~s** los diez mandamientos

commando /kə'mændəʊ ‖kə'mɑːndəʊ/ *n (pl* **-dos** *or* **-does)** comando *m*

commemorate /kə'meməreɪt/ *vt* conmemorar

commence /kə'mens/ *vi* (frml) «session/ celebration» dar* comienzo (frml); «person» comenzar*
■ **~** *vt* (frml) ⟨work/discussion⟩ dar* comienzo a (frml)

commend /kə'mend/ *vt* **1 (a)** (praise) elogiar **(b)** (recommend) recomendar* **2** (frml) (entrust) **to ~ sb/sth TO sb** encomendar(le)* algn/algo A algn

commendable /kə'mendəbəl/ *adj* loable, encomiable

commendation /'kɑːmən'deɪʃən ‖,kɒmən'deɪʃən/ *n* **(a)** (praise) (frml) encomio *m* (frml), elogios *mpl* **(b)** (award) mención *f* de honor, accésit *m*

comment¹ /'kɑːment ‖'kɒment/ *n* **(a)** (remark) comentario *m* **(b)** (reaction) comentarios *mpl*; **no ~** sin comentarios

comment² *vi* **to ~ (ON sth)** hacer* comentarios (SOBRE algo)
■ **~** *vt* comentar

commentary /'kɑːmənteri ‖'kɒməntəri, -tri/ *n (pl* **-ries)** (Rad, Sport, TV) comentarios *mpl*, crónica *f*; (analysis) comentario *m*

commentator /'kɑːmənteɪtər ‖'kɒmənteɪtə(r)/ *n* comentarista *mf*

commerce /'kɑːmərs ‖'kɒmɜːs/ *n* comercio *m*

commercial¹ /kə'mɜːrʃəl ‖kə'mɜːʃəl/ *adj* comercial

commercial² *n* spot *m* publicitario, anuncio *m*, aviso *m* (AmL), comercial *m* (AmL)

commercialize /kə'mɜːrʃəlaɪz ‖kə'mɜːʃəlaɪz/ *vt* comercializar*

commiserate /kə'mɪzəreɪt/ *vi*: **I ~d with him about losing his job** le dije cuánto sentía que se hubiera quedado sin trabajo

commiseration /kə'mɪzə'reɪʃən/ *n* (often *pl*) conmiseración *f*

commission¹ /kə'mɪʃən/ *n* **1** (group)

comisión *f* **2** (for sales) comisión *f* **3 (a)** (for music, painting, building) encargo *m*, comisión *f* (esp AmL) **(b)** (office) (Govt) cargo *m*

commission² *vt* **1 (a) to ~ sb to +** INF ⟨artist/writer/researcher⟩ encargarle* a algn que (+ *subj*) **(b)** ⟨painting/novel/study⟩ encargar*, comisionar (esp AmL) **2 (a)** (Mil) nombrar oficial; **~ed officer** oficial *mf* (del ejército) (con grado de teniente o superior a teniente) **(b)** (Naut) ⟨ship⟩ poner* en servicio

commissioner /kə'mɪʃənər ‖kə'mɪʃənə(r)/ *n* **(a)** (commission member) comisionado, -da *m,f*, miembro *mf* de la comisión **(b)** (of police) (BrE) inspector, -tora *m,f* jefe

commit /kə'mɪt/ **-tt-** *vt* **1** (perpetrate) ⟨crime/ error/sin⟩ cometer **2** (assign) ⟨funds/time/ resources⟩ asignar **3** (send): **to ~ sb to an asylum** internar a algn en un manicomio
■ *v refl* **to ~ (oneself) TO -ING/+ INF** comprometerse (A + INF)

commitment /kə'mɪtmənt/ *n* **1 (a)** (responsibility) responsabilidad *f*; (obligation) obligación *f* **(b)** (engagement) compromiso *m* **2** (dedication) dedicación *f*

committed /kə'mɪtəd ‖kə'mɪtɪd/ *adj* ⟨Christian/feminist⟩ comprometido; ⟨teacher/ worker⟩ entregado a su trabajo

committee /kə'mɪti/ *n* (of club, society) comité *m*, comisión *f*; (of parliament) comisión *f*

commodity /kə'mɑːdəti ‖kə'mɒdəti/ *n (pl* **-ties) (a)** (product) artículo *m*, producto *m*, mercadería *f* (AmS) **(b)** (Fin) materia *f* prima

common¹ /'kɑːmən ‖'kɒmən/ *adj* **1 (a)** (widespread, prevalent) común; **the ~ cold** el resfriado común **(b)** (average, normal) ⟨soldier⟩ raso; **the ~ people** la gente común y corriente **(c)** (low-class, vulgar) ordinario **2 (a)** (shared, mutual) común **(b)** (public): **it's ~ knowledge** todo el mundo lo sabe

common² *n* **1** (in phrases) **in common** en común; **to have sth in ~ (with sb)** tener* algo en común (con algn); *see also* COMMONS **2** (in UK) terreno perteneciente al municipio

common: ~ law *n* derecho *m* consuetudinario; *(before n)* **common-law wife** concubina *f*, conviviente *f* (Chi); **C~ Market** *n* the **C~ Market** el Mercado Común; **~-or-garden** /'kɑːmənɔːr'gɑːrdn ‖'kɒmənɔː'gɑːdn/ *adj* (BrE colloq) vulgar *or* común y corriente

commonplace /'kɑːmənpleɪs ‖'kɒmənpleɪs/ *adj* (ordinary) común; (trite) banal

Commons /'kɑːmənz ‖'kɒmənz/ *n* (in UK) (+ *sing or pl vb*) **the ~** la Cámara de los Comunes

common sense *n* sentido *m* común

Commonwealth /'kɑːmənwelθ ‖'kɒmənwelθ/ *n* **the ~** la *or* el Commonwealth

commotion /kə'məʊʃən/ *n* (no *pl*) **(a)** (outrage) conmoción *f*; **to cause (a) ~** producir* una conmoción **(b)** (noise) alboroto *m*

communal /kə'mjuːnl ‖'kɒmjʊnl, kə'mjuːnl/

adj (a) ⟨*land/ownership*⟩ comunal; ⟨*kitchen/ bathroom*⟩ común; ⟨*life*⟩ comunitario (b) (between groups) ⟨*violence*⟩ interno

commune /'kɑːmjuːn ‖ 'kɒmjuːn/ *n* comuna *f*

communicate /kə'mjuːnɪkeɪt/ *vi* comunicarse*
■ ~ *vt* comunicar*

communication /kə'mjuːnə'keɪʃən ‖ kəˌmjuːnɪ'keɪʃən/ *n* **1** (act) comunicación *f* **2** **communications** *pl* comunicaciones *fpl*

communicative /kə'mjuːnəkeɪtɪv ‖ kə'mjuːnɪkətɪv/ *adj* comunicativo

communion /kə'mjuːnjən/ *n* **1** (Holy C~) la Santa *or* Sagrada Comunión **2** (exchange of ideas, fellowship) (frml) comunión *f*

communism, Communism /'kɑːmjənɪzəm ‖ 'kɒmjʊnɪzəm/ *n* comunismo *m*

communist¹, Communist /'kɑːmjənəst ‖ 'kɒmjʊnɪst/ *adj* comunista

communist², Communist *n* comunista *mf*

community /kə'mjuːnəti/ *n* (*pl* **-ties**) comunidad *f*; **the city's black ~** la población *or* comunidad negra de la ciudad

community: ~ **center,** (BrE) ~ **centre** *n* centro *m* social; ~ **chest** *n* (in US) *fondos reunidos voluntariamente por la comunidad, destinados a beneficencia y bienestar social*; ~ **service** trabajo *m* comunitario ⟨*prestado en lugar de cumplir una pena de prisión*⟩

commute /kə'mjuːt/ *vi* viajar todos los días ⟨*entre el lugar de residencia y el de trabajo*⟩
■ ~ *vt* ⟨*sentence/punishment*⟩ conmutar

commuter /kə'mjuːtər ‖ kə'mjuːtə(r)/ *n*: *persona que viaja diariamente una distancia considerable entre su lugar de residencia y el de trabajo*

compact¹ /kəm'pækt/ *adj* compacto

compact² /kəm'mpækt ‖ 'kɒmpækt/ *n* **1** (**powder**) ~ polvera *f* **2** (agreement) (frml) pacto *m*

compact disc, compact disk /'kɑːmpækt ‖ 'kɒmpækt/ *n* disco *m* compacto, compact-disc *m*; (*before n*) ~ ~ **player** (reproductor *m* de) compact-disc *m*

companion /kəm'pænjən/ *n* compañero, -ra *m,f*

companionship /kəm'pænjənʃɪp/ *n* compañía *f*

company /'kʌmpəni/ (*pl* **-nies**) *n* **1** (companionship, companions) compañía *f*; **to keep sb ~** hacerle* compañía a algn; **to part ~** separarse; **she's excellent ~** es muy agradable (*or* divertido *etc*) estar con ella; **we've got ~** tenemos visita **2** (Busn) compañía *f*, empresa *f*; (*before n*) ⟨*car*⟩ de la compañía *or* empresa **3** (a) (Theat) compañía *f* (b) (Mil) compañía *f* (c) (Naut): **ship's ~** tripulación *f*, dotación *f*

comparable /'kɑːmpərəbəl ‖ 'kɒmpərəbəl/ *adj* comparable

comparative¹ /kəm'pærətɪv/ *adj* relativo; ⟨*literature/linguistics*⟩ comparado; ⟨*analysis/ study*⟩ comparativo

comparative² *n* (Ling) comparativo *m*

compare /kəm'per ‖ kəm'peə(r)/ *vt* (a) (make comparison between) comparar; **to ~ sth/sb TO o**

WITH sth/sb comparar algo/a algn CON algo/algn (b) (liken) **to ~ sth/sb TO sth/sb** comparar algo/a algn CON *or* A algo/algn
■ ~ *vi*: **how do the two models ~ for speed?** en cuanto a velocidad ¿qué diferencia hay entre los dos modelos?; **this novel ~s favorably with the previous one** esta novela no desmerece de la anterior

comparison /kəm'pærəsən ‖ kəm'pærɪsən/ *n* comparación *f*

compartment /kəm'pɑːrtmənt ‖ kəm'pɑːtmənt/ *n* (a) (of bag, desk, refrigerator) compartimento *m*, compartimiento *m* (b) (in train) (BrE Rail) compartimento *m*, compartimiento *m*

compass /'kʌmpəs/ *n* (a) (magnetic ~) brújula *f* (b) (Math) (*often pl*) compás *m*

compassion /kəm'pæʃən/ *n* compasión *f*

compassionate /kəm'pæʃənət/ *adj* compasivo

compatible /kəm'pætəbəl/ *adj* (a) ⟨*people/ ideas/principles*⟩ compatible (b) (Comput) compatible; **an IBM ~ computer** una computadora *or* (Esp tb) un ordenador compatible con IBM

compel /kəm'pel/ *vt* **-ll-** **to ~ sb to + INF** obligar* a algn A + INF

compelling /kəm'pelɪŋ/ *adj* ⟨*argument*⟩ convincente; ⟨*book*⟩ absorbente

compendium /kəm'pendiəm/ *n* (*pl* **-diums** *or* **-dia** /-dɪə/) (BrE) (a) (book) compendio *m* (b) (of games) juegos *mpl* reunidos

compensate /'kɑːmpənseɪt ‖ 'kɒmpenseɪt/ *vt* indemnizar*, compensar; **to ~ sb FOR sth** indemnizar* *or* compensar a algn POR algo
■ ~ *vi* **to ~ FOR sth** compensar algo

compensation /'kɑːmpən'seɪʃən ‖ 'kɒmpen'seɪʃən/ *n* (a) (recompense) indemnización *f*, compensación *f*; **I received $20,000 as o in ~ for the damage** me dieron 20.000 dólares de indemnización *or* en compensación por los daños (b) (remuneration) (AmE) remuneración *f*

compete /kəm'piːt/ *vi* competir*; **to ~ FOR sth** competir* POR algo

competence /'kɑːmpətəns ‖ 'kɒmpɪtəns/ *n* competencia *f*

competent /'kɑːmpətənt ‖ 'kɒmpɪtənt/ *adj* competente

competition /'kɑːmpə'tɪʃən ‖ kɒmpə'tɪʃən/ *n* **1** (a) (competing) competencia *f*; **to be in ~ with sb/sth** competir* con algn/algo (b) (opposition) competencia *f* **2** (contest) concurso *m*; (Sport) competencia *f* (AmL), competición *f* (Esp)

competitive /kəm'petɪtɪv ‖ kəm'petɪtɪv/ *adj* competitivo

competitiveness /kəm'petɪtɪvnəs ‖ kəm'petɪtɪvnɪs/ *n* (a) (of business, economy) competitividad *f* (b) (of person) espíritu *m* competitivo

competitor /kəm'petətər ‖ kəm'petɪtə(r)/ *n* (a) (contestant) participante *mf*, concursante *mf* (b) (rival) (Busn) competidor, -dora *m,f*, rival *mf*; (Sport) contrincante *mf*

compile /kəm'paɪl/ *vt* (a) ⟨*dictionary/index*⟩ compilar (b) ⟨*information*⟩ recopilar, reunir*

complacent /kəm'pleɪsn̩t/ *adj* ⟨*person*⟩ satisfecho de sí mismo; ⟨*attitude*⟩ displicente

complain /kəm'pleɪn/ vi/t quejarse

complaint /kəm'pleɪnt/ n (a) (grievance) queja f, reclamo m (AmL); **to make a** ~ quejarse (b) (ailment) dolencia f (frml)

complement¹ /'kɑːmpləmənt ‖ 'kɒmplɪmənt/ n ☐ ~ (TO sth) complemento m (DE algo) ② (full number): **the orchestra had the full** ~ **of strings** la orquesta contaba con una sección de cuerdas completa

complement² vt complementar

complementary /'kɑːmplə'mentri ‖ ,kɒmplɪ'mentri/ adj complementario

complete¹ /kəm'pliːt/ adj ☐ (a) (entire) completo (b) (finished) terminado, concluido ② (thorough, absolute) (as intensifier) total, completo; **it came as a** ~ **surprise** fue una auténtica sorpresa

complete² vt (a) (finish) (building/education) acabar, terminar; (sentence) cumplir; (investigations) completar, concluir* (b) (make whole) (set/collection) completar (c) (fill in) (frml) (form) llenar, rellenar

completely /kəm'pliːtli/ adv completamente, totalmente

completion /kəm'pliːʃən/ n finalización f, terminación f

complex¹ /'kɑːmpleks ‖ 'kɒmpleks/ adj complejo

complex² n ☐ (buildings) complejo m ② (Psych) complejo m

complexion /kəm'plekʃən/ n cutis m; (in terms of color) tez f

complexity /kəm'pleksəti/ n (pl -ties) complejidad f

complicate /'kɑːmpləkeɪt ‖ 'kɒmplɪkeɪt/ vt complicar*

complicated /'kɑːmpləkeɪtəd ‖ 'kɒmplɪkeɪtɪd/ adj complicado

complication /'kɑːmplə'keɪʃən ‖ ,kɒmplɪ'keɪʃən/ n complicación f; ~s set in (Med) surgieron complicaciones

compliment¹ /'kɑːmpləmənt ‖ 'kɒmplɪmənt/ n (a) (expression of praise) cumplido m, halago m; **to pay sb a** ~ hacerle* un cumplido a algn, halagar* a algn (b) **compliments** pl (best wishes) saludos mpl; **with the** ~**s of the management** gentileza de la casa

compliment² vt **to** ~ **sb** (ON sth) felicitar a algn (POR algo)

complimentary /'kɑːmplə'mentəri ‖ ,kɒmplɪ'mentri/ adj (a) (flattering) elogioso, halagüeño (b) (free) (copy) de obsequio or regalo; ~ **ticket** invitación f

comply /kəm'plaɪ/ vi -plies, -plying, -plied: **to** ~ **with a request/an order** acceder a una solicitud/cumplir una orden

component¹ /kəm'pəʊnənt/ n componente m; (Auto) pieza f; (Electron) componente m

component² adj componente; (element) constituyente; ~ **part** componente m

compose /kəm'pəʊz/ vt ☐ (constitute) (usu pass) **to be** ~**d OF sth** estar* compuesto DE algo ② (music) componer*; (letter) redactar ③ (calm, control) (liter): **to** ~ **oneself** serenarse, recobrar la compostura

composed /kəm'pəʊzd/ adj sereno

composer /kəm'pəʊzər ‖ kəm'pəʊzə(r)/ n compositor, -tora m,f

composition /'kɑːmpə'zɪʃən ‖ ,kɒmpə'zɪʃən/ n composición f

compost /'kɑːmpəʊst ‖ 'kɒmpɒst/ n abono m orgánico

composure /kəm'pəʊʒər ‖ kəm'pəʊʒə(r)/ n compostura f

compound¹ /'kɑːmpaʊnd ‖ 'kɒmpaʊnd/ adj (number/interest) compuesto

compound² /'kɑːmpaʊnd ‖ 'kɒmpaʊnd/ n ☐ (a) (Chem) compuesto m (b) (word) palabra f compuesta ② (residence) complejo m habitacional; (for prisoners etc) barracones mpl

compound³ /kə'm'paʊnd ‖ kəm'paʊnd/ vt (problem) agravar; (risk/difficulties) acrecentar*

comprehend /'kɑːmprɪ'hend ‖ ,kɒmprɪ'hend/ vt comprender

comprehension /'kɑːmprɪ'hentʃən ‖ ,kɒmprɪ'henʃən/ n (a) (understanding) comprensión f (b) (school exercise) (BrE) ejercicio m de comprensión

comprehensive /'kɑːmprɪ'hensɪv ‖ ,kɒmprɪ'hensɪv/ adj (a) (survey/report) exhaustivo, global; (view) integral, de conjunto; (list/range) completo; (insurance/cover) contra todo riesgo (b) (Educ) (in UK) relativo al sistema educativo en el cual no se separa a los alumnos según su nivel de aptitud

comprehensive (**school**) n (in UK) instituto de segunda enseñanza para alumnos de cualquier nivel de aptitud

compress¹ /kəm'pres/ vt comprimir

compress² /'kɑːmpres ‖ 'kɒmpres/ n compresa f

comprise /kəm'praɪz/ vt (a) (consist of) comprender (b) (constitute, make up) componer*

compromise¹ /'kɑːmprəmaɪz ‖ 'kɒmprəmaɪz/ n acuerdo m mutuo, arreglo m, compromiso m

compromise² vi transigir*, transar (AmL) ■ ~ vt (a) (discredit) comprometer; **to** ~ **oneself** ponerse* en una situación comprometida (b) (endanger) comprometer

compromising /'kɑːmprəmaɪzɪŋ ‖ 'kɒmprəmaɪzɪŋ/ adj (evidence) comprometedor; (situation) comprometido

compulsion /kəm'pʌlʃən/ n (a) (force, duress) coacción f (b) (obsession) compulsión f

compulsive /kəm'pʌlsɪv/ adj (a) (compelling): **the book is** ~ **reading** es uno de esos libros que se empiezan y no se pueden dejar (b) (obsessive) (behavior) compulsivo; **he's a** ~ **eater/liar** come/miente por compulsión

compulsory /kəm'pʌlsəri/ adj (attendance) obligatorio; (retirement) forzoso; ~ **education** enseñanza f obligatoria

computer /kəm'pjuːtər ‖ kəm'pjuːtə(r)/ n computadora f (esp AmL), computador m (esp AmL), ordenador m (Esp); (before n) (society/age/revolution) de la informática; (program/game) de computadora (or ordenador etc)

computer: ~ **crime** n delito m informático; ~ **dating** n citas fpl por computadora or (Esp tb) ordenador

computerize /kəm'pju:təraɪz/ vt
computarizar*, computerizar*; ⟨company/
department⟩ informatizar*

computer: ~-literate adj capacitado para
operar un ordenador; ~ **programmer** n
programador, -dora m,f; ~ **programming** n
programación f; ~ **science** n informática f; ~
studies n informática f, computación f

computing /kəm'pju:tɪŋ/ n informática f,
computación f

comrade /'kɑːmræd ‖'kɒmreɪd/ n compañero,
-ra m,f, camarada mf

con[1] /kɑːn ‖kɒn/ n [1] (fraud) (colloq) timo m
(fam), estafa f [2] (convict) (sl) preso, -sa m,f
[3] (colloq) (objection) contra m; see also PRO 2

con[2] vt -nn- (colloq) timar (fam), estafar

concave /'kɑːnkeɪv ‖'kɒŋkeɪv/ adj cóncavo

conceal /kən'siːl/ vt ⟨object/facts⟩ ocultar;
⟨emotions⟩ disimular; to ~ sth FROM sb
ocultar(le) algo A algn

concede /kən'siːd/ vt (a) (admit) reconocer* (b)
(allow) ⟨right/privilege⟩ conceder (c) (give away)
⟨game/penalty⟩ conceder

conceit /kən'siːt/ n engreimiento m,
presunción f

conceited /kən'siːtəd ‖kən'siːtɪd/ adj
engreído, presuntuoso

conceivable /kən'siːvəbəl/ adj imaginable

conceive /kən'siːv/ vt [1] (a) (devise) ⟨plan⟩
concebir* (b) (imagine) imaginar; (consider)
considerar [2] ⟨child⟩ concebir*
■ ~ vi concebir*

concentrate[1] /'kɑːnsəntreɪt/
vt to ~ sth (ON sth) concentrar algo (EN algo)
■ ~ vi ⟨person⟩ concentrarse; ⟨talks⟩ centrarse;
~ on getting this finished concéntrate en
terminar esto

concentrate[2] n concentrado m

concentrated /'kɑːnsəntreɪtəd
‖'kɒnsəntreɪtɪd/ adj (a) ⟨effort⟩ intenso y
continuado (b) ⟨solution/juice⟩ concentrado

concentration /'kɑːnsən'treɪʃən
‖,kɒnsən'treɪʃən/ n concentración f

concentration camp n campo m de
concentración

concept /'kɑːnsept ‖'kɒnsept/ n concepto m

conception /kən'sepʃən/ n [1] (idea) noción f
[2] (of baby, plan) concepción f

concern[1] /kən'sɜːrn ‖kən'sɜːn/ n [1] (business,
affair) asunto m; that's no ~ of yours eso no es
asunto tuyo [2] (a) (anxiety) preocupación f,
inquietud f (b) (interest) ~ FOR sb/sth interés m
POR algn/algo; to be of ~ to sb importarle a algn
[3] (firm) empresa f; ▶ GOING[2]

concern[2] vt [1] (affect, involve) concernir*,
incumbir; to be ~ed WITH sth ocuparse DE algo;
as far as I'm ~ed en lo que a mí respecta, por mi
parte; to whom it may ~ (fml) a quien
corresponda (fml) [2] (a) (interest) interesar (b)
(worry, bother) preocupar, inquietar [3] (relate to):
item one ~s the new office el primer punto trata
de la nueva oficina

concerned /kən'sɜːrnd ‖kən'sɜːnd/ adj
⟨person⟩ preocupado; ⟨look⟩ de preocupación; to
be ~ ABOUT/FOR sb/sth estar* preocupado POR
algn/algo

concerning /kən'sɜːrnɪŋ ‖kən'sɜːnɪŋ/ prep
sobre, acerca de, con respecto a

concert[1] /'kɑːnsərt ‖'kɒnsət/ n concierto m;
in ~ en vivo, en concierto; ⟨before n⟩ ~ hall sala
f de conciertos, auditorio m

concert[2] /kən'sɜːrt ‖kən'sɜːt/ vt (fml)
concertar*, coordinar; we made a ~ed effort to ...
coordinamos or concertamos nuestros esfuerzos
para ...

concerto /kən'tʃertəʊ ‖kən'tʃɜːtəʊ,
kən'tʃeətəʊ/ n (pl -tos or -ti /-ti/) concierto m

concession /kən'seʃən/ n concesión f

conciliation /kən'sɪli'eɪʃən/ n conciliación f

conciliatory /kən'sɪliətɔːri ‖kən'sɪliətəri/ adj
conciliador, conciliatorio

concise /kən'saɪs/ adj conciso

conclude /kən'kluːd/ vt [1] (a) (end) concluir*
(fml), finalizar* (b) (settle) ⟨deal⟩ cerrar*;
⟨agreement⟩ llegar* a; ⟨treaty⟩ firmar; ⟨alliance⟩
pactar [2] (infer) concluir* (fml)
■ ~ vi concluir* (fml), terminar

conclusion /kən'kluːʒən/ n [1] (end)
conclusión f; in ~ (as linker) para concluir
[2] (decision, judgment) conclusión f; to come to o
reach a ~ llegar* a una conclusión; to jump to
~s precipitarse (a sacar conclusiones)

conclusive /kən'kluːsɪv/ adj ⟨evidence/
argument⟩ concluyente; ⟨victory⟩ decisivo

concoct /kən'kɑːkt ‖kən'kɒkt/ vt ⟨meal/drink⟩
preparar; ⟨excuse/story⟩ inventarse; ⟨plan⟩
tramar

concrete[1] /kɑːn'kriːt, 'kɑːnkriːt ‖'kɒnkriːt/
adj concreto

concrete[2] /'kɑːnkriːt ‖'kɒnkriːt/ n hormigón
m, concreto m (AmL)

concur /kən'kɜːr ‖kən'kɜː(r)/ vi -rr- (fml) to ~
(WITH sb/sth) coincidir (CON algn/algo)

concuss /kən'kʌs/ vt (usu pass): to be ~ed
sufrir una conmoción (cerebral) or una
concusión

concussion /kən'kʌʃən/ n conmoción f
cerebral, concusión f

condemn /kən'dem/ vt [1] (a) (sentence)
condenar (b) (censure) condenar [2] (a) (declare
unusable) ⟨building⟩ declarar ruinoso (b) (in US:
convert to public use) ⟨building⟩ expropiar (por
causa de utilidad pública)

condemnation /'kɑːndem'neɪʃən
‖,kɒndem'neɪʃən/ n condena f

condensation /'kɑːnden'seɪʃən
‖,kɒnden'seɪʃən/ n (a) (process) condensación f
(b) (on windows etc) vapor m, vaho m

condense /kən'dens/ vt [1] (abridge) ⟨book/
article⟩ condensar [2] (Chem) condensar

condensed /kən'densd/ adj condensado; ~
milk leche f condensada

condescend /'kɑːndɪ'send ‖,kɒndɪ'send/ vi to
~ to + INF dignarse or condescender* A + INF

condescending /'kɑːndɪ'sendɪŋ
‖,kɒndɪ'sendɪŋ/ adj ⟨tone/smile⟩ condescendiente

condiment /'kɑːndəmənt ‖'kɒndɪmənt/ n
(seasoning) condimento m, aliño m; (relish) salsa f
(para condimentar)

condition[1] /kən'dɪʃən/ n [1] (stipulation,
requirement) condición f; on ~ that con la
condición de que [2] (a) (state) (no pl) estado m, ···⟩

condiciones *fpl*; **in good ~** en buen estado **(b)**
(state of fitness): **to be in/out of ~** estar*/no estar*
en forma **(c)** (Med) afección *f* (frml), enfermedad *f*
3 conditions *pl* **(a)** (circumstances) condiciones
fpl; **working/housing ~s** condiciones de trabajo/
vivienda **(b)** (Meteo): **weather ~s are good** el
estado del tiempo es bueno

condition² *vt* **(a)** (influence, determine)
condicionar **(b)** (hair) acondicionar

conditional /kənˈdɪʃnəl ‖ kənˈdɪʃənl/ *adj* **(a)**
(provisional) condicional **(b)** (Ling) condicional

conditioner /kənˈdɪʃnər ‖ kənˈdɪʃnə(r)/ *n* (hair
~) acondicionador *m*, enjuague *m* (AmL),
suavizante *m* (Esp), bálsamo *m* (Chi); (fabric ~)
suavizante *m*

conditioning /kənˈdɪʃnɪŋ/ *n* (Psych)
condicionamiento *m*

condo /ˈkɑːndəʊ ‖ ˈkɒndəʊ/ *n* (AmE colloq) ▶
CONDOMINIUM

condolences /kənˈdəʊlənsɪz/ *pl n* (frml)
condolencias *fpl* (frml)

condom /ˈkɑːndəm ‖ ˈkɒndɒm/ *n* preservativo
m, condón *m*

condominium /ˌkɑːndəˈmɪniəm
‖ ˌkɒndəˈmɪniəm/ *n* (*pl* ~s) (AmE) apartamento
m, piso *m* (Esp) (*en régimen de propiedad
horizontal*)

condone /kənˈdəʊn/ *vt* aprobar*

conduct¹ /ˈkɑːndʌkt ‖ ˈkɒndʌkt/ *n* conducta *f*

conduct² /kənˈdʌkt/ *vt* **(a)** (inquiry/
experiment/business) llevar a cabo, realizar*;
(conversation) mantener* **(b)** (Mus) dirigir* **(c)**
(visitor/tour/party) guiar* **(d)** (heat/electricity)
conducir*

conductor /kənˈdʌktər ‖ kənˈdʌktə(r)/ *n*
1 (Mus) director, -tora *m,f* (de orquesta) **2** (on
bus) cobrador, -dora *m,f*, guarda *mf* (RPl); (on train)
(AmE) cobrador, -dora *m,f* **3** (Elec, Phys)
conductor *m*

cone /kəʊn/ *n* **(a)** (Auto, Math) cono *m* **(b)**
(ice-cream ~) cucurucho *m* or barquillo *m* or (Ven)
barquilla *f* or (Col) cono *m*

confectionery /kənˈfekʃəneri
‖ kənˈfekʃənəri/ *n* productos *mpl* de confitería

confer /kənˈfɜːr ‖ kənˈfɜː(r)/ **-rr-** *vt* (bestow)
conceder, conferir* (frml); **to ~ sth ON** *o* **UPON sb/
sth** concederle *or* (frml) conferirle* algo A algn/
algo
■ ~ *vi* (discuss) consultar

conference /ˈkɑːnfrəns ‖ ˈkɒnfərəns/ *n* **(a)**
(large assembly, convention) congreso *m*, conferencia
f; (*before n*) **~ center** *o* (BrE) **centre** centro *m* de
conferencias **(b)** (meeting, discussion) conferencia *f*;
(*before n*) **~ room** sala *f* de juntas

confess /kənˈfes/ *vt* confesar*
■ ~ *vi* **(a)** (admit) confesar* **(b)** (Relig) confesarse*

confession /kənˈfeʃən/ *n* **(a)** (statement)
confesión *f* **(b)** (Relig) confesión *f*

confetti /kənˈfeti/ *n* confeti *m* or (Chi) chaya *f*
or (RPl) papel *m* picado or (Ven) papelillos *mpl*

confide /kənˈfaɪd/ *vi* (tell secrets) **to ~ IN sb**
confiarse* A algn
■ ~ *vt* **to ~ sth TO sb** confiarle* algo A algn

confidence /ˈkɑːnfədəns ‖ ˈkɒnfɪdəns/ *n* **1**
(a) (trust, faith) confianza *f* **(b)** (self-confidence)
confianza *f* en sí mismo **2** (confidentiality): **he took
her into his ~** se confió a ella; **in ~** en confianza

confidence game *n* (AmE), **confidence
trick** *n* estafa *f*, timo *m* (fam)

confident /ˈkɑːnfədənt ‖ ˈkɒnfɪdənt/ *adj* **(a)**
(sure) (statement/forecast) hecho con confianza; **to
be ~ OF sth** confiar* EN algo **(b)** (self-confident)
(person) seguro de sí mismo

confidential /ˌkɑːnfəˈdentʃəl ‖ ˌkɒnfɪˈdenʃəl/
adj confidencial

confidentiality /ˌkɑːnfəˈdentʃiˈæləti
‖ ˌkɒnfɪdenʃiˈræləti/ *n* confidencialidad *f*

confine /kənˈfaɪn/ *vt* **(a)** (limit, restrict) **to ~ sth
TO sth** limitar algo A algo **(b)** (shut in, imprison)
(person) confinar, recluir*; (animal) encerrar*

confined /kənˈfaɪnd/ *adj* (space) limitado

confinement /kənˈfaɪnmənt/ *n* **(a)** (act, state)
reclusión *f*, confinamiento *m* **(b)** (in childbirth)
parto *m*

confines /ˈkɑːnfaɪnz ‖ ˈkɒnfaɪnz/ *pl n* confines
mpl

confirm /kənˈfɜːrm ‖ kənˈfɜːm/ *vt* **1** **(a)**
(substantiate) (report/reservation) confirmar **(b)**
confirmed *past p* (bachelor/liar) empedernido
2 (Relig) confirmar

confirmation /ˌkɑːnfərˈmeɪʃən
‖ ˌkɒnfəˈmeɪʃən/ *n* **1** **(a)** (substantiation)
confirmación *f* **(b)** (ratification) (frml) ratificación *f*
2 (Relig) confirmación *f*

confiscate /ˈkɑːnfəskeɪt ‖ ˈkɒnfɪskeɪt/ *vt*
confiscar*

conflict¹ /ˈkɑːnflɪkt ‖ ˈkɒnflɪkt/ *n* conflicto *m*

conflict² /kənˈflɪkt/ *vi* discrepar

conflicting /kənˈflɪktɪŋ/ *adj* (interests)
opuesto; (views/accounts/emotions) contradictorio

conform /kənˈfɔːrm ‖ kənˈfɔːm/ *vi* **(a)** (be in
accordance) **to ~ TO** *o* **WITH sth** ajustarse A *or*
cumplir CON algo **(b)** (act in a conformist way) ser*
conformista; **he usually ~s to their wishes** por lo
general se aviene a sus deseos

confound /kənˈfaʊnd/ *vt* **(a)** (perplex) (person)
confundir **(b)** (thwart) (atttempt) frustrar

confront /kənˈfrʌnt/ *vt* **(a)** (come face to face
with) (danger/problem) afrontar, enfrentar; **police
were ~ed by a group of demonstrators** la policía
se vio enfrentada a un grupo de manifestantes
(b) (face up to) (enemy/fear/crisis) hacer* frente a

confrontation /ˈkɑːnfrʌnˈteɪʃən
‖ ˌkɒnfrʌnˈteɪʃən/ *n* **(a)** (conflict) enfrentamiento
m, confrontación *f* **(b)** (encounter) confrontación *f*

confuse /kənˈfjuːz/ *vt* **1** **(a)** (bewilder)
confundir **(b)** (blur) (situation) complicar* **2** (mix
up, be unable to distinguish) (ideas/sounds) confundir

confused /kənˈfjuːzd/ *adj* **(a)** (perplexed)
confundido; **to get ~** confundirse **(b)** (unclear)
(argument) confuso

AmC	América Central	Arg	Argentina	Cu	Cuba	Per	Perú
AmL	América Latina	Bol	Bolivia	Ec	Ecuador	RPl	Río de la Plata
AmS	América del Sur	Chi	Chile	Esp	España	Ur	Uruguay
Andes	Región andina	CS	Cono Sur	Méx	México	Ven	Venezuela

confusing /kən'fju:zɪŋ/ *adj* confuso

confusion /kən'fju:ʒən/ *n* **(a)** (turmoil) confusión *f* **(b)** (disorder) desorden *m*

congeal /kən'dʒi:l/ *vi* «*fat*» solidificarse*; ~ed blood sangre *f* coagulada

congested /kən'dʒestəd ‖ kən'dʒestɪd/ *adj* **(a)** (with traffic) congestionado; (with people) abarrotado de gente **(b)** (Med) congestionado

congestion /kən'dʒestʃən/ *n* **(a)** (with traffic) congestión *f*; (with people) abarrotamiento *m* **(b)** (Med) congestión *f*

Congo /'kɑːŋgəʊ ‖ 'kɒŋgəʊ/ *n* el Congo

congratulate /kən'grætʃəleɪt ‖ kən'grætjʊleɪt/ *vt* felicitar; **to ~ sb on sth/-ING** felicitar *or* darle* la enhorabuena a algn **POR** algo/+ INF

congratulation /kən'grætʃə'leɪʃən ‖ kən,grætjʊ'leɪʃən/ *n* **(a)** (praise) felicitación *f* **(b)** **congratulations** *pl* enhorabuena *f*, felicitaciones *fpl*; (*as interj*) ~**s!** ¡enhorabuena!, ¡felicitaciones! (AmL)

congregate /'kɑːŋgrɪgeɪt ‖ 'kɒŋgrɪgeɪt/ *vi* congregarse*

congregation /'kɑːŋgrɪ'geɪʃən ‖ ,kɒŋgrɪ'geɪʃən/ *n* (Relig) (attending service) fieles *mpl*; (parishioners) feligreses *mpl*

congress /'kɑːŋgrəs ‖ 'kɒŋgres/ *n* **(a)** (conference) congreso *m* **(b)** **Congress** (in US) el Congreso (de los Estados Unidos)

congress: ~**man** /'kɑːŋgrəsmən ‖ 'kɒŋgresmən/ *n* (*pl* **-men** /-mən/) (in US) miembro *m* del Congreso; ~**woman** *n* (in US) miembro *f* del Congreso

conifer /'kɑːnəfər ‖ 'kɒnɪfə(r)/ *n* conífera *f*

conjecture¹ /kən'dʒektʃər ‖ kən'dʒektʃə(r)/ *n*: **it's pure ~** no son más que conjeturas

conjecture² *vt/i* (frml) conjeturar

conjugal /'kɑːndʒəgəl ‖ 'kɒndʒʊgəl/ *adj* (frml) conyugal

conjunctivitis /kən'dʒʌŋktɪ'vaɪtəs ‖ kən,dʒʌŋktɪ'vaɪtɪs/ *n* conjuntivitis *f*

conjurer /'kɑːndʒərər ‖ 'kʌndʒərə(r)/ *n* prestidigitador, -dora *m,f*, mago, -ga *m,f*

conjure up /'kɑːndʒər ‖ 'kʌndʒə(r)/ [*v + o + adv, v + adv + o*] (evoke) evocar*; **it ~s ~ images of ...** hace pensar en ...

conjuror *n* ▶ CONJURER

con man *n* estafador *m*, timador *m*

Conn = Connecticut

connect /kə'nekt/ *vt* **[1]** **(a)** (attach) **to ~ sth** (**TO sth**) conectar algo (**A** algo) **(b)** (link together) «*rooms/buildings*» comunicar*; «*towns*» conectar **(c)** (Telec): **I'm trying to ~ you** un momento que lo comunico *or* (Esp) le pongo con el número **(d)** «*phone/gas*» conectar **[2]** (associate) «*people/ideas/events*» relacionar
■ ~ *vi* **[1]** **(a)** (be joined together) «*rooms*» comunicarse*; «*pipes*» empalmar **(b)** (be fitted) **to ~** (**TO sth**) estar* conectado (a algo) **[2]** (Transp) **to ~ WITH sth** «*train/flight*» enlazar* CON algo, conectar CON algo (AmL)
■ **connect up** [*v + o + adv, v + adv + o*] «*wires/apparatus*» conectar **[2]** [*v + adv*] «*wires*» conectarse*; **it all ~s up** todo está relacionado

connected /kə'nektəd ‖ kə'nektɪd/ *adj* «*ideas/ events*» relacionado; **to be ~ed WITH sth** estar* relacionado CON algo

connection /kə'nekʃən/ *n* **[1]** **(a)** (link) ~ (**WITH sth**) enlace *m or* conexión *f* (CON algo) **(b)** (Elec) conexión *f* **[2]** (Transp) ~ (**WITH sth**) conexión *f or* enlace *m* (CON algo) **[3]** (relation) relación *f or* conexión *f* **[4]** **connections** *pl* (links, ties) lazos *mpl*; (influential people) contactos *mpl*, conexiones *fpl* (AmL)

connive /kə'naɪv/ *vi* **(a)** (plot) **to ~** (**WITH sb**) actuar* en complicidad (CON algn) **(b)** (cooperate) **to ~ AT sth** ser* cómplice EN algo

connoisseur /'kɑːnə'sɜːr ‖ ,kɒnə'sɜː(r)/ *n* entendido, -da *m,f*

connotation /'kɑːnəʊ'teɪʃən ‖ ,kɒnə'teɪʃən/ *n* connotación *f*

conquer /'kɑːŋkər ‖ 'kɒŋkə(r)/ *vt* «*country/ mountain*» conquistar; «*enemy/fear*» vencer

conqueror /'kɑːŋkərər ‖ 'kɒŋkərə(r)/ *n* conquistador, -dora *m,f*

conquest /'kɑːŋkwest ‖ 'kɒŋkwest/ *n* conquista *f*

conscience /'kɑːntʃəns ‖ 'kɒnʃəns/ *n* conciencia *f*; **to have a clear ~** tener* la conciencia tranquila

conscientious /'kɑːntʃi'entʃəs ‖ ,kɒnʃi'enʃəs/ *adj* «*work*» concienzudo; «*student*» aplicado

conscientious objector *n* /əb'jektər ‖ əb'jektə(r)/ objetor, -tora *m,f* de conciencia

conscious /'kɑːntʃəs ‖ 'kɒnʃəs/ *adj* **[1]** **(a)** (awake, alert) (*no comp*) consciente **(b)** (aware) (*pred*) **to be ~ OF sth** ser* *or* (Chi, Méx tb) estar* consciente DE algo **[2]** (deliberate) «*decision*» deliberado; **she made a ~ effort to be nice** se esforzó por ser amable

consciousness /'kɑːntʃəsnəs ‖ 'kɒnʃəsnɪs/ *n* **(a)** (state of being awake, alert) conocimiento *m* **(b)** (awareness) conciencia *f*

conscript¹ /'kɑːnskrɪpt ‖ 'kɒnskrɪpt/ *n* recluta *mf*, conscripto, -ta *m,f* (AmL)

conscript² /kən'skrɪpt/ *vt* reclutar

conscription /kən'skrɪpʃən/ *n* conscripción *f* (esp AmL), reclutamiento *m* (*para el servicio militar obligatorio en casos de guerra*)

consecrate /'kɑːnsəkreɪt ‖ 'kɒnsɪkreɪt/ *vt* consagrar

consecutive /kən'sekjətɪv ‖ kən'sekjʊtɪv/ *adj* «*numbers*» consecutivo; **he was absent on three ~ days** faltó tres días seguidos

consensus /kən'sensəs/ *n* consenso *m*

consent¹ /kən'sent/ *vi* acceder; **to ~ TO sth** acceder A *or* consentir* EN algo

consent² *n* consentimiento *m* de común acuerdo; **age of ~** (Law) *edad a partir de la cual es válido el consentimiento que se da para tener relaciones sexuales*

consequence /'kɑːnsəkwens ‖ 'kɒnsɪkwəns/ *n* **[1]** (result) consecuencia *f* **[2]** (importance) trascendencia *f*

consequently /'kɑːnsəkwentli ‖ 'kɒnsɪkwəntli/ *adv* consiguientemente, por consiguiente

conservation /ˌkɑːnsərˈveɪʃən ‖ˌkɒnsəˈveɪʃən/ n protección f or conservación f del medio ambiente

conservationist /ˌkɑːnsərˈveɪʃənəst ‖ˌkɒnsəˈveɪʃənɪst/ n conservacionista mf

conservative /kənˈsɜːrvətɪv ‖kənˈsɜːvətɪv/ adj (a) (traditional) conservador (b)
Conservative (in UK) (before n) conservador (c) (cautious) cauteloso; **a ~ estimate** un cálculo por lo bajo
Conservative n (in UK) conservador, -dora m,f

conservatory /kənˈsɜːrvətɔːri ‖kənˈsɜːvətri/ n (pl **-ries**) (a) (greenhouse) jardín m de invierno (b) (school of music) conservatorio m

conserve /kənˈsɜːrv ‖kənˈsɜːv/ vt (a) (preserve) ⟨wildlife/rivers⟩ proteger*, conservar (b) (save) ⟨energy/resources⟩ conservar

consider /kənˈsɪdər ‖kənˈsɪdə(r)/ vt (a) (think about, of) considerar; **we're ~ing moving house** estamos pensando en mudarnos; **~ yourself lucky** puedes darle por afortunado (b) (take into account) tener* en cuenta, considerar; **all things ~ed, I think that …** bien considerado, creo que …

considerable /kənˈsɪdərəbəl/ adj ⟨achievement/risk⟩ considerable; ⟨sum⟩ importante; **with ~ difficulty** con bastante dificultad

considerably /kənˈsɪdərəbli/ adv bastante, considerablemente

considerate /kənˈsɪdərət/ adj atento, considerado

consideration /kənˌsɪdəˈreɪʃən/ n ① (a) (attention, thought): **their case has been given careful ~** su caso ha sido estudiado or considerado detenidamente; **to take sth into ~** tener* algo en cuenta (b) (factor): **a major ~ is the cost** un factor muy a tener en cuenta es el costo ② (thoughtfulness) consideración f ③ (importance): **of little/no ~** de poca/ninguna importancia

considering[1] /kənˈsɪdərɪŋ/ prep teniendo en cuenta

considering[2] conj: **~ (that) she's only two years old** teniendo en cuenta que tiene solo dos años

consignment /kənˈsaɪnmənt/ n (a) (goods sent) envío m, remesa f (b) (sending) envío m

consist /kənˈsɪst/ vi **to ~ of sth** constar DE algo

consistency /kənˈsɪstənsi/ n (pl **-cies**) (a) (regularity) regularidad f (b) (of mixture) consistencia f

consistent /kənˈsɪstənt/ adj (a) (compatible) **to be ~ (WITH sth)** ⟨statements/beliefs⟩ concordar* (CON algo) (b) (constant) ⟨excellence/failure⟩ constante; ⟨denial⟩ sistemático

consistently /kənˈsɪstəntli/ adv (a) (without change) ⟨argue⟩ coherentemente; ⟨behave⟩ consecuentemente (b) (constantly) ⟨claim/refuse⟩ sistemáticamente

consolation /ˌkɑːnsəˈleɪʃən ‖ˌkɒnsəˈleɪʃən/ n consuelo m; (before n) **~ prize** premio m de consolación, premio m (de) consuelo (CS)

console[1] /ˈkɑːnsəʊl ‖ˈkɒnsəʊl/ n consola f

console[2] /kənˈsəʊl/ vt consolar*

consolidate /kənˈsɑːlədeɪt ‖kənˈsɒlɪdeɪt/ vt (a) (reinforce) ⟨support/position⟩ consolidar (b) (combine) ⟨companies⟩ fusionar; ⟨debts⟩ consolidar

consonant /ˈkɑːnsənənt ‖ˈkɒnsənənt/ n consonante f

consort /ˈkɑːnsɔːrt ‖ˈkɒnsɔːt/ n (frml) consorte mf (frml)

consortium /kənˈsɔːrʃjəm ‖kənˈsɔːtɪəm/ n (pl **-tia** /-tɪə/ or **-tiums**) consorcio m

conspicuous /kənˈspɪkjuəs/ adj ⟨hat/badge⟩ llamativo; ⟨differences/omissions⟩ manifiesto, evidente; **to make oneself ~** llamar la atención; **to be ~ by one's absence** brillar por su (or mi etc) ausencia

conspiracy /kənˈspɪrəsi/ n (pl **-cies**) conspiración f

conspirator /kənˈspɪrətər ‖kənˈspɪrətə(r)/ n conspirador, -dora m,f

conspire /kənˈspaɪr ‖kənˈspaɪə(r)/ vi conspirar; **to ~ to + INF** conspirar PARA + INF

constable /ˈkɑːnstəbəl ‖ˈkʌnstəbəl/ n (BrE) agente mf de policía

constant /ˈkɑːnstənt ‖ˈkɒnstənt/ adj (a) (continual) ⟨pain/complaints⟩ constante (b) (unchanging) ⟨temperature/speed⟩ constante (c) (loyal) (liter) fiel, leal

constantly /ˈkɑːnstəntli ‖ˈkɒnstəntli/ adv constantemente

constellation /ˌkɑːnstəˈleɪʃən ‖ˌkɒnstəˈleɪʃən/ n constelación f

constipated /ˈkɑːnstəpeɪtəd ‖ˈkɒnstɪpeɪtɪd/ adj estreñido

constipation /ˌkɑːnstəˈpeɪʃən ‖ˌkɒnstɪˈpeɪʃən/ n estreñimiento m

constituency /kənˈstɪtʃuənsi ‖kənˈstɪtjuənsi/ n (pl **-cies**) (area) circunscripción f or distrito m electoral; (supporters) electores mpl potenciales (de una circunscripción electoral)

constituent[1] /kənˈstɪtʃuənt ‖kənˈstɪtjuənt/ n ① (Pol) elector, -tora m,f ② (component) (frml) componente m, elemento m constitutivo or constituyente

constituent[2] adj (before n) ⟨part/element⟩ constituyente, constitutivo

constitute /ˈkɑːnstətuːt ‖ˈkɒnstɪtjuːt/ vt (frml) constituir* (frml)

constitution /ˌkɑːnstəˈtuːʃən ‖ˌkɒnstɪˈtjuːʃən/ n ① (of country) constitución f; (of association, party) estatutos mpl ② (of person) constitución f

constitutional /ˌkɑːnstəˈtuːʃnəl ‖ˌkɒnstɪˈtjuːʃənl/ adj constitucional

constrain /kənˈstreɪn/ vt (often pass) obligar*

constraint /kənˈstreɪnt/ n (a) (compulsion) coacción f (b) (restriction) (often pl) restricción f, limitación f

constrict /kənˈstrɪkt/ vt ⟨opening/channel⟩ estrechar; ⟨flow/breathing⟩ dificultar; ⟨freedom⟩ coartar

construct /kənˈstrʌkt/ vt (a) (build) (frml) construir* (b) (put together) ⟨model⟩ armar, montar

construction /kənˈstrʌkʃən/ n ① (a) (of building) construcción f; (before n) ⟨industry/worker⟩ de la construcción (b) (Ling, Math) construcción f ② (structure) estructura f

constructive /kən'strʌktɪv/ *adj* constructivo

consul /'kɑːnsəl ‖'kɒnsəl/ *n* cónsul *mf*

consulate /'kɑːnsələt ‖'kɒnsjʊlət/ *n* consulado *m*

consult /kən'sʌlt/ *vt* consultar
■ ∼ *vi*: I ought to ∼ with my wife first primero debería consultárselo a mi mujer

consultancy /kən'sʌltənsi/ *n* (*pl* -**cies**) (Busn) asesoría *f*, consultoría *f*

consultant /kən'sʌltənt/ *n* (adviser) asesor, -sora *m,f*, consultor, -tora *m,f*; (BrE Med) especialista *mf*

consultation /'kɑːnsəl'teɪʃn ‖,kɒnsəl'teɪʃən/ *n* (a) (with doctor, lawyer) consulta *f* (b) (of dictionary, notes) consulta *f* (c) (discussion): **there was no** ∼ **with the tenants** no se consultó a los inquilinos; **in** ∼ **with sb** en conferencia con algn

consulting /kən'sʌltɪŋ/ *adj* (*before n*) (Med): ∼ **room** consultorio *m*, consulta *f*

consume /kən'suːm ‖kən'sjuːm/ *vt* consumir; **he was** ∼**d by** *o* **with jealousy** lo consumían los celos

consumer /kən'suːmər ‖kən'sjuːmə(r)/ *n* consumidor, -dora *m,f*; (*before n*) ∼ **goods** artículos *mpl* *o* bienes *mpl* de consumo; **the** ∼ **society** la sociedad de consumo

consummate¹ /'kɑːn,səmət ‖'kɒnsəmət/ *adj* (frml) (*before n*) ⟨actor/liar⟩ consumado

consummate² /'kɑːnsəmeɪt ‖'kɒnsəmeɪt/ *vt* consumar

consumption /kən'sʌmpʃən/ *n* consumo *m*

contact¹ /'kɑːntækt ‖'kɒntækt/ *n* (a) (physical) contacto *m*; **to come into** ∼ **with sth** hacer* contacto con algo (b) (communication) contacto *m*; **to come in/into** ∼ **with sb** tratar a algn; **to be/get in** ∼ **with sb** estar*/ponerse* en contacto con algn

contact² *vt* ponerse* en contacto con

contact lens *n* lente *f* *or* (AmL) lente *m* de contacto, lentilla *f* (Esp)

contagious /kən'teɪdʒəs/ *adj* contagioso

contain /kən'teɪn/ *vt* [1] (hold) contener* [2] ⟨enemy/fire/epidemic⟩ contener*; ⟨anger/laughter⟩ contener*; **to** ∼ **oneself** contenerse*

container /kən'teɪnər ‖kən'teɪnə(r)/ *n* (receptacle) recipiente *m*; (as packaging) envase *m*; (Transp) contenedor *m*, contáiner *m*; (*before n*) ∼ **ship** buque *m* portacontenedores

contaminate /kən'tæmɪnert ‖kən'tæmɪnert/ *vt* contaminar

contamination /kən'tæmə'neɪʃən ‖kən,tæmɪ'neɪʃən/ *n* contaminación *f*

contd (= **continued**) sigue

contemplate /'kɑːntəmpleɪt ‖'kɒntəmpleɪt/ *vt* contemplar; **I** ∼**d phoning her** pensé (en) llamarla

contemporary¹ /kən'tempəreri ‖kən'tempərəri/ *adj* (a) (of the same period) ⟨person⟩ contemporáneo, coetáneo; ⟨object⟩ de la época (b) (present-day) contemporáneo, actual

contemporary² *n* (*pl* -**ries**) (a) (sb living at same time) contemporáneo, -nea *m,f*, coetáneo, -na *m,f* (b) (sb of same age): **he looks older than his contemporaries** parece mayor que la gente de su edad

contempt /kən'tempt/ *n* desprecio *m*; **to be beneath** ∼ ser* despreciable; ∼ **(of court)** (Law) desacato *m* al tribunal

contemptible /kən'temptəbəl/ *adj* despreciable

contemptuous /kən'temptʃuəs ‖kən'temptʃʊəs/ *adj* despectivo

contend /kən'tend/ *vi* (a) (compete) **to** ∼ (**WITH sb**) (**FOR sth**) competir* (**CON algn**) (**POR algo**) (b) (face) **to** ∼ **WITH sth** lidiar **CON** algo
■ ∼ *vt* argüir*

contender /kən'tendər ‖kən'tendə(r)/ *n* ∼ (**FOR sth**) aspirante *mf* (**A** algo)

content¹ /'kɑːntent ‖'kɒntent/ *n* [1] **contents** *pl* (of box, bottle) contenido *m*; ∼**s** (of book) índice *m* de materias; (in magazine) sumario *m* [2] (amount contained) contenido *m*

content² /kən'tent/ *adj* (*pred*) contento

content³ /kən'tent/ *v* *refl* **to** ∼ **oneself WITH sth/-ING** contentarse **CON** algo/+ INF

contented /kən'tentɪd ‖kən'tentɪd/ *adj* ⟨sigh/purr⟩ de satisfacción; ⟨person/workforce⟩ satisfecho; **to be** ∼ **WITH sth** contentarse **CON** algo

contention /kən'tentʃən ‖kən'tenʃən/ *n* [1] (dispute): **there is considerable** ∼ **over ...** existe un gran desacuerdo sobre ... [2] (assertion) opinión *f*; **it is her** ∼ **that ...** ella sostiene que ...

contentious /kən'tentʃəs ‖kən'tenʃəs/ *adj* ⟨issue⟩ polémico

contentment /kən'tentmənt/ *n* satisfacción *f*

contest¹ /'kɑːntest ‖'kɒntest/ *n* (a) (competition) (Games) concurso *m*; (Sport) competencia *f* (AmL), competición *f* (Esp); (in boxing) combate *m* (b) (struggle) lucha *f*

contest² /kən'test/ *vt* (a) ⟨allegation⟩ refutar; ⟨will⟩ impugnar; ⟨decision⟩ protestar contra (b) ⟨election⟩ presentarse como candidato a

contestant /kən'testənt/ *n* concursante *mf*

context /'kɑːntekst ‖'kɒntekst/ *n* contexto *m*

continent /'kɑːntɪnənt ‖'kɒntɪnənt/ *n* continente *m*; **the C∼** Europa *f* (continental)

continental /'kɑːntɪ'nent ‖,kɒntɪ'nentl/ *adj* continental; **C∼** (European) de Europa (continental)

continental: ∼ **breakfast** *n* desayuno *m* continental (desayuno de café o té y bollos con mantequilla y mermelada); ∼ **quilt** *n* (BrE) ▶ DUVET

contingency /kən'tɪndʒənsi/ *n* (*pl* -**cies**) (eventuality) contingencia *f*; (*before n*) ⟨fund⟩ (para casos) de emergencia; **a** ∼ **plan** un plan para prever

continual /kən'tɪnjuəl/ *adj* continuo, constante

continually /kən'tɪnjuəli/ *adv* continuamente, constantemente

continuation /kən'tɪnju'eɪʃən/ *n* continuación *f*

continue /kən'tɪnjuː/ *vi* continuar*, seguir*; **we** ∼**d on our way** reanudamos el camino
■ ∼ *vt* (a) (keep on) continuar*, seguir* con; **to** ∼ **-ING/to + INF** continuar* *or* seguir* + GER (b) (resume) continuar*, seguir* con, proseguir* (frml); **to be** ∼**d** continuará (c) (extend, prolong) prolongar*

continuity /ˌkɑːntn̩'uːəti ‖ˌkɒntrɪ'njuːɪti/ n
continuidad f

continuous /kən'tɪnjuəs/ adj continuo; ~
assessment (Educ) evaluación f continua

continuously /kən'tɪnjuəsli/ adv
continuamente, sin interrupción

contort /kən'tɔːrt ‖kən'tɔːt/ vt ⟨face⟩ contraer*;
to ~ oneself contorsionarse
■ ~ vi crisparse

contortion /kən'tɔːrʃən ‖kən'tɔːʃən/ n
contorsión f

contour /'kɑːntʊr ‖'kɒntʊə(r)/ n contorno m;
(before n) ~ line curva f de nivel, cota f

contraband /'kɑːntrəbænd ‖'kɒntrəbænd/ n
contrabando m

contraception /ˌkɑːntrə'sepʃən
‖ˌkɒntrə'sepʃən/ n anticoncepción f,
contracepción f

contraceptive /ˌkɑːntrə'septɪv
‖ˌkɒntrə'septɪv/ n anticonceptivo m,
contraconceptivo m

contract¹ /'kɑːntrækt ‖'kɒntrækt/ n
(agreement, document) contrato m; (for public works)
contrata f; ~ killer asesino, -na m,f a sueldo,
sicario, -ria m,f

contract² /kən'trækt/ vt also /'kɑːntrækt/ (a)
(place under contract) ⟨person⟩ contratar (b) ⟨debt/
disease⟩ contraer* (frml) (c) ⟨muscle⟩ contraer*
■ ~ vi (become smaller/tighter) contraerse*
■ **contract out** /'kɑːntrækt ‖'kɒntrækt/ [v + o
+ adv, v + adv + o] ⟨job/work⟩ subcontratar

contraction /kən'trækʃən/ n contracción f

contractor /'kɑːntræktər ‖kən'træktə(r)/ n
contratista m

contradict /ˌkɑːntrə'dɪkt ‖ˌkɒntrə'dɪkt/ vt
contradecir*

contradiction /ˌkɑːntrə'dɪkʃən
‖ˌkɒntrə'dɪkʃən/ n contradicción f; a ~ in terms
un contrasentido

contradictory /ˌkɑːntrə'dɪktəri
‖ˌkɒntrə'dɪktəri/ adj contradictorio

contralto /kən'træltəʊ/ n (pl ~s) contralto f

contraption /kən'træpʃən/ n (colloq) artilugio
m

contrary¹ adj [1] /'kɑːntreri ‖'kɒntrəri/ (a)
(opposed, opposite) contrario (b) ~ to (as prep)
contrariamente a, al contrario de [2] /'kɑːntreri,
kən'treri ‖kən'treəri/ (obstinate): he's so ~
siempre tiene que llevar la contraria

contrary² /'kɑːntreri ‖'kɒntrəri/ n (pl -ries):
the ~ lo contrario; on the ~ (as linker) al
contrario

contrast¹ /'kɑːntræst ‖'kɒntrɑːst/ n contraste
m; by ~ (as linker) por contraste; in ~ to o with
(as prep) en contraste con

contrast² /kən'træst ‖kən'trɑːst/ vt contrastar
■ ~ vi (a) (differ) contrastar (b) **contrasting**
pres p ⟨opinions/approaches⟩ contrastante

contribute /kən'trɪbjət, -bjuːt/ vt (a) ⟨money/
time⟩ contribuir* con, aportar, hacer* una

aportación or (esp AmL) un aporte de;
⟨suggestions/ideas⟩ aportar (b) ⟨article/poem/
paper⟩ escribir*
■ ~ vi (a) (play significant part) to ~ (TO sth)
contribuir* (A algo) (b) (give money) contribuir*
(c) (participate) to ~ TO sth participar EN algo (d)
(Journ) to ~ TO sth escribir* PARA algo

contribution /ˌkɑːntrə'bjuːʃən
‖ˌkɒntrɪ'bjuːʃən/ n (a) (participation, part played)
contribución f (b) (payment, donation) contribución
f; (to a fund) aportación f, aporte m (esp AmL)

contributor /kən'trɪbjətər ‖kən'trɪbjʊtə(r)/ n
(a) (writer) colaborador, -dora m,f (b) (donor)
donante mf

contrive /kən'traɪv/ vt (a) (manage) to ~ to +
INF lograr + INF/QUE (+ subj), ingeniárselas or
arreglárselas PARA + INF/PARA QUE (+ subj) (b)
(create) ⟨method/device⟩ idear

contrived /kən'traɪvd/ adj artificioso

control¹ /kən'trəʊl/ vt -ll- controlar; ⟨traffic⟩
dirigir*; to ~ oneself controlarse

control² n [1] control m; to be in o of sth
dominar algo; to gain ~ of sth hacerse* con;
circumstances beyond our ~ circunstancias
ajenas a nuestra voluntad; to be out of ~ estar*
fuera de control; to get out of ~ descontrolarse
[2] price ~(s) control m de precios [3] **controls**
pl (of vehicle) mandos mpl [4] (mastery) dominio m

controlled /kən'trəʊld/ adj ⟨voice/emotion⟩
contenido; ⟨response⟩ mesurado; ⟨conditions/
experiment⟩ controlado

controller /kən'trəʊlər ‖kən'trəʊlə(r)/ n
director, -tora m,f

control: ~ room n (Mil, Naut) centro m de
operaciones; (Audio, Rad, TV) sala f de control; ~
tower n torre f de control

controversial /ˌkɑːntrə'vɜːrʃəl
‖ˌkɒntrə'vɜːʃəl/ adj controvertido

controversy /'kɑːntrəvɜːrsi ‖'kɒntrəvɜːsi,
kən'trɒvəsi/ n (pl -sies) controversia f

conundrum /kə'nʌndrəm/ n adivinanza f

conurbation /ˌkɑːnɜːr'beɪʃən ‖ˌkɒnɜː'beɪʃən/
n conurbación f

convalesce /ˌkɑːnvə'les ‖ˌkɒnvə'les/ vi
recuperarse, convalecer*

convene /kən'viːn/ vi reunirse*

convenience /kən'viːniəns/ n (a) (comfort,
practicality) conveniencia f; at your ~ cuando le
resulte conveniente (b) (amenity, appliance): with
every modern ~ con todas las comodidades
modernas

convenience food n comida f de
preparación rápida

convenient /kən'viːniənt/ adj (a) (opportune,
suitable) conveniente (b) (practical) práctico; a very
~ way of storing things una manera muy
práctica de guardar las cosas (c) (handy, close): it's
very ~ having the school so near resulta muy
práctico tener la escuela tan cerca

conveniently /kən'viːniəntli/ adv (a) (handily)
convenientemente (b) (expediently): the

government ~ forgets its election promises le resulta muy cómodo al gobierno olvidarse de sus promesas electorales

convent /'kɑːnvənt ‖'kɒnvənt/ n convento m

convention /kən'ventʃən ‖kən'venʃən/ n **1** **(a)** (social code) convenciónes fpl, convencionalismos mpl **(b)** (established practice) convención f **2** (agreement) convención f **3** (conference) convención f, congreso m

conventional /kən'ventʃnəl ‖kən'venʃənl̩/ adj convencional

converge /kən'vɜːrdʒ ‖kən'vɜːdʒ/ vi «lines/roads» converger*, convergir*; «crowd/armies» reunirse*

conversation /'kɑːnvər'seɪʃən ‖ˌkɒnvə'seɪʃən/ n conversación f

conversational /'kɑːnvər'seɪʃnəl ‖ˌkɒnvə'seɪʃənl̩/ adj familiar, coloquial

converse /kən'vɜːrs ‖kən'vɜːs/ vi conversar

conversion /kən'vɜːrʒən ‖kən'vɜːʃən/ n **1** **(a)** (change) conversión f **(b)** (of house): to do a ~ transformar una casa **(c)** (Relig) conversión f **2** (in rugby) conversión f, transformación f

convert[1] /'kɑːnvɜːrt ‖'kɒnvɜːt/ n converso, -sa m,f

convert[2] /kən'vɜːrt ‖kən'vɜːt/ vt **1** ⟨building⟩ remodelar; ⟨vehicle⟩ transformar; to ~ sth INTO sth convertir* algo EN algo **2** (cause to change view, religion) convertir* **3** (in rugby) transformar, convertir*
■ ~ vi (Pol, Relig) convertirse*

convertible[1] /kən'vɜːrtəbəl ‖kən'vɜːtəbəl/ adj convertible

convertible[2] n (Auto) descapotable m, convertible m (AmL)

convex /'kɑːnveks ‖'kɒnveks/ adj convexo

convey /kən'veɪ/ vt ⟨goods/people⟩ transportar; ⟨feeling⟩ expresar; ⟨thanks⟩ hacer* llegar

conveyor (belt) /kən'veɪər ‖kən'veɪə(r)/ n cinta f or correa f transportadora, banda f transportadora (Méx)

convict[1] /'kɑːnvɪkt ‖'kɒnvɪkt/ n recluso, -sa m,f, presidiario, -ria m,f

convict[2] /kən'vɪkt/ vt (often pass) declarar culpable, condenar; to be ~ed OF sth ser* condenado POR algo

conviction /kən'vɪkʃən/ n **1** (Law) condena f **2** (certainty) convicción f

convince /kən'vɪns/ vt convencer*; to ~ sb THAT convencer* a algn DE QUE

convinced /kən'vɪnst/ adj (persuaded) (pred): to be ~ OF sth/THAT estar* convencido DE algo/DE QUE

convincing /kən'vɪnsɪŋ/ adj convincente

convivial /kən'vɪviəl/ adj ⟨atmosphere⟩ cordial; ⟨person⟩ simpático

convoy /'kɑːnvɔɪ ‖'kɒnvɔɪ/ n convoy m

convulsion /kən'vʌlʃən/ n convulsión f

coo /kuː/ vi ⟨dove/pigeon⟩ arrullar

cook[1] /kʊk/ n cocinero, -ra m,f; he's a good ~ cocina muy bien, es muy buen cocinero

cook[2] vt ⟨food/meal⟩ hacer*, preparar
■ ~ vi **(a)** (prepare food) cocinar, guisar **(b)** (become ready) ⟨food⟩ hacerse*

cookbook /'kʊkbʊk/ n libro m de cocina or de recetas

cooker /'kʊkər ‖'kʊkə(r)/ n (BrE) (stove) cocina f or (Col, Méx) estufa f

cookery /'kʊkəri/ n cocina f; (before n) ~ book (BrE) ▶ COOKBOOK

cookie /'kʊki/ n (AmE Culin) galleta f, galletita f (RPl)

cooking /'kʊkɪŋ/ n: to do the ~ cocinar; it is used in ~ se usa para cocinar; home ~ la comida casera; Spanish ~ la cocina española

cooky n ▶ COOKIE

cool[1] /kuːl/ adj -er, -est **1** (cold) fresco; it's ~ today hace or está fresco hoy **2** (reserved, hostile) ⟨reception/behavior⟩ frío **3** (calm) sereno, tranquilo; keep ~! ¡tranquilo!, no te pongas nervioso; he's a very ~ customer tiene una sangre fría impresionante **4** (sl) (trendy, laid-back): he's really ~ es muy en la onda (fam)

cool[2] n **1** (low temperature): let's stay here in the ~ quedémonos aquí al fresco **2** (composure) calma f; to keep/lose one's ~ mantener*/perder* la calma

cool[3] vt ⟨air/room⟩ refrigerar; ⟨engine/food/enthusiasm⟩ enfriar*
■ ~ vi ⟨air/room⟩ refrigerarse*; ⟨engine/food/enthusiasm⟩ enfriarse*
■ **cool down** [v + adv] **(a)** (become cooler) ⟨food/iron⟩ enfriarse*; ⟨person⟩ refrescarse* **(b)** (become calmer) calmarse
■ **cool off** [v + adv] **(a)** (become cooler) ⟨person⟩ refrescarse* **(b)** (become calmer) calmarse

coolly /'kuːlli/ adv **(a)** (calmly) con serenidad or calma **(b)** (boldly) descaradamente, con la mayor frescura **(c)** (with reserve, hostility) fríamente, con frialdad

coop /kuːp/ n: chicken/hen ~ gallinero m
■ **coop up** [v + o + adv, v + adv + o] (usu passive) encerrar*

co-op /'kəʊɑːp ‖'kəʊɒp/ n cooperativa f

cooperate /kəʊ'ɑːpəreɪt ‖kəʊ'ɒpəreɪt/ vi cooperar, colaborar

cooperation /kəʊˌɑːpə'reɪʃən ‖kəʊˌɒpə'reɪʃən/ n cooperación f, colaboración f

cooperative[1] /kəʊ'ɑːpərətɪv ‖kəʊ'ɒpərətɪv/ adj **(a)** ⟨attitude⟩ de colaboración, cooperativo **(b)** ⟨effort/venture⟩ conjunto

cooperative[2] n cooperativa f

co-opt /kəʊ'ɑːpt ‖kəʊ'ɒpt/ vt: to ~ sb onto a committee invitar a algn a formar parte de una comisión

coordinate[1] /kəʊ'ɔːrdneɪt ‖ˌkəʊ'ɔːdmeɪt/ vt coordinar

coordinate[2] /kəʊ'ɔːrdnət ‖kəʊ'ɔːdmət/ n **1** (Math) coordenada f **2** **coordinates** pl prendas fpl para combinar, coordinados mpl

coordination /kəʊˌɔːrdn'eɪʃən ‖kəʊˌɔːdɪ'neɪʃən/ n coordinación f

coordinator /kəʊ'ɔːrdneɪtər ‖kəʊ'ɔːdmeɪtə(r)/ n coordinador, -dora m,f

coowner /'kəʊˈəʊnər ‖kəʊ'əʊnə(r)/ n copropietario, -ria m,f

cop /kɑːp ‖kɒp/ n (colloq) poli mf (fam), tira mf (Méx fam), cana mf (RPl arg), cachaco, -ca m,f (Per fam), paco, -ca m,f (Chi fam)

cope /kəʊp/ vi: I can't ~ with all this work no doy abasto or no puedo con tanto trabajo; how do you ~ without a washing machine? ¿cómo te las ⋯⋙

arreglas sin lavadora?; **how is he coping on his own?** ¿qué tal se las arregla solo?; **these are some of the problems they have to ~ with** estos son algunos de los problemas a los que tienen que enfrentarse

Copenhagen /'kəupən'heigən/ n Copenhague m

copious /'kəupiəs/ adj copioso

copper /'kɑːpər ‖'kɒpə(r)/ n [1] **(a)** (metal) cobre m **(b) coppers** pl (coins) (colloq) peniques mpl, perras fpl (Esp fam), quintos mpl (Méx fam), chauchas fpl (Chi fam), vintenes mpl (Ur fam) **(c)** (color) color m cobre; (before n) cobrizo [2] (police officer) (colloq) ▶ COP

co-production /'kəuprə,dʌkʃən/ n coproducción f

copy¹ /'kɑːpi ‖'kɒpi/ n (pl **copies**) [1] (of painting, document) copia f [2] (of newspaper, book) ejemplar m [3] (text): **he/she must be able to produce clear ~** debe saber redactar con claridad

copy² copies, copying, copied vt [1] **(a)** (reproduce, transcribe) copiar **(b)** (photocopy) fotocopiar [2] (imitate) ⟨painter/singer⟩ copiarle a; ⟨style/behavior⟩ copiar

copy: ~**cat** n (colloq) copión, -piona m,f (fam), imitamonos mf (Méx fam); ~**right** n copyright m, derechos mpl de reproducción

coral /'kɔːrəl ‖'kɒrəl/ n coral m

cord /kɔːrd ‖kɔːd/ n [1] **(a)** (string, rope) cuerda f; (of pajamas, curtains) cordón m **(b)** (AmE Elec) cordón m, cable m **(c)** (Anat) ▶ SPINAL CORD, UMBILICAL CORD, VOCAL CORDS [2] (Tex) pana f, corderoy m (AmS), cotelé m (Chi)

cordial¹ /'kɔːrdʒəl ‖'kɔːdiəl/ adj cordial

cordial² n refresco m (concentrado)

cordless /'kɔːrdləs ‖'kɔːdlɪs/ adj inalámbrico

cordon /'kɔːrdn ‖'kɔːdn/ n cordón m

■ **cordon off** [v + o + adv, v + adv + o] acordonar

corduroy /'kɔːrdərɔɪ ‖'kɔːdərɔɪ/ n pana f, corderoy m (AmS), cotelé m (Chi)

core¹ /kɔːr ‖kɔː(r)/ n (of apple, pear) corazón m; (of Earth) centro m; (of nuclear reactor) núcleo; (of problem) meollo m

core² vt ⟨apple⟩ quitarle el corazón a

coriander /'kɔːriændər ‖,kɒri'ændə(r)/ n cilantro m, culantro m

cork /kɔːrk ‖kɔːk/ n corcho m

corkscrew /'kɔːrkskruː ‖'kɔːkskruː/ n sacacorchos m, tirabuzón m

corn /kɔːrn ‖kɔːn/ n [1] **(a)** (cereal crop — in general) grano m; (maize) (AmE) maíz m; (wheat) (BrE) trigo m; (oats) (BrE) avena f **(b)** (foodstuff) maíz m, choclo m (AmS); ~ **on the cob** mazorca f de maíz or (AmS) de choclo, elote f (Méx) [2] (on toe) callo m

corner¹ /'kɔːrnər ‖'kɔːnə(r)/ n [1] **(a)** (inside angle — of room, cupboard) rincón m; (— of field) esquina f; (— of mouth) comisura f; (— of page) ángulo m **(b)** (outside angle — of street, page) esquina f; (— of table) esquina f, punta f; (bend in road) curva f; **I'll meet you on** o **at the ~** te veo en la esquina; **to cut ~s** (financially) hacer* economías; (in a process) simplificar*; (before n) ~ **shop** (BrE) tienda f de la esquina; (local shop) tienda f de barrio

[2] (in soccer) (~ kick) córner m, tiro m or saque m de esquina
[3] (in boxing) esquina f

corner² vt [1] (trap) acorralar [2] (monopolize) acaparar

■ ~ vi tomar una curva; **this car ~s well** este coche tiene buen agarre en las curvas

cornerstone /'kɔːrnərstəun ‖'kɔːnəstəun/ n piedra f angular

corn: ~**flakes** pl n copos mpl or hojuelas fpl de maíz; ~**flour** n (BrE) maizena® f

Cornish /'kɔːrnɪʃ ‖'kɔːnɪʃ/ adj de Cornualles

cornstarch /'kɔːrnstɑːrtʃ ‖'kɔːnstɑːtʃ/ n (AmE) maizena® f

Cornwall /'kɔːrnwɔːl ‖'kɔːnwɔːl/ n Cornualles m

corny /'kɔːrni ‖'kɔːni/ adj **-nier, -niest** (colloq) **(a)** ⟨song/movie⟩ cursi, sensiblero **(b)** (BrE) ⟨joke⟩ malo

coronary¹ /'kɔːrəneri ‖'kɒrənri/ adj coronario

coronary² n (pl **-ries**) infarto m (de miocardio)

coronation /'kɔːrə'neiʃən ‖,kɒrə'neiʃən/ n coronación f

coroner /'kɔːrənər ‖'kɒrənə(r)/ n: funcionario encargado de investigar las causas de muertes violentas, repentinas o sospechosas, ≈ juez mf de instrucción

corporal /'kɔːrprəl ‖'kɔːpərəl/ n cabo m

corporal punishment n castigos mpl corporales

corporate /'kɔːrpərət ‖'kɔːpərət/ adj [1] **(a)** (of a company) ⟨headquarters/lawyer⟩ de la empresa or compañía **(b)** ⟨mentality/jargon⟩ empresarial [2] (joint, collective) ⟨action/decision⟩ colectivo

corporation /'kɔːrpə'reiʃən ‖,kɔːpə'reiʃən/ n (company — in US) sociedad f anónima; (— in UK) compañía f, empresa f, corporación f

corpse /kɔːrps ‖kɔːps/ n cadáver m

corpuscle /'kɔːrpʌsəl ‖'kɔːpʌsəl/ n corpúsculo m

corral /kə'ræl ‖kʊ'rɑːl/ n corral m

correct¹ /kə'rekt/ vt corregir*

correct² adj correcto

correction /kə'rekʃən/ n corrección f

correctly /kə'rektli/ adv correctamente

correlate /'kɔːrəleit ‖'kɒr-/ vi **to ~ (with sth)** estar* correlacionado (con algo)

correlation /,kɔːrə'leiʃən ‖,kɒrə'leiʃən/ n correlación f (frml)

correspond /'kɔːrə'spɑːnd ‖,kɒrə'spɒnd/ vi [1] (tally) **to ~ (with sth)** corresponderse or concordar* (con algo) **(b)** (be equivalent) **to ~ (to sth)** equivaler* or corresponder (a algo) [2] (communicate by letter) **to ~ (with sb)** mantener* correspondencia (con algn)

correspondence /'kɔːrə'spɑːndəns ‖,kɒrə'spɒndəns/ n [1] (agreement) correspondencia f [2] (letters, letter writing) correspondencia f

correspondence course n curso m por correspondencia

correspondent /ˌkɔːrəˈspɑːndənt ‖ˌkɒrəˈspɒndənt/ n (a) (letter writer) corresponsal mf (b) (Journ) corresponsal mf

corridor /ˈkɔːrədər ‖ˈkɒrɪdɔː(r)/ n pasillo m, corredor m

corroborate /kəˈrɑːbəreɪt ‖kəˈrɒbəreɪt/ vt corroborar

corrode /kəˈrəʊd/ vt corroer*
■ ~ vi corroerse*

corrosion /kəˈrəʊʒən/ n (a) (action) corrosión f (b) (substance) herrumbre f, orín m

corrosive /kəˈrəʊsɪv/ adj corrosivo

corrugated /ˈkɔːrəgeɪtəd ‖ˈkɒrəgeɪtɪd/ adj ondulado; ~ cardboard cartón m corrugado; ~ iron chapa f de zinc, calamina f (Chi, Per)

corrupt¹ /kəˈrʌpt/ vt (deprave) corromper; (bribe) sobornar; (Comput) corromper

corrupt² adj ⟨person/government⟩ corrompido, corrupto

corruption /kəˈrʌpʃən/ n corrupción f

corset /ˈkɔːrsət ‖ˈkɔːsɪt/ n (often pl) corsé m

cosmetic /kɑːzˈmetɪk ‖kɒzˈmetɪk/ adj (a) (beautifying) (before n) ⟨powder/cream⟩ cosmético; ~ surgery cirugía f estética (b) (superficial) ⟨reforms/changes⟩ superficial

cosmetics /kɑːzˈmetɪks ‖kɒzˈmetɪks/ pl n cosméticos mpl

cosmic /ˈkɑːzmɪk ‖ˈkɒzmɪk/ adj cósmico

cosmonaut /ˈkɑːzmənɔːt ‖ˈkɒzmənɔːt/ n cosmonauta mf

cosmopolitan /ˌkɑːzməˈpɑːlətn̩ ‖ˌkɒzməˈpɒlɪtn̩/ adj cosmopolita

cosmos /ˈkɑːzməʊs ‖ˈkɒzmɒs/ n the ~ el cosmos

cost¹ /kɔːst ‖kɒst/ n [1] (a) (expense) (often pl) costo m (esp AmL), coste m (Esp); to cut ~s reducir* los gastos (b) costs pl (Law) costas fpl [2] (loss, sacrifice): she helped me out, at great ~ to herself sacrificó mucho al ayudarme; at all ~s a toda costa

cost² vt [1] (past & past p cost) (a) «article/service» costar* (b) (cause to lose) costar*; one slip ~ him the title un error le costó el título [2] (past & past p costed) (calculate cost of) calcular el costo or (Esp) coste de

co-star /ˈkəʊstɑːr ‖ˈkəʊstɑː(r)/ n coprotagonista mf

Costa Rica /ˌkɔːstəˈriːkə ‖ˌkɒstəˈriːkə/ n Costa Rica f

Costa Rican¹ /ˌkɔːstəˈriːkən ‖ˌkɒstəˈriːkən/ adj costarricense

Costa Rican² n costarricense mf

cost-effective /ˈkɔːstɪˈfektɪv ‖ˌkɒstɪˈfektɪv/ adj rentable

costly /ˈkɔːstli ‖ˈkɒstli/ adj -lier, -liest costoso

cost: of living n costo m or (Esp) coste m de (la) vida; ~ price n precio m de costo or (Esp) de coste

costume /ˈkɑːstuːm ‖ˈkɒstjuːm/ n (a) (style of dress) traje m; (for parties, disguise) disfraz m (b) (wardrobe) (Theat) vestuario m; (individual outfit) traje m (c) (swimming ~) traje m de baño

costume jewelry, (BrE) **costume jewellery** n bisutería f, alhajas fpl de fantasía

cosy¹ /ˈkəʊzi/ adj cosier, cosiest (BrE) ▶ cozy¹

cosy² n (pl cosies) (BrE) ▶ cozy²

cot /kɑːt ‖kɒt/ n (a) (campbed) (AmE) catre m (b) (for child) (BrE) cuna f, cama f (con barandas)

cottage /ˈkɑːtɪdʒ ‖ˈkɒtɪdʒ/ n casita f

cottage cheese n requesón m

cotton /ˈkɑːtn̩ ‖ˈkɒtn̩/ n (a) (cloth) algodón m; (before n) ⟨dress/sheet/print⟩ de algodón (b) (thread) (BrE) hilo m (de coser) (c) (absorbent ~) (AmE) algodón m (hidrófilo)

cotton wool n (BrE) algodón m (hidrófilo)

couch /kaʊtʃ/ n (sofa) sofá m; (doctor's, psychoanalyst's) diván m

couch potato /kaʊtʃ/ n (colloq) teleadicto, -ta m,f (fam)

cough¹ /kɔːf ‖kɒf/ n tos f; (before n) ~ mixture jarabe m para la tos

cough² vi toser
■ ~ vt ~ (up) expectorar
■ **cough up** [1] [v + adv + o] (pay) (colloq) ⟨money⟩ soltar* (fam), aflojar (fam) [2] [v + adv] (pay) soltar* la plata or (Esp) la pasta or (AmL tb) la lana (fam)

could /kʊd/ v mod [1] past of CAN³ [2] (indicating possibility) poder*; I would help you if I ~ te ayudaría si pudiera; you ~ have killed us all! ¡podrías or podías habernos matado a todos!; you ~ be right puede (ser) que tengas razón [3] (a) (asking permission): ~ I use your bathroom? ¿podría or me permitiría pasar al baño? (b) (in requests): ~ you sign here please? ¿quiere firmar aquí, por favor? [4] (a) (in suggestions) poder*; you ~ try doing it this way podrías tratar de hacerlo de esta manera (b) (indicating strong desire) poder*; I ~ have killed her la hubiera matado, la podría or podía haber matado

couldn't /ˈkʊdn̩t/ = **could not**

council /ˈkaʊnsəl/ n (a) (advisory group) consejo m (b) (Govt) ayuntamiento m, municipio m; ~ housing (BrE) viviendas de alquiler subvencionadas por el ayuntamiento

councillor n (BrE) ▶ COUNCILOR

Council of Europe n the ~ ~ ~ el Consejo de Europa

councilor, (BrE) **councillor** /ˈkaʊnsələr ‖ˈkaʊnsələ(r)/ n concejal, -jala m,f

council tax n (in UK) ≈ contribución f (municipal or inmobiliaria)

counsel¹ /ˈkaʊnsəl/ n (pl ~) (no art) (Law) abogado, -da m,f; ~ for the defense abogado defensor, abogada defensora m,f; ~ for the prosecution fiscal mf

counsel² vt, (BrE) **-ll-** (fml) aconsejar

counseling, (BrE) **counselling** /ˈkaʊnsəlɪŋ/ n (Educ, Psych) orientación f psicopedagógica

counselor, (BrE) **counsellor** /ˈkaʊnsələr ‖ˈkaʊnsələ(r)/ n (a) (Educ, Psych) consejero, -ra m,f, orientador, -dora m,f (b) (AmE Law) abogado, -da m,f

count¹ /kaʊnt/ n [1] (a) (act of counting) recuento m, cómputo m; (of votes) escrutinio m, recuento m, cómputo m, conteo m (Andes, Ven); to keep/lose ~ of sth llevar/perder* la cuenta de algo (b) (total) total m; the final ~ (of votes) el recuento or ⋯⋯⋯

cómputo final **2** (point): **it has been criticized on several ~s** ha sido criticado por varios motivos **3** (rank) conde *m*

count² *vt* **1** (enumerate, add up) contar* **2** (include) contar*; **not ~ing the driver** sin contar al conductor **3** (consider) considerar; **to ~ oneself lucky** darse* por afortunado

■ ~ *vi* **1** (enumerate) contar* **2** (be valid, matter) contar*; **that doesn't ~** eso no cuenta *or* no vale; **every minute ~s** cada minuto cuenta

■ **count for** [*v + prep + o*] contar*; **your opinion ~s for a great deal/won't ~ for much** tu opinión importa mucho/no va a contar mucho

■ **count on** [*v + prep + o*] **(a)** (rely on) ⟨*friend/help*⟩ contar* con **(b)** (expect) esperar; **we hadn't ~ed on that happening** no esperábamos que fuera a pasar eso

■ **count out 1** [*v + o + adv*]: **you can ~ me out** a mí no me incluyan, no cuenten conmigo **2** [*v + o + adv, v + adv + o*] ⟨*money/objects*⟩ contar* (*uno por uno*)

countdown /'kaʊntdaʊn/ *n* cuenta *f* atrás *or* regresiva, conteo *m* regresivo (Andes, Ven)

counter¹ /'kaʊntər ‖'kaʊntə(r)/ *n* **1** (in shop) mostrador *m*; (in café) barra *f*; (in bank, post office) ventanilla *f*; (in kitchen) (AmE) encimera *f* **2** (Games) ficha *f*

counter² *vt* **(a)** (oppose) ⟨*deficiency/trend*⟩ contrarrestar **(b)** (in debate) ⟨*idea/statement*⟩ rebatir, refutar; **to ~ THAT** responder *or* replicar* QUE

counter³ *adv*: **to run** *o* **go ~ to sth** ser* contrario a *or* oponerse* a algo

counteract /'kaʊntər'ækt/ *vt* contrarrestar

counterattack¹ /'kaʊntərə'tæk/ *n* contraataque *m*

counterattack² *vi* contraatacar*

counterbalance /'kaʊntər'bæləns ‖'kaʊntə,bæləns/ *n* contrapeso *m*

counterclockwise /'kaʊntər'klɑːkwaɪz ‖,kaʊntə'klɒkwaɪz/ *adj/adv* (AmE) en sentido contrario a las agujas del reloj

counterfeit¹ /'kaʊntərfɪt ‖'kaʊntəfɪt/ *n* falsificación *f*

counterfeit² *adj* ⟨*money*⟩ falso

counter: **~foil** *n* talón *m* (AmL), matriz *f* (Esp); **~part** *n* (person) homólogo, -ga *m,f*; (thing) equivalente *m*; **~point** *n* (Mus) contrapunto *m*; **~productive** /'kaʊntərprə'dʌktɪv ‖,kaʊntəprə'dʌktɪv/ *adj* contraproducente

countess /'kaʊntəs ‖'kaʊntɪs/ *n* condesa *f*

countless /'kaʊntləs ‖'kaʊntlɪs/ *adj* ⟨*stars/hours*⟩ incontables, innumerables

country /'kʌntri/ *n* (*pl* **-tries**) **1** (nation) país *m*; (people) pueblo *m*; (native land) patria *f* **2** (rural area) **the ~** el campo; (*before n*) ⟨*people*⟩ del campo; ⟨*cottage*⟩ de campo **3** (region) terreno *m* **4** (Mus) (música *f*) country *m*

country: **~-and-western** /'kʌntriən'westərn

~-and-western /'kʌntriən'westərn/ *n* (música *f*) country *m*; **~ dancing** *n* (esp BrE) danzas *fpl* folklóricas; **~ house** *n* casa *f* solariega; **~man** /'kʌntrimən/ *n* (*pl* **-men** /-mən/) (fellow ~man) (liter) compatriota *m*; **~side** *n* campiña *f*, campo *m*; **~wide** /'kʌntri'waɪd/ *adj/adv* a escala nacional

county /'kaʊnti/ *n* (*pl* **-ties**) condado *m*

county: **~ council** *n* (in UK) corporación *de gobierno a nivel de condado*; **~ court** *n* (in US) juzgado *m* comarcal; (in UK) juzgado *m* comarcal (*que conoce de causas de derecho civil*)

coup /kuː/ *n* (*pl* **~s** /kuːz/) **1** (successful action) golpe *m* maestro **2** (~ **d'état**) /deɪtɑː/ (Pol) golpe *m* (de estado)

couple¹ /'kʌpəl/ *n* **1** (two people) (+ *sing o pl vb*) pareja *f*; **a married ~** un matrimonio **2** (two or small number): **a ~ (of sth)** (+ *pl vb*) un par (de algo)

couple² *vt* **(a)** (connect) (Rail) enganchar; ⟨*theories/events*⟩ asociar; **to ~ sth/sb WITH sth/sb** asociar algo/a algn CON algo/algn **(b)** (combine) (*often pass*): **the fall in demand, ~d with competition from abroad** el descenso de la demanda, unido a la competencia extranjera

coupon /'kuːpɑn ‖'kuːpɒn/ *n* **(a)** (voucher — for discount) vale *m*; (— in rationing) cupón *m* de racionamiento **(b)** (form — in advertisement) cupón *m*; (— for competition) boleto *m*

courage /'kʌrɪdʒ ‖'kʌrɪdʒ/ *n* valor *m*, coraje *m*

courageous /kə'reɪdʒəs/ *adj* ⟨*person*⟩ valiente, corajudo; ⟨*words*⟩ valiente; ⟨*act*⟩ valeroso

courgette /kʊr'ʒet ‖kɔː'ʒet/ *n* (BrE) ▶ ZUCCHINI

courier /'kʊriər ‖'kʊriə(r)/ *n* **(a)** (guide) guía *mf* **(b)** (messenger) (BrE) mensajero, -ra *m,f*, correo *mf*, rutero, -ra *m,f*

course /kɔːrs ‖kɔːs/ *n* **1 (a)** (of river) curso *m*; (of road) recorrido *m* **(b)** (way of proceeding): **the best ~ of action** las mejores medidas que se pueden tomar **(c)** (progress, direction) (*no pl*): **in the normal ~ of events** normalmente; **in due ~** a su debido tiempo; **it changed the ~ of history** cambió el curso de la historia **2 of course** claro, desde luego, por supuesto; **of ~ not** claro *or* por supuesto que no **3** (Aviat, Naut) rumbo *m*; **to go off ~** desviarse* de rumbo; **to change ~** cambiar de rumbo **4 (a)** (Educ) curso *m*; **~ IN/ON sth** curso DE/SOBRE algo; **to take a ~** hacer* un curso **(b)** (Med) **a ~ of treatment** un tratamiento **5** (part of a meal) plato *m*; **main ~** plato principal *or* fuerte; **a three-~ meal** una comida de dos platos y postre **6** (Sport) (race~) hipódromo *m*, pista *f* (de carreras); (golf ~) campo *m or* (CS *tb*) cancha *f* (de golf)

court¹ /kɔːrt ‖kɔːt/ *n* **1** (Law) **(a)** (tribunal) tribunal *m*; **to take sb to ~** demandar a algn, llevar a algn a juicio; (*before n*) **~ case** causa *f*, juicio *m* **(b)** (building) juzgado *m* **2** (of sovereign) corte *f* **3** (Sport) cancha *f* (AmL), pista *f* (Esp) **4** (courtyard) patio *m*

court² /kɔːt/ *vt* (a) ‹*girl*› (dated) cortejar (ant), hacerle* la corte a (ant) (b) (seek) ‹*danger/favor*› buscar*; ‹*danger*› exponerse* a

courteous /ˈkɜːtiəs ‖ˈkɜːtiəs/ *adj* cortés

courtesy /ˈkɜːrtəsi ‖ˈkɜːtəsi/ *n* cortesía *f*; ~ **of** por atención de

courthouse /ˈkɔːrthaʊs ‖ˈkɔːthaʊs/ *n* juzgado *m*

courtier /ˈkɔːrtiər ‖ˈkɔːtiə(r)/ *n* cortesano, -na *m,f*

court-martial¹ /ˈkɔːrtˈmɑːrʃəl ‖ˌkɔːtˈmɑːʃəl/ *n* (*pl* **courts-martial** /ˈkɔːrts-/) consejo *m* de guerra

court-martial² *vt*, (BrE) **-ll-** formarle consejo de guerra a

court: ~**room** *n* sala *f* (*de un tribunal*); ~ **shoe** *n* (BrE) zapato *m* (de) salón; ~**yard** *n* patio *m*

cousin /ˈkʌzn̩/ *n* primo, -ma *m,f*; **first** ~ primo hermano *or* carnal, prima hermana *or* carnal; **second** ~ primo segundo, prima segunda

cove /kəʊv/ *n* cala *f*, caleta *f*

covenant /ˈkʌvənənt/ *n* pacto *m*

cover¹ /ˈkʌvər ‖ˈkʌvə(r)/ *n* [1] (a) (lid, casing) tapa *f*, cubierta *f*; (for cushion, sofa, typewriter) funda *f*; (for book) forro *m* (b) **covers** *pl* (bedclothes) the ~s las mantas, las cobijas (AmL), las frazadas (AmL)

[2] (of book) tapa *f*, cubierta *f*; (of magazine) portada *f*, carátula *f* (Andes); (front ~) portada *f*; **to read sth from** ~ **to** ~ leer* algo de cabo a rabo

[3] (a) (shelter, protection): **to take** ~ guarecerse*, ponerse* a cubierto; **to run for** ~ correr a guarecerse *or* a ponerse a cubierto; **under** ~ **of darkness** al abrigo de la oscuridad (b) (front, pretense) tapadera *f*, pantalla *f*; **to blow sb's** ~ desenmascarar a algn

[4] (insurance) (BrE) cobertura *f*

cover² *vt* [1] (a) (overlay) cubrir*; **to be** ~**ed IN sth** estar* cubierto DE algo (b) ‹*hole/saucepan*› tapar (c) ‹*cushion*› ponerle* una funda a; ‹*book*› forrar; ‹*sofa*› tapizar*, recubrir* (d) ‹*passage/terrace*› techar, cubrir*

[2] (a) (extend over) ‹*area/floor*› cubrir*; ‹*page*› llenar (b) (travel) ‹*distance*› recorrer

[3] (a) (deal with) ‹*syllabus*› cubrir*; ‹*topic*› tratar (b) (report on) (Journ) cubrir*

[4] (a) (hide) tapar; **to** ~ **one's head** cubrirse* (la cabeza) (b) (mask) ‹*surprise/ignorance*› disimular; ‹*mistake*› ocultar

[5] (a) (guard, protect) cubrir* (b) (point gun at) apuntarle a (c) (Sport) ‹*opponent*› marcar*; ‹*shot/base*› cubrir*

[6] (Fin) (a) ‹*costs/expenses*› cubrir*; ‹*liabilities*› hacer* frente a; **will $100** ~ **it?** ¿alcanzará con 100 dólares? (b) (insurance) cubrir*

■ ~ *vi* (a) (deputize) **to** ~ FOR sb sustituir* a algn (b) (conceal truth) **to** ~ FOR sb encubrir* a algn

■ **cover up** [1] [*v* + *o* + *adv*, *v* + *adv* + *o*] (a) (cover completely) cubrir*, tapar (b) (conceal) ‹*facts/truth*› ocultar; ‹*mistake*› disimular

[2] [*v* + *adv*] (conceal error) disimular; (conceal truth) **to** ~ **up** FOR sb encubrir* a algn

coverage /ˈkʌvərɪdʒ/ *n* (Journ) cobertura *f*

cover-alls /ˈkʌvərɔːlz/ *pl n* (AmE) overol *m* (AmL), mono *m* (Esp, Méx)

covering letter /ˈkʌvərɪŋ/ *n* carta *f* adjunta

covert /ˈkəʊvərt ‖ˈkʌvət, ˈkəʊ-/ *adj* encubierto

cover-up /ˈkʌvərʌp/ *n* (of crime) encubrimiento *m*

covet /ˈkʌvət/ *vt* codiciar

cow /kaʊ/ *n* (a) (Agr) vaca *f* (b) (female whale, elephant, seal) hembra *f*

coward /ˈkaʊərd ‖ˈkaʊəd/ *n* cobarde *mf*

cowardice /ˈkaʊərdəs ‖ˈkaʊədɪs/ *n* cobardía *f*

cowardly /ˈkaʊərdli ‖ˈkaʊədli/ *adj* cobarde

cowboy /ˈkaʊbɔɪ/ *n* (in Western US) vaquero *m*; (in Wild West) vaquero *m*, cowboy *m*

cower /ˈkaʊər ‖ˈkaʊə(r)/ *vi* encogerse* (de miedo)

coworker /ˈkəʊˈwɜːrkər ‖ˈkəʊˈwɜːkə(r)/ *n* (esp AmE) (workmate) colega *mf*, compañero, -ra *m,f* de trabajo; (collaborator) colaborador, -dora *m,f*

coy /kɔɪ/ *adj* **coyer, coyest** (shy) tímido; (evasive) evasivo

coyote /kaɪˈəʊti ‖kɔɪˈəʊti/ *n* (*pl* **-otes** *or* **-ote**) coyote *m*

cozy¹, (BrE) **cosy** /ˈkəʊzi/ *adj* **cozier, coziest** (a) ‹*room*› acogedor (b) ‹*chat*› íntimo y agradable

cozy², (BrE) **cosy** *n* (*pl* **-ies**) (tea ~) cubreteteras *m*

CPA *n* (in US) = **Certified Public Accountant**

crab /kræb/ *n*(animal, meat) cangrejo *m*, jaiba *f* (AmL)

crack¹ /kræk/ *n* [1] (a) (in ice, wall, pavement) grieta *f*; (in glass, china) rajadura *f* (b) (chink, slit) rendija *f* [2] (sound — of whip, twig) chasquido *m*; (— of rifle shot) estallido *m*; (— of thunder) estruendo *m* [3] (blow) golpe *m* [4] (instant): **at the** ~ **of dawn** al amanecer [5] (attempt) (colloq) intento *m*; **to have a** ~ **at sth** intentar algo [6] (colloq) (wisecrack) comentario *m* socarrón [7] (drug) crack *m*

crack² *adj* (*before n*) ‹*shot/troops*› de primera

crack³ *vt* [1] ‹*cup/glass*› rajar; ‹*ground/earth/skin*› agrietar; **he** ~**ed a rib** se fracturó una costilla

[2] (a) (break open) ‹*egg/nut*› cascar*; ‹*safe*› forzar*; ‹*drugs ring/spy ring*› desmantelar (b) (decipher, solve) ‹*code*› descifrar; ‹*problem*› resolver*

[3] (make cracking sound with) ‹*whip*› hacer*) chasquear; ‹*finger/knuckle*› hacer* crujir

[4] (hit sharply) pegar*

[5] ‹*joke*› (colloq) contar*

■ ~ *vi* [1] (a) ‹*cup/glass*› rajarse; «*rock/paint/skin*» agrietarse (b) (make cracking sound) «*whip*» chasquear; «*bones/twigs*» crujir (c) ‹*voice*› quebrarse* (d) (break down): **she** ~**ed under the strain** sufrió una crisis nerviosa a causa de la tensión

[2] (be active, busy): **to get** ~**ing** (colloq) poner(se)* manos a la obra

■ **crack down** [*v* + *adv*] **to** ~ **down** ON sb/sth tomar medidas enérgicas CONTRA algn/algo

■ **crack up** [*v* + *adv*] (a) (break down) (colloq) «*person*» sufrir un ataque de nervios, sucumbir a la presión (b) (burst out laughing) (colloq) soltar* una carcajada

cracked /krækt/ *adj* (a) ‹*cup/glass*› rajado; ‹*rib*› fracturado; ‹*wall/ceiling*› con grietas; ‹*lips*› partido; ‹*skin*› agrietado (b) (crazy) (colloq) ‹*person*› loco, chiflado (fam) (c) ‹*voice*› cascado

cracker /'krækər ‖'krækə(r)/ n [1] (biscuit) cracker f, galleta f (salada) [2] (a) (fire∼) petardo m (b) (BrE) sorpresa f (que estalla al abrirla) [3] (Comput colloq) intruso, -sa m,f

crackle¹ /'krækəl/ vi «fire» crepitar; «twigs/paper» crujir

crackle² n (of twigs, paper) crujido m; (of fire) chisporroteo m

cradle¹ /'kreɪdl/ n cuna f

cradle² vt «baby» acunar, mecer*

craft /kræft ‖krɑːft/ n [1] (a) (trade) oficio m; (skill) arte m (b) **crafts** pl artesanía f; see also ART 1B [2] (guile, deceit) (liter) artimañas fpl [3] (pl ∼) (Naut) embarcación f; (Aerosp, Aviat) nave f

craftsman /'kræftsmən ‖'krɑːftsmən/ n (pl **-men** /mən/) artesano m, artífice m

crafty /'kræfti ‖'krɑːfti/ adj **-tier, -tiest** «person» astuto; «methods/tactics» hábil

craggy /'krægi/ adj **-gier, -giest** escarpado; he had a ∼, weather-beaten face tenía un rostro curtido y de facciones bien marcadas

cram /kræm/ **-mm-** vt (stuff) meter; the room was ∼med with books la habitación estaba abarrotada de libros; I ∼med three meetings into one morning logré asistir a tres reuniones en una mañana
■ ∼ vi (for exam) empollar (Esp fam), zambutir (Méx), tragar* (RPl fam), matearse (Chi fam), empacarse* (Col fam)

cramp¹ /kræmp/ n (in leg) calambre m, rampa f (Esp); stomach ∼s retorcijones mpl or (Esp) retortijones mpl en el estómago

cramp² vt (limit) «work/progress» entorpecer*; to ∼ sb's style cortarle los vuelos a algn

cramped /kræmpt/ adj «handwriting» apretado; they work in ∼ conditions están muy estrechos en el trabajo; they live in ∼ conditions viven hacinados

cranberry /'kræn,beri ‖'krænbəri/ n (pl **-ries**) arándano m (rojo y agrio)

crane¹ /kreɪn/ n [1] (for lifting) grúa f [2] (Zool) grulla f

crane² vt: to ∼ one's neck estirar el cuello

crank /kræŋk/ n [1] (a) (Mech Eng) cigüeñal m (b) ∼ (**handle**) (Auto) manivela f (de arranque) [2] (colloq) (a) (eccentric) maniático, -ca m,f (b) (bad-tempered person) (AmE) cascarrabias mf

cranny /'kræni/ n (pl **-nies**) ranura f; ▶ NOOK

crap /kræp/ n (a) (excrement) (vulg) mierda f (vulg) (b) (nonsense) (sl) estupideces fpl, gilipolleces fpl (Esp fam o vulg), pendejadas fpl (AmL exc CS fam), huevadas fpl (Andes, Ven vulg), boludeces fpl (Col, RPl vulg)

crash¹ /kræʃ/ n (a) (loud noise) estrépito m (b) (collision, accident) accidente m, choque m (c) (financial failure) crac m, crack m

crash² vt [1] (smash): he ∼ed the car tuvo un accidente con el coche, chocó [2] (colloq) to ∼ a party colarse* en una fiesta (fam)
■ ∼ vi (a) (collide) to ∼ (INTO sth) estrellarse or chocar* (CONTRA algo) (b) (make loud noise) «thunder» retumbar; the dishes ∼ed to the floor los platos se cayeron al suelo estrepitosamente (c) (Fin) «shares» caer* a pique

crash³ adj (before n) «program/course» intensivo; ∼ diet régimen m muy estricto

crash: ∼ **barrier** n barrera f de protección; ∼ **helmet** n casco m (protector); ∼**-landing** /'kræʃ'lændɪŋ/ n aterrizaje m forzoso

crate /kreɪt/ n cajón m (de embalaje), jaba f (Chi)

crater /'kreɪtər ‖'kreɪtə(r)/ n cráter m

cravat /krə'væt/ n pañuelo m de cuello (de caballero)

crave /kreɪv/ vt «admiration» ansiar*; «affection» tener* ansias de; «food/drink» morirse* por (fam)

craving /'kreɪvɪŋ/ n (a) (strong desire) ansias fpl (b) (in pregnancy) antojo m

crawfish /'krɔːfɪʃ/ n (pl **-fish** or **-fishes**) ▶ CRAYFISH

crawl¹ /krɔːl/ vi [1] (a) (creep) arrastrarse; «baby» gatear, ir* a gatas; «insect» andar* (b) (go slowly) «traffic/train» avanzar* muy lentamente [2] (teem): the beach was ∼ing with tourists la playa estaba plagada de turistas [3] (demean oneself) (colloq) arrastrarse

crawl² n [1] (slow pace) (no pl): to go at a ∼ avanzar* muy lentamente [2] (swimming stroke) crol m

crayfish /'kreɪfɪʃ/ n (pl **-fish** or **-fishes**) (freshwater) ástaco m, cangrejo m de río; (marine) langosta f (pequeña), cigala f

crayon /'kreɪɑːn ‖'kreɪən/ n (pencil) lápiz m de color; (wax ∼) crayola® f, crayón m (Méx, RPl), lápiz m de cera (Chi)

craze /kreɪz/ n (fashion) moda f; (fad) manía f

crazy /'kreɪzi/ adj **-zier, -ziest** loco; to go ∼ volverse* loco; to be ∼ ABOUT o (AmE) FOR o (AmE) OVER sb estar* loco POR algn (fam)

creak /kriːk/ vi «door» chirriar*; «bedsprings/floorboards/joints» crujir

cream¹ /kriːm/ n [1] (Culin) crema f (de leche) (esp AmL), nata f (Esp) [2] (lotion) crema f [3] (elite) the ∼ of society la flor y nata de la sociedad [4] (color) color m crema

cream² adj color crema adj inv

cream³ vt «butter/sugar» batir (hasta obtener una consistencia cremosa); ∼ed potatoes puré m de papas or (Esp) patatas

cream cheese n queso m crema (AmL), queso m para untar (Esp)

creamer /'kriːmər ‖'kriːmə(r)/ n [1] (jug) (AmE) jarrita f para crema [2] (powder) leche f en polvo

creamy /'kriːmi/ adj **-mier, -miest** (containing cream) con crema; (smooth) cremoso

crease¹ /kriːs/ n (in paper, clothes) arruga f; (in trousers) raya f, pliegue m (Méx, Ven)

crease² vi arrugarse*
■ ∼ vt «clothes» arrugar*; «paper» doblar, plegar*

create /kri'eɪt/ vt crear; «impression» producir*

creation /kri'eɪʃən/ n creación f

creative /kri'eɪtɪv/ adj creativo

creativity /ˌkriːeɪ'tɪvəti/ n creatividad f

creator /kri'eɪtər ‖kri'eɪtə(r)/ n creador, -dora m,f

creature /'kriːtʃər ‖'kriːtʃə(r)/ n (a) (animate being) criatura f; ∼ sea ∼ animal m marino (b) (person) ser m, criatura f

creche, crèche /kreʃ/ n (a) (hospital for foundlings) (AmE) orfanato m, orfelinato m,

orfanatorio *m* **(b)** (day nursery) (BrE) guardería *f*
(infantil) (*puede ser en el lugar de trabajo para
los empleados etc.*)

credentials /krɪ'dentʃəlz ‖krɪ'denʃəlz/ *pl n*
(of ambassador) cartas *fpl* credenciales; (references)
referencias *fpl*; (identifying papers) documentos *mpl*
(de identidad)

credibility /ˌkredə'bɪləti/ *n* credibilidad *f*

credible /'kredəbəl/ *adj* creíble

credit¹ /'kredət ‖'kredɪt/ *n* $\boxed{1}$ (Fin) **(a)** (in store)
crédito *m*; **on ∼** a crédito **(b)** (in banking): **to keep
one's account in ∼** mantener* un saldo positivo;
(*before n*) **∼ balance** saldo *m* positivo; **∼ limit**
límite *m* de crédito **(c)** (on balance sheet) saldo *m*
acreedor *or* a favor
$\boxed{2}$ (honor, recognition) mérito *m*; **Jim must take the
∼ for the excellent organization** la excelente
organización es obra de Jim; **your children are a
∼ to you** puedes estar orgulloso de tus hijos
$\boxed{3}$ (Educ) **(a)** (for study) crédito *m* (*unidad de valor
de una asignatura dentro de un programa de
estudios*) **(b)** (grade) ≈notable *m*
$\boxed{4}$ **credits** *pl* (Cin, TV, Video) créditos *mpl*

credit² *vt* $\boxed{1}$ **to ∼ money to an account** abonar
or ingresar dinero en una cuenta $\boxed{2}$ **(a)** (ascribe
to) **please, ∼ me with some intelligence**
reconóceme algo de inteligencia, por favor; **they
are ∼ed with having invented the game** se les
atribuye la invención del juego **(b)** (believe) creer*

credit card *n* tarjeta *f* de crédito

creditor /'kredətər ‖'kredɪtə(r)/ *n* acreedor,
-dora *m,f*

creed /kriːd/ *n* credo *m*

creek /kriːk/ *n* **(a)** (stream) (AmE) arroyo *m*,
riachuelo *m* **(b)** (inlet) (BrE) cala *f*

creep¹ /kriːp/ (*past & past p* **crept**) *vi* (+ *adv
compl*) **(a)** (crawl) arrastrarse **(b)** (move stealthily):
to ∼ into a room entrar en un cuarto
sigilosamente; **a note of suspicion crept into his
voice** se empezó a notar un elemento de sospecha
en su voz

creep² *n* (colloq) **(a)** (unpleasant person) asqueroso,
-sa *m,f* **(b)** (favor-seeking person) adulador, -dora
m,f, pelota *mf* (Esp fam), chupamedias *mf* (CS, Ven
fam), lambiscón, -cona *m,f* (Méx fam), lambón,
-bona *m,f* (Col fam)

creeper /'kriːpər ‖'kriːpə(r)/ *n* planta *f*
trepadora

cremate /'kriːmeɪt ‖krɪ'meɪt/ *vt* incinerar,
cremar

cremation /krɪ'meɪʃən/ *n* incineración *f*,
cremación *f*

crematorium /ˌkriːmə'tɔːriəm
‖ˌkremə'tɔːriəm/ *n* (*pl* **-riums** *or* **-ria** /-riə/)
crematorio *m*

crepe, crêpe /kreɪp/ *n* $\boxed{1}$ (fabric) crep *m*, crepé
m $\boxed{2}$ (pancake) (Culin) crep *m*, crêpe *f*, panqueque
m (AmC, CS), crepa *f* (Méx)

crepe paper *n* papel *m* crepé *or* crep

crept /krept/ *past & past p of* CREEP¹

crescendo /krə'ʃendəʊ ‖krɪ'ʃendəʊ/ *n* (*pl*
-dos) (Mus) crescendo *m*; (climax) punto *m*
culminante

crescent /'kresn̩t/ *n* $\boxed{1}$ (moon) creciente *m*
$\boxed{2}$ **(a)** (shape) media luna *f* **(b)** (street) *calle en
forma de media luna*

cress /kres/ *n* mastuerzo *m*

crest /krest/ *n* $\boxed{1}$ (Zool) (of skin) cresta *f*; (of
feathers) penacho *m* $\boxed{2}$ (in heraldry) emblema *m*,
divisa *f* $\boxed{3}$ (of wave) cresta *f*; (of mountain) cima *f*

crestfallen /'krest,fɔːlən/ *adj* alicaído

crevice /'krevəs ‖'krevɪs/ *n* grieta *f*

crew /kruː/ *n* **(a)** (Aviat, Naut) tripulación *f* **(b)**
(team) equipo *m*; **film ∼** (Cin) equipo *m* de rodaje
(c) (gang, band) banda *f*, pandilla *f*

crew: ∼ cut *n* pelo *m* cortado al rape; **∼
neck** *n* cuello *m* redondo

crib /krɪb/ *n* $\boxed{1}$ **(a)** (child's bed) (AmE) cuna *f* **(b)**
(Nativity scene) nacimiento *m*, pesebre *m*, belén *m*
(Esp) $\boxed{2}$ (Agr) **(a)** (manger) pesebre *m* **(b)** (for storing
grain) (AmE) granero *m*

crick /krɪk/ *vt*: **to ∼ one's neck** hacer* un mal
movimiento con el cuello

cricket /'krɪkət ‖'krɪkɪt/ *n* $\boxed{1}$ (Zool) grillo *m*
$\boxed{2}$ (Sport) críquet *m*

cricketer /'krɪkətər ‖'krɪkɪtə(r)/ *n* jugador,
-dora *m,f* de críquet

crime /kraɪm/ *n* **(a)** (wrongful act) delito *m*;
(murder) crimen *m* **(b)** (criminal activity) delincuencia
f; **∼ wave** ola *f* delictiva

criminal¹ /'krɪmənl̩ ‖'krɪmml̩/ *n* delincuente
mf; (serious offender) criminal *mf*

criminal² *adj* ‹act› delictivo; ‹organization/
mind› criminal; **∼ court** juzgado *m* en lo penal;
∼ law derecho *m* penal; **∼ offense** delito *m*

criminal record *n* antecedentes *mpl* penales,
prontuario *m* (CS)

crimson¹ /'krɪmzən/ *n* carmesí *m*

crimson² *adj* carmesí *adj inv*

cringe /krɪndʒ/ *vi* **(a)** (shrink, cower) encogerse*
(b) (grovel) arrastrarse

crinkle /'krɪŋkəl/ **∼ (up)** *vt* arrugar*
■ **∼** *vi* arrugarse*

cripple¹ /'krɪpəl/ *n* lisiado, -da *m,f*

cripple² *vt* **(a)** (lame, disable): **he was ∼d for life**
quedó lisiado de por vida; **he's ∼d with arthritis**
la artritis lo tiene casi inmovilizado **(b)** (make
inactive, ineffective) ‹ship/plane› inutilizar*;
‹industry› paralizar*

crippling /'krɪplɪŋ/ *adj* ‹costs/debts› agobiante;
‹losses/strike› de consecuencias catastróficas;
‹pain› atroz

crisis /'kraɪsəs ‖'kraɪsɪs/ *n* (*pl* **-ses** /-siːz/)
crisis *f*; (*before n*) **to reach ∼ point** hacer* crisis

crisp¹ /krɪsp/ *adj* **-er, -est** $\boxed{1}$ **(a)** (crunchy)
‹toast/bacon› crujiente, crocante (RPl); ‹lettuce›
fresco; ‹apple/snow› crujiente **(b)** ‹sheets› limpio
y almidonado **(c)** (cold) ‹air› frío y vigorizante
$\boxed{2}$ (brisk, concise) ‹manner› seco; ‹style› escueto

crisp² *n* (potato ∼) (BrE) papa *f or* (Esp) patata *f*
frita (*de bolsa*), papa *f* chip (Ur)

crisscross¹ /'krɪskrɔːs ‖'krɪskrɒs/ *adj*
entrecruzado

crisscross² *vt* entrecruzar*

criterion /kraɪ'tɪriən ‖kraɪ'tɪəriən/ *n* (*pl* **-ria**
/-riə/) criterio *m*

critic /'krɪtɪk/ *n* (Art, Theat, Lit) crítico, -ca *m,f*;
(detractor) detractor, -tora *m,f*

critical /'krɪtɪkəl/ *adj* $\boxed{1}$ ‹remark/report›
crítico $\boxed{2}$ **(a)** (very serious) ‹condition/shortage›
crítico **(b)** (crucial) ‹period› crítico

critically /'krɪtɪkli/ adv **1** ⟨ill⟩ gravemente **2** (a) (as a critic): she looked ~ at her reflection miró con ojo crítico la imagen que le devolvía el espejo (b) (censoriously): she spoke rather ~ of him habló de él en tono de crítica

criticism /'krɪtəsɪzəm ‖'krɪtɪsɪzəm/ n crítica f

criticize /'krɪtəsaɪz ‖'krɪtɪsaɪz/ vt criticar*

croak¹ /krəʊk/ n (of frog) croar m; (of raven) graznido m; (of person) voz f ronca

croak² vi «frog» croar; «raven» graznar; «person» hablar con voz ronca
■ ~ vt decir* con voz ronca

Croat /'krəʊæt/ n croata mf

Croatia /krəʊ'eɪʃə/ n Croacia f

Croatian /krəʊ'eɪʃən/ adj croata

crochet¹ /krəʊ'ʃeɪ ‖'krəʊʃeɪ/ vt tejer a crochet or a ganchillo; (before n) ~ hook aguja f de crochet, ganchillo m, crochet m (Chi)

crochet² n crochet m, ganchillo m

crockery /'krɑːkəri ‖'krɒkəri/ n vajilla f, loza f

crocodile /'krɑːkədaɪl ‖'krɒkədaɪl/ n cocodrilo m

crocus /'krəʊkəs/ n (pl -cuses) azafrán m de primavera

crook /krʊk/ n sinvergüenza mf

crooked /'krʊkəd ‖'krʊkɪd/ adj (a) ⟨line/legs⟩ torcido, chueco (AmL); ⟨back⟩ encorvado; ⟨path⟩ sinuoso (b) (dishonest) (colloq) ⟨person/deal⟩ deshonesto, chueco (Chi, Méx fam)

crop¹ /krɑːp ‖krɒp/ n **1** (a) (quantity of produce) cosecha f (b) (type of produce) cultivo m **2** (haircut) corte m de pelo muy corto **3** (riding ~) fusta f, fuete m (AmL exc CS)

crop² -pp- vt ⟨hair⟩ cortar muy corto
■ **crop up** [v + adv] (colloq) surgir*

croquet /krəʊ'keɪ ‖'krəʊkeɪ/ n croquet m

croquette /krəʊ'ket/ n (potato ~) rollito de puré de papa envuelto en pan rallado y frito

cross¹ /krɔːs/ n **1** (a) (Relig) cruz f (b) (mark, sign) cruz f **2** (hybrid) cruce m, cruza f (AmL) **3** (Sport) (a) (in soccer) pase m cruzado (b) (in boxing) cruzado m, cross m

cross² vt **1** (go across) ⟨road/river/desert⟩ cruzar*; it ~ed my mind that ... se me ocurrió que ... **2** ⟨arms/legs⟩ cruzar* **3** ⟨plants/breeds⟩ cruzar* **4** (go against) ⟨person⟩ contrariar*; ⟨plans⟩ frustrar
■ ~ vi (a) (walk across road) cruzar* (b) «paths/letters» cruzarse*
■ v refl to ~ oneself persignarse, santiguarse*
■ **cross out** [v + o + adv, v + adv + o] tachar

cross³ adj -er, -est (esp BrE) enojado (esp AmL), enfadado (esp Esp); to get ~ enojarse (esp AmL), enfadarse (esp Esp)

cross: ~bar n (on bicycle) barra f; (of goal) larguero m; ~bow /'krɔːsbəʊ ‖'krɒsbəʊ/ n ballesta f; ~breed vt (past & past p -bred) cruzar*; ~-Channel /'krɔːs'tʃæn ‖,krɒs'tʃæn/ adj (before n) ⟨ferry/traffic⟩ que cruza el Canal de la Mancha; ~-check /'krɔːs'tʃek ‖,krɒs'tʃek/ vt

⟨facts/references⟩ verificar* (consultando otras fuentes); to ~-check sth AGAINST sth cotejar algo con algo; ~-country /'krɔːs'kʌntri ‖krɒs'kʌntri/ adj ⟨route/drive⟩ campo a través; ~-examination /'krɔːsɪg,zæmə'neɪʃən ‖,krɒsɪg,zæmɪ'neɪʃən/ n repreguntas fpl, contrainterrogación f (Chi); ~-examine /'krɔːsɪg'zæmən ‖'krɒsɪg'zæmɪn/ vt ⟨witness⟩ repreguntar; ~-eyed /'krɔːs'aɪd ‖'krɒsaɪd/ adj bizco; ~fire n fuego m cruzado

crossing /'krɔːsɪŋ ‖'krɒsɪŋ/ n **1** (across sea) travesía f, cruce m (AmS) **2** (for pedestrians) cruce m peatonal or de peatones

cross: ~-legged /'krɔːs'legd ‖,krɒs'legd/ adv con las piernas cruzadas (en el suelo); ~-purposes /'krɔːs'pɜːrpəsəz ‖,krɒs'pɜːpəsɪz/ pl n: we're (talking) at ~-purposes estamos hablando de cosas distintas; ~-question /'krɔːs'kwestʃən ‖,krɒs'kwestʃən/ vt interrogar*; ~-reference /'krɔːs'refrəns ‖,krɒs'refrəns/ n remisión f, cruce m (pl ~-roads) cruce m, encrucijada f (liter); ~ section, (BrE) ~-section /'krɔːs'sekʃən ‖,krɒs'sekʃən/ n (Biol, Eng) sección f, corte m transversal; ~walk n (AmE) cruce m peatonal or de peatones; ~word (puzzle) n crucigrama f, palabras fpl cruzadas (CS)

crotch /krɑːtʃ ‖krɒtʃ/ n entrepierna f

crotchet /'krɑːtʃət ‖'krɒtʃɪt/ n (BrE Mus) negra f

crouch /kraʊtʃ/ vi agacharse, ponerse* en cuclillas

croupier /'kruːpiər ‖'kruːpiə(r)/ n crupier mf, croupier mf

crow¹ /krəʊ/ n cuervo m; as the ~ flies en línea recta

crow² vi (a) «cock» cacarear (b) (exult) alardear

crowbar /'krəʊbɑːr ‖'krəʊbɑː(r)/ n palanca f

crowd¹ /kraʊd/ n (a) (gathering of people) muchedumbre f, multitud f; the game attracted a good ~ el partido atrajo mucho público (b) (masses, average folk) (pej): to follow the ~ seguir* (a) la manada; to stand out from the ~ destacar(se)* (c) (group, set) (colloq): they are a nice ~ son gente simpática

crowd² vi aglomerarse
■ ~ vt ⟨hall/entrance⟩ llenar, abarrotar

crowded /'kraʊdəd ‖'kraʊdɪd/ adj ⟨street/room/bus⟩ abarrotado, atestado; the beach gets very ~ la playa se llena de gente

crown¹ /kraʊn/ n **1** (of monarch) corona f **2** (top — of hill) cima f; (— of tree) copa f; (— of tooth) corona f; (— of head) coronilla f; (— of hat) copa f **3** (Fin) corona f

crown² vt **1** (make monarch) coronar **2** (be culmination of) coronar; to ~ it all, I lost my wallet y para rematarla, perdí la billetera

crown court n (in UK) juzgado m (que conoce de causas de derecho penal)

crowning /'kraʊnɪŋ/ adj (before n) ⟨success/achievement⟩ supremo, mayor

---

AmC	Central America	Arg	Argentina	Cu	Cuba	Per	Peru
AmL	Latin America	Bol	Bolivia	Ec	Ecuador	RPI	River Plate Area
AmS	South America	Chi	Chile	Esp	Spain	Ur	Uruguay
Andes	Andean Region	CS	Southern Cone	Méx	Mexico	Ven	Venezuela

crown: ~ jewels pl n joyas fpl de la corona; **~ prince** n príncipe m heredero

crow's feet pl n patas fpl de gallo

crucial /'kru:ʃəl/ adj crucial, decisivo

crucifixion /ˌkru:sə'fɪkʃən ‖ˌkru:sɪ'fɪkʃən/ n crucifixión f

crucify /'kru:səfaɪ ‖'kru:sɪfaɪ/ vt (past & past p **-fied**) crucificar*

crude /kru:d/ adj **-der, -dest (a)** (vulgar) ordinario, grosero **(b)** (unsophisticated) rudimentario, burdo **(c)** (containing impurities) (before n) ‹oil› crudo

cruel /'kru:əl/ adj **crueller, cruellest** cruel

cruelty /'kru:əlti/ n (pl **-ties**) crueldad f

cruet /'kru:ət ‖'kru:ɪt/ n (Culin) vinagrera f, aceitera f, alcuza f (Chi)

cruise¹ /kru:z/ vi ① **(a)** (Naut) hacer* un crucero **(b)** ‹police car› patrullar ② (travel at steady speed) ‹plane› volar*; ‹car› ir* (a una velocidad constante)

cruise² n crucero m

cruiser /'kru:zər ‖'kru:zə(r)/ n (warship) crucero m; (cabin ~) lancha f

crumb /krʌm/ n miga f

crumble /'krʌmbəl/ vi ‹cake/soil› desmenuzarse*; ‹wall› desmoronarse; ‹democracy/resolve› desmoronarse
■ ~ vt ‹earth/cake› desmenuzar*; ‹bread› desmigajar

crummy /'krʌmi/ adj **-mier, -miest** (colloq) malo, horrible

crumpet /'krʌmpət ‖'krʌmpɪt/ n (Culin) panecillo de levadura que se come tostado

crumple /'krʌmpəl/ vt ‹paper/clothes› arrugar*; ‹metal› abollar; **she ~d the sheet of paper into a ball** hizo una bola estrujando la hoja de papel

crunch¹ /krʌntʃ/ vt **(a)** (eat noisily) mascar*, ronchar **(b)** (crush) aplastar (haciendo crujir)

crunch² n ① (noise) crujido m ② (crisis): **when it comes to the ~** a la hora de la verdad

crunchy /'krʌntʃi/ adj **-chier, -chiest** crujiente

crusade /kru:'seɪd/ n **(a)** (Hist) also **Crusade** cruzada f **(b)** (campaign) cruzada f

crush¹ /krʌʃ/ vt ① (squash) ‹box/car/person/ fingers› aplastar; ‹grapes› prensar; ‹dress/suit› arrugar* ② (subdue) ‹resistance/enemy› aplastar

crush² n ① (crowd) (no pl) aglomeración f ② (infatuation) (colloq) enamoramiento m; **to have a ~ on sb** estar* chiflado por algn (fam)

crush barrier n valla f de protección

crushing /'krʌʃɪŋ/ adj ‹defeat› aplastante; ‹reply/contempt› apabullante

crust /krʌst/ n **(a)** (on bread) corteza f **(b)** (thin outer layer) costra f, corteza f; **the earth's ~** la corteza terrestre

crustacean /krʌ'steɪʃən/ n crustáceo m

crusty /'krʌsti/ adj **-tier, -tiest (a)** (crispy) ‹bread› crujiente **(b)** (irascible) malhumorado

crutch /krʌtʃ/ n ① (walking aid) muleta f ② (BrE) ▶ CROTCH

crux /krʌks/ n (no pl) **the ~** (of the matter) el quid (de la cuestión)

cry¹ /kraɪ/ n (pl **cries**) ① **(a)** (exclamation) grito m; **to be a far ~ from sth** ser* muy distinto

de or a algo **(b)** (of street vendor) pregón m **(c)** (no pl) (call of seagull) chillido m ② (weep) (colloq) (no pl) llanto m; **to have a ~** llorar

cry² **cries, crying, cried** vi ① (weep) llorar ② (call) ‹bird› chillar; ‹person› gritar
■ **cry out** [v + adv] **(a)** (call out) gritar **(b)** (need) **to ~ out FOR sth** pedir* algo a gritos

crypt /krɪpt/ n cripta f

cryptic /'krɪptɪk/ adj enigmático

crystal /'krɪstl/ n **(a)** (Chem) cristal m **(b)** ~ (glass) cristal m

crystal: ~ ball n bola f de cristal; **~-clear** /'krɪstl'klɪr ‖ˌkrɪstl'klɪə(r)/ adj ‹water› (liter) cristalino; ‹sound/image› nítido, claro

crystallize /'krɪstəlaɪz/ vt **(a)** (Chem, Geol) cristalizar*; ‹idea/plan› materializar* **(b)** (Culin) ‹fruit› confitar, escarchar, abrillantar (RPl), cristalizar* (Méx)

CS gas /'si:'es/ n gas m lacrimógeno

CST (in US) = **Central Standard Time**

CT = **Connecticut**

cub /kʌb/ n **(a)** (young animal) cachorro m **(b)** **Cub (Scout)** lobato m

Cuba /'kju:bə/ n Cuba f

Cuban¹ /'kju:bən/ adj cubano

Cuban² n cubano, -na m,f

cubbyhole /'kʌbihəʊl/ n cuchitril m

cube¹ /kju:b/ n (solid, shape) cubo m; (of meat, cheese) dado m, cubito m; (of sugar) terrón m

cube² vt (Math) elevar al cubo, cubicar*

cubic /'kju:bɪk/ adj (of measure, shape) cúbico; ~ **capacity** volumen m; (of engine) cilindrada f, cubicaje m

cubicle /'kju:bɪkəl/ n (in dormitory, toilets) cubículo m; (booth) cabina f; (in store) probador m

cuckoo /'ku:ku: ‖'kʊku:/ n (pl **cuckoos**) cuco m, cucú m, cuclillo m

cuckoo clock n reloj m de cuco or cucú

cucumber /'kju:kʌmbər ‖'kju:kʌmbə(r)/ n pepino m

cud /kʌd/ n: **to chew the ~** (lit) ‹cow› rumiar; ‹person› rumiar el asunto

cuddle¹ /'kʌdl/ vt abrazar*

cuddle² n abrazo m

cuddly /'kʌdli/ adj **-dlier, -dliest** adorable; ~ **toy** muñeco m de peluche

cudgel /'kʌdʒəl/ n garrote m, porra f

cue /kju:/ n ① (Mus) entrada f; (Theat) pie m; **right on ~** en el momento justo ② (in snooker) taco m

cuff¹ /kʌf/ n ① **(a)** (of sleeve) puño m; (of pants) (AmE) vuelta f or (Chi) bastilla f or (Méx) valenciana f or (RPl) botamanga f **(b)** (in phrases) **off the cuff** (as adv): **he spoke off the ~** habló improvisando; (as adj): **an off-the-~ speech** un discurso improvisado ② (blow — on side of head) cachete m, bofetón m, cachetada f (AmL); (— on head) coscorrón m

cuff² vt darle* un cachete (or coscorrón etc) a

cuff link n gemelo m or (Col) mancorna f or (Chi) collera f or (Méx) mancuernilla or mancuerna f

cuisine /kwɪ'zi:n/ n cocina f

cul-de-sac /'kʌldɪsæk/ n calle f sin salida or (Col) ciega or (RPl) cortada

cull /kʌl/ vt sacrificar de forma selectiva

culminate /ˈkʌlməneɪt ‖ˈkʌlmɪneɪt/ vi (reach peak) **to ~ IN** sth culminar EN algo

culprit /ˈkʌlprət ‖ˈkʌlprɪt/ n culpable mf

cult /kʌlt/ n (belief, worship) culto m; (sect) secta f; (before n) **~ figure** ídolo m

cultivate /ˈkʌltəveɪt ‖ˈkʌltɪveɪt/ vt cultivar

cultural /ˈkʌltʃərəl/ adj cultural

culture¹ /ˈkʌltʃər ‖ˈkʌltʃə(r)/ n **1** (civilization) cultura f; (before n) **~ shock** choque m cultural or de culturas **2** (Agr, Biol) cultivo m

culture² vt cultivar

cultured /ˈkʌltʃərd ‖ˈkʌltʃəd/ adj ⟨person/mind⟩ culto; ⟨tastes⟩ refinado

cumbersome /ˈkʌmbərsəm ‖ˈkʌmbəsəm/ adj ⟨movements/gait⟩ pesado y torpe

cumin /ˈkʌmən ‖ˈkʌmɪn/ n comino m

cumulative /ˈkjuːmjələtɪv ‖ˈkjuːmjʊlətɪv/ adj acumulativo

cunning /ˈkʌnɪŋ/ adj (a) (clever, sly) astuto; ⟨smile⟩ malicioso (b) (ingenious) ⟨device⟩ ingenioso

cup¹ /kʌp/ n **1** (a) (container, contents, cupful) taza f; **paper ~** vaso m de papel (b) (goblet) copa f **2** (trophy) copa f

cup² vt -pp-: **to ~** one's hands (to drink) ahuecar* las manos; (to shout) hacer* bocina (con las manos)

cupboard /ˈkʌbərd ‖ˈkʌbəd/ n (a) (cabinet) armario m; (in dining-room) aparador m (b) (full-length, built-in) (BrE) armario m or (AmL exc RPl) clóset m or (RPl) placard m

curable /ˈkjʊrəbəl ‖ˈkjʊərəbəl/ adj curable

curate /ˈkjʊrət ‖ˈkjʊərət/ n coadjutor m

curator /kjʊˈreɪtər ‖kjʊəˈreɪtə(r)/ n (of museum, art gallery) conservador, -dora m,f; (of exhibition) comisario, -ria m,f

curb¹ /kɜːrb ‖kɜːb/ n **1** (restraint) freno m **2** **curb**, (BrE) **kerb** (in street) bordillo m (de la acera), borde m de la banqueta (Méx), cuneta f (Chi), sardinel m (Col), cordón m de la vereda (RPl)

curb² vt (control) ⟨anger⟩ dominar, refrenar; ⟨spending/prices⟩ poner* freno a, frenar

curd /kɜːrd ‖kɜːd/ n (often pl) cuajada f

curdle /ˈkɜːrdl ‖ˈkɜːdl/ vi (a) (go bad, separate) ⟨⟨milk/sauce⟩⟩ cortarse (b) (form curds) ⟨⟨milk⟩⟩ cuajarse

cure¹ /kjʊr ‖kjʊə(r)/ vt **1** (Med) curar **2** ⟨meat⟩ curar

cure² n cura f

curfew /ˈkɜːrfjuː ‖ˈkɜːfjuː/ n toque m de queda

curiosity /ˌkjʊriˈɑːsəti ‖ˌkjʊərɪˈɒsəti/ n (pl -ties) curiosidad f

curious /ˈkjʊriəs ‖ˈkjʊərɪəs/ adj (a) (inquisitive) curioso (b) (strange) curioso, extraño

curiously /ˈkjʊriəsli ‖ˈkjʊərɪəsli/ adv (with curiosity) con curiosidad; (strangely) curiosamente; **~ enough**, ... (indep) curiosamente, ...

curl¹ /kɜːrl ‖kɜːl/ n rizo m, rulo m (CS), chino m (Méx); (ringlet) bucle m, tirabuzón m

curl² vt ⟨hair⟩ rizar*, encrespar (CS), enchinar (Méx), enrular (RPl)
~ vi ⟨⟨hair⟩⟩ rizarse*, encresparse (CS), enchinarse (Méx), enrularse (RPl); ⟨⟨paper/leaf/edge⟩⟩ ondularse

curl up [v + adv] (twist) ⟨⟨leaf/pages⟩⟩ ondularse; ⟨⟨cat⟩⟩ hacerse* un ovillo; **to ~ up in a chair** acurrucarse* en un sillón

curler /ˈkɜːrlər ‖ˈkɜːlə(r)/ n (for hair) rulo m, rulero m (RPl), marrón m (Col), tubo m (Chi, Méx)

curling irons, curling tongs /ˈkɜːrlɪŋ ‖ˈkɜːlɪŋ/ pl n tenacillas fpl (para rizar el pelo)

curly /ˈkɜːrli ‖ˈkɜːli/ adj -lier, -liest ⟨hair⟩ rizado, crespo (CS), chino (Méx); ⟨tail⟩ enroscado

currant /ˈkɜːrənt ‖ˈkʌrənt/ n pasa f de Corinto

currency /ˈkɜːrənsi ‖ˈkʌrənsi/ n (pl -cies) moneda f; **foreign ~** moneda f extranjera, divisas fpl

current¹ /ˈkɜːrənt ‖ˈkʌrənt/ adj **1** (before n) (a) (existing) ⟨situation/prices⟩ actual; ⟨year⟩ en curso (b) (most recent) ⟨issue⟩ último **2** (a) (valid) ⟨license/membership⟩ vigente (b) (prevailing) ⟨opinion/practice⟩ corriente

current² n (Elec) corriente f

current: ~ account n (BrE) cuenta f corriente; **~ affairs** pl n sucesos mpl de actualidad

currently /ˈkɜːrəntli ‖ˈkʌrəntli/ adv (a) (at present) actualmente (b) (commonly) comúnmente

curriculum /kəˈrɪkjələm ‖kəˈrɪkjʊləm/ n (pl -lums or -la /-lə/) (a) (range of courses) plan m de estudios (b) (for single course) programa m (de estudio), currículo m, curriculum m (AmL)

curriculum vitae /ˈviːtaɪ/ n (pl curricula vitae) (BrE) currículum m (vitae), historial m personal

curry¹ /ˈkɜːri ‖ˈkʌri/ n (pl curries) curry m

curry² vt -ries, -rying, -ried **1** (Culin) preparar al curry; **curried chicken** pollo m al curry **2** ▶ FAVOR¹ 1A

curse¹ /kɜːrs ‖kɜːs/ n (a) (evil spell) maldición f (b) (oath) maldición f, palabrota f

curse² vt/i maldecir*

cursor /ˈkɜːrsər ‖ˈkɜːsə(r)/ n cursor m

cursory /ˈkɜːrsəri ‖ˈkɜːsəri/ adj ⟨glance⟩ rápido; ⟨description⟩ somero; ⟨interest⟩ superficial

curt /kɜːrt ‖kɜːt/ adj cortante, seco

curtail /kɜːrˈteɪl ‖kɜːˈteɪl/ vt (cut short) abreviar; (restrict) restringir*; (reduce) reducir*

curtain /ˈkɜːrtn ‖ˈkɜːtn/ n (at window) cortina f; (Theat) telón m

curtain call n salida f a escena (para saludar), telón m (Méx)

curtsey¹ n (pl -seys) (esp BrE) ▶ CURTSY¹

curtsey² vi -seys, -seying, -seyed (BrE) ▶ CURTSY²

curtsy¹ /ˈkɜːrtsi ‖ˈkɜːtsi/ n (pl -sies) reverencia f (que hacen las mujeres agachándose)

curtsy² vi -sies, -sying, -sied hacer* una reverencia

curve¹ /kɜːrv ‖kɜːv/ n curva f

curve² vi ⟨⟨surface⟩⟩ estar* curvado; ⟨⟨river/ball⟩⟩ describir* una curva

curved /kɜːrvd ‖kɜːvd/ adj curvo

cushion¹ /ˈkʊʃən/ n almohadón m; (before n) **~ cover** funda f de almohadón

cushion² vt ⟨blow⟩ amortiguar*; (protect) **to ~ sb AGAINST** sth proteger* a algn CONTRA algo

cuss /kʌs/ (esp AmE colloq) vi (a) (complain) despotricar* (b) (swear) maldecir*

custard /'kʌstərd ‖ 'kʌstəd/ n (a) (sauce) (BrE) crema f; (cold, set) ≈ natillas fpl (b) (egg ∿) *especie de flan*

custodian /kʌ'stəʊdiən/ n (a) (of morals, tradition) guardián, -diana m,f, custodio, -dia m,f (b) (of museum, building) conservador, -dora m,f

custody /'kʌstədi/ n [1] (detention): **to be in** (**police**) ∿ estar* detenido [2] (of child) custodia f

custom /'kʌstəm/ n [1] (convention, tradition, habit) costumbre f [2] (patronage) (esp BrE) **I'll take my** ∿ **elsewhere** dejaré de ser su cliente [3] **customs** pl aduana f

customary /'kʌstəməri/ adj (a) (traditional) tradicional; **it is** ∿ **to + INF** es la costumbre + INF (b) (habitual) habitual, acostumbrado

custom-built /'kʌstəm'bɪlt/ adj ⟨car⟩ hecho de encargo; ⟨house⟩ construido según las especificaciones del cliente

customer /'kʌstəmər ‖ 'kʌstəmə(r)/ n cliente, -ta m,f; ⟨before n⟩ **©** **customer services** información y reclamaciones

customize /'kʌstəmaɪz/ vt ⟨car/program⟩ hacer* (or adaptar etc) según los requisitos del cliente

custom-made /'kʌstəm'meɪd/ adj hecho de encargo; ⟨suit/shoes⟩ a la medida

cut¹ /kʌt/ n [1] (a) (wound) tajo m, corte m (b) (incision) corte m [2] (a) (reduction): **to make** ∿**s in essential services** hacer* recortes en los servicios esenciales (b) (in text, film) corte m (c) (power ∿) apagón m [3] (a) (hair∿) corte m de pelo (b) (of suit) corte m [4] (of meat — type) corte m; (— piece) trozo m [5] (share) (colloq) tajada f (fam), parte f [6] (blow — with knife) cuchillada f

cut² ⟨pres p **cutting**; past & past p **cut**⟩ vt [1] ⟨wood/paper/wire/rope⟩ cortar; **to** ∿ **sth in half** cortar algo por la mitad; **I** ∿ **my finger** me corté el dedo; **to cut sb's throat** degollar* a algn; see also SHORT² 1
[2] (a) (trim) ⟨hair/nails⟩ cortar; ⟨grass/corn⟩ cortar, segar*; **to get one's hair** ∿ cortarse el pelo (b) (shape) ⟨glass/stone⟩ tallar; ⟨key⟩ hacer* [3] (reduce) ⟨level/number⟩ reducir*; ⟨budget⟩ recortar; ⟨price/rate⟩ rebajar; ⟨service/workforce⟩ hacer* recortes en [4] (a) (shorten) ⟨text⟩ acortar (b) (remove) ⟨scene⟩ cortar (c) ⟨film⟩ (edit) editar; «censors» hacer* cortes en [5] (in cards) ⟨deck⟩ cortar [6] (colloq) (cease): ∿ **the jokes!** ¡basta ya de bromas!
∎ ∿ vi [1] «knife/scissors» cortar; **the rope** ∿ **into her wrists** la cuerda le estaba cortando las muñecas [2] (Cin, Rad): ∿**!** ¡corte(n)! [3] (in cards) cortar
∎ **cut across** [v + prep + o] (a) (take shortcut across) cortar por (b) (cross boundaries of) trascender*
∎ **cut back** [1] [v + o + adv, v + adv + o] (a) (prune) ⟨hedge⟩ podar (b) (reduce) ⟨spending⟩ recortar [2] [v + adv] (make reductions) hacer* economías; **to** ∿ **back ON sth** reducir* algo
∎ **cut down** [1] [v + o + adv, v + adv + o] (a) (fell) ⟨tree⟩ cortar, talar (b) (kill) matar [2] [v + adv] (make reductions): **cigarette? — no, thanks, I'm trying to** ∿ **down** ¿un cigarrillo? —

no, gracias, estoy tratando de fumar menos; **you should** ∿ **down on carbohydrates** debería reducir el consumo de hidratos de carbono
∎ **cut in** [v + adv] (a) (interrupt) interrumpir (b) (Auto) atravesarse*
∎ **cut off** [1] [v + o + adv, v + adv + o] (sever) ⟨branch/limb⟩ cortar [2] [v + o + adv, v + adv + o] (interrupt, block) ⟨supply/route⟩ cortar [3] [v + o + adv] (a) (isolate) aislar*; **to feel** ∿ **off** sentirse* aislado; **the town was** ∿ **off** la ciudad quedó sin comunicaciones (b) (on telephone): **we were** ∿ **off** se cortó la comunicación
∎ **cut out** [1] [v + o + adv, v + adv + o] ⟨article/ photograph⟩ recortar [2] [v + o + adv, v + adv + o] (a) ⟨dress/cookies⟩ cortar (b) (exclude) ⟨noise/carbohydrates⟩ eliminar; **he** ∿ **me out of his will** me excluyó de su testamento; ∿ **it out!** (colloq) ¡basta ya! [3] (suit): **to be** ∿ **out FOR sth** estar* hecho para algo [4] [v + adv] «engine» pararse
∎ **cut up** [v + o + adv, v + adv + o] ⟨vegetables/ wood⟩ cortar en pedazos

cut³ adj ⟨before n⟩ ⟨flowers⟩ cortado; ⟨glass⟩ tallado

cutback /'kʌtbæk/ n recorte m

cute /kjuːt/ adj **cuter, cutest** (a) (sweet) ⟨baby/face⟩ mono (fam), cuco (fam), rico (CS fam) (b) (attractive) (AmE) guapo

cut-glass /'kʌt'glæs ‖ 'kʌt'glɑːs/ adj de cristal tallado

cuticle /'kjuːtɪkəl/ n cutícula f

cutlery /'kʌtləri/ n cubiertos mpl, cubertería f, cuchillería f (Chi)

cutlet /'kʌtlət ‖ 'kʌtlɪt/ n chuleta f (pequeña)

cut- ∿**off** (point) n límite m; ∿**price** /'kʌt'praɪs/ adj (BrE) ▶ ∿-RATE; ∿**-rate** /'kʌt'reɪt/ adj (AmE) a precio rebajado; ∿**throat** adj ⟨competition⟩ feroz, salvaje

cutting¹ /'kʌtɪŋ/ n [1] (from newspaper) (BrE) recorte m (b) (from plant) esqueje m [2] (for road, railway) (BrE) zanja f

cutting² adj (a) ⟨before n⟩ ⟨tool/blade⟩ cortante (b) (cold) ⟨wind⟩ cortante (c) (hurtful) ⟨remark⟩ hiriente

CV n = **curriculum vitae**

cwt n = **hundredweight**

cyanide /'saɪənaɪd/ n cianuro m

cybercafé /'saɪbər,kæfeɪ ‖ 'saɪbə,kæfeɪ/ n cibercafé m

cyberspace /'saɪbərspeɪs ‖ 'saɪbəspeɪs/ n ciberespacio m

cycle¹ /'saɪkəl/ n [1] (process) ciclo m [2] (Elec, Comput) ciclo m [3] (bicycle) bicicleta f

cycle² vi ir* en bicicleta

cycling /'saɪklɪŋ/ n ciclismo m

cyclist /'saɪklɪst ‖ 'saɪklɪst/ n ciclista mf

cyclone /'saɪkləʊn/ n ciclón m

cylinder /'sɪləndər ‖ 'sɪlɪndə(r)/ n [1] (Math) cilindro m [2] (a) (of engine) cilindro m (b) (container — for liquid gas) tanque m or (Esp) bombona f or (RPl) garrafa f or (Chi) balón m

cymbal /'sɪmbəl/ n platillo m, címbalo m

cynic /'sɪnɪk/ n cínico, -ca m,f

cynical /'sɪnɪkəl/ adj cínico

cynicism /'sɪnəsɪzəm/ n cinismo m
cypher n (esp BrE) ▶ CIPHER
cypress /'saɪprəs/ n ciprés m
Cyprus /'saɪprəs/ n Chipre f
cyst /sɪst/ n quiste m
cystic fibrosis /ˌsɪstɪkfaɪ'brəʊsəs
  ‖ˌsɪstɪkfaɪ'brəʊsɪs/ n fibrosis f cística or
  pancreática
cystitis /sɪ'staɪtəs ‖sɪ'staɪtɪs/ n cistitis f
czar /zɑːr ‖zɑː(r)/ n (esp AmE) ▶ TSAR

Czech¹ /tʃek/ adj checo
Czech² n (a) (person) checo, -ca m,f (b)
  (language) checo m
Czechoslovakia /ˌtʃekəslə'vɑːkiə
  ‖ˌtʃekəslə'vækiə/ n (Hist) Checoslovaquia f
Czechoslovakian /ˌtʃekəslə'vɑːkiən
  ‖ˌtʃekəslə'vækiən/ adj (Hist) checoslovaco
Czech Republic n the ∼ ∼ la República
  Checa

Dd

D, d /diː/ n (a) (letter) D, d f (b) (Mus) re m
d' = **do**; d'you go there often? ¿vas ahí a
  menudo?
'd /d/ (a) = **had** (b) = **would** (c) = **did**
DA n (in US) = **district attorney**
dab /dæb/ vt: ∼ the stain with a damp cloth frote
  suavemente la mancha con un trapo húmedo; ∼
  antiseptic on the cut dese unos toques de
  antiséptico en la herida
dabble /'dæbəl/ vi: to ∼ in politics/journalism
  tener* escarceos con la política/el periodismo
dad /dæd/ n (colloq) papá m (fam)
daddy /'dædi/ n papi m (fam)
daddy longlegs /'lɔːŋlegz ‖'lɒŋlegz/ n (pl ∼
  ∼) (colloq) (a) (harvestman) (AmE) segador m,
  falangio m (b) (cranefly) (BrE) típula f
daffodil /'dæfədɪl/ n narciso m
daft /dæft ‖dɑːft/ adj -er, -est (esp BrE colloq)
  tonto, bobo (fam)
dagger /'dægər ‖'dægə(r)/ n daga f, puñal m
dahlia /'dæljə ‖'deɪliə/ n dalia f
daily¹ /'deɪli/ adj (before n) ‹newspaper/prayers›
  diario; ‹walk/visit› diario, cotidiano
daily² adv a diario, diariamente
daily³ n (pl -lies) diario m, periódico m
dainty /'deɪnti/ adj -tier, -tiest ‹flowers/vase›
  delicado; ‹appearance› delicado, refinado
dairy /'deri ‖'deəri/ n (pl -ries) (a) (on farm)
  lechería f; (before n) ‹produce› lácteo; ‹butter/
  cream› de granja; ‹cow/industry› lechero (b)
  (shop) lechería f; (company) central f lechera
daisy /'deɪzi/ n (pl -sies) (cultivated) margarita
  f; (wild) margarita f de los prados, maya f
dally /'dæli/ vi -lies, -lying, -lied perder* el
  tiempo
dam¹ /dæm/ n dique m, presa f, represa f (AmS)
dam² vt -mm- construir* una presa or (AmS)
  una represa en

damage¹ /'dæmɪdʒ/ n ⬚1⬚ (to object) daño m; (to
  reputation, cause) daño m, perjuicio m
  ⬚2⬚ **damages** pl (Law) daños y perjuicios mpl
damage² vt ‹building/vehicle› dañar; ‹health›
  perjudicar*, ser* perjudicial para; ‹reputation/
  cause› perjudicar*, dañar
damaging /'dæmɪdʒɪŋ/ adj perjudicial
dame /deɪm/ n ⬚1⬚ **Dame** (title in UK) Dame
  (título honorífico) ⬚2⬚ (woman) (AmE sl) tipa f (fam),
  tía f (Esp fam)
damn¹ /dæm/ vt (a) (Relig) condenar (b)
  (condemn) condenar
damn² n (colloq) (no pl): not to give a ∼: I don't
  give a ∼ what they think me importa un bledo lo
  que piensen (fam), me vale madres lo que piensen
  (Méx vulg)
damn³ interj (colloq) ¡caray! (fam & euf)
damn⁴ adj (colloq) (before n) (as intensifier)
  condenado (fam), maldito (fam), pinche (Méx fam)
damnation /dæm'neɪʃən/ n condenación f
damned /dæmd/ ▶ DAMN⁴
damning /'dæmɪŋ/ adj (a) (condemnatory)
  ‹evidence› condenatorio (b) (critical) ‹appraisal›
  crítico
damp¹ /dæmp/ adj -er, -est húmedo; to smell
  ∼ oler* a humedad
damp² n humedad f
damp³ vt ∼ (down) ‹fire› sofocar*; ‹enthusiasm/
  excitement› apagar*, enfriar*
damp course n membrana f aislante
dampen /'dæmpən/ vt ⬚1⬚ (moisten) humedecer*,
  mojar ⬚2⬚ (discourage) ‹hopes› hacer* perder;
  ‹enthusiasm› hacer* perder, apagar*
damper /'dæmpər ‖'dæmpə(r)/ n (of piano)
  sordina f; to put a ∼ on sth (colloq): the bad news
  put a ∼ on the celebrations la mala noticia
  estropeó las fiestas
damp: ∼-proof vt proteger* contra la
  humedad; **∼-proof course** n ▶ DAMP COURSE
damson /'dæmzən/ n ciruela f damascena

AmC	América Central	Arg	Argentina	Cu	Cuba	Per	Perú
AmL	América Latina	Bol	Bolivia	Ec	Ecuador	RPI	Río de la Plata
AmS	América del Sur	Chi	Chile	Esp	España	Ur	Uruguay
Andes	Región andina	CS	Cono Sur	Méx	México	Ven	Venezuela

dance¹ /dæns ‖dɑːns/ n **(a)** (act, occasion) baile m; (before n) ‹music› de baile, bailable **(b)** (set of steps) baile m, danza f **(c)** (art form) danza f, baile m

dance² vi [1] **(a)** (to music) bailar **(b)** (skip) dar* saltos [2] «eyes/flames» (liter) bailar, danzar* (liter);
■ ~ vt ‹waltz/tango› bailar

dancer /'dænsər ‖'dɑːnsə(r)/ n bailarín, -rina m,f

dancing /'dænsɪŋ ‖'dɑːnsɪŋ/ n baile m; (before n) ‹lesson/shoes› de baile

dandelion /'dændəlaɪən ‖'dændɪlaɪən/ n diente m de león

dandruff /'dændrʌf/ n caspa f; (before n) ~ shampoo champú m anti-caspa

Dane /deɪn/ n danés, -nesa m,f, dinamarqués, -quesa m,f

danger /'deɪndʒər ‖'deɪndʒə(r)/ n peligro m; in ~ en peligro or en riesgo; to be in ~ of -ING correr peligro or riesgo de + INF; (before n) to be on the ~ list encontrarse* en estado grave; ~ signal señal f

dangerous /'deɪndʒərəs/ adj peligroso

dangerously /'deɪndʒərəsli/ adv peligrosamente

dangle /'dæŋgəl/ vi colgar*, pender
■ ~ vt hacer* oscilar

Danish¹ /'deɪnɪʃ/ adj danés, dinamarqués

Danish² n danés m

Danish (**pastry**) n: bollo cubierto de azúcar glaseado

dank /dæŋk/ adj frío y húmedo

dapper /'dæpər ‖'dæpə(r)/ adj atildado, pulcro

dare¹ /der ‖deə(r)/ n reto m, desafío m

dare² v mod atreverse a, osar (liter); how ~ you! ¡cómo te atreves!; I ~ say you've had enough estarás harto(, me imagino)
■ ~ vt [1] (be so bold) to ~ to + INF atreverse a + INF, osar + INF (liter) [2] (challenge) to ~ sb to + INF retar or desafiar* a algn a + INF or A QUE (+ subj)

daredevil /'der‚devl ‖'deə‚devl/ n corajudo, -da m,f (fam); (before n) ‹feat/exploit› temerario

daring¹ /'derɪŋ ‖'deərɪŋ/ adj **(a)** ‹explorer/pilot› osado; ‹plan› audaz **(b)** ‹dress/film› atrevido

daring² n **(a)** (courage) arrojo m, coraje m **(b)** (audacity) audacia f

dark¹ /dɑːrk ‖dɑːk/ adj **-er, -est** [1] (unlit) ‹room/night› oscuro; it's getting ~ está oscureciendo, se está haciendo de noche [2] **(a)** (in color) oscuro; ~ chocolate chocolate m sin leche; ~ glasses anteojos mpl oscuros (esp AmL), gafas fpl negras (Esp) **(b)** (in complexion) moreno

dark² n (absence of light) the ~ la oscuridad; to wait until ~ esperar hasta que anochezca; to keep sb in the ~ about sth ocultarle algo a algn

Dark Ages pl n the ~ la Alta Edad Media, la Edad de las tinieblas

darken /'dɑːrkən ‖'dɑːkən/ vt **(a)** (make dark) oscurecer* **(b)** (make somber) ensombrecer*
■ ~ vi **(a)** (grow dark) «room/color/sky» oscurecerse* **(b)** (grow somber) ensombrecerse*

darkness /'dɑːrknəs ‖'dɑːknɪs/ n oscuridad f

darkroom /'dɑːrkruːm, -rʊm ‖'dɑːkruːm, -rʊm/ n cuarto m oscuro

darling¹ /'dɑːrlɪŋ ‖'dɑːlɪŋ/ n (as form of address) cariño

darling² adj (before n) querido

darn¹ /dɑːrn ‖dɑːn/ vt zurcir*

dart¹ /dɑːrt ‖dɑːt/ n **(a)** (weapon) dardo m **(b)** (Games) dardo m **(c)** (Clothing) pinza f

dart² vi: to ~ into/out of a room entrar como una flecha en/salir* como una flecha de una habitación
■ ~ vt ‹look› lanzar*

dartboard /'dɑːrtbɔːrd ‖'dɑːtbɔːd/ n diana f

darts /dɑːrts ‖dɑːts/ n (+ sing vb) dardos mpl

dash¹ /dæʃ/ n [1] (small amount) poquito m; a ~ of milk un chorrito de leche [2] (punctuation mark) guion m

dash² vt [1] (hurl) tirar*; she ~ed the plate to pieces hizo añicos or trizas el plato; the ship was ~ed against the rocks el barco se estrelló contra las rocas [2] (disappoint) ‹hopes› (usu pass) defraudar
■ ~ vi: I ~ed to the rescue me lancé al rescate; she ~ed out salió disparada
■ **dash off** [1] [v + o + adv, v + adv + o] (write hurriedly) escribir* corriendo [2] [v + adv] (leave hastily) irse* corriendo

dashboard /'dæʃbɔːrd ‖'dæʃbɔːd/ n tablero m de mandos, salpicadero m (Esp)

data /'deɪtə/ n [1] (facts, information) (+ pl vb) datos mpl, información f [2] (Comput) (+ sing vb) datos mpl

data: ~base n base f de datos; ~ **highway** n (Comput) autopista f de datos

date¹ /deɪt/ n [1] (of appointment, battle) fecha f; what's the ~ today? ¿a qué fecha estamos?; to ~ hasta la fecha, hasta el momento [2] (colloq) (appointment) cita f; Greg has a ~ with Ana on Sunday Greg sale con Ana el domingo [3] (fruit) dátil m

date² vt [1] **(a)** (mark with date) fechar **(b)** (give date to) ‹remains/pottery/fossil› datar, determinar la antigüedad de [2] (betray age) (colloq): that really ~s you eso delata tu edad, eso demuestra lo viejo que eres
■ ~ vi [1] (originate in) datar; it ~s from the 14th century data del siglo XIV; his title ~s back to the 14th century los orígenes de su título se remontan al siglo XIV [2] (become old-fashioned) pasar de moda

dated /'deɪtəd ‖'deɪtɪd/ adj ‹fashion/word› anticuado; his plays are ~ sus obras han perdido actualidad

date: ~ rape n violación f (cometida durante una cita); ~ **stamp** n (instrument) fechador m; (date) fecha f; **~-stamp** vt fechar

daub /dɔːb/ vt (smear) to ~ sth WITH sth embadurnar algo DE algo

daughter /'dɔːtər ‖'dɔːtə(r)/ n hija f

daughter-in-law /'dɔːtərɪnlɔː/ n (pl **daughters-in-law**) nuera f

daunt /dɔːnt/ vt (usu pass) amilanar, intimidar

daunting /'dɔːntɪŋ/ adj ‹prospect› desalentador, sobrecogedor; ‹task› de enormes proporciones

dawdle /'dɔːdl/ vi entretenerse*

dawn¹ /dɔːn/ n amanecer m; at ~ al amanecer, al alba (liter)

dawn² *vi* (liter) «*day*» amanecer*, clarear, alborear (liter); «*new age*» alborear (liter), nacer*
∎ **dawn on** [*v* + *prep* + *o*]: **it gradually ∼ed on me that ...** fui cayendo en la cuenta de que ...

dawn chorus *n* **the ∼ ∼** el trino de los pájaros al amanecer

day /deɪ/ *n* **1** día *m*; (working day) jornada *f*, día *m*; **twice a ∼** dos veces al día; **all ∼** todo el día; **every ∼** todos los días; **one of these ∼s** un día de estos; **∼ by ∼** día a día, de día en día; **it's not my/his ∼** no es mi/su día; **to take a ∼ off** (from work) tomarse un día libre; **in this ∼ and age** hoy (en) día, el día de hoy; **these ∼s** hoy (en) día; **that'll be the ∼** (colloq & iro) cuando las ranas críen cola; **have a good o nice ∼!** (AmE) ¡que le vaya bien!; **to call it a ∼** (temporarily) dejarlo para otro día; (permanently) dejar de trabajar (*or* estudiar *etc*); **to make someone's ∼** (colloq) alegrarle la vida a algn
2 days (*as adv*): **to work ∼s** trabajar durante el día

day: ∼break *n* alba *f*‡ (liter), amanecer *m*; **∼-care center** *n* (AmE) guardería *f* infantil

daydream¹ /'deɪdriːm/ *n* ensueño *m*, ensoñación *f*

daydream² *vi* soñar* despierto, fantasear

day: ∼light *n* luz *f* (del día); **∼light** (saving) **time** *n* (AmE) hora *f* de verano; **∼ release** *n* (in UK) *sistema que permite a un empleado ausentarse regularmente de su trabajo para seguir estudios relacionados con el mismo*; **∼room** *n*: *sala de estar comunal en hospitales, prisiones etc*; **∼time** *n*: **in** *o* **during the ∼time** de día *or* durante el día; **∼-to-∼** /'deɪtə'deɪ/ *adj* (*before n*) «*occurrence*» cotidiano, diario; «*chores/difficulties*» de cada día; «*existence*» diario; **∼ trip** *n* excursión *f* de un día; **∼-tripper** /,trɪpər ‖,trɪpə(r)/ *n* excursionista *mf*

daze /deɪz/ *n* (*no pl*) aturdimiento *m*; **to go about in a ∼** estar* en las nubes

dazed /deɪzd/ *adj* aturdido

dazzle /'dæzəl/ *vt* «*light*» deslumbrar, encandilar; «*beauty/wit*» deslumbrar

dazzling /'dæzlɪŋ/ *adj* (bright) «*light/glare*» deslumbrante, resplandeciente, que encandila; (impressive) «*wit/looks*» deslumbrante, deslumbrador

DC (a) (= **direct current**) CC **(b)** = **District of Columbia**

D-day /'diːdeɪ/ *n* **(a)** (in World War II) día *m* D (*día del desembarco aliado en Normandía*) **(b)** (important day) el día señalado

DE = **Delaware**

DEA *n* (= **Drug Enforcement Administration**) DEA *f*

deacon /'diːkən/ *n* diácono *m*

deaconess /'diːkənəs ‖,diːkə'nes, 'diːkənɪs/ *n* diaconisa *f*

dead¹ /ded/ *adj* **1** (no longer alive) muerto; **he's ∼** está muerto; **to drop ∼** caerse* muerto; **I wouldn't be seen ∼ in that dress** (colloq) yo no me pondría ese vestido ni muerta *or* ni loca; ▶ **BODY** 1c **2** (numb) (*usu pred*) dormido; **to go ∼** «*limb*» dormirse* **3** (very tired, ill) (colloq) muerto (fam) **4** (obsolete) «*language*» muerto; «*custom*» en desuso **5 (a)** (not functioning) «*wire/circuit*»

desconectado; «*telephone*» desconectado, cortado; «*battery*» descargado **(b)** (not alight) «*fire/match*» apagado **(c)** (not busy) «*town/hotel/party*» muerto

dead² *adv* **1 (a)** (exactly) justo **(b)** (directly) justo, directamente; **∼ ahead** justo delante **(c)** (suddenly) en seco **2** (colloq) «*straight/level*» completamente; **∼ slow** lentísimo; **to be ∼ certain** estar* totalmente seguro; **it was ∼ easy** estuvo regalado *or* tirado (fam)

dead³ *pl n*: **the ∼** los muertos

deaden /'dedn/ *vt* «*impact*» amortiguar; «*noise/vibration*» reducir*; «*pain*» atenuar*, aliviar; «*nerve*» insensibilizar*; «*faculties*» entorpecer*

dead: ∼ end *n* callejón *m* sin salida; **∼-end** /'ded'end/ *adj* «*street*» sin salida, ciego (Andes, Ven); **a ∼-end job** (colloq) un trabajo sin porvenir *or* futuro; **∼line** *n* fecha *f* tope *or* límite, plazo *m* de entrega; **∼lock** *n* (*no pl*) punto *m* muerto

deadly¹ /'dedli/ *adj* **-lier, -liest 1** (fatal) «*disease/poison*» mortal; «*weapon*» mortífero **2** (dull) (colloq) aburridísimo, terriblemente aburrido (AmE)

deadly² *adv* (*as intensifier*) «*dull*» terriblemente

dead: ∼pan *adj* «*expression*» de póquer *or* (fam) de palo; «*voice/delivery*» deliberadamente inexpresivo; **D∼ Sea** *n* **the D∼ Sea** el Mar Muerto; **∼ weight** *n* peso *m* muerto

deaf /def/ *adj* sordo; **to go ∼** quedarse sordo; **∼ and dumb** sordomudo

deaf-aid /'defeɪd/ *n* (BrE) audífono *m*

deafen /'defən/ *vt* ensordecer*

deafening /'defənɪŋ/ *adj* ensordecedor

deaf-mute /'defmjuːt/ *n* sordomudo, -da *m,f*

deafness /'defnəs ‖'defnɪs/ *n* sordera *f*

deal¹ /diːl/ *n* **1** (indicating amount): **it makes a great/good ∼ of difference** cambia mucho/ bastante las cosas; **we've seen a great ∼ of her lately** la hemos visto mucho *or* muy a menudo últimamente
2 (a) (agreement) trato *m*, acuerdo *m*; **to do a ∼ with sb** llegar* a un acuerdo con algn, hacer* un trato *or* un pacto con algn; **it's no big ∼** no es nada del otro mundo **(b)** (financial arrangement) acuerdo *m* **(c)** (bargain): **you'll get a better ∼ if you shop around** lo conseguirás más barato si vas a otras tiendas
3 (treatment) trato *m*; **she's had a raw ∼ in life** la vida la ha tratado muy mal

deal² (*past & past p* **dealt**) *vt/i* (Games) dar*, repartir
∎ **deal in** [*v* + *prep* + *o*] (Busn) dedicarse* a la compra y venta de, comerciar en
∎ **deal out** [*v* + *o* + *adv*, *v* + *adv* + *o*] «*gifts/ money*» repartir, distribuir*
∎ **deal with** [*v* + *prep* + *o*] **1** (do business with) «*company*» tener* relaciones comerciales con; **I prefer to ∼ with her** yo prefiero tratar con ella **2 (a)** (tackle, handle) «*complaint*» ocuparse de, atender*; «*situation*» manejar **(b)** (be responsible for) ocuparse *or* encargarse* de **3** «*issue*» (discuss, treat) tratar; (have as subject) tratar de

dealer /'diːlər ‖'diːlə(r)/ *n* **1 (a)** (trader): **she's a car ∼** se dedica a la compra-venta de coches; **visit your local Hoover ∼** visite a su representante Hoover más próximo; **drug ∼**

traficante *mf* de drogas **(b)** (Fin) corredor, -dora
m,f de bolsa *or* de valores **2** (Games): **the ∼** el
que da *or* reparte las cartas

dealing /'di:lɪŋ/ *n* **1 (a)** (business methods): **the
company has a reputation for honest/shady ∼** la
empresa tiene fama de honradez en los negocios/
de hacer negocios turbios **(b) dealings** *pl*
(contacts, relations) relaciones *fpl*, trato *m*
2 (trafficking) tráfico *m*

dealt /delt/ *past & past p of* DEAL²

dean /di:n/ *n* **1** (Relig) deán *m* **2 (a)** (in
university) decano, -na *m,f* **(b)** (in college, secondary
school) (AmE) *docente a cargo del asesoramiento y
de la disciplina de los estudiantes*

dear¹ /dɪr ‖ dɪə(r)/ *adj* **dearer, dearest**
1 (loved) querido **2** (in direct address) **(a)** (in
speech): **my ∼ Mrs Harper, I can assure you that ...**
mi buena señora (Harper), le aseguro que ... **(b)**
(in letter writing): **D∼ Mr Jones** Estimado Sr. Jones;
D∼ Sir or Madam Estimado/a Señor(a), Muy
señor mío/señora mía; **D∼ Jimmy** Querido
Jimmy **3** (lovable) adorable **4** (expensive) caro

dear² *interj*: oh ∼! ¡ay!, ¡qué cosa!

dear³ *n* (*as form of address*) querido, -da,
cariño; **(you) poor ∼!** ¡pobre ángel!, ¡pobrecito!

dearly /'dɪrli ‖ 'dɪəli/ *adv* **1** (*as intensifier*): **I
love him ∼** lo quiero mucho *or* de verdad; **∼
beloved** (frml) (Relig) (amados) hermanos **2** (at
great cost) caro *adj*

death /deθ/ *n* muerte *f*, fallecimiento *m* (frml); **to
put sb to ∼** ejecutar a algn; **to be worried to ∼**
(colloq) estar* preocupadísimo

death: ∼bed *n* lecho *m* de muerte; **∼
certificate** *n* certificado *m* de defunción; **∼
penalty** *n* the ∼ pena la pena de muerte; **∼
row** /rəʊ/ *n* (*no art*) pabellón *m* de los
condenados a muerte, corredor *m* de la muerte;
∼ sentence *n*: the ∼ sentence la pena de
muerte; **∼ squad** *n* escuadrón *m* de la muerte;
∼ toll *n* número *m* de víctimas (mortales) *or* de
muertos; **∼ trap** *n*: edificio, vehículo etc muy
poco seguro; **∼ warrant** *n* sentencia *f* de
muerte; **∼ wish** *n* (*no pl*) (Psych) pulsión *f* de
muerte

debar /dɪ'bɑːr ‖ dɪ'bɑː(r)/ *vt* **-rr-** (frml) **the fact
that she didn't have a degree ∼red her from
promotion** el hecho de no tener un título
universitario le impedía ascender; **he was ∼red
from taking his final exam** se le prohibió rendir el
examen final

debase /dɪ'beɪs/ *vt* **(a)** (devalue) ⟨*ideal/principle*⟩
degradar, envilecer*; ⟨*language*⟩ corromper,
viciar **(b)** (demean) ⟨*person*⟩ degradar, rebajar

debate¹ /dɪ'beɪt/ *n* **(a)** (public, parliamentary)
debate *m* **(b)** (discussion) debate *m*, discusión *f*

debate² *vt* **(a)** ⟨*question/topic/motion*⟩ debatir,
discutir **(b)** (weigh up) ⟨*idea/possibility*⟩ darle*
vueltas a, considerar

debauchery /dɪ'bɔːtʃəri/ *n* disipación *f*,
libertinaje *m*

debenture /dɪ'bentʃər ‖ dɪ'bentʃə(r)/ *n* ∼
(bond) (Fin) obligación *f*, bono *m*

debilitating /dɪ'bɪlɪteɪtɪŋ/ *adj*
⟨*disease*⟩ debilitante; ⟨*climate*⟩ extenuante

debit¹ /'debət ‖ 'debɪt/ *n* débito *m*, cargo *m*;
(*before n*) **∼ card** tarjeta *f* de cobro automático

debit² *vt* (Fin) debitar, cargar*

debonair /ˌdebə'ner ‖ ˌdebə'neə(r)/ *adj* (suave)
elegante y desenvuelto; (courteous) cortés, afable

debriefing /'diː'briːfɪŋ/ *n*: **they were sent for ∼**
los llamaron para que rindiesen informe *or*
diesen parte de su misión

debris /də'briː ‖ 'debriː, 'deɪbriː/ *n* **(a)** (rubble)
escombros *mpl*; (of plane, ship) restos *mpl*; (rubbish)
desechos *mpl* **(b)** (Geol) detritos *mpl*

debt /det/ *n* **(a)** (indebtedness) endeudamiento *m*;
I'm $200 in ∼ debo 200 dólares, tengo deudas por
200 dólares; **to be in ∼ to sb** (frml) estarle* en
deuda a algn, estar* en deuda con algn; **to get
into ∼** endeudarse, llenarse *or* cargarse* de
deudas **(b)** (money owing) deuda *f*; **bad ∼s** deudas
incobrables

debtor /'detər ‖ 'detə(r)/ *n* deudor, -dora *m,f*

debunk /'diː'bʌŋk/ *vt* (colloq) desacreditar

debut, début /'deɪbjuː, 'de-/ (*pl* **-buts** /-bjuːz/)
n debut *m*

decade /'dekeɪd/ *n* década *f*

decadence /'dekədəns/ *n* decadencia *f*

decadent /'dekədənt/ *adj* decadente

decaffeinated /'diː'kæfəneɪtəd
‖ ˌdiː'kæfɪneɪtɪd/ *adj* descafeinado

decanter /dɪ'kæntər ‖ dɪ'kæntə(r)/ *n* licorera *f*

decapitate /dɪ'kæpɪteɪt/ *vt* decapitar

decathlon /dɪ'kæθlən/ *n* decatlón *m*

decay¹ /dɪ'keɪ/ *vi* «*foodstuffs/corpse*»
descomponerse*, pudrirse*; «*wood*» pudrirse*;
«*tooth*» cariarse, picarse*; «*building/machine*»
deteriorarse*; «*empire/culture/civilization*»
decaer*, declinar

decay² *n* (of organic matter) descomposición *f*;
(tooth ∼) caries *f*; (of building) deterioro *m*; (of
culture) decadencia *f*

deceased¹ /dɪ'siːst/ *n* (*pl* ∼) (frml) **the ∼** el
difunto, la difunta; (*pl*) los difuntos, las difuntas
(frml)

deceased² *adj* (frml) difunto

deceit /dɪ'siːt/ *n* engaño *m*

deceitful /dɪ'siːtfəl/ *adj* ⟨*person*⟩ falso,
embustero; ⟨*action*⟩ engañoso

deceive /dɪ'siːv/ *vt* engañar

deceiver /dɪ'siːvər ‖ dɪ'siːvə(r)/ *n* impostor,
-tora *m,f*

decelerate /'diː'seləreɪt/ *vi* (frml) «*vehicle/
driver*» reducir* *or* aminorar la velocidad

December /dɪ'sembər ‖ dɪ'sembə(r)/ *n*
diciembre *m*

decency /'diːsnsi/ *n* **(a)** (of dress, conduct)
decencia *f*, decoro *m* **(b)** (propriety) buena
educación *f*, consideración *f*; **she didn't even
have the ∼ to ask me** ni siquiera tuvo la
consideración de preguntarme

decent /'diːsnt/ *adj* **1** (appropriate, respectable)
decente, decoroso **2** (acceptable) ⟨*person*⟩ pasable,
aceptable; ⟨*meal/housing*⟩ decente, como es
debido

decently /'diːsntli/ *adv* **1** (respectably) ⟨*dress/
behave*⟩ decentemente, con decencia
2 (acceptably) ⟨*perform/cook*⟩ bastante bien

decentralize /diː'sentrəlaɪz/ *vt*
descentralizar*

deception /dɪ'sepʃən/ *n* engaño *m*

··· decibel ···✦ deduction

decibel /'desəbəl ‖'desɪbel/ n decibelio m, decíbel m

decide /dɪ'saɪd/ vt **1** (make up one's mind) decidir; **to ~ to + INF** decidir or resolver + INF **2** (settle) ⟨question/issue⟩ decidir; ⟨outcome⟩ determinar
■ ~ vi decidirse

decided /dɪ'saɪdəd ‖dɪ'saɪdɪd/ adj **(a)** (definite) (before n) ⟨improvement/advantage⟩ claro, marcado **(b)** (determined) ⟨character/tone⟩ decidido

deciduous /dɪ'sɪdʒuəs ‖dɪ'sɪdjʊəs/ adj de hoja caduca, caducifolio (téc)

decimal¹ /'desɪməl ‖'desɪməl/ adj decimal

decimal² n decimal m

decimalization /desəmələ'zeɪʃən ‖ˌdesɪməlaɪ'zeɪʃən/ n decimalización f, conversión f al sistema decimal

decimal point n ≈ coma f (decimal o de los decimales), punto m decimal

decimate /'desəmeɪt ‖'desɪmeɪt/ vt diezmar

decipher /dɪ'saɪfər ‖dɪ'saɪfə(r)/ vt descifrar

decision /dɪ'sɪʒən/ n decisión f; **to make** o (BrE also) **take a ~** tomar una decisión

decision-making /dɪ'sɪʒən,meɪkɪŋ/ n toma f de decisiones; (before n) ⟨body/process⟩ decisorio

decisive /dɪ'saɪsɪv/ adj **1** (conclusive) ⟨battle/factor⟩ decisivo; ⟨victory⟩ contundente **2** (purposeful) ⟨person⟩ decidido, resuelto; ⟨leadership/answer⟩ firme

deck¹ /dek/ n **1** **(a)** (Naut) cubierta f **(b)** (of stadium) (AmE) nivel m **(c)** (sun ~) terraza f **(d)** (of bus) (BrE) piso m **2** (Audio) deck m (AmL), pletina f (Esp) **3** (AmE Games) ~ **(of cards)** baraja f, mazo m (de naipes or cartas) (esp AmL)

deck² vt **1** (adorn) **to ~ sth (out) WITH sth** engalanar or adornar algo CON algo; **he was all ~ed out in his Sunday best** iba muy endomingado **2** (knock down) (AmE colloq) tumbar (fam)

deckchair /'dektʃer ‖'dektʃeə(r)/ n silla f de playa, perezosa f (Col, Per), reposera f (RPl)

declaim /dɪ'kleɪm/ vt/i declamar

declaration /deklə'reɪʃən/ n **1** (statement) declaración f **2** (Law) (finding) pronunciamiento m (oficial); (statement) declaración f

declare /dɪ'kler ‖dɪ'kleə(r)/ vt **(a)** (state, announce) ⟨intention⟩ declarar; ⟨opinion⟩ manifestar*; **to ~ war** declarar la guerra; **to ~ war on sb/sth** declararle la guerra a algn/algo **(b)** (Tax) ⟨goods/income⟩ declarar

decline¹ /dɪ'klaɪn/ n (no pl) **(a)** (decrease) descenso m, disminución f **(b)** (downward trend) declive m, decadencia f, deterioro m; **to be in ~** estar* en declive or en decadencia

decline² vi **1** **(a)** (decrease) «production/strength» disminuir*, decrecer*; «interest» disminuir*, decaer* **(b)** (deteriorate) «health» deteriorarse*; «industry/region/standards» decaer* **(c) declining** pres p ⟨industry/region/

standards⟩ en declive, en decadencia **2** (refuse): **I invited him, but he ~d** lo invité, pero rehusó or declinó mi invitación
■ ~ vt ⟨offer/invitation⟩ rehusar, declinar

decode /ˌdiː'kəʊd/ vt ⟨signal⟩ descodificar*; ⟨message⟩ descifrar

decompose /ˌdiːkəm'pəʊz/ vi descomponerse*, pudrirse*

decor, décor /deɪ'kɔːr ‖'deɪkɔː(r)/ n (furnishings) decoración f

decorate /'dekəreɪt/ vt **(a)** ⟨room/house⟩ (with paint) pintar; (with wallpaper) empapelar **(b)** ⟨Christmas tree⟩ adornar, decorar (AmL); ⟨cake⟩ decorar

decoration /dekə'reɪʃən/ n **1** **(a)** (act) decoración f **(b)** (ornamentation) decoración f **(c)** (ornament) adorno m **2** (Mil) condecoración f

decorative /'dekərətɪv/ adj ⟨object⟩ ornamental, de adorno

decorator /'dekəreɪtər ‖'dekəreɪtə(r)/ n **(a)** (painter) pintor, -tora m,f; (paperhanger) empapelador, -dora m,f **(b)** (designer) decorador, -dora m,f, interiorista mf

decorous /'dekərəs/ adj (frml) decoroso

decorum /dɪ'kɔːrəm/ n decoro m

decoy /'diːkɔɪ/ n (lure) señuelo m; (in hunting) señuelo m, reclamo m

decrease¹ /dɪ'kriːs, 'diːkriːs/ vi **(a)** (in quantity) «amount/numbers» disminuir*, decrecer*; «prices» bajar; «speed» disminuir* **(b)** (in intensity) «quality» disminuir*, bajar; «power/effectiveness» disminuir*, decrecer*; «interest» disminuir*, decaer*
■ ~ vt disminuir*, reducir*

decrease² /'diːkriːs, dɪ'kriːs/ n disminución f, descenso m

decree¹ /dɪ'kriː/ n decreto m

decree² vt decretar

decrepit /dɪ'krepət ‖dɪ'krepɪt/ adj **(a)** (dilapidated) ⟨bus/furniture⟩ destartalado; ⟨house⟩ deteriorado, viejo y en mal estado **(b)** (infirm) ⟨person/animal⟩ decrépito

decriminalize /ˌdiː'krɪmɪnəlaɪz/ vt despenalizar*

dedicate /'dedɪkeɪt/ vt **(a)** (devote) **to ~ sth TO sth/-ING** dedicar* algo A algo/+ INF **(b)** ⟨poem/book⟩ dedicar*

dedicated /'dedɪkeɪtəd ‖'dedɪkeɪtɪd/ adj **1** ⟨musician/nurse/teacher⟩ de gran dedicación, dedicado or entregado a su (or mi etc) trabajo; **to be ~ TO sth** estar* dedicado or entregado A algo **2** (Comput) (before n) dedicado

dedication /dedɪ'keɪʃən/ n **1** (devotion) dedicación f, entrega f **2** (written message) dedicatoria f

deduce /dɪ'duːs ‖dɪ'djuːs/ vt deducir*, inferir*

deduct /dɪ'dʌkt/ vt deducir*, descontar*

deduction /dɪ'dʌkʃən/ n **1** (subtraction) deducción f, descuento m **2** (reasoning, conclusion) deducción f

AmC Central America	Arg Argentina	Cu Cuba	Per Peru
AmL Latin America	Bol Bolivia	Ec Ecuador	RPl River Plate Area
AmS South America	Chi Chile	Esp Spain	Ur Uruguay
Andes Andean Region	CS Southern Cone	Méx Mexico	Ven Venezuela

deed /diːd/ n **1** (action) hecho m **2** (Law) escritura f

deed poll n (BrE): **to change one's name by** ∼   ∼ ≈cambiarse el apellido oficialmente

deem /diːm/ vt (fml) considerar, juzgar*

deep¹ /diːp/ adj **-er, -est 1** (a) ⟨water⟩ profundo; ⟨hole/pit⟩ profundo, hondo; ⟨gash⟩ profundo; ⟨dish⟩ hondo; ⟨pan⟩ alto; **the ditch is 6 ft** ∼ la zanja tiene 6 pies de profundidad **(b)** (horizontally) ⟨shelf⟩ profundo; **the soldiers were standing 12** ∼ los soldados formaban columnas de 12 en fondo **2** ⟨sigh/groan⟩ profundo, hondo; **take a** ∼ **breath** respire hondo **3** (a) ⟨voice⟩ profundo, grave; ⟨note⟩ grave **(b)** ⟨color⟩ intenso, subido **4** (a) (intense) ⟨sleep/love/impression⟩ profundo; **it is with** ∼ **regret that** ... es con gran or profundo pesar que ... **(b)** ⟨thoughts⟩ profundo **(c)** ⟨mystery/secret⟩ profundo

deep² adv **-er, -est** (of penetration): **to dig** ∼ cavar hondo; **feelings run very** ∼ **among the population** hay un sentir muy fuerte entre la población; **he looked** ∼ **into her eyes** la miró fijamente a los ojos; **to go** ∼**er (into sth)** ahondar or profundizar* más (en algo) **2** (situated far from edge): ∼ **in the forest** en lo profundo del bosque; ∼ **down you know I'm right** en el fondo sabes que tengo razón

deepen /ˈdiːpən/ vt **1** ⟨canal/well⟩ hacer* más profundo or hondo **2** ⟨knowledge⟩ profundizar* or ahondar en; ⟨concern⟩ aumentar; ⟨friendship⟩ estrechar
■ ∼ vi **1** «gorge/river» hacerse* or volverse* más hondo or profundo **2** «concern/love» hacerse* más profundo; «friendship» estrecharse; «mystery» crecer*, aumentar; «crisis» acentuarse*

deep: ∼ **end** n **the** ∼ **end** (of swimming pool) la parte honda, lo hondo (fam); **to throw sb in (at) the** ∼ **end** meter a algn de lleno en lo más difícil; ∼ **freeze** n congelador m, freezer f (AmL); ∼**-fry** /ˈdiːpˈfraɪ/ vt **-fries, -frying, -fried** freír* (en abundante aceite)

deeply /ˈdiːpli/ adv **1** ⟨sigh⟩ profundamente; **to breathe** ∼ respirar hondo **2** ⟨think⟩ a fondo; ⟨concerned⟩ profundamente; ⟨interested⟩ sumamente

deep: ∼**-sea** /ˈdiːpˈsiː/ adj (before n) ∼**-sea diving** buceo m de altura or en alta mar; ∼**-sea fishing** pesca f de altura; ∼**-seated** /ˈdiːpˈsiːtəd ‖ˌdiːpˈsiːtɪd/ adj ⟨prejudice/conviction⟩ profundamente arraigado; ⟨problem⟩ de raíces profundas; ∼**-set** /ˈdiːpˈset/ adj ⟨eyes⟩ hundido

deer /dɪr ‖ dɪə(r)/ n (pl ∼) ciervo m, venado m

deface /dɪˈfeɪs/ vt ⟨wall/notice⟩ pintarrajear

defamation /ˌdefəˈmeɪʃən/ n (fml) difamación f

default¹ /dɪˈfɔːlt/ n **1** (omission) omisión f; (on payments) mora f; (failure to appear) incomparecencia f; (Law) rebeldía f **2** (lack) falta f; **he was elected by** ∼ fue elegido por ausencia de otros candidatos; (before n) ∼ **option** (Comput) opción f por defecto

default² vi (a) (Fin) **to** ∼ **(on sth)** no pagar* (algo) **(b)** (Law) estar* en rebeldía **(c)** (Sport) no presentarse

defeat¹ /dɪˈfiːt/ n **1** (by opponent) derrota f **2** (of motion, bill) (Adm, Govt) rechazo m

defeat² vt **1** ⟨opponent⟩ derrotar, vencer* **2** ⟨hopes/plans⟩ frustrar; **that would** ∼ **the object of the exercise** eso iría en contra de lo que se pretende lograr **3** (Adm, Govt) ⟨opposition⟩ derrotar; ⟨bill/motion⟩ rechazar* **4** (baffle) (colloq): **it** ∼**s me** no alcanzo a comprenderlo

defeatist /dɪˈfiːtəst ‖ dɪˈfiːtɪst/ adj derrotista

defect¹ /ˈdiːfekt/ n defecto m; **a speech** ∼ un defecto en el habla

defect² /dɪˈfekt/ vi (Pol) desertar*, defeccionar (period)

defective /dɪˈfektɪv/ adj defectuoso

defector /dɪˈfektər ‖dɪˈfektə(r)/ n desertor, -tora m,f

defence etc (BrE) ▶ **DEFENSE** etc

defend /dɪˈfend/ vt defender*
■ ∼ vi **1** (Law) actuar* por la defensa **2** (Sport): **he's better at** ∼**ing** juega mejor como defensa

defendant /dɪˈfendənt/ n (Law) (in civil case) demandado, -da m,f; (in criminal case) acusado, -da m,f

defender /dɪˈfendər ‖dɪˈfendə(r)/ n (a) (of cause, course of action, opinion) defensor, -sora m,f **(b)** (Sport) defensa mf

defending /dɪˈfendɪŋ/ adj: **the** ∼ **champion** el actual campeón (que defiende su título)

defense, (BrE) **defence** /dɪˈfens, ˈdiːfens ‖dɪˈfens/ n **1** (a) (Mil) defensa f **(b)** (on personal level) defensa f **2** (a) (protection) defensa f, protección f **(b)** (apologia) defensa f **3 defenses** pl (Mil, Med, Psych) defensas fpl **4** (Law) defensa f **5** (a) (Sport) defensa f **(b)** (in chess) defensa f

defenseless, (BrE) **defenceless** /dɪˈfensləs ‖dɪˈfenslɪs/ adj indefenso

defensive /dɪˈfensɪv/ adj defensivo

defer /dɪˈfɜːr ‖dɪˈfɜː(r)/ **-rr-** vt (fml) diferir* (fml), aplazar*, postergar* (esp AmL)
■ **defer to** [v + prep + o] (fml) deferir* a (fml)

deference /ˈdefərəns/ n (fml) deferencia f

deferential /ˈdefəˈrentʃəl ‖ˌdefəˈrenʃəl/ adj deferente

deferment /dɪˈfɜːrmənt ‖dɪˈfɜːmənt/ n (fml) aplazamiento m

defiance /dɪˈfaɪəns/ n **an act of** ∼ un desafío, un acto de rebeldía; **in** ∼ **of her orders** haciendo caso omiso de sus órdenes

defiant /dɪˈfaɪənt/ adj ⟨attitude/tone⟩ desafiante; ⟨person⟩ rebelde

deficiency /dɪˈfɪʃənsi/ n (pl **-cies**) deficiencia f

deficient /dɪˈfɪʃənt/ adj (fml) deficiente, insuficiente

deficit /ˈdefəsɪt ‖ˈdefɪsɪt/ n déficit m

define /dɪˈfaɪn/ vt (a) (state meaning of, describe) ⟨word/position⟩ definir **(b)** ⟨powers/duties⟩ delimitar **(c)** (characterize) distinguir*

definite /ˈdefənət, ˈdefnət ‖ˈdefɪnɪt/ adj **1** (a) (final) ⟨date/price/offer⟩ definitivo, en firme **(b)** (certain) seguro, confirmado **(c)** (firm, categorical) ⟨tone⟩ firme, terminante **(d)** (distinct): **it's a** ∼ **advantage/possibility** es, sin duda, una ventaja/posibilidad **2** (Ling): ∼ **article** artículo m determinado or definido

definitely /ˈdefənətli, ˈdefnətli ‖ˈdefɪnɪtli/ adv **(a)** (without doubt): **it's** ∼ **true** es indudablemente ···⟩

cierto; **he ~ said we should meet here** seguro que dijo que nos encontráramos aquí **(b)** (definitively) ⟨*arrange/agree*⟩ definitivamente

definition /ˌdefəˈnɪʃən ‖ˌdefrˈnɪʃən/ *n* **1** **(a)** (statement of meaning) definición *f*; **by ~** por definición **(b)** (categorization) definición *f*, delimitación *f*

definitive /dɪˈfɪnətɪv/ *adj* (*no comp*) **(a)** (final) ⟨*verdict/victory*⟩ definitivo **(b)** (authoritative) ⟨*biography/study*⟩ de mayor autoridad

deflate /dɪˈfleɪt/ *vt* **(a)** ⟨*balloon/tire*⟩ desinflar **(b)** (humble): **to ~ sb** bajarle los humos a algn **(c)** (depress) deprimir; **I felt ~d** me sentí por los suelos

deflation /dɪˈfleɪʃən/ *n* deflación *f*

deflect /dɪˈflekt/ *vt* **to ~ sth** (**FROM sth**) desviar* algo (**DE** algo)
■ **~** *vi* desviarse*

defogger /ˈdiːˈfɔːɡər ‖ˌdiːˈfɒɡə(r)/ *n* (AmE) desempañador *m*

deforestation /diːˌfɔːrəˈsteɪʃən ‖ˌdiːˌfɒrɪˈsteɪʃən/ *n* deforestación *f*, despoblación *f* forestal (Esp)

deformed /dɪˈfɔːrmd ‖dɪˈfɔːmd/ *adj* deforme

deformity /dɪˈfɔːrməti ‖dɪˈfɔːməti/ *n* (*pl* **-ties**) deformidad *f*

defraud /dɪˈfrɔːd/ *vt* ⟨*person*⟩ estafar

defray /dɪˈfreɪ/ *vt* (frml) ⟨*cost*⟩ sufragar* (frml)

defrost /diːˈfrɔːst ‖diːˈfrɒst/ *vt* ⟨*food*⟩ descongelar; ⟨*refrigerator*⟩ deshelar*, descongelar
■ **~** *vi* «*meat*» descongelarse; «*refrigerator*» deshelarse*, descongelarse

deft /deft/ *adj* **-er, -est** ⟨*movement*⟩ hábil, diestro

deftly /ˈdeftli/ *adv* hábilmente, con destreza

defunct /dɪˈfʌŋkt/ *adj* ⟨*idea/theory*⟩ caduco; ⟨*institution*⟩ desaparecido, extinto, fenecido (frml)

defuse /ˌdiːˈfjuːz/ *vt* ⟨*bomb*⟩ desactivar; ⟨*situation*⟩ distender*; ⟨*crisis*⟩ calmar

defy /dɪˈfaɪ/ *vt* **defies, defying, defied (a)** (disobey) ⟨*order/authority*⟩ desacatar, desobedecer* **(b)** (resist): **to ~ understanding/description** ser* incomprensible/indescriptible **(c)** (ignore) ⟨*danger/death*⟩ desafiar*

degenerate¹ /dɪˈdʒenəreɪt/ *vi* degenerar; «*health*» deteriorarse

degenerate² /dɪˈdʒenərət/ *adj* degenerado

degeneration /dɪˌdʒenəˈreɪʃən/ *n* **(a)** (deterioration) degeneración *f*, deterioro *m* **(b)** (Med) (of tissue, organs) degeneración *f*

degrade /dɪˈɡreɪd/ *vt* degradar

degrading /dɪˈɡreɪdɪŋ/ *adj* degradante

degree /dɪˈɡriː/ *n* **1** (level, amount) grado *m*, nivel *m*; **there's a ~ of truth in what she says** hay cierta verdad en lo que dice; **to a ~** (extremely) en grado sumo; (to some extent) hasta cierto punto **2** (grade, step) grado *m*; **first/third ~ burns** quemaduras *fpl* de primer/tercer grado; **first/second ~ murder** (in US) homicidio *m* en primer/segundo grado; **by ~s** gradualmente, paulatinamente

3 (Math, Geog, Meteo, Phys) grado *m*; **12 ~s below zero** 12 grados bajo cero; **this wine is 12 ~s proof** este vino es de *or* tiene 12 grados

4 (Educ) título *m*; **first ~** licenciatura *f*; **he has** *o* (frml) **holds a ~ in chemistry** es licenciado en química

dehydrated /ˈdiːhaɪˈdreɪtəd ‖ˌdiːhaɪˈdreɪtɪd/ *adj* deshidratado; **to become ~** deshidratarse

dehydration /ˌdiːhaɪˈdreɪʃən/ *n* deshidratación *f*

deign /deɪn/ *vi* **to ~ to + INF** dignarse (A) + INF

deity /ˈdiːəti/ *n* (*pl* **-ties**) deidad *f*

dejected /dɪˈdʒektəd ‖dɪˈdʒektɪd/ *adj* abatido, desalentado

Del = **Delaware**

delay¹ /dɪˈleɪ/ *vt* **1** (make late, hold up) retrasar, demorar (esp AmL) **2** (defer) ⟨*decision/payment*⟩ retrasar, demorar (esp AmL)
■ **~** *vi* tardar, demorar (esp AmL)

delay² *n* **(a)** (waiting) tardanza *f*, dilación *f*, demora *f* (esp AmL) **(b)** (holdup) retraso *m*, demora *f* (esp AmL); **~s can be expected on major roads** se puede esperar embotellamientos en las principales carreteras

delayed action /dɪˈleɪd/ *n* acción *f* retardada

delectable /dɪˈlektəbəl/ *adj* **(a)** (delicious) delicioso, exquisito **(b)** (delightful) delicioso, encantador

delegate¹ /ˈdelɪɡeɪt/ *vt/i* delegar*

delegate² /ˈdelɪɡət/ *n* delegado, -da *m,f*

delegation /ˌdelɪˈɡeɪʃən/ *n* delegación *f*

delete /dɪˈliːt/ *vt* suprimir, eliminar; (by crossing out) tachar; (Comput) borrar, suprimir

delete key *n* (Comput) tecla *f* de borrar, tecla *f* de borrado

deliberate¹ /dɪˈlɪbərət, -brət/ *adj* **1** (intentional) ⟨*act/attempt*⟩ deliberado, intencionado **2** **(a)** (considered) reflexivo **(b)** (unhurried) pausado, lento

deliberate² /dɪˈlɪbəreɪt/ *vi* (frml) **to ~** (**ABOUT/ON sth**) deliberar (SOBRE algo)
■ **~** *vt* (frml) deliberar sobre

deliberately /dɪˈlɪbərətli, -brətli/ *adv* **1** (intentionally) adrede, a propósito **2** (unhurriedly) pausadamente, con parsimonia

deliberation /dɪˌlɪbəˈreɪʃən/ *n* (frml) **(a)** (consideration) deliberación *f* **(b)** **deliberations** *pl* (decision-making) deliberaciones *fpl*

delicacy /ˈdelɪkəsi/ *n* (*pl* **-cies**) **1** **(a)** (fineness, intricacy) delicadeza *f*, lo delicado; (fragility) fragilidad *f*, lo delicado **(b)** (tact) delicadeza *f* **(c)** (subtleness) lo delicado **2** (choice food) manjar *m*, exquisitez *f*

delicate /ˈdelɪkət/ *adj* **1** **(a)** (fine, intricate) ⟨*lace/features*⟩ delicado; ⟨*workmanship*⟩ fino, esmerado **(b)** (fragile, needing care) delicado **2** **(a)** (needing skill, tact) delicado **(b)** (tactful) delicado, discreto **3** (subtle) ⟨*shade/taste*⟩ delicado

delicately /ˈdelɪkətli/ *adv* **1** ⟨*carve/paint*⟩ con delicadeza, delicadamente **2** ⟨*treat*⟩ con delicadeza **3** ⟨*patterned/perfumed*⟩ delicadamente

delicatessen /ˌdelɪkəˈtesən/ *n* charcutería *f*, rotisería *f* (CS), salsamentaria *f* (Col), salchichonería *f* (Méx)

delicious /dɪˈlɪʃəs/ *adj* delicioso

delight¹ /dɪˈlaɪt/ *n* **(a)** (joy) placer *m*, deleite *m*; **to take ~ in sth** disfrutar *or* gozar* con algo **(b)** (source of joy) placer *m*

delight² *vt* **(a)** (make very happy) llenar de

alegría; **his success** ~ed **them** su éxito los llenó de alegría **(b)** (give pleasure to) deleitar; **the clown** ~ed **the children** el payaso hizo las delicias de *or* deleitó a los niños
■ ~ *vi* **to** ~ **IN** -**ING** deleitarse + GER

delighted /dɪˈlaɪtɪd ‖dɪˈlaɪtɪd/ *adj* ⟨*grin/look*⟩ de alegría; **I'm** ~ (**that**) **you can come** me alegra mucho que puedas venir; **to be** ~ **WITH** sth/sb estar* encantado CON algo/algn

delightful /dɪˈlaɪtfəl/ *adj* ⟨*weather/evening*⟩ muy agradable, delicioso; ⟨*person*⟩ encantador; ⟨*dress*⟩ precioso

delineate /dɪˈlɪnieɪt/ *vt* (fml) **(a)** (draw) trazar*, delinear **(b)** (describe) ⟨*problem*⟩ definir

delinquency /dɪˈlɪŋkwənsi/ *n* (Law, Sociol) delincuencia *f*

delinquent /dɪˈlɪŋkwənt/ *n* delincuente *mf*

delirious /dɪˈlɪriəs/ *adj* **(a)** (Med) delirante; **to be** ~ delirar, desvariar* **(b)** (wildly excited, happy) (colloq) loco de alegría (fam)

deliver /dɪˈlɪvər ‖dɪˈlɪvə(r)/ *vt* **1** **(a)** (hand over) entregar* **(b)** (distribute) repartir ⟨*a domicilio*⟩ **2** **(a)** (administer) ⟨*blow/punch*⟩ propinar, asestar **(b)** (issue) ⟨*ultimatum/lecture/sermon*⟩ dar*; ⟨*warning*⟩ hacer*; ⟨*speech*⟩ pronunciar; ⟨*judgment*⟩ dictar, pronunciar, emitir **(c)** (produce, provide): **he promised much, but** ~ed **little** cumplió muy poco de lo mucho que había prometido **(d)** (Sport) ⟨*ball*⟩ lanzar* **(e)** (in elections) (AmE) ⟨*state*⟩ ganar **3** (Med): **her husband** ~ed **the baby** su marido la asistió en el parto
■ ~ *vi* **1** (Busn): **we** ~ **free of charge** hacemos reparto(s) a domicilio gratuitamente **2** (produce the necessary) (colloq) cumplir

delivery /dɪˈlɪvəri/ *n* (*pl* -**ries**) **1** **(a)** (act) entrega *f*; (*before n*) ~ **charges** gastos *mpl* de envío *or* transporte; ~ **man** repartidor *m*; ~ **truck** *o* (BrE) **van** camioneta *f or* furgoneta *f* de los repartos **(b)** (occasion) reparto *m*; **is there a** ~ **on Saturdays?** ¿hay reparto los sábados? **(c)** (consignment) partida *f*, remesa *f* **2** (of baby) parto *m*, alumbramiento *m* (fml) **3** (manner of speaking) expresión *f* oral

delta /ˈdeltə/ *n* delta *m*

delude /dɪˈluːd/ *vt* engañar

deluge /ˈdeljuːdʒ/ *n* **1** **(a)** (flood) inundación *f* **(b)** (downpour) diluvio *m* **2** **(a)** (of protests, questions, letters) aluvión *m*, avalancha *f*

delusion /dɪˈluːʒən/ *n* (mistaken idea) error *m*; (vain hope) falsa ilusión *f*

deluxe /dəˈlʊks/ *adj* de lujo

delve /delv/ *vi* (liter) **to** ~ **INTO** sth ahondar EN algo; **to** ~ **into the past** hurgar* en el pasado

demand[1] /dɪˈmænd ‖dɪˈmɑːnd/ *vt* **1** «*person*» (call for, insist on) exigir*; **the unions are** ~ing **better conditions** los sindicatos reclaman mejores condiciones **2** (require) ⟨*determination/perseverance*⟩ exigir*, requerir*

demand[2] *n* **1** (claim) exigencia *f*; (Lab Rel, Pol) reivindicación *f*, reclamo *m*; (request) petición *f*, pedido *m* (AmL); **the** ~s **of the job** las exigencias del trabajo; **abortion on** ~ libre aborto *m* **2** (requirement) demanda *f*; **he's in great** ~ está muy solicitado, es popular

demanding /dɪˈmændɪŋ ‖dɪˈmɑːndɪŋ/ *adj* ⟨*job*⟩ que exige mucho; ⟨*book/music*⟩ difícil; ⟨*teacher*⟩ exigente

demarcation /ˌdiːmɑːrˈkeɪʃən ‖ˌdiːmɑːˈkeɪʃən/ *n* demarcación *f*; (*before n*) ~ **line** línea *f* de demarcación

demean /dɪˈmiːn/ *vt* (fml) degradar

demeaning /dɪˈmiːnɪŋ/ *adj* degradante

demeanor, (BrE) **demeanour** /dɪˈmiːnər ‖dɪˈmiːnə(r)/ *n* (fml) **(a)** (behavior) comportamiento *m*, conducta *f* **(b)** (bearing) porte *m*

demented /dɪˈmentəd ‖dɪˈmentɪd/ *adj* ⟨*person*⟩ demente; ⟨*screams/mutterings*⟩ enloquecido

dementia /dɪˈmentʃə ‖dɪˈmenʃə/ *n* demencia *f*

demerara (**sugar**) /ˈdeməˈrɑːrə ‖ˌdeməˈreərə/ *n* (BrE) azúcar *f* morena, azúcar *m* moreno

demerit /diːˈmerət ‖diːˈmerɪt/ *n* (fml) demérito *m* (fml)

demise /dɪˈmaɪz/ *n* (*no pl*) (fml) **(a)** (death) fallecimiento *m* (fml), deceso *m* (AmL fml) **(b)** (end) desaparición *f*

demister /ˈdiːˈmɪstər ‖ˌdiːˈmɪstə(r)/ *n* (BrE) desempañador *m*

demo /ˈdeməʊ/ *n* (*pl* **demos**) **1** (Mus) demostración *f*; (*before n*) ~ **tape** cinta *f* de demostración **2** (protest) (BrE colloq) manifestación *f*

demobilize /dɪˈməʊbəlaɪz ‖diːˈməʊbɪlaɪz/ *vt* desmovilizar*

democracy /dɪˈmɑːkrəsi ‖dɪˈmɒkrəsi/ *n* (*pl* -**cies**) democracia *f*

democrat /ˈdeməkræt/ *n* **(a)** (believer in democracy) demócrata *mf* **(b)** **Democrat** (in US) demócrata *mf*

democratic /ˌdeməˈkrætɪk/ *adj* **(a)** ⟨*country/election*⟩ democrático **(b)** **Democratic** (in US) demócrata

demographic /ˈdeməˈgræfɪk/ *adj* demográfico

demography /dɪˈmɑːgrəfi ‖dɪˈmɒgrəfi/ *n* demografía *f*

demolish /dɪˈmɑːlɪʃ ‖dɪˈmɒlɪʃ/ *vt* ⟨*structure/building*⟩ demoler*, derribar, echar abajo; ⟨*argument/theory*⟩ demoler*, echar por tierra

demolition /ˌdeməˈlɪʃən/ *n* (of building) demolición *f*, derribo *m*; (of theory) demolición *f*, destrucción *f*

demon /ˈdiːmən/ *n* demonio *m*

demonstrate /ˈdemənstreɪt/ *vt* **(a)** (show) ⟨*need/ability*⟩ demostrar* **(b)** (Marketing) hacer* una demostración de
■ ~ *vi* (Pol) manifestarse*

demonstration /ˌdemənˈstreɪʃən/ *n* **1** **(a)** (expression) muestra *f*, demostración *f* **(b)** (display) demostración *f* **2** (Pol) manifestación *f*

demonstrative /dɪˈmɑːnstrətɪv ‖dɪˈmɒnstrətɪv/ *adj* efusivo, expresivo, demostrativo (AmL)

demonstrator /ˈdemənstreɪtər ‖ˈdemənstreɪtə(r)/ *n* manifestante *mf*

demoralize /dɪˈmɔːrəlaɪz ‖dɪˈmɒrəlaɪz/ *vt* desmoralizar*

demoralizing /dɪˈmɔːrəlaɪzɪŋ ‖dɪˈmɒrəlaɪzɪŋ/ *adj* desalentador, desmoralizante

d

demote /dɪˈməʊt, ˈdiː-/ vt (in organization) bajar de categoría; (Mil) degradar

demotion /dɪˈməʊʃən, diː-/ n (in organization) descenso m de categoría; (Mil) degradación f

demur /dɪˈmɜːr ‖ dɪˈmɜː(r)/ vi -rr- (fml) objetar

demure /dɪˈmjʊr ‖ dɪˈmjʊə(r)/ adj recatado

den /den/ n [1] (of animals, thieves) guarida f [2] (room) (colloq) cuarto m de estar; (for study, work) estudio m

denial /dɪˈnaɪəl/ n [1] (of accusation, fact): **to issue a ~ of sth** desmentir* algo [2] (of request, rights) denegación f [3] (repudiation) negación f, rechazo m [4] (abstinence) renuncia f

denier /ˈdenjər ‖ ˈdeniə(r)/ n denier m

denigrate /ˈdenɪgreɪt/ vt (fml) ⟨character/person⟩ denigrar; ⟨effort⟩ menospreciar

denim /ˈdenəm ‖ ˈdenɪm/ n(Tex) tela f vaquera or de jeans, mezclilla f (Chi, Méx); (before n) ⟨jacket/skirt⟩ vaquero, tejano (Esp), de mezclilla (Chi, Méx)

Denmark /ˈdenmɑːrk ‖ ˈdenmɑːk/ n Dinamarca f

denomination /dɪˌnɑːməˈneɪʃən ‖ dɪˌnɒmɪˈneɪʃən/ n [1] (Relig) confesión f [2] (of currency) valor m, denominación f (AmL)

denominator /dɪˈnɑːməneɪtər ‖ dɪˈnɒmɪneɪtə(r)/ n (Math) denominador m

denote /dɪˈnəʊt/ vt denotar

denouement /ˌdeɪnuːˈmɑːn ‖ deɪˈnuːmɒːn/ n desenlace m

denounce /dɪˈnaʊns/ vt denunciar

dense /dens/ adj **denser, densest** [1] (a) (closely spaced) ⟨forest/jungle⟩ espeso; ⟨population/traffic⟩ denso; ⟨crowd⟩ compacto, apretado (b) (thick) ⟨fog/mist/smoke⟩ denso, espeso (c) (Phys) denso (d) (complicated) ⟨prose/article⟩ denso [2] (stupid) (colloq) burro (fam), duro de entendederas (fam)

densely /ˈdensli/ adv ⟨populated/forested⟩ densamente; ⟨packed⟩ apretadamente

density /ˈdensəti/ n (pl **-ties**) densidad f; (of fog) lo espeso, densidad f

dent¹ /dent/ n (in metal) abolladura f, abollón m; (in wood) marca f

dent² vt ⟨metal⟩ abollar; ⟨wood⟩ hacer* una marca en; ⟨popularity⟩ afectar; ⟨pride⟩ hacer* mella en

dental /ˈdentl/ adj dental; ⟨school⟩ de odontología

dental floss /flɑːs ‖ flɒs/ n hilo m or seda f dental

dentist /ˈdentəst ‖ ˈdentɪst/ n dentista mf, odontólogo, -ga m,f (fml)

dentistry /ˈdentəstri ‖ ˈdentɪstri/ n odontología f

dentures /ˈdentʃərz ‖ ˈdentʃəz/ pl n dentadura f postiza

deny /dɪˈnaɪ/ vt **denies, denying, denied** [1] ⟨accusation/fact⟩ negar*; ⟨rumors⟩ desmentir* [2] (refuse) ⟨request⟩ denegar*

deodorant /diːˈəʊdərənt/ n desodorante m

depart /dɪˈpɑːrt ‖ dɪˈpɑːt/ vi (Transp) salir*, partir (frml); «person» (frml) partir (frml), salir*

department /dɪˈpɑːrtmənt ‖ dɪˈpɑːtmənt/ n [1] (of store) sección f; (of company) departamento m, sección f [2] (a) (Govt) ministerio m, secretaría f (Méx) (b) (AmE Adm): **the police/fire ~** el cuerpo de policía/bomberos [3] (Educ) departamento m

department store n (grandes) almacenes mpl, tienda f de departamentos (Méx)

departure /dɪˈpɑːrtʃər ‖ dɪˈpɑːtʃə(r)/ n(Transp) salida f, partida f (frml); (of person) salida f (frml), ida f; **point of ~** punto m de partida; **a ~ from the norm** una desviación de la norma; (before n) **~ lounge** sala f de embarque

depend /dɪˈpend/ vi **to ~ on** sb/sth depender DE algn/algo

dependable /dɪˈpendəbəl/ adj ⟨person⟩ formal, digno de confianza; ⟨ally/workman⟩ digno de confianza

dependant, (AmE also) **dependent** /dɪˈpendənt/ n carga f familiar, familiar mf a su (or mi etc) cargo

dependence /dɪˈpendəns/ n dependencia f

dependent¹ /dɪˈpendənt/ adj **(a)** (reliant) (pred) **to be ~ on** sth/sb depender DE algo/algn **(b)** (conditional) (pred) **to be ~ on** sth depender DE algo

dependent² n (AmE) ▶ DEPENDANT

depict /dɪˈpɪkt/ vt (fml) **(a)** (portray) representar **(b)** (describe) describir*, pintar

depiction /dɪˈpɪkʃən/ n (fml) **(a)** (representation) representación f **(b)** (description) descripción f

depilatory /dɪˈpɪlətɔːri ‖ dɪˈpɪlətri/ n (pl **-ries**) depilatorio m

deplete /dɪˈpliːt/ vt (reduce) ⟨supply/stock⟩ reducir*; (exhaust) ⟨energy source⟩ agotar

deplorable /dɪˈplɔːrəbəl/ adj **(a)** (disgraceful) deplorable, vergonzoso **(b)** (regrettable) lamentable

deplore /dɪˈplɔːr ‖ dɪˈplɔː(r)/ vt (fml) **(a)** (condemn) deplorar, condenar **(b)** (regret) deplorar, lamentar

deploy /dɪˈplɔɪ/ vt [1] (position) (Mil) desplegar* [2] (distribute, use) ⟨resources⟩ utilizar*, hacer* uso de

deport /dɪˈpɔːrt ‖ dɪˈpɔːt/ vt deportar

deportation /ˌdiːpɔːrˈteɪʃən ‖ ˌdiːpɔːˈteɪʃən/ n deportación f

deportment /dɪˈpɔːrtmənt ‖ dɪˈpɔːtmənt/ n (fml) **(a)** (carriage) porte m **(b)** (conduct) conducta f

depose /dɪˈpəʊz/ vt ⟨dictator/ruler⟩ deponer*, derrocar*; ⟨champion/king⟩ destronar

deposit¹ /dɪˈpɑːzət ‖ dɪˈpɒzɪt/ vt [1] **(a)** (set down) depositar, poner* **(b)** (Geol) ⟨silt⟩ depositar [2] **(a)** (leave) depositar **(b)** ⟨money⟩ depositar, ingresar (Esp)

deposit² n [1] **(a)** (payment into account) depósito m, ingreso m (Esp); (before n) **~ account** cuenta f de ahorros **(b)** (down payment — on large amounts) depósito m, entrega f inicial; (— on small amounts) depósito m, señal f, seña f (RPI) **(c)** (security)

---

depósito *m*, fianza *f* **2** (accumulation — of silt, mud)
depósito *m*; (— of dust) capa *f* **3** (Min) (of gas)
depósito *m*; (of gold, copper) yacimiento *m*

depot /'di:pəʊ ‖'depəʊ/ *n* **1** **(a)** (storehouse)
depósito *m*, almacén *m* **(b)** (Mil) depósito *m*
2 (esp AmE) (bus station) terminal *f* or (Chi) *m*,
estación *f* de autobuses; (train station) estación *f*
3 (esp BrE) (storage area) **(a)** (for buses) garage *m*
(esp AmL), cochera *f* (Esp), depósito *m* (Chi) **(b)** (for
trains) depósito *m* de locomotoras

depraved /dɪ'preɪvd/ *adj* depravado

depravity /dɪ'prævəti/ *n* depravación *f*

deprecating /'deprɪkeɪtɪŋ/ *adj* (frml) **(a)**
(disapproving) ⟨remark⟩ de desaprobación,
reprobatorio **(b)** (belittling) ⟨smile/laugh⟩ de
desprecio

depreciate /dɪ'pri:ʃieɪt/ *vt* (Fin) depreciar
■ ~ *vi* (Fin) depreciarse

depress /dɪ'pres/ *vt* **1** (sadden) deprimir,
abatir **2** (press down) (frml) ⟨lever⟩ bajar; ⟨button⟩
pulsar (frml) **3** (Econ) ⟨market⟩ deprimir; ⟨prices/
wages⟩ reducir*, hacer* bajar

depressed /dɪ'prest/ *adj* **1** (dejected)
deprimido, abatido; **to get** ~ deprimirse, dejarse
abatir **2** (Econ) ⟨economy/market/area⟩
deprimido

depressing /dɪ'presɪŋ/ *adj* deprimente

depression /dɪ'preʃən/ *n* **1** (despondency)
depresión *f*, abatimiento *m* **2** (in flat surface)
depresión *f* **3** (Econ) depresión *f*, crisis *f*

deprivation /'deprə'veɪʃən ‖,deprɪ'veɪʃən/ *n*
(lack, loss) privación *f*; (hardship) privaciones *fpl*,
penurias *fpl*

deprive /dɪ'praɪv/ *vt*: **to** ~ **sb** **OF** **sth** privar a
algn DE algo

deprived /dɪ'praɪvd/ *adj* ⟨child⟩ carencido,
desventajado; ⟨region⟩ carenciado

dept (= **department**) Dpto.

depth /depθ/ *n* **1** **(a)** (of hole, water)
profundidad *f*; **out of one's** ~: **when it comes to
computers I'm out of my** ~ estoy muy flojo en
informática; **don't go out of your** ~ (in water) no
vayas donde no haces pie or no tocas fondo **(b)**
(of shelf, cupboard) profundidad *f*, fondo *m*; (of hem)
ancho *m*
2 (of emotion, knowledge) profundidad *f*; **to study
sth in** ~ estudiar algo a fondo or en profundidad
3 (of voice) profundidad *f*; (of sound) intensidad *f*
4 **depths** *pl n*: **in the** ~**s of the ocean** en las
profundidades del océano; **in the** ~**s of despair** en
lo más hondo de la desesperación

deputation /'depjə'teɪʃən ‖,depjʊ'teɪʃən/ *n*
delegación *f*

deputy /'depjəti/ *n* (*pl* **-ties**) **1** **(a)**
(second-in-command) segundo, -da *m,f*; (substitute)
suplente *mf*, reemplazo *mf* **(b)** ~ **(sheriff)** (AmE
Law) ayudante *mf* del sheriff **2** (Govt) diputado,
-da *m,f*

derail /dɪ'reɪl/ *vt* **(a)** ⟨train⟩ hacer* descarrilar
(b) (upset) ⟨plan⟩ desbaratar

deranged /dɪ'reɪndʒd/ *adj* trastornado

derby /'dɜ:rbi ‖'dɑ:bi/ *n* (*pl* **derbies**)
1 (Sport): **the D**~ (in UK) el Derby, el clásico de
Epsom; **the Kentucky D**~ el Derby de Kentucky
2 (hat) (AmE) bombín *m*, sombrero *m* de hongo

deregulate /'di:'regjəleɪt ‖,di:'regjʊleɪt/ *vt*
desregular, liberalizar*

deregulation /'di:'regjə'leɪʃən
‖di:,regjʊ'leɪʃən/ *n* desregulación *f*,
liberalización *f*

derelict /'derəlɪkt/ *adj* abandonado y en ruinas

deride /dɪ'raɪd/ *vt* ridiculizar*, burlarse de

derision /dɪ'rɪʒən/ *n* escarnio *m* (frml), irrisión
f (frml)

derisive /dɪ'raɪsɪv/ *adj* ⟨smile/laughter⟩ burlón;
⟨attitude/remark⟩ desdeñoso y burlón

derisory /dɪ'raɪzəri/ *adj* ⟨sum/offer⟩ irrisorio

derivative¹ /dɪ'rɪvətɪv/ *adj* (unoriginal) ⟨novel⟩
carente de originalidad; ⟨plot/theme⟩ manido,
trillado; ⟨artist/writer⟩ adocenado

derivative² *n* (in industry) derivado *m*

derive /dɪ'raɪv/ *vt* children can ~ great
enjoyment from the simplest things las cosas más
simples pueden dar enorme placer a un niño; **the
name is** ~**d from the Greek** el nombre viene or
deriva del griego
■ ~ *vi* **to** ~ **FROM sth** «attitude/problem»
provenir* DE algo; «idea» tener* su origen EN
algo; (Ling) derivar(se) DE algo

dermatitis /'dɜ:rmə'taɪtəs ‖,dɜ:mə'taɪtɪs/ *n*
dermatitis *f*

derogatory /dɪ'rɑ:gətɔ:ri ‖dɪ'rɒgətri/ *adj*
despectivo, peyorativo

descant /'deskænt/ *n* contrapunto *m*

descend /dɪ'send/ *vi* (move downwards)
descender* (frml), bajar; **in** ~**ing order of
importance** en orden decreciente or descendente
de importancia; **don't** ~ **to his level** no te pongas
a su nivel
■ ~ *vt* descender* (frml), bajar

descendant /dɪ'sendənt/ *n* descendiente *mf*

descended /dɪ'sendəd ‖dɪ'sendɪd/ *adj* (pred)
to be ~ **FROM sb** ser* descendiente DE algn,
descender* DE algn

descendent *n* (AmE) ▶ DESCENDANT

descent /dɪ'sent/ *n* **1** **(a)** (by climbers, plane)
descenso *m*, bajada *f* **(b)** (in terrain) pendiente *f*,
bajada *f* **2** (decline) caída *f* **3** (lineage)
ascendencia *f*

describe /dɪ'skraɪb/ *vt* describir*; **he** ~**s
himself as a socialist** se define como socialista

description /dɪ'skrɪpʃən/ *n* descripción *f*; **of
every** ~ de todo tipo, de toda clase

descriptive /dɪ'skrɪptɪv/ *adj* descriptivo

desecrate /'desɪkreɪt/ *vt* profanar

desert¹ /'dezərt ‖'dezət/ *n* (Geog) desierto *m*;
(before n) ⟨region/climate⟩ desértico; ⟨tribe/sand⟩
del desierto

desert² /dɪ'zɜ:rt ‖dɪ'zɜ:t/ *vt* **(a)** (frml) ⟨place⟩
abandonar, huir* de **(b)** ⟨family⟩ abandonar;
⟨cause⟩ desertar de
■ ~ *vi* (Mil) desertar

deserted /dɪ'zɜ:rtəd ‖dɪ'zɜ:tɪd/ *adj* **(a)** ⟨streets/
village⟩ desierto **(b)** ⟨husband/wife⟩ abandonado

deserter /dɪ'zɜ:rtər ‖dɪ'zɜ:tə(r)/ *n* desertor,
-tora *m,f*

desertion /dɪ'zɜ:rʃən ‖dɪ'zɜ:ʃən/ *n* **(a)** (Mil)
deserción *f* **(b)** (of family, place) abandono *m*

desert island /'dezərt ‖'dezət/ *n* isla *f*
desierta

deserts /dɪ'zɜ:rts ‖dɪ'zɜ:ts/ *pl n*: **to get one's
just** ~ recibir su (or tu *etc*) merecido

deserve /dɪˈzɜːrv ‖dɪˈzɜːv/ *vt* merecer(se)*; **they got what they ~d** se llevaron su merecido

deserving /dɪˈzɜːrvɪŋ ‖dɪˈzɜːvɪŋ/ *adj* ⟨*cause/case*⟩ meritorio; **the ~ poor** los pobres dignos de ayuda

desiccated /ˈdesɪkeɪtəd ‖ˈdesɪkeɪtɪd/ *adj* seco; **~ coconut** coco *m* rallado

design¹ /dɪˈzaɪn/ *n* **1** **(a)** (of product, car, machine) diseño *m*; (drawing) diseño *m*, boceto *m* **(b)** (pattern, decoration) diseño *m*, motivo *m*, dibujo *m* **(c)** (product, model) modelo *m* **2** **(a)** (Art) diseño *m* **(b)** (style) estilo *m*, líneas *fpl* **3** **(a)** (plan) (liter) plan *m*; **by ~** deliberadamente **(b)** **designs** *pl n* (intentions) propósitos *mpl*, designios *mpl* (liter)

design² *vt* ⟨*house/garden*⟩ diseñar, proyectar; ⟨*dress/product*⟩ diseñar; ⟨*course/program*⟩ planear, estructurar; **a statement ~ed to reassure the public** una declaración destinada a tranquilizar al público

designate¹ /ˈdezɪgneɪt/ *vt* **1** (name officially) nombrar, designar **2** (call) (frml) designar

designate² /ˈdezɪgneɪt, -nət ‖ˈdezɪgnət/ *adj* (*after n*): **the governor ~** quien ha sido nombrado gobernador

designer /dɪˈzaɪnər ‖dɪˈzaɪnə(r)/ *n* diseñador, -dora *m,f*; (*before n*) ⟨*clothes/jeans*⟩ de diseño exclusivo; ⟨*furniture/pen*⟩ de diseño

desirable /dɪˈzaɪrəbəl ‖dɪˈzaɪərəbəl/ *adj* **(a)** ⟨*property/location*⟩ atractivo **(b)** (sexually) ⟨*man/woman*⟩ atractivo, deseable, apetecible **(c)** ⟨*outcome*⟩ deseable, conveniente; ⟨*option*⟩ conveniente, aconsejable

desire¹ /dɪˈzaɪr ‖dɪˈzaɪə(r)/ *n* **1** (wish) deseo *m*, anhelo *m* (liter) **2** (lust) deseo *m*

desire² *vt* **(a)** (want) ⟨*happiness/success*⟩ desear; **to leave a lot to be ~d** dejar bastante que desear **(b)** (lust after) ⟨*person*⟩ desear

desirous /dɪˈzaɪrəs ‖dɪˈzaɪərəs/ *adj* (frml) (*pred*): **we are ~ of your success** le deseamos éxito

desist /dɪˈzɪst/ *vi* (frml) **to ~** (**FROM** sth/-ING) (cease) desistir (DE algo/+ INF); (abstain) abstenerse* (DE algo/+ INF)

desk /desk/ *n* **(a)** (table) escritorio *m*, mesa *f* de trabajo; (in school) pupitre *m*; (*before n*) ⟨*lamp*⟩ de escritorio, de (sobre)mesa; **a ~ job** un trabajo de oficina **(b)** (service counter) mostrador *m* **(c)** (Journ) sección *f*

desktop /ˈdesktɑːp ‖ˈdesktɒp/ *adj* (*before n*) ⟨*calculator/computer*⟩ de escritorio, de (sobre)mesa; **~ publishing** autoedición *f*, edición *f* electrónica

desolate /ˈdesələt/ *adj* **1** (deserted) ⟨*place/landscape*⟩ desierto, desolado **2** ⟨*person*⟩ desconsolado, desolado; ⟨*outlook/existence*⟩ sombrío, lúgubre

despair¹ /dɪˈsper ‖dɪˈspeə(r)/ *n* desesperación *f*; **to be in ~** estar* desesperado

despair² *vi* perder* las esperanzas, desesperar(se); **honestly, I ~ of you!** ¡francamente, eres un caso perdido!

despairing /dɪˈsperɪŋ ‖dɪˈspeərɪŋ/ *adj* ⟨*look/cry*⟩ de desesperación

despatch /dɪˈspætʃ/ *vt/n* ▶ DISPATCH¹,²

desperate /ˈdespərət/ *adj* **1** (frantic) ⟨*person/*

attempt⟩ desesperado; **to be ~** estar* desesperado **2** (critical) ⟨*state/situation*⟩ grave, desesperado; ⟨*need*⟩ apremiante

desperately /ˈdespərətli/ *adv* ⟨*struggle*⟩ desesperadamente; ⟨*need*⟩ urgentemente, con urgencia

desperation /ˌdespəˈreɪʃən/ *n* desesperación *f*

despicable /dɪˈspɪkəbəl/ *adj* vil, despreciable

despise /dɪˈspaɪz/ *vt* despreciar (profundamente)

despite /dɪˈspaɪt/ *prep* a pesar de

despondent /dɪˈspɑːndənt ‖dɪˈspɒndənt/ *adj* abatido, descorazonado

despot /ˈdespɑːt ‖ˈdespɒt/ *n* déspota *mf*

dessert /dɪˈzɜːrt ‖dɪˈzɜːt/ *n* postre *m*

dessertspoon /dɪˈzɜːrtspuːn ‖dɪˈzɜːtspuːn/ *n* cuchara *f* de postre

destabilize /diːˈsteɪbəlaɪz/ *vt* desestabilizar*

destination /ˌdestəˈneɪʃən, ˌdestɪˈneɪʃən/ *n* **(a)** (end of journey) destino *m* **(b)** (purpose) meta *f*

destined /ˈdestənd ‖ˈdestɪnd/ *adj* (*pred*) **1** (fated) **to be ~ to** + INF estar* (pre)destinado A + INF **2** **(a)** (intended) **~ FOR sth** destinado A algo **(b)** (bound, on way): **~ for the West Indies** con destino al Caribe

destiny /ˈdestəni ‖ˈdestɪni/ *n* (*pl* **-nies**) destino *m*, sino *m* (liter)

destitute /ˈdestətuːt ‖ˈdestɪtjuːt/ *adj* indigente

destroy /dɪˈstrɔɪ/ *vt* **(a)** (ruin, wreck) ⟨*building/forest*⟩ destruir*; ⟨*reputation/confidence*⟩ acabar con; ⟨*life*⟩ arruinar **(b)** ⟨*animal*⟩ sacrificar* (euf)

destroyer /dɪˈstrɔɪər ‖dɪˈstrɔɪə(r)/ *n* destructor *m*

destruction /dɪˈstrʌkʃən/ *n* **1** (of city, books, forest) destrucción *f*; (of reputation, civilization) ruina *f*, destrucción *f*; (slaughter) exterminación *f* **2** (cause of downfall) (frml) ruina *f*, perdición *f* **3** (damage) destrucción *f*, estragos *mpl*, destrozos *mpl*

destructive /dɪˈstrʌktɪv/ *adj* ⟨*storm/weapon*⟩ destructor; ⟨*tendency*⟩ destructivo; ⟨*child*⟩ destrozón; ⟨*criticism*⟩ destructivo, negativo

desultory /ˈdesəltɔːri ‖ˈdezəltəri/ *adj* ⟨*effort/attempt*⟩ desganado

detach /dɪˈtætʃ/ *vt* (separate) separar, quitar; (unstick) despegar*; **the headrest can be ~ed** el apoyacabezas se puede desmontar *or* quitar

detachable /dɪˈtætʃəbəl/ *adj* ⟨*cover*⟩ de quita y pon, de quitar y poner; ⟨*lining*⟩ desmontable

detached /dɪˈtætʃt/ *adj* **1** ⟨*person/manner*⟩ (aloof) distante, indiferente; (objective) objetivo, imparcial **2** (BrE) ⟨*house*⟩ no adosado

detachment /dɪˈtætʃmənt/ *n* **1** (aloofness) distancia *f*, indiferencia *f*; (objectivity) objetividad *f*, imparcialidad *f* **2** (act of detaching) (frml) desprendimiento *m* **3** (Mil) destacamento *m*

detail¹ /dɪˈteɪl, ˈdiːteɪl ‖ˈdiːteɪl/ *n* **1** **(a)** (particular) detalle *m*, pormenor *m*; **he asked for further ~s** pidió más información *or* información más detallada **(b)** (embellishment) detalle *m* **(c)** (insignificant matter) minucia *f*, detalle *m* (sin importancia) **2** (minutiae) detalles *mpl*; **to go into ~** entrar en detalles *or* pormenores; **to explain sth in ~** explicar* algo detalladamente *or* minuciosamente

detail² *vt* **1** (describe) exponer* en detalle, detallar **2** (Mil) destacar*

detailed /ˈdiːteɪld/ adj ⟨description⟩ detallado, minucioso, pormenorizado; ⟨examination⟩ minucioso, detenido

detain /dɪˈteɪn/ vt (a) (delay) (frml): don't let me ~ you no quiero entretenerlo or demorarlo (b) (in custody) detener*

detect /dɪˈtekt/ vt ⟨object/substance⟩ detectar

detection /dɪˈtekʃən/ n [1] (of error) descubrimiento m; (of act, crime, criminal): to escape ~ pasar desapercibido or inadvertido [2] (of substance) detección f

detective /dɪˈtektɪv/ n (private) detective mf; (in police force) agente mf, oficial mf; (before n) ~ story novela f policíaca or policial

detector /dɪˈtektər ‖dɪˈtektə(r)/ n detector m

detente /deɪˈtɑːnt/ n (Pol) distensión f

detention /dɪˈtenʃən ‖dɪˈtenʃən/ n [1] (in custody) detención f [2] (Educ): to be in ~ estar* castigado

deter /dɪˈtɜːr ‖dɪˈtɜː(r)/ vt -rr- ⟨person⟩ disuadir, hacer* disuadir; ⟨crime/war⟩ impedir*; to ~ sb FROM sth/-ING disuadir a algn DE algo/ + INF

detergent /dɪˈtɜːrdʒənt ‖dɪˈtɜːdʒənt/ n (Chem) detergente m; (for clothes) detergente m; (for dishes) lavavajillas m

deteriorate /dɪˈtɪriəreɪt ‖dɪˈtɪəriəreɪt/ vi «health/relationship/material» deteriorarse; «weather/work» empeorar

deterioration /dɪˌtɪriəˈreɪʃən ‖dɪˌtɪəriəˈreɪʃən/ n deterioro m

determination /dɪˌtɜːrməˈneɪʃən ‖dɪˌtɜːmɪˈneɪʃən/ n determinación f, resolución f

determine /dɪˈtɜːrmən ‖dɪˈtɜːmɪn/ vt [1] (ascertain) establecer*, determinar [2] (a) (influence) determinar, condicionar (b) (mark) ⟨boundary/limit⟩ definir, demarcar* [3] (liter) (resolve) decidir; to ~ to + INF decidir + INF, tomar la determinación DE + INF

determined /dɪˈtɜːrmənd ‖dɪˈtɜːmɪnd/ adj ⟨mood/person⟩ decidido, resuelto; to be ~ to + INF estar* decidido A + INF, estar* empeñado EN + INF; to be ~ THAT estar* resuelto or decidido A QUE (+ subj)

deterrent /dɪˈterənt/ n: it may act as a ~ to thieves puede servir para disuadir a los ladrones; the nuclear ~ las armas nucleares como fuerza disuasoria

detest /dɪˈtest/ vt detestar, odiar

dethrone /dɪˈθrəʊn/ vt destronar

detonate /ˈdetəneɪt/ vt hacer* detonar

detour¹ /ˈdiːtʊr ‖ˈdiːtʊə(r)/ n (a) (deviation) rodeo m, vuelta f; to make a ~ dar* un rodeo, desviarse* (b) (AmE Transp) desvío m, desviación f

detour² vt (AmE) ⟨traffic⟩ desviar*

detract /dɪˈtrækt/ vi: I didn't wish to ~ from her achievement no quise quitarle méritos or restarle valor a su logro; it ~s from the beauty of the painting desmerece la belleza del cuadro

detractor /dɪˈtræktər ‖dɪˈtræktə(r)/ n detractor, -tora m,f

detriment /ˈdetrəmənt ‖ˈdetrɪmənt/ n (frml) detrimento m, perjuicio m; to the ~ of sb/sth en detrimento or perjuicio de algn/algo

devalue /ˈdiːˈvæljuː/ vt (Fin) devaluar*

devastate /ˈdevəsteɪt/ vt (a) (lay waste) devastar, asolar* (b) (overwhelm) ⟨opposition/

argument⟩ aplastar, demoler*; I was ~d when I heard quedé deshecho or anonadado cuando me enteré

devastating /ˈdevəsteɪtɪŋ/ adj (a) ⟨punch/ shock⟩ devastador (b) ⟨accuracy/logic⟩ abrumador, apabullante; ⟨reply/defeat⟩ demoledor, aplastante; ⟨beauty⟩ irresistible

devastation /ˈdevəˈsteɪʃən/ n devastación f

develop /dɪˈveləp/ vt [1] (a) (elaborate, devise) desarrollar (b) (improve) ⟨skill/ability/quality⟩ desarrollar (c) (exploit) ⟨land/area⟩ urbanizar* (d) (expand) ⟨business/range⟩ ampliar* (e) (create) ⟨drug/engine⟩ crear [2] (acquire) ⟨immunity/ resistance⟩ desarrollar; ⟨disease⟩ contraer* (frml); the machine ~ed a fault la máquina empezó a funcionar mal [3] (Phot) revelar
■ ~ vi [1] (a) (grow) «person/industry» desarrollarse; «interest» crecer*, aumentar (b) (evolve) to ~ INTO sth convertirse* or transformarse EN algo [2] (appear) «problem/ complication» surgir*, aparecer*; «crisis» producirse*

developer /dɪˈveləpər ‖dɪˈveləpə(r)/ n [1] (of land, property) promotor inmobiliario, promotora inmobiliaria m,f [2] (Phot) revelador m

developing /dɪˈveləpɪŋ/ adj ⟨country⟩ en vías de desarrollo

development /dɪˈveləpmənt/ n [1] (of person, idea, situation) desarrollo m [2] (of drug, engine) creación f [3] (of land, area) urbanización f [4] (housing ~) complejo m habitacional, fraccionamiento m (Méx), urbanización f (Esp) [5] (Econ) desarrollo m [6] (happening, event) acontecimiento m, suceso m

deviant /ˈdiːviənt/ adj ⟨practices/conduct⟩ desviado, que se aparta de la norma; ⟨person/ personality⟩ anormal

deviate /ˈdiːvieɪt/ vi to ~ FROM sth ⟨from course⟩ desviarse* DE algo; ⟨from truth/norm⟩ apartarse DE algo

deviation /ˈdiːviˈeɪʃən/ n desviación f

device /dɪˈvaɪs/ n [1] (gadget, tool) artefacto m, dispositivo m, aparato m; (mechanism) dispositivo m, mecanismo m [2] (stratagem) recurso m, estratagema f; to leave sb to her/his own ~s dejar que algn se las arregle solo

devil /ˈdevl/ n [1] (a) (Relig) diablo m, demonio m (b) (evil spirit) demonio m [2] (colloq) (person): he's a little ~! ¡es un diablillo!; poor ~! ¡pobre diablo!

devious /ˈdiːviəs/ adj (a) (underhand) ⟨person⟩ taimado, artero (b) (roundabout) ⟨route/path⟩ tortuoso, sinuoso

devise /dɪˈvaɪz/ vt ⟨plan/system⟩ idear, crear, concebir*; ⟨machine/tool⟩ inventar

devoid /dɪˈvɔɪd/ adj (pred) (frml) to be ~ OF sth carecer* DE algo

devolution /ˈdevəˈluːʃən ‖ˌdiːvəˈluːʃən/ n (a) (delegation) delegación f, transferencia f (b) (BrE Govt) transferencia de competencias del gobierno central a un gobierno regional

devolve /dɪˈvɑːlv ‖dɪˈvɒlv/ vt (frml) ⟨power⟩ delegar*, transferir*; ⟨privilege/right⟩ conceder

devote /dɪˈvəʊt/ vt to ~ sth TO sth/-ING dedicar* algo A algo/ + INF
■ v refl to ~ oneself TO sth/-ING dedicarse* A algo/ + INF

devoted /dɪˈvəʊtəd ‖dɪˈvəʊtɪd/ adj (a) (loving) ⟨couple/family⟩ unido; **to be ~ TO sb** sentir* devoción POR algn (b) (dedicated) ⟨before n⟩ ⟨follower/admirer⟩ ferviente, devoto; ⟨service/friendship⟩ leal

devotion /dɪˈvəʊʃən/ n (love) devoción f; (loyalty) lealtad f

devour /dɪˈvaʊr ‖dɪˈvaʊə(r)/ vt devorar

devout /dɪˈvaʊt/ adj (a) (Relig) devoto, piadoso (b) (earnest) (frml) ⟨before n⟩ ⟨supporter⟩ ferviente

dew /du: ‖dju:/ n rocío m

dexterity /dekˈsterəti/ n (manual) destreza f, habilidad f; (skill) habilidad f

diabetes /ˌdaɪəˈbiːtiːz/ n diabetes f

diabetic¹ /ˌdaɪəˈbetɪk/ adj diabético; ⟨jam/chocolate⟩ para diabéticos

diabetic² n diabético, -ca m,f

diabolical /ˌdaɪəˈbɑːlɪkəl ‖ˌdaɪəˈbɒlɪkəl/ adj ⟨machinations⟩ diabólico, satánico; ⟨cruelty⟩ perverso, satánico

diagnose /ˈdaɪəgnəʊs, -əʊz ‖ˈdaɪəgnəʊz/ vt ⟨illness⟩ diagnosticar*; ⟨cause/fault⟩ determinar

diagnosis /ˌdaɪəgˈnəʊsəs ‖ˌdaɪəgˈnəʊsɪs/ n (pl **-ses** /-siːz/) diagnóstico m

diagonal /daɪˈægənl/ adj ⟨line⟩ diagonal; ⟨path⟩ en diagonal

diagram /ˈdaɪəgræm/ n diagrama m, esquema m, gráfico m

dial¹ /ˈdaɪl ‖ˈdaɪəl/ n (on clock, watch) esfera f; (on measuring instrument) cuadrante m; (of telephone) disco m; (on radio) dial m

dial², (BrE) **-ll-** vt/i (Telec) marcar*, discar* (AmL)

dialect /ˈdaɪəlekt/ n dialecto m

dialling tone /ˈdaɪlɪŋ ‖ˈdaɪəlɪŋ/ n (BrE) ▶ DIAL TONE

dialogue, (AmE also) **dialog** /ˈdaɪələːg ‖ˈdaɪəlɒg/ n diálogo m

dial tone n tono m de marcar or (AmL) de discado

diameter /daɪˈæmətər ‖daɪˈæmɪtə(r)/ n diámetro m

diamond /ˈdaɪəmənd/ n ① (Min) diamante m; (cut) brillante m, diamante m ② (shape) rombo m ③ (Games) **diamonds** (suit) (+ sing or pl vb) diamantes mpl

diaper /ˈdaɪpər ‖ˈdaɪəpə(r)/ n (AmE) pañal m

diaphragm /ˈdaɪəfræm/ n ① (Anat) diafragma m ② (contraceptive) diafragma m

diarrhea, (BrE) **diarrhoea** /ˌdaɪəˈriːə ‖ˌdaɪəˈrɪə/ n diarrea f

diary /ˈdaɪəri/ n (pl **-ries**) ① (personal record) diario m ② (book for appointments) agenda f

dice¹ /daɪs/ n (pl ~) dado m

dice² pl of DIE² and of DICE¹

dice³ vt (Culin) cortar en dados or cubitos

dictate /ˈdɪkteɪt ‖dɪkˈteɪt/ vt ① (read out) dictar ② (prescribe, lay down) ⟨law⟩ establecer*, dictar; ⟨common sense⟩ dictar

dictation /dɪkˈteɪʃən/ n (Corresp, Educ) dictado m

dictator /ˈdɪkteɪtər ‖dɪkˈteɪtə(r)/ n dictador, -dora m,f

dictatorial /ˌdɪktəˈtɔːriəl/ adj dictatorial

dictatorship /dɪkˈteɪtərʃɪp ‖dɪkˈteɪtəʃɪp/ n dictadura f

diction /ˈdɪkʃən/ n dicción f

dictionary /ˈdɪkʃəneri ‖ˈdɪkʃənri, ˈdɪkʃənəri/ n (pl **-ries**) diccionario m

did /dɪd/ past of DO¹

didactic /daɪˈdæktɪk/ adj didáctico

diddle /ˈdɪdl/ vt (colloq) estafar, timar (fam)

didn't /ˈdɪdnt/ = **did not**

die¹ /daɪ/ **dies, dying, died** vi (a) (stop living) morir*; (violently) matarse, morir*; **to be dying FOR sth** (colloq) morirse* POR algo; **to be dying to + INF** (colloq) morirse* POR + INF, morirse* de ganas de + INF (b) (stop functioning) ⟨engine/motor⟩ apagarse*, dejar de funcionar
  ■ ~ vt: **to ~ a natural death** morir* de muerte natural; **to ~ a violent death** tener* or sufrir una muerte violenta
  ■ **die away** [v + adv] ⟨storm/wind⟩ amainar; ⟨anger⟩ pasar
  ■ **die down** [v + adv] ⟨fire/noise⟩ irse* apagando; ⟨storm/wind⟩ amainar; ⟨anger/excitement⟩ calmarse
  ■ **die out** [v + adv] ⟨race/species⟩ extinguirse*; ⟨custom⟩ morir*, caer* en desuso

die² n (pl **dice**) (Games) dado m

diehard /ˈdaɪhɑːrd ‖ˈdaɪhɑːd/ n intransigente mf; ⟨before n⟩ intransigente, acérrimo

diesel¹ /ˈdiːzəl/ n (a) (vehicle) coche m (or camión m etc) diesel, diesel m (b) (fuel) diesel m, gasóleo m, gas-oil m

diesel² adj ⟨before n⟩ diesel adj inv

diet¹ /ˈdaɪət/ n (a) (special food) régimen m, dieta f; **to be/go on a ~** estar*/ponerse* a régimen or a dieta; ⟨before n⟩ ⟨cola⟩ light adj inv (b) (nourishment) alimentación f, dieta f (alimenticia); **they live on a ~ of rice and fish** se alimentan de arroz y pescado

diet² vi hacer* régimen or dieta

differ /ˈdɪfər ‖ˈdɪfə(r)/ vi ① (a) (be at variance) diferir*; **how do they ~?** ¿en qué difieren? (b) (be unlike) ser* distinto or diferente; **to ~ FROM sb/sth** diferenciarse or diferir* DE algn/algo ② (disagree) discrepar, diferir* (frml)

difference /ˈdɪfrəns/ n diferencia f; **to tell the ~** notar or ver* la diferencia; **it could make a ~ in** (BrE) **to the outcome** podría influir en el resultado; **it will make no ~ to you** a ti no te va a afectar

different /ˈdɪfrənt/ adj (a) (not the same) distinto, diferente; **~ FROM** o **TO** o (AmE also) **THAN sth/sb** distinto or diferente DE or A algo/algn (b) (unusual) diferente, original

differential /ˌdɪfəˈrentʃəl ‖ˌdɪfəˈrenʃəl/ n diferencial m

differentiate /ˌdɪfəˈrentʃieɪt ‖ˌdɪfəˈrenʃieɪt/ vi distinguir*

■ ~ *vt* (frml): **to ~ sth (FROM sth)** diferenciar *or* distinguir* algo (DE algo)

differently /'dɪfrəntli/ *adv*: they think ~ no piensan igual *or* del mismo modo; **I view things** ~ yo veo las cosas de otra forma *or* otro modo

difficult /'dɪfɪkəlt/ *adj* difícil; **the ~ part is ...** lo difícil es ..., la dificultad está en ...; **he's finding it ~ to give up smoking** le está resultando difícil dejar de fumar, le está costando dejar de fumar

difficulty /'dɪfɪkəlti/ *n* (*pl* **-ties**) **(a)** (of situation, task) dificultad *f*; **she had great ~ walking** caminaba con mucha dificultad **(b)** (problem) dificultad *f*, problema *m*; **to get into difficulties** meterse en líos

diffident /'dɪfədənt ‖'dɪfɪdənt/ *adj* ⟨person⟩ poco seguro de sí mismo; ⟨smile⟩ tímido

diffuse¹ /dɪ'fju:z/ *vt* ⟨heat⟩ esparcir*; ⟨light⟩ tamizar*, difuminar; ⟨knowledge⟩ (frml) difundir

diffuse² /dɪ'fju:s/ *adj* difuso

dig¹ /dɪg/ (*pres p* **digging**; *past & past p* **dug**) *vt* ☐1 ⟨ground⟩ cavar; ⟨hole/trench⟩ (by hand) cavar; (by machine) excavar ☐2 (jab, thrust) **to ~ sth INTO sth** clavar algo EN algo

■ ~ *vi* ☐1 (excavate — by hand) cavar; (— by machine) excavar; «*dog*» escarbar; **to ~ for oil** hacer* prospecciones petrolíferas ☐2 (search) buscar*; **she dug in her pockets for the key** buscó la llave en los bolsillos

■ **dig up** [*v + o + adv, v + adv + o*] **(a)** ⟨lawn⟩ levantar; ⟨weeds/tree⟩ arrancar* **(b)** ⟨body/ treasure⟩ desenterrar* **(c)** ⟨facts⟩ (colloq) sacar* a la luz

dig² *n* ☐1 (Archeol) excavación *f* ☐2 (jab — with elbow) codazo *m*; (— with pin) pinchazo *m* ☐3 (critical remark) (colloq) pulla *f*; (hint) indirecta *f*; **to have a ~ at sb/sth** meterse con algn/algo

digest¹ /daɪ'dʒest, də- ‖daɪ'dʒest, dɪ-/ *vt* ⟨food⟩ digerir*; (assimilate mentally) asimilar, digerir* (fam)

digest² /'daɪdʒest/ *n* (summary) compendio *m*; (journal) boletín *m*, revista *f*

digestible /daɪ'dʒestəbəl, də- ‖daɪ'dʒestəbəl, dɪ-/ *adj* (Physiol) digerible; (comprehensible) fácil de asimilar *or* (fam) digerir

digestion /daɪ'dʒestʃən, də- ‖daɪ'dʒestʃən, dɪ-/ *n* digestión *f*

digestive /daɪ'dʒestɪv, də- ‖daɪ'dʒestɪv, dɪ-/ *adj* digestivo

digger /'dɪgər ‖'dɪgə(r)/ *n* (machine) excavadora *f*; (person) excavador, -dora *m,f*

digit /'dɪdʒət ‖'dɪdʒɪt/ *n* ☐1 (Math) dígito *m* (frml) ☐2 (Anat) dedo *m*

digital /'dɪdʒətəl ‖'dɪdʒɪtl/ *adj* digital

digital: ~ **camera** *n* cámara *f* (fotográfica) digital; ~ **video disc** *n* videodisco *m* digital

dignified /'dɪgnəfaɪd ‖'dɪgnɪfaɪd/ *adj* **(a)** ⟨person/reply⟩ digno, circunspecto; ⟨silence/ attitude⟩ digno **(b)** (stately) majestuoso

dignity /'dɪgnəti/ *n* (of person) dignidad *f*; (of occasion) solemnidad *f*

digress /daɪ'gres/ *vi*: but I ~ pero estoy divagando; **to ~ FROM sth** apartarse DE algo

digression /daɪ'greʃən/ *n* digresión *f*

dike /daɪk/ *n* ☐1 **(a)** (to keep out water) dique *m* **(b)** (causeway) terraplén *m* **(c)** (ditch) acequia *f* ☐2 ▶ DYKE 2

dilapidated /də'læpədeɪtəd ‖dɪ'læpɪdeɪtɪd/ *adj* ⟨building⟩ ruinoso; ⟨car⟩ destartalado

dilate /daɪ'leɪt/ *vi* dilatarse

dilemma /də'lemə, daɪ- ‖dɪ'lemə, daɪ-/ *n* dilema *m*

diligence /'dɪlədʒəns ‖'dɪlɪdʒəns/ *n* diligencia *f*

diligent /'dɪlədʒənt ‖'dɪlɪdʒənt/ *adj* ⟨worker⟩ diligente, cumplidor; ⟨student⟩ aplicado, diligente; ⟨work/study⟩ esmerado, concienzudo

dilute /daɪ'lu:t ‖daɪ'lju:t/ *vt* diluir*

dim¹ /dɪm/ *adj* **-mm-** ☐1 **(a)** (dark) ⟨room⟩ oscuro, poco iluminado; ⟨light⟩ débil, tenue **(b)** (indistinct) ⟨memory/shape⟩ borroso; ⟨idea⟩ vago **(c)** (gloomy) ⟨prospects⟩ nada halagüeño, nada prometedor ☐2 (stupid) (colloq) corto (de luces) (fam), tonto (fam)

dim² *vt* **-mm-** ⟨lights⟩ atenuar*; **to ~ one's headlights** (AmE) poner* las (luces) cortas *or* de cruce *or* (AmL tb) las (luces) bajas

dime /daɪm/ *n* (AmE colloq) moneda de diez centavos

dimension /de'mentʃən, daɪ- ‖dɪ'menʃən, daɪ-/ *n* dimensión *f*

dime store *n* (AmE) tienda que vende artículos de bajo precio, ≈baratillo *m*

diminish /də'mɪnɪʃ ‖dɪ'mɪnɪʃ/ *vi* «*cost/ number*» disminuir*, reducirse*; «*enthusiasm*» disminuir*, apagarse*

■ ~ *vt* ⟨size/cost⟩ reducir*, disminuir*; ⟨enthusiasm⟩ disminuir*

diminutive /də'mɪnjətɪv ‖dɪ'mɪnjʊtɪv/ *adj* diminuto, minúsculo

dimly /'dɪmli/ *adv* ⟨shine⟩ débilmente; **a ~ lit room** una habitación poco iluminada *or* iluminada por una luz tenue

dimmer /'dɪmər ‖'dɪmə(r)/ *n* potenciómetro *m*, dimmer *m*

dimple /'dɪmpəl/ *n* (in cheeks, chin) hoyuelo *m*

dimwit /'dɪmwɪt/ *n* (colloq) tarado, -da (mental) *m,f* (fam)

din /dɪn/ *n* (colloq) (*no pl*) (of conversation, voices) barullo *m* (fam), bulla *f* (fam); (of drill, traffic) estruendo *m*, ruido *m*

dine /daɪn/ *vi* (frml) cenar

diner /'daɪnər ‖'daɪnə(r)/ *n* ☐1 (person) comensal *mf* ☐2 **(a)** (restaurant) (AmE) cafetería *f* **(b)** ▶ DINING CAR

dinghy /'dɪŋgi, 'dɪŋi/ *n* (*pl* **-ghies**) (sailing boat) bote *m*; (inflatable *or* rubber ~) bote *m* neumático

dingy /'dɪndʒi/ *adj* **-gier, -giest** ⟨building/ room⟩ lúgubre, ⟨furnishings⟩ deslucido; (dirty) sucio

dining /'daɪnɪŋ/**:** ~ **car** *n* coche *m* restaurante, coche *m* comedor; ~ **room** *n* comedor *m*; ~ **table** *n* mesa *f* (de comedor)

dinner /'dɪnər ‖'dɪnə(r)/ *n* **(a)** (in evening) cena *f*, comida *f* (AmL); **to eat o have ~** cenar, comer (AmL) **(b)** (formal) cena *f* (de gala) **(c)** (at midday) almuerzo *m*, comida *f* (esp Esp, Méx); **to eat o** have ~ almorzar*, comer (esp Esp, Méx)

dinner: ~ **dance** *n* cena *f* con baile, comida *f* bailable (esp AmL), cena-baile *f* (Méx); ~ **jacket** *n* (esp BrE) esmoquin *m*, smoking *m*; ~ **party** *n* cena *f*, comida *f* (AmL); ~ **plate** *n* plato *m* llano *or* (Méx) plano *or* (RPl tb) playo *or* (Chi) bajo; ~ ⋯⟶

service n vajilla f; **~ table** n mesa f; **~time** n (in evening) hora f de cenar or (esp AmL) de comer; (at midday) hora f de almorzar or (esp Esp, Méx) de comer

dinosaur /'daɪnəsɔːr ‖'daɪnəsɔː(r)/ n dinosaurio m

dint /dɪnt/ n: **by ~ of sth** a fuerza de algo

diocese /'daɪəsəs ‖'daɪəsɪs/ n diócesis f

dip¹ /dɪp/ **-pp-** vt **1** **to ~ sth IN(TO) sth** meter algo EN algo; (into liquid) mojar algo EN algo **2** (Agr) ⟨sheep⟩ desinfectar (haciendo pasar por un baño) **3** **(a)** (lower) ⟨head⟩ agachar, bajar **(b)** (BrE Auto): **to ~ one's headlights** poner* las (luces) cortas or de cruce or (AmL tb) las (luces) bajas
■ **~** vi **(a)** (decrease) «sales/prices» bajar **(b)** (move downward) «aircraft/bird» bajar en picada or (Esp) en picado

dip² n **1** (swim) (colloq) (no pl) chapuzón m (fam) **2** (Agr) baño m desinfectante **3** (depression, hollow) hondonada f **4** (in sales, production) caída f, descenso m **5** (Culin) salsa en la que se mojan diferentes bocaditos (en una fiesta etc)

diphthong /'dɪfθɔːŋ ‖'dɪfθɒŋ/ n diptongo m

diploma /də'pləʊmə ‖dɪ'pləʊmə/ n diploma m

diplomacy /də'pləʊməsi ‖dɪ'pləʊməsi/ n diplomacia f

diplomat /'dɪpləmæt/ n diplomático, -ca m,f

diplomatic /ˌdɪplə'mætɪk/ adj **(a)** (Govt) (before n) diplomático; **~ immunity** inmunidad f diplomática **(b)** (tactful) diplomático

dipstick /'dɪpstɪk/ n varilla f (medidora) del aceite

dire /daɪr ‖'daɪə(r)/ adj **direr, direst** **1** **(a)** ⟨news/consequences⟩ funesto, nefasto; **to be in ~ straits** estar* en una situación desesperada **(b)** (very bad) (BrE colloq) espantoso (fam), atroz **2** (ominous) ⟨warning⟩ serio, grave **3** (desperate) ⟨need/misery⟩ extremo

direct¹ /də'rekt, daɪ- ‖daɪ'rekt, dɪ-/ adj **1** **(a)** ⟨route/flight⟩ directo; ⟨contact⟩ directo; ⟨cause/consequence⟩ directo **(b)** (Ling) (before n) ⟨question/command⟩ en estilo directo; **~ discourse** o (BrE) **speech** estilo m directo **2** (frank, straightforward) ⟨person/manner⟩ franco, directo; ⟨question⟩ directo

direct² adv **1** ⟨write/phone⟩ directamente; ⟨go/travel⟩ (BrE) directo, directamente **2** (straight) directamente; **~ from Paris** (Rad, TV) en directo desde París

direct³ vt **1** **(a)** (give directions to) indicarle* el camino a **(b)** (address) ⟨letter/parcel⟩ mandar, dirigir* **2** (aim) dirigir*; **it was ~ed at us** iba dirigido a nosotros ⟨play/orchestra/traffic⟩ dirigir* **4** (order) (fml) ordenar; **to ~ sb to +** INF ordenarle A algn QUE (+ subj)
■ **~** vi (Cin, Theat) dirigir*

direct: ~ billing /'bɪlɪŋ/ n (AmE) débito m bancario or (Esp) domiciliación f de pagos; **~ current** n corriente f continua; **~ debit** n ▶ BILLING; **~ dialing,** (BrE) **~ dialling** n discado m directo or automático

direction /də'rekʃən, daɪ- ‖daɪ'rekʃən, dɪ-/ n **1** (course, compass point) dirección f; **sense of ~** sentido m de (la) orientación; **in the ~ of** en dirección a **2** (purpose): **he lacks ~** no tiene un

norte **3** (supervision) dirección f **4** **directions** pl (for route) indicaciones fpl; (for task, use, assembly) instrucciones fpl, indicaciones fpl

directive /də'rektɪv, daɪ- ‖daɪ'rektɪv, dɪ-/ n directriz f, directiva f (esp AmL)

directly /də'rektli, daɪ- ‖daɪ'rektli, dɪ-/ adv **1** **(a)** (without stopping) ⟨go/drive/fly⟩ directamente, directo **(b)** (without intermediaries) ⟨report/deal⟩ directamente; **he's ~ responsible** es el responsable directo **(c)** (exactly) ⟨opposite/above⟩ justo **(d)** (in genealogy) ⟨related/descended⟩ por línea directa **2** (frankly, straightforwardly) ⟨ask⟩ directamente; ⟨speak⟩ con franqueza **3** (now, at once) inmediatamente, ahora mismo

director /də'rektər, daɪ- ‖daɪ'rektə(r), dɪ-/ n **1** (of company) directivo, -tiva m,f; (of department, project) director, -tora m,f; see also MANAGING DIRECTOR **2** (Cin, Theat) director, -tora m,f; (esp AmE Mus) director, -tora m,f

directory /də'rektəri, daɪ- ‖daɪ'rektəri, dɪ-/ n (pl **-ries**) **(a)** (telephone **~**) guía f telefónica or de teléfonos, directorio m telefónico (Col, Méx) **(b)** (index, yearbook) directorio m, guía f

dirt /dɜːrt ‖dɜːt/ n suciedad f, mugre f

dirty¹ /'dɜːrti ‖'dɜːti/ adj **-tier, -tiest** **1** (soiled) sucio; **to get ~** ensuciarse **2** **(a)** (obscene) ⟨story/book⟩ cochino (fam), guarro (Esp fam); ⟨leer/grin⟩ lascivo; ⟨joke⟩ verde or (Méx) colorado; ⟨magazine⟩ porno adj inv **(b)** (shameful) ⟨job/work⟩ sucio; **to do sb's ~ work** hacerle* el trabajo sucio a algn

dirty² vt **dirties, dirtying, dirtied** ensuciar

dirty old man n (colloq) viejo m verde (fam)

disability /ˌdɪsə'bɪləti/ n (pl **-ties**) **(a)** (state) invalidez f, discapacidad f; (before n) ⟨pension/allowance⟩ por invalidez **(b)** (particular handicap) problema m

disable /dɪs'eɪbəl/ vt **(a)** «illness/accident/injury» dejar inválido (or lisiado or ciego etc) **(b)** ⟨machine/weapon⟩ (Mil) inutilizar*

disabled /dɪs'eɪbəld/ adj discapacitado, minusválido

disabuse /ˌdɪsə'bjuːz/ vt (fml) desengañar; **I tried to ~ him of the notion that ...** intenté sacarlo del error de que ...

disadvantage /ˌdɪsəd'væntɪdʒ ‖ˌdɪsəd'vɑːntɪdʒ/ n desventaja f, inconveniente m; **to be at a ~** estar* en desventaja

disadvantageous /dɪsˌædvæn'teɪdʒəs ‖dɪsˌædvən'teɪdʒəs/ adj desventajoso, desfavorable

disaffected /ˌdɪsə'fektəd ‖ˌdɪsə'fektɪd/ adj desafecto

disagree /ˌdɪsə'griː/ vi **1** **(a)** (differ in opinion) **to ~ (WITH sb/sth)** no estar* de acuerdo (CON algn/algo), discrepar (DE algn/algo) (fml) **(b)** (conflict) ⟨figures/accounts⟩ no coincidir, discrepar **2** (cause discomfort) «food» **to ~ WITH sb** sentarle* or caerle* mal A algn

disagreeable /ˌdɪsə'griːəbəl/ adj ⟨smell/experience/person⟩ desagradable; ⟨task/job⟩ ingrato, desagradable

disagreement /ˌdɪsə'griːmənt/ n **(a)** (difference of opinion) desacuerdo m, disconformidad f **(b)** (quarrel) discusión f **(c)** (disparity) discrepancia f

disallow /ˌdɪsə'laʊ/ vt (fml) ⟨claim/evidence⟩ (Law) rechazar*, desestimar; ⟨goal⟩ anular

disappear /ˌdɪsəˈpɪr ‖ ˌdɪsəˈpɪə(r)/ vi (a) (become invisible) desaparecer* (b) (go away) «pain/ problems» desaparecer*, irse*; «worries/fears» desvanecerse*

disappearance /ˌdɪsəˈpɪrəns ‖ ˌdɪsəˈpɪərəns/ n desaparición f

disappoint /ˌdɪsəˈpɔɪnt/ vt ‹person› decepcionar; ‹hopes/desires› defraudar

disappointed /ˌdɪsəˈpɔɪntəd ‖ ˌdɪsəˈpɔɪntɪd/ adj (pred) to be ~ estar* desilusionado or decepcionado; I'm ~ with the results los resultados me han decepcionado

disappointing /ˌdɪsəˈpɔɪntɪŋ/ adj decepcionante

disappointment /ˌdɪsəˈpɔɪntmənt/ n (a) (emotion) desilusión f, decepción f (b) (letdown) decepción f, chasco m

disapproval /ˌdɪsəˈpruːvəl/ n desaprobación f

disapprove /ˌdɪsəˈpruːv/ vi: he ~s of smoking está en contra del tabaco or del cigarrillo; she ~s of her son's fiancée no tiene buen concepto de la novia de su hijo

disapproving /ˌdɪsəˈpruːvɪŋ/ adj ‹tone/look› de reproche

disarm /dɪsˈɑːrm ‖ dɪsˈɑːm/ vt ① ‹troops/ opposition› desarmar; ‹bomb/mine› desactivar; ‹criticism› desbaratar ② (win confidence of) desarmar
■ ~ vi desarmarse

disarmament /dɪsˈɑːrməmənt ‖ dɪsˈɑːməmənt/ n desarme m

disarming /dɪsˈɑːrmɪŋ ‖ dɪsˈɑːmɪŋ/ adj que desarma

disarray /ˌdɪsəˈreɪ/ n (of political party) desorganización f; (of appearance) desaliño m; her papers were in total ~ sus papeles estaban completamente desordenados

disassociate /ˌdɪsəˈsəʊʃɪeɪt, -sɪert/ vt ▶ DISSOCIATE

disaster /dɪˈzæstər ‖ dɪˈzɑːstə(r)/ n ① (flood, earthquake) catástrofe f, desastre m; (crash, sinking) siniestro m, desastre m; (before n) ~ fund fondo m para los damnificados ② (a) (fiasco) desastre m (b) (hopeless person) (colloq) desastre m (fam) ③ (misfortune): ~ struck ocurrió or se produjo una catástrofe

disaster area n zona f siniestrada, zona f de desastre; my room is a real ~ ~ (colloq & hum) mi habitación está hecha un desastre (fam)

disastrous /dɪˈzæstrəs ‖ dɪˈzɑːstrəs/ adj desastroso, catastrófico

disband /dɪsˈbænd/ vt ‹organization› disolver*; ‹army› licenciar
■ ~ vi «organization» disolverse*; «group» desbandarse

disbelief /ˌdɪsbəˈliːf/ n incredulidad f

disbelieve /ˌdɪsbəˈliːv/ vt (frml) ‹statement› no creer*; ‹person› no creerle* a

disc /dɪsk/ n (esp BrE) ▶ DISK

discard /dɪsˈkɑːrd ‖ dɪsˈkɑːd/ vt (a) (dispose of) desechar, deshacerse* de (b) ‹idea/belief› desechar (c) (shed) ‹skin/leaves› mudar (d) (take off) ‹clothing› desembarazarse* de

discern /dɪˈsɜːrn ‖ dɪˈsɜːn/ vt (frml) distinguir*, percibir

discerning /dɪˈsɜːrnɪŋ ‖ dɪˈsɜːnɪŋ/ adj ‹reader/ customer› exigente, con criterio; ‹palate/taste› exigente, fino; ‹ear/eye› educado

discharge¹ /dɪsˈtʃɑːrdʒ ‖ dɪsˈtʃɑːdʒ/ vt ① (a) (release) ‹prisoner› liberar, poner* en libertad; ‹patient› dar* de alta; ‹juror› dispensar; ‹bankrupt› rehabilitar (b) (dismiss) (frml) despedir* ② (a) (send out) ‹fumes› despedir*; ‹electricity› descargar*; ‹sewage/waste› verter* (b) (unload) ‹cargo› descargar* (c) (shoot) ‹volley/ broadside› descargar* ③ (a) ‹duty› cumplir con (b) ‹debt› saldar, liquidar

discharge² /ˈdɪstʃɑːrdʒ ‖ ˈdɪstʃɑːdʒ/ n ① (release — from army) baja f; (— from hospital) alta f; (— from prison) puesta f en libertad ② (a) (Med) secreción f; (vaginal ~) flujo m (vaginal) (b) (of toxic fumes, gases) emisión f; (of sewage, waste) vertido m (c) (Elec) descarga f ③ (of debt, liabilities) liquidación f, pago m; (of duty) (frml) cumplimiento m

disciple /dɪˈsaɪpəl/ n (Relig) discípulo, -la m,f; (adherent) seguidor, -dora m,f

disciplinary /ˈdɪsəplənəri ‖ ˌdɪsɪˈplɪnəri/ adj disciplinario

discipline¹ /ˈdɪsəplən ‖ ˈdɪsɪplɪn/ n disciplina f

discipline² vt (a) (control) ‹child/pupils› disciplinar; ‹emotions› controlar (b) (punish) ‹employee› sancionar (c) (train) ‹body/mind› disciplinar

disc jockey n disc(-)jockey mf, pinchadiscos mf (Esp fam)

disclaim /dɪsˈkleɪm/ vt (deny): she ~ed all knowledge of his whereabouts negó conocer su paradero; he ~ed any connection with him negó tener ninguna relación con él

disclaimer /dɪsˈkleɪmər ‖ dɪsˈkleɪmə(r)/ n (Law) descargo m de responsabilidad

disclose /dɪsˈkləʊz/ vt revelar

disclosure /dɪsˈkləʊʒər ‖ dɪsˈkləʊʒə(r)/ n revelación f

disco /ˈdɪskəʊ/ n (pl -cos) discoteca f, disco f (fam)

discolor, (BrE) **discolour** /dɪsˈkʌlər ‖ dɪsˈkʌlə(r)/ vt (fade) decolorar; (stain) dejar amarillento, manchar

discomfort /dɪsˈkʌmfərt ‖ dɪsˈkʌmfət/ n (a) (lack of comfort) incomodidad f; (pain) molestia(s) f(pl), malestar m (b) (emotional, mental) inquietud f, desasosiego m

disconcert /ˌdɪskənˈsɜːrt ‖ ˌdɪskənˈsɜːt/ vt desconcertar*

disconcerting /ˌdɪskənˈsɜːrtɪŋ ‖ ˌdɪskənˈsɜːtɪŋ/ adj desconcertante

disconnect /ˌdɪskəˈnekt/ vt desconectar; I didn't pay my bills, so I was ~ed me cortaron el teléfono (or el gas etc) por no pagar

discontent /ˌdɪskənˈtent/ n descontento m

discontented /ˌdɪskənˈtentəd ‖ ˌdɪskənˈtentɪd/ adj descontento

discontinue /ˌdɪskənˈtɪnjuː/ vt ‹production› suspender; ‹model› discontinuar*, descontinuar*; ‹action/suit› (Law) desistir de

discord /ˈdɪskɔːrd ‖ ˈdɪskɔːd/ n ① (conflict) ⋯▷

discordia /dɪs'kɔːrdiə/ f [2] (Mus) **(a)** (lack of harmony) discordancia f, disonancia f **(b)** (chord) acorde m disonante

discotheque /'dɪskətek/ n ▶ DISCO

discount¹ /'dɪskaʊnt/ n descuento m; **at a ~** ⟨sell⟩ con descuento, a precio reducido; (before n) ⟨store⟩ de saldos; ⟨goods⟩ de saldo

discount² /'dɪskaʊnt, dɪs'kaʊnt ‖dɪs'kaʊnt/ vt [1] (Busn) **(a)** ⟨amount⟩ descontar* **(b)** ⟨goods⟩ rebajar **(c)** ⟨price⟩ reducir* [2] (disregard) ⟨possibility⟩ descartar; ⟨claim/criticism⟩ pasar por alto

discourage /dɪs'kɜːrɪdʒ ‖dɪs'kʌrɪdʒ/ vt **(a)** (depress) desalentar*, desanimar **(b)** (deter) ⟨crime/speculation⟩ poner* freno a; ⟨burglar⟩ ahuyentar, disuadir **(c)** (dissuade) **to ~ sb FROM -ING: she ~d me from taking the exam** trató de convencerme de que no me presentara al examen

discouraging /dɪs'kɜːrɪdʒɪŋ ‖dɪs'kʌrɪdʒɪŋ/ adj ⟨news/result⟩ desalentador, descorazonador

discourse /'dɪskɔːrs ‖'dɪskɔːs/ n (fml) **(a)** (dissertation) disertación f **(b)** (talk) conversación f

discourteous /dɪs'kɜːrtiəs/ adj descortés

discover /dɪs'kʌvər ‖dɪs'kʌvə(r)/ vt descubrir*

discoverer /dɪs'kʌvərər ‖dɪs'kʌvərə(r)/ n descubridor, -dora m,f

discovery /dɪs'kʌvəri/ n (pl **-ries**) descubrimiento m

discredit¹ /dɪs'kredət ‖dɪs'kredɪt/ vt desacreditar

discredit² n descrédito m

discreet /dɪs'kriːt/ adj **(a)** (tactful) ⟨person/inquiries⟩ discreto **(b)** (restrained) ⟨elegance/colors⟩ discreto, sobrio

discreetly /dɪs'kriːtli/ adv discretamente, con discreción

discrepancy /dɪs'krepənsi/ n (pl **-cies**) discrepancia f

discretion /dɪs'kreʃən/ n [1] (tact) discreción f [2] (judgment) criterio m; **at the committee's ~** a criterio or a discreción de la comisión

discretionary /dɪs'kreʃəneri ‖dɪs'kreʃənəri, -ənri/ adj discrecional

discriminate /dɪs'krɪmənet ‖dɪ'skrɪmɪneɪt/ vi [1] (act with prejudice) hacer* discriminaciones, discriminar; **to ~ AGAINST sb** discriminar a algn [2] **(a)** (distinguish) distinguir*, discriminar **(b)** (be discerning) discernir*, utilizar* el sentido crítico

discriminating /dɪs'krɪmənetɪŋ ‖dɪ'skrɪmɪneɪtɪŋ/ adj (discerning) ⟨critic/customer⟩ exigente; ⟨judgment⟩ sagaz; ⟨taste⟩ refinado, educado

discrimination /dɪs'krɪmə'neɪʃən ‖dɪˌskrɪmɪ'neɪʃən/ n [1] (unfair treatment) discriminación f [2] (discernment) criterio m, discernimiento m

discus /'dɪskəs/ n (pl **-cuses**) disco m

discuss /dɪs'kʌs/ vt (talk about) ⟨person⟩ hablar de; ⟨topic⟩ hablar de, tratar; ⟨debate⟩ debatir; ⟨plan/problem⟩ discutir

discussion /dɪs'kʌʃən/ n discusión f, debate m

disdain /dɪs'deɪn/ n desdén m

disdainful /dɪs'deɪnfəl/ adj ⟨manner/tone⟩ despectivo, desdeñoso

disease /dɪ'ziːz/ n enfermedad f, dolencia f (fml)

diseased /dɪ'ziːzd/ adj ⟨organ/tissue⟩ afectado; ⟨plant/animal⟩ enfermo

disembark /'dɪsəm'bɑːrk ‖ˌdɪsɪm'bɑːk/ vi desembarcar*

disembodied /'dɪsəm'bɑːdid ‖ˌdɪsɪm'bɒdid/ adj incorpóreo

disembowel /'dɪsəm'baʊəl ‖ˌdɪsɪm'baʊəl/ vt, (BrE) **-ll-** destripar

disenchanted /'dɪsɪn'tʃæntəd ‖ˌdɪsɪn'tʃɑːntɪd/ adj **to be ~ WITH sb/sth** estar* desilusionado CON or DE algn/DE algo

disenfranchise /'dɪsɪn'fræntʃaɪz ‖ˌdɪsɪn'fræntʃaɪz/ vt ⟨person⟩ privar del derecho al voto; ⟨place⟩ privar del derecho de representación

disengage /'dɪsɪn'geɪdʒ ‖ˌdɪsɪn'geɪdʒ/ vt [1] **(a)** (extricate) soltar* **(b)** (Mil) ⟨troops/forces⟩ retirar [2] (Tech) ⟨gears/mechanism⟩ desconectar

disentangle /'dɪsɪn'tæŋgəl ‖ˌdɪsɪn'tæŋgəl/ vt ⟨rope/hair/wool⟩ desenredar, desenmarañar; ⟨mystery⟩ esclarecer*, desentrañar

disfavor, (BrE) **disfavour** /dɪs'feɪvər ‖dɪs'feɪvə(r)/ n (fml) desaprobación f

disfigure /dɪs'fɪgjər ‖dɪs'fɪgə(r)/ vt ⟨face/person⟩ desfigurar; ⟨landscape/building⟩ afear, estropear

disgrace¹ /dɪs'greɪs/ n vergüenza f; **she was sent upstairs in ~** la mandaron arriba castigada

disgrace² vt **(a)** (bring shame on) ⟨person/family/school⟩ deshonrar **(b)** (destroy reputation of) ⟨enemy/politician⟩ desacreditar

disgraceful /dɪs'greɪsfəl/ adj vergonzoso

disgruntled /dɪs'grʌntld/ adj ⟨child/look⟩ contrariado; ⟨employee⟩ descontento

disguise¹ /dɪs'gaɪz/ vt **(a)** ⟨person⟩ disfrazar*; ⟨voice⟩ cambiar **(b)** (conceal) ⟨mistake⟩ ocultar; ⟨disapproval/contempt⟩ disimular

disguise² n disfraz m; **in ~** disfrazado

disgust¹ /dɪs'gʌst/ vt darle* asco a

disgust² n (revulsion) indignación f; (physical, stronger) asco m, repugnancia f; **she stormed out of the meeting in ~** salió indignada or furiosa de la reunión

disgusted /dɪs'gʌstəd ‖dɪs'gʌstɪd/ adj indignado; (stronger) asqueado

disgusting /dɪs'gʌstɪŋ/ adj **(a)** ⟨smell/taste/food⟩ asqueroso, repugnante **(b)** ⟨conduct/attitude⟩ vergonzoso

dish /dɪʃ/ n [1] **(a)** (plate) plato m; (serving ~) fuente f; **to wash the ~es** lavar los platos **(b)** (amount) plato m [2] (Culin) plato m [3] (Telec, TV) antena f parabólica

AmC	América Central	Arg	Argentina
AmL	América Latina	Bol	Bolivia
AmS	América del Sur	Chi	Chile
Andes	Región andina	CS	Cono Sur

Cu	Cuba	Per	Perú
Ec	Ecuador	RPI	Río de la Plata
Esp	España	Ur	Uruguay
Méx	México	Ven	Venezuela

■ **dish up** [*v* + *o* + *adv*, *v* + *adv* + *o*] [*v* + *adv*] (Culin) servir*

dishcloth /ˈdɪʃklɔːθ ‖ˈdɪʃklɑːθ/ *n* (a) (for drying) paño *m* de cocina, repasador *m* (RPl), limpión *m* (Col) (b) (BrE) ▶ DISHRAG

disheartening /dɪsˈhɑːrtnɪŋ ‖dɪsˈhɑːtnɪŋ/ *adj* descorazonador, desalentador

disheveled, (BrE) **dishevelled** /dɪˈʃevəld/ *adj* despeinado

dishonest /dɪsˈɑːnəst ‖dɪsˈɒnɪst/ *adj* ‹person/answer› deshonesto; ‹dealings/means› fraudulento, deshonesto

dishonesty /dɪsˈɑːnəsti ‖dɪsˈɒnɪsti/ *n* deshonestidad *f*, falta *f* de honradez; (of statement) falsedad *f*; (of dealings) fraudulencia *f*

dishonor, (BrE) **dishonour** /dɪsˈɑːnər ‖dɪsˈɒnə(r)/ *n* deshonra *f*, deshonor *m*

dishonorable, (BrE) **dishonourable** /dɪsˈɑːnərəbəl ‖dɪsˈɒnərəbəl/ *adj* deshonroso

dish: ~**rag** *n* (AmE) trapo *m*, bayeta *f*, fregón *m* (RPl); ~ **soap** *n* (AmE) lavavajillas *m*, detergente *m*; ~**towel** *n* ▶ DISHCLOTH A; ~**washer** /ˈdɪʃˌwɔːʃər ‖ˈdɪʃˌwɒʃə(r)/ *n* (machine) lavaplatos *m*, lavavajillas *m*; ~**washing liquid** /ˈdɪʃˌwɔːʃɪŋ ‖ˈdɪʃˌwɒʃɪŋ/ *n* (AmE) ▶ ◀ SOAP; ~**water** *n* agua *f*; de fregar *or* de lavar los platos

disillusion /ˌdɪsəˈluːʒən ‖ˌdɪsɪˈluːʒən/ *vt* desilusionar

disillusionment /ˌdɪsəˈluːʒənmənt ‖ˌdɪsɪˈluːʒənmənt/ *n* desilusión *f*

disinfect /ˌdɪsɪnˈfekt ‖ˌdɪsɪnˈfekt/ *vt* desinfectar

disinfectant /ˌdɪsɪnˈfektənt ‖ˌdɪsɪnˈfektənt/ *n* desinfectante *m*

disinformation /ˌdɪsɪnfərˈmeɪʃən ‖ˌdɪsɪnfəˈmeɪʃən/ *n* desinformación *f*

disinherit /ˌdɪsɪnˈherət ‖ˌdɪsɪnˈherɪt/ *vt* desheredar

disintegrate /dɪsˈɪntəɡreɪt ‖dɪsˈɪntɪɡreɪt/ *vi* desintegrarse

disintegration /dɪsˌɪntəˈɡreɪʃən ‖dɪsˌɪntɪˈɡreɪʃən/ *n* desintegración *f*

disinterested /dɪsˈɪntrəstəd ‖dɪsˈɪntrəstɪd/ *adj* ‹decision/advice› imparcial; ‹action› desinteresado

disjointed /dɪsˈdʒɔɪntəd ‖dɪsˈdʒɔɪntɪd/ *adj* inconexo, deshilvanado

disk /dɪsk/ *n* (a) (flat, circular object) disco *m* (b) (Comput, Audio, Anat) disco *m*

disk drive *n* unidad *f* de disco

diskette /dɪsˈket/ *n* disquete *m*

dislike¹ /dɪsˈlaɪk/ *vt*: I ~ dogs no me gustan los perros; **he** ~**s wearing a tie** le desagrada *or* no le gusta llevar corbata

dislike² *n* (a) (emotion): **I have a strong** ~ **of dogs** no me gustan nada los perros, (les) tengo aversión a los perros; **to take a** ~ **to sb** tomarle antipatía a algn (b) (sth disliked): **you'll have to tell us all your likes and** ~**s** tendrás que decirnos lo que te gusta y lo que no te gusta

dislocate /ˈdɪsləkeɪt/ *vt* (Med) dislocarse*

dislodge /dɪsˈlɑːdʒ ‖dɪsˈlɒdʒ/ *vt* (shift, remove) sacar*; **the wind** ~**d some tiles** el viento causó que se soltaran varias tejas

disloyal /dɪsˈlɔɪəl/ *adj* desleal

dismal /ˈdɪzməl/ *adj* (a) (gloomy) ‹place/tone›

sombrío, deprimente, lúgubre (b) (very bad) ‹news/prophecy› funesto; ‹future› muy negro; ‹weather› malísimo; ‹results/performance› pésimo

dismantle /dɪsˈmæntl/ *vt* ‹machinery/furniture› desmontar; ‹organization› desmantelar

dismay¹ /dɪsˈmeɪ/ *n* consternación *f*, **they looked at him in** *o* **with** ~ lo miraron consternados; **much to my/his** ~ para mi/su desgracia

dismay² *vt* consternar

dismember /dɪsˈmembər ‖dɪsˈmembə(r)/ *vt* ‹animal› descuartizar*; ‹corpse› desmembrar*

dismiss /dɪsˈmɪs/ *vt* 1 (a) ‹employee› despedir*; ‹executive, minister› destituir* (b) (send away) ‹class› dejar salir 2 ‹possibility/suggestion› descartar, desechar; ‹request/petition/claim› desestimar, rechazar; 3 (Law) ‹charge/appeal› desestimar; **to** ~ **a case** sobreseer* una causa

dismissal /dɪsˈmɪsəl/ *n* (a) (of employee) despido *m*; (of executive, minister) destitución *f* (b) (sending away) autorización *f* para retirarse (c) (of theory, request) rechazo *m* (d) (Law) desestimación *f*

dismount /dɪsˈmaʊnt/ *vi* desmontar

disobedience /ˌdɪsəˈbiːdiəns/ *n* desobediencia *f*

disobedient /ˌdɪsəˈbiːdiənt/ *adj* desobediente

disobey /ˌdɪsəˈbeɪ/ *vt/i* desobedecer*

disorder /dɪsˈɔːrdər ‖dɪsˈɔːdə(r)/ *n* 1 (a) (confusion) desorden *m* (b) (unrest) desórdenes *mpl*, disturbios *mpl* 2 (Med) afección *f* (frml), problema *m*

disorderly /dɪsˈɔːrdərli ‖dɪsˈɔːdəli/ *adj* (a) (untidy) desordenado (b) (unruly) ‹crowd› alborotado; ‹person› revoltoso; ~ **conduct** alteración *f* del orden público

disorganized /dɪsˈɔːrɡənaɪzd ‖dɪsˈɔːɡənaɪzd/ *adj* desorganizado

disorient /dɪsˈɔːrient/, **disorientate** /dɪsˈɔːriənteɪt/ *vt* desorientar

disown /dɪsˈəʊn/ *vt* (a) (repudiate) renegar* de, repudiar (b) (deny responsibility for) no reconocer* como propio

disparaging /dɪsˈpærədʒɪŋ/ *adj* desdeñoso, despreciativo

disparity /dɪsˈpærəti/ *n* (inequality) disparidad *f*; (difference) discrepancia *f*

dispassionate /dɪsˈpæʃənət/ *adj* ‹account› desapasionado, objetivo; ‹adjudication/onlooker› imparcial

dispatch¹ /dɪˈspætʃ/ *vt* 1 (send) despachar, enviar* 2 (a) (carry out) (frml) ‹task/duty› despachar (b) (kill) (euph) ‹person/animal› despachar (euf) (c) (consume) (hum) ‹food/drink› despacharse (hum)

dispatch² *n* 1 (message) despacho *m*; (Mil) parte *m* 2 (sending) despacho *m*, envío *m*, expedición *f*

dispel /dɪˈspel/ *vt* **-ll-** (a) ‹doubts/fear› disipar, hacer* desvanecer (b) ‹fog› disipar

dispensary /dɪˈspensəri/ *n* (*pl* **-ries**) (in hospital) dispensario *m*, farmacia *f*; (in school) enfermería *f*

dispensation /ˌdɪspənˈseɪʃən/ *n* 1 (a) (exemption) exención *f* (b) (Relig) dispensa *f* 2 (of justice) administración *f*

dispense /dɪ'spens/ vt **1** (a) ⟨grants/alms⟩ dar*; ⟨advice⟩ ofrecer*, dar*; ⟨favors⟩ conceder* (b) «machine» ⟨coffee/soap⟩ expender **2** ⟨drugs/ prescription⟩ despachar, preparar **3** (administer) ⟨justice⟩ administrar
■ **dispense with** [v + prep + o] prescindir de

dispenser /dɪ'spensər ‖dɪ'spensə(r)/ n (device): **a cash ~** un cajero automático; **a soap ~** un dispositivo que suministra jabón

disperse /dɪ'spɜːrs ‖dɪ'spɜːs/ vt dispersar
■ **~** vi dispersarse

dispirited /dɪ'spɪrətəd ‖dɪ'spɪrɪtɪd/ adj ⟨person⟩ desanimado, abatido

displace /dɪs'pleɪs/ vt (a) (Phys) ⟨liquid/ volume⟩ desplazar* (b) (replace) reemplazar* (c) (force from home) ⟨refugees/workers⟩ desplazar*

display¹ /dɪ'spleɪ/ vt (a) (put on show) ⟨exhibit⟩ exponer*; ⟨data/figures⟩ (Comput) visualizar* (b) (flaunt) ⟨finery/erudition⟩ hacer* despliegue or gala de; ⟨muscles⟩ lucir*, hacer* alarde de (c) (reveal) ⟨anger/interest⟩ demostrar*, manifestar*; ⟨feelings⟩ exteriorizar*, demostrar*; ⟨tendencies/ symptoms⟩ mostrar*; ⟨skill/courage⟩ demostrar*

display² n **1** (a) (exhibition) exposición f, muestra f; (show) show m; **to be on ~** «painting/ wares» estar* expuesto; (before n) ~ **cabinet** vitrina f (b) (of feeling) exteriorización f, demostración f; (of courage, strength, knowledge) despliegue m; (of ignorance) demostración f **2** (Comput, Electron) display m, visualizador m **3** (Journ, Print) (before n) ~ **advertising** anuncios mpl destacados

displease /dɪs'pliːz/ vt desagradar, contrariar*

displeasure /dɪs'pleʒər ‖dɪs'pleʒə(r)/ n desagrado m

disposable /dɪ'spəʊzəbəl/ adj **1** ⟨cup/razor/ pen⟩ desechable, de usar y tirar **2** ⟨income⟩ disponible

disposal /dɪ'spəʊzəl/ n **1** (removal, riddance): **the problem of the ~ of waste** el problema de cómo deshacerse de residuos; **arrangements were made for the ~ of the body** se hicieron arreglos para que el cadáver fuera inhumado (or trasladado al crematorio etc) **2** (power to use) disposición f; **to have sth at one's ~** disponer* de algo, tener* algo a su (or mi etc) disposición

disposed /dɪ'spəʊzd/ adj (pred) (a) (inclined) **to be ~ to + INF** estar* dispuesto A + INF (b) (liable) (frml) **to be ~ TO sth** ser* propenso A algo, tener* propensión A algo

dispose of /dɪ'spəʊz/ [v + prep + o] **1** (a) (get rid of) ⟨refuse/evidence⟩ deshacerse* de; ⟨rival/ opponent⟩ deshacerse* de, liquidar (fam) (b) (sell) ⟨house/car/land⟩ vender, enajenar (frml) (c) (deal with) ⟨problem/question/objection⟩ despachar **2** (have use of) (frml) ⟨funds/resources⟩ disponer* de

disposition /dɪspə'zɪʃən/ n **1** (a) (personality) manera f or modo m de ser, temperamento m (b) (inclination) (no pl) (frml) ~ **TO sth** predisposición f A algo **2** (arrangement) disposición f

dispossess /dɪspə'zes/ vt (frml) **to ~ sb OF sth** desposeer or despojar a algn DE algo (frml)

disproportionate /dɪsprə'pɔːrʃənət ‖dɪsprə'pɔːʃənət/ adj ⟨number/size⟩ desproporcionado

disprove /dɪs'pruːv/ vt ⟨claim/assertion/charge⟩ desmentir*; ⟨doctrine/theory⟩ rebatir, refutar

dispute¹ /dɪ'spjuːt/ n (a) (controversy, clash) polémica f, controversia f (b) (debate) discusión f; (quarrel) disputa f (c) (Lab Rel) conflicto m (laboral)

dispute² vt **1** (a) (contest) discutir, cuestionar (b) ⟨will/decision⟩ impugnar (c) (argue) ⟨point/ question⟩ debatir, discutir (d) **disputed** past p ⟨decision⟩ discutido, polémico; ⟨territory⟩ en litigio **2** (fight for) ⟨possession/victory/territory⟩ disputarse

disqualify /dɪs'kwɑːləfaɪ ‖dɪs'kwɒlɪfaɪ/ vt **-fies, -fying, -fied** (a) (make ineligible): **as a professional she was disqualified from entering the Olympics** el hecho de ser profesional le impedía participar en las Olimpíadas; **a criminal record disqualifies you from jury service** tener antecedentes penales inhabilita para ser miembro de un jurado (b) (debar) (Sport) descalificar

disquiet /dɪs'kwaɪət/ n (frml) inquietud f, intranquilidad f, desasosiego m

disregard¹ /dɪsrɪ'gɑːrd ‖dɪsrɪ'gɑːd/ vt ⟨danger/difficulty⟩ ignorar, despreciar; ⟨advice⟩ hacer* caso omiso de, no prestar atención a; ⟨feelings/wishes⟩ no tener* en cuenta

disregard² n ~ **FOR sth/sb** indiferencia f HACIA algo/algn

disrepair /dɪsrɪ'per ‖dɪsrɪ'peə(r)/ n mal estado m; **to be in (a state of) ~** estar* en mal estado

disreputable /dɪs'repjətəbəl ‖dɪs'repjʊtəbəl/ adj ⟨person/firm⟩ de dudosa reputación, de mala fama; ⟨nightclub/district⟩ de mala fama; ⟨conduct/ action⟩ vergonzoso

disrepute /dɪsrɪ'pjuːt/ n (frml): **to fall into ~** caer* en descrédito; **to bring sth into ~** desacreditar algo

disrespect /dɪsrɪ'spekt/ n ~ (**FOR sth**) falta f de respeto (HACIA algo); **I meant no ~** no fue mi intención ofenderlo, no quise faltarle al or (CS) el respeto

disrespectful /dɪsrɪ'spektfəl/ adj ⟨person⟩ irrespetuoso; ⟨attitude⟩ irreverente

disrupt /dɪs'rʌpt/ vt ⟨meeting/class⟩ perturbar el desarrollo de; ⟨traffic/communications⟩ crear problemas de, afectar a; ⟨plans⟩ desbaratar, trastocar*

disruption /dɪs'rʌpʃən/ n trastorno m

disruptive /dɪs'rʌptɪv/ adj ⟨influence⟩ perjudicial, negativo; **a ~ pupil** un alumno problema

dissatisfaction /dɪsˌsætəs'fækʃən ‖dɪsˌsætɪs'fækʃən/ n descontento m, insatisfacción f

dissatisfied /dɪs'sætəsfaɪd ‖dɪ'sætɪsfaɪd/ adj descontento, insatisfecho

dissect /dɪ'sekt, daɪ-/ vt ⟨animal/body⟩ diseccionar, hacer* la disección de

disseminate /dɪ'seməneɪt ‖dɪ'semɪneɪt/ vt (frml) diseminar

dissent /dɪ'sent/ n (frml) desacuerdo m

dissertation /dɪsər'teɪʃən ‖dɪsə'teɪʃən/ n (in US: for PhD) tesis f (doctoral); (in UK: for lower degree) tesis f, tesina f

disservice /'dɪs'sɜːrvəs ‖dɪs'sɜːvɪs/ n (fml): **this report does him a** ∼ este informe no le hace justicia

dissident /'dɪsədənt ‖'dɪsɪdənt/ n disidente *mf*

dissimilar /dɪ'sɪmələr ‖dɪ'sɪmɪlə(r)/ adj distinto, diferente

dissipate /'dɪsəpeɪt ‖'dɪsɪpeɪt/ vt (fml) **(a)** (squander) ⟨inheritance⟩ disipar, dilapidar; ⟨energy/talents⟩ desperdiciar **(b)** (dispel) ⟨anxiety⟩ disipar, hacer* desvanecer
■ ∼ vi (fml) «anger/doubts» disiparse, desvanecerse*

dissociate /dɪ'səʊʃieɪt, -sieɪt/ vt **(a)** (separate) disociar **(b)** (distance) **to** ∼ **oneself FROM sb/sth** desvincularse DE algn/algo

dissolute /'dɪsəluːt/ adj disoluto

dissolve /dɪ'zɑːlv ‖dɪ'zɒlv/ vt disolver*
■ ∼ vi disolverse*

dissuade /dɪ'sweɪd/ vt **to** ∼ **sb** (**FROM sth**) disuadir a algn (DE algo); **I managed to** ∼ **her from leaving** logré convencerla de que no se fuera

distance¹ /'dɪstəns/ n distancia *f*; **in the** (**far**) ∼ en la distancia *or* lejanía, a lo lejos; **to keep one's** ∼ (remain aloof) guardar las distancias; (lit: keep away) no acercarse*

distance² v refl **to** ∼ **oneself** (**FROM sb/sth**) (emotionally) distanciarse (DE algn/algo); (deny involvement) desvincularse (DE algn/algo)

distance learning n enseñanza *f* a distancia

distant /'dɪstənt/ adj ⟨spot/country⟩ distante, lejano; ⟨relative⟩ lejano; **in the** ∼ **past** en el pasado remoto

distantly /'dɪstəntli/ adv ⟨hear/see⟩ en la lejanía; **we are** ∼ **related** somos parientes lejanos

distaste /dɪs'teɪst/ n desagrado *m*

distasteful /dɪs'teɪstfəl/ adj **(a)** (unpleasant) ⟨task/chore⟩ desagradable **(b)** (offensive) ⟨remark/picture⟩ de mal gusto

distend /dɪ'stend/ vt dilatar, hinchar
■ ∼ vi dilatarse, hincharse

distill, (BrE) **distil** vt **-ll-** /dɪ'stɪl/ destilar

distillery /dɪ'stɪləri/ n (pl **-ries**) destilería *f*

distinct /dɪ'stɪŋkt/ adj **1** ⟨shape/outline⟩ definido, claro, nítido; ⟨likeness⟩ obvio, marcado; ⟨improvement⟩ decidido, marcado; ⟨possibility⟩ nada desdeñable **2** (different, separate) distinto, bien diferenciado **we are talking about English people as** ∼ **from British people** nos referimos a los ingleses en particular y no a los británicos

distinction /dɪ'stɪŋkʃən/ n **1** **(a)** (difference) distinción *f*; **we must make** *o* **draw a** ∼ **between** ... debemos distinguir entre ... **(b)** (act of differentiating) distinción *f*; **without** ∼ **of race or creed** sin distinción de raza o credo **2** **(a)** (merit, excellence): **a writer of** ∼ un distinguido *or* destacado escritor; **a car of** ∼ un coche de categoría **(b)** (distinguished appearance) distinción *f* **(c)** (mark of recognition) honor *m*, distinción *f* **(d)** (BrE Educ) mención *f* especial

distinctive /dɪ'stɪŋktɪv/ adj ⟨marking/plumage⟩ distintivo, característico; ⟨gesture/laugh⟩ personal, inconfundible; ⟨decor/dress⟩ particular

distinctly /dɪ'stɪŋktli/ adv **(a)** ⟨speak/

enunciate⟩ con claridad **(b)** ⟨hear⟩ perfectamente, claramente; **I** ∼ **remember telling you** me acuerdo perfectamente *or* muy bien de que te lo dije

distinguish /dɪ'stɪŋgwɪʃ/ vt **1** **(a)** (differentiate) distinguir*, diferenciar **(b)** **distinguishing** pres p ⟨feature/mark⟩ distintivo, característico **2** (make out) distinguir*
■ ∼ vi distinguir*

distinguished /dɪ'stɪŋgwɪʃt/ adj distinguido

distort /dɪ'stɔːrt ‖dɪ'stɔːt/ vt **(a)** (deform) ⟨metal/object⟩ deformar **(b)** (Opt) ⟨image/reflection⟩ deformar, distorsionar **(c)** (Electron) ⟨signal/sound⟩ distorsionar **(d)** (misrepresent) ⟨facts/statement⟩ tergiversar, distorsionar

distortion /dɪ'stɔːrʃən ‖dɪ'stɔːʃən/ n **(a)** (of metal, object) deformación *f*; (of features) distorsión *f* **(b)** (Opt) deformación *f*, distorsión *f* **(c)** (of facts, news) tergiversación *f*, distorsión *f*

distract /dɪ'strækt/ vt **(a)** (divert) ⟨person⟩ distraer* **(b)** (amuse) entretener*, distraer*

distraction /dɪ'strækʃən/ n **1** **(a)** (interruption) distracción *f* **(b)** (entertainment) (fml) entretenimiento *m*, distracción *f* **2** (madness): **to drive sb to** ∼ sacar* a algn de quicio

distraught /dɪ'strɔːt/ adj ⟨voice/person⟩ consternado, angustiado

distress¹ /dɪ'stres/ n angustia *f*, aflicción *f*; **he was in great** ∼ sufría mucho

distress² vt (upset) afligir*; (grieve) consternar

distressed /dɪ'strest/ adj afligido

distressing /dɪ'stresɪŋ/ adj ⟨news/circumstance⟩ penoso, angustiante

distribute /dɪ'strɪbjət, -bjuːt ‖dɪ'strɪbjuːt/ vt distribuir*; ⟨profits⟩ repartir

distribution /'dɪstrɪ'bjuːʃən/ n distribución *f*, reparto *m*; (of dividends) reparto *m*

distributor /dɪ'strɪbjətər ‖dɪ'strɪbjutə(r)/ n **1** (Busn) distribuidor *m*; (Cin) distribuidora *f* **2** (Auto, Elec) distribuidor *m* (del encendido)

district /'dɪstrɪkt/ n **1** **(a)** (region) zona *f*, región *f* **(b)** (locality) barrio *m* **2** (Govt) (in US: of state, city) distrito *m*

district: ∼ **attorney** n (in US) fiscal *mf* del distrito; ∼ **court** n (in US) tribunal *m* de distrito; ∼ **nurse** n (in UK) enfermero que tiene a su cuidado a los pacientes de un distrito

distrust¹ /dɪs'trʌst/ vt desconfiar* de, no fiarse* de

distrust² n desconfianza *f*, recelo *m*

distrustful /dɪs'trʌstfəl/ adj desconfiado, receloso

disturb /dɪ'stɜːrb ‖dɪ'stɜːb/ vt **1** **(a)** (interrupt): **the noise** ∼**ed my concentration** el ruido me hizo perder la concentración; **the calm was** ∼**ed by the arrival of the tourists** la llegada de los turistas vino a perturbar la calma **(b)** (inconvenience) molestar **(c)** (burst in upon) ⟨thief⟩ sorprender **2** (disarrange): **she found that her papers had been** ∼**ed** notó que alguien había tocado sus papeles **3** (trouble) perturbar, inquietar, llenar de inquietud

disturbance /dɪ'stɜːrbəns ‖dɪ'stɜːbəns/ n **1** **(a)** (noisy disruption): **to cause/create a** ∼ provocar*/armar un alboroto **(b)** (interruption) interrupción *f* **2** (of routine) alteración *f* **3** (riot) disturbio *m*

disturbed /dɪ'stɜːrbd ‖dɪ'stɜːbd/ adj [1] (a) (Psych) ⟨person/mind⟩ trastornado (b) (perturbed) (pred): I was greatly ~ to hear of his misfortune la noticia de su desgracia me impresionó or afectó muchísimo [2] (restless) ⟨sleep⟩ agitado, inquieto

disturbing /dɪ'stɜːrbɪŋ ‖dɪ'stɜːbɪŋ/ adj (worrying, upsetting) inquietante, perturbador; (alarming) alarmante

disuse /dɪs'juːs ‖dɪs'juːs/ n desuso m

disused /dɪʃ'uːzd ‖dɪs'juːzd/ adj ⟨factory/quarry⟩ abandonado; ⟨machinery⟩ en desuso

ditch¹ /dɪtʃ/ n zanja f; (at roadside) cuneta f; (for irrigation) acequia f

ditch² vt [1] (abandon) (colloq) ⟨girlfriend/boyfriend⟩ plantar (fam), botar (AmC, Chi fam); ⟨object⟩ deshacerse* de, botar (AmL exc RPl), tirar (Esp, RPl); ⟨plan⟩ abandonar, desechar [2] (Aviat): to ~ a plane hacer* un amaraje or amarizaje or amerizaje (forzoso)

dither /'dɪðər ‖'dɪðə(r)/ vi (colloq) (a) (become agitated) (AmE) ponerse* muy nervioso (b) (be indecisive) titubear, vacilar

ditto /'dɪtəʊ/ adv (colloq): I'm fed up — ditto! estoy harto — ¡y yo ídem de ídem! (fam)

divan /dɪ'væn/ n (a) (sofa) diván m, canapé m (b) ~ (bed) cama f turca

dive¹ /daɪv/ vi (past dived or (AmE also) dove; past p dived) (a) (from height) zambullirse*, tirarse (al agua), tirarse or echarse un clavado (AmL) (b) (from surface) «person/whale» sumergirse*, zambullirse*; «submarine» sumergirse* (c) (swoop) «plane/bird» bajar en picada or (Esp) en picado

dive² n [1] (a) (into water) zambullida f, clavado m (AmL); (Sport) salto m (de trampolín), clavado m (AmL) (b) (of submarine, whale) inmersión f (c) (swoop) descenso m en picada or (Esp) en picado [2] (lunge, sudden movement) (colloq): he made a ~ for the gun se abalanzó sobre la pistola [3] (disreputable club, bar) (colloq) antro m

dive-bomb /'daɪvbɑːm ‖'daɪvbɒm/ vt bombardear en picada or (Esp) en picado

diver /'daɪvər ‖'daɪvə(r)/ n (a) (from diving board etc) saltador, -dora m,f, clavadista mf (b) (deep-sea) buzo mf, submarinista mf

diverge /daɪ'vɜːrdʒ ‖daɪ'vɜːdʒ/ vi (a) «lines/paths» separarse (b) «opinions/explanations» divergir*

diverse /daɪ'vɜːrs ‖daɪ'vɜːs/ adj (a) (varied) ⟨interests/tastes⟩ diversos, variados; plant life in the area is extremely ~ la vegetación en la zona es muy variada (b) (unlike) diferentes, distintos

diversion /də'vɜːrʒən ‖daɪ'vɜːʃən/ n [1] (a) (of river) desviación f (b) (of funds) malversación f (c) (BrE Transp) desvío m, desviación f [2] (distraction) (Mil) diversión f, divertimiento m estratégico [3] (amusement) (frml) diversión f, entretenimiento m

diversity /də'vɜːrsəti ‖daɪ'vɜːsəti/ n diversidad f

divert /də'vɜːrt ‖daɪ'vɜːt/ vt [1] (a) (redirect) ⟨stream/flow⟩ desviar*; ⟨traffic⟩ (BrE) desviar* (b) (ward off) ⟨blow/attack⟩ eludir, esquivar [2] (distract) ⟨attention/thoughts⟩ distraer* [3] (amuse) (frml) divertir*, entretener*

divest /daɪ'vest/ vt (frml) to ~ sb OF sth despojar a algn DE algo (frml)

divide /də'vaɪd ‖dɪ'vaɪd/ vt [1] (a) (split up) dividir; to ~ sth INTO sth dividir algo EN algo (b) (separate) to ~ sth FROM sth separar algo DE algo (c) (share) ⟨cake/money/work⟩ repartir [2] (cause to disagree) dividir [3] (Math) dividir; ▶ FOUR¹
■ ~ vi [1] (a) (fork) «road/river» dividirse (b) (split) «group/particles/cells» dividirse [2] (Math) dividir
■ **divide up** [1] [v + o + adv, v + adv + o] dividir [2] [v + adv] dividirse

divided /də'vaɪdəd ‖dɪ'vaɪdɪd/ adj ⟨opinion⟩ dividido

divided highway n (AmE) autovía f, carretera f de doble pista

dividend /'dɪvədend ‖'dɪvɪdend/ n dividendo m; to pay ~s dar* dividendos, reportar beneficios

divider /də'vaɪdər ‖dɪ'vaɪdə(r)/ n (a) (screen) mampara f; (in filing system) separador m (b) **dividers** pl (Math) compás m de puntas fijas

dividing line /də'vaɪdɪŋ ‖dɪ'vaɪdɪŋ/ n línea f divisoria

divine¹ /də'vaɪn ‖dɪ'vaɪn/ adj [1] (before n) ⟨intervention/inspiration⟩ divino [2] (wonderful) divino, precioso

divine² vt (a) (discover, guess) (liter) adivinar (b) ⟨water/minerals⟩ descubrir* (con una varita de zahorí)

diving /'daɪvɪŋ/ n (a) (from height) saltos mpl de trampolín, clavados mpl (AmL) (b) (under water) submarinismo m, buceo m

diving: ~ **board** n trampolín m; ~ **suit** n escafandra f, traje m de buzo

divinity /də'vɪnəti ‖dɪ'vɪnəti/ n (pl -ties) (frml) (a) (divine nature, being) divinidad f (b) (theology) teología f

division /də'vɪʒən ‖dɪ'vɪʒən/ n [1] (a) (distribution) reparto m, división f (b) (boundary) división f; class ~s divisiones de clase (c) (part) división f [2] (disagreement) desacuerdo m [3] (department) división f, sección f [4] (Mil) división f [5] (Sport) (a) (in boxing) categoría f (b) (in US: area) zona f (c) (in UK: by standard) división f [6] (Math) división f

divisive /də'vaɪsɪv ‖dɪ'vaɪsɪv/ adj divisivo

divorce¹ /də'vɔːrs ‖dɪ'vɔːs/ n divorcio m

divorce² vt (Law) divorciarse de; to get ~d divorciarse
■ ~ vi divorciarse

divorcee /dɪˌvɔːr'seɪ ‖dɪˌvɔː'siː/ n divorciado, -da m,f

divulge /daɪ'vʌldʒ/ vt divulgar*; to ~ sth TO sb revelarle algo A algn

DIY n (BrE) (= **do-it-yourself**) bricolaje m

AmC	Central America	Arg	Argentina	Cu	Cuba	Per Peru
AmL	Latin America	Bol	Bolivia	Ec	Ecuador	RPl River Plate Area
AmS	South America	Chi	Chile	Esp	Spain	Ur Uruguay
Andes	Andean Region	CS	Southern Cone	Méx	Mexico	Ven Venezuela

dizzy /'dɪzi/ adj **-zier, -ziest (a)** (giddy)
⟨sensation⟩ de mareo; **to feel ~** estar* mareado
(b) (causing dizziness) ⟨speed⟩ vertiginoso; ⟨height⟩
de vértigo

DJ n = **disc jockey**

DNA n (= **deoxyribonucleic acid**) ADN m

do¹ /duː, weak form dʊ, də/ (3rd pers sing pres
does; pres **doing**; past **did**; past p **done**) vt
1 hacer*; **to have something/nothing to ~** tener*
algo/no tener* nada que hacer; **it was a silly thing
to ~** fue una estupidez; **can I ~ anything to help?**
¿puedo ayudar en algo?

2 (carry out) ⟨job/task⟩ hacer*; **to ~ the cooking**
cocinar; **well done!** ¡muy bien!

3 (achieve, bring about): **she's done it: it's a new
world record** lo ha logrado: es una nueva marca
mundial; **it was climbing those stairs that did it**
fue por subir esa escalera; **that mustache really
does something for him** la verdad es que le queda
muy bien el bigote

4 (a) (fix, arrange, repair): **I have to ~ my nails** me
tengo que arreglar las uñas; **she had her hair
done** se hizo peinar **(b)** (clean) ⟨dishes⟩ lavar;
⟨brass/windows⟩ limpiar

5 (make, produce) ⟨meal⟩ preparar, hacer*;
⟨drawing/translation⟩ hacer*

6 (travel): **he was ~ing 100 mph** iba a 100 millas
por hora; **the car has only done 4,000 miles** el
coche solo tiene hecho 4.000 millas

■ **~** vi **1** (act, behave) hacer*; **~ as you're told!**
¡haz lo que se te dice!; **his concern to ~ well by
his son** su preocupación por hacer todo lo
posible por su hijo

2 (get along, manage): **how are you ~ing?** (colloq)
¿qué tal estás or andas or te va?; **how do you ~?**
(as greeting) mucho gusto, encantado; **how are we
~ing for time?** ¿cómo or qué tal vamos or
andamos de tiempo?; **she did well in her exams** le
fue bien en los exámenes; **he's done well for
himself** ha sabido abrirse camino

3 (go on, happen) (colloq) (in -ing form): **there's
nothing ~ing in town** no pasa nada en el pueblo;
nothing ~ing! ¡ni hablar!, ¡ni lo sueñes!

4 (be suitable, acceptable): **look, this won't ~!**
¡mira, esto no puede ser!; **it's not ideal, but it'll ~**
no es lo ideal, pero sirve; **this box will ~ for** o **as
a table** esta caja nos servirá de mesa

5 (be enough) ser* suficiente, alcanzar*, bastar;
that'll ~! ¡basta! ¡cállate la boca!

■ **~** v aux [El verbo auxiliar DO se usa para
formar el negativo (I 1) y el interrogativo (I 2),
para agregar énfasis (I 3) o para sustituir a un
verbo usado anteriormente (II)]

I 1 (used to form negative, interrogative,
exclamations): **I ~ not** o **don't know** no sé; **not
only does it cost more, it also ...** no solo cuesta
más, sino que también ...; **did I frighten you?** ¿te
asusté?; **doesn't it make you sick!** ¡dime si no es
asqueante!

2 (emphasizing): **you ~ exaggerate!** ¡cómo
exageras!; **you must admit, she did look ill** tienes
que reconocer que tenía mala cara

II 1 (in elliptical uses): **~ you live here?** — **yes,
I ~/no, I don't** ¿vives aquí? — sí/no; **she says she
understands, but she doesn't** dice que
comprende, pero no es así

2 (in tag questions): **you know Bob, don't you?**
conoces a Bob, ¿no? or ¿verdad? or ¿no es cierto?;
I told you, didn't I? te lo dije ¿no? or ¿no es
cierto?

■ **do away with** [v + adv + prep + o] **(a)** (abolish)
⟨privilege/tax⟩ abolir*, suprimir; ⟨need⟩ eliminar,
acabar con **(b)** (kill) (colloq) eliminar, liquidar
(fam)

■ **do up** [v + o + adv, v + adv + o] **(a)** (fasten) ⟨coat/
necklace/button⟩ abrochar; ⟨zipper⟩ subir; **to ~ up
one's shoes** atarse los cordones or (Méx) las
agujetas or (Per) los pasadores (de los zapatos) **(b)**
(wrap up) ⟨parcel⟩ envolver* **(c)** (dress up) (colloq):
she was all done up estaba muy elegante **(d)** (colloq)
⟨house⟩ arreglar (pintando, empapelando etc)

■ **do with** [v + prep + o] **1** (benefit from) (with
can, could): **that door could ~ with a coat of paint**
no le vendría mal una mano de pintura a esa
puerta; **you could ~ with a change** te hace falta
or te vendría bien un cambio

2 (expressing connection) **I don't want to have
anything to ~ with him/this business** yo no
quiero tener nada que ver con él/este asunto; **it's
nothing to ~ with you!** no es nada que te
concierna or que te importe a ti

■ **do without 1** [v + prep + o]: **to ~ without sth/
sb** prescindir de or arreglárselas sin algo/algn
2 [v + adv] arreglárselas

do² /duː/ n (pl **dos**) **1** (party, gathering) (colloq)
fiesta f, reunión f **2** **do's and don'ts** (rules)
normas fpl

do³ /dəʊ/ n (pl **dos**) (Mus) do m

docile /'dɑːsəl ‖'dəʊsaɪl/ adj dócil, sumiso

dock¹ /dɑːk ‖dɒk/ n **1** (Naut) **(a)** (wharf, quay)
muelle m; (for cargo ships) dársena f; (before n)
⟨worker/strike⟩ portuario **(b)** **docks** pl puerto m
2 (Law) (no pl) the **~** el banquillo de los
acusados **3** (Bot) acedera f

dock² vt **1 (a)** ⟨tail⟩ cortar **(b)** ⟨wages⟩
descontar* dinero de **2** ⟨vessel/ship⟩ fondear,
atracar*

■ **~** vi **(a)** (Naut) «ship/vessel» atracar*, fondear
(b) (Aerosp) acoplarse

docker /'dɑːkər ‖'dɒkə(r)/ n (BrE) estibador,
-dora m,f

dockyard /'dɑːkjɑːrd ‖'dɒkjɑːd/ n (often pl)
astillero m

doctor¹ /'dɑːktər ‖'dɒktə(r)/ n **1** (Med)
médico, -ca m,f, doctor, -tora m,f, facultativo, -va
m,f (fml); **D~ Jones** el doctor Jones **2** (Educ)
doctor, -tora m,f

doctor² vt (pej) **(a)** ⟨food/drink⟩ adulterar **(b)**
⟨text⟩ arreglar **(c)** ⟨results/evidence⟩ falsificar*

doctoral /'dɑːktərəl ‖'dɒktərəl/ adj ⟨thesis/
dissertation⟩ doctoral

doctorate /'dɑːktərət ‖'dɒktərət/ n doctorado
m

doctrine /'dɑːktrən ‖'dɒktrɪn/ n doctrina f

document¹ /'dɑːkjəmənt ‖'dɒkjumənt/ n
documento m

document² vt /'dɑːkjəment ‖'dɒkjument/
documentar

documentary¹ /'dɑːkjə'mentəri
‖ˌdɒkjuˈmentri/ adj documental

documentary² n (pl **-ries**) documental m

documentation /'dɑːkjəmən'teɪʃən
‖ˌdɒkjumenˈteɪʃən/ n documentación f

dodge /dɑːdʒ ‖dɒdʒ/ vt **(a)** ⟨blow⟩ esquivar;
⟨pursuer⟩ eludir **(b)** ⟨question⟩ esquivar,
soslayar; ⟨problem/issue⟩ soslayar; ⟨work/
responsibility⟩ eludir; ⟨tax⟩ evadir

■ ~ *vi* echarse a un lado, apartarse; **she ~d behind the car** se escondió rápidamente detrás del coche

dodgem (car) /ˈdɑːdʒəm ‖ˈdɒdʒəm/ *n* ▶ BUMPER CAR

dodger /ˈdɑːdʒər ‖ˈdɒdʒə(r)/ *n*: **tax ~** evasor, -sora *m,f* de impuestos; **fare ~** *persona que intenta viajar sin pagar en un medio de transporte público*

doe /dəʊ/ *n* (of deer) hembra *f* de gamo, gama *f*; (of rabbit) coneja *f*

does /dʌz, *weak form* dəz/ *3rd pers sing pres of* DO[1]

doesn't /ˈdʌznt/ = **does not**

dog[1] /dɔːɡ ‖dɒɡ/ *n* (Zool) perro, -rra *m,f*; (male canine) macho *m*; **it's ~ eat ~** hay una competencia brutal; **let sleeping ~s lie** mejor no revolver el asunto; (*before n*) **~ show** exposición *f* canina

dog[2] *vt* **-gg-** (*often pass*) perseguir*

dog-eared /ˈdɔːɡɪrd ‖ˈdɒɡɪəd/ *adj* sobado y con las esquinas dobladas

dogged /ˈdɔːɡəd ‖ˈdɒɡɪd/ *adj* obstinado

doggedly /ˈdɔːɡədli ‖ˈdɒɡɪdli/ *adv* obstinadamente

doggerel /ˈdɔːɡərəl ‖ˈdɒɡərəl/ *n* ripios *mpl*

doghouse /ˈdɔːɡhaʊs ‖ˈdɒɡhaʊs/ *n* (AmE) casa *f* or casilla *f* or (Esp) caseta *f* or (Chi) casucha *f* del perro, perrera *f* (Col); **to be in the ~** (also BrE colloq) haber* caído en desgracia

dogma /ˈdɔːɡmə ‖ˈdɒɡmə/ *n* dogma *m*

dogmatic /dɔːɡˈmætɪk ‖dɒɡˈmætɪk/ *adj* dogmático

do-gooder /ˈduːˌɡʊdər ‖duːˈɡʊdə(r)/ *n* (*pej*) hacedor, -dora *m,f* de buenas obras (hum)

dog: **~ paddle** *n* estilo *m* perro *or* perrito; **~sbody** *n* (esp BrE colloq): **I'm just the general ~sbody around here** yo aquí no soy más que el botones

doh /dəʊ/ *n* (Mus) do *m*

doily /ˈdɔɪli/ *n* (*pl* **-lies**) (a) (on plate) blonda *f* (b) (under plate, ornament) tapete *m*, pañito *m*, carpeta *f* (Col, CS)

doing /ˈduːɪŋ/ *n* [1] (action): **that takes some ~** eso no es nada fácil; **it was none of our ~** nosotros no tuvimos nada que ver [2] **doings** *pl* (activities, events) actividades *fpl*

do-it-yourself /ˈduːətʃərˈself ‖ˌduːɪtjɔːˈself/ *n* bricolaje *m*

doldrums /ˈdəʊldrəmz, ˈdɑːl- ‖ˈdɒldrəmz/ *pl n*: **to be in the ~** estar* de capa caída

dole /dəʊl/ *n* (BrE): **to be on the ~** estar* cobrando subsidio de desempleo *or* (Chi tb) de cesantía, estar* en el paro (Esp)

■ **dole out** [v + o + adv, v + adv + o] ⟨food/money⟩ dar*, repartir

doleful /ˈdəʊlfəl/ *adj* ⟨face/look⟩ compungido, triste; ⟨sound/voice⟩ plañidero, lúgubre

doll /dɑːl ‖dɒl/ *n* muñeca *f*

■ **doll up** [v + o + adv] (colloq): **to get (all) ~ed up** emperifollarse (fam)

dollar /ˈdɑːlər ‖ˈdɒlə(r)/ *n* dólar *m*; **you can bet your bottom ~** (colloq) puedes estar seguro, te lo doy firmado (fam); (*before n*) **~ bill** billete *m* de un dólar; **~ sign** signo *m* or símbolo *m* del dólar

dollhouse /ˈdɑːlhaʊs ‖ˈdɒlhaʊs/ (AmE) *n* casa *f* de muñecas

dollop /ˈdɑːləp ‖ˈdɒləp/ *n* (colloq) (served with a spoon) cucharada *f*; (serving, measure) porción *f*

doll's house *n* (BrE) casa *f* de muñecas

dolly /ˈdɑːli ‖ˈdɒli/ *n* (*pl* **-lies**) (used to or by children) muñequita *f*

dolphin /ˈdɑːlfən ‖ˈdɒlfɪn/ *n* (*pl* **~s** *or* **~**) delfín *m*

domain /dəˈmeɪn, dəʊ-/ *n* (a) (sphere of influence, activity) campo *m*, esfera *f*; **in the public ~** de(l) dominio público (b) (Comput) dominio *m*

dome /dəʊm/ *n* (Archit) cúpula *f*

domestic /dəˈmestɪk/ *adj* [1] (a) (of the home) ⟨life/problems⟩ doméstico; **~ violence** violencia *f* en el hogar (b) (home-loving) casero, hogareño [2] ⟨animal⟩ doméstico [3] (Econ, Pol) ⟨affairs/policy/market⟩ interno; ⟨produce/flight⟩ nacional

domesticated /dəˈmestɪkeɪtəd ‖dəˈmestɪkeɪtɪd/ *adj* ⟨animal/species⟩ domesticado

domesticity /ˌdəʊmesˈtɪsəti ‖ˌdɒmesˈtɪsəti, dəʊ-/ *n* (frml or hum) domesticidad *f*

domestic science *n* economía *f* doméstica, hogar *m* (Esp)

domicile /ˈdɑːməsaɪl ‖ˈdɒmɪsaɪl/ *n* (frml) domicilio *m* (frml)

dominance /ˈdɑːmənəns ‖ˈdɒmɪnəns/ *n* (a) (supremacy) dominio *m*, dominación *f* (b) (predominance) predominio *m*, preponderancia *f*

dominant /ˈdɑːmənənt ‖ˈdɒmɪnənt/ *adj* (a) (more powerful) ⟨nation/influence⟩ dominante (b) (predominant) ⟨crop/industry⟩ predominante, preponderante (c) (Biol, Ecol) dominante

dominate /ˈdɑːməneɪt ‖ˈdɒmɪneɪt/ *vt* dominar

domination /ˌdɑːməˈneɪʃən ‖ˌdɒmɪˈneɪʃən/ *n* dominación *f*

domineering /ˌdɑːməˈnɪrɪŋ ‖ˌdɒmɪˈnɪərɪŋ/ *adj* dominante

Dominican Republic /dəˈmɪnɪkən/ *n* **the ~** la República Dominicana

dominion /dəˈmɪnjən/ *n* (liter) dominio *m*

domino /ˈdɑːmənəʊ ‖ˈdɒmɪnəʊ/ *n* (*pl* **-noes**) (a) (counter) ficha *f* de dominó (b) **dominoes** (+ *sing vb*) dominó *m*

don /dɑːn ‖dɒn/ *vt* **-nn-** (put on) (liter) ponerse*

donate /ˈdəʊneɪt, dəʊˈneɪt/ *vt* donar

donation /dəʊˈneɪʃən/ *n* (a) (gift) donativo *m*, donación *f* (b) (act) donación *f*

done[1] /dʌn/ *past p of* DO[1]

done[2] *adj* (*no comp*) [1] (*pred*) (a) (finished) hecho (b) (cooked) cocido [2] (accepted): **it's not ~** *o* **not the ~ thing** no está bien visto

donkey /ˈdɑːŋki ‖ˈdɒŋki/ *n* (*pl* **-keys**) burro *m*, asno *m*

donor /ˈdəʊnər ‖ˈdəʊnə(r)/ *n* donante *mf*

don't /dəʊnt/ = **do not**

doodle /ˈduːdl̩/ *vi/t* garabatear, garrapatear

doom[1] /duːm/ *vt* (*usu pass*) condenar

doom[2] *n* (a) (fate) sino *m* (liter); (death) muerte *f* (b) (ruin) fatalidad *f*

doomsday /ˈduːmzdeɪ/ *n* (arch) día *m* del Juicio Final

door /dɔːr ‖dɔː(r)/ *n* puerta *f*; **double ~s** puerta de dos hojas; **there's someone at the ~** llaman a la puerta; **tickets are available at the** ~ se pueden comprar las localidades en la puerta *or* a la entrada; **he's not allowed out of** ~**s** no le permiten salir; *to show sb the* ~ mostrarle* *or* enseñarle la puerta a algn, echar a algn

door: ~**bell** *n* timbre *m*; ~ **knob** *n* pomo *m* (de la puerta); ~**man** /'dɔːrmən ‖'dɔːmən/ *n* (*pl* -**men** /-mən/) portero *m*; ~**mat** *n* felpudo *m*; ~**step** *n* umbral *m*; ~**stop** *n* cuña *f* (*para mantener la puerta abierta*); ~**-to-~** /'dɔːrtə'dɔːr ‖,dɔːtə'dɔː(r)/ *adj* ⟨*delivery/service*⟩ de puerta a puerta; **a** ~**-to-~ salesman** un vendedor ambulante (*que va de puerta a puerta*); ~**way** *n* entrada *f*

dope¹ /dəʊp/ *n* [1] **(a)** (drugs) (sl) droga *f*, pichicata *f* (CS, Per fam); (cannabis) hachís *m*, chocolate *m* (Esp arg) **(b)** (Sport) estimulante *m*, droga *f*, doping *m*; (*before n*) ⟨*test*⟩ antidoping *adj inv* [2] (information) (sl) información *f* [3] (stupid person) (colloq) imbécil *mf*, tarugo *mf* (fam)

dope² *vt* (colloq) ⟨*person/racehorse*⟩ dopar (fam), drogar*; ⟨*food/drink*⟩ poner* droga en

dopey, dopy /'dəʊpi/ *adj* **dopier, dopiest** (colloq) **(a)** (stupid) lelo (fam), bobo (fam) **(b)** (befuddled) atontado, grogui (fam)

dormant /'dɔːrmənt ‖'dɔːmənt/ *adj* [1] **(a)** ⟨*animal/plant*⟩ aletargado **(b)** ⟨*volcano*⟩ inactivo [2] (frml) ⟨*idea/emotion*⟩ latente

dormice /'dɔːrmaɪs ‖'dɔːmaɪs/ *pl of* DORMOUSE

dormitory /'dɔːrmətɔːri ‖'dɔːmɪtri/ *n* (*pl* -**ries**) **(a)** (in school, hostel) dormitorio *m*; (*before n*) ~ **town** (BrE) ciudad *f* dormitorio **(b)** (students' residence) (AmE) residencia *f* de estudiantes

dormouse /'dɔːrmaʊs ‖'dɔːmaʊs/ *n* (*pl* -**mice** /-maɪs/) lirón *m*

dorsal /'dɔːrsəl ‖'dɔːsəl/ *adj* dorsal

DOS /dɑːs ‖dɒs/ *n* (= **disk-operating system**) DOS *m*

dosage /'dəʊsɪdʒ/ *n* dosis *f*

dose¹ /dəʊs/ *n* (of medication) dosis *f*; **a bad** ~ **of flu** (colloq) una gripe *or* (Col, Méx) una gripa muy mala

dose² *vt*: **I'm all** ~**d up with painkillers** me he tomado no sé cuántos analgésicos

dossier /'dɔːsieɪ ‖'dɒsɪə(r), -ieɪ/ *n* dossier *m*, expediente *m*

dot¹ /dɑːt ‖dɒt/ *n* punto *m*; ~ ~ ~ puntos suspensivos; **on the** ~ en punto

dot² *vt* -**tt**- [1] (add dot) puntuar*; **to sign on the** ~**ted line** firmar la línea punteada *or* de puntos [2] (scatter) (*usu pass*) salpicar*; **her family is** ~**ted about all over Europe** su familia está desperdigada por toda Europa

dot.com /kɑːm ‖kɒm/ *n* (Comput) punto *m* com; (*before n*) ⟨*company*⟩ punto com

dote /dəʊt/ *vi* **to** ~ **on sb** adorar a algn

doting /'dəʊtɪŋ/ *adj*: **his** ~ **mother** su madre, que lo adora

dotty /'dɑːti ‖'dɒti/ *adj* -**tier, -tiest** (colloq) ⟨*person*⟩ chiflado (fam); ⟨*idea*⟩ descabellada

double¹ /'dʌbəl/ *adj* double; (*bed*) de matrimonio, de dos plazas (AmL); **it's** ~ **that** es el doble de eso; **my number is** ~ **three seven** ~ **four eight** (esp BrE) mi número es tres tres siete, cuatro cuatro ocho; **it's spelled with a** ~ **'t'** se escribe con dos tes; ~ **bend** curva *f* en S (*read as: curva en ese*); **inflation reached** ~ **figures** la inflación alcanzó/rebasó el 10%

double² *adv* ⟨*pay/earn/cost*⟩ el doble; **she spends** ~ **what she earns** gasta el doble de lo que gana; **to see** ~ ver* doble

double³ *n* [1] **(a)** (hotel room) doble *f* **(b)** (of spirits): **I'll have a** ~ (deme) uno doble [2] (lookalike) doble *mf* [3] (Sport) (double win) doblete *m* [4] (pace): **at** *o* **on the** ~ (Mil) a paso ligero

double⁴ *vt* **(a)** (increase twofold) ⟨*earnings/profits*⟩ doblar, duplicar*; ⟨*efforts*⟩ redoblar **(b)** (Games) ⟨*stake/call/bid*⟩ doblar
■ ~ *vi* [1] (increase twofold) «*price/amount*» duplicarse*, doblarse
[2] (have dual role): **the table** ~**s as a desk** la mesa también se usa como escritorio; **somebody** ~**d for him in the dangerous scenes** alguien lo doblaba en las escenas peligrosas
■ **double back** [*v* + *adv*] «*person/animal*» volver* sobre sus pasos; **the path** ~**d back on itself** el camino doblaba sobre sí mismo
■ **double up** [*v* + *adv* (+ *o*)] **(a)** (bend): **to** ~ **up with laughter** morirse* *or* desternillarse de risa; **he was** ~**d up with pain** se retorcía de dolor **(b)** (redouble) (AmE) doblar

double: ~ **act** *n*: **they are a** ~ **act** actúan en pareja; ~**-barreled**, (BrE) ~**-barrelled** /'dʌbəl'bærəld/ *adj* **(a)** ⟨*shotgun*⟩ de dos cañones **(b)** (BrE) ⟨*surname*⟩ compuesto; ~ **bass** *n* contrabajo *m*; ~**-book** /'dʌbəl'bʊk/ *vt* (BrE): **the room had been** ~**-booked** la habitación había sido reservada para dos personas distintas; ~**-breasted** /'dʌbəl'brestəd ‖,dʌbəl'brestɪd/ *adj* cruzado; ~**-check** /'dʌbəl'tʃek/ *vi* volver* a mirar, verificar* dos veces ■ ~ *vt* ⟨*facts/information*⟩ volver* a revisar; ~ **chin** *n* papada *f*; ~**-click** /'dʌbəl'klɪk/ *vi* (Comput) hacer* doble click; ~ **cream** *n* (BrE) crema *f* doble, nata *f* para montar (Esp), doble crema *f* (Méx); ~**-cross** /'dʌbəl'krɔːs ‖,dʌbəl'krɒs/ *vt* traicionar; ~**-decker** /'dʌbəl'dekər ‖,dʌbəl'dekə(r)/ *n* ~**-decker (bus)** (esp BrE) autobús *m* de dos pisos; ~ **Dutch** *n* (colloq) chino *m* (fam); ~**-edged** /'dʌbəl'edʒd/ *adj* ⟨*knife/blade/scheme*⟩ de doble filo; ⟨*remark/comment*⟩ de doble sentido; ~ **glazing** /'ɡleɪzɪŋ/ *n* (BrE) doble ventana *f*; ~**-jointed** /'dʌbəl'dʒɔɪntəd ‖,dʌbəl'dʒɔɪntɪd/ *adj*: **he's** ~**-jointed** tiene articulaciones dobles

doubles /'dʌbəlz/ *pl n* dobles *mpl*

double standard *n*: **to have** ~ **s** aplicar* una ley para unos y otra para otros

doubly /'dʌbli/ *adv* ⟨*difficult/dangerous/ interesting*⟩ doblemente

doubt¹ /daʊt/ *n* (uncertainty) duda *f*; **no** ~ **she will phone** con seguridad que llama, seguro que llama; **if in** ~**, don't go** si estás en (la) duda, no vayas; **I have my** ~**s** tengo mis dudas

doubt² *vt* **(a)** ⟨*fact/truth*⟩ dudar de **(b)** (consider unlikely) dudar; **to** ~ (THAT) *o* **if** *o* **whether** dudar QUE (+ *subj*)

doubtful /'daʊtfəl/ *adj* **(a)** (full of doubt) ⟨*expression/tone*⟩ de indecisión *or* duda, dubitativo; **I am** ~ **as to its value** tengo mis dudas acerca de su valor **(b)** (in doubt) dudoso; **the outcome remains** ~ el resultado sigue siendo dudoso *or* incierto

··· doubtfully ···▷ doze

doubtfully /'daʊtfəli/ adv ‹say› sin convicción; ‹agree› con reserva

doubtless /'daʊtləs ‖'daʊtlɪs/ adv sin duda, indudablemente

dough /dəʊ/ n **1** (Culin) masa f **2** (money) (sl) guita f (arg), lana f (AmL fam), plata f (AmS fam), pasta f (Esp fam)

doughnut /'dəʊnʌt/ n donut m, rosquilla f

dour /daʊr, dʊr ‖dʊə(r)/ adj adusto

douse /daʊs/ vt ‹flames› sofocar*

dove[1] /dʌv/ n paloma f

dove[2] /dəʊv/ (AmE) past of DIVE[1]

dovetail /'dʌvteɪl/ vi encajar

dowager /'daʊədʒər ‖'daʊədʒə(r)/ n: viuda de un noble

dowdy /'daʊdi/ adj **-dier, -diest** ‹woman› sin gracia, sin estilo

down[1] /daʊn/ adv **1** (a) (in downward direction): to go ~ bajar; to look ~ mirar (hacia or para) abajo; from the waist ~ desde la cintura para abajo; ~ with tyranny! ¡abajo la tiranía! (b) (downstairs): can you come ~? ¿puedes bajar? **2** (a) (of position) abajo; two floors ~ dos pisos más abajo; ~ here/there aquí/allí (abajo) (b) (downstairs): I'm ~ in the cellar estoy aquí abajo, en el sótano (c) (lowered, pointing downward) bajado; face ~ boca abajo (d) (prostrate): I was ~ with flu all last week estuve con gripe toda la semana pasada **3** (of numbers, intensity): my temperature is ~ to 38° C la fiebre me ha bajado a 38° C; they were two goals ~ iban perdiendo por dos goles **4** (a) (in, toward the south): to go/come ~ south ir*/venir* al sur (b) (at, to another place) (esp BrE): ~ on the farm en la granja; I'm going ~ to the library voy a la biblioteca **5** (a) (dismantled, removed): the room looks bare with the pictures ~ la habitación queda desnuda sin los cuadros; once this wall is ~ una vez que hayan derribado esta pared (b) (out of action): the telephone lines are ~ las líneas de teléfono están cortadas; the system is ~ (Comput) el sistema no funciona **6** down to (a) (as far as) hasta; ~ to the present day hasta nuestros días (b) (reduced to): we're ~ to our last can of tomatoes nos queda solo una lata de tomates

down[2] prep **1** (in downward direction): we ran ~ the slope corrimos cuesta abajo; it fell ~ a hole se cayó por un agujero; halfway ~ the page hacia la mitad de la página **2** (along): we drove on ~ the coast seguimos por la costa; the library is just ~ the street la biblioteca está un poco más allá

down[3] adj **1** (before n) (going downward): the ~ escalator la escalera mecánica de bajada or para bajar **2** (depressed) (colloq) (pred) deprimido

down[4] n (a) (on bird) plumón m (b) (on face, body) vello m, pelusilla f (c) (on plant, fruit) pelusa f

down[5] vt (a) (drink) beberse or tomarse rápidamente (b) (knock down) ‹person› tumbar, derribar

down: ~ and out adj (colloq) (pred): to be ~

and out estar* en la miseria; **~cast** adj (a) (dejected) alicaído, abatido (b) (directed downward): with ~cast eyes con la mirada baja; **~fall** n (of person) perdición f, ruina f; (of king, dictator) caída f; **~grade** ‹employee/hotel› bajar de categoría; **~hearted** /'daʊn'hɑːrtəd ‖,daʊn'hɑːtɪd/ adj desanimado, desmoralizado; **~hill** /'daʊn'hɪl/ adv ‹walk/run› cuesta abajo; to go ~hill ir* cuesta abajo, ir* de mal en peor

Downing Street /'daʊnɪŋ/ n Downing Street (calle de Londres donde se encuentra la residencia oficial del primer ministro británico)

download /'daʊn'ləʊd/ vt (Comput) trasvasar

downmarket[1] /'daʊn'mɑːrkət ‖,daʊn'mɑːkɪt/ adv: the paper has gone ~ el diario ha perdido categoría; (deliberately) el diario se dirige ahora a un sector más popular del público

downmarket[2] adj ‹newspaper› popular; ‹store› barato

down: ~ payment n cuota f or entrega f inicial, entrada f (Esp), pie m (Chi); **~pour** n aguacero m, chaparrón m

downright[1] /'daʊnraɪt/ adj ‹lie/insolence› descarado; ‹crook/liar/rogue› redomado, de tomo y lomo (fam); ‹madness› total y absoluto

downright[2] adv: it was ~ dangerous! ¡fue peligrosísimo!; he was ~ rude! ¡estuvo de lo más grosero!

downriver /'daʊn'rɪvər ‖,daʊn'rɪvə(r)/ adv río abajo

Down's syndrome /daʊnz/ n síndrome m de Down; (before n) ‹child› afectado por el síndrome de Down

downstairs[1] /'daʊn'sterz ‖,daʊn'steəz/ adv abajo; he went ~ to open the door bajó a abrir la puerta

downstairs[2] n planta f baja; (before n) ‹neighbor/toilet› (del piso) de abajo

down: ~stream /'daʊn'striːm/ adv río abajo; **~-to-earth** /'daʊntʊ'ɜːr θ ‖,daʊntə'ɜː θ/ adj (pred ~ to earth) realista, práctico

downtown[1] /'daʊn'taʊn/ n (AmE) centro m (de la ciudad); (before n) ~ New York el centro de Nueva York

downtown[2] adv (AmE): to go/live ~ ir* al/ vivir en el centro

downtrodden /'daʊn'trɑːdn̩ ‖'daʊn,trɒdn̩/ adj oprimido

downward[1] /'daʊnwərd ‖'daʊnwəd/ adj ‹direction/pressure› hacia abajo; ‹movement/ spiral› descendente; ‹tendency› (Fin) a la baja

downward[2] /'daʊnwərd ‖'daʊnwəd/, (esp BrE) **downwards** /-z/ adv hacia abajo

downwind /'daʊn'wɪnd/ adv en la dirección del viento

dowry /'daʊəri/ n (pl **-ries**) dote f

doze /dəʊz/ vi dormitar

■ **doze off** [v + adv] quedarse dormido, dormirse*

dozen¹ /'dʌzn/ n (pl ~ or ~s) docena f; **four dollars a** o **per** ~ cuatro dólares la docena; **I got** ~**s of cards** recibí montones de tarjetas (fam)

dozen² adj docena f de; **a** ~/**two** ~ **eggs** una docena/dos docenas de huevos

dozy /'dəʊzi/ adj **dozier, doziest** amodorrado, adormilado

Dr /'dɑːktər ǁ 'dɒktə(r)/ (title) (= **Doctor**) Dr., Dra.

drab /dræb/ adj ‹clothing/decor/appearance› soso, sin gracia; ‹life/occupation› gris, monótono

draft¹ /dræft ǁ drɑːft/ n [1] (BrE) **draught** (cold air) corriente f de aire [2] (formulation) versión f [3] (Fin) cheque m or efecto m bancario [4] (AmE) **the** ~ (Mil) el llamamiento or (AmL tb) llamado a filas

draft² vt [1] (formulate) ‹document/contract/letter› redactar el borrador de; ‹speech› preparar [2] (conscript) (AmE) reclutar, llamar a filas

draftproof /'dræftpruːf ǁ 'drɑːftpruːf/ adj hermético

draftsman, (BrE) **draughtsman** /'dræftsmən ǁ 'drɑːftsmən/ n (pl **-men** /-mən/) dibujante mf

drafty, (BrE) **draughty** /'dræfti ǁ 'drɑːfti/ adj **-tier, -tiest** con corrientes de aire

drag¹ /dræg/ **-gg-** vt [1] (haul) arrastrar, llevar a rastras; **I couldn't** ~ **myself away** (colloq) no tenía fuerzas para irme [2] (allow to trail) ‹tail/garment/anchor› arrastrar; **to** ~ **one's feet** o **heels** dar(le)* largas al asunto [3] (Comput) ~ **(and drop)** arrastrar (y soltar)
■ ~ vi [1] (a) (trail) «anchor» garrar; «coat» arrastrar (b) (lag) rezagarse* [2] (go on slowly) «work/conversation» hacerse* pesado; «film/play» hacerse* largo
■ **drag on** [v + adv] alargarse* (interminablemente)

drag² n (no pl) [1] (tiresome thing): **what a** ~! ¡qué lata! (fam) [2] (resistant force) resistencia f al avance [3] (women's clothes): **in** ~ vestido de mujer

dragon /'drægən/ n dragón m

dragonfly /'drægənflaɪ/ n (pl **-flies**) libélula f, caballito m del diablo, matapiojos m (Andes)

drain¹ /dreɪn/ n [1] (a) (pipe) sumidero m, resumidero m (AmL); **the** ~**s** (of town) el alcantarillado; (of building) las tuberías de desagüe (b) (grid) (BrE) sumidero m, resumidero m (AmL) [2] (plughole) desagüe m [3] (no pl) (cause of depletion) **a** ~ **on the country's resources** una sangría para el país; **the extra work is an enormous** ~ **on my energy** el trabajo extra me está agotando

drain² vt [1] (a) ‹container/tank› vaciar*; ‹land/swamp› drenar, avenar; ‹blood› drenar; ‹sap/water› extraer* (b) (Culin) ‹vegetables/pasta› escurrir, colar* (c) (Med) drenar [2] (drink up) ‹glass/cup› vaciar*, apurar [3] (consume, exhaust) ‹resources/strength› agotar, consumir
■ ~ vi (a) (dry) ‹dishes› escurrirse* (b) (disappear): **all the strength seemed to** ~ **from my limbs** los brazos y las piernas se me quedaron como sin fuerzas (c) (discharge) «pipes/river» desaguar*

drainage /'dreɪnɪdʒ/ n (a) (of household waste) desagüe m (de aguas residuales); (of rainwater)

canalización f (de agua de lluvia); (before n) ~ **system** (red f de) alcantarillado m (b) (of fields, marshes) drenaje m, avenamiento m

drainboard /'dreɪnbɔːrd ǁ 'dreɪnbɔːd/ n (AmE) escurridero m

draining board /'dreɪnɪŋ/ n (BrE) escurridero m

drainpipe /'dreɪnpaɪp/ n tubo m or caño m del desagüe, bajante f

drake /dreɪk/ n pato m (macho)

drama /'drɑːmə/ n (pl **-mas**) [1] (Theat) (a) (play) obra f dramática, drama m (b) (plays collectively) teatro m, drama m; (dramatic art) arte m dramático [2] (excitement) dramatismo m

dramatic /drə'mætɪk/ adj [1] (Theat) (before n) dramático, teatral [2] (a) (striking) ‹change/improvement› espectacular, drástico; ‹increase› espectacular (b) (momentous) ‹events/development› dramático

dramatically /drə'mætɪkli/ adv (a) (exaggeratedly) ‹pause/announce› dramáticamente, de manera teatral or histriónica (b) (strikingly) ‹change/improve/increase› de manera espectacular

dramatics /drə'mætɪks/ n (Theat) (+ sing vb): amateur ~ teatro m amateur or de aficionados

dramatist /'dræmətɪst/ n dramaturgo, -ga m,f

dramatize /'dræmətaɪz/ vt [1] ‹story/novel› (Theat) dramatizar*, hacer* una adaptación teatral de; (Cin) llevar al cine [2] (exaggerate) ‹situation/event› dramatizar*, exagerar

drank /dræŋk/ past of DRINK²

drape /dreɪp/ vt (a) (arrange): **they** ~**d a flag over the tomb** colocaron una bandera formando pliegues sobre la tumba; **she** ~**d herself over the sofa** se tendió sobre el sofá (b) (cover) cubrir*

drapes /dreɪps/ pl n (AmE) cortinas fpl

drastic /'dræstɪk/ adj drástico, radical

drastically /'dræstɪkli/ adv drásticamente

draught /dræft ǁ drɑːft/ n [1] (storage under pressure): **beer on** ~ cerveza f de barril; (before n) ‹beer/cider› de barril [2] (liter) (of water, beer) trago m [3] (BrE) ▶ DRAFT¹ 1

draughtproof /'dræftpruːf ǁ 'drɑːftpruːf/ adj (BrE) ▶ DRAFTPROOF

draughts /dræfts ǁ drɑːfts/ n (BrE) (+ sing vb) damas fpl

draughtsman /'dræftsmən ǁ 'drɑːftsmən/ n (BrE) ▶ DRAFTSMAN

draughty /'dræfti ǁ 'drɑːfti/ adj (BrE) ▶ DRAFTY

draw¹ /drɔː/ (past **drew**; past p **drawn**) vt [1] (a) (move by pulling) ‹curtains/bolt› (open) descorrer; (shut) correr; **he drew her to one side** la llevó a un lado, la llevó aparte (b) (pull along) ‹cart/sled› tirar de, arrastrar [2] (a) (pull out) ‹tooth/cork› sacar*, extraer* (fml); ‹gun› desenfundar, sacar*; ‹sword› desenvainar, sacar* (b) (cause to flow) sacar*; **to** ~ **blood** sacar* sangre, hacer* sangrar; **to** ~ **breath** respirar [3] (a) (Fin) ‹salary/pension› cobrar, percibir (fml); ‹check› girar, librar (b) (derive) ‹strength/lesson› sacar* [4] (establish) ‹distinction/parallel› establecer* [5] (a) (attract) ‹customers/crowd› atraer*; **to be**

∼n to sb/sth sentirse* atraído por algn/algo **(b)** (elicit) ⟨*praise*⟩ conseguir*; ⟨*criticism/protest*⟩ provocar*, suscitar
6 (sketch) ⟨*flower/picture*⟩ dibujar; ⟨*line*⟩ trazar*
7 (BrE Games, Sport) empatar
■ **∼** *vi* **1** (move): **to ∼ close to sth/sb** acercarse* a algo/algn; **to ∼ to a close** terminar, finalizar* (frml); **the train drew out of/into the station** el tren salió de/entró en la estación; **to ∼ ahead of sb/ sth** adelantarse a algn/algo
2 (Art) dibujar
3 (BrE Games, Sport) empatar; (in chess game) hacer* tablas
■ **draw back** [*v + adv*] **(a)** (retreat) retirarse **(b)** (recoil) retroceder
■ **draw in** **1** [*v + o + adv, v + adv + o*] **(a)** (retract) ⟨*claws*⟩ esconder, retraer* **(b)** (into quarrel, war) involucrar; (into conversation) darle* participación a
2 [*v + adv*] **(a)** (arrive) «*train*» llegar* **(b)** «*days/nights*» hacerse* más corto
■ **draw on** [*v + prep + o*] (make use of) ⟨*resources/ reserves*⟩ recurrir a, hacer* uso de; **she drew on her own experiences** se inspiró en sus propias experiencias
■ **draw out** **1** [*v + adv*] **(a)** (depart) «*train*» salir* **(b)** (become longer) hacerse* más largo
2 [*v + o + adv, v + adv + o*] **(a)** (prolong) alargar*, estirar **(b)** (extract, remove) ⟨*tooth/thorn*⟩ sacar*, extraer* (frml); ⟨*wallet/handkerchief*⟩ sacar*; ⟨*information*⟩ sacar*, sonsacar*; ⟨*confession*⟩ arrancar* **(c)** (withdraw) ⟨*money*⟩ sacar*
■ **draw up** **1** [*v + adv*] «*car*» detenerse*, parar
2 [*v + o + adv, v + adv + o*] **(a)** (prepare, draft) ⟨*contract/treaty*⟩ redactar, preparar; ⟨*list/plan*⟩ hacer* **(b)** (arrange in formation) ⟨*troops/competitors*⟩ alinear, formar **(c)** (bring near) ⟨*chair*⟩ acercar*, arrimar
draw² *n* **1** (raffle) sorteo *m* **2** (tie) (Games, Sport) empate *m*
draw: ∼back *n* inconveniente *m*, desventaja *f*; **∼bridge** *n* puente *m* levadizo
drawer *n* /drɔːr ‖'drɔː(r)/ **1** (in furniture) cajón *m*, gaveta *f* (esp AmC, Méx) **2** **drawers** *pl* (Clothing) calzones *mpl*
drawing /'drɔːɪŋ/ *n* dibujo *m*
drawing: ∼ pin *n* (BrE) ▶ THUMBTACK; **∼ room** *n* sala *f*, salón *m*
drawl /drɔːl/ *n*: acento caracterizado por la longitud de las vocales
drawn¹ /drɔːn/ *past p of* DRAW¹
drawn² *adj* ⟨*features/face*⟩ demacrado
drawstring /'drɔːstrɪŋ/ *n* cordón *m* (*del que se tira para cerrar algo*); (before n) ⟨*bag/waist*⟩ fruncido con un cordón o una cinta
dread¹ /dred/ *vt* tenerle* terror *or* pavor a
dread² *n* terror *m*
dreadful /'dredfəl/ *adj* ⟨*news/experience/ weather*⟩ espantoso, terrible; **I feel ∼** me siento pésimo
dreadfully /'dredfəli/ *adv* (as intensifier) ⟨*upset/late*⟩ terriblemente, enormemente
dream¹ /driːm/ *n* sueño *m*; **a ∼ come true** un sueño hecho realidad; (before n) **he lives in a ∼ world** vive de ilusiones, vive en las nubes
dream² (*past & past p* **dreamed** *or* (BrE also)

dreamt /dremt/) *vi* soñar*; **to ∼ ABOUT sth/sb** soñar* CON algo/algn; **would you do that? — I wouldn't ∼ of it!** ¿harías eso? — ¡ni pensarlo!
■ **∼** *vt* soñar*; **I never ∼ed he'd be so rude** nunca (me) imaginé que iba a ser tan grosero
■ **dream up** [*v + o + adv, v + adv + o*] ⟨*plan*⟩ idear
dreamer /'driːmər ‖'driːmə(r)/ *n* soñador, -dora *m,f*
dreamt /dremt/ (BrE) *past & past p of* DREAM²
dreamy /'driːmi/ *adj* **-mier, -miest (a)** (abstracted) ⟨*person*⟩ soñador, fantasioso; ⟨*gaze*⟩ distraído **(b)** ⟨*music*⟩ etéreo, sutil
dreary /'drɪri ‖'drɪəri/ *adj* **-rier, -riest (a)** ⟨*room/landscape*⟩ deprimente, lóbrego, sombrío; ⟨*weather*⟩ gris, deprimente **(b)** ⟨*work/routine*⟩ monótono, aburrido, aburridor (AmL)
dredge /dredʒ/ *vt* dragar*
■ **dredge up** [*v + o + adv, v + adv + o*] ⟨*mud/ sand*⟩ dragar*; ⟨*story/scandal*⟩ desenterrar*
dredger /'dredʒər ‖'dredʒə(r)/ *n* (machine) draga *f*; (vessel) dragador *m*, draga *f*
dregs /dregz/ *pl n* posos *mpl*, cunchos *mpl* (Col), conchos *mpl* (Chi); **the ∼ of society** la escoria de la sociedad
drench /drentʃ/ *vt* (usu pass) empapar
dress¹ /dres/ *n* **1** (for woman, girl) vestido *m* **2** (style of dressing): **they adopted Western ∼** adoptaron el modo de vestir *or* la vestimenta occidental; (before n) **she has no ∼ sense** tiene mal gusto para vestirse
dress² *vt* **1** (put clothes on) vestir*; **to get ∼ed** vestirse*; **he was ∼ed in white** iba (vestido) de blanco **2** (Culin) **(a)** (prepare) ⟨*chicken/fish*⟩ preparar **(b)** (season) ⟨*salad*⟩ aliñar **3** (Med) ⟨*wound*⟩ vendar
■ **∼** *vi* vestirse*
■ **dress up** [*v + adv*] **(a)** (dress smartly) ponerse* elegante **(b)** (in fancy dress) disfrazarse*; **to ∼ up AS sth** disfrazarse* DE algo
dresser /'dresər ‖'dresə(r)/ *n* **1** (person): **he's a stylish ∼** (se) viste con mucho estilo **2 (a)** (in bedroom) (AmE) tocador *m* **(b)** (in kitchen) (BrE) aparador *m*
dressing /'dresɪŋ/ *n* **1** (Med) apósito *m*, gasa *f*; (bandage) vendaje *m* **2** (Culin) (for salad) aliño *m*, aderezo *m*; (stuffing) (AmE) relleno *m*
dressing: ∼ gown *n* bata *f*, salto *m* de cama (CS); **∼ room** *n* (Theat) camerino *m*; (in house) vestidor *m*; **∼ table** *n* tocador *m*
dress: ∼maker *n* modista *mf*; (designer) modisto, -ta *m,f*; **∼ rehearsal** *n* ensayo *m* general; **∼ suit** *n* traje *m* de etiqueta
dressy /'dresi/ *adj* **-sier, -siest** elegante
drew /druː/ *past of* DRAW¹
dribble /'drɪbəl/ *vi* **1** (drool) babear **2** (Sport) driblar, driblear
dribs and drabs /'drɪbzən'dræbz/ *pl n*: **in ∼ ∼ ∼** poquito a poco
dried /draɪd/ *adj* ⟨*figs/flowers*⟩ seco; ⟨*fish*⟩ salado, seco; ⟨*milk/eggs*⟩ en polvo
drier /'draɪər ‖'draɪə(r)/ *n* ▶ DRYER
drift¹ /drɪft/ *vi* **1 (a)** (on water) *moverse empujado por la corriente* **(b)** (be adrift) «*boat/ person*» ir* a la deriva **(c)** (in air) «*balloon*» *moverse empujado por el viento* **2** (proceed

aimlessly): **the crowd began to ~ away** la muchedumbre comenzó a dispersarse; **to ~ apart** «*couple/friends*» distanciarse ③ (pile up) «*sand/snow*» amontonarse

drift² n ① (of sand) montón m; (of snow) ventisquero m ② (meaning) (no pl) sentido m; **I didn't quite catch your ~** no entendí or capté muy bien lo que querías decir ③ (movement): **the ~ from the land** el éxodo rural

driftwood /'drɪftwʊd/ n madera, tablas etc que flotan en el mar a la deriva o que arrastra el mar hasta la playa

drill¹ /drɪl/ n ① (electric o power ~) taladradora f, taladro m; (hand ~) taladro m (manual); (Dent) torno m, fresa f; (Eng, Min) perforadora f, barreno m; (drill head) broca f ② (a) (Mil) instrucción f (b) (Educ) ejercicio m

drill² vt ① (hole) hacer*, perforar; (wood/metal) taladrar, perforar, barrenar; (tooth) trabajar or limpiar con la fresa ② (Mil) (soldiers) instruir*
■ ~ vi perforar, hacer* perforaciones; **to ~ for oil** perforar en busca de petróleo

drily /'draɪli/ adv secamente, con sequedad

drink¹ /drɪŋk/ n ① (a) (any liquid) bebida f (b) (alcohol) bebida f ② (a) (amount drunk, served, sold): **have a ~ of water/milk** bebe or (esp AmL) toma un poco de agua/leche (b) (alcoholic) copa f, trago m (fam); **to have a ~** tomar una copa

drink² (past **drank**; past p **drunk**) vt/i beber, tomar (esp AmL)
■ **drink up** ① [v + adv] bebérselo or (esp AmL) tomárselo todo, terminar su (or mi etc) copa (or leche etc) ② [v + o + adv, v + adv + o] beberse, tomarse (esp AmL)

drinkable /'drɪŋkəbəl/ adj (water) potable

drink-driving /ˌdrɪŋk'draɪvɪŋ/ n BrE ▶ DRUNK DRIVING

drinker /'drɪŋkər ‖ 'drɪŋkə(r)/ n: **he's a heavy ~** es un gran bebedor or un bebedor empedernido; **I'm a beer ~ myself** yo prefiero la cerveza

drinking /'drɪŋkɪŋ/ n (a) (of liquid) beber (b) (of alcohol): **his ~ is causing concern** lo mucho que bebe está causando preocupación

drinking: **~ chocolate** n chocolate m en polvo; **~ water** n agua f⁌ potable

drip¹ /drɪp/ vi -pp- «*washing/hair*» chorrear, gotear; «*faucet/tap*» gotear; **water was ~ping from the ceiling** el techo goteaba, caían gotas del techo

drip² n ① (of rainwater, tap) (no pl) goteo m ② (Med) suero m, gota a gota m ③ (ineffectual person) (colloq) soso, -sa m,f (fam)

drip-dry /'drɪp'draɪ/ adj (fabric/garment) de lava y pon, de lavar y poner

dripping /'drɪpɪŋ/ adj (colloq) empapado; (as intensifier) **to be ~ wet** estar* chorreando or empapado

drive¹ /draɪv/ (past **drove**; past p **driven**) vt ① (Transp) (a) (car/bus/train) manejar or (Esp) conducir* (b) (convey in vehicle) llevar en coche ② (a) (cause to move) (+ adv compl): **the Indians were ~n off their land** los indios fueron expulsados de sus tierras; **we drove them away with sticks** los ahuyentamos con palos (b) (Sport) (ball) mandar, lanzar* (c) (provide power for, operate) hacer* funcionar, mover*

③ (make penetrate) (nail) clavar; (stake) hincar* ④ (a) (cause to become) volver*; **to ~ sb mad** volver* loco a algn; **she is ~ me crazy with his incessant chatter** me saca de quicio con su constante cháchara (b) (compel to act) **to ~ sb to + INF** llevar or empujar a algn A + INF; **she is ~n by ambition** la impulsa or motiva la ambición (c) (overwork): **he drove them mercilessly** los hizo trabajar como esclavos; **she ~s herself too hard** se exige demasiado a sí misma
■ ~ vi manejar or (Esp) conducir*; **she ~s to work** va a trabajar en coche
■ **drive out** [v + o + adv, v + adv + o] expulsar

drive² n ① (in vehicle): **to go for a ~** ir* a dar un paseo or una vuelta en coche; **it's a three-hour ~** es un viaje de tres horas en coche ② (a) (leading to house) camino m, avenida f (que lleva hasta una casa) (b) (in front of house) entrada f (para coches) ③ (in golf, tennis) golpe m fuerte ④ (a) (energy) empuje m, dinamismo m (b) (compulsion) (Psych) impulso m, instinto m; **the sex ~** el apetito sexual ⑤ (a) (organized effort) campaña f (b) (attacking move) (Mil) ofensiva f, avanzada f (c) (in US football) ataque m ⑥ (a) (propulsion system) transmisión f, propulsión f (b) (Auto): **front-wheel/rear-wheel ~** tracción f delantera/trasera

drive-in /'draɪvɪn/ n (AmE) (cinema) autocine m; (restaurant) drive in m (restaurante que sirve a los clientes en el propio automóvil)

drivel /'drɪvəl/ n tonterías fpl, estupideces fpl

driven /'drɪvən/ past p of DRIVE¹

driver /'draɪvər ‖ 'draɪvə(r)/ n (of car, truck, bus) conductor, -ra m,f, chofer m or (Esp) chófer mf; (of racing car) piloto mf; **she's a good ~** maneja or (Esp) conduce bien

driver's license n (AmE) licencia f or (Esp) permiso m de conducción; (less formally) carné m or permiso m (de conducir) (Esp), carné m (Chi) (Ur) libreta f or (AmC, Méx, Ven) licencia f or (Col) pase m (de manejar), registro m (Arg), brevete m (Per)

driving¹ /'draɪvɪŋ/ n (Auto) conducción f (frml)

driving² adj (a) (rain) torrencial; (wind) azotador (b) (dynamic): **the ~ force behind the project** es el alma-máter or la impulsora del proyecto

driving: **~ instructor** n instructor, -tora m,f de autoescuela; **~ licence** n (BrE) ▶ DRIVER'S LICENSE; **~ test** n examen m de conducir or (AmL tb) de manejar

drizzle¹ /'drɪzəl/ n llovizna f, garúa f (AmL)

drizzle² v impers lloviznar, garuar* (AmL)

droll /drəʊl/ adj (a) (comic) gracioso, con chispa (b) (quaint, curious) curioso

drone¹ /drəʊn/ n ① (bee) zángano m ② (sound — of bees, traffic, aircraft) zumbido m; (— of voice) cantinela f (fam), sonsonete m

drone² vi «*bee/engine/plane*» zumbar; **she ~d (on) for hours** estuvo horas con la misma perorata (fam)

drool /druːl/ vi «*dog/baby*» babear; **we ~ed at the sight of the cakes** se nos hizo la boca agua or agua la boca al ver los pasteles

droop /druːp/ vi (a) (sag) «*flowers*» ponerse* ···⯈

mustio; **his shoulders ~ed** se encorvó **(b)** ⟨flag⟩
«*spirits*» flaquear, decaer*; «*person*»
desfallecer*, decaer* **(c) drooping** *pres p* ⟨*head*⟩
gacho; ⟨*flowers*⟩ mustio

drop¹ /drɑːp ‖drɒp/ *n* **1 (a)** (of liquid) gota *f*,
she's had a ~ too much ha bebido más de la
cuenta **(b) drops** *pl* (Med) gotas *fpl*; **nose ~s**
gotas para la nariz **(d)** (candy): **acid ~s** caramelos
mpl ácidos; **chocolate ~s** pastillas *fpl* de
chocolate **2** (fall) (*no pl*) (in temperature) descenso
m; (in prices) caída *f*, baja *f*; **a sheer ~** una caída a
plomo; **at the ~ of a hat** en cualquier momento

drop² -pp- *vt* **1 (a)** (accidentally): **I/he ~ped the
cup** se me/le cayó la taza; **don't ~ it!** ¡que no se
te caiga! **(b)** (deliberately) ⟨*cup/vase*⟩ dejar caer,
tirar; ⟨*bomb/supplies*⟩ lanzar*; **~ that gun!** ¡suelta
ese revólver!
2 (lower) ⟨*hem*⟩ alargar*, bajar; ⟨*eyes/voice*⟩ bajar
3 (a) (set down) ⟨*passenger/cargo*⟩ dejar **(b)**
(deliver) pasar a dejar
4 (send) (colloq) ⟨*card/letter*⟩ mandar; **~ me a line**
a ver si me mandas *or* me escribes unas líneas
5 (utter) ⟨*hint/remark*⟩ soltar*, dejar caer; **to let it
~ that** … (inadvertently) dejar escapar que …;
(deliberately) dejar caer que …
6 (a) (omit) ⟨*letter/syllable/word*⟩ omitir; **to ~ sb
from a team** sacar* a algn de un equipo **(b)** (give
up, abandon) ⟨*case*⟩ abandonar; ⟨*charges*⟩ retirar;
⟨*plan/idea*⟩ abandonar, renunciar a; ⟨*friend/
associate*⟩ dejar de ver a; **to ~ the subject** dejar
el tema
■ **~** *vi* **1 (a)** (fall) «*object*» caer(se)*; «*plane*»
bajar, descender*; **he ~ped to the ground**
(deliberately) se tiró al suelo; (fell) cayó de un golpe
(b) (collapse) desplomarse
2 (a) (decrease) «*wind*» amainar;
«*temperature*» bajar, descender*; «*prices*»
bajar, experimentar un descenso (frml); «*voice*»
bajar **(b)** (in height) «*terrain*» caer*
■ **drop in** [*v + adv*] (colloq) pasar; **to ~ in on sb**
pasar a ver a algn, caerle* a algn (fam)
■ **drop off 1** [*v + adv*] **(a)** (fall off) caerse* **(b)**
(fall asleep) dormirse*, quedarse dormido **(c)**
(decrease) «*sales/numbers*» disminuir*
2 [*v + o + adv*] ⟨*person/goods*⟩ dejar
■ **drop out** [*v + adv*]: **to ~ out of school**
abandonar los estudios; **to ~ out** (of a
competition/race) (before event) no presentarse (a
un concurso/una carrera); (during event)
abandonar (un curso/una carrera); **to ~ out** (of
society) marginarse, convertirse* en un
marginado

drop-dead /'drɑːpded ‖'drɒpded/ *adv*: **~
gorgeous** que te caes de espaldas de guapo

droplet /'drɑːplət ‖'drɒplɪt/ *n* gotita *f*

dropper /'drɑːpər ‖'drɒpə(r)/ *n* cuentagotas *m*,
gotero *m*

droppings /'drɑːpɪŋz ‖'drɒpɪŋz/ *pl n* (of bird,
flies) excremento *m* (frml), cagadas *fpl* (fam); (of
rabbit, sheep) cagarrutas *fpl*

dross /drɑːs ‖drɒs/ *n* **(a)** (waste) basura *f* **(b)**
(Metall) escoria *f*

drought /draʊt/ *n* sequía *f*

drove¹ /drəʊv/ *past of* DRIVE¹

drove² *n* **(a)** (of animals) manada *f* **(b) droves**
pl (of people) hordas *fpl*, manadas *fpl*

drown /draʊn/ *vt* **1** ⟨*person/animal*⟩ ahogar*
2 ~ (out) (make inaudible) ⟨*noise/cries/screams*⟩
ahogar*
■ *vi* ahogarse*, morir* ahogado

drowsy /'draʊzi/ *adj* **-sier, -siest**
somnoliento, adormilado

drudge /drʌdʒ/ *n* esclavo, -va *m,f*

drudgery /'drʌdʒəri/ *n*: **this job is sheer ~** este
trabajo es una pesadez

drug¹ /drʌg/ *n* **(a)** (narcotic) droga *f*,
estupefaciente *m* (frml); **to be on ~s** drogarse* **(b)**
(medication) medicamento *m*, medicina *f*, fármaco
m (frml)

drug² *vt* **-gg-** drogar*

drug addict *n* drogadicto, -ta *m,f*

druggist /'drʌgɪst/ *n* (AmE) farmacéutico, -ca
m,f

drug: ~store *n* (AmE) establecimiento que vende
*medicamentos, cosméticos, periódicos y una gran
variedad de artículos*; **~-taker** /ˌteɪkər
‖ˌteɪkə(r)/ *n* consumidor, -dora *m,f* de drogas;
~-taking *n* consumo *m* de drogas

drum¹ /drʌm/ *n* **1** (Mus) **(a)** tambor *m* **(b)
drums** *pl* (in band) batería *f* **2 (a)** (container)
bidón *m* **(b)** (machine part) tambor *m* **(c)** (spool)
tambor *m*

drum² **-mm-** *vt* ⟨*table/floor*⟩ golpetear; **to ~
one's fingers** tamborilear con los dedos
■ **~** *vi* **(a)** (Mus) tocar* el tambor **(b)** (beat, tap)
«*person*» dar* golpecitos, tamborilear; «*rain/
hail/hooves*» repiquetear
■ **drum up** [*v + adv + o*] ⟨*support*⟩ conseguir*,
obtener*

drum: ~beat *n* son *m* del tambor; **~kit** *n*
batería *f*

drummer /'drʌmər ‖'drʌmə(r)/ *n* (pop, jazz)
batería *mf*, baterista *mf* (AmL); (military) tambor *m*

drumstick /'drʌmstɪk/ *n* **1** palillo *m* (de
tambor), baqueta *f* **2** (Culin) muslo *m*, pata *f*

drunk¹ /drʌŋk/ *past p of* DRINK¹

drunk² *adj* (pred) borracho; **to get ~**
emborracharse; **~ and disorderly** (Law) en estado
de embriaguez y alterando el orden público (frml)

drunk³ *n* borracho, -cha *m,f*

drunkard /'drʌŋkərd ‖'drʌŋkəd/ *n* (frml & pej)
borracho, -cha *m,f*, beodo, -da *m,f* (frml)

drunk driving *n* (AmE) conducción *f* de un
vehículo bajo los efectos del alcohol

drunken /'drʌŋkən/ *adj* (before n) ⟨*person/mob*⟩
borracho; ⟨*orgy/brawl*⟩ de borrachos

drunkenness /'drʌŋkənnəs ‖'drʌŋkənnɪs/ *n*
borrachera *f*, embriaguez *f* (frml)

dry¹ /draɪ/ *adj* **drier, driest 1 (a)** (not wet)
⟨*ground/washing*⟩ seco **(b)** (lacking natural moisture)
⟨*leaves/skin/hair*⟩ seco; ⟨*cough*⟩ seco **(c)** (dried-up)
⟨*well/river*⟩ seco; **to run ~** «*river/well*» secarse*
(d) (not rainy, not humid) ⟨*climate/weather/heat*⟩
seco; **tomorrow will be ~** mañana no lloverá

AmC	Central America	Arg	Argentina	Cu	Cuba	Per	Peru
AmL	Latin America	Bol	Bolivia	Ec	Ecuador	RPI	River Plate Area
AmS	South America	Chi	Chile	Esp	Spain	Ur	Uruguay
Andes	Andean Region	CS	Southern Cone	Méx	Mexico	Ven	Venezuela

2 (not sweet) ‹wine/sherry› seco **3** (ironic) ‹humor/wit› mordaz **4** (dull, boring) ‹lecture/book› árido

dry² dries, drying, dried vt secar*; to ~ one's eyes secarse* or (liter) enjugarse* las lágrimas
■ ~ vi secarse*
■ **dry up** [v + adv] **(a)** «stream/pond» secarse* (completamente) **(b)** «funds/resources/ inspiration» agotarse

dry: ~ **clean** vt limpiar en seco; ~ **cleaner('s)** n tintorería f; ~ **dock** n dique m seco

dryer /'draɪər ‖'draɪə(r)/ n **(a)** (for clothes — machine) secadora f; (— rack) tendedor m, tendedero m; (spin ~) secadora f (centrífuga); (tumble ~) secadora f (de aire caliente) **(b)** ▶ HAIRDRIER

dry: ~ **goods** pl n **(a)** (clothing) (AmE) artículos mpl or prendas fpl de confección; (before n) ~ **goods store** tienda f de confecciones **(b)** (groceries) (BrE) comestibles mpl no perecederos; ~ **ice** n hielo m seco

dryly adv ▶ DRILY

dryness /'draɪnəs ‖'draɪnɪs/ n **1** (of ground, hair, skin, climate) sequedad f **2** (of wine, sherry) lo seco **3** (of humor, wit) lo mordaz

dry: ~ **rot** n putrefacción de la madera producida por un hongo; ~ **wall**, (BrE) ~**-stone wall** n muro m de mampostería sin mortero

dual /'duːəl ‖'djuːəl/ adj (before n) ‹role/ function› doble; ‹nationality› doble

dual: ~ **carriageway** /'kærɪdʒweɪ/ n (BrE) autovía f, carretera f de doble pista; ~**-control** /'duːələn'trəʊl ‖,djuːələn'trəʊl/ adj ‹car/ brakes› de doble mando or control; ~**-purpose** /'duːəl'pɜːpəs ‖,djuːəl'pɜːpəs/ adj ‹utensil› de doble uso; ‹cleaner› de doble acción; ‹furniture› de doble función or uso

dub /dʌb/ vt **-bb-** **1** (nickname) apodar **2** **(a)** (Cin) ‹film› doblar **(b)** (Audio) mezclar

dubious /'duːbiəs ‖'djuːbiəs/ adj **(a)** (questionable) ‹honor/achievement› dudoso, discutible; ‹past› turbio; ‹motives/person› sospechoso **(b)** (doubtful) to be ~ (ABOUT sth/sb) tener* reservas or dudas (SOBRE or ACERCA DE algo/algn)

duchess /'dʌtʃəs ‖'dʌtʃɪs/ n duquesa f

duchy /'dʌtʃi/ n (pl **duchies**) ducado m

duck¹ /dʌk/ n pato, -ta m,f

duck² vi (bow down) agacharse; (hide): I ~ed behind a pillar me escondí rápidamente detrás de una columna
■ ~ vt **1** (lower) ‹head› agachar, bajar **2** (submerge) hundir **3** (dodge) ‹question› eludir, esquivar; ‹responsibility› evadir, eludir

duckling /'dʌklɪŋ/ n patito m, anadón m

duct /dʌkt/ n (Tech, Anat) conducto m

dud¹ /dʌd/ n (colloq) **(a)** (useless thing) birria f (fam), porquería f (fam) **(b)** (useless person) calamidad f, inútil mf

dud² adj (colloq) **(a)** (useless, valueless) ‹note/coin› falso; ‹check› sin fondos **(b)** (Mil) ‹shell/bomb› que no estalla

dude /duːd ‖djuːd/ n (AmE sl) tipo m (fam), tío m (Esp fam)

dudgeon /'dʌdʒən/ n: in high ~ indignadísimo, lleno de indignación

due¹ /duː ‖djuː/ adj **1** (pred): the rent is ~ hay que pagar el alquiler; the respect ~ to one's elders el respeto que se les debe a los mayores; it's all ~ to you todo gracias a ti, te lo debemos todo a ti; when is the next train ~? ¿cuándo llega el próximo tren?; she's ~ back tomorrow vuelve mañana, su regreso está previsto para mañana **2** (before n) ‹consideration/regard› debido; with all ~ respect con el debido respeto **3** due to (as prep) (crit) debido a

due² adv: the fort is ~ west of the town el fuerte está justo or exactamente al oeste del pueblo; we headed ~ north nos dirigimos derecho hacia el norte

due³ n **1** to give him his ~, he is efficient tienes que reconocer que es eficiente **2** **dues** pl n (subscription) cuota f

duel /'duːəl ‖'djuːəl/ n duelo m

duet /duː'et ‖dju'et/ n dúo m

duffel bag, (BrE) **duffle bag** /'dʌfəl/ n talego m, tula f (Col), bolso m marinero (RPl)

duffel coat, (BrE) **duffle coat** /'dʌfəl/ n trenca f, montgomery m (CS)

dug /dʌg/ past & past p of DIG¹

dugout /'dʌgaʊt/ n **1** (Mil) refugio m subterráneo **2** ~ (**canoe**) piragua f **3** (in baseball) dogaut m, caseta f

duke /duːk ‖djuːk/ n duque m

dull¹ /dʌl/ adj **1** **(a)** (not bright) ‹color› apagado; ‹light/glow› pálido; ‹eyes/complexion› sin brillo **(b)** (not shiny) ‹finish› mate; ‹hair› sin brillo **(c)** (overcast) ‹day/morning› gris, feo **2** (boring) ‹speech/person› aburrido **3** **(a)** ‹faculties› torpe, lerdo; ‹pain/ache› sordo; ‹sound› sordo, amortiguado **(b)** ‹edge/blade› romo, embotado

dull² vt **(a)** (make less bright) ‹color/surface› quitar el brillo a, opacar* (b) (make less sharp) ‹pain› aliviar, calmar; ‹senses› entorpecer*, embotar

dully /'dʌlli/ adv **(a)** (dimly) ‹glow/shine› débilmente, pálidamente **(b)** (boringly) ‹talk/write› de manera aburrida

duly /'duːli ‖'djuːli/ adv debidamente; permission was ~ granted el permiso fue concedido, como era de esperar

dumb /dʌm/ adj **1** (unable to speak) mudo; to be struck ~ quedarse mudo or sin habla **2** (stupid) (colloq) bobo (fam)
■ **dumb down** [v + adv + o, v + o + adv] bajar el nivel intelectual de

dumb: ~**bell** n pesa f, mancuerna f; ~**found** /'dʌm'faʊnd/ vt (usu pass) anonadar; ~**struck** adj estupefacto; ~**waiter** /'dʌm'weɪtər ‖,dʌm'weɪtə(r)/ n (elevator) montaplatos m; (table) mesita f rodante

dummy¹ /'dʌmi/ n **1** **(a)** (in window display, for dressmaker) maniquí m **(b)** (in tests, stunts) muñeco m **(c)** (in US football) domi m **2** (for baby) (BrE) ▶ PACIFIER **3** (fool) (colloq) bobo, -ba m,f (fam)

dummy² adj ‹gun/telephone› de juguete

dump¹ /dʌmp/ n **1** (place for waste) vertedero m (de basura), basural m (AmL), tiradero m (Méx) **2** (temporary store) (Mil) depósito m **3** (unpleasant place) (colloq) lugar m de mala muerte **4** to be (down) in the ~s (colloq) estar* or andar* con la depre (fam)

··· **dump** ···▶ **dyslexic**

dump² /dʌmp/ vt ⓵ (get rid of) ‹waste/refuse› tirar, botar (AmL exc RPl); ‹boyfriend/girlfriend› (colloq) plantar (fam), botar (AmS exc RPl fam), largar* (RPl fam) ⓶ (a) (set on ground) ‹load/sand› descargar*, verter*; **where can I ~ my things?** (colloq) ¿dónde puedo dejar or poner mis cosas? (b) (Comput) ‹data/disks› volcar*

dumper (truck) /'dʌmpər ǁ'dʌmpə(r)/ n ▶ DUMP TRUCK

dumpling /'dʌmplɪŋ/ n: bola de masa que se come en sopas o guisos

Dumpster® /'dʌmpstər ǁ'dʌmpstə(r)/ n (AmE) contenedor m (para escombros)

dump truck n volquete m, camión m volteador (RPl) or (Méx) de volteo, volqueta f (Col)

dumpy /'dʌmpi/ adj **-pier, -piest** regordete

dunce /dʌns/ n (pej) burro, -rra m,f

dune /duːn ǁdjuːn/ n duna f

dung /dʌŋ/ n (a) (feces) boñiga f, bosta f (b) (manure) (esp BrE) estiércol m

dungarees /ˌdʌŋɡə'riːz/ pl n (workman's) overol m; (fashion) pantalón m de peto m

dungeon /'dʌndʒən/ n mazmorra f, calabozo m

duo /'duːəʊ ǁ'djuːəʊ/ n (pl **-os**) dúo m

dupe¹ /duːp ǁdjuːp/ vt engañar, embaucar*

dupe² n inocentón, -tona m,f, primo, -ma m,f (Esp fam)

duplex /'duːpleks ǁ'djuːpleks/ n (AmE) ~ (apartment) dúplex m; ~ (house) casa de dos viviendas adosadas

duplicate¹ /'duːplɪkət ǁ'djuːplɪkət/ adj (before n): **a ~ copy** un duplicado; **a ~ key** un duplicado or una copia de una llave

duplicate² /'duːplɪkət ǁ'djuːplɪkət/ n duplicado m, copia f

duplicate³ /'duːplɪkeɪt ǁ'djuːplɪkeɪt/ vt (a) (copy) ‹letter/document› hacer* copias de (b) (repeat) ‹work/efforts› repetir* (en forma innecesaria)

durable /'dʊrəbəl ǁ'djʊərəbəl/ adj durable

duration /dʊ'reɪʃən ǁdjʊə'reɪʃən/ n duración f

duress /dʊ'res ǁdjʊə'res/ n: **under ~** bajo coacción

during /'dʊrɪŋ ǁ'djʊərɪŋ/ prep durante

dusk /dʌsk/ n anochecer m

dust¹ /dʌst/ n polvo m; **to bite the ~** «person» morder* el polvo

dust² vt ⓵ (remove dust from): **to ~ the furniture** quitarles el polvo a los muebles, sacudir los muebles (CS, Méx) ⓶ (sprinkle) **to ~ sth WITH sth** espolvorear algo CON algo

dust: **~bin** /'dʌstbɪn, 'dʌsbɪn/ n (BrE) cubo m or (CS, Per) tacho m or (Méx) tambo m or (Col) caneca f or (Ven) tobo m de la basura; **~cart** /'dʌstkɑːr, 'dʌskɑːrt ǁ'dʌstkɑːt, dʌskɑːt/ or (CS, Méx) camión m de la basura; **~ cloth** n (AmE) trapo m del polvo, trapo m de sacudir (CS, Méx), sacudidor m (Méx)

duster /'dʌstər ǁ'dʌstə(r)/ n ⓵ (Clothing) (housecoat) (AmE) guardapolvo m ⓶ (BrE) (a) (for blackboard) borrador m (b) ▶ DUST CLOTH

dust: **~ jacket** n sobrecubierta f; **~man** /'dʌstmən, 'dʌsmən/ n (pl **-men** /-mən/) (BrE) basurero m; **~pan** /'dʌstpæn, 'dʌspæn/ n pala f, recogedor m

dusty /'dʌsti/ adj **-tier, -tiest** ‹furniture› cubierto de polvo; ‹road/plain› polvoriento

Dutch¹ /dʌtʃ/ adj holandés; **to go ~** pagar* a escote (fam), pagar* or ir* a la americana (AmL), pagar* or ir* a la inglesa (Chi fam)

Dutch² n (a) (language) holandés m (b) (people) (+ pl vb) **the ~** los holandeses

Dutch: **~man** /'dʌtʃmən/ n (pl **-men** /-mən/) holandés m; **~woman** n holandesa f

dutiful /'duːtɪfəl ǁ'djuːtɪfəl/ adj consciente de sus deberes

duty /'duːti ǁ'djuːti/ n (pl **duties**) ⓵ (obligation) deber m, obligación f ⓶ (a) (service) servicio m; **to do ~ as sth** hacer* las veces de algo, servir* de algo (b) (in phrases) **to be on/off ~** «nurse/doctor» estar*/no estar* de turno or guardia; «policeman/fireman» estar*/no estar* de servicio (c) **duties** pl n (responsibilities) (frml) funciones fpl, responsabilidades fpl ⓷ (Tax) (often pl) impuesto m

duty: **~-free** /'duːtiˈfriː ǁ,djuːtiˈfriː/ adj libre de impuestos; **~-free shop** n duty free m, tienda f libre de impuestos

duvet /'duːveɪ/ n (BrE) edredón m (nórdico)

DVD n = digital video disc

dwarf¹ /dwɔːrf ǁdwɔːf/ n (pl **~s** or **dwarves** /dwɔːrvz/) enano, -na m,f; (before n) ‹tree/species› enano

dwarf² vt ‹building› hacer* parecer pequeño

dwell /dwel/ (past & past p **dwelt** or **dwelled**) vi (liter) morar (liter), vivir
■ **dwell on** [v + prep + o]: **try not to ~ on the past** trata de no pensar demasiado en el pasado; **the documentary ~s excessively on ...** el documental se detiene demasiado or hace demasiado hincapié en ...

dwelling /'dwelɪŋ/ n (a) (habitation) (liter) morada f (liter) (b) (house) (frml) vivienda f

dwelt /dwelt/ past & past p of DWELL

dwindle /'dwɪndl/ vi (a) «numbers/population» disminuir*, menguar*, reducirse* (b) **dwindling** pres p: **dwindling resources** recursos mpl cada vez más limitados

dye¹ /daɪ/ n tintura f, tinte m

dye² dyes, dyeing, dyed vt teñir*

dying /'daɪɪŋ/ adj (before n) (a) (near death, extinction) ‹person/animal› moribundo, agonizante; ‹race/art› en vías de extinción (b) (related to time of death) ‹wish/words/breath› último, postrero (liter)

dyke /daɪk/ n ⓵ ▶ DIKE 1 ⓶ (lesbian) (sl & often pej) tortillera f (arg)

dynamic /daɪ'næmɪk/ adj dinámico

dynamism /'daɪnəmɪzəm/ n dinamismo m

dynamite /'daɪnəmaɪt/ n dinamita f

dynamo /'daɪnəməʊ/ n (pl **-mos**) dínamo m or dinamo m (AmL), dinamo f or dínamo f (Esp)

dynasty /'daɪnəsti ǁ'dɪnəsti/ n (pl **-ties**) dinastía f

dysentery /'dɪsənteri ǁ'dɪsəntri/ n disentería f

dysfunction /dɪs'fʌŋkʃən/ n disfunción f

dysfunctional /dɪs'fʌŋkʃənəl ǁdɪs'fʌŋkʃənl/ adj disfuncional

dyslexia /dɪs'leksiə/ n dislexia f

dyslexic /dɪs'leksɪk/ adj disléxico

Ee

E, e /iː/ n (a) (letter) E, e f (b) (Mus) mi m
E (= **east**) E
each¹ /iːtʃ/ adj cada adj inv
each² pron 1 cada uno, cada una; **he questioned ~ of them in turn** les preguntó uno por uno 2 **each other: they are always criticizing ~ other** siempre se están criticando el uno al otro; (if more than two people) siempre se están criticando unos a otros; **their respect for ~ other** su mutuo respeto
each³ adv: **we were paid \$10 ~** nos pagaron 10 dólares a cada uno; **the apples are 20 cents ~** las manzanas valen 20 centavos por pieza or cada una
eager /ˈiːgər ‖ ˈiːgə(r)/ adj (excited, impatient) impaciente, ansioso; (keen) entusiasta; **he's ~ to please** está deseoso de complacer; **she is ~ for change** tiene muchos deseos de cambio
eagerly /ˈiːgərli ‖ ˈiːgəli/ adv ⟨accept/agree⟩ con entusiasmo; ⟨await⟩ ansiosamente, con ansiedad e impaciencia; ⟨listen/read⟩ con avidez
eagle /ˈiːgəl/ n águila f‡
ear /ɪr ‖ ɪə(r)/ n 1 (a) (Anat) oreja f; (organ) oído m (b) (sense of hearing) (no pl) oído m; **to play sth by ~** tocar* algo de oído 2 (of corn) espiga f
ear: ~ache n dolor m de oído; **~drum** n tímpano m
earl /ɜːrl ‖ ɜːl/ n conde m
early¹ /ˈɜːrli ‖ ˈɜːli/ adj -lier, -liest 1 (before expected time) ⟨arrival/elections⟩ anticipado; **to be ~** ⟨person⟩ llegar* temprano; **the bus was ~** el autobús pasó (or salió etc) antes de la hora 2 (a) (before normal time): **to have an ~ night** acostarse* temprano; **~ retirement** jubilación f anticipada (b) ⟨crop/variety⟩ temprano, tempranero 3 (far back in time): **~ man** el hombre primitivo; **his earliest memories** sus primeros recuerdos 4 (toward beginning of period): **it's too ~ to tell** es demasiado pronto para saber; **in ~ June** a principios de junio; **he was in his ~ twenties** tenía poco más de veinte años
early² adv -lier, -liest 1 (before expected time) temprano 2 (before usual time) temprano, pronto (Esp) 3 (toward beginning of period): **~ in the morning** por la mañana temprano; **~ in the year** a principios de año; **~ (on) in her career** en los comienzos de su carrera 4 (soon) pronto; **they won't be here till nine at the earliest** por temprano que lleguen no estarán aquí antes de las nueve
ear: ~mark vt ⟨money/funds⟩ destinar; **~muffs** pl n orejeras fpl
earn /ɜːrn ‖ ɜːn/ vt 1 ⟨money/wages⟩ ganar; ⟨interest⟩ dar* 2 ⟨respect/gratitude⟩ ganarse; ⟨promotion⟩ ganar
earnest¹ /ˈɜːrnəst ‖ ˈɜːnɪst/ adj (a) (sincere) (frml) ⟨effort/attempt⟩ serio; ⟨wish⟩ ferviente (b) (serious) serio
earnest² n **in ~** en serio

earnings /ˈɜːrnɪŋz ‖ ˈɜːnɪŋz/ pl n ingresos mpl
ear: ~plug n tapón m para el oído; **~ring** n arete m (AmL), aro m (CS), pendiente m (Esp), caravana f (Ur); **~shot** n: **to be within/out of ~shot** estar*/no estar* lo suficientemente cerca como para oír
earth /ɜːrθ ‖ ɜːθ/ n 1 (a) (Astron, Relig) tierra f; **the ~** o **E~** la Tierra (b) (as intensifier): **why on ~ didn't you warn me?** ¿por qué diablos no me avisaste? 2 (land, soil) tierra f 3 (BrE Elec) tierra f
earthenware /ˈɜːrθənwer ‖ ˈɜːθənweə(r)/ n (material) barro m (cocido); (dishes) vajilla f de barro (cocido)
earth: ~quake n terremoto m; **~worm** n lombriz f (de tierra)
earwig /ˈɪrwɪg ‖ ˈɪəwɪg/ n tijereta f, cortapicos m
ease¹ /iːz/ n 1 (facility) facilidad f; **~ of operation** facilidad de manejo; **for ~ of access** para facilitar el acceso; **with ~** fácilmente 2 (a) (freedom from constraint): **at ~** a gusto; **to put sb at his/her ~** hacer* que algn se sienta a gusto (b) (Mil): **(stand) at ~!** ¡descansen!
ease² vt 1 (a) (relieve) ⟨pain⟩ calmar, aliviar; ⟨tension⟩ hacer* disminuir, aliviar; ⟨burden⟩ aligerar; **to ~ sb's mind** tranquilizar* a algn (b) (make easier) ⟨situation⟩ paliar; ⟨transition⟩ facilitar; **to ~ the way for sth** preparar el terreno para algo 2 (a) ⟨rules/restrictions⟩ relajar (b) ⟨belt/rope⟩ aflojar 3 (move with care) (+ adv compl): **they ~d him into the wheelchair** lo sentaron con cuidado en la silla de ruedas; **he ~d the key into the lock** introdujo la llave en la cerradura con cuidado
■ ~ vi ⟨pain⟩ aliviarse, calmarse; ⟨tension⟩ disminuir*
■ **ease off** [v + adv] ⟨rain⟩ amainar; ⟨pain⟩ aliviarse, calmarse; ⟨pressure/traffic⟩ disminuir*
■ **ease up** [v + adv] (slacken pace — of life) tomarse las cosas con más calma; (— of work, activity) bajar el ritmo
easel /ˈiːzəl/ n caballete m
easily /ˈiːzəli ‖ ˈiːzɪli/ adv 1 (a) (without difficulty) fácilmente, con facilidad (b) (readily) ⟨break/stain/cry⟩ con facilidad 2 (by far) con mucho, (de) lejos (AmL fam); **there's ~ enough for everybody** hay de sobra para todos
east¹ /iːst/ n 1 (point of the compass, direction) este m; **the ~, the E~** (region) el este 2 **the East** (the Orient) (el) Oriente
east² adj (before n) este adj inv, oriental; ⟨wind⟩ del este
east³ adv al este
east: ~bound adj que va (or iba etc) en dirección este or hacia el este; **E~ End** n (in UK) **the E~ End of** (London) barrio del este de Londres de tradición obrera

Easter /ˈiːstər ‖ ˈiːstə(r)/ *n* Pascua *f* (de Resurrección); (*before n*) ∼ **Day** *o* **Sunday** (el) Domingo de Pascua *or* Resurrección; ∼ **egg** huevo *m* de Pascua

easterly /ˈiːstərli ‖ ˈiːstəli/ *adj* ⟨*wind*⟩ del este; **in an** ∼ **direction** hacia el este, en dirección este

eastern /ˈiːstərn ‖ ˈiːstən/ *adj* (a) (Geog) (*before n*) oriental, este *adj inv*; **heavy rain over** ∼ **England** fuertes lluvias en *or* sobre el este de Inglaterra; **the** ∼ **states** los estados del este; **E**∼ **Europe** Europa Oriental *or* del Este (b) (oriental) ⟨*appearance/custom*⟩ oriental

eastward¹ /ˈiːstwərd ‖ ˈiːstwəd/ *adj* (*before n*): **in an** ∼ **direction** en dirección este, hacia el este

eastward², (BrE) **eastwards** /-z/ *adv* hacia el este

easy¹ /ˈiːzi/ *adj* **easier, easiest** 1 (not difficult) fácil; **it's** ∼ **to see that …** es fácil ver que …; **she was an** ∼ **winner** ganó sin problemas 2 (undemanding) ⟨*life*⟩ fácil; **to be** ∼ **on the eye** ser* agradable a la vista

easy² *adv* 1 (without difficulty): **money doesn't come** ∼ el dinero no es fácil de conseguir; ∼ **come,** ∼ **go** así como viene se va 2 (slowly, calmly) despacio, con calma; ∼ **does it** despacito; **to take it** ∼ tomárselo con calma

easy: ∼ **chair** *n* sillón *m*, poltrona *f*, butaca *f*; ∼**going** /ˈiːziˈɡəʊɪŋ/ *adj*: **she's very** ∼**going** es una persona de trato fácil *or* sin complicaciones

eat /iːt/ (*past* **ate**; *past p* **eaten**) *vt/i* comer

■ **eat away** [*v + o + adv, v + adv + o*] ⟨*rats/ mice*⟩ roer*; ⟨*moths*⟩ picar*, comerse; ⟨*acid*⟩ corroer*

■ **eat into** [*v + prep + o*] ⟨*acid/rust*⟩ corroer*; ⟨*profits/savings*⟩ comerse

■ **eat up** 1 [*v + o + adv, v + adv + o*] (finish) ⟨*meal/food*⟩ comerse 2 [*v + adv*] (finish meal) terminar (de comer) 3 [*v + adv + o*] (consume) ⟨*fuel/electricity*⟩ consumir, gastar 4 [*v + o + adv*] ⟨*curiosity/ambition*⟩ consumir

eaten /ˈiːtn̩/ *past p of* EAT

eater /ˈiːtər ‖ ˈiːtə(r)/ *n*: **he's a big** ∼ come mucho, es muy comelón *or* (CS, Esp) comilón (fam); **we're big meat** ∼**s** comemos mucha carne

eaves /iːvz/ *pl n* alero *m*

eavesdrop /ˈiːvzdrɑːp ‖ ˈiːvzdrɒp/ *vi* **-pp-** **to** ∼ (ON **sth/sb**) escuchar (algo/a algn) a escondidas

ebb¹ /eb/ *n* reflujo *m*; **the** ∼ **and flow of the tide** el flujo y reflujo de la marea; **to be at a low** ∼ ⟨*person*⟩ estar* decaído; ⟨*diplomatic relations*⟩ estar* en un punto bajo

ebb² *vi* (a) ⟨*tide*⟩ bajar, retroceder; **to** ∼ **and flow** fluir* y refluir* (b) (dwindle) decaer*

■ **ebb away** [*v + adv*]: **his life was** ∼**ing away** se consumía poco a poco; **I felt my strength** ∼**ing away** sentí que me abandonaban las fuerzas

ebb tide *n* reflujo *m*

ebony /ˈebəni/ *n* (a) (wood) ébano *m* (b) (color) color *m* (de) ébano; (*before n*) ⟨*hair/skin*⟩ negro como el ébano

EC *n* (= **European Community**) CE *f*

eccentric¹ /ɪkˈsentrɪk, ek-/ *adj* excéntrico

eccentric² *n* excéntrico, -ca *m,f*

eccentricity /ˌeksenˈtrɪsəti/ *n* (*pl* **-ties**) excentricidad *f*

ecclesiastical /ɪˌkliːziˈæstɪkəl/ *adj* eclesiástico

echo¹ /ˈekəʊ/ *n* (*pl* **-oes**) eco *m*

echo² *vi* ⟨*footsteps/voices*⟩ hacer* eco

eclair /eɪˈkleə(r), ɪˈkleə(r)/ *n*: **pastel** *individual* relleno de crema

eclipse¹ /ɪˈklɪps/ *n* eclipse *m*

eclipse² *vt* eclipsar

eco-friendly /ˈiːkəʊˌfrendli/ *adj* ecológico, que no daña el medio ambiente

ecological /ˌiːkəˈlɑːdʒəkəl ‖ ˌiːkəˈlɒdʒɪkəl/ *adj* ecológico

ecologist /ɪˈkɑːlədʒəst ‖ iːˈkɒlədʒɪst/ *n* (student of ecology) ecólogo, -ga *m,f*; (conservationist) ecologista *mf*

ecology /ɪˈkɑːlədʒi ‖ iːˈkɒlədʒi/ *n* ecología *f*

e-commerce /ˈiːkɑːmərs ‖ iːˈkɒmɜːs/ *n*. comercio *m* electrónico, e-comercio

economic /ˌekəˈnɑːmɪk, ˌiːk- ‖ ˌiːkəˈnɒmɪk, ˌek-/ *adj* económico

economical /ˌekəˈnɑːmɪkəl, ˌiːk- ‖ ˌiːkəˈnɒmɪkəl, ˌek-/ *adj* económico

economics /ˌekəˈnɑːmɪks, ˌiːk- ‖ ˌiːkəˈnɒmɪks, ˌek-/ *n* (a) (+ *sing vb*) economía *f* (b) (financial aspect) (+ *pl vb*) aspecto *m* económico

economist /ɪˈkɑːnəməst ‖ ɪˈkɒnəmɪst/ *n* economista *mf*

economize /ɪˈkɑːnəmaɪz ‖ ɪˈkɒnəmaɪz/ *vi* economizar*; **to** ∼ ON **sth** economizar* algo

economy /ɪˈkɑːnəmi, iː- ‖ ɪˈkɒnəmi/ *n* (*pl* **-mies**) 1 (economic state or system of country) economía *f* 2 (a) (saving): **to make economies** economizar*, hacer* economía(s) (b) (thrift) economía *f*; (*before n*) ⟨*pack/size*⟩ familiar; ∼ **class** clase *f* turista

ecosystem /ˈiːkəʊˌsɪstəm/ *n* ecosistema *m*

ecstasy /ˈekstəsi/ *n* (*pl* **-sies**) (a) (state) éxtasis *m* (b) (drug) éxtasis *m*

ecstatic /ɪkˈstætɪk/ *adj* ⟨*look/expression*⟩ extasiado, extático; ⟨*applause*⟩ clamoroso

ECU /ˈiːkjuː, eɪˈkuː/ *n* (*pl* **ECUs**) ecu *m*

Ecuador /ˈekwədɔːr ‖ ˈekwədɔː(r)/ *n* Ecuador *m*

Ecuadorean¹ /ˈekwəˈdɔːriən/ *adj* ecuatoriano

Ecuadorean² *n* ecuatoriano, -na *m,f*

eczema /ɪɡˈziːmə, ˈeɡzəmə ‖ ˈeksɪmə/ *n* eczema *m*

eddy¹ /ˈedi/ *n* (*pl* **eddies**) remolino *m*, torbellino *m*

eddy² *vi* **eddies, eddying, eddied** ⟨*water*⟩ formar remolinos; ⟨*smoke/dust*⟩ arremolinarse

Eden /ˈiːdn̩/ *n* Edén *m*

edge /edʒ/ *n* 1 (a) (no *pl*) (border, brink — of town) afueras *fpl*; (— of forest) lindero *m*, borde *m*; (— of river, lake) orilla *f*, margen *m*; (— of cliff) borde *m* (b) (of plate, table, chair) borde *m*; (of coin)

---

canto *m*; (of page) margen *m* **2** (cutting part) filo *m*;
to be on ~ estar* nervioso, tener* los nervios de
punta (fam)

edge² *vt*: the collar was ~d with fur el cuello
estaba ribeteado de piel; the paper was ~d in
black el papel tenía un borde negro
■ ~ *vi* (+ *adv compl*): to ~ forward/closer/away ir*
avanzando/acercándose/alejándose (poco a poco)

edging /'edʒɪŋ/ *n* borde *m*

edgy /'edʒi/ *adj* tenso, con los nervios de punta

edible /'edəbəl/ *adj* (safe to eat) comestible;
(eatable) pasable, comible

edifying /'edəfaɪŋ ‖'edɪfaɪŋ/ *adj* edificante

Edinburgh /'edṇˌbɜːrə, -rəʊ ‖'edɪmbrə/ *n*
Edimburgo *m*

edit /'edət ‖'edɪt/ *vt* **1** ‹manuscript› (correct)
corregir*, editar; (cut) recortar, editar **2** ‹movie/
tape› editar **3** (manage) ‹newspaper/magazine›
dirigir*

edition /ɪ'dɪʃən/ *n* edición *f*

editor /'edətər ‖'edɪtə(r)/ *n* **1** (of text) redactor,
-tora *m,f*, editor, -tora *m,f*; (of collected works, series)
editor, -tora *m,f* **2** (of newspaper, magazine)
director, -tora *m,f*, redactor, -tora *m,f*
responsable **3** (of movie, radio show) editor, -tora
m,f

editorial¹ /'edə'tɔːriəl ‖,edɪ'tɔːriəl/ *adj* (a)
(Publ) ‹assistant/director› de redacción (b) (Journ)
‹comment/decision/freedom› editorial

editorial² *n* editorial *m*

EDT (in US) = **Eastern Daylight Time**

educate /'edʒəkeɪt ‖'edjʊkeɪt/ *vt* (a) (teach,
school) educar* (b) (make aware) concientizar* *or*
(Esp) concienciar

educated /'edʒəkeɪtəd ‖'edjʊkeɪtɪd/ *adj*
‹person› culto; **to make an** ~ **guess** hacer* una
conjetura hecha con cierta base

education /'edʒə'keɪʃən ‖,edjʊ'keɪʃən/ *n*
educación *f*; (before *n*) ‹system/policy› educativo

educational /'edʒə'keɪʃnəl ‖,edjʊ'keɪʃənl/ *adj*
(a) ‹establishment› docente, de enseñanza; ‹toy›
educativo (b) (instructive) instructivo

Edwardian /ed'wɔːrdiən ‖ed'wɔːdiən/ *adj*
eduardiano

EEC *n* (= **European Economic
Community**) CEE *f*

eel /iːl/ *n* anguila *f*

e'er /er ‖eə(r)/ *adv* (poet & arch) ▶ EVER

eerie /'ɪri ‖'ɪəri/ *adj* **eerier, eeriest**
‹atmosphere/silence/cry› inquietante,
espeluznante; ‹phenomenon› efecto *m*

efface /ɪ'feɪs/ *vt* (fml) borrar

effect¹ /ɪ'fekt/ *n* **1** (a) (consequence) efecto *m*;
to take ~ surtir efecto (b) **in effect** de hecho,
realmente (c) (phenomenon) efecto *m*
2 (impression) impresión *f*; **he only did it for** ~ lo
hizo sólo para llamar la atención
3 (applicability, operation): **to come into** ~, **to take** ~
entrar en vigor or en vigencia
4 (meaning): **a statement was issued to the** ~ **that
…** (fml) se hizo público un comunicado
anunciando que …; **he said it wasn't true, or
words to that** ~ dijo que no era verdad o algo de
ese tenor

5 **effects** *pl* (a) (special ~s) (Cin, TV) efectos
mpl especiales (b) (belongings) (frml) efectos *mpl*
(frml)

effect² *vt* (frml) ‹reconciliation/cure› lograr;
‹escape› llevar a cabo; ‹repairs/payment›
efectuar* (frml)

effective /ɪ'fektɪv/ *adj* (a) (producing the desired
result) ‹method/treatment› eficaz, efectivo (b)
(striking) ‹design/contrast› de mucho efecto (c)
(real) (before *n*) ‹control/leader› efectivo

effectively /ɪ'fektɪvli/ *adv* (a) ‹manage/spend›
con eficacia, eficazmente (b) ‹contrast/decorate›
con mucho gran efecto; ‹speak›
convincentemente (c) (in effect) (indep) de hecho

effeminate /ə'femənət ‖ɪ'femɪnət/ *adj*
afeminado

effervescent /'efər'vesənt ‖,efə'vesənt/ *adj*
‹liquid/personality› efervescente

efficiency /ɪ'fɪʃənsi/ *n* (*pl* **-cies**) (of person,
system) eficiencia *f*; (Mech Eng, Phys) rendimiento
m

efficient /ɪ'fɪʃənt/ *adj* ‹person/system› eficiente;
‹machine/engine› de buen rendimiento

efficiently /ɪ'fɪʃəntli/ *adv* eficientemente

effigy /'efədʒi ‖'efɪdʒi/ *n* (*pl* **-gies**) efigie *f*

effluent /'efluənt/ *n* (liquid waste) vertidos *mpl*;
(sewage) aguas *fpl* residuales

effort /'efərt ‖'efət/ *n* esfuerzo *m*; **to make an** ~
hacer* un esfuerzo, esforzarse*; **it's not worth the**
~ no merece *or* vale la pena

effortless /'efərtləs ‖'efətlɪs/ *adj* ‹grace›
natural; ‹prose/style› fluido

e.g. (for example) p. ej. *or* vg. *or* e.g.; (in speech) por
ejemplo

egalitarian /ɪ'gælə'teriən ‖ɪ,gælɪ'teəriən/ *adj*
igualitario

egg /eg/ *n* huevo *m*
■ **egg on** [*v* + *o* + *adv*, *v* + *adv* + *o*] incitar

egg: ~**cup** *n* huevera *f*; ~**plant** *n* (AmE)
berenjena *f*; ~**shell** *n* cáscara *f* de huevo; ~
timer *n* (with sand) reloj *m* de arena (*de tres
minutos*); (clockwork) avisador *m*; ~ **white** *n*
clara *f* de huevo; ~ **yolk** *n* yema *f* de huevo

ego /'iːgəʊ, 'egəʊ/ *n* (*pl* **egos**) (a) (Psych) the ~
el yo, el ego (b) (self-regard) amor *m* propio, ego *m*

ego trip *n* (colloq): **his autobiography is simply
an** ~ ~ su autobiografía es un regodeo ególatra

Egypt /'iːdʒəpt ‖'iːdʒɪpt/ *n* Egipto *m*

Egyptian¹ /ɪ'dʒɪpʃən/ *adj* egipcio

Egyptian² *n* egipcio, -cia *m,f*

eiderdown /'aɪdərdaʊn ‖'aɪdədaʊn/ *n* edredón
m

eight /eɪt/ *adj/n* ocho *adj inv/m*; *see also* FOUR¹

eighteen /'eɪ'tiːn/ *adj/n* dieciocho *adj inv/m*; *see
also* FOUR

eighteenth¹ /'eɪ'tiːnθ/ *adj* decimoctavo

eighteenth² *adv* en decimoctavo lugar

eighteenth³ *n* (a) (Math) dieciochoavo *m*;
(part) dieciochoava parte *f* (b) (birthday): **it's her** ~
today hoy cumple dieciocho años

eighth¹ /eɪtθ/ *adj* octavo

eighth² *adv* en octavo lugar

eighth³ *n* (Math) octavo *m*; (part) octava parte *f*

eighth note *n* (AmE) corchea *f*

eightieth¹ /'eɪtiəθ/ *adj* octogésimo

eightieth² *adv* en octogésimo lugar

eightieth³ *n* (Math) ochentavo *m*; (part) ochentava *or* octogésima parte *f*

eighty /'eɪti/ *adj/n* ochenta *adj inv/m*; *see also* FOUR¹

Eire /'erə ‖'eərə/ *n* Eire *m*, Irlanda *f*

either¹ /'iːðər, 'aɪðər ‖'iːðə(r), 'aɪðə(r)/ *conj* either ... or ... o ... o ...

■ **Note** In the usual translation of *either ... or*, *o ... o*, *o* becomes *u* when it precedes a word beginning with *o* or *ho*.

either² *adj*: you can take ~ route puedes tomar cualquiera de las dos rutas; on ~ side of the path a ambos lados del camino

either³ *pron* (esp BrE) cualquiera; (with neg) ninguno, -na; (in questions) alguno, -na

either⁴ *adv* (with neg) she can't ~ cook and he can't ~ ella no sabe cocinar y él tampoco

ejaculate /ɪ'dʒækjəleɪt ‖ɪ'dʒækjʊleɪt/ *vi* (Physiol) eyacular

eject /ɪ'dʒekt/ *vt* ‹troublemaker/cassette› expulsar

■ ~ *vi* (Aviat) eyectarse

eke out /iːk/ [v + adv + o, v + o + adv] (a) (make last) ‹resources/funds› estirar, hacer* alcanzar (b) (barely obtain): to ~ out a living ganarse la vida a duras penas

elaborate¹ /ɪ'læbərət/ *adj* ‹decoration/design/ hairstyle› complicado; ‹meal› de mucho trabajo; ‹plan› minucioso

elaborate² /ɪ'læbəreɪt/ *vt* elaborar

■ ~ *vi* dar* (más) detalles

elapse /ɪ'læps/ *vi* transcurrir

elastic¹ /ɪ'læstɪk/ *n* (a) (Tex) elástico *m* (b) (garter) (AmE) liga *f* (c) (AmE) ▶ ELASTIC BAND

elastic² *adj* ‹waistband/garter› de elástico; ‹stocking› elastizado; ‹fiber/properties› elástico

elastic band *n* (esp BrE) goma *f* (elástica), gomita *f*, liga *f* (Méx), caucho *m* (Col), elástico *m* (Chi), banda *f* elástica (Ven)

elated /ɪ'leɪtəd ‖ɪ'leɪtɪd/ *adj* eufórico

elbow¹ /'elbəʊ/ *n* codo *m*

elbow² *vt* darle* un codazo a; they ~ed us out of the way nos apartaron a empujones

elbow: ~ **grease** *n* (colloq): put some ~ grease into it! ¡dale con más fuerza! (fam); ~ **room** *n* espacio *m*

elder¹ /'eldər ‖'eldə(r)/ *adj* mayor

elder² *n* [1] (a) (older person): she's my ~ by two years me lleva dos años, es dos años mayor que yo (b) (senior person): the village/tribal ~s los ancianos del pueblo/de la tribu (c) (Relig) miembro *m* del consejo [2] (Bot) saúco *m*

elderberry /'eldər,beri ‖'eldəberi/ *n* (pl -ries) baya *f* del saúco

elderly¹ /'eldərli ‖'eldəli/ *adj* mayor, de edad

elderly² *pl n* the ~ los ancianos

eldest /'eldəst ‖'eldɪst/ *adj* (before n) ‹brother/ sister/child› mayor; the ~ (as pron) el/la mayor, el/la de más edad

elect¹ /ɪ'lekt/ *vt* [1] (Adm, Govt) elegir* [2] (choose) (frml) to ~ to + INF optar POR + INF

elect² *adj* (after n): the president ~ el presidente electo, la presidenta electa

election /ɪ'lekʃən/ *n* (a) (event) elecciones *fpl*;

to call/hold an ~ convocar*/celebrar elecciones; (before n) ‹campaign/speech› electoral; ‹day/ results› de las elecciones (b) (act) elección *f*

elector /ɪ'lektər ‖ɪ'lektə(r)/ *n* elector, -tora *m,f*

electoral /ɪ'lektərəl/ *adj* (usu before n) ‹system/reform› electoral; ~ **register** *o* **roll** padrón *m* (AmL) *or* (Esp) censo *m or* (Chi, Ven) registro *m or* (Col) planilla *f* electoral

electorate /ɪ'lektərət/ *n* (+ sing or pl vb) electorado *m*

electric /ɪ'lektrɪk/ *adj* eléctrico; ‹fence› electrificado; ‹performance/atmosphere› electrizante

electrical /ɪ'lektrɪkəl/ *adj* eléctrico

electric: ~ **blanket** *n* manta *f or* (AmL exc CS) cobija *f or* (CS) frazada *f* eléctrica; ~ **chair** *n* silla *f* eléctrica

electrician /ɪ,lek'trɪʃən/ *n* electricista *mf*

electricity /ɪ,lek'trɪsəti/ *n* electricidad *f*

electric shock *n* descarga *f* eléctrica

electrify /ɪ'lektrəfaɪ ‖ɪ'lektrɪfaɪ/ *vt* **-fies, -fying, -fied** electrificar*; (excite, thrill) electrizar*

electrocute /ɪ'lektrəkjuːt/ *vt* electrocutar

electrode /ɪ'lektrəʊd/ *n* electrodo *m*

electrolysis /ɪ'lek'trɑːləsɪs ‖ɪ,lek'trɒləsɪs/ *n* electrólisis *f*

electron /ɪ'lektrɑːn ‖ɪ'lektrɒn/ *n* electrón *m*

electronic /ɪ'lek'trɑːnɪk ‖ɪ,lek'trɒnɪk/ *adj* electrónico

electronic mail *n* correo *m* electrónico

electronics /ɪ'lek'trɑːnɪks ‖ɪ,lek'trɒnɪks/ *n* (a) (subject) (+ sing vb) electrónica *f*; (before n) ‹industry› electrónico (b) (circuitry) (+ sing or pl vb) sistema *m* electrónico

elegance /'elɪgəns/ *n* elegancia *f*

elegant /'elɪgənt/ *adj* elegante

element /'eləmənt ‖'elɪmənt/ *n* [1] (a) (part, group) elemento *m*; an ~ of doubt algo de duda; extremist ~s in society elementos extremistas de la sociedad (b) elements *pl* (rudiments): the basic ~s of self-defense los principios elementales de la defensa personal [2] (Chem) elemento *m* [3] elements *pl* (weather) (liter) the ~s los elementos [4] (preferred environment) elemento *m*; to be in one's ~ estar* en su (or mi etc) elemento [5] (of kettle, heater) resistencia *f*, elemento *m* (CS)

elementary /'elə'mentəri ‖,elɪ'mentri/ *adj* elemental

elementary: ~ **school** *n* (in US) escuela *f* (de enseñanza) primaria; ~ **teacher** *n* (in US) maestro, -tra *m,f* de enseñanza primaria

elephant /'eləfənt ‖'elɪfənt/ *n* elefante, -ta *m,f*

elevate /'eləveɪt ‖'elɪveɪt/ *vt* (a) (promote): to ~ sb to the peerage concederle a algn el título de lord/lady; he's been ~d to the position of manager (hum) lo han ascendido a director (b) (frml) ‹spirit› elevar (c) ‹load/platform› elevar (frml), subir

elevated railroad /'eləveɪtəd ‖'elɪveɪtɪd/ *n* (AmE) ferrocarril *m* elevado

elevation /'elə'veɪʃən ‖,elɪ'veɪʃən/ *n* [1] (promotion) elevación *f* [2] (angle) elevación *f* [3] (altitude) altura *f*

elevator /'eləveɪtər ‖'elɪveɪtə(r)/ n **(a)** (for passengers) (AmE) ascensor m, elevador m (Méx) **(b)** (for goods) elevador m, montacargas m

eleven[1] /ɪ'levən/ n **(a)** (number) once m; see also FOUR[1] **(b)** (in soccer, field hockey) equipo m, once m (period)

eleven[2] adj once adj inv

eleventh[1] /ɪ'levənθ/ adj undécimo

eleventh[2] adv en undécimo lugar

eleventh[3] n (Math) onceavo m; (part) onceava parte f

elf /elf/ n (pl **elves**) geniecillo m, elfo m

elicit /ɪ'lɪsət ‖ɪ'lɪsɪt/ vt ⟨laughter/smile⟩ provocar*; to ~ sth (FROM sb) ⟨explanation/reply⟩ obtener* algo (DE algn)

eligible /'elədʒəbəl ‖'elɪdʒəbəl/ adj **(a)** (qualified, suitable) ⟨applicant/candidate⟩ que reúne los requisitos necesarios; **he's ~ for a grant** tiene derecho a solicitar una beca; **he is not ~ to compete** no reúne los requisitos necesarios para competir **(b)** (marriageable): **an ~ bachelor** un buen partido

eliminate /ɪ'lɪməneɪt ‖ɪ'lɪmɪneɪt/ vt eliminar; ⟨possibility/suspect⟩ descartar

elimination /ɪ'lɪmə'neɪʃən ‖ɪ,lɪmɪ'neɪʃən/ n (getting rid of) eliminación f; (ruling out) descarte m; **by a process of ~** por (un proceso de) eliminación or descarte

elite[1] /eɪ'li:t, i-/ n (+ sing or pl vb) elite f, élite f

elite[2] adj (before n) selecto, de elite or élite

elitism /eɪ'li:tɪzəm, i-/ n elitismo m

elitist /eɪ'li:tɪst, i-/ adj elitista

elixir /ɪ'lɪksər ‖ɪ'lɪksə(r)/ n elixir m

Elizabethan /ɪ'lɪzə'bi:θən/ adj isabelino

elk /elk/ n (pl **~s** or **~**) (European animal) alce m; (American animal) uapití m

elm /elm/ n ~ (**tree**) olmo m

elocution /elə'kju:ʃən/ n dicción f, elocución f

elongated /ɪ'lɔːŋgeɪtəd ‖'i:lɒŋgeɪtɪd/ adj alargado

elope /ɪ'ləʊp/ vi fugarse* (con un amante, novio para casarse)

eloquent /'eləkwənt/ adj elocuente

El Salvador /el'sælvədɔːr ‖,el'sælvədɔː(r)/ n El Salvador

else /els/ adv **1** (after pron): **somebody** o **someone ~** otra persona; **everybody** o **everyone ~** todos los demás; **everything ~** lo todo los demás; **there's not much ~ we can do** no podemos hacer mucho más; **nobody ~** nadie más; **they have nowhere ~ to go** no tienen ningún otro sitio or lugar adonde ir; **anything ~?** ¿algo más? **2** (with interrog): **what/who ~?** ¿qué/quién más?; **what can you expect from her?** ¿qué otra cosa se puede esperar de ella? **3** **or else** (as conj) si no

elsewhere /'elswher ‖,els'weə(r)/ adv: **to go ~** ir* a otro sitio or lugar; **~ in Europe** en otras partes or otros lugares de Europa

elude /i:'lu:d ‖ɪ'lu:d/ vt (avoid) eludir; (escape from) escaparse de

elusive /i:'lu:sɪv ‖i'lu:sɪv/ adj ⟨enemy/prey⟩ escurridizo, difícil de aprehender; ⟨goal/ agreement⟩ difícil de alcanzar

elves /elvz/ pl of ELF

emaciated /ɪ'meɪʃieɪtəd ‖ɪ'meɪsieɪtɪd/ adj ⟨person/animal⟩ escuálido; ⟨body/face⟩ consumido

E-mail, e-mail /'i:meɪl/ n correo m electrónico

emanate /'eməneɪt/ vi **to ~ FROM sth** ⟨gas/ light/sound⟩ emanar DE algo; ⟨ideas/ suggestions⟩ provenir* DE algo

emancipate /ɪ'mænsəpeɪt ‖ɪ'mænsɪpeɪt/ vt (frml) emancipar

emancipated /ɪ'mænsəpeɪtəd ‖ɪ'mænsɪpeɪtɪd/ adj emancipado; ⟨viewpoint/ lifestyle⟩ independiente y progresista

emancipation /ɪ,mænsə'peɪʃən ‖ɪ,mænsɪ'peɪʃən/ n (frml) emancipación f

embankment /ɪm'bæŋkmənt/ n (for road, railroad) terraplén m; (as protection) muro m de contención

embargo /ɪm'bɑːrgəʊ ‖ɪm'bɑːgəʊ/ n (pl **-goes**) embargo m, prohibición f; **to put an ~ on sth** imponer* un embargo sobre algo

embark /ɪm'bɑːrk ‖ɪm'bɑːk/ vi **(a)** (on ship, plane) embarcar(se)* **(b)** (start) **to ~ ON** o **UPON sth** ⟨on career/new life⟩ emprender algo; ⟨on adventure/undertaking⟩ embarcarse* EN algo

embarrass /ɪm'bærəs/ vt hacerle* pasar vergüenza a, avergonzar*

embarrassed /ɪm'bærəst/ adj: **an ~ silence** un silencio violento; **I'm ~** me da vergüenza, me da pena (AmL exc CS)

embarrassing /ɪm'bærəsɪŋ/ adj ⟨situation/ question⟩ embarazoso; **how ~!** ¡qué vergüenza or (AmL exc CS) pena!

embarrassment /ɪm'bærəsmənt/ n **(a)** (shame) bochorno m, vergüenza f, pena f (AmL exc CS) **(b)** (cause of shame): **he's an ~ to his friends** les hace pasar vergüenza a sus amigos

embassy /'embəsi/ n (pl **-sies**) embajada f

embed /ɪm'bed/ vt **-dd-** (in rock, wood) enterrar*; **the bullet was ~ded in his arm** la bala quedó alojada en el brazo

ember /'embər ‖'embə(r)/ n brasa f, ascua f

embezzle /ɪm'bezəl/ vt desfalcar*, malversar

embittered /ɪm'bɪtərd ‖ɪm'bɪtəd/ adj ⟨person⟩ amargado; ⟨fighting/rivalry⟩ enconado

emblem /'embləm/ n emblema m

embody /ɪm'bɑːdi ‖ɪm'bɒdi/ vt **-dies, -dying, -died (a)** (personify) encarnar, personificar* **(b)** (express) ⟨thought/idea⟩ plasmar, expresar

emboss /ɪm'bɑːs, ɪm'bɔːs ‖ɪm'bɒs/ vt **(a)** ⟨leather/metal⟩ repujar **(b) embossed** past p ⟨stationery⟩ con membrete en relieve; ⟨wallpaper⟩ estampado en relieve

embrace[1] /ɪm'breɪs/ vt **(a)** (hug) abrazar* **(b)** ⟨idea/principle⟩ abrazar*; ⟨lifestyle/religion⟩ adoptar
■ ~ vi abrazarse*

embrace[2] n abrazo m

embrocation /'embrə'keɪʃən/ n linimento m, embrocación f (ant)

embroider /ɪm'brɔɪdər ‖ɪm'brɔɪdə(r)/ vt ⟨cloth/design⟩ bordar; ⟨story⟩ adornar

embroidery /ɪm'brɔɪdəri/ n (pl **-ries**) bordado m

embroil /ɪm'brɔɪl/ vt: **to be/become ~ed in sth** estar*/verse* envuelto en algo

embryo /'embriəʊ/ n (pl **-os**) embrión m

emend /i:'mend ‖ɪ'mend/ vt (frml) enmendar*

emerald /'emərəld/ n (a) (gem) esmeralda f; (b) (color) verde m esmeralda

emerge /ɪ'mɜːrdʒ ‖ɪ'mɜːdʒ/ vi (a) (come out) salir*, aparecer* (b) (become evident, known) «*problem*» surgir*; «*pattern*» dibujarse; «*truth*» revelarse; «*facts*» salir* a la luz

emergency /ɪ'mɜːrdʒənsi ‖ɪ'mɜːdʒənsi/ n (pl **-cies**) (a) (serious situation) emergencia f; in an ∼ o in case of ∼ en una emergencia or en caso de emergencia (b) (Med) urgencia f; (before n) «*case/operation*» de urgencia (c) (Govt): a state of ∼ was declared se declaró el estado de excepción

emergency: ∼ **exit** n salida f de emergencia; ∼ **landing** n aterrizaje m forzoso; ∼ **stop** n parada f de emergencia

emery /'eməri/‡ ∼ **board** n lima f de esmeril; ∼ **paper** n papel m de lija

emigrant /'eməgrənt ‖'emɪgrənt/ n emigrante mf

emigrate /'eməgreɪt ‖'emɪgreɪt/ vi emigrar

emigration /emə'greɪʃən ‖emɪ'greɪʃən/ n emigración f

eminent /'emənənt ‖'emɪnənt/ adj eminente, ilustre

emission /iː'mɪʃən ‖ɪ'mɪʃən/ n emisión f

emit /iː'mɪt ‖i'mɪt/ vt **-tt-** «*gas/smell/vapor*» despedir*; «*heat/light/radiation/sound*» emitir

emotion /ɪ'məʊʃən/ n (a) (feeling) sentimiento m (b) (strength of feeling) emoción f

emotional /ɪ'məʊʃnəl ‖ɪ'məʊʃənḷ/ adj (a) «*disorder*» emocional (b) (sensitive) «*person/nature*» emotivo (c) (upset) emocionado; to get ∼ emocionarse (d) (moving) «*speech/experience/scene*» emotivo

empathize /'empəθaɪz/ vi to ∼ **WITH** sb establecer* lazos de empatía CON algn, identificarse* CON algn

empathy /'empəθi/ n empatía f

emperor /'empərər ‖'empərə(r)/ n emperador m

emphasis /'emfəsəs ‖'emfəsɪs/ n (pl **-ses** /-siːz/) énfasis m; to lay o put ∼ on sth hacer* hincapié or poner* énfasis en la importancia de algo

emphasize /'emfəsaɪz/ vt «*phrase/word*» enfatizar*; «*fact/point/warning*» recalcar*, hacer* hincapié en; «*fault/value*» poner* de relieve; «*shape/feature*» resaltar, hacer* resaltar

emphatic /ɪm'fætɪk/ adj «*gesture/tone*» enérgico, enfático; «*assertion/refusal*» categórico

empire /'empaɪr ‖'empaɪə(r)/ n imperio m

employ /ɪm'plɔɪ/ vt (a) «*person*» (take on) contratar, emplear; (have working) emplear, dar* empleo a (b) «*method/tactics/tool*» emplear

employee /ɪm'plɔɪiː/ n empleado, -da m,f

employer /ɪm'plɔɪər ‖ɪm'plɔɪə(r)/ n empleador, -dora m,f; (of domestic worker etc) patrón, -trona m,f

employment /ɪm'plɔɪmənt/ n (a) (work) trabajo m; to be in ∼ tener* trabajo; (before n) ∼ **agency** agencia f de trabajo (b) (availability of work) empleo m; full ∼ pleno empleo m

empress /'emprəs ‖'emprɪs/ n emperatriz f

empty¹ /'empti/ adj **-tier, -tiest** «*container/table*» vacío; «*words/gesture/life*» vacío; «*threat/promise*» vano

empty² **-ties, -tying, -tied** vt «*container/warehouse*» vaciar*; she emptied the contents all over the floor vació la caja (or el bolso etc) en el suelo
■ ∼ vi «*room/street*» vaciarse*; «*river/stream*» to ∼ **INTO** sth desaguar* EN algo
■ **empty out** [v + o + adv, v + adv + o] «*bag/drawer/pockets*» vaciar*; «*garbage*» tirar, botar (AmL exc RPl)

empty³ n (pl **-ties**) (colloq) (bottle) envase m (vacío), casco m (Esp, Méx)

empty-handed /'empti'hændəd ‖empti'hændɪd/ adj con las manos vacías

emu /'iːmjuː/ n emú m

emulate /'emjəleɪt ‖'emjʊleɪt/ vt emular

emulsion /ɪ'mʌlʃən/ n ∼ (**paint**) pintura f al agua

enable /ɪn'eɪbəl/ vt (a) (provide means for) to ∼ sb to + INF permitir(le) A algn + INF (b) (make possible) posibilitar, permitir

enact /ɪn'ækt/ vt [1] (Govt, Law) «*law*» promulgar* [2] «*play/role*» representar

enamel /ɪ'næməl/ n esmalte m

enamored, (BrE) **enamoured** /ɪ'næmərd ‖ɪ'næməd/ adj (frml) to be ∼ **OF** sb estar* enamorado or prendado DE algn; I'm not very ∼ of the idea no estoy muy entusiasmado con la idea

enc (= **enclosed**) anexo

encampment /ɪn'kæmpmənt/ n campamento m

encase /ɪn'keɪs/ vt revestir*, recubrir*; ∼d **IN** sth revestido or recubierto DE algo

enchant /ɪn'tʃænt ‖ɪn'tʃɑːnt/ vt (delight, charm) cautivar; (Occult) hechizar*

enchanting /ɪn'tʃæntɪŋ ‖ɪn'tʃɑːntɪŋ/ adj encantador

encircle /ɪn'sɜːrkəl ‖ɪn'sɜːkəl/ vt «*camp/house*» rodear; «*waist/wrist*» ceñir*

enclave /'enkleɪv/ n enclave m

enclose /ɪn'kləʊz/ vt [1] (a) (surround) encerrar*; (fence in) cercar* (b) **enclosed** past p «*area/space*» cerrado [2] (in letter) adjuntar, acompañar

enclosure /ɪn'kləʊʒər ‖ɪn'kləʊʒə(r)/ n recinto m; a fenced ∼ un cercado

encode /ɪn'kəʊd, en-/ vt codificar*, cifrar

encompass /ɪn'kʌmpəs/ vt (fml) abarcar*

encore /'ɑːnkɔːr ‖'ɒŋkɔː(r)/ n bis m; (as interj) ¡otra!

encounter¹ /ɪn'kaʊntər ‖ɪn'kaʊntə(r)/ vt (a)

AmC	Central America	Arg	Argentina	Cu	Cuba	Per	Peru
AmL	Latin America	Bol	Bolivia	Ec	Ecuador	RPl	River Plate Area
AmS	South America	Chi	Chile	Esp	Spain	Ur	Uruguay
Andes	Andean Region	CS	Southern Cone	Méx	Mexico	Ven	Venezuela

(be faced with) ⟨danger/difficulty/opposition⟩
encontrar*, encontrarse* con **(b)** (come across)
tropezar* or toparse con

encounter² n encuentro m

encourage /ɪn'kɜːrɪdʒ ‖ɪn'kʌrɪdʒ/ vt **(a)** (give
hope, courage to) animar, alentar*; **she/it** ∼**d me to
carry on** me animó a seguir adelante **(b)**
⟨industry/competition/growth⟩ fomentar

encouragement /ɪn'kɜːrɪdʒmənt
‖ɪn'kʌrɪdʒmənt/ n ánimo m

encouraging /ɪn'kɜːrɪdʒɪŋ ‖ɪn'kʌrɪdʒɪŋ/ adj
alentador

encroach /ɪn'krəʊtʃ/ vi to ∼ **ON** o **UPON** sth
⟨on land⟩ invadir algo; ⟨on rights⟩ cercenar algo

encrypt /en'krɪpt/ vt (Comput) cifrar

encumber /ɪn'kʌmbər ‖ɪn'kʌmbə(r)/ vt
cargar*

encyclopedia, (BrE also) **encyclopaedia**
/ɪn'saɪkləˈpiːdiə/ n enciclopedia f

end¹ /end/ n **1** **(a)** (extremity — of rope, stick)
extremo m, punta f; (— of nose) punta f; (— of
street) final m; **for weeks on** ∼ durante semanas y
semanas, durante semanas enteras; **it measures
five feet (from)** ∼ **to** ∼ mide cinco pies de un
lado al otro or de punta a punta; **to make** ∼**s
meet** llegar* a fin de mes **(b)** (remaining part) final
m, resto m
2 **(a)** (finish, close) fin m, final m; **at the** ∼ **of
January** a fines or a finales de enero; **in the** ∼ al
final; **to put an** ∼ **to** sth poner* fin or poner*
punto final a algo **(b)** (death, destruction) final m,
fin m **(c)** (outcome) final m
3 (purpose) fin m; **to this** ∼ (frml) con este fin
(frml)

end² vt **(a)** (stop) ⟨argument/discussion/fight⟩
terminar; ⟨gossip/speculation⟩ acabar or terminar
con **(b)** (conclude) terminar
■ ∼ vi acabar, terminar
■ **end up** [v + adv] terminar, acabar

endanger /ɪn'deɪndʒər ‖ɪn'deɪndʒə(r)/ vt **(a)**
⟨life⟩ poner* en peligro; ⟨chances/reputation⟩
hacer* peligrar **(b)** **endangered** past p
⟨species⟩ en peligro

endear /ɪn'dɪr ‖ɪn'dɪə(r)/ vt to ∼ **oneself** **TO** sb
granjearse el cariño de algn

endearing /ɪn'dɪrɪŋ ‖ɪn'dɪərɪŋ/ adj atractivo

endearment /ɪn'dɪrmənt ‖ɪn'dɪəmənt/ n
expresión f de cariño

endeavor¹, (BrE) **endeavour** /ɪn'devər
‖ɪn'devə(r)/ n (frml) esfuerzo m, intento m

endeavor², (BrE) **endeavour** vi (frml) to ∼ **to
+ INF** intentar por todos los medios + INF,
esforzarse* POR + INF

ending /'endɪŋ/ n **(a)** (conclusion) final m,
desenlace m **(b)** (Ling) desinencia f, terminación f

endless /'endləs ‖'endlɪs/ adj **(a)** ⟨journey/
meeting⟩ interminable; ⟨plain/patience⟩ sin
límites; ⟨chatter/complaining⟩ continuo **(b)**
(innumerable) innumerable; **the possibilities are** ∼
las posibilidades son infinitas

endorse /ɪn'dɔːrs ‖ɪn'dɔːs/ vt **1** (approve)
⟨statement/decision⟩ aprobar* **2** (sign) ⟨check/bill⟩
endosar

endorsement /ɪn'dɔːrsmənt ‖ɪn'dɔːsmənt/ n
1 **(a)** (approval) aval m, aprobación f **(b)** (Pol)
refrendo m **2** (on driving licence) (BrE) anotación f
(de una infracción de tráfico)

endow /ɪn'daʊ/ vt **(a)** (provide) (usu pass) ∼**ed
WITH** sth dotado DE algo **(b)** (provide income for)
⟨college/school/hospital⟩ dotar DE (fondos) a

endowment /ɪn'daʊmənt/ n (Fin) donación f

end product n producto m final

endurance /ɪn'dʊrəns ‖ɪn'djʊərəns/ n
(physical) resistencia f; (mental) entereza f; (before
n) ∼ **test** prueba f de resistencia

endure /ɪn'dʊr ‖ɪn'djʊə(r)/ vt soportar
■ ∼ vi «fame/friendship/memories» perdurar

enemy /'enəmi/ n (pl **-mies**) enemigo, -ga m,f

energetic /'enərˈdʒetɪk ‖ˌenəˈdʒetɪk/ adj
⟨person⟩ lleno de energía; ⟨exercise⟩ enérgico

energy /'enərdʒi ‖'enədʒi/ n energía f; (power,
effort) energías fpl

enforce /ɪn'fɔːrs ‖ɪn'fɔːs/ vt ⟨law/regulation⟩
hacer* respetar or cumplir; ⟨claim/right⟩ hacer*
valer

engage /ɪn'geɪdʒ/ vt **1** ⟨attention/interest⟩
captar **2** ⟨cog/wheel⟩ engranar con; ⟨gear⟩
engranar **3** (hire) ⟨staff/performer⟩ contratar
■ ∼ vi (take part) to ∼ **IN** sth ⟨in politics/voluntary
work/study⟩ dedicarse* A algo; **they** ∼**d in a
variety of activities** participaron en una variedad
de actividades

engaged /ɪn'geɪdʒd/ adj **1** (betrothed)
prometido, comprometido (AmL); **to be** ∼ **TO** sb
estar* prometido A algn, estar* comprometido
CON algn (AmL); **to get** ∼ prometerse,
comprometerse (AmL) **2** (pred) **(a)** (occupied) (frml)
ocupado; **I'm otherwise** ∼ tengo otro compromiso;
they are ∼ **in a new business venture** tienen un
nuevo negocio entre manos **(b)** (BrE) ⟨toilet⟩
ocupado **(c)** (BrE Telec) ocupado, comunicando
(Esp); **the** ∼ **tone** o **signal** la señal de ocupado or
(Esp) de comunicando

engagement /ɪn'geɪdʒmənt/ n **1** (pledge to
marry) compromiso m; (period) noviazgo m; (before
n) ∼ **ring** anillo m de compromiso **2** (appointment)
compromiso m

engine /'endʒən ‖'endʒɪn/ n **(a)** (motor) motor
m **(b)** (locomotive) locomotora f, máquina f

engine driver n (BrE) maquinista mf

engineer¹ /'endʒə'nɪr ‖ˌendʒə'nɪə(r)/ n **1** **(a)**
(graduate) ingeniero, -ra m,f **(b)** (for maintenance)
(BrE) técnico mf, ingeniero, -ra m,f (Méx) **2** (AmE
Rail) maquinista mf

engineer² vt ⟨plan⟩ urdir, tramar; ⟨defeat/
downfall⟩ fraguar*

engineering /'endʒə'nɪrɪŋ ‖ˌendʒɪ'nɪərɪŋ/ n
ingeniería f

England /'ɪŋglənd/ n Inglaterra f

English¹ /'ɪŋglɪʃ/ adj inglés

English² n **(a)** (language) inglés m; (before n)
⟨lesson/teacher⟩ de inglés **(b)** (people) (+ pl vb) **the**
∼ los ingleses

English: ∼**man** /'ɪŋglɪʃmən/ n (pl **-men**
/-mən/) inglés m; ∼**woman** n inglesa f

engrave /ɪn'greɪv/ vt grabar

engraving /ɪn'greɪvɪŋ/ n grabado m

engross /ɪn'grəʊs/ vt absorber*; **to be** ∼**ed IN**
sth estar* absorto EN algo

engulf /ɪn'gʌlf/ vt «flames/fire/waves»
envolver*; «lava» sepultar; «feeling» asaltar

enhance /ɪnˈhæns ‖ɪnˈhɑːns/ vt ⟨beauty/taste⟩ realzar*; ⟨value⟩ aumentar; ⟨reputation/ performance⟩ mejorar

enigma /ɪˈnɪgmə/ n (pl **-mas**) enigma m

enigmatic /ˈenɪgˈmætɪk/ adj enigmático

enjoy /ɪnˈdʒɔɪ/ vt ⟨1⟩ (like): I ~ traveling/music me gusta viajar/la música; I ~ed the party lo pasé bien en la fiesta ⟨2⟩ (have, experience) ⟨good health⟩ disfrutar de, gozar* de
- v refl to ~ oneself divertirse*, pasarlo or pasarla bien

enjoyable /ɪnˈdʒɔɪəbəl/ adj agradable

enjoyment /ɪnˈdʒɔɪmənt/ n placer m

enlarge /ɪnˈlɑːrdʒ ‖ɪnˈlɑːdʒ/ vt ⟨hole/area⟩ agrandar; ⟨gland/heart⟩ dilatar; ⟨room/office⟩ ampliar*; ⟨print/photograph⟩ ampliar*

enlighten /ɪnˈlaɪtn̩/ vt ⟨people/population⟩ ilustrar (frml); would you care to ~ me? ¿te importaría explicarme?

enlightened /ɪnˈlaɪtn̩d/ adj ⟨person/view⟩ progresista; ⟨decision⟩ inteligente

Enlightenment /ɪnˈlaɪtn̩mənt/ n (Hist) the (Age of) ~ la Ilustración, el Siglo de las Luces

enlist /ɪnˈlɪst/ vi alistarse
- ~ vt ⟨soldiers/helpers/members⟩ reclutar, alistar; ⟨sailors⟩ enrolar; ⟨support/aid⟩ conseguir*

enlisted man /ɪnˈlɪstəd ‖ɪnˈlɪstɪd/ n (AmE) soldado m raso

en masse /ɑːnˈmæs ‖ɒnˈmæs/ adv en masa

enmity /ˈenməti/ n (pl **-ties**) (frml) enemistad f

enormous /ɪˈnɔːrməs ‖ɪˈnɔːməs/ adj enorme, inmenso

enormously /ɪˈnɔːrməsli ‖ɪˈnɔːməsli/ adv ⟨enjoy/benefit⟩ enormemente; he's ~ fat es gordísimo

enough¹ /ɪˈnʌf/ adj bastante, suficiente; (pl) bastantes, suficientes; they had more than ~ time tuvieron tiempo de sobra

enough² pron: they don't pay us ~ no nos pagan bastante or lo suficiente; I've had ~! ¡ya estoy harto!

enough³ adv you don't go out ~ no sales lo suficiente; make sure it's big ~ asegúrate de que sea lo suficientemente grande; curiously ~ curiosamente

---

- Note Where the meaning ... enough to ... is being translated, the translation uses the structure lo bastante or lo suficiente ... como para ...: you aren't eating enough (to stay healthy) no estás comiendo lo suficiente or lo bastante (como para mantenerte saludable).

---

enquire etc (BrE) /ɪnˈkwaɪr ‖ɪnˈkwaɪə(r)/ ▶ INQUIRE etc

enrage /ɪnˈreɪdʒ/ vt enfurecer*

enrich /ɪnˈrɪtʃ/ vt enriquecer*

enroll, (BrE) **enrol** /ɪnˈrəʊl/ vi-**ll-** matricularse, inscribirse*
- ~ vt matricular, inscribir*

enrollment, (BrE) **enrolment** /ɪnˈrəʊlmənt/ n inscripción f, matrícula f

en route /ɑːnˈruːt ‖ɒnˈruːt/ adv por el camino, de camino

ensemble /ɑːnˈsɑːmbəl ‖ɒnˈsɒmbəl/ n ⟨1⟩ (group of performers) conjunto m ⟨2⟩ (Clothing) conjunto m

enslave /ɪnˈsleɪv/ vt esclavizar*

ensue /ɪnˈsuː ‖ɪnˈsjuː/ vi seguir*; in the ensuing fight en la pelea que tuvo lugar a continuación

en suite /ˌɑːnˈswiːt ‖ˌɒnˈswiːt/ adj adjunto, en suite

ensure /ɪnˈʃʊr ‖ɪnˈʃʊə(r), ɪnˈʃɔː(r)/ vt asegurar

entail /ɪnˈteɪl/ vt ⟨risk⟩ implicar*, suponer*; ⟨expense⟩ acarrear, suponer*; ⟨responsibility⟩ conllevar

entangle /ɪnˈtæŋgəl/ vt enredar

enter /ˈentər ‖ˈentə(r)/ vt ⟨1⟩ (a) ⟨room/house/ country⟩ entrar en, entrar a (esp AmL) (b) (penetrate) entrar en ⟨2⟩ (begin) ⟨period/phase⟩ entrar en ⟨3⟩ (a) (join) ⟨army⟩ alistarse en, entrar en; ⟨firm/organization⟩ entrar en, incorporarse a (b) (begin to take part in) ⟨war/negotiations⟩ entrar en; ⟨debate/dispute⟩ sumarse a (c) ⟨student/ candidate⟩ presentar (d) ⟨race⟩ inscribirse* (para tomar parte) en; to ~ a competition presentarse a un concurso ⟨4⟩ (a) (record — in register) inscribir*; (— in ledger, book) anotar (b) (Comput) dar* entrada a
- ~ vi ⟨1⟩ entrar ⟨2⟩ to ~ (FOR sth) ⟨for competition/race⟩ inscribirse* (EN algo); ⟨for examination⟩ presentarse (A algo)

enterprise /ˈentərpraɪz ‖ˈentəpraɪz/ n ⟨1⟩ (a) (project) empresa f (b) (initiative, daring) empuje m ⟨2⟩ (a) (company) empresa f (b) (business activity): free ~ la libre empresa; private ~ la iniciativa privada; (sector) el sector privado

entertain /ˈentərˈteɪn ‖ˌentəˈteɪn/ vt ⟨1⟩ (amuse) ⟨audience⟩ entretener* ⟨2⟩ (frml) ⟨idea/suggestion⟩ contemplar; ⟨doubt/suspicions⟩ abrigar* (frml)
- ~ vi ⟨1⟩ (provide entertainment) entretener* ⟨2⟩ (have guests) recibir

entertainer /ˈentərˈteɪnər ‖ˌentəˈteɪnə(r)/ n artista mf (del mundo del espectáculo); (presenter of program) (Rad, TV) animador, -dora m,f

entertaining /ˈentərˈteɪnɪŋ ‖ˌentəˈteɪnɪŋ/ adj ⟨book/movie/anecdote⟩ entretenido; ⟨person⟩ divertido

entertainment /ˈentərˈteɪnmənt ‖ˌentəˈteɪnmənt/ n (a) (amusement) entretenimiento m (b) (show) espectáculo m

enthrall, (BrE) **enthral** /ɪnˈθrɔːl/ vt -**ll-** cautivar

enthusiasm /ɪnˈθuːziæzəm ‖ɪnˈθjuːziæzəm/ n entusiasmo m

enthusiast /ɪnˈθuːziæst ‖ɪnˈθjuːziæst/ n entusiasta mf

enthusiastic /ɪnˈθuːziˈæstɪk ‖ɪnˌθjuːziˈæstɪk/ adj entusiasta

entice /ɪnˈtaɪs/ vt atraer*

entire /ɪnˈtaɪr ‖ɪnˈtaɪə(r)/ adj (a) (whole) (before n) entero (b) (intact) (pred) intacto

entirely /ɪnˈtaɪrli ‖ɪnˈtaɪəli/ adv totalmente, completamente

entirety /ɪnˈtaɪrəti ‖ɪnˈtaɪərəti/ n: in its ~ íntegramente, en su totalidad

entitle /ɪnˈtaɪtl̩/ vt ⟨1⟩ (give right) to ~ sb TO sth darle* a algn derecho A algo; to be ~d TO sth tener* derecho A algo ⟨2⟩ (name) (frml) (often pass) titular

entity /ˈentəti/ n (pl **-ties**) entidad f

entourage /ˈɑːntʊˈrɑːʒ ‖ˌɒntʊˈrɑːʒ/ n séquito m

entrails /'entreɪlz/ *pl n* (of person) entrañas *fpl*; (of animal) vísceras *fpl*

entrance¹ /'entrəns/ *n* **1** **(a)** (way in) entrada *f* **(b)** (foyer) hall *m*; (*before n*) ∼ **hall** hall *m*, vestíbulo *m* **(c)** (access) (frml) entrada *f* **2** (admission — to club, museum) entrada *f*; (— to school, university) ingreso *m*; (*before n*) ∼ **fee** (for entry) (precio *m* de) entrada *f*; (to join club) cuota *f* de ingreso *or* inscripción; (for exam, competition) cuota *f or* tasa *f* de inscripción **3** (act of entering) entrada *f*; (Theat) entrada *f* en escena

entrance² /ɪn'trɑːns ‖ ɪn'træns/ *vt* embelesar, extasiar*

entrant /'entrənt/ *n* (in competition) participante *mf*; (for exam) candidato, -ta *m,f*

entreat /ɪn'triːt/ *vt* (liter) suplicar*, rogar*

entreaty /ɪn'triːti/ *n* (*pl* **-ties**) (liter) súplica *f*, ruego *m*

entrepreneur /ˌɑːntrəprə'nɜːr ‖ ˌɒntrəprə'nɜː(r)/ *n* empresario, -ria *m,f*

entrust /ɪn'trʌst/ *vt to* ∼ **sth TO sb** encomendarle* *or* confiarle* algo a algn

entry /'entri/ *n* (*pl* **entries**) **1** (coming, going in) entrada *f* **2** (access) entrada *f*, acceso *m*; **⊝ no entry** (on door) prohibida la entrada; (on road sign) prohibido el paso **3 (a)** (in accounts) entrada *f*, asiento *m* **(b)** (in diary) anotación *f*, entrada *f* **(c)** (in dictionary — headword) entrada *f*; (in encyclopedia — article) artículo *m* **4** (in contest): **the winning** ∼ **in the painting competition** el ejemplar ganador del concurso de pintura; **there were 20 entries** hubo 20 inscripciones **5** (door, gate) (AmE) entrada *f*

entryphone /'entrifəʊn/ *n* (BrE) portero *m* eléctrico *or* (Esp) automático, interfón *m* (Méx), intercomunicador *m* (Ven)

entwine /ɪn'twaɪn/ *vt* (liter) entrelazar*

envelop /ɪn'veləp/ *vt* envolver*

envelope /'envələʊp/ *n* sobre *m*

enviable /'enviəbəl/ *adj* envidiable

envious /'enviəs/ *adj* envidioso*; *⟨expression⟩* (lleno) de envidia

environment /ɪn'vaɪrənmənt ‖ ɪn'vaɪərənmənt/ *n* **(a)** (Ecol) **the** ∼ el medio ambiente **(b)** (surroundings): **she's studying gorillas in their natural** ∼ estudia a las gorilas en su entorno *or* hábitat natural; **the home** ∼ el ambiente del hogar

environmental /ɪnˌvaɪrən'mentḷ ‖ ɪnˌvaɪərən'mentḷ/ *adj* **(a)** (Ecol) *⟨factor⟩* ambiental; *⟨damage⟩* al medio ambiente, medioambiental; ∼ **groups** grupos *mpl* ecologistas **(b)** (of surroundings) *⟨factor⟩* ambiental; *⟨influence⟩* del ambiente *or* entorno

environment-friendly /ɪn'vaɪrənmənt,frendli ‖ ɪn'vaɪərənmənt,frendli/ *adj*: ∼ **products** productos *mpl* ecológicos, productos *mpl* que no dañan al medio ambiente

environs /ɪn'vaɪrənz ‖ ɪn'vaɪərənz/ *pl n* alrededores *mpl*, entorno *m*

envisage /ɪn'vɪzɪdʒ/ *vt* **(a)** (foresee) prever* *vt* **(b)** (visualize) imaginarse

envision /ɪn'vɪʒən/ *vt* (AmE) prever*

envoy /'envoɪ/ *n* enviado, -da *m,f*

envy¹ /'envi/ *n* envidia *f*

envy² *vt* **envies, envying, envied** envidiar

enzyme /'enzaɪm/ *n* enzima *f*

epic¹ /'epɪk/ *adj* (*usu before n*) *⟨poem/poetry/film⟩* épico; *⟨achievement/struggle⟩* colosal, de epopeya

epic² *n* (poem) poema *m* épico; (film) superproducción *f*; (novel) epopeya *f*

epidemic /'epə'demɪk ‖ ˌepɪ'demɪk/ *n* epidemia *f*

epigram /'epəgræm ‖ 'epɪgræm/ *n* epigrama *m*

epilepsy /'epəlepsi ‖ 'epɪlepsi/ *n* epilepsia *f*

epileptic /'epə'leptɪk ‖ ˌepɪ'leptɪk/ *adj* *⟨fit/attack⟩* epiléptico, de epilepsia; **she's** ∼ es epiléptica

epilogue, (AmE also) **epilog** /'epəlɔːg ‖ 'epɪlɒg/ *n* epílogo *m*

Epiphany /ɪ'pɪfəni/ *n* **the** ∼ la Epifanía (del Señor)

episode /'epəsəʊd ‖ 'epɪsəʊd/ *n* episodio *m*

epistle /ɪ'pɪsəl/ *n* epístola *f*

epitaph /'epətæf ‖ 'epɪtɑːf/ *n* epitafio *m*

epitome /ɪ'pɪtəmi/ *n* (embodiment) personificación *f*; (typical example) arquetipo *m*

epitomize /ɪ'pɪtəmaɪz/ *vt* tipificar*; *«person»* ser* la personificación de

epoch /'epək ‖ 'iːpɒk/ *n* era *f*, época *f*

equal¹ /'iːkwəl/ *adj* igual; ∼ **opportunities** igualdad *f* de oportunidades; **he doesn't feel** ∼ **to the task** no se siente capaz de hacerlo

equal² *n* igual *mf*

equal³ *vt*, (BrE) **-ll-** **1** (Math) ser* igual a; **three times three** ∼**s nine** tres por tres son nueve *or* es igual a nueve **2** *⟨record/time⟩* igualar

equality /ɪ'kwɑːləti ‖ ɪ'kwɒləti/ *n* igualdad *f*

equalize /'iːkwəlaɪz/ *vt* *⟨pressure/weight⟩* igualar; *⟨incomes⟩* equiparar

■ ∼ *vi* (Sport) empatar

equalizer /'iːkwəlaɪzər ‖ 'iːkwəlaɪzə(r)/ *n* (Sport) gol *m* de la igualada *or* del empate

equally /'iːkwəli/ *adv* **1 (a)** (in equal amounts) *⟨divide/share⟩* por igual **(b)** (without bias) *⟨treat⟩* de la misma manera, (por) igual **2** (to an equal degree) igualmente; **to** ∼ **easily** con igual *or* con la misma facilidad **3** (indep) **(a)** (just as possibly) ∼ (well) de igual modo **(b)** (at the same time) (as linker) al mismo tiempo

equate /ɪ'kweɪt/ *vt* (compare) equiparar; (identify) identificar*

equation /ɪ'kweɪʒən/ *n* ecuación *f*

equator /ɪ'kweɪtər ‖ ɪ'kweɪtə(r)/ *n* **the** ∼ *o* **E**∼ el ecuador

equilibrium /'iːkwə'lɪbriəm ‖ ˌiːkwɪ'lɪbriəm/ *n* (*pl* **-riums** *or* **-ria** /-riə/) equilibrio *m*

equinox /'iːkwənɑːks, 'ek- ‖ 'iːkwɪnɒks, 'ek-/ *n* equinoccio *m*

equip /ɪ'kwɪp/ *vt* **-pp-** **(a)** (furnish, supply) *⟨troops/laboratory⟩* equipar; **to** ∼ **sth/sb WITH sth** proveer* algo/a algn DE algo **(b)** (prepare, make capable) preparar

equipment /ɪ'kwɪpmənt/ *n* equipo *m*; **office** ∼ mobiliario, máquinas y material de oficina; **sports** ∼ artículos *mpl* deportivos

equity /'ekwəti/ *n* **1** (fairness) (frml) equidad *f* (frml) **2** (Busn, Fin) **(a)** (shareholders' interest in company) patrimonio *m* neto **(b) equities** *pl n* (shares) valores *mpl* de renta variable

equivalent¹ /ɪ'kwɪvələnt/ *adj* **(a)** (equal) *⟨size⟩* ⋯✧

value⟩ equivalente; **to be ~ TO sth/-ING**
equivaler* A algo/+ INF **(b)** (corresponding)
⟨*position/term*⟩ equivalente

equivalent² *n* equivalente *m*

era /'ɪrə, 'erə ‖'ɪərə/ *n* era *f*, época *f*

eradicate /ɪ'rædəkeɪt ‖ɪ'rædɪkeɪt/ *vt*
erradicar*

erase /ɪ'reɪs ‖ɪ'reɪz/ *vt* borrar

eraser /ɪ'reɪsər ‖ɪ'reɪzə(r)/ *n* goma *f* (de borrar)

erect¹ /ɪ'rekt/ *adj* **1** ⟨*bearing/posture*⟩ erguido
2 (Physiol) erecto

erect² *vt* ⟨*altar/monument*⟩ erigir* (frml),
levantar; ⟨*barricade/wall*⟩ levantar; ⟨*tent*⟩ armar

erection /ɪ'rekʃən/ *n* **1** (frml) **(a)** (of building,
monument) construcción *f*; (of barricade)
levantamiento *m* **(b)** (building) construcción *f*
2 (Physiol) erección *f*

erode /ɪ'rəʊd/ *vt* «*water/wind/waves*»
erosionar; «*acid*» corroer*; ⟨*confidence/faith*⟩
minar

erosion /ɪ'rəʊʒən/ *n* (by water, wind, waves)
erosión *f*; (by acid) corrosión *f*; (of confidence, power,
rights) menoscabo *m*

erotic /ɪ'rɑːtɪk ‖ɪ'rɒtɪk/ *adj* erótico

err /er ‖ɜː(r)/ *vi* (frml): **to ~ IN sth** equivocarse*
EN algo; **to ~ on the side of caution** pecar* de
cauteloso

errand /'erənd/ *n* mandado *m* (esp AmL), recado
m (Esp); **to run an ~ for sb** hacerle* un mandado
or (Esp) recado a algn

erratic /ɪ'rætɪk/ *adj* ⟨*performance/work*⟩
desigual; ⟨*person/moods*⟩ imprevisible; ⟨*course*⟩
errático

erroneous /ɪ'rəʊniəs/ *adj* erróneo

error /'erər ‖'erə(r)/ *n* error *m*

error message *n* (Comput) mensaje *m* de
error

erstwhile /'ɜːrstʰwaɪl ‖'ɜːstwaɪl/ *adj* (liter)
antiguo

erudite /'erjədaɪt ‖'eruːdaɪt/ *adj* (frml) erudito

erupt /ɪ'rʌpt/ *vi* **(a)** «*volcano/geyser*» entrar en
erupción **(b)** (break out) «*violence/fighting*»
estallar

eruption /ɪ'rʌpʃən/ *n* **(a)** (of volcano) erupción *f*
(b) (of violence) brote *m*; (of anger) estallido *m*

escalate /'eskəleɪt/ *vi* **(a)** «*fighting/violence/
dispute*» intensificarse*; «*prices/claims*»
aumentar **(b) escalating** *pres p* ⟨*dispute/
tension*⟩ creciente

escalator /'eskəleɪtər ‖'eskəleɪtə(r)/ *n*
escalera *f* mecánica

escapade /'eskəpeɪd/ *n* aventura *f*

escape¹ /ɪ'skeɪp/ *vi* **1** **(a)** (flee) escaparse;
«*prisoner*» fugarse*; **to ~ FROM sth** ⟨*from
prison*⟩ fugarse* DE algo; ⟨*from cage/zoo*⟩
escaparse DE algo; ⟨*from danger/routine*⟩ escapar
DE algo **(b)** ⟨*air/gas/water*⟩ escaparse **2** (from
accident, danger) salvarse
■ ~ *vt* ⟨*pursuer/police*⟩ escaparse de; ⟨*capture*⟩

salvarse de; ⟨*responsibilities/consequences*⟩
librarse de; **that detail had ~d my notice** se me
había escapado ese detalle

escape² *n* **(a)** (from prison) fuga *f*, huida *f*; **to
make one's ~** escaparse **(b)** (from accident, danger):
to have a miraculous ~ salvarse milagrosamente;
there's no ~ no hay escapatoria posible **(c)** (of
gas, air, water) escape *m* **(d)** (from reality) evasión *f*
(e) (Comput): **press ~** pulse la tecla de escape;
⟨*before n*⟩ **~ key** tecla *f* de escape

escapist /ɪ'skeɪpəst ‖ɪ'skeɪpɪst/ *adj* escapista

escort¹ /'eskɔːrt ‖'eskɔːt/ *n* **1** (guard) escolta *f*;
under police ~ escoltado por la policía
2 (companion) acompañante *mf*; (male companion)
(frml) acompañante *m*

escort² /ɪ'skɔːrt ‖ɪ'skɔːt/ *vt* **(a)** (accompany)
acompañar; ⟨*prisoner/intruder*⟩ llevar **(b)** (for
protection) ⟨*politician/procession/ship*⟩ escoltar

Eskimo *n* (*pl* **-mos**) esquimal *mf*

esoteric /'esə'terɪk ‖ˌiːsəʊ'terɪk, ˌesəʊ-/ *adj*
esotérico

espadrille /ˌespə'drɪl/ *n* alpargata *f*

especially /ɪ'speʃli/ *adv* especialmente;
everyone was bored, ~ me estaba todo el mundo
aburrido, sobre todo *or* especialmente yo

espionage /'espiənɑːʒ/ *n* espionaje *m*

Esquire /ɪ'skwaɪr ‖ɪ'skwaɪə(r)/ *n* (as title):
Frederick Saunders, ~ Sr. Frederick Saunders,
Sr Don Frederick Saunders (esp Esp)

essay /'eseɪ/ *n* (literary composition) ensayo *m*;
(academic composition) trabajo *m*, ensayo *m*;
(language exercise) composición *f*, redacción *f*

essence /'esns/ *n* **1** **(a)** (central feature, quality)
esencia *f*; **in ~** en esencia **(b)** (personification)
personificación *f* **2** (Culin): **vanilla ~** esencia *f* de
vainilla

essential¹ /ɪ'sentʃəl ‖ɪ'senʃəl/ *adj* esencial

essential² *n* **(a)** (sth indispensable) imperativo
m, elemento *m* esencial **(b) essentials** *pl n*
(fundamental features) puntos *mpl* esenciales

essentially /ɪ'sentʃəli ‖ɪ'senʃəli/ *adv*
esencialmente; (indep) en lo esencial

EST (in US) = **Eastern Standard Time**

establish /ɪ'stæblɪʃ/ *vt* **(a)** ⟨*colony/company*⟩
establecer*, fundar; ⟨*committee/fund*⟩ instituir*,
crear **(b)** ⟨*procedure/diplomatic relations*⟩
establecer* **(c)** (prove) ⟨*guilt/innocence*⟩
establecer*; (ascertain) ⟨*motive/fact/identity*⟩
establecer*

established /ɪ'stæblɪʃt/ *adj* **1** ⟨*expert/
company*⟩ de reconocido prestigio; ⟨*star*⟩ de
renombre; ⟨*reputation*⟩ sólido; ⟨*practice*⟩
establecido; ⟨*fact*⟩ comprobado **2** ⟨*church/
religion*⟩ oficial

establishment /ɪ'stæblɪʃmənt/ *n* **1** **(a)** (of
colony, business) fundación *f*; (of committee) creación
f **(b)** (of criteria, relations) establecimiento *m*
2 (club, hotel, shop) establecimiento *m* **3 the
Establishment** la clase dirigente, el establishment

estate /ɪ'steɪt/ *n* **1** **(a)** (land, property) finca *f*,
propiedad *f* **(b)** (group of buildings): **a private ~** un

AmC	América Central		Arg	Argentina		Cu	Cuba		Per	Perú
AmL	América Latina		Bol	Bolivia		Ec	Ecuador		RPI	Río de la Plata
AmS	América del Sur		Chi	Chile		Esp	España		Ur	Uruguay
Andes	Región andina		CS	Cono Sur		Méx	México		Ven	Venezuela

complejo habitacional, una urbanización (Esp), un fraccionamiento (Méx) **2** (Law) patrimonio *m*; (of deceased person) sucesión *f* **3** ~ (**car**) (BrE) ▶ STATION WAGON

estate agent *n* (BrE) agente *mf* de la propiedad inmobiliaria

esteem /ɪˈstiːm/ *n* estima *f*; **I hold him in high** ~ lo aprecio mucho

esthetic /ˈesθetɪk ‖ ˈiːsθetɪk/ *adj* estético

estimate¹ /ˈestəmeɪt ‖ ˈestɪmeɪt/ *vt* **(a)** (calculate approximately) ⟨price/number/age⟩ calcular **(b) estimated** *past p* ⟨cost/speed⟩ aproximado; ~**d time of arrival** hora *f* de llegada previsto **(c)** (form judgment of) ⟨outcome/ability⟩ juzgar*, valorar

estimate² /ˈestəmət ‖ ˈestɪmət/ *n* **(a)** (rough calculation) cálculo *m* aproximado **(b)** (of costs) (Busn) presupuesto *m*

estimation /ˌestəˈmeɪʃən ‖ ˌestɪˈmeɪʃən/ *n* **(a)** (judgment, opinion) juicio *m*, valoración *f* **(b)** (esteem): **to go up/down in sb's** ~ ganarse/ perder* la estima de algn

Estonia /eˈstəʊniə/ *n* Estonia *f*

Estonian /eˈstəʊniən/ *adj* estonio

estrange /ɪˈstreɪndʒ/ *vt*: **his** ~**d wife** su mujer, de quien está separado

estuary /ˈestʃueri ‖ ˈestjʊəri/ *n* (*pl* **-ries**) estuario *m*

etc (= **et cetera**) etc.

et cetera /ɪtˈsetrə/ *adv* etcétera

etch /etʃ/ *vt* (Art, Print) grabar

etching /ˈetʃɪŋ/ *n* grabado *m*

eternal /ɪˈtɜːrnl ‖ ɪˈtɜːnl/ *adj* eterno; (colloq) ⟨noise/complaints⟩ constante

eternity /ɪˈtɜːrnəti ‖ ɪˈtɜːnəti/ *n* (*pl* **-ties**) eternidad *f*

ethereal /ɪˈθɪriəl ‖ ɪˈθɪəriəl/ *adj* (liter) etéreo (liter)

ethical /ˈeθɪkəl/ *adj* ⟨dilemma⟩ ético; ⟨code⟩ de conducta

ethics /ˈeθɪks/ *n* **1** (Phil) (+ *sing vb*) ética *f* **2** (+ *pl vb*) (morality) ética *f*

Ethiopia /ˌiːθiˈəʊpiə/ *n* Etiopía *f*

Ethiopian /ˌiːθiˈəʊpiən/ *adj* etíope

ethnic /ˈeθnɪk/ *adj* ⟨origin/group⟩ étnico; ⟨culture/art/vote⟩ de las minorías étnicas; **an** ~ **minority** una minoría étnica; ~ **cleansing** limpieza *f* étnica

etiquette /ˈetɪket/ *n* etiqueta *f*

etymology /ˌetəˈmɒlədʒi ‖ ˌetɪˈmɒlədʒi/ *n* (*pl* **-gies**) etimología *f*

EU *n* = **European Union**

eucalyptus /ˌjuːkəˈlɪptəs/ *n* (*pl* **-tuses**) eucalipto *m*

Eucharist /ˈjuːkərəst ‖ ˈjuːkərɪst/ *n* Eucaristía *f*

eulogy /ˈjuːlədʒi/ *n* (*pl* **-gies**) (liter) elogio *m*, loa *f* (liter)

eunuch /ˈjuːnək/ *n* eunuco *m*

euphemism /ˈjuːfəmɪzəm/ *n* eufemismo *m*

euphemistic /ˌjuːfəˈmɪstɪk/ *adj* eufemístico

euphoria /juːˈfɔːriə/ *n* euforia *f*

euphoric /juːˈfɔːrɪk ‖ juːˈfɒrɪk/ *adj* eufórico

euro /ˈjʊərəʊ ‖ ˈjʊərəʊ/ *n* (*pl* **euros**) euro *m*

eurocheque /ˈjʊərəʊtʃek ‖ ˈjʊərəʊtʃek/ *n* (BrE) eurocheque *m*

Europe /ˈjʊərəp ‖ ˈjʊərəp/ *n* **(a)** (Geog) Europa *f* **(b)** (the EC) (BrE) Europa *f*

European¹ /ˌjʊərəˈpiːən ‖ ˌjʊərəˈpiən/ *adj* europeo

European² *n* europeo, -pea *m,f*

European: ~ **Commission** *n* Comisión *f* Europea, Comisión *f* de las Comunidades Europeas; ~ **Currency Unit** *n* unidad *f* monetaria europea; ~ (**Economic**) **Community** *n* Comunidad *f* (Económica) Europea; ~ **Union** *n* Unión *f* Europea

euthanasia /ˌjuːθəˈneɪzə ‖ ˌjuːθəˈneɪziə/ *n* eutanasia *f*

evacuate /ɪˈvækjueɪt/ *vt* evacuar*

evacuation /ɪˌvækjuˈeɪʃən/ *n* evacuación *f*

evade /ɪˈveɪd/ *vt* ⟨arrest/enemy/responsibility⟩ eludir, evadir; ⟨question/issue⟩ eludir; ⟨regulations/military service⟩ eludir; ⟨taxes⟩ evadir

evaluate /ɪˈvæljueɪt/ *vt* **(a)** ⟨ability/data⟩ evaluar* **(b)** (value) (AmE) valorar, tasar, avaluar* (AmL)

evangelical /ˌiːvænˈdʒelɪkəl/ *adj* evangélico

evaporate /ɪˈvæpəreɪt/ *vi* «liquid/support/ opposition» evaporarse; «hope/fear» desvanecerse*; «confidence» esfumarse

evaporated milk /ɪˈvæpəreɪtəd ‖ ɪˈvæpəreɪtɪd/ *n* leche *f* evaporada, leche *f* condensada (sin azúcar)

evasion /ɪˈveɪʒən/ *n* evasión *f*

evasive /ɪˈveɪsɪv/ *adj* ⟨reply⟩ evasivo

eve /iːv/ *n* (day, night before) (liter or journ) víspera *f*

even¹ /ˈiːvən/ *adv* **1** **(a)** hasta, incluso **(b)** (with neg): **he can't** ~ **sew a button on** no sabe ni pegar un botón; **you're not** ~ **trying** ni siquiera lo estás intentando **(c)** (with comparative) aún, todavía **2** (in phrases) **even if** aunque (+ *subj*); **even so** aun así; **even though** aun cuando, a pesar de que

even² *adj* **1** **(a)** (flat, smooth) ⟨ground/surface⟩ plano; ⟨coat of paint⟩ uniforme **(b)** (regular, uniform) ⟨color/lighting⟩ uniforme, parejo (AmL); ⟨breathing⟩ acompasado; ⟨temperature⟩ constante **2** (equal) ⟨distribution⟩ equitativo; **to break** ~ recuperar los gastos; **to get** ~ desquitarse; **I'll get** ~ **with her** me las pagará **3** (divisible by two) ⟨number⟩ par

even³ *vt* **1** (level) ⟨surface⟩ allanar, nivelar **2** (make equal) ⟨score⟩ igualar; ⟨contest/situation⟩ equilibrar

■ **even out** **1** [*v* + *o* + *adv*, *v* + *adv* + *o*] compensar, nivelar **2** [*v* + *adv*] compensarse, nivelarse

■ **even up** [*v* + *o* + *adv*, *v* + *adv* + *o*] ⟨numbers/ amounts⟩ equilibrar

evening /ˈiːvnɪŋ/ *n* **1** **(a)** (after dark) noche *f*; (before dark) tarde *f*; **good** ~ (early on) buenas tardes; (later) buenas noches; (before n) ~ **meal** cena *f* **(b)** (period of entertainment) velada *f* (frml), noche *f* **2** **evenings** (as adv) (before dark) por la tarde, en la tarde (AmL), a la tarde or de tarde (RPl); (after dark) por la noche, de noche, en la noche (AmL)

evening: ∼ **class** n clase f nocturna; ∼ **dress** n (a) (for woman) traje m de noche (b) (formal wear) traje m de etiqueta

evenly /'iːvənli/ adv ① (equally) ⟨distribute/ divide⟩ equitativamente; ⟨spread⟩ uniformemente ② (a) (calmly) ⟨say/speak⟩ sin alterar la voz (b) (steadily) ⟨breathe⟩ con regularidad

event /ɪ'vent/ n ① (a) (happening, incident) acontecimiento m (b) (Sport) prueba f ② (in phrases) **in the event: in the** ∼ **of the reactor becoming overheated** en caso de que el reactor se recalentara; **in any event** en todo caso; **at all events** de cualquier modo

eventful /ɪ'ventfəl/ adj ⟨week⟩ lleno de incidentes; ⟨life⟩ rico en experiencias

eventuality /ɪ'ventʃu'æləti/ n (pl -ties) eventualidad f

eventually /ɪ'ventʃuəli/ adv finalmente, al final

ever /'evər ǁ 'evə(r)/ adv ① (at any time): **have you** ∼ **visited London?** ¿has estado en Londres (alguna vez)?; **nobody** ∼ **comes to see me** nunca viene nadie a verme; **hardly** ∼ casi nunca ② (after comp or superl): **these are our worst** ∼ **results** estos son los peores resultados que hemos tenido hasta ahora; **the situation is worse than** ∼ la situación está peor que nunca ③ (always, constantly) **as ever** como siempre; **ever since:** ∼ **since we first saw her** desde que la vimos por primera vez; **we've been friends** ∼ **since** somos amigos desde entonces; **for ever** para siempre ④ (as intensifier): **when will you** ∼ **learn?** ¿cuándo vas a aprender?; **thanks** ∼ **so much** (esp BrE colloq) muchísimas gracias

ever-: ∼**green** adj ⟨tree/shrub⟩ de hoja perenne; ∼**lasting** /evər'læstɪŋ ǁ evə'lɑːstɪŋ/ adj eterno

every /'evri/ adj ① (each): ∼ **room was searched** se registraron todas las habitaciones; ∼ **minute is precious** cada minuto es precioso; **she comes** ∼ **month** viene todos los meses ② (indicating recurrence) cada; ∼ **three days**, ∼ **third day** cada tres días; ∼ **other day** un día sí, otro no, día por medio (CS, Per); ∼ **so often** cada tanto, de vez en cuando ③ (very great, all possible): **they have** ∼ **confidence in us** confían plenamente en nosotros; **she made** ∼ **effort to satisfy him** hizo lo indecible por satisfacerlo

everybody /'evri,bɑːdi ǁ 'evri,bɒdi/ pron todos; **is that** ∼? ¿están todos?, ¿está todo el mundo?

everyday /'evri'deɪ/ adj (before n) ⟨occurrence/ problems/activities⟩ de todos los días, cotidiano; ⟨suit/clothes⟩ de diario; ⟨expression⟩ corriente, de todos los días; ⟨life⟩ diario , cotidiano

everyone /'evriwʌn/ pron ▶ EVERYBODY

everything /'evriθɪŋ/ pron todo

everywhere /'evrihwer ǁ 'evriweə(r)/ adv ⟨be⟩ en todas partes; **I've looked** ∼ **for it** lo he buscado por todas partes or por todos lados; **they go** ∼ **by car** van a todos lados or a todas partes en coche

evict /ɪ'vɪkt/ vt ⟨tenant/squatter⟩ desahuciar, desalojar; ⟨demonstrators⟩ desalojar

eviction /ɪ'vɪkʃən/ n (of tenant, squatter) desalojo m, desahucio m

evidence /'evədəns ǁ 'evɪdəns/ n ① (Law) (a) (proof) pruebas fpl (b) (testimony) testimonio m; **to give** ∼ declarar declaración ② (sign, indication) indicio m, señal f

evident /'evədənt ǁ 'evɪdənt/ adj evidente

evidently /'evədəntli ǁ 'evɪdəntli/ adv (a) (embarrassed/unsuitable) claramente, obviamente (b) (indep) aparentemente, según parece

evil¹ /'iːvəl/ adj ⟨demon/wizard⟩ malvado; ⟨deeds/thoughts/character⟩ de gran maldad; ⟨influence⟩ maléfico; ⟨plan/suggestion⟩ diabólico; ⟨spirit⟩ maligno

evil² n mal m

evildoer /'iːvəl'duːər ǁ 'iːvəl,duːə(r)/ n malhechor, -chora m,f

evocative /ɪ'vɑːkətɪv ǁ ɪ'vɒkətɪv/ adj evocador

evoke /ɪ'vəʊk/ vt ⟨response/admiration/ sympathy⟩ provocar*; ⟨memories/associations⟩ evocar*

evolution /evə'luːʃən ǁ ,iːvə'luːʃən/ n evolución f

evolve /ɪ'vɑːlv ǁ ɪ'vɒlv/ vi evolucionar

ewe /juː/ n oveja f (hembra)

ex- /'eks/ pref ex(-); ∼**wife** ex(-)esposa

exact¹ /ɪg'zækt/ adj (a) (precise) ⟨number/size/ time/date⟩ exacto (b) (accurate) ⟨description/ definition⟩ preciso

exact² vt ⟨promise⟩ arrancar*; **he** ∼**ed his revenge** se vengó

exacting /ɪg'zæktɪŋ/ adj ⟨work/job⟩ que exige mucho; ⟨supervisor/employer⟩ exigente; ⟨standards/conditions⟩ riguroso

exactly /ɪg'zæktli/ adv ⟨measure/calculate⟩ exactamente; **at** ∼ **six-thirty** a las seis y media en punto

exaggerate /ɪg'zædʒəreɪt/ vi/t exagerar

exaggeration /ɪg'zædʒə'reɪʃən/ n exageración f

exalt /ɪg'zɔːlt/ vt (fml) (a) (elevate) exaltar (fml), elevar (b) (praise) ensalzar*, exaltar (fml)

exam /ɪg'zæm/ n ▶ EXAMINATION 1

examination /ɪg'zæmə'neɪʃən ǁ ɪg,zæmɪ'neɪʃən/ n ① (Educ) (fml) examen m ② (a) (inspection — of accounts) revisión f, inspección f; (— of passports) control m; (— by doctor) reconocimiento m, examen m, revisación f (RPl) (b) (study, investigation) examen m; **on closer** ∼ al examinarlo más de cerca

examine /ɪg'zæmən ǁ ɪg'zæmɪn/ vt ① (a) (inspect) examinar; ⟨accounts⟩ inspeccionar, revisar; ⟨baggage⟩ registrar, revisar (AmL) (b) (Med, Dent) examinar, revisar (AmL) (c) (study, investigate) examinar, estudiar ② (a) (Educ) examinar (b) (Law) ⟨witness/accused⟩ interrogar*

examiner /ɪg'zæmənər ǁ ɪg'zæmɪnə(r)/ n examinador, -dora m,f

example /ɪg'zæmpəl ǁ ɪg'zɑːmpəl/ n ① (specimen, sample) ejemplo m; **for** ∼ por ejemplo ② (a) (model) ejemplo m (b) (warning): **to make an** ∼ **of sb** darle* un castigo ejemplar a algn

exasperated /ɪg'zæspəreɪtəd ǁ ɪg'zæspəreɪtɪd/ adj exasperado

exasperating /ɪg'zæspəreɪtɪŋ/ adj exasperante

exasperation /ɪg'zæspə'reɪʃən/ n exasperación f

excavate /'ekskəveɪt/ vt/i excavar

excavation /ˌekskə'veɪʃən/ n excavación f

exceed /ɪk'siːd/ vt (a) (be greater than) exceder de (b) (go beyond) ⟨limit/minimum⟩ rebasar; ⟨expectations/hopes⟩ superar; ⟨powers⟩ (frml) excederse en

excel /ɪk'sel/ -ll- vi to ~ AT/IN sth destacar* EN algo
■ v refl to ~ oneself lucirse*

excellence /'eksələns/ n excelencia f

excellent /'eksələnt/ adj excelente; (Educ) sobresaliente

except /ɪk'sept/ prep (a) (apart from): ~ (for) menos, excepto, salvo (b) ~ for (if it weren't for) si no fuera por

exception /ɪk'sepʃən/ n 1 excepción f 2 (offense): to take ~ to sth ofenderse por algo

exceptional /ɪk'sepʃnəl ‖ɪk'sepʃənl/ adj excepcional

excerpt /'eksɜːrpt ‖'eksɜːpt/ n pasaje m

excess¹ /ɪk'ses/ n 1 (no pl) exceso m 2 (surplus) excedente m; in ~ of superior a

excess² /ɪk'ses ‖'ekses/ adj: ~ baggage/weight exceso m de equipaje/de peso

excessive /ɪk'sesɪv/ adj ⟨price/charges⟩ excesivo; ⟨demands/pressure/interest⟩ exagerado

exchange¹ /ɪks'tʃeɪndʒ/ n 1 (a) (of information, greetings, insults) intercambio m; (of prisoners, hostages) canje m; in ~ for sth a cambio de algo (b) (of students) intercambio m (c) (dialogue) intercambio m de palabras (d) (of currency) cambio m 2 (Telec) (telephone ~) central f telefónica

exchange² vt (a) (give in place of) to ~ sth FOR sth cambiar algo por algo (b) ⟨information/addresses⟩ intercambiar(se); ⟨blows⟩ darse*; ⟨insults⟩ intercambiar; ⟨prisoners/hostages⟩ canjear

exchange rate n tasa f or (esp Esp) tipo m de cambio

Exchequer /'ekstʃekər ‖ɪks'tʃekə(r)/ n (in UK) the ~ el tesoro público, el erario público; see also CHANCELLOR A

excise /'eksaɪz/ n impuestos mpl internos

excitable /ɪk'saɪtəbəl/ adj excitable

excite /ɪk'saɪt/ vt 1 (a) (make happy, enthusiastic) entusiasmar; (make impatient, boisterous) ⟨children⟩ alborotar (b) (sexually) excitar 2 ⟨interest/admiration⟩ despertar*; ⟨envy/curiosity⟩ provocar*

excited /ɪk'saɪtəd ‖ɪk'saɪtɪd/ adj (a) (happy, enthusiastic) ⟨person⟩ entusiasmado, excitado; ⟨shouts⟩ de excitación or entusiasmo; to get ~ entusiasmarse (b) (nervous, worried) ⟨person⟩ excitado, agitado; ⟨voice/gesture⟩ vehemente, ansioso (c) (impatient, boisterous) ⟨children⟩ excitado, alborotado (d) (sexually) excitado

excitement /ɪk'saɪtmənt/ n (enthusiasm, happiness) excitación f, entusiasmo m; (agitation) agitación f, alboroto m

exciting /ɪk'saɪtɪŋ/ adj ⟨events/experience⟩ emocionante; ⟨film/story⟩ apasionante

exclaim /ɪk'skleɪm/ vi/t exclamar

exclamation /ˌeksklə'meɪʃən/ n exclamación f

exclamation point, (BrE) **exclamation mark** n signo m de admiración

exclude /ɪk'skluːd/ vt excluir*

excluding /ɪk'skluːdɪŋ/ prep sin incluir, excluyendo

exclusion /ɪk'skluːʒən/ n exclusión f

exclusive /ɪk'skluːsɪv/ adj 1 ⟨rights/ownership/privileges⟩ exclusivo; ⟨story/interview⟩ en exclusiva 2 ⟨club/gathering⟩ selecto, exclusivo

excommunicate /ˌekskə'mjuːnəkeɪt ‖ˌekskə'mjuːnɪkeɪt/ vt excomulgar*

excrement /'ekskrəmənt ‖'ekskrɪmənt/ n (frml) excremento m (frml)

excruciating /ɪk'skruːʃieɪtɪŋ/ adj ⟨pain⟩ atroz; ⟨boredom/embarrassment⟩ espantoso

excursion /ɪk'skɜːrʒən ‖ɪk'skɜːʃən/ n excursión f

excuse¹ /ɪk'skjuːz/ vt 1 (a) (forgive) ⟨mistake/misconduct⟩ disculpar, perdonar; ~ me! ¡perdón!; ~ me, please (con) permiso (b) (justify) ⟨conduct/rudeness⟩ excusar, justificar* 2 (release from obligation) disculpar; to ~ sb (FROM) sth dispensar a algn DE algo

excuse² /ɪk'skjuːs/ n excusa f; to make ~s poner* excusas

ex-directory /'eksdaɪˈrektəri, -də- ‖ˌeksdaɪˈrektəri, -dɪ-/ adj (BrE Telec) que no figura en la guía telefónica, privado (Méx)

execute /'eksɪkjuːt/ vt 1 (a) (carry out, perform) ejecutar; ⟨duties⟩ desempeñar 2 (put to death) ejecutar

execution /ˌeksɪ'kjuːʃən/ n 1 (of order, plan) ejecución f; (of duties) desempeño m 2 (putting to death) ejecución f

executioner /'eksɪˈkjuːʃnər ‖ˌeksɪ'kjuːʃənə(r)/ n verdugo m

executive¹ /ɪg'zekjʊtɪv ‖ɪg'zekjʊtɪv/ adj 1 (Adm, Busn) (managerial) ejecutivo; ⟨washroom/suite/jet⟩ para ejecutivos; ⟨car/briefcase⟩ de ejecutivo 2 (Govt) ⟨powers/branch⟩ ejecutivo

executive² n 1 (manager) ejecutivo, -va m,f 2 (a) (branch of government) the ~ el (poder) ejecutivo (b) (~ committee) (esp BrE) comisión f directiva

executor /ɪg'zekjətər ‖ɪg'zekjʊtə(r)/ n albacea mf, testamentario, -ria m,f

exemplify /ɪg'zempləfaɪ ‖ɪg'zemplɪfaɪ/ vt -fies, -fying, -fied (a) (give example of) ejemplificar* (b) (be example of) demostrar*

exempt /ɪg'zempt/ adj: to be ~ FROM sth estar* exento DE algo

exemption /ɪg'zempʃən/ n ~ FROM sth exención f or exoneración f DE algo

exercise¹ /'eksərsaɪz ‖'eksəsaɪz/ n 1 (physical) ejercicio m; to take ~ hacer* ejercicio 2 (Sport, Educ) ejercicio m; (Mil) ejercicios mpl, maniobras fpl 3 (undertaking): a public relations ~ una operación de relaciones públicas 4 (use — of rights, power) (frml) ejercicio m; (— of caution, patience) uso m

exercise² vt 1 ⟨body⟩ ejercitar; ⟨dog⟩ pasear; ⟨horse⟩ ejercitar 2 ⟨power/control/right⟩ ejercer*; ⟨patience/tact⟩ hacer* uso de
■ ~ vi hacer* ejercicio

exercise book n cuaderno m

exert /ɪgˈzɜːrt ‖ɪgˈzɜːt/ vt ejercer*; ‹force› emplear
■ v refl to ~ oneself hacer* un (gran) esfuerzo
exertion /ɪgˈzɜːrʃən ‖ɪgˈzɜːʃən/ n (often pl) esfuerzo m
exhale /eksˈheɪl/ vi espirar
exhaust[1] /ɪgˈzɔːst/ n (a) (~ pipe) tubo m or (RPl) caño m de escape, mofle m (AmC, Méx), exhosto m (Col) (b) (system) escape m, exhosto m (Col) (c) (fumes) gases mpl del tubo de escape
exhaust[2] vt agotar
exhausted /ɪgˈzɔːstəd ‖ɪgˈzɔːstɪd/ adj agotado
exhausting /ɪgˈzɔːstɪŋ/ adj agotador
exhaustion /ɪgˈzɔːstʃən/ n agotamiento m
exhaustive /ɪgˈzɔːstɪv/ adj (frml) exhaustivo
exhibit[1] /ɪgˈzɪbət ‖ɪgˈzɪbɪt/ vt [1] ‹goods/paintings› exponer* [2] (frml) ‹skill/dexterity› demostrar*; ‹fear/courage› mostrar*; ‹symptoms› presentar
exhibit[2] n (a) (in gallery, museum) objeto en exposición (b) (Law) documento u objeto que se exhibe en un juicio como prueba (c) (exhibition) (AmE) exposición f
exhibition /ˌeksəˈbɪʃən ‖ˌeksɪˈbɪʃən/ n (of paintings, goods) exposición f; to make an ~ of oneself dar* un espectáculo
exhilarate /ɪgˈzɪləreɪt/ vt (a) (make happy) llenar de júbilo (b) (stimulate) tonificar*
exhilarating /ɪgˈzɪləreɪtɪŋ/ adj ‹experience› excitante; ‹climate› tonificante
exile[1] /ˈeksaɪl/ n (a) (person — voluntary) exiliado, -da m,f, exilado, -da m,f; (— expelled) desterrado, -da m,f, exiliado, -da m,f, exilado, -da m,f (b) (state) exilio m, destierro m
exile[2] vt desterrar*, exiliar, exilar
exist /ɪgˈzɪst/ vi [1] (be real) existir [2] (survive) subsistir
existence /ɪgˈzɪstəns/ n [1] (being) existencia f; this is the only copy in ~ este es el único ejemplar existente [2] (life) vida f, existencia f
existing /ɪgˈzɪstɪŋ/ adj existente
exit /ˈegzət ‖ˈeksɪt/ n salida f
exodus /ˈeksədəs/ n (no pl) éxodo m
exorbitant /ɪgˈzɔːrbətənt ‖ɪgˈzɔːbɪtənt/ adj (frml) ‹price/rent› exorbitante
exorcize /ˈeksɔːrsaɪz ‖ˈeksɔːsaɪz/ vt exorcizar*
exotic /ɪgˈzɑːtɪk ‖ɪgˈzɒtɪk/ adj exótico
expand /ɪkˈspænd/ vt [1] (enlarge) expandir; ‹lungs› ensanchar; ‹chest› desarrollar; ‹horizons› ampliar*; ‹influence/role› extender* [2] ‹story/summary› ampliar*
■ ~ vi (a) «metal/gas» expandirse; «elastic/rubber band» estirarse (b) **expanding** pres p ‹industry/market» en expansión
expanse /ɪkˈspæns/ n extensión f
expansion /ɪkˈspæntʃən ‖ɪkˈspænʃən/ n expansión f
expatriate /eksˈpeɪtriət ‖eksˈpætriət/ n expatriado, -da m,f
expect /ɪkˈspekt/ vt [1] (anticipate) esperar; is he

coming tonight? — I ~ so ¿va a venir esta noche? — supongo que sí; we're not ~ing any trouble no creemos que vaya a haber problemas; to ~ to + INF: she ~s to win the match espera ganar el partido [2] (imagine) suponer*, imaginarse [3] (await) esperar; I'll ~ you at eight te espero a las ocho; to be ~ing a baby esperar un bebé [4] (require): he ~ed me to pay esperaba que yo pagara; that's the least you'd ~ es lo menos que se puede esperar
■ ~ vi (colloq): she's ~ing está esperando (familia)
expectancy /ɪkˈspektənsi/ n expectación f; life ~ esperanza f or expectativas fpl de vida
expectant /ɪkˈspektənt/ adj expectante
expectation /ˌekspekˈteɪʃən/ n [1] (anticipation): in ~ of victory previendo la victoria; an atmosphere of great ~ un ambiente de gran expectación [2] **expectations** pl (of inheritance, promotion) expectativas fpl
expedient[1] /ɪkˈspiːdiənt/ adj (frml) (usu pred) conveniente
expedient[2] n (frml) recurso m, expediente m (frml)
expedition /ˌekspəˈdɪʃən ‖ˌekspɪˈdɪʃən/ n expedición f
expel /ɪkˈspel/ vt -ll- expulsar
expendable /ɪkˈspendəbəl/ adj prescindible
expenditure /ɪkˈspendɪtʃər ‖ɪkˈspendɪtʃə(r)/ n (amount) gastos mpl, (spending) gasto m
expense /ɪkˈspens/ n [1] (cost, outlay) gasto m; they had a good laugh at my ~ se partieron de risa a costa mía; at the ~ of sth/sb (with the loss of) a expensas de algo/algn [2] **expenses** pl (Busn) (incidental costs) gastos mpl
expense account n cuenta f de gastos de representación
expensive /ɪkˈspensɪv/ adj caro
experience[1] /ɪkˈspɪriəns ‖ɪkˈspɪəriəns/ n experiencia f
experience[2] vt ‹loss/setback/delays› sufrir; ‹difficulty› tener*; ‹change/improvement/pleasure/pain› experimentar
experienced /ɪkˈspɪriənst ‖ɪkˈspɪəriənst/ adj ‹secretary/chef› con experiencia; ‹driver› experimentado
experiment[1] /ɪkˈsperəmənt ‖ɪkˈsperɪmənt/ n experimento m
experiment[2] vi to ~ ON sth/sb experimentar CON algo/algn; to ~ WITH sth experimentar CON algo
experimental /ɪkˌsperəˈmentl̩ ‖ɪkˌsperɪˈmentl̩/ adj experimental
expert[1] /ˈekspɜːrt ‖ˈekspɜːt/ n experto, -ta m,f
expert[2] adj experto; ~ witness perito, -ta m,f
expertise /ˌekspɜːrˈtiːz ‖ˌekspɜːˈtiːz/ n pericia f
expire /ɪkˈspaɪr ‖ɪkˈspaɪə(r)/ vi (run out) «visa/passport/ticket» caducar*; «lease/contract» vencer*

expiry /ɪkˈspaɪri ‖ɪkˈspaɪəri/ n vencimiento m, caducidad f

explain /ɪkˈspleɪn/ vt.explicar*
■ v refl to ∼ oneself explicarse*
■ **explain away** [v + o + adv, v + adv + o] ⟨fact/ result⟩ encontrar* una explicación convincente para

explanation /ˈekspləˈneɪʃən/ n explicación f

explanatory /ɪkˈsplænətɔːri ‖ɪkˈsplænətri/ adj explicativo

explicit /ɪkˈsplɪsət ‖ɪkˈsplɪsɪt/ adj explícito; ⟨denial/refutation⟩ categórico

explode /ɪkˈspləʊd/ vi (a) «gunpowder/bomb» estallar, hacer* explosión, explotar; «vehicle» hacer* explosión; (with emotion) explotar, estallar (b) «population/costs» dispararse
■ ∼ vt [1] ⟨bomb/dynamite⟩ explosionar, hacer* explotar or estallar [2] (discredit) ⟨theory⟩ rebatir; ⟨myth⟩ destruir*

exploit[1] /ɪkˈsplɔɪt/ vt explotar; ⟨situation/ relationship⟩ aprovecharse de

exploit[2] /ˈeksplɔɪt/ n hazaña f

exploitation /ˈeksplɔɪˈteɪʃən/ n explotación f

exploration /ˈekspləˈreɪʃən/ n exploración f

exploratory /ɪkˈsplɔːrətɔːri ‖ɪkˈsplɒrətəri/ adj ⟨talks⟩ preliminar; ⟨surgery⟩ exploratorio

explore /ɪkˈsplɔːr ‖ɪkˈsplɔː(r)/ vt ⟨territory/ town⟩ explorar; ⟨topic/possibility⟩ investigar*

explorer /ɪkˈsplɔːrər ‖ɪkˈsplɔːrə(r)/ n (a) (traveler) explorador, -dora m,f (b) **Explorer** (in US) boy scout m (mayor de 14 años)

explosion /ɪkˈspləʊʒən/ n (of bomb, gas) explosión f, estallido m; (of anger) estallido m, explosión f

explosive[1] /ɪkˈspləʊsɪv/ adj explosivo

explosive[2] n explosivo m

exponent /ɪkˈspəʊnənt/ n (of idea, theory) defensor, -sora m,f; (of art style) exponente mf

export[1] /ekˈspɔːrt ‖ɪkˈspɔːt/ vt exportar

export[2] /ˈekspɔːrt ‖ˈekspɔːt/ n (a) (item exported) artículo m or producto m de exportación (b) (act of exporting) exportación f

exporter /ekˈspɔːrtər ‖ɪkˈspɔːtə(r)/ n exportador, -dora m,f

expose /ɪkˈspəʊz/ vt [1] (lay bare) ⟨nerve/wire/ wound⟩ exponer*; to ∼ oneself to criticism exponerse* a las críticas [2] (uncover) ⟨secret/ scandal⟩ poner* al descubierto, sacar* a la luz; ⟨inefficiency/weaknesses⟩ poner* en evidencia; ⟨criminal⟩ desenmascarar [3] (Phot) exponer*

exposition /ˈekspəˈzɪʃən/ n exposición f

exposure /ɪkˈspəʊʒər ‖ɪkˈspəʊʒə(r)/ n [1] (a) (contact) ∼ ᴛᴏ sth exposición f ᴀ algo (b) (Med) congelación f; to die from ∼ morir* de frío [2] (a) (unmasking): she was threatened with public ∼ amenazaron con ponerla al descubierto (b) (publicity) publicidad f [3] (Phot) exposición f

expound /ɪkˈspaʊnd/ vt (fml) exponer*

express[1] /ɪkˈspres/ vt expresar

express[2] n (train) expreso m, rápido m; (bus) directo m

express[3] adj [1] (fast) ⟨train⟩ expreso, rápido; ⟨bus⟩ directo; ⟨delivery/letter⟩ exprés adj inv [2] (specific) (fml) ⟨intention/wish⟩ expreso

expression /ɪkˈspreʃən/ n expresión f

expressive /ɪkˈspresɪv/ adj expresivo

expressly /ɪkˈspresli/ adv (fml) expresamente

expressway /ɪkˈspresweɪ/ n (AmE) autopista f; (urban) vía f rápida

expropriate /eksˈprəʊprieɪt/ vt expropiar

expulsion /ɪkˈspʌlʃən/ n expulsión f

exquisite /ekˈskwɪzət ‖ˈekskwɪzɪt/ adj (a) ⟨dress/meal/taste⟩ exquisito; ⟨carving/brooch⟩ de exquisita factura; ⟨work/workmanship⟩ intrincado (b) ⟨pleasure⟩ infinito

ex-serviceman /ˈeksˈsɜːrvəsmən ‖ˌeksˈsɜːvɪsmən/ n (pl **-men** /-mən/) soldado (or marinero etc) m retirado

extend /ɪkˈstend/ vt [1] (a) (stretch out) ⟨limbs/ wings/telescope⟩ extender*; ⟨rope/wire⟩ tender* (b) (lengthen) ⟨road/line/visit⟩ prolongar*; ⟨lease/ contract/deadline⟩ prorrogar* (c) (enlarge) ⟨house/ room⟩ ampliar*; ⟨range/scope/influence⟩ extender* [2] (offer) (fml): to ∼ an invitation to sb invitar a algn; (of written invitations) cursarle invitación a algn (fml)
■ ∼ vi (a) (stretch) «fence/property/influence» extenderse* (b) (in time) «talks» prolongarse* (c) (become extended) «ladder/antenna» extenderse*

extension /ɪkˈstentʃən ‖ɪkˈstenʃən/ n [1] (a) (of power, meaning) extensión f (b) (lengthening) prolongación f; (of deadline) prórroga f, extensión f [2] (to building) ampliación f [3] (Telec) (a) (line) extensión f, interno m (RPl), anexo m (Chi) (b) (telephone) supletorio m

extension cord, (BrE) **extension lead** n extensión f, alargador m, alargue m (RPl)

extensive /ɪkˈstensɪv/ adj ⟨area/field⟩ extenso; ⟨knowledge⟩ vasto; ⟨experience/coverage⟩ amplio; ⟨search/inquiries⟩ exhaustivo; ⟨damage/repairs⟩ de consideración

extensively /ɪkˈstensɪvli/ adv (a) (widely): he's traveled ∼ ha viajado por todas partes; this technique is used ∼ esta técnica es de uso extendido (b) (thoroughly, at length) ⟨research/ investigate⟩ exhaustivamente

extent /ɪkˈstent/ n [1] (size, area) extensión f [2] (range, degree — of knowledge) amplitud f; (— of problem) alcance m; to some ∼ hasta cierto punto; to a large ∼ en gran parte

extenuate /ɪkˈstenjueɪt/ vt (fml) atenuar*; extenuating circumstances circunstancias fpl atenuantes, atenuantes mpl or fpl

exterior[1] /ekˈstɪriər ‖ɪkˈstɪəriə(r)/ adj ⟨wall/ surface⟩ exterior

exterior[2] n exterior m

exterminate /ɪkˈstɜːrməneɪt ‖ɪkˈstɜːmɪneɪt/ vt exterminar

external /ekˈstɜːrn̩ ‖ɪkˈstɜːn̩/ adj (a) (exterior) ⟨appearance/sign⟩ externo, exterior; ⟨wall⟩ exterior; ⟨wound/treatment⟩ externo (b) ⟨aid/ influence⟩ del exterior; ⟨pressure/evidence⟩ externo (c) (foreign) ⟨affairs/trade/policy⟩ exterior

extinct /ɪkˈstɪŋkt/ adj ⟨animal/species⟩ extinto, desaparecido; ⟨volcano⟩ extinto, apagado

extinction /ɪkˈstɪŋkʃən/ n extinción f

extinguish /ɪkˈstɪŋgwɪʃ/ vt (a) ⟨fire⟩ extinguir*; ⟨candle/cigar⟩ apagar* (b) (liter) ⟨hope/ memory⟩ apagar* (liter); ⟨passion/life⟩ extinguir* (liter)

extinguisher /ɪkˈstɪŋgwɪʃər ‖ɪkˈstɪŋgwɪʃə(r)/ n (fire ∼) extinguidor m (AmL), extintor m (Esp)

extortion /ɪk'stɔːrʃən ‖ɪk'stɔːʃən/ *n* extorsión *f*

extortionate /ɪk'stɔːrʃənət ‖ɪk'stɔːʃənət/ *adj* ⟨*fee/price*⟩ abusivo; ⟨*demand*⟩ excesivo

extra¹ /'ekstrə/ *adj* **(a)** (additional) (*before n*) de más; **we need ∼ staff** necesitamos más personal; **at no ∼ charge** sin cargo adicional; **they organized three ∼ flights** organizaron tres vuelos adicionales; **∼ time** (in soccer) prórroga *f* **(b)** (especial) (*before n*) ⟨*care/caution*⟩ especial

extra² *adv* **(a)** (*as intensifier*): **∼ long** extralargo; **I worked ∼ hard** trabajé más que nunca **(b)** (more): **to charge ∼ for sth** cobrar algo aparte

extra³ *n* **1** (additional payment or expense) extra *m*; **optional ∼s** (Auto) equipamiento *m* opcional, **extras** *mpl* **2** (Cin) extra *mf*

extract¹ /ɪk'strækt/ *vt* extraer*

extract² /'ekstrækt/ *n* **1** (excerpt) fragmento *m* **2** (concentrate) extracto *m*

extraction /ɪk'strækʃən/ *n* **1** **(a)** (Dent) extracción *f* **(b)** (of mineral, juice) extracción *f* **2** (ancestry) extracción *f*; **of Polish ∼** de extracción polaca

extradite /'ekstrədaɪt/ *vt* extraditar

extradition /'ekstrə'dɪʃən/ *n* extradición *f*; (*before n*) ⟨*order/treaty*⟩ de extradición

extraordinary /ɪk'strɔːrdneri ‖ɪk'strɔːdnṛi/ *adj* **1** (exceptional) extraordinario; (very odd) ⟨*sight/appearance*⟩ insólito; (incredible) increíble **2** (frml) (Adm, Govt) ⟨*powers/meeting*⟩ extraordinario

extrapolate /ɪk'stræpəleɪt/ *vt* (frml) extrapolar

extrasensory /'ekstrə'sensəri/ *adj* extrasensorial; **∼ perception** percepción *f* extrasensorial

extravagance /ɪk'strævəgəns/ *n* **1** **(a)** (lavishness, wastefulness) despilfarro *m*, derroche *m* **(b)** (luxury) lujo *m* **2** (of gestures, dress) extravagancia *f*; (of claim, story) lo insólito

extravagant /ɪk'strævəgənt/ *adj* **(a)** (lavish, wasteful) ⟨*person*⟩ derrochador, despilfarrador; ⟨*lifestyle*⟩ de lujo **(b)** ⟨*claim/notions*⟩ insólito; ⟨*praise/compliments*⟩ exagerado; ⟨*behavior/dress/ gesture*⟩ extravagante

extravaganza /ɪk'strævə'gænzə/ *n* gran espectáculo *m* (*realizado con alarde de color, fantasía y dinero*)

extreme¹ /ɪk'striːm/ *adj* **(a)** (very great) ⟨*poverty/caution/urgency*⟩ extremo; ⟨*annoyance/ relief*⟩ enorme; ⟨*heat*⟩ extremado **(b)** (not moderate) ⟨*action/measure*⟩ extremo; ⟨*opinion*⟩ extremista **(c)** (outermost) (*before n*): **in the ∼ north/south** en la zona más septentrional/meridional

extreme² *n* extremo *m*; **∼s of temperature** temperaturas *fpl* extremas

extremely /ɪk'striːmli/ *adv* (*as intensifier*) sumamente; **it's ∼ difficult** es dificilísimo

extremist /ɪk'striːməst ‖ɪk'striːmɪst/ *n* extremista *mf*

extremity /ɪk'streməti/ *n* (*pl* **-ties**) **1** **(a)** (farthest point) extremo *m* **(b)** **extremities** *pl* (Anat) extremidades *fpl* **2** (critical degree, situation) (frml) extremo *m*

extricate /'ekstrəkeɪt ‖'ekstrɪkeɪt/ *vt* sacar* (*con dificultad*)

extrovert¹ /'ekstrəvɜːrt ‖'ekstrəvɜːt/ *adj* extrovertido

extrovert² /'ekstrəvɜːrt ‖'ekstrəvɜːt/ *n* extrovertido, -da *m,f*

exude /ɪg'zuːd ‖ɪg'zjuːd/ *vt* ⟨*resin/fluid*⟩ exudar; ⟨*charm/confidence*⟩ emanar

exult /ɪg'zʌlt/ *vi* (frml) exultar (frml)

exultation /'egzʌl'teɪʃən/ *n* (frml) exultación *f* (frml)

eye¹ /aɪ/ *n* **1** **(a)** (Anat) ojo *m*; **as far as the ∼ can/could see** hasta donde alcanza/alcanzaba la vista; **I can't believe my ∼s** si no lo veo, no lo creo; **to see ∼ to ∼ with sb** (*usu with neg*) estar* de acuerdo con algn; **to be up to one's ∼s in sth** estar* hasta aquí de algo (fam) **(b)** (look, gaze) mirada *f*; **before my very ∼s** ante mis propios ojos; **nothing caught my ∼ in the store** no vi nada que me llamara la atención en la tienda; **to keep an ∼ on sth/sb** vigilar or cuidar algo/a algn **(c)** (attention): **the company has been in the public ∼ a lot recently** últimamente se ha hablado mucho de la compañía; **to have one's ∼ on sth** echarle el ojo a algo (fam) **(d)** (ability to judge) ojo *m*; **to have an ∼ for design** tener* ojo para el diseño **2** **(a)** (of needle) ojo *m* **(b)** (of hurricane, storm) ojo *m* **(c)** (in potato) ojo *m*

eye² *vt* (*pres p* **eying** *or* (BrE) **eyeing**) mirar

eye: ∼ball /'aɪbɔːl/ *n* globo *m* ocular; **∼brow** *n* ceja *f*; **to raise one's ∼brows** arquear las cejas; **to raise one's ∼brows at sth** asombrarse ante algo; **∼catching** *adj* llamativo; **∼drops** *pl n* colirio *m*

eyeful /'aɪfʊl/ *n*: **I got an ∼ of dust** se me llenó el ojo de polvo

eye: ∼glasses *pl n* (AmE) gafas *fpl*, anteojos *mpl* (esp AmL), lentes *mpl* (esp AmL); **∼lash** *n* pestaña *f*

eyelet /'aɪlət ‖'aɪlɪt/ *n* ojete *m*

eye: ∼lid *n* párpado *m*; **∼liner** *n* delineador *m* (de ojos); **∼opener** *n* (colloq) (*no pl*) revelación *f*; **∼shadow** *n* sombra *f* de ojos; **∼sight** *n* vista *f*; **∼sore** *n* monstruosidad *f*, adefesio *m*; **∼strain** *n* fatiga *f* visual; **∼wash** *n* colirio *m*; **it's a lot of ∼wash** (colloq) es un cuento chino (fam); **∼witness** /'aɪ'wɪtnəs ‖'aɪwɪtnɪs/ *n* testigo *mf* ocular

Ff

F, f /ef/ n (a) (letter) F, f f (b) (Mus) fa m
F (= **Fahrenheit**) F
fa /fɑ:/ n (Mus) fa m
FA n (in UK) = **Football Association**
fable /'feɪbəl/ n fábula f
fabric /'fæbrɪk/ n (a) (Tex) tela f (b) (of building, society) estructura f
fabricate /'fæbrɪkeɪt/ vt (a) (invent) inventar(se) (b) (manufacture) fabricar*
fabulous /'fæbjələs ‖'fæbjʊləs/ adj (a) (wonderful) (colloq) magnífico (b) (imaginary) fabuloso
facade, façade /fə'sɑ:d/ n fachada f
face¹ /feɪs/ n [1] (of person, animal) cara f, rostro m; **a new ~** una cara nueva; **in the ~ of stiff opposition** en medio de una fuerte oposición; **to fall flat on one's ~** caerse* de bruces; **to keep a straight ~**: **I could hardly keep a straight ~** casi no podía aguantarme (de) la risa; **to make** o (BrE also) **pull a ~** poner* mala cara; **to put a brave ~ on it** poner(le)* al mal tiempo buena cara; **to sb's ~** a o en la cara
[2] (a) (appearance, nature) (no pl) fisonomía f; **on the ~ of it** aparentemente (b) (dignity): **to lose ~** desprestigiarse; **to save ~** guardar las apariencias
[3] (of coin, medal, solid) cara f; (of clock, watch) esfera f, carátula f (Méx)
[4] (of cliff) pared f; **to disappear off the ~ of the earth** desaparecer* de la faz de la tierra
face² vt [1] (be opposite): **she turned to ~ him** se volvió hacia él; **the hotel ~s the sea** el hotel está frente al mar
[2] (confront) enfrentarse a; **to be ~d with sth** estar* or verse* frente a algo
[3] (a) (be presented with) ‹problem/increase› enfrentarse a (b) (bear): **I can't ~ going through all that again** no podría volver a pasar por todo eso; **I can't ~ food first thing in the morning** no puedo ni oler la comida temprano por la mañana
■ **~** vi: **the house ~s north** la casa está orientada al norte; **I was facing the other way** miraba para el otro lado
■ **face up to** [v + adv + prep + o] afrontar
face: **~cloth,** (BrE also) **~ flannel** n toallita f (para lavarse); **~ lift** n lifting m, estiramiento m (facial); **the building was given a ~ lift** remozaron el edificio; **~ pack** n mascarilla f (de belleza)
facet /'fæsət ‖'fæsɪt/ n faceta f
facetious /fə'si:ʃəs/ adj burlón
face: **~ to ~** adv cara a cara; **~ value** n valor m nominal; **to take sb/sth at ~ value**: **I took her/what she said at ~ value** me fie de ella/yo me creí lo que dijo
facial /'feɪʃəl/ adj facial
facile /'fæsaɪl ‖'fæsɪl/ adj superficial, simplista
facilitate /fə'sɪləteɪt ‖fə'sɪlɪteɪt/ vt (frml) facilitar
facility /fə'sɪləti/ n (pl **-ties**) [1] **facilities** pl:

facilities for the disabled instalaciones fpl para minusválidos; **the hotel has conference facilities** el hotel dispone de sala(s) de conferencia
[2] (building) (AmE) complejo m, centro m
-facing /'feɪsɪŋ/ suff: **north/south~** que da al norte/sur
facsimile /fæk'sɪməli/ n facsímil(e) m
fact /fækt/ n [1] (sth true) hecho m; **hard ~s** datos mpl concretos; **to face (the) ~s** aceptar la realidad [2] (reality): **this novel is based on ~** esta novela está basada en hechos reales; **in ~** de hecho, en realidad; **the ~ of the matter is (that)** ... el hecho es que ...
fact: **~-finding** /'fækt,faɪndɪŋ/ adj (before n) de investigación, investigador; **~ sheet** n resumen m de datos esenciales
faction /'fækʃən/ n facción f
factor /'fæktər ‖'fæktə(r)/ n factor m
factory /'fæktri, -təri/ n (pl **-ries**) fábrica f
factory: **~ farming** n (BrE) cría f intensiva; **~ ship** n buque m factoría
factual /'fæktʃuəl/ adj ‹account› que se atiene a los hechos
faculty /'fækəlti/ n (pl **-ties**) [1] (sense) facultad f [2] (Educ) (a) (of university, college) facultad f (b) (academic personnel) (AmE) cuerpo m docente
fad /fæd/ n moda f pasajera
fade /feɪd/ vi [1] ‹color› apagarse*; ‹fabric› perder* color, desteñirse* [2] (a) (disappear) ‹hope/memories› desvanecerse*; ‹beauty› marchitarse; ‹interest› decaer*; ‹sound› debilitarse (b) ‹flower/plant› ajarse
■ **~** vt ‹fabric› desteñir*, hacer* perder el color a
■ **fade away** [v + adv] irse* apagando
faded /'feɪdəd ‖'feɪdɪd/ adj ‹color› apagado; ‹fabric› desteñido
faeces /'fi:si:z/ pl n (BrE frml) ▶ FECES
fag /fæg/ n [1] (male homosexual) (AmE sl & pej) maricón m (fam & pey) [2] (cigarette) (BrE colloq) cigarrillo m, pitillo m (fam)
fah /fɑ:/ n (BrE Mus) fa m
Fahrenheit /'færənhaɪt/ adj Fahrenheit adj inv
fail¹ /feɪl/ vi [1] (not succeed) ‹marriage/business/plan› fracasar; **if all else ~s** como último recurso; **he ~ed to live up to our expectations** no dio todo lo que se esperaba de él [2] (a) ‹brakes/lights› fallar (b) ‹crop› perderse*, malograrse (c) **failing** pres p: **he could no longer read because of his ~ing eyesight** la vista se le había deteriorado tanto que ya no podía leer; **he retired because of ~ing health** se retiró porque su salud se había deteriorado mucho
[3] (in exam) ser* reprobado (AmL), suspender (Esp)
■ **~** vt [1] (a) ‹exam› no pasar, ser* reprobado en ····▷

(AmL), suspender (Esp), reprobar* (Méx), perder*
(Col, Ur), salir* mal en (Chi) **(b)** ‹student›
reprobar* or (Esp) suspender
2 (let down): **his courage ∼ed him** le faltó valor;
words ∼ me! ¡es el colmo!

fail² n **1** (in exam, test) (BrE) reprobado m or (Esp)
suspenso m or (RPl) aplazo m **2** **without ∼** sin
falta

failing¹ /'feɪlɪŋ/ n defecto m

failing² prep: **∼ that, try bleach** si eso no
resulta, prueba con lejía

fail-safe /'feɪlseɪf/ adj ‹mechanism› de
seguridad

failure /'feɪljər ‖ 'feɪljə(r)/ n (unsuccessful thing,
act, person) fracaso m; **engine ∼** falla f mecánica
or (Esp) fallo m mecánico; **power ∼** apagón m;
heart ∼ insuficiencia f cardíaca; **∼ to carry out
orders** el incumplimiento de las órdenes

faint¹ /feɪnt/ adj **-er, -est** ‹line› apenas visible;
‹light› débil; ‹noise› apenas perceptible; ‹hope/
smile› ligero; **I feel ∼** estoy mareado; **I haven't
the ∼est (idea)** (colloq) no tengo la más mínima
idea

faint² vi desmayarse

faint³ n desmayo m

faintly /'feɪntli/ adv **(a)** (barely perceptibly) ‹see/
hear› apenas; ‹shine› débilmente **(b)** (slightly)
‹amused› ligeramente; ‹amusing/ridiculous› algo

fair¹ /fer ‖ feə(r)/ adj **-er, -est** **1** (just) ‹person/
decision› justo; ‹contest/election› limpio; **∼
enough** bueno, está bien; **I've had my ∼ share of
problems recently** ya he tenido bastantes
problemas últimamente; **∼ and square**: **he won
∼ and square** ganó en buena ley **2** ‹hair›
rubio, güero (Méx), mono (Col), catire (Ven); ‹skin›
blanco **3** (beautiful) (liter) hermoso, bello **4** **(a)**
(quite good) ‹work› pasable; **we have a ∼ chance
of winning** tenemos bastantes posibilidades de
ganar **(b)** (considerable) ‹before n› ‹number/
amount› bueno **5** (Meteo): **the weather tomorrow
will be ∼** mañana va a hacer buen tiempo

fair² adv (impartially) ‹play› limpio, limpiamente

fair³ n **1** (market) feria f; (trade ∼) feria f
industrial/comercial **2** (funfair) (BrE) feria f

fair: **∼ground** n (funfair) (BrE) feria f; (fairground)
parque m de diversiones or (Esp) atracciones;
∼-haired /'fer'herd ‖ ˌfeə'heəd/ adj (BrE) rubio,
güero (Méx), mono (Col), catire (Ven)

fairly /'ferli ‖ 'feəli/ adv **1** (justly) ‹play› limpio;
‹judge› con imparcialidad; ‹divide›
equitativamente **2** (moderately) bastante; **I'm ∼
sure** estoy casi segura

fairness /'fernəs ‖ 'feənɪs/ n imparcialidad f; **in
all ∼** sinceramente

fair: **∼ play** n juego m limpio; **∼-sized**
/'fer'saɪzd ‖ ˌfeə'saɪzd/ adj ‹before n› bastante
grande

fairy /'feri ‖ 'feəri/ n (pl **-ries**) hada f‡

fairy: **∼ godmother** n hada f‡ madrina;
∼land n el país de las hadas; **∼ story, ∼ tale**
n cuento m de hadas

faith /feɪθ/ n **1** (trust) confianza f; **to have ∼ IN
sb/sth** tener* confianza or fe EN algn/algo
2 (Relig) fe f

faithful /'feɪθfəl/ adj fiel

faithfully /'feɪθfəli/ adv **(a)** (in letters): **yours ∼**
(esp BrE) (le saluda) atentamente **(b)** ‹serve/
record› fielmente

faith healer /'hiːlər ‖ 'hiːlə(r)/ n curandero,
-ra m,f

fake¹ /feɪk/ n (object) falsificación f; (person)
farsante mf

fake² adj ‹jewel/document› falso; ‹fur› sintético

fake³ vt ‹document/signature› falsificar*;
‹results/evidence› falsear
■ ∼ vi fingir*

falcon /'fælkən ‖ 'fɔːlkən/ n halcón m

Falkland Islands /'fɔːlklənd/, **Falklands**
/'fɔːlkləndz/ pl n **the ∼∼,the ∼** las (Islas)
Malvinas

fall¹ /fɔːl/ n **1** (tumble, collapse) caída f
2 (autumn) (AmE) otoño m **3** (decrease): **a ∼ in
temperature** un descenso de (las) temperaturas; **a
∼ in prices** una bajada de precios **4** (of snow)
nevada f; (of rocks) desprendimiento m **5** **falls**
pl (waterfall) cascada f; (higher) catarata f

fall² (past **fell**; past p **fallen**) vi **1** **(a)** (tumble)
caerse*; **I fell over a piece of wood** tropecé con un
trozo de madera; **I fell down the stairs** me caí por
la escalera **(b)** (descend) ‹night/rain› caer*
2 ‹temperature/price› bajar; **his face fell** puso
cara larga
3 (be captured, defeated) **to ∼ (TO sb)** ‹city/
country› caer* (en manos de algn)
4 (pass into specified state): **to ∼ ill** o (esp AmE) **sick**
caer* or (Esp tb) ponerse* enfermo, enfermarse
(AmL); **to ∼ silent** callarse
5 (land): **Christmas ∼s on a Thursday this year**
este año Navidad cae en (un) jueves; **the burden
will ∼ on the poor** los pobres serán los que
sufrirán la carga
■ **fall apart** [v + adv] ‹clothing› deshacerse*;
‹system› venirse* abajo; ‹relationship› irse* a
pique
■ **fall back** [v + adv] ‹troops› replegarse*
■ **fall back on** [v + adv + prep + o] ‹one's
parents› recurrir a; ‹resources› echar mano de
■ **fall behind** [v + adv] [v + prep + o] (in class,
race) rezagarse*, quedarse atrás; **to ∼ behind
WITH sth** ‹with payments› atrasarse EN algo
■ **fall down** [v + adv] ‹person/tree› caerse*;
‹house/wall› venirse* abajo
■ **fall for** [v + prep + o] **(a)** (be attracted to) ‹man/
woman› enamorarse de **(b)** (be deceived by) ‹trick/
story› tragarse* (fam)
■ **fall in** [v + adv] **(a)** (tumble in) caerse* (a un
pozo, al agua etc) **(b)** (collapse) ‹roof› venirse*
abajo **(c)** (form ranks) (Mil) formar filas
■ **fall off** [v + adv] **(a)** (tumble down) caerse* (de
una bicicleta, un caballo etc) **(b)** (break off)
‹button/handle› caerse* **(c)** (decline)
‹production/attendance› decaer*

■ **fall out** [v + adv] **(a)** (drop out) caerse* **(b)** (break ranks) (Mil) romper* filas **(c)** (quarrel) «*friends*» pelearse

■ **fall over** [v + adv] «*person/object*» caerse*

■ **fall through** [v + adv] (fail) no salir* adelante

fallacy /'fæləsi/ n (pl **-cies**) falacia f

fallen /'fɔːlən/ past p of FALL²

fallible /'fæləbəl/ adj falible

falling /'fɔːlɪŋ/: ~**-off** /'fɔːlɪŋ'ɔːf ‖ ˌfɔːlɪŋ'ɒf/ n
▶ FALLOFF; ~**-out** /'fɔːlɪŋ'aʊt/ n (AmE) pelea f

falloff /'fɔːlɔːf ‖'fɔːlɒf/ n (no pl) (in speed) disminución f

Fallopian tube /fə'ləʊpiən/ n trompa f de Falopio

fallout /'fɔːlaʊt/ n lluvia f radiactiva; (before n) ~ **shelter** refugio m antinuclear

fallow /'fæləʊ/ adj ‹land› en barbecho

false /fɔːls/ adj ‹statement/pride/name› falso; ‹belief› erróneo; ‹eyelashes/fingernails› postizo; **true or ~?** ¿verdadero o falso?

false alarm n falsa alarma f

falsehood /'fɔːlshʊd/ n (frml) falsedad f

falsely /'fɔːlsli/ adv ‹accuse› falsamente

false: ~ start n (Sport) salida f en falso; (to career, speech) intento m fallido; ~ **teeth** pl n dentadura f postiza

falsify /'fɔːlsəfaɪ ‖'fɔːlsɪfaɪ/ vt **-fies, -fying, -fied** ‹accounts/evidence› falsificar*; ‹truth› falsear

falter /'fɔːltər ‖'fɔːltə(r)/ vi **(a)** (speak hesitantly) titubear, balbucear **(b)** «*enthusiasm/interest*» decaer*; «*courage/resolve*» flaquear

fame /feɪm/ n fama f

familiar /fə'mɪljər ‖fə'mɪliə(r)/ adj **(a)** (well-known) ‹sound/face› familiar, conocido; **the name sounds ~** el nombre me suena **(b)** (having knowledge of) **to be ~ WITH sth/sb** estar* familiarizado CON algo/algn

familiarity /fəˌmɪli'ærəti/ n (pl **-ties**) **(a)** (knowledge): **she claimed extensive ~ with the method** dijo estar muy familiarizada con el método; **some ~ with computers would be an asset** se valorará la experiencia previa con computadoras f; (of person, book, landscape) familiaridad f; ~ **breeds contempt** lo que se tiene no se aprecia

familiarize /fə'mɪljəraɪz ‖fə'mɪliəraɪz/ vt **to ~ oneself WITH sth** familiarizarse* CON algo

family /'fæmli, 'fæməli ‖'fæmɪli, 'fæmli/ n (pl **-lies**) (relatives) familia f; (before n) ‹business› familiar; ‹fortune› de la familia

family: ~ planning n planificación f familiar; ~ **tree** n árbol m genealógico

famine /'fæmən/ n hambruna f

famished /'fæmɪʃt/ adj famélico; **I'm ~!** (colloq) ¡estoy muerto de hambre! (fam)

famous /'feɪməs/ adj famoso

fan¹ /fæn/ n **1** (hand-held) abanico m; (mechanical) ventilador m **2** (of group, actor) fan mf; (of football team) hincha mf

fan² **-nn-** vt ‹person› abanicar*; ‹interest/ curiosity› avivar

■ **fan out** [v + adv] «*searchers*» abrirse* en abanico

fanatic /fə'nætɪk/ n fanático, -ca m,f

fanatical /fə'nætɪkəl/ adj ‹believer› fanático; ‹belief› ciego

fan belt n correa f or (Méx) banda f del ventilador

fanciful /'fænsɪfəl/ adj **(a)** (impractical) ‹idea› extravagante **(b)** (elaborate) ‹design› imaginativo

fan club n club m de fans

fancy¹ /'fænsi/ vt **fancies, fancying, fancied** (esp BrE) **1** (expressing surprise) (in interj): (just) ~ **that!** ¡pues mira tú!; ~ **meeting them here!** ¡qué casualidad encontrarnos con ellos aquí! **2** (feel desire for) (colloq): **I really ~ an ice-cream** ¡qué ganas de tomarme un helado!; **do you ~ going to see a movie?** ¿tienes ganas de ir al cine? **3** (be physically attracted to) (colloq): **I ~ her/ him** me gusta mucho **4** (imagine) (frml) **to ~** (THAT): **she fancied she saw his face in the crowd** creyó ver su cara entre la multitud

fancy² adj **-cier, -ciest** **(a)** (elaborate) elaborado **(b)** (superior) (pej) ‹hotel› de campanillas; ‹car› lujoso; ‹ideas› extravagante

fancy³ n (pl **-cies**) **1** (liking) (no pl): **to take a ~ to sb**: **she seems to have taken a ~ to you** parece que le has caído en gracia; **to tickle sb's ~**: **the idea rather tickled my ~** la idea me resultó atractiva **2** (imagination) imaginación f

fancy: ~ dress n (BrE) disfraz m; (before n) ~**-dress party** fiesta f de disfraces; ~**-free** /'fænsi'friː/ adj ▶ FOOTLOOSE; ~ **goods** pl n (Busn) artículos mpl para regalo

fanfare /'fænfer ‖'fænfeə(r)/ n fanfarria f

fang /fæŋ/ n (of dog) colmillo m; (of snake) diente m

fan heater n electroconvector m

fanny /'fæni/ n (pl **-nies**) (buttocks) (AmE sl) culo m (fam: en algunas regiones vulg), traste m (CS fam), poto m (Chi, Per fam)

fantasize /'fæntəsaɪz/ vi fantasear

fantastic /fæn'tæstɪk/ adj **(a)** (wonderful) (colloq) fantástico **(b)** (incredible) ‹story› absurdo

fantasy /'fæntəsi/ n (pl **-sies**) **(a)** (unreality) fantasía f **(b)** (daydream) sueño m

FAQ pl n (Comput) = **frequently asked questions**

far¹ /fɑːr ‖fɑː(r)/ adv **1** (comp **further** or **farther**; superl **furthest** or **farthest**) **(a)** (in distance) lejos; **how ~ is it?** ¿a qué distancia está?; ~ **away in the distance** a lo lejos **(b)** (in progress): **the plans are now quite ~ advanced** los planes están ya muy avanzados; **that girl will go ~** esa chica va a llegar lejos **(c)** (in time): **Christmas isn't ~ away o off now** ya falta poco para Navidad; **I can't remember that ~ back** no recuerdo cosas tan lejanas **(d)** (in extent, degree): **the new legislation doesn't go ~ enough** la nueva legislación no tiene el alcance necesario; **his jokes went a bit too ~** se pasó un poco con esos chistes
2 (very much): ~ **better** mucho mejor
3 (in phrases) **as o so far as: as o so ~ as I know** que yo sepa; **by far: their team was by ~ the worst** su equipo fue con mucho el peor; **so far: so ~, everything has gone according to plan** hasta ahora todo ha salido de acuerdo a lo planeado

far² adj (comp **farther**; superl **farthest**) **(a)** (distant) lejano **(b)** (most distant, extreme) (before n, ···✦

no comp): **at the ~ end of the room** en el otro extremo de la habitación; **the ~ left/right** (Pol) la extrema izquierda/derecha

faraway /ˈfɑːrəˈweɪ/ *adj* (*before n*) ‹*lands*› lejano; ‹*look*› ausente

farce /fɑːrs ‖ fɑːs/ *n* farsa *f*

farcical /ˈfɑːrsɪkəl ‖ ˈfɑːsɪkəl/ *adj* ridículo

fare /fer ‖ feə(r)/ *n* [1] (cost of travel — by air) pasaje *m or* (Esp) billete *m*; (— by bus, train) boleto *m or* (esp Esp) billete *m*; **~s will rise again next year** las tarifas subirán de nuevo en el próximo año [2] (food and drink) comida *f*

Far East *n* **the ~ ~** el Lejano *or* Extremo Oriente

farewell¹ /ˈferˈwel ‖ ˌfeəˈwel/ *n* despedida *f*

farewell² *interj* (liter) adiós

far-fetched /ˈfɑːrˈfetʃt ‖ ˌfɑːˈfetʃt/ *adj* exagerado

farm¹ /fɑːrm ‖ fɑːm/ *n* (small) granja *f*, chacra *f* (CS, Per); (large) hacienda *f*, cortijo *m* (Esp), rancho *m* (Méx), estancia *f* (RPl), fundo *m* (Chi); (*before n*) ‹*machinery/worker*› agrícola

farm² *vt* ‹*land*› cultivar
■ **farm out** [*v + o + adv, v + adv + o*] ‹*work*› encargar* (*a terceros*)

farmer /ˈfɑːrmər ‖ ˈfɑːmə(r)/ *n* agricultor, -tora *m,f*, granjero, -ra *m,f*, chacarero, -ra *m,f* (CS, Per); (owner of large farm) hacendado, -da *m,f*, ranchero, -ra *m,f* (Méx), estanciero, -ra *m,f* (RPl), dueño, -ña *m,f* de fundo (Chi)

farm: ~hand *n* peón *m or* (Esp) mozo *m* de labranza; **~house** *n* casa *f* de labranza, alquería *f* (en Esp), ≈casco *m* de la estancia (en RPl)

farming /ˈfɑːrmɪŋ ‖ ˈfɑːmɪŋ/ *n* (of land) labranza *f*, (of animals) crianza *f*, (*before n*) ‹*community*› agrícola; ‹*methods*› de labranza

farm: ~land *n* tierras *fpl* de labranza; **~yard** *n* corral *m*

far: ~-off /ˈfɑːrˈɔːf ‖ ˈfɑːˈrɒf/ *adj* (*pred* **~ off**) (in space) remoto; (in time) distante; **~-reaching** /ˈfɑːrˈriːtʃɪŋ ‖ ˌfɑːˈriːtʃɪŋ/ *adj* de gran alcance; **~-sighted** /ˈfɑːrˈsaɪtəd ‖ ˌfɑːˈsaɪtɪd/ *adj* (a) (showing foresight) con visión de futuro (b) (AmE Med) hipermétrope

fart¹ /fɑːrt ‖ fɑːt/ *n* (vulg) pedo *m* (fam)

fart² *vi* (vulg) tirarse *or* echarse un pedo (fam)

farther¹ /ˈfɑːrðər ‖ ˈfɑːðə(r)/ *adv comp of* FAR¹ 1

farther² *adj comp of* FAR²

farthest¹ /ˈfɑːrðəst ‖ ˈfɑːðɪst/ *adv superl of* FAR¹ 1

farthest² *adj superl of* FAR²

fascinate /ˈfæsəneɪt ‖ ˈfæsɪneɪt/ *vt* fascinar

fascinated /ˈfæsəneɪtəd ‖ ˈfæsɪneɪtɪd/ *adj* fascinado

fascinating /ˈfæsəneɪtɪŋ ‖ ˈfæsɪneɪtɪŋ/ *adj* fascinante

fascination /ˌfæsənˈeɪʃən ‖ ˌfæsɪˈneɪʃən/ *n* fascinación *f*

fascism /ˈfæʃɪzəm/ *n* fascismo *m*

fascist¹ /ˈfæʃəst ‖ ˈfæʃɪst/ *n* fascista *mf*

fascist² *adj* fascista

fashion¹ /ˈfæʃən/ *n* [1] (vogue) moda *f*; **to be in/out of ~** estar* de moda/estar* pasado de moda; (*before n*) **~ designer** diseñador, -dora *m,f* de

modas [2] (custom) costumbre *f* [3] (manner) manera *f*; *after a ~*: **can you swim? — well, after a ~** ¿sabes nadar? — bueno, a mi manera

fashion² *vt* crear

fashionable /ˈfæʃnəbəl/ *adj* ‹*clothes/designs*› a la moda; ‹*restaurant/people/idea*› de moda

fashionably /ˈfæʃnəbli/ *adv* a la moda

fashion show *n* desfile *m* de modas

fast¹ /fæst ‖ fɑːst/ *adj* **-er, -est** [1] (a) (speedy) rápido (b) (of clock, watch) (*pred*): **my watch is five minutes ~** mi reloj (se) adelanta cinco minutos [2] (permanent) ‹*color*› inalterable

fast² *adv* [1] (quickly) rápidamente, rápido [2] (firmly): **the car was stuck ~ in the mud** el coche estaba atascado en el barro completamente; **to be ~ asleep** estar* profundamente dormido

fast³ *vi* ayunar

fast⁴ *n* ayuno *m*

fasten /ˈfæsn ‖ ˈfɑːsn/ *vt* (a) (attach) sujetar; (tie) atar (b) (do up, close) ‹*case*› cerrar*; ‹*coat/seat belt*› abrochar
■ ~ *vi* «*suitcase*» cerrar*; «*skirt/necklace*» abrocharse

fastener /ˈfæsnər ‖ ˈfɑːsnə(r)/ *n* cierre *m*

fast: ~ food *n* comida *f* rápida; **~-forward** /ˈfæstˈfɔːrwərd ‖ ˌfɑːstˈfɔːwəd/ *vt/i* avanzar*

fastidious /fæsˈtɪdiəs/ *adj* (a) (demanding) muy exigente (b) (fussy) maniático, mañoso (AmL)

fast track *n* vía *f* rápida

fat¹ /fæt/ *adj* **-tt-** ‹*person/animal*› gordo; ‹*book/cigar*› grueso; **to get ~** engordar; **a ~ lot of good that'll do!** (iro) ¡para lo que va a servir!

fat² *n* grasa *f*

fatal /ˈfeɪtl/ *adj* (a) (causing death) mortal (b) (disastrous) ‹*decision/mistake*› fatídico

fatalistic /ˌfeɪtlˈɪstɪk ‖ ˌfeɪtəˈlɪstɪk/ *adj* fatalista

fatality /ferˈtæləti ‖ fəˈtæləti/ *n* (*pl* **-ties**) muerto *m*

fatally /ˈfeɪtli ‖ ˈfeɪtəli/ *adv* mortalmente

fate /feɪt/ *n* (a) (destiny) destino *m* (b) (*no pl*) (one's lot, end) suerte *f*

fated /ˈfeɪtəd ‖ ˈfeɪtɪd/ *adj* (destined) **to be ~ to +** INF (liter) estar* predestinado A + INF

fateful /ˈfeɪtfəl/ *adj* (a) (momentous) ‹*day/decision*› fatídico (b) (prophetic) ‹*words*› profético

father¹ /ˈfɑːðər ‖ ˈfɑːðə(r)/ *n* padre *m*

father² *vt* ‹*child*› engendrar, tener*

Father Christmas *n* (BrE) Papá *m* Noel, viejo *m* Pascuero (Chi)

fatherhood /ˈfɑːðərhʊd ‖ ˈfɑːðəhʊd/ *n* paternidad *f*

father: ~-in-law *n* (*pl* **~s-in-law**) suegro *m*; **~land** *n* patria *f*

fatherly /ˈfɑːðərli ‖ ˈfɑːðəli/ *adj* paternal

fathom¹ /ˈfæðəm/ *n* braza *f*

fathom² *vt* ~ (out) entender*

fatigue /fəˈtiːg/ *n* fatiga *f*

fatten /ˈfætn/ *vt* ~ (up) ‹*animal*› cebar

fattening /ˈfætnɪŋ/ *adj*: **cakes are extremely ~** los pasteles engordan muchísimo

fatty /ˈfæti/ *adj* **-tier, -tiest** ‹*food/substance*› graso, grasoso (AmL)

faucet /'fɔːsət/ *n* (AmE) llave *f or* (Esp) grifo *m or* (RPl) canilla *f or* (Per) caño *m or* (AmC) paja *f*, chorro *m* (AmC, Ven)

fault¹ /fɔːlt/ *n* **1** (responsibility, blame) culpa *f*; they're always finding ∼ with me todo lo que hago les parece mal **2** (a) (failing) defecto *m*; **she is generous to a** ∼ es generosa en extremo (b) (in machine) avería *f*; (in goods) defecto *m* **3** (Geol) falla *f* **4** (in tennis, show jumping) falta *f*

fault² *vt* encontrarle* defectos a

faultless /'fɔːltləs ‖'fɔːltlɪs/ *adj* impecable

faulty /'fɔːlti/ *adj* **-tier, -tiest** ⟨goods/design⟩ defectuoso; ⟨workmanship⟩ imperfecto

faux pas /ˌfəʊ'pɑː/ *n* (*pl* ∼ ∼ /-z/) metedura *f or* (AmL tb) metida *f* de pata (fam)

favor¹, (BrE) **favour** /'feɪvər ‖'feɪvə(r)/ *n* **1** (approval): to find ∼ with sb (frml) tener* buena acogida por parte de algn (frml); **to curry ∼ with sb** tratar de congraciarse con algn **2** in ∼ a favor; **to be in ∼ of sth** estar* a favor de algo **3** (act of kindness) favor *m*; **to do/ask sb a ∼** hacerle*/pedirle* un favor a algn

favor², (BrE) **favour** *vt* (a) (be in favor of) estar* a favor de (b) (benefit) favorecer* (c) (treat preferentially) favorecer*

favorable, (BrE) **favourable** /'feɪvrəbəl/ *adj* favorable; **to be ∼ TO sth** favorecer* algo

favorite¹, (BrE) **favourite** /'feɪvrət ‖'feɪvərɪt/ *adj* preferido

favorite², (BrE) **favourite** *n* (a) (person, thing) preferido, -da *m,f*; (Sport) favorito, -ta *m,f* (b) (of teacher, ruler) favorito, -ta *m,f*

favoritism, (BrE) **favouritism** /'feɪvrətɪzəm ‖'feɪvərɪtɪzəm/ *n* favoritismo *m*

fawn¹ /fɔːn/ *n* **1** (young deer) cervato *m* **2** (color) beige *m*, beis *m* (Esp); (before n) ⟨sweater/coat⟩ beige *adj inv*, beis *adj inv* (Esp)

fawn² *vi* (flatter) **to ∼ ON sb** ⟨person⟩ (pej) adular a algn

fax¹ /fæks/ *n* fax *m*; (before n) ∼ **machine** fax *m*

fax² *vt* faxear

faze /feɪz/ *vt* (colloq) perturbar

FBI *n* (in US) (= **Federal Bureau of Investigation**) FBI *m*

FDA *n* (in US) = **Food and Drug Administration**

fear¹ /fɪr ‖fɪə(r)/ *n* miedo *m*, temor *m*; ∼ **of heights** miedo a las alturas; **no ∼!** (as interj) (colloq) ¡ni loco! *or* ¡ni muerto!

fear² *vt* (a) (dread) temer (b) (suspect) **to ∼ (THAT)** temerse QUE
 ■ ∼ *vi* temer; **to ∼ FOR sb/sth** temer POR algn/algo

fearful /'fɪrfəl ‖'fɪəfəl/ *adj* **1** (frightening) aterrador **2** (timid) miedoso

fearless /'fɪrləs ‖'fɪəlɪs/ *adj* intrépido

fearsome /'fɪrsəm ‖'fɪəsəm/ *adj* ⟨enemy⟩ aterrador; ⟨task⟩ tremendo

feasibility /ˌfiːzə'bɪləti/ *n* viabilidad *f*; (before n) ∼ **study** estudio *m* de viabilidad

feasible /'fiːzəbəl/ *adj* (practicable) viable; (possible) posible

feast¹ /fiːst/ *n* **1** (banquet) banquete *m* **2** (Relig) fiesta *f*; (before n) ∼ **day** día *m* festivo

feast² *vi* festejar
 ■ ∼ *vt* **to ∼ one's eyes ON sth** regalarse los ojos CON algo

feat /fiːt/ *n* hazaña *f*

feather /'feðər ‖'feðə(r)/ *n* pluma *f*; **as light as a** ∼ ligero *or* (esp AmL) liviano como una pluma; (before n) ∼ **bed** colchón *m* de plumas; ∼ **duster** plumero *m*

feature¹ /'fiːtʃər ‖'fiːtʃə(r)/ *n* **1** (a) (of face) rasgo *m* (b) (of character, landscape, machine, style) característica *f* **2** (a) ∼ **(film)** película *f* (b) (Journ) artículo *m* (Rad, TV) documental *m*

feature² *vt* **1** (Journ, Cin): he was ∼d in 'The Globe' recently 'The Globe' publicó un artículo sobre él hace poco; featuring John Ball con la actuación de John Ball **2** (a) (have as feature) «hotel/house» ofrecer* (b) (depict) mostrar*
 ■ ∼ *vi* figurar; rice ∼s prominently in their diet el arroz ocupa un lugar importante en su alimentación

February /'februeri ‖'februəri/ *n* febrero *m*

feces, (BrE) **faeces** /'fiːsiːz/ *pl n* (frml) heces *fpl* (frml)

fed /fed/ past & past p of FEED¹

federal /'fedərəl/ *adj* federal

federal: F∼ Republic of Germany *n* the **F∼ Republic of Germany** la República Federal de Alemania; **F∼ Reserve Board** *n* (in US) la Junta de Gobernadores de la Reserva Federal

federation /ˌfedə'reɪʃən/ *n* federación *f*

fed up *adj* (colloq) (usu pred) **to be ∼ ∼ (WITH sb/sth/-ING)** estar* harto (DE algn/algo/+ INF)

fee /fiː/ *n* (a) (payment — to doctor, lawyer) honorarios *mpl*; (— to actor, singer) caché *m* (b) (charge) (often pl): **on payment of a small ∼** por una módica suma; **membership ∼(s)** cuota *f* (de socio)

feeble /'fiːbəl/ *adj* **-bler** /-blər ‖-blə(r)/, **-blest** /-bləst ‖-blɪst/ (a) (weak) débil (b) (poor) ⟨joke⟩ flojo; ⟨excuse⟩ pobre

feed¹ /fiːd/ (past & past p **fed**) *vt* **1** (a) (give food to) dar* de comer a; ⟨baby⟩ (breastfeed) darle* el pecho a; (with a bottle) darle* el biberón *or* (CS, Per) la mamadera *or* (Col, Ven) el tetero a (b) (provide food for) alimentar (c) (give as food) **to ∼ sth TO sb** dar* algo (de comer) A algn **2** (insert) **to ∼ sth INTO sth** ⟨into a machine⟩ introducir* algo EN algo **3** (sustain) ⟨imagination/rumor⟩ avivar; ⟨hope/fire⟩ alimentar
 ■ ∼ *vi* comer; **to ∼ ON sth** alimentarse DE algo

feed² *n* (a) (act of feeding): **it's time for the baby's ∼** es hora de darle de comer al niño (b) (food) alimento *m*; (for cattle) pienso *m*

feedback /'fiːdbæk/ *n* (reaction) reacción *f*; (Audio, Electron) retroalimentación *f*

feeding bottle /'fiːdɪŋ/ *n* (BrE) biberón *m*, mamila *f* (Méx), mamadera *f* (CS, Per), tetero *m* (Col)

feel¹ /fiːl/ (past & past p **felt**) *vi* **1** (physically, emotionally) sentirse*; **to ∼ hot/cold/hungry/thirsty** tener* calor/frío/hambre/sed **2** (have opinion): **it's something I ∼ strongly about** es algo que me parece muy importante; **how do you ∼ about these changes?** ¿qué opinas de estos cambios? **3** **to ∼ like -ING** (be in the mood for) tener* ganas DE + INF **4** (seem): **your hands ∼ cold** tienes las manos frías; **how does that ∼? — it's still too tight** ¿cómo lo sientes? — todavía me queda apretado ⋯⋙

5 (grope) to ∼ **FOR sth** buscar* algo a tientas

■ ∼ *vt* **1** (touch) tocar*; *to* ∼ *one's way* ir* a tientas

2 ⟨sensation/movement/shame⟩ sentir*; **I couldn't** ∼ **my fingers** no sentía los dedos

3 (consider) considerar; **I** ∼ **that** ... me parece que ...

feel² *n (no pl)* **1 (a)** (sensation) sensación *f* **(b)** (sense of touch) tacto *m* **2 (a)** (atmosphere — of house, room) ambiente *m* **(b)** (instinct): **to have a** ∼ **for sth** tener* sensibilidad para algo; **to get the** ∼ **of sth** acostumbrarse a algo

feeler /'fiːlər ‖'fiːlə(r)/ *n* **(a)** (Zool) (antenna) antena *f*; (tentacle) tentáculo *m* **(b)** (tentative approach): **to put out** ∼**s** tantear el terreno

feeling /'fiːlɪŋ/ *n* **1 (a)** (physical sensitivity) sensibilidad *f* **(b)** (physical, emotional sensation) sensación *f* **2 (a)** (sincere emotion) sentimiento *m* **(b) feelings** *pl* (sensitivity) sentimientos *mpl* **3** (opinion) opinión *f* **4** *(no pl)* (impression) impresión *f*; **I've a** ∼ **that he knows already** tengo *or* me da la sensación de que ya lo sabe

feet /fiːt/ *n pl of* FOOT¹

feign /feɪn/ *vt* fingir*

feline /'fiːlaɪn/ *adj* felino

fell¹ /fel/ *past of* FALL²

fell² *vt* ⟨tree⟩ talar; ⟨person⟩ derribar

fellow¹ /'feləʊ/ *n* **1** (man) tipo *m* (fam), hombre *m* **2** (member — of college) *miembro del cuerpo docente y de la junta rectora de una universidad*; (— of learned society) miembro *mf* de número

fellow² *adj (before n)*: ∼ **worker/traveler** compañero, -ra *m,f* de trabajo/viaje; ∼ **citizen** conciudadano, -na *m,f*; **he has no love for his** ∼ **men** no le tiene amor al prójimo

fellow feeling *n* camaradería *f*

fellowship /'feləʊʃɪp/ *n* **1** (Educ) **(a)** (at university) título *m* de FELLOW¹ 2 **(b)** (endowment) beca *f* de investigación **2 (a)** (companionship) (liter) hermandad *f* (liter) **(b)** (fraternity) fraternidad *f*

felon /'felən/ *n* (in US law) delincuente *mf* (*que ha cometido un delito grave*)

felony /'feləni/ *n (pl* **-nies)** (in US Law) delito *m* grave

felt¹ /felt/ *n* fieltro *m*

felt² *past & past p of* FEEL¹

felt pen, felt-tip (pen) /'felttɪp/ *n* rotulador *m*, marcador *m* (AmL)

female¹ /'fiːmeɪl/ *adj* ⟨sex⟩ femenino; ⟨animal/plant⟩ hembra; **the victim was** ∼ la víctima era una mujer

female² *n* hembra *f*; (woman, girl) mujer *f*

feminine /'femənən ‖'femɪnɪn/ *adj* femenino

femininity /,femə'nɪnəti ‖,femɪ'nɪnəti/ *n* feminidad *f*, feminidad *f*

feminism /'femənəzəm ‖'femɪnɪzəm/ *n* feminismo *m*

feminist¹ /'femənəst ‖'femɪnɪst/ *n* feminista *mf*

feminist² *adj* feminista

fence¹ /fens/ *n* **1 (a)** (barrier) cerca *f*, cerco *m* (AmL); **to sit on the** ∼ nadar entre dos aguas **(b)** (in showjumping) valla *f* **2** (receiver of stolen goods) (colloq) *persona que comercia con objetos robados*, reducidor, -dora *m,f* (AmS)

fence² *vt* cercar*

■ ∼ *vi* (Sport) practicar* la esgrima

■ **fence in** [*v + adv + o, v + o + adv*] cercar*

■ **fence off** [*v + adv + o, v + o + adv*] separar con una cerca

fencer /'fensər ‖'fensə(r)/ *n* esgrimista *mf*

fencing /'fensɪŋ/ *n* **1** (Sport) esgrima *f* **2 (a)** (material) *materiales para cercos o vallas* **(b)** (fence) cerca *f*

fend /fend/ *vi*: **to** ∼ **for oneself** valerse* por sí mismo

■ **fend off** [*v + o + adv, v + adv + o*] ⟨attack/enemy⟩ rechazar*; ⟨blow⟩ esquivar; ⟨questions⟩ eludir

fender /'fendər ‖'fendə(r)/ *n* **1** (around fireplace) rejilla *f* **2** (on car) (AmE) guardabarros *m or* (Méx) salpicadera *f or* (Chi, Per) tapabarro(s) *m*; (on boat) defensa *f*

fennel /'fenl/ *n* hinojo *m*

ferment /fər'ment ‖fə'ment/ *vi* fermentar

fern /fɜːrn ‖fɜːn/ *n* helecho *m*

ferocious /fə'rəʊʃəs/ *adj* feroz

ferocity /fə'rɑːsəti ‖fə'rɒsəti/ *n* ferocidad *f*

ferret /'ferət ‖'ferɪt/ *n* hurón *m*

■ **ferret around, ferret about** [*v + adv*] husmear

■ **ferret out** [*v + o + adv, v + adv + o*] (colloq) descubrir*

ferry¹ /'feri/ *n (pl* **-ries)** (boat) transbordador *m*, ferry *m*; (smaller) balsa *f*

ferry² *vt* **-ries, -rying, -ried** llevar; **we** ∼ **the children to and from school in the car** llevamos a los niños al colegio y los vamos a buscar en coche

fertile /'fɜːrtl ‖'fɜːtaɪl/ *adj* ⟨woman/animal/plant/soil⟩ fértil; ⟨seed/egg⟩ fecundado; ⟨imagination⟩ fértil

fertility /fər'tɪləti ‖fə'tɪləti/ *n* fertilidad *f*

fertilize /'fɜːrtlaɪz ‖'fɜːtɪlaɪz/ *vt* ⟨egg/plant/cell⟩ fecundar; ⟨soil/crop⟩ abonar

fertilizer /'fɜːrtlaɪzər ‖'fɜːtɪlaɪzə(r)/ *n* fertilizante *m*

fervent /'fɜːrvənt ‖'fɜːvənt/ *adj* ferviente

fervor, (BrE) **fervour** /'fɜːrvər ‖'fɜːvə(r)/ *n* fervor *m*

fester /'festər ‖'festə(r)/ *vi* enconarse

festival /'festəvəl ‖'festɪvl/ *n* **(a)** (Relig) fiesta *f* **(b)** (Cin, Mus, Theat) festival *m* **(c)** (celebration) fiesta *f*

festive /'festɪv/ *adj* festivo; **the** ∼ **season** (set phrase) las Navidades

festivity /fes'tɪvəti/ *n (usu pl)* celebración *f*

festoon /fe'stuːn/ *vt* **to** ∼ **sth/sb (WITH sth)** adornar algo/a algn (CON algo)

fetch /fetʃ/ vt **1** (bring) traer*, ir* a por (Esp) **2** (sell for) (colloq): **the car ~ed $4,000** el coche se vendió en 4.000 dólares

■ **~** vi: **to ~ and carry** ser* el recadero/la recadera

fetching /'fetʃɪŋ/ adj ⟨smile⟩ atractivo; ⟨dress/hat⟩ sentador, que sienta bien (Esp)

fete, fête /feɪt/ n **(a)** (fund-raising event) (BrE) feria f (benéfica), kermesse f (CS, Méx), bazar m (Col) **(b)** (party) (AmE) fiesta f (en un jardín)

fetish /'fetɪʃ/ n fetiche m

fetter /'fetər ‖'fetə(r)/ vt (liter) encadenar; **he felt ~ed by convention** se sentía prisionero de los convencionalismos

fetters /'fetərz ‖'fetəz/ pl n (liter) grillos mpl

fettle /'fetl/ n: **to be in fine ~** estar* en (buena) forma

fetus, (BrE) **foetus** /'fiːtəs/ n feto m

feud¹ /fjuːd/ n contienda f (frml)

feud² vi contender* (frml)

feudal /'fjuːdl/ adj feudal

fever /'fiːvər ‖'fiːvə(r)/ n fiebre f

feverish /'fiːvərɪʃ/ adj (Med) con fiebre; (frantic) febril

fever pitch n: **to reach ~ ~** llegar* al paroxismo

few¹ /fjuː/ adj **-er, -est** pocos, -cas; **the last ~ days have been difficult** estos últimos días han sido difíciles; **there were ~er people than usual** había menos gente de costumbre; **I've been there a ~ times** he estado allí unas cuantas veces

few² pron **-er, -est** pocos, -cas; **the privileged ~** la minoría privilegiada; **a ~ of us complained** algunos (de nosotros) nos quejamos

fiancé /'fiːɑːnˈseɪ, fiːˈɑːnseɪ ‖fiːˈɒnseɪ/ n prometido m

fiancée /'fiːɑːnˈseɪ, fiːˈɑːnseɪ ‖fiːˈɒnseɪ/ n prometida f

fiasco /fiˈæskəʊ/ n (pl **-cos** or **-coes**) fracaso m

fib¹ /fɪb/ n (colloq) mentirilla f, bola f (fam)

fib² vi **-bb-** (colloq) mentir*, decir* mentirillas or (fam) bolas

fiber, (BrE) **fibre** /'faɪbər ‖'faɪbə(r)/ n fibra f; (dietary) **~** fibra f

fiberglass /'faɪbərglæs ‖'faɪbəglɑːs/ n fibra f de vidrio

fickle /'fɪkəl/ adj veleidoso

fiction /'fɪkʃən/ n ficción f

fictional /'fɪkʃnəl ‖'fɪkʃənl/ adj ficticio

fictitious /fɪkˈtɪʃəs/ adj **(a)** (false) ⟨name⟩ ficticio **(b)** (imaginary) imaginario

fiddle¹ /'fɪdl/ n **1** (violin) violín m; **as fit as a ~** rebosante de salud **2** (cheat) (BrE colloq) chanchullo m (fam)

fiddle² vt (BrE colloq) ⟨accounts⟩ hacer* chanchullos con (fam); ⟨results⟩ amañar

■ **~** vi (fidget) **to ~ WITH sth** juguetear CON algo

fiddler /'fɪdlər ‖'fɪdlə(r)/ n violinista mf

fidelity /fəˈdeləti ‖fɪˈdeləti/ n fidelidad f

fidget /'fɪdʒət ‖'fɪdʒɪt/ vi: **stop ~ing** ¡estate quieto!

field¹ /fiːld/ n **1** (Agr) campo m **2** (Sport) **(a)** (area of play) campo m, cancha f (AmL) **(b)** (competitors) (+ sing o pl vb): **to lead the ~** llevar la delantera; **our products lead the ~** nuestros

productos son los líderes del mercado **3** (of study, work) campo m; (of activities) esfera f **4** (Opt, Phot, Phys) campo m; **~ of vision** campo visual

field² vt (Sport) fildear

field: ~ day n: **to have a ~ day** hacer* su agosto; **~ glasses** pl n gemelos mpl, prismáticos mpl; **~ hockey** n (AmE) hockey m (sobre hierba); **~ marshal** n mariscal m de campo; **~ trip** n viaje m de estudio; **~work** n trabajo m de campo

fiend /fiːnd/ n **(a)** (demon) demonio m **(b)** (cruel person) (journ or hum) desalmado, -da m,f

fiendish /'fiːndɪʃ/ adj **(a)** (wicked) diabólico **(b)** (very difficult) (colloq) endemoniado (fam)

fierce /fɪrs ‖fɪəs/ adj **fiercer, fiercest (a)** ⟨dog/lion⟩ fiero; ⟨temper⟩ feroz **(b)** ⟨hatred/love⟩ intenso; ⟨fighting⟩ encarnizado; ⟨criticism/opposition⟩ violento **(c)** ⟨storm⟩ violento; ⟨wind⟩ fortísimo; **the ~ tropical sun** el implacable sol del trópico

fiercely /'fɪrsli ‖'fɪəsli/ adv **(a)** ⟨growl⟩ con ferocidad **(b)** ⟨fight⟩ con fiereza; ⟨criticize⟩ duramente; ⟨competitive/independent⟩ extremadamente

fiery /'faɪri ‖'faɪəri/ adj **-rier, -riest** ⟨glow⟩ ardiente; ⟨red⟩ encendido; ⟨heat/sun⟩ abrasador; ⟨liquor⟩ muy fuerte; ⟨temper⟩ exaltado; ⟨speech⟩ fogoso

FIFA /'fiːfə/ n (no art) la FIFA

fifteen /fɪfˈtiːn/ adj/n quince adj inv/m; see also FOUR¹

fifteenth¹ /fɪfˈtiːnθ/ adj decimoquinto

fifteenth² adv en decimoquinto lugar

fifteenth³ n (Math) quinceavo m; (part) quinceava parte f

fifth¹ /fɪfθ/ adj quinto

fifth² adv en quinto lugar

fifth³ n **1** **(a)** (Math) quinto m; (part) quinta parte f, quinto m **(b)** (Mus) quinta f **(c)** (in competition): **he finished a disappointing ~** llegó en un deslucido quinto lugar **2** **~** **(gear)** (no art) quinta f

fiftieth¹ /'fɪftiəθ/ adj quincuagésimo

fiftieth² adv en quincuagésimo lugar

fiftieth³ n (Math) cincuentavo m; (part) cincuentava or quincuagésima parte f

fifty /'fɪfti/ adj/n cincuenta adj inv/m; see also FOUR¹

fifty-fifty¹ /'fɪftiˈfɪfti/ adv (colloq) a medias

fifty-fifty² adj (colloq): **a ~ chance** un 50% de posibilidades; **on a ~ basis** a medias

fig /fɪg/ n higo m; (before n) **~ tree** higuera f

fight¹ /faɪt/ (past & past p **fought**) vi «army/country/animal» luchar; «person» pelear; **to ~ FOR/AGAINST sb/sth** luchar POR/CONTRA algn/algo; **to ~ OVER sth** pelearse POR algo

■ **~** vt **1** **(a)** ⟨army/country⟩ luchar contra **(b)** ⟨fire/disease/measure⟩ combatir **2** **(a)** (conduct): **they fought a long war against the rebels** lucharon contra los rebeldes durante largo tiempo **(b)** ⟨contest⟩ ⟨election⟩ presentarse a; **we intend to ~ the case** (Law) pensamos llevar el caso a los tribunales (or defendernos etc)

■ **fight back 1** [v + adv] defenderse*; **to ~ back AGAINST sb/sth** luchar CONTRA algn/algo ···⫶

2 [v + o + adv, v + adv + o] ⟨tears⟩ contener*; ⟨anger⟩ reprimir

■ **fight off** [v + o + adv, v + adv + o] ⟨attack/enemy⟩ rechazar*; ⟨cold⟩ combatir

■ **fight out** [v + o + adv]: you'll have to ~ it out among yourselves tendrán que resolverlo entre ustedes

fight² n **1** **(a)** (between persons) pelea f; (between armies, companies) lucha f **(b)** (boxing match) pelea f **2** **(a)** (struggle) lucha f **(b)** (quarrel) pelea f

fighter /'faɪtər ‖ 'faɪtə(r)/ n **1** **(a)** (person) luchador, -dora m,f **(b)** (boxer) boxeador, -dora m,f **2** (plane) caza m; (before n) ~ **pilot** piloto m de caza

fighting /'faɪtɪŋ/ n (Mil) enfrentamientos mpl; (brawling, arguing) peleas fpl

figment /'fɪgmənt/ n: a ~ of the imagination (un) producto de la imaginación

figurative /'fɪgjərətɪv ‖ 'fɪgərətɪv/ adj figurado

figure¹ /'fɪgjər ‖ 'fɪgə(r)/ n **1** (digit) cifra f; recent ~s show that … estadísticas recientes muestran que … **2** **(a)** (person) figura f; a public ~ un personaje público **(b)** (body shape) figura f **3** (Art, Math, Mus) figura f

figure² vi **1** (feature) figurar; **to ~ prominently** destacarse* **2** (make sense) (colloq): it just doesn't ~ no me lo explico

■ ~ vt (reckon) (AmE colloq) calcular

■ **figure on** [v + prep + o] (AmE colloq) contar* con

■ **figure out** [v + o + adv, v + adv + o] **(a)** (understand) entender* **(b)** (calculate) ⟨sum/result⟩ calcular; ⟨problem⟩ resolver*

figure: ~**head** n (Naut) mascarón m de proa; he's merely a ~**head** no es más que una figura decorativa; ~ **of speech** n figura f retórica; ~ **skating** n patinaje m artístico

Fiji /'fi:dʒi:/ n Fiji

filament /'fɪləmənt/ n filamento m

filch /fɪltʃ/ vt (colloq) birlar (fam)

file¹ /faɪl/ n **1** (tool) lima f **2** **(a)** (folder) carpeta f; (box ~) clasificador m; (for card index) fichero m **(b)** (collection of documents) archivo m; (of a particular case) expediente m **(c)** (Comput) archivo m

file² vt **1** (sort) ⟨papers⟩ archivar **2** ⟨application/suit⟩ presentar **3** ⟨metal⟩ limar; **to ~ one's nails** limarse las uñas

■ ~ vi **1** (walk in line) (+ adv compl): they ~d into the room entraron en la habitación en fila; the crowd ~d past the tomb la multitud desfiló ante la tumba **2** (Law): **to ~ for divorce** presentar una demanda de divorcio

file: ~ **card** n (AmE) ficha f; ~ **clerk** n (AmE) administrativo, -va m,f (encargado de archivar)

filing /'faɪlɪŋ/ n: there's a lot of ~ to do hay mucho que archivar

filing: ~ **cabinet** n archivador m; ~ **clerk** n (BrE) ▸ FILE CLERK

Filipino /ˌfɪlə'pi:nəʊ ‖ ˌfɪlɪ'pi:nəʊ/ adj filipino

fill¹ /fɪl/ vt **1** **(a)** (make full) **to ~ sth** (WITH sth) llenar algo (DE algo); ⟨cake/sandwich⟩ rellenar algo (DE algo) **(b)** (plug) ⟨hole/crack⟩ rellenar; ⟨tooth⟩ empastar, tapar (Andes), emplomar (RPl), calzar* (Col)

2 ⟨vacancy⟩ cubrir*

■ ~ vi «bath/auditorium» **to ~** (WITH sth) llenarse (DE algo)

■ **fill in 1** [v + o + adv, v + adv + o] **(a)** ⟨hole/outline⟩ rellenar **(b)** ⟨form⟩ rellenar

2 [v + o + adv] (inform) (colloq) **to ~ sb in** (ON sth) poner* a algn al corriente (DE algo)

3 [v + adv] (deputize) **to ~ in** FOR sb sustituir* a algn

■ **fill out** [v + o + adv, v + adv + o] ⟨form⟩ rellenar

■ **fill up 1** [v + o + adv, v + adv + o] **(a)** (make full) llenar **(b)** (Auto): ~ **her up!** ¡llénelo! **2** [v + adv] **(a)** (become full) llenarse **(b)** (buy fuel) echar gasolina

fill² n: to eat one's ~ of sth (liter) comer algo hasta saciarse; to have had one's ~ of sth estar* harto de algo

filler /'fɪlər ‖ 'fɪlə(r)/ n (for cracks) masilla f

fillet¹ /'fɪlət ‖ 'fɪlɪt/ n (of beef) filete m, solomillo m (Esp), lomo m (AmS); (of pork) lomo m; (of fish) filete m; (before n) **a ~ steak** un filete, un solomillo de ternera (Esp), un bife de lomo (RPl)

fillet² vt ⟨meat⟩ cortar en filetes; ⟨fish⟩ quitarle la espina a

filling¹ /'fɪlɪŋ/ n **1** (Dent) empaste m, tapadura f (Chi, Méx), emplomadura f (RPl), calza f (Col) **2** (Culin) relleno m

filling² adj: pasta's very ~ la pasta llena mucho

filling station n ▸ GAS STATION

filly /'fɪli/ n (pl **-lies**) n potra f

film¹ /fɪlm/ n **1 (a)** (Phot) película f (fotográfica) **(b)** (movie) película f, film(e) m (period); (before n) ~ **star** estrella f de cine **2 (a)** (thin covering) película f **(b)** (wrap) film m transparente

film² vt ⟨scene⟩ filmar; ⟨novel/play⟩ llevar al cine

■ ~ vi rodar*; ~**ing starts tomorrow** el rodaje empieza mañana

filmstrip /'fɪlmstrɪp/ n: película o serie de filminas para proyección fija

Filofax® /'faɪləfæks/ n filofax® m

filter¹ /'fɪltər ‖ 'fɪltə(r)/ n **1** (device) filtro m; (before n) ~ **coffee** café m americano **2** (BrE Transp) flecha f (que autoriza el giro a derecha o izquierda en algunos semáforos); (before n) ~ **lane** carril m de giro

filter² vt filtrar

■ ~ vi «gas/light/sound» filtrarse

filter-tipped /'fɪltərtɪpt ‖ ˌfɪltə'tɪpt/ adj con filtro

filth /fɪlθ/ n mugre f

filthy /'fɪlθi/ adj **-thier, -thiest** **(a)** (dirty) mugriento **(b)** (obscene) ⟨language⟩ obsceno **(c)** (unpleasant) (BrE colloq) ⟨weather/habit⟩ asqueroso (fam)

fin /fɪn/ n aleta f

final¹ /'faɪnl/ adj **1** (last) (before n) último; a ~ **demand** (for payment) (Busn) un último aviso de pago **2** (definitive) final; the judges' decision is ~ (frml) la decisión del jurado es inapelable

final² n **1** (Games, Sport) (often pl) final f **2** **finals** pl (Educ) exámenes mpl finales

finale /fə'næli ‖ fɪ'nɑ:li/ n **(a)** (Mus) final m **(b)** (Theat) apoteosis f

finalist /'faɪnləst ‖ 'faɪnəlɪst/ n finalista mf

finalize /'faɪnlaɪz ‖ 'faɪnəlaɪz/ vt ultimar

finally /'faɪnli ‖ 'faɪnəli/ adv **(a)** (lastly) ⟨indep⟩ por último **(b)** (at last) por fin

finance¹ /fə'næns, faɪ- ‖'fæmæns, far'næns/ *n*
(a) (banking, business) finanzas *fpl* (b) **finances**
pl recursos *mpl* financieros (c) (funding)
financiación *f*, financiamiento *m* (esp AmL)

finance² *vt* financiar

financial /fə'nænt∫əl ‖faɪ'nænʃəl/ *adj* ⟨system/
risk⟩ financiero; ⟨difficulties/independence⟩
económico; ⟨news⟩ de economía, de negocios; ~
advice asesoría *f* económica; ~ **management**
gestión *f* financiera

financial year *n* (BrE) (of company) ejercicio
m; (of government) año *m* fiscal

financier /'fɪnən'sɪr ‖far'nænsɪə(r)/ *n*
financiero, -ra *m,f*

find¹ /faɪnd/ (past & past p **found**) *vt*
encontrar*; **I can't ~ it** no lo encuentro; **I found
(that) it was easier to do it this way** descubrí que
era más fácil hacerlo así; **I ~ that hard to believe!**
¡me cuesta creerlo!; **to ~ sb guilty/not guilty** (Law)
declarar a algn culpable/inocente
■ *v refl* **to ~ oneself** encontrarse* a sí (*or* mí *etc*)
mismo
■ **find out** ⏢1⏢ [*v + o + adv, v + adv + o*] (discover)
⟨truth⟩ descubrir*; ⟨information⟩ (by making
enquiries) averiguar*
⏢2⏢ [*v + adv*] (a) (learn) enterarse; **to ~ out ABOUT
sth** enterarse DE algo (b) (make inquiries)
averiguar*

find² *n* hallazgo *m*

findings /'faɪndɪŋz/ *pl n* conclusiones *fpl*

fine¹ /faɪn/ *adj* **finer, finest** ⏢1⏢ (*usu before n*)
(a) (excellent) ⟨house/speech/example⟩ magnífico;
⟨difficulties/ingredients⟩ de primera calidad (b) (fair)
⟨weather⟩ bueno ⏢2⏢ (colloq) (*pred*) (a) (in good
health) muy bien (b) (OK) bien; (perfect) perfecto
⏢3⏢ (thin, delicate) ⟨hair/china/point⟩ fino ⏢4⏢ (subtle)
⟨distinction/nuance⟩ sutil; ⟨balance⟩ delicado;
⟨adjustment⟩ preciso

fine² *adv* (adequately) bien; (very well) muy bien

fine³ *n* multa *f*

fine⁴ *vt* multar

fine art *n* arte *m*; **the ~ ~s** las bellas artes; **to
have (got) sth down to a ~ ~** hacer* algo a la
perfección

finely /'faɪnli/ *adv* (a) (in small pieces): **to chop
sth ~** picar* algo muy fino (b) (subtly) ⟨adjust⟩
con precisión

fine print *n* (AmE) **the ~ ~** la letra pequeña *or*
menuda, la letra chica (AmL)

finery /'faɪnəri/ *n*: **in all their ~** con sus mejores
galas

finesse /fə'nes ‖fɪ'nes/ *n* (a) (refinement) finura *f*
(b) (tact) diplomacia *f*

fine-tooth(ed) comb /faɪn'tu:θ(t)/ *n*: **to go
over sth with a ~-tooth(ed) comb** mirar algo con
lupa

finger¹ /'fɪŋgər ‖'fɪŋgə(r)/ *n* (of hand, glove) dedo
m; **index ~** (dedo) índice *m*; **middle ~** (dedo)
corazón *m or* medio *m*; **ring ~** (dedo) anular *m*;
little ~ (dedo) meñique *m*; **to cross one's ~s: I'll
keep my ~s crossed for you** ojalá (que) tengas
suerte; **to snap one's ~s** chasquear *or* (Méx)
tronar* los dedos

finger² *vt* toquetear, tentalear (Méx)

finger: ~nail *n* uña *f*; **~print** *n* huella *f*
digital; **~tip** *n* yema *f* del dedo

finish¹ /'fɪnɪʃ/ *vt* ⏢1⏢ (a) (complete) terminar,
acabar; **we ~ work at four o'clock today** hoy
salimos a las cuatro; **to ~ -ING** terminar *or*
acabar DE + INF (b) (consume) ⟨drink/rations⟩
terminar, acabar
⏢2⏢ ⟨cloth/porcelain⟩ terminar; ⟨wood⟩ pulir
⏢3⏢ (destroy) (colloq) acabar con
■ ~ *vi* terminar, acabar
■ **finish off** ⏢1⏢ [*v + o + adv, v + adv + o*] (a)
(complete) terminar, acabar (b) (exhaust) dejar
agotado (c) (consume) terminar (d) (kill) matar
⏢2⏢ [*v + adv*] (conclude) terminar, acabar
■ **finish up** ⏢1⏢ [*v + o + adv, v + adv + o*] ⟨food/
paint⟩ terminar
⏢2⏢ [*v + adv*] (end up) acabar

finish² *n* ⏢1⏢ (*no pl*) (end) fin *m*, final *m*; (of race)
llegada *f* ⏢2⏢ (surface texture) acabado *m*

finished /'fɪnɪʃt/ *adj* (*pred*) (a) (complete,
achieved): **to get sth ~** terminar *or* acabar algo;
I'm ~ with the scissors no necesito más la tijera
(b) (ruined) acabado

finishing /'fɪnɪʃɪŋ/ **: ~ line** *n* (BrE) ▶ FINISH
LINE**; ~ school** *n*: colegio privado para
señoritas donde se aprende a comportarse en
sociedad**; ~ touch** *n*: **to put the ~ touch(es) to
sth** darle* los últimos toques a algo

finish line, (BrE) **finishing line** *n* meta *f*,
línea *f* de llegada

finite /'faɪnaɪt/ *adj* finito

Finland /'fɪnlənd/ *n* Finlandia *f*

Finn /fɪn/ *n* finlandés, -desa *m,f*, finés, -nesa *m,f*

Finnish¹ /'fɪnɪʃ/ *adj* finlandés, finés

Finnish² *n* finlandés *m*

fiord /fi'ɔ:rd ‖'fi'ɔ:d/ *n* fiordo *m*

fir /fɜ:r ‖fɜ:(r)/ *n* abeto *m*

fire¹ /faɪr ‖'faɪə(r)/ *n* ⏢1⏢ (a) (flames) fuego *m*; **to
be on ~** estar* en llamas; **to set sth on ~** *o* **to set
~ to sth** prenderle fuego a algo; **to catch ~**
prender fuego (b) (outdoors) hoguera *f*; (in hearth)
fuego *m* ⏢2⏢ (blaze which destroys a building) incendio
m; (*as interj*) ~! ¡fuego!; (*before n*) ~ **curtain**
telón *m* contra incendios; **this is a ~ hazard** esto
podría causar un incendio ⏢3⏢ (heater) estufa
f ⏢4⏢ (of guns) fuego *m*; **to open ~ on sb/sth** abrir*
fuego sobre algn/algo

fire² *vt* ⏢1⏢ ⟨gun/shot⟩ disparar; ⟨rocket⟩ lanzar*;
to ~ questions at sb hacerle* preguntas a algn
⏢2⏢ (dismiss) (colloq) echar, despedir*
⏢3⏢ ⟨imagination⟩ avivar
■ ~ *vi* (shoot) disparar; **to ~ AT sb/sth** disparar
CONTRA algn/algo; **ready, aim, ~!** apunten ¡fuego!

fire: ~ alarm *n* (apparatus) alarma *f* contra
incendios; (signal) alarma *f*; **~arm** *n* arma *f*; de
fuego; ~ **department**, (BrE) ~ **brigade** *n*
cuerpo *m* de bomberos; ~ **drill** *n* simulacro *m* de
incendio; ~ **engine** *n* (BrE) ▶ ~ TRUCK; ~
escape *n* escalera *f* de incendios; ~
extinguisher *n* extinguidor *m* (de incendios)
(AmL), extintor *m* (Esp); ~**fighter** *n* bombero *mf*;
~ **guard** *n* rejilla *f* (de chimenea); ~**lighter** *n*:
líquido o pastilla utilizados para facilitar el
encendido del fuego de leña o carbón; ~**man**
/'faɪrmən ‖'faɪəmən/ *n* (*pl* **-men** /-mən/) *n*
bombero *m*; ~**place** *n* chimenea *f*; ~**proof** *adj*
ignífugo; ~**side** *n* hogar *m*; ~ **station** *n*
estación *f* or (Esp) parque *m* or (RPl) cuartel *m* de ⸱⸱⸱❖

bomberos, bomba f (Chi); ∼ **truck** n (AmE) carro
m or (Esp) coche m de bomberos, autobomba m
(RPl), bomba f (Chi); ∼**wood** n leña f; ∼**works**
pl n fuegos mpl artificiales

firing /'faɪrɪŋ ‖ 'faɪrɪŋ/ : ∼ **line** n: **to be on o**
(BrE) **in the** ∼ **line** (exposed to criticism) estar*
expuesto a las críticas; (Mil) estar* en la línea de
combate; ∼ **squad** n pelotón m de fusilamiento

firm¹ /fɜːrm ‖ fɜːm/ adj **1 (a)** (secure) ⟨grasp⟩
firme **(b)** (not yielding) ⟨surface/muscles⟩ firme;
⟨mattress⟩ duro; ⟨foundation⟩ sólido **2 (a)**
(steadfast) ⟨friendship⟩ sólido; ⟨support⟩ firme **(b)**
(strict) estricto **3** (definite) ⟨offer/date⟩ en firme

firm² n empresa f, firma f

firmly /'fɜːrmli ‖ 'fɜːmli/ adv ⟨grasp/believe⟩ con
firmeza; ⟨fixed/supported⟩ firmemente

first¹ /fɜːrst ‖ fɜːst/ adj

■ **Note** The usual translation of *first*, *primero*,
becomes *primer* when it precedes a masculine
singular noun.

1 (initial) primero; **the** ∼ **president of the USA** el
primer presidente de los EE UU; **who's going to
be** ∼? ¿quién va a ser el primero?; ∼ **things first**
primero lo más importante
2 (elliptical use): **he'll be arriving on the** ∼ (of the
month) llegará el primero or (Esp tb) el uno (del
mes); **she was the** ∼ **to arrive** fue la primera en
llegar
3 (in phrases) **at first** al principio; **from first to
last** de(l) principio a(l) fin

first² adv **1 (a)** (ahead of others) primero; **he
came** ∼ **in the exam** sacó la mejor nota en el
examen; **I always put my children** ∼ para mí
antes que nada están mis hijos; **ladies** ∼ primero
las damas **(b)** (before other actions, events) primero
(c) (beforehand) antes **(d)** (for the first time) por
primera vez **2** (in phrases) **first and foremost**
ante todo; **first and last** por encima de todo; **first
of all** en primer lugar

first³ (a) ∼ **(gear)** (Auto) (no art) primera f **(b)**
(original idea, accomplishment) primicia f

first: ∼ **aid** n primeros auxilios mpl; (before n)
∼**aid kit** botiquín m (de primeros auxilios);
∼**aid station** o (BrE) **post** puesto m de primeros
auxilios; ∼ **class** adv ⟨travel⟩ en primera
(clase); ∼**class** /'fɜːrst'klæs ‖ ,fɜːst'klɑːs/ adj
(pred ∼ **class**) **(a)** (of highest grade) ⟨hotel/ticket⟩
de primera clase; ⟨travel⟩ en primera (clase) **(b)**
(excellent) de primera **(c)** (BrE Corresp) ∼**class mail**
*correspondencia enviada a una tarifa superior,
que garantiza una rápida entrega*; ∼**hand**
/'fɜːrst'hænd ‖ ,fɜːst'hænd/ adj ⟨news⟩ de primera
mano; ∼ **lady** n primera dama f

firstly /'fɜːrstli ‖ 'fɜːstli/ adv (as linker) en
primer lugar

first: ∼ **name** n nombre m de pila; ∼**rate**
/'fɜːrst'reɪt ‖ ,fɜːst'reɪt/ adj de primera; ∼**time
buyer** n: *persona que compra algo, gen una
vivienda, por primera vez*

fiscal /'fɪskəl/ adj fiscal

fiscal year n (AmE) año m fiscal

fish¹ /fɪʃ/ n (pl **fish** or **fishes**) **(a)** (Zool) pez m;
(before n) ∼ **pond** estanque m; ∼ **tank** pecera f
(b) (Culin) pescado m; ∼ **and chips** (esp BrE)
pescado m frito con papas or (Esp) patatas fritas

fish² vi pescar*; **to go** ∼**ing** ir* de pesca; **to** ∼
FOR sth ⟨for trout⟩ pescar* algo; ⟨for compliments⟩
andar* a la caza de algo; **to** ∼ (around) **in one's
pockets/bag** rebuscar* en los bolsillos/la bolsa
■ **fish out** [v + o + adv, v + adv + o] sacar*

fish: ∼**bone** n espina f (de pez); ∼**cake** n
≈ croqueta f (de pescado y papas)

fisherman /'fɪʃərmən ‖ 'fɪʃəmən/ n (pl **-men**
/-mən/) pescador m

fishery /'fɪʃəri/ n (pl **-eries**) **1** ▶ FISH FARM
2 fisheries pl (industry) industria f pesquera,
pesca f

fish: ∼ **farm** n piscifactoría f; ∼ **finger** n
(BrE) ▶ FISH STICK; ∼**hook** n anzuelo m

fishing /'fɪʃɪŋ/ n pesca f; (before n) ⟨industry/
port/vessel/fleet⟩ pesquero

fishing: ∼ **net** n red f de pesca; ∼ **pole** n
(AmE), ∼ **rod** n caña f de pescar

fish: ∼**monger** /'fɪʃ,mɑːŋgər ‖ 'fɪʃ,mʌŋgə(r)/ n
(BrE) pescadero, -ra m,f; **at the** ∼**monger('s)** en
la pescadería; ∼**net** n **(a)** (AmE) ▶ FISHING NET
(b) (Tex) red f; (before n) ⟨stockings⟩ de malla
gruesa or de red; ∼ **slice** n (BrE) espumadera f,
∼ **stick** n (AmE) palito m de bacalao (or
merluza etc) (trozo de pescado rebozado y frito)

fishy /'fɪʃi/ adj **fishier, fishiest 1** ⟨smell/
taste⟩ a pescado **2** (suspicious) (colloq) sospechoso

fission /'fɪʃən/ n fisión f

fist /fɪst/ n puño m

fistfight /'fɪstfaɪt/ n pelea f (a puñetazos)

fit¹ /fɪt/ adj **-tt-** **1 (a)** (healthy) en forma; **to keep** ∼
mantenerse* en forma; **to be** ∼ **to** + INF ⟨to play/
travel⟩ estar* en condiciones DE + INF **2** (suitable)
⟨person/conduct⟩ adecuado; **this isn't** ∼ **to eat**
(harmful) esto no está en buenas condiciones;
(unappetizing) esto está incomible; **he's not** ∼ **to be
a father** no es digno de ser padre; **he did not see**
∼ **to reply to our letter** ni se dignó contestar a
nuestra carta

fit² **-tt-** vt **1 (a)** (Clothing): **the dress** ∼**s you
perfectly** el vestido te queda perfecto; **the jacket
doesn't** ∼ **me** la chaqueta no me queda bien **(b)**
(be right size, shape for) ⟨socket⟩ encajar en **(c)**
(correspond to) ⟨theory⟩ concordar* con; **to** ∼ **a
description** responder a una descripción
2 (install) (esp BrE) ⟨carpet/lock⟩ poner*; ⟨double
glazing⟩ instalar
3 (accommodate) **to** ∼ **sth INTO sth** meter algo EN
algo
■ ∼ vi **(a)** (Clothing): **these shoes don't** ∼ estos
zapatos no me quedan bien; **to make sth** ∼
ajustar algo **(b)** (be right size, shape) «lid» ajustar;
«key/peg» encajar **(c)** (correspond) «facts/
description» encajar
■ **fit in** **1** [v + adv] **(a)** (have enough room) caber*
(b) (accord) «detail/event» **to** ∼ **in** (WITH sth)
concordar* (CON algo) **(c)** (belong): **she doesn't** ∼

in **here** esto no es para ella **(d)** (conform to): **he'll have to** ∼ **in with our plans** tendrá que amoldarse a nuestros planes
2 [*v* + *o* + *adv*, *v* + *adv* + *o*] **(a)** (find space for) acomodar **(b)** (find time for): **I can** ∼ **you in at ten o'clock** puedo atenderla a las diez; **she hoped to** ∼ **in some sightseeing** esperaba tener un poco de tiempo para salir a conocer el lugar
■ **fit out** [*v* + *o* + *adv*, *v* + *adv* + *o*] equipar; **to** ∼ **sb out WITH sth** ⟨*with boots/equipment*⟩ equipar a algn CON algo; ⟨*with uniform*⟩ proveer* a algn DE algo

fit³ *n* **1** **(a)** (attack) ataque *m*; **epileptic** ∼ ataque epiléptico; **to have a** ∼ (colloq): **I nearly had a** ∼ casi me da un ataque (fam) **(b)** (short burst): **a** ∼ **of coughing** un acceso de tos; **in** ∼**s and starts** a los tropezones **2** (of clothes) (*no pl*): **my new jacket is a good** ∼ la chaqueta nueva me queda bien; **it's a tight** ∼ es muy entallado

fitful /'fɪtfəl/ *adj* ⟨*progress/sunshine*⟩ intermitente; ⟨*sleep*⟩ irregular

fitfully /'fɪtfəli/ *adv* de manera irregular

fitness /'fɪtnəs ‖'fɪtnɪs/ *n* **1** (healthiness) salud *f*; **(physical)** ∼ (buena) forma *f* física **2** (suitability) aptitud *f*

fitted /'fɪtəd ‖'fɪtɪd/ *adj* **(a)** ⟨*cupboard*⟩ empotrado; ⟨*shelves*⟩ hecho a medida; ⟨*sheet*⟩ ajustable, de cajón (Méx); ∼ **carpet** (esp BrE) alfombra *f* de pared a pared, moqueta *f* (Esp) **(b)** ⟨*kitchen*⟩ integral

fitter /'fɪtər ‖'fɪtə(r)/ *n* **1** (Clothing) probador, -dora *m,f* **2** (mechanic — in garage) mecánico, -ca *m,f*; (— in car industry, shipbuilding) operario, -ria *m,f*

fitting¹ /'fɪtɪŋ/ *adj* ⟨*conclusion*⟩ adecuado; ⟨*tribute*⟩ digno

fitting² *n* **1** (Clothing) **(a)** (trying on) prueba *f* **(b)** (BrE) (size — of clothes) medida *f*; (— of shoe) horma *f* **2** **(a)** (accessory) accesorio *m* **(b)** **fittings** *pl* (esp BrE Const) accesorios *mpl*; **electrical** ∼**s** instalaciones *fpl* eléctricas; **bathroom** ∼**s** grifería *f* y accesorios *mpl* de baño

fitting room *n* probador *m*

five /faɪv/ *adj/n* cinco *adj inv/m*; *see also* FOUR¹

fiver /'faɪvər ‖'faɪvə(r)/ *n* **(a)** ($5) (AmE sl) cinco dólares *mpl* **(b)** (£5) (BrE colloq) cinco libras *fpl*

fix¹ /fɪks/ *vt*
I **1** ⟨*plank/shelf*⟩ sujetar; **to** ∼ **a notice on a door** poner* un anuncio en una puerta; **to** ∼ **sth in one's memory** grabar algo en la memoria **2** (direct steadily): **his eyes were** ∼**ed on the road ahead** tenía la mirada fija en la carretera; **he** ∼**ed her with a stony gaze** clavó en ella una mirada glacial
II **1** ⟨*date/time/price*⟩ fijar **2** (repair) (colloq) arreglar **3** (prepare) (esp AmE colloq) preparar **4** (colloq) ⟨*election/contest*⟩ amañar (fam)
■ ∼ *vi* (make plans) (AmE): **we're** ∼**ing to go fishing on Sunday** estamos planeando ir de pesca el domingo
■ **fix up** [*v* + *o* + *adv*, *v* + *adv* + *o*] **(a)** (provide for): **I need somewhere to stay: can you** ∼ **me up?** necesito alojamiento ¿me lo puedes arreglar?; **she** ∼**ed me up with a job** me encontró un trabajo **(b)** (repair) ⟨*house/room*⟩ (AmE) arreglar

fix² *n* (predicament) (colloq) aprieto *m*, apuro *m*

fixation /fɪk'seɪʃən/ *n* obsesión *f*

fixed /fɪkst/ *adj* **1** ⟨*price/rate/ideas*⟩ fijo; ⟨*principles/position*⟩ rígido; **a** ∼**-term contract** un contrato a plazo fijo **2** ⟨*gaze*⟩ fijo; ⟨*smile*⟩ petrificado

fixed: ∼ **assets** *pl n* activo *m* fijo; ∼**-rate** /'fɪkst'reɪt/ *adj* a una tasa de interés fija *or* (esp Esp) a tipo de interés fijo

fixture /'fɪkstʃər ‖'fɪkstʃə(r)/ *n* **1** **(a)** (in building) *elemento de la instalación, como los artefactos del baño, cocina etc* **(b)** (permanent feature) parte *f* integrante **2** (BrE Sport) encuentro *m*

fizz /fɪz/ *vi* ⟨*champagne/cola*⟩ burbujear

fizzle out /'fɪzəl/ [*v* + *adv*] ⟨*fire/firework*⟩ apagarse*; ⟨*excitement*⟩ esfumarse

fizzy /'fɪzi/ *adj* **-zier, -ziest** gaseoso, efervescente; ∼ **water** (colloq) agua *f‡* mineral con gas

fjord /fi'ɔːrd ‖fɪ'ɔːd/ *n* fiordo *m*

FL, Fla = Florida

flabbergasted /'flæbərˌgæstəd ‖'flæbəˌgɑːstɪd/ *adj* estupefacto

flabby /'flæbi/ *adj* **-bier, -biest** ⟨*stomach*⟩ fofo; ⟨*muscle*⟩ flojo

flag¹ /flæg/ *n* bandera *f*

flag² **-gg-** *vi* ⟨⟨*person/animal*⟩⟩ desfallecer*; ⟨⟨*interest/conversation/spirits*⟩⟩ decaer*; ⟨⟨*attendance*⟩⟩ disminuir*
■ ∼ *vt* **(a)** (mark with flags) marcar* con banderas **(b)** (mark for special attention) marcar*
■ **flag down** [*v* + *o* + *adv*, *v* + *adv* + *o*] parar (haciendo señas)

flagpole /'flæɡpəʊl/ *n* asta *f‡* de (la) bandera

flagrant /'fleɪɡrənt/ *adj* flagrante

flag: ∼**ship** *n* (Naut) buque *m* insignia; (showpiece) producto *m* (*or* programa *m etc*) bandera; ∼**stone** *n* losa *f*

flair /fler ‖fleə(r)/ *n* **(a)** (natural aptitude) (*no pl*): **a** ∼ **for languages/business** facilidad *f* para los idiomas/olfato *m* para los negocios **(b)** (stylishness) estilo *m*

flak /flæk/ *n* **(a)** (Aviat, Mil) fuego *m* antiaéreo **(b)** (criticism) críticas *fpl*

flake¹ /fleɪk/ *n* (of snow, cereals) copo *m*; (of paint, rust, skin) escama *f*

flake² *vi* ⟨⟨*paint/plaster*⟩⟩ descascararse

flaky, flakey /'fleɪki/ *adj* **-kier, -kiest** ⟨*piecrust*⟩ hojaldrado; ⟨*paint/plaster*⟩ que se desconcha; ∼ **pastry** masa tipo hojaldre

flamboyant /flæm'bɔɪənt/ *adj* **(a)** (dashing) ⟨*style/person*⟩ exuberante; ⟨*gesture*⟩ ampuloso **(b)** (brilliant) ⟨*color*⟩ vistoso; ⟨*hat/dress*⟩ llamativo

flame /fleɪm/ *n* **(a)** (flame) llama *f*; **to be in** ∼**s** estar* (envuelto) en llamas; **to go up in** ∼**s** incendiarse **(b)** (lover): **he's an old** ∼ **of mine** es un antiguo enamorado mío

flame: ∼**proof** *adj* ⟨*fabric*⟩ ininflamable; ⟨*dish*⟩ resistente al fuego; ∼**thrower** /'fleɪm'θrəʊər ‖'fleɪmˌθrəʊə(r)/ *n* lanzallamas *m*

flamingo /flə'mɪŋɡəʊ/ *n* (*pl* **-gos** *or* **-goes**) flamenco *m*

flammable /'flæməbəl/ *adj* inflamable, flamable (Méx)

flan /flæn/ *n* (sweet) tarta *f*, kuchen *m* (Chi); (individual) tartaleta *f*, tarteleta *f* (RPl)

flank¹ /flæŋk/ n (a) (of animal) ijada f, ijar m; (of person) costado m (b) (Mil, Sport) flanco m

flank² vt (often pass) flanquear

flannel /'flænl/ n ⓵ (a) (fabric) franela f; (before n) ⟨shirt/nightgown⟩ de franela (b) **flannels** pl (trousers) pantalón m de franela ⓶ (face ∼) (BrE) toallita f (para lavarse)

flap¹ /flæp/ n ⓵ (a) (cover) tapa f; (of pocket, envelope) solapa f; (of table) hoja f; (of jacket, coat) faldón m; (of tent) portezuela f; (ear ∼) orejera f; **a cat ∼** una gatera (b) (Aviat) alerón m ⓶ (motion) aletazo m ⓷ (commotion, agitation) (colloq): **to be in/ get into a ∼** estar*/ponerse* como loco (fam)

flap² -pp- vi ⟨⟨sail/curtain⟩⟩ agitarse; ⟨⟨flag⟩⟩ ondear
■ ∼ vt ⟨wings⟩ batir; ⟨arms⟩ agitar

flapjack /'flæpdʒæk/ n ⓵ (pancake) (esp AmE) crepe o panqueque pequeño y grueso ⓶ (cookie) (BrE) tipo de galleta dulce de avena

flare /fler ‖fleə(r)/ n ⓵ (a) (marker light) bengala f; (on runway, road) baliza f (b) (sudden light) destello m; (flame) llamarada f ⓶ (Clothing) (a) (on jacket) vuelo m (b) **flares** (BrE) pantalones mpl acampanados
■ **flare up** [v + adv] (a) ⟨⟨fire⟩⟩ llamear; ⟨⟨fighting⟩⟩ estallar (b) ⟨⟨infection/disease⟩⟩ recrudecer* (c) (lose temper) explotar

flared /flerd ‖fleəd/ adj ⟨skirt⟩ con mucho vuelo, evasé (RPl); ⟨trousers⟩ acampanado

flare-up /'flerʌp ‖'fleəʌp/ n (of violence) brote m

flash¹ /flæʃ/ n ⓵ (a) (of light) destello m; (from explosion) fogonazo m; **a ∼ of inspiration** un ramalazo de inspiración; (as) **quick as a ∼** como un rayo; **in a ∼**: **it came to me in a ∼** de repente lo vi claro (b) (Phot) flash m ⓶ (news ∼) avance m informativo

flash² vt ⓵ (direct): **they ∼ed a light in my face** me enfocaron la cara con una luz; **to ∼ one's headlights at sb** hacerle* una señal con los faros a algn ⓶ (show) ⟨card⟩ mostrar*, enseñar (esp Esp); **she loves ∼ing her money around** le encanta ir por ahí haciendo ostentación de su dinero
■ ∼ vi ⓵ (a) (emit sudden light) destellar (b) (Auto) hacer* una señal con los faros (c) **flashing** pres p ⟨sign/light⟩ intermitente; ⟨eyes/smile⟩ brillante ⓶ (move fast) (+ adv compl): **a message ∼ed across the screen** un mensaje apareció fugazmente en la pantalla; **to ∼ by** o **past** ⟨⟨train/ car/person⟩⟩ pasar como una bala

flash: ∼**back** n (Cin, Lit) flashback m; ∼**bulb** n (Phot) lámpara f de flash; ∼**cube** n (Phot) cubo m (de) flash; ∼ **gun** n flash m electrónico; ∼**light** n (AmE) linterna f

flashy /'flæʃi/ adj **-shier, -shiest** llamativo

flask /flæsk ‖flɑːsk/ n (bottle) frasco m; (in laboratory) matraz m; (hip ∼) petaca f, nalguera f (Méx); (vacuum ∼) (BrE) termo m

flat¹ /flæt/ adj **-tt-** ⓵ (a) ⟨surface⟩ plano; ⟨countryside⟩ llano; ∼ **feet** pies mpl planos; **I was ∼ on my back for two months** estuve en cama durante dos semanas (b) ⟨dish⟩ llano, bajo (Chi), playo (RPl); ∼ **shoes** zapatos mpl bajos, zapatillas ʃpi de piso (Méx) (c) (deflated) ⟨ball⟩ desinflado,

ponchado (Méx); **you have a ∼ tire** o (BrE) **tyre** tienes un neumático desinflado or (Méx) una llanta ponchada
⓶ (a) ⟨lemonade/beer⟩ sin efervescencia (b) ⟨battery⟩ descargado
⓷ (dull, uninteresting) ⟨conversation/party⟩ soso (fam); ⟨joke⟩ sin gracia; ⟨voice⟩ monótono; **to fall ∼** ⟨⟨play/project⟩⟩ fracasar*; **the joke fell very ∼** el chiste no hizo ni pizca de gracia
⓸ (total, firm) ⟨denial/refusal⟩ rotundo
⓹ (Mus) (referring to key) bemol; **A ∼** la m bemol
⓺ (fixed) (before n) ⟨rate⟩ fijo

flat² adv ⓵ (a) ⟨refuse/turn down⟩ de plano (b) (exactly): **it took him two hours ∼** tardó dos horas justas ⓶ (Mus) demasiado bajo

flat³ n ⓵ (apartment) (BrE) apartamento m, departamento m (AmL), piso m (Esp) ⓶ (a) (surface — of sword) cara f de la hoja; (— of hand) palma f (b) (level ground) llano m ⓷ (Mus) bemol m

flatly /'flætli/ adv de plano

flatmate /'flætmeɪt/ n (BrE) compañero, -ra m,f de apartamento or (Esp) de piso

flat out¹ adj (colloq) (pred) (prostrate) tirado

flat out² adv (at full speed) (colloq) a toda máquina

flat-rate /'flætreɪt/ adj (BrE) a una tasa de interés fija or (esp Esp) a tipo de interés fijo

flatten /'flætn/ vt ⟨surface⟩ aplanar; ⟨path/ lawn⟩ allanar; ⟨city⟩ arrasar

flatter /'flætər ‖'flætə(r)/ vt (a) (gratify) halagar* (b) (show to advantage) favorecer*

flattering /'flætərɪŋ/ adj (a) ⟨words/speech⟩ halagador (b) ⟨clothes/hairstyle⟩ favorecedor

flattery /'flætəri/ n halagos mpl

flaunt /flɔːnt/ vt ⟨possessions⟩ hacer* ostentación de; ⟨knowledge⟩ alardear de

flavor¹, (BrE) **flavour** /'fleɪvər ‖'fleɪvə(r)/ n sabor m, gusto m

flavor², (BrE) **flavour** vt sazonar; **chocolate-∼ed** con sabor or gusto a chocolate

flavoring, (BrE) **flavouring** /'fleɪvərɪŋ/ n condimento m

flaw /flɔː/ n (in material, character) defecto m; (in argument) error m

flawless /'flɔːləs ‖'flɔːlɪs/ adj ⟨performance/ logic⟩ impecable; ⟨conduct⟩ intachable; ⟨complexion/gem⟩ perfecto

flax /flæks/ n lino m

flay /fleɪ/ vt desollar*

flea /fliː/ n pulga f; (before n) ⟨collar/powder⟩ antipulgas adj inv

flea market n mercado m de las pulgas or (CS) de pulgas, rastro m (Esp)

fleck¹ /flek/ n (of dust) mota f; (of paint, mud) salpicadura f

fleck² vt (with mud) salpicar*; **beige ∼ed with brown** beige moteado de marrón

fled /fled/ past & past p of FLEE

fledgling, fledgeling /'fledʒlɪŋ/ n polluelo m; (before n) **a ∼ democracy** una democracia en ciernes

flee /fliː/ (past & past p **fled**) vi huir*
■ ∼ vt huir* de

fleece¹ /fliːs/ n (on sheep) lana f; (from sheep) vellón m

fleece² *vt* (colloq) desplumar (fam)

fleet /fliːt/ *n* **(a)** (naval unit, body of shipping) flota *f* **(b)** (navy) armada *f* **(c)** (of cars) parque *m* móvil, flota *f*

fleeting /'fliːtɪŋ/ *adj* (*usu before n*) fugaz

Flemish¹ /'flemɪʃ/ *adj* flamenco

Flemish² *n* flamenco *m*

flesh /fleʃ/ *n* carne *f*; **in the ~** en persona; **~ and blood**: after all, I'm only **~ and blood** después de todo, soy de carne y hueso

fleshy /'fleʃi/ *adj* **-shier, -shiest** *adj* ‹arms/ person› rollizo; ‹plant/leaf› carnoso

flew /fluː/ *past of* FLY²

flex¹ /fleks/ *vt* ‹arm/knees/body› doblar; **to ~ one's muscles** (to warm up) hacer* ejercicios de calentamiento; (in body building) mostrar* los músculos; «*regime*» mostrar* su poderío

flex² *n* (BrE) cable *m* (eléctrico)

flexible /'fleksəbəl/ *adj* flexible

flextime /'flekstaɪm/, (BrE) **flexitime** /'fleksɪtaɪm/ *n* horario *m* flexible

flick¹ /flɪk/ *vt* **(a)** (strike lightly): **she ~ed a piece of bread at me** me tiró un pedazo de pan **(b)** (remove): **he ~ed the ash off his lapel** se sacudió la ceniza de la solapa
■ **flick through** [*v + prep + o*] ‹book› hojear; ‹pages› pasar

flick² *n* (of tail) coletazo *m*; (of wrist) giro *m*

flicker¹ /'flɪkər ‖'flɪkə(r)/ *vi* parpadear

flicker² *n* parpadeo *m*

flier /'flaɪər ‖'flaɪə(r)/ *n* **1 (a)** (pilot) aviador, -dora *m,f* **(b)** (passenger) usuario -ria *m,f* (regular) del avion **2** (handbill) (AmE) folleto *m* (publicitario), volante *m* (AmL)

flight /flaɪt/ *n* **1 (a)** (of bird, aircraft) vuelo *m*; (of ball, projectile) trayectoria *f*; **in ~** en vuelo **(b)** (air journey) vuelo *m*; (*before n*) **~ path** ruta *f*; **~ recorder** caja *f* negra **2** (group of birds) bandada *f* **3** (of stairs) tramo *m* **4** (act of fleeing) huida *f*; **to take ~** darse* a la fuga

flight: **~ attendant** *n* auxiliar *mf* de vuelo; **~ deck** *n* (on plane) cabina *f* de mando; (on aircraft carrier) cubierta *f* de vuelo

flimsy /'flɪmzi/ *adj* **-sier, -siest** **(a)** ‹material/ garment› ligerísimo **(b)** ‹construction/object› endeble **(c)** ‹excuse› pobre; ‹argument/evidence› poco sólido

flinch /flɪntʃ/ *vi* estremecerse*

fling¹ /flɪŋ/ *vt* (*past & past p* **flung**) lanzar*, aventar* (Col, Méx, Per)

fling² *n* (colloq) **(a)** (love affair) aventura *f*; **to have a ~** tener* una aventurilla **(b)** (wild time) juerga *f* (fam); **to have a ~** irse* de juerga

flint /flɪnt/ *n* **(a)** (Geol) sílex *m*, pedernal *m*; (piece of stone) pedernal *m* **(b)** (for cigarette lighter) piedra *f*

flip /flɪp/ **-pp-** *vt* tirar, aventar* (Méx); **we'll ~ a coin to decide** vamos a echarlo a cara o cruz *or* (Andes, Ven) a cara o sello *or* (Arg) a cara o ceca, vamos a echar un volado (Méx)
■ **~** *vi* (sl) (lose self-control) perder* la chaveta (fam)

flip-flop /'flɪpflɑːp ‖'flɪpflɒp/ *n* (BrE) ▶ THONG B

flippant /'flɪpənt/ *adj* ‹remark› frívolo; ‹attitude› displicente

flipper /'flɪpər ‖'flɪpə(r)/ *n* aleta *f*

flip side *n* **the ~ ~** (Audio) la cara B; (of a situation) (colloq) la otra cara de la moneda (fam)

flirt¹ /flɜːrt ‖flɜːt/ *vi* flirtear

flirt² *n*: **he is a terrible ~** le encanta flirtear

flirtation /flɜːr'teɪʃən ‖flɜː'teɪʃən/ *n* **(a)** (relationship) flirt *m* **(b)** (coquetry) flirteo *m*

flit /flɪt/ *vi* **-tt-** «*bird/butterfly/bat*» revolotear

float¹ /fləʊt/ *vi* **(a)** (on water) flotar; **to ~ (up) to the surface** salir* a flote **(b)** «*cloud/smoke*» flotar en el aire
■ **~** *vt* **1** ‹ship/boat› poner* a flote; ‹raft/logs› llevar **2** (Fin) **(a)** (establish): **to ~ a company** introducir* una compañía en Bolsa **(b)** ‹shares/ stock› emitir* **(c)** ‹currency› dejar flotar **3** (circulate) ‹idea› presentar

float² *n* **1 (a)** (for fishing, for buoyancy) flotador *m* **(b)** (in cistern, carburetor) flotador *m* **(c)** (raft, platform) plataforma *f* (flotante) **2 (a)** (in parade) carroza *f*, carro *m* alegórico (CS, Méx) **(b)** (milk ~) (BrE) furgoneta *f* (*del reparto de leche*) **3** (ready cash) caja *f* chica; (Busn, Fin) fondo *m* fijo

floating /'fləʊtɪŋ/ *adj* (*before n*) **1** ‹harbor/ restaurant› flotante **2** (Fin) ‹currency› flotante; ‹assets› circulante **3** ‹population› flotante; ‹voter› (BrE) indeciso

flock¹ /flɑːk ‖flɒk/ *n* (+ *sing or pl vb*) (of sheep) rebaño *m*; (of birds) bandada *f*; (of people) (*often pl*) tropel *m*, multitud *f*

flock² *vi* acudir (*en gran número, en masa*)

floe /fləʊ/ *n* témpano *m* de hielo

flog /flɑːg ‖flɒg/ *vt* **-gg-** **1** (beat) azotar **2** (sell) (BrE sl) vender

flood¹ /flʌd/ *n* (of water) inundación *f*; (of complaints, calls) avalancha *f*; **she was in ~s of tears** estaba hecha un mar de lágrimas

flood² *vt* inundar; ‹engine› ahogar*; **to ~ the market with imports** (Busn) inundar el mercado de productos importados
■ **~** *vi* ‹river/sewers› desbordarse; «*mine/ basement*» inundarse; (Auto) ahogarse*; **to ~ in** «*sunshine*» entrar a raudales; **donations came ~ing in** llovieron los donativos

flooding /'flʌdɪŋ/ *n* inundación *f*

floodlight¹ /'flʌdlaɪt/ *n* reflector *m*, foco *m*

floodlight² *vt* (*past & past p* **floodlit** /'flʌdlɪt/) **(a)** iluminar (*con reflectores o focos*) **(b)**
floodlit *past p* ‹arena/building› iluminado*; ‹game› que se juega con luz artificial

flood: **~ tide** *n* pleamar *f*; **~water** *n* (*often pl*) crecida *f*

floor¹ /flɔːr ‖flɔː(r)/ *n* **1 (a)** (of room, vehicle) suelo *m*, piso *m* (AmL) **(b)** (for dancing) pista *f* (de baile) **(c)** (of ocean, valley, forest) fondo *m* **2** (storey) piso *m*; **we live on the first/second ~** (AmE) vivimos en la planta baja/el primer piso *or* (Chi) en el primer/segundo piso; (BrE) vivimos en el primer/segundo piso *or* (Chi) en el segundo/tercer piso

floor² *vt* **(a)** (knock down) derribar **(b)** (nonplus) (colloq) dejar helado (fam)

floorboard /'flɔːrbɔːrd ‖'flɔːbɔːd/ *n* tabla *f* del suelo, duela *f* (Méx)

flooring /'flɔːrɪŋ/ *n* revestimiento *m* para suelos

floor show *n* espectáculo *m* (*de cabaret*)

flop¹ /flɑːp ‖flɒp/ *vi* **-pp-** **1** (fall, move slackly) (+ ····>

··· **flop** ···▷ **fly**

630

adv compl): **she ~ped down into a chair** se dejó
caer en un sillón; **he ~ped down exhausted onto
the bed** se desplomó en la cama muerto de
cansancio **2** (fail) (colloq) fracasar
estrepitosamente

flop² *n* (colloq) fracaso *m*

floppy¹ /ˈflɑːpi ‖ ˈflɒpi/ *adj* ‹hat/bag› flexible;
‹ears/tail› caído

floppy² *n* (*pl* **-pies**) (colloq) ▶ FLOPPY DISK

floppy disk *n* disquete *m*, floppy (disk) *m*

floral /ˈflɔːrəl/ *adj* ‹fabric/dress› floreado; **a ~
print** un estampado de flores

florid /ˈflɔːrəst ‖ ˈflɒrɪd/ *adj* **(a)** (red)
‹complexion› rubicundo **(b)** (ornate) ‹decoration/
style› recargado; ‹language› florido

florist /ˈflɔːrəst ‖ ˈflɒrɪst/ *n* (person) florista *mf*;
is there a ~'s near here? ¿hay una floristería *or*
(AmL tb) florería cerca de aquí?

flotation /fləʊˈteɪʃən/ *n* (of company) salida *f* a
Bolsa; (of shares) emisión *f*

flotsam /ˈflɑːtsəm ‖ ˈflɒtsəm/ *n* restos *mpl*
flotantes (de un naufragio); **~ and jetsam**
desechos *mpl*

flounce¹ /flaʊns/ *vi* (+ *adv compl*): **to ~ in/out**
entrar/salir* indignado (*or* airado *etc*)

flounce² *n* (ruffle) volante *m*, elán *m* (Méx),
volado *m* (RPl), vuelo *m* (Chi)

flounder /ˈflaʊndər ‖ ˈflaʊndə(r)/ *vi* **(a)** (in
water) luchar para mantenerse a flote **(b)**
‹speaker› quedarse sin saber qué decir

flour /flaʊər ‖ ˈflaʊə(r)/ *n* harina *f*

flourish¹ /ˈflɜːrɪʃ ‖ ˈflʌrɪʃ/ *vi* ‹arts/trade›
florecer*; ‹business› prosperar; ‹plant› darse*
or crecer* bien
■ **~** *vt* ‹stick/letter› blandir

flourish² *n* **(a)** (showy gesture) floreo *m* **(b)**
(embellishment) floritura *f*, firulete *m* (AmL); (in
signature) rúbrica *f*

flourishing /ˈflɜːrɪʃɪŋ ‖ ˈflʌrɪʃɪŋ/ *adj* ‹business›
próspero

flout /flaʊt/ *vt* desobedecer* abiertamente

flow¹ /fləʊ/ *vi* **(a)** ‹liquid/electric current›
fluir*; ‹tide› subir; ‹blood› correr; (from wound)
manar **(b)** (run smoothly, continuously) ‹traffic›
circular con fluidez; ‹music/words› fluir*

flow² *n* **1** **(a)** (of liquid, current) flujo *m* **(b)** (of
traffic, information) circulación *f*; (of capital, money)
movimiento *m* **2** (stream — of water, lava)
corriente *f*

flow chart, flow diagram *n* organigrama *m*

flower¹ /flaʊər ‖ ˈflaʊə(r)/ *n* flor *f*

flower² *vi* florecer*, florear (Chi, Méx)

flower: ~bed *n* arriate *m* (Esp, Méx), parterre
m (Esp), cantero *m* (Cu, RPl); **~pot** *n* maceta *f*,
tiesto *m* (Esp), macetero *m* (AmS)

flowery /ˈflaʊri ‖ ˈflaʊəri/ *adj* ‹pattern›
floreado; ‹meadow› florido; ‹style/prose› florido

flowing /ˈfləʊɪŋ/ *adj* **(a)** ‹beard/robe› largo y
suelto **(b)** ‹handwriting/movement› fluido

flown /fləʊn/ *past p of* FLY²

flu /fluː/ *n* gripe *f*, gripa *f* (Col, Méx)

fluctuate /ˈflʌktʃueɪt ‖ ˈflʌktjʊeɪt/ *vi* fluctuar*

fluctuation /ˌflʌktʃuˈeɪʃən ‖ ˌflʌktjʊˈeɪʃən/ *n*
fluctuación *f*

flue /fluː/ *n* tiro *m*

fluency /ˈfluːənsi/ *n* fluidez *f*

fluent /ˈfluːənt/ *adj*: **to speak ~ Italian** hablar
italiano con fluidez

fluently /ˈfluːəntli/ *adv* con fluidez

fluff /flʌf/ *n* pelusa *f*

fluffy /ˈflʌfi/ *adj* **-fier, -fiest** ‹fabric/garment›
suave y esponjoso; ‹fur/hair› suave y sedoso

fluid¹ /ˈfluːəd ‖ ˈfluːɪd/ *n* fluido *m*

fluid² *adj* fluido

fluke /fluːk/ *n* (colloq) chiripa *f* (fam)

flummox /ˈflʌməks/ *vt* (colloq) desconcertar*

flung /flʌŋ/ *past & past p of* FLING¹

fluorescent /ˌflʊˈresənt ‖ ˌfluəˈresənt, flɔː-/ *adj*
fluorescente; **~ light** tubo *m* fluorescente,
tubolux® *m* (RPl)

fluoride /ˈflʊraɪd ‖ ˈflɔːraɪd/ *n* (Chem) fluoruro
m; (Dent) flúor *m*; (before *n*) **~ toothpaste**
dentífrico *m* con flúor

flurry /ˈflɜːri ‖ ˈflʌri/ *n* (*pl* **-ries**) **1** (of snow,
wind) ráfaga *f*; (of rain) chaparrón *m* **2** (sudden
burst): **a ~ of excitement/activity** una oleada de
emoción/un frenesí de actividad

flush¹ /flʌʃ/ *n* **1** **(a)** (blush) rubor *m* **(b)** (of
anger, passion) arrebato *m*; **in the first ~ of
success** con la euforia del triunfo **2** (in cards)
flor *f*

flush² *vt* **1** ‹toilet›: **to ~ the toilet** tirar de la
cadena, jalarle (a la cadena) (AmL exc CS) **2** (drive
out) **~ (out)** ‹person/criminal› hacer* salir
■ **~** *vi* **1** ‹toilet› funcionar **2** (blush) ‹person/
face› (with anger) enrojecer*; (with embarrassment)
ruborizarse*

flush³ *adj* alineado

flushed /flʌʃt/ *adj* ‹cheeks› colorado; **~ with
success** exaltado por el éxito

fluster /ˈflʌstər ‖ ˈflʌstə(r)/ *vt* poner* nervioso;
to get ~ed ponerse* nervioso

flute /fluːt/ *n* flauta *f*

flutter¹ /ˈflʌtər ‖ ˈflʌtə(r)/ *vi* ‹bird/butterfly›
revolotear; ‹flag› ondear, agitarse; ‹heart›
latir con fuerza
■ **~** *vt* ‹wings› batir, sacudir

flutter² *n* **~** (of wings) (no *pl*) aleteo *m*

flux /flʌks/ *n*: **to be in (a state of) ~** estar* en
un estado de cambio

fly¹ /flaɪ/ *n* (*pl* **flies**) **1** (insect) mosca *f* **2** (on
trousers) (often *pl* in BrE) bragueta *f*, marrueco *m*
(Chi)

fly² (3rd pers sing pres **flies**; pres p **flying**; past
flew; past p **flown**) *vi* **1** **(a)** volar*;
‹passenger› ir* en avión; **to ~ away** irse*
volando; **to ~ in/out** ‹bird/bee› entrar/salir*
volando; ‹plane/pilot› llegar*/salir* (en avión)
(b) ‹flag› ondear
2 **(a)** (rush) ‹person› correr, ir* (*or* salir* *etc*)

AmC	Central America	Arg	Argentina	Cu	Cuba	Per	Peru
AmL	Latin America	Bol	Bolivia	Ec	Ecuador	RPl	River Plate Area
AmS	South America	Chi	Chile	Esp	Spain	Ur	Uruguay
Andes	Andean Region	CS	Southern Cone	Méx	Mexico	Ven	Venezuela

volando; **to ~ AT sb** lanzarse* SOBRE algn; **to ~ into a rage** ponerse* hecho una furia **(b)** (move, be thrown) volar*; **I tripped and went ~ing** tropecé y salí volando **(c)** (pass quickly) «*time*» pasar volando
■ **~** *vt* ⓵ **(a)** (control) ⟨*plane/glider/balloon*⟩ pilotar; ⟨*kite*⟩ hacer* volar *or* encumbrar (Andes), remontar (RPl) **(b)** (carry) ⟨*cargo*⟩ transportar (*en avión*); ⟨*person*⟩ llevar (*en avión*) **(c)** (travel over) ⟨*distance*⟩ recorrer (*en avión*)
⓶ ⟨*flag*⟩ izar*, enarbolar

flyer /'flaɪər ‖ 'flaɪə(r)/ *n* ▶ FLIER

flying¹ /'flaɪŋ/ *adj* (before *n*) **(a)** (hurried): **a ~ visit** una visita relámpago **(b)** ⟨*glass/debris*⟩ que vuela (por los aires)

flying² *n* **(a)** (as pilot) pilotaje *m*; (before *n*) ⟨*time/lesson*⟩ de vuelo; ⟨*helmet/jacket*⟩ de piloto **(b)** (as passenger): **I hate ~** odio viajar en avión

flying: ~ saucer *n* platillo *m* volador *or* (Esp) volante; **~ start** *n* salida *f* lanzada; **to get off to a ~ start** «*person/business*» empezar* con muy buen pie

fly: ~leaf *n* guarda *f*; **~-on-the-wall** *adj* ⟨*documentary*⟩ en el que las cámaras son meras espectadoras de la acción; **~over** *n* (BrE Transp) paso *m* elevado, paso *m* a desnivel (Méx); **~ spray** *n* insecticida *m* (*en aerosol*); **~swatter** /'flaɪˌswɔːtər ‖ 'flaɪˌswɒtə(r)/ *n* matamoscas *m*; **~wheel** *n* volante *m*

FM *n* (= **frequency modulation**) FM *f*

foal /fəʊl/ *n* (male) potro *m*, potrillo *m*; (female) potranca *f*, potra *f*

foam¹ /fəʊm/ *n* espuma *f*

foam² *vi* «*sea/waves*» hacer* espuma; **to ~ at the mouth** echar espuma por la boca

foam rubber *n* goma espuma *f*, hule *m* espuma (Méx)

fob /fɑːb ‖ fɒb/ *n* (watchchain) leontina *f*; (before *n*) **~ watch** reloj *m* de bolsillo
■ **fob off: -bb-** [*v* + *o* + *adv*] (placate) **to ~ sb off** (WITH sth) engatusar* a algn (CON algo)

focal /'fəʊkəl/ *adj* (before *n*) **(a)** (Opt) focal **(b)** ⟨*issue*⟩ central

focal point *n* **(a)** (Opt) foco *m* **(b)** (of attention, activity) centro *m*

focus¹ /'fəʊkəs/ *n* (*pl* **-cuses** *or* **foci** /'fəʊsaɪ/) ⓵ (Opt, Phot) foco *m*; **to be in/out of ~** estar* enfocado/desenfocado ⓶ (central point) centro *m*

focus² **-s-** *or* **-ss-** *vt* **(a)** (Opt, Phot) enfocar* **(b)** (concentrate) **to ~ sth** (ON sth) ⟨*attention*⟩ centrar algo (EN algo)
■ **~** *vi* **(a)** «*camera/eyes*» enfocar* **(b)** «*lecturer/ chapter/attention*» **to ~ ON sth/sb** centrarse EN algo/algn

focus group *n* grupo *m* analizado

fodder /'fɑːdər ‖ 'fɒdə(r)/ *n* forraje *m*

foe /fəʊ/ *n* (liter) enemigo, -ga *m,f*

foetus /'fiːtəs/ *n* (BrE) ▶ FETUS

fog /fɔːg ‖ fɒg/ *n* (Meteo) niebla *f*

fogbound /'fɔːgbaʊnd ‖ 'fɒgbaʊnd/ *adj* ⟨*airport/road*⟩ afectado por la niebla; ⟨*plane/ ferry*⟩ retenido a causa de la niebla

foggy /'fɔːgi ‖ 'fɒgi/ *adj* **-gier, -giest** **(a)** ⟨*day*⟩ de niebla; ⟨*weather*⟩ nebuloso; **it's ~** hay niebla **(b)** (confused) confuso

fog: ~horn *n* sirena *f* (*de niebla*); **~ light,** (BrE) **~ lamp** *n* faro *m* antiniebla

foible /'fɔɪbəl/ *n* debilidad *f*

foil¹ /fɔɪl/ *n* **(a)** (metal sheet) lámina *f* de metal **(b)** (Culin) (kitchen **~**) papel *m* de aluminio *or* de plata

foil² *vt* ⟨*plan/attempt*⟩ frustrar

foist /fɔɪst/ *vt* **to ~ sth** (OFF) ON *o* ONTO **sb** endilgarle* algo a algn

fold¹ /fəʊld/ *vt* ⓵ **(a)** (bend, bring together) ⟨*paper/ sheet*⟩ doblar; **to ~ one's arms** cruzar* los brazos ⓶ (Culin) **to ~ sth** INTO sth incorporar algo A algo
■ **~** *vi* ⓵ **(a)** «*chair/table*» plegarse*; «*map/ poster*» doblarse **(b) folding** *pres p* ⟨*chair/table*⟩ plegable ⓶ (fail) ⟨*project*⟩ venirse* abajo; «*play*» bajar de cartel; «*business*» cerrar* (sus puertas)
■ **fold up** [*v* + *o* + *adv*, *v* + *adv* + *o*] ⟨*sheet/ newspaper*⟩ doblar; ⟨*chair/table*⟩ plegar*

fold² *n* ⓵ (crease) doblez *m* ⓶ (sheep pen) redil *m*

-fold /fəʊld/ *suff*: **his income increased five~** sus ingresos se multiplicaron por cinco *or* se quintuplicaron; **the problem is three~** el problema tiene tres aspectos

folder /'fəʊldər ‖ 'fəʊldə(r)/ *n* **(a)** (for papers) carpeta *f* **(b)** (Comput) carpeta *f*

foliage /'fəʊliɪdʒ/ *n* follaje *m*

folio /'fəʊliəʊ/ *n* (*pl* **folios**) (sheet) pliego *m*; (numbered leaf) folio *m*

folk /fəʊk/ *n* ⓵ **(a)** *also* **folks** *pl* (people) (colloq) gente *f* **(b) folks** *pl* (esp AmE colloq) (relatives) familia *f*; (parents) padres *mpl*, viejos *mpl* (fam) ⓶ (+ *pl vb*) (Anthrop) pueblo *m*; (before *n*) ⟨*art/ medicine*⟩ popular; ⟨*dancing*⟩ folklórico

folk: ~lore *n* folklore *m*; **~ music** *n* (traditional) música *f* folklórica; (modern) música *f* folk; **~ song** *n* (traditional) canción *f* popular; (modern) canción *f* folk

follow /'fɑːloʊ ‖ 'fɒləʊ/ *vt* ⓵ (go, come after) seguir*; **the lecture was ~ed by a discussion** después de la conferencia hubo un debate ⓶ (keep to, conform to) ⟨*road*⟩ seguir* (por); ⟨*trail*⟩ seguir*; ⟨*instructions*⟩ seguir*; ⟨*order*⟩ cumplir; ⟨*fashion/example*⟩ seguir* ⓷ (pay close attention to) ⟨*movement/progress*⟩ seguir* de cerca; ⟨*news*⟩ mantenerse* al tanto de; ⟨*TV serial*⟩ seguir* ⓸ ⟨*argument/reasoning*⟩ entender*
■ **~** *vi* ⓵ (come after): **you go first, and I'll ~** tú ve delante que yo te sigo; **the winners were as ~s ...** los ganadores fueron ... ⓶ (be logical consequence) deducirse*; **that doesn't necessarily ~** una cosa no implica la otra ⓷ (understand) entender*
■ **follow up** [*v* + *o* + *adv*, *v* + *adv* + *o*] seguir*

follower /'fɑːloʊər ‖ 'fɒləʊə(r)/ *n* seguidor, -dora *m,f*

following¹ /'fɑːloʊŋ ‖ 'fɒləʊŋ/ *adj* (before *n*) (next) siguiente; (on) **the ~ day** al día siguiente

following² *n* ⓵ (followers) seguidores *mpl*; (admirers) admiradores *mpl* ⓶ (what, who comes next) **the ~ are to play in tomorrow's game ...** los siguientes jugarán en el partido de mañana ...; **the letter said the ~ ...** la carta decía lo siguiente ...

follow-up /'fɑːləʊʌp ‖'fɒləʊʌp/ n (sequel) continuación f; (before n): **she sent a ∼ letter** mandó una segunda (or tercera etc) carta

folly /'fɑːli ‖'fɒli/ n (pl **-lies**) locura f

fond /fɑːnd ‖fɒnd/ adj **-er, -est** [1] (pred): **she's very ∼ of Sue** le tiene mucho cariño a Sue; **he was ∼ of chocolate** le gustaba el chocolate [2] (before n) (loving) ⟨gesture/look⟩ cariñoso

fondle /'fɑːndḷ ‖'fɒndḷ/ vt acariciar

fondly /'fɑːndli ‖'fɒndli/ adv **(a)** (lovingly) cariñosamente; ⟨remember⟩ con cariño **(b)** (foolishly) ingenuamente

fondness /'fɑːndnəs ‖'fɒndnɪs/ n (love) cariño m; (liking) afición f

font /fɑːnt ‖fɒnt/ n [1] (baptismal) pila f bautismal [2] **(a)** (Print) fuente f **(b)** (Comput) font m, fuente f, juego m de caracteres

food /fuːd/ n **(a)** (in general) comida f; (before n) ⟨shortage/exports⟩ de alimentos **(b)** (specific kind) alimento m

food: ∼ poisoning n intoxicación f (por alimentos); **∼ processor** /'prɑːsesər, prəʊ‖'prəʊsesə(r)/ n robot m de cocina; **∼stuffs** pl n productos mpl alimenticios

fool¹ /fuːl/ n idiota mf; **to make a ∼ of oneself** hacer* el ridículo

fool² vt engañar

■ **fool around,** (BrE also) **fool about** [v + adv] hacer* payasadas, hacer* el tonto (Esp)

foolhardy /'fuːlhɑːrdi ‖'fuːlhɑːdi/ adj imprudente

foolish /'fuːlɪʃ/ adj ⟨person/prank⟩ tonto; ⟨look/grin⟩ de tonto; ⟨decision/plan⟩ insensato

fool: ∼proof adj ⟨idea/plan⟩ infalible; ⟨machine⟩ sencillo de manejar; **∼scap** /'fuːlskæp/ n pliego de aprox 33 x 22 cm

foot¹ /fʊt/ n (pl **feet**) [1] (of person) pie m; (of animal) pata f; (on sewing machine) pie m; **to be on one's feet** estar* de pie, estar* parado (AmL); **to go/come on ∼** ir*/venir* a pie; **to find one's feet: it didn't take him long to find his feet in his new school** no tardó en habituarse a la nueva escuela; **to put one's ∼ down** (be firm) imponerse*; (accelerate vehicle) (colloq) apretar* el acelerador, meterle (AmL fam); **to put one's ∼ in it** (colloq) meter la pata (fam); **under sb's feet: the cat keeps getting under my feet** el gato siempre me anda alrededor [2] (lower end) (no pl) pie m; **the ∼ of the bed** los pies de la cama [3] (measure) (pl **foot** or **feet**) pie m

foot² vt: **to ∼ the bill** pagar*

footage /'fʊtɪdʒ/ n (Cin) secuencias fpl (filmadas)

foot-and-mouth (disease) /ˌfʊtṇ'maʊθ/ n fiebre f aftosa, glosopeda f

football /'fʊtbɔːl/ n [1] **(a)** (American ∼) fútbol m or (AmC, Méx) futbol m americano **(b)** (soccer) fútbol m or (AmC, Méx) futbol m; (before n) **∼ match** partido m de fútbol or (AmC, Méx) futbol; **∼ player** ▶ FOOTBALLER [2] (ball) balón m or (esp AmL) pelota f de fútbol or (AmC, Méx) futbol

footballer /'fʊtbɔːlər ‖'fʊtbɔːlə(r)/ n (BrE) futbolista mf, jugador, -dora m,f de fútbol or (AmC, Méx) futbol

football: ∼ pool n (AmE) apuesta f colectiva, polla f (AmL); **∼ pools** pl n (BrE) **the ∼ pools**

juego de apuestas en que se trata de acertar los resultados de los partidos de la liga de fútbol, ≈el pronóstico deportivo (en Méx), ≈las quinielas (en Esp), ≈el prode (en Arg), ≈el totogol (en Col), ≈la polla-gol (en Chi), ≈la polla (en Per)

-footed /'fʊtəd ‖'fʊtɪd/ suff: **four∼** de cuatro patas; **light∼** ligero de pies

foot: ∼hills pl n estribaciones fpl; **∼hold** n punto m de apoyo (para el pie); **to gain a ∼hold** «ideology» prender*

footing /'fʊtɪŋ/ n (no pl) [1] (balance) equilibrio m; **to miss one's ∼** resbalar [2] (basis): **on an equal ∼** en igualdad de condiciones

foot: ∼lights pl n candilejas fpl; **∼loose** adj libre y sin compromiso; **∼loose and fancy-free** libre como el viento; **∼man** /'fʊtmən/ n (pl **-men** /-mən/) lacayo m; **∼note** n nota f a pie de página; **∼path** n (path) sendero m; (pavement) (BrE) acera f, banqueta f (Méx), vereda f (CS, Per); **∼print** n huella f; **∼step** n paso m; **∼wear** n calzado m

for¹ /fɔːr ‖fɔː(r), weak form fər ‖fə(r)/ prep

I [1] (intended for) para; **is there a letter ∼ me?** ¿hay carta para mí?; **my love ∼ her** mi amor por ella

[2] **(a)** (on behalf of, representing): **I did it ∼ you** lo hice por ti; **he plays ∼ England** forma parte de or juega en la selección inglesa; **D ∼ David** D de David **(b)** (as): **we're having chicken ∼ dinner** vamos a cenar pollo; **I can see him now ∼ what he is** ahora me doy cuenta de cómo es en realidad **(c)** (in favor of) a favor de

[3] (indicating purpose): **what's that ∼?** ¿para qué es eso?; **it's ∼ decoration** es de adorno; **it's ∼ your own good!** ¡es por tu (propio) bien!

[4] (giving reason) por; **∼ that reason** por esa razón; **if it weren't ∼ Joe …** si no fuera por Joe …

[5] (in exchange for) por; **I bought the book ∼ $10** compré el libro por 10 dólares; **she left him ∼ somebody else** lo dejó por otro

[6] (as concerns) para; **it's too cold ∼ me here** aquí hace demasiado frío para mí

[7] **(a)** (in spite of): **∼ all her faults, she's been very kind to us** tendrá sus defectos, pero con nosotros ha sido muy buena **(b)** (with infinitive clause): **it's unusual ∼ me to forget a name** es raro que se me olvide un nombre; **it's not ∼ me to decide** no me corresponde a mí decidir

II [1] (in the direction of) para; **the plane ∼ New York** el avión para or de Nueva York

[2] **(a)** (indicating duration): **he spoke ∼ half an hour** habló (durante) media hora; **I've only been here ∼ a day** solo llevo un día aquí; **how long are you going ∼?** ¿por cuánto tiempo vas? **(b)** (on the occasion of) para; **he gave it to me ∼ my birthday** me lo regaló para mi cumpleaños **(c)** (by, before) para; **we have to be there ∼ six o'clock** tenemos que estar allí a las seis

[3] (indicating distance): **we drove ∼ 20 miles** hicimos 20 millas; **we could see ∼ miles** se podía ver hasta muy lejos

for² conj (liter) pues (liter), puesto que (frml)

forage /'fɔːrɪdʒ ‖'fɒrɪdʒ/ vi **(a)** «animal» forrajear **(b)** (for supplies) **to ∼ FOR sth** buscar* algo

foray /'fɔːreɪ ‖'fɒreɪ/ n (Mil) incursión f

forbid /fər'bɪd ‖fə'bɪd/ vt ⟨past **forbad(e)** /fər'bæd, -'beɪd ‖fə'bæd, -'beɪd/; past p

forbidden /fər'bɪdn̩ ‖fəbɪdn̩/) (not allow) prohibir*; **to ~ sb to + INF** prohibirle* A algn + INF, prohibirle* A algn QUE (+ *subj*)

force¹ /fɔːrs ‖fɔːs/ *n* fuerza *f*; **the (armed) ~s** las fuerzas armadas; **a ~ eight gale** vientos de fuerza ocho; **to join ~s with sb** unirse a algn; **to come into ~** entrar en vigor *or* vigencia; **to be in ~** estar* en vigor *or* vigencia

force² *vt* ① (compel) **to ~ sb to + INF** obligar* a algn A + INF ② (push, drive) ⟨*door/link*⟩ forzar*; **they ~d their way in** entraron por la fuerza
■ **force down** [*v + o + adv*, *v + adv + o*] **(a)** ⟨*aircraft/pilot*⟩ aterrizar **(b)** ⟨*food*⟩ tragar* (*a duras penas*)

forced /fɔːrst ‖fɔːst/ *adj* (*before n*) ⟨*labor/smile*⟩ forzado; ⟨*landing/stopover*⟩ forzoso

force-feed /'fɔːrs'fiːd ‖'fɔːsfiːd/ *vt* (*past & past p* **-fed**) alimentar por la fuerza

forceful /'fɔːrsfəl ‖'fɔːsfəl/ *adj* **(a)** (vigorous) ⟨*person*⟩ con carácter; ⟨*personality*⟩ fuerte **(b)** (persuasive) ⟨*words/argument*⟩ convincente

forceps /'fɔːrsəps ‖'fɔːseps/ *pl n* fórceps *m*

forcible /'fɔːrsəbəl ‖'fɔːsəbəl/ *adj* forzoso

ford /fɔːrd ‖fɔːd/ *n* vado *m*

fore /fɔːr ‖fɔː(r)/ *n*: **to come to the ~** «*issue*» saltar a primera plana

forearm /'fɔːrɑːrm ‖'fɔːrɑːm/ *n* antebrazo *m*

foreboding /fɔːr'bəʊdɪŋ ‖fɔː'bəʊdɪŋ/ *n* **(a)** (apprehension) aprensión *f* **(b)** (presentiment) premonición *f*

forecast¹ /'fɔːrkæst ‖'fɔːkɑːst/ *n* (weather ~) pronóstico *m* del tiempo; (prediction) previsión *f*

forecast² *vt* (*past & past p* **forecast** *or* **forecasted**) ⟨*weather*⟩ pronosticar*; ⟨*result/ trend*⟩ prever*

forecourt /'fɔːrkɔːrt ‖'fɔːkɔːt/ *n* patio *m* delantero

forefathers /'fɔːr,fɑːðərz ‖'fɔːfɑːðəz/ *pl n* (liter) antepasados *mpl*

forefinger /'fɔːr,fɪŋgər ‖'fɔːfɪŋgə(r)/ *n* índice *m*

forefront /'fɔːrfrʌnt ‖'fɔːfrʌnt/ *n*: **in** *o* **at the ~ of sth** al frente de algo; (in the vanguard) a la vanguardia de algo

forego /fɔːr'gəʊ ‖fɔː'gəʊ/ *vt* (*3rd pers sing pres* **-goes**; *pres p* **-going**; *past* **-went**; *past p* **-gone**) ▶ FORGO

foregone /'fɔːrgɑːn ‖'fɔːgɒn/ *adj*: **the result was a ~ conclusion** el resultado era de prever

foreground /'fɔːrgraʊnd ‖'fɔːgraʊnd/ *n*: **in the ~** en primer plano

forehand /'fɔːrhænd ‖'fɔːhænd/ *n* golpe *m* de derecho

forehead /'fɑːrəd, 'fɔːrhed ‖'fɒrɪd, 'fɔːhed/ *n* frente *f*

foreign /'fɔːrən, 'fɑː- ‖'fɒrən/ *adj* ① **(a)** ⟨*custom/country/language*⟩ extranjero **(b)** ⟨*policy/ trade/relations*⟩ exterior; **~ debt** deuda *f* externa ② (Med) extraño; **a ~ body** un cuerpo extraño

foreigner /'fɔːrənər, 'fɑː- ‖'fɒrənə(r)/ *n* extranjero, -ra *m,f*

foreign: **~ exchange** *n* divisas *fpl*; **F~ minister** *n* ministro, -tra *or* (Méx) secretario, -ria *m,f* de relaciones *or* (Esp) asuntos exteriores, canciller *mf* (AmS); **F~ Office** *n* (in UK) the **F~**

Office el Foreign Office, el ministerio de relaciones exteriores de Gran Bretaña; **F~ Secretary** *n* (in UK) **F~** ▶ MINISTER

foreleg /'fɔːrleg ‖'fɔːleg/ *n* pata *f* delantera

foreman /'fɔːrmən ‖'fɔːmən/ *n* (*pl* **-men** /-mən/) **(a)** (supervisor) capataz *m* **(b)** (of jury) presidente *m*

foremost¹ /'fɔːrməʊst ‖'fɔːməʊst/ *adj* más importante

foremost² *adv* en primer lugar

forename /'fɔːrneɪm ‖'fɔːneɪm/ *n* nombre *m* (de pila)

forensic /fə'rensɪk/ *adj* (*before n*) forense

forerunner /'fɔːr,rʌnər ‖'fɔː,rʌnə(r)/ *n* precursor, -sora *m,f*

foresee /fɔːr'siː ‖fɔː'siː/ *vt* (*past* **foresaw**; *past p* **foreseen**) prever*

foreshore /'fɔːrʃɔːr ‖'fɔːʃɔː(r)/ *n*: parte de la playa entre la pleamar y la bajamar

foresight /'fɔːrsaɪt ‖'fɔːsaɪt/ *n* previsión *f*

foreskin /'fɔːrskɪn ‖'fɔːskɪn/ *n* prepucio *m*

forest /'fɔːrəst ‖'fɒrɪst/ *n* (wood) bosque *m*; (tropical) selva *f*; (*before n*) forestal

forestall /fɔːr'stɔːl ‖fɔː'stɔːl/ *vt* **(a)** (prevent) prevenir* **(b)** (preempt) adelantarse a

forestry /'fɔːrəstri ‖'fɒrɪstri/ *n* silvicultura *f*

foretaste /'fɔːrteɪst ‖'fɔːteɪst/ *n* anticipo *m*

foretell /fɔːr'tel ‖fɔː'tel/ *vt* (*past & past p* **foretold**) predecir*

forever /fə'revər ‖fə'revə(r)/ *adv*: **those days are gone ~** esos días no volverán; **nothing lasts ~** nada dura eternamente

forewarn /fɔːr'wɔːrn ‖fɔː'wɔːn/ *vt* **to ~ sb OF sth** advertir* A algn DE algo

forewent /fɔːr'went ‖fɔː'went/ *past of* FOREGO

foreword /'fɔːrwɜːrd ‖'fɔːwɜːd/ *n* prólogo *m*

forfeit¹ /'fɔːrfət ‖'fɔːfɪt/ *vt* ⟨*property*⟩ perder* el derecho a; ⟨*rights/respect/game*⟩ perder*

forfeit² *n* **(a)** (penalty) multa *f* **(b)** (Games) prenda *f*

forgave /fər'geɪv ‖fə'geɪv/ *past of* FORGIVE

forge¹ /fɔːrdʒ ‖fɔːdʒ/ *vt* ① ⟨*metal/bond*⟩ forjar ② (counterfeit) falsificar*

forge² *n* **(a)** (smithy) forja *f* **(b)** (furnace) fragua *f*

forger /'fɔːrdʒər ‖'fɔːdʒə(r)/ *n* falsificador, -dora *m,f*

forgery /'fɔːrdʒəri ‖'fɔːdʒəri/ *n* (*pl* **-ries**) falsificación *f*

forget /fər'get ‖fə'get/ (*pres p* **forgetting**; *past* **forgot**; *past p* **forgotten**) *vt* olvidarse de, olvidar
■ ~ *vi*: **to ~ (ABOUT sth)** olvidarse (DE algo)

forgetful /fər'getfəl ‖fə'getfəl/ *adj* olvidadizo

forget-me-not /fər'getmiːnɑːt ‖fə'getmɪnɒt/ *n* nomeolvides *f*

forgive /fər'gɪv ‖fə'gɪv/ *vt* (*past* **forgave**; *past p* **forgiven**) perdonar; **to ~ sb FOR sth** perdonarle algo a algn

forgiveness /fər'gɪvnəs ‖fə'gɪvnɪs/ *n* (quality) clemencia *f*; **to ask sb's ~ for sth** pedirle* perdón a algn por algo

forgo /fɔːr'gəʊ ‖fɔː'gəʊ/ *vt* (*3rd pers sing pres* **-goes**; *pres p* **-going**; *past* **-went**; *past p* **-gone**) (frml) privarse de

forgot /fər'gɑːt ‖fə'gɒt/ *past of* FORGET

forgotten /fəˈrˈgɑːtn̩ ‖fəˈgɒtn̩/ *past p of* FORGET

fork¹ /fɔːrk ‖fɔːk/ *n* (Culin) tenedor *m*; (for gardening) horca *f*

fork² *vi* **(a)** (split) «*branch/road/river*» bifurcarse* **(b)** (turn): **to ~ (to the) right** desviarse* a la derecha

forklift (**truck**) /ˈfɔːrkˈlɪft ‖ˈfɔːklɪft/ *n* carretilla *f* elevadora (*de horquilla*)

forlorn /fərˈlɔːrn ‖fəˈlɔːn/ *adj* **(a)** «*glance/smile*» triste; «*appearance*» de tristeza y desamparo **(b)** «*attempt*» desesperado

form¹ /fɔːrm ‖fɔːm/ *n* **1** (shape, manner) forma *f* **2** (type, kind) tipo; **other ~s of life** otras formas de vida **3** (fitness, ability) forma *f*; **to be on ~** estar* en forma **4** (document) formulario *m*, forma *f* (Méx) **5** (BrE Educ) (class) clase *f*; (year) curso *m*

form² *vt* «*character/shape/company/basis*» formar; «*opinion*» formarse; «*habit*» adquirir* ■ ~ *vi* «*idea/plan*» tomar forma; «*ice/fog*» formarse

formal /ˈfɔːrməl ‖ˈfɔːməl/ *adj* «*reception/dinner/language*» formal; «*manner/person*» ceremonioso; **~ dress** traje *m* de etiqueta

formality /fɔːrˈmæləti ‖fɔːˈmæləti/ *n* (*pl* **-ties**) **1** (formal quality) ceremonia *f* **2** (convention) formalidad *f*

formalize /ˈfɔːrmələɪz ‖ˈfɔːmələɪz/ *vt* formalizar*

formally /ˈfɔːrməli ‖ˈfɔːməli/ *adv* «*invite/reprimand*» formalmente

format¹ /ˈfɔːrmæt ‖ˈfɔːmæt/ *n* formato *m*

format² *vt* **-tt-** formatear

formation /fɔːrˈmeɪʃən ‖fɔːˈmeɪʃən/ *n* formación *f*

former¹ /ˈfɔːrmər ‖ˈfɔːmə(r)/ *adj* **1** (previous) antiguo **2** (first-mentioned) primero

former² *n* **the ~** el primero, la primera; (*pl*) los primeros, las primeras

formerly /ˈfɔːrmərli ‖ˈfɔːməli/ *adv* antes

formidable /ˈfɔːrmədəbəl ‖ˈfɔːmɪdəbəl, fɔːˈmɪdəbəl/ *adj* «*task*» imponente; «*problem/obstacle*» tremendo; «*opponent*» temible

formula /ˈfɔːrmjələ ‖ˈfɔːmjʊlə/ *n* (*pl* **-las** o (frml) **-lae** /-liː/) fórmula *f*; **~ one** (motor racing) fórmula uno

formulate /ˈfɔːrmjələɪt ‖ˈfɔːmjʊleɪt/ *vt* formular

fornication /ˌfɔːrnəˈkeɪʃən ‖ˌfɔːnɪˈkeɪʃən/ *n* (frml) fornicación *f* (frml)

for-profit /fərˈprɑːfət ‖fəˈprɒfɪt/ *adj* comercial, con fines de lucro

forsake /fərˈseɪk ‖fəˈseɪk/ *vt* (*past* **forsook** /fərˈsʊk ‖fəˈsʊk/; *past p* **forsaken** /fərˈseɪkən ‖fəˈseɪkən/) (liter) **(a)** (abandon) abandonar **(b)** (relinquish) «*pleasure/habits*» renunciar a

fort /fɔːrt ‖fɔːt/ *n* fuerte *m*; (small) fortín *m*

forte /ˈfɔːrteɪ ‖ˈfɔːteɪ/ *n* fuerte *m*

forth /fɔːrθ ‖fɔːθ/ *adv* (liter) **(a)** (out): **~ he went**

to battle with his enemy marchó a luchar con su enemigo **(b)** (in time): **from this day ~** de hoy en adelante

forthcoming /ˈfɔːrθˈkʌmɪŋ ‖ˌfɔːθˈkʌmɪŋ/ *adj* **1** **(a)** (approaching) (*usu before n*) «*event*» próximo **(b)** (about to appear) «*article/record*» de próxima aparición; «*film*» a estrenarse próximamente **2** (available) (*pred*): **no explanation was ~** no dieron (*or* dio *etc*) ninguna explicación **3** (open, helpful): **he was not very ~** no estuvo muy comunicativo

forthright /ˈfɔːrθˈraɪt ‖ˈfɔːθˈraɪt/ *adj* directo

forthwith /ˈfɔːrθˈwɪð ‖ˌfɔːθˈwɪθ/ *adv* (frml *or* liter) inmediatamente

fortieth¹ /ˈfɔːrtiəθ ‖ˈfɔːtiəθ/ *adj* cuadragésimo

fortieth² *adv* en cuadragésimo lugar

fortieth³ *n* (Math) cuarentavo *m*; (part) cuarentava *or* cuadragésima parte *f*

fortification /ˌfɔːrtəfəˈkeɪʃən ‖ˌfɔːtɪfɪˈkeɪʃən/ *n* (Mil) fortificación *f*

fortify /ˈfɔːrtəfər ‖ˈfɔːtɪfaɪ/ *vt* **-fies, -fying, -fied** «*town/building*» fortificar*; «*person/determination*» fortalecer*; «*argument*» reforzar*; **fortified wine** vino *m* fortificado

fortnight /ˈfɔːrtnaɪt ‖ˈfɔːtnaɪt/ *n* (esp BrE) quince días, dos semanas

fortnightly¹ /ˈfɔːrtnaɪtli ‖ˈfɔːtnaɪtli/ *adv* (esp BrE) cada dos semanas

fortnightly² *adj* (esp BrE) quincenal

fortress /ˈfɔːrtrəs ‖ˈfɔːtrɪs/ *n* fortaleza *f*

fortuitous /fɔːrˈtuːɪtəs ‖fɔːˈtjuːɪtəs/ *adj* fortuito

fortunate /ˈfɔːrtʃənət ‖ˈfɔːtʃənət/ *adj* afortunado; **it was ~ that he came** fue una suerte que viniera

fortunately /ˈfɔːrtʃn̩ətli ‖ˈfɔːtʃənətli/ *adv* (*indep*) afortunadamente

fortune /ˈfɔːrtʃən ‖ˈfɔːtʃən, ˈfɔːtʃuːn/ *n* **1** (money, prosperity) fortuna *f*; (a lot of money) (colloq) (*no pl*) dineral *m*, platal *m* (AmL fam), pastón *m* (Esp fam) **2** (destiny) destino *m*; **to tell sb's ~** decirle* la buenaventura a algn **3** (luck) **good ~** suerte *f*

fortune-teller /ˈfɔːrtʃən̩ˌtelər ‖ˈfɔːtʃənˌtelə(r), ˈfɔːtʃuːn-/ *n* adivino, -na *m,f*

forty /ˈfɔːrti ‖ˈfɔːti/ *adj/n* cuarenta *adj inv/m*; *see also* FOUR¹

forum /ˈfɔːrəm/ *n* foro *m*

forward¹ /ˈfɔːrward ‖ˈfɔːwəd/, (esp BrE) **forwards** /ˈfɔːrwardz ‖ˈfɔːwədz/ *adv* **(a)** «*bend/slope/lean*» hacia adelante **(b)** (in time) (frml) en adelante; **from this day ~** desde hoy en adelante

forward² *adj* **1** (*before n*) «*movement*» hacia adelante **2** (advance): **~ planning** planificación *f* **3** (assertive) atrevido

forward³ *vt* (send) (Busn) enviar*; **☺ please forward** hacer* seguir

forward⁴ *n* (Sport) delantero *mf*

forwent /fɔːrˈwent ‖fɔːˈwent/ *past of* FORGO

fossil /ˈfɑːsəl ‖ˈfɒsəl/ *n* fósil *m*

AmC	América Central	Arg	Argentina	Cu	Cuba	Per	Perú
AmL	América Latina	Bol	Bolivia	Ec	Ecuador	RPI	Río de la Plata
AmS	América del Sur	Chi	Chile	Esp	España	Ur	Uruguay
Andes	Región andina	CS	Cono Sur	Méx	México	Ven	Venezuela

fossil fuel ⸳⸳⸳⟡ frankly ⸳⸳⸳

fossil fuel *n* combustible *m* fósil

foster¹ /'fɔstər ‖'fɒstə(r)/ *vt* **1** ⟨*child*⟩ (BrE) acoger en el hogar sin adoptarlo legalmente **2** ⟨*suspicion/talent*⟩ fomentar; ⟨*reconciliation*⟩ promover*

foster² *adj* ⟨*child*⟩ ≈adoptivo; ~ **home** casa *f* de acogida de menores

fought /fɔːt/ *past & past p of* FIGHT¹

foul¹ /faʊl/ *adj* **-er, -est** **1** (offensive) ⟨*smell*⟩ nauseabundo; ⟨*taste*⟩ repugnante **2** (horrible) (colloq) ⟨*person*⟩ asqueroso (fam); ⟨*weather*⟩ pésimo **3** (obscene) ⟨*language/gesture*⟩ ordinario

foul² *n* falta *f*, faul *m or* foul *m* (AmL)

foul³ *vt* **1** (pollute) contaminar **2** (a) (block) ⟨*drain/chimney*⟩ obstruir* (b) (entangle) ⟨*rope/chain*⟩ enredar **3** (Sport) cometer una falta *or* (AmL tb) un foul *or* faul contra, faulear (AmL)

foul: ~-mouthed /faʊl'maʊðd/ *adj* malhablado; ~ **play** *n* (a) (Law): they suspect ~ play sospechan que se trata de un crimen (b) (Sport) juego *m* sucio

found¹ /faʊnd/ *past & past p of* FIND¹

found² *vt* **1** (a) (establish) fundar (b) **founding** *pres p* fundador **2** (base) **to ~ sth ON** sth fundar algo EN algo

foundation /faʊn'deɪʃən/ *n* **1** (a) (establishing) fundación *f* (b) (institution) fundación *f* **2** (often *pl*) (a) (Const) cimientos *mpl* (b) (groundwork, basis) fundamentos *mpl*; (before *n*) ~ **course** curso *m* preparatorio **3** (grounds) fundamento *m* **4** (cosmetic) base *f* de maquillaje

founder¹ /'faʊndər ‖'faʊndə(r)/ *n* fundador, -dora *m,f*

founder² *vi* «*ship*» hundirse; «*plan/project*» irse* a pique

foundry /'faʊndri/ *n* (*pl* **-ries**) fundición *f*

fountain /'faʊntn̩ ‖'faʊntɪn/ *n* (a) (ornamental) fuente *f* (b) (drinking ~) fuente *f*, bebedero *m* (CS, Méx)

fountain pen *n* pluma *f* (estilográfica), pluma *f* fuente (AmL), estilográfica *f*, lapicera *f* fuente (CS)

four¹ /fɔːr ‖fɔː(r)/ *n* cuatro *m*; **4 + 1 = 5** (*léase: four plus one equals o is five*) 4 + 1 = 5 (*read as: cuatro más uno es igual a cinco*); **4 - 1 = 3** (*léase: four minus one equals o is three*) 4 - 1 = 3 (*read as: cuatro menos uno es igual a tres*); **3 x 4 = 12** (*léase: three times four equals o is twelve, o three fours are twelve*) 3 x 4 = 12 (*read as: tres (multiplicado) por cuatro (son) doce*); **4 ÷ 2 = 2** (*léase: four divided by two equals o is two*) 4 ÷ 2 = 2 (*read as: cuatro dividido por dos es (igual a) dos*); **on all ~s** en *or* a cuatro patas, a gatas

four² *adj* cuatro *adj inv*

four: ~-by-~ *n* todoterreno *m*; **~-poster (bed)** /'fɔːr'pəʊstər ‖,fɔː'pəʊstə(r)/ *n*: cama con cuatro columnas, gen con dosel; **~-seater** /'fɔːr'siːtər ‖'fɔː,siːtə(r)/ *n* coche *m*/avión *m* de cuatro plazas

foursome /'fɔːrsəm ‖'fɔːsəm/ *n*: grupo de cuatro personas

fourteen /'fɔːr'tiːn ‖,fɔː'tiːn/ *adj/n* catorce *adj inv/m*; *see also* FOUR¹

fourteenth¹ /'fɔːr'tiːnθ ‖,fɔː'tiːnθ/ *adj* decimocuarto

fourteenth² *adv* en decimocuarto lugar

fourteenth³ *n* (Math) catorceavo *m*; (part) catorceava parte *f*

fourth¹ /fɔːrθ ‖fɔːθ/ *adj* cuarto

fourth² *adv* (a) (in position, time, order) en cuarto lugar (b) (fourthly) en cuarto lugar

fourth³ *n* **1** (part) cuarto *m* **2** ~ (gear) (Auto) (no art) cuarta *f*

fourthly /'fɔːrθli ‖'fɔːθli/ *adv* (indep) en cuarto lugar

four-wheel drive /'fɔːrhwiːl ‖'fɔːwiːl/ *n* tracción *f* integral

fowl /faʊl/ *n* (*pl* ~**s** *or* ~) ave *f*✝ (de corral)

fox¹ /fɑːks ‖fɒks/ *n* zorro *m*

fox² *vt* (colloq) confundir

fox: ~glove *n* dedalera *f*, digital *f*; **~-hunting** *n* caza *f* del zorro

foyer /'fɔɪeɪ/ *n* (of theatre) foyer *m*; (of hotel) vestíbulo *m*

fracas /'freɪkəs, 'frækəs ‖'frækɑː/ *n* (*pl* **fracases** *or* (BrE) **fracas** /-z/) (liter) altercado *m*

fraction /'frækʃən/ *n* fracción *f*

fracture¹ /'fræktʃər ‖'fræktʃə(r)/ *n* fractura *f*

fracture² *vt* fracturar

fragile /'frædʒəl ‖'frædʒaɪl/ *adj* (a) ⟨*object/china/glass*⟩ frágil; ⟨*relationship/link/agreement*⟩ precario (b) ⟨*person*⟩ débil; ⟨*health*⟩ delicado

fragment /'frægmənt/ *n* fragmento *m*

fragrance /'freɪgrəns/ *n* (smell) fragancia *f*; (perfume) perfume *m*

fragrant /'freɪgrənt/ *adj* fragante

frail /freɪl/ *adj* **-er, -est** (a) (physically delicate) ⟨*person*⟩ débil; ⟨*health*⟩ delicado (b) (morally weak) débil (c) (fragile) precario

frame¹ /freɪm/ *n* (a) (structure — of building, ship, plane) armazón *m or f*; (— of car, motorcycle, bed, door) bastidor *m*; (— of bicycle) cuadro *m*, marco *m* (Chi, Col) (b) (edge — of picture, window, door) marco *m* (c) **frames** *pl* (for spectacles) montura *f*

frame² *vt* **1** ⟨*picture/photograph*⟩ enmarcar*; ⟨*plan/policy/question*⟩ formular, elaborar **2** (incriminate unjustly) (colloq): I was ~d me tendieron una trampa para incriminarme

frame: ~ of mind *n* (*pl* ~**s of mind**) estado *m* de ánimo; **~work** *n* (basis) marco *m*; (plan) esquema *m*; (Eng) armazón *m or f*

franc /fræŋk/ *n* franco *m*

France /fræns ‖frɑːns/ *n* Francia *f*

franchise /'fræntʃaɪz/ *n* **1** (Busn) (a) (right — to operate retail outlet) franquicia *f*; (— to market product, service) concesión *f* (b) (retail outlet) franquicia *f* **2** (Pol frml) **the** ~ el derecho de *or* al voto

frank¹ /fræŋk/ *adj* **-er, -est** (a) (candid) sincero (b) (outspoken) franco

frank² *vt* (a) ⟨*letter/parcel/envelope*⟩ franquear (b) (postmark) ⟨*stamp/letter*⟩ matasellar

frankfurter /'fræŋkfɜːrtər ‖'fræŋkfɜːtə(r)/ *n* salchicha *f* de Frankfurt *or* (Arg, Col) de Viena, frankfurter *m* (Ur), vienesa *f* (Chi), salchicha *f* alemana (Ven)

frankincense /'fræŋkɪnsens ‖'fræŋkɪnsens/ *n* incienso *m*

frankly /'fræŋkli/ *adv* francamente

frantic /'fræntɪk/ adj (a) (very worried)
desesperado (b) (frenzied) ⟨activity⟩ frenético

fraternal /frə'tɜːnl̩/ adj ⟨love⟩
fraternal, fraterno; ⟨jealousy⟩ entre hermanos

fraternity /frə'tɜːrnəti ‖frə'tɜːnəti/ n (pl
-ties) [1] (virtue of brotherhood) fraternidad f [2] (a)
(Relig) hermandad f (b) (university club) asociación f
estudiantil

fraternize /'frætərnaɪz ‖'frætənaɪz/ vi
confraternizar*

fraud /frɔːd/ n [1] (deception) fraude m [2] (person)
farsante mf

fraudulent /'frɔːdʒələnt ‖'frɔːdjʊlənt/ adj
fraudulento

fraught /frɔːt/ adj (a) (pred) to be ~ WITH sth
⟨with danger/problems⟩ estar* lleno de algo (b)
(tense) ⟨atmosphere/relationship⟩ tirante

fray¹ /freɪ/ vi ⟨cloth/collar/rope⟩ deshilacharse;
⟨wire⟩ pelarse

fray² n refriega f

frayed /freɪd/ adj (a) ⟨collar/cloth⟩
deshilachado; ⟨rope/wire⟩ desgastado (b) ⟨nerves⟩
crispado; **tempers were getting ~** se estaban
exaltando los ánimos

freak¹ /friːk/ n (a) (abnormal specimen) fenómeno
m; (monster) monstruo m (b) (unnatural event)
fenómeno m

freak² adj (before n) ⟨weather⟩ inusitado;
⟨happening⟩ inesperado
■ **freak out** (sl) [1] [v + adv] flipar (arg),
friquear(se) (Méx arg) [2] [v + o + adv] alucinar
(fam), friquear (Méx arg)

freckle /'frekəl/ n peca f

free¹ /friː/ adj freer /'friːər ‖'friːə(r)/, freest
/'friːəst ‖'friːɪst/ [1] (a) (at liberty) (usu pred)
libre; **to set sb ~** dejar or poner* a algn en
libertad (b) ⟨country/people/press⟩ libre; **the right
of ~ speech** la libertad de expresión (c) (loose)
suelto; **to work ~** soltarse* [2] (pred) (without, rid
of) ~ **FROM** o **OF sth** libre DE algo; ~ **of** o **from
additives** sin aditivos; ~ **of charge** gratis
[3] (costing nothing) ⟨ticket/sample⟩ gratis adj inv;
⟨schooling/health care⟩ gratuito [4] (not occupied)
⟨table/time⟩ libre

free² adv (a) (without payment) gratuitamente; **I
got in for ~** (colloq) entré gratis (b) (without
restriction) ⟨roam/run⟩ a su (or mi etc) antojo

free³ vt [1] (liberate) ⟨prisoner/hostage⟩ poner* or
dejar en libertad; ⟨animal⟩ soltar*; ⟨nation/slave⟩
liberar [2] (a) (release) ⟨bound person⟩ soltar*;
⟨trapped person⟩ rescatar (b) (loose, clear) ⟨sth
stuck or caught⟩ desenganchar

-free /'friː/ suff: **trouble~** sin problemas;
nuclear~ zone zona f desnuclearizada

freedom /'friːdəm/ n libertad f

freedom fighter n guerrillero, -ra m,f

free: ~-for-all /'friːfər'ɔːl/ n gresca f; **~hold**
adj (esp BrE): **~hold property** bien m raíz (que se
compra o vende en plena propiedad junto con el
suelo sobre el que está edificado); ~ **kick** n (in
soccer) tiro m libre; (in rugby) patada f libre

freelance¹ /'friːlæns ‖'friːlɑːns/ adj por
cuenta propia, por libre (Esp)

freelance² adv por cuenta propia, por libre
(Esp)

freely /'friːli/ adv [1] (a) (without restriction)

libremente (b) (openly) ⟨speak/write⟩ con libertad
(c) (willingly) ⟨offer⟩ de buen grado [2] (a)
(generously) ⟨spend/give⟩ a manos llenas (b)
(copiously) ⟨flow/pour⟩ profusamente

free: F~mason /'friːmeɪsən ‖'friːmeɪsən/ n
masón, -sona m,f, francmasón, -sona m,f;
~-range /'friːˈreɪndʒ/ adj (BrE) ⟨chicken/eggs⟩ de
granja; **~style** n estilo m libre; ~ **trade** n
libre comercio m; **~ware** n (Comput) programas
mpl de libre distribución; **~way** n (AmE)
autopista f (sin peaje); **~wheel** /'friːˈhwiːl
‖ˌfriːˈwiːl/ vi: **he ~wheeled down the hill** (on bike)
bajó la cuesta sin pedalear; (in car) bajó la cuesta
en punto muerto; ~ **will** n: **of one's own ~ will**
por su (or mi etc) propia voluntad

freeze¹ /friːz/ (past froze; past p frozen) vi
[1] «pipe/lock/ground/person» helarse*; **I'm
freezing!** ¡estoy helado! [2] (stand still) quedarse
inmóvil
■ ~ vt ⟨water/stream/pipe⟩ helar*; ⟨food⟩ congelar
[2] (Fin) ⟨assets/account/prices⟩ congelar
■ ~ v impers helar*
■ **freeze over** [v + adv] helarse*
■ **freeze up** [v + adv] helarse*

freeze² n congelación f; **a wage/price ~** una
congelación salarial/de precios

freezer /'friːzər ‖'friːzə(r)/ n (deep freeze)
freezer m; (freezing compartment) congelador m

freezing¹ /'friːzɪŋ/ adj ⟨temperatures⟩ bajo
cero; ⟨weather⟩ con temperaturas bajo cero;
⟨hands/feet⟩ helado; **it's ~ (cold) in here** aquí
hace un frío que pela (fam)

freezing² n [1] ~ **(point)** punto m de
congelación; **three degrees below ~** tres grados
sobre/bajo cero [2] (process) congelación f

freight /freɪt/ n (a) (goods transported) carga f (b)
(transportation) transporte m, flete m (AmL)

freighter /'freɪtər ‖'freɪtə(r)/ n buque m de
carga

freight train n tren m de carga

French¹ /frentʃ/ adj francés

French² n (a) (language) francés m (b) (people)
+ pl vb **the ~** los franceses

French: ~ bean pl n (BrE) ▶ GREEN BEAN; **~
doors** pl n (AmE) ▶ ~ WINDOWS; **~ dressing** n
aliño para ensaladas a base de aceite, vinagre y
mostaza; (AmE) aderezo (para ensaladas) a base
de aceite, vinagre y tomate; ~ **fries** pl n papas
fpl or (Esp) patatas fpl fritas, papas fpl a la
francesa (Col, Méx); **~man** /'frentʃmən/ n (pl
-men /-mən/) francés m; ~ **windows** pl n
puerta f ventana, cristalera f (Esp); **~woman** n
francesa f

frenetic /frə'netɪk/ adj ⟨activity⟩ frenético;
⟨attempt⟩ desesperado

frenzy /'frenzi/ n (no pl) frenesí m

frequency /'friːkwənsi/ n (pl **-cies**)
frecuencia f

frequent¹ /'friːkwənt/ adj ⟨attempts/journeys⟩
frecuente; ⟨visitor⟩ asiduo

frequent² /friː'kwent/ vt frecuentar

frequently /'friːkwəntli/ adv con frecuencia, a
menudo

fresh /freʃ/ adj **-er, -est** [1] (a) (not stale, frozen
or canned) ⟨food⟩ fresco; **to get some ~ air** tomar
el fresco (b) (not tired) ⟨complexion/appearance⟩

fresco [2] (not salty): ~ **water** agua f; dulce [3] **(a)** (new, clean) ⟨clothes/linen⟩ limpio **(b)** (new, additional) ⟨supplies/initiative⟩ nuevo

freshen /'freʃən/ vt refrescar*

■ **freshen up** [v + adv] lavarse

fresher /'freʃər ‖ 'freʃə(r)/ n (BrE colloq) ▶ FRESHMAN

freshly /'freʃli/ adv recién

freshman /'freʃmən/ n (pl **-men** /-mən/) (Educ) estudiante mf de primer año, mechón, -chona m,f (Chi fam)

freshness /'freʃnəs ‖ 'freʃnɪs/ n frescura f

freshwater /'freʃ'wɔːtər ‖ 'freʃ,wɔːtə(r)/ adj (before n) de agua dulce

fret /fret/ vi **-tt-** preocuparse

fretful /'fretfəl/ adj **(a)** (querulous) quejoso **(b)** (anxious) inquieto

friar /'fraɪər ‖ 'fraɪə(r)/ n fraile m

friction /'frɪkʃən/ n [1] (Phys, Tech) rozamiento m, fricción f [2] (discord) tirantez f

Friday /'fraɪdeɪ, -di/ n viernes m; see also MONDAY

fridge /frɪdʒ/ n (colloq) nevera f, refrigerador m, frigorífico m (Esp), heladera f (RPl), refrigeradora f (Col, Per)

fried /fraɪd/ adj frito; **a ~ egg** un huevo frito or (Méx) estrellado

friend /frend/ n amigo, -ga m,f; **he soon made ~s with her** en poco tiempo se hizo amigo suyo

friendliness /'frendlinəs ‖ 'frendlinɪs/ n simpatía f

friendly /'frendli/ adj **-lier, -liest (a)** ⟨person/pet⟩ simpático; ⟨place/atmosphere⟩ agradable; ⟨welcome⟩ cordial; **to be ~ WITH sb** ser* amigo, -ga DE algn **(b)** (good-natured) ⟨rivalry/match⟩ amistoso

friendship /'frendʃɪp/ n amistad f

frieze /friːz/ n (on building, wall) friso m; (on wallpaper) greca f

frigate /'frɪgət ‖ 'frɪgɪt/ n fragata f

fright /fraɪt/ n **(a)** (fear) miedo m; **to take ~ at sth** asustarse por algo **(b)** (shock) susto m

frighten /'fraɪtn̩/ vt asustar

■ **frighten away, frighten off** [v + o + adv, v + adv + o] espantar

frightened /'fraɪtn̩d/ adj ⟨person/animal⟩ asustado; **to be ~ OF sb/sth** tenerle* miedo A algn/algo

frightening /'fraɪtn̩ɪŋ/ adj ⟨experience⟩ espantoso; (stronger) aterrador

frightful /'fraɪtfəl/ adj [1] (horrific) aterrador [2] (BrE colloq) (very unpleasant) horroroso

frigid /'frɪdʒəd ‖ 'frɪdʒɪd/ adj frígido

frill /frɪl/ n volante m or (RPl) volado m or (Méx) olán m or (Chi) vuelo m; **a ceremony with no ~s** una ceremonia sencilla

frilly /'frɪli/ adj **-lier, -liest** ⟨dress/petticoat⟩ de volantes or (RPl) de volados or (Méx) de olanes or (Chi) de vuelos

fringe /frɪndʒ/ n [1] (on shawl, carpet, tablecloth) fleco m [2] (of hair) (BrE) flequillo m, cerquillo m (AmL), fleco m (Méx), chasquilla f (Chi), capul m (Col), pollina f (Ven) [3] (periphery) (often pl): **to live on the ~(s) of society** vivir al margen de la sociedad; (before n) ⟨area/group⟩ marginal; ⟨music/medicine⟩ alternativo

fringe benefit n **(a)** (Lab Rel) incentivo m **(b)** (incidental advantage) ventaja f adicional

frisk /frɪsk/ vt cachear, catear (Méx)

frisky /'frɪski/ adj **-kier, -kiest** retozón

fritter /'frɪtər ‖ 'frɪtə(r)/ n buñuelo m, fruta f de sartén (Esp)

■ **fritter away** [v + o + adv, v + adv + o] ⟨money⟩ malgastar; ⟨fortune⟩ dilapidar; ⟨time⟩ desperdiciar

frivolous /'frɪvələs/ adj frívolo

frizzy /'frɪzi/ adj **-zier, -ziest** crespo, chino (Méx), como mota (CS)

frock /frɑːk ‖ frɒk/ n vestido m

frog /frɔːg ‖ frɒg/ n rana f; **to have a ~ in the o one's throat** tener* carraspera

frog: ~man /'frɔːgmæn ‖ 'frɒgmən/ n (pl **-men** /-mən/) hombre m rana; **~spawn** n (BrE) huevos mpl de rana

frolic /'frɑːlɪk ‖ 'frɒlɪk/ vi **-ck-** retozar*

from /frɑːm ‖ frɒm, weak form frəm/ prep [1] (indicating starting point) desde; **~ the beginning** desde el principio [2] (indicating distance): **2cm ~ the edge** a 2cm del borde; **we're still three hours ~ Tulsa** todavía faltan tres horas para llegar a Tulsa [3] (after): **~ today** a partir de hoy; **50 years ~ now** dentro de 50 años [4] (indicating origin) de; **I'm ~ Texas** soy de Texas; **the flight ~ Madrid** el vuelo procedente de Madrid; **a letter ~ my lawyer** una carta de mi abogado [5] **from ... to ...:** **they flew ~ New York to Lima** volaron de Nueva York a Lima; **they stretch ~ Derbyshire to the borders of Scotland** se extienden desde el condado de Derbyshire hasta el sur de Escocia; **we work ~ nine to five** trabajamos de nueve a cinco; **~ $50 to $100** entre 50 y 100 dólares [6] (as a result of) de; **his eyes were red ~ crying** tenía los ojos rojos de tanto llorar; **~ experience I would say that ...** según mi experiencia diría que ... [7] (out of, off) de; **~ the cupboard/shelf** del armario/estante; **if you take 5 ~ 10** si le restas 5 a 10 [8] (with preps & advs): **~ above/below** desde arriba/abajo; **he crawled out ~ under the table** salió gateando de debajo de la mesa

frond /frɑːnd ‖ frɒnd/ n (of fern) fronda f; (of palm) hoja f

front¹ /frʌnt/ n [1] (forward part) frente m; (of building) frente m, fachada f; (of dress) delantera f; **you sit in the ~** tú siéntate delante or (esp AmL) adelante [2] (in phrases) **in front** (as adv) delante, adelante (esp AmL); **in front of sb/sth** delante or (esp AmL) adelante de algn/algo; (facing) enfrente de algn/algo [3] (Meteo, Mil, Pol) frente m [4] (outward show) fachada f; **(— for illegal activity)** pantalla f [5] (overlooking sea) paseo m marítimo, malecón m (AmL), rambla f (RPl)

front² adj (at front) ⟨seat/wheel/leg⟩ delantero, de delante or (esp AmL) de adelante; **the ~ door** la puerta de (la) calle; **the ~ yard** o (BrE) **garden** el jardín del frente; **a ~-row seat** un asiento en primera fila

frontbencher /'frʌnt'bentʃər ⋯⟫

‖ˌfrʌnt'bentʃə(r)/ n (BrE) diputado con cargo ministerial en el gobierno o en el gabinete *fantasma*

frontier /frʌn'tɪr ‖'frʌntɪə(r)/ n frontera f; (before n) ⟨guard/zone⟩ fronterizo

frontispiece /'frʌntɪspiːs/ n frontispicio m

front room n salón m, living m (esp AmL)

frost¹ /frɔːst ‖frɒst/ n **(a)** (sub-zero temperature) helada f **(b)** (frozen dew) escarcha f

frost² vt **1** (Meteo) helar*; ⟨plant⟩ quemar **2** (AmE Culin) bañar

frostbite /'frɔːstbaɪt ‖'frɒstbaɪt/ n congelación f

frosting /'frɔːstɪŋ ‖'frɒstɪŋ/ n (AmE Culin) baño m

frosty /'frɔːsti ‖'frɒsti/ adj **-tier, -tiest** ⟨weather/air⟩ helado; ⟨night⟩ de helada; ⟨manner/reception⟩ glacial

froth /frɔːθ ‖frɒθ/ n espuma f

frothy /'frɔːθi ‖'frɒθi/ adj **frothier, frothiest** espumoso

frown¹ /fraʊn/ vi fruncir* el ceño; **to ~ AT sb** mirar a algn con el ceño fruncido
■ **frown on, frown upon** [v + prep + o]: **that sort of thing is ~ed upon** eso está muy mal visto

frown² n ceño m fruncido

froze /frəʊz/ past of FREEZE¹

frozen¹ /'frəʊzn̩/ past p of FREEZE¹

frozen² adj **1 (a)** ⟨water/lock/pipe/food⟩ congelado; ⟨region⟩ helado; **my feet are ~** (colloq) tengo los pies helados **(b)** (Fin) ⟨prices/incomes⟩ congelado **2** (motionless): **I stood there ~ (to the spot)** me quedé allí clavado, paralizado por el terror

frugal /'fruːɡəl/ adj frugal

fruit /fruːt/ n **1 (a)** (collectively) fruta f; **dried ~** (BrE) fruta f seca; (before noun) **~ juice** jugo m or (Esp) zumo m de frutas; **~ tree** árbol m frutal **(b)** (type — as food) fruta f; (Bot) fruto m **2 (a)** (product) fruto m; **to bear ~** dar* (su) fruto

fruit: ~cake n plum-cake m, ponqué m de frutas (Col), fruit cake m (Méx), budín m inglés (RPI); **~ cocktail** n (dish) ensalada f or macedonia f or cóctel m de frutas; **~ cup** n (AmE) ▶ ~ COCKTAIL

fruitful /'fruːtfəl/ adj provechoso, fructífero

fruition /fruː'ɪʃən/ n (fml): **their plan never came to ~** su plan nunca cristalizó

fruitless /'fruːtləs ‖'fruːtlɪs/ adj infructuoso

fruit: ~ machine n (BrE) máquina f tragamonedas or (Esp tb) tragaperras; **~ salad** n **(a)** (AmE) ensalada f de frutas, gen en gelatina **(b)** (BrE) ▶ FRUIT COCKTAIL

frustrate /frʌ'streɪt ‖frʌs'treɪt/ vt frustrar

frustrated /frʌ'streɪtəd ‖frʌs'treɪtɪd/ adj **(a)** (thwarted) frustrado **(b)** (dissatisfied) descontento; (sexually) ~ sexualmente frustrado

frustrating /frʌ'streɪtɪŋ ‖frʌs'treɪtɪŋ/ adj frustrante

frustration /frʌs'treɪʃən/ n frustración f

fry¹ /fraɪ/ **fries, frying, fried** vt freír*
■ **~** vi freírse*

fry² n (pl **fries**) **1 fries** pl (French fries) papas or (Esp) patatas fritas, papas fpl a la francesa (Col, Méx) **2 (a)** (+ pl vb) (Zool) alevines mpl, majuga f (Ur) **(b)** (people): **small ~** gente f de poca monta

frying pan /'fraɪɪŋ/, (AmE also) **fry pan** n sartén f, sartén m or f (AmL)

ft = foot/feet

FTP n (Comput) (= **file transfer protocol**) FTP m

fuchsia /'fjuːʃə/ n (Bot) fucsia f, aljaba f (RPI)

fuck /fʌk/ vt (vulg) (copulate with) joder (vulg), tirarse (vulg), follarse (Esp vulg), coger* (Méx, RPI, Ven vulg)
■ **~** vi (vulg) joder (vulg), tirar (vulg), coger* (Méx, RPI, Ven vulg), follar (Esp vulg), cachar (Chi, Per vulg)
■ **fuck off** [v + adv] (vulg): **~ off!** ¡vete a la mierda! (vulg), ¡vete a tomar por (el) culo! (Esp vulg), ¡vete a la chingada! (Méx vulg), ¡andá a cagar! (RPI vulg)

fucking /'fʌkɪŋ/ adj (vulg) (before n): **~ hell!** ¡puta madre! (vulg)

fudge¹ /fʌdʒ/ n (Culin) especie de caramelo de dulce de leche

fudge² vt (colloq) **(a)** (falsify) ⟨figures⟩ amañar **(b)** (evade) ⟨issue⟩ esquivar

fuel¹ /'fjuːəl/ n combustible m

fuel² vt (BrE) **-ll- 1** ⟨ship/plane⟩ abastecer* de combustible; ⟨stove/furnace⟩ alimentar **2** ⟨hope/passion⟩ alimentar; ⟨debate⟩ avivar; ⟨fear⟩ exacerbar

fuel oil n fuel-oil m

fugitive /'fjuːdʒətɪv/ n fugitivo, -va m,f

fulfill, (BrE) **fulfil** /fʊl'fɪl/ **-ll-** vt **1 (a)** (carry out) ⟨duty⟩ cumplir con; ⟨task⟩ llevar a cabo **(b)** (obey, keep) ⟨order/promise/contract⟩ cumplir **(c)** (serve) ⟨need⟩ satisfacer* **(d)** (meet) ⟨requirements⟩ satisfacer* **2** (realize) ⟨ambition⟩ hacer* realidad; ⟨potential⟩ alcanzar* **3** (make content) ⟨person⟩ satisfacer*
■ **v refl to ~ oneself** realizarse*

fulfilled /fʊl'fɪld/ adj (usu pred) realizado

fulfillment, (BrE) **fulfilment** /fʊl'fɪlmənt/ n **(a)** (of duty, promise) cumplimiento m **(b)** (satisfaction): **her family gave her a sense of ~** su familia la hacía sentirse realizada

full¹ /fʊl/ adj **-er, -est 1** (filled) lleno; **I'm ~ (up)** estoy lleno; **~ OF sth** lleno de algo **2 (a)** (complete) ⟨report/description⟩ detallado; ⟨name/answer⟩ completo; **you have my ~ support** tienes todo mi apoyo; **to lead a very ~ life** llevar una vida muy activa **(b)** (maximum): **at ~ speed** a toda velocidad; **~ employment** (Econ) pleno empleo m **3** ⟨figure⟩ regordete

full² adv **1** (as intensifier) **~ well** muy bien **2** (directly): **the sun was shining ~ in my face** el sol me daba de lleno en la cara **3 in full: write your name in ~** escriba su nombre completo; **it will be paid in ~** será pagado en su totalidad

full: ~-blown /'fʊl'bləʊn/ adj (before n)

verdadero; **~-fledged** /'fʊl'fledʒd/ adj (AmE) 1 ⟨chick⟩ capaz de volar; 2 ⟨lawyer/nurse⟩ hecho y derecho; **~-grown** /'fʊl'grəʊn/ adj ⟨before n⟩ totalmente desarrollado; **~ house** n (Cin, Theat) lleno m; **~-length** /'fʊl'leŋθ/ adj ⟨portrait/mirror⟩ de cuerpo entero; ⟨dress/skirt⟩ largo

fullness /'fʊlnəs ‖'fʊlnɪs/ n plenitud f; **in the ~ of time** con el tiempo

full: ~-scale /'fʊl'skeɪl/ adj 1 (actual size) a escala natural; 2 (major) ⟨work⟩ de envergadura; ⟨investigation⟩ a fondo; ⟨test⟩ a escala real; ⟨war⟩ declarado; **~-size** /'fʊl'saɪz/, **~-sized** /-d/ adj (a) (life-size) de tamaño natural (b) (of adult size) ⟨bicycle/bed⟩ de adulto; **~ stop** n (BrE) punto m

full-time¹ /'fʊltaɪm/ adj ⟨student/soldier⟩ de tiempo completo; ⟨employment/post⟩ de jornada completa

full-time² /fʊl'taɪm/ adv a tiempo completo

fully /'fʊli/ adv 1 (a) (completely): **I ~ understand** comprendo muy bien; **she's a ~ trained nurse** es una enfermera diplomada (b) (in full) enteramente 2 (at least) por lo menos, como poco

fully-fledged /'fʊli'fledʒd/ adj (BrE) ▶ FULL-FLEDGED

fulsome /'fʊlsəm/ adj ⟨praise⟩ empalagoso; ⟨manner⟩ excesivamente efusivo

fumble /'fʌmbəl/ vi: **she ~d in her pockets** revolvió en sus bolsillos; **he ~d for the right words** tartamudeó, tratando de encontrar las palabras adecuadas; **she ~d with her buttons** intentó torpemente abrocharse/desabrocharse

fume /fjuːm/ vi 1 (smoke) (Chem) despedir* gases 2 (be angry) (colloq): **she was absolutely fuming** estaba que echaba humo

fumes /fjuːmz/ pl n gases mpl

fumigate /'fjuːməgeɪt ‖'fjuːmɪgeɪt/ vt fumigar*

fun /fʌn/ n diversión f; **to have ~** divertirse*; **he's good ~** es muy divertido; **to do sth for ~** hacer* algo por gusto; **to make ~ of sb/sth** reírse* de algn/algo

function¹ /'fʌŋkʃən/ n 1 (of tool, organ, person) función f; **to carry out/perform a ~** cumplir/ desempeñar una función 2 (reception, party) recepción f 3 (Comput, Math) función f; ⟨before n⟩ **~ key** tecla f de función

function² vi (a) (operate) ⟨machine/organ⟩ funcionar (b) (serve) **to ~ AS sth** ⟨object/ building⟩ hacer* (las veces) DE algo

functional /'fʌŋkʃnəl ‖'fʌŋkʃənl/ adj (a) (functioning) ⟨machine/part⟩ en buen estado (de funcionamiento) (b) (practical) ⟨furniture/design⟩ funcional

fund¹ /fʌnd/ n (a) (money reserve) fondo m (b) **funds** pl (resources, money) fondos mpl

fund² vt (a) (finance) ⟨research/organization⟩ financiar (b) (Fin) ⟨debt⟩ consolidar

fundamental /ˌfʌndə'mentl/ adj (a) (basic) ⟨principle/error/concept⟩ fundamental (b) (essential) ⟨skill/constituent⟩ esencial (c) (intrinsic, innate) ⟨absurdity/truth⟩ intrínseco

fundamentalism /ˌfʌndə'mentəlɪzəm/ n integrismo m, fundamentalismo m

fundamentalist /ˌfʌndə'mentləst ‖ˌfʌndə'mentəlɪst/ n integrista mf, fundamentalista mf

fundamentally /ˌfʌndə'mentli ‖ˌfʌndə'mentəli/ adv (a) (radically) ⟨different/ mistaken⟩ fundamentalmente (b) (in essence) ⟨correct/justified⟩ esencialmente

fundamentals /ˌfʌndə'mentlz/ pl n fundamentos mpl

funding /'fʌndɪŋ/ n (act) financiación f; (resources) fondos mpl

fund-raising /'fʌnd'reɪzɪŋ ‖'fʌnd,reɪzɪŋ/ n recaudación f de fondos

funeral /'fjuːnərəl/ n funerales mpl

funeral: ~ director n (frml) director, -tora m,f de una funeraria; **~ home** (AmE), **~ parlour** (BrE) n funeraria f

funfair /'fʌnfer ‖'fʌnfeə(r)/ n (BrE) (traveling) feria f; (permanent) parque m de diversiones or (Esp) de atracciones

fungus /'fʌŋgəs/ n (pl **fungi** /'fʌŋgaɪ/) hongo m

funnel /'fʌnl/ n (a) (for pouring) embudo m (b) (on steamship, steam engine) (BrE) chimenea f

funnily /'fʌnli ‖'fʌnɪli/ adv (a) (strangely) (esp BrE) de modo extraño (b) **~ enough** (indep) casualmente

funny /'fʌni/ adj **-nier, -niest** 1 (amusing) ⟨joke⟩ gracioso; ⟨person⟩ divertido 2 (strange) raro; (it's) **~ (that) you should mention it** es curioso que lo menciones; **to taste/smell ~** saber*/oler* raro 3 (colloq) (unwell): **I feel a bit ~** me siento medio mal

fur /fɜːr ‖fɜː(r)/ n (a) (of animal) (Zool) pelo m, pelaje m; (Clothing) piel f; ⟨before n⟩ **~ coat** abrigo m de piel or (Esp tb) de pieles (b) (pelt) piel f

furious /'fjʊriəs ‖'fjʊəriəs/ adj (a) (angry) furioso (b) (violent, intense) ⟨struggle⟩ feroz; ⟨speed⟩ vertiginoso; ⟨storm⟩ violento; ⟨activity⟩ febril

furiously /'fjʊriəsli ‖'fjʊəriəsli/ adv (a) (angrily) con furia (b) (violently, intensely) frenéticamente

furlough /'fɜːrləʊ ‖'fɜːləʊ/ n (AmE) permiso m, licencia f; **on ~** de permiso, con licencia

furnace /'fɜːrnəs ‖'fɜːnɪs/ n (in industry) horno m; (for heating) caldera f

furnish /'fɜːrnɪʃ ‖'fɜːnɪʃ/ vt 1 (a) ⟨house/ room⟩ amueblar, amoblar* (AmL) (b) **furnished** past p ⟨room/apartment⟩ amueblado, amoblado (AmL) 2 (supply) (frml) proporcionar; **to ~ sb WITH sth** ⟨with information⟩ proporcionarle algo a algn

furnishings /'fɜːrnɪʃɪŋz ‖'fɜːnɪʃɪŋz/ pl n: mobiliario, cortinas, alfombras, etc

furniture /'fɜːrnɪtʃər ‖'fɜːnɪtʃə(r)/ n (in home, office) muebles mpl, mobiliario m; **a piece of ~** un mueble; ⟨before n⟩ **~ mover** o (BrE) **remover** empresa f de mudanzas; **~ polish** cera f para muebles

furor /'fjʊrɔːr ‖'fjʊərɔː(r)/, (BrE) **furore** /fjʊ'rɔːri ‖fjʊə'rɔːri/ n escándalo m

furrow /'fɜːrəʊ ‖'fʌrəʊ/ n surco m

furry /'fɜːri/ adj **-rier, -riest** ⟨animal⟩ peludo; ⟨toy⟩ de peluche; ⟨covering/lining⟩ afelpado

further¹ /'fɜːrðər ‖'fɜːðə(r)/ adv 1 comp of FAR¹ 1 (a) (in distance): **they live even ~ away** ellos viven aún más lejos; **how much ~ is it?** ¿cuánto camino nos queda por hacer?; **~ on, there's another set of traffic lights** más adelante, hay otro semáforo (b) (in progress): **the legislation should have gone ~** la legislación debería haber ido ···⊱

más lejos; **have you got any ∼ with that essay?** ¿has adelantado ese trabajo? **(c)** (in time): **we must look back even ∼** tenemos que retroceder aún más en el tiempo; **this vase dates back even ∼** este jarrón es aún más antiguo **(d)** (in extent, degree): **I'll look ∼ into that possibility** voy a estudiar esa posibilidad más a fondo; **the situation is ∼ complicated by her absence** el hecho de que ella no esté complica aún más la situación

2 further to (Corresp) (as prep): **∼ to your letter of June 6,** ... con relación a su carta del 6 de junio, ...

3 (furthermore) (as linker) además

further² adj más; **have you any ∼ questions?** ¿tienen más preguntas?; **until ∼ notice** hasta nuevo aviso

further³ vt ⟨cause/aims⟩ promover*; ⟨career/interests⟩ favorecer*

further education n (BrE) programa de cursos de extensión cultural para adultos

furthermore /'fɜːrðərmɔːr ‖ ˌfɜːðə'mɔː(r)/ adv además

furthest /'fɜːrðəst ‖ 'fɜːðɪst/ adv superl of FAR¹ 1

furtive /'fɜːrtɪv ‖ 'fɜːtɪv/ adj **(a)** (stealthy) ⟨movement/look⟩ furtivo; ⟨person⟩ solapado **(b)** (suspicious, shifty) ⟨appearance⟩ sospechoso; ⟨manner⟩ solapado

furtively /'fɜːrtɪvli ‖ 'fɜːtɪvli/ adv ⟨creep⟩ sigilosamente; ⟨peep/listen⟩ a hurtadillas

fury /'fjʊri ‖ 'fjʊəri/ n (pl **furies**) ira f

fuse¹ /fjuːz/ n **1** (Elec) fusible m, plomo m (Esp), tapón m (CS) **2** (for explosives) mecha f

fuse² vt **1** (Elec) **(a)** (short-circuit) (BrE): **to ∼ the**

lights hacer* saltar los fusibles or (CS tb) los tapones, fundir los plomos (Esp) **(b) fused** past p con fusible **2 (a)** (melt together) alear **(b)** (merge) fusionar

fuse box n caja f de fusibles or (Esp tb) de plomos or (CS tb) de tapones

fuselage /'fjuːzəlɑːʒ/ n fuselaje m

fusion /'fjuːʒən/ n fusión f

fuss¹ /fʌs/ n alboroto m; **to kick up a ∼** armar un lío, montar un número (Esp fam); **to make o** (AmE also) **raise a ∼** hacer* un escándalo

fuss² vi preocuparse

fussbudget /'fʌsˌbʌdʒɪt/, (BrE also) **fusspot** /'fʌspɑːt ‖ 'fʌspɒt/ n maniático, -ca m,f, mañoso, -sa m,f (AmL)

fussy /'fʌsi/ adj **-sier, -siest** exigente; **I'm a ∼ eater** soy muy maniático or (AmL tb) mañoso para comer

futile /'fjuːtl ‖ 'fjuːtaɪl/ adj ⟨attempt⟩ inútil; ⟨suggestion/question⟩ trivial

futility /fjʊ'tɪləti/ n inutilidad f

future¹ /'fjuːtʃər ‖ 'fjuːtʃə(r)/ n **1** (time ahead) **the ∼** el futuro; **in ∼** de ahora en adelante **2** (prospects) futuro m; **a job with a ∼** un trabajo con futuro **3** (Ling) futuro m **4 futures** pl (Fin) futuros mpl

future² adj (before n) **(a)** ⟨husband/home⟩ futuro **(b)** (Ling): **the ∼ tense** el futuro

futuristic /ˌfjuːtʃə'rɪstɪk/ adj futurista

fuze /fjuːz/ n (AmE) ▶ FUSE¹ 2

fuzzy /'fʌzi/ adj **-zier, -ziest 1** ⟨hair⟩ muy rizado; ⟨beard⟩ enmarañado **2** (blurred) ⟨sound⟩ confuso; ⟨picture/outline⟩ borroso

Gg

G, g /dʒiː/ n **(a)** (letter) G, g f **(b)** (Mus) sol m

g (= **gram(s)**) g., gr.

G (in US) (Cin) (= **general**) apta para todo público

GA, Ga = **Georgia**

gab /gæb/ vi **-bb-** (colloq) charlar (fam)

gabble /'gæbəl/ vi (speak incoherently) hablar atropelladamente, farfullar; (speak quickly) parlotear (fam)

gable /'geɪbəl/ n gablete m; **∼ (end)** hastial m

gadget /'gædʒət ‖ 'gædʒɪt/ n (colloq) aparato m, chisme m (Esp fam)

Gaelic /'geɪlɪk/ n gaélico m

gaffe /gæf/ n metedura f or (AmL tb) metida f de pata (fam)

gag¹ /gæg/ n **1** (for mouth) mordaza f **2** (joke) (colloq) chiste m, gag m

gag² **-gg-** vt amordazar*
■ **∼** vi hacer* arcadas

gage /geɪdʒ/ vt/n (AmE) ▶ GAUGE¹,²

gaggle /'gægəl/ n (of geese) bandada f

gain¹ /geɪn/ vt **1** (acquire) ⟨control⟩ conseguir*; ⟨experience⟩ adquirir*; ⟨recognition⟩ obtener* **2** (increase) ⟨strength/speed⟩ ganar **3** ⟨time⟩ ganar; **my watch is ∼ing ten minutes a day** mi reloj (se) adelanta diez minutos por día
■ **∼** vi **1 (a)** (improve) **to ∼ in value** subir or aumentar de valor; **she's gradually ∼ing in confidence** poco a poco va adquiriendo confianza en sí misma **(b)** (benefit) beneficiarse **2 (a)** (go fast) «clock/watch» adelantar(se) **(b)** (move nearer) **to ∼ ON sb** acortar (las) distancias con respecto a algn

gain² n **1** (profit) ganancia f **2** (increase) aumento m

gainful /'geɪnfəl/ adj retribuido

gait /geɪt/ n (no pl) modo m de andar

gala /'gælə, 'geɪlə ‖ 'gɑːlə/ n fiesta f

Galapagos Islands /gə'lɑːpəgəs ‖ gə'læpəgəs/ pl n **the ∼ ∼** las Islas Galápagos

galaxy /'gæləksi/ n (pl **-xies**) galaxia f

gale /geɪl/ n vendaval f; ⟨before n⟩ **∼ force winds** vientos mpl (huracanados)

Galicia /gəˈlɪʃiə, gəˈlɪsiə/ n Galicia f

Galician¹ /gəˈlɪʃiən, gəˈlɪsiən/ n (a) (person) gallego, -ga m,f (b) (language) gallego m

Galician² adj gallego

gallant adj (a) /ˈɡælənt/ (brave) (liter) aguerrido (liter) (b) /gəˈlænt/ (chivalrous) galante

gall bladder /ˈɡɔːl/ n vesícula f (biliar)

galleon /ˈɡæliən/ n galeón m

gallery /ˈɡæləri/ n (pl **-ries**) **1** (Art) museo m (de Bellas Artes); (commercial) galería f (de arte) **2** (Archit) galería f; (for press, spectators) tribuna f

galley /ˈɡæli/ n **1** (ship) galera f **2** (kitchen on boat, plane) cocina f

gallon /ˈɡælən/ n galón m (EEUU: 3,78 litros, RU: 4,55 litros)

gallop¹ /ˈɡæləp/ n galope m

gallop² vi galopar

gallows /ˈɡæləʊz/ n (pl ∼) (+ sing o pl vb) horca f

gallstone /ˈɡɔːlstəʊn/ n cálculo m biliar

galore /gəˈlɔːr ‖gəˈlɔː(r)/ adj (after n) en abundancia

galvanize /ˈɡælvənaɪz/ vt **1** (rouse) to ∼ sb (INTO sth/-ING) impulsar a algn (A algo /+ INF) **2** **galvanized** past p ⟨iron/steel⟩ galvanizado

Gambia /ˈɡæmbiə/ n Gambia f

gambit /ˈɡæmbət ‖ˈɡæmbɪt/ n (stratagem) táctica f; (in chess) gambito m

gamble¹ /ˈɡæmbəl/ vi jugar*; to ∼ on a horse apostar* a un caballo
  ■ ∼ vt jugarse*

gamble² n (no pl) (a) (bet) apuesta f (b) (risk): to take a ∼ arriesgarse*

gambler /ˈɡæmblər ‖ˈɡæmblə(r)/ n jugador, -dora m,f

gambling /ˈɡæmblɪŋ/ n juego m

gambol /ˈɡæmbəl/ vi, (BrE) **-ll-** retozar*

game¹ /ɡeɪm/ n **1** (a) (amusement) juego m (b) (type of sport) deporte m **2** (a) (complete match) (Sport) partido m; (in board games, cards) partida f (b) (part of tennis, squash match) juego m **3** (underhand scheme, ploy) juego m **4** (in hunting) caza f; big ∼ caza mayor **5** (Culin) caza f

game² adj we're going swimming, are you ∼? vamos a nadar ¿te apuntas?; she's ∼ for anything se apunta a todo

game: ∼keeper n guardabosque(s) mf; ∼ reserve n coto m de caza; ∼ show n programa m concurso

gammon /ˈɡæmən/ n (esp BrE) jamón m fresco

gamut /ˈɡæmət/ n gama f; to run the (whole) ∼ of sth cubrir* toda la gama de algo

gander /ˈɡændər ‖ˈɡændə(r)/ n (Zool) ganso m (macho)

gang /ɡæŋ/ n (of criminals) banda f; (of youths, children) pandilla f
  ■ **gang up** [v + adv] (colloq) to ∼ up AGAINST o ON sb ponerse*/estar* en contra de algn

gang: ∼land n (journ) hampa f‡, mundo m del crimen organizado; ∼plank n plancha f

gangrene /ˈɡæŋɡriːn/ n gangrena f

gangster /ˈɡæŋstər ‖ˈɡæŋstə(r)/ n gángster mf

gangway /ˈɡæŋweɪ/ n **1** (walkway) pasarela f **2** (between rows of seats) (BrE) pasillo m

gantlet /ˈɡɔːntlət/ n (AmE) ▶ GAUNTLET

gaol /dʒeɪl/ n/vt (esp BrE) ▶ JAIL¹, ²

gap /ɡæp/ n **1** (space) espacio m; (in fence, hedge) hueco m **2** (a) (in knowledge) laguna f (b) (in time) intervalo m, interrupción f (c) (disparity) distancia f, brecha f (d) (void) vacío m

gape /ɡeɪp/ vi **1** (stare) mirar boquiabierto **2** (be open) estar* abierto

gaping /ˈɡeɪpɪŋ/ adj ⟨wound⟩ abierto; ⟨hole⟩ enorme

garage /gəˈrɑːʒ ‖ˈɡærɑːdʒ, -ɪdʒ/ n **1** (for parking) garaje m, garage m (esp AmL) **2** (a) (for repairs) taller m (mecánico), garaje m, garage m (esp AmL) (b) (for fuel) (BrE) ▶ GAS STATION

garb /ɡɑːrb ‖ɡɑːb/ n (liter o hum) atuendo m (liter o hum)

garbage /ˈɡɑːrbɪdʒ ‖ˈɡɑːbɪdʒ/ n (a) (AmE) (refuse) basura f; (before n) ∼ dump vertedero m (de basuras), basurero m, basural m (AmL) (b) (junk) (colloq) trastos mpl, cachivaches mpl (fam), porquerías fpl (fam); this book is absolute ∼ este libro es una auténtica porquería

garbage: ∼ bag n (AmE) bolsa f de la basura; ∼ can n (AmE) cubo m or (CS) tacho m or (Col) caneca f or (Méx) bote m or (Ven) tobo m de la basura; ∼man /ˈɡɑːrbɪdʒmæn/ n (pl -men /-men/) (AmE) basurero m; ∼ truck n (AmE) camión m de la basura

garbled /ˈɡɑːrbəld ‖ˈɡɑːbəld/ adj ⟨account⟩ confuso; ⟨message⟩ incomprensible

garden¹ /ˈɡɑːrdn ‖ˈɡɑːdn/ n (a) (for ornamental plants) jardín m; (for vegetables) huerta f, huerto m (b) **gardens** pl (public, on private estate) jardines mpl, parque m

garden² vi trabajar en el jardín

garden center, (BrE) **garden centre** n vivero m, centro m de jardinería

gardener /ˈɡɑːrdnər ‖ˈɡɑːdnə(r)/ n jardinero, -ra m,f

gardening /ˈɡɑːrdnɪŋ ‖ˈɡɑːdnɪŋ/ n jardinería f; (vegetable growing) horticultura f; he does the ∼ él se encarga del jardín

garden: ∼ party n recepción f al aire libre; ∼-variety adj (AmE colloq) (before n) vulgar or común y corriente

gargle /ˈɡɑːrɡəl ‖ˈɡɑːɡəl/ vi hacer* gárgaras

gargoyle /ˈɡɑːrɡɔɪl ‖ˈɡɑːɡɔɪl/ n gárgola f

garish /ˈɡeərɪʃ ‖ˈɡeərɪʃ/ adj ⟨color⟩ chillón, charro (AmL fam); ⟨garment⟩ estridente, charro (AmL fam)

garland /ˈɡɑːrlənd ‖ˈɡɑːlənd/ n guirnalda f

garlic /ˈɡɑːrlɪk ‖ˈɡɑːlɪk/ n ajo m

garment /ˈɡɑːrmənt ‖ˈɡɑːmənt/ n prenda f (de ropa)

garnet /ˈɡɑːrnət ‖ˈɡɑːnɪt/ n granate m

garnish¹ /ˈɡɑːrnɪʃ ‖ˈɡɑːnɪʃ/ vt adornar

garnish² n adorno m, aderezo m; (more substantial) guarnición f

garret /ˈɡærət/ n buhardilla f

garrison /ˈɡærəsən ‖ˈɡærɪsən/ n (a) (place) plaza f fuerte or de armas (b) (troops) guarnición f

garrulous /ˈɡærələs/ adj charlatán

garter /ˈɡɑːrtər ‖ˈɡɑːtə(r)/ n liga f

gas¹ /ɡæs/ n (pl **gases** or **gasses**) **1** (Phys)⋯⟶

gas *m* ⟨2⟩ **(a)** (fuel) gas *m*; (before n) ⟨ring/heater⟩ de *or* a gas **(b)** (anesthetic) gas *m* ⟨3⟩ (gasoline) (AmE) ▶ GASOLINE ⟨4⟩ (flatulence) (AmE) gases *mpl*

gas² *vt* **-ss-** (Mil) gasear; (kill) asfixiar con gas; (in gas chamber) ejecutar en la cámara de gas

gas chamber *n* cámara *f* de gas

gaseous /'gæsɪəs/ *adj* gaseoso

gash¹ /gæʃ/ *n* tajo *m*, corte *m* profundo

gash² *vt* hacer* un tajo en, cortar (*profundamente*)

gasket /'gæskət ‖'gæskɪt/ *n* junta *f*

gas: ~light *n* (illumination) luz *f* de gas; **~ mask** *n* máscara *f* antigás

gasoline /'gæsəli:n/ *n* (AmE) gasolina *f*, nafta *f* (RPl), bencina *f* (Andes)

gasp¹ /gæsp ‖gɑ:sp/ *vi* **(a)** (inhale sharply) dar* un grito ahogado **(b)** (pant) respirar entrecortadamente, jadear
■ **~** *vt* decir* jadeando

gasp² *n* exclamación *f*, grito *m* (*entrecortado o ahogado*)

gas: ~ pedal *n* (esp AmE) acelerador *m*; **~ pump** *n* (in service station) surtidor *m*, bomba *f* bencinera (Andes); **~ station** *n* (AmE) estación *f* de servicio *or* (RPl tb) de nafta, gasolinera *f*, bomba *f* (Andes, Ven), grifo *m* (Per); **~ tank** *n* (AmE) depósito *m* *or* tanque *m* de gasolina *or* (RPl) de nafta *or* (Andes) de bencina

gastric /'gæstrɪk/ *adj* gástrico

gastroenteritis /ˌgæstrəʊˌentəˈraɪtəs ‖ˌgæstrəʊˌentəˈraɪtɪs/ *n* gastroenteritis *f*

gasworks /'gæswɜːks ‖'gæswɜːks/ *n* (*pl* **~**) (+ *sing o pl vb*) fábrica *f* de gas

gate /geɪt/ *n* **(a)** (to garden — wooden) puerta *f* (del jardín); (— wrought-iron) verja *f*, cancela *f* (Esp); (to field) tranquera *f* (AmL), portillo *m* (Esp) **(b)** (to castle, city) (*usu pl*) puerta *f* **(c)** (controlling admission) entrada *f* **(d)** (at airport) puerta *f* (de embarque)

gate: ~crash *vi* colarse*; **~way** *n* verja *f*, portalón *m*

gather¹ /'gæðər ‖'gæðə(r)/ *vi* congregarse*, reunirse*
■ **~** *vt* ⟨1⟩ **(a)** (collect) ⟨wood/berries⟩ recoger*, coger* (esp Esp); ⟨information⟩ reunir*, juntar; ⟨people⟩ reunir*; **to ~ dust** juntar *or* acumular polvo **(b)** ⟨thoughts⟩ poner* en orden; ⟨strength⟩ juntar, hacer* acopio de **(c)** ⟨speed⟩ ir* adquiriendo ⟨2⟩ (conclude) deducir*; **I ~ you're moving** tengo entendido que te mudas (de casa) ⟨3⟩ (by sewing) fruncir*
■ **gather in** [*v + o + adv, v + adv + o*] recoger*

gather² *n* fruncido *m*, frunce *m*

gathering¹ /'gæðərɪŋ/ *n* (meeting) reunión *f*; (group of people) concurrencia *f*

gathering² *adj* (before n) creciente; **the ~ storm** la tormenta que se avecinaba

gaudy /'gɔːdi/ *adj* chillón, charro (AmL fam)

gauge¹, (AmE also) **gage** /geɪdʒ/ *vt* **(a)** (estimate) ⟨size⟩ calcular **(b)** (judge) ⟨effects⟩ evaluar* **(c)** (measure) medir*

gauge², (AmE also) **gage** *n* ⟨1⟩ (instrument) indicador *m* ⟨2⟩ (measure, indication) indicio *m* ⟨3⟩ (Rail): **narrow ~** vía *f* estrecha, trocha *f* angosta (CS)

gaunt /gɔːnt/ *adj* ⟨person⟩ descarnado, delgado y adusto; (from illness, tiredness) demacrado

gauntlet /'gɔːntlət ‖'gɔːntlɪt/ *n* guante *m* (*con el puño largo*); (of suit of armor) guantelete *m*, manopla *f*

gauze /gɔːz/ *n* (Tex, Med) gasa *f*; (fine mesh) malla *f*

gave /geɪv/ *past of* GIVE¹

gavel /'gævəl/ *n* mazo *m* *or* martillo *m* (*usado por jueces, subastadores etc*)

gay /geɪ/ *adj* ⟨1⟩ (homosexual) gay *adj inv* ⟨2⟩ (dated) (merry) alegre

gaze¹ /geɪz/ *vi* mirar (larga y fijamente); **to ~ AT sth/sb** mirar algo/a algn

gaze² *n* mirada *f* (*larga y fija*)

gazelle /gəˈzel/ *n* (*pl* **~s** *or* **~**) gacela *f*

gazette /gəˈzet/ *n* gaceta *f*

gazetteer /ˌgæzəˈtɪr ‖ˌgæzəˈtɪə(r)/ *n* índice *m* geográfico

GB = **Great Britain**

GCSE *n* (in UK) = **General Certificate of Secondary Education** ≈ bachillerato *m* elemental (*exámenes que se toman en diferentes asignaturas alrededor de los 16 años*)

gear¹ /gɪr ‖'gɪə(r)/ *n* ⟨1⟩ (Mech Eng) engranaje *m*; (Auto) marcha *f*, velocidad *f*, cambio *m*; **to shift** *o* (BrE) **change ~** cambiar de marcha, cambiar de velocidad, hacer* un cambio ⟨2⟩ **(a)** (equipment) equipo *m*; (tools) herramientas *fpl*; (fishing **~**) aparejo(s) *m(pl)* de pesca **(b)** (miscellaneous items) (colloq) cosas *fpl*

gear² *vt* orientar; (to be) **~ed TO/TOWARD sth/sb** (estar*) dirigido A algo/algn
■ **gear up** ⟨1⟩ [*v + adv*] (prepare) prepararse ⟨2⟩ [*v + o + adv, v + adv + o*] preparar

gearbox /'gɪrbɑːks ‖'gɪəbɒks/ *n* (Auto) caja *f* de cambios *or* velocidades

gee /dʒiː/ *interj* (AmE colloq): **~, I'm sorry to hear that you**, lo siento; **~, thanks!** ¡pero … gracias!

geese /giːs/ *pl of* GOOSE

gel¹ /dʒel/ *n* gel *m*

gel² *vi* **-ll-** **(a)** ⟨liquid⟩ gelificarse* **(b)** (BrE) ⟨plans/ideas⟩ cuajar

gelatin /'dʒelətn ‖'dʒelətɪn/, **gelatine** /'dʒeləti:n/ *n* gelatina *f*

gem /dʒem/ *n* **(a)** (stone) gema *f*, piedra *f* preciosa/semipreciosa; (jewel) joya *f*, alhaja *f* **(b)** (wonderful example) joya *f*

Gemini /'dʒemənaɪ, -ni:/ *n* **(a)** (sign) (*no art*) Géminis **(b)** (person) Géminis *or* géminis *mf*, geminiano, -na *m,f*

gender /'dʒendər ‖'dʒendə(r)/ *n* **(a)** (Ling) género *m* **(b)** (sex) sexo *m*

gene /dʒiːn/ *n* gen *m*, gene *m*

genealogy /ˌdʒiːniˈælədʒi/ *n* genealogía *f*

general¹ /'dʒenrəl/ *adj* ⟨1⟩ (not detailed or specific)

AmC América Central	Arg Argentina	Cu Cuba	Per Perú
AmL América Latina	Bol Bolivia	Ec Ecuador	RPl Río de la Plata
AmS América del Sur	Chi Chile	Esp España	Ur Uruguay
Andes Región andina	CS Cono Sur	Méx México	Ven Venezuela

general; **in** ～ en general **2** (widespread) ‹tendency› generalizado **3** (usual) general; **as a** ～ **rule** por lo general, por regla general **4** (chief) ‹manager› general **5** (Med) ‹anesthetic› general

general² n (Mil) general mf

general: ～ **delivery** n (AmE) lista f de correos, poste f restante (AmL); ～ **election** n elecciones fpl generales

generalization /ˌdʒenrələˈzeɪʃən ‖ˌdʒenrəlaɪˈzeɪʃən/ n generalización f

generalize /ˈdʒenrəlaɪz/ vi/t generalizar*

general knowledge n cultura f general

generally /ˈdʒenrəli/ adv (a) (usually, as a rule) generalmente, por lo general (b) (broadly) (indep) ～ **(speaking)** por lo general, en general (c) (as a whole) en general

general: ～ **practitioner** n médico, -ca m,f de medicina general; ～ **public** n the ～ **public** el público en general, el gran público; ～**-purpose** adj ‹tool› para todo uso; ‹dictionary› de uso general; ～ **store** n (AmE) tienda f (que vende todo tipo de artículos en una comunidad pequeña), almacén m (CS); ～ **strike** n huelga f general, paro m general (AmL)

generate /ˈdʒenəreɪt/ vt generar

generation /ˌdʒenəˈreɪʃən/ n **1** generación f; **the older** ～ la gente de más edad; **first-～ computers** computadoras fpl or (Esp tb) ordenadores mpl de primera generación **2** (act of generating) generación f

generation gap n brecha f generacional

generator /ˈdʒenəreɪtər ‖ˈdʒenəreɪtə(r)/ n generador m, grupo m electrógeno

generic /dʒəˈnerɪk/ adj ‹term› genérico

generosity /ˌdʒenəˈrɑːsəti ‖ˌdʒenəˈrɒsəti/ n generosidad f

generous /ˈdʒenrəs ‖ˈdʒenərəs/ adj **(a)** (open-handed) generoso **(b)** (ample, large) abundante, generoso

genetic /dʒəˈnetɪk ‖dʒɪˈnetɪk/ adj genético

genetically /dʒəˈnetɪkli/ adv genéticamente; ～ **modified** transgénico, genéticamente modificado

genetics /dʒəˈnetɪks ‖dʒɪˈnetɪks/ n (+ sing vb) genética f

genial /ˈdʒiːnjəl ‖ˈdʒiːniəl/ adj ‹person› simpático; ‹welcome/smile› cordial

genie /ˈdʒiːni/ n genio m

genitals /ˈdʒenətlz ‖ˈdʒenɪtlz/ pl n genitales mpl

genius /ˈdʒiːniəs/ n **1** (clever person) genio m **2** (brilliance) genialidad f

genre /ˈʒɑːnrə ‖ʒɒnrə/ n género m

gent /dʒent/ n (BrE colloq) caballero m; **🄖 Gents** Caballeros

gentle /ˈdʒentl/ adj **gentler** /ˈdʒentlər ‖ˈdʒentlə(r)/, **gentlest** /ˈdʒentləst ‖ˈdʒentlɪst/ **1 (a)** ‹person› dulce; ‹character› suave **(b)** (of voice): **in a** ～ **voice** en un tono suave or dulce **2** ‹murmur/breeze› suave; ‹exercise› moderado; ‹slope› poco empinado; ‹reminder› discreto

gentleman /ˈdʒentlmən/ n (pl **-men** /-mən/) **(a)** (man) caballero m, señor m **(b)** (well-bred man) caballero m

gently /ˈdʒentli/ adv **(a)** (not roughly or violently)

‹handle› con cuidado; ‹tap› ligeramente; ‹hint› con tacto **(b)** (tenderly) dulcemente; (tactfully) con delicadeza

gentry /ˈdʒentri/ n (+ sing o pl vb) alta burguesía f, pequeña nobleza f

genuine /ˈdʒenjuan ‖ˈdʒenjʊɪn/ adj **(a)** ‹interest/person› genuino, sincero; ‹inquiry/buyer/mistake› serio; **it was a** ～ **mistake** fue realmente un error **(b)** ‹antique› auténtico; ‹leather› legítimo

genuinely /ˈdʒenjuənli ‖ˈdʒenjʊmli/ adv **(a)** (sincerely) sinceramente **(b)** (really) realmente

geographical /ˌdʒiːəˈgræfɪkəl ‖ˌdʒiəˈgræfɪkəl/ adj geográfico

geography /dʒiˈɑːgrəfi ‖dʒiˈɒgrəfi/ n geografía f

geological /ˌdʒiːəˈlɑːdʒɪkəl ‖ˌdʒiəˈlɒdʒɪkəl/ adj geológico

geologist /dʒiˈɑːlədʒəst ‖dʒiˈɒlədʒɪst/ n geólogo, -ga m,f

geology /dʒiˈɑːlədʒi ‖dʒiˈɒlədʒi/ n geología f

geometrical /ˌdʒiːəˈmetrɪkəl ‖ˌdʒiəˈmetrɪkəl/ adj geométrico

geometry /dʒiˈɑːmətri ‖dʒiˈɒmətri/ n geometría f

Georgia /ˈdʒɔːrdʒə ‖ˈdʒɔːdʒə/ n **(a)** (republic in the Caucasus) Georgia f **(b)** (US state) Georgia f

Georgian¹ /ˈdʒɔːrdʒən ‖ˈdʒɔːdʒən/ adj **(a)** (of Georgia in the Caucasus) georgiano **(b)** (of Georgia in USA) georgiano **(c)** (in architecture, UK history) georgiano

Georgian² n **(a)** (from the Caucasus) georgiano, -na m,f **(b)** (language) georgiano m **(c)** (from USA) georgiano, -na m,f

geriatric /ˈdʒeriˈætrɪk/ adj (Med) ‹patient› anciano; ‹ward› de geriatría

geriatrician /ˌdʒeriəˈtrɪʃən/ n geriatra mf

germ /dʒɜːrm ‖dʒɜːm/ n **1** (Med) microbio m, germen m **2** (Biol, Bot) germen m

German¹ /ˈdʒɜːrmən ‖ˈdʒɜːmən/ adj alemán

German² n **(a)** (language) alemán m **(b)** (person) alemán, -mana m,f

German: ～ **measles** n (+ sing vb) rubéola f, rubeola f; ～ **shepherd (dog)** n pastor m or (CS) ovejero m alemán

Germany /ˈdʒɜːrməni ‖ˈdʒɜːməni/ n Alemania f

germinate /ˈdʒɜːrməneɪt ‖ˈdʒɜːmɪneɪt/ vi germinar

gerund /ˈdʒerənd/ n gerundio m

gestation /dʒeˈsteɪʃən/ n gestación f

gesticulate /dʒeˈstɪkjələt ‖dʒeˈstɪkjʊleɪt/ vi gesticular

gesture¹ /ˈdʒestʃər ‖ˈdʒestʃə(r)/ n **(a)** (of body) gesto m, ademán m **(b)** (token, expression) gesto m; **a** ～ **of good will** un gesto de buena voluntad; **it was a nice** ～ fue todo un detalle

gesture² vi hacer* gestos

get /get/ (pres p **getting**; past **got**; past p **got** or (AmE also) **gotten**) vt

I 1 (a) (obtain) conseguir*, obtener*; ‹job/staff› conseguir*; ‹idea› sacar*; **where did you** ～ **that beautiful rug?** ¿dónde conseguiste esa alfombra tan preciosa? **(b)** (buy) comprar; **I got it from Harrods** lo compré en Harrods **(c)** (achieve, win) ‹prize/grade› sacar*, obtener* (frml) **(d)** (on the ⋯▸

telephone) ⟨person⟩ lograr comunicarse con; **you've got the wrong number** se ha equivocado de número

2 **(a)** (receive) ⟨letter/reward/reprimand⟩ recibir; **I got a stereo for my birthday** me regalaron un estéreo para mi cumpleaños **(b)** (be paid) ⟨salary/pay⟩ ganar; **I got £200 for the piano** me dieron 200 libras por el piano **(c)** (experience) ⟨shock/surprise⟩ llevarse; **I ~ the feeling that ...** tengo la sensación de que ... **(d)** (suffer): **how did you ~ that bump on your head?** ¿cómo te hiciste ese chichón en la cabeza?

3 (fetch) ⟨hammer/scissors⟩ traer*, ir* a buscar; ⟨doctor/plumber⟩ llamar; **~ your coat** anda or vete a buscar tu abrigo

4 **(a)** (take hold of) agarrar, coger* (esp Esp) **(b)** (catch, trap) pillar (fam), agarrar (AmL), coger* (esp Esp)

5 (contract) ⟨cold/flu⟩ agarrar, pescar* (fam), pillar (fam), coger* (esp Esp)

6 (catch) ⟨bus/train⟩ tomar, coger* (Esp)

7 (colloq) **(a)** (irritate) fastidiar **(b)** (puzzle): **what ~s me is how ...** lo que no entiendo es cómo ...

8 **(a)** (understand) (colloq) entender*; **don't ~ me wrong** no me malentiendas **(b)** (take note of): **did you ~ the number?** ¿tomaste nota del número?

9 (possess) **to have got** ▶ HAVE *vt*

II **1** (bring, move, put) (+ *adv compl*): **we'll ~ it there by two o'clock** lo tendremos allí antes de las dos; **they couldn't ~ it up the stairs** no lo pudieron subir por las escaleras

2 (cause to be) (+ *adj compl*): **he got the children ready** preparó a los niños; **I can't ~ the window open** no puedo abrir la ventana; **they got their feet wet** se mojaron los pies

3 **to ~ sb/sth + *pp*** **(a)** (with action carried out by subject): **we must ~ some work done** tenemos que trabajar un poco; **to ~ oneself organized** organizarse* **(b)** (with action carried out by somebody else): **he got the house painted** hizo pintar la casa; **I must ~ this watch fixed** tengo que llevar a or (AmL tb) mandar (a) arreglar este reloj

4 (arrange, persuade, force) **to ~ sb/sth to + INF**: **I'll ~ him to help you** (order) le diré que te ayude; (ask) le pediré que te ayude; (persuade) lo convenceré de que te ayude; **I can't ~ it to work** no puedo hacerlo funcionar

■ **~ *vi* 1** (reach) (+ *adv compl*): **can you ~ there by train?** ¿se puede ir en tren?

2 (become): **to ~ tired** cansarse; **to ~ dressed** vestirse*; **he got very angry** se puso furioso; ▶ MARRIED, COLD *etc*

3 **to ~ to + INF** **(a)** (come to) llegar* a + INF; **I never really got to know him** nunca llegué a conocerlo de verdad **(b)** (have opportunity to): **in this job you ~ to meet many interesting people** en este trabajo uno tiene la oportunidad de conocer a mucha gente interesante; **when do we ~ to open the presents?** ¿cuándo podemos abrir los regalos?

4 (start) **to ~ -ING** empezar* a + INF, ponerse* a + INF

■ **get about** [v + adv] [v + prep + o] (BrE) ▶ GET AROUND I 1

■ **get above** [v + prep + o]: **to ~ above oneself** llenarse de ínfulas

■ **get across** **1** [v + prep + o] [v + adv] (cross) ⟨river⟩ atravesar*, cruzar*; ⟨road⟩ cruzar*

2 [v + o + adv, v + adv + o] ⟨meaning/concept⟩ hacer* entender

3 [v + adv] (be understood) «teacher/speaker» hacerse* entender

■ **get ahead** [v + adv] **(a)** (get in front) «student/worker» adelantar **(b)** (progress, succeed) progresar

■ **get along** [v + adv] **1** (manage, cope) arreglárselas

2 (progress) «work/patient» marchar, andar*; **he's ~ting along just fine at school** le va muy bien en el colegio

3 (be on good terms) **to ~ along** (WITH sb) llevarse bien (CON algn)

■ **get around**

I **1** [v + adv] **(a)** (walk, move about) caminar, andar*; (using transport, car) desplazarse* **(b)** (travel) viajar **(c)** (circulate): **it** o **word got around that ...** pronto corrió el rumor de que ...

2 [v + prep + o] (gather in circle): **we can't all ~ around this table** no cabemos todos alrededor de esta mesa

II [v + prep + o] **(a)** (avoid, circumvent) ⟨difficulty/obstacle⟩ sortear, evitar; ⟨rule/law⟩ eludir el cumplimiento de **(b)** (persuade) ⟨person⟩ engatusar

III [v + adv] (go) ir*; (come) venir*

■ **get around to** [v + adv + prep + o]: **I meant to write to you, I just never got around to it** tenía intenciones de escribirte pero nunca llegué a hacerlo; **I must ~ around to writing those letters** debo ponerme a escribir esas cartas

■ **get at** [v + prep + o] **1** **(a)** (reach) ⟨pipe/wire⟩ llegar* a **(b)** (ascertain) ⟨facts/truth⟩ establecer*

2 (nag, criticize) (colloq) criticar*, meterse con (fam)

3 (hint at, mean) (colloq): **what are you ~ting at?** ¿qué quieres decir?

■ **get away** [v + adv] **1** (escape) escaparse

2 **(a)** (leave) salir* **(b)** (go on vacation) irse* de vacaciones; **to ~ away from it all** alejarse del mundanal ruido

■ **get away with** [v + adv + prep + o] **1** (make off with) llevarse, escaparse con

2 **(a)** (go unpunished for): **you won't ~ away with this** esto no va a quedar así; **don't let them ~ away with it** no dejes que se salgan con la suya **(b)** (be let off with) ⟨fine/warning⟩ escaparse or librarse con

■ **get back** **1** [v + adv] **(a)** (return) volver*, regresar; (arrive home) llegar* (a casa) **(b)** (retreat): **~ back!** ¡atrás!

2 [v + o + adv, v + adv + o] (regain possession of) ⟨property⟩ recuperar; ⟨health⟩ recobrar; **we never got our money back** nos devolvieron el dinero

■ **get behind** **1** [v + adv] (fall behind) **to ~ behind** (WITH sth) atrasarse (CON algo)

2 [v + prep + o] (move to rear of) ponerse* detrás de; (fall behind) rezagarse*, quedarse atrás

■ **get by** [v + adv] (manage) arreglárselas; **I speak enough French to ~ by** me defiendo en francés; **to ~ by ON sth** arreglárselas CON algo

■ **get down** **1** [v + adv] **(a)** (descend) bajar **(b)** (crouch) agacharse

2 [v + o + adv, v + adv + o] **(a)** (take, lift, bring down) bajar **(b)** (write down) anotar, tomar nota de

3 [v + o + adv] **(a)** (reduce) ⟨costs/inflation⟩ reducir*; ⟨blood pressure⟩ bajar **(b)** (depress) deprimir

4 [v + prep + o] (descend) ‹stairs› bajar; ‹ladder›
bajarse de; ‹rope› bajar por
■ **get down to** [v + adv + prep + o] (start work on)
ponerse* a
■ **get in** **1** (a) [v + adv] (enter) entrar (b) [v +
prep + o] ▶ GET INTO 1A
2 [v + adv] (a) (arrive) «person/train» llegar*
(b) (gain admission to, be selected for) entrar, ser*
admitido (c) (be elected) (Pol) ganar, resultar
elegido
3 [v + o + adv, v + adv + o] (a) (bring in, collect up)
‹washing/chairs› entrar; ‹harvest› recoger* (b)
(buy, obtain) (BrE) ‹wood/coal/food› aprovisionarse
de (c) (call out) ‹doctor/plumber› llamar (d)
(interpose) ‹blow/kick› dar*; ‹remark› hacer*
■ **get into** **1** [v + prep + o] (a) (enter) ‹house›
entrar en or (AmL tb) a; ‹car› subir a; ‹hole›
meterse en (b) (arrive at) ‹station/office› llegar* a
(c) (be selected for, elected to) ‹college/club/
Congress› entrar en or (AmL tb) a (d) (put on)
‹coat/robe› ponerse*; (fit into) **I can't ~ into this
dress any more** este vestido ya no me entra (e)
(into a given state): **to ~ into a rage/a mess**
ponerse* furioso/meterse en un lío; (f) (affect): **I
don't know what's got into him lately** no sé qué le
pasa últimamente
2 [v + o + prep + o] (a) (bring, take, put in) meter
(b) (involve): **you got me into this** tú me metiste en
esto
■ **get off** **1** [v + adv] [v + prep + o] (a) (alight,
dismount) bajarse; **to ~ off a train/horse/bicycle**
bajarse de un tren/de un caballo/de una bicicleta
(b) (remove oneself from) ‹flowerbed/lawn› salir* de
(c) (finish) ‹work/school› salir* de
2 [v + adv] (a) (leave) «person/letter» salir* (b)
(escape unpunished) «person accused» salir* libre;
he got off lightly o (AmE also) **easy** no recibió el
castigo que se merecía; **he got off with a fine** se
escapó con solo una multa
3 [v + prep + o] (a) (get up from) ‹floor›
levantarse de (b) (deviate from) ‹track/tourist
routes› salir* or alejarse de; ‹point› desviarse* or
irse* de; **I tried to ~ him off the subject** intenté
hacerlo cambiar de tema (c) (evade) ‹duty›
librarse or salvarse de
4 [v + o + adv] (remove) ‹lid/top/stain› quitar
5 [v + o + adv] (send, see off): **we got the children
off to school** mandamos a los niños a la escuela
6 (save from punishment) salvar
■ **get on**
I [v + adv] **1** (move on) seguir* adelante; **to ~ on
TO sth** pasar A algo; **~ on with what you're doing**
sigue con lo que estás haciendo
2 (a) (fare): **how's Joe ~ting on nowadays?**
¿qué tal anda Joe?; **how did he ~ on at the
interview?** ¿cómo le fue en la entrevista? (b)
(succeed) tener* éxito; **to ~ on in life** tener éxito
en la vida
3 (be friends, agree) **to ~ on** (WITH sb) llevarse
bien (CON algn)
4 (in -ing form) (a) (in time) **it's ~ting on** se está
haciendo tarde (b) (in age): **she's ~ting on** (in
years) está vieja, ya no es joven
II [v + adv] [v + prep + o] (climb on, board)
subirse; **to ~ on the bus/a horse** subirse al
autobús/subirse a un caballo
III [v + o + adv] [v + prep + o] (place, fix on)
poner; **I can't ~ the top on** (it) no puedo ponerle
la tapa

IV [v + o + adv] (put on) ‹clothes› ponerse*
■ **get on for** [v + adv + prep + o] (approach) (BrE)
(usu in -ing form): **it's ~ting on for six o'clock**
van a ser las seis; **he must be ~ting on for 40**
debe (de) andar rondando los 40
■ **get onto** [v + prep + o] **1** (a) (contact) ‹person/
department› ponerse* en contacto con (b) (begin
discussing) ‹subject› empezar* a hablar de
2 (mount, board) ‹table/bus/train› subirse a;
‹horse/bicycle› montarse en
■ **get out**
I [v + adv] **1** (a) (of car, bus, train) bajar(se); (of
hole) salir*; (of bath) salir*; **to ~ out of bed**
levantarse (de la cama) (b) (of room, country) salir*;
~ out! ¡fuera (de aquí)!
2 (a) (escape) «animal/prisoner» escaparse (b)
(become known) «news/truth» saberse*
II [v + o + adv, v + adv + o] (a) (remove, extract)
‹stopper/nail› sacar*; ‹stain› quitar, sacar* (esp
AmL) (b) (take out) ‹knife/map› sacar* (c)
(withdraw) ‹money› sacar* (d) (borrow) ‹library
book› sacar*
III [v + o + adv] **1** (remove) ‹tenant› echar; **~
that dog out of here!** ¡saquen a ese perro de
aquí!; **I can't ~ you out of this mess** no te puedo
sacar de este lío
2 (send for) ‹doctor/repairman› llamar
■ **get out of** **1** [v + adv + prep + o] (a) (avoid)
‹obligation› librarse or salvarse de; **to ~ out of**
-ING librarse or salvarse de + INF (b) (give up):
you must ~ out of that bad habit tienes que
sacarte esa mala costumbre; **I'd got out of the
habit of setting my alarm clock** había perdido la
costumbre de poner el despertador
2 [v + o + adv + prep + o] (a) (extract)
‹information/truth› sonsacar*, sacar* (b) (derive,
gain) ‹money/profit› sacar*
■ **get over** **1** [v + prep + o] ‹river/chasm›
cruzar*; ‹wall/fence› pasar por encima de; ‹hill/
ridge› atravesar*; ‹obstacle› superar
2 [v + prep + o] ‹loss/tragedy/difficulty› superar;
‹illness/shock› reponerse* de; **he's very
disappointed — he'll ~ over it** ha quedado muy
decepcionado — ya se le pasará
3 [v + o + adv] (cause to come, take): **~ those
documents over to Wall Street right away** manda
esos documentos a Wall Street enseguida; **to ~
sth over with**: **I'd like to ~ it over with as quickly
as possible** quisiera salir de eso or quitarme eso
de encima lo más pronto posible
4 [v + o + adv] (communicate) ‹emotion›
comunicar*
■ **get past** **1** [v + adv] (move past) pasar
2 [v + prep + o] (a) (move past) ‹vehicle› pasar,
adelantarse a; ‹opponent/attacker› eludir (b) (get
beyond) ‹obstacle› superar; ‹semifinals› pasar
■ **get round** (esp BrE) ▶ GET AROUND
■ **get through**
I [v + prep + o] [v + adv + o] (a) (pass through) ‹gap/
hole› pasar por (b) (ordeal) superar; ‹winter/
difficult time› pasar (c) (Sport) ‹heat› pasar
II [v + adv] **1** (a) (reach destination) ‹supplies/
messenger› llegar* a destino; «news/report»
llegar* (b) (on the telephone) **to ~ through** (TO sb/
sth) comunicarse* (CON algn/algo) (c) (make
understand): **am I ~ting through to you?** ¿me
entiendes?; **I can't ~ through to him** no logro
hacerme entender con él
2 (finish) (AmE) terminar, acabar

III [v + prep + o] **(a)** (use up) (BrE) ‹money› gastarse; ‹materials› usar; ‹shoes› destrozar* **(b)** (deal with): **I've only got ten more pages to ~ through** me quedan solo diez páginas por leer (or estudiar etc)

IV [v + o + adv] [v + o + prep + o] (bring through) pasar; **to ~ sth through customs** pasar algo por la aduana

V [v + o + adv] **(a)** (send) ‹supplies/message› hacer* llegar **(b)** (make understood) hacer* entender

■ **get together** 1 [v + adv] **(a)** (meet up) reunirse*, quedar (Esp); (have a family reunion) juntarse, reunirse* **(b)** (join forces) «nations/unions» unirse **(c)** (become couple, team) (colloq) juntarse

2 [v + o + adv, v + adv + o] (assemble) ‹people/money› reunir*; **~ your things together** junta or recoge tus cosas

■ **get up** 1 [v + prep + o] [v + adv] (climb up) subir; **to ~ up ON sth** subir(se) A algo

2 [v + adv] **(a)** (out of bed) levantarse **(b)** (stand up) levantarse

3 [v + o + adv] (raise, lift) ‹person› levantar

4 [v + o + adv, v + adv + o] (develop, arouse) ‹appetite/enthusiasm› despertar*; ‹speed› agarrar, coger* (esp Esp); **she didn't want to ~ their hopes up** no quería esperanzarlos

■ **get up to** [v + adv + prep + o] 1 (reach): **when he got up to them ...** cuando los alcanzó ...; **we got up to page 161** llegamos hasta la página 161

2 (be involved in) (colloq) hacer*; **to ~ up to mischief** hacer* travesuras or de las suyas

get: **~away** n huida f, fuga f; **to make one's ~away** escaparse, huir*; **~-together** n (colloq) reunión f

geyser /'gaɪzər ‖'giːzə(r)/ n (Geog) géiser m

Ghana /'gɑːnə/ n Ghana f

Ghanaian /gɑː'neɪən/ adj ghanés

ghastly /'gæstli ‖'gɑːstli/ adj **(a)** (very bad, awful) (colloq) espantoso, horrendo (fam) **(b)** (horrible, hideous) horrible, espantoso

gherkin /'gɜːrkən ‖'gɜːkɪn/ n pepinillo m

ghetto /'getəʊ/ n (pl **-tos** or **-toes**) gueto m

ghost /gəʊst/ n fantasma m, espíritu m

ghostly /'gəʊstli/ adj **-lier, -liest** fantasmal, fantasmagórico

ghoul /guːl/ n **(a)** (person) morboso, -sa m,f **(b)** (evil spirit) demonio m necrófago

GI n (colloq) soldado m estadounidense

giant[1] /'dʒaɪənt/ n gigante, -ta m,f

giant[2] adj (before n) ‹organization› gigantesco; ‹insect› gigante; ‹stride› gigantesco

gibber /'dʒɪbər ‖'dʒɪbə(r)/ vi farfullar

gibberish /'dʒɪbərɪʃ/ n galimatías m; **to talk ~** decir* sandeces (fam)

gibe /dʒaɪb/ n pulla f

giblets /'dʒɪbləts ‖'dʒɪblɪts/ pl n menudillos mpl, menudos mpl

Gibraltar /dʒə'brɔːltər ‖dʒɪ'brɔːltə(r)/ n Gibraltar

giddy /'gɪdi/ adj **-dier, -diest** ‹sensation› de mareo or aturdimiento; **to feel ~** sentirse* mareado

gift /gɪft/ n 1 (present) regalo m; **it was a ~ me** lo regalaron, es un regalo 2 (talent) don m; **she has a ~ for poetry** tiene talento para la poesía

gift certificate n (AmE) vale m (canjeable por artículos en una tienda), cheque regalo m

gifted /'gɪftəd ‖'gɪftɪd/ adj ‹person› de talento, talentoso

gift: **~ token**, **~ voucher** n (BrE) ▶ GIFT CERTIFICATE; **~-wrap** vt **-pp-** envolver* para regalo or (frml) obsequio

gig /gɪg/ n (sl) actuación f

gigabyte /'gɪɡəbaɪt/ n gigabyte m

gigantic /dʒaɪ'ɡæntɪk/ adj gigantesco; ‹success/appetite› enorme; ‹effort› titánico

giggle[1] /'gɪɡəl/ vi reírse* tontamente

giggle[2] n risita f

gild /gɪld/ vt dorar

gill n 1 /dʒɪl/ medida para líquidos equivalente a la cuarta parte de una pinta o 0,142 l 2 /gɪl/ (Zool) agalla f, branquia f

gilt /gɪlt/ n dorado m

gimmick /'gɪmɪk/ n **(a)** (ingenious idea, device) truco m **(b)** (catch, snag) (AmE) trampa f

gin /dʒɪn/ n ginebra f, gin m

ginger[1] /'dʒɪndʒər ‖'dʒɪndʒə(r)/ n jengibre m

ginger[2] adj ‹hair› color zanahoria; ‹cat› rojizo

ginger: **~ ale** n ginger ale m, refresco m de jengibre; **~ beer** n cerveza f de jengibre; **~bread** n (cake) pan m de jengibre; (cookie) galleta f de jengibre

gipsy, Gipsy /'dʒɪpsi/ n ▶ GYPSY

giraffe /dʒə'ræf ‖dʒɪ'rɑːf/ n jirafa f

girder /'gɜːrdər ‖'gɜːdə(r)/ n viga f (de metal)

girdle /'gɜːrdl̩ ‖'gɜːdl̩/ n faja f

girl /gɜːrl ‖gɜːl/ n 1 **(a)** (baby, child) niña f, nena f (esp RPl) **(b)** (young woman) chica f, muchacha f 2 (daughter) hija f, niña f

girl: **~friend** n **(a)** (of man) novia f **(b)** (of woman) (esp AmE) amiga f; (in lesbian couple) compañera f; **~ guide** (BrE) ▶ GIRL SCOUT

girlish /'gɜːrlɪʃ ‖'gɜːlɪʃ/ adj de niña

girl scout n (AmE) guía f (de los scouts), exploradora f

giro /'dʒaɪrəʊ/ n (pl **-ros**) (in UK) (system) transferencia f, giro m

girth /gɜːrθ ‖gɜːθ/ n 1 (of person, object) circunferencia f 2 (Equ) cincha f

gist /dʒɪst/ n lo esencial; **to get the ~ of sth** captar lo esencial de algo

give[1] /gɪv/ (past **gave**; past p **given**) vt

I 1 **(a)** (hand, pass) dar*; **~ her/me/them a glass of water** dale/dame/dales un vaso de agua **(b)** (as gift) regalar*; **to ~ sb a present** hacerle* un regalo a algn, regalarle algo a algn **(c)** (donate) dar*, donar **(d)** (dedicate, devote) ‹love/affection› dar*;

⟨attention⟩ prestar; **I'll ∼ it some thought** lo pensaré **(e)** (sacrifice) ⟨life⟩ dar*, entregar* **(f)** ⟨injection/sedative⟩ dar*, administrar (frml)
2 (a) (supply, grant) ⟨help⟩ dar*, brindar; ⟨idea⟩ dar* **(b)** (allow, concede) ⟨opportunity/permission⟩ dar*, conceder (frml)
3 (a) (cause) ⟨pleasure/shock⟩ dar*; ⟨cough⟩ dar* **(b)** (yield) ⟨results/fruit⟩ dar*
4 (a) (award, allot) ⟨title/authority/right⟩ dar*, otorgar* (frml); ⟨contract⟩ dar*, adjudicar*; ⟨mark⟩ dar*, poner* **(b)** (entrust) ⟨task/responsibility⟩ dar*, confiar*
5 (pay, exchange) dar*; **I'd ∼ anything for a cigarette** no sé qué daría por un cigarrillo
6 (care) (colloq): **I don't ∼ a damn** me importa un bledo (fam)
II **1** (convey, state) ⟨apologies/information⟩ dar*; **she gave a detailed description of the place** describió el lugar detalladamente
2 (make sound, movement) ⟨cry/jump⟩ dar*; ⟨laugh⟩ soltar*
3 (indicate) ⟨speed/temperature⟩ señalar
4 (hold) ⟨party/dinner⟩ dar*, ofrecer* (frml); ⟨concert⟩ dar*; ⟨speech⟩ decir*
■ ∼ *vi* **1 (a)** (yield under pressure) ceder, dar* de sí **(b)** (break, give way) ⟨planks/branch⟩ romperse*
2 (make gift) dar*; **to ∼ to charity** dar* dinero a organizaciones de caridad
■ **give away** [v + o + adv, v + adv + o] **1 (a)** (free of charge) regalar **(b)** ⟨prizes⟩ hacer* entrega de
2 (a) (disclose) revelar; **he didn't ∼ anything away** no dejó entrever nada **(b)** (betray) delatar
3 ⟨bride⟩ entregar* en matrimonio
■ **give back** [v + o + adv, v + adv + o] devolver*
■ **give in** [v + adv] (surrender, succumb) ceder; (in guessing games) rendirse*; **we will not ∼ in to terrorists** no vamos a ceder frente a los terroristas
■ **give off** [v + adv + o] ⟨smell/fumes⟩ despedir*, largar* (RPl fam); ⟨heat⟩ dar*; ⟨radiation⟩ emitir
■ **give out** **1** [v + o + adv, v + adv + o] ⟨leaflets⟩ repartir, distribuir*
2 [v + adv + o] **(a)** (let out) ⟨cry/yell⟩ dar* **(b)** (emit) ⟨heat⟩ dar*; ⟨signal⟩ emitir
■ **give up**
I [v + o + adv, v + adv + o] **1 (a)** (renounce, cease from) ⟨alcohol⟩ dejar; ⟨fight⟩ abandonar; **to ∼ up hope** perder* las esperanzas; **to ∼ up -ING** dejar DE + INF **(b)** (relinquish, hand over) ⟨territory/position⟩ ceder; **to ∼ up one's seat for sb** cederle el asiento a algn
2 (surrender): **to ∼ oneself up** entregarse*
II [v + adv] **(a)** (cease fighting, trying) rendirse*; **I've ∼n up on them** yo con ellos no insisto más, no pierdo más tiempo **(b)** (stop doing sth) dejar
III [v + o + adv] (abandon hope for): **to ∼ sb up for lost** dar* a algn por desaparecido
give² n elasticidad f

give: ∼-and-take /'gɪvən'teɪk/ n concesiones fpl mutuas, toma y daca m; **∼away** n
1 (evidence): **her accent is a real ∼away** el acento la delata or (fam) la vende; **2 (a)** (free gift) regalo m; (before n) **at ∼away prices** a precio de regalo **(b)** (sth easily done, obtained): **the last question was a ∼away** la última pregunta estaba regalada or tirada (fam)
given¹ /'gɪvən/ past p of GIVE¹
given² adj ⟨amount/time⟩ determinado, dado

given³ prep **1** (in view of) dado **2** (as conj) ∼ (THAT) dado que
given name n (AmE) nombre m de pila
glacé /glæ'se ‖'glæseɪ/ adj (before n) glaseado
glacier /'gleɪʃər ‖'glæsɪə(r), 'gleɪsɪə(r)/ n glaciar m
glad /glæd/ adj -dd- (pred) to be ∼ (ABOUT sth) alegrarse DE algo; **to be ∼ (THAT)** alegrarse DE QUE (+ subj); **I'm only too ∼ to help** es un placer poder ser útil
gladden /'glædn/ vt (liter) llenar de alegría or (liter) de gozo
gladly /'glædli/ adv con mucho gusto
glamor /'glæmər ‖'glæmə(r)/ n (AmE) ▶ GLAMOUR
glamorous /'glæmərəs/ adj ⟨person/dress⟩ glamoroso; ⟨lifestyle⟩ sofisticado; ⟨job⟩ rodeado de glamour
glamour, (AmE also) **glamor** /'glæmər ‖'glæmə(r)/ n glamour m
glance¹ /glæns ‖glɑːns/ n mirada f; **to take a ∼ at sth** echarle un vistazo or una ojeada a algo; **at first ∼** a primera vista
glance² vi mirar; **to ∼ AT sth** echarle una ojeada or un vistazo A algo; **to ∼ AT sb** echarle una mirada A algn
glancing /'glænsɪŋ ‖'glɑːnsɪŋ/ adj (before n): **to strike sb a ∼ blow** pegarle* a algn de refilón
gland /glænd/ n **(a)** (organ) glándula f **(b)** (lymph node) ganglio m
glandular fever /'glændjələr ‖'glændjʊlə(r)/ n mononucleosis f (infecciosa)
glare¹ /gler ‖gleə(r)/ n **1** (stare) mirada f (hostil, feroz, de odio etc) **2** (light) resplandor m
glare² vi **1** (stare) **to ∼ AT sb** fulminar a algn con la mirada **2** (shine) brillar
glaring /'glerɪŋ ‖'gleərɪŋ/ adj **(a)** ⟨light⟩ deslumbrante **(b)** (flagrant) (before n) ⟨error⟩ mayúsculo
glass /glæs ‖glɑːs/ n **1** (material) vidrio m, cristal m (Esp) **2** (vessel) vaso m; (with stem) copa f; **a ∼ of wine** una copa de vino **3** **glasses** pl (spectacles) gafas fpl, lentes mpl (esp AmL), anteojos mpl (esp AmL) **4** (magnifying ∼) lupa f, lente f de aumento
glassblowing /'glæs,bləʊɪŋ ‖'glɑːs,bləʊŋ/ n soplado m del vidrio
glassy /'glæsi ‖'glɑːsi/ adj **(a)** (like glass) vítreo **(b)** (dull, lifeless) ⟨stare⟩ vidrioso
glaze¹ /gleɪz/ n **(a)** (on pottery) vidriado m **(b)** (Culin) glaseado m
glaze² vt **1** (fit with glass) ⟨window/door⟩ acristalar; **to ∼ a window** ponerle* vidrio(s) or (Esp) cristal(es) a **2** (make shiny, glossy) **(a)** ⟨pottery⟩ vidriar **(b)** (Culin) glasear
■ ∼ vi ∼ (over) «eyes» vidriarse
glazed /gleɪzd/ adj **1** (fitted with glass) ⟨window/door⟩ con vidrio or (Esp) cristal **2 (a)** (Culin) glaseado **(b)** ⟨expression⟩ vidrioso
glazier /'gleɪʒər ‖'gleɪzɪə(r)/ n vidriero, -ra m,f, cristalero, -ra m,f (Esp)
gleam¹ /gliːm/ vi «metal» relucir*
gleam² n (on metal, water) reflejo m; **he had a wicked ∼ in his eyes** sus ojos despedían un destello maleficioso
gleaming /'gliːmɪŋ/ adj reluciente

glean /gliːn/ vt ⟨information⟩ recoger*

glee /gliː/ n regocijo m

gleeful /'gliːfəl/ adj lleno de alegría

glen /glen/ n cañada f

glib /glɪb/ adj **-bb-** ⟨remark/answer⟩ simplista; ⟨salesman/politician⟩ con mucha labia

glide /glaɪd/ vi ❙1❙ (move smoothly over a surface) deslizarse* ❙2❙ ⟨bird/plane⟩ planear

glider /'glaɪdər ‖'glaɪdə(r)/ n planeador m

glimmer¹ /'glɪmər ‖'glɪmə(r)/ vi brillar con luz trémula

glimmer² n luz f débil; **a ~ of hope** un rayo de esperanza

glimpse¹ /glɪmps/ n: **I caught a ~ of the room** pude ver brevemente la habitación; **a ~ of life in rural England** una visión de la vida en la Inglaterra rural

glimpse² vt alcanzar* a ver

glint¹ /glɪnt/ vi destellar

glint² n (of metal, light) destello m; (in eye) (no pl) chispa f, brillo m

glisten /'glɪsən/ vi brillar

glitter¹ /'glɪtər ‖'glɪtə(r)/ vi relumbrar

glitter² n (a) (sparkle) (no pl) destello m (b) (superficial attractiveness) oropel m (c) (decoration) purpurina f, brillantes mpl (Arg), brillantina f (Ur, Ven), brillo m (Chi)

gloat /gləʊt/ vi **to ~** ⟨OVER sth⟩ regodearse ⟨CON algo⟩

global /'gləʊbəl/ adj (a) (worldwide) a escala mundial, global; **~ warming** calentamiento m global (b) (overall, comprehensive) global

globe /gləʊb/ n (a) (world) **the ~** el globo (b) (model) globo m terráqueo

globe: ~ artichoke n alcachofa f, alcuacil m (RPl); **~trotter** /'gləʊb,trɑːtər ‖'gləʊb,trɒtə(r)/ n trotamundos mf

globule /'glɑːbjuːl ‖'glɒbjuːl/ n glóbulo m

gloom /gluːm/ n (a) (darkness) penumbra f, oscuridad f (b) (melancholy) melancolía f

gloomily /'gluːməli ‖'gluːmɪli/ adv ⟨sigh/stare⟩ tristemente; ⟨predict⟩ con pesimismo

gloomy /'gluːmi/ adj **-mier, -miest** (a) (dark) ⟨day/place⟩ sombrío (b) (dismal) ⟨person⟩ lúgubre, fúnebre; ⟨prospect⟩ nada halagüeño; ⟨prediction⟩ pesimista

glorify /'glɔːrəfaɪ ‖'glɔːrɪfaɪ/ vt **-fies, -fying, -fied** ⟨person⟩ ensalzar*; ⟨violence/war⟩ exaltar

glorious /'glɔːriəs/ adj (a) (deserving glory) glorioso (b) (wonderful) ⟨view/weather⟩ maravilloso

glory¹ /'glɔːri/ n (pl **-ries**) (a) (fame) gloria f (b) (beauty, magnificence) esplendor m

glory² vi **-ries, -rying, -ried: to ~ IN sth** (take pleasure) disfrutar DE algo; (in unpleasant way) regodearse CON algo

gloss /glɑːs ‖glɒs/ n (a) (shine) brillo m; ⟨before n⟩ **~ finish** acabado m brillante (b) **~ (paint)** (pintura f al or de) esmalte m

■ **gloss over** [v + adv + o] (make light of) quitarle importancia a; (ignore) pasar por alto

glossary /'glɑːsəri ‖'glɒsəri/ n (pl **-ries**) glosario m

glossy /'glɑːsi ‖'glɒsi/ adj **-sier, -siest** ⟨coat of animal⟩ brillante, lustroso; ⟨hair⟩ brillante,

brilloso (AmL); ⟨photograph⟩ brillante; **~ magazine** revista f ilustrada (impresa en papel satinado)

glove /glʌv/ n guante m

glove compartment n guantera f

glow¹ /gləʊ/ vi ⟨fire⟩ brillar; ⟨metal⟩ estar* al rojo vivo; **to ~ with health** rebosar (de) salud; **to be ~ing with happiness** estar* radiante de felicidad

glow² n (no pl) brillo m; **he felt a ~ of pride** sintió una oleada de orgullo

glower /'glaʊər ‖'glaʊə(r)/ vi tener* el ceño fruncido; **to ~ AT sb** lanzarle* miradas fulminantes/una mirada fulminante A algn

glowing /'gləʊɪŋ/ adj (a) (shining) ⟨before n⟩ ⟨cheeks⟩ encendido; **the ~ embers** las brasas (b) (expressing praise) ⟨report⟩ elogioso

glucose /'gluːkəʊs, -kəʊz/ n glucosa f

glue¹ /gluː/ n goma f de pegar, pegamento m

glue² vt **glues, glueing, glued** (a) (stick) pegar* (b) (fix): **he was ~d to the television** estaba pegado a la televisión

glum /glʌm/ adj **-mm-** apesadumbrado

glut /glʌt/ n superabundancia f

glutton /'glʌtn̩/ n glotón, -tona m,f

gluttony /'glʌtn̩i ‖'glʌtəni/ n glotonería f

glycerin /'glɪsərən ‖'glɪsərɪn/, **glycerine** /'glɪsərən ‖'glɪsəriːn/ n glicerina f

GM adj **= genetically modified**

GMO n **(= genetically modified organism)** OGM m

GMT **(= Greenwich Mean Time)** GMT

gnarled /nɑːrld ‖nɑːld/ adj ⟨wood/fingers⟩ nudoso; ⟨tree⟩ retorcido

gnash /næʃ/ vt: **to ~ one's teeth** hacer* rechinar los dientes

gnat /næt/ n jején m; (general usage) mosquito m

gnaw /nɔː/ vt roer*

■ **~** vi **to ~ AT sth** roer* algo

gnome /nəʊm/ n gnomo m

go¹ /gəʊ/ (3rd pers sing pres **goes**; past **went**; past p **gone**) vi

I ❙1❙ (a) (move, travel) ir*; **where do we ~ from here?** ¿y ahora qué hacemos? (b) (start moving, acting): **ready, (get) set, ~!** preparados or en sus marcas, listos ¡ya!; **let's ~!** ¡vamos!; **here ~es!** ¡allá vamos (or voy etc)!

❙2❙ (past p **gone/been**) (a) (travel to) ir*; **she's gone to France** se ha ido a Francia; **I have never been abroad** no he estado nunca en el extranjero; **to ~ by car/bus** ir* en coche/autobús; **to ~ on foot** ir* a pie; **to ~ for a walk** ir* a dar un paseo; **~ and see what she wants** anda or vete a ver qué quiere (b) (attend) ir*; **to ~ on a course** hacer* un curso; **to ~ -ING** ir* A + INF; **to ~ swimming** ir* a nadar

❙3❙ (attempt, make as if to) **to ~ to + INF** ir* A + INF

II ❙1❙ (leave, depart) ⟨visitor⟩ irse*, marcharse (esp Esp); ⟨bus/train⟩ salir*; ▶ LET² 1c

❙2❙ (a) (pass) ⟨time⟩ pasar; **the time ~es quickly** el tiempo pasa volando (b) (disappear) ⟨headache/pain/fear⟩ pasarse or irse* ⟨+ me/te/le etc⟩ (c) ⟨money⟩ (be spent) irse*; (be used up) acabarse

❙3❙ (a) (be disposed of): **that sofa will have to ~**

nos vamos (*or* se van *etc*) a tener que deshacer de ese sofá **(b)** (be sold) venderse; **the painting went for £1,000** el cuadro se vendió en 1.000 libras
④ **(a)** (cease to function, wear out) «*bulb/fuse*» fundirse; «*thermostat/fan/exhaust*» estropearse; **her memory/eyesight is ∼ing** está fallándole la memoria/la vista; **my legs went (from under me)** me fallaron las piernas **(b)** (die) (colloq) morir*

⑤ **to go (a)** (remaining): **only two weeks to ∼ till he comes** solo faltan dos semanas para que llegue; **I still have 50 pages to ∼** todavía me faltan *or* me quedan 50 páginas **(b)** (take away) (AmE): **two burgers to ∼** dos hamburguesas para llevar

III ① **(a)** (lead) «*path/road*» ir*, llevar **(b)** (extend, range) «*road/railway line*» ir*; **it only ∼es as far as Croydon** solo va hasta Croydon ② (have place) ir*; (fit) caber*; *see also* GO IN, GO INTO

IV ① **(a)** (become): **to ∼ blind** quedarse ciego; **to ∼ crazy** volverse* loco; **her face went red** se puso colorada **(b)** (be, remain): **to ∼ barefoot** ir* *or* andar* descalzo; **to ∼ hungry** pasar hambre ② (turn out, proceed, progress) ir*; **how are things ∼ing?** ¿cómo van *or* andan las cosas? ③ **(a)** (be available) (*only in -ing form*): **I'll take any job that's ∼ing** estoy dispuesto a aceptar el trabajo que sea **(b)** (be in general): **it's not expensive as dishwashers ∼** no es caro, para lo que cuestan los lavavajillas

V ① **(a)** (function, work) «*heater/engine/clock*» funcionar **(b) to get going: the car's OK once it gets ∼ing** el coche marcha bien una vez que arranca; **we'd better get ∼ing** más vale que nos vayamos; **we tried to get a fire ∼ing** tratamos de hacer fuego **(c) to keep going** (continue to function) aguantar; (not stop) seguir*; **to keep a project ∼ing** mantener* a flote un proyecto ② (continue, last out) seguir*; **the club's been ∼ing for 12 years now** el club lleva 12 años funcionando ③ **(a)** (sound) «*bell/siren*» sonar* **(b)** (make sound, movement) hacer* ④ **(a)** (contribute): **everything that ∼es to make a good school** todo lo que contribuye a que una escuela sea buena; **it just ∼es to show: we can't leave them on their own** está visto que no los podemos dejar solos **(b)** (be used) **all their savings are ∼ing toward the trip** van a gastar todos sus ahorros en el viaje; **the money will ∼ to pay the workmen** el dinero se usará para pagar a los obreros ⑤ (run, be worded) decir*; **how does the song ∼?** ¿cómo es la (letra/música de la) canción? ⑥ **(a)** (be permitted): **anything ∼es** todo vale **(b)** (be necessarily obeyed, believed): **what the boss says ∼es** lo que dice el jefe, va a misa **(c)** (match, suit) pegar*, ir*

■ ∼ *v aux* (*only in -ing form*) **to be ∼ing to + INF** (expressing intention, prediction) ir* A + INF

■ **go about** [*v + prep + o*] **(a)** (tackle) «*task*» acometer; **how would you ∼ about solving this equation?** ¿cómo harías para resolver esta ecuación? **(b)** (occupy oneself with): **to ∼ about one's business** ocuparse de sus (*or* mis *etc*) cosas

■ **go after** [*v + prep + o*] (pursue, chase) perseguir*, dar* caza a

■ **go against** [*v + prep + o*] **(a)** (oppose, resist)

⟨*instructions/policy/person*⟩ oponerse* a, ir* en contra de **(b)** (be unfavorable to): **the decision went against them** la decisión les fue desfavorable

■ **go ahead** [*v + adv*] (proceed, begin) **to ∼ ahead (WITH sth)** seguir* adelante (CON algo); **may I ask you a question? — ∼ ahead!** ¿le puedo hacer una pregunta? — por supuesto *or* (AmL tb) pregunte nomás

■ **go along** [*v + adv*] **(a)** (accompany, be present) ir* **(b)** (proceed, progress) ir*; **I usually make corrections as I ∼ along** normalmente hago correcciones sobre la marcha **(c)** (acquiesce): **to ∼ along with a proposal** secundar una propuesta

■ **go around**, (BrE also) **go round**
I [*v + prep + o*] ① **(a)** (turn) ⟨*corner*⟩ doblar, dar* la vuelta a, dar* vuelta (CS); ⟨*bend*⟩ tomar **(b)** (make detour) ⟨*obstacle*⟩ rodear
② (visit, move through) ⟨*country/city*⟩ recorrer; ⟨*museum/castle*⟩ visitar; **to ∼ around the world** dar* la vuelta al mundo
II [*v + adv*] ① **(a)** (move, travel, be outdoors) andar*; **to ∼ around -ING** ir* por ahí + GER **(b)** (circulate) «*joke/rumor*» correr **(c)** (be sufficient for everybody): **there aren't enough to ∼ around** no alcanzan
② (revolve) «*wheel/world*» dar* vueltas
③ (visit) ir*; **I'll ∼ around and see him** iré a verlo

■ **go away** [*v + adv*] **(a)** (depart, leave) irse* **(b)** (from home): **I'm ∼ing away this weekend** voy a salir este fin de semana; **to ∼ away on vacation** irse* de vacaciones **(c)** (disappear, fade away) «*smell*» irse*; «*pain*» pasarse *or* irse* (+ *me/te/le etc*)

■ **go back** [*v + adv*] ① (return) volver*; **∼ back!** ¡vuelve atrás!, ¡retrocede!
② **(a)** (date, originate) «*tradition/dynasty*» remontarse; **we ∼ back a long way** (colloq) nos conocemos desde hace mucho **(b)** «*clocks*» atrasarse

■ **go back on** [*v + adv + prep + o*] ⟨*one's promise*⟩ dejar de cumplir; ⟨*one's word*⟩ faltar a

■ **go before** [*v + prep + o*] ⟨*court/committee*⟩ presentarse ante

■ **go by** ① [*v + adv*] **(a)** (move past) pasar; **to let an opportunity ∼ by** dejar pasar una oportunidad **(b)** (elapse) «*days/years*» pasar; **as time goes by** con el tiempo
② [*v + prep + o*] **(a)** (be guided by) ⟨*instinct*⟩ dejarse llevar por; ⟨*rules*⟩ seguir* **(b)** (base judgment on) ⟨*appearances*⟩ guiarse* *or* dejarse llevar por; **if previous experience is anything to ∼ by** a juzgar por lo que ha sucedido en otras ocasiones

■ **go down** [*v + adv*] ① **(a)** (descend) «*person*» bajar; «*sun*» ponerse*; «*curtain*» (Theat) caer* **(b)** (fall) «*boxer/horse*» caerse*; «*plane*» caer*, estrellarse **(c)** (sink) «*ship*» hundirse **(d)** «*computer*» dejar de funcionar, descomponerse (AmL) **(e)** (be defeated) (Sport) perder*; **to ∼ down fighting** caer* luchando
② **(a)** (decrease) «*temperature/exchange rate*» bajar; «*population/unemployment*» disminuir*; **to ∼ down in value** perder* valor **(b)** (decline) «*standard/quality*» empeorar **(c)** (abate) «*wind/storm*» amainar; «*floods/swelling*» bajar; **his temperature's gone down** le ha bajado la fiebre **(d)** (deflate) «*tire*» perder* aire
③ (extend): **this road ∼es down to the beach** ⋯✺

este camino baja a *or* hasta la playa; **the skirt ∼es down to her ankles** la falda le llega a los tobillos

⸤**4**⸣ **(a)** (be swallowed): **it just won't ∼ down** no lo puedo tragar; **it went down the wrong way** se me fue por el otro camino **(b)** «*present/proposal/ remarks*»: **how did the announcement ∼ down?** ¿qué tipo de acogida tuvo el anuncio?; **that won't ∼ down too well with your father** eso no le va a caer muy bien a tu padre

⸤**5**⸣ (be recorded, written): **all these absences will ∼ down on your record** va a quedar constancia de estas faltas en tu ficha; **to ∼ down in history as sth** pasar a la historia como algo

■ **go down with** [*v + adv + prep + o*] (BrE): **to ∼ down with flu/hepatitis** caer* en cama con gripe/ caer* enfermo de hepatitis

■ **go for** [*v + prep + o*] ⸤**1**⸣ **(a)** (head toward, reach for): **he went for his gun** fue a echar mano de la pistola **(b)** (attack): **he went for Bill** se le echó encima a Bill

⸤**2**⸣ (choose) decidirse por

⸤**3**⸣ (aim at): **∼ for it!** ¡haz la tentativa!, ¡a por ello! (Esp)

■ **go in** [*v + adv*] ⸤**1**⸣ **(a)** (enter) entrar **(b)** «*screw/ key*» entrar; **the big case won't ∼** la maleta grande no cabe **(c)** (go to work) ir* a trabajar

⸤**2**⸣ (be obscured) «*sun/moon*» ocultarse

■ **go in for** [*v + adv + prep + o*] **(a)** (enter) ⟨*competition*⟩ participar en; ⟨*exam/test*⟩ presentarse a **(b)** (take up, practice): **he'd thought of ∼ing in for teaching** había pensado dedicarse a la enseñanza

■ **go into** [*v + prep + o*] ⸤**1**⸣ **(a)** (enter) ⟨*room/ building*⟩ entrar en, entrar a (AmL) **(b)** (crash into) ⟨*car/wall*⟩ chocar* contra **(c)** (fit into) entrar en

⸤**2**⸣ **(a)** (start, embark on) ⟨*phase/era*⟩ entrar en **(b)** (enter certain state) ⟨*coma/trance*⟩ entrar en **(c)** (enter profession) ⟨*television/Parliament*⟩ entrar en

⸤**3**⸣ **(a)** (discuss, explain) entrar en; **I don't want to ∼ into that** no quiero entrar en ese tema **(b)** (investigate, analyze) ⟨*problem/motives*⟩ analizar*

⸤**4**⸣ (be devoted to): **after all the money/work that has gone into this!** ¡después de todo el dinero/ trabajo que se ha metido en esto!

■ **go off**

I [*v + adv*] ⸤**1**⸣ (depart) irse*, marcharse (esp Esp); **to ∼ off with sth** llevarse algo

⸤**2**⸣ «*milk/meat/fish*» echarse a perder

⸤**3**⸣ **(a)** «*bomb/firework*» estallar; «*gun*» dispararse **(b)** «*alarm*» sonar*

⸤**4**⸣ (stop operating) «*heating/lights*» apagarse*

II [*v + prep + o*] (lose liking for) (BrE): **to ∼ off one's food** perder* el apetito; **I've gone off the idea** ya no me atrae la idea

■ **go on** [*v + adv*] ⸤**1**⸣ **(a)** (go further) seguir*; **I can't ∼ on** no puedo más **(b)** (go ahead): **you ∼ on, we'll follow** tú vete que nosotros ya iremos; **he went on ahead to look for a hotel** él fue antes para buscar hotel

⸤**2**⸣ (continue) «*fight/struggle*» continuar*; **we can't ∼ on like this** no podemos seguir así; **the**

discussion went on for hours la discusión duró horas; **to ∼ on -ING** seguir* + GER; **he went on to become President** llegó a ser presidente; **to ∼ on with sth** seguir* con algo; **∼ on!** (encouraging, urging) ¡dale!, ¡vamos!, ¡ándale! (Méx), ¡ándele! (Col), ¡venga! (Esp)

⸤**3**⸣ **(a)** (continue speaking) seguir*, continuar* **(b)** (talk irritatingly) (pej): **he went on and on** siguió dale que dale; **to ∼ on about sth** hablar insistentemente DE algo

⸤**4**⸣ (happen): **what's ∼ing on?** ¿qué pasa?; **is there anything ∼ing on between them?** ¿hay algo entre ellos?; **how long has this been ∼ing on?** ¿desde cuándo viene sucediendo esto?

⸤**5**⸣ **(a)** (onto stage) salir* a escena; (onto field of play) salir* al campo **(b)** (fit, be placed): **the lid won't ∼ on** no lo puedo (*or* podemos *etc*) poner la tapa

■ **go out** [*v + adv*] ⸤**1**⸣ **(a)** (leave, exit) salir*; **to ∼ out hunting/shopping** salir* de caza/de compras **(b)** (socially, for entertainment) salir*; **to ∼ out for a meal** salir* a comer fuera **(c)** (as boyfriend, girlfriend) **to ∼ out** (WITH sb) salir* (CON algn)

⸤**2**⸣ **(a)** (be broadcast) «*TV, radio program*» emitirse **(b)** (be issued, distributed): **a warrant has gone out for her arrest** se ha ordenado su detención; **the invitations have already gone out** ya se han mandado las invitaciones

⸤**3**⸣ (be extinguished) «*fire/cigarette/light*» apagarse*

⸤**4**⸣ «*tide*» bajar

⸤**5**⸣ (become outmoded) «*clothes/style*» pasar de moda

■ **go over**

I [*v + prep + o*] ⸤**1**⸣ (check) ⟨*text/figures/work*⟩ revisar; ⟨*car*⟩ revisar; ⟨*house/premises*⟩ inspeccionar

⸤**2**⸣ (revise, review) ⟨*notes/chapter*⟩ repasar

II [*v + adv*] ⸤**1**⸣ (make one's way, travel) ir*; **she went over to Jack and took his hand** se acercó a Jack y le tomó la mano

⸤**2**⸣ (change sides) pasarse

■ **go past** [*v + adv*] [*v + prep + o*] pasar

■ **go round** (BrE) ▶ GO AROUND

■ **go through**

I [*v + prep + o*] ⸤**1**⸣ **(a)** (pass through) ⟨*process/ stage*⟩ pasar por **(b)** (perform): **let's ∼ through the procedure once more** repitamos otra vez todos los pasos del procedimiento **(c)** (endure) ⟨*ordeal/ hard times*⟩ pasar por

⸤**2**⸣ **(a)** (search) ⟨*attic/suitcase*⟩ registrar, revisar (AmL); ⟨*drawers/desk*⟩ hurgar* en; **to ∼ through sb's mail** abrirle* las cartas a algn **(b)** ▶ GO OVER I 2

⸤**3**⸣ (consume, use up) ⟨*money/fortune*⟩ gastarse; **he ∼es through ten shirts a week** ensucia diez camisas por semana

II [*v + adv*] **(a)** (be carried out) «*changes/ legislation*» ser* aprobado; «*business deal*» llevarse a cabo; **when his divorce ∼es through** cuando obtenga el divorcio **(b)** (Sport): **to ∼ through to the next round** pasar a la siguiente etapa

■ **go through with** [*v + adv + prep + o*] ⟨*threat/ plans*⟩ llevar a cabo

■ **go together** [*v + adv*] «*colors/patterns*» combinar; **lamb and mint sauce ∼ well together** el cordero queda muy bien con salsa de menta

■ **go under** [*v* + *adv*] **(a)** (sink) «*ship*» hundirse; «*submarine/diver*» sumergirse* **(b)** (fail, go bankrupt) hundirse

■ **go up** [*v* + *adv*] **1** **(a)** (ascend) «*person*» subir; «*balloon/plane*» subir; «*curtain*» (Theat) levantarse **(b)** (approach) **to ~ up to sb/sth** acercarse* A algn/algo
2 **(a)** (increase) «*temperature/price/cost*» subir, aumentar; **to ~ up in price** subir *or* aumentar de precio **(b)** (improve) «*standard*» mejorar
3 (burst into flames) prenderse fuego; (explode) estallar; **to ~ up in flames** incendiarse

■ **go with** [*v* + *prep* + *o*] **(a)** (be compatible with): **this sauce ~es well with hamburgers** esta salsa queda muy bien con hamburguesas; **choose a tie to ~ with your shirt** elija una corbata que quede bien con su camisa **(b)** (accompany, be associated with): **the house ~es with the job** la casa va con el puesto

■ **go without (a)** [*v* + *prep* + *o*] (do without) pasar sin; **she often went without food** a menudo pasaba sin comer; **they went without food/sleep for days** (not by choice) no comieron nada/no durmieron durante días **(b)** [*v* + *adv*]: **in order to feed her children she herself often went without** para darles de comer a los niños a menudo pasaba privaciones; **there's no coffee left, you'll just have to ~** si no queda café, así que tendrás que pasar sin él

go² *n* (*pl* **goes**) **1** **(a)** (attempt): **at one ~** (AmE), **in one ~** (BrE) «*empty/eat*» de un tirón (fam); «*drink*» de un trago; **she succeeded in lifting it at the third ~** consiguió levantarlo al tercer intento; **I want to have a ~ at learning Arabic** quiero intentar aprender árabe; **have a ~** prueba a ver, inténtalo; **to have a ~ at sb** (colloq): **she had a ~ at me for not having told her** se la agarró conmigo por no habérselo dicho (fam) **(b)** (turn): **whose ~ is it?** ¿a quién le toca?; **it's my ~** me toca a mí
2 (energy, drive) empuje *m*; (**to be**) **on the ~**: **I've been on the ~ all morning** no he parado en toda la mañana

goad /ɡəʊd/ *vt* «*person*» acosar; «*animal*» aguijonear

go-ahead /'ɡəʊəhed/ *n*: **to give sb/sth the ~** darle* luz verde a algn/algo

goal /ɡəʊl/ *n* **1** (Sport) **(a)** (structure) portería *f*, arco *m* (AmL) **(b)** (point) gol *m* **2** (aim) meta *f*

goal: ~keeper *n* portero, -ra *m,f*, guardameta *mf*, arquero, -ra *m,f* (AmL); **~post** *n* poste *m* de la portería *or* (AmL tb) del arco; **~tender** *n* (AmE) ▶ **KEEPER**

goat /ɡəʊt/ *n* (Zool) cabra *f*

gobble /'ɡɑːbəl ‖'ɡɒbəl/ *vt* engullirse*

■ **gobble up** [*v* + *o* + *adv*, *v* + *adv* + *o*] tragarse*

gobbledygook /'ɡɑːbəldi'ɡuːk ‖'ɡɒbəldi,ɡuːk/ *n* (colloq & pej) jerigonza *f*

go-between /'ɡəʊbɪtwiːn/ *n* (intermediary) intermediario, -ria *m,f*; (messenger) mensajero, -ra *m,f*

goblet /'ɡɑːblət ‖'ɡɒblɪt/ *n* copa *f*

goblin /'ɡɑːblən ‖'ɡɒblɪn/ *n* duende *m* travieso, trasgo *m*

god /ɡɑːd ‖ɡɒd/ *n* **1** **God** Dios *m*; **G~ bless (you)** que Dios te bendiga; **G~!** ¡Dios (santo)! **2** (deity, idol) dios *m*

god: ~child *n* ahijado, -da *m,f*; **~dam, ~damn** *adj* (AmE sl) (*before n*) condenado (fam); **~daughter** /'ɡɑːd'dɔːtər ‖'ɡɒd,dɔːtə(r)/ *n* ahijada *f*

goddess /'ɡɑːdəs ‖'ɡɒdɪs/ *n* diosa *f*

god: ~father /'ɡɑːd'fɑːðər ‖'ɡɒd,fɑːðə(r)/ *n* padrino *m*; **~mother** /'ɡɑːd'mʌðər ‖'ɡɒd,mʌðə(r)/ *n* madrina *f*; **~parent** /'ɡɑːd'perənt ‖'ɡɒd,peərənt/ *n* (man) padrino *m*; (woman) madrina *f*; **my ~parents** mis padrinos; **~send** *n* bendición *f* (del cielo); **~son** *n* ahijado *m*

goggle /'ɡɑːɡəl ‖'ɡɒɡəl/ *vi* (pej) **to ~ AT sth/sb** mirar algo/a algn con los ojos desorbitados

goggles /'ɡɑːɡəlz ‖'ɡɒɡəlz/ *pl n* (Sport) gafas *fpl* *or* anteojos *mpl* (esp AmL) de esquí (*or* natación *etc*); (for welders) gafas *fpl* protectoras, anteojos *mpl* protectores (esp AmL)

going¹ /'ɡəʊɪŋ/ *n* (*no pl*) **1** (progress): **once at the top, the ~ was easier** una vez en la cima, la marcha fue más fácil; **I found that lecture hard ~** me resultó difícil seguir la conferencia; **the novel was heavy ~** la novela era pesada **2** (departure) partida *f* **3** (situation) situación *f*; **if I were you, I'd buy it while the ~ is good** yo que tú lo compraría ahora, aprovechando el buen momento; **when the ~ got tough** cuando las cosas se pusieron difíciles

going² *adj* (*before n*) **(a)** (in operation) en marcha; **a ~ concern** (Busn) un negocio *or* una empresa en marcha **(b)** (present, current): **that's the ~ rate** es lo que se suele cobrar/pagar

gold /ɡəʊld/ *n* **1** (metal) oro *m*; (money) (monedas *fpl* de) oro *m*; (*before n*) «*ring/medal*» de oro **2** (color) dorado *m*, color *m* (de) oro

gold dust *n* oro *m* en polvo

golden /'ɡəʊldən/ *adj* **1** **(a)** (made of gold) de oro **(b)** (in color) dorado **2** **(a)** (happy, prosperous) «*years*» dorado **(b)** (excellent): **a ~ opportunity** una excelente oportunidad

golden: ~ age *n* época *f* dorada, edad *f* de oro; **~ wedding (anniversary)** *n* bodas *fpl* de oro

gold: ~fish *n* (*pl* **-fish** *or* **-fishes**) pececito *m* (rojo); (plural) peces *mpl* de colores; **~ leaf** *n* oro *m* batido, pan *m* de oro; **~ mine** *n* mina *f* de oro; **~-plated** /'ɡəʊld'pleɪtəd ‖,ɡəʊld'pleɪtɪd/ *adj* chapado en oro; **~ rush** *n* fiebre *f* del oro; **~smith** *n* orfebre *mf*

golf /ɡɑːlf ‖ɡɒlf/ *n* golf *m*

golf: ~ ball *n* (Sport) pelota *f* de golf; **~ club** **(a)** (stick) palo *m* de golf **(b)** (place) club *m* de golf; **~ course** *n* campo *m* *or* (AmL tb) cancha *f* de golf

golfer /'ɡɑːlfər ‖'ɡɒlfə(r)/ *n* golfista *mf*

gone¹ /ɡɔːn ‖ɡɒn/ *past p of* GO¹

gone² *adj* (*pred*) **(a)** (not here): **my briefcase is ~!** ¡se me ha desaparecido la cartera!; **how long has she been ~?** ¿cuánto hace que se fue? **(b)** (past): **those days are (long) ~** de eso hace ya mucho, ha llovido mucho desde entonces **(c)** (used up): **the money is all ~** se ha acabado el dinero, no queda nada de dinero

gone³ *prep* (BrE): **it's just ~ five** acaban de dar las cinco

gong /ɡɑːŋ ‖ɡɒŋ/ *n* gong *m*

gonna /'ɡənə ‖'ɡɒnə/ (colloq) (= **going to**) ▶ GO¹ *v aux*

gonorrhea, (BrE) **gonorrhoea** /ˌgɑːnəˈriːə ‖ˌgɒnəˈriə/ n gonorrea f

goo /guː/ n (colloq) mugre f

good[1] /gʊd/ adj

■ Note The usual translation of good, bueno, becomes buen when it precedes a masculine singular noun.

(comp **better**; superl **best**) [1] ⟨food/quality/book/work/reputation⟩ bueno; **it smells ~** huele bien; **her French is very ~** habla muy bien (el) francés; **is this a ~ time to phone?** ¿es buena hora para llamar?; **it's ~ to be back home** ¡qué alegría estar otra vez en casa!; **I had a ~ night's sleep** dormí bien [2] (advantageous, useful) ⟨deal/offer/advice⟩ bueno; **burn it; that's all it's ~ for** quémalo, no sirve para otra cosa; **~ idea!, ~ thinking!** ¡buena idea! [3] (healthy) ⟨diet/habit/exercise⟩ bueno; **I'm not feeling too ~** (colloq) no me siento bien; **spinach is ~ for you** las espinacas son buenas para la salud [4] (attractive): **it looks ~** tiene buen aspecto; **that dress looks really ~ on her** ese vestido le queda or le sienta muy bien [5] **(a)** (in interj phrases): **~! now to the next question** bien, pasemos ahora a la siguiente pregunta; **~ for you!** ¡bien hecho! **(b)** (for emphasis) (colloq): **I'll do it when I'm ~ and ready to** lo haré cuando me parezca; **the water's ~ and hot** el agua está bien caliente **(c)** as good as: **it's as ~ as new** está como nuevo; **he as ~ as admitted it** prácticamente lo admitió [6] (skilled, competent) bueno; **he's no ~ in emergencies** en situaciones de emergencia no sabe qué hacer; **to be ~ at languages** tener* facilidad para los idiomas; **he is ~ with children** tiene buena mano con los niños; **she is ~ with her hands** es muy habilidosa [7] (well-behaved, virtuous) bueno; **~ boy!** ¡muy bien! [8] (kind) bueno; **she was very ~ to me** fue muy amable conmigo [9] (valid) ⟨argument/excuse⟩ bueno; **this ticket is ~ for another week** este billete vale para una semana más; **it's simply not ~ enough!** ¡esto no puede ser! [10] (substantial, considerable) ⟨meal/salary/distance⟩ bueno; **there were a ~ many people there** había bastante gente allí [11] (not less than): **it'll take a ~ hour** va a llevar su buena hora or una hora larga; **a ~ half of all the people interviewed** más de la mitad de los entrevistados

good[2] n [1] (moral right) bien m; **to do ~** hacer* el bien; **there is some ~ in everyone** todos tenemos algo bueno; **to be up to no ~** (colloq) estar* tramando algo, traerse* algo entre manos [2] **(a)** (benefit) bien m; **no ~ will come of it** nada bueno saldrá de ello; **to do sb ~** hacerle* bien a algn **(b)** (use): **this knife is no ~ (at all)** este cuchillo no sirve (para nada); **this book is no ~** este libro no vale nada **(c)** for good para siempre [3] **goods** pl **(a)** (merchandise) artículos mpl, mercancías fpl, mercaderías fpl (AmS); **manufactured ~s** productos mpl manufacturados, manufacturas fpl **(b)** (property) (frml) bienes mpl

goodbye[1] /ˌgʊdˈbaɪ/ interj ¡adiós!, ¡chao! or ¡chau! (esp AmL)

goodbye[2] n: **to say ~ to sb** decirle* adiós a algn

good: G~ **Friday** n Viernes m Santo; **~-humored,** (BrE) **~-humoured** /ˈgʊdˈhjuːmərd ‖ˌgʊdˈhjuːməd/ adj ⟨person⟩ (permanent characteristic) alegre, jovial; (in good mood) de buen humor; ⟨joke⟩ sin mala intención; **~-looking** /ˈgʊdˈlʊkɪŋ/ adj ⟨man⟩ buen mozo (esp AmL), guapo (esp Esp); **a ~-looking woman** una mujer bonita or (esp Esp) guapa; **~-natured** /ˈgʊdˈneɪtʃərd ‖ˌgʊdˈneɪtʃəd/ adj (as permanent characteristic) bueno, de natural bondadoso

goodness /ˈgʊdnəs ‖ˈgʊdnɪs/ n [1] **(a)** (moral worth) bondad f **(b)** (of food) valor m nutritivo [2] (in interj phrases, as intensifier): **(my) ~!** ¡Dios (mío)!; **~ me!** ¡Dios mío!, ¡válgame Dios!

goodwill /ˈgʊdˈwɪl/ n **(a)** (benevolence) buena voluntad f **(b)** (Busn, Fin) fondo m de comercio, llave f (CS)

goofy /ˈguːfi/ adj **-fier, -fiest** (AmE sl) ⟨person⟩ memo (fam); ⟨smile⟩ bobalicón (fam)

goose /guːs/ n (pl **geese**) **(a)** (Zool) oca f, ganso m **(b)** (Culin) ganso m

goose: **~berry** /ˈguːsˌberi ‖ˈgʊzbəri/ n [1] (Bot) grosella f espinosa, uva f espina; [2] (unwanted third person) (BrE colloq) carabina f (fam), chaperón, -rona m,f, violinista mf (Chi fam); **to play ~berry** hacer* de carabina (Esp fam), tocar* el violín (Chi fam); **~ bumps** pl n (AmE colloq), **~flesh** n, **~ pimples** pl n carne f de gallina

gore[1] /gɔːr ‖gɔː(r)/ vt cornear

gorge[1] /gɔːrdʒ ‖gɔːdʒ/ n (Geog) desfiladero m, cañón m

gorge[2] v refl **to ~ oneself** atiborrarse de comida

gorgeous /ˈgɔːrdʒəs ‖ˈgɔːdʒəs/ adj **(a)** (lovely) (colloq) ⟨girl⟩ precioso, guapísimo; ⟨dress⟩ precioso, divino; ⟨day⟩ maravilloso, espléndido **(b)** (splendid) ⟨color⟩ magnífico

gorilla /gəˈrɪlə/ n gorila m

gorse /gɔːrs ‖gɔːs/ n aulaga f, tojo m

gory /ˈgɔːri/ adj **gorier, goriest** (colloq) sangriento

gosh /gɑːʃ ‖gɒʃ/ interj (colloq) ¡(mi) Dios!, ¡Dios mío!

gospel /ˈgɑːspəl ‖ˈgɒspəl/ n **(a)** **Gospel** (in New Testament) evangelio m **(b)** (Christian teaching) (no pl) Evangelio m; (before n) **it's ~ (truth)** es la pura verdad **(c)** **~ (music)** (Mus) gospel m

gossamer /ˈgɑːsəmər ‖ˈgɒsəmə(r)/ n (liter) telaraña f; (before n) ⟨threads⟩ tenue

gossip[1] /ˈgɑːsəp ‖ˈgɒsɪp/ n **(a)** (speculation, scandal) chismorreo m (fam), cotilleo m (Esp fam); **an interesting piece of ~** un chisme interesante; (before n) **~ column** crónica f de sociedad **(b)** (chat): **to have a ~ with sb** chismorrear (fam) or (Esp tb) cotillear con algn **(c)** (person) chismoso, -sa m,f (fam), cotilla mf (Esp fam)

gossip[2] vi **(a)** (chatter) chismorrear (fam), cotillear (Esp fam) **(b)** (spread tales) contar* chismes

got /gɑːt ‖gɒt/ [1] past & past p of GET [2] (crit) pres of HAVE

Gothic /ˈgɑːθɪk ‖ˈgɒθɪk/ adj (Archit, Lit) gótico

gotta /ˈgɑːtə ‖ˈgɒtə/ (sl) = **have got to**

gotten /ˈgɑːtn̩ ‖ˈgɒtn̩/ (AmE) past p of GET

gouge /gaʊdʒ/ vt ‹hole› abrir*
■ **gouge out** [v + o + adv, v + adv + o] sacar*
gourd /gʊrd, gɔːrd ‖ gʊəd/ n (Bot) calabaza f, jícaro m (AmC, Col, Méx)
gourmet /'gʊrmeɪ ‖ 'gʊəmeɪ/ n gourmet mf, gastrónomo, -ma m,f
gout /gaʊt/ n gota f
govern /'gʌvərn ‖ 'gʌvən/ vt (a) ‹rule› gobernar* (b) ‹determine› determinar (c) **governing** pres p ‹party› de gobierno; ‹principle› rector; ∼ing body organismo m rector
■ ∼ vi gobernar*
governess /'gʌvərnəs ‖ 'gʌvənɪs/ n institutriz f
government /'gʌvərnmənt ‖ 'gʌvənmənt/ n gobierno m; (before n) ∼ **policy** política f gubernamental
governor /'gʌvənər ‖ 'gʌvənə(r)/ n [1] (of state, province, colony) gobernador, -dora m,f [2] (of institution): **prison** ∼ (BrE) director, -tora m,f de una cárcel; **school** ∼ (BrE) miembro de un consejo escolar
gown /gaʊn/ n [1] (a) (dress) vestido m; **evening** ∼ traje m de fiesta (b) (night∼) (AmE) camisón m [2] (a) (Educ, Law) toga f (b) (Med) bata f
GP n (= **general practitioner**) médico, -ca m,f de medicina general; **my** ∼ mi médico de cabecera
gr (= **gram(s)**) gr., g.
grab /græb/ -bb- vt (a) (seize) ‹rope/hand› agarrar; ‹chance› aprovechar (b) (appropriate) ‹land› apropiarse de; ‹money› llevarse (c) (appeal to) (colloq) ‹idea› atraer*; **how does that** ∼ **you?** ¿qué te parece?
■ ∼ vi: **to** ∼ **AT sth: she** ∼**bed at the rope** trató de agarrar la cuerda
grace /greɪs/ n [1] (elegance — of movement) gracia f, garbo m; (— of expression, form) elegancia f
[2] (a) (courtesy) cortesía f, gentileza f (b) (good nature): **to do sth with good/bad** ∼ hacer* algo de buen talante/a regañadientes (c) (good quality): **her saving** ∼ **is her sense of humor** lo que la salva es que tiene sentido del humor; **social** ∼**s** modales mpl
[3] (Relig) (a) (mercy) gracia f; **by the** ∼ **of God** ... gracias a Dios ... (b) (prayer): **to say** ∼ (before a meal) bendecir* la mesa
[4] (respite) gracia f; **16 days'** ∼ (BrE Law) 16 días de gracia
graceful /'greɪsfəl/ adj ‹dancer/movement› lleno de gracia, grácil (liter); ‹style› elegante
gracefully /'greɪsfəli/ adv con gracia or garbo
gracious¹ /'greɪʃəs/ adj (a) ‹smile/act› gentil, cortés (b) (merciful) misericordioso
gracious² interj: (good o goodness) ∼! (expressing surprise) ¡Dios Santo!; (expressing exasperation) ¡por favor!
graciously /'greɪʃəsli/ adv ‹smile/apologize› gentilmente
grade¹ /greɪd/ n [1] (a) (quality) calidad f; ∼ **A tomatoes** tomates mpl de la mejor calidad (b) (degree, level): **it divides hotels into four** ∼**s** divide a los hoteles en cuatro categorías (c) (in seniority) grado m (del escalafón); (Mil) rango m [2] (Educ) (a) (class) (AmE) grado m, año m, curso m (b) (in exam) nota f

grade² vt [1] (a) (classify) clasificar* (b) (order in ascending scale) ‹exercise/questions› ordenar por grado de dificultad (c) (mark) (AmE) ‹test/exercise› corregir* y calificar* (d) **graded** past p ‹produce› clasificado [2] (make more level) ‹surface/soil› (AmE) nivelar
grade: ∼ **crossing** n (AmE) paso m a nivel, crucero m (Méx); ∼ **school** n (AmE) escuela f primaria
gradient /'greɪdiənt/ n (slope) pendiente f, gradiente f (AmL)
gradual /'grædʒuəl/ adj ‹improvement› gradual; ‹slope› no muy empinado
gradually /'grædʒuəli/ adv ‹improve› gradualmente, poco a poco; ‹rise/slope› suavemente
graduate¹ /'grædʒueɪt/ vi [1] (Educ) (a) (from a college, university) terminar la carrera, recibirse (AmL), graduarse*; (obtain bachelor's degree) licenciarse (b) (from high school) (AmE) terminar el bachillerato, recibirse de bachiller (AmL) [2] (progress) **to** ∼ (**FROM sth) TO sth** pasar (DE algo) A algo
graduate² /'grædʒuət/ n (a) (from higher education) persona con título universitario; (with a bachelor's degree) licenciado, -da m,f; (before n) ‹course/student› de posgrado or postgrado; **he went to** ∼ **school** (AmE) hizo un curso de posgrado (b) (from high school) (AmE) bachiller mf
graduated /'grædʒueɪtəd ‖ 'grædʒueɪtɪd/ adj (a) (progressive) ‹scale› graduado; ‹payments› escalonado (b) (calibrated) ‹flask/test tube› graduado
graduation /grædʒu'eɪʃən/ n (Educ) graduación f
graffiti /grə'fiːti/ n (+ sing o pl vb) graffiti mpl
graft¹ /græft ‖ grɑːft/ vt (Hort) injertar
graft² n [1] (Hort, Med) injerto m [2] (bribery, corruption) (AmE colloq) chanchullos mpl (fam)
grain /greɪn/ n [1] (of cereal, salt, sugar, sand) grano m [2] (Agr) grano m, cereal m [3] (of wood — pattern) veta f, veteado m; (— texture) grano m; **to go against the** ∼: **it goes against the** ∼ **for me to support them** apoyarlos va en contra de mis principios
gram, (BrE also) **gramme** /græm/ n gramo m
grammar /'græmər ‖ 'græmə(r)/ n gramática f
grammar school n (a) (in US) ▶ ELEMENTARY SCHOOL (b) (in UK) colegio de enseñanza secundaria para ingresar al cual hay que aprobar un examen de aptitud
grammatical /grə'mætɪkəl/ adj (a) (of grammar) gramatical (b) (correct) gramaticalmente correcto
gramme /græm/ n (BrE) ▶ GRAM
granary /'greɪnəri, 'grænəri ‖ 'grænəri/ n (pl -ries) granero m
grand /grænd/ adj -er, -est [1] (a) (impressive) magnífico (b) (ostentatious) ‹gesture› grandilocuente; ‹entrance› triunfal (c) (ambitious, lofty) ‹vision› grandioso; ‹ideal› elevado (d) (overall) (before n, no comp) global; **the** ∼ **total** el total [2] (formal, ceremonial) ‹opening/occasion› solemne [3] (very good) (colloq) ‹day/weather› espléndido
grandad /'grændæd/ n abuelo m

grand: G~ **Canyon** *n* the G~ Canyon el Cañón del Colorado; ~**child** /'ɡræntʃaɪld/ *n* nieto, -ta *m,f*; ~**dad** /'ɡrændæd/ *n* abuelo *m*; ~**daughter** /'ɡræn,dɔːtər ‖'ɡræn,dɔːtə(r)/ *n* nieta *f*

grandeur /'ɡrændʒər ‖'ɡrændʒə(r)/ *n* grandiosidad *f*

grandfather /'ɡræn,fɑːðər ‖'ɡræn,fɑːðə(r)/ *n* abuelo *m*; (*before n*) ~ **clock** reloj *m* de pie

grandiose /'ɡrændiəʊs/ *adj* ‹*claim/scheme/notion*› fatuo; ‹*speech*› altisonante

grand: ~ **jury** *n* (in US) jurado *m* de acusación (*jurado que decide si hay suficientes pruebas para procesar*); ~**ma** /'ɡrænmɑː/ *n* (colloq) abuela *f*; ~**mother** /'ɡræn,mʌðər ‖'ɡræn,mʌðə(r)/ *n* abuela *f*; ~**pa** /'ɡrænpɑː/ *n* (colloq) abuelo *m*; ~**parent** /'ɡræn,perənt ‖'ɡræn,peərənt/ *n* abuelo, -la *m,f*; **my** ~**parents** mis abuelos; ~ **piano** *n* piano *m* de cola; ~**son** /'ɡrænsʌn/ *n* nieto *m*; ~**stand** *n* tribuna *f*; (*before n*) ‹*ticket/seat*› de tribuna

granite /'ɡrænət ‖'ɡrænɪt/ *n* granito *m*

granny, grannie /'ɡræni/ *n* (*pl* -**nies**) abuelita *f* (fam)

grant¹ /ɡrænt ‖ɡrɑːnt/ *vt* **1** (a) ‹*desire/request*› conceder (b) ‹*interview/asylum*› conceder (c) ‹*land/pension*› otorgar* **2** (admit) reconocer* **3** **granted** *past p* (admittedly): ~**ed**, **it's very expensive, but ...** de acuerdo, es muy caro, pero ...; **to take sth for** ~**ed** dar* algo por sentado

grant² *n* (subsidy — to body, individual) subvención *f*, subsidio *m* (AmL); (— to student) (esp BrE) beca *f*

granulated /'ɡrænjəlertəd ‖'ɡrænjʊlertɪd/ *adj*: ~ **sugar** azúcar *f* granulada, azúcar *m* granulado

granule /'ɡrænjuːl/ *n* gránulo *m*

grape /ɡreɪp/ *n* (fruit) uva *f*; **it's sour** ~**s** (set phrase) las uvas están verdes (fr hecha)

grape: ~**fruit** *n* (*pl* -**fruit** *or* -**fruits**) toronja *f* (AmL exc CS), pomelo *m* (CS, Esp); ~**vine** *n* (a) (Agr, Bot) parra *f* (b) (source of information) (colloq): **I heard it on** *o* **through the** ~**vine** me lo dijo un pajarito (fam), lo he escuchado en radio macuto (Esp fam)

graph /ɡræf ‖ɡrɑːf/ *n* gráfico *m*, gráfica *f*

graphic /'ɡræfɪk/ *adj* **1** (vivid) ‹*account/description*› muy gráfico; **in** ~ **detail** con todo lujo de detalles **2** (Art) gráfico; ~ **design** diseño *m* gráfico

graphics /'ɡræfɪks/ *pl n* **1** (graphic design) diseño *m* gráfico **2** (Comput) gráficos *mpl*

graph paper *n* papel *m* milimetrado *or* (Méx) cuadriculado

grapple /'ɡræpl/ *vi* **to** ~ (WITH sb/sth) forcejear (CON algn/algo); **to** ~ **with one's conscience** tener* escrúpulos de conciencia

grasp¹ /ɡræsp ‖ɡrɑːsp/ *vt* **1** (a) (seize) ‹*object/person*› agarrar; ‹*opportunity/offer*› aprovechar (b) (hold tightly) tener* agarrado **2** (understand) ‹*concept*› captar

■ ~ *vi* **to** ~ **AT sth** tratar de agarrar algo; ‹*opportunity*› aprovechar

grasp² *n* (*no pl*) **1** (a) (grip): **he tightened his** ~ **on my arm** me apretó más el brazo (b) (reach) alcance *m* **2** (understanding) comprensión *f*; (knowledge) conocimientos *mpl*

grasping /'ɡræspɪŋ ‖'ɡrɑːspɪŋ/ *adj* avaricioso

grass /ɡræs ‖ɡrɑːs/ *n* **1** (a) (as pasture) pasto *m*, zacate *m* (Méx); (lawn) césped *m*, hierba *f*, pasto *m* (AmL), grama (AmC, Ven); **the** ~ **is always greener on the other side** nadie está contento con su suerte (b) (Bot) hierba *f* **2** (marijuana) (sl) maría *f* (arg), hierba *f* (arg), monte *m* (AmC, Col, Ven arg), mota *f* (Méx arg)

grass: ~**hopper** /'ɡræs,hɑːpər ‖'ɡrɑːs,hɒpə(r)/ *n* saltamontes *m*; ~ **roots** *pl n* (ordinary members) (*before n*) ‹*support/opinion*› de las bases

grassy /'ɡræsi ‖'ɡrɑːsi/ *adj* -**sier**, -**siest** cubierto de hierba

grate¹ /ɡreɪt/ *vt* (Culin) rallar; ~**d cheese** queso *m* rallado

■ ~ *vi* (a) (irritate) ser* crispante (b) (make harsh noise) chirriar*

grate² *n* (metal frame in fireplace) rejilla *f*; (fireplace) chimenea *f*

grateful /'ɡreɪtfəl/ *adj* agradecido; **I'm very** ~ **to you for your advice** le agradezco mucho sus consejos

grater /'ɡreɪtər ‖'ɡreɪtə(r)/ *n* rallador *m*

gratify /'ɡrætəfaɪ ‖'ɡrætɪfaɪ/ *vt* -**fies**, -**fying**, -**fied** (a) (fulfill) satisfacer* (b) (give satisfaction) complacer*

grating¹ /'ɡreɪtɪŋ/ *adj* (a) (harsh) ‹*noise/sound*› chirriante (b) (irritating) crispante

grating² *n* rejilla *f*

gratitude /'ɡrætətuːd ‖'ɡrætɪtjuːd/ *n* gratitud *f*

gratuitous /ɡrəˈtuːətəs ‖ɡrəˈtjuːtəs/ *adj* (pej) gratuito

grave¹ /ɡreɪv/ *adj* **graver, gravest** **1** ‹*error/danger/voice*› grave **2** /ɡrɑːv/ (Ling) ‹*accent*› grave

grave² *n* tumba *f*, sepultura *f*

gravedigger /'ɡreɪv,dɪɡər ‖'ɡreɪv,dɪɡə(r)/ *n* sepulturero, -ra *m,f*

gravel /'ɡrævəl/ *n* grava *f*; (finer) gravilla *f*

gravely /'ɡreɪvli/ *adv* (a) (seriously) gravemente (b) (solemnly) con gravedad

grave: ~**stone** *n* lápida *f*; ~**yard** *n* cementerio *m*, panteón *m* (Méx)

gravitate /'ɡrævəteɪt ‖'ɡrævɪteɪt/ *vi*: **people of similar interests naturally** ~ **toward each other** uno tiende a acercarse a gente con intereses afines; **young people tend to** ~ **toward the big cities** las grandes ciudades son un polo de atracción para los jóvenes

gravity /'ɡrævəti/ *n* **1** (Phys) gravedad *f* **2** (seriousness) gravedad *f*

gravy /'ɡreɪvi/ *n* (Culin) *salsa hecha con el jugo de la carne asada*

gray¹, (BrE) **grey** /ɡreɪ/ *adj* -**er**, -**est** gris; ‹*outlook/future*› poco prometedor; **a** ~ **hair** una cana; **she has** ~ **hair** es canosa

---

AmC	Central America	Arg	Argentina	Cu	Cuba
AmL	Latin America	Bol	Bolivia	Ec	Ecuador
AmS	South America	Chi	Chile	Esp	Spain
Andes	Andean Region	CS	Southern Cone	Méx	Mexico

Per	Peru
RPl	River Plate Area
Ur	Uruguay
Ven	Venezuela

gray², (BrE) **grey** n gris m

graze¹ /greɪz/ vt (a) (cut, injure) rasguñarse (b) (touch, brush) rozar*

■ ~ vi (Agr) pastar

graze² n rasguño m

grease¹ /griːs/ n grasa f

grease² vt (a) (lubricate) ⟨machinery/hinge⟩ engrasar (b) (Culin): to ~ (with butter) enmantequillar, enmantecar* (RPl); to ~ (with oil) aceitar

grease: ~paint n maquillaje m teatral; **~proof paper** n (BrE) papel m encerado or (Esp) parafinado, papel m manteca (RPl), papel m mantequilla (Chi)

greasy /ˈgriːsi/ adj **-sier, -siest** (a) (soiled) ⟨hands⟩ grasiento; ⟨overalls⟩ cubierto de grasa (b) (containing grease) ⟨food⟩ graso; (pej) grasiento (c) ⟨hair/skin⟩ graso, grasoso (esp AmL)

great¹ /greɪt/ adj [1] (before n) (large in size, number, quantity) (sing) gran (delante del n); (pl) grandes (delante del n); **a ~ many people** muchísima gente [2] (before n) (a) (important) ⟨landowner/occasion⟩ (sing) gran (delante del n); (pl) grandes (delante del n); **Catherine the G~** Catalina la Grande (b) (genuine, real) ⟨friend/rival⟩ (sing) gran (delante del n); (pl) grandes (delante del n) [3] (excellent) (colloq) ⟨goal/movie/meal⟩ sensacional; **he's a really ~ guy** es un tipo or (Esp tb) tío sensacional (fam); (as interj) (that's) ~! ¡fenomenal!, ¡estupendo! (fam)

great² adv (esp AmE colloq) fenomenal (fam)

great: ~aunt /ˈgreɪtˈænt ǁˌgreɪtˈɑːnt/ n tía f abuela; **G~ Britain** n Gran Bretaña f; **G~ Dane** n gran danés m; **~granddaughter** /ˈgreɪtˈgrænˌdɔːtər ǁˌgreɪtˈgrænˌdɔːtə(r)/ n bisnieta f, biznieta f; **~grandfather** /ˈgreɪtˈgrænˌfɑːðər ǁˌgreɪtˈgrænˌfɑːðə(r)/ n bisabuelo m; **~grandmother** /ˈgreɪtˈgrænˌmʌðər ǁˌgreɪtˈgrænˌmʌðə(r)/ n bisabuela f, **~grandson** /ˈgreɪtˈgrænsʌn/ n bisnieto m, biznieto m

greatly /ˈgreɪtli/ adv (as intensifier) ⟨admire/improve⟩ enormemente

great-uncle /ˈgreɪtˈʌŋkəl/ n tío m abuelo

Greece /griːs/ n Grecia f

greed /griːd/ n (a) (for food) gula f, angurria f (CS) (b) (for power, money) codicia f

greedy /ˈgriːdi/ adj **-dier, -diest** (a) (for food, drink) glotón, angurriento (CS) (b) (for power, wealth) **to be ~ FOR sth** tener* ansias DE algo

Greek¹ /griːk/ adj griego

Greek² n (a) (language) griego m (b) (person) griego, -ga m,f

green¹ /griːn/ adj **-er, -est** [1] (in color) verde; **he was ~ with envy** se moría de envidia; **to have a ~ thumb** o (BrE) ~ **fingers** tener* mano para las plantas [2] (a) (unripe) verde (b) (colloq) ⟨pred⟩ (inexperienced) verde (fam) [3] (Pol) verde, ecologista

green² n [1] (color) verde m [2] (in village, town) ≈ plaza f (con césped) [3] **greens** pl (vegetables) verdura f (de hoja verde)

green: ~back n (AmE colloq) dólar m, verde m (esp AmL fam); ~ **bean** n habichuela f or (Esp) judía f verde or (Méx) ejote m or (RPl) chaucha f or (Chi) poroto m verde or (Ven) vainita f; ~ **belt** n (esp BrE) zona f verde; ~ **card** n (in US)

permiso m de residencia y trabajo; **~field site** n: terreno en zona rural; **~fly** n (pl **-flies** or **-fly**) (BrE) pulgón m; **~grocer** n (BrE) verdulero, -ra m,f; **the ~grocer('s)** la verdulería; **~house** n invernadero m; (before n) **the ~house effect** (Ecol) el efecto invernadero; **G~land** /ˈgriːnlənd/ n Groenlandia f; ~ **onion** n (AmE) cebolleta f, cebollino m; ~ **pepper** n ▶ PEPPER¹ 2

Greenwich Mean Time /ˈgrenɪdʒ, ˈgrenɪtʃ/ n hora f de Greenwich

greet /griːt/ vt [1] (a) (welcome, receive) ⟨guest/client⟩ recibir (b) (say hello to) saludar [2] (reactto) acoger* [3] (meet): **a strange sight ~ed our eyes** un extraño espectáculo se ofreció a nuestra vista

greeting /ˈgriːtɪŋ/ n (a) (spoken) saludo m; (as interj) ~! (arch or hum) ¡buenas! (fam) (b) (message) (usu pl): **❂ birthday/Christmas greetings** feliz cumpleaños/Navidad; (before n) **a ~ o** (BrE also) **~s card** una tarjeta de felicitación

gregarious /grɪˈgeriəs ǁgrɪˈgeəriəs/ adj ⟨person⟩ sociable; (Zool) gregario

Grenada /grəˈneɪdə/ n Granada f

grenade /grəˈneɪd/ n granada f

grew /gruː/ past of GROW

grey adj/n (BrE) ▶ GRAY¹,²

greyhound /ˈgreɪhaʊnd/ n galgo m

grid /grɪd/ n [1] (grating over opening) rejilla f [2] (on map) (Geog) cuadriculado m; (before n) ~ **reference** coordenadas fpl cartográficas

griddle /ˈgrɪdl/ n plancha f

grid: ~iron /ˈgrɪdˌaɪərn ǁˈgrɪdaɪən/ n [1] (Culin) parrilla f; [2] (in US football) campo m, cancha f (AmL), emparrillado m (Méx); **~lock** n (esp AmE) paralización f total del tráfico; **~locked** /ˈgrɪdlɑːkt ǁˈgrɪdlɒkt/ adj colapsado, paralizado

grief /griːf/ n dolor m, profunda pena f; **to come to ~** «plans» fracasar, irse* al traste (fam); **he'll come to ~ one day** va a acabar mal

grievance /ˈgriːvəns/ n (a) (ground for complaint) motivo m de queja; **to air one's ~s** quejarse (b) (Lab Rel) queja f formal; (before n) ~ **procedure** procedimiento m conciliatorio

grieve /griːv/ vi sufrir; **to ~ FOR sb** llorar a algn

■ ~ vt apenar

grievous /ˈgriːvəs/ adj (liter) ⟨loss⟩ doloroso; ⟨wound/injury⟩ de extrema gravedad; ~ **bodily harm** (Law) lesiones fpl (corporales) graves

grill¹ /grɪl/ vt [1] (BrE Culin) (in electric, gas grill) hacer* al grill; (over hot fire) hacer* a la parrilla [2] (interrogate) (colloq) interrogar*

grill² n (a) (on stove) (esp BrE) grill m, gratinador m (b) (on barbecue) parrilla f

grille /grɪl/ n (a) (partition) reja f (b) (protective covering) (Tech) rejilla f; (Auto) calandra f

grim /grɪm/ adj **-mm-** ⟨person/expression⟩ adusto; (gloomy) ⟨outlook/situation⟩ nefasto; **she carried on with ~ determination** siguió adelante, resuelta a no dejarse vencer

grimace¹ /ˈgrɪməs, grɪˈmeɪs/ n mueca f

grimace² vi hacer* una mueca

grime /graɪm/ n mugre f

grimy /ˈgraɪmi/ adj **-mier, -miest** mugriento

grin¹ /grɪn/ vi **-nn-** sonreír* (abiertamente o burlonamente); **to ~ and bear it** aguantarse

grin² n sonrisa f

grind¹ /ɡraɪnd/ (past & past p **ground**) vt ‹coffee/wheat› moler*; (in mortar) machacar*; ‹meat› (AmE) moler* or (Esp, RPl) picar*; ‹crystals/ore› triturar; **he ~s his teeth in his sleep** le rechinan los dientes cuando duerme
■ ~ vi (move with friction) rechinar, chirriar*; **to ~ to a halt o standstill** ‹vehicle› pararse or detenerse* con un chirrido; «negotiations» llegar* a un punto muerto

grind² n (a) (drudgery) (colloq) (no pl): **the daily ~** el monótono trajín diario (b) (over-conscientious worker) (AmE colloq): **she's the office ~** es la niña aplicada de la oficina (iró)

grinder /'ɡraɪndər/ n (machine) molinillo m; **a coffee ~** un molinillo de café

grindstone /'ɡraɪnstəʊn, 'ɡraɪndstəʊn ‖'ɡraɪndstəʊn/ n muela f, piedra f de afilar; **back to the ~!** ¡de vuelta al yugo!

grip¹ /ɡrɪp/ n 1 (a) (hold): **she held his arm in a strong ~** lo tenía agarrado or asido fuertemente del brazo; **he kept a firm ~ on expenses** llevaba un rígido control de los gastos; **get a ~ on yourself!** ¡contrólate!; **the region is in the ~ of an epidemic** una epidemia azota la región; **to come to ~s with sth** ‹idea/situation› aceptar or asumir algo; **to get to ~s with sth** ‹subject› entender* algo; ‹new system› aprender algo (b) (of tires) adherencia f
2 (on handle) empuñadura f
3 (hair ~) (BrE) horquilla f, pinche (Chi), pasador m (Méx)

grip² vt -pp- 1 (take hold of) agarrar; (have hold of) tener* agarrado 2 (of feelings, attention): **the audience was ~ped by the play** la obra captó la atención del público

gripping /'ɡrɪpɪŋ/ adj apasionante

grisly /'ɡrɪzli/ adj -lier, -liest truculento

gristle /'ɡrɪsəl/ n cartílago m

grit¹ /ɡrɪt/ n 1 (a) (dirt) polvo m (b) (gravel) arenilla f 2 (courage) (colloq) agallas fpl (fam) 3 **grits** pl (hominy ~s) (AmE Culin) sémola f de maíz

grit² vt -tt- (a) (BrE) ‹road› echar arenilla en (b) ▶ TOOTH A

grizzly /'ɡrɪzli/ n (pl -lies), **grizzly bear** oso m pardo

groan¹ /ɡrəʊn/ vi 1 (a) (with pain, suffering) gemir* (b) (with dismay) gruñir* (c) (creak) «door/timber» crujir 2 (grumble) (colloq) refunfuñar (fam)

groan² n (a) (of pain, suffering) quejido m (b) (of dismay) gruñido m (c) (creak) crujido m

grocer /'ɡrəʊsər/ n tendero, -ra m,f, almacenero, -ra m,f (esp CS); **the ~'s** (BrE) la tienda de comestibles or de ultramarinos, la bodega (Cu, Per, Ven), la tienda de abarrotes (AmC, Andes, Méx), el almacén (esp CS)

grocery /'ɡrəʊsəri/ n (pl -ries) (a) (shop) tienda f de comestibles or de ultramarinos, bodega f (Cu, Per, Ven), tienda f de abarrotes (AmC, Andes, Méx), almacén m (esp CS) (b) **groceries** pl (provisions) comestibles mpl, provisiones fpl

groggy /'ɡrɑːɡi ‖'ɡrɒɡi/ adj -gier, -giest (colloq) grogui (fam)

groin /ɡrɔɪn/ n (Anat) ingle f

groom¹ /gruːm/ vt (a) ‹dog› cepillar; ‹horse›

cepillar, almohazar* (b) (make neat, attractive) (usu pass): **well ~ed** bien arreglado (c) (prepare) preparar; **to ~ sb for sth** preparar a algn para algo

groom² n 1 (Equ) mozo m de cuadra 2 (bride~) novio m

groove /gruːv/ n ranura f; (Audio) surco m

grope /ɡrəʊp/ vi andar* a tientas; **to ~ FOR sth** buscar* algo a tientas
■ ~ vt ‹person› (colloq) manosear, meterle mano a (fam)

gross¹ /ɡrəʊs/ adj 1 (extreme, flagrant) (before n) ‹disregard/injustice› flagrante; ‹exaggeration› burdo 2 (total) ‹weight/profit/income› bruto; **~ national product** (Econ) producto m nacional bruto 3 (a) (fat) obeso (b) (disgusting) ‹person› asqueroso; ‹language/joke› soez

gross² vt «worker/earner» tener* una entrada bruta de; **their profits ~ed 2 million** tuvieron beneficios brutos de 2 millones

gross³ n 1 (pl ~) (144) gruesa f 2 (pl **grosses**) (gross profit) (AmE) ingresos mpl brutos

grossly /'ɡrəʊsli/ adv ‹exaggerated/unfair› terriblemente

grotesque /ɡrəʊ'tesk/ adj grotesco

grotto /'ɡrɑːtəʊ ‖'ɡrɒtəʊ/ n (pl **-toes** or **-tos**) gruta f

ground¹ /ɡraʊnd/ n 1 (land, terrain) terreno m; **to gain/lose ~** ganar/perder* terreno; **to stand one's ~** (in argument) mantenerse* firme; (in battle) no ceder terreno
2 **grounds** pl (premises) terreno m; (gardens) jardines mpl
3 (surface of the earth) suelo m; (soil) tierra f; **to break new ~** abrir* nuevos caminos; **to get off the ~** «plan/project» llegar* a concretarse; «talks» empezar* a encaminarse; **to get sth off the ~** ‹project› poner* algo en marcha; **to suit sb down to the ~** (colloq) «arrangement» venirle* de perlas a algn (fam); «hat» quedarle que ni pintado a algn (fam)
4 (matter, subject): **we covered a lot of ~ in our discussions** tratamos muchos puntos en nuestras conversaciones
5 (outdoor site): **football ~** (BrE) campo m de fútbol, cancha f de fútbol (AmL); **recreation ~** parque m (donde se practican deportes)
6 (AmE Elec) tierra f
7 (justification) (usu pl) motivo m; **~s for divorce** causal f de divorcio; **on ~s of ill health** por motivos de salud; **they refused, on the ~s that ...** se negaron, alegando que ...
8 **grounds** pl (dregs): **coffee ~s** posos mpl de café

ground² vt 1 (usu pass) (a) (base) ‹argument/theory› fundar (b) (instruct): **we were well ~ed in German** se nos dio una sólida base en alemán 2 (a) ‹plane› retirar del servicio (b) ‹child/teenager› (esp AmE colloq): **I can't go out tonight; I'm ~ed** no puedo salir esta noche, estoy castigado or no me dejan 3 (Naut) ‹ship› hacer* encallar

ground³ past & past p of GRIND¹

ground⁴ adj ‹coffee/pepper› molido; **~ beef** (AmE) carne f molida or (Esp, RPl) picada

ground: ~cloth, (BrE) **~sheet** n suelo m

impermeable (de una tienda de campaña); **~ control** n control m de tierra; **~ floor** n (BrE) the **~ floor** la planta baja, el primer piso (Chi)

grounding /'graʊndɪŋ/ n (no pl) base f

groundless /'graʊndləs ‖'graʊndlɪs/ adj infundado

ground: **~ level** n: at **~ level** a ras del suelo; **above ~ level** sobre el nivel del suelo; **below ~ level** bajo tierra; **~ rule** n **1** (guiding principle) directriz f; **2** (AmE Sport) regla f de terreno or de campo, regla local (Ven); **~sheet** n (BrE) ▶ GROUNDCLOTH; **~work** n trabajo m preliminar or de base

group¹ /gruːp/ n **1** (+ sing o pl vb) **(a)** (of people) grupo m; **a women's/gay ~** una agrupación de mujeres/gay; (before n) ⟨discussion/visit⟩ en grupo; ⟨portrait⟩ de conjunto **(b)** (Mus) grupo m, conjunto m **2** (Busn, Chem, Math) grupo m

group² vt agrupar
■ **~** vi: **to ~ together** agruparse

grouse¹ /graʊs/ n (pl **~**) (bird) urogallo m

grouse² vi (colloq) gruñir* (fam); **to ~ ABOUT sb/sth** quejarse DE algn/algo

grout /graʊt/ vt ⟨tiles⟩ enlechar

grove /grəʊv/ n (of trees) bosquecillo m; **an orange ~** un naranjal

grovel /'grɑːvəl ‖'grɒvəl/ vi, (BrE) **-ll-** (physically) postrarse; (abase oneself) arrastrarse

grow /grəʊ/ (past **grew**; past p **grown**) vi **1** (get bigger) crecer*; (develop emotionally) madurar; (expand, increase) ⟨city/company/influence⟩ crecer*; ⟨quantity/population/membership⟩ aumentar; **his hair has ~n** le creció el pelo; **the economy is ~ing again** la economía vuelve a experimentar un período de crecimiento or expansión
2 (a) (become): **to ~ careless** volverse* descuidado; **to ~ old** envejecer* **(b)** (get) **to ~ to + INF**: **she grew to love him** llegó a quererlo
■ **~** vt ⟨flowers/plants/crops⟩ cultivar; **to ~ a beard** dejarse (crecer) la barba; **to ~ one's hair (long)** dejarse crecer el pelo
■ **grow into** [v + prep + o] **(a)** (become) convertirse* en **(b)** (grow to fit): **she will soon ~ into these dresses** pronto podrá usar estos vestidos
■ **grow on** [v + prep + o] (colloq): **it ~s on you** ⟨music/place⟩ llega a gustar con el tiempo
■ **grow out of** [v + adv + prep + o] **(a)** ⟨habit⟩ perder*, quitarse (con el tiempo o la edad); **it's just a phase, she'll ~ out of it** son cosas de la edad, ya se le pasará **(b)** ⟨clothes⟩: **she's ~n out of those shoes already** esos zapatos ya le quedan chicos or (Esp) le están pequeños
■ **grow up** [v + adv] **(a)** (spend childhood) criarse*, crecer* **(b)** (become adult) hacerse* mayor; **when I ~ up** cuando sea grande; **~ up!** ¡no seas infantil! **(c)** (arise) ⟨friendship/custom/feeling⟩ surgir*; ⟨settlement/town⟩ desarrollarse

grower /'grəʊər ‖'grəʊə(r)/ n cultivador, -dora m,f

growing /'grəʊɪŋ/ adj (before n) **(a)** ⟨quantity/reputation⟩ cada vez mayor; ⟨influence⟩ creciente **(b)** ⟨child⟩: **you need a lot to eat; you're a ~ boy** tienes que comer mucho, estás creciendo **(c)** ⟨plant/stem/vegetable⟩ que está creciendo

growl¹ /graʊl/ vi gruñir*

growl² n gruñido m

grown¹ /grəʊn/ past p of GROW

grown² adj: **he's a ~ man** es un hombre hecho y derecho; **when the young are fully ~** (Zool) cuando las crías han alcanzado su pleno desarrollo

grown-up¹ /'grəʊnʌp/ n persona f mayor

grown-up² adj **(a)** (adult) mayor **(b)** (mature) (colloq) maduro, adulto

growth /grəʊθ/ n **1** (of animals, plants, humans) crecimiento m **2** (of population, city, business) crecimiento m; (of quantity, profits) aumento m; (in popularity) aumento m **3 (a)** (what grows): **new ~** brotes mpl nuevos; **several days' ~ of beard** una barba de varios días **(b)** (Med) bulto m, tumor m

growth industry n industria f en crecimiento or en expansión

grub /grʌb/ n **1** (Zool) larva f **2** (food) (colloq) comida f, papeo m (Esp arg), morfe m (CS arg)

grubby /'grʌbi/ adj **-bier, -biest** mugriento

grudge¹ /grʌdʒ/ n rencilla f; **to bear sb a ~** tenerle* or guardarle rencor a algn

grudge² vt ▶ BEGRUDGE

grueling, (BrE) **gruelling** /'gruːəlɪŋ/ adj ⟨journey⟩ extenuante; ⟨experience/ordeal⟩ penoso

gruesome /'gruːsəm/ adj truculento

gruff /grʌf/ adj **-er, -est** ⟨voice⟩ áspero; ⟨manner/reply⟩ brusco

grumble /'grʌmbəl/ vi refunfuñar (fam), rezongar*; **to ~ ABOUT sth/sb** quejarse DE algo/algn

grumpy /'grʌmpi/ adj **-pier, -piest** ⟨person⟩ gruñón; ⟨remark/voice⟩ malhumorado

grunt¹ /grʌnt/ vi gruñir*

grunt² n gruñido m

guarantee¹ /ˌgærən'tiː/ n garantía f

guarantee² vt garantizar*

guarantor /'gærəntɔːr ‖ˌgærən'tɔː(r)/ n garante mf

guard¹ /gɑːrd ‖gɑːd/ vt **(a)** ⟨building/prisoner⟩ vigilar; ⟨person/reputation⟩ proteger*; ⟨secret⟩ guardar **(b)** (AmE Sport) marcar*
■ **guard against** [v + prep + o] ⟨injury/temptation⟩ evitar; ⟨risk⟩ protegerse* contra

guard² n **1 (a)** (sentry, soldier) guardia mf; **security ~** guarda mf de seguridad; **prison ~** (AmE) carcelero, -ra m,f, oficial mf de prisiones **(b)** (squad) (no pl) guardia f **(c)** (Sport) (in US football) defensa mf; (in basketball) escolta mf **2** (surveillance) guardia f; **to be on ~** estar* de guardia; (before n) **~ duty** guardia f, posta f (AmC) **3** (in boxing, fencing) guardia f; **to be on/off (one's) ~** estar* alerta/desprevenido **4 (a)** (fire ~) guardallama(s) m **(b)** (on machinery) cubierta f (or dispositivo m etc) de seguridad **5** (BrE Rail) jefe, -fa m,f de tren

guard dog n perro m guardián

guarded /'gɑːrdəd ‖'gɑːdɪd/ adj ⟨reply/admission⟩ cauteloso; ⟨optimism⟩ cauto

guardian /'gɑːrdiən ‖'gɑːdiən/ n **(a)** (of child) tutor, -tora m,f **(b)** (protector) defensor, -sora m,f, custodio, -dia m,f

guardian angel *n* ángel *m* de la guarda, ángel *m* custodio

guard: ~**rail** *n* (in staircase) barandilla *f*; (in roads etc) barrera *f* de seguridad; ~**'s van** *n* (BrE Rail) furgón *m* de cola

Guatemala /ˈgwɑːtəˈmɑːlə/ *n* Guatemala *f*

Guatemalan¹ /ˈgwɑːtəˈmɑːlən/ *adj* guatemalteco

Guatemalan² *n* guatemalteco, -ca *m,f*

Guernsey /ˈgɜːrnzi ‖ˈgɜːnzi/ *n* Guernesey

guerrilla /gəˈrɪlə/ *n* guerrillero, -ra *m,f*; *(before n)* ⟨*tactics/leader*⟩ guerrillero; ~ **warfare** guerrilla *f*

guess¹ /ges/ *n*: **have a** ~**!** ¡a ver si adivinas!; **your** ~ **is as good as mine** quién sabe, vete tú a saber

guess² *vt* (a) (conjecture, estimate) adivinar; ~ **what!** ¿sabes qué?; **you'll never** ~ **what he said** no te puedes imaginar lo que dijo (b) (suppose) (esp AmE colloq) suponer*; **I** ~ **so** supongo (que sí)
■ ~ *vi*: **how did you** ~**?** ¿cómo adivinaste? *or* (Esp) ¿cómo lo has adivinado?; **to** ~ **right** acertar*, adivinar, atinar(le) (Méx)

guesswork /ˈgeswɜːrk ‖ˈgeswɜːk/ *n* conjeturas *fpl*

guest /gest/ *n* (visitor) invitado, -da *m,f*; (in hotel) huésped *mf*, cliente, -ta *m,f*; *(before n)* ~ **list** lista *f* de invitados; ~ **speaker** conferenciante invitado, -da *m,f*, ~ **star** estrella *f* invitada

guest: ~**house** *n* (a) (in US, attached to mansion) pabellón *m* de huéspedes (b) (Tourism) (in UK) casa *f* de huéspedes, pensión *f*; ~**room** *n* cuarto *m* de huéspedes *or* (Chi) de alojados

guffaw¹ /ɡʌˈfɔː/ *n* risotada *f*

guffaw² *vi* reírse* a carcajadas

guidance /ˈgaɪdn̩s/ *n* orientación *f*; **he needs** ~ necesita que lo orienten; *(before n)* ~ **counselor** (AmE) orientador, -dora *m,f* vocacional

guide¹ /gaɪd/ *n* ① (a) (Tourism) (person) guía *mf*; (publication) guía *f* (b) (adviser) consejero, -ra *m,f* ② **Guide** (BrE) exploradora *f*, guía *f* ③ (indicator) guía *f*; **to use** *o* **take sth as a** ~ guiarse* por algo

guide² *vt* (a) ⟨*tourist/stranger*⟩ guiar*; **a priest** ~**d them round the cathedral** un sacerdote les hizo de guía en la catedral (b) (help, advise) guiar*, aconsejar (c) (steer, manipulate) (+ *adv compl*): **the captain** ~**d the ship between the rocks** el capitán condujo *or* guio el barco por entre las rocas

guide: ~**book** *n* guía *f*; ~ **dog** *n* perro *m* guía, perro *m* lazarillo

guided tour /ˈgaɪdəd ‖ˈgaɪdɪd/ *n* visita *f* guiada

guideline /ˈgaɪdlaɪn/ *n* pauta *f*

guild /gɪld/ *n* (a) (of workers) gremio *m* (b) (club, society) asociación *f*

guile /gaɪl/ *n* astucia *f*

guillotine /ˈgɪləti:n/ *n* guillotina *f*

guilt /gɪlt/ *n* (a) (blame) culpa *f*; (Law) culpabilidad *f* (b) (Psych) culpa *f*

guilty /ˈgɪlti/ *adj* **-tier, -tiest** (a) (Law) *(no comp)* culpable; **to be** ~ **of sth** ser* culpable DE algo (b) (ashamed, remorseful) culpable (c) (shameful) *(before n)* ⟨*secret*⟩ vergonzoso

guinea /ˈgɪni/ *n* guinea *f*

guinea pig *n* (a) (Zool) cobayo *m*, cobaya *f*, conejillo *m* de Indias, cuy *m* (AmS) (b) (person) conejillo *m* de Indias

guise /gaɪz/ *n*: **under the** ~ **of friendship** bajo una apariencia de amistad; **in many different** ~**s** de muchas formas distintas

guitar /gəˈtɑːr ‖gɪˈtɑː(r)/ *n* guitarra *f*

guitarist /gəˈtɑːrəst ‖gɪˈtɑːrɪst/ *n* guitarrista *mf*

gulf /gʌlf/ *n* (a) (Geog) golfo *m* (b) (gap) abismo *m*

gull /gʌl/ *n* (Zool) gaviota *f*

gullet /ˈgʌlət ‖ˈgʌlɪt/ *n* garganta *f*

gulley /ˈgʌli/ *n* (*pl* **-leys**) ▶ GULLY

gullible /ˈgʌləbəl/ *adj* crédulo

gully /ˈgʌli/ *n* (*pl* **-lies**) (a) (small valley) barranco *m* (b) (channel) surco *m*, cauce *m*

gulp¹ /gʌlp/ *vi* tragar* saliva
■ ~ *vt* ~ **(down)** ⟨*food*⟩ engullir*; ⟨*drink/medicine*⟩ beberse de un trago

gulp² *n* (of liquid) trago *m*; (of air) bocanada *f*: **in one** ~ de un trago

gum /gʌm/ *n* ① (Anat) encía *f* ② (chewing ~) chicle *m*, goma *f* de mascar ③ (a) (glue) (BrE) goma *f* de pegar (b) (from plant) resina *f*

gun /gʌn/ *n* (pistol) pistola *f*, revólver *m*; (shotgun, rifle) escopeta *f*, fusil *m*, rifle *m*; (artillery piece) cañón *m*
■ **gun down** [*v + o + adv, v + adv + o*] abatir a tiros

gun: ~**dog** *n* perro *m* de caza; ~**fight** *n* tiroteo *m*, balacera *f* (AmL); ~**fire** *n* disparos *mpl*; (from heavy artillery) cañoneo *m*, cañonazos *mpl*; ~**man** /ˈgʌnmən/ *n* (*pl* **-men** /-mən/) pistolero *m*, gatillero *m* (Méx); ~**point** *n*: **at** ~**point a punta de pistola; ~**powder** *n* pólvora *f*, ~**running** *n* tráfico *m* de armas; ~**shot** *n* disparo *m*; *(before n)* ~**shot wound** herida *f* de bala; ~**smith** *n* armero, -ra *m,f*

gurgle¹ /ˈgɜːrgəl ‖ˈgɜːgəl/ *vi* «*water/brook*» borbotar; «*baby*» gorjear

gurgle² *n* (of water, liquid) borboteo *m*; (of delight) gorjeo *m*

gush /gʌʃ/ *vi* «*liquid*» salir* a borbotones

gushing /ˈgʌʃɪŋ/ *adj* (pej) demasiado efusivo

gusset /ˈgʌsət ‖ˈgʌsɪt/ *n* entretela *f*

gust /gʌst/ *n* ráfaga *f*

gusto /ˈgʌstəʊ/ *n* entusiasmo *m*; **with** ~ ⟨*eat*⟩ con ganas; ⟨*sing/play*⟩ con brío

gusty /ˈgʌsti/ *adj* **-tier, -tiest** ⟨*wind*⟩ racheado; ⟨*weather/day*⟩ ventoso

gut¹ /gʌt/ *n* (a) (intestine) intestino *m* (b) (belly) (colloq) barriga *f* (fam); *(before n)* ⟨*reaction*⟩ instintivo

AmC	América Central	Arg	Argentina	Cu	Cuba
AmL	América Latina	Bol	Bolivia	Ec	Ecuador
AmS	América del Sur	Chi	Chile	Esp	España
Andes	Región andina	CS	Cono Sur	Méx	México

Per	Perú
RPI	Río de la Plata
Ur	Uruguay
Ven	Venezuela

gut² *vt* -tt- (a) ⟨*fish/chicken/rabbit*⟩ limpiar (b) ⟨*building*⟩ destruir* el interior de

guts /gʌts/ *n* ❶ (+ *pl vb*) (colloq) (bowels) tripas *fpl* (fam) ❷ (+ *sing o pl vb*) (courage) (colloq) agallas *fpl* (fam)

gutter /'gʌtər ‖ 'gʌtə(r)/ *n* (a) (on roof) canaleta *f*, canalón *m* (Esp) (b) (in street) alcantarilla *f* (c) (lowest section of society) **the ~** el arroyo; (*before n*) **the ~ press** la prensa sensacionalista

guttural /'gʌtərəl/ *adj* gutural

guy /gaɪ/ *n* (colloq) (a) (man) tipo *m* (fam), tío *m* (Esp fam), chavo *m* (Méx fam) (b) **guys** *pl* (people) (AmE) gente *f*

Guyana /gaɪˈænə/ *n* Guyana *f*, Guayana *f*

Guyanese /ˌgaɪəˈniːz/ *adj* guyanés, guayanés

guzzle /'gʌzəl/ *vt* (a) (drink greedily) chupar (fam) (b) (eat greedily) (BrE) engullirse*, tragarse*

gym /dʒɪm/ *n* (a) (gymnasium) gimnasio *m* (b) (gymnastics) gimnasia *f*

gymnasium /dʒɪmˈneɪziəm/ *n* (*pl* -**siums** *or* -**sia** /-ziə/) gimnasio *m*

gymnast /'dʒɪmnæst/ *n* gimnasta *mf*

gymnastics /dʒɪmˈnæstɪks/ *n* (a) (activity) (+ *sing vb*) gimnasia *f* (b) (exercises) (+ *pl vb*) gimnasia *f*

gynecologist, (BrE) **gynaecologist** /'gaɪnəˈkɑːlədʒəst ‖ ˌgaɪnəˈkɒlədʒɪst/ *n* ginecólogo, -ga *m,f*

gynecology, (BrE) **gynaecology** /'gaɪnəˈkɑːlədʒi ‖ ˌgaɪnəˈkɒlədʒi/ *n* ginecología *f*

gypsy, Gypsy /'dʒɪpsi/ *n* (*pl* -**sies**) gitano, -na *m,f*

gyrate /'dʒaɪreɪt ‖ dʒaɪˈreɪt/ *vi* girar

h

Hh

H, h /eɪtʃ/ *n* H, h *f*

haberdashery /'hæbərˌdæʃəri ‖ 'hæbəˌdæʃəri/ *n* (a) (clothes) (AmE) ropa *f* y accesorios *mpl* para caballeros (b) (sewing materials) (BrE) (artículos *mpl* de) mercería *f*

habit /'hæbət ‖ 'hæbɪt/ *n* ❶ (a) (usual piece of behavior) costumbre *f*, hábito *m*; (bad) vicio *m*, mala costumbre *f*, mal hábito *m*; **to get out of/ into the ~ of doing sth** perder*/tomar la costumbre de hacer algo (b) (customary behavior) costumbre *f*; **by** *or* **out of** *or* **from force of ~** por fuerza de la costumbre ❷ (Clothing) hábito *m*

habitat /'hæbətæt ‖ 'hæbɪtæt/ *n* hábitat *m*

habitation /'hæbəˈteɪʃən ‖ ˌhæbɪˈteɪʃən/ *n* (frml): **unfit for human ~** inhabitable

habitual /həˈbɪtʃuəl/ *adj* (a) (usual) habitual, acostumbrado (b) (compulsive) ⟨*liar/gambler*⟩ empedernido

hack¹ /hæk/ *vt* cortar a tajos, tajear (Andes)
■ ~ *vi* ❶ (to cut): **to ~ at sth** darle* (golpes) a algo; **we ~ed through the undergrowth** nos abrimos paso a machetazos (*or* hachazos *etc*) a través de la espesura ❷ (Comput colloq) **to ~ into** ⟨*system*⟩ piratear

hack² *n* ❶ (*pej or hum*) (writer) escritorzuelo, -la *m,f* (pey); (journalist) gacetillero, -ra *m,f* (pey) ❷ (horse — for hire) caballo *m* de alquiler; (— worn-out) jaco *m*, jamelgo *m* ❸ (AmE colloq) (a) (taxi driver) taxista *mf*, tachero, -ra *m,f* (RPl fam), ruletero, -ra *m,f* (Méx fam) (b) (taxi) taxi *m*, tacho *m* (RPl fam)

hacker /'hækər ‖ 'hækə(r)/ *n* (Comput colloq) pirata informático, -ca *m,f*

hacking /'hækɪŋ/ *adj* ⟨*cough*⟩ áspero

hackles /'hækəlz/ *pl n* **to make sb's ~ rise** poner* furioso a algn; **his ~ rose** se enfureció

hackneyed /'hæknid/ *adj* manido, trillado

hacksaw /'hæksɔː/ *n* sierra *f* de arco (*para metales*)

had /hæd, *weak form* həd, əd/ *past & past p of* HAVE

haddock /'hædək/ *n* (*pl* ~) (a) (Zool) eglefino *m* (b) (Culin) abadejo *m*

hadn't /'hædn̩t/ = **had not**

haem- *etc* (BrE) ▶ HEM- *etc*

hag /hæg/ *n* bruja *f*, arpía *f*

haggard /'hægərd ‖ 'hægəd/ *adj* demacrado

haggis /'hægəs ‖ 'hægɪs/ *n* (*pl* -**gis** *or* -**gises**) plato escocés hecho con vísceras de cordero y avena

haggle /'hægəl/ *vi* regatear

Hague /heɪg/ *n* **The ~** La Haya

hail¹ /heɪl/ *n* (a) (Meteo) granizo *m*, pedrisco *m* (b) (of bullets, insults) (*no pl*) lluvia *f*

hail² *v impers* (Meteo) granizar*
■ ~ *vt* ❶ (call to) ⟨*person*⟩ llamar; ⟨*ship*⟩ saludar; ⟨*taxi*⟩ hacerle* señas a ❷ (acclaim, welcome) ⟨*king/ leader*⟩ aclamar; **it was ~ed as a major breakthrough** fue acogido como un importantísimo avance
■ ~ *vi* **to ~ FROM** «*person*» ser* DE

hail: H~ Mary /'meri ‖ 'meəri/ *n* Avemaría *m*; **~stone** *n* granizo *m*, piedra *f* (de granizo)

hair /her ‖ heə(r)/ *n* (a) (on human head) pelo *m*, cabello *m* (frml o liter); **to have one's ~ done** peinarse (*en la peluquería*); (*before n*) ⟨*gel/ lacquer/oil*⟩ para el pelo; ⟨*transplant*⟩ capilar (b) (on human body) vello *m*; (on animal, plant) pelo *m* (c) (single strand) pelo *m*

hair: ~band (elastic) cinta *f*, huincha *f* (Bol, Chi, Per), balaca *f* (Col), banda *f* (Méx), vincha *f* (RPl, Ven); (rigid) diadema *f*, cintillo *m*, vincha *f* (RPl, Ven); **~brush** *n* cepillo *m* (*del pelo*); **~clip** *n* (BrE) horquilla *f*, pinche *m* (Chi), pasador *m* (Méx); **~cut** *n* corte *m* de pelo; **~do** *n* (colloq) peinado *m*; **~dresser** *n* peluquero, -ra *m,f*; **the ~dresser's** la peluquería; **~drier, ~dryer** *n* secador *m* *or* (Méx) secadora *f*; **~grip** *n* (BrE) horquilla *f*, pinche *m* (Chi), pasador *m* (Méx); ···⟩

∼line n **(a)** (where hair begins) nacimiento m del pelo **(b)** (fine line) línea f delgada; (before n) **a ∼line fracture** una pequeña fisura; **∼net** n redecilla f; **∼piece** n postizo m; **∼pin** n horquilla f (de moño); (before n) **∼pin turn** o (BrE) **bend** curva f muy cerrada; **∼-raising** /ˈherˌreɪzɪŋ ‖ˈheəˌreɪzɪŋ/ adj espeluznante; **∼'s breadth, ∼sbreadth** n (no pl): **by a ∼'s breadth** por un pelo (fam); **∼slide** n (BrE) ▶ BARRETTE; **∼spray** n laca f, fijador m (para el pelo); **∼style** n peinado m, corte m de pelo

hairy /ˈheri ‖ˈheəri/ adj **-rier, -riest** ⟨legs/chest⟩ peludo, velludo

Haiti /ˈheɪti/ n Haití m

Haitian /ˈheɪʃən/ adj haitiano

hake /heɪk/ n (pl ∼) merluza f

halal /hɑːˈlɑːl/ adj (Culin) ⟨meat⟩ de animales faenados or (Esp) sacrificados según la ley musulmana

hale /heɪl/ adj (liter): **∼ and hearty** (fuerte) como un roble

half¹ /hæf ‖hɑːf/ n (pl **halves**) **1** **(a)** (part) mitad f; **to break sth in ∼** romper* algo por la mitad or en dos; **to go halves** (colloq) pagar* a medias **(b)** (Math) medio m **(c)** (elliptical usage): **an hour and a ∼** una hora y media; **it's ∼ past ten** son las diez y media **2** (Sport) **(a)** (period) tiempo m **(b)** (of pitch) campo m **(c)** (interval) (AmE) descanso m, medio tiempo m (AmL)

half² pron la mitad

half³ adj medio, -dia; **∼ a pint of milk** media pinta de leche; **one and a ∼ hours** una hora y media

half⁴ adv medio; **she was ∼ asleep** estaba medio dormida or semidormida; **the work is only ∼ done** el trabajo está a medio hacer; **she is ∼ Italian, ∼ Greek** es hija de italianos y griegos; **they are paid ∼ as much as we are** les pagan la mitad que a nosotros

half- /ˈhæf ‖ˈhɑːf/ pref: **∼closed/∼open** entreabierto; **∼starved** medio muerto de hambre

half: ∼ a dozen n (no pl) media docena f; **∼ a dozen eggs** media docena de huevos; **∼ an hour** n media hora f; **∼ brother** n hermanastro m, medio hermano m; **∼hearted** /ˈhæfˈhɑːrtəd ‖ˌhɑːfˈhɑːtɪd/ adj poco entusiasta; **∼-hour** /ˈhæfˈaʊr ‖ˌhɑːfˈaʊə(r)/ n media hora f; **∼-light** n penumbra f; **∼-mast** /ˈhæfˈmæst ‖ˌhɑːfˈmɑːst/ n: **at ∼-mast** a media asta; **∼ measures** pl n medias tintas fpl; **∼-moon** /ˈhæfˈmuːn ‖ˌhɑːfˈmuːn/ n media luna f; **∼ note** n (AmE) blanca f; **∼penny** /ˈheɪpni/ n (Hist) **(a)** (pl **-pennies**) (coin) medio penique m **(b)** (pl **-pence** /ˈheɪpəns/) (value) medio penique m; **∼ price** n mitad f de precio; **it's ∼ price** está a mitad de precio; **∼ sister** n hermanastra f, media hermana f; **∼staff** n (AmE) ▶ ∼-MAST; **∼ term** n (in UK) vacaciones fpl de mitad de trimestre; **∼-time** n (a) (Sport) descanso m, medio tiempo m (AmL); **(b)** (Busn, Lab Rel) media jornada f

half-way¹ /ˈhæfˈweɪ ‖ˌhɑːfˈweɪ/ adv (at, to mid point) a mitad de camino; **I'm about ∼ through** voy por la mitad; **to meet sb ∼** (compromise) llegar* a una solución intermedia con algn; (lit: journey) encontrarse* con algn a mitad de camino

half-way² adj (before n) ⟨point⟩ medio; ⟨stage⟩ intermedio; **the ∼ mark** el punto medio, la mitad

half-yearly /ˈhæfˈjɪrli ‖ˌhɑːfˈjɪəli/ adj semestral

hall /hɔːl/ n **1** **(a)** (vestibule) vestíbulo m, entrada f **(b)** (corridor) (AmE) pasillo m, corredor m **2** **(a)** (for gatherings) salón m **(b)** (in castle, mansion) sala f **3** (student residence) (BrE) residencia f universitaria or de estudiantes, colegio m mayor (Esp) **4** (large country house) (BrE) casa f solariega

halleluja /ˌhælɪˈluːjə ‖ˌhælɪˈluːjə/ interj ¡aleluya!

hallmark /ˈhɔːlmɑːrk ‖ˈhɔːlmɑːk/ n **(a)** (on gold, silver) contraste m, sello m (de contraste) **(b)** (distinguishing characteristic) distintivo m, sello m

hallo /həˈləʊ/ interj ▶ HELLO

hall of residence n (pl **∼s of residence**) (BrE) ▶ HALL 3

Halloween, Hallowe'en /ˌhæləʊˈiːn/ n víspera f del día de Todos los Santos

hallucination /həˌluːsɪˈneɪʃən ‖həˈluːsɪˈneɪʃən/ n alucinación f

hallway /ˈhɔːlweɪ/ n ▶ HALL 1

halo /ˈheɪləʊ/ n (pl **-los** or **-loes**) **(a)** (Art, Relig) aureola f, halo m **(b)** (Astron, Opt) halo m

halt¹ /hɔːlt ‖hɒlt, hɔːlt/ n: **to come to a ∼** pararse

halt² vi detenerse* (frml); **∼!** (Mil) ¡alto! ■ **∼** vt ⟨vehicle/troops⟩ detener* (frml); ⟨process⟩ atajar, detener* (frml); ⟨work/production⟩ interrumpir

halter /ˈhɔːltər ‖ˈhɒltə(r), ˈhɔː-/ n cabestro m, ronzal m

halve /hæv ‖hɑːv/ vt **(a)** (reduce by half) ⟨expense/time/length⟩ reducir* a la mitad or en un 50%; ⟨number⟩ dividir por dos **(b)** (divide into halves) partir por la mitad ■ **∼** vi reducirse* a la mitad or en un 50%

halves /hævz ‖hɑːvz/ pl of HALF¹

ham /hæm/ n **1** (Culin) (cured) jamón m (crudo), jamón m serrano (Esp); (cooked) jamón m (cocido), jamón m (de) York (Esp) **2** (Theat) actor extravagante m histriónico

hamburger /ˈhæmbɜːrgər ‖ˈhæmbɜːgə(r)/ n hamburguesa f

hamlet /ˈhæmlət ‖ˈhæmlɪt/ n aldea f, caserío m

hammer¹ /ˈhæmər ‖ˈhæmə(r)/ n martillo m

hammer² vt ⟨nail⟩ clavar (con un martillo); ⟨metal⟩ martillar, batir ■ **∼** vi (strike) dar* golpes; (with hammer) dar* martillazos; **to ∼ at or on the door** golpear la puerta ■ **hammer home** [v + o + adv, v + adv + o] ⟨nail⟩ remachar; ⟨point⟩ recalcar*, machacar* ■ **hammer out** [v + o + adv, v + adv + o] ⟨metal/dent⟩ alisar a martillazos; ⟨compromise/deal⟩ negociar (con mucho toma y daca)

hammock /ˈhæmək/ n hamaca f, hamaca f paraguaya (RPl); (Naut) coy m

hamper¹ /ˈhæmpər ‖ˈhæmpə(r)/ vt dificultar

hamper² n cesta f, canasta f

hamster /ˈhæmstər ‖ˈhæmstə(r)/ n hámster m

hamstring /ˈhæmstrɪŋ/ n (of person) ligamento m de la corva; (of horse) tendón m del corvejón or jarrete

hand¹ /hænd/ n **1** (Anat) mano f; ~s off! ¡quita las manos de ahí!; ~s up all those in favor que levanten la mano los que estén a favor; ~s up! ¡manos arriba!

2 (in phrases) at hand: help was at ~ la ayuda estaba en camino; by hand ⟨make/write/wash⟩ a mano; hand in hand (tomados or agarrados or (esp Esp) cogidos) de la mano; **poverty and disease go ~ in ~** la pobreza y la enfermedad van de la mano; on hand: the police were on ~ la policía estaba cerca; to have sth on ~ tener* algo a mano; out of hand: the situation is getting out of ~ la situación se nos (or les etc) va de las manos; to reject sth out of ~ rechazar* algo de plano; to hand (BrE) (within reach) al alcance de la mano, a (la) mano; (available) disponible; *to beat sb/win* ~s down ganarle a algn/ganar sin problemas; *to get one's* ~s on sb/ sth: just wait till I get my ~s on him! ¡vas a ver cuando lo agarre!; she can't wait to get her ~s on the new computer se muere por usar la computadora nueva; *to give sb/have a free* ~ darle* a algn/tener* carta blanca; *to know a place like the back of one's* ~ conocer* un sitio al dedillo; *to try one's* ~ (at sth) probar* (a hacer algo)

3 (a) (agency) mano f; to have a ~ in sth tener* parte en algo; the town had suffered at the ~s of invaders la ciudad había sufrido a manos de los invasores (b) (assistance) (colloq): to give sb a ~ echarle or darle* una mano a algn; if you need a ~ si necesitas ayuda (c) hands pl (possession, control, care): to change ~s cambiar de dueño; in good/capable ~s en buenas manos; my life is in your ~s mi vida depende de ti; we've got a problem on our ~s tenemos un problema; the matter is out of my ~s el asunto no está en mis manos

4 (side): on sb's right/left ~ a la derecha/ izquierda de algn; on the one ~ ... on the other (~) ... por un lado ... por otro (lado) ...

5 (Games) (a) (set of cards) mano f, cartas fpl (b) (round of card game) mano f

6 (a) (worker) obrero, -ra m,f; (farm ~) peón m (b) (Naut) marinero m (c) (experienced person): an old ~ un veterano, una veterana

7 (applause) (colloq) (no pl): a big ~ for ... un gran aplauso para ...

8 (handwriting) (liter) letra f

9 (on clock) manecilla f, aguja f, puntero m (Andes)

hand² vt to ~ sb sth, to ~ sth TO sb pasarle algo A algn

▪ **hand around,** (BrE also) **hand round** [v + o + adv, v + adv + o] (distribute) repartir, distribuir*; (offer round) ⟨cakes⟩ ofrecer*

▪ **hand down** [v + o + adv, v + adv + o] (pass down) ⟨custom/heirloom/story⟩ transmitir; ⟨clothes⟩ pasar

▪ **hand in** [v + o + adv, v + adv + o] ⟨homework/ form/ticket⟩ entregar*; ⟨resignation⟩ presentar

▪ **hand on** [v + o + adv, v + adv + o] ⟨skills/ knowledge⟩ transmitir, pasar; ⟨object/photograph⟩ pasar

▪ **hand out** [v + o + adv, v + adv + o] repartir, distribuir*; ⟨advice⟩ dar*

▪ **hand over** [v + o + adv, v + adv + o] (a) (relinquish) entregar* (b) (transfer) transferir*

▪ **hand round** (BrE) ▶ HAND AROUND

hand: ~bag n (used by women) cartera f or (Esp) bolso m or (Méx) bolsa f; (small suitcase) (AmE) maletín m; ~ baggage, (BrE) ~ luggage n equipaje m de mano; ~ball n (a) (game — in US) frontón m, pelota f; (— in Europe) balonmano m, handball m (AmL) (b) (in soccer) mano f; ~book n manual m; ~brake n (on bicycle) (AmE) freno m (de pastilla); (BrE Auto) freno m de mano; ~craft n ▶ HANDICRAFT; ~ cream n crema f de manos or para las manos; ~cuff vt esposar, ponerle* esposas a; ~cuffs pl n esposas fpl

handful /ˈhændfʊl/ n (a) (amount) puñado m (b) (small number) (+ sing o pl vb) puñado m; a ~ of people unas cuantas personas (c) (troublesome person or group) (no pl): that child is a real ~ ese niño da mucho trabajo

hand grenade n granada f (de mano)

handicap¹ /ˈhændɪkæp/ n **1** (a) (disability): physical ~ impedimento m físico; mental ~ retraso m mental (b) (disadvantage) desventaja f **2** (Sport) (in golf, polo) hándicap m; (penalty) desventaja f

handicap² vt -pp- ⟨person/chances⟩ perjudicar*

handicapped /ˈhændɪkæpt/ adj disminuido, discapacitado, minusválido; mentally/physically ~ disminuido or discapacitado or minusválido psíquico/físico

handicraft /ˈhændɪkræft ‖ˈhændɪkrɑːft/, **handcraft** n (a) (skill) artesanía f, trabajo m artesanal (b) (product) producto m de artesanía

handiwork /ˈhændiwɜːrk ‖ˈhændiwɜːk/ n (a) (craftsmanship) trabajo m (b) (product) artesanías fpl, objetos mpl artesanales (c) (doing) (pej) obra f; it looks like Laura's ~ to me a mí me parece obra de Laura

handkerchief /ˈhæŋkərtʃəf, -tʃiːf ‖ˈhæŋkətʃɪf, -tʃiːf/ n (pl **-chieves** /-tʃiːvz/ or **-chiefs**) pañuelo m

handle¹ /ˈhændl/ n (of cup, jug, bag) asa f; (of door) picaporte m; (knob) pomo m; (of drawer) tirador m, manija f; (of broom, knife, spade) mango m; (of wheelbarrow) brazo m; (of pump) manivela f

handle² vt **1** (a) (touch) tocar*; ❺ handle with care frágil (b) (manipulate, manage) ⟨vehicle/ weapon⟩ manejar; ⟨chemicals⟩ manipular **2** (deal with) ⟨people⟩ tratar; ⟨situation/affair⟩ manejar; he can't ~ the job (colloq) no puede con el trabajo **3** (a) (be responsible for) ⟨business/financial matters⟩ encargarse* or ocuparse de, llevar (b) (do business in) ⟨goods/commodities⟩ comerciar con (c) «computer» ⟨data⟩ procesar

handlebar /ˈhændlbɑːr ‖ˈhændlbɑː(r)/ n (often pl) ~(s) manillar m, manubrio m (AmL)

handling /ˈhændlɪŋ/ n **1** (treatment — of situation) manejo m; (— of subject) tratamiento m **2** (a) (Busn) porte m (b) (Aviat) handling m (c) (Auto) manejo m

handling charge n cargo m por tramitación

hand: ~ luggage n (BrE) equipaje m de mano; ~made /ˈhændˈmeɪd/ adj hecho a mano; ~-me-down n: prenda usada o heredada; ~out n (a) (of money, food) dádiva f (b) (advertising ⋯⟶

leaflet) folleto *m* **(c)** (at lecture, in class) notas *fpl* (*que se distribuyen a los asistentes*); **~-picked** /'hænd,pıkt/ *adj* cuidadosamente seleccionado; **~rail** *n* (on stairs, slope) pasamanos *m*; (on bridge, ship) baranda *f*, barandilla *f*; **~set** *n* auricular *m*, tubo *m* (RPI); **~shake** *n* apretón *m* de manos; **~ signal** *n* (Auto) señal *f* (*hecha con la mano*); (by referee, coach) (AmE) señal *f*

handsome /'hænsəm/ **handsomer, handsomest** *adj* **(a)** (attractive) ‹man› apuesto, buen mozo (AmL), guapo (esp Esp, Méx) **(b)** ‹gift/ offer› generoso

hand: **~s-on** /'hændz'ɑ:n ‖'hændz,ɒn/ *adj* (*before n*) **(a)** ‹instruction/experience› práctico **(b)** (Comput) manual; **~stand** *n*: **to do a ~stand** hacer* la vertical *or* (Esp) el pino, pararse de manos (AmL); **~-to-mouth** /'hændtə'maυθ/ *adj* pobre, precario; **~-wash** /'hænd'wɔ:ʃ ‖'hænd,wɒʃ/ *vt* lavar a mano; **~writing** *n* letra *f*, **~written** /'hænd'rıtn/ *adj* manuscrito, escrito a mano

handy /'hændi/ *adj* **-dier, -diest** (colloq) **[1]** (*pred*) **(a)** (readily accessible) a mano **(b)** (conveniently situated) cerca, a mano **[2]** (useful) práctico; **to come in ~** venir* bien, resultar útil **[3]** ‹person› hábil, habilidoso

handyman /'hændimæn/ *n* (*pl* **-men** /-men/) hombre habilidoso para trabajos de carpintería, albañilería etc

hang¹ /hæŋ/ *vt* **[1]** (*past & past p* hung) **(a)** (suspend) ‹coat/picture› colgar* **(b)** (put in position) ‹door/gate› colocar* **(c)** to ~ **one's head** bajar la cabeza
[2] (*past & past p* **hanged** *or* **hung**) (execute) ahorcar*

■ *vi* **[1]** (*past p* hung) **(a)** (be suspended) colgar*, estar* colgado; **to ~ BY/FROM/ON sth** colgar* DE algo; **it's ~ing on the wall** está colgado en la pared **(b)** (hover) ‹fog/smoke› flotar; «*bird*» planear, cernerse*; **he still has the court case ~ing over him** todavía tiene el juicio pendiente **(c)** «*clothing/fabric*» caer*
[2] (*past & past p* **hanged** *or* **hung**) (be executed): **he should ~ for his crime** debería ir a la horca por este crimen

■ **hang about** [*v + adv*] ▶ HANG AROUND

■ **hang around** (colloq) [*v + adv*] **(a)** (wait) esperar **(b)** (stay) quedarse **(c)** (spend time idly): **they just ~ around on street corners** pasan el tiempo en la calle, holgazaneando; **to ~ around WITH sb** andar* *or* juntarse CON algn

■ **hang on [1]** [*v + adv*] **(a)** (wait) esperar **(b)** (keep hold) **to ~ on TO sth: you ~ on to this end of the rope** tú sostén esta punta de la cuerda **(c)** (keep) (colloq) **to ~ on TO sth** conservar *or* guardar algo **(d)** (in a crisis) aguantar, resistir
[2] [*v + prep + o*] (depend on) «*outcome/decision*» depender de

■ **hang out [1]** [*v + o + adv, v + adv + o*] ‹washing› tender*, colgar*; ‹flag› poner*
[2] [*v + adv*] (dangle) «*wires*» estar* suelto; **with his shirt/tongue ~ing out** con la camisa/la lengua afuera

■ **hang up [1]** [*v + adv*] (put down receiver) colgar*, cortar (CS)
[2] [*v + o + adv, v + adv + o*] ‹coat› colgar*

hang² *n* (*no pl*) **to get the ~ of sth** (colloq) agarrarle la onda a algo (AmL fam), cogerle* el tranquillo a algo (Esp fam), agarrarle la mano a algo (CS fam)

hangar /'hæŋər ‖'hæŋə(r)/ *n* hangar *m*

hanger /'hæŋər ‖'hæŋə(r)/ *n* (clothes or coat ~) percha *f*, gancho *m* (para la ropa) (AmL)

hang: ~ glider *n* ala *f*, delta, deslizador *m* (Méx); **~ gliding** /'ɡlaıdıŋ/ *n* vuelo *m* con ala delta *or* (Méx) en deslizador

hanging /'hæŋıŋ/ *n* **[1]** (execution) ejecución *f* (*en la horca*) **[2]** (wall ~) tapiz *m*

hanging basket *n*: cesto colgante para plantas

hang: ~man *n* (*pl* **-men** /-mən/) verdugo *m*; **~over** *n* **(a)** (from drinking) resaca *f*, cruda *f* (AmC, Méx fam), guayabo *m* (Col fam), ratón *m* (Ven fam) **(b)** (something surviving) vestigio *m*, reliquia *f*; **~-up** *n* (colloq) complejo *m*, trauma *m*

hanker /'hæŋkər ‖'hæŋkə(r)/ *vi* **to ~ AFTER** *o* **FOR sth** anhelar *or* ansiar* algo

hanky, hankie /'hæŋki/ *n* (*pl* **-kies**) (colloq) pañuelo *m*

Hanukkah, Hanukah /'hɑ:nəkə/ *n* Januká *m*, Hanukkah *m* (*fiesta judía de la dedicación del Templo*)

haphazard /'hæp'hæzərd ‖,hæp'hæzəd/ *adj* **(a)** (random): **they promote people in a very ~ way** ascienden a la gente caprichosamente *or* al azar **(b)** (without order): **his approach is very ~** no es coherente en su enfoque

hapless /'hæpləs ‖'hæplıs/ *adj* (*before n*) (liter *or* journ) desafortunado, desventurado (liter)

happen /'hæpən/ *vi* **[1]** (occur) pasar, suceder, ocurrir **(b)** (befall, become of) **to ~ TO sb** pasarle a algn **[2]** **to ~ to + INF: she ~ed to be there** dio la casualidad de que estaba ahí; **if you ~ to see her ...** si por casualidad la ves ...
■ **~** *v impers*: **it (just) so ~s that ...** da la casualidad de que ...

happening /'hæpənıŋ/ *n* suceso *m*

happily /'hæpəli/ *adv* **[1] (a)** ‹smile/ laugh› alegremente; **to be ~ married** ser* feliz en el matrimonio **(b)** (gladly) (*usu before vb*) ‹help› con mucho gusto **[2]** (fortunately) (*indep*) por suerte, afortunadamente

happiness /'hæpines ‖'hæpınıs/ *n* felicidad *f*

happy /'hæpi/ *adj* **-pier, -piest [1] (a)** (joyful, content) ‹person/home› feliz; ‹smile› de felicidad, alegre **(b)** (pleased) (*pred*) **to be ~** alegrarse **(c)** (satisfied) (*pred*) **to be ~ (WITH sth)** estar* contento (CON algo) **[2]** ‹days/occasion› feliz; **~ birthday** feliz cumpleaños

happy-go-lucky /'hæpigəυ'lʌki/ *adj* despreocupado

harangue /hə'ræŋ/ *vt* arengar*

harass /'hærəs, hə'ræs/ *vt* **(a)** (persistently annoy) acosar **(b)** (Mil) hostigar*

663

harassment ··· **harpoon** ···

harassment /'hærəsmənt, hə'ræs-/ n acoso
m; **racial** ~ hostilidad f racial; **sexual** ~ acoso m
sexual
harbor¹, (BrE) **harbour** /'hɑːrbər ‖ 'hɑːbə(r)/ n
puerto m
harbor², (BrE) **harbour** vt (a) (shelter)
⟨fugitive⟩ albergar*, dar* refugio a (b) ⟨desire/
suspicion⟩ albergar* (liter); **to ~ a grudge** guardar
rencor
hard¹ /hɑːrd ‖ hɑːd/ adj **-er, -est** 1 (a) (firm,
solid) ⟨object/surface⟩ duro (b) (forceful) ⟨push/
knock⟩ fuerte
2 (a) (difficult) ⟨question/subject⟩ difícil; ⟨task⟩
arduo; **I find that ~ to believe** me cuesta creerlo;
to learn sth the ~ way aprender algo a base de
cometer errores (b) (severe) ⟨winter/climate/
master⟩ duro, severo; **to give sb a ~ time**
hacérselas* pasar mal a algn; **don't be too ~ on**
him no seas demasiado duro con él; ~ **luck** mala
suerte (c) (tough, cynical) ⟨person/attitude⟩ duro
3 (concentrated, strenuous) ⟨work⟩ duro; **children**
are very ~ work los niños dan mucho trabajo;
he's a ~ worker es muy trabajador
4 (definite) ⟨evidence⟩ concluyente
5 (sharp, harsh) ⟨light/voice⟩ fuerte
6 (a) (in strongest form): ~ **drugs** drogas fpl
duras; ~ **liquor** bebidas fpl (alcohólicas) fuertes;
~ **porn** porno m duro (b) ⟨water⟩ duro
hard² adv **-er, -est** 1 (a) (with force) ⟨pull/
push⟩ con fuerza; ⟨hit⟩ fuerte (b) (strenuously)
⟨work⟩ mucho, duro (c) (intently) ⟨listen⟩
atentamente 2 (heavily) ⟨rain/snow⟩ fuerte,
mucho; ⟨pant/breathe⟩ pesadamente 3 (severely):
to be ~ hit ser* muy afectado; **to feel ~ done by**:
she feels ~ done by piensa que la han tratado
injustamente
hard: ~-and-fast /'hɑːrdṇ'fæst ‖ 'hɑːdən'fɑːst/
adj (no comp, usu before n) absoluto; ~**back** n
(book) libro m de tapa dura or en cartoné; ~**ball**
n (AmE) béisbol m; ~**board** n cartón m madera;
~-**boiled** /'hɑːrd'bɔɪld ‖ hɑːd'bɔɪld/ adj (a)
⟨egg⟩ duro (b) (unsentimental) endurecido; ~ **disk**
n disco m duro (b) ⟨water⟩ duro ~-**earned** /'hɑːrd'ɜːrnd
‖ 'hɑːd,ɜːnd/ adj (usu before n) ⟨cash⟩ ganado con
el sudor de la frente
harden /'hɑːrdṇ ‖ 'hɑːdṇ/ vt (a) (make hard)
⟨clay/cement/skin⟩ endurecer*; ⟨steel/glass⟩
templar (b) (make tough, unfeeling) ⟨person⟩
endurecer*; **you must ~ your heart and tell him**
to go tienes que hacerte fuerte y decirle que se
vaya
■ ~ vi (a) (become hard, rigid) endurecerse* (b)
(become inflexible) ⟨attitude⟩ volverse* inflexible
hardened /'hɑːrdṇd ‖ 'hɑːdṇd/ adj (before n)
⟨sinner/drinker⟩ empedernido; ⟨criminal⟩
habitual
hard: ~ **hat** n (Clothing, Const) casco m;
~-**headed** /'hɑːrd'hedəd ‖ hɑːd'hedɪd/ adj (a)
(practical, realistic) práctico, realista (b) (stubborn)
(AmE) testarudo, cabezota (fam); ~-**hearted**
/'hɑːrd'hɑːrtəd ‖ hɑːd'hɑːtɪd/ adj duro de
corazón; ~-**hitting** /'hɑːrd'hɪtɪŋ ‖ hɑːd'hɪtɪŋ/
adj implacable, feroz; ~ **labor,** (BrE) ~ **labour**
n trabajos mpl forzados; ~-**liner** /'hɑːrd'laɪnər
‖ hɑːd'laɪnə(r)/ n partidario, -ria m,f de la línea
dura
hardly /'hɑːrdli ‖ 'hɑːdli/ adv (a) (scarcely): ~
anyone/anything casi nadie/nada; ~ **ever** casi

nunca; **he ~ knew her** apenas la conocía (b)
(surely not): **it's ~ what you'd call a masterpiece** no
es precisamente una obra maestra
hardness /'hɑːrdnəs ‖ 'hɑːdnɪs/ n dureza f
hard: ~ **of hearing** adj duro de oído;
~-**pressed** /'hɑːrd'prest ‖ hɑːd'prest/ adj ⟨pred
~ **pressed**⟩ ⟨industry/nation/staff⟩ en apuros;
~ **sell** n (no pl) venta f agresiva
hardship /'hɑːrdʃɪp ‖ 'hɑːdʃɪp/ n: **to experience**
o **suffer great ~** pasar muchos apuros; **the ~s of**
the journey las penurias del viaje
hard: ~ **shoulder** n (BrE) arcén m, berma f
(Andes), acotamiento m (Méx), banquina f (RPl),
hombrillo m (Ven); ~ **up** adj (colloq) ⟨pred⟩ **to be**
~ **up** estar* mal de dinero; ~**ware** /'hɑːrdwer
‖ hɑːd'dweə(r)/ n (a) (ironmongery) ferretería f;
(before n) ~**ware store** ferretería f (b) (Mil):
military ~**ware** armamento m (c) (Comput)
hardware m, soporte m físico, equipo m;
~-**wearing** /'hɑːrd'werɪŋ ‖ hɑːd'weərɪŋ/ adj
(BrE) resistente; ~-**working** /'hɑːrd'wɜːrkɪŋ
‖ hɑːd'wɜːkɪŋ/ adj trabajador
hardy /'hɑːrdi ‖ 'hɑːdi/ adj **-dier, -diest**
⟨person/animal⟩ fuerte; ⟨plant⟩ resistente (a las
heladas etc)
hare /her ‖ heə(r)/ n liebre f
haricot (bean) /'hærɪkəʊ/ n frijol m or (Esp)
alubia f or judía f or (CS) poroto m (de color
blanco)
hark back /hɑːrk ‖ hɑːk/ vi **to ~ ~ TO sth**
⟨⟨person⟩⟩ rememorar algo; ⟨⟨book⟩⟩ evocar* algo
harm¹ /hɑːrm ‖ hɑːm/ n daño m; **to do ~ to sb/**
sth hacerle* daño a algn/algo; **there's no ~ in**
asking con preguntar no se pierde nada; **he won't**
come to any ~ no le va a pasar nada; **to be out**
of ~'s way estar* a salvo
harm² vt ⟨person/object⟩ hacerle* daño a;
⟨reputation/career⟩ perjudicar*
harmful /'hɑːrmfəl ‖ 'hɑːmfəl/ adj ⟨substance⟩
nocivo; ⟨influence⟩ pernicioso, dañino; ⟨effect⟩
perjudicial
harmless /'hɑːrmləs ‖ 'hɑːmlɪs/ adj ⟨animal/
person⟩ inofensivo; ⟨substance⟩ inocuo; ⟨joke/
suggestion/fun⟩ inocente
harmonica /hɑːr'mɑːnɪkə ‖ hɑː'mɒnɪkə/ n
armónica f
harmonious /hɑːr'məʊniəs ‖ hɑː'məʊniəs/ adj
armonioso
harmonize /'hɑːrmənaɪz ‖ 'hɑːmənaɪz/ vi (Mus)
cantar en armonía; (be in accord) ⟨⟨colors/ideas⟩⟩
armonizar*
■ ~ vt ⟨policies/plans⟩ armonizar*
harmony /'hɑːrməni ‖ 'hɑːməni/ n (pl **-nies**)
(Mus) armonía f; **in ~** en armonía
harness¹ /'hɑːrnəs ‖ 'hɑːnɪs/ n (a) (for horse)
arnés m, arreos mpl (b) (for baby, on parachute)
arnés m (c) (safety ~) arnés m de seguridad
harness² vt (a) (put harness on) ⟨horse⟩
enjaezar*, ponerle* los arreos or el arnés a (b)
(utilize) ⟨energy/resources⟩ aprovechar, utilizar*
harp /hɑːrp ‖ hɑːp/ n arpa f;
■ **harp on** [v + adv] (colloq) **to ~ on ABOUT sth**
insistir SOBRE algo
harpoon¹ /hɑːr'puːn ‖ hɑː'puːn/ n arpón m
harpoon² vt arponear

harrowing /ˈhærəʊɪŋ/ adj ⟨experience⟩ angustioso, terrible; ⟨tale⟩ desgarrador

harry /ˈhæri/ vt **-ries, -rying, -ried (a)** (raid) ⟨enemy⟩ hostilizar* **(b)** (pester) hostigar*, acosar

harsh /hɑːrʃ ‖ hɑːʃ/ adj ⟨punishment⟩ duro, severo; ⟨words/conditions⟩ duro; ⟨light⟩ fuerte; ⟨climate⟩ riguroso; ⟨contrast⟩ violento; ⟨color⟩ chillón; ⟨sound⟩ discordante; ⟨tone/texture⟩ áspero

harshly /ˈhɑːrʃli ‖ ˈhɑːʃli/ adv ⟨judge/punish/speak⟩ severamente, con severidad

harvest¹ /ˈhɑːrvəst ‖ ˈhɑːvɪst/ n **(a)** (of grain) cosecha f, siega f; (of fruit, vegetables) cosecha f, recolección f; (of grapes) vendimia f **(b)** (yield) cosecha f

harvest² vt ⟨crop/wheat⟩ cosechar; ⟨grapes⟩ vendimiar; ⟨field⟩ realizar* la cosecha en

harvester /ˈhɑːrvəstər ‖ ˈhɑːvɪstə(r)/ n **(a)** (machine) cosechadora f **(b)** (person) segador, -dora m,f

has /hæz, weak form həz, əz/ 3rd pers sing pres of HAVE

has-been /ˈhæzbɪn ‖ ˈhæzbiːn/ n (colloq & pej) nombre m del pasado

hash /hæʃ/ n **(a)** (Culin) plato de carne y verduras picadas y doradas **(b)** (muddle): **to make a ~ of sth** (colloq) hacer* algo muy mal

hash browns pl n (AmE colloq) papas y cebolla doradas en la sartén

hashish /ˈhæʃiːʃ/ n hachís m

hasn't /ˈhæznt/ = **has not**

hassle¹ /ˈhæsəl/ n (colloq) lío m (fam), rollo m (fam)

hassle² vt (colloq) fastidiar, jorobar (fam)

haste /heɪst/ n prisa f, apuro m (AmL)

hasten /ˈheɪsn/ vt ⟨process⟩ acelerar; ⟨defeat/death⟩ adelantar
■ ~ vi apresurarse, apurarse (AmL)

hastily /ˈheɪstəli ‖ ˈheɪstɪli/ adv **(a)** (quickly) ⟨built/thought up⟩ a toda prisa, apresuradamente **(b)** (rashly) ⟨speak/act⟩ con precipitación, precipitadamente

hasty /ˈheɪsti/ adj **-tier, -tiest (a)** (quick) ⟨glance/meal⟩ rápido **(b)** (rash) ⟨move/decision/judgment⟩ precipitado; **I think you're being rather ~** creo que te precipitas

hat /hæt/ n sombrero m

hatch¹ /hætʃ/ vt **(a)** ⟨egg⟩ incubar **(b)** **~ (out)** ⟨chick⟩ empollar **(c)** (devise) (pej) ⟨plot/scheme⟩ tramar, urdir
■ ~ vi **(a)** ⟨egg⟩ romperse* **(b)** **~ (out)** ⟨chick⟩ salir* del cascarón, nacer*

hatch² n **(a)** (opening, cover) trampilla f; (Aviat, Naut) escotilla f **(b)** (serving ~) ventanilla f (que comunica cocina y comedor)

hatchback /ˈhætʃbæk/ n (car) coche m con tres/cinco puertas; (door) puerta f trasera

hatchet /ˈhætʃət ‖ ˈhætʃɪt/ n hacha f‡, hachuela f; **to bury the ~** enterrar* el hacha de guerra

hate¹ /heɪt/ vt odiar, detestar

hate² n **(a)** (hatred) odio m **(b)** (object of hatred) ▶ PET² B

hatred /ˈheɪtrəd ‖ ˈheɪtrɪd/ n odio m

hat trick n: **to score a ~ ~** marcar* tres goles (or tantos etc) en un partido

haughty /ˈhɔːti/ adj **-tier, -tiest** altivo, altanero

haul¹ /hɔːl/ vt **(a)** (drag) ⟨logs/load⟩ llevar arrastrando; **the fishermen ~ed in their nets** los pescadores cobraron las redes **(b)** (Transp) transportar

haul² n **1** (catch — of fish) redada f; (— of stolen goods) botín m **2** (distance) (Transp) recorrido m, trayecto m

haulage /ˈhɔːlɪdʒ/ n **(a)** (activity) transporte m; (before n) **~ contractor** transportista mf **(b)** (charge) (gastos mpl de) transporte m

hauler /ˈhɔːlər ‖ ˈhɔːlə(r)/, (BrE) **haulier** /ˈhɔːljə(r)/ n (person) transportista mf; (business) empresa f de transportes

haunch /hɔːntʃ/ n (usu pl) (of animal) anca f‡; (of horse) grupa f, anca f‡; (of person) cadera f

haunt¹ /hɔːnt/ vt ⟨ghost⟩ rondar; «memory/idea» perseguir*

haunt² n: **we went to all her old ~s** fuimos a todos los sitios a los que solía ir

haunted /ˈhɔːntəd ‖ ˈhɔːntɪd/ adj ⟨house⟩ embrujado; ⟨look⟩ angustiado

haunting /ˈhɔːntɪŋ/ adj evocador e inquietante

Havana /həˈvænə/ n La Habana

have /hæv, weak forms həv, əv/ (3rd pers sing pres **has**; past & past p **had**) vt
I 1 (possess) tener*; **I ~ o** (esp BrE) **I've got two cats** tengo dos gatos
2 (hold, have at one's disposal) tener*; **can I ~ a sheet of paper?** ¿me das una hoja de papel?; **I've (got) a lot to do** tengo mucho que hacer
3 (a) (receive) ⟨letter/news⟩ tener*, recibir; **to ~ had it** (colloq): **I've had it** (I'm in trouble) estoy frito (AmL), me la he cargado (Esp fam); (I've lost my chance) la he fastidiado (fam); **to ~ it in for sb** (colloq) tenerle* manía or tirria a algn (fam) **(b)** (obtain) conseguir*; **they were the only seats to be had** eran los únicos asientos que había
4 (consume) ⟨steak/spaghetti⟩ comer, tomar (Esp); ⟨champagne/beer⟩ tomar; ⟨cigarette⟩ fumar(se); **to ~ something to eat/drink** comer/beber algo; **to ~ breakfast** desayunar; **to ~ lunch** almorzar* or (esp Esp, Méx) comer; **to ~ dinner** cenar, comer (AmL)
5 (a) (experience, undergo) ⟨accident⟩ tener*; **~ a nice day!** ¡adiós! ¡que le (or te etc) vaya bien!; **we had a very pleasant evening** pasamos una noche muy agradable; **she had a heart attack** le dio un ataque al corazón **(b)** (organize) ⟨party⟩ hacer*, dar*; ⟨meeting⟩ tener* **(c)** (suffer from) ⟨cancer/diabetes/flu⟩ tener*; **to ~ a cold** estar* resfriado
6 (give birth to) ⟨baby⟩ tener*
7 (colloq) (swindle, dupe): **you've been had!** ¡te han timado or engañado!
II 1 (causative use): **we'll ~ it clean in no time** enseguida lo limpiamos or lo dejamos limpio; **he had them all in tears** los hizo llorar a todos; **you had me worried** me tenías preocupado; **to ~ sth +** PAST P: **we had it repaired** lo hicimos arreglar, lo mandamos (a) arreglar (AmL); **to ~ one's hair cut** cortarse el pelo
2 (indicating what happens to sb): **to have sth +** PAST P: **he had his bicycle stolen** le robaron la bicicleta
3 (a) (allow) (with neg) tolerar, consentir*; **I**

won't ~ **it!** ¡no lo consentiré *or* toleraré! **(b)** (accept, believe) aceptar, creer*; **she wouldn't** ~ **it** no lo quiso aceptar *or* creer

4 (indicating state, position) tener*; **I had the radio on** tenía la radio puesta

■ ~ *v aux*

I 1 (*used to form perfect tenses*) haber*; **I** ~/**had seen her** la he/había visto; ~ **you been waiting long?** ¿hace mucho que esperas?; **if I'd known that ...** si hubiera sabido que ...; **when he had finished, she ...** cuando terminó *or* (liter) cuando hubo terminado, ella ...

2 **(a)** (in tags): **you've met Joe,** ~**n't you?** conoces a Joe ¿no? *or* ¿no es cierto? *or* ¿no es verdad?; **you** ~**n't lost the key,** ~ **you?** ¡no habrás perdido la llave ...! **(b)** (elliptical use): **you may** ~ **forgiven him, but I** ~**n't** puede que tú lo hayas perdonado, pero yo no; **the clock has stopped — so it has!** el reloj se ha parado — ¡es verdad! *or* ¡es cierto!; **you've forgotten something** ~ **I?** ¿te has olvidado de algo — ¿sí?

II (expressing obligation): **to** ~ **to** + INF tener* QUE + INF; **you don't** ~ **to be an expert to realize that** no hay que *or* no se necesita ser un experto para darse cuenta de eso

■ **have back** 1 [*v + o + adv, v + adv + o*] (receive back): **can I** ~ **the ring back?** ¿me devuelves el anillo?

2 [*v + o + adv*] ⟨*guests*⟩ **to** ~ **sb back** (invite again) volver* a invitar a algn; (reciprocate invitation) devolverle* a algn una invitación

■ **have on** [*v + o + adv*] (tease) (colloq) **to** ~ **sb on** tomarle el pelo a algn (fam)

■ **have out** [*v + o + adv*] **(a)** (have removed): **to** ~ **a tooth out** sacarse* una muela; **she had her tonsils out** la operaron de las amígdalas **(b)** (discuss forcefully) **to** ~ **it out WITH sb** ponerle* las cosas claras A algn

haven /ˈheɪvən/ *n* **(a)** (refuge) refugio *m* **(b)** (port) (liter) puerto *m*

haven't /ˈhævənt/ = **have not**

haversack /ˈhævɑrsæk ‖ˈhævəsæk/ *n* mochila *f*, morral *m*

haves /hævz/ *pl n* **the** ~ **and the have-nots** los ricos y los pobres *or* los desposeídos

havoc /ˈhævək/ *n*: **the accident caused** ~ el accidente creó gran confusión; **the children created** ~ los niños armaron un lío tremendo (fam); **to play** ~ **with sth** trastocar* *or* desbaratar algo

Hawaii /həˈwaɪiː/ *n* Hawai *m*

Hawaiian /həˈwaɪən/ *adj* hawaiano

hawk¹ /hɔːk/ *n* halcón *m*

hawk² *vt* ⟨*goods/wares*⟩ vocear, pregonar

hawthorn /ˈhɔːθɔːrn ‖ˈhɔːθɔːn/ *n* espino *m*

hay /heɪ/ *n* heno *m*

hay: ~ **fever** *n* fiebre *f* del heno; ~**rick** /ˈherrɪk/ *n* almiar *m*; ~**seed** *n* (AmE sl) ▶ YOKEL; ~**stack** *n* almiar *m*; ~**wire** *adj* (colloq) (*pred*): **to go** ~**wire** «*person*» perder* la chaveta (fam); «*machine*» estropearse, descomponerse* (AmL)

hazard¹ /ˈhæzərd ‖ˈhæzəd/ *n* peligro *m*, riesgo *m*

hazard² *vt* (frml) ⟨*remark/question*⟩ aventurar; **to** ~ **a guess** aventurar una respuesta

hazard lights, (BrE also) **hazard warning lights** *pl n* (Auto) luces *fpl* de emergencia

hazardous /ˈhæzərdəs ‖ˈhæzədəs/ *adj* peligroso, arriesgado

haze /heɪz/ *n* (*no pl*) (due to humidity) neblina *f*, bruma *f*; (due to heat) calima *f*

hazel /ˈheɪzl/ *n* **(a)** (plant) avellano *m* **(b)** (wood) (madera *f* de) avellano *m* **(c)** (color) color *m* avellana; (*before n*) ⟨*eyes*⟩ color avellana *adj inv*

hazelnut /ˈheɪzlnʌt/ *n* avellana *f*

hazy /ˈheɪzi/ *adj* **hazier, haziest (a)** ⟨*day*⟩ (due to humidity) neblinoso, brumoso; (due to heat) de calima **(b)** ⟨*memory/idea/distinction*⟩ vago, confuso

he /hiː, *weak form* i/ *pron* él

■ **Note** Although *él* is given as the main translation of *he*, it is in practice used only for emphasis, or to avoid ambiguity: *he went to the theater* fue al teatro; *she went to the theater, he went to the cinema* ella fue al teatro y él fue al cine; *he did it* él lo hizo.

head¹ /hed/ *n* 1 (Anat) cabeza *f*; **a fine** ~ **of hair** una buena cabellera; **from** ~ **to foot** *o* **toe** de pies a cabeza, de arriba (a) abajo; ~ *over heels*: **she tripped and went** ~ **over heels down the steps** tropezó y cayó rodando escaleras abajo; **to be** ~ **over heels in love** estar* locamente enamorado; *to go to sb's* ~ subírsele a la cabeza a algn; *to make* ~ *or tail o* (AmE also) ~**s or tails of sth** entender* algo

2 (mind, brain) cabeza *f*; **I said the first thing that came into my** ~ dije lo primero que se me ocurrió; **she added it up in her** ~ hizo la suma mentalmente; **she has a good** ~ **for business** tiene cabeza para los negocios; **I've no** ~ **for heights** sufro de vértigo; **it never entered my** ~ **that ...** ni se me pasó por la cabeza que ...; *to keep/lose one's* ~ mantener*/perder* la calma

3 **(a)** (of nail, tack, pin) cabeza *f*; (of spear, arrow) punta *f*; (of hammer) cabeza *f*; (on beer) espuma *f* **(b)** (top end — of bed, table) cabecera *f*; (— of page, letter) encabezamiento *m*; (— of procession, line) cabeza *f*

4 **(a)** (chief) director, -tora *m,f*; ~ **of state** jefe, -fa *m,f* de Estado; **the** ~ **of the household** el/la cabeza de familia; (*before n*) ~ **waiter** maître *m*, capitán *m* de meseros (Méx) **(b)** (~ **teacher**) (esp BrE) director, -tora *m,f* (de colegio)

5 (person): **$15 per** ~ 15 dólares por cabeza *or* persona

6 (crisis): **to come to a** ~ hacer* crisis

7 **(a)** (magnetic device) (Audio, Comput) cabeza *f*, cabezal *m* **(b)** (of drill) cabezal *m*

8 (Geog) cabo *m*

head² *vt* 1 **(a)** ⟨*march/procession*⟩ encabezar*, ir* a la cabeza de **(b)** ⟨*revolt*⟩ acaudillar; ⟨*team*⟩ capitanear; ⟨*expedition/department*⟩ dirigir*

2 (direct) (+ *adv compl*) ⟨*vehicle/ship*⟩ dirigir*

3 (in soccer) ⟨*ball*⟩ cabecear

4 ⟨*page/chapter*⟩ encabezar*

■ ~ *vi*: **to** ~ **west/north** ir* en dirección oeste/norte

■ **head for** [*v + prep + o*] **(a)** (go toward) «*ship*» ir* con rumbo a; **to** ~ **for home** ponerse* en camino a casa; **the car was** ~**ing straight for me** el coche venía derecho hacia mí **(b)** (be in danger of): **to be** ~**ed** *o* ~**ing for sth** ir* camino de algo

■ **head off** 1 [*v + adv*] (set out) salir*

2 [*v + o + adv, v + adv + o*] **(a)** (get in front of) atajar, cortarle el paso a **(b)** (prevent, forestall) ⟨*criticism/threat*⟩ prevenir*

head: ∼**ache** n dolor m de cabeza; **I've got a** ∼**ache** tengo dolor de cabeza, me duele la cabeza; ∼**band** n cinta f del pelo, vincha f (AmS), huincha f (Bol, Chi, Per); ∼**board** n cabecera f; ∼**dress** n tocado m

headed /'hedəd ‖'hedɪd/ adj ⟨notepaper⟩ con membrete, membretado, membreteado (Andes)

header /'hedər ‖'hedə(r)/ n (in soccer) cabezazo m

head: ∼**first** /'hed'fɜːrst ‖,hed'fɜːst/ adv (a) (with head foremost) de cabeza (b) (over-hastily) precipitadamente; ∼**hunt** vt ofrecerle* un puesto a; ∼**hunter** n (Busn) cazatalentos m

heading /'hedɪŋ/ n (title) encabezamiento m, título m, acápite m (AmL); (letterhead) membrete m

head: ∼**lamp** n faro m; ∼**land** /'hedlənd/ n cabo m; ∼**light** n faro m; ∼**line** n titular m; **the news** ∼**lines** el resumen informativo or de noticias; ∼**long** adv (a) (hastily) precipitadamente (b) (with head foremost) de cabeza; ∼**master** /'hed'mæstər ‖,hed'mɑːstə(r)/ n director m (de colegio); ∼**mistress** /'hed'mɪstrəs ‖,hed'mɪstrɪs/ n directora f (de colegio); ∼ **office** n (oficina f) central f; ∼**on** /'hed'ɑːn ‖,hed'ɒn/ adj ⟨crash/collision⟩ frontal, de frente; ∼**phones** pl n auriculares mpl, cascos mpl; ∼**quarters** /'hed'kwɔːrtərz ‖,hed'kwɔːtəz/ n (pl ∼**quarters**) (+ sing or pl vb) oficina f central; (Mil) cuartel m general; ∼**rest** n reposacabezas m, apoyacabezas m; ∼**room** n altura f

heads /hedz/ adv (on coin) cara f, águila f‡ (Méx); ∼ **or tails?** ¿cara o cruz, ¿águila o sol? (Méx), ¿cara o sello? (Andes, Ven), ¿cara o ceca? (Arg)

head: ∼**scarf** n pañuelo m (de cabeza); ∼**set** n auriculares mpl, cascos mpl; ∼**stand** n: **to do a** ∼**stand** pararse de cabeza (AmL), hacer* el pino (Esp); ∼ **start** n ventaja f; ∼**stone** n lápida f; ∼**strong** adj testarudo, obstinado; ∼**teacher** /'hed'tiːtʃər ‖,hed'tiːtʃə(r)/ n (BrE) director, -tora m,f (de colegio); ∼**way** n: **to make** ∼**way** hacer* progresos, avanzar*

heady /'hedi/ adj **-dier, -diest** ⟨scent⟩ embriagador; ⟨wine⟩ que se sube a la cabeza

heal /hiːl/ vt curar
■ ∼ vi cicatrizar*, cerrarse*

health /helθ/ n salud f; **to be in good/poor** ∼ estar* bien/mal de salud; **your (good)** ∼! (proposing a toast) ¡salud!; (before n) ⟨policy/ services⟩ sanitario, de salud pública; ⟨inspector/ regulations⟩ de sanidad; ∼ **hazard** riesgo m or peligro m para la salud

health: ∼ **care** n asistencia f sanitaria or médica; ∼ **centre** n (BrE) centro m médico or de salud; ∼ **food** n alimentos mpl naturales; **insurance** n seguro m de enfermedad; ∼ **service** n (in UK) ▶ NATIONAL HEALTH (SERVICE)

healthy /'helθi/ adj **-thier, -thiest** [1] (a) (in good health) ⟨person/animal/complexion⟩ sano; **she has a** ∼ **appetite** tiene buen apetito (b) (promoting

good health) ⟨diet/living/environment⟩ sano, saludable (c) (sound) ⟨respect⟩ sano [2] ⟨economy/ finances⟩ próspero

heap¹ /hiːp/ n (a) (pile) montón m, pila f (b) (car) (colloq) cacharro m (fam)

heap² vt (a) (make pile) amontonar, apilar (b) (supply liberally): **she** ∼**ed his plate with food** le llenó el plato de comida; **a** ∼**ing** (AmE) o (BrE) ∼**ed spoonful** (Culin) una cucharada colmada

hear /hɪr ‖hɪə(r)/ ⟨past & past p **heard** /hɜːrd ‖hɜːd/⟩ vt [2] (get to know) oír*; **I've** ∼**d so much about you** me han hablado tanto de ti, he oído hablar tanto de ti; **he's very ill, I** ∼ me han dicho que está muy enfermo [3] (listen to) (a) ⟨lecture/broadcast/views⟩ escuchar, oír* (b) (Law) ⟨case⟩ ver*; ⟨charge⟩ oír*
■ ∼ vi [1] (perceive) oír*; ∼, ∼! ¡eso, eso!, ¡bien dicho! [2] (get news): **have you** ∼**d?** ¿te has enterado?; **to** ∼ ABOUT sth enterarse DE algo; **I haven't** ∼**d from them for months** hace meses que no sé nada de ellos or que no tengo noticias suyas
■ **hear of** [v + prep + o] (a) (encounter, come to know of): **I've** ∼**d of him** he oído hablar de él; **if you** ∼ **of anything interesting, let me know** si te enteras de algo interesante, me lo dices (b) (have news of) tener* noticias or saber* de (c) (allow): **I won't** ∼ **of it!** ¡ni hablar!
■ **hear out** [v + o + adv, v + adv + o] escuchar (hasta el final)

hearing /'hɪrɪŋ ‖'hɪərɪŋ/ n [1] (sense) oído m [2] (a) (consideration) **to give sb a** ∼ escuchar a algn (b) (Law) vista f

hearing aid n audífono m

hearsay /'hɪrseɪ ‖'hɪəseɪ/ n habladurías fpl

hearse /hɜːrs ‖hɜːs/ n coche m fúnebre

heart /hɑːrt ‖hɑːt/ n [1] (Anat) corazón m; (before n) ⟨disease⟩ del corazón, cardíaco; ⟨operation⟩ de(l) corazón [2] (seat of emotions): **to have a kind** ∼ tener* buen corazón, ser* de buen corazón; **to have sb's interests at** ∼ preocuparse por algn; **to learn/ know sth by** ∼ aprender/saber* algo de memoria; **my/her/his** ∼ **wasn't in it** lo hacía sin ganas; **to take sth to** ∼ tomarse algo a pecho [3] (courage, morale) ánimos mpl; **to lose** ∼ descorazonarse, desanimarse; **to take** ∼ animarse; **not to have the** ∼ **to do sth: I didn't have the** ∼ **to tell him** no tuve valor para decírselo [4] (a) (central part): **the** ∼ **of the city/country** el corazón or centro de la ciudad/del país; **the** ∼ **of the matter** el meollo del asunto (b) (of cabbage, lettuce) cogollo m [5] (Games) **hearts** (suit) (+ sing or pl vb) corazones mpl

heart: ∼**ache** n pena f, dolor m; ∼ **attack** n ataque m al corazón, infarto m; ∼**beat** n latido m (del corazón); ∼**break** n (a) (grief) congoja f, sufrimiento m (b) (cause of grief) desengaño m; ∼**breaking** adj desgarrador; ∼**broken** adj

⟨look/sobs⟩ desconsolado; **she was ∼broken when
he died** su muerte la dejó destrozada; **∼burn** n
ardor m de estómago; **∼felt** adj sincero

hearth /hɑːθ ‖hɑːθ/ n chimenea f, hogar m

heartily /'hɑːtḷi ‖'hɑːtɪli/ adv (a) (warmly)
⟨congratulate/greet⟩ efusivamente (b) (with
enthusiasm) ⟨laugh/eat⟩ con ganas

heartless /'hɑːtləs ‖'hɑːtlɪs/ adj ⟨person⟩ sin
corazón; ⟨refusal⟩ cruel

heart: ∼-shaped adj ⟨card/cake⟩ con forma de
corazón; ⟨face⟩ en forma de corazón; **∼-to-∼** n
(colloq) charla f íntima

hearty /'hɑːrti ‖'hɑːti/ adj **-tier, -tiest**
⟨person⟩ campechano; ⟨welcome⟩ caluroso;
⟨appetite⟩ bueno

heat¹ /hiːt/ n ⟨1⟩ **(a)** (warmth) calor m **(b)** (for
cooking) fuego m ⟨2⟩ **in the ∼ of the moment** en
un momento de enojo (or exaltación etc)
⟨3⟩ (estrus) celo m; **to be in** o (BrE) **on ∼** estar* en
celo ⟨4⟩ (Sport) (prueba) eliminatoria f

heat² vt calentar*; ⟨house⟩ calentar*,
calefaccionar*

■ **heat up** ⟨1⟩ [v + adv] calentarse* ⟨2⟩ [v + o +
adv, v + adv + o] calentar*

heated /'hiːtəd ‖'hiːtɪd/ adj **(a)** (warmed) ⟨pool⟩
climatizado; ⟨seat/rear window⟩ térmico **(b)**
(impassioned) ⟨argument⟩ acalorado; **to get ∼**
acalorarse

heater /'hiːtər ‖'hiːtə(r)/ n calentador m, estufa
f; (water ∼) calentador m (de agua)

heath /hiːθ/ n brezal m, monte m

heathen /'hiːðən/ n pagano, -na m,f

heather /'heðər ‖'heðə(r)/ n brezo m

heating /'hiːtɪŋ/ n calefacción f

heat wave n ola f de calor

heave¹ /hiːv/ vt ⟨1⟩ **(a)** (move with effort): **we ∼d
the box onto the shelf** con esfuerzo logramos
subir la caja al estante; **they ∼d it into place** lo
colocaron empujando/levantándolo **(b)** (throw)
(colloq) tirar ⟨2⟩ (utter): **to ∼ a sigh** suspirar

■ **∼** vi ⟨1⟩ (pull) tirar, jalar (AmL exc CS) ⟨2⟩ (rise and
fall): **his chest ∼d** respiraba agitadamente

heave² n (pull) tirón m, jalón m (AmL exc CS);
(push) empujón m

heaven /'hevən/ n cielo m; **(good) ∼s!** ¡Dios
mío!; **thank ∼** gracias a Dios

heavenly /'hevnli/ adj **(a)** (Relig) celestial **(b)**
(Astron) celeste **(c)** (superb) (colloq) divino (fam)

heavily /'hevəli ‖'hevɪli/ adv ⟨1⟩ **(a)** ⟨tread/
fall⟩ pesadamente; **to be ∼ built** ser* corpulento;
to breathe ∼ jadear **(b)** (thickly) ⟨underlined⟩ con
trazo grueso; **she was ∼ made-up** iba muy
maquillada ⟨2⟩ **(a)** (copiously) ⟨rain/snow⟩ mucho
(b) (immoderately) ⟨drink/smoke⟩ en exceso **(c)**
(greatly): **to borrow ∼** contraer* considerables
deudas; **∼ pregnant** en avanzado estado de
gravidez (frml) or (period) de gestación

heavy¹ /'hevi/ adj **-vier, -viest** ⟨1⟩ **(a)**
(weighty) ⟨load/suitcase/weight⟩ pesado; ⟨fabric/
garment⟩ grueso, pesado; ⟨saucepan⟩ de fondo
grueso; ⟨boots⟩ fuerte; ⟨work⟩ pesado; **it's very ∼**
es muy pesado, pesa mucho **(b)** (large-scale)
(before n) ⟨artillery/machinery⟩ pesado ⟨2⟩ **(a)**
(ponderous) ⟨tread/footstep/fall⟩ pesado; ⟨thud⟩
sordo **(b)** ⟨features⟩ tosco; ⟨irony⟩ poco sutil
⟨3⟩ **(a)** (oppressive) ⟨clouds/sky⟩ pesado **(b)** (loud)
⟨sigh⟩ profundo ⟨4⟩ **(a)** (bigger than usual)

⟨expenditure⟩ cuantioso **(b)** (intense) ⟨book⟩
pesado, denso; ⟨rain⟩ fuerte; ⟨traffic⟩ denso;
⟨schedule⟩ apretado; **to be a ∼ drinker/smoker**
beber/fumar mucho **(c)** (severe) ⟨sentence⟩ severo;
⟨casualties⟩ numeroso; ⟨blow⟩ duro, fuerte

heavy² n (pl **-vies**) (colloq) matón m (fam)

heavy: ∼ cream n (AmE) crema f doble, nata f
para montar (Esp), doble crema f (Méx); **∼-duty**
/'hevi'duːti ‖,hevi'djuːti/ adj ⟨material/sacks⟩
muy resistente; ⟨machine⟩ para uso industrial;
⟨clothing/overalls⟩ de trabajo; **∼-handed**
/'hevi'hændəd ‖,hevi'hændid/ adj torpe; **∼
metal** n (Mus) heavy m (metal), rock m duro

heavyweight¹ /'heviweit/ n (Sport) peso mf
pesado; **a political ∼** un peso pesado de la
política

heavyweight² adj **(a)** (Sport) (before n)
⟨boxer/wrestler⟩ de la categoría de los pesos
pesados; ⟨title⟩ de los pesos pesados **(b)** (Tex)
⟨cotton/denim⟩ grueso y resistente

Hebrew¹ /'hiːbruː/ adj hebreo

Hebrew² n hebreo m

Hebrides /'hebrədiːz ‖'hebrɪdiːz/ pl n **the ∼**
las (islas) Hébridas

heck /hek/ n (colloq & euph): **∼!** ¡caray! (fam &
euf); **what the ∼!** ¡qué diablos! (fam)

heckle /'hekḷ/ vt interrumpir (con preguntas o
comentarios molestos)

heckler /'heklər ‖'heklə(r)/ n: persona que
interrumpe a un orador para molestar

hectare /'hekter ‖'hekteə(r)/ n hectárea f

hectic /'hektɪk/ adj ⟨day/week⟩ ajetreado,
agitado; ⟨journey/pace⟩ agotador; ⟨activity⟩
frenético, febril

he'd /hiːd/ **(a)** = **he had (b)** = **he would**

hedge¹ /hedʒ/ n seto m (verde o vivo)

hedge² vt ⟨field/garden⟩ cercar* (con seto)
■ **∼** vi (evade the issue) dar* rodeos

hedgehog /'hedʒhɒɡ ‖'hedʒhɒɡ/ n erizo m

hedgerow /'hedʒrəʊ/ n (usu pl) seto m (verde
or vivo)

hedonism /'hiːdṇɪzəm ‖'hiːdənɪzəm/ n
hedonismo m

hedonist /'hiːdṇəst ‖'hiːdənɪst/ n hedonista mf

heed¹ /hiːd/ n: **to take ∼** tener* cuidado

heed² vt prestar atención a, hacer* caso de

heedless /'hiːdləs ‖'hiːdlɪs/ adj (frml) **∼ of**
sth: ∼ of the danger ... haciendo caso omiso del
peligro ...

heel¹ /hiːl/ n **(a)** (Anat) talón m **(b)** (of shoe)
tacón m, taco m (CS)

heel² vt ⟨shoes⟩ ponerles* tacones or (CS) tacos
nuevos a; ⟨high-heeled shoes⟩ ponerles* tapas or
(Chi) tapillas a

hefty /'hefti/ adj **-tier, -tiest** (colloq) **(a)** (large
and heavy) ⟨person⟩ robusto, fornido, corpulento;
⟨load/case⟩ pesado **(b)** (strong) fuerte **(c)**
(substantial) ⟨price/salary⟩ alto; ⟨fine⟩ considerable

heifer /'hefər ‖'hefə(r)/ n vaquilla f, novilla f

height /hait/ n ⟨1⟩ **(a)** (tallness — of object) altura
f; (— of person) estatura f, talla f; **what ∼ are you?**
¿cuánto mides? **(b)** (Aviat) altura f; **to gain/lose ∼**
ganar/perder* altura
⟨2⟩ (peak) (no pl): **to be at the ∼ of one's power**
estar* en la cima or en la cumbre or en la

cúspide de su (or mi etc) poder; **at the ~ of the
season** en plena temporada; **it's the ~ of
stupidity** es el colmo de la estupidez
[3] **heights** pl (a) (high ground) cerros mpl,
cumbres fpl (b) **to be afraid of ~s** sufrir de
vértigo

heighten /'haɪtn/ vt ⟨effect/impression⟩
destacar*, realzar*; ⟨suspense/admiration/respect⟩
aumentar

heinous /'heməs/ adj (fml) atroz, abyecto

heir /er ‖eə(r)/ n heredero, -ra m,f; **~ TO sth** (to
fortune, title) heredero DE algo; (to throne) heredero A
algo

heiress /'erəs ‖'eəres/ n heredera f

heirloom /'erluːm ‖'eəluːm/ n reliquia f

heist /haɪst/ n (AmE colloq) golpe m (fam), atraco
m

held /held/ past & past p of HOLD¹

helicopter /'helɪkɑːptər ‖'helɪkɒptə(r)/ n
helicóptero m

heliport /'helɪpɔːrt ‖'helɪpɔːt/ n helipuerto m

helium /'hiːliəm/ n helio m

hell /hel/ n [1] (Relig) infierno m; **three months of
sheer ~** tres meses infernales; **to make sb's life
~** (colloq) hacerle* la vida imposible a algn
[2] (colloq) (as intensifier): **how/why the ~ ...?**
¿cómo/por qué demonios or diablos ...? (fam); **he's
a o one ~ of a guy** un tipo sensacional (fam);
to run like ~ correr como un loco (fam); **oh, well,
what the ~!** bueno ¡qué importa! (fam)

he'll /hiːl/ (a) = **he will** (b) = **he shall**

hello /hə'ləʊ/ interj (a) (greeting) ¡hola! (b)
(answering the telephone) sí, aló (AmS), diga or
dígame (Esp), bueno (Méx), olá (RPl)

helm /helm/ n (Naut) timón m

helmet /'helmət ‖'helmɪt/ n (headgear) casco m;
(armor) yelmo m

help¹ /help/ vt [1] (assist) ayudar; **to ~ sb (to) +
INF** ayudar a algn A + INF
[2] (avoid, prevent) (usu neg or interrog): **I can't ~ it**
no lo puedo remediar; **they can't ~ being poor** no
tienen la culpa de ser pobres
■ **~** vi ⟨person/remark⟩ ayudar; ⟨tool⟩ servir*
■ v refl **to ~ oneself** [1] (assist) ayudarse (a sí
mismo)
[2] (resist impulse) (usu neg) controlarse; **I can't ~
myself** no me puedo controlar
[3] (take) **to ~ oneself (TO sth)** ⟨to food/a drink⟩
servirse* (algo)
■ **help out** [1] [v + o + adv, v + adv + o] ayudar
[2] [v + adv] ayudar

help² n (a) (rescue) ayuda f; (as interj) **~!**
¡socorro!, ¡auxilio! (b) (assistance) ayuda f; **can I
be of (any) ~ to you?** ¿la/lo puedo ayudar (en
algo)?

help desk n servicio m de asistencia, ayuda f
al usuario

helper /'helpər ‖'helpə(r)/ n ayudante, -ta m,f

helpful /'helpfəl/ adj (a) (obliging) ⟨person/
attitude⟩ servicial, amable (b) (useful) ⟨advice⟩
útil

helping /'helpɪŋ/ n porción f (esp AmL), ración f
(esp Esp)

helpless /'helpləs ‖'helplɪs/ adj (a)
(defenseless) ⟨prey/victim⟩ indefenso (b) (powerless)

⟨look/expression⟩ de impotencia; **to be ~ to + INF**
ser* incapaz DE + INF (c) (incapacitated): **to leave sb
~** dejar a algn sin recursos

helplessly /'helpləsli ‖'helplɪsli/ adv ⟨look on/
stand by⟩ sin poder hacer nada; ⟨struggle/try⟩ en
vano, inútilmente

helpline /'helplaɪn/ n servicio m telefónico de
asistencia, línea f directa

helter-skelter /'heltər'skeltər
‖,heltə'skeltə(r)/ adv atropelladamente, a la
desbanda

hem /hem/ n dobladillo m, basta f (Chi)
■ **hem in: -mm-** [v + o + adv, v + adv + o]
encerrar*

hemisphere /'heməsfɪr ‖'hemɪsfɪə(r)/ n
(Geog) hemisferio m

hemline /'hemlaɪn/ n bajo m, ruedo m

hemoglobin, (BrE) **haemoglobin**
/'hiːmə,gləʊbən ‖,hiːmə'gləʊbɪn/ n hemoglobina f

hemophilia, (BrE) **haemophilia**
/'hiːmə'fɪliə/ n hemofilia f

hemophiliac, (BrE) **haemophiliac**
/,hiːmə'fɪliæk/ n hemofílico, -ca m,f

hemorrhage¹, (BrE) **haemorrhage**
/'hemərɪdʒ/ n (Med) hemorragia f

hemorrhage², (BrE) **haemorrhage** vi
«patient» tener* or (fml) sufrir una hemorragia;
«wound/blood vessel» sangrar mucho

hemorrhoids, (BrE) **haemorrhoids**
/'hemərɔɪdz/ pl n hemorroides fpl, almorranas
fpl

hemp /hemp/ n (fiber) cáñamo m; (drug)
marihuana f, cannabis m; (plant) cannabis m,
cáñamo m índico or de la India

hen /hen/ n (chicken) gallina f; (female bird)
hembra f

hence /hens/ adv [1] (a) (that is the reason for) de
ahí (b) (therefore) por lo tanto, por consiguiente
[2] (from now) (frml): **a few years ~** dentro de
algunos años

henceforth /'hens'fɔːrθ ‖,hens'fɔːθ/ adv (liter)
a partir de ahora, de ahora en adelante

henchman /'hentʃmən/ n (pl **-men** /-mən/)
secuaz m

henna /'henə/ n henna f

hen: ~ night, hen party n (a) (all-female
celebration) fiesta f de mujeres (b) (before wedding)
despedida f de soltera; **~pecked** /'henpekt/ adj
(colloq): **a ~pecked husband** un marido dominado
por su mujer, un mandilón (Méx fam), un
calzonazos (Esp fam)

hepatitis /'hepə'taɪtəs ‖,hepə'taɪtɪs/ n
hepatitis f

her¹ /hɜːr ‖hɜː(r), weak form ər ‖ə(r)/ pron
[1] (a) (as direct object) la; **I can't stand ~** no la
soporto; **call ~** llámala (b) (as indirect object) le;
(with direct object pronoun present) se; **I wrote ~ a
letter** le escribí una carta (c) (after preposition) ella
[2] (emphatic use) ella; **it's ~** es ella

her² adj

■ **Note** The translation su agrees in number with the
noun which it modifies: her is translated by su, sus,
according to what follows: her father/mother su padre/
madre; her books/magazines sus libros/revistas.

(sing) su; (pl) sus; **she took ~ hat off** se quitó el
sombrero; **she broke ~ arm** se rompió el brazo

herald¹ /'herəld/ n (Hist) heraldo m

herald² vt anunciar

heraldry /'herəldri/ n heráldica f

herb /ɜːrb, 'hɜːrb ‖hɜːb/ n hierba f, yuyo m (Per, RPl)

herbal /'ɜːrbəl, 'hɜːrbəl‖'hɜːbəl/ adj ⟨shampoo⟩ de hierbas; ~ **tea** (esp BrE) ▶ HERB TEA

herb tea n infusión f, agua f‡ (AmC, Andes), té m de yuyos (Per, RPl)

herd¹ /hɜːrd ‖hɜːd/ n (a) (of cattle) manada f, vacada f; (of goats) rebaño m; (of pigs) piara f, manada f; (of wild animals) manada f (b) (of people) (pej) tropel m

herd² vt ⟨animals⟩ arrear, arriar (RPl); **the refugees were ~ed into trucks** metieron a los refugiados en camiones como si fueran ganado

here /hɪr ‖hɪə(r)/ adv **1** (a) (at, to this place) aquí, acá (esp AmL); (less precise) acá (b) (in phrases) here and there aquí y allá; here, there and everywhere por todas partes **2** (calling attention to sth, sb): ~'s £20 toma 20 libras; ~ he is aquí está **3** (a) (present): he isn't ~ today hoy no está (b) (arrived): they're ~! ¡ya llegaron!, ¡ya están aquí! **4** (as interj): ~, let me do it trae, deja que lo haga yo

hereabouts /'hɪrə'baʊts ‖,hɪərə'baʊts/ adv por aquí, por acá

hereafter /,hɪr'æftər ‖,hɪər'ɑːftə(r)/ adv (frml: used esp in legal texts) (from now on) de aquí en adelante; (in the future) en el futuro, en lo sucesivo

hereditary /hə'redəteri ‖hɪ'redɪtri/ adj hereditario

heredity /hə'redəti ‖hɪ'redəti/ n herencia f

heresy /'herəsi/ n (pl -sies) herejía f

heretic /'herətɪk/ n hereje mf

heritage /'herətɪdʒ ‖'herɪtɪdʒ/ n (no pl) patrimonio m

hermetically /hɜːr'metɪkli ‖hɜː'metɪkli/ adv: ~ **sealed** herméticamente cerrado

hermit /'hɜːrmət ‖'hɜːmɪt/ n ermitaño, -ña m,f, eremita mf

hernia /'hɜːrniə ‖'hɜːnɪə/ n hernia f

hero /'hiːrəʊ ‖'hɪərəʊ/ n (pl **heroes**) héroe m; (of novel, film) protagonista mf

heroic /hɪ'rəʊɪk/ adj heroico

heroin/'herəʊɪn/ n heroína f; (before n) ~ **addict** heroinómano, -na m,f

heroine /'herəʊɪn/ n (brave, admirable woman) heroína f; (of novel, film) protagonista f

heroism /'herəʊɪzəm/ n heroísmo m

heron /'herən/ n garza f (real)

hero worship n adoración f ⟨de alguien a quien se tiene como ídolo⟩

herpes /'hɜːrpiːz ‖'hɜːpiːz/ n herpes m, herpe f

herring /'herɪŋ/ n (pl **herrings** or **herring**) arenque m

hers /hɜːrz ‖hɜːz/ pron

■ **Note** The translation suyo reflects the gender and number of the noun it is standing for; hers is translated by el suyo, la suya, los suyos, las suyas, depending on what is being referred to.

(sing) suyo, -ya; (pl) suyos, -yas, de ella; **they're** ~ son suyos/suyas, son de ella; ~ **is blue** el suyo/la suya es azul, el/la de ella es azul; **a friend of** ~ un amigo suyo or de ella

herself /hər'self ‖hə'self/ pron (a) (reflexive): **she cut** ~ se cortó; **she bought** ~ **a hat** se compró un sombrero; **she only thinks of** ~ solo piensa en sí misma; **by** ~ sola; **she was talking to** ~ estaba hablando sola (b) (emphatic use) ella misma; **she told me so** ~ me lo dijo ella misma (c) (normal self): **she's not** ~ no es la de siempre

he's /hiːz/ (a) = **he is** (b) = **he has**

hesitant /'hezətənt ‖'hezɪtənt/ adj ⟨voice⟩ vacilante; ⟨manner⟩ inseguro; ⟨steps⟩ vacilante; **he seemed a little** ~ parecía un poco indeciso

hesitate /'hezəteɪt ‖'hezɪteɪt/ vi vacilar, titubear

hesitation /heza'teɪʃən ‖,hezɪ'teɪʃən/ n vacilación f

heterosexual¹ /'hetərəʊ'sekʃuəl/ adj heterosexual

heterosexual² n heterosexual mf

heterosexuality /'hetərəʊ'sekʃu'æləti/ n heterosexualidad f

hew /hjuː/ vt (past **hewed**; past p **hewed** or **hewn** /hjuːn/) (extract) extraer*; (fashion) ⟨stone⟩ labrar

hexagon /'heksəgɑːn ‖'heksəgən/ n hexágono m

hey /heɪ/ interj (a) (calling attention) ¡eh! (b) (expressing dismay, protest, indignation) ¡oye!, ¡oiga(n)!

heyday /'heɪdeɪ/ n apogeo m, auge m; **in his** ~ en sus buenos tiempos

HGV n (BrE) (= **heavy goods vehicle**) vehículo m pesado

hi /haɪ/ interj (colloq) ¡hola! (fam)

HI = Hawaii

hiatus /haɪ'eɪtəs/ n (pl -**tuses**) (frml) paréntesis m (frml)

hibernate /'haɪbərneɪt ‖'haɪbəneɪt/ vi hibernar

hibernation /'haɪbər'neɪʃən ‖,haɪbə'neɪʃən/ n hibernación f; **to go into** ~ entrar en estado de hibernación

hiccough /'hɪkʌp/ n/vi ▶ HICCUP¹,²

hiccup¹ /'hɪkʌp/ n (a) (hipo) hipo m; **to have (the)** ~**s** tener* hipo (b) (brief interruption) dificultad f

hiccup² vi, (BrE also) -**pp**- hipar

hick /hɪk/ n (AmE colloq & pej) pueblerino, -na m,f, paleto, -ta m,f (Esp fam & pey), pajuerano, -na m,f (RPl fam & pey)

hid /hɪd/ (a) past of HIDE¹ (b) (arch) past p of HIDE¹

hidden¹ /'hɪdn̩/ adj ⟨entrance/camera/reserves⟩ oculto; ⟨cost⟩ no aparente

hidden² past p of HIDE¹

hide¹ /haɪd/ (past **hid** /hɪd/; past p **hidden** or (arch) **hid**) vt (a) (conceal) esconder; **she hid the money from the police** escondió el dinero para que no lo encontrara la policía; **to** ~ **oneself** esconderse (b) (keep secret) ⟨feelings/thoughts⟩ ocultar; **to** ~ **sth FROM sb** ocultarle algo A algn (c) (mask, screen) tapar

■ ~ vi esconderse

■ **hide away 1** [v + adv] esconderse **2** [v + o + adv, v + adv + o] esconder

hide² n (raw) piel f; (tanned) cuero m

hide: hide-and-seek~-**and-seek** /'haɪdn̩'siːk/, (AmE & Scot also) ~-**and-go-seek** /'haɪdŋgəʊ'siːk/ n: **to play** ~-**and-seek** jugar* al ⸱⸱⸱⸢⸣

escondite, jugar* a las escondidas (AmL);
~away n **(a)** (hiding place) (AmE) escondite m **(b)**
(secluded spot) rincón m

hideous /'hɪdiəs/ adj ⟨monster/sight⟩
horroroso, horrible; ⟨crime/fate⟩ espantoso;
⟨color/furniture⟩ (colloq) horrendo, espantoso

hideout /'haɪdaʊt/ n guarida f

hiding /'haɪdɪŋ/ n **1** (concealment): **to be in ~/go
into ~** estar* escondido/esconderse; ⟨before n⟩ **~
place** escondite m, escondrijo m **2** (beating)
(colloq) paliza f, tunda f

hierarchy /'haɪərɑːrki ‖ 'haɪərɑːki/ n ⟨pl
-chies⟩ jerarquía f

hieroglyphics /ˌhaɪərə'glɪfɪks/ pl n
jeroglíficos mpl

hi-fi /'haɪfaɪ/ n **(a)** (equipment) alta fidelidad f **(b)**
(set) equipo m de alta fidelidad, hi-fi m

higgledy-piggledy /ˌhɪgəldi'pɪgəldi/ adv
(colloq) sin orden ni concierto, de cualquier
manera

high¹ /haɪ/ adj **-er, -est** **1** **(a)** (tall) ⟨wall/
mountain⟩ alto; **how ~ is it?** ¿qué altura tiene?;
the tower is 40 m ~ la torre tiene 40 m de alto or
de altura **(b)** (high up) ⟨window/balcony⟩ alto;
⟨plateau⟩ elevado; **at a ~ altitude** a gran altitud;
~ cheekbones pómulos mpl salientes **(c)** (in
status) ⟨office/rank⟩ alto; **he has friends in ~
places** tiene amigos muy bien situados; **~
society** la alta sociedad **(d)** (morally, ethically)
⟨ideals/principles⟩ elevado **(e)** (in pitch) ⟨voice⟩
agudo; ⟨note⟩ alto
2 (greater than usual) ⟨temperature/speed/pressure⟩
alto; ⟨wind⟩ fuerte; **unemployment is very ~** hay
mucho desempleo; **to be ~ in vitamins** ser* rico
en vitaminas
3 (climactic) culminante; **the ~ point** el punto
culminante
4 **(a)** (happy, excited): **she was in ~ spirits** estaba
muy animada **(b)** (intoxicated) (colloq) drogado,
colocado (Esp fam)
5 (of time): **~ noon** mediodía m; **in ~ summer** en
pleno verano
6 ⟨meat⟩ pasado; ⟨game⟩ que tiene un olor
fuerte

high² adv **-er, -est** **1** ⟨fly⟩ alto; **~ up** arriba,
en lo alto; **to search ~ and low (for sth)** remover*
cielo y tierra (para encontrar algo) **2** (in pitch)
⟨sing⟩ alto

high³ n **1** (level) récord m **2** (Meteo) (anticyclone)
zona f de altas presiones; (high temperature)
máxima f **3** (top gear) (AmE Auto) (no art) directa
f

high- /haɪ/ pref. **~quality** de alta calidad, de
gran calidad; **~speed** ⟨train⟩ de alta velocidad

high: ~brow adj (colloq) ⟨tastes⟩ de intelectual;
⟨art/music⟩ para intelectuales; **~chair** n silla f
alta (para niño); **~class** /'haɪˈklæs ‖ haɪˈklɑːs/
adj ⟨restaurant/hotel⟩ de lujo; ⟨merchandise⟩ de
primera calidad; **H~ Court** n (in England and
Wales) una de las dos ramas del Tribunal
Supremo, con competencia para conocer de causas
civiles cuyo coste excede cierta cuantía

higher /'haɪər ‖ 'haɪə(r)/ adj **(a)** comp of HIGH¹
(b) ⟨before n⟩ ⟨mammals/organs⟩ superior

higher education n enseñanza f superior

high: ~ finance n altas finanzas fpl; **~flier,
~flyer** /'haɪˈflaɪər ‖ ˌhaɪˈflaɪə(r)/ n persona f
muy prometedora; **~flown** adj altisonante;
~frequency /'haɪˈfriːkwənsi/ adj de alta
frecuencia; **~grade** adj de calidad superior;
~handed /'haɪˈhændəd ‖ ˌhaɪˈhændɪd/ adj
arbitrario; **~heeled** /'haɪˈhiːld/ adj de tacón or
(CS) de taco alto; **~ jump** n salto m de altura,
salto m alto (AmL); **~lands** /'haɪləndz/ pl n **(a)**
(uplands) tierras fpl altas, altiplanicie f **(b)** (in
Scotland) **the H~lands** las or los Highlands, las
tierras altas; **~level** /'haɪˈlevəl/ adj **(a)** ⟨talks/
delegation⟩ de alto nivel **(b)** ⟨bridge/road⟩
elevado **(c)** (Comput) de alto nivel

highlight¹ /'haɪlaɪt/ vt ⟨past & past p
-lighted⟩ **1** (call attention to) ⟨problem/question⟩
destacar*, poner* de relieve **2** (Art, Phot)
realzar*, dar* realce a

highlight² n **1** (most memorable part) lo más
destacado; **her performance was the ~ of the
evening** su actuación fue el plato fuerte de la
velada **2** **(a)** (Art, Phot) toque m de luz **(b)**
highlights pl (in hair) reflejos mpl, claritos mpl
(RPl), visos mpl (Chi), luces fpl (Méx), mechones
mpl (Col)

highlighter /'haɪlaɪtər ‖ 'haɪlaɪtə(r)/ n **(a)**
(makeup) sombra f clara de ojos **(b)** (pen)
rotulador m, marcador m (AmL)

highly /'haɪli/ adv **(a)** (to a high degree): **~
unlikely** muy poco probable; **~ intelligent**
inteligentísimo; **~ trained** altamente capacitado
(b) (favorably): **his boss speaks/thinks very ~ of**
him su jefe habla muy bien/tiene muy buena
opinión de él **(c)** (at a high rate): **a ~ paid job** un
trabajo muy bien pagado

highly-strung /ˌhaɪliˈstrʌŋ/ adj (BrE) ▶
HIGH-STRUNG

Highness /'haɪnəs ‖ 'haɪnɪs/ n: **Her/His/Your**
(Royal) ~ Su Alteza (Real)

high: ~pitched /'haɪˈpɪtʃt/ adj ⟨voice/sound⟩
agudo; ⟨instrument⟩ de tono agudo or alto;
~powered /'haɪˈpaʊərd ‖ ˌhaɪˈpaʊəd/ adj ⟨car/
machine⟩ muy potente, de gran potencia;
⟨executive/campaign⟩ dinámico, enérgico; ⟨job⟩ de
alto(s) vuelo(s); **~profile** /'haɪˈprəʊfaɪl/ adj
prominente; **~ranking** /'haɪˈrænkɪŋ/ adj
⟨officer⟩ de alto rango; ⟨official⟩ alto, de alta
jerarquía; **~ rise** n (esp AmE) torre f (de
apartamentos or (Esp) pisos); **~rise** /'haɪˈraɪz/
adj ⟨before n⟩ ⟨building/block⟩ alto, de muchas
plantas; ⟨apartment⟩ de una torre, de un edificio
alto; **~risk** /'haɪˈrɪsk/ adj de alto riesgo;
~road n carretera f; **~ school** n colegio m
secundario, ≈instituto m (en Esp), ≈liceo m (en
CS, Ven); **~ season** n temporada f alta;
~spirited /'haɪˈspɪrətəd ‖ ˌhaɪˈspɪrɪtɪd/ adj
lleno de vida, brioso; **~ street** n (BrE) calle f
principal, calle f mayor (Esp); **~strung**
/'haɪˈstrʌŋ/, (BrE) **highly-strung** adj ⟨person⟩

AmC	Central America	Arg	Argentina	Cu	Cuba	Per	Peru
AmL	Latin America	Bol	Bolivia	Ec	Ecuador	RPl	River Plate Area
AmS	South America	Chi	Chile	Esp	Spain	Ur	Uruguay
Andes	Andean Region	CS	Southern Cone	Méx	Mexico	Ven	Venezuela

nervioso; ‹dog/horse› muy excitable; **~-tech**
/'haɪtek/ adj de alta tecnología; ‹era› high tech
adj inv; **~-up** n (esp AmE colloq) gerifalte mf,
capo, -pa m,f (fam); **~way** n (main road) carretera
f; (public way) vía f públiċa; (before n) ‹patrol/
patrolman› (AmE) de carretera; **H~way Code**
n (in UK) Código m de la Circulación;
~wayman /'haɪweɪmən/ n (pl **-men** /-mən/)
salteador m de caminos, bandolero m; **~ wire** n
cuerda f floja

hijack¹ /'haɪdʒæk/ vt secuestrar

hijack² n secuestro m

hijacker /'haɪdʒækər ‖ 'haɪdʒækə(r)/ n
secuestrador, -dora m,f; (of planes) pirata áereo,
-rea m,f

hike¹ /haɪk/ n **1** (long walk) caminata f,
excursión f **2** (increase) subida f

hike² vi (walk) ir* de caminata or de excursión;
to go hiking hacer* excursionismo

hiker /'haɪkər ‖ 'haɪkə(r)/ n excursionista mf

hilarious /hɪ'leriəs ‖ hɪ'leəriəs/ adj
divertidísimo, comiquísimo

hill /hɪl/ n (low) colina f, cerro m, collado m;
(higher) montaña f; (slope, incline) cuesta f

hill: ~billy n (AmE colloq) rústico, -ca m,f,
paleto, -ta m,f (Esp fam & pey), pajuerano, -na m,f
(RPl fam & pey); **~side** n ladera f; **~top** n cima
f, cumbre f

hilly /'hɪli/ adj **-lier, -liest** accidentado

hilt /hɪlt/ n empuñadura f, puño m

him /hɪm, weak form ɪm/ pron **1** (a) (as direct
object) lo, le (Esp); **I saw ~** lo or (Esp tb) le vi; **call
~** llámalo, llámale (Esp) (b) (as indirect object) le;
(with direct object pronoun present) se; **I sent ~ a card**
le mandé una tarjeta (c) (after preposition) él
2 (emphatic use) él; **it's ~** es él

Himalayas /'hɪmə'leɪəz/ pl n **the ~** el
Himalaya

himself /hɪm'self/ pron (a) (reflexive): **he cut/
hurt ~** se cortó/lastimó; **he bought ~ a hat** se
compró un sombrero; **he only thinks of ~** solo
piensa en sí mismo; **by ~** solo; **he was talking to
~** estaba hablando solo (b) (emphatic use) él
mismo; **he told me so ~** me lo dijo él mismo (c)
(normal self): **he's not ~** no es el de siempre

hind /haɪnd/ adj (before n, no comp) ‹legs›
trasero

hinder /'hɪndər ‖ 'hɪndə(r)/ vt dificultar

Hindi /'hɪndi/ n indi m, hindi m

hindrance /'hɪndrəns/ n estorbo m

hindsight /'haɪndsaɪt/ n: **with (the benefit of)
~** a posteriori, en retrospectiva

Hindu¹ /'hɪnduː/ n hindú mf

Hindu² adj hindú

Hinduism /'hɪnduːɪzəm/ n hinduismo m

hinge¹ /hɪndʒ/ n (of door, window, gate) bisagra f,
gozne m; (of box, lid) bisagra f

hinge² hinges, hinging, hinged vi **to ~ on**
sth (turn) girar SOBRE algo; (be fixed) ir* asegurado
con bisagras A algo; (depend) depender DE algo

hint¹ /hɪnt/ n **1** (a) (oblique reference)
insinuación f, indirecta f; (clue) pista f; **to drop a
~ to sb** lanzarle* una indirecta a algn; **to take
the ~** captar or (Esp tb) coger* la indirecta (b)

(trace – of bitterness, sadness) dejo m; (– of color)
toque m, matiz m; (– of garlic, lemon) dejo m, gusto
m **2** (tip) consejo m

hint² vt insinuar*, dar* a entender
■ **~** vi lanzar* indirectas; **to ~ AT** sth insinuar*
or dar* a entender algo

hip¹ /hɪp/ n cadera f

hip² interj: **~, ~, hooray** o **hurrah!** ¡hurra!, ¡viva!

hippie /'hɪpi/ n ▶ HIPPY

hippo /'hɪpəʊ/ n (pl **-pos**) (colloq) hipopótamo m

hippopotamus
‖ ,hɪpə'pɒtəməs/ n (pl **-muses** or **-mi** /-maɪ/)
hipopótamo m

hippy, hippie /'hɪpi/ n (pl **-pies**) hippy mf

hire¹ /haɪr ‖ 'haɪə(r)/ vt **1** (a) ‹hall/boat/suit›
alquilar, arrendar* (b) (Busn, Lab Rel) ‹staff/
person› contratar (c) **hired** past p ‹car›
alquilado **2** ▶ HIRE OUT
■ **hire out** [v + o + adv, v + adv + o] (BrE)
alquilar, arrendar*

hire² n **1** (of hall/car/suit) alquiler m, arriendo m;
❺ **for hire** se alquila or se arrienda; (on taxis)
libre **2** (payment) alquiler m, arriendo m

hire purchase n (BrE) compra f a plazos; **to
buy** sth **on ~ ~** comprar algo a plazos, comprar
algo en cuotas (esp AmL)

his¹ /hɪz, weak form ɪz/ adj
■ **Note** The translation su agrees in number with the
noun which it modifies; his is translated by su, sus,
according to what follows: his father/mother su padre/
madre; his books/magazines sus libros/revistas.

(sing) su; (pl) sus; **he injured ~ knee** se lesionó
la rodilla

his² pron
■ **Note** The translation suyo reflects the gender and
number of the noun it is standing for; his is translated
by el suyo, la suya, los suyos, las suyas, depending
on what is being referred to.

(sing) suyo, -ya; (pl) suyos, -yas, de él; **they're ~**
son suyos/suyas, son de él; **~ is blue** el suyo/la
suya es azul; el/la de él es azul; **a friend of ~** un
amigo suyo or de él

Hispanic¹ /hɪ'spænɪk/ adj hispánico, hispano;
‹community/voter› (in US) hispano

Hispanic² n (esp AmE) hispano, -na m,f

hiss¹ /hɪs/ vi silbar; «cat» bufar
■ **~** vt decir* entre dientes

hiss² n (of snake, audience) silbido m; (of cat)
bufido m

historian /hɪ'stɔːriən/ n historiador, -dora m,f

historic /hɪ'stɒrɪk ‖ hɪ'stɒrɪk/ adj (a)
(momentous) ‹event/moment› memorable (b) (old)
‹house/building› histórico

historical /hɪ'stɒrɪkəl ‖ hɪ'stɒrɪkəl/ adj (a)
(relating to history) histórico (b) (crit) ▶ HISTORIC

history /'hɪstəri/ n (pl **-ries**) **1** historia f; **the
worst earthquake in ~** el peor terremoto de la
historia **2** (record, background) historial m

hit¹ /hɪt/ (pres p **hitting**; past & past p **hit**) vt
1 (a) (deal blow to) ‹door/table› dar* un golpe en,
golpear; ‹person› pegarle* a (b) (strike) golpear;
the truck ~ a tree el camión chocó con or contra
un árbol; **the house was ~ by a bomb** una bomba
cayó sobre la casa; **the bullet ~ him in the leg** la ⋯▸

bala le dio *or* lo alcanzó en la pierna; **to ~ one's
head on sth** darse* un golpe en la cabeza contra
algo; **to ~ it off with sb** congeniar con algn
[2] **(a)** (strike accurately) ‹*target*› dar* en **(b)** (attack)
‹*opponent/enemy*› atacar* **(c)** (score) (Sport)
anotarse, marcar*
[3] (affect adversely) afectar (a)
[4] **(a)** (meet with, run into) ‹*difficulty/problem*›
toparse con **(b)** (reach) llegar* a, alcanzar*
[5] (occur to): **suddenly it ~ me: why had he … ?**
de repente se me ocurrió: ¿por qué había … ?
■ **hit back (a)** [*v + adv*] (strike in return) devolver*
el golpe; **she ~ back at her critics** arremetió
contra sus detractores **(b)** [*v + o + adv*]
devolverle* el golpe a
■ **hit on** [*v + prep + o*] ‹*solution*› dar* con
■ **hit out** [*v + adv*] **(a)** (strike) **to ~ out (AT sb)**
(once) lanzar*(le) un golpe (A algn); (repeatedly)
tirar(le) golpes (A algn) **(b)** (attack verbally) **to ~
out AT** *o* **AGAINST sth/sb** atacar* algo/a algn
■ **hit upon** ▶ HIT ON

hit² *n* [1] **(a)** (blow, stroke) (Sport) golpe *m* **(b)** (in
shooting) blanco *m* [2] (success) (colloq) éxito *m*
[3] (Comput) impacto *m*

hit: ~-and-miss /'hɪtən'mɪs/ *adj* (*pred* ▶ **and
miss**) ▶ HIT-OR-MISS; **~-and-run** /'hɪtən'rʌn/
adj (*before n*) ‹*driver*› que se da a la fuga tras
atropellar a algn

hitch¹ /hɪtʃ/ *n* [1] (difficulty) complicación *f*,
problema *m*, pega *f* (Esp fam); **a technical ~** un
problema técnico [2] (limp) (AmE) cojera *f*,
renguera *f* (AmL)

hitch² *vt* **(a)** (attach) **to ~ sth TO sth** enganchar
algo A algo [2] (thumb) (colloq): **to ~ a ride** *o* (BrE
also) **a lift** hacer* dedo (fam), hacer* autostop, ir*
de aventón (Col, Méx fam), pedir* cola (Ven fam)
■ **~** *vi* ▶ HITCHHIKE

hitch: ~hike *vi* hacer* autostop, hacer* dedo
(fam), ir* de aventón (Col, Méx fam), pedir* cola
(Ven fam); **~hiker** *n* autoestopista *mf*

hi-tech /'haɪ'tek/ *adj* ▶ HIGH-TECH

hitherto /'hɪðər'tu: ‖ ˌhɪðə'tu:/ *adv* (fml) hasta
ahora, hasta la fecha

hit: ~ list *n* (colloq) (murder list) lista *f* de
sentenciados; (blacklist) lista *f* negra; **~ man** *n*
(colloq) (assassin) asesino *m* a sueldo, sicario *m*;
~-or-miss /'hɪtər'mɪs ‖ ˌhɪtɔ:'mɪs/ *adj* (*pred* ▶
or miss) ‹*method/approach*› poco científico

hitter /'hɪtər ‖ 'hɪtə(r)/ *n* (in baseball) bateador,
-dora *m,f*; (in US football) liniero, -ra *m,f*

HIV *n* (= **Human Immunodeficiency
Virus**) VIH *m*, virus *m* del sida; **he's ~ positive**
es seropositivo

hive /haɪv/ *n* (home of bees) colmena *f*; (bee colony)
enjambre *m*

hives /haɪvz/ *n* (Med) urticaria *f*

HM (= **Her/His Majesty**) S.M.

HMS (in UK) = **Her/His Majesty's Ship**

hoard¹ /hɔːrd ‖ hɔːd/ *n* (of food) reserva *f*; **a ~
of treasure** un tesoro escondido

hoard² *vt* acumular, juntar; (anticipating a
shortage) acaparar

hoarding /'hɔːrdɪŋ ‖ 'hɔːdɪŋ/ *n* [1] (anticipating a
shortage) acaparamiento *m* [2] (billboard) (BrE) valla
f publicitaria, barda *f* de anuncios (Méx)

hoarse /hɔːrs ‖ hɔːs/ *adj* **hoarser, hoarsest**
ronco

hoax /həʊks/ *n* (deception) engaño *m*; (joke)
broma *f*; (tall story) patraña *f*

hob /hɑːb ‖ hɒb/ *n* **(a)** (beside open fire) placa *f* **(b)**
(of cooker) (BrE) hornillas *fpl* (AmL exc CS),
hornillos *mpl* (Esp), hornallas *fpl* (RPl), platos
mpl (Chi)

hobble /'hɑːbəl ‖ 'hɒbəl/ *vi* cojear, renguear
(AmL)

hobby /'hɑːbi ‖ 'hɒbi/ *n* (*pl* **-bies**) hobby *m*,
pasatiempo *m*, afición *f*

hobnailed /'hɑːbneɪld ‖ 'hɒbneɪld/ *adj* con
tachuelas

hobo /'həʊbəʊ/ *n* (*pl* **-boes** *or* **-bos**) (AmE
colloq) vagabundo, -da *m,f*, linyera *mf* (CS fam)

hockey /'hɑːki ‖ 'hɒki/ *n* **(a)** (ice ~) (AmE)
hockey *m* sobre hielo **(b)** (played on grass) (BrE)
hockey *m* (sobre hierba)

hod /hɑːd ‖ hɒd/ *n* (for bricks) capacho *m* (*para
acarrear ladrillos*)

hoe¹ /həʊ/ *n* azada *f*, azadón *m*

hoe² *vt* azadonar, pasar la azada por

hog¹ /hɔːg ‖ hɒg/ *n* [1] (AmE Agr, Zool) cerdo, -da
m,f, puerco, -ca *m,f*, chancho, -cha *m,f* (AmL)
[2] (person) (colloq) tragón, -gona *m,f* (fam),
angurriento, -ta *m,f* (CS fam)

hog² *vt* **-gg-** (colloq) ‹*food/bathroom/limelight*›
acaparar; ‹*discussion*› monopolizar*

Hogmanay /'hɑːgmənei ‖ 'hɒgmənei/ *n* (Scot)
Nochevieja *f*, noche *f* de fin de año

hoist¹ /hɔɪst/ *vt* (lift) levantar, alzar*; ‹*sail/flag*›
izar*

hoist² *n* (elevator) montacargas *m*; (crane, derrick)
grúa *f*

hokum /'həʊkəm/ *n* (colloq) **(a)** (nonsense)
paparruchas *fpl* (fam) **(b)** (corny material) (AmE)
recursos efectistas de tipo melodramático o cómico

hold¹ /həʊld/ (*past & past p* **held**) *vt* [1] **(a)**
(have in one's hand(s)) tener* (en la mano); **will you
~ this for me?** ¿me puedes tener *or* (esp AmL)
agarrar esto por favor? **(b)** (clasp): **~ it with both
hands** sujétalo *or* (esp AmL) agárralo con las dos
manos; **he was ~ing her hand** la tenía agarrada
or (esp Esp) cogida de la mano **(c)** (grip) (Auto)
agarrar, adherirse*
[2] (have room for) ‹*cup/jug*› tener* una capacidad
de; ‹*stadium*› tener* capacidad *or* cabida para;
this report ~s all the answers to … este informe
contiene todas las respuestas a …; **who knows what
the future ~s** quién sabe qué nos deparará el futuro
[3] **(a)** (keep in position) ‹*ladder*› sujetar, sostener*
(b) (maintain) ‹*attention/interest*› mantener*; **she
held the lead throughout the race** se mantuvo a la
cabeza durante toda la carrera
[4] **(a)** (keep) ‹*tickets/room*› reservar, guardar **(b)**
(detain, imprison): **she is being held at the police
station for questioning** está detenida en la
comisaría para ser interrogada **(c)** (restrain)
detener* **(d)** (control) ‹*troops/rebels*› ocupar
[5] **(a)** (have) ‹*passport/permit*› tener*, estar* en
posesión de (frml); ‹*degree/shares*› tener*; ‹*record*›
ostentar, tener*; ‹*post/position*› tener*, ocupar;
he ~s the view that … sostiene *or* mantiene que
… **(b)** (consider) considerar; (assert) sostener*,
mantener*; **to ~ sb responsible for sth**
responsabilizar* a algn de algo **(c)** (conduct)
‹*meeting/elections*› celebrar; ‹*demonstration*›
hacer*; ‹*party*› dar*; ‹*conversation*› mantener*

6 (stop): **~ it!** ¡espera!

■ **~** *vi* **1** (clasp, grip): **~ tight!** ¡agárrate fuerte!
2 (a) (stay firm) «*rope/door*» aguantar, resistir
(b) (continue) «*weather*» seguir* *or* continuar*
bueno; **if our luck ~s** si nos sigue acompañando
la suerte

■ **hold against** [*v* + *o* + *prep* + *o*]: **I won't ~ that
against him** no se lo voy a tomar en cuenta

■ **hold back** [*v* + *o* + *adv, v* + *adv* + *o*] **(a)**
(restrain) «*crowds/water/tears*» contener* **(b)**
(withhold, delay) «*information*» no revelar;
«*payment*» retrasar
2 [*v* + *adv*] (restrain oneself) contenerse*, frenarse

■ **hold down** [*v* + *o* + *adv, v* + *adv* + *o*] **(a)** (force,
press down) «*lid/papers*» sujetar; «*person*»
inmovilizar **(b)** «*job*»: **he can't ~ down a job** es
incapaz de tener un trabajo y cumplir con él **(c)**
(limit) «*price/increase*» moderar, contener*

■ **hold in** [*v* + *o* + *adv, v* + *adv* + *o*] «*stomach*»
meter; «*feelings/laughter*» contener*

■ **hold off** **1** [*v* + *o* + *adv, v* + *adv* + *o*] **(a)** (resist)
«*attack/enemy*» resistir **(b)** (defeat) «*challenger/
rival*» derrotar
2 [*v* + *adv*] (be delayed): **if the rain ~s off** si no
empieza a llover

■ **hold on** [*v* + *adv*] **(a)** (wait) esperar **(b)** (survive)
resistir, aguantar **(c)** (clasp, grip) agarrarse; **to ~
on** TO **sth/sb** agarrarse A *or* DE algo/algn **(d)**
(keep) **to ~ on** TO **sth** «*receipt/photo*» conservar *or*
guardar algo

■ **hold out** **1** [*v* + *o* + *adv, v* + *adv* + *o*] (extend)
«*hands/arms*» tender*, alargar*
2 [*v* + *adv* + *o*] **(a)** (offer) «*possibility*» ofrecer*;
«*hope*» dar* **(b)** (have, retain) «*hope*» tener*; **I don't
~ out much hope of getting the job** no tengo
muchas esperanzas de que me den el trabajo
3 [*v* + *adv*] (survive, last) «*person*» aguantar
(b) (resist, make a stand) «*army/town*» resistir

■ **hold over** [*v* + *o* + *adv, v* + *adv* + *o*] (postpone)
«*meeting/decision*» aplazar*, postergar* (esp AmL)

■ **hold together** **1** [*v* + *adv*] «*arguments*»
tener* lógica *or* solidez; «*people*» mantenerse*
unidos
2 [*v* + *o* + *adv*] (keep united) «*family/group*»
mantener* unido

■ **hold up** **1** [*v* + *o* + *adv, v* + *adv* + *o*] **(a)** (raise)
«*hand/banner*» levantar; «*head*» mantener*
erguido **(b)** (support) «*roof/walls*» sostener* **(c)**
(delay) «*person/arrival*» retrasar; «*progress*»
entorpecer* **(d)** (rob) atracar*, asaltar
2 [*v* + *adv*] «*theory/argument*» resultar válido

■ **hold with** [*v* + *prep* + *o*] (*usu neg*) estar* de
acuerdo con

hold² *n* **1 (a)** (grip, grasp): **to catch** *o* **grab** *o*
take ~ of sth agarrar *or* (esp Esp) coger* algo; (so
as not to fall etc) agarrarse *or* asirse de *or* a algo; **to
get ~ of sb** (find) localizar *or* (AmL tb) ubicar* a
algn; **to get ~ of sth** (manage to get) conseguir*
algo **(b)** (control): **the ~ they have over the
members of the sect** el dominio que ejercen sobre
los miembros de la secta
2 (a) (in wrestling, judo) llave *f*; **with no ~s barred**
sin ningún tipo de restricciones **(b)** (in
mountaineering) asidero *m*
3 (delay, pause) demora *f*; **I've got Mr Brown on ~**
(Telec) el Sr Brown está esperando para hablar
con usted; **to put sth on ~** «*project*» dejar algo
aparcado

4 (of ship, aircraft) bodega *f*

holdall /'həʊldɔːl/ *n* (BrE) bolso *m* de viaje,
bolsón *m* (RPl)

holder /'həʊldər ‖'həʊldə(r)/ *n* **1** (of permit,
passport, job) titular *mf*; (of ticket) poseedor, -dora
m,f; (of bonds etc) titular *mf*, tenedor, -dora *m,f*;
(of title, cup) poseedor, -dora *m,f* **2** (wallet) funda *f*

holdup /'həʊldʌp/ *n* **(a)** (delay) demora *f*, retraso
m; (in traffic) atasco *m*, embotellamiento *m* **(b)**
(armed robbery) atraco *m*

hole /həʊl/ *n* **1 (a)** (in belt, material, clothing)
agujero *m*; (in ground) hoyo *m*, agujero *m*; (in road)
bache *m*; (in wall) boquete *m*; **to make a ~ in sth**
hacer* un agujero en algo, agujerear algo **(b)** (in
argument, proposal) punto *m* débil; **to pick ~s in sth**
encontrarle* defectos *or* faltas a algo **(c)** (of
animal) madriguera *f* **2** (in golf) hoyo *m*
3 (unpleasant place) (colloq): **this town is a real ~!**
¡qué pueblo de mala muerte! (fam)

holiday /'hɑːlədeɪ ‖'hɒlədeɪ/ *n* **(a)** (day) fiesta *f*,
día *m* festivo, (día *m*) feriado *m* (AmL) **(b)** (period
away from work) (esp BrE) vacaciones *fpl*,
licencia *f* (Col, Méx, RPl); **to go/be on ~** irse*/
estar* de vacaciones; (*before n*) «*mood/spirit*»
festivo; «*cottage*» de vacaciones **(c)** (BrE Educ)
(*often pl*) vacaciones *fpl*

holiday: **~ camp** *n* (BrE) colonia *f* de
vacaciones; **~maker** *n* (BrE) turista *mf*; (on
summer holidays) veraneante *mf*; **~ resort** *n*
centro *m* turístico

Holland /'hɑːlənd ‖'hɒlənd/ *n* Holanda *f*

holler /'hɑːlər ‖'hɒlə(r)/ *vt/i* (AmE colloq) gritar

hollow¹ /'hɑːləʊ ‖'hɒləʊ/ *adj* **1** «*tree/tooth/
wall*» hueco; «*sound*» hueco; «*voice*» apagado;
«*cheeks/eyes*» hundido **2** «*success/triumph*» vacío;
«*person*» vacío, vacuo; «*promises/threats*» vano,
falso; «*words*» hueco, vacío

hollow² *n* **(a)** (empty space) hueco *m*; (depression)
hoyo *m*, depresión *f* **(b)** (dell, valley) hondonada *f*

■ **hollow out** [*v* + *o* + *adv, v* + *adv* + *o*] vaciar*,
ahuecar*

holly /'hɑːli ‖'hɒli/ *n* acebo *m*

holocaust /'hɑːləkɔːst, 'hɑː- ‖'hɒləkɔːst/ *n*
hecatombe *f*, desastre *m*; **nuclear ~** holocausto *m*
nuclear; **the H~** el Holocausto

hologram /'həʊləɡræm, 'hɑː- ‖'hɒləɡræm/ *n*
holograma *m*

holster /'həʊlstər ‖'həʊlstə(r)/ *n* pistolera *f*,
funda *f* de pistola (*or* revólver *etc*)

holy /'həʊli/ *adj* **-lier, -liest** «*ground/place*»
sagrado, santo; «*day*» de precepto, de guardar;
«*water*» bendito; «*person/life/virtue*» santo; **the H~
Bible** la Sagrada *or* Santa Biblia; **H~ Week**
Semana Santa

holy: **H~ Ghost** *n* **the H~ Ghost** el Espíritu
Santo; **H~ Spirit** *n* **the H~ Spirit** el Espíritu
Santo

homage /'hɑːmɪdʒ ‖'hɒmɪdʒ/ *n* (frml) homenaje
m; **to pay ~ to sb/sth** rendir* homenaje a algn/
algo

home¹ /həʊm/ *n* **1** (of person) **(a)** (dwelling) casa
f **(b)** (in wider sense): **New York is my ~ now**
Nueva York es donde vivo ahora; **~ sweet ~**
hogar dulce hogar; **to leave ~** irse* de casa **(c)**
(family environment) hogar *m*
2 (of animal, plant) (Bot, Zool) hábitat *m*
3 **at home (a)** (in house) en casa **(b)** (at ease): ⋯⋗

make yourself at ~ ponte cómodo, estás en tu casa **(c)** (not abroad): **at** ~ **and abroad** dentro y fuera del país **(d)** (Sport) en casa ▢4 (institution) (for children) asilo *m* (AmL), orfanatorio *m* (Méx), centro *m* de acogida de menores (Esp); (for old people) residencia *f* de ancianos; **dogs'** ~ (BrE) perrera *f*

■ **home in** [*v* + *adv*] **to** ~ **in** ON sth localizar* y dirigirse* HACIA algo

home² *adv* ▢1 (where one lives) ⟨come/arrive⟩ a casa; **I'll be** ~ **at five** estaré en casa a las cinco ▢2 (to desired place): **to hit** ~ dar* en el blanco; **to drive sth** ~ (**to sb**) hacer(le)* entender algo (a algn)

home³ *adj* (before n) **(a)** ⟨address/telephone number⟩ particular; ⟨background/environment⟩ familiar; ⟨cooking/perm⟩ casero; ~ **delivery** (of purchases) entrega *f* a domicilio;~ **visit** (by doctor) (BrE) visita *f* a domicilio **(b)** (of origin): ~ **state** (in US) estado *m* natal *or* de procedencia **(c)** (not foreign) ⟨affairs/market⟩ nacional **(d)** (Sport) ⟨team⟩ de casa, local; ⟨game⟩ en casa

home: ~ **base** *n* (AmE) **(a)** (Busn, Mil) base *f* de operaciones **(b)** (in baseball) ▶ HOME PLATE; ~**boy** *n* (AmE sl) compinche *m* (fam), cuate *m* (Méx fam); ~ **brew** *n* cerveza hecha en casa; ~**coming** *n* **(a)** (return home) regreso *m*, vuelta *f* (*a casa, a la patria etc*) **(b)** (at school, college) (AmE) *fiesta estudiantil al comienzo del año académico con asistencia de ex-alumnos*; **H**~ **Counties** *pl n* (in UK) the **H**~ **Counties** *los condados de los alrededores de Londres*; ~**-grown** /'həʊm'grəʊn/ *adj* (from one's own garden) de la huerta propia; (not foreign) del país, local, nacional; ~ **help** *n* (BrE) auxiliar *mf*; ~**land** *n* patria *f*, tierra *f* natal

homeless /'həʊmləs ‖ 'həʊmlɪs/ *adj* sin hogar, sin techo

homely /'həʊmli/ *adj* **-lier, -liest (a)** (characteristic of home) ⟨meal/food⟩ casero; ⟨atmosphere/room⟩ acogedor, hogareño **(b)** (plain) (AmE) feo

home: ~**-made** /'həʊm'meɪd/ *adj* ⟨clothes⟩ hecho en casa; ⟨food⟩ casero; ~**-maker** *n* ama *f*‡ de casa; ~ **movie** *n* película *f* casera; ~ **office** *n* (AmE) oficina *f* central; **H**~ **Office** *n* (in UK) the **H**~ **Office** el Home Office, el Ministerio del Interior británico

homeopathic, (BrE) **homoeopathic** /'həʊmɪə'pæθɪk/ *adj* homeopático

home: ~ **owner** *n* propietario, -ria *m,f* (*de una vivienda*); ~ **page** *n* (Comput) página *f* frontal, página *f* inicial; ~ **plate** *n* home *m*, pentágono *m* (Méx)

homer /'həʊmər ‖ 'həʊmə(r)/ *n* (AmE colloq) ▶ HOME RUN

home: ~**room** *n* (AmE Educ) clase *f* or aula *f*‡ del curso; ~ **rule** *n* autogobierno *m*; ~ **run** *n* cuadrangular *m*, jonrón *m* (AmL); **H**~ **Secretary** *n* (in UK) ministro, -tra *m,f* del Interior; ~**sick** *adj*: **I am** *o* **feel** ~**sick** echo de menos *or* (AmL tb) extraño a mi familia (*or mi país etc*)

homestead /'həʊmsted/ *n* (AmE) casa *f* (*en una granja, hacienda etc*)

home: ~ **straight,** ~ **stretch** *n* (Sport) recta *f* final *or* de llegada; ~**town** /'həʊm'taʊn/ *n* ciudad *f*/pueblo *m* natal; ~ **truth** *n* (*usu pl*) verdad *f* (*desagradable*)

homeward¹ /'həʊmwərd ‖ 'həʊmwəd/ **(a)** (BrE also) **homewards** /-z/ *adv* ⟨travel/journey/sail⟩ de vuelta a casa **(b)** **to be** ~ **bound** ir* de camino *or* de vuelta a casa

homeward² *adj* (before n) ⟨journey⟩ de vuelta *or* de regreso

homework /'həʊmwɜ:rk ‖ 'həʊmwɜ:k/ *n* deberes *mpl*, tarea *f*

homey /'həʊmi/ *adj* **homier, homiest** (AmE colloq) ⟨atmosphere/place⟩ hogareño, acogedor; ⟨manner⟩ campechano

homicidal /'hɑ:mə'saɪdl ‖ ,hɒmɪ'saɪdl̩/ *adj* ⟨tendency⟩ homicida; ⟨rage⟩ asesino

homicide /'hɑ:məsaɪd ‖ 'hɒmɪsaɪd/ *n* **(a)** (crime, act) homicidio *m* **(b)** (murderer) (frml) homicida *mf*

homing /'həʊmɪŋ/ *adj* (before n) ⟨instinct⟩ de volver al hogar; ⟨device/missile⟩ buscador; ~ **pigeon** paloma *f* mensajera

homoeopathic /'həʊmɪə'pæθɪk/ *adj* (BrE) ▶ HOMEOPATHIC

homogeneous /'həʊmə'dʒi:nɪəs ‖ ,hɒmə'dʒi:nɪəs/ *adj* homogéneo

homosexual¹ /'həʊmə'sekʃʊəl ‖ ,həʊmə'sekʃʊəl, ,hɒmə-/ *adj* homosexual

homosexual² *n* homosexual *mf*

homosexuality /'həʊmə'sekʃʊ'æləti ‖ ,həʊməsekʃʊ'æləti, ,hɒmə-/ *n* homosexualidad *f*

Hon /hɒn/ (in UK) = **Honourable**

Honduran¹ /hɑ:n'dʊrən ‖ hɒn'djʊərən/ *adj* hondureño

Honduran² *n* hondureño, -ña *m,f*

Honduras /hɑ:n'dʊrəs ‖ hɒn'djʊərəs/ *n* Honduras *f*

hone /həʊn/ *vt* ⟨blade/edge⟩ afilar; ⟨style/skill⟩ afinar

honest /'ɑ:nəst ‖ 'ɒnɪst/ *adj* **(a)** (trustworthy, upright) ⟨person/action⟩ honrado, honesto; ⟨face⟩ de persona honrada *or* honesta **(b)** (sincere) ⟨appraisal/opinion⟩ sincero; **to be** ~ **with you** ... si quieres que te diga la verdad ...

honestly /'ɑ:nəstli ‖ 'ɒnɪstli/ *adv* **(a)** (sincerely) ⟨answer/say/state⟩ sinceramente, francamente **(b)** (indep) en serio, de verdad **(c)** (as interj) (expressing exasperation) ¡por favor! **(d)** (legitimately) ⟨act/earn⟩ con honradez, honradamente

honesty /'ɑ:nəsti ‖ 'ɒnɪsti/ *n* **(a)** (probity) honradez *f*, honestidad *f*, rectitud *f* **(b)** (truthfulness) franqueza *f*, sinceridad *f*; **in all** ~ ... para ser sincero ...

honey /'hʌni/ *n* (*pl* **honeys**) ▢1 miel *f* ▢2 (*as form of address*) (colloq) cariño (fam)

honey: ~ **bee** *n* abeja *f*; ~**comb** *n* panal *m*; ~**moon** *n* luna *f* de miel; ~**suckle** *n* madreselva *f*

Hong Kong /ˈhɑːŋˈkɑːŋ ‖ˌhɒŋˈkɒŋ/ n
Hong-Kong m

honk vi (hoot) «goose» graznar; «driver» tocar*
el claxon, pitar

honor¹, (BrE) **honour** /ˈɑːnər ‖ˈɒnə(r)/ n
1 (good name) honor m **2** (privilege, mark of
distinction) honor m; **to have the ~ to +** INF o of
-ING (frml) tener* el honor DE + INF (frml); **a
reception in ~ of the delegates** una recepción en
honor de los delegados **3 Honor** (as title) **Your/
His H~** Su Señoría **4 honors** pl (a) (special
mention) (before n) **~s list** (AmE) cuadro m de
honor **(b)** (Educ): **to graduate with ~s** licenciarse
con matrícula (de honor) or con honores; (before
n) **an honours degree** (BrE) ≈una licenciatura

honor², (BrE) **honour** vt **1** (show respect)
honrar **2 (a)** (keep to) «agreement/obligation»
cumplir (con) **(b)** (Fin) «bill/debt» satisfacer*
(frml), pagar*; «check/draft» pagar*, aceptar

honorable, (BrE) **honourable** /ˈɑːnərəbəl
‖ˈɒnərəbəl/ adj **1 (a)** (honest, respectable)
«person/action» honorable **(b)** (creditable) «peace/
settlement» honroso **2 Honourable** (in UK)
tratamiento dado a representantes parlamentarios
y a hijos de vizcondes, barones y condes

honorary /ˈɑːnəreri ‖ˈɒnərəri/ adj honorario;
«doctorate» honoris causa

honour etc (BrE) ▶ HONOR etc

hood /hʊd/ n **1** (on coat, jacket) capucha f;
(pointed) capirote m; (of monk) capucha f,
capuchón m **2 (a)** (on chimney, cooker) campana f;
(on machine) cubierta f **(b)** (AmE Auto) capó m **(c)**
(folding cover) (BrE) capota f

hoodlum /ˈhuːdləm/ n **(a)** (thug) (AmE) matón,
-tona m,f (fam), gorila mf **(b)** (rowdy youth)
vándalo, -la m,f, gamberro, -rra m,f (Esp)

hoodwink /ˈhʊdwɪŋk/ vt engañar; **to ~ sb
INTO -ING** engañar a algn PARA QUE (+ subj)

hoof /hʊf ‖huːf/ n (pl **hoofs** or **hooves**) (of
horse) casco m, vaso m (RPl), pezuña f (Méx); (of
cow) pezuña f

hoof-and-mouth disease /ˈhʊfənˈmaʊθ
‖ˌhuːfənˈmaʊθ/ n (AmE) fiebre f aftosa, glosopeda
f (téc)

hook¹ /hʊk/ n **1 (a)** (gancho m; (for hanging
clothes) percha f, gancho m; (for fishing) anzuelo m;
to take the phone off the ~ descolgar* el teléfono;
to let sb off the ~ dejar salir a algn del
atolladero **(b)** (Clothing) corchete m, ganchito m;
~s and eyes corchetes (macho y hembra) **2** (in
boxing) gancho m

hook² vt (grasp, secure) enganchar
■ **hook up 1** [v + o + adv, v + adv + o] **(a)**
(fasten) «dress/bra» abrochar **(b)** (connect, link)
enganchar **2** [v + adv] **(a)** (Rad, TV) conectarse,
transmitir en cadena **(b)** (fasten) «dress»
abrocharse

hooked /hʊkt/ adj **1** (hook-shaped) «tool» en
forma de gancho; «beak» ganchudo; «nose»
aguileño **2** (addicted) (colloq) **to be/get ~ ON sth**
estar* enviciado/enviciarse CON algo, estar
enganchado/engancharse A algo (Esp)

hooker /ˈhʊkər ‖ˈhʊkə(r)/ n (esp AmE colloq)
prostituta f, puta f (vulg)

hooky, hookey /ˈhʊki/ n: **to play ~** (esp AmE
colloq) faltar a clase, hacer* novillos or (Méx) irse*

de pinta or (RPl) hacerse* la rata or la rabona or
(Per) la vaca or (Chi) hacer* la cimarra or (Col)
capar clase or (Ven) jubilarse (fam)

hooligan /ˈhuːlɪgən/ n vándalo, -la m,f,
gamberro, -rra m,f (Esp)

hoop /huːp/ n aro m

hooray /hʊˈreɪ/ interj ¡hurra!

hoot¹ /huːt/ n (of owl) grito m, ululato m; **~s of
laughter** risotadas fpl, carcajadas fpl

hoot² vi «owl» ulular; «car/driver» tocar* el
claxon, pitar

hooter /ˈhuːtər ‖ˈhuːtə(r)/ n (BrE) **(a)** (siren)
sirena f **(b)** (horn) claxon m, bocina f

hoover /ˈhuːvər ‖ˈhuːvə(r)/ (BrE) vt pasar la
aspiradora or el aspirador por, aspirar (AmL)

Hoover®, hoover /ˈhuːvər ‖ˈhuːvə(r)/ n (BrE)
aspiradora f, aspirador m

hooves /hʊvz ‖huːvz/ pl of HOOF

hop¹ /hɑːp ‖hɒp/ n **1** (jump — of person) salto m
a la pata coja, brinco m de cojito (Méx); (— of
rabbit) salto m, brinco m; (— of bird) saltito m
2 (Bot, Culin) (usu pl) lúpulo m

hop² -pp- vi **(a)** «frog/rabbit» brincar*, saltar;
«bird» dar* saltitos **(b)** «person/child» saltar a
la pata coja, brincar* de cojito (Méx) **(c)** (move
quickly) (colloq): **~ in, I'll take you to the station**
súbete, que te llevo a la estación; **to ~ on a bus**
tomarse un autobús
■ **~** vt (AmE colloq) «flight/train» tomar, pillar (fam)

hope¹ /həʊp/ n esperanza f; **she did it in the ~
of a reward** lo hizo con la esperanza de obtener
una recompensa

hope² vi esperar; **I ~ so/not** espero que sí/que
no; **we're hoping for good weather** esperamos
tener buen tiempo
■ **~** vt **to ~** (THAT) esperar QUE (+ subj); **to ~ to +**
INF esperar + INF

hope chest n (AmE) baúl m or arcón m del
ajuar

hopeful¹ /ˈhəʊpfəl/ adj **(a)** «person»
esperanzado, optimista **(b)** (promising)
esperanzador, prometedor

hopeful² n aspirante mf, candidato, -ta m,f

hopefully /ˈhəʊpfəli/ adv **(a)** (in hopeful way):
can you pay me in dollars? she asked ~ —
¿puedes pagarme en dólares? —preguntó
esperanzada **(b)** (crit) (indep): **when do you leave?
— ~, on Friday** ¿cuándo te vas? — el viernes,
espero

hopeless /ˈhəʊpləs ‖ˈhəʊplɪs/ adj **1** (allowing
no hope) «situation» desesperado; «task» imposible;
he's a ~ case «patient» está desahuciado;
(colloq) «pupil» no tiene remedio **2** (incompetent,
inadequate) (colloq): **you're ~!** ¡eres un inútil!; **the
train service on this line is ~** el servicio de
trenes en esta línea es desastroso or es un
desastre; **to be ~ AT sth** ser* negado PARA algo

hopelessly /ˈhəʊpləsli ‖ˈhəʊplɪsli/ adv **(a)**
(irredeemably) (as intensifier): **to be ~ lost/in love**
estar* completamente perdido/perdidamente
enamorado **(b)** (without hope) sin esperanzas

hopelessness /ˈhəʊpləsnəs ‖ˈhəʊplɪsnɪs/ n
(a) (of situation) lo desesperado **(b)** (despair)
desesperanza f

hopping /ˈhɑːpɪŋ ‖ˈhɒpɪŋ/ adj: **to be ~ mad**
(colloq) estar* furioso

h

hopscotch /'hɑ:pskɑ:tʃ ‖'hɒpskɒtʃ/ *n*: to play ~ jugar* al tejo *or* (Méx) al avión *or* (RPI) a la rayuela *or* (Col) a la golosa *or* (Chi) al luche

horde /hɔːrd ‖hɔːd/ *n* (colloq) multitud *f*, horda *f*

horizon /həˈraɪzən/ *n* (Geog) the ~ el horizonte

horizontal /ˌhɔːrəˈzɑːntl̩ ‖ˌhɒrɪ'zɒntl̩/ *adj* horizontal

hormone /'hɔːrməʊn ‖'hɔːməʊn/ *n* hormona *f*; *(before n)* ~ **replacement therapy** terapia *f* hormonal sustitiva

horn /hɔːrn ‖hɔːn/ *n* **1** (Zool) (of animal) cuerno *m*, asta *f̣*, cacho *m* (AmS), guampa *f* (CS) **2** (Mus) **(a)** (wind instrument) cuerno *m* **(b)** (French ~) trompa *f* **3** (Auto) claxon *m*, bocina *f̣*; (Naut) sirena *f*

hornet /'hɔːrnət ‖'hɔːnɪt/ *n* avispón *m*

horoscope /'hɔːrəskəʊp ‖'hɒrəskəʊp/ *n* horóscopo *m*

horrendous /hɔːˈrendəs ‖hɒˈrendəs/ *adj* **(a)** (horrifying) *‹crime/account›* horrendo, horroroso **(b)** (dreadful) (colloq) *‹price/mistake›* terrible

horrible /'hɔːrəbəl ‖'hɒrɪbəl/ *adj* horrible, horroroso

horrid /'hɔːrəd ‖'hɒrɪd/ *adj* (esp BrE colloq) *‹weather/taste›* horroroso

horrific /hɔːˈrɪfɪk ‖hɒˈrɪfɪk, hə-/ *adj* horroroso, espantoso

horrify /'hɔːrəfaɪ ‖'hɒrɪfaɪ/ *vt* **-fies, -fying, -fied** horrorizar*

horrifying /'hɔːrəfaɪɪŋ ‖'hɒrɪfaɪɪŋ/ *adj* horroroso, horrendo, horripilante

horror /'hɔːrər ‖'hɒrə(r)/ *n* horror *m*; *(before n)* *‹movie/story›* de terror

horror-struck /'hɔːrərstrʌk ‖'hɒrəstrʌk/ *adj* horrorizado

hors d'oeuvre /ɔːrˈdɜːrv ‖ɔːˈdɜːvrə/ *n* (*pl* **hors d'oeuvres** /-'dɜːrv ‖-'dɜːvrə/) entremés *m*, botana *f* (Méx)

horse /hɔːrs ‖hɔːs/ *n* **1** (Zool) caballo *m*; *I could eat a* ~ tengo un hambre canina; *(before n)* ~ **riding** (BrE) equitación *f* **2** (vaulting ~) potro *m*, caballo *m* (Méx)

horse: ~**back** *n*: on ~**back** a caballo; *(before n)* ~**back riding** (AmE) equitación *f̣*; ~**box** *n* (BrE) ▶ ~**CAR**; ~**car** *n* (AmE) (for transporting horses) remolque *m or* trailer *m* (*para transportar caballos*); ~ **chestnut** *n* **(a)** (tree) castaño *m* de Indias **(b)** (fruit) castaña *f* de Indias; ~**-drawn** *adj* tirado por caballos; ~**fly** *n* tábano *m*; ~**man** /'hɔːrsmən ‖'hɔːsmən/ *n* (*pl* **-men** /-mən/) jinete *m*; ~**power** *n* caballo *m* (de fuerza); ~ **racing** *n* carreras *fpl* de caballos, hípica *f*; ~**radish** /'hɔːrsˈrædɪʃ ‖'hɔːsrædɪʃ/ *n* rábano *m* picante; ~**shoe** *n* herradura *f̣*; ~ **show** *n* concurso *m* hípico

horticulture /'hɔːrtəˌkʌltʃər ‖'hɔːtɪˌkʌltʃə(r)/ *n* horticultura *f*

hose /həʊz/ *n* **1** (~pipe) manguera *f*, manga *f*; (Auto) manguito *m* **2** (Clothing) (+ *pl vb*) **(a)** (tights) pantis *mpl* (Hist, Theat) calzas *fpl*, malla *f* **(b)** (AmE) ▶ PANTYHOSE

■ **hose down** [*v + o + adv, v + adv + o*] lavar (*con manguera*)

hosepipe /'həʊzpaɪp/ *n* (esp BrE) ▶ HOSE 1

hosiery /'həʊʒəri ‖'həʊʒɪəri/ *n* (frml) calcetería *f*

hospice /'hɑːspəs ‖'hɒspɪs/ *n*: residencia para *enfermos desahuciados*

hospitable /hɑːˈspɪtəbəl ‖hɒˈspɪtəbəl/ *adj* hospitalario

hospital /'hɑːspɪt̩l ‖'hɒspɪt̩l/ *n* hospital *m*

hospitality /ˌhɑːspəˈtæləti ‖ˌhɒspɪˈtæləti/ *n* hospitalidad *f*

hospitalize /'hɑːspɪt̩laɪz ‖'hɒspɪt̩laɪz/ *vt* hospitalizar*, internar (CS, Méx)

host¹ /həʊst/ *n* **1** **(a)** (person dispensing hospitality) anfitrión, -triona *m*,*f̣*; *(before n)* *‹country/government›* anfitrión **(b)** (Rad, TV) presentador, -dora *m*,*f* **2** (of parasite) huésped *m* **3** (multitude) gran cantidad *f* **4** **the Host** (Relig) la Sagrada Hostia

host² *vt* **(a)** (be the venue for) *‹conference/event›* ser* la sede de **(b)** (Rad, TV) *‹program›* presentar

hostage /'hɑːstɪdʒ ‖'hɒstɪdʒ/ *n* rehén *m*

hostel /'hɑːst̩l ‖'hɒst̩l/ *n* **(a)** (youth ~) albergue *m* juvenil *or* de juventud **(b)** (for students) (BrE) residencia *f̣*; (for homeless people, battered wives etc) hogar *m*

hostess /'həʊstəs ‖'həʊstes/ *n* **(a)** (in private capacity) anfitriona *f* **(b)** (air ~) (esp BrE) ▶ STEWARDESS B **(c)** (on TV show) (presenter) presentadora *f̣*; (assistant) azafata *f*

hostile /'hɑːst̩l ‖'hɒstaɪl/ *adj* hostil

hostility /hɑːˈstɪləti ‖hɒˈstɪləti/ *n* hostilidad *f*

hot /hɑːt ‖hɒt/ *adj* **-tt-** **1** **(a)** *‹food/water›* caliente; *‹weather/day/country›* caluroso; *‹climate›* cálido; it's ~ today hoy hace calor; I'm ~ tengo calor; to be ~ «*object*» estar* caliente; to get ~ *‹oven/iron/radiator›* calentarse* **(b)** (spicy) picante, picoso (Méx) **2** **(a)** (fresh) *‹news/scent›* reciente, fresco **(b)** (current) *‹story/issue›* de plena actualidad **(c)** (popular, in demand) *‹product›* de gran aceptación; *‹play/movie›* taquillero **3** (colloq) (knowledgeable, keen): he's very ~ on current affairs está muy al tanto en temas de actualidad; she's ~ on punctuality le da mucha importancia a la puntualidad

hot: ~ **air** *n* palabrería *f̣*; ~**-air balloon** /ˈhɑːt̩er ‖ˈhɒt̩eə/ *n* globo *m* de aire caliente; ~**bed** *n* (of crime, unrest) semillero *m*; ~**-blooded** /ˈhɑːt̩ˈblʌdəd ‖ˌhɒt̩ˈblʌdɪd/ *adj* apasionado; ~ **dog** *n* perro *m or* perrito *m* caliente, pancho *m* (RPI)

hotel /həʊˈtel/ *n* hotel *m*

hotelier /həʊˈteljər ‖həʊˈtelɪə(r)/ *n* hotelero, -ra *m*,*f*

hot: ~ **flush**, (AmE) ~ **flash** *n* sofoco *m*, bochorno *m*, calor *m* (RPI fam); ~**headed** /ˈhɑːt̩ˈhedəd ‖ˌhɒt̩ˈhedɪd/ *adj* exaltado; ~**house** *n* invernadero *m*; *(before n)* *‹plant/flowers›* de invernadero; ~ **line** *n* (Pol) teléfono *m* rojo; (for public) línea *f* directa

hotly /'hɑːtli ‖'hɒtli/ *adv* *‹dispute/deny›* con vehemencia; *‹debated›* acaloradamente

hot: ~ **pepper** *n* (AmE) pimiento *m* picante, ají *m* picante (AmS), chile *m* (Méx); ~**plate** *n* (for cooking) placa *f*, hornilla *f* (AmL exc CS), hornalla *f* (RPI), plato *m* (Chi); (for keeping food warm) calientaplatos *m*; ~ **seat** *n* (colloq): to be in the ~ seat estar* en la línea de fuego; ~**shot** *n* personaje *m*; ~ **spot** *n* (colloq) **(a)** (Pol) punto *m* conflictivo **(b)** (night club) club *m* nocturno; ~ **spring** *n* fuente *f* termal; ~**-tempered**

677

hot-water bottle ···❖ hull

/'hɑ:t'tempərd ‖,hɒt'tempəd/ adj irascible;
~-water bottle /'hɑ:t'wɔ:tər ‖,hɒt'wɔ:tə/ n
bolsa f de agua caliente

hound¹ /haʊnd/ n perro m de caza, sabueso m

hound² vt acosar

hour /aʊr ‖aʊə(r)/ n (a) (60 minutes) hora f (b)
(time of day) hora f; **on the ~** a la hora en punto;
at 1600 ~s a las 16:00 horas (c) (particular moment)
momento m; **her finest ~** su mejor momento

hourly¹ /'aʊrli ‖'aʊəli/ adj ‹rate/wage› por
hora

hourly² adv (a) (every hour) ‹run/broadcast›
cada hora (b) (by the hour) ‹pay/charge› por
hora(s)

house¹ /haʊs/ n (pl **houses** /'haʊzəz
‖'haʊzɪz/) 1 (dwelling, household) casa f; **to put
one's (own) ~ in order** poner* sus (or mis etc)
asuntos en orden; **to set up ~** poner* casa
2 (Govt) Cámara f; **the H~ of Representatives** (in
US) la Cámara de Representantes or de
Diputados; **the H~ of Commons/of Lords** (in UK)
la Cámara de los Comunes/de los Lores; **the H~s
of Parliament** (in UK) el Parlamento
3 (Busn) casa f, empresa f; **publishing ~**
editorial f; **drinks are on the ~** invita la casa;
(before n) **~ wine** vino m de la casa
4 (Theat) (a) (auditorium) sala f (b) (audience)
público m

house² /haʊz/ vt (a) (accommodate) ‹person/
family› alojar (b) (contain) ‹office/museum›
albergar*

house /haʊs/: **~ arrest** n arresto m
domiciliario; **~boat** n casa f flotante; **~bound**
adj: **she's 85 and completely ~bound** tiene 85
años y está completamente confinado a su casa;
~broken adj (AmE) ‹pet› enseñado; **~fly** n
mosca f común or doméstica

household /'haʊshəʊld/ n casa f, **~s with
more than one wage earner** las familias or (fml)
los hogares donde trabajan dos o más personas;
(before n) **a ~ name** un nombre muy conocido

householder /'haʊshəʊldər ‖'haʊshəʊldə(r)/
n dueño, -ña m,f de casa

house /haʊs/: **~-hunt** vi (usu in -ing form)
buscar* casa (para comprar o alquilar);
~husband n (hum) hombre que se ocupa de la
casa mientras su mujer sale a trabajar, amo m de
casa (hum); **~keeper** n (woman) ama f‡ de llaves;
(in hotel) gobernanta f; (man) encargado m de la
casa; **~keeping** n (a) (running of home) gobierno
m de la casa (b) **~keeping (money)** dinero m
(para los gastos) de la casa; **~maid** n criada f,
mucama f (AmL); **~plant** n planta f de interior;
~-proud adj (esp BrE) muy meticuloso (en la
limpieza y el arreglo de la casa); **~-to-~**
/'haʊstə'haʊs/ adj ‹inquiries/search› puerta a
puerta; **~-trained** adj (BrE) ‹pet› enseñado;
~warming (party) /'haʊs,wɔ:rmɪŋ
‖'haʊs,wɔ:mɪŋ/ n: fiesta de inauguración de una
casa; **~wife** n ama f‡ de casa; **~work** n tareas
fpl domésticas, trabajo m de la casa

housing /'haʊzɪŋ/ n (a) (dwellings) viviendas fpl
(b) (provision of houses): **the government's policy
on ~** la política del gobierno en cuanto al
problema de la vivienda

housing: ~ association n (in UK) asociación
que construye o renueva viviendas para
alquilarlas a precios módicos; **~ development**

n (AmE) complejo m habitacional, urbanización f
(Esp), fraccionamiento m (Méx); **~ estate** n
(BrE) (a) (council estate) urbanización de viviendas
de alquiler subvencionadas por el ayuntamiento
(b) (privately owned) ▶ ~ DEVELOPMENT; **~
project** n (in US) complejo m de viviendas
subvencionadas

hovel /'hʌvəl ‖'hɒvəl/ n casucha f, rancho m
(RPl)

hover /'hʌvər ‖'hɒvə(r)/ vi «helicopter»
sostenerse* en el aire (sin avanzar); «bird»
cernerse*; **the temperature ~ed around 20°** la
temperatura rondaba los 20°; **the waiter ~ed
around, waiting for a tip** el mesero estuvo
rodando la mesa, esperando una propina

hovercraft /'hʌvərkræft ‖'hɒvəkrɑ:ft/ n (pl
-craft or **-crafts**) aerodeslizador m

how /haʊ/ adv 1 (in questions) cómo; **~ are you?**
¿cómo estás?
2 (with adjs, advs) (a) (in questions): **~ wide is it?**
¿cuánto mide or tiene de ancho?, ¿qué tan ancho
es? (AmL exc CS); **~ heavy is it?** ¿cuánto pesa?; **~
often do you meet?** ¿con qué frecuencia se
reúnen?; **~ old are you?** ¿cuántos años tienes?
(b) (in exclamations) qué; **~ strange/rude!** ¡qué
raro/grosero!
3 (in phrases) **how about** o (colloq) **how's about
sth: Thursday's no good; ~ about Friday?** el
jueves no puede ser ¿qué te parece el viernes?; **I'd
love to go; ~ about you?** me encantaría ir ¿y a
ti?; **how come** (colloq): **~ come the door's locked?**
¿cómo es que la puerta está cerrada con llave?

however /haʊ'evər ‖haʊ'evə(r)/ adv 1 (as
linker) sin embargo, no obstante (fml) 2 (used
before adj or adv) (no matter how): **~ hard she tried
...** por más que trataba ... 3 (interrog) cómo

howl¹ /haʊl/ vi (a) «dog/wolf» aullar*;
«person» dar* alaridos; «wind/gale» aullar*,
bramar (b) (weep noisily) (colloq) berrear (fam)

howl² n (of dog, wolf) aullido m; (of person)
alarido m, aullido m

hp (= **horsepower**) CV, HP

HP n (BrE) = **hire purchase**

HQ n = **headquarters**

hr (= **hour**) h.

HRH (in UK) (= **Her/His Royal Highness**)
S.A.R.

HRT n = **hormone replacement therapy**

HTML n (Comput) (= **hypertext markup
language**) HTML m

hub /'hʌb/ n (a) (of wheel) cubo m (b) (focal point)
centro m

hub cap n tapacubos m, taza f (RPl)

huddle¹ /'hʌdl/ vi (a) **~ (together)** (crowd
together) apiñarse (b) **~ (up)** (curl up) acurrucarse*

huddle² n (tight group) grupo m, corrillo m; (in
US football) timbac m, jol m

hue /hju:/ n (liter) (color) color m; (shade) tono m

hue and cry n (no pl) revuelo m

huff /hʌf/ n (no pl): **to be in a ~** estar*
enfurruñado, estar* con mufa (RPl fam)

hug¹ /hʌg/ vt **-gg-** (a) (embrace) abrazar* (b)
(keep close to) ir* pegado a

hug² n abrazo m

huge /'hju:dʒ/ adj enorme

hull /hʌl/ n (of ship, plane, tank) casco m

hullo /həˈləʊ ‖hʌˈləʊ/ (esp BrE) ► HELLO

hum¹ /hʌm/ -mm- vi «machinery/bee/wire» zumbar; «person» tararear (con la boca cerrada) ■ ~ vt ‹tune› tararear (con la boca cerrada)

hum² n (no pl) (of bees, machinery) zumbido m; (of voices, traffic) murmullo m

human¹ /ˈhjuːmən/ adj humano

human² n ser* m humano

human being n ser m humano

humane /hjuːˈmeɪn/ adj humanitario, humano

humanism /ˈhjuːmənɪzəm/ n humanismo m

humanist /ˈhjuːmənəst ‖ˈhjuːmənɪst/ n humanista mf

humanitarian /hjuːˌmænəˈteəriən ‖hjuːˌmænɪˈteəriən/ adj humanitario

humanities /hjuːˈmænətiz/ n (a) (+ pl vb) the ~ las humanidades, las artes y las letras (b) (discipline) (+ sing vb) humanidades fpl

humanity /hjuːˈmænəti/ n humanidad f

human: ~ nature n naturaleza f humana; **~ rights** pl n derechos mpl humanos

humble /ˈhʌmbəl/ adj humilde

humbly /ˈhʌmbli/ adv humildemente

humdrum /ˈhʌmdrʌm/ adj monótono, rutinario

humid /ˈhjuːməd ‖ˈhjuːmɪd/ adj húmedo

humidity /hjuːˈmɪdəti/ n humedad f

humiliate /hjuːˈmɪlieɪt/ vt humillar

humiliating /hjuːˈmɪlieɪtɪŋ/ adj humillante

humiliation /hjuːˌmɪliˈeɪʃən/ n humillación f

humility /hjuːˈmɪləti/ n humildad f

humor¹, (BrE) **humour** /ˈhjuːmər ‖ˈhjuːmə(r)/ n humor m

humor², (BrE) **humour** vt seguirle* la corriente a

humorless, (BrE) **humourless** /ˈhjuːmərləs ‖ˈhjuːmələs/ adj ‹person› sin sentido del humor

humorous /ˈhjuːmərəs/ adj ‹novel/play/speech› humorístico; ‹situation› cómico, gracioso

humour n/vt (BrE) ► HUMOR¹,²

hump /hʌmp/ n (a) (of camel) joroba f, giba f; (of person) joroba f (b) (in ground) montículo m

hunch¹ /hʌntʃ/ vt ‹back/shoulders› encorvar

hunch² n (intuitive feeling) (colloq) presentimiento m, pálpito m, corazonada f

hunch: ~back n (person) jorobado, -da m,f; (hump) joroba f; **~backed** /ˈhʌntʃbækt/ adj jorobado

hundred /ˈhʌndrəd/ n cien m; a/one ~ cien; a/one ~ and one ciento uno; two ~ doscientos; five ~ quinientos; five ~ pages quinientas páginas; in (the year) fifteen ~ en el (año) mil quinientos; she lived in the seventeen ~s vivió en el siglo XVIII; ten ~s are a thousand diez centenas son un millar; they are sold by the ~ o in ~s se venden de a cien or (Esp) de cien en cien; a/one ~ thousand/million cien mil/millones; ~s of times cientos de veces

hundredfold /ˈhʌndrədfəʊld/ adj/adv ► -FOLD

hundredth¹ /ˈhʌndrədθ/ adj centésimo

hundredth² adv en centésimo lugar

hundredth³ n (Math) centésimo m; (part) centésima parte f

hundredweight /ˈhʌndrədweɪt/ n (pl ~) unidad de peso equivalente a 45,36kg. en EEUU y a 50,80kg. en RU

hung /hʌŋ/ past & past p of HANG¹

Hungarian¹ /hʌŋˈgeriən ‖hʌŋˈgeəriən/ adj húngaro

Hungarian² n (a) (language) húngaro m (b) (person) húngaro, -ra m,f

Hungary /ˈhʌŋgəri/ n Hungría f

hunger /ˈhʌŋgər ‖ˈhʌŋgə(r)/ n (a) (physical) hambre f; (b) (strong desire) (no pl): a ~ for adventure un ansia f or (liter) hambre de aventura

hunger strike n huelga f de hambre

hung: ~ jury n: jurado que se disuelve al no ponerse de acuerdo sus miembros; **~over** /hʌŋˈəʊvər‖hʌŋˈəʊvə(r)/ adj to be ~over tener* resaca or (Col fam) guayabo or (AmL, Méx fam) cruda or (Ven fam) ratón

hungrily /ˈhʌŋgrəli ‖ˈhʌŋgrɪli/ adv ávidamente

hungry /ˈhʌŋgri/ adj -grier, -griest hambriento; to be ~ tener* hambre; to be ~ FOR sth estar* ávido DE algo

hunk /hʌŋk/ n (a) (chunk) trozo m, pedazo m (b) (man) (colloq): he's a real ~ está buenísimo (fam)

hunt¹ /hʌnt/ vt [1] ‹game/fox› cazar* [2] (search for) buscar* ■ ~ vi (a) (pursue game) cazar*; to go ~ing ir* de caza or de cacería (b) (search) to ~ (FOR sth) buscar* (algo) ■ **hunt down** [v + o + adv, v + adv + o] ‹animal/fugitive› darle* caza a

hunt² n [1] (a) (chase) caza f, cacería f (b) (hunters) partida f de caza, cacería f [2] (search) búsqueda f

hunter /ˈhʌntər ‖ˈhʌntə(r)/ n (person) cazador, -dora m,f; (horse) caballo m de caza

hunting /ˈhʌntɪŋ/ n (Sport) caza f, cacería f

hurdle /ˈhɜːrdl̩ ‖ˈhɜːdl̩/ n (a) (Sport) (obstacle) obstáculo m, valla f; see also HURDLES (b) (problem) obstáculo m

hurdles /ˈhɜːrdlz ‖ˈhɜːdlz/ n (+ sing vb) vallas fpl

hurl /hɜːrl ‖hɜːl/ vt tirar, arrojar, lanzar*

hurrah /hʊˈrɑː/, **hurray** /hʊˈreɪ/ interj ► HOORAY

hurricane /ˈhɜːrəkeɪn ‖ˈhʌrɪkən, -keɪn/ n huracán m

hurry¹ /ˈhɜːri ‖ˈhʌri/ n (no pl) prisa f, apuro m (AmL); I'm in a ~ tengo prisa, estoy apurado (AmL); he wrote it in a ~ lo escribió deprisa (fam)

hurry² -ries, -rying, -ried vi (a) (make haste) darse* prisa, apurarse (AmL) (b) (move hastily) (+ adv compl): she hurried after him corrió tras él; he hurried back/in/out volvió/entró/salió corriendo

■ ~ *vt* (a) ⟨*person*⟩ meterle prisa a, apurar (AmL)
(b) ⟨*work*⟩ hacer* apresuradamente
■ **hurry away, hurry off** [*v* + *adv*] alejarse
rápidamente
■ **hurry up** ① [*v* + *adv*] darse* prisa, apurarse
(AmL) ② [*v* + *o* + *adv*, *v* + *adv* + *o*] ⟨*person*⟩
meterle prisa a, apurar (AmL); ⟨*work*⟩ acelerar,
apurar (AmL)

hurt¹ /hɜːrt ‖ˈhɜːt/ (*past* & *past p* **hurt**) *vt*
① (a) (cause pain): **you're ~ing her/me!** ¡le/me
estás haciendo daño!, ¡la/me estás lastimando!
(esp AmL) (b) (injure): **I ~ my ankle** me hice daño
en el tobillo, me lastimé el tobillo (esp AmL); **to ~
oneself, to get ~** hacerse* daño, lastimarse (esp
AmL)
② (distress emotionally): **I've been ~ too often** me
han hecho sufrir demasiadas veces; **to ~ sb's
feelings** herir* los sentimientos de algn
■ ~ *vi* ① (be source of pain) doler*; **my leg ~s** me
duele la pierna
② (have adverse effects): **it won't ~ to postpone it
for a while** no pasa nada si lo dejamos por el
momento
③ (suffer adverse effects) (AmE colloq): **to be ~ing**
estar* pasándola *or* pasándolo mal (fam)

hurt² *n* (emotional) dolor *m*, pena *f*

hurt³ *adj* (a) (physically) ⟨*finger/foot*⟩ lastimado;
she was badly ~ estaba gravemente herida (b)
(emotionally) ⟨*feelings/pride*⟩ herido; ⟨*tone/
expression*⟩ dolido; **to feel/be ~** sentirse*/estar*
dolido

hurtful /ˈhɜːrtfəl ‖ˈhɜːtfəl/ *adj* hiriente

hurtle /ˈhɜːrtl̩ ‖ˈhɜːtl̩/ *vi* (+ *adv compl*): **to ~
along/past** ir*/pasar volando *or* a toda velocidad

husband /ˈhʌzbənd/ *n* marido *m*, esposo *m*

hush¹ /hʌʃ/ *n* (*no pl*) silencio *m*

hush² *vt* (quieten) hacer* callar; (calm down)
calmar
■ **hush up** ① [*v* + *o* + *adv*, *v* + *adv* + *o*] ⟨*scandal/
story*⟩ acallar ② [*v* + *adv*] (be quiet) (AmE colloq)
callarse

hush³ *interj*: ~! ¡shh!, ¡chitón!

hushed /hʌʃt/ *adj* (*before n*) silencioso; **in ~
tones** en voz muy baja, en murmullos

hush-hush *adj* (colloq) super secreto (fam)

husk /hʌsk/ *n* (of wheat, rice) cáscara *f*, cascarilla
f; (of maize) chala *f or* (Esp) farfolla *f*

husky¹ /ˈhʌski/ *adj* **-kier, -kiest** ronco

husky² *n* (*pl* **-kies**) husky *mf*, perro, -rra *m,f*
esquimal

hustings /ˈhʌstɪŋz/ *pl n* **the ~** la campaña
electoral

hustle¹ /ˈhʌsəl/ *vt* ① (a) (move hurriedly) (+ *adv
compl*): **she was ~d into the car** la metieron en el
coche a empujones; **he was ~d away by his
bodyguards** sus guardaespaldas se lo llevaron
precipitadamente (b) (pressure) apremiar, meterle
prisa a, apurar (AmL) ② (AmE colloq) (a) (obtain
aggressively) hacerse* con (b) (hawk, sell) vender

hustle² *n* ① (hurry) ajetreo *m*; **the ~ and bustle
of the big city** el ajetreo y bullicio de la gran
ciudad ② (trick, swindle) (AmE colloq) chanchullo *m*
(fam)

hustler /ˈhʌslər ‖ˈhʌslə(r)/ *n* (AmE) (a) (hard
worker) (colloq) persona *f* trabajadora (b) (swindler)
(sl) estafador, -dora *m,f* (c) (prostitute) (sl) puto, -ta
m,f (vulg)

hut /hʌt/ *n* (a) (cabin) cabaña *f*; (of mud, straw)
choza *f* (b) (hovel) casucha *f*

hutch /ˈhʌtʃ/ *n* (rabbit ~) conejera *f*

hyaena /haɪˈiːnə/ *n* ▶ HYENA

hybrid /ˈhaɪbrəd ‖ˈhaɪbrɪd/ *n* híbrido *m*

hydrant /ˈhaɪdrənt/ *n* boca *f* de riego, toma *f* de
agua, hidrante *m* (AmC, Col); (fire ~) boca *f* de
incendios *or* (Esp) de riego, toma *f* de agua,
hidrante *m* de incendios (AmC, Col), grifo *m* (Chi)

hydraulic /haɪˈdrɔːlɪk ‖haɪˈdrɔːlɪk, haɪˈdrɒlɪk/
adj hidráulico

hydrocarbon /ˌhaɪdrəʊˈkɑːrbən
‖ˌhaɪdrəˈkɑːbən/ *n* hidrocarburo *m*

hydroelectric /ˈhaɪdrəʊɪˈlektrɪk/ *adj*
hidroeléctrico

hydrofoil /ˈhaɪdrəfɔɪl/ *n* (vessel) hidrodeslizador
m, aliscafo *m*

hydrogen /ˈhaɪdrədʒən/ *n* hidrógeno *m*

hyena /haɪˈiːnə/ *n* hiena *f*

hygiene /ˈhaɪdʒiːn/ *n* higiene *f*

hygienic /haɪˈdʒiːnɪk/ *adj* higiénico

hymn /hɪm/ *n* (Relig) cántico *m*, himno *m*

hype¹ /haɪp/ *n* (colloq) despliegue *m or* bombo *m*
publicitario

hype² *vt* (colloq) promocionar con bombos y
platillos *or* (Esp) a bombo y platillo
■ **hype up** [*v* + *adv* + *o*, *v* + *o* + *adv*] (colloq)
⟨*movie*⟩ promocionar con bombos y platillos *or*
(Esp) a bombo y platillo; ⟨*person*⟩ poner* nervioso

hyperactive /ˈhaɪpərˈæktɪv/ *adj* hiperactivo

hypermarket /ˈhaɪpərˌmɑːrkət
‖ˈhaɪpəmɑːkɪt/ *n* (BrE) hipermercado *m*

hypertension /ˈhaɪpərˈtenʃən
‖ˈhaɪpəˈtenʃən/ *n* hipertensión *f*

hypertext markup language
/ˈhaɪpərtekst ‖ˈhaɪpətekst/ *n* (Comput) lenguaje *m*
de marcado de hipertexto

hyperventilate /ˈhaɪpərˈventɪleɪt
‖ˌhaɪpəˈventɪleɪt/ *vi* hiperventilarse

hyphen /ˈhaɪfən/ *n* guion *m*

hypnosis /hɪpˈnəʊsəs ‖hɪpˈnəʊsɪs/ *n* hipnosis *f*

hypnotic /hɪpˈnɑːtɪk ‖hɪpˈnɒtɪk/ *adj*
⟨*suggestion/state*⟩ hipnótico; ⟨*voice/eyes/rhythm*⟩
hipnotizador, hipnotizante

hypnotism /ˈhɪpnətɪzəm/ *n* hipnotismo *m*

hypnotist /ˈhɪpnətəst ‖ˈhɪpnətɪst/ *n*
hipnotizador, -dora *m,f*

hypnotize /ˈhɪpnətaɪz/ *vt* hipnotizar*

hypoallergenic /ˈhaɪpəʊˌæler'dʒenɪk
‖ˌhaɪpəʊˌælə'dʒenɪk/ *adj* hipoalérgeno

hypochondriac /ˈhaɪpəˈkɑːndriæk
‖ˌhaɪpəˈkɒndriæk/ *n* hipocondríaco, -ca *m,f*

hypocrisy /hɪˈpɑːkrəsi ‖hɪˈpɒkrəsi/ *n* (*pl*
-sies) hipocresía *f*

hypocrite /ˈhɪpəkrɪt/ *n* hipócrita *mf*

hypocritical /ˈhɪpəˈkrɪtɪkəl/ *adj* hipócrita

hypodermic¹ /ˈhaɪpəˈdɜːrmɪk ‖ˌhaɪpəˈdɜːmɪk/
adj hipodérmico

hypodermic² *n* (aguja *f*) hipodérmica *f*

hypothermia /ˈhaɪpəˈθɜːrmiə ‖ˌhaɪpəˈθɜːmiə/
n hipotermia *f*

hypothesis /haɪˈpɑːθəsəs ‖haɪˈpɒθəsɪs/ *n* (*pl*
-ses /-siːz/) hipótesis *f*

hypothetical /ˈhaɪpəˈθetɪkəl/ *adj* hipotético

h

hysterectomy /ˈhɪstəˈrektəmi/ n (pl **-mies**) histerectomía f

hysteria /hɪˈstɪriə ‖ hɪˈstɪəriə/ n histerismo m, histeria f

hysterical /hɪˈsterɪkəl/ adj (a) (Psych) histérico (b) (very funny) (colloq) para morirse de (la) risa

hysterics /hɪˈsterɪks/ pl n (a) (nervous agitation) histeria f, histerismo m; **to go into** or **have ~** ponerse* histérico (b) (laughter) (colloq) **to be in ~** estar* como loco

I i

I, i /aɪ/ n I, i f

I /aɪ/ pron yo

■ Note Although yo is given as the main translation of I, it is in practice used only for emphasis, or to avoid ambiguity: I went to the theater fui al teatro; I was singing, he was playing the piano yo cantaba y él tocaba el piano; I did it yo lo hice.

IA = Iowa

IBA n (in UK) = **Independent Broadcasting Authority**

Iberian /aɪˈbɪriən ‖ aɪˈbɪəriən/ adj ibérico

ice¹ /aɪs/ n **1** (frozen water) hielo m; **to break the ~** (overcome reserve) romper* el hielo; (make a start) (AmE) dar* los primeros pasos **2** (sherbet) (AmE) sorbete m, helado m de agua (AmL), nieve f (Méx)

ice² vt ‹cake› bañar ‹con fondant›

Ice Age n: **the ~ ~** la edad de hielo

iceberg /ˈaɪsbɜːrg ‖ ˈaɪsbɜːg/ n iceberg m

ice: ~box n (a) (refrigerator) (AmE colloq & dated) refrigerador m, nevera f, heladera f (RPl) (b) (freezing compartment) (BrE) congelador m; **~ cream** n helado m; **~ cube** n cubito m de hielo

iced /aɪst/ adj **1** (chilled) helado **2** (Culin) glaseado

ice hockey n hockey m sobre hielo

Iceland /ˈaɪslənd/ n Islandia f

Icelandic¹ /aɪsˈlændɪk/ adj islandés

Icelandic² n islandés m

ice: ~ lolly n (BrE) paleta f helada or (Esp) polo m or (RPl) palito m helado or (CS) chupete m helado; **~ rink** n (BrE) pista f de (patinaje sobre) hielo; **~ skating** n patinaje m sobre hielo

icicle /ˈaɪsɪkəl/ n carámbano m (de hielo)

icing /ˈaɪsɪŋ/ n (Culin) glaseado m

icing sugar n (BrE) azúcar m or f glas(é) or (RPl) impalpable or (Chi) flor or (Col) en polvo

icon /ˈaɪkɑːn ‖ ˈaɪkɒn/ n icono m, ícono m

icy /ˈaɪsi/ adj **icier, iciest** (a) ‹wind/rain› helado, glacial; ‹feet/hands› helado; (as adv) **~ cold** helado (b) ‹stare/reception› glacial (c) ‹roads/ground› cubierto de hielo

ID (a) = **identification** (b) = **Idaho**

idea /aɪˈdiːə ‖ aɪˈdɪə/ n idea f; **I had an ~** se me ocurrió una idea; **that's the general ~** de eso se trata; **that's not my ~ of fun** eso no es lo que yo entiendo por diversión; **where is he? — (I've) no ~!** ¿dónde está? — (no tengo) ni idea

ideal¹ /aɪˈdiːəl/ adj ideal

ideal² n ideal m

idealism /aɪˈdiːəlɪzəm/ n idealismo m

idealist /aɪˈdiːələst ‖ aɪˈdiːəlɪst/ n idealista mf

idealistic /aɪˈdiːəˈlɪstɪk ‖ ˌaɪdiəˈlɪstɪk/ adj idealista

idealize /aɪˈdiːəlaɪz ‖ aɪˈdiəlaɪz/ vt idealizar*

ideally /aɪˈdiːəli ‖ aɪˈdɪəli/ adv ‹located/placed/equipped› inmejorablemente; **they are ~ suited** están hechos el uno para el otro; **~, no one would have to do it** (indep) lo ideal sería que nadie tuviera que hacerlo

identical /aɪˈdentɪkəl/ adj idéntico; **~ twins** gemelos mpl univitelinos (téc), gemelos mpl (AmL), gemelos mpl idénticos (Esp); **to be ~ TO** o **WITH sth** ser* idéntico A algo

identification /aɪˈdentəfəˈkeɪʃən ‖ aɪˌdentɪfɪˈkeɪʃən/ n (a) (act of identifying) identificación f (b) (evidence of identity): **have you got any ~?** ¿tiene algún documento que acredite su identidad?

identification parade n (BrE) rueda f de identificación or de sospechosos

identify /aɪˈdentəfaɪ ‖ aɪˈdentɪfaɪ/ **-fies, -fying, -fied** vt identificar*
■ v refl (reveal identity) **to ~ oneself** identificarse*
■ ~ vi **to ~ WITH sb/sth** identificarse* CON algn/algo

Identikit® /aɪˈdentəkɪt ‖ aɪˈdentɪkɪt/ n: **~ picture** Identikit® m, retrato m hablado (AmS) or (Méx) reconstruido or (Esp) robot

identity /aɪˈdentəti/ n (pl **-ties**) identidad f; (before n) **~ card** carné m or (AmL tb) cédula f de identidad

ideological /ˈaɪdiəˈlɑːdʒɪkəl ‖ ˌaɪdiəˈlɒdʒɪkəl/ adj ideológico

ideology /ˈaɪdiˈɑːlədʒi ‖ ˌaɪdiˈɒlədʒi/ n (pl **-gies**) ideología f

idiom /ˈɪdiəm/ n modismo m

idiomatic /ˈɪdiəˈmætɪk/ adj idiomático

idiosyncrasy /ˈɪdiəˈsɪŋkrəsi/ n (pl **-sies**) idiosincrasia f

idiosyncratic /ˈɪdiəsɪŋˈkrætɪk ‖ ˌɪdiəsɪŋˈkrætɪk/ adj idiosincrásico

idiot /ˈɪdiət/ n idiota mf

idiotic /ˈɪdiˈɑːtɪk ‖ ˌɪdiˈɒtɪk/ adj idiota

idle¹ /ˈaɪdl/ adj **idler** /ˈaɪdlər ‖ ˈaɪdlə(r)/, **idlest** /ˈaɪdləst ‖ ˈaɪdlɪst/ **1** (a) (not in use or employment): **to be ~** «worker» no tener* trabajo; «machine/

factory» estar* parado **(b)** (unoccupied) ‹*hours/ moment*› de ocio **2** (lazy) holgazán **3** (frivolous): **it was ~ curiosity** era pura curiosidad; **~ speculation** conjeturas *fpl* inútiles

idle² *vi* **(a)** (be lazy) holgazanear **(b)** (Auto) «*engine*» andar* al ralentí

idleness /'aɪdlnəs ‖'aɪdlnɪs/ *n* **(a)** (involuntary inactivity) inactividad *f* **(b)** (laziness) holgazanería *f*

idol /'aɪdl̩/ *n* ídolo *m*

idolize /'aɪdl̩aɪz/ *vt* idolatrar

idyll /'aɪdl̩ ‖'ɪdɪl/ *n* idilio *m*

idyllic /aɪ'dɪlɪk ‖ɪ'dɪlɪk/ *adj* idílico

i.e. /'aɪ'iː/ (that is) (in writing) i.e.; (in speech) esto es

if /ɪf/ *conj* **1** (on condition that) si; **~ I were you, I wouldn't do it it** yo en tu lugar *or* yo que tú, no lo haría; **she was very offhand, ~ not downright rude** estuvo muy brusca, por no decir verdaderamente grosera; **~ nothing else** aunque no sea más que eso; **~ so** (*as linker*) si es así **2** (whether) si **3** (though) aunque, si bien

igloo /'ɪgluː/ *n* iglú *m*

ignite /ɪg'naɪt/ *vt* prenderle fuego a ∎ **~** *vi* ‹*fuel/paper*» prenderse fuego

ignition /ɪg'nɪʃən/ *n* **(a)** (act) encendido *m* **(b)** (mechanism) (Auto) encendido *m*; (*before n*) **~ key** llave *f* de contacto *or* (AmL tb) del arranque

ignorance /'ɪgnərəns/ *n* ignorancia *f*

ignorant /'ɪgnərənt/ *adj* (lacking knowledge) ignorante; **to be ~ oF sth** ignorar algo

ignore /ɪg'nɔːr ‖ɪg'nɔː(r)/ *vt* ‹*person/remark*» ignorar; (*warning*) hacer* caso omiso de; **we can't ~ the fact that ...** no podemos dejar de tener en cuenta el hecho de que ...

IL = **Illinois**

ilk /ɪlk/ *n* tipo *m*

ill¹ /ɪl/ *adj* **1** -**er, -est** (unwell) enfermo; **to feel ~ sentirse* mal** **2** (bad) (*before n*): **~ effects** efectos *mpl* negativos; **his ~ health** su mala salud

ill² *adv* (*no comp*) **(a)** (hardly): **I can ~ afford to buy a new car** mal puedo yo permitirme comprar un coche nuevo **(b)** (badly) (frml) mal; **to speak ~ of sb** hablar mal de algn

ill³ *n* mal *m*

Ill = **Illinois**

I'll /aɪl/ = **I will, I shall**

ill: ~-advised /'ɪləd'vaɪzd/ *adj* ‹*action*» desacertado; **you would be ~-advised to go** no sería aconsejable que fueras; **~ at ease** *adj* (*pred*) (uncomfortable) incómodo; (anxious) inquieto; **~-bred** /'ɪl'bred/ *adj* sin educación

illegal /ɪ'liːgəl/ *adj* **(a)** (unlawful) ilegal **(b)** (AmE Sport) antirreglamentario

illegible /ɪ'ledʒəbəl/ *adj* ilegible

illegitimate /ɪlɪ'dʒɪtəmət ‖ɪlɪ'dʒɪtɪmət/ *adj* ilegítimo

ill: ~-fated /'ɪl'feɪtəd ‖ɪl'feɪtɪd/ *adj* infortunado; **~ feeling** *n* resentimiento *m*, rencor *m*; **~-gotten** /'ɪl'gɑːtn̩ ‖ɪl'gɒtn̩/*adj*: **~-gotten gains** dinero *m* mal habido

illicit /ɪ'lɪsət ‖ɪ'lɪsɪt/ *adj* ilícito

ill-informed /'ɪlɪn'fɔːrmd ‖ɪlɪn'fɔːmd/ *adj* mal informado

illiteracy /ɪ'lɪtərəsi/ *n* analfabetismo *m*

illiterate /ɪ'lɪtərət/ *adj* analfabeto

illness /'ɪlnəs ‖'ɪlnɪs/ *n* enfermedad *f*

illogical /ɪ'lɑːdʒɪkəl ‖ɪ'lɒdʒɪkəl/ *adj* ilógico

ill: ~-treat /'ɪl'triːt/ *vt* maltratar; **~-treatment** /'ɪl'triːtmənt/ *n* malos tratos *mpl*

illuminate /ɪ'luːməneɪt ‖ɪ'luːmɪneɪt/ *vt* iluminar

illumination /ɪ'luːmə'neɪʃən ‖ɪ,luː'mɪ'neɪʃən/ *n* iluminación *f*

illusion /ɪ'luːʒən/ *n* **(a)** (false appearance): **to give** *o* **create an ~ of sth** dar* la impresión de algo; (Art) crear la ilusión de algo; **an optical ~** una ilusión óptica **(b)** (false idea) ilusión *f*

illustrate /'ɪləstreɪt/ *vt* **1** ‹*book/magazine*» ilustrar **2** **(a)** (explain by examples) ilustrar **(b)** (show) poner* de manifiesto

illustration /'ɪlə'streɪʃən/ *n* **1** (picture, technique) ilustración *f* **2** (example) ejemplo *m*

illustrator /'ɪləstreɪtər ‖'ɪləstreɪtə(r)/ *n* ilustrador, -dora *m,f*

illustrious /ɪ'lʌstriəs/ *adj* (liter) ilustre

ill will *n* **(a)** (hostility) animadversión *f* **(b)** (spite) rencor *m*

I'm /aɪm/ = **I am**

image /'ɪmɪdʒ/ *n* imagen *f*; **to be the (spitting) ~** *o* **spit and ~ of sb** ser* la viva imagen de algn

imagery /'ɪmɪdʒəri/ *n* imaginería *f*, imágenes *fpl*

imaginable /ɪ'mædʒənəbəl ‖ɪ'mædʒɪnəbəl/ *adj* imaginable

imaginary /ɪ'mædʒəneri ‖ɪ'mædʒɪnəri/ *adj* imaginario

imagination /ɪ'mædʒə'neɪʃən ‖ɪ,mædʒɪ'neɪʃən/ *n* imaginación *f*

imaginative /ɪ'mædʒənətɪv ‖ɪ'mædʒɪnətɪv/ *adj* imaginativo

imagine /ɪ'mædʒən ‖ɪ'mædʒɪn/ *vt* **(a)** (picture to oneself) imaginarse; **I can just ~ her saying that** ya me la imagino diciendo eso **(b)** (fancy mistakenly): **you're imagining things** son imaginaciones *or* figuraciones tuyas **(c)** (assume) imaginarse; **I ~ she's very tired** me imagino que estará muy cansada

imbalance /ɪm'bæləns/ *n* desequilibrio *m*

imbecile /'ɪmbəsəl ‖'ɪmbəsiːl/ *n* imbécil *mf*

imbed /ɪm'bed/ *vt* **-dd-** (AmE) ▶ EMBED

IMF *n* (= **International Monetary Fund**) FMI *m*

imitate /'ɪməteɪt ‖'ɪmɪteɪt/ *vt* imitar

imitation¹ /'ɪmə'teɪʃən ‖,ɪmɪ'teɪʃən/ *n* imitación *f*

imitation² *adj* ‹*gold/pearls*› de imitación

immaculate /ɪ'mækjələt ‖ɪ'mækjʊlət/ *adj* impecable

immaterial /'ɪmə'tɪriəl ‖,ɪmə'tɪəriəl/ *adj* irrelevante

immature /'ɪmə'tʊr ‖,ɪmə'tjʊə(r)/ *adj* **(a)** ‹*tree/ animal*› joven; ‹*fruit*› verde, inmaduro **(b)** (childish) ‹*person/attitude*› inmaduro

immaturity /'ɪmə'tʊrəti ‖,ɪmə'tjʊərəti/ *n* inmadurez *f*

immediate /ɪ'miːdiət/ *adj* **1** **(a)** (instant, prompt) inmediato **(b)** ‹*problem/need*› urgente, apremiante **2** (*before n*) (close): **in the ~ future** en el futuro inmediato; **in the ~ vicinity** en las inmediaciones

immediately /ɪˈmiːdiətli/ adv **1** (at once)
inmediatamente **2** ‹before/after/above/below›
justo

immemorial /ˈɪməˈmɔːriəl/ adj (liter)
inmemorial (liter)

immense /ɪˈmens/ adj inmenso, enorme

immensely /ɪˈmensli/ adv ‹enjoy/like›
enormemente; ‹popular/powerful› inmensamente

immerse /ɪˈmɜːrs ‖ɪˈmɜːs/ vt **(a)** (submerge) to
~ sth/sb (IN sth) sumergir* algo/a algn (EN algo)
(b) (absorb, involve) to be ~d IN sth estar* absorto
EN algo

immersion heater /ɪˈmɜːrʒən ‖ɪˈmɜːʃən/ n
calentador m eléctrico (de agua), termo m (Chi),
termofón m (RPl)

immigrant /ˈɪməɡrənt ‖ˈɪmɪɡrənt/ n
inmigrante mf; ‹before n› ‹worker/population›
inmigrante

immigration /ˈɪməˈɡreɪʃən ‖ˌɪmɪˈɡreɪʃən/ n
inmigración f

imminent /ˈɪmənənt ‖ˈɪmɪnənt/ adj inminente

immobile /ɪˈməʊbaɪl ‖ɪˈməʊbaɪl/ adj inmóvil

immobilize /ɪˈməʊbəlaɪz ‖ɪˈməʊbɪlaɪz/ vt
inmovilizar*

immoderate /ɪˈmɑːdərət ‖ɪˈmɒdərət/ adj
‹demands/appetite› desmedido

immodest /ɪˈmɑːdəst ‖ɪˈmɒdɪst/ adj **(a)**
(conceited) presuntuoso, inmodesto **(b)** (indecent)
‹behavior/suggestion› impúdico, inmodesto

immoral /ɪˈmɔːrəl ‖ɪˈmɒrəl/ adj inmoral

immorality /ˈɪmɔːˈræləti ‖ˌɪməˈræləti/ n
inmoralidad f

immortal /ɪˈmɔːrtl ‖ɪˈmɔːtl/ adj inmortal

immortality /ˈɪmɔːrˈtæləti ‖ˌɪmɔːˈtæləti/ n
inmortalidad f

immortalize /ɪˈmɔːrtlaɪz ‖ɪˈmɔːtlaɪz/ vt
inmortalizar*

immune /ɪˈmjuːn/ adj **(a)** (not susceptible) to be
~ TO sth ser* inmune A algo **(b)** ‹before n›
‹system/response› inmunológico

immunity /ɪˈmjuːnəti/ n inmunidad f

immunization /ˈɪmjənəˈzeɪʃən ‖ˌɪmjʊnaɪˈzeɪʃən/ n inmunización f

immunize /ˈɪmjənaɪz ‖ˈɪmjʊnaɪz/ vt
inmunizar*

imp /ɪmp/ n diablillo m (fam)

impact /ˈɪmpækt/ n impacto m

impair /ɪmˈper ‖ɪmˈpeə(r)/ vt afectar; ~ed
vision/hearing problemas mpl de vista/audición

impale /ɪmˈpeɪl/ vt to ~ sth/sb ON sth
atravesar* algo/a algn CON algo

impart /ɪmˈpɑːrt ‖ɪmˈpɑːt/ vt (fml) ‹news›
comunicar*; ‹knowledge› impartir; ‹feeling/
quality› conferir* (fml)

impartial /ɪmˈpɑːrʃəl ‖ɪmˈpɑːʃəl/ adj imparcial

impassable /ɪmˈpæsəbəl ‖ɪmˈpɑːsəbəl/ adj
‹river/barrier› infranqueable; ‹road›
intransitable

impasse /ˈɪmpæs ‖ˈæmpæs/ n impasse m

impassioned /ɪmˈpæʃənd/ adj apasionado

impassive /ɪmˈpæsɪv/ adj impasible

impatience /ɪmˈpeɪʃəns/ n impaciencia f

impatient /ɪmˈpeɪʃənt/ adj ‹person›
impaciente; ‹gesture/voice› de impaciencia

impatiently /ɪmˈpeɪʃəntli/ adv con
impaciencia

impeach /ɪmˈpiːtʃ/ vt (Law) acusar a un alto
cargo de delitos cometidos en el desempeño de sus
funciones

impeccable /ɪmˈpekəbəl/ adj impecable

impecunious /ˈɪmpɪˈkjuːniəs/ adj (liter or hum)
sin peculio (liter o hum)

impede /ɪmˈpiːd/ vt dificultar

impediment /ɪmˈpedəmənt ‖ɪmˈpedɪmənt/ n
(a) (hindrance) impedimento m **(b)** (physical defect)
defecto m; a speech ~ un defecto del habla

impel /ɪmˈpel/ vt -ll- impeler

impending /ɪmˈpendɪŋ/ adj ‹before n›
inminente

impenetrable /ɪmˈpenətrəbəl/ adj
impenetrable

imperative¹ /ɪmˈperətɪv/ adj **1 (a)** (essential)
imprescindible, fundamental **(b)** ‹need›
imperioso, imperativo **2** (Ling) ‹mood›
imperativo; ‹sentence› en imperativo

imperative² n imperativo m

imperceptible /ˈɪmpərˈseptəbəl ‖ˌɪmpəˈseptəbəl/ adj imperceptible

imperfect¹ /ɪmˈpɜːrfɪkt ‖ɪmˈpɜːfɪkt/ adj
imperfecto

imperfect² n imperfecto m

imperfection /ˈɪmpərˈfekʃən ‖ˌɪmpəˈfekʃən/
n imperfección f

imperial /ɪmˈpɪriəl ‖ɪmˈpɪəriəl/ adj (of empire)
‹before n› imperial, del imperio

imperialism /ɪmˈpɪriəlɪzəm ‖ɪmˈpɪəriəlɪzəm/
n imperialismo m

imperialist /ɪmˈpɪriələst ‖ɪmˈpɪəriəlɪst/ n
imperialista mf

imperil /ɪmˈperəl ‖ɪmˈperɪl, ɪmˈperəl/ vt, (BrE)
-ll- poner* en peligro

imperious /ɪmˈpɪriəs ‖ɪmˈpɪəriəs/ adj
imperioso

impermeable /ɪmˈpɜːrmiəbəl ‖ɪmˈpɜːmiəbəl/
adj impermeable

impersonal /ɪmˈpɜːrsnəl ‖ɪmˈpɜːsənl/ adj
impersonal

impersonate /ɪmˈpɜːrsəneɪt ‖ɪmˈpɜːsəneɪt/ vt
(a) (pretend to be) hacerse* pasar por **(b)** (mimic)
imitar, impersonar (Méx)

impersonator /ɪmˈpɜːrsəneɪtər
‖ɪmˈpɜːsəneɪtə(r)/ n imitador, -dora m,f,
impersonador, -dora m,f (Méx)

impertinent /ɪmˈpɜːrtnənt ‖ɪmˈpɜːtɪnənt/ adj
impertinente

impervious /ɪmˈpɜːrviəs ‖ɪmˈpɜːviəs/ adj **(a)**
‹rock/material› impermeable **(b)** (unaffected) to be
~ TO sth ‹to criticism/doubt› ser* impermeable A
algo

impetuous /ɪmˈpetʃuəs/ adj ⟨person⟩ impetuoso; ⟨action/decision⟩ impulsivo

impetus /ˈɪmpətəs ‖ ˈɪmpɪtəs/ n ímpetu m

impinge /ɪmˈpɪndʒ/ vi to ~ ON o UPON sth ⟨privacy/freedom⟩ vulnerar algo

implacable /ɪmˈplækəbəl/ adj implacable

implant /ɪmˈplænt ‖ ɪmˈplɑːnt/ vt (a) ⟨idea/ideal⟩ inculcar* (b) ⟨embryo/hair⟩ implantar

implausible /ɪmˈplɔːzəbəl/ adj inverosímil

implement¹ /ˈɪmpləmənt ‖ ˈɪmplɪmənt/ vt implementar

implement² /ˈɪmpləmənt ‖ ˈɪmplɪmənt/ n instrumento m, implemento m (AmL)

implicate /ˈɪmpləkeɪt ‖ ˈɪmplɪkeɪt/ vt implicar*

implication /ˌɪmpləˈkeɪʃən ‖ ˌɪmplɪˈkeɪʃən/ n [1] (consequence, significance) repercusión f, implicación f [2] (involvement) implicación f

implicit /ɪmˈplɪsət ‖ ɪmˈplɪsɪt/ adj (a) ⟨threat⟩ implícito (b) ⟨confidence/trust⟩ incondicional, total

implode /ɪmˈpləʊd/ vi implosionar

implore /ɪmˈplɔːr ‖ ɪmˈplɔː(r)/ vt implorar

imply /ɪmˈplaɪ/ vt **implies, implying, implied** [1] (suggest, hint) dar* a entender, insinuar* [2] (involve) implicar*, suponer*

impolite /ˌɪmpəˈlaɪt/ adj maleducado, descortés

import¹ /ˈɪmpɔːrt ‖ ˈɪmpɔːt/ n [1] (Busn) (a) (act) importación f (b) (article): a foreign ~ un artículo de importación [2] (significance) (fml) importancia f

import² /ɪmˈpɔːrt ‖ ɪmˈpɔːt/ vt importar

importance /ɪmˈpɔːrtn̩s ‖ ɪmˈpɔːtn̩s/ n importancia f

important /ɪmˈpɔːrtn̩t ‖ ɪmˈpɔːtn̩t/ adj importante

importer /ɪmˈpɔːrtər ‖ ɪmˈpɔːtə(r)/ n importador, -dora m,f

impose /ɪmˈpəʊz/ vt imponer*
■ ~ vi molestar; **to ~ on sb's goodwill** abusar de la buena voluntad de algn

imposing /ɪmˈpəʊzɪŋ/ adj imponente

imposition /ˌɪmpəˈzɪʃən/ n (a) (enforcement) imposición f (b) (taking unfair advantage) abuso m

impossibility /ɪmˌpɑːsəˈbɪləti ‖ ɪmˌpɒsəˈbɪləti/ n imposibilidad f

impossible¹ /ɪmˈpɑːsəbəl ‖ ɪmˈpɒsəbəl/ adj (a) ⟨job/request⟩ imposible; **it's ~ for me to arrive by twelve** me es imposible llegar para las doce (b) (intolerable) intolerable

impossible² n **to ask/attempt the ~** pedir*/intentar lo imposible

impostor /ɪmˈpɑːstər ‖ ɪmˈpɒstə(r)/ n impostor, -tora m,f

impotence /ˈɪmpətəns/ n impotencia f

impotent /ˈɪmpətənt/ adj impotente

impound /ɪmˈpaʊnd/ vt (a) ⟨possessions/assets⟩ incautar(se de) (b) ⟨vehicle⟩ llevar al depósito municipal

impoverished /ɪmˈpɑːvərɪʃt ‖ ɪmˈpɒvərɪʃt/ adj (financially, spiritually) empobrecido; ⟨soil/diet⟩ pobre

impractical /ɪmˈpræktɪkəl/ adj poco práctico

impregnable /ɪmˈpregnəbəl/ adj ⟨fortress⟩ inexpugnable; ⟨organization⟩ impenetrable

impregnate /ˈɪmpregneɪt ‖ ˈɪmpregneɪt/ vt [1] (saturate) **to ~ sth WITH sth** impregnar algo CON o DE algo [2] (make pregnant) (fml) fecundar

impresario /ˌɪmprəˈsɑːriəʊ ‖ ˌɪmprɪˈsɑːriəʊ/ (pl **-os**) n empresario, -ria m,f teatral

impress /ɪmˈpres/ vt [1] (make impression on): **we were ~ed by your work** tu trabajo nos causó muy buena impresión; **he only did it to ~ her** lo hizo sólo para impactarla [2] (emphasize) **to ~ sth ON o UPON sb** recalcarle* algo a algn
■ ~ vi impresionar

impression /ɪmˈpreʃən/ n [1] (a) (idea, image) impresión f; **to be under the ~ (that) … creer* or pensar* que …** (b) (effect) impresión f; **to make o create a good/bad ~ on sb** causarle a algn una buena/mala impresión [2] (imprint) impresión f, huella f [3] (impersonation) imitación f

impressionable /ɪmˈpreʃnəbəl/ adj (a) (easily influenced) influenciable (b) (easily frightened, upset) impresionable

impressionism /ɪmˈpreʃənɪzəm/ n impresionismo m

impressionist /ɪmˈpreʃənəst ‖ ɪmˈpreʃənɪst/ n (a) (Art) impresionista mf (b) (impersonator) imitador, -dora m,f

impressive /ɪmˈpresɪv/ adj ⟨record/work⟩ admirable; ⟨building/ceremony⟩ imponente

imprint¹ /ˈɪmprɪnt/ n marca f, huella f

imprint² /ɪmˈprɪnt/ vt (physically) imprimir*; (on mind) grabar

imprison /ɪmˈprɪzən/ vt (Law) encarcelar

imprisonment /ɪmˈprɪzənmənt/ n (act) encarcelamiento m; (state) prisión f; **life ~** cadena f perpetua

improbable /ɪmˈprɑːbəbəl ‖ ɪmˈprɒbəbəl/ adj (a) (unlikely) improbable (b) (implausible) inverosímil

impromptu /ɪmˈprɑːmptu ‖ ɪmˈprɒmptjuː/ adj improvisado

improper /ɪmˈprɑːpər ‖ ɪmˈprɒpə(r)/ adj [1] ⟨behavior/language⟩ indecoroso; ⟨suggestion⟩ deshonesto [2] (incorrect) (fml) ⟨use⟩ indebido; ⟨term⟩ incorrecto

improve /ɪmˈpruːv/ vt (a) ⟨design/results⟩ mejorar; ⟨chances⟩ aumentar; **to ~ one's mind** cultivarse (b) ⟨property⟩ hacer* mejoras en
■ ~ vi «situation/weather/health» mejorar; «chances» aumentar

improvement /ɪmˈpruːvmənt/ n (in design, situation) mejora f; (in health) mejoría f

improvise /ˈɪmprəvaɪz/ vi/t improvisar

imprudent /ɪmˈpruːdn̩t/ adj (fml) imprudente

impudence /ˈɪmpjədəns ‖ ˈɪmpjʊdəns/ n insolencia f

impudent /ˈɪmpjədənt ‖ ˈɪmpjʊdənt/ adj insolente

impulse /ˈɪmpʌls/ n impulso m; **I did it on ~** lo hice sin pensarlo

impulsive /ɪmˈpʌlsɪv/ adj impulsivo

impunity /ɪmˈpjuːnəti/ n (fml) impunidad f

impure /ˈɪmˈpjʊr ‖ ɪmˈpjʊə(r)/ adj impuro

impurity /ɪmˈpjʊrəti ‖ ɪmˈpjʊərəti/ n (pl **-ties**) impureza f

in¹ /ɪn/ prep [1] (a) (indicating place, location) en; ~ **Japan** en (el) Japón; **he went ~ the shop** entró en la tienda; **who's that ~ the photo?** ¿quién es ese ⋯❱

de la foto?; ~ **here/there** aquí/allí dentro *or* (esp AmL) adentro; ~ **the rain** bajo la lluvia **(b)** (*with superl*) de; **the highest mountain** ~ **Italy** la montaña más alta de Italia; **the worst storm** ~ **living memory** la peor tormenta que se recuerda
2 (indicating time) en; ~ **spring/January/1924** en primavera/enero/1924; **at four o'clock** ~ **the morning** a las cuatro de la mañana; **she did it** ~ **three hours** lo hizo en tres horas; ~ **two months' time** dentro de dos meses
3 (a) (indicating manner) en; ~ **dollars** en dólares; ~ **French** en francés; ~ **twos** de dos en dos, de a dos (AmL); **cut it** ~ **half** córtalo por la mitad; **they came** ~ **their thousands** vinieron miles y miles **(b)** (wearing): **he turned up** ~ **a suit** apareció de traje; **are you going** ~ **that dress?** ¿vas a ir con ese vestido?
4 (indicating circumstances, state): **the company is** ~ **difficulties** la empresa está pasando dificultades; **to be** ~ **a good mood** estar* de buen humor; **he's** ~ **pain** está dolorido; **low** ~ **calories** bajo en calorías
5 (indicating ratio): **one** ~ **four** uno de cada cuatro; **she's one** ~ **a million** es única
6 (a) (+ *gerund*): ~ **so doing, they set a precedent** al hacerlo, sentaron precedente **(b)** **in that** (*as conj*): **the case is unusual** ~ **that ...** el caso es poco común en el sentido de que ...

in² *adv* **1 (a)** (inside): **is the cat** ~? ¿el gato está dentro *or* (esp AmL) adentro?; ~ **you go!** ¡entra! **(b)** (at home, work): **is Lisa** ~? ¿está Lisa?; **there was nobody** ~ no había nadie **2 (a)** (in position): **she had her curlers** ~ llevaba *or* tenía los rulos puestos **(b)** (at destination): **the train isn't** ~ **yet** el tren no ha llegado todavía; **application forms must be** ~ **by October 5** las solicitudes deben entregarse antes del 5 de octubre
3 (involved): **we were** ~ **on the planning stage** participamos en la planificación; *to be* ~ *for sth*: **it looks like we're** ~ **for some rain** parece que va a llover; **you're** ~ **for a big surprise** te vas a llevar una buena sorpresa

in³ *adj* **1 (a)** (fashionable) (*colloq*) (*no comp*): **black is** ~ **this season** el negro está de moda esta temporada; **the** ~ **place** el lugar *in* (fam) **(b)** (exclusive, private) (*before n*): **an** ~ **joke** un chiste para iniciados **2** (*pred*) (in tennis, badminton, etc): **the ball was** ~ la pelota fue buena *or* cayó dentro *or* (esp AmL) adentro

in⁴ *n*: **the** ~**s and outs (of sth)** los pormenores (de algo)

in⁵ (*pl* **in** *or* **ins**) = **inch(es)**

IN = **Indiana**

inability /ˌɪnəˈbɪləti/ *n* incapacidad *f*; ~ **to +** INF incapacidad PARA + INF

inaccessible /ˈɪnəkˈsesəbəl ‖ˌɪnækˈsesəbəl/ *adj* inaccesible

inaccurate /ɪnˈækjərət/ *adj* **(a)** ⟨*translation/ estimate*⟩ inexacto **(b)** ⟨*aim/shot*⟩ impreciso

inactive /ɪnˈæktɪv/ *adj* inactivo

inactivity /ˌɪnækˈtɪvəti/ *n* inactividad *f*

inadequate /ɪnˈædɪkwət/ *adj* **(a)** ⟨*resources/ measures*⟩ insuficiente **(b)** ⟨*person*⟩ inepto

inadvertently /ˌɪnədˈvɜːrtntli ‖ˌɪnədˈvɜːtntli/ *adv* sin querer

inadvisable /ˌɪnədˈvaɪzəbəl/ *adj* desaconsejable

inane /ɪˈneɪn/ *adj* estúpido, idiota

inanimate /ɪnˈænəmət ‖ɪnˈænɪmət/ *adj* inanimado

inapplicable /ɪnˈæplɪkəbəl, ˌɪnəˈplɪkəbəl/ *adj* inaplicable, no aplicable

inappropriate /ˈɪnəˈprəʊpriət/ *adj* ⟨*measure/ dress*⟩ inadecuado; ⟨*moment*⟩ inoportuno

inarticulate /ˈɪnɑːˈtɪkjələt ‖ˌɪnɑːˈtɪkjʊlət/ *adj* ⟨*babbling/grunt*⟩ inarticulado; ⟨*person*⟩ con dificultad para expresarse

inasmuch as /ˈɪnəzˈmʌtʃ/ *conj* (frml) **(a)** (since, seeing that) ya que, puesto que **(b)** ▶ INSOFAR AS

inattentive /ˈɪnəˈtentɪv/ *adj* ⟨*pupil/listener*⟩ distraído, poco atento

inaudible /ɪnˈɔːdəbəl/ *adj* inaudible

inaugural /ɪnˈɔːɡjərəl ‖ɪˈnɔːɡjʊrəl/ *adj* **(a)** ⟨*speech/lecture*⟩ inaugural **(b)** (of official) ⟨*speech*⟩ de toma de posesión; ⟨*ceremony*⟩ de investidura

inaugurate /ɪnˈɔːɡjəreɪt ‖ɪˈnɔːɡjʊreɪt/ *vt* **(a)** (begin, open) inaugurar **(b)** (frml) ⟨*president*⟩ investir*

inauguration /ɪnˌɔːɡjəˈreɪʃən ‖ɪˌnɔːɡjʊˈreɪʃən/ *n* **(a)** (investiture) investidura *f*; (before n) **I~ Day** (in US) *día de la toma de posesión del presidente de los EEUU* **(b)** (opening) inauguración *f*

inbreeding /ˈɪnˌbriːdɪŋ/ *n* endogamia *f*

Inc /ɪŋk/ (AmE) = **Incorporated**

Inca¹ /ˈɪŋkə/ *adj* incaico, inca

Inca² *n* inca *mf*

incapable /ɪnˈkeɪpəbəl/ *adj* (*pred*) **(a)** (not able) **to be** ~ **OF** -ING ser* incapaz DE + INF **(b)** (helpless) inútil, incapaz

incapacitate /ˈɪnkəˈpæsəteɪt ‖ˌɪnkəˈpæsɪteɪt/ *vt* **(a)** (disable) incapacitar **(b)** (Law) inhabilitar

incarcerate /ɪnˈkɑːrsərəɪt ‖ɪnˈkɑːsəreɪt/ *vt* encarcelar

incarnate /ɪnˈkɑːrnət ‖ɪnˈkɑːnət/ *adj* (liter) (*usu pred*) encarnado

incarnation /ˈɪnkɑːrˈneɪʃən ‖ˌɪnkɑːˈneɪʃən/ *n* encarnación *f*

incendiary /ɪnˈsendiəri ‖ɪnˈsendiəri/ *adj* incendiario

incense¹ /ˈɪnsens/ *n* incienso *m*

incense² /ɪnˈsens/ *vt* indignar

incentive /ɪnˈsentɪv/ *n* incentivo *m*

inception /ɪnˈsepʃən/ *n* (frml) inicio *m*

incessant /ɪnˈsesnt/ *adj* incesante

incessantly /ɪnˈsesntli/ *adv* sin cesar

incest /ˈɪnsest/ *n* incesto *m*

incestuous /ɪnˈsestʃuəs ‖ɪnˈsestjʊəs/ *adj* incestuoso

inch¹ /ɪntʃ/ *n* pulgada *f* (*2,54 centímetros*); **I've searched every** ~ **of the house** he buscado hasta en el último rincón de la casa; **she wouldn't budge** *o* **give an** ~ no cedió ni un ápice

inch² *vi*: **to** ~ **forward** avanzar* lentamente

incidence /ˈɪnsədəns ‖ˈɪnsɪdəns/ *n* **1** (frequency) índice *m* **2** (Opt, Phys) incidencia *f*

incident /ˈɪnsədənt ‖ˈɪnsɪdənt/ *n* incidente *m*

incidental /ˈɪnsəˈdentl ‖ˌɪnsɪˈdentl/ *adj* **(a)** (accompanying) ⟨*effect*⟩ secundario; ⟨*advantage/ benefit*⟩ adicional; ⟨*expenses*⟩ imprevisto **(b)** (minor) incidental

incidentally /ˈɪnsəˈdentli ‖ˌɪnsɪˈdentli/ *adv* (*indep*) a propósito

incinerate /ɪnˈsɪnəreɪt/ *vt* incinerar

incinerator /ɪnˈsɪnəreɪtər ‖ɪnˈsɪnəreɪtə(r)/ *n* incinerador *m*

incision /ɪnˈsɪʒən/ *n* incisión *f*

incisor /ɪnˈsaɪzər ‖ɪnˈsaɪzə(r)/ *n* incisivo *m*

incite /ɪnˈsaɪt/ *vt* ‹hatred/violence› instigar* a, incitar a; ‹person› to ~ sb **to** sth/+ **inf** instigar* or incitar a algn **a** algo/+ **inf**

inclination /ˌɪnklɪˈneɪʃən ‖ˌɪnklɪˈneɪʃən/ *n* **(a)** (leaning) tendencia *f* **(b)** (desire) to have an/no ~ **to** + **inf** tener*/no tener* deseos de + **inf**

incline[1] /ɪnˈklaɪn/ *vt* (frml) ‹head› inclinar
■ ~ *vi* (frml) to ~ **to** sth: she ~s to the opposite view se inclina a pensar lo contrario

incline[2] /ˈɪnklaɪn/ *n* (frml) pendiente *f*

inclined /ɪnˈklaɪnd/ *adj* (disposed) ~ to + **inf**: I'm ~ to agree yo me inclino a pensar lo mismo; she's ~ to be irritable in the morning tiende a estar de mal humor por la mañana

include /ɪnˈkluːd/ *vt* incluir*; (with letter) adjuntar; service isn't ~d el servicio no está incluido

including /ɪnˈkluːdɪŋ/ *prep*: up to and ~ page 25 hasta la página 25 inclusive; not ~ insurance sin incluir el seguro

inclusion /ɪnˈkluːʒən/ *n* inclusión *f*

inclusive /ɪnˈkluːsɪv/ *adj* ‹price/charge› global; to be ~ **of** sth incluir* algo

incognito /ˌɪnkɑːɡˈniːtəʊ ‖ˌɪnkɒɡˈniːtəʊ/ *adv* de incógnito

incoherent /ˌɪnkəʊˈhɪrənt ‖ˌɪnkəʊˈhɪərənt/ *adj* incoherente

income /ˈɪnkʌm/ *n* ingresos *mpl*

income: ~ **support** *n* (in UK) *subsidio otorgado a personas de bajos ingresos;* ~ **tax** *n* impuesto *m* sobre *or* a la renta, impuesto *m* a los réditos (Arg)

incoming /ˈɪnˌkʌmɪŋ/ *adj* (before n) **(a)** (inbound): the area has been closed to ~ traffic no se permite la entrada de vehículos a la zona; the secretary takes all ~ calls la secretaria atiende todas las llamadas **(b)** (about to take office) ‹president› entrante

incommunicado /ˌɪnkəˈmjuːnəˈkɑːdəʊ ‖ˌɪnkəˌmjuːnɪˈkɑːdəʊ/ *adj* (pred) to be ~ estar* incomunicado

incomparable /ɪnˈkɑːmpərəbəl ‖ɪnˈkɒmpərəbəl/ *adj* (liter) incomparable

incompatibility /ˌɪnkəmpætəˈbɪləti/ *n* incompatibilidad *f*

incompatible /ˌɪnkəmˈpætəbəl/ *adj* incompatible

incompetence /ɪnˈkɑːmpətəns ‖ɪnˈkɒmpɪtəns/ *n* incompetencia *f*

incompetent /ɪnˈkɑːmpətənt ‖ɪnˈkɒmpɪtənt/ *adj* ‹person› incompetente; ‹work› deficiente

incomplete /ˈɪnkəmˈpliːt/ *adj* **(a)** (with sth or sb missing) incompleto **(b)** (unfinished) inacabado

incomprehensible /ɪnˌkɑːmprəˈhensəbəl ‖ɪnˌkɒmprɪˈhensəbəl/ *adj* incomprensible

incomprehension /ɪnˌkɑːmprɪˈhentʃən ‖ɪnˌkɒmprɪˈhenʃən/ *n* incomprensión *f*

inconceivable /ˌɪnkənˈsiːvəbəl/ *adj* inconcebible

inconclusive /ˌɪnkənˈkluːsɪv/ *adj* ‹evidence/ findings› no concluyente

incongruous /ɪnˈkɑːŋɡruəs ‖ɪnˈkɒŋɡrəʊəs/ *adj* ‹behavior/remark› fuera de lugar, inapropiado; ‹appearance› extraño, raro

inconsequential /ˌɪnkɑːnsəˈkwentʃəl ‖ˌɪnˌkɒnsɪˈkwenʃəl/ *adj* intrascendente

inconsiderate /ˈɪnkənˈsɪdərət/ *adj* desconsiderado

inconsistent /ˈɪnkənˈsɪstənt/ *adj* **(a)** (contradictory) contradictorio; to be ~ **with** sth no concordar* **con** algo; ‹with principles/ideas› no compadecerse* **con** algo **(b)** (changeable) ‹person/ attitude› inconsecuente

inconspicuous /ˈɪnkənˈspɪkjuəs/ *adj* que no llama la atención

incontinent /ɪnˈkɑːntɪnənt ‖ɪnˈkɒntɪnənt/ *adj* (Med) incontinente

inconvenience[1] /ˈɪnkənˈviːniəns/ *n* **(a)** (unsuitability, troublesomeness) inconveniencia *f* **(b)** (trouble) molestias *fpl* **(c)** (drawback, nuisance) inconveniente *m*

inconvenience[2] *vt* causarle molestias a

inconvenient /ˈɪnkənˈviːniənt/ *adj* ‹moment› poco conveniente; ‹position› poco práctico

incorporate /ɪnˈkɔːrpəreɪt ‖ɪnˈkɔːpəreɪt/ *vt* **1 (a)** (take in) ‹idea/plan› incorporar; to ~ sth **into** sth incorporar algo **a** algo **(b)** (include, contain) incluir* **2** (Busn, Law) ‹business/ enterprise› constituir* (en sociedad)

incorrect /ˈɪnkəˈrekt/ *adj* ‹answer/spelling› incorrecto; ‹statement/belief› equivocado

incorrigible /ɪnˈkɔːrədʒəbəl ‖ɪnˈkɒrɪdʒəbəl/ *adj* incorregible

increase[1] /ɪnˈkriːs/ *vi* «number/size/prices/ output» aumentar; «influence/popularity» crecer*; to ~ in size aumentar de tamaño; to ~ in number crecer* en número; to ~ in value aumentar de valor
■ ~ *vt* aumentar

increase[2] /ˈɪnkriːs/ *n* aumento *m*; to be on the ~ estar* or ir* en aumento

increasing /ɪnˈkriːsɪŋ/ *adj* (before n) creciente

increasingly /ɪnˈkriːsɪŋli/ *adv*: ~ difficult cada vez más difícil; it is becoming ~ clear that ... resulta cada vez más claro que ...

incredible /ɪnˈkredəbəl/ *adj* increíble

incredibly /ɪnˈkredəbli/ *adv* (colloq) (as intensifier) increíblemente

incredulous /ɪnˈkredʒələs ‖ɪnˈkredjʊləs/ *adj* de incredulidad

increment /ˈɪnkrəmənt/ *n* (in salary) incremento *m* (salarial) (frml)

incriminate /ɪnˈkrɪməneɪt ‖ɪnˈkrɪmɪneɪt/ *vt* incriminar (frml)

incriminating /ɪnˈkrɪməneɪtɪŋ ‖ɪnˈkrɪmɪneɪtɪŋ/ *adj* ‹evidence/document› comprometedor

incubate /ˈɪŋkjəbeɪt ‖ˈɪŋkjʊbeɪt/ *vt* incubar
■ ~ *vi* «bird» empollar; «egg/bacteria» incubarse

incubation /ˌɪŋkjəˈbeɪʃən ‖ˌɪŋkjʊˈbeɪʃən/ *n* incubación *f*

incubator /ˈɪŋkjəbeɪtər ‖ˈɪŋkjʊbeɪtə(r)/ *n* incubadora *f*

inculcate /ˈɪŋkʌlkeɪt/ *vt* (frml) to ~ sth **in(to)** sb, to ~ sb **with** sth inculcarle* algo **a** algn, inculcar* algo **en** algn

incumbent¹ /ɪnˈkʌmbənt/ *adj* (fml) to be ~ ON *o* UPON sb incumbirle A algn

incumbent² *n* titular *mf* del cargo

incur /ɪnˈkɜːr ‖ ɪnˈkɜː(r)/ *vt* **-rr-** (fml) ‹*anger*› provocar*, incurrir en (fml); ‹*penalty*› acarrear; ‹*damage/loss*› sufrir; ‹*debt/liability*› contraer*; ‹*expense*› incurrir en (fml)

incurable /ɪnˈkjʊrəbəl ‖ ɪnˈkjʊərəbəl/ *adj* ‹*illness*› incurable; ‹*optimist/romantic*› empedernido

incursion /ɪnˈkɜːrʒən ‖ ɪnˈkɜːʃən/ *n* incursión *f*

Ind = **Indiana**

indebted /ɪnˈdetɪd ‖ ɪnˈdetɪd/ *adj* to be ~ TO sb (FOR sth) estar* en deuda CON algn (POR algo)

indecency /ɪnˈdiːsn̩si/ *n* indecencia *f*

indecent /ɪnˈdiːsn̩t/ *adj* indecente

indecent assault *n* abusos *mpl* deshonestos

indecipherable /ˈɪndɪˈsaɪfərəbəl/ *adj* indescifrable

indecision /ˈɪndɪˈsɪʒən/ *n* indecisión *f*

indecisive /ˈɪndɪˈsaɪsɪv/ *adj* **(a)** (hesitant) indeciso **(b)** (inconclusive) no decisivo

indeed /ɪnˈdiːd/ *adv* **1** (*as intensifier*): thank you very much ~ muchísimas gracias; this is ~ a great privilege este es un auténtico *or* verdadero privilegio **2** (in fact): the wheel was ~ loose en efecto, la rueda estaba suelta; if ~ he is right si es que tiene razón

indefensible /ˈɪndɪˈfensəbəl/ *adj* inexcusable

indefinite /ɪnˈdefənət ‖ ɪnˈdefmət/ *adj* **1** **(a)** ‹*number/period/outline*› indefinido **2** (Ling): ~ article artículo *m* indefinido

indelible /ɪnˈdeləbəl/ *adj* indeleble

indelicate /ɪnˈdelɪkət ‖ ɪnˈdelɪkət/ *adj* **(a)** (vulgar) indelicado **(b)** (tactless) indiscreto

indemnify /ɪnˈdemnəfaɪ ‖ ɪnˈdemnɪfaɪ/ *vt* **-fies, -fying, -fied (a)** (insure) asegurar **(b)** (compensate) indemnizar*

indemnity /ɪnˈdemnəti/ *n* (*pl* **-ties**) **(a)** (insurance) indemnidad *f* **(b)** (compensation) indemnización *f*

indent /ɪnˈdent/ *vt* **(a)** ‹*line/paragraph*› sangrar **(b)** ‹*surface/edge*› marcar*

independence /ˈɪndɪˈpendəns/ *n* independencia *f*

Independence Day *n* día *m* de la Independencia

independent /ˈɪndɪˈpendənt/ *adj* independiente

in-depth /ˈɪnˈdepθ/ *adj* (before *n*) a fondo

indescribable /ˈɪndɪˈskraɪbəbəl/ *adj* indescriptible

indestructible /ˈɪndɪˈstrʌktəbəl/ *adj* indestructible

indeterminate /ˈɪndɪˈtɜːrmənət ‖ ˌɪndɪˈtɜːmɪnət/ *adj* indeterminado

index¹ /ˈɪndeks/ *n* **1** (*pl* **indexes**) **(a)** (in book, journal) índice *m* **(b)** (list) lista *f*; (before *n*) ~ card ficha *f* **2** (*pl* **indexes** *o* **indices**) (Econ, Fin) índice *m* **3** (*pl* **indices**) (Math) índice *m*

index² *vt* **1** (Publ) **(a)** (provide with index) ponerle* un índice a **(b)** (enter in index) incluir* en un índice **2** (Econ, Fin) ‹*prices/wages*› indexar

index: ~ **finger** *n* (dedo *m*) índice *m*; ~**-linked** /ˈɪndeksˈlɪŋkt/ *adj* (esp BrE) indexado

India /ˈɪndiə/ *n* la India

Indian¹ /ˈɪndiən/ *adj* **1** (of India) indio **2** (of America) indígena, indio

Indian² *n* **1** (person from India) indio, -dia *m,f* **2** (American ~) indígena *mf*, indio, -dia *m,f*

Indian: ~ **Ocean** *n* the ~ Ocean el (Océano) Índico; ~ **summer** *n* (in northern hemisphere) ≈ veranillo *m* de San Martín *or* de San Miguel; (in southern hemisphere) ≈ veranillo *m* de San Juan

indicate /ˈɪndəkeɪt ‖ ˈɪndɪkeɪt/ *vt* **1** **(a)** (point out) señalar **(b)** (Auto) indicar* **2** **(a)** (show) ‹*change/condition*› ser* indicio de **(b)** (state) señalar

■ ~ *vi* (BrE Auto) indicar*, señalizar*, poner* el intermitente *or* (Col, Méx) las direccionales *or* (Chi) el señalizador

indication /ˈɪndəˈkeɪʃən ‖ ˌɪndɪˈkeɪʃən/ *n* **(a)** (sign, hint) indicio *m* **(b)** (Med) indicación *f*

indicative¹ /ɪnˈdɪkətɪv/ *adj* **1** (revealing) (fml) to be ~ OF sth ser* indicio DE algo **2** (Ling) ‹*mood/form*› indicativo

indicative² *n* (Ling) indicativo *m*

indicator /ˈɪndəkeɪtər ‖ ˈɪndɪkeɪtə(r)/ *n* **1** **(a)** (pointer) indicador *m* **(b)** (instrument) indicador *m* **2** (Auto) intermitente *m*, direccional *f* (Col, Méx), señalizador *m* (de viraje) (Chi) **3** (sign) indicador *m*

indices /ˈɪndəsiːz ‖ ˈɪndɪsiːz/ *pl* of INDEX¹ 2,3

indict /ɪnˈdaɪt/ *vt* (Law) acusar

indictment /ɪnˈdaɪtmənt/ *n* **1** (Law) acusación *f* **2** (criticism): the report was an ~ of his management el informe censuraba su gestión

indifference /ɪnˈdɪfrəns/ *n* indiferencia *f*

indifferent /ɪnˈdɪfrənt/ *adj* **1** (uninterested) indiferente **2** (mediocre) mediocre

indigenous /ɪnˈdɪdʒənəs/ *adj* ‹*population/ language*› indígena, autóctono; ‹*species*› autóctono

indigestible /ˈɪndaɪˈdʒestəbəl, -də- ‖ ˌɪndɪˈdʒestəbəl/ *adj* (impossible to digest) no digerible; (hard to digest) indigesto

indigestion /ˈɪndaɪˈdʒestʃən, -də- ‖ ˌɪndɪˈdʒestʃən/ *n* indigestión *f*

indignant /ɪnˈdɪɡnənt/ *adj* indignado

indignation /ˈɪndɪɡˈneɪʃən/ *n* indignación *f*

indignity /ɪnˈdɪɡnəti/ *n* (*pl* **-ties**) humillación *f*

indigo /ˈɪndɪɡəʊ/ *n* índigo *m*, añil *m*; (before *n*) ‹*ink/sea*› color añil *adj inv*

indirect /ˈɪndəˈrekt, -daɪ- ‖ ˌɪndɪˈrekt, -daɪ-/ *adj* **1** **(a)** ‹*route/method*› indirecto; ‹*result/benefit*› indirecto **(b)** (Ling) ‹*statement/question*› indirecto; ~ **discourse** *o* (BrE) **speech** estilo *m* indirecto **2** (Fin) ‹*costs/taxes*› indirecto

indirectly /ˈɪndəˈrektli, -daɪ- ‖ˌɪndɪˈrektli, -daɪ-/ *adv* indirectamente

indiscreet /ˈɪndɪsˈkriːt/ *adj* indiscreto

indiscretion /ˈɪndɪsˈkreʃən/ *n* indiscreción *f*

indiscriminate /ˈɪndɪsˈkrɪmənət ‖ˌɪndɪˈskrɪmɪnət/ *adj* indiscriminado

indispensable /ˈɪndɪsˈpensəbəl/ *adj* indispensable

indisposed /ˈɪndɪˈspəʊzd/ *adj* (frml) (*pred*) (ill) **to be ~** estar* indispuesto (frml)

indisputable /ˈɪndɪˈspjuːtəbəl/ *adj* ‹evidence/proof› irrefutable; ‹leader/winner› indiscutible

indistinct /ˈɪndɪˈstɪŋkt/ *adj* ‹sound/shape› poco definido; ‹speech› poco claro

indistinguishable /ˈɪndɪˈstɪŋgwɪʃəbəl/ *adj* **~ (FROM sth)** indistinguible (DE algo)

individual[1] /ˈɪndəˈvɪdʒuəl ‖ˌɪndɪˈvɪdjʊəl/ *adj* [1] (*before n*) (*no comp*) **(a)** (for one person) ‹portion› individual; ‹tuition› personal **(b)** (single, separate): **you can purchase the whole set or ~ items** se puede comprar el juego o cada pieza por separado **(c)** (particular, personal) ‹style› personal [2] (distinctive) personal

individual[2] *n* **(a)** (single person, animal) individuo *m* **(b)** (person) (colloq) individuo, -dua *m,f*

indivisible /ˈɪndəˈvɪzəbəl ‖ˌɪndɪˈvɪzəbəl/ *adj* indivisible

indoctrinate /ɪnˈdɑːktrəneɪt ‖ɪnˈdɒktrɪneɪt/ *vt* adoctrinar

indolent /ˈɪndələnt/ *adj* (frml) indolente

Indonesia /ˈɪndəˈniːʒə ‖ˌɪndəˈniːziə/ *n* Indonesia *f*

Indonesian[1] /ˈɪndəˈniːʒən ‖ˌɪndəˈniːziən/ *adj* indonesio

Indonesian[2] *n* **(a)** (person) indonesio, -sia *m,f* **(b)** (language) indonesio *m*

indoor /ˈɪndɔːr ‖ˈɪndɔː(r)/ *adj* (*before n*) ‹clothes/shoes› para estar en casa; ‹plants› de interior(es); ‹swimming pool› cubierto, techado

indoors /ˈɪnˈdɔːrz ‖ˌɪnˈdɔːz/ *adv* dentro, adentro (esp AmL)

induce /ɪnˈduːs ‖ɪnˈdjuːs/ *vt* [1] (persuade) **to ~ sb to + INF** inducir* a algn A + INF [2] (Med) ‹sleep/labor› inducir*

inducement /ɪnˈduːsmənt ‖ɪnˈdjuːsmənt/ *n* incentivo *m*

induction /ɪnˈdʌkʃən/ *n* [1] (introduction) **~ (INTO sth)** iniciación *f* (EN algo); (*before n*) ‹course/period› introductorio [2] (Med) (of labor) inducción *f*

indulge /ɪnˈdʌldʒ/ *vt* ‹child› consentir*, mimar; ‹desire› satisfacer*; **it doesn't hurt to ~ oneself every now and again** es bueno darse algún gusto de vez en cuando
■ **~** *vi* **to ~ IN sth** permitirse algo

indulgence /ɪnˈdʌldʒəns/ *n* **(a)** (extravagance): **an occasional cigar is my only ~** un puro de vez en cuando es el único lujo que me permito **(b)** (partaking): **too much ~ in anything is bad** es malo abusar de cualquier placer

indulgent /ɪnˈdʌldʒənt/ *adj* indulgente

industrial /ɪnˈdʌstriəl/ *adj* ‹town/production/engineering› industrial; **~ dispute** conflicto *m* laboral

industrial estate *n* (BrE) zona *f* industrial, polígono *m* industrial (Esp)

industrialist /ɪnˈdʌstriələst ‖ɪnˈdʌstriəlɪst/ *n* industrial *mf*

industrialize /ɪnˈdʌstriəlaɪz/ *vt* industrializar*

industrial: ~ park *n* (AmE) zona *f* industrial, polígono *m* industrial (Esp); **I~ Revolution** *n* **the I~ Revolution** la Revolución Industrial

industrious /ɪnˈdʌstriəs/ *adj* ‹worker› trabajador; ‹student› aplicado

industry /ˈɪndəstri/ *n* (*pl* **-tries**) industria *f*; **the steel ~** la industria siderúrgica; **the tourist ~** el turismo

inebriated /ɪˈniːbrieɪtəd ‖ɪˈniːbrieɪtɪd/ *adj* (frml) ‹person› beodo (frml), ebrio (frml); ‹state› de embriaguez (frml)

inedible /ɪnˈedəbəl/ *adj* (impossible to eat) no comestible; (unpalatable) incomible

ineffective /ˈɪnəˈfektɪv ‖ˌɪnɪˈfektɪv/ *adj* ‹measure› ineficaz; ‹attempt› infructuoso; ‹person› incompetente

inefficiency /ˈɪnəˈfɪʃənsi ‖ˌɪnɪˈfɪʃənsi/ *n* (of machinery) falta *f* de eficiencia; (of persons, method) ineficiencia *f*

inefficient /ˈɪnəˈfɪʃənt ‖ˌɪnɪˈfɪʃənt/ *adj* ineficiente

ineligible /ɪnˈelədʒəbəl ‖ɪnˈelɪdʒəbəl/ *adj* (*usu pred*) ‹candidate› inelegible; **she was ~ to vote** no tenía derecho a votar

inept /ɪˈnept/ *adj* ‹person› inepto; ‹conduct› torpe

inequality /ˈɪnɪˈkwɑːləti ‖ˌɪnɪˈkwɒləti/ *n* (*pl* **-ties**) desigualdad *f*

inert /ɪˈnɜːrt ‖ɪˈnɜːt/ *adj* inerte

inertia /ɪˈnɜːrʃə ‖ɪˈnɜːʃə/ *n* inercia *f*

inevitable[1] /ɪnˈevətəbəl ‖ɪnˈevɪtəbəl/ *adj* inevitable

inevitable[2] *n* **the ~** lo inevitable

inevitably /ɪˈnevətəbli ‖ɪnˈevɪtəbli/ *adv* inevitablemente

inexact /ˈɪnɪɡˈzækt/ *adj* inexacto

inexcusable /ˈɪnɪkˈskjuːzəbəl/ *adj* imperdonable

inexpensive /ˈɪnɪkˈspensɪv/ *adj* económico

inexperience /ˈɪnɪkˈspɪriəns ‖ˌɪnɪkˈspɪəriəns/ *n* inexperiencia *f*, falta *f* de experiencia

inexperienced /ˈɪnɪkˈspɪriənst ‖ˌɪnɪkˈspɪəriənst/ *adj* ‹nurse/pilot› sin experiencia; ‹swimmer/driver› inexperto, novato

inexpert /ɪnˈeks03ːrt ‖ɪnˈekspɜːt/ *adj* inexperto

inexplicable /ˈɪnɪkˈsplɪkəbəl/ *adj* inexplicable

inextricably /ˈɪnɪkˈstrɪkəbli/ *adv* inextricablemente

infallibility /ˈɪnˌfæləˈbɪləti/ *n* infalibilidad *f*

infallible /ɪnˈfæləbəl/ *adj* infalible

infamous /ˈɪnfəməs/ *adj* **(a)** (notorious) de triste fama **(b)** (shameful) infame

infancy /ˈɪnfənsi/ *n* primera infancia *f*

infant /ˈɪnfənt/ *n* **(a)** (baby) bebé *m*, niño, -ña *m,f*; (*before n*) **~ mortality** mortalidad *f* infantil **(b)** (BrE Educ) niño, -ña *m,f* (entre cinco y siete años de edad); (*before n*) **~ school** (in UK) escuela para niños de entre cinco y siete años de edad

infantile /ˈɪnfəntaɪl/ *adj* pueril, infantil

infantry /'ɪnfəntri/ n (+ sing or pl vb)
infantería f

infatuated /ɪn'fætʃuertəd ‖ɪn'fætjuertɪd/ adj
to be ~ WITH sb estar* encaprichado CON or (Esp
tb) DE algn

infatuation /ɪn'fætʃu'eɪʃən ‖ɪnˌfætjʊ'eɪʃən/ n
encaprichamiento m

infect /ɪn'fekt/ vt ⟨wound/cut⟩ infectar; ⟨person/
animal⟩ contagiar; **the wound became ~ed** la
herida se infectó

infection /ɪn'fekʃən/ n **(a)** (disease) infección f
(b) (of wound) infección f; (of person) contagio m

infectious /ɪn'fekʃəs/ adj ⟨disease⟩ infeccioso,
contagioso; ⟨laughter/enthusiasm⟩ contagioso

infer /ɪn'fɜːr ‖ɪn'fɜː(r)/ vt **-rr-** (deduce) **to ~ sth**
(FROM sth) inferir* or deducir* algo (DE algo)

inferior¹ /ɪn'frɪər ‖ɪn'fɪərɪə(r)/ adj (no comp)
⟨product⟩ (de calidad) inferior; ⟨workmanship/
rank⟩ inferior

inferior² n inferior mf

inferiority /ɪnˌfɪri'ɔːrəti ‖ɪnˌfɪərɪ'ɒrəti/ n
inferioridad f; (before n) **~ complex** complejo m
de inferioridad

inferno /ɪn'fɜːrnəʊ ‖ɪn'fɜːnəʊ/ n (pl **-noes**)
(journ): **the building was a blazing ~** el edificio
estaba totalmente envuelto en llamas

infertile /ɪn'fɜːrtl ‖ɪn'fɜːtaɪl/ adj ⟨land⟩ estéril,
infecundo; ⟨woman/man/animal⟩ estéril

infertility /ˈɪnfɜr'tɪləti ‖ˌɪnfə'tɪləti/ n (Agr)
infecundidad f; (Biol) esterilidad f

infest /ɪn'fest/ vt infestar

infidelity /ˈɪnfə'deləti ‖ˌɪnfɪ'deləti/ n (pl **-ties**)
infidelidad f

infighting /'ɪnˌfaɪtɪŋ/ n luchas fpl internas

infiltrate /ɪn'fɪltreɪt ‖'ɪnfɪltreɪt/ vt infiltrarse
en

infiltrator /ɪn'fɪltreɪtər ‖'ɪnfɪltreɪtə(r)/ n
infiltrado, -da m,f

infinite /'ɪnfənət ‖'ɪnfɪnət/ adj infinito

infinitesimal /'ɪnfɪnə'tesɪml ‖ˌɪnfɪnɪ'tesɪml/
adj infinitesimal

infinitive /ɪn'fɪnətɪv/ n infinitivo m

infinity /ɪn'fɪnəti/ n **(a)** (Math) infinito m **(b)**
(endless space) infinito m **(c)** (vast number, quantity)
(liter) (no pl) infinidad f

infirm /ɪn'fɜːrm ‖ɪn'fɜːm/ adj (weak) endeble; (ill)
enfermo

infirmary /ɪn'fɜːrməri ‖ɪn'fɜːməri/ n (pl **-ries**)
(used in titles) hospital m

infirmity /ɪn'fɜːrməti ‖ɪn'fɜːməti/ n (pl **-ties**)
dolencia f (frml), padecimiento m

inflame /ɪn'fleɪm/ vt ⟨person/passion⟩
encender*; ⟨situation⟩ exacerbar

inflamed /ɪn'fleɪmd/ adj inflamado; **to become**
~ inflamarse

inflammable /ɪn'flæməbəl/ adj inflamable,
flamable (Méx)

inflammation /ˈɪnflə'meɪʃən/ n inflamación f

inflate /ɪn'fleɪt/ vt (with air, gas) inflar, hinchar
(Esp)

inflation /ɪn'fleɪʃən/ n inflación f

inflexible /ɪn'fleksəbəl/ adj ⟨personality/
regulations⟩ inflexible; ⟨material⟩ rígido

inflict /ɪn'flɪkt/ vt ⟨pain/damage⟩ causar;

⟨punishment⟩ imponer*; **to ~ sth ON sb: the**
suffering which he ~ed on his family el
sufrimiento que le causó a su familia

influence¹ /'ɪnfluəns/ n influencia f: **to be**
under the ~ of sb/sth estar* bajo la influencia de
algn/algo; **she's a good/bad ~ on him** ejerce
buena/mala influencia sobre él

influence² vt influir* en, influenciar

influential /'ɪnflu'entʃəl ‖ˌɪnflʊ'enʃəl/ adj
influyente

influenza /'ɪnflu'enzə/ n (Med) gripe f or (Chi tb)
influenza f or (Col, Méx) gripa f

influx /'ɪnflʌks/ n (of people) afluencia f; (of
goods) entrada f; (of ideas) llegada f

inform /ɪn'fɔːrm ‖ɪn'fɔːm/ vt informar; **to keep**
sb ~ed mantener* a algn informado or al
corriente
■ ~ vi **to ~ ON sb** delatar or denunciar a algn

informal /ɪn'fɔːrməl ‖ɪn'fɔːməl/ adj informal

informality /'ɪnfɔːr'mæləti ‖ˌɪnfɔː'mæləti/ n
falta f de ceremonia, informalidad f

informally /ɪn'fɔːrməli ‖ɪn'fɔːməli/ adv **(a)**
(casually) ⟨talk/dress⟩ de manera informal **(b)**
(unofficially) ⟨meet/discuss⟩ informalmente

informant /ɪn'fɔːrmənt ‖ɪn'fɔːmənt/ n
informante mf

information /'ɪnfər'meɪʃən ‖ˌɪnfə'meɪʃən/ n
información f; **a piece of ~** un dato; (before n) **~**
desk información f

information: ~ highway n (Comput)
autopista f de información, infovía f; **~**
technology n informática f

informative /ɪn'fɔːrmətɪv ‖ɪn'fɔːmətɪv/ adj
⟨article/lecture⟩ instructivo, informativo;
⟨guidebook⟩ lleno de información, informativo

informed /ɪn'fɔːrmd ‖ɪn'fɔːmd/ adj ⟨source⟩
bien informado; ⟨criticism/approach⟩ bien
fundado

informer /ɪn'fɔːrmər ‖ɪn'fɔːmə(r)/ n
informante mf

infrared /'ɪnfrə'red/ adj infrarrojo

infrastructure /'ɪnfrə'strʌktʃər
‖'ɪnfrəˌstrʌktʃə(r)/ n infraestructura f

infrequent /ɪn'friːkwənt/ adj poco frecuente

infringe /ɪn'frɪndʒ/ vt ⟨contract⟩ no cumplir
(con); ⟨treaty/rule⟩ infringir*
■ ~ vi **to ~ ON o UPON sth** violar algo

infringement /ɪn'frɪndʒmənt/ n (of law)
contravención f, violación f; (of contract)
incumplimiento m; (Sport) falta f; (of rights)
violación f

infuriate /ɪn'fjʊriert ‖ɪn'fjʊəriert/ vt
enfurecer*

infuriating /ɪn'fjʊrieɪtɪŋ ‖ɪn'fjʊərieɪtɪŋ/ adj
exasperante

infuse /ɪn'fjuːz/ vt ⟨tea/herb⟩ hacer* una
infusión de

infusion /ɪn'fjuːʒən/ n infusión f

ingenious /ɪn'dʒiːnjəs ‖ɪn'dʒiːniəs/ adj
ingenioso

ingenuity /ˌɪndʒə'nuːəti ‖ˌɪndʒə'njuːəti/ n (of
person) ingenio m; (of gadget, idea) lo ingenioso

ingenuous /ɪn'dʒenjuəs/ adj ingenuo

ingot /'ɪŋɡət/ n lingote m

ingrained /ɪnˈɡreɪnd/ adj (a) ‹belief/habit› arraigado (b) ‹dirt› incrustado

ingratiate /ɪnˈɡreɪʃieɪt/ v refl to ~ oneself (WITH sb) congraciarse (CON algn)

ingratitude /ɪnˈɡrætətuːd ‖ɪnˈɡrætɪtjuːd/ n ingratitud f

ingredient /ɪnˈɡriːdiənt/ n (a) (Culin) ingrediente m (b) (Pharm) componente m (c) (element) elemento m

ingrowing /ˈɪnˈɡrəʊɪŋ/ adj (BrE) ‹toenail› encarnado

ingrown /ˈɪnɡrəʊn/ adj ‹toenail› encarnado

inhabit /ɪnˈhæbət ‖ɪnˈhæbɪt/ vt habitar (frml), vivir en

inhabitant /ɪnˈhæbətənt ‖ɪnˈhæbɪtənt/ n habitante mf

inhale /ɪnˈheɪl/ vi aspirar

inhaler /ɪnˈheɪlər ‖ɪnˈheɪlə(r)/ n inhalador m

inherent /ɪnˈhɪrənt, -ˈher- ‖ɪnˈhɪərənt, -ˈher-/ adj inherente; to be ~ IN sth ser* inherente A algo

inherit /ɪnˈherət ‖ɪnˈherɪt/ vt heredar

inheritance /ɪnˈherətəns ‖ɪnˈherɪtəns/ n (a) (sth inherited) herencia f (b) (act) sucesión f

inhibit /ɪnˈhɪbət ‖ɪnˈhɪbɪt/ vt (frml) inhibir

inhibited /ɪnˈhɪbətəd ‖ɪnˈhɪbɪtɪd/ adj inhibido

inhibition /ˈɪnəˈbɪʃən ‖ˌɪnhɪˈbɪʃən/ n inhibición f

inhospitable /ˌɪnhɑːˈspɪtəbəl ‖ɪnhɒˈspɪtəbəl/ adj ‹person› poco hospitalario; ‹climate/region› inhóspito

in-house /ˈɪnhaʊs/ adj ‹training› en la empresa (or organización etc); ‹staff› interno

inhuman /ɪnˈhjuːmən/ adj inhumano

inhumane /ˈɪnhjuːˈmeɪn/ adj ‹treatment› inhumano; ‹person› cruel

inhumanity /ˈɪnhjuːˈmænəti/ n (pl -ties) (a) (cruelty) crueldad f (b) (cruel act) atrocidad f

inimitable /ɪnˈɪmətəbəl ‖ɪˈnɪmɪtəbəl/ adj inimitable

initial¹ /ɪˈnɪʃəl/ adj inicial

initial² n inicial f

initial³ vt, (BrE) **-ll-** inicialar

initially /ɪˈnɪʃəli/ adv inicialmente

initiate /ɪˈnɪʃieɪt/ vt ⟨1⟩ (start) (frml) ‹talks› iniciar (frml); ‹reform/plan› poner* en marcha ⟨2⟩ (admit, introduce) to ~ sb (INTO sth) iniciar a algn (EN algo)

initiation /ɪˈnɪʃiˈeɪʃən/ n ⟨1⟩ (admission) iniciación f; (before n) ~ ceremony ceremonia f iniciática ⟨2⟩ (of plan, talks) inicio m (frml)

initiative /ɪˈnɪʃətɪv/ n iniciativa f; on one's own ~ por iniciativa propia; to take the ~ tomar la iniciativa

inject /ɪnˈdʒekt/ vt ‹drug› inyectar; to ~ sth (INTO sth) ‹capital/resources› inyectarle algo (A algo)

injection /ɪnˈdʒekʃən/ n inyección f

injunction /ɪnˈdʒʌŋkʃən/ n (Law) mandamiento m judicial

injure /ˈɪndʒər ‖ˈɪndʒə(r)/ vt (a) ‹person/ feelings› herir* (b) **injured** past p: she gave me an ~d look me miró con expresión ofendida; I am the ~d party soy yo quien sufrió el agravio

injurious /ɪnˈdʒʊriəs ‖ɪnˈdʒʊəriəs/ adj (frml) perjudicial

injury /ˈɪndʒəri/ n (pl -ries) herida f; (before n) ~ time (BrE Sport) tiempo m de descuento

injustice /ɪnˈdʒʌstəs ‖ɪnˈdʒʌstɪs/ n injusticia f; to do sb an ~ cometer una injusticia con algn

ink /ɪŋk/ n tinta f

inkling /ˈɪŋklɪŋ/ n: I had an ~ something had gone wrong tuve el presentimiento or (CS, Per tb) el pálpito de que algo había salido mal

inkwell /ˈɪŋkwel/ n tintero m (empotrado en un escritorio)

inlaid¹ /ˈɪnˈleɪd/ past & past p of INLAY²

inlaid² adj ‹design› de marquetería; ‹box/lid› con incrustaciones

inland¹ /ˈɪnlənd/ adj (before n) ‹town› del interior; ‹sea› interior

inland² /ˈɪnˈlænd/ adv tierra adentro

Inland Revenue /ˈɪnlənd/ n (in UK) the ~ ~ ≈Hacienda, ≈ la Dirección General Impositiva (en RPl), ≈ Impuestos Internos (en Chi)

in-laws /ˈɪnlɔːz/ pl n (colloq) (spouse's parents) suegros mpl; (spouse's family) parientes mpl políticos

inlay¹ /ˈɪnleɪ/ n (of wood, metal, ivory) incrustación f

inlay² /ɪnˈleɪ/ vt (past & past p **inlaid**) to ~ sth WITH sth hacer* incrustaciones de algo EN algo

inlet /ˈɪnlet/ n (in coastline) ensenada f, entrada f; (of river, sea) brazo m

inmate /ˈɪnmeɪt/ n (of asylum) interno, -na m,f; (of prison) preso, -sa m,f; (of hospital) paciente hospitalizado, -da m,f

inmost /ˈɪnməʊst/ adj ▶ INNERMOST

inn /ɪn/ n (tavern) taberna f; (hotel) hostal m

innards /ˈɪnərdz ‖ˈɪnədz/ pl n tripas fpl (fam)

innate /ɪˈneɪt/ adj innato

inner /ˈɪnər ‖ˈɪnə(r)/ adj (before n, no comp) (a) ‹room/part› interior; the ~ city la zona del centro urbano habitada por familias de escasos ingresos, caracterizada por problemas sociales etc (b) (of person) ‹life› interior; ‹thoughts› íntimo

innermost /ˈɪnərməʊst ‖ˈɪnəməʊst/ adj ‹part/ chamber› más recóndito; ‹thoughts› más íntimo

inner tube n cámara f

inning /ˈɪnɪŋ/ n (in baseball) entrada f, manga f

innings /ˈɪnɪŋz/ n (pl ~) (in cricket) entrada f

innkeeper /ˈɪnˌkiːpər ‖ˈɪnˌkiːpə(r)/ n posadero, -ra m,f

innocence /ˈɪnəsəns/ n inocencia f

innocent /ˈɪnəsənt/ adj inocente

innocuous /ɪˈnɑːkjuəs ‖ɪˈnɒkjuəs/ adj ‹drug› inocuo; ‹person/comment› inofensivo

innovation /ˈɪnəˈveɪʃən/ n innovación f

innovative /ˈɪnəveɪtɪv ‖ˈɪnəvətɪv/ adj innovador

innuendo /ˈɪnjuˈendəʊ/ n (pl **-dos** or **-does**) indirecta f, insinuación f

innumerable /ɪˈnuːmərəbəl ‖ɪˈnjuːmərəbəl/ adj innumerable

inoculate /ɪˈnɑːkjəleɪt ‖ɪˈnɒkjʊleɪt/ vt inocular

inoculation /ɪˈnɑːkjəˈleɪʃən ‖ɪˌnɒkjʊˈleɪʃən/ n inoculación f

inoffensive /ˌɪnəˈfensɪv/ adj inofensivo

inordinate /ɪˈnɔːrdɪnət ‖ɪnˈɔːdɪnət/ adj: an ~ amount of money una cantidad exorbitante de dinero; **they are making ~ demands** lo que piden es excesivo

inpatient /ˈɪnˌpeɪʃənt/ n paciente hospitalizado, -da m,f

input¹ /ˈɪnpʊt/ n [1] (a) (of resources) aportación f, aporte m (esp AmL) (b) (contribution) aportación f, aporte m (esp AmL) [2] (Comput) entrada f

input² vt (pres p **inputting**; past & past p **input** or **inputted**) ⟨data⟩ entrar

inquest /ˈɪnkwest/ n investigación f

inquire, (BrE) **enquire** /ɪnˈkwaɪr ‖ɪnˈkwaɪə(r)/ vt preguntar

■ ~ vi preguntar; **to ~ ABOUT sth** informarse ACERCA DE algo

inquiring, (BrE) **enquiring** /ɪnˈkwaɪrɪŋ ‖ɪnˈkwaɪərɪŋ/ adj (before n) ⟨mind⟩ curioso; ⟨look⟩ inquisitivo

inquiry, (BrE) **enquiry** /ɪnˈkwaɪri, ˈɪnkwəri ‖ɪnˈkwaɪəri/ n (pl **-ries**) (a) (question): we made inquiries about o into his past hicimos averiguaciones sobre su pasado; **all inquiries to** ... para cualquier información dirigirse a ...; ❸ **inquiries** información (b) (investigation) investigación f

inquisition /ˌɪnkwəˈzɪʃən ‖ˌɪnkwɪˈzɪʃən/ n (a) (severe questioning) interrogatorio m (b) **the Spanish I~** la (Santa) Inquisición, el Santo Oficio

inquisitive /ɪnˈkwɪzətɪv/ adj ⟨mind⟩ inquisitivo; ⟨person/animal⟩ muy curioso

inroads /ˈɪnrəʊdz/ pl n: **we are making ~ into the Japanese market** estamos haciendo avances en el mercado japonés; **this made substantial ~ into her savings** esto le comió buena parte de los ahorros

INS n (in US) = **Immigration and Naturalization Service**

insane /ɪnˈseɪn/ adj (mad) demente; (foolish) insensato

insanitary /ɪnˈsænəteri ‖ɪnˈsænɪtəri/ adj malsano, insanitorio

insanity /ɪnˈsænəti/ n demencia f

insatiable /ɪnˈseɪʃəbəl/ adj insaciable

inscribe /ɪnˈskraɪb/ vt **to ~ sth (ON sth)** ⟨letters⟩ inscribir* algo (EN algo); ⟨design⟩ grabar algo (EN algo)

inscription /ɪnˈskrɪpʃən/ n inscripción f

insect /ˈɪnsekt/ n insecto m

insecticide /ɪnˈsektəsaɪd ‖ɪnˈsektɪsaɪd/ n insecticida m

insecure /ˌɪnsɪˈkjʊr ‖ˌɪnsɪˈkjʊə(r)/ adj (a) (unsafe, exposed) inseguro (b) (not firmly fixed) poco seguro (c) (not confident) inseguro

insecurity /ˌɪnsɪˈkjʊrəti ‖ˌɪnsɪˈkjʊərəti/ n (pl **-ties**) inseguridad f

insemination /ɪnˌseməˈneɪʃən ‖ɪnˌsemɪˈneɪʃən/ n inseminación f

insensible /ɪnˈsensəbəl/ adj (fml) (a) (unconscious) inconsciente (b) (without sensation) insensible

insensitive /ɪnˈsensətɪv/ adj ⟨person⟩ insensible; ⟨behavior⟩ falto de sensibilidad

insensitivity /ɪnˌsensəˈtɪvəti/ n falta f de sensibilidad

inseparable /ɪnˈsepərəbəl/ adj inseparable

insert /ɪnˈsɜːrt ‖ɪnˈsɜːt/ vt ⟨coin/token⟩ introducir*; ⟨zipper⟩ poner*; ⟨word/paragraph⟩ insertar

insertion /ɪnˈsɜːrʃən ‖ɪnˈsɜːʃən/ n introducción f

inshore¹ /ˈɪnˈʃɔːr ‖ˌɪnˈʃɔː(r)/ adj costero

inshore² adv hacia la costa

inside¹ /ˈɪnsaɪd/ n [1] (interior part) interior m; (inner side, surface) parte f de dentro or (esp AmL) de adentro [2] **insides** fpl (fam) tripas fpl (fam) [3] **inside out** adv: **turn it ~ out** ponlo de adentro para fuera; **you've got your socks on ~ out** llevas los calcetines del or al revés

inside² prep (a) (within) dentro de; **we did the journey ~ 3 hours** (colloq) hicimos el viaje en menos de 3 horas (b) (into): **he followed her ~ the bar** la siguió al interior del bar

inside³ adv (a) (within, indoors) dentro, adentro (esp AmL); **come ~** entra, pasa (b) (in prison) (colloq) entre rejas (fam), a la sombra (fam)

inside⁴ adj (before n) (a) ⟨pages⟩ interior; ⟨pocket⟩ interior, de adentro (esp AmL) (b) **the ~ lane** (Auto) el carril de la derecha; (in UK etc) el carril de la izquierda; (Sport) el carril (AmL) or (Esp) la calle número uno (c) (from within group) ⟨information⟩ de dentro, de adentro (esp AmL)

insider /ɪnˈsaɪdər ‖ɪnˈsaɪdə(r)/ n: persona que pertenece a una organización determinada o que tiene acceso a información confidencial

insidious /ɪnˈsɪdiəs/ adj insidioso

insight /ˈɪnsaɪt/ n (a) (perceptiveness) perspicacia f (b) (comprehension): **to gain an ~ into sth** llegar* a comprender bien algo

insignia /ɪnˈsɪɡniə/ n (pl ~ or ~s) insignia f

insignificant /ˌɪnsɪɡˈnɪfɪkənt/ adj ⟨person/amount⟩ insignificante; ⟨detail⟩ nimio

insincere /ˌɪnsɪnˈsɪr ‖ˌɪnsɪnˈsɪə(r)/ adj ⟨offer⟩ poco sincero; ⟨person/smile⟩ falso

insincerity /ˌɪnsɪnˈserəti/ n falta f de sinceridad

insinuate /ɪnˈsɪnjuert/ vt insinuar*

insinuation /ɪnˌsɪnjuˈeɪʃən/ n insinuación f

insipid /ɪnˈsɪped ‖ɪnˈsɪpɪd/ adj ⟨food/drink⟩ insípido; ⟨person/novel⟩ insulso

insist /ɪnˈsɪst/ vt (a) (demand) **to ~ (THAT)** insistir EN QUE (+ subj) (b) (maintain) **to ~ (THAT)** insistir EN QUE

■ ~ vi insistir

■ **insist on** [v + prep + o] **to ~ on -ING** insistir EN + INF/EN QUE (+ subj)

insistence /ɪnˈsɪstəns/ n insistencia f

AmC	América Central	Arg	Argentina	Cu	Cuba	Per	Perú
AmL	América Latina	Bol	Bolivia	Ec	Ecuador	RPI	Río de la Plata
AmS	América del Sur	Chi	Chile	Esp	España	Ur	Uruguay
Andes	Región andina	CS	Cono Sur	Méx	México	Ven	Venezuela

insistent /ɪnˈsɪstənt/ adj (a) (persistent) insistente; **to be ~ THAT** insistir EN QUE (b) (pressing) ⟨need⟩ apremiante

insofar as /ˌɪnsəˈfɑːr ‖ ˌɪnsəˈfɑː(r)/ conj (fml) en la medida en que

insole /ˈɪnsəʊl/ n plantilla f

insolence /ˈɪnsələns/ n insolencia f

insolent /ˈɪnsələnt/ adj insolente

insolvent /ɪnˈsɑːlvənt ‖ ɪnˈsɒlvənt/ adj insolvente

insomnia /ɪnˈsɑːmniə ‖ ɪnˈsɒmniə/ n insomnio m

insomniac /ɪnˈsɑːmniæk ‖ ɪnˈsɒmniæk/ n insomne mf

inspect /ɪnˈspekt/ vt (a) (look closely at) ⟨car/camera⟩ revisar, examinar; (examine officially) ⟨school/restaurant/equipment⟩ inspeccionar (b) ⟨troops⟩ pasar revista a

inspection /ɪnˈspekʃən/ n (a) (official examination) inspección f (b) (of troops) revista f (c) (scrutiny) examen m, revisión f

inspector /ɪnˈspektər ‖ ɪnˈspektə(r)/ n (a) (official) inspector, -tora m,f (b) (police officer) inspector, -tora m,f (de policía)

inspiration /ˌɪnspəˈreɪʃən/ n inspiración f

inspire /ɪnˈspaɪr ‖ ɪnˈspaɪə(r)/ vt inspirar; ⟨hope/courage⟩ infundir; **what ~d you to do that?** ¿qué te movió or te llevó a hacer eso?

inspired /ɪnˈspaɪrd ‖ ɪnˈspaɪəd/ adj inspirado

inspiring /ɪnˈspaɪrɪŋ ‖ ɪnˈspaɪərɪŋ/ adj inspirador

instability /ˌɪnstəˈbɪləti/ n inestabilidad f

install, instal /ɪnˈstɔːl/ vt -ll- instalar

installation /ˌɪnstəˈleɪʃən/ n instalación f

installment, (BrE) **instalment** /ɪnˈstɔːlmənt/ n 1 (payment) plazo m, cuota f (esp AmL); **to pay in** o **by ~s** pagar* a plazos, pagar* en cuotas (esp AmL) 2 (of publication) entrega f; (of TV, radio serial) episodio m

installment plan n (AmE) plan m de financiación; **to buy sth on an ~** ~ comprar algo a plazos, comprar algo en cuotas (esp AmL)

instance /ˈɪnstəns/ n (a) (example) ejemplo m; **for ~** por ejemplo (b) (case) caso m; **in this ~** en este caso

instant¹ /ˈɪnstənt/ adj instantáneo

instant² n (a) (precise moment) instante m (b) (short time) momento m

instantaneous /ˌɪnstənˈteɪniəs/ adj instantáneo

instantly /ˈɪnstəntli/ adv al instante

instant replay n repetición f (de la jugada)

instead /ɪnˈsted/ adv: I couldn't go, so she went ~ no pude ir, así que fue ella (en vez de mí); **~ of** (as prep) en vez de, en lugar de

instep /ˈɪnstep/ n (of foot — arch) arco m (del pie); (— upper surface) empeine m

instigate /ˈɪnstəgeɪt ‖ ˈɪnstɪgeɪt/ vt ⟨rebellion/mutiny⟩ instigar* a

instigation /ˌɪnstəˈgeɪʃən ‖ ˌɪnstɪˈgeɪʃən/ n instigación f; **it was carried out at the director's ~** se llevó a cabo a instancias del director

instill, instil /ɪnˈstɪl/ vt -ll-: **to ~ sth IN/INTO sb** ⟨habit/attitude⟩ inculcarle* algo A algn; ⟨courage/fear⟩ infundirle algo A algn

instinct /ˈɪnstɪŋkt/ n instinto m

instinctive /ɪnˈstɪŋktɪv/ adj instintivo

institute¹ /ˈɪnstətuːt ‖ ˈɪnstɪtjuːt/ vt (fml) ⟨search/inquiry⟩ iniciar; ⟨proceedings⟩ entablar

institute² n instituto m

institution /ˌɪnstəˈtuːʃən ‖ ˌɪnstɪˈtjuːʃən/ n 1 (established practice) institución f 2 (a) (organization) organismo m; (building) institución f (b) (hospital, asylum, home) establecimiento sanitario, penitenciario o de asistencia social

institutional /ˌɪnstəˈtuːʃnəl ‖ ˌɪnstɪˈtjuːʃənl/ adj institucional

instruct /ɪnˈstrʌkt/ vt 1 (command) **to ~ sb to + INF** ordenar a algn QUE (+ subj) 2 (fml) (teach) **to ~ sb IN sth** enseñarle algo a algn

instruction /ɪnˈstrʌkʃən/ n instrucción f; ❸ **instructions** (for use) instrucciones; **they were acting on the ~s of the chief of police** cumplían órdenes del jefe de policía

instructive /ɪnˈstrʌktɪv/ adj instructivo

instructor /ɪnˈstrʌktər ‖ ɪnˈstrʌktə(r)/ n (a) (teacher) (Mil) instructor, -tora m,f (b) (in US colleges) profesor, -sora m,f auxiliar

instrument /ˈɪnstrəmənt ‖ ˈɪnstrʊmənt/ n 1 (musical ~) instrumento m (musical) 2 (a) (piece of equipment) instrumento m (b) **instruments** pl n (Aviat) instrumentos mpl; (Auto) instrumentación f

instrumental /ˌɪnstrəˈment ‖ ˌɪnstrʊˈment/ adj 1 (serving as a means) **to be ~ IN sth** jugar* un papel decisivo EN algo 2 (Mus) instrumental

instrument panel n (Auto) tablero m de mandos, salpicadero m (Esp); (Aviat) tablero m de mandos

insubordination /ˌɪnsəbɔːrdnˈeɪʃən ‖ ˌɪnsəbɔːdɪˈneɪʃən/ n insubordinación f

insubstantial /ˌɪnsəbˈstænʃəl ‖ ˌɪnsəbˈstænʃəl/ adj ⟨structure/object⟩ frágil; ⟨evidence/argument⟩ inconsistente

insufferable /ɪnˈsʌfrəbəl/ adj (fml) ⟨person/rudeness⟩ insufrible; ⟨heat/noise⟩ insoportable

insufficient /ˌɪnsəˈfɪʃənt/ adj insuficiente

insular /ˈɪnsələr ‖ ˈɪnsjʊlə(r)/ adj ⟨mentality⟩ cerrado; ⟨person⟩ estrecho de miras

insulate /ˈɪnsəleɪt ‖ ˈɪnsjʊleɪt/ vt aislar*

insulation /ˌɪnsəˈleɪʃən ‖ ˌɪnsjʊˈleɪʃən/ n aislamiento m

insulin /ˈɪnsələn ‖ ˈɪnsjʊlɪn/ n insulina f

insult¹ /ɪnˈsʌlt/ vt insultar

insult² /ˈɪnsʌlt/ n insulto m

insulting /ɪnˈsʌltɪŋ/ adj insultante

insurance /ɪnˈʃʊrəns ‖ ɪnˈʃʊərəns, ɪnˈʃɔːrəns/ n seguro m; **to take out ~** hacerse* un seguro; (before n) **~ company** compañía f de seguros

insure /ɪnˈʃʊr ‖ ɪnˈʃʊə(r), ɪnˈʃɔː(r)/ vt 1 (Fin) asegurar 2 (AmE) ▶ ENSURE

insurer /ɪnˈʃʊrər ‖ ɪnˈʃʊərə(r), ɪnˈʃɔːrə(r)/ n (company) compañía f de seguros; (person) asegurador, -dora m,f

insurgent /ɪnˈsɜːrdʒənt ‖ ɪnˈsɜːdʒənt/ adj (fml) insurgente (fml)

insurmountable /ˌɪnsərˈmaʊntəbəl ‖ ˌɪnsəˈmaʊntəbəl/ adj (fml) ⟨difficulty⟩ insalvable

insurrection /ˌɪnsəˈrekʃən/ n (fml) insurrección f (fml)

intact /ɪnˈtækt/ adj (usu pred) intacto

intake /ˈɪnteɪk/ n [1] (of water, air) entrada f; (of calories, protein) consumo m [2] (Tech) (pipe, vent) toma f (de aire, agua etc)

intangible /ɪnˈtændʒəbəl/ adj intangible

integral /ˈɪntɪɡrəl/ adj ‹part/feature› integral

integrate /ˈɪntəɡreɪt ‖ ˈɪntɪɡreɪt/ vt integrar
■ ~ vi integrarse

integrated /ˈɪntəɡreɪtəd ‖ ˈɪntɪɡreɪtɪd/ adj (a) ‹system/network› integrado (b) (not separate) ‹component/feature› incorporado (c) (nonsegregated) no segregacionista

integration /ˈɪntəˈɡreɪʃən ‖ ˌɪntɪˈɡreɪʃən/ n integración f

integrity /ɪnˈteɡrəti/ n integridad f

intellect /ˈɪntlekt ‖ ˈɪntəlekt/ n intelecto m

intellectual¹ /ˈɪntəˈlektʃuəl/ adj intelectual

intellectual² n intelectual mf

intelligence /ɪnˈtelədʒəns ‖ ɪnˈtelɪdʒəns/ n [1] (mental capacity) inteligencia f [2] (Govt, Mil) (a) (information) inteligencia f (b) (department) servicio m de información

intelligent /ɪnˈtelədʒənt ‖ ɪnˈtelɪdʒənt/ adj inteligente

intelligible /ɪnˈtelədʒəbəl ‖ ɪnˈtelɪdʒəbəl/ adj inteligible

intemperate /ɪnˈtempərət/ adj ‹climate› inclemente, riguroso

intend /ɪnˈtend/ vt: no insult was ~ed no fue mi intención ofender; to ~ -ING o to ~ to + INF pensar* + INF; to ~ sb/sth to + INF querer* QUE algn/algo (+ subj)

intense /ɪnˈtens/ adj intenso

intensely /ɪnˈtensli/ adv (as intensifier) ‹moving› profundamente, sumamente; I dislike him ~ siento una profunda antipatía hacia él

intensify /ɪnˈtensəfaɪ ‖ ɪnˈtensɪfaɪ/ -fies, -fying, -fied vt ‹search› intensificar*; ‹efforts› redoblar
■ ~ vi «pain» agudizarse*; «search» intensificarse*; «fighting» recrudecer*

intensity /ɪnˈtensəti/ n intensidad f

intensive /ɪnˈtensɪv/ adj intensivo

intensive care n cuidados mpl intensivos, terapia f intensiva (Méx, RPl)

intent¹ /ɪnˈtent/ adj (a) (determined) (pred) to be ~ ON sth/-ING estar* decidido or resuelto A + INF (b) (attentive, concentrated) ‹expression› de viva atención; ‹look› penetrante, fijo; to be ~ ON sth estar* abstraído EN algo

intent² n propósito m; to all ~s and purposes a efectos prácticos

intention /ɪnˈtentʃən ‖ ɪnˈtenʃən/ n intención f; I have every ~ of going tengo la firme intención de ir

intentional /ɪnˈtentʃnəl ‖ ɪnˈtenʃənl/ adj ‹destruction› intencional; ‹insult/cruelty› deliberado

intently /ɪnˈtentli/ adv ‹listen› atentamente; he was staring ~ at them tenía la mirada fija en ellos

inter /ɪnˈtɜːr ‖ ɪnˈtɜː(r)/ vt -rr- (fml or liter) inhumar (fml)

interact /ˈɪntərˈækt/ vi «people/organizations» relacionarse

interaction /ˈɪntərˈækʃən/ n interacción f

interactive /ˈɪntərˈæktɪv/ adj interactivo

intercede /ˈɪntərˈsiːd ‖ ˌɪntəˈsiːd/ vi interceder

intercept /ˈɪntərˈsept ‖ ˌɪntəˈsept/ vt interceptar; they were ~ed before they reached the building les cerraron el paso antes de llegar al edificio

interchange¹ /ˈɪntərˈtʃeɪndʒ ‖ ˌɪntəˈtʃeɪndʒ/ vt intercambiar

interchange² /ˈɪntərtʃeɪndʒ ‖ ˈɪntətʃeɪndʒ/ n [1] (exchange) intercambio m [2] (on road system) enlace m, intercambiador m (Esp)

interchangeable /ˈɪntərˈtʃeɪndʒəbəl ‖ ˌɪntəˈtʃeɪndʒəbəl/ adj intercambiable

intercity /ˈɪntərˈsɪti ‖ ˌɪntəˈsɪti/ adj rápido interurbano

intercom /ˈɪntərkɑːm ‖ ˈɪntəkɒm/ n (a) (on plane, ship, in office) interfono m (b) (at building entrance) (AmE) portero m eléctrico or (Esp) automático, interfón m (Méx), intercomunicador m (Ven)

intercourse /ˈɪntərkɔːrs ‖ ˈɪntəkɔːs/ n (sexual ~) coito m (fml), acto m sexual; to have ~ with sb tener* relaciones sexuales con algn

interest¹ /ˈɪntrəst/ n [1] (a) (enthusiasm) interés m; to take (an) ~ IN sth/sb interesarse POR algo/algn (b) (hobby) interés m [2] (a) (stake) participación f; he has a number of business ~s abroad tiene varios negocios en el extranjero (b) (advantage) (often pl) interés m; it was not in our ~(s) to intervene no nos convenía intervenir [3] (Fin) interés m; (before n) ~ rate tasa f or (esp Esp) tipo m de interés

interest² vt interesar

interested /ˈɪntrəstəd ‖ ˈɪntrəstɪd/ adj interesado; I am ~ in astronomy me interesa la astronomía; ~ party parte f interesada

interesting /ˈɪntrəstɪŋ/ adj interesante

interface /ˈɪntərfeɪs ‖ ˈɪntəfeɪs/ n (Comput) interface f or m, interfaz f or m, interfase f or m

interfere /ˈɪntərˈfɪr ‖ ˌɪntəˈfɪə(r)/ vi [1] (get involved) to ~ (IN sth) entrometerse (EN algo) [2] (a) (disrupt) to ~ WITH sth afectar (A) algo (b) (tamper) to ~ WITH sth tocar* algo

interference /ˈɪntərˈfɪrəns ‖ ˌɪntəˈfɪərəns/ n (a) (interfering) intromisión f (b) (Phys, Rad, Telec) interferencia f

interfering /ˈɪntərˈfɪrɪŋ ‖ ˌɪntəˈfɪərɪŋ/ adj entrometido

interim¹ /ˈɪntərəm ‖ ˈɪntərɪm/ adj (before n) ‹measure› provisional, provisorio (AmS); an ~ period un período intermedio

interim² n: in o during the ~ en el interín or ínterin

interior¹ /ɪnˈtɪriər ‖ ɪnˈtɪəriə(r)/ n [1] (a) (of building) interior m (b) (Cin) interior m [2] (a) (Geog) the ~ el interior (b) (Govt) the Ministry/Department of the I~ el Ministerio/Departamento del Interior

interior² adj [1] (a) (inside) ‹walls› interior (b) (mental) interior [2] (inland) del interior

interior: ~ **decorator** n (painter) pintor, -tora m,f; (designer) interiorista mf, decorador, -dora m,f (de interiores); ~ **design** n interiorismo m

interjection /ˈɪntərˈdʒekʃən ‖ ˌɪntəˈdʒekʃən/ n (Ling) interjección f; (exclamation) exclamación f

interloper /'ɪntərləʊpər ‖'ɪntələʊpə(r)/ n
intruso, -sa m,f

interlude /'ɪntəlu:d ‖'ɪntəlu:d/ n [1] (intervening
period) intervalo m [2] **(a)** (Theat) (intermission)
entreacto m **(b)** (Mus) interludio m

intermediary /'ɪntər'mi:dieri ‖,ɪntə'mi:diəri/
n (pl **-ries**) (fml) intermediario, -ria m,f

intermediate /'ɪntər'mi:diət ‖,ɪntə'mi:diət/
adj ⟨stage/step⟩ intermedio; ⟨size/weight/level⟩
medio; ⟨course⟩ de nivel medio or intermedio

intermediate school n (in US) **(a)**
(secondary) escuela donde se cursa el primer ciclo
de la enseñanza secundaria **(b)** (primary) escuela
donde se cursa segundo ciclo de la enseñanza
primaria

interminable /ɪn'tɜ:rmənəbəl ‖ɪm'tɜ:mɪnəbəl/
adj interminable

intermission /'ɪntər'mɪʃən ‖,ɪntə'mɪʃən/ n
intermedio m

intermittent /'ɪntər'mɪtn̩t ‖,ɪntə'mɪtənt/ adj
intermitente

intern¹ /ɪn'tɜ:rn ‖ɪn'tɜ:n/ vt recluir*, confinar

intern² /'ɪntɜ:rn ‖'ɪntɜ:n/ n (AmE) **(a)** (Med)
interno, -na m,f **(b)** (Educ) profesor, -sora m,f en
prácticas

internal /ɪn'tɜ:rnl̩ ‖ɪn'tɜ:nl̩/ adj interno

Internal Revenue Service n (in US) the
∼ ∼ ∼ ≈ Hacienda, ≈ la Dirección General
Impositiva (en RPl), ≈ Impuestos Internos (en
Chi)

international¹ /'ɪntər'næʃnəl ‖,ɪntə'næʃənl̩/
adj internacional

international² n (Sport) **(a)** (event) partido m
internacional **(b)** (player) internacional mf

internationally /'ɪntər'næʃnəli
‖,ɪntə'næʃnəli/ adv **(a)** ⟨expand/trade⟩
internacionalmente **(b)** ⟨famous/known⟩
mundialmente

International Monetary Fund n the ∼
∼ ∼ el Fondo Monetario Internacional

Internet /'ɪntərnet ‖'ɪntənet/ n the ∼ el
Internet

Internet service provider /prə'vaɪdər
‖prə'vaɪdə(r)/ n proveedor m de servicios
Internet

internment /ɪn'tɜ:rnmənt ‖ɪn'tɜ:nmənt/ n
internamiento m

interpret /ɪn'tɜ:rprət ‖ɪn'tɜ:prɪt/ vt interpretar
■ ∼ vi (Ling) (translate) traducir* (oralmente),
interpretar

interpretation /ɪn'tɜ:rprə'teɪʃən
‖ɪn,tɜ:prɪ'teɪʃən/ n interpretación f

interpreter /ɪn'tɜ:rprətər ‖ɪn'tɜ:prɪtə(r)/ n
intérprete mf

interrogate /ɪn'terəgeɪt/ vt interrogar*

interrogation /ɪn'terə'geɪʃən/ n
interrogatorio m

interrogation point n (AmE fml) signo m de
interrogación

interrogative /'ɪntə'rɑ:gətɪv ‖,ɪntə'rɒgətɪv/
adj interrogativo

interrupt /'ɪntə'rʌpt/ vt/i interrumpir

interruption /'ɪntə'rʌpʃən/ n interrupción f

intersect /'ɪntər'sekt ‖,ɪntə'sekt/ vi ⟨roads/
paths⟩ cruzarse*

intersection /'ɪntər'sekʃən ‖,ɪntə'sekʃən/ n
(a) (Transp) cruce m **(b)** (Geog, Math) intersección f

intersperse /'ɪntər'spɜ:rs ‖,ɪntə'spɜ:s/ vt
intercalar

interstate (highway) /'ɪntərsteɪt
‖'ɪntəsteɪt/ n (AmE) carretera f interestatal

intertwine /'ɪntər'twaɪn ‖,ɪntə'twaɪn/ vi
⟨fingers/plants⟩ entrelazarse*; ⟨paths/
destinies⟩ entrecruzarse*
■ ∼ vt ⟨fingers⟩ entrelazar*

interval /'ɪntərvəl ‖'ɪntəvəl/ n [1] (time, distance)
intervalo m [2] (pause) (BrE Cin, Mus) intermedio
m; (BrE Theat) entreacto m; (Sport) descanso m,
entretiempo m (Chi) [3] (Mus) intervalo m

intervene /'ɪntər'vi:n ‖,ɪntə'vi:n/ vi **(a)**
(interpose oneself) intervenir* **(b)** **intervening**
pres p: in the intervening period en el interín or
ínterin

intervention /'ɪntər'ventʃən ‖,ɪntə'venʃən/ n
intervención f

interview¹ /'ɪntərvju: ‖'ɪntəvju:/ n entrevista
f

interview² vt entrevistar

interviewee /'ɪntərvju:'i: ‖,ɪntəvju:'i:/ n
entrevistado, -da m,f

interviewer /'ɪntərvju:ər ‖'ɪntəvju:ə(r)/ n
entrevistador, -dora m,f

interweave /'ɪntər'wi:v ‖,ɪntə'wi:v/ vt (past
-wove or -weaved; past p -woven or
-weaved) entretejer; their lives were interwoven
sus vidas estaban inextricablemente unidas

intestate /ɪn'testeɪt/ adj intestado

intestine /ɪn'testən ‖ɪn'testɪn/ n (often pl)
intestino m; the small/large ∼ el intestino
delgado/grueso

intimacy /'ɪntəməsi ‖'ɪntɪməsi/ n intimidad f

intimate /'ɪntəmət ‖'ɪntɪmət/ adj ⟨friend/
atmosphere⟩ íntimo; ⟨talk⟩ de carácter íntimo;
⟨knowledge⟩ profundo; to be on ∼ terms with sb
ser* íntimo de algn

intimation /'ɪntə'meɪʃən ‖,ɪntɪ'meɪʃən/ n (sign)
indicio m; (inkling) presentimiento m

intimidate /ɪn'tɪmədeɪt ‖ɪn'tɪmɪdeɪt/ vt
intimidar

intimidating /ɪn'tɪmədeɪtɪŋ ‖ɪn'tɪmɪdeɪtɪŋ/
adj intimidante

intimidation /ɪn'tɪmə'deɪʃən ‖ɪn,tɪmɪ'deɪʃən/
n intimidación f

into /'ɪntu, before consonant 'ɪntə/ prep [1] **(a)**
(indicating motion, direction): to walk ∼ a building
entrar en or (esp AmL) a un edificio; they helped
him ∼ the chair lo ayudaron a sentarse en el
sillón; she sat staring ∼ space estaba sentada
mirando al vacío; to translate sth ∼ Spanish
traducir* algo al español **(b)** (against): she walked
∼ a tree se dio contra un árbol; he drove ∼ the
other car chocó con el otro coche
[2] (in time, distance): ten minutes ∼ the game a los
diez minutos de empezar el partido; they
penetrated deep ∼ the jungle entraron en el
corazón de la selva
[3] (indicating result of action): we split ∼ two groups
nos dividimos en dos grupos; roll the dough ∼ a
ball haga una bola con la masa
[4] (involved in) (colloq) they're ∼ drugs se drogan;
at two, children are ∼ everything a los dos años,
los niños son muy inquietos

intolerable /ɪnˈtɑ:lərəbəl ‖ɪnˈtɒlərəbəl/ *adj* intolerable

intolerance /ɪnˈtɑ: lərəns ‖ɪnˈtɒlərəns/ *n* intolerancia *f*

intolerant /ɪnˈtɑ:lərənt ‖ɪnˈtɒlərənt/ *adj* intolerante

intonation /ˌɪntəˈneɪʃən/ *n* entonación *f*

intone /ɪnˈtəʊn/ *vt* ⟨*psalm/Gloria*⟩ entonar

intoxicated /ɪnˈtɑ:ksəkeɪtəd ‖ɪnˈtɒksɪkeɪtɪd/ *adj* (frml) en estado de embriaguez (frml)

intoxicating /ɪnˈtɑ:ksəkeɪtɪŋ ‖ɪnˈtɒksɪkeɪtɪŋ/ *adj* (frml) ⟨*substance*⟩ estupefaciente; ∼ **liquor** bebida *f* alcohólica

intractable /ɪnˈtræktəbəl/ *adj* (frml) **(a)** ⟨*temperament*⟩ obstinado; ⟨*child*⟩ incorregible **(b)** ⟨*problem/dilemma*⟩ inextricable (frml)

intransigent /ɪnˈtrænsədʒənt ‖ɪnˈtrænsɪdʒənt/ *adj* intransigente

intransitive /ɪnˈtrænsətɪv/ *adj* intransitivo

intrauterine device /ˈɪntrəˈjuːtərən ‖ˌɪntrəˈjuːtəraɪn/ *n* dispositivo *m* intrauterino; (in the shape of a coil) espiral *f*

intravenous /ˈɪntrəˈviːnəs/ *adj* intravenoso

intrepid /ɪnˈtrepəd ‖ɪnˈtrepɪd/ *adj* intrépido

intricacy /ˈɪntrɪkəsi/ *n* **(a)** (of pattern, embroidery) lo intrincado **(b) intricacies** *pl* (complexities) complejidades *fpl*

intricate /ˈɪntrɪkət/ *adj* complicado

intrigue¹ /ˈɪntriːg/ *n* intriga *f*

intrigue² /ɪnˈtriːg/ *vt* intrigar*

intriguing /ɪnˈtriːgɪŋ/ *adj* ⟨*problem/text*⟩ intrigante; ⟨*possibility*⟩ fascinante; ⟨*person*⟩ interesante

intrinsic /ɪnˈtrɪnzɪk/ *adj* intrínseco

introduce /ˈɪntrəˈduːs ‖ˌɪntrəˈdjuːs/ *vt* **1** **(a)** (acquaint) presentar; **allow me to** ∼ **myself/my mother** (frml) permítame que me presente/le presente a mi madre; **to** ∼ **sb TO sb** presentarle a algn A algn **(b)** (initiate) **to** ∼ **sb TO sth** introducir* a algn A algo, iniciar a algn EN algo **(c)** (present) ⟨*speaker/program*⟩ presentar; ⟨*meeting/article*⟩ iniciar **2** (bring in) ⟨*subject/custom/legislation*⟩ introducir*; ⟨*product*⟩ lanzar*, sacar*

introduction /ˈɪntrəˈdʌkʃən/ *n* **1** **(a)** (to person) presentación *f* **(b)** (to activity, experience) ∼ **TO sth** introducción *f* A algo **(c)** (of speaker, performer) presentación *f* **2** (of species, practice, legislation) introducción *f* **3** (insertion, entry) (frml) introducción *f* **4** **(a)** (to meeting, lecture) presentación *f* **(b)** (in book) introducción *f* **(c)** (Mus) introducción *f* **5** (elementary instruction) introducción *f*, iniciación *f*

introductory /ˈɪntrəˈdʌktəri/ *adj* **(a)** (opening) ⟨*notes/remarks*⟩ preliminar; ⟨*lecture/chapter*⟩ de introducción; ⟨*offer*⟩ (Busn) de lanzamiento **(b)** (elementary) ⟨*course/lesson*⟩ de introducción

introspective /ˈɪntrəˈspektɪv/ *adj* introspectivo

introvert /ˈɪntrəvɜːrt ‖ˈɪntrəvɜːt/ *n* introvertido, -da *m,f*

introverted /ˈɪntrəvɜːrtəd ‖ˈɪntrəvɜːtɪd/ *adj* introvertido

intrude /ɪnˈtruːd/ *vi* (disturb) importunar; (interfere) inmiscuirse*; **to** ∼ **on sb's privacy** inmiscuirse* en la vida privada de algn

intruder /ɪnˈtruːdər ‖ɪnˈtruːdə(r)/ *n* intruso, -sa *m,f*

intrusion /ɪnˈtruːʒən/ *n* intrusión *f*

intrusive /ɪnˈtruːsɪv/ *adj* **(a)** ⟨*noise/smell*⟩ molesto **(b)** ⟨*questioning/reporter*⟩ impertinente

intuition /ˈɪntuːˈɪʃən ‖ˌɪntjuːˈɪʃən/ *n* intuición *f*

intuitive /ɪnˈtuːətɪv ‖ɪnˈtjuːɪtɪv/ *adj* intuitivo

Inuit /ˈɪnuːt ‖ˈɪnjuːɪt/ *n* (*pl* ∼ *or* ∼**s**) **(a)** (person) esquimal *mf* **(b)** (Ling) esquimal *m*

inundate /ˈɪnʌndeɪt/ *vt* inundar

invade /ɪnˈveɪd/ *vt/i* invadir

invader /ɪnˈveɪdər ‖ɪnˈveɪdə(r)/ *n* invasor, -sora *m,f*

invalid¹ /ɪnˈvæləd ‖ɪnˈvælɪd/ *adj* inválido

invalid² /ˈɪnvəlɪd ‖ˈɪnvəliːd, ˈɪnvəlɪd/ *n* inválido, -da *m,f*

invalidate /ɪnˈvælədeɪt ‖ɪnˈvælɪdeɪt/ *vt* (frml) invalidar

invalidity /ˈɪnvəˈlɪdəti/ *n* (frml) invalidez *f*

invaluable /ɪnˈvæljuəbəl/ *adj* inapreciable, invalorable (AmL)

invariable /ɪnˈveriəbəl ‖ɪnˈveəriəbəl/ *adj* invariable

invariably /ɪnˈveriəbli ‖ɪnˈveəriəbli/ *adv* invariablemente, siempre

invasion /ɪnˈveɪʒən/ *n* invasión *f*

invective /ɪnˈvektɪv/ *n* **(a)** (abuse) invectivas *fpl* (frml) **(b)** (condemnation) invectiva *f* (frml)

invent /ɪnˈvent/ *vt* inventar

invention /ɪnˈventʃən ‖ɪnˈvenʃən/ *n* **1** **(a)** (device) invento *m* **(b)** (action) invención *f* **2** (imagination): ⟨*powers of*⟩ ∼ inventiva *f*

inventive /ɪnˈventɪv/ *adj* ingenioso

inventor /ɪnˈventər ‖ɪnˈventə(r)/ *n* inventor, -tora *m,f*

inventory /ˈɪnvəntɔːri ‖ˈɪnventri/ *n* (*pl* **-ries**) inventario *m*

inverse /ˈɪnvɜːrs, ˈɪnvɜːrs ‖ˌɪnvɜːs, ˈɪnvɜːs/ *adj* (*usu before n*) inverso; **in** ∼ **proportion to sth** en proporción inversa a algo

inversion /ɪnˈvɜːrʒən ‖ɪnˈvɜːʃən/ *n* inversión *f*

invert /ɪnˈvɜːrt ‖ɪnˈvɜːt/ *vt* invertir*

invertebrate /ɪnˈvɜːrtəbrət ‖ɪnˈvɜːtɪbrət/ *n* invertebrado, -da *m,f*

inverted commas /ɪnˈvɜːrtəd ‖ɪnˈvɜːtɪd/ *pl n* (BrE) comillas *fpl*

invest /ɪnˈvest/ *vt* **to** ∼ **sth** (**IN sth**) ⟨*money/time*⟩ invertir* algo (EN algo)
■ ∼ *vi* **to** ∼ **in** (**IN sth**) invertir* (EN algo)

investigate /ɪnˈvestəgeɪt ‖ɪnˈvestɪgeɪt/ *vt* **(a)** ⟨*crime/cause*⟩ investigar*; ⟨*complaint/possibility*⟩ estudiar **(b)** (do research on) hacer* una investigación sobre
■ ∼ *vi* investigar*

investigation /ɪnˌvestəˈɡeɪʃən ‖ ɪnˌvestɪˈɡeɪʃən/ n **(a)** (detailed examination) estudio m **(b)** (official, scientific) investigación f

investigator /ɪnˈvestəɡeɪtər ‖ ɪnˈvestɪɡeɪtə(r)/ n **(a)** (private ∼) investigador privado, investigadora privada m,f **(b)** (official) inspector, -tora m,f

investiture /ɪnˈvestətʃʊr ‖ ɪnˈvestɪtʃə(r)/ n investidura f

investment /ɪnˈvestmənt/ n inversión f

investor /ɪnˈvestər ‖ ɪnˈvestə(r)/ n inversor, -sora m,f, inversionista mf

inveterate /ɪnˈvetərət/ adj (fml) (usu before n) ‹thief/liar› empedernido

invigorating /ɪnˈvɪɡəreɪtɪŋ/ adj ‹weather/walk› vigorizante; ‹environment/change› estimulante

invisible /ɪnˈvɪzəbəl/ adj invisible

invitation /ˌɪnvəˈteɪʃən ‖ ˌɪnvɪˈteɪʃən/ n invitación f; at the ∼ of invitado por, por invitación de

invite /ɪnˈvaɪt/ vt to ∼ sb (TO sth)/to + INF invitar a algn (A algo)/A + INF or A QUE (+ subj); to ∼ sb in/out invitar a algn a pasar/a salir; his work ∼s comparison with the classics su obra sugiere comparación con los clásicos

inviting /ɪnˈvaɪtɪŋ/ adj ‹prospect/offer› atractivo

in vitro /ɪnˈviːtrəʊ/ adj in vitro adj inv

invoice¹ /ˈɪnvɔɪs/ n factura f

invoice² vt to ∼ sb (FOR sth) pasarle A algn factura (POR algo)

invoke /ɪnˈvəʊk/ vt invocar*

involuntary /ɪnˈvɑːlənteri ‖ ɪnˈvɒləntri/ adj involuntario

involve /ɪnˈvɑːlv ‖ ɪnˈvɒlv/ vt **1** **(a)** (entail, comprise) suponer*; what exactly does your work ∼? ¿en qué consiste exactamente tu trabajo? **(b)** (affect, concern): where national security is ∼d ... cuando se trata de la seguridad nacional ...; it's my reputation that's ∼d here es mi reputación lo que está en juego
2 to ∼ sb IN sth/-ING (implicate) implicar* or involucrar a algn EN algo; (allow to participate) darle* participación a algn EN algo
3 **involved** past p **(a)** (implicated): I was ∼d in an accident last year el año pasado me vi envuelto en un accidente; several high-ranking officials were ∼d in the affair había varios oficiales de alto rango implicados en el asunto; the people you're ∼d with la gente con la que andas metido **(b)** be ∼d in sth (engrossed) estar* absorto EN algo; (busy) estar* ocupado CON algo **(c)** (emotionally): she doesn't want to get too ∼d with him no quiere llegar a una relación muy seria con él

involved /ɪnˈvɑːlvd ‖ ɪnˈvɒlvd/ adj enrevesado, complicado

involvement /ɪnˈvɑːlvmənt ‖ ɪnˈvɒlvmənt/ n **(a)** n (entanglement) participación f; they deny any ∼ in terrorist attacks niegan estar implicados en ningún ataque terrorista **(b)** (relationship) relación f (sentimental)

inward¹ /ˈɪnwərd ‖ ˈɪnwəd/ adj **(a)** (toward inside) ‹curve› hacia adentro **(b)** (private, mental) ‹torment/serenity› interior

inward², (BrE also) **inwards** adv **(a)** (toward inside) ‹move/bend› hacia adentro; ‹travel› hacia

el interior **(b)** (toward mind, spirit): **meditation involves looking** ∼ la meditación exige introspección

iodine /ˈaɪədaɪn ‖ ˈaɪədiːn/ n yodo m

ion /ˈaɪən, ˈaɪɑːn ‖ ˈaɪən/ n ión m

iota /aɪˈəʊtə/ n (usu with neg) pizca f, ápice m

IOU n (= I owe you) pagaré m

IQ n (= intelligence quotient) CI m

IRA n (= Irish Republican Army) IRA m

Iran /ɪˈrɑːn, ɪˈræn/ n Irán m

Iranian¹ /ɪˈreɪniən/ adj iraní

Iranian² n iraní mf

Iraq /ɪˈrɑːk, ɪˈræk/ n Irak m

Iraqi¹ /ɪˈrɑːki, ɪˈræki/ adj iraquí

Iraqi² n iraquí mf

irascible /ɪˈræsəbəl/ adj irascible

irate /aɪˈreɪt/ adj airado

ire /aɪr ‖ ˈaɪə(r)/ n (liter) ira f, cólera f

Ireland /ˈaɪrlənd ‖ ˈaɪələnd/ n (the island) Irlanda f; (the Republic) Irlanda f, (el) Eire

iris /ˈaɪrəs ‖ ˈaɪərɪs/ n (Bot) lirio m

Irish¹ /ˈaɪrɪʃ ‖ ˈaɪərɪʃ/ adj irlandés; the ∼ Sea el Mar de Irlanda

Irish² n **(a)** (people) (+ pl vb) the ∼ los irlandeses **(b)** (language) irlandés m

Irish: ∼man /ˈaɪrɪʃmən ‖ ˈaɪərɪʃmən/ n (pl -men /-mən/) irlandés m; ∼woman n irlandesa f

irk /ɜːrk ‖ ɜːk/ vt fastidiar, irritar

iron¹ /ˈaɪərn ‖ ˈaɪən/ n **1** **(a)** (metal) hierro m, fierro m (AmL) **(b)** (in food) hierro m **2** (for clothes) plancha f **3** (golf club) hierro m **4** **irons** pl (fetters) grilletes mpl, grillos mpl

iron² adj **(a)** (made of iron) de hierro **(b)** (strong) (before n) ‹constitution› de hierro; ‹will/resolve› férreo, de hierro

iron³ vt/i planchar
■ **iron out** [v + o + adv, v + adv + o] ‹problems› resolver*; ‹difficulties› allanar

Iron Curtain n the ∼ ∼ la cortina de hierro (AmL), el telón de acero (Esp)

ironic /aɪˈrɑːnɪk ‖ aɪˈrɒnɪk/ adj irónico

ironically /aɪˈrɑːnɪkli ‖ aɪˈrɒnɪkli/ adv irónicamente

ironing /ˈaɪərnɪŋ ‖ ˈaɪənɪŋ/ n to do the ∼ planchar

ironing board n tabla f or (Méx) burro m de planchar

ironmonger /ˈaɪərnˌmɑːŋɡər ‖ ˈaɪənˌmʌŋɡə(r)/ n (BrE) ferretero, -ra m,f; at the ∼'s en la ferretería

irony /ˈaɪrəni/ n (pl -nies) ironía f

irrational /ɪˈræʃnəl ‖ ɪˈræʃənl/ adj irracional

irreconcilable /ɪˈrekənˌsaɪləbəl/ adj irreconciliable

irrefutable /ɪˈrefjətəbəl, ˈɪrɪˈfjuː- ‖ ˌɪrɪˈfjuːtəbəl/ adj irrefutable

irregular /ɪˈreɡjələr ‖ ɪˈreɡjʊlə(r)/ adj **1** (in shape, positioning, time) irregular **2** (contrary to rules) inadmisible, contrario a las normas **3** (Ling) irregular

irregularity /ɪˌreɡjəˈlærəti ‖ ɪˌreɡjʊˈlærəti/ n (pl -ties) **1** (in shape, positioning, time)

irregularidad *f* **2** (of action) lo inadmisible; **several irregularities** varias contravenciones de las normas

irrelevant /ɪˈreləvənt/ *adj* ‹fact/detail› irrelevante; **to be ~ TO sth** no tener* relación *or* no tener* que ver CON algo

irreparable /ɪˈrepərəbəl/ *adj* irreparable

irreplaceable /ɪrɪˈpleɪsəbəl/ *adj* irreemplazable

irrepressible /ɪrɪˈpresəbəl/ *adj* ‹laughter› incontenible; ‹desire› irreprimible

irresistible /ɪrɪˈzɪstəbəl/ *adj* irresistible

irrespective /ɪrɪˈspektɪv/ *adv* **~ OF sth**: **~ of what you say** independientemente de lo que usted diga; **~ of age or sex** sin distinción de edad o sexo

irresponsible /ɪrɪˈspɑːnsəbəl ‖ ɪrɪˈspɒnsəbəl/ *adj* irresponsable

irreverent /ɪˈrevrənt, ɪˈrevərənt/ *adj* irreverente

irreversible /ɪrɪˈvɜːrsəbəl ‖ ɪrɪˈvɜːsəbəl/ *adj* ‹decision› irrevocable; ‹process/event› irreversible

irrigate /ˈɪrəgeɪt ‖ ˈɪrɪgeɪt/ *vt* irrigar*, regar*

irrigation /ɪrəˈgeɪʃən ‖ ɪrɪˈgeɪʃən/ *n* irrigación *f*, riego *m*

irritable /ˈɪrətəbəl ‖ ˈɪrɪtəbəl/ *adj* **1** (bad-tempered) ‹person/mood› irritable; ‹reply› irritado **2** (sensitive) ‹skin/scalp› sensible

irritant /ˈɪrətənt ‖ ˈɪrɪtənt/ *n* **(a)** (Med) agente *m* irritante **(b)** (person, thing) fastidio *m*

irritate /ˈɪrəteɪt ‖ ˈɪrɪteɪt/ *vt* irritar

irritated /ˈɪrəteɪtəd ‖ ˈɪrɪteɪtɪd/ *adj* **1** ‹look/frown› de impaciencia; **to be ~ WITH** *o* **AT sth/WITH sb** estar* irritado POR algo/CON algn **2** ‹skin/hands› irritado

irritating /ˈɪrəteɪtɪŋ ‖ ˈɪrɪteɪtɪŋ/ *adj* irritante

irritation /ɪrəˈteɪʃən ‖ ɪrɪˈteɪʃən/ *n* irritación *f*

IRS *n* (in US) = **Internal Revenue Service**

is /ɪz/ *3rd pers sing pres of* BE

ISBN *n* (= **International Standard Book Number**) ISBN *n*

-ish /ɪʃ/ *suff*: **long~** más bien largo; **green~** verdoso; **tennish** a eso de las diez

Islam /ˈɪzlɑːm, ɪzˈlɑːm/ *n* el Islam

Islamic /ɪzˈlæmɪk, ɪzˈlɑːmɪk/ *adj* islámico

island /ˈaɪlənd/ *n* isla *f*

islander /ˈaɪləndər ‖ ˈaɪləndə(r)/ *n* isleño, -ña *m,f*

isle /aɪl/ *n* **(a)** (poet) isla *f*, ínsula *f* (liter) **(b)** (in place names): **the I~ of Wight** la Isla de Wight

Isles of Scilly /ˈaɪlzəvˈsɪli/ *pl n* **the ~ ~ ~** las islas Scilly *or* Sorlingas

isn't /ˈɪznt/ = **is not**

isolate /ˈaɪsəleɪt/ *vt* aislar*

isolated /ˈaɪsəleɪtəd ‖ ˈaɪsəleɪtɪd/ *adj* aislado

isolation /aɪsəˈleɪʃən/ *n* aislamiento *m*

ISP *n* (= **Internet service provider**) ISP *m*

Israel /ˈɪzreɪəl/ *n* Israel *m*

Israeli¹ /ɪzˈreɪli/ *adj* israelí

Israeli² *n* israelí *mf*

issue¹ /ˈɪʃuː ‖ ˈɪʃjuː, ˈɪsjuː/ *n* **1** (subject discussed) tema *m*, cuestión *f*, asunto *m*; **to take ~ with sb/sth** discrepar de *or* con algn/en *or* de algo **2 (a)** (of documents) expedición *f*; (of library books)

préstamo *m*; (of tickets) venta *f* **(b)** (of stamps, shares, bank notes) emisión *f* **(c)** (of newspaper, magazine) número *m*

issue² *vt* (give out) ‹statement/report› hacer* público; ‹instructions› dar*; ‹guidelines› establecer*; ‹tickets/visas› expedir*; ‹library books› prestar; ‹bank notes/stamps/shares› emitir; ‹summons› dictar; **we can ~ you with the necessary documents** le podemos proporcionar los documentos necesarios
■ ~ *vi* (frml) **1** (result) **to ~ FROM sth** derivar(se) DE algo (frml) **2** (emerge) salir*; «liquid» fluir*

it /ɪt/ *pron* **1** (replacing noun — as direct object) lo, la; (— as indirect object) le; (— as subject, after prep) *gen not translated*; **~'s enormous** es enorme; **there's nothing behind ~** no hay nada detrás **2** (introducing person, thing, event): **who is ~?** ¿quién es?; **~'s me** soy yo; **I'll see to ~** yo me encargo (de ello); **~'s his attitude that I don't like** su actitud es lo que no me gusta; **a little higher up ... that's ~!** un poco más arriba ... ¡ahí está! *or* ¡eso es!; **one more and that's ~** uno más y ya está *or* se acabó **3** (in impersonal constructions): **~'s raining** está lloviendo; **~'s two o'clock** son las dos; **~ says here that ...** aquí dice que ...; **~ is known that ...** se sabe que ...

Italian¹ /ɪˈtæljən/ *adj* italiano

Italian² *n* **(a)** (person) italiano, -na *m,f* **(b)** (language) italiano *m*

italics /ɪˈtælɪks/ *pl n* (letra *f*) cursiva *f*

Italy /ˈɪtli ‖ ˈɪtəli/ *n* Italia *f*

itch¹ /ɪtʃ/ *vi* **1** «scalp/toe» picar* (+ *me/te/le etc*) **(b)** (be impatient, eager) (colloq) **to be ~ing to + INF: he was ~ing to tell her** estaba que se moría por decírselo (fam) **2** «wool/underwear» (cause irritation) picar*

itch² *n* **(a)** (irritation) picor *m*, picazón *f* **(b)** (desire) ansia *f*‡

itchy /ˈɪtʃi/ *adj* **itchier, itchiest (a)** (feeling irritation): **I've got an ~ nose/scalp** me pica la nariz/la cabeza **(b)** (causing irritation) ‹garment/material› que pica

it'd /ˈɪtəd/ **(a)** = **it had (b)** = **it would**

item /ˈaɪtəm/ *n* **(a)** (article) (Busn) artículo *m*; (in collection) pieza *f*; (on agenda) punto *m*: **~s of clothing** prendas *fpl* de vestir **(b)** (in newspaper) artículo *m*; **news ~** noticia *f*

itemize /ˈaɪtəmaɪz/ *vt* (break down) detallar; (list) hacer* una lista de

itinerant /aɪˈtɪnərənt/ *adj* (frml) ‹worker/judge› itinerante (frml); ‹salesman/musician› ambulante

itinerary /aɪˈtɪnəreri ‖ aɪˈtɪnərəri/ *n* (*pl* **-ries**) itinerario *m*

it'll /ˈɪtl/ = **it will**

its /ɪts/ *adj* (*sing*) su; (*pl*) sus
■ **Note** The translation *su* agrees in number with the noun which it modifies; *its* is translated by *su, sus*, depending on what follows: *its snout/head* su hocico/cabeza; *its problems/difficulties* sus problemas/dificultades.

it's /ɪts/ **(a)** = **it is (b)** = **it has**

itself /ɪtˈself/ *pron* **(a)** (reflexive): **it has earned ~ a reputation** se ha hecho fama; **another problem**

presented ∼ se presentó otro problema **(b)**
(emphatic use): **the town ∼ is small** la ciudad en sí
or propiamente dicha es pequeña
ITV n (in UK) (no art) = **Independent
Television**
IUD n (= **intrauterine device**) DIU m
I've /aɪv/ = **I have**

ivory /'aɪvəri/ n (pl **-ries**) **(a)** (material) marfil m
(b) (color) (color m) marfil m
Ivory Coast n Costa f de Marfil
ivy /'aɪvi/ n hiedra f
Ivy League n (AmE) **the ∼** ∼ grupo de ocho
universidades prestigiosas de EEUU

J, j /dʒeɪ/ n J, j f
jab¹ /dʒæb/ vt **-bb-**: I ∼bed myself with the
needle me pinché con la aguja, me piqué con la
aguja (Méx); she ∼bed me with her fork me clavó
con el tenedor
jab² n **(a)** (prick) pinchazo m; (blow) golpe m; (with
elbow) codazo m **(b)** (in boxing) jab m, corto m **(c)**
(injection) (BrE colloq) inyección f
jabber /'dʒæbər ‖'dʒæbə(r)/ vi/t farfullar
jack /dʒæk/ n **(a)** (lifting device) gato m **(b)** (socket)
enchufe m hembra **(c)** (in French pack of cards) jota
f, valet m; (in Spanish pack) sota f
▪ **jack up** [v + o + adv, v + adv + o] ⟨car⟩
levantar (con el gato)
jackal /'dʒækəl/ n chacal m
jackdaw /'dʒækdɔ:/ n grajilla f
jacket /'dʒækət ‖'dʒækɪt/ n **1** (Clothing)
chaqueta f; (sports ∼) americana f, saco m (sport)
(AmL) **2** (of book) sobrecubierta f; (of record) (AmE)
funda f, carátula f **3** (of potato) (BrE): ∼ **potatoes**
papas fpl asadas (con la cáscara) (AmL), patatas
fpl asadas (con la piel) (Esp)
jack: ∼**hammer** n martillo m neumático;
∼**-in-the-box** /'dʒækəndə'bɑ:ks
‖'dʒækɪndə,bɒks/ n caja f de sorpresas (con
muñeco a resorte); ∼**knife** vi ⟨truck⟩ plegarse*;
∼ **of all trades** /'dʒækəv'ɔ:ltreɪdz/ n (pl ∼**s
of all trades**) hombre m or mujer f orquesta,
manitas mf (Esp, Méx fam); ∼**pot** n (in bingo, lottery)
bote m, pozo m; ∼**rabbit** n: tipo de liebre de
Norteamérica
Jacuzzi®, jacuzzi /dʒə'ku:zi/ n Jacuzzi® m
jade /dʒeɪd/ n **(a)** (Min) jade m **(b)** (color) verde
m jade
jaded /'dʒeɪdəd ‖'dʒeɪdɪd/ adj hastiado
jagged /'dʒægəd ‖'dʒægɪd/ adj ⟨edge/cut⟩
irregular; ⟨rock/cliff⟩ recortado, con picos
jaguar /'dʒægwɑ:r ‖'dʒægjʊə(r)/ n jaguar m
jail¹ /dʒeɪl/ n cárcel f, prisión f; he went to ∼ lo
metieron preso
jail² vt encarcelar
jailer, jailor /'dʒeɪlər ‖'dʒeɪlə(r)/ n carcelero,
-ra m,f
jailhouse /'dʒeɪlhaʊs/ n (AmE) cárcel f
jam¹ /dʒæm/ n **1** (Culin) mermelada f, dulce m
(RPl) **2** (difficult situation) (colloq) aprieto m
jam² -mm- vt **1** **(a)** (cram) to ∼ sth INTO sth
meter algo a la fuerza EN algo **(b)** (congest, block)
⟨road⟩ atestar; the switchboard was ∼med with

calls la centralita estaba saturada de llamadas
2 (wedge firmly): he ∼med his foot in the door
metió el pie entre la puerta y el marco **3** (Rad)
interferir*
▪ ∼ vi ⟨brakes⟩ bloquearse; ⟨machine⟩
trancarse*; ⟨switch/lock⟩ trabarse; ⟨gun⟩
encasquillarse
▪ **jam on** [v + o + adv, v + adv + o]: to ∼ on the
brakes dar* un frenazo
Jamaica /dʒə'meɪkə/ n Jamaica f
Jamaican /dʒə'meɪkən/ adj jamaicano
jamb /dʒæm/ n jamba f
jam: ∼ **jar** n (BrE) tarro m or bote m para
mermelada; ∼**-packed** /'dʒæm'pækt/ adj (colloq)
repleto, atestado (de gente); ∼ **session** n:
sesión de un grupo de músicos de jazz o rock que
se reúnen para improvisar
jangle /'dʒæŋgəl/ vi hacer* ruido (metálico)
janitor /'dʒænətər ‖'dʒænɪtə(r)/ n conserje m
January /'dʒænjueri ‖'dʒænjʊəri/ n enero m
Japan /dʒə'pæn/ n (el) Japón m
Japanese¹ /'dʒæpə'ni:z/ adj japonés
Japanese² n (pl ∼) **(a)** (language) japonés m
(b) (person) japonés, -nesa m,f
jar¹ /dʒɑ:r ‖dʒɑ:(r)/ n **1** (container) tarro m, bote
m **2** (jolt) sacudida f
jar² -rr- vi **(a)** (clash) desentonar **(b)** (irritate): it
∼s on my nerves me crispa los nervios, me
enerva
▪ ∼ vt sacudir
jargon /'dʒɑ:rgən ‖'dʒɑ:gən/ n jerga f
jarring /'dʒɑ:rɪŋ/ adj ⟨sound⟩ discordante
jasmine /'dʒæzmən ‖'dʒæsmɪn/ n jazmín m
jaundice /'dʒɔ:ndəs ‖'dʒɔ:ndɪs/ n ictericia f
jaundiced /'dʒɔ:ndəst ‖'dʒɔ:ndɪst/ adj **(a)**
(Med) ⟨skin/baby⟩ ictérico **(b)** ⟨view/opinion⟩
negativo
jaunt /dʒɔ:nt/ n excursión f
jaunty /'dʒɔ:nti/ adj **-tier, -tiest** (usu before n)
⟨air⟩ garboso; ⟨tune⟩ alegre
javelin /'dʒævlən ‖'dʒævlɪn/ n jabalina f
jaw /dʒɔ:/ n **(a)** (of person, animal) mandíbula f;
(esp of animal) quijada f; his ∼ dropped se quedó
boquiabierto **(b)** jaws pl fauces fpl
jawbone /'dʒɔ:bəʊn/ n mandíbula f, maxilar m;
(of an animal) quijada f
jay /dʒeɪ/ n arrendajo m

jay: ∼**walk** vi cruzar* la calzada imprudentemente; ∼**walker** n peatón m imprudente

jazz /dʒæz/ n (Mus) jazz m

■ **jazz up** [v + o + adv, v + adv + o] (colloq) **(a)** ⟨music⟩ tocar* con ritmo sincopado **(b)** ⟨room⟩ alegrar, darle* vida a

jazzy /ˈdʒæzi/ adj **jazzier, jazziest** 1 (flashy) (colloq) llamativo 2 (Mus) ⟨rhythm⟩ de jazz

jealous /ˈdʒeləs/ adj **(a)** ⟨husband/wife⟩ celoso; **to be** ∼ estar* celoso, tener* celos **(b)** (envious) envidioso; **to be** ∼ **OF sb** tenerle* envidia A algn

jealousy /ˈdʒeləsi/ n (pl **-sies**) **(a)** (fear of rivalry) celos mpl **(b)** (envy) envidia f

jeans /dʒiːnz/ pl n vaqueros mpl, jeans mpl, bluyines mpl (Andes)

Jeep®, jeep /dʒiːp/ n Jeep® m

jeer /dʒɪr ‖ dʒɪə(r)/ vi: **to** ∼ **AT sth/sb** (boo) abuchear (algo/a algn); (mock) burlarse (DE algo/algn)

Jehovah /dʒəˈhəʊvə/ n Jehová

Jehovah's Witness n testigo mf de Jehová

jell /dʒel/ vi ▶ GEL²

Jell-O® /ˈdʒeləʊ/ n (AmE) gelatina f ⟨con sabor a frutas⟩

jelly /ˈdʒeli/ n (pl **-lies**) 1 (Culin) **(a)** (clear jam) jalea f **(b)** (as dessert) (BrE) gelatina f ⟨con sabor a frutas⟩ 2 (gelatinous substance) gelatina f

jellyfish /ˈdʒeliˌfɪʃ/ n (pl **-fish** or **-fishes**) medusa f, malagua f (Per), aguaviva f (RPl), aguamala f (Col, Méx)

jeopardize /ˈdʒepərdaɪz ‖ ˈdʒepədaɪz/ vt poner* en peligro, hacer* peligrar

jeopardy /ˈdʒepərdi ‖ ˈdʒepədi/ n: **in** ∼ en peligro

jerk¹ /dʒɜːrk ‖ dʒɜːk/ vi «leg/arm» hacer* un movimiento brusco; (repeatedly) «legs/arms» agitarse; **the train** ∼**ed to a stop** el tren se detuvo con una sacudida

■ ∼ vt: **the impact** ∼**ed him forward** el impacto lo propulsó hacia adelante

jerk² n 1 **(a)** (tug) tirón m **(b)** (sudden movement) sacudida f 2 (contemptible person) (colloq) estúpido, -da m,f, pendejo, -ja m,f (AmL exc CS fam), gilipollas mf (Esp fam), huevón, -ona m,f (Andes, Ven fam)

jerky /ˈdʒɜːrki ‖ ˈdʒɜːki/ adj **-kier, -kiest** ⟨speech⟩ entrecortado; **it was a** ∼ **ride** fuimos (or fueron etc) dando botes por el camino

jerry /ˈdʒeri/: ∼**-built** adj mal construido; ∼ **can** n bidón m

jersey /ˈdʒərzi ‖ ˈdʒɜːzi/ n (pl **-seys**) 1 **(a)** (sports shirt) camiseta f **(b)** (Tex) jersey m **(c)** (BrE) ▶ SWEATER 2 **Jersey** (la isla de) Jersey

Jerusalem /dʒəˈruːsələm/ n Jerusalén m

jest /dʒest/ n (arch) broma f, chanza f (arc); **in** ∼ en broma

jester /ˈdʒestər ‖ ˈdʒestə(r)/ n bufón m

Jesuit /ˈdʒezuət ‖ ˈdʒezjʊɪt/ n jesuita m

Jesus /ˈdʒiːzəs/ n Jesús; ∼ **Christ** Jesucristo

jet¹ /dʒet/ n 1 (Aviat) avión m ⟨con motor a reacción⟩ 2 (of water, air, gas) chorro m 3 (Min) azabache m

jet² vi **-tt-** (fly) (colloq) volar*

jet: ∼**-black** /ˈdʒet'blæk/ adj (pred ∼ **black**) negro azabache adj inv; ∼ **lag** n jet lag m, desfase m horario

jetsam /ˈdʒetsəm/ n echazón f; see also FLOTSAM

jet set n the ∼ ∼ el jet set (AmL), la jet set (Esp)

jettison /ˈdʒetəsən ‖ ˈdʒetɪsən/ vt (Naut) echar por la borda; (Aviat) deshacerse* de

jetty /ˈdʒeti/ n (pl **-ties**) embarcadero m, malecón m

Jew /dʒuː/ n judío, -día m,f

jewel /ˈdʒuːəl/ n (gem) piedra f preciosa; (piece of jewelry) alhaja f, joya f; (in watch) rubí m; (sb, sth wonderful) joya f

jeweler, (BrE) **jeweller** /ˈdʒuːələr ‖ ˈdʒuːələ(r)/ n joyero, -ra m,f; **a** ∼**'s (shop)** una joyería

jewelry, (BrE) **jewellery** /ˈdʒuːəlri/ n joyas fpl, alhajas fpl; (before n) ∼ **box** joyero m; ∼ **store** (AmE) joyería f

Jewish /ˈdʒuːɪʃ/ adj judío

jibe /dʒaɪb/ n pulla f

jiffy /ˈdʒɪfi/ n (colloq) (no pl) segundo m

jig /dʒɪg/ n 1 (dance) giga f 2 (Tech) plantilla f de guía

jiggle /ˈdʒɪgəl/ vt mover*, sacudir

jigsaw /ˈdʒɪgsɔː/ n 1 ∼ **(puzzle)** rompecabezas m, puzzle m 2 (saw) sierra f de vaivén or de puñal

jilt /dʒɪlt/ vt dejar plantado

jingle¹ /ˈdʒɪŋgəl/ n 1 (sound) (no pl) tintineo m; (of harness bells) cascabeleo m, tintineo m 2 (Marketing) jingle m (publicitario)

jingle² vi tintinear

jingoism /ˈdʒɪŋgəʊɪzəm/ n patriotería f, jingoísmo m

jinx¹ /dʒɪŋks/ n: **there's a** ∼ **on this project** a este proyecto le han echado una maldición

jinx² vt traer* mala suerte a

jitters /ˈdʒɪtərz ‖ ˈdʒɪtəz/ pl n (colloq): **he got the** ∼ se puso nervioso, le dio el tembleque (fam)

jittery /ˈdʒɪtəri/ adj nervioso

Jnr (BrE) (= **Junior**) (h), Jr.

job /dʒɑːb ‖ dʒɒb/ n 1 **(a)** (occupation, post) trabajo m, empleo m; **is he the right person for the** ∼**?** ¿es la persona idónea para el puesto?; (before n) ∼ **creation** creación f de empleo **(b)** (duty, responsibility): **it's your** ∼ **to make the tea** tú eres el encargado de hacer el té; **I'm only doing my** ∼ sólo cumplo con mi deber 2 **(a)** (task, piece of work) trabajo m; (Comput) trabajo m; **you're doing a fine** ∼ lo estás haciendo muy bien; **a good** ∼ (BrE colloq) menos mal; **it's a good** ∼ **I did it yesterday** menos mal que lo hice ayer; **to give sth up as a bad** ∼ dejar algo por imposible; **to make the best of a bad** ∼

apechugar* y hacer* lo que se pueda **(b)** (difficult task) (colloq): **I had a (terrible) ~ getting that nail out** me dio mucho trabajo sacar ese clavo

job: J~centre n (in UK) agencia f de colocaciones, oficina f de empleo; **~ description** n descripción f del puesto; **~-hunt** vi (usu in -ing form) buscar* trabajo

jobless /'dʒɑːbləs ǀǀ'dʒɒblɪs/ adj (journ) desempleado, en paro (Esp), cesante (Chi)

job: ~ lot n lote m; **~share** n puesto m de trabajo compartido (entre dos); **~ sharing** /'ʃerɪŋ ǀǀ'ʃeərɪŋ/ n sistema en el cual dos personas comparten un puesto de trabajo

jockey /'dʒɑːki ǀǀ'dʒɒki/ n (pl **~s**) jockey mf, jinete mf

Jockey shorts® /'dʒɑːki ǀǀ'dʒɒki/ pl n (AmE) calzoncillos mpl, calzones mpl (Méx), interiores mpl (Col, Ven)

jockstrap /'dʒɑːkstræp ǀǀ'dʒɒkstræp/ n suspensorio m, suspensor m (Per, RPI)

jocular /'dʒɑːkjələr ǀǀ'dʒɒkjʊlə(r)/ adj jocoso

jodhpurs /'dʒɑːdpərz ǀǀ'dʒɒdpəz/ pl n pantalones mpl de montar, breeches mpl (Col, RPI)

jog¹ /dʒɑːg ǀǀdʒɒg/ **-gg-** vt (table) mover*; she **~ged his elbow** le dio en el codo; **to ~ sb's memory** refrescarle* la memoria a algn
■ **~** vi **(a)** (run) correr **(b)** (Leisure) hacer* footing or jogging; **to go ~ging** salir* a hacer footing or jogging

jog² n (no pl) (Leisure): **to go for a ~** hacer* footing or jogging

jogger /'dʒɑːgər ǀǀ'dʒɒgə(r)/ n: persona que hace footing

jogging /'dʒɑːgɪŋ ǀǀ'dʒɒgɪŋ/ n footing m, jogging m

john /dʒɑːn ǀǀdʒɒn/ n **1** (toilet) (AmE colloq) baño m, váter m (Esp fam) **2** **John Doe** (AmE) (Law) persona f inidentificada; (colloq) el típico americano

join¹ /dʒɔɪn/ vt **1** (fasten, link) (ropes/wires) unir; (put together) (tables) juntar; **to ~ two things together** unir dos cosas; **to ~ hands** tomarse or (esp Esp) cogerse* de la mano
2 (meet, keep company with): **we're going for a drink, will you ~ us?** vamos a tomar algo ¿nos acompañas?; **you go ahead, I'll ~ you later** ustedes vayan que ya iré yo luego; **may I ~ you?** ¿le importa si me siento aquí?
3 **(a)** (become part of) unirse a, sumarse a; **I ~ed the line** me puse en la cola **(b)** (become member of) (club) hacerse* socio de; (union) afiliarse a; (army) alistarse en; (firm) entrar en or (AmL tb) entrar a
■ **~** vi **1 to ~ (together)** «parts/groups» unirse **2** (merge) «streams» confluir*; «roads» empalmar
■ **join in 1** [v + adv] participar, tomar parte **2** [v + adv + o] (celebrations) participar or tomar parte en
■ **join up** [v + adv] **(a)** (enlist) alistarse **(b)** (fit together) «pieces/parts» encajar **(c)** (team up) «people» unirse

join² n juntura f, unión f

joiner /'dʒɔɪnər ǀǀ'dʒɔɪnə(r)/ n carpintero, -ra m,f (de obra)

joint¹ /dʒɔɪnt/ n **1** (Anat) articulación f **2** (Const) (point of joining) unión f, junta f; (in woodwork) ensambladura f **3** (Culin) trozo m de carne (para asar) **4** (of marijuana) (colloq) porro m (Esp arg), canuto m (Esp arg), toque m (Méx arg), varillo m (Col arg), pito m (Chi arg)

joint² adj (before n) (action) conjunto; **~ owner** copropietario, -ria m,f; **it was a ~ effort** fue un trabajo realizado en conjunto

joint account n cuenta f conjunta

jointly /'dʒɔɪntli/ adv (decide/act) conjuntamente

joint: ~ stock company n sociedad f por acciones; **~ venture** n empresa f conjunta

joist /dʒɔɪst/ n viga f

joke¹ /dʒəʊk/ n **(a)** (verbal) chiste m; (directed at sb) broma f; **he can't take a ~** no sabe aceptar una broma **(b)** (practical ~) broma f

joke² vi bromear; **you must be joking!** ¡tú debes estar loco!; **I was only joking** lo dije en broma

joker /'dʒəʊkər ǀǀ'dʒəʊkə(r)/ n **1** (cards) comodín m **2** (prankster) bromista mf; (contemptible person) (colloq) tipo, -pa m,f (fam)

jokey /'dʒəʊki/ adj ▶ JOKY

joky /'dʒəʊki/ adj jokier, jokiest jocoso

jolly¹ /'dʒɑːli ǀǀ'dʒɒli/ adj **-lier, -liest** (person) jovial; (laugh/tune) alegre

jolly² adv (BrE colloq) (as intensifier): **you were ~ lucky!** ¡qué suerte tuviste!; **~ good!** ¡muy bien!

jolly³ vt **-lies, -lying, -lied** (colloq): **to ~ sb along** animar a algn

jolt¹ /dʒəʊlt/ vi «train/bus» dar* or pegar* una sacudida; (repeatedly) dar* tumbos
■ **~** vt: **she ~ed his arm** le movió el brazo

jolt² n sacudida f

Jordan /'dʒɔːrdn ǀǀ'dʒɔːdn/ n **(a)** (country) Jordania f **(b)** **the ~, the ~ River** (AmE), **the River ~** (BrE) el Jordán

Jordanian /dʒɔːr'deɪniən ǀǀdʒɔː'deɪniən/ adj jordano

jostle /'dʒɑːsəl ǀǀ'dʒɒsəl/ vt empujar
■ **~** vi: **people were jostling trying to get out** la gente se empujaba tratando de salir

jot /dʒɑːt ǀǀdʒɒt/ n (no pl, usu with neg): **it doesn't make a o one ~ of difference** da exactamente igual
■ **jot down: -tt-** [v + o + adv, v + adv + o] apuntar or anotar (rápidamente)

journal /'dʒɜːrnl ǀǀ'dʒɜːnl/ n **(a)** (periodical) revista f, publicación f; (newspaper) periódico m **(b)** (diary) (fml) diario m

journalism /'dʒɜːrnlɪzəm ǀǀ'dʒɜːnəlɪzəm/ n periodismo m

journalist /'dʒɜːrnləst ǀǀ'dʒɜːnəlɪst/ n periodista mf

journey /'dʒɜːrni ǀǀ'dʒɜːni/ n (pl **-neys**) viaje m; **to go on o make a ~** hacer* un viaje

joust /dʒaʊst/ vi justar

jovial /'dʒəʊviəl/ adj jovial

jowls /dʒaʊlz/ pl n (sometimes sing) parte inferior de los carrillos, que a veces cuelga de la mandíbula

joy /dʒɔɪ/ n **(a)** (emotion) alegría f, dicha f; **to jump for ~** saltar de alegría **(b)** (source of pleasure): **she's a ~ to teach** es un verdadero placer or da gusto tenerla como alumna

joyful /'dʒɔɪfəl/ adj (event) feliz; (dance/news) alegre

joyless /'dʒɔɪləs ‖'dʒɔɪlɪs/ adj ‹occasion› falto de alegría; ‹existence› sombrío

joyous /'dʒɔɪəs/ adj ‹expression› de dicha; ‹occasion› feliz

joy: ~**rider** n: joven que roba un coche para dar una vuelta; ~**stick** n (Aviat) palanca f de mando; (Electron, Comput) mando m, joystick m

Jr (esp AmE) (= **Junior**) (h), Jr.

jubilant /'dʒuːbələnt ‖'dʒuːbɪlənt/ adj ‹expression› de júbilo (liter); ‹speech› exultante (liter); **to be** ~ estar* radiante de alegría

jubilee /'dʒuːbəliː ‖'dʒuːbɪliː/ n: **the Queen's silver** ~ el vigésimo quinto aniversario de la reina

Judaism /'dʒuːdəɪzəm ‖'dʒuːdeɪɪzəm/ n judaísmo m

judge¹ /dʒʌdʒ/ n **1** (Law) juez mf, juez, jueza m,f; (of competition) juez mf; (Sport) juez mf **2** (appraiser): **he's a good** ~ **of character** es muy buen psicólogo; **let me be the** ~ **of that** eso lo decidiré yo

judge² vt **1** (Law) ‹case/person› juzgar*; ‹contest› ser* el juez de **2** (a) (estimate) ‹size/speed› calcular (b) (assess) ‹situation/position› evaluar*; ‹person› juzgar* (c) (deem) juzgar*
3 (censure, condemn) juzgar*
■ ~ vi juzgar*; **judging by** a juzgar por

judgment, judgement /'dʒʌdʒmənt/ n **1** (Law) fallo m, sentencia f; (in arbitration) fallo m; **to pass** ~ **on sth/sb** juzgar* algo/a algn **2** (a) (estimation) cálculo m (b) (view) opinión f **3** (sense, discernment): **an error of** ~ una equivocación; **I lent him the money against my better** ~ le presté el dinero sabiendo que era un error

judgmental, judgemental /dʒʌdʒ'mentl/ adj ‹attitude/assessment› sentencioso

judicial /dʒuː'dɪʃəl/ adj judicial

judiciary /dʒuː'dɪʃieri ‖dʒuː'dɪʃəri/ n (judges) judicatura f; (arm of government) poder m judicial

judicious /dʒuː'dɪʃəs/ adj ‹decision› acertado; ‹historian› de criterio

judo /'dʒuːdəʊ/ n judo m

jug /dʒʌg/ n (large) jarra f; (for milk, cream) jarrita f

juggernaut /'dʒʌgərnɔːt ‖'dʒʌgənɔːt/ n (BrE) camión m grande

juggle /'dʒʌgəl/ vi hacer* malabarismos
■ ~ vt hacer* malabarismos con

juggler /'dʒʌglər ‖'dʒʌglə(r)/ n malabarista mf

Jugoslavia /ˌjuːgəʊ'slɑːviə, ˌjuːgə'slɑːviə/ etc ▶ YUGOSLAVIA etc

jugular /'dʒʌgjələr ‖'dʒʌgjʊlə(r)/ n (vena f) yugular f

juice /dʒuːs/ n (fruit drink) jugo m, zumo m; (from fruit, meat) jugo m; (Physiol) jugo m

juicer /'dʒuːsər ‖'dʒuːsə(r)/ n exprimidor m (gen eléctrico), juguera f (CS)

juicy /'dʒuːsi/ adj -**cier**, -**ciest** (a) (Culin) jugoso (b) ‹gossip/details› sabroso (fam)

jukebox /'dʒuːkbɑːks ‖'dʒuːkbɒks/ n máquina f de discos, rocola f (AmL)

July /dʒʊ'laɪ/ n julio m

jumble¹ /'dʒʌmbəl/ vt ~ (**up**) ‹cards/pieces› mezclar; **the clothes were all** ~**d up in the drawer** la ropa estaba toda revuelta en el cajón

jumble² n (no pl) (of clothes, papers) revoltijo m; (of facts, data) embrollo m

jumble sale n (BrE) mercadillo de beneficencia donde se venden artículos de segunda mano

jumbo /'dʒʌmbəʊ/ adj (before n) ‹packet/size› gigante

jumbo (**jet**) n jumbo m

jump¹ /dʒʌmp/ vi **1** (a) (leap) saltar; **the horse** ~**ed over the gate** el caballo saltó la verja (b) (move quickly): **I** ~**ed out of bed** me levanté (de la cama) de un salto; **they'll** ~ **at the chance** no van a dejar pasar la oportunidad **2** (a) (change, skip) saltar (b) (increase, advance suddenly) subir de un golpe **3** (a) (jerk) saltar (b) (in alarm) sobresaltarse; **you made me** ~! ¡qué susto me diste!
■ ~ vt **1** (leap over) ‹hurdle› saltar, brincar* (Méx); **to** ~ **rope** (AmE) saltar a la cuerda or (Esp tb) a la comba or (Chi) al cordel, brincar* la reata (Méx) **2** (a) (spring out of) ‹rails/tracks› salirse* de (b) (disregard) saltarse; **to** ~ **the lights** pasar el semáforo en rojo, pasarse el alto (Méx); **to** ~ **the line** o (BrE) **queue** colarse* **3** (ambush, attack) ‹colloq› asaltar, atacar*

jump² n **1** (a) (leap) salto m; **I sat up with a** ~ me incorporé sobresaltado (b) (fence) valla f **2** (a) (sudden transition) salto m (b) (increase, advance) aumento m

jumper /'dʒʌmpər ‖'dʒʌmpə(r)/ n (a) (dress) (AmE) jumper m or f (AmL), pichi m (Esp) (b) (BrE) ▶ SWEATER

jumper cables pl n (AmE) cables mpl de arranque

jump: ~ **jet** n avión m de despegue vertical; ~ **leads** /liːdz/ pl n (BrE) ▶ JUMPER CABLES; ~ **rope** n (AmE) cuerda f or (Méx) reata f or (Chi) cordel m (de saltar), comba f (Esp); ~**start** vt: hacer arrancar un coche ya sea empujándolo o haciendo un puente; ~ **suit** n mono m, enterito m (RPl)

jumpy /'dʒʌmpi/ adj -**pier**, -**piest** nervioso

junction /'dʒʌŋkʃən/ n (a) (meeting point — of roads, rails) cruce m; (— of rivers) confluencia f (b) (Elec) empalme m

juncture /'dʒʌŋktʃər ‖'dʒʌŋktʃə(r)/ n coyuntura f; **at this** ~ en este momento

June /dʒuːn/ n junio m

jungle /'dʒʌŋgəl/ n selva f, jungla f

junior¹ /'dʒuːnjər ‖'dʒuːniə(r)/ adj **1** (a) (lower in rank) ‹official› subalterno; ‹position› de subalterno (b) (younger) más joven; **James D. Clark J**~ (AmE) James D. Clark, hijo or junior **2** (AmE Educ) (before n) de tercer año

junior² n **1** (a) (younger person): **he is two years my** ~ tiene dos años menos que yo (b) (person of lower rank) subalterno, -na m,f **2** (Educ) (in US) estudiante de tercer año de colegio secundario o universidad; (in UK) alumno de primaria o de los primeros años de secundaria

junior: ~ **college** n (in US) establecimiento universitario donde se estudian los primeros años de la carrera; ~ **high** (**school**) n (in US) colegio en el que se imparten los dos o tres primeros años de la enseñanza secundaria; ~ **school** n (in UK) escuela f primaria (para niños de 7 a 11 años)

junk /dʒʌŋk/ n **1** (a) (discarded items) trastos mpl (viejos); (before n) ~ **shop** tienda f de viejo

(c) (worthless stuff) (colloq) basura f (fam); (before n) ~ **mail** propaganda f que se recibe por correo ⏹2 (boat) junco m

junk food n comida f basura, alimento m chatarra (Méx)

junkie /'dʒʌŋki/ n (colloq) yonqui mf (fam), drogadicto, -ta m,f, pichicatero, -ra (CS, Per fam)

junkyard /'dʒʌŋk.jɑːrd ‖'dʒʌŋk.jɑːd/ n depósito m de chatarra, deshuesadero m (Méx)

junta /'hʊntə ‖'dʒʌntə/ n junta f militar

Jupiter /'dʒuːpətər ‖'dʒuːpɪtə(r)/ n Júpiter m

jurisdiction /'dʒʊrəs'dɪkʃən ‖,dʒʊərɪs'dɪkʃən/ n jurisdicción f

juror /'dʒʊrər ‖'dʒʊərə(r)/ n jurado mf

jury /'dʒʊri ‖'dʒʊəri/ n (pl **-ries**) jurado m

just¹ /dʒʌst/ adj justo

just² adv ⏹1 **(a)** (in recent past): **she's ~ left** se acaba de ir, recién se fue (AmL) **(b)** (at the moment): **I was ~ about to leave when he called** estaba a punto de salir cuando llamó ⏹2 **(a)** (barely) justo; **I arrived ~ in time** llegué justo a tiempo; **I ~ missed him** no lo vi por poco or por apenas unos minutos **(b)** (a little): **~ above the knee** justo or apenas encima de la rodilla ⏹3 **(a)** (only) solo; **she was ~ three when her father died** tenía apenas or solo tres años cuando murió su padre; **would you like some more? — ~ a little, please** ¿quieres más? — bueno, un poquito **(b)** (simply): **I ~ stopped by to say hello** pasé para saludarte; **that's ~ gossip** no son más que chismes; **~ because he's famous doesn't mean he can be rude** (colloq) el hecho de que sea famoso no le da derecho a ser grosero ⏹4 **(a)** (exactly, precisely): **it's ~ what I wanted** es justo or precisamente or exactamente lo que quería; **the temperature was ~ right** la

temperatura era la perfecta **(b)** (equally): **the desserts were ~ as good as the rest of the meal** los postres estuvieron tan buenos como el resto de la comida; **it's ~ as well you're leaving** menos mal que te vas ⏹5 (emphatic use): **I ~ can't understand it** simplemente no lo entiendo; **~ leave it here** déjelo aquí, déjelo aquí nomás (AmL)

justice /'dʒʌstəs ‖'dʒʌstɪs/ n justicia f; **to do sb/sth ~: the photo doesn't do her ~** la foto no le hace justicia; **he couldn't do ~ to the meal** no pudo hacerle honor a la comida; **she didn't do herself ~ in the exam** no rindió a la altura de su capacidad en el examen

Justice of the Peace n (pl ~**s** ~ ~ ~) juez mf de paz, juez, jueza m,f de paz

justifiable /'dʒʌstəfaɪəbəl ‖'dʒʌstɪfaɪəbəl/ adj justificable

justification /'dʒʌstəfə'keɪʃən ‖,dʒʌstɪfɪ'keɪʃən/ n justificación f

justified /'dʒʌstəfaɪd ‖'dʒʌstɪfaɪd/ adj justificado

justify /'dʒʌstəfaɪ ‖t'dʒʌstɪfaɪ/ vt **-fies, -fying, -fied** justificar*

jut /dʒʌt/ **-tt-** vi sobresalir*
■ **jut out** [v + adv] sobresalir*

jute /dʒuːt/ n yute m

juvenile¹ /'dʒuːvənaɪl, -vənl ‖'dʒuːvənaɪl/ adj **(a)** (Law) (before n) ⟨court⟩ de menores; ⟨delinquent⟩ juvenil **(b)** (childish) (pej) infantil **(c)** ⟨literature⟩ (AmE) infantil y juvenil

juvenile² n (Law) menor mf

juxtapose /'dʒʌkstəpəʊz ‖,dʒʌkstə'pəʊz/ vt yuxtaponer*

k

Kk

K, k /keɪ/ n K, k f

K (Comput) (= **kilobyte**) K

kale /keɪl/ n col f rizada

kaleidoscope /kə'laɪdəskəʊp/ n caleidoscopio m

Kampuchea /,kæmpuː'tʃiə/ n Kampuchea f

kangaroo /'kæŋgə'ruː/ n (pl **-roos**) canguro m

Kans = **Kansas**

karaoke /'kæri'əʊki/ n karaoke m

karat n (AmE) ▶ CARAT A

karate /kə'rɑːti/ n kárate m, karate m (AmL)

kayak /'kaɪæk/ n kayak m

Kazakhstan /,kɑːzɑːk'stɑːn/ n Kazajstán m

kebab /'kəbɑːb ‖kɪ'bæb/ n pincho m, anticucho m (Bol, Chi, Per), brocheta f (Esp, Méx)

keel /kiːl/ n quilla f
■ **keel over** [v + adv] **(a)** (capsize) «ship» volcar(se)* **(b)** (collapse) (colloq) «person» caer* redondo (fam)

keen /kiːn/ adj **-er, -est** ⏹1 (enthusiastic) ⟨photographer⟩ entusiasta; ⟨student⟩ aplicado; **he was ~ to start work** tenía muchas ganas de empezar a trabajar; **he's ~ to take part** tiene mucho interés en participar; **to be ~ ON sth/sb/-ING** (BrE): **I'm ~ on golf** me encanta el golf; **she's very ~ on him** le gusta muchísimo; **they're ~ on joining the club** tienen muchas ganas de hacerse socios del club ⏹2 **(a)** (sharp) ⟨blade⟩ afilado, filoso (AmL), filudo (Chi, Per) **(b)** (acute) ⟨hearing⟩ muy fino; ⟨sight/sense of smell/intelligence⟩ agudo **(c)** (intense) ⟨competition⟩ muy reñido; ⟨interest⟩ vivo

keep¹ /kiːp/ n ⏹1 (living) sustento m ⏹2 **for ~s** (colloq) para siempre ⏹3 (in castle, fortress) torre f del homenaje

keep² (past & past p **kept**) vt ⏹1 **(a)** (not throw away) ⟨receipt/ticket⟩ guardar; (not give back) quedarse con; (not lose) conservar; **~ the change** quédese (con) el cambio **(b)** (look after, reserve) **to ~ sth (FOR sb)** guardar(le) algo (A algn) ····❖

② (store) guardar; **I always ~ a first-aid kit in the car** me gusta tener un botiquín en el coche
③ (reserve for future use) guardar
④ **(a)** (raise) ‹pigs/bees› criar* **(b)** (manage, run) ‹stall/guesthouse› tener*
⑤ **(a)** (support) mantener* **(b)** (maintain): **I've kept a note o record of everything** he tomado nota de todo
⑥ **(a)** (cause to remain, continue) mantener*; **try and ~ it clean** trata de mantenerlo limpio; **the noise kept me awake** el ruido no me dejó dormir **(b)** (detain): **don't let me ~ you** no te quiero entretener; **what kept you?** ¿qué te retuvo?; **they kept her in hospital** la dejaron ingresada *or* (CS, Méx tb) internada
⑦ (adhere to, fulfill) ‹promise/vow› cumplir; ‹secret› guardar
■ **~** *vi* ① (remain) mantenerse*: **to ~ fit** mantenerse* en forma; **to ~ awake** mantenerse* despierto; **~ still!** ¡estate quieto!
② **(a)** (continue) seguir*; **~ left** siga por la izquierda; **to ~-ING** seguir* + GER; **to ~ at it** seguir* dándole (fam) **(b)** (repeatedly): **he ~s interfering** está continuamente entrometiéndose; **I ~ forgetting to bring it** nunca me acuerdo de traerlo
③ ‹food› conservarse (fresco)
④ (be in certain state of health) (colloq): **how are you ~ing?** ¿qué tal estás? (fam)
■ **keep away** [v + adv] **to ~ away (FROM sb/sth)** no acercarse* (A algn/algo)
■ **keep back**
Ⅰ [v + adv]: **~ back!** ¡atrás!; **~ well back from the edge** mantente bien alejado del borde
Ⅱ [v + o + adv, v + adv + o] **(a)** ‹crowd/floodwaters› contener* **(b)** ‹tears/sobs› contener*
② (not reveal) ‹information/facts› ocultar
■ **keep down** [v + o + adv] **(a)** (not raise): **~ your head/voice down** no levantes la cabeza/la voz **(b)** ‹food› retener*
② [v + o + adv, v + adv + o] (not allow to increase) ‹prices› mantener* al mismo nivel; ‹weeds› contener*
■ **keep from** [v + o + prep + o] ① (restrain, prevent): **I don't want to ~ you from your work** no quiero distraerte de tu trabajo; **I managed to ~ myself from laughing** pude aguantar la risa
② (not reveal to) ocultar; **he kept vital information from them/us** les/nos ocultó información vital
■ **keep in** [v + o + adv, v + adv + o] (detain): **the teacher kept me in after school** el maestro me hizo quedar después de clase; **he was kept in for observation** lo dejaron ingresado *or* (CS, Méx tb) internado en observación **(b)** ‹anger/feelings› contener*
■ **keep off** ① [v + prep + o] **(a)** (stay away from) ‹land/property› mantenerse* alejado de; **⊖ keep off the grass** prohibido pisar el césped **(b)** (avoid) ‹cigarettes/subject› evitar
② [v + o + prep + o] **~ your hands off me!** ¡quítame las manos de encima!
■ **keep on** ① [v + adv] **(a)** (continue) seguir*; **to ~ on -ING** seguir* + GER **(b)** (repeatedly): **I ~ on forgetting to tell him** siempre me olvido de

decírselo; **she kept on interrupting him** lo interrumpía constantemente **(c)** (talk incessantly): **she ~s on at me about my weight** me está siempre encima con que estoy muy gordo
② [v + o + adv, v + adv + o] (continue to employ) no despedir*
③ [v + o + adv] (continue to wear): **~ your coat on** no te quites el abrigo
■ **keep out** ① [v + adv] (not enter): **⊖ keep out** prohibido el paso; **~ out of the kitchen** no entres en la cocina
② [v + o + adv, v + adv + o] (prevent from entering, exclude) ‹rain/sun› impedir* que entre
■ **keep out of** [v + adv + prep + o] ‹danger› no exponerse* a; ‹trouble/argument› no meterse en
■ **keep to** ① [v + prep + o] **(a)** (adhere to, fulfill) ‹plan› ceñirse* a; ‹promise› cumplir **(b)** (not deviate from) ‹path› seguir* por; ‹script› ceñirse* a **(c)** (stay on): **~ to the right** (Auto) mantenga su derecha
② [v + o + prep + o] (not divulge): **to ~ sth to oneself** guardarse algo
③ [v + prep + o] [v + o + prep + o]: **to ~ (oneself) to oneself** no ser* muy sociable
■ **keep up**
Ⅰ [v + adv] ① (not stop) ‹rain/noise› seguir*, continuar*; **to ~ up WITH sth** seguir* *or* continuar* CON algo
② **(a)** (maintain pace) **to ~ up WITH sb** seguirle* el ritmo A algn; **he's finding it difficult to ~ up in class** le está resultando difícil mantenerse al nivel de la clase **(b)** (remain informed) **to ~ up WITH sth** mantenerse* al tanto *or* al corriente DE algo
Ⅱ [v + o + adv, v + adv + o] ① (maintain at present level) mantener*
② (continue, not stop) ‹payments› mantenerse* al día con; ‹friendship› mantener*
Ⅲ [v + o + adv] ① ‹trousers/socks› sujetar
② (prevent from sleeping): **I hope we're not ~ing you up** espero que no te estemos quitando el sueño; **the baby kept me up all night** el niño me tuvo toda la noche en vela

keeper /'ki:pər ‖ 'ki:pə(r)/ *n* (in zoo) guarda *mf*, cuidador, -dora *m,f*; (in museum) (BrE) conservador, -dora *m,f*

keep-fit /'ki:p'fɪt/ *n* (BrE) gimnasia *f* (de mantenimiento)

keeping /'ki:pɪŋ/ *n* **(a)** (conformity): **in ~ with** ‹with law/tradition› en conformidad con **(b)** (trust, care): **to leave sth in sb's ~** dejar algo al cuidado de algn

keepsake /'ki:pseɪk/ *n* recuerdo *m*

keg /keg/ *n* barril *m*

kennel /'kenl/ *n* **(a)** (AmE) (for boarding) residencia *f* canina; (for breeding) criadero *m* de perros **(b)** (BrE) (hut) casa *f* del perro

kennels /'kenlz/ *n* (pl **~**) (BrE) (+ *sing vb*) ▶ KENNEL A

Kenya /'kenjə, 'ki:-/ *n* Kenia *f*

Kenyan /'kenjən, 'ki:-/ *adj* keniano

kept /kept/ *past & past p of* KEEP²

kerb /kɜːrb ‖ kɜːb/ *n* (BrE) ▶ CURB¹ 2

kernel /'kɜːrnl̩ ‖'kɜːnl̩/ n (of nut, fruit) almendra f; (of corn, wheat) grano m

kerosene /'kerəsiːn/ n queroseno m, kerosene m

kestrel /'kestrəl/ n cernícalo m

ketchup /'ketʃəp ‖'ketʃʌp/ n salsa f de tomate, ketchup m, catsup m

kettle /'ketl̩/ n pava f or (Bol, Ur) caldera f or (Andes, Méx) tetera f

kettledrum /'ketl̩drʌm/ n timbal m

key¹ /kiː/ n (pl ~**s**) ⒈ (for lock) llave f; (on can) llave f, abridor m; (before n) ~ **ring** llavero m ⒉ **(a)** (to puzzle, code etc) clave f **(b)** (to map) explicación f de los signos convencionales **(c)** (answers) soluciones fpl ⒊ (crucial element) clave f; **patience is the** ~ la paciencia es el factor clave or la clave ⒋ (of typewriter, piano) tecla f; (of wind instrument) llave f ⒌ (Mus) tono m; **to be off** ~ no estar* en el tono

key² adj ⟨man/question⟩ clave adj inv
■ **key in** [v + o + adv, v + adv + o] ⟨text/data⟩ teclear

key: ~**board** n teclado m; ~**hole** n ojo m de la cerradura; (before noun) ~hole **surgery** cirugía f no invasiva; ~**note** n (Mus) tónica f; (central idea) tónica f or ~**pad** n (Comput, Telec, TV) teclado m numérico; ~**word** n palabra f clave

kg (= **kilo(s)** o **kilogram(s)**) Kg.

khaki /'kæki ‖'kɑːki/ adj caqui adj inv

kibbutz /kɪ'bʊts/ n (pl -**butzim** /-bʊtsɪm/) kibbutz m

kick¹ /kɪk/ n ⒈ (by person) patada f, puntapié m; (by horse) coz f ⒉ (colloq) (thrill, excitement): **to get a** ~ **out of doing sth** deleitarse haciendo algo; **just for** ~**s** nada más que por divertirse

kick² vi ⟨person⟩ dar* patadas; ⟨swimmer⟩ patalear; ⟨horse⟩ cocear
■ ~ vt ⒈ ⟨ball⟩ patear, darle* una patada or un puntapié a; ⟨person⟩ pegarle* una patada a ⒉ (stop) (colloq) ⟨habit⟩ dejar
■ **kick around,** (BrE also) **kick about** (colloq) [v + o + adv] **(a)** (treat badly) maltratar **(b)** ⟨idea⟩ estudiar **(c)** **to** ~ **a ball around** pelotear
■ **kick down** [v + o + adv, v + adv + o] ⟨door⟩ echar abajo (a patadas)
■ **kick off** ⒈ [v + adv] **(a)** (in football): **they** ~ **off at three** el partido empieza a las tres **(b)** (begin) (colloq) ⟨person/meeting⟩ empezar* ⒉ [v + adv + o] (begin) ⟨discussion⟩ iniciar, empezar*
■ **kick out** [v + o + adv] echar
■ **kick up** ⒈ [v + o + adv, v + adv + o] ⟨leaves/dust⟩ levantar ⒉ [v + adv + o]: **to** ~ **up a fuss** o **row** armar una bronca (fam); **to** ~ **up a din** armar un escándalo

kick: ~**off** n (Sport) saque m or puntapié m inicial, patada f de inicio; ~**start** vt ⟨engine⟩ arrancar* (con el pedal de arranque)

kid¹ /kɪd/ n ⒈ (colloq) **(a)** (child) niño, -ña m,f, chaval, -vala m,f (Esp fam), chavalo, -vala m,f (AmC, Méx fam), escuincle, -cla (Méx fam), pibe, -ba m,f (RPI fam), cabro, -bra m,f (Chi fam) **(b)** (young person) chico, -ca m,f ⒉ **(a)** (goat) cabrito, -ta m,f, choto, -ta m,f **(b)** (leather) cabritilla f

kid² -**dd**- vi (colloq) bromear

■ ~ vt **(a)** (tease) **to** ~ **sb** (**ABOUT sth**) tomarle el pelo a algn (**CON algo**) **(b)** (deceive) engañar; **don't** ~ **yourself!** ¡no te hagas ilusiones!

kidnap /'kɪdnæp/ vt -**pp**- or (AmE) -**p**-secuestrar, raptar

kidnapper, (AmE also) **kidnaper** /'kɪdnæpər ‖'kɪdnæpə(r)/ n secuestrador, -dora m,f, raptor, -tora m,f

kidnapping, (AmE also) **kidnaping** /'kɪdnæpɪŋ/ n secuestro m, rapto m

kidney /'kɪdni/ n (pl -**neys**) (Anat, Culin) riñón m; (before n) ⟨disease/stone⟩ renal; ~ **machine** riñón m artificial

kidney bean n frijol m or (Esp) judía f or (CS) poroto m (con forma de riñón)

kill¹ /kɪl/ vt ⒈ (cause death of) ⟨person/animal⟩ matar; **she was** ~**ed in a car crash** se mató or murió en un accidente de coche ⒉ **(a)** (destroy) ⟨hopes⟩ acabar con **(b)** (spoil) ⟨flavor/taste⟩ estropear **(c)** (deaden) ⟨pain⟩ calmar **(d)** (use up): **to** ~ **time** matar el tiempo
■ ~ vi matar
■ **kill off** [v + o + adv, v + adv + o] matar

kill² n **(a)** (act): **he went in for the** ~ entró a matar **(b)** (animal, animals killed) presa f

killer /'kɪlər ‖'kɪlə(r)/ n (person) asesino, -na m,f; (before n) ⟨shark⟩ asesino; ⟨disease⟩ mortal

killer whale n orca f

killing /'kɪlɪŋ/ n (of person) asesinato m; (of animal) matanza f; **to make a** ~ hacer* un gran negocio, forrarse (fam)

killjoy /'kɪldʒɔɪ/ n aguafiestas mf

kiln /kɪln/ n horno m

kilo /'kiːləʊ/ n (pl -**los**) kilo m

kilobyte /'kɪləbaɪt/ n kilobyte m, kilocteto m

kilogram, (BrE also) **kilogramme** /'kɪləgræm/ n kilogramo m

kilometer, (BrE) **kilometre** /'kɪləmiːtər ‖kɪ'lɒmɪtə(r), 'kɪləmiːtə(r)/ n kilómetro m

kilowatt /'kɪləwɑːt ‖'kɪləwɒt/ n kilovatio m

kilt /kɪlt/ n falda f or (CS) pollera f escocesa

kimono /kə'məʊnəʊ ‖kɪ'məʊnəʊ/ n (pl -**nos**) kimono m, quimono m

kin /kɪn/ n (+ pl vb) familiares mpl, parientes mpl

kind¹ /kaɪnd/ n ⒈ (sort, type) **(a)** (of things) tipo m, clase f; **of all** ~**s** de todo tipo, de toda clase **(b)** (of people) clase f, tipo m ⒉ (sth approximating to) especie f; **she was overcome by a** ~ **of yearning** la invadió una especie de añoranza ⒊ (in phrases) **in kind** ⟨pay⟩ en especie; **kind of** (colloq): **he seemed** ~ **of stupid** parecía como tonto (fam); **of a kind: they served a meal, of a** ~ sirvieron una especie de comida, si se le puede llamar así; **they're two of a** ~ son tal para cual

kind² adj -**er**, -**est** ⟨offer⟩ amable; **he's very** ~ es muy buena persona; **she's always been** ~ **to me** siempre ha sido muy amable conmigo; **it's very** ~ **to your skin** no daña la piel; **would you be** ~ **enough to accompany me?** ¿tendría la amabilidad de acompañarme?

kindergarten /'kɪndərˌɡɑːrtn̩ ‖'kɪndəgɑːtn̩/ n jardín m de infancia or de niños

kind-hearted /'kaɪnd'hɑːrtəd ‖kaɪnd'hɑːtɪd/ adj de buen corazón

kindle /'kɪndl/ vt ⟨fire⟩ encender*; ⟨interest⟩ despertar*; ⟨passion⟩ encender*

kindly¹ /'kaɪndli/ adv **1 (a)** (generously) amablemente **(b)** (adding polite emphasis) (frml): **passengers are ~ requested to ...** se ruega a los pasajeros tengan la amabilidad de ...
2 (favorably): **they didn't take ~ to my suggestions** no recibieron demasiado bien mis sugerencias; **she doesn't take ~ to being contradicted** no le hace ninguna gracia que la contradigan

kindly² adj **-lier, -liest** bondadoso

kindness /'kaɪndnəs ‖'kaɪndnɪs/ n **(a)** (quality) ~ **(TO o TOWARD sb)** amabilidad f (PARA CON algn) **(b)** (act) favor m

kindred /'kɪndrəd ‖'kɪndrɪd/ adj ⟨before n⟩ (similar) similar; ~ **spirits** almas fpl gemelas

king /kɪŋ/ n rey m

kingdom /'kɪŋdəm/ n reino m; **the animal ~** el reino animal

king: ~fisher /'kɪŋ.fɪʃər ‖'kɪŋ.fɪʃə(r)/ n martín m pescador; **~-size, ~-sized** /'kɪŋsaɪzd/ adj ⟨cigarette⟩ extralargo; ⟨bed⟩ de matrimonio (extragrande)

kink /kɪŋk/ n (in rope, wire) vuelta f, curva f; (in hair) onda f

kinky /'kɪŋki/ adj **-kier, -kiest** (colloq) pervertidillo (fam)

kinship /'kɪnʃɪp/ n parentesco m

kiosk /'kiːɒsk ‖'kiːɒsk/ n (stall) quiosco m

kipper /'kɪpər ‖'kɪpə(r)/ n arenque m salado y ahumado

Kirghizia /kʊr'giːziə ‖kɪə'gɪziə/, **Kirghizstan** /ˌkɪrgiːˈstɑːn ‖kɪəgɪˈstɑːn/ n Kirguizistán m

kiss¹ /kɪs/ vt ⟨person⟩ besar; **to ~ sb goodbye/ goodnight** darle* un beso de despedida/de buenas noches a algn
 ■ ~ vi besarse

kiss² n beso m; **to give sb a ~** darle* un beso a algn; **she gave him the ~ of life** le hizo (la) respiración artificial

kit /kɪt/ n **1 (a)** (set of items): **first-aid ~** botiquín m de primeros auxilios; **tool ~** caja f de herramientas **(b)** (parts for assembly) kit m **2 (a)** (personal effects) cosas fpl; (Mil) petate m **(b)** (Clothing) (esp BrE) **gym ~** (Sport) equipo m de gimnasia

kitchen /'kɪtʃən ‖'kɪtʃɪn/ n cocina f

kitchen garden n huerto m

kite /kaɪt/ n cometa f or (RPI tb) barrilete m or (AmC, Méx) papalote m or (Ven) papagayo m or (Chi) volantín m

kitten /'kɪtn/ n gatito, -ta m,f

kitty /'kɪti/ n (pl **-ties**) (colloq) bote m, fondo m común

kiwi /'kiːwiː/ n **(a)** (Zool) kiwi m **(b)** ~ **(fruit)** kiwi m

kleptomaniac /ˌkleptəˈmeɪniæk/ n cleptómano, -na m,f

klutz /klʌts/ n (AmE colloq) torpe mf, patoso, -sa m,f (Esp fam)

km (= **kilometer(s)** o (BrE) **kilometre(s)**) Km.

knack /næk/ n: **there's a ~ to making omelettes** hacer tortillas tiene su truco o (Méx) su chiste;

I'll never get the ~ of this! ¡nunca le voy a agarrar la onda (AmL fam) or (Esp) coger el tranquillo a esto!

knapsack /'næpsæk/ n mochila f

knave /neɪv/ n **(a)** (rogue) (arch) truhán m (ant) **(b)** (in French pack of cards) jota f; (in Spanish pack) sota f

knead /niːd/ vt (Culin) amasar

knee¹ /niː/ n (Anat, Clothing) rodilla f; **to be on one's ~s** estar* arrodillado; **to go o get down on one's ~s** ponerse* de rodillas

knee² vt darle* or pegarle* un rodillazo a

knee: ~cap n rótula f; **~-deep** /'niːˈdiːp/ adj ⟨pred⟩: **the water is ~-deep** el agua llega hasta la(s) rodilla(s); **they were ~-deep in mud** estaban con el barro hasta las rodillas; **~-high** /'niːˈhaɪ/ adj ⟨sock⟩ largo

kneel /niːl/ vi (past & past p **kneeled** or **knelt**) (get down on one's knees) arrodillarse; (be on one's knees) estar* arrodillado; **to ~ down** arrodillarse

knee-length /'niːleŋθ/ adj ⟨sock⟩ largo; ⟨skirt⟩ hasta la rodilla; ⟨boot⟩ alto

knelt /nelt/ past & past p of KNEEL

knew /nuː ‖njuː/ past of KNOW

knickerbockers /'nɪkərbɑːkərz ‖'nɪkəbɒkəz/ pl n pantalones mpl bombachos

knickers /'nɪkərz ‖'nɪkəz/ pl n **1** (AmE) ▶ KNICKERBOCKERS **2** (BrE) (undergarment) calzones mpl (AmS), bragas fpl (Esp), pantaletas fpl (AmC, Ven), bombacha f (RPI)

knickknack /'nɪknæk/ n chuchería f

knife¹ /naɪf/ n (pl **knives**) cuchillo m; (penknife) navaja f, cortaplumas m or f; (dagger) puñal m

knife² vt acuchillar

knife: ~ edge n filo m (de cuchillo, navaja etc); **to be on a ~ edge** pender de un hilo; **~-point** n: **he was robbed at ~-point** le robaron amenazándolo con un cuchillo

knight¹ /naɪt/ n **(a)** (Hist) caballero m **(b)** (holder of title) sir m **(c)** (in chess) caballo m

knight² vt conceder el título de sir a

knighthood /'naɪthʊd/ n título m de sir

knit /nɪt/ (pres.p **knitting**; past & past p **knitted** or **knit**) vt **1 (a)** ⟨sweater⟩ (by hand) hacer*, tejer; (with machine) tejer, tricotar (Esp) **(b)** ⟨knitted o (esp AmE) knit⟩ past p ⟨jacket/cuffs⟩ de punto, tejido **2** (join, unite) ⟨bones⟩ soldar*; **a tightly ~ family** una familia muy unida
 ■ ~ vi (by hand) tejer, hacer* punto or calceta (Esp); (with machine) tejer, tricotar (Esp)

knitting /'nɪtɪŋ/ n **(a)** (piece of work) tejido m, punto m (Esp) **(b)** (activity): **I like ~** me gusta tejer, me gusta hacer* punto or calceta (Esp)

knitting: ~ machine n máquina f de tejer, tricotosa f (Esp); **~ needle** n aguja f de tejer or (Esp) de hacer punto, palillo m (Chi)

knives /naɪvz/ pl of KNIFE¹

knob /nɑːb ‖nɒb/ n **(a)** (on door) pomo m, perilla f (AmL); (on drawer) tirador m, perilla f (AmL); (on walking stick) puño m; (on radio, TV) botón m **(b)** (lump) bulto m **(c)** (small piece) (esp BrE): **a ~ of butter** un trocito or una nuez de mantequilla

knobbly /'nɑːbli ‖'nɒbli/ adj **-lier, -liest** ⟨tree/fingers⟩ nudoso; ⟨knees⟩ huesudo

knock¹ /nɑːk ‖nɒk/ *n* (sound) golpe *m*; (blow to head, on door) golpe *m*

knock² *vt* ① (strike, push): **to ~ one's head on/against sth** darse* (un golpe) en la cabeza con/contra algo; **she ~ed the vase off the shelf** tiró el jarrón de la repisa; **they ~ed a large hole in the wall** hicieron un gran boquete en la pared
② (criticize) (colloq) criticar*
■ **~** *vi* **(a)** (on door) llamar, golpear (AmL), tocar* (AmL) **(b)** (collide) **to ~ AGAINST/INTO sb/sth** darse* *or* chocar* CONTRA algn/algo
■ **knock about, knock around** (colloq) [*v + o + adv*] pegarle* a
■ **knock back** [*v + o + adv, v + adv + o*] (colloq) ⟨*drink*⟩ beberse, tomarse
■ **knock down** [*v + o + adv, v + adv + o*] ① **(a)** (cause to fall) ⟨*door/fence*⟩ tirar abajo; ⟨*obstacle*⟩ derribar*; **he ran into her and ~ed her down** chocó con ella y la hizo caer **(b)** «*vehicle/driver*» atropellar **(c)** (demolish) echar abajo
② (colloq) (reduce) ⟨*price/charge*⟩ rebajar
■ **knock off** ① [*v + adv*] [*v + prep + o*] (stop work) (colloq): **when do you ~ off (work)?** ¿a qué hora sales del trabajo?, ¿hasta qué hora trabajas?; **let's ~ off for lunch** vamos a parar para comer
② [*v + o + adv, v + adv + o*] (stop) (colloq) dejar de; **~ it off, will you!** ¡déjala ya! (fam)
③ [*v + o + adv, v + adv + o*] (deduct, eliminate) (colloq) rebajar; **I'll ~ off 25% for you** le hago un descuento del 25%
■ **knock out** ① [*v + o + adv, v + adv + o*] (make unconscious) dejar sin sentido, hacer* perder el conocimiento; (in boxing) dejar K.O., noquear; **she hit her head and ~ed herself out** se dio un golpe en la cabeza y perdió el conocimiento
② [*v + o + adv, v + adv + o*] (of competition) eliminar
■ **knock over** [*v + o + adv, v + adv + o*] **(a)** (cause to fall) tirar **(b)** «*vehicle*» atropellar
■ **knock up** [*v + o + adv, v + adv + o*] (colloq) (assemble hurriedly) improvisar

knocker /ˈnɑːkər ‖ˈnɒkə(r)/ *n* aldaba *f*, llamador *m*

knocking /ˈnɑːkɪŋ ‖ˈnɒkɪŋ/ *n* **(a)** (noise) (no pl) golpes *mpl* **(b)** (Auto) golpeteo *m*, cascabeleo *m* (AmL)

knock: **~-kneed** /ˈnɑːkˈniːd ‖nɒkˈniːd/ *adj* patizambo; **~-on effect** /ˈnɑːkˈɑːn ‖nɒkˈɒn/ *n* repercusiones *fpl*; **~out** *n* (in boxing) nocaut *m*, K.O. *m* (*read as: nocaut or* (Esp) cao)

knoll /nəʊl/ *n* loma *f*, montículo *m*

knot¹ /nɑːt ‖nɒt/ *n* ① (in string, hair, wood) nudo *m*; (in muscles) nódulo *m* ② (measure of speed) nudo *m*

knot² *vt* **-tt-** hacer* un nudo en

know¹ /nəʊ/ (*past* **knew**; *past p* **known**) *vt* ① **(a)** (have knowledge of, be aware of) saber*; **I don't ~ his name/how old he is** no sé cómo se llama/cuántos años tiene; **it is well ~n that ...** todo el mundo sabe que ...; **to let sb ~ sth** decirle* algo a algn; (warn) avisarle algo a algn; **without our ~ing** sin saberlo nosotros; **there's no ~ing what he might do** quién sabe qué hará; **I ~ what: let's go skating!** ¡tengo una idea: vayamos a patinar!; **to ~ sth backwards** ⟨*part/play*⟩

saber* algo al dedillo *or* al revés y al derecho **(b)** (have skill, ability) **to ~ how to + INF** saber* + INF
② (be acquainted with) ⟨*person/place*⟩ conocer*; **how did they get to ~ each other?** ¿cómo se conocieron?; **to get to ~ sth** ⟨*subject/job*⟩ familiarizarse* con algo
③ **(a)** (recognize, identify) reconocer*; **to ~ sth/sb BY sth** reconocer* algo/a algn POR algo **(b)** (distinguish) **to ~ sth/sb FROM sth/sb** distinguir* algo/a algn DE algo/algn
■ **~** *vi* saber*; **how do you ~?** ¿cómo lo sabes?; **I ~!** ¡ya sé!, ¡tengo una idea!; **you never ~** nunca se sabe; **I'm not stupid, you ~** oye, que no soy tonto ¿eh? *or* ¿sabes?; **did you ~ about John?** ¿sabías lo de John?; **to get to ~ about sth** enterarse de algo; **she knew of their activities** tenía conocimiento *or* estaba enterada de sus actividades; **not that I ~ of** que yo sepa, no; **do you ~ of a good carpenter?** ¿conoces a *or* sabes de algún carpintero bueno?

know² *n*: **to be in the ~** estar* enterado

know: **~-all** *n* (BrE) ► KNOW-IT-ALL; **~how** *n* know-how *m*, conocimientos *mpl* *y* experiencia

knowing /ˈnəʊɪŋ/ *adj* ⟨*smile*⟩ de complicidad; **she gave me a ~ look** me miró dándome a entender que ya lo sabía

knowingly /ˈnəʊɪŋli/ *adv* **(a)** ⟨*smile/nod*⟩ de manera cómplice **(b)** (deliberately) ⟨*hurt/lie*⟩ a sabiendas

know-it-all /ˈnəʊɪtɔːl/ *n* (colloq) sabelotodo *mf* (fam)

knowledge /ˈnɑːlɪdʒ ‖ˈnɒlɪdʒ/ *n* ① (awareness) conocimiento *m*; **to the best of my ~** que yo sepa; **it is common ~ that ...** todo el mundo sabe que ... ② (facts known) saber *m*; (by particular person) conocimientos *mpl*

knowledgeable /ˈnɑːlɪdʒəbəl ‖ˈnɒlɪdʒəbəl/ *adj* (about current affairs) informado; (about given subject) entendido; (in general) culto

known¹ /nəʊn/ *past p of* KNOW

known² *adj* ⟨*fact*⟩ conocido, sabido; **a little-~ artist** un artista poco conocido; **to be ~ AS sth** (have reputation) tener* fama DE algo; **better ~ as ...** más conocido como ...; **for reasons best ~ to herself** por motivos que ella conocerá; **he's better ~ for his work in films** se le conoce mejor por su trabajo cinematográfico

knuckle /ˈnʌkəl/ *n* **(a)** (finger joint) nudillo *m* **(b)** (of pork) codillo *m*; (of veal) morcillo *m*, jarrete *m*
■ **knuckle down** [*v + adv*] ponerse* a trabajar en serio
■ **knuckle under** [*v + adv*] ceder*, pasar por el aro

knuckleduster /ˈnʌkəlˌdʌstər ‖ˈnʌkəlˌdʌstə(r)/ *n* (BrE) ► BRASS KNUCKLES

koala /kəʊˈɑːlə/ *n* **~ (bear)** koala *m*

kooky /ˈkuːki/ *adj* **-kier, -kiest** (AmE colloq) chiflado (fam)

Koran /kəˈrɑːn/ *n* **the ~** el Corán

Korea /kəˈriːə/ *n* Corea *f*

Korean¹ /kəˈriːən/ *adj* coreano

Korean² *n* **(a)** (person) coreano, -na *m,f* **(b)** (language) coreano *m*

kosher /ˈkəʊʃər ‖ˈkəʊʃə(r)/ *adj* ⟨*food/butcher*⟩ kosher *adj inv*

Kosovo /ˈkɑːsəvəʊ ‖ˈkɒsəvəʊ/ *n* Kosovo *m*

kowtow /'kaʊ'taʊ/ *vi* to ~ TO sb doblar la
cerviz ANTE algn
kph (= **kilometers** *o* (BrE) **kilometres per
hour**) Km/h.
KS = **Kansas**
kung fu /'kʌŋ'fuː/ *n* kung fu *m*

Kurd /kɜːrd ‖kɜːd/ *n* kurdo, -da *m,f*
Kurdish /'kɜːrdɪʃ ‖'kɜːdɪʃ/ *adj* kurdo
Kuwait /kə'weɪt ‖kʊ'weɪt/ *n* Kuwait *m*
Kuwaiti /kə'weɪti ‖kʊ'weɪti/ *adj* kuwaití
KY, Ky = **Kentucky**

• •

L l

• •

L, l /el/ *n* L, l *f*
l (= **liter(s)** *or* (BrE) **litre(s)**) l.
L (a) (BrE Auto) Ⓢ **L** (= **learner**) L (*conductor en
aprendizaje*) (b) (Clothing) (= **large**) G (*talla
grande*)
la /lɑː/ *n* (Mus) la *m*
La = **Louisiana**
LA (a) = **Los Angeles** (b) = **Louisiana**
lab /læb/ *n* (colloq) laboratorio *m*
label¹ /'leɪbəl/ *n* etiqueta *f*
label² *vt*, (BrE) **-ll- (a)** ⟨*bottle/luggage*⟩ ponerle*
una etiqueta a **(b)** (categorize) to ~ sth/sb (AS) sth
catalogar* algo/a algn DE algo
labor¹, (BrE) **labour** /'leɪbər ‖'leɪbə(r)/ *n* [1]
(a) (work) trabajo *m*; (before *n*) ⟨*dispute/laws*⟩
laboral **(b)** (workers) mano *f* de obra [2] **Labour**
(in UK) (Pol) (*no art, + sing or pl vb*) los laboristas,
el Partido Laborista [3] **(a)** (effort) esfuerzos *mpl*,
trabajo *m* **(b)** (task) labor *f*, tarea *f* [4] (Med) parto
m; **to be in** ~ estar* de parto; (before *n*) ~ **pains**
dolores *mpl or* contracciones *fpl* del parto
labor², (BrE) **labour** *vt*: **to** ~ **a point** insistir
excesivamente sobre un punto
■ ~ *vi* (toil) trabajar; **he** ~**ed up the hill** subió
trabajosamente *or* penosamente la cuesta
laboratory /'læbərətɔːri ‖lə'bɒrətri/ *n* (*pl*
-ries) laboratorio *m*
Labor Day *n* Día *m* del Trabajo *or* de los
trabajadores
labored, (BrE) **laboured** /'leɪbərd ‖'leɪbəd/
adj ⟨*breathing*⟩ dificultoso, fatigoso; ⟨*metaphor/
joke*⟩ forzado, torpe
laborer, (BrE) **labourer** /'leɪbərər ‖'leɪbərə(r)/
n peón *m*; **farm** ~ peón *m*, trabajador *m* agrícola
laborious /lə'bɔːriəs/ *adj* ⟨*task/process*⟩
laborioso; ⟨*style*⟩ farragoso
labor union *n* (AmE) sindicato *m*
labour *etc* (BrE) ▶ LABOR *etc*
labrador /'læbrədɔːr ‖'læbrədɔː(r)/ *n* labrador
m
labyrinth /'læbərɪnθ/ *n* laberinto *m*
lace¹ /leɪs/ *n* [1] (fabric) encaje *m*; (as border)
puntilla *f* [2] (shoe~) cordón *m* (de zapato),
agujeta *f* (Méx), pasador *m* (Per)

lace² *vt* [1] ⟨*shoes/boots*⟩ ponerles* los cordones
or (Méx) las agujetas *or* (Per) los pasadores a
[2] (fortify): **he** ~**d my drink with vodka** me echó un
chorro de vodka en la bebida
lacerate /'læsəreɪt/ *vt* lacerar
lack¹ /læk/ *n* ~ OF sth falta *f or* (frml) carencia *f*
DE algo
lack² *vt* no tener*, carecer* de (frml); **it** ~**s
originality** le falta *or* no tiene originalidad, carece
de originalidad (frml)
lacking /'lækɪŋ/ *adj* (pred) **(a)** (absent): **the
necessary resources are** ~ faltan los recursos
necesarios **(b)** (deficient) **to be** ~ IN sth no tener*
algo, carecer DE algo (frml)
lackluster, (BrE) **lacklustre** /'læk,lʌstər
‖'læk,lʌstə(r)/ *adj* **(a)** ⟨*eyes*⟩ apagado; ⟨*hair*⟩
opaco **(b)** (mediocre) ⟨*performance/campaign*⟩
deslucido; ⟨*candidate*⟩ mediocre
laconic /lə'kɑːnɪk ‖lə'kɒnɪk/ *adj* lacónico
lacquer /'lækər ‖'lækə(r)/ *n* **(a)** (varnish) laca *f*
(b) (hair ~) laca *f or* fijador *m* (para el pelo)
lad /læd/ *n* muchacho *m*, chaval *m* (Esp fam),
pibe *m* (RPI fam), chavo *m* (Méx, Ven fam), chavalo
m (AmC, Méx fam), cabro *m* (Chi fam)
ladder /'lædər ‖'lædə(r)/ *n* [1] (Const) escalera *f*
(de mano) [2] (in stocking, tights) (BrE) carrera *f*
laden /'leɪdn/ *adj* ~ WITH sth cargado DE algo
ladies /'leɪdiz/ *n* (BrE) ▶ LADIES' ROOM
ladies' room /'leɪdiz/ *n* (AmE) baño *m or* (esp
Esp) servicio *m* de señoras; Ⓢ **Ladies (Room)**
Señoras, Damas
ladle /'leɪdl/ *n* cucharón *m*
lady /'leɪdi/ *n* (*pl* **ladies**) [1] **(a)** (woman) señora
f; **ladies and gentlemen** señoras y señores, damas
y caballeros **(b)** (refined woman) señora *f*, dama *f*
[2] (noblewoman or wife of a knight) lady *f*
lady: ~**bug** (AmE), ~**bird** (BrE) *n* mariquita *f*,
catarina *f* (Méx), petaca *f* (Col), chinita *f* (Chi), San
Antonio *m* (Ur), vaca *f* de San Antón (Arg);
~**-in-waiting** /'leɪdim'weɪtɪŋ/ *n* (*pl*
ladies-in-waiting) dama *f* de honor; ~**like**
adj fino
ladyship /'leɪdiʃɪp/ *n*: **Her/Your L**~ la señora
lag¹ /læg/ *n* (interval) lapso *m*, intervalo *m*; (delay)
retraso *m*, demora *f* (esp AmL)

• •

lag² **-gg-** *vi* to ~ **(behind)** quedarse atrás; **to ~ behind sb/sth** ir* a la zaga de algn/algo
■ ~ *vt* ⟨*pipes*⟩ revestir* con aislantes

lager /'lɑːgər ‖ 'lɑːgə(r)/ *n* cerveza *f* (rubia)

lagoon /lə'guːn/ *n* laguna *f*

lah /lɑː/ *n* (BrE Mus) la *m*

laid /leɪd/ *past & past p of* LAY²

laid-back /'leɪd'bæk/ *adj* (colloq) ⟨*person*⟩ tranquilo y relajado; ⟨*atmosphere*⟩ relajado

lain /leɪn/ *past p of* LIE² II

lair /ler ‖ leə(r)/ *n* guarida *f*

lake /leɪk/ *n* lago *m*

Lake District *n* the ~ ~ el Lake District (*región de lagos al noroeste de Inglaterra*)

lamb /læm/ *n* cordero *m*; ⟨*before n*⟩ ~ **chop** chuleta *f* de cordero

lame¹ /leɪm/ *adj* 1 (in foot, leg) cojo, rengo (AmL); **to go ~** quedarse cojo *or* (AmL tb) rengo 2 (weak) ⟨*excuse*⟩ pobre, malo

lame² *vt* lisiar

lament¹ /lə'ment/ *n* lamento *m*

lament² *vt* **(a)** ⟨*misfortune/failure*⟩ lamentar **(b)** (liter) ⟨*death/loss*⟩ llorar

lamentable /'læməntəbəl/ *adj* lamentable

lamp /læmp/ *n* lámpara *f*; (Auto) luz *f*

lamplight /'læmplaɪt/ *n* (of table lamp) luz *f* de (la) lámpara; (of streetlamp) luz *f* de(l) farol

lampoon /læm'puːn/ *vt* satirizar*

lamp: ~**post** *n* farol *m*; ~**shade** *n* pantalla *f* (*de lámpara*)

lance¹ /læns ‖ lɑːns/ *n* lanza *f*

lance² *vt* abrir* con lanceta

lancet /'lænsət ‖ 'lɑːnsɪt/ *n* lanceta *f*

land¹ /lænd/ *n* 1 (Geog, Agr) tierra *f*; ⟨*before n*⟩ ⟨*animal/defenses*⟩ de tierra; ~ **reform** reforma *f* agraria 2 (country, realm) (liter) país *m*; (kingdom) reino *m*

land² *vi* 1 **(a)** (Aerosp, Aviat) aterrizar*; (on the moon) alunizar* **(b)** (fall) caer* 2 (arrive, end up) (colloq) ir* a parar (fam) 3 (Naut) ⟨*ship*⟩ atracar*; ⟨*traveler/troops*⟩ desembarcar*
■ ~ *vt* 1 **(a)** (from sea) ⟨*passengers*⟩ desembarcar*; ⟨*cargo*⟩ descargar* **(b)** (from air) ⟨*plane*⟩ hacer* aterrizar; ⟨*troops*⟩ desembarcar*; ⟨*supplies*⟩ descargar* 2 ⟨*fish*⟩ sacar* del agua; ⟨*contract/job*⟩ conseguir* 3 (burden) (colloq) **to ~ sb WITH sth/sb, to ~ sth/sb ON sb** endilgarle* algo/a algn a algn (fam)

landing /'lændɪŋ/ *n* 1 **(a)** (Aerosp, Aviat) aterrizaje *m*; (on moon) alunizaje *m*; ⟨*before n*⟩ ~ **strip** pista *f* de aterrizaje **(b)** (Mil, Naut) desembarco *m* **(c)** (of cargo) descarga *f*; (of troops) desembarco *m* 2 (on staircase) rellano *m*, descanso *m* (Col, CS)

land: ~**lady** *n* **(a)** (of rented dwelling) casera *f* **(b)** (of small hotel) dueña *f* **(c)** (BrE) (of pub — owner) dueña *f*; (— manager) encargada *f*; ~**locked** /'lændlɑːkt ‖ 'lændlɒkt/ *adj* sin salida al mar; ~**lord** *n* **(a)** (of landed estate) terrateniente *m* **(b)** (of rented dwelling) casero *m*, dueño *m* **(c)** (BrE) (of pub — owner) dueño *m*; (— manager) encargado *m*; ~**mark** *n* monumento *m* (or edificio *m etc*) famoso; ~ **mine** *n* mina *f* (de tierra); ~**owner** *n* terrateniente *mf*; ~**scape** /'lændskeɪp/ *n* paisaje *m*; ⟨*before n*⟩ ~**scape gardener** jardinero,

-ra *m,f* paisajista; ~**slide** *n* **(a)** (Geog) derrumbamiento *m or* desprendimiento *m* de tierras **(b)** (Pol) victoria *f* aplastante

lane /leɪn/ *n* 1 (in countryside) camino *m*, sendero *m*; (alleyway) callejón *m* 2 (Transp) **(a)** (for road traffic) carril *m or* (Chi) pista *f or* (RPl) senda *f*; **bus/bicycle ~** carril *m* de autobuses/bicicletas **(b)** (for ships) ruta *f* 3 (in athletics) carril *m* (AmL), calle *f* (Esp)

language /'læŋgwɪdʒ/ *n* 1 (means of communication, style of speech) lenguaje *m*; **bad ~** palabrotas *fpl* 2 **(a)** (particular tongue) idioma *m*, lengua *f* **(b)** (Comput) lenguaje *m*

languid /'læŋgwəd ‖ 'læŋgwɪd/ *adj* lánguido

languish /'læŋgwɪʃ/ *vi* (liter) languidecer*; (in prison) pudrirse*

lank /læŋk/ *adj* lacio

lanky /'læŋki/ *adj* **-kier, -kiest** desgarbado

lantern /'læntərn ‖ 'læntən/ *n* farol *m*

Laos /laʊs ‖ 'lɑːɒs, laʊs/ *n* Laos *m*

lap¹ /læp/ *n* 1 (of body) rodillas *fpl* 2 **(a)** (Sport) vuelta *f* **(b)** (stage) etapa *f*

lap² **-pp-** *vt* 1 (Sport) sacarle* una vuelta de ventaja a 2 ⟨*water/milk*⟩ beber a lengüetazos
■ ~ *vi* chapalear; **to ~ AGAINST sth** lamer *or* besar algo (liter)
■ **lap up** [*v + o + adv, v + adv + o*] beber a lengüetazos

lapel /lə'pel/ *n* solapa *f*

Lapland /'læplænd/ *n* Laponia *f*

lapse¹ /læps/ *n* 1 (fault, error) falla *f*, fallo *m* (Esp) 2 (interval) lapso *m*, período *m*

lapse² *vi* 1 (fall, slip): **standards have ~d** el nivel ha decaído; **to ~ into bad habits** adquirir* malos hábitos 2 **(a)** (cease) ⟨*project*⟩ cancelarse; ⟨*practice*⟩ perderse* **(b)** ⟨*membership/contract*⟩ caducar*, vencer* 3 ⟨*time*⟩ transcurrir

laptop /'læptɑːp ‖ 'læptɒp/ *n* (~ computer) laptop *f or* (Esp) *m*

lapwing /'læpwɪŋ/ *n* avefría *f*‡

larceny /'lɑːrsəni ‖ 'lɑːsəni/ *n* (in US) robo *m*

larch /lɑːrtʃ ‖ lɑːtʃ/ *n* alerce *m*

lard /lɑːrd ‖ lɑːd/ *n* manteca *f or* (RPl) grasa *f* de cerdo

larder /'lɑːrdər ‖ 'lɑːdə(r)/ *n* despensa *f*

large¹ /lɑːrdʒ ‖ lɑːdʒ/ *adj*

■ **Note** The usual translation of *large*, *grande*, becomes *gran* when it precedes a singular noun.

larger, largest grande; **the ~st collection of stamps in the world** la mayor colección de sellos del mundo

large² *n* **at large (a)** (as a whole) en general; **the public at ~** el público en general **(b)** (at liberty): **to be at ~** andar* suelto

largely /'lɑːrdʒli ‖ 'lɑːdʒli/ *adv* en gran parte

lark /lɑːrk ‖ lɑːk/ *n* alondra *f*

larva /'lɑːrvə ‖ 'lɑːvə/ *n* (*pl* **-vae** /-viː/) larva *f*

laryngitis /ˌlærən'dʒaɪtəs ‖ ˌlærɪn'dʒaɪtɪs/ *n* laringitis *f*

larynx /'lærɪŋks/ *n* (*pl* **larynxes** *or* **larynges** /lə'rɪndʒiːs/) laringe *f*

laser /'leɪzər ‖ 'leɪzə(r)/ *n* láser *m*; ⟨*before n*⟩ ~ **beam** rayo *m* láser; ~ **printer** impresora *f* láser

lash¹ /læʃ/ n **1** (eye~) pestaña f **2** (whip) látigo m

lash² vt **1** (a) (whip) ‹person› azotar; ‹horse› fustigar* (b) (beat against) azotar **2** (bind) **to ~ sth/sb TO sth** amarrar algo/a algn A algo ∎ **lash out** [v + adv (+ prep + o)] atacar*; **to ~ out AT/AGAINST sb** (physically) emprenderla a golpes (or patadas etc) CON algn; (verbally) arremeter CONTRA algn

lass /læs/ n (liter or dial) muchacha f

lasso /'læsəʊ, læ'suː/ n (pl **-sos** or **-soes**) lazo m

last¹ /læst ‖lɑːst/ adj **1** (a) (in series) último; **the ~ door but one** la penúltima puerta; **to be ~** (in race, on arrival) ser* el último (en llegar); **to be ~ to + INF** ser* el último EN + INF (b) (final, ultimate) ‹chance/day› último; **at the very ~ minute** en el último momento, a última hora (c) (only remaining) último; **I'm down to my ~ few dollars** solo me quedan unos pocos dólares **2** (previous, most recent) (before n): **~ Tuesday** el martes pasado; **in my ~ letter** en mi última carta **3** (least likely): **that was the ~ thing I expected to hear from you** es lo que menos me esperaba que me dijeras; **that's the ~ thing I'd do!** ¡no se me ocurriría hacer eso!

last² pron **1** (a) (in series) último, -ma m,f; **the ~ to + INF** el último/la última/los últimos/las últimas EN + INF; **the ~ I remember** lo último que recuerdo (b) (only remaining): **the ~ of its kind** el último de su clase; **that's the ~ of the jam** esa es toda la mermelada que queda (c) (in phrases) (liter) **at the last** al final; **to the ~** hasta el último momento **2** (preceding one): **the night before ~** anteanoche, antenoche (AmL); **each hill seemed steeper than the ~** cada colina parecía más empinada que la anterior

last³ adv **1** (a) (at the end): **I went in ~** fui el último en entrar; **our team finished ~** nuestro equipo quedó en último lugar (b) (finally): **~ of all** por último; **and ~ but not least** y por último, pero no por eso menos importante (c) (in phrases) **at last** por fin, al fin; **at long last** por fin, finalmente **2** (most recently): **she was ~ seen a year ago** la última vez que se la vio fue hace un año; **when did you ~ see him?** ¿cuándo fue la última vez que lo viste?

last⁴ vi/t durar

last-ditch /'læst'dɪtʃ ‖'lɑːst'dɪtʃ/ adj (before n) desesperado

lasting /'læstɪŋ ‖'lɑːstɪŋ/ adj duradero

lastly /'læstli ‖'lɑːstli/ adv (as linker) por último

last-minute /'læst'mɪnət ‖,lɑːst'mɪnɪt/ adj (before n) de última hora

latch /lætʃ/ n pasador m, pestillo m; (on lock) seguro m ∎ **latch on** [v + adv (+ prep + o)] (understand) (colloq) agarrar or (Esp) coger* la onda; **to ~ on TO sth** entender* algo; (realize) darse* cuenta DE algo

late¹ /leɪt/ adj **later, latest 1** (after correct, scheduled time): **the ~ arrival of the train** el retraso en la llegada del tren; **to be ~** «person» llegar* tarde; **the train was an hour ~** el tren llegó con una hora de retraso; **you'll be ~ for work** vas a llegar tarde al trabajo **2** (a) (after usual time): **to have a ~ night**

acostarse* tarde; **Spring is ~ this year** la primavera se ha atrasado este año (b) ‹chrysanthemum/potatoes› tardío **3** (a) (far on in time): **it's ~** es tarde; **it's getting ~** se está haciendo tarde (b) (before n) ‹shift/bus› último; **at this ~ stage** a estas alturas; **in ~ April** a finales de abril; **she's in her ~ forties** tiene cerca de cincuenta años **4** (before n) (deceased) difunto (frml); **the ~ John Doe** el difunto John Doe

late² adv **later, latest 1** (after correct, scheduled time) tarde; **the trains are running 20 minutes ~** los trenes llevan 20 minutos de retraso; **better ~ than never** más vale tarde que nunca **2** (after usual time) ‹work/sleep› hasta tarde; ‹mature› tarde **3** (recently): **as ~ as the thirteenth century** aún en el siglo trece; **of ~** últimamente **4** (toward end of period): **~ in the afternoon** a última hora de la tarde; **~ in the year** a finales del año; **~ in her career** hacia el final de su carrera **5** (far on in time): **don't leave it too ~** no lo dejes para muy tarde; **we stayed up ~** nos quedamos levantados hasta tarde

lately /'leɪtli/ adv últimamente

latent /'leɪtnt/ adj latente

later¹ /'leɪtər ‖'leɪtə(r)/ adj posterior

later² adv después, más tarde; **~ that day** más tarde or posteriormente ese día; **not o no ~ than May 14** a más tardar el 14 de mayo; **~ on** más tarde, después; **see you ~!** ¡hasta luego!

lateral /'lætərəl/ adj lateral

latest /'leɪtəst ‖'leɪtɪst/ adj (a) (superl of LATE¹) último (b) (most up to date) (before n) último

latex /'leɪteks/ n látex m

lathe /leɪð/ n torno m

lather¹ /'læðər ‖'lɑːðə(r), læðə(r)/ n (no pl) espuma

lather² vt enjabonar

Latin¹ /'lætn ‖'lætɪn/ adj latino

Latin² n (a) (language) latín m (b) (person) latino, -na m,f

Latin America n América f Latina, Latinoamérica f

Latin American¹ adj latinoamericano

Latin American² n latinoamericano, -na m,f

latitude /'lætətuːd ‖'lætɪtjuːd/ n (a) (Geog) latitud f (b) (freedom to choose) libertad f

latter¹ /'lætər ‖'lætə(r)/ n (pl ~) **the ~** este, -ta; (pl) estos, -tas

latter² adj (before n) (a) (second of two) segundo, último (b) (later, last): **in the ~ part of the season** hacia el final de la temporada; **in his ~ years** (frml) en sus últimos años

lattice /'lætəs ‖'lætɪs/ n entramado m, enrejado m

Latvia /'lætviə/ n Letonia f

Latvian /'lætviən/ adj letón

laugh¹ /læf ‖lɑːf/ n risa f; ; **she's a good ~** es muy divertida; **to do/say sth for a ~** hacer*/decir* algo por divertirse; **to have a ~** (about/at sth) reírse* (de algo)

laugh² vi reír(se)*; **to burst out ~ing** soltar* una carcajada; **to ~ AT sb/sth** reírse* DE algn/algo

laughing ⋯⟫ lead ⋯

■ **laugh off** [v + o + adv, v + adv + o] tomar a broma

laughing /'læfɪŋ ‖ 'lɑːfɪŋ/ adj risueño; **this is no ∼ matter** no es motivo de risa

laughingstock /'læfɪŋstɑːk ‖ 'lɑːfɪŋstɒk/ n hazmerreír m; **he made a ∼ of his opponent** dejó or puso a su contrincante en ridículo

laughter /'læftər ‖ 'lɑːftə(r)/ n risas fpl

launch¹ /lɔːntʃ/ vt [1] (a) (new vessel) botar; (lifeboat) echar al agua (b) (satellite/missile) lanzar*; (attack) emprender [2] (product/campaign) lanzar*; (company) fundar*

launch² n [1] (motorboat) lancha f (a motor) [2] (a) (of new vessel) botadura f; (of lifeboat) lanzamiento m (al agua) (b) (of rocket, missile) lanzamiento m [3] (of product, campaign) lanzamiento m

launching pad /'lɔːntʃɪŋ/, **launchpad** /'lɔːntʃpæd/ n (a) (Aerosp) rampa f de lanzamiento (b) (for ideas, career) trampolín m

launder /'lɔːndər ‖ 'lɔːndə(r)/ vt (a) (wash and iron) (fml) lavar y planchar (b) (money) blanquear, lavar (AmL)

launderette /'lɔːndə'ret ‖ lɔːn'dret/ n lavandería f automática

Laundromat®, laundromat /'lɔːndrəmæt/ n (AmE) lavandería f automática

laundry /'lɔːndri/ n (pl **-dries**) (a) (commercial) lavandería f, lavadero m (RPl); (in home) lavadero m (b) (dirty clothes) ropa f sucia or para lavar; (washed clothes) ropa f limpia or lavada; (before n) **∼ basket** canasto m or cesto m de la ropa sucia

laurel /'lɔːrəl ‖ 'lɒrəl/ n laurel m

lava /'lɑːvə/ n lava f

lavatory /'lævətɔːri ‖ 'lævətri/ n (pl **-ries**) (a) (room in house) (cuarto m de) baño m (b) (public) (often pl) baños mpl, servicios mpl (Esp) (c) (receptacle) taza f, inodoro m

lavender /'lævəndər ‖ 'lævəndə(r)/ n lavanda f, espliego m

lavish¹ /'lævɪʃ/ adj (lifestyle) de derroche; (gift/meal) espléndido; (production) fastuoso

lavish² vt to ∼ sth ON sb prodigar(le)* algo A algn

lavishly /'lævɪʃli/ adv (give) con esplendidez; (decorated/illustrated) magníficamente

law /lɔː/ n (a) (rule, principle) ley f (b) (collectively): **the ∼** la ley; **to break the ∼** violar or contravenir* or infringir* la ley; **it is against the ∼** es ilegal; **under French ∼** según la ley francesa; **to lay down the ∼** dar* órdenes (c) (as field, discipline) derecho m; (profession) abogacía f; (before n) **∼ school** facultad f de Derecho

law: **∼-abiding** /'lɔːəˌbaɪdɪŋ/ adj respetuoso de la ley; **∼ and order** n (+ sing o pl vb) el orden público

lawful /'lɔːfəl/ adj (ruler/heir) legítimo; (contract) válido, legal; (conduct) lícito

lawless /'lɔːləs ‖ 'lɔːlɪs/ adj (mob) desmandado; (region) anárquico, donde no rige la ley

lawn /lɔːn/ n césped m, pasto m (AmL), grama f (AmC, Ven)

lawnmower /'lɔːnˌməʊər ‖ 'lɔːnˌməʊə(r)/n máquina f de cortar el césped or (AmL tb) el pasto, cortadora f de césped or (AmL tb) de pasto, cortacésped m (Esp), cortagrama m (AmC, Ven)

lawsuit /'lɔːsuːt/ n juicio m

lawyer /'lɔːjər ‖ 'lɔːjə(r)/ n abogado, -da m,f

lax /læks/ adj (discipline/supervision) poco estricto; (standards) laxo

laxative /'læksətɪv/ n laxante m

lay¹ /leɪ/ past of LIE² II

lay² (past & past p **laid**) vt [1] (put) poner*; **∼ the cloth flat on the table** extiende la tela sobre la mesa
[2] (put in position) (bricks/carpet) poner*, colocar*; (cable/pipes) tender*; (mines) sembrar*
[3] (prepare) (trap) tender*; (plans) hacer*; **to ∼ the table** poner* la mesa
[4] (cause to be): **one blow laid him flat on his back** de un golpe quedó tendido de espaldas en el suelo; **to ∼ sb low**: **he was laid low by malaria** estuvo postrado con malaria
[5] (Zool): **to ∼ eggs** «bird/reptile» poner* huevos; «fish/insects» desovar*
■ ∼ vi [1] «hen» poner* huevos
[2] (crit) ▶ LIE² II

■ **lay down** [v + o + adv, v + adv + o] (a) (tools/weapons) dejar (a un lado) (b) (guidelines/procedure) establecer*

■ **lay off** [v + adv + o, v + o + adv] despedir*; (BrE) suspender temporalmente por falta de trabajo

■ **lay on** [v + adv + o, v + o + adv] (transport/food) hacerse* cargo de; (entertainment) ofrecer*

■ **lay out** [v + o + adv, v + adv + o] [1] (a) (park/garden) diseñar; (town) hacer* el trazado de; (objects) disponer* (b) (page) diseñar
[2] (spend) gastar; (invest) invertir*
[3] (knock unconscious) dejar sin sentido
[4] (dead body) amortajar

lay³ adj (before n) (a) (secular) laico; **∼ preacher** predicador, -dora m,f seglar (b) (not expert): **the ∼ reader** el lector profano en la materia

lay-by /'leɪbaɪ/ n (BrE) área f; de reposo

layer¹ /'leɪər ‖ 'leɪə(r)/ n (of dust, paint, snow) capa f; (of rock, sediment) capa f, estrato m

layer² vt: **I had my hair ∼ed** me corté el pelo en or (Esp) a capas, me rebajé el pelo (RPl)

lay: **∼man** /'leɪmən/ n (pl **-men** /-mən/) (non-expert): **a book written for the ∼man** un libro dirigido al gran público; **in ∼man's terms** en lenguaje accesible; **∼out** n (a) (of house) distribución f; (of town, garden) trazado m (b) (in magazine, newspaper) diseño m

laze /leɪz/ vi haraganear

lazily /'leɪzəli ‖ 'leɪzɪli/ adv perezosamente

lazy /'leɪzi/ adj **lazier, laziest** perezoso

lazybones /'leɪzibəʊnz/ n (pl **∼**) (colloq) haragán, -gana m,f

lb = **pound(s)**

LCD n = **liquid crystal display**

lead¹ n
I /led/ [1] (metal) plomo m; (before n) **∼ poisoning** intoxicación f por plomo; (chronic disease) saturnismo m [2] (in pencil) mina f
II /liːd/ [1] (in competition) (no pl): **to be in/take the ∼** llevar/tomar la delantera [2] (example, leadership) (no pl) ejemplo m; **to follow sb's ∼** seguir* el ejemplo de algn [3] (clue) pista f [4] (a) (for dog) (BrE) correa f (b) (Elec) cable m [5] (a) (main role) papel m principal (b) (Mus) solista mf; (before n) (guitar/singer) principal

lead² /liːd/ (*past & past p* **led**) *vt* **1** (conduct)
⟨*person/animal*⟩ llevar, guiar*; **to ∼ sb TO sth/sb**
conducir* *or* llevar a algn A algo/ANTE algn; **to ∼
sb away** llevarse a algn; **I was led to believe that
…** me dieron a entender que …; **he's easily led** se
deja llevar fácilmente
2 (head, have charge of) ⟨*discussion*⟩ conducir*;
the expedition was led by Smith la expedición iba
al mando de Smith
3 (a) (be at front of) ⟨*parade/attack*⟩ encabezar*
(b) (in race, competition) aventajar
4 ⟨*life*⟩ llevar
■ ∼ *vi* **1** **to ∼ TO sth** «*road/steps*» llevar *or*
conducir* *or* dar* A algo; **to ∼ TO sth**
2 (a) (be leader): **you ∼, we'll follow** ve delante
or (esp AmL) adelante, que te seguimos **(b)** (in race,
competition) ir* a la cabeza, puntear (AmL); **they are
∼ing by three goals** van ganando por tres goles
■ **lead on** **1** [*v + adv*]: **∼ on!** ¡adelante! (¡te
seguimos!)
2 [*v + o + adv*] (raise false hopes) engañar
■ **lead to** [*v + prep + o*] llevar *or* conducir* a

leaded /ˈledəd ‖ˈledɪd/ *adj* ⟨*fuel*⟩ con plomo

leader /ˈliːdər ‖ˈliːdə(r)/ *n* **(a)** (of group, political
party) líder *mf*; (of expedition) jefe, -fa *m,f*; (of gang)
cabecilla *mf* **(b)** (in race, competition) primero, -ra
m,f; (in league) líder *m*

leadership /ˈliːdərʃɪp ‖ˈliːdəʃɪp/ *n* **(a)**
(direction, control — of party) liderazgo *m*; (— of
country) conducción *f* **(b)** (quality) autoridad *f*, dotes
fpl de mando **(c)** (leaders) (+ *sing o pl vb*)
dirigentes *mpl*

lead-free /ˈledˈfriː/ *adj* ⟨*fuel*⟩ sin plomo

leading /ˈliːdɪŋ/ *adj* (*before n*) **(a)** (principal)
⟨*scientist/playwright*⟩ destacado; ⟨*brand/
company*⟩ líder *adj inv* **(b)** (in front) ⟨*runner/horse/
driver*⟩ que va a la cabeza

leading: ∼ lady *n* (Cin) protagonista *f*; (Theat)
primera actriz *f*; **∼ light** *n* estrella *f*

leaf /liːf/ *n* (*pl* **leaves**) **1** (of plant) hoja *f*
2 (page, sheet) hoja *f*; **to turn (over) a new ∼**
reformarse **3** (of table) ala *f*‡; (of door, shutter)
hoja *f*
■ **leaf through** [*v + prep + o*] hojear

leaflet /ˈliːflət ‖ˈliːflɪt/ *n* (Print) folleto *m*; (Pol)
panfleto *m*

leafy /ˈliːfi/ *adj* **-fier, -fiest** ⟨*boughs*⟩ frondoso;
⟨*lane*⟩ arbolado

league /liːg/ *n* **1** (alliance) liga *f*; **to be in ∼
(with sb)** estar* aliado (con algn) **2** (a) (Sport)
liga *f* **(b)** (level, category): **not to be in the same ∼
as sb/sth** no estar* a la misma altura que algn/
algo **3** (measure of distance) legua *f*

leak¹ /liːk/ *vi* **(a)** «*bucket/tank*» gotear, perder*
(RPl), salirse* (Chi, Méx); «*shoes/tent*» dejar pasar
el agua; «*faucet*» gotear; «*pen*» perder* tinta;
the roof is ∼ing hay una gotera/hay goteras en el
techo **(b)** (escape) «*liquid*» escaparse
■ ∼ *vt* **(a)** ⟨*liquid/gas*⟩ perder*, botar (AmL exc RPl)
(b) ⟨*information*⟩ filtrar

leak² *n* **(a)** (in bucket, boat, pipe) agujero *m*; (in
roof) gotera *f* **(b)** (escaping liquid, gas) escape *m* **(c)**
(of information) filtración *f*

leakage /ˈliːkɪdʒ/ *n* escape *m*

leaky /ˈliːki/ *adj* **-kier, -kiest** agujereado

lean¹ /liːn/ (*past & past p* **leaned** *or* (BrE also)
leant /lent/) *vi* **(a)** (bend, incline): **she ∼ed back
in her chair** se echó hacia atrás en la silla; **don't
∼ out of the window** no te asomes por la ventana
(b) (support oneself) apoyarse; **to ∼ AGAINST sth**
apoyarse CONTRA algo; **to ∼ ON sth/sb** apoyarse
EN algo/algn
■ ∼ *vt* apoyar

lean² *adj* ⟨*person*⟩ delgado; ⟨*animal*⟩ flaco
(b) ⟨*meat*⟩ magro

leant /lent/ (BrE) *past & past p of* LEAN¹

leap¹ /liːp/ *vi/t* (*past & past p* **leaped** *or* (BrE
also) **leapt** /lept/) saltar

leap² *n* salto *m*, brinco *m*; **by ∼s and bounds** a
pasos agigantados

leapfrog /ˈliːpfrɔːg ‖ˈliːpfrɒg/ *n*: **to play ∼**
jugar* a la pídola, brincar* al burro (Méx), jugar*
al rango (RPl)

leapt /lept/ (BrE) *past & past p of* LEAP¹

leap year *n* año *m* bisiesto

learn /lɜːrn ‖lɜːn/ (*past & past p* **learned** *or*
(BrE also) **learnt**) *vt* **1** **(a)** (gain knowledge of)
aprender; **to ∼ to + INF** aprender A + INF **(b)**
(memorize) aprender de memoria **2** (become
informed about) enterarse de
■ ∼ *vi* **1** (gain knowledge) aprender **2** (become
informed) **to ∼ ABOUT** *o* **OF sth** enterarse DE algo

learned /ˈlɜːrnɪd ‖ˈlɜːnɪd/ *adj* docto

learner /ˈlɜːrnər ‖ˈlɜːnə(r)/ *n*: **he's a fast/slow
∼** aprende con mucha rapidez/tiene dificultades
de aprendizaje; (*before n*) **∼ (driver)** (esp BrE)
persona que está aprendiendo a conducir

learning /ˈlɜːrnɪŋ ‖ˈlɜːnɪŋ/ *n* **(a)** (knowledge)
saber *m*; (education) educación *f*; **a man of ∼** un
erudito **(b)** (act) aprendizaje *m*; (*before n*) **∼
difficulties** dificultades *fpl* de aprendizaje

learnt /lɜːrnt ‖lɜːnt/ (BrE) *past & past p of*
LEARN

lease¹ /liːs/ *n* ≈ contrato *m* de arrendamiento;
(of real estate) ≈ usufructo *m*

lease² *vt* **(a)** **∼ (out)** (grant use of) arrendar*;
⟨*real estate*⟩ dar* en usufructo **(b)** (hold under
lease) arrendar*; ⟨*real estate*⟩ tener* el usufructo
de

leasehold /ˈliːshəʊld/ *n* arrendamiento *m*

leash /liːʃ/ *n* correa *f*

least¹ /liːst/ *adj* **1** (*superl of* LITTLE¹ II): **she
has the ∼ money** es quien menos dinero tiene
2 (smallest, slightest) más mínimo; **that's the ∼ of
my worries** eso es lo que menos me preocupa

least² *pron* **1** (*superl of* LITTLE²) **to say the ∼**
por no decir más; **it's the ∼ I can do** es lo menos
que puedo hacer **2** (in adv phrases) **at least** por lo
menos; **in the least** en lo más mínimo

AmC	Central America	Arg	Argentina	Cu	Cuba	Per	Peru
AmL	Latin America	Bol	Bolivia	Ec	Ecuador	RPl	River Plate Area
AmS	South America	Chi	Chile	Esp	Spain	Ur	Uruguay
Andes	Andean Region	CS	Southern Cone	Méx	Mexico	Ven	Venezuela

least³ *adv* **1** (*superl of* LITTLE³): ∼ **of all you** tú menos que nadie; **when you** ∼ **expect it** cuando menos te lo esperas **2** (*before adj, adv*) menos

leather /'leðər ‖'leða(r)/ *n* cuero *m*, piel *f* (Esp, Méx)

leave¹ /li:v/ *n* **1** (authorized absence) permiso *m*, licencia *f* (esp AmL); (Mil) licencia *f*; **to be/go on** ∼ estar*/salir* de permiso *or* (esp AmL) de licencia **2** (permission) (frml) permiso *m* **3** (departure) (frml): **to take** ∼ **of sb** despedirse* de algn; **have you taken** ∼ **of your senses?** ¿te has vuelto loco?

leave² (*past & past p* **left**) *vt* **1** (a) (go away from): **she** ∼**s home at 6** sale de casa a las 6; **I left her reading a book** la dejé leyendo un libro; **to** ∼ **school** terminar el colegio; **she left home at the age of 17** se fue de casa a los 17 años **(b)** (withdraw from) ⟨*profession/organization/politics*⟩ dejar **2** (abandon) dejar; **she left her husband for another man** dejó a su marido por otro (hombre) **3** (a) (deposit in specified place) dejar; **to** ∼ **sth FOR sb** dejarle algo A algn **(b)** (not take — deliberately) dejar; **(— inadvertently)** olvidarse de, dejarse **(c)** (not eat) ⟨*food*⟩ dejar **4** (allow, cause to remain) dejar; **please** ∼ **the window open** por favor dejen la ventana abierta **5** (have as aftereffect) ⟨*stain/scar*⟩ dejar **6** (a) (not attend to) dejar **(b)** (not disturb) dejar; ∼ **her to finish on her own** déjala terminar sola **7** (entrust): ∼ **it to me!** ¡déjalo por mi cuenta!; **we must** ∼ **nothing to chance** no debemos dejar nada (librado) al azar **8** (after deduction, elimination): **6 from 10** ∼**s 4** si a 10 le quitamos 6, quedan 4; **there isn't much time left** no queda mucho tiempo **9** (bequeath) **to** ∼ **sth TO sb/sth** dejar(le) algo A algn/algo

■ ∼ *vi* irse*, marcharse (esp Esp); **the train** ∼**s at 5 o'clock** el tren sale a las 5 en punto

■ **leave behind** [*v + o + adv, v + adv + o*] **(a)** (not take or bring — deliberately) dejar; **(— inadvertently)** olvidarse de, dejarse **(b)** ⟨*worries/cares*⟩ dejar atrás

■ **leave on** [*v + o + adv, v + adv + o*] **(a)** ⟨*light/machine/television*⟩ dejar encendido *or* (AmL tb) prendido **(b)** (keep wearing) no quitarse

■ **leave out 1** [*v + o + adv, v + adv + o*] [*v + o + adv (+ prep + o)*] **(a)** (omit) omitir **(b)** (exclude) excluir* **2** [*v + o + adv*] **(a)** (leave outside) dejar fuera *or* (esp AmL) afuera **(b)** (not put away) ⟨*clothes/toys*⟩ no guardar **(c)** (leave available) dejar preparado

■ **leave over** [*v + o + adv, v + adv + o*] (*usu pass*): **tomorrow we can eat what's left over** mañana podemos comer lo que sobre *or* quede

leaves /li:vz/ *pl of* LEAF

leaving /'li:vɪŋ/ *adj* (*before n*) ⟨*present*⟩ de despedida; ∼ **party** despedida *f*

Lebanese /'lebə'ni:z/ *adj* libanés

Lebanon /'lebənɑn ‖'lebənən/ *n* (el) Líbano

lecherous /'letʃərəs/ *adj* libidinoso

lectern /'lektərn ‖'lektɜ:n/ *n* atril *m*; (in church) facistol *m*

lecture¹ /'lektʃər ‖'lektʃə(r)/ *n* (public address) conferencia *f*; (Educ) clase *f*; (*before n*) ∼ **theater** auditorio *m*

lecture² *vi* (Educ) dar* clase, dictar clase (AmL frml), hacer* clase (Chi)

■ ∼ *vt* (scold) sermonear

lecturer /'lektʃərər ‖'lektʃərə(r)/ *n* **(a)** (speaker) conferenciante *mf*, conferencista *mf* (AmL) **(b)** (esp BrE Educ) profesor universitario, profesora universitaria *m,f*

led /led/ *past & past p of* LEAD²

LED *n* = **light-emitting diode**

ledge /ledʒ/ *n* **(a)** (on wall) cornisa *f*; (window ∼) (exterior) alféizar *m* (de la ventana); (interior) repisa *f* (de la ventana) **(b)** (on cliff) saliente *m or f*

ledger /'ledʒər ‖'ledʒə(r)/ *n* libro *m* de contabilidad

leech /li:tʃ/ *n* sanguijuela *f*

leek /li:k/ *n* puerro *m*

leer /lɪr ‖lɪə(r)/ *vi* **to** ∼ **AT sb** lanzarle* una mirada lasciva A algn

leeway /'li:weɪ/ *n*: **I am given a lot of** ∼ me dan mucha libertad de acción; **there isn't much** ∼ **in the budget** el presupuesto tiene poco margen de flexibilidad

left¹ /left/ *past & past p of* LEAVE²

left² /left/ *n* **1** (a) (left side) izquierda *f*; **on the** ∼ a la izquierda; **to drive on the** ∼ manejar *or* (esp Esp) conducir* por la izquierda **(b)** (left turn): **to make** *o* (BrE) **take a** ∼ girar a la izquierda **(c)** (Sport) (hand) izquierda *f* **2** (Pol) **the** ∼ la izquierda

left³ *adj* (*before n*) izquierdo

left⁴ *adv* a *or* hacia la izquierda

left: ∼**-hand** *adj* (*before n*) de la izquierda; **on the** ∼**-hand side** a mano izquierda; ∼**-handed** /'left'hændəd ‖,left'hændɪd/ *adj* ⟨*person*⟩ zurdo; ⟨*tool*⟩ para zurdos; ∼**-luggage** (**office**) /'left'lʌgɪdʒ/ *n* (BrE) consigna *f*; ∼**over** *adj* (*before n*) sobrante; ∼**overs** /'left,əʊvərz ‖'left,əʊvəz/ *pl n* sobras *fpl*; ∼ **wing** *n* **(a)** (Pol) (+ *sing or pl vb*) (ala *f*) izquierda *f* **(b)** (Sport) ala *f*; izquierda; ∼**-wing** /'left'wɪŋ/ *adj* (Pol) izquierdista; ∼**-winger** /'left'wɪŋər ‖,left'wɪŋə(r)/ *n* (Pol) izquierdista *mf*

leg /leg/ *n* **1** (Anat) (of person) pierna *f*; (of animal, bird) pata *f*; **to pull sb's** ∼ (colloq) tomarle el pelo a algn (fam) **2** (a) (Culin) (of lamb, pork) pierna *f*; (of chicken) pata *f*, muslo *m* **b** (Clothing) pierna *f* **(c)** (of chair, table) pata *f* **3** (stage — of competition, race) manga *f*; (— of journey) etapa *f*

legacy /'legəsi/ *n* (*pl* **-cies**) legado *m*

legal /'li:gəl/ *adj* **1** (a) (allowed) legal; ⟨*tackle/move*⟩ reglamentario **(b)** (founded upon law) ⟨*contract/requirement*⟩ legal **2** (relating to legal system, profession) (*before n*) jurídico; **we will be forced to take** ∼ **action** nos veremos obligados a poner el asunto en manos de nuestro(s) abogado(s)

legal holiday *n* (AmE) día *m* festivo oficial, feriado *m* oficial (esp AmL)

legalization /,li:gələ'zeɪʃən ‖,li:gəlaɪ'zeɪʃən/ *n* legalización *f*

legalize /'li:gəlaɪz/ *vt* legalizar*

legally /'li:gəli/ *adv* legalmente

legal tender *n* moneda *f* de curso legal

legend /'ledʒənd/ *n* leyenda *f*

legendary /'ledʒənderi ‖'ledʒəndri/ *adj* legendario

leggings /'legɪnz/ *pl n* **(a)** (pants, trousers) leggings *mpl*, mallas *fpl*, calzas *fpl* (RPl) **(b)** (for lower leg) polainas *fpl*

legible /'ledʒəbəl/ *adj* legible

legion /'li:dʒən/ n legión f
legislate /'ledʒəsleɪt ‖'ledʒɪsleɪt/ vi legislar
legislation /'ledʒəs'leɪʃən ‖,ledʒɪs'leɪʃən/ n legislación f
legislative /'ledʒəsleɪtɪv ‖'ledʒɪslətɪv/ adj (before n) legislativo
legislator /'ledʒəsleɪtər ‖'ledʒɪsleɪtə(r)/ n legislador, -dora m,f
legislature /'ledʒɪsleɪtʃər ‖'ledʒɪsleɪtʃə(r)/ n asamblea f legislativa
legitimate /lɪ'dʒɪtəmət ‖lɪ'dʒɪtɪmət/ adj legítimo
legitimize /lɪ'dʒɪtəmaɪz ‖lɪ'dʒɪtɪmaɪz/ vt legitimar
legroom /'legru:m, -rʊm/ n espacio m para las piernas
leisure /'li:ʒər ‖'leʒə(r)/ n tiempo m libre; **read it at your ~** léalo cuando le venga bien; (before n) ‹activity› de tiempo libre; **~ center** (AmE) centro m recreativo; **~ centre** (BrE) centro m deportivo
leisurely /'li:ʒərli ‖'leʒəli/ adj lento, pausado; **at a ~ pace** sin prisas
lemon /'lemən/ n **(a)** (fruit) limón m, limón m francés (Méx, Ven); (before n) ‹squeezer (BrE) exprimelimones m, exprimidor m; **~ tea** té m con limón **(b) ~ (tree)** limonero m **(c)** (color) amarillo m limón; (before n) amarillo limón adj inv
lemonade /'lemə'neɪd/ n **(a)** (with fresh lemons) limonada f **(b)** (fizzy drink) (BrE) (bebida f) gaseosa f
lemon cheese, lemon curd n crema f de limón (en conserva)
lend /lend/ vt (past & past p **lent**) prestar; **this ~s an air of mystery to the scene** esto le da un aire de misterio a la escena
lender /'lendər ‖'lendə(r)/ n (institution) entidad f crediticia; (person) prestamista mf
length /leŋθ/ n **1** **(a)** (of line, surface) longitud f; (of sleeve, coat) largo m; **it's 5m in ~** mide 5 metros de largo; **he traveled the ~ and breadth of the country** viajó a lo largo y a (lo ancho) del país; **he'd go to any ~s to get what he wants** es capaz de hacer cualquier cosa con tal de obtener lo que se propone **(b)** (of book, list) extensión f **2** **(a)** (duration) (of movie, play) duración f; **after a considerable ~ of time** después de mucho tiempo **(b) at length** (finally) finalmente; (for a long time) extensamente; (in detail) detenidamente; **to talk at ~** hablar largo y tendido **3** (section — of wood, pipe) trozo m; (— of river, road) tramo m **4** **(a)** (in swimming) largo m **(b)** (in horse, dog racing) cuerpo m; (in rowing) largo m
lengthen /'leŋθən/ vt ‹skirt/novel› alargar*; ‹line/visit› alargar*
lengthwise /'leŋθwaɪz/, (esp BrE) **lengthways** /-weɪz/ adv a lo largo
lengthy /'leŋθi/ adj **-thier -thiest** (long) largo; (tedious) largo y pesado
lenient /'li:niənt/ adj ‹attitude/view› indulgente; ‹sentence› poco severo
lens /lenz/ n (pl **lenses**) **(a)** (Opt) lente f **(b)** (for magnifying) lupa f **(c)** (in spectacles) cristal m **(d)** ▶ CONTACT LENS **(e)** (Phot) lente f
lent /lent/ past & past p of LEND

Lent /lent/ n Cuaresma f
lentil /'lentl/ n lenteja f
Leo /'li:əʊ/ n (pl **-os**) **(a)** (sign) (no art) Leo **(b)** (person) Leo or leo mf
leopard /'lepərd ‖'lepəd/ n leopardo m
leotard /'li:ətɑ:rd ‖'li:ətɑ:d/ n malla f
leper /'lepər ‖'lepə(r)/ n leproso, -sa m,f
leprosy /'leprəsi/ n lepra f
lesbian /'lezbiən/ n lesbiana f
lesion /'li:ʒən/ n lesión f
less¹ /les/ adj (comp of LITTLE¹ II) menos; **~ and ~ money** cada vez menos dinero
less² pron (comp of LITTLE²) menos; **a sum of ~ than $1,000** una suma inferior a los 1.000 dólares
less³ adv (comp of LITTLE³) menos; **the situation is no ~ serious than it was** la situación sigue siendo tan grave como antes
-less /ləs ‖lɪs/ suff sin; **hat~** sin sombrero
lessen /'lesn/ vt ‹pain› aliviar; ‹cost/risk› reducir*
■ ~ vi «noise» disminuir*; «pain» aliviarse; «interest» decrecer*
lesser /'lesər ‖'lesə(r)/ adj (before n) menor; **to a ~ extent** en menor grado
lesson /'lesn/ n **1** (Educ) **(a)** (class) clase f **(b)** (in textbook) lección f **2** (from experience) lección f; **to learn one's ~** aprender la lección
lest /lest/ conj (liter) no sea que (+ subj); **~ we forget** para que no olvidemos
let /let/ (pres p **letting**; past & past p **let**) vt **1** (no pass) (allow to) dejar; **he ~ his hair grow** se dejó crecer el pelo; **~ me help you** deja que te ayude; **~ me see** ¿a ver?; **don't ~ me catch you here again!** ¡que no te vuelva a pescar por aquí! **(b)** (cause to, make): **~ me know if there are any problems** avísame si hay algún problema; **he ~ it be known that ...** hizo saber que ... **(c)** to **~ go** soltar*; **~ go of my hand!** ¡suéltame la mano!; **to ~ oneself go** (enjoy oneself) soltarse*; (neglect oneself) abandonarse **2** (+ adv compl): **to ~ sth/sb by o past** dejar pasar algo/a algn; **she ~ herself into the house** abrió la puerta y entró en la casa **3** [Used to form 1st pers pl imperative] **~'s go** vamos, vámonos; **~'s ask Chris** vamos a preguntarle a Chris, preguntémosle a Chris; **don't ~'s o ~'s not argue** no discutamos; **~ us pray** (frml) oremos **4** [Used to form 3rd pers imperative, gen translated by QUE + SUBJ in Spanish] **~ that be a lesson to you** que te sirva de lección; **just ~ them try!** ¡que se atrevan! **5** (rent) (esp BrE) alquilar; **❺ to let** se alquila
■ **let down** [v + o + adv, v + adv + o] **1** **(a)** (lower) ‹rope/bucket› bajar **(b)** (lengthen) ‹skirt› alargar*; (lower) ‹hem› bajar, sacar **(c)** ‹tire/balloon› desinflar **2** (disappoint) fallar; **her spelling ~s her down** su ortografía no le hace justicia a su trabajo
■ **let in** [v + o + adv, v + adv + o] dejar entrar
■ **let off**
I **1** **(a)** [v + o + adv] (forgive, not punish) perdonar; **she was ~ off with a reprimand** solo le hicieron una amonestación **(b)** [v + o + adv] [v + o + prep + o] (excuse from) perdonar
2 [v + o + adv] (allow to go) dejar salir

II [v + o + adv, v + adv + o] ‹fireworks› hacer*
estallar; ‹rocket/cracker› tirar
■ **let on** [v + adv] [v + adv + o]: you mustn't ∼
on about this to Jim no le vayas a decir nada de
esto a Jim; don't ∼ on (that) you know me! no
digas que me conoces
■ **let out**
I [v + o + adv, v + adv + o] [1] (disclose) ‹secret›
revelar
[2] (rent out) (esp BrE) alquilar
[3] (make wider) ‹skirt/dress› ensanchar, agrandar
II [v + o + adv, v + adv + o] [v + o + adv (+ prep
+ o)] (allow to leave) dejar salir; someone ∼ the air
out of my tires alguien me desinfló los
neumáticos
III [v + adv + o] ‹scream/yell› soltar*
■ **let up** [v + adv] ‹wind/storm› amainar;
‹‹pressure/work›› disminuir*
letdown /'letdaʊn/ n decepción f
lethal /'li:θəl/ adj mortal, letal; ‹weapon›
mortífero
lethargic /lə'θɑːrdʒɪk ‖lɪ'θɑːdʒɪk/ adj
aletargado
let's /lets/ (= **let us**) ▶ **LET²** 3
letter /'letər ‖'letə(r)/ n [1] (written message)
carta f [2] (of alphabet) letra f
letter: ∼ **bomb** n carta f bomba; ∼ **box** n
buzón m
lettuce /'letəs ‖'letɪs/ n lechuga f
let-up /'letʌp/ n interrupción f
leukemia, (esp BrE) **leukaemia** /luːˈkiːmiə/ n
leucemia f
level¹ /'levəl/ n nivel m; at eye ∼ a la altura de
los ojos; a top-∼ meeting una reunión de or a
alto nivel
level² adj [1] ‹ground/surface› plano, llano; a ∼
spoonful una cucharada rasa; to do one's ∼ best
hacer* todo lo posible [2] (a) (at same height) to be
∼ (WITH sth) estar* al nivel (DE algo) (b) (abreast,
equal): the two teams were ∼ at half-time al medio
tiempo los dos equipos iban empatados; to draw
∼ with sb (in a race) alcanzar* a algn
[3] (unemotional, calm) desapasionado
level³, (BrE) **-ll-** vt [1] (a) (make flat) ‹ground/
surface› nivelar (b) (raze) ‹building/town› arrasar
[2] (make equal) igualar [3] (direct) to ∼ sth AT sb/
sth ‹weapon› apuntarle A algn/A algo con algo; to
∼ an accusation at sb acusar a algn
■ ∼ vi (be honest; colloq) to ∼ WITH sb ser* franco
CON algn
■ **level off** [v + adv] (a) ‹‹aircraft›› nivelarse,
enderezarse* (b) ‹‹prices/growth/inflation››
estabilizarse*
level: ∼ **crossing** n (BrE) paso m a nivel,
crucero m (Méx); ∼**-headed** /'levəl'hedəd
‖,levəl'hedɪd/ adj sensato
lever¹ /'levər ‖'liːvə(r)/ n palanca f
lever² vt (+ adv compl): to ∼ sth open abrir*
algo haciendo palanca
levy¹ /'levi/ vt **levies, levying, levied** (a)
‹tax/duty› (impose) imponer*; (collect) recaudar (b)
‹fee/charge› cobrar (c) ‹fine› imponer*
levy² n (pl **levies**) (a) (raising of tax, contributions):
the strike was funded by a ∼ on all members la
huelga se financió mediante el cobro de una
cuota a todos los miembros (b) (tax) impuesto m
lewd /luːd ‖ljuːd/ adj **-er, -est** lascivo

liability /ˌlaɪə'bɪləti/ n (pl **-ties**)
[1] (responsibility) responsabilidad f [2] **liabilities**
pl (debt) (Fin) pasivo m [3] (disadvantage) (no pl):
she's a positive ∼ es un verdadero lastre; the car
turned out to be a ∼ el coche terminó dándonos
más problemas que otra cosa
liable /'laɪəbəl/ adj (pred) [1] (responsible)
responsable; to be ∼ FOR sth ser* responsable DE
algo [2] (likely): I'm ∼ to forget es probable que me
olvide; the earlier model was ∼ to overheat el
modelo anterior tenía tendencia a recalentarse
liaise /li'eɪz/ vi (esp BrE) to ∼ (WITH sb) actuar*
de enlace (CON algn); the departments will ∼
closely los departamentos mantendrán un
estrecho contacto
liaison /li'eɪzɑːn ‖li'eɪzn̩/ n [1] (coordination)
enlace m [2] (affair) (liter) affaire m
liar /'laɪər ‖'laɪə(r)/ n mentiroso, -sa m,f
libel¹ /'laɪbəl/ n (defamation) difamación f; (where
a crime is implied) calumnia f
libel² vt, (BrE) **-ll-** (defame) difamar; (where a crime
is implied) calumniar
liberal¹ /'lɪbərəl/ adj [1] (a) (tolerant) ‹ideas›
liberal; ‹interpretation› libre (b) **Liberal** (Pol)
del Partido Liberal; L∼ **Democrat** (in UK)
demócrata mf liberal [2] (generous) generoso
liberal² n (a) (progressive thinker) liberal mf (b)
Liberal (party member) liberal mf
liberalism /'lɪbərəlɪzəm/ n liberalismo m
liberalize /'lɪbərəlaɪz/ vt liberalizar*
liberally /'lɪbərəli/ adv (a) (generously)
generosamente (b) (not strictly) libremente
liberate /'lɪbəreɪt/ vt liberar
liberation /ˌlɪbə'reɪʃən/ n liberación f
Liberia /laɪ'bɪriə ‖laɪ'bɪəriə/ n Liberia f
Liberian /laɪ'bɪriən ‖laɪ'bɪəriən/ adj liberiano
liberty /'lɪbərti ‖'lɪbəti/ n (pl **-ties**) libertad f;
I'm not at ∼ to tell you no se lo puedo decir; to
take the ∼ of -ING (esp BrE) tomarse la libertad DE
+ INF
Libra /'liːbrə, 'laɪbrə ‖'liːbrə/ n (a) (sign) (no
art) Libra (b) (person) Libra or Libra mf
librarian /laɪ'breriən ‖laɪ'breəriən/ n
bibliotecario, -ria m,f
library /'laɪbreri ‖'laɪbrəri/ n (pl **-ries**)
biblioteca f
libretto /lə'bretəʊ ‖lɪ'bretəʊ/ n (pl **-tos** or **-ti**
/-tiː/) libreto m
Libya /'lɪbiə/ n Libia f
Libyan /'lɪbiən/ adj libio
lice /laɪs/ pl of **LOUSE**
license¹, (BrE) **licence** /'laɪsn̩s/ n [1] (a)
(permit) permiso m; import/export ∼ permiso de
importación/exportación; (before n) ∼ number
(AmE Auto) número m de matrícula or (CS) de
patente; ∼ plate matrícula f, placa f (AmL),
patente f (CS), chapa f (RPI) (b) ▶ DRIVER'S
LICENSE [2] (a) (freedom): poetic ∼ licencia f
poética (b) (excessive freedom) (frml) libertinaje m
license² /'laɪsn̩s/ vt otorgarle* un permiso a
licensed /'laɪsn̩st/ adj ‹practitioner› autorizado
para ejercer; ‹premises› (BrE) autorizado para
vender bebidas alcohólicas
licentious /laɪ'sentʃəs ‖laɪ'senʃəs/ adj
licencioso
lichen /'laɪkən, 'lɪtʃən/ n liquen m

lick /lɪk/ vt lamer; ‹stamp› pasarle la lengua a

licorice, (BrE) **liquorice** /'lɪkərɪʃ, -ɪs/ n
regaliz f, orozuz m

lid /lɪd/ n **1** (of container) tapa f **2** (eye ∼)
párpado m

lie¹ /laɪ/ n (untruth) mentira f; **to tell** ∼**s** decir*
mentiras, mentir*

lie² vi

I (3rd pers sing pres **lies**; pres p **lying**; past &
past p **lied**) (tell untruths) mentir*

II (3rd pers sing pres **lies**; pres p **lying**; past
lay; past p **lain**) **1** (a) (lie down) echarse,
tenderse* (b) (be in lying position) estar* tendido; **I
lay awake for hours** estuve horas sin poder
dormir (c) (be buried) yacer* (liter); **❺ here lies
John Brown** aquí yacen los restos de John Brown
2 (be) «object» estar*; **the snow lay two feet
deep** la nieve tenía dos pies de espesor
3 (be located) «building/city» encontrarse*; **a
group of islands lying off the west coast** un
conjunto de islas situadas cerca de la costa
occidental
4 «problem/difference» radicar*; «answer»
estar*

■ **lie down** [v + adv] (a) (adopt lying position)
echarse, tenderse* (b) (be lying) estar* tendido

lie detector n detector m de mentiras

lieu /lu: ‖lju:/ n (frml): **in** ∼ en lugar de, en
vez de; **time off in** ∼ horas fpl/días mpl libres a
cambio

lieutenant /lu:'tenənt ‖lef'tenənt/ n (a) (in
navy) teniente mf de navío, teniente mf primero
(en Chi) (b) (in other services) teniente mf

life /laɪf/ n (pl **lives**) **1** vida f; **animal/plant** ∼
vida animal/vegetal; **in later** ∼ más tarde or más
adelante; **it brings the history of this period to** ∼
hace cobrar vida a este período de la historia; **to
bring sb back to** ∼ resucitar a algn; **to come to**
∼ «party» animarse; «puppet» cobrar vida; **he
was fighting for his life** se debatía entre la vida y
la muerte; **to have the time of one's** ∼ divertirse*
como nunca; **run for your lives!** ¡sálvese quien
pueda!; **to save sb's** ∼ salvarle la vida a algn; **to
be the** ∼ o (esp BrE) **the** ∼ **and soul of the party**
ser* el alma de la fiesta; **to live the** ∼ **of Riley**
darse* la gran vida; **to take one's** ∼ **in one's
hands** jugarse* la vida; (before n) «member/
president» vitalicio; **his** ∼ **story** la historia de su
vida
2 (duration — of battery) duración f; (— of agreement)
vigencia f
3 (imprisonment) (colloq) cadena f perpetua

life: ∼ **assurance** n (BrE) ▶ ∼ INSURANCE; ∼
belt n (BrE) salvavidas m; ∼**boat** n (on ship)
bote m salvavidas; (shore-based) lancha f de
salvamento; ∼ **buoy** n salvavidas m; ∼ **cycle**
n ciclo m vital; ∼**guard** n salvavidas mf,
socorrista mf; ∼ **insurance** n seguro m de
vida; ∼ **jacket** n chaleco m salvavidas

lifeless /'laɪfləs ‖'laɪflɪs/ adj (dead) sin vida,
inánime (frml), exánime (liter); (unconscious) inerte

life: ∼**like** adj verosímil; ∼**line** n (rope) cuerda

f de salvamento; **his letters were my** ∼**line** sus
cartas eran lo único que me mantenía viva;
∼**long** adj (before n): **a** ∼**long friend** un amigo
de toda la vida; ∼ **preserver** /prɪ'zɜːrvər
‖prɪ'zɜːvə(r)/ n (AmE) (a) ▶ LIFE BUOY (b) ▶ LIFE
JACKET; ∼ **raft** n balsa f salvavidas; ∼ **ring** n
(AmE) salvavidas m; ∼**saver** /'laɪf,seɪvər
‖'laɪf,seɪvə(r)/ n (a) ▶ LIFEGUARD (b) (from bad
situation) salvación f; ∼**saving** adj (before n) que
salva vidas; ∼**size** /'laɪf'saɪz/, ∼**sized** /-d/ adj
(de) tamaño natural; ∼ **span** n (of living creature)
vida f; (of project) duración f; (of equipment) vida f
útil; ∼**style** n estilo m de vida; ∼**time** n vida
f; **the chance of a** ∼**time** la oportunidad de su (or
mi etc) vida; (before n) ‹appointment/post›
vitalicio; ∼**time guarantee** garantía f para toda la
vida; ∼ **vest** n (AmE) chaleco m salvavidas

lift¹ /lɪft/ n **1** (boost) impulso m **2** (ride): **can I
give you a** ∼? ¿quieres que te lleve or (Per fam)
jale?, ¿quieres que te dé un aventón (Méx) or (Col
fam) una palomita? **3** (elevator) ascensor m

lift² vt **1** (raise) levantar **2** (end) ‹ban/siege›
levantar

■ ∼ vi (a) (rise) ‹curtain› levantarse (b) (clear)
«mist» disiparse

■ **lift off** [v + adv] «rocket» despegar*

■ **lift up** [v + o + adv, v + adv + o] levantar

lift-off /'lɪftɔːf ‖'lɪftɒf/ n (Aerosp) despegue m

ligament /'lɪgəmənt/ n ligamento m

ligature /'lɪgətʃər ‖'lɪgətʃə(r)/ n ligadura f

light¹ /laɪt/ n **1** luz f; **by the** ∼ **of the moon** a
la luz de la luna; **to come to** ∼ salir* a la luz; **to
see the** ∼ abrir* los ojos
2 (a) (source of light) luz f; (lamp) lámpara f;
(before n) ∼ **switch** interruptor m (b) (of car,
bicycle) luz f (c) (traffic ∼) semáforo m
3 (a) (aspect) (no pl): **to see sth/sb in a good/
bad/new** ∼ **different** ∼ ver* algo o algn con
buenos/malos/otros ojos (b) **in the** ∼ **of** o (AmE
also) **in** ∼ **of** (as prep) a la luz de, en vista de
4 (for igniting): **have you got a** ∼? ¿tienes fuego?;
to set ∼ **to sth** prender fuego a algo

light² adj **-er, -est**
I **1** (not heavy) ligero, liviano (esp AmL); ‹voice›
suave **2** (a) (Meteo) ‹breeze/wind› suave; ∼ **rain**
llovizna f (b) (sparse): **the losses were fairly** ∼ las
pérdidas fueron de poca consideración (c) (not
strenuous) ‹work/duties› ligero, liviano (esp AmL)
3 (not serious) ‹music/comedy/reading› ligero; **to
make** ∼ **of sth** quitarle or restarle importancia a
algo
II (a) (pale) ‹green/brown› claro (b) (bright): **it
gets** ∼ **very early these days** ahora amanece muy
temprano; **it's already** ∼ ya es de día

light³ adv: **to travel** ∼ viajar con el mínimo de
equipaje

light⁴ vt **1** (past & past p **lighted** or **lit**) (set
alight) encender* **2** (past & past p **lit**) (illuminate)
iluminar

■ ∼ vi (past & past p **lighted** or **lit**) encenderse*

■ **light up** (past & past p **lit**) **1** [v + adv] (a)
«eyes/face» iluminarse (b) «smoker» encender*

un cigarrillo (*or* un puro *etc*) **2** [*v* + *o* + *adv*, *v* + *adv* + *o*] **(a)** ‹*street/square*› iluminar **(b)** ‹*cigar/ pipe*› encender*

light: ~ **bulb** *n* ▶ BULB 2; ~ **cream** *n* (AmE) crema *f* líquida, nata *f* líquida (Esp); ~**-emitting diode** /'daɪəʊd/ *n* diodo *m* emisor de luz

lighten /'laɪtn̩/ *vt* **1** ‹*load/workload*› aligerar; ‹*responsibility/conscience*› descargar* **2** **(a)** ‹*room*› dar* más luz a; ‹*sky*› iluminar **(b)** ‹*color/ hair*› aclarar
■ ~ *vi* **1** «*load/weight*» hacerse* más ligero *or* (esp AmL) liviano, aligerarse **2** «*sky*» despejarse; «*face*» iluminarse; «*atmosphere*» relajarse

lighter /'laɪtər ‖'laɪtə(r)/ *n* (cigarette ~) encendedor *m*, mechero *m* (Esp)

light: ~**-fingered** /'laɪt'fɪŋɡərd ‖,laɪt'fɪŋɡəd/ *adj* (colloq): **to be** ~**-fingered** tener* (la) mano larga (fam); ~**-hearted** /'laɪt'hɑːrtəd ‖,laɪt'hɑːtɪd/ *adj* alegre, desenfadado; ~**house** *n* faro *m*

lighting /'laɪtɪŋ/ *n* iluminación *f*, (on streets) alumbrado *m*

lightly /'laɪtli/ *adv* **1** **(a)** ‹*touch*› suavemente; ‹*snow*› ligeramente **(b)** ‹*grill/beat*› ligeramente **2** **(a)** (frivolously) a la ligera **(b)** (not severely): **they were let off** ~ los trataron con indulgencia

lightning¹ /'laɪtnɪŋ/ *n*: **a bolt of** ~ un relámpago; **a flash of** ~ un relámpago; **a streak of** ~ un rayo; **like greased** ~ como un relámpago; (*before n*) ~ **conductor** *o* **rod** pararrayos *m*

lightning² *adj* relámpago *adj inv*: **with** ~ **speed** como un rayo

lightweight¹ /'laɪtweɪt/ *adj* ligero, liviano (esp AmL); ‹*writer/performance*› de poco peso

lightweight² *n* (in boxing, wrestling) peso *m* ligero; (minor figure) persona *f* de poco peso

light year *n* año *m* luz

likable /'laɪkəbəl/ *adj* agradable, simpático

like¹ /laɪk/ *vt* **1** (enjoy, be fond of): **I** ~ **tennis** me gusta el tenis; **she** ~**s him, but she doesn't love him** le resulta simpático pero no lo quiere; **do as** *o* **what you** ~ haz lo que quieras; **I** ~ **dancing** me gusta bailar; **I don't** ~ **to mention it, but …** no me gusta (tener que) decírtelo pero …
2 (in requests, wishes) querer*; **we would just** ~ **to say how grateful we are** queríamos decirle lo agradecidos que estamos; **would you** ~ **a cup of tea?** ¿quieres una taza de té?
■ ~ *vi* querer*; **if you** ~ si quieres

like² *n* **1** (sth liked): **her/his** ~**s and dislikes** sus preferencias **2** (similar thing, person) **the** ~: **judges, lawyers and the** ~ jueces, abogados y (otra) gente por el estilo; **I've never heard the** ~ **(of this)** nunca he oído cosa igual

like³ *adj* (dated *or* frml) parecido

like⁴ *prep* **1** **(a)** (similar to) como; **what's she** ~? ¿cómo es?; **she's very** ~ **her mother** se parece mucho a su madre **(b)** (typical of): **that's not** ~ **her** es muy raro en ella; **it's just** ~ **you to think of food** ¡típico!, ¡cuándo no!; ¡tú pensando en comida! **2** (indicating manner): ~ **this/that** así; **to run** ~ **mad** correr como un loco **3** (such as, for example) como

like⁵ *conj* (crit) **(a)** (as if): **she looks** ~ **she knows**

what she's doing parece que sabe lo que hace; **they stared at him** ~ **he was crazy** se quedaron mirándolo como si estuviera loco **(b)** (as, in same way) como

-like /laɪk/ *suff*: **prison**~ parecido a una prisión; **snake**~ *(appearance)* (como) de serpiente; ‹*movement*› serpenteante

likeable *adj* ▶ LIKABLE

likelihood /'laɪklihʊd/ *n* probabilidad *f*, posibilidad *f*; **there is every** ~ **that she'll agree** es muy probable que acepte

likely¹ /'laɪkli/ *adj* **-lier, -liest** **(a)** (probable) ‹*outcome/winner*› probable; **it's more than** ~ **that she's out** lo más seguro es que no esté; **a** ~ **story!** (iro) ¡cuéntame otra! (iró); **it is** ~ **to be a tough match** lo más probable es que sea un partido difícil **(b)** (promising): **she's the most** ~ **applicant** es la candidata con más posibilidades; **this is a** ~ **place to find a telephone** aquí tiene que haber un teléfono

likely² *adv*: **most** ~ **she'll forget** lo más probable es que se olvide; **not** ~! (colloq) ¡ni hablar! (fam)

liken /'laɪkən/ *vt* **to** ~ **sth/sb** TO **sth/sb** comparar algo/a algn CON *or* A algo/algn

likeness /'laɪknəs ‖'laɪknɪs/ *n* **(a)** (resemblance) parecido *m* **(b)** (referring to a portrait): **it's a good** ~ es un buen retrato

likewise /'laɪkwaɪz/ *adv* **(a)** (in the same way) asimismo **(b)** (the same): **to do** ~ hacer* lo mismo

liking /'laɪkɪŋ/ *n* (fondness) ~ (FOR sth) afición *f* (A algo); **to take a** ~ **to sb/sth** tomarle *or* (esp Esp) cogerle* simpatía a algn/gusto a algo **(b)** (satisfaction) gusto *m*; **to be to sb's** ~ ser* del gusto de algn

lilac /'laɪlək/ *n* **(a)** ~ (**bush**) lila *f*, lilo *m*; (*before n*) ~ **flower** lila *f* **(b)** (color) lila *m*; (*before n*) lila *adj inv*

lilt /lɪlt/ *n* (of song, tune) cadencia *f*; **to speak with a** ~ hablar con un tono cantarín

lilting /'lɪltɪŋ/ *adj* ‹*voice*› cantarín, musical; ‹*melody*› cadencioso

lily /'lɪli/ *n* (*pl* **lilies**) (Bot) liliácea *f*; (white ~) azucena *f*, lirio *m* blanco

lily-of-the-valley /'lɪliəvðə'væli/ *n* (*pl* **lilies-of-the-valley**) lirio *m* de los valles, muguete *m*

limb /lɪm/ *n* **(a)** (Anat) miembro *m*; **to tear sb** ~ **from** ~ despedazar* a algn **(b)** (of tree) rama *f* (*principal*); **to go out on a** ~ aventurarse

limber up /'lɪmbər ‖'lɪmbə(r)/ [*v* + *adv*] hacer* ejercicios de calentamiento

lime /laɪm/ *n* **1** (calcium oxide) cal *f* **2** **(a)** (fruit) lima *f* **(b)** (tree) limero *m*, lima *f* **(c)** (color) verde *m* lima; (*before n*) verde lima *adj inv* **3** (linden) (BrE) tilo *m*

lime: ~**-green** /'laɪm'ɡriːn/ *adj* (*pred* ~ **green**) verde lima *adj inv*; ~**light** *n*: **to be in the** ~**light** estar* en primer plano; **to steal the** ~**light** acaparar la atención del público

limerick /'lɪmərɪk/ *n*: poema humorístico de cinco versos

limestone /'laɪmstəʊn/ *n* (piedra *f*) caliza *f*

limit¹ /'lɪmət ‖'lɪmɪt/ *n* **1** **(a)** (boundary) límite ⋯⊹

m **(b)** (furthest extent): **she pushes herself to the ~** se esfuerza al máximo; **that's the ~!** (colloq) ¡es el colmo! (fam) **2** (restriction, maximum) límite *m*

limit² *vt* limitar; **to ~ oneself TO sth/-ING** limitarse A algo/+ INF

limitation /ˌlɪməˈteɪʃən ‖ ˌlɪmɪˈteɪʃən/ *n* limitación *f*

limited /ˈlɪmətəd ‖ ˈlɪmɪtɪd/ *adj* **(a)** ⟨*number/ experience/scope*⟩ limitado **(b)** (AmE Transp) ⟨*express/train/bus*⟩ semi-directo **(c)** (Busn) ⟨*liability*⟩ limitado; **public ~ company** (BrE) sociedad *f* anónima

limitless /ˈlɪmətləs ‖ ˈlɪmɪtlɪs/ *adj* ilimitado, sin límites

limousine /ˈlɪməziːn, lɪməˈziːn/ *n* limusina *f*

limp¹ /lɪmp/ *vi* cojear, renguear (AmL)

limp² *n* cojera *f*, renguera *f* (AmL); **she walks with a ~** cojea *or* (AmL tb) renguea

limp³ *adj* ⟨*handshake*⟩ flojo; ⟨*lettuce*⟩ mustio; ⟨*hair*⟩ lacio y sin vida

limpet /ˈlɪmpət ‖ ˈlɪmpɪt/ *n* lapa *f*

linden /ˈlɪndən/ *n* (AmE) tilo *m*

line¹ /laɪn/ *n* **1** **(a)** (mark, trace) línea *f*; (Math) recta *f*; **to be on the ~** (colloq) estar* en peligro, peligrar; (before *n*) **~ drawing** dibujo *m* lineal **(b)** (on face, palm) línea *f*; (wrinkle) arruga *f* **2** **(a)** (boundary, border) línea *f*; **the county/state ~** (AmE) (la línea de) la frontera del condado/estado **(b)** (Sport) línea *f*; (before *n*) **~ judge** juez *mf* de línea **(c)** (contour) línea *f* **3** **(a)** (cable, rope) cuerda *f*; (clothes o washing **~**) cuerda (de tender la ropa); (fishing **~**) sedal *m*; **power ~** cable *m* eléctrico **(b)** (Telec) línea *f*; **hold the ~, please** no cuelgue *or* (CS tb) no corte, por favor; **it's a very bad ~** se oye muy mal **4** (Transp) **(a)** (company, service) línea *f*; **shipping ~** línea de transportes marítimos **(b)** (Rail) línea *f*; (track) (BrE) vía *f* **5** **(a)** (path) línea *f*; **it was right in my ~ of vision** me obstruía la visual **(b)** (attitude, policy) postura *f*, línea *f*; **to take a hard ~ (with sb/on sth)** adoptar una postura *or* línea dura (con algn/ con respecto a algo) **(c)** (method, style): **~ of inquiry** línea *f* de investigación; **I was thinking of something along the ~s of ...** pensaba en algo del tipo de ... **6** **(a)** (row) fila *f*; (queue) (AmE) cola *f*; **to wait in ~** (AmE) hacer* cola; **to get in ~** (AmE) ponerse* en la cola; **to cut in ~** (AmE) colarse* (fam), brincarse* *or* saltarse la cola (Méx fam); **in/into ~ with sth**: **the new measures are in ~ with government policy** las nuevas medidas siguen la línea de la política del gobierno; **he needs to be brought into ~** hay que llamarlo al orden **(b)** (series) serie *f*; **he's the latest in a long ~ of radical leaders** es el último de una larga serie de dirigentes radicales **(c)** (succession) línea *f*; **he's next in ~ to the throne** es el siguiente en la línea de sucesión al trono **7** (Mil) línea *f* **8** **(a)** (of text) línea *f*, renglón *m*; (of poem) verso *m*; **to read between the ~s** leer* entre líneas **(b)** **lines** *pl* (Theat): **to learn one's ~s** aprenderse el papel; **he forgot his ~s** se le olvidó de lo que le tocaba decir **(c)** (note): **to drop sb a ~** escribirle* a algn unas líneas

line² *vt* **1** **(a)** ⟨*skirt/box*⟩ forrar **(b)** (form lining along) cubrir* **2** (border): **the avenue is ~d with**

trees la avenida está bordeada de árboles; **crowds ~d the route** cientos de personas estaban alineadas a ambos lados del camino

■ **line up 1** [*v + adv*] (form line, row) ponerse* en fila; (queue up) (AmE) hacer* cola **2** [*v + o + adv, v + adv + o*] **(a)** (form into line) ⟨*soldiers/prisoners*⟩ poner* en fila **(b)** (arrange): **we've a busy program ~d up for you** le tenemos preparada una apretada agenda **(c)** (align) alinear

lineage /ˈlɪniɪdʒ/ *n* linaje *m*

linear /ˈlɪniər ‖ ˈlɪniə(r)/ *adj* lineal

lined /laɪnd/ *adj* **(a)** ⟨*paper*⟩ con renglones *or* (Chi) reglones **(b)** ⟨*jacket/boots/curtains*⟩ forrado **(c)** (Tech) revestido **(d)** ⟨*face/skin*⟩ arrugado

linen /ˈlɪnən/ *n* **1** (cloth) hilo *m*, lino *m* **2** (bed **~**) ropa *f* blanca *or* de cama; (table **~**) mantelerías *fpl*; (before *n*) **~ basket** canasto *m or* cesto *m* de la ropa sucia

liner /ˈlaɪnər ‖ ˈlaɪnə(r)/ *n* **1** (ship) buque *m* (de pasaje *or* pasajeros); (ocean **~**) transatlántico *m* **2** **(a)** (lining) forro *m*; (dust)bin **~** (BrE) bolsa *f* de la basura **(b)** (of record) (AmE) funda *f*, carátula *f*

line: ~sman /ˈlaɪnzmən/ *n* (*pl* **-men** /-mən/) (Sport) juez *m* de línea; **~up** *n* **(a)** (Sport) alineación *f*; **the band's original ~up** la integración original del grupo **(b)** (of suspects) (AmE) rueda *f* de identificación *or* de sospechosos

linger /ˈlɪŋɡər ‖ ˈlɪŋɡə(r)/ *vi* **(a)** (delay leaving) quedarse (un rato) **(b)** **~ (on)** ⟨*aftertaste/smell*⟩ persistir; ⟨*tradition*⟩ perdurar, sobrevivir **(c)** (take one's time): **her eyes ~ed on the child** se quedó largo rato mirando al niño; **they ~ed over their coffee** se entretuvieron tomando el café

lingering *pres p* persistente, que no desaparece

lingerie /ˈlɑːnʒəˈreɪ ‖ ˈlænʒəri/ *n* lencería *f*

linguist /ˈlɪŋɡwəst ‖ ˈlɪŋɡwɪst/ *n* lingüista *mf*

linguistic /lɪŋˈɡwɪstɪk/ *adj* lingüístico

linguistics /lɪŋˈɡwɪstɪks/ *n* (+ *sing vb*) lingüística *f*

lining /ˈlaɪnɪŋ/ *n* forro *m*

link¹ /lɪŋk/ *n* **1** **(a)** (in chain) eslabón *m* **(b)** ▶ CUFF LINK **2** **(a)** (connection) conexión *f* **(b)** (tie, bond) vínculo *m*, lazo *m* **(c)** (Telec, Transp) conexión *f*, enlace *m*

link² *vt* **(a)** ⟨*components*⟩ unir; ⟨*terminals*⟩ conectar; **to ~ arms** tomarse *or* (esp Esp) cogerse* del brazo **(b)** ⟨*buildings/towns*⟩ unir, conectar **(c)** ⟨*facts/events*⟩ relacionar

■ **link up 1** [*v + adv*] conectar; ⟨*spacecraft*⟩ acoplarse **2** [*v + o + adv, v + adv + o*] conectar

links /lɪŋks/ *n* (*pl* **~**) (+ *sing o pl vb*) campo *m* de golf (*esp a orillas del mar*)

linkup /ˈlɪŋkʌp/ *n* **(a)** (connection) conexión *f*; (of spacecraft) acoplamiento *m* **(b)** (Rad, TV) conexión *f*, enlace *m*

linoleum /lɪˈnəʊliəm/ *n* linóleo *m*

linseed /ˈlɪnsiːd/ *n* linaza *f*; (before *n*) **~ oil** aceite *m* de linaza

lint /lɪnt/ *n* hilas *fpl*

lion /ˈlaɪən/ *n* león *m*

lioness /ˈlaɪənəs ‖ ˈlaɪənes/ *n* leona *f*

lion tamer /ˈteɪmər ‖ ˈteɪmə(r)/ *n* domador, -dora *m,f* de leones

lip /lɪp/ *n* **(a)** (Anat) labio *m* **(b)** (of cup, tray) borde *m*

lip: ~ **gloss** n brillo m de labias; ~**read** (past & past p **-read**) vi /-red/) leer* los labios; ~ **salve** n bálsamo m labial; ~ **service** n: he just pays ~ service to feminism es feminista de los dientes para afuera; ~**stick** n (a) (stick) lápiz m or barra f de labios, lápiz m labial (AmL), pintalabios m (Esp fam) (b) (substance) rouge m

liquefy /'lɪkwəfaɪ ‖'lɪkwɪfaɪ/ **-fies, -fying, -fied** vi licuarse*
■ ~ vt licuar*

liqueur /lɪ'kɜːr ‖lɪ'kjʊə(r)/ n licor m

liquid[1] /'lɪkwəd ‖'lɪkwɪd/ n líquido m

liquid[2] adj líquido

liquidation /ˌlɪkwə'deɪʃən ‖ˌlɪkwɪ'deɪʃən/ n liquidación f

liquid crystal display n pantalla f de cristal líquido

liquidize /'lɪkwədaɪz ‖'lɪkwɪdaɪz/ vt licuar*

liquidizer /'lɪkwədaɪzər ‖'lɪkwɪdaɪzə(r)/ n (BrE) licuadora f

liquor /'lɪkər ‖'lɪkə(r)/ n alcohol m, bebidas fpl alcohólicas; (before n) ~ **cabinet** (AmE) mueble-bar m

liquorice (BrE) ▶ LICORICE

liquor store n (AmE) ≈ tienda f de vinos y licores, botillería f (Chi)

Lisbon /'lɪzbən/ n Lisboa f

lisp[1] /lɪsp/ n ceceo m

lisp[2] vi cecear

list[1] /lɪst/ n lista f

list[2] vt (a) (enumerate) hacer* una lista de; (verbally) enumerar (b) ⟨securities/stocks⟩ cotizar*
■ ~ vi (Naut) escorar

listen /'lɪsn/ vi escuchar; **to** ~ **TO sth/sb** escuchar algo/a algn

listener /'lɪsnər ‖'lɪsnə(r)/ n (a) (Rad) oyente mf, radioyente mf (b) (in conversation): **he's a good** ~ es una persona que sabe escuchar

listing /'lɪstɪŋ/ n lista f; ~**s magazine** guía f de espectáculos, ≈ guía f del ocio (en Esp)

listless /'lɪstləs ‖'lɪstlɪs/ adj (lacking enthusiasm) apático; (lacking energy) lánguido

lit /lɪt/ past & past p of LIGHT[4]

litany /'lɪtəni/ n (pl **-nies**) letanía f

liter, (BrE) **litre** /'liːtər ‖'liːtə(r)/ n litro m

literacy /'lɪtərəsi/ n alfabetismo m

literal /'lɪtərəl/ adj literal

literally /'lɪtərəli/ adv literalmente; **I didn't mean it** ~ no lo decía en sentido literal

literary /'lɪtərəri ‖'lɪtrərəri/ adj literario

literate /'lɪtərət/ adj alfabetizado

literature /'lɪtərətʃur ‖'lɪtrətʃə(r)/ n (a) (art) literatura f (b) (promotional material) folletos mpl

lithe /laɪð/ adj **lither, lithest** ágil

lithograph /'lɪθəgræf ‖'lɪθəgrɑːf/ n litografía f

Lithuania /ˌlɪθju'eɪniə/ n Lituania f

Lithuanian /ˌlɪθju'eɪniən/ adj lituano

litigation /ˌlɪtə'geɪʃən ‖ˌlɪtɪ'geɪʃən/ n litigio m

litmus /'lɪtməs/: ~ **paper** n papel m (de) tornasol; ~ **test** n (Chem) prueba f de acidez or de tornasol

litre /'liːtər ‖'liːtə(r)/ n (BrE) ▶ LITER

litter[1] /'lɪtər ‖'lɪtə(r)/ n [1] (refuse) basura f [2] (offspring) (Zool) camada f, cría f [3] (for horses, cows) lecho m de paja; (for cats) arena f higiénica

litter[2] vt: newspapers ~ed the floor el suelo estaba cubierto de papeles; **to be** ~**ed WITH sth** estar* lleno DE algo

litter: ~ **bin** n (BrE) papelera f or (AmL tb) papelero m or (Col) caneca f; ~**bug** n: persona que tira basura en lugares públicos; ~ **lout** n (BrE) ▶ ~BUG

little[1] /'lɪtl/ adj
I (comp **littler** /'lɪtlər ‖'lɪtlə(r)/; superl **littlest** /'lɪtləst ‖'lɪtlɪst/) (small, young) pequeño, chico (esp AmL); **a** ~ **while** un ratito; **my** ~ **sister/brother** mi hermanita/hermanito
II (comp **less**; superl **least**) (a) (not much) poco; **there is very** ~ **bread left** queda muy poco pan (b) **a little** (some) un poco de

little[2] pron (comp **less**; superl **least**) (a) (not much) poco, -ca; ~ **by** ~ poco a poco (b) **a little** (some) un poco, algo

little[3] adv (comp **less**; superl **least**) poco; ~ **did he know that ...** lo que menos se imaginaba era que ...; **a little** (somewhat) un poco; **I'm feeling a** ~ **tired** estoy algo or un poco cansado

live[1] /lɪv/ vi vivir; **she** ~**d to be 100** llegó a cumplir 100 años; **she had three months to** ~ le quedaban tres meses de vida; **where do you** ~? ¿dónde vives?; **long** ~ **the king!** ¡viva el rey!; ~ **and let** ~ (set phrase) vive y deja vivir a los demás
■ ~ vt vivir; **she** ~**s a happy life** lleva una vida feliz, vive feliz; **to** ~ **life to the full** vivir la vida al máximo
■ **live down** [v + o + adv, v + adv + o]: **if they see you wearing that, you'll never** ~ **it down** si te ven con eso no lo van a olvidar nunca
■ **live for** [v + prep + o]: **she** ~**s for her work** vive para su trabajo; **I've nothing left to** ~ **for** ya no tengo nada por lo que vivir
■ **live off** [v + prep + o] (a) (be supported by) ⟨family/friends⟩ vivir a costa de; ⟨crime/the land⟩ vivir de (b) (feed on) ⟨fruits/seeds⟩ alimentarse de
■ **live on** [1] [v + adv] «memory» seguir* presente; «tradition» seguir* existiendo [2] [v + prep + o] (a) (feed on) alimentarse de (b) (support oneself with): **she** ~**s on $75 a week** vive con 75 dólares a la semana
■ **live through** [v + prep + o] ⟨war/experience⟩ vivir
■ **live together** [v + adv] (a) (cohabit) vivir juntos (b) (coexist) convivir
■ **live up** [v + o + adv]: **to** ~ **it up** (colloq) darse* la gran vida (fam)
■ **live up to** [v + adv + prep + o]: **it didn't** ~ **up to its reputation** no estuvo a la altura de su reputación; **they** ~ **up to their name** hacen honor a su nombre

live[2] /laɪv/ adj [1] (alive) vivo [2] (of current interest) ⟨issue⟩ candente [3] (Rad, TV): **the show was** ~ el programa era en directo; **the program is recorded before a** ~ **audience** el programa se graba con público en la sala

live[3] /laɪv/ adv ⟨broadcast⟩ en directo

live-in /'lɪvɪn/ adj (before n) ⟨staff⟩ residente; ⟨nanny/maid⟩ con cama, de planta (Méx), puertas adentro (Chi); **she has a** ~ **lover** su amante vive con ella

livelihood /ˈlaɪvlihʊd/ n (no pl): farming is their ∼ viven de la agricultura; **to earn one's ∼** ganarse la vida

lively /ˈlaɪvli/ adj **-lier, -liest** ⟨place/debate⟩ animado; ⟨music⟩ alegre; ⟨account⟩ vívido

liven up /ˈlaɪvən/ **1** [v + adv] animarse **2** [v + o + adv, v + adv + o] animar

liver /ˈlɪvər ‖ ˈlɪvə(r)/ n hígado m; (before n) ⟨transplant⟩ de hígado; ∼ **disease** enfermedad f del hígado

lives /laɪvz/ pl of LIFE

livestock /ˈlaɪvstɑːk ‖ ˈlaɪvstɒk/ n (+ sing or pl vb) animales mpl (de cría); (cattle) ganado m

livid /ˈlɪvəd ‖ ˈlɪvɪd/ adj **1** (furious) (colloq) furioso **2** ⟨bruise⟩ amoratado; ⟨face⟩ lívido

living¹ /ˈlɪvɪŋ/ n **1** (livelihood) (no pl): **to earn o make one's ∼** ganarse la vida; **to work for a ∼** trabajar para vivir; **what does he do for a ∼?** ¿en qué trabaja? **2** (style of life) vida f; (before n) ⟨space/area⟩ destinado a vivienda; ∼ **standards** nivel m de vida

living² adj (before n) vivo

living room n sala f (de estar) , living m (esp AmS), salón m (esp Esp)

lizard /ˈlɪzərd ‖ ˈlɪzəd/ n lagarto m; (wall ∼) lagartija f

'll /l/ (a) = **will** (b) = **shall**

llama /ˈlɑːmə/ n llama f

LLB n = **Bachelor of Laws**

lo /ləʊ/ interj (arch or hum): ∼ **and behold** ¡y quién lo iba a decir!

load¹ /ləʊd/ n **1** (cargo, burden) carga f; **four ∼s of washing** cuatro lavados or (Esp) coladas **2** (often pl) (colloq) (much, many) cantidad f, montón m (fam); **the play is a ∼ of rubbish** la obra es una porquería (fam) **3** (Civil Eng) carga f; ⊙ **maximum load 15 tons** peso máximo: 15 toneladas

load² vt/i cargar*
■ **load up 1** [v + o + adv, v + adv + o] cargar* **2** [v + adv] cargar*

loaded /ˈləʊdəd ‖ ˈləʊdɪd/ adj (a) ⟨vehicle/gun/camera⟩ cargado (b) (richly provided) (pred) **to be ∼ WITH sth** estar* repleto DE algo (c) (weighted) ⟨dice⟩ cargado; ⟨question⟩ tendencioso

loaf¹ /ləʊf/ n (pl **loaves**): **a ∼** (of bread) un pan; (of French bread) una barra de pan, una flauta (CS); (baked in tin) un pan de molde

loaf² vi (colloq): **to ∼** (around o about) holgazanear

loan¹ /ləʊn/ n préstamo m

loan² vt prestar

loath /ləʊθ/ adj (pred) **to be ∼ to + INF** resistirse A + INF

loathe /ləʊð/ vt odiar, detestar

loathsome /ˈləʊðsəm/ adj repugnante

loaves /ləʊvz/ pl of LOAF¹

lob¹ /lɑːb ‖ lɒb/ vt **-bb-** lanzar* por lo alto

lob² n globo m, lob m

lobby¹ /ˈlɑːbi ‖ ˈlɒbi/ n (pl **-bies**) **1** (entrance hall) vestíbulo m; (in theater) foyer m **2** (pressure group) grupo m de presión

lobby² **-bies, -bying, -bied** vt ejercer* presión sobre
■ ∼ vi **to ∼ FOR sth** ejercer* presión para obtener algo

lobe /ləʊb/ n (ear∼) lóbulo m (de la oreja)

lobster /ˈlɑːbstər ‖ ˈlɒbstə(r)/ n langosta f, bogavante m (Esp)

local¹ /ˈləʊkəl/ adj **1** ⟨dialect/newspaper⟩ local; ⟨council/election⟩ ≈municipal; **a ∼ call** una llamada urbana; **he's a ∼ man** es de aquí (or de allí) **2** (Med) ⟨anesthetic⟩ local; ⟨infection⟩ localizado

local² n (a) (inhabitant): **he's not a ∼** no es de aquí (or de allí); **the ∼s say it's true** los (vecinos) del lugar dicen que es verdad (b) (pub) (BrE colloq): **our ∼** el bar de nuestro barrio (or de nuestra zona etc)

locale /ləʊˈkæl ‖ ləʊˈkɑːl/ n escenario m

local government n ≈administración f municipal; (before n) ⟨elections⟩ ≈municipal

locality /ləʊˈkæləti/ n (pl **-ties**) (frml) localidad f

localize /ˈləʊkəlaɪz/ vt localizar*

locally /ˈləʊkəli/ adv ⟨live/work⟩ en la zona

locate /ˈləʊkeɪt ‖ ləʊˈkeɪt/ vt **1** (find) ⟨fault/leak⟩ localizar*, ubicar* (esp AmL) **2** (position) ⟨building/business⟩ situar*, ubicar* (esp AmL)

location /ləʊˈkeɪʃən/ n **1** (position) posición f, ubicación f (esp AmL) **2** (Cin) lugar m de filmación; **we were filming on ∼ in Italy** estábamos rodando los exteriores en Italia

loch /lɑːk, lɑːx ‖ lɒk, lɒx/ n lago

lock¹ /lɑːk ‖ lɒk/ n **1** (device) cerradura f, chapa f (AmL) **2** (on canal) esclusa f **3** (of hair) mechón m

lock² vt ⟨door/car⟩ cerrar* (con llave); **to ∼ sb in a room** encerrar* a algn en una habitación
■ **lock in** [v + o + adv, v + adv + o] encerrar*
■ **lock out** [v + o + adv, v + adv + o]: **I ∼ed myself out (of the house)** me quedé afuera sin llaves
■ **lock up** [v + o + adv, v + adv + o] (a) ⟨valuables⟩ guardar bajo llave; ⟨person⟩ encerrar* (b) ⟨house/shop⟩ cerrar* con llave

locker /ˈlɑːkər ‖ ˈlɒkə(r)/ n armario m, locker m (AmL); (at bus, railway station) (casilla f de la) consigna f automática

locker room n (esp AmE) vestuario m

locket /ˈlɑːkət ‖ ˈlɒkɪt/ n relicario m

lock: ∼out n cierre m patronal, paro m patronal (AmL); **∼smith** n cerrajero, -ra m,f

locomotive /ˌləʊkəˈməʊtɪv/ n locomotora f

locust /ˈləʊkəst/ n langosta f

lode /ləʊd/ n veta f, filón m

lodge¹ /lɑːdʒ ‖ lɒdʒ/ n **1** (a) (for gatekeeper) (BrE) casa f del guarda (b) (for porter) portería f (c) (on private estate) pabellón m (d) (at resort) (AmE) hotel m **2** (branch, meeting place) logia f

lodge ····❖ **longstanding** ····

lodge² vt 1 ⟨appeal⟩ interponer*; ⟨complaint⟩ presentar 2 (deposit) depositar
■ ~ vi 1 (become stuck): **the bullet had ~d in his spine** la bala se le había alojado en la columna 2 (live as lodger) alojarse, hospedarse

lodger /'lɑːdʒər ‖ 'lɒdʒə(r)/ n inquilino, -na m,f (de una habitación en una casa particular)

lodging /'lɑːdʒɪŋ ‖ 'lɒdʒɪŋ/ n **(a)** (accommodations) alojamiento m **(b) lodgings** pl (rented): **to live in ~s** vivir en una habitación alquilada (or en una pensión etc)

loft /lɔːft ‖ lɒft/ n (BrE) desván m, altillo m (esp AmL), zarzo m (Col)

loftily /'lɔːftəli ‖ 'lɒftɪli/ adv con altivez, altaneramente

lofty /'lɔːfti ‖ 'lɒfti/ adj **-tier, -tiest (a)** (elevated) ⟨ideals/sentiments⟩ noble, elevado **(b)** (haughty) altivo, altanero **(c)** (high) (liter) alto, majestuoso (liter)

log¹ /lɔːg ‖ lɒg/ n 1 (wood) tronco m; (as fuel) leño m; **to sleep like a ~** dormir* como un tronco (fam) 2 (record) diario m 3 (Math) logaritmo m

log² -gg- vt ⟨speed/position/time⟩ registrar, anotar; ⟨call⟩ registrar
■ **log in, log on** [v + adv] (Comput) entrar (al sistema)
■ **log off, log out** [v + adv] (Comput) salir* (del sistema)

loganberry /'lɔːgənˌberi ‖ 'lɔːgənbəri/ n (pl -ries) frambuesa f de Logan

logarithm /'lɔːgərɪðəm ‖ 'lɒgərɪðəm/ n logaritmo m

logbook /'lɔːgbʊk ‖ 'lɒgbʊk/ n (register) diario m; (Naut) diario m de navegación or de a bordo; (Aviat) diario m de vuelo

loggerheads /'lɔːgərhedz ‖ 'lɒgəhedz/ pl n: **they were constantly at ~** siempre estaban en desacuerdo

logic /'lɑːdʒɪk ‖ 'lɒdʒɪk/ n lógica f

logical /'lɑːdʒɪkəl ‖ 'lɒdʒɪkəl/ adj lógico

logistics /lə'dʒɪstɪks/ n **(a)** (Mil) (+ sing vb) logística f **(b)** (practicalities) (+ pl vb) problemas mpl logísticos

logo /'ləʊgəʊ, 'lɑː- ‖ 'ləʊgəʊ/ n (pl **logos**) logo m

loin /lɔɪn/ n **(a)** (meat) lomo m **(b) loins** pl (Anat) (liter) entrañas fpl (liter)

loincloth /'lɔɪnklɔːθ ‖ 'lɔɪnklɒθ/ n taparrabos m

loiter /'lɔɪtər ‖ 'lɔɪtə(r)/ vi perder* el tiempo

lollipop /'lɑːlipɑːp ‖ 'lɒlipɒp/ n piruleta f or (Esp) Chupa Chups®, chupachup(s) m or (Andes, Méx) paleta f or (RPI) chupetín m or (Col) colombina f or (Chi, Per) chupete m

lolly /'lɑːli ‖ 'lɒli/ n (pl **-lies**) (BrE) (ice ~) paleta f (helada) or (Esp) polo m or (RPI) palito m or (CS) chupete m helado

London /'lʌndən/ n Londres; (before n) londinense

lone /ləʊn/ adj solitario; ⟨explorer/sailor⟩ en solitario

loneliness /'ləʊnlinəs ‖ 'ləʊnlinɪs/ n soledad f

lonely /'ləʊnli/ adj **-lier, -liest (a)** (feeling alone): **to feel ~** sentirse* solo **(b)** (isolated) solitario, aislado

loner /'ləʊnər ‖ 'ləʊnə(r)/ n: **she's a bit of a ~** le gusta estar sola

lonesome /'ləʊnsəm/ adj (esp AmE) ► LONELY

long¹ /lɔːŋ ‖ lɒŋ/ adj **longer** /'lɔːŋgər ‖ 'lɒŋgə(r)/, **longest** /'lɔːŋgəst ‖ 'lɒŋgɪst/ 1 (in space) ⟨distance/hair/list⟩ largo; **how ~ do you want the skirt?** ¿cómo quieres la falda de larga?; **the wall is 200 m ~** el muro mide 200 m de largo; **the book is over 300 pages ~** el libro tiene más de 300 páginas 2 (in time) largo; **two months isn't ~ enough** dos meses no son suficientes; **she's been gone a ~ time** hace tiempo que se fue

long² adv **-er, -est** 1 (in time): **how ~ have you been living here?** ¿cuánto hace que vives aquí?; **people live ~er now** ahora la gente vive más (años); **it won't be ~ before they get here** no tardarán en llegar; **not ~ afterwards** poco después; **not ~ ago** no hace mucho 2 **(a)** (in phrases) **before long: you'll be an aunt before ~** dentro de poco serás tía; **for long: she wasn't gone for ~** no estuvo fuera mucho tiempo; **no longer, not any longer: I can't stand it any ~er** ya no aguanto más; **they no ~er live here** ya no viven aquí **(b) as long as, so long as** (as conj) (for the period) mientras; (providing that) con tal de que (+ subj); **for as ~ as I can remember** desde que tengo memoria

long³ vi **to ~ to +** INF estar* deseando + INF
■ **long for** [v + prep + o] ⟨mother/friend⟩ echar de menos, extrañar (esp AmL); **she ~ed for Friday to arrive** estaba deseando que llegara el viernes

long-distance¹ /'lɔːŋ'dɪstəns ‖ ˌlɒŋ'dɪstəns/ adj ⟨truck driver⟩ que hace largos recorridos; ⟨train⟩ de largo recorrido; ⟨race/runner⟩ de fondo; **a ~ telephone call** una llamada de larga distancia, una conferencia (interurbana) (Esp)

long-distance² adv (esp AmE): **to call ~** hacer* una llamada de larga distancia, poner* una conferencia (Esp)

longevity /lɑːn'dʒevəti ‖ lɒn'dʒevəti/ n (fml) longevidad f

long: ~-haired /'lɔːŋ'herd ‖ ˌlɒŋ'heəd/ adj de pelo largo; **~hand** n: **in ~hand** en escritura normal (no en taquigrafía); **~-haul** /'lɔːŋ'hɔːl ‖ ˌlɒŋ'hɔːl/ adj (before n) de larga distancia

longing /'lɔːŋɪŋ ‖ 'lɒŋɪŋ/ n (nostalgia) añoranza f; (desire) vivo deseo m

longitude /'lɑːndʒətuːd ‖ 'lɒŋgɪtjuːd, 'lɒndʒɪtjuːd/ n longitud f

long: ~ johns /dʒɑːnz ‖ dʒɒnz/ pl n calzoncillos mpl largos; **~ jump** n salto m de longitud, salto m (en) largo (AmL); **~-lost** /'lɔːŋ'lɔːst ‖ 'lɒŋlɒst/ adj (before n): **she had a ~-lost uncle in Australia** tenía un tío en Australia a quien había perdido de vista hacía mucho tiempo; **~-playing record** /'lɔːŋ'pleɪŋ ‖ 'lɒŋˌpleɪŋ/ n disco m de larga duración; **~-range** /'lɔːŋ'reɪndʒ ‖ 'lɒŋreɪndʒ/ adj (before n) ⟨missile⟩ de largo alcance; ⟨aircraft⟩ para vuelos largos; **~-running** /'lɔːŋ'rʌnɪŋ ‖ 'lɒŋˌrʌnɪŋ/ adj ⟨musical/farce⟩ que lleva tiempo en cartelera; ⟨feud/controversy⟩ que viene (or venía etc) de largo; **~shoreman** /'lɔːŋ'ʃɔːrmən ‖ 'lɒŋˌʃɔːmən/ n (pl **-men** /-mən/) (AmE) estibador m, changador m (RPI); **~sighted** /'lɔːŋ'saɪtəd ‖ 'lɒŋ'saɪtɪd/ adj hipermétrope; **~-sleeved** /'lɔːŋ'sliːvd ‖ 'lɒŋsliːvd/ adj de manga larga; **~standing** /'lɔːŋ'stændɪŋ

‖ˌlɒŋˈstændɪŋ/ adj antiguo, que viene (or venía etc) de largo; ~-**suffering** /ˈlɔːŋˈsʌfərɪŋ/ ‖ˌlɒŋˈsʌfərɪŋ/ adj sufrido; ~-**term** /ˈlɔːŋˈtɜːrm ‖ˈlɒŋtɜːm/ adj (usu before n) **(a)** (in the future) ⟨effects/benefits⟩ a largo plazo **(b)** (for a long period) ⟨solution⟩ duradero; ⟨effects⟩ prolongado; ⟨unemployment⟩ de larga duración; ~ **wave** n onda f larga; ~-**winded** /ˈlɔːŋˈwɪndɪd ‖ˌlɒŋˈwɪndɪd/ adj ⟨speech/article⟩ denso, prolijo

loo /luː/ n (BrE colloq) baño m (esp AmL), váter m (Esp fam)

look¹ /lʊk/ n **1** (glance) mirada f; **to have o take a ~** at sth/sb echarle un vistazo a algo/algn **2** (search, examination): **have a ~ for my pipe, will you?** mira a ver si me encuentras la pipa, por favor; **do you mind if I take a ~ around?** ¿le importa si echo un vistazo? **3** **(a)** (expression) cara f **(b)** (appearance) aire m; **I don't like the ~ of his friend** no me gusta el aspecto or (fam) la pinta de su amigo **(c)** (Clothing) moda f, look m **(d)** **looks** pl (beauty) belleza f; **she was attracted by his good ~s** la atrajo lo guapo or (AmL tb) lo buen mozo que era

look² vi **I** **1** (see, glance) mirar; **I ~ed around (behind)** me volví a mirar or miré hacia atrás; (all around) miré a mi alrededor; **to ~ away** apartar la vista; **to ~ down** (lower eyes) bajar la vista; (from tower, clifftop) mirar hacia abajo; **~ out (of) the window** mira por la ventana; **to ~ up** (raise eyes) levantar la vista; (toward ceiling, sky) mirar hacia arriba; **to ~ on the bright side of sth** ver* el lado bueno or positivo de algo **2** (search, investigate) mirar, buscar* **II** (seem, appear): **he ~s well** tiene buena cara; **he ~s like his father** se parece a su padre; **I wanted to ~ my best** quería estar lo mejor posible

■ ~ vt mirar; **to ~ sb up and down** mirar a algn de arriba (a) abajo; **~ where you're going!** ¡mira por dónde vas!

■ **look after** [v + prep + o] **(a)** (care for) ⟨invalid/child/animal⟩ cuidar (de); ⟨guest⟩ atender* **(b)** (keep watch on) cuidar **(c)** (be responsible for) encargarse* de

■ **look ahead** [v + adv] (in space) mirar hacia adelante; (into the future) mirar hacia el futuro

■ **look at** [v + prep + o] **1** ⟨person/picture⟩ mirar **2** (consider) considerar; **~ at it from my point of view** míralo desde mi punto de vista; **the program ~s at university life** el programa enfoca la vida universitaria **3** (check) ⟨patient/arm⟩ examinar; ⟨car/pump⟩ revisar

■ **look back** [v + adv] **(a)** (in space) mirar (hacia) atrás **(b)** (into the past): **~ing back, it seems foolish** mirándolo ahora, parece una locura; **the program ~s back over the last 20 years** el programa es una retrospectiva de los últimos veinte años

■ **look down on** [v + adv + prep + o] mirar por encima del hombro a

■ **look for** [v + prep + o] buscar*

■ **look forward to** [v + adv + prep + o]: **I'm ~ing forward to my birthday** estoy deseando que llegue mi cumpleaños; **I'm really ~ing forward to the trip** tengo muchas ganas de hacer el viaje; **I ~ forward to hearing from you soon** (Corresp) esperando tener pronto noticias suyas

■ **look into** [v + prep + o] ⟨matter/case⟩ investigar*; ⟨possibility⟩ estudiar

■ **look on** [v + adv] mirar

■ **look out** [v + adv] **(a)** (be careful) tener* cuidado; **~ out!** ¡cuidado! **(b)** (overlook) **to ~ out ON o OVER** sth dar* A algo

■ **look out for** [v + adv + prep + o]: **~ out for her at the station** fíjate a ver si la ves en la estación; **we were warned to ~ out for thieves** nos advirtieron que tuviéramos cuidado con los ladrones

■ **look over** [v + o + adv, v + adv + o] ⟨work/contract⟩ revisar; ⟨building⟩ inspeccionar

■ **look to** [v + prep + o] (rely on): **they are ~ing to you for guidance** esperan que tú los guíes

■ **look up** **1** [v + o + adv, v + adv + o] **(a)** ⟨word⟩ buscar* (en el diccionario) **(b)** ⟨person⟩ ir* a ver **2** [v + adv] (improve) mejorar

■ **look up to** [v + adv + prep + o] admirar

look-alike /ˈlʊkəˌlaɪk/ n (colloq) (person) doble mf

looking glass /ˈlʊkɪŋˌglæs ‖ˈlʊkɪŋˌglɑːs/ n (dated) espejo m

lookout /ˈlʊkaʊt/ n **(a)** (watch) (no pl): **to be on the ~ for** sth/sb andar* a la caza de algo/algn **(b)** (person) (Mil) vigía mf

loom¹ /luːm/ n telar m

loom² vi **(a)** (be imminent) avecinarse **(b)** (look threatening): **the mountain ~ed high above them** la montaña surgió imponente ante ellos; **the problem ~ed large in his mind** el problema dominaba sus pensamientos

■ **loom up** [v + adv]: **a figure ~ed up in the darkness** una figura surgió de entre las tinieblas

loop¹ /luːp/ n **1** **(a)** (shape) curva f; (in river) meandro m **(b)** (in string) lazada f **(c)** (in sewing) presilla f **(d)** (Aviat): **to loop the ~** rizar* el rizo **2** **(a)** (circuit) circuito m cerrado **(b)** (Comput) bucle m

loop² vt: **~ the wool** haz una lazada con la lana; **I ~ed the dog's lead over the post** enganché la correa del perro en el poste

■ ~ vi ⟨road⟩ serpentear

loophole /ˈluːphəʊl/ n: **a legal ~** una laguna jurídica (que se presta a trampas)

loose¹ /luːs/ adj **looser**, **loosest** **1** **(a)** (not tight) ⟨garment⟩ suelto **(b)** (not secure) ⟨screw/knot⟩ flojo; ⟨thread/end⟩ suelto; ⟨hair⟩ suelto; **to be at a ~ end** no tener* nada que hacer **(c)** (separate, not packaged) ⟨cigarettes⟩ suelto; ⟨tea/lentils⟩ a granel, suelto; **~ change** calderilla f **2** (free) (pred) suelto; **to let o set o turn sb ~** soltar* a algn; **to be on the ~** andar* suelto **3** ⟨definition⟩ poco preciso; ⟨translation⟩ libre

loose² vt (liter) **(a)** ⟨prisoner⟩ poner* en libertad; ⟨horse⟩ soltar* **(b)** ⟨arrow⟩ lanzar*; ⟨violence/wrath⟩ desatar

loose: ~-**fitting** /ˈluːsˈfɪtɪŋ/ adj suelto; ⟨clothes⟩ holgado; ~-**leaf** /ˈluːsˈliːf/ adj ⟨binder⟩ de anillas

loosely /ˈluːsli/ adv **1** (not tightly) ⟨tie/bandage⟩ sin apretar; **the dress fits ~** el vestido no es entallado **2** (not precisely) ⟨define⟩ sin excesivo rigor; ⟨translate⟩ libremente; **~ speaking** (indep) (hablando) en términos generales

loosen /ˈluːsn/ vt **(a)** ⟨tooth⟩ aflojar **(b)** ⟨collar/

knot/bolt⟩ aflojar, soltar*; **she ～ed her grip on the steering wheel** dejó de apretar con tanta fuerza el volante
■ ～ *vi* «*knot/bolt*» aflojarse

loot¹ /luːt/ *n* **(a)** (plunder) botín *m* **(b)** (money) (sl) guita *f* (arg), lana *f* (AmL fam), pasta *f* (Esp fam)

loot² *vt/i* saquear

looter /ˈluːtər ‖ˈluːtə(r)/ *n* saqueador, -dora *m,f*

looting /ˈluːtɪŋ/ *n* saqueo *m*

lop /lɑːp ‖lɒp/ *vt* **-pp-** **(a)** ⟨*tree*⟩ podar **(b)** ～ **(off)** ⟨*branch*⟩ cortar

lope /ləʊp/ *vi* «*wolf/dog*» trotar

lopsided /ˈlɑːpˈsaɪdəd ‖ˌlɒpˈsaɪdɪd/ *adj* **(a)** (not straight) torcido, chueco (AmL) **(b)** (asymmetric) ⟨*face/smile*⟩ torcido; ⟨*shape*⟩ asimétrico

lord /lɔːrd ‖lɔːd/ *n* **1** **(a)** (nobleman) señor *m*, noble *m* **(b) Lord** (in UK) lord *m*; **the (House of) L～s** la cámara de los lores **(c) my L～** (addressing judge) (BrE) (su) señoría **2 Lord** (God): **the L～** el Señor; **the L～'s Prayer** el Padrenuestro

lordship /ˈlɔːrdʃɪp ‖ˈlɔːdʃɪp/ *n*: **His/Your L～** (of or to peers, judges) (su) señoría; (of or to bishops) (su) Ilustrísima

lore /lɔːr ‖lɔː(r)/ *n*: **French peasant ～** las tradiciones rurales francesas

lorry /ˈlɔːri ‖ˈlɒri/ *n* (*pl* **-ries**) (BrE) camión *m*; (*before n*) ⟨*driver*⟩ camionero, -ra *m,f*

lose /luːz/ *vt* (*past & past p* **lost**)
I **1** (mislay) perder*
2 (be deprived of) ⟨*sight/territory/right*⟩ perder*; **to ～ one's voice** quedarse afónico
3 (rid oneself of) ⟨*inhibitions*⟩ perder*; **to ～ weight** adelgazar*, perder* peso
4 (cause to lose) costar*; **their hesitation lost them the contract** la falta de decisión les costó *or* les hizo perder el contrato
5 (let pass) ⟨*time/opportunity*⟩ perder*; **my watch ～s three minutes every day** mi reloj (se) atrasa tres minutos por día
II (fail to win) ⟨*game/battle/election*⟩ perder*
■ ～ *vi* **1** **(a)** (be beaten) «*team/contestant/party*» perder*; **they're losing 3-1** van perdiendo 3 a 1; **to ～ TO sb** perder* FRENTE A algn **(b)** **losing** *pres p* ⟨*team/party*⟩ perdedor
2 (suffer losses) perder*
3 «*watch/clock*» atrasar, atrasarse

loser /ˈluːzər ‖ˈluːzə(r)/ *n* perdedor, -dora *m,f*

loss /lɔːs ‖lɒs/ *n* pérdida *f*; **to be a dead ～** (colloq): **this typewriter is a dead ～** esta máquina de escribir no sirve para nada *or* (fam) es una porquería; **to be at a ～**: **I was at a ～ for words** no supe qué decir; **to cut one's ～es** cortar por lo sano; (Fin) reducir* las pérdidas

lost¹ /lɔːst ‖lɒst/ *past & past p of* LOSE

lost² *adj*
I **1** (mislaid, missing) perdido; **to get ～** perderse*, extraviarse* (frml); **get ～!** (sl) ¡vete al diablo! (fam), ¡andá a pasear! (RPl fam) **2** (wasted) ⟨*time*⟩ perdido; ⟨*opportunity*⟩ desperdiciado, perdido; **to be ～ on sb: these subtleties are ～ on him** se le escapan estas sutilezas **4** (*pred*) (absorbed) **to be ～ IN sth** estar* ensimismado EN algo; **to be ～ in thought** estar* absorto *or* ensimismado
II (not won) ⟨*battle/election*⟩ perdido

lost: ～ and found /ˈlɔːstənˈfaʊnd ‖ˌlɒstənˈfaʊnd/ *n* (AmE) objetos *mpl* perdidos; **～ property** *n* (esp BrE) objetos *mpl* perdidos

lot /lɑːt ‖lɒt/ *n* **1** (large number, quantity) **(a)** (*no pl*): **a ～ of wine** mucho vino; **I've seen a ～ of her recently** la he visto mucho últimamente; **what a ～ of books you've got!** ¡cuántos libros tienes! **(b) a ～** (*as adv*) mucho **(c) lots** *pl* (colloq): **how many seats are there left?** — **lots** ¿cuántos asientos quedan? — muchos *or* (fam) montones; **～s of people liked it** a mucha gente le gustó **2** **(a)** (group, mass of things) montón *m*, pila *f* **(b)** (group of people) (colloq): **they're a funny ～** son raros, son gente rara; **come on, you ～!** ¡vamos, ustedes *or* (Esp) vosotros! **(c) the ～** (esp BrE): **they ate the ～** se lo comieron todo (*or* se las comieron todas *etc*) **3** (at auction) lote *m*

loth /ləʊθ/ *adj* ▶ LOATH

lotion /ˈləʊʃən/ *n* loción *f*

lottery /ˈlɑːtəri ‖ˈlɒtəri/ *n* (*pl* **-ries**) lotería *f*

lotus /ˈləʊtəs/ *n* (*pl* **～es**) loto *m*

loud¹ /laʊd/ *adj* **-er, -est** **(a)** ⟨*noise*⟩ fuerte; **he said it in a ～ voice** lo dijo en voz alta **(b)** (vigorous) ⟨*protests*⟩ enérgico **(c)** (ostentatious) ⟨*color*⟩ llamativo, chillón

loud² *adv* **-er, -est** ⟨*speak*⟩ alto; **she laughed (the) ～est of all** fue la que se rió más fuerte

loudly /ˈlaʊdli/ *adv* **(a)** ⟨*shout*⟩ fuerte; ⟨*speak*⟩ alto, en voz alta **(b)** ⟨*complain*⟩ a voz en grito

loud: ～mouth *n* (colloq) gritón, -tona *m,f*; **～speaker** /ˈlaʊdˈspiːkər ‖ˌlaʊdˈspiːkə(r)/ *n* altavoz *m*, altoparlante *m* (AmL)

lounge¹ /laʊndʒ/ *n* (on ship, in hotel) salón *m*; (in house) (BrE) sala *f* (de estar), living *m* (esp AmS), salón *m* (esp Esp)

lounge² *vi*: **to ～ around** *o* **about** no hacer* nada

louse /laʊs/ *n* (*pl* **lice**) (Zool) piojo *m*

lousy /ˈlaʊzi/ *adj* **-sier, -siest** (colloq) ⟨*food/weather*⟩ asqueroso (fam); **a ～ movie** una película malísima

lout /laʊt/ *n* patán *m* (fam), gandalla *m* (Méx fam), jallán *m* (AmC)

louver, (BrE) **louvre** /ˈluːvər ‖ˈluːvə(r)/ *n* lama *f*, listón *m* (de persiana); (*before n*) ⟨*door/window*⟩ de lamas, tipo persiana

lovable /ˈlʌvəbəl/ *adj* adorable, amoroso (AmL)

love¹ /lʌv/ *n* **1** **(a)** (emotional attachment) amor *m*; **to fall/be in ～ with sb/sth** enamorarse/estar* enamorado de algn/algo; **to make ～ to sb** hacer* el amor con algn **(b)** (enthusiasm, interest) **～ OF** *or* **sth** amor *m* A *or* POR algo **2** **(a)** (greetings, regards): **give my ～ to your parents** (dale) recuerdos a tus padres (de mi parte) **(b)** (in letters) **～ from John** *o* **～, John** un abrazo, John **3** (person loved) amor *m*; (thing loved) pasión *f* **4** (colloq) (*as form of address*) cariño **5** (in tennis) cero *m*

love² *vt* querer*, amar (liter); **I ～ music/reading** me encanta la música/leer; **I'd ～ a cup of tea** una taza de té me vendría de maravilla

loveable *adj* ▶ LOVABLE

loveless /ˈlʌvləs ‖ˈlʌvlɪs/ *adj* sin amor

lovely /ˈlʌvli/ *adj* **-lier, liest** ⟨*appearance*⟩ precioso, lindo (esp AmL); ⟨*person/nature*⟩ encantador, amoroso (AmL); ⟨*meal/taste*⟩ (BrE) riquísimo; **the weather was ～** hacía un tiempo buenísimo

lover /'lʌvər ‖'lʌvə(r)/ *n* **1** (partner in love) amante *mf* **2** (fan) ~ **OF** sth amante *mf* DE algo

loving /'lʌvɪŋ/ *adj* cariñoso; **with** ~ **care** con tierno cuidado

lovingly /'lʌvɪŋli/ *adv* ‹gaze/whisper› tiernamente; ‹handwritten/prepared› con amor *or* cariño; ‹restored› con el mayor cuidado

low¹ /ləʊ/ *adj* **-er, -est** **1** (in height) bajo; **the dress had a very** ~ **back** el vestido era muy escotado por la espalda **2 (a)** (in volume) ‹voice› bajo; ‹sound/whisper› débil; **turn the radio down** ~ bájale al radio (AmL exc CS), baja la radio (CS, Esp) **(b)** ‹key/note/pitch› grave **3** (in intensity, amount, quality) bajo; ‹proportion› pequeño; **cook on a** ~ **flame** *o* **heat** cocinar a fuego lento; **he has a** ~ **opinion of doctors** no tiene muy buena opinión de los médicos; **a** ~ **point in his career** un momento bajo en su carrera **4** (in short supply): **stocks are running** ~ se están agotando las existencias

low² *adv* **-er, -est** **1** bajo; **to fly** ~ volar* bajo *or* a poca altura **2** (in volume, pitch) bajo

low³ *n* punto *m* más bajo; **relations between the two countries are at an all-time** ~ las relaciones entre los dos países nunca han sido peores

low⁴ *vi* mugir*

low- /ləʊ/ *pref*: **~priced** de bajo precio; **~income** de bajos ingresos

low: **~-alcohol** /'ləʊˈælkəhɔːl ‖'ləʊˌælkəhɒl/ *adj* de baja graduación alcohólica; **~-calorie** /'ləʊˈkæləri/ *adj* bajo en calorías; **~-class** /'ləʊˈklæs ‖ˌləʊˈklɑːs/ *adj* ‹place› de mala muerte (fam); ‹clientele› de poca categoría; **~-cut** /'ləʊˈkʌt/ *adj* escotado; **~down** *n* (colloq): **to give sb the ~down (on sth)** poner* a algn al tanto (de algo)

lower¹ /'ləʊər ‖'ləʊə(r)/ *adj* **1 (a)** (spatially, numerically) ‹jaw/lip› inferior; ~ **age limit** edad *f* mínima **(b)** (in rank, importance) inferior, más bajo **(c)** ‹life form› inferior **2** (Geog) bajo; **the** ~ **reaches of the Nile** el curso bajo del Nilo

lower² /'ləʊər ‖'ləʊə(r)/ *vt* **1** ‹blind/flag› bajar; **he** ~ed **himself into his chair** se sentó en el sillón **2** ‹temperature/volume/price/voice› bajar ■ *v refl* **to** ~ **oneself** rebajarse

lower: ~ **class** *n* (often pl) clase *f* baja; **~-class** /ˌləʊərˈklæs ‖ˌləʊəˈklɑːs/ *adj* de clase baja

lowest common denominator /'ləʊəst ‖'ləʊɪst/ *n* (Math) mínimo común denominador *m*; **a series aimed at the** ~ ~ ~ una serie dirigida al público de nivel más bajo

low: **~-fat** /'ləʊˈfæt/ *adj* de bajo contenido graso; **~-flying** /'ləʊˈflaɪŋ/ *adj* ‹aircraft› que vuela bajo; **~-grade** /'ləʊˈɡreɪd/ *adj* ‹oil› de baja calidad; ‹ore› pobre; **~-key** /'ləʊˈkiː/ *adj* ‹speech› mesurado; ‹ceremony› sencillo; **~-land** /'ləʊlənd/ *adj* (before n) de las tierras bajas; (in tropical countries) de tierra caliente; **~lands** /'ləʊləndz/ *pl n* tierras *fpl* bajas; (in tropical

countries) tierras *fpl* calientes; **~-level** /'ləʊˈlevəl/ *adj* **(a)** ‹talks› a bajo nivel **(b)** ‹radiation› de baja intensidad **(c)** (Comput): **~-level language** lenguaje *m* de bajo nivel

lowly /'ləʊli/ *adj* **-lier, -liest** humilde

low: **~-lying** /'ləʊˈlaɪŋ/ *adj* bajo; **~-necked** /'ləʊˈnekt/ *adj* escotado; **~-paid** /'ləʊˈpeɪd/ *adj* mal remunerado; **~-profile** /'ləʊˈprəʊfaɪl/ *adj* poco prominente; **~-rise** /'ləʊˈraɪz/ *adj* de poca altura; **~-risk** /'ləʊˈrɪsk/ *adj* ‹business› poco arriesgado; ‹investment› de poco *or* bajo riesgo; ~ **season** *n* (BrE) temporada *f* baja

loyal /'lɔɪəl/ *adj* ‹friend/customer› fiel; **to be** ~ **TO sth** ‹to the state/party› ser* leal A algo; ‹to one's ideals› ser* fiel A algo; **he is** ~ **to his friends** es un amigo leal *or* fiel

loyalist /'lɔɪələst ‖'lɔɪəlɪst/ *n* partidario, -ria *m,f* del régimen

loyalty /'lɔɪəlti/ *n* (*pl* **-ties**) lealtad *f*

loyalty card *n* tarjeta *f* de cliente (que otorga puntos)

lozenge /'lɑːzɪndʒ ‖'lɒzɪndʒ/ *n* (Med) pastilla *f*

LP *n* (= **long-playing record**) LP *m*, elepé *m*

L-plate /'elpleɪt/ *n* (in UK) placa *f* de la L *or* de prácticas (placa que se debe exhibir en el coche cuando se aprende a conducir)

LSD *n* (= **lysergic acid diethylamide**) LSD *m*

LST (in US) = **Local Standard Time**

Ltd (= **Limited**) Ltda., S.A.

lubricant /'luːbrɪkənt/ *n* lubricante *m*

lubricate /'luːbrɪkeɪt/ *vt* lubricar*

lucid /'luːsəd ‖'luːsɪd/ *adj* lúcido

luck /lʌk/ *n* suerte *f*; **good** ~! ¡buena suerte!; **a piece** *o* **stroke of** ~ un golpe de suerte; **to be down on one's** ~ estar* de mala racha; **to push one's** ~ desafiar* a la suerte

luckily /'lʌkəli ‖'lʌkɪli/ *adv* (indep) por suerte

lucky /'lʌki/ *adj* **luckier, luckiest (a)** ‹person› con suerte, suertudo (AmL fam); **he's** ~ **to be alive** tuvo suerte de no matarse; ~ **you!** (colloq) ¡qué suerte (tienes)! **(b)** (fortuitous): **he had a** ~ **escape** se salvó de milagro; **it was** ~ **you were there** fue una suerte que estuvieras ahí **(c)** (bringing luck): ~ **charm** amuleto *m* (de la suerte); **seven is my** ~ **number** el siete es mi número de la suerte

lucrative /'luːkrətɪv/ *adj* lucrativo

ludicrous /'luːdɪkrəs/ *adj* ridículo

lug /lʌɡ/ *vt* **-gg-** (colloq) arrastrar

luggage /'lʌɡɪdʒ/ *n* equipaje *m*

luggage: ~ **checkroom** *n* (AmE) consigna *f* (de equipajes); ~ **rack** *n* **(a)** (Rail) rejilla *f* (portaequipajes) **(b)** (Auto) baca *f*, parrilla *f* (Andes)

lugubrious /loˈɡuːbriəs/ *adj* lúgubre

lukewarm /luːkˈwɔːrm ‖luːkˈwɔːm/ *adj* **(a)** ‹water/milk› tibio **(b)** ‹support/reaction› poco entusiasta

lull¹ /lʌl/ *vt* **(a)** ‹baby›: **to** ~ **a baby to sleep**

arrullar a un niño hasta dormirlo **(b)** ⟨*fears*⟩ calmar, ⟨*suspicions*⟩ desvanecer **(c)** (deceive): **we were ~ed into a false sense of security** nos confiamos demasiado

lull² *n* (in activity) período *m* de calma; (in fighting) tregua *f*; (in conversation) pausa *f*

lullaby /'lʌləbaɪ/ *n* (*pl* **-bies**) canción *f* de cuna

lumbago /lʌm'beɪɡəʊ/ *n* lumbago *m*

lumber¹ /'lʌmbər ‖'lʌmbə(r)/ *n* **(a)** (timber) (AmE) madera *f* **(b)** (junk) cachivaches *mpl*

lumber² *vt* (colloq) **to ~ sb with sth** enjaretarle algo ᴀ algn (fam)
■ ~ *vi* **(a)** (move awkwardly) avanzar* pesadamente **(b) lumbering** *pres p* ⟨*gait*⟩ torpe

lumber: ~jack *n* leñador *m*; **~yard** *n* (AmE) almacén *m* de maderas, barraca *f* (CS)

luminous /'lu:mənəs ‖'lu:mɪnəs/ *adj* luminoso

lump¹ /lʌmp/ *n* **⏍** (swelling, protuberance) bulto *m*; (as result of knock) chichón *m*; **a ~ in one's throat** un nudo en la garganta **⏎** (piece — of coal, iron, clay, cheese) trozo *m*, pedazo *m*; (— of sugar) terrón *m*

lump² *vt* **(a)** (put up with) (colloq): **to ~ it** aguantarse (fam); **if you don't like it, (you can) ~ it** si no te gusta, te aguantas **(b)** (place together): **to ~ sth together: you can ~ all those items together under one heading** todo eso puede ir junto bajo el mismo epígrafe; **they can't all be ~ed together as reactionaries** no se puede tachar a todos indiscriminadamente de reaccionarios

lump sum *n* cantidad *f* global (*que se paga o recibe para saldar totalmente una obligación*)

lumpy /'lʌmpi/ *adj* **-pier, -piest (a)** ⟨*sauce*⟩ lleno de grumos **(b)** ⟨*mattress/cushion*⟩ lleno de bultos

lunacy /'lu:nəsi/ *n* (*pl* **-cies**) locura *f*

lunar /'lu:nər ‖'lu:nə(r)/ *adj* lunar

lunatic /'lu:nətɪk/ *n* loco, -ca *m,f*

lunch /lʌntʃ/ *n* almuerzo *m*, comida *f* (esp Esp, Méx); **to have ~** almorzar*, comer (esp Esp, Méx)

lunchbox /'lʌntʃbɑːks ‖'lʌntʃbɒks/ *n* lonchera *f* (AmL), fiambrera *f* (Esp)

luncheon /'lʌntʃən/ *n* (frml) almuerzo *m*

lunchtime /'lʌntʃtaɪm/ *n* hora *f* de almorzar, hora *f* de comer (esp Esp, Méx)

lung /lʌŋ/ *n* (*often pl*) pulmón *m*; (*before n*) **~ cancer** cáncer *m* de pulmón

lunge¹ /lʌndʒ/ *vi* embestir*; **to ~ ᴀᴛ sb/sth** arremeter ᴄᴏɴᴛʀᴀ algn/algo

lunge² *n* arremetida *f*

lurch¹ /lɜːrtʃ ‖lɜːtʃ/ *vi* ⟨*vehicle*⟩ dar* bandazos; ⟨*person*⟩ tambalearse

lurch² *n* bandazo *m*; **to leave sb in the ~** (colloq) dejar a algn plantado

lure /lʊr ‖ljʊə(r), lʊə(r)/ *vt* atraer*

lurid /'lʊrəd ‖'lʊərɪd/ *adj* **(a)** (sensational) ⟨*details/imagination*⟩ morboso **(b)** (garish) ⟨*color/garment*⟩ chillón

lurk /lɜːrk ‖lɜːk/ *vi* merodear

luscious /'lʌʃəs/ *adj* **(a)** ⟨*girl*⟩ seductora **(b)** ⟨*scent/sweetness*⟩ exquisito

lush /lʌʃ/ *adj* **-er, -est** ⟨*vegetation*⟩ exuberante

lust¹ /lʌst/ *n* **(a)** (sexual) lujuria *f* **(b)** (craving) deseo *m*

lust² *vi* **to ~ ᴀғᴛᴇʀ sb** desear a algn; **to ~ ᴀғᴛᴇʀ sth** codiciar algo

luster, (BrE) **lustre** /'lʌstər ‖'lʌstə(r)/ *n* (liter) lustre *m*

lustful /'lʌstfəl/ *adj* lujurioso

lustre /'lʌstər ‖'lʌstə(r)/ *n* (BrE) ▶ ʟᴜsᴛᴇʀ

lusty /'lʌsti/ *adj* **-tier, tiest** sano

Luxembourg, Luxemburg /'lʌksəmbɜːrg ‖'lʌksəmbɜːg/ *n* Luxemburgo *m*

luxuriant /lʌg'ʒʊriənt ‖lʌg'zjʊəriənt/ *adj* ⟨*vegetation/growth*⟩ exuberante; ⟨*hair*⟩ hermoso y abundante

luxuriate /lʌg'ʒʊrieɪt ‖lʌg'zjʊərieɪt/ *vi* (revel) **to ~ ɪɴ sth** deleitarse ᴄᴏɴ algo

luxurious /lʌg'ʒʊriəs ‖lʌg'zjʊəriəs/ *adj* lujoso

luxury /'lʌkʃəri/ *n* (*pl* **-ries**) lujo *m*; (*before n*) ⟨*car/hotel*⟩ de lujo

lying¹ /'laɪŋ/ *n* mentiras *fpl*

lying² *adj* (*before n*) mentiroso

lymph /lɪmf/ *n* linfa *f*; (*before n*) **~ gland** glándula *f* linfática

lynch /lɪntʃ/ *vt* linchar

lynx /lɪŋks/ *n* (*pl* **~es** *or* **~**) lince *m*

lyre /'laɪr ‖'laɪə(r)/ *n* lira *f*

lyric /'lɪrɪk/ *n* **(a)** (poem) poema *m* lírico **(b) lyrics** *pl n* (Mus) letra *f*

lyrical /'lɪrɪkəl/ *adj* (Lit) lleno de lirismo

M m

M, m /em/ *n* M, m *f*

m (a) (= **million(s)**) m **(b)** (= **meter(s)** *o* (BrE) **metre(s)**) m **(c)** (= **male**) de sexo masculino **(d)** (Ling) (= **masculine**) m

M (a) (Clothing) (= **medium**) M, talla *f* mediana *or* (RPl) talle *m* mediano **(b)** (in UK) (Transp) (= **motorway**) indicador de autopista

ma /mɑː/ *n* (colloq) mamá *f*

MA /'em'eɪ/ *n* **(a)** = **Master of Arts (b)** = **Massachusetts**

macabre /mə'kɑːbrə/ *adj* macabro

macaroni /'mækə'rəʊni/ *n* macarrones *mpl*

mace /meɪs/ *n* **⏍** (Art, Hist, Mil) maza *f* **⏎** (Culin) macis *f* **⏏ Mace®** (tear gas) (AmE) gas para defensa personal

Macedonia /ˌmæsə'dəʊniə/ *n* Macedonia *f*

machete /mə'ʃeti, mə'tʃeti/ *n* machete *m*

machinations /ˌmækəˈneɪʃənz, ˈmæʃ-
‖ˌmækɪˈneɪʃənz, ˈmæʃ-/ *pl n* (liter) maquinaciones
fpl

machine /məˈʃiːn/ *n* máquina *f*; (washing ∼)
lavadora *f*, máquina *f* (de lavar), lavarropas *m*
(RPl)

machine gun *n* ametralladora *f*

machinery /məˈʃiːnəri/ *n* (machines)
maquinaria *f*; (working parts) mecanismo *m*

macho /ˈmɑːtʃəʊ ‖ˈmætʃəʊ/ *adj* ⟨behavior/
attitude⟩ machista; ⟨image⟩ de macho

macintosh *n* ▶ MACKINTOSH

mackerel /ˈmækrəl/ *n* (*pl* ∼ *or* ∼s) caballa *f*

mackintosh /ˈmækəntɒʃ ‖ˈmækɪntɒʃ/ *n*
impermeable *m*

macro /ˈmækrəʊ/ *n* (*pl* -ros) (Comput) macro *m*

mad /mæd/ *adj* -dd- ① (a) (insane) loco; to go
∼ volverse* loco; to work/run like ∼ trabajar/
correr como un loco (b) ⟨rush⟩ loco; we made a
∼ dash for the airport salimos como locos para el
aeropuerto (c) ⟨scheme/idea⟩ disparatado
② (angry) (esp AmE) (*pred*) to be ∼ (WITH/AT sb)
estar* furioso *or* (esp AmL) enojadísimo *or* (esp
Esp) enfadadísimo (CON algn); to get ∼ ponerse*
furioso ③ (very enthusiastic) (colloq) (*pred*) to be ∼
ABOUT sb estar* loco POR algn; she's ∼ about *o*
on African music la música africana la vuelve
loca

Madagascar /ˌmædəˈɡæskər
‖ˌmædəˈɡæskə(r)/ *n* Madagascar *m*

madam /ˈmædəm/ *n* (as title) señora *f*

madden /ˈmædn̩/ *vt* (make angry) enfurecer*;
(drive mad) enloquecer*

made¹ /meɪd/ *past & past p of* MAKE¹

made² *adj* (*pred*) (a) (assured of success) to have
it ∼ tener* el éxito asegurado (b) (ideally suited):
they were ∼ for each other estaban hechos el uno
para el otro

Madeira /məˈdɪrə ‖məˈdɪərə/ *n* Madeira *f*,
Madera *f*

made-to-measure /ˌmeɪdtəˈmeʒər
‖ˌmeɪdtəˈmeʒə(r)/ *adj* (*pred* **made to
measure**) hecho a (la) medida

madly /ˈmædli/ *adv* (a) (frantically) ⟨rush/work⟩
como un loco; ⟨love⟩ locamente (b) (very) (as
intensifier): ∼ in love locamente enamorado

madman /ˈmædmən/ *n* (*pl* -men /-mən/) loco
m

madness /ˈmædnəs ‖ˈmædnɪs/ *n* locura *f*

Madrid /məˈdrɪd/ *n* Madrid *m*; (before n)
madrileño

Mafia /ˈmɑːfiə, ˈmæ- ‖ˈmæfiə/ *n* Mafia *f*

magazine /ˌmæɡəˈziːn/ *n* ① (a) (Publ) revista
f; (before n) ∼ rack revistero *m* (b) ∼
(**program**) (Rad, TV) programa *m* de entrevistas
y variedades ② (on gun — compartment) recámara
f; (— bullet case) cargador *m*

maggot /ˈmæɡət/ *n* gusano *m*

magic¹ /ˈmædʒɪk/ *n* magia *f*

magic² *adj* (a) ⟨power/potion⟩ mágico; ⟨trick⟩
de magia (b) (enchanting) ⟨moment/beauty⟩ mágico

magical /ˈmædʒɪkəl/ *adj* mágico

magician /məˈdʒɪʃən/ *n* (sorcerer) mago *m*;
(conjurer) mago, -ga *m,f*, prestidigitador, -dora *m,f*

magistrate /ˈmædʒəstreɪt ‖ˈmædʒɪstreɪt/ *n* (in
UK) *juez que conoce de faltas y asuntos civiles de
menor importancia*

magnanimous /mæɡˈnænəməs
‖mæɡˈnænɪməs/ *adj* magnánimo

magnesium /mæɡˈniːziəm/ *n* magnesio *m*

magnet /ˈmæɡnət ‖ˈmæɡnɪt/ *n* imán *m*

magnetic /mæɡˈnetɪk/ *adj* magnético;
⟨personality⟩ lleno de magnetismo

magnetism /ˈmæɡnətɪzəm ‖ˈmæɡnɪtɪzəm/ *n*
magnetismo *m*

magnificent /mæɡˈnɪfəsənt ‖mæɡˈnɪfɪsənt/
adj magnífico

magnify /ˈmæɡnəfaɪ ‖ˈmæɡnɪfaɪ/ *vt* -fies,
-fying, -fied ⟨image⟩ ampliar*, aumentar de
tamaño; ⟨problem/difficulty⟩ exagerar

magnifying glass /ˈmæɡnəfaɪŋ
‖ˈmæɡnɪfaɪŋ/ *n* lupa *f*

magnitude /ˈmæɡnətuːd ‖ˈmæɡnɪtjuːd/ *n*
(size) magnitud *f*; (importance) envergadura *f*

magpie /ˈmæɡpaɪ/ *n* urraca *f*, picaza *f*

mahogany /məˈhɑːɡəni ‖məˈhɒɡəni/ *n* caoba *f*

maid /meɪd/ *n* ① (a) (servant) sirvienta *f*, criada
f, mucama *f* (AmL); (parlor/lady's ∼) (primera)
doncella *f* (b) (in hotel) camarera *f*, mucama *f*
(AmL) (c) (occasional housekeeper) (AmE) señora *f* de
la limpieza, limpiadora *f* ② (young woman) (arch *or*
liter) doncella *f* (arc *o* liter)

maiden¹ /ˈmeɪdn̩/ *n* (arch *or* liter) doncella *f* (arc
o liter)

maiden² *adj* (before n) ⟨flight/speech⟩
inaugural

maiden name *n* apellido *m* de soltera

mail¹ /meɪl/ *n* ① (a) (system) correo *m*; by ∼
por correo (b) (letters, parcels) correspondencia *f*,
correo *m* ② (armor) malla *f*

mail² *vt* (esp AmE) ⟨letter/parcel⟩ echar al correo;
(drop in mailbox) echar al buzón; to ∼ sth TO sb
mandarle *or* enviarle* algo por correo A algn

mail: ∼**box** *n* (a) (for receiving mail) (AmE) buzón
m, casillero *m* (Ven) (b) (for sending mail) (AmE)
buzón *m* (de correos) (c) (electronic) buzón *m*; ∼
carrier *n* (AmE) cartero, -ra *m,f*

mailing list /ˈmeɪlɪŋ/ *n* (Marketing) banco *m or*
lista *f* de direcciones

mail: ∼**man** /ˈmeɪlmæn/ *n* (*pl* **-men** /-men/)
(AmE) cartero *m*; ∼ **order** *n* venta *f* por correo;
(before n) ∼-order catalog catálogo *m* de venta
por correo

maim /meɪm/ *vt* (cripple) lisiar; (mutilate) mutilar

main¹ /meɪn/ *adj* (before n, no comp) principal;
the ∼ thing lo principal; ∼ course plato *m*
principal *or* fuerte; ∼ street calle *f* principal

main² *n* (a) (pipe) cañería *f or* tubería *f*
principal; (cable) cable *m* principal (b) (supply) the
∼ *o* (BrE) the ∼s la red de suministro; to turn the
water/gas off at the ∼ *o* (BrE) the ∼s cerrar la
llave (principal) del agua/del gas

main: ∼**frame** *n* unidad *f* central,
computadora *f or* (Esp tb) ordenador *m* central;
∼**land** /ˈmeɪnlənd, -lænd/ *n*: the ∼land *la masa
territorial de un país o continente excluyendo sus
islas*; (before n) ∼land China (la) China
continental; ∼ **line** *n* (Rail) línea *f* principal

mainly /ˈmeɪnli/ *adv* principalmente

main: ∼ **road** *n* (BrE) carretera *f* principal;

~**stream** adj ⟨culture⟩ establecido; ~**stream politics** la política a nivel de los partidos mayoritarios

maintain /mem'tem/ vt 1 (a) ⟨speed/lead⟩ mantener*; ⟨silence⟩ guardar (b) ⟨house/machine⟩ ocuparse del mantenimiento de; ⟨aircraft⟩ mantener* (c) ⟨family/dependents⟩ mantener* 2 (claim) mantener*

maintenance /'meintnəns ‖'meintənəns/ n 1 (repairs) mantenimiento m 2 (money) (BrE Law) pensión f alimenticia

maisonette /'meizə'net ‖,meizə'net/ n (BrE) (apartment) dúplex m; (house) vivienda independiente de dos pisos que forma parte de una casa

maize /meiz/ n (a) (plant) maíz m (b) (grains) maíz m, choclo m (CS, Per), elote m (Méx)

majestic /mə'dʒestik/ adj majestuoso

majesty /'mædʒəsti/ n (pl -ties) (a) (of appearance, landscape) majestuosidad f (b) (as title) Her/Your M~ su Majestad

major[1] /'meidʒər ‖'meidʒə(r)/ adj 1 ⟨change/client⟩ muy importante; ⟨setback⟩ serio; ⟨revision⟩ a fondo 2 (Mus) mayor

major[2] n 1 (Mil) mayor mf (en AmL), comandante mf (en Esp) 2 (AmE Educ) asignatura f principal

major[3] vi (AmE Educ) to ~ IN sth especializarse* EN algo

Majorca /mə'jɔːrkə ‖mə'jɔːkə, mə'dʒɔːkə/ n Mallorca f

majority /mə'dʒɔːrəti ‖mə'dʒɒrəti/ n (pl -ties) (greater number) (+ sing o pl vb) mayoría f; (before n) ⟨decision/party⟩ mayoritario

major league n (Sport) liga f nacional

make[1] /meik/ (past & past p **made**) vt
I 1 (create, produce) hacer*; to ~ a note of sth anotar algo; she made the dress out of an old sheet se hizo el vestido con una sábana vieja; it's made of wood es de madera; see also DIFFERENCE, FUSS[1], MESS 1 etc
2 (a) (carry out) ⟨repairs/payment/journey⟩ hacer*; ~ a left (turn) here (AmE) dobla a la izquierda aquí (b) ⟨remark/announcement⟩ hacer*
II 1 (cause to be): I'll ~ you happy te haré feliz; that made me sad eso me entristeció; the work made me thirsty el trabajo me dio sed; what ~s me angry is ... lo que me da rabia es ...; they've made him supervisor lo han nombrado supervisor; if nine o'clock is too early, ~ it later si las nueve es muy temprano, podemos reunirnos (or encontrarnos etc) más tarde
2 (a) (cause to) hacer*; whatever made you do it? ¿por qué lo hiciste? (b) (compel) obligar* a, hacer*; she was made to apologize la obligaron a or la hicieron pedir perdón (c) (in phrases) to make believe: you can't just ~ believe it never happened no puedes hacer como si no hubiera sucedido; to make do (WITH sth) arreglárselas (CON algo)
III 1 (a) (constitute, be) ser*; it would ~ a nice change sería un cambio agradable; they ~ a nice couple hacen buena pareja (b) (amount to) ser*; five plus five ~s ten cinco y or más cinco son diez
2 (calculate): I ~ it 253 (a mí) me da 253; what time do you ~ it? ¿qué hora tienes?

3 (a) (understand): I could ~ nothing of the message no entendí el mensaje; ~ of that what you will tú saca tus propias conclusiones (b) (think) to ~ sth OF sb/sth: what did you ~ of him? ¿qué te pareció?; I don't know what to ~ of it no sé qué pensar
IV 1 (a) (gain, earn) ⟨money⟩ hacer* (b) (acquire) ⟨friends⟩ hacer*; to ~ a name for oneself hacerse* un nombre
2 (colloq) (manage to attend, reach): we just made the 3 o'clock train llegamos justo a tiempo para el tren de las tres; he'll never ~ it as a doctor nunca será un buen médico
3 (assure success of): to ~ or break sth/sb ser* el éxito o la ruina de algo/algn
■ **make for** [v + prep + o] 1 (head toward) dirigirse* hacia/a
2 (encourage, promote) contribuir* a
■ **make out**
I [v + o + adv, v + adv + o] 1 (a) (discern) ⟨object/outline⟩ distinguir*; (from a distance) divisar*; ⟨sound⟩ distinguir*; ⟨writing⟩ descifrar (b) (figure out) (colloq) entender*
2 (write) ⟨list/invoice/receipt⟩ hacer*; ~ the check out to P. Jones haga el cheque pagadero a P. Jones
II (claim, pretend) [v + adv + o]: she made out it was her own work dio a entender que lo había hecho ella misma; you're not as ill as you ~ out no estás tan enfermo como pretendes
■ **make up**
I [v + o + adv, v + adv + o] 1 ⟨story/excuse⟩ inventar
2 (prepare) ⟨prescription/food parcel⟩ preparar; ⟨agenda/list⟩ hacer*
3 (a) (complete, add) completar; she came along to ~ up the numbers vino para completar el grupo (b) (compensate for): I'll take the afternoon off, and ~ up the time later me tomaré la tarde libre y ya recuperaré el tiempo más tarde
II [v + adv + o] (constitute) formar; it is made up of three parts está compuesto de tres partes
III [v + adv, v + o + adv] (achieve reconciliation) to ~ (it) up (WITH sb) hacer* las paces (CON algn)

make[2] n marca f

make: ~**believe** n fantasía f; don't be frightened, it's only ~believe no te asustes, es de mentira; ~**over** n (AmE) maquillaje m; to have a (cosmetic) ~over maquillarse

maker /'meikər ‖'meikə(r)/ n fabricante mf

make: ~**shift** adj ⟨repair⟩ provisional, provisorio (AmS); ⟨bed⟩ improvisado; ~**up** n 1 (cosmetics) maquillaje m; to put on one's ~up maquillarse, pintarse; (before n) ~up remover desmaquillador m; 2 (no pl) (of person) carácter m; 3 (AmE Educ) examen m de recuperación

making /'meikiŋ/ n (a) (production, creation): a book about the ~ of the TV series un libro que trata de cómo se hizo la serie de televisión; this is history in the ~ esto va a pasar a la historia (b) **makings** pl: you have the ~s of a good story there allí tienes material para una buena historia; she has the ~s of a great actress es una gran actriz en ciernes

maladjusted /,mælə'dʒʌstəd ‖,mælə'dʒʌstɪd/ adj (Psych) inadaptado

maladjustment /,mælə'dʒʌstmənt/ n (Psych) inadaptación f

malaria ⋯✦ maneuver

malaria /mə'leriə ‖mə'leəriə/ n malaria f, paludismo m

Malawi /mə'lɑ:wi/ n Malaui m, Malawi m

Malawian /mə'lɑ:wiən/ adj malauiano

Malaysia /mə'leɪʒə ‖mə'leɪziə/ n Malaisia f; (continental part) Malasia f

Malaysian¹ /mə'leɪʒən ‖mə'leɪziən/ adj malaisio; (from continental part) malasio

Malaysian² n malaisio, -sia m,f; (from continental part) malasio, -sia m,f

Maldive Islands /'mɔ:ldi:v, -daɪv/, **Maldives** /-z/ pl n the ~ ~ las (islas) Maldivas

male¹ /meɪl/ adj ⟨animal/plant⟩ macho; ⟨attitude⟩ masculino; **there were several ~ applicants** se presentaron varios candidatos varones

male² n (animal) macho m; (person) varón m

malevolent /mə'levələnt/ adj ⟨grin⟩ malévolo; ⟨deity⟩ maligno

malformation /ˌmælfɔ:r'meɪʃən ‖ˌmælfɔ:'meɪʃən/ n deformación f (esp congénita), malformación f

malfunction¹ /ˌmæl'fʌŋkʃən/ n (a) (defective functioning) mal funcionamiento m (b) (failure) falla f or (Esp) fallo m

malfunction² vi (Med, Tech) fallar, funcionar mal

malice /'mælɪs ‖'mælɪs/ n mala intención f

malicious /mə'lɪʃəs/ adj ⟨person/gossip⟩ malicioso; ⟨damage⟩ doloso

malignant /mə'lɪɡnənt/ adj maligno

malinger /mə'lɪŋɡər ‖mə'lɪŋɡə(r)/ vi hacerse* el enfermo

mall /mɔ:l ‖mæl, mɔ:l/ n (a) (for shopping) centro m comercial (b) (avenue) paseo m

mallet /'mælət ‖'mælɪt/ n mazo m

malnutrition /ˌmælnu:'trɪʃən ‖ˌmælnju:'trɪʃən/ n desnutrición f

malpractice /ˌmæl'præktəs ‖ˌmæl'præktɪs/ n mala práctica f (en el ejercicio de la profesión)

malt /mɔ:lt/ n (a) (grain) malta f (b) ~ (**whisky**) whisky m de malta

Malta /'mɔ:ltə/ n Malta f

Maltese¹ /'mɔ:l'ti:z/ adj maltés

Maltese² n (pl ~) (a) (person) maltés, -tesa m,f (b) (language) maltés m

mamma /'mæmə ‖'mʌmə/ n ▶ MOMMA

mammal /'mæməl/ n mamífero m

mammoth¹ /'mæməθ/ n mamut m

mammoth² adj ⟨building/cost⟩ gigantesco; ⟨task⟩ de titanes

man¹ /mæn/ n (pl men /men/) **1** (a) (adult male) hombre m (b) (husband/boyfriend): **her new ~** su nueva pareja (or su nuevo compañero etc); **to live together as ~ and wife** vivir como marido y mujer (c) (type): **he's a local ~** es del lugar; **he's a family ~** es un padre de familia **2** (a) (person) persona f; **every ~ for himself** (set phrase) sálvese quien pueda (fr hecha) (b) also **Man** (mankind) (no art) el hombre

3 men pl: the men (troops) los soldados; (employees) los trabajadores **4** (in chess) pieza f; (in draughts) ficha f **5** (as form of address) (colloq): **hey, ~!** ¡oiga, amigo!, ¡oye, tío (Esp) or (AmL exc CS) mano or (Chi) gallo! (fam), ¡oíme, che! (RPI fam)

man² vt **-nn-** ⟨switchboard⟩ encargarse* de; ⟨ship⟩ tripular; **soldiers ~ned the barricades** había soldados apostados en las barricadas

manacles /'mænəkəlz/ pl n (for wrists) esposas fpl; (for legs) grillos mpl

manage /'mænɪdʒ/ vt **1** (Busn) ⟨company/bank⟩ dirigir*, administrar, gerenciar (AmL); ⟨staff/team⟩ dirigir*; ⟨land/finances⟩ administrar **2** (handle, cope with) ⟨children⟩ manejar; ⟨household⟩ llevar; **she can't ~ the stairs** no puede subir la escalera **3** (achieve): **he ~d a smile** esbozó una sonrisa forzada; **I can't ~ the meeting** no puedo ir a la reunión; **to ~ to + INF** lograr + INF
■ ~ vi **1** (Busn) dirigir*, administrar **2** (cope): **can I help you? — thank you, I can ~** ¿me permite que la ayude? — gracias, yo puedo sola; **they have to ~ on $300 a week** tienen que arreglarse con 300 dólares a la semana

manageable /'mænɪdʒəbəl/ adj ⟨child/animal/hair⟩ dócil; ⟨task/goal⟩ posible de alcanzar; ⟨size/amount⟩ razonable

management /'mænɪdʒmənt/ n **1** (act) (a) (Busn) dirección f, administración f (b) (handling, control) manejo m **2** (managers) (a) (as group) (no art, + sing o pl vb) directivos mpl; **senior ~** altos cargos mpl (b) (of particular company) dirección f, gerencia f

manager /'mænɪdʒər ‖'mænɪdʒə(r)/ n (Busn) (of company, department) director, -tora m,f, gerente mf; (of store, restaurant) gerente mf, encargado, -da m,f; (of estate, fund) administrador, -dora m,f; (of pop group, boxer) manager mf; (Sport) agente mf; (in soccer) entrenador, -dora m,f, director técnico, directora técnica m,f (AmL)

manageress /'mænɪdʒərəs ‖ˌmænɪdʒə'res/ n (esp BrE) encargada f

managerial /ˌmænə'dʒɪriəl ‖ˌmænɪ'dʒɪəriəl/ adj directivo, gerencial (AmL)

managing director /'mænədʒɪŋ ‖'mænɪdʒɪŋ/ n (esp BrE) director ejecutivo, directora ejecutiva m,f

mandarin /'mændərən ‖'mændərɪn/ n ~ (**orange**) mandarina f

mandate /'mændeɪt/ n mandato m

mandatory /'mændətɔ:ri ‖'mændətəri/ adj (frml) obligatorio

mane /meɪn/ n (of horse) crin(es) f(pl); (of lion) melena f

maneuver¹, (BrE) **manoeuvre** /mə'nu:vər ‖mə'nu:və(r)/ n maniobra f

maneuver², (BrE) **manoeuvre** vt: **they ~ed the piano up the stairs** subieron trabajosamente el piano por la escalera; **she ~ed the car out of the garage** sacó el coche del garaje maniobrando
■ ~ vi ⟨⟨vehicle/driver⟩⟩ maniobrar, hacer* una

AmC	Central America	Arg	Argentina	Cu	Cuba	Per	Peru
AmL	Latin America	Bol	Bolivia	Ec	Ecuador	RPI	River Plate Area
AmS	South America	Chi	Chile	Esp	Spain	Ur	Uruguay
Andes	Andean Region	CS	Southern Cone	Méx	Mexico	Ven	Venezuela

maniobra; **to have room to ~** «*driver*» tener* espacio para maniobrar; «*diplomat*» tener* libertad de acción

manger /'meɪndʒər ‖'meɪndʒə(r)/ n pesebre m

mangle¹ /'mæŋgəl/ vt destrozar*

mangle² n rodillo m (escurridor)

mango /'mæŋgəʊ/ n (pl **-goes** or **-gos**) mango m

mangy /'meɪndʒi/ adj **-gier, -giest** ‹cat› sarnoso

man: ~handle vt (move by hand) mover* a pulso; (treat roughly) maltratar; **~hole** n registro m, pozo m de inspección; (into sewer) boca f de alcantarilla

manhood /'mænhʊd/ n **(a)** (adulthood) madurez f **(b)** (virility) hombría f

man: ~hour n hora f hombre; **~hunt** n persecución f

mania /'meɪniə/ n (pl **-nias**) manía f

maniac /'meɪniæk/ n maniaco, -ca m,f, maníaco, -ca m,f

manic /'mænɪk/ adj ‹behavior› maniaco, maníaco; ‹activity› frenético

manic-depressive /'mænɪkdɪ'presɪv/ n maniacodepresivo, -va m,f

manicure¹ /'mænəkjʊr ‖'mænɪkjʊə(r)/ n manicura f, manicure f (AmL exc RPl)

manicure² vt arreglarle las manos or las uñas a

manifest¹ /'mænəfest ‖'mænɪfest/ v refl (fml) **to ~ itself** «ghost» aparecerse*; «disease/fear» manifestarse*

■ **~** vt (express) manifestar*

manifest² adj manifiesto

manifestation /'mænəfə'steɪʃən ‖,mænɪfə'steɪʃən/ n manifestación f; (of ghost) aparición f

manifesto /'mænə'festəʊ ‖,mænɪ'festəʊ/ n (pl **-toes** or **-tos**) manifiesto m; (for a specific election) (esp BrE) plataforma f electoral

manifold¹ /'mænəfəʊld ‖'mænɪfəʊld/ adj (fml) múltiples

manifold² n colector m

manipulate /mə'nɪpjələrt ‖mə'nɪpjʊleɪt/ vt manipular

manipulative /mə'nɪpjələtɪv ‖mə'nɪpjʊlətɪv/ adj manipulador

mankind /mæn'kaɪnd/ n humanidad f, género m humano

manly /'mænli/ adj **-lier, -liest** ‹physique/ pursuits› varonil, masculino

man-made /'mæn'meɪd/ adj ‹lake› artificial; ‹material› sintético

manna /'mænə/ n maná m

manner /'mænər ‖'mænə(r)/ n [1] (way, fashion) forma f, modo m, manera f; **in a ~ of speaking** en cierto modo [2] (bearing, demeanor) actitud f; **a good telephone ~ is essential** es imprescindible tener buen trato por teléfono [3] (variety) tipo m, suerte f, clase f; **all ~ of things** todo tipo or toda suerte or toda clase de cosas [4] **manners** pl (personal conduct) modales mpl, educación f

mannerism /'mænərɪzəm/ n (peculiarity, habit) peculiaridad f; (gesture) gesto m

manoeuvre n/vt/vi (BrE) ▶ MANEUVER¹,²

manor /'mænər ‖'mænə(r)/ n **~ (house)** casa f solariega

manpower /'mænpaʊər ‖'mænpaʊə(r)/ n (workers) personal m; (blue-collar) mano f de obra

mansion /'mænʃən/ n mansión f

manslaughter /'mæn,slɔːtər ‖'mæn,slɔːtə(r)/ n homicidio m sin premeditación

mantelpiece /'mæntlpiːs/ n repisa f de la chimenea

mantle /'mæntl/ n [1] (covering) (liter) manto m (liter) [2] (Geol) manto m, sima f

manual¹ /'mænjuəl/ adj manual

manual² n manual m

manufacture¹ /'mænjə'fæktʃər ‖,mænjʊ'fæktʃə(r)/ vt ‹cars/toys› fabricar*; ‹clothes› confeccionar; ‹foodstuffs› elaborar

manufacture² n (act) fabricación f; (of clothes) confección f; (of foodstuffs) elaboración f

manufacturer /'mænjə'fæktʃərər ‖,mænjʊ'fæktʃərə(r)/ n fabricante mf

manufacturing /'mænjə'fæktʃərɪŋ ‖,mænjʊ'fæktʃərɪŋ/ adj ‹sector/town› manufacturero; ‹output/capacity› industrial; **~ industry** industria f manufacturera

manure /mə'nʊr ‖mə'njʊə(r)/ n estiércol m

manuscript /'mænjəskrɪpt ‖'mænjʊskrɪpt/ n manuscrito m

Manx /mæŋks/ adj manés, de la isla de Man 🅜

many¹ /'meni/ adj muchos, -chas; **how ~ plates/cups?** ¿cuántos platos/cuántas tazas?; **I've had as ~ jobs as you** he tenido tantos trabajos como tú; **too ~ problems** demasiados problemas

many² pron muchos, -chas; **how ~ of you smoke?** ¿cuántos/cuántas de ustedes fuman?; **would ten be too ~?** ¿diez serían demasiados?

Maori /'maʊri/ n maorí mf

map¹ /mæp/ n (of country, region) mapa m; (of town, subway, building) plano m

map² **-pp-** vt trazar* el mapa de

■ **map out** [v + o + adv, v + adv + o] ‹itinerary/ holiday› planear

maple /'meɪpəl/ n **~ (tree)** arce m; (before n) **~ syrup** jarabe m or sirope m de arce

mar /mɑːr ‖mɑː(r)/ vt **-rr-** estropear

marathon /'mærəθɑːn ‖'mærəθən/ n maratón m or f

marauder /mə'rɔːdər ‖mə'rɔːdə(r)/ n (criminal) maleante mf; (prowler) merodeador, -dora m,f

marble /'mɑːrbəl ‖'mɑːbəl/ n [1] (Min) mármol m [2] (Games) canica f or (AmS) bolita f

march¹ /mɑːrtʃ ‖mɑːtʃ/ n [1] **(a)** (Mil, Mus) marcha f **(b)** (demonstration) marcha f (de protesta) [2] (of time) paso m; (of science, technology) avance m

march² vi ‹troops› marchar; **when Saddam ~ed on Kuwait** cuando Saddam invadió Kuwait; **she ~ed into the office** entró con paso firme en or (esp AmL) a la oficina

■ **~** vt hacer* marchar; **the prisoner was ~ed in** hicieron entrar al prisionero

March /mɑːrtʃ ‖mɑːtʃ/ n marzo m

mare /mer ‖meə(r)/ n yegua f

margarine /'mɑːrdʒərən ‖,mɑːdʒə'riːn/ n margarina f

margin /'mɑːrdʒən ‖'mɑːdʒɪn/ n [1] (on page, typewriter) margen m [2] **(a)** (leeway) margen m **(b)** ⋯

(Busn) (of profit) margen *m* (de ganancia) **3** (fringe — of lake) (*often pl*) margen *f*; (— of society) margen *m*

marginal /'mɑːrdʒnəl ‖'mɑːdʒɪnl/ *adj* ⟨difference⟩ mínimo; ⟨role⟩ menor

marginally /'mɑːrdʒnəli ‖'mɑːdʒɪnli/ *adv* ligeramente

marigold /'mærəgəʊld ‖'mærɪgəʊld/ *n* caléndula *f*, maravilla *f*

marijuana, marihuana /'mærə'wɑːnə, -'hwɑː- ‖,mæri'wɑːnə/ *n* marihuana *f*

marinade, marinate /'mærəneɪd, -eɪt ‖'mærɪneɪd, -eɪt/ *vt* dejar en adobo

marine¹ /mə'riːn/ *n also* **Marine** (Mil) ≈ infante *m* de marina

marine² *adj* ⟨before n⟩ ⟨biology⟩ marino; ⟨engineering⟩ naval; ⟨insurance⟩ marítimo

marital /'mærət̬l ‖'mærɪtl/ *adj* ⟨problems⟩ matrimonial; ⟨bliss⟩ conyugal; ~ **status** estado *m* civil

marjoram /'mɑːrdʒərəm ‖'mɑːdʒərəm/ *n* mejorana *f*

mark¹ /mɑːrk ‖mɑːk/ *n* **1** (sign, symbol) marca *f*; (stain) mancha *f*; (imprint) huella *f*; (on body) marca *f*; **as a ~ of respect** en señal de respeto; **to make one's ~** dejar su impronta **2** (Educ) nota *f*; (Sport) punto *m*; **to get a good ~** sacar* una buena nota **3** (a) (indicator): **the cost has reached the $100,000 ~** el costo ha llegado a los 100.000 dólares; **to overstep the ~** pasarse de la raya (b) (for race) línea *f* de salida; **on your ~s!** ¡a sus marcas! **4** (target) blanco *m*; **to be wide of the ~:** his estimate was wide of the ~ erró por mucho en su cálculo **5** *also* **Mark** (type, version) modelo *m* **6** (Fin) marco *m*

mark² *vt* **1** (stain, scar) manchar **2** (indicate) señalar, marcar* **3** ⟨anniversary⟩ celebrar; ⟨beginning⟩ marcar*, señalar **4** ⟨exam⟩ (make corrections in) corregir*; (grade) poner(le)* nota a **5** (BrE Sport) ⟨opponent⟩ marcar*
■ **mark down** [v + o + adv, v + adv + o] (a) (Busn) ⟨goods⟩ rebajar (b) (BrE Educ) ⟨person/work⟩ bajarle la nota a
■ **mark out** [v + o + adv, v + adv + o] (a) ⟨sports ground⟩ marcar* (b) (select) señalar (c) (distinguish) distinguir*

marked /mɑːrkt ‖mɑːkt/ *adj* ⟨improvement⟩ marcado; ⟨contrast⟩ acusado

marker /'mɑːrkər ‖'mɑːkə(r)/ *n* (a) (to show position) indicador *m* (b) ~ (**pen**) rotulador *m*

market¹ /'mɑːrkət ‖'mɑːkɪt/ *n* mercado *m*; (street ~) mercado *m or* mercadillo *m or* (CS, Per) feria *f*; **to come on (to) the ~** salir* a la venta; **we put the house on the ~ at $320,000** pusimos la casa en venta en $320.000; ⟨before n⟩ ~ **forces** fuerzas *fpl* del mercado **2** (Fin) (stock ~) bolsa *f* (de valores); **to corner the ~** (*in sth*) hacerse* con el mercado (de algo)

market² *vt* comercializar*

market garden *n* (BrE) huerta *f*

marketing /'mɑːrkətɪŋ ‖'mɑːkɪtɪŋ/ *n* marketing *m*

market: ~**place** *n* (in town) mercado *m*, plaza *f* del mercado; (Busn) mercado *m*; ~ **research** *n* estudio *m or* investigación *f* de mercado

marking /'mɑːrkɪŋ ‖'mɑːkɪŋ/ *n* (a) (on animal, plant) mancha *f* (b) (manmade) marca *f*; **road** ~**s** líneas *fpl* de señalización vial

marksman /'mɑːrksmən ‖'mɑːksmən/ *n* (*pl* **-men** /-mən/) tirador *m*

marmalade /'mɑːrməleɪd ‖'mɑːməleɪd/ *n* mermelada *f* (de cítricos)

maroon¹ /mə'ruːn/ *adj* granate *adj inv*

maroon² *vt* (*usu pass*) ⟨castaway⟩ abandonar (en una isla desierta)

marquee /mɑːr'kiː ‖mɑː'kiː/ *n* (a) (canopy) (AmE) marquesina *f* (b) (tent) (BrE) entoldado *m*

marriage /'mærɪdʒ/ *n* **1** (a) (act) casamiento *m*, matrimonio *m*; ⟨before n⟩ ~ **certificate** certificado *m* de matrimonio (b) (relationship) matrimonio *m*; **her ~ to the poet lasted two years** estuvo dos años casada con el poeta **2** (union) (liter) (*no pl*) maridaje *m*, unión *f*

married /'mærid/ *adj* ⟨man/woman⟩ casado; **a ~ couple** un matrimonio; **they have been ~ for two years** llevan dos años casados; **to get ~** (**to sb**) casarse (con algn)

marrow /'mærəʊ/ *n* **1** (bone ~) médula *f* **2** ~ **squash** *o* (BrE) ~ (Culin) tipo de calabaza alargada y de cáscara verde

marry /'mæri/ **-ries, -rying, -ried** *vt* (a) (get married to) casarse con (b) (perform ceremony) casar (c) (unite, combine) unir
■ *vi* casarse
■ **marry off** [v + o + adv, v + adv + o] casar

Mars /mɑːrz ‖mɑːz/ *n* Marte *m*

marsh /mɑːrʃ ‖mɑːʃ/ *n* (*often pl*) pantano *m*; (on coast) marisma *f*

marshal¹ /'mɑːrʃəl ‖'mɑːʃəl/ *n* **1** (as title) (Mil) mariscal *m* **2** (as title) (AmE) (a) (police chief) jefe, -fa *m,f* de policía (b) (Law) supervisor de los tribunales de un distrito judicial **3** (at public gathering) miembro *m* del servicio de vigilancia

marshal² *vt*, (BrE) **-ll-** ⟨troops/crowd⟩ reunir*; ⟨thoughts⟩ poner* en orden; ⟨evidence⟩ reunir*

martial /'mɑːrʃəl ‖'mɑːʃəl/ *adj* marcial

martial: ~ **arts** *pl n* artes *fpl* marciales; ~ **law** *n* ley *f* marcial

martyr /'mɑːrtər ‖'mɑːtə(r)/ *n* mártir *mf*

martyrdom /'mɑːrtərdəm ‖'mɑːtədəm/ *n* martirio *m*

marvel¹ /'mɑːrvəl ‖'mɑːvəl/ *n* maravilla *f*

marvel², (BrE) **-ll-** *vi* **to ~** (**at sth**) maravillarse (**de algo**)

marvelous, (BrE) **marvellous** /'mɑːrvləs ‖'mɑːvələs/ *adj* maravilloso

Marxism /'mɑːrksɪzəm ‖'mɑːksɪzəm/ *n* marxismo *m*

Marxist¹ /'mɑːrksəst ‖'mɑːksɪst/ *n* marxista *mf*

Marxist² *adj* marxista

marzipan /'mɑːrzəpɑːn ‖'mɑːzɪpæn, ,mɑːziˈpæn/ *n* mazapán *m*

mascara /mæ'skærə ‖mæ'skɑːrə/ *n* rímel® *m*

mascot /'mæskɑːt ‖'mæskət, -skɒt/ *n* mascota *f*

masculine /'mæskjələn ‖'mæskjʊlɪn/ *adj* masculino

mash¹ /mæʃ/ *n*(BrE colloq) puré *m* de papas *or* (Esp) de patatas

mash² *vt* hacer* puré de, moler* (Chi, Méx), pisar (RPl, Ven), espichar (Col); ∼ed potato(es) puré *m* de papas *or* (Esp) de patatas

mask¹ /mæsk ‖mɑːsk/ *n* (for disguise, ritual) máscara *f*; (in fencing, ice hockey) careta *f*; (used by doctors) mascarilla *f*, barbijo *m*; (for diving) gafas *fpl or* anteojos *mpl* de bucear; (against dust, fumes) mascarilla *f*

mask² *vt* (a) (conceal) ocultar (b) (cover) cubrir*

masking tape /ˈmæskɪŋ ‖ˈmɑːskɪŋ/ *n* cinta *f* adhesiva protectora, cinta *f* de enmascarar (Col), tirro *m* (Ven)

masochist /ˈmæsəkəst ‖ˈmæsəkɪst/ *n* masoquista *mf*

mason /ˈmeɪsn̩/ *n* (a) (Const) albañil *mf*; (stone ∼) mampostero *m* (b) *also* **Mason** (Free∼) masón *m*, francmasón *m*

masquerade¹ /ˌmæskəˈreɪd ‖ˌmɑːskəˈreɪd, ˌmæ-/ *n* mascarada *f*

masquerade² *vi* to ∼ AS sb hacerse* pasar POR algn

mass¹ /mæs/ *n* [1] (bulk, body) masa *f*; **her hair was a ∼ of curls** tenía la cabeza cubierta de rizos [2] **masses** *pl* (a) (great quantity) (BrE colloq): **we received ∼es of complaints** recibimos montones de quejas (fam) (b) **the ∼es** las masas [3] (Phys) masa *f* [4] *also* **Mass** (Mus, Relig) misa *f*

mass² *vi* «*crowd/clouds*» concentrarse

mass³ *adj* (*before n*) «*culture/market*» de masas; «*hysteria/suicide*» colectivo; «*protest*» masivo; «*unemployment*» generalizado; **a ∼ meeting** una reunión de todo el personal (*or* el estudiantado *etc*); ∼ **transit** (AmE) transporte *m* público

Mass = Massachusetts

massacre¹ /ˈmæsəkər ‖ˈmæsəkə(r)/ *vt* masacrar

massacre² *n* matanza *f*, masacre *f*

massage¹ /məˈsɑːʒ ‖ˈmæsɑːʒ/ *vt* masajear

massage² *n* masaje *m*

massive /ˈmæsɪv/ *adj* «*wall*» sólido; «*support/ task*» enorme; «*heart attack/overdose*» masivo

mass: ∼ **media** *pl n* **the** ∼ **media** los medios de comunicación (de masas); ∼-**produce** /ˈmæsprəˈduːs ‖ˌmæsprəˈdjuːs/ *vt* fabricar* en serie

mast /mæst ‖mɑːst/ *n* (a) (Naut) mástil *m* (b) (flagpole) mástil *m* (c) (relay ∼) antena *f* repetidora, repetidor *m*

mastectomy /mæˈstektəmi/ *n* (*pl* -**mies**) mastectomía *f*

master¹ /ˈmæstər ‖ˈmɑːstə(r)/ *n* [1] (of household) señor *m*, amo *m*; (of animal) amo *m*, dueño *m*; (of servant) amo *m*, patrón *m* [2] (expert) ∼ OF sth maestro, -tra *m,f* DE algo [3] (Educ) (a) (degree) ∼'s (degree) máster *m*, maestría *f*; M∼ of **Arts/Science** *poseedor de una maestría en Humanidades/Ciencias* (b) (BrE) (in secondary school) profesor *m* [4] (Naut) capitán *m* [5] (∼ copy) (Audio, Comput, Print) original *m*

master² *vt* «*technique/subject*» llegar* a dominar

master³ *adj* (*before n, no comp*) (a) (expert): ∼ **baker/builder** maestro *m* panadero/de obras (b) (main) «*switch/key*» maestro (c) (original) «*tape*» original, matriz; ∼ **plan** plan *m* general

mastermind¹ /ˈmæstərmaɪnd ‖ˈmɑːstəmaɪnd/ *n* cerebro *m*

mastermind² *vt* planear y organizar*

master: ∼ **of ceremonies** *n* maestro, -tra *m,f* de ceremonias; ∼**piece** *n* obra *f* maestra

mastery /ˈmæstəri ‖ˈmɑːstəri/ *n* (a) (expertise, skill) maestría *f*; (of language, technique) dominio *m* (b) (control) dominio *m*

masturbate /ˈmæstərbeɪt ‖ˈmæstəbeɪt/ *vi* masturbarse

mat¹ /mæt/ *n* (of rushes, straw) estera *f*, esterilla *f*; (door ∼) felpudo *m*, tapete *m* (Col, Méx); (table∼) (individual) (mantel *m*) individual *m*; (in center of table) salvamanteles *m*, posafuentes *m* (CS)

mat² *adj* (AmE) ▶ MATT

match¹ /mætʃ/ *n* [1] (for fire) fósforo *m*, cerilla *f* (Esp), cerillo *m* (AmC, Méx) [2] (Sport): **boxing** ∼ combate *m* de boxeo; **tennis** ∼ partido *m* de tenis; **football** ∼ (BrE) partido *m* de fútbol [3] (equal) (*no pl*): **to be a∼/no** ∼ **for sb** estar*/no estar* a la altura de algn

match² *vt* [1] (equal) igualar [2] (a) (correspond to) «*description*» ajustarse a, corresponder a (b) (harmonize with) hacer* juego con (c) (make correspond, find equivalent for): ∼ **the words with the pictures** encuentra la palabra que corresponda a cada dibujo; **to be well** ∼**ed** «*competitors*» ser* del mismo nivel, ser* muy parejos (esp AmL); «*couple*» hacer* buena pareja (d) **matching** *pres p* haciendo juego, a juego (Esp)

■ ∼ *vi* (a) (go together) «*clothes/colors*» hacer* juego; **a demanding job with a salary to** ∼ un trabajo que exige mucho con un salario acorde (b) (tally) coincidir

match: ∼**book** *n* (AmE) librito *m* de fósforos *or* (Esp) de cerillas *or* (AmC, Méx tb) de cerillos; ∼**box** *n* caja *f* de fósforos *or* (Esp) de cerillas *or* (AmC, Méx tb) de cerillos; ∼**maker** *n* casamentero, -ra *m,f*; ∼ **point** *n* punto *m* de partido; ∼**stick** *n* (a) ▶ MATCH¹ 1 (b) (stick) palillo *m*

mate¹ /meɪt/ *n* [1] (a) (assistant) ayudante *mf* (b) (Naut) oficial *mf* de cubierta; **first** ∼ primer oficial *m* [2] (a) (Zool) (male) macho *m*; (female) hembra *f* (b) (of person) pareja *f* [3] (BrE colloq) amigo, -ga *m,f*, cuate, -ta *m,f* (Méx fam) [4] (check∼) (jaque∼) mate *m*

mate² *vi* aparearse

material¹ /məˈtɪriəl ‖məˈtɪəriəl/ *n* [1] (a) (used in manufacturing etc) material *m* (b) **materials** *pl* (equipment) material *m* [2] (cloth) tela *f*, género *m*, tejido *m* [3] (a) (for book, show etc) material *m* (b) (potential, quality): **this is bestseller** ∼ este es un bestseller en potencia; **she's champion** ∼ tiene madera de campeona

material² *adj* material

materialistic /məˌtɪriəˈlɪstɪk ‖məˌtɪəriəˈlɪstɪk/ *adj* materialista

materialize /məˈtɪriəlaɪz ‖məˈtɪəriəlaɪz/ *vi* «*object/ghost*» aparecer*; «*hope/idea*» hacerse* realidad

maternal /məˈtɜːrnl̩ ‖məˈtɜːnl̩/ *adj* (a) (motherly) maternal (b) (on mother's side) (*before n*) materno

maternity /mə'tɜːrnəti ‖mə'tɜːnəti/ n
maternidad f; (before n) ‹clinic/ward› de
obstetricia; ‹dress/clothes› de embarazada,
premamá adj inv (Esp); ‹pay/leave› por
maternidad; ~ **hospital** maternidad f

math /mæθ/ n (AmE) matemática(s) f(pl)

mathematical /'mæθə'mætɪkəl/ adj
matemático

mathematician /'mæθəmə'tɪʃən/ n
matemático, -ca m,f

mathematics /'mæθə'mætɪks/ n (+ sing vb)
matemática(s) f(pl)

maths /mæθs/ n (BrE) (+ sing vb) matemática(s)
f(pl)

matinee, matinée /'mætn̩'eɪ ‖'mætɪneɪ/ n
(Cin) primera sesión f (de la tarde), matiné(e) f
(AmS); (Theat) función f de tarde, matiné(e) f
(AmS)

matrices /'meɪtrəsiːz, 'mæt- ‖'meɪtrɪsiːz/ pl of
MATRIX

matriculate /mə'trɪkjəleɪt ‖mə'trɪkjʊleɪt/ vi
(frml) matricularse

matrimony /'mætrəməʊni ‖'mætrɪməni/ n
(frml) matrimonio m

matrix /'meɪtrɪks/ n (pl **matrices** or ~**es**)
matriz f

matron /'meɪtrən/ n (a) (dignified woman)
matrona f (b) (in prison) (AmE) matrona f (c) (in
hospital) (BrE dated) enfermera f jefe or jefa f (d) (in
school) ≈ enfermera f

matt, (AmE also) **matte, mat** /mæt/ adj mate;
a ~ **finish** un acabado mate

matted /'mætəd ‖'mætɪd/ adj enmarañado y
apelmazado

matter¹ /'mætər ‖'mætə(r)/ n [1] (a)
(substance) (Phil, Phys) materia f (b) (discharge) (Med)
pus m, materia f (c) (subject ~) temática f, tema
m (d) (written, printed material): **printed** ~ impresos
mpl; **reading** ~ material m de lectura
[2] (a) (question, affair) asunto m, cuestión f; **it's
only a** ~ **of time** solo es cuestión de tiempo;
that's a ~ **of opinion** eso es discutible (b)
matters pl: **to make** ~**s worse** para colmo (de
males); **that didn't help** ~**s** aquello no ayudó a
mejorar la situación (c) (in phrases) **as a matter
of fact: as a** ~ **of fact, I've never been to Spain** la
verdad es que nunca he estado en España; **for
that matter** en realidad; **no matter** (as interj) no
importa; (as conj): **no** ~ **how hard I try** por
mucho que me esfuerce
[3] (problem, trouble): **what's the** ~? ¿qué pasa?;
what's the ~ **with Jane?** ¿qué le pasa a Jane?

matter² vi importar

matter-of-fact /'mætərəv'fækt/ adj ‹person›
práctico; **he explained it in a very** ~ **way** lo
explicó con total naturalidad

mattress /'mætrəs ‖'mætrɪs/ n colchón m

mature¹ /mə'tʊr ‖mə'tjʊə(r)/ adj (a) (developed)
‹animal/tree› adulto; ‹fruit/artist/ideas› maduro
(b) (sensible) maduro

mature² vi (a) (develop) «plant/animal/person»

desarrollarse; «artist/work» madurar; «wine»
añejarse (b) (become sensible) madurar (c) (Fin)
«bond/policy» vencer*

maturity /mə'tʊrəti ‖mə'tjʊərəti/ n madurez f

maudlin /'mɔːdlən ‖'mɔːdlɪn/ adj llorón

maul /mɔːl/ vt atacar* (y herir*)

mausoleum /'mɔːsə'liːəm/ n (pl -**ums**)
mausoleo m

mauve /məʊv/ adj malva adj inv

maverick /'mævərɪk/ n inconformista mf; (Pol)
disidente mf

maxim /'mæksəm ‖'mæksɪm/ n máxima f

maximize /'mæksəmaɪz ‖'mæksɪmaɪz/ vt
maximizar*

maximum¹ /'mæksəməm ‖'mæksɪməm/ n
máximo m

maximum² adj (before n) máximo

may /meɪ/ v mod (past **might**) [1] (asking, granting
permission) poder*; ~ **I smoke?** ¿puedo fumar?; ~ **I
have your name and address, please?** ¿quiere
darme su nombre y dirección, por favor?
[2] (indicating probability) [El grado de probabilidad
que indica MAY es mayor que el que expresan
MIGHT O COULD]: **we** ~ **increase the price** quizás
aumentemos el precio; **it** ~ **or** ~ **not be true**
puede o no ser cierto
[3] (indicating sth is natural): **you** ~ **well ask!** ¡buena
pregunta!
[4] (conceding): **he** ~ **not be clever, but he's very
hard-working** no será inteligente, pero es muy
trabajador; **that's as** ~ **be** puede ser

May /meɪ/ n mayo m

Maybe /'meɪbi/ adv quizá(s), tal vez; ~ **I'll
come later** quizá(s) or tal vez venga luego

May: ~ **Day** n el primero de mayo; (in some
countries) el día del trabajo; **m~fly** n efímera f,
cachipolla f

mayhem /'meɪhem/ n caos m

mayonnaise /'meɪə'neɪz, 'meɪəneɪz
‖,meɪə'neɪz/ n mayonesa f, mahonesa f

mayor /'meɪər ‖meə(r)/ n alcalde, -desa m,f,
intendente mf (municipal) (RPl)

mayoress /'meɪərəs ‖'meəres/ n (BrE) (female
mayor) alcaldesa f, intendente f (RPl); (mayor's wife)
alcaldesa f

maze /meɪz/ n laberinto m

MB (= megabyte(s)) Mb.

MBA n = **Master of Business
Administration**

MC n = **master of ceremonies**

Md = **Maryland**

me¹ /miː, weak form mi/ pron [1] (a) (as direct
object) me; **she helped** ~ me ayudó; **help** ~
ayúdame (b) (as indirect object) me; **he bought** ~
flowers me compró flores (c) (after prep) mí; **for/
behind** ~ para mí/detrás de mí; **come with** ~ ven
conmigo; **she's older than** ~ es mayor que yo
[2] (emphatic use) yo; **it's** ~ soy yo

me² /miː/ n (Mus) mi m

ME **1** (Geog) = **Maine** **2** = **myalgic encephalomyelitis**

meadow /'medəʊ/ n prado m, pradera f

meager, (BrE) **meagre** /'mi:gər ‖'mi:gə(r)/ adj ‹portion/salary› escaso; ‹existence› precario

meal /mi:l/ n **1** (Culin) comida f **2** (Agr, Culin) harina f ‹de avena, maíz etc›

mealtime /'mi:ltaɪm/ n hora f de comer

mean¹ /mi:n/ vt (past & past p **meant**)
1 (represent, signify) «word/symbol» significar*, querer* decir; **that ∼s trouble** eso quiere decir que va a haber problemas; **does the number 0296 ∼ anything to you?** ¿el número 0296 te dice algo?; **fame ∼s nothing to her** la fama la tiene sin cuidado
2 (a) (refer to, intend to say) «person» querer* decir; **what do you ∼?** ¿qué quieres decir (con eso)?; **do you know what I ∼?** ¿me entiendes?; **I know who you ∼** ya sé de quién hablas **(b)** (be serious about) decir* en serio
3 (equal, entail) significar*; **that would ∼ repainting the kitchen** eso supondría volver a pintar la cocina
4 (a) (intend): **he didn't ∼ (you) any harm** no quiso hacerte daño; **to ∼ to + INF: I ∼ to succeed** mi intención es triunfar; **I ∼t to do it but I forgot** tenía toda la intención de hacerlo pero me olvidé **(b) to be ∼t to + INF** (supposed, intended): **you weren't ∼t to hear that** no pensaron (or pensé etc) que tú estarías escuchando; **I was never ∼t to be a teacher** yo no estoy hecho para enseñar

mean² adj **1** (miserly) ‹person› tacaño; ‹portion› mezquino **2** (a) (unkind, nasty) malo; **it was really ∼ of you** fue una maldad (de tu parte) **(b)** (excellent) (esp AmE sl) genial **3** (inferior, humble) (liter) humilde; **that's no ∼ feat** no es poca cosa **4** (Math) (before n) medio

mean³ n media f, promedio m; see also MEANS

meander /mi'ændər ‖mɪ'ændə(r)/ vi «river» serpentear; «person» deambular, vagar*

meaning /'mi:nɪŋ/ n significado m

meaningful /'mi:nɪŋfəl/ adj ‹look/experience/relationship› significativo; ‹explanation› con sentido; ‹discussions› positivo

meaningless /'mi:nɪŋləs ‖'mi:nɪŋlɪs/ adj sin sentido

means /mi:nz/ n (pl ∼) **1** (+ sing vb) (a) (method) medio m; **a ∼ to an end** un medio para lograr un fin; **∼ of transport** medio de transporte; see also WAYS AND MEANS **(b)** (in phrases) **by all means** por supuesto, ¡cómo no! (esp AmL); **by no means, not by any means: we are by no ∼ rich** no somos ricos ni mucho menos; **it's not a perfect film by any ∼** de ninguna manera es una película perfecta; **by means of** (as prep) por medio de, mediante
2 (frml) (+ pl vb) (wealth) medios mpl (económicos); (income) ingresos mpl

means test n: investigación de los ingresos de una persona para determinar si tiene derecho o no a ciertas prestaciones

meant /ment/ past & past p of MEAN¹

meantime /'mi:ntaɪm/ n: **in the ∼** (while sth else happens) mientras tanto, entretanto; (in the intervening period) en el ínterin or interín; **for the ∼** por ahora

meanwhile /'mi:nhwaɪl ‖'mi:nwaɪl/ adv mientras tanto, entretanto

measles /'mi:zəlz/ n (+ sing or pl vb) (Med) sarampión m

measure¹ /'meʒər ‖'meʒə(r)/ n **1** (a) (system) medida f **(b)** (unit) medida f **(c)** (amount) cantidad f; **with a (certain) ∼ of success** con cierto éxito **2** (device) medida f **3** (step) medida f; **to take ∼s to + INF** tomar medidas para + INF **4** (AmE Mus) compás m

measure² vt **1** ‹length/speed/waist› medir*; ‹weight› pesar **2** (assess) calcular; **to ∼ sth AGAINST sth** comparar algo CON algo
■ **∼** vi medir*
■ **measure out** [v + o + adv, v + adv + o] ‹length› medir*; ‹weight› pesar
■ **measure up** [v + adv] estar* a la altura de las circunstancias; **to ∼ up TO sth** estar* a la altura DE algo

measurement /'meʒərmənt ‖'meʒəmənt/ n **(a)** (act) medición f **(b)** (dimension) medida f

measuring /'meʒərɪŋ/: **∼ cup,** (BrE) **∼ jug** n jarra f graduada; **∼ spoon** n cuchara f de medir

meat /mi:t/ n **(a)** carne f; (before n) ‹product› cárnico **(b)** (substance) sustancia f

meat: **∼ball** n albóndiga f; **∼loaf** n pan m de carne

meaty /'mi:ti/ adj **-tier, -tiest** ‹taste/smell› a carne; ‹soup/stew› con mucha carne

Mecca /'mekə/ n **(a)** La Meca **(b)** also **mecca** (center of attraction) meca f

mechanic /mə'kænɪk ‖mɪ'kænɪk/ n mecánico, -ca m,f; see also MECHANICS

mechanical /mə'kænɪkəl ‖mɪ'kænɪkəl/ adj mecánico, maquinal; ‹action/reply› mecánico

mechanics /mə'kænɪks ‖mɪ'kænɪks/ n **1** (+ sing vb) (Phys, Mech Eng) mecánica f **2** (+ pl vb) **the ∼** (practical details) los aspectos prácticos; (mechanical parts) el mecanismo

mechanism /'mekənɪzəm/ n mecanismo m

mechanize /'mekənaɪz/ vt mecanizar*

medal /'medl/ n medalla f

medalist, (BrE) **medallist** /'medləst ‖'medəlɪst/ n medallista m,f; **gold/silver ∼** medalla mf de oro/plata

medallion /mə'dæljən/ n medallón m

medallist (BrE) ▶ MEDALIST

meddle /'medl/ vi **(a)** (interfere) **to ∼ (IN/WITH sth)** meterse or entrometerse (EN algo) **(b)** (tamper) **to ∼ WITH sth** toquetear algo

media¹ /'mi:diə/ n: **the ∼** (+ pl or (crit) sing vb) los medios de comunicación

media² pl of MEDIUM¹ 1, 2

mediaeval /'mi:di'i:vəl, 'me- ‖,medi'i:vəl/ ▶ MEDIEVAL

median¹ /'mi:diən/ adj (Math) medio

median² n **1** (Math) mediana f **2** **∼ (strip)** (AmE) mediana f, bandejón m (central) (Chi), camellón m (Méx)

mediate /'mi:dieɪt/ vi mediar

mediator /'mi:dieɪtər ‖'mi:dieɪtə(r)/ n mediador, -dora m,f

Medicaid /'medɪkeɪd/ n (in US) organismo y programa estatal de asistencia sanitaria a personas de bajos ingresos

medical¹ /'medɪkəl/ adj ‹care/examination/ insurance› médico; ‹student› de medicina; ~ **school** facultad f de medicina

medical² n revisión f médica

Medicare /'medɪkər ‖'medɪkeə(r)/ n (in US) organismo y programa estatal de asistencia sanitaria a personas mayores de 65 años

medicated /'medəkeɪtəd ‖'medɪkeɪtɪd/ adj medicinal

medication /,medə'keɪʃən ‖,medr'keɪʃən/ n **(a)** (substance) medicamento m **(b)** (drugs) medicación f

medicinal /mə'dɪsnəl ‖mɪ'dɪsɪnl̩/ adj medicinal

medicine /'medəsən ‖'medsən, 'medəsən/ n **1** (substance) medicamento m, medicina f, remedio m (esp AmL) **2** (science) medicina f

medieval /,mi:di'i:vəl, 'me- ‖,medi'i:vəl/ adj medieval, medioeval

mediocre /'mi:di'əukər ‖,mi:dɪ'əukə(r)/ adj mediocre

mediocrity /,mi:di'ɑːkrəti ‖,mi:dɪ'ɒkrəti/ n (pl **-ties**) **(a)** (quality) mediocridad f **(b)** (person) mediocre mf

meditate /'medəteɪt ‖'medɪteɪt/ vi meditar

meditation /,medə'teɪʃən ‖,medɪ'teɪʃən/ n meditación f

Mediterranean¹ /'medətə'reɪniən ‖,medɪtə'reɪniən/ adj mediterráneo

Mediterranean² n the ~ (Sea) el (mar) Mediterráneo

medium¹ /'mi:diəm/ adj **1** (intermediate) ‹size› mediano **2** (Culin) **(a)** ‹steak› a punto, término medio (Méx) **(b)** (as adv): ~ **rare** ‹steak› poco hecho, a la inglesa (Méx); ~ **dry** ‹wine› semi-seco

medium² n **1** (pl **media**) (means, vehicle) medio m **2** (pl **media**) (environment) medio m (ambiente) **3** (middle position) (no pl) punto m medio; **to strike a happy** ~ lograr un término medio **4** (pl **mediums**) (Occult) médium mf

medium: ~**-size** /'mi:diəm'saɪz/, (BrE also) ~**-sized** /-d/ adj ‹book/house› de tamaño mediano; ‹person› de talla media or mediana; ~**-term** /'mi:diəm'tɜːrm ‖,mi:diəm'tɜːm/ adj (before n) a medio plazo; ~ **wave** n (BrE) (no pl) onda f media

medley /'medli/ n **(a)** (mixture) mezcla f **(b)** (Mus) popurrí m

meek /mi:k/ adj **-er, -est** dócil, sumiso

meet¹ /mi:t/ (past & past p **met**) vt **1 (a)** (encounter) encontrarse* con **(b)** (welcome) recibir; (collect on arrival) ir* a buscar; **she ran to** ~ **me** corrió a mi encuentro
2 (make acquaintance of) conocer*; **pleased to** ~ **you** encantado de conocerlo
3 (come up against, experience) encontrar*; **there's more to this than** ~**s the eye** esto es más complicado de lo que parece
4 ‹demands/wishes/debt› satisfacer*; ‹deadline/ quota/obligation› cumplir con; ‹requirements› reunir*; ‹cost› hacerse* cargo de
■ ~ vi **1 (a)** (encounter each other) encontrarse*; **we arranged to** ~ **at three** quedamos en or (AmL tb) quedamos de encontrarnos a las tres, quedamos a las tres (esp Esp) **(b)** (hold meeting)

«club» reunirse*; «heads of state/ministers» entrevistarse **(c)** (make acquaintance) conocerse*; **have you two already met?** ¿ya se conocen? **2** (come into contact): **the vehicles met head on** los vehículos chocaron de frente; **their eyes met** sus miradas se cruzaron
■ **meet up** [v + adv] **to** ~ **up (WITH sb)** encontrarse* (CON algn)
■ **meet with** [v + prep + o] **(a)** ‹opposition/ hostility› ser* recibido con; **she met with an unfortunate accident** le ocurrió un lamentable accidente **(b)** (meet) (AmE) encontrarse* con

meet² n **(a)** (AmE Sport) encuentro m **(b)** (in hunting) partida f (de caza)

meeting /'mi:tɪŋ/ n **1** (assembly) reunión f; **to call/hold a** ~ convocar*/celebrar una reunión; **political** ~ mitin m, mítin m **2** (encounter) encuentro m; (between presidents) entrevista f **3** (BrE Sport) encuentro m

megabyte /'megəbaɪt/ n megabyte m, megaocteto m

megalomaniac /'megələu'meɪniæk/ n megalómano, -na m,f

megaphone /'megəfəun/ n megáfono m

melancholy /'melənkɑːli ‖'melənkəli/ adj ‹person/mood› melancólico; ‹sound› triste

mellow¹ /'meləu/ adj **-er, -est (a)** ‹fruit› maduro; ‹wine› añejo; ‹sound/voice› dulce; ‹light/ color› tenue **(b)** ‹person/mood› apacible

mellow² vt suavizar*
■ ~ vi ‹color/voice› suavizarse*; **he has** ~**ed with age** se le ha suavizado el carácter con los años

melodrama /'melədrɑːmə/ n melodrama m

melodramatic /,melədrə'mætɪk/ adj melodramático

melody /'melədi/ n (pl **-dies**) melodía f

melon /'melən/ n melón m

melt /melt/ vi ‹ice/butter» derretirse*; «metal/ wax» fundirse; «anger» desaparecer*; **they** ~**ed into the crowd** se perdieron en la muchedumbre
■ ~ vt ‹snow/butter» derretir*; **their cries** ~**ed her heart** su llanto la conmovió
■ **melt away** [v + adv] ‹ice/snow» derretirse*; «mist/fog» levantarse; «fear/suspicion» disiparse; «confidence» desvanecerse*; «resistance/opposition» desaparecer*; **they** ~**ed away into the woods** desaparecieron ocultándose en el bosque
■ **melt down** [v + o + adv, v + adv + o] ‹gold/ coins› fundir

member /'membər ‖'membə(r)/ n **1** (of committee, board) miembro mf; (of club) socio, -cia m,f; ~ **of staff** empleado, -da m,f; **a** ~ **of the audience** un espectador; **the offer is open to any** ~ **of the public** la oferta está abierta al público en general; (before n) ~ **states** países mpl miembros **2** (limb) (arch) miembro m

Member: ~ **of Congress** n (in US) miembro mf del Congreso; ~ **of Parliament** n (in UK etc) diputado, -da m,f, parlamentario, -ria m,f

membership /'membərʃɪp ‖'membəʃɪp/ n **(a)** (being a member): ~ **of the club is restricted to residents** solo los residentes pueden hacerse socios del club; **to apply for** ~ solicitar el ingreso en un club (or partido etc); (before n) ~ **card**

carné *m* de socio **(b)** (members) (+ *sing or pl vb*) socios *mpl* (*or* afiliados *mpl etc*); (number of members) número *m* de socios (*or* afiliados *etc*)

membrane /'membreɪn/ *n* membrana *f*

memento /mə'mentəʊ ‖mɪ'mentəʊ/ *n* (*pl* **-tos** *or* **-toes**) recuerdo *m*

memo /'meməʊ/ *n* (*pl* **-os**) memorándum *m*

memoirs /'memwɑːrz ‖'memwɑːz/ *pl n* memorias *fpl*

memorabilia /ˌmemərə'bɪliə/ *pl n* objetos *mpl* de interés

memorable /'memərəbəl/ *adj* memorable

memorandum /ˌmemə'rændəm/ *n* (*pl* **-dums** *or* **-da** /-də/) memorándum *m*

memorial¹ /mə'mɔːriəl/ *n* monumento *m*

memorial² *adj* conmemorativo

Memorial Day *n* (in US) el último lunes de mayo, día en que se recuerda a los caídos en la guerra

memorize /'meməraɪz/ *vt* memorizar*

memory /'meməri/ *n* (*pl* **-ries**) [1] **(a)** (faculty) memoria *f* **(b)** (period): **the worst storm in living** ~ la peor tormenta que se recuerde [2] **(a)** (recollection) recuerdo *m*; **his** ~ **will live on** su recuerdo permanecerá vivo **(b)** (remembrance) memoria *f*; **in** ~ **of sb/sth** a la memoria de algn/ en conmemoración de algo [3] (Comput) memoria *f*

men /men/ *pl of* MAN¹

menace /'menəs ‖'menɪs/ *n* [1] **(a)** (threatening quality): **the** ~ **in his voice** el tono amenazador de su voz **(b)** (threat) amenaza *f* [2] (danger) amenaza *f*

menacing /'menəsɪŋ ‖'menɪsɪŋ/ *adj* amenazador

menagerie /mə'nædʒəri/ *n* colección *f* de animales salvajes

mend¹ /mend/ *vt* ⟨garment⟩ coser; ⟨shoe/clock/roof⟩ arreglar, reparar; **to** ~ **one's ways** enmendarse*

■ ~ *vi* (heal) ⟨injury⟩ curarse; ⟨fracture/bone⟩ soldarse*

mend² *n* remiendo *m*; **to be on the** ~ (colloq) ir* mejorando

menial /'miːniəl/ *adj* de ínfima importancia

meningitis /ˌmenən'dʒaɪtəs ‖ˌmenɪn'dʒaɪtɪs/ *n* meningitis *f*

menopause /'menəpɔːz/ *n* **the** ~ la menopausia

men's room *n* (AmE) baño *m or* servicios *mpl* de caballeros

menstruate /'menstrueɪt/ *vi* menstruar*

menswear /'menzwer ‖'menzweə(r)/ *n* ropa *f* de caballero

mental /'mentl/ *adj* (before n) ⟨powers/illness⟩ mental; ⟨hospital/patient⟩ psiquiátrico

mental arithmetic *n* cálculos *mpl* mentales

mentality /men'tæləti/ *n* (*pl* **-ties**) mentalidad *f*

mentally /'mentəli/ *adv* mentalmente; **he's** ~ **ill/handicapped** es un enfermo mental/un disminuido psíquico

menthol /'menθɒl ‖'menθɒl/ *n* mentol *m*; (before n) ⟨cigarettes⟩ mentolado

mentholated /'menθəleɪtəd ‖'menθəleɪtɪd/ *adj* mentolado

mention¹ /'mentʃən ‖'menʃən/ *vt* mencionar; **I won't** ~ **any names** no daré nombres; **there's the problem of time, not to** ~ **the cost** está el problema del tiempo y no digamos ya el costo; **don't** ~ **it** (on being thanked) no hay de qué, de nada

mention² *n* mención *f*

mentor /'mentɔːr ‖'mentɔː(r)/ *n* (liter) mentor, -tora *m,f* (liter)

menu /'menjuː/ *n* **(a)** (in restaurant) carta *f*, menú *m* (esp AmL) **(b)** (Comput) menú *m*

meow¹ /mi'aʊ/ *n* maullido *m*

meow² *vi* maullar*

MEP *n* (= **Member of the European Parliament**) eurodiputado, -da *m,f*

mercenary /'mɜːrsəneri ‖'mɜːsənəri/ *n* (*pl* **-ries**) mercenario, -ria *m,f*

merchandise /'mɜːrtʃəndaɪz ‖'mɜːtʃəndaɪz/ *n* mercancía *f*, mercadería *f* (AmS)

merchant /'mɜːrtʃənt ‖'mɜːtʃənt/ *n* **(a)** (retailer) comerciante *mf* **(b)** (Hist) mercader *m*

merchant marine, (BrE also) **merchant navy** *n* marina *f* mercante

merciful /'mɜːrsɪfəl ‖'mɜːsɪfəl/ *adj* misericordioso

merciless /'mɜːrsɪləs ‖'mɜːsɪlɪs/ *adj* despiadado

mercury /'mɜːrkjəri ‖'mɜːkjʊri/ *n* mercurio *m*

Mercury /'mɜːrkjəri ‖'mɜːkjʊri/ *n* Mercurio *m*

mercy /'mɜːrsi ‖'mɜːsi/ *n* (*pl* **-cies**) **(a)** (clemency) misericordia *f*; **to have** ~ **(on sb)** tener* misericordia (de algn), apiadarse (de algn); **at the** ~ **of the elements** a merced de los elementos **(b)** (blessing) bendición *f*; **it's a** ~ **that** … colloq) es una suerte que …; **let's be thankful for small mercies** (set phrase) seamos positivos, podría haber sido peor

mere /mɪr ‖mɪə(r)/ *adj* (*superl* **merest**) (before n) simple, mero

merely /'mɪrli ‖'mɪəli/ *adv* simplemente

merge /mɜːrdʒ ‖mɜːdʒ/ *vi* ⟨roads/rivers⟩ confluir*; ⟨colors⟩ fundirse; ⟨companies⟩ fusionarse; **he** ~**d into the crowd** se perdió entre el gentío

■ ~ *vt* ⟨companies/organizations⟩ fusionar; ⟨colors⟩ combinar

merger /'mɜːrdʒər ‖'mɜːdʒə(r)/ *n* **(a)** (Busn) fusión *f* **(b)** (of organizations etc) fusión *f*

meringue /mə'ræŋ/ *n* merengue *m*

merit¹ /'merət ‖'merɪt/ *n* mérito *m*; **each case is judged on its (own)** ~**s** se juzga cada caso individualmente

merit² *vt* merecer*

mermaid /'mɜːrmeɪd ‖'mɜːmeɪd/ *n* sirena *f*

merrily /'merəli ‖'merɪli/ *adv* **(a)** (joyfully) alegremente **(b)** (unconcernedly) tranquilamente

merriment /'merɪmənt/ *n* (joy) alegría *f*; (laughter) risas *fpl*

merry /'meri/ *adj* **-rier, -riest** alegre; ~ **Christmas!** ¡feliz Navidad!, ¡felices Pascuas!

merry-go-round /'merigəʊˌraʊnd/ *n* carrusel *m*, tiovivo *m* (Esp), calesita *f* (Per, RPl)

mesh /meʃ/ *n* malla *f*

mesmerize /'mezməraɪz/ *vt* **(a)** (fascinate) cautivar **(b)** (hypnotize) (dated) hipnotizar*

mess /mes/ n **1** (a) (no pl) (untidiness) desorden m; **the bedroom was (in) a ~** el dormitorio estaba todo desordenado; **my hair is a ~** (colloq) tengo el pelo hecho un desastre (b) (dirt): **what a ~!** ¡qué desastre or (RPl tb) enchastre! (fam); **they made a ~ on the carpet** dejaron la alfombra hecha un asco (fam)
2 (no pl) (confused, troubled state): **the country is (in) a complete ~** la situación del país es caótica; **my life's a ~** mi vida es un desastre; **to make a ~ of sth: you made a real ~ of this job** hiciste muy mal este trabajo
3 (Mil): **officers' ~** casino m or comedor m de oficiales
■ **mess around,** (BrE also) **mess about** (colloq) [v + adv] (a) (misbehave) «children» hacer* travesuras (b) (interfere): **stop ~ing around with my things!** ¡deja mis cosas tranquilas!; **don't ~ around with me** no juegues conmigo
■ **mess up** [v + o + adv, v + adv + o] (a) (make untidy) desordenar (b) (make dirty) ensuciar (c) (spoil) «plans» estropear

message /'mesɪdʒ/ n mensaje m; **would you like to leave a ~?** ¿quiere dejar algún recado or (esp AmL) mensaje?, ¿quiere dejar algo dicho? (CS); **to get the ~** (colloq) entender*, darse* cuenta

messenger /'mesn̩dʒər ‖ 'mesɪndʒə(r)/ n mensajero, -ra m,f

Messiah /mə'saɪə/ n Mesías m

Messrs /'mesərz ‖ 'mesəz/ pl of **Mr** Sres.

messy /'mesi/ adj **-sier, -siest** (a) (untidy) «room» desordenado; «writing» sucio y descuidado, desprolijo (CS) (b) (dirty) sucio; **he's a ~ eater** no sabe comer (c) (unpleasant, confused) «business» turbio

met /met/ past & past p of **MEET**[1]

metabolism /mə'tæbəlɪzəm ‖ mə'tæbəlɪzəm/ n metabolismo m

metal /'metl̩/ n (Chem, Metall) metal m; (before n) «box» metálico

metallic /mə'tælɪk/ adj metálico

metamorphosis /'metə'mɔːrfəsəs ‖ ˌmetə'mɔːfəsɪs/ n (pl **-phoses** /-fəsiːz/) metamorfosis f

metaphor /'metəfɔːr, -fər ‖ 'metəfɔː(r), -fə(r)/ n metáfora f

metaphorical /ˌmetə'fɔːrɪkəl ‖ ˌmetə'fɒrɪkəl/ adj metafórico

mete /miːt/ ▶ **METE OUT**

meteor /'miːtiər, -ɔːr ‖ 'miːtiə(r), -ɔː(r)/ n meteorito m

meteoric /ˌmiːti'ɔːrɪk ‖ ˌmiːtɪ'ɒrɪk/ adj «rise/progress» meteórico; **~ rock** piedra f meteórica

meteorite /'miːtiəraɪt/ n meteorito m

meteorology /ˌmiːtiə'rɑːlədʒi ‖ ˌmiːtiə'rɒlədʒi/ n meteorología f

mete out [v + o + adv, v + adv + o] «fine/punishment» imponer*

meter[1] /'miːtər ‖ 'miːtə(r)/ n **1** (a) (measuring device): **gas/electricity/water ~** contador m or (AmL

tb) medidor m de gas/electricidad/agua (b) (parking ~) parquímetro m **2** (AmE Mus) compás m **3** (BrE) **metre** (measure) metro m

meter[2] vt medir* (con contador)

methane /'meθeɪn ‖ 'miːθeɪn/ n metano m

method /'meθəd/ n método m

methodical /mə'θɑːdɪkəl ‖ mɪ'θɒdɪkəl/ adj metódico

Methodism /'meθədɪzəm/ n metodismo m

Methodist /'meθədəst ‖ 'meθədɪst/ n metodista mf

methylated spirit(s) /'meθəleɪtəd ‖ 'meθəleɪtɪd/ n (+ sing vb) alcohol m desnaturalizado

meticulous /mə'tɪkjələs ‖ mə'tɪkjʊləs/ adj meticuloso

metre (BrE) ▶ **METER**[1] 3

metric /'metrɪk/ adj métrico

metro /'metrəʊ/ n (pl **-ros**) (Rail, Transp) metro m, subterráneo m (RPl)

metropolitan /ˌmetrə'pɑːlətn̩ ‖ ˌmetrə'pɒlɪtən/ adj (frml) metropolitano

mettle /'metl̩/ n temple m; **to be on one's ~** estar* dispuesto a dar lo mejor de sí

mew /mjuː/ vi maullar*

Mexican[1] /'meksɪkən/ adj mexicano, mejicano

Mexican[2] n mexicano, -na m,f, mejicano, -na m,f

Mexico /'meksɪkəʊ/ n México m, Méjico m

Mexico City n (ciudad f de) México m or Méjico m

mezzanine /'mezəniːn/ n (a) **~ (floor)** entresuelo m, mezzanine f or m (AmL) (b) (AmE Theat) platea f alta

mi /miː/ n (Mus) mi m

MI = **Michigan**

miaow /mi'aʊ/ n/vi ▶ **MEOW**[1,2]

mice /maɪs/ pl of **MOUSE**

Mich = **Michigan**

microbe /'maɪkrəʊb/ n microbio m

microchip /'maɪkrəʊtʃɪp/ n (micro)chip m, pastilla f de silicio

microcomputer /'maɪkrəʊkəmˌpjuːtər ‖ ˌmaɪkrəʊkəm'pjuːtə(r)/ n microcomputadora f (esp AmL), microordenador m (Esp)

microfilm /'maɪkrəʊfɪlm/ n microfilm m, microfilme m

microlight /'maɪkrəʊlaɪt/ n aeroligero m

microphone /'maɪkrəfəʊn/ n micrófono m

microprocessor /'maɪkrəʊˈprɑːsesər ‖ ˌmaɪkrəʊˌprəʊsesə(r)/ n microprocesador m

microscope /'maɪkrəskəʊp/ n microscopio m

microscopic /ˌmaɪkrə'skɑːpɪk ‖ ˌmaɪkrə'skɒpɪk/ adj microscópico, al microscopio

microwave /'maɪkrəʊweɪv, 'maɪkrə-/ n **~ (oven)** (horno m de) microondas m

AmC	Central America	Arg	Argentina	Cu	Cuba	Per	Peru
AmL	Latin America	Bol	Bolivia	Ec	Ecuador	RPl	River Plate Area
AmS	South America	Chi	Chile	Esp	Spain	Ur	Uruguay
Andes	Andean Region	CS	Southern Cone	Méx	Mexico	Ven	Venezuela

mid- /mɪd/ *pref*: in ~**January** a mediados de enero; ~**morning** a media mañana; **she was in her** ~**forties** tenía alrededor de 45 años

midair /'mɪd'er ‖,mɪd'eə(r)/ *n*: in ~ en el aire

midday /'mɪd'deɪ/ *n* mediodía *m*

middle¹ /'mɪdl/ *n* **1** (of object, place — center) centro *m*, medio *m*; (— half-way line) mitad *f*; **it stood in the** ~ **of the room** estaba en el centro *or* en (el) medio de la habitación; **in the** ~ **of nowhere** quién sabe dónde, en el quinto pino (Esp fam), donde el diablo perdió el poncho (AmS fam) **2** (of period, activity): **in the** ~ **of the week/January** a mediados de semana/de enero; **it's the** ~ **of winter** estamos en pleno invierno; **in the** ~ **of the night** en la mitad de la noche; **I'm in the** ~ **of a really exciting novel at the moment** en este momento estoy leyendo una novela muy interesante; **I'm in the** ~ **of cooking dinner** estoy preparando la cena **3** (waist) cintura *f*

middle² *adj* (*before n*): **the** ~ **house of the three** de las tres, la casa de en medio *or* del medio

middle: ~**-aged** /'mɪdl'eɪdʒd/ *adj* de mediana edad; **M**~ **Ages** *pl n* **the M**~ **Ages** la Edad Media; ~ **class** *n* (*often pl*) clase *f* media; ~**-class** /'mɪdl'klæs ‖,mɪdl'klɑːs/ *adj* de clase media; ~**-distance** /'mɪdl'dɪstəns/ *adj* (*before n*) ⟨*running/race*⟩ de medio fondo; ~**-distance runner** mediofondista *mf*; **M**~ **East** *n* **the M**~ **East** el Oriente Medio, el Medio Oriente; ~**man** /'mɪdlmæn/ *n* (*pl* **-men** /-men/) intermediario *m*; ~ **management** *n* mandos *mpl* (inter)medios; ~ **name** *n* segundo nombre *m*; ~**-of-the-road** /'mɪdlǝvðǝ'rǝud/ *adj* ⟨*politician/views*⟩ moderado; ⟨*artist*⟩ del montón; ~ **school** *n* (in US) colegio para niños de 12 a 14 años; (in UK) colegio para niños de 9 a 13 años

midge /mɪdʒ/ *n*: especie de mosquito pequeño

midget /'mɪdʒǝt ‖'mɪdʒɪt/ *n* enano, -na *m,f* (*de proporciones normales*)

midnight /'mɪdnaɪt/ *n* medianoche *f*

midst /mɪdst/ *n*: in the ~ of sth en medio de algo; in our ~ entre nosotros

midsummer /'mɪd'sʌmǝr ‖,mɪd'sʌmǝ(r)/ *n* pleno verano *m*; **M**~**'s Day** el solsticio estival *or* vernal; (in the Northern hemisphere) el día de San Juan

midtown /'mɪd'taʊn/ *n* casco *m*, centro *m*; (*before n*) ⟨*apartment/hotel*⟩ de la periferia del centro

midway /'mɪd'weɪ/ *adv* ⟨*stop*⟩ a mitad de camino; ~ **through the morning** a media mañana

midweek¹ /'mɪd'wiːk/ *n*: around ~ a mediados de semana; (*before n*) ⟨*concert/flight*⟩ de entre semana

midweek² *adv* entre semana

Midwest /'mɪd'west/ *n* **the** ~ *la región central de los EEUU*

midwife /'mɪdwaɪf/ *n* (*pl* **-wives**) partera *f*

midwinter /'mɪd'wɪntǝr ‖,mɪd'wɪntǝ(r)/ *n* pleno invierno *m*

might¹ /maɪt/ *v mod* **1** *past of* MAY
2 **(a)** (asking permission) (esp BrE) podría (*or* podríamos *etc*); ~ **I make a suggestion?** si se me permite (hacer) una sugerencia … **(b)** (in suggestions, expressing annoyance, regret) poder*; **you** ~ **at least listen** al menos podrías escuchar

3 (indicating possibility) [*La posibilidad que indica* MIGHT *es más remota que la que expresan* MAY *o* COULD]: **somebody** ~ **have found it** pudiera ser que alguien lo hubiera encontrado; **it** ~ (**well**) **have been disastrous if the police hadn't arrived** podría haber sido catastrófico si no hubiera llegado la policía
4 (indicating sth is natural): **he rang to apologize — and well he** ~! llamó para pedir perdón — ¡era lo menos que podía hacer!
5 (conceding): **the house** ~ **not be big, but** … la casa no será grande pero …

might² *n* poder *m*

mighty¹ /'maɪti/ *adj* **-tier, -tiest (a)** (powerful) ⟨*empire/ruler*⟩ poderoso; ⟨*kick/blow*⟩ fortísimo **(b)** (imposing) ⟨*ocean/river*⟩ imponente

mighty² *adv* (colloq) (*as intensifier*) muy

migraine /'maɪɡreɪn ‖'miːɡreɪn, 'maɪ-/ *n* jaqueca *f*, migraña *f*

migrant¹ /'maɪɡrǝnt/ *n* **(a)** (Zool) (species) especie *f* migratoria; (bird) ave *f*; migratoria **(b)** (person) trabajador, -dora *m,f* itinerante

migrant² *adj* **(a)** (Zool) migratorio **(b)** (*before n*) ⟨*worker*⟩ itinerante; (foreign) extranjero

migrate /'maɪɡreɪt ‖maɪ'ɡreɪt/ *vi* emigrar

migration /maɪ'ɡreɪʃǝn/ *n* migración *f*

mike /maɪk/ *n* (colloq) micro *m* (fam)

milage *n* ▶ MILEAGE

mild /maɪld/ *adj* **-er, -est 1 (a)** (gentle) ⟨*person*⟩ afable; ⟨*manner/criticism*⟩ suave **(b)** (not serious or potent) ⟨*attack/form*⟩ ligero, leve; ⟨*discomfort*⟩ ligero **2** ⟨*climate*⟩ templado; ⟨*winter*⟩ no muy frío; **it's very** ~ **today** hoy no hace nada de frío **3** ⟨*cheese/tobacco/detergent/ sedative*⟩ suave

mildew /'mɪldu ‖'mɪldju/ *n* (on plants) mildeu *m*, mildiu *m*; (on wall, fabric) moho *m*

mildly /'maɪldli/ *adv* **(a)** (gently) ⟨*rebuke*⟩ suavemente; **to put it** ~ por no decir algo peor **(b)** (slightly) ligeramente

mile /maɪl/ *n* milla *f* (*1.609 metros*); **that's** ~**s away from here** (colloq) eso está lejísimos de aquí; **it sticks** *o* **stands out a** ~ se ve a la legua

mileage /'maɪlɪdʒ/ *n* **1** (Auto) distancia *f* recorrida (*en millas*), ≈ kilometraje *m* **2** (advantage, profit): **they want to extract maximum** ~ **from the Pope's visit** quieren explotar al máximo la visita del Papa

mileometer /maɪ'lɑːmǝtǝr ‖maɪ'lɒmɪtǝ(r)/ *n* (BrE) ≈ cuentakilómetros *m*

milestone /'maɪlstǝun/ *n* (on road) mojón *m*; (significant event) hito *m*, jalón *m*

militant¹ /'mɪlɪtǝnt/ *adj* militante

militant² *n* militante *mf*

military¹ /'mɪlǝteri ‖'mɪlɪtri/ *adj* militar; ~ **academy** (in US) escuela *f* militar; **to do** ~ **service** hacer* el servicio militar

military² *n* **the** ~ los militares

military police *n* policía *f* militar

militia /mǝ'lɪʃǝ ‖mɪ'lɪʃǝ/ *n* (+ *sing or pl vb*) milicia *f*

milk¹ /mɪlk/ *n* **(a)** leche *f*; (*before n*) ⟨*production/bottle*⟩ de leche; ⟨*product*⟩ lácteo; ~ **chocolate** chocolate *m* con leche **(b)** (lotion) (BrE) leche *f*

milk² *vt* **(a)** ‹*cow/herd*› ordeñar **(b)** (exploit) explotar

milk: **∼man** /'mɪlkmən/ *n* (*pl* **-men** /-mən/) lechero *m*; **∼ shake** *n* batido *m*, (leche *f*) malteada *f* (AmL), licuado *m* con leche (AmL)

milky /'mɪlki/ *adj* **-kier, -kiest** lechoso; ‹*coffee/tea*› con mucha leche

Milky Way *n* the **∼ ∼** la Vía Láctea

mill¹ /mɪl/ *n* 1 **(a)** (building, machine) molino *m* **(b)** (for pepper etc) molinillo *m* 2 (cotton **∼**) fábrica *f* de tejidos de algodón

mill² *vt* ‹*flour*› moler*

■ **mill about, mill around** [*v* + *adv*] «*crowd*» dar* vueltas

millennium /mɪ'leniəm/ *n* (*pl* **-niums** *or* **-nia** /-niə/) milenio *m*

millennium bug *n* efecto *m* dos mil

miller /'mɪlər ‖'mɪlə(r)/ *n* molinero, -ra *m,f*

milligram /'mɪləgræm ‖'mɪlɪgræm/ *n* miligramo *m*

millimeter, (BrE) **millimetre** /'mɪlə,miːtər ‖'mɪlɪmiːtə(r)/ *n* milímetro *m*

milliner /'mɪlənər ‖'mɪlɪnə(r)/ *n* sombrerero, -ra *m,f* de señoras

million /'mɪljən/ *n* millón *m*; **a ∼ people** un millón de personas

millionaire /,mɪljə'ner ‖,mɪljə'neə(r)/ *n* millonario, -ria *m,f*

milometer /mar'lɑːmətər ‖mar'lɒmɪtə(r)/ *n* ▶ MILEOMETER

mime¹ /maɪm/ *n* **(a)** (technique) mímica *f* **(b)** **∼** (**artist**) mimo *mf* **(c)** (performance) pantomima *f*

mime² *vt* imitar, hacer* la mímica de
■ **∼** *vi* hacer* la mímica

mimic /'mɪmɪk/ *vt* **-ck-** imitar

mince¹ /mɪns/ *vt* ‹*onions*› picar* (*en trozos menudos*); ‹*meat*› moler* *or* (Esp, RPl) picar*; *not to* **∼** (*one's*) *words* no andar(se)* con rodeos
■ **∼** *vi* caminar con afectación

mince² *n* (BrE) carne *f* molida *or* (Esp, RPl) picada

mincemeat /'mɪnsmiːt/ *n* picadillo *m de frutos secos, grasa y especias usado en pastelería*

mind¹ /maɪnd/ *n* 1 **(a)** (Psych) mente *f*; **to bear** *o* **keep sth/sb in ∼** tener* algo/a algn en cuenta; **to bring** *o* **call sth to ∼** recordar(le)* algo (a algn); **to have sth/sb in ∼** tener* algo/a algn en mente; **with that in ∼** pensando en eso; **what's on your ∼?** ¿qué es lo que te preocupa?; **that put my ∼ at rest** con eso me tranquilicé; **put it out of your ∼!** ¡no pienses más en eso!; **I can't get him/the thought out of my ∼** no puedo quitarme de la cabeza; **to read sb's ∼** adivinarle *or* leerle* el pensamiento a algn **(b)** (mentality) mentalidad *f* 2 (attention): **my ∼ was on other things** tenía la cabeza en otras cosas; **he needs something to take his ∼ off** it necesita algo que lo distraiga 3 **(a)** (opinion): **to change one's ∼** cambiar de opinión; **to make up one's ∼** decidirse; **to my ∼** a mi parecer **(b)** (will, intention): **he has a ∼ of his own** (he is obstinate) es muy empecinado; (he knows his own mind) sabe muy bien lo que quiere; **I've a good ∼ to complain to the manager** tengo ganas de ir a quejarme al gerente 4 (mental faculties) juicio *m*, razón *f*; **to be/go out of one's ∼** estar*/volverse* loco

mind² *vt* 1 (look after) ‹*children*› cuidar, cuidar de; ‹*seat/place*› guardar; ‹*shop/office*› atender* 2 (*usu in imperative*) **(a)** (be careful about): **∼ your head!** ¡ojo *or* cuidado con la cabeza!; **∼ (that) you don't forget!** procura no olvidarte **(b)** (concern oneself about) preocuparse por; **never ∼ him!** ¡no le hagas caso! 3 (object to) (*usu neg or interrog*): **I don't ∼ the noise** no me molesta *or* no me importa el ruido; **I don't ∼ him, but I can't stand her** él no me disgusta, pero a ella no la soporto; **I don't ∼ what you do** me da igual lo que hagas; **would you ∼ waiting?** ¿le importaría esperar?
■ **∼** *vi* 1 (*in imperative*) (concern oneself): **never ∼** no importa, no te preocupes (*or* no se preocupen *etc*); **never you ∼!** ¡(a ti) qué te importa! 2 (object) (*usu neg or interrog*): **I don't ∼** me da igual; **do you ∼ if I open the window?** ¿le importa *or* le molesta si abro la ventana?; **do you ∼ if I smoke? — yes, I do ∼!** ¿te importa si fumo? — ¡sí que me importa!

-minded /'maɪndəd ‖'maɪndɪd/ *suff*: **business∼** con mentalidad para los negocios; **liberal∼** liberal

mindless /'maɪndləs ‖'maɪndlɪs/ *adj* ‹*activity*› mecánico; ‹*violence/obedience*› ciego

mine¹ /maɪn/ *n* 1 (Min) mina *f*; **to be a ∼ of information** ser* una mina de información 2 (Mil) mina *f*

mine² *pron*

■ **Note** The translation *mío* reflects the gender and number of the noun it is standing for; *mine* is translated by *el mío, la mía, los míos, las mías*, depending on what is being referred to.

(*sing*) mío, mía; (*pl*) míos, mías; **∼ is here** el mío/la mía está aquí; **a friend of ∼** un amigo mío; **it's a hobby of ∼** es uno de mis hobbies

mine³ *vt* 1 (Min) ‹*gold/coal*› extraer* 2 (Mil) minar

minefield /'maɪnfiːld/ *n* campo *m* minado

miner /'maɪnər ‖'maɪnə(r)/ *n* minero, -ra *m,f*

mineral /'mɪnərəl/ *n* mineral *m*

mineral water *n* agua *f*‡ mineral

mingle /'mɪŋgəl/ *vi* **(a)** «*people*» mezclarse; (at a party etc) circular **(b)** «*liquids*» mezclarse; «*sounds*» fundirse
■ **∼** *vt* **to ∼ sth WITH sth** mezclar algo CON algo

miniature¹ /'mɪnɪtʃʊr ‖'mɪnɪtʃə(r)/ *n* miniatura *f*

miniature² *adj* (before n) ‹*portrait*› en miniatura; ‹*poodle*› enano

minibus /'mɪnɪbʌs/ *n* microbús *m*, micro *m*

minicab /'mɪnɪkæb/ *n* (BrE) taxi *m* (*que se pide por teléfono*)

minim /'mɪnɪm ‖'mɪnɪm/ *n* (BrE) blanca *f*

minimal /'mɪnəməl ‖'mɪnɪməl/ *adj* mínimo

minimize /'mɪnəmaɪz ‖'mɪnɪmaɪz/ *vt* ‹*risk/cost*› reducir* (al mínimo)

minimum¹ /'mɪnəməm ‖'mɪnɪməm/ *n* mínimo *m*

minimum² *adj* (before n) mínimo

mining /'maɪnɪŋ/ *n* minería *f*; (before n) ‹*company/town*› minero

miniskirt /'mɪnɪskɜːrt ‖'mɪnɪskɜːt/ *n* minifalda *f*

minister¹ /'mɪnəstər ‖'mɪnɪstə(r)/ n **1** (Relig) pastor, -tora m,f **2** (Pol) ministro, -tra m,f, secretario, -ria m,f (Méx)

minister² vi to ∼ TO sb cuidar DE algn

ministry /'mɪnəstri ‖'mɪnɪstri/ n (pl **-tries**) (Pol) ministerio m, secretaría f (Méx)

mink /mɪŋk/ n (pl ∼s or ∼) **(a)** (animal) visón m **(b)** (fur) visón m

Minn = Minnesota

minor¹ /'maɪnər ‖'maɪnə(r)/ adj **1** (unimportant) ⟨poet/work⟩ menor; ⟨role⟩ secundario; ⟨operation⟩ de poca importancia or gravedad **2** (Mus) menor

minor² n **1** (Law) menor mf (de edad) **2** (AmE Educ) asignatura f secundaria

Minorca /mə'nɔːrkə ‖mɪ'nɔːkə/ n Menorca f

minority /mə'nɔːrəti ‖maɪ'nɒrɪti/ n (pl **-ties**) **(a)** (smaller number) (+ sing o pl vb) minoría f; (before n) ⟨group/vote⟩ minoritario **(b)** (in US) (Govt) oposición f

minor league n (in US) (Sport) liga f menor

minstrel /'mɪnstrəl/ n trovador m

mint¹ /mɪnt/ n **1** (Bot, Culin) **(a)** (spear∼) menta f (verde) **(b)** (pepper∼) menta f, hierbabuena f **(c)** (confection) pastilla f de menta **2** (Fin) casa f de la moneda

mint² vt ⟨coin⟩ acuñar

mint³ adj (before n) ⟨coin/stamp⟩ sin usar; in ∼ condition en perfecto estado

minus¹ /'maɪnəs/ n (pl **-nuses** or **-nusses**) **(a)** ∼ (sign) (signo m de) menos m **(b)** (disadvantage) (colloq) desventaja f

minus² adj **(a)** (disadvantageous) (colloq) (before n) on the ∼ side, … un factor negativo es que … **(b)** (negative) (before n) ⟨number⟩ negativo

minus³ prep **(a)** (Math) menos ▶ FOUR¹ **(b)** (without, missing) (colloq) sin

minuscule /'mɪnəskjuːl/ adj minúsculo

minute¹ /'mɪnət ‖'mɪnɪt/ n **1** **(a)** (unit of time) minuto m; (before n) ∼ hand minutero m **(b)** (short period) minuto m, momento m **(c)** (instant) minuto m; any ∼ (now) de un momento a otro **2** **(a)** (memorandum) acta f **(b)** (of meeting): **the ∼s** el acta

minute² /maɪ'njuːt ‖maɪ'njuːt/ adj ⟨amount⟩ mínimo; ⟨object⟩ diminuto

miracle /'mɪrɪkəl ‖'mɪrəkəl/ n milagro m; (before n) ⟨drug/cure⟩ milagroso

miraculous /mə'rækjələs ‖mɪ'rækjʊləs/ adj milagroso

mirage /mə'rɑːʒ ‖'mɪrɑːʒ, mɪ'rɑːʒ/ n espejismo m

mirror¹ /'mɪrər ‖'mɪrə(r)/ n espejo m; (driving ∼) (espejo m) retrovisor m

mirror² vt reflejar

mirth /mɜːrθ ‖mɜːθ/ n (liter) regocijo m (liter)

misadventure /ˌmɪsəd'ventʃər ‖ˌmɪsəd'ventʃə(r)/ n desventura f

misapprehension /ˌmɪsæprɪ'hentʃən ‖ˌmɪsæprɪ'henʃən/ n (fml) malentendido m

misappropriate /ˌmɪsə'prəʊprieɪt/ vt malversar

misbehave /ˌmɪsbɪ'heɪv/ vi portarse mal

miscalculation /ˌmɪskælkjə'leɪʃən ‖ˌmɪskælkjʊ'leɪʃən/ n error m de cálculo

miscarriage /'mɪsˌkærɪdʒ/ n **1** (Med) aborto m espontáneo or no provocado; **to have a ∼** tener* un aborto **2** a ∼ of justice una injusticia

miscarry /'mɪskæri/ vi **-ries, -rying, -ried** **(a)** (Med) abortar (espontáneamente), tener* un aborto **(b)** (liter) ⟨plan⟩ malograrse (liter)

miscellaneous /ˌmɪsə'leɪniəs/ adj ⟨collection/crowd⟩ heterogéneo; ⟨assortment⟩ variado

mischance /'mɪs'tʃæns ‖ˌmɪs'tʃɑːns/ n infortunio m

mischief /'mɪstʃəf ‖'mɪstʃɪf/ n **(a)** (naughtiness): **to get up to ∼** hacer* travesuras **(b)** (trouble, harm) daño m; **to make ∼** causar daños

mischievous /'mɪstʃəvəs ‖'mɪstʃɪvəs/ adj ⟨child⟩ travieso; ⟨grin⟩ pícaro

misconception /ˌmɪskən'sepʃən/ n error m

misconduct /ˌmɪs'kɑːndʌkt ‖ˌmɪs'kɒndʌkt/ n (fml) mala conducta f

misconstrue /ˌmɪskən'struː/ vt (fml) malinterpretar

misdemeanor, (BrE) **misdemeanour** /ˌmɪsdɪ'miːnər ‖ˌmɪsdɪ'miːnə(r)/ n (Law) delito m menor

miser /'maɪzər ‖'maɪzə(r)/ n avaro, -ra m,f

miserable /'mɪzərəbəl/ adj **1** **(a)** (in low spirits) abatido **(b)** (depressing) ⟨weather⟩ deprimente; ⟨prospect⟩ triste **2** **(a)** (mean-spirited) miserable **(b)** (wretched, poor) mísero **(c)** ⟨episode/failure⟩ lamentable

miserably /'mɪzərəbli/ adv **(a)** (unhappily) con abatimiento **(b)** ⟨fail⟩ de manera lamentable

miserly /'maɪzərli ‖'maɪzəli/ adj mezquino

misery /'mɪzəri/ n sufrimiento m; **to make sb's life a ∼** amargarle* la vida a algn

misfire /'mɪs'faɪr ‖ˌmɪs'faɪə(r)/ vi «gun/engine/plan» fallar

misfit /'mɪsfɪt/ n: **a social ∼** un inadaptado social

misfortune /ˌmɪs'fɔːrtʃən ‖ˌmɪs'fɔːtʃən, ˌmɪs'fɔːtʃuːn/ n (fml) desgracia f; **to have the ∼ to + INF** tener* la desgracia DE + INF

misgiving /mɪs'gɪvɪŋ/ n recelo m

misguided /'mɪs'gaɪdəd ‖ˌmɪs'gaɪdɪd/ adj equivocado

mishandle /'mɪs'hændl̩/ vt (deal with ineptly) llevar mal

mishap /'mɪshæp/ n percance m

mishear /'mɪs'hɪr ‖ˌmɪs'hɪə(r)/ (past & past p **-heard**) vt/i entender* mal

misinform /ˌmɪsɪn'fɔːrm ‖ˌmɪsɪn'fɔːm/ vt (fml) informar mal, malinformar (CS fml)

misinterpret /ˌmɪsɪn'tɜːrprət ‖ˌmɪsɪn'tɜːprɪt/ vt ⟨statement/action⟩ interpretar mal; (deliberately) tergiversar

misjudge /'mɪs'dʒʌdʒ/ vt **(a)** (judge unfairly) juzgar* mal **(b)** (miscalculate) calcular mal

mislay /'mɪs'leɪ/ vt (past & past p **-laid**) perder* (momentáneamente)

mislead /'mɪs'liːd/ vt (past & past p **-led**) engañar; ⟨court/parliament⟩ inducir* a error

mismanage /'mɪs'mænɪdʒ/ vt ⟨affair⟩ llevar mal; ⟨company⟩ administrar mal

misogynist /mɪ'sɑːdʒənəst ‖mɪ'sɒdʒɪnɪst/ n misógino m

misplace /'mɪs'pleɪs/ vt perder* (*momentáneamente*)

misprint /'mɪsprɪnt/ n errata f

misrepresent /'mɪsreprɪ'zent/ vt ‹*event*› deformar; ‹*remarks/views*› tergiversar

miss¹ /mɪs/ n **1 Miss** (as title) señorita f; **M~ Jane Smith** la señorita Jane Smith; (in correspondence) Sra Jane Smith **2** (failure to hit) fallo m; **to give sth a ~** (colloq): **I think I'll give swimming a ~ this afternoon** creo que esta tarde no voy a ir a a nadar

miss² vt
I 1 (a) (fail to hit): **the bomb ~ed its target** la bomba no cayó en el blanco; **the bullet just ~ed him** la bala le pasó rozando (b) (overlook, fail to notice): **you ~ed three mistakes** se te pasaron (por alto) tres errores; **you can't ~ it** lo va a ver enseguida, no tiene pérdida (Esp) (c) (fail to hear, understand) no oír*; **he's ~ed the point** no ha entendido (d) ‹*chance*› perder*
2 (fail to catch) ‹*bus/flight*› perder*; **sorry, you've just ~ed him** lo siento, acaba de irse
3 (a) (fail to experience) perderse*; **you didn't ~ much** no te perdiste nada (b) (fail to attend) ‹*meeting*› faltar a; ‹*party/show*› perderse*
II (a) (regret absence of) ‹*friend/country/activity*› echar de menos, extrañar (esp AmL) (b) (notice absence of) echar en falta; **when did you first ~ the necklace?** ¿cuándo echaste en falta el collar?
■ ~ vi ‹*marksman*› errar* el tiro, fallar; ‹*bullet*› no dar* en el blanco
■ **miss out 1** [v + o + adv, v + adv + o] ‹*line/paragraph*› saltarse
2 [v + adv] **to ~ out ON sth** perderse* algo

Miss = **Mississippi**

misshapen /'mɪs'ʃeɪpən/ adj deforme

missile /'mɪsəl ‖'mɪsaɪl/ n (Mil) misil m; (sth thrown) proyectil m

missing /'mɪsɪŋ/ adj: **the ~ papers** los papeles que faltan; **~ person** desaparecido, -da m,f; **to be ~** faltar; **to go ~** (BrE) desaparecer*

mission /'mɪʃən/ n misión f

missionary /'mɪʃəneri ‖'mɪʃənəri/ n misionero, -ra m,f

misspent /'mɪs'spent/ adj (before n) ‹*money*› malgastado; ‹*hours*› perdido; **a ~ youth** (set phrase) una juventud disipada

mist /mɪst/ n (a) (Meteo) neblina f; **sea ~** bruma f (b) (condensation) vaho m (c) (spray) vaporización f
■ **mist over** [v + adv] ‹*eyes*› empañarse; ‹*glass/mirror*› empañarse
■ **mist up** [v + adv] ‹*glass/mirror*› empañarse

mistake¹ /mə'steɪk ‖mɪ'steɪk/ n error m; **to make a ~** cometer un error; **by ~** por equivocación, por error

mistake² vt (past **-took**; past p **-taken**) confundir; **to ~ sth/sb FOR sth/sb** confundir algo/a algn CON algo/algn

mistaken /mə'steɪkən ‖mɪ'steɪkən/ adj ‹*impression/idea*› equivocado; **unless I'm (very) much ~** si no me equivoco

mistletoe /'mɪsəltəʊ/ n muérdago m

mistook /mɪ'stʊk/ past of MISTAKE²

mistreat /'mɪs'triːt/ vt maltratar

mistress /'mɪstrəs ‖'mɪstrɪs/ n (a) (of dog) dueña f, ama f; (of servant) señora f (b) (lover) amante f

mistrust¹ /'mɪs'trʌst/ vt desconfiar* de, recelar de

mistrust² n desconfianza f, recelo m

mistrustful /'mɪs'trʌstfəl/ adj desconfiado, receloso

misty /'mɪsti/ adj **-tier, -tiest** ‹*day/morning*› neblinoso; **it's ~** hay neblina; (it's drizzling) (AmE) está llloviznando

misunderstand /'mɪsʌndər'stænd ‖,mɪs,ʌndə'stænd/ (past & past p **-stood**) vt ‹*idea/instructions*› entender* or comprender mal; ‹*remark/motives*› malinterpretar; ‹*artist/work*› interpretar mal

misunderstanding /'mɪsʌndər'stændɪŋ ‖,mɪs,ʌndə'stændɪŋ/ n malentendido m

misunderstood /'mɪsʌndər'stʊd ‖,mɪs,ʌndə'stʊd/ past & past p of MISUNDERSTAND

misuse¹ /'mɪs'juːs/ n (of word) mal uso m; (of power) abuso m; (of funds) malversación f; (of resources) despilfarro m

misuse² /'mɪs'juːz/ vt ‹*language/tool*› utilizar* or emplear mal; ‹*resources*› despilfarrar; ‹*funds*› malversar

mite /maɪt/ n (Zool) ácaro m

miter, (BrE) **mitre** /'maɪtər ‖'maɪtə(r)/ n mitra f

mitigate /'mɪtɪgeɪt ‖'mɪtɪgeɪt/ vt (frml) (a) (soften, lessen) mitigar* (frml) (b) **mitigating** pres p ‹*factor*› atenuante; **mitigating circumstances** (circunstancias fpl) atenuantes fpl or mpl

mitre /'maɪtər ‖'maɪtə(r)/ n (BrE) ▶ MITER

mitt /mɪt/ n (a) (mitten) mitón m (b) (in baseball) manopla f, guante m (de béisbol)

mitten /'mɪtn/ n mitón m

mix¹ /mɪks/ n (a) (mixture, ingredients) mezcla f; **cake ~** preparado comercial para hacer pasteles (b) (Audio) mezcla f

mix² vt (a) ‹*ingredients/paint*› mezclar; ‹*cocktail*› preparar (b) (Audio) mezclar
■ ~ vi (a) (combine) ‹*substances*› mezclarse (b) (go together) ‹*foods/colors*› combinar (bien) (c) (socially): **she doesn't ~ well at parties** le cuesta entablar conversación con la gente en una reunión; **to ~ WITH sb** tratarse CON algn
■ **mix up**
I [v + o + adv, v + adv + o] **1** (throw into confusion) desordenar **2** (confuse) confundir
II (usu pass) (a) (involve) **to get ~ed up IN sth** meterse EN algo (b) (confuse): **to get ~ed up** confundirse

mixed /mɪkst/ adj (a) (various) mezclado; **~ spice** mezcla f de especias (b) (male and female) ‹*sauna/bathing*› mixto (c) (ambivalent) ‹*fortunes*› desigual; **I have ~ feelings about it** no sé muy bien qué pensar sobre el asunto

mixer /'mɪksər ‖'mɪksə(r)/ n (a) (Culin) batidora f (b) (Audio, Cin, TV) (person) operador, -dora m,f de sonido; (machine) mezcladora f (c) (sociable person) persona f sociable (d) (dance) (AmE) baile m (e) (drink) refresco m (para mezclar con alcohol)

mixing bowl /'mɪksɪŋ/ n bol m (grande, para mezclar ingredientes)

mixture /'mɪkstʃər ‖'mɪkstʃə(r)/ n mezcla f

mix-up /'mɪksʌp/ n (colloq) lío m (fam)

mm (= millimeter(s) o (BrE) millimetre(s)) mm.

MN = Minnesota

MO = Missouri

moan¹ /məʊn/ vi (a) (make sound) «person/wind» gemir* (b) (complain) (pej) to ~ (ABOUT sth) quejarse (DE algo)

moan² n (a) (sound) gemido m (b) (complaint) (colloq) (no pl) queja f

moat /məʊt/ n foso m

mob¹ /mɑːb ‖mɒb/ n turba f; (before n) ~ rule la ley de la calle

mob² vt -bb- atacar* en grupo

mobile¹ /'məʊbəl ‖'məʊbaɪl/ adj (a) (library/shop) ambulante (b) (able to move): we try and get the patient ~ as soon as possible tratamos de que el paciente recupere su movilidad lo más pronto posible

mobile² n móvil m

mobile: ~ home n trailer m (AmL), caravana f fija (Esp); ~ phone n (teléfono m) celular m (AmL), (teléfono m) móvil m (Esp)

mobilize /'məʊbəlaɪz ‖'məʊbɪlaɪz/ vt movilizar*

mock¹ /mɑːk ‖mɒk/ vt burlarse de

mock² adj (before n) (examination/interview) de práctica; (anger/outrage) fingido

mockery /'mɑːkəri ‖'mɒkəri/ n (a) (ridicule) burla f (b) (travesty) (no pl) farsa f; to make a ~ of sth ridiculizar* algo

mocking /'mɑːkɪŋ ‖'mɒkɪŋ/ adj burlón

mod cons /ˌmɑːd'kɑːnz ‖ˌmɒd'kɒnz/ pl n (= modern conveniences) (BrE colloq & journ) comodidades fpl

mode /məʊd/ n 1 (a) (means) medio m; (kind) modo m (b) (operating method) (Comput, Tech) modalidad f 2 (Math) modo m 3 (Clothing) moda f

model¹ /'mɑːdl̩ ‖'mɒdl̩/ n 1 (reproduction) maqueta f, modelo m 2 (paragon, example) modelo m 3 (design) modelo m 4 (person) modelo mf

model², (BrE) -ll- vt 1 (clay/shape) modelar 2 (base): their education system was ~ed on that of France su sistema educativo se inspiró en el francés; to ~ oneself on sb tomar a algn como modelo 3 (garment): she ~s sportswear es modelo de ropa sport

model³ adj (before n, no comp) 1 (miniature) (railway/village) en miniatura 2 (ideal) (citizen/husband/pupil) modelo adj inv; (answer) tipo adj inv

modem /'məʊdem/ n módem m

moderate¹ /'mɑːdərət ‖'mɒdərət/ adj moderado

moderate² /'mɑːdəreɪt ‖'mɒdəreɪt/ vt moderar

moderate³ /'mɑːdərət ‖'mɒdərət/ n moderado, -da m,f

moderation /ˌmɑːdə'reɪʃən ‖ˌmɒdə'reɪʃən/ n moderación f; drinking is not harmful, in ~ beber no es nocivo, si se hace con moderación

modern /'mɑːdərn ‖'mɒdn̩/ adj moderno

modernization /ˌmɑːdərnaɪ'zeɪʃən ‖ˌmɒdənaɪ'zeɪʃən/ n modernización f

modernize /'mɑːdərnaɪz ‖'mɒdənaɪz/ vt modernizar*

modest /'mɑːdəst ‖'mɒdɪst/ adj (a) (not boastful) (person/remark) modesto (b) (income/gift) modesto; (improvement/success) moderado (c) (chaste) pudoroso

modesty /'mɑːdəsti ‖'mɒdɪsti/ n (a) (absence of conceit) modestia f (b) (propriety) recato m, pudor m

modicum /'mɑːdɪkəm ‖'mɒdɪkəm/ n (no pl) (frml) a ~ OF sth un atisbo DE algo (frml), un mínimo DE algo

modification /ˌmɑːdəfə'keɪʃən ‖ˌmɒdɪfɪ'keɪʃən/ n modificación f

modify /'mɑːdəfaɪ ‖'mɒdɪfaɪ/ vt -fies, -fying, -fied modificar*

modular /'mɑːdʒələr ‖'mɒdjʊlə(r)/ adj (design/furniture) modular; (degree/course) dividido en módulos

modulate /'mɑːdʒəleɪt ‖'mɒdjʊleɪt/ vt modular

modulation /ˌmɑːdʒə'leɪʃən ‖ˌmɒdjʊ'leɪʃən/ n modulación f; frequency ~ frecuencia f modulada

module /'mɑːdʒuːl ‖'mɒdjuːl/ n módulo m

Mohammed /məʊ'hæməd ‖məʊ'hæmɪd/ n Mahoma

moist /mɔɪst/ adj (climate/soil) húmedo; (cake) no seco

moisten /'mɔɪsn̩/ vt humedecer*

moisture /'mɔɪstʃər ‖'mɔɪstʃə(r)/ n humedad f

moisturize /'mɔɪstʃəraɪz/ vt hidratar

moisturizer /'mɔɪstʃəraɪzər ‖'mɔɪstʃəraɪzə(r)/, **moisturizing cream** /'mɔɪstʃəraɪzɪŋ/ n crema f hidratante

molar /'məʊlər ‖'məʊlə(r)/ n muela f

molasses /mə'læsəz ‖mə'læsɪz/ n (+ sing vb) melaza f

mold¹, (BrE) **mould** /məʊld/ n 1 (a) (hollow vessel) molde m (b) (dish) timbal m 2 (fungus) moho m

mold², (BrE) **mould** vt (steel/plastic) moldear; (character/attitudes) formar

Moldavia /mɑːl'deɪvjə ‖mɒl'deɪvɪə/ n Moldavia f

Moldova /mɑːl'dəʊvə ‖mɒl'dəʊvə/ n Moldova f

moldy, (BrE) **mouldy** /'məʊldi/ adj mohoso; to become o (BrE) go ~ enmohecerse*

mole /məʊl/ n 1 (Zool) topo m 2 (on skin) lunar m

molecule /'mɑːlɪkjuːl ‖'mɒlɪkjuːl/ n molécula f

molest /mə'lest/ vt (a) (sexually) abusar (sexualmente) de (b) (harass) importunar

mollusk, mollusc /'mɑːləsk ‖'mɒləsk/ n molusco m

mollycoddle /'mɑːlikɑːdl̩ ‖'mɒlɪkɒdl̩/ vt (colloq & pej) mimar

molt, (BrE) **moult** /məʊlt/ vi «snake» mudar de piel; «bird» mudar de plumas; «dog/cat» pelechar, mudar de pelo

molten /'məʊltən/ adj ‹rock/metal› fundido; ‹lava› líquido

mom /mɑːm ‖mɒm/ n (AmE colloq) mamá f (fam)

moment /'məʊmənt/ n momento m; **at the ∼** en este momento; **for the ∼** de momento; **to have one's ∼s** tener* sus (or mis etc) buenos momentos

momentary /'məʊmənteri ‖'məʊməntri/ adj ‹feeling/glimpse› momentáneo

momentous /məʊ'mentəs/ adj ‹occasion/ decision› trascendental; ‹day› memorable

momentum /məʊ'mentəm/ n (pl **-ta** /-tə/ or **-tums**) (a) (Phys) momento m (b) (speed) velocidad f; **to gather ∼** ir* adquiriendo velocidad

momma /'mɑːmə ‖'mɒmə/ n (AmE) (colloq) mamá f (fam)

mommy /'mɑːmi ‖'mɒmi/ n (pl **-mies**) (AmE colloq) mami f (fam), mamita f (fam)

Monaco /'mɑːnəkəʊ, mə'nɑː- ‖'mɒnəkəʊ/ n Mónaco m

monarch /'mɑːnərk ‖'mɒnək/ n monarca mf

monarchist /'mɑːnərkəst ‖'mɒnəkɪst/ n monárquico, -ca m,f

monarchy /'mɑːnərki ‖'mɒnəki/ n monarquía f

monastery /'mɑːnəsteri ‖'mɒnəstri/ n (pl **-ries**) monasterio m

Monday /'mʌndeɪ, -di/ n 1 (day) lunes m; **on ∼** el lunes; **next ∼** el próximo lunes or el lunes que viene; **(on) ∼s** los lunes; **the ∼ after next** el lunes que viene no, el siguiente; (before n) **∼ afternoon/morning** la tarde por la tarde/mañana, la tarde/mañana del lunes 2 **Mondays** (as adv) los lunes

monetarism /'mɑːnətərɪzəm ‖'mʌnɪtərɪzəm/ n monetarismo m

monetary /'mɑːnəteri ‖'mʌnɪtəri/ adj monetario

money /'mʌni/ n (pl **-nies** or **-neys**) dinero m; (currency) moneda f, dinero m; **their European operation is making a lot of ∼** su operación europea está dando mucho; **to put ∼ into sth** invertir* dinero en algo; **∼ talks** poderoso caballero es don Dinero

money: ∼ belt n faltriquera f, **∼box** n alcancía f (AmL), hucha f (Esp); **∼lender** n prestamista mf; **∼-making** adj lucrativo; **∼ order** n ≈ giro m postal; **∼ supply** n the **∼ supply** la masa monetaria

Mongolia /mɑːn'gəʊliə ‖mɒŋ'gəʊliə/ n Mongolia f

Mongolian /mɑːn'gəʊliən ‖mɒŋ'gəʊliən/ adj mongol

mongrel /'mɑːngrəl ‖'mʌŋgrəl/ n: perro mestizo, chucho, -cha m,f (fam), gozque mf (Col), quiltro, -tra m,f (Chi fam)

monitor¹ /'mɑːnətər ‖'mɒnɪtə(r)/ n 1 (a) (screen) monitor m (b) (for measuring) monitor m 2 (listener) escucha mf 3 (Educ) encargado, -da m,f, monitor, -tora m,f (CS)

monitor² vt (a) ‹elections› observar; ‹process/ progress› seguir*; (esp electronically) monitorizar* (b) ‹radio station› escuchar

monk /mʌŋk/ n monje m

monkey /'mʌŋki/ n mono, -na m,f

monkey wrench n llave f inglesa; **to throw a ∼ in the works** o **the machinery** (AmE) fastidiarlo todo

mono /'mɑːnəʊ ‖'mɒnəʊ/ n (Audio) monofonía f

monochrome /'mɑːnəkrəʊm ‖'mɒnəkrəʊm/ adj ‹picture› monocromático, monocromo

monogamy /mə'nɑːgəmi ‖mə'nɒgəmi/ n monogamía f

monologue, (AmE also) **monolog** /'mɑːnəlɔːg ‖'mɒnəlɒg/ n monólogo m

monopolize /mə'nɑːpəlaɪz ‖mə'nɒpəlaɪz/ vt ‹market/industry› monopolizar*; ‹conversation/ television› acaparar

monopoly /mə'nɑːpəli ‖mə'nɒpəli/ n (pl **-lies**) monopolio m

monosyllable /'mɑːnə,sɪləbəl ‖'mɒnəsɪləbəl/ n monosílabo m

monotone /'mɑːnətəʊn ‖'mɒnətəʊn/ n tono m monocorde

monotonous /mə'nɑːtn̩əs ‖mə'nɒtənəs/ adj monótono

monotony /mə'nɑːtn̩i ‖mə'nɒtəni/ n monotonía f

monsoon /mɑːn'suːn ‖mɒn'suːn/ n monzón m

monster /'mɑːnstər ‖'mɒnstə(r)/ n monstruo m

monstrous /'mɑːnstrəs ‖'mɒnstrəs/ adj (a) (huge) gigantesco (b) (shocking) monstruoso

Mont = Montana

month /mʌnθ/ n mes m; **$900 a ∼** 900 dólares mensuales or por mes or al mes; **in a ∼'s time** dentro de un mes

monthly¹ /'mʌnθli/ adj ‹journal/event› mensual; **∼ payment** mensualidad f, cuota f mensual (esp AmL)

monthly² adv mensualmente, una vez al or por mes

monthly³ n (pl **-lies**) publicación f mensual

monument /'mɑːnjəmənt ‖'mɒnjʊmənt/ n monumento m

monumental /ˌmɑːnjə'mentl̩ ‖ˌmɒnjʊ'mentl̩/ adj monumental

moo /muː/ vi **moos, mooing, mooed** mugir*

mood /muːd/ n 1 (a) (state of mind) humor m; **to be in a good/bad ∼** estar* de buen/de mal humor; **I'm not in the ∼** no tengo ganas; **I'm not in the ∼ for dancing** no tengo ganas de bailar (b) (atmosphere) atmósfera f 2 (Ling) modo m

moody /'muːdi/ adj **-dier, -diest** (a) (irritable, sulky) de mal humor; (gloomy) deprimido (b) (changeable) ‹person› temperamental

moon /muːn/ n luna f; **once in a blue ∼** muy de vez en cuando

moonbeam /'muːnbiːm/ n rayo m de luna

moonlight¹ /'muːnlaɪt/ n luz f de la luna

moonlight² vi tener* un segundo empleo; **he ∼s as a cab driver** trabaja además como taxista

moon: ∼lighting n pluriempleo m; **∼lit** adj iluminado por la luna

moor¹ /mʊr ‖mʊə(r), mɔː(r)/ n **(a)** (boggy area) llanura f anegadiza **(b)** (high exposed area) (esp BrE) páramo m; (covered with heather) brezal m

moor² vt amarrar
■ ~ vi echar amarras

mooring /'mʊrɪŋ ‖'mʊərɪŋ, 'mɔːrɪŋ/ n **(a)** (place) amarradero m **(b) moorings** pl (ropes) amarras fpl

moose /muːs/ n (pl **moose**) alce m americano or de América

mop¹ /mɑːp ‖mɒp/ n **(a)** (for floor) trapeador m (AmL), fregona f (Esp) **(b)** ~ **of hair** mata f de pelo

mop² -pp- vt ⟨floor/room⟩ limpiar, trapear (AmL), pasarle la fregona a (Esp); **to** ~ **one's brow** secarse* la frente
■ **mop up** [v + o + adv, v + adv + o] ⟨water⟩ secar*; ⟨mess⟩ limpiar

mope /məʊp/ vi (colloq) estar* deprimido

moped /'məʊped/ n ciclomotor m

moral¹ /'mɒrəl ‖'mɔːrəl/ adj moral

moral² n [1] (message) moraleja f [2] **morals** pl (principles) moralidad f

morale /mə'ræl ‖mə'rɑːl/ n moral f

morality /mə'ræləti/ n (pl **-ties**) moralidad f

morally /'mɒrəli ‖'mɔːrəli/ adv moralmente

morbid /'mɔːbəd ‖'mɔːbɪd/ adj morboso

more¹ /mɔːr ‖mɔː(r)/ adj más; **there'll be no** ~ **talking** se acabó la charla; **how much** ~ **flour?** ¿cuánta harina más?; **for** ~ **information call 387-73-51;** ~ **and** ~ **people** cada vez más gente; **I eat** ~ **meat than you** yo como más carne que tú

more² pron más; **let's say no** ~ **about it** no hablemos más del asunto; **the** ~ **she eats, the thinner she gets** cuanto más come, más adelgaza; **you eat** ~ **than me** tú comes más que yo

more³ adv más; **you watch television** ~ **than I do** tú ves más televisión que yo; ~ **or less** más o menos; **could you please speak** ~ **clearly?** ¿podría hacer el favor de hablar más claro?; ~ **often** con más frecuencia; **I don't eat meat any** ~ ya no como carne

moreover /mɔːr'əʊvər ‖mɔːr'rəʊvə(r)/ adv (frml) (as linker) además

morgue /mɔːrg ‖mɔːg/ n depósito m de cadáveres, morgue f (AmL)

Mormon /'mɔːrmən ‖'mɔːmən/ n mormón, -mona m,f

morning /'mɔːrnɪŋ ‖'mɔːnɪŋ/ n [1] (time of day) mañana f; **yesterday/tomorrow** ~ ayer/mañana por la mañana or (AmL tb) en la mañana or (RPl tb) a la mañana or de mañana; **we'll do it first thing in the** ~ lo haremos por la mañana a primera hora; **(good)** ~**!** ¡buenos días!, ¡buen día! (RPl) [2] **mornings** (as adv) por las mañanas, en las mañanas (AmL), a la or de mañana (RPl)

morning: ~ **coat** n chaqué m, frac m; ~ **sickness** n náuseas fpl (matinales) (del embarazo)

Moroccan /mə'rɑːkən ‖mə'rɒkən/ adj marroquí

Morocco /mə'rɑːkəʊ ‖mə'rɒkəʊ/ n Marruecos m

moron /'mɔːrɑːn ‖'mɔːrɒn/ n (colloq & pej) imbécil mf, tarado, -da m,f (fam)

morose /mə'rəʊs/ adj taciturno

morphine /'mɔːrfiːn ‖'mɔːfiːn/ n morfina f

Morse /mɔːrs ‖mɔːs/ n morse m; **in** ~ **(code)** en (código) morse

morsel /'mɔːrsəl ‖'mɔːsəl/ n bocado m

mortal¹ /'mɔːrtl ‖'mɔːtl/ adj **(a)** (subject to death) mortal **(b)** (liter) ⟨blow/injury/sin⟩ mortal

mortal² n mortal mf

mortality /mɔːr'tæləti ‖mɔː'tæləti/ n **(a)** (death rate) mortalidad f **(b)** (loss of life) mortandad f **(c)** (condition) mortalidad f

mortar /'mɔːrtər ‖'mɔːtə(r)/ n [1] (cement) argamasa f, mortero m [2] (weapon) mortero m [3] (bowl) mortero m, molcajete m (Méx)

mortgage¹ /'mɔːrgɪdʒ ‖'mɔːgɪdʒ/ n (charge) hipoteca f; (loan) préstamo m hipotecario, hipoteca f; **to take out a** ~ **on a property** hipotecar* una propiedad

mortgage² vt hipotecar*

mortician /mɔːr'tɪʃən ‖mɔː'tɪʃən/ n (AmE) (employee) persona que trabaja en una funeraria; (funeral director) director, -tora m,f de pompas fúnebres

mortified /'mɔːrtəfaɪd ‖'mɔːtɪfaɪd/ adj: **I was** ~ me dio mucha vergüenza, me dio mucha pena (AmL exc CS)

mortuary /'mɔːrtʃueri ‖'mɔːtjʊəri/ n (pl **-ries**) depósito m de cadáveres, morgue f (AmL)

mosaic /məʊ'zeɪɪk/ n mosaico m

Moscow /'mɑːskaʊ ‖'mɒskəʊ/ n Moscú m

Moslem /'mɑːzləm ‖'mɒzləm/ n/adj ▶ MUSLIM¹,²

mosque /mɑːsk ‖mɒsk/ n mezquita f

mosquito /mə'skiːtəʊ ‖mɒs'kiːtəʊ/ n (pl **-toes** or **-tos**) mosquito m, zancudo m (AmL)

moss /mɔːs ‖mɒs/ n musgo m

most¹ /məʊst/ adj **(a)** (nearly all) la mayoría de, la mayor parte de; ~ **days** casi todos los días **(b)** (as superl): **who eats (the)** ~ **meat in your family?** ¿quién es el que come más carne de tu familia?

most² pron **(a)** (nearly all) la mayoría, la mayor parte; **I read** ~ **of it** lo leí casi todo **(b)** (as superl): **she ate the** ~ fue la que más comió; **at (the)** ~ como máximo; **to make the** ~ **of sth** sacar* el mejor provecho posible de algo **(c)** (people) la mayoría

most³ adv [1] **(a)** (to greatest extent) más; **I enjoyed the last act** ~ **of all** el último acto fue el que más me gustó **(b)** (before adj, adv) más; **which is the** ~ **expensive?** ¿cuál es el más caro? [2] (as intensifier): **what happened was** ~ **interesting** lo que sucedió fue de lo más interesante; ~ **likely** muy probablemente [3] (almost) (AmE colloq) casi

mostly /'məʊstli/ adv: **her friends are** ~ **students** la mayoría de sus amigos son estudiantes; **the land is** ~ **flat** el terreno es en su mayor parte llano

motel /məʊ'tel/ n motel m

moth /mɔːθ ‖mɒθ/ n mariposa f de la luz, palomilla f; (clothes ~) polilla f

mother¹ /'mʌðər ‖'mʌðə(r)/ n madre f; (before n) ~ **country** madre patria f

mother² vt mimar

motherhood /'mʌðərhʊd ‖'mʌðəhʊd/ n maternidad f

Mothering Sunday /'mʌðərɪŋ/ n (BrE) ▶
MOTHER'S DAY

mother: ~**-in-law** n (pl ~**s-in-law**) suegra f;
~**land** n patria f

motherly /'mʌðəli ‖'mʌðəli/ adj maternal

mother: ~**-of-pearl** /'mʌðərəv'pɜːrl
‖'mʌðərəv'pɜːl/ n nácar m, madreperla f, concha
f nácar (Méx), concha f de perla (Chi); **M~'s Day**
n el día de la Madre (el segundo domingo de mayo
en EEUU y el cuarto domingo de Cuaresma en
GB); **M~ Superior** n Madre f Superiora;
~**-to-be**) /,mʌðərtə'biː ‖,mʌðətə'biː/ n (pl
~**s-to-be**) futura madre f, futura mamá f; ~
tongue n lengua f materna

motif /məʊ'tiːf/ n (a) (theme) tema m (b) (design)
motivo m

motion¹ /'məʊʃən/ n [1] (a) (movement)
movimiento m; **to be in** ~ estar* en movimiento;
to set o **put sth in** ~ ⟨wheel⟩ poner* algo en
movimiento; ⟨project/plan⟩ poner* algo en
marcha (b) (action, gesture) gesto m; **to go through
the** ~**s**: he went through the ~s of interviewing
them los entrevistó por pura fórmula [2] (for vote)
moción f

motion² vi: she ~ed to her assistant le hizo
una señal a su ayudante; they ~ed to us to sit
down nos hicieron señas para que nos
sentáramos

motionless /'məʊʃənləs ‖'məʊʃənlɪs/ adj
inmóvil

motion picture n película f

motivate /'məʊtəveɪt ‖'məʊtɪveɪt/ vt motivar

motivation /'məʊtə'veɪʃən ‖,məʊtɪ'veɪʃən/ n
(a) (drive) motivación f (b) (motive) motivo m

motive /'məʊtɪv/ n motivo m

motley /'mɑːtli ‖'mɒtli/ adj variopinto

motor¹ /'məʊtər ‖'məʊtə(r)/ n motor m

motor² adj (before n) [1] (Auto, Mech Eng) ⟨parts⟩
de automóvil; ⟨mechanic⟩ de automóviles; ~
show salón m del automóvil; ~ **vehicle** (vehículo
m) automóvil m (frml) [2] (Physiol) ⟨neuron/nerve⟩
motor [The feminine of MOTOR is MOTRIZ or
MOTORA]

motor: ~**bike** n moto f; ~**boat** n lancha f a
motor; ~**car** n (frml) automóvil m (frml);
~**cycle** n motocicleta f; ~**cyclist** n
motociclista mf, motorista mf

motoring /'məʊtərɪŋ/ n automovilismo m

motorist /'məʊtərəst ‖'məʊtərɪst/ n
automovilista mf, conductor, -tora m,f

motorway /'məʊtərweɪ ‖'məʊtəweɪ/ n (BrE)
autopista f

mottled /'mɑːtld ‖'mɒtld/ adj ⟨skin⟩
manchado; ⟨marble⟩ veteado

motto /'mɑːtəʊ ‖'mɒtəʊ/ n (pl **-toes**) (of family,
school) lema m

mould etc (BrE) ▶ MOLD etc

moult vi (BrE) ▶ MOLT

mound /maʊnd/ n (a) (hillock) montículo m (b)
(man-made) túmulo m; **burial** ~ túmulo funerario
(c) (heap) montón m

mount¹ /maʊnt/ n [1] (mountain) (liter) monte m
[2] (Equ) montura f [3] (for machine, gun) soporte m;
(for picture — surround) passepartú m, marialuisa f
(Méx); (— backing) fondo m; (for slide) marco m; (for
stamp) fijasellos m; (for jewel) montura f, engaste m

mount² vt [1] (a) ⟨horse⟩ montar, montarse en
(b) ⟨platform/throne⟩ subir a [2] ⟨gun/picture⟩
montar; ⟨stamp/butterfly⟩ fijar; ⟨gem⟩ engarzar*,
montar [3] ⟨attack/offensive⟩ preparar;
⟨campaign/event⟩ organizar*
■ ~ vi [1] (a) ⟨cost/temperature⟩ subir;
⟨excitement/alarm⟩ crecer* (b) **mounting** pres
p ⟨cost/fears/tension⟩ cada vez mayor, creciente
[2] (climb onto horse) montar
■ **mount up** [v + adv] ⟨bills⟩ irse* acumulando

mountain /'maʊntn ‖'maʊntɪn/ n (Geog)
montaña f; (before n) ⟨stream/path⟩ de montaña;
⟨scenery⟩ montañoso; ~ **range** cordillera f,
(shorter) sierra f

mountain bike n bicicleta f de montaña

mountaineer /'maʊntn'ɪr ‖,maʊntɪ'nɪə(r)/ n
alpinista mf, andinista mf (AmL)

mountaineering /'maʊntn'ɪrɪŋ
‖,maʊntɪ'nɪərɪŋ/ n alpinismo m, andinismo m
(AmL)

mountainous /'maʊntnəs ‖'maʊntɪnəs/ adj
montañoso

mountaintop /'maʊntn,tɑːp ‖'maʊntɪn,tɒp/ n
cima f or cumbre f (de la montaña)

mounted /'maʊntəd ‖'maʊntɪd/ adj montado:
~ **police** policía f montada

mourn /mɔːrn ‖mɔːn/ vt ⟨loss/tragedy⟩ llorar
■ ~ vi **to** ~ **FOR sb** llorar a algn

mourner /'mɔːrnər ‖'mɔːnə(r)/ n doliente mf

mournful /'mɔːrnfəl ‖'mɔːnfəl/ adj ⟨expression/
glance⟩ de profunda tristeza; ⟨sigh/cry⟩ lastimero

mourning /'mɔːrnɪŋ ‖'mɔːnɪŋ/ n (action, period)
duelo m, luto m; **to be in** ~ **for sb** estar* de luto
por algn

mouse /maʊs/ n (pl **mice**) [1] (animal) ratón m,
laucha f (CS) [2] (Comput) ratón m; (before n) ~
mat alfombrilla f para ratón

mousey adj ▶ MOUSY

mousse /muːs/ n (a) (Culin) mousse f or m (b)
(for hair) mousse f

moustache n (BrE) ▶ MUSTACHE

mousy /'maʊsi/ adj **-sier, -siest** ⟨hair⟩
castaño desvaído adj inv

mouth¹ /maʊθ/ n (pl **mouths** /maʊðz/) [1] (of
person, animal) boca f; **down in the** ~ alicaído; **to
make sb's** ~ **water**: it made my ~ water se me
hizo agua la boca or (Esp) se me hizo la boca
agua [2] (of bottle) boca f; (of tunnel, cave) entrada f;
(of river) desembocadura f

mouth² /maʊð/ vt (silently): it's him, she ~ed —
es él —me/le dijo articulando para que le leyera
los labios

mouthful /'maʊθfʊl/ n (of food) bocado m; (of
drink) trago m; (of air) bocanada f

mouth: ~ **organ** n armónica f; ~**piece** n
[1] (of telephone) micrófono m; (Mus) boquilla f;

AmC	Central America	Arg	Argentina	Cu	Cuba
AmL	Latin America	Bol	Bolivia	Ec	Ecuador
AmS	South America	Chi	Chile	Esp	Spain
Andes	Andean Region	CS	Southern Cone	Méx	Mexico

Per	Peru
RPI	River Plate Area
Ur	Uruguay
Ven	Venezuela

2 (spokesperson) portavoz *mf*; **~-to-~**
/'maʊθtə'maʊθ/ *adj* (*before n*) boca a boca;
~wash *n* enjuague *m* (bucal); **~-watering**
/'maʊθ,wɔːtərɪŋ/ *adj* delicioso

move¹ /muːv/ *n* **1** (movement) movimiento *m*;
on the **~**: *she's always on the* **~** siempre está de
un lado para otro **2** (change — of residence)
mudanza *f*, trasteo *m* (Col); (— of premises)
traslado *m* **3** **(a)** (action, step) paso *m*; (measure)
medida *f*; *what's the next* **~**? ¿cuál es el siguiente
paso? **(b)** (in profession, occupation): *it would be a
good career* **~** sería un cambio muy provechoso
para mi (*or* su *etc*) carrera profesional **4** (Games)
movimiento *m*; *whose* **~** *is it?* ¿a quién le toca
mover?

move² *vi* **1** **(a)** (change place): *he* **~d** *nearer
the fire* se acercó al fuego; *to* **~** *to a new job*
cambiar de trabajo **(b)** (change location, residence)
mudarse
2 (change position) moverse*
3 (proceed, go): *the vehicle began to* **~** el
vehículo se puso en marcha; *the police kept the
crowds moving* la policía hacía circular a la
multitud; *the earth* **~s** *around the sun* la Tierra
gira alrededor del sol; *we* **~d** *to one side* nos
apartamos, nos hicimos a un lado
4 (advance, develop): *events* **~d** *rapidly* los
acontecimientos se desarrollaron rápidamente; *to
* **~** *with the times* mantenerse* al día; *to* **~** *into
the lead* pasar a ocupar el primer lugar
5 (carry oneself) moverse*
6 (go fast) (colloq) correr
7 (take steps, act): *we must* **~** *now* tenemos que
actuar ahora; *she* **~d** *quickly to scotch rumors*
inmediatamente tomó medidas para acallar los
rumores
■ **~** *vt* **1** (transfer, shift position of): **~** *your chair a
little* corre un poco la silla; *ask him to* **~** *the
boxes out of the way* dile que quite las cajas de
en medio; *I can't* **~** *my leg* no puedo mover la
pierna
2 **(a)** (transport) transportar **(b)** (relocate, transfer)
trasladar **(c)** (change residence, location): *the firm
that* **~d** *us* la compañía que nos hizo la mudanza;
to **~** *house* (BrE) mudarse de casa
3 **(a)** (arouse emotionally) conmover*; *to* **~** *sb to
tears* hacer* llorar a algn de la emoción **(b)**
(prompt) *to* **~** *sb to* + INF: *this* **~d** *her to
remonstrate* esto la indujo a protestar
4 (propose) (Adm, Govt) proponer*
■ **move along** **1** [*v + adv*] **(a)** (go further along)
correrse **(b)** (disperse) circular
2 [*v + o + adv*] (cause to disperse) hacer*
circular
■ **move around,** (BrE also) **move about** [*v +
adv*] **(a)** (walk) andar* **(b)** (change residence)
mudarse (*a menudo*); (change job) cambiar de
trabajo (*a menudo*)
■ **move away** [*v + adv*] **(a)** (move house)
mudarse (*de la ciudad, el barrio etc*) **(b)** ▶ MOVE
OFF
■ **move down** **1** [*v + adv*] bajar
2 [*v + o + adv*] bajar
■ **move in** [*v + adv*] **(a)** (set up home) mudarse (*a
una casa etc*); *to* **~** *in* WITH *sb* irse* a vivir CON
algn **(b)** (draw closer) acercarse* **(c)** (go into action)
«*police*» intervenir*; (Mil) atacar*
■ **move off** [*v + adv*] «*procession*» ponerse* en
marcha; «*car*» arrancar*
■ **move on**

I [*v + adv*] **1** (walk further) seguir* adelante;
(continue journey) continuar* el viaje
2 **(a)** (proceed) pasar **(b)** (progress) progresar
II [*v + o + adv*] (cause to disperse) hacer* circular
■ **move out** [*v + adv*] (make move) (*de una casa etc*)
■ **move over** [*v + adv*] (make room) correrse
■ **move up** **1** [*v + adv*] **(a)** (rise) subir **(b)** (make
room) correrse
2 [*v + o + adv*] ‹*picture/shelf*› subir; *they* **~d**
him up a class lo pusieron en la clase
inmediatamente superior

movement /'muːvmənt/ *n* **1** **(a)** (motion)
movimiento *m* **(b)** **movements** *pl* (activities,
whereabouts) desplazamientos *mpl*, movimientos
mpl **2** **(a)** (transportation) movimiento *m* **(b)**
(travel) desplazamiento *m* **3** (Art, Pol, Relig)
movimiento *m*

mover /'muːvər ‖ 'muːvə(r)/ *n* (of furniture,
belongings) (AmE): *a firm of* **~s** una compañía de
mudanzas

movie /'muːvi/ *n* (esp AmE) **1** (film) película *f*,
film(e) *m* (period); (*before n*) ‹*actor/director*› de
cine **2** **movies** *pl* (esp AmE) *the* **~s** el cine

movie camera *n* (esp AmE) filmadora *f or*
(Esp) tomavistas *m*; (large, professional) cámara *f*
cinematográfica

moving /'muːvɪŋ/ *adj* **1** (emotionally) emotivo,
conmovedor **2** (in motion) (*before n*) **~** *part* pieza *f*
movible **3** (AmE) (*before n*) ‹*van/company*› de
mudanzas

mow /məʊ/ *vt* (*past* **mowed**; *past p* **mown** *or*
mowed) ‹*hay*› segar*; ‹*lawn*› cortar
■ **mow down** [*v + o + adv, v + adv + o*]
acribillar

mower /'məʊər ‖ 'məʊə(r)/ *n* **(a)** (Hort) ▶
LAWNMOWER **(b)** (on farm) segadora *f*

mown /məʊn/ *past p of* MOW

Mozambique /'məʊzəm'biːk ‖ ,məʊzæm'biːk/
n Mozambique *m*

MP *n* **(a)** (in UK) (Govt) = **Member of
Parliament (b)** (= military police) PM *f*

mph = **miles per hour**

Mr /'mɪstər ‖ 'mɪstə(r)/ (= **Mister**) Sr.

Mrs /'mɪsəs ‖ 'mɪsɪz/ Sra.

Ms /mɪz ‖ məz/ ≈Sra. (*tratamiento que se da a
las mujeres y que no indica su estado civil*)

MS *n* **(a)** *also* **ms** (*pl* **MSS** *or* **mss**)
(= **manuscript**) ms. **(b)** (= **multiple
sclerosis**) E.M. *f* **(c)** (AmE) = **Master of
Science (d)** = **Mississippi**

MSc *n* (BrE) = **Master of Science**

MST (in US) = **Mountain Standard Time**

Mt (= **Mount**) **~** *Rushmore* el monte Rushmore

MT = **Montana**

much¹ /mʌtʃ/ *adj* mucho, -cha; *how* **~** *coffee/
milk?* ¿cuánto café/cuánta leche?; *I do as* **~** *work
as anybody* trabajo tanto como cualquiera; *too* **~**
coffee demasiado café

much² *pron* mucho, -cha; *do you see* **~** *of the
Smiths?* ¿ves mucho a los Smith?; *how* **~** *does it
cost?* ¿cuánto cuesta?; *I've done as* **~** *as I can* he
hecho todo lo que he podido; *and as* **~** *again* y
otro tanto; *you've drunk too* **~** has bebido
demasiado

much³ *adv* mucho; *I'd very* **~** *like to meet her*
me gustaría mucho conocerla; *you deserve the* ⋯⟶

prize just as ~ as I do te mereces el premio tanto como yo; **so ~ the better** tanto mejor; **you talk too ~** hablas demasiado; **this church is ~ the larger of the two** de las dos iglesias esta es, con mucho, la más grande; **I'm ~ too busy to do it** estoy demasiado ocupada para hacerlo

muck /mʌk/ n (dung) estiércol m; (dirt) mugre f
■ **muck out** [v + o + adv, v + adv + o] limpiar

mucus /'mjuːkəs/ n mucosidad f

mud /mʌd/ n barro m, fango m, lodo m; (before n) ‹brick/hut› de barro, de adobe

muddle¹ /'mʌdl/ n lío m, follón m (Esp fam); **to be in a ~** ‹papers› estar* (todo) revuelto; «person» estar* liado or hecho un lío (fam)

muddle² vt ▶ MUDDLE UP
■ **muddle up** [v + o + adv, v + adv + o] (a) ‹papers› entreverar (b) (mix up) confundir (c) (bewilder) confundir; **to get ~d up** confundirse

muddled /'mʌdld/ adj confuso; **to get ~** hacerse* un lío (fam)

muddy /'mʌdi/ adj **-dier, -diest** ‹boots/hands/road› lleno or cubierto de barro or de lodo; ‹water› turbio

mudguard /'mʌdgɑːrd ‖ 'mʌdgɑːd/ n guardabarros m, salpicadera f (Méx), tapabarros m (Chi, Per)

muesli /'mjuːzli, 'muː- ‖ 'mjuːzli/ n (esp BrE) musli m, muesli m

muff¹ /mʌf/ vt (colloq) ‹shot› errar*; ‹chance› desperdiciar

muff² n (Clothing) manguito m

muffin /'mʌfən ‖ 'mʌfɪn/ n (AmE) mollete m (bollo dulce hecho con huevos); (BrE) bollo de pan que suele servirse tostado

muffle /'mʌfl/ vt [1] ‹sound› amortiguar* [2] ~ (up): **her face was ~d (up) in a scarf** una bufanda casi le tapaba la cara

muffler /'mʌflər ‖ 'mʌflə(r)/ n [1] (scarf) bufanda f [2] (a) (Mus) sordina f (b) (AmE Auto) silenciador m, mofle m (AmC, Méx)

mug¹ /mʌg/ n [1] (cup) taza f (alta y sin platillo), tarro m (Méx, Ven) [2] (gullible person) (BrE colloq) idiota mf [3] (face) (sl) cara f, jeta f (arg), careto m (Esp arg)

mug² vt **-gg-** atracar*

mugger /'mʌgər ‖ 'mʌgə(r)/ n atracador, -dora m,f

mugging /'mʌgɪŋ/ n atraco m

muggy /'mʌgi/ adj **-gier, -giest** ‹weather/day› pesado

mug shot n (colloq) foto f (de archivo policial)

Muhammad /mə'hæməd ‖ mə'hæmɪd/ n Mahoma

mulberry /'mʌlˌberi ‖ 'mʌlbəri/ n (pl **-ries**) (tree) morera f; (fruit) mora f (de morera)

mule /mjuːl/ n mula f ‹cruce de burro y yegua›; **stubborn as a ~** más terco que una mula

mull /mʌl/ vt (a) (Culin): **~ed wine** ponche caliente de vino y especias (b) (AmE) ▶ MULL OVER
■ **mull over** [v + o + adv, v + adv + o] reflexionar sobre

multicolored, (BrE) **multi-coloured** /'mʌltiˌkʌlərd ‖ ˌmʌltɪ'kʌləd/ adj multicolor

multicultural /ˌmʌltɪ'kʌltʃərəl/ adj multicultural

multilevel /'mʌltiˌlevl/ adj (AmE) de varias plantas, de varios pisos

multinational¹ /ˌmʌltɪ'næʃnəl ‖ ˌmʌltɪ'næʃənl/ adj multinacional

multinational² n multinacional f

multiple¹ /'mʌltəpəl ‖ 'mʌltɪpəl/ adj (a) (involving many elements) múltiple (b) (many) múltiples

multiple² n múltiplo m

multiple: ~-choice /'mʌltəpəl'tʃɔɪs ‖ ˌmʌltɪpəl'tʃɔɪs/ adj de opción múltiple, tipo test; **~ sclerosis** /sklə'rəʊsəs/ n esclerosis f múltiple

multiplication /'mʌltəpləˈkeɪʃən ‖ ˌmʌltɪplɪ'keɪʃən/ n multiplicación f

multiply /'mʌltəplaɪ ‖ 'mʌltɪplaɪ/ **-plies, -plying, -plied** vt (a) (Math) multiplicar* algo (POR algo) (b) (increase) multiplicar*
■ vi (a) (Math) multiplicar* (b) (increase, reproduce) multiplicarse*

multipurpose /'mʌltiˈpɜːrpəs ‖ ˌmʌltiˈpɜːpəs/ adj ‹tool/appliance› multiuso adj inv

multistory, (BrE) **multistorey** /'mʌltiˈstɔːri/ adj de varias plantas, de varios pisos

multitude /'mʌltətuːd ‖ 'mʌltɪtjuːd/ n (a) (large number) (frml) (no pl) a ~ of problems innumerables or múltiples problemas (b) (crowd) (arch or liter) multitud f

mum /mʌm/ n [1] (mother) (BrE colloq) mamá f (fam) [2] (silence) (colloq): **~'s the word** ¡punto en boca! (fam); **to keep ~** no decir* ni pío (fam)

mumble /'mʌmbəl/ vi hablar entre dientes
■ ~ vt mascullar

mumbo jumbo /'mʌmbəʊ'dʒʌmbəʊ/ n (pej): **religion, he said, was a lot of ~** dijo que la religión no era más que supercherías

mummy /'mʌmi/ n (pl **-mies**) [1] (mother) (BrE colloq: esp used by children) mami f (fam), mamita f (fam) [2] (Archeol) momia f

mumps /mʌmps/ n paperas fpl

munch /mʌntʃ/ vt/i mascar*

mundane /mʌn'deɪn/ adj ‹existence› prosaico; ‹activity› rutinario

municipal /mjʊ'nɪsəpəl ‖ mjuː'nɪsɪpəl/ adj (usu before n) municipal

munitions /mjʊ'nɪʃənz ‖ mjuː'nɪʃənz/ pl n municiones fpl

mural /'mjʊrəl ‖ 'mjʊərəl/ n mural m

murder¹ /'mɜːrdər ‖ 'mɜːdə(r)/ n asesinato m; (Law) homicidio m; **to get away with ~:** **she lets them get away with ~** les permite cualquier cosa

murder² vt (a) (kill) asesinar (b) (ruin) ‹music/play› destrozar*
■ ~ vi matar

murderer /'mɜːrdərər ‖ 'mɜːdərə(r)/ n asesino, -na m,f

murderous /'mɜːrdərəs ‖ 'mɜːdərəs/ adj ‹instinct/look› asesino; ‹individual› de instintos asesinos

murky /'mɜːrki ‖ 'mɜːki/ adj **-kier, -kiest** ‹water› turbio; ‹green/brown› sucio; ‹past› turbio

murmur¹ /'mɜːrmər ‖ 'mɜːmə(r)/ n murmullo m

murmur² vt murmurar

muscle /'mʌsəl/ n (a) (Anat) músculo m (b) (power) fuerza f
■ **muscle in** [v + adv] (colloq) meterse por medio (con prepotencia); **a rival company ~d in on their market** una compañía de la competencia se introdujo en su sector del mercado

muscular /'mʌskjələr ‖'mʌskjʊlə(r)/ adj (a) ⟨arms/build⟩ musculoso (b) ⟨strain/contraction⟩ muscular

muscular dystrophy /'dɪstrəfi/ n distrofia f muscular

muse¹ /mjuːz/ vi to ~ (ON o UPON sth) cavilar or reflexionar (SOBRE algo)

muse², Muse n musa f

museum /mjʊ'ziːəm/ n museo m

mush /mʌʃ/ n papilla f, pasta f

mushroom¹ /'mʌʃrʊm, -ruːm/ n hongo m (esp AmL), seta f (esp Esp), callampa f (Chi); (rounded, white) champiñón m

mushroom² vi «town/population» crecer* rápidamente; «companies/buildings» aparecer* como hongos or (Chi) como callampas, multiplicarse*

mushy /'mʌʃi/ adj mushier, mushiest ⟨vegetables/fruit⟩ blando

music /'mjuːzɪk/ n (a) (art form) música f; to face the ~ afrontar las consecuencias (b) (written notes) partitura f, música f

musical¹ /'mjuːzɪkəl/ adj (a) (Mus) (before n) ⟨ability/tradition⟩ musical (b) (musically gifted) con aptitudes para la música (c) (melodious) ⟨voice/laugh⟩ musical

musical² n musical m

musical chairs n (+ sing vb): to play ~ jugar* a las sillitas

music: ~ **box** n caja f de música; ~ **hall** n (a) (entertainment) music hall m, ≈revista f de variedades (b) (building) teatro m de variedades

musician /mjʊ'zɪʃən/ n músico, -ca m,f

musk /mʌsk/ n almizcle m

musket /'mʌskət ‖'mʌskɪt/ n mosquete m

Muslim¹ /'mʊzləm ‖'mʊzlɪm/ n musulmán, -mana m,f

Muslim² adj musulmán

muslin /'mʌzlən ‖'mʌzlɪn/ n muselina f (de algodón)

muss /mʌs/ vt ~ (up) (AmE colloq) ⟨room⟩ desordenar; **she ~ed her hair** se despeinó

mussel /'mʌsəl/ n mejillón m

must¹ /mʌst, weak form məst/ v mod
⌐1⌐ (expressing obligation) tener* que or deber; **it ~ be remembered that ...** hay que recordar que ..., tenemos que or debemos recordar que ...; **she ~ not know that I am here** no debe enterarse de que estoy aquí, no se entere de que estoy aquí; **I ~ say, everywhere looks very tidy** tengo que reconocer que está todo muy ordenado
⌐2⌐ (expressing certainty, supposition) deber (de) or (esp AmL) haber* de; **it ~ be six o'clock** deben (de) ser or (esp AmL) han de ser las seis, serán las seis

must² /mʌst/ n (essential thing, activity): **a car is a ~ here** aquí es indispensable tener coche; **this book is a ~** este es un libro que hay que leer

mustache /'mʌstæʃ/, (BrE) **moustache** /mə'stɑːʃ/ n bigote(s) m(pl); **to grow a ~** dejarse bigote(s) or el bigote

mustard /'mʌstərd ‖'mʌstəd/ n mostaza f

muster /'mʌstər ‖'mʌstə(r)/ vt (a) (Mil) ⟨soldiers⟩ reunir*, llamar a asamblea (b) (succeed in raising) **to ~ (up)** ⟨team/army⟩ lograr formar; **if they can ~ enough support** si logran el apoyo que necesitan

mustn't /'mʌsn̩t/ = must not

musty /'mʌsti/ adj -tier, tiest que huele a humedad or a moho

mutate /'mjuːteɪt ‖mjuː'teɪt/ vi (a) (Biol, Ling) mutar (b) (change) (frml) sufrir una transformación/transformaciones

mutation /mjuː'teɪʃən/ n (a) (Biol, Ling) mutación f (b) (change) (frml) transformación f

mute /mjuːt/ adj mudo

muted /'mjuːtəd ‖'mjuːtɪd/ adj ⟨sound⟩ sordo; ⟨voice⟩ apagado; ⟨trumpet⟩ con sordina; ⟨shade⟩ apagado; ⟨protest/reaction⟩ débil

mutilate /'mjuːtl̩eɪt ‖'mjuːtɪleɪt/ vt mutilar

mutiny¹ /'mjuːtni ‖'mjuːtɪni/ n (pl -nies) (a) (instance) motín m, amotinamiento m (b) (offense) amotinamiento m

mutiny² vi -nies, -nying, -nied amotinarse

mutt /mʌt/ n (AmE colloq) (dog) chucho m (fam), gozque m (Col fam), quiltro m (Chi fam), pichicho m (RPl fam)

mutter /'mʌtər ‖'mʌtə(r)/ vi hablar entre dientes
■ ~ vt mascullar

mutton /'mʌtn̩/ n carne f de ovino (de más de un año), añojo m (Esp), capón m (RPl)

mutual /'mjuːtʃuəl/ adj (a) (reciprocal) mutuo (b) (shared, common) (before n) ⟨friend/enemy⟩ común

muzzle /'mʌzəl/ n (a) (snout) hocico m (b) (for dog) bozal m (c) (of gun) boca f

my /maɪ/ adj
■ **Note** The translation mi agrees in number with the noun which it modifies; my is translated by mi, mis, according to what follows: my father/mother mi padre/madre; my books/magazines mis libros/revistas.

(sing) mi; (pl) mis; **I put ~ hat on** me puse el sombrero; **I broke ~ arm** me rompí el brazo

myalgic encephalomyelitis /maɪˈældʒɪkenˌsefələʊmaɪəˈlaɪtəs ‖maɪˌældʒɪkenˌsefələʊˌmaɪəˈlaɪtɪs/ n encefalomielitis f miálgica

myriad /'mɪriəd/ adj (liter): **the ~ varieties of butterfly** los miles tipos de mariposas

myrrh /mɜːr ‖mɜː(r)/ n mirra f

myself /maɪˈself/ pron (a) (reflexive): **I cut/hurt ~** me corté/lastimé; **I was talking to ~** estaba hablando solo/sola; **I was by ~** estaba solo/sola (b) (emphatic use) yo mismo, yo misma; **I made it ~** lo hice yo mismo/misma (c) (normal self): **I haven't been feeling ~ lately** no me encuentro muy bien últimamente

mysterious /mɪˈstɪriəs ‖mɪˈstɪəriəs/ adj misterioso

mystery /'mɪstəri/ n (pl -ries) ⌐1⌐ (a) (puzzle) misterio m (b) (quality) misterio m; (before n) ⟨guest/tour⟩ sorpresa adj inv ⌐2⌐ (Cin, Lit, Theat) película f (or novela f etc) de misterio or de suspenso or (Esp) de suspense

mystical /'mɪstɪkəl/ adj místico
mystify /'mɪstəfaɪ ‖'mɪstɪfaɪ/ vt **-fies, -fying, -fied** desconcertar*

myth /mɪθ/ n mito m
mythology /mɪ'θɑːlədʒi ‖mɪ'θɒlədʒi/ n (pl **-gies**) mitología f

N n

N, n /en/ n **(a)** (letter) N, n f **(b)** (indeterminate number) (Math) (número m) n

'n' /ən/ = **and**

N (= **north**) N

NAACP /'endʌbəl'eɪsiː'piː/ n (in US) = **National Association for the Advancement of Colored People**

nab /næb/ vt **-bb-** (colloq) **(a)** (catch) ⟨person⟩ pescar* (fam) **(b)** (snatch) agarrar or (esp Esp) coger*

nadir /'neɪdɪr ‖'neɪdɪə(r)/ n (Astron) nadir m; (lowest point) punto m más bajo

nag /næg/ **-gg-** vt **(a)** (pester) fastidiar **(b)** (criticize): he's always ∼ging her for being untidy siempre le está encima con que es desordenada ■ ∼ vi **1** **(a)** (pester) fastidiar **(b)** (criticize) rezongar* **2** **nagging** pres p ⟨doubt/worry⟩ persistente; ⟨husband/wife⟩ rezongón (fam)

nail¹ /neɪl/ n **1** (Const) clavo m; (smaller) puntilla f; **to be as hard as** ∼**s** ser* muy duro (de corazón) **2** (Anat) uña f; (before n) ∼ **polish** o (BrE also) **varnish** esmalte m de uñas

nail² vt **1** (fix) clavar **2** (colloq) (apprehend) agarrar or (esp Esp) coger*
■ **nail down** [v + o + adv, v + adv + o] clavar, asegurar con clavos

nail: ∼**brush** n cepillo m de uñas; ∼ **clippers** pl n cortaúñas m; ∼ **file** n lima f (de uñas)

naive, naïve /nɑː'iːv, naɪ'iːv/ adj ingenuo

naked /'neɪkəd ‖'neɪkɪd/ adj **(a)** (unclothed) desnudo **(b)** ⟨sword/blade⟩ desenvainado; **visible/ invisible to the** ∼ **eye** que se puede ver/invisible a simple vista

name¹ /neɪm/ n **1** (of person, thing) nombre m; (surname) apellido m; **what's your** ∼? ¿cómo te llamas?, ¿cómo se llama (Ud)?; **my** ∼ **is John Baker** me llamo John Baker; **he knows them all by** ∼ los conoce a todos por su nombre; **in** ∼ **only** solo de nombre; **mentioning no** ∼**s** sin mencionar a nadie; **to call sb** ∼**s** insultar a algn; (before n) ∼ **tag** etiqueta f de identificación **2** **(a)** (reputation) fama f; **to give sb/sth a bad** ∼ darle* mala fama a algn/algo **(b)** (person) figura f; (company) nombre m; **to drop** ∼**s** mencionar a gente importante (para darse tono)

name² vt **1** (give name to) ⟨company/town⟩ ponerle* nombre a; ⟨boat⟩ bautizar*; **a man** ∼**d Smith** un hombre llamado Smith; **they** ∼**d her**

after o (AmE also) **for Ann's mother** le pusieron el nombre de la madre de Ann **2** (identify, mention): **police have** ∼**d the suspect** la policía ha dado el nombre del sospechoso; **to** ∼ **but a few** por mencionar a unos pocos; **you** ∼ **it, she's done it** ha hecho de todo lo habido y por haber **3** (appoint) nombrar

nameless /'neɪmləs ‖'neɪmlɪs/ adj **1** (not specified) anónimo **2** ⟨fear/yearning⟩ indescriptible

namely /'neɪmli/ adv (frml) a saber (frml)

namesake /'neɪmseɪk/ n tocayo, -ya m,f

nanny /'næni/ n (pl **-nies**) **1** (nursemaid) (esp BrE) niñera f **2** (granny) (used to or by children) abuelita f (fam) **3** ∼ **goat** cabra f

nap /næp/ n sueñecito m (fam), sueñito m (esp AmL fam); (esp in the afternoon) siesta f

nape /neɪp/ n nuca f

napkin /'næpkɪn/ n servilleta f

nappy /'næpi/ n (pl **-pies**) (BrE) pañal m

narcotic /nɑːr'kɑːtɪk ‖nɑː'kɒtɪk/ n estupefaciente m, narcótico m

narrate /'næreɪt ‖nə'reɪt/ vt **(a)** (Lit frml) ⟨story/ events⟩ narrar **(b)** ⟨film/documentary⟩ hacer* el comentario de

narrative¹ /'nærətɪv/ adj narrativo

narrative² n **(a)** (story) (frml) narración f **(b)** (Lit) (narrated part) narración f

narrator /'næreɪtər ‖nə'reɪtə(r)/ n **(a)** (Lit) narrador, -dora m,f **(b)** (Cin, Theat, TV) comentarista mf

narrow¹ /'nærəʊ/ adj **1** **(a)** (not wide) ⟨path/ opening/hips⟩ estrecho, angosto (esp AmL) **(b)** (slender) ⟨margin⟩ escaso; ⟨win/victory⟩ conseguido por un escaso margen; **to have a** ∼ **escape** salvarse de milagro **2** (restricted) ⟨range/ view⟩ limitado; ⟨attitude/ideas⟩ cerrado

narrow² vt **(a)** (reduce width of) estrechar, angostar (esp AmL) **(b)** (restrict) ⟨range/field⟩ restringir*
■ ∼ vi **(a)** ⟨road/river/valley⟩ estrecharse, angostarse (esp AmL) **(b)** ⟨options/odds⟩ reducirse*
■ **narrow down** [v + o + adv, v + adv + o]: they've ∼ed their investigation down to this area han restringido su investigación a esta área; **we**

~ed it down to only three candidates fuimos descartando candidatos hasta quedar con solo tres

narrowly /'nærəʊli/ *adv* por poco

narrow-minded /ˌnærəʊ'maɪndəd ‖ˌnærəʊ'maɪndɪd/ *adj* de mentalidad cerrada

NASA /'næsə/ *n* (in US) (*no art*) (= **National Aeronautics and Space Administration**) la NASA

nasal /'neɪzəl/ *adj* (Anat, Ling) nasal; ⟨voice/accent⟩ gangoso, de timbre nasal

nasty /'næsti ‖'nɑːsti/ *adj* **-tier, -tiest** [1] ⟨taste/smell/medicine⟩ asqueroso; ⟨habit⟩ feo [2] (spiteful) ⟨person⟩ malo [3] (a) (severe) ⟨cut/injury/cough⟩ feo; ⟨accident⟩ serio; (stronger) horrible (b) (unpleasant) ⟨situation/experience⟩ desagradable

nation /'neɪʃn/ *n* nación *f*

national¹ /'næʃnəl ‖'næʃənl/ *adj* nacional

national² *n* ciudadano, -na *m,f*

national: N~ Health (Service) *n* (in UK) **the N~ Health (Service)** *servicio de asistencia sanitaria de la Seguridad Social*; **N~ Insurance** *n* (in UK) Seguridad *f* Social

nationalism /'næʃnəlɪzəm/ *n* nacionalismo *m*

nationalist¹ /'næʃnələst ‖'næʃnəlɪst/ *adj* nacionalista

nationalist² *n* nacionalista *mf*

nationality /ˌnæʃə'næləti/ *n* (*pl* **-ties**) nacionalidad *f*; **what's your?, what ~ are you?** ¿de qué nacionalidad eres?

nationalize /'næʃnəlaɪz/ *vt* nacionalizar*

nationally /'næʃnəli/ *adv* a escala nacional

national park *n* parque *m* nacional

nationwide¹ /ˈneɪʃənwaɪd/ *adj* ⟨campaign⟩ a escala nacional; ⟨appeal⟩ a toda la nación

nationwide² *adv* ⟨distribute/operate⟩ a escala nacional

native¹ /'neɪtɪv/ *adj* [1] (a) (of or by birth) ⟨country/town⟩ natal; ⟨customs⟩ nativo; ⟨language⟩ materno; **his ~ land** su patria, su tierra natal; **a ~ speaker of ...** un hablante nativo de ... (b) (innate) ⟨ability/wit/charm⟩ innato [2] (indigenous) ⟨plant/animal⟩ autóctono

native² *n* (a) (Anthrop) nativo, -va *m,f*, indígena *mf* (b) (plant, animal): **the dingo is a ~ of Australia** el dingo es originario de Australia

Native American *n* indio americano, india americana *m,f*

nativity /nə'tɪvəti/ *n*: **The N~** (Relig) la Natividad

NATO /'neɪtəʊ/ *n* (*no art*) (= **North Atlantic Treaty Organization**) la OTAN

natural /'nætʃrəl/ *adj* [1] (as in nature) natural [2] (a) ⟨talent/propensity⟩ innato; ⟨leader⟩ nato (b) ⟨reaction/response⟩ natural; ⟨successor⟩ lógico [3] (not forced) ⟨warmth/style⟩ natural

natural history *n* historia *f* natural

naturalist /'nætʃrələst ‖'nætʃrəlɪst/ *n* naturalista *mf*

naturalization /ˌnætʃrələ'zeɪʃən ‖ˌnætʃrələr'zeɪʃən/ *n* naturalización *f*

naturalized /'nætʃrəlaɪzd/ *adj* (a) ⟨citizen/American⟩ naturalizado (b) (Bot, Zool) aclimatado

naturally /'nætʃrəli/ *adv* [1] (a) (inherently)

⟨shy/tidy⟩ por naturaleza (b) (unaffectedly) ⟨smile/behave/speak⟩ con naturalidad [2] (without artifice) ⟨form/heal⟩ de manera natural [3] (indep) (of course) naturalmente, por supuesto

nature /'neɪtʃər ‖'neɪtʃə(r)/ *n* [1] (universe, way of things) naturaleza *f* [2] (a) (of people) carácter *m*; **by ~** por naturaleza (b) (of things, concepts) naturaleza *f*

nature reserve *n* reserva *f* natural

naturist /'neɪtʃərəst ‖'neɪtʃərɪst/ *n* (esp BrE) nudista *mf*; (before n) ⟨beach/camp⟩ nudista

naught /nɔːt/ *n* (esp AmE) cero *m*

naughty /'nɔːti/ *adj* **-tier, -tiest** malo, travieso

nausea /'nɔːsɪə, -zɪə/ *n* náusea *f*

nauseating /'nɔːsɪeɪtɪŋ, 'nɔːz-/ *adj* ⟨violence/brutality⟩ repugnante; ⟨smell⟩ nauseabundo

nauseous /'nɔːʃəs, 'nɔːzɪəs ‖'nɔːsɪəs, nɔːz-/ *adj* (bilious): **to feel ~** sentir* náuseas

nautical /'nɔːtɪkl ‖'nɔːtɪkəl/ *adj* náutico, marítimo; **~ mile** milla *f* marina

naval /'neɪvəl/ *adj* naval; ⟨officer⟩ de marina

nave /neɪv/ *n* nave *f*

navel /'neɪvəl/ *n* ombligo *m*

navigable /'nævɪgəbəl/ *adj* navegable

navigate /'nævəgeɪt ‖'nævɪgeɪt/ *vi* (a) (Aviat, Naut) navegar* (b) (in car) hacer* de copiloto ■ ~ *vt* (a) (steer) ⟨ship/plane⟩ conducir*, llevar (b) (travel across, along) ⟨sea/river⟩ navegar* por

navigation /ˌnævə'geɪʃən ‖ˌnævɪ'geɪʃən/ *n* navegación *f*; (in car) dirección *f*

navigator /'nævəgeɪtər ‖'nævɪgeɪtə(r)/ *n* [1] (crew member) (Naut) oficial *mf* de derrota; (Aviat) navegante *mf* [2] (explorer) navegante *mf*

navy¹ /'neɪvi/ *n* (*pl* **navies**) [1] (Mil, Naut) marina *f* de guerra [2] **~ (blue)** azul *m* marino

navy², navy-blue /'neɪvi'bluː/ (*pred* **navy blue**) *adj* azul marino *adj inv*

Nazi¹ /'nɑːtsi/ *n* nazi *mf*, nazista *mf*

Nazi² *adj* nazi, nazista

NB (= **nota bene**) NB

NBC *n* (in US) (*no art*) (= **National Broadcasting Company**) la NBC

NC = North Carolina

NCO *n* = **noncommissioned officer**

ND, N Dak = North Dakota

NE (a) (= **northeast**) NE (b) = **Nebraska**

near¹ /nɪr ‖nɪə(r)/ *adj* **-er, -est** [1] (a) (in position, time) cercano, próximo (b) ⟨relative⟩ cercano [2] (virtual) (before n): **there was ~ panic when the alarms sounded** casi se produjo el pánico cuando sonaron las alarmas; **in a state of ~ exhaustion** prácticamente en estado de agotamiento

near² *adv* **-er, -est** [1] (in position) cerca; **from ~ and far** de todas partes [2] (nearly) casi

near³ *prep* **-er, -est** (a) (in position) cerca de; **don't go too ~ the fire** no te acerques demasiado al fuego (b) (in time): **we're getting very ~ Christmas** falta muy poco para Navidad (c) (in approximation): **I'd say he's ~er 70 than 60** yo diría que está más cerca de los 70 que de los 60

near⁴ *vt* acercarse* a; **the project is ~ing completion** el proyecto se está por acabar

near- /'nɪr ‖'nɪə(r)/ *pref* casi

nearby¹ /'nɪrbaɪ ‖nɪə'baɪ/ *adj* cercano

nearby² *adv* cerca

nearly /'nɪrli ‖'nɪəli/ *adv* casi; **she very ~ died** por poco *or* casi se muere

nearsighted /'nɪr'saɪtəd ‖,nɪə'saɪtɪd/ *adj* miope, corto de vista

neat /niːt/ *adj* **-er, -est** **1** (tidy, orderly) ‹appearance› arreglado, cuidado, prolijo (RPl); ‹person› pulcro, prolijo (RPl); ‹garden› muy cuidado **2** (good, nice) (AmE colloq) fantástico (fam), padre (Méx fam), chévere (AmL exc CS fam), chulo (Esp fam), encachado (Chi fam) **3** (BrE) ‹brandy/ alcohol› solo

neatly /'niːtli/ *adv* **(a)** (tidily): **the papers were ~ organized into piles** los papeles estaban cuidadosamente apilados; **she was ~ dressed** iba bien arreglada **(b)** (snugly): **the table fits ~ into the alcove** la mesa cabe perfectamente en el hueco **(c)** ‹explain/evade› hábilmente

Neb, Nebr = **Nebraska**

necessarily /'nesə'serəli ‖,nesə'serɪli/ *adv* forzosamente, necesariamente

necessary /'nesəseri ‖'nesəsəri / *adj* necesario

necessitate /nə'sesɪteɪt ‖nɪ'sesɪteɪt/ *vt* (fml) exigir*

necessity /nə'sesəti ‖nɪ'sesəti/ *n* (*pl* **-ties**) **1** (imperative need) (*no pl*) necesidad *f*; **~ FOR sth** necesidad DE algo; **out of ~** por necesidad **2** (necessary item): **the bare necessities** lo indispensable; **a car is a ~ for me** para mí tener coche es una necesidad

neck /nek/ *n* **1** (Anat) (of person) cuello *m*; (of animal) cuello *m*, pescuezo *m*; **they were ~ and ~** iban a la par, iban parejos (esp AmL); **to be up to one's ~ in sth** (colloq): **she's up to her ~ in work** está hasta aquí de trabajo (fam); **they're up to their ~s in debt** deben hasta la camisa (fam) **2** (Clothing) cuello *m*, escote *m*; (measurement) cuello *m* **3** (of pork, beef, lamb) (esp BrE) cuello *m* **4** (of bottle, vase) cuello *m*; (of guitar, violin) mástil *m*; **a ~ of land** un istmo

necklace /'nekləs ‖'neklɪs/ *n* collar *m*

neck: **~line** *n* escote *m*; **~tie** *n* (AmE) corbata *f*

nectar /'nektər ‖'nektə(r)/ *n* néctar *m*

nectarine /'nektəriːn ‖'nektərɪn, -riːn/ *n* nectarina *f*, pelón *m* (RPl), durazno *m* pelado (Chi)

née /neɪ/ *adj* de soltera

need¹ /niːd/ *n* **1** (requirement, necessity) necesidad *f*, **~ FOR sth/to + INF** necesidad DE algo/DE + INF; **there's no ~ to tell her** no hay ninguna necesidad de decírselo; **if ~ be** si hace falta; **the house is badly in ~ of renovation** a la casa le hacen muchísima falta unos arreglos **2** **(a)** (emergency): **he abandoned them in their hour of ~** los abandonó cuando más falta les hacía **(b)** (poverty) necesidad *f*; **those in ~** los necesitados

need² *vt* necesitar; **the plants ~ watering** hay que regar las plantas; **to ~ to + INF** tener* QUE + INF

■ **~** *v mod* (*usu with neg or interrog*) (be obliged to): **you ~n't come if you don't want to** no hay necesidad de que vengas si no tienes ganas; **that ~n't mean that ...** eso no significa necesariamente que ...

needle¹ /'niːdl/ *n* **(a)** (for sewing, on syringe) aguja

f; (on record player) aguja *f*, púa *f* (RPl); (knitting ~) aguja *f* de tejer *or* (Esp) de hacer punto, palillo *m* (Chi); **to look for a ~ in a haystack** buscar* una aguja en un pajar **(b)** (on gauge) aguja *f* **(c)** (Bot) aguja *f*

needle² *vt* pinchar (fam)

needless /'niːdləs ‖'niːdlɪs/ *adj* innecesario; **~ to say, no one asked me** de más está decir que nadie me preguntó

needlework /'niːdlwɜːrk ‖'niːdlwɜːk/ *n* (activity, skill) labores *fpl* de aguja

needn't /'niːdnt/ = **need not**

needy¹ /'niːdi/ *adj* **-dier, -diest** necesitado

needy² *pl n* **the ~** los necesitados

negative¹ /'negətɪv/ *adj* negativo

negative² *n* **1** **(a)** (word, particle) negación *f* **(b)** (no) negativa *f* **2** (Phot) negativo *m*

neglect¹ /nɪ'glekt/ *vt* **(a)** (leave uncared-for) ‹family/child› desatender*; ‹house/health› descuidar **(b)** (not carry out) ‹duty/obligations› desatender*; ‹studies/business› descuidar

neglect² *n* (lack of care) abandono *m*; (negligence) negligencia *f*

neglected /nɪ'glektəd ‖nɪ'glektɪd/ *adj* ‹building/garden› abandonado, descuidado; ‹appearance› dejado, abandonado

neglectful /nɪ'glektfəl/ *adj* negligente

negligee /'neglə'ʒeɪ ‖'neglɪʒeɪ/ *n* negligé *m*

negligence /'neglɪdʒəns/ *n* negligencia *f*

negligent /'neglɪdʒənt/ *adj* negligente

negligible /'neglɪdʒəbəl/ *adj* insignificante

negotiable /nɪ'gəʊʃəbəl/ *adj* **(a)** (subject to negotiation) ‹contract/claim/salary› negociable **(b)** (passable) ‹road› transitable; ‹obstacle› superable

negotiate /nɪ'gəʊʃɪeɪt/ *vi* negociar
■ **~** *vt* **1** (obtain by discussion) ‹contract/treaty› negociar; ‹loan› gestionar **2** (pass, deal with) ‹obstacle› sortear; ‹difficulty› superar

negotiation /nɪ'gəʊʃi'eɪʃən/ *n* (*sometimes pl*) negociación *f*

negotiator /nɪ'gəʊʃɪeɪtər ‖nɪ'gəʊʃɪeɪtə(r)/ *n* negociador, -dora *m,f*

Negro /'niːgrəʊ/ *n* (*pl* **Negroes**) (often offensive) negro, -gra *m,f*

neigh /neɪ/ *vi* relinchar

neighbor, (BrE) **neighbour** /'neɪbər ‖'neɪbə(r)/ *n* vecino, -na *m,f*

neighborhood, (BrE) **neighbourhood** /'neɪbrhʊd ‖'neɪbəhʊd/ *n* **(a)** (residential area) barrio *m*; (before n) ‹school/policeman› del barrio **(b)** (inhabitants) vecindario *m* **(c)** (vicinity) zona *f*; **in the ~** en los alrededores

neighboring, (BrE) **neighbouring** /'neɪbərɪŋ/ *adj* ‹country› vecino; **the town and the ~ villages** la ciudad y los pueblos de los alrededores

neither¹ /'niːðər, 'naɪ- ‖'naɪðə(r), 'niːð-/ *conj* **1** **neither ... nor ...** ni ... ni ... **2** (nor) tampoco; **I don't want to go — ~ do I** *o* (colloq) **me ~** no quiero ir — yo tampoco *or* ni yo

neither² *adj*: **~ proposal was accepted** no se aceptó ninguna de las (dos) propuestas

neither³ *pron* ninguno, -na

neo- /'niːəʊ/ *pref* neo-

neon /'niːɑːn ‖'niːɒn/ n neón m; (before n) ⟨glow/lighting/sign⟩ de neón

Nepal /nəˈpɔːl ‖nɪˈpɔːl/ n Nepal m

Nepalese /ˌnepəˈliːz/ adj nepalés

nephew /'nefjuː ‖'nevjuː, 'nef-/ n sobrino m

nepotism /'nepətɪzəm/ n nepotismo m

Neptune /'neptuːn ‖'neptjuːn/ n Neptuno m

nerve /nɜːrv ‖nɜːv/ n **1** (Anat, Bot) nervio m; (before n) ⟨fiber/ending⟩ nervioso **2 nerves** pl (a) (emotional constitution) nervios mpl; **to get on sb's ∼s** (colloq) ponerle* los nervios de punta a algn (b) (anxiety) nervios mpl **3** (a) (resolve) valor m; **to lose one's ∼** perder* el valor (b) (effrontery) (colloq) ⟨no pl⟩ frescura f (fam); **to have the ∼ to +** INF tener* la frescura de + INF (fam)

nerve-racking /'nɜːrvˈrækɪŋ ‖'nɜːvˌrækɪŋ/ adj que destroza los nervios

nervous /'nɜːrvəs ‖'nɜːvəs/ adj **1** (apprehensive, tense) nervioso; **to feel/get ∼** estar*/ponerse* nervioso; **to make sb ∼** poner* nervioso a algn **2** ⟨system/tissue/tension⟩ nervioso; **she's a ∼ wreck** (colloq) es un manojo de nervios

nervously /'nɜːrvəsli ‖'nɜːvəsli/ adv nerviosamente

nest¹ /nest/ n nido m

nest² vi anidar

nest egg n (colloq) ahorros mpl

nestle /'nesəl/ vi (snuggle) acurrucarse*; **the village ∼s at the foot of the hill** el pueblo está enclavado al pie de la montaña

net¹ /net/ n **1** red f **2** (Sport) red f **3** (fabric) tela f de visillos; (before n) **∼ curtains** visillos mpl

net² vt **-tt-** **1** (catch) ⟨butterfly⟩ cazar* (con red); ⟨fish⟩ pescar* (con red) **2** (earn) «company/sale» producir*; **he ∼ted $50,000** se embolsó 50.000 dólares limpios (fam)

net³ adj ⟨income/profit⟩ neto; ⟨effect/result⟩ global

netball /'netbɔːl/ n (in UK) deporte similar al baloncesto jugado esp por mujeres

Netherlands /'neðərləndz ‖'neðələndz/ n (+ sing or pl vb) **the ∼** los Países Bajos

nett adj (BrE) ▶ NET³

netting /'netɪŋ/ n redes fpl; **wire ∼** tela f metálica, tejido m metálico (RPl), anjeo m (Col)

nettle /'netl/ n ortiga f; (stinging ∼) ortiga f (romana)

network¹ /'netwɜːrk ‖'netwɜːk/ n **(a)** (system) red f **(b)** (Elec) red f **(c)** (Rad, TV) cadena f; (before) **∼ television** (in US) emisiones fpl televisivas en cadena

network² vt **1** (BrE Rad, TV) transmitir en cadena **2** (link together) (Comput) interconectar

neuralgia /nʊˈrældʒə ‖njʊəˈrældʒə/ n neuralgia f

neurosis /nʊˈrəʊsəs ‖njʊəˈrəʊsɪs/ n (pl **-roses** /-'rəʊsiːz/) neurosis f

neurotic /nʊˈrɑːtɪk ‖njʊəˈrɒtɪk/ adj neurótico

neuter¹ /'nuːtər ‖'njuːtə(r)/ adj neutro

neuter² vt castrar

neutral¹ /'nuːtrəl ‖'njuːtrəl/ adj **(a)** (impartial) neutral **(b)** (not bright) ⟨shade/tone⟩ neutro **(c)** (Chem, Elec, Ling) neutro

neutral² n (Auto): **to be in ∼** estar* en punto muerto

neutralize /'nuːtrəlaɪz ‖'njuːtrəlaɪz/ vt neutralizar*

neutron /'nuːtrɑːn ‖'njuːtrɒn/ n neutrón m

Nev = Nevada

never /'nevər ‖'nevə(r)/ adv nunca; (more emphatic) jamás; **as ∼ before** como nunca; **she said she'd call but she ∼ did** dijo que llamaría pero no llamó; **this will ∼ do!** ¡esto no puede ser!

never: ∼-ending /'nevərˈendɪŋ/ adj (pred ∼ **ending**) ⟨dispute/saga⟩ interminable; ⟨devotion/ supply⟩ inagotable; **∼theless** /ˌnevərðəˈles ‖ˌnevəðəˈles/ adv sin embargo, no obstante (frml)

new¹ /nuː ‖njuː/ adj **-er, -est** nuevo; **after the shower I felt like a ∼ man** la ducha me dejó como nuevo

new² adv recién

new: N∼ Age adj New Age, de la Nueva Era; **∼born** /'nuːbɔːrn ‖'njuːbɔːn/ adj recién nacido; **∼comer** /'nuːkʌmər ‖'njuːkʌmə(r)/ n recién llegado, -da m,f, **∼fangled** /'nuːˈfæŋgəld ‖'njuːˈfæŋgəld/ adj (before n) (pej) moderno; **∼found** /'nuːfaʊnd ‖'njuːfaʊnd/ adj nuevo, recién descubierto

newlyweds /'nuːliwedz ‖'njuːliwedz/ pl n recién casados mpl

news /nuːz ‖njuːz/ n **1** (fresh information): **a piece of ∼** una noticia; **I have (some) good/bad ∼** tengo buenas/malas noticias **2** (Journ, Rad, TV) noticias fpl; (before n) **∼ bulletin** boletín m informativo

news: ∼agent n (BrE) dueño o empleado de una tienda que vende prensa, caramelos etc; **∼caster** n locutor, -tora m,f, presentador, -dora m,f (de un informativo); **∼ flash** n (BrE) información f de última hora; **∼ group** n grupo m de noticias; **∼letter** n boletín m informativo

newspaper /'nuːzˌpeɪpər ‖'njuːsˌpeɪpə(r)/ n periódico m, diario m

news: ∼print n papel m de prensa; **∼reel** n noticiario m or (AmL tb) noticiero m (cinematográfico), nodo m (Esp); **∼stand** n kiosco m de periódicos

newt /nuːt ‖njuːt/ n tritón m

new: N∼ Year n Año m Nuevo; **N∼ Year's Day** n día m de Año Nuevo; **N∼ Year's Eve** n la noche de Fin de Año, la Nochevieja (Esp); **N∼ York** /jɔːrk ‖jɔːk/ n Nueva York f; (before n) neoyorquino; **N∼ Zealand** /'ziːlənd/ n Nueva Zelanda; (before n) neocelandés

next¹ /nekst/ adj **(a)** (in time — talking about the future) próximo; (— talking about the past) siguiente; **I'll see you ∼ Thursday** nos vemos el jueves que viene or el jueves próximo; **the matter was discussed at the ∼ meeting** el asunto se trató en la reunión siguiente; **the week after ∼** la semana que viene no, la otra or la siguiente **(b)** (in position) siguiente; **take the ∼ turning on the right** tome la próxima or la siguiente a la derecha **(c)** (in sequence): **who's ∼?** ¿quién sigue?; **you're the ∼ to speak** luego te toca a ti hablar

next² adv **1 (a)** (then) luego, después **(b)** (now): **what shall we do ∼?** ¿y ahora qué hacemos?; **what comes ∼?** ¿qué sigue (ahora)?; **whatever ∼!** ¡adónde vamos (a ir) a parar! ····⊱

2 (second): **Tom is the tallest in the class, Bob the ~ tallest** Tom es el más alto de la clase y (a Tom) le sigue Bob; **it's the ~ best thing to champagne** después del champán, es lo mejor que hay

3 next to (a) (beside) al lado de; **come and sit ~ to me** ven y siéntate a mi lado **(b)** (compared with) al lado de **(c)** (second): **the ~ to last page** la penúltima página **(d)** (almost, virtually): **I bought it for ~ to nothing** lo compré por poquísimo dinero; **I'll have it ready in ~ to no time** lo termino en un segundo

next: **~ door** adv al lado; **~ door TO sb/sth** al lado DE algn/algo; **~ door** ‖'neks'dɔːr‖ adj (before n) de al lado; **~ of kin** n (pl ~ of kin) familiar(es) m(pl) más cercano(s)

NH = **New Hampshire**

NHS n (in UK) = **National Health Service**

nib /nɪb/ n plumín m, pluma f

nibble /'nɪbəl/ vt **(a)** (bite) mordisquear **(b)** (eat, pick at) picar*
■ ~ vi **(a)** (bite, gnaw) **to ~ AT/ON sth** mordisquear algo **(b)** (eat) picar*

Nicaragua /'nɪkə'rɑːgwə ‖ ˌnɪkə'rægjʊə/ n Nicaragua f

Nicaraguan¹ /'nɪkə'rɑːgwən ‖ ˌnɪkə'rægjʊən/ adj nicaragüense

Nicaraguan² n nicaragüense mf

nice /naɪs/ adj **nicer, nicest** **1 (a)** (kind, amiable) amable; (kind-hearted) bueno; (friendly) simpático; **to be ~ TO sb** ser* amable CON algn **(b)** (attractive, appealing) ⟨place/dress/face⟩ bonito, lindo (esp AmL); ⟨food⟩ bueno, rico; **the soup smells ~** la sopa huele bien **(c)** (enjoyable) ⟨walk/ surprise⟩ agradable, lindo (esp AmL)
2 (as intensifier): **I had a ~ hot shower** me di una buena ducha caliente; **her apartment is ~ and sunny** tiene un apartamento muy or de lo más soleado
3 (respectable, decent): **he seemed such a ~ boy** parecía tan buen chico; **it isn't a very ~ area** es un barrio bastante feo

nicely /'naɪsli/ adv **1 (a)** (amiably) ⟨treat/smile⟩ amablemente **(b)** (politely, respectably) con buenos modales **2** (attractively) ⟨presented/dressed⟩ bien

niceties /'naɪsətiz/ pl n sutilezas fpl

niche /nɪtʃ, niːʃ/ n nicho m, hornacina f

nick¹ /nɪk/ n (in wood) muesca f, (in blade) mella f; **did you cut yourself? — it's just a little ~** ¿te cortaste? — es solo un rasguño; **in the ~ of time** justo a tiempo

nick² vt **1** (notch) hacer* una muesca en; **I ~ed myself shaving** me corté al afeitarme **2** (steal) (BrE colloq) afanar (arg), volar* (Méx, Ven fam), robar

nickel /'nɪkəl/ **1** n (Chem, Metall) níquel m **2** (US coin) moneda de cinco centavos

nickname¹ /'nɪkneɪm/ n apodo m; (relating to personal characteristics) mote m

nickname² vt apodar

nicotine /'nɪkətiːn/ n nicotina f

nicotine patch n parche m de nicotina

niece /niːs/ n sobrina f

Nigeria /naɪ'dʒɪəriə ‖ naɪ'dʒɪəriə/ n Nigeria f

Nigerian /naɪ'dʒɪriən ‖ naɪ'dʒɪəriən/ adj nigeriano

niggle /'nɪgəl/ vt: **something's niggling him** algo le preocupa

niggling /'nɪglɪŋ/ adj ⟨doubt/worry⟩ constante

night /naɪt/ n **1** noche f; **at ~** por la noche, de noche; **~ and day** día y noche; **last ~** anoche; **the ~ before last** anteanoche, antenoche (AmL); **we stayed (for) the ~** nos quedamos a dormir; **we haven't had a ~ out for ages** hace muchísimo que no salimos por la noche; **good ~** buenas noches; (before n) ⟨flight/patrol⟩ nocturno **2 nights** (as adv) por las noches

night: **~cap** n **(a)** (clothing) gorro m de dormir **(b)** (drink) bebida alcohólica o caliente tomada antes de acostarse; **~clothes** pl n ropa f de dormir; **~club** n club m nocturno; **~dress** n camisón m; **~fall** n anochecer m; **at ~fall** al anochecer; **~gown** n camisón m

nightingale /'naɪtɪŋgeɪl ‖ 'naɪtɪŋgeɪl/ n ruiseñor m

nightlife /'naɪtlaɪf/ n vida f nocturna

nightly¹ /'naɪtli/ adj diario, de todas las noches

nightly² adv todas las noches

nightmare /'naɪtmer ‖ 'naɪtmeə(r)/ n pesadilla f

night: **~ school** n clases fpl nocturnas; **~time** n noche f; **~ watchman** n sereno m

nil /nɪl/ n **(a)** (nothing): **its food value is virtually ~** su valor nutritivo es casi nulo **(b)** (BrE Sport) cero m

Nile /naɪl/ n **the ~** el Nilo

nimble /'nɪmbəl/ adj **-bler** /-blər/, **-blest** /-bləst/ ⟨person/step/mind⟩ ágil; ⟨fingers⟩ diestro

nine¹ /naɪn/ n nueve m; see also FOUR¹

nine² adj nueve adj inv; **~ times out of ten he's late/right** casi siempre llega tarde/tiene razón

ninefold /'naɪnfəʊld/ adj/adv ▶ -FOLD

nineteen /'naɪn'tiːn/ adj/n diecinueve adj inv/ m; **to talk ~ to the dozen** hablar (hasta) por los codos or como una cotorra (fam); see also FOUR¹

nineteenth¹ /'naɪn'tiːnθ/ adj decimonoveno

nineteenth² adv en decimonoveno lugar

nineteenth³ n (Math) diecinueveavo m; (part) diecinueveava parte f

ninetieth¹ /'naɪntiəθ/ adj nonagésimo

ninetieth² adv en nonagésimo lugar

ninetieth³ n (Math) noventavo m; (part) noventava or nonagésima parte f

nine-to-five /'naɪntə'faɪv/ adj ⟨job/worker⟩ de oficina (con horario de nueve a cinco)

ninety /'naɪnti/ adj/n noventa adj inv/m; see also FOUR¹

ninth¹ /naɪnθ/ adj noveno

ninth² adv en noveno lugar

ninth³ n (Math) noveno m; (part) novena parte f

nip¹ /nɪp/ n **(a)** (pinch) pellizco m; (bite) mordisco m **(b)** (chill): there's a ~ in the air hace bastante fresco

nip² vt **-pp-** (pinch) pellizcar*; (bite) mordisquear

nipple /'nɪpəl/ n **(a)** (on breast — of woman) pezón m; (— of man) tetilla f **(b)** (on bottle) (AmE) tetina f, chupón m (Méx)

nippy /'nɪpi/ adj **-pier, -piest** (colloq) frío; it's ~ hace frío

nit /nɪt/ n (Zool) liendre f

nit: ~**pick** vi encontrarle* defectos a todo; ~**picking** adj quisquilloso

nitrate /'naɪtreɪt/ n nitrato m

nitrogen /'naɪtrədʒən/ n nitrógeno m

NJ = **New Jersey**

NM, N Mex = **New Mexico**

no¹ /nəʊ/ adj **1** **(a)** (+ pl n): they have ~ **children** no tienen hijos; **the room has ~ windows** la habitación no tiene ninguna ventana or no tiene ventanas **(b)** (+ uncount n): there's ~ **food left** no queda nada de comida; there's ~ **time for that now** no tenemos tiempo para eso ahora; I'll be finished in ~ time (at all) termino enseguida **(c)** (+ sing count n): this cup has ~ **handle** esta taza no tiene asa; ~ **intelligent person would do that** ninguna persona inteligente haría eso

2 (in understatements): I'm ~ expert, but ... no soy ningún experto, pero ...; she told him what she thought in ~ uncertain terms le dijo lo que pensaba muy claramente

3 **(a)** (prohibiting, demanding): ❸ no smoking prohibido fumar **(b)** (with -ing form): there's ~ **pleasing some people** no hay manera de complacer a cierta gente; there'll be ~ stopping **them now** ahora no hay quien los pare

no² adv (before adj or adv): my house is ~ larger than yours mi casa no es más grande que la tuya; ~ fewer than 200 guests are expected se espera nada menos que a unos 200 invitados

no³ interj no; to say ~ decir* que no; have you seen John? — ~, I haven't ¿has visto a John? — no

no⁴ n (pl **noes**) no m

no⁵ (pl **nos**) (= **number**) n°, N°

Nobel Prize /nəʊ'bel/ n the a ~ el Premio Nobel

nobility /nəʊ'bɪləti/ n nobleza f; the ~ la nobleza

noble¹ /'nəʊbəl/ adj **nobler** /-blər/, **noblest** /-bləst/ noble

noble² n noble mf

nobleman /'nəʊbəlmən/ n (pl **-men** /-mən/) noble m

nobody¹ /'nəʊ,bɑːdi ‖ 'nəʊbədi/ pron nadie

nobody² n (pl **-dies**): to be (a) ~ ser* un don nadie

nocturnal /nɑːk'tɜːrnl̩ ‖ nɒk'tɜːnl̩/ adj nocturno

nod¹ /nɑːd ‖ nɒd/ n: he greeted her with a ~ la saludó con un movimiento de cabeza; to give sb/ sth the ~ darle* luz verde a algn/algo

nod² **-dd-** vt: he ~ded his head (in agreement) asintió con la cabeza

■ ~ vi: she smiled at me and I ~ed to her me sonrió y la saludé con la cabeza; they ~ded in assent asintieron con la cabeza

■ nod off [v + adv] (colloq) dormirse*

nodule /'nɑːdʒuːl ‖ 'nɒdjuːl/ n nódulo m

no-fly zone /nəʊ'flaɪ/ n zona f de exclusión aérea

no-good /'nəʊ'gʊd/ adj (AmE colloq) maldito (fam)

noise /nɔɪz/ n ruido m

noisily /'nɔɪzəli ‖ 'nɔɪzɪli/ adv ruidosamente

noisy /'nɔɪzi/ adj **-sier, -siest** ⟨machine/office/ street⟩ ruidoso; ⟨person/child/party⟩ bullicioso

nomad /'nəʊmæd/ n nómada mf, nómade mf (CS)

no-man's land /'nəʊmænzlænd/ n tierra f de nadie

nominal /'nɑːmənl̩ ‖ 'nɒmɪnl̩/ adj **(a)** (in name) nominal **(b)** (token) ⟨fee/rent⟩ simbólico

nominate /'nɑːməneɪt ‖ 'nɒmɪneɪt/ vt **(a)** (propose) to ~ sb (FOR sth) ⟨for a post⟩ proponer* or (AmL tb) postular a algn (PARA algo) **(b)** (appoint, choose) nombrar; ⟨candidate⟩ (AmE Pol) proclamar

nomination /ˌnɑːmə'neɪʃən ‖ ˌnɒmɪ'neɪʃən/ n **(a)** (choice, appointment) nombramiento m; (of candidate) (AmE Pol) proclamación f **(b)** (proposal) propuesta f, postulación f (AmL)

nominee /ˌnɑːmə'niː ‖ ˌnɒmɪ'niː/ n **(a)** (person proposed) candidato, -ta m,f **(b)** (person appointed) persona f nombrada; (candidate) (AmE Pol) candidato, -ta m,f

non- /nɑːn ‖ nɒn/ pref no; ~swimmers must ... las personas que no saben nadar deben ...

nonchalant /'nɑːnʃə'lɑːnt ‖ 'nɒnʃələnt/ adj (casual) despreocupado; (indifferent) indiferente

noncommissioned officer /ˌnɑːnkə'mɪʃənd ‖ ˌnɒnkə'mɪʃənd/ n ≈ suboficial mf

noncommittal /ˌnɑːnkə'mɪtl̩ ‖ ˌnɒnkə'mɪtl̩/ adj ⟨reply⟩ evasivo

nondescript /'nɑːndɪ'skrɪpt ‖ 'nɒndɪskrɪpt/ adj (not unusual or outstanding) anodino; (dull) insulso

none¹ /nʌn/ pron **1** (not any, not one) (referring to count n) ninguno, ninguna; I tried to get tickets, but there were ~ left traté de comprar entradas pero no quedaba ninguna or ni una; ~ of us know o knows her ninguno de nosotros la conoce **2** (no amount or part) (referring to uncount n): did you buy any milk? there's ~ left ¿comprasté leche? no hay más

none² adv **(a)** none the (not, in no way) (with comp): I was ~ the wiser after his explanation su explicación no me aclaró nada **(b)** none too (not very) (with adj or adv): she was ~ too pleased to see me no le hizo demasiada gracia verme

nonentity /nɑː'nentəti ‖ nɒ'nentəti/ n (pl **-ties**) persona f insignificante

nonetheless /ˌnʌnðə'les/ adv ▶ NEVERTHELESS

non-existent /ˌnɑːnɪg'zɪstənt ‖ ˌnɒnɪg'zɪstənt/ adj inexistente

nonfiction /ˌnɑːn'fɪkʃən ‖ ˌnɒn'fɪkʃən/ n no ficción f (ensayos, biografías, obras de divulgación etc)

no-nonsense /'nəʊ'nɑːnsens ‖ ˌnəʊ'nɒnsəns/ adj (before n) ⟨approach/attitude⟩ sensato

nonplused, nonplussed /nɑːnˈplʌst ‖ˌnɒnˈplʌst/ adj desconcertado

nonprofit /ˈnɑːnˈprɑːfət ‖ˌnɒnˈprɒfɪt/, (BrE) **non-profitmaking** /ˈnɑːnˈprɑːfətˌmeɪkɪŋ ‖ˌnɒnˈprɒfɪtmeɪkɪŋ/ adj sin fines lucrativos

nonsense /ˈnɑːnsens ‖ˈnɒnsəns/ n tonterías fpl

nonsensical /nɑːnˈsensɪkəl ‖nɒnˈsensɪkəl/ adj disparatado

nonsmoker /ˈnɑːnˈsməʊkər ‖ˌnɒnˈsməʊkə(r)/ n no fumador, -dora m,f

nonsmoking /nɑːnˈsməʊkɪŋ ‖nɒnˈsməʊkɪŋ/ adj para no fumadores

nonstick /ˈnɑːnˈstɪk ‖nɑːnˈstɪk/ adj antiadherente, de teflón®, de tefal®

nonstop /ˈnɑːnˈstɑːp ‖ˌnɒnˈstɒp/ adv **(a)** ⟨work/talk⟩ sin parar **(b)** ⟨sail/fly⟩ sin hacer escalas

noodle /ˈnuːdl/ n fideo m

nook /nʊk/ n rincón m; **to search every ~ and cranny** mirar/buscar* hasta en el último rincón

noon /nuːn/ n mediodía m; **at ~** a mediodía

no one pron ▶ NOBODY[1]

noose /nuːs/ n soga f, dogal m

noplace /ˈnəʊpleɪs/ adv (AmE) ▶ NOWHERE[1] 1

nor /nər, nɔːr ‖nɔː(r)/ conj **(a) neither ... nor ...** ▶ NEITHER[1] 1 **(b)** (usu with neg) tampoco

norm /nɔːrm ‖nɔːm/ n norma f

normal /ˈnɔːrməl ‖ˈnɔːməl/ adj normal; **when things get back to ~** cuando todo vuelva a la normalidad

normality /nɔːrˈmæləti ‖nɔːˈmæləti/ n normalidad f

normally /ˈnɔːrməli ‖ˈnɔːməli/ adv normalmente

north[1] /nɔːrθ ‖nɔːθ/ n (point of the compass, direction) norte m; **the ~, the N~** (region) el norte

north[2] adj (before n) norte adj inv, septentrional; ⟨wind⟩ norte adj inv

north[3] adv al norte

north: N~ America n Norteamérica f, América f del Norte; **N~ American** adj de América del Norte, norteamericano; **~bound** adj ⟨traffic/train⟩ que va (or iba etc) en dirección norte

northeast[1], Northeast /ˈnɔːrθˈiːst ‖ˌnɔːθˈiːst/ n **the ~** el nor(d)este or Nor(d)este

northeast[2] adj nor(d)este adj inv, del nor(d)este, nororiental

northeast[3] adv hacia el nor(d)este, en dirección nor(d)este

northeasterly /ˈnɔːrθˈiːstərli ‖ˌnɔːθˈiːstəli/ adj ⟨wind⟩ del nor(d)este

northeastern /ˈnɔːrθˈiːstərn ‖ˌnɔːθˈiːstən/ adj nor(d)este adj inv, del nor(d)este, nororiental

northerly /ˈnɔːrðərli ‖ˈnɔːðəli/ adj ⟨wind⟩ del norte; ⟨latitude⟩ norte adj inv; **in a ~ direction** hacia el or en dirección norte

northern /ˈnɔːrðərn ‖ˈnɔːðən/ adj ⟨region/ country⟩ del norte, septentrional, norteño, nortino (Chi, Per); **~ England** el norte de Inglaterra; **the ~ states** (in US) los estados del norte

Northern Ireland n Irlanda f del Norte

north: N~ Sea n Mar m del Norte; **N~ Star** n estrella f polar

northward[1] /ˈnɔːrθwərd ‖ˈnɔːθwəd/ adj (before n): **in a ~ direction** en dirección norte, hacia el norte

northward[2], (BrE) **northwards** /-z/ adv hacia el norte

northwest[1], Northwest /ˈnɔːrθˈwest ‖ˌnɔːθˈwest/ n **the ~** el noroeste or Noroeste

northwest[2] adj noroeste adj inv, del noroeste

northwest[3] adv hacia el noroeste, en dirección noroeste

northwesterly /ˈnɔːrθˈwestərli ‖ˌnɔːθˈwestəli/ adj ⟨wind⟩ del noroeste

northwestern /ˈnɔːrθˈwestərn ‖ˌnɔːθˈwestən/ adj noroccidental, noroeste adj inv, del noroeste

Norway /ˈnɔːrweɪ ‖ˈnɔːweɪ/ n Noruega f

Norwegian[1] /nɔːrˈwiːdʒən ‖nɔːˈwiːdʒən/ adj noruego

Norwegian[2] n **(a)** (person) noruego, -ga m,f **(b)** (language) noruego m

nose[1] /nəʊz/ n [1] (of person, animal) nariz f; **to look down one's ~ at sb** mirar a algn por encima del hombro; **to poke o stick one's ~ in** (colloq) meter las narices en algo (fam); **to turn one's ~ up at sth/sb** (colloq) despreciar algo/a algn [2] (of plane, car) parte f delantera, trompa f (RPl)

nose[2] vi (rummage, pry) entrometerse; **to ~ around o about in sth** husmear en algo

nose: ~bleed n hemorragia f nasal (frml); **I've got a ~bleed** me sangra la nariz; **~dive** vi **(a)** (Aviat) ⟨plane/pilot⟩ descender* or bajar en picada or (Esp) en picado **(b)** (drop sharply) ⟨prices⟩ caer* en picada or (Esp) en picado

nosey /ˈnəʊzi/ adj (BrE) ▶ NOSY

no-smoking /ˈnəʊˈsməʊkɪŋ/ adj ⟨compartment/section⟩ para no fumadores

nostalgia /nɑːˈstældʒə ‖nɒˈstældʒə/ n nostalgia f

nostalgic /nɑːˈstældʒɪk ‖nɒˈstældʒɪk/ adj nostálgico

nostril /ˈnɑːstrəl ‖ˈnɒstrɪl/ n ventana f de la nariz

nosy, (BrE also) **nosey** /ˈnəʊzi/ adj **nosier, nosiest** (colloq) ⟨person⟩ entrometido, metiche (AmL fam), metido (AmL fam); ⟨question⟩ impertinente

not /nɑːt ‖nɒt/ adv **(a)** no; **I asked them ~ to tell anyone** les pedí que no se lo dijeran a nadie **(b) not that** (as conj): **I'm going to London, ~ that it's any business of yours** voy a Londres, no es que a ti te importe, pero ... **(c)** (emphatic) ni; **~ a penny more** ni un penique más **(d)** (replacing clause): **I hope ~** espero que no; **are you going to help me or ~?** ¿me vas a ayudar o no?

notable /ˈnəʊtəbəl/ adj ⟨author/actor⟩ distinguido; ⟨success⟩ señalado; ⟨improvement/ difference⟩ notable

notably /ˈnəʊtəbli/ adv **(a)** (noticeably) notablemente **(b)** (in particular) particularmente, en particular

notch /nɑːtʃ ‖nɒtʃ/ n (in wood, metal) muesca f; (on belt) agujero m
■ **notch up** [v + adv + o] (colloq) apuntarse

note[1] /nəʊt/ n [1] (record, reminder) nota f; **to**

make a ~ of sth anotar *or* apuntar algo; **to make ~s** hacer* anotaciones; **to take ~s** tomar apuntes *or* notas; **to compare ~s** cambiar impresiones **2** (message) nota *f*
3 **(a)** (Mus) nota *f* **(b)** (tone): **I detected a ~ of sarcasm in his voice** percibí un tono de sarcasmo en su voz; **the evening ended on a sad ~** la velada terminó con una nota triste
4 (esp BrE) (bank~) billete *m*
5 (attention): **take ~ of what he says** toma nota de *or* presta atención a lo que dice

note² *vt* **(a)** (observe, notice) observar **(b)** (record) ⟨*information*⟩ apuntar, anotar
■ **note down** [*v + adv + o, v + o + adv*] apuntar

notebook /ˈnəʊtbʊk/ *n* cuaderno *m*

noted /ˈnəʊtəd ‖ˈnəʊtɪd/ *adj* ⟨*historian/surgeon*⟩ renombrado, de nota

note: **~pad** *n* bloc *m*; **~paper** *n* papel *m* de carta(s)

nothing /ˈnʌθɪŋ/ *pron* **1** nada; **there's ~ to eat** no hay nada de comer **2** (*in phrases*) **for nothing: she gave it to me for ~** me lo dio gratis; **it was all for ~** todo fue en vano; **if nothing else** al menos, por lo menos; **nothing but: she's caused ~ but trouble** no ha causado (nada) más que problemas; **nothing like: there's ~ like a shower to freshen you up** no hay (nada) como una ducha para refrescarse; **nothing much: ~ much happened** no pasó gran cosa

notice¹ /ˈnəʊtəs ‖ˈnəʊtɪs/ *n* **1** **(a)** (written sign) letrero *m* **(b)** (item of information) anuncio *m*
2 (attention): **it has come/been brought to my ~ that ...** (frml) ha llegado a mi conocimiento que .../ se me ha señalado que ... (frml); **she took no ~** no hizo caso; **don't take any ~ of him** no le hagas caso
3 **(a)** (notification) aviso *m*; **until further ~** hasta nuevo aviso; **it's impossible to do it at such short ~** es imposible hacerlo a tan corto plazo **(b)** (of termination of employment) previsio *m*; **I have to give (the company) a month's ~** tengo que dar un mes de previsio; **to give** *o* **hand in one's ~** presentar su (*or* mi *etc*) renuncia

notice² *vt* notar; **nobody ~d him put it in his pocket** nadie lo vio ponérselo en el bolsillo
■ **~** *vi* (realize, observe) darse* cuenta

noticeable /ˈnəʊtəsəbəl ‖ˈnəʊtɪsəbəl/ *adj* perceptible

noticeboard /ˈnəʊtəsbɔːrd ‖ˈnəʊtɪsbɔːd/ *n* (esp BrE) tablero *m or* (Esp) tablón *m* de anuncios, cartelera *f* (AmL), diario *m* mural (Chi)

notification /ˌnəʊtəfəˈkeɪʃən ‖ˌnəʊtɪfɪˈkeɪʃən/ *n* notificación *f*

notify /ˈnəʊtəfaɪ ‖ˈnəʊtɪfaɪ/ *vt* **-fies, -fying, -fied** (inform) informar; (in writing) notificar*; **to ~ sb** OF **sth** comunicarle* algo A algn

notion /ˈnəʊʃən/ *n* **1** (idea) idea *f* **2** (concept) concepto *m* **3** **notions** *pl* **(a)** (in sewing) artículos *mpl* de mercería **(b)** (AmE): **household/ gift ~s** artículos *mpl* para el hogar/de regalo

notorious /nəʊˈtɔːriəs/ *adj* ⟨*thief/womanizer/ gossip*⟩ (bien) conocido; ⟨*place*⟩ de mala fama

notwithstanding¹ /ˌnɑːtwɪðˈstændɪŋ ‖ˌnɒtwɪθˈstændɪŋ/ *prep* (frml) a pesar de, no obstante (frml)

notwithstanding² *adv* (frml) no obstante (frml)

nougat /ˈnuːɡət ‖ˈnuːɡɑː, ˈnʌɡət/ *n* ≈turrón *m*

nought /nɔːt/ *n* (esp BrE) cero *m*

noun /naʊn/ *n* sustantivo *m*, nombre *m*

nourish /ˈnɜːrɪʃ ‖ˈnʌrɪʃ/ *vt* nutrir

nourishing /ˈnɜːrɪʃɪŋ ‖ˈnʌrɪʃɪŋ/ *adj* nutritivo

nourishment /ˈnɜːrɪʃmənt ‖ˈnʌrɪʃmənt/ *n* alimento *m*

nouveau riche /ˌnuːvəʊˈriːʃ/ *n* (*pl* **~x ~s** /ˈnuːvəʊˈriːʃ/) (pej) nuevo rico, nueva rica *m,f* (pey)

novel¹ /ˈnɑːvəl ‖ˈnɒvəl/ *n* novela *f*

novel² *adj* original, novedoso (esp AmL)

novelist /ˈnɑːvələst ‖ˈnɒvəlɪst/ *n* novelista *mf*

novelty /ˈnɑːvəlti ‖ˈnɒvəlti/ *n* (*pl* **-ties**) **(a)** (newness): **the ~ will soon wear off** pronto dejará de ser novedad *or* (esp AmL) novedoso **(b)** (new thing, situation) novedad *f*

November /nəʊˈvembər ‖nəʊˈvembə(r)/ *n* noviembre *m*

novice /ˈnɑːvəs ‖ˈnɒvɪs/ *n* principiante *mf*, novato, -ta *m,f*

now¹ /naʊ/ *adv* **1** **(a)** (at this time) ahora; **you can come in ~** ya puedes entrar; **any minute ~** en cualquier momento; **~'s your chance** esta es tu oportunidad **(b)** (at that time): **it was ~ time to say goodbye** había llegado el momento de decir adiós **(c)** (nowadays) hoy en día, actualmente **(d)** (*in phrases*) **(every) now and then** *o* **again** de vez en cuando; **for now** por ahora
2 **(a)** (at once, immediately) ahora (mismo); **it's ~ or never!** ¡ahora o nunca! **(b)** (*in phrases*) **just now: he's talking to a client just ~** en este momento está hablando con un cliente; **right now** (immediately) ahora mismo, inmediatamente; (at present) ahora mismo, en este momento
3 **(a)** (showing length of time) ya; **we've been living here for 40 years ~** ya hace 40 años que vivimos aquí **(b)** (*after prep*): **between ~ and Friday** de aquí al viernes; **she should be here by ~** ya debería estar aquí; **(up) until** *o* **till ~, up to ~** hasta ahora
4 **(a)** (indicating pause, transition): **~, who's next?** bueno ¿(ahora) a quién le toca? **(b)** (emphasizing command, request, warning, advice): **~ look here!** ¡espera un momento! **(c)** (*in phrases*) **now, now** ¡vamos, vamos!; **now then ...** a ver ...

now² *conj* **~ (that)** ahora que

nowadays /ˈnaʊədeɪz/ *adv* hoy (en) día, actualmente

nowhere¹ /ˈnəʊhwer ‖ˈnəʊweə(r)/ *adv* **1** : **where did you go last night? — nowhere** ¿adónde fuiste anoche? — a ningún lado *or* a ninguna parte; **she was ~ to be found/seen** no se la encontraba/se la veía por ningún lado *or* por ninguna parte; **to get ~** no conseguir* nada
2 **nowhere near: Warsaw is ~ near Moscow** Varsovia está lejísimos de Moscú; **I'm ~ near finished** me falta mucho para terminar

nowhere² *pron*: **he had ~ to go** no tenía dónde ir; **the car just appeared from ~** el coche apareció de la nada

noxious /ˈnɑːkʃəs ‖ˈnɒkʃəs/ *adj* (frml) nocivo

nozzle /ˈnɑːzəl ‖ˈnɒzəl/ *n* (on hose) boca *f*; (on fire extinguisher) boquilla *f*

NSPCC *n* (in UK) (= **National Society for the Prevention of Cruelty to Children**) ≈Asociación *f* de protección a la infancia

n

nuance /'nu:a:ns ‖'nju:a:ns/ *n* matiz *m*
nuclear /'nu:kliər ‖'nju:kliə(r)/ *adj* nuclear; ~ **power** energía *f* nuclear; ~ **power station** central *f* nuclear

nuclear: ~ **family** *n* familia *f* nuclear; ~**-powered** /'nu:kliər'pauərd ‖'nju:kliə'pauəd/ *adj* nuclear
nucleus /'nu:kliəs ‖'nju:kliəs/ *n* (*pl* **-clei** /-kliaɪ/) núcleo *m*
nude¹ /nu:d ‖nju:d/ *n* (Art) desnudo *m*; **in the** ~ desnudo
nude² *adj* desnudo
nudge¹ /nʌdʒ/ *vt* codear (ligeramente)
nudge² *n* golpe *m* (suave) con el codo
nudist /'nu:dəst ‖'nju:dɪst/ *n* nudista *mf*; (*before n*) ⟨*beach/camp*⟩ nudista
nudity /'nu:dəti ‖'nju:dəti/ *n* desnudez *f*
nugget /'nʌgət ‖'nʌgɪt/ *n* (Min) pepita *f*
nuisance /'nu:sn̩s ‖'nju:sn̩s/ *n* (a) (occurrence, thing): **to be a** ~ ser* una molestia, ser* un incordio (Esp) (b) (person) pesado, -da *m,f*, incordio *m* (Esp fam); **he's always making a** ~ **of** himself siempre está dando la lata (fam)
null /nʌl/ *adj* (Law): **to declare sth** ~ **and void** declarar nulo algo
numb¹ /nʌm/ *adj* **-er, -est** (with cold) entumecido; **the injection made my gums go** ~ la inyección me durmió las encías
numb² *vt* ⟨*cold*⟩ entumecer*; ⟨*drug*⟩ dormir*
number¹ /'nʌmbər ‖'nʌmbə(r)/ *n* número *m*; (telephone ~) número de teléfono; **wrong** ~ número equivocado; **student** ~**s** el número de estudiantes; **on a** ~ **of occasions** en varias ocasiones
number² *vt* (a) (assign number to) ⟨*houses/pages/ items*⟩ numerar (b) (amount to): **the spectators** ~**ed 50,000** había (un total de) 50.000 espectadores (c) (count) contar*; **his days are** ~**ed** tiene los días contados
numberplate /'nʌmbərpleɪt'nʌmbəpleɪt/ *n* (BrE) matrícula *f*, placa *f* (AmL), patente *f* (CS), chapa *f* (RPl)
numeral /'nu:mərəl ‖'nju:mərəl/ *n* número *m*
numerical /nʊ'merɪkəl ‖nju:'merɪkəl/ *adj* numérico

numerous /'nu:mərəs ‖'nju:mərəs/ *adj* numeroso
nun /nʌn/ *n* monja *f*, religiosa *f* (frml)
nurse¹ /nɜrs ‖nɜ:s/ *n* (a) (Med) enfermero, -ra *m,f* (b) (nanny) niñera *f*
nurse² *vt* 1 (Med) ⟨*patient*⟩ atender*; **he** ~**d her** **back to health** la atendió hasta que se repuso 2 (cradle) ⟨*baby*⟩ arrullar 3 (suckle) ⟨*baby*⟩ amamantar
nursery /'nɜrsri ‖'nɜ:səri/ *n* (*pl* **-ries**) (a) (day ~) guardería *f* (b) (room in house) cuarto *m* or habitación *f* de los niños (c) (Agr, Hort) vivero *m*
nursery: ~ **rhyme** *n* canción *f* infantil; ~ **school** *n* jardín *m* de infancia, jardín *m* infantil (AmL), kindergarten *m* (AmL); (preschool) pre-escolar *m*
nursing /'nɜrsɪŋ ‖'nɜ:sɪŋ/ *n* (a) (profession) enfermería *f* (b) (care) atención *f*
nursing home *n* (for the aged) residencia *f* de ancianos ⟨*con mayor nivel de asistencia médica*⟩; (for convalescence) clínica *f*, casa *f* de reposo or (Ur) de salud
nurture /'nɜrtʃər ‖'nɜ:tʃə(r)/ *vt* ⟨*child/person*⟩ criar*; ⟨*plant/crop*⟩ cuidar; ⟨*friendship*⟩ cultivar
nut /nʌt/ *n* 1 (Agr, Bot, Culin) fruto *m* seco (nuez, almendra, avellana etc) 2 (Tech) tuerca *f*
nut: ~**case** *n* (colloq) chiflado, -da *m,f* (fam); ~**crackers** *pl n* (BrE) cascanueces *m*
nutmeg /'nʌtmeg/ *n* nuez *f* moscada
nutrient /'nu:triənt ‖'nju:triənt/ *n* nutriente *m*
nutrition /nʊ'trɪʃən ‖nju:'trɪʃən/ *n* nutrición *f*
nutritious /nʊ'trɪʃəs ‖nju:'trɪʃəs/ *adj* nutritivo
nuts /nʌts/ *adj* (colloq) (pred) chiflado (fam)
nutshell /'nʌtʃel/ *n* cáscara *f* de nuez; **in a** ~ en dos or en pocas palabras
nutty /'nʌti/ *adj* **-tier, -tiest** 1 ⟨*taste*⟩ a nueces (or almendras etc) 2 (colloq) (eccentric) ⟨*professor*⟩ chiflado (fam); ⟨*idea*⟩ de loco
NVQ *n* (in UK) = **National Vocational** **Qualification**
NW (= **northwest**) NO
NY = **New York**
nylon /'naɪlɑːn ‖'naɪlɒn/ *n* nylon *m*
nymph /nɪmf/ *n* (Myth, Zool) ninfa *f*

Oo

O, o /əʊ/ n O, o f

oaf /əʊf/ n zoquete mf (fam)

oak /əʊk/ n (a) ~ (**tree**) roble m (b) (wood) roble m

OAP n (BrE) = **old age pensioner**

oar /ɔːr ‖ɔː(r)/ n remo m

OAS n (= **Organization of American States**) OEA f

oasis /əʊˈeɪsɪs/ n (pl **oases** /əʊˈeɪsiːz/) oasis m

oat /əʊt/ n (a) (plant) avena f (b) **oats** pl (cereal) avena f, copos mpl de avena

oath /əʊθ/ n (pl ~**s** /əʊðz/) (a) (promise) juramento m; **under** o (BrE also) **on** ~ (Law) bajo juramento (b) (curse) (liter) juramento m (liter)

oatmeal /ˈəʊtmiːl/ n (Culin) (flour) harina f de avena; (flakes) (AmE) avena f (en copos)

obedience /əˈbiːdiəns, əʊ-/ n obediencia f

obedient /əˈbiːdiənt, əʊ-/ adj obediente

obese /əʊˈbiːs/ adj obeso

obesity /əʊˈbiːsəti/ n obesidad f

obey /əˈbeɪ, əʊ-/ vt/i obedecer*

obituary /əˈbɪtʃʊəri ‖əˈbɪtʃʊəri/ n (pl **-ries**) obituario m, nota f necrológica

object¹ /ˈɒbdʒɪkt ‖ˈɒbdʒɪkt/ n **1** (a) (thing) objeto m (b) no ~: **money's no** ~ **for them** el dinero no les preocupa (c) (of actions, feelings) objeto m **2** (aim, purpose) objetivo m **3** (Ling) complemento m

object² /əbˈdʒekt/ vi **to** ~ (**to sth**) oponerse* (A algo); I ~! ¡protesto!; **if you don't** ~ si no le molesta
■ ~ vt objetar

objection /əbˈdʒekʃən/ n (a) (argument against) objeción f (b) (Law) protesta f; ~! ¡protesto! (c) (disapproval, dislike): **I have no** ~ **to her** no tengo nada en contra de ella

objectionable /əbˈdʒekʃnəbəl/ adj ⟨attitude/remark⟩ censurable; ⟨person/tone⟩ desagradable

objective¹ /ɑːbˈdʒektɪv ‖əbˈdʒektɪv/ adj objetivo

objective² n objetivo m

objectively /ɑːbˈdʒektɪvli ‖əbˈdʒektɪvli/ adv objetivamente

obligate /ˈɑːbləgeɪt ‖ˈɒbləgeɪt/ vt (esp AmE frml) **to** ~ **sb to + INF** obligar* a algn A + INF; **to be/feel** ~**d** (**to + INF**) estar*/sentirse* obligado (A + INF)

obligation /ɑːbləˈgeɪʃən ‖ˌɒblɪˈgeɪʃən/ n obligación f; ~ **to + INF** obligación DE + INF; **I understand that I am under no** ~ entiendo que no contraigo ninguna obligación

obligatory /əˈblɪgətɔːri ‖əˈblɪgətri/ adj obligatorio

oblige /əˈblaɪdʒ/ vt **1** (require, compel) **to** ~ **sb to + INF** obligar* a algn A + INF; **to be** ~**d to + INF** estar* obligado A + INF **2** (do favor for): **I'd be much** ~**d if you could help me** le quedaría muy agradecido si pudiera ayudarme

■ ~ vi: **he's always willing to** ~ siempre está dispuesto a hacer un favor

obliging /əˈblaɪdʒɪŋ/ adj atento

oblique /əˈbliːk, əʊ- ‖əˈbliːk/ adj ⟨line/angle⟩ oblicuo; ⟨reply/reference⟩ indirecto

obliterate /əˈblɪtəreɪt/ vt (a) (destroy) arrasar (b) (obscure, erase) borrar

oblivion /əˈblɪviən/ n (a) (obscurity) olvido m (b) (unconsciousness) inconsciencia f

oblivious /əˈblɪviəs/ adj (pred): **she was quite** ~ **of** o **to her surroundings** estaba totalmente ajena a lo que la rodeaba; ~ **of** o **to the danger** (unaware of) ignorante del peligro; (not mindful of) haciendo caso omiso del peligro

oblong¹ /ˈɑːblɔːŋ ‖ˈɒblɒŋ/ adj alargado

oblong² n rectángulo m

obnoxious /ɑːbˈnɑːkʃəs ‖əbˈnɒkʃəs/ adj detestable

oboe /ˈəʊbəʊ/ n oboe m

obscene /ɑːbˈsiːn ‖əbˈsiːn/ adj obsceno

obscenity /ɑːbˈsenəti ‖əbˈsenəti/ n (pl **-ties**) obscenidad f

obscure¹ /əbˈskjʊr ‖əbˈskjʊə(r)/ adj obscurer, obscurest (a) (not easily understood) ⟨meaning⟩ oscuro; ⟨message/reference⟩ críptico (b) (little known) ⟨writer/journal⟩ oscuro

obscure² vt ⟨object/beauty/sun⟩ ocultar; ⟨sky⟩ oscurecer*; ⟨issue⟩ impedir* ver claramente

obscurity /əbˈskjʊrəti ‖əbˈskjʊərəti/ n (pl **-ties**) oscuridad f

obsequious /əbˈsiːkwiəs/ adj servil

observant /əbˈzɜːrvənt ‖əbˈzɜːvənt/ adj observador

observation /ˈɑːbzərˈveɪʃən ‖ˌɒbzəˈveɪʃən/ n (all senses) observación f

observatory /əbˈzɜːrvətɔːri ‖əbˈzɜːvətri/ n (pl **-ries**) observatorio m

observe /əbˈzɜːrv ‖əbˈzɜːv/ vt **1** (watch, notice) observar; ⟨patient⟩ observar **2** (comment) (liter) observar

observer /əbˈzɜːrvər ‖əbˈzɜːvə(r)/ n observador, -dora m,f

obsess /əbˈses/ vt obsesionar

obsessed /əbˈsest/ adj (pred) obsesionado

obsession /əbˈseʃən/ n obsesión f

obsessive /əbˈsesɪv/ adj obsesivo

obsolete /ˈɑːbsəliːt ‖ˈɒbsəliːt/ adj obsoleto

obstacle /ˈɑːbstɪkəl ‖ˈɒbstəkəl/ n obstáculo m

obstetrics /əbˈstetrɪks/ n (+ sing vb) obstetricia f, tocología f

obstinate /ˈɑːbstənət ‖ˈɒbstɪnət/ adj obstinado

obstinately /ˈɑːbstənətli ‖ˈɒbstɪnətli/ adv (stubbornly) obstinadamente; (determinedly) tenazmente

obstruct /əbˈstrʌkt/ vt (a) (block) obstruir* (b) (impede, hinder) ⟨traffic⟩ bloquear (c) (Sport) obstruir*

obstruction /əb'strʌkʃən/ n **(a)** (in traffic, pipeline) obstrucción f; (Med) obstrucción f, oclusión f **(b)** (Sport) obstrucción f

obtain /əb'teɪn/ vt conseguir*, obtener* (frml)

obtrusive /əb'truːsɪv/ adj ‹presence/building› demasiado prominente; ‹noise› molesto; ‹smell› penetrante

obtuse /ɑːb'tuːs ‖ɒb'tjuːs/ adj **1** (Math) ‹angle› obtuso **2** (frml) (stupid) obtuso

obvious /'ɑːbviəs ‖'ɒbviəs/ adj **(a)** (evident) ‹answer/advantage/difference› obvio **(b)** (unmistakable) (before n) ‹candidate/choice› indiscutible

obviously /'ɑːbviəsli ‖'ɒbviəsli/ adv obviamente; **they're ~ not coming** está visto que no van a venir; **the two ideas are ~ not related** es evidente que las dos ideas no tienen relación; **~, I'm sad, but what can I do?** (indep) como es lógico estoy triste pero ¿qué puedo hacer?

OCAS (= **Organization of Central American States**) n ODECA f

occasion /ə'keɪʒən/ n ocasión f

occasional /ə'keɪʒnəl ‖ə'keɪʒənl/ adj ‹showers/sunny spells› aislado; **I like an o the ~ glass of wine** de tanto en tanto me gusta tomarme un vaso de vino

occasionally /ə'keɪʒŋəli/ adv de vez en cuando

occult¹ /ə'kʌlt ‖ɒ'kʌlt/ n **the ~** las ciencias ocultas

occult² adj ‹arts/powers› oculto; ‹ritual› ocultista

occupant /'ɑːkjəpənt ‖'ɒkjʊpənt/ n (of building, room, vehicle) ocupante mf; (tenant) inquilino, -na m,f

occupation /ɑːkjə'peɪʃən ‖ɒkjʊ'peɪʃən/ n **(a)** (profession, activity) ocupación f **(b)** (Mil) ocupación f **(c)** (of accommodations) ocupación f

occupational /ˌɑːkjə'peɪʃnəl ‖ˌɒkjʊ'peɪʃənl/ adj ‹training› ocupacional; ‹disease› profesional; **it's an ~ hazard** son riesgos de la profesión/del oficio

occupational therapy n terapia f ocupacional

occupier /'ɑːkjəpaɪər ‖'ɒkjʊpaɪə(r)/ n (BrE) ocupante mf

occupy /'ɑːkjəpaɪ ‖'ɒkjʊpaɪ/ vt **-pies, -pying, -pied** ocupar; **to keep sb occupied** mantener* a algn ocupado

occur /ə'kɜːr ‖ə'kɜː(r)/ vi **-rr- 1 (a)** (take place) (frml) «event/incident» tener* lugar (frml); «change» producirse* (frml) **(b)** (appear, be found) «disease/species» darse*, encontrarse* **2** (come to mind) **to ~ TO sb** (to + INF) ocurrírsele A algn (+ INF)

occurrence /ə'kɜːrəns ‖ə'kʌrəns/ n **(a)** (event, instance): **it is a rare ~** no es algo frecuente **(b)** (incidence) incidencia f

ocean /'əʊʃən/ n océano m

ocean-going /'əʊʃən,gəʊɪŋ/ adj ‹vessel› transatlántico

o'clock /ə'klɑːk ‖ə'klɒk/ adv: **it's four ~** son las cuatro; **it's one ~** es la una; **at ten ~** a las diez

octagon /'ɑːktəgɑːn ‖'ɒktəgən/ n octágono m, octógono m

octane /'ɑːkteɪn ‖'ɒkteɪn/ n octano m

octave /'ɑːktɪv ‖'ɒktɪv/ n (Lit, Mus) octava f

October /ɑːk'təʊbər ‖ɒk'təʊbə(r)/ n octubre m

octopus /'ɑːktəpəs ‖'ɒktəpəs/ n (pl **-puses**) pulpo m

odd /ɑːd ‖ɒd/ adj **-er, -est 1** (strange) raro, extraño **2** (occasional, random) (no comp): **she smokes the ~ cigarette** se fuma algún or alguno que otro cigarrillo **3** (no comp) **(a)** (unmatched, single) desparejado, sin pareja; **the ~ one out** la excepción **(b)** (Math) ‹number› impar

oddball /'ɑːdbɔːl ‖'ɒdbɔːl/ n (colloq) bicho m raro (fam)

oddity /'ɑːdəti ‖'ɒdɪti/ n (pl **-ties**) rareza f

odd-job man /'ɑːd'dʒɑːbmæn ‖,ɒd'dʒɒbmæn/ n (pl **-men** /-men/) hombre que hace pequeños trabajos o arreglos

oddly /'ɑːdli ‖'ɒdli/ adv ‹dress/behave› de una manera rara or extraña

oddment /'ɑːdmənt ‖'ɒdmənt/ n: **~s of fabric o material** retazos mpl or (Esp) retales mpl

odds /ɑːdz ‖ɒdz/ pl n **1** (in betting) proporción en que se ofrece pagar una apuesta, que refleja las posibilidades de acierto de la misma **2** (likelihood, chances) probabilidades fpl, posibilidades fpl; **the ~ are against her winning** tiene pocas probabilidades or posibilidades de ganar; **the pilot survived against all (the) ~** aunque parezca increíble, el piloto sobrevivió **3** (variance): **those two are always at ~ with each other** esos dos siempre están en desacuerdo; **that's at ~ with the official version** eso no concuerda con la versión oficial

odds and ends /'ɑːdzən'endz ‖,ɒdzən'endz/ pl n (colloq) cosas fpl sueltas; (trinkets) chucherías fpl; (junk) cachivaches mpl

odious /'əʊdiəs/ adj (frml) detestable

odometer /əʊ'dɑːmətər ‖ɒ'dɒmɪtə(r), əʊ-/ n (AmE) cuentarrevoluciones m

odor, (BrE) **odour** /'əʊdər ‖'əʊdə(r)/ n olor m; (pleasant) aroma m

of /ɑːv ‖ɒv, weak form əv/ prep **1** (indicating relationship, material, content) de; **it's made ~ wood** es de madera; **a colleague ~ mine/his** un colega mío/suyo **2** (descriptive use): **a boy ~ ten** un niño de diez años; **a woman ~ courage** una mujer valiente **3 (a)** (partitive use): **there were eight ~ us** éramos ocho; **six ~ them survived** seis de ellos sobrevivieron **(b)** (with superl) de; **the wisest ~ men** el más sabio de los hombres; **most ~ all** más que nada **4 (a)** (indicating date) de; **the sixth ~ October** el seis de octubre **(b)** (indicating time): **it's ten (minutes) ~ five** (AmE) son las cinco menos diez, son diez para las cinco (AmL exc RPl); **Jane, his wife ~ six months ...** Jane, con la que lleva/ llevaba casado seis meses ... **5** (on the part of): **it was very kind ~ you** fue muy amable de su parte **6** (indicating cause): **it's a problem ~ their own making** es un problema que ellos mismos se han creado; **what did he die ~?** ¿de qué murió?

off¹ /ɔːf ‖ɒf/ prep **1** (from) de; **she picked it up ~ o** (crit) **~ of the floor** lo recogió del suelo; **he bought it ~ a friend** (colloq) se lo compró a un amigo

2 (a) (distant from): **3 ft ~ the ground** a 3 pies del suelo; **just ~ the coast of Florida** a poca distancia de la costa de Florida **(b)** (leading from): **it's just ~ Oxford Street** está en una bocacalle de Oxford Street; **the bathroom's ~ the bedroom** el baño da al dormitorio
3 (a) (absent from): **I've been ~ work for a week** hace una semana que no voy a trabajar **(b)** (indicating dislike, abstinence) (BrE): **he's ~ his food** anda sin apetito; **is he ~ drugs now?** ¿ha dejado las drogas?

off² *adv* **1** (a) (removed): **the lid was ~** la tapa no estaba puesta; **20% ~** 20% de descuento **(b) off and on** ▶ ON² 2c **2** (indicating departure): **I must be ~** me tengo que ir **3** (distant): **some way ~** a cierta distancia; **my birthday is a long way ~** falta mucho para mi cumpleaños

off³ *adj* **1** (*pred*) (a) (not turned on): **to be ~** «*TV/light*» estar* apagado **(b)** (canceled): **the game/wedding is ~** el partido/la boda se ha suspendido; **the deal is ~** ya no hay trato **2** (absent, not on duty) libre; **a day ~** *o* (AmE also) **an ~ day** un día libre **3** (poor, unsatisfactory) (*before n*) malo; **to have an ~ day** tener* un mal día **4** (Culin) (*pred*) **to be ~** «*meat/fish*» estar* malo *or* pasado; «*milk*» estar* cortado; «*butter/cheese*» estar* rancio

offal /'ɔːfəl ‖'ɒfəl/ *n* (Culin) despojos *mpl*, achuras *fpl* (RPl), interiores *mpl* (Chi)

off: ~beat *adj* poco convencional; **~-chance** *n*: **on the ~-chance** por si acaso; **~-color**, (BrE) **~-colour** /'ɔːfˈkʌlər ‖ˌɒfˈkʌlə(r)/ *adj* (*pred ~ color*) **(a)** (unwell) (*pred*): **to feel ~ color** no encontrarse* muy bien **(b)** (risqué) (esp AmE) ‹*joke*› subido de tono; **~cut** *n* (of leather, fabric, paper, wood) recorte *m*; (of meat) resto *m*

offence /ə'fens/ *n* ▶ OFFENSE

offend /ə'fend/ *vt* ofender
■ **~** *vi* **(a)** (cause displeasure) «*person/action/remark*» ofender **(b) offending** *pres p*: **he rewrote it omitting the ~ing paragraph** volvió a escribirlo omitiendo el párrafo que había causado controversia **(c)** (Law frml) infringir* a la ley (*or* el reglamento *etc*); (criminally) cometer un delito

offender /ə'fendər ‖ə'fendə(r)/ *n* (against regulations) infractor, -tora *m,f*; (criminal) delincuente *mf*; **young ~** menor *mf* (*que ha cometido un delito*)

offense, (BrE) **offence** /ə'fens/ *n* **1** (breach of law, regulations) infracción *f*; (criminal ~) delito *m* **2** (a) (cause of outrage) (*no pl*) atentado *m* **(b)** (resentment, displeasure): **to take ~ at sth** ofenderse *or* sentirse* ofendido por algo **3** (AmE) *also* /'ɑːfens/ **(a)** (attack) ataque *m* **(b)** (Sport) (línea *f* de) ataque *m*

offensive¹ /ə'fensɪv/ *adj* **1** ‹*language/gesture*› ofensivo; ‹*sight/smell*› desagradable **2** (a) ‹*strategy*› ofensivo **(b)** (AmE Sport) ‹*play/tactics*› de ataque

offensive² *n* ofensiva *f*

offer¹ /'ɔːfər ‖'ɒfə(r)/ *vt* **1** (a) (proffer) ofrecer* **(b)** (show willingness) **to ~ to + INF** ofrecerse* A + INF **2** (put forward) ‹*idea/solution*› proponer* **3** (provide) ‹*reward*› ofrecer*; ‹*opportunity*› brindar
■ **~** *vi* (show willingness) ofrecerse*

offer² *n* **1** (a) (proposal — of job, money) oferta *f*;

(— of help, mediation) ofrecimiento *m* **(b)** (bid) oferta *f*; **$650 or nearest ~** 650 dólares negociables **2** (bargain, reduced price) oferta *f*; **on ~** (BrE) (at reduced price) de oferta

offering /'ɔːfərɪŋ ‖'ɒfərɪŋ/ *n* ofrenda *f*

offhand¹ /'ɔːfˈhænd ‖ˌɒfˈhænd/ *adj*: **to say sth in a very ~ way** *o* manner decir* algo muy a la ligera; **she was very ~ with me** estuvo muy brusca conmigo

offhand² *adv* así de pronto, en ese momento

office /'ɔːfəs ‖'ɒfɪs/ *n* **1** (room) oficina *f*, despacho *m*; (building, set of rooms) oficina *f*, oficinas *fpl*; (staff) oficina *f*; (doctor's ~) (AmE) consultorio *m*, consulta *f*; (*before n*) ‹*work/furniture*› de oficina; ‹*block/building*› de oficinas; **during ~ hours** en horas de oficina; **~ worker** oficinista *mf*, empleado, -da *m,f* de oficina **2** (post, position) cargo *m*; **he was in ~ for three years** ocupó el cargo durante tres años

officer /'ɑːfəsər ‖'ɒfɪsə(r)/ *n* (a) (Mil, Naut) oficial *mf* **(b)** (police ~) policía *mf*, agente *mf* de policía; (*as form of address*) agente

official¹ /ə'fɪʃəl/ *adj* oficial

official² *n* (government ~) funcionario, -ria *m,f* del Estado *or* gobierno; (party/union ~) dirigente *mf* (del partido/sindicato)

officially /ə'fɪʃəli/ *adv* oficialmente

officiate /ə'fɪʃieɪt/ *vi* **to ~ AT sth** ‹*at mass/at a wedding*› oficiar (EN) *or* celebrar algo

officious /ə'fɪʃəs/ *adj* oficioso

offing /'ɔːfɪŋ ‖'ɒfɪŋ/ *n*: **in the ~** en perspectiva

off: ~ key *adv*: **to play/sing ~ key** desafinar; **~-licence** *n* (in UK) ≈tienda *f* de vinos y licores, botillería *f* (Chi); **~ limits** /'lɪməts ‖'lɪmɪts/ *adv*: **to go/be ~ limits** entrar/estar* en zona prohibida; **~-line** /'ɔːfˈlaɪn ‖ˌɒfˈlaɪn/ *adj* (*pred ~ line*) ‹*storage/printer*› autónomo; **~-peak** /'piːk /*adj* (*before noun*) ‹*travel/fare/tariffs*› fuera de las horas pico *or* (Esp) punta; (Elec) fuera de (las) horas pico *or* (Esp) punta; **~-putting** /'ɔːfˈpʊtɪŋ ‖ˌɒfˈpʊtɪŋ/ *adj* (BrE) (disagreeable) desagradable; (discouraging) desmoralizador; **~-road** *adj*: **~-road vehicle** todoterreno *m*; **~-set** /'ɔːfˈset ‖'ɒfset/ *vt* (*pres -sets*; *pres p -setting*; *past & past p -set*) compensar; **~-shoot** *n* (a) (of plant, tree) retoño *m* **(b)** (of company, organization) filial *f*; **~-shore** /'ɔːfˈʃɔːr ‖ˌɒfˈʃɔː(r)/ *adj* ‹*oilfield/pipeline*› submarino; ‹*exploration/drilling*› off-shore *adj inv*

offside¹ /ˌɔːfˈsaɪd ‖ˌɒfˈsaɪd/ *adj* (Sport) ‹*player*› en fuera de juego *or* (AmL tb) de lugar

offside² *adv* (Sport) fuera de juego *or* (AmL tb) de lugar

off: ~spring *n* (*pl* **~spring**) **(a)** (animal) cría *f* **(b)** (hum) (child) hijo, -ja *m,f*, crío, cría *m,f* (fam); (children) prole *f* (fam & hum), críos *mpl* (fam); **~stage** /'ɔːfˈsteɪdʒ ‖ˌɒfˈsteɪdʒ/ *adv* fuera del escenario; **~-the-peg** /'ɔːfˈðəˈpeg ‖ˌɒfˈðəˈpeg/ *adj* (*pred ~ the peg*) (esp BrE) ▶ **~-THE-RACK**; **~-the-rack** /'ɔːfˈðəˈræk ‖ˌɒfˈðəˈræk/ *adj* (*pred ~ the rack*) (AmE) ‹*suit*› de confección; **~-white** /'ɔːfˈhwaɪt ‖ˌɒfˈwaɪt/ *adj* color hueso *adj inv*

often /'ɔːfən, 'ɔːftən ‖'ɒfən, 'ɒftən/ *adv* a menudo; **how ~ do you see her?** ¿con qué frecuencia la ves?

ogle /'əʊgəl/ vt comerse con los ojos

ogre /'əʊgər ‖'əʊgə(r)/ n ogro m

oh /əʊ/ interj: ~, it's you ah, eres tú; ~ no, not him again! ¡ay no, es él otra vez!

OH = Ohio

oil¹ /ɔɪl/ n **1** **(a)** (petroleum) petróleo m; (before n) ~ **refinery** refinería f de petróleo; ~ **tanker** (ship) petrolero m; (truck) camión m cisterna (para petróleo) **(b)** (lubricant) aceite m **(c)** (fuel ~) fuel-oil m **2** (Culin) aceite m **3** **oils** pl (paints): he paints in ~s pinta al óleo

oil² vt lubricar*, aceitar

oil: ~**can** n aceitera f; ~**cloth** n hule m; ~**field** n yacimiento m petrolífero; ~ **paint** n óleo m; ~ **painting** n óleo m; ~ **rig** n plataforma f petrolífera; (derrick) torre f de perforación; ~ **slick** n marea f negra; ~ **well** n pozo m petrolero

oily /'ɔɪli/ adj **oilier, oiliest** ⟨substance⟩ oleaginoso; ⟨food⟩ aceitoso; ⟨skin/hair⟩ graso (AmL)

ointment /'ɔɪntmənt/ n pomada f

OK¹**, okay** /'əʊ'keɪ/ interj (colloq) ¡bueno!, ¡okey! (esp AmL fam), ¡vale! (Esp fam), ¡vaya (pues)! (AmC)

OK²**, okay** adj (all right) (colloq) ⟨pred⟩: how are you? — ~, thanks ¿qué tal estás? — bien, gracias; the job's ~, but ... el trabajo no está mal, pero ...

OK³**, okay** vt (pres **OK's**; pres p **OK'ing**; past & past p **OK'ed**) (colloq) darle* el visto bueno a

OK⁴**, Okla** = Oklahoma

old /əʊld/ adj **1** (of certain age): he's 10 years ~ tiene 10 años; how ~ are you? ¿cuántos años tienes?; she's two years ~er than me me lleva dos años
2 (not young) mayor; (less polite) viejo; ~ o ~er people los ancianos, las personas mayores or de edad; to get o grow ~/~er envejecer*
3 **(a)** (not new) ⟨clothes/car/custom⟩ viejo; ⟨city/civilization⟩ **(b)** (longstanding, familiar) (before n) ⟨friend/enemy/rivalry⟩ viejo; ⟨injury/problem⟩ antiguo
4 (former, previous) (before n) antiguo
5 (colloq) (before n) (as intensifier): just wear any ~ thing ponte cualquier cosa; this book is a load of ~ rubbish este libro es una porquería (fam)

old: ~ **age** n vejez f; ~ **age pensioner** n (BrE) pensionista mf (de la tercera edad)

olden /'əʊldən/ adj (liter): in ~ days o times antaño (liter)

old: ~**fashioned** /'əʊld'fæʃənd/ adj (outdated) anticuado; (traditional) tradicional; ~ **people's home** n residencia f de ancianos; ~ **wives' tale** n cuento m de viejas

olive¹ /'ɑːlɪv ‖'ɒlɪv/ n **(a)** (Culin) aceituna f; (before n) ~ **oil** aceite m de oliva **(b)** ~ **tree** olivo m

olive² adj color aceituna adj inv; ⟨skin⟩ aceitunado

Olympic /ə'lɪmpɪk/ adj olímpico

Olympic Games pl n the ~ ~ los juegos Olímpicos

Olympics /ə'lɪmpɪks/ pl n the ~ las Olimpiadas or Olimpíadas

ombudsman /'ɑːmbʊdzmən ‖'ɒmbʊdzmən/ n (pl **-men** /-mən/) defensor m del pueblo, ombudsman m

omelet, (BrE) **omelette** /'ɑːmlət ‖'ɒmlɪt/ n omelette f or (Esp) tortilla f francesa

omen /'əʊmən/ n presagio m; it's a good/bad ~ es un buen/mal augurio

ominous /'ɑːmənəs ‖'ɒmɪnəs/ adj: there was an ~ silence se hizo un silencio que no presagiaba nada bueno; there are some ~ clouds on the horizon hay nubes que no auguran nada bueno

omission /əʊ'mɪʃən ‖ə'mɪʃən/ n omisión f

omit /əʊ'mɪt ‖ə'mɪt/ vt **-tt-** (leave out) omitir; (accidentally) olvidar incluir

omnibus /'ɑːmnɪbəs ‖'ɒmnɪbəs/ n (pl **-buses**) **1** (Publ) antología f **2** (Transp dated) ómnibus m (ant exc en Per y RPI)

omnipotent /ɑːm'nɪpətənt ‖ɒm'nɪpətənt/ adj (fml) omnipotente

omnivorous /ɑːm'nɪvərəs ‖ɒm'nɪvərəs/ adj omnívoro

on¹ /ɑːn ‖ɒn/ prep **1** **(a)** (indicating position); en; put it ~ the table ponlo en or sobre la mesa; ~ the ground en el suelo; he hung it ~ a hook lo colgó de un gancho **(b)** (belonging to) de; the handle ~ the cup el asa de la taza **(c)** (against): I hit my head ~ the shelf me di con la cabeza contra el estante; he cut his hand ~ the glass se cortó la mano con el vidrio
2 **(a)** (of clothing): it looks better ~ you than me te queda mejor a ti que a mí **(b)** (about one's person): I didn't have any cash ~ me no llevaba dinero encima
3 (indicating means of transport): I went ~ the bus fui en autobús; ~ a bicycle/horse en bicicleta/a caballo; ~ foot a pie
4 **(a)** (playing instrument) a; George Smith ~ drums George Smith a la or en la batería **(b)** (Rad, TV): I heard it ~ the radio lo oí por la radio; I was ~ TV last night anoche salí por televisión; the play's ~ channel 4 la obra la dan en el canal 4
5 **(a)** (using equipment): who's ~ the computer? ¿quién está usando la computadora?; you've been ~ the phone an hour! ¡hace una hora que estás hablando por teléfono! **(b)** (contactable via): call us ~ 800 7777 llámenos al 800 7777
6 (a member of): she's ~ the committee está en la comisión; ~ a team (AmE) en un equipo
7 (indicating time): ~ Monday el lunes; ~ Wednesdays los miércoles; ~ -ING al + INF; ~ hearing the news al enterarse de la noticia
8 (about, concerning) sobre
9 (working on, studying): we're ~ page 45 vamos por la página 45; I'm still ~ question 1 todavía estoy con la pregunta número 1

10 (taking, consuming): **she's ~ antibiotics** está tomando antibióticos; **he's ~ heroin** es heroinómano

11 (talking about income, available funds): **I manage ~ less than that** yo me las arreglo con menos de eso

12 (at the expense of): **this round's ~ me** a esta ronda invito yo

13 (in comparison with): **profits are up ~ last year** los beneficios han aumentado respecto al año pasado

on² *adv* **1** **(a)** (worn): **she had a blue dress ~** llevaba (puesto) un vestido azul; **I had nothing ~** estaba desnudo **(b)** (in place): **the lid's not ~ properly** la tapa no está bien puesta **2** (indicating progression) **(a)** (in space): **further ~** un poco más allá; **go ~ up; I'll follow in a minute** tú ve subiendo que yo voy **(b)** (in time, activity): **from then ~** a partir de ese momento; **from now ~** de ahora en adelante **(c) on and off, off and on: we still see each other ~ and off** todavía nos vemos de vez en cuando; **it rained ~ and off** *o* **off and ~ all week** estuvo lloviendo y parando toda la semana

on³ *adj* **1** (*pred*) **(a)** (functioning): **to be ~** «*light/ TV/radio*» estar* encendido, estar* prendido (AmL); «*faucet*» estar* abierto; **the electricity/ water isn't ~ yet** la electricidad/el agua todavía no está conectada **(b)** (on duty): **we work four hours ~, four hours off** trabajamos cuatro horas y tenemos otras cuatro de descanso **2** (*pred*) **(a)** (taking place): **there's a lecture ~ in there** hay una conferencia allí; **while the conference is ~** mientras dure el congreso **(b)** (due to take place): **the party's definitely ~ for Friday** la fiesta es el viernes seguro; **I don't have anything ~ that day** no tengo ningún compromiso ese día **(c)** (being presented): **what's ~ at the Renoir?** (Cin, Rad, Theat, TV) ¿qué dan *or* (Esp tb) ponen en el Renoir?; **the exhibition is still ~** la exposición sigue abierta **3** (indicating agreement, acceptance) (colloq): **you teach me Spanish and I'll teach you French — you're ~!** tú me enseñas español y yo te enseño francés — ¡trato hecho!; **that sort of thing just isn't ~** (esp BrE) ese tipo de cosa no se puede tolerar

once¹ /wʌns/ *adv* **1** **(a)** (one time, on one occasion) una vez; **~ a week** una vez por semana **(b)** (formerly): **a health care system which was ~ the pride of the nation** un sistema de asistencia sanitaria que antes era el orgullo de la nación; **upon a time there was ...** érase una vez ... **2** (*in phrases*) **at once: come here at ~!** ¡ven aquí inmediatamente!; **don't all shout at ~** no griten todos al mismo tiempo; **for once** por una vez; **once again** *o* **once more** otra vez; **once (and) for all** de una vez por todas; **(every) once in a while** de vez en cuando; **once or twice** una o dos veces

once² *conj* una vez que; (with verb omitted) una vez

once- /wʌns/ *pref* otrora (liter)

oncoming /ˈɑːnˌkʌmɪŋ ‖ˈɒnkʌmɪŋ/ *adj* (before n) «*vehicle*» que viene (*or* venía) en dirección contraria

one¹ /wʌn/ *n* **1** **(a)** (number) uno *m*; *see also* FOUR¹ **(b)** (elliptical use): **he's nearly ~** tiene casi un año; **it was interesting in more ways than ~** fue interesante en más de un sentido/en muchos sentidos **2** (*in phrases*) **as one: they rose as ~** se pusieron de pie todos a la vez; **for one** por lo pronto; **one by one** uno a *or* por uno

one² *adj* **1** (stating number) un, una; **~ button/ pear** un botón/una pera; **~ window looks out over the park** una de las ventanas da al parque **2** (single): **she was the ~ person I trusted** era la única persona en quien confiaba; **there is not ~ shred of evidence** no existe ni la más mínima prueba; **the ~ and only Frank Sinatra** el incomparable Frank Sinatra **3** (unspecified) un, una; **you must come over ~ evening** tienes que venir una noche **4** (with names): **in the name of ~ John Smith/ Sarah Brown** a nombre de un tal John Smith/una tal Sarah Brown

one³ *pron* **1** (thing): **this ~** este/esta; **that ~** ese/ esa; **which ~?** ¿cuál?; **the ~ on the right/left** el/la de la derecha/izquierda; **the ~s on the table** los/ las que están en la mesa; **the blue ~s** los/las azules; **I want the big ~** quiero el/la grande; **~ of the oldest cities in Europe** una de las ciudades más antiguas de Europa **2** (person): **the ~ on the right's my cousin** el/la de la derecha es mi primo/prima; **I'm not ~ to gossip, but ...** no me gustan los chismes pero ...; **~ after another** *o* **the other** uno tras otro *or* detrás de otro

one⁴ *pron* uno, una; **~ simply never knows** realmente nunca se sabe; **~ another** = **each other, ▸** EACH² 2

one: **~-armed** /ˈwʌnˈɑːrmd ‖ˈwʌnˌɑːmd/ *adj* manco; **~-man** /ˈwʌnˈmæn/ *adj* (before n) ‹*business*› unipersonal; ‹*operation*› dirigido por una sola persona; **~-off** /ˈwʌnˈɔːf ‖ˌwʌnˈɒf/ *n* (BrE colloq): **this payment is strictly a ~-off** este pago es una excepción; **~ on ~** *adv* (AmE) uno a uno; **~-piece** /ˈwʌnpiːs/ *adj* ‹*swimsuit*› entero

onerous /ˈəʊnərəs/ *adj* ‹*task*› pesado

one: **~-self** /wʌnˈself/ *pron* (frml) (reflexive) se; (after prep) sí mismo; (emphatic use) uno mismo; **to cut ~self** cortarse; **~-sided** /ˈwʌnˈsaɪdəd ‖ˌwʌnˈsaɪdɪd/ *adj* ‹*account/version*› parcial; ‹*game/contest*› desigual; **~-stop shopping** *n* compras *fpl* en un mismo sitio; **~-time** *adj* antiguo; **~-to-~** /ˈwʌntəˈwʌn/ *adj* ‹*teaching/ attention*› individualizado; ‹*discussion*› mano a mano; **on a ~-to-~ basis** de uno a uno

one-upmanship /ˈwʌnˈʌpmənʃɪp/ *n* (colloq) arte de colocarse siempre en una situación de superioridad con respecto a los demás

one-way /ˈwʌnˈweɪ/ *adj* **(a)** ‹*street*› de sentido único **(b)** (for one journey): **~ or round trip?** ¿ida solo o ida y vuelta?, ¿sencillo o redondo? (Méx)

ongoing /ˈɑːnˌɡəʊɪŋ ‖ˈɒnɡəʊɪŋ/ *adj*: **the ~ talks** las conversaciones en curso; **the investigations have been ~ for several months** se están llevando a cabo investigaciones desde hace meses

onion /ˈʌnjən/ *n* cebolla *f*

on: **~ line** *adv*: **to edit/work ~ line** (Comput) editar/trabajar en línea; **~-line** /ˈɑːnˈlaɪn ‖ˌɒnˈlaɪn/ *adj* (*pred* **~ line**) (Comput) conectado, en línea; **~looker** /ˈɑːnlʊkər ‖ˈɒnlʊkə(r)/ *n* espectador, -dora *m,f*

only¹ /ˈəʊnli/ *adv* **(a)** (merely, no more than) solo, solamente; **you'll ~ make matters worse** lo único que vas a lograr es empeorar las cosas **(b)**

(exclusively) solo, solamente, únicamente **(c)** (no longer ago than): ~ **last week the very same problem came up** la semana pasada, sin ir más lejos, surgió el mismo problema **(d)** (*in phrases*) **if only: if ~ I were rich!** ¡ojalá fuera rico!; **if ~ I'd known** si lo hubiera sabido; **only just: they've ~ just arrived** ahora mismo acaban de llegar; **will it fit in?** — **~ just** ¿cabrá? — apenas *or* (fam) justito; **not only … , but also …** no solo … , sino también …

only² *adj* (*before* n) único; **she's an ~ child** es hija única

only³ *conj* (colloq) pero

-only /'əʊnli/ *suff*: **a men~/women~ session** una sesión solo *or* exclusivamente para hombres/mujeres

on: **~set** n (of winter, rains) llegada f; (of disease) aparición f; **~shore** /'ɑːnʃɔːr ‖'ɒnʃɔː(r)/ *adj* **(a)** ⟨*wind*⟩ que sopla desde el mar **(b)** (on land) ⟨*oil terminal/location*⟩ en tierra

onslaught /'ɑːnslɔːt ‖'ɒnslɔːt/ n ataque m

onstage /'ɑːnsteɪdʒ ‖,ɒn'steɪdʒ/ *adv*: **to come ~** salir* a escena

onto /'ɑːntuː ‖'ɒntuː, *before consonant* 'ɑːntə ‖'ɒntə/ *prep* [1] (on): **it fell ~ the table** cayó sobre la mesa; **he climbed ~ the cart** se subió al carro [2] (aware of) (colloq) **the police are ~ her** la policía anda tras ella; **I think we're ~ something big** creo que hemos dado con algo gordo (fam)

onus /'əʊnəs/ n (frml) responsabilidad f, **the ~ is on him to prove his theory** le corresponde a él probar su teoría

onward¹ /'ɑːnwərd ‖'ɒnwəd/ *adj* (*before* n) hacia adelante

onward², (BrE also) **onwards** /-z/ *adv* (hacia) adelante; **from now ~** de ahora en adelante

ooh /uː/ *interj*: **~, what a beautiful sunset!** ¡ah, qué puesta de sol tan bonita!; **~, that hurt** ¡ay, eso me dolió!

oops /ʊps ‖uːps/ *interj* (colloq) ¡uy! (fam)

ooze /uːz/ *vi*: **blood ~d from his wound** le salía sangre de la herida; **to ~ with sth: the walls were oozing with damp** las paredes rezumaban humedad

■ ~ *vt*: **the wound ~d pus** la herida (le) supuraba; **he ~s charm** irradia simpatía

opal /'əʊpəl/ n ópalo m

opaque /əʊ'peɪk/ *adj* opaco

OPEC /'əʊpek/ n (*no art*) (= **Organization of Petroleum Exporting Countries**) la OPEC *or* la OPEP

open¹ /'əʊpən/ *adj* [1] **(a)** (not shut, sealed, fastened) abierto; **he pushed the door ~** abrió la puerta de un empujón **(b)** (not folded) ⟨*flower/newspaper/book*⟩ abierto [2] (not enclosed) abierto; **~ prison** cárcel f en régimen abierto; **on the ~ seas** en alta mar [3] **(a)** (not covered) ⟨*carriage*⟩ abierto; ⟨*sewer*⟩ a cielo abierto; **an ~ fire** una chimenea, un hogar **(b)** (exposed, vulnerable) **~ TO sth** ⟨*to elements/enemy attack*⟩ expuesto A algo [4] (*pred*) (ready for business) **to be ~** ⟨*shop/museum*⟩ estar* abierto [5] (unrestricted) ⟨*membership*⟩ abierto al público en general; ⟨*meeting*⟩ a puertas abiertas; ⟨*ticket/reservation*⟩ abierto [6] (not decided): **let's leave things ~ for the time**

being no descartemos ninguna posibilidad de momento; **~ verdict** *veredicto que se emite cuando no se puede establecer la causa de la muerte de una persona* [7] **(a)** (receptive) abierto; **I'm ~ to suggestions** estoy abierto a todo tipo de sugerencias **(b)** (frank, candid): **to be ~ WITH sb** ser* sincero *or* franco CON algn [8] (not concealed) ⟨*resentment/hostility*⟩ abierto

open² *vt* [1] **(a)** ⟨*door/box/bottle*⟩ abrir*; **to ~ one's mouth/eyes** abrir* la boca/los ojos **(b)** (unfold) ⟨*newspaper/book*⟩ abrir* [2] (clear) ⟨*road/channel*⟩ abrir* [3] (set up, start) ⟨*shop*⟩ abrir* [4] (begin) ⟨*debate/meeting*⟩ abrir*; ⟨*bidding*⟩ iniciar; ⟨*talks*⟩ entablar

■ ~ *vi* [1] **(a)** «*door/window/wound*» abrirse* **(b)** (unfold) «*flower/parachute*» abrirse* [2] (give access) **to ~ ONTO/INTO sth** dar* A algo [3] (for business) «*shop/museum*» abrir* [4] (begin) «*play/book*» comenzar*, empezar*

■ **open up**
I [v + o + adv, v + adv + o] abrir*
II [v + adv] [1] (become open) abrirse* [2] (become accessible, available) «*country/market*» abrirse* [3] (start up) «*business/factory/store*» abrir*

open³ n: **in the ~** (in open space or country) al aire libre; (Mil) al descubierto; **I feel better now it's all out in the ~** me siento mejor ahora que todo el mundo lo sabe

open: **~ air** n: **in the ~ air** al aire libre; **~-and-shut** /'əʊpənən'ʃʌt/ *adj*: **an ~-and-shut case** un caso clarísimo; **~ day** n (BrE) *día en que un establecimiento educativo, científico etc puede ser visitado por el público*; **~-ended** /'əʊpən'endəd ‖,əʊpən'endɪd/ *adj* ⟨*contract/lease*⟩ de duración indefinida; ⟨*discussion*⟩ abierto

opener /'əʊpnər ‖,əʊpnə(r)/ n (for bottle) abridor m, abrebotellas m, destapador m (AmL); (for can) abrelatas m

open house n [1] (*no art*): **to keep ~ ~** tener* las puertas siempre abiertas a todos; [2] (AmE) *día en que un establecimiento educativo, científico etc puede ser visitado por el público*

opening /'əʊpnɪŋ/ n [1] (in hedge, fence) abertura f [2] (beginning, initial stage) apertura f [3] (of exhibition, building) inauguración f; (Cin, Theat) estreno m; (*before* n) ⟨*speech*⟩ inaugural; **~ night** noche f del estreno [4] (period when open): **hours of ~** (of shop) horario m comercial; (of bank, office) horario m de atención al público [5] (favorable opportunity) oportunidad f

openly /'əʊpənli/ *adv* abiertamente

open: **~-minded** /'əʊpən'maɪndəd ‖,əʊpən'maɪndɪd/ *adj* ⟨*person*⟩ de actitud abierta; ⟨*approach*⟩ imparcial; **~-mouthed** /'əʊpən'maʊðd/ *adj* boquiabierto; **~-plan** /'əʊpən'plæn/ *adj* abierto, de planta abierta; **~ university** n universidad f a distancia, universidad f abierta (Méx); **the O~ U~** (in UK) *la universidad a distancia del Reino Unido*

opera /'ɑːprə ‖'ɒprə/ n (*pl* **-ras**) ópera f

operate /'ɑːpəreɪt ‖'ɒpəreɪt/ *vi* [1] «*machine/mechanism*» funcionar [2] (be applicable) «*rules/laws*» regir* [3] (pursue one's business) «*company/airline/gang*» operar [4] (Med) operar, intervenir* (frml); **to ~ ON sb** (**FOR sth**) operar A algn (DE algo)

■ ~ vt [1] ‹machine/controls› manejar [2] (manage, run) ‹business› llevar; ‹bus service› tener*

operatic /ˌɑːpəˈrætɪk ‖ˌɒpəˈrætɪk/ adj operístico

operating /ˈɑːpəreɪtɪŋ ‖ˈɒpəreɪtɪŋ/ adj (before n) [1] (Busn) ‹profit/loss/costs› de explotación [2] (Med): ~ room o (BrE) theatre quirófano m, sala f de operaciones; ~ table mesa f de operaciones

operation /ˌɑːpəˈreɪʃən ‖ˌɒpəˈreɪʃən/ n [1] (functioning) funcionamiento m; to be in ~ «machine» estar* en funcionamiento; «system» regir* [2] (using, running of machine) manejo m [3] (activity, series of activities) operación f [4] (Med) operación f, intervención f quirúrgica (frml)

operative /ˈɑːpərətɪv ‖ˈɒpərətɪv/ adj to be ~ «rules/measures» estar* en vigor; the ~ word la palabra clave

operator /ˈɑːpəreɪtər ‖ˈɒpəreɪtə(r)/ n (a) (Telec) operador, -dora m,f (b) (of equipment) operario, -ria m,f; (Comput) operador, -dora m,f

ophthalmic optician /ɑːpˈθælmɪk, ɑːf-‖ˌɒfˈθælmɪk/ n ≈ oculista mf

opinion /əˈpɪnjən/ n opinión f; what's your ~? ¿qué opinas?, ¿qué te parece?; in my ~ en mi opinión, a mi parecer; I'd like a second ~ me gustaría consultarlo con otro especialista

opinionated /əˈpɪnjəneɪtəd ‖əˈpɪnjəˌneɪtɪd/ adj dogmático, aferrado a sus (or tus etc) opiniones

opinion poll n sondeo m or encuesta f de opinión

opium /ˈəʊpiəm/ n opio m

opponent /əˈpəʊnənt/ n (a) (of a regime, policy) opositor, -tora m,f; (in debate) adversario, -ria m,f (b) (Games, Sport) contrincante mf, rival mf

opportune /ˌɑːpərˈtuːn ‖ˈɒpətjuːn/ adj (frml) oportuno

opportunist¹ /ˌɑːpərˈtuːnəst ‖ˌɒpəˈtjuːnɪst/ n oportunista mf

opportunist², opportunistic /-tuːˈnɪstɪk ‖-tjuː-/ adj oportunista

opportunity /ˌɑːpərˈtuːnəti ‖ˌɒpəˈtjuːnəti/ n (pl -ties) oportunidad f, ocasión f; ~ to + INF/OF -ING oportunidad DE + INF; there was little ~ for sightseeing hubo poco tiempo para hacer turismo

oppose /əˈpəʊz/ vt (a) (be against) ‹measure/policy/actions› oponerse* a (b) (resist) ‹decision/plan› combatir

opposed /əˈpəʊzd/ adj [1] (against, in disagreement with) (pred) to be ~ TO sth oponerse* A algo [2] as opposed to a diferencia de

opposing /əˈpəʊzɪŋ/ adj (before n) ‹viewpoint/faction/team› contrario; ‹army› enemigo

opposite¹ /ˈɑːpəzət ‖ˈɒpəzɪt/ adj [1] (facing) ‹side/wall/page› de enfrente [2] (contrary) ‹opinions/news› opuesto; we set off in ~ directions partimos en direcciones opuestas; it was coming in the ~ direction venía en dirección contraria; the ~ sex el sexo opuesto

opposite² adv enfrente

opposite³ prep enfrente de, frente a

opposite⁴ n: the ~ lo contrario

opposite number n homólogo, -ga m,f

opposition /ˌɑːpəˈzɪʃən ‖ˌɒpəˈzɪʃən/ n

[1] (antagonism, resistance) oposición f [2] (+ sing or pl vb) (a) (rivals, competitors) (Busn) competencia f; (Sport) adversarios mpl (b) (Pol) oposición f

oppress /əˈpres/ vt oprimir

oppression /əˈpreʃən/ n (Pol) opresión f; (feeling) agobio m

oppressive /əˈpresɪv/ adj (Pol) opresivo; ‹heat/humidity› agobiante

opt /ɑːpt ‖ɒpt/ vi optar; to ~ FOR sth optar POR algo; to ~ to + INF optar POR + INF

■ opt out [v + adv] to ~ out (OF sth) decidir no tomar parte (EN algo); (when already involved) dejar de tomar parte (EN algo)

optical /ˈɑːptɪkəl ‖ˈɒptɪkəl/ adj óptico

optician /ɑːpˈtɪʃən ‖ɒpˈtɪʃən/ n óptico, -ca m,f; (esp in UK) ≈ oculista mf

optics /ˈɑːptɪks ‖ˈɒptɪks/ n (+ sing vb) óptica f

optimism /ˈɑːptəmɪzəm ‖ˈɒptɪmɪzəm/ n optimismo m

optimist /ˈɑːptəməst ‖ˈɒptɪmɪst/ n optimista mf

optimistic /ˌɑːptəˈmɪstɪk ‖ˌɒptɪˈmɪstɪk/ adj optimista

optimum /ˈɑːptəməm ‖ˈɒptɪməm/ adj (before n) óptimo

option /ˈɑːpʃən ‖ˈɒpʃən/ n opción f; (Educ) (asignatura f) optativa f

optional /ˈɑːpʃənl ‖ˈɒpʃənl/ adj ‹accessories/features› opcional; ‹course/subject› optativo

opulence /ˈɑːpjələns ‖ˈɒpjʊləns/ n opulencia f

opulent /ˈɑːpjələnt ‖ˈɒpjʊlənt/ adj opulento

opus /ˈəʊpəs/ n obra f; (Mus) opus m

or /ər, ɔːr ‖ɔː(r)/ conj

■ Note The usual translation of or, o, becomes u when it precedes a word beginning with o or ho.

o; either … or … ▶ EITHER¹; five minutes ~ so unos cinco minutos; do as I say, ~ else! ¡haz lo que digo o vas a ver!

OR = Oregon

oracle /ˈɔːrəkəl ‖ˈɒrəkəl/ n oráculo m

oral¹ /ˈɔːrəl/ adj (usu before n) oral

oral² n (examen m) oral m

orange¹ /ˈɑːrɪndʒ ‖ˈɒrɪndʒ/ n (a) (fruit) naranja f; (before n) ~ juice jugo m or (Esp) zumo m de naranja (b) (tree) naranjo m (c) (color) naranja m

orange² adj naranja adj inv, de color naranja

orangeade /ˌɑːrɪndʒˈeɪd ‖ˌɒrɪndʒˈeɪd/ n naranjada f

orator /ˈɔːrətər ‖ˈɒrətə(r)/ n orador, -dora m,f

orbit¹ /ˈɔːrbət ‖ˈɔːbɪt/ n órbita f

orbit² vt girar or orbitar alrededor de

■ ~ vi orbitar

orchard /ˈɔːrtʃərd ‖ˈɔːtʃəd/ n huerto m (de árboles frutales)

orchestra /ˈɔːrkəstrə ‖ˈɔːkɪstrə/ n [1] (Mus) orquesta f [2] (AmE Theat) platea f, patio m de butacas

orchestral /ɔːrˈkestrəl ‖ɔːˈkestrəl/ adj ‹music› orquestal; ‹piece› para orquesta

orchestrate /ˈɔːrkəstreɪt ‖ˈɔːkɪstreɪt/ vt orquestar

orchid /ˈɔːrkəd ‖ˈɔːkɪd/ n orquídea f

ordain ···⟫ Oscar

ordain /ɔːˈdeɪn ‖ɔːˈdeɪn/ *vt* **1** (Relig) ordenar **2** (a) (decree) (frml) **to ~ THAT** decretar QUE (+ *subj*) (b) (predestine) predestinar

ordeal /ɔːˈdiːl ‖ɔːˈdiːl/ *n* terrible experiencia *f*

order¹ /ˈɔːrdər ‖ˈɔːdə(r)/ *n*
I 1 (command) orden *f*; **~ to + INF** orden DE + inf **2** (request, goods requested) pedido *m*; **the books are on ~** los libros están pedidos; **we make them to ~** los hacemos por encargo; **the waiter took my ~** el camarero tomó nota de lo que quería
II 1 (sequence) orden *m*; **to put sth in(to) ~** poner* algo en orden **2** (satisfactory condition) orden *m*; **I'm trying to put my affairs in ~** estoy tratando de poner mis asuntos en orden; **the car was in perfect working ~** el coche funcionaba perfectamente bien **3** (harmony, discipline) orden *m*; **to keep ~** mantener* el orden **4** (in phrases) (a) in order: **are her papers in ~?** ¿tiene los papeles en regla?; **an apology would seem to be in ~** parecería que lo indicado sería disculparse (b) in order to para (c) in order that para que (+ *subj*) (d) out of order (not in sequence) desordenado; (not working) averiado, descompuesto (AmL); Ⓢ **out of order** no funciona
III 1 (Biol) orden *m* **2** (of monks, nuns) orden *f*

order² *vt* **1** (a) (command) ordenar; **to ~ sb to + INF** ordenarle a algn QUE (+ *subj*) (b) (Med) mandar **2** (request) pedir*; ⟨*goods*⟩ encargar* **3** (put in order) ordenar
■ **~** *vi* (in restaurant): **are you ready to ~?** ¿ya han decidido qué van a tomar?

order book *n* libro *m* de pedidos

ordered /ˈɔːrdərd ‖ˈɔːdəd/ *adj* ordenado

orderly¹ /ˈɔːrdərli ‖ˈɔːdəli/ *adj* (a) ⟨*life/mind*⟩ ordenado (b) ⟨*crowd*⟩ disciplinado

orderly² *n* (*pl* **-lies**) (a) (in hospital) camillero *m* (b) (Mil) ordenanza *m*

ordinal (number) /ˈɔːrdnəl ‖ˈɔːdɪnəl/ *n* (número *m*) ordinal *m*

ordinarily /ˈɔːrdn̩ˈerəli ‖ˈɔːdənrəli/ *adv* (a) (usually) normalmente (b) (averagely) medianamente

ordinary¹ /ˈɔːrdn̩eri ‖ˈɔːdənri/ *adj* (a) (average, normal) normal, corriente (b) (usual) normal

ordinary² *n* (average): **out of the ~** fuera de lo común

ore /ɔːr ‖ɔː(r)/ *n* mena *f*, mineral *m* metalífero

Ore, Oreg = **Oregon**

oregano /əˈreɡənəʊ ‖ˌɒrɪˈɡɑːnəʊ/ *n* orégano *m*

organ /ˈɔːrɡən ‖ˈɔːɡən/ *n* **1** (Anat) órgano *m* **2** (Mus) órgano *m*

organic /ɔːrˈɡænɪk ‖ɔːˈɡænɪk/ *adj* orgánico; ⟨*farming*⟩ ecológico; ⟨*vegetable*⟩ biológico, cultivado sin pesticidas ni fertilizantes artificiales

organism /ˈɔːrɡənɪzəm ‖ˈɔːɡənɪzəm/ *n* organismo *m*

organization /ˌɔːrɡənəˈzeɪʃən ‖ˌɔːɡənaɪˈzeɪʃən/ *n* (a) (group) organización *f*; (*before n*) **~ chart** organigrama *m* (b) (organizing) organización *f*

organize /ˈɔːrɡənaɪz ‖ˈɔːɡənaɪz/ *vt* **1** (arrange, set up) organizar* **2** (systematize) ⟨*ideas/life*⟩ ordenar; **to get oneself ~d** organizarse* **3** (Lab Rels) sindicalizar* (esp AmL), sindicar* (esp Esp)

organized /ˈɔːrɡənaɪzd ‖ˈɔːɡənaɪzd/ *adj* **1** (methodical) organizado **2** (Lab Rels) sindicalizado (esp AmL), sindicado (esp Esp) **3** ⟨*crime*⟩ organizado

organizer /ˈɔːrɡənaɪzər ‖ˈɔːɡənaɪzə(r)/ *n* organizador, -dora *m,f*

orgasm /ˈɔːrɡæzəm ‖ˈɔːɡæzəm/ *n* orgasmo *m*

orgy /ˈɔːrdʒi ‖ˈɔːdʒi/ *n* (*pl* **orgies**) orgía *f*

orient¹, Orient /ˈɔːriənt/ *n* **the ~** (el) Oriente

orient² *vt* (esp AmE) orientar

oriental /ˌɔːriˈentl̩/ *adj* oriental

orientate /ˈɔːrienteɪt/ *vt* (esp BrE) ▶ ORIENT²

orientation /ˌɔːriənˈteɪʃən/ *n* (a) (leanings, preference) tendencia *f* (b) (guidance) orientación *f*

orienteering /ˌɔːriənˈtɪrɪŋ ‖ˌɔːriənˈtɪərɪŋ/ *n* orientación *f*

orifice /ˈɔːrəfəs ‖ˈɒrɪfɪs/ *n* orificio *m*

origin /ˈɔːrədʒən ‖ˈɒrɪdʒɪn/ *n* origen *m*

original¹ /əˈrɪdʒənl̩/ *adj* **1** (first) original; **the ~ inhabitants** los primeros habitantes **2** (a) (not copied) original (b) (unusual) original

original² *n* (document, painting) original *m*

originality /əˌrɪdʒəˈnæləti/ *n* originalidad *f*

originally /əˈrɪdʒənl̩i/ *adv* (a) (in the beginning) originariamente (b) (unusually) con originalidad

originate /əˈrɪdʒəneɪt ‖əˈrɪdʒɪneɪt/ *vi* (a) (begin) «*custom*» originarse; «*fire*» empezar* (b) **to ~ from sth** (develop from) tener* su origen en algo (c) (AmE Transp) salir* de

originator /əˈrɪdʒəneɪtər ‖əˈrɪdʒɪneɪtə(r)/ *n* creador, -dora *m,f*

Orkney Islands /ˈɔːrkni ‖ˈɔːkni/, **Orkneys** /-z/ *pl n* (Islas *fpl*) Órcadas *fpl*

ornament /ˈɔːrnəmənt ‖ˈɔːnəmənt/ *n* adorno *m*

ornamental /ˌɔːrnəˈmentl̩ ‖ˌɔːnəˈmentl̩/ *adj* ornamental

ornate /ɔːrˈneɪt ‖ɔːˈneɪt/ *adj* ornamentado; (pej) recargado

ornithologist /ˌɔːrnəˈθɑːlədʒəst ‖ˌɔːnɪˈθɒlədʒɪst/ *n* ornitólogo, -ga *m,f*

ornithology /ˌɔːrnəˈθɑːlədʒi ‖ˌɔːnɪˈθɒlədʒi/ *n* ornitología *f*

orphan¹ /ˈɔːrfən ‖ˈɔːfən/ *n* huérfano, -na *m,f*

orphan² *vt* (*usu pass*): **she was ~ed at the age of two** quedó huérfana a los dos años

orphanage /ˈɔːrfənɪdʒ ‖ˈɔːfənɪdʒ/ *n* orfanato *m*

orthodox /ˈɔːrθədɑːks ‖ˈɔːθədɒks/ *adj* ortodoxo

orthopedic, (BrE) **orthopaedic** /ˌɔːrθəˈpiːdɪk ‖ˌɔːθəˈpiːdɪk/ *adj* ortopédico

Oscar /ˈɑːskər ‖ˈɒskə(r)/ *n* oscar *m*

AmC	América Central	Arg	Argentina	Cu	Cuba	Per	Perú
AmL	América Latina	Bol	Bolivia	Ec	Ecuador	RPI	Río de la Plata
AmS	América del Sur	Chi	Chile	Esp	España	Ur	Uruguay
Andes	Región andina	CS	Cono Sur	Méx	México	Ven	Venezuela

oscillate /'ɑːsəleɪt ‖'ɒsɪleɪt/ *vi* (Elec, Phys)
oscilar

ostensible /ɑːs'tensəbəl ‖ɒ'stensəbəl/ *adj*
aparente

ostensibly /ɑːs'tensəbli ‖ɒ'stensəbli/ *adv*
aparentemente

ostentatious /ˌɑːstən'teɪʃəs ‖ˌɒsten'teɪʃəs/
adj ostentoso

osteopath /'ɑːstiəpæθ ‖'ɒstiəpæθ/ *n* osteópata
mf

ostracize /'ɑːstrəsaɪz ‖'ɒstrəsaɪz/ *vt* hacerle*
el vacío a

ostrich /'ɑːstrɪtʃ ‖'ɒstrɪtʃ/ *n* avestruz *m*

other¹ /'ʌðər ‖'ʌðə(r)/ *adj* otro, otra; (*pl*) otros,
otras; **he doesn't relate easily to ~ people** no se
relaciona fácilmente con los demás; **the ~ day** el
otro día

other² *pron* (*pl* **others**) ⓵ (a) (different,
alternative one or ones) otro, otra; **~s** otros, otras;
I'll think of some excuse or ~ ya me inventaré
alguna excusa (u otra); **he was called Richard
something or ~** se llamaba Richard no sé cuánto
(fam) (b) (the remaining one or ones) otro, otra; **~s**
otros, otras; **what do the ~s think?** ¿qué piensan
los demás? (c) (additional one or ones) otro, otra; **~s**
otros, otras; **answer the first three questions and
one ~** conteste las tres primeras preguntas y
otra más
⓶ **other than** (apart from) aparte de; (different from)
distinto (*or* distinta etc) de *or* a; **it was none ~
than Bob** no era ni más ni menos que Bob

other³ *adv*: **somehow or ~** de alguna manera;
somewhere or ~ en algún sitio; **where would you
like to live? — anywhere ~ than London** ¿dónde
te gustaría vivir? — en cualquier (otro) sitio
menos en Londres

otherwise /'ʌðəwaɪz ‖'ʌðəwaɪz/ *adv* ⓵ (if
not) (*as linker*) si no ⓶ (in other respects) por lo
demás ⓷ (a) (in a different way): **he could not have
done ~** no podía haber hecho otra cosa; **~
agreed, payments …** a menos que se convenga
otra cosa, los pagos … (b) (other, different): **there
are many problems, legal and ~** hay muchos
problemas, legales y de otro tipo

otter /'ɑːtər ‖'ɒtə(r)/ *n* nutria *f*

ouch /aʊtʃ/ *interj* (colloq) ¡ay!

ought /ɔːt/ *v mod* **~ to + INF** debería (*or*
deberías *etc*) + INF, debiera (*or* debieras *etc*) +
INF; **she ~ not to have said that** no debería haber
dicho eso

ounce /aʊns/ *n* (a) (unit) onza *f* (*28,35 gramos*)
(b) (small quantity) (*no pl*): **if you had an ~ of
decency/sense …** si tuvieras una pizca de
vergüenza/sentido común …

our /aʊr ‖'aʊə(r)/ *adj*

■ **Note** The translation *nuestro* agrees in number and
gender with the noun which it modifies; *our* is
translated by *nuestro, nuestra, nuestros, nuestras*,
according to what follows: *our father/mother* nuestro
padre/nuestra madre; *our books/magazines* nuestros
libros/nuestras revistas.

(*sing*) nuestro, -tra; (*pl*) nuestros, -tras; **we were
washing ~ hair** nos lavábamos el pelo

ours /aʊrz ‖'aʊəz/ *pron*

■ **Note** The translation *nuestro* reflects the gender and

number of the noun it is standing for; *ours* is
translated by *el nuestro, la nuestra, los nuestros, las
nuestras*, depending on what is being referred to.

(*sing*) nuestro, -tra; (*pl*) nuestros, -tras; **~ is blue**
el nuestro/la nuestra es azul; **a friend of ~** un
amigo nuestro

ourselves /aʊr'selvz ‖aʊə'selvz, ɑː-/ *pron* (a)
(reflexive) **we behaved ~** nos portamos bien; **we
thought only of ~** solo pensamos en nosotros
mismos/nosotras mismas; **we were by ~**
estábamos solos/solas (b) (emphatic use): **we did it
~** lo hicimos nosotros mismos/nosotras mismas

oust /aʊst/ *vt* (rival/leader) desbancar*;
(government) derrocar*

out¹ /aʊt/ *adv*
Ⅰ ⓵ (a) (outside) fuera, afuera (esp AmL) (b) (not at
home, work): **tell him I'm ~** dile que no estoy; **I was
~ most of the day** estuve (a)fuera casi todo el
día; **to eat ~** cenar/comer fuera *or* (esp AmL)
afuera; **~ and about: you must get ~ and about
more** tienes que salir más
⓶ (removed): **I'm having my stitches ~ next week**
la semana que viene me sacan los puntos
⓷ (a) (indicating movement, direction): **~! ¡fuera!; ⓢ
out** salida; **she went over to the window and
looked ~** se acercó a la ventana y miró para
afuera (b) (outstretched, projecting): **the dog had its
tongue ~** el perro tenía la lengua fuera *or* (esp
AmL) afuera
⓸ (indicating distance): **~ here in Japan** aquí en
Japón; **we live ~ Brampton way** vivimos en la
dirección de Brampton
⓹ (from hospital, jail): **he's been ~ for a month now**
ya hace un mes que salió
⓺ (in phrases) **out for: Lewis was ~ for revenge**
Lewis quería vengarse; **out to + INF: she's ~ to
beat the record** está decidida a batir el récord;
they're only ~ to make money su único objetivo
es hacer dinero; *see also* OUT OF
Ⅱ ⓵ (a) (displayed, not put away): **are the plates ~
yet?** ¿están puestos ya los platos? (b) (in blossom)
en flor (c) (shining): **when the sun's ~** cuando hay
or hace sol
⓶ (published, produced): **a report ~ today points
out that …** un informe publicado hoy señala que
…; **their new album will be ~ by April** sacarán el
nuevo disco para abril

out² *adj* ⓵ (*pred*) (a) (extinguished) **to be ~**
«fire/light/pipe» estar* apagado (b) (unconscious)
inconsciente ⓶ (*pred*) (a) (at an end): **before the
month/year is ~** antes de que acabe el mes/año
(b) (out of fashion) pasado de moda ⓷ (Sport) (a)
(eliminated) **to be ~** (batter/batsman) quedar out;
(team) quedar eliminado (b) (outside limit) (*pred*)
fuera; **~!** (call) ¡out!

out³ *prep*: **he looked ~ the window** miró (hacia
afuera) por la ventana; *see also* OUT OF 1

out: **~-and-~** /'aʊtn'aʊt/ *adj* (as intensifier)
(villain/liar) consumado; (radical/feminist)
acérrimo; (defeat/disgrace) total; **~back** *n* **the
~back** el interior (zona despoblada de Australia);
~bid /'aʊt'bɪd/ *vt* (pres p **-bidding**; past **-bid**;
past p **-bid** *or* (AmE also) **-bidden**) **to ~bid sb
(FOR sth)** pujar más que algn (POR algo);
~board (motor) *n* motor *m* fuera de borda,
fueraborda *m*; **~break** *n* (of war) estallido *m*; (of
hostilities) comienzo *m*; (of cholera, influenza, violence)
brote *m*; **~building** *n* edificación *f* anexa; ⋯⋮

∼**burst** n (of emotion) arrebato m; ∼**cast** n paria mf; ∼**come** n (result) resultado m; (consequences) consecuencias fpl; ∼**crop** n afloramiento m; ∼**cry** n protesta f (enérgica); **there was a public** ∼**cry** hubo protestas generalizadas; ∼**dated** /'aʊt'deɪtəd ‖,aʊt'deɪtɪd/ adj ⟨style/custom⟩ pasado de moda; ⟨idea/theory⟩ anticuado; ∼**did** /'aʊt'dɪd/ past of ∼DO; ∼**distance** /'aʊt'dɪstəns/ vt dejar atrás; ∼**do** /'aʊt'duː/ vt (3rd pers sing pres **-does**; past **-did**; past p **-done**) superar; ⟨person/team⟩ superar; ⟨result/achievement⟩ mejorar; ∼**door** /'aʊtdɔːr ‖'aʊtdɔː(r)/ adj (before n) ⟨clothes⟩ de calle; ⟨plants⟩ de exterior; ⟨swimming pool⟩ descubierto; ∼**doors** /'aʊt'dɔːrz ‖,aʊt'dɔːz/ adv al aire libre

outer /'aʊtər ‖'aʊtə(r)/ adj (before n) exterior; ∼ **space** el espacio sideral

out: ∼**fit** n (a) (clothes) conjunto m, tenida f (Chi) (b) (equipment) equipo m; ∼**flow** n (of water) desagüe m, flujo m; ∼**go** n (AmE) salida f; ∼**going** adj [1] (sociable) sociable; [2] ⟨president/administration⟩ saliente; ∼**goings** pl n (esp BrE) gastos mpl; ∼**grow** /'aʊt'grəʊ/ vt (past **-grew**; past p **-grown**): **he's already** ∼**grown his new shoes** los zapatos nuevos ya le han quedado chicos or (Esp) ya se le han quedado pequeños; **she's** ∼**grown these toys** ya está grande para jugar con esos juguetes; ∼**house** n (a) (building) (BrE) edificación f anexa (b) (outdoor privy) (AmE) excusado m exterior

outing /'aʊtɪŋ/ n excursión f

outlandish /aʊt'lændɪʃ/ adj ⟨clothes⟩ extravagante; ⟨idea/suggestion⟩ descabellado

outlast /'aʊt'læst ‖,aʊt'lɑːst/ vt (a) (last longer than) durar más que (b) (survive) sobrevivir a

outlaw¹ /'aʊtlɔː/ n forajido, -da m,f, bandido, -da m,f

outlaw² vt ⟨activity/product⟩ prohibir*, declarar ilegal; ⟨organization⟩ proscribir*; ⟨person⟩ declarar fuera de la ley

out: ∼**lay** n desembolso m; ∼**let** n [1] (a) (for liquid, gas) salida f (b) (AmE Elec) toma f de corriente, tomacorriente m (AmL); [2] (means of expression): **she found an** ∼**let for her feelings** encontró una manera de canalizar sus sentimientos; [3] (Busn, Marketing) punto m de venta; **retail** ∼**let** tienda f al por menor

outline¹ /'aʊtlaɪn/ n [1] (a) (contour) contorno m (b) (shape) perfil m [2] (summary) resumen m; (plan of project, article) esquema m

outline² vt (a) (sketch) ⟨shape⟩ bosquejar; ⟨map⟩ trazar* (b) (summarize) esbozar*

out: ∼**live** /'aʊt'lɪv/ vt sobrevivir a; ∼**look** n (a) (attitude) punto m de vista (b) (prospects) perspectivas fpl; ∼**lying** adj (before n) ⟨villages/islands⟩ alejado; ⟨area/hills/suburbs⟩ de la periferia; ∼**number** /'aʊt'nʌmbər ‖,aʊt'nʌmbə(r)/ vt superar en número a

out of prep [1] (from inside): **it fell** ∼ ∼ **her hand** se le cayó de la mano; (come) ∼ ∼ **there!** ¡salgan de ahí!; **to look** ∼ ∼ **the window** mirar (hacia afuera) por la ventana

[2] (outside): **I was** ∼ ∼ **the room for two minutes** estuve dos minutos fuera or (AmL tb) afuera de la habitación

[3] (eliminated, excluded): **Korea is** ∼ ∼ **the tournament** Corea ha quedado eliminada; **he was left** ∼ ∼ **the team** no lo incluyeron en el equipo [4] (a) (indicating substance, makeup) de; **made** ∼ ∼ **steel** hecho de acero (b) (indicating motive) por; ∼ **charity** por caridad [5] (from among) de; **eight** ∼ **ten people** ocho de cada diez personas [6] (indicating lack): **we're** ∼ ∼ **bread** nos hemos quedado sin pan

out: ∼**-of-date** /'aʊtəv'deɪt/ adj (pred ∼ **of date**) ⟨ideas/technology⟩ desfasado, perimido (RPl); ⟨ticket/check⟩ caducado, vencido (AmL); ⟨clothes⟩ pasado de moda; ∼**-of-the-way** /'əʊtəvðə'weɪ/ adj ⟨place⟩ apartado; ∼**patient** n paciente externo, -na m,f; ∼**post** n (a) (Mil) avanzada f (b) (settlement) puesto m de avanzada; ∼**put** n (of factory, writer, artist) producción f; (of worker, machine) rendimiento m; (Comput) salida f; (Elec) salida f

outrage¹ /'aʊtreɪdʒ/ n (a) (cruel act) atrocidad f (b) (scandal) escándalo m (c) (feeling) ∼ (**AT** sth) indignación f (**ANTE** algo)

outrage² vt (a) (offend) indignar (b) (scandalize) escandalizar*

outrageous /aʊt'reɪdʒəs/ adj (a) (scandalous) ⟨behavior/state of affairs⟩ vergonzoso; ⟨demands/price⟩ escandaloso; **how dare you! this is** ∼! ¡cómo te atreves! ¡esto es intolerable! (b) (unconventional) ⟨clothes⟩ extravagante

outran /'aʊt'ræn/ past of OUTRUN

outright¹ /'aʊtraɪt/ adj (before n) ⟨refusal/opposition⟩ rotundo; ⟨hostility⟩ declarado; ⟨winner⟩ indiscutido; ⟨lie⟩ descarado

outright² adv (a) (completely) ⟨refuse/reject⟩ rotundamente; ⟨win⟩ indiscutiblemente (b) (directly, frankly) ⟨ask/say⟩ abiertamente (c) (instantly) ⟨kill⟩ en el acto

out: ∼**run** /'aʊt'rʌn/ vt (pres p **-running**; past **-ran**; past p **-run**) dejar atrás; ∼**set** n: **from the** ∼**set** desde el principio; ∼**shine** /'aʊt'ʃaɪn/ vt (past & past p **-shone**) eclipsar

outside¹ /'aʊt'saɪd/ n (exterior part) exterior m; (surface) parte f de fuera or (esp AmL) de afuera; **at the (very)** ∼ como máximo

outside² adv fuera, afuera (esp AmL); **to run** ∼ salir* corriendo

outside³ prep fuera de; **it's just** ∼ **London** está en las afueras de Londres; **it's** ∼ **my responsibilities** no está dentro de mis responsabilidades

outside⁴ adj (before n) (a) (exterior, outward) exterior (b) (outdoor) ⟨toilet⟩ fuera de la vivienda, exterior (c) (outer) exterior; **the** ∼ **lane** (Auto) (in UK etc) el carril de la izquierda; (in US etc) el carril de la derecha; (Sport) el carril (AmL) or (Esp) la calle número ocho (or seis etc) (d) (external) ⟨interference/pressure⟩ externo

outsider /'aʊt'saɪdər ‖,aʊt'saɪdə(r)/ n (a) (person not belonging) persona f de fuera, afuerano, -na m,f (b) (in competition): **he was beaten by an** ∼ fue derrotado por un desconocido (un competidor que se consideraba tenía pocas probabilidades de ganar)

out: ∼**size** /'aʊt'saɪz/, (esp AmE) ∼**-sized** /-d/ adj (Clothing) de talla or (RPl) talle gigante; (very large) gigantesco; ∼**skirts** pl n afueras fpl,

alrededores *mpl*; **~smart** /'aʊt'smɑːrt
‖,aʊt'smɑːt/ *vt* (esp AmE colloq) burlar; **~source**
vt adquirir* … de fuentes externas; **~spoken**
/'aʊt'spəʊkən/ *adj* directo, franco; **~spread**
/'aʊt'spred/ *adj* ‹*wings*› extendido; **~standing**
/aʊt'stændɪŋ/ *adj* ①(a) (excellent) ‹*ability*/
beauty› extraordinario; ‹*achievement*/*performer*›
destacado (b) (prominent) (before n) ‹*feature*›
destacado; ② ‹*debt*› pendiente (de pago); **~stay**
/'aʊt'steɪ/ *vt*: I think we've **~stayed our welcome**
creo que nos hemos quedado más de la cuenta;
~stretched /'aʊt'stretʃt/ *adj* extendido;
~strip /'aʊt'strɪp/ *vt* **-pp-** (run faster than)
tomarle la delantera a; (exceed) sobrepasar;
~vote /'aʊt'vəʊt/ *vt*: to be **~voted** perder* la
votación

outward¹ /'aʊtwərd ‖'aʊtwəd/ *adj* (before n)
(a) ‹*appearance*› exterior; ‹*sign*› externo (b)
‹*journey*/*flight*› de ida

outward², (BrE also) **outwards** /-z/ *adv* hacia
afuera

outwardly /'aʊtwərdli ‖'aʊtwədli/ *adv* en
apariencia

out: ~weigh /'aʊt'weɪ/ *vt* ser* mayor que;
~wit /'aʊt'wɪt/ *vt* **-tt-** burlar

oval¹ /'əʊvəl/ *n* óvalo *m*

oval² *adj* ovalado, oval

ovary /'əʊvəri/ *n* (*pl* **-ries**) ovario *m*

ovation /əʊ'veɪʃən/ *n* (frml) ovación *f* (frml); he
got a standing **~** los delegados se pusieron de pie
para aplaudirlo

oven /'ʌvən/ *n* horno *m*; (before n) **~ glove**
guante *m* para el horno

oven: ~proof *adj* refractario; **~-ready**
/'ʌvən'redi/ *adj* listo para el horno

over¹ /'əʊvər ‖'əʊvə(r)/ *adv*
I ① (a) (across): come **~** here! ¡ven aquí!; look **~**
there! ¡mira allí!; she called me **~** me llamó
(desde el otro lado); he reached **~** and took the
money se estiró y tomó el dinero (b) (overhead)
por encima
② (a) (in another place): she was sitting **~** there
estaba sentada allí; how long are you **~** (here)
for? ¿cuánto tiempo te vas a quedar (aquí)? (b)
(on other page, TV station etc): see **~** véase al dorso;
for the latest news, **~** to New York para las
últimas noticias, conectamos ahora con Nueva
York (c) (Rad, Telec) corto; **~** and out! corto y
fuera
③ (out of upright position): to knock sth **~** tirar or
(AmL exc RPl) botar algo (de un golpe); to tip sth **~**
volcar* algo
II ① (finished): the film was **~** by 11 o'clock la
película terminó antes de las 11; it's all **~**
between us lo nuestro se ha acabado; *to be* **~**
(*and done*) *with* haber* terminado
② (remaining): if you have any material **~** si te
sobra tela; 3 into 10 goes 3 and 1 **~** 10 dividido
(por) 3 cabe a 3 y sobra 1
③ (a) (*as intensifier*): twice/ten times **~** dos/diez
veces (b) (again) (AmE) otra vez; we had to start **~**
tuvimos que volver a empezar
④ (more) más
⑤ (excessively) demasiado
III (*in phrases*) ① all over (everywhere) por todas
partes; I'm aching all **~** me duele todo (el
cuerpo); that's her all **~** (colloq) eso es típico de
ella

② (all) over again: to start (all) **~** again volver* a
empezar (desde cero)
③ over and over (repeatedly) una y otra vez

over² *prep*
I ① (across): he jumped **~** the fence saltó (por
encima de) la valla; they built a bridge **~** the river
construyeron un puente sobre el río; she peered
~ his shoulder atisbó por encima de su hombro
② (above) encima de
③ (covering, on): snow was falling **~** the
countryside nevaba sobre la campiña; my room
looks out **~** the square mi habitación da a la
plaza; he put a coat on **~** his pajamas se puso un
abrigo encima del pijama; she hit me **~** the head
with her stick me dio con el bastón en la cabeza
④ (a) (through, all around): **~** an area of 50km² en
un área de 50km²; I've been **~** the details with her
he repasado los detalles con ella (b) (referring to
experiences, illnesses): is she **~** her measles yet?
¿ya se ha repuesto del sarampión?; we're **~** the
worst now ya hemos pasado lo peor
⑤ (during, in the course of): **~** the past/next few
years en los últimos/próximos años; we can
discuss it **~** lunch podemos hablarlo mientras
comemos
⑥ (by the medium of) por; **~** the loudspeaker por
el altavoz
⑦ (about, on account of): to cry **~** sth llorar por
algo; they argued **~** money discutieron por
asuntos de dinero
⑧ all over: there are black marks all **~** the floor
hay marcas negras por todo el suelo; all **~** town
por toda la ciudad
II ① (a) (more than) más de (b) over and above
(in addition to) además de
② (a) (senior to) por encima de (b) (indicating
superiority) sobre; to have control **~** sb/sth tener*
control sobre algн/algo

over³ *n* (in cricket) over *m* (*serie de seis
lanzamientos*)

over- /'əʊvər ‖'əʊvə(r)/ *pref* (a) (excessively)
demasiado (b) (in deliberate understatement): she
wasn't **~enthusiastic** no demostró mucho
entusiasmo que digamos

overact /'əʊvər'ækt/ *vi* sobreactuar*

overall¹ /'əʊvərɔːl/ *adj* (before n) ‹*length*› total;
‹*result*/*cost*› global; the **~** impression la
impresión general

overall² *n*. ① (protective garment) (esp BrE) bata *f*
② **overalls** *pl* (a) (dungarees) (AmE) overol *m*
(AmL), (pantalones *mpl* de) peto *m* (Esp),
mameluco *m* (CS) (b) (boiler suit) (BrE) overol *m*
(AmL), mono *m* (Esp, Méx)

over: ~arm *adv* (esp BrE) por encima de la
cabeza; **~ate** /'əʊvər'et/ *past of* **~EAT; ~awe**
/'əʊvər'ɔː/ *vt* intimidar; **~balance**
/'əʊvər'bæləns ‖,əʊvə'bæləns/ *vi* perder* el
equilibrio; **~board** *adv*: they threw him **~board**
lo echaron por la borda; *to go* **~board** (colloq —
exaggerate) exagerar; (— be excessively enthusiastic,
generous) pasarse (fam); **~came** /'əʊvər'keɪm
‖,əʊvə'keɪm/ *past of* **~COME; ~cast** *adj* ‹*sky*›
cubierto; ‹*day*› nublado; it's **~cast** está nublado
or cubierto; **~charge** /'əʊvər'tʃɑːrdʒ
‖,əʊvə'tʃɑːdʒ/ *vt* to **~charge sb** (FOR sth)
cobrarle de más a algн (POR algo); **~coat** *n*
abrigo *m*, sobretodo *m* (esp RPl); **~come**
/'əʊvər'kʌm ‖,əʊvə'kʌm/ (*past* **-came**; *past p* ⋯⟶

-come vt (a) ⟨opponent⟩ reducir*; ⟨fear⟩
superar; ⟨inhibitions⟩ vencer* (b) (overwhelm)
invadir; **he was ~come by fatigue** lo venció la
fatiga; **to be ~come WITH sth** ⟨with guilt/
remorse⟩ sentirse* ⟨abrumado POR algo ■ ∗ vi:
we shall ~come venceremos; **~crowded**
/'əʊvər'kraʊdəd ‖ˌəʊvə'kraʊdɪd/ adj abarrotado
(de gente); ⟨country⟩ superpoblado; **~crowding**
/'əʊvər'kraʊdɪŋ ‖ˌəʊvə'kraʊdɪŋ/ n: **they
complained about the ~crowding on the trains** se
quejaron de lo aborrotados que iban los trenes;
the severe ~crowding in our prisons el
hacinamiento en nuestras cárceles; **~do**
/'əʊvər'duː ‖ˌəʊvə'duː/ vt (3rd pers sing pres
-does; past **-did**; past p **-done**) ① (exaggerate)
exagerar; **to ~do it** (go too far) írsele la mano a
algn; (overexert oneself) exigir* demasiado;
② (Culin) cocinar demasiado, recocer*; **~dose** n
sobredosis f; **~draft** n descubierto m; **~draw**
/'əʊvər'drɔː ‖ˌəʊvə'drɔː/ vt (past **-drew**; past p
-drawn) (Fin): **I'm ~drawn** tengo un descubierto;
~drive /'əʊvərdraɪv ‖'əʊvədraɪv/ n
superdirecta f; **~due** /'əʊvər'duː ‖ˌəʊvə'djuː/
adj: **the book is a month ~due** el plazo de
devolución del libro venció hace un mes; **such
measures are long ~due** tales medidas deberían
haberse adoptado mucho antes; **~eat** /'əʊvər'iːt/
vi (past **-ate**; past p **-eaten**) comer demasiado;
~excited /'əʊvərɪk'saɪtəd ‖ˌəʊvərɪk'saɪtɪd/ adj
sobreexcitado; **~feed** /'əʊvər'fiːd ‖ˌəʊvə'fiːd/ vt
(past & past p **-fed**) sobrealimentar

overflow¹ /'əʊvər'fləʊ ‖ˌəʊvə'fləʊ/ vi «liquid»
derramarse; «bucket/bath/river» desbordarse;
the house is ~ing with junk la casa está hasta el
techo de cachivaches

overflow² /'əʊvərfləʊ ‖'əʊvəfləʊ/ n (a)
(excess): **we put a bowl there to catch the ~**
pusimos un bol para recoger el líquido que se
derramaba (b) (outlet) rebosadero m

over: ~grown /'əʊvər'grəʊn ‖ˌəʊvə'grəʊn/ adj
(a) ⟨garden⟩ lleno de maleza (b) (too big)
demasiado grande; **~hand** adv (AmE) por
encima de la cabeza; **~hang** /'əʊvər'hæŋ
‖ˌəʊvə'hæŋ/ (past & past p **-hung**) vt
sobresalir* por encima de ∎ ∗ vi sobresalir*

overhaul¹ /'əʊvər'hɔːl ‖ˌəʊvə'hɔːl/ vt revisar

overhaul² /'əʊvərhɔːl ‖'əʊvəhɔːl/ n revisión f
(general), overjol m (AmC)

overhead¹ /'əʊvər'hed ‖ˌəʊvə'hed/ adv: **the
sun was directly ~** el sol caía de pleno; **a plane
flew ~** pasó un avión

overhead² /'əʊvərhed ‖'əʊvəhed/ adj ⟨cable⟩
aéreo; ⟨railway⟩ elevado

overhead³ /'əʊvərhed ‖'əʊvəhed/ n (AmE)
gastos mpl indirectos

over: ~heads /'əʊvərhedz ‖'əʊvəhedz/ pl n
(BrE) ▶ OVERHEAD³; **~hear** /'əʊvər'hɪr
‖ˌəʊvə'hɪə(r)/ vt (past & past p **-heard**) oír*
(por casualidad); **~heat** /'əʊvər'hiːt ‖ˌəʊvə'hiːt/
vi recalentarse*; **~hung** past & past p of
OVERHANG; **~joyed** /'əʊvər'dʒɔɪd ‖ˌəʊvə'dʒɔɪd/
adj encantado; **~kill** n exageración f; **~land**

adj/adv por tierra; **~lap** /'əʊvər'læp ‖ˌəʊvə'læp/
vi **-pp-** (a) «tiles/planks» estar* montados unos
sobre otros, traslaparse (b) «responsibilities»
coincidir en parte; **~leaf** /'əʊvər'liːf ‖ˌəʊvə'liːf/
adv al dorso; **~load** /'əʊvər'ləʊd ‖ˌəʊvə'ləʊd/ vt
sobrecargar*; **~look** /'əʊvər'lʊk ‖ˌəʊvə'lʊk/ vt
① (a) (not notice) pasar por alto (b) (disregard)
disculpar; ② (have view over): **a room ~looking
the sea** una habitación con vista al mar or que
da al mar

overly /'əʊvərli ‖'əʊvəli/ adv demasiado

overnight¹ /'əʊvər'naɪt ‖ˌəʊvə'naɪt/ adv (a)
(through the night): **to stay ~** quedarse a pasar la
noche; **there had been a heavy fall of snow ~**
durante la noche había nevado mucho; **soak the
chickpeas ~** ponga los garbanzos en remojo la
noche anterior (b) (suddenly) ⟨change/disappear⟩
de la noche a la mañana

overnight² /'əʊvərnaɪt ‖'əʊvənaɪt/adj (a)
(through the night) ⟨journey⟩ de noche; ⟨stay⟩ de una
noche (b) (sudden) ⟨change/success⟩ repentino

over: ~paid /'əʊvər'peɪd ‖ˌəʊvə'peɪd/ adj:
she's ~paid le pagan demasiado **~pass** n paso
m elevado, paso m a desnivel (Méx);
~population /ˌəʊvərˌpɑːpjə'leɪʃən
‖ˌəʊvəˌpɒpjʊ'leɪʃən/ n superpoblación f,
sobrepoblación f (AmL); **~power** /'əʊvər'paʊər
‖ˌəʊvə'paʊə(r)/ vt (a) (render helpless) dominar (b)
(affect greatly) «smell» marear; «heat» sofocar*;
«emotion» abrumar; **~powering**
/'əʊvər'paʊrɪŋ ‖ˌəʊvə'paʊərɪŋ/ adj (a) ⟨smell⟩
muy fuerte; ⟨heat⟩ aplastante; ⟨desire⟩ irresistible
(b) ⟨personality⟩ apabullante; **~priced**
/'əʊvər'praɪst ‖ˌəʊvə'praɪst/ vt: **it's ~priced** es
caro para lo que es; **~ran** /'əʊvər'ræn
‖ˌəʊvə'ræn/ past of ~RUN; **~rated**
/'əʊvər'reɪtəd ‖ˌəʊvə'reɪtɪd/ adj sobrevalorado;
~reach /'əʊvər'riːtʃ ‖ˌəʊvə'riːtʃ/ v refl: **to
~reach oneself** intentar hacer demasiado;
~react /'əʊvərri'ækt ‖ˌəʊvəri'ækt/ vi
reaccionar en forma exagerada; **~ride**
/'əʊvər'raɪd ‖ˌəʊvə'raɪd/ vt (past **-rode**; past p
-ridden) ⟨decision/recommendation⟩ invalidar;
⟨wishes/advice⟩ hacer* caso omiso de; **~ripe**
/'əʊvər'raɪp ‖ˌəʊvə'raɪp/ adj demasiado maduro;
~rode /'əʊvər'rəʊd ‖ˌəʊvə'rəʊd/ past of ~RIDE;
~rule /'əʊvər'ruːl ‖ˌəʊvə'ruːl/ vt ⟨decision/
verdict⟩ anular; ⟨objection⟩ rechazar*; **~run**
/'əʊvər'rʌn ‖ˌəʊvə'rʌn/ vt (past **-ran**; past p
-run) (a) (invade, swarm over) invadir; **to be ~run
WITH sth** estar* plagado DE algo (b) (exceed)
exceder; **~saw** /'əʊvər'sɔː ‖ˌəʊvə'sɔː/ past of
OVERSEE

overseas¹ /'əʊvər'siːz ‖ˌəʊvəˌsiːz/ adj (before
n) ⟨trade⟩ exterior; ⟨investments/branches⟩ en el
exterior; ⟨student/visitor⟩ extranjero; ⟨news⟩ del
exterior

overseas² /'əʊvər'siːz ‖ˌəʊvə'siːz/ adv ⟨live⟩
en el extranjero; ⟨travel/send⟩ al extranjero

over: ~see /'əʊvər'siː ‖ˌəʊvə'siː/ vt (past
-saw; past p **-seen**) supervisar; **~seer**
/'əʊvər'sɪr, -'siːər ‖'əʊvəsiːə(r)/ n capataz mf;
~shadow /'əʊvər'ʃædəʊ ‖ˌəʊvə'ʃædəʊ/ vt

eclipsar; ~**shoot** /'əʊvər'ʃuːt ‖,əʊvə'ʃuːt/ vt (past & past p -**shot**) ⟨runway⟩ salirse* de; ⟨turning⟩ pasarse de; ⟨target/budget⟩ exceder; ~**sight** /'əʊvərsaɪt ‖'əʊvəsaɪt/ n descuido m; ~**sleep** /'əʊvər'sliːp ‖,əʊvə'sliːp/ vi (past & past p -**slept**) quedarse dormido; ~**spend** /'əʊvər'spend ‖,əʊvə'spend/ vi (past & past p -**spent**) gastar más de la cuenta; ~**spill** n excedente m de población; ~**staffed** /'əʊvər'stæft ‖,əʊvə'stɑːft/ adj con exceso de personal or (Esp tb) de plantilla; ~**state** /'əʊvər'steɪt ‖,əʊvə'steɪt/ vt exagerar; ~**stay** /'əʊvər'steɪ ‖,əʊvə'steɪ/ vt ▶ OUTSTAY; ~**step** /'əʊvər'step ‖,əʊvə'step/ vt -**pp**- sobrepasar

overt /əʊ'vɜːrt ‖'əʊvɜːt/ adj ⟨hostility⟩ declarado; ⟨criticism⟩ abierto

over: ~**take** /'əʊvər'teɪk ‖,əʊvə'teɪk/ (past -**took**; past p -**taken**) vt (a) (go past) adelantar, rebasar (Méx) (b) (surpass) superar ■ ~ vi (BrE) adelantar, rebasar (Méx); ~**tax** /'əʊvər'tæks ‖,əʊvə'tæks/ vt (a) (strain) poner* a prueba (b) (Tax) gravar en exceso (con impuestos); ~**throw** /'əʊvər'θrəʊ ‖,əʊvə'θrəʊ/ vt (past -**threw**; past p -**thrown**) ⟨government⟩ derrocar*; ~**time** n [1] (extra work hours) horas fpl extra(s), sobretiempo m (Chi, Per); [2] (AmE Sport) prórroga f; ~**tone** n (suggestion, hint) (usu pl) dejo m, deje m (Esp); ~**took** /'əʊvər'tʊk ‖,əʊvə'tʊk/ past of ~TAKE

overture /'əʊvərtʃʊr ‖'əʊvətjʊə(r)/ n [1] (Mus) obertura f [2] **overtures** pl (approaches) (fml) intento m de acercamiento; (sexual) insinuación f

over: ~**turn** /'əʊvər'tɜːrn ‖,əʊvə'tɜːn/ vt (a) (tip over) ⟨table/boat⟩ darle* la vuelta a, dar* vuelta (CS) (b) (depose) ⟨government⟩ derrocar* ■ ~ vi «vehicle» volcar*; ~**weight** /'əʊvər'weɪt ‖,əʊvə'weɪt/ adj ⟨person⟩ demasiado gordo; I am 10lb ~**weight** peso 10 libras de más, tengo un sobrepeso de 10 libras (Chi, Méx)

overwhelm /'əʊvər'hwelm ‖,əʊvə'welm/ vt (a) (emotionally) abrumar (b) (defeat) aplastar (c) (swamp): **they've been ~ed with applications/complaints** han recibido infinidad de solicitudes/quejas

overwhelming /'əʊvər'hwelmɪŋ ‖,əʊvə'welmɪŋ/ adj ⟨grief⟩ inconsolable; ⟨urge⟩ irresistible; ⟨anger⟩ incontenible; ⟨boredom⟩ insoportable; ⟨defeat⟩ aplastante

overwind /'əʊvər'waɪnd ‖,əʊvə'waɪnd/ vt (past & past p -**wound** /-waʊnd/) dar* demasiada cuerda a

overwork[1] /'əʊvər'wɜːrk ‖,əʊvə'wɜːk/ vt hacer* trabajar demasiado

overwork[2] n agotamiento m

ovulate /'ɑːvjəleɪt ‖'ɒvjʊleɪt/ vi ovular

ovulation /'ɑːvjə'leɪʃən ‖,ɒvjʊ'leɪʃən/ n ovulación f

owe /əʊ/ vt (a) (financially) deber; **to ~ sb sth, ~ sth TO sb** deberle algo A algn (b) (be obliged to give, do) ⟨explanation/apology/favor⟩ deber

owing /'əʊɪŋ/ adj [1] (pred): **the money still ~** el dinero que aún se debe [2] **owing to** (as prep) debido a

owl /aʊl/ n búho m, tecolote m (Méx); (barn ~) lechuza f

own[1] /əʊn/ vt ⟨property⟩ tener*
■ **own up** [v + adv]: **no one ~ed up** nadie reconoció tener la culpa; **no one would ~ up to having left the window open** nadie quiso reconocer que había sido quien dejó la ventana abierta

own[2] adj **my/her/your** etc ~: **in our ~ house** en nuestra propia casa; **she makes her ~ clothes** se hace la ropa ella misma

own[3] pron **my/her/your** etc ~: **it isn't a company car, it's her ~** no es un coche de la empresa, es suyo (propio); **she wanted a room of her ~** quería una habitación para ella sola; **on one's ~** solo; **to get one's ~ back** (BrE colloq) desquitarse

owner ?/'əʊnər ‖'əʊnə(r)/ n (of house, car) dueño, -ña m,f, propietario, -ria m,f; (of pet) dueño, -ña m,f

ownership /'əʊnərʃɪp ‖'əʊnəʃɪp/ n propiedad f

own goal n autogol m, gol m en contra (CS)

ox /ɑːks ‖ɒks/ n (pl **oxen**) buey m

oxen /'ɑːksən ‖'ɒksən/ pl of ox

oxide /'ɑːksaɪd ‖'ɒksaɪd/ n óxido m

oxtail /'ɑːksteɪl ‖'ɒksteɪl/ n rabo m de buey

oxygen /'ɑːksədʒən ‖'ɒksɪdʒən/ n oxígeno m; (before n) ~ **mask** (Aviat, Med) mascarilla f de oxígeno

oyster /'ɔɪstər ‖'ɔɪstə(r)/ n ostra f, ostión m (Méx)

oz = **ounce(s)**

ozone /'əʊzəʊn/ n (Chem) ozono m; (before n) **the ~ layer** la capa de ozono

Pp

P, p /piː/ n P, p f

p (in UK) (= **penny/pence**) penique(s) m(pl)

p. (pl **pp.**) (= **page**) pág., p.; **pp. 12-48** págs. 12 a 48

pa[1] /pɑː/ n (colloq) papá m

pa[2], **p.a.** /'piː'eɪ/ = **per annum**

PA n (a) /'piː'eɪ/ ~ (**system**) = **public-address system** (b) /piː'eɪ/ (BrE) = **personal assistant** (c) also **Pa** = **Pennsylvania**

pace[1] /peɪs/ n [1] (stride) paso m; **to put sb through her/his ~s** poner* a algn a prueba [2] (speed) (no pl) ritmo m; **to keep ~ with sb** ⋯⋗

seguirle* el ritmo lento a algn; **to set the ~** marcar* la pauta

pace² /vi/: **to ~ up and down** caminar or (esp Esp) andar de un lado para otro

pace: ~maker n (Sport) liebre f; (Med) marcapasos m; **~setter** /'peɪsˌsetə(r) ‖'peɪsˌsetə(r)/ n (Sport) liebre f; (pioneer) líder mf

Pacific /pə'sɪfɪk/ n the ~ (**Ocean**) el (Océano) Pacífico

pacifier /'pæsəfaɪər ‖'pæsɪfaɪə(r)/ n (AmE) chupete m, chupón m (AmL exc CS), chupo m (Col), chupa f (Ven)

pacifism /'pæsəfɪzəm ‖'pæsɪfɪzəm/ n pacifismo m

pacifist /'pæsəfəst ‖'pæsɪfɪst/ n pacifista mf

pacify /'pæsəfaɪ ‖'pæsɪfaɪ/ vt **-fies, -fying, -fied** (a) (calm, satisfy) apaciguar* (b) (restore to peace) pacificar*

pack¹ /pæk/ n **1** (bundle, load) fardo m; (rucksack) mochila f **2** (a) (package) paquete m; (of cigarettes) paquete m, cajetilla f (b) (of cards) (BrE) baraja f, mazo m (esp AmL) **3** (a) (of wolves) manada f; **a ~ of hounds** (Sport) una jauría (b) (in race) pelotón m **4** (of thieves, fools) (pej) partida f (pey); **a ~ of lies** una sarta de mentiras

pack² vt **1** (a) (Busn) ⟨goods/products⟩ (put into container) envasar; (make packets with) empaquetar; (for transport) embalar (b) (put into suitcase, bag): **have you ~ed your toothbrush?** ¿llevas el cepillo de dientes?; **to ~ one's suitcase** hacer* la maleta or (RPl) la valija, empacar (AmL); **she takes a ~ed lunch to work** se lleva el almuerzo or (esp Esp, Méx) la comida al trabajo

2 (a) (press tightly together): **~ the soil** (down) firmly apisone bien la tierra (b) (cram): **the book is ~ed with useful information** el libro está lleno de información útil; **we ~ed a lot into a short time** hicimos un montón de cosas en poco tiempo fam

■ ~ vi (fill suitcase) hacer* la(s) maleta(s) or (RPl) la(s) valija(s), empacar* (AmL)

■ **pack in** [v + o + adv, v + adv + o] **1** (quit) (colloq) ⟨job/course⟩ dejar
2 (cram in): **we managed to ~ in 50 people** pudimos meter a 50 personas

■ **pack off** [v + o + adv, v + adv + o] despachar, mandar; **she ~ed the children off to school** mandó a los niños al colegio

■ **pack up 1** [v + adv] (a) (assemble belongings) liar* el petate, hacer* su itacate (Méx) (b) (stop) (colloq): **let's ~ up for the day** dejémoslo por hoy (c) (break down) (colloq) ⟨⟨motor/radio⟩⟩ dejar de funcionar, descomponerse* (esp AmL), tronarse* (Méx fam)
2 [v + o + adv, v + adv + o] (a) ⟨tools/belongings⟩ recoger* (b) ▶ PACK IN 1

package /'pækɪdʒ/ n paquete m

package: ~ holiday (BrE) ▶ ~ VACATION; **~ store** n (AmE) tienda f de bebidas alcohólicas; **~ tour** n viaje m organizado (en el que se recorren diferentes localidades); **~ vacation** n (AmE) vacaciones fpl organizadas

packaging /'pækɪdʒɪŋ/ n (a) (packing) embalaje m (b) (wrapping) envoltorio m (c) (Marketing) presentación f

packed /pækt/ adj ⟨hall/restaurant⟩ lleno de gente, repleto

packet /'pækət ‖'pækɪt/ n (esp BrE) paquete m; (before n) ⟨soup/cake mix⟩ de sobre

packing /'pækɪŋ/ n (a) (of suitcase): **to do one's ~** hacer* la(s) maleta(s) or (RPl) la(s) valija(s), empacar* (AmL) (b) (in factory) embalaje m

packing case n caja f de embalaje

pact /pækt/ n pacto m

pad¹ /pæd/ n **1** (cushioning) almohadilla f; **shoulder ~s** hombreras fpl; **knee ~s** rodilleras fpl **2** (of paper) bloc m

pad² vt **-dd-** **1** (a) (line) ⟨seat/panel⟩ acolchar, enguatar (Esp) (b) **padded** past p ⟨jacket⟩ acolchado, enguatado (Esp); ⟨bra⟩ con relleno; ⟨envelope⟩ acolchado; **~ded cell** celda f de aislamiento **2** ~ (out) ⟨essay⟩ rellenar, meter* paja en (fam)

padding /'pædɪŋ/ n (material) relleno m, guata f (Esp); (for protection) almohadillas fpl

paddle¹ /'pædl/ n **1** (oar) zagual m, pala f **2** (no pl): **to go for a ~** ir* a mojarse los pies

paddle² vi **1** (wet feet) mojarse los pies (en la orilla) **2** (a) (in canoe) remar (con pala o zagual) (b) (swim) ⟨⟨duck/dog⟩⟩ chapotear
■ ~ vt ⟨boat/canoe⟩ llevar (remando con pala o zagual)

paddling pool /'pædlɪŋ/ n (BrE) (in park) estanque m; (inflatable) piscina f or (Méx) alberca f inflable (para niños)

paddock /'pædək/ n prado m

paddy /'pædi/ n (pl **-dies**) ~ (**field**) arrozal m

padlock¹ /'pædlɑːk ‖'pædlɒk/ n candado m

padlock² vt cerrar* con candado

paediatric etc (BrE) ▶ PEDIATRIC etc

paedophile n (BrE) ▶ PEDOPHILE

pagan¹ /'peɪgən/ n pagano, -na m,f

pagan² adj pagano

page¹ /peɪdʒ/ n **1** (of book, newspaper) página f; **on ~ four** en la página cuatro **2** (attendant) paje m; (in hotel) botones m

page² vt (over loudspeaker) llamar por megafonía; (by beeper) llamar por buscapersonas or (Méx) bip or (Chi) bíper

pageant /'pædʒənt/ n (a) (show, ceremony) festividades fpl (b) (historical show) espectáculo histórico al aire libre

pageboy /'peɪdʒbɔɪ/ n ▶ PAGE¹ 2

pager /'peɪdʒər ‖'peɪdʒə(r)/ n buscapersonas m, bip m (Méx), bíper m (Chi)

paid¹ /peɪd/ past & past p of PAY¹

paid² adj ⟨employment⟩ remunerado; ⟨worker⟩ asalariado; ⟨vacation⟩ pagado; ⟨leave⟩ con goce de sueldo

pail /peɪl/ n balde m, cubo m (Esp), cubeta f (Méx)

pain /peɪn/ n **1** (a) (physical) dolor m; **she was in great ~** estaba muy dolorida or (AmL tb) adolorida; **to be a ~ in the neck** ser* un pesado (b) (annoying person or thing) (colloq) lata f (fam) **2** **pains** pl (effort): **that's all you get for your ~s** así te pagan la molestia; **I went to great ~s to explain it to them carefully** puse mucho esmero en explicárselo

painful /'peɪnfəl/ adj (a) (physically) doloroso; **it's very ~** duele mucho (b) (mentally) ⟨task⟩ desagradable; ⟨reminder⟩ doloroso

painfully /ˈpeɪnfəli/ *adv*: she dragged herself ∼ along se iba arrastrando con mucho dolor; she's ∼ shy es tan tímida que da pena

painkiller /ˈpeɪnˌkɪlər ‖ ˈpeɪnˌkɪlə(r)/ *n* analgésico *m*

painless /ˈpeɪnləs ‖ ˈpeɪnlɪs/ *adj* **(a)** (causing no pain) indoloro; ∼ **childbirth** parto *m* sin dolor **(b)** (easy, pleasant) ‹colloq› ‹*method*› sencillo

painstaking /ˈpeɪnzˌteɪkɪŋ/ *adj* ‹*research/ efforts*› concienzudo; ‹*person/personality*› meticuloso

paint¹ /peɪnt/ *n* pintura *f*

paint² *vt/i* pintar

paint: ∼**box** *n* caja *f* de acuarelas; ∼**brush** *n* pincel *m*; (large, for walls) brocha *f*

painter /ˈpeɪntər ‖ ˈpeɪntə(r)/ *n* (Art, Const) pintor, -tora *m,f*

painting /ˈpeɪntɪŋ/ *n* **(a)** (picture) cuadro *m*, pintura *f* **(b)** (Art) pintura *f*

paintwork /ˈpeɪntwɜːrk ‖ ˈpeɪntwɜːk/ *n* pintura *f*

pair /per ‖ peə(r)/ *n* **1 (a)** (of shoes, socks, gloves) par *m*; a ∼ of trousers unos pantalones; a ∼ of scissors unas tijeras **(b)** (in cards) pareja *f*, par *m* **2** (couple) pareja *f*
∎ **pair up** [*v + adv*] formar parejas

pajamas, (BrE) **pyjamas** /pəˈdʒɑːməz/ *pl n* pijama *m*, piyama *m* or *f* (AmL)

Pakistan /ˈpækɪstæn ‖ ˌpɑːkɪˈstɑːn, ˌpækɪ-/ *n* Pakistán *m*, Paquistán *m*

Pakistani¹ /ˈpækɪstæni ‖ ˌpɑːkɪˈstɑːni, ˌpækɪ-/ *adj* pakistaní, paquistaní

Pakistani² *n* pakistaní *mf*, paquistaní *mf*

pal /pæl/ *n* ‹colloq› amigo *m*, compinche *m* (fam), cuate *m* (Méx fam)

palace /ˈpæləs ‖ ˈpælɪs/ *n* palacio *m*

palatable /ˈpælətəbəl/ *adj* agradable

palate /ˈpælət/ *n* paladar *m*

pale¹ /peɪl/ *adj* **(a)** ‹*skin/person*› (naturally) blanco; (pallid) pálido **(b)** ‹*blue/pink*› pálido

pale² *vi* **(a)** «*person*» palidecer* **(b)** (seem minor) to ∼ BESIDE *o* BEFORE sb/sth palidecer* JUNTO A algn/algo

pale³ *n*: to be beyond the ∼ ser* intolerable

Palestine /ˈpæləstaɪn/ *n* Palestina *f*

Palestinian¹ /ˈpæləˈstɪniən/ *adj* palestino

Palestinian² *n* palestino, -na *m,f*

palette /ˈpælət ‖ ˈpælɪt/ *n* paleta *f*

pall¹ /pɔːl/ *n*: to cast a ∼ on *o* over sth empañar algo

pall² *vi* hacerse* pesado

pallid /ˈpæləd ‖ ˈpælɪd/ *adj* pálido

palm /pɑːm/ *n* **1 (a)** ∼ (**tree**) palmera *f* **(b)** (leaf, branch) palma *f* **2** (Anat) palma *f*
∎ **palm off** [*v + o + adv*] to ∼ sth off ON *o* ONTO sb encajarle algo a algn (fam); to ∼ sb off WITH sth quitarse a algn de encima CON algo

palmistry /ˈpɑːməstri ‖ ˈpɑːmɪstri/ *n* quiromancia *f*

Palm Sunday *n* Domingo *m* de Ramos

palpable /ˈpælpəbəl/ *adj* ‹frml› palmario, palpable

palpitate /ˈpælpəteɪt ‖ ˈpælpɪteɪt/ *vi* palpitar

palpitation /ˌpælpəˈteɪʃən ‖ ˌpælpɪˈteɪʃən/ *n* (Med) palpitación *f*

paltry /ˈpɔːltri/ *adj* **-trier -triest** ‹*sum/ amount*› mísero; ‹*excuse*› malo

pamper /ˈpæmpər ‖ ˈpæmpə(r)/ *vt* mimar

pamphlet /ˈpæmflət ‖ ˈpæmflɪt/ *n* (informative) folleto *m*; (political) panfleto *m*

pan¹ /pæn/ *n* **1** (Culin) cacerola *f*, (large, with two handles) olla *f*, (small) cacerola *f*, cazo *m* (Esp); (frying ∼) sartén *f* **2** (of toilet) (BrE) taza *f*

pan² *vi* **-nn-** **1** (Min): to ∼ for gold lavar oro **2** (Cin): the camera ∼s across to the two figures la cámara recorre hasta enfocar en las dos figuras

panacea /ˌpænəˈsiːə/ *n* ‹frml› panacea *f*

panache /pəˈnæʃ/ *n* garbo *m*

Panama /ˈpænəmɑː/ *n* Panamá *m*; ‹before *n*› the ∼ Canal el Canal de Panamá

Panamanian¹ /ˈpænəˈmeɪniən/ *adj* panameño

Panamanian² *n* panameño, -ña *m,f*

pancake /ˈpænkeɪk/ *n* (Culin) crep(e) *m*, panqueque *m* (AmL), crepa *f* (Méx), panqué *m* (AmC, Col), panqueca *f* (Ven)

pancreas /ˈpæŋkriəs/ *n* páncreas *m*

panda /ˈpændə/ *n* (oso, osa *m,f*) panda *mf*

pandemonium /ˌpændəˈməʊniəm/ *n* pandemonio *m*, pandemónium *m*

pander /ˈpændər ‖ ˈpændə(r)/ *vi*: to ∼ to sb's whims consentirle* los caprichos a algn

pane /peɪn/ *n* (hoja *f* de) vidrio *m*, cristal *m* (Esp)

panel¹ /ˈpænl̩/ *n* **1 (a)** (of door, car body, plane wing) panel *m*; (of garment) pieza *f* **(b)** (instrument ∼) tablero *m* (de instrumentos); (control ∼) tablero *m* (de control) **2** (in discussion, interview) panel *m* or (Col, Ven) pánel *m*; (in quiz, contest) equipo *m*; (in exam) mesa *f*, comisión *f* (Chi)

panel² *vt*, (BrE) **-ll-** **(a)** ‹*room/wall*› revestir* con paneles **(b) paneled**, (BrE) **panelled** *past p* ‹*door*› de paneles

pang /pæŋ/ *n* punzada *f*; ∼s of hunger retorcijones *mpl or* (Esp) retortijones *mpl* de hambre

panhandler /ˈpænˌhændlər ‖ ˈpænˌhændlə(r)/ *n* (AmE colloq) mendigo *m*

panic¹ /ˈpænɪk/ *n* (fear, anxiety) pánico *m*; ‹before *n*› ∼ button botón *m* de alarma

panic² *vi* **-ck-** dejarse llevar por el pánico; don't ∼! ¡tranquilo!

panicky /ˈpænɪki/ *adj* ‹*person*› muy nervioso; ‹*behavior/decision*› precipitado

panic-stricken /ˈpænɪkˌstrɪkən/ *adj* aterrorizado

pannier /ˈpæniər ‖ ˈpæniə(r)/ *n* alforja *f*; (on cycle) maletero *m*

panorama /ˌpænəˈræmə ‖ ˌpænəˈrɑːmə/ *n* panorama *m*

panoramic /ˌpænəˈræmɪk/ *adj* panorámico

pansy /ˈpænzi/ *n* (*pl* **-sies**) (Bot) pensamiento *m*

pant¹ /pænt/ *vi* jadear

pant² *n* jadeo *m*; see also PANTS

pantheon /ˈpænθiːɑːn ‖ ˈpænθiən/ *n* panteón *m*

panther /ˈpænθər ‖ ˈpænθə(r)/ *n* pantera *f*

panties /ˈpæntiz/ *pl n* calzones *mpl* (AmL), bragas *fpl* (Esp), pantaletas *fpl* (Méx, Ven), bombacha *f* (RPl), calzoneta *f* (AmC)

pantihose /'pæntihəʊz/ *pl n* ▸ PANTYHOSE

pantomime /'pæntəmaɪm/ *n* **(a)** (mime) pantomima *f* **(b)** (in UK) *comedia musical navideña, basada en cuentos de hadas*

pantry /'pæntri/ *n* (*pl* **-tries**) despensa *f*

pants /pænts/ *pl n* [1] (trousers) (AmE) pantalón *m*, pantalones *mpl* **(b)** (underwear) (BrE) **(a)** (men's) calzoncillos *mpl*, calzones *mpl* (Méx), interiores *mpl* (Col, Ven) **(b)** (women's) ▸ PANTIES

pantsuit /'pæntsu:t/, **pants suit** *n* (AmE) traje *m* pantalón

pantyhose /'pæntihəʊz/ *pl n* (AmE) medias *fpl*, pantimedias *fpl* (Méx), medias *fpl* bombacha (RPl) *or* (Col) pantalón *or* (Ven) panty

papa *n* **(a)** /'pɑːpə/ (AmE) papá *m* **(b)** /pə'pɑː/ (BrE dated) padre *m* (ant)

paper[1] /'peɪpər ‖ 'peɪpə(r)/ *n* [1] **(a)** (material) papel *m*; (*before n*) ⟨*towel/handkerchief/bag*⟩ de papel **(b)** (wrapper) (esp BrE) envoltorio *m* [2] (newspaper) diario *m*, periódico *m* [3] (for journal) trabajo *m*; (at conference) ponencia *f* [4] (exam ⟨∼⟩) (BrE) examen *m*; (part) parte *f* [5] **papers** *pl* (documents) documentos *mpl*

paper[2] *vt* ⟨*wall/room*⟩ empapelar *or* (Méx tb) tapizar*

paper: **∼back** *n* libro *m* en rústica *or* (Méx) de pasta blanda; **∼clip** *n* clip *m*, sujetapapeles *m*; **∼weight** *n* pisapapeles *m*; **∼work** *n* papeleo *m* (fam), trabajo *m* administrativo

paprika /pə'priːkə ‖ 'pæprɪkə/ *n* pimentón *m* dulce, paprika *f*

Pap smear, Pap test /pæp/ *n* (AmE) citología *f*, frotis *m*, Papanicolau *m* (AmL)

Papua New Guinea /'pɑːpuə ‖ 'pæpjʊə/ *n* Papua Nueva Guinea *f*

papyrus /pə'paɪrəs/ *n* (*pl* **-ruses** *or* **-ri** /-raɪ/) papiro *m*

par /pɑːr ‖ pɑː(r)/ *n* [1] **(a)** (equal level) on a ∼: the two athletes are on a ∼ los dos atletas son del mismo nivel; this puts us on a ∼ with workers in other countries esto nos pone en igualdad de condiciones con los trabajadores de otros países **(b)** (accepted standard): your work is below *o* not up to ∼ tu trabajo no está a la altura de lo que se esperaba; to feel below *o* under∼ no sentirse* del todo bien [2] (in golf) par *m*

parable /'pærəbəl/ *n* parábola *f*

parachute[1] /'pærəʃuːt/ *n* paracaídas *m*

parachute[2] *vi* saltar en *or* con paracaídas

parachutist /'pærəʃuːtəst ‖ 'pærəʃuːtɪst/ *n* paracaidista *mf*

parade[1] /pə'reɪd/ *n* **(a)** (procession) desfile *m* **(b)** (assembly) (Mil) formación *f*

parade[2] *vt* **(a)** (display) ⟨*wealth*⟩ hacer* ostentación de **(b)** (march, walk) ⟨*streets*⟩ desfilar por **(c)** (assemble) ⟨*troops*⟩ hacer* formar
■ ∼ *vi* **(a)** (march, walk) desfilar **(b)** (assemble) (Mil) formar

paradise /'pærədaɪs/ *n* **(a)** (heaven) paraíso *m* **(b)** **Paradise** (Garden of Eden) Paraíso *m* (Terrenal)

paradox /'pærədɑːks ‖ 'pærədɒks/ *n* paradoja *f*

paraffin /'pærəfən ‖ 'pærəfɪn/ *n* **(a)** ∼ (wax) parafina *f* **(b)** ∼ (oil) (BrE) queroseno *m*, kerosene *m*, parafina *f* (Chi)

paragliding /'pærə,glaɪdɪŋ/ *n* parapente *m*

paragon /'pærəgɑːn ‖ 'pærəgən/ *n*: a ∼ of virtue (set phrase) un dechado de virtudes (fr hecha)

paragraph /'pærəgræf ‖ 'pærəgrɑːf/ *n* párrafo *m*

Paraguay /'pærəgwaɪ/ *n* Paraguay *m*

Paraguayan[1] /'pærə'gwaɪən/ *adj* paraguayo

Paraguayan[2] *n* paraguayo, -ya *m,f*

parallel[1] /'pærəlel/ *adj* paralelo

parallel[2] *n* [1] (Math) (line) paralela *f* [2] (similarity) paralelismo *m*, paralelo *m*; without ∼ sin parangón

parallel[3] *vt* **-l-** *or* (BrE also) **-ll-** (fml) ser* análogo *or* paralelo a

parallel bars *pl n* (barras *fpl*) paralelas *fpl*

paralysis /pə'ræləsəs ‖ pə'ræləsɪs/ *n* (*pl* **-ses** /-siːz/)(Med) parálisis *f*

paralyze /'pærəlaɪz/ *vt* paralizar*

paramedic /'pærə'medɪk/ *n*: *profesional conectado con la medicina, como enfermero, kinesiólogo etc*

parameter /pə'ræmətər ‖ pə'ræmɪtə(r)/ *n* parámetro *m*

paramilitary /'pærə'mɪləteri ‖ ,pærə'mɪlɪtəri/ *adj* paramilitar

paramount /'pærəmaʊnt/ *adj* (fml) primordial

paranoia /'pærə'nɔɪə/ *n* paranoia *f*

paranoid /'pærənɔɪd/ *adj* paranoico

parapet /'pærəpət ‖ 'pærəpɪt/ *n* parapeto *m*

paraphernalia /'pærəfər'neɪljə ‖ ,pærəfə'neɪliə/ *n* parafernalia *f*

paraphrase /'pærəfreɪz/ *vt* parafrasear

paraplegic /,pærə'pliːdʒɪk/ *n* parapléjico, -ca *m,f*

parasailing /'pærəseɪlɪŋ/ *n* parasailing *m*

parasite /'pærəsaɪt/ *n* parásito *m*

parasol /'pærəsɔːl ‖ 'pærəsɒl/ *n* sombrilla *f*, quitasol *m*

paratrooper /'pærə,truːpər ‖ 'pærə,truːpə(r)/ *n* (Mil) paracaidista *mf* (*del ejército*)

parcel /'pɑːrsəl ‖ 'pɑːsəl/ *n* (BrE) paquete *m*

parched /pɑːrtʃt ‖ pɑːtʃt/ *adj* **(a)** (very dry) reseco *f* **(b)** (very thirsty) (colloq) (*pred*) muerto de sed (fam)

parchment /'pɑːrtʃmənt ‖ 'pɑːtʃmənt/ *n* pergamino *m*

pardon[1] /'pɑːrdn ‖ 'pɑːdn/ *n* [1] **(a)** (forgiveness) perdón *m* **(b)** (*as interj*): ∼? *o* (fml) I beg your ∼? (requesting repetition) ¿cómo?, ¿mande? (Méx); I beg your ∼ (apologizing) perdón [2] (Law) indulto *m*

pardon[2] *vt* [1] (forgive) perdonar*; ∼ me! (apologizing) ¡perdón!; ∼ me? (requesting repetition) (esp AmE) ¿cómo? [2] (Law) ⟨*offender*⟩ indultar

pare /per ‖ peə(r)/ *vt* **(a)** (peel) pelar **(b)** ⟨*nails*⟩ cortar

---

AmC	América Central	Arg	Argentina	Cu	Cuba	Per	Perú
AmL	América Latina	Bol	Bolivia	Ec	Ecuador	RPl	Río de la Plata
AmS	América del Sur	Chi	Chile	Esp	España	Ur	Uruguay
Andes	Región andina	CS	Cono Sur	Méx	México	Ven	Venezuela

■ **pare down** [*v* + *o* + *adv, v* + *adv* + *o*] reducir*

parent /ˈpeərənt ‖ˈpeərənt/ *n*: **my/his** ~**s** mis/sus padres; **the responsibility of being a** ~ las responsabilidades que conlleva el ser padre/madre; (*before n*) ~ **company** sociedad *f* matriz

parental /pəˈrentl/ *adj* de los padres

parenthesis /pəˈrenθəsəs ‖pəˈrenθəsɪs/ *n* (*pl* **-theses** /-θəsiːz/) paréntesis *m*; **in parentheses** entre paréntesis

parenthood /ˈperənθʊd ‖ˈpeərənθʊd/ *n* el ser padre/madre

parenting /ˈperəntɪŋ ‖ˈpeərəntɪŋ/ *n* crianza *f* de los hijos

Paris /ˈpærəs ‖ˈpærɪs/ *n* París *m*

parish /ˈpærɪʃ/ *n* 1 (Relig) parroquia *f*; (*before n*) ~ **church** parroquia *f*, iglesia *f* parroquial 2 (Govt) distrito *m*

parishioner /pəˈrɪʃənər ‖pəˈrɪʃənə(r)/ *n* feligrés, -gresa *m,f* (*de una parroquia*)

Parisian /pəˈrɪʒən ‖pəˈrɪzɪən/ *n* parisino, -na *m,f*, parisiense *mf*, parisién *mf*

parity /ˈpærəti/ *n*(equality) (frml) igualdad *f*, paridad *f*

park¹ /pɑːrk ‖pɑːk/ *n* parque *m*; (*before n*) ~ **bench** banco *m or* (Méx) banca *f* (de plaza)

park² *vt* ⟨*car*⟩ estacionar (esp AmL), aparcar* (Esp), parquear (AmL)
■ ~ *vi* (Auto) estacionar (esp AmL), aparcar* (Esp), parquear (AmL), estacionarse (Chi, Méx)

parking /ˈpɑːrkɪŋ ‖ˈpɑːkɪŋ/ *n* estacionamiento *m* (esp AmL), aparcamiento *m* (Esp); ❾ **no parking** prohibido estacionar (esp AmL) *or* (Esp) aparcar *or* (AmL) parquear; (*before n*) ~ **place** *o* **space** un lugar para estacionar (*or* aparcar *etc*); ~ **ticket** multa *f* (por estacionamiento indebido)

parking: ~ **garage** *n* (AmE) estacionamiento *m* (esp AmL), aparcamiento *m* (Esp), parking *m* (Esp); ~ **lot** *n* (AmE) estacionamiento *m* (esp AmL), aparcamiento *m* (Esp), parking *m* (Esp), parqueadero *m* (Col); ~ **meter** *n* parquímetro *m*

Parkinson's Disease /ˈpɑːrkənsənz ‖ˈpɑːkɪnsənz/ *n* enfermedad *f* de Parkinson, Parkinson *m*

parkway /ˈpɑːrkweɪ ‖ˈpɑːkweɪ/ *n* (AmE) carretera *f*/avenida *f* ajardinada

parliament /ˈpɑːrləmənt ‖ˈpɑːləmənt/ *n* (a) (assembly) parlamento *m* (b) **Parliament** (in UK etc) Parlamento *m*

parliamentary /ˌpɑːrləˈmentəri ‖ˌpɑːləˈmentri/ *adj* parlamentario

parlor, (BrE) **parlour** /ˈpɑːrlər ‖ˈpɑːlə(r)/ *n* 1 (dated in BrE) (in house) salón *m* (esp Esp), sala *f* (de estar) 2 (for business) (AmE) sala *f*; **ice-cream** ~ heladería *f*

Parmesan (cheese) /ˈpɑːrməzɑːn ‖ˈpɑːmɪzæn/ *n* (queso *m*) parmesano *m*

parochial /pəˈrəʊkiəl/ *adj* (a) (pej) ⟨*person/attitude/outlook*⟩ provinciano (b) (Relig) parroquial

parody¹ /ˈpærədi/ *n* (*pl* **-dies**) parodia *f*

parody² *vt* **-dies, -dying, -died** parodiar

parole /pəˈrəʊl/ *n* libertad *f* condicional

paroxysm /ˈpærəksɪzəm/ *n* (Med) paroxismo *m*; **the news sent them into** ~**s** **of laughter** la noticia los hizo desternillarse de risa

parquet /pɑːrˈkeɪ ‖ˈpɑːkeɪ/ *n* 1 (Const) parqué *m*, parquet *m* 2 (AmE Theat) platea *f*

parrot /ˈpærət/ *n* loro *m*, papagayo *m*

parry /ˈpæri/ *vt* **-ries, -rying, -ried** ⟨*blow/thrust*⟩ parar; ⟨*attack*⟩ rechazar*; ⟨*question*⟩ eludir

parsley /ˈpɑːrsli ‖ˈpɑːsli/ *n* perejil *m*

parsnip /ˈpɑːrsnəp ‖ˈpɑːsnɪp/ *n* chirivía *f*, pastinaca *f*

parson /ˈpɑːrsn ‖ˈpɑːsn/ *n* clérigo *m*; (vicar) ≈(cura *m*) párroco *m*

part¹ /pɑːrt ‖pɑːt/ *n* 1 (a) (section) parte *f* (b) (in phrases) **in part** en parte; **for the most part** en su mayor parte; **for my part** por mi parte, por mi lado 2 (component) pieza *f*; (spare ~) repuesto *m or* (Méx) refacción *f* 3 (a) (in play) papel *m* (b) (role, share) papel *m*; **she had** *o* **played a major** ~ **in ...** tuvo *or* desempeñó un papel fundamental en ...; **to take** ~ **in sth** tomar parte en algo 4 (episode of TV, radio serial) episodio *m*; (Publ) fascículo *m* 5 (Mus) (vocal, instrumental line) parte *f* 6 (in hair) (AmE) raya *f*, carrera *f* (Col, Ven), partidura *f* (Chi) 7 **parts** *pl* (area): **in/around these** ~**s** por aquí; **in foreign** ~**s** en el extranjero

part² *vt* (separate) separar
■ ~ *vi* (a) (separate) ⟨*lovers*⟩ separarse; **they** ~**ed on bad terms** quedaron disgustados (b) ⟨*curtains/lips*⟩ (open up) abrirse*
■ **part with** [*v* + *prep* + *o*] desprenderse de

part³ *adv* en parte

part⁴ *adj* (before n) ⟨*payment*⟩ parcial

part exchange *n* (esp BrE): **in** ~ ~ a cuenta *or* como parte del pago

partial /ˈpɑːrʃəl ‖ˈpɑːʃəl/ *adj* 1 (not complete) parcial 2 (a) (fond) (*pred*) **to be** ~ **to sth** tener* debilidad POR algo (b) (biased) (frml) parcial

partially /ˈpɑːrʃəli ‖ˈpɑːʃəli/ *adv* (a) (partly) parcialmente (b) (with bias) con parcialidad

participant /pərˈtɪsəpənt, pɑːr- ‖pɑːˈtɪsɪpənt/ *n* participante *mf*

participate /pərˈtɪsəpeɪt, pɑːr- ‖pɑːˈtɪsɪpeɪt/ *vi* **to** ~ (IN sth) participar (EN algo)

participation /pərˌtɪsəˈpeɪʃən, pɑːr- ‖pɑːˌtɪsɪˈpeɪʃən/ *n* participación *f*

participle /ˈpɑːrtəsɪpəl ‖ˈpɑːtɪsɪpəl/ *n* participio *m*

particle /ˈpɑːrtɪkəl ‖ˈpɑːtɪkəl/ *n* partícula *f*

particular¹ /pərˈtɪkjələr ‖pəˈtɪkjʊlə(r)/ *adj* 1 (specific, precise): **this** ~ **one** este en especial; **is there any** ~ **style you'd prefer?** ¿tiene preferencia por algún estilo determinado?; **for no** ~ **reason** por nada en especial 2 (special) ⟨*interest/concern*⟩ especial 3 (fastidious) (*pred*) **to be** ~ (ABOUT sth): **she's very** ~ **about what she eats** es muy especial con la comida

particular² *n* (a) (detail) (frml) (*usu pl*) detalle *m* 2 **in particular** en particular

particularly /pərˈtɪkjələrli ‖pəˈtɪkjʊləli/ *adv* (a) (specifically) específicamente (b) (especially) particularmente

parting¹ /'pɑːrtɪŋ ‖'pɑːtɪŋ/ n **1** (separation) despedida f **2** (in hair) (BrE) raya f, carrera f (Col, Ven), partidura f (Chi)

parting² adj (before n) ⟨kiss/words⟩ de despedida

partisan¹ /'pɑːrtəzən ‖'pɑːtɪzæn/ n **(a)** (guerrilla) partisano, -na m,f **(b)** (supporter) partidario, -ria m,f

partisan² adj ⟨crowd/decision⟩ partidista

partition¹ /pər'tɪʃən, pɑːr- ‖pɑː'tɪʃən/ n **1** **(a)** (screen) tabique m; **a glass ~** una mampara de vidrio or (Esp) de cristal **(b)** (divider) separador m **2** (of country, territory) división f

partition² vt **(a)** ⟨country/territory⟩ dividir **(b)** ⟨room⟩ dividir con un tabique/con una mampara

partly /'pɑːrtli ‖'pɑːtli/ adv en parte

partner¹ /'pɑːrtnər ‖'pɑːtnə(r)/ n **(a)** (in an activity) compañero, -ra m,f; (in dancing, tennis) pareja f **(b)** (Busn) socio, -cia m,f; **~s in crime** cómplices mpl or fpl **(c)** (in personal relationship) pareja f, compañero, -ra m,f

partner² vt bailar (or jugar* etc) en pareja con

partnership /'pɑːrtnərʃɪp ‖'pɑːtnəʃɪp/ n **(a)** (relationship) asociación f **(b)** (Busn) sociedad f (colectiva)

part of speech n (pl ~s ~ ~) categoría f gramatical

partridge /'pɑːrtrɪdʒ ‖'pɑːtrɪdʒ/ n (pl ~s or ~) perdiz f

part-time¹ /'pɑːrt'taɪm ‖,pɑː't'taɪm/ adj de medio tiempo (AmL), a tiempo parcial (Esp)

part-time² adv de medio tiempo (AmL), a tiempo parcial (Esp)

party¹ /'pɑːrti ‖'pɑːti/ n **1** (event) fiesta f; **I was invited to a tea ~** me invitaron a un té **2** (Pol) partido m **3** (group) grupo m; (in hunting) partida f **4** (person or body involved) parte f; **the guilty/innocent ~** el culpable/inocente

party² vi (esp AmE colloq) (to go to parties) ir* a fiestas; (have fun) divertirse*

party line n (Pol) **the ~ ~** la línea del partido

pass¹ /pæs ‖pɑːs/ n **1** (document, permit) pase m; (ticket) abono m **2** (Geog) paso m; (narrow) desfiladero m **3** (in test, examination) (BrE) aprobado m **4** (Sport) pase m **5** (sexual advance): **to make a ~ at sb** intentar besar a algn

pass² vt

I 1 (a) (go by, past) ⟨shop/house⟩ pasar por; **I ~ed him in the street** me crucé con él en la calle **(b)** (overtake) rebasar (Méx) **2 (a)** (cross, go beyond) ⟨limit⟩ pasar; ⟨frontier⟩ pasar, cruzar* **(b)** (surpass) sobrepasar **3** (spend) ⟨time⟩ pasar; **to ~ the time** pasar el rato

II (a) (convey, hand over) **to ~ sb sth, to ~ sth TO sb** pasarle algo A algn **(b)** (Sport) ⟨ball⟩ pasar

III (a) (succeed in) ⟨exam/test⟩ aprobar*, salvar (Ur) **(b)** (approve) ⟨candidate/work⟩ aprobar* **(c)** ⟨law/motion⟩ aprobar*

■ **~** vi

I 1 (move, travel) pasar **2 (a)** (go, move past) pasar; **I was just ~ing** pasaba por aquí; **they ~ed on the stairs** se cruzaron en la escalera **(b)** (overtake) adelantarse, rebasar (Méx) **3 (a)** (elapse) «time» pasar **(b)** (disappear) «feeling/pain» pasarse

4 (be transferred) «title/estate/crown» pasar **5** (decline chance to play) pasar; (as interj) ¡paso! **6** (Sport) **to ~ (TO sb)** pasar(le) la pelota (or el balón etc) (A algn)

II (a) (be acceptable) pasar **(b)** (in an exam) aprobar*

■ **pass away** [v + adv] (frml & euph) fallecer* (frml)

■ **pass by 1** [v + adv] (go past) pasar **2** [v + o + adv] (not affect): **he felt life had ~ed him by** sentía que no había vivido

■ **pass down** [v + o + adv, v + adv + o] (often pass) ⟨heirloom⟩ pasar; ⟨story/tradition⟩ transmitir

■ **pass for** [v + prep + o] pasar por

■ **pass off** [v + o + adv, v + adv + o] (represent falsely) hacer* pasar; **she ~ed herself off as a journalist** se hizo pasar por periodista

■ **pass on 1** [v + o + adv, v + adv + o] ⟨information⟩ pasar; ⟨infection⟩ contagiar **2** [v + adv] **(a) to ~ on TO sth** pasar A algo **(b)** ▶ PASS AWAY **1**

■ **pass out 1** [v + adv] (become unconscious) desmayarse, perder* el conocimiento **2** [v + o + adv, v + adv + o] (distribute) repartir

■ **pass over 1** [v + adv + o] (omit) ⟨fact/detail⟩ pasar por alto **2** [v + o + adv] (disregard for promotion) (usu pass) pasarle por encima a

■ **pass through (a)** [v + adv] pasar; **we're just ~ing through** estamos solo de paso **(b)** [v + prep + o] ⟨town/area⟩ pasar por

■ **pass up** [v + o + adv, v + adv + o] (colloq) ⟨opportunity⟩ dejar pasar

passable /'pæsəbəl ‖'pɑːsəbəl/ adj **(a)** (adequate) pasable **(b)** ⟨road/route⟩ transitable

passage /'pæsɪdʒ/ n **1 (a)** (alleyway) callejón m, pasaje m; (narrow) pasadizo m **(b)** (corridor) (esp BrE) pasillo m **(c)** (Anat) conducto m **2** (lapse): **the ~ of time** el paso del tiempo **3** (voyage) viaje m; (fare) pasaje m **4** (extract) pasaje m

passageway /'pæsɪdʒweɪ/ n pasillo m

passenger /'pæsɪndʒər ‖'pæsɪndʒə(r)/ n pasajero, -ra m,f

passer-by /'pæsər'baɪ ‖,pɑːsə'baɪ/ n (pl **passers-by**) transeúnte mf

passing¹ /'pæsɪŋ ‖'pɑːsɪŋ/ adj (before n) **1** (going past): **she hailed a ~ taxi** llamó a un taxi que pasaba **2 (a)** ⟨fad/fashion⟩ pasajero; ⟨glance⟩ rápido **(b)** (casual): **it was only a ~ thought** simplemente fue algo que se me ocurrió

passing² n **in passing** al pasar, de pasada

passing lane n (AmE) carril m de adelantamiento

passion /'pæʃən/ n pasión f

passionate /'pæʃənət/ adj ⟨love⟩ apasionado; ⟨hatred⟩ mortal; ⟨admirer⟩ ardiente; ⟨speech⟩ vehemente

passionately /'pæʃənətli/ adv ⟨love⟩ apasionadamente; ⟨believe⟩ fervientemente; ⟨desire⟩ ardientemente

passion fruit n granadilla f, maracuyá m, parchita f (Ven)

passive¹ /'pæsɪv/ adj pasivo

passive² n voz f pasiva

pass: ~ key n llave f maestra; **P~over** n

Pascua f (*judía*); ~**port** n pasaporte m; ~**word** n (a) (secret word or phrase) contraseña f (b) (Comput) clave f de acceso

past¹ /pæst ‖pɑːst/ adj 1 (a) (former) anterior; ⟨*life*⟩ pasado; (old) antiguo (b) (most recent) ⟨*week/ month/year*⟩ último (c) (finished, gone) (pred): what's ~ **is** ~ lo pasado, pasado 2 (Ling): **the** ~ **tense** el pasado, el pretérito

past² n 1 (a) (former times) pasado m; **steam trains are a thing of the** ~ las locomotoras de vapor han pasado a la historia; **in the** ~, **women … antes** *or* antiguamente las mujeres …; **that's all in the** ~ eso forma parte del pasado (b) (of person) pasado m; (of place) historia f 2 (Ling) pasado m, pretérito m

past³ prep 1 (a) (by the side of): **I go** ~ **their house every morning** paso por (delante de) su casa todas las mañanas; **she walked straight** ~ **him** pasó de largo por su lado (b) (beyond): **it's just** ~ **the school** queda un poco más allá de la escuela
2 (a) (after) (esp BrE): **it's ten** ~ **six/half** ~ **two** son las seis y diez/las dos y media; **it was** ~ **eleven** eran las once pasadas; **it's** ~ **your bedtime** ya deberías estar acostado (b) (older than): **I'm** ~ **the age/stage when …** ya he pasado la edad/ superado la etapa en que …
3 (outside, beyond): **to be** ~ **-ING**: **I'm** ~ **caring** ya no me importa; **I wouldn't put it** ~ **her** no me extrañaría que lo hiciera; **to be** ~ **it** (colloq) estar* para el arrastre (fam)

past⁴ adv (a) (with verbs of motion): **to fly/cycle/ drive** ~ pasar volando/en bicicleta/en coche; **he hurried** ~ pasó a toda prisa (b) (giving time) (esp BrE): **it's twenty-five** ~ son y veinticinco

pasta /'pɑːstə ‖'pæstə/ n pasta(s) f(*pl*)

paste /peɪst/ n (a) (thick mixture) pasta f (b) (glue) engrudo m; (wallpaper ~) pegamento m, cola f (c) (imitation gem) estrás m

pastel /pæs'tel ‖'pæstl/ n (a) (Art) (crayon) pastel m (b) (pale shade) tono m pastel; (before n) ⟨*shades/color*⟩ pastel adj inv

pasteurize /'pæstʃəraɪz ‖'pɑːstʃəraɪz/ vt pasteurizar*, pasterizar*

pastille /pæs'tiːl ‖'pæstl/ n pastilla f

pastime /'pæstaɪm ‖'pɑːstaɪm/ n pasatiempo m

pastor /'pæstər ‖'pɑːstə(r)/ n pastor, -tora m,f

pastoral /'pæstərəl ‖'pɑːstərəl/ adj (a) ⟨*painting/scene*⟩ pastoril (b) (Relig) ⟨*care/duties*⟩ pastoral

pastry /'peɪstri/ n (*pl* **-tries**) (a) (substance) masa f (b) (cake) pastelito m *or* (RPl) masa f

pasture¹ /'pæstʃər ‖'pɑːstʃə(r)/ n (a) (grazing land) pastos mpl (b) (grass) pasto m, pastura f

pasture² vt apacentar*, pastar

pasty /'pæsti/ n (*pl* **-ties**) (esp BrE) empanada f (AmL), empanadilla f (Esp)

pat¹ /pæt/ vt **-tt-** darle* palmaditas a

pat² n 1 (tap) palmadita f; (touch) toque m 2 (of butter) porción f

pat³ adj (pej) ⟨*answer*⟩ fácil

pat⁴ adv (by heart): **to have** *o* **know sth down** (AmE) *o* (BrE) **off** ~ saberse* algo al dedillo

patch¹ /pætʃ/ n 1 (a) (for mending clothes) remiendo m, parche m; (for reinforcing) refuerzo m;

(on knee) rodillera f; (on elbow) codera f (b) (eye ~) parche m (*en el ojo*) 2 (a) (damaged area): **she slipped on a** ~ **of ice/oil** resbaló en el hielo/en una mancha de aceite; **a damp** ~ una mancha de humedad; **to go through a bad** *o* **rough** *o* **sticky** ~ (BrE) pasar por una mala racha (b) (of land): **a** ~ **of ground** un área de terreno; **a vegetable** ~ un huerto (c) (territory) (BrE colloq): **my/his** ~ mi/su territorio

patch² vt remendar*, parchar (esp AmL)

■ **patch up** [v + o + adv, v + adv + o] (a) (mend) ⟨*roof/furniture*⟩ hacerle* un arreglo a (*provisionalmente*); ⟨*clothes*⟩ remendar*, parchar (esp AmL); ⟨*hole*⟩ ponerle* un parche a (b) (resolve, settle): **I tried to help** ~ **things up betweem them** quise ayudar para que hicieran las paces

patchwork /'pætʃwɜːrk ‖'pætʃwɜːk/ n patchwork m, labor f de retazos *or* (Esp) retales; (before n) ⟨*quilt*⟩ de patchwork, de retazos *or* (Esp) retales

patchy /'pætʃi/ adj **-chier, -chiest** ⟨*paintwork/color*⟩ disparejo; ⟨*coverage*⟩ incompleto; ⟨*description*⟩ fragmentario; ⟨*performance/work*⟩ irregular; ~ **fog** zonas fpl de niebla

pâté /pɑː'teɪ ‖'pæteɪ/ n paté m

patent¹ /'pætnt ‖'peɪtnt, 'pætnt/ n patente f

patent² /'pætnt ‖'peɪtnt, 'pætnt/ vt patentar

patent³ adj /'peɪtnt, 'pæt- ‖'peɪtnt/ (frml) patente

patent leather /'pætnt ‖'peɪtnt, 'pæt-/ n charol m

patently /'peɪtntli, 'pæt- ‖'peɪtntli/ adv: **it's** ~ **clear** *o* **obvious that …** salta a la vista que …

paternal /pə'tɜːrnl ‖pə'tɜːnl/ adj (a) (fatherly) ⟨*affection*⟩ paternal; ⟨*pride*⟩ de padre; ⟨*trait/ inheritance*⟩ paterno (b) (on father's side) (before n) por parte de padre

paternity /pə'tɜːrnəti ‖pə'tɜːnəti/ n (frml) paternidad f

path /pæθ ‖pɑːθ/ n (a) (track, walkway) sendero m, senda f (b) (of missile) trayectoria f; (of the sun) recorrido m

pathetic /pə'θetɪk/ adj (a) (pitiful) patético (b) (feeble) (colloq): **what a** ~ **excuse!** ¡qué excusa más pobre!; **don't be so** ~ no seas tan pusilánime

pathological /ˌpæθə'lɑːdʒɪkəl ‖ˌpæθə'lɒdʒɪkəl/ adj patológico

pathologist /pə'θɑːlədʒəst ‖pə'θɒlədʒɪst/ n patólogo, -ga m,f

pathology /pə'θɑːlədʒi ‖pə'θɒlədʒi/ n patología f

pathos /'peɪθɑːs ‖'peɪθɒs/ n patetismo m

pathway /'pæθweɪ ‖'pɑːθweɪ/ n camino m, sendero m

patience /'peɪʃəns/ n (a) (quality) paciencia f (b) (cards) (BrE) solitario m

patient¹ /'peɪʃənt/ adj paciente; **to be** ~ **WITH sb** tener* paciencia CON algn

patient² n paciente mf

patiently /'peɪʃəntli/ adv pacientemente

patio /'pætiəʊ/ n patio m

patriot /'peɪtriət ‖'pætriət, 'peɪ-/ n patriota mf

patriotic /ˌpeɪtri'ɑːtɪk ‖ˌpætri'ɒtɪk, 'peɪ-/ adj patriótico

patriotism /'peɪtriətɪzəm ‖'pætriətɪzəm, 'peɪ-/ n patriotismo m

patrol¹ /pə'trəʊl/ n **(a)** (act) patrulla f; **to be on ~** estar* patrullando, estar* de patrulla; (before n) **~ car** coche m patrulla, patrullero m (RPl), auto m patrulla (Chi) **(b)** (group) patrulla f

patrol² vt/i **-ll-** patrullar

patron /'peɪtrən/ n **(a)** (sponsor) patrocinador, -dora f, a **~ of the arts** un mecenas **(b)** (customer) (frml) cliente, -ta m,f

patronize /'peɪtrənaɪz ‖'pætrənaɪz/ vt **1** (condescend to) tratar con condescendencia **2** (frequent) (frml) ⟨shop/hotel⟩ ser* cliente de; ⟨theater/cinema⟩ frecuentar

patronizing /'peɪtrənaɪzɪŋ ‖'pætrənaɪzɪŋ/ adj condescendiente

patter¹ /'pætər ‖'pætə(r)/ vi golpetear

patter² n **1** (of rain) golpeteo m **2** (talk): **he has a good sales ~** tiene mucha labia para vender

pattern /'pætərn ‖'pætən/ n **1 (a)** (decoration) diseño m, dibujo m; (on fabric) diseño m, estampado m **(b)** (order, arrangement): **it follows the normal ~** sigue las pautas normales; **the murders all seem to follow a ~** todos los asesinatos parecen responder al mismo patrón **2 (a)** (model) modelo m **(b)** (in dressmaking) patrón m, molde m (CS) **(c)** (sample) muestra f

patterned /'pætərnd ‖'pætənd/ adj con dibujos; ⟨fabric⟩ estampado

paunch /pɔːntʃ/ n panza f (fam)

pauper /'pɔːpər ‖'pɔːpə(r)/ n pobre mf

pause¹ /pɔːz/ n pausa f; **without ~** sin interrupción

pause² vi (in speech) hacer* una pausa; (in movement) detenerse*

pave /peɪv/ vt (with concrete) pavimentar; (with flagstones) enlosar; (with stones) empedrar*

pavement /'peɪvmənt/ n **(a)** (paved area) pavimento m **(b)** (beside road) (BrE) ▶ SIDEWALK

pavilion /pə'vɪljən/ n **(a)** (tent, stand) pabellón m **(b)** (BrE Sport) caseta f

paving /'peɪvɪŋ/ n **(a)** (pavimento m; (of flagstones) enlosado m, (of stones) empedrado m; (before n) **~ stone** losa f

paw¹ /pɔː/ n pata f

paw² vt ⟨animal⟩ tocar* con la pata; **to ~ the ground** ⟨horse⟩ piafar

pawn¹ /pɔːn/ n **(a)** (in chess) peón m **(b)** (manipulated person) títere m

pawn² vt empeñar

pawnbroker /'pɔːn,brəʊkər ‖'pɔːn,brəʊkə(r)/ n prestamista mf

pay¹ /peɪ/ (past & past p **paid**) vt **1 (a)** ⟨tax/rent/sum/debt⟩ pagar*; **how much did you ~ for the painting?** ¿cuánto te costó el cuadro? **(b)** ⟨employee/creditor/tradesperson⟩ pagarle a; **to ~ sb FOR sth** pagarle* algo A algn **2** ⟨respects⟩ presentar; ⟨attention⟩ prestar ■ **~** vi **1 (a)** ⟨person⟩ pagar* **(b)** ⟨work/activity⟩ pagarse*; **teaching doesn't ~ very well** la enseñanza no está muy bien pagada

2 (suffer) **to ~ for sth** pagar* algo; **he paid for the mistake with his life** el error le costó la vida ■ **~** v impers convenir*

■ **pay back** [v + o + adv, v + adv + o] **1** (repay) ⟨money⟩ devolver*, regresar (AmL exc CS); ⟨loan/mortgage⟩ pagar*; **to ~ sb back** devolverle or (AmL exc CS) regresarle el dinero a algn **2** (take revenge on): **I'll ~ you back!** ¡ya me las vas a pagar!

■ **pay in** [v + o + adv, v + adv + o] (BrE) ⟨money⟩ depositar or (Esp) ingresar or (Col) consignar

■ **pay off 1** [v + o + adv, v + adv + o] ⟨debt⟩ cancelar, saldar; ⟨worker⟩ liquidarle el sueldo (or jornal etc) a (al despedirlo) **2** [v + adv] (prove worthwhile) valer* la pena; ⟨gamble⟩ resultar

■ **pay out** [v + o + adv, v + adv + o] pagar*

■ **pay up** [v + adv] pagar*

pay² n (of manual worker) paga f; (of employee) sueldo m; **equal ~** igualdad f salarial; (before n) **~ increase** aumento m salarial

payable /'peɪəbəl/ adj (frml) (pred) pagadero; **the rent becomes ~ on the first of the month** el alquiler vence el primero de mes; **make the check ~ to ...** extienda el cheque a nombre de ...

pay: ~check, (BrE) **~ cheque** n cheque m del sueldo; (salary) sueldo m; **~day** n día m de paga

payee /peɪ'iː/ n beneficiario, -ria m,f

payment /'peɪmənt/ n **(a)** (of debt, money, wage) pago m; **he received no ~ for what he did** no recibió remuneración por lo que hizo (frml) **(b)** (installment) plazo m, cuota f (AmL)

pay: ~ phone n teléfono m público, monedero m (público) (Ur); **~roll** n **(a)** (list) nómina f, planilla f (de sueldos) (AmL), plantilla f (Esp) **(b)** (wages) nómina f, **~ slip** n nómina f, recibo m del sueldo

PC¹ n **1** = **personal computer 2** (in UK) = **police constable**

PC² adj = **politically correct**

PD n (in US) = **Police Department**

PE n = **physical education**

pea /piː/ n arveja f or (Esp) guisante m or (AmC, Méx) chícharo m

peace /piːs/ n **1** paz f; **in o at ~** en paz; (before n) para la paz; ⟨proposal/initiative/treaty⟩ de paz; ⟨talks/march/campaign⟩ por la paz; **the ~ movement** el movimiento pacifista; **as a ~ offering** en señal de reconciliación **2** (Law): **to keep the ~** mantener* el orden **3** (tranquillity) paz f, **I went to the library for some ~ and quiet** me fui a la biblioteca para poder estar tranquilo; **I turned off the gas for my own ~ of mind** apagué el gas para quedarme tranquilo

peaceful /'piːsfəl/ adj **(a)** (calm, quiet) ⟨place⟩ tranquilo **(b)** (non-violent) ⟨protest⟩ pacífico; **they are a ~ people** son un pueblo amante de la paz

peacefully /'piːsfəli/ adv ⟨sleep⟩ plácidamente; ⟨read/sit⟩ tranquilamente

peace: ∼**keeping** adj (before n): ∼**keeping forces** fuerzas fpl de paz; ∼**maker** n conciliador, -dora m,f; ∼**time** n época f de paz

peach /piːtʃ/ n durazno m (esp AmL), melocotón m (Esp); (before n) ∼ **tree** duraznero m (esp AmL), melocotonero m (Esp)

peacock /'piːkɑːk ‖'piːkɒk/ n pavo m real

peak¹ /piːk/ n **(a)** (of mountain) cima f, cumbre f; (mountain) pico m; (of cap) visera f **(b)** (highest point): **at the** ∼ **of her career** en el apogeo de su carrera

peak² adj (before n) **(a)** (maximum) ⟨level/power⟩ máximo; **to be in** ∼ **condition** «athlete/horse» estar* en plena forma **(b)** (busiest): **during** ∼ **hours** durante las horas de mayor demanda (or consumo etc); ∼ **rate** tarifa f alta

peal /piːl/ n: ∼ **of bells** (sound) repique m de campanas; (set) carillón m; ∼**s of laughter** carcajadas fpl; **a** ∼ **of thunder** un trueno

peanut /'piːnʌt/ n **(a)** (Agr, Culin) maní m or (Esp) cacahuete m or (Méx) cacahuate m **(b) peanuts** pl (small sum) (colloq) una miseria (fam)

peanut butter n mantequilla f de maní or (Esp) de cacahuete or (Méx) de cacahuate, manteca f de maní (RPl)

pear /per ‖peə(r)/ n pera f; ∼ **(tree)** peral m

pearl /pɜːrl ‖pɜːl/ n **(a)** (jewel) perla f; ∼**s of wisdom** sabias palabras fpl; (iro) joyitas fpl (iró) **(b)** (mother-of-∼) nácar m, madreperla f, concha f nácar (Méx), concha f de perla (Chi)

peasant /'pezn̩t/ n campesino, -na m,f

peat /piːt/ n turba f

pebble /'pebəl/ n guijarro m

pecan /pɪ'kæn ‖'piːkən/ n pacana f, nuez f (Méx)

peck¹ /pek/ n **(a)** (of bird) picotazo m **(b)** (kiss) beso m

peck² vt picotear

pecking order /'pekɪŋ/ n jerarquía f

peckish /'pekɪʃ/ adj (esp BrE colloq) (pred) **to be** o **feel** ∼ tener* un poco de hambre

peculiar /pɪ'kjuːljər ‖pɪ'kjuːliə(r)/ adj **(a)** (strange) raro, extraño **(b)** (particular, exclusive) peculiar, característico

peculiarity /pɪˌkjuːli'jærəti ‖pɪˌkjuːli'ærəti/ n (pl **-ties**) (sth unusual) rasgo m singular; (oddity) rareza f

pedal¹ /'pedl̩/ n pedal m

pedal² vi, (BrE) **-ll-** pedalear

pedal bin n (BrE) cubo m or (Méx) bote m or (CS) tacho m or (Ven) tobo m or (Col) caneca f de la basura (con pedal)

pedantic /pɪ'dæntɪk/ adj pedante

peddle /'pedl̩/ vt vender (en las calles o de puerta en puerta); **to** ∼ **drugs** traficar* con drogas

peddler /'pedlər ‖'pedlə(r)/ n vendedor, -dora ambulante m,f; (in former times) buhonero m; **a drug** ∼ un traficante de drogas

pedestal /'pedəst̩l ‖'pedɪstl̩/ n pedestal m

pedestrian¹ /pə'destriən ‖pɪ'destriən/ n peatón, -tona m,f; (before n) ∼ **crossing** cruce m peatonal or de peatones; ∼ **mall** o (BrE) **precinct** zona f peatonal

pedestrian² adj pedestre

pediatric, (BrE also) **paediatric** /'piːdi'ætrɪk/ adj ⟨hospital⟩ pediátrico; ⟨specialist⟩ en pediatría

pediatrician, (BrE also) **paediatrician** /'piːdiə'trɪʃən/ n pediatra mf

pedicure /'pedɪkjʊr ‖'pedɪkjʊə(r)/ n: **to have a** ∼ arreglarse/hacerse* arreglar los pies

pedigree /'pedəgriː ‖'pedɪgriː/ n **(a)** (ancestry — of animal) pedigrí m; (— of person) linaje m; (before n) ⟨bull/dog⟩ de raza **(b)** (certificate, document) pedigrí m

pedlar /'pedlər ‖'pedlə(r)/ n (BrE) ▶ PEDDLER

pedophile, (BrE) **paedophile** /'piːdəfaɪl/ n pedófilo, -la m,f

pee¹ /piː/ vi (past & past p **peed**) (colloq) hacer* pis or pipí (fam), hacer* del uno (Méx, Per fam & euf)

pee² n (colloq) (no pl) pis m (fam), pipí m (fam)

peek¹ /piːk/ vi ∼ (**AT sth/sb**) mirar (algo/a algn) (a hurtadillas), vichar (algo/a algn) (RPl fam)

peek² n **to take** o **have a** ∼ **at sth** echar(le) una miradita a algo, vichar algo (RPl fam)

peel¹ /piːl/ vt ⟨apple/potato⟩ pelar

■ ∼ vi «person» pelarse; «paint» desconcharse; «wallpaper» despegarse*

■ **peel off** **1** [v + adv] «wallpaper/label» despegarse*; ⟨paint⟩ desconcharse **2** [v + o + adv, v + adv + o] ⟨stamp/sticker⟩ despegar*; ⟨paint/bark⟩ quitar

peel² n (of potato, apple) piel f, cáscara f (esp AmL); (of orange, lemon) cáscara f

peelings /'piːlɪŋz/ pl n cáscaras fpl, peladuras fpl

peep¹ /piːp/ vi **(a)** (watch) espiar*, vichar (RPl fam); (look quickly) mirar (a hurtadillas), vichar (RPl fam) **(b)** (show, stick out) ∼ (**out**) asomar

■ ∼ vt (colloq): **I** ∼**ed the horn** toqué la bocina or el claxon

peep² n **1** (quick or furtive look) vistazo m; **to have a** ∼ **AT sth** echarle un vistazo A algo **2** (of bird) pío m; (of car horn) pitido m

peephole /'piːphəʊl/ n mirilla f

peer¹ /pɪr ‖pɪə(r)/ n **1 (a)** (equal) par mf **(b)** (contemporary) coetáneo, -nea m,f **2** (lord) (in UK) par m

peer² vi: **to** ∼ **AT sth/sb** (with difficulty) mirar algo/a algn con ojos de miope; (closely) mirar algo/a algn detenidamente

peerage /'pɪrɪdʒ ‖'pɪərɪdʒ/ n **the** ∼ la nobleza

peer group n grupo m paritario (fml)

peeved /piːvd/ adj ⟨expression/look⟩ de fastidio; **to be** o **feel** ∼ estar* molesto

peevish /'piːvɪʃ/ adj ⟨remark⟩ desagradable, malhumorado; **to be** ∼ estar* fastidioso

peg¹ /peg/ n **1 (a)** (in ground) estaca f; (on violin, guitar) clavija f; (tent ∼) estaquilla f; (on board game) pieza o ficha que encaja en un tablero **(b)** (clothes-∼) (BrE) ▶ CLOTHESPIN **2** (hook, hanger) colgador m, perchero m, gancho m

peg² vt **-gg-** (attach, secure) sujetar, asegurar (con estaquillas etc)

pejorative /pɪ'dʒɔːrətɪv ‖pɪ'dʒɒrətɪv/ adj peyorativo

Peking /'piː'kɪŋ/ n Pekín m

pelican /'pelɪkən/ n pelícano m

pellet /'pelət ‖'pelɪt/ *n* **(a)** (of bread, paper) bolita *f* **(b)** (ammunition) perdigón *m*

pelt¹ /pelt/ *vt*: **to ~ sb with tomatoes** lanzarle* tomates a algn
■ ~ *vi* (colloq) **1** (rush): **they came ~ing down the hill** bajaron la cuesta (corriendo) a toda velocidad **2** (fall heavily): **it was ~ing with rain** llovía a cántaros

pelt² *n* (animal skin) piel *f*; (stripped) cuero *m*

pelvis /'pelvəs ‖'pelvɪs/ *n* (*pl* **-vises**) pelvis *f*

pen /pen/ *n* **1** (fountain ~) pluma *f* estilográfica, pluma *f* fuente (AmL); (ballpoint ~) bolígrafo *m*, boli *m* (Esp fam), birome *f* (RPl), pluma *f* atómica (Méx), lápiz *m* de pasta (Chi); (felt ~) rotulador *m* **2** (Agr) (sheep ~) redil *m*; (cattle ~) corral *m*

penal /'piːnl/ *adj* penal

penalize /'piːnlaɪz ‖'piːnəlaɪz/ *vt* **(a)** (punish) ⟨*player*⟩ sancionar **(b)** (make punishable, illegal) penalizar*

penalty /'penlti/ *n* (*pl* **-ties**) **1** (punishment) pena *f*; (fine) multa *f*; **to pay the ~** pagar* las consecuencias **2** (Sport) (in rugby) penalty *m*; (in US football) castigo *m*; ~ **(kick)** (in soccer) penalty *m*, penalti *m*, penal (AmL), pénal *m* (Andes); (*before n*) ~ **area** (in soccer) área *f*; de penalty

penance /'penəns/ *n* **(a)** (Relig) penitencia *f* **(b)** (punishment) (hum) castigo *m*

pence /pens/ *n pl* of PENNY 1A

penchant /'pentʃənt ‖'pɒnʃɒŋ/ *n* (frml) ~ **(FOR sth)** inclinación *f* (POR algo)

pencil /'pensəl/ *n* lápiz *m*; **in ~** con lápiz
pencil: ~ **case** *n* estuche *m* (para lápices), plumier *m* (Esp), chuspa *f* (Col), cartuchera *f* (RPl); ~ **sharpener** *n* sacapuntas *m*, tajalápiz *m* (Col)

pendant /'pendənt/ *n* colgante *m*

pending¹ /'pendɪŋ/ *adj* **(a)** (awaiting action) (*pred*): **to be ~** estar* pendiente **(b)** (imminent) próximo

pending² *prep* (frml) en espera de

pendulum /'pendʒələm ‖'pendjuləm/ *n* (*pl* **-lums**) péndulo *m*

penetrate /'penətreɪt ‖'penɪtreɪt/ *vt* **(a)** ⟨*membrane/defenses*⟩ penetrar (en); ⟨*armor*⟩ atravesar*; ⟨*enemy lines*⟩ adentrarse en; ⟨*territory*⟩ penetrar en; ⟨*organization*⟩ infiltrarse en; ⟨*market*⟩ introducirse* en **(b)** ⟨*liquid*⟩ penetrar (en)
■ ~ *vi* **(a)** ⟨*arrow/water/light*⟩ penetrar **(b)** (sink in mentally): **it took a long time to ~** tardé (*or* tardó *etc*) en entenderlo

penetrating /'penətreɪtɪŋ ‖'penɪtreɪtɪŋ/ *adj* penetrante

penetration /,penə'treɪʃən ‖,penɪ'treɪʃən/ *n* penetración *f*

pen friend *n* (esp BrE) ▶ PEN PAL

penguin /'peŋgwən ‖'peŋgwɪn/ *n* pingüino *m*

penicillin /,penə'sɪlən ‖,penɪ'sɪlɪn/ *n* penicilina *f*

peninsula /pə'nɪnsələ ‖pə'nɪnsjulə/ *n* península *f*

penis /'piːnəs ‖'piːnɪs/ *n* pene *m*

penitent /'penətənt ‖'penɪtənt/ *adj* arrepentido

penitentiary /,penə'tentʃəri ‖,penɪ'tenʃəri/ *n* (*pl* **-ries**) (AmE) prisión *f*

penknife /'pennaɪf/ *n* (*pl* **-knives**) navaja *f*

Penn, Penna = Pennsylvania

pen name *n* seudónimo *m*

penniless /'penɪləs ‖'penɪlɪs/ *adj* pobre, sin un céntimo

penny /'peni/ *n* **1** (in UK) **(a)** (*pl* **pence**) penique *m* **(b)** (*pl* **pennies**) (coin) penique *m* **2** (*pl* **pennies**) (cent coin) (in US, Canada) (colloq) (moneda *f* de un) centavo *m*

penny-pinching /'peni,pɪntʃɪŋ/ *adj* cicatero (fam)

pen pal /'penpæl/ *n* (esp AmE) amigo, -ga *m,f* por correspondencia

pension /'pentʃən ‖'penʃən/ *n* pensión *f*; (retirement ~) pensión de jubilación

pensioner /'pentʃənər ‖'penʃənə(r)/ *n* pensionado, -da *m,f*, pensionista *mf*; (retired person) jubilado, -da *m,f*

pensive /'pensɪv/ *adj* pensativo

pentagon /'pentəgɑːn ‖'pentəgən/ *n* **(a)** (Math) pentágono *m* **(b)** (in US) **the Pentagon** el Pentágono

pentathlon /pen'tæθlən/ *n* pentatlón *m*

Pentecost /'pentəkɔːst ‖'pentɪkɒst/ *n* Pentecostés *m*

penthouse /'penthaʊs/ *n* penthouse *m*

pent-up /'pent'ʌp/ *adj* (*pred* **pent up**) ⟨*emotions*⟩ contenido; ⟨*energy*⟩ acumulado

penultimate /prʲ'nʌltəmət ‖pen'ʌltɪmət/ *adj* (*before n*) penúltimo

people¹ /'piːpəl/ *n* **1** (+ *pl vb*, no *art*) **(a)** (in general) gente *f*; ~ **say that ...** dicen que ..., se dice que ...; **some ~ don't like it** a algunos no les gusta **(b)** (individuals) personas *fpl* **(c)** (specific group): **tall/rich ~** la gente alta/rica, los altos/ ricos; **young ~** los jóvenes **2** **(a)** (inhabitants) (+ *pl vb*): **the ~ of this country** la gente de este país; **the country and its ~** el país y su(s) gente(s) **(b)** (citizens, nation) (+ *pl vb*) **the ~** el pueblo **(c)** (race) (+ *sing vb*) pueblo *m*

people² *vt* poblar*

pepper¹ /'pepər ‖'pepə(r)/ *n* **1** (spice) pimienta *f*; **black/white ~** pimienta negra/blanca **2** (capsicum fruit, plant) pimiento *m*, pimentón *m* (AmS exc RPl), ají *m* (RPl); **green ~** pimiento (*or* pimentón *etc*) verde; **red ~** pimiento (*or* pimentón *etc*) rojo *or* colorado, ají *m* morrón (RPl)

pepper² *vt* (intersperse) **to ~ sth WITH sth** salpicar* algo DE algo

pepper: ~**box** *n* (AmE) pimentero *m*; ~**mint** *n* **(a)** (plant) menta *f*; (*before n*) ⟨*tea/oil*⟩ de menta; ⟨*flavor*⟩ a menta **(b)** (sweet) caramelo *m* de menta; ~**pot** *n* (BrE) pimentero *m*

pep /pep/: ~ **talk** *n*: **he gave them a ~ talk** les habló para levantarles la moral/infundirles ánimo; ~ **up**: **-pp-** [*v* + *o* + *adv*, *v* + *adv* + *o*] (colloq) ⟨*person*⟩ animar; (physically) darle* energía a

per /pɜːr ‖pɜː(r)/ *prep* (for each) por; **£10 ~ head** 10 libras por cabeza; **at $25 ~ kilo** a 25 dólares el kilo; **30 miles ~ hour** 30 millas por hora

per: ~ **annum** /pər'ænəm/ *adv* al año, por año; ~ **capita** /pər'kæpətə ‖pə'kæpɪtə/ *adv* per cápita

777

perceive ⋯⟶ permanent ⋯

perceive /pər'siːv ‖pə'siːv/ *vt* **(a)** ‹object/ sound› percibir **(b)** (realize) percatarse de **(c)** (regard) ver*

percent¹, per cent /pər'sent ‖pə'sent/ *n* (*no pl*) porcentaje *m*

percent², per cent *adv* por ciento

percentage /pər'sentɪdʒ ‖pə'sentɪdʒ/ *n* porcentaje *m*

perceptible /pər'septəbəl ‖pə'septəbəl/ *adj* perceptible

perception /pər'sepʃən ‖pə'sepʃən/ *n* **(a)** (faculty) percepción *f* **(b)** (idea) idea *f*; (image) imagen *f* **(c)** (insight) perspicacia *f*

perceptive /pər'septɪv ‖pə'septɪv/ *adj* perspicaz

perch¹ /pɜːrtʃ ‖pɜːtʃ/ *n* **1** (in birdcage) percha *f* **2** (*pl* ~ *or* ~**es**) (fish) perca *f*

perch² *vi* «*bird*» posarse; **he ~ed on the edge of the table** se sentó en el borde de la mesa

percolate /'pɜːrkəleɪt ‖'pɜːkəleɪt/ *vi* **(a)** (filter) filtrarse **(b)** (Culin) «*coffee*» hacerse*

percolator /'pɜːrkəleɪtər ‖'pɜːkəleɪtə(r)/ *n* cafetera *f* eléctrica

percussion /pər'kʌʃən ‖pə'kʌʃən/ *n* percusión *f*

perennial¹ /pə'reniəl/ *adj* **(a)** (Bot) perenne **(b)** (recurring) perenne, perpetuo

perennial² *n* planta *f* perenne *or* vivaz

perfect¹ /'pɜːrfɪkt ‖'pɜːfɪkt/ *adj* **1** (flawless, ideal) perfecto; ‹day/opportunity› ideal; **he speaks ~ French** habla francés perfectamente **2** (complete) (*before n*): **he's a ~ stranger to me** me es totalmente desconocido

perfect² /pər'fekt ‖pə'fekt/ *vt* perfeccionar

perfect³ /'pɜːrfɪkt ‖'pɜːfɪkt/ *n*: **the future/ present ~** el futuro/pretérito perfecto; **the past ~** el pluscuamperfecto

perfection /pər'fekʃən ‖pə'fekʃən/ *n* **(a)** (state, quality) perfección *f* **(b)** (act) perfeccionamiento *m*

perfectionist /pər'fekʃənəst ‖pə'fekʃənɪst/ *n* perfeccionista *mf*

perfectly /'pɜːrfɪktli ‖'pɜːfɪktli/ *adv* **1** (exactly) ‹round/straight› totalmente; ‹fit/match› perfectamente **(b)** (faultlessly, ideally) perfectamente **2** (completely, utterly) ‹safe/ridiculous› totalmente; **he knows ~ well that ...** sabe perfectamente que ...

perforate /'pɜːrfəreɪt ‖'pɜːfəreɪt/ *vt* perforar

perforation /pɜːrfə'reɪʃən ‖pɜːfə'reɪʃən/ *n* perforación *f*; ~**s** (on sheet of stamps etc) perforado *m*

perform /pər'fɔːrm ‖pə'fɔːm/ *vi* **1** (Mus, Theat) «*actor/comedian*» actuar*; «*singer*» cantar; «*musician*» tocar*; «*dancer*» bailar **2** (work, produce results) «*student/worker*» rendir*, trabajar; «*team/athlete/vehicle*» responder; «*company/stocks*» rendir*
■ ~ *vt* **1** (Mus, Theat) ‹play› representar; ‹symphony› tocar* **2** (carry out, fulfill) ‹function› desempeñar; ‹role› desempeñar; ‹task› ejecutar; ‹experiment› realizar*; ‹ceremony› celebrar; ‹rites› practicar*

performance /pər'fɔːrməns ‖pə'fɔːməns/ *n* **1** (Cin, Mus, Theat) **(a)** (session) (Theat) representación *f*, función *f*; (Cin) función *f* **(b)** (of symphony, song) interpretación *f*; (of play)
representación *f* **(c)** (of actor) interpretación *f*; (of pianist, tenor) interpretación *f*; (of entertainer) actuación *f* **2** (of employee) rendimiento *m*, desempeño *m* (AmL); (of student) rendimiento *m*; (of team, athlete) actuación *f*, performance *f* (AmL period); (of machine, vehicle) comportamiento *m*, performance *f* (AmL); (of company) resultados *mpl*

performer /pər'fɔːrmər ‖pə'fɔːmə(r)/ *n* (Theat, Cin) actor, -triz *m,f*; (entertainer) artista *mf*

performing /pər'fɔːrmɪŋ ‖pə'fɔːmɪŋ/ *adj* (*before n*) **(a)** (Mus, Theat): **the ~ arts** las artes interpretativas **(b)** ‹seal/dog› amaestrado

perfume¹ /'pɜːrfjuːm ‖'pɜːfjuːm/ *n* perfume *m*

perfume² /pər'fjuːm ‖'pɜːfjuːm/ *vt* perfumar

perfunctory /pər'fʌŋktəri ‖pə'fʌŋktəri/ *adj* ‹inspection/description› somero; ‹greeting› mecánico

perhaps /pər'hæps ‖pə'hæps/ *adv* quizá(s), tal vez; ~ **they'll come later** tal vez *or* quizá(s) vengan más tarde

peril /'perəl ‖'perɪl, 'perəl/ *n* peligro *m*

perilous /'perələs ‖'perɪləs, 'perələs/ *adj* peligroso

perimeter /pə'rɪmətər ‖pə'rɪmɪtə(r)/ *n* perímetro *m*

period¹ /'pɪriəd ‖'pɪəriəd/ *n* [*the forms* PERÍODO *and* PERIODO *are equally acceptable in Spanish where this translation applies*] **1 (a)** (interval, length of time) período *m*; (when specifying a time limit) plazo *m*; **for a ~ of five hours/12 months** por un espacio de cinco horas/período de 12 meses **(b)** (epoch) época *f* **2** (menstruation) periodo *m*, regla *f* **3** (in school) hora *f* (*de clase*) **4** (in punctuation) (AmE) punto *m*

period² *adj* ‹costume/furniture› de época

periodic /pɪri'ɑːdɪk ‖pɪəri'ɒdɪk/ *adj* periódico

periodical¹ /pɪri'ɑːdɪkəl ‖pɪəri'ɒdɪkəl/ *n* publicación *f* periódica

periodical² *adj* ▶ PERIODIC

peripheral /pə'rɪfərəl/ *adj* **(a)** (minor, secondary) secundario **(b)** (Comput) ‹device/unit› periférico

periphery /pə'rɪfəri/ *n* (*pl* -**ries**) (frml) (of city) periferia *f*; (of society) margen *m*

periscope /'perəskəʊp ‖'perɪskəʊp/ *n* periscopio *m*

perish /'perɪʃ/ *vi* **(a)** (die) (liter) perecer* (liter) **(b)** (decay) «*rubber/leather*» deteriorarse; «*foodstuffs*» echarse a perder

perishable /'perɪʃəbəl/ *adj* perecedero

perjure /'pɜːrdʒər ‖'pɜːdʒə(r)/ *v refl* (Law) **to ~ oneself** perjurar(se), cometer perjurio

perjury /'pɜːrdʒəri ‖'pɜːdʒəri/ *n* perjurio *m*

perk /pɜːrk ‖pɜːk/ *n* (colloq) (of job) (beneficio *m*) extra *m*; (particular advantage) ventaja *f*
■ **perk up** [*v + adv*] «*person*» animarse; «*business/weather*» mejorar

perky /'pɜːrki ‖'pɜːki/ *adj* -**kier**, -**kiest** alegre

perm¹ /pɜːrm ‖pɜːm/ *n* permanente *f or* (Méx) *m*

perm² *vt*: **to have one's hair ~ed** hacerse* la *or* (Méx) un permanente

permanent¹ /'pɜːrmənənt ‖'pɜːmənənt/ *adj* permanente; ‹address/job› fijo, permanente; ‹dye/ ink› indeleble

permanent² *n* (AmE) ▶ PERM¹

permanently /ˈpɜːrmənəntli ‖ˈpɜːmənəntli/ *adv* ⟨work/settle⟩ permanentemente; ⟨marked/disfigured⟩ para siempre

permeate /ˈpɜːrmieɪt ‖ˈpɜːmieɪt/ *vt* «liquid» calar; «smoke/smell» impregnar

permissible /pərˈmɪsəbəl ‖pəˈmɪsəbəl/ *adj* (permitted) permisible; (acceptable) tolerable

permission /pərˈmɪʃən ‖pəˈmɪʃən/ *n* permiso *m*; **she gave me ~** me dio (su) permiso

permissive /pərˈmɪsɪv ‖pəˈmɪsɪv/ *adj* permisivo

permit¹ /pərˈmɪt ‖pəˈmɪt/ **-tt-** *vt* permitir; **photography is not ~ted** no se permite tomar fotografías; **to ~ sb to + INF** permitirle a algn que (+ subj)
■ ~ *vi*: **weather ~ting** si hace buen tiempo

permit² /ˈpɜːrmɪt ‖ˈpɜːmɪt/ *n* permiso *m* (por escrito); **work/residence ~** permiso de trabajo/de residencia; **gun ~** (AmE) licencia *f* de armas

permutation /ˌpɜːrmjuˈteɪʃən ‖ˌpɜːmjuˈteɪʃən/ *n* (a) (arrangement) variante *f* (b) (Math) permutación *f*

peroxide /pərˈɑːksaɪd ‖pəˈrɒksaɪd/ *n* peróxido *m*

perpendicular /ˌpɜːrpənˈdɪkjələr ‖ˌpɜːpənˈdɪkjʊlə(r)/ *adj* (a) (vertical) ⟨wall/surface⟩ perpendicular al horizonte (b) (Math) **~ TO sth** perpendicular A algo

perpetrate /ˈpɜːrpətreɪt ‖ˈpɜːpɪtreɪt/ *vt* (fml) perpetrar

perpetrator /ˈpɜːrpətreɪtər ‖ˈpɜːpɪtreɪtə(r)/ *n* (fml or hum) autor, -tora *m,f* (de un crimen etc)

perpetual /pərˈpetʃuəl ‖pəˈpetjuəl/ *adj* eterno, perpetuo

perpetuate /pərˈpetʃueɪt ‖pəˈpetjʊeɪt/ *vt* perpetuar*

perplex /pərˈpleks ‖pəˈpleks/ *vt* dejar perplejo

perplexed /pərˈplekst ‖pəˈplekst/ *adj* perplejo

per se /ˈpɜːrˈseɪ ‖ˌpɜːˈseɪ/ *adv* en sí, per se

persecute /ˈpɜːrsɪkjuːt ‖ˈpɜːsɪkjuːt/ *vt* perseguir*

persecution /ˌpɜːrsɪˈkjuːʃən ‖ˌpɜːsɪˈkjuːʃən/ *n* persecución *f*

perseverance /ˌpɜːrsəˈvɪrəns ‖ˌpɜːsɪˈvɪərəns/ *n* perseverancia *f*

persevere /ˌpɜːrsəˈvɪr ‖ˌpɜːsɪˈvɪə(r)/ *vi* perseverar

Persia /ˈpɜːrʒə ‖ˈpɜːʃə/ *n* Persia *f*

Persian /ˈpɜːrʒən ‖ˈpɜːʃən/ *adj* persa; **the ~ Gulf** el Golfo Pérsico

persist /pərˈsɪst ‖pəˈsɪst/ *vi* persistir; **to ~ IN sth/-ING: they ~ed in the belief** o **in believing that …** persistieron en la creencia de que …

persistence /pərˈsɪstəns ‖pəˈsɪstəns/ *n* perseverancia *f*

persistent /pərˈsɪstənt ‖pəˈsɪstənt/ *adj* (a) (unceasing) ⟨demands/warnings⟩ continuo, constante; ⟨cough/fog⟩ persistente; ⟨rain⟩ continuo (b) (undaunted) ⟨salesman/suitor⟩ insistente

person /ˈpɜːrsn̩ ‖ˈpɜːsn̩/ *n* ⓵ (*pl* **people** o (fml) **persons**) persona *f*; **Sue's the ~ to ask** a quien hay que preguntarle es a Sue; **in ~** en persona ⓶ (Ling) (*pl* **persons**) persona *f*

personable /ˈpɜːrsṇəbəl ‖ˈpɜːsṇəbəl/ *adj* agradable

personal /ˈpɜːrsṇəl ‖ˈpɜːsənl/ *adj* ⓵ (a) (own) ⟨experience/preference⟩ personal; ⟨property⟩ privado (b) (private) personal; **a ~ call** una llamada particular; **don't ask ~ questions** no hagas preguntas indiscretas (c) (individual) ⟨account/loan⟩ personal ⓶ (a) (in person) ⟨appearance⟩ en persona (b) (physical) ⟨hygiene⟩ íntimo; ⟨appearance⟩ personal (c) (directed against individual): **it's nothing ~, but …** no tengo nada contra ti (or ella etc), pero …

personal: ~ assistant *n* (Busn) secretario, -ria *m,f* personal; **~ computer** *n* computadora *f* or (Esp tb) ordenador *m* personal

personality /ˌpɜːrsṇˈæləti ‖ˌpɜːsəˈnæləti/ *n* (*pl* **-ties**) personalidad *f*

personally /ˈpɜːrsṇəli ‖ˈpɜːsṇəli/ *adv* personalmente

personal organizer *n* agenda *f* de uso múltiple, Filofax® *m*

personification /pərˌsɑːnəfəˈkeɪʃən ‖pəˌsɒnɪfɪˈkeɪʃən/ *n* personificación *f*

personify /pərˈsɑːnəfaɪ ‖pəˈsɒnɪfaɪ/ *vt* **-fies, -fying, -fied** personificar*

personnel /ˌpɜːrsṇˈel ‖ˌpɜːsəˈnel/ *n* (a) (staff) (+ *pl vb*) personal *m*; (before *n*) **~ manager** jefe *m,f* de personal (b) **Personnel** (department) (+ *sing vb*) sección *f* de personal

perspective /pərˈspektɪv ‖pəˈspektɪv/ *n* perspectiva *f*; **you have to keep things in ~** no tienes que perder de vista la verdadera dimensión de las cosas

Perspex® /ˈpɜːrspeks ‖ˈpɜːspeks/ *n* (BrE) acrílico *m*, plexiglás® *m* (Esp)

perspiration /ˌpɜːrspəˈreɪʃən ‖ˌpɜːspɪˈreɪʃən/ *n* transpiración *f*

perspire /pərˈspaɪr ‖pəˈspaɪə(r)/ *vi* transpirar

persuade /pərˈsweɪd ‖pəˈsweɪd/ *vt* ⟨person⟩ convencer*, persuadir; **to ~ sb to + INF** convencer* or persuadir a algn DE QUE or PARA QUE (+ subj)

persuasion /pərˈsweɪʒən ‖pəˈsweɪʒən/ *n* (a) (act) persuasión *f* (b) (Relig) (fml): **people of all ~s** gente de todas las creencias

persuasive /pərˈsweɪsɪv ‖pəˈsweɪsɪv/ *adj* ⟨person/manner⟩ persuasivo; ⟨argument⟩ convincente

pert /pɜːrt ‖pɜːt/ *adj* ⟨reply⟩ descarado; ⟨hat/dress⟩ coqueto

pertinent /ˈpɜːrtṇənt ‖ˈpɜːtɪnənt/ *adj* (fml) pertinente; **to be ~ TO sth** guardar relación CON algo

perturb /pərˈtɜːrb ‖pəˈtɜːb/ *vt* (usu pass) perturbar

Peru /pəˈruː/ *n* (el) Perú *m*

peruse /pə'ru:z/ vt **(a)** (read through) (frml or hum) leer* detenidamente **(b)** (examine, study) (frml) examinar

Peruvian[1] /pə'ru:viən/ adj peruano

Peruvian[2] n peruano, -na m,f

pervade /pər'veɪd ‖pə'veɪd/ vt «idea/mood» dominar; «smell» llenar

pervasive /pər'veɪsɪv ‖pə'veɪsɪv/ adj «smell» penetrante; «idea/mood» dominante; «influence» omnipresente

perverse /pər'vɜ:rs ‖pə'vɜ:s/ adj (stubborn) obstinado; (wayward, contrary) retorcido

perversion /pər'vɜ:rʒən ‖pə'vɜ:ʃən/ n **(a)** (distortion): **a ~ of justice** una deformación de la justicia **(b)** (Psych) perversión f

pervert[1] /pər'vɜ:rt ‖pə'vɜ:t/ vt pervertir*

pervert[2] /'pɜ:rvɜ:rt ‖'pɜ:vɜ:t/ n pervertido, -da m,f

peseta /pə'seɪtə/ n peseta f

pesky /'peski/ adj **-kier, -kiest** (AmE colloq) latoso (fam)

peso /'peɪsəʊ/ n (pl ~s) peso m

pessimism /'pesəmɪzəm ‖'pesɪmɪzəm/ n pesimismo m

pessimist /'pesəməst ‖'pesɪmɪst/ n pesimista mf

pessimistic /pesə'mɪstɪk ‖,pesɪ'mɪstɪk/ adj pesimista

pest /pest/ n **(a)** (Agr, Hort) plaga f **(b)** (person, thing) (colloq) peste f (fam)

pester /'pestər ‖'pestə(r)/ vt molestar

pesticide /'pestəsaɪd ‖'pestɪsaɪd/ n pesticida m

pestle /'pesəl/ n mano f de mortero

pet[1] /pet/ n **(a)** (animal) animal m doméstico or de compañía; (before n) ~ **food** comida f para animales; ~ **shop** ≈ pajarería f **(b)** (favorite): **he's teacher's ~** es el niño mimado de la maestra

pet[2] adj (before n) **(a)** (kept as pet): **his ~ budgie** su periquito **(b)** (favorite) «subject/theory» favorito; **my ~ hate** lo que más odio

pet[3] -tt- vt «animal» acariciar
■ ~ vi acariciarse, manosearse (pey)

petal /'petl/ n pétalo m

peter out /'pi:tər/ [v + adv] «supplies» irse* agotando; «conversation» apagarse*

petition /pə'tɪʃən/ n **(a)** (written document) petición f **(b)** (Law) demanda f

pet name n apodo m

petrified /'petrɪfaɪd/ adj **(a)** (terrified) muerto de miedo **(b)** (Geol) petrificado

petrochemical /'petrəʊ'kemɪkəl/ n producto m petroquímico; (before n) «industry/plant» petroquímico

petrol /'petrəl/ n (BrE) gasolina f, bencina f (Andes), nafta f (RPl); (before n) ~ **pump** surtidor m; ~ **station** estación f de servicio, gasolinera f, bomba f (Andes, Ven), estación f de nafta (RPl), bencinera f (Andes), grifo m (Per)

petroleum /pə'trəʊliəm/ n petróleo m; (before n) ~ **jelly** vaselina f

petticoat /'petikəʊt/ n **(a)** (underskirt) enagua f or (Méx) fondo m **(b)** (slip) (BrE) combinación f, viso m

petty /'peti/ adj **-tier, -tiest** **(a)** (unimportant) «details» insignificante, nimio; ~ **thief** ladronzuelo, -la m,f **(b)** (small-minded) mezquino

petty cash n caja f chica, dinero m para gastos menores

petulant /'petʃələnt ‖'petjʊlənt/ adj de mal genio

pew /pju:/ n banco m (de iglesia)

pewter /'pju:tər ‖'pju:tə(r)/ n peltre m

PG (= **parental guidance**) menores acompañados

PG-13 (in US) mayores de 13 años o menores acompañados

phantom[1] /'fæntəm/ n (liter) fantasma m

phantom[2] adj **(a)** (ghostly) (liter) (before n) «shape» fantasmal; «horseman» fantasma adj inv **(b)** (imaginary) ilusorio

Pharaoh /'ferəʊ ‖'feərəʊ/ n faraón m

pharmaceutical /'fɑ:rmə'su:tɪkəl ‖,fɑ:mə'sju:tɪkəl/ adj farmacéutico

pharmacist /'fɑ:rməsəst ‖'fɑ:məsɪst/ n farmacéutico, -ca m,f, farmaceuta mf (Col, Ven)

pharmacy /'fɑ:rməsi ‖'fɑ:məsi/ n (pl **-cies**) **(a)** (discipline) química f farmacéutica, farmacia f **(b)** (dispensary) farmacia f

phase /feɪz/ n fase f
■ **phase out** [v + o + adv, v + adv + o] «service» retirar paulatinamente; «old model» dejar de producir

PhD n (= **Doctor of Philosophy**) (award) doctorado m; (person) Dr., Dra.

pheasant /'fezn̩t/ n (pl ~s or ~) faisán m

phenomena /fɪ'nɑ:mənə ‖fə'nɒmɪnə/ pl of PHENOMENON

phenomenal /fɪ'nɑ:mənl ‖fə'nɒmɪnl/ adj (colloq) «success/achievement» espectacular; «strength» increíble

phenomenon /fɪ'nɑ:mənɑ:n ‖fə'nɒmɪnən/ n (pl **-mena**) fenómeno m

phew /fju:/ interj (colloq) ¡uf!

philanderer /fə'lændərər ‖fɪ'lændərə(r)/ n (pej) mujeriego m (pey)

philanthropic /'fɪlən'θrɑ:pɪk ‖,fɪlən'θrɒpɪk/ adj filantrópico

philanthropist /fə'lænθrəpəst ‖fɪ'lænθrəpɪst/ n filántropo, -pa m,f

philately /fə'lætli ‖fɪ'lætəli/ n (frml) filatelia f

Philippine /'fɪləpi:n ‖'fɪlɪpi:n/ adj filipino

Philippines /'fɪləpi:nz ‖'fɪlɪpi:nz/ pl n **the ~** (las) Filipinas

philistine /'fɪləsti:n, -aɪn ‖'fɪlɪstaɪn/ n ignorante mf

philosopher /fə'lɑ:səfər ‖fɪ'lɒsəfə(r)/ n filósofo, -fa m,f

philosophic /'fɪlə'sɑ:fɪk ‖,fɪlə'sɒfɪk/, **-ical** /-ɪkəl/ adj filosófico; **to be ~ ABOUT sth** tomarse algo con filosofía

philosophy /fə'lɑ:səfi ‖fɪ'lɒsəfi/ n filosofía f

phlegm /flem/ n flema f

phobia /'fəʊbiə/ n fobia f

phoenix /'fi:nɪks/ n Ave f; Fénix, fénix m or f

phone[1] /fəʊn/ n teléfono m; **to be on the ~** (be speaking) estar* hablando por teléfono; (subscribe) (BrE) tener* teléfono; (before n) ~ **call** llamada f (telefónica); ~ **number** (número m de) teléfono m

phone² vt ⟨person⟩ llamar (por teléfono), telefonear, hablar (Méx); ⟨place/number⟩ llamar (por teléfono) a
■ **phone up** [v + adv + o, v + o + adv] llamar, telefonear

phone: ~ **book** n (colloq) guía f (telefónica or de teléfonos) or (Col, Méx) directorio m; ~ **booth,** (BrE) ~ **box** n cabina f telefónica; ~**card** n tarjeta f telefónica

phonetics /fə'netɪks/ n (+ sing vb) fonética f

phoney¹, (AmE also) **phony** /'fəʊni/ adj **-nier, -niest** (colloq & pej) falso

phoney², (AmE also) **phony** n (pl **-neys** or **-nies**) (colloq & pej) (person) farsante mf (fam); (thing) falsificación f

phosphate /'fɑːsfeɪt ‖ 'fɒsfeɪt/ n fosfato m

phosphorus /'fɑːsfərəs ‖ 'fɒsfərəs/ n fósforo m

photo /'fəʊtəʊ/ n (pl **-tos**) (colloq) foto f; **to take a** ~ **(of sb/sth)** sacar(le)* or (Esp tb) hacer(le)* una foto (a algn/algo)

photocopier /'fəʊtəʊˌkɑːpiər ‖ 'fəʊtəʊˌkɒpiə(r)/ n fotocopiadora f

photocopy¹ /'fəʊtəʊˌkɑːpi ‖ 'fəʊtəʊˌkɒpi/ n (pl **-copies**) fotocopia f

photocopy² vt **-copies, -copying, -copied** fotocopiar

photo: ~ **finish** n foto(-)finish f; **P~fit®** n (BrE): **P~fit (picture)** retrato m hablado (AmS) or (Esp) robot or (Méx) reconstruido

photogenic /ˌfəʊtə'dʒenɪk/ adj fotogénico

photograph¹ /'fəʊtəɡræf ‖ 'fəʊtəɡrɑːf/ n fotografía f, foto f; **to take a** ~ **(of sb/sth)** sacar(le)* or (Esp tb) hacer(le)* una foto or una fotografía (a algn/algo)

photograph² vt fotografiar*, sacarle* or (Esp tb) hacerle* una foto or una fotografía a

photographer /fə'tɑːɡrəfər ‖ fə'tɒɡrəfə(r)/ n fotógrafo, -fa m,f

photographic /ˌfəʊtə'ɡræfɪk/ adj ⟨copy/ evidence/memory⟩ fotográfico; ⟨shop/equipment⟩ de fotografía

photography /fə'tɑːɡrəfi ‖ fə'tɒɡrəfi/ n fotografía f

photosynthesis /ˌfəʊtəʊ'sɪnθəsəs ‖ ˌfəʊtəʊ'sɪnθəsɪs/ n fotosíntesis f

phrasal verb /'freɪzl/ n verbo m con partícula(s)

phrase¹ /freɪz/ n frase f

phrase² vt expresar

phrase book n manual m de conversación, ≈guía m de bolsillo para el viajero

physical¹ /'fɪzɪkəl/ adj **1** (bodily) físico; ⟨illness⟩ orgánico; ~ **education** educación f física **2** (material) ⟨world⟩ material

physical² n reconocimiento m médico

physically /'fɪzɪkli/ adv ⟨attractive⟩ físicamente; ⟨demanding⟩ desde el punto de vista físico; **it's** ~ **impossible** es materialmente imposible

physical therapist n (AmE) ▶ PHYSIOTHERAPIST

physical therapy n (AmE) ▶ PHYSIOTHERAPY

physician /fə'zɪʃən ‖ fɪ'zɪʃən/ n (frml) médico, -ca m,f

physicist /'fɪzəsəst ‖ 'fɪzɪsɪst/ n físico, -ca m,f

physics /'fɪzɪks/ n (+ sing vb) física f

physiological /ˌfɪziə'lɑːdʒɪkəl ‖ ˌfɪziə'lɒdʒɪkəl/ adj fisiológico

physiology /ˌfɪzi'ɑːlədʒi ‖ ˌfɪzi'ɒlədʒi/ n fisiología f

physiotherapist /ˌfɪziəʊ'θerəpəst ‖ ˌfɪziəʊ'θerəpɪst/ n fisioterapeuta mf, kinesiólogo, -ga m,f

physiotherapy /ˌfɪziəʊ'θerəpi/ n (discipline) kinesiología f; (treatment) fisioterapia f, kinesiterapia f

physique /fə'ziːk ‖ fɪ'ziːk/ n físico m

pianist /'piːænəst ‖ 'piənɪst/ n pianista mf

piano /pi'ænəʊ/ n (pl **-os**) piano m

pick¹ /pɪk/ n **1** (a) ▶ PICKAX (b) (ice ~) piolet m (c) (plectrum) púa f, plectro m, uñeta f (CS), uña f (Méx, Ven) **2** (choice) (no pl): **take your** ~ elige or escoge el (or los etc) que quieras

pick² vt **1** (a) (choose, select) ⟨number/color⟩ elegir*, escoger*; ⟨team/crew⟩ seleccionar (b) (provoke): **to** ~ **a fight with sb** meterse con algn **2** (gather) ⟨flower⟩ cortar, coger* (esp Esp); ⟨fruit/ cotton/tea⟩ recoger*, coger* (esp Esp), pizcar* (Méx)
3 (a) (remove matter from): **to** ~ **one's nose** meterse el dedo en la nariz, hurgarse* la nariz; **don't** ~ **your spots** no te toques los granitos; **to** ~ **sb's pocket** robarle la billetera (or las llaves etc) a algn del bolsillo, bolsear a algn (Mex fam), carterear a algn (Chi fam) (b) (open) ⟨lock⟩ abrir* con una ganzúa (or una horquilla etc)
■ ~ vi (a) : **to** ~ **and choose** ser exigente (b) (take bits): **he was** ~**ing at his dinner** comía desganado
■ **pick on** [v + prep + o] (colloq) meterse con, agarrársela(s) con (AmL fam)
■ **pick out** [v + o + adv, v + adv + o] **1** (choose, select) elegir*, escoger* **2** (a) (recognize, identify) reconocer* (b) (discern) distinguir*
■ **pick up**
I [v + o + adv, v + adv + o] **1** (gather off floor, ground) recoger*; (take) tomar, agarrar (esp AmL), coger* (esp Esp); (lift up) levantar
2 (learn) ⟨language⟩ aprender; ⟨habit⟩ adquirir, agarrar (esp AmL), coger* (esp Esp)
3 (a) (collect, fetch) recoger* (b) (take on board) ⟨passenger⟩ recoger* (c) (colloq) ⟨man/woman⟩ ligarse* (fam), levantar (AmS fam)
4 (receive) ⟨signal⟩ captar
II [v + adv + o] (gain) ⟨speed⟩ agarrar, coger* (esp Esp)
III [v + o + adv] (a) (revive) reanimar (b) (correct) corregir*
IV [v + adv] (improve) «prices/sales» subir; «economy/business» repuntar; «invalid» mejorar; «weather» mejorar

pickax, (BrE) **pickaxe** /'pɪkæks/ n pico m, piqueta f

picket¹ /'pɪkət ‖ 'pɪkɪt/ n (group) piquete m; (before n) ~ **line** piquete m

picket² vt ⟨factory/workplace⟩ formar un piquete frente a, piquetear (esp AmL)

pickings /'pɪkɪŋz/ pl n (a) (profits) ganancias fpl (b) (food) sobras fpl

pickle¹ /'pɪkəl/ n (a) (dill ~) (AmE) pepinillo m

en vinagre al eneldo (b) ~s (vegetables) encurtidos *mpl*, pickles *mpl* (CS) (c) (relish) ⟨BrE⟩ *condimento a base de encurtidos en una salsa*

pickle² *vt* conservar en vinagre *or* (Chi tb) en escabeche, encurtir

pick: ~-me-up *n* (colloq) estimulante *m*; ~**pocket** *n* carterista *mf*, bolsista *mf* (Méx); ~**up** (truck) *n* camioneta *f* (de reparto)

picky /'pɪki/ *adj* **pickier, pickiest** (colloq) quisquilloso

picnic /'pɪknɪk/ *n* picnic *m*; **to go for** *o* **on a ~** ir* de picnic

pictorial /pɪk'tɔːriəl/ *adj* ⟨representation⟩ pictórico; ⟨account/history⟩ en imágenes; ⟨magazine⟩ ilustrado

picture¹ /'pɪktʃər ‖ 'pɪktʃə(r)/ *n* ❶ (a) (illustration) ilustración *f*; (drawing) dibujo *m*; (painting) cuadro *m*, pintura *f*; (print) cuadro *m*, lámina *f*; (portrait) retrato *m* (b) (photo) foto *f*; **to take a ~ of sth/sb** sacarle* *or* (Esp tb) hacerle* una foto a algo/algn ❷ (situation) panorama *m*; **to put sb in the ~** poner* a algn al tanto (de la situación) ❸ (idea) idea *f* ❹ (TV) imagen *f* ❺ (Cin) (a) (movie) película *f* (b) **pictures** *pl* (cinema) (BrE dated) **the ~s** el cine

picture² *vt* imaginarse

picturesque /ˌpɪktʃə'resk/ *adj* pintoresco

pie /paɪ/ *n* (savory) empanada *f*; (sweet) pastel *m*, pay *m* (AmC, Méx)

piece /piːs/ *n* ❶ (a) (part of sth broken, torn, cut, divided) pedazo *m*, trozo *m*; **she ripped the letter into ~s** rompió la carta en pedacitos; **to come** *o* **fall to ~s** hacerse* pedazos; **a ~ of land** un terreno, una parcela; **in one ~** (safe) sano y salvo; (unbroken) intacto; **to go to ~s** perder* el control; **to pull sth/sb to ~s** destrozar* algo/a algn; **to say one's ~** dar* su (*or* mi etc) opinión (b) (component) pieza *f*, parte *f*; **to take sth to ~s** desarmar algo

❷ (item): **a ~ of advice** un consejo; **a ~ of furniture** un mueble; **a ~ of paper** un papel; **an excellent ~ of work** un trabajo excelente; **to give sb a ~ of one's mind** cantarle las cuarenta a algn ❸ (a) (Mus): **a ~ (of music)** una pieza (de música) (b) (Journ) artículo *m* ❹ (coin) moneda *f* ❺ (in board games) ficha *f*; (in chess) figura *f*

■ **piece together** [v + o + adv, v + adv + o] ⟨fragments⟩ juntar*; ⟨events/facts⟩ reconstruir*

piecemeal¹ /'piːsmiːl/ *adj* poco sistemático

piecemeal² *adv* (gradually) poco a poco; (unsystematically) de manera poco sistemática

piecework /'piːswɜːrk ‖ 'piːswɜːk/ *n* trabajo *m* a destajo

pier /pɪr ‖ pɪə(r)/ *n* (a) (landing place) embarcadero *m*, muelle *m* (b) (with amusements) *paseo con juegos y atracciones sobre un muelle*

pierce /pɪrs ‖ pɪəs/ *vt* (a) (make a hole in) agujerear; (go through) atravesar*; **she's had her ears ~d** se ha hecho hacer agujeros en las orejas (b) ⟨sound/light⟩ (liter) rasgar* (liter)

piercing /'pɪrsɪŋ ‖ 'pɪəsɪŋ/ *adj* ⟨eyes/look⟩ penetrante; ⟨scream⟩ desgarrador

piety /'paɪəti/ *n* piedad *f*

pig¹ /pɪg/ *n* ❶ (Agr, Zool) cerdo *m*, chancho *m*

(AmL) ❷ (a) (obnoxious person) (colloq) cerdo, -da *m,f* (fam) (b) (glutton) (colloq) glotón, -tona *m,f*, angurriento, -ta *m,f* (CS fam)

pigeon /'pɪdʒən ‖ 'pɪdʒɪn, 'pɪdʒən/ *n* (Zool) paloma *f*; (Culin) pichón *m*

pigeonhole /'pɪdʒənhəʊl ‖ 'pɪdʒɪnhəʊl, 'pɪdʒən-/ *n* (a) (on wall, desk) casillero *m* (b) (category) casilla *f*

piggy /'pɪgi/ *n* (*pl* **-gies**) (used to or by children) cerdito *m*, chanchito *m* (AmL)

piggy: ~**back** *n*: **to give sb a ~back** llevar a algn a caballo; ~**bank** *n* alcancía *f* (AmL), hucha *f* (Esp) (*en forma de cerdito*)

pigheaded /'pɪg'hedəd ‖ ˌpɪg'hedɪd/ *adj* terco

piglet /'pɪglət ‖ 'pɪglɪt/ *n* cochinillo *m*, lechón *m*, chanchito *m* (AmL)

pigment /'pɪgmənt/ *n* pigmento *m*

pigmy /'pɪgmi/ *n* ▶ PYGMY

pig: ~**pen** (AmE) ▶ ~STY; ~**sty** *n* pocilga *f*, chiquero *m* (AmL); ~**tail** *n* (bunch) coleta *f*, chape *m* (Chi); (plait) trenza *f*

pike /paɪk/ *n* (a) (*pl* ~) (Zool) lucio *m* (b) (turn~) (AmE) carretera *f*

pilchard /'pɪltʃərd ‖ 'pɪltʃəd/ *n* sardina *f* (grande)

pile¹ /paɪl/ *n* ❶ (stack, heap) montón *m* ❷ (Tex) pelo *m* ❸ **piles** *pl* (BrE Med) hemorroides *fpl*, almorranas *fpl*

pile² *vt* amontonar

■ **pile in** [v + adv] (colloq) meterse

■ **pile into** [v + prep + o] (colloq) (a) (squeeze into) ⟨car⟩ meterse en (b) (attack) arremeter contra (c) (crash into) ⟨vehicle⟩ estrellarse contra

■ **pile up** ❶ [v + adv] (accumulate) amontonarse ❷ [v + o + adv, v + adv + o] (form into pile) apilar

pileup /'paɪlʌp/ *n* choque *m* múltiple

pilfering /'pɪlfərɪŋ/ *n* robos *mpl*, hurtos *mpl*

pilgrim /'pɪlgrəm ‖ 'pɪlgrɪm/ *n* peregrino, -na *m,f*; (before *n*) **the P~ Fathers** *los primeros colonizadores de Nueva Inglaterra*

pilgrimage /'pɪlgrəmɪdʒ ‖ 'pɪlgrɪmɪdʒ/ *n* peregrinación *f*

pill /pɪl/ *n* (a) (tablet) pastilla *f*, píldora *f* (b) (contraceptive) **the P~** la píldora (anticonceptiva); **to be on the P~** tomar la píldora

pillage¹ /'pɪlɪdʒ/ *n* pillaje *m*

pillage² *vt/i* saquear

pillar /'pɪlər ‖ 'pɪlə(r)/ *n* pilar *m*; **he is a ~ of the community** es uno de los pilares *or* baluartes de la comunidad

pillar box *n* (BrE) buzón *m*

pillion¹ /'pɪljən ‖ 'pɪliən/ *n* (Auto) asiento *m* trasero (de una moto)

pillion² *adv* ⟨ride⟩ en el asiento trasero

pillory /'pɪləri/ *n* (*pl* **-ries**) picota *f*

pillow /'pɪləʊ/ *n* almohada *f*

pillowcase /'pɪləʊkeɪs/, (BrE also) **pillow slip** *n* funda *f*, almohadón *m* (Esp)

pilot¹ /'paɪlət/ *n* ❶ (Aerosp, Aviat) piloto *mf* ❷ (Naut) práctico *mf* (de puerto) ❸ (Rad, TV) programa *m* piloto

pilot² *adj* (before *n*) piloto *adj inv*

pilot³ *vt* ❶ (Aviat, Naut) pilotar, pilotear (AmL) ❷ (test) poner* a prueba

pilot light *n* piloto *m*

pimple /'pɪmpəl/ n grano m, espinilla f (AmL)

pin¹ /pɪn/ n **1** (for cloth, paper) alfiler m
2 (brooch, badge) (AmE) insignia f **3** (a) (on plug)
(BrE Elec) clavija f, borne m **(b)** (peg) (Tech) perno
m

pin² -nn- vt **1** (fasten, attach) ⟨dress/seam⟩
prender con alfileres; **I ∼ned the papers together**
sujeté los papeles con un alfiler; **she had ∼ned
her hopes on getting a scholarship** había
depositado sus esperanzas en conseguir una beca;
they tried to ∼ the blame on him trataron de
hacerle cargar con la culpa
2 (hold motionless) inmovilizar*
■ **pin down** [v + o + adv, v + adv + o] **1** (prevent
from moving): **they ∼ned him down** (se echaron
sobre él y) lo inmovilizaron
2 (a) (define) ⟨cause/identity⟩ definir;
something's wrong with me, but I can't ∼ it down
algo tengo, pero no sabría decir exactamente qué
(b) (force to state position): **I managed to ∼ him
down to a definite date** conseguí que se
comprometiera para una fecha concreta

PIN /pɪn/ n (= **personal identification
number**) PIN m

pinafore /'pɪnəfɔːr ‖ 'pɪnəfɔː(r)/ n **(a) ∼
(dress)** (sleeveless dress) jumper m or (Esp) pichi
m **(b)** (apron) (BrE) delantal m or (esp Méx) mandil
m ⟨con peto⟩ **(c)** (protective overdress) delantal m

pinball /'pɪnbɔːl/ n ⟨before n⟩ ∼ **machine** flipper
m

pincer /'pɪnsər ‖ 'pɪnsə(r)/ n **(a)** (Zool) pinza f
(b) pincers pl (tool) tenaza(s) f(pl)

pinch¹ /pɪntʃ/ n **(a)** (act) pellizco m; **in** o (BrE) **at
a ∼** si fuera necesario **(b)** (small quantity) pizca f

pinch² vt **1** «person» pellizcar*; «shoes»
apretar* **2** (BrE colloq) (steal) robar

pinched /pɪntʃt/ adj: **faces ∼ with grief** caras
transidas de dolor

pincushion /'pɪn,kʊʃən/ n alfiletero m

pine¹ /paɪn/ n **(a) ∼ (tree)** pino m; ⟨before n⟩
∼ **cone** piña f; ∼ **needle** hoja f de pino **(b)** (wood)
(madera f de) pino m

pine² vi estar* triste; **to ∼ FOR sth** suspirar POR
algo
■ **pine away** [v + adv] languidecer* de añoranza

pineapple /'paɪn,æpəl/ n piña f or (esp RPl)
ananá f

Ping-Pong®, ping-pong /'pɪŋpɑːŋ ‖ 'pɪŋpɒŋ/
n ping-pong m

pinion /'pɪnjən/ vt ⟨person⟩ inmovilizar* (esp
sujetándole los brazos)

pink¹ /pɪŋk/ adj **-er, -est** rosa adj inv, rosado
(AmL); ⟨cheeks⟩ sonrosado

pink² n rosa m, rosado m (AmL)

pinking shears /'pɪŋkɪŋ/ pl n tijeras fpl
dentadas

pin money n dinero para gastos personales

pinnacle /'pɪnəkəl ‖ 'pɪnəkəl/ n **(a)** (Archit)
pináculo m **(b)** (mountain peak) cumbre f, cima f

pin: ∼point vt ⟨position⟩ localizar* or (AmL tb)
ubicar* con exactitud; **to ∼point the causes of**
the problem establecer* con exactitud cuáles son
las causas del problema; **∼prick** n pinchazo m;
∼s and needles pl n hormigueo m;
∼stripe, ∼striped adj: **∼stripe(d) suit** traje m
oscuro de raya diplomática

pint /paɪnt/ n pinta f (EEUU: 0,47 litros, RU: 0,57
litros)

pinup /'pɪnʌp/ n foto f (de chica atractiva, actor
famoso etc); ⟨person⟩ pin-up mf

pioneer¹ /'paɪə'nɪr ‖ ,paɪə'nɪə(r)/ n pionero, -ra
m,f

pioneer² vt **(a)** ⟨policy⟩ promover*; ⟨technique⟩
ser* el primero (or la primera etc) en aplicar **(b)**

pioneering pres p ⟨research⟩ pionero

pious /'paɪəs/ adj piadoso; (sanctimonious) beato

pip /pɪp/ n **1** (seed) pepita f **2** (BrE Rad, Telec)
pitido m

pipe¹ /paɪp/ n **1** (for liquid, gas) caño m **2** (for
tobacco) pipa f **3** (Mus) **(a)** (wind instrument)
caramillo m **(b)** (of organ) tubo m **(c) pipes** pl
gaita f

pipe² vt (transport by pipe) ⟨+ adv compl⟩ llevar
⟨por tuberías, gasoducto, oleoducto⟩
■ **pipe down** [v + adv] (colloq) (usu in imperative)
callarse la boca (fam)

piped music /paɪpt/ n música f ambiental,
hilo m musical (Esp)

pipe: ∼ dream n quimera f, sueño m guajiro
(Méx); **∼line** n conducto m, ducto m (Méx); **it's in
the ∼line** está proyectado

piper /'paɪpər ‖ 'paɪpə(r)/ n gaitero, -ra m,f

piping¹ /'paɪpɪŋ/ n cañería f, tubería f

piping² adv (as intensifier): **∼ hot** bien caliente

pique¹ /piːk/ n despecho m

pique² vt: **he was ∼d by her lack of interest** se
resintió por su falta de interés

piracy /'paɪrəsi/ n piratería f

pirate /'paɪrət/ n **(a)** (at sea) pirata mf **(b)**
⟨before n⟩ ⟨tape/video/radio station⟩ pirata adj inv

pirouette¹ /'pɪru'et/ n giro m; (in ballet) pirueta
f

pirouette² vi girar

Pisces /'paɪsiːz/ n **(a)** (sign) (no art) Piscis **(b)**
⟨person⟩ Piscis or piscis mf

piss¹ /pɪs/ n (sl) **(a)** (act) (no pl) meada f (vulg)
(b) (urine) meados mpl (vulg)

piss² vi (sl) mear (vulg)
■ **piss off** (sl) **1** [v + adv] (go away) (BrE): **∼ off!**
¡vete a la mierda! (vulg) **2** [v + o + adv] (anger): **it
∼es me off** me revienta (fam), me encabrona (Esp,
Méx vulg)

pissed /pɪst/ adj (sl) **(a)** (AmE) (fed up) cabreado
(fam), encabronado (Esp, Méx vulg), choreado (Chi
fam) **(b)** (drunk) (BrE) como una cuba (fam), tomado
(AmL fam)

pistachio /pɪ'stæʃiəʊ/ n ∼ **(nut)** pistacho m,
pistache m (Méx)

pistol /'pɪstl/ n pistola f

piston /'pɪstən/ n émbolo m, pistón m

pit¹ /pɪt/ n **1** (hole — in ground) hoyo m; (— for

AmC	Central America	Arg	Argentina	Cu	Cuba	Per	Peru
AmL	Latin America	Bol	Bolivia	Ec	Ecuador	RPl	River Plate Area
AmS	South America	Chi	Chile	Esp	Spain	Ur	Uruguay
Andes	Andean Region	CS	Southern Cone	Méx	Mexico	Ven	Venezuela

burying) fosa *f*; (— as trap) trampa *f*; (**inspection**) ~
(Auto) foso *m or* (RPl) fosa *f* **2** (coalmine) mina *f*
(*de carbón*); (quarry) cantera *f* **3** (orchestra) ~ foso
m orquestal *or* de la orquesta **4** **pits** *pl* (the very
worst) (sl) **the ~s** lo peor que hay (fam) **5** (in fruit)
(AmE) hueso *m*, carozo *m* (CS), pepa *f* (Col)

pit² -tt- *vt* ‹*surface/metal*› picar*
■ **pit against** [*v* + *o* + *prep* + *o*] enfrentar a; **to
~ oneself against sb** enfrentarse a algn

pitch¹ /pɪtʃ/ *n* **(a)** (level, degree) (*no pl*) punto *m*,
extremo *m* **(b)** (Mus) tono *m* **(c)** (in baseball)
lanzamiento *m* **(d)** (Sport) (playing area) (BrE)
campo *m*, cancha *f* (AmL) **(e)** (position, site) (BrE)
lugar *m*, sitio *m*; (in market, fair) puesto *m* **(f)**
(substance) brea *f*

pitch² *vt* **1** (set up) ‹*tent*› armar, montar;
‹*camp*› montar, hacer* **2** (Sport) ‹*ball*› lanzar*,
pichear **3** (aim, set, address): **she doesn't know at
what level to ~ her talk** no sabe qué nivel darle a
la charla
■ **~** *vi* **(a)** (fall) (+ *adv compl*) caerse* **(b)** (lurch)
‹*ship/plane*› cabecear
■ **pitch in** [*v* + *adv*] (colloq) arrimar el hombro

pitch-black /ˈpɪtʃˈblæk/, **pitch-dark**
/ˈpɪtʃˈdɑːrk ‖ˌpɪtʃˈdɑːk/ *adj* ‹*night*› (oscuro)
como boca de lobo (fam), muy oscuro; ‹*surface*›
negro como el azabache

pitched battle /pɪtʃt/ *n* batalla *f* campal

pitcher /ˈpɪtʃər ‖ˈpɪtʃə(r)/ *n* **1** (for pouring)
jarra *f*, pichel *m* (AmC); (of clay) (BrE) cántaro *m*
2 (in baseball) lanzador, -dora *m,f*, pítcher *mf*

pitchfork /ˈpɪtʃfɔːrk ‖ˈpɪtʃfɔːk/ *n* horca *f*,
horquilla *f*, horqueta *f* (Chi)

pitfall /ˈpɪtfɔːl/ *n* (difficulty) dificultad *f*; (risk)
riesgo *m*

pith /pɪθ/ *n* tejido blanco fibroso que recubre el
interior de la cáscara de los cítricos

pithy /ˈpɪθi/ *adj* **pithier, pithiest** ‹*remark/
reply*› sucinto *or* conciso y expresivo

pitiful /ˈpɪtɪfəl/ *adj* **(a)** (arousing pity) ‹*cry/moan*›
lastimero; ‹*sight*› lastimoso **(b)** (wretched,
inadequate) lamentable

pittance /ˈpɪtns/ *n* miseria *f*

pituitary gland /pəˈtuːəteri ‖pɪˈtjuːɪtəri/ *n*
glándula pituitaria *f*

pity¹ /ˈpɪti/ *n* **1** (*no pl*) (cause of regret) lástima *f*,
pena *f*; **it's a ~** (THAT) es una lástima *or* una
pena QUE (+ *subj*); **what a ~!** ¡qué lástima!, ¡que
pena! **2** (compassion) piedad *f*; **to take ~ on sb/
sth** apiadarse de algn/algo

pity² *vt* **pities, pitying, pitied** tenerle*
lástima a

pivot /ˈpɪvət/ *vi* (Mech Eng) pivotar; **he ~ed on
his heel** giró sobre sus talones

pixie /ˈpɪksi/ *n* (elf) duendecillo *m*; (fairy) hadita
f

pizza /ˈpiːtsə/ *n* pizza *f*

pizzeria /ˈpiːtsəˈriːə/ *n* pizzería *f*

placard /ˈplækɑːrd ‖ˈplækɑːd/ *n* letrero *m*; (at
demonstration) pancarta *f*

placate /ˈpleɪkeɪt ‖pləˈkeɪt/ *vt* apaciguar*

place¹ /pleɪs/ *n* **1** **(a)** (spot, position, area) lugar
m, sitio *m*; **to have friends in high ~s** tener*
amigos influyentes; **all over the ~** por todas
partes; **to fall into ~** aclararse **(b)** (specific location)
lugar *m*; **~ of birth** lugar de nacimiento **(c)** (in

phrases) **in place: to hold sth in ~** sujetar algo;
out of place: to look out of ~ ‹*furniture*› quedar
mal; **to feel out of ~** sentirse* fuera de lugar
2 **(a)** (building, shop, restaurant etc) sitio *m*, lugar
m **(b)** (home): **my/his ~** mi/su casa
3 **(a)** (position, role) lugar *m*; **I wouldn't change
~s with her for anything** no me cambiaría por
ella por nada; **nobody can ever take your ~** nadie
podrá jamás ocupar tu lugar **(b)** **in place of** (*as
prep*) en lugar de **(c)** **to take place** (occur) ocurrir;
‹*meeting/concert/wedding*› tener* lugar
4 **(a)** (seat): **save me a ~** guárdame un asiento
(b) (at table) cubierto *m*; **to lay/set a ~ for sb**
poner* un cubierto para algn
5 (in contest, league) puesto *m*; **your social life will
have to take second ~** tu vida social va a tener
que pasar a un segundo plano
6 (in book, sequence): **you've made me lose my ~**
me has hecho perder la página (*or* la línea *etc*)
por donde iba
7 **(a)** (job) puesto *m* **(b)** (BrE Educ) plaza *f* **(c)**
(on team) puesto *m*
8 (in argument) lugar *m*; **in the first/second ~** en
primer/segundo lugar

place² *vt* **1** (put, position) ‹*object*› poner*;
(carefully, precisely) colocar* **2** (in race): **this victory
~s her among the top three** este triunfo la sitúa
entre las tres primeras **3** **(a)** (find a home, job for)
colocar* **(b)** ‹*advertisement*› poner*; ‹*phone call*›
pedir*; **we ~d an order with Acme Corp** hicimos
un pedido a Acme Corp **4** (identify) ‹*tune*›
identificar*, ubicar* (AmL); **her face is familiar,
but I can't quite ~ her** su cara me resulta
conocida pero no sé de dónde *or* (AmL tb) pero no
la ubico

placebo /pləˈsiːbəʊ/ *n* (*pl* ~**s** *or* ~**es**) placebo
m

place mat *n* (mantel *m*) individual *m*

placement /ˈpleɪsmənt/ *n* **(a)** (in employment)
colocación *f* **(b)** (positioning) colocación *f*,
ubicación *f* (esp AmL)

place name *n* topónimo *m*

placenta /pləˈsentə/ *n* (*pl* ~**s** *or* ~**e** /-tiː/)
placenta *f*

placid /ˈplæsəd ‖ˈplæsɪd/ *adj* plácido

plagiarism /ˈpleɪdʒərɪzəm/ *n* plagio *m*

plagiarize /ˈpleɪdʒəraɪz/ *vt* plagiar

plague¹ /pleɪg/ *n* **(a)** (disease) peste *f* **(b)** (horde
— of locusts, tourists) plaga *f*

plague² *vt* **(a)** (afflict): **a country ~d by strikes**
un país asolado por constantes huelgas; **~d with
problems** plagado de problemas **(b)** (pester)
acosar

plaice /pleɪs/ *n* (*pl* ~) platija *f*

plaid /plæd/ *n* (pattern) cuadros *mpl* escoceses;
(material) tela *f* escocesa

plain¹ /pleɪn/ *adj* **-er, -est** **1** **(a)** (unadorned)
‹*decor/cooking/language*› sencillo; ‹*fabric*› liso
(b) (Culin): **~ chocolate** (BrE) chocolate *m* sin
leche; **~ flour** harina *f* común **2** **(a)** (clear) claro;
the reasons are ~ to see las razones saltan a la
vista **(b)** (blunt): **the ~ truth** la pura verdad
3 (not good-looking) feo, poco agraciado

plain² *adv* (*as intensifier*) totalmente; **that's just
~ stupid** eso es una completa estupidez

plain³ *n* llanura *f*

plain clothes *pl n*: **in ~ ~** de civil *or* (Esp tb) de paisano

plainly /'pleɪnli/ *adv* **(a)** (obviously, visibly) claramente **(b)** (clearly) ⟨*explain*⟩ claramente; ⟨*remember*⟩ perfectamente **(c)** (bluntly) ⟨*speak*⟩ claramente **(d)** ⟨*dress*⟩ con sencillez

plaintiff /'pleɪntəf ‖'pleɪntɪf/ *n* demandante *mf*

plaintive /'pleɪntɪv/ *adj* lastimero

plait¹ /plæt/ *n* trenza *f*

plait² *vt* trenzar*

plan¹ /plæn/ *n* **1 (a)** (diagram, map) plano *m* **(b)** (of book, essay) esquema *m* **2** (arrangement, scheme) plan *m*; **do you have any ~s for tonight?** ¿tienes algún plan para esta noche?

plan² **-nn-** *vt* ⟨*journey/raid*⟩ planear; ⟨*garden/house*⟩ diseñar; ⟨*economy/strategies*⟩ planificar*; ⟨*essay*⟩ hacer* un esquema de; ⟨*surprise*⟩ preparar; **as ~ned** según lo planeado; **to ~ to +** INF: **where are you ~ning to spend Christmas?** ¿dónde tienes pensado pasar las Navidades?
■ **~** *vi*: **to ~ ahead** planear las cosas de antemano
■ **plan on** [*v + prep + o*] **(a)** (intend) pensar* **(b)** (expect, count on) contar* con

plane¹ /pleɪn/ *n* **1** (aircraft) avión *m* **2** **~ (tree)** plátano *m* **3** (tool) cepillo *m* de carpintero; (longer) garlopa *f* **4** (surface) plano *m*

plane² *vt* ⟨*wood/surface*⟩ cepillar

planet /'plænət ‖'plænɪt/ *n* planeta *m*

planetary /'plænəteri ‖'plænɪtəri/ *adj* (*before n*) planetario

plank /plæŋk/ *n* tabla *f*, tablón *m*

plankton /'plæŋktən/ *n* plancton *m*

planned /plænd/ *adj* planeado; **~ parenthood** (AmE) planificación *f* familiar

planner /'plænər ‖'plænə(r)/ *n* **(a)** (of project) planificador, -dora *m,f* **(b)** (town **~**) urbanista *mf*

planning /'plænɪŋ/ *n* **(a)** (of project) planificación *f* **(b)** (town **~**) urbanismo *m*; (*before n*) **~ permission** (BrE) permiso *m* de obras

plant¹ /plænt ‖plɑːnt/ *n* **1** (Bot) planta *f* **2 (a)** (factory, installation) planta *f* **(b)** (equipment) maquinaria *f*

plant² *vt* **1** ⟨*flower/trees*⟩ plantar; ⟨*seeds*⟩ sembrar* **2** (place) ⟨*bomb*⟩ colocar*; ⟨*kiss*⟩ dar*, plantar (fam); **she herself right next to me** se me plantó justo al lado (fam) **3** ⟨*drugs/evidence*⟩ colocar*; ⟨*agent/informer*⟩ infiltrar

plantain /'plæntɪn ‖'plæntɪn/ *n* plátano *m* grande (*para cocinar*), plátano *m* (Col, Ven), plátano *m* macho (Méx)

plantation /plæn'teɪʃən ‖plæn'teɪʃən, plɑːn-/ *n* plantación *f*

plaque /plæk/ *n* **1** (tablet) placa *f* **2** (Dent) sarro *m*, placa *f* (dental)

plasma /'plæzmə/ *n* plasma *m*

plaster¹ /'plæstər ‖'plɑːstə(r)/ *n* **1 (a)** (Const) (powder, mixture) yeso *m*; (on walls) revoque *m* **(b)** **~ (of Paris)** (Art, Med) yeso *m*, escayola *f* (Esp); **to have one's leg in ~** tener* la pierna enyesada *or* (Esp) escayolada **2** (sticking **~**) (BrE) ▶ BAND-AID

plaster² *vt* (Const) ⟨*wall/room*⟩ revocar*; ⟨*cracks*⟩ rellenar con yeso

plaster cast *n* **(a)** (Med) yeso *m or* (Esp) escayola *f* **(b)** (Art) molde *m* de yeso, escayola *f* (Esp)

plastic¹ /'plæstɪk/ *n* plástico *m*; (*before n*) de plástico

plastic² *adj* **1** (artificial) (pej) ⟨*smile/people*⟩ de plástico (pey) **2 (a)** (malleable) (Tech) plástico, moldeable **(b)** (Art) plástico

plastic: ~ bullet *n* bala *f* de plástico; **~ explosive** *n* explosivo *m* plástico, goma dos *f*

Plasticine® /'plæstəsiːn/ *n* plastilina® *f*, plasticina® *f* (CS)

plastic: ~ surgeon *n* cirujano plástico, cirujana plástica *m,f* (AmL), especialista *mf* en cirugía estética *or* plástica; **~ surgery** *n* cirugía *f* estética *or* plástica

plate¹ /pleɪt/ *n* **1 (a)** (dish) plato *m* **(b)** (dishes) vajilla *f* (de plata *u oro*) **2** (of metal) chapa *f*; (thin) lámina *f*; (of glass) placa *f* **3 (a)** (Phot) placa *f* **(b)** (Art, Print) plancha *f* **(c)** (illustration) ilustración *f*, lámina *f*

plate² *vt* (Metall) **to ~ sth WITH sth** recubrir* algo DE algo

plateau /plæ'təʊ ‖'plætəʊ/ *n* (*pl* **-teaus** *or* **-teaux** /-z/) meseta *f*

platform /'plætfɔːrm ‖'plætfɔːm/ *n* **(a)** (raised structure) plataforma *f*, (for orator) estrado *m*, tribuna *f* **(b)** (Rail) andén *m* **(c)** (Pol) (opportunity to air views) plataforma *f*, tribuna *f*

platinum /'plætnəm ‖'plætɪnəm/ *n* platino *m*

platitude /'plætətuːd ‖'plætɪtjuːd/ *n* lugar *m* común

platonic /plə'tɑːnɪk ‖plə'tɒnɪk/ *adj* platónico

platoon /plə'tuːn/ *n* (Mil) sección *f*

platter /'plætər ‖'plætə(r)/ *n* fuente *f*

platypus /'plætɪpəs/ *n* (*pl* **~es**) (duck-billed **~**) ornitorrinco *m*

plausible /'plɔːzəbəl/ *adj* ⟨*argument/story*⟩ verosímil; ⟨*liar*⟩ convincente

play¹ /pleɪ/ *n* **1 (a)** (recreation) juego *m* **(b)** (Sport) juego *m* **2** (interplay) juego *m* **3** (slack) (Tech) juego *m* **4** (Theat) obra *f* (de teatro), pieza *f* (teatral), comedia *f* **5** (pun): **a ~ on words** un juego de palabras, un albur (Méx)

play² *vt*
I 1 (a) ⟨*cards/hopscotch*⟩ jugar* a; **to ~ a joke/trick on sb** hacerle* o gastarle una broma/una jugarreta a algn **(b)** ⟨*football/chess*⟩ jugar* (AmL exc RPl), jugar* a (Esp, RPl)
2 (a) (compete against) ⟨*opponent*⟩ jugar* contra **(b)** ⟨*card*⟩ tirar, jugar*; ⟨*piece*⟩ mover* **(c)** (in particular position) jugar* de
II 1 (Theat) **(a)** ⟨*villain/Hamlet*⟩ representar el papel de; **to ~ the innocent** hacerse* el inocente **(b)** ⟨*theater/town*⟩ actuar* en
2 (Mus) ⟨*instrument/note/piece*⟩ tocar*
3 (Audio) ⟨*tape/record*⟩ poner*
■ **~** *vi*
I 1 (amuse oneself) «*children*» jugar*; **to ~ AT sth** jugar* A algo
2 (Games, Sport) jugar*
II 1 (a) (Theat) «*cast*» actuar*; «*show*» ser* representado **(b)** (pretend): **to ~ dead** hacerse* el muerto; **to ~ hard to get** hacerse* el (*or* la *etc*) interesante
2 (Mus) «*musician*» tocar*; **music was ~ing in the background** se escuchaba una música de fondo
■ **play along 1** [*v + adv*] (cooperate): **I refuse to**

~ **along with him/his schemes** me niego a hacerle el juego/a tener nada que ver con sus enjuagues (fam)
[2] [*v* + *o* + *adv*] (deceive, manipulate) manipular
■ **play around** [*v* + *adv*] jugar*, juguetear (fam & pey)
■ **play back** [*v* + *o* + *adv*, *v* + *adv* + *o*] poner* (*una grabación*)
■ **play down** [*v* + *o* + *adv*, *v* + *adv* + *o*] ⟨*importance*⟩ minimizar*; ⟨*risk/achievement*⟩ quitarle importancia a
■ **play off** [*v* + *o* + *adv*] oponer*; **to ~ sb off against sb: she ~s her parents off against each other** hace pelear a sus padres para lograr sus propósitos
■ **play up** [1] [*v* + *adv*] (BrE) (cause trouble) (colloq) «*child*» dar* guerra (fam); «*car/TV*» no funcionar bien
[2] [*v* + *o* + *adv*] (cause trouble) (BrE colloq) «*child*» darle* guerra a (fam); «*shoulder/back*» darle* problemas a (fam)

play: ~**back** *n* play-back *m*; ~**boy** *n* playboy *m*; ~**-by-~** /'pleɪbaɪ'pleɪ/ *adj* (AmE Sport) (*before* -*n*) jugada a jugada

player /'pleɪər ‖ 'pleɪə(r)/ *n* [1] (Games, Sport) jugador, -dora *m,f* [2] (Mus) músico *mf*, músico, -ca *m,f*

playful /'pleɪfəl/ *adj* (a) (boisterous) juguetón (b) (not serious) pícaro

playfully /'pleɪfəli/ *adv* (a) (boisterously) juguetonamente (b) (humorously) ⟨*remark/slap*⟩ en broma

play: ~**ground** *n* (BrE) patio *m* (de recreo); ~**group** *n*: grupo de actividades lúdico-educativas para niños de edad preescolar

playing /'pleɪɪŋ/: ~ **card** *n* naipe *m*, carta *f*; ~ **field** *n* (BrE) (*often pl*) campo *m* de juego, cancha *f* de deportes (esp AmL)

play: ~**mate** *n* compañero, -ra *m,f* de juegos; ~**off** *n* desempate *m*; ~**pen** *n* corral *m*, parque *m* (Esp); ~**room** *n* cuarto *m* de los juguetes; ~**thing** *n* juguete *m*; ~**time** *n* (*no art*) (BrE) recreo *m*; ~**wright** /'pleɪraɪt/ *n* dramaturgo, -ga *m,f*

plaza /'plæzə ‖ 'plɑːzə/ *n* (a) (square) plaza *f*; (in front of big building) explanada *f* (b) (complex) (AmE) centro *m* comercial

plc, Plc (in UK) (= **public limited company**) ≈ S.A.

plea /pliː/ *n* [1] (appeal) (frml) petición *f*; (in supplication) ruego *m* [2] (Law): **to enter a ~ of guilty/not guilty** declararse culpable/inocente

plead /pliːd/ (*past & past p* **pleaded** *or* (AmE also) **pled**) *vt* alegar*; **she's not coming, she ~ed poverty** no viene, dijo que no tenía dinero
■ ~ *vi* (a) (implore, beg) suplicar*; **to ~ FOR sth** suplicar* algo; **to ~ WITH sb to + INF** suplicarle* a algn QUE (+ *subj*) (b) (Law): **to ~ guilty/not guilty** declararse culpable/inocente

pleasant /'plezn̩t/ *adj* **-er, -est** agradable; ⟨*person*⟩ simpático, agradable

pleasantly /'plezn̩tli/ *adv* ⟨*say/speak*⟩ en tono agradable; ⟨*smile*⟩ con simpatía; **I was ~ surprised by the changes** los cambios me causaron una grata sorpresa

pleasantry /'plezn̩tri/ *n* (*pl* **-ries**) cortesía *f*

please¹ /pliːz/ *interj* por favor; **yes, ~** sí, gracias

please² *vt* (make happy) complacer*; (satisfy) contentar
■ ~ *vi* (a) (satisfy): **we do our best to ~** hacemos todo lo posible por complacer al cliente (*or* a todo el mundo *etc*) (b) (choose) querer*; **do as you ~** haz lo que quieras
■ *v refl* **to ~ oneself: ~ yourself** haz lo que quieras

pleased /pliːzd/ *adj* (satisfied) satisfecho; (happy) contento; **I'm very ~ for you!** me alegro mucho por ti; **she was very ~ with herself** estaba muy ufana; **I am ~ to inform you that ...** (frml) tengo el placer de comunicarle que ... (frml); **~ to meet you** encantado (de conocerlo), mucho gusto

pleasing /'pliːzɪŋ/ *adj* (a) (pleasant) agradable (b) (gratifying) ⟨*news*⟩ grato

pleasurable /'pleʒərəbəl/ *adj* placentero

pleasure /'pleʒər ‖ 'pleʒə(r)/ *n* [1] (happiness, satisfaction) placer *m*; **it's a ~ to listen to her** es un placer escucharla; **it gives me great ~ to introduce ...** es un placer para mí presentarles ...; **to take ~ in sth** disfrutar con algo [2] (a) (recreation) placer *m*; **I play just for ~** toco sólo porque me gusta (b) (source of happiness) placer *m*; **Jane is a real ~ to teach** da gusto darle clases a Jane

pleasure boat *n* (steamer) barco *m* de recreo; (small craft) bote *m* de recreo

pleat /pliːt/ *n* pliegue *m*; (wide) tabla *f*

plectrum /'plektrəm/ *n* (*pl* **-trums** *or* **-tra** /-trə/) púa *f*, plectro *m*, uñeta *f* (CS), uña *f* (Méx, Ven)

pled /pled/ (AmE) *past & past p of* PLEAD

pledge¹ /pledʒ/ *vt* ⟨*support/funds*⟩ prometer

pledge² *n* (a) (promise) promesa *f*; **to make a ~ to + INF** prometer + INF (b) (of money) cantidad *f* prometida

plentiful /'plentɪfəl/ *adj* abundante

plenty¹ /'plenti/ *n* abundancia *f*

plenty² *pron* [1] (a) (large, sufficient number) muchos, -chas (b) plenty of muchos, -chas [2] (a) (large, sufficient quantity) mucho, -cha; **$50 is ~** 50 dólares es más que suficiente (b) plenty of mucho, -cha; **~ of time** tiempo de sobra

plethora /'pleθərə/ *n* (*no pl*) **a ~ OF sth** una plétora DE algo

Plexiglas® /'pleksɪglæs ‖ 'pleksɪglɑːs/ *n* (AmE) acrílico *m*, plexiglás® *m* (Esp)

pliable /'plaɪəbəl/, **pliant** /'plaɪənt/ *adj* ⟨*material/substance*⟩ maleable; ⟨*person/attitude*⟩ flexible

pliers /'plaɪərz ‖ 'plaɪəz/ *pl n* alicate(s) *m(pl)*, pinza(s) *f(pl)* (Méx, RPl)

plight /plaɪt/ *n* (*no pl*) situación *f* difícil

plimsoll /'plɪmsəl/ *n* (BrE) zapatilla *f* de lona, tenis *m*, playera *f* (Esp)

plinth /plɪnθ/ *n* (of pillar, column) plinto *m*; (of statue) pedestal *m*

plod /plɑːd ‖ plɒd/ *vi* **-dd-** (a) (walk) caminar lenta y pesadamente (b) (work): **she's still ~ding away at her thesis** sigue lidiando con la tesis

plonk¹ /plɑːŋk ‖ plɒŋk/ *vt* (BrE colloq) ▶ PLUNK

plonk² *n* (colloq) vino *m* peleón (fam)

plot¹ /plɑːt ‖plɒt/ n **1** (conspiracy) complot m **2** (story) argumento m **3** (piece of land) terreno m, solar m, parcela f

plot² **-tt-** vt **1** (mark out) ⟨curve/graph⟩ trazar*; ⟨position⟩ determinar **2** (plan) ⟨rebellion/revenge⟩ tramar

■ ~ vi to ~ (AGAINST sb) conspirar (CONTRA algn)

plotter /'plɑːtər ‖'plɒtə(r)/ n **1** (conspirator) conspirador, -dora m,f **2** (Comput, Tech) trazador m de gráficos

plough etc /plaʊ/ (BrE) ▶ PLOW etc

plow¹, (BrE) **plough** /plaʊ/ n (Agr) arado m

plow², (BrE) **plough** vt arar

■ ~ vi arar la tierra

■ **plow back,** (BrE) **plough back** [v + o + adv, v + adv + o] ⟨profits⟩ reinvertir*

■ **plow into,** (BrE) **plough into** [v + prep + o] ⟨vehicle/wall⟩ estrellarse contra

■ **plow through,** (BrE) **plough through** [v + prep + o] ⟨mud/snow⟩ abrirse* camino a través de; I'm still ~ing through the book todavía estoy tratando de leer el libro, pero me cuesta

plowman, (BrE) **ploughman** /'plaʊmən/ n (pl **-men** /-mən/) labrador m

ploy /plɔɪ/ n treta f

pluck¹ /plʌk/ vt (a) ⟨chicken⟩ desplumar; to ~ one's eyebrows depilarse las cejas (b) ⟨fruit/flower⟩ arrancar*; to ~ up (the) courage to + INF armarse de valor para + INF (c) (Mus) ⟨string/guitar⟩ puntear

pluck² n valor m

plucky /'plʌki/ adj **pluckier, pluckiest** valiente

plug¹ /plʌg/ n **1** (stopper) tapón m **2** (Elec) (a) (attached to lead) enchufe m; (socket) toma f de corriente, enchufe m, tomacorriente(s) m (AmL) (b) (spark ~) bujía f

plug² **-gg-** vt **1** ⟨hole/gap⟩ tapar **2** (promote) ⟨record/book⟩ hacerle* propaganda a

■ **plug in 1** [v + o + adv, v + adv + o] enchufar **2** [v + adv] enchufarse

plughole /'plʌghəʊl/ n (BrE) desagüe m

plum /plʌm/ n ciruela f

plumage /'pluːmɪdʒ/ n plumaje m

plumb¹ /plʌm/ adv (colloq) justo

plumb² vt **1** (fathom) ⟨mystery⟩ dilucidar **2** (Naut) sondar, sondear

plumber /'plʌmər ‖'plʌmə(r)/ n plomero, -ra m,f or (AmC, Esp) fontanero, -ra m,f or (Per) gasfitero, -ra m,f or (Chi) gásfiter mf

plumbing /'plʌmɪŋ/ n (pipes) cañerías fpl, tuberías fpl; (installation) instalación f de agua

plume /pluːm/ n pluma f; (cluster of feathers) penacho m

plummet /'plʌmət ‖'plʌmɪt/ vi caer* en picada or (Esp) en picado

plump /plʌmp/ adj **-er, -est** ⟨person/face⟩ (re)llenito; ⟨chicken/rabbit⟩ gordo

■ **plump for** [v + prep + o] (colloq) decidirse por

■ **plump up** [v + o + adv, v + adv + o] ⟨pillow/cushion⟩ ahuecar*

plunder¹ /'plʌndər ‖'plʌndə(r)/ vt (a) (steal from) ⟨village⟩ saquear (b) (steal) ⟨treasure/wealth⟩ robar

plunder² n (a) (objects) botín m (b) (action) saqueo m

plunge¹ /plʌndʒ/ vt to ~ sth INTO sth (a) (immerse, thrust) ⟨into liquid⟩ sumergir* algo EN algo; she ~d the knife into his heart le hundió el cuchillo en el corazón (b) (into state, condition) sumir algo/a algn EN algo

■ ~ vi **1** (dive) zambullirse*; (fall) caer* **2** (a) (slope downward steeply) ⟨road/path⟩ descender* bruscamente (b) (drop) ⟪price/temperature/popularity⟫ caer* en picada or (Esp) en picado

plunge² n (in water) zambullida f; to take the ~ (take a risk) arriesgarse*, jugarse* el todo por todo; (get married) casarse, darse* el paso

plunger /'plʌndʒər ‖'plʌndʒə(r)/ n (a) (for unblocking drain) desatascador m, chupona f (Esp), destapador m (de caño) (Méx), sopapa f (RPl), sopapo m (Chi), chupa f (Col), goma f (Ven) (b) (in syringe) émbolo m

plunk /plʌŋk/ vt (AmE) poner*, plantificar* (fam)

pluperfect /'pluːpɜːrfɪkt ‖,pluː'pɜːfɪkt/ n pluscuamperfecto m

plural¹ /'plʊrəl ‖'plʊərəl/ adj (Ling) en plural

plural² n plural m; in the ~ en plural

plus¹ /plʌs/ n (pl **~es** or **~ses**) (a) ~ (sign) (signo m de) más m (b) (advantage, bonus) (colloq) ventaja f

plus² adj (a) (advantageous, colloq) (before n) ⟨point⟩ positivo (b) (and more) (pred): children aged 13 ~ niños de 13 años para arriba

plus³ prep más; ~ the fact that ... aparte de que ...; ▶ FOUR¹

plush /plʌʃ/ adj lujoso

Pluto /'pluːtəʊ/ n Plutón m

plutonium /pluː'təʊniəm/ n plutonio m

ply¹ /plaɪ/ n (pl **plies**) (a) (of wood) chapa f (b) (of wool, yarn) cabo m; three-~ wool lana f de tres cabos

ply² **plies, plying, plied** vt (a) (carry out): to ~ one's trade ejercer* su oficio (b) ⟨oar⟩ mover*; ⟨tools⟩ manejar (c) ⟨ship⟩ ⟨sea⟩ navegar* por

■ ~ vi (frml) ⟪ship/plane/bus⟫ hacer* el trayecto

■ **ply with** [v + o + prep + o]: he kept ~ing me with whiskey estaba constantemente sirviéndome whisky

plywood /'plaɪwʊd/ n contrachapado m (tablero en varias capas)

pm (after midday) p.m.; at 2 ~ a las 2 de la tarde, a las 2 p.m.

PM (BrE) n = **prime minister**

PMS n = **premenstrual syndrome**

PMT (BrE) n = **premenstrual tension**

pneumatic drill /nʊ'mætɪk ‖nju:'mætɪk/ n martillo m neumático

pneumonia /nʊ'məʊnjə ‖nju:'məʊnɪə/ n pulmonía f, neumonía f

poach /pəʊtʃ/ vt **1** (Culin) ‹egg› escalfar; ‹fish› cocer* a fuego lento **2** (steal) ‹game› cazar* furtivamente; ‹staff/ideas› robar
■ ~ vi (hunt game) cazar* furtivamente

poacher /'pəʊtʃər ‖ 'pəʊtʃə(r)/ n cazador furtivo, cazadora furtiva m,f

PO box n Apdo. postal, Apdo. de correos, C.C. (CS)

pocket¹ /'pɑ:kət ‖ 'pɒkɪt/ n **1 (a)** (in garment) bolsillo m **(b)** (on billiard, snooker, pool table) tronera f **2** (small area) bolsa f; ~s of resistance bolsas fpl de resistencia

pocket² vt **(a)** (put in pocket) meterse en el bolsillo **(b)** (steal, gain) (colloq) embolsarse (fam)

pocket³ adj (before n) de bolsillo

pocket: ~**book** /'pɑ:kətbʊk ‖ 'pɒkɪtbʊk/ n **(a)** (handbag) (AmE) cartera f or (Esp) bolso m or (Méx) bolsa f **(b)** (wallet) (AmE) cartera f, billetera f **(c)** (paperback) (AmE) libro m en rústica **(d)** (notebook) (BrE) cuaderno m; ~ **money** n (spending money) dinero m para gastos personales; (for children) (BrE) dinero m de bolsillo, ≈ mesada f (AmL), domingo m (Méx), propina f (Per)

pod /pɑ:d ‖ pɒd/ n (of peas, beans) vaina f

podiatrist /pə'daɪətrəst ‖ pə'daɪətrɪst/ n (AmE) pedicuro, -ra m,f, podólogo, -ga, m,f (frml)

podium /'pəʊdiəm/ n estrado m

poem /'pəʊəm ‖ 'pəʊɪm/ n poema m

poet /'pəʊət ‖ 'pəʊɪt/ n poeta mf

poetic /pəʊ'etɪk/ adj poético

poet laureate, Poet Laureate /'lɔːriət ‖ 'lɒriət/ n (pl ~s ~) poeta laureado, poeta laureada m,f

poetry /'pəʊətri ‖ 'pəʊɪtri/ n poesía f

poignant /'pɔɪnjənt/ adj ‹story/moment› conmovedor; ‹look/plea› patético; ‹reminder› doloroso

point¹ /pɔɪnt/ n
I 1 (a) (dot) punto m **(b)** (decimal ~) ≈ coma f, punto m decimal (AmL) (the point is used instead of the comma in some Latin American countries) **2 (a)** (in space) punto m; the ~s of the compass los puntos cardinales; the ~ of no return: we've reached the ~ of no return ahora ya no nos podemos echar atrás **(b)** (on scale) punto m; you're right, up to a ~ hasta cierto punto tienes razón **3** (in time) momento m; at this ~ in time en este momento; to be on the ~ of -ING estar* a punto de + INF **4** (in contest, exam) punto m
II 1 (a) (item, matter) punto m; to bring up o raise a ~ plantear una cuestión; to make a ~ of -ING: I'll make a ~ of watching them closely me encargaré de vigilarlos de cerca **(b)** (argument): yes, that's a ~ sí, ese es un punto interesante; to make a ~: that was a very interesting ~ you made lo que señalaste es muy interesante; all right, you've made your ~! sí, bueno, ya has dicho lo que querías decir; ~ taken de acuerdo **2** (no pl) (central issue, meaning): to come/get to the ~ ir* al grano; she was brief and to the ~ fue breve y concisa; that's beside the ~ eso no tiene nada que ver; eso no viene al caso; the ~ is that ... el hecho es que ...; that's not the ~ no se trata de eso **3** (purpose): what's the ~ of going on? ¿qué

sentido tiene seguir?; there's no ~ o there isn't any ~ (in) feeling sorry for yourself no sirve de nada compadecerse **4** (feature, quality): strong ~ fuerte m; bad ~s defectos mpl; he has many good ~s tiene muchos puntos a su favor
III 1 (a) (sharp end, tip) punta f **(b)** (promontory) (Geog) punta f **2** **points** pl (BrE Rail) agujas fpl **3** (socket) (BrE) (electrical o power) ~ toma f de corriente, enchufe m, tomacorriente m (AmL)

point² vt (aim, direct) señalar, indicar*; to ~ sth AT sb/sth: he ~ed his finger at me me señaló con el dedo; she ~ed the gun at him le apuntó con la pistola
■ ~ vi **(a)** (with finger, stick etc) señalar; it's rude to ~ es de mala educación señalar con el dedo; to ~ AT/TO sth/sb señalar algo/a algn **(b)** (call attention) to ~ TO sth señalar algo **(c)** (indicate) to ~ TO sth ‹facts/symptoms› indicar* algo
■ **point out** [v + o + adv, v + adv + o] **1** (show) señalar; I'll ~ it/her out to you te lo/la señalaré **2** (make aware of) ‹problem/advantage› señalar

point: ~ **blank** adv ‹shoot› a quemarropa; ~-**blank** /'pɔɪntblæŋk/ adj: at ~-blank range a quemarropa

pointed /'pɔɪntəd ‖ 'pɔɪntɪd/ adj **1** (with a point) ‹stick/leaf› acabado en punta, puntudo (Andes); ‹arch› ojival; ‹chin/nose› puntiagudo, puntudo (Andes); ‹shoe› de punta, puntudo (Andes); ‹hat› de pico **2** (deliberate) ‹remark/comment› mordaz

pointer /'pɔɪntər ‖ 'pɔɪntə(r)/ n **1** (on dial, gage) aguja f **2 (a)** (clue, signal) pista f; ~ TO sth indicador m DE algo **(b)** (tip) idea f

pointless /'pɔɪntləs ‖ 'pɔɪntlɪs/ adj ‹attempt› vano, inútil; ‹existence› sin sentido; it's ~ arguing with him no tiene sentido discutir con él

point of view n (pl ~s ~) punto m de vista

poise /pɔɪz/ n **(a)** (bearing) porte m **(b)** (composure) desenvoltura f

poised /pɔɪzd/ adj **1** (balanced, suspended): ~ in the air suspendido en el aire; they were waiting with pencils ~ esperaban, lápiz en mano **(b)** (ready) listo **2** (self-assured): she is very ~ tiene mucho aplomo

poison¹ /'pɔɪzn/ n veneno m

poison² vt **(a)** (with poison) envenenar; (make ill) intoxicar*; ‹river/soil› contaminar **(b)** (corrupt) ‹mind/society› corromper; ‹relationship/ atmosphere› dañar

poisoning /'pɔɪznɪŋ/ n envenenamiento m

poisonous /'pɔɪznəs/ adj venenoso

poison-pen letter /'pɔɪzn'pen/ n anónimo m ponzoñoso

poke¹ /pəʊk/ vt **(a)** (jab): to ~ sb's eye out sacarle* un ojo a algn; she ~d him in the ribs le dio en el costado; (with elbow) le dio un codazo en el costado **(b)** (thrust): she ~d her head around the door asomó la cabeza por la puerta; he ~d his finger through the crack metió el dedo por la ranura
■ ~ vi (project) asomar; her feet were poking out of the sheets los pies le asomaban por entre las sábanas; a few shoots were poking up out of the soil unos cuantos brotes asomaban en la tierra ⋯⟶

■ **poke about, poke around** [v + adv] fisgonear

poke² n golpe m; (with elbow) codazo m

poker /'pəʊkər ‖'pəʊkə(r)/ n **1** (for fire) atizador m **2** (game) póker m, póquer m

poky /'pəʊki/ adj **pokier, pokiest** (colloq) **(a)** (cramped) diminuto **(b)** (slow) (AmE) lerdo

Poland /'pəʊlənd/ n Polonia f

polar /'pəʊlər ‖'pəʊlə(r)/ adj polar

polar bear n oso m polar

polarize /'pəʊləraɪz/ vt polarizar*

pole /pəʊl/ n **1** (fixed support) poste m; (flag~) mástil m; (tent ~) palo m **2** **(a)** (Geog) polo m; **the North/South P~** el Polo Norte/Sur **(b)** (Phys) polo m

Pole n (a) polaco, -ca m,f

polecat n **(a)** (of weasel family) turón m **(b)** (AmE) ▶ SKUNK

polemical /pə'lemɪkəl/ adj polémico

pole: ~star, (BrE) **P~ Star** n estrella f polar; **~-vault** n salto m con garrocha or (Esp) con pértiga

police¹ /pə'liːs/ n (force) (+ sing or pl vb) **the ~** la policía; (before n) ⟨escort/patrol⟩ policial; **~ car** coche m patrulla or de policía; **~ constable** (in UK) agente mf; **~ department** (in US) distrito m policial; **the ~ force** la policía; **~ officer** agente mf, policía mf; **to have a ~ record** estar* fichado or (CS tb) prontuariado

police² vt (keep order in) ⟨streets⟩ patrullar; ⟨region/area⟩ mantener* una fuerza policial en

police: ~ dog n perro m policía; **~man** /pə'liːsmən/ n (pl **-men** /-mən/) policía m, agente m; **~ state** n estado m policía; **~ station** n comisaría f, **~woman** n agente f, policía f, mujer f policía

policy /'pɑːləsi ‖'pɒləsi/ n (pl **-cies**) **1** **(a)** (Pol) política f; **(b)** (standard practice, plan) (Busn) política f; **it is good/bad ~** es/no es recomendable **2** (insurance ~) ⟨contract⟩ seguro m; (document) póliza f de seguros

policyholder /'pɑːləsi.həʊldər ‖'pɒləsi,həʊldə(r)/ n asegurado, -da m,f

polio /'pəʊliəʊ/ n polio f

poliomyelitis /ˌpəʊliəʊ'maɪə'laɪtəs ‖ˌpəʊliəʊ,maɪə'laɪtɪs/ n poliomielitis f

polish¹ /'pɑːlɪʃ ‖'pɒlɪʃ/ n **(a)** (shoe ~) betún m, pomada f (RPl), pasta f (Chi); (furniture ~) cera f para muebles, lustramuebles m (CS); (metal ~) limpiametales m; (floor ~) (esp BrE) abrillantador m (de suelos); (wax ~) cera f (abrillantadora) **(b)** (sheen) brillo m **(c)** (refinement): **he lacks ~** tiene que pulir su estilo

polish² vt **(a)** ⟨floor/table/car/brass⟩ darle* or sacarle* brillo a; ⟨shoes⟩ limpiar, lustrar (esp AmL), bolear (Méx), embolar (Col); ⟨lens/mirror⟩ limpiar; ⟨stone⟩ (by abrasion) pulir **(b)** (refine) pulir

■ **polish off** [v + o + adv, v + adv + o] (colloq) ⟨food⟩ liquidarse (fam)

Polish¹ /'pəʊlɪʃ/ adj polaco

Polish² n polaco m

polished /'pɑːlɪʃt ‖'pɒlɪʃt/ adj **(a)** (shiny) ⟨metal/marble⟩ pulido; ⟨wood⟩ brillante, lustrado (esp AmL) **(b)** (refined) ⟨manners/accent⟩ refinado; ⟨performance/translation⟩ pulido

polite /pə'laɪt/ adj **politer, politest** ⟨manner/

person⟩ cortés; **they were making ~ conversation** conversaban tratando de ser agradables; **it's not ~ to shout** gritar es una falta de educación

politely /pə'laɪtli/ adv ⟨behave⟩ correctamente; ⟨ask/refuse⟩ con buenos modales

politeness /pə'laɪtnəs ‖pə'laɪtnɪs/ n cortesía f

political /pə'lɪtɪkəl/ adj político

politically correct /pə'lɪtɪkli/ adj ⟨term⟩ usado por gente de ideología progresista

politician /ˌpɑːlə'tɪʃən ‖ˌpɒlɪ'tɪʃən/ n político, -ca m,f

politics /'pɑːlətɪks ‖'pɒlətɪks/ n **1** (+ sing vb) (science, activity) política f **2** (+ pl vb) (political relations) política f

polka /'pəʊlkə ‖'pɒlkə, 'pəʊlkə/ n polca f, polka f

polka dot /'pəʊkə, pəʊlkə ‖'pɒlkə, 'pəʊlkə/ n lunar m, topo m (Esp)

poll¹ /pəʊl/ n **1** **(a)** (ballot) votación f **(b)** (opinion ~) encuesta f or sondeo m (de opinión) **2** **polls** pl (polling stations) **the ~s: to go to the ~s** ir* or acudir a las urnas

poll² vt (Pol) ⟨votes⟩ (obtain) obtener*; (cast) emitir

pollen /'pɑːlən ‖'pɒlən/ n polen m

pollinate /'pɑːlənət ‖'pɒlənet/ vt polinizar*

polling /'pəʊlɪŋ/ n votación f; (before n) **~ place** o (BrE) **station** centro m electoral

pollutant /pə'luːtṇt/ n (agente m) contaminante m

pollute /pə'luːt/ vt (Ecol) contaminar

pollution /pə'luːʃən/ n contaminación f

polo /'pəʊləʊ/ n polo m

polo: ~ neck n (BrE) **(a)** (style of neck) cuello m alto **(b)** ▶ ~ NECK SWEATER; **~ neck sweater** n (BrE) suéter m de cuello alto, polera f (RPl)

poly- /'pɑːli ‖'pɒli/ pref poli-

polyester /ˌpɑːli'estər ‖ˌpɒli'estə(r)/ n poliéster m

polyethylene /ˌpɑːli'eθəliːn ‖ˌpɒli'eθəliːn/ n (esp AmE) polietileno m

polygamy /pə'lɪgəmi/ n poligamia f

Polynesia /ˌpɑːlə'niːʒə ‖ˌpɒlɪ'niːʒə/ n (la) Polinesia

Polynesian /ˌpɑːlə'niːʒən ‖ˌpɒlɪ'niːʒən/ adj polinesio

polystyrene /ˌpɑːli'staɪriːn ‖ˌpɒli'staɪriːn/ n poliestireno m

polythene /'pɑːləθiːn ‖'pɒlɪθiːn/ n (BrE) plástico m, polietileno m (téc)

pomegranate /'pɑːməgrænət ‖'pɒmɪgrænɪt/ n granada f

pomp /pɑːmp ‖pɒmp/ n pompa f, fausto m

pompom /'pɑːmpɑːm ‖'pɒmpɒm/ n (on hat) borla f, pompón m

pompous /'pɑːmpəs ‖'pɒmpəs/ adj pomposo

pond /pɑːnd ‖pɒnd/ n (man-made) estanque m; (natural) laguna f

ponder /'pɑːndər ‖'pɒndə(r)/ vt considerar

ponderous /'pɑːndərəs ‖'pɒndərəs/ adj ⟨movement⟩ lento y pesado; ⟨explanation/speech⟩ pesado

pong¹ /pɑːŋ ‖pɒŋ/ n (BrE colloq) peste f (fam)

pong² vi (BrE colloq) apestar (fam)

pontiff /'pɑːntəf ‖'pɒntɪf/ n pontífice m

pony /'pəʊni/ n (pl **ponies**) poni m

ponytail /'pəʊniteɪl/ n cola f de caballo

poodle /'puːdl̩/ n caniche m

pooh-pooh /ˌpuːˈpuː/ vt (colloq) reírse* de

pool¹ /puːl/ n **1** **(a)** (collection of water) charca f **(b)** (swimming ∼) piscina f, pileta f (RPl), alberca f (esp Méx) **(c)** (puddle) charco m **2** (common reserve of money) fondo m común **3** **pools** pl (BrE) ▸ FOOTBALL POOLS **4** (billiards) billar m americano, pool m

pool² vt hacer* un fondo común de

pooped (out) /puːpt/ adj (AmE sl) (pred) reventado (fam)

poor /pɔːr ‖pɔːr, pʊə(r)/ adj **-er, -est** **1** (not wealthy) pobre **2** (unsatisfactory, bad) ⟨harvest⟩ pobre, escaso; ⟨diet/quality⟩ malo; ⟨imitation⟩ burdo **3** (unfortunate) (before n) pobre; **you ∼ thing!** ¡pobrecito!

poorly¹ /'pʊrli ‖'pɔːli, 'pʊəli/ adj (pred) (esp BrE) mal

poorly² adv ⟨perform/play⟩ mal

pop¹ /pɑːp ‖pɒp/ n **1** (noise): **to go ∼** hacer 'pum', (burst) reventar* **2** (Mus) música f pop **3** (Culin) gaseosa f **4** (father) (AmE colloq) papá m (fam)

pop² -pp- vi **1** «balloon» estallar, reventar(se)*; «cork» saltar; **my ears ∼ped** se me destaparon los oídos **2** (spring) saltar; **his eyes were ∼ping (out of his head)** los ojos se le salían de las órbitas **3** (go casually) (colloq): **to ∼ out** salir* un momento; **he just ∼ped in to say hello** pasó un minuto a saludar
■ ∼ vt **1** (burst) ⟨balloon⟩ reventar*, hacer* estallar **2** (put quickly, casually): **she ∼ped her head around the door** asomó la cabeza por la puerta; **∼ it into your pocket** métetelo en el bolsillo
■ **pop up** [v + adv] (colloq) **(a)** (rise) «toast» saltar; **his head ∼ped up from behind the wall** asomó la cabeza por encima del muro **(b)** (appear) aparecer*

pop³ adj **(a)** (popular) ⟨sociology/culture⟩ popular; ⟨music/singer⟩ (AmE) popular **(b)** (BrE Mus) pop adj inv

popcorn /'pɑːpkɔːrn ‖'pɒpkɔːn/ n palomitas fpl (de maíz), cabritas fpl (de maíz) (Chi), pororó m (RPl), maíz m pira or tote (Col)

pope /pəʊp/ n papa m

poplar /'pɑːplər ‖'pɒplə(r)/ n álamo m (blanco)

poppa /'pɑːpə ‖'pɒpə/ n (AmE) papá m (fam)

poppy /'pɑːpi ‖'pɒpi/ n (pl **-pies**) amapola f, adormidera f

Popsicle® /'pɑːpsɪkəl ‖'pɒpsɪkəl/ n (AmE) paleta f (helada) or (Esp) polo m or (RPl) palito m or (CS) chupete m helado

populace /'pɑːpjələs ‖'pɒpjʊləs/ n (+ sing o pl vb) **the ∼** (common people) el pueblo; (population) la población

popular /'pɑːpjʊlər ‖'pɒpjʊlə(r)/ adj **1** **(a)** (well-liked) popular; **she is ∼ with her students** goza de popularidad entre sus alumnos **(b)** ⟨resort/restaurant⟩ muy frecuentado; ⟨brand/product⟩ popular **2** **(a)** (not highbrow, specialist) ⟨music/literature⟩ popular **(b)** (of populace) ⟨feeling⟩ popular; ⟨rebellion⟩ del pueblo, popular;

by ∼ demand/request a petición or (AmL tb) a pedido del público **(c)** (widespread) ⟨belief/notion⟩ generalizado

popularity /ˌpɑːpjəˈlærəti ‖ˌpɒpjʊˈlærəti/ n popularidad f

popularize /'pɑːpjələraɪz ‖'pɒpjʊləraɪz/ vt **(a)** (make popular) popularizar* **(b)** (make accessible) divulgar*

populate /'pɑːpjəleɪt ‖'pɒpjʊleɪt/ vt poblar*

population /ˌpɑːpjəˈleɪʃən ‖ˌpɒpjʊˈleɪʃən/ n población f; (before n) ∼ **explosion** explosión f demográfica

porcelain /'pɔːrsələn ‖'pɔːsələm/ n porcelana f

porch /pɔːrtʃ ‖pɔːtʃ/ n **(a)** (covered entrance) porche m **(b)** (veranda) (AmE) porche m, galería f

porcupine /'pɔːrkjəpaɪn ‖'pɔːkjʊpaɪn/ n puercoespín m

pore /pɔːr ‖pɔː(r)/ n poro m
■ **pore over** [v + prep + o] estudiar minuciosamente

pork /pɔːrk ‖pɔːk/ n (carne f de) cerdo m, (carne f de) puerco m (Méx), chancho m (Chi, Per), marrano m (Col); (before n) ∼ **chop** chuleta f de cerdo (or de chancho etc), costilla f de cerdo (RPl)

pornographic /ˌpɔːrnəˈɡræfɪk ‖ˌpɔːnəˈɡræfɪk/ adj pornográfico

pornography /pɔːrˈnɑːɡrəfi ‖pɔːˈnɒɡrəfi/ n pornografía f

porous /'pɔːrəs/ adj poroso

porpoise /'pɔːrpəs ‖'pɔːpəs/ n marsopa f

porridge /'pɔːrɪdʒ ‖'pɒrɪdʒ/ n avena f (cocida), gachas fpl (de avena) (Esp); (before n) ∼ **oats** copos mpl de avena

port¹ /pɔːrt ‖pɔːt/ n **1** (for ships) puerto m; (before n) ⟨authority/tax/regulation⟩ portuario **2** (left side) babor m **3** **(a)** (for loading) (Aviat, Naut) porta f **(b)** (Comput) puerto m **4** (Culin) oporto m, vino m de Oporto

port² adj (before n) ⟨lights⟩ de babor

portable /'pɔːrtəbəl ‖'pɔːtəbəl/ adj portátil

portcullis /pɔːrtˈkʌləs ‖pɔːtˈkʌlɪs/ n rastrillo m

portend /pɔːrˈtend ‖pɔːˈtend/ vt (liter) augurar

portent /'pɔːrtent ‖'pɔːtent/ n augurio m, presagio m

porter /'pɔːrtər ‖'pɔːtə(r)/ n **1** (at station, airport) maletero m, changador m (RPl); (on expedition) porteador m; (in hospital) (BrE) camillero m **2** (in hotel, apartment block) portero m

portfolio /pɔːrtˈfəʊliəʊ ‖pɔːtˈfəʊliəʊ/ n (pl **-lios**) **1** **(a)** (case) portafolio(s) m **(b)** (samples of work) carpeta f de trabajos **2** (Pol) cartera f

porthole /'pɔːrthəʊl ‖'pɔːthəʊl/ n (Naut) ojo m de buey, portilla f

portion /'pɔːrʃən ‖'pɔːʃən/ n **(a)** (of food) porción f (esp AmL), ración f (esp Esp) **(b)** (share, part) parte f

portrait /'pɔːrtrət, -treɪt ‖'pɔːtrɪt, -treɪt/ n retrato m

portray /pɔːrˈtreɪ ‖pɔːˈtreɪ/ vt **(a)** (depict) «picture» representar **(b)** (describe, represent) ⟨person/scene⟩ describir*

portrayal /pɔːrˈtreɪəl ‖pɔːˈtreɪəl/ n (Art) representación f; (Lit) descripción f; (Theat) interpretación f

Portugal /'pɔːrtʃɪɡəl ‖'pɔːtjʊɡl̩/ n Portugal m

Portuguese¹ /ˌpɔːrtʃəˈɡiːz ‖ˌpɔːtjʊˈɡiːz/ adj
portugués

Portuguese² n (pl ~) (a) (language)
portugués m (b) (person) portugués, -guesa m,f

pose¹ /pəʊz/ vt ⟨threat⟩ representar; ⟨problem/
question⟩ plantear
■ ~ vi (a) (Art, Phot) posar (b) (put on an act)
hacerse* el interesante (c) (pretend to be) **to ~ AS
sb/sth** hacerse* pasar POR algn/algo

pose² n (a) (position of body) pose f, postura f (b)
(assumed manner) pose f, afectación f

poser /ˈpəʊzər ‖ˈpəʊzə(r)/ n (a) (question)
pregunta f difícil; (problem) dilema m (b) (person)
(BrE colloq) ▶ POSEUR

poseur /pəʊˈzɜːr ‖pəʊˈzɜː(r)/ n: he's a real ~
todo en él es pura pose or afectación

posh /pɑːʃ ‖pɒʃ/ adj **-er, -est** (esp BrE colloq)
elegante, pijo (Esp fam), posudo (Col fam), pituco
(CS fam), cheto (RPI fam), sifrino (Ven fam), popoff
(Méx fam)

position¹ /pəˈzɪʃən/ n ① (a) (location) posición
f, ubicación f (esp AmL) (b) (Sport) posición f
② (a) (posture) posición f (b) (stance, point of view)
postura f ③ (a) (in league) puesto m (b) (job, post)
(frml) puesto m ④ (situation, circumstances) situación
f; **I'm not in a ~ to help them** no estoy en
condiciones de prestarles ayuda

position² vt colocar*, poner*

positive /ˈpɑːzətɪv ‖ˈpɒzətɪv/ adj ① ⟨number/
quantity⟩ positivo; ⟨electrode⟩ positivo; **the test
was ~** (Med) el análisis dio positivo
② (constructive) ⟨attitude⟩ positivo; ⟨criticism⟩
constructivo ③ (definite): **there is no ~ evidence**
no hay pruebas concluyentes ④ (absolute) ⟨before
n⟩ ⟨disgrace/outrage⟩ auténtico ⑤ (sure) (colloq)
(pred): **are you sure? — positive** ¿estás seguro? —
segurísimo

positively /ˈpɑːzətɪvli ‖ˈpɒzətɪvli/ adv
① (constructively): **to think ~** ser* positivo; **they
reacted ~** tuvieron una reacción/respuesta
positiva (b) (absolutely) ⟨delighted/furious⟩
verdaderamente

posse /ˈpɑːsi ‖ˈpɒsi/ n (in US) partida f (al
mando de un sheriff)

possess /pəˈzes/ vt ① (own) tener*, poseer*
(frml) ② (influence) «anger/fear» apoderarse de;
whatever can gave ~ed him to say such a thing?
¿qué lo habrá llevado a decir semejante cosa?

possessed /pəˈzest/ adj (pred) **to be ~ (by
the devil)** estar* endemoniado

possession /pəˈzeʃən/ n (a) (sth owned) bien
m (b) (ownership) posesión f; (of arms) tenencia f

possessive /pəˈzesɪv/ adj posesivo

possessor /pəˈzesər ‖pəˈzesə(r)/ n dueño, -ña
m,f, poseedor, -dora m,f

possibility /ˌpɑːsəˈbɪləti ‖ˌpɒsəˈbɪləti/ n
posibilidad f

possible /ˈpɑːsəbəl ‖ˈpɒsəbəl/ adj posible; **get
here by eight if ~** llega antes de las ocho, si es
posible; **as little as ~** lo menos posible

possibly /ˈpɑːsəbli ‖ˈpɒsəbli/ adv (a)
(conceivably): **I couldn't ~ eat any more** me es
totalmente imposible comer nada más; **could you
~ give me a hand with this?** ¿sería tan amable de
ayudarme con esto? (b) (perhaps) (indep)
posiblemente

post¹ /pəʊst/ n ① (pole) poste m ② (mail) (esp
BrE) correo m; **to send sth by ~** o through the ~
mandar or enviar* algo por correo; **it's in the ~**
ya ha sido enviado; **the first/second ~** (delivery) el
primer/segundo reparto; (collection) la primera/
segunda recogida ③ (job) puesto m

post² vt ① (a) (position) ⟨policeman/soldier⟩
apostar (b) (send) ⟨employee/diplomat⟩ destinar
② (mail) (esp BrE) ⟨letter/parcel⟩ echar al correo;
(drop in postbox) echar al buzón; **to ~ sth to sb**
mandarle or enviarle* algo a algn (por correo)

post- /pəʊst/ pref post-, pos-

postage /ˈpəʊstɪdʒ/ n franqueo m; **~ and
handling** (AmE), **~ and packing** (BrE) gastos mpl
de envío

postage: ~ paid adv con franqueo pagado;
~ stamp n (frml) sello m (de correos),
estampilla f (AmL), timbre m (Méx)

postal /ˈpəʊstl/ adj ⟨before n⟩ postal

postal order n (BrE) ≈ giro m postal

post: ~box n (BrE) buzón m; **~card** n tarjeta
f postal, postal f; **~code** n (BrE) código m postal

postdate /ˈpəʊstˈdeɪt/ vt ⟨contract/check⟩
posfechar, diferir* (RPI)

poster /ˈpəʊstər ‖ˈpəʊstə(r)/ n cartel m, póster
m

posterity /pɑːˈsterəti ‖pɒˈsterəti/ n posteridad
f

postgraduate /ˌpəʊstˈɡrædʒuət/ n estudiante
mf de postgrado; ⟨before n⟩ ⟨student/research⟩ de
postgrado

posthumous /ˈpɑːstʃəməs ‖ˈpɒstjʊməs/ adj
póstumo

posting /ˈpəʊstɪŋ/ n destino m

postman /ˈpəʊstmən/ n (pl **-men** /-mən/) (esp
BrE) cartero m

postmark¹ /ˈpəʊstmɑːrk ‖ˈpəʊstmɑːk/ n
matasellos m

postmark² vt matasellar

postmortem /ˌpəʊstˈmɔːrtəm ‖ˌpəʊstˈmɔːtəm/
n (esp BrE Med) autopsia f

postnatal /ˈpəʊstˈneɪtl/ adj postnatal

post office n oficina f de correos, correo m
(AmL), estafeta f de correos (Esp)

postpone /pəʊsˈpəʊn ‖pəˈspəʊn/ vt aplazar*,
posponer*, postergar* (esp AmL)

postponement /pəʊsˈpəʊnmənt
‖pəˈspəʊnmənt/ n aplazamiento m, postergación
f (esp AmL)

postscript /ˈpəʊstskrɪpt/ n (to letter) postdata f;
(to book) epílogo m

posture /ˈpɑːstʃər ‖ˈpɒstʃə(r)/ n postura f

postwar /ˈpəʊstˈwɔːr ‖ˌpəʊstˈwɔː(r)/ adj ⟨before
n⟩ de la posguerra

posy /'pəʊzi/ n (pl **posies**) ramillete m

pot¹ /pɑːt ‖pɒt/ n **1** **(a)** (cooking ~) olla f; ~**s and pans** cacharros mpl (fam), trastes mpl (Méx); **to go to** ~ (colloq) echarse a perder **(b)** (for jam, honey etc) tarro m, bote m (Esp) **(c)** (tea~) tetera f; (coffee~) cafetera f **(d)** (in pottery) vasija f **2** (flower~) maceta f, tiesto m (Esp)

pot² vt -tt- ⟨plant⟩ plantar (en una maceta)

potash /'pɑːtæʃ ‖'pɒtæʃ/ n potasa f

potassium /pə'tæsiəm/ n potasio m

potato /pə'teɪtəʊ/ n (pl **-toes**) papa f or (Esp) patata f; (before n) ~ **chips** o (BrE) **crisps** papas fpl or (Esp) patatas fpl fritas; ~ **peeler** pelapapas m or (Esp) pelapatatas m

potbelly /'pɑːtbeli ‖'pɒtbeli /n barriga f (fam), panza f (fam), guata f (Chi fam)

potency /'pəʊtn̩si/ n **(a)** (of drink) lo fuerte **(b)** (sexual ~) potencia f sexual

potent /'pəʊtn̩t/ adj **1** ⟨drink/drug/medicine⟩ fuerte **2** (Physiol) potente

potential¹ /pə'tentʃəl ‖pə'tenʃəl/ n (capacity) potencial m; (possibilities) posibilidades fpl

potential² adj (before n) ⟨danger⟩ potencial; ⟨leader⟩ en potencia

potentially /pə'tentʃəli ‖pə'tenʃəli/ adv potencialmente

pot: ~**hole** n **(a)** (cave) cueva f subterránea; (hole) sima f **(b)** (in road) bache m; ~**holing** /'pɑːt.həʊlɪŋ ‖'pɒt.həʊlɪŋ/ n (BrE) espeleología f

potion /'pəʊʃən/ n poción f, pócima f

pot: ~**luck** /'pɑːt'lʌk ‖.pɒt'lʌk/ n: **to take** ~**luck** conformarse con lo que haya; ~ **plant** n planta f (cultivada en una maceta), mata f (Col, Ven); ~**shot** n (Sport) tiro m al azar

potted /'pɑːtəd ‖'pɒtɪd/ adj (before n) **(a)** ⟨plant⟩ en maceta or tiesto **(b)** ⟨account/version⟩ resumido

potter¹ /'pɑːtər ‖'pɒtə(r)/ n alfarero, -ra m,f

potter² vi (BrE) (+ adv compl) ▶ PUTTER²

pottery /'pɑːtəri ‖'pɒtəri/ n (pl **-ries**) **(a)** (vessels) cerámica f **(b)** (workshop) alfarería f **(c)** (craft) alfarería f

potty¹ /'pɑːti ‖'pɒti/ n (pl **-ties**) (colloq) orinal m (para niños) (fam), bacinica f (AmL exc RPl), pelela f (CS fam); **he's** ~**-trained** ya no usa pañales

potty² adj -**tier**, -**tiest** (BrE colloq) chiflado (fam)

pouch /paʊtʃ/ n **1** **(a)** (small bag) bolsa f **(b)** (for correspondence) (AmE) valija f **2** (Anat, Zool) bolsa f

poultice /'pəʊltəs ‖'pəʊltɪs/ n cataplasma f

poultry /'pəʊltri/ n **(a)** (birds) (+ pl vb) aves fpl de corral **(b)** (meat) carne f de ave

pounce /paʊns/ vi saltar; **to** ~ ON/UPON sb/sth abalanzarse* SOBRE algn/algo

pound¹ /paʊnd/ n **1** (measure) libra f (454 gramos) **2** (Fin) libra f; (before n) **a** ~ **coin** una moneda de (una) libra **3** (enclosure — for cars) depósito m; (— for dogs) perrera f

pound² vt **(a)** ⟨corn/spices⟩ machacar*; ⟨garlic/ chili⟩ majar **(b)** ⟨table/door⟩ aporrear; **the waves** ~**ed the wall** las olas batían contra el muro
■ ~ vi **(a)** (strike, beat) aporrear **(b)** «heart» palpitar; «sound» retumbar; **my head is** ~**ing** tengo la cabeza a punto de reventar

pour /pɔːr ‖pɔː(r)/ vt **(a)** (+ adv compl) ⟨liquid⟩ verter*, echar; ⟨salt/powder⟩ echar; **he** ~**ed the tea down the sink** tiró el té por el fregadero **(b)** ~ (out) (serve) ⟨drink⟩ servir*
■ ~ vi (+ adv compl) «blood» manar; «water/ sweat» salir*
■ ~ v impers diluviar, llover* a cántaros
■ **pour out 1** [v + o + adv, v + adv + o] **(a)** ▶ POUR vt **(b)** (emotionally): **he** ~**ed out his feelings** reveló sus sentimientos; **she** ~**ed her heart out to him** se desahogó con él **2** [v + adv] salir*

pouring /'pɔːrɪŋ/ adj: **he went out in the** ~ **rain** salió en medio de una lluvia torrencial

pout /paʊt/ vi hacer* un mohín

poverty /'pɑːvərti ‖'pɒvəti/ n pobreza f

poverty-stricken /'pɑːvərti.strɪkən ‖'pɒvəti.strɪkən/ adj pobrísimo

POW n = **prisoner of war**

powder¹ /'paʊdər ‖'paʊdə(r)/ n **(a)** polvo m **(b)** (face ~) polvo(s) m(pl) (de tocador); (before n) ~ **puff** borla f, cisne m (RPl)

powder² vt **1** (cover) empolvar; **to** ~ **one's nose** retocarse* el maquillaje; (euph) lavarse las manos (euf) **2** **powdered** past p ⟨milk/eggs⟩ en polvo; ~**ed sugar** (AmE) azúcar m or f glas, azúcar m or f flor (Chi), azúcar m or f impalpable (RPl), azúcar m or f en polvo (Col)

powdery /'paʊdəri/ adj como polvo

power¹ /'paʊər ‖'paʊə(r)/ n **1** **(a)** (control, influence) poder m; (of country) poderío m, poder m; **to be in** ~ estar* en el poder **(b)** (official authority) poder m; ~ **to** + INF poder PARA + INF **2** **(a)** (nation) potencia f **(b)** (person, group): **the** ~**s that be** los que mandan; **the** ~**s of darkness** las fuerzas del mal **3** **(a)** (physical strength, force) fuerza f **(b)** (of engine, loudspeaker, transmitter) potencia f **4** **(a)** (ability, capacity): **I did everything in my** ~ hice todo lo que estaba en mi(s) mano(s) **(b)** (specific faculty) (often pl): **he lost the** ~ **of speech** perdió el habla; ~**(s) of concentration** capacidad f de concentración **5** **(a)** (Eng, Phys) potencia f; (particular source of energy) energía f **(b)** (electricity) electricidad f; (before n) ~ **lines** cables mpl de alta tensión; ~ **point** (BrE) toma f de corriente, enchufe m, tomacorriente m (AmL) **6** **(a lot)** (colloq): **to do sb a** ~ **of good** hacerle* a algn mucho bien

power² vt: **the plane is** ~**ed by four engines** el avión está propulsado por cuatro motores

power: ~**boat** n lancha f de motor, lancha f motora (Esp); ~ **cut** n apagón m

powerful /'paʊərfəl ‖'paʊəfəl/ adj **(a)** ⟨country⟩ poderoso **(b)** ⟨shoulders/arms⟩ fuerte **(c)** ⟨performance/image⟩ impactante; ⟨argument⟩ poderoso; ⟨incentive⟩ poderoso **(d)** ⟨engine/ weapon/drug⟩ potente; ⟨smell/current⟩ fuerte

powerless /'paʊərləs ‖'paʊəlɪs/ adj impotente; **they were** ~ **to prevent it** no pudieron hacer nada para impedirlo

power: ~ **of attorney** n (pl ~**s of attorney**) (Law) poder m (notarial); ~ **plant** n (AmE) ▶ ~ STATION; ~ **station** n central f eléctrica, usina f eléctrica (AmS)

pp. (= **pages**) págs.

PR¹ n (a) = **public relations** (b)
= **proportional representation**

PR² = **Puerto Rico**

practicable /'præktɪkəbəl/ adj factible

practical¹ /'præktɪkəl/ adj (a) práctico; **for all
~ purposes** a efectos prácticos (b) (feasible)
factible

practical² n (Educ) práctica f

practicality /'præktɪ'kæləti/ n ① (of scheme/
idea) lo práctico ② **practicalities** pl aspectos
mpl prácticos

practical joke n broma f

practically /'præktɪkli/ adv ① (virtually) casi,
prácticamente ② (in a practical way) ‹consider/
think› con sentido práctico

practice¹ /'præktəs ‖ 'præktɪs/ n ① (training,
repetition) práctica f; **he's out of ~** le falta
práctica; **piano ~** ejercicios mpl de piano; **~
teaching** o (BrE) **teaching ~** prácticas fpl de
magisterio; **~ makes perfect** la práctica hace al
maestro ② (a) (carrying out, implementing) práctica
f; **to put sth into ~** llevar algo a la práctica; **in ~**
en la práctica (b) (exercise of profession) ejercicio m
③ (custom, procedure) costumbre f ④ (Med)
consultorio m

practice², (BrE) **practise** vt ① (rehearse)
practicar*; ‹song/act› ensayar ② «doctor/
lawyer» ejercer* ③ **practicing** pres p (a)
‹doctor/lawyer› en ejercicio (de su profesión) (b)
‹Catholic› practicante
■ **~ vi** ① (rehearse, train) practicar*
② (professionally) ejercer*

practitioner /præk'tɪʃnər ‖ præk'tɪʃnə(r)/ n
médico, -ca m,f

pragmatic /præg'mætɪk/ adj pragmático

pragmatism /'prægmətɪzəm/ n pragmatismo
m

Prague /prɑːg/ n Praga f

prairie /'preri ‖ 'preəri/ n pradera f; **the ~(s)**
(in US) la Pradera

prairie dog n perro m de las praderas

praise¹ /preɪz/ n (a) (credit, applause) elogios
mpl; **to sing sth's/sb's ~s** poner* algo/a algn por
las nubes (b) (Relig) alabanza f

praise² vt (a) (compliment) elogiar (b) (Relig)
alabar

praiseworthy /'preɪz,wɜːrði ‖ 'preɪz,wɜːði/
adj digno de elogio

pram /præm/ n (BrE) cochecito m

prance /præns ‖ prɑːns/ vi (a) «horse»
brincar* (b) (pej) «person»: **she ~d into the
room wearing her new dress** entró meneándose
con el vestido nuevo
■ **prance about** [v + adv] brincar*

prank /præŋk/ n broma f, (of child) travesura f

prat /præt/ n (BrE sl) imbécil mf

prattle /'prætl/ vi «adult» cotorrear (fam);
«child» balbucear

prawn /prɔːn/ n (large) langostino m, camarón
m (AmL); (medium) camarón m (AmL), gamba f (esp
Esp), langostino m (CS); (small) camarón m,
quisquilla f (Esp)

pray /preɪ/ vi rezar*, orar (frml)

prayer /prer ‖ preə(r)/ n oración f

pre- /'priː/ pref (a) (in advance): **~planned**
planeado de antemano (b) (before): **a ~dinner
drink** una copa antes de cenar

preach /priːtʃ/ vt (a) (Relig) predicar*; ‹sermon›
dar* (b) (advocate) ‹doctrine/ideas› preconizar*
■ **~ vi** predicar*

preacher /'priːtʃər ‖ 'priːtʃə(r)/ n (a) (one who
preaches) predicador, -dora m,f (b) (minister) (AmE)
pastor, -tora m,f

prearrange /'priːə'reɪndʒ/ vt (a) (arrange in
advance) concertar* de antemano (b)
prearranged past p ‹meeting› concertado de
antemano; ‹signal/place/time› convenido

precarious /prɪ'keriəs ‖ prɪ'keəriəs/ adj
precario

precaution /prɪ'kɔːʃən/ n precaución f; **as a
~** por o como precaución

precautionary /prɪ'kɔːʃəneri ‖ prɪ'kɔːʃənəri/
adj preventivo

precede /prɪ'siːd/ vt (frml) preceder a
■ **~ vi** (a) (come before) preceder (b) **preceding**
pres p anterior

precedence /'presədəns/ n precedencia f

precedent /'presədənt/ n precedente m; **to set
a ~ (for sth)** sentar* precedente (para algo)

precept /'priːsept/ n precepto m

precinct /'priːsɪŋkt/ n ① (a) (delimited zone)
(BrE): **shopping ~** centro m/zona f comercial (b)
(AmE) (police district) distrito m policial; (police
station) comisaría f (c) (voting district) (AmE)
circunscripción f, distrito m electoral
② **precincts** pl (of city) límites mpl; (of cathedral,
castle, hospital) recinto m, predio(s) m(pl) (esp AmL)

precious¹ /'preʃəs/ adj ① (a) (valuable) ‹jewel/
object› precioso; **~ metal** metal m precioso; **~
stone** piedra f preciosa (b) (dear) querido (c) (iro):
her ~ son su queridísimo hijo (iró) ② (affected)
preciosista

precious² adv (colloq) (as intensifier): **~ few**
muy pocos; **she's done ~ little to help** bien poco
ha hecho para ayudar

precipice /'presəpəs ‖ 'presɪpɪs/ n precipicio
m

precipitate /prɪ'sɪpəteɪt ‖ prɪ'sɪpɪteɪt/ vt (frml)
precipitar

precipitation /prɪ'sɪpə'teɪʃən ‖ prɪ,sɪpɪ'teɪʃən/
n (a) (Meteo) precipitaciones fpl (b) (Chem)
precipitación f

precis, précis /preɪ'siː, 'preɪsiː ‖ 'preɪsiː/ n (pl
~ /-z/) resumen m

precise /prɪ'saɪs/ adj (a) (accurate)
‹calculations/measurements› exacto; ‹description/
instructions› preciso (b) (specific) preciso; **there
were about 60, 59 to be ~** había unos 60, 59 para
ser exacto or preciso (c) (meticulous) minucioso

precisely /prɪ'saɪsli/ adv (a) (accurately)
‹calculate/measure/describe› con precisión (b)
(exactly): **we have ~ one hour** tenemos
exactamente una hora; **at two o'clock ~** a las dos
en punto; **precisely!** ¡exacto!, ¡justamente!

precision /prɪ'sɪʒən/ n precisión f; (before n)
‹instrument/tool› de precisión

preclude /prɪ'kluːd/ vt (frml) ‹possibility›
excluir*

precocious /prɪ'kəʊʃəs/ adj precoz

preconceived /ˈpriːkənˈsiːvd/ adj (before n) preconcebido

preconception /ˈpriːkənˈsepʃən/ n idea f preconcebida

precondition /ˈpriːkənˈdɪʃən/ n condición f previa

precursor /prɪˈkɜːrsər ‖ prɪˈkɜːsə(r)/ n (fml) precursor, -sora m,f

predate /ˈpriːˈdeɪt/ vt (fml) (a) (precede) ser* anterior a (b) ⟨document/letter⟩ antedatar (fml)

predator /ˈpredətər ‖ ˈpredətə(r)/ n depredador m, predador m

predatory /ˈpredətɔːri ‖ ˈpredətri/ adj ⟨animal⟩ predador, depredador; ⟨person⟩ rapaz

predecessor /ˈpredəsesər ‖ ˈpriːdɪsesə(r)/ n predecesor, -sora m,f

predestine /ˈpriːˈdestən ‖ ˌpriːˈdestɪn/ vt predestinar

predetermine /ˈpriːdɪˈtɜːrmən ‖ ˌpriːdɪˈtɜːmɪn/ vt predeterminar

predicament /prɪˈdɪkəmənt/ n aprieto m

predicative /prɪˈdɪkətɪv/ adj predicativo

predict /prɪˈdɪkt/ vt predecir*

predictable /prɪˈdɪktəbəl/ adj ⟨result/outcome⟩ previsible; you're so ~ siempre sales con lo mismo

predictably /prɪˈdɪktəbli/ adv de manera previsible

prediction /prɪˈdɪkʃən/ n (forecast) pronóstico m, predicción f; (prophecy) profecía f

predispose /ˈpriːdɪsˈpəʊz/ vt (fml) predisponer*

predominance /prɪˈdɑːmənəns ‖ prɪˈdɒmɪnəns/ n predominio m

predominant /prɪˈdɑːmənənt ‖ prɪˈdɒmɪnənt/ adj predominante

predominantly /prɪˈdɑːmənəntli ‖ prɪˈdɒmɪnəntli/ adv predominantemente

predominate /prɪˈdɑːməneɪt ‖ prɪˈdɒmɪneɪt/ vi predominar

pre-eminent /priːˈemənənt ‖ priːˈemɪnənt/ adj (fml) preeminente

pre-empt /priːˈempt/ vt ⟨attack/move⟩ adelantarse a

pre-emptive /priːˈemptɪv/ adj ⟨strike/attack⟩ preventivo

preen /priːn/ vt ⟨feathers⟩ arreglar con el pico ■ v refl to ~ oneself «bird» arreglarse las plumas con el pico; «person» acicalarse

pre-exist /ˈpriːɪgˈzɪst/ vi (fml) (a) preexistir (b) **pre-existing** pres p preexistente

prefab /ˈpriːfæb/ n (colloq) vivienda f prefabricada

prefabricated /ˈpriːˈfæbrɪkeɪtəd ‖ ˌpriːˈfæbrɪkeɪtɪd/ adj prefabricado

preface /ˈprefəs ‖ ˈprefɪs/ n (to book, speech) prefacio m; (to event) prólogo m

prefect /ˈpriːfekt/ n [1] (BrE Educ) alumno encargado de la disciplina, ≈ monitor, -tora m,f [2] (official) prefecto m

prefer /prɪˈfɜːr ‖ prɪˈfɜː(r)/ vt -rr- preferir*; to ~ sth TO sth preferir* algo A algo; to ~ to + INF preferir* + INF

preferable /ˈprefərəbəl/ adj preferible

preferably /ˈprefərəbli/ adv (indep) preferentemente; I'd like a size 10, ~ in red quisiera la talla 10, de ser posible en rojo

preference /ˈprefərəns/ n preferencia f; ~ FOR sth preferencia POR algo

preferential /ˈprefəˈrentʃəl ‖ ˌprefəˈrenʃəl/ adj (before n) preferente, preferencial; to give ~ treatment to sb dar* trato preferente or preferencial a algn

prefix /ˈpriːfɪks/ n prefijo m

pregnancy /ˈpregnənsi/ n (pl -cies) (of woman) embarazo m; (of animal) preñez f

pregnant /ˈpregnənt/ adj [1] ⟨woman⟩ embarazada; ⟨cow/mare⟩ preñada [2] (liter) (meaningful) ⟨pause/silence⟩ elocuente, preñado de significado (liter)

preheat /ˈpriːˈhiːt/ vt precalentar*

prehistoric /ˈpriːhɪˈstɔːrɪk ‖ ˌpriːhɪˈstɒrɪk/ adj prehistórico

prejudge /ˈpriːˈdʒʌdʒ/ vt prejuzgar*

prejudice¹ /ˈpredʒədəs ‖ ˈpredʒʊdɪs/ n prejuicio m

prejudice² vt [1] (influence) predisponer* [2] (harm) ⟨case/claim⟩ perjudicar*

prejudiced /ˈpredʒədəst ‖ ˈpredʒʊdɪst/ adj lleno de prejuicios, prejuiciado (AmL)

preliminary¹ /prɪˈlɪməneri ‖ prɪˈlɪmɪnəri/ adj preliminar

preliminary² n (pl -ries) (a) (preamble) prolegómeno m (b) **preliminaries** pl (Sport) etapa f de clasificación previa, preliminares mpl or fpl

prelude /ˈpreljuːd/ n (a) (introduction) ~ (TO sth) preludio m (DE algo) (b) (Mus) preludio m

premature /ˈpriːməˈtʊr ‖ ˈpremətjʊə(r)/ adj prematuro

prematurely /ˈpriːməˈtʊrli ‖ ˈpremətjʊəli/ adv prematuramente

premeditated /ˈpriːˈmedətertəd ‖ ˌpriːˈmedɪteɪtɪd/ adj premeditado

premenstrual /ˈpriːˈmenstruəl/ adj premenstrual; ~ syndrome/tension síndrome m/ tensión f premenstrual

premier /prɪˈmɪr ‖ ˈpremiə(r)/ n primer ministro, primera ministra m,f, premier mf

premiere¹, première /prɪˈmɪr ‖ ˈpremieə(r)/ n estreno m

premiere², première vt ⟨play/film⟩ estrenar ■ ~ vi «play/film» estrenarse

premise /ˈpreməs ‖ ˈpremɪs/ n [1] (Phil) premisa f [2] **premises** pl (building, site) local m; they've moved to new ~s se han mudado a un nuevo local (or a nuevas oficinas etc); meals are cooked on the ~s las comidas se preparan en el mismo establecimiento

premium /ˈpriːmiəm/ n (Fin) (a) (insurance ~) prima f (de seguro) (b) (surcharge) recargo m; to be at a ~ (in short supply) escasear; (lit: above par) estar* por encima de la par (c) (bonus) prima f

Premium Bond n (in UK) bono del Estado que permite ganar dinero participando en sorteos mensuales

premonition /ˈpriːməˈnɪʃən, ˈprem-/ n premonición f

prenatal /ˈpriːˈneɪtl̩/ adj (esp AmE) ▶ ANTENATAL

preoccupation /priːˈɑːkjəˈpeɪʃən ‖ ˌpriːˌɒkjʊˈpeɪʃən/ n **1** (obsession) obsesión f **2** (concern): my main ~ was not to offend my parents mi mayor preocupación/lo que más me importaba era no ofender a mis padres

preoccupied /priːˈɑːkjəpaɪd ‖ priːˈɒkjʊpaɪd/ adj (absorbed) absorto; (worried) preocupado

preoccupy /priːˈɑːkjəpaɪ ‖ priːˈɒkjʊpaɪ/ vt -pies, -pying, -pied preocupar

prepaid /priːˈpeɪd/ adj ⟨envelope⟩ con franqueo pagado; ⟨advertisement/insertion⟩ pagado por adelantado

preparation /ˌprepəˈreɪʃən/ n **1** (a) (act) preparación f (b) **preparations** pl (arrangements) preparativos mpl **2** (substance) preparado m

preparatory /prɪˈpærətɔːri ‖ prɪˈpærətri/ adj preparatorio

preparatory school n (frml) (a) (in US) colegio secundario privado (b) (in UK) colegio primario privado

prepare /prɪˈpeə(r) ‖ prɪˈpeə(r)/ vt preparar ■ ~ vi to ~ (FOR sth) prepararse (PARA algo)

prepared /prɪˈpeəd ‖ prɪˈpeəd/ adj (a) (ready in advance) ⟨speech/statement⟩ preparado; I wasn't ~ for this no contaba con esto (b) (willing) ⟨pred⟩ to be ~ to + INF estar* dispuesto A + INF

preposition /ˌprepəˈzɪʃən/ n preposición f

prepossessing /ˌpriːpəˈzesɪŋ/ adj (frml) (usu neg) atractivo

preposterous /prɪˈpɑːstərəs ‖ prɪˈpɒstərəs/ adj absurdo

prep school /prep/ n ▶ PREPARATORY SCHOOL B

prerequisite /ˌpriːˈrekwəzət ‖ ˌpriːˈrekwɪzɪt/ n requisito m esencial

prerogative /prɪˈrɑːgətɪv ‖ prɪˈrɒgətɪv/ n prerrogativa f; that's your ~ estás en todo tu derecho

Pres (title) = **President**

Presbyterian¹ /ˌprezbəˈtɪriən ‖ ˌprezbrˈtɪəriən/ n presbiteriano, -na m,f

Presbyterian² adj presbiteriano

preschool¹ /ˈpriːskuːl/ adj ⟨before n⟩ ⟨child⟩ de edad preescolar; ⟨education⟩ preescolar

preschool² n (AmE) jardín m de infancia, kindergarten m (AmL), jardín m de niños (Méx), jardín m de infantes (RPl), jardín m infantil (Chi)

prescribe /prɪˈskraɪb/ vt (a) ⟨drug⟩ recetar; ⟨rest⟩ recomendar* (b) (order) (frml) prescribir* (frml); ~d reading libros mpl de lectura obligatoria

prescription /prɪˈskrɪpʃən/ n receta f; available on ~ only en venta solamente bajo receta

presence /ˈprezns/ n presencia f; to make one's ~ felt hacerse* sentir

presence of mind n presencia f de ánimo

present¹ /prɪˈzent/ vt **1** (a) (give, hand over) to ~ sth TO sb entregarle* algo A algn; to ~ sb

WITH sth obsequiar a algn CON algo (frml), obsequiarle algo A algn (esp AmL frml) (b) (confront): we were ~ed with a very difficult situation nos vimos frente a una situación muy difícil **2** ⟨ticket/passport/account/ideas⟩ presentar **3** (Cin, Theat, Rad, TV) presentar **4** (introduce) (frml) presentar

present² /ˈpreznt/ adj **1** (at scene) ⟨pred⟩ to be ~ estar* presente **2** ⟨before n⟩ (a) (current) actual; at the ~ time en este momento (b) (Ling): the ~ tense el presente

present³ /ˈpreznt/ n **1** (a) (current time): the ~ el presente; at ~ en este momento (b) (Ling) the ~ el presente **2** (gift) regalo m

presentable /prɪˈzentəbəl/ adj presentable

presentation /ˌpriːzenˈteɪʃən, ˌprezənˈteɪʃən ‖ ˌprezənˈteɪʃən/ n **1** (of gift, prize) entrega f **2** (a) (of document, bill, proposal) presentación f (b) (display) (Busn) presentación f **3** (manner of presenting) presentación f

present-day /ˈprezntˈdeɪ/ adj ⟨before n⟩ actual

presenter /prɪˈzentər ‖ prɪˈzentə(r)/ n (BrE) presentador, -dora m,f

presently /ˈprezntli/ adv (a) (now) en este momento (b) (soon afterwards, in past) pronto (c) (soon, in future) poco después

preservation /ˌprezərˈveɪʃən ‖ ˌprezəˈveɪʃən/ n conservación f

preservative /prɪˈzɜːrvətɪv ‖ prɪˈzɜːvətɪv/ n conservante m

preserve¹ /prɪˈzɜːrv ‖ prɪˈzɜːv/ vt (a) ⟨food/specimen⟩ conservar (b) (Culin) ⟨fruit/vegetables⟩ hacer* conserva de (c) ⟨building/traditions⟩ conservar

preserve² n **1** (a) (exclusive privilege, sphere): to be a male ~ ser* terreno exclusivamente masculino (b) (restricted area): game ~ coto m de caza; wildlife ~ (AmE) reserva f de animales **2** (Culin) ⟨jam, jelly⟩ confitura f, mermelada f

preside /prɪˈzaɪd/ vi presidir; to ~ over a meeting presidir una reunión

presidency /ˈprezədənsi ‖ ˈprezɪdənsi/ n presidencia f

president /ˈprezədənt ‖ ˈprezɪdənt/ n (a) (of state, society) presidente, -ta m,f (b) (of bank, corporation) (esp AmE) director, -tora m,f, presidente, -ta m,f (c) (of university) (AmE) rector, -tora m,f

presidential /ˌprezəˈdentʃəl ‖ ˌprezɪˈdenʃəl/ adj ⟨before n⟩ presidencial

press¹ /pres/ n **1** (newspapers, journalists) prensa f; the ~ la prensa; ⟨before n⟩ ~ agency (BrE) agencia f de prensa; ~ photographer reportero gráfico, reportera gráfica m,f; ~ release comunicado m de prensa **2** (a) (printing ~) prensa f, imprenta f; to go to ~ entrar en prensa (b) (publishing house) editorial f **3** (for pressing — grapes, flowers, machine parts) prensa f; (— trousers) prensa f plancha-pantalones

press² vt **1** (a) (push) ⟨button/doorbell⟩ apretar*; ⟨pedal/footbrake⟩ pisar **2** (a) (squeeze) apretar*

(a) (in press) ⟨grapes/olives/flowers⟩ prensar **(c)** ⟨disk/album⟩ imprimir* **(d)** ⟨clothes⟩ planchar ③ **(a)** (put pressure on) presionar **(b)** (pursue): to ~ charges against sb presentar cargos en contra de algn
■ ~ vi ① (exert pressure): ~ firmly presione con fuerza ② (urge, pressurize) presionar
■ **press on** [v + adv] to ~ on (WITH sth) seguir* adelante (CON algo)

press conference n rueda f de prensa

pressed /prest/ adj (pred): to be ~ for time estar* or andar* escaso de tiempo

pressing /'presɪŋ/ adj ⟨engagements/concerns⟩ urgente; ⟨need/desire⟩ apremiante

press: ~ **stud** n (BrE) broche m or botón m de presión (AmL), (cierre m) automático m (Esp); **~-up** n (BrE) flexión f (de brazos or de pecho), fondo m, lagartija f (Méx)

pressure¹ /'preʃər ‖ 'preʃə(r)/ n presión f; to put ~ on sth/sb hacer* presión sobre algo/ presionar a algn; the ~s of city life las presiones a las que somete la vida urbana; I've been under a lot of ~ recently últimamente he estado muy agobiado

pressure² vt presionar; to ~ sb to + INF presionar a algn PARA QUE (+ subj)

pressure: ~ **cooker** n olla f a presión or (Esp tb) olla f exprés or (Méx) olla f presto; ~ **group** n grupo m de presión; ~ **pan** n (AmE) ▶ ~ COOKER

pressurize /'preʃəraɪz/ vt **(a)** (Aerosp, Aviat) presurizar* **(b)** (urge) (BrE) ▶ PRESSURE²

prestige /pre'stiːʒ/ n prestigio m

prestigious /pre'stɪdʒəs/ adj prestigioso

presumably /prɪ'zuːməbli ‖ prɪ'zjuːməbli/ adv (indep): you've taken the necessary steps, ~ supongo or me imagino que habrás tomado las medidas pertinentes

presume /prɪ'zuːm ‖ prɪ'zjuːm/ vt **(a)** (assume) suponer*; I ~ so supongo or me imagino que sí **(b)** (dare) to ~ to + INF atreverse A + INF

presumption /prɪ'zʌmpʃən/ n **(a)** (boldness) atrevimiento m **(b)** (assumption) suposición f

presumptuous /prɪ'zʌmptʃəs ‖ prɪ'zʌmptʃʊəs/ adj impertinente

presuppose /'priːsə'pəʊz/ vt presuponer*

pretence n (BrE) ▶ PRETENSE

pretend¹ /prɪ'tend/ vt/i fingir*

pretend² adj (used to or by children) ⟨money/ gun⟩ de mentira (fam)

pretender /prɪ'tendər ‖ prɪ'tendə(r)/ n ~ (TO sth) pretendiente mf (A algo)

pretense, (BrE) **pretence** /'priːtens, prɪ'tens ‖ prɪ'tens/ n: her air of confidence is a ~ ese aire de seguridad suyo es fingido; let's drop this ~! ¡vamos a dejarnos de fingir!; under false ~s de manera fraudulenta

pretension /prɪ'tentʃən ‖ prɪ'tenʃən/ n (often pl) pretensión f

pretentious /prɪ'tentʃəs ‖ prɪ'tenʃəs/ adj ⟨person/language/film⟩ pretencioso; ⟨house/decor⟩ presuntuoso

pretext /'priːtekst/ n pretexto m; on o under the ~ of con el pretexto de

pretty¹ /'prɪti/ adj -tier, -tiest bonito, lindo (AmL)

pretty² adv (rather, quite) bastante; (emphatic) bien

prevail /prɪ'veɪl/ vi ① (triumph) ⟨justice/common sense⟩ prevalecer*; ⟨enemy⟩ imponerse* ② (predominate) ⟨attitude/pessimism⟩ preponderar; ⟨situation⟩ reinar

prevailing /prɪ'veɪlɪŋ/ adj (before n) ⟨wind⟩ preponderante; ⟨trend/view⟩ imperante; ⟨uncertainty⟩ reinante

prevalence /'prevələns/ n **(a)** (widespread occurrence) preponderancia f **(b)** (predominance) predominio m

prevalent /'prevələnt/ adj frecuente, corriente; ⟨disease⟩ común

prevaricate /prɪ'værəkeɪt ‖ prɪ'værɪkeɪt/ vi **(a)** (not answer directly) andarse* con rodeos **(b)** (lie) (AmE) mentir*

prevent /prɪ'vent/ vt **(a)** (hinder) impedir*; to ~ sb/sth (FROM) -ING impedir* QUE algn/algo (+ subj) **(b)** (forestall) ⟨crime/disease/accident⟩ prevenir*, evitar

preventative /prɪ'ventətɪv/ adj ▶ PREVENTIVE

prevention /prɪ'ventʃən ‖ prɪ'venʃən/ n prevención f

preventive /prɪ'ventɪv/ adj preventivo

preview /'priːvjuː/ n **(a)** (advance showing) preestreno m **(b)** (trailer) avance m, trailer m (Esp), sinopsis f (CS)

previous /'priːviəs/ adj (earlier) (before n) ⟨occasion/attempt/page⟩ anterior; ⟨experience/ knowledge⟩ previo; on the ~ day el día anterior; I had a ~ engagement ya tenía un compromiso

previously /'priːviəsli/ adv antes

prewar /'priː'wɔːr ‖ ,priː'wɔː(r)/ adj de antes de la guerra

prey /preɪ/ n presa f
■ **prey on, prey upon** [v + prep + o] **(a)** ⟨animal⟩ (hunt) cazar*; (feed on) alimentarse de; it's been ~ing on my mind me ha estado preocupando **(b)** (exploit) explotar

price¹ /praɪs/ n ① (cost) precio m; to go up/ down in ~ subir/bajar de precio; to pay a/the ~ for sth pagar* algo caro; (before n) ~ list lista f de precios; it's out of my ~ range cuesta más de lo que puedo pagar ② (value) (liter) precio m; one cannot put a ~ on freedom la libertad no tiene precio

price² vt **(a)** (fix price of) (often pass): their products are reasonably ~d sus productos tienen precios razonables; they have ~d themselves out of the market han subido tanto los precios que se han quedado sin compradores (or clientes etc) **(b)** (mark price on) ponerle* el precio a

priceless /'praɪsləs ‖ 'praɪslɪs/ adj inestimable, invalorable (CS)

price tag n etiqueta f (del precio), precio m

pricey, pricy /'praɪsi/ adj pricier, priciest (colloq) ⟨item⟩ carito (fam); ⟨store⟩ carero (fam)

prick¹ /prɪk/ vt ① (pierce, wound) pinchar, picar* (Méx); that ~ed his conscience eso hizo que le remordiera la conciencia ② ~ up ⟨ears⟩ ⟨dog⟩ levantar, parar (AmL); she ~ed up her ears at the mention of France aguzó el oído or (AmL fam) paró la oreja al oír hablar de Francia
■ ~ vi pinchar

prick² n **(a)** (act) pinchazo m, piquete m (Méx) **(b)** (mark) agujero m

prickle¹ /ˈprɪkəl/ n **(a)** (thorn) espina f **(b)** (sensation) picor m

prickle² vi «wool» picar*; «beard» pinchar, picar* (Méx); «skin/scalp» picar*

prickly /ˈprɪkli/ adj **-lier, -liest (a)** (with prickles) «plant» espinoso; «animal» con púas **(b)** (scratchy) «wool» que pica; «beard» que pincha or (Méx) pica

pride¹ /praɪd/ n **1 (a)** (self-respect) orgullo m; false ~ vanidad f; she takes great ~ in her work se toma muy en serio su trabajo; **to swallow one's ~** tragarse* el orgullo **(b)** (conceit) orgullo m **2** (source of pride) orgullo m; she is her mother's ~ and joy es el orgullo de su madre. **3** (of lions) manada f

pride² v refl **to ~ oneself ON sth/-ING** enorgullecerse* DE algo/+ INF

priest /priːst/ n sacerdote m; (parish ~) cura m (párroco), párroco m

priestess /ˈpriːstəs ‖ ˈpriːstes/ n sacerdotisa f

priesthood /ˈpriːsthʊd/ n **(a)** (office) sacerdocio m **(b)** (clergy) clero m

prig /prɪg/ n mojigato, -ta m,f

prim /prɪm/ adj **-mer, -mest (a)** (prudish) mojigato; (affected) remilgado, repipi (Esp fam); she's so ~ and proper! es tan correcta y formal **(b)** (neat) cuidado

prima ballerina /ˈpriːmə/ n primera bailarina f

primaevel adj (BrE) ▶ PRIMEVAL

primarily /praɪˈmerəli ‖ ˈpraɪmərɪli/ adv fundamentalmente

primary /ˈpraɪmeri ‖ ˈpraɪməri/ adj **1** (principal) «purpose/role/aim» primordial **2 (a)** (first, basic) «source/energy» primario; «industry» de base **(b)** «education» primario

primary: ~ color, (BrE) **colour** n color m primario; **~ school** n escuela f (de enseñanza) primaria

primate n **1** /ˈpraɪmeɪt/ (Zool) primate m **2** /ˈpraɪmeɪt, -ət/ (Relig) primado m

prime¹ /praɪm/ adj (no comp) **(a)** (major) principal **(b)** (first-rate) «example/location» excelente; «cut» de primera (calidad)

prime² (in best time): **to be in one's ~ o in the ~ of life** estar* en la flor de la vida

prime³ vt **(a)** (prepare for painting) «wood/metal» aplicar* una capa de imprimación a; «canvas» preparar **(b)** «pump/gun» cebar **(c)** (brief) preparar

prime minister n primer ministro, primera ministra m,f

primer /ˈpraɪmər ‖ ˈpraɪmə(r)/ n **1 (a)** (paint) imprimación f **(b)** (explosive) cebo m **2** (textbook) manual m

prime time n horas fpl de máxima audiencia

primeval, (BrE) **primaeval** /praɪˈmiːvəl/ adj primigenio

primitive /ˈprɪmətɪv ‖ ˈprɪmɪtɪv/ adj primitivo; «urges/instincts» primario

primrose /ˈprɪmrəʊz/ n primavera f, prímula f

Primus® **(stove)** /ˈpraɪməs/ n hornillo m de queroseno, Primus® m

prince /prɪns/ n príncipe m

princess /ˈprɪnsəs ‖ ˈprɪnses/ n princesa f

principal¹ /ˈprɪnsəpəl/ adj (before n) principal

principal² n (of school) director, -tora m,f; (of university) rector, -tora m,f

principally /ˈprɪnsəpli/ adv principalmente

principle /ˈprɪnsəpəl/ n **1** (basic fact, law) principio m; **in ~** en principio **2** (rule of conduct) principio m; **I never borrow money, on ~** nunca pido dinero prestado, por principio; **it is against my ~s** va contra mis principios

print¹ /prɪnt/ n **1** (Print) **(a)** (lettering) letra f **(b)** (text): **in ~** (published) publicado; (available) a la venta; **out of ~** agotado **2 (a)** (Art, Print) grabado m **(b)** (Phot) copia f **3** (of foot, finger) huella f **4** (fabric) estampado m

print² vt **1 (a)** «letter/text/design» imprimir* **(b)** «fabric» estampar **(c)** (publish) publicar* **(d)** **printed** past p impreso **2** (write clearly) escribir* con letra de imprenta **3** (Phot) «negative» imprimir*

■ ~ vi **(a)** (Print) imprimir* **(b)** (write without joining the letters) escribir* con letra de imprenta or de molde

■ **print out** [v + adv + o, v + o + adv] imprimir*

printer /ˈprɪntər ‖ ˈprɪntə(r)/ n **(a)** (worker) tipógrafo, -fa m,f, impresor, -sora m,f **(b)** (business) imprenta f **(c)** (machine) impresora f

printing /ˈprɪntɪŋ/ n **(a)** (act, process, result) impresión f **(b)** (quantity printed) edición f **(c)** (trade) imprenta f

printing press n imprenta f, prensa f

print: ~out n listado m; **~ run** n tirada f

prior¹ /ˈpraɪər ‖ ˈpraɪə(r)/ adj (before n) «knowledge/warning» previo; **I had a ~ engagement** ya tenía un compromiso; **prior to** (as prep) antes de

prior² n prior m

priority /praɪˈɔːrəti ‖ praɪˈɒrɪti/ n (pl -ties) **(a)** (precedence) prioridad f; **to have/take ~ (over sth)** tener* prioridad (sobre algo) **(b)** (important matter, aim): **you have to get your priorities right** tienes que saber decidir qué es lo más importante **(c)** (in traffic) (BrE) preferencia f

priory /ˈpraɪəri/ n (pl -ries) priorato m

prise /praɪz/ vt (BrE) ▶ PRIZE³ 2

prism /ˈprɪzəm/ n prisma m

prison /ˈprɪzn/ n prisión f, cárcel f; (before n) «system/reform» carcelario, penitenciario; **~ officer** (BrE) funcionario, -ria m,f de prisiones

prison camp n campo m de prisioneros

prisoner /ˈprɪznər ‖ ˈprɪznə(r)/ n **(a)** (captive) prisionero, -ra m,f; **to take sb ~** tomar or (esp Esp) coger* a algn prisionero **(b)** (in jail) preso, -sa m,f **(c)** (person arrested) detenido, -da m,f **(d)** (accused) reo mf, acusado, -da m,f

prisoner of war n (pl ~s o ~) prisionero, -ra m,f de guerra

prissy /ˈprɪsi/ adj **-sier, -siest** (colloq) remilgado, repipi (Esp fam)

pristine /ˈprɪstiːn, -taɪn/ adj (frml & liter) inmaculado, prístino (liter)

privacy /ˈpraɪvəsi ‖ ˈprɪvəsi/ n privacidad f

private¹ /ˈpraɪvət ‖ ˈpraɪvɪt/ adj **1 (a)** (confidential) «conversation/matter» privado; «letter» personal **(b) in private:** she told me in ~ me lo dijo confidencialmente; **can we talk in ~?** ¿podemos hablar en privado? **2** (for own use, in own possession) «road/lesson/

secretary› particular; ‹*income*› personal; ~ **property** propiedad *f* privada; ~ **income** rentas *fpl*

3 (a) (not official) ‹*visit/correspondence*› privado; their ~ **life** su vida privada **(b)** (unconnected to the state) ‹*school*› privado, de pago (Esp); ‹*ward*› reservado; ‹*patient*› particular; ~ **enterprise** la empresa privada; **the** ~ **sector** el sector privado **4 (a)** ‹*thoughts/doubts*› íntimo; **it's a** ~ **joke** es un chiste que los dos entendemos/entienden **(b)** ‹*person*› reservado

private² *n* soldado *mf* raso

private: ~ **detective** *n* detective *mf* privado; ~ **eye** *n* (esp AmE colloq) sabueso *mf*

privately /'praɪvətli ǁ 'praɪvɪtli/ *adv* **1** (in private) en privado **2** (not by state): **she had the operation done** ~ (BrE) la operaron en una clínica privada; **this land is** ~ **owned** esta tierra es de particulares

private parts *pl n* (euph & hum) partes *fpl* pudendas (euf & hum)

privation /praɪ'veɪʃən/ *n* (frml) privación *f*

privatization /ˌpraɪvətə'zeɪʃən ǁ ˌpraɪvɪtaɪ'zeɪʃən/ *n* privatización *f*

privatize /'praɪvətaɪz ǁ 'praɪvɪtaɪz/ *vt* privatizar*

privilege /'prɪvəlɪdʒ/ *n* privilegio *m*

privileged /'prɪvəlɪdʒd/ *adj* **(a)** (having advantages) ‹*position*› privilegiado **(b)** (honored) (*pred*) **to be** ~ **to + INF** tener* el privilegio *or* el honor DE + INF

privy /'prɪvi/ *adj* (frml) (*pred*) **to be** ~ **TO sth** tener* conocimiento DE algo

prize¹ /praɪz/ *n* premio *m*

prize² *adj* (before n) premiado

prize³ *vt* **1** (value) valorar (mucho) **2** (BrE) **prise**: **to** ~ **information out of sb** arrancarle* información a algn; **he** ~**d the lid off the crate** le arrancó la tapa a la caja haciendo palanca

prize: ~ **money** *n* premio *m* (en metálico); ~**winner** *n* ganador, -dora *m,f* (de un premio)

pro /prəʊ/ *n* **1** (professional) (colloq) profesional *mf* **2 pros** *pl* (advantages): **the** ~**s and cons** los pros y los contras

pro- /prəʊ/ *pref* pro(-)

proactive /prəʊ'æktɪv/ *adj* proactivo

probability /ˌprɑːbə'bɪləti ǁ ˌprɒbə'bɪlɪti/ *n* (*pl* -**ties**) probabilidad *f*

probable /'prɑːbəbəl ǁ 'prɒbəbəl/ *adj* probable; ‹*reason*› posible

probably /'prɑːbəbli ǁ 'prɒbəbli/ *adv* (indep) probablemente (+ *subj*)

probation /prəʊ'beɪʃən ǁ prə'beɪʃən/ *n* **1** (Law) libertad *f* condicional; **to be on** ~ estar* en libertad condicional **2** (trial period) período *m* de prueba

probationary /ˌprəʊ'beɪʃəneri ǁ prə'beɪʃənəri/ *adj* ‹*period*› de prueba

probe¹ /prəʊb/ *vt* **(a)** (physically) sondar **(b)** (investigate) investigar*; ‹*mind/subconscious*› explorar
■ ~ *vi* investigar*

probe² *n* **(a)** (Med, Elec) sonda *f* **(b)** (investigation) investigación *f*

probing /'prəʊbɪŋ/ *adj* ‹*question*› sagaz; ‹*study*› a fondo

problem /'prɑːbləm ǁ 'prɒbləm/ *n* problema *m*; **no** ~**!** (colloq) ¡no hay problema!; **what's the** ~**?** ¿qué pasa?; (before n) ‹*family/child*› difícil

problematic /ˌprɑːblə'mætɪk ǁ ˌprɒblə'mætɪk/, -**ical** /-ɪkəl/ *adj* problemático

procedure /prə'siːdʒər ǁ prə'siːdjə(r)/ *n* (practice) procedimiento *m*; (step) trámite *m*

proceed /prəʊ'siːd, prə- ǁ prə'siːd, prəʊ-/ *vi* **(a)** (move forward) (frml) «*person/vehicle*» avanzar* **(b)** (continue) continuar*; **to** ~ **to + INF: she** ~**ed to tell us why** pasó a explicarnos por qué **(c)** (act) (frml) proceder **(d)** (progress) marchar

proceedings /prəʊ'siːdɪŋz, prə-/ *pl n* **(a)** (events): ~ **began late** la reunión (*or* el acto *etc*) empezó tarde **(b)** (measures) medidas *fpl*; (Law) juicio *m*

proceeds /'prəʊsiːdz/ *pl n*: **the** ~ (from charity sale, function) lo recaudado

process¹ /'prɑːses, 'prəʊ- ǁ 'prəʊses/ *n* **(a)** (series of actions, changes) proceso *m*; **the** ~ **of obtaining a permit** el trámite para obtener un permiso; **I am in the** ~ **of writing to him right now** en este preciso momento le estoy escribiendo **(b)** (method) proceso *m*, procedimiento *m*

process² *vt* ‹*raw materials/waste*› procesar, tratar; ‹*film*› revelar; ‹*applications*› dar* curso a; ‹*order*› tramitar; ‹*data*› procesar

process cheese (AmE), **processed cheese** /'prɑːsest ǁ 'prəʊsest/ (BrE) *n* queso *m* fundido

processing /'prɑːsesɪŋ, 'prəʊ- ǁ 'prəʊsesɪŋ/ *n* **(a)** (of materials, waste) tratamiento *m*, procesamiento *m*; (of film) revelado *m* **(b)** (of an order, an application) tramitación *f* **(c)** (Comput) procesamiento *m*

procession /prə'seʃən/ *n* desfile *m*; (Relig) procesión *f*; **a funeral** ~ un cortejo fúnebre

proclaim /prəʊ'kleɪm, prə- ǁ prə'kleɪm/ *vt* (frml) ‹*independence*› proclamar; ‹*love*› declarar

proclamation /ˌprɑːklə'meɪʃən ǁ ˌprɒklə'meɪʃən/ *n* (frml) proclamación *f*

procrastinate /prəʊ'kræstɪneɪt ǁ prəʊ'kræstɪneɪt/ *vi* dejar las cosas para más tarde

procreation /ˌprəʊkri'eɪʃən/ *n* (frml) procreación *f*

procure /prə'kjʊr ǁ prə'kjʊə(r)/ *vt* (frml) procurar (frml)

prod¹ /prɑːd ǁ prɒd/ *vt* -**dd**- (with elbow) darle* un codazo a; (with sth sharp) pinchar

prod² *n* (with elbow) codazo *m*; (with sth sharp) pinchazo *m*

prodigal /'prɑːdɪgəl ǁ 'prɒdɪgəl/ *adj* pródigo

prodigious /prə'dɪdʒəs/ *adj* ‹*amount/cost*› enorme; ‹*efforts/strength*› prodigioso

prodigy /'prɑːdədʒi ǁ 'prɒdɪdʒi/ *n* (*pl* -**gies**) prodigio *m*; **child** ~ niño, -ña *m,f* prodigio

produce¹ /prə'duːs ǁ prə'djuːs/ *vt* **1 (a)** (manufacture, yield) ‹*cars/cloth*› producir*, fabricar*; ‹*coal/grain/beef*› producir*; ‹*fruit*› «*country/region*» producir*; «*tree/bush*» dar*, producir* **(b)** (create, give) ‹*energy/sound*› producir* **(c)** (cause) ‹*effect*› surtir, producir* **(d)** (give birth to) ‹*young*› tener* **2** (show, bring out) ‹*ticket/document/evidence*› presentar, aportar; ‹*gun*/

knife⟩ sacar* **3** **(a)** (Cin, TV) producir*; (Theat)
⟨*play*⟩ poner* en escena; ⟨*show*⟩ montar **(b)** (Rad,
Theat) (direct) dirigir*

produce² /'prɑːduːs ‖'prɒdjuːs/ n productos
mpl (alimenticios)

producer /prə'duːsər ‖prə'djuːsə(r)/ n
1 (manufacturer) fabricante *mf* **2** **(a)** (Cin, TV,
Theat) productor, -tora *m,f* **(b)** (Rad, Theat) (director)
director, -tora *m,f*

product /'prɑːdəkt ‖'prɒdʌkt/ n producto *m*

production /prə'dʌkʃən/ n **1** **(a)** (manufacture)
fabricación *f* **(b)** (output) producción *f* **2** (showing)
presentación *f* **3** (staging, version) (Theat, Cin)
producción *f*; **4** **(a)** (act of producing) (Cin, TV)
producción *f*; (Theat) puesta *f* en escena **(b)**
(direction) (Rad, Theat) dirección *f*

production line n cadena *f* de fabricación

productive /prə'dʌktɪv/ adj ⟨*land/factory/
mine*⟩ productivo; ⟨*meeting*⟩ fructífero

productively /prə'dʌktɪvli/ adv
productivamente; **I didn't spend my time very ∼**
no saqué buen partido del tiempo

productivity /ˌprəʊdʌk'tɪvəti ‖ˌprɒdʌk'tɪvəti/
n productividad *f*

profane /prə'feɪn/ adj **(a)** (blasphemous)
irreverente **(b)** (secular) profano

profanity /prə'fænəti/ n (pl **-ties**) **(a)**
(blasphemy, vulgarity) irreverencia *f* **(b)** (swearword)
blasfemia *f*

profess /prə'fes/ vt **(a)** (claim) (frml) ⟨*desire/
belief*⟩ manifestar*; **he ∼ed to be an expert** se
preciaba de ser un experto **(b)** (Relig) profesar

profession /prə'feʃən/ n **1** **(a)** (occupation)
profesión *f*; **by ∼** de profesión **(b)** (members) (*no
pl*): **the medical ∼** el cuerpo médico; **the teaching
∼** la enseñanza **2** (declaration) (frml) profesión *f*

professional¹ /prə'feʃnəl ‖prə'feʃənl/ adj
(before n) ⟨*musician/golfer*⟩ profesional; ⟨*soldier*⟩
de carrera; **to take ∼ advice** asesorarse con un
profesional (*or* un experto, técnico *etc*)

professional² n profesional *mf*; (competent
person) experto, -ta *m,f*

professionalism /prə'feʃnəlɪzəm
‖prə'feʃənlˌɪzəm/ n profesionalidad *f*

professionally /prə'feʃnəli/ adv **(a)** (as
livelihood) ⟨*sing/act*⟩ profesionalmente **(b)** (by
qualified person): **we had the job done ∼** hicimos
hacer el trabajo por un experto (*or* por un pintor,
albañil *etc*) **(c)** (in a professional way) con
profesionalidad

professor /prə'fesər ‖prə'fesə(r)/ n (of the
highest academic rank) catedrático, -ca *m,f*; (any
university teacher) (AmE) profesor universitario,
profesora universitaria *m,f*

proffer /'prɑːfər ‖'prɒfə(r)/ vt (frml) ofrecer*

proficiency /prə'fɪʃənsi/ n competencia *f*

proficient /prə'fɪʃənt/ adj muy competente

profile¹ /'prəʊfaɪl/ n perfil *m*; **to keep a low ∼**
tratar de pasar desapercibido

profile² vt ⟨*situation*⟩ hacer* un esbozo de; **to ∼
sb's life** hacer* una reseña biográfica de algn

profit¹ /'prɑːfət ‖'prɒfɪt/ n (Busn, Econ)
ganancias *fpl*, utilidades *fpl* (AmL); **to sell sth at a
∼** vender algo con ganancia

profit² vi **to ∼ FROM sth** sacar* provecho DE
algo

profitable /'prɑːfətəbəl ‖'prɒfɪtəbəl/ adj **(a)**
(Busn) ⟨*company/investment/crop*⟩ rentable **(b)**
⟨*day/journey*⟩ provechoso

profitably /'prɑːfətəbli ‖'prɒfɪtəbli/ adv **(a)**
(Busn) ⟨*trade/operate*⟩ de manera rentable; ⟨*sell*⟩
con ganancia **(b)** (fruitfully) provechosamente

profiteer /ˌprɑːfə'tɪr ‖ˌprɒfɪ'tɪə(r)/ n
especulador, -dora *m,f*

profiteering /ˌprɑːfə'tɪrɪŋ ‖ˌprɒfɪ'tɪərɪŋ/ n
especulación *f*

profit-making /'prɑːfətˌmeɪkɪŋ
‖'prɒfɪtˌmeɪkɪŋ/ adj (profitable) rentable; (which
aims to make a profit) con fines lucrativos

profound /prə'faʊnd/ adj **-er, -est** profundo

profoundly /prə'faʊndli/ adv profundamente

profuse /prə'fjuːs/ adj abundante; ⟨*bleeding*⟩
intenso

profusely /prə'fjuːsli/ adv ⟨*bleed*⟩
profusamente; ⟨*thank*⟩ efusivamente; **he
apologized ∼** se deshizo en disculpas

profusion /prə'fjuːʒən/ n profusión *f*

prognosis /prɑːg'nəʊsəs ‖prɒg'nəʊsɪs/ n (pl
-ses /-siːz/) pronóstico *m*

program¹, (BrE) **programme** /'prəʊɡræm/ n
1 **(a)** (schedule, plan) programa *m* **(b)** (for concert,
performance) programa *m* **(c)** (esp AmE Educ)
(course) curso *m* **2** (Rad, TV) programa *m*
3 **program** (Comput) programa *m*

program² vt **-mm-** *or* **-m-** **1** (BrE also)
programme **(a)** (schedule) ⟨*activities*⟩
programar, planear **(b)** (instruct) programar
2 (Comput) programar

programmer, (AmE also) **programer**
/'prəʊɡræmər ‖'prəʊɡræmə(r)/ n (Comput)
programador, -dora *m,f*

progress¹ /'prɑːɡrəs ‖'prəʊɡres/ n
1 (advancement) progreso *m*; (of situation, events)
desarrollo *m*; **to make ∼** ⟨*pupil*⟩ adelantar,
hacer* progresos; «*patient*» mejorar **2** **in
progress:** talks are in **∼ between the two parties**
los dos partidos están manteniendo
conversaciones; **while the examination is in ∼**
mientras dure el examen **3** (forward movement)
avance *m*

progress² /prə'ɡres/ vi «*work/science/
technology*» progresar; «*patient*» mejorar

progression /prə'ɡreʃən/ n **(a)** (advance)
evolución *f* **(b)** (Math, Mus) progresión *f*

progressive /prə'ɡresɪv/ adj **1** ⟨*attitude/
thinker/measure*⟩ progresista **2** ⟨*illness/
deterioration/improvement*⟩ progresivo

prohibit /prəʊ'hɪbɪt ‖prə'hɪbɪt/ vt **(a)** (forbid)
prohibir* **(b)** (prevent) impedir*

prohibition /ˌprəʊə'bɪʃən ‖ˌprəʊhɪ'bɪʃən/ n **(a)**
prohibición *f* **(b)** **Prohibition** (in US history) (*no
art*) la Ley seca, la Prohibición

AmC	Central America	Arg	Argentina	Cu	Cuba	Per	Peru
AmL	Latin America	Bol	Bolivia	Ec	Ecuador	RPl	River Plate Area
AmS	South America	Chi	Chile	Esp	Spain	Ur	Uruguay
Andes	Andean Region	CS	Southern Cone	Méx	Mexico	Ven	Venezuela

prohibitive /prəʊˈhɪbətɪv ‖ prəˈhɪbətɪv/ *adj* ⟨*price/cost*⟩ prohibitivo

project¹ /ˈprɒdʒekt ‖ ˈprɒdʒekt/ *n* (a) (scheme) proyecto *m* (b) (Educ) trabajo *m* (c) (housing ∼) (in US) complejo *m* de viviendas subvencionadas

project² /prəˈdʒekt/ *vt* **1** (a) ⟨*beam/shadow/ image*⟩ proyectar (b) (convey) ⟨*personality/image/ voice*⟩ proyectar **2** (fml) ⟨*missile*⟩ lanzar* **3** (forecast) pronosticar*; ⟨*costs/trends*⟩ hacer* una proyección de; **the ∼ed figure** la cifra prevista
■ ∼ *vi* (jut out) sobresalir*

projection /prəˈdʒekʃən/ *n* **1** (of image, slide) proyección *f* **2** (forecast) proyección *f*, pronóstico *m* **3** (protuberance) saliente *f or m*

projector /prəˈdʒektər ‖ prəˈdʒektə(r)/ *n* proyector *m*

proletarian /ˌprəʊləˈteriən ‖ ˌprəʊləˈteəriən/ *adj* proletario

pro-life *adj* pro-vida

proliferate /prəˈlɪfəreɪt/ *vi* proliferar

prolific /prəˈlɪfɪk/ *adj* prolífico

prologue, (AmE also) **prolog** /ˈprəʊlɔ:g ‖ ˈprəʊlɒg/ *n* prólogo *m*

prolong /prəˈlɔ:ŋ ‖ prəˈlɒŋ/ *vt* prolongar*

prom /prɑ:m ‖ prɒm/ *n* (a) (ball) (in US) (colloq) baile *m* del colegio (*or* de la facultad *etc*) (b) (esplanade) (BrE colloq) ▶ PROMENADE¹

promenade¹ /ˌprɑ:məˈneɪd ‖ ˈprɒmənɑ:d/ *n* (at seaside) (esp BrE) paseo *m* marítimo, malecón *m* (AmL), costanera *f* (CS)

promenade² *vi* pasear(se)

prominence /ˈprɑ:mənəns ‖ ˈprɒmɪnəns/ *n* (conspicuousness) prominencia *f*; (eminence, importance) importancia *f*

prominent /ˈprɑ:mənənt ‖ ˈprɒmɪnənt/ *adj* ⟨*position*⟩ destacado; ⟨*role/politician*⟩ prominente, destacado (b) ⟨*jaw/nose*⟩ prominente

prominently /ˈprɑ:mənəntlɪ ‖ ˈprɒmɪnəntlɪ/ *adv*: **it was ∼ displayed** ocupaba un lugar prominente *or* destacado; **he figured ∼ in the negotiations** desempeñó un papel prominente *or* destacado en las negociaciones

promiscuity /ˌprɑ:məsˈkju:ətɪ ‖ ˌprɒmɪsˈkju:əti/ *n* promiscuidad *f*

promiscuous /prəˈmɪskjuəs/ *adj* promiscuo

promise¹ /ˈprɑ:məs ‖ ˈprɒmɪs/ *n* **1** (pledge) promesa *f* **2** (potential): **his work showed great *o* a lot of ∼** su trabajo prometía mucho

promise² *vt/i* prometer; **to ∼ to + INF** prometer + INF

promising /ˈprɑ:məsɪŋ ‖ ˈprɒmɪsɪŋ/ *adj* ⟨*pupil/ writer/career*⟩ prometedor; ⟨*future*⟩ halagüeño

promote /prəˈməʊt/ *vt* **1** (a) (raise in rank) ⟨*employee*⟩ ascender* (b) (AmE Educ) promover* **2** (a) (encourage) promover*; ⟨*growth*⟩ estimular (b) (advocate) promover* **3** ⟨*product/service*⟩ promocionar

promoter /prəˈməʊtər ‖ prəˈməʊtə(r)/ *n* (a) (Busn) promotor, -tora *m,f* (b) (Sport) empresario, -ria *m,f*

promotion /prəˈməʊʃən/ *n* **1** (advancement in rank) ascenso *m*; **she got** (a) **∼** la ascendieron **2** (a) (of research, peace, trade) promoción *f* (b) (advocacy) promoción *f* **3** (publicity) promoción *f*

promotional /prəˈməʊʃnəl ‖ prəˈməʊʃənl/ *adj* de promoción, promocional

prompt¹ /prɑ:mpt ‖ prɒmpt/ *vt* **1** ⟨*response/ outcry*⟩ provocar*; **to ∼ sb to + INF** mover* a algn A + INF **2** ⟨*actor/orator*⟩ apuntarle a

prompt² *adj* **-er, -est** rápido

prompt³ *adv* (BrE): **at ten o'clock ∼** a las diez en punto

prompt⁴ *n* (a) (reminder) apunte *m* (b) (Comput) presto *m*

prompter /ˈprɑ:mptər ‖ ˈprɒmptə(r)/ *n* apuntador, -dora *m,f*

promptly /ˈprɑ:mptlɪ ‖ ˈprɒmptli/ *adv* (a) (on time) puntualmente (b) (speedily) ⟨*pay/deliver*⟩ sin demora (c) (instantly) de inmediato

prone /prəʊn/ *adj* **1** (liable, disposed) (*pred*) **to be ∼ TO sth** ser* propenso A algo; **to be ∼ to + INF** ser* propenso a + INF **2** (face downward) (tendido) boca abajo

prong /prɔ:ŋ ‖ prɒŋ/ *n* diente *m*

pronoun /ˈprəʊnaʊn/ *n* pronombre *m*

pronounce /prəˈnaʊns/ *vt* (a) ⟨*sound/word/ syllable*⟩ pronunciar (b) ⟨*judgment/sentence*⟩ pronunciar (c) (declare) (frml): **the doctor ∼d him dead** el médico dictaminó que estaba muerto

pronounced /prəˈnaʊnst/ *adj* pronunciado

pronouncement /prəˈnaʊnsmənt/ *n* declaración *f*

pronunciation /prəˌnʌnsiˈeɪʃən/ *n* pronunciación *f*

proof¹ /pru:f/ *n* **1** (conclusive evidence) prueba *f* **2** (Print) prueba *f* (de imprenta) **3** (alcoholic strength) graduación *f* alcohólica

proof² *adj* (*pred*) **to be ∼ AGAINST sth** ser* a prueba DE algo

proof: **∼read** (*past & past p* **-read** /-red/) *vt* *corregir ■ ∼ *vi* corregir* pruebas; **∼reader** *n* corrector, -tora *m,f* de pruebas

prop¹ /prɑ:p ‖ prɒp/ *n* **1** (holding up roof etc) puntal *m* **2** (Cin, Theat) accesorio *m*, objeto *m* de utilería *or* (Esp, Méx) del attrezzo

prop² **-pp-** *vt* **to ∼ sth AGAINST sth** apoyar algo EN *or* CONTRA algo
■ **prop up** [*v + o + adv, v + adv + o*] (a) (support) ⟨*wall/building*⟩ sostener* (b) (lean) apoyar

propaganda /ˌprɑ:pəˈgændə ‖ ˌprɒpəˈgændə/ *n* propaganda *f*

propagate /ˈprɑ:pəgeɪt ‖ ˈprɒpəgeɪt/ *vt* propagar*

propel /prəˈpel/ *vt* **-ll-** ⟨*plane/ship*⟩ propulsar

propeller /prəˈpelər ‖ prəˈpelə(r)/ *n* hélice *f*

proper /ˈprɑ:pər ‖ ˈprɒpə(r)/ *adj* **1** (before n, no comp) (correct) ⟨*treatment/procedure*⟩ apropiado; ⟨*pronunciation*⟩ correcto **2** (before n, no comp) (genuine) ⟨*chance*⟩ verdadero; ⟨*meal*⟩ como Dios manda; ⟨*vacation*⟩ de verdad **3** (a) ⟨*behavior/ person*⟩ correcto (b) (overly decorous) recatado **4** (in the strict sense) (after n) propiamente dicho

properly /ˈprɑ:pərlɪ ‖ ˈprɒpəli/ *adv* (a) ⟨*write/ spell/fit*⟩ correctamente; ⟨*work/concentrate/eat*⟩ bien (b) (appropriately) apropiadamente

proper name, proper noun *n* nombre *m* propio

property /ˈprɑ:pərtɪ ‖ ˈprɒpəti/ *n* (*pl* **-ties**) **1** (possessions) propiedad *f* **2** (a) (buildings, land) ·····⟶

propiedades *fpl*, bienes *mpl* raíces (frml); (*before n*) ~ **developer** promotor inmobiliario, promotora inmobiliaria *m,f*; ~ **tax** (in US) impuesto *m* sobre la propiedad inmobiliaria **(b)** (building) inmueble *m* (frml); (*piece of land*) terreno *m*, solar *m*, parcela *f* **3** (quality) propiedad *f*

prophecy /'prɑːfəsi ‖'prɒfəsi/ *n* (*pl* **-cies**) profecía *f*

prophesy /'prɑːfəsaɪ ‖'prɒfəsaɪ/ *vt* **-sies, -sying, -sied** predecir*; (Relig) profetizar*

prophet /'prɑːfət ‖'prɒfɪt/ *n* profeta, -tisa *m,f*

prophetic /prə'fetɪk/ *adj* profético

proportion /prə'pɔːrʃən ‖prə'pɔːʃən/ *n* **1** (part) (*no pl*) parte *f* **2** (ratio) proporción *f*; **in equal ~s** por partes iguales; **in ~ to sth** en proporción a algo **3** (proper relation) proporción *f*; **let's keep things in ~** no exageremos; **to blow sth up out of all ~** exagerar algo desmesuradamente **4 proportions** *pl* (size) proporciones *fpl*

proportional /prə'pɔːrʃnəl ‖prə'pɔːʃənl/ *adj* proporcional; **~ representation** representación *f* proporcional

proportionate /prə'pɔːrʃnət ‖prə'pɔːʃənət/ *adj* proporcional

proposal /prə'pəʊzəl/ *n* **(a)** (suggestion) propuesta *f* **(b)** (of marriage) proposición *f* matrimonial

propose /prə'pəʊz/ *vt* **1** **(a)** (suggest) proponer*; **to ~ -ING/(THAT)** proponer* QUE (+ *subj*) **(b) proposed** *past p*: **the ~d cuts** los recortes que se proponen implementar **(c)** (in meeting) (*amendment*) proponer*; (*motion*) presentar **2** (intend) **to ~ to + INF, to ~ -ING** pensar* + INF
∎ ~ *vi* **to ~ TO sb** proponerle* matrimonio a algn

proposition¹ /ˌprɑːpə'zɪʃən ‖ˌprɒpə'zɪʃən/ *n* **1** (suggestion) propuesta *f*; (offer) oferta *f* **2** (prospect): **it's not a viable ~** no es viable

proposition² *vt* hacerle* proposiciones deshonestas a (euf)

proprietary /prə'praɪəteri ‖prə'praɪətri/ *adj* (*device/software/drug*) de marca registrada

proprietor /prə'praɪətər ‖prə'praɪətə(r)/ *n* propietario, -ria *m,f*, dueño, -ña *m,f*

propulsion /prə'pʌlʃən/ *n* propulsión *f*

pro rata /ˌprəʊ'rɑːtə/ *adv* a prorrata

prosaic /prəʊ'zeɪɪk/ *adj* prosaico

proscribe /prəʊ'skraɪb ‖prə'skraɪb/ *vt* proscribir*

prose /prəʊz/ *n* (Lit) prosa *f*

prosecute /'prɑːsɪkjuːt ‖'prɒsɪkjuːt/ *vt* (Law) **to ~ sb FOR sth** procesar a algn POR algo
∎ ~ *vi* iniciar procedimiento criminal; **prosecuting attorney** (in US) fiscal *mf*

prosecution /ˌprɑːsɪ'kjuːʃən ‖ˌprɒsɪ'kjuːʃən/ *n* (Law) **(a)** (bringing to trial) interposición *f* de una acción judicial **(b)** (prosecuting side) **the ~** la acusación

prosecutor /'prɑːsɪkjuːtər ‖'prɒsɪkjuːtə(r)/ *n* fiscal *mf*; (in private prosecutions) abogado, -da *m,f* de *or* por la acusación

prospect¹ /'prɑːspekt ‖'prɒspekt/ *n* **1** **(a)** (possibility) posibilidad *f*; **~ OF sth** posibilidades *fpl* DE algo **(b)** (situation envisaged) perspectiva *f* **(c)**

prospects *pl* (chances) perspectivas *fpl*; **a job with no ~s** un trabajo sin futuro **2** (potential customer) posible cliente, -ta *m,f*

prospect² /'prɑːspekt ‖prə'spekt/ *vi* **to ~ FOR sth** buscar* algo

prospective /prə'spektɪv/ *adj* (*before n*) (*customer*) posible; (*husband*) futuro

prospector /'prɑːspektər ‖prə'spektə(r)/ *n* prospector, -tora *m,f*, cateador, -dora *m,f* (AmS)

prospectus /prə'spektəs/ *n* (*pl* ~**es**) (Educ) folleto *m* informativo

prosper /'prɑːspər ‖'prɒspə(r)/ *vi* prosperar

prosperity /prɑː'sperəti ‖prɒ'sperəti/ *n* prosperidad *f*

prosperous /'prɑːspərəs ‖'prɒspərəs/ *adj* próspero

prostate (gland) /'prɑːsteɪt ‖'prɒsteɪt/ *n* próstata *f*

prostitute¹ /'prɑːstətuːt ‖'prɒstɪtjuːt/ *n* prostituta *f*; **male ~** prostituto *m*

prostitute² *vt* prostituir*; **to ~ oneself** prostituirse*

prostitution /ˌprɑːstə'tuːʃən ‖ˌprɒstɪ'tjuːʃən/ *n* prostitución *f*

prostrate /'prɑːstreɪt ‖'prɒstreɪt/ *adj* postrado

protagonist /prəʊ'tægənəst ‖prə'tægənɪst/ *n* (Lit) protagonista *mf*

protect /prə'tekt/ *vt* proteger*

protection /prə'tekʃən/ *n* protección *f*; (*before n*) ~ **racket** chantaje *m* (*que se practica a propietarios de comercios*)

protectionism /prə'tekʃənɪzəm/ *n* proteccionismo *m*

protective /prə'tektɪv/ *adj* **(a)** (*headgear/ covering*) protector; (*clothing*) de protección **(b)** (*attitude/feelings*) protector

protector /prə'tektər ‖prə'tektə(r)/ *n* protector, -tora *m,f*

protein /'prəʊtiːn/ *n* proteína *f*

protest¹ /'prəʊtest/ *n* **(a)** (expression of disagreement) protesta *f*; **in ~** (against sth) en señal de protesta (contra algo); **under ~** bajo protesta **(b)** (complaint) protesta *f* **(c)** (demonstration) manifestación *f* de protesta

protest² /prə'test/ *vi* protestar; **to ~ AGAINST/ ABOUT sth** protestar CONTRA/ACERCA DE algo
∎ ~ *vt* **1** **(a)** (complain) **to ~ THAT** quejarse DE QUE, protestar QUE **(b)** (object to) (AmE) (*decision/ action*) protestar (contra) **2** (assert) (*love*) declarar; (*innocence/loyalty*) hacer* protestas de

Protestant¹ /'prɑːtəstənt ‖'prɒtɪstənt/ *n* protestante *mf*

Protestant² *adj* protestante

Protestantism /'prɑːtəstəntɪzəm ‖'prɒtɪstəntɪzəm/ *n* protestantismo *m*

protester /prə'testər ‖prə'testə(r)/ *n* manifestante *mf*

protocol /'prəʊtəkɔːl ‖'prəʊtəkɒl/ *n* protocolo *m*

prototype /'prəʊtətaɪp/ *n* prototipo *m*

protracted /prə'træktəd ‖prə'træktɪd/ *adj* prolongado

protrude /prə'truːd/ *vi* (frml) **(a)** «*nail/ledge*»

sobresalir* **(b) protruding** *pres p* ‹*chin*›
prominente; ‹*teeth*› salido; ‹*nail*› que sobresale;
protruding eyes ojos *mpl* saltones

proud /praʊd/ *adj* **-er, -est (a)** (pleased)
‹*parent/winner*› orgulloso; ‹*smile/moment*› de
orgullo; **to be ~ OF** sb/sth estar* orgulloso DE
algn/algo **(b)** (having self-respect) ‹*nation/race*›
digno **(c)** (arrogant, haughty) orgulloso

proudly /'praʊdli/ *adv* **(a)** (with pleasure,
satisfaction) con orgullo **(b)** (arrogantly)
orgullosamente

prove /pruːv/ (*past* **proved**; *past p* **proved** or
proven) *vt* ‹*theory/statement/innocence*› probar*,
demostrar*; ‹*loyalty/courage*› demostrar*
  ■ *v refl* **to ~** oneself: **he was given three months to
~ himself** le dieron tres meses para que
demostrara su valía; **to ~ oneself to be sth**
demostrarse* ser algo
  ■ **~** *vi* resultar

proven /'pruːvən/ *adj* ‹*experience/ability*›
probado; ‹*method*› de probada eficacia

proverb /'prɑːvɜːrb ‖'prɒvɜːb/ *n* refrán *m*,
proverbio *m*

proverbial /prə'vɜːrbiəl ‖prə'vɜːbiəl/ *adj*
proverbial

provide /prə'vaɪd/ *vt* (supply) proporcionar;
‹*accommodation*› dar*; **to ~** sb WITH sth proveer*
a algn DE algo
  ■ **provide for** [*v* + *prep* + *o*] **(a)** (support) ‹*family*›
mantener* **(b)** (make arrangements for): **I have to ~
for my old age** tengo que asegurarme el bienestar
en la vejez

provided /prə'vaɪdəd ‖prə'vaɪdɪd/ *conj* **~
(that)** siempre que (+ *subj*)

providence /'prɑːvədəns ‖'prɒvɪdəns/ *n* **(a)**
(Relig) providencia *f* **(b)** (fate, chance): **it was sheer
~ that ...** fue providencial que ...

providing /prə'vaɪdɪŋ/ *conj* ▶ PROVIDED

province /'prɑːvəns ‖'prɒvɪns/ *n*
[1] (administrative unit) provincia *f* [2] **(a)** (area of
knowledge, activity) terreno *m* **(b)** (area of responsibility)
competencia *f*

provincial /prə'vɪntʃəl ‖prə'vɪnʃəl/ *adj*
[1] (Govt) provincial [2] **(a)** ‹*town*› de provincia(s)
(b) (pej) ‹*outlook*› provinciano

provision /prə'vɪʒən/ *n* [1] (of funding) provisión
f; (of food, supplies) suministro *m* [2] (preparatory
arrangements) previsiones *fpl* [3] (stipulation) (Govt,
Law) disposición *f* [4] **provisions** *pl* provisiones
fpl, víveres *mpl*

provisional /prə'vɪʒnəl ‖prə'vɪʒən/ *adj*
provisional, provisorio (AmS)

proviso /prə'vaɪzəʊ/ *n* (*pl* **-sos**) condición *f*

provocation /ˌprɑːvə'keɪʃən ‖ˌprɒvə'keɪʃən/
n provocación *f*

provocative /prə'vɑːkətɪv ‖prə'vɒkətɪv/ *adj*
[1] (causing trouble) provocador [2] (seductive)
provocativo

provoke /prə'vəʊk/ *vt* [1] ‹*person/animal*›
provocar*; **I was ~d into hitting him** tanto me
provocó, que le pegué [2] ‹*argument/revolt/
criticism*› provocar*; ‹*discussion/debate*› motivar;
‹*interest/curiosity*› despertar*

prow /praʊ/ *n* proa *f*

prowess /'praʊəs ‖'praʊɪs/ *n* destreza *f*

prowl /praʊl/ *vi* merodear

proximity /prɑːk'sɪməti ‖prɒk'sɪməti/ *n* (frml)
proximidad *f*

proxy /'prɑːksi ‖'prɒksi/ *n* (*pl* **-xies**) **(a)**
(person) representante *mf* **(b)** (authorization) poder
m; **by ~** por poder *or* (Esp) por poderes

prude /pruːd/ *n* mojigato, -ta *m,f*

prudence /'pruːdn̩s/ *n* prudencia *f*

prudent /'pruːdn̩t/ *adj* prudente

prudish /'pruːdɪʃ/ *adj* mojigato

prune[1] /pruːn/ *n* ciruela *f* pasa *or* (CS) seca

prune[2] *vt* **(a)** (Hort) podar **(b)** ‹*costs/workforce*›
reducir*

pry /praɪ/ **pries, prying, pried** *vi* curiosear;
to ~ INTO sth entrometerse EN algo
  ■ **~** *vt* (esp AmE) (+ *adv compl*): **she pried the lid
off** levantó la tapa (haciendo palanca)

PS *n* (postscript) P.D.

psalm /sɑːm/ *n* salmo *m*

pseudonym /'suːdn̩ɪm ‖'sjuːdənɪm/ *n*
(p)seudónimo *m*

PST (in US) = **Pacific Standard Time**

psychiatric /ˌsaɪki'ætrɪk/ *adj* (p)siquiátrico

psychiatrist /sə'kaɪətrəst ‖saɪ'kaɪətrɪst/ *n*
(p)siquiatra *mf*

psychiatry /sə'kaɪətri ‖saɪ'kaɪətri/ *n*
(p)siquiatría *f*

psychic /'saɪkɪk/ *adj* **(a)** (Occult)
para(p)sicológico **(b)** (Psych) (p)síquico

psychoanalysis /ˌsaɪkəʊə'næləsəs
‖ˌsaɪkəʊə'næləsɪs/ *n* (p)sicoanálisis *m*

psychological /ˌsaɪkə'lɑːdʒɪkəl
‖ˌsaɪkə'lɒdʒɪkəl/ *adj* (p)sicológico

psychologist /saɪ'kɑːlədʒəst ‖saɪ'kɒlədʒɪst/ *n*
(p)sicólogo, -ga *m,f*

psychology /saɪ'kɑːlədʒi ‖saɪ'kɒlədʒi/ *n* (*pl*
-gies) (p)sicología *f*

psychopath /'saɪkəpæθ ‖'saɪkəʊpæθ/ *n*
(p)sicópata *mf*

psychosis /saɪ'kəʊsəs ‖saɪ'kəʊsɪs/ *n* (*pl* **-ses**
/-siːz/) (p)sicosis *f*

psychosomatic /ˌsaɪkəsə'mætɪk
‖ˌsaɪkəʊsə'mætɪk/ *adj* (p)sicosomático

psychotherapy /ˌsaɪkəʊ'θerəpi/ *n*
(p)sicoterapia *f*

psychotic /saɪ'kɑːtɪk ‖saɪ'kɒtɪk/ *adj*
(p)sicótico

PTO (= **please turn over**) sigue al dorso

pub /pʌb/ *n* (BrE) ≈ bar *m*; (before *n*) **to go on a
~ crawl** ir* de bar en bar tomando copas

puberty /'pjuːbərti ‖'pjuːbəti/ *n* pubertad *f*

pubic /'pjuːbɪk/ *adj* ‹*hair*› púbico, pubiano;
‹*region/bone*› pubiano

public[1] /'pʌblɪk/ *adj* público; **it is ~ knowledge**
es de dominio público; **at ~ expense** con fondos
públicos; **the ~ sector** el sector público; **~
speaking** oratoria *f*

public[2] *n* (+ *sing* or *pl vb*) **(a)** (people in general)
the ~ el público **(b)** (audience) público *m* **(c) in
public** en-público

public-address system /'pʌblɪkə'dres/ *n*
(sistema *m* de) megafonía *f*, altoparlantes *mpl*
(AmL)

publican /'pʌblɪkən/ *n* (BrE) dueño, -ña *m,f* de
un bar

public assistance n (AmE) ayuda estatal a los sectores más necesitados de la población; **to be on ~ ~** recibir ayuda estatal

publication /ˌpʌbləˈkeɪʃən ‖ˌpʌblɪˈkeɪʃən/ n publicación f

public: ~ **health** n salud f or sanidad f pública; ~ **holiday** n fiesta f oficial, (día m) feriado m (AmL); ~ **house** n (BrE) ≈ bar m

publicity /pʌbˈlɪsəti/ n publicidad f

publicize /ˈpʌbləsaɪz ‖ˈpʌblɪsaɪz/ vt hacer* público

publicly /ˈpʌblɪkli/ adv (a) públicamente (b) (Govt) ⟨funded/maintained⟩ con fondos públicos

public: ~ **relations** n relaciones fpl públicas; ~ **school** n (in US) escuela f pública; (in UK) colegio m privado; (— boarding school) internado m privado; ~ **service** n (communal provision) servicio m público; ~**-spirited** /ˈpʌblɪkˈspɪrətəd ‖ˌpʌblɪkˈspɪrɪtɪd/ adj solidario; ~ **transportation** (AmE), ~ **transport** (BrE) n transporte m público

publish /ˈpʌblɪʃ/ vt (a) ⟨book/newspaper/article⟩ publicar* (b) (make known) hacer* público

publisher /ˈpʌblɪʃər ‖ˈpʌblɪʃə(r)/ n (a) (company) editorial f (b) (job title) editor, -tora m,f

publishing /ˈpʌblɪʃɪŋ/ n mundo m editorial; (before n) ~ **house** editorial f

pucker /ˈpʌkər ‖ˈpʌkə(r)/ vt fruncir*

pudding /ˈpʊdɪŋ/ n (a) (baked, steamed) budín m, pudín m (b) (dessert) (BrE) postre m

puddle /ˈpʌdl/ n charco m

Puerto Rican¹ /ˈpwertəˈriːkən ‖ˌpwɜːtəʊˈriːkən/ adj portorriqueño, puertorriqueño

Puerto Rican² n portorriqueño, -ña m,f, puertorriqueño, -ña m,f

Puerto Rico /ˈpwertəˈriːkəʊ ‖ˌpwɜːtəʊˈriːkəʊ/ n Puerto Rico m

puff¹ /pʌf/ n (a) (of wind, air) ráfaga f; **a ~ of** smoke una nube de humo (b) (action) soplo m; (on cigarette) chupada f, pitada f (AmL), calada f (Esp) (c) (sound) resoplido m

puff² vt (a) (blow) soplar (b) (smoke) ⟨cigarette/cigar/pipe⟩ dar* chupadas or (AmL tb) pitadas or (Esp tb) caladas a
■ ~ vi **1** (blow) soplar (b) (smoke) **to ~ on** o **AT sth** ⟨on cigarette/cigar/pipe⟩ dar* chupadas or (AmL tb) pitadas or (Esp tb) caladas **A** algo **2** (pant) resoplar
■ **puff out** [v + o + adv, v + adv + o] ⟨cheeks⟩ inflar, hinchar (Esp); ⟨feathers⟩ erizar*
■ **puff up** [v + adv] hincharse

puffed /pʌft/ adj ⟨sleeve⟩ abombado

puffed-up /ˈpʌftˈʌp/ adj ⟨pred **puffed up**⟩ (a) (swollen) hinchado (b) (conceited) engreído

puffin /ˈpʌfən ‖ˈpʌfɪn/ n frailecillo m

puff paste, (BrE) **puff pastry** n hojaldre m

puffy /ˈpʌfi/ adj **-fier, -fiest** hinchado

puke /pjuːk/ vi (colloq) vomitar, devolver*

pull¹ /pʊl/ vt **1** (a) (draw) tirar de, jalar (AmL

exc CS); (drag) arrastrar (b) (in specified direction) (+ adv compl): **he was ~ed from the rubble alive** lo sacaron vivo de entre los escombros; **the current ~ed him under** la corriente lo arrastró al fondo **2** (a) (tug) tirar de, jalar (AmL exc CS) (b) (tear, detach): **he ~ed the toy to bits** rompió el juguete **3** (a) ⟨tooth⟩ sacar* (b) ⟨gun⟩ sacar* **4** (colloq) ⟨crowd/audience⟩ atraer* **5** (Med) ⟨muscle/tendon⟩ desgarrarse
■ ~ vi **1** (drag, tug) tirar, jalar (AmL exc CS) **2** ⟨vehicle⟩ (move) (+ adv compl): **to ~ off the road** salir* de la carretera; **to ~ into the station** entrar en la estación
■ **pull apart** [v + o + adv] (a) (separate) separar (b) (pull to pieces) destrozar*, hacer* pedazos
■ **pull away** [v + adv] (a) (free oneself) soltarse* (b) (move off) ⟨train/car⟩ arrancar*
■ **pull back** [v + adv] (a) (retreat) ⟨troops/enemy⟩ retirarse (b) (withdraw) echarse atrás
■ **pull down** [v + o + adv, v + adv + o] (a) (lower) ⟨blind⟩ bajar (b) (demolish) ⟨building⟩ echar, tumbar (Méx)
■ **pull in**
I [v + o + adv, v + adv + o] **1** (draw in) ⟨nets/rope⟩ recoger*; ⟨claws⟩ retraer* **2** (attract) ⟨customers⟩ atraer*
II [v + adv] **1** (arrive) ⟨train/bus⟩ llegar* **2** (a) (move over) ⟨ship/car⟩ arrimarse (b) (stop) (BrE) ⟨car/truck⟩ parar
■ **pull off** [v + o + adv, v + adv + o] **1** (remove) ⟨cover/lid⟩ quitar **2** (achieve) (colloq) conseguir*
■ **pull out**
I [v + adv] **1** ⟨vehicle/driver⟩ (a) (depart) arrancar* **2** (enter traffic): **he ~ed out right in front of me** se me metió justo delante **2** (withdraw) ⟨troops/partner⟩ retirarse
II [v + o + adv, v + adv + o] **1** (a) (extract, remove) ⟨tooth/nail/plug⟩ sacar*; ⟨weeds/page⟩ arrancar* (b) (produce) ⟨wallet/gun⟩ sacar* **2** (withdraw) ⟨team/troops⟩ retirar
■ **pull over** (a) [v + adv] ⟨driver/car⟩ hacerse* a un lado; (to stop) acercarse* a la acera (or al arcén etc) y parar (b) [v + o + adv] parar
■ **pull through** [v + adv] (a) (recover) reponerse* (b) (survive) salir* adelante
■ **pull together 1** [v + adv] (cooperate) trabajar codo con codo **2** [v + o + adv] (control oneself): **to ~ oneself together** calmarse
■ **pull up 1** [v + o + adv, v + adv + o] (a) (draw up) levantar, subir; **to ~ one's socks up** subirse los calcetines (b) (uproot) ⟨plant⟩ arrancar* **2** [v + o + adv] (reprimand) **to ~ sb up (ON sth)** regañar or (CS) retar a algn (POR algo) **3** [v + adv] (stop) ⟨car/driver⟩ parar

pull² n **1** (tug) tirón m, jalón m (AmL exc CS) **2** (a) (pulling force) fuerza f (b) (influence) influencia f

pulley /ˈpʊli/ n (pl ~s) polea f

pull: ~**-out** n (a) (withdrawal) retirada f (b) (Journ) suplemento m; ~**over,** (AmE also) ~**over sweater** n ▸ SWEATER

---

pulp /pʌlp/ n **(a)** (of fruit, vegetable) pulpa f, carne f; (of wood, paper) pasta f (de papel) **(b)** (crushed material) pasta f

pulpit /ˈpʊlpɪt/ n púlpito m

pulsate /pʌlˈseɪt ‖pʌlˈseɪt/ vi «heart» latir; «light/current» oscilar

pulse¹ /pʌls/ n **1 (a)** (Physiol) pulso m; (before n) ~ **rate** número m de pulsaciones **(b)** (throbbing) cadencia f **(c)** (Phys) pulsación f **2** (Agr, Culin) legumbre f (como los garbanzos, las lentejas etc)

pulse² vi latir

pulverize /ˈpʌlvəraɪz/ vt pulverizar*

puma /ˈpuːmə ‖ˈpjuːmə/ n puma m, león m (Chi, Méx)

pummel /ˈpʌməl/ vt, (BrE) **-ll-** darle* una paliza a

pump¹ /pʌmp/ n **1** bomba f; (gasoline o (BrE) petrol ~) surtidor m **2** (AmE Clothing) zapato m (de) salón

pump² vt **(a)** (supply) bombear; **to ~ sth INTO sth** «water/oil» bombear algo A algo **(b)** (drain) **to ~ sth OUT OF sth** sacar* algo de algo con una bomba; **to ~ sb's stomach out** hacerle* un lavado de estómago a algn **(c)** (ask; colloq): **he was ~ing me for information** me estaba tratando de (son)sacar información
■ ~ vi «machine/heart» bombear
■ **pump up** [v + o + adv, v + adv + o] (inflate) «tire» inflar, hinchar (Esp)

pumpkin /ˈpʌmpkən ‖ˈpʌmpkɪn/ n calabaza f, zapallo m (CS, Per)

pun /pʌn/ n juego m de palabras, albur m (Méx)

punch¹ /pʌntʃ/ n **1 (a)** (blow) puñetazo m **(b)** (vigor) garra f (fam), fuerza f **2** (for paper) perforadora f; (for metal, leather) sacabocados m **3** (Culin) **(a)** ponche m; (before n) ~ **bowl** ponchera f **(b)** (in US) refresco m de frutas

punch² vt **(a)** (hit) pegarle* a **(b)** (perforate) «ticket» picar*, ponchar (Méx); «leather/metal» perforar*; **to ~ a hole in sth** hacerle* un agujero a algo
■ **punch in** [v + adv] (AmE) fichar, marcar* or (Méx) checar* tarjeta (al entrar al trabajo)
■ **punch out** [v + adv] (AmE) fichar, marcar* or (Méx) checar* tarjeta (al salir del trabajo)

punch: ~**-drunk** adj grogui (fam), atontado; ~ **line** n remate m (de un chiste); ~**-up** n (BrE colloq) bronca f (fam)

punctual /ˈpʌŋktʃuəl ‖ˈpʌŋktjəl, ˈpʌŋktʃəl/ adj puntual

punctuality /ˌpʌŋktʃuˈæləti ‖ˌpʌŋktjuˈæləti, ˌpʌŋktʃuˈæləti/ n puntualidad f

punctually /ˈpʌŋktʃuəli ‖ˈpʌŋktjuəli, ˈpʌŋktʃuəli/ adv puntualmente

punctuate /ˈpʌŋktʃueɪt ‖ˈpʌŋktjueɪt, ˈpʌŋktʃueɪt/ vt **(a)** «writing/text» puntuar* **(b)** (intersperse) salpicar*

punctuation /ˌpʌŋktʃuˈeɪʃən ‖ˌpʌŋktjuˈeɪʃən, ˌpʌŋktʃuˈeɪʃən/ n puntuación f; (before n) ~ **mark** signo m de puntuación

puncture¹ /ˈpʌŋktʃər ‖ˈpʌŋktʃə(r)/ n (in tire, ball) pinchazo m, pinchadura f (AmL), ponchadura f (Méx); **we had a ~ on the way there** pinchamos por el camino, se nos ponchó una llanta en el camino (Méx)

puncture² vt «tire/ball» pinchar, ponchar (Méx)

pungent /ˈpʌndʒənt/ adj «taste/smell» acre

punish /ˈpʌnɪʃ/ vt castigar*

punishable /ˈpʌnɪʃəbəl/ adj punible; ~ **BY sth** penado CON algo

punishing /ˈpʌnɪʃɪŋ/ adj «schedule/treatment» duro; «pace» agotador, extenuante

punishment /ˈpʌnɪʃmənt/ n **(a)** (chastisement) castigo m **(b)** (rough treatment): **it's taken a lot of ~** ha sido muy maltratado

punk /pʌŋk/ n **1 (a)** (person) ~ (**rocker**) punk mf, punki mf **(b)** ~ (**rock**) punk m **2** (young hoodlum) (AmE colloq) vándalo, -la m,f, gamberro, -rra m,f (Esp)

punt¹ /pʌnt/ n (Fin) libra f (irlandesa)

punt² /pʌnt/ vi (in boat): **to go ~ing** salir* de paseo en batea

puny /ˈpjuːni/ adj punier, puniest (pej) «person» enclenque; «effort» lastimoso

pup /pʌp/ n cría f; (of dog) cachorro, -rra m,f

pupil /ˈpjuːpəl ‖ˈpjuːpɪl/ n **1** (Educ) alumno, -na m,f, educando, -da m,f (frml) **2** (of eye) pupila f

puppet /ˈpʌpət ‖ˈpʌpɪt/ n **1 (a)** (marionette) marioneta f, títere m **(b)** (glove puppet) títere m **2** (stooge) títere m; (before n) «regime/leader» títere

puppy /ˈpʌpi/ n (pl **-pies**) cachorro, -rra m,f

purchase¹ /ˈpɜːrtʃəs ‖ˈpɜːtʃəs/ n (frml) adquisición f (frml)

purchase² vt (frml) adquirir* (frml)

purchaser /ˈpɜːrtʃəsər ‖ˈpɜːtʃəsə(r)/ n (frml) comprador, -dora m,f

pure /pjʊr ‖pjʊə(r)/ adj purer, purest puro

puree, purée /pjʊˈreɪ ‖ˈpjʊəreɪ/ n puré m; **tomato ~** concentrado m de tomate

purely /ˈpjʊrli ‖ˈpjʊəli/ adv «decorative» puramente; ~ **by chance** por pura casualidad

purgatory /ˈpɜːrgətɔːri ‖ˈpɜːgətəri/ n purgatorio m

purge¹ /pɜːrdʒ ‖pɜːdʒ/ vt **(a)** (cleanse) purgar* **(b)** (Pol) «party/government/committee» hacer* una purga en

purge² n (Med, Pol) purga f

purify /ˈpjʊrəfaɪ ‖ˈpjʊərɪfaɪ/ vt **-fies, -fying, -fied** purificar*; «water» depurar

purist /ˈpjʊrəst ‖ˈpjʊərɪst/ n purista mf

puritan /ˈpjʊrətn̩ ‖ˈpjʊərɪtən/ n puritano, -na m,f

puritanical /ˌpjʊrəˈtænɪkəl ‖ˌpjʊərɪˈtænɪkəl/ adj puritano

purity /ˈpjʊrəti ‖ˈpjʊərəti/ n pureza f

purl¹ /pɜːrl ‖pɜːl/ n punto m (al or del) revés

purl² vt tejer al or del revés

purple¹ /ˈpɜːrpəl ‖ˈpɜːpəl/ adj (bluish) morado; (reddish) púrpura

purple² n (bluish) morado m, violeta m; (reddish) púrpura m

purport /pərˈpɔːrt ‖pəˈpɔːt/ vt (frml) **to ~ to +** INF pretender + INF

purpose /ˈpɜːrpəs ‖ˈpɜːpəs/ n **1 (a)** (intention, reason) propósito m; **for one's own ~s** por su (or mi etc) propio interés; **the machine is good enough for our ~s** la máquina sirve para lo que nos proponemos hacer con ella; **on ~** a propósito **(b)** (use): **to serve a (useful) ~** servir* de algo **2** (resolution) determinación f

purposeful /'pɜ:rpəsfəl ‖'pɜ:pəsfəl/ adj
⟨person/stride⟩ resuelto; ⟨expression⟩ de
determinación

purposely /'pɜ:rpəsli ‖'pɜ:pəsli/ adv
⟨facetious/hurtful⟩ deliberadamente; ⟨say/do⟩ a
propósito

purr¹ /pɜ:r ‖pɜ:(r)/ vi ronronear

purr² n ronroneo m

purse¹ /pɜ:rs ‖pɜ:s/ n **1** (a) (for money)
monedero m, portamonedas m **(b)** (funds) fondos
mpl **2** (handbag) (AmE) cartera f or (Esp) bolso m
or (Méx) bolsa f

purse² vt to ~ one's lips fruncir* la boca

purser /'pɜ:rsər ‖'pɜ:sə(r)/ n sobrecargo mf

pursue /pər'su: ‖pə'sju:/ vt **1** (chase)
perseguir*; ⟨pleasure/happiness⟩ buscar*
2 ⟨policy/course of action⟩ continuar* con;
⟨research/study⟩ continuar* con; ⟨profession⟩
ejercer*

pursuer /pər'su:ər ‖pə'sju:ə(r)/ n perseguidor,
-dora m,f

pursuit /pər'su:t ‖pə'sju:t/ n **1** (chase)
persecución f; she set off in ~ of the thief salió
en persecución del ladrón; the ~ of happiness la
búsqueda de la felicidad **2** (pastime) actividad f

pus /pʌs/ n pus m

push¹ /pʊʃ/ n empujoncito m; (violent) empujón
m; she gave the door a ~ empujó la puerta; at
the ~ of a button con solo apretar un botón; at a
~ (colloq): at a ~, I could finish it by Friday si me
apuras, podría terminarlo para el viernes

push² vt **1** (a) ⟨person/car/table⟩ empujar; I
~ed the door to o shut cerré la puerta
empujándola **(b)** (press) ⟨button⟩ apretar* **(c)**
(force): to ~ prices up/down hacer* que suban/
bajen los precios; I tried to ~ the thought to the
back of my mind traté de no pensar en ello
2 (put pressure on): you're ~ing him/yourself too
hard le/te exiges demasiado; to ~ed for time/
money (colloq) andar* corto de tiempo/de dinero
(fam)
3 (a) (promote) promocionar **(b)** (sell) (colloq)
⟨drugs⟩ pasar (fam), transar (CS arg)
4 (approach) (colloq) (only in -ing form): to be
~ing forty rondar los cuarenta
■ ~ vi **1** (give a push) empujar
2 (apply pressure) presionar
■ **push back** [v + o + adv, v + adv + o] **(a)** (force
back) ⟨person/object⟩ empujar hacia atrás; ⟨crowd/
army⟩ hacer* retroceder **(b)** (extend) ⟨limits⟩
ampliar*
■ **push in** [v + adv] colarse* (fam)
■ **push off** [v + adv] **(a)** (in boat) desatracar* **(b)**
(leave, go) (colloq) largarse* (fam)
■ **push on** [v + adv] **(a)** (continue journey) seguir*
el viaje **(b)** (continue working) seguir* adelante
■ **push through** [v + o + adv, v + adv + o]
⟨legislation⟩ hacer* aprobar
push: ~**bike** n (BrE) bicicleta f; ~**button**
adj (before n) ⟨controls/telephone⟩ de botones;
~**chair** n (BrE) sillita f (de paseo), carreola f
(Méx)

pusher /'pʊʃər ‖'pʊʃə(r)/ n (colloq) camello
mf (arg), jíbaro mf (Col, Ven arg), conecte m,f
(Mex arg)

push: ~**over** n: to be a ~**over** «task/game»
ser* pan comido (fam), estar* chupado (Esp fam);

«person» ser* un incauto; ~**start**
/'pʊʃ'stɑ:rt ‖,pʊʃ'stɑ:t/ vt ⟨car⟩ arrancar* empujando; ~**up**
n flexión f (de brazos o de pecho), fondo m,
lagartija f (Méx)

pushy /'pʊʃi/ adj **pushier, pushiest** (colloq)
prepotente

pussy /'pʊsi/ (pl -**sies**), **pussycat** /'pʊsikæt/
n (colloq) minino, -na m,f (fam), gatito, -ta m,f
(fam)

put /pʊt/ (pres p **putting**; past & past p **put**) vt
I **1** (place) poner*; (with care, precision etc)
colocar*; (inside sth) meter*; he ~ it in his mouth se
lo puso en la boca
2 (a) (thrust): he ~ his arms around her la
abrazó; she ~ her head out of the window asomó
la cabeza por la ventana **(b)** (Sport) to ~ the shot
lanzar* el peso
3 (a) (rank) poner*; she ~s herself first se pone
ella primero; he ~s his art before everything else
antepone su arte a todo **(b)** (in competition, league):
this victory ~s them in o into the lead con esta
victoria pasan a ocupar la delantera
II **1** (cause to be) poner*; the doctor ~ me on a
diet el doctor me puso a régimen
2 (make undergo) to ~ sb TO sth: I don't want to
~ you to any trouble no quiero causarle ninguna
molestia
III **1** (a) (attribute, assign): I ~ a high value on
our friendship valoro mucho nuestra amistad **(b)**
(impose) to ~ sth ON sth/sb: to ~ the blame on sb
echarle la culpa a algn; it ~ a great strain on
their relationship eso sometió su relación a una
gran tensión
2 (a) (invest) to ~ sth INTO sth ⟨money⟩ invertir*
algo EN algo; she had ~ a lot of thought into it lo
había pensado mucho **(b)** (bet, stake) to ~ sth
ON sth ⟨money⟩ apostar* algo A algo **(c)** (contribute)
to ~ sth TOWARD sth contribuir* CON algoA
algo
IV **1** (present) ⟨views/case⟩ exponer*; ⟨proposal⟩
presentar
2 (write, indicate, mark) poner*
3 (express) decir*; ~ it this way: I wouldn't invite
him again te digo lo siguiente: no lo volvería a
invitar; to ~ sth well/badly expresar algo bien/
mal
■ **put about** [v + o + adv] (colloq) ⟨story/rumor⟩
hacer* correr
■ **put across** [v + o + adv, v + adv + o] ⟨idea/
message⟩ comunicar*
■ **put aside** [v + o + adv, v + adv + o] **(a)** (lay to
one side) dejar a un lado **(b)** (reserve) ⟨money⟩
guardar; ⟨goods/time⟩ reservar **(c)** ⟨differences⟩
dejar de lado
■ **put away** [v + o + adv, v + adv + o] **(a)** (put in
cupboard, drawer) ⟨dishes/tools/clothes⟩ guardar **(b)**
(save) ⟨money⟩ guardar, ahorrar **(c)** (consume)
(colloq) ⟨food/drink⟩ zamparse (fam) **(d)** (confine)
(colloq) ⟨criminal/lunatic⟩ encerrar* **(e)** (destroy)
(AmE euph) ⟨animal⟩ sacrificar* (euf)
■ **put back** [v + o + adv, v + adv + o] **(a)** (replace)
volver* a poner **(b)** (reset) ⟨clocks⟩ atrasar **(c)**
(delay, retard) ⟨project⟩ retrasar **(d)** (postpone)
posponer*, aplazar*, postergar* (AmL)
■ **put by** [v + o + adv, v + adv + o] ⟨money⟩
ahorrar
■ **put down**
I [v + o + adv, v + adv + o] **1** (a) (set down)

⟨bag/pen⟩ dejar; ⟨telephone⟩ colgar* **(b)** (lay) ⟨tiles/carpet⟩ poner*, colocar* **(c)** (lower) bajar **(d)** ⟨passenger⟩ dejar

2 (a) (suppress) ⟨rebellion⟩ sofocar* **(b)** (destroy) (BrE euph) ⟨animal⟩ sacrificar* (euf)

3 (a) (write down) ⟨thoughts⟩ anotar, escribir*; ⟨name⟩ poner*, escribir* **(b)** (attribute) **to ~ sth down TO sth** atribuirle* algo A algo

4 (in part payment) ⟨sum⟩ entregar*; ⟨deposit⟩ dejar

II [v + o + adv] (belittle) rebajar

■ **put forward** [v + o + adv, v + adv + o] **1 (a)** ⟨theory/plan⟩ presentar; ⟨suggestion⟩ hacer* **(b)** ⟨candidate⟩ proponer*, postular (AmL)

2 (a) ⟨clocks⟩ adelantar **(b)** ⟨trip/meeting⟩ adelantar

■ **put in**
I [v + o + adv, v + adv + o] **1** (install) ⟨central heating/shower unit⟩ poner*, instalar **2** (enter, submit) ⟨claim/request/tender⟩ presentar

3 (invest): **how much time can you put in?** ¿cuánto tiempo puedes dedicarle?

4 (insert, add) ⟨word/chapter/scene⟩ poner*
II [v + adv] **1** (Naut) hacer* escala
2 (apply) **to ~ in FOR sth** solicitar algo

■ **put off**
I [v + o + adv, v + adv + o] **1 (a)** (postpone) ⟨meeting/visit/decision⟩ aplazar*, posponer*, postergar* (AmL); **I keep ~ting off going to the dentist** siempre estoy aplazando ir al dentista **(b)** (stall) ⟨visitor/creditor⟩: **if Saturday isn't convenient, I can ~ them off** si el sábado no es conveniente, puedo decirles que lo dejen para más adelante

2 (turn off) (BrE) ⟨light⟩ apagar*
II [v + o + adv, v + adv + o] **1** (discourage): **the thought of the journey ~s me off going to see them** pensar en el viaje me quita las ganas de ir a visitarlos

2 (distract) distraer*; (disconcert) desconcertar*

■ **put on**
I [v + o + adv, v + adv + o] **1** ⟨jacket/sweater⟩ ponerse*; **to put one's clothes on** vestirse*, ponerse* la ropa; **to ~ one's shoes on** ponerse* los zapatos, calzarse*

2 ⟨light/radio/oven⟩ encender*, prender* (AmL); ⟨music⟩ poner*

3 (gain): **I've ~ on four pounds** he engordado cuatro libras; **to ~ on weight** engordar

4 ⟨exhibition⟩ organizar*; ⟨play/show⟩ presentar
5 (assume) ⟨expression⟩ adoptar; **he's just ~ting it on** está haciendo teatro

II [v + o + adv] **1 (a)** (alert) **to ~ sb on TO sb:** **somebody had ~ the police on to them** alguien había puesto a la policía sobre su pista **(b)** (introduce) **to ~ sb on TO sb: I can ~ you on to someone who ...** puedo ponerte en contacto con una persona que ...

2 (tease) (AmE colloq) tomarle el pelo a (fam)

■ **put out**
I [v + o + adv, v + adv + o] **1 (a)** (put outside) ⟨washing/cat⟩ sacar* **(b)** (set out) disponer* **(c)** (extend) ⟨arm/tongue⟩ sacar* **(d)** (dislocate) dislocarse*, zafarse (Chi, Méx)

2 (a) (extinguish) ⟨fire/light/cigarette⟩ apagar* **(b)** (anesthetize) (colloq) dormir*

3 (offend, inconvenience) molestar

4 (a) (issue, publish) ⟨statement⟩ publicar* **(b)** (broadcast) transmitir
II [v + adv] (Naut) salir*; **to ~ out to sea** hacerse* a la mar

■ **put over (a)** ▶ PUT ACROSS **(b)** (AmE) ▶ PUT OFF I 1A

■ **put past** [v + o + prep + o]: **not to ~ it past sb:** **I wouldn't ~ it past her** no me extrañaría nada or la creo muy capaz

■ **put through 1** [v + o + prep + o] (make undergo) someter a
2 [v + o + adv, v + adv + o] (Telec): **to ~ sb through (TO sb)** pasar or (AmL) comunicar* or (Esp) poner* a algn CON algn

■ **put together** [v + o + adv, v + adv + o] **1 (a)** (assemble) armar; ⟨collection⟩ reunir* **(b)** (create) ⟨team⟩ formar; ⟨magazine⟩ producir*; ⟨meal⟩ preparar; (quickly) improvisar

2 (combine) juntar, reunir*; **more than everything else ~ together** más que todo los demás junto

■ **put up**
I [v + o + adv, v + adv + o] **1 (a)** ⟨hotel⟩ levantar; ⟨tent⟩ armar **(b)** ⟨decorations/curtains/notice⟩ poner* **(c)** ⟨umbrella⟩ abrir* **(d)** ⟨hand⟩ levantar

2 ⟨price/fare⟩ aumentar
3 ⟨candidate⟩ proponer*, postular (AmL)
4 (in accommodation) alojar; **they ~ us up for the night** nos quedamos a dormir en su casa
II [v + adv + o] **(a)** (present): **to ~ up resistance/a struggle/a fight** ofrecer* resistencia **(b)** ⟨money/capital⟩ poner*
III [v + adv] (stay) quedarse

■ **put up to** [v + o + adv + prep + o]: **somebody must have ~ them up to it** alguien debe haberlos empujado a ello

■ **put up with** [v + adv + prep + o] aguantar

put: **~-down** n (colloq) desprecio m; **~ out** adj (pred) **to be ~ out** estar* molesto

putrid /'pju:trəd ‖'pju:trɪd/ adj putrefacto, pútrido

putt /pʌt/ vi golpear la bola, potear (AmL)
■ ~ vt golpear

putter¹ /'pʌtər ‖'pʌtə(r)/ n (club) putter m

putter² vi (AmE) (+ adv compl): **to ~ around** o **about in the garden** entretenerse trabajando en el jardín; **I've been ~ing around the house all day** me he pasado el día haciendo un poco de esto y un poco de aquello en la casa

putting green /'pʌtɪŋ/ n putting green m

putty /'pʌti/ n masilla f

puzzle¹ /'pʌzəl/ n **(a)** (game,toy) rompecabezas m; (riddle) adivinanza f **(b)** (mystery) misterio m

puzzle² vt: **one thing ~s me** hay algo que no entiendo

puzzled /'pʌzəld/ adj ⟨expression/tone⟩ de desconcierto; **I'm ~ about it** me tiene perplejo

PVC n PVC m

pygmy /'pɪgmi/ n (pl **-mies**) **(a)** (Anthrop) also **Pygmy** pigmeo, -mea m,f **(b)** (Zool) (before n) enano

pyjamas /pə'dʒɑːməz/ n (BrE) ▶ PAJAMAS

pylon /'paɪlɑːn, -lən ‖'paɪlɒn, -lən/ n torre f de alta tensión

pyramid /'pɪrəmɪd/ n pirámide f

pyre /paɪr ‖'paɪə(r)/ n pira f

Pyrenees /'pɪrə'niːz ‖,pɪrə'niːz/ *pl* in the ~ los Pirineos

Pyrex® /'paɪreks/ *n* pyrex® *m*, arcopal® *m*

python /'paɪθɑːn ‖'paɪθən/ *n* (serpiente *f*) pitón *f*

Qq

Q, q /kjuː/ *n* Q, q *f*

QC *n* (in UK) (= **Queen's Counsel**) *título conferido a ciertos abogados de prestigio*

QED (= **quod erat demonstrandum**) Q.E.D. (fml), *que es lo que había que demostrar*

quack¹ /kwæk/ *vi* graznar

quack² *n* (pej) 1 (charlatan) charlatán, -tana *m,f*; (professing medical skill) (~ doctor) curandero, -ra *m,f* 2 (of duck) graznido *m*

quad /kwɑːd ‖kwɒd/ *n* (colloq) 1 (quadruplet) cuatrillizo, -za *m,f* 2 (of college) ▶ QUADRANGLE 1

quadrangle /'kwɑːdræŋɡəl ‖'kwɒdræŋɡəl/ *n* 1 (BrE Archit) patio *m* interior 2 (Math) ▶ QUADRILATERAL

quadrant /'kwɑːdrənt ‖'kwɒdrənt/ *n* cuadrante *m*

quadrilateral /'kwɑːdrə'lætərəl ‖,kwɒdrɪ'lætərəl/ *n* cuadrilátero *m*

quadruped /'kwɑːdrʊped ‖'kwɒdrʊped/ *n* cuadrúpedo *m*

quadruple¹ /kwɑː'druːpḷ ‖'kwɒdrʊpḷ/ *adj* cuádruple, cuádruplo

quadruple² /kwɑː'druːpḷ ‖kwɒ'druːpḷ/ *vi* cuadruplicarse*

quadruplet /kwɑː'druːplət ‖'kwɒdrʊplət/ *n* cuatrillizo, -za *m,f*

quaff /kwɑːf ‖kwɒf/ *vt* (hum) beberse, zamparse (fam)

quagmire /'kwæɡmaɪr, 'kwɑːg- ‖'kwɒɡmaɪə(r), 'kwæg-/ *n* (a) (bog) lodazal *m*, barrial *m* (AmL) (b) (situation) atolladero *m*

quail¹ /kweɪl/ *vi* temblar*; she ~ed at the idea la idea le daba pavor

quail² *n* (*pl* quails *or* quail) codorniz *f*

quaint /kweɪnt/ *adj* **-er, -est** (a) (charming, picturesque) pintoresco (b) (odd) extraño

quake¹ /kweɪk/ *vi* temblar*

quake² *n* (colloq) (earthquake) terremoto *m*

Quaker /'kweɪkər ‖'kweɪkə(r)/ *n* cuáquero, -ra *m,f*

qualification /'kwɑːləfə'keɪʃən ‖,kwɒlɪfɪ'keɪʃən/ *n* 1 (a) (Educ): she has a teaching ~ tiene título de maestra/profesora; his ~s are very good está muy bien calificado *or* (Esp) cualificado (b) (skill, necessary attribute) requisito *m* 2 (a) (eligibility) derecho *m* (b) (being accepted) clasificación *f* 3 (reservation) reserva *f*

qualified /'kwɑːləfaɪd ‖'kwɒlɪfaɪd/ *adj* (a) (trained) titulado; to be ~ to + INF tener* la titulación necesaria PARA + INF (b) (competent) (*pred*) capacitado; to be ~ to + INF estar* capacitado PARA + INF (c) (eligible) (*pred*) to be ~ to + INF reunir* los requisitos PARA + INF

qualify /'kwɑːləfaɪ ‖'kwɒlɪfaɪ/ **-fies, -fying, -fied** *vt* 1 (equip, entitle): this degree qualifies you to practice anywhere in Europe este título te habilita para ejercer en cualquier parte de Europa; their low income qualifies them for some benefits sus bajos ingresos les dan derecho a recibir ciertas prestaciones 2 (a) (limit): I'd like to ~ the statement I made earlier quisiera matizar lo que expresé anteriormente haciendo algunas salvedades (*or* puntualizaciones *etc*) (b) (Ling) calificar*
■ ~ *vi* (a) (gain professional qualification) titularse, recibirse (AmL) (b) (Sport) clasificarse* (c) (be entitled) to ~ (FOR sth) tener* derecho (A algo)

quality /'kwɑːləti ‖'kwɒləti/ *n* (*pl* **-ties**) calidad *f*

qualm /kwɑːm/ *n* (*often pl*) (a) (scruple) reparo *m*; to have no ~s about sth no tener* ningún reparo en algo (b) (misgiving) duda *f*

quandary /'kwɑːndri ‖'kwɒndri/ *n* (*pl* **-ries**) (*usu sing*) dilema *m*

quango /'kwæŋɡəʊ/ *n* (*pl* **-gos**) (BrE) (= **quasi-autonomous non-governmental organization**) organismo *m* or ente *m* semi-autónomo

quantify /'kwɑːntəfaɪ ‖'kwɒntɪfaɪ/ *vt* **-fies, -fying, -fied** cuantificar*

quantity /'kwɑːntəti ‖'kwɒntəti/ *n* (*pl* **-ties**) cantidad *f*

quantity surveyor *n*: ingeniero o técnico que se ocupa de mediciones y cálculo de materiales

quarantine¹ /'kwɔːrəntiːn ‖'kwɒrənti:n/ *n* cuarentena *f*

quarantine² *vt* poner* en cuarentena

quarrel¹ /'kwɔːrəl ‖'kwɒrəl/ *n* (a) (argument) pelea *f*, riña *f*; to have a ~ with sb pelearse con algn (b) (disagreement) discrepancia *f*

quarrel² *vi*, (BrE) **-ll-** (argue) pelearse, discutir

quarrelsome /'kwɔːrəlsəm ‖'kwɒrəlsəm/ *adj* peleador, peleón (Esp fam)

AmC Central America	Arg Argentina	Cu Cuba	Per Peru
AmL Latin America	Bol Bolivia	Ec Ecuador	RPI River Plate Area
AmS South America	Chi Chile	Esp Spain	Ur Uruguay
Andes Andean Region	CS Southern Cone	Méx Mexico	Ven Venezuela

quarry¹ /'kwɔːri ‖'kwɒri/ n (pl **-ries**)
1 (excavation) cantera f **2** (prey) presa f

quarry² vt **-ries, -rying, -ried** ⟨stone/slate⟩ extraer* (de una cantera); ⟨land/hillside⟩ abrir* una cantera en

quart /kwɔːrt ‖kwɔːt/ n cuarto m de galón (EEUU: 0,94 litros, RU: 1,14 litros)

quarter /'kwɔːrtər ‖'kwɔːtə(r)/ n **1** (fourth part) cuarta parte f, cuarto m; **a ~ of a mile** un cuarto de milla
2 (US, Canadian coin) moneda f de 25 centavos
3 (a) (in telling time) cuarto m; **a ~ of an hour** un cuarto de hora; **it's a ~ to one** es la una menos cuarto or (AmL exc RPl) un cuarto para la una; **a ~ after** o (BrE) **past one** la una y cuarto **(b)** (three months) trimestre m
4 (a) (district of town) barrio m **(b)** (area) parte f; **at close ~s** de cerca
5 **quarters** pl (accommodations): **the servants' ~s** las habitaciones de la servidumbre

quarterfinal /'kwɔːrtərˌfaɪnḷ ‖ˌkwɔːtəˈfaɪnḷ/ n cuarto m de final

quarterly¹ /'kwɔːrtərli ‖'kwɔːtəli/ adj trimestral

quarterly² adv trimestralmente

quarter note n (AmE) negra f

quartet /kwɔːrˈtet ‖kwɔːˈtet/ n cuarteto m

quartz /kwɔːrts ‖kwɔːts/ n cuarzo m

quash /kwɑːʃ ‖kwɒʃ/ vt **(a)** (Law) ⟨verdict/sentence⟩ anular **(b)** (suppress) ⟨revolt⟩ sofocar*; ⟨protest⟩ acallar

quaver¹ /'kweɪvər ‖'kweɪvə(r)/ n **(a)** (in voice) temblor m **(b)** (BrE Mus) corchea f

quaver² vi «voice» (in singing) vibrar; (in speech) temblar*

quay /kiː/ n muelle m

quayside /'kiːsaɪd/ n muelle m

queasy /'kwiːzi/ adj **-sier, -siest** mareado

queen /kwiːn/ n reina f

queen: ~ bee n (Zool) abeja f reina; **~ mother** n reina f madre

queer¹ /kwɪr ‖kwɪə(r)/ adj **1** (odd) raro, extraño **2** (male homosexual) (colloq & sometimes pej) maricón (fam & pey), gay

queer² n (colloq & sometimes pej) maricón m (fam & pey), gay m

quell /kwel/ vt ⟨revolt⟩ sofocar*; ⟨criticism⟩ acallar

quench /kwentʃ/ vt **(a)** ⟨thirst⟩ quitar, saciar (liter) **(b)** ⟨flames⟩ sofocar*

querulous /'kwerələs ‖'kwerʊləs/ adj quejumbroso

query¹ /'kwɪri ‖'kwɪəri/ n (pl **-ries**) (doubt) duda f; (question) pregunta f

query² vt **-ries, -rying, -ried** cuestionar

quest /kwest/ n búsqueda f; **~ FOR sth** búsqueda DE algo

question¹ /'kwestʃən/ n **(a)** (inquiry) pregunta f; **to ask a ~** hacer* una pregunta **(b)** (in quiz, exam) pregunta f **(c)** (issue, problem) cuestión f, asunto m; **the person in ~** la persona en cuestión; **if it's a ~ of money ...** si es cuestión or se trata de dinero ... **(d)** (doubt) duda f; **beyond ~** fuera de duda **(e)** (possibility) posibilidad f; **it is completely out of the ~** es totalmente imposible

question² vt **(a)** ⟨person⟩ hacerle* preguntas a; ⟨suspect/student⟩ interrogar* **(b)** (doubt) ⟨integrity/motives⟩ poner* en duda

questionable /'kwestʃənəbəl/ adj cuestionable

questioner /'kwestʃənər ‖'kwestʃənə(r)/ n interrogador, -dora m,f

questioning¹ /'kwestʃənɪŋ/ adj ⟨expression/voice⟩ inquisidor; ⟨mind⟩ inquisitivo

questioning² n interrogatorio m

question mark n signo m de interrogación

questionnaire /'kwestʃəˈner ‖ˌkwestʃəˈneə(r)/ n cuestionario m

queue¹ /kjuː/ n (BrE) cola f; **to form a ~** hacer* cola; **to jump the ~** colarse* (fam), brincarse* or saltarse la cola (Méx fam)

queue² vi **queues, queueing, queued ~ (up)** (BrE) hacer* cola

quibble¹ /'kwɪbəl/ n objeción f (de poca monta)

quibble² vi hacer* problemas por nimiedades

quick¹ /kwɪk/ adj **quicker, quickest (a)** (speedy) ⟨action/movement⟩ rápido; **I'll be as ~ as I can** volveré (or lo haré etc) lo más rápido que pueda; **that was ~!** ¡qué rapidez! **(b)** (brief) (before n, no comp) ⟨calculation/question⟩ rápido; (mod) breve; **he'd like a ~ word with you** quiere hablar contigo un momento **(c)** (easily roused): **she has a ~ temper** tiene mucho genio **(d)** (prompt): **he's ~ to take offense** se ofende por lo más mínimo

quick² adv **quicker, quickest** rápido, rápidamente

quick³ n the **~**: **her nails were bitten to the ~** tenía las uñas en carne viva de mordérselas; **to cut sb to the ~** herir* a algn en lo más vivo

quicken /'kwɪkən/ vt acelerar
■ **~** vi acelerarse

quickly /'kwɪkli/ adv **(a)** (speedily) ⟨move/recover⟩ rápidamente, rápido **(b)** (promptly) ⟨understand/reply⟩ pronto

quickness /'kwɪknəs ‖'kwɪknɪs/ n rapidez f

quick: ~sand n (often pl) arenas fpl movedizas; **~-tempered** /'kwɪkˈtempərd ‖ˌkwɪkˈtempəd/ adj ⟨person⟩ de genio vivo, irascible; **~-witted** /'kwɪkˈwɪtəd ‖ˌkwɪkˈwɪtɪd/ adj agudo

quid /kwɪd/ n (pl **~**) (pound) (BrE colloq) libra f

quiet¹ /'kwaɪət/ adj **1** **(a)** (silent) ⟨street⟩ silencioso; **be ~!** (to one person) ¡cállate!; (to more than one person) ¡cállense! or (Esp tb) ¡callaros or callaos!, ¡silencio!; **I kept ~ about the bill** no dije nada de lo de la factura **(b)** (not loud) ⟨engine⟩ silencioso; **he has a very ~ voice** habla muy bajo **(c)** (not boisterous) ⟨manner⟩ tranquilo; **you're very ~ today** hoy estás muy callada **2** **(a)** (peaceful) tranquilo; **they had a ~ wedding** la boda se celebró en la intimidad **(b)** (not busy) ⟨day⟩ tranquilo

quiet² n **(a)** (silence) silencio m **(b)** (peace, tranquillity) tranquilidad f

quiet³ (AmE) vt **(a)** (silence) ⟨uproar/protests⟩ acallar; ⟨class⟩ hacer* callar **(b)** (calm) ⟨horse/person⟩ tranquilizar*; ⟨fear/suspicion⟩ disipar
■ **quiet down** (AmE) ▶ QUIETEN DOWN

quieten /'kwaɪətn̩/ vt (esp BrE) ▶ QUIET³
■ **quieten down** **1** [v + o + adv, v + adv + o] ⋯⟶

⟨person⟩ calmar; ⟨rumors/clamor⟩ acallar **2** [v + adv] «person» calmarse; (with maturity) sentar* la cabeza; «rumors» acallarse

quietly /'kwaɪətli/ adv **1** (silently, not loudly) ⟨move⟩ silenciosamente; ⟨say/speak⟩ en voz baja **2 (a)** (peacefully) ⟨sleep/rest⟩ tranquilamente **(b)** (unobtrusively) ⟨dress/mention/slip away⟩ discretamente

quill /kwɪl/ n pluma f (de oca or ganso)

quilt /kwɪlt/ n edredón m, acolchado m (RPl), cobija f (Méx)

quilted /'kwɪltəd ‖'kwɪltɪd/ adj acolchado, guateado (Esp)

quin /kwɪn/ n (BrE colloq) ▶ QUINTUPLET

quince /kwɪns/ n membrillo m

quint /kwɪnt/ n (AmE colloq) ▶ QUINTUPLET

quintessential /'kwɪntə'sentʃəl ‖,kwɪntɪ'senʃəl/ adj (usu before n) por excelencia

quintet /kwɪn'tet/ n quinteto m

quintuplet /kwɪn'tuːplət ‖'kwɪntjʊplət/ n quintillizo, -za m,f, quintuple mf (Chi, Ven)

quip¹ /kwɪp/ n ocurrencia f, salida f

quip² vt **-pp-** decir* bromeando

quirk /kwɜːrk ‖kwɜːk/ n **(a)** (of circumstance) singularidad f **(b)** (of person) rareza f

quit /kwɪt/ ⟨ pres p **quitting**; past & past p **quit** or **quitted**⟩ vt (esp AmE) ⟨job/habit⟩ dejar; ⟨contest⟩ abandonar; **to ~ -ING** dejar DE + INF
■ **~** vi **(a)** (stop) (esp AmE) parar **(b)** (give in) abandonar **(c)** (leave): **notice to ~** notificación f de desahucio

quite /kwaɪt/ adv **1 (a)** (completely, absolutely) completamente, totalmente; **is this what you wanted? — not ~** ¿es esto lo que buscaba? — no exactamente; **there isn't ~ enough** falta un poquito; **there's nothing ~ like champagne** realmente no hay como el champán; **~ the opposite** todo lo contrario **(b)** (as intensifier): it

makes ~ a difference hace bastante diferencia; **~ a few of them** muchos de ellos; **that was ~ a game!** ¡fue un partidazo! (fam), ¡fue flor de partido! (CS fam)
2 (fairly) (BrE) bastante; **it's ~ warm today** hoy hace bastante calor; **there were ~ a few** había bastantes, había unos cuantos

quits /kwɪts/ adj **to be ~** estar* en paz or (AmL) a mano; **to call the money and call it ~** toma el dinero y dejémoslo de una vez

quiver¹ /'kwɪvər ‖'kwɪvə(r)/ vi «person/lips» temblar*; «leaves» agitarse

quiver² n **1** (for arrows) carcaj m, aljaba f **2** (movement) temblor m

quiz¹ /kwɪz/ n (pl **~es**) **(a)** (competition) concurso m; (before n) **~ show** programa m concurso **(b)** (test) (AmE) prueba f

quiz² vt **-zz-** **(a)** (question) ⟨suspect⟩ interrogar* **(b)** (test) (AmE) ⟨students⟩ poner* or hacer* una prueba a

quizzical /'kwɪzɪkəl/ adj socarrón, burlón

quorum /'kwɔːrəm/ n quórum m

quota /'kwəʊtə/ n (pl **~s**) (EC, Econ) cuota f

quotation /kwəʊ'teɪʃən/ n **1** (passage) cita f **2** (estimate) presupuesto m

quotation marks pl n comillas fpl

quote¹ /kwəʊt/ vt **1 (a)** ⟨writer/passage⟩ citar*; ⟨reference number⟩ indicar* **(b)** ⟨example⟩ dar*; ⟨instance⟩ citar **2 (a)** (price) dar*, ofrecer* **(b)** (Fin) cotizar*
■ **~** vi (repeat, recite): **he was quoting from the Bible** citaba de la Biblia; **she said, and I ~** ... dijo, y yo repito textualmente ..., sus palabras textuales fueron ...

quote² n (colloq) **1** (passage) cita f **2** (estimate) presupuesto m

quotient /'kwəʊʃənt/ n (Math) cociente m

Rr

R, r /ɑːr ‖ɑː(r)/ n R, r f

R (in US) (Cin) (= **restricted**) menores acompañadas

rabbi /'ræbaɪ/ n (pl **-bis**) rabino, -na m,f; (as title) rabí mf

rabbit /'ræbət ‖'ræbɪt/ n **(a)** (Zool) conejo, -ja m,f **(b)** (meat) conejo m

rabble /'ræbəl/ n **(a)** (mob) muchedumbre f **(b)** (common people) (pej) **the ~** la chusma (pey)

rabid /'ræbəd ‖'ræbɪd/ adj rabioso

rabies /'reɪbiːz/ n rabia f

RAC n (in UK) = **Royal Automobile Club**

raccoon /ræ'kuːn ‖rə'kuːn/ n mapache m

race¹ /reɪs/ n **1** (contest) carrera f **2** (Anthrop) raza f; **the human ~** el género humano; (before n) **~ relations** pl n relaciones fpl raciales

race² vi **(a)** (rush) (+ adv compl): **she ~d down the hill on her bike** bajó la cuesta en bicicleta a

toda velocidad **(b)** (in competition) correr, competir* **(c)** «pulse/heart» latir aceleradamente
■ **~** vt ⟨person⟩ echarle or (RPl) jugarle* una carrera a

race: ~course n (stadium) hipódromo m; (track) pista f (de carreras); **~horse** n caballo m de carrera(s)

racial /'reɪʃəl/ adj racial

racially /'reɪʃəli/ adv ⟨pure/mixed/motivated/ prejudiced⟩ racialmente

racing¹ /'reɪsɪŋ/ n **(a)** (horse ~) carreras fpl de caballos **(b)** (sport, pastime) carreras fpl

racing² adj ⟨person⟩ ⟨bicycle/car⟩ de carrera(s)

racism /'reɪsɪzəm/ n racismo m

racist¹ /'reɪsəst ‖'reɪsɪst/ n racista mf

racist² adj racista

rack¹ /ræk/ n **1** (shelf) estante m; (for baggage)

rejilla *f*; (clothes ∿) perchero *m*; (drying ∿) tendedero *m* **2** (for torture) potro *m* (de tortura); **to go to ∿ and ruin** venirse* abajo

rack² *vt* (shake): **to be ∿ed with pain** sufrir dolores atroces; **to be ∿ed with guilt** estar* atormentado por el remordimiento

racket /'rækət ‖'rækɪt/ *n* **1** (Sport) raqueta *f* **2** (noise) (colloq) jaleo *m* (fam) **3** (business) (colloq) tinglado *m* (fam)

racketeer /ˌrækə'tɪr ‖ˌrækə'tɪə(r)/ *n* mafioso, -sa *m,f*

racquet /'rækət ‖'rækɪt/ *n* ▶ RACKET 1

racy /'reɪsi/ *adj* **racier, raciest** (a) (lively) animado (b) (risqué) ⟨*story/joke*⟩ subido de tono

radar /'reɪdɑːr ‖'reɪdɑː(r)/ *n* radar *m*

radiant /'reɪdiənt/ *adj* ⟨*smile/look*⟩ radiante; ⟨*sun/blue*⟩ resplandeciente

radiate /'reɪdieɪt/ *vt* irradiar

radiation /ˌreɪdi'eɪʃən/ *n* radiación *f*; (before *n*) ∿ **sickness** radiotoxemia *f*

radiator /'reɪdieɪtər ‖'reɪdieɪtə(r)/ *n* radiador *m*

radical /'rædɪkəl/ *adj* radical; ⟨*writer*⟩ de ideas radicales

radically /'rædɪkli/ *adv* radicalmente

radii /'reɪdiaɪ/ *pl of* RADIUS

radio¹ /'reɪdiəʊ/ *n* (*pl* **-os**) (a) (receiver) radio *m* (AmL exc CS), radio *f* (CS, Esp); **I heard it on the ∿** lo oí por el *or* (CS, Esp) la radio (b) (medium) radio *f*

radio² (*3rd pers sing pres* **radios**; *pres p* **radioing**; *past & past p* **radioed**) *vt* ⟨*person*⟩ llamar por radio; ⟨*message*⟩ transmitir por radio

radio: ∿**active** /'reɪdiəʊ'æktɪv/ *adj* radiactivo; ∿**activity** /'reɪdiəʊæk'tɪvəti/ *n* radiactividad *f*; ∿**controlled** /'reɪdiəʊkən'trəʊld/ *adj* teledirigido

radiographer /'reɪdi'ɑːɡrəfər ‖ˌreɪdi'ɒɡrəfə(r)/ *n* radiógrafo, -fa *m,f*

radiologist /'reɪdi'ɑːlədʒəst ‖ˌreɪdi'ɒlədʒɪst/ *n* radiólogo, -ga *m,f*

radiotherapy /'reɪdiəʊ'θerəpi/ *n* radioterapia *f*

radish /'rædɪʃ/ *n* rabanito *m*, rábano *m*

radius /'reɪdiəs/ *n* (*pl* **radiuses** *or* **radii**) radio *m*

RAF /'ɑːˌrer'ef/ (in UK) (= **Royal Air Force**) **the ∿** la Fuerza Aérea británica

raffle¹ /'ræfəl/ *n* rifa *f*

raffle² *vt* rifar, sortear

raft /ræft ‖rɑːft/ *n* balsa *f*

rafter /'ræftər ‖'rɑːftə(r)/ *n* viga *f*

rag /ræɡ/ *n* **1** (a) (piece of cloth) trapo *m* (b) **rags** *pl* (tattered clothes) harapos *mpl*, andrajos *mpl*; **dressed in ∿s** harapiento, andrajoso **2** (newspaper) (colloq & pej) periodicucho *m* (pey)

ragamuffin /'ræɡəˌmʌfən ‖'ræɡəˌmʌfɪn/ *n* pilluelo, -la *m,f*

rag doll *n* muñeca *f* de trapo

rage¹ /reɪdʒ/ *n* **1** (a) (violent anger) furia *f* (b) (fit of fury): **to be in a ∿** estar* furioso **2** (fashion) (colloq): **to be (all) the ∿** hacer* furor

rage² *vi* (a) ⟨*storm/sea*⟩ rugir*; ⟨*fire*⟩ arder

furiosamente (b) ⟨*person*⟩ rabiar (c) ⟨*raging pres p* ⟨*storm*⟩ rugiente; ⟨*sea*⟩ embravecido; ⟨*headache*⟩ enloquecedor; ⟨*argument*⟩ enconado

ragged /'ræɡəd ‖'ræɡɪd/ *adj* ⟨*clothes/ appearance*⟩ harapiento, andrajoso; ⟨*edge*⟩ irregular

raid¹ /reɪd/ *n* (a) (Mil) asalto *m* (b) (air ∿) bombardeo *m* aéreo (c) (by thieves) atraco *m* (d) (by police) redada *f*, allanamiento *m* (AmL)

raid² *vt* (a) (Mil) asaltar (b) ⟨*bank*⟩ asaltar (c) ⟨*police*⟩ ⟨*house/building*⟩ hacer* una redada en, allanar (AmL)

raider /'reɪdər ‖'reɪdə(r)/ *n* asaltante *mf*

rail /reɪl/ *n* **1** (a) (bar) riel *m* (b) (hand ∿) pasamanos *m* (c) (barrier) baranda *f* **2** (a) (for trains, trams) riel *m*, raíl *m* (Esp) (b) (railroad) ferrocarril *m*; **by ∿** en *or* por ferrocarril

railing /'reɪlɪŋ/ *n* (*often pl*) reja *f*

rail: ∿**road** *n* (AmE) (a) (system) ferrocarril *m* (b) (track) vía *f* férrea; ∿**way** (BrE) ▶ ∿ROAD

rain¹ /reɪn/ *n* lluvia *f*

rain² *v impers* llover*; **it's** ∿**ing** está lloviendo, llueve

rainbow /'reɪnbəʊ/ *n* arco *m* iris

rain: ∿**coat** *n* impermeable *m*; ∿**drop** *n* gota *f* de lluvia; ∿**fall** *n* precipitaciones *fpl*, lluvia *f*; ∿ **forest** *n* selva *f* tropical (húmeda); ∿**water** *n* agua *f*; de lluvia

rainy /'reɪni/ *adj* **-nier, -niest** lluvioso

raise¹ /reɪz/ *vt*

I **1** (a) ⟨*head/hand*⟩ levantar, alzar*; ⟨*eyebrows*⟩ arquear; ⟨*flag*⟩ izar* (b) (make higher) ⟨*shelf/level*⟩ subir **2** (a) (set upright) levantar (b) (erect) ⟨*monument/building*⟩ levantar, erigir* (fml) **3** (a) ⟨*pressure/temperature*⟩ aumentar, elevar; ⟨*price/salary*⟩ subir, aumentar; **to ∿ one's voice** levantar la voz (b) ⟨*consciousness*⟩ aumentar

II **1** (a) ⟨*money/funds*⟩ recaudar (b) ⟨*army*⟩ reclutar **2** ⟨*fears/doubt*⟩ suscitar; **he managed to ∿ a smile** pudo sonreír; **to ∿ the alarm** dar* la alarma **3** ⟨*subject*⟩ sacar*; ⟨*question*⟩ formular; **to ∿ an objection** poner* una objeción **4** (a) ⟨*family*⟩ criar* (b) ⟨*cattle*⟩ dedicarse* a la cría de

raise² *n* (AmE) aumento *m or* subida *f* de sueldo

raisin /'reɪzn̩/ *n* (uva *f*) pasa *f*, pasa *f* (de uva)

rake¹ /reɪk/ *n* (tool) rastrillo *m*

rake² *vt* rastrillar

rakish /'reɪkɪʃ/ *adj* (casual, jaunty) desenfadado

rally¹ /'ræli/ *n* (*pl* **-lies**) **1** (mass meeting) concentración *f*; **political** ∿ mitin *m*, mítin *m* **2** (Auto) rally *m* **3** (in tennis, badminton) peloteo *m*

rally² **-lies, -lying, -lied** *vi* **1** (unite) unirse; (gather) congregarse* **2** (a) (recover) ⟨*person*⟩ recuperarse, reponerse* (b) (Fin) ⟨⟨*currency/ price*⟩⟩ repuntar, recuperarse

■ *vt* **1** ⟨*support/vote*⟩ conseguir* **2** ⟨*strength/ spirits*⟩ recobrar

■ **rally round** [*v + adv*]: **all the neighbors rallied round to help** todos los vecinos se juntaron para ayudar

ram¹ /ræm/ *n* (Zool) carnero *m*

ram² **-mm-** *vt* (a) (force) (+ *adv compl*): **he** ∿**med the stake into the ground** hincó la estaca en la tierra; **he** ∿**med his fist through the door** atravesó la puerta de un puñetazo (b) (crash into) chocar* con; (deliberately) embestir* contra   ┄┅➤

■ **ram home** [v + o + adv, v + adv + o] ⟨point/ message⟩ hacer* entender a la fuerza

RAM /ræm/ n (Comput) (= **random access memory**) RAM f

Ramadan /ˈrɑːmədɑːn ‖ˌræməˈdæn/ n Ramadán m

ramble¹ /ˈræmbəl/ n paseo m; (BrE Sport) excursión f ⟨a pie⟩

ramble² vi (a) (walk) pasear; **to go rambling** (BrE) hacer* excursionismo (b) (in speech, writing) irse* por las ramas

■ **ramble on** [v + adv] divagar*

rambler /ˈræmblər ‖ˈræmblə(r)/ n excursionista mf

rambling /ˈræmblɪŋ/ adj (a) ⟨essay/lecture⟩ que se va por las ramas (b) ⟨streets⟩ laberíntico; **a ~ old house** una vieja casona llena de recovecos (c) ⟨rose⟩ trepador

ramp /ræmp/ n (a) (slope) rampa f; **entrance o on ~** (AmE) vía f de acceso; **exit o off ~** (AmE) vía f de salida (b) (on ship, aircraft) (for passengers) escalerilla f; (for vehicles) rampa f (c) (platform) elevador m (d) (hump) (BrE) desnivel m

rampage /ˈræmpeɪdʒ/ n: **to be/go on the ~** empezar* a arrasarlo todo

rampant /ˈræmpənt/ adj ⟨inflation⟩ galopante; ⟨growth⟩ desenfrenado; ⟨crime⟩ endémico

rampart /ˈræmpɑːrt ‖ˈræmpɑːt/ n (bank) terraplén m; (wall) muralla f

ram: ~ raid n asalto ⟨rompiendo el escaparate con un vehículo⟩; **~-raid** vt asaltar ⟨rompiendo el escaparate con un vehículo⟩

ramshackle /ˈræmˌʃækəl/ adj destartalado

ran /ræn/ past of RUN¹

ranch /ræntʃ ‖rɑːntʃ/ n: **cattle ~** finca f (ganadera), hacienda f (ganadera) (esp AmL), rancho m ganadero (Méx), estancia f (CS)

rancher /ˈræntʃər ‖ˈrɑːntʃə(r)/ n hacendado, -da m,f, estanciero, -ra m,f(CS), ranchero, -ra m,f (Méx); **cattle ~** ganadero, -ra m,f

rancid /ˈrænsəd ‖ˈrænsɪd/ adj rancio

rancor, (BrE) **rancour** /ˈræŋkər ‖ˈræŋkə(r)/ n rencor m

rand /rænd/ n (pl ~) rand m

random /ˈrændəm/ adj (a) ⟨testing/choice⟩ al azar; ⟨sample⟩ aleatorio (b) **at random** (as adv) al azar

rang /ræŋ/ past of RING²

range¹ /reɪndʒ/ n ① (a) (scope) ámbito m (b) (Mus) registro m (c) (bracket): **within/out of our price ~** dentro de/fuera de nuestras posibilidades ② (a) (variety) gama f (b) (selection) línea f ③ (a) (of gun, transmitter) alcance m; **at close/long ~** de cerca/lejos; **to come/be within ~** ponerse*/estar* a tiro (b) (of vehicle, missile) autonomía f ④ (for shooting) campo m de tiro ⑤ (chain) cadena f; **a mountain ~** una cordillera ⑥ (stove) cocina f económica, estufa f (Col, Méx)

range² vi: **their ages ~ from 12 to 20** tienen entre 12 y 20 años

ranger /ˈreɪndʒər ‖ˈreɪndʒə(r)/ n guarda mf forestal, guardabosques mf

rank¹ /ræŋk/ n ① (line) fila f ② (status) categoría f; (Mil) grado m, rango m ③ (taxi ~) (BrE) parada f de taxis, sitio m (Méx)

rank² vt: **he's ~ed fourth** está clasificado cuarto

■ **~** vi (a) (be classed) estar*; **it ~s among the best** está entre los mejores (b) (hold rank): **to ~ above/ below sb** estar* por encima/por debajo de algn

rank³ adj ① (before n) (complete) ⟨beginner⟩ absoluto; ⟨injustice⟩ flagrante ② ⟨smell⟩ fétido

rank and file n (Mil) (+ pl vb) tropa f; **the ~ ~ of the union** las bases del sindicato

rankle /ˈræŋkəl/ vi doler*

ransack /ˈrænsæk/ vt ⟨room/drawer⟩ revolver*; ⟨house/premises⟩ (search) registrar (de arriba a abajo); (pillage) saquear

ransom /ˈrænsəm/ n rescate m; **to hold sb to o** (AmE also) **for ~** exigir* un rescate por algn

rant /rænt/ vi despotricar*

rap¹ /ræp/ n ① (blow) golpe m ② **to take the ~ for sth** (esp AmE colloq) cargar* con la culpa de algo ③ (a) (chat) (colloq) cháchara f (fam) (b) (Mus) rap m

rap² -pp- vi dar* un golpe

■ **~** vt: **he ~ped my knuckles** me pegó en los nudillos

rape¹ /reɪp/ n ① (a) (sexual violation) violación f; (of a minor) estupro m (b) (of the countryside) (liter) expoliación f (liter) ② (plant) colza f

rape² vt ⟨person⟩ violar

rapid /ˈræpəd ‖ˈræpɪd/ adj rápido

rapidly /ˈræpədli ‖ˈræpɪdli/ adv rápidamente

rapids /ˈræpədz ‖ˈræpɪdz/ pl n rápidos mpl

rapist /ˈreɪpəst ‖ˈreɪpɪst/ n violador, -dora m,f

rapport /ræˈpɔːr ‖ræˈpɔː(r)/ n relación f de comunicación

rapt /ræpt/ adj (liter) ⟨expression/smile⟩ embelesado

rapture /ˈræptʃər ‖ˈræptʃə(r)/ n éxtasis m, arrobamiento m (liter)

rapturous /ˈræptʃərəs/ adj ⟨applause/welcome⟩ calurososísimo

rare /rer ‖reə(r)/ adj **rarer** /ˈrerər ‖ˈreərər/, **rarest** /ˈrerəst ‖ˈreərɪst/ ① (a) (uncommon) raro (b) (liter) ⟨talent/beauty⟩ excepcional ② (Culin) ⟨steak⟩ vuelta y vuelta

rarely /ˈrerli ‖ˈreəli/ adv rara vez

raring /ˈrerɪŋ ‖ˈreərɪŋ/ adj: **to be ~ to go**: **he's ~ to go** está que ya no se aguanta

rarity /ˈrerəti ‖ˈreərɪti/ n (pl **-ties**) algo poco común

rascal /ˈræskəl ‖ˈrɑːskəl/ n granuja mf

rash¹ /ræʃ/ n sarpullido m

rash² adj **-er**, **-est** precipitado

rasher /ˈræʃər ‖ˈræʃə(r)/ n loncha f, lonja f

rashly /ˈræʃli/ adv ⟨act⟩ precipitadamente

rasp¹ /ræsp ‖rɑːsp/ n escofina f

rasp² vt ⟨wood⟩ raspar, escofinar

AmC	América Central	Arg	Argentina	Cu	Cuba	Per	Perú
AmL	América Latina	Bol	Bolivia	Ec	Ecuador	RPl	Río de la Plata
AmS	América del Sur	Chi	Chile	Esp	España	Ur	Uruguay
Andes	Región andina	CS	Cono Sur	Méx	México	Ven	Venezuela

raspberry /'ræz,beri ‖'rɑːzbəri/ n (pl **-ries**) frambuesa f

rasping /'ræspɪŋ ‖'rɑːspɪŋ/ adj ‹sound/voice› áspero

Rastafarian /ˌræstə'feriən ‖ˌræstə'feəriən/ n rastafari mf

rat /ræt/ n **(a)** (Zool) rata f; (before n) ∼ **poison** raticida m **(b)** (person) (colloq) rata f de alcantarilla (fam)

rate¹ /reɪt/ n **1** **(a)** (speed) velocidad; (rhythm) ritmo m; **at this** ∼ a este paso; **at any** ∼ (at least) por lo menos; (in any case) en todo caso **(b)** (level, ratio): **birth** ∼ índice m de natalidad; **death** ∼ mortalidad f; ∼ **of inflation** tasa f de inflación; **interest** ∼ tasa f or (esp Esp) tipo m de interés; ∼ **of exchange** tipo m de cambio **(c)** (price, charge) tarifa f; **that's the going** ∼ eso es lo que se suele pagar **2** (local tax) (formerly, in UK) (often pl) ≈ contribución f (municipal or inmobiliaria)

rate² vt **1** (rank, consider): **I** ∼ **her work very highly** tengo una excelente opinión de su trabajo; **I** ∼ **her as the best woman tennis player** yo la considero la mejor tenista **2** (deserve) merecer*

rather /'ræðər ‖'rɑːðə(r)/ adv **1** **(a)** (stating preference): **I'd** ∼ **walk than go by bus** prefiero andar a ir en autobús; ∼ **you than me!** ¡menos mal que eres tú y no yo! **(b)** (more precisely): **or** ∼ o mejor dicho **2** (fairly) bastante; (somewhat) algo

ratification /ˌrætəfə'keɪʃən ‖ˌrætɪfɪ'keɪʃən/ n (frml) ratificación f

ratify /'rætəfaɪ ‖'rætɪfaɪ/ vt **-fies, -fying, -fied** (frml) ratificar*

rating /'reɪtɪŋ/ n **(a)** (evaluation): **credit** ∼ clasificación f crediticia **(b)** **ratings** pl (Rad, TV) índice m de audiencia

ratio /'reɪʃəʊ, -ʃiəʊ ‖'reɪʃiəʊ/ n (pl **ratios**) proporción f, ratio m (téc); **in a** ∼ **of two to one** en una proporción de dos a uno

ration¹ /'ræʃən/ n **(a)** (allowance) ración f **(b)** **rations** pl víveres mpl

ration² vt racionar

rational /'ræʃnəl ‖'ræʃənl/ adj **(a)** (able to reason) ‹being› racional **(b)** (sane, lucid) **to be** ∼ estar* en su (or mi etc) sano juicio **(c)** (sensible) ‹suggestion› razonable

rationale /ˌræʃə'næl ‖ˌræʃə'nɑːl/ n (no pl) base f, razones fpl

rationalize /'ræʃnəlaɪz/ vt racionalizar*

rationally /'ræʃnəli/ adv ‹think› racionalmente; ‹behave› con sensatez

rationing /'ræʃənɪŋ/ n racionamiento m

rat run n (Auto) atajo m (para evitar el tráfico de una calle principal en horas punta)

rattle¹ /'rætl/ n **1** (no pl) (noise) ruido m; (of train, carriage) traqueteo m **2** (baby's) ∼ sonajero m, sonaja f (Méx)

rattle² vi **(a)** (make noise) «chains/bottles/keys» repiquetear; «window/engine» vibrar **(b)** (move) (+ adv compl) traquetear
 ■ ∼ vt ‹keys/chain› hacer* repiquetear; ‹door/window› «wind» hacer* vibrar
 ■ **rattle off** [v + o + adv, v + adv + o] recitar
 ■ **rattle on** [v + adv] hablar or (fam) parlotear sin parar

rattlesnake /'rætlsneɪk/ n serpiente f (de) cascabel, cascabel f

raucous /'rɔːkəs/ adj (loud) estentóreo; (shrill) estridente

raunchy /'rɔːntʃi/ adj **-chier, -chiest** (colloq) ‹humor› picante; ‹joke› escabroso

ravage /'rævɪdʒ/ vt (plunder) saquear; **a country** ∼**d by war** un país asolado por la guerra

ravages /'rævɪdʒəz ‖'rævɪdʒɪz/ pl n estragos mpl

rave¹ /reɪv/ vi **(a)** (talk deliriously) delirar **(b)** (talk, write enthusiastically): **to** ∼ **about sth** poner* a algo por las nubes **(c)** (talk angrily) despotricar*

rave² n (colloq) **1** (before n) (full of praise) ∼ **reviews** críticas fpl muy favorables **2** (BrE) (party) fiesta con música acid

raven /'reɪvən/ n cuervo m

ravenous /'rævənəs/ adj hambriento; **to be** ∼ (colloq) tener* un hambre canina (fam)

ravine /rə'viːn/ n barranco m, quebrada f

raving¹ /'reɪvɪŋ/ adj (colloq) (before n, as intensifier): **he's a** ∼ **lunatic** está loco de atar (fam); (as adv) **he's** ∼ **mad** está como una cabra (fam)

raving² n (often pl) desvarío m

ravish /'rævɪʃ/ vt (liter) violar

ravishing /'rævɪʃɪŋ/ adj deslumbrante

raw /rɔː/ adj **1** **(a)** ‹meat/vegetables› crudo **(b)** ‹silk› crudo; ‹sugar› sin refinar; ‹sewage› sin tratar **2** (sore): **my fingers were** ∼ tenía los dedos en carne viva **3** (inexperienced) verde (fam); ‹recruit› novato

raw material n materia f prima

ray /reɪ/ n **1** (beam) rayo m **2** (Mus) re m **3** (Zool) raya f

rayon /'reɪɑːn ‖'reɪɒn/ n rayón m

raze /reɪz/ vt: **to** ∼ **sth** (to the ground) arrasar algo

razor /'reɪzər ‖'reɪzə(r)/ n **(a)** (safety ∼) cuchilla f or máquina f or maquinilla f de afeitar, rastrillo m (Méx); (before n) ∼ **blade** cuchilla f, hoja f de afeitar **(b)** (electric) máquina f or maquinilla f de afeitar, máquina f de rasurar (esp Méx)

razzmatazz /'ræzmə'tæz/ n (colloq) bulla f; (publicity) alarde m publicitario

Rd = **Road**

re¹ /reɪ/ n (Mus) re m

re² /riː/ prep con relación a, con referencia a

re- /riː/ pref re-

RE n (BrE) (= **religious education**) religión f

reach¹ /riːtʃ/ n **1** **(a)** (distance) alcance m **(b)** (in phrases) **within reach** a mi (or tu etc) alcance; **out of reach** fuera de su (or mi etc) alcance **2** (of river) tramo m

reach² vt **1** (with hand) alcanzar* **(b)** (extend to) llegar* a **2** ‹destination/limit/age› llegar* a; ‹stage/agreement› llegar* a, alcanzar* **3** (contact) ponerse* en contacto con
 ■ ∼ vi **(a)** (extend hand, arm): **he** ∼**ed for his gun** echó mano a la pistola; **she** ∼**ed across the table for the salt** agarró or (esp Esp) cogió la sal, que estaba al otro lado de la mesa **(b)** (stretch far enough) alcanzar*; **I can't** ∼! ¡no alcanzo! **(c)** (extend) extenderse*
 ■ **reach out** [v + adv] alargar* la mano

react /ri'ækt/ vi reaccionar

reaction /ri'ækʃən/ n reacción f

reactionary /riˈækʃəneri ‖riˈækʃənri/ adj
(pej) reaccionario (pey)

reactor /riˈæktər ‖riˈæktə(r)/ n (nuclear ~)
reactor m (nuclear)

read¹ /riːd/ (past & past p **read** /red/) vt
[1] (a) ⟨book/map/music/meter⟩ leer* (b) (interpret)
⟨sign/mood/situation⟩ interpretar [2] (a) «⟨sign/
notice⟩» decir* (b) (indicate) «⟨thermometer/gauge⟩»
marcar*
- ~ vi leer*
- **read out** [v + o + adv, v + adv + o] leer* (en
voz alta)
- **read over, read through** [v + o + adv] leer*
(por entero)
- **read up** [v + adv] to ~ up (ON sth) estudiar
(algo)

read² /red/ adj: to be well ~ ser* muy leído

readable /ˈriːdəbəl/ adj ⟨book/style⟩ ameno;
⟨writing⟩ legible

reader /ˈriːdər ‖ˈriːdə(r)/ n [1] (person) lector,
-tora m,f; she's a fast/slow ~ lee muy rápido/
lento [2] (Educ, Publ) libro m de lectura

readership /ˈriːdərʃɪp ‖ˈriːdəʃɪp/ n lectores
mpl; it has a ~ of over 10 million tiene una tirada
de 10 millones

readily /ˈredli ‖ˈredɪli/ adv (a) (willingly): she ~
agreed accedió de buena gana (b) (easily)
⟨understand⟩ fácilmente; they are ~ available se
pueden conseguir fácilmente

reading /ˈriːdɪŋ/ n [1] (a) (activity, skill) lectura f;
(before n) ⟨glasses⟩ para leer; ~ list lista f de
lecturas recomendadas; ~ room sala f de lectura
(b) (event): poetry ~ recital m de poesía [2] (on
dial, gauge) lectura f

readjust /ˌriːəˈdʒʌst/ vt reajustar
- ~ vi «person» to ~ (TO sth) readaptarse (A
algo)

ready¹ /ˈredi/ adj **-dier, -diest** [1] (a) (having
completed preparations) (pred) to be ~ estar* listo,
estar* pronto (RPl); to be ~ to + INF estar* listo
PARA + INF; to get ~ (prepare oneself) prepararse,
aprontarse (CS); (get dressed, made up etc)
arreglarse, aprontarse (CS) (b) (mentally prepared)
(pred) to be ~ FOR sth/to + INF estar* preparado
PARA algo/PARA + INF [2] (willing) dispuesto
[3] (easy, available): ~ money o cash dinero m (en
efectivo)

ready² n at the ~ listo

ready³ vt **-dies, -dying, -died** preparar

ready: ~-**made** /ˈrediˈmeɪd/ adj ⟨suit⟩ de
confección; ⟨soup/sauce⟩ preparado; ~-**to-wear**
/ˈrediˈtəˈwer ‖ˌrediˈtəˈweə(r)/ adj (before n)
⟨clothes⟩ de confección

reaffirm /ˌriːəˈfɜːrm ‖ˌriːəˈfɜːm/ vt reiterar,
reafirmar

real¹ /riːl, rɪl ‖riːl, rɪəl/ adj (a) (actual, not
imaginary) real, verdadero (b) (actual, true) (before
n) ⟨reason/name⟩ verdadero (c) (genuine, not fake)
⟨fur/leather⟩ auténtico; ⟨gold⟩ de ley (d) (as
intensifier) auténtico

real² adv (AmE colloq) (as intensifier) muy

real estate n (esp AmE) bienes mpl raíces or
inmuebles, propiedad f inmobiliaria; (before n) ~
~ agent ▶ REALTOR

realism /ˈriːəlɪzəm/ n realismo m

realist /ˈriːələst ‖ˈriːəlɪst/ n realista mf

realistic /ˈriːəˈlɪstɪk ‖rɪəˈlɪstɪk/ adj realista

reality /riˈæləti/ n (pl **-ties**) realidad f; in ~
en realidad

realization /ˈriːələˈzeɪʃən ‖ˌriːəlaɪˈzeɪʃən/ n
[1] (understanding) comprensión f [2] (of plan)
realización f

realize /ˈriːəlaɪz/ vt [1] (a) (become aware of)
darse* cuenta de, comprender, caer* en la cuenta
de (b) (know, be aware of) saber* [2] (achieve)
⟨ambition⟩ hacer* realidad; ⟨potential⟩
desarrollar
- ~ vi darse* cuenta

really /ˈriːəli ‖ˈriːəli, ˈrɪəli/ adv (a) (in fact): I ~
did see him! ¡de verdad que lo vi!; the tomato is
~ a fruit el tomate en realidad es una fruta (b)
(as intensifier): it's ~ good/old es buenísimo/
viejísimo (c) (as interj): (oh,) ~? (expressing
interest) ¿ah sí?; really? (expressing surprise) ¿de
verdad?

realm /relm/ n (a) (kingdom) (frml) reino m (b)
(sphere) (often pl) mundo m

realtor /ˈriːəltər ‖ˈrɪəltə(r)/ n (AmE) agente
inmobiliario, -ria m,f

ream /riːm/ n (Print) resma f

reamer /ˈriːmər ‖ˈriːmə(r)/ n (AmE)
exprimelimones m, exprimidor m

reap /riːp/ vt (Agr) cosechar, recoger*; to ~ the
benefits of sth cosechar los beneficios de algo

reappear /ˈriːəˈpɪr ‖rɪəˈpɪə(r)/ vi volver* a
aparecer

rear¹ /rɪr ‖rɪə(r)/ n (a) (back part) (no pl) parte f
trasera or de atrás (b) (of column, procession) (no
pl) the ~ la retaguardia (c) (buttocks) (colloq)
trasero m (fam)

rear² adj ⟨window/wheel⟩ de atrás, trasero

rear³ vt ⟨child/cattle⟩ criar*
- ~ vi ~ (up) «horse» encabritarse

rearguard /ˈrɪrɡɑːrd ‖ˈrɪəɡɑːd/ n retaguardia f

rearm /ˈriːˈɑːrm ‖ri:ˈɑːm/ vt rearmar
- ~ vi rearmarse

rearrange /ˈriːəˈreɪndʒ/ vt (a) ⟨furniture⟩
cambiar de lugar (b) (change time of)
⟨appointment⟩ cambiar la fecha/la hora de

rear-view mirror /ˈrɪrvjuː ‖ˈrɪəvjuː/ n
(espejo m) retrovisor m

reason¹ /ˈriːzn/ n [1] (cause) razón f, motivo m;
~ FOR sth razón or motivo de algo; I left it there
for a ~ por algo lo dejé ahí [2] (faculty) razón f
[3] (good sense): to listen to ~ atender* a razones;
it stands to ~ es lógico

reason² vt pensar*
- ~ vi razonar, discurrir

reasonable /ˈriːznəbəl/ adj (a) ⟨offer/request/
person⟩ razonable (b) ⟨price/sum⟩ razonable,
moderado

reasonably /ˈriːznəbli/ adv (a) ⟨behave/argue⟩
razonablemente (b) (fairly): I'm ~ certain estoy
casi seguro

reasoning /ˈriːznɪŋ/ n razonamiento m

reassemble /ˈriːəˈsembl/ vt (a) ⟨people/
group⟩ volver* a reunir, reunir* (b) ⟨parts/
engine⟩ reensamblar
- ~ vi «meeting/group» volverse* a reunir,
reunirse*

reassurance /ˈriːəˈʃʊrəns ‖riːəˈʃʊərəns,
ˌriːəˈʃɔːrəns/ n (a) (feeling): he drew ~ from his
wife's words lo que le dijo su mujer lo confortó

or lo tranquilizó **(b)** (words, support): **he gave us countless ∼s that ...** nos tranquilizó asegurándonos repetidamente que ...

reassure /ˌriːəˈʃʊr ‖ˌriːəˈʃʊə(r), ˌriːəˈʃɔː(r)/ *vt* tranquilizar*

reassuring /ˈriːəˈʃʊrɪŋ ‖ˌriːəˈʃʊərɪŋ, ˌriːəˈʃɔːrɪŋ/ *adj ⟨voice/manner/answer⟩* tranquilizador; **it's ∼ to know that ...** tranquiliza saber que ...

rebate /ˈriːbeɪt/ *n* (repayment) reembolso *m*; (discount) descuento *m*

rebel¹ /ˈrebəl/ *n* rebelde *mf*

rebel² /rɪˈbel/ *vi* **-ll-** rebelarse, sublevarse

rebellion /rɪˈbeljən/ *n* rebelión *f*

rebellious /rɪˈbeljəs/ *adj* rebelde

rebirth /ˈriːˈbɜːθ ‖ˌriːˈbɜːθ/ *n* renacimiento *m*

reboot /riːˈbuːt/ *vt* (Comput) reiniciar

rebound¹ /rɪˈbaʊnd/ *n*: **she married him on the ∼** se casó con él por despecho

rebound² /rɪˈbaʊnd/ *vi ⟨ball⟩* rebotar

rebuff¹ /rɪˈbʌf/ *n*: **to meet with/receive a ∼** ser* rechazado

rebuff² *vt* rechazar*

rebuild /riːˈbɪld/ *vt* (*past & past p* **rebuilt**) *⟨building/economy⟩* reconstruir*; **he tried to ∼ his life** intentó rehacer su vida

rebuke¹ /rɪˈbjuːk/ *vt* reprender

rebuke² *n* reprimenda *f*

rebut /rɪˈbʌt/ *vt* **-tt-** (fml) rebatir

recall¹ /rɪˈkɔːl, ˈriːkɔːl/ *n* **1** (memory) memoria *f*; **to have total ∼** tener* una memoria excelente **2** (of goods, ambassador) retirada *f*

recall² /rɪˈkɔːl/ *vt* **1** (remember) recordar* **2 (a)** *⟨faulty goods⟩* retirar (del mercado) **(b)** *⟨ambassador⟩* retirar; (temporarily) llamar; *⟨troops⟩* llamar

recant /rɪˈkænt/ *vi* retractarse; (Relig) abjurar

recap¹ /ˈriːkæp/ *n* (colloq) resumen *m*

recap² /riːˈkæp/ **-pp-** *vt* **1** (summarize) (colloq) resumir, recapitular **2** (AmE Auto) ▸ RETREAD¹
■ ∼ *vi* (colloq) resumir

recapitulate /ˈriːkəˈpɪtʃəleɪt ‖ˌriːkəˈpɪtjʊleɪt/ *vt/i* (fml) recapitular, resumir

recapture /riːˈkæptʃər ‖riːˈkæptʃə(r)/ *vt ⟨convict/animal⟩* capturar; *⟨youth/beauty⟩* recuperar

recede /rɪˈsiːd/ *vi* **(a)** (move back) *⟨tide⟩* retirarse; **to ∼ into the distance** perderse en la distancia **(b)** *⟨danger⟩* alejarse; *⟨prospect⟩* desvanecerse* **(c) receding** *pres p ⟨chin⟩* hundido; **he has a receding hairline** tiene entradas

receipt /rɪˈsiːt/ *n* **(a)** (paper) recibo *m* **(b)** (act) recibo *m*, recepción *f*

receive /rɪˈsiːv/ *vt* **1 (a)** *⟨letter/award/visit⟩* recibir; *⟨payment⟩* recibir, cobrar, percibir (frml); *⟨stolen goods⟩* comerciar con, reducir* (AmS); *⟨serve/ball⟩* recibir; *⟨injuries⟩* sufrir; *⟨blow⟩* recibir **(b)** (react to) *⟨news/idea⟩* recibir **2** (welcome, admit) (fml) *⟨person⟩* recibir, acoger* **3** (Rad, TV) *⟨signal⟩* recibir, captar

receiver /rɪˈsiːvər ‖rɪˈsiːvə(r)/ *n* **1** (Telec) auricular *m* **2** (Rad, TV) receptor *m* **3** (of stolen goods) comerciante *mf* de mercancía robada

receivership /rɪˈsiːvərʃɪp ‖rɪˈsiːvəʃɪp/ *n* **to go into/be in ∼** ser* declarado/estar* en suspensión *or* en cesación de pagos

recent /ˈriːsn̩t/ *adj* reciente; **in ∼ years/months** en los últimos años/meses; **in the ∼ past** en los últimos tiempos

recently /ˈriːsn̩tli/ *adv* recientemente; **until quite ∼** hasta hace bien poco

receptacle /rɪˈseptɪkəl/ *n* (frml) recipiente *m*, receptáculo *m*

reception /rɪˈsepʃən/ *n* **(a)** (reaction) (*no pl*) recibimiento *m*, acogida *f* **(b)** (in hotel, office) (*no art*) recepción *f*; (*before n*) **∼ desk** recepción *f* **(c)** (social event) recepción *f* **(d)** (Rad, TV) recepción *f*

receptionist /rɪˈsepʃənəst ‖rɪˈsepʃənɪst/ *n* recepcionista *mf*

receptive /rɪˈseptɪv/ *adj* receptivo

recess /ˈriːses/ *n* **1 (a)** (of legislative body) receso *m* (AmL), suspensión *f* de actividades (Esp); (of committee etc) intermedio *m* **(b)** (AmE Educ) recreo *m* **2** (alcove) hueco *m*, entrada *f*

recession /rɪˈseʃn̩ ‖rɪˈseʃən/ *n* (Econ) recesión *f*

recharge /ˈriːˈtʃɑːrdʒ ‖ˌriːˈtʃɑːdʒ/ *vt* volver* a cargar, recargar*

rechargeable /ˈriːˈtʃɑːrdʒəbəl ‖ˌriːˈtʃɑːdʒəbəl/ *adj* recargable

recipe /ˈresəpi/ *n* receta *f*; (*before n*) **∼ book** libro *m* de cocina; (personal) cuaderno *m* de recetas (de cocina)

recipient /rɪˈsɪpiənt/ *n* (fml) (of letter) destinatario, -ria *m,f*; (of an organ) (Med) receptor, -tora *m,f*

reciprocal /rɪˈsɪprəkəl/ *adj* recíproco

reciprocate /rɪˈsɪprəkeɪt/ *vt* corresponder a, reciprocar* (AmL)
■ ∼ *vi* corresponder, reciprocar* (AmL)

recital /rɪˈsaɪtl/ *n* (Mus) recital *m*

recite /rɪˈsaɪt/ *vt* **(a)** (declaim) *⟨poem⟩* recitar **(b)** (list) *⟨names⟩* enumerar

reckless /ˈrekləs ‖ˈreklɪs/ *adj* imprudente, temerario

reckon /ˈrekən/ *vt* **(a)** (calculate) calcular **(b)** (consider) considerar **(c)** (think) (colloq) creer*; **what do you ∼?** ¿tú qué opinas?, ¿y a ti qué te parece?
■ **reckon on** [*v + prep + o*] contar con

reckoning /ˈrekənɪŋ/ *n* cálculos *mpl*

reclaim /rɪˈkleɪm/ *vt* **(a)** (claim back): **I filled in a form to ∼ tax** llené un formulario para que me devolvieran parte de los impuestos; **to ∼ one's luggage** (Aviat) recoger* el equipaje; (at left luggage) (pasar a) retirar el equipaje **(b)** (recover) recuperar; **∼ed land** terreno *m* ganado al mar

recline /rɪˈklaɪn/ *vi* **(a)** (lean back) recostarse*, reclinarse; (rest) apoyarse **(b)** *⟨chair⟩* reclinarse **(c) reclining** *pres p ⟨chair/seat⟩* reclinable, abatible; *⟨figure⟩* yacente (liter), recostado

recluse /rɪˈkluːs/ *n* ermitaño, -ña *m,f*

reclusive /rɪˈkluːsɪv/ *adj* dado a recluirse

recognition /ˌrekəgˈnɪʃən/ *n* reconocimiento *m*; **in ∼ of** (fml) en reconocimiento a *or* por (fml)

recognizable /ˈrekəgnaɪzəbəl/ *adj* reconocible; *⟨difference⟩* apreciable

recognize /ˈrekəgnaɪz/ *vt* **(a)** *⟨voice/person⟩* reconocer* **(b)** (acknowledge) reconocer*, admitir

r

recoil¹ /rɪ'kɔɪl/ vi (shrink back) retroceder; **to ~ FROM sth** rehuir* algo

recoil² /'riːkɔɪl/ n retroceso m

recollect /rekə'lekt/ vt recordar*

recollection /rekə'lekʃən/ n recuerdo m

recommend /rekə'mend/ vt **(a)** (praise, declare acceptable) recomendar* **(b)** (advise) **to ~ sth/-ING** aconsejar or recomendar* algo/+ INF; **~ed** (retail) **price** precio m de venta recomendado

recommendation /rekəmen'deɪʃən/ n recomendación f

recompense /'rekəmpens/ n (frml) recompensa f

reconcile /'rekənsaɪl/ vt **(a)** ‹enemies› reconciliar **(b)** ‹theories/ideals› conciliar **(c) to become ~d TO sth** resignarse A algo

reconciliation /'rekənsɪli'eɪʃən/ n reconciliación f

recondition /riːkən'dɪʃən/ vt reacondicionar

reconnaissance /rə'kɑːnəzəns, -səns ‖rɪ'kɒnɪsəns/ n (Mil) reconocimiento m

reconnoiter, (BrE) reconnoitre /'riːkə'nɔɪtər, 're- ‖rekə'nɔɪtə(r)/ vt reconocer*

reconquer /'riːkɑːŋkər ‖riː'kɒŋkə(r)/ vt reconquistar

reconsider /'riːkən'sɪdər ‖riːkən'sɪdə(r)/ vt reconsiderar

reconstruct /'riːkən'strʌkt/ vt reconstruir*

reconstruction /'riːkən'strʌkʃən/ n **(a)** (rebuilding) reconstrucción f **(b)** (re-creation) reconstitución f

record¹ /'rekərd ‖'rekɔːd/ n **1 (a)** (document) documento m; (of attendances etc) registro m; (file) archivo m; (minutes) acta f‡; (note) nota f; **medical ~s** historial m médico; **keep a ~ of your expenses** anote sus gastos; **according to our ~s** según nuestros datos **(b)** (in phrases) **off the record** extraoficialmente; **on record: the hottest summer on ~** el verano más caluroso del que se tienen datos **2 (a)** (of performance, behavior): **he has a good academic ~** tiene un buen currículum académico; **our products have an excellent safety ~** nuestros productos son de probada seguridad **(b)** (criminal ~) antecedentes mpl (penales) **3** (highest, lowest, best, worst) récord m, marca f **4** (Audio, Mus) disco m; (before n) **~ store** disquería f, tienda f de discos

record² /rɪ'kɔːrd ‖rɪ'kɔːd/ vt **1 (a)** «person» (write down) anotar; (in minutes) hacer* constar **(b)** (register) «instrument» registrar **2** ‹song/program/album› grabar

record³ /'rekərd ‖'rekɔːd/ adj (before n, no comp) récord adj inv

record card n ficha f

recorded /rɪ'kɔːrdəd ‖rɪ'kɔːdɪd/ adj **(a)** ‹music› grabado **(b)** ‹history› escrito, documentado

recorder /rɪ'kɔːrdər ‖rɪ'kɔːdə(r)/ n (Mus) flauta f dulce

recording /rɪ'kɔːrdɪŋ ‖rɪ'kɔːdɪŋ/ n grabación f

record player n tocadiscos m

recount /rɪ'kaʊnt/ vt narrar, contar*

re-count /'riːkaʊnt/ vt volver* a contar; ‹votes› hacer* un segundo escrutinio de, recontar*

recoup /rɪ'kuːp/ vt ‹costs› recuperar; ‹losses› resarcirse* de

recourse /'riːkɔːrs ‖rɪ'kɔːs/ n **to have ~ to sth/sb** recurrir a algo/algn

recover /rɪ'kʌvər ‖rɪ'kʌvə(r)/ vt **(a)** ‹consciousness/strength› recuperar, recobrar; ‹investment/lead› recuperar **(b)** (retrieve) rescatar ■ ~ vi **(a)** «person» reponerse*, restablecerse*, recuperarse **(b)** «economy» recuperarse, repuntar

recovery /rɪ'kʌvəri/ n (pl **-ries**) **1 (a)** (return to health) recuperación f, restablecimiento m **(b)** (of economy) recuperación f **2** (of stolen goods, missing documents) recuperación f; (retrieval) rescate m

re-create /'riːkri'eɪt/ vt recrear

recreation /rekri'eɪʃən/ n **(a)** (leisure) esparcimiento m **(b)** (in school, prison) (BrE) recreo m

recreational /'rekri'eɪʃnəl ‖rekri'eɪʃənl/ adj recreativo; **~ drug** droga f recreativa

recrimination /rɪ'krɪmə'neɪʃən/ n (often pl) recriminación f

recruit¹ /rɪ'kruːt/ n (Mil) recluta mf

recruit² vt reclutar; ‹staff› contratar

recruitment /rɪ'kruːtmənt/ n reclutamiento m

rectangle /'rektæŋgəl/ n rectángulo m

rectangular /rek'tæŋgələr ‖rek'tæŋgjʊlə(r)/ adj rectangular

rectify /'rektəfaɪ ‖'rektɪfaɪ/ vt **-fies, -fying, -fied** rectificar*

rector /'rektər ‖'rektə(r)/ n **(a)** (Relig) rector, -tora m,f, ≈ párroco m **(b)** (in US) (Educ) rector, -ra m,f

rectum /'rektəm/ n (pl **rectums** or **recta** /'rektə/) recto m

recuperate /rɪ'kuːpəreɪt/ vi recuperarse, reponerse*

recuperation /rɪ'kuːpə'reɪʃən/ n recuperación f, restablecimiento m

recur /rɪ'kɜːr ‖rɪ'kɜː(r)/ vi **-rr- (a)** «phenomenon» volver* a ocurrir or a suceder, repetirse*; «symptom» volver* a presentarse **(b) recurring** pres p recurrente

recurrence /rɪ'kɜːrəns ‖rɪ'kʌrəns/ n (of symptoms) reaparición f; (of incident) repetición f

recurrent /rɪ'kɜːrənt ‖rɪ'kʌrənt/ adj recurrente

recycle /riː'saɪkəl/ vt reciclar

recycling /riː'saɪklɪŋ/ n reciclaje m

red¹ /red/ adj **redder, reddest** ‹rose/dress› rojo, colorado; ‹flag/signal› rojo; ‹meat› rojo; ‹wine› tinto; **her eyes were ~** tenía los ojos enrojecidos or rojos

AmC	Central America	Arg	Argentina	Cu	Cuba
AmL	Latin America	Bol	Bolivia	Ec	Ecuador
AmS	South America	Chi	Chile	Esp	Spain
Andes	Andean Region	CS	Southern Cone	Méx	Mexico

Per	Peru
RPI	River Plate Area
Ur	Uruguay
Ven	Venezuela

red² n rojo m, colorado m; **to see ~** ponerse*
hecho una furia or un basilisco; **to be in the ~**
estar* en números rojos

red: **~ admiral** n vanesa f roja; **~ carpet** n:
to roll out the **~ carpet for sb** recibir* a algn con
bombos y platillos or (Esp) a bombo y platillo;
R~ Cross n Cruz f Roja

redden /'redn̩/ vi enrojecerse*

redecorate /ˌriː'dekəreɪt/ vt/i pintar (y
empapelar)

redeem /rɪ'diːm/ vt **1** (a) ⟨good name⟩
rescatar (b) ⟨sinners⟩ redimir (c) **redeeming**
pres p: he has no **~ing features** no tiene ningún
punto a su favor **2** (from pawnshop) desempeñar

redefine /ˌriːdɪ'faɪn/ vt redefinir

redemption /rɪ'dempʃən/ n (saving) salvación
f; (Relig) redención f

redeploy /ˌriːdɪ'plɔɪ/ vt ⟨resources⟩ reorientar;
⟨staff⟩ asignar un nuevo destino a, reubicar*
(AmL); ⟨troops⟩ cambiar la disposición de

redevelop /ˌriːdɪ'veləp/ vt reurbanizar*

red: **~-haired** /'red'herd ǁ ˌred'heəd/ adj
pelirrojo; **~-handed** /'red'hændəd
ǁ ˌred'hændɪd/ adj: **to catch sb ~-handed** agarrar
or (esp Esp) coger* a algn con las manos en la
masa; **~head** n pelirrojo, -ja m,f, **~ herring** n
(in detective story) pista f falsa; **~-hot** /'red'hɑːt
ǁ ˌred'hɒt/ adj (pred **~ hot**) al rojo vivo

redial /'riː'daɪl ǁ ˌriː'daɪəl/ vi/t, (BrE) **-ll-** volver*
a marcar or (AmS tb) a discar

redirect /ˌriːdɪ'rekt, -daɪ- ǁ ˌriːdaɪ'rekt, -də-/ vt
(often pass) ⟨mail⟩ enviar* a una nueva
dirección; ⟨traffic⟩ desviar*

rediscover /ˌriːdɪ'skʌvər ǁ ˌriːdɪ'skʌvə(r)/ vt
redescubrir*, volver* a descubrir

redistribute /ˌriːdɪ'strɪbjət ǁ ˌriːdɪ'strɪbjuːt/ vt
redistribuir*

red: **~ light** n luz f roja, semáforo m en rojo,
alto m (Méx); **~-light district** /'red'laɪt/ n zona
f de tolerancia, zona f roja (AmL); **~neck** n (in
US) (pej) sureño reaccionario de la clase baja
rural

redo /ˌriː'duː/ vt (3rd pers sing pres **redoes**;
past **redid**; past p **redone**) rehacer*, volver* a
hacer

redouble /ˌriː'dʌbəl/ vt ⟨efforts⟩ redoblar

red pepper n (capsicum) ▶ PEPPER¹ 2

redraft /'riː'drɑːft ǁ ˌriː'drɑːft/ vt volver* a
redactar

redress¹ /rɪ'dres/ n reparación f

redress² vt ⟨wrong⟩ reparar; ⟨imbalance⟩
corregir*

red: **R~ Sea** n the R~ Sea el Mar Rojo; **~
tape** n (bureaucracy) trámites mpl burocráticos,
papeleo m (fam)

reduce /rɪ'duːs ǁ rɪ'djuːs/ vt **1** ⟨number/
amount⟩ reducir*; ⟨pressure/speed⟩ disminuir*,
reducir*; ⟨price/taxes⟩ reducir*, rebajar; ⟨pain⟩
aliviar; ⊖ reduce speed now disminuya la
velocidad **2** (break down, simplify) **to ~ sth TO sth**
reducir* algo A algo **3** **to ~ sb to tears** hacer*
llorar a algn

reduced /rɪ'duːst ǁ rɪ'djuːst/ adj reducido

reduction /rɪ'dʌkʃən/ n reducción f; (in prices,
charges) rebaja f

redundancy /rɪ'dʌndənsi/ n (pl **-cies**) (BrE
Lab Rel) despido m, cese m; (before n) **~ money** o
pay indemnización f (por despido or cese)

redundant /rɪ'dʌndənt/ adj (a) (superfluous)
superfluo (b) (esp BrE Lab Rel): **she was made ~**
la despidieron por reducción de planilla or (Esp)
de plantilla

reed /riːd/ n (a) (Bot) carrizo m, junco m (b)
(Mus) lengüeta f

reeducate /ˌriː'edʒəkeɪt ǁ ˌriː'edjʊkeɪt/ vt
reeducar*

reef /riːf/ n (Geog) arrecife m; (seen as hazard)
escollo m, arrecife m

reek /riːk/ vi (a) (stink) **to ~ (OF sth)** apestar or
heder* (A algo) (b) (have air of) **to ~ OF sth** ⟨of
corruption/fraud⟩ oler* A algo

reel¹ /riːl/ n (a) (for wire, thread, tape) carrete m
(b) (of film) rollo m, carrete m (esp Esp) (c) (fishing)
carrete m, carretel m

reel² vi tambalearse; **my head was ~ing** todo
me daba vueltas
▪ **reel in** [v + o + adv, v + adv + o] ⟨line⟩ enrollar
▪ **reel off** [v + o + adv, v + adv + o] recitar de un
tirón

reelect /ˌriːə'lekt ǁ ˌriːɪ'lekt/ vt reelegir*

reemerge /ˌriːə'mɜːrdʒ ǁ ˌriːɪ'mɜːdʒ/ vi (a)
(reappear) volver* a salir (b) (regain prominence)
resurgir*

reenact /ˌriːə'nækt ǁ ˌriːɪ'nækt/ vt ⟨historical
event⟩ recrear; ⟨crime⟩ reconstruir*

reenter /ˌriː'entər ǁ ˌriː'entə(r)/ vt volver* a
entrar en or (esp AmL) a

reexamine /ˌriːɪg'zæmən ǁ ˌriːɪg'zæmɪn/ vt
volver* a examinar

ref¹ /ref/ n (colloq) (= **referee**) árbitro, -tra m,f,
réferi mf (AmL)

ref² /ref/ (= **reference**) ref.

refectory /rɪ'fektəri/ n (pl **-ries**) comedor m

refer /rɪ'fɜːr ǁ rɪ'fɜː(r)/ **-rr-** vt remitir; **to ~ sb to
a specialist** (Med) mandar or (AmL) derivar a algn
a un especialista
▪ **refer to** [v + prep + o] (a) (mention) hacer*
referencia a, aludir a (b) (allude to) referirse* a
(c) ⟨dictionary/notes⟩ consultar

referee¹ /ˌrefə'riː/ n **1** (a) (Sport) árbitro, -tra
m,f, réferi mf (AmL) (b) (in dispute) árbitro -tra m,f
2 (for job candidate) (BrE): **you need two ~s**
necesitas el aval de dos personas

referee² vt/i arbitrar

reference /'refrəns, 'refərəns/ n **1** (allusion)
alusión f, referencia f; **with ~ to** con referencia
or relación a **2** (a) (consultation) consulta f;
(before n) **~ book/library** obra f/biblioteca f de
consulta or de referencia (b) (indicator) referencia
f; (before n) **~ number** número m de referencia
3 (for job candidate — testimonial) referencia f,
informe m; (— person giving testimonial) (AmE): **you
need two ~s** necesitas el aval de dos personas

referendum /ˌrefə'rendəm/ n (pl **-dums** or
-da /-də/) referéndum m, referendo m

refill¹ /'riːfɪl/ n (for pen) repuesto m, recambio m;
(for lighter) carga f

refill² /'riː'fɪl/ vt volver* a llenar, rellenar

refine /rɪ'faɪn/ vt (a) ⟨sugar/oil⟩ refinar (b)
(improve) ⟨design/style⟩ pulir, perfeccionar

r

refined /rɪˈfaɪnd/ *adj* **(a)** ⟨person/manners⟩ refinado, fino **(b)** ⟨sugar/oil⟩ refinado

refinement /rɪˈfaɪnmənt/ *n* **(a)** (gentility, elegance) refinamiento *m*, finura *f* **(b)** (improvement) mejora *f*

refinery /rɪˈfaɪnəri/ *n* (*pl* **-ries**) refinería *f*

reflect /rɪˈflekt/ *vt* reflejar
■ ~ *vi* **1** (think) **to** ~ **(ON sth)** reflexionar *or* meditar (SOBRE algo) **2** «light/heat» reflejarse
■ **reflect on, reflect upon** [*v + prep + o*] repercutir en; **to** ~ **badly on sth/sb** perjudicar* algo/a algn

reflection /rɪˈflekʃən/ *n* **1** **(a)** (Opt, Phys) reflexión *f* **(b)** (image) reflejo *m*; (of situation, feeling) reflejo *m* **2** **(a)** (contemplation) reflexión *f*; **on** *o* **upon** ~ … pensándolo bien … **(b)** (comment) observación *f*

reflector /rɪˈflektər ‖rɪˈflektə(r)/ *n* (of light, heat) reflector *m*; (Auto) catafaros *m*

reflex /ˈriːfleks/ *n* reflejo *m*

reflexive /rɪˈfleksɪv/ *adj* reflexivo

reform¹ /rɪˈfɔːrm ‖rɪˈfɔːm/ *n* reforma *f*

reform² *vt* reformar

reformation /refərˈmeɪʃən ‖refəˈmeɪʃən/ *n* reforma *f*; **the Reformation** (Relig) la Reforma

reformatory /rɪˈfɔːrmətɔːri ‖rɪˈfɔːmətəri/ *n* (*pl* **-ries**, in US) reformatorio *m*

refrain¹ /rɪˈfreɪn/ *vi* (frml) **to** ~ **(FROM sth/-ING)** abstenerse* (DE algo/+ INF)

refrain² *n* (Lit, Mus) estribillo *m*

refresh /rɪˈfreʃ/ *vt* refrescar*

refreshing /rɪˈfreʃɪŋ/ *adj* ⟨drink/bath⟩ refrescante; ⟨sleep⟩ reparador; ⟨enthusiasm⟩ reconfortante

refreshments /rɪˈfreʃmənts/ *pl n* refrigerio *m*

refrigerate /rɪˈfrɪdʒəreɪt/ *vt* refrigerar

refrigerator /rɪˈfrɪdʒəreɪtər ‖rɪˈfrɪdʒəreɪtə(r)/ *n* nevera *f*, refrigerador *m*, frigorífico *m* (Esp), heladera *f* (RPl), refrigeradora *f* (Col, Per)

refuel /riːˈfjuːəl/, (BrE) **-ll-** *vt* reabastecer* de combustible
■ ~ *vi* repostar, reabastecerse* de combustible

refuge /ˈrefjuːdʒ/ *n* refugio *m*; **to take** ~ refugiarse

refugee /refjʊˈdʒiː/ *n* refugiado, -da *m,f*; ⟨before n⟩ ~ **camp** campamento *m* de refugiados

refund¹ /rɪˈfʌnd/ *vt* ⟨expenses/postage⟩ reembolsar

refund² /ˈriːfʌnd/ *n* reembolso *m*

refurbish /riːˈfɜːrbɪʃ ‖riːˈfɜːbɪʃ/ *vt* renovar*, hacer* reformas en; (restore) restaurar

refusal /rɪˈfjuːzəl/ *n* (of permission, request) denegación *f*; (of offer) rechazo *m*; (to do sth) negativa *f*

refuse¹ /rɪˈfjuːz/ *vt* ⟨offer/gift⟩ rechazar*, no aceptar, rehusar*; **to** ~ **to** + INF negarse* A + INF
■ ~ *vi* negarse*

refuse² /ˈrefjuːs/ *n* residuos *mpl*

refute /rɪˈfjuːt/ *vt* refutar, rebatir

regain /rɪˈgeɪn, ˈriː-/ *vt* recuperar, recobrar

regal /ˈriːgəl/ *adj* majestuoso, regio

regalia /rɪˈgeɪlɪə ‖rɪˈgeɪliːə/ *pl n* ropajes *mpl*

regard¹ /rɪˈgɑːrd ‖rɪˈgɑːd/ *vt* **1** **(a)** (consider) considerar; **he is very highly** ~**ed within the** profession está muy bien considerado en esa profesión **(b)** **as regards** en lo que se refiere a, en lo que atañe a **2** (look at) (liter) contemplar

regard² *n* **1** **(a)** (esteem): **to have a high** ~ **for sb** tener* muy buena opinión de algn, tener* a algn en gran estima **(b)** (consideration) consideración *f* **2** **regards** *pl* (greeting) saludos *mpl*, recuerdos *mpl* **3** (*in phrases*) **with regard to** (con) respecto a, con relación a, en relación con

regarding /rɪˈgɑːrdɪŋ ‖rɪˈgɑːdɪŋ/ *prep* (frml) en lo que concierne *or* respecta a, en lo que se refiere a

regardless /rɪˈgɑːrdləs ‖rɪˈgɑːdlɪs/ *adv* **(a)** (in spite of everything): **to carry on** ~ seguir* como si no pasara nada *or* (fam) como si tal cosa **(b)** **regardless of** ⟨as prep⟩: ~ **of the cost** cueste lo que cueste

regatta /rɪˈgætə/ *n* regata *f*

regenerate /rɪˈdʒenəreɪt/ *vt* (revive) revitalizar*; (Biol) regenerar

regent /ˈriːdʒənt/ *n* (ruler) regente *mf*

reggae /ˈregeɪ/ *n* reggae *m*

regime, régime /reɪˈʒiːm/ *n* **(a)** (rule) régimen *m* **(b)** (system) sistema *m*

regiment /ˈredʒəmənt ‖ˈredʒɪmənt/ *n* regimiento *m*

regimental /redʒəˈmentl ‖redʒɪˈmentl/ *adj* ⟨before n⟩ ⟨mascot/band⟩ del regimiento

region /ˈriːdʒən/ *n* **(a)** (Anat, Geog) (area) región *f*, zona *f* **(b)** **in the region of** alrededor de

regional /ˈriːdʒənl/ *adj* regional

register¹ /ˈredʒəstər ‖ˈredʒɪstə(r)/ *n* **(a)** (record, list) registro *m*; (in school) (BrE) lista *f*; **to take** *o* **call the** ~ (BrE Educ) pasar lista **(b)** (Mus) registro *m*

register² *vt* **1** (record) ⟨death/birth⟩ inscribir*, registrar; ⟨ship/car⟩ matricular **2** (Post) mandar certificado *or* (Méx) registrado **3** **registered** *past p*: **(a)** (Fin, Adm) ~**ed trademark** marca *f* registrada; ~**ed nurse** enfermero titulado, enfermera titulada *m,f* **(b)** (Post) certificado *or* (Méx) registrado **4** **(a)** (make known) ⟨complaint⟩ presentar **(b)** «dial» registrar, marcar*
■ ~ *vi* **1** (enroll) inscribirse*; (Educ) matricularse, inscribirse*; (at a hotel) registrarse **2** (show, be revealed) ser* detectado **3** (be understood, remembered): **eventually it** ~**ed who he was** al final caí en la cuenta de quién era

registrar /ˈredʒəstrɑːr ‖redʒɪsˈtrɑː(r), ˈredʒɪstrɑː(r)/ *n* **(a)** (Soc Adm) funcionario encargado de llevar los registros de nacimientos, defunciones, etc **(b)** (in university, college) secretario, -ria *m,f* de admisiones

registration /redʒəˈstreɪʃən ‖redʒɪsˈtreɪʃən/ *n* **(a)** (enrollment) inscripción *f*, matrícula *f*; (Educ) inscripción *f*, matriculación *f* **(b)** (BrE Auto) ⟨before n⟩ ~ **number** (número *m* de) matrícula *f*

registry /ˈredʒəstri ‖ˈredʒɪstri/ *n* (*pl* **-tries**) registro *m*; (at university) secretaría *f*; (at church) ≈ sacristía *f*

registry office *n* (in UK) ≈ juzgado *m* (de paz)

regret¹ /rɪˈgret/ *vt* **-tt-** arrepentirse* de, lamentar; **we** ~ **to inform you that** … lamentamos comunicarle *or* informarle que …

regret² *n* (sadness) pesar *m*; (remorse) arrepentimiento *m*

regretful /rɪ'gretfəl/ *adj* ‹*expression*› de pesar

regretfully /rɪ'gretfəli/ *adv* con pesar; ‹*indep*› muy a mi *(or* nuestro *etc)* pesar, lamentablemente

regrettable /rɪ'gretəbəl/ *adj* lamentable

regrettably /rɪ'gretəbli/ *adv* lamentablemente

regroup /'ri:'gru:p/ *vi* reagruparse

regular¹ /'regjələr ǁ'regjʊlə(r)/ *adj* **1** **(a)** ‹*pulse*› regular; ‹*breathing*› acompasado; **at ~ intervals** (in time) con regularidad; (in space) a intervalos regulares **(b)** ‹*customer/reader*› habitual, asiduo; **a ~ income** una fuente regular de ingresos; **on a ~ basis** con regularidad **(c)** (customary) habitual **2** (even, symmetrical) ‹*shape*› regular **3** (Ling) ‹*verb/plural*› regular **4** (colloq) ‹*as intensifier*› verdadero

regular² *n* cliente *mf* habitual, asiduo, -dua *m,f*

regularity /'regjə'lærəti ǁ,regjʊ'lærəti/ *n* regularidad *f*

regularly /'regjələrli ǁ'regjʊləli/ *adv* con regularidad, regularmente; (frequently) con frecuencia

regulate /'regjəleɪt ǁ'regjʊleɪt/ *vt* regular

regulation /'regjə'leɪʃən ǁ,regjʊ'leɪʃən/ *n* **1** (rule) norma *f*, regla *f*; ‹*before n*› ‹*dress/haircut*› reglamentario **2** (control, adjustment) regulación *f*

regurgitate /rɪ'gɜ:rdʒəteɪt ǁrɪ'gɜ:dʒɪteɪt/ *vt* ‹*food*› regurgitar; ‹*information*› repetir* mecánicamente

rehabilitate /'ri:hə'bɪləteɪt, 'ri:ə- ǁ,ri:hə'bɪlɪteɪt, ,ri:ə-/ *vt* rehabilitar

rehabilitation /'ri:hə'bɪlə'teɪʃən, 'ri:ə- ǁ,ri:hə,bɪlɪ'teɪʃən, ,ri:ə-/ *n* rehabilitación *f*

rehearsal /rɪ'hɜ:rsəl ǁrɪ'hɜ:səl/ *n* ensayo *m*

rehearse /rɪ'hɜ:rs ǁrɪ'hɜ:s/ *vt/i* ensayar

reheat /'ri:'hi:t/ *vt* recalentar*

rehouse /'ri:'haʊz/ *vt* realojar

reign¹ /reɪn/ *n* reinado *m*

reign² *vi* **(a)** «*monarch*» reinar **(b)** **reigning** *pres p* ‹*monarch*› reinante; ‹*champion*› actual

reimburse /'ri:ɪm'bɜ:rs ǁ,ri:ɪm'bɜ:s/ *vt* reembolsar

rein /reɪn/ *n* (Equ) rienda *f*; **to give free ~ to sb** darle* carta blanca a algn

reincarnation /'ri:ɪnkɑ:r'neɪʃən ǁ,ri:ɪnkɑ:'neɪʃən/ *n* reencarnación *f*

reindeer /'reɪndɪr ǁ'reɪndɪə(r)/ *n* (*pl* ~) reno *m*

reinforce /'ri:ɪn'fɔ:rs ǁ,ri:ɪn'fɔ:s/ *vt* reforzar*

reinforcement /'ri:ɪn'fɔ:rsmənt ǁ,ri:ɪn'fɔ:smənt/ *n* **(a)** (strengthening) refuerzo *m* **(b)** **reinforcements** *pl* refuerzos *mpl*

reinstate /'ri:ɪn'steɪt/ *vt* ‹*worker*› reintegrar, reincorporar; ‹*official*› restituir* en el cargo

reintegrate /ri:'ɪntəgreɪt/ *vt* reintegrar; **they must be ~d into society** es preciso reinsertarlos en la sociedad

reintegration /'ri:,ɪntə'greɪʃən/ *n* reintegración *f*; (into society) reinserción *f* social

reissue /'ri:'ɪʃu:/ *vt* ‹*book/record*› reeditar; ‹*document*› reexpedir*

reiterate /ri:'ɪtəreɪt/ *vt* (frml) reiterar, repetir*

reject¹ /rɪ'dʒekt/ *vt* rechazar*

reject² /'ri:dʒekt/ *n* (flawed product) artículo *m* (*or* producto *m etc*) defectuoso

rejection /rɪ'dʒekʃən/ *n* rechazo *m*; (following job application) respuesta *f* negativa

rejoice /rɪ'dʒɔɪs/ *vi* alegrarse mucho, regocijarse (liter)

rejoin /'ri:'dʒɔɪn/ *vt* ‹*regiment/team*› reincorporarse a; ‹*firm*› reincorporarse a, reintegrarse a

rejuvenate /rɪ'dʒu:vəneɪt/ *vt* rejuvenecer*

rekindle /'ri:'kɪndl/ *vt* ‹*fire*› reavivar; ‹*desire*› reavivar

relapse¹ /'ri:læps/ *n* recaída *f*

relapse² /rɪ'læps/ *vi* recaer*, tener* *or* sufrir una recaída

relate /rɪ'leɪt/ *vt* **1** (link) **to ~ sth TO sth** relacionar algo CON algo **2** (tell) (frml) ‹*story*› relatar, referir* (liter)
■ ~ *vi* **1** **(a)** (be connected with) **to ~ TO sth** estar* relacionado CON algo **(b) relating to** ‹*as prep*› relativo a, relacionado con **2** (understand, sympathize with) **to ~ TO sb** sintonizar* CON algn; **to ~ TO sth** identificarse* CON algo

related /rɪ'leɪtəd ǁrɪ'leɪtɪd/ *adj* **(a)** (of same family) ‹*pred*› **to be ~ (TO sb)** ser* pariente (DE algn), estar* emparentado (CON algn) **(b)** ‹*ideas/questions/subjects*› relacionado, afín

relation /rɪ'leɪʃən/ *n* **1** (relative) pariente *mf*, pariente, -ta *m,f*, familiar *m* **2** **(a)** (connection) relación *f* **(b) in relation to** ‹*as prep*› en relación con, con relación a **3 relations** *pl* relaciones *fpl*; **sexual ~s** relaciones sexuales

relationship /rɪ'leɪʃənʃɪp/ *n* **1** (between people) relación *f* **2** (between things, events) relación *f* **3** (kinship) (TO sb) parentesco *m* (CON algn)

relative¹ /'relətɪv/ *n* pariente *mf*, pariente, -ta *m,f*, familiar *mf*

relative² *adj* **(a)** (comparative): **the ~ merits of** los pros y los contras de **(b)** (not absolute) relativo; **it's all ~** (set phrase) todo es relativo (fr hecha) **(c) relative to** (compared to) en comparación con

relatively /'relətɪvli/ *adv* relativamente

relax /rɪ'læks/ *vi* relajarse
■ ~ *vt* relajar; **she ~ed her grip** sujetó con menos fuerza

relaxation /'ri:læk'seɪʃən/ *n* (rest) relax *m*; (recreation) esparcimiento *m*, distracción *f*

relaxed /rɪ'lækst/ *adj* ‹*manner/person*› relajado; ‹*atmosphere/party*› informal

relaxing /rɪ'læksɪŋ/ *adj* relajante

relay¹ /'ri:leɪ/ *n* **(a)** (team) relevo *m*; **to work in ~s** trabajar en *or* por relevos **(b)** ~ **(race)** (Sport) carrera *f* de relevos *or* (AmL) de postas

relay² /'ri:leɪ, rɪ'leɪ/ *vt* transmitir

release¹ /rɪ'li:s/ *vt* **1** ‹*prisoner/hostage*› poner* en libertad, liberar **2** ‹*information*› hacer* público; ‹*record/book*› sacar* (a la venta); ‹*movie*› estrenar **3** (emit) ‹*gas*› despedir* **4** ‹*brake/clutch*› soltar*

release² *n* **1** (from prison, captivity) puesta *f* en libertad, liberación *f* **2** (of record) salida *f* al mercado; (of movie) estreno *m*; **in** *o* (BrE) **on general ~** en todos los cines

relegate /'releɡeɪt ǁ'relɪɡeɪt/ *vt* **(a)** (consign, ⋯⋗

demote) relegar* **(b)** (BrE Sport) (usu pass): **the team was ∼d to the third division** el equipo descendió or bajó a tercera división

relent /rɪ'lent/ vi «person» transigir*, ceder

relentless /rɪ'lentləs ‖rɪ'lentlɪs/ adj ‹enemy/ pursuer› implacable; ‹pursuit› incesante

relentlessly /rɪ'lentləsli ‖rɪ'lentlɪsli/ adv implacablemente

relevance /'reləvəns/ n (connection) relación f; (importance) relevancia f

relevant /'reləvənt/ adj ‹document/facts› pertinente, relevante

reliability /rɪˌlaɪə'bɪləti/ n (of worker) formalidad f, responsabilidad f; (of sources) fiabilidad f; (of vehicle) fiabilidad f

reliable /rɪ'laɪəbəl/ adj **(a)** ‹information/source› fidedigno; ‹witness› fiable, confiable (esp AmL) **(b)** ‹worker› responsable, de confianza; ‹vehicle› fiable

reliably /rɪ'laɪəbli/ adv: **I am ∼ informed that ...** sé de fuentes fidedignas que ..., sé de buena fuente que ...

reliant /rɪ'laɪənt/ adj (pred) **to be ∼ ON sth/sb** depender DE algo/algn

relic /'relɪk/ n reliquia f

relief /rɪ'liːf/ n **1** (from worry, pain) alivio m; **it's a ∼ that** the rain's stopped at last menos mal que ha parado de llover **2** (aid) ayuda f, auxilio m (de emergencia); **to be on ∼** (AmE) recibir prestaciones de la seguridad social **3** (replacement) relevo m **4** (Art, Geog) relieve m

relieve /rɪ'liːv/ vt **(a)** ‹pain› calmar, aliviar; ‹suffering› mitigar*, aliviar; ‹tension› aliviar; **to ∼ sb of his/her duties** relevar a algn de su cargo **(b)** ‹town/fortress› liberar **(c)** ‹guard/driver› relevar
■ v refl **to ∼ oneself** (euph) orinar

relieved /rɪ'liːvd/ adj aliviado; **to feel ∼** sentir* un gran alivio, sentirse* aliviado

religion /rɪ'lɪdʒən/ n religión f

religious /rɪ'lɪdʒəs/ adj religioso

religiously /rɪ'lɪdʒəsli/ adv religiosamente

relinquish /rɪ'lɪŋkwɪʃ/ vt renunciar a

relish¹ /'relɪʃ/ vt ‹meal/joke/success› saborear; **I don't ∼ the prospect of ...** no me entusiasma or no me hace ninguna gracia la perspectiva de ...

relish² n **1** (Culin) salsa o conserva que se come con carnes **2** (enjoyment): **with ∼** ‹eat/drink› con gusto, con fruición; ‹read/listen to› con placer, con deleite

relive /riː'lɪv/ vt revivir

relocate /'riːləʊ'keɪt/ vt trasladar
■ vi «company» trasladarse; «employee» mudarse or trasladarse de domicilio

reluctance /rɪ'lʌktəns/ n renuencia f (fml)

reluctant /rɪ'lʌktənt/ adj reacio, renuente

reluctantly /rɪ'lʌktəntli/ adv a su (or mi etc) pesar, a regañadientes

rely /rɪ'laɪ/ vi relies, relying, relied **(a)** (have confidence) **to ∼ ON** or **UPON sb/sth** contar* CON

algn/algo; **you can ∼ on me** puedes contar conmigo; **she can't be relied (up)on to help** no se puede contar con or confiar en que vaya a ayudar **(b)** (be dependent) **to ∼ ON sb/sth FOR sth** depender* DE algn/algo (PARA algo)

remain /rɪ'meɪn/ vi **1 (a)** (+ adj or adv compl) (continue to be) seguir*, continuar*; **her condition ∼s critical** su estado sigue siendo crítico; **he ∼ed silent** se mantuvo en silencio **(b)** (stay) quedarse, permanecer* (fml); **to ∼ behind** quedarse **2 (a)** (be left) quedar; **what still ∼s to be done?** ¿qué queda por hacer? **(b)**: **that ∼s to be seen** eso está por verse **(b) remaining** pres p: **the ∼ing ten pounds** las diez libras restantes or que quedan

remainder /rɪ'meɪndər ‖rɪ'meɪndə(r)/ n **the ∼** el resto

remains /rɪ'meɪnz/ pl n restos mpl; (of meal) sobras fpl, restos mpl

remake¹ /'riːmeɪk/ n nueva versión f

remake² /'riːˈmeɪk/ vt (past & past p **remade**) volver* a hacer, rehacer*

remand¹ /rɪ'mænd ‖rɪ'mɑːnd/ vt: **to be ∼ed on bail** quedar en libertad bajo fianza; **he was ∼ed in custody** se decretó su prisión preventiva

remand² n: **to be on ∼** (in detention) estar* en prisión preventiva

remand centre, **remand home** n (in UK) centro para menores en prisión preventiva

remark¹ /rɪ'mɑːrk ‖rɪ'mɑːk/ n comentario m, observación f

remark² vi **to ∼ ON** o **UPON sth** hacer* un comentario/comentarios ACERCA DE algo
■ ∼ vt observar, comentar

remarkable /rɪ'mɑːrkəbəl ‖rɪ'mɑːkəbəl/ adj ‹ability/likeness› notable; ‹achievement› sorprendente; ‹coincidence› extraordinario; ‹person› excepcional

remarkably /rɪ'mɑːrkəbli ‖rɪ'mɑːkəbli/ adv **(a)** (surprisingly) sorprendentemente **(b)** (exceptionally) ‹stupid› increíblemente

remarry /'riːˈmæri/ vi **-ries, -rying, -ried** volver* a casarse

remedial /rɪ'miːdiəl/ adj de recuperación

remedy¹ /'remədi/ n (pl **-dies**) remedio m

remedy² vt **-dies, -dying, -died** ‹mistake/ situation› remediar; ‹injustice/evil› reparar

remember /rɪ'membər ‖rɪ'membə(r)/ vt **1** (recall) acordarse* de, recordar*; **I ∼ him saying something about ...** me acuerdo de or recuerdo que dijo algo de ... **2 (a)** (be mindful of, not forget): **to ∼ to + INF** acordarse* DE + INF **(b)** (commemorate) ‹dead› recordar* **(c)** (send regards): **∼ me to your mother** dale recuerdos or saludos a tu madre (de mi parte)
■ ∼ vi **(a)** (recall) acordarse*, recordar*; **try to ∼!** ¡haz memoria! **(b)** (be mindful, not forget) no olvidarse

remembrance /rɪ'membrəns/ n (liter or frml) recuerdo m, remembranza f (liter); **in ∼ of sth/sb** en memoria de algo/algn; (before n) **R∼ Sunday**

(in UK) *domingo de noviembre en que se conmemora a los caídos en las dos guerras mundiales*

remind /rɪ'maɪnd/ *vt* recordarle* a; **oh, that ~s me** ¡ah! por cierto ..., y a propósito ...; **to ~ sb + INF** recordarle* A algn QUE (+ *subj*); **he ~s me of my grandfather** me recuerda a mi abuelo

reminder /rɪ'maɪndər ‖ rɪ'maɪndə(r)/ *n* **(a) to serve as a ~ of sth** recordar* algo **(b)** (requesting payment) recordatorio *m* de pago

reminisce /'remə'nɪs ‖ ,remɪ'nɪs/ *vi* rememorar los viejos tiempos; **to ~ ABOUT sth** rememorar algo

reminiscences /'remə'nɪsnsɪz ‖ ,remɪ'nɪsnsɪz/ *pl n* recuerdos *mpl*, memorias *fpl*

reminiscent /'remə'nɪsnt ‖ ,remɪ'nɪsnt/ *adj* (*pred*) **to be ~ OF sb/sth** recordar* a algn/(a) algo

remiss /rɪ'mɪs/ *adj* (*fml*) (*pred*) negligente

remission /rɪ'mɪʃən/ *n* remisión *f*

remit /rɪ'mɪt/ *vt* **-tt-** (*fml*) **1** (send) remitir (*fml*) **2** (Law) (*sentence*) perdonar, condonar (*fml*)

remnant /'remnənt/ *n* **(a)** (leftover): **a ~ of the past** una reliquia del pasado; **the ~s of a meal** los restos de una comida **(b)** (Tex) retazo *m*, retal *m* (Esp)

remonstrate /rɪ'mɑːnstreɪt, 'remən- ‖ 'remənstreɪt/ *vi* protestar, quejarse; **to ~ with sb about sth** reprocharle algo a algn

remorse /rɪ'mɔːrs ‖ rɪ'mɔːs/ *n* remordimiento *m*

remorseful /rɪ'mɔːrsfəl ‖ rɪ'mɔːsfəl/ *adj* arrepentido

remorseless /rɪ'mɔːrsləs ‖ rɪ'mɔːslɪs/ *adj* despiadado

remote /rɪ'məʊt/ *adj* **-ter, -test** remoto

remote: ~ control *n* mando *m* a distancia, control *m* remoto; **~-controlled** /rɪ'məʊtkən'trəʊld/ *adj* (*pred* **~ controlled**) ⟨*TV/hi-fi*⟩ con mando a distancia *or* con control remoto; ⟨*model/toy*⟩ de control remoto

remotely /rɪ'məʊtli/ *adv* (at all, in the least) (*usu with neg*) remotamente

remould¹ /'riː'məʊld/ *vt* (BrE Auto) ▶ RETREAD¹

remould² /'riː'məʊld/ *n* (BrE Auto) ▶ RETREAD²

removable /rɪ'muːvəbəl/ *adj* ⟨*hood/lining*⟩ de quita y pon; ⟨*handle/shelf*⟩ desmontable

removal /rɪ'muːvəl/ *n* **1** (of contents) extracción *f*; (of appendix, tonsils) extirpación *f* **2** (of stain, unwanted hair) eliminación *f* **3** **(a)** (moving, taking away) traslado *m* **(b)** (from house to house) (BrE) mudanza *f*

remove /rɪ'muːv/ *vt* **1** **(a)** (take off) quitar, sacar* **(b)** (take out) ⟨*contents*⟩ sacar*; ⟨*tonsils/appendix*⟩ extirpar (*fml*); ⟨*bullet*⟩ extraer* (*fml*) **2** **(a)** (get rid of) ⟨*stain/grease*⟩ quitar; ⟨*unwanted hair*⟩ eliminar **(b)** ⟨*doubt*⟩ disipar; ⟨*threat*⟩ eliminar **3** (take away, move) ⟨*object*⟩ quitar; ⟨*person*⟩ sacar* **4** (dismiss from post, position) destituir*

remover /rɪ'muːvər ‖ rɪ'muːvə(r)/ *n* (substance): **makeup ~** desmaquillador *m*; **nail polish** *o* (BrE also) **nail varnish ~** quitaesmalte *m*

remuneration /rɪ'mjuːnə'reɪʃən/ *n* (*fml*) remuneración *f*

renaissance /'renə'sɑːns ‖ rɪ'neɪsəns/ *n* **(a) Renaissance** Renacimiento *m* **(b)** (revival) (liter) renacimiento *m*

rename /'riː'neɪm/ *vt* dar* un nuevo nombre a

render /'rendər ‖ 'rendə(r)/ *vt* **1** (make): **to ~ sth useless** hacer* que algo resulte inútil **2** (give, proffer) (*fml*) ⟨*thanks*⟩ dar*; ⟨*assistance*⟩ prestar; **for services ~ed** por servicios prestados **3** (translate) traducir*

rendezvous /'rɑːndeɪvuː ‖ 'rɒndɪvuː, -deɪvuː/ *n* (*pl* ~ /-z/) (meeting) encuentro *m*, cita *f*; (place) lugar *m* señalado para un encuentro *or* una cita

rendition /ren'dɪʃən/ *n* interpretación *f*

renegade /'renɪgeɪd/ *n* renegado, -da *m,f*

renew /rɪ'nuː ‖ rɪ'njuː/ *vt* **(a)** ⟨*hope/promise*⟩ renovar*; ⟨*efforts/friendship*⟩ reanudar; ⟨*library book*⟩ renovar* **(b)** renewed *past p* renovado

renewal /rɪ'nuːəl ‖ rɪ'njuːəl/ *n* renovación *f*

renounce /rɪ'naʊns/ *vt* **(a)** (cede) (*fml*) ⟨*claim/title*⟩ renunciar a **(b)** (reject) ⟨*religion*⟩ renunciar a

renovate /'renəveɪt/ *vt* renovar*

renovation /'renə'veɪʃən/ *n* renovación *f*

renown /rɪ'naʊn/ *n* renombre *m*, fama *f*

renowned /rɪ'naʊnd/ *adj* de renombre

rent¹ /rent/ *n* **(a)** (for accommodations, office) alquiler *m*, arrendamiento *m*, arriendo *m*, renta *f* (esp Méx) **(b)** (for boat, suit) (esp AmE) alquiler *m*, arriendo *m* (esp Andes), renta *f* (Méx)

rent² *vt* (a) (pay for) **to ~ sth** (FROM sb) alquilarle *or* arrendarle* *or* (Méx tb) rentarle algo (A algn) **(b)** ▶ RENT OUT
- **~ out** [v + o + adv, v + adv + o] alquilar, arrendar*

rental /'rentl/ *n* **(a)** (act of renting) alquiler *m*, arriendo *m* **(b)** (charge) alquiler *m*, renta *f* (Méx), arriendo *m* (esp Andes)

renunciation /rɪ'nʌnsi'eɪʃən/ *n* (*fml*) **(a)** (of faith) rechazo *m* **(b)** (of claim, right, title) renuncia *f*

reopen /'riː'əʊpən ‖ ,riː'əʊpən/ *vt* ⟨*book/road*⟩ volver* a abrir; ⟨*negotiations/hostilities*⟩ reanudar; ⟨*criminal case*⟩ reabrir*
- **~** *vi* abrir* de nuevo

reorganize /'riː'ɔːrgənaɪz ‖ ,riː'ɔːgənaɪz/ *vt* reorganizar*

rep /rep/ *n* (sales ~) representante *mf or* agente *mf* (comercial); **a union ~** un/una representante *or* (Esp) un/una enlace sindical

repair¹ /rɪ'per ‖ rɪ'peə(r)/ *vt* ⟨*machinery/roof*⟩ arreglar, reparar; ⟨*shoes/clothes*⟩ arreglar

repair² *n* arreglo *m*, reparación *f*; **the museum is closed for ~s** el museo está cerrado por obras; **in a good/bad state of ~, in good/bad ~** en buen/mal estado

repairer /rɪ'perər ‖ rɪ'peərə(r)/ *n* técnico, -ca *m,f*; **watch ~** (BrE) relojero, -ra *m,f*

repairman /rɪ'permæn ‖ rɪ'peəmæn/ *n* (*pl* **-men** /-men/-men) técnico *m*

repatriate /'riː'peɪtrieɪt ‖ ,riː'pætrieɪt/ *vt* repatriar

repay /'riː'peɪ/ *vt* (*past & past p* **repaid**) **(a)** ⟨*money/loan*⟩ devolver*; ⟨*debt*⟩ pagar*, cancelar **(b)** ⟨*kindness/favor*⟩ pagar*, corresponder a

repayment /'riː'peɪmənt/ *n* **(a)** (act of repaying) pago *m* **(b)** (installment) plazo *m*, cuota *f* (AmI)

repeal¹ /rɪ'piːl/ *vt* (Govt, Law) revocar*

repeal² n revocación f

repeat¹ /rɪ'piːt/ vt **1** **(a)** (say again) repetir* **(b)** (divulge) contar* **2** (do again) repetir*
■ v refl to ~ oneself repetirse*
■ ~ vi repetir*

repeat² n repetición f

repeated /rɪ'piːtəd ‖rɪ'piːtɪd/ adj (before n) ⟨attempts⟩ repetido, reiterado; ⟨requests⟩ reiterado

repeatedly /rɪ'piːtədli ‖rɪ'piːtɪdli/ adv repetidamente, reiteradamente

repel /rɪ'pel/ vt **-ll-** **(a)** ⟨enemy/army⟩ repeler; ⟨attack⟩ repeler, rechazar* **(b)** ⟨insects⟩ repeler, ahuyentar **(c)** (disgust) repeler, repugnar

repellant /rɪ'pelənt/ n: **insect ~** repelente m para insectos

repellent /rɪ'pelənt/ adj repelente

repent /rɪ'pent/ vi arrepentirse*

repentance /rɪ'pentns/ n arrepentimiento m

repentant /rɪ'pentnt/ adj arrepentido

repercussions /ˌriːpər'kʌʃənz ‖ˌriːpə'kʌʃənz/ pl n repercusiones fpl

repertoire /'repərtwɑːr ‖ 'repətwɑː(r)/ n repertorio m

repertory /'repərtɔːri ‖ 'repətəri/ n: **to be/act/ work in ~** trabajar en una compañía de repertorio

repetition /ˌrepə'tɪʃən/ n repetición f

repetitious /ˌrepə'tɪʃəs/ adj repetitivo

repetitive /rɪ'petətɪv/ adj repetitivo

repetitive strain injury n lesión f por fatiga crónica

rephrase /ˌriː'freɪz/ vt expresar de otra manera

replace /rɪ'pleɪs/ vt **1** **(a)** (take the place of) sustituir*, reemplazar* **(b)** ⟨lost item⟩ reponer*; ⟨broken window/battery⟩ cambiar **2** (put back in its place) volver* a poner or colocar; ⟨lid⟩ volver* a poner; ⟨receiver⟩ colgar*

replacement /rɪ'pleɪsmənt/ n **(a)** (act) sustitución f, reemplazo m **(b)** (person) sustituto, -ta m,f **(c)** (object): **I'll buy you a ~** te compraré uno nuevo

replay¹ /ˌriː'pleɪ/ vt **(a)** (Sport) ⟨game/match⟩ volver* a jugar, repetir* **(b)** (Audio, Video) volver* a poner

replay² /'riːpleɪ/ n (Sport) repetición f (de la jugada)

replenish /rɪ'plenɪʃ/ vt ⟨stock⟩ reponer*

replete /rɪ'pliːt/ adj (liter) ~ **WITH sth** repleto DE algo

replica /'replɪkə/ n (pl **-cas**) réplica f, reproducción f

reply¹ /rɪ'plaɪ/ n (pl **replies**) (spoken, written) respuesta f, contestación f; **in ~ to your letter** en respuesta a su carta

reply² vi/t replies, replying, replied responder, contestar

report¹ /rɪ'pɔːrt ‖rɪ'pɔːt/ n **1** **(a)** (account) informe m; (piece of news) noticia f; (in newspaper) reportaje m, crónica f **(b)** (evaluation) informe m, reporte m (Méx); **medical ~** parte m médico; **(school) ~** boletín m or (Méx) boleta f de calificaciones **2** (sound) estallido m

report² vt **1** **(a)** (relate, announce): **several**

people ~ed seeing the tiger varias personas dijeron haber visto al tigre; **he is ~ed to be very rich** se dice que es muy rico **(b)** (Journ) «reporter/ media» informar sobre
2 **(a)** (notify) ⟨accident⟩ informar de, dar* parte de; ⟨crime⟩ denunciar, dar* parte de, reportar (AmL); **to ~ sth TO sb** dar* parte DE algo A algn **(b)** (denounce) denunciar, reportar (AmL)
■ ~ vi **1** (Journ) «reporter» informar
2 (present oneself) presentarse, reportarse (AmL); **to ~ sick** dar* parte de enfermo
■ **report back** [v + adv] **(a)** (return): **to ~ back (to base)** regresar a la base **(b)** (give report) **to ~ back (TO sb)** presentar un informe (A algn)

report card n (AmE Educ) boletín m or (Méx) boleta f de calificaciones

reported speech /rɪ'pɔːrtəd ‖rɪ'pɔːtɪd/ n estilo m indirecto

reporter /rɪ'pɔːrtər ‖rɪ'pɔːtə(r)/ n periodista mf, reportero, -tera m,f

repose /rɪ'pəʊz/ n (liter) reposo m

repossess /ˌriːpə'zes/ vt ⟨car/house⟩ recuperar la posesión de (por falta de pago)

reprehensible /ˌreprɪ'hensəbəl/ adj reprensible

represent /ˌreprɪ'zent/ vt **1** **(a)** (stand for) representar **(b)** (constitute) representar, constituir* **2** (act as representative for) ⟨client⟩ representar **3** (fml) (describe) presentar

representation /ˌreprɪzen'teɪʃən/ n representación f

representative¹ /ˌreprɪ'zentətɪv/ n **(a)** representante mf **(b)** (in US) (Govt) representante mf, diputado, -da m,f **(c)** (sales ~) representante mf or agente mf comercial

representative² adj representativo

repress /rɪ'pres/ vt reprimir

repression /rɪ'preʃən/ n represión f

repressive /rɪ'presɪv/ adj represivo

reprieve¹ /rɪ'priːv/ n (Law) indulto m

reprieve² vt indultar

reprimand¹ /'reprəmænd ‖ 'reprɪmɑːnd/ n reprimenda f

reprimand² vt reprender

reprint¹ /'riːprɪnt/ n (Publ) reimpresión f; (Phot) copia f

reprint² /ˌriː'prɪnt/ vt (Publ) reimprimir*

reprisal /rɪ'praɪzəl/ n represalia f

reproach¹ /rɪ'prəʊtʃ/ vt **to ~ sb FOR -ING**: **he ~ed her for not having written to him** le reprochó que no le hubiera escrito

reproach² n reproche m; **above o beyond ~** irreprochable, intachable

reproachful /rɪ'prəʊtʃfəl/ adj (lleno) de reproche

reproduce /ˌriːprə'duːs ‖ˌriːprə'djuːs/ vt reproducir*
■ ~ vi (Biol) reproducirse*

reproduction /ˌriːprə'dʌkʃən/ n reproducción f

reproductive /ˌriːprə'dʌktɪv/ adj reproductor

reproof /rɪ'pruːf/ n (fml) reprobación f

reprove /rɪ'pruːv/ vt (fml) **to ~ sb (FOR sth)** reprender or (fml) reconvenir* a algn (POR algo)

reptile /'reptl, -taɪl ‖ 'reptaɪl/ n reptil m

republic /rɪˈpʌblɪk/ n república f

republican¹ /rɪˈpʌblɪkən/ adj (a) (of a republic) republicano (b) **Republican** (in US) republicano

republican² n (a) (supporter of republic) republicano, -na m,f (b) **Republican** (in US) republicano, -na m,f

repudiate /rɪˈpjuːdieɪt/ vt (a) (deny) ‹accusation› rechazar*, negar* (b) ‹violence/family› repudiar

repugnance /rɪˈpʌgnəns/ n repugnancia f

repugnant /rɪˈpʌgnənt/ adj repugnante

repulse /rɪˈpʌls/ vt repeler, rechazar*

repulsion /rɪˈpʌlʃən/ n (frml) repulsión f

repulsive /rɪˈpʌlsɪv/ adj repulsivo, repugnante

reputable /ˈrepjətəbəl ‖ˈrepjʊtəbəl/ adj acreditado (frml), reputado (frml)

reputation /ˌrepjəˈteɪʃən ‖ˌrepjʊˈteɪʃən/ n reputación f; good/bad ∼ buena/mala reputación or fama; a ∼ **FOR** sth fama DE algo

repute /rɪˈpjuːt/ n (frml) reputación f, fama f; of ∼ de renombre

reputed /rɪˈpjuːtəd ‖rɪˈpjuːtɪd/ adj presunto, supuesto; she is ∼ to be the best in the world está considerada como la mejor del mundo

reputedly /rɪˈpjuːtədli ‖rɪˈpjʊtɪdli/ adv (indep) según se dice or cree

request¹ /rɪˈkwest/ n (a) (polite demand) petición f, pedido m (esp AmL), solicitud f (frml); ∼ **FOR** sth petición (or pedido etc) DE algo (b) (for song) petición f, pedido m (esp AmL)

request² vt pedir*, solicitar (frml)

requiem /ˈrekwiəm/ n réquiem m

require /rɪˈkwaɪr ‖rɪˈkwaɪə(r)/ vt [1] (a) (need) necesitar; (call for) ‹patience/dedication› requerir*, exigir* (b) (demand) to ∼ sb/sth to + INF requerir* que algn/algo (+ subj); I shall do all that is ∼d of me haré todo lo que me corresponda [2] **required** past p (a) ‹dose/amount› necesario (b) (compulsory) ‹reading/viewing› obligado

requirement /rɪˈkwaɪrmənt ‖rɪˈkwaɪəmənt/ n (a) (usu pl) (need) necesidad f (b) (condition) requisito m

requisite /ˈrekwəzət ‖ˈrekwɪzɪt/ adj (frml) necesario, requerido

requisition /ˌrekwəˈzɪʃən ‖ˌrekwɪˈzɪʃən/ vt requisar

reroute /ˌriːˈruːt/ vt desviar*

reschedule /ˌriːˈskedʒuːl ‖ˌriːˈʃedjuːl/ vt ‹meeting› cambiar la hora/fecha de

rescind /rɪˈsɪnd/ vt (frml) ‹contract› rescindir*; ‹order/ruling› revocar*; ‹law› derogar*

rescue¹ /ˈreskjuː/ n rescate m; they went to his ∼ acudieron a socorrerlo (liter), fueron or (liter) acudieron en su auxilio

rescue² vt rescatar, salvar

rescuer /ˈreskjuər ‖ˈreskjuːə(r)/ n salvador, -dora m,f

research¹ /rɪˈsɜːrtʃ, ˈriːsɜːrtʃ ‖rɪˈsɜːtʃ/ n investigación f; ∼ **INTO/ON** sth investigación SOBRE algo

research² vi investigar*
■ ∼ vt ‹causes/problem› investigar*, estudiar; this article is well ∼ed este artículo está bien documentado

researcher /rɪˈsɜːrtʃər ‖rɪˈsɜːtʃə(r)/ n investigador, -dora m,f

resemblance /rɪˈzembləns/ n parecido m, semejanza f; ∼ **TO** sb/sth parecido CON algn/algo

resemble /rɪˈzembəl/ vt parecerse* a

resent /rɪˈzent/ vt ‹person› guardarle rencor a; he ∼ed her success le molestaba que ella tuviera éxito; I ∼ having to help him me molesta tener que ayudarle

resentful /rɪˈzentfəl/ adj ‹person› resentido, rencoroso; ‹air/look› de resentimiento

resentment /rɪˈzentmənt/ n resentimiento m, rencor m

reservation /ˌrezərˈveɪʃən ‖ˌrezəˈveɪʃən/ n (a) (booking) reserva f, reservación f (AmL) (b) (doubt, qualification) reserva f; without ∼ sin reservas (c) (land) (in US) reserva f, reservación f (AmL)

reserve¹ /rɪˈzɜːrv ‖rɪˈzɜːv/ n [1] (stock) reserva f; to keep sth in ∼ ‹money/food› tener* algo reservado [2] (Sport) reserva mf [3] **reserves** pl (Mil) reservas fpl [4] (land) coto m, reserva f [5] (self-restraint) reserva f, cautela f

reserve² vt (a) (book) ‹room/table› reservar (b) (keep, save) reservar, guardar; to ∼ (one's) judgment reservarse la opinión

reserved /rɪˈzɜːrvd ‖rɪˈzɜːvd/ adj reservado

reservoir /ˈrezərvwɑːr ‖ˈrezəvwɑː(r)/ n embalse m, presa f, represa f (AmS)

reset /ˈriːˈset/ vt (pres p **resetting**; past & past p **reset**) (a) ‹alarm clock› (volver* a) poner*; ‹counter/dial› volver* a cero (b) (Med) ‹bone› colocar*

reshuffle /ˈriːˈʃʌfəl/ n reorganización f; cabinet ∼ remodelación f del gabinete

reside /rɪˈzaɪd/ vi (frml) residir (frml)

residence /ˈrezədəns ‖ˈrezɪdəns/ n [1] (a) (in a country) residencia f (b) (in building) (frml) residencia f; to take up ∼ instalarse (c) ∼ hall (AmE) residencia f universitaria or estudiantes, colegio m mayor (Esp) [2] (home) residencia f

resident¹ /ˈrezədənt ‖ˈrezɪdənt/ n (a) (in country) residente mf (b) (of district) vecino, -na m,f

resident² adj residente

residential /ˌrezəˈdentʃəl ‖ˌrezɪˈdenʃəl/ adj ‹area/suburb› residencial; ‹course› con alojamiento para los asistentes

residue /ˈrezəduː ‖ˈrezɪdjuː/ n residuo m

resign /rɪˈzaɪn/ vi renunciar, dimitir; to ∼ **FROM** sth renunciar A algo, dimitir algo
■ v refl to ∼ oneself (**TO** sth/-ING) resignarse (A algo/+ INF)

resignation /ˌrezɪgˈneɪʃən/ n [1] (from job, position) renuncia f, dimisión f [2] (acceptance, submission) resignación f

resigned /rɪˈzaɪnd/ adj resignado

resilience /rɪˈzɪliəns ‖rɪˈzɪliːəns/ n (a) (of person) capacidad f de recuperación, resistencia f (b) (of material) elasticidad f

resilient /rɪˈzɪliənt ‖rɪˈzɪlɪənt/ adj (a) ‹person› fuerte, con capacidad de recuperación (b) ‹material› elástico

resin /ˈrezn ‖ˈrezɪn/ n resina f

resist /rɪ'zɪst/ vt resistir; ‹change/plan› oponer* resistencia a; **I can't ~ chocolate** el chocolate me vuelve loco; **to ~ -ING** resistirse A + INF

resistance /rɪ'zɪstəns/ n resistencia f; **the ~** la resistencia

resistant /rɪ'zɪstənt/ adj resistente

resit¹ /'riːsɪt/ vt (pres p **resitting**; past & past p **resat** /'riː'sæt/) (BrE) ‹examination› volver* a presentarse a

resit² /'riːsɪt/ n (BrE): **to do a ~** volver* a examinarse

resolute /'rezəluːt/ adj resuelto, decidido

resolution /rezə'luːʃən/ n (a) (decision) determinación f, propósito m; **New Year's ~s** buenos propósitos de Año Nuevo (b) (in US, passed by legislature) resolución f

resolve¹ /rɪ'zɑːlv ‖ rɪ'zɒlv/ n resolución f

resolve² vt (a) (clear up) ‹difficulty› resolver*; ‹differences› saldar, resolver (b) (decide) **to ~ (to + INF)** resolver* or decidir (+ INF)

resonance /'reznəns ‖ 'rezənəns/ n resonancia f

resonant /'reznənt ‖ 'rezənənt/ adj resonante

resort /rɪ'zɔːrt ‖ rɪ'zɔːt/ n **1** (for vacations) centro m turístico or vacacional; **a seaside ~** un centro turístico costero, un balneario (AmL); **a ski ~** una estación de esquí **2** (recourse) recurso m; **as a/the last ~** como último recurso

■ **resort** [v + prep + o]: **to ~ to force/violence** recurrir a la fuerza/violencia; **they had to ~ to strike action** no les quedó más remedio que ir a la huelga

resound /rɪ'zaʊnd/ vi retumbar, resonar*

resounding /rɪ'zaʊndɪŋ/ adj (before n) (a) ‹cheers/explosion› retumbante, resonante (b) ‹success/failure› rotundo

resource /'riːsɔːrs ‖ rɪ'zɔːs/ n recurso m; **natural/human ~s** recursos naturales/humanos

resourceful /rɪ'sɔːrsfəl ‖ rɪ'zɔːsfəl/ adj de recursos

respect¹ /rɪ'spekt/ n **1** (a) (esteem) respeto m; **to have ~ for sb** respetar algn (b) (consideration) consideración f, respeto m (c) **respects** pl respetos mpl **2** (a) (way, aspect) sentido m, respecto m; **in this ~** en cuanto a esto, en este sentido (b) **with respect to** (frml) (introducing subject) en lo que concierne a (frml); (in relation to) con respecto a

respect² vt respetar

respectable /rɪ'spektəbəl/ adj **1** (socially acceptable) ‹person/conduct› decente, respetable **2** (a) (quite large) ‹amount/salary› respetable (b) (reasonably good) ‹performance/score› digno, aceptable

respected /rɪ'spektəd ‖ rɪ'spektɪd/ adj respetado

respectful /rɪ'spektfəl/ adj respetuoso

respecting /rɪ'spektɪŋ/ prep (frml) en lo que concierne a (frml)

respective /rɪ'spektɪv/ adj (before n) respectivo

respiration /respə'reɪʃən ‖ respɪ'reɪʃən/ n respiración f

respirator /'respəreɪtər ‖ 'respɪreɪtə(r)/ n (a) (Med) respirador m (b) (mask) máscara f de oxígeno

respiratory /'respərətɔːri ‖ rɪ'spɪrətəri/ adj respiratorio

respite /'respət ‖ 'respaɪt/ n (no pl) respiro m, descanso m; **without ~** sin respiro

resplendent /rɪ'splendənt/ adj resplandeciente

respond /rɪ'spɑːnd ‖ rɪ'spɒnd/ vi (a) (reply) responder, contestar (b) (react) responder, reaccionar

response /rɪ'spɑːns ‖ rɪ'spɒns/ n (a) (reply) respuesta f (b) (reaction) respuesta f; (to news) reacción f

responsibility /rɪspɑːnsə'bɪləti ‖ rɪspɒnsə'bɪləti/ n (pl **-ties**) (a) (task, duty) responsabilidad f (b) (authority, accountability) responsabilidad f; **to take ~ for sth** responsabilizarse* or encargarse* de algo (c) (liability, blame) responsabilidad f; **they took full ~ for the disaster** aceptaron ser responsables del desastre

responsible /rɪ'spɑːnsəbəl ‖ rɪ'spɒnsəbəl/ adj (a) (accountable) (pred) **to be ~ (FOR sth)**: **who's ~?** ¿quién es el responsable?; **a build-up of gas was ~ for the explosion** una acumulación de gas fue la causa de la explosión; **to hold sb ~ for sth** responsabilizar* or hacer* responsable a algn de algo (b) (in charge) (pred) **to be ~ FOR sth** ser* responsable DE algo (c) (trustworthy) responsable, formal (d) (before n) ‹post› de responsabilidad

responsibly /rɪ'spɑːnsəbli ‖ rɪ'spɒnsɪbli/ adv con responsabilidad, responsablemente

responsive /rɪ'spɑːnsɪv ‖ rɪ'spɒnsɪv/ adj ‹brakes/engine› sensible; ‹person/audience› receptivo

rest¹ /rest/ n

I **1** (a) (break) descanso m; **to have a ~** tomarse un descanso (b) (relaxation) descanso m, reposo m; **try to get some ~** trata de descansar un poco **2** (motionlessness) **to come to ~** detenerse* **3** (support) apoyo m **4** (Mus) silencio m

II (remainder) **the ~**: **the ~ of the money** el resto del dinero; **the ~ of the children** los demás niños

rest² vi **1** (relax) descansar **2** (a) (be supported) **to ~ ON sth** (Const) descansar or apoyarse EN or SOBRE algo (b) (be based, depend) **to ~ ON sth** «argument/theory» descansar SOBRE algo (c) (stop) **to ~ ON sth/sb** «eyes/gaze» detenerse* SOBRE algo/algn **3** (be responsible of) **to ~ WITH sb** «responsibility» recaer* SOBRE algn

■ **~ vt** **1** (relax) descansar **2** (place for support) apoyar

■ **rest up** [v + adv] (AmE) descansar

rest area n (AmE) área f‡ de reposo

restaurant /'restərənt ‖ 'restrɒnt/ n restaurante m, restorán m

restaurant car n (BrE) coche-comedor m, vagón m restaurante

restful /'restfəl/ adj tranquilo, apacible
restless /'restləs/ adj ⟨person/manner⟩ inquieto; ⟨waves/wind⟩ (liter) agitado
restoration /ˌrestə'reɪʃən/ n **1** **(a)** (of order, peace) restablecimiento m **(b)** (to throne, power) restauración f, reinstauración f **2** (of building, painting) restauración f
restore /rɪ'stɔːr ‖rɪ'stɔː(r)/ vt **1** **(a)** (re-establish) ⟨order/peace⟩ restablecer*; ⟨confidence/health/energy⟩ devolver*; ⟨monarchy/king⟩ restaurar, reinstaurar **(b)** (give back) (frml) restituir* (frml) **2** ⟨building/painting⟩ restaurar
restrain /rɪ'streɪn/ vt contener*
▪ v refl to ~ oneself contenerse*, refrenarse
restrained /rɪ'streɪnd/ adj ⟨person/behavior⟩ moderado, comedido; ⟨colors/style⟩ sobrio
restraint /rɪ'streɪnt/ n **(a)** (self-control) compostura f, circunspección f **(b)** (restriction) limitación f, restricción f
restrict /rɪ'strɪkt/ vt ⟨power/freedom/access⟩ restringir*, limitar; ⟨imports/movements⟩ restringir*
restricted /rɪ'strɪktəd ‖rɪ'strɪktɪd/ adj **(a)** ⟨number/space⟩ limitado **(b)** ⟨information⟩ confidencial; ~ area (Mil) zona f restringida
restriction /rɪ'strɪkʃən/ n restricción f
restrictive /rɪ'strɪktɪv/ adj restrictivo
rest room n (AmE) baño m, servicio(s) m(pl)
restructure /ˌriː'strʌktʃər ‖ˌriː'strʌktʃə(r)/ vt reestructurar
rest stop (AmE) ▶ REST AREA
result¹ /rɪ'zʌlt/ n **1** **(a)** (consequence) resultado m; the company collapsed, with the ~ that … la compañía quebró, y como consecuencia … **(b)** (of calculation, exam, contest) resultado m **2** **(a)** as a result (as linker) por consiguiente, por ende (frml) **(b)** as a result of (as prep) a raíz de
result² vi: to ~ in traer* como consecuencia, resultar en; it could ~ in his dismissal podría ocasionar or acarrear su despido
resultant /rɪ'zʌltənt/, **resulting** /rɪ'zʌltɪŋ/ adj (before n) consiguiente, resultante
resume /rɪ'zuːm ‖rɪ'zjuːm/ vt ⟨work/journey⟩ reanudar
▪ ~ vi «negotiations/work» reanudarse, continuar*
resumé /'rezəmeɪ, ˌrezə'meɪ ‖'rezjʊmeɪ/ n **(a)** (summary) resumen m **(b)** (of career) (AmE) currículum m (vitae), historial m personal
resurgence /rɪ'sɜːrdʒəns ‖rɪ'sɜːdʒəns/ n resurgimiento m, renacer m
resurrect /ˌrezə'rekt/ vt desenterrar*, resucitar
resurrection /ˌrezə'rekʃən/ n resurrección f
resuscitate /rɪ'sʌsəteɪt ‖rɪ'sʌsɪteɪt/ vt (Med) resucitar
resuscitation /rɪˌsʌsə'teɪʃən ‖rɪˌsʌsɪ'teɪʃən/ n (Med) resucitación f
retail¹ /'riːteɪl/ vt vender al por menor or al detalle
▪ ~ vi venderse al por menor
retail² n venta f al por menor or al detalle; (before n) ~ price precio m de venta al público, precio m al por menor
retailer /'riːteɪlər ‖'riːteɪlə(r)/ n minorista mf, detallista mf

retail price index n (BrE) índice m de precios al consumo
retain /rɪ'teɪn/ vt ⟨property/money⟩ quedarse con; ⟨authority/power⟩ retener*; ⟨heat⟩ conservar; ⟨moisture/water⟩ retener*; ⟨information⟩ retener*
retake¹ /'riːteɪk/ vt (past **retook**; past p **retaken**) (Educ) volver* a presentarse a, volver* a presentar
retake² /'riːteɪk/ n (of exam): to do a ~ volver* a examinarse
retaliate /rɪ'tælieɪt/ vi (Mil) tomar represalias
retaliation /rɪˌtæli'eɪʃən/ n represalias fpl
retarded /rɪ'tɑːrdəd ‖rɪ'tɑːdɪd/ adj (sometimes offensive) retrasado
retch /retʃ/ vi hacer* arcadas
retention /rɪ'tentʃən ‖rɪ'tenʃən/ n retención f
retentive /rɪ'tentɪv/ adj ⟨memory⟩ retentivo
rethink /ˌriː'θɪŋk/ vt (past & past p **rethought**) reconsiderar, replantearse
reticence /'retəsəns ‖'retɪsəns/ n reticencia f
reticent /'retəsənt ‖'retɪsənt/ adj reticente
retina /'retnə ‖'retɪnə/ n (pl **-nas** or **-nae** /-niː/) retina f
retinue /'retnuː ‖'retɪnjuː/ n séquito m, comitiva f
retire /rɪ'taɪr ‖rɪ'taɪə(r)/ vi **1** (from occupation) jubilarse, retirarse; «soldier/athlete» retirarse **2** **(a)** (retreat, withdraw) (frml) retirarse **(b)** (go to bed) (frml or hum) retirarse a sus (or mis etc) aposentos (frml o hum)
retired /rɪ'taɪrd ‖rɪ'taɪəd/ adj jubilado, retirado
retirement /rɪ'taɪrmənt ‖rɪ'taɪəmənt/ n (from job) jubilación f, retiro m
retiring /rɪ'taɪrɪŋ ‖rɪ'taɪərɪŋ/ adj (shy) retraído
retort¹ /rɪ'tɔːrt ‖rɪ'tɔːt/ vt replicar* (liter), contestar
retort² n réplica f (liter), contestación f
retrace /'riːtreɪs/ vt to ~ one's steps volver* sobre sus (or mis etc) pasos
retract /rɪ'trækt/ vt **(a)** ⟨allegation/statement⟩ retirar **(b)** ⟨undercarriage⟩ replegar*, levantar
retrain /ˌriː'treɪn/ vi hacer* un curso de reciclaje or recapacitación
retread¹ /ˌriː'tred/ vt (past and past p **~ed**) ⟨tire⟩ recauchutar, recauchar, reencauchar (AmC, Ven)
retread² /'riːtred/ n neumático m recauchutado or recauchado or (AmC, Ven) reencauchado, llanta f vulcanizada (AmL)
retreat¹ /rɪ'triːt/ vi retirarse
retreat² n **1** (Mil) retirada f, repliegue m **2** **(a)** (place) refugio m **(b)** (Relig) retiro m espiritual
retrial /ˌriː'traɪəl/ n nuevo juicio m
retribution /ˌretrə'bjuːʃən ‖ˌretrɪ'bjuːʃən/ n castigo m
retrieve /rɪ'triːv/ vt ⟨object/data⟩ recuperar
retriever /rɪ'triːvər ‖rɪ'triːvə(r)/ n perro m cobrador
retrograde /'retrəgreɪd/ adj retrógrado
retrospect /'retrəspekt/ n: in ~ mirando hacia atrás, en retrospectiva
retrospective¹ /ˌretrə'spektɪv/ adj retrospectivo

r

retrospective² n (exposición f)
retrospectiva f

return¹ /rɪ'tɜːrn ‖rɪ'tɜːn/ vi **(a)** (to place)
volver*, regresar; **to ~ to** sth (to former activity,
state) volver* A algo **(b)** (reappear) «symptom»
volver* a aparecer; «doubts/suspicions»
resurgir*

■ **~ vt 1 (a)** (give back) devolver*, regresar (AmL
exc CS), restituir* (frml) **(b)** (reciprocate) «affection»
corresponder a; «blow/favor» devolver*; «greeting»
devolver*, corresponder a; **to ~ sb's call**
devolverle* la llamada a algn **(c)** (Sport) «ball»
devolver* **2** (Law) «verdict» emitir

return² n **1 (a)** (to place) regreso m, vuelta f,
retorno m (frml o liter) **(b)** (reappearance)
reaparición f; **many happy ~s of the day!** ¡que
cumplas muchos más! **2** (to owner) devolución f,
regreso m (AmL) **3** (in phrases) **in ~** (**FOR** sth) a
cambio (DE algo) **4** (profit) rendimiento m **5** (tax
~) declaración f (de la renta or de impuestos)
6 (ticket) (BrE) boleto m or (Esp) billete m de ida y
vuelta, boleto m de viaje redondo (Méx)

return³ adj (before n) «journey/flight» de vuelta,
de regreso; «ticket/fare» (BrE) de ida y vuelta, de
viaje redondo (Méx)

returnable /rɪ'tɜːrnəbəl ‖rɪ'tɜːnəbəl/ adj
«deposit» reembolsable, reintegrable; «bottle»
retornable

reunion /riː'juːnjən/ n reunión f, reencuentro
m; **a family ~** una reunión familiar

reunite /'riːjʊ'naɪt/ vt «family/party» volver* a
unir; **to be ~d with** sb reencontrarse* con algn

reusable /riː'juːzəbəl/ adj reutilizable

reuse /riː'juːz/ vt reutilizar*, volver* a usar

rev¹ /rev/ n revolución f

rev² vt -**vv**- **~** (up) «engine/car» acelerar (sin
desplazarse)

revalue /riː'væljuː/, (AmE also) **revaluate**
/-jueɪt/ vt «currency» revalorizar*, revaluar* (esp
AmL); «house» reevaluar*, revalorar

revamp /'riː'væmp/ vt «kitchen/interior»
reformar; (modernize) modernizar*; «image»
cambiar; «organization» modernizar*

reveal /rɪ'viːl/ vt **(a)** (disclose) revelar, develar
(AmL), desvelar (Esp) **(b)** (bring to view) dejar ver

revealing /rɪ'viːlɪŋ/ adj revelador

revel /'revəl/ vi, (BrE) -**ll**- (enjoy greatly) **to ~ IN**
sth deleitarse CON or EN algo

revelation /revə'leɪʃən/ n **(a)** (disclosure)
revelación f **(b)** (Bib): (the Book of) **Revelations** el
Apocalipsis

reveler, (BrE) **reveller** /'revələr ‖'revələ(r)/ n
(liter) juerguista mf (fam)

revelry /'revəlri/ n (pl -**ries**) jolgorio m

revenge¹ /rɪ'vendʒ/ n venganza f; **to take ~**
vengarse*, desquitarse

revenge² vt vengar*

revenue /'revənuː ‖'revənjuː/ n **(a)** (Tax)
rentas fpl públicas **(b) revenues** pl ingresos
mpl

reverberate /rɪ'vɜːrbəreɪt ‖rɪ'vɜːbəreɪt/ vi
retumbar

revere /rɪ'vɪr ‖rɪ'vɪə(r)/ vt (frml) reverenciar
(frml)

reverence /'revrəns, 'revərəns/ n reverencia f

Reverend adj (in titles) reverendo

reverent /'revrənt, 'revərənt/ adj reverente

reverie /'revəri/ n ensueño m

reversal /rɪ'vɜːrsəl ‖rɪ'vɜːsəl/ n **(a)** (inversion)
inversión f **(b)** (of trend, policy) cambio m completo
or total **(c)** (setback) (frml) revés m

reverse¹ /rɪ'vɜːrs ‖rɪ'vɜːs/ n **1** (of picture,
paper) reverso m, dorso m; (of cloth, garment) revés
m; (of coin) reverso m **2** (no pl) (opposite) **the ~** lo
contrario **3 ~** (**gear**) (no art) marcha f atrás,
reversa f (Col, Méx) **4** (setback) (frml) revés m

reverse² vt **1 (a)** (transpose) «roles/positions»
invertir*; **to ~ the charges** (BrE Telec) llamar a
cobro revertido or (Chi, Méx) por cobrar **(b)** (invert)
«order/process» invertir* **2** (undo, negate) «policy»
cambiar radicalmente; «trend» invertir* el
sentido de; «ruling» revocar* **3** «vehicle»: **she ~d**
her car around the corner dobló la esquina dando
marcha atrás or (Col, Méx) en reversa

■ **~ vi** «vehicle/driver» dar* marcha atrás, meter
reversa (Col, Méx)

reverse³ adj (before n) **(a)** (backward, opposite)
«movement/direction/trend» contrario, inverso; **in**
~ order en orden inverso **(b)** (back): **the ~ side**
(of cloth) el revés; (of paper) el reverso, el dorso

reverse-charge call /rɪ'vɜːrs'tʃɑːrdʒ
‖rɪ'vɜːs'tʃɑːdʒ/ n (BrE) llamada f a cobro
revertido or (Chi, Méx) por cobrar

reversible /rɪ'vɜːrsəbəl ‖rɪ'vɜːsəbəl/ adj
reversible

reversion /rɪ'vɜːrʒən ‖rɪ'vɜːʃən/ n (to former
state, practice) vuelta f, reversión f (frml)

revert /rɪ'vɜːrt ‖rɪ'vɜːt/ vi: **to ~ to** volver* a

review¹ /rɪ'vjuː/ n **1 (a)** (of book, film) crítica
f, reseña f **(b)** (report, summary) resumen m, reseña
f **2 (a)** (reconsideration) revisión f **(b)** (for exam)
(AmE) repaso m

review² vt **1 (a)** (consider) «situation»
examinar, estudiar **(b)** (reconsider) «policy/case»
reconsiderar; «salary» reajustar **2 (a)**
(summarize) «news/events» resumir, reseñar **(b)**
«book/play» hacer* (or escribir* etc) la crítica de,
reseñar **3** (for exam) (AmE) repasar

revise /rɪ'vaɪz/ vt **(a)** (alter) modificar* **(b)** (for
exam) (BrE) repasar

■ **~ vi** (BrE) repasar

revision /rɪ'vɪʒən/ n **1 (a)** (alteration)
modificación f **(b)** (text) edición f corregida **2** (for
exam) (BrE) repaso m

revitalize /'riː'vaɪtlaɪz/ vt vigorizar*, darle*
vitalidad a; «economy» estimular, reactivar

revival /rɪ'vaɪvəl/ n **(a)** (renewal, upsurge): **a ~ of**
interest in ... un renovado interés por ...;
economic ~ reactivación f económica; **a religious**
~ un renacer or un renacimiento religioso **(b)**
(Med) reanimación f

revive /rɪ'vaɪv/ vt **(a)** (Med) reanimar, resucitar
(b) (revitalize) «economy» reactivar, estimular;
«interest/friendship» hacer* renacer, reavivar **(c)**
«custom/practice» restablecer*

■ **~ vi** «trade» reactivarse, repuntar; «hope/
interest» renacer, resurgir*; «patient»
reanimarse; «plant» revivir

revoke /rɪ'vəʊk/ vt revocar*

revolt¹ /rɪ'vəʊlt/ n revuelta f, sublevación f

revolt² vi sublevarse

■ **~ vt** darle* asco a

revolting /rɪˈvəʊltɪŋ/ adj (nauseating) repugnante; (horrible) (colloq) asqueroso, horrible

revolution /ˌrevəˈluːʃən/ n revolución f

revolutionary¹ /ˌrevəˈluːʃənerɪ ‖ˌrevəˈluːʃənərɪ/ adj revolucionario

revolutionary² n (pl -ries) revolucionario, -ria m,f

revolutionize /ˌrevəˈluːʃənaɪz/ vt revolucionar

revolve /rɪˈvɑːlv ‖rɪˈvɒlv/ vi (a) (rotate) girar (b) **revolving** pres p ⟨chair/door⟩ giratorio

revolver /rɪˈvɑːlvər ‖rɪˈvɒlvə(r)/ n revólver m

revue /rɪˈvjuː/ n revista f

revulsion /rɪˈvʌlʃən/ n repugnancia f, asco m

reward¹ /rɪˈwɔːrd ‖rɪˈwɔːd/ n recompensa f

reward² vt premiar, recompensar

rewarding /rɪˈwɔːrdɪŋ ‖rɪˈwɔːdɪŋ/ adj gratificante

rewind /riːˈwaɪnd/ vt (past & past p **rewound**) rebobinar

rewire /riːˈwaɪr ‖ˌriːˈwaɪə(r)/ vt ⟨house⟩ renovar* la instalación eléctrica de

reword /riːˈwɜːrd ‖ˌriːˈwɜːd/ vt ⟨question⟩ formular de otra manera; ⟨statement⟩ volver* a redactar

rewound /riːˈwaʊnd/ past & past p of REWIND

rewrite /riːˈraɪt/ vt (past **rewrote**; past p **rewritten**) volver* a escribir or redactar

rhapsody /ˈræpsədɪ/ n (pl -dies) rapsodia f

rhetoric /ˈretərɪk/ n retórica f

rhetorical /rɪˈtɔːrɪkəl ‖rɪˈtɒrɪkəl/ adj retórico

rheumatic /ruːˈmætɪk/ adj reumático

rheumatism /ˈruːmətɪzəm/ n reumatismo m

Rhine /raɪn/ n the ~ el Rin

rhino /ˈraɪnəʊ/ n (pl ~ or ~s) rinoceronte m

rhinoceros /raɪˈnɑːsrəs, -sərəs ‖raɪˈnɒsərəs, -srəs/ n (pl -oses or ~) rinoceronte m

rhubarb /ˈruːbɑːrb ‖ˈruːbɑːb/ n ruibarbo m

rhyme¹ /raɪm/ n (a) (correspondence of sound) rima f (b) (poem) rima f, poema m

rhyme² vi/t rimar

rhythm /ˈrɪðəm/ n ritmo m

rhythmic /ˈrɪðmɪk/, **-mical** /-mɪkəl/ adj rítmico

RI = Rhode Island

rib /rɪb/ n (Anat, Culin) costilla f

ribald /ˈrɪbəld/ adj ⟨comments/humor⟩ procaz, picaresco

ribbed /rɪbd/ adj ⟨neck/sleeves⟩ en punto elástico, en canalé, en resorte (AmC, Col, Méx)

ribbon /ˈrɪbən/ n (a) (strip of fabric) cinta f, listón m (Méx) (b) (as insignia, award) galón m (c) (of typewriter, printer etc) cinta f (d) **ribbons** pl (shreds) jirones mpl

ribcage /ˈrɪbkeɪdʒ/ n caja f torácica

rice /raɪs/ n arroz m; (before n) ~ **pudding** arroz con leche

rice: ~**field** n arrozal m; ~ **paper** n papel m de arroz

rich /rɪtʃ/ adj -**er**, -**est** [1] (a) (wealthy) rico (b) (opulent) ⟨banquet⟩ suntuoso; ⟨furnishings⟩ lujoso, suntuoso (c) (abundant) ⟨harvest/supply⟩ abundante; ⟨reward⟩ generoso; ⟨history/

experience⟩ rico [2] (a) ⟨food⟩ con alto contenido de grasas, huevos, azúcar etc (b) ⟨soil⟩ rico; ⟨color⟩ cálido e intenso

riches /ˈrɪtʃəz ‖ˈrɪtʃɪz/ pl n riquezas fpl

richness /ˈrɪtʃnəs ‖ˈrɪtʃnɪs/ n riqueza f

rickety /ˈrɪkətɪ/ adj desvencijado

rickshaw /ˈrɪkʃɔː/ n: calesa oriental de dos ruedas tirada por un hombre

ricochet /ˈrɪkəʃeɪ/ vi -**chets** /-ʃeɪz/, -**cheting** /-ʃeɪɪŋ/, -**cheted** /-ʃeɪd/ to ~ (OFF sth) rebotar (EN algo)

rid /rɪd/ vt (pres p **ridding**; past & past p **rid**): they ~ **the country of corruption** libraron al país de la corrupción; **to get ~ of** ⟨unwanted object⟩ deshacerse* de; ⟨person, cold⟩ quitarse de encima; ⟨smell⟩ quitar

riddance /ˈrɪdns/ n: **good ~!** (colloq) ¡adiós y buen viaje! (fam & iró)

ridden /ˈrɪdn/ past p of RIDE¹

riddle¹ /ˈrɪdl/ n (a) (puzzle) adivinanza f, acertijo m (b) (mystery) enigma m, misterio m

riddle² vt (perforate) (often pass) **to be ~d WITH sth: his body was ~d with bullets** lo habían acribillado a balazos; **she was ~d with cancer** tenía cáncer por todo el cuerpo

ride¹ /raɪd/ (past **rode**; past p **ridden**) vt [1] (a) **to ~ a horse** montar a caballo; **to ~ a bicycle/motorbike** montar or (AmL tb) andar* en bicicleta/moto (b) (AmE) ⟨bus/subway/train⟩ ir* en [2] (be carried upon) ⟨waves/wind⟩ dejarse llevar por

■ ~ vi (a) (on horse) montar or (AmL tb) andar* a caballo; **to go riding** ir* a montar or (AmL tb) a andar a caballo (b) (on bicycle, in vehicle) ir*; **we rode into town** fuimos al centro en bicicleta (or en moto etc)

■ **ride out** [v + o + adv, v + adv + o] aguantar, sobrellevar

■ **ride up** [v + adv] subirse

ride² n (on horse, in vehicle etc): **let's go for a ~ on our bikes/in your car** vamos a dar una vuelta or un paseo en bicicleta/en tu coche; **it was a long ~** fue un viaje largo; **to give sb a ~** (esp AmE) llevar a algn en coche, darle* un aventón (Méx) or (Col fam) una palomita a algn; **to take sb for a ~** (colloq) tomarle el pelo a algn (fam)

rider /ˈraɪdər ‖ˈraɪdə(r)/ n [1] (a) (on horseback) jinete mf; (on bicycle) ciclista mf; (on motorbike) motociclista mf, motorista mf (b) (of subway, bus) (AmE) pasajero, -ra m,f [2] (appended statement) cláusula f adicional; (condition) condición f

ridge /rɪdʒ/ n (of hills) cadena f; (hilltop) cresta f

ridicule¹ /ˈrɪdəkjuːl ‖ˈrɪdɪkjuːl/ n burlas fpl

ridicule² vt ridiculizar*, burlarse de

ridiculous /rɪˈdɪkjələs ‖rɪˈdɪkjʊləs/ adj ridículo

riding /ˈraɪdɪŋ/ n equitación f; (before n) ⟨school/lesson⟩ de equitación; ⟨breeches/boots⟩ de montar

rife /raɪf/ adj (pred) extendido; **disease is ~** cunden las enfermedades; **corruption is ~** reina la corrupción

riffraff /ˈrɪfræf/ n (+ sing or pl vb) chusma f

rifle¹ /ˈraɪfl/ n rifle m, fusil m

rifle² vi **to ~ THROUGH sth** hojear algo

■ **ring off** [v + adv] (BrE) colgar*, cortar (CS)

■ **ring out** [v + adv] «shot/voice» oírse*, resonar*; «bells» sonar*, resonar*

■ **ring up** ⟨1⟩ [v + o + adv, v + adv + o] (BrE) ▶ RING² vt 1B

⟨2⟩ [v + adv] (BrE) ▶ RING² vi 2

ring binder n archivador m, carpeta f de anillos or (Esp) de anillas

ringing /'rɪŋɪŋ/ n (a) (of bell) repique m, toque m (b) (of doorbell, telephone) timbre m (c) (in ears) zumbido m

ringleader /'rɪŋ,liːdər ‖ 'rɪŋ,liːdə(r)/ n cabecilla mf

ringlet /'rɪŋlət/ n tirabuzón m, rizo m

ring road n (BrE) carretera f de circunvalación

rink /rɪŋk/ n (ice ∼) pista f de hielo; (skating ∼) pista f de patinaje

rinse¹ /rɪns/ vt (a) (wash) ⟨cutlery/hands⟩ enjuagar*; ⟨rice/mushrooms⟩ lavar (b) (to remove soap) ⟨clothes/hair⟩ enjuagar*, aclarar (Esp); ⟨dishes⟩ enjuagar*

rinse² n (a) (wash) enjuague m (b) (to remove soap — from clothes) enjuague m, aclarado m (Esp); (— from dishes) enjuague m (c) (tint) tintura f (no permanente)

riot¹ /'raɪət/ n (a) (disorder) disturbio m; (mutiny) motín m; **to run ∼** «fans» descontrolarse, desmadrarse (fam); **she let her imagination run ∼** dio rienda suelta a su imaginación; (before n) ⟨gear/shield⟩ antidisturbios adj inv; **the ∼ squad** la brigada antidisturbios (b) (profusion): **a ∼ of color** un derroche or una profusión de color

riot² vi causar disturbios or desórdenes; «prisoners» amotinarse

rioter /'raɪətər ‖ 'raɪətə(r)/ n alborotador, -dora m,f

rioting /'raɪətɪŋ/ n disturbios mpl

riotous /'raɪətəs/ adj (a) ⟨crowd/behavior⟩ descontrolado, desenfrenado (b) ⟨occasion⟩ desenfrenado

rip¹ /rɪp/ **-pp-** vt ⟨cloth⟩ rasgar*, romper*; ⟨skirt/trousers⟩ hacerse* un rasgón en; **she ∼ped the letter open** abrió la carta de un rasgón

■ **∼** vi rasgarse*

■ **rip off** [v + o + adv, v + adv + o] ⟨1⟩ (remove) arrancar* ⟨2⟩ (sl) (a) (cheat) timar, estafar, tracalear (Méx, Ven fam) (b) (steal) afanar (arg), robar

■ **rip up** [v + o + adv, v + adv + o] romper*, hacer* pedazos

rip² n rasgón m, desgarrón m

RIP (= rest in peace) R.I.P.

rip cord n cordón m de apertura

ripe /raɪp/ adj ⟨fruit⟩ maduro; ⟨cheese⟩ a punto

ripen /'raɪpən/ vi madurar

■ **∼** vt hacer* madurar

rip-off /'rɪpɔːf ‖ 'rɪpɒf/ n (colloq) (con) timo m, estafa f; (theft) robo m; (copy) plagio m

ripple¹ /'rɪpəl/ n (on water) onda f; **a ∼ of applause** un breve aplauso

ripple² vi (a) «water» rizarse*; «wheat/grass» mecerse* (b) **rippling** pres p ⟨muscles⟩ tensado

rise¹ /raɪz/ n ⟨1⟩ (a) (upward movement — of tide, level) subida f; (— in pitch) elevación f (b) (increase — in prices, interest rates) subida f, aumento m, alza f‡ (fml); (— in pressure, temperature) aumento m,

subida f; (— in number, amount) aumento m (c) (in pay) (BrE) aumento m, incremento m (fml); **a pay ∼** un aumento or (fml) un incremento salarial

⟨2⟩ (advance) (to fame, power) ascenso m, ascensión f; (of movement, ideology) surgimiento m; **to give ∼ to sth** ⟨to belief⟩ dar* origen or lugar a algo; ⟨to dispute⟩ ocasionar or causar algo; ⟨to ideas⟩ suscitar algo

⟨3⟩ (slope) subida f, cuesta f

rise² (past **rose**; past p **risen** /'rɪzn/) vi ⟨1⟩ (a) (come, go up) subir; «sun/moon» salir*; «river» crecer*; «cake» subir; **to ∼ to the surface** salir* or subir a la superficie (b) (increase) «price/temperature/pressure» subir, aumentar; «wind» arreciar; «wage/amount» aumentar; «tension» crecer*, aumentar (c) «sound» (become louder) aumentar de volumen; (become higher) subir de tono (d) (improve) «standard» mejorar; **their spirits rose** se les levantó el ánimo, se animaron ⟨2⟩ (a) (slope upward) «ground/land» elevarse (b) (extend upwards) «building/hill» levantarse, alzarse*

⟨3⟩ (a) (stand up) «person/audience» (fml) ponerse* de pie, levantarse, pararse (AmL) (b) (out of bed) levantarse

⟨4⟩ (in rank): **she has ∼n in my estimation** ha ganado en mi estima

⟨5⟩ (revolt) **to ∼ (up)** levantarse, alzarse*

⟨6⟩ (originate) «river» (fml) nacer*

■ **rise above** [v + prep + o] ⟨disability⟩ sobreponerse* a; ⟨difficulty⟩ superar

■ **rise to** [v + prep + o] (respond to): **to ∼ to the challenge** aceptar el reto; **to ∼ to the occasion** estar* a la altura de las circunstancias

rising¹ /'raɪzɪŋ/ n (rebellion) levantamiento m

rising² adj (before n) (a) ⟨tide/level⟩ creciente; **the ∼ sun** el sol naciente (b) (increasing) ⟨number⟩ creciente; ⟨temperature⟩ creciente, en aumento; ⟨prices/interest rates⟩ en alza or en aumento (c) (sloping) en pendiente

rising damp n humedad f (que sube de los cimientos por las paredes)

risk¹ /rɪsk/ n riesgo m; **those most at ∼ from the disease** los que corren mayor riesgo or peligro de contraer la enfermedad; **at the ∼ of** -ING a riesgo de + INF; **to take a ∼** correr un riesgo; **to take ∼s** arriesgarse, correr riesgos

risk² vt (a) (put in danger) arriesgar*, poner* en peligro (b) (expose oneself to) arriesgarse* a; **to ∼** -ING arriesgarse* A or correr el riesgo DE + INF

risky /'rɪski/ adj **-kier, -kiest** arriesgado, riesgoso (AmL)

risqué /rɪ'skeɪ, 'rɪskeɪ/ adj atrevido, subido de tono

rite /raɪt/ n rito m

ritual¹ /'rɪtʃuəl/ n ritual m

ritual² adj ritual

rival¹ /'raɪvəl/ n rival mf

rival² adj (before n) ⟨company⟩ rival, competidor

rival³ vt, (BrE) **-ll-**: **his voice ∼s that of the lead singer** su voz no tiene nada que envidiarle a la del cantante principal

rivalry /'raɪvəlri/ n (pl **-ries**) rivalidad f, competencia f

river /'rɪvər ‖ 'rɪvə(r)/ n río m; (before n) ⟨traffic/port⟩ fluvial; ⟨mouth/basin⟩ del río

river: ∼bank n ribera f, margen f (de un río); ⋯⋮

r

~bed *n* lecho *m* (*de un río*); **R~ Plate** *n* Río *m* de la Plata; **~side** *n* ribera *f*, margen *f* (*de un río*); (*before n*) ⟨*café*⟩ a orillas del río

rivet¹ /'rɪvət ‖'rɪvɪt/ *n* remache *m*, roblón *m*

rivet² *vt* (a) (attach) remachar (b) (fix) (*usu pass*): **my eyes were ~ed to the screen** estaba absorto, con los ojos clavados en la pantalla; **their eyes were ~ed on her** no le quitaban los ojos de encima (c) (fascinate) (*usu pass*) fascinar

riveting /'rɪvətɪŋ/ *adj* fascinante

Riviera /ˌrɪvi'erə ‖ˌrɪvi'eərə/ *n*: **the (French) ~** la Costa Azul; **the Italian ~** la Riviera

RN *n* (in UK) = **Royal Navy**

RNA *n* (= **ribonucleic acid**) RNA *m*, ARN *m*

road /rəʊd/ *n* **1** (for vehicles — in town) calle *f*; (— out of town) carretera *f*; (— minor) camino *m*; **by ~** por carretera, por tierra; (*before n*) ⟨*accident*⟩ de tráfico *or* (AmL tb) de tránsito; **~ safety** seguridad *f* en la carretera; **~ sign** señal *f* vial *or* de tráfico *or* (AmL tb) de tránsito; **~ tax** impuesto *m* de rodaje

2 (route, way) camino *m*; **the economy is on the ~ to recovery** la economía está en vías de recuperación

3 to be on the road «*car*» estar* en circulación; **we've been on the ~ for four days** llevamos cuatro días viajando

road: ~block *n* control *m* (de carretera); **~ hog** *n* (colloq) loco, -ca *m*,*f* del volante; **~ hump** *n* badén *m*, tope *m* (Méx), lomo *m* de burro (RPl); **~map** *n* mapa *m* de carreteras; **~ rage** *n* (Auto) agresión *f* (*provocada por el estrés que supone conducir en condiciones difíciles*); **~side** *n* borde *m* de la carretera/del camino; **~ sweeper** *n* (person) barrendero, -ra *m*,*f*; (machine) barredera *f*, barredora *f*; **~works** *pl n* (BrE) obras *fpl* (de vialidad); **~worthy** *adj* **-thier, -thiest** apto para circular

roam /rəʊm/ *vt* vagar* *or* deambular por
■ ~ *vi* vagar*, errar* (liter)

roar¹ /rɔːr ‖rɔː(r)/ *vi* «*lion/engine*» rugir*; «*sea/wind/fire*» bramar, rugir*; **to ~ with laughter** reírse* a carcajadas

roar² *n* (of lion, tiger) rugido *m*; (of person) rugido *m*, bramido *m*; (of thunder) estruendo *m*; (of traffic, engine, guns) estruendo *m*; (of crowd) clamor *m*

roaring /'rɔːrɪŋ/ *adj* (*before n*) ⟨*waves*⟩ rugiente; ⟨*traffic*⟩ estruendoso

roast¹ /rəʊst/ *adj* asado; **~ beef** rosbif *m*, rosbeef *m*

roast² *n* asado *m* (*al horno*)

roast³ *vt* ⟨*meat/potatoes*⟩ asar; ⟨*coffee beans*⟩ tostar*, torrefaccionar; ⟨*peanuts*⟩ tostar*
■ ~ *vi* asarse

roasting /'rəʊstɪŋ/ *adj* (colloq): **it's absolutely ~** hace un calor que te asas (fam)

rob /rɑːb ‖rɒb/ *vt* **-bb-** (a) (steal from) ⟨*person*⟩ robarle a; ⟨*bank*⟩ asaltar, atracar*, robar (b) (deprive) **to ~ sb/sth OF sth** privar a algn/algo DE algo

robber /'rɑːbər ‖'rɒbə(r)/ *n* ladrón, -drona *m*,*f*; **bank ~** atracador, -dora *m*,*f* *or* asaltante *mf* de bancos

robbery /'rɑːbəri ‖'rɒbəri/ *n* (*pl* **-ries**) robo *m*, asalto *m*; **bank ~** asalto *m* *or* atraco *m* a un banco

robe /rəʊb/ *n* (a) (worn by magistrates) (*often pl*) toga *f* (b) (worn in house) bata *f*, salto *m* de cama (CS)

robin /'rɑːbən ‖'rɒbɪn/ *n* (European) petirrojo *m*; (N. American) ceón *m*, tordo *m* norteamericano

robot /'rəʊbɑːt ‖'rəʊbɒt/ *n* robot *m*

robust /rəʊ'bʌst/ *adj* ⟨*person/animal*⟩ robusto; ⟨*health*⟩ de hierro; ⟨*material*⟩ resistente, sólido

rock¹ /rɑːk ‖rɒk/ *n* **1** (substance) roca *f* **2** (a) (crag, cliff) peñasco *m*, peñón *m* (b) (in sea) roca *f*, escollo *m*; **on the ~s** ⟨*whisky*⟩ con hielo; **their marriage is on the ~s** su matrimonio anda muy mal (c) (boulder) roca *f* (d) (stone) (esp AmE) piedra *f* **3** (music) rock *m*

rock² *vt* (a) (gently) ⟨*cradle*⟩ mecer*; ⟨*child*⟩ acunar (b) (violently) sacudir, estremecer*; «*scandal*» convulsionar, conmocionar
■ ~ *vi* (gently) mecerse*, balancearse

rock: ~ and roll *n* ▶ ROCK'N'ROLL; **~bottom** /'rɑːk'bɑːtəm ‖'rɒk'bɒtəm/ *n*: **to hit/reach ~bottom** tocar* fondo; **~ climbing** /'rɑːk'klaɪmɪŋ ‖'rɒk'klaɪmɪŋ/ *n* escalada *f* en roca

rocket¹ /'rɑːkət ‖'rɒkɪt/ *n* (a) (spacecraft) cohete *m* espacial (b) (missile) cohete *m*, misil *m*; (*before n*) ~ **launcher** lanzacohetes *m*, lanzamisiles *m*

rocket² *vi* «*price*» dispararse, ponerse* por las nubes

rock: ~face *n* pared *f* rocosa; **~-hard** /'rɑːk'hɑːrd ‖'rɒk'hɑːd/ *adj* (duro) como una piedra

rocking /'rɑːkɪŋ ‖'rɒkɪŋ/: **~ chair** *n* mecedora *f*; **~ horse** *n* caballito *m* mecedor *or* de balancín

rock'n'roll /'rɑːkən'rəʊl ‖'rɒkən'rəʊl/ *n* rocanrol *m*, rock and roll *m*

rocky /'rɑːki ‖'rɒki/ *adj* **rockier, rockiest** **1** ⟨*ground*⟩ rocoso; ⟨*path*⟩ pedregoso **2** (unsteady) ⟨*period*⟩ de incertidumbre; ⟨*base*⟩ nada sólido, tambaleante

Rocky Mountains *pl n* **the ~ ~** las Montañas Rocallosas *or* Rocosas

rod /rɑːd ‖rɒd/ *n* (a) (bar) varilla *f*, barra *f* (b) (fishing ~) caña *f* (de pescar) (c) (for punishment) vara *f*

rode /rəʊd/ *past of* RIDE¹

rodent /'rəʊdnt/ *n* roedor *m*

rodeo /'rəʊdiəʊ, rə'deɪəʊ/ *n* (*pl* **-os**) rodeo *m*

roe /rəʊ/ *n* **1** (of fish) hueva *f* **2** ~ **deer** corzo, -za *m*,*f*

rogue /rəʊg/ *n* pícaro, -ra *m*,*f*, pillo, -lla *m*,*f*

roguish /'rəʊgɪʃ/ *adj* pícaro

role, rôle /rəʊl/ *n* (a) (Cin, Theat) papel *m* (b) (function) papel *m*, rol *m*; (*before n*) ~ **model** modelo *m* de conducta

role-play /'rəʊlpleɪ/ *n* teatro *m* improvisado; (Psych) psicodrama *m*

roll¹ /rəʊl/ *n* **1** (Culin) (bread) ~ pancito *m* *or* (Esp) panecillo *m* *or* (Méx) bolillo *m* **2** (of paper, wire, fabric) rollo *m*; (of banknotes) fajo *m*; **a ~ of film** un rollo *or* un carrete (de fotos) **3** (sound — of drum) redoble *m*; (— of thunder) retumbo *m* **4** (list) lista *f*; **to call the ~** pasar lista

roll² *vi* **1** (a) (rotate) «*ball/barrel*» rodar* (b) (turn over): **the car ~ed over three times** el coche dio tres vueltas de campana; ~ **(over) onto your**

back ponte boca arriba, date la vuelta or (CS) date vuelta; **to be ~ing in money** o in it (colloq) estar* forrado (de oro) (fam) **(c)** (sway) «ship» bambolearse

2 (move) (+ adv compl): **the car began to ~ down the hill** el coche empezó a deslizarse cuesta abajo; **tears ~ed down his cheeks** las lágrimas le corrían por las mejillas

3 (begin operating) «camera» empezar* a rodar
4 (make noise) «drum» redoblar; «thunder» retumbar

5 **rolling** pres p «countryside/hills» ondulado
■ ~ vt 1 **(a)** «ball/barrel» hacer* rodar; «dice» tirar **(b) to ~ one's eyes** poner* los ojos en blanco

2 «cigarette» liar*; **it ~ed itself into a ball** se hizo un ovillo; **to ~ up one's sleeves** arremangarse
3 «dough/pastry» estirar
4 (Ling) **to ~ one's 'r's** hacer* vibrar las erres
■ **roll in** [v + adv] (arrive in large quantities) llover*
■ **roll on** [v + adv] **(a)** (pass) «time/months» pasar **(b)** (arrive) (colloq): **~ on vacation time!** ¡que lleguen pronto las vacaciones!
■ **roll out** [v + o + adv, v + adv + o] «dough/pastry» estirar
■ **roll up** [v + adv] (arrive) (colloq) aparecer*

roll call n **(a)** (calling of roll): **~ is 9 a.m.** pasan lista a las nueve de la mañana **(b)** (list) lista f

rolled gold /rəʊld/ n metal m (en)chapado en oro

roller /ˈrəʊlər ‖ˈrəʊlə(r)/ n 1 (for lawn, in machine, for applying paint) rodillo m 2 (for hair) rulo m 3 (caster) ruedecita f, ruedita f (esp AmL) 4 (wave) ola f grande

roller: R~blade® n patín m en línea; **~ blind** n persiana f or cortina f de enrollar; **~ coaster** n montaña f rusa; **~ skate** n patín m (de ruedas); **~-skate** /ˈrəʊlərskeɪt ‖ˈrəʊləskeɪt/ vi patinar (sobre ruedas)

rolling pin /ˈrəʊlɪŋ/ n rodillo m, rollo m pastelero (Esp)

roll-on /ˈrəʊlɑːn ‖ˈrəʊlɒn/adj (before n) «deodorant» de bola

ROM /rɑːm ‖rɒm/ n (= **read-only memory**) ROM f

Roman¹ /ˈrəʊmən/ adj **(a)** (of, from Rome) romano **(b) roman** «numeral» romano; «alphabet» latino

Roman² n romano, -na m,f

Roman Catholic¹ n católico, -ca m,f

Roman Catholic² adj católico

romance /rəˈmæns, ˈrəʊmæns ‖rəʊˈmæns/ n 1 **(a)** (affair) romance m, idilio m **(b)** (feeling) romanticismo m 2 (Lit) (love story) novela f romántica

Romance /rəˈmæns, ˈrəʊmæns ‖rəʊˈmæns/ adj «languages» romance, románico

Romania /rəʊˈmeɪnɪə/ n Rumania f, Rumanía f

Romanian¹ /rəʊˈmeɪnɪən/ adj rumano

Romanian² n **(a)** (language) rumano m **(b)** (person) rumano, -na m,f

romantic¹ /rəʊˈmæntɪk, rə-/ adj romántico

romantic² n romántico, -ca m,f

romanticize /rəʊˈmæntəsaɪz, rə- ‖rəʊˈmæntɪsaɪz/ vt idealizar*

Romany /ˈrɑːməni, ˈrəʊ- ‖ˈrɒməni, ˈrəʊ-/ n (pl **-nies**) **(a)** (person) gitano, -na m,f **(b)** (language) romaní m

Rome /rəʊm/ n Roma f

romp¹ /rɑːmp ‖rɒmp/ n **(a)** (frolic) retozo m **(b)** (sexual) revolcón m (fam)

romp² vi (frolic) retozar*

rompers /ˈrɑːmpərz ‖ˈrɒmpəz/ pl n, (BrE also) **romper suit** /ˈrɑːmpər ‖ˈrɒmpə(r)/ n mameluco m (AmL), pelele m (Esp)

roof¹ /ruːf/ n (pl **~s** /ruːfs/) **(a)** (of building) tejado m, techo m (AmL); (before n) **~ garden** terraza f or azotea f ajardinada **(b)** (of car) techo m; (before n) **~ rack** baca f, portaequipajes m, parrilla f (AmL) **(c) the ~ of the mouth** el paladar

roof² vt techar

roofing /ˈruːfɪŋ/ n materiales mpl para techar

rooftop /ˈruːftɑːp ‖ˈruːftɒp/ n tejado m, techo m (AmL)

rook /rʊk/ n **(a)** (Zool) grajo m **(b)** (in chess) torre f

rookie /ˈrʊki/ n (colloq) **(a)** (novice) novato, -ta m,f **(b)** (military recruit) recluta m

room /ruːm, rʊm/ n 1 (in house, building) habitación f, pieza f (esp AmL); (bedroom) habitación f, dormitorio m, cuarto m, pieza f (esp AmL), recámara f (Méx); (for meeting) sala f; (before n) **~ temperature** temperatura f ambiente 2 (space) espacio m, lugar m; **there's ~ for improvement** se puede mejorar

room-: ~ clerk n (AmE) recepcionista mf; **~mate** n (sharing apartment) compañero, -ra m,f de apartamento or (Esp) de piso; **~ service** n servicio m a las habitaciones

roomy /ˈruːmi, ˈrʊmi/ adj **-mier, -miest** amplio

roost /ruːst/ vi posarse (para pasar la noche)

rooster /ˈruːstər ‖ˈruːstə(r)/ n (esp AmE) gallo m

root¹ /ruːt/ n **(a)** raíz f; **to take ~** «plant» echar raíces, arraigar*; «idea» arraigarse* **(b) roots** pl (background) raíces fpl

root² vi 1 «pig» hozar* 2 (Bot) echar raíces, arraigar*
■ **root for** [v + prep + o] (encourage) animar, alentar; (support) apoyar
■ **root out** [v + o + adv, v + adv + o] (remove) arrancar* de raíz, erradicar*

root beer n refresco hecho con distintas raíces

rooted /ˈruːtəd ‖ˈruːtɪd/ adj: **a deeply ~ prejudice** un prejuicio profundamente arraigado; **he stood ~ to the spot** se quedó como clavado donde estaba

rope¹ /rəʊp/ n cuerda f, soga f; (Naut) cabo m; **to show sb the ~s: Mike will show you the ~s** Mike te enseñará cómo funciona todo

rope² vt **(a)** (tie) atar, amarrar (AmL exc RPI) (con una cuerda) **(b)** (lasso) (AmE) «steer/cattle» enlazar* or (Méx) lazar* or (CS) lacear
■ **rope in** [v + o + adv, v + adv + o] (colloq) (usu pass) agarrar (fam)

rope ladder n escala f or escalera f de cuerda or de soga

ropey, ropy /ˈrəʊpi/ adj **ropier, ropiest** (BrE ···÷

colloq) ⟨wine⟩ malo, chungo (Esp arg); **I feel a bit ~** me siento bastante mal, estoy bastante pachucho (Esp fam)

rosary /'rəʊzəri/ n (pl **-ries**) rosario m

rose¹ /rəʊz/ past of RISE²

rose² /rəʊz/ n **1** (Bot) (flower) rosa f; (plant) rosal m; (before n) ~ **bush** rosal m **2** (on watering can) roseta f

rosé /'rəʊ'zeɪ ‖'rəʊzeɪ/ n (vino m) rosado m

rose: ~**bud** n capullo m or pimpollo m de rosa; ~**hip** n escaramujo m

rosemary /'rəʊz,meri ‖'rəʊzməri/ n romero m

rosette /rəʊ'zet/ n escarapela f

roster /'rɑːstər ‖'rɒstə(r)/ n **(a)** (duty ~) lista f de turnos **(b)** (list) lista f

rostrum /'rɑːstrəm ‖'rɒstrəm/ n (pl **-trums** or **-tra** /-trə/) (for public speaking) tribuna f, estrado m; (for orchestra conductor) podio m

rosy /'rəʊzi/ adj **rosier, rosiest** ⟨cheeks⟩ sonrosado; ⟨outlook⟩ halagüeño, optimista

rot¹ /rɑːt ‖rɒt/ n (Biol) podredumbre f, putrefacción f; **the ~ set in** las cosas empezaron a decaer or a venirse abajo

rot² -tt- vi pudrirse*; **to ~ away** pudrirse* ■ ~ vt ⟨wood/tree⟩ pudrir*, ⟨teeth⟩ picar*

rota /'rəʊtə/ n (BrE) lista f (de turnos)

rotary /'rəʊtəri/ adj rotatorio, rotativo

rotate /'rəʊteɪt ‖rəʊ'teɪt/ vi girar, rotar ■ ~ vt **(a)** (turn, spin) (hacer*) girar, dar* vueltas a **(b)** (alternate) ⟨crops⟩ alternar, rotar

rotation /rəʊ'teɪʃən/ n rotación f

rote /rəʊt/ n: **by ~** de memoria

rotten /'rɑːtn̩ ‖'rɒtn̩/ adj **(a)** (decayed) podrido; ⟨tooth⟩ picado **(b)** (bad) (colloq) ⟨weather⟩ horrible; ⟨food⟩ pésimo; **to feel ~** (ill) sentirse* mal or pésimo or (Esp fam) fatal

rotund /rəʊ'tʌnd/ adj (hum & euph) voluminoso

rouble /'ruːbəl/ n (BrE) rublo m

rouge /ruːʒ/ n colorete m

rough¹ /rʌf/ adj -**er, -est 1 (a)** (not smooth) ⟨surface/texture/skin⟩ áspero, rugoso; ⟨cloth⟩ basto; ⟨hands⟩ áspero, basto **(b)** (uneven) ⟨ground/road⟩ desigual; ⟨terrain⟩ agreste, escabroso **(c)** ⟨sea⟩ agitado, picado **2** (colloq) **(a)** (unpleasant, hard) ⟨life⟩ duro **(b)** (ill): **I feel a bit ~** no estoy muy bien, me siento bastante mal **3** (not gentle) brusco; ⟨neighborhood⟩ peligroso **4** (crude, unpolished) tosco, rudo; **a ~ draft** un borrador **(b)** (approximate) aproximado

rough² adv ⟨sleep⟩ a la intemperie

rough³ vt: **to ~ it** (colloq) pasar sin comodidades

roughage /'rʌfɪdʒ/ n fibra f (de los alimentos)

rough-and-ready /'rʌfən'redi/ adj improvisado

roughen /'rʌfən/ vt poner* áspero

roughly /'rʌfli/ adv **(a)** (approximately) aproximadamente **(b)** (not gently) ⟨play⟩ bruscamente, de manera violenta **(c)** (crudely) toscamente

roughshod /'rʌfʃɑːd ‖'rʌfʃɒd/ adv: **to ride ~**

over sth: he rides ~ **over other people's feelings** no tiene la menor consideración para con los sentimientos de los demás; **to ride ~ over sb** llevarse por delante a algn

roulette /ruː'let/ n ruleta f

Roumania /ruː'meɪniə/ etc ▶ ROMANIA etc

round¹ /raʊnd/ adj redondo

round² n **1** (circle) círculo m, redondel m **2 (a)** (series) serie f; ~ **of talks** ronda f de conversaciones **(b)** (burst): **let's have a ~ of applause for ...** un aplauso para ... **3** (Sport, Games) (of tournament, quiz) vuelta f, (in boxing, wrestling) round m, asalto m; (in golf) vuelta f, recorrido m; (in showjumping) recorrido m; (in card games) partida f **4 (a)** (of visits) (often pl): **the doctor is off making his ~s** o (BrE) **is on his ~s** el doctor está haciendo visitas a domicilio or visitando pacientes **(b)** (of watchman) ronda f; (of postman, milkman) (BrE) recorrido m **5** (of drinks) ronda f, vuelta f **6** (shot) disparo m; (bullet) bala f **7** (of bread) (BrE): **a ~ of toast** una tostada or (Méx) un pan tostado; **a ~ of sandwiches** un sándwich **8** (Mus) canon m

round³ vt ⟨corner⟩ doblar ■ **round off 1** [v + o + adv, v + adv + o] **(a)** ⟨sharp edge⟩ redondear **(b)** (end suitably) ⟨day/ meal⟩ terminar, rematar **(c)** ⟨number⟩ redondear **2** [v + adv] concluir*, terminar ■ **round on** [v + prep + o] volverse* contra ■ **round up** [v + o + adv, v + adv + o] ⟨sheep/ cattle⟩ rodear; ⟨criminals⟩ hacer* una redada de

round⁴ adv (esp BrE) **1 (a)** (in a circle): **we walked all the way ~** dimos toda la vuelta; **all year ~** durante todo el año **(b)** (so as to face in different direction): **she spun ~** dio media vuelta; see also TURN ROUND **(c)** (on all sides) alrededor **2 (a)** (from one place, person to another): **the curator took us ~** el conservador nos mostró or nos enseñó el museo (or la colección etc); **a list was handed ~** se hizo circular una lista **(b)** (in every respect) en todos los sentidos; (for everybody) a todos

round⁵ prep (esp BrE) **1** (encircling) alrededor de; **the wall ~ the garden** el muro que rodea el jardín; ~ **the corner** a la vuelta (de la esquina) **2 (a)** (in the vicinity of) cerca de, en los alrededores de; **she lives ~ here** vive por aquí **(b)** (within, through): **he does odd jobs ~ the house** hace arreglitos en la casa; **we had a look ~ the cathedral** (le) echamos un vistazo a la catedral

round- /'raʊnd/ pref: ~**faced** de cara redonda; ~**shouldered** cargado de espaldas, encorvado

roundabout¹ /'raʊndəbaʊt/ n (BrE) **(a)** ▶ MERRY-GO-ROUND **(b)** (Transp) rotonda f, glorieta f

roundabout² adj ⟨route⟩ indirecto; **he said it in a very ~ way** lo dijo con muchos rodeos or circunloquios

rounded /'raʊndəd ‖'raʊndɪd/ adj redondeado

rounders /'raʊndərz ‖ 'raʊndəz/ n (in UK)
(+ *sing vb*) juego parecido al béisbol

round: ∼ **table** n mesa f redonda; ∼ **the
clock** adv las 24 horas, día y noche; ∼ **trip** n
(a) (there and back) (viaje m de) ida f y vuelta,
viaje m redondo (Méx) **(b)** (return fare) (AmE) tarifa
f de ida y vuelta or (Méx) de viaje redondo;
(*before n*) **round-trip ticket** pasaje m or (Esp)
billete m de ida y vuelta, boleto m redondo (Méx);
∼**-up** n **(a)** (of livestock) rodeo m **(b)** (summary)
resumen m

rouse /raʊz/ vt despertar*

rousing /'raʊzɪŋ/ adj ⟨speech⟩ enardecedor

rout¹ /raʊt/ n derrota f aplastante

rout² vt (defeat) derrotar or vencer* de forma
aplastante; (put to flight) poner* en fuga

route /ruːt, raʊt ‖ruːt/ n **(a)** (way) camino m,
ruta f; (of bus) ruta f, recorrido m; **air/sea** ∼ ruta
aérea/marítima **(b)** (highway) (AmE) carretera f

routine¹ /ruːˈtiːn/ n [1] (regular pattern) rutina f
[2] (of skater, comedian) número m

routine² adj **(a)** (usual) ⟨procedure/inquiries⟩ de
rutina **(b)** (ordinary, dull) rutinario

roving /'rəʊvɪŋ/ adj (before n) errante

row¹ n
I /rəʊ/ [1] **(a)** (straight line) hilera f; (of people,
seats) fila f **(b)** (in knitting) vuelta f [2] (succession)
serie f; **four times in a** ∼ cuatro veces seguidas
II /raʊ/ **(a)** (noisy argument) pelea f, riña f; **to have
a** ∼ **with sb** pelearse or reñir* con algn **(b)** (about
a public matter) disputa f **(c)** (noise) (no pl) bulla f
(fam)

row² vt /rəʊ/: **he** ∼**ed the boat towards the
shore** remó hacia la orilla
■ ∼ vi
I /rəʊ/ remar; **to go** ∼**ing** salir* or ir* a remar
II /raʊ/ pelearse, reñir*

rowboat /'rəʊbəʊt/, (BrE) **rowing boat**
/'rəʊɪŋ/ n bote m a remo or de remos

rowdy /'raʊdi/ adj **-dier, -diest** ⟨person⟩
escandaloso, alborotador; (quarrelsome)
pendenciero

row house /'rəʊ/ n (AmE) casa adosada en una
hilera de casas idénticas

rowing /'rəʊɪŋ/ n (Sport) remo m

rowing boat /'rəʊɪŋ/ n (BrE) ▶ ROWBOAT

royal /'rɔɪəl/ adj **(a)** (monarchic) real **(b)**
(magnificent) espléndido, regio

royal: ∼**-blue** /'rɔɪəl'bluː/ adj (pred ∼ **blue**)
azul real adj inv; **R**∼ **Highness** n: Her/Your
R∼ Highness Su/Vuestra Alteza Real

royalist /'rɔɪəlɪst/ adj monárquico

royalty /'rɔɪəlti/ n (pl **-ties**) [1] (status) realeza
f [2] **royalties** mpl derechos mpl de autor,
regalías fpl

rpm (= **revolutions per minute**) r.p.m.

RSI n = **repetitive strain injury**

RSPCA n (in UK) (= **Royal Society for the
Prevention of Cruelty to Animals**)
≈ Asociación f protectora de animales

RSVP (please reply) s.r.c., se ruega contestación

rub /rʌb/ **-bb-** vt **(a)** (with hand, finger) frotar;
(firmly) restregar*; (massage) masajear, friccionar;
to ∼ **one's eyes** restregarse* or refregarse* or
(Méx) tallarse los ojos **(b)** (with a cloth) frotar

■ **rub down** [v + o + adv, v + adv + o] **(a)**
⟨horse⟩ almohazar* **(b)** (using sandpaper) lijar

■ **rub in** [v + o + adv, v + adv + o] ⟨cream/lotion⟩
aplicar* frotando

■ **rub off** [v + o + adv, v + adv + o] ⟨dirt/marks⟩
quitar frotando or restregando or refregando;
(from blackboard) (BrE) borrar

■ **rub out** [v + o + adv, v + adv + o] borrar

■ **rub up** [v + o + adv, v + adv + o]: **to** ∼ **sb up
the wrong way** caerle* mal a algn

rubber /'rʌbər ‖ 'rʌbə(r)/ n **(a)** (substance) goma
f, caucho m, hule m (Méx); (before n) ∼ **ring**
flotador m **(b)** (eraser) (BrE) goma f (de borrar)

rubber: ∼ **band** n goma f (elástica), gomita f
(RPl); ∼ **bullet** n bala f de goma or caucho; ∼
plant n ficus m, gomero m (CS); ∼ **stamp** n
(device) sello m; (approval) visto m bueno; ∼ **tree**
n árbol m del caucho, hule m (Méx)

rubbery /'rʌbəri/ adj ⟨texture⟩ gomoso;
⟨material⟩ parecido a la goma or al caucho or
(Méx) al hule

rubbish /'rʌbɪʃ/ n **(a)** (refuse) basura f; (before
n) ∼ **bag** bolsa f de la basura; ∼ **bin** (BrE) cubo m
or (CS) tacho m or (Méx) bote m or (Col) caneca f
or (Ven) tobo m de la basura **(b)** (junk) (colloq)
porquerías fpl (fam) **(c)** (nonsense) (colloq) tonterías
fpl

rubble /'rʌbəl/ n escombros mpl

ruble, (BrE) **rouble** /'ruːbəl/ n rublo m

ruby /'ruːbi/ n (pl **rubies**) rubí m

rucksack /'rʌksæk, 'rʊk-/ n mochila f, morral
m

ructions /'rʌkʃənz/ pl n (colloq) jaleo m (fam)

rudder /'rʌdər ‖ 'rʌdə(r)/ n timón m

ruddy /'rʌdi/ adj **-dier, -diest** ⟨cheeks⟩
rubicundo

rude /ruːd/ adj **(a)** (bad-mannered) ⟨person⟩
maleducado, grosero; ⟨remark⟩ grosero,
descortés; **to be** ∼ **TO sb** ser* grosero CON algn
(b) (vulgar) (esp BrE) grosero

rudely /'ruːdli/ adv groseramente

rudeness /'ruːdnəs ‖ 'ruːdnɪs/ n grosería f,
mala educación f

rudimentary /ruːdəˈmentri ‖ ruːdɪˈmentri/
adj rudimentario

rudiments /'ruːdəmənts ‖ 'ruːdɪmənts/ pl n
rudimentos mpl, nociones fpl elementales

rue /ruː/ vt lamentar, arrepentirse* de

rueful /'ruːfəl/ adj atribulado, compungido

ruff /rʌf/ n (collar) gorguera f; (on animal, bird)
collar m

ruffian /'rʌfiən/ n rufián m, villano m

ruffle¹ /'rʌfəl/ n (frill) volante m or (RPl) volado
m or (Chi) vuelo m

ruffle² vt ⟨hair⟩ alborotar; ⟨feathers⟩ erizar*;
⟨clothes⟩ arrugar* **(b)** ⟨person⟩ alterar, contrariar

rug /rʌg/ n **(a)** (small carpet) alfombra f,
alfombrilla f, tapete m (Col, Méx) **(b)** (blanket)
manta f de viaje

rugby /'rʌgbi/ n rugby m

rugged /'rʌgəd ‖ 'rʌgɪd/ adj **(a)** ⟨rocks/coast⟩
escarpado; ⟨terrain⟩ escabroso **(b)** ⟨face⟩ de
facciones duras

ruin¹ /'ruːən ‖ 'ruːɪn/ n **(a)** (sth ruined) (often pl) ····❖

ruina *f*; **his career was in ∼s** su carrera estaba
arruinada **(b)** (cause) (*no pl*) ruina *f*, perdición *f*
(c) (state) ruina *f*

ruin² *vt* **1** (destroy) ⟨*city/building*⟩ destruir*;
⟨*career/plans*⟩ arruinar; ⟨*person*⟩ (financially)
arruinar **2** (spoil) ⟨*dress/carpet/toy*⟩ estropear;
⟨*party/surprise*⟩ echar a perder, estropear,
arruinar

rule¹ /ruːl/ *n* **1** (regulation, principle) regla *f*,
norma *f*; **it's against the ∼s** está prohibido; **∼s
and regulations** reglamento *m*; **to work to ∼** (Lab
Rel) hacer* huelga de celo **2 as a ∼** por lo
general, generalmente **3** (government) gobierno *m*;
(of monarch) reinado *m*; **to be under foreign ∼**
estar* bajo dominio extranjero

rule² *vt* **1** (govern, control) ⟨*country*⟩ gobernar*,
administrar; ⟨*person*⟩ dominar **2** (pronounce)
dictaminar **3** (draw) ⟨*line*⟩ trazar* con una regla
■ ∼ *vi* **1** (govern) gobernar*; ⟨*monarch*⟩ reinar
2 (pronounce) **to ∼** (**ON** sth) fallar *or* resolver*
(**EN** algo)
■ **rule out** [*v + o + adv, v + adv + o*] ⟨*possibility*⟩
descartar; ⟨*course of action*⟩ hacer* imposible

ruler /ˈruːlər ‖ˈruːlə(r)/ *n* **1** (leader) gobernante
mf; (sovereign) soberano, -na *m,f* **2** (measure)
regla *f*

ruling¹ /ˈruːlɪŋ/ *n* fallo *m*, resolución *f*

ruling² *adj* (*before n*) ⟨*monarch*⟩ reinante; **the ∼
classes** las clases dirigentes

rum /rʌm/ *n* ron *m*

Rumania /ruːˈmeɪniə/ *etc* ▶ ROMANIA *etc*

rumble¹ /ˈrʌmbl/ *n* (sound) ruido *m* sordo; (of
thunder) estruendo *m*; (of stomach) ruido *m* de
tripas (fam)

rumble² *vi* ⟨*guns/drums*⟩ hacer* un ruido
sordo; ⟨*thunder*⟩ retumbar; **my stomach's
rumbling** me suenan las tripas (fam)

ruminate /ˈruːmɪneɪt ‖ˈruːmɪneɪt/ *vi* **(a)** (Zool)
rumiar **(b)** (ponder) **to ∼ ON/ABOUT sth** cavilar
SOBRE algo, rumiar algo

rummage /ˈrʌmɪdʒ/ *vi* hurgar*

rumor¹, (BrE) **rumour** /ˈruːmər ‖ˈruːmə(r)/ *n*
rumor *m*

rumor², (BrE) **rumour** *vt* (*usu pass*) rumorear;
it is ∼ed that ... se rumorea que ...

rump /rʌmp/ *n* **(a)** (Culin) cadera *f*; (*before n*)
∼ steak filete *m* de cadera, churrasco *m* de cuadril
(RPl) **(b)** (bottom) (colloq & hum) traste *m* (fam)

rumpus /ˈrʌmpəs/ *n* (*pl* ∼**es**) lío *m*, escándalo
m

run¹ /rʌn/ (*pres p* **running**; *past* **ran**; *past p*
run) *vi*
I 1 correr; **he ran downstairs/indoors** bajó/entró
corriendo
2 (colloq) (drive) ir* (*en coche*)
3 (Transp): **the trains ∼ every half hour** hay
trenes cada media hora
4 (flow) ⟨*water/oil*⟩ correr; **she left the water
∼ning** dejó la llave abierta (AmL) *or* (Esp) el grifo
abierto; **my nose is ∼ning** me gotea la nariz
5 (Pol) ⟨*candidate*⟩ presentarse, postularse
(AmL)
II (operate, function): **with the engine ∼ning** con el
motor encendido *or* en marcha *or* (AmL tb)
prendido; **it ∼s off batteries** funciona con pilas *or*
a pila(s)
III 1 (extend) **(a)** (in space): **the streets ∼ parallel**

to each other las calles corren paralelas; **the path
∼s across the field** el sendero atraviesa el campo
(b) «*show*» estar* en cartel
2 (a) (be, stand): **feelings are ∼ning high** los
ánimos están caldeados; **inflation is ∼ning at 4%**
la tasa de inflación es del 4%; **it ∼s in the family**
es de familia **(b)** (become): **stocks are ∼ning low**
se están agotando las existencias; *see also* DRY¹ 1c
3 (melt, merge) «*paint/makeup*» correrse;
«*color*» desteñir*, despintarse (Méx)
■ ∼ *vt*
I 1 ⟨*race/marathon*⟩ correr, tomar parte en
2 (a) (push, move) pasar **(b)** (drive) ⟨*person*⟩
(colloq) llevar (*en coche*)
3 to ∼ a bath preparar un baño
4 (a) (extend) ⟨*cable/wire*⟩ tender* **(b)** (pass)
(hacer*) pasar
II 1 (operate) ⟨*engine*⟩ hacer* funcionar;
⟨*program*⟩ (Comput) pasar, ejecutar
2 (manage) ⟨*business*⟩ dirigir*, llevar
3 ⟨*course*⟩ organizar*; ⟨*article*⟩ publicar*; ▶
TEMPERATURE B
■ **run about** ▶ RUN AROUND
■ **run across** [*v + prep + o*] **(a)** (meet) ⟨*person*⟩
encontrarse* *or* toparse con **(b)** (find) ⟨*object*⟩
encontrar*
■ **run after** [*v + prep + o*] (pursue) correr detrás
de *or* tras; (romantically) andar* detrás de,
perseguir*
■ **run along** [*v + adv*] irse*
■ **run around** [*v + adv*] «*children*» corretear
■ **run away** [*v + adv*] huir*, escaparse, fugarse*;
(run off) salir* corriendo; **she ran away from home**
se escapó de casa
■ **run away with** [*v + adv + prep + o*] **1 (a)**
⟨*race/contest*⟩ ganar fácilmente **(b)** (take over): **she
lets her imagination ∼ away with her** se deja
llevar por la imaginación
2 (elope with) escaparse *or* fugarse* *or* irse*
con
■ **run down**
I [*v + o + adv, v + adv + o*] **1** (disparage) (colloq)
criticar*, hablar mal de
2 ⟨*pedestrian*⟩ atropellar
II [*v + adv*] **(a)** «*battery*» (Auto) descargarse*
(b) «*business/factory*» venirse* abajo **(c)**
«*stocks*» agotarse
■ **run in** [*v + o + adv*] (BrE Auto) ⟨*car/engine*⟩
hacer* el rodaje de
■ **run into** [*v + prep + o*] **(a)** ⟨*vehicle*⟩ chocar*
con **(b)** ⟨*person/table*⟩ toparse con
■ **run off 1** [*v + o + adv, v + adv + o*] (produce)
⟨*copies*⟩ tirar*; ⟨*photocopies*⟩ sacar*
2 [*v + adv*] (depart) salir* corriendo
■ **run off with** [*v + adv + prep + o*] ▶ RUN AWAY
WITH 2
■ **run out** [*v + adv*] **(a)** (exhaust supplies): **to ∼ out
OF sth** quedarse SIN algo **(b)** «*money*» acabarse;
«*supplies/stock*» acabarse, agotarse; «*lease/
policy*» vencer*, caducar*
■ **run over 1** [*v + o + adv, v + adv + o*]
⟨*pedestrian*⟩ atropellar
2 [*v + prep + o*] (review) ⟨*details/plan*⟩ repasar;
(rehearse) ⟨*scene*⟩ ensayar
■ **run through** [*v + prep + o*] ▶ RUN OVER 2
■ **run up 1** [*v + adv + o*] **(a)** ⟨*total/debts*⟩ ir*
acumulando **(b)** ⟨*flag*⟩ izar*
2 [*v + o + adv, v + adv + o*] ⟨*dress*⟩ hacer*
(*rápidamente*)

■ **run up against** [*v* + *adv* + *prep* + *o*] ⟨*difficulty/obstacle*⟩ toparse *or* tropezar* con

run² *n* **1** (on foot): **to go for a ~** salir* a correr; **on the ~:** he's on the ~ está prófugo; **after seven years on the ~** después de estar siete años huyendo de la justicia; **to make a ~ for it** escaparse **2 (a)** (trip, outing) vuelta *f*, paseo *m* (*en coche*) **(b)** (journey): **it's only a short ~** está muy cerca **3 (a)** (sequence): **a ~ of good/bad luck** una racha de buena/mala suerte, una buena/mala racha **(b)** (period of time): **in the long ~** a la larga **4** (heavy demand) **~ ON sth:** there's been a ~ on these watches estos relojes han estado muy solicitados **5** (Cin, Theat) temporada *f* **6** (track) pista *f*; **ski ~** pista de esquí **7** (in stocking, knitted garment) carrera *f* **8** (in baseball, cricket) carrera *f*

runaway¹ /ˈrʌnəweɪ/ *n* fugitivo, -va *m,f*

runaway² *adj* (*before n*) ⟨*slave/prisoner*⟩ fugitivo

run: ~down *n* resumen *m*; **~-down** /ˈrʌnˈdaʊn/ *adj* (*pred* ~ **down**) **(a)** (tired, sickly) (*usu pred*) **to be/feel ~ down** estar*/sentirse* cansado *or* débil **(b)** (dilapidated) ⟨*district/hotel*⟩ venido a menos

rung¹ /rʌŋ/ *past p of* RING²

rung² *n* **(a)** (of ladder, chair) travesaño *m* **(b)** (in career, organization) peldaño *m*

runner /ˈrʌnər ‖ ˈrʌnə(r)/ *n* **1** (in race, baseball) corredor, -dora *m,f*; (taking messages) mensajero, -ra *m,f* **2 (a)** (on sled) patín *m* **(b)** (for drawer) riel *m*, guía *f*

runner: ~ bean *n* (esp BrE) habichuela *f* (Col) *or* (Esp) judía *f* verde *or* (Chi) poroto *m* verde *or* (RPl) chaucha *f or* (Ven) vainita *f or* (Méx) ejote *m*; **~-up** /ˈrʌnərˈʌp/ *n* (*pl* **~s-up**): **to be ~-up** quedar en segundo lugar *or* puesto

running¹ /ˈrʌnɪŋ/ *n* **(a)** (exercise): **~ is a good form of exercise** correr es muy buen ejercicio; **there are five candidates in the ~ for the post** hay cinco candidatos compitiendo *or* en liza por el puesto **(b)** (of machine) funcionamiento *m*, marcha *f* **(c)** (management) gestión *f*

running² *adj* (*before n, no comp*) **1 (a) to take a ~ jump** saltar tomando carrera *or* (Esp) carrerilla **(b)** (continuous) ⟨*joke*⟩ continuo; **~ water** agua *f* corriente **2** (discharging) ⟨*sore*⟩ supurante

running³ *adv*: **the third day ~** el tercer día consecutivo *or* seguido

running costs *pl n* (of car) gastos *mpl* de mantenimiento; (of company) costos *mpl or* (Esp) costes *mpl* corrientes

runny /ˈrʌni/ *adj* **-nier, -niest (a)** ⟨*eyes*⟩ lloroso; **I've got a ~ nose** me gotea la nariz **(b)** ⟨*sauce*⟩ líquido

run-of-the-mill /ˈrʌnəvðəˈmɪl/ *adj* (*pred* **run of the mill**) ⟨*job/car*⟩ común *or* normal y corriente

runt /rʌnt/ *n* (Agr) animal más pequeño de una camada

run: ~-up *n* (preparatory period) **~-up TO** período *m* previo A algo; **~way** *n* (Aviat) pista *f*; (at fashion show) (AmE) pasarela *f*

rupee /ˈruːpiː, ruːˈpiː/ *n* rupia *f*

rupture¹ /ˈrʌptʃər ‖ ˈrʌptʃə(r)/ *n* ruptura *f*

rupture² *vt* romper*

rural /ˈrʊrəl ‖ ˈrʊərəl/ *adj* rural

ruse /ruːs, ruːz ‖ ruːz/ *n* artimaña *f*, treta *f*

rush¹ /rʌʃ/ *n* **1 (a)** (haste) (*no pl*) prisa *f*, apuro *m* (AmL); **I'm in a ~** tengo prisa, ando *or* estoy apurado (AmL) **(b)** (movement): **a ~ of air** una ráfaga de aire; **there was a ~ for the exit** todo el mundo se precipitó hacia la salida **2** (Bot) junco *m*

rush² *vi* **(a)** (hurry) darse* prisa, apurarse (AmL); **she ~ed through the first course** se comió el primer plato a todo correr *or* a la carrera **(b)** (run) (+ *adv compl*): **he ~ed in/out** entró/salió corriendo; **to ~ around** ir* de acá para allá, correr de un lado para otro **(c)** (surge, flow): **blood ~ed to his face** (from anger) se le subió la sangre a la cabeza

■ ~ *vt* **(a)** ⟨*job*⟩ hacer* a todo correr *or* a la carrera, hacer* deprisa y corriendo; ⟨*person*⟩ meterle prisa a, apurar (AmL) **(b)** (take hastily): **she was ~ed to hospital** la llevaron rápidamente al hospital

■ **rush into** [*v* + *prep* + *o*]: **she ~ed into marriage** se precipitó al casarse; **don't ~ into anything** no te precipites

rush: ~ hour *n* hora *f* pico (AmL), hora *f* punta (Esp); **~ job** *n* (colloq) (urgent) trabajo *m* urgente; (hastily done): **it was a ~ job** se hizo a todo correr *or* deprisa y corriendo *or* a la(s) carrera(s)

rusk /rʌsk/ *n* galleta *f* (dura, para bebés)

Russia /ˈrʌʃə/ *n* Rusia *f*

Russian¹ /ˈrʌʃən/ *adj* ruso

Russian² *n* **(a)** (language) ruso *m* **(b)** (person) ruso, -sa *m,f*

Russian roulette *n* ruleta *f* rusa

rust¹ /rʌst/ *n* óxido *m*, herrumbre *f*, orín *m*

rust² *vi* oxidarse, herrumbrarse

rustic /ˈrʌstɪk/ *adj* rústico

rustle¹ /ˈrʌsəl/ *vi* ⟨*leaves*⟩ susurrar; ⟨*paper*⟩ crujir

■ ~ *vt* **1** ⟨*wind*⟩ ⟨*leaves*⟩ hacer* susurrar **2** (steal) ⟨*cattle/horses*⟩ robar

rustle² *n* (of leaves) susurro *m*; (of paper) crujido *m*; (of silk) frufrú *m*

rustler /ˈrʌslər ‖ ˈrʌslə(r)/ *n* ladrón, -drona *m,f* de ganado

rustproof /ˈrʌstpruːf/ *adj* ⟨*surface/metal*⟩ inoxidable; ⟨*coating*⟩ anticorrosivo, antioxidante

rusty /ˈrʌsti/ *adj* **-tier, -tiest** oxidado, herrumbrado; **to get** *o* (BrE also) **go ~** oxidarse, herrumbrarse; **my German is a bit ~** tengo muy olvidado el alemán

rut /rʌt/ *n* **1** (groove) surco *m*, rodada *f*; **to be in a ~** estar* anquilosado; **to get into a ~** anquilosarse **2** (Zool) celo *m*

rutabaga /ˈruːtəbeɪgə ‖ ˌruːtəˈbeɪgə/ *n* (AmE) nabo *m* sueco

ruthless /ˈruːθləs ‖ ˈruːθlɪs/ *adj* ⟨*person*⟩ despiadado; ⟨*persecution*⟩ implacable, inexorable

Rwanda /rʊˈændə/ *n* Ruanda *f*

Rwandan /rʊˈændən/ *adj* ruandés

rye /raɪ/ *n* **(a)** (plant, grain) centeno *m* **(b) ~ (bread)** pan *m* de centeno

Ss

S, s /es/ n S, s f

S (a) (Geog) (= **south**) S **(b)** (Clothing) (= **small**) P

Sabbath /'sæbəθ/ n (Jewish) sábado m; (Christian) domingo m

sabbatical /sə'bætɪkəl/ n (year) año m sabático; (period) período m sabático

saber, (BrE) **sabre** /'seɪbər ‖'seɪbə(r)/ n sable m

sabotage¹ /'sæbətɑːʒ/ n sabotaje m

sabotage² vt sabotear

saboteur /ˌsæbə'tɜːr ‖ˌsæbə'tɜː(r)/ n saboteador, -dora m,f

sabre n (BrE) ▶ SABER

saccharin /'sækərən ‖'sækərɪn/ n sacarina f

sachet /sæ'ʃeɪ ‖'sæʃeɪ/ n (of shampoo, cream) sachet m; (of powder, sugar) (BrE) sobrecito m

sack¹ /sæk/ n **1 (a)** (large bag) saco m **(b)** (paper bag) (AmE) bolsa f (de papel) **2** (dismissal) (BrE colloq): **to give sb the ~** echar a algn (del trabajo), botar a algn (del trabajo) (AmL fam)

sack² vt **1** (dismiss) (BrE colloq) ⟨person/ employee⟩ echar (del trabajo), botar (del trabajo) (AmL fam) **2** (destroy) ⟨town/city⟩ saquear

sacrament /'sækrəmənt/ n sacramento m

sacred /'seɪkrəd ‖'seɪkrɪd/ adj sagrado

sacrifice¹ /'sækrəfaɪs ‖'sækrɪfaɪs/ n **1** (Occult, Relig) **(a)** (practice, act) sacrificio m **(b)** (offering) ofrenda f **2** (giving up) sacrificio m; **to make ~s** sacrificarse*

sacrifice² vt sacrificar*

sacrilege /'sækrəlɪdʒ ‖'sækrɪlɪdʒ/ n sacrilegio m

sad /sæd/ adj **-dd-** triste; **~ to say** lamentablemente

sadden /'sædn̩/ vt entristecer*

saddle¹ /'sædl̩/ n (on horse) silla f (de montar); (on bicycle) sillín m

saddle² vt **(a)** ~ **(up)** ⟨horse⟩ ensillar **(b)** (burden) (colloq) **to ~ sb WITH sth** endilgarle* or (esp AmL) encajarle algo A algn

saddle-bag /'sædlbæg/ n (on horse) alforja f; (on bicycle) maletero m

sadist /'seɪdast ‖'seɪdɪst/ n sádico, -ca m,f

sadly /'sædli/ adv **(a)** (sorrowfully) ⟨smile/speak⟩ tristemente, con tristeza **(b)** (regrettably): **you are ~ mistaken** estás totalmente equivocado **(c)** (unfortunately) ⟨indep⟩ lamentablemente

sadness /'sædnəs ‖'sædnɪs/ n tristeza f

sae, SAE n (BrE) (= **stamped, addressed envelope**) ▶ SASE

safari /sə'fɑːri/ n safari m; (before n) ~ **park** safari-park m

safe¹ /seɪf/ adj **safer, safest** **1** (secure from danger) seguro; ⟨haven/place⟩ seguro; **you are not ~ here** corres peligro aquí; **keep these documents ~** guarda estos documentos en un lugar seguro; **they're ~** están a salvo; **they were found ~ and well** o ~ **and sound** los encontraron sanos y salvos **2** (not dangerous) ⟨ladder⟩ seguro **3** (not risky) ⟨investment/sex/method⟩ seguro; **to be on the ~ side** por si acaso; **better (to be) ~ than sorry** más vale prevenir que curar

safe² n caja f fuerte, caja f de caudales

safe: ~-conduct /ˌseɪf'kɑːndʌkt ‖ˌseɪf'kɒndʌkt/ n protección f; ~**-deposit (box)** /'seɪfdɪ'pɑːzət ‖'seɪfdɪ'pɒzɪt/ n caja f de seguridad

safeguard¹ /'seɪfgɑːrd ‖'seɪfgɑːd/ n salvaguarda f

safeguard² vt salvaguardar

safe: ~ house n piso m franco; ~**keeping** n: **he gave her the watch for ~keeping** le dio el reloj para que lo guardara en lugar seguro or (esp Esp frml) para que lo pusiera a buen recaudo

safely /'seɪfli/ adv **1 (a)** (without mishap, unharmed): **we got home ~** llegamos a casa sin novedad **(b)** (without danger) sin peligro; **drive ~** conduzca con prudencia or cuidado **2** (with certainty) ⟨say/assume⟩ sin temor a equivocarse (or equivocarnos etc)

safety /'seɪfti/ n (pl **-ties**)(security, freedom from risk) seguridad f; (before n) ⟨device/precautions/ regulations⟩ de seguridad

safety: ~ belt n cinturón m de seguridad; ~ **catch** (on gun) seguro m; ~ **net** n (for acrobats) red f de seguridad; (protection) protección f; ~ **pin** n imperdible m, gancho m (Andes), alfiler m de gancho (CS, Ven), gancho m de nodriza (Col), seguro m (Méx)

saffron /'sæfrən/ n azafrán m

sag /sæg/ vi **-gg-** **(a)** ⟨beams/ceiling⟩ combarse; ⟨bed⟩ hundirse **(b)** (hang down, droop): ~**ging breasts** pechos mpl caídos

saga /'sɑːgə/ n (Lit) saga f; (long story) historia f, saga f

sage /seɪdʒ/ n **1** (Bot, Culin) salvia f **2** (wise man) sabio m

Sagittarius /ˌsædʒə'teriəs ‖ˌsædʒɪ'teəriəs/ n **(a)** (sign) ⟨no art⟩ Sagitario **(b)** (person) Sagitario or sagitario mf, sagitariano, -na m,f

Sahara /sə'hærə ‖sə'hɑːrə/ n **the ~** el Sahara or (Esp) el Sáhara

said /sed/ past & past p of SAY¹

sail¹ /seɪl/ n (of ship, boat) vela f; **to set ~** (start journey) zarpar, hacerse* a la mar; «*yacht/ galleon*» hacerse* a la vela

sail² vt ‹*boat/ship*› gobernar*
■ ~ vi (a) (travel) «*ship/boat*» navegar*; «*person/ passenger*» ir* en barco; **to go ~ing** salir a navegar (b) (depart) «*person/ship*» zarpar, salir*
■ **sail through** [v + prep + o]: you'll ~ **through the exam** aprobarás el examen con los ojos cerrados

sailboat /'seɪlbəʊt/ n (AmE) velero m, barco m de vela

sailing /'seɪlɪŋ/ n (a) (skill) navegación f (b) (Sport) vela f

sailing: ~ boat n (BrE) ▶ SAILBOAT; **~ ship** n velero m, barco m de vela

sailor /'seɪlər ‖'seɪlə(r)/ n (a) (seaman) marinero m (b) (Sport) navegante mf

saint /seɪnt/ n

■ **Note** Although the usual translation for *saint* as a title is *san* for a man or *santa* for a woman, *santo* is used before *Domingo*, *Tomás*, *Tomé* and *Toribio*.

(a) (canonized person) santo, -ta m,f (b) **Saint** /seɪnt ‖sənt/ (before name) san, santa

sake /seɪk/ n (a) (benefit, account): **for my/their ~** por mí/ellos; **for your own ~** por tu propio bien (b) (purpose, end): **art for art's ~** el arte por el arte; **for argument's ~** pongamos por caso (c) (in interj phrases): **for goodness' o heaven's ~!** ¡por Dios!; **for God's ~!** ¡por el amor de Dios!

salad /'sæləd/ n ensalada f; (before n) **~ bowl** ensaladera f; **~ dressing** aliño m para ensalada

salad cream n (BrE) aliño para ensalada *parecido a la mayonesa*

salami /sə'lɑːmi/ n (pl **-mis**) salami o (CS) salame m

salary /'sæləri/ n (pl **-ries**) sueldo m

sale /seɪl/ n **1** (a) (act of selling) venta f (b) (individual transaction) venta f (c) (auction) subasta f, remate m (AmL)
2 (in phrases) **for sale:** ➌ **for sale** se vende; **on sale** (at reduced price) (AmE) **toys are on ~ this week** esta semana los juguetes están rebajados; (offered for sale) (BrE): **on ~ now at leading stores** ya está a la venta en los principales comercios **3** (clearance) liquidación f; (seasonal reductions) rebajas fpl; (before n) ‹*price*› de liquidación **4** **sales** (a) (volume sold) (sometimes sing) (volumen m de) ventas fpl (b) (department) (+ sing o pl vb) ventas (+ sing vb)

saleroom /'seɪlruːm, -rʊm/ n (BrE) ▶ SALESROOM A

sales /seɪlz/: **~clerk** n (AmE) vendedor, -dora m,f, dependiente, -ta m,f; **~man** /'seɪlzmən/ n (pl **-men** /-mən/) (in shop) vendedor m; (representative) representante m, corredor m (RPl); **~room** n (AmE) (a) (for auctions) sala f de subastas, sala f de remates (AmL) (b) (showroom) salón m de exposición (y ventas); **~ slip** n (AmE) recibo m; **~woman** /-wʊmən/ n (in shop) vendedora f; (representative) representante f, corredora f (RPl)

saliva /sə'laɪvə/ n saliva f

sallow /'sæləʊ/ adj **-er**, **-est** cetrino

salmon /'sæmən/ n (pl ~) salmón m

salon /sə'lɑːn ‖'sælɒn/ n (business): hairdressing **~** peluquería f; **beauty ~** salón m de belleza

saloon /sə'luːn/ n **1** (bar) (AmE) bar m (del Lejano Oeste) **2** ~ (**car**) (BrE) sedán m

salt¹ /sɔːlt/ n sal f

salt² vt (a) (put salt on) ‹*vegetables/meat*› salar, ponerle* o echarle sal a; ‹*road*› echar sal en (b) **salted** past p salado

salt: ~ cellar n salero m; **~water** adj ‹*lake*› de agua salada; ‹*fish*› de mar, de agua salada

salty /'sɔːlti/ adj **-tier**, **-tiest** salado

salubrious /sə'luːbriəs/ adj (a) (healthy) (frml) saludable, salubre (b) (wholesome) (usu neg): **not a very ~ district** un barrio muy poco recomendable

salutary /'sæljətəri ‖'sæljʊtri/ adj saludable

salute¹ /sə'luːt/ n (a) (gesture) saludo m, venia f (RPl) (b) (firing of guns) salva f (c) (tribute) homenaje m

salute² vt (a) (Mil) ‹*officer*› saludar (b) (acknowledge, pay tribute) (frml) ‹*courage/achievement*› rendir* homenaje a
■ ~ vi (Mil) **to ~** (**to sb**) hacerle* el saludo or (RPl) la venia (A algn)

Salvadorean¹, Salvadorian /'sælvə'dɔːriən/ adj salvadoreño

Salvadorean², Salvadorian n salvadoreño, -ña m,f

salvage /'sælvɪdʒ/ vt rescatar

salvation /sæl'veɪʃən/ n salvación f

Salvation Army n Ejército m de Salvación

salve¹ /sæv ‖sælv/ n (ointment) bálsamo m, ungüento m

salve² vt: **to ~ one's conscience** acallar la voz de su (or mi etc) conciencia

Samaritan /sə'mærətn ‖sə'mærɪtən/ n (Bib) samaritano, -na m,f; **the good ~** el buen samaritano

same¹ /seɪm/ adj (before n) mismo, misma; **the ~ address/mistake** la misma dirección/el mismo error; **the two boxes are exactly the ~** las dos cajas son exactamente iguales; **that dress is the ~ as mine** ese vestido es igual al mío; **the ~ thing happened to me** a mí me pasó lo mismo; **on that very ~ day** ese mismísimo día

same² pron (a) : **the ~** lo mismo; **have a nice vacation! — ~ to you!** ¡felices vacaciones! — ¡igualmente! (b) **all the same, just the same** igual; (as linker) de todas formas or maneras; **it's all the ~ to me/you/them** me/te/les da lo mismo, me/te/ les da igual

same³ adv: **the ~** igual

sample¹ /'sæmpəl ‖'sɑːmpəl/ n muestra f

sample² vt ‹*food*› degustar

sanatorium /'sænə'tɔːriəm/ n (pl **-riums** or **-ria** /-riə/) sanatorio m (para convalecientes)

sanctify /'sæŋktɪfaɪ/ vt **-fies**, **-fying**, **-fied** santificar*

sanctimonious /'sæŋktə'məʊniəs ‖,sæŋktɪ'məʊniəs/ adj (frml) moralista, gazmoño, mojigato

sanction¹ /'sæŋkʃən/ n **1** (authorization) autorización f, sanción f **2** **sanctions** pl (coercive measures) sanciones fpl

sanction² vt ‹*act/initiative*› sancionar (frml), aprobar*; ‹*injustice*› consentir*

sanctity /'sæŋktəti/ n (a) (inviolability) inviolabilidad f (b) (holiness) santidad f

sanctuary /'sæŋktʃueri ‖'sæŋktjʊəri/ n (pl -ries) (a) (protection, safety) asilo m, refugio m (b) (place of refuge) santuario m

sand¹ /sænd/ n arena f

sand² vt ~ (**down**) ⟨wood/furniture⟩ lijar; ⟨floor⟩ pulir

sandal /'sændl/ n sandalia f

sand: ~**bank** n banco m de arena; ~**box** n (AmE) cajón m de arena (en parques y jardines); ~**castle** n castillo m de arena; ~**paper** n papel m de lija; ~**pit** n (BrE) ▶ ~BOX; ~**stone** n arenisca f; ~**storm** n tormenta f de arena

sandwich¹ /'sænwɪtʃ ‖'sændwɪdʒ/ n (pl ~es) sándwich m, emparedado m, ≈ bocadillo m (Esp)

sandwich² vt (usu pass): **I was ~ed between two fat men** estaba apretujado entre dos gordos

sandy /'sændi/ adj -dier, -diest (a) ⟨beach/path⟩ de arena; ⟨soil⟩ arenoso (b) (in color) ⟨hair⟩ rubio rojizo adj inv

sane /seɪn/ adj **saner, sanest** (a) (not mad) cuerdo (b) (sensible) sensato

sang /sæŋ/ past of SING

sanitarium /ˌsænə'teriəm ‖ˌsænɪ'teəriəm/ n (AmE) ▶ SANATORIUM

sanitary /'sænəteri ‖'sænɪtri/ adj (a) (concerning health) (before n) ⟨conditions/regulations⟩ sanitario; ⟨inspector⟩ de sanidad (b) (hygienic) higiénico

sanitary napkin, (BrE) **sanitary towel** n compresa f, paño m higiénico

sanitation /ˌsænə'teɪʃən ‖ˌsænɪ'teɪʃən/ n (a) (hygiene) condiciones fpl de salubridad (b) (waste disposal system) servicios mpl sanitarios

sanitize /'sænətaɪz ‖'sænɪtaɪz/ vt (a) (disinfect) desinfectar (b) (make inoffensive) (pej) hacer* potable; **a ~d version** una versión aséptica

sanity /'sænəti/ n (a) (mental health) razón f, cordura f (b) (good sense) sensatez f

sank /sæŋk/ past of SINK¹

Santa Claus /'sæntəklɔːz/ n Papá Noel, San Nicolás, Santa Claus, Viejo m Pascuero (Chi)

sap¹ /sæp/ n savia f

sap² vt -pp- minar

sapling /'sæplɪŋ/ n árbol m joven

sapphire /'sæfaɪr ‖'sæfaɪə(r)/ n zafiro m

sarcasm /'sɑːrkæzəm ‖'sɑːkæzəm/ n sarcasmo m

sarcastic /sɑːr'kæstɪk ‖sɑː'kæstɪk/ adj sarcástico

sardine /sɑːr'diːn ‖sɑː'diːn/ n sardina f

sardonic /sɑːr'dɑːnɪk ‖sɑː'dɒnɪk/ adj sardónico

sari /'sɑːri/ n (pl ~s) sari m

SASE n (AmE) (= **self-addressed stamped envelope**): **I enclose an ~** adjunto sobre franqueado (a mi nombre)

sash /sæʃ/ n ① (on dress) faja f; (on uniform — around waist) fajín m; (— over shoulder) banda f ② (of window) marco m

sassy /'sæsi/ adj -sier, -siest (AmE colloq) (a) (impertinent) caradura (fam) (b) (brash) ⟨hat/style⟩ llamativo y atrevido

sat /sæt/ past & past p of SIT

Satan /'seɪtn/ n Satanás

satanic /sə'tænɪk/ adj satánico

satchel /'sætʃəl/ n cartera f (de colegial)

sate /seɪt/ vt (liter) (usu pass) ⟨appetite/lust⟩ saciar (liter)

satellite /'sætlaɪt ‖'sætəlaɪt/ n ① (a) (Aerosp) satélite m (artificial); (before n) ~ **TV** televisión f por or vía satélite (b) (Astron) satélite m ② (dependent body, state) satélite m; (before n) **a ~ town** una ciudad satélite

satin /'sætn ‖'sætɪn/ n satén m, satín m (AmL)

satire /'sætaɪr ‖'sætaɪə(r)/ n sátira f

satirical /sə'tɪrɪkəl/ adj satírico

satirize /'sætəraɪz/ vt satirizar*

satisfaction /ˌsætəs'fækʃən ‖ˌsætɪs'fækʃən/ n satisfacción f

satisfactory /ˌsætəs'fæktri ‖ˌsætɪs'fæktəri/ adj satisfactorio

satisfied /'sætəsfaɪd ‖'sætɪsfaɪd/ adj ⟨expression/customer⟩ satisfecho; ⟨smile⟩ de satisfacción

satisfy /'sætəsfaɪ ‖'sætɪsfaɪ/ vt -fies, -fying, -fied ① (a) (please) satisfacer* (b) (meet) ⟨requirements⟩ llenar; ⟨demand⟩ satisfacer* ② (convince) (often pass) **to ~ sb OF sth** convencer* a algn DE algo

satisfying /'sætəsfaɪɪŋ ‖'sætɪsfaɪɪŋ/ adj (a) (pleasing) ⟨result/job⟩ satisfactorio (b) (filling) ⟨meal⟩ que llena

satsuma /sæt'suːmə/ n satsuma f (tipo de mandarina)

saturate /'sætʃəreɪt/ vt ① (drench) empapar ② (fill) ⟨market/mind/place⟩ saturar ③ (Chem, Phys) saturar

saturation /ˌsætʃə'reɪʃən/ n ① (Busn, Marketing) saturación f ② (Chem, Phys) saturación f

Saturday /'sætərdeɪ, -di ‖'sætədeɪ, -di/ n sábado m; see also MONDAY

Saturn /'sætərn ‖'sætən/ n Saturno m

sauce /sɔːs/ n salsa f

saucepan /'sɔːspæn ‖'sɔːspən/ n cacerola f, cazo m (Esp); (large) olla f

saucer /'sɔːsər ‖'sɔːsə(r)/ n platillo m

saucy /'sɔːsi, 'sɔːsi ‖'sɔːsi/ adj -cier, -ciest insolente, fresco (fam)

Saudi¹ /'saʊdi/ adj saudita, saudí

Saudi² n saudita mf, saudí mf

Saudi Arabia /ə'reɪbiə/ n Arabia f Saudita, Arabia f Saudí

sauna /'sɔːnə/ n sauna f, sauna m (AmL)

saunter /'sɔːntər ‖'sɔːntə(r)/ vi pasear; **she ~ed in/out** entró/salió andando despacio

sausage /'sɔːsɪdʒ ‖'sɒsɪdʒ/ n (for cooking) salchicha f; (cold, cured) embutido m

sauté /sɔː'teɪ ‖'səʊteɪ/ vt -tés, -téeing or -téing, -téed or -téd saltear

savage¹ /'sævɪdʒ/ adj (a) (fierce, wild) ⟨beast/attack⟩ salvaje; ⟨blow⟩ violento (b) (uncivilized) ⟨tribe/people⟩ salvaje

savage² n salvaje mf

savage³ vt atacar* salvajemente a

savagely /'sævɪdʒli/ adv salvajemente

savagery /'sævɪdʒri/ n ferocidad f

save¹ /seɪv/ vt ① (a) (preserve) ⟨life/person/job⟩ salvar; ⟨possessions⟩ rescatar; **firefighters ~d 20 people** bomberos rescataron a 20 personas (b)

837

save ···❖ scapegoat

(redeem) ⟨soul/sinner⟩ salvar **2** **(a)** (be economical with) ⟨money/fuel/space/time⟩ ahorrar **(b)** (spare, avoid) ⟨trouble/expense/embarrassment⟩ ahorrar, evitar **3** **(a)** (keep, put aside) guardar; ⟨money⟩ ahorrar; **don't eat it now;** ∼ **it for later** no te lo comas ahora; déjalo para luego; **to** ∼ **one's energy** guardar las energías **(b)** (Comput) guardar **4** (Sport) ⟨shot/penalty⟩ salvar
■ ∼ *vi* ahorrar
■ **save up** **1** [v + adv] ahorrar **2** [v + o + adv, v + adv + o] ahorrar

save² *n* parada *f*

save³ *prep* (frml) (apart from) ∼ **(for)** salvo, excepto

saving¹ /'seɪvɪŋ/ *n* **(a)** (economy) ahorro *m* **(b)** **savings** *pl* ahorros *mpl*; (before n) ∼**s account** cuenta *f* de ahorros

saving² *adj* (before n) ▶ GRACE 2c

savings /'seɪvɪŋz/: ∼ **and loan** *n* ∼ ∼ ∼ **(association/company)** (AmE) sociedad *f* de ahorro y préstamos; ∼ **bank** *n* caja *f* de ahorros

savior, (BrE) **saviour** /'seɪvjər ‖'seɪvjə(r)/ *n* salvador, -dora *m,f*

savor¹, (BrE) **savour** /'seɪvər ‖'seɪvə(r)/ *vt* saborear

savor², (BrE) **savour** *n* (taste) sabor *m*; (hint, trace) dejo *m*

savory, (BrE) **savoury** /'seɪvəri/ *adj* (tasty) sabroso; (wholesome) (*usu with neg*) limpio

savour *vt/n* (BrE) ▶ SAVOR¹,²

savoury /'seɪvəri/ *adj* (BrE) **(a)** ▶ SAVORY² **(b)** (not sweet) salado

saw¹ /sɔː/ *past of* SEE

saw² *n* (manual) sierra *f*; (— with one handle) serrucho *m*; (power-driven) sierra *f* mecánica

saw³ *vt* (*past p* **sawed** *or* (esp BrE) **sawn**) (with handsaw) cortar (con serrucho), serruchar (AmL); (with a larger saw) cortar (con sierra), serrar*, aserrar*

sawdust /'sɔːdʌst/ *n* serrín *m*, aserrín *m* (esp AmL)

sawed-off /'sɔːdˈɔːf ‖'sɔːdɒf/, (BrE) **sawn-off** /'sɔːnˈɔːf ‖'sɔːnɒf/ *adj*: ∼ **shotgun** escopeta *f* recortada

sawn /sɔːn/ *past p of* SAW³

sawn-off *adj* (BrE) ▶ SAWED-OFF

saxophone /'sæksəfəʊn/ *n* saxofón *m*, saxófono *m*

say¹ /seɪ/ (*pres* **says** /sez/; *past & past p* **said** /sed/) *vt* **1** (utter, express in speech) ⟨word/sentence⟩ decir*; ⟨prayer⟩ rezar*; **I said yes/no** dije que sí/no; **to** ∼ **sth TO sb** decirle* algo A algn; **why didn't you** ∼ **so before?** haberlo dicho antes; **that's to** ∼ es decir; **to** ∼ **the least** como mínimo; **what have you got to** ∼ **for yourself?** a ver, explícate; ∼ **no more** no me digas más; **you can** ∼ **that again!** ¡y que lo digas!; **it goes without** ∼**ing that** ... huelga decir que ...; **that's easier said than done** del dicho al hecho hay mucho trecho; **no sooner said than done** dicho y hecho; **when all's said and done** al fin y al cabo **2** «watch/dial» marcar* **3** (suppose) (colloq) suponer*; (let's) ∼ **that** ... supongamos que ... **4** (allege) decir*; ..., **or so he** ∼**s** ..., al menos eso es lo que dice

■ ∼ *vi* decir*; **I'd rather not** ∼ prefiero no decirlo; **it's hard to** ∼ es difícil decirlo

say² *interj* (AmE colloq) ¡oye! (fam)

say³ *n* (no pl) **(a)** (statement of view): **to have one's** ∼ dar* su (or mi etc) opinión **(b)** (power): **I have no** ∼ **in the matter** yo no tengo ni voz ni voto en el asunto

saying /'seɪɪŋ/ *n* refrán *m*, dicho *m*

SC = **South Carolina**

scab /skæb/ *n* **1** (on wound) costra *f* **2** (strikebreaker) (pej) esquirol *mf* (pey), carnero, -ra *m,f* (RPl fam & pey)

scaffold /'skæfəld, -fəʊld/ *n* (for execution) patíbulo *m*, cadalso *m*

scaffolding /'skæfəldɪŋ, '-fəʊldɪŋ/ *n* andamiaje *m*

scald /skɔːld/ *vt* escaldar

scale¹ /skeɪl/ *n*
I **1** (no pl) **(a)** (extent, size) escala *f*; **on a large/small** ∼ en gran/pequeña escala **(b)** (of map, diagram) escala *f*; (before n) ⟨model/drawing⟩ a escala **2** (on measuring instrument) escala *f* **3** (Mus) escala *f* **4** (for weighing) (*usu pl*) balanza *f*, pesa *f*; **bathroom** ∼**s** una báscula *or* pesa (de baño) **II** **1** (on fish) escama *f* **2** (deposit in kettle, pipes) sarro *m*

scale² *vt* ⟨mountain/wall⟩ escalar; ⟨ladder⟩ subir
■ **scale down** [v + o + adv, v + adv + o] ⟨drawing⟩ reducir* (a escala); ⟨operation⟩ recortar

scallion /'skæljən/ *n* (AmE) **(a)** (young onion) cebolleta *f*, cebollino *m* **(b)** (shallot) chalote *m*, chalota *f*

scallop /'skæləp/ *n* vieira *f*, ostión *m* (CS)

scalp¹ /skælp/ *n* (Anat) cuero *m* cabelludo

scalp² *vt*: **to** ∼ **sb** arrancarle* la cabellera a algn

scalpel /'skælpəl/ *n* bisturí *m*, escalpelo *m*

scaly /'skeɪli/ *adj* **-lier, -liest** ⟨skin⟩ escamoso

scamper /'skæmpər ‖'skæmpə(r)/ *vi* corretear; **she** ∼**ed off** se fue correteando

scampi /'skæmpi/ *pl n* langostinos *mpl* (gen rebozados)

scan¹ /skæn/ *vt* **-nn-** **1** **(a)** ⟨horizon⟩ escudriñar **(b)** ⟨noticeboard/newspaper⟩ recorrer con la vista; ⟨report⟩ echarle un vistazo a **2** (Med) ⟨body/brain⟩ hacer* un escáner de; (with ultrasound scanner) hacer* una ecografía de

scan² *n* (Med) escáner *m*; (ultrasound) ecografía *f*

scandal /'skændl/ *n* **(a)** (outrage) escándalo *m* **(b)** (gossip) chismorreo *m*

scandalize /'skændlaɪz/ *vt* escandalizar*

scandalous /'skændləs/ *adj* escandaloso

Scandinavia /ˌskændəˈneɪviə ‖ˌskændɪˈneɪviə/ *n* Escandinavia *f*

Scandinavian¹ /ˌskændəˈneɪviən ‖ˌskændɪˈneɪviən/ *adj* escandinavo

Scandinavian² *n* escandinavo, -va *m,f*

scanner /'skænər ‖'skænə(r)/ *n* (Med) escáner *m*, scanner *m*

scanty /'skænti/ *adj* **-tier, -tiest** ⟨information⟩ insuficiente; ⟨meal⟩ poco abundante, frugal; ⟨costume⟩ breve

scapegoat /'skeɪpgəʊt/ *n* chivo *m* expiatorio

scar¹ /skɑːr ‖skɑː(r)/ n cicatriz f

scar² vt **-rr-**: his face was badly ~red le quedó una enorme cicatriz en el rostro; **she'll be ~red for life** (physically) le va a quedar (la) cicatriz; (emotionally) va a quedar marcada

scarce /skers ‖skeəs/ adj escaso; **to be ~** escasear

scarcely /'skersli ‖'skeəsli/ adv apenas

scarcity /'skersəti ‖'skeəsəti/ n (pl **-ties**) escasez f

scare¹ /sker ‖skeə(r)/ vt asustar
■ **scare away, scare off** [v + o + adv, v + adv + o] espantar

scare² n (a) (fright, shock) susto m (b) (panic) (Journ): **bomb ~** amenaza f de bomba

scarecrow /'skerkrəʊ ‖'skeəkrəʊ/ n espantapájaros m

scared /skerd ‖skeəd/ adj asustado; **I'm ~** tengo miedo; **to be ~ OF sth/sb** tenerle* miedo A algo/algn

scarf /skɑːrf ‖skɑːf/ n (pl ~**s** or **scarves**) (a) (muffler) bufanda f (b) (square) pañuelo m

scarlet /'skɑːrlət ‖'skɑːlət/ adj (rojo) escarlata adj inv

scarlet fever n escarlatina f

scarves /skɑːrvz ‖skɑːvz/ pl of SCARF

scathing /'skeɪðɪŋ/ adj mordaz

scatter /'skætər ‖'skætə(r)/ vt **1** ⟨salt/grit⟩ esparcir*; ⟨seeds⟩ sembrar* (a voleo) **2** (disperse) ⟨crowd/group⟩ dispersar; **they are ~ed all over the country** están desperdigados por todo el país
■ ~ vi ⟨crowd/light⟩ dispersarse

scatterbrained /'skætərbreɪnd ‖'skætəbreɪnd/ adj atolondrado, despistado

scattered /'skætərd ‖'skætəd/ adj (before n) ⟨fighting/applause/outbreak⟩ aislado; ⟨community⟩ diseminado; ~ **showers** chubascos mpl aislados

scavenge /'skævəndʒ ‖'skævɪndʒ/ vi **to ~ FOR sth** escarbar or hurgar* en busca de algo

scavenger /'skævəndʒər ‖'skævɪndʒə(r)/ n (a) (animal, bird) carroñero, -ra m,f (b) (person) persona que busca comida etc hurgando en los desperdicios

scenario /səˈneriəʊ, -ˈnæ- ‖sɪˈnɑːriəʊ/ n (pl **-os**) (a) (Cin, TV) guion m (b) (of future) perspectiva f, escenario m (period)

scene /siːn/ n **1** (a) (view, situation) escena f (b) (of incident, crime) escena f; **it was the ~ of violent demonstrations** fue el escenario de violentas manifestaciones; **to appear on the ~** aparecer*; **to set the ~ (for sth)** situar* la escena (de algo) **2** (in play, book etc) escena f **3** (stage setting) decorado m; **behind the ~s** entre bastidores **4** (fuss, row) escena f **5** (sphere) ámbito m; **it's not my ~** (colloq) no es lo mío

scenery /'siːnəri/ n (a) (surroundings) paisaje m (b) (Theat) escenografía f

scenic /'siːnɪk/ adj pintoresco

scent¹ /sent/ n (a) (fragrance) perfume m (b) (perfume) (BrE) perfume m (c) (trail) rastro m; **to put o throw sb off the ~** despistar a algn

scent² vt (a) (sense) ⟨danger/victory⟩ intuir* (b) (perfume) ⟨air/room/skin⟩ perfumar (c) **scented** past p ⟨writing paper⟩ perfumado; ⟨rose⟩ fragante

scepter, (BrE) **sceptre** /'septər ‖'septə(r)/ n cetro m

sceptic etc (BrE) ▶ SKEPTIC etc

sceptre n (BrE) ▶ SCEPTER

schedule¹ /'skedʒuːl ‖'ʃedjuːl/ n **1** (plan) programa m; **the flight is due to arrive on ~** el vuelo llegará a la hora prevista; **to be ahead of/ behind ~** estar* adelantado/atrasado con respecto al programa **2** (a) (list) (frml) lista f (b) (AmE) (timetable — for transport) horario m; (— for classes) horario m (de clases)

schedule² vt (timetable, plan) (usu pass) programar; **the conference is ~d to take place in August** la conferencia está planeada para el mes de agosto

scheduled /'skedʒuːld ‖'ʃedjuːld/ adj (before n) (a) (planned) ⟨meeting/visit⟩ previsto, programado (b) ⟨flight/service⟩ regular

scheme¹ /skiːm/ n (plan) plan m; (underhand) ardid m; (plot) confabulación f, conspiración f

scheme² vi intrigar*; (plot) conspirar

scheming¹ /'skiːmɪŋ/ adj intrigante

scheming² n maquinaciones fpl, intrigas fpl

schism /'sɪzəm, 'skɪzəm/ n cisma m

schizophrenia /ˌskɪtsəˈfriːniə ‖ˌskɪtsəˈfriːniə/ n esquizofrenia f

schizophrenic /ˌskɪtsəˈfrenɪk, -ˈfriːnɪk ‖ˌskɪtsəʊˈfrenɪk, -ˈfriːnɪk/ adj esquizofrénico

schmaltz /ʃmɔːlts/ n (colloq) sensiblería f

schmaltzy /'ʃmɔːltsi/ adj **-zier, -ziest** (colloq) sensiblero

scholar /'skɑːlər ‖'skɒlə(r)/ n (a) (learned person) erudito, -ta m,f (b) (holder of scholarship) becario, -ria m,f

scholarly /'skɑːlərli ‖'skɒləli/ adj ⟨person⟩ erudito, docto; ⟨attainments⟩ en el campo académico

scholarship /'skɑːlərʃɪp ‖'skɒləʃɪp/ n **1** (grant) beca f **2** (scholarliness) erudición f

school¹ /skuːl/ n **1** (a) (in primary, secondary education) colegio m, escuela f; **to go to ~** ir* al colegio or a la escuela; (within) ⟨uniform/rules⟩ del colegio; ⟨bus⟩ escolar; ~ **fees** cuotas que se pagan en un colegio particular, colegiatura f (Méx); ~ **year** año m escolar or lectivo (b) (college, university) (AmE) universidad f (c) (department) facultad f **2** (other training establishment) academia f, escuela f **3** (of fish) cardumen m, banco m; (of dolphins, whales) grupo m

school² vt ⟨person⟩ instruir*; (train) capacitar

school: ~**boy** n colegial m, escolar m; ~**child** n colegial, -giala m,f, escolar mf; ~**girl** n colegiala f, escolar f

schooling /'skuːlɪŋ/ n educación f, estudios mpl

school: ∼-leaver /'liːvər ‖'liːvə(r)/ n (BrE)
joven mf que termina el colegio; **∼master** n
(BrE frml) (in primary school) maestro m; (in secondary
school) profesor m; **∼mistress** n (BrE frml) (in
primary school) maestra; (in secondary school)
profesora f, **∼teacher** n (in primary school)
maestro, -tra m,f; (in secondary school) profesor,
-sora m,f

science /'saɪəns/ n ciencia f

science fiction n ciencia ficción f

scientific /ˌsaɪən'tɪfɪk/ adj científico

scientist /'saɪəntəst ‖'saɪəntɪst/ n científico,
-ca m,f

sci-fi /'saɪ'faɪ/ n (colloq) ciencia ficción f

Scillies /'sɪliz/ pl n ▶ ISLES OF SCILLY

scintillating /'sɪntleɪtɪŋ ‖'sɪntɪleɪtɪŋ/ adj
⟨wit/conversation⟩ chispeante

scissors /'sɪzərz ‖'sɪzəz/ n (+ pl vb) tijeras fpl,
tijera f

scoff /skɑːf ‖skɒf/ vi to ∼ (AT sb/sth) burlarse
(DE algn/algo)
■ ∼ vt (eat greedily) (BrE colloq) engullirse*

scold /skəʊld/ vt reprender, regañar, retar (CS)

scone /skəʊn, skɑːn ‖skɒn, skəʊn/ n (in UK)
bollito que se come untado de mantequilla,
mermelada etc, scone m (CS), bísquet m (Méx)

scoop /skuːp/ n **1 (a)** (for grain, ice cream) pala f
(b) (measure — of ice cream) bola f **2** (Journ)
primicia f
■ **scoop out 1** [v + o + adv, v + adv + o] ⟨flour/
rice/soil⟩ sacar* (con pala, cuchara etc) **2** [v +
adv + o] (hollow) ⟨hole/tunnel⟩ excavar
■ **scoop up** [v + o + adv, v + adv + o] recoger*
(con pala, cuchara etc)

scooter /'skuːtər ‖'skuːtə(r)/ n **(a)** (motor ∼)
escúter m, Vespa® f **(b)** (toy) patinete m

scope /skəʊp/ n (of law, regulations) alcance m; (of
influence) ámbito m; (of investigation) campo m

scorch /skɔːrtʃ ‖skɔːtʃ/ vt ⟨fabric⟩
chamuscar*; ⟨sun⟩ ⟨plant⟩ quemar, abrasar

score¹ /skɔːr ‖skɔː(r)/ n **1 (a)** (in game): the
final ∼ el resultado final; what's the ∼? ¿cómo
van? **(b)** (in competition, test etc) puntuación f,
puntaje m (AmL) **2 (a)** (account): I have no
worries on that ∼ en lo que a eso se refiere, no
me preocupo; to have a ∼ to settle with sb tener*
que arreglar cuentas con algn **(b)** (situation)
(colloq): to know the ∼ saber cómo son las cosas
3 (Mus) **(a)** (notation) partitura f **(b)** (music for
show, movie) música f **4** (twenty) veintena f; there
were ∼s of people there había muchísima gente

score² vt **1 (a)** (Sport) ⟨goal⟩ marcar*,
anotar(se) (AmL); you ∼ 20 points for that eso te
da or (AmL tb) con eso te anotas 20 puntos **(b)** (in
competition, test) ⟨person⟩ sacar* **(c)** (win) ⟨success⟩
lograr, conseguir* **2** (cut, mark) ⟨surface/paper⟩
marcar*
■ ∼ vi (Sport) marcar*, anotar(se) un tanto (AmL)

scoreboard /'skɔːrbɔːrd ‖'skɔːbɔːd/ n
marcador m

scorn¹ /skɔːrn ‖'skɔːn/ n desdén m; to pour ∼
on sth desdeñar algo

scorn² vt (reject, despise) desdeñar

scornful /'skɔːrnfəl ‖'skɔːnfəl/ adj desdeñoso;
to be ∼ of sth desdeñar algo

Scorpio /'skɔːrpiəʊ ‖'skɔːpiəʊ/ n (pl -os) **(a)**

(sign) (no art) Escorpio, Escorpión **(b)** (person)
Escorpio or escorpio mf, Escorpión or escorpión
mf, escorpión, -na m,f

scorpion /'skɔːrpiən ‖'skɔːpiən/ n escorpión
m, alacrán m

Scot /skɑːt ‖skɒt/ n escocés, -cesa m,f

scotch¹ /skɑːtʃ ‖skɒtʃ/ vt ⟨plan/efforts⟩ echar
por tierra; ⟨rumors⟩ acallar

scotch², Scotch n whisky m or güisqui m
(escocés)

Scotch: ∼ egg n: huevo duro envuelto en
carne de salchicha y rebozado; **∼ tape**® n (AmE)
cinta f Scotch®, cel(l)o® m (Esp), (cinta f) durex®
m (AmL)

scot-free /'skɑːt'friː ‖ˌskɒt'friː/ adj (pred): to
get away ∼ quedar impune

Scotland /'skɑːtlənd ‖'skɒtlənd/ n Escocia f

Scots /skɑːts ‖skɒts/ adj ⟨person etc⟩ escocés

Scots: ∼man /'skɑːtsmən ‖'skɒtsmən/ n (pl
-men /-mən/) escocés m; **∼woman** n escocesa
f

Scottish /'skɑːtɪʃ ‖'skɒtɪʃ/ adj escocés

scoundrel /'skaʊndrəl/ n (dated) sinvergüenza
mf

scour /skaʊr ‖'skaʊə(r)/ vt **1** (rub hard) fregar*
2 (search thoroughly) registrar

scourge /skɜːrdʒ ‖skɜːdʒ/ n azote m

scouring powder /'skaʊrɪŋ ‖'skaʊərɪŋ/ n
polvo m limpiador, limpiador m en polvo,
pulidor m (RPl)

scout /skaʊt/ n **1** (person) explorador, -dora
m,f **2** also **Scout** (boy ∼) explorador m, (boy)
scout m; (girl ∼) exploradora f, (girl) scout f
■ **scout around** [v + adv] to ∼ around (FOR sth)
buscar* (algo)

scowl¹ /skaʊl/ n ceño m fruncido

scowl² vi fruncir* el ceño; to ∼ AT sb mirar a
algn con el ceño fruncido

scrabble /'skræbəl/ vi «dog/chicken»
escarbar; he was scrabbling about in the drawers
of the desk estaba hurgando en los cajones del
escritorio

scraggy /'skrægi/ adj -gier, -giest **(a)**
(scrawny) esmirriado **(b)** (tough) ⟨meat⟩ duro

scram /skræm/ vi -mm- (colloq): go on, ∼!
¡fuera or largo de aquí! (fam)

scramble¹ /'skræmbəl/ n (no pl) **(a)** (chaotic
rush): barullo m; there was a last-minute ∼ for
tickets a último momento hubo una rebatiña
para conseguir entradas **(b)** (difficult climb) subida f
difícil

scramble² vi (+ adv compl): we ∼d through
the bushes nos abrimos paso con dificultad a
través de los arbustos
■ ∼ vt **(a)** (mix) mezclar **(b)** ⟨message⟩ codificar*

scrambled egg /'skræmbəld/ n (Culin)
huevos mpl revueltos

scrap¹ /skræp/ n **1 (a)** (of paper, cloth, leather)
pedacito m, trocito m **(b)** (single bit) ⟨with neg, no
pl⟩: it doesn't make a ∼ of difference what you
think lo que tú pienses no importa en lo más
mínimo **2 scraps** pl sobras fpl, sobros mpl
(AmC) **3** (reusable waste) chatarra f, (before n) ∼
paper papel m para borrador

scrap² *vt* -**pp**- **(a)** (abandon) ⟨*idea*⟩ desechar; ⟨*plan*⟩ abandonar **(b)** (throw away) tirar a la basura, botar ⟨AmL exc RPl⟩

scrapbook /'skræpbʊk/ *n* álbum *m* de recortes

scrape¹ /skreɪp/ *n* (colloq) lío *m* (fam)

scrape² *vt* 1 **(a)** (rub against) rozar*; (grate against) rascar* **(b)** (damage, graze) ⟨*paintwork*⟩ rayar; ⟨*knee/elbow*⟩ rasparse, rasguñarse 2 **(a)** (clean) ⟨*carrot/potato*⟩ pelar; ⟨*woodwork*⟩ raspar, rascar*; **to ~ sth off** ⟨*paint/wallpaper*⟩ quitar algo (con una rasqueta/un cuchillo); **~ the mud off your boots** quítales el barro a las botas (con un cuchillo, contra una piedra etc) **(b)** ⟨*bowl/pan*⟩ fregar*

■ **scrape through** [v + adv] [v + prep + o] ⟨*exam*⟩ aprobar* raspando *or* (fam) por los pelos

scraper /'skreɪpər ‖ 'skreɪpə(r)/ *n* (tool) rasqueta *f*, espátula *f*

scrap: **~heap** *n*: **to throw sth on the ~heap** desechar algo; **at 50 he found himself on the ~heap** a los 50 años se vio sin trabajo y sin perspectivas de futuro; **~yard** *n* chatarrería *f*, (for cars) cementerio *m* de automóviles, desguace *m or* (Méx) deshuesadero *m*

scratch¹ /skrætʃ/ *n* 1 rasguño *m*, arañazo *m*; (on paint, record, furniture) rayón *m* 2 (in phrases) **from scratch: to start from ~** empezar* desde cero; **to be up to ~** (colloq) dar* la talla

scratch² *vt* **(a)** ⟨*paint/record/furniture*⟩ rayar **(b)** (with claws, nails) arañar **(c)** ⟨*name/initials*⟩ marcar* **(d)** (to relieve itch) rascarse*

■ ~ *vi* **(a)** (damage, wound) arañar **(b)** (to relieve itching) rascarse*

■ **scratch out** [v + o + adv, v + adv + o] **(a)** (gouge): **to ~ sb's eyes out** sacarle* los ojos a algn **(b)** (strike out) ⟨*name/sentence*⟩ tachar; (on ticket) rascar*

scratch: **~ card** *n* número *m* de la lotería (con sección que se raspa); **~ pad** *n* (AmE) bloc *m* (para borrador o apuntes)

scrawl¹ /skrɔːl/ *n* garabatos *mpl*

scrawl² *vt/i* garabatear

scrawny /'skrɔːni/ *adj* -**nier**, -**niest** ⟨*person*⟩ escuálido; ⟨*arms/legs*⟩ esquelético

scream¹ /skriːm/ *n* grito *m*, chillido *m*; (louder) alarido *m*

scream² *vi* gritar, chillar; «*baby*» llorar a gritos

■ ~ *vt* ⟨*insult*⟩ gritar, soltar*; ⟨*command*⟩ dar* a voces *or* a gritos

screech¹ /skriːtʃ/ *n* (of terror, pain) alarido *m*; (of joy) chillido *m*; (of brakes) chirrido *m*; (of bird) chillido *m*

screech² *vi* «*person/animal*» chillar; «*brakes/tires*» chirriar*

screen¹ /skriːn/ *n* 1 (folding) biombo *m*; (as partition) mampara *f*, (protective, defensive) cortina *f* 2 (Cin, Comput, Phot, TV) pantalla *f*

screen² *vt* 1 **(a)** (conceal) ocultar, tapar **(b)** (protect) proteger* 2 ⟨*TV program*⟩ emitir; ⟨*film*⟩ proyectar 3 (check, examine) ⟨*blood donor*⟩ someter a una revisión (médica); ⟨*applicants*⟩ someter a una investigación de antecedentes

■ **screen off** [v + o + adv, v + adv + o] aislar*, separar (con un biombo o una mampara)

screen: **~ door** *n* puerta *f* mosquitera;

~play *n* guion *m*; **~ saver** /'seɪvər ‖ 'seɪvə(r)/ *n* (Comput) protector *m* de pantalla, salvapantallas *m*; **~ test** *n* prueba *f* (cinematográfica)

screw¹ /skruː/ *n* (Const, Tech) tornillo *m*; **to have a ~ loose** (colloq & hum): **he's/you've got a ~ loose** le/te falta un tornillo (fam & hum)

screw² *vt* (Const, Tech) atornillar; **to ~ sth down** (securely) atornillar (bien) algo; **~ the lid on tight** enrosca bien la tapa

■ **screw up** [v + o + adv, v + adv + o] 1 (tighten) ⟨*bolt*⟩ apretar* 2 (crumple) ⟨*letter/paper*⟩ arrugar* 3 (spoil, botch) (sl) fastidiar (fam)

screw: **~ball** *n* (eccentric person) (AmE colloq) excéntrico, -ca *mf*, chiflado, -da *m,f* (fam); **~driver** *n* destornillador *m*, desarmador *m* (Méx), desatornillador *m* (AmC, Chi); **~top** *adj* ⟨*bottle*⟩ con tapón de rosca; ⟨*jar*⟩ con tapa de rosca

scribble¹ /'skrɪbəl/ *n* garabato *m*

scribble² *vt* garabatear; **to ~ sth down** anotar algo rápidamente

■ ~ *vi* garabatear

scrimp /skrɪmp/ *vi*: **to ~ on sth** escatimar EN algo; **to ~ and save** cuidar mucho el dinero

script /skrɪpt/ *n* 1 **(a)** (handwriting) letra *f* **(b)** (style of writing) caligrafía *f* **(c)** (alphabet) escritura *f* 2 (text of film, broadcast) guion *m*

scripture /'skrɪptʃər ‖ 'skrɪptʃə(r)/ *n*: **the (Holy) S~s** las (Sagradas) Escrituras

scriptwriter /'skrɪptˌraɪtər ‖ 'skrɪptˌraɪtə(r)/ *n* guionista *mf*

scroll¹ /skroʊl/ *n* rollo *m*

scroll² *vi* (Comput): **to ~ up/down** hacer* avanzar/retroceder el texto que aparece en pantalla

scroll bar *n* (Comput) barra *f* de enrollar

scrounge /skraʊndʒ/ (colloq) *vt* **to ~ sth FROM/OFF sb** gorronearle *or* gorrearle *or* (RPl) garronearle *or* (Chi) bolsearle algo A algn (fam)

■ ~ *vi* gorronear *or* gorrear *or* (RPl) garronear *or* (Chi) bolsear (fam)

scrub¹ /skrʌb/ *n* 1 (vegetation) matorrales *mpl* 2 (act) (no pl): **to give sth a good ~** fregar* *or* (Méx) tallar algo bien (con cepillo); (before n) **~ brush** (AmE) cepillo *m* de fregar

scrub² *vt* -**bb**- ⟨*floor/table*⟩ fregar*; ⟨*knees/hands*⟩ restregar*

scrubbing brush /'skrʌbɪŋ/ *n* cepillo *m* de fregar

scruff /skrʌf/ *n*: **by the ~ of the neck** por el pescuezo

scruffy /'skrʌfi/ *adj* -**fier**, -**fiest** (colloq) ⟨*person*⟩ dejado, desaliñado; **a ~-looking building** un edificio de aspecto destartalado

scrum /skrʌm/, **scrummage** /'skrʌmɪdʒ/ *n* (in rugby) melé *f* (ordenada), scrum *m*

scrumptious /'skrʌmpʃəs/ *adj* (colloq) ⟨*meal*⟩ para chuparse los dedos (fam)

scruple /'skruːpəl/ *n* (usu pl) escrúpulo *m*

scrupulous /'skruːpjələs ‖ 'skruːpjʊləs/ *adj* escrupuloso

scrupulously /'skruːpjələsli ‖ 'skruːpjʊləsli/ *adv* escrupulosamente; **~ clean** impecable

scrutinize /'skruːtnaɪz ‖ 'skruːtɪnaɪz/ *vt* ⟨*document*⟩ inspeccionar; ⟨*face*⟩ escudriñar

scrutiny /'skru:tɲi ‖'skru:tɪni/ n (pl **-nies**) examen m

scuba diving /'sku:bə/ n buceo m, submarinismo m

scuff /skʌf/ vt ⟨floor⟩ dejar marcas en; ⟨leather⟩ raspar

scuffle /'skʌfəl/ n refriega f

scullery /'skʌləri/ n (pl **-ries**) habitación anexa a la cocina donde se fregaba, se preparaban las verduras etc

sculpt /skʌlpt/ vt/i esculpir

sculptor /'skʌlptər ‖'skʌlptə(r)/ n escultor, -tora m,f

sculpture¹ /'skʌlptʃər ‖'skʌlptʃə(r)/ n escultura f

sculpture² vt esculpir

scum /skʌm/ n [1] (on liquid) capa f de suciedad [2] (colloq) (people) escoria f; **the ~ of the earth** la escoria de la sociedad

scupper /'skʌpər ‖'skʌpə(r)/ vt (BrE) ⟨ship⟩ hundir; ⟨plan/talks⟩ echar por tierra

scurry /'skɜːri ‖'skʌri/ vi: **he scurried away** o **off** salió disparado; **to ~ around** «mice» corretear

scuttle¹ /'skʌtl/ n (coal ~) cubo m para el carbón

scuttle² vt ⟨ship⟩ hundir; ⟨plans/talks⟩ echar por tierra

■ ~ vi: **the children ~d away** o **off** los niños se escabulleron rápidamente

scythe /saɪð/ n guadaña f

SD, S Dak = **South Dakota**

SE (= **southeast**) SE

sea /siː/ n [1] (often pl) (ocean) mar m [The noun MAR is feminine in literary language and in some set idiomatic expressions]; **to go/travel by ~** ir*/ viajar en barco; ⟨before n⟩ ⟨route/transport⟩ marítimo; ⟨battle⟩ naval; **the ~ breeze** la brisa del mar; **~ crossing** travesía f [2] (large mass, quantity) (no pl): **a ~ of faces** una multitud de rostros

sea: ~ anemone n anémona f or ortiga f de mar; **~bed** n the **~bed** el lecho marino; **~ bird** n ave f; marina; **~food** n mariscos mpl, marisco m (Esp); **~front** n paseo m marítimo, malecón m (AmL), costanera f (CS); **~gull** n gaviota f; **~horse** n caballito m de mar

seal¹ /siːl/ n [1] (implement, impression) sello m; **he gave the plan his ~ of approval** dio su aprobación al plan [2] **(a)** (security device) precinto m **(b)** (airtight closure) cierre m hermético; (on glass jar) aro m de goma [3] (Zool) foca f

seal² vt [1] **(a)** ⟨envelope/parcel⟩ cerrar*; (with tape) precintar; (with wax) lacrar; **my lips are ~ed** (set phrase) soy una tumba **(b)** ⟨jar/container⟩ cerrar* herméticamente; ⟨tomb/door⟩ precintar; ⟨wood⟩ sellar [2] (affix seal to) ⟨document/treaty⟩ sellar [3] (seal, determine) ⟨victory/outcome⟩ decidir; **their fate was ~ed** su destino estaba escrito

■ **seal off** [v + o + adv, v + adv + o] ⟨area/road/ building⟩ acordonar; ⟨exit⟩ cerrar*

sea level n nivel m del mar

sealing wax /'siːlɪŋ/ n lacre m

sea lion n león m marino

seam /siːm/ n [1] (stitching) costura f [2] (of coal, gold) veta f, filón m

seaman /'siːmən/ n (pl **-men** /-mən/) (sailor) marinero m; (officer) marino m

seamy /'siːmi/ adj **-mier, -miest** sórdido

seance /'seɪɑːns/ n sesión f de espiritismo

sear /sɪr ‖sɪə(r)/ vt **(a)** ⟨flesh⟩ quemar; ⟨meat⟩ (Culin) dorar rápidamente a fuego muy vivo **(b)** (wither) «heat» secar*, abrasar

search¹ /sɜːrtʃ ‖sɜːtʃ/ vt ⟨building⟩ registrar, escular* (AmL exc CS); ⟨person⟩ registrar, cachear, catear (Méx); ⟨luggage⟩ registrar, revisar (AmL), esculcar* (AmL exc CS); ⟨records/files⟩ buscar* en

■ ~ vi buscar*; **to ~ FOR sth/sb** buscar* algo/a algn

search² n **(a)** (hunt, quest) ~ (FOR sth/sb) búsqueda f (DE algo/algn) **(b)** (of building, pockets) registro m, esculque m (Col, Méx); (of records, documents) inspección f **(c)** (Comput) búsqueda f

search engine n (Comput) buscador m

searching /'sɜːrtʃɪŋ ‖'sɜːtʃɪŋ/ adj ⟨look⟩ inquisitivo; ⟨question⟩ perspicaz

search: ~light n reflector m; **~ party** n partida f de rescate

sea: ~scape /'siːskeɪp/ n marina f; **~shell** n concha f (de mar); **~shore** n orilla f del mar; **~sick** adj mareado; **~sickness** n mareo m (en los viajes por mar); **~side** n costa f, playa f; **we spent two weeks at the ~side** pasamos dos semanas en la costa or en la playa

season¹ /'siːzn/ n [1] (division of year) estación f [2] (for specific activity, event, crop) temporada f [3] (in phrases) **in season** (of female animal) en celo; (of fresh food, game): **cherries are in ~** es época or temporada de cerezas; **out of season** fuera de temporada

season² vt [1] (Culin) condimentar, sazonar; (with salt and pepper) salpimentar* [2] ⟨wood⟩ secar*, curar

seasonal /'siːznəl ‖'siːzənl/ adj ⟨variations/ fluctuations⟩ estacional; ⟨vegetables⟩ del tiempo; ⟨demand⟩ de estación

seasoned /'siːznd/ adj [1] (experienced) ⟨troops/ traveler⟩ avezado, experimentado [2] ⟨food⟩ condimentado, sazonado [3] ⟨wood⟩ seco, curado

seasoning /'siːznɪŋ/ n (Culin) condimento m, sazón f

season ticket n abono m (de temporada)

seat¹ /siːt/ n [1] (place to sit) asiento m; **please have** o **take a ~** tome asiento, por favor (frml), siéntese, por favor; **there aren't any ~s left** (in cinema) no quedan localidades [2] (of chair) asiento m [3] **(a)** (Govt) escaño m, banca f (RPl), curul m (Col, Méx) **(b)** (constituency) (BrE) distrito m electoral [4] (center) sede f; **the ~ of government** la sede del gobierno

seat² vt **(a)** ⟨child⟩ sentar*; **to remain ~ed** permanecer* sentado **(b)** (have room for) «auditorium» tener* cabida or capacidad para

seat belt n cinturón m de seguridad

seating /'siːtɪŋ/ n número m de asientos; ⟨before n⟩ **~ capacity** aforo m

sea: ~ urchin n erizo m de mar; **~water** n ····⟶

S

agua f‡ de mar, agua f‡ salada; **~way** n ruta f marítima; **~weed** n alga f‡ marina; **~worthy** adj ‹ship› en condiciones de navegar

secluded /sɪ'kluːdəd ‖sɪ'kluːdɪd/ adj ‹house/area› apartado, aislado; ‹life/existence› solitario

seclusion /sɪ'kluːʒən/ n aislamiento m

second¹ /'sekənd/ adj **1** segundo; **~ language** segundo idioma m; **our service is ~ to none** nuestro servicio es insuperable **2** (elliptical use): **I leave on the ~ (of the month)** me voy el (día) dos

second² adv **(a)** (in position, time, order) en segundo lugar **(b)** (secondly) en segundo lugar **(c)** (with superl): **the ~ highest building** el segundo edificio en altura

second³ n **1** (of time) segundo m; **it doesn't take a ~** no lleva ni un segundo; (before n) **~ hand** segundero m **2** **(a)** **~ (gear)** (Auto) ‹no art› segunda f **(b)** (in competition): **he finished a good/poor ~** quedó en un honroso/deslucido segundo lugar **3** (substandard product) artículo m con defectos de fábrica **4** **seconds** pl (second helping) (colloq): **to have ~s** repetir*

second⁴ vt **1** (support) ‹motion/candidate› secundar **2** /sɪ'kɒnd/ (attach) (BrE) **to ~ sb** (**TO sth**) trasladar a algn temporalmente (**A** algo)

secondary /'sekənderi ‖'sekəndri/ adj **1** **(a)** (subordinate) ‹matter› de interés secundario; ‹road› secundario **(b)** (not primary, original) ‹source› de segunda mano; ‹industry› derivado **2** ‹teacher/pupils› de enseñanza secundaria

secondary school n instituto m or colegio m de enseñanza secundaria, liceo m (CS, Ven)

second: **~ best** n: **he won't accept ~ best** solo se conforma con lo mejor; **~ class** adv ‹travel/go› en segunda (clase); **~-class** /'sekənd'klæs ‖,sekənd'klɑːs/ adj (pred **~ class**) **(a)** (inferior) ‹goods/service› de segunda (clase or categoría), de calidad inferior **(b)** (Post): **~-class mail** (in UK) servicio regular de correos, que tarda más en llegar a destino que el de primera clase **(c)** (in UK) (Transp) ‹travel/ticket/compartment› de segunda (clase)

second-hand¹ /'sekənd'hænd/ adj (pred **second hand**) ‹car/clothes› de segunda mano, usado; ‹bookstore› de viejo; ‹shop› de artículos de segunda mano; ‹information› de segunda mano

second-hand² adv **to buy sth ~** comprar algo de segunda mano

second-in-command /'sekəndɪnkə'mænd ‖,sekəndɪnkə'mɑːnd/ n (pl **seconds-in-command**) número dos mf (persona directamente por debajo de la autoridad máxima de una organización, departamento etc)

secondly /'sekəndli/ adv (indep) en segundo lugar

second-rate /'sekənd'reɪt/ adj mediocre

secrecy /'siːkrəsi/ n secreto m

secret¹ /'siːkrət ‖'siːkrɪt/ n secreto m; **in ~** en secreto; **to make no ~ of sth** no esconder algo

secret² adj secreto

secretarial /'sekrə'teriəl ‖,sekrə'teəriəl/ adj ‹job› de oficina, de secretaria/secretario; ‹course› de secretariado

secretary /'sekrəteri ‖'sekrətri/ n (pl **-ries**) **1** (in office, of committee, of society) secretario, -ria m,f **2** (Govt) ministro, -tra m,f, secretario, -ria m,f (Méx)

Secretary of State n (pl **Secretaries of State**) (Govt) **(a)** (in US) secretario, -ria m,f de Estado (de los Estados Unidos); **(b)** (in UK) ministro, -tra m,f, secretario, -ria m,f (Méx)

secrete /sɪ'kriːt/ vt **1** (Biol, Physiol) segregar*, secretar **2** (hide) (frml) ocultar

secretive /'siːkrətɪv/ adj reservado

secret: **~ police** n policía f secreta; **~ service** n (intelligence service) servicio m secreto

sect /sekt/ n secta f

sectarian /sek'teriən ‖sek'teəriən/ adj ‹views/violence› sectario; ‹schooling/school› confesional

section /'sekʃən/ n **1** (of object, newspaper, orchestra) sección f; (of machine, piece of furniture) parte f; (of road) tramo m; (of city, population) sector m **2** (department) sección f **3** (in geometry, drawing) sección f

sector /'sektər ‖'sektə(r)/ n sector m

secular /'sekjələr ‖'sekjələ(r)/ adj ‹education› laico; ‹society/art› secular

secure¹ /sɪ'kjʊr ‖sɪ'kjʊə(r)/ adj **1** **(a)** (safe) ‹fortress/hideaway› seguro **(b)** (emotionally) ‹childhood/home› estable **(c)** (assured) ‹job/investment› seguro **2** ‹foothold/shelf› firme; ‹foundation› sólido

secure² vt **1** (obtain) ‹job/votes/support› conseguir* **2** (fasten, fix firmly) ‹door/shelf› asegurar

security /sɪ'kjʊrəti ‖sɪ'kjʊərəti/ n (pl **-ties**) **1** (against crime, espionage etc) seguridad f; (before n) **~ guard** guarda jurado, guarda jurada m,f **2** **(a)** (safety, certainty) seguridad f **(b)** (protection) seguro m **3** (Fin) **(a)** (guarantee) garantía f **(b)** **securities** pl (Fin) valores mpl, títulos mpl

Security Council n **the (United Nations) ~** el Consejo de Seguridad (de las Naciones Unidas)

sedan /sɪ'dæn/ n **1** (car) (AmE) sedán m **2** **~ (chair)** palanquín m, silla f de manos

sedate¹ /sɪ'deɪt/ adj reposado, tranquilo

sedate² vt (Med) sedar

sedation /sɪ'deɪʃən/ n sedación f; **to be under ~** estar* bajo el efecto de los sedantes

sedative /'sedətɪv/ n sedante m

sediment /'sedəmənt ‖'sedɪmənt/ n **(a)** (in wine, coffee) poso m, asiento m **(b)** (Geol) sedimento m

seduce /sɪ'duːs ‖sɪ'djuːs/ vt seducir*

seduction /sɪ'dʌkʃən/ n seducción f

seductive /sɪ'dʌktɪv/ adj seductor

see /siː/ (past **saw**; past p **seen**) vt **1** (regard, perceive) ver*; **I can't ~ a thing!** ¡no veo nada!; **I saw her cross the street** la vi cruzar la calle; **I**

thought I was ~ing things pensé que estaba viendo visiones; ~ **page 20** ver página 20; **I don't know what she ~s in him** no sé qué es lo que le ve; **anyone can ~ she's upset** cualquiera se da cuenta de que está disgustada; **the way I ~ it, as I ~ it** a mi modo de ver; **can you ~ him as a teacher?** ¿te lo imaginas de profesor?; **I'll ~ what I can do** veré qué puedo hacer; **that remains to be ~** n eso está por verse

2 (understand) ver*; **do you ~ what I mean?** ¿entiendes?

3 (ensure) **to ~ THAT** asegurarse DE QUE; **~ that it doesn't happen again** que no vuelva a suceder

4 **(a)** (meet, visit) ver*; **I'm ~ing him on Tuesday** lo voy a ver el martes **(b)** (go out with) (colloq): salir* con **(c)** (saying goodbye) (colloq): **~ you!** ¡hasta luego!, ¡hasta la vista!; **~ you later/soon!** ¡hasta luego/pronto!

5 **(a)** (consult) ‹doctor/manager› ver* **(b)** (receive) ver*, atender*; **the doctor will ~ you now** el doctor lo verá or lo atenderá ahora

6 (escort, accompany) acompañar; **to ~ sb to the door** acompañar a algn a la puerta

■ ~ *vi* ver*; **~ for yourself!** ¡compruébalo tú mismo!; **as far as I can ~** por lo que yo veo; **I ~** (expressing realization) ya veo; (accepting explanation) entiendo; **let's ~** vamos a ver, veamos; **will it work? — try it and ~** ¿funcionará? — prueba a ver; **~ing is believing** ver para creer

■ **see off** [v + o + adv, v + adv + o] **1** (say goodbye to) despedir*, despedirse* de **2** (get rid of) deshacerse* de

■ **see out** [v + o + adv, v + adv + o] ‹person› acompañar (hasta la puerta); **I can ~ myself out** no hace falta que me acompañes

■ **see through 1** [v + prep + o] (not be deceived by) calar
2 [v + o + adv] [v + o + prep + o] (last): **make sure this ~s you through** con esto te tienes que alcanzar; **$20 should ~ me through the week** con 20 dólares me alcanza hasta el fin de semana **3** [v + o + adv] (carry to completion) terminar

■ **see to** [v + prep + o] (attend to) ocuparse de

seed /siːd/ n **1** (of plant) semilla f; (of orange, grape) (AmE) pepita f, semilla f; **to go to ~** estar* en decadencia **2** (Sport) cabeza mf de serie, sembrado, -da m,f (Méx)

seedless /ˈsiːdləs ‖ ˈsiːdlɪs/ adj sin pepitas or semillas

seedling /ˈsiːdlɪŋ/ n planta f de semillero

seedy /ˈsiːdi/ adj **-dier, -diest** ‹nightclub/bar› sórdido, de mala muerte (fam), cutre (Esp fam); ‹appearance› desastrado

seeing /ˈsiːɪŋ/ conj (colloq) **~ (that)** o **~ as** ya que

seek /siːk/ (past & past p **sought**) vt **(a)** (search for) (frml) ‹person/object› buscar* **(b)** (try to obtain) ‹work/companionship› buscar*; ‹solution/explanation› tratar de encontrar **(c)** (request) ‹approval/help› pedir* **(d)** (try to bring about) (frml) ‹reconciliation› buscar*

■ **seek out** [v + o + adv, v + adv + o] ‹person› buscar*; ‹opinion› pedir*

seem /siːm/ vi parecer*; **strange as it may ~** por raro que parezca; **she ~s to like you** parece que le caes bien; **so it ~s, so it would ~** eso parece, así parece; **I ~ to remember that you ...** creo recordar que tú ...; **it ~s to me/him/them**

that ... me/le/les parece que ...; **I can't ~ to remember where I put it** no logro acordarme de dónde lo puse

seen /siːn/ past p of SEE

seep /siːp/ vi «liquid/moisture» filtrarse

seesaw /ˈsiːsɔː/ n balancín m, subibaja m

seethe /siːð/ vi **(a)** (be agitated) bullir*; **the town was seething with tourists** la ciudad estaba plagada de turistas **(b)** (be angry) estar* furioso; **I was absolutely seething** me hervía la sangre

see-through /ˈsiːθruː/ adj transparente

segment /ˈsɛgmənt/ n **(a)** (Math) (of circle, sphere, line) segmento m **(b)** (of citrus fruit) gajo m; **(c)** (section) sector m

segregate /ˈsɛgrɪgeɪt/ vt ‹races/sexes› segregar*; ‹rival groups› mantener* aparte

segregation /ˌsɛgrɪˈgeɪʃən/ n segregación f

seize /siːz/ vt **1** (grab, snatch) ‹hand/object› agarrar; ‹opportunity› aprovechar; ‹power› tomar **2** **(a)** (capture) ‹town/fortress› tomar; ‹person› detener* **(b)** ‹assets/property› (confiscate) confiscar*; (impound) embargar*; ‹cargo/contraband› confiscar*; ‹drugs/arms› incautar

■ **seize on, seize upon** [v + prep + o] ‹chance› aprovechar

■ **seize up** [v + adv] «engine» agarrotarse, fundirse (AmL); «muscles» agarrotarse; «traffic» paralizarse*

seizure /ˈsiːʒər ‖ ˈsiːʒə(r)/ n **1** (of property, contraband) confiscación f **2** (Med) ataque m

seldom /ˈsɛldəm/ adv rara vez, pocas veces

select¹ /sɪˈlɛkt/ vt ‹gift/book/wine› elegir*, escoger*; ‹candidate/team member› seleccionar

select² adj **(a)** (exclusive) ‹school› de élite; ‹district› distinguido **(b)** (choice) ‹fruit/wine› selecto **(c)** (especially chosen) ‹group› selecto

selection /sɪˈlɛkʃən/ n **1** (act, thing chosen) selección f **2** (Busn) (of chocolates, buttons, yarns) surtido m; **a wide ~ of new and used cars** una amplia gama de coches nuevos y usados

selective /sɪˈlɛktɪv/ adj **(a)** ‹control/recruitment› selectivo; ‹reporting› parcial **(b)** (discriminating) **he's fairly ~ about who he mixes with** elige or escoge mucho sus amistades

self /sɛlf/ n (pl **selves**): **she's her old ~ again** vuelve a ser la de antes; **you're not your usual cheerful ~** no estás tan alegre como de costumbre

self- /sɛlf/ pref **(a)** (concerning the self): **~doubt** duda f de sí mismo **(b)** (with no outside agency) auto-; **~financing** autofinanciado

self: **~-addressed** /ˈsɛlfəˈdrɛst/ adj: con el nombre y la dirección del remitente; **send a ~-addressed envelope to ...** envíe un sobre con su nombre y dirección a ...; **~-adhesive** /ˈsɛlfədˈhiːsɪv/ adj autoadhesivo; **~-assured** /ˈsɛlfəˈʃʊərd ‖ ˌsɛlfəˈʃɔːd/ adj seguro de sí mismo; **~-catering** /ˈsɛlfˈkeɪtərɪŋ/ adj (BrE) ‹accommodation› equipado con cocina; **~-centered,** (BrE) **~-centred** /ˈsɛlfˈsɛntərd ‖ ˌsɛlfˈsɛntəd/ adj egocéntrico; **~-confessed** /ˈsɛlfkənˈfɛst/ adj (before n) confeso; **~-confidence** /ˈsɛlfˈkɑːnfədəns ‖ ˌsɛlfˈkɒnfɪdəns/ n confianza f en sí mismo; **~-confident** /ˈsɛlfˈkɑːnfədənt ‖ ˌsɛlfˈkɒnfɪdənt/ adj seguro de sí mismo; **~-conscious** /ˈsɛlfˈkɑːntʃəs ‖ ˌsɛlfˈkɒntʃəs/ adj **1** (shy,

embarrassed) ⟨person/manner⟩ tímido; **to feel
~-conscious** sentirse* cohibido; **2** (unspontaneous,
unnatural) (pej) afectado; **~-contained**
/ˌselfkən'teɪnd/ adj **(a)** ⟨flat⟩ (BrE) con cocina y
cuarto de baño propios **(b)** ⟨person⟩
independiente; **~-control** /ˌselfkən'trəʊl/ n
dominio m de sí mismo; **~-defense,** (BrE)
~-defence /ˌselfdɪ'fens/ n **(a)** (Law): **to act in
~-defense** actuar* en defensa propia **(b)** (fighting
technique) defensa f personal; **~-destruct**
/ˌselfdɪ'strʌkt/ vi autodestruirse*;
~-destructive /ˌselfdɪ'strʌktɪv/ adj
autodestructivo; **~-determination**
/ˌselfdɪˌtɜːrmə'neɪʃən ‖ˌselfdɪˌtɜːmɪ'neɪʃən/ n
autodeterminación f; **~-discipline**
/'selfdɪsəplɪn ‖ˌselfdɪsɪplɪn/ n autodisciplina f;
~-employed /'selfɪm'plɔɪd/ adj autónomo;
~-esteem /'selfɪ'stiːm/ n autoestima f;
~-evident /'selfˈevədənt ‖ˌselfˈevɪdənt/ adj
⟨truth⟩ manifiesto; ⟨conclusion⟩ evidente;
~-explanatory /'selfɪk'splænətɔːri
‖ˌselfɪk'splænətri/ adj: **the instructions are
~-explanatory** las instrucciones son muy claras;
~-government /ˌselfˈgʌvərnmənt
‖ˌselfˈgʌvənmənt/ n autogobierno m, autonomía
f; **~-help** /'selfhelp/ n autoayuda f; **~-image**
/'selfˈɪmɪdʒ/ n imagen f de sí mismo;
~-important /'selfɪm'pɔːrtṇt ‖ˌselfɪm'pɔːtṇt/
adj engreído, presumido; **~-imposed**
/'selfɪm'pəʊzd/ adj voluntario, autoimpuesto;
~-indulgent /ˌselfɪn'dʌldʒənt/ adj
demasiado indulgente consigo mismo;
~-interest /'selfˈɪntrəst ‖ˌselfˈɪntrɪst/ n interés
m (personal)

selfish /'selfɪʃ/ adj egoísta

selfishly /'selfɪʃli/ adv egoístamente

selfishness /'selfɪʃnəs ‖'selfɪʃnɪs/ n egoísmo
m

self: ~-made /'selfˈmeɪd/ adj (before n) ⟨man/
woman⟩ que ha alcanzado su posición gracias a
sus propios esfuerzos; **~-pity** /'selfˈpɪti/ n
autocompasión f; **~-portrait** /'selfˈpɔːrtrət
‖ˌselfˈpɔːtrɪt/ n autorretrato m;
~-preservation /'selfˈprezərˈveɪʃən
‖ˌselfprezəˈveɪʃən/ n: **the instinct of
~-preservation** el instinto de conservación;
~-raising /'selfˈreɪzɪŋ/ adj (BrE) ▶ ~-RISING;
~-reliant /'selfrɪ'laɪənt/ adj independiente;
~-respect /'selfrɪ'spekt/ n dignidad f, amor m
propio; **~-respecting** /'selfrɪ'spektɪŋ/ adj
(before n): **no ~-respecting editor would work for
them** ningún editor que se precie trabajaría para
ellos; **~-righteous** /'selfˈraɪtʃəs/ adj ⟨person⟩
con pretensiones de superioridad moral;
~-rising /'selfˈraɪzɪŋ/ adj (AmE) ⟨flour⟩ con
polvos de hornear (AmL), con levadura (Esp),
leudante (RPl); **~-same** adj (before n)
mismísimo; **~-satisfied** /'selfˈsætəsfaɪd
‖ˌselfˈsætɪsfaɪd/ adj ufano, satisfecho de sí
mismo; ⟨expression/grin⟩ de (auto)suficiencia;
~-service /'selfˈsɜːrvəs ‖ˌselfˈsɜːvɪs/, (esp AmE)
self-serve /'-ˈsɜːrv/ adj: **~-service restaurant**
autoservicio m, self-service m; **~-sufficiency**
/ˌselfsə'fɪʃənsi/ n independencia f; (Econ)
autosuficiencia f; **~-sufficient** /'selfsə'fɪʃənt/
adj ⟨person⟩ independiente; ⟨country⟩
autosuficiente; **~-taught** /'selfˈtɔːt/ adj
autodidacta, autodidacto

sell /sel/ (past & past p **sold**) vt vender; **to ~
sth TO sb, to ~ sb sth** venderle algo A algn; **to ~
sth FOR sth** vender algo EN or POR algo
■ ~ vi **(a)** «person/company» vender **(b)** (be sold)
«product» venderse; **to ~ AT/FOR sth** venderse
A/POR algo
■ **sell off** [v + o + adv, v + adv + o] vender;
(cheaply) liquidar
■ **sell out** **1** [v + adv + o] (sell all of) ⟨stock⟩
agotar; ⟨article⟩ agotar las existencias de
2 [v + adv] **(a)** (sell all stock) «shop» **to ~ out
(OF sth)**: **we've o we're sold out of umbrellas** los
paraguas están agotados, se agotaron los
paraguas **(b)** (be sold) «stock/tickets» agotarse **(c)**
(be traitor) «leader/artist» venderse
sell-by date /'selbaɪ/ n (BrE) fecha f límite de
venta
seller /'selər ‖'selə(r)/ n vendedor, -dora m,f
selling /'selɪŋ/ n ventas fpl; (before n) **~ price**
precio m de venta
Sellotape® /'seləteɪp/ n (BrE) ▶ SCOTCH TAPE
sell-out /'selaʊt/ n **1** (performance) éxito m de
taquilla **2** (betrayal) capitulación f
selves /selvz/ pl of SELF
semaphore /'seməfɔːr ‖'seməfɔː(r)/ n código
m de señales
semblance /'sembləns/ n (frml) **~ OF sth**
apariencia f DE algo
semen /'siːmən/ n semen m
semester /sə'mestər ‖sɪ'mestə(r)/ n (in US)
semestre m (lectivo)
semi- /'semi, 'semaɪ ‖'semi/ pref semi-
semibreve /'semibriːv/ n (BrE) semibreve f,
redonda f
semicircle /'semiˌsɜːrkəl ‖'semiˌsɜːkəl/ n
semicírculo m
semicolon /'semiˈkəʊlən/ n punto y coma m
semiconscious /'semiˈkɑːntʃəs
‖ˌsemiˈkɒnʃəs/ adj semiconsciente
semidetached /ˌsemidɪ'tætʃt/ adj: **a ~
house** una casa pareada or adosada
semifinal /'semiˈfaɪnl/ n semifinal f
seminar /'semənɑːr ‖'semɪnɑː(r)/ n seminario
m
semiquaver /'semiˌkweɪvər ‖'semiˌkweɪvə(r)/
n (BrE) semicorchea f
semiskilled /'semi'skɪld/ adj semicalificado
or (Esp) semicualificado
semitone /'semitəʊn/ n semitono m
semitrailer /'semiˌtreɪlər ‖'semiˌtreɪlə(r)/ n
(AmE) camión m con remolque or (CS tb) con
acoplado, tráiler m (Esp), trailer m (Méx)
senate /'senət ‖'senɪt/ n **the Senate** (Govt) el
senado or Senado
senator /'senətər ‖'senətə(r)/ n senador, -dora
m,f
send /send/ (past & past p **sent**) vt mandar,
enviar*; **to ~ sb to prison** mandar a algn a la
cárcel; **the blow sent him reeling** el golpe lo dejó
tambaleándose; **she sent everything flying** lo hizo
saltar todo por los aires; **to ~ sb to sleep**
dormir* a algn
■ **send away** **1** [v + o + adv, v + adv + o] **(a)**
(dismiss) despachar; **don't ~ me away** no me digas
que me vaya **(b)** (send elsewhere) mandar, enviar*
2 [v + adv] ▶ SEND OFF 3

■ **send for** [*v* + *prep* + *o*] **(a)** (ask to come) ‹*doctor/ambulance*› mandar a buscar, mandar llamar (AmL) **(b)** (order) ‹*catalog/application form*› pedir*; ‹*books/tapes/clothes*› encargar*

■ **send in** [*v* + *o* + *adv*, *v* + *adv* + *o*] **(a)** ‹*troops*› enviar*, mandar **(b)** (by post) ‹*entry/coupon/application*› mandar, enviar* **(c)** (into room) ‹*person*› hacer* pasar; ~ **him in** hágalo pasar

■ **send off** ⟦1⟧ [*v* + *o* + *adv*, *v* + *adv* + *o*] (dispatch) ‹*letter/parcel/goods*› despachar, mandar; ‹*person*› mandar
⟦2⟧ [*v* + *o* + *adv*, *v* + *adv* + *o*] (BrE Sport) expulsar
⟦3⟧ [*v* + *adv*] **to ~ off FOR sth**: **I sent off for a brochure** escribí pidiendo un folleto, mandé pedir un folleto (AmL)

■ **send on** [*v* + *o* + *adv*, *v* + *adv* + *o*] ‹*luggage*› enviar* *or* mandar por adelantado; ‹*mail*› hacer* seguir

■ **send out** [*v* + *o* + *adv*, *v* + *adv* + *o*] **(a)** (emit) ‹*heat*› despedir*, irradiar; ‹*signal/radio waves*› emitir **(b)** (on errand) mandar **(c)** ‹*invitations*› mandar, enviar*

■ **send up** [*v* + *o* + *adv*, *v* + *adv* + *o*] ⟦1⟧ (to prison) (AmE) meter preso
⟦2⟧ (satirize) (BrE colloq) parodiar

sender /'sendər ‖'sendə(r)/ *n* remitente *mf*

send: ~**-off** *n* (colloq) despedida *f*; ~**-up** *n* (esp BrE colloq) parodia *f*

Senegal /'senɪ'gɔːl/ *n* (el) Senegal

Senegalese /'senɪgə'liːz/ *adj* senegalés

senile /'siːnaɪl/ *adj* senil

senile dementia *n* demencia *f* senil

senior[1] /'siːnjər ‖'siːniə(r)/ *adj* **(a)** (superior in rank): **a ~ officer in the Army** un oficial de alto rango del Ejército; **~ lecturer** (BrE) ≈profesor adjunto, profesora adjunta *m,f*; **she's ~ to him** es su superior **(b)** (older): **the ~ members of a club** los socios más antiguos de un club; **Robert King, S~** (esp AmE) Robert King, padre *or* sénior

senior[2] *n* ⟦1⟧ **(a)** (older person): **he's five years my ~** me lleva cinco años **(b)** (person of higher rank) superior *m* **(c)** (AmE) ▶ SENIOR CITIZEN
⟦2⟧ (Educ) estudiante *mf* del último año *or* curso

senior: ~ **citizen** *n* persona *f* de la tercera edad; ~ **high (school)** *n* (in US) *colegio donde se imparten los tres últimos años de la enseñanza secundaria*

seniority /siːn'jɔːrəti ‖,siːni'ɒrəti/ *n* **(a)** (in rank) jerarquía *f* **(b)** (in length of service) antigüedad *f*

sensation /sen'seɪʃən/ *n* ⟦1⟧ (feeling, impression) sensación *f* ⟦2⟧ **(a)** (furor) sensación *f* **(b)** (success): **to be a ~** «*play/show*» ser* todo un éxito

sensational /sen'seɪʃnəl ‖sen'seɪʃənl/ *adj* **(a)** (causing furor) que causa sensación **(b)** (sensationalist) sensacionalista **(c)** (very good) (colloq) sensacional (fam)

sensationalist /sen'seɪʃənələst ‖sen'seɪʃənəlɪst/ *adj* sensacionalista

sense[1] /sens/ *n* ⟦1⟧ **(a)** (physical faculty) sentido *m*; **the ~ of hearing/smell/taste/touch** el (sentido del) oído/olfato/gusto/tacto **(b) senses** *pl* (rational state): **to come to one's ~s** entrar en razón
⟦2⟧ **(a)** (impression) (*no pl*) sensación *f* **(b)**

(awareness) sentido *m*; ~ **of direction/humor** sentido de la orientación/del humor; **I lost all ~ of time** perdí completamente la noción del tiempo
⟦3⟧ (common ~) sentido *m* común; **she had the (good) ~ to leave her phone number** tuvo la sensatez de dejar su número de teléfono; **I can't make him see ~** no puedo hacerlo entrar en razón
⟦4⟧ **(a)** (meaning) sentido *m*; **in every ~ of the word** en todo sentido **(b)** (aspect, way): **in a ~ they're both correct** en cierto modo ambos tienen razón
⟦5⟧ **to make ~ (a)** (be comprehensible) tener* sentido **(b)** (be sensible): **what he said made a lot of ~** lo que dijo era muy razonable; **to make ~ of sth** entender* algo

sense[2] *vt* **(a)** (be aware of) sentir*, notar **(b)** (detect) (Tech) detectar

senseless /'sensləs ‖'senslɪs/ *adj* ⟦1⟧ (pointless) ‹*act/destruction*› sin sentido ⟦2⟧ (unconscious) inconsciente

sensible /'sensəbəl/ *adj* ‹*person/approach*› sensato; ‹*decision*› prudente; ‹*clothes/shoes*› cómodo y práctico

sensitive /'sensətɪv/ *adj* ⟦1⟧ **(a)** (emotionally responsive) ‹*person*› sensible; ‹*performance*› lleno de sensibilidad **(b)** (touchy) ‹*person*› susceptible
⟦2⟧ (physically responsive) ‹*skin/instrument*› sensible
⟦3⟧ (requiring tact) ‹*topic/issue*› delicado

sensor /'sensər ‖'sensə(r)/ *n* sensor *m*

sensual /'sentʃuəl ‖'senʃʊəl/ *adj* sensual

sensuous /'sentʃuəs ‖'sensjʊəs/ *adj* sensual

sent /sent/ *past & past p of* SEND

sentence[1] /'sentəns ‖'sentəns/ *n* ⟦1⟧ (Ling) oración *f*, frase *f* ⟦2⟧ (Law) (judgment) sentencia *f*; (punishment) pena *f*; **to pass ~ (on sb)** dictar *or* pronunciar sentencia (contra algn); **a life ~** una condena a cadena perpetua

sentence[2] *vt* **to ~ sb (TO sth)** condenar *or* sentenciar a algn (A algo)

sentiment /'sentɪmənt/ *n* **(a)** (feeling) sentir *m*, sentimiento *m* **(b)** (view) opinión *f*; **my ~s exactly** estoy totalmente de acuerdo

sentimental /sentɪ'mentl/ *adj* sentimental

sentry /'sentri/ *n* (*pl* -**tries**) centinela *m*

Seoul /səʊl/ *n* Seúl *m*

separate[1] /'sepərət/ *adj* **(a)** (individual) separado **(b)** (physically apart) aparte *adj inv*; ~ **FROM sth** separado DE algo **(c)** (distinct, different): **it has three ~ meanings** tiene tres significados distintos; **answer each question on a ~ sheet of paper** conteste cada pregunta en una hoja aparte

separate[2] /'sepərert/ *vt* **(a)** (set apart) separar **(b)** (distinguish) distinguir*; **to ~ sth FROM sth** distinguir* algo DE algo
■ ~ *vi* separarse

separately /'seprətli, 'sepərətli/ *adv* **(a)** (apart) por separado **(b)** (individually) separadamente

separation /sepə'reɪʃən/ *n* separación *f*

separatism /'seprətɪzəm, 'sepərətɪzəm/ *n* separatismo *m*

separatist /'seprətəst, 'sepə- ‖'sepərətɪst, 'seprə-/ *n* separatista *mf*; (*before n*) ‹*group/movement*› separatista

September /sep'tembər ‖sep'tembə(r)/ *n* septiembre *m*, setiembre *m*

S

septic /'septɪk/ adj séptico; **to go ~** infectarse

sequel /'si:kwəl/ n **(a)** (Cin, Lit, TV) continuación f **(b)** (later events) secuela f

sequence /'si:kwəns/ n **1** (order): the police established the ~ of events la policía estableció cómo se sucedieron los hechos; **it's better to look at the pictures in ~** es mejor ver las fotos en or por orden **2 (a)** (series) serie f **(b)** (Math, Mus) secuencia f **3** (Cin, TV) secuencia f

sequin /'si:kwən/ ‖'si:kwɪn/ n lentejuela f

Serb /sɜːrb ‖sɜːb/ adj/n ▶ SERBIAN[1,2]

Serbia /'sɜːrbiə ‖'sɜːbiə/ n Serbia f, Servia f

Serbian[1] /'sɜːrbiən ‖'sɜːbiən/ adj serbio, servio

Serbian[2] n serbio, -bia m,f, servio, -via m,f

Serbo-Croat /'sɜːrbəʊ'krəʊæt ‖,sɜːbəʊ'krəʊæt/ n serbocroata m

serenade[1] /'serə'neɪd/ n serenata f

serenade[2] vt darle* (una) serenata a

serene /sə'riːn ‖sɪ'riːn/ adj sereno

sergeant /'sɑːrdʒənt ‖'sɑːdʒənt/ n sargento mf

sergeant major n ≈ brigada mf

serial /'sɪriəl ‖'sɪəriəl/ n **(a)** (Rad, TV) serie f, serial m or (CS) serial f **(b)** (Publ): it was published as a ~ se publicó por entregas

serialize /'sɪriəlaɪz ‖'sɪəriəlaɪz/ vt serializar*

serial: ~ killer n asesino, -na m,f en serie; **~ number** n número m de serie

series /'sɪriːz ‖'sɪəriːz/ n (pl ~) **(a)** (succession) serie f **(b)** (TV, Rad) serie f, serial m or (CS) f

serious /'sɪriəs ‖'sɪəriəs/ adj **1 (a)** (in earnest, sincere) serio; **I'm ~** lo digo en serio **(b)** (committed) (before n) ⟨student/worker⟩ dedicado **(c)** (not lightweight) (before n) ⟨newspaper/play/music⟩ serio **2** (grave) ⟨injury/illness⟩ grave; **I have ~ doubts about him** tengo mis serias dudas acerca de él

seriously /'sɪriəsli ‖'sɪəriəsli/ adv **1 (a)** (not frivolously) seriamente; **to take sth/sb ~** tomar(se) algo/a algn en serio **(b)** (genuinely, sincerely): **you can't ~ mean that** no lo puedes estar diciendo en serio **2** (gravely) ⟨ill/injured⟩ gravemente

seriousness /'sɪriəsnəs ‖'sɪəriəsnəs/ n seriedad f; **he said it in all ~** lo dijo muy en serio

sermon /'sɜːrmən ‖'sɜːmən/ n sermón m

serpent /'sɜːrpənt ‖'sɜːpənt/ n (liter) sierpe f (liter)

serrated /'sə'reɪtəd ‖sə'reɪtɪd/ adj ⟨edge/knife⟩ serrado

serum /'sɪrəm ‖'sɪərəm/ n suero m

servant /'sɜːrvənt ‖'sɜːvənt/ n criado, -da m,f, sirviente, -ta m,f

serve[1] /sɜːrv ‖sɜːv/ vt **1** (work for) ⟨God/country⟩ servir* a **2** (help, be useful to) servir*; **it ~s no useful purpose** no sirve para nada (útil); **to ~ sb right** (colloq): **it ~s her right!** ¡se lo merece!, ¡le está bien empleado! (Esp) **3 (a)** (Culin) ⟨food/drink⟩ servir* **(b)** (in shop) (BrE) atender* **4** (Law) ⟨summons/notice/order⟩ entregar*

5 (complete) ⟨apprenticeship⟩ hacer*; ⟨sentence⟩ cumplir

■ ~ vi **1 (a)** (be servant) (liter) servir* **(b)** (BrE) atender* **(c)** (distribute food) servir* **2** (spend time, do duty): **to ~ in the army** servir* en el ejército **3** (have effect, function) **to ~ to + INF** servir* PARA + INF **4** (Sport) sacar*, servir*

serve[2] n servicio m, saque m

server /'sɜːrvər ‖'sɜːvə(r)/ n **1** (Sport) jugador que tiene el saque **2** (Comput) servidor m

service[1] /'sɜːrvəs ‖'sɜːvɪs/ n **1 (a)** (duty, work) servicio m **(b)** (given by a tool, machine): **you'll get years of ~ from this iron** esta plancha te durará años **2** (of professional, tradesman, company) servicio m; **we no longer require your ~s** ya no precisamos sus servicios **3** (assistance) servicio m; **she has done us all a ~** nos ha hecho a todos un favor or servicio; **how can I be of ~ to you?** ¿en qué puedo ayudarlo or servirlo? **4** (organization, system) servicio m; **telephone/postal ~** servicio telefónico/postal **5** (Mil): **the ~s** las fuerzas armadas **6** (in shop, restaurant) servicio m **7** (overhaul, maintenance) revisión f, servicio m (AmL), service m (RPl) **8** (Relig) oficio m religioso **9** (in tennis) servicio m, saque m **10** (dinner ~) vajilla f

service[2] vt ⟨car⟩ hacerle* una revisión or (AmL) un servicio a; ⟨machine/appliance⟩ hacerle* el mantenimiento a

service: ~ charge n **(a)** (in restaurant) servicio m **(b)** (for maintenance — of apartment) gastos mpl comunes or (Esp) de comunidad; (— of office) gastos mpl de mantenimiento; **~ industry** n sector m (de) servicios; **~man** /'sɜːrvəsmən ‖'sɜːvɪsmən/ n (pl **-men** /-mən/) militar m, soldado m; **~ station** n estación f de servicio

serviette /'sɜːrvi'et ‖,sɜːvi'et/ n (BrE) servilleta f

serving /'sɜːrvɪŋ ‖'sɜːvɪŋ/ n porción f, ración f; (before n) **~ dish** fuente f; **~ spoon** cuchara f de servir

session /'seʃən/ n **1** (Adm, Govt, Law) (single meeting) sesión f; **to be in ~** estar* en sesión, estar* sesionando (esp AmL) **2** (period of time) sesión f; **a recording ~** una sesión de grabación

set[1] /set/ n **1** (of tools, golf clubs, pens, keys) juego m; (of books, records) colección f; (of stamps) serie f; **a matching ~ of sheets and pillowcases** un juego de cama **2** (TV) aparato m, televisor m; (Rad) aparato m, receptor m **3** (in tennis, squash) set m **4 (a)** (Theat) (stage) escenario m; (scenery) decorado m **(b)** (Cin) plató m **5** (in hairdressing) marcado m

set[2] adj **1** (established, prescribed) ⟨wage/price⟩ fijo; **there are no ~ times for visiting** no hay horas de visita establecidas; **a ~ phrase** una frase hecha; **we ordered the ~ menu** (BrE) pedimos el menú del día

2 (*pred*) **(a)** (ready, prepared): **to be ~** estar* listo, estar* pronto (RPl) **(b)** (likely, about to) (*journ*) **to be ~ to + INF** llevar camino de + INF **(c)** (determined, resolute): **she's absolutely ~ on that bicycle** está empeñada en que tiene que ser esa bicicleta; **he's dead ~ on going to college** está resuelto a ir a la universidad sea como sea

3 (rigid, inflexible): **to be ~ in one's ways** tener* costumbres muy arraigadas

set³ (*pres p* **setting**; *past & past p* **set**) *vt*
1 (put, place) poner*, colocar*
2 (cause to be, become): **to ~ sb free** poner* en libertad a algn; **to ~ fire to sth, to ~ sth on fire** prenderle* fuego a algo
3 (a) (prepare) ⟨*trap*⟩ tender*; ⟨*table*⟩ poner* **(b)** (Med) ⟨*bone*⟩ encajar, componer* (AmL) **(c)** ⟨*hair*⟩ marcar*
4 (adjust) ⟨*oven/alarm clock/watch*⟩ poner*
5 (a) (arrange, agree on) ⟨*date/time*⟩ fijar **(b)** (impose, prescribe) ⟨*target*⟩ establecer* **(c)** (allot) ⟨*task*⟩ asignar; ⟨*homework*⟩ mandar; ⟨*exam/test/ problem*⟩ poner*; ⟨*text*⟩ prescribir* **(d)** (establish) ⟨*precedent*⟩ sentar*; ⟨*record/standard*⟩ establecer*; **to ~ a good example** dar* buen ejemplo
6 (cause to do, start): **she ~ them to work in the garden** los puso a trabajar en el jardín; **to ~ sth going** poner* algo en marcha
7 (*usu pass*) ⟨*book/film*⟩ ambientar; **the novel is ~ in Japan** la novela está ambientada en el Japón
8 (mount, insert) ⟨*gem*⟩ engarzar*, engastar; ⟨*stake*⟩ hincar*, clavar; **the posts are ~ in concrete** los postes están puestos en hormigón
■ **~** *vi* **1** (go down) ⟨⟨*sun/moon*⟩⟩ ponerse*
2 (a) (become solid, rigid) ⟨⟨*jelly*⟩⟩ cuajar(se); ⟨⟨*cement*⟩⟩ fraguar* **(b)** ⟨*bone*⟩ soldarse*
■ **set about** [*v + prep*] **(a)** ⟨*task*⟩ (begin) emprender; (tackle) acometer **(b) to ~ about -ING** ponerse* a + INF **(c)** (attack) atacar*
■ **set apart** [*v + o + adv*] distinguir*
■ **set aside** [*v + o + adv, v + adv + o*] **(a)** (save, reserve) ⟨*food/goods*⟩ guardar, apartar; ⟨*time*⟩ dejar; ⟨*money*⟩ guardar, ahorrar **(b)** (put to one side, shelve) ⟨*book/project*⟩ dejar (de lado) **(c)** (disregard) ⟨*hostility*⟩ dejar de lado; ⟨*rules/ formality*⟩ prescindir de
■ **set back** [*v + o + adv, v + adv + o*] ⟨*progress*⟩ retrasar, atrasar; ⟨*clock*⟩ atrasar
■ **set in** [*v + adv*] ⟨*infection*⟩ declararse
■ **set off** **1** [*v + adv*] (begin journey) salir*
2 [*v + o + adv, v + adv + o*] **(a)** (activate) ⟨*bomb/ mine*⟩ hacer* explotar; ⟨*alarm*⟩ hacer* sonar; ⟨*firework*⟩ lanzar*, tirar **(b)** (enhance) hacer* resaltar
■ **set out** **1** [*v + adv*] **(a)** (begin journey) salir* **(b)** (begin, intend): **I didn't ~ out with that intention** no empecé con esa intención; **she had failed in what she had ~ out to achieve** no había logrado lo que se había propuesto
2 [*v + o + adv, v + adv + o*] **(a)** ⟨*argument/ theory*⟩ exponer* **(b)** ⟨*goods*⟩ exponer*; ⟨*chess pieces*⟩ colocar*
■ **set to** [*v + adv*] ponerse* a trabajar
■ **set up** [*v + o + adv, v + adv + o*] **1 (a)** (erect, assemble) ⟨*monument*⟩ levantar; ⟨*machine/tent*⟩

montar, armar; **they ~ up camp near the river** acamparon cerca del río **(b)** (arrange, plan) ⟨*meeting*⟩ convocar* a
2 (institute, found) ⟨*committee/commission*⟩ crear; ⟨*inquiry*⟩ abrir*; ⟨*business*⟩ montar
3 (establish): **she ~ herself up as a photographer** se estableció como fotógrafa
4 (colloq) **(a)** (frame) tenderle* una trampa a **(b)** (rig) arreglar

set: **~back** *n* revés *m*; **~ square** *n* escuadra *f*; (with two equal sides) cartabón *m*

settee /se'tiː/ *n* sofá *m*

setting /'setɪŋ/ *n* **1** (of dial, switch) posición *f* **2 (a)** (of novel, movie) escenario *m* **(b)** (surroundings) marco *m*, entorno *m* **(c)** (for gem) engarce *m*, engaste *m*, montura *f* **3** (place ~) cubierto *m*

settle /'setl/ *vt* **1 (a)** ⟨*price/terms/time*⟩ acordar*; **it's all been ~d, we're going to Miami** ya está (todo) decidido, nos vamos a Miami; **that ~s it: I never want to see him again** ya no me cabe duda: no lo quiero volver a ver **(b)** (resolve) ⟨*dispute/differences*⟩ resolver*
2 ⟨*bill/account*⟩ pagar*; ⟨*debt*⟩ saldar, liquidar
3 ⟨*country/region*⟩ colonizar*
4 (make comfortable) ⟨*patient/child*⟩ poner* cómodo
5 (make calm) ⟨*child*⟩ calmar; ⟨*doubts*⟩ disipar; ⟨*stomach*⟩ asentar*
■ **~** *vi* **1** (come to live) establecerse*
2 (become calm) ⟨⟨*person*⟩⟩ tranquilizarse*
3 (a) (make oneself comfortable) ponerse* cómodo **(b)** ⟨⟨*bird*⟩⟩ posarse
4 (a) ⟨⟨*dust*⟩⟩ asentarse*; ⟨⟨*snow*⟩⟩ cuajar **(b)** (sink) ⟨⟨*soil/foundations*⟩⟩ asentarse*; ⟨⟨*sediment*⟩⟩ depositarse
5 (a) (pay) saldar la cuenta (*or* la deuda *etc*) **(b)** (Law): **to ~ out of court** resolver* una disputa extrajudicialmente
■ **settle down** **1** [*v + adv*] **(a)** (become calm): **things have ~d down now** las cosas ya se han apaciguado; **~ down please, children** niños, por favor, tranquilos **(b)** (get comfortable): **we ~d down for the night** nos acomodamos para pasar la noche **(c)** (in place, activity): **she's settling down well in her new school** se está adaptando bien a su nueva escuela; **you should get a job and ~ down** deberías conseguirte un trabajo y establecerte *or* echar raíces en algún sitio **(d)** (become more responsible) sentar* (la) cabeza
2 [*v + o + adv*] (make calm) calmar, tranquilizar*
■ **settle for** [*v + prep + o*] conformarse con
■ **settle in** [*v + adv*]: **I'll come and see you when you've ~d in** te vendré a ver cuando estés instalado; **she's settling in well in her new job** se está adaptando bien a su nuevo trabajo
■ **settle into** [*v + prep + o*] ⟨*school/job*⟩ adaptarse a; ⟨*routine*⟩ acostumbrarse a
■ **settle on** [*v + prep + o*] ⟨*date/place*⟩ decidirse por
■ **settle up** [*v + adv*] (colloq) arreglar (las) cuentas

settled /'setld/ *adj* **(a)** (established) ⟨*habits/life*⟩ ordenado; ⟨*order*⟩ estable **(b)** ⟨*weather*⟩ estable

settlement /'setlmənt/ *n* **1** (agreement) acuerdo *m*, convenio *m*; **wage ~** (agreement) convenio *m* (laboral), acuerdo *m* salarial; (increase) aumento *m* (salarial) **2 (a)** (of account, ⋯⊱

bill) pago m; (of debt) liquidación f, satisfacción f
(b) (payment) pago m **3** (of dispute) resolución f
4 (village) asentamiento m
settler /'setlər ‖'setlə(r)/ n colono, -na m,f
set-up /'setʌp/ n (colloq) (situation, arrangement)
sistema f; (pej) tinglado m (fam & pey)
seven /'sevən/ adj/n siete adj inv/m; see also
FOUR¹
sevenfold /'sevənfəʊld/ adj/adv ▶ -FOLD
seventeen /'sevən'ti:n/ adj/n diecisiete adj
inv/m; see also FOUR¹
seventeenth¹ /'sevən'ti:nθ/ adj
decimoséptimo
seventeenth² adv en decimoséptimo lugar
seventeenth³ n (Math) diecisieteavo m; (part)
diecisieteava parte f
seventh¹ /'sevənθ/ adj séptimo
seventh² adv en séptimo lugar
seventh³ n (Math) séptimo m; (part) séptima
parte f
seventieth¹ /'sevəntiəθ/ adj septuagésimo
seventieth² adv en septuagésimo lugar
seventieth³ n (Math) setentavo m; (part)
setentava or septuagésima parte f
seventy /'sevənti/ adj/n setenta adj inv/m; see
also FOUR¹
sever /'sevər ‖'sevə(r)/ vt **(a)** (cut) ⟨rope/chain⟩
cortar; **the saw ~ed his finger** la sierra le cortó
or le amputó el dedo **(b)** (break off)
⟨communications⟩ cortar; ⟨relations⟩ romper*
several¹ /'sevrəl/ adj varios, -rias
several² pron varios, varias
severance /'sevərəns/ n **(a)** (of relations, links)
ruptura f **(b)** (Lab Rel) cese m; (before n) ~ **pay**
indemnización f por cese
severe /sə'vɪr ‖sɪ'vɪə(r)/ adj **severer,
severest 1 (a)** (strict, harsh) ⟨punishment/
judge⟩ severo; ⟨discipline⟩ riguroso **(b)** (austere)
⟨style/colors⟩ austero **2 (a)** (serious, bad) ⟨illness/
injury⟩ grave; ⟨pain⟩ fuerte; ⟨winter⟩ severo;
⟨weather conditions⟩ muy malo **(b)** (difficult,
rigorous) ⟨conditions⟩ estricto
severely /sə'vɪrli ‖sɪ'vɪəli/ adv con severidad,
severamente
severity /sə'verəti ‖sɪ'verəti/ n severidad f; (of
illness, injury) gravedad f; (of pain) intensidad f
sew /səʊ/ (past **sewed**; past p **sewn** or
sewed) vt coser; ⟨seam/hem⟩ hacer*; **to ~ sth
on** coser algo
■ ~ vi coser
■ **sew up** [v + o + adv, v + adv + o] coser
sewage /'su:ɪdʒ ‖'su:ɪdʒ, 'sju:ɪdʒ/ n aguas fpl
negras or residuales, aguas fpl servidas (CS)
sewer /'su:ər ‖'su:ə(r), 'sju:ə(r)/ n **(a)**
(underground) alcantarilla f, cloaca f **(b)** (drain)
(AmE) boca f de (la) alcantarilla, sumidero m
sewing /'səʊɪŋ/ n costura f
sewing machine n máquina f de coser
sewn /səʊn/ past p of SEW
sex /seks/ n **1 (a)** (sexual matters) sexo m;
(before n) ~ **education** educación f sexual; ~
symbol sex symbol mf **(b)** (intercourse) relaciones
fpl sexuales **2 (a)** (gender) sexo m **(b)** (men,
women collectively) sexo m; (before n) ~
discrimination discriminación f sexual

sexism /'seksɪzəm/ n sexismo m
sexist¹ /'seksəst ‖'seksɪst/ n sexista mf
sexist² adj sexista
sextet /seks'tet/ n sexteto m
sexual /'sekʃuəl/ adj sexual
sexuality /sekʃu'æləti/ n sexualidad f
sexually /'sekʃuəli/ adv sexualmente; a ~
transmitted disease una enfermedad de
transmisión sexual
sexy /'seksi/ adj **sexier, sexiest (a)** (sexually
attractive) sexy **(b)** (erotic) ⟨book/film/talk⟩ erótico
sh /ʃ/ interj ¡sh!
shabby /'ʃæbi/ adj **-bier, -biest (a)** ⟨carpet/
sofa/jacket⟩ gastado; (threadbare) raído **(b)** (bad,
unfair): **what a ~ way to treat him** qué manera más
fea de tratarlo
shack /ʃæk/ n choza f, casucha f, rancho m
(AmL), jacal m (Méx), bohío m (AmC, Col)
shackles /'ʃækəlz/ pl n grilletes mpl
shade¹ /ʃeɪd/ n **1** (dark place) sombra f; **in the
~** a la sombra **2** (over window) (AmE) persiana f,
estor m (Esp) **3 (a)** (of color) tono m **(b)** (degree of
difference, nuance) matiz m
shade² vt ⟨eyes/face⟩ proteger* del sol/de la luz;
her seat was ~d from the sun su asiento estaba
resguardado del sol
shadow¹ /'ʃædəʊ/ n sombra f; **she was a ~ of
her former self** no era ni sombra de lo que había
sido; **without a ~ of (a) doubt** sin la más mínima
duda
shadow² vt seguir* de cerca a
shadowy /'ʃædəʊi/ adj **(a)** (indistinct) ⟨form⟩
impreciso **(b)** (full of shadows) ⟨place/forest⟩ oscuro
shady /'ʃeɪdi/ adj **-dier, -diest (a)** (giving
shade) ⟨place/garden⟩ sombreado; ⟨tree⟩ que da
mucha sombra **(b)** (disreputable) (colloq) ⟨deal/
business⟩ turbio; ⟨character⟩ sospechoso
shaft /ʃæft ‖ʃɑːft/ n **1 (a)** (of arrow, spear) asta
f‡, astil m; (of hammer, ax) mango m **(b)** (of light)
rayo m **2** (Mech Eng) eje m **3** (of elevator) hueco
m; (of mine) pozo m, tiro m
shaggy /'ʃægi/ adj **-gier, -giest** ⟨dog⟩ lanudo,
peludo; ⟨beard/hair⟩ enmarañado, greñudo
shake¹ /ʃeɪk/ (past **shook**; past p **shaken**)
vt **1 (a)** (cause to move, agitate) ⟨bottle/cocktail⟩
agitar; ⟨person/building⟩ sacudir; ⟨dice⟩ agitar,
revolver* (AmL); **she shook the sand out of the
towel** sacudió la toalla para quitarle la arena; **to
~ hands with sb, to ~ sb's hand** darle* or
estrecharle la mano a algn; **they shook hands** se
dieron la mano; **to ~ one's head** negar* con la
cabeza; (meaning yes) (AmE) asentir* con la cabeza
(b) (brandish) ⟨sword/stick⟩ agitar; **to ~ one's fist
at sb** amenazar* a algn con el puño
2 (a) (undermine, impair) ⟨courage/nerve⟩ hacer*
flaquear; ⟨faith⟩ debilitar **(b)** (shock, surprise)
⟨person⟩ impresionar
■ ~ vi **1** (move, tremble) «earth/hand/voice»
temblar*; **he was shaking with fear/cold/rage**
estaba temblando de miedo/frío/rabia
2 (shake hands) (colloq): **they shook on it** sellaron
el acuerdo con un apretón de manos
■ **shake off** [v + o + adv, v + adv + o] ⟨pursuer/
reporter⟩ deshacerse* de; ⟨habit⟩ quitarse; ⟨cold⟩
quitarse de encima
■ **shake up** [v + o + adv, v + adv + o] **1** ⟨liquid⟩
agitar

2 (colloq) ⟨*industry/personnel*⟩ reorganizar* totalmente
3 (disturb, shock) (colloq): **he's a bit ~n up** está un poco alterado

shake² n **1** (act) sacudida f; (violent) sacudida f violenta, sacudón m (AmL); **he replied with a ~ of the head** contestó negando con la cabeza **2** (milk ~) (AmE) batido m, (leche f) malteada f (AmL), licuado m con leche (AmL)

shaken /'ʃeɪkən/ *past p of* SHAKE¹

shaker /'ʃeɪkər ‖ 'ʃeɪkə(r)/ n (a) (for cocktails) coctelera f (b) (for salt) salero m; (for pepper) pimentero m; (for sugar) azucarero m (c) (for dice) cubilete m, cacho m (Andes)

shaky /'ʃeɪki/ adj **-kier, -kiest** (a) (trembling) ⟨*hands/voice*⟩ tembloroso; ⟨*writing*⟩ de trazo poco firme (b) (unsteady) ⟨*table*⟩ poco firme; ⟨*structure*⟩ tambaleante; ⟨*health*⟩ delicado; ⟨*currency/government*⟩ débil; ⟨*theory/start*⟩ flojo

shale /ʃeɪl/ n esquisto m, pizarra f

shall /ʃæl, *weak forms* ʃl, ʃəl/ v mod (*past should*) **1** (with 1st person) (a) (in statements about the future): **I ~ be very interested to see what happens** tendré mucho interés en ver qué sucede; **we shan't be able to come** (BrE) no podremos venir (b) (making suggestions, asking for assent) [*The present tense is used in this type of question in Spanish*] **~ I open the window?** ¿abro la ventana?; **~ we go out tonight?** ¿qué te (*or* le *etc*) parece si salimos esta noche? **2** (with 2nd and 3rd persons) (in commands, promises etc): **they ~ not pass** no pasarán

shallot /ʃə'lɑːt ‖ ʃə'lɒt/ n chalote m, chalota f

shallow /'ʃæləʊ/ adj **-er, -est** (a) (not deep) ⟨*water/pond/river*⟩ poco profundo; ⟨*dish*⟩ llano, plano; ⟨*breathing*⟩ superficial (b) (superficial) ⟨*person*⟩ superficial

shallows /'ʃæləʊz/ pl n bajío m

sham¹ /ʃæm/ n farsa f

sham² adj (pej) (no comp) fingido

sham³ vt/i **-mm-** fingir*

shame¹ /ʃeɪm/ n **1** (feeling) vergüenza f, pena f (AmL exc CS); **~ on you!** ¡qué vergüenza!; **to put sb to ~: she's such a good hostess, she puts me to ~** es tan buena anfitriona que me hace sentir culpable **2** (pity) (no pl) lástima f, pena f; **what a ~!** ¡qué lástima!; **it's a ~ you can't go** es una pena que no puedas ir

shame² vt avergonzar*, apenar (AmL exc CS); **they ~d us into paying** nos hicieron avergonzarnos de tal manera que al final pagamos

shamefaced /'ʃeɪm'feɪst/ adj avergonzado

shameful /'ʃeɪmfəl/ adj vergonzoso

shameless /'ʃeɪmləs ‖ 'ʃeɪmlɪs/ adj ⟨*lie/exploitation*⟩ descarado; ⟨*liar/cheat*⟩ desvergonzado

shampoo¹ /ʃæm'puː/ n (pl **-poos**) champú m

shampoo² vt **-poos, -pooing, -pooed** ⟨*hair*⟩ lavar; ⟨*carpet/upholstery*⟩ limpiar

shan't /ʃænt ‖ ʃɑːnt/ = **shall not**

shanty /'ʃænti/ n (pl **-ties**) **1** (hut) casucha f, rancho m (AmL), chabola f (Esp) **2** (sea ~) (BrE) canción f de marineros

shantytown /'ʃænti.taʊn/ n barriada f (AmL), chabolas fpl (Esp), población f callampa (Chi), villa f miseria (Arg), ciudad f perdida (Méx), cantegril m (Ur), ranchos mpl (Ven)

shape¹ /ʃeɪp/ n **1** (a) (visible form) forma f; **it is triangular in ~** tiene forma triangular; **in the ~ of a cross** en forma de cruz; **to take ~** tomar forma (b) (general nature, outline) conformación f; **the ~ of things to come** lo que nos espera **2** (guise): **assistance in the ~ of food stamps** ayuda consistente en vales canjeables por comida; **I won't tolerate bribery in any ~ or form** no pienso tolerar sobornos de ningún tipo **3** (condition, order): **she's in pretty good/bad ~** está bastante bien/mal (de salud); **to keep in ~** mantenerse* en forma

shape² vt (a) ⟨*object/material*⟩ darle* forma a (b) (influence) ⟨*events*⟩ determinar; ⟨*character/ideas*⟩ formar
■ **~** vi «*project*» tomar forma; «*plan*» desarrollarse
■ **shape up** [v + adv] (a) ▶ SHAPE² vi (b) (improve, pull oneself together) entrar en vereda (fam)

-shaped /ʃeɪpt/ suff: **L~/heart~** con or en forma de L/corazón

shapeless /'ʃeɪpləs ‖ 'ʃeɪplɪs/ adj informe, sin forma

shapely /'ʃeɪpli/ adj **-lier, -liest** ⟨*figure*⟩ bien modulado, hermoso; ⟨*legs*⟩ torneado

share¹ /ʃer ‖ ʃeə(r)/ n **1** (portion) parte f; **she must take her ~ of the blame** debe aceptar que tiene parte de la culpa **2** (Busn, Fin) (a) (held by partner) (no pl) participación f (b) (held by shareholder) acción f

share² vt **1** (a) (use jointly) **to ~ sth (WITH sb)** compartir algo (CON algn) (b) (have in common) ⟨*interest/opinion*⟩ compartir; ⟨*characteristics*⟩ tener* en común **2** (a) (divide) dividir (b) (communicate) ⟨*experience/knowledge*⟩ intercambiar
■ **~** vi (a) (use jointly) compartir; **to ~ and ~ alike** compartir las cosas (b) (have a part) **to ~ IN sth** compartir algo, participar DE algo
■ **share out** [v + o + adv, v + adv + o] repartir, distribuir*

shareholder /'ʃerhəʊldər ‖ 'ʃeəhəʊldə(r)/ n accionista mf

shark /ʃɑːrk ‖ ʃɑːk/ n (Zool) tiburón m

sharp¹ /ʃɑːrp ‖ ʃɑːp/ adj **-er, -est** **1** (a) ⟨*knife/edge/scissors*⟩ afilado, filoso (AmL), filudo (Chi, Per); ⟨*features*⟩ anguloso; ⟨*pencil*⟩ con punta; **it has a ~ point** es muy puntiagudo (b) (pain) agudo (c) ⟨*wind*⟩ cortante; ⟨*frost*⟩ crudo, fuerte (d) ⟨*taste*⟩ ácido **2** (a) (abrupt, steep) ⟨*bend/angle*⟩ cerrado; ⟨*turn*⟩ brusco; ⟨*rise/fall*⟩ brusco (b) (sudden) repentino, súbito **3** (a) (keen) ⟨*eyesight*⟩ agudo; ⟨*hearing*⟩ fino, agudo (b) (acute) ⟨*wit/mind*⟩ agudo **4** (clear, unblurred) ⟨*photo/TV picture*⟩ nítido; ⟨*outline*⟩ definido; ⟨*contrast*⟩ marcado **5** (harsh) ⟨*retort*⟩ cortante; **to have a ~ tongue** ser* muy mordaz, tener* una lengua muy afilada **6** (clever, shrewd) ⟨*person*⟩ listo, astuto; ⟨*move*⟩ astuto **7** (Mus) (referring to key) sostenido; **C ~** do m sostenido

sharp² adv **1** (exactly): **at six o'clock ~** a las ⋯⟶

seis en punto **2** (abruptly): **turn ∼ right** gire a la
derecha en curva cerrada **3** (Mus) ⟨play⟩
demasiado alto

sharp³ n (Mus) sostenido m

sharpen /'ʃɑːrpən ‖'ʃɑːpən/ vt ⟨knife/claws⟩
afilar; ⟨pencil⟩ sacarle* punta a

sharpener /'ʃɑːrpnər ‖'ʃɑːpnə(r)/ n (knife ∼)
afilador m; (pencil ∼) sacapuntas m

sharply /'ʃɑːrpli ‖'ʃɑːpli/ adv **1** (a) (steeply,
abruptly) ⟨drop/fall/increase⟩ bruscamente; ⟨bend⟩
repentinamente (b) (suddenly, swiftly) de repente
2 ⟨outlined/defined⟩ claramente, nítidamente
3 ⟨answer⟩ con dureza

shat /ʃæt/ past & past p of SHIT²

shatter /'ʃætər ‖'ʃætə(r)/ vt ⟨window/plate⟩
hacer* añicos or pedazos; ⟨health/nerves⟩
destrozar*; ⟨confidence/hopes⟩ destruir*; ⟨silence⟩
romper*; **she was ∼ed by the news** la noticia la
dejó destrozada
■ ∼ vi hacerse* añicos or pedazos

shave¹ /ʃeɪv/ vt **1** ⟨person⟩ afeitar or (esp Méx)
rasurar **2** (touch in passing) rozar*
■ ∼ vi ⟨person⟩ afeitarse or (esp Méx) rasurarse

shave² n afeitada f or (esp Méx) rasurada f; **to
have a ∼** afeitarse or (esp Méx) rasurarse; *a close
∼* (colloq): **we won in the end, but it was a pretty
close ∼** al final ganamos, pero por los pelos or
por un pelo (fam)

shaven /'ʃeɪvən/ adj ⟨head⟩ rapado

shaver /'ʃeɪvər ‖'ʃeɪvə(r)/ n (electric ∼)
máquina f de afeitar, afeitadora f or (esp Méx)
rasuradora f

shaving /'ʃeɪvɪŋ/ n (a) (before n) ⟨cream/soap⟩
de afeitar or (esp Méx) de rasurar; **∼ brush**
brocha f de afeitar (b) **shavings** pl (pieces)
virutas fpl

shawl /ʃɔːl/ n chal m

she /ʃiː, weak form ʃi/ pron ella

■ Note Although *ella* is given as the main translation
of *she*, it is in practice used only for emphasis, or to
avoid ambiguity: *she went to the theater* fue al teatro;
she went to the theater, he went to the cinema ella
fue al teatro y él fue al cine; **she** *did it* ella lo hizo.

∼'s a writer/my sister es escritora/mi hermana;
∼ didn't say it, I did no fue ella quien lo dijo,
sino yo

sheaf /ʃiːf/ n (pl **sheaves**) (a) (Agr) gavilla f
(b) (of notes) fajo m; (of arrows) haz m

shear /ʃɪr ‖ʃɪə(r)/ vt (past **sheared**; past p
shorn) ⟨sheep⟩ esquilar

shears /ʃɪrz ‖ʃɪəz/ pl n (for grass, hedge) tijeras
fpl; (for shearing sheep) tijeras fpl de esquilar

sheath /ʃiːθ/ n (pl ∼s /ʃiːðz/) (for sword, knife)
funda f, vaina f

sheaves /ʃiːvz/ pl of SHEAF

shed¹ /ʃed/ vt (pres p **shedding**; past & past p
shed) **1** (a) ⟨tears/blood⟩ derramar (b) ⟨leaves/
skin⟩ mudar; ⟨clothing⟩ despojarse de (frml)
2 (send out) ⟨light⟩ emitir

shed² n (a) (hut) cabaña f; (garden ∼) cobertizo
m (b) (larger building) nave f

she'd /ʃiːd/ (a) = **she would** (b) = **she had**

sheen /ʃiːn/ n brillo m, lustre m

sheep /ʃiːp/ n (pl ∼) oveja f

sheepdog /'ʃiːpdɔːg ‖'ʃiːpdɒg/ n perro m
pastor

sheepish /'ʃiːpɪʃ/ adj avergonzado

sheepskin /'ʃiːpskɪn/ n piel f de borrego or de
cordero

sheer /ʃɪr ‖ʃɪə(r)/ adj **sheerer, sheerest**
1 (pure, absolute) (as intensifier) puro; **the ∼ size
of the problem** la mera magnitud del problema
2 (vertical) ⟨drop⟩ a pique; ⟨cliff⟩ escarpado
3 (fine) ⟨stockings/fabric⟩ muy fino

sheet /ʃiːt/ n **1** (on bed) sábana f **2** (of paper)
hoja f; (of wrapping paper) pliego m, hoja f; (of
stamps) pliego m **3** (a) (of metal) chapa f, plancha
f, lámina f; **a ∼ of glass** un vidrio (b) (of ice)
capa f; (before n) **∼ lightning** relámpagos mpl
difusos

sheet: ∼ metal n metal m en planchas or
chapas; **∼ music** n partituras fpl

sheik, sheikh /ʃiːk ‖ʃeɪk/ n jeque m

shelf /ʃelf/ n (pl **shelves**) **1** (in cupboard,
bookcase) estante m, balda f (Esp); **a set of shelves**
unos estantes, una estantería f **2** (Geol):
continental ∼ plataforma f continental

shell¹ /ʃel/ n **1** (a) (of egg, nut) cáscara f; (of
sea mollusk) concha f; (of tortoise, turtle, snail,
crustacean) caparazón m or f (b) (of building, vehicle)
armazón m or f **2** (Mil) proyectil m, obús m

shell² vt **1** (Culin) ⟨peas/nuts/eggs⟩ pelar;
⟨mussel/clam⟩ quitarle la concha a **2** (Mil)
⟨position/troops/city⟩ bombardear

she'll /ʃiːl, weak form ʃil/ = **she will**

shell: ∼fish n (pl **∼fish**) (a) (creature) marisco
m (b) (collectively) mariscos mpl, marisco m (Esp);
∼shock n neurosis f de guerra

shelter¹ /'ʃeltər ‖'ʃeltə(r)/ n **1** (building)
refugio m **2** (a) (protection): **to take ∼** refugiarse
(b) (accommodations): **they need food and ∼**
necesitan alimentos y albergue

shelter² vt (a) (protect from weather) resguardar
(b) ⟨criminal/fugitive⟩ darle* cobijo a
■ ∼ vi **to ∼ (from sth)** refugiarse or resguardarse
(DE algo)

sheltered /'ʃeltərd ‖'ʃeltəd/ adj ⟨valley/
harbor⟩ abrigado; ⟨life⟩ protegido

shelve /ʃelv/ vt ⟨plan/project⟩ archivar

shelves /ʃelvz/ pl of SHELF

shelving /'ʃelvɪŋ/ n estantería f

shepherd /'ʃepərd ‖'ʃepəd/ n pastor m

sherbet /'ʃɜːrbət ‖'ʃɜːbət/ n (a) (sorbet) (AmE)
sorbete m (b) (powder) (BrE) polvos efervescentes
con sabor a frutas, sidral® m (Esp)

sheriff /'ʃerəf ‖'ʃerɪf/ n (in US) sheriff mf

sherry /'ʃeri/ n (pl **-ries**) jerez m

she's /ʃiːz, weak form ʃɪz/ (a) = **she is** (b)
= **she has**

shield¹ /ʃiːld/ n **1** (Hist, Mil) escudo m
2 (protective cover on machine) revestimiento m

shield² vt to ~ sth/sb (FROM sb/sth) proteger*
algo/a algn (DE algn/algo)

shift¹ /ʃɪft/ vt **(a)** (change position of) ⟨object/
furniture⟩ correr, mover* **(b)** (transfer): they tried
to ~ the responsibility onto us trataron de
cargarnos la responsabilidad

■ ~ vi **1** (change position, direction) «cargo»
correrse; (change direction) «wind» cambiar; he ~ed uneasily in
his chair se movía intranquilo en la silla; the
focus of attention has ~ed to Europe el foco de
atención ha pasado a Europa **2** (change gear)
(AmE) cambiar de marcha or de velocidad

shift² n **1** (change in position) cambio m **2** (work
period) turno m; to work the day/night ~ hacer* el
turno de día/de noche; (before n) ~ work trabajo
m por turnos **3** (AmE Auto) palanca m de cambio
or (Méx) de velocidades

shift key n tecla f de las mayúsculas

shifty /ˈʃɪfti/ adj **-tier, -tiest** ⟨expression/eyes⟩
furtivo; ⟨appearance⟩ sospechoso

shilling /ˈʃɪlɪŋ/ n chelín m

shimmer /ˈʃɪmər ‖ ˈʃɪmə(r)/ vi «water/silk»
brillar; «lights» titilar; (in water) rielar (liter)

shin /ʃɪn/ n espinilla f, canilla f

shine¹ /ʃaɪn/ n brillo m

shine² (past & past p **shone**) vi **(a)** (gleam,
glow) «star/sun/eyes» brillar; «metal/shoes»
relucir*, brillar **(b)** (excel) to ~ (AT sth)
destacar(se*) (EN algo)

■ ~ vt (+ adv compl): to ~ a light on sth alumbrar
algo con una luz

shingle /ˈʃɪŋɡəl/ n guijarros mpl

shingles /ˈʃɪŋɡəlz/ n (Med) (+ sing vb) herpes
m, culebrilla f

shining /ˈʃaɪnɪŋ/ adj ⟨eyes⟩ brillante, luminoso;
⟨hair/metal⟩ brillante, reluciente

shiny /ˈʃaɪni/ adj **-nier, -niest** ⟨hair/fabric/
shoe⟩ brillante; ⟨coin⟩ reluciente

ship¹ /ʃɪp/ n barco m, buque m

ship² vt **-pp- (a)** (send by sea) enviar* or mandar
por barco **(b)** (send) enviar*, despachar

ship: ~building n construcción f naval;
~load n cargamento m

shipment /ˈʃɪpmənt/ n (goods) envío m, remesa
f

shipping /ˈʃɪpɪŋ/ n **(a)** (ships) barcos mpl,
embarcaciones fpl (frml); (before n) ⟨lane/route⟩ de
navegación **(b)** (transportation of freight) transporte
m

shipshape /ˈʃɪpʃeɪp/ adj (pred) limpio y
ordenado

shipwreck¹ /ˈʃɪprek/ n naufragio m

shipwreck² vt (usu pass): to be ~ed
naufragar*

shipyard /ˈʃɪpjɑːrd ‖ ˈʃɪpjɑːd/ n (often pl)
astillero m

shirk /ʃɜːrk ‖ ʃɜːk/ vt ⟨task/duty⟩ eludir, rehuir*

shirt /ʃɜːrt ‖ ʃɜːt/ n camisa f

shirtsleeve /ˈʃɜːrtsliːv ‖ ˈʃɜːtsliːv/ n manga f
de camisa; in (one's) ~s en mangas de camisa

shit¹ /ʃɪt/ n (vulg) mierda f (vulg)

shit² vi (pres p **shitting**; past & past p **shit** or
shat) (vulg) cagar* (vulg)

shit³ interj (vulg) ¡carajo! (vulg), ¡mierda! (vulg)

shiver¹ /ˈʃɪvər ‖ ˈʃɪvə(r)/ n escalofrío m; the
scream sent ~s o a ~ down my spine el grito me
produjo escalofríos

shiver² vi (with cold) temblar*; (with fear)
temblar*; (with anticipation) estremecerse*

shivery /ˈʃɪvəri/ adj: to feel ~ tener*
escalofríos

shmaltz, shmalz etc ▶ SCHMALTZ etc

shoal /ʃəʊl/ n **1** (of fish) cardumen m, banco m
2 (sandbank) bajío m, banco m de arena

shock¹ /ʃɑːk ‖ ʃɒk/ n **1 (a)** (of impact) choque
m; (of earthquake, explosion) sacudida f **(b)** (electric
~) descarga f (eléctrica) **2 (a)** (Med) shock m; to
be in (a state of) ~ estar* en estado de shock **(b)**
(distress, surprise) shock m; to get a ~ llevarse un
shock; the news came as a great ~ to us la
noticia nos conmocionó **(c)** (scare) susto m; to get
a ~ llevarse un susto **3** (bushy mass): a ~ of hair
una mata de pelo

shock² vt (stun, appal) horrorizar*; (scandalize)
escandalizar*

shock absorber /əbˈsɔːrbər ‖ əbˈzɔːbə(r)/ n
amortiguador m

shocked /ʃɑːkt ‖ ʃɒkt/ adj **(a)** (appalled)
horrorizado **(b)** (scandalized): I was ~ to hear that
… me indigné cuando me enteré de que …

shocking /ˈʃɑːkɪŋ ‖ ˈʃɒkɪŋ/ adj **(a)** ⟨news/
report⟩ espeluznante **(b)** ⟨behavior/language⟩
escandaloso

shock wave n (Phys) onda f expansiva

shod /ʃɑːd ‖ ʃɒd/ past & past p of SHOE²

shoddy /ˈʃɑːdi ‖ ˈʃɒdi/ adj **-dier, -diest**
⟨goods/workmanship⟩ de muy mala calidad

shoe¹ /ʃuː/ n **(a)** (Clothing) zapato m; (before n)
~ polish betún m; ~ repairer zapatero, -ra m,f
(b) (for horse) herradura f **(c)** (brake ~) zapata f

shoe² vt (pres **shoes**; pres p **shoeing**; past &
past p **shod**) ⟨horse⟩ herrar*

shoe: ~brush n cepillo m de los zapatos;
~horn n calzador m; ~lace n cordón m (de
zapato), agujeta f (Méx), pasador m (Per)

shone /ʃəʊn, ʃɑːn ‖ ʃɒn/ past & past p of SHINE²

shoo¹ /ʃuː/ interj ¡fuera!, ¡úscale! (Méx)

shoo² vt shoos, shooing, shooed: I ~ed
the birds off o away espanté a los pájaros

shook /ʃʊk/ past of SHAKE¹

shoot¹ /ʃuːt/ n **1** (Bot) brote m **2** (shooting
expedition) cacería f **3** (Cin) rodaje m

shoot² (past & past p **shot**) vt **1 (a)** ⟨person/
animal⟩ pegarle* un tiro a; **they shot him dead,
they shot him to death** (AmE) lo mataron a tiros/
de un tiro; to ~ oneself pegarse* un tiro **(b)**
(hunt) ⟨duck/deer⟩ cazar*
2 (fire) ⟨bullet⟩ disparar, tirar; ⟨arrow/missile⟩
lanzar*, arrojar; ⟨glance⟩ lanzar*
3 (pass swiftly): to ~ the rapids salvar los rápidos
4 (Cin) rodar*

■ ~ vi **1 (a)** (fire weapon) disparar; to ~ AT sb/sth
dispararle A algn/algo **(b)** (hunt) cazar*
2 (move swiftly): she shot past pasó como una
bala (fam); he shot out of his seat saltó del
asiento
3 (Sport) tirar, disparar

■ **shoot down** [v + o + adv, v + adv + o] ⟨plane⟩
derribar, abatir ⸱⸱⸱⸦

■ **shoot out** [v + adv] (emerge quickly) salir* disparado or (fam) como un bólido

■ **shoot up** [v + adv] (grow tall) crecer* mucho **(b)** (go up quickly) «*prices/temperature*» dispararse; «*flames*» alzarse*

shoot³ *interj* (AmE colloq) ¡miércoles! (fam & euf)

shooting /ˈʃuːtɪŋ/ *n* **(a)** (exchange of fire) tiroteo *m*, balacera *f* (AmL); (shots) tiros *mpl*, disparos *mpl* **(b)** (killing) asesinato *m*

shooting star *n* estrella *f* fugaz

shoot-out /ˈʃuːtaʊt/ *n* tiroteo *m*, balacera *f* (AmL), baleo *m* (Chi)

shop¹ /ʃɑːp ‖ ʃɒp/ *n* **(a)** (retail outlet) tienda *f*, negocio *m* (CS), comercio *m* (frml); **to go to the** ∼ ir* de compras **(b)** (business) (colloq): **to talk** ∼ hablar del trabajo

shop² **-pp-** *vi* hacer* compras; **to go** ∼**ping** ir* de compras

shopaholic /ˌʃɑːpəˈhɒlɪk ‖ ˌʃɒpəˈhɒlɪk/ *n* (colloq) persona *f* adicta a las compras

shop: ∼ **assistant** *n* (BrE) dependiente, -ta *m,f*, empleado, -da *m,f* (de tienda) (AmL), vendedor, -dora *m,f* (CS); ∼ **floor** *n* (part of factory) taller *m*; (workers) obreros *mpl*, trabajadores *mpl*; (as union members) bases *fpl* sindicales; ∼**keeper** *n* comerciante *mf*, tendero, -ra *m,f*, ∼**lifter** /ˈʃɑːpˌlɪftər ‖ ˈʃɒpˌlɪftə(r)/ *n* ladrón, -drona *m,f* (*que roba en las tiendas*); ∼**lifting** /ˈʃɑːpˌlɪftɪŋ ‖ ˈʃɒpˌlɪftɪŋ/ *n* hurto *m* (*en las tiendas*)

shopper /ˈʃɑːpər ‖ ˈʃɒpə(r)/ *n* comprador, -dora *m,f*

shopping /ˈʃɑːpɪŋ ‖ ˈʃɒpɪŋ/ *n* **(a)** (act): **to do the** ∼ hacer* la compra or (AmS) las compras, hacer* el mercado (Col, Ven), hacer* el mandado (Méx); (*before it*) ⟨*basket*⟩ de la compra or (AmS) de las compras **(b)** (purchases) compras *fpl*

shopping: ∼ **bag** *n* **(a)** (given by store) (AmE) bolsa *f* (*de plástico, papel etc*) **(b)** (owned by customer) (BrE) bolsa *f* (de la compra or (AmS) de las compras); ∼ **cart** *n* (AmE) carrito *m* (de la compra or (AmS) de las compras); ∼ **center**, (BrE) ∼ **centre** ▸ → MALL; ∼ **list** *n* lista *f* de la compra or (AmS) de las compras or (Col, Ven) del mercado or (Méx) del mandado; ∼ **mall** *n* (esp AmE) centro *m* comercial; ∼ **trolley** *n* (BrE) **(a)** ▸ → CART **(b)** (bag on wheels) carrito *m*, changuito *m* (RPl)

shop: ∼**-soiled** *adj* ⟨*goods*⟩ deteriorado; ∼ **window** *n* escaparate *m*, vitrina *f* (AmL), aparador *m* (AmC, Col, Méx); ∼**worn** *adj* (AmE) ⟨*goods*⟩ deteriorado

shore /ʃɔːr ‖ ʃɔː(r)/ *n* **1** **(a)** (of sea, lake) orilla *f* **(b)** (coast) costa *f*, ribera *f* **2** (land): **to go on** ∼ bajar a tierra (firme)

■ **shore up** [v + o + adv, v + adv + o] apuntalar

shorn /ʃɔːrn ‖ ʃɔːn/ *past p of* SHEAR

short¹ /ʃɔːrt ‖ ʃɔːt/ *adj* **-er, -est** **1** (of length, height, distance) corto; ⟨*person*⟩ bajo

2 **(a)** (brief) ⟨*visit/trip*⟩ corto; **the days are getting** ∼**er** los días van acortándose; **a** ∼ **time ago** hace poco (tiempo); **we call him Rob for** ∼ lo llamamos Rob para abreviar **(b)** **in short** (briefly) (*as linker*) en resumen

3 (brusque) ⟨*manner*⟩ brusco; **she has a** ∼ **temper** tiene muy mal genio

4 (inadequate, deficient) escaso; **to be in** ∼ **supply** escasear; **we're six people** ∼ todavía nos faltan seis personas; **(to be)** ∼ **OF sth/sb: we're very** ∼ **of time** estamos muy cortos de tiempo; **they were** ∼ **of staff** no tenían suficiente personal

short² *adv* **1** (suddenly, abruptly): **he cut** ∼ **his vacation** interrumpió sus vacaciones; **he stopped** ∼ **when he saw me** se paró en seco cuando me vio **2** (below target, requirement): **to fall** ∼ «*shell/arrow*» quedarse corto; **we never went** ∼ **of food** nunca nos faltó la comida

short³ *n* **1** (Cin) cortometraje *m*, corto *m* **2** (drink) (BrE) copa *f* de bebida alcohólica de las que se sirven en pequeñas cantidades, como el whisky o el coñac **3** **shorts** *pl* **(a)** (short trousers) shorts *mpl*, pantalones *mpl* cortos **(b)** (men's underwear) (AmE) calzoncillos *mpl*

short⁴ *vi* (Elec) hacer* un cortocircuito

■ **short out** (AmE Elec) [v + adv] «*fuse*» fundirse; «*iron/hairdryer*» hacer* (un) cortocircuito

shortage /ˈʃɔːrtɪdʒ ‖ ˈʃɔːtɪdʒ/ *n* ∼ (OF sth/sb) falta *f or* escasez *f* (DE algo/algn)

short: ∼**bread** *n* galleta dulce de mantequilla; ∼**change** /ˈʃɔːrtˈtʃeɪndʒ ‖ ˈʃɔːtˈtʃeɪndʒ/ *vt* (in shop): **he** ∼**changed me** me dio mal el cambio or (AmL tb) el vuelto; ∼ **circuit** *n* cortocircuito *m*; ∼**circuit** /ˈʃɔːrtˈsɜːrkət ‖ ˈʃɔːtˈsɜːkɪt/ *vt* (Elec) provocar* un cortocircuito en ■ ∼ *vi* (Elec) hacer* (un) cortocircuito; ∼**coming** *n* defecto *m*, deficiencia *f*; ∼**crust (pastry)** *n* (BrE) pasta *f* quebradiza (*tipo de masa para empanadas, tartas etc*); ∼ **cut** *n* atajo *m*; **there are no** ∼ **cuts to success** no hay fórmulas mágicas para el éxito

shorten /ˈʃɔːrtn ‖ ˈʃɔːtn/ *vt* ⟨*skirt/sleeves*⟩ acortar; ⟨*text/report*⟩ acortar, abreviar

short: ∼**fall** *n* ∼**fall** (IN sth): **a** ∼**fall of 7% in revenues** un déficit de 7% en los ingresos; ∼**-haired** /ˈʃɔːrtherd ‖ ˈʃɔːtˈheəd/ *adj* de pelo corto; ∼**hand** *n* taquigrafía *f*; ∼ **list** *n* lista *f* de candidatos preseleccionados; ∼**list** *vt* preseleccionar; ∼**-lived** /ˈʃɔːrtˈlɪvd ‖ ˈʃɔːtˈlɪvd/ *adj* ⟨*success/enthusiasm*⟩ efímero; ⟨*recovery*⟩ pasajero

shortly /ˈʃɔːrtli ‖ ˈʃɔːtli/ *adv* dentro de poco; ∼ **before/after midnight** poco antes/después de la medianoche

short: ∼**sighted** /ˈʃɔːrtˈsaɪtəd ‖ ˈʃɔːtˈsaɪtɪd/ *adj* **(a)** (esp BrE Med) miope, corto de vista **(b)** ⟨*attitude/policy*⟩ corto de miras; ∼**sleeved** /ˈʃɔːrtˈsliːvd ‖ ˈʃɔːtˈsliːvd/ *adj* de manga corta; ∼**staffed** /ˈʃɔːrtˈstæft ‖ ˈʃɔːtˈstɑːft/ *adj*: **they/we were** ∼**staffed** les/nos faltaba personal; ∼ **story** *n* cuento *m*, relato *m* breve; ∼**tempered** /ˈʃɔːrtˈtempərd ‖ ˈʃɔːtˈtempəd/ *adj* de mal genio; ∼**term** /ˈʃɔːrtˈtɜːrm ‖ ˈʃɔːtˈtɜːm/ *adj* a corto plazo; ∼**wave** /ˈʃɔːrtˈweɪv ‖ ˈʃɔːtˈweɪv/ *n* onda *f* corta

shot¹ /ʃɑːt ‖ ʃɒt/ *past & past p of* SHOOT²

shot² *n* **1** **(a)** (from gun, rifle) disparo *m*, tiro *m*; (from cannon) cañonazo *m*; **she fired three** ∼**s** disparó tres veces; **she was off like a** ∼ salió disparada **(b)** (marksman): **a good/poor** ∼ un buen/mal tirador

2 (colloq) (attempt, try): **it costs $50 a** ∼ son 50 dólares por vez; **I'd like another** ∼ **at it** me gustaría volver a intentarlo

3 (Phot) foto *f*; (Cin) toma *f*

4 (pellets): **(lead)** ∼ perdigones *mpl*

5 (used in shotput) bala *f*, peso *m* (Esp)
6 (in soccer) disparo *m*, tiro *m*; (in basketball) tiro *m*, tirada *f*; (in golf, tennis) tiro *m*
7 (injection) inyección *f*

shot: ∼**gun** *n* escopeta *f*; ∼**put** *n* (event) lanzamiento *m* de bala *or* (Esp) de peso

should[1] /ʃʊd/ *past of* SHALL

should[2] *v mod* **1** (expressing desirability) debería (*or* deberías *etc*), debiera (*or* debieras *etc*); **you** ∼ **have thought of that before** deberías *or* debieras haber pensado en eso antes **2** (indicating probability, logical expectation) debería (*or* deberías *etc*) (de), debiera (*or* debieras *etc*) (de); **it** ∼ **add up to 100** debería (de) *or* debiera (de) dar 100 **3** (*with first person only*) **(a)** (conditional use) (BrE fml): **I** ∼ **like to see her** me gustaría verla **(b)** (venturing a guess) (BrE): **I** ∼ **think she must be over 80** yo diría que debe tener más de 80 **(c)** (expressing indignation): **I** ∼ **think so too!** ¡(no) faltaría más! **4** (subjunctive use) (*with all persons*): **it's natural that he** ∼ **want to go with her** es natural que quiera ir con ella; **if you** ∼ **happen to pass a bookshop …** si pasaras por una librería …

shoulder[1] /ˈʃəʊldər ‖ˈʃəʊldə(r)/ *n* **1** (Anat, Clothing) hombro *m* **2** (of road) arcén *m*, berma *f* (Andes), acotamiento *m* (Méx), banquina *f* (RPl), hombrillo *m* (Ven)

shoulder[2] *vt* ⟨*knapsack*⟩ ponerse* *or* echarse al hombro; ⟨*blame/responsibility*⟩ cargar* con

shoulder: ∼ **bag** *n* bolso *m or* (CS) cartera *f or* (Méx) bolsa *f* (*con correa larga para colgar del hombro*); ∼ **blade** *n* omóplato *m*; ∼**length** /ˈʃəʊldərˌleŋθ ‖ˈʃəʊldəˈleŋθ/ *adj*: ∼**length hair** pelo *m* hasta los hombros; ∼ **strap** *n* (of garment) tirante *m or* (CS) bretel *m* (of bag) correa *f*

shouldn't /ˈʃʊdnt/ = **should not**

shout[1] /ʃaʊt/ *n* grito *m*

shout[2] *vi* gritar; **to** ∼ **AT sb** gritarle A algn
■ ∼ *vt* gritar
■ **shout out 1** [v + o + adv, v + adv + o] ⟨*answer*⟩ gritar **2** [v + adv] dar* un grito

shouting /ˈʃaʊtɪŋ/ *n* griterío *m*

shove[1] /ʃʌv/ *vt* **(a)** (push roughly) empujar; **they** ∼**d her out of the way** la quitaron de en medio a empellones *or* a empujones **(b)** (put) (colloq) poner*, meter
■ ∼ *vi* empujar

shove[2] *n* empujón *m*, empellón *m*

shovel[1] /ˈʃʌvəl/ *n* pala *f*

shovel[2] *vt*, (BrE) **-ll-** ⟨*coal*⟩ palear; ⟨*snow*⟩ espalar

show[1] /ʃəʊ/ (*past* **showed**; *past p* **shown** *or* **showed**) *vt* **1** **(a)** ⟨*photograph/passport*⟩ mostrar*, enseñar; **to** ∼ **sb sth, to** ∼ **sth TO sb** mostrarle* algo A algn **(b)** ⟨*feelings*⟩ demostrar*; ⟨*interest/enthusiasm*⟩ demostrar*, mostrar*; ⟨*courage*⟩ demostrar* (tener); **could you** ∼ **me the way?** ¿me podría indicar el camino? **(c)** (allow to be seen): **this carpet** ∼**s every mark** en esta alfombra se notan todas las marcas; **he's started to** ∼ **his age** se le han empezado a notar los años **2** (record, register) ⟨*barometer/dial/indicator*⟩ marcar*, señalar; ⟨*profit/loss*⟩ arrojar

3 (a) (demonstrate) ⟨*truth/importance*⟩ demostrar*; **it just goes to** ∼ **how wrong you can be** eso te demuestra lo equivocado que puedes estar **(b)** (teach) enseñar; **I** ∼**ed her how to do it** le enseñé cómo se hacía **4** (by accompanying) (+ *adv compl*): **he** ∼**ed us to our seats** nos llevó hasta nuestros asientos; **to** ∼ **sb in** hacer* pasar a algn; **to** ∼ **sb out** acompañar a algn a la puerta **5 (a)** (screen) ⟨*movie*⟩ dar*, pasar, poner* (Esp); ⟨*program*⟩ dar*, poner* (Esp); ⟨*slides*⟩ pasar **(b)** (exhibit) ⟨*paintings/sculpture*⟩ exponer*; ⟨*horse/dog*⟩ presentar
■ ∼ *vi* **1** (be visible) «*dirt/stain*» verse*; «*emotion/scar*» notarse; **your petticoat is** ∼**ing** se te ve la enagua **2** (be screened) (Cin): **it's** ∼**ing at the Trocadero** la están dando en el Trocadero, la ponen en el Trocadero (Esp)
■ *v refl* **to** ∼ **oneself (a)** (become visible) «*person*» asomarse **(b)** (prove to be) demostrar* ser; (turn out to be) resultar ser
■ **show off 1** [v + adv] lucirse*; **stop** ∼**ing off** déjate de hacer tonterías **2** [v + o + adv, v + adv + o] **(a)** (display for admiration) ⟨*car/girlfriend*⟩ lucir*, presumir de (Esp); ⟨*wealth/knowledge*⟩ presumir de **(b)** (display to advantage) ⟨*beauty/complexion*⟩ hacer* resaltar
■ **show up 1** [v + o + adv, v + adv + o] **(a)** (reveal) ⟨*mistake/deception*⟩ poner* de manifiesto (fml) **(b)** (embarrass) ⟨*parents/friends*⟩ hacer* quedar mal **2** [v + adv] **(a)** (be visible) «*imperfection*» notarse **(b)** (arrive) (colloq) aparecer* (fam)

show[2] *n* **1** (exhibition) (Art) exposición *f*; **to be on** ∼ estar* expuesto; **to put sth on** ∼ exponer* algo **2 (a)** (stage production) espectáculo *m*; **to steal the** ∼ robarse* el espectáculo **(b)** (on television, radio) programa *m* **3** (*no pl*) **(a)** (display) muestra *f*, demostración *f*; **a** ∼ **of force** un despliegue de fuerza **(b)** (outward appearance): **I made a** ∼ **of enthusiasm** fingí estar entusiasmado; **their plush office is simply for** ∼ su elegante oficina es solo para darse tono **4** (colloq) (*no pl*) (activity, organization) asunto *m*; **to run the** ∼ llevar la voz cantante (fam)

show: ∼ **business** (colloq) *n* mundo *m* del espectáculo; ∼**case** *n* **(a)** (cabinet) vitrina *f* **(b)** (for products, ideologies) escaparate *m*; ∼**down** *n* enfrentamiento *m*

shower[1] /ˈʃaʊər ‖ˈʃaʊə(r)/ *n* **1** (in bathroom) ducha *f*, regadera *f* (Méx); **to take** *o* (BrE) **have a** ∼ ducharse; (*before n*) ∼ **cap** gorro *m* de ducha **2** (Meteo) chaparrón *m*, chubasco *m* **3** (party) (AmE) fiesta *f* en la que los invitados obsequian a la homenajeada con motivo de su próxima boda, el nacimiento de su niño etc

shower[2] *vt* **(a)** (spray) regar*; **to** ∼ **sb WITH sth** tirarle algo A algn **(b)** (bestow lavishly) **to** ∼ **sb WITH sth**: **he** ∼**ed her with gifts** la llenó de regalos; **the country** ∼**ed him with honors** el país lo colmó de honores
■ ∼ *vi* **(a)** (wash) ducharse **(b)** (be sprayed) «*water/leaves/stones*» caer*; «*letters/congratulations/protests*» llover*

show jumping /ˈdʒʌmpɪŋ/ *n* concursos *mpl* hípicos

shown /ʃəʊn/ *past p of* SHOW[1]

S

show: ~-off n (colloq) fanfarrón, -rrona m,f, fantasma mf (Esp fam); **~room** n (often pl) salón m de exposición (y ventas)

showy /'ʃəʊi/ adj **showier, showiest (a)** (gaudy) llamativo **(b)** (attractive) vistoso

shrank /ʃræŋk/ past of SHRINK

shrapnel /'ʃræpnl/ n metralla f

shred¹ /ʃred/ n (of paper, fabric) tira f, trozo m; **not a (single) ~ of evidence** ni una (sola) prueba; **not a ~ of truth** ni pizca de verdad; **to be in ~s** «clothes/fabric» estar* hecho jirones or tiras; «argument/reputation» estar* destrozado

shred² vt **-dd-** cortar en tiras; ‹documents› destruir*, triturar

shredder /'ʃredər ‖'ʃredə(r)/ n (for paper) trituradora f; (for vegetables) cortadora f

shrew /ʃruː/ n (Zool) musaraña f

shrewd /ʃruːd/ adj **-er, -est** ‹person› astuto; ‹move/investment/assessment› hábil

shriek¹ /ʃriːk/ n (of delight, terror) grito m, chillido m; (of pain) grito m, alarido m; **we could hear ~s of laughter** oíamos risotadas

shriek² vi/t gritar, chillar

shrift /ʃrɪft/ n: **to give sth short ~** ‹idea/suggestion› desestimar algo de plano; **to give sb short ~** echar a algn con cajas destempladas

shrill /ʃrɪl/ adj **-er, -est** ‹whistle/laugh› agudo, estridente; ‹voice› agudo, chillón

shrimp /ʃrɪmp/ n (pl ~ or (BrE also) ~s) (large) (AmE) langostino m; (medium) camarón m (AmL), gamba f (esp Esp); (small) (BrE) camarón m, quisquilla f (Esp)

shrine /ʃraɪn/ n (holy place) santuario m; (in out-of-the-way place) ermita f

shrink /ʃrɪŋk/ (past **shrank** or **shrunk**; past p **shrunk** or **shrunken**) vi **1** (diminish in size) «clothes/fabric» encoger(se)*; «meat» achicarse*; «wood» contraerse*; «area/amount» reducirse* **2** (recoil) retroceder; **to ~ back o away from sth/sb** echarse atrás or retroceder ante algo/algn

■ ~ vt ‹clothes/fabric› encoger*

shrinkage /'ʃrɪŋkɪdʒ/ n (of clothes, fabric) encogimiento m; (of wood, metal) contracción f

shrivel /'ʃrɪvl/, (BrE) **-ll- ~ (up)** vi «leaf/plant» marchitarse, secarse*; «fruit/vegetables» resecarse* y arrugarse*; «skin» ajarse

■ vt ‹leaf/plant› secar*, marchitar

shroud¹ /ʃraʊd/ n mortaja f

shroud² vt envolver*; **a case ~ed in mystery** (journ) un caso envuelto en un velo de misterio

Shrove Tuesday /ʃrəʊv/ n martes m de Carnaval

shrub /ʃrʌb/ n arbusto m, mata f

shrubbery /'ʃrʌbəri/ n arbustos mpl, matas fpl

shrug¹ /ʃrʌg/ n: **with a ~** (of her shoulders) encogiéndose de hombros

shrug² **-gg-** vi encogerse* de hombros

■ ~ vt: **to ~ one's shoulders** encogerse* de hombros

■ **shrug off** [v + o + adv, v + adv + o] ‹misfortune/disappointment› superar; ‹criticism› hacer* caso omiso de

shrunk /ʃrʌŋk/ past & past p of SHRINK

shrunken¹ /'ʃrʌŋkən/ past p of SHRINK

shrunken² adj ‹body› consumido

shudder¹ /'ʃʌdər ‖'ʃʌdə(r)/ vi **(a)** «person» estremecerse* **(b)** «bus/train/plane» dar* sacudidas; **to ~ to a halt** pararse abruptamente

shudder² n **(a)** (of person) estremecimiento m **(b)** (of vehicle, engine) sacudida f

shuffle /'ʃʌfəl/ vt **1** **to ~ one's feet** arrastrar los pies **2** ‹cards/papers› barajar

■ ~ vi caminar or andar* arrastrando los pies

shun /ʃʌn/ vt **-nn-** ‹person/society› rechazar*, rehuir*; ‹publicity/limelight› evitar, rehuir*

shunt /ʃʌnt/ vt (Rail) cambiar de vía

shush¹ /ʃʊʃ/ vt acallar

shush² interj: **~!** ¡chitón!, ¡silencio!

shut¹ /ʃʌt/ (pres p **shutting**; past & past p **shut**) vt **1 (a)** ‹window/book/eyes› cerrar* **(b)** ‹store/business› cerrar* **2** (confine) **to ~ sb in sth** encerrar* a algn EN algo; **he ~ himself in his room** se encerró en su cuarto

■ ~ vi **1** «door/window» cerrar(se)* **2** (esp BrE) (cease business — for day) cerrar*; (— permanently) cerrar* (sus puertas)

■ **shut down** **1** [v + adv] «factory/business» cerrar*; «machinery» apagarse* **2** [v + o + adv, v + adv + o] ‹factory/business› cerrar*; ‹machinery› apagar*

■ **shut in** [v + o + adv, v + adv + o] encerrar*

■ **shut off** [v + o + adv, v + adv + o] **(a)** ‹water/electricity› cortar; ‹engine› apagar* **(b)** (isolate) (often pass) ‹place/person› aislar*

■ **shut out** [v + o + adv, v + adv + o] **(a)** ‹person/animal› dejar (a)fuera; ‹light/heat› no dejar entrar; **to ~ oneself out** quedarse (a)fuera **(b)** (AmE Sport) ‹team/pitcher› ganarle a (sin conceder ni un gol o carrera etc)

■ **shut up** **1** [v + o + adv, v + adv + o] **(a)** (close) ‹house/office› cerrar* **(b)** (confine) ‹dog› encerrar* **2** [v + o + adv] (silence) (colloq) hacer* callar **3** [v + adv] **(a)** (close business) cerrar* **(b)** (stop talking) (colloq) callarse

shut² adj (pred) cerrado

shutdown /'ʃʌtdaʊn/ n (of hospital, college) cierre m; (of power) corte m; (of services) paralización f

shutter /'ʃʌtər ‖'ʃʌtə(r)/ n **1** (on window) postigo m **2** (Phot) obturador m

shuttle¹ /'ʃʌtl/ n **1** (in loom, sewing machine) lanzadera f **2 (a)** (Aviat) puente m aéreo; (bus, train service) servicio m (regular) de enlace **(b)** (space ~) transbordador m or lanzadera f espacial

shuttle² vi: **to ~ back and forth** ir* y venir*

■ ~ vt ‹passengers› transportar, llevar

AmC	Central America	Arg	Argentina	Cu	Cuba	Per	Peru
AmL	Latin America	Bol	Bolivia	Ec	Ecuador	RPI	River Plate Area
AmS	South America	Chi	Chile	Esp	Spain	Ur	Uruguay
Andes	Andean Region	CS	Southern Cone	Méx	Mexico	Ven	Venezuela

shuttlecock /'ʃʌtļkɑːk ‖'ʃʌtļkɒk/ n volante m, plumilla f, rehilete m, gallito m (Col, Méx)

shy¹ /ʃaɪ/ adj **shyer, shyest** ‹person› tímido; ‹animal› huraño

shy² vi **shies, shying, shied** «horse» respingar*

shyly /'ʃaɪli/ adv tímidamente, con timidez

shyness /'ʃaɪnəs ‖'ʃaɪnɪs/ n timidez f

Siamese /saɪə'miːz/ n (pl ~) ~ **(cat)** gato m siamés

Siamese twins pl n (hermanos) siameses mpl, (hermanas) siamesas fpl

sibling /'sɪblɪŋ/ n (frml) (brother) hermano m; (sister) hermana f

sick /sɪk/ adj **-er, -est** [1] (ill) enfermo; **to be off ~** estar* ausente por enfermedad [2] (nauseated) ‹pred›: **to feel ~** (dizzy, unwell) estar* mareado; (about to vomit) tener* ganas de vomitar; **to be ~** vomitar; **he makes me ~** me da asco [3] **(a)** (disturbed, sickened) ‹pred›: **to be ~ with fear/worry** estar* muerto de miedo/preocupación **(b)** (weary, fed up) **to be ~ OF sth/-ING** estar* harto DE algo/+ INF; **I'm ~ and tired of hearing that** estoy absolutamente harto de oír eso [4] (gruesome) ‹person/mind› morboso; ‹humor/joke› de muy mal gusto

sick: ~ bay n enfermería f; **~bed** n (liter) lecho m de enfermo (liter)

sicken /'sɪkən/ vt dar* rabia, enfermar (AmL); (stronger) asquear
■ ~ vi (BrE) **to be ~ing FOR sth** estar* incubando algo

sickening /'sɪkənɪŋ/ adj **(a)** (appalling): **it's ~, isn't it?** da mucha rabia ¿no?; (stronger) da asco ¿no? **(b)** ‹smell/sight› nauseabundo

sickle /'sɪkəl/ n hoz f

sick leave n permiso m or (Esp) baja f or (RPl) licencia f por enfermedad

sickly¹ /'sɪkli/ adj **-lier, -liest (a)** ‹complexion/child› enfermizo **(b)** ‹taste/smell› empalagoso; ‹color› horrible, asqueroso

sickly² adv: ~ **sweet** demasiado empalagoso

sickness /'sɪknəs ‖'sɪknɪs/ n **(a)** (disease) (liter) enfermedad f **(b)** (nausea) náuseas fpl; (vomiting) vómitos mpl

sick pay n salario que se percibe mientras se está con permiso por enfermedad

side¹ /saɪd/ n [1] (surface — of cube, record, coin, piece of paper) lado m, cara f; (— of building, cupboard) lado m, costado m; (— of mountain, hill) ladera f, falda f
[2] (boundary, edge): **they were playing by the ~ of the pool** estaban jugando junto a or al lado de la piscina
[3] **(a)** (of person) costado m; (of animal) ijada f, ijar m; **Roy stood at her ~** Roy estaba a su lado; **they sat ~ by ~** estaban sentados uno junto al otro **(b)** (Culin) a ~ **of beef** media res f
[4] (contrasted area, part, half) lado m; **from ~ to ~** de un lado al otro; **on the ~:** **he repairs cars on the ~** arregla coches como trabajo extra
[5] **(a)** (faction): **to take ~s** tomar partido; **whose ~ are you on?** ¿tú de parte de quién estás? **(b)** (Sport) equipo m
[6] (area, aspect) lado m, aspecto m; **you must**

listen to both ~s of the story hay que oír las dos versiones; **it's a little on the short ~** es un poco corto
■ **side with** [v + prep + o] ponerse* de parte de

side² adj (before n, no comp) **(a)** ‹door/entrance/wall› lateral; **a ~ street** una calle lateral, una lateral **(b)** (incidental, secondary) ‹issue› secundario **(c)** (Culin): ~ **dish** acompañamiento m; **a ~ salad** una ensalada (como acompañamiento)

side: ~**board** n [1] (piece of furniture) aparador m, seibó m (Ven); [2] ~**boards** pl (BrE) ▶ ~BURNS; ~**burns** pl n patillas fpl; ~**car** n sidecar m; ~ **effect** n (of drug, treatment) efecto m secundario; (incidental result) consecuencia f indirecta; ~**kick** n (colloq) adlátere mf; ~**line** n [1] (Sport) línea f de banda; [2] (subsidiary activity) actividad f suplementaria; ~**long** adj (before n) ‹glance› de reojo, de soslayo; ~**saddle** adv a mujeriegas (con las dos piernas hacia el mismo lado); ~**show** n (at fair) puesto m; ~**step** vt -pp- ‹blow/opponent› esquivar; ‹problem/question› eludir; ~**track** vt **(a)** (from subject) hacer* desviar del tema **(b)** (from purpose): **sorry, I got ~tracked** perdón, me entretuve haciendo otra cosa; ~**walk** n (AmE) acera f, banqueta f (Méx), andén m (AmC, Col), vereda f (CS, Per)

sideways¹ /'saɪdweɪz/ adv **(a)** ‹glance› de reojo, de soslayo; ‹walk› de lado, de costado **(b)** (with side part forward) de lado

sideways² adj ‹look› de reojo, de soslayo; ‹movement› lateral, de lado

siding /'saɪdɪŋ/ n (Rail) apartadero m

sidle /'saɪdļ/ vi **to ~ up to sb** acercársele* sigilosamente a algn

siege /siːdʒ/ n sitio m; **the city was under ~** la ciudad estaba sitiada

Sierra Leone /si'erəliˈəʊn/ n Sierra Leona f

siesta /si'estə/ n siesta f; **to have a ~** dormir* or echarse una siesta

sieve¹ /sɪv/ n (Culin) (for flour etc) tamiz m, cedazo m, cernidor m

sieve² vt ‹flour› (BrE) tamizar*, cernir*, cerner*

sift /sɪft/ vt **(a)** ‹sugar/flour› tamizar*, cernir*, cerner*; (sprinkle) espolvorear **(b)** ‹facts/evidence› pasar por el tamiz or la criba

sigh¹ /saɪ/ vi suspirar; **he ~ed with relief/contentment** suspiró aliviado/satisfecho

sigh² n suspiro m; **she breathed o heaved a ~ of relief** dio un suspiro de alivio

sight¹ /saɪt/ n [1] (eye) vista f
[2] (range of vision): **to come into ~** aparecer*; **to lose ~ of sth/sb** perder* algo/a algn de vista; **the finishing line was now in ~** ya se veía la meta; **she watched until they were out of ~** los siguió con la mirada hasta que los perdió de vista
[3] (act of seeing, view) (no pl): **at first ~** a primera vista; **it was love at first ~** fue amor a primera vista; **to catch o get ~ of sth/sb** ver* algo/a algn; (in distance) avistar algo/a algn; **to know sb by ~** conocer* a algn de vista; **to play at o by ~** (Mus) tocar* a primera vista; **I can't stand the ~ of him** (colloq) no lo puedo ver (fam)
[4] **(a)** (thing seen): **the sparrow is a familiar ~ in our gardens** el gorrión se ve con frecuencia en nuestros jardines; **it's not a pretty ~** (colloq) no es ···‹›

muy agradable de ver **(b)** **sights** *pl* (famous
places): **to see the ~s** visitar los lugares de
interés

⑤ **(a)** (of gun) mira *f* **(b)** **sights** *pl* (ambition): **to
have sth in one's ~s** tener* la mira puesta en
algo

sight² *vt* ‹*land/ship*› divisar; ‹*person/animal*›
ver*

sighted /'saɪtəd ‖'saɪtɪd/ *adj* vidente; **he's
partially ~** tiene visión parcial

sight: **~read** /'saɪt'riːd/ (*past & past p* **-read**
/-red/) *vt/i* repentizar*; **~seeing** /'saɪt,siːɪŋ/ *n*:
to go ~seeing ir* a visitar los lugares de interés;
~seer /'saɪt,siːər/ *n* turista *mf*, visitante *mf*

sign¹ /saɪn/ *n* ① **(a)** (indication) señal *f*, indicio
m; **it's a ~ of the times** es un indicio de los
tiempos que corren **(b)** (omen) presagio *m*
② (gesture) seña *f*, señal *f* ③ **(a)** (notice, board)
letrero *m*, cartel *m*; (in demonstration) pancarta *f*
(b) (road ~) señal *f* (vial) ④ **(a)** (symbol) símbolo
m; (Math) signo *m* **(b)** (Astrol) signo *m*

sign² *vt* **(a)** (write signature on) firmar **(b)** (hire)
‹*actor*› contratar; ‹*player*› fichar
■ **~** *vi* firmar

■ **sign for** [*v + prep + o*] ‹*goods/parcel*› firmar el
recibo de

■ **sign on** [*v + adv*] **(a)** (enlist) «*recruit*»
alistarse, enlistarse (AmC, Col, Ven) **(b)** (in UK) (Soc
Adm) *anotarse para recibir el seguro de desempleo*,
apuntarse al paro (Esp)

■ **sign up** ① [*v + adv*] (for a course) inscribirse*,
matricularse; (to join the army) alistarse, enlistarse
(AmC, Col, Ven) ② [*v + o + adv*, *v + adv + o*]
‹*soldiers*› reclutar; ‹*player*› fichar

signal¹ /'sɪgnl/ *n* señal *f*

signal², (BrE) **-ll-** *vt* señalar
■ **~** *vi* **(a)** (gesture) **to ~** (**TO sb**) hacer(le)* señas/
una seña (a algn) **(b)** (Auto) señalizar*, poner* el
intermitente *or* (Col, Méx) la direccional *or* (CS) el
señalizador

signature /'sɪgnətʃʊr ‖'sɪgnətʃə(r)/ *n*
① (written name) firma *f* ② (Mus): **time ~** compás
m, tiempo *m*

signature tune *n* (BrE) sintonía *f* (del
programa), cortina *f* musical (CS)

significance /sɪg'nɪfɪkəns/ *n* importancia *f*

significant /sɪg'nɪfɪkənt/ *adj* **(a)** (important)
importante **(b)** (meaningful) ‹*look/smile*› expresivo;
‹*fact/remark*› significativo

significantly /sɪg'nɪfɪkəntli/ *adv*
considerablemente

signify /'sɪgnəfaɪ ‖'sɪgnɪfaɪ/ *vt* **-fies, -fying,
-fied** significar*

signing /'saɪnɪŋ/ *n* **(a)** (act of signing) firma *f* **(b)**
(Sport) fichaje *m*

sign language *n* lenguaje *m* gestual

signpost¹ /'saɪmpəʊst/ *n* señal *f*, poste *m*
indicador

signpost² *vt* (BrE Auto) ‹*way/route*› señalizar*

Sikh¹ /siːk/ *n* sij *mf*

Sikh² *adj* sij *adj inv*

silage /'saɪlɪdʒ/ *n* ensilaje *m*, ensilado *m*
(*forraje fermentado en silos*)

silence¹ /'saɪləns/ *n* silencio *m*; **in ~** en
silencio

silence² *vt* ‹*cries/voice*› acallar; ‹*child/animal*›
hacer* callar; ‹*opposition/criticism*› silenciar

silencer /'saɪlənsər ‖'saɪlənsə(r)/ *n* **(a)** (on gun)
silenciador *m* **(b)** (on car) (BrE) silenciador *m*,
mofle *m* (AmC, Méx)

silent /'saɪlənt/ *adj* **(a)** (noiseless, still) ‹*night/
forest*› silencioso **(b)** (not speaking) ‹*gesture/
protest*› mudo; **the 'h' is ~** la hache es muda; **a ~
movie** una película muda

silently /'saɪləntli/ *adv* **(a)** (noiselessly) ‹*creep/
glide/enter*› silenciosamente **(b)** (without speaking)
‹*pray/stand/listen*› en silencio, calladamente

silent partner *n* socio, -cia *m,f* capitalista

silhouette /ˌsɪlu'et/ *n* silueta *f*

silicon /'sɪlɪkən ‖'sɪlɪkən/ *n* silicio *m*; (*before
n*) **~ chip** (Comput) pastilla *f* de silicio

silk /sɪlk/ *n* seda *f*

silky /'sɪlki/ **-kier, -kiest** *adj* ‹*fabric/fur*›
sedoso

sill /sɪl/ *n* (window~) alféizar *m*, antepecho *m*

silly /'sɪli/ *adj* **-lier, -liest** ‹*person/idea/
mistake*› tonto; ‹*name/hat*› ridículo

silo /'saɪləʊ/ *n* (*pl* **-los**) silo *m*

silt /sɪlt/ *n* cieno *m*, limo *m*

silver¹ /'sɪlvər ‖'sɪlvə(r)/ *n* ① (metal) plata *f*
② **(a)** (household items) platería *f*, plata *f* **(b)**
(coins) monedas *fpl* (*de plata, aluminio etc*)

silver² *adj* **(a)** (made of silver) de plata **(b)** (in
color) plateado **(c)** (representing 25 years) (*before n*):
~ jubilee el vigésimo quinto aniversario; **~
wedding** (BrE) bodas *fpl* de plata

silver: **~ foil** *n* (BrE Culin) papel *m* de aluminio
or de plata; **~plate** /'sɪlvər'pleɪt ‖,sɪlvə'pleɪt/
vt dar*(le) un baño de plata a, platear; **~smith**
n platero, -ra *m,f*, orfebre *mf*; **~ware**
/'sɪlvərwer ‖'sɪlvəweə(r)/ *n* platería *f*, plata *f*

similar /'sɪmələr ‖'sɪmɪlə(r)/ *adj* similar,
parecido, semejante; **to be ~ TO sth** parecerse* A
algo

similarity /ˌsɪmə'lærəti ‖,sɪmɪ'lærəti/ *n* (*pl*
-ties) **(a)** (likeness — between things) similitud *f*,
parecido *m*, semejanza *f*; (— between persons)
parecido *m* **(b)** (common feature) semejanza *f*,
similitud *f*

similarly /'sɪmələrli ‖'sɪmɪləli/ *adv* **(a)** (in a
similar way) de modo parecido *or* similar **(b)**
(equally) igualmente **(c)** (*as linker*) asimismo

simile /'sɪməli ‖'sɪmɪli/ *n* símil *m*

simmer /'sɪmər ‖'sɪmə(r)/ *vt/i* hervir* a fuego
lento

simple /'sɪmpəl/ *adj* **simpler** /-plər/,
simplest /-pləst/ ① (uncomplicated) ‹*task/
problem*› sencillo, simple ② (plain, unpretentious)
‹*dress/food*› sencillo, simple ③ **(a)** (unsophisticated,
humble) simple **(b)** (backward) simple

simplicity /sɪm'plɪsəti/ *n* simplicidad *f*,
sencillez *f*

simplify /'sɪmpləfaɪ ‖'sɪmplɪfaɪ/ *vt* **-fies,
-fying, -fied** simplificar*

simplistic /sɪm'plɪstɪk/ *adj* simplista

simply /'sɪmpli/ *adv* ① (only, merely)
simplemente, sencillamente ② **(a)** (plainly) con
sencillez, sencillamente **(b)** (in simple language)
simplemente, sencillamente

simulate /'sɪmjəleɪt ‖'sɪmjʊleɪt/ *vt* simular

simultaneous /ˌsaɪməlˈteɪniəs ‖ ˌsɪməlˈteɪniəs/ *adj* simultáneo

simultaneously /ˌsaɪməlˈteɪniəsli ‖ ˌsɪməlˈteɪniəsli/ *adv* simultáneamente, a la vez

sin¹ /sɪn/ *n* pecado *m*

sin² *vi* **-nn-** pecar*

since¹ /sɪns/ *conj* **1** (in time) desde que; ∼ **coming to London** desde que vino (*or* vine *etc*) a Londres **2** (introducing a reason) ya que; ∼ **you can't go, can I have your ticket?** ya que no puedes ir ¿me das tu entrada?

since² *prep* desde; **they've worked there** ∼ **1970** han trabajado allí desde 1970; **how long is it** ∼ **your operation?** ¿cuánto (tiempo) hace de tu operación?

since³ *adv* desde entonces; **she has lived here ever** ∼ desde entonces que vive aquí

sincere /sɪnˈsɪr ‖ sɪnˈsɪə(r)/, **sincerer, sincerest** *adj* sincero

sincerely /sɪnˈsɪrli ‖ sɪnˈsɪəli/ *adv* sinceramente; ∼ **(yours)** *o* (BrE) **yours** ∼ (in letters) (saluda) a usted atentamente

sincerity /sɪnˈserəti/ *n* sinceridad *f*

sinew /ˈsɪnjuː/ *n* tendón *m*; (in meat) nervio *m*

sinful /ˈsɪnfəl/ *adj* ‹person› pecador; ‹act› pecaminoso

sing /sɪŋ/ (*past* **sang**; *past p* **sung**) *vt/i* cantar
∎ **sing along** [*v* + *adv*] **to** ∼ **along** (WITH **sb**) cantar (CON algn)

Singapore /ˈsɪŋɡəˈpɔːr /ˌsɪŋəˈpɔː(r)/ *n* Singapur *m*

singe /sɪndʒ/ *vt* **singes, singeing, singed** chamuscar*

singer /ˈsɪŋər ‖ ˈsɪŋə(r)/ *n* cantante *mf*

singing /ˈsɪŋɪŋ/ *n* canto *m*; (*before n*) **a good** ∼ **voice** una buena voz (para el canto)

single¹ /ˈsɪŋɡəl/ *adj* **1** (just one) (*before n*) solo; **the largest** ∼ **shareholder** el mayor accionista individual; **every** ∼ **day** todos los días sin excepción; (*with neg*) **not a** ∼ **house was left standing** no quedó ni una sola casa en pie **2** (*before n*) **(a)** (for one person) ‹room› individual; ‹bed/sheet› individual, de una plaza (AmL) **(b)** (not double): **in** ∼ **file** en fila india **(c)** (BrE Transp) ‹fare/ticket› de ida, sencillo **3** (unmarried) soltero
∎ **single out** [*v* + *o* + *adv*, *v* + *adv* + *o*]: **to** ∼ **sb out** (select) escoger* a algn en particular; (identify) señalar a algn en particular; **she was** ∼**d out for criticism/praise** se la criticó/elogió a ella en particular

single² *n* **1** (Mus) single *m*, (disco *m*) sencillo *m* **2** (ticket) (BrE) boleto *m or* (Esp) billete *m* de ida

single: ∼**-breasted** /ˈsɪŋɡəlˈbrestəd ‖ ˌsɪŋɡəlˈbrestɪd/ *adj* (de una fila de botones, derecho (AmL); ∼ **cream** *n* (BrE) crema *f* líquida, nata *f* líquida (Esp); ∼**-handed** /ˈsɪŋɡəlˈhændəd ‖ ˌsɪŋɡəlˈhændɪd/ *adv* sin (la) ayuda de nadie; ∼ **market** *n* mercado *m* único; ∼**-minded** /ˈsɪŋɡəlˈmaɪndəd ‖ ˌsɪŋɡəlˈmaɪndɪd/ *adj* decidido, resuelto; ∼ **parent** *n*: **he's/she's a** ∼ **parent** es un padre/una madre que cría a su(s) hijo(s) sin pareja

singles /ˈsɪŋɡəlz/ *pl n* (Sport) individuales *mpl*, singles *mpl* (AmL)

singsong /ˈsɪŋsɔːŋ ‖ ˈsɪŋsɒŋ/ *adj* ‹voice/accent› cantarín

singular¹ /ˈsɪŋɡjələr ‖ ˈsɪŋɡjʊlə(r)/ *adj* singular

singular² *n* singular *m*; **in the** ∼ en singular

sinister /ˈsɪnɪstər ‖ ˈsɪnɪstə(r)/ *adj* siniestro

sink¹ /sɪŋk/ (*past* **sank**; *past p* **sunk**) *vi* **1 (a)** ‹ship/stone› hundirse **(b)** (subside) **to** ∼ (INTO sth) ‹building/foundations› hundirse (EN algo); **he sank back into the chair** se arrellanó en el sillón **2** (fall, drop) ‹water/level› descender*, bajar; ‹price/value› caer* a pique; ‹attendance/output› decaer*; **my heart sank** se me cayó el alma a los pies **3** (degenerate) degradarse; **I'd never** ∼ **so low** nunca caería tan bajo
∎ *vt* **1** ‹ship› hundir **2** (bury, hide) ‹pipe/cable› enterrar* **3 (a)** (drive in): **the dog sank its teeth into my thigh** el perro me clavó los dientes en el muslo **(b)** (excavate) ‹shaft› abrir*; ‹well› perforar
∎ **sink in** [*v* + *adv*] (colloq): **it finally sank in that ...** finalmente nos dimos cuenta de que ...

sink² *n* **(a)** (in kitchen) fregadero *m*, lavaplatos *m* (Andes) **(b)** (washbasin) (AmE) lavabo *m*, lavamanos *m*, lavatorio *m* (CS), pileta *f* (RPl)

sinner /ˈsɪnər ‖ ˈsɪnə(r)/ *n* pecador, -dora *m,f*

sinus /ˈsaɪnəs/ *n* (*pl* **-nuses**) seno *m*

sip¹ /sɪp/ *vt* **-pp-** sorber, beber *or* tomar a sorbos

sip² *n* sorbo *m*

siphon /ˈsaɪfən/ *n* sifón *m*
∎ **siphon off** [*v* + *o* + *adv*, *v* + *adv* + *o*] ‹liquid/fuel› sacar* con sifón; ‹money› desviar*

sir /sɜːr ‖ sɜː(r)/ *n* **1 (a)** (as form of address — to male customer) señor, caballero; (— to male teacher) (BrE) profesor, señor **(b)** (Corresp): **Dear Sir** De mi mayor consideración:, Muy señor mío: **2 Sir** (as title) sir *m*

siren /ˈsaɪrən/ *n* sirena *f*

sirloin /ˈsɜːrlɔɪn ‖ ˈsɜːlɔɪn/ *n* preciado corte de carne vacuna del cuarto trasero

sirup *n* (AmE) ▶ SYRUP

sister /ˈsɪstər ‖ ˈsɪstə(r)/ *n* **1** (sibling) hermana *f*, (*before n*) ‹company› afiliado; ∼ **ship** buque *m* gemelo **2 (a)** (nun) hermana *f*, monja *f* **(b)** (nurse) (BrE) enfermera *f* jefe *or* jefa (*a cargo de una o más salas*)

sisterhood /ˈsɪstərhʊd ‖ ˈsɪstəhʊd/ *n* **(a)** (association of women) asociación *f* de mujeres **(b)** (Relig) congregación *f* **(c)** (sisterly relationship) solidaridad *f* (*entre mujeres*)

sister-in-law /ˈsɪstərənlɔː ‖ ˈsɪstərɪnlɔː/ *n* (*pl* **sisters-in-law**) cuñada *f*

sisterly /ˈsɪstərli ‖ ˈsɪstəli/ *adj* (propio) de hermana

sit /sɪt/ (*pres p* **sitting**; *past & past p* **sat**) *vi* **1 (a)** (sit down) sentarse* **(b)** (be seated) estar* sentado **2** (be in session) ‹committee/court› reunirse* en sesión, sesionar (esp AmE) **3 sitting** *pres p* ‹figure› sentado
∎ *vt* **1** (cause to be seated) ‹person› sentar*; ‹object› poner*, colocar* (*en posición vertical*) **2** (BrE Educ): **to** ∼ **an exam** hacer* *or* dar* *or* (CS) rendir* *or* (Méx) tomar un examen, examinarse

                                                  ⋯❖

■ **sit around** [v + adv]: he ~s around all day doing nothing se pasa el día sentado sin hacer nada

■ **sit back** [v + adv] (colloq) recostarse*

■ **sit down** [v + adv] sentarse*

■ **sit in** [v + adv] **to ~ in on a class** asistir a una clase como oyente (or observador etc)

■ **sit out** [v + o + adv, v + adv + o] **(a)** (wait until end of) ‹siege› aguantar; **to ~ it out** aguantarse **(b)** (not participate in) ‹dance› no bailar; ‹game› no tomar parte en

■ **sit up** [v + adv] **(a)** (in upright position) «person/ patient» incorporarse; «dog» sentarse* sobre las patas traseras; **that should make them ~ up and take notice** eso debería alertarlos **(b)** (with straight back) ponerse* derecho, enderezarse* **(c)** (not go to bed): **we sat up talking** nos quedamos (levantados) conversando

sitcom /'sɪtkɑːm ‖ 'sɪtkɒm/ n (colloq) ▶ SITUATION COMEDY

site /saɪt/ n **(a)** (location) emplazamiento m (frml); (piece of land) terreno m, solar m **(b)** (building ~) obra f **(c)** (archeological ~) yacimiento m (arqueológico) **(d)** (camp~) camping m

sit-in /'sɪtɪn/ n (demonstration) sentada f, sitin m (Méx); (strike) encierro m, ocupación f or toma f (del lugar de trabajo)

sitting /'sɪtɪŋ/ n **(a)** (for meal etc) turno m; **I watched three movies in a single ~** vi tres películas de una sentada (fam) **(b)** (of committee, parliament) sesión f

sitting: ~ **duck** n (colloq) presa f fácil, blanco m seguro; ~ **room** n (BrE) sala f de estar, living m (esp AmL); salón m (esp Esp)

situate /'sɪtʃuert ‖ 'sɪtjuert/ vt (locate) (often pass) ‹building/town› situar*, ubicar* (esp AmL)

situation /sɪtʃu'eɪʃən ‖ sɪtju'eɪʃən/ n **1** (circumstances, position) situación f **2** (job) (frml) empleo m; **☉ situations vacant** ofertas de empleo

situation comedy n comedia f (acerca de situaciones de la vida diaria)

sit-up /'sɪtʌp/ n (ejercicio m) abdominal m (levantando el torso del suelo)

six¹ /sɪks/ n seis m; **it's ~ of one and half a dozen of the other** (colloq) (it makes no difference) da lo mismo; (both parties are to blame) los dos tienen parte de la culpa; see also FOUR¹

six² adj seis adj inv

sixteen /'sɪks'tiːn/ adj/n dieciséis adj inv/m; see also FOUR¹

sixteenth¹ /'sɪks'tiːnθ/ adj decimosexto

sixteenth² adv en decimosexto lugar

sixteenth³ n diecisieisavo m; (part) dieciseisava parte f

sixteenth note n (AmE) semicorchea f

sixth¹ /sɪksθ/ adj sexto

sixth² adv en sexto lugar

sixth³ n (Math) sexto m; (part) sexta parte f, sexto m

sixth: ~ **form** n (in UK) los dos últimos años de la enseñanza secundaria; ~ **sense** n sexto sentido m

sixtieth¹ /'sɪkstɪəθ/ adj sexagésimo

sixtieth² adv en sexagésimo lugar

sixtieth³ n (Math) sesentavo m; (part) sesentava or sexagésima parte f

sixty /'sɪksti/ adj/n sesenta adj inv/m; see also FOUR¹

sizable /'saɪzəbəl/ adj ‹fortune› considerable; ‹property› de proporciones considerables

size /saɪz/ n **1** (dimensions) tamaño m; (of problem, task) magnitud f; **what ~ is it?** ¿de qué tamaño es?; **to cut sb down to ~** poner* a algn en su sitio, bajarle los humos a algn (fam) **2** (of clothes) talla f or (RPl) talle m; (of shoes, gloves) número m; **what ~ do you take?** ¿qué talla or (RPl) talle tiene or usa?; **I take (a) ~ 10 in shoes** calzo or (Esp tb) gasto el número 10

■ **size up** [v + o + adv, v + adv + o] (colloq) ‹problem› evaluar*; **she ~d him up immediately** enseguida lo caló ▶

sizeable adj ▶ SIZABLE

sizzle /'sɪzəl/ vi chisporrotear

skate¹ /skeɪt/ n **1** (ice ~) patín m (para patinaje sobre hielo); (roller ~) patín m (de ruedas) **2** (pl ~ or ~s) (Culin, Zool) raya f

skate² vi patinar

skate: ~**board** n monopatín m or (CS, Méx, Ven) patineta f; ~**boarding** n deporte m del monopatín or (CS, Méx, Ven) de la patineta

skater /'skeɪtər ‖ 'skeɪtə(r)/ n patinador, -dora m,f

skating /'skeɪtɪŋ/ n (ice ~) patinaje m sobre hielo; (roller ~) patinaje m sobre ruedas; (before n) ~ **rink** pista f de patinaje

skeleton /'skelətn ‖ 'skelɪtn/ n **(a)** (Anat) esqueleto m **(b)** (of building, vehicle) armazón m or f

skeleton key n llave f maestra

skeptic, (BrE) **sceptic** /'skeptɪk/ n escéptico, -ca m,f

skeptical, (BrE) **sceptical** /'skeptɪkəl/ adj ‹person/attitude› escéptico

skepticism, (BrE) **scepticism** /'skeptɪsɪzəm/ n escepticismo m

sketch¹ /sketʃ/ n **1** (drawing) bosquejo m, esbozo m **2** (Theat, TV) sketch m, apunte m

sketch² vt hacer* un bosquejo de, bosquejar ■ ~ vi hacer* bosquejos or bocetos

sketch: ~**book** n cuaderno m de bocetos; ~**pad** n bloc m de dibujo

sketchy /'sketʃi/ adj -chier, -chiest ‹account/treatment› muy superficial; ‹knowledge› muy básico

skewer /'skjuːər ‖ 'skjuːə(r)/ n pincho m, brocheta f

ski¹ /skiː/ n esquí m

ski² vi **skis, skiing, skied** esquiar*; **to go ~ing** ir* a esquiar

AmC	América Central	Arg	Argentina
AmL	América Latina	Bol	Bolivia
AmS	América del Sur	Chi	Chile
Andes	Región andina	CS	Cono Sur

Cu	Cuba	Per	Perú
Ec	Ecuador	RPl	Río de la Plata
Esp	España	Ur	Uruguay
Méx	México	Ven	Venezuela

skid¹ /skɪd/ n (Auto) patinazo m, patinada f (AmL)

skid² vi **-dd-** «car/plane/wheels» patinar; «person» resbalarse; «object» deslizarse*

skier /'skiːər ‖'skiːə(r)/ n esquiador, -dora m,f

skiing /'skiːɪŋ/ n esquí m

skilful adj (BrE) ▶ SKILLFUL

skilift /'skiːlɪft/ n telesquí m

skill /skɪl/ n **(a)** (ability) habilidad f; **technical** ~ destreza f **(b)** (technique): **typing is a very useful** ~ **to have** saber escribir a máquina es muy útil; **social** ~s don m de gente

skilled /skɪld/ adj «negotiator» hábil; «pilot» diestro; «worker/labor» calificado or (Esp) cualificado; «work» de especialista

skillful, (BrE) **skilful** /'skɪlfəl/ adj «liar/play» hábil; «surgeon/mechanic» diestro; (at sewing, craftwork) habilidoso

skim /skɪm/ **-mm-** vt [1] (Culin) «milk» descremar, desnatar (Esp); «soup» espumar [2] **(a)** «water/treetops» pasar casi rozando **(b)** (throw): **to** ~ **stones** hacer* cabrillas [3] (read quickly) leer* por encima
■ ~ vi [1] (glide): **the speedboat** ~**med over the sea** la lancha apenas rozaba la superficie del mar [2] (read quickly) leer* por encima

skim milk, (BrE) **skimmed milk** /skɪmd/ n leche f descremada or (Esp tb) desnatada

skimp /skɪmp/ vi (colloq) **to** ~ (**ON sth**) escatimar (algo)

skimpy /'skɪmpi/ adj **-pier, -piest** «meal/portion» mezquino, pobre; «funds» escaso; «nightdress/bikini» brevísimo

skin¹ /skɪn/ n **(a)** (of person) piel f; (esp of face; in terms of quality, condition) cutis m, piel f; (in terms of color) tez f, piel f; **to have a thick/thin** ~ ser* insensible/muy sensible a las críticas **(b)** (of animal, bird, fish) piel f **(c)** (of tomatoes, plums, sausage) piel f; (of potatoes, bananas) piel f, cáscara f **(d)** (on milk, custard) nata f; (on paint) capa f dura

skin² vt **-nn-** «animal» despellejar, desollar*

skin: ~**deep** /'skɪn'diːp/ adj (pred) superficial; ~**dive** /'skɪndaɪv/ vi hacer* submarinismo, bucear; **to go** ~**diving** ir* a hacer submarinismo, ir* a bucear; ~**diver** n buzo m, submarinista mf; ~**diving** n submarinismo m, buceo m; ~**head** n cabeza mf rapada

skinny /'skɪni/ adj **-nier, -niest** flaco, flacucho (fam)

skintight /'skɪn'taɪt/ adj muy ceñido, muy ajustado

skip¹ /skɪp/ n [1] (jump) brinco m, saltito m [2] (BrE) (container) contenedor m (para escombros, basura etc)

skip² **-pp-** vi **(a)** (move lightly and quickly) brincar, dar* saltitos **(b)** (with rope) (BrE) ▶ vt 2
■ ~ vt [1] **(a)** (omit) «page/chapter» saltarse **(b)** (not attend) «class/meeting» faltar a [2] (jump) (AmE): **to** ~ **rope** saltar a la cuerda or (Esp tb) a la comba

skipper /'skɪpər ‖'skɪpə(r)/ n (colloq) **(a)** (of boat) patrón, -trona m,f, capitán, -tana m,f; (of plane) capitán, -tana m,f **(b)** (Sport) (coach) entrenador, -dora m,f; (captain) capitán, -tana m,f

skip rope, (BrE) **skipping rope** /'skɪpɪŋ/ n ▶ JUMP ROPE

skirmish /'skɜːrmɪʃ ‖'skɜːmɪʃ/ n escaramuza f

skirt¹ /skɜːrt ‖skɜːt/ n falda f, pollera f (CS)

skirt² vt **(a)** (run alongside) bordear **(b)** ▶ SKIRT AROUND
■ **skirt around,** (BrE also) **skirt round** [v + prep + o] **(a)** «mountain/lake» bordear **(b)** «issue/problem» eludir

skittle /'skɪtl/ n bolo m

skittles /'skɪtlz/ n (+ sing vb) bolos mpl

skive off /skaɪv/ [v + adv] (BrE colloq) **(a)** (disappear) escurrir el bulto (fam), escaparse, pirarse (Esp fam) **(b)** (stay away — from school) hacer* novillos (fam); (— from work) no ir* a trabajar, capear (Chi) or (Col) capar trabajo (fam)

skulk /skʌlk/ vi: **I saw him** ~**ing in the background** lo vi al fondo, tratando de pasar desapercibido; **to** ~ **around** merodear

skull /skʌl/ n cráneo m

skullcap /'skʌlkæp/ n casquete m; (Relig) solideo m

skunk /skʌŋk/ n mofeta f, zorrillo m (AmL), zorrino m (CS), mapurite m (AmC, Ven)

sky /skaɪ/ n (pl **skies**) cielo m

sky: ~**diving** n paracaidismo m (en la modalidad de caída libre); ~**high** /'skaɪ'haɪ/ adj: **prices are** ~**high** los precios están por las nubes; ~**lark** n alondra f; ~**light** n tragaluz m, claraboya f; ~**line** n (a) (horizon) (línea f del) horizonte m **(b)** (of city): **the Manhattan** ~**line** los edificios de Manhattan recortados contra el horizonte; ~**scraper** n rascacielos m

slab /slæb/ n (of stone) losa f; (of concrete) bloque m; (of wood) tabla f; (of cake, bread) pedazo m, trozo m (grueso)

slack¹ /slæk/ adj **-er, -est** [1] (loose) «rope/cable» flojo [2] (lax, negligent) «student» poco aplicado; «piece of work» flojo [3] (not busy) «period» de poca actividad

slack² n: **there's too much** ~ **in the rope** la cuerda está demasiado floja; **to take up the** ~ **in sth** tensar algo

slack³ vi (colloq) haraganear, flojear (fam)

slacken /'slækən/ vi **(a)** (become looser) «rope/wire» aflojarse **(b)** (diminish) ▶ SLACKEN OFF 1
■ ~ vt **(a)** (loosen) ▶ SLACKEN OFF 2 **(b)** (reduce) «speed» reducir*; «pace» aflojar
■ **slacken off** [1] [v + adv] «wind» amainar, aflojar; «student» aflojar el ritmo de trabajo; «speed/rate» disminuir*; «trade/demand» decaer*, disminuir* [2] [v + o + adv, v + adv + o] «rope/wire» aflojar

slacks /slæks/ n pantalones mpl (de sport)

slag /slæg/ n (Metall) escoria f; (Min) escombro m, escoria f; (before n) ~ **heap** escorial m, escombrera f

slain /sleɪn/ past p of SLAY

slake /sleɪk/ vt (liter) «thirst» saciar

slalom /'slɑːləm/ n slalom m

slam /slæm/ **-mm-** vt [1] **(a)** (close violently): **to** ~ **the door** dar* un portazo **(b)** (put with force): **he** ~**med the book down on the table** tiró el libro sobre la mesa [2] (criticize) (journ) atacar* violentamente
■ ~ vi «door» cerrarse* de un portazo

slander¹ /'slændər ‖'slɑːndə(r)/ n calumnia f, difamación f

slander² vt calumniar, difamar

slang /slæŋ/ n argot m

slant[1] /slænt ‖slɑːnt/ n [1] (slope) inclinación f; (of roof, floor) pendiente f [2] (point of view) enfoque m; (bias) sesgo m

slant[2] vi (a) inclinarse (b) **slanting** pres p inclinado; ‹eyes› rasgado

slap[1] /slæp/ vt **-pp-** [1] (hit): to ~ sb (on face) pegarle* or darle* una bofetada or (AmL tb) una cachetada a algn; (on arm, leg) pegarle* or darle* una palmada a algn [2] (a) (put with force) tirar (b) (put, apply carelessly): he ~ped some paint on it le dio una mano de pintura rápidamente; she ~ped on some makeup se maquilló de cualquier manera

slap[2] n (on face) bofetada f, cachetada f (AmL); (on back, leg) palmada f

slap: ~**dash** adj ‹work› chapucero (fam); ~**stick** n bufonadas fpl; (before n) ~**stick comedy** astracanada f

slash[1] /slæʃ/ n [1] (cut — on body) cuchillada f, tajo m; (— in tire, cloth) raja f, corte m [2] (oblique) barra f (oblicua)

slash[2] vt [1] ‹person/face› acuchillar, tajear (AmL); ‹tires/coat› rajar; he ~ed his wrists se cortó las venas [2] (reduce) ‹prices/taxes› rebajar drásticamente

slat /slæt/ n (of wood) listón m, tablilla f; (of other material) tira f

slate[1] /sleɪt/ n pizarra f

slate[2] vt [1] ‹roof› empizarrar [2] (criticize) ‹book/film/writer› poner* por los suelos

slaughter[1] /'slɔːtər ‖'slɔːtə(r)/ n [1] (cut) matanza f; (massacre) matanza f, carnicería f

slaughter[2] vt ‹animal› matar, carnear (CS); ‹people› matar salvajemente

slaughterhouse /'slɔːtərhaʊs ‖'slɔːtəhaʊs/ n matadero m

Slav /slɑːv/ n eslavo, -va m,f

slave[1] /sleɪv/ n esclavo, -va m,f

slave[2] vi (colloq): I've been slaving away all day he estado trabajando como un negro todo el día (fam)

slave: ~ **driver** n (colloq) negrero, -ra m,f (fam); ~ **labor**, (BrE) ~ **labour** n el trabajo de los esclavos

slaver /'slævər ‖'slævə(r)/ vi babear

slavery /'sleɪvəri/ n esclavitud f

slaw /slɔː/ n (AmE) ensalada de repollo, zanahoria y cebolla con mayonesa

slay /sleɪ/ vt (past **slew**; past p **slain**) (liter or journ) dar* muerte a

sleazy /'sliːzi/ adj **-zier, -ziest** ‹district/bar› sórdido; ‹character/type› de mala pinta

sled[1] /sled/ n (AmE) trineo m

sled[2] vi **-dd-** (AmE) ir* en trineo

sledge /sledʒ/ n/vi ▶ SLED[1,2]

sledgehammer /'sledʒˌhæmər ‖'sledʒˌhæmə(r)/ n mazo m, almádena f

sleek /sliːk/ adj **-er, -est** (a) (glossy) ‹hair/fur› lacio y brillante (b) (well-groomed) acicalado

sleep[1] /sliːp/ n [1] sueño m; to go to ~ dormirse*; my foot has gone to ~ se me ha dormido el pie; the cat had to be put to ~ (euph) hubo que sacrificar al gato (euf); to talk in one's ~ hablar dormido [2] (in eyes) lagañas fpl, legañas fpl

sleep[2] (past & past p **slept**) vi dormir*
- ~ vt: the hotel ~s 200 guests el hotel tiene 200 camas
- ■ **sleep around** [v + adv] (colloq & pej) acostarse* con cualquiera
- ■ **sleep in** [v + adv] (a) (sleep late) dormir* hasta tarde (b) «servant/nurse» vivir en (la) casa (or hospital etc)
- ■ **sleep on** [v + prep + o] ‹decision/problem› consultar con la almohada
- ■ **sleep through** [v + prep + o]: he slept through the alarm clock no oyó el despertador y siguió durmiendo; she slept through the whole film durmió durante toda la película
- ■ **sleep together** [v + adv] (euph) tener* relaciones (sexuales)
- ■ **sleep with** [v + prep + o] (euph) acostarse* con (euf)

sleeper /'sliːpər ‖'sliːpə(r)/ n [1] (person): to be a heavy/light ~ tener* el sueño pesado/ligero [2] (Rail) (a) (berth) litera f (b) (train) tren m con coches camas or (CS) coches dormitorio [3] (on track) (Rail) durmiente m or (Esp) traviesa f

sleeping /'sliːpɪŋ/: ~ **bag** n saco m de dormir; ~ **car** n (Rail) coche m cama, coche m dormitorio (CS); ~ **partner** n (BrE) socio, -cia m,f capitalista; ~ **pill**, ~ **tablet** (BrE) n somnífero m

sleepless /'sliːpləs ‖'sliːplɪs/ adj: to have a ~ night pasar la noche en blanco

sleepwalk /'sliːpwɔːk/ vi caminar dormido

sleepy /'sliːpi/ adj **-pier, -piest** ‹expression› adormilado, somnoliento; to be/feel ~ tener* sueño

sleet /sliːt/ n aguanieve f

sleeve /sliːv/ n (a) (of garment) manga f; to have sth up one's ~ (colloq) tener* algo planeado (b) (of record) (BrE) funda f, carátula f

sleeveless /'sliːvləs ‖'sliːvlɪs/ adj sin mangas

sleigh /sleɪ/ n trineo m

sleight of hand /slaɪt/ n prestidigitación f

slender /'slendər ‖'slendə(r)/ adj **-derer, -derest** (a) ‹person/figure› delgado, esbelto; ‹waist/neck› fino, delgado (b) ‹means› escaso; ‹majority› estrecho

slept /slept/ past & past p of SLEEP[2]

sleuth /sluːθ/ n sabueso mf

slew /sluː/ past of SLAY

slice[1] /slaɪs/ n (piece — of bread, cheese) rebanada f; (— of cake) trozo m; (— of lemon, cucumber) rodaja f; (— of meat) tajada f, (— of ham) loncha f, lonja f; (— of melon) raja f

slice[2] vt ‹bread› cortar (en rebanadas); ‹meat› cortar (en tajadas); ‹cake› cortar (en trozos); ‹lemon/cucumber› cortar (en rodajas); ‹ham› cortar (en lonchas)

slick[1] /slɪk/ adj **-er, -est** [1] (a) ‹book/program› ingenioso pero insustancial (b) ‹person› (glib) de mucha labia; (clever) hábil; ‹reply› fácil (c) ‹performance/production› muy logrado or pulido [2] (slippery) (AmE) ‹surface› resbaladizo

slick[2] n (oil ~) marea f negra

slide[1] /slaɪd/ (past & past p **slid** /slɪd/) vi deslizarse*

■ ~ *vt* (+ *adv compl*): **she slid the book across the table to him** le pasó el libro deslizándolo por la mesa; **to ~ the bolt back** correr el cerrojo

slide² *n* [1] (in playground) tobogán *m* [2] (action — accidental) resbalón *m*, resbalada *f*; (— deliberate) deslizamiento *m* [3] (a) (Phot) diapositiva *f*; (*before n*) ~ **projector** proyector *m* de diapositivas; (for microscope — glass plate) portaobjetos *m*; (— specimen) muestra *f* [4] (for hair) (BrE) ▶ BARRETTE

slide rule *n* regla *f* de cálculo

sliding /'slaɪdɪŋ/: ~ **door** puerta *f* corrediza; ~ **scale** *n* escala *f* móvil

slight¹ /slaɪt/ *adj* **-er, -est** [1] (a) ⟨*improvement/accent/scent*⟩ ligero, leve; **she has a ~ temperature** tiene un poco de fiebre; **I haven't the ~est idea** no tengo (ni) la menor idea; **he's not the ~est bit interested** no le interesa en lo más mínimo (b) (minimal) ⟨*chance/hope*⟩ escaso [2] (slim) delgado, menudo

slight² *vt* (frml) desairar

slight³ *n* (frml) desaire *m*

slightly /'slaɪtli/ *adv* ligeramente

slim¹ /slɪm/ *adj* **-mm-** ⟨*person/figure*⟩ esbelto, delgado; ⟨*waist*⟩ fino; ⟨*chance*⟩ escaso; ⟨*majority*⟩ estrecho

slim² *vi* **-mm-** (a) (become slimmer) adelgazar*, bajar de peso (b) (BrE) (diet) hacer* régimen

slime /slaɪm/ *n* (thin mud) limo *m*, cieno *m*; (of snail, slug etc) baba *f*

slimmer /'slɪmər ‖'slɪmə(r)/ *n* (BrE) persona *f* que está a régimen

slimy /'slaɪmi/ *adj* **-mier, -miest** (a) ⟨*substance/surface*⟩ viscoso (b) ⟨*person*⟩ excesivamente obsequioso, falso

sling¹ /slɪŋ/ *n* (a) (Med) cabestrillo *m* (b) (for carrying a baby) canguro *m* (c) (for lifting) eslinga *f*

sling² *vt* (*past & past p* **slung**) (colloq) tirar, lanzar*, aventar* (Col, Méx, Per)

slink /slɪŋk/ *vi* (*past & past p* **slunk**) (+ *adv compl*): **to ~ off** *o* **away** escabullirse*

slip¹ /slɪp/ *n* [1] (slide) resbalón *m*, resbalada *f* (AmL); **to give sb the ~** (colloq) lograr zafarse de algn [2] (mistake) error *m*; **a ~ of the tongue/pen** un lapsus (linguae/cálami) [3] **a ~ of paper** un papelito, un papel [4] (undergarment) (full-length) combinación *f*; (half-length) enagua *f*, fondo *m* (Méx)

slip² **-pp-** *vi* [1] (a) (slide, shift position) «*person*» resbalar(se); «*clutch*» patinar; **it just ~ped out of my hands** se me resbaló de las manos (b) «*standards/service*» decaer* [2] (a) (move unobtrusively) (+ *adv compl*): **he ~ped out the back door** se deslizó por la puerta trasera; **we managed to ~ past the guards** logramos pasar sin que nos vieran las guardias (b) (escape, be lost): **to let ~ an opportunity** dejar escapar una oportunidad; **to ~ through one's fingers** escapársele a algn de las manos; **I didn't mean to say that: it just ~ped out** no quería decirlo, pero se me escapó

■ ~ *vt* [1] (a) (put unobtrusively) (+ *adv compl*) poner*, meter, deslizar*; **she ~ped a coin into his hand** le deslizó una moneda (b) (pass) **to ~ sth TO sb** pasarle algo A algn con disimulo

[2] **to ~ sb's mind**: **it ~ped my mind** me olvidé, se me olvidó

■ **slip away** «*person/opportunity*» escabullirse*; «*hours/time*» pasar

■ **slip in** [*v + o + adv, v + adv + o*] ⟨*comment/ reference*⟩ incluir*

■ **slip off** [1] [*v + o + adv, v + adv + o*] ⟨*clothes/ shoes*⟩ quitarse [2] [*v + adv*] escabullirse*

■ **slip on** [*v + o + adv, v + adv + o*] ⟨*clothes/ shoes*⟩ ponerse*

■ **slip up** [*v + adv*] equivocarse*

slipped disc /slɪpt/ *n* hernia *f* de disco

slipper /'slɪpər ‖'slɪpə(r)/ *n* zapatilla *f*, pantufla *f* (esp AmL)

slippery /'slɪpəri/ *adj* (a) ⟨*surface/soap*⟩ resbaladizo, resbaloso (AmL) (b) ⟨*person*⟩ (elusive) escurridizo; (untrustworthy) que no es de fiar

slip: **~-road** *n* (BrE) vía *f* de acceso; **~-up** *n* error *m*

slit¹ /slɪt/ *n* (opening) rendija *f*; (cut) raja *f*

slit² *vt* (*pres p* **slitting**; *past & past p* **slit**) cortar, rajar (Méx); **to ~ sb's throat** degollar a algn

slither /'slɪðər ‖'slɪðə(r)/ *vi* «*snake*» deslizarse*

sliver /'slɪvər ‖'slɪvə(r)/ *n* (a) (of glass, wood) astilla *f* (b) (thin slice) tajada *f* (*or* rodaja *f etc*) fina; *see also* SLICE¹

slob /slɑːb ‖slɒb/ *n* (colloq) vago, -ga *m,f* (fam)

slobber /'slɑːbər ‖'slɒbə(r)/ *vi* babear

slog /slɑːg ‖slɒg/ *n* (colloq) (*no pl*): **we've got a long ~ ahead of us** tenemos un largo y arduo camino por delante

■ **slog away**: **-gg-** [*v + adv*] (BrE colloq) sudar tinta (fam), trabajar duro (esp AmL)

slogan /'sləʊgən/ *n* (Busn) slogan *m*, eslogan *m*; (Pol) lema *m*, consigna *f*

slop /slɑːp ‖slɒp/ *vi* **-pp-** (colloq) (spill) derramarse, volcarse*

slope¹ /sləʊp/ *n* (a) (sloping ground) cuesta *f*, pendiente *f*, barranca *f* (RPl) (b) (of mountain) ladera *f*, falda *f* (c) (for skiing) pista *f* de esquí, cancha *f* de esquí (CS)

slope² *vi*: **to ~ down** ⟨*hill/road*⟩ tener* un declive; **her handwriting ~s backward/forward** tiene la letra inclinada hacia atrás/adelante

sloping /'sləʊpɪŋ/ *adj* ⟨*field/floor*⟩ en declive; ⟨*roof/handwriting*⟩ inclinado

sloppy /'slɑːpi ‖'slɒpi/ *adj* **-pier, -piest** [1] (careless) ⟨*manners/work*⟩ descuidado; ⟨*presentation*⟩ descuidado, desprolijo (CS) [2] ⟨*kiss*⟩ baboso

slosh /slɑːʃ ‖slɒʃ/ *vt* (splash) echar

■ ~ *vi* **to ~ around** *o* **about** «*person*» chapotear; «*liquid*» agitarse haciendo ruido

slot¹ /slɑːt ‖slɒt/ *n* [1] (opening, groove) ranura *f* [2] (Rad, TV) espacio *m*

slot² **-tt-** *vt* (insert) **to ~ sth INTO sth** encajar algo EN algo

■ **slot in** [1] [*v + adv*] «*shelf/part*» encajar [2] [*v + o + adv, v + adv + o*] ⟨*component*⟩ hacer* encajar

sloth /sləʊθ/ *n* (Zool) perezoso *m*

slot machine *n* (a) (vending machine) distribuidor *m* automático, máquina *f* expendedora (b) (for gambling) máquina *f* tragamonedas *or* (Esp tb) tragaperras

S

slouch /slaʊtʃ/ vi (a) (droop shoulders) encorvarse; **don't ∼!** ¡ponte derecho! **(b)** (walk) (+ adv compl): **he ∼ed out of the room** salió de la habitación arrastrando los pies

Slovak /'sləʊvæk/ n **(a)** (person) eslovaco, -ca m,f **(b)** (language) eslovaco m

Slovakia /sləʊ'vɑːkiə ‖sləʊ'vækiə/ n Eslovaquia f

Slovene /sləʊviːn/ n **(a)** (person) esloveno, -na m,f **(b)** (language) esloveno m

Slovenia /sləʊ'viːnjə/ n Eslovenia f

slovenly /'slʌvənli/ adj **-lier, -liest** ⟨work⟩ descuidado; ⟨person⟩ desaliñado

slow¹ /sləʊ/ adj **-er, -est** **1** ⟨speed/rate/ reactions⟩ lento; **to be ∼ to + INF** tardar EN + INF **2 (a)** (not lively) ⟨novel/plot⟩ lento **(b)** (stupid) (euph) poco despierto (euf) **3** (of clock, watch) ⟨pred⟩: **my watch is five minutes ∼** mi reloj está cinco minutos atrasado

slow² vi: **the train ∼ed to a stop** el tren fue disminuyendo la velocidad hasta detenerse
■ ∼ vt: **bad weather ∼ed their progress** el mal tiempo los retrasó
■ **slow down 1** [v + adv] **(a)** (go more slowly) ⟨runner⟩ aflojar el paso; ⟨vehicle/driver⟩ reducir* la velocidad; ⟨speaker⟩ hablar más despacio **(b)** (be less active) (colloq) tomarse las cosas con más calma **2** [v + o + adv, v + adv + o] **(a)** ⟨process⟩ hacer* más lento **(b)** ⟨vehicle/ engine⟩ reducir* la velocidad de
■ **slow up** ▶ SLOW DOWN

slow³ adv lentamente, despacio

slowly /'sləʊli/ adv lentamente, despacio

slow motion n cámara f lenta; **in ∼** en or (Esp) a cámara lenta

sludge /slʌdʒ/ n lodo m, fango m

slug /slʌɡ/ n (Zool) babosa f

sluggish /'slʌɡɪʃ/ adj **(a)** (slow-moving) lento; ⟨stream/river⟩ de aguas mansas **(b)** ⟨growth⟩ lento

sluice /sluːs/ n **(a)** (channel) canal m, conducto m (de esclusa) **(b)** (sluicegate) compuerta f

sluicegate /'sluːsɡeɪt/ n compuerta f (de esclusa)

slum /slʌm/ n **(a)** (poor urban area) (often pl) barrio m bajo, barriada f (AmL exc CS), barrio m de conventillos (CS) **(b)** (filthy place) (colloq & pej) pocilga f

slumber¹ /'slʌmbər ‖'slʌmbə(r)/ n (liter) (often pl) sueño m

slumber² vi (liter) dormir*

slump¹ /slʌmp/ n **(a)** (economic depression) depresión f **(b)** (in prices, sales) caída f or baja f repentina; (in attendance, interest) disminución f

slump² vi **1** (collapse) (+ adv compl) desplomarse; **they found her ∼ed over her desk** la encontraron desplomada sobre su escritorio **2** ⟨prices/output/sales⟩ caer* or bajar repentinamente

slung /slʌŋ/ past & past p of SLING²

slunk /slʌŋk/ past & past p of SLINK

slur¹ /slɜːr ‖slɜː(r)/ n **1** (insult): **a racist ∼** un comentario racista; **to cast a ∼ on sb** injuriar a algn **2** (Mus) ligado m

slur² vt **-rr-** **1** (pronounce unclearly): **to ∼ one's words** arrastrar las palabras **2** (Mus) ligar*

slurp /slɜːrp ‖slɜːp/ vt sorber (haciendo ruido)

slurred /slɜːrd ‖slɜːd/ adj: **her speech was ∼** arrastraba las palabras

slush /slʌʃ/ n **(a)** (snow) nieve f fangosa or medio derretida **(b)** (sentimental trash) sensiblería f

sly /slaɪ/ adj **-er, -est** ⟨person⟩ astuto; ⟨look/ grin⟩ malicioso; **on the ∼** a hurtadillas

smack¹ /smæk/ n manotazo m, palmada f (AmL)

smack² vt **(a)** (slap) ⟨child⟩ pegarle* a (con la mano) **(b) to ∼ one's lips** relamerse
■ ∼ vi **to ∼ OF sth** oler* A algo

smack³ adv (colloq): **∼ in the middle** justo en el medio; **he went ∼ into a tree** se dio contra un árbol

small¹ /smɔːl/ adj **-er, -est** pequeño, chico (esp AmL); ⟨sum/price⟩ módico, reducido; ⟨mistake/problem⟩ pequeño, de poca importancia; **to feel ∼** sentirse* insignificante

small² n **the ∼ of the back** región baja de la espalda, que corresponde al segmento dorsal de la columna vertebral

small: ∼ ad n (BrE) anuncio m (clasificado), aviso m (clasificado) (AmL); **∼ change** n cambio m, (dinero m) suelto m, sencillo m (AmL), feria f (Méx fam); **∼ hours** pl n **the ∼ hours** (of the morning) la madrugada; **∼-minded** /'smɔːl'maɪndəd ‖,smɔːl'maɪndɪd/ adj cerrado, de miras estrechas; **∼pox** /'smɔːlpɑːks ‖'smɔːlpɒks/ n viruela f; **∼ print** n (BrE) **the ∼ print** la letra pequeña or menuda, la letra chica (esp AmL); **∼ talk** n charla f sobre temas triviales; **∼-time** /'smɔːl'taɪm/ adj de poca monta; **∼-town** /'smɔːl'taʊn/ adj pueblerino

smart¹ /smɑːrt ‖smɑːt/ adj **-er, -est** **1** (esp BrE) (neat, stylish) ⟨appearance/dress/hotel/ neighborhood⟩ elegante **2** (clever, shrewd) ⟨child⟩ listo; ⟨answer⟩ inteligente **3 (a)** (brisk, prompt) ⟨pace⟩ rápido **(b)** (forceful) ⟨blow/tap⟩ seco, fuerte

smart² vi ⟨eyes/wound⟩ escocer*

smarten up /'smɑːrtən ‖'smɑːtən/ **(a)** [v + o + adv, v + adv + o] ⟨house/town⟩ arreglar **(b)** [v + adv] ⟨person⟩ mejorar su (or mi etc) aspecto

smash¹ /smæʃ/ n **1 (a)** (sound) estrépito m, estruendo m **(b)** (collision) (BrE) choque m **2 (a)** (blow) golpe m **(b)** (Sport) smash m, remate m, remache m **3** (success) (colloq) exitazo m (fam)

smash² vt **1** (break) ⟨furniture⟩ romper*; ⟨car⟩ destrozar*; ⟨glass⟩ romper*; (into small pieces) hacer* añicos **2** (destroy) ⟨rebellion⟩ aplastar; ⟨drug racket/spy ring⟩ acabar con **3** (Sport) rematar, remachar
■ ∼ vi (shatter) hacerse* pedazos
■ **smash up** [v + o + adv] (colloq) destrozar*

smash: ∼ hit n (colloq) exitazo m (fam); **∼up** n (colloq) choque m violento

smattering /ˈsmætərɪŋ/ n (no pl) nociones fpl

smear¹ /smɪr ‖smɪə(r)/ n **1** (stain) mancha f **2** (slander, slur) calumnia f; (before n) ~ campaign campaña f difamatoria **3** (Med) ~ (**test**) citología f, frotis m cervical, Papanicolau m (AmL)

smear² vt **1** to ~ sth ON(TO)/OVER sth ⟨paint/grease⟩ embadurnar algo de algo; ⟨butter⟩ untar algo con algo **2** (slander, libel) difamar
■ ~ vi «ink/lipstick» correrse

smell¹ /smel/ n **(a)** (odor) olor m **(b)** (sense of smell) olfato m

smell² (past & past p **smelled** or (BrE) also) **smelt**) vt **(a)** (sense) oler*; **we could ~ gas/burning** olía a gas/quemado; **to ~ danger** olfatear el peligro **(b)** (sniff at) ⟨person⟩ oler*; ⟨animal⟩ olfatear
■ ~ vi oler*; **to ~ OF sth** oler* A algo

smelling salts /ˈsmelɪŋ/ pl n sales fpl (aromáticas)

smelly /ˈsmeli/ adj **-lier, -liest** que huele mal

smelt¹ /smelt/ (BrE) past & past p of SMELL²

smelt² vt fundir

smile¹ /smaɪl/ n sonrisa f

smile² vi sonreír*; **to ~ AT sb** sonreírle* A algn

smirk¹ /smɜːrk ‖smɜːk/ n sonrisita f (de suficiencia, de complicidad, etc)

smirk² vi sonreírse* (con suficiencia, complicidad etc)

smith /smɪθ/ n herrero, -ra m,f

smithereens /ˈsmɪðəˈriːnz/ pl n: **to smash sth to ~** hacer* algo pedazos or añicos

smock /smɑːk ‖smɒk/ n **(a)** (of fisherman, artist) blusón m, bata f **(b)** (dress) vestido m amplio

smog /smɑːg ‖smɒg/ n smog m

smoke¹ /sməʊk/ n humo m; **to go up in ~** «books/papers» quemarse; «hopes» esfumarse; «ambitions/plans» quedar en agua de borrajas

smoke² vi **1** ⟨person⟩ fumar **2** (give off smoke) echar humo
■ ~ vt **1** ⟨cigarettes/tobacco⟩ fumar; **he ~s a pipe** fuma en pipa **2** (cure) ⟨fish/cheese⟩ ahumar*

smoke-bomb /ˈsməʊkbɑːm ‖ˈsməʊkbɒm/ n bomba f de humo

smoked /sməʊkt/ adj ahumado

smoke detector n detector m de humo

smokeless /ˈsməʊkləs ‖ˈsməʊklɪs/ adj ⟨fuel⟩ que arde sin humo; **~ zone** (in UK) zona donde está prohibido usar combustibles que produzcan humo

smoker /ˈsməʊkər ‖ˈsməʊkə(r)/ n fumador, -dora m,f; **he's a heavy ~** fuma mucho

smoke: ~screen n cortina f de humo; **~ signal** n señal f de humo

smoking /ˈsməʊkɪŋ/ n ⊗ **no smoking** prohibido fumar; **to give up ~** dejar de fumar

smoking: ~ car n (AmE) vagón m or (Chi, Méx) carro m de fumadores; **~ compartment** n compartimento m de fumadores

smoky /ˈsməʊki/ adj **-kier, -kiest** ⟨fire/chimney⟩ que echa humo; ⟨room⟩ lleno de humo; ⟨atmosphere⟩ cargado de humo

smolder, (BrE) **smoulder** /ˈsməʊldər ‖ˈsməʊldə(r)/ vi ⟨fire⟩ arder (sin llama); «eyes» arder

smooth¹ /smuːð/ adj **-er, -est** **1** **(a)**

⟨texture/stone⟩ liso, suave; ⟨skin⟩ suave, terso; ⟨sea⟩ tranquilo **(b)** (of consistency) ⟨sauce⟩ sin grumos **(c)** (of taste) ⟨wine⟩ suave **2** **(a)** (of movement) ⟨take-off⟩ suave; ⟨flight⟩ cómodo **(b)** (trouble-free) ⟨journey⟩ sin complicaciones **3** **(a)** (easy, polished) ⟨performance⟩ fluido **(b)** (glib, suave) (pej) poco sincero, falso; **he's a ~ talker** tiene mucha labia

smooth² vt **(a)** ⟨dress/sheets/hair⟩ alisar, arreglar **(b)** (polish) pulir
■ **smooth out** [v + o + adv, v + adv + o] **(a)** ⟨sheets/creases⟩ alisar **(b)** ⟨difficulties/problems⟩ allanar
■ **smooth over** [v + o + adv, v + adv + o] ⟨differences⟩ dejar de lado

smoothly /ˈsmuːðli/ adv **1** **(a)** (of movement) ⟨take off/drive⟩ suavemente **(b)** (without problems) sin problemas **2** (glibly, suavely) (pej) ⟨talk⟩ con mucha labia

smother /ˈsmʌðər ‖ˈsmʌðə(r)/ vt **(a)** (stifle) ⟨person⟩ asfixiar, ahogar*; ⟨flames⟩ sofocar* **(b)** (suppress) ⟨yawn/giggle⟩ reprimir **(c)** (cover profusely): **she ~ed him with kisses** lo cubrió de besos

smoulder vi (BrE) ▶ SMOLDER

smudge¹ /smʌdʒ/ n mancha f

smudge² vt correr; (deliberately) difuminar

smug /smʌg/ adj **-gg-** ⟨expression⟩ de suficiencia, petulante; ⟨person⟩ pagado de sí mismo, petulante

smuggle /ˈsmʌgəl/ vt ⟨tobacco/drugs⟩ contrabandear, pasar de contrabando; **I ~d her into my room** la hice entrar a mi habitación a escondidas

smuggler /ˈsmʌglər ‖ˈsmʌglə(r)/ n contrabandista mf

smuggling /ˈsmʌglɪŋ/ n contrabando m

snack /snæk/ n tentempié m; **to have a ~** comer algo ligero or (esp AmL) liviano, tomar(se) un tentempié

snack bar n bar m, cafetería f

snag¹ /snæg/ n **(a)** (difficulty) inconveniente m, pega f (Esp fam) **(b)** (in fabric, stocking) enganchón m

snag² vt **-gg-** enganchar

snail /sneɪl/ n caracol m; **at a ~'s pace** a paso de tortuga

snake /sneɪk/ n culebra f, serpiente f; (poisonous) víbora f

snake: ~bite n mordedura f de serpiente; **~ charmer** /ˈtʃɑːrmər ‖ˈtʃɑːmə(r)/ n encantador, -dora m,f de serpientes

snap¹ /snæp/ n **1** (sound) chasquido m **2** ~ (**fastener**) (AmE) (on clothes) broche m or botón m de presión (AmL), (cierre m) automático m (Esp) **3** (photo) (colloq) foto f, instantánea f **4** (Meteo): **a cold ~** una ola de frío

snap² **-pp-** vt **1** **(a)** (break) partir **(b)** (cause to make sharp sound): **she ~ped the lid/book shut** cerró la tapa/el libro de un golpe; ▶ FINGER¹ **2** (utter sharply) decir* bruscamente **3** (photograph) ⟨person/thing⟩ sacarle* una foto a
■ ~ vi **1** (bite) **to ~ AT sth** intentar morder algo **2** **(a)** (break) ⟨twigs/branch⟩ romperse*, quebrarse* (esp AmL); «elastic» romperse* **(b)** (click): **to ~ shut** cerrarse* (con un clic) **3** (speak sharply) hablar con brusquedad

⋯▸

4 (move quickly): **to ~ out of it** (of depression) animarse; (of lethargy, inertia) espabilarse
■ **snap up** [v + o + adv, v + adv + o] ‹offer› no dejar escapar

snap³ adj ‹decision› precipitado, repentino

snappy /'snæpi/ adj **-pier, -piest (a)** ‹person› irascible; ‹retort› brusco **(b)** ‹pace› (colloq) ágil

snapshot /'snæpʃɑːt ‖'snæpʃʊt/ n foto f, instantánea f

snare¹ /sner ‖sneə(r)/ n trampa f

snare² vt atrapar

snarl¹ /snɑːrl ‖snɑːl/ n gruñido m

snarl² vi/t gruñir*
■ **snarl up** [v + adv + o] (usu pass) ‹ball of wool› enmarañar, enredar; ‹traffic› atascar*

snatch¹ /snætʃ/ vt **1 (a)** (grab) ‹~ sth FROM sb› arrebatarle algo a algn; **she ~ed the letter out of my hand** me arrancó la carta de las manos **(b)** (steal) (colloq & journ) robar ‹arrebatando› **(c)** (kidnap) (journ) secuestrar, raptar **2** (take hurriedly) ‹opportunity› no dejar pasar

snatch² n **1** (robbery) (BrE journ) robo m **2 (a)** (fragment) fragmento m **(b)** (brief spell) rato m; **to sleep in ~es** dormir* (de) a ratos

sneak /sniːk/ (past & past p **sneaked** or (AmE also) **snuck**) vt **(a)** (smuggle) (+ adv compl): **he ~ed the files out of the office** sacó los archivos de la oficina a escondidas; **she tried to ~ him in without paying** trató de colarlo sin pagar **(b)** (take furtively): **to ~ a look at sth/sb** mirar algo/a algn con disimulo
■ ~ vi (+ adv compl): **to ~ in** entrar a hurtadillas; **to ~ away** escabullirse*
■ **sneak up** [v + adv] **to ~ up** (ON sb) acercarse* sigilosamente (A algn)

sneakers /'sniːkərz ‖'sniːkəz/ pl n zapatillas fpl (de deporte), tenis mpl, playeras fpl (Esp)

sneak: **~ preview** n (Cin, TV) preestreno m; **~ thief** n ratero, -ra m,f

sneaky /'sniːki/ adj **-kier, -kiest** (colloq) ‹person› artero, taimado; ‹behavior› solapado

sneer¹ /snɪr ‖snɪə(r)/ vi adoptar un aire despectivo; (with facial expression) hacer* una mueca de desprecio

sneer² n expresión f desdeñosa

sneeze¹ /sniːz/ vi estornudar

sneeze² n estornudo m

snide /snaɪd/ adj insidioso

sniff /snɪf/ vt **(a)** (smell) «person» oler*; «animal» olfatear **(b)** ‹glue› inhalar, esnifar
■ ~ vi «animal» husmear, olfatear; «person» sorberse la nariz

sniffer dog /'snɪfər ‖'snɪfə(r)/ n (BrE) perro m rastreador

sniffle /'snɪfəl/ vi (due to cold) sorberse la nariz; (when crying) gimotear

snigger¹ /'snɪgər ‖'snɪgə(r)/ n risilla f, risita f

snigger² vi reírse* (por lo bajo)

snip¹ /snɪp/ n (act) tijeretazo m; (sound) tijereteo m

snip² vt **-pp-** cortar (con tijera)

sniper /'snaɪpər ‖'snaɪpə(r)/ n francotirador, -dora m,f

snippet /'snɪpət ‖'snɪpɪt/ n (of conversation) trozo m; **~s of information** (algunos) datos aislados

snivel /'snɪvəl/ vi, (BrE) **-ll-** lloriquear

snob /snɑːb ‖snɒb/ n (e)snob mf

snobbery /'snɑːbəri ‖'snɒbəri/ n (e)snobismo m

snobbish /'snɑːbɪʃ ‖'snɒbɪʃ/ adj (e)snob

snooker /'snʊkər ‖'snuːkə(r)/ n snooker m (modalidad de billar que se juega con 15 bolas rojas y 6 de otro color)

snoop /snuːp/ vi (colloq) husmear, fisgonear

snooper /'snuːpər ‖'snuːpə(r)/ n (colloq) fisgón, -gona m,f

snooze¹ /snuːz/ vi (colloq) dormitar

snooze² n (colloq) sueñecito m (fam), sueñito m (esp AmL fam); **to have a ~** echar una cabezada (fam)

snore¹ /snɔːr ‖snɔː(r)/ vi roncar*

snore² n ronquido m

snoring /'snɔːrɪŋ/ n ronquidos mpl

snorkel /'snɔːrkəl ‖'snɔːkəl/ n esnórkel m

snort¹ /snɔːrt ‖snɔːt/ vi bufar, resoplar
■ ~ vt (utter) bramar, gruñir*

snort² n bufido m, resoplido m

snout /snaʊt/ n hocico m, morro m

snow¹ /snəʊ/ n **(a)** nieve f **(b)** (snowfall) nevada f

snow² v impers nevar*
■ **snow in** [v + o + adv]: **to be ~ed in** estar* aislado por la nieve
■ **snow under** [v + o + adv]: **I'm ~ed under with work** estoy agobiada or desbordada de trabajo

snowball¹ /'snəʊbɔːl/ n (Meteo) bola f de nieve

snowball² vi «problems» agravarse

snow: **~board** n snowboard m; **~boarding** n snowboard m; **~bound** adj bloqueado por la nieve; **~drift** n: nieve acumulada durante una ventisca; **~drop** n campanilla f de invierno; **~fall** n nevada f; **~flake** n copo m de nieve; **~man** /'snəʊmæn/ n (pl **-men** /-men/) muñeco m de nieve; **~plow**, (BrE) **~plough** n quitanieves m; **~shoe** n raqueta f; **~storm** n tormenta f de nieve

snowy /'snəʊi/ adj **snowier, snowiest** nevoso

snub¹ /snʌb/ vt **-bb- (a)** ‹person› desairar; (ignore) ignorar; (treat coldly) tratar fríamente (CS) **(b)** (reject) ‹offer› desdeñar, rechazar*

snub² n desaire m

snub³ adj ‹nose› respingón, respingado (AmL)

snub-nosed /'snʌb'nəʊzd/ adj de nariz respingona or (AmL tb) respingada

snuck /snʌk/ (AmE colloq) past & past p of SNEAK

snuff /snʌf/ n rapé m
■ **snuff out** [v + o + adv, v + adv + o] ‹candle› apagar*

snuffbox /'snʌfbɑːks ‖'snʌfbɒks/ n caja f de rapé

snug /snʌg/ adj **(a)** (cosy) cómodo y acogedor **(b)** (close-fitting) ceñido, ajustado

snuggle /'snʌgəl/ vi acurrucarse*; **he ~d up against her** se le arrimó

so¹ /səʊ/ adv **1 (a)** (very) tan; **she's ~ tall** es tan alta; **he did it ~ quickly** lo hizo tan rápido; **thank you ~ much** muchísimas gracias **(b)** so **much/many** (as adj) tanto, -ta/tantos, -tas; **~**

much space/food tanto espacio/tanta comida; ∼ many things tantas cosas **(c) so much** (*as pronoun*) tanto; **he eats** ∼ **much** come tanto **2** or so más o menos

3 (with clauses of result or purpose) ∼ ... (that) tan ... que; **he was** ∼ **rude (that) she slapped him** fue tan grosero, que le dio una bofetada

4 (a) (thus, in this way): **the street was** ∼ **named because** ... se le puso ese nombre a la calle porque ...; **hold the bat like** ∼ agarra el bate así **(b)** (as stated) así; **that is** ∼ (frml) así es; **if** ∼, **they're lying** si es así or de ser así, están mintiendo **(c) and so on (and so forth)** etcétera (etcétera)

5 (*replacing clause, phrase, word*): **I expect** ∼ me imagino que sí; **I got a bit dirty — ∼ I see** me ensucié un poco — sí, ya veo; **I told you** ∼ ¿no te lo dije?

6 (*with v aux*) **(a)** (also, equally): **Peter agrees and** ∼ **does Bill** Peter está de acuerdo y Bill también **(b)** (indeed): **you promised — ∼ I did!** lo prometiste — ¡es verdad! or ¡tienes razón!

7 **(a)** (indicating pause or transition) bueno; ∼ **here we are again** bueno, aquí estamos otra vez **(b)** (querying, eliciting information): ∼ **now what do we do?** ¿y ahora qué hacemos? **(c)** (summarizing, concluding) así que; ∼ **now you know** así que ya sabes **(d)** (expressing surprised reaction) así que, conque; ∼ **that's what he's after!** ¡así que or conque eso es lo que quiere! **(e)** (challenging): ∼ **what?** ¿y qué?

so² *conj* **1** (*in clauses of purpose or result*) **(a) so (that)** (expressing purpose) para que (+ *subj*); (expressing result) de manera que or de manera que (+ *indic*); **she said it slowly,** ∼ **(that) we'd all understand** lo dijo despacio, para que todos entendiéramos; **she said it slowly,** ∼ **(that) we all understood** lo dijo despacio, así que or de manera que todos entendimos **(b) so as to +** INF para + INF **2** (therefore, consequently) así que, de manera que

so³ *n* (Mus) sol *m*

soak /səʊk/ *vt* **(a)** ⟨*lentils/clothes*⟩ (immerse) poner* en or a remojo; (leave immersed) dejar en or a remojo **(b)** (drench) empapar; **to be ∼ed (to the skin)** estar* empapado, estar* calado hasta los huesos

■ ∼ *vi* **(a)** (lie in liquid): **to leave sth to** ∼ dejar algo en or a remojo **(b)** (penetrate) (+ *adv compl*): **to** ∼ **into/through sth** calar algo

■ **soak up** [*v + o + adv, v + adv + o*] ⟨*liquid/information*⟩ absorber; ⟨*sun*⟩ empaparse de

soaking /'səʊkɪŋ/ *adj* empapado; (*as adv*) **it's** ∼ **wet** está empapado

so-and-so /'səʊənsəʊ/ *n* (colloq) (unspecified person) (*no art*) fulano, -na *m,f*

soap /səʊp/ *n* **1** jabón *m*; (*before n*) ∼ **dish** jabonera *f* **2** ▶ SOAP OPERA

soap: ∼**flakes** *pl n* jabón *m* en escamas; ∼ **opera** *n* (TV) telenovela *f*, culebrón *m*; (Rad) radionovela *f*, comedia *f* (AmL); ∼ **powder** *n* (BrE) jabón *m* en polvo, detergente *m* (*en polvo*); ∼**suds** *pl n* espuma *f* (*de jabón*)

soapy /'səʊpi/ *adj* **-pier, -piest (a)** ⟨*water*⟩ jabonoso; ⟨*cloth/hands*⟩ enjabonado **(b)** ⟨*smell/taste*⟩ a jabón

soar /sɔːr ‖sɔːr/ *vi* **1** **(a)** (fly) «*bird/glider*» planear **(b)** (rise) «*bird/kite*» elevarse; «*prices/costs*» dispararse; «*hopes*» aumentar;

«*popularity*» aumentar **(c)** (tower) «*skyscraper/mountain*» alzarse* **2** **soaring** *pres p* ⟨*inflation*⟩ galopante, de ritmo vertiginoso; ⟨*popularity*⟩ en alza; **caused by** ∼ **temperatures** causado por una subida vertiginosa de las temperaturas

sob¹ /sɑːb ‖sɒb/ *vi* **-bb-** sollozar*

sob² *n* sollozo *m*

sober /'səʊbər ‖'səʊbə(r)/ *adj* **1** (not drunk) sobrio **2** **(a)** (serious) grave; ⟨*young man*⟩ serio; ⟨*occasion*⟩ formal **(b)** (subdued) ⟨*dress/colors*⟩ sobrio

■ **sober up** **1** [*v + adv*]: **he's** ∼**ed up now** ya está sobrio **2** [*v + o + adv, v + adv + o*] despejar

sobriety /səʊ'braɪəti, sə- ‖sə'braɪəti/ *n* seriedad *f*, sensatez *f*; (*before n*) ∼ **test** (AmE) prueba *f* del alcohol or de la alcoholemia

so-called /'səʊ'kɔːld/ *adj* (*usu before n*) **(a)** (commonly named) (así) llamado **(b)** (indicating skeptical attitude) ⟨*expert*⟩ supuesto, presunto

soccer /'sɑːkər ‖'sɒkə(r)/ *n* fútbol *m* or (AmC, Méx) futbol *m*

sociable /'səʊʃəbəl/ *adj* sociable

social /'səʊʃəl/ *adj* social; **he has no** ∼ **graces** no sabe cómo comportarse; ∼ **life** vida *f* social

social democrat *n* socialdemócrata *mf*

socialism /'səʊʃəlɪzəm/ *n* socialismo *m*

socialist¹, Socialist /'səʊʃəlɪst ‖'səʊʃəlɪst/ *adj* socialista

socialist², Socialist *n* socialista *mf*

socialize /'səʊʃəlaɪz/ *vi* alternar; (at party) circular

socially /'səʊʃəli/ *adv* **(a)** (relating to the community) ⟨*divisive/useful*⟩ socialmente; (*indep*) desde el punto de vista social **(b)** (in social situations): **it's not** ∼ **acceptable** está mal visto, no se considera correcto

social: ∼ **science** *n* ciencia *f* social; ∼ **security** *n* (BrE) seguridad *f* social; ∼ **service** *n* **(a)** (welfare work) (AmE) asistencia *f* or trabajo *m* social **(b)** (in UK) servicio *m* social; ∼ **work** *n* asistencia *f* social; ∼ **worker** *n* (Soc Adm) asistente, -ta *m,f* social, trabajador, -dora *m,f* social (Méx), visitador, -dora *m,f* social (Chi)

society /sə'saɪəti/ *n* (*pl* **-ties**) **1** **(a)** (community) sociedad *f*; **in polite** ∼ entre la gente educada **(b)** (fashionable elite) (alta) sociedad *f* **2** (association, club) sociedad *f*

sociologist /ˌsəʊsi'ɑːlədʒəst, -ʃi- ‖ˌsəʊsi'ɒlədʒɪst, -ʃi-/ *n* sociólogo, -ga *m,f*

sociology /ˌsəʊsi'ɑːlədʒi, -ʃi- ‖ˌsəʊsi'ɒlədʒi, -ʃi-/ *n* sociología *f*

sociopath /'səʊsiəpæθ, -ʃi-/ *n* (p)sicópata *mf*

sock /sɑːk ‖sɒk/ *n* calcetín *m*, media *f* (AmL)

socket /'sɑːkət ‖'sɒkɪt/ *n* **(a)** (Anat) (of eye) cuenca *f*, órbita *f*; (of joint) fosa *f*, hueco *m* **(b)** (Elec) (for plug) enchufe *m*, toma *f* de corriente, tomacorriente *m* (AmL) **(c)** (Tech) encaje *m*

sod /sɑːd ‖sɒd/ *n* **1** (piece of turf) tepe *m*, champa *f* (Andes) **2** (BrE vulg) (obnoxious person) cabrón, -brona *m,f* (vulg)

soda /'səʊdə/ *n* **1** **(a)** (soda water) soda *f*, agua *f*‡ de seltz **(b)** (flavored) (AmE) refresco *m*, fresco *m* (AmL) **(c)** (ice-cream soda) (AmE) ice-cream soda *m* (AmL) (*refresco con helado*) **2** (Chem) soda *f*, sosa *f*

S

soda: ~ **pop** n (AmE) refresco m; ~ **water** n soda f, agua f̣ de seltz

sodden /'sɒːdn̩ ‖'sɒdn̩/ adj empapado

sodium /'səʊdiəm/ n sodio m

sodium bicarbonate n bicarbonato m sódico or de sodio

sofa /'səʊfə/ n sofá m

soft /sɒːft ‖sɒft/ adj **-er, -est** ⒈ (a) (not hard) blando; ⟨metal⟩ maleable; **to go** ~ ablandarse (b) (smooth) ⟨fur/fabric/skin⟩ suave ⒉ (mild, subdued) ⟨light/color/music⟩ suave ⒊ (lenient) blando, indulgente ⒋ ⟨drugs/pornography⟩ blando ⒌ (Chem) ⟨water⟩ blando

soft: ~**ball** n softball m (especie de béisbol que se juega con pelota blanda); ~ **drink** n refresco m (bebida no alcohólica)

soften /'sɒːfən ‖'sɒfən/ vt (a) ⟨butter/leather⟩ ablandar; ⟨skin⟩ suavizar*; ⟨light/color⟩ suavizar*; ⟨contours⟩ difuminar (b) (mitigate) ⟨effect⟩ atenuar*, mitigar*; **to** ~ **the blow** suavizar* el golpe (c) ⟨water⟩ ablandar, descalcificar*

■ ~ vi (a) «butter/leather» ablandarse; «skin» suavizarse* (b) (become gentler) ablandarse; (become more moderate) volverse* menos intransigente

■ **soften up** [v + o + adv, v + adv + o] ablandar

softener /'sɒːfnər ‖'sɒfnə(r)/ n (a) (for water) descalcificador m (b) (for fabric) suavizante m

softly /'sɒːftli ‖'sɒftli/ adv (a) (gently) ⟨touch⟩ suavemente (b) (quietly) ⟨speak⟩ bajito

soft: ~**-spoken** /'sɒːft'spəʊkən ‖,sɒft'spəʊkən/ adj de voz suave; ~ **top** n (AmE) (car) descapotable m, convertible m (AmL); (roof) capota f; ~**ware** /'sɒːftwer ‖'sɒftweə(r)/ n software m

soggy /'sɑːgi ‖'sɒgi/ adj **-gier, -giest** ⟨ground/grass⟩ empapado; ⟨vegetables⟩ pasado

soh /səʊ/ n (Mus) sol m

soil¹ /sɔɪl/ n (a) (earth) tierra f (b) (filth, dirt) (AmE) suciedad f

soil² vt ensuciar

soiled /sɔɪld/ adj ⟨linen⟩ sucio; ⟨goods⟩ dañado

sol /səʊl ‖sɒl/ n (Mus) sol m

solace /'sɑːləs ‖'sɒlɪs/ n (liter) consuelo m

solar /'səʊlər ‖'səʊlə(r)/ adj solar

solar system n the ~ ~ el sistema solar

sold /səʊld/ past & past p of SELL

solder /'sɑːdər ‖'səʊldə(r)/ vt soldar*

soldier /'səʊldʒər ‖'səʊldʒə(r)/ n soldado mf; (officer) militar mf

■ **soldier on** [v + adv] (BrE colloq) seguir* al pie del cañón

sole¹ /səʊl/ n ⒈ (of foot) planta f; (of shoe) suela f ⒉ (fish) (pl ~ or ~**s**) lenguado m

sole² adj (before n) (a) (only) único (b) (exclusive) ⟨rights⟩ exclusivo

sole³ vt (usu pass): **to have one's shoes** ~**d and heeled** hacerles* poner suelas y tacones or (CS, Per) tacos a los zapatos

solely /'səʊlli/ adv (a) (wholly) únicamente, exclusivamente (b) (only, simply) solo, solamente, únicamente

solemn /'sɑːləm ‖'sɒləm/ adj (a) (serious, formal) ⟨occasion/silence⟩ solemne (b) (grave) ⟨person⟩ serio; ⟨face⟩ solemne

sol-fa /'səʊl'fɑː ‖,sɒl'fɑː/ n solfa f

solicit /sə'lɪsət ‖sə'lɪsɪt/ vt (frml) ⟨information/help⟩ solicitar (frml)

■ ~ vi «prostitute» ejercer la prostitución callejera (abordando a posibles clientes)

solicitor /sə'lɪsətər ‖sə'lɪsɪtə(r)/ n (a) (in US and in UK) abogado responsable de los asuntos legales de un municipio o de un departamento gubernamental (b) (in UK) abogado, -da m,f (que prepara causas legales y desempeña también funciones de notario)

solid¹ /'sɑːləd ‖'sɒlɪd/ adj **-er, -est** ⒈ (a) (not liquid or gaseous) sólido (b) (not hollow) ⟨rubber/tire⟩ macizo ⒉ (a) (unbroken) ⟨line/row⟩ continuo, ininterrumpido (b) (continuous) (colloq) ⟨month/year⟩ seguido ⒊ (a) (physically sturdy) ⟨furniture/house⟩ sólido; ⟨meal⟩ consistente (b) (substantial) ⟨reason⟩ sólido ⒋ (pure) ⟨metal/wood⟩ macizo, puro; ⟨rock⟩ vivo

solid² n ⒈ (Chem, Phys) sólido m ⒉ **solids** pl (food) alimentos mpl sólidos

solid³ adv: **to be packed/jammed** ~ estar* lleno hasta el tope or hasta los topes

solidarity /'sɑːlə'dærəti ‖,sɒlɪ'dærəti/ n solidaridad f

solidify /sə'lɪdəfaɪ/ vi **-fies, -fying, -fied** solidificarse*

solidly /'sɑːlədli ‖'sɒlɪdli/ adv (a) (sturdily) ⟨fixed/grounded⟩ firmemente; ⟨made⟩ sólidamente (b) (unanimously) unánimemente

solitaire /'sɑːlɪter ‖'sɒlɪ,teə(r)/ n ⒈ ~ ⟨diamond⟩ solitario m ⒉ (Games) solitario m

solitary /'sɑːləteri ‖'sɒlɪtəri/ adj (a) (alone) ⟨person/life/place⟩ solitario (b) (single) (before n) solo

solitary confinement n incomunicación f; **he's in** ~ ~ lo han incomunicado

solitude /'sɑːlətuːd ‖'sɒlɪtjuːd/ n soledad f

solo¹ /'səʊləʊ/ n (pl **-los**) solo m

solo² adj (a) (Mus) ⟨violin/voices⟩ solista; ⟨album⟩ en solitario (b) ⟨flight⟩ en solitario

solo³ adv en solitario

soloist /'səʊləʊəst ‖'səʊləʊɪst/ n solista mf

so long interj (colloq) hasta luego, hasta la vista

solstice /'sɑːlstəs ‖'sɒlstɪs/ n solsticio m

soluble /'sɑːljəbəl ‖'sɒljʊbəl/ adj soluble

solution /sə'luːʃən/ n solución f

solve /sɑːlv ‖sɒlv/ vt ⟨mystery/equation⟩ resolver*; ⟨crossword puzzle⟩ sacar*; ⟨crime⟩ esclarecer*; ⟨riddle⟩ encontrar* la solución a

solvent¹ /'sɑːlvənt ‖'sɒlvənt/ adj solvente

solvent² n disolvente m, solvente m

Somali /sə'mɑːli/ adj somalí

Somalia /sə'mɑːliə/ n Somalia f

AmC	América Central	Arg	Argentina	Cu	Cuba
AmL	América Latina	Bol	Bolivia	Ec	Ecuador
AmS	América del Sur	Chi	Chile	Esp	España
Andes	Región andina	CS	Cono Sur	Méx	México

Per	Perú
RPI	Río de la Plata
Ur	Uruguay
Ven	Venezuela

somber, (BrE) **sombre** /'sɑːmbər ‖'sɒmbə(r)/ *adj* **(a)** (dark) sombrío **(b)** (melancholy) ⟨*mood/ thought*⟩ sombrío; ⟨*music*⟩ lúgubre

some¹ /sʌm, *weak form* səm/ *adj* **1** **(a)** (unstated number or type) (+ *pl n*) unos, unas; **there were ~ children in the park** había unos niños en el parque; **would you like ~ cherries?** ¿quieres (unas) cerezas? **(b)** (unstated quantity or type) (+ *uncount n*): **~ paint fell on my head** me cayó (un poco de) pintura en la cabeza; **would you like ~ coffee?** ¿quieres café? **2** (a, one) (+ *sing count noun*) algún, -guna; **~ day I'll get my revenge** ya me vengaré algún día **3** (particular, not all) (+ *pl n*) algunos, -nas; **I like ~ modern artists** algunos artistas modernos me gustan; **in ~ ways** en cierto modo **4** **(a)** (not many, a few) ⟨*lemons/apples*⟩ algunos, -nas **(b)** (not much, a little) ⟨*meat/rice*⟩ un poco de **5** **(a)** (several, many): **she's been bedridden for ~ years now** hace algunos años que está postrada en cama **(b)** (large amount of): **we've known each other for quite ~ time now** ya hace mucho (tiempo) que nos conocemos **6** (colloq) **(a)** (expressing appreciation): **that's ~ car you've got!** ¡vaya coche que tienes! **(b)** (stressing remarkable, ridiculous nature): **that was ~ exam!** ¡vaya examen! **(c)** (expressing irony): **~ friend you are!** ¡qué buen amigo eres! (iró)

some² *pron* **1** **(a)** (a number of things or people) algunos, -nas **(b)** (an amount): **there's no salt left; we'll have to buy ~** no queda sal; vamos a tener que comprar; **the coffee's ready: would you like ~?** el café está listo: ¿quieres? **2** (certain people) algunos, -nas; **~ say that ...** algunos dicen que ...

some³ *adv* (approximately) unos, unas, alrededor de

somebody¹ /'sʌm,bɑːdi ‖'sʌmbədi/ *pron* alguien; **~'s coming** viene alguien; **who was it? — John** ¿quién era? — John algo *or* John no sé cuánto (fam)

somebody² *n* (*no pl*): **to be ~** ser* alguien

somehow /'sʌmhaʊ/ *adv* **(a)** (by some means) de algún modo, de alguna manera; **~ or other** de algún modo u otro **(b)** (in some way, for some reason): **it isn't the same, ~** no sé por qué, pero no es lo mismo

someone /'sʌmwʌn/ *pron* ▶ SOMEBODY¹

someplace /'sʌmpleɪs/ *adv* (AmE) ▶ SOMEWHERE¹ 1

somersault¹ /'sʌmərsɔːlt ‖'sʌməsɒlt, -sɔːlt/ *n* (on ground) voltereta *f*, vuelta *f* (de) carnero (CS); (in air) (salto *m*) mortal *m*

somersault² *vi* (on ground) hacer* volteretas, dar* vueltas (de) carnero (CS); (in air) dar* un (salto) mortal

something /'sʌmθɪŋ/ *pron* **1** algo; **have ~ to eat/drink** come/bebe algo; **it's not ~ to be proud of** no es como para estar orgulloso; **that was ~ I hadn't expected** eso no me lo esperaba; **is it ~ I said?** ¿qué pasa? ¿qué he dicho? **2** **(a)** (in vague statements or approximations): **she's 30 ~** tiene treinta y pico años (fam); **he said it was because of the traffic or ~** dijo que era por el tráfico o qué se yo **(b)** (something like): **~ like 200 spectators** alrededor de *or* unos 200 espectadores **(c)** something of (rather): **she's ~ of an eccentric** es algo excéntrica; **it came as ~ of a surprise** me (*or* nos *etc*) sorprendió un poco

3 (sth special): **it was quite ~ for him to reach that position** era todo un logro que él alcanzara esa posición

sometime¹ /'sʌmtaɪm/ *adv* (at unspecified time): **I'll get around to it ~** ya lo haré en algún momento; **we'll have to finish it ~ or another** algún día habrá que terminarlo; **~ next week** un día de la semana que viene

sometime² *adj* (*before n*) (frml) ex, antiguo

sometimes /'sʌmtaɪmz/ *adv* a veces, algunas veces

someway /'sʌmweɪ/ *adv* (AmE) ▶ SOMEHOW

somewhat /'sʌmhwɑːt ‖'sʌmwɒt/ *adv* algo, un tanto

somewhere¹ /'sʌmhwer ‖'sʌmweə(r)/ *adv* **1** (in, at a place) en algún lado *or* sitio *or* lugar; (to a place) a algún lado *or* sitio *or* lugar; **to get ~** avanzar*, adelantar **2** (in approximations): **~ around $10,000** cerca de *or* alrededor de 10.000 dólares

somewhere² *pron*: **will there be ~ open?** ¿habrá algo (*or* algún sitio *etc*) abierto?; **she's found ~ to live** ha encontrado casa (*or* habitación *etc*)

son /sʌn/ *n* hijo *m*

sonata /sə'nɑːtə/ *n* (*pl* **-tas**) (Mus) sonata *f*

song /sɔːŋ ‖sɒŋ/ *n* **(a)** (piece) canción *f* **(b)** (of bird) canto *m*

song: **~bird** *n* pájaro *m* cantor; **~writer** *n* compositor, -tora *m,f* (*de canciones*)

sonic /'sɑːnɪk ‖'sɒnɪk/ *adj* sónico

son-in-law /'sʌnɪnlɔː/ *n* (*pl* **sons-in-law**) yerno *m*, hijo *m* político

sonnet /'sɑːnət ‖'sɒnɪt/ *n* soneto *m*

son of a bitch *n* (*pl* **sons of bitches**) (esp AmE sl) hijo *m* de puta, hijo *m* de la chingada (Méx vulg)

soon /suːn/ *adv* **-er, -est** **1** (shortly, after a while) pronto, dentro de poco; **~ afterward** poco después; **it'll ~ be spring** ya falta poco para que empiece) la primavera; **~er or later** tarde o temprano **2** **(a)** (early, quickly) pronto; **how ~ can you be here?** ¿cuándo puedes llegar?, ¿qué tan pronto puedes llegar? (AmL); **I finished ~er than I expected** terminé antes de lo que esperaba; **not a minute *o* moment too ~** no antes de tiempo; **to speak too ~** hablar antes de tiempo; **as ~ as possible** lo antes posible, cuanto antes; **the ~er the better** cuanto antes mejor **(b)** (as conj): **as ~ as** en cuanto, tan pronto como; **as ~ as you've finished, you can go** en cuanto hayas terminado *or* tan pronto como hayas terminado, te puedes ir; **no ~er had we set out than it began to rain** apenas nos habíamos puesto en camino cuando empezó a llover; **no ~er said than done** dicho y hecho **3** (*in phrases*) as soon ... (as): **I'd just as ~ stay at home (as go out)** no me importaría quedarme en casa, tanto me da quedarme en casa (como salir)

soot /sʊt/ *n* hollín *m*

soothe /suːð/ *vt* ⟨*person/nerves*⟩ calmar; ⟨*pain/ cough*⟩ aliviar

soothing /'suːðɪŋ/ *adj* **(a)** ⟨*voice/words*⟩ tranquilizador; ⟨*music/bath*⟩ relajante **(b)** ⟨*ointment/syrup*⟩ balsámico; ⟨*medicine*⟩ calmante

sophisticated /səˈfɪstəkeɪtəd ‖səˈfɪstɪkeɪtɪd/ *adj* (a) ⟨appearance/person⟩ sofisticado (b) ⟨machine/technique⟩ complejo, altamente desarrollado

sophomore /ˈsɑːfəmɔːr ‖ˈsɒfəmɔː(r)/ *n* (AmE) estudiante *mf* de segundo curso (en una universidad o colegio secundario estadounidense)

sopping¹ /ˈsɑːpɪŋ ‖ˈsɒpɪŋ/ *adj* empapado

sopping² *adv* (as intensifier) ~ **wet** (of people) calado hasta los huesos; (of clothes) chorreando

soprano¹ /səˈprænəʊ ‖səˈprɑːnəʊ/ *n* (pl **-nos**) soprano *mf*

soprano² *adj* ⟨voice/recorder⟩ soprano; ⟨part/role⟩ de soprano

sorbet /sɔːrˈbeɪ, ˈsɔːrbət ‖ˈsɔːbeɪ/ *n* sorbete *m*

sorcerer /ˈsɔːrsərər ‖ˈsɔːsərə(r)/ *n* (liter) hechicero *m*, brujo *m*

sordid /ˈsɔːrdəd ‖ˈsɔːdɪd/ *adj* (a) (base) ⟨method/deal⟩ vergonzoso (b) (squalid) ⟨hotel/conditions⟩ sórdido

sore¹ /sɔːr ‖sɔː(r)/ *adj* **sorer** /ˈsɔːrər ‖ˈsɔːrə(r)/, **sorest** /ˈsɔːrəst ‖ˈsɔːrɪst/ (a) (painful) ⟨finger/foot⟩ dolorido; ⟨eye⟩ irritado; ⟨lips⟩ reseco; **she has a ~ throat** le duele la garganta; **a ~ point/subject** un punto/tema delicado (b) (angry) (AmE colloq) **to be ~ AT** *o* **WITH sb** estar* picado CON algn (fam)

sore² *n* llaga *f*, úlcera *f*

sorority /səˈrɔːrəti ‖səˈrɒrəti/ *n* (pl **-ties**) (in US) asociación *f* femenina de estudiantes (en universidades norteamericanas)

sorrow /ˈsɑːrəʊ ‖ˈsɒrəʊ/ *n* pesar *m*, pena *f*

sorrowful /ˈsɑːrəfəl ‖ˈsɒrəfəl/ *adj* afligido, triste

sorry /ˈsɑːri ‖ˈsɒri/ *adj* **-rier, -riest** [1] (pred) (a) (grieved, sad): **I'm ~** lo siento; **I'm very ~, but I can't help you** lo siento mucho, pero no te puedo ayudar; **to feel** *o* **be ~ FOR sb: I feel so ~ for you/him** te/lo compadezco; **to feel ~ for oneself** lamentarse de su (*or* tu *etc*) suerte; **I'm ~ to have to tell you that …** siento tener que decirte que …; **to be ~ (THAT)** sentir* QUE (+ *subj*) (b) (apologetic, repentant): **to say ~** pedir* perdón, disculparse; **I'm ~, I didn't mean to …** perdóname *or* lo siento *or* disculpa, no fue mi intención …; **I'm very sorry, but I can't help you** lo siento mucho, pero no te puedo ayudar; **to be ~ ABOUT sth** arrepentirse* DE algo; **I'm ~ I didn't make it to your party** siento no haber podido ir a tu fiesta [2] (as interj) perdón, lo siento [3] (pitiful, miserable) (before n) ⟨tale⟩ lamentable; **he was a ~ sight** tenía un aspecto lamentable

sort¹ /sɔːrt ‖sɔːt/ *n* [1] (kind, type) tipo *m*, clase *f*, **what ~ of car is it?** ¿qué tipo *or* clase de coche es?; **she's not the ~ to let you down** no es de las que te fallan; **a ~ of** *o* **~ of a** una especie de; **I didn't say anything of the ~** no dije nada semejante [2] (in phrases) sort of (colloq): **it's ~ of sad to think of him all alone** da como pena pensar que está solo (fam); **do you want to go? — well, ~ of** ¿quieres ir? — bueno, en cierto modo sí

sort² *vt* (a) (classify) ⟨papers/letters⟩ clasificar* (b) (mend) arreglar
■ **sort out** [v + o + adv, v + adv + o] [1] (a) (put in order) ⟨books/photos/desk/room⟩ ordenar; ⟨finances⟩ organizar* (b) (separate out) separar

[2] (a) (arrange) (BrE) ⟨date⟩ fijar; ⟨deal⟩ llegar* a (b) (resolve) ⟨problem/dispute⟩ solucionar; ⟨misunderstanding⟩ aclarar
■ **sort through** [v + prep + o] ⟨papers/files⟩ revisar

SOS *n* S.O.S. *m*

so-so /ˈsəʊsəʊ/ *adj* (colloq) así así (fam)

soufflé /suːˈfleɪ ‖ˈsuːfleɪ/ *n* suflé *m*

sought /sɔːt/ *past & past p of* SEEK

sought-after /ˈsɔːtˈæftər ‖ˈsɔːtˌɑːftə(r)/ *adj* (pred **sought after**) ⟨product⟩ solicitado, en demanda; ⟨prize⟩ codiciado; ⟨area⟩ en demanda

soul /səʊl/ *n* [1] (Relig) alma *f‡* [2] (person): **I won't tell a ⟨living⟩ ~** no se lo diré a nadie; **poor old ~!** ¡pobrecilla!, ¡pobrecita! [3] **~ (music)** soul *m*

soul-destroying /ˈsəʊldɪˈstrɔɪŋ/ *adj* desmoralizador

soulful /ˈsəʊlfəl/ *adj* enternecedor, conmovedor

soul: ~mate *n* alma *f‡* gemela; **~searching** /ˈsəʊlˌsɜːrtʃɪŋ ‖ˈsəʊlˌsɜːtʃɪŋ/ *n* introspección *f*

sound¹ /saʊnd/ *n* [1] (noise) sonido *m*; (unpleasant, disturbing) ruido *m*; (before n) **the ~ barrier** la barrera del sonido; **~ effects** efectos *mpl* sonoros [2] (impression conveyed) (colloq) (no pl): **I don't like the ~ of that at all** eso no me huele nada bien; **by** *o* **from the ~ of it, everything's going very well** parece que *or* por lo visto todo marcha muy bien

sound² *vi* [1] (a) (give impression) sonar*; **you ~ as if** *o* **as though you could do with a rest** me da la impresión de que no te vendría mal un descanso; **that ~s like Susan now** esa debe (de) ser Susan (b) (seem) parecer*; **how does that ~ to you?** ¿qué te parece?; **it ~s as if** *o* **as though you had a great time** parece que lo pasaste fenomenal [2] (make noise, resound) «bell/alarm» sonar*
■ *vt* ⟨trumpet/horn⟩ tocar*, hacer* sonar
■ **sound out** [v + o + adv, v + adv + o] tantear, sondear

sound³ *adj* **-er, -est** [1] (a) (healthy) sano; **being of ~ mind** (estando) en pleno uso de sus facultades (b) (in good condition) ⟨basis/foundation⟩ sólido, firme; ⟨timber⟩ en buenas condiciones [2] (valid) ⟨reasoning/knowledge⟩ sólido; ⟨advice/decision⟩ sensato

sound⁴ *adv* **-er, -est:** **~ asleep** profundamente dormido

sound bite *n* (Journ, Pol) frase *f* corta (que suena bien en los titulares y en los discursos)

soundiy /ˈsaʊndli/ *adv* [1] ⟨sleep⟩ profundamente [2] (solidly, validly) sólidamente

soundproof¹ /ˈsaʊndpruːf/ *adj* insonorizado

soundproof² *vt* insonorizar*

sound: ~ system *n* equipo *m* de sonido; **~track** *n* banda *f* sonora

soup /suːp/ *n* sopa *f*; **clear ~** caldo *m*, consomé *m*

sour¹ /saʊər ‖saʊə(r)/ *adj* **sourer, sourest** (a) (sharp, acid) ácido, agrio (b) (spoiled) ⟨milk⟩ agrio, cortado (c) (bad-tempered, disagreeable) agrio, avinagrado

sour² *vt* ⟨relationship/occasion⟩ amargar*

source /sɔːrs ‖sɔːs/ *n* [1] (origin, supply) fuente *f*,

s

(of river) nacimiento *m*; ~ **of income** fuente de ingresos **2** (providing information) **(a)** (person) (journ) fuente *f* **(b)** (text, document) fuente *f*

sourdough /'sauərdəu ‖'sauədou/ *n* (AmE) masa *f* fermentada (*para hacer pan*)

south¹ /sauθ/ *n* (point of the compass, direction) sur *m*; **the ~, the S~** (region) el sur

south² *adj* (*before n*) sur *adj inv*, meridional; (*wind*) del sur

south³ *adv* al sur

South Africa *n* Sudáfrica *f*, Suráfrica *f*

South African *adj* sudafricano, surafricano

South America *n* América *f* del Sur *or* del Sud, Sudamérica *f*, Suramérica *f*

South American¹ *adj* sudamericano, suramericano

South American² *n* sudamericano, -na *m,f*, suramericano, -na *m,f*

southbound /'sauθbaund/ *adj* (*traffic/train*) que va (*or* iba *etc*) hacia el sur *or* en dirección sur

southeast¹, Southeast /'sauθ'i:st/ *n* **the ~** el sudeste *or* Sudeste, el sureste *or* Sureste

southeast² *adj* sudeste *adj inv*, sureste *adj inv*, del sudeste *or* sureste, sudoriental

southeast³ *adv* hacia el sudeste *or* sureste, en dirección sudeste *or* sureste

south: ~easterly /'sauθ'i:stərli ‖,sauθ'i:stəli/ *adj* (*wind*) del sudeste *or* sureste; **~eastern** /'sauθ'i:stərn ‖,sauθ'i:stən/ *adj* sudeste *adj inv*, sureste *adj inv*, del sudeste *or* sureste, sudoriental

southerly /'sʌðərli ‖'sʌðəli/ *adj* (*wind*) del sur; (*latitude*) sur *adj inv*; **in a ~ direction** hacia el sur, en dirección sur

southern /'sʌðərn ‖'sʌðən/ *adj* (*region*) del sur, meridional, sur *adj inv*; (*country*) del sur, meridional; **~ Italy** el sur de Italia; **the ~ states** (in US) los estados del sur

southward¹ /'sauθwərd ‖'sauθwəd/ *adj* (*before n*): **in a ~ direction** hacia el sur, en dirección sur

southward², (BrE also) southwards /-z/ *adv* hacia el sur

southwest¹, Southwest /'sauθ'west/ *n* **the ~** el sudoeste *or* Sudoeste, el suroeste *or* Suroeste

southwest² *adj* sudoeste *adj inv*, suroeste *adj inv*, del sudoeste *or* suroeste

southwest³ *adv* hacia el sudoeste *or* suroeste, en dirección sudoeste *or* suroeste

south: ~westerly /'sauθ'westərli ‖,sauθ'westəli/ *adj* (*wind*) del sudoeste *or* suroeste; **~western** /'sauθ'westərn ‖,sauθ'westən/ *adj* sudoeste *adj inv*, sudoccidental, sudoeste *adj inv*, suroeste *adj inv*, del sudoeste *or* suroeste

souvenir /'su:vənɪr ‖,su:və'nɪə(r)/ *n* recuerdo *m*, souvenir *m*

sovereign¹ /'sɑ:vrən ‖'sɒvrɪn/ *n* **1** (monarch) soberano, -na *m,f* **2** (coin) soberano *m*, libra *f* (de oro)

sovereign² *adj* soberano

sovereignty /'sɑ:vrənti ‖'sɒvrənti/ *n* soberanía *f*

Soviet /'səuviet, 'sɑ:viət ‖'səuviət/ *adj* (Hist) soviético

Soviet Union *n* (Hist) **the ~ ~** la Unión Soviética

sow¹ /səu/ *vt/i* (*past* **sowed**; *past p* **sowed** *or* **sown**) sembrar*

sow² /sau/ *n* cerda *f*, puerca *f*

sown /səun/ *past p of* sow¹

soy /sɔɪ/, (BrE) **soya** /'sɔɪə/ *n* soya *f* (AmL), soja *f* (Esp)

soy: ~ bean, (BrE) **soya bean** *n* soya *f* (AmL), soja *f* (Esp); **~ sauce** *n* salsa *f* de soya (AmL) *or* (Esp) soja

spa /spɑ:/ *n* **(a)** (resort) balneario *m* **(b)** (spring) manantial *m* (*de agua mineral*) **(c)** (health club) (AmE) gimnasio *m*

space¹ /speɪs/ *n* **1 (a)** (Phys) espacio *m* **(b)** (Aerosp) espacio *m*; (*before n*) (*station/program*) espacial **2 (a)** (room) espacio *m*, lugar *m* **(b)** (empty area) espacio *m*; **let's clear a ~ for it first** hagámosle (un) sitio primero **3** (of time) (*no pl*) espacio *m*; **in the ~ of one hour** en el espacio *or* lapso de una hora **4** (Print) espacio *m*

space² *vt* **~ (out)** espaciar

space: ~-age *adj* (*technology*) futurista, espacial; **~craft** *n* (*pl* **~craft**) nave *f* espacial; **~man** /'speɪsmæn/ *n* (*pl* **-men** /-men/) astronauta *m*, cosmonauta *m*; **~ship** *n* nave *f* espacial, astronave *f*

spacing /'speɪsɪŋ/ *n* (Print) espaciado *m*

spacious /'speɪʃəs/ *adj* (*house/room*) amplio, espacioso; (*park*) grande, extenso

spade /speɪd/ *n* **1** (tool) pala *f*; **to call a ~ a ~** llamar al pan, pan y al vino, vino **2** (Games) **spades** *pl* (suit) (+ *sing or pl vb*) picas *fpl*

spaghetti /spə'geti/ *n* espaguetis *mpl*, spaghetti *mpl*

Spain /speɪn/ *n* España *f*

span¹ /spæn/ *n* **(a)** (of hand) palmo *m*; (of wing) envergadura *f*; (of bridge, arch) luz *f* **(b)** (part of bridge) arco *m* **(c)** (of time) lapso *m*; ▶ LIFE SPAN

span² *vt* **-nn- (a)** (extend over) abarcar* **(b)** (cross) «*bridge*» «*river*» extenderse* sobre

Spaniard /'spænjərd ‖'spænjəd/ *n* español, -ñola *m,f*

spaniel /'spænjəl/ *n* spaniel *m*

Spanish¹ /'spænɪʃ/ *adj* español; (*language*) castellano, español

Spanish² *n* **(a)** (language) castellano *m*, español *m* **(b)** (people) (+ *pl vb*) **the ~** los españoles

Spanish omelet, (BrE) **Spanish omelette** *n* tortilla *f* de papas *or* (Esp) patatas, tortilla *f* española

spank /spæŋk/ *vt* pegarle* a (*en las nalgas*)

spanner /'spænər ‖'spænə(r)/ *n* (BrE) (adjustable ~) llave *f* inglesa; (box ~) llave *f* de tubo; **to throw a ~ in the works** fastidiarlo todo

spar¹ /spɑ:r ‖spɑ:r/ *n* (Naut) palo *m*

spar² *vi* **-rr-** (in boxing) entrenarse; (argue) discutir

spare¹ /sper ‖speə(r)/ *adj* **(a)** (not in use) (*umbrella/pen*) de más; **have you got any ~ paper?** ¿tienes un poco de papel que no te haga falta? **(b)** (*before n*) (*key/cartridge*) de repuesto **(c)** (free) libre; **if you've got a ~ minute** si tienes un minuto (libre)

spare² *n*: **I'll take a ~ just in case** llevaré uno de repuesto por si acaso

spare³ vt **1** (a) (do without): can you ∼ your dictionary for a moment? ¿me permites el diccionario un momento, si no lo necesitas?; **if you can ∼ the time** si tienes or dispones de tiempo **(b)** (give) **to ∼ (sb) sth**: can you ∼ me a pound? ¿tienes una libra que me prestes/des?; can you ∼ me a few minutes? ¿tienes unos minutos? **(c)** to spare (as adj): **there's food to ∼** hay comida de sobra; **have you got a few minutes to ∼?** ¿tienes unos minutos?

2 (a) (keep from using, stint) (usu neg): **to ∼ no effort** no escatimar esfuerzos; **to ∼ no expense** no reparar en gastos **(b)** (save, relieve) **to ∼ sb sth** ⟨trouble/embarrassment⟩ ahorrarle algo a algn **(c)** (show mercy, consideration toward) perdonar

spare: ∼ **part** n repuesto m or (Méx) refacción f; ∼ **room** n cuarto m de huéspedes or (Esp) de los invitados, recámara f de visitas (Méx); ∼ **time** n tiempo m libre; ∼ **tire**, (BrE) ∼ **tyre** n rueda f de repuesto or (Esp tb) de recambio, llanta f de refacción (Méx)

sparingly /'sperŋli ǁ'speərŋli/ adv ⟨use⟩ con moderación

spark¹ /spɑːrk ǁspɑːk/ n chispa f

spark² vt, (BrE also) **spark off** ⟨rioting/revolution⟩ hacer* estallar; ⟨interest⟩ suscitar; ⟨criticism⟩ provocar*

sparking plug /'spɑːrkɪŋ ǁ'spɑːkɪŋ/ n (BrE) ▸ SPARK PLUG

sparkle¹ /'spɑːrkəl ǁ'spɑːkəl/ vi ⟨gem/glass⟩ centellear, destellar, brillar; ⟨eyes⟩ brillar

sparkle² n (a) (no pl) (of gem, glass) destello m, brillo m; (of eyes) brillo m (b) (animation) chispa f, brillo m

sparkler /'spɑːrklər ǁ'spɑːklə(r)/ n (firework) luz f de Bengala, bengala f

sparkling /'spɑːrklɪŋ ǁ'spɑːklɪŋ/ adj (a) (shining) ⟨gems/stars⟩ centelleante; ⟨eyes⟩ chispeante (b) ⟨wit/conversation⟩ chispeante (c) (effervescent) ⟨wine⟩ espumoso

spark plug n bujía f, chispero m (AmC)

sparrow /'spærəʊ/ n gorrión m

sparse /spɑːrs ǁspɑːs/ adj ⟨population/vegetation/furniture⟩ escaso; ⟨beard/hair⟩ ralo

sparsely /'spɑːrsli ǁ'spɑːsli/ adv: **the area was ∼ populated** la zona estaba escasamente poblada; **the room is ∼ furnished** la habitación tiene pocos muebles

spartan /'spɑːrtn ǁ'spɑːtn/ adj espartano

spasm /'spæzəm/ n espasmo m

spasmodic /spæz'mɑːdɪk ǁspæz'mɒdɪk/ adj (a) ⟨growth/activity⟩ irregular (b) (Med) ⟨pain/cough⟩ espasmódico

spat /spæt/ past & past p of SPIT²

spate /speɪt/ n racha f, serie f; **to be in (full) ∼** (BrE) ⟨river⟩ estar* crecido

spatial /'speɪʃəl/ adj (before n) espacial

spatter /'spætər ǁ'spætə(r)/ vt/i salpicar*

spatula /'spætʃələ ǁ'spætjʊlə/ n (a) (Culin) (for turning, serving) pala f (de servir); (for scraping out bowls) espátula f (b) (Pharm, Med) espátula f

spawn¹ /spɔːn/ n (of fish) hueva(s) f(pl); (of frogs) huevas fpl

spawn² vt (journ) generar, producir* ∎ ∼ vi «frogs/fish» desovar

SPCA n (in US) (= **Society for the Prevention of Cruelty to Animals**) ≈ Asociación f protectora de animales

SPCC n (in US) (= **Society for the Prevention of Cruelty to Children**) ≈ Asociación f de protección a la infancia

speak /spiːk/ (past **spoke**; past p **spoken**) vi **1** (a) (say sth) hablar; **to ∼ TO o** (esp AmE) **WITH sb** hablar CON algn, hablarle A algn; **they are not ∼ing** (to each other) no se hablan; **to ∼ OF sth/sb/-ING** hablar DE algo/algn/+ INF; **so to ∼** por así decirlo **(b)** (on telephone): hello, Barbara Mason ∼ing ... buenas tardes, habla or (Esp tb) soy Barbara Mason; **could I ∼ to Mrs Hodges, please?** — ∼ing! ¿podría hablar con la Sra. Hodges, por favor? — con ella (habla) or (Esp tb) soy yo

2 (make speech) hablar; **to ∼ ON o ABOUT sth** hablar ACERCA DE or SOBRE algo
∎ ∼ vt **(a)** (say, declare): nobody spoke a word nadie dijo nada; **to ∼ one's mind** hablar claro; **to ∼ the truth** decir* la verdad **(b)** ⟨language⟩ hablar

∎ **speak for** [v + prep + o] (a): we'd love to meet him — ∼ for yourself! nos encantaría conocerlo — ¡eso lo dirás por ti!; **the facts ∼ for themselves** los hechos son elocuentes

∎ **speak out** [v + adv]: **to ∼ out AGAINST sth** denunciar algo

∎ **speak up** [v + adv] **(a)** (speak loudly, clearly) hablar más fuerte or más alto **(b)** (speak boldly) decir* lo que se piensa; **to ∼ up FOR sb** defender* a algn

speaker /'spiːkər ǁ'spiːkə(r)/ n **1** (a) (in public) orador, -dora m,f **(b)** (of language) hablante mf **(c)** (Govt) presidente, -ta m,f **2** (Audio) (a) (loudspeaker) altavoz m, (alto)parlante m (AmS) **(b)** (of hi-fi) baf(f)le m, parlante m (AmS)

speaking /'spiːkɪŋ/ n (before n): **a good ∼ voice** una voz muy clara (or potente etc); **to be on ∼ terms with sb** estar* en buenas relaciones con algn

-speaking /ˌspiːkɪŋ/ suff -hablante, -parlante; **Spanish∼** hispanohablante, hispanoparlante; **French∼** francófono; **English∼** de habla inglesa

spear¹ /spɪr ǁ'spɪə(r)/ n (a) (weapon) lanza f (b) (for fishing) arpón m

spear² vt ⟨fish⟩ arponear

spear: ∼**head** vt (Mil) encabezar*; ∼**mint** n menta f verde

spec /spek/ n: **on ∼** (colloq) por si acaso

special /'speʃəl/ adj (a) (exceptional) (before n) ⟨favor/request⟩ especial **(b)** (for specific purpose) (before n) ⟨arrangements/fund⟩ especial **(c)** (particular, individual) especial, particular; **children with ∼ needs** (Educ) niños que requieren una atención diferenciada

special: ∼ **delivery** n correo m exprés or expreso; ∼ **effects** pl n efectos mpl especiales

specialist /'speʃələst ‖'speʃəlɪst/ n especialista mf; (before n) ⟨knowledge/shop⟩ especializado

speciality /ˌspeʃi'æləti/ n (pl **-ties**) (BrE) ▶ SPECIALTY¹

specialize /'speʃəlaɪz/ vi to ∼ (IN sth) especializarse* (EN algo)

specialized /'speʃəlaɪzd/ adj especializado

specially /'speʃəli/ adv (a) (specifically) especialmente, expresamente (b) (especially) ⟨long/difficult⟩ particularmente

specialty¹ /'speʃəlti/ n (pl **-ties**) (AmE) especialidad f

specialty² adj (AmE) (before n: no comp) ⟨merchandise/store⟩ especializado

species /'spiːʃiːz/ n (pl ∼) especie f

specific /spɪ'sɪfɪk ‖spə'sɪfɪk/ adj (a) (particular, individual) específico; ⟨example⟩ concreto (b) (exact, precise) preciso

specifically /spɪ'sɪfɪkli ‖spə'sɪfɪkli/ adv (a) (explicitly) ⟨state/mention⟩ explícitamente (b) (specially, particularly) ⟨built/designed⟩ específicamente

specification /ˌspesəfə'keɪʃən ‖ˌspesɪfɪ'keɪʃən/ n (often pl) especificación f

specify /'spesəfaɪ ‖'spesɪfaɪ/ vt **-fies, -fying, -fied** especificar*

specimen /'spesəmən ‖'spesɪmən/ n (a) (sample — of rock, plant, tissue) muestra f, espécimen m; (— of blood, urine) muestra f; (— of work, handwriting) muestra f (b) (individual example) ejemplar m, espécimen m

speck /spek/ n (of dust) mota f; (in distance) punto m; (dirt stain) manchita f

speckle /'spekəl/vt (usu pass) motear; **a** ∼**d hen** una gallina pinta or (RPl) bataraza

spectacle /'spektɪkəl ‖'spektəkəl/ n **1** (show, sight) espectáculo m **2** **spectacles** pl gafas fpl, anteojos mpl (esp AmL), lentes mpl (esp AmL)

spectacular /spek'tækjələr ‖spek'tækjʊlə(r)/ adj espectacular

spectator /'spekteɪtər ‖spek'teɪtə(r)/ n espectador, -dora m,f

specter, (BrE) **spectre** /'spektər ‖'spektə(r)/ n (liter) espectro m

spectra /'spektrə/ pl of SPECTRUM

spectre /'spektər/ n (BrE) ▶ SPECTER

spectrum /'spektrəm/ n (pl **-tra**) **1** (Opt, Phys) espectro m **2** (range) espectro m, gama f; **the political** ∼ el espectro político

speculate /'spekjələrt ‖'spekjʊlert/ vi **1** (Fin) especular **2** (guess, conjecture) to ∼ (ON o ABOUT sth) hacer* conjeturas o especular (SOBRE algo)

speculation /ˌspekjə'leɪʃən ‖ˌspekjʊ'leɪʃən/ n especulación f

speculative /'spekjələtɪv ‖'spekjʊlətɪv/ adj especulativo

sped /sped/ past & past p of SPEED² vi A

speech /spiːtʃ/ n **1** (a) (act, faculty) habla f; (b) (manner of speaking) forma f de hablar (c) (language, dialect) habla f; **2** (a) (oration) discurso m; **to make a** ∼ dar* un discurso (b) (Theat) parlamento m

speechless /'spiːtʃləs ‖'spiːtʃlɪs/ adj: **she was** ∼ **with rage** enmudeció de rabia; **I'm** ∼**!** no sé qué decir

speech therapy n foniatría f, logopedia f

speed¹ /spiːd/ n **1** (a) (rate of movement, progress) velocidad f (b) (relative quickness) rapidez f **2** (Phot): **film** ∼ sensibilidad f de la película; **shutter** ∼ tiempo m de exposición **3** (gear) velocidad f, marcha f **4** (amphetamine) (sl) anfetas fpl (fam)

speed² vi (a) (past & past p **sped**) (go, pass quickly) (+ adv compl): **to** ∼ **off** o **away** alejarse a toda velocidad; **he sped by** o **past in his new sports car** nos pasó a toda velocidad con su nuevo coche deportivo; **the hours sped by** las horas pasaron volando (b) (past & past p **speeded**) (drive too fast) ir* a velocidad excesiva
■ ∼ vt (past & past p **speeded**) (hasten) acelerar
■ **speed up** (past & past p **speeded**) **1** [v + adv] (a) (move faster) ⟨vehicle/driver⟩ acelerar; ⟨walker⟩ apretar* el paso (b) ⟨process/production⟩ acelerarse
2 [v + o + adv, v + adv + o] (a) ⟨vehicle⟩ acelerar (b) ⟨work/production⟩ acelerar

speed: ∼**boat** n (lancha f) motora f; ∼ **bump** n badén m, guardia m tumbado (Esp), tope m (Méx), policía m acostado (Col), lomo m de burro (RPl), baden m (Chi); ∼ **limit** n velocidad f máxima, límite m de velocidad

speedometer /spɪ'dɑːmətər ‖spiː'dɒmɪtə(r)/ n velocímetro m, indicador m de velocidad

speedway /'spiːdweɪ/ n (a) (sport) carreras fpl de motocicletas (b) (AmE Transp) autopista f

speedy /'spiːdi/ adj **-dier, -diest** ⟨reply/delivery⟩ rápido; ⟨solution⟩ pronto, rápido

spell¹ /spel/ n **1** (magic) ∼) encanto m, hechizo m, encantamiento m; **evil** ∼ maleficio m; **to cast a** ∼ **over** o **to put a** ∼ **on sth/sb** hechizar* or embrujar algo/a algn **2** (a) (of weather) período m (b) (of work, activity) período m, temporada f; **a bad** ∼ una mala racha

spell² (past & past p **spelled** or (BrE also) **spelt**) vt **1** (write) escribir*; (orally) deletrear; **how do you** ∼ **Zimbabwe?** ¿cómo se escribe Zimbabwe?; **could you** ∼ **it for me?** ¿me lo deletrea? **2** (mean) significar*; (foretell) anunciar, augurar
■ ∼ vi: **he can't** ∼ tiene mala ortografía
■ **spell out** [v + o + adv, v + adv + o] (a) ⟨word⟩ deletrear (b) (explain) explicar* en detalle

spell: ∼**binding** adj ⟨speech/film⟩ fascinante; ∼**bound** adj embelesado, maravillado; ∼**checker** n (Comput) corrector m ortográfico

spelling /'spelɪŋ/ n (a) (system, ability) ortografía f; **to be good/bad at** ∼ tener* buena/mala ortografía; (before n) ∼ **mistake** falta f de ortografía, error m ortográfico (b) (of a word) grafía f, ortografía f

spelt /spelt/ (BrE) past & past p of SPELL²

spelunking /spɪ'lʌŋkɪŋ/ n (AmE) espeleología f

spend /spend/ vt (past & past p **spent**) **1** (a) ⟨money⟩ gastar (b) (expend) **to** ∼ **sth** (ON sth) dedicarle* algo A algo; **don't** ∼ **too long on each question** no le dediquen mucho tiempo a cada pregunta **2** (pass) ⟨period of time⟩ pasar **3** (exhaust) agotar

S

spending /'spendɪŋ/ n gastos mpl; public ∼ el gasto público; (before n) ∼ **power** poder m adquisitivo

spending money n dinero m para gastos personales

spendthrift /'spendθrɪft/ n despilfarrador, -dora m,f

spent /spent/ past & past p of SPEND

sperm /spɜːrm ‖spɜːm/ n (pl ∼ or ∼s) (a) (seminal liquid) esperma m or f (b) (gamete) espermatozoide m, espermatozoo m

spew /spjuː/ vi (a) «water» salir* a borbotones (b) (vomit) (BrE sl) vomitar, lanzar* (fam)
■ ∼ vt «lava/flames» arrojar

sphere /sfɪr ‖sfɪə(r)/ n esfera f

spherical /'sfɪrɪkəl ‖'sferɪkəl/ adj esférico

Sphinx /sfɪŋks/ n the ∼ la Esfinge

spice¹ /spaɪs/ n (a) (seasoning) especia f (b) (zest, interest) sabor m

spice² vt (a) (Culin) (often pass) condimentar, sazonar* (b) (add excitement to): **to ∼ up a story** darle* más sabor a un relato

spick-and-span /'spɪkən'spæn/ adj (colloq) (pred) limpio y ordenado

spicy /'spaɪsi/ adj -cier, -ciest (a) «sauce/ food» (with spices) con muchas especias; (hot, peppery) picante (b) (racy) «story/account» sabroso; (with sexual connotations) picante

spider /'spaɪdər ‖'spaɪdə(r)/ n araña f

spike¹ /spaɪk/ n [1] (a) (pointed object) punta f, púa f, pincho m or (Arg) pinche m; (on track shoes) clavo m or (Chi, Ven) púa f or (Col) carramplón m
[2] **spikes** pl (running shoes) zapatillas fpl de clavos or (Chi, Ven) de púas or (Col) con carramplones, picos mpl (Méx)

spike² vt [1] (pierce) pinchar, clavar [2] (add sth to) (colloq): **they ∼d his lemonade with vodka** le echaron vodka en la limonada

spiky /'spaɪki/ adj -kier, -kiest (a) (having spikes) con puntas or púas or pinchos (b) (sharp, pointed) puntiagudo, puntudo (Col, CS) (c) «hair» de punta

spill /spɪl/ n (past & past p **spilled** or **spilt** /spɪlt/) vt «liquid» derramar, verter*; (knock over) volcar*
■ ∼ vi «liquid» derramarse; **people ∼ed (out) into the streets** la gente se volcó or se echó a las calles

■ **spill over** [v + adv] «container» desbordarse; «liquid» rebosar; «fighting/conflict» extenderse*

spillage /'spɪlɪdʒ/ n vertido m, derrame m

spilt /spɪlt/ past & past p of SPILL

spin¹ /spɪn/ n [1] (on ball) (Sport) efecto m, chanfle m (AmL) [2] (a) (of aircraft) barrena f (b) (Auto) trompo m [3] (ride) (colloq): **to go for a ∼** ir* a dar un paseo en coche (or en moto etc), ir* a dar un garbeo (Esp fam)

spin² (pres p **spinning**; past & past p **spun**) vt «wheel/top» hacer* girar [2] (a) «wool/ cotton» hilar (b) «web» tejer
■ ∼ vi [1] (a) (rotate) «wheel/top» girar; **my head is ∼ning** la cabeza me da vueltas [2] «washing machine» centrifugar* (c) (move rapidly) (+ adv compl): **the car spun out of control** el coche giró fuera de control [2] (Tex) hilar

■ **spin out** [v + o + adv, v + adv + o] «money» estirar; «vacation/story» alargar*, prolongar*

spina bifida /'spaɪnə'bɪfədə ‖,spaɪnə'bɪfɪdə/ n espina f bífida

spinach /'spɪnɪtʃ ‖'spɪnɪdʒ, -ɪtʃ/ n (Bot) espinaca f; (Culin) espinaca(s) f(pl)

spinal /'spaɪnl/ adj de la columna vertebral

spinal: ∼ **column** n columna f vertebral; ∼ **cord** n médula f espinal

spindle /'spɪndl/ n (a) (Mech Eng) eje m (b) (Tex) huso m

spindly /'spɪndli/ adj -dlier, -dliest «legs» largo y flaco; «plant» alto y débil

spin: ∼ **doctor** n (esp Pol) portavoz mf (contratado para dar a la prensa, TV, etc, una interpretación favorable de los hechos); ∼ **drier** n centrifugadora f (de ropa); ∼**-dry** /'spɪn'draɪ/ vt -**dries, -drying, -dried** centrifugar*; ∼ **dryer** n ▶ ∼ DRIER

spine /spaɪn/ n [1] (a) (Anat) columna f (vertebral) (b) (of book) lomo m [2] (on animal) púa f; (on plant) espina f

spine-chilling /'spaɪn,tʃɪlɪŋ/ adj espeluznante

spineless /'spaɪnləs ‖'spaɪnlɪs/ adj (a) (cowardly, weak) débil, sin carácter (b) (Zool) invertebrado

spinning /'spɪnɪŋ/ n (Tex) hilado m

spinning wheel n rueca f

spin-off /'spɪnɔːf ‖'spɪnɒf/ n (product) producto m derivado; (result) resultado m indirecto

spinster /'spɪnstər ‖'spɪnstə(r)/ n soltera f

spiral¹ /'spaɪrəl ‖'spaɪərəl/ n (a) (shape, movement) espiral f (b) (of smoke) voluta f, espiral f

spiral² adj «shape» de espiral, acaracolado; ∼ **staircase** escalera f de caracol

spiral³ vi, (BrE) -**ll-** «unemployment» escalar; «prices» dispararse

spire /spaɪr ‖'spaɪə(r)/ n aguja f, chapitel m

spirit /'spɪrət ‖'spɪrɪt/ n [1] (a) (life force, soul) espíritu m (b) (Occult) espíritu m [2] (vigor, courage) espíritu m, temple m; **to break sb's ∼** quebrantarle el espíritu a algn [3] (mental attitude, mood) (no pl) espíritu m; **the party/Christmas ∼** el espíritu festivo/navideño [4] **spirits** pl (emotional state): **to be in good ∼s** estar* animado; **keep your ∼s up** ¡arriba ese ánimo! [5] **spirits** pl (alcohol) bebidas fpl alcohólicas (de alta graduación), licores mpl

spirited /'spɪrətəd ‖'spɪrɪtɪd/ adj «horse/child» brioso; «reply» enérgico; «defense» ardiente

spirit level n nivel m (de burbuja or de aire)

spiritual¹ /'spɪrɪtʃuəl ‖'spɪrɪtjuəl/ adj espiritual

spiritual² n (negro ∼) espiritual m (negro)

spiritualism /'spɪrɪtʃuəlɪzəm ‖'spɪrɪtjuəlɪzəm/ n (Occult) espiritismo m; (Phil) espiritualismo m

spit¹ /spɪt/ n [1] (saliva) saliva f [2] (for roasting) asador m (en forma de varilla), espetón m

spit² vi (pres p **spitting**; past & past p **spat** or (AmE esp) **spit**) (a) «person/animal» escupir; **to ∼ AT sb** escupirle a algn; ▶ IMAGE (b) «fire/ fat» chisporrotear (c) «cat» bufar
■ ∼ vt (past & past p **spat**) «food/blood» escupir

■ ~ *v impers* (colloq): **it's** ~**ting** caen algunas gotas (de lluvia), está chispeando (fam)

■ **spit out** [*v* + *o* + *adv*, *v* + *adv* + *o*] escupir

spite[1] /spaɪt/ *n* [1] (malice) maldad *f*; (resentment) rencor *m*, resentimiento *m* [2] **in spite of** (*as prep*) a pesar de

spite[2] *vt* molestar, fastidiar

spiteful /'spaɪtfəl/ *adj* ⟨remark⟩ malicioso; ⟨person⟩ malo; (resentful) rencoroso

spittle /'spɪtl/ *n* baba *f*

splash[1] /splæʃ/ *n* [1] (a) (spray) salpicadura *f* (b) (sound): **we heard a** ~ oímos el ruido de algo al caer al agua (c) (paddle, swim) (*no pl*) chapuzón *m* [2] (a) (of milk, paint) (*no pl*) **a** ~ un poco (b) (mark, patch) salpicadura *f*, manchón *m*

splash[2] *vt* salpicar*; **to** ~ **sth/sb WITH sth** salpicar* algo/a algn DE algo

■ ~ *vi* (a) ⟨water/paint⟩ salpicar* (b) ⟨person/animal⟩ chapotear

■ **splash out** (BrE colloq) [*v* + *adv*] darse* un lujo; **to** ~ **out ON sth** gastar(se) un dineral EN algo (fam)

splashguard /'splæʃgɑːrd ‖'splæʃgɑːd/ *n* (AmE) guardabarros *m*, salpicadera *f* (Méx), tapabarros *m* (Chi, Per)

splatter /'splætər ‖'splætə(r)/ *vt/i* ▸ SPATTER

splay /spleɪ/ *vt* ~ (out) ⟨fingers⟩ abrir*, separar; **to** ~ **one's legs** abrir* de piernas

spleen /spliːn/ *n* (Anat) bazo *m*

splendid /'splendəd ‖'splendɪd/ *adj* (a) (very good) ⟨idea/opportunity/meal⟩ espléndido (b) (imposing) ⟨clothes/building⟩ magnífico; ⟨ceremony⟩ lleno de esplendor

splendor, (BrE) **splendour** /'splendər ‖'splendə(r)/ *n* esplendor *m*

splice /splaɪs/ *vt* ~ (together) ⟨ropes⟩ coser; ⟨tape/film⟩ unir

splint /splɪnt/ *n* tablilla *f*

splinter[1] /'splɪntər ‖'splɪntə(r)/ *n* (of wood) astilla *f*; (of glass, bone, metal) esquirla *f*, astilla *f*; (*before n*) ~ **group** grupo *m* escindido

splinter[2] *vi* (a) (break into pieces) ⟨wood/bone⟩ astillarse (b) ⟨political party/society⟩ escindirse

■ ~ *vt* ⟨wood/bone⟩ astillar

split[1] /splɪt/ *n* [1] (a) (in garment, cloth — in seam) descosido *m*; (— part of design) abertura *f*, raja *f* (b) (in wood, glass) rajadura *f*, grieta *f* [2] (a) (Pol) escisión *f*; (Relig) cisma *m*, escisión *f* (b) (breakup) ruptura *f*, separación *f* [3] **splits** *pl*: **to do the** ~**s** abrirse* completamente de piernas, hacer* el spagat (Esp)

split[2] *adj* [1] (damaged) ⟨wood⟩ rajado, partido; ⟨lip⟩ partido [2] (a) (divided): ~ **personality** doble personalidad *f*; ~ **shift** horario *m* (de trabajo) partido (b) (in factions) dividido

split[3] (*pres p* **splitting**; *past & past p* **split**) *vt* [1] (a) (break) ⟨wood/stone⟩ partir; **to** ~ **the atom** fisionar el átomo (b) (burst) ⟨pants/trousers⟩ reventar* (c) (divide into factions) ⟨nation/church⟩ dividir

[2] (divide, share) ⟨cost/food⟩ dividir

■ ~ *vi* [1] (crack, burst) ⟨wood/rock⟩ partirse, rajarse; ⟨leather/seam⟩ abrirse*, romperse*; **I've got a** ~**ting headache** tengo un dolor de cabeza espantoso

[2] ⟨political party/church⟩ dividirse, escindirse

[3] (leave) (sl) abrirse* (arg), largarse* (fam)

■ **split away, split off** [*v* + *adv*] **to** ~ **away** *o* **off FROM sth** escindirse *or* separarse DE algo

■ **split up** [1] [*v* + *adv*] ⟨couple/band⟩ separarse; ⟨crowd⟩ dispersarse

[2] [*v* + *o* + *adv*, *v* + *adv* + *o*] ⟨wrestlers/boxers⟩ separar; ⟨lovers⟩ hacer* que se separen; ~ **them up into groups** divídelos en grupos

split: ~ **end** *n* (of hair): **I've got** ~ **ends** tengo las puntas abiertas *or* (CS) florecidas, tengo horquillas (Col) *or* (Méx) orzuela *or* (Ven) horquetillas; ~**-level** /'splɪt'levəl/ *adj* ⟨apartment⟩ en dos niveles; ~**-second** *n* fracción *f* de segundo; (*before n*) ~**-second timing** sincronización *f* perfecta

splutter /'splʌtər ‖'splʌtə(r)/ *vi* (a) ⟨fire/fat⟩ chisporrotear; ⟨engine⟩ resoplar (b) ⟨person⟩ resoplar; (in anger, embarrassment etc) farfullar

spoil /spɔɪl/ (*past & past p* **spoiled** *or* (BrE also) **spoilt**) *vt* [1] ⟨party/surprise⟩ echar a perder, estropear; **I don't want to** ~ **your fun but ...** no les quiero aguar la fiesta pero ...; **it will** ~ **your appetite** te quitará el apetito [2] (overindulge) ⟨child⟩ consentir*, malcriar*; **to be** ~**ed for choice** tener* mucho de donde elegir

■ ~ *vi* [1] ⟨food/meal⟩ echarse a perder, estropearse [2] (be eager) (colloq): **to be** ~**ing for a fight** estar* *or* andar* buscando pelea

spoiled /spɔɪld/, (BrE also) **spoilt** /spɔɪlt/ *adj* mimado

spoils /spɔɪlz/ *pl n* botín *m*

spoilsport /'spɔɪlspɔːrt ‖'spɔɪlspɔːt/ *n* (colloq) aguafiestas *mf* (fam)

spoilt[1] /spɔɪlt/ (BrE) *past & past p of* SPOIL

spoilt[2] *adj* (BrE) ▸ SPOILED

spoke[1] /spəʊk/ *n* rayo *m* (de una rueda)

spoke[2] *past of* SPEAK

spoken[1] /'spəʊkən/ *past p of* SPEAK

spoken[2] *adj* (*before n*) hablado, oral

spokesman /'spəʊksmən/ *n* (*pl* **-men** /-mən/) portavoz *m*, vocero *m* (esp AmL)

spokesperson /'spəʊks,pɜːrsn ‖'spəʊks,pɜːsn/ *n* portavoz *mf*, vocero, -ra *m,f* (esp AmL)

spokeswoman /'spəʊks,wʊmən/ (*pl* **-women**) *n* portavoz *f*, vocera *f* (esp AmL)

sponge[1] /spʌndʒ/ *n* [1] (a) (Zool) esponja *f* (b) (for bath) esponja *f* [2] (Culin) ~ (**cake**) bizcocho *m*, bizcochuelo *m* (CS)

sponge[2] *vt* pasar una esponja por

■ ~ *vi*: **he lives by sponging on** *o* **off his relatives** vive a costillas de sus parientes

sponsor[1] /'spɑːnsər ‖'spɒnsə(r)/ *n* (a) (of program, show, sporting event) patrocinador, -dora *m,f*, espónsor *mf*; (for the arts) mecenas *mf* (b) (for membership): **you need two members to act as** ~**s** te tienen que presentar dos socios (c) (of bill, motion) proponente *mf*

sponsor[2] *vt* (a) ⟨event/festival⟩ patrocinar; ⟨research/expedition⟩ subvencionar (b) ⟨applicant/application⟩ apoyar (c) ⟨bill/motion⟩ (present) presentar, proponer*; (support) apoyar

sponsorship /'spɑːnsərʃɪp ‖'spɒnsəʃɪp/ *n* patrocinio *m*; (of the arts) mecenazgo *m*

spontaneous /spɑːn'teɪniəs ‖spɒn'teɪniəs/ *adj* espontáneo

S

spontaneously /spɑːnˈtemɪəsli ‖spɒnˈtemɪəsli/ *adv* espontáneamente

spoof /spuːf/ *n* (colloq) parodia *f*, burla *f*

spooky /ˈspuːki/ *adj* **-kier, -kiest** (colloq) espeluznante

spool /spuːl/ *n* carrete *m*, carretel *m* (AmL)

spoon /spuːn/ *n* cuchara *f*; (small) cucharita *f*

spoonfeed /ˈspuːnfiːd/ *vt* (past & past p **-fed**) ⟨baby⟩ darle* de comer en la boca a; **she ~s her students** se lo da todo mascado a sus alumnos

spoonful /ˈspuːnfʊl/ *n* (*pl* **~s** *or* **spoonsful**) cucharada *f*; (small) cucharadita *f*

sporadic /spəˈrædɪk/ *adj* esporádico

sport¹ /spɔːrt ‖spɔːt/ *n* **1** deporte *m* **2** (person): **to be a good ~** (to be sporting) tener* espíritu deportivo; (to be understanding) ser* comprensivo

sport² *vt* ⟨clothes/hairstyle⟩ lucir*

sport³ *adj* (AmE) **(a)** (Sport) ⟨equipment⟩ de deportes **(b)** (casual) ⟨clothes⟩ sport *adj inv*, de sport

sporting /ˈspɔːrtɪŋ ‖ˈspɔːtɪŋ/ *adj* **1** (fair) ⟨spirit⟩ deportivo; **it's very ~ of you** es muy amable de tu parte **2** (*no comp*) (relating to sport) ⟨press/interests⟩ deportivo

sports /spɔːrts ‖spɔːts/ *adj* **(a)** (Sport) ⟨page/ program⟩ de deportes; **~ complex** polideportivo *m* **(b)** (casual) ⟨clothes/shirt⟩ sport *adj inv*

sports: ~ car *n* coche *m* deportivo, carro *m* sport (AmL exc CS), auto *m* sport *or* deportivo (CS); **~man** /ˈspɔːrtsmən ‖ˈspɔːtsmən/ *n* (*pl* **-men** /-mən/) deportista *m*

sportsmanship /ˈspɔːrtsmənʃɪp ‖ˈspɔːtsmənʃɪp/ *n* espíritu *m* deportivo

sportswoman /ˈspɔːrtswʊmən ‖ˈspɔːtswʊmən/ *n* deportista *f*

sporty /ˈspɔːrti ‖ˈspɔːti/ *adj* **-tier, -tiest** **(a)** ⟨person⟩ deportista **(b)** (Auto) deportivo

spot¹ /spɑːt ‖spɒt/ *n* **1 (a)** (dot — on material) lunar *m*, mota *f*; (— on animal's skin) mancha *f* **(b)** (blemish, stain) mancha *f* **(c)** (pimple) (BrE) grano *m*, espinilla *f* **2 (a)** (location, place) lugar *m*, sitio *m*; **on the ~: he had to decide on the ~** tuvo que decidir en ese mismo momento; **they were killed on the ~** los mataron allí mismo; **on-the-~ fine** multa que se paga en el acto **(b)** (difficult situation): **to be in a** ⟨tight⟩ **~** estar* en apuros **3 (a)** (drop) gota *f* **(b)** (small amount) (BrE colloq) (*no pl*): **do you fancy a ~ of supper?** ¿quieres cenar algo?

spot² *vt* **-tt-** **1** ⟨error⟩ descubrir*; ⟨bargain⟩ encontrar*; **he ~ted her in the crowd** la vio *or* (AmL tb) la ubicó entre el gentío **2** (mark) (*usu pass*) manchar

spot check *n*: control o inspección realizada al azar

spotless /ˈspɑːtləs ‖ˈspɒtlɪs/ *adj* ⟨clothes⟩ impecable; ⟨house⟩ limpísimo; ⟨reputation/record⟩ intachable

spotlight /ˈspɑːtlaɪt ‖ˈspɒtlaɪt/ *n* (in theater) foco *m*; (on building) reflector *m*

spotted /ˈspɑːtəd ‖ˈspɒtɪd/ *adj* ⟨tie/material⟩ de *or* a lunares *or* motas

spotty /ˈspɑːti ‖ˈspɒti/ *adj* **-tier, -tiest** (BrE) ⟨skin⟩ lleno de granos; ⟨youth⟩ con la cara llena de granos

spouse /spaʊs/ *n* (frml or hum) cónyuge *mf* (frml)

spout¹ /spaʊt/ *n* **(a)** (of teapot, kettle) pico *m*, pitorro *m* (Esp) **(b)** (pipe — on gutter) canalón *m*; (— on fountain, gargoyle) caño *m* **(c)** (jet) chorro *m*

spout² *vt* ⟨oil/liquid⟩ arrojar *or* expulsar chorros de
■ ~ *vi* ⟨liquid⟩ salir* a chorros; ⟨whale⟩ expulsar chorros de agua

sprain¹ /spreɪn/ *n* esguince *m*, distensión *f*

sprain² *vt* hacerse* un esguince en, distenderse*

sprang /spræŋ/ *past of* SPRING¹

sprawl¹ /sprɔːl/ *vi* ⟨person⟩ sentarse* (*or* tumbarse *etc*) de forma poco elegante

sprawl² *n* (of built-up area) expansión *f*

spray¹ /spreɪ/ *vt* **(a)** ⟨liquid⟩ pulverizar*, aplicar* con atomizador; ⟨paint⟩ aplicar* con pistola pulverizadora **(b)** ⟨plants⟩ rociar* (con atomizador)

spray² *n* **1 (a)** (fine drops) rocío *m* **(b)** (liquid in spray form) espray *m*; (before *n*) ⟨deodorant/polish⟩ en aerosol, en espray, en atomizador **(c)** (implement) rociador *m* **2** (bunch) ramillete *m*

spread¹ /spred/ (*past & past p* **spread**) *vt* **1** (extend) ⟨arms/legs⟩ extender*; ⟨map/sails/ wings⟩ desplegar*; **you can ~ the cost over five years** se puede pagar el costo a lo largo de cinco años **2 (a)** ⟨paint/glue⟩ extender*; ⟨seeds/sand⟩ esparcir*; **to ~ butter on a piece of toast** untar una tostada con mantequilla **(b)** ⟨knowledge/ news⟩ difundir*; ⟨influence⟩ extender*; ⟨rumor⟩ hacer* correr; ⟨disease⟩ propagar*; ⟨fear⟩ sembrar*; ⟨ideas/culture⟩ diseminar
■ ~ *vi* **1** ⟨disease⟩ propagarse*; ⟨liquid/fire⟩ extenderse*; ⟨ideas/culture⟩ diseminarse*; ⟨panic/fear⟩ cundir; ⟨influence/revolt⟩ extenderse* **2** (extend in space, time) extenderse* **3** ⟨paint⟩ extenderse*; ⟨butter⟩ untarse
■ **spread out** [*v* + *adv*] **(a)** (move apart) ⟨troops⟩ desplegarse* **(b)** (extend) extenderse*

spread² *n* **1** (diffusion — of disease) propagación *f*; (— of ideas) difusión *f*, diseminación *f*; (— of fire) propagación *f* **2** (of wings, sails) envergadura *f* **3** (Culin) **(a)** (meal) (colloq) festín *m*, banquete *m* **(b)** (paste) pasta para extender sobre pan, tostadas *etc* **4** (Journ, Print): **it was advertised in a full-page ~** venía anunciado a plana entera

spread-: ~-eagled /ˈspredˈiːgəld/ *adj* con los brazos y piernas abiertos; **~sheet** *n* hoja *f* de cálculo; (before *n*) **~sheet program** hoja *f* electrónica

spree /spriː/ *n*: **to go on a shopping ~** ir* de expedición a las tiendas

---

sprig /sprɪg/ n ramito m

sprightly /'spraɪtli/ adj **-lier, -liest** ⟨person⟩ lleno de brío; ⟨walk/step⟩ ágil

spring¹ /sprɪŋ/ (past **sprang** or (esp AmE) **sprung**; past p **sprung**) vi [1] (leap) saltar; **to ~ into action** entrar en acción [2] (a) (liter) «stream» surgir*, nacer*; «shoots» brotar (b) **to ~ FROM sth** «ideas/doubts» surgir* DE algo; «problem» provenir* DE algo
■ **~** vt (a) (produce suddenly): **to ~ a surprise on sb** darle* una sorpresa a algn (b) **to ~ a leak** empezar* a hacer agua
■ **spring up** [v + adv] «stores/housing estates» surgir*; «plant» brotar; «wind» levantarse

spring² n [1] (season) primavera f; **in (the) ~** en primavera; (before n) «weather/showers» primaveral [2] (Geog) manantial m, fuente f [3] (jump) salto m, brinco m [4] (a) (in watch, toy) resorte m; (in mattress) muelle m, resorte m (AmL) (b) (elasticity) (no pl) elasticidad f

spring: **~board** n trampolín m; **~clean** /'sprɪŋ'kliːn/ vt hacer* limpieza general; **~cleaning** /'sprɪŋ'kliːnɪŋ/ n (no pl) limpieza f general; **~ onion** n (BrE) cebolleta f, cebollino m; **~time** n primavera f

springy /'sprɪŋi/ adj **-gier, -giest** ⟨mattress/grass⟩ mullido; ⟨floor⟩ elástico

sprinkle /'sprɪŋkəl/ vt (a) (scatter) **to ~ sth ON sth: to ~ water on the plants** rociar* las plantas con agua; **to ~ sugar on sth** espolvorear algo con azúcar (b) (cover) **to ~ sth WITH sth: ~ the board with flour** espolvorea la tabla con harina

sprinkler /'sprɪŋklər ‖ 'sprɪŋklə(r)/ n (a) (garden **~**) aspersor m (b) (for firefighting) (usu pl) rociador m; (before n) **~ system** sistema m de rociadores

sprint¹ /sprɪnt/ n (a) (fast run) (e)sprint m (b) (short race) (Sport) carrera f corta

sprint² vi (a) (Sport) (e)sprintar (b) (run fast): **I ~ed after him** salí corriendo tras él a toda velocidad

sprout¹ /spraʊt/ vt ⟨leaves/shoots⟩ echar
■ **~** vi «plant» echar retoños, retoñar; «leaf» brotar, salir*; «seeds» germinar

sprout² n (a) (Brussels **~**) col f or (AmS) repollito m de Bruselas (b) (shoot) brote m

spruce¹ /spruːs/ n (tree) picea f, abeto m falso

spruce² adj **sprucer, sprucest** ⟨appearance⟩ cuidado, acicalado; ⟨garden⟩ cuidado, arreglado
■ **spruce up** [v + o + adv, v + adv + o] ⟨garden/room⟩ arreglar

sprung /sprʌŋ/ past p & (esp AmE) past of SPRING¹

spry /spraɪ/ adj **-er, -est** lleno de vida, dinámico

spud /spʌd/ n (colloq) papa f or (Esp) patata f

spun¹ /spʌn/ past & past p of SPIN²

spun² adj ⟨silk/cotton⟩ hilado

spur¹ /spɜːr ‖ spɜː(r)/ n (a) (Equ) espuela f; **on the ~ of the moment** sin pensarlo (b) (stimulus) acicate m

spur² vt **-rr-** (a) (Equ) ⟨horse⟩ espolear (b) **~** (on) ⟨person/team⟩ estimular

spurious /'spjʊəriəs ‖ 'spjʊəriəs/ adj ⟨document⟩ falso, espurio; ⟨argument⟩ falaz, espurio

spurn /spɜːrn ‖ spɜːn/ vt desdeñar, rechazar*

spurt¹ /spɜːrt ‖ spɜːt/ n (a) (of speed, activity) racha f; **to put on a ~** acelerar (b) (jet) chorro m

spurt² vi «liquid/steam» salir* a chorros

spy¹ /spaɪ/ n (pl **spies**) espía mf; (before n) ⟨story⟩ de espías, de espionaje; **~ ring** red f de espionaje

spy² **spies, spying, spied** vi espiar*; **to ~ ON sb** espiar* a algn
■ **~** vt descubrir*, ver*

sq adj (= square): **220 ~ m** 220 m²

Sq (= **Square**) Pza.

squabble /'skwɑːbəl ‖ 'skwɒbəl/ vi pelear(se), reñir*

squad /skwɑːd ‖ skwɒd/ n (a) (Mil) pelotón m; (of workmen) cuadrilla f (b) (of policemen) brigada f, **drug ~** brigada f antidroga (c) (Sport) equipo m

squad car n (AmE) coche m or (AmL tb) auto m patrulla, patrullero m (CS, Per)

squadron /'skwɑːdrən ‖ 'skwɒdrən/ n (Mil, Aviat) escuadrón m; (Naut) escuadra f

squalid /'skwɑːləd ‖ 'skwɒlɪd/ adj (a) (dirty) ⟨existence/house⟩ miserable (b) (sordid) ⟨story/business⟩ sórdido

squall /skwɔːl/ n borrasca f, turbión m

squalor /'skwɑːlər ‖ 'skwɒlə(r)/ n miseria f

squander /'skwɑːndər ‖ 'skwɒndə(r)/ vt ⟨money⟩ despilfarrar; ⟨opportunity⟩ desaprovechar

square¹ /skwer ‖ skweə(r)/ n [1] (a) (shape) cuadrado m; (in fabric design) cuadro m (b) (on chessboard) casilla f, escaque m; (in crossword) casilla f, **to go back to ~ one** volver* a empezar desde cero [2] (in town, city) plaza f [3] (Math) cuadrado m

square² adj **squarer, squarest** [1] (a) ⟨box/table/block⟩ cuadrado; **the room is 15 feet ~** la habitación mide 15 (pies por 15 (pies)) (b) (having right angles) ⟨corner/edges⟩ en ángulo recto (c) ⟨face⟩ cuadrado; ⟨jaw⟩ angular [2] (Math) (before n) ⟨yard/mile⟩ cuadrado [3] (a) (fair, honest): **he'll give you a ~ deal** no te va a engañar (b) (large and wholesome) (before n) ⟨meal⟩ decente

square³ vt [1] (make square) ⟨angle/side⟩ cuadrar [2] (Math) elevar al cuadrado [3] (a) (settle, make even) ⟨debts/accounts⟩ pagar*, saldar (b) (reconcile) ⟨facts/principles⟩ conciliar
■ **~** vi «ideas/arguments» concordar*
■ **square up** [v + adv] (settle debts) (colloq) **to ~ up** (**WITH sb**) arreglar cuentas (CON algn)

square root n raíz f cuadrada

squash¹ /skwɑːʃ ‖ skwɒʃ/ n [1] (Sport) squash m [2] (drink) (BrE) refresco a base de extractos; **orange ~** naranjada f [3] (Bot, Culin) nombre genérico de varios tipos de calabaza y zapallo

squash² vt [1] (a) (crush) ⟨fruit/insect⟩ aplastar (b) (squeeze): **to ~ sth/sb in** meter algo/a algn (apretando) [2] (suppress, silence) (colloq) ⟨protests/rumors⟩ acallar
■ **~** vi (+ adv compl): **we all ~ed into his study** nos metimos todos en su despacho

squashy /'skwɑːʃi ‖ 'skwɒʃi/ adj **-shier, -shiest** ⟨fruit⟩ blando; ⟨ground⟩ húmedo y mullido

squat¹ /skwɑːt ‖skwɒt/ vi -tt- ① (crouch)
agacharse, ponerse* en cuclillas ② (in building, on
land) ocupar un inmueble ajeno sin autorización

squat² adj -tt- ⟨person⟩ rechoncho y bajo;
⟨building/church⟩ achaparrado

squatter /'skwɑːtər ‖'skwɒtə(r)/ n (in building)
ocupante mf ilegal, ocupa or okupa mf (Esp),
paracaidista mf (Méx)

squawk¹ /skwɔːk/ n (of bird) graznido m

squawk² vi «bird» graznar; «person» chillar

squeak¹ /skwiːk/ n (of animal, person) chillido m;
(of hinge) chirrido m; (of shoes) crujido m

squeak² vi «animal/person» chillar; «hinge»
chirriar*; «shoes» crujir

squeaky /'skwiːki/ adj -kier, kiest ⟨hinge/
pen⟩ chirriante; ⟨voice⟩ chillón, de pito

squeal¹ /skwiːl/ vi (a) (make noise) «person/
animal» chillar; «brakes/tires» chirriar* (b)
(inform) (colloq) cantar (fam), chivarse (Esp fam),
sapear (Ven fam)

squeal² n (of animal) chillido m; (of person) grito
m, chillido m; (of brakes, tires) chirrido m

squeamish /'skwiːmɪʃ/ adj impresionable,
aprensivo

squeeze¹ /skwiːz/ n ① (a) (application of
pressure) apretón m; he gave her hand a ∼ le dio
un apretón de manos (b) (restrictions): a credit ∼
una restricción crediticia (c) (confined, restricted condition) (colloq) (no pl): it will
be a (tight) ∼ vamos (or van etc) a estar
apretados

squeeze² vt (a) (press) ⟨tube/pimple⟩ apretar*,
espichar (Col); ⟨lemon⟩ exprimir; to ∼ a cloth
(out) retorcer* un trapo (b) (extract) ⟨liquid/juice⟩
extraer*, sacar*; he tried to ∼ more money out of
them trató de sacarles más dinero (c) (force, fit)
meter; I can ∼ you in tomorrow morning le puedo
hacer un huequito mañana por la mañana
■ ∼ vi: he ∼d in through the hole se metió por el
agujero

squelch /skweltʃ/ vi «shoes/hooves» hacer* un
ruido como de succión

squid /skwɪd/ n (pl ∼) calamar m

squiggle /'skwɪgəl/ n garabato m

squint¹ /skwɪnt/ n bizquera f, estrabismo m

squint² vi (a) (attempting to see) entrecerrar* los
ojos (b) (be cross-eyed) bizquear, torcer* la vista

squire /skwaɪr ‖'skwaɪə(r)/ n (a) (Hist, Mil)
escudero m (b) (in UK: landowner) señor m

squirm /skwɜːrm ‖skwɜːm/ vi retorcerse*; she
∼ed with embarrassment le dio mucha
vergüenza, no sabía dónde meterse de la
vergüenza

squirrel /skwɜːrl ‖'skwɪrəl/ n ardilla f

squirt¹ /skwɜːrt ‖skwɜːt/ n ① (stream) chorrito
m ② (person) (colloq) mequetrefe m (fam)

squirt² vt ⟨liquid⟩ echar un chorro de
■ ∼ vi «liquid» salir* a chorros

Sr (= Senior) Sr.

Sri Lanka /sriː'lɑːŋkə, ʃriː- ‖srɪˈlæŋkə, ʃrɪ-/ n
Sri Lanka m

St (a) (= Saint) S(an), Sta.; ∼ Thomas Sto.
Tomás **(b)** (= Street) c/

stab¹ /stæb/ n (a) (with knife) puñalada f,

cuchillada f; to have a ∼ at sth intentar algo **(b)**
(sudden sensation): a ∼ of pain una punzada de
dolor

stab² vt -bb- apuñalar, acuchillar; he had been
∼bed to death había muerto apuñalado or
acuchillado

stabbing¹ /'stæbɪŋ/ n apuñalamiento m

stabbing² adj ⟨pain/sensation⟩ punzante

stability /stə'bɪləti/ n estabilidad f

stabilize /'sterbəlaɪz/ vt estabilizar*
■ ∼ vi estabilizarse*

stable¹ /'sterbəl/ adj -bler, -blest (a) (firm,
steady) estable **(b)** (Psych) equilibrado

stable² n (often pl) (for horses) caballeriza f,
cuadra f; (for other livestock) establo m

staccato /stə'kɑːtəʊ/ adj (Mus) staccato

stack¹ /stæk/ n (a) (pile) montón m, pila f **(b)**
(many, much) (colloq) (often pl) montón m (fam), pila
f (AmS fam)

stack² vt ∼ (up) amontonar, apilar

stadium /'sterdiəm/ n (pl -diums or -dia
/-diə/) estadio m

staff¹ /stæf ‖stɑːf/ n ① (a) (as group) (+ sing o
pl vb) personal m; the teaching ∼ el personal
docente; a member of ∼ un empleado **(b)** (as
individuals) (BrE) (pl ∼) (+ pl vb) empleados mpl
② (pl staffs or staves /stervz/) (stick) bastón
m; (of bishop) báculo m, cayado m ③ (Mus) ▶
STAVE 2

staff² vt proveer* de personal

staffroom /'stæfruːm, -ruːm ‖'stɑːfruːm, -rʊm/
n (BrE) sala f de profesores

stag /stæg/ n ciervo m, venado m

stage¹ /sterdʒ/ n ① (a) (platform) tablado m; (in
theater) escenario m; (before n) ∼ door entrada f
de artistas **(b)** (medium, profession) the ∼ el teatro;
(before n) ∼ name nombre m artístico ② (in
development, activity) fase f, etapa f; at some ∼ en
algún momento

stage² vt ① (a) ⟨event⟩ organizar*, montar;
⟨strike/demonstration⟩ hacer*; ⟨attack⟩ llevar a
cabo; ⟨coup⟩ dar* **(b)** (engineer, arrange) arreglar,
orquestar ② (Theat) ⟨play⟩ poner* en escena

stage: ∼coach n diligencia f; ∼ fright n
miedo m a salir a escena; ∼hand n tramoyista
mf; ∼manage vt ⟨event⟩ orquestar, arreglar; ∼
manager n director, -tora m,f de escena

stagger /'stægər ‖'stægə(r)/ vi tambalearse
■ ∼ vt ① (amaze) dejar estupefacto ② ⟨shifts/
payments⟩ escalonar

staggering /'stægərɪŋ/ adj asombroso

stagnant /'stægnənt/ adj estancado

stagnate /'stægneɪt ‖stæg'neɪt/ vi «water/
economy» estancarse*; «person» anquilosarse

stag: ∼ night n (for men only) ▶ ∼ PARTY b; ∼
party n (a) (before wedding) despedida f de soltero
(b) (all-male celebration) fiesta f para hombres,
noche f de cuates (Méx)

staid /steɪd/ adj -er, -est serio, formal;
⟨clothes⟩ serio, sobrio; (pej) aburrido

stain¹ /steɪn/ n (a) (dirty mark) mancha f **(b)**
(dye) tintura f, tinte m **(c)** (on character) mancha f

stain² vt (a) ⟨clothes/skin⟩ manchar **(b)** (dye)
⟨wood⟩ teñir*
■ ∼ vi manchar

S

stained glass /steɪnd/ n vidrio m or cristal m de colores; (before n) ~ ~ **window** vitral m, vidriera f (de colores)

stainless steel /'steɪnləs ‖'steɪnlɪs/ n acero m inoxidable

stain remover n quitamanchas m

stair /ster ‖stea(r)/ n **(a) stairs** pl (flight of stairs, stairway) escalera(s) f(pl) **(b)** (single step) escalón m, peldaño m

stair: ~**case,** ~**way** n escalera(s) f(pl); ~**well** n caja f or hueco m or (Méx) cubo m de la escalera

stake¹ /steɪk/ n **1** (pole) estaca f **2 (a)** (bet) apuesta f; **to be at a** ~ estar* en juego **(b)** (interest): **to have a** ~ **in a company** tener* participación or intereses en una compañía

stake² vt **1** (risk) ‹money/reputation› jugarse* **2 (a)** (mark with stakes) marcar* con estacas, estacar*; **the government was quick to** ~ **its claim** el gobierno se apresuró a reclamar su parte **(b)** ‹tree/plant› arrodrigar*

stalactite /stə'læktaɪt ‖'stæləktaɪt/ n estalactita f

stalagmite /stə'lægmaɪt ‖'stæləgmaɪt/ n estalagmita f

stale /steɪl/ adj **staler, stalest** ‹bread› no fresco; ‹butter/cheese› rancio; ‹beer› pasado; ‹air› viciado; ‹joke› añejo, viejo; ‹ideas› trasnochado

stalemate /'steɪlmeɪt/ n (in chess) tablas fpl (por ahogar al rey); **to be at a** ~ estar* en un punto muerto

stalk¹ /stɔːk/ n (of plant) tallo m; (of leaf, flower) pedúnculo m, tallo m; (of fruit) rabillo m

stalk² vt acechar
■ ~ vi: **to** ~ **off** irse* ofendido/indignado

stall¹ /stɔːl/ n **1** (in market) puesto m, tenderete m **2 stalls** pl (in theater, movie house) (BrE) platea f, patio m de butacas **3** (in stable) compartimiento m

stall² vi **1** ‹engine/car› pararse, calarse (Esp), atascarse* (Méx) **2** (play for time) (colloq): **quit** ~**ing** no andes con rodeos or con evasivas
■ ~ vt **1** ‹engine/car› parar, calar (Esp), atascar* (Méx) **2** (delay) (colloq) entretener*

stallion /'stæljən/ n semental m

stalwart /'stɔːlwərt ‖'stɔːlwət/ adj ‹supporter› incondicional, fiel

stamina /'stæmənə ‖'stæmɪnə/ n resistencia f

stammer¹ /'stæmər ‖'stæmə(r)/ n tartamudeo m

stammer² vi tartamudear

stamp¹ /stæmp/ n **1** (postage ~) sello m, estampilla f (AmL), timbre m (Méx); (before n) ~ **collecting** filatelia f; ~ **collector** coleccionista mf de sellos (or estampillas etc), filatelista mf **2 (a)** (instrument) sello m **(b)** (printed mark) sello m **3** (character) impronta f; **she left her** ~ **on the institute** dejó su impronta en el instituto

stamp² vt **1** (with foot) ‹ground› dar* una patada en; **to** ~ **one's foot** dar* una patada en el suelo **2** ‹letter/parcel› franquear, ponerle* sellos (or estampillas etc) a, estampillar (AmL), timbrar (Méx); **a** ~**ed addressed envelope** un sobre franqueado or (AmL tb) estampillado or (Méx) timbrado con su dirección

3 (a) ‹passport/ticket› sellar **(b)** ‹coin› acuñar
■ ~ vi «person» dar* patadas en el suelo; «horse» piafar; **he** ~**ed on the spider** le dio un pisotón a la araña
■ **stamp out** [v + o + adv, v + adv + o] **(a)** ‹fire› apagar* (con los pies) **(b)** (suppress) ‹resistance› aplastar; ‹rebellion› sofocar*; ‹crime› erradicar*

stampede¹ /stæm'piːd/ n estampida f

stampede² vi salir* en estampida

stance /stæns ‖stɑːns/ n postura f

stand¹ /stænd/ n **1 (a)** (position) lugar m **(b)** (attitude) postura f **(c)** (resistance) resistencia f; **to make a** ~ **against** sth oponer* resistencia a algo **2 (a)** (base) pie m, base f **(b)** (for coats, hats) perchero m **3** (at fair, exhibition) stand m, caseta f; **newspaper** ~ puesto m de periódicos; **a hot-dog** ~ (esp AmE) un puesto de perritos calientes **4** (for spectators) (often pl) tribuna f **5** (witness box) (AmE) estrado m

stand² (past & past p **stood**) vi **1 (a)** (be, remain upright) «person» estar* de pie, estar* parado (AmL) **(b)** (rise) «person» levantarse, ponerse* de pie, pararse (AmL); **her hair stood on end** se le pusieron los pelos de punta, se le pararon los pelos (AmL); see also STAND UP **2** (move, take up position) ponerse*, pararse (AmL) ~ **over there** ponte or (AmL tb) párate allí; **to** ~ **aside** hacerse* a un lado; **to** ~ **on one's head** pararse de cabeza (AmL), hacer* el pino (Esp) **3 (a)** (be situated, located): **a church stood here long ago** hace mucho tiempo aquí había una iglesia; **I won't** ~ **in your way** no seré yo quien te lo impida **(b)** (hold position): **where do you** ~ **on this issue?** ¿cuál es tu posición en cuanto a ese problema?; **you never know where you** ~ **with him** con él uno nunca sabe a qué atenerse **(c)** (be mounted, fixed): **a hut** ~**ing on wooden piles** una choza construida sobre pilotes de madera **4 (a)** (stop, remain still) «person»: **they stood and stared** se quedaron mirando; **time stood still** el tiempo se detuvo **(b)** (Culin) «batter/water»: **leave to** ~ dejar reposar **(c)** (survive, last): **the tower is still** ~**ing** la torre sigue en pie **5** (remain unchanged, valid) «law/agreement» seguir* vigente; **the offer still** ~s la oferta sigue en pie **6 (a)** (be currently): **as things** ~ tal (y) como están las cosas **(b)** (be likely to): **to** ~ **to + INF**: **he** ~**s to lose a fortune** puede llegar a perder una fortuna; **what does she** ~ **to gain out of this?** ¿qué es lo que puede ganar con esto ? **7** (for office, election) (BrE) presentarse (como candidato)
■ ~ vt **1** (place) poner*; (carefully, precisely) colocar* **2 (a)** (tolerate, bear) (with CAN, CAN'T, WON'T) ‹pain/noise› aguantar, soportar; **I can't** ~ **him** no lo aguanto or soporto; **I can't** ~ **it any longer!** ¡no puedo más!; **she can't** ~ **being interrupted** no soporta que la interrumpan **(b)** (withstand) ‹heat/strain› soportar
■ **stand back** [v + adv] (move away) **to** ~ **back** (FROM sth) apartarse (DE algo)
■ **stand by** [v + adv] **1 (a)** (remain uninvolved) mantenerse* al margen; **people just stood by and did nothing** la gente estaba allí mirando sin hacer nada **(b)** (be at readiness) «army/troops» estar* en estado de alerta **2** [v + prep + o] **(a)** ‹promise› mantener*; ‹decision› atenerse* a **(b)** (support) ‹friend› apoyar ·····✦

■ **stand down** [v + adv] (relinquish position) retirarse; (resign) renunciar, dimitir

■ **stand for** [v + prep + o] (a) (represent) «*initials/symbol*» significar*; CTI ~s for ... CTI son las siglas de ...; **he has betrayed everything he once stood for** ha traicionado todo aquello con lo que solía identificar (b) (put up with) (*usu with neg*) consentir*

■ **stand in** [v + adv] to ~ in FOR sb sustituir* a algn

■ **stand out** [v + adv] (a) (project) to ~ out (FROM sth) sobresalir* (DE algo) (b) (be conspicuous, contrast) sobresalir*, destacar(se)*; «*color*» resaltar

■ **stand up** ①[v + adv] (a) (get up) ponerse* de pie, levantarse, pararse (AmL) (b) (be, remain standing): ~ **up straight** ponte derecho (c) (endure, withstand wear) resistir; **to ~ up TO sth** (*to cold/pressure*) resistir *or* soportar algo; *see also* STAND UP TO
② [v + o + adv] (a) (set upright) poner* de pie, levantar (b) (not keep appointment with) (colloq) dejar plantado a (fam)

■ **stand up for** [v + adv + prep + o] defender*; **I can ~ up for myself** me puedo defender solo

■ **stand up to** [v + adv + prep + o] (*person/threats*) hacerle* frente a; *see also* STAND UP 1C

standard[1] /ˈstændərd ‖ ˈstændəd/ n ① (a) (level) nivel m; (quality) calidad f; ~ **of living** nivel m *or* estándar m de vida (b) (norm): **she sets very high ~s** exige un estándar *or* nivel muy alto; **the product was below ~** el producto no era de la calidad requerida (c) (official measure) estándar m ② (a) (yardstick) criterio m, parámetro m (b) **standards** pl (moral principles) principios mpl ③ (flag, emblem) estandarte m

standard[2] adj ① (normal) «*size*» estándar *adj inv*, normal; «*model*» (Auto) estándar *adj inv*, de serie; «*procedure*» habitual; «*reaction*» típico; ~ **rate** tarifa f normal ② (officially established) «*weight/measure*» estándar *adj inv*, oficial; ~ **time** hora f oficial

standardization /ˌstændərdəˈzeɪʃən ‖ ˌstændədaɪˈzeɪʃən/ n estandarización f

standardize /ˈstændərdaɪz ‖ ˈstændədaɪz/ vt estandarizar*

standard lamp n (BrE) lámpara f de pie

standby[1] /ˈstændbaɪ/ n (pl **-bys**) (a) (thing one can turn to): **frozen meals are a useful ~** las comidas congeladas son muy socorridas (b) (state of readiness): **to be on ~** «*police/squadron*» estar* en estado de alerta (c) (Aviat) stand-by m

standby[2] adj (before n) (a) (ready for emergency) de emergencia; **to be on ~ duty** estar* de guardia (b) (Aviat) «*passenger/ticket/fare*» stand-by *adj inv*

stand-in /ˈstændɪn/ n suplente *mf*; (Cin) doble *mf*

standing[1] /ˈstændɪŋ/ n (a) (position) posición f; (prestige) prestigio m (b) (duration): **friends of more than 20 years' ~** amigos desde hace más de 20 años

standing[2] adj (before n, no comp) (a) (permanent) permanente; ~ **charge** cuota f fija; (for utilities) cuota f abono; **it's a ~ joke that he never pays for a single drink** tiene fama de no invitar nunca a una copa (b) (upright, not seated) «*passenger*» de pie, parado (AmL)

standing order n (a) (with bank) (BrE) orden f permanente de pago (b) (with supplier) pedido m fijo

stand: ~**off** n (AmE) (a) (tie, draw) empate m (b) (deadlock) callejón m sin salida; ~**point** n punto m de vista; ~**still** n (no pl): **to be at a ~still** «*traffic*» estar* paralizado; **to come to a ~still** «*vehicle*» parar; «*city/factory*» quedar paralizado

stank /stæŋk/ *past of* STINK[2]

staple[1] /ˈsteɪpəl/ n ① (for fastening paper, cloth etc) grapa f, ganchito m, corchete m (Chi) ② (a) (basic food) alimento m básico (b) (principal product) producto m principal

staple[2] adj «*food/ingredient*» básico; «*industry*» principal; **rice is their ~ diet** se alimentan principalmente a base de arroz

staple[3] vt grapar, engrapar (AmL), corchetear (Chi)

stapler /ˈsteɪplər ‖ ˈsteɪplə(r)/ n grapadora f, engrapadora f (AmL), corchetera f (Chi)

star[1] /stɑːr ‖ stɑː(r)/ n ① (in sky) estrella f; (Astrol, Astron) astro m; (before n) ~ **sign** signo m del zodíaco ② (symbol) estrella f; (asterisk) asterisco m; **a four-~ hotel** un hotel de cuatro estrellas; **four-~ petrol** (BrE) gasolina f *or* (RPI) nafta f súper, bencina f especial (Andes) ③ (celebrity) estrella f

star[2] **-rr-** vt: **the famous film which ~red Bogart and Bergman** la famosa película que tuvo como protagonistas a Bogart y Bergman; **'2005', ~ring Mike Kirnon** '2005', con (la actuación estelar de) Mike Kirnon
■ ~ vi: **to ~ in a film** protagonizar* una película

starboard[1] /ˈstɑːrbərd ‖ ˈstɑːbəd/ n estribor m

starboard[2] adj (before n) de estribor

starch /stɑːrtʃ ‖ stɑːtʃ/ n (a) (in food, for clothes) almidón m (b) (starchy food) fécula f, almidón m

starchy /ˈstɑːrtʃi ‖ ˈstɑːtʃi/ adj **-chier, -chiest** «*diet*» a base de féculas *or* de almidones

stardom /ˈstɑːrdəm ‖ ˈstɑːdəm/ n estrellato m

stare[1] /ster ‖ steə(r)/ vi mirar (fijamente); **to ~ AT sth/sb** mirar algo/a algn fijamente

stare[2] n mirada f (fija)

starfish /ˈstɑːrfɪʃ ‖ ˈstɑːfɪʃ/ n (pl **-fish**) estrella f de mar

stark[1] /stɑːrk ‖ stɑːk/ adj **-er, -est** «*landscape*» agreste; «*truth*» escueto; «*realism*» descarnado

stark[2] adv: ~ **naked** completamente desnudo

starlet /ˈstɑːrlət ‖ ˈstɑːlɪt/ n starlet(te) f (*joven actriz que aspira al estrellato*)

starling /ˈstɑːrlɪŋ ‖ ˈstɑːlɪŋ/ n estornino m

starry /ˈstɑːri/ adj **-rier, -riest** estrellado

starry-eyed /ˌstɑːriˈaɪd/ adj (a) (full of illusions) «*person*» iluso, soñador (b) (dreamy): **she gazed at him all ~** lo miraba arrobada

AmC	Central America	Arg	Argentina	Cu	Cuba
AmL	Latin America	Bol	Bolivia	Ec	Ecuador
AmS	South America	Chi	Chile	Esp	Spain
Andes	Andean Region	CS	Southern Cone	Méx	Mexico

Per	Peru
RPI	River Plate Area
Ur	Uruguay
Ven	Venezuela

star: S∼s and Stripes n the S∼s and Stripes
la bandera de las barras y las estrellas;
∼-**spangled** /'stɑːr,spæŋgəld ‖'stɑː,spæŋgəld/
adj (liter) ⟨sky/heavens⟩ tachonado de estrellas
(liter); **S∼-Spangled Banner** n the S∼
Spangled Banner el himno de las barras y las
estrellas (himno nacional de EEUU)

start¹ /stɑːrt ‖stɑːt/ n **1** (a) (beginning)
principio m, comienzo m; from ∼ to finish del
principio al fin; **to make a** ∼ (ON sth) empezar*
(algo); **to make an early** ∼ empezar* temprano;
(on a journey) salir* temprano **(b) for a** ∼ (as
linker) para empezar **2** (Sport) **(a)** (of race) salida
f **(b)** (lead, advantage) ventaja f **3** (jump): **to give
sb a** ∼ darle* or pegarle* un susto a algn; **I woke
up with a** ∼ me desperté sobresaltado

start² vt **1** (begin) empezar*, comenzar*; **I** ∼
work at eight empiezo a trabajar a las ocho; **to** ∼
-**ING, to** ∼ **to** + INF empezar* A + INF
2 (cause to begin) ⟨race⟩ dar* comienzo a, largar*
(CS, Méx); ⟨fire/epidemic⟩ provocar*; ⟨argument/
fight⟩ empezar*; ⟨war⟩ «incident» desencadenar
3 (establish) ⟨business⟩ abrir*; ⟨organization⟩
fundar
4 (cause to operate) ⟨engine/dishwasher⟩
encender*, prender (AmL); ⟨car⟩ arrancar*
■ ∼ vi
I 1 (a) (begin) empezar*, comenzar*; **to get** ∼**ed**
empezar*, comenzar*; **to** ∼ **BY** -ING empezar* POR
+ INF; ∼**ing (from) next January** a partir del
próximo mes de enero **(b) to** ∼ **with** (as linker)
primero, para empezar
2 (originate) empezar*, originarse
3 (set out) (+ adv compl): **to** ∼ **back** emprender
el regreso; **we** ∼ **from the hotel at six** salimos del
hotel a las seis
4 (begin to operate) «car» arrancar*
II (move suddenly) dar* un respingo; (be frightened)
asustarse, sobresaltarse
■ **start off 1** [v + adv] **(a)** ▶ START OUT A **(b)**
(begin moving) arrancar* **(c)** (begin) empezar*
2 [v + o + adv, v + adv + o] (begin) ⟨discussion/
concert⟩ empezar*
3 [v + o + adv] (get sb started): **I'll do the first one,
just to** ∼ **you off** yo haré el primero, para
ayudarte a empezar
■ **start out** [v + adv] **(a)** (set out) salir* **(b)** (in life,
career) empezar* **(c)** (begin) **to** ∼ **out (BY)** -ING: **we**
∼**ed out (by) thinking it would be easy**
empezamos pensando que sería fácil
■ **start over** (AmE) [v + adv] [v + o + adv]
volver* a empezar
■ **start up 1** [v + adv] **(a)** ▶ START vi I 4 **(b)**
(begin business) empezar*
2 [v + o + adv, v + adv + o] **(a)** ⟨engine/car/
machinery⟩ arrancar*, poner* en marcha **(b)**
⟨business⟩ montar **(c)** ⟨conversation⟩ entablar;
⟨discussion⟩ empezar*

starter /'stɑːrtər ‖'stɑːtə(r)/ n **1** (Culin) entrada
f, primer plato m, entrante m (Esp) **2** (Auto) (∼
motor) motor m de arranque

starting /'stɑːrtɪŋ/**:** ∼ **line** n línea f de salida;
∼ **point** n ∼ **point** (FOR sth) punto m de partida
(DE/PARA algo)

startle /'stɑːrtl ‖'stɑːtl/ vt sobresaltar, asustar

startling /'stɑːrtlɪŋ ‖'stɑːtlɪŋ/ adj **(a)** (surprising)
asombroso; ⟨similarity/coincidence⟩
extraordinario **(b)** (alarming) ⟨report/increase⟩
alarmante

starvation /stɑːr'veɪʃən ‖stɑː'veɪʃən/ n
hambre f‡, inanición f

starve /stɑːrv ‖stɑːv/ vt **(a)** (deny food) privar
de comida a; **I'm** ∼**d** (AmE colloq) me muero de
hambre **(b)** (deprive) **to** ∼ **sth/sb** OR **sth** privar
algo/a algn DE algo
■ ∼ vi (die) morirse* de hambre or de inanición;
(feel hungry) pasar hambre; **I'm starving** (BrE colloq)
me muero de hambre

starving /'stɑːrvɪŋ ‖'stɑːvɪŋ/ adj hambriento,
famélico

stash /stæʃ/ vt ∼ (**away**) (colloq) (hide) esconder;
(save) ir* ahorrando

state¹ /steɪt/ n
I 1 (a) (nation) estado m; (before n) ∼ **visit** visita
f oficial **(b)** (division of country) estado m; **the S∼s**
los Estados Unidos
2 (Govt) estado m; (before n) (esp BrE) ⟨control/
funding⟩ estatal; ∼ **school** escuela f pública or
estatal
3 (pomp): **to lie in** ∼ yacer* en capilla ardiente
II (condition) estado m; ∼ **of war/emergency**
estado de guerra/emergencia; ∼ **of mind** estado
de ánimo; **I was in no (fit)** ∼ **to make a decision**
no estaba en condiciones de tomar una decisión;
the kitchen is in a ∼ (colloq) la cocina está hecha
un asco (fam)

state² vt «person» ⟨facts/case⟩ exponer*;
⟨problem⟩ plantear; ⟨name/address⟩ (in writing)
escribir*; (orally) decir*; «law/document»
establecer*; **he** ∼**d that he had seen her there
earlier** afirmó haberla visto antes allí

State Department n (in US) **the** ∼ ∼ el
Departamento de Estado de los EEUU, ≈ el
Ministerio de Asuntos Exteriores or de
Relaciones Exteriores

stately /'steɪtli/ adj majestuoso

stately home n (in UK) casa f solariega

statement /'steɪtmənt/ n **1 (a)** (declaration)
declaración f, afirmación f; **official** ∼ comunicado
m oficial **(b)** (to police, in court) declaración f
2 (bank ∼) estado m or extracto m de cuenta

state: ∼-**of-the-art** /'steɪtəvðiˈɑːrt
‖,steɪtəvðiˈɑːt/ adj último modelo adj inv;
S∼side, ∼**side** adv (AmE colloq) en/a/hacia los
Estados Unidos

statesman /'steɪtsmən/ n (pl -**men** /-mən/)
estadista m, hombre m de estado

static¹ /'stætɪk/ adj **1** ⟨situation⟩ estacionario
2 ⟨electricity⟩ estático

static² n **(a)** (electricity) electricidad f estática
(b) (interference) estática f

station¹ /'steɪʃən/ n **1 (a)** (Rail) estación f **(b)**
(bus ∼) estación f or terminal f de autobuses
2 (place of operations) **research** ∼ centro m de
investigación; see also FIRE STATION, POLICE
STATION etc **3** (TV) canal m; (Rad) emisora f or
(AmL tb) estación f (de radio)

station² vt **(a)** (position) ⟨sentries⟩ apostar* **(b)**
(post) (usu pass) ⟨personnel⟩ destinar; ⟨fleet/
troops⟩ emplazar*

stationary /'steɪʃənəri ‖'steɪʃənri/ adj ⟨object/
vehicle⟩ estacionario

stationery /'steɪʃənəri ‖'steɪʃənəri/ n **(a)**
(writing materials) artículos mpl de papelería or de
escritorio **(b)** (writing paper) papel m y sobres mpl
de carta

S

station: ~ **house** n (AmE) (a) (police station) comisaría f (b) ▶ FIRE STATION; ~**master** n jefe, -fa m, f de estación; ~ **wagon** n (AmE) ranchera f, (coche m) familiar m, camioneta f (AmL)

statistic /stə'tɪstɪk/ n estadística f; **the** ~**s show that ...** las estadísticas demuestran que ...

statistical /stə'tɪstɪkəl/ adj estadístico

statistics /stə'tɪstɪks/ n (+ sing vb) estadística f

statue /'stætʃu; II'stætju:, 'stætʃu:/ n estatua f

stature /'stætʃər II'stætʃə(r)/ n (a) (status) talla f (b) (height) (frml) estatura f, talla f

status /'stætəs II'steɪtəs/ n (pl -**tuses**) (a) (category, situation): **the group has no official** ~ el grupo no está oficialmente reconocido como tal; **financial** ~ situación f económica (b) (social ~) posición f social, estatus m (c) (kudos) estatus m; (before n) ~ **symbol** símbolo m de estatus

status quo /kwəʊ/ n statu quo m

statute /'stætʃu:t II'stætju:t, 'stætʃu:t/ n ley f

statutory /'stætʃu:tɔ:ri II'stætʃʊtəri, 'stætʃu:təri/ adj ‹right/obligation› legal; ‹penalty› establecido por la ley

staunch /stɔ:ntʃ/ adj -**er**, -**est** ‹supporter› incondicional; ‹Protestant› acérrimo

stave /steɪv/ n ① (of barrel, hull) duela f ② (Mus) pentagrama m
■ **stave off** [v + o + adv, v + adv + o] ‹defeat/disaster› evitar; ‹danger› conjurar

staves (a) pl of STAFF¹ 2A (b) pl of STAVE

stay¹ /steɪ/ vi ① (a) (in specified place, position) quedarse; ~ **there** quédate ahí; **to** ~ **put** quedarse (in specified state): ~ **still** quédate quieto; **we** ~**ed friends** seguimos siendo amigos ② (a) (remain, not leave) quedarse (b) (reside temporarily) quedarse; (in a hotel etc) hospedarse, alojarse, quedarse; **he's** ~**ing with us over Easter** va a pasar la Semana Santa con nosotros
■ **stay away** [v + adv] (to) ~ **away FROM** sth/sb no acercarse* A algo/algn
■ **stay in** [v + adv] (remain in position) quedarse en su sitio; (remain indoors) quedarse en casa
■ **stay on** [v + adv] (a) (remain in position) «hat/top» quedarse en su sitio (b) (at school, in job) quedarse
■ **stay out** [v + adv] (a) (not come home): **to** ~ **out late** quedarse fuera hasta tarde; **he usually** ~**s out late** normalmente no vuelve hasta tarde (b) (out of doors) quedarse fuera
■ **stay out of** [v + adv + prep + o] (a) (avoid) ‹trouble› no meterse en; ~ **out of the sun** quédate a la sombra (b) (not get involved in) ‹argument› no meterse en
■ **stay up** [v + adv] (a) (not fall or sink) «tent/pole» sostenerse* (b) (not go to bed) quedarse levantado

stay² n ① (time) estadía f (AmL), estancia f (Esp, Méx); **during her** ~ **in hospital** mientras estuvo en el hospital ② (Law): ~ **of execution** suspensión f del cumplimiento de la sentencia

staying power /'steɪɪŋ/ n resistencia f, aguante m

stead /sted/ n: **in sb's** ~ (liter) en lugar de algn; **to stand sb in good** ~ resultarle muy útil a algn

steadfast /'stedfæst II'stedfɑ:st/ adj (liter) ‹refusal› firme, categórico; ‹resolve› inquebrantable

steadily /'stedɪli II'stedɪli/ adv (a) (constantly, gradually) ‹breathe/beat/work› regularmente (b) (incessantly) ‹rain/work› sin cesar, sin parar (c) (not shaking) ‹gaze› fijamente; ‹walk› con paso seguro

steady¹ /'stedi/ adj -**dier**, -**diest** ① (not shaky) ‹gaze› fijo; ‹chair/table/ladder› firme, seguro; **with a** ~ **hand** con pulso firme; **hold the camera** ~ no muevas la cámara ② (a) (constant) ‹rain/speed/pace› constante; ‹flow/stream› continuo (b) (regular) (before n) ‹job› fijo; ‹income› regular; ~ **boyfriend** novio m; ~ **girlfriend** novia f (c) (dependable) ‹person/worker› serio, formal

steady² vt -**dies**, -**dying**, -**died** (a) (make stable) ‹table/ladder› (by holding) sujetar (para que no se mueva) (b) (make calm) calmar, tranquilizar*

steak /steɪk/ n (a) bistec m, filete m, churrasco m (CS), bife m (RPl, Bol) (b) (cut) carne f para filete (or bistec etc)

steal /sti:l/ (past **stole**; past p **stolen**) vt ① ‹object/idea› robar; **to** ~ sth **FROM** sb robarle algo a algn; **to** ~ **a glance at** sth/sb (liter) echar una mirada furtiva a algo/algn ② **stolen** past p ‹money/property› robado
■ ~ vi ① robar ② (go stealthily) (+ adv compl): **to** ~ **away** o **off** escabullirse*; **they stole into the room** entraron en la habitación a hurtadillas

stealth /stelθ/ n sigilo m

stealthy /'stelθi/ adj -**thier**, -**thiest** ‹movement/departure› furtivo; ‹footsteps› sigiloso

steam¹ /sti:m/ n vapor m; **to let off** ~ desahogarse*; **to run out of** ~ perder* ímpetu

steam² vt (Culin) ‹vegetables/rice› cocinar or cocer* al vapor; ‹pudding› cocinar or cocer* al baño (de) María
■ ~ vi (give off steam) echar vapor; «hot food» humear
■ **steam up** [v + adv] «window/glass» empañarse

steam: ~**boat** n vapor m, barco m de or a vapor; ~ **engine** n (a) (Mech Eng) motor m de or a vapor (b) (esp BrE Rail) locomotora f or máquina f de or a vapor

steamer /'sti:mər II'sti:mə(r)/ n ① (Naut) vapor m, buque m or barco m de or a vapor ② (cooking vessel) vaporera f

steam: ~**roller** n apisonadora f, aplanadora f (AmL); ~**ship** n ▶ STEAMER 1

steamy /'sti:mi/ adj -**mier**, -**miest** ‹room/atmosphere› lleno de vapor; ‹window/glass› empañado

steel¹ /sti:l/ n (Metall) acero m

steel² v refl **to** ~ **oneself FOR** sth/**to** + INF armarse de valor PARA algo/PARA + INF

steel wool n lana f de acero, virulana® f (Arg), fibra f metálica (Méx)

steely /'sti:li/ adj -**lier**, -**liest** ‹gaze/expression› duro; ‹determination› férreo

steep¹ /sti:p/ adj -**er**, -**est** ① (a) ‹slope› empinado; ‹drop› brusco; ‹descent› en picada or (Esp) en picado (b) (large) ‹increase/decline› considerable ② (colloq) ‹prices› alto, excesivo

steep² vt (to soften, clean) remojar; (to flavor) macerar

steeple /'sti:pəl/ n aguja f, campanario m

steeple: ~**chase** n carrera f de obstáculos; ~**jack** n: *persona que repara chimeneas, torres etc*

steeply /'sti:pli/ adv (a) ‹slope/rise/fall› abruptamente (b) ‹increase/decline› considerablemente

steer¹ /stɪr ‖stɪə(r)/ n (a) (castrated bull) buey m (b) (young bull) novillo m

steer² vt (a) ‹vehicle/plane› dirigir*, conducir*; ‹ship› gobernar* (b) (guide) llevar, conducir*
■ ~ vi (Naut) estar* or ir* al timón; (Auto) ir* al volante; **to ~ clear of sth/sb** evitar algo/a algn

steering /'stɪrɪŋ ‖'stɪərɪŋ/ n dirección f

steering wheel n (Auto) volante m

stem¹ /stem/ n ①(of plant) tallo m; (of leaf) peciolo m, pecíolo m; (of fruit) pedúnculo m ②(of glass) pie m

stem² -mm- vt ‹flow/bleeding› contener*; ‹outbreak/decline› detener*
■ ~ vi **to ~ FROM sth** provenir* DE algo

stench /stentʃ/ n fetidez f

stencil¹ /'stensəl ‖'stensɪl/ n (a) (for lettering, decoration) plantilla f, troquel m (b) (for duplicating) stencil m, cliché m (Esp)

stencil² vt, (BrE) -**ll**- ‹design/pattern› escribir, dibujar o pintar utilizando una plantilla

stenographer /stə'nɑ:grəfər ‖stə'nɒgrəfə(r)/ n (esp AmE) taquígrafo, -fa m,f, estenógrafo, -fa m,f

stenography /stə'nɑ:grəfi ‖stə'nɒgrəfi/ n (AmE) taquigrafía f, estenografía f

step¹ /step/ n ①(footstep, pace) paso m; **to take a ~ forward** dar* un paso adelante; **to watch one's ~** andarse* con cuidado ②(a) (of dance) paso m (b) (in marching, walking) paso m; **to be in/out of ~** llevar/no llevar el paso ③(measure) medida f; **to take ~s (to + INF)** tomar medidas (PARA + INF) ④(on stair) escalón m, peldaño m; (on ladder) travesaño m, escalón m ⑤(AmE Mus): **whole ~** tono m; **half ~** semitono m

step² -pp- vi: would you ~ inside/outside for a moment? ¿quiere pasar/salir un momento?; **to ~ off a plane** bajarse de un avión; **to ~ IN/ON sth** pisar algo
■ **step aside** [v + adv] hacerse* a un lado
■ **step back** [v + adv] (a) (move back) dar* un paso atrás (b) (become detached) **to ~ back (FROM sth)** distanciarse (DE algo)
■ **step down** [v + adv] (a) (get down) bajar (b) (resign) renunciar, dimitir
■ **step forward** [v + adv] (a) (move forward) dar* un paso adelante (b) (present oneself) ofrecerse*
■ **step in** [v + adv] intervenir*
■ **step up** [v + o + adv, v + adv + o] ‹production/ campaign› intensificar*; ‹efforts/security/attacks› redoblar

step: ~**brother** n hermanastro m; ~ **by ~** adv (one stage at a time) paso a paso; (gradually) poco a poco; ~-**by-**~ /'stepbar'step/ adj ‹instructions› detallado, paso a paso; ~**child** n (son) hijastro m; (daughter) hijastra f; ~**daughter** n hijastra f; ~**father** n padrastro m; ~**ladder** n escalera f de mano or de tijera; ~**mother** n madrastra f

stepping-stone /'stepɪŋstəʊn/ n: cada una

---

de las piedras que se colocan para cruzar un arroyo, un pantano etc; **a ~ to success** un peldaño en el camino del éxito

step: ~**sister** n hermanastra f; ~**son** n hijastro m

stereo¹ /'steriəʊ/ n (pl -**os**) (a) (player) estéreo m (b) (sound) estéreo m

stereo² adj estéreo adj inv

stereotype¹ /'steriətaɪp/ n estereotipo m

stereotype² vt catalogar*, estereotipar

sterile /'sterəl ‖'steraɪl/ adj estéril

sterility /stə'rɪləti/ n esterilidad f

sterilize /'sterəlaɪz/ vt esterilizar*

sterling¹ /'stɜ:rlɪŋ ‖'stɜ:lɪŋ/ n la libra (esterlina)

sterling² adj: **the pound ~** la libra esterlina

stern¹ /stɜ:rn ‖stɜ:n/ n popa f

stern² adj -**er**, -**est** severo

steroid /'stɪrɔɪd, 'ste- ‖'stɪərɔɪd, 'ste-/ n esteroide m

stethoscope /'steθəskəʊp/ n estetoscopio m

stevedore /'sti:vədɔːr ‖'sti:vədɔː(r)/ n estibador, -dora m,f

stew¹ /stu: ‖stju:/ n estofado m, guiso m

stew² vt ‹meat› estofar, guisar; ‹fruit› hacer* compota de

steward /'stu:ərd ‖'stju:əd/ n ①(a) (on ship) camarero m (b) (on plane) auxiliar (m) de vuelo, sobrecargo (m), aeromozo (m) (AmL) ②(a) (manager of estate) administrador, -dora m,f (b) (at public gatherings) (BrE) persona encargada de supervisar al público en manifestaciones

stewardess /'stu:ərdəs ‖'stu:ədes/ n (a) (on ship) camarera f (b) (on plane) auxiliar f de vuelo, azafata f, sobrecargo f, aeromoza f (AmL)

stick¹ /stɪk/ n ①(a) (of wood) palo m, vara f; (twig) ramita f, (for fire) astilla f (b) (walking ~) bastón m (b) (hockey ~) palo m ③(of celery, rhubarb) rama f, penca f; (of dynamite) cartucho m; (of rock, candy) palo m; **a ~ of chalk** una tiza; **a ~ of chewing gum** un chicle ④ **sticks** pl **the ~s** (colloq): **to live out in the ~s** vivir en la Cochinchina or (Esp tb) en las Batuecas

stick² (past & past p **stuck**) vt ①(attach, glue) pegar*
②(a) (thrust) ‹needle/knife/sword› clavar (b) (impale) **to ~ sth ON sth** clavar algo EN algo ③(put, place) (colloq) poner* ④(tolerate) (esp BrE colloq) aguantar, soportar
■ ~ vi ①(adhere) «glue» pegar*; «food» pegarse*; **to ~ TO sth** pegarse* or (frml) adherirse* A algo; **the two pages have stuck together** las dos páginas se han pegado; **the song stuck in my mind** la canción se me quedó grabada ②(become jammed) atascarse*; see also **STUCK²**
■ **stick at** [v + prep + o] (colloq) seguir* con; ~ **at it** sigue así
■ **stick by** [v + prep + o] ‹friend› no abandonar; ‹promise› mantener* en pie
■ **stick out** ① [v + adv] (a) (protrude) sobresalir* (b) (be obvious) resaltar; **he really ~s out in a crowd** uno enseguida lo nota en un grupo de gente ② [v + o + adv, v + adv + o] (stretch out) (colloq) ‹hand› extender*; ‹tongue› sacar*
■ **stick to** [v + prep + o] (a) (hold to) ‹road/path› ···❖

seguir* por; ⟨*principles*⟩ mantener*; ⟨*rules*⟩
ceñirse* a, atenerse* a; **I'll ~ to my original plan**
seguiré con mi plan original **(b)** (not digress from)
⟨*subject/facts*⟩ ceñirse* a **(c)** (restrict oneself to)
limitarse a
■ **stick together** [*v* + *adv*] no separarse; (support
each other) mantenerse* unidos
■ **stick up** ⒈ [*v* + *o* + *adv*, *v* + *adv* + *o*] **(a)** (on
wall) ⟨*notice*⟩ colocar*, poner* **(b)** (raise) ⟨*hand*⟩
levantar
⒉ [*v* + *adv*] (project): **something was ~ing up out**
of the ground algo sobresalía del suelo; **her hair**
was ~ing up tenía el pelo de punta, tenía el pelo
parado (AmL)
■ **stick up for** [*v* + *adv* + *prep* + *o*] ⟨*person*⟩
sacar* la cara por, defender*; **to ~ up for oneself**
hacerse* valer

sticker /'stɪkər ‖'stɪkə(r)/ *n* (label) etiqueta *f*;
(with slogan etc) pegatina *f*, adhesivo *m*

sticking plaster /'stɪkɪŋ/ *n* (BrE) **(a)**
(individual strip) curita® *f* (AmL), tirita® *f* (Esp) **(b)**
(tape) esparadrapo *m*, cinta *f* adhesiva

stick: ~ insect *n* insecto *m* palo;
~-in-the-mud *n* (colloq): **don't be such a**
~-in-the-mud no seas tan rutinario e inflexible

stickler /'stɪklər ‖'stɪklə(r)/ *n*: **he's a ~ for**
discipline insiste mucho en la disciplina

stick: ~-on *adj* adhesivo; **~ shift** *n* (AmE) **(a)**
(lever) palanca *f* de cambio(s) *or* (Méx) de
velocidades **(b)** (car) coche *m* (de transmisión)
estándar *or* manual; **~up** *n* (colloq) atraco *m*,
asalto *m*

sticky /'stɪki/ *adj* **stickier, stickiest** ⒈ **(a)**
⟨*label*⟩ engomado, autoadhesivo; ⟨*surface*⟩
pegajoso **(b)** ⟨*weather*⟩ bochornoso ⒉ (difficult)
(colloq) ⟨*problem/issue*⟩ peliagudo; ⟨*situation*⟩
violento

stiff¹ /stɪf/ *adj* **-er, -est** ⒈ **(a)** ⟨*collar/bristles*⟩
duro; ⟨*fabric*⟩ tieso, duro; ⟨*corpse*⟩ rígido;
⟨*muscles*⟩ entumecido, agarrotado; **to have a ~**
neck tener* tortícolis; **I'm ~ after that walk** estoy
dolorido *or* (esp AmL) adolorido despues de la
caminata **(b)** ⟨*paste/dough*⟩ consistente; ⟨*egg*
white⟩ firme ⒉ ⟨*test/climb*⟩ difícil, duro;
⟨*resistance*⟩ férreo; ⟨*penalty*⟩ fuerte; ⟨*breeze/*
drink⟩ fuerte ⒊ ⟨*person/manner*⟩ estirado; ⟨*bow/*
smile⟩ forzado

stiff² *adv* (colloq): **I'm frozen ~** estoy helado
hasta los huesos (fam); **we were bored ~** nos
aburrimos como ostras (fam); **scared ~** muerto de
miedo

stiffen /'stɪfən/ *vt* **(a)** (with starch) almidonar;
(with fabric underneath) armar **(b) ~ (up)** ⟨*resolve*⟩
fortalecer*
■ **~** *vi* **(a) ~ (up)** (become rigid) ⟨⟨*person/muscles/*
joint⟩⟩ agarrotarse **(b)** (become firm) endurecerse*
(c) (in manner, reaction) ponerse* tenso

stiffly /'stɪfli/ *adv* **(a)** ⟨*walk/move*⟩ rígidamente,
con rigidez **(b)** ⟨*greet*⟩ fríamente; ⟨*bow*⟩ con fría
formalidad

stifle /'staɪfəl/ *vt* ⒈ (suffocate) (*often pass*)
⟨*person*⟩ sofocar* ⒉ (suppress) ⟨*flames*⟩ sofocar*;
⟨*yawn/anger*⟩ contener*; ⟨*noise*⟩ ahogar*

stifling /'staɪflɪŋ/ *adj* ⟨*heat*⟩ sofocante

stigma /'stɪɡmə/ *n* (*pl* **-mas**) estigma *m*

stile /staɪl/ *n*: *escalones que permiten pasar por*
encima de una cerca

stiletto /strɪ'letəʊ/ *n* (*pl* **-tos** *or* **-toes**) **~**
(heel) tacón *m* de aguja, taco *m* aguja *or* alfiler
(CS)

still¹ /stɪl/ *adv*

■ **Note** Spanish has two words for *still*: *todavía* and
aún. Both can go at the beginning or end of the
sentence: *I still haven't seen him* todavía *or* aún no lo
he visto *or* no lo he visto todavía *or* aún. The
distinction in English between *he hasn't arrived yet*
and *he still hasn't arrived* is not expressed verbally in
Spanish. Both can be translated by *todavía* or *aún no*
ha llegado, or *no ha llegado todavía* or *aún*. The
degree of intensity, surprise, or annoyance is often
expressed by intonation. Note that the verb *seguir* can
be used to express continuation: *I still don't*
understand why sigo sin entender por qué; *he's still*
looking for a job sigue buscando trabajo.

⒈ (even now, even then) todavía, aún; **there's ~**
plenty left todavía *or* aún queda mucho; **are we ~**
friends? ¿seguimos siendo amigos?
⒉ (as intensifier) aún, todavía; **the risk is greater**
~ el riesgo es aún *or* todavía mayor
⒊ (as linker): **they say it's safe, but I'm ~ scared**
dicen que no hay peligro pero igual *or* aun así
tengo miedo; **~, it could have been worse** de
todos modos, podría haber sido peor

still² *adj* **(a)** (motionless) ⟨*lake/air*⟩ en calma,
quieto, tranquilo; **sit/stand ~** quédate quieto; **her**
heart stood ~ for a moment se le paró
el corazón se le paró
un momento **(b)** ⟨*drink*⟩ sin gas, no efervescente

still³ *n* ⒈ (Cin, Phot) fotograma *m* ⒉ (distillery)
destilería *f*; (distilling apparatus) alambique *m*

still: ~born /'stɪl'bɔːrn ‖'stɪlbɔːn/ *adj* nacido
muerto; **~ life** *n* (*pl* **~ lifes**) naturaleza *f*
muerta

stilt /stɪlt/ *n* zanco *m*

stilted /'stɪltəd ‖'stɪltɪd/ *adj* **(a)** ⟨*conversation/*
manner⟩ forzado **(b)** ⟨*language/writing*⟩
rebuscado; ⟨*acting*⟩ acartonado

stimulate /'stɪmjʊleɪt ‖'stɪmjʊleɪt/ *vt*
estimular

stimulating /'stɪmjəleɪtɪŋ ‖'stɪmjʊleɪtɪŋ/ *adj*
estimulante

stimulation /ˌstɪmjə'leɪʃən ‖ˌstɪmjʊ'leɪʃən/ *n*
estímulo *m*

stimulus /'stɪmjələs ‖'stɪmjʊləs/ *n* (*pl* **-li**
/-laɪ/) estímulo *m*

sting¹ /stɪŋ/ *n* ⒈ **(a)** (of bee, wasp) aguijón *m*
(b) (action, wound) picadura *f* ⒉ (*no pl*) (pain)
escozor *m*, ardor *m* (CS)

sting² (*past* & *past p* **stung**) *vt* ⒈ ⟨⟨*bee/*
nettle⟩⟩ picar* ⒉ (cause pain) hacer* escocer,
hacer* arder (CS)

■ ~ *vi* **1** «*insect/nettle*» picar* **2** (hurt physically) «*ointment*» hacer* escocer, hacer* arder (CS); «*cut*» escocer*, arder (CS)

stinging nettle /'stɪŋɪŋ/ *n* ortiga *f*

stingy /'stɪndʒi/ *adj* **-gier -giest** ‹*person*› tacaño; ‹*portion*› mezquino

stink¹ /stɪŋk/ *n* **(a)** (bad smell) hediondez *f*, mal olor *m*, peste *f* (fam) **(b)** (fuss) (colloq) escándalo *m*, lío *m* (fam), follón *m* (Esp fam); **to make** *o* **kick up a** ~ armar un lío (*or* un escándalo *etc*)

stink² *vi* (*past* **stank** *or* **stunk**; *past p* **stunk**) «*person/place/breath*» apestar; **the whole business** ~**s** (colloq) todo el asunto da asco

stink bomb *n* bomba *f* fétida

stinking /'stɪŋkɪŋ/ *adj* (before *n*) hediondo, fétido, apestoso; **I've got a** ~ **cold** (colloq) tengo un resfriado espantoso

stint¹ /stɪnt/ *n* **(a)** (fixed amount, share): **I've done my** ~ **for today** hoy ya he hecho mi parte **(b)** (period) período *m*; **he did a five-year** ~ **in the army** pasó (un período de) cinco años en el ejército

stint² *vi* **to** ~ **ON sth** escatimar algo

stipulate /'stɪpjəleɪt/ *vt* estipular

stipulation /ˌstɪpjə'leɪʃən ‖ˌstɪpjʊ'leɪʃən/ *n* condición *f*, estipulación *f*

stir¹ /stɜːr ‖stɜː(r)/ *n* **(a)** (action) **to give sth a** ~ revolver* *or* (Esp) remover* algo **(b)** (excitement) revuelo *m*, conmoción *f*

stir² **-rr-** *vt* **1** (mix) ‹*liquid/mixture*› revolver*, remover* (Esp) **2** **(a)** (move slightly) agitar, mover* **(b)** (get moving) (colloq) mover* **(c)** (waken) despertar* **3** **(a)** (arouse) ‹*imagination*› estimular **(b)** (move, affect) conmover* **(c)** (provoke, incite) **to** ~ **sb into action** empujar *or* incitar a algn a la acción

■ ~ *vi* **(a)** (change position) moverse*, agitarse **(b)** (venture out) moverse*, salir* **(c)** (wake up) despertarse*; (get up) levantarse

■ **stir up** [*v* + *adv, v* + *adv* + *o*] ‹*mud/waters*› revolver*, remover* (Esp); ‹*hatred/unrest/revolt*› provocar*; ‹*discontent*› promover*; **to** ~ **up trouble** armar lío (fam)

stir-fry /'stɜːr'fraɪ ‖'stɜː'fraɪ/ *vt* **-fries, -frying, -fried** freír en poco aceite y revolviendo constantemente

stirring /'stɜːrɪŋ/ *adj* conmovedor

stirrup /'stɜrəp ‖'stɪrəp/ *n* estribo *m*

stitch¹ /stɪtʃ/ *n* **1** **(a)** (in sewing) puntada *f* **(b)** (in knitting) punto *m* **(c)** (Med) punto *m* **2** (pain) (*no pl*) punzada *f* *or* (CS) puntada *f* (en el costado), flato *m* (Esp)

stitch² *vt* **(a)** (sew) coser **(b)** (embroider) bordar **(c)** (Med) suturar

stoat /stəʊt/ *n* armiño *m*

stock¹ /stɑːk ‖stɒk/ *n* **1** **(a)** (supply) (*often pl*) reserva *f* (of shop, business) existencias *fpl*, estoc *m*; **we're out of** ~ **of green ones** las verdes se han agotado; **to take** ~ **of sth** hacer* un balance de algo **2** (Fin) **(a)** (shares) acciones *fpl*, valores *mpl*; (government securities) bonos *mpl* *or* papel *m* del Estado **(b)** ~**s and bonds** *o* (BrE) ~**s and shares** acciones *fpl* **3** (livestock) ganado *m* **4** (descent) linaje *m*, estirpe *f* **5** (Culin) caldo *m*

6 **stocks** *pl* (Hist) **the** ~**s** el cepo **7** (Am Theat) repertorio *m*

stock² *vt* **1** (Busn) vender **2** (fill) ‹*store*› surtir, abastecer*; ‹*larder/freezer*› llenar

■ **stock up** [*v* + *adv*] abastecerse*; (Busn) hacer* un estoc; **we'd better** ~ **up on coffee before it goes up** más vale que compremos bastante café antes de que suba

stock³ *adj* (before *n*) ‹*size*› estándar *adj inv*; ‹*model*› de serie

stock: ~**broker** *n* corredor, -dora *m,f* de valores *or* de Bolsa, agente *mf* de Bolsa; ~ **company** *n* (AmE) **(a)** (Fin) sociedad *f* anónima **(b)** (Theat) compañía *f* de repertorio; ~ **cube** *n* cubito *m* de caldo; ~ **exchange** *n* bolsa *f* (de valores), Bolsa *f*; ~**holder** *n* accionista *mf*

Stockholm /'stɑːkhəʊlm ‖'stɒkhəʊm/ *n* Estocolmo

stocking /'stɑːkɪŋ ‖'stɒkɪŋ/ *n* media *f*

stock-in-trade /'stɑːkɪn'treɪd ‖'stɒkɪn'treɪd/ *n* especialidad *f*

stockist /'stɑːkəst ‖'stɒkɪst/ *n* (BrE) proveedor, -dora *m,f*, distribuidor, -dora *m,f*

stock market *n* mercado *m* de valores, mercado *m* (bursátil)

stockpile¹ /'stɑːkpaɪl ‖'stɒkpaɪl/ *n* reservas *fpl*

stockpile² *vt* almacenar

stock: ~**room** *n* almacén *m*, depósito *m*, bodega *f* (Méx); ~**-still** /'stɑːk'stɪl ‖,stɒk'stɪl/ *adj* inmóvil; ~**taking** /'stɑːk,teɪkɪŋ ‖'stɒk,teɪkɪŋ/ *n* (esp BrE Busn): ☉ **closed for stocktaking** cerrado por inventario

stocky /'stɑːki ‖'stɒki/ *adj* **stockier, stockiest** bajo y fornido

stockyard /'stɑːkjɑːrd ‖'stɒkjɑːd/ *n* (AmE) corral *m*

stodgy /'stɑːdʒi ‖'stɒdʒi/ *adj* **-dgier, -dgiest** (BrE) ‹*food*› feculento, pesado

stoical /'stəʊɪkəl/ *adj* estoico

stoke /stəʊk/ *vt* echarle carbón (*or* leña *etc*) a

stole¹ /stəʊl/ *past of* STEAL

stole² *n* estola *f*

stolen /'stəʊlən/ *past p of* STEAL

stolid /'stɑːləd ‖'stɒlɪd/ *adj* impasible

stomach¹ /'stʌmək/ *n* **(a)** (organ) estómago *m*; **on an empty** ~ con el estómago vacío, en ayunas **(b)** (belly) barriga (fam), panza *f* (fam)

stomach² *vt* (*usu neg*) ‹*insults/insolence/person*› soportar, aguantar

stomach: ~**ache** *n* dolor *m* de estómago; (in lower abdomen) dolor *m* de barriga *or* (frml) de vientre; ~ **pump** *n* bomba *f* estomacal

stomp /stɑːmp ‖stɒmp/ *vi* (+ *adv compl*): **to** ~ **in/out** entrar/salir* pisando fuerte

stone¹ /stəʊn/ *n* **1** (substance, piece) piedra *f* **2** **(a)** (gem) piedra *f* **(b)** (in kidney) cálculo *m*, piedra *f* **(c)** (of fruit) hueso *m*, cuesco *m* **3** (*pl* ~ *or* ~**s**) (in UK) *unidad de peso equivalente a 14 libras o 6,35 kg*

stone² *vt* apedrear, lapidar

stone: **S**~ **Age** *n* Edad *f* de Piedra; ~**-cold** /'stəʊn'kəʊld/ *adj* (colloq) helado

stoned /stəʊnd/ *adj* (colloq) (*usu pred*) (from ⋯✦

drugs) volado, pacheco (Méx), colocado (Esp fam); **to get ~** volarse*, ponerse* pacheco (Méx), colocarse* (Esp fam)

stone: ~-deaf /'stəʊn'def/ *adj* (colloq) sordo como una tapia (fam); **~mason** *n* picapedrero *m*, cantero *m*; **~wall** /'stəʊn'wɔːl/ *vi* (be evasive) andarse* con evasivas; (be obstructive) utilizar* tácticas obstruccionistas

stony /'stəʊni/ *adj* **-nier, -niest** [1] ⟨ground/ path⟩ pedregoso [2] ⟨look/person⟩ frío, glacial; ⟨silence⟩ sepulcral

stood /stʊd/ *past & past p of* STAND²

stool /stuːl/ *n* taburete *m*, banco *m*

stoop¹ /stuːp/ *vi* [1] (have a stoop): **he ~s a little** es un poco cargado de espaldas *or* encorvado [2] (bend over) agacharse [3] (demean oneself): **how could he ~ so low?** ¿cómo pudo llegar tan bajo?; **to ~ TO sth** rebajarse A algo

stoop² *n* (*no pl*): **she walks with a ~** camina encorvada

stop¹ /stɑːp ‖stɒp/ *n* [1] (halt): **to come to a ~** ⟨vehicle/aircraft⟩ detenerse*; ⟨production/ conversation⟩ interrumpirse; **to put a ~ to sth** ⟨to mischief/malpractice⟩ poner* fin a algo [2] (a) (break on journey) parada *f* (b) (stopping place) parada *f*, paradero *m* (AmL exc RPl)

stop² **-pp-** *vt* [1] (a) (halt) ⟨taxi/bus⟩ parar; ⟨person⟩ parar, detener* (b) (switch off) ⟨machine/ engine⟩ parar [2] (a) (bring to an end, interrupt) ⟨decline/inflation⟩ detener*, parar; ⟨discussion/abuse⟩ poner* fin a, acabar con; **~ that noise!** ¡deja de hacer ruido! (b) (cease): **~ what you're doing and listen to me** deja lo que estás haciendo y escúchame; **~ it!** ¡basta ya!; **to ~ -ING** dejar DE + INF [3] (prevent): **what's ~ping you?** ¿qué te lo impide?; **I had to tell him, I couldn't ~ myself** tuve que decírselo, no pude contenerme; **to ~ sb (FROM) -ING** (esp BrE) impedirle* a algn + INF, impedir* QUE algn (+ *subj*); **to ~ sth happening** impedir* que ocurra algo [4] (cancel, withhold) ⟨subscription⟩ cancelar; ⟨payment⟩ suspender [5] (block) ⟨hole⟩ tapar; ⟨gap⟩ rellenar [6] (parry) ⟨blow/punch⟩ parar, detener*
■ **~** *vi* [1] (a) (halt) ⟨vehicle/driver⟩ parar, detenerse*; **~ or I'll shoot!** ¡alto o disparo! (b) (interrupt journey) ⟨train/bus⟩ parar (c) (cease operating) ⟨watch/clock/machine⟩ pararse [2] (a) (cease): **the rain has ~ped** ha dejado *or* parado de llover, ya no llueve; **the pain/bleeding has ~ped** ya no le (*or* me *etc*) duele/sale sangre (b) (interrupt activity) parar; **I didn't ~ to think** no me detuve a pensar [3] (colloq) (stay) quedarse
■ **stop by** [*v + adv*] [*v + prep + o*]: **I ~ped by (at) the store for some milk** pasé por la tienda para comprar leche
■ **stop off** [*v + adv*]: **I ~ped off at home to change** pasé por casa para cambiarme; **we ~ped off in San Juan for a few hours** paramos unas horas en San Juan
■ **stop over** [*v + adv*] (a) (overnight) hacer* noche (b) (Aviat) ⟨plane⟩ hacer* escala
■ **stop up** [*v + o + adv, v + adv + o*] (fill) ⟨hole/ crack⟩ tapar, rellenar

stop: ~gap *n* recurso *m* provisional *or* (AmS tb) provisorio; **~over** *n* (break in journey) parada *f*; (Aviat) escala *f*

stoppage /'stɑːpɪdʒ ‖'stɒpɪdʒ/ *n* [1] (a) (in play, production) interrupción *f* (b) (strike) huelga *f*, paro *m* (AmL) (c) (cancellation) suspensión *f* [2] (blockage) obstrucción *f*

stopper /'stɑːpər ‖'stɒpə(r)/ *n* tapón *m*

stopping train /'stɑːpɪŋ ‖'stɒpɪŋ/ *n* (BrE) tren con parada en todas las estaciones

stop: ~ press *n* noticias *fpl* de última hora; **~watch** *n* cronómetro *m*

storage /'stɔːrɪdʒ/ *n* (a) (of goods) depósito *m*, almacenamiento *m*, almacenaje *m*; (before *n*) **~ space** lugar *m* *or* espacio *m* para guardar cosas (b) (Comput) almacenamiento *m*

store¹ /stɔːr ‖stɔː(r)/ *n* [1] (a) (stock, supply) reserva *f*, provisión *f*; **in ~: there's a surprise in ~ for her** la espera una sorpresa; **who knows what the future has in ~?** ¿quién sabe lo que nos deparará el futuro?; **to set great/little ~ by sth** dar* mucho/poco valor a algo (b) **stores** *pl* (Mil, Naut) pertrechos *mpl* [2] (warehouse, storage place) (often *pl*) almacén *m*, depósito *m*, bodega *f* (Méx) [3] (a) (shop) (esp AmE) tienda *f* (b) (department **~**) grandes almacenes *mpl*, tienda *f*

store² *vt* (a) (keep) ⟨food/drink/supplies⟩ guardar; (Busn) almacenar; ⟨information⟩ almacenar; ⟨electricity⟩ acumular (b) (Comput) ⟨data/program⟩ almacenar
■ **store up** [*v + o + adv, v + adv + o*] (a) ⟨supplies⟩ almacenar (b) ⟨resentment⟩ ir* acumulando

store: ~house *n* (a) (warehouse) almacén *m*, depósito *m*, bodega *f* (Méx) (b) (source) mina *f*; **~keeper** *n* tendero, -ra *m,f*; **~room** *n* almacén *m*, depósito *m*, bodega *f* (Méx); (for food) despensa *f*

storey /'stɔːri/ *n* (BrE) ▶ STORY II

stork /stɔːrk ‖stɔːk/ *n* cigüeña *f*

storm¹ /stɔːrm ‖stɔːm/ *n* [1] (Meteo) tormenta *f*; **a ~ at sea** una tempestad; **to take sth by ~** ⟨city/fortress⟩ tomar algo por asalto; **she took New York's audiences by ~** cautivó al público neoyorquino [2] (of protest) ola *f*, tempestad *f*

storm² *vi* [1] (move violently) (+ *adv compl*): **she ~ed into the office** irrumpió en la oficina [2] (express anger) despotricar*, vociferar
■ **~** *vt* ⟨city/fortress⟩ tomar por asalto; ⟨house⟩ irrumpir en

stormy /'stɔːrmi ‖'stɔːmi/ *adj* **-mier, -miest** (a) (Meteo) tormentoso; ⟨sea⟩ tempestuoso (b) (turbulent) ⟨relationship⟩ tempestuoso

story /'stɔːri/ *n* (*pl* **-ries**)
I [1] (a) (account) historia *f*, relato *m*; (genre) cuento *m*; **to cut a long ~ short** en pocas palabras (b) (anecdote) anécdota *f* [2] (plot) argumento *m*, trama *f* [3] (Journ) artículo *m* [4] (lie) (colloq) cuento *m* (fam), mentira *f*
II (BrE) **storey** (of building) piso *m*, planta *f*

story: ~book *n* libro *m* de cuentos; **~ line** *n* argumento *m*; **~teller** *n* narrador, -dora *m,f*

stout¹ /staʊt/ *adj* **-er, -est** ⟨person/figure⟩ robusto, corpulento; ⟨door⟩ sólido

stout² *n* cerveza *f* negra

stove /stəʊv/ *n* (a) (for cooking) cocina *f*, estufa *f* (Col, Méx) (b) (for warmth) estufa *f*

stow /stəʊ/ vt ⟨put away⟩ guardar, poner*; ⟨hide⟩ esconder; (Naut) estibar
■ **stow away** [v + adv] viajar de polizón

stowaway /'stəʊə,weɪ/ n polizón mf

straddle /'strædl/ vt ⟨horse⟩ sentarse* a horcajadas sobre; **he ∼d the chair** se sentó a caballo or a horcajadas en la silla

straggle /'strægəl/ vi [1] (spread untidily) «*plant*» crecer* desordenadamente [2] (lag behind, fall away) rezagarse*

straggler /'stræglər ‖'stræglə(r)/ n rezagado, -da m,f

straggly /'strægli/ adj **-glier, -gliest** ⟨hair⟩ desordenado, desgreñado; ⟨beard⟩ descuidado

straight¹ /streɪt/ adj **-er, -est** [1] (a) (not curved or wavy) recto; ⟨hair⟩ lacio, liso (b) (level, upright, vertical) (pred) **to be ∼** estar* derecho; **is my tie ∼?** ¿tengo la corbata derecha or bien puesta?
[2] (in order) (pred): **I have to put my room ∼** tengo que ordenar mi cuarto; **let's get this ∼** a ver si nos entendemos; **to set the record ∼** dejar las cosas en claro
[3] (a) (direct, clear) ⟨denial/refusal⟩ rotundo, categórico (b) (unmixed) ⟨gin/vodka⟩ solo
[4] (honest, frank) ⟨question⟩ directo; ⟨answer⟩ claro
[5] (successive): **he won in ∼ sets** (Sport) ganó sin conceder or sin perder ningún set; **she's had five ∼ wins** ha ganado cinco veces seguidas
[6] (a) (serious) ⟨play/actor⟩ dramático, serio (b) (conventional) (colloq) convencional (c) (heterosexual) (colloq) heterosexual

straight² adv [1] (a) (in a straight line) ⟨walk⟩ en línea recta; **she looked ∼ ahead** miró al frente; **the truck was coming ∼ at me** el camión venía derecho hacia mí; **he made ∼ for the bar** se fue derecho al bar; **keep ∼ on** until you come to the lights sigue derecho hasta llegar al semáforo (b) (erect) ⟨sit/stand⟩ derecho; **sit up ∼** ponte derecho
[2] (a) (directly) directamente; **I came ∼ home from work** vine directamente or derecho a casa después del trabajo (b) (immediately): **I came ∼ after dinner** inmediatamente después de cenar; **I'll bring it ∼ back** enseguida lo devuelvo; **I'll come ∼ to the point** iré derecho al grano; **∼ away** ▶
STRAIGHTAWAY
[3] (colloq) (frankly) con franqueza; **she told him ∼ out** se lo dijo sin rodeos
[4] (clearly) ⟨see/think⟩ con claridad

straight: ∼ and narrow n **the ∼ and narrow** el buen camino, el camino recto; **∼away** /'streɪtə,weɪ/, **∼ away** adv enseguida, inmediatamente

straighten /'streɪtn/ vt (a) ⟨nail/wire/picture⟩ enderezar*; ⟨hair⟩ alisar; **he ∼ed his tie** se enderezó la corbata (b) (tidy) ⟨room/papers⟩ arreglar, ordenar
■ **straighten out** [v + o + adv, v + adv + o] ⟨confusion/misunderstanding⟩ aclarar; ⟨problem⟩ resolver*
■ **straighten up** [1] [v + o + adv, v + adv + o] (tidy) ⟨room/papers⟩ ordenar, arreglar; ⟨bed⟩ arreglar [2] [v + adv] (stand up straight) ponerse* derecho

straight: ∼faced /'streɪt'feɪst/ adj: **he said it completely ∼faced** lo dijo muy serio; **∼forward** /'streɪt'fɔːrwərd ‖,streɪt'fɔːwəd/ adj (a) (honest, frank) ⟨person/answer⟩ franco (b) (uncomplicated) ⟨problem/question⟩ sencillo; **∼jacket** n ▶
STRAITJACKET

strain¹ /streɪn/ n [1] (tension) tensión f; (pressure) presión f; **it puts ∼ on the spine** ejerce presión sobre la columna vertebral; **the incident put a ∼ on Franco-German relations** las relaciones franco-alemanas se volvieron tirantes a raíz del incidente [2] (Med) (resulting from wrench, twist) torcedura f; (on a muscle) esguince m [3] **strains** pl (tune): **the ∼s** el sonido de; **to the ∼s of the violin** al son del violín [4] (a) (type — of plant) variedad f; (— of virus) cepa f; (— of animal) raza f (b) (streak) (no pl) veta f

strain² vt [1] (exert): **to ∼ one's eyes/voice** forzar* la vista/voz; **he ∼ed every muscle to lift the weight** usó todas sus fuerzas para levantar el peso [2] (a) (overburden) ⟨beam/support⟩ ejercer* demasiada presión sobre (b) (injure): **to ∼ one's back** hacerse* daño en la espalda; **to ∼ a muscle** hacerse* un esguince (c) (overtax, stretch) ⟨relations⟩ someter a demasiada tensión; ⟨patience⟩ poner* a prueba [3] (filter) filtrar; (Culin) colar*; ⟨vegetables/rice⟩ escurrir
■ ∼ vi: **to ∼ AT sth** tirar DE algo; **to ∼ to + INF** hacer* un gran esfuerzo PARA + INF

strained /streɪnd/ adj [1] (tense) ⟨relations/atmosphere⟩ tenso, tirante; ⟨expression⟩ tenso, crispado; ⟨voice⟩ forzado [2] (Med) **a ∼ muscle** un esguince

strainer /'streɪnər ‖'streɪnə(r)/ n (Culin) colador m

strait /streɪt/ n [1] (Geog) (often pl) estrecho m [2] **straits** pl (difficulties, difficult position): **to be in dire ∼s** estar* en grandes apuros

strait: ∼jacket n camisa f de fuerza, chaleco m de fuerza (CS); **∼laced** /'streɪt'leɪst/ adj puritano

strand¹ /strænd/ n (of rope, string) ramal m; (of thread, wool) hebra f; (of wire) filamento m; **a ∼ of hair** un pelo

strand² vt (usu pass): **to be ∼ed** «*ship*» quedar encallado; «*whale*» quedar varado; **they left me ∼ed** me abandonaron a mi suerte, me dejaron tirado or (AmL exc RPl) botado (fam)

strange /streɪndʒ/ adj **stranger, strangest** [1] (odd) raro, extraño; **it is ∼ (THAT)** es raro QUE (+ subj) [2] (a) (unfamiliar, unaccustomed) ⟨faces/handwriting⟩ desconocido (b) (alien) (liter): **in a ∼ land** en tierras extrañas

strangely /'streɪndʒli/ adv ⟨behave/act⟩ de una manera rara or extraña; **∼ enough** (indep) aunque parezca mentira

stranger /'streɪndʒər ‖'streɪndʒə(r)/ n desconocido, -da m,f; (from another place) forastero, -ra m,f; **I'm a ∼ here myself** yo tampoco soy de aquí

strangle /'stræŋgəl/ vt (a) ⟨person⟩ estrangular (b) **strangled** past p ⟨cry/voice⟩ ahogado

stranglehold /'stræŋgəlhəʊld/ n (a) (Sport) llave f al cuello (b) (absolute control) poder m, dominio m

strap¹ /stræp/ n (a) (of leather) correa f; (of canvas) asa f‡ (b) (shoulder ∼) tirante m, bretel m (CS)

strap² vt **-pp-** (tie) atar or sujetar con una correa, amarrar con una correa (AmL exc RPl)

strapless /'stræpləs ‖'stræplɪs/ *adj* sin
tirantes, sin breteles (CS)

strapping /'stræpɪŋ/ *adj* robusto, fornido

Strasbourg /'strɑːsbʊrg ‖'stræzbɜːg/ *n*
Estrasburgo *m*

strata /'streɪtə, 'strætə ‖'strɑːtə, 'streɪtə/ *pl of*
STRATUM

stratagem /'strætədʒəm/ *n* estratagema *f*

strategic /strə'tiːdʒɪk/ *adj* estratégico

strategy /'strætədʒi/ *n* (*pl* **-gies**) estrategia *f*

stratify /'strætɪfaɪ ‖'strætɪfaɪ/ *vt* **-fies,
-fying, -fied** (*usu pass*) estratificar*

stratum /'streɪtəm, 'stræ- ‖'strɑːtəm, 'streɪ-/ *n*
(*pl* **-ta**) estrato *m*

straw /strɔː/ *n* **(a)** (material, single stem) paja *f*; **to
be the last o final ~** ser* el colmo; **to clutch o
grasp at ~s** aferrarse desesperadamente a una
esperanza **(b)** (for drinking) pajita *f*, paja *f*, caña *f*
(Esp), pitillo *m* (Col), popote *m* (Méx)

strawberry /'strɔːberi ‖'strɔːbəri/ *n* (*pl*
-ries) fresa *f*, frutilla *f* (Bol, CS); (large) fresón *m*

stray¹ /streɪ/ *vi* **(a)** (wander away) apartarse,
alejarse; (get lost) extraviarse*, perderse* **(b)**
(digress) apartarse, desviarse*

stray² *adj* **(a)** ⟨dog⟩ (ownerless) callejero; (lost)
perdido; ⟨sheep⟩ descarriado **(b)** (random, scattered)
⟨bullet⟩ perdido; ⟨hair⟩ suelto

stray³ *n* (ownerless animal) perro *m*/gato *m*
callejero; (lost animal) perro *m*/gato *m* perdido

streak¹ /striːk/ *n* **1** **(a)** (line, band) lista *f*, raya
f; (in hair) reflejo *m*, mechón *m*; (in marble) veta *f*;
(of ore) veta *f*, filón *m* **(b)** (in personality) veta *f*
2 (spell) racha *f*; **to be on a winning ~** tener*
una buena racha

streak² *vi* (+ *adv compl*): **to ~ past** pasar como
una centella
■ **~** *vt*: **tears ~ed her face** tenía el rostro surcado
de lágrimas; **to have one's hair ~ed** hacerse*
mechas *or* reflejos *or* (RPl) claritos *or* (Méx) luces
or (Chi) visos (en el pelo)

streaky /'striːki/ *adj* **-kier, -kiest (a)** (uneven)
⟨paint⟩ no uniforme, disparejo (AmL) **(b)** (BrE
Culin): **~ bacon** tocino *m* or (Esp) bacon *m* or (RPl)
panceta *f*

stream¹ /striːm/ *n* **1** **(a)** (small river) arroyo *m*,
riachuelo *m* **(b)** (current) corriente *f* **2** (flow): **a
thin ~ of water** un chorrito de agua; **a ~ of
abuse** una sarta de insultos; **there is a
continuous ~ of traffic** pasan vehículos
continuamente

stream² *vi* **1** (flow) (+ *adv compl*): **blood ~ed
from the wound** salía *or* manaba mucha sangre
de la herida; **tears were ~ing down her cheeks**
lloraba a lágrima viva; **the sunlight was ~ing in
through the window** el sol entraba a raudales por
la ventana; **I've got a ~ing cold** tengo un
resfriado muy fuerte **2** (wave) ⟨flag/hair⟩
ondear
■ **~** *vt* (BrE Educ) dividir (a los alumnos) en grupos
según su aptitud para una asignatura

streamer /'striːmər ‖'striːmə(r)/ *n* **(a)** (banner)
banderín *m* **(b)** (of paper) serpentina *f*

stream: ~line *vt* ⟨car/plane⟩ hacer* más
aerodinámico el diseño de, aerodinamizar*;
⟨organization/production⟩ racionalizar*; **~lined**
adj ⟨car/plane⟩ aerodinámico; ⟨methods/
production⟩ racionalizado

street /striːt/ *n* calle *f*; **it's on o** (BrE) **in Elm S~**
queda en la calle Elm; (before n) ⟨musician/
theater⟩ callejero; **~ corner** esquina *f*; **~ map o
plan** plano *m* de la ciudad, callejero *m* (Esp); **~
market** mercado *m* al aire libre, feria *f* (CS)

street: ~car *n* (AmE) tranvía *m*; **~ cleaner**
n (AmE) barrendero, -ra *m,f*; **~ lamp** *n* farol *m*;
~ level *n*: **at ~ level** a nivel de la calle; **~
light** *n* ► **~ LAMP; ~ sweeper** *n* (person)
barrendero, -ra *m,f*; (machine) (máquina *f*)
barredora *f*

strength /streŋθ/ *n* **1** (of persons) **(a)** (physical
energy) fuerza(s) *f(pl)*; (health) fortaleza *f* física; **to
get one's ~ back** recobrar las fuerzas **(b)**
(emotional, mental) fortaleza *f*
2 (of economy, currency) solidez *f*
3 **(a)** (of materials) resistencia *f*; (of wind, current)
fuerza *f*; (of drug, solution) concentración *f*; (of
alcoholic drink) graduación *f* **(b)** (of sound, light)
potencia *f*; (of emotions) intensidad *f* **(c)** (of
argument, evidence) lo convincente; (of protests) lo
enérgico
4 (strong point) virtud *f*, punto *m* fuerte
5 (force in numbers): **their fans were there in ~** sus
hinchas estaban allí en bloque *or* en masa

strengthen /'streŋθən/ *vt* ⟨muscle/limb⟩
fortalecer*; ⟨wall/furniture/glass⟩ reforzar*;
⟨support⟩ aumentar
■ **~** *vi* ⟨limb/muscle⟩ fortalecerse*; ⟨opposition/
support⟩ aumentar

strenuous /'strenjuəs/ *adj* **(a)** ⟨activity⟩
agotador **(b)** ⟨denial⟩ vigoroso; ⟨opposition⟩ tenaz

stress¹ /stres/ *n* **1** **(a)** (tension) tensión *f*; (Med)
estrés *m*, tensión *f*; **she's under a lot of ~** está
sometida a muchas presiones **(b)** (Phys, Tech)
tensión *f* **2** **(a)** (emphasis) énfasis *m*, hincapié *m*
(b) (Ling, Lit) acento *m* (tónico)

stress² *vt* **(a)** (emphasize) poner* énfasis *or*
hacer* hincapié en, enfatizar* **(b)** (Ling)
acentuar*

stressful /'stresfəl/ *adj* ⟨life/job⟩ estresante

stretch¹ /stretʃ/ *vt* **1** ⟨arm/leg⟩ estirar,
extender*; ⟨wing⟩ extender*, desplegar*
2 ⟨sheet/canvas⟩ extender*
3 (eke out) ⟨money/resources⟩ estirar
4 **(a)** (make demands on) exigirle* a; **she's not
being ~ed at school** en el colegio no le exigen de
acuerdo a su capacidad **(b)** (strain): **our resources
are ~ed to the limit** nuestros recursos están
empleados al máximo
5 ⟨truth/meaning⟩ forzar*; ⟨rules⟩ apartarse un
poco de
■ **~** *vi* **1** ⟨person⟩ estirarse*; (when sleepy)
desperezarse*

2 **(a)** (reach, extend) «*sea/influence/power*» extenderse* **(b)** (in time): **to ~ over a period** alargarse* *or* prolongarse* durante un período 3 **(a)** (be elastic) «*elastic/rope*» estirarse **(b)** (become loose, longer) «*garment*» estirarse 4 (be enough) «*money/resources/supply*» alcanzar*, llegar*

■ *v refl* **to ~ oneself** (physically) estirarse; (when sleepy) desperezarse*

■ **stretch out** 1 [*v + o + adv, v + adv + o*] (extend) estirar
  2 [*v + adv*] **(a)** (lie full length) tenderse* **(b)** (extend — in space) extenderse*; (— in time) alargarse*

stretch² *n* 1 (act of stretching) (*no pl*): **to have a ~** estirarse; (when sleepy) desperezarse* 2 **(a)** (expanse — of road, river) tramo *m*, trecho *m* **(b)** (period) período *m*; **at a ~** (without a break) sin parar 3 (elasticity) elasticidad *f*

stretch³ *adj* (*before n, no comp*) ‹*fabric/pants*› elástico; **~ limo** (colloq) limusina *f* (*grande*)

stretcher /'stretʃər ‖'stretʃə(r)/ *n* (Med) camilla *f*

stretch marks *pl n* estrías *fpl*

stretchy /'stretʃi/ *adj* **-chier, -chiest** elástico

strew /struː/ *vt* (*past* **strewn** /struːn/ *past p* **strewn** *or* **strewed** -/d/) ‹*gravel/seeds*› esparcir*; ‹*objects*› (untidily) desparramar

stricken /'strɪkən/ *adj* **(a)** (afflicted) **~ WITH sth: a country ~ with famine** un país asolado por el hambre; **I was suddenly ~ with remorse** de pronto me empezó a remorder la conciencia **(b)** ‹*vessel*› siniestrado (frml), dañado; ‹*area*› damnificado, afectado

strict /strɪkt/ *adj* **-er, -est (a)** (severe) estricto, severo **(b)** (rigorous) ‹*vegetarian*› estricto, riguroso **(c)** (exact) (*before n*) estricto, riguroso; **in the ~ sense of the word** en el sentido estricto *or* riguroso de la palabra **(d)** (complete) (*before n*) absoluto; **in ~est secrecy** en el más absoluto secreto

strictly /'strɪktli/ *adv* **(a)** (severely) con severidad, severamente, rigurosamente **(b)** (rigorously): **smoking is ~ prohibited** fumar está terminantemente prohibido; **~ (speaking)** (*indep*) en rigor, en sentido estricto **(c)** (exactly) totalmente; **that's not ~ true** eso no es totalmente cierto **(d)** (exclusively) exclusivamente; **this is ~ between ourselves** que quede entre nosotros

stride¹ /straɪd/ *vi* (*past* **strode**; *past p* **stridden** /'strɪdn/) (+ *adv compl*): **he strode across the room** cruzó la habitación a grandes zancadas

stride² *n* zancada *f*, tranco *m*; **to take sth in one's ~** tomarse algo con calma

strident /'straɪdnt/ *adj* estridente

strife /straɪf/ *n* (journ *or* frml) conflictos *mpl*; (armed) luchas *fpl*

strike¹ /straɪk/ (*past & past p* **struck**) *vt*
  1 **(a)** (hit) ‹*person*› pegarle* a, golpear; ‹*blow*› dar*, pegar*; ‹*key*› pulsar **(b)** (collide with, fall on) «*vehicle*» chocar* *or* dar* contra; «*stone/ball*» pegar* *or* dar* contra; «*lightning/bullet*» alcanzar*; **I struck my head on the beam** me di (un golpe) en la cabeza contra la viga; **he was struck by lightning** le cayó un rayo
  2 **(a)** (cause to become): **to be struck blind/dumb**

quedarse ciego/mudo; **to ~ sb dead** matar a algn **(b)** (introduce): **to ~ fear into sb** infundirle miedo a algn
  3 **(a)** (occur to) ocurrírsele (+ *me/te/le etc*); **it ~s me (that)** ... me da la impresión de que ..., se me ocurre que ... **(b)** (impress) parecerle* a; **it ~s me as odd** me parece raro; **I was struck by his changed appearance** me llamó la atención lo cambiado que estaba
  4 ‹*oil/gold*› encontrar*, dar* con
  5 ‹*match/light*› encender*
  6 **(a)** (Mus) ‹*note*› dar* **(b)** «*clock*» dar*; **the clock struck five** el reloj dio las cinco
  7 (enter into, arrive at): **to ~ a deal** llegar* a un acuerdo, cerrar*, cerrar* un trato; **to ~ a balance between** ... encontrar* el justo equilibrio entre ...
  8 (adopt) ‹*pose/attitude*› adoptar
  9 (delete) suprimir; **his name was struck off the register** se borró su nombre del registro; *see also* STRIKE OFF

■ **~** *vi* 1 (hit) «*person*» golpear; «*lightning*» caer*
  2 **(a)** (attack) atacar* **(b)** (happen suddenly) «*illness/misfortune*» sobrevenir*; «*disaster*» ocurrir
  3 (withdraw labor) hacer* huelga, declararse en huelga *or* (esp AmL) en paro
  4 «*clock*» dar* la hora

■ **strike back** [*v + adv*] (Mil) contraatacar*; **he struck back at his critics** devolvió el golpe a sus detractores

■ **strike down** [*v + o + adv, v + adv + o*] (liter): **she was struck down with cholera** fue abatida por el cólera (liter)

■ **strike off** [*v + o + adv, v + adv + o*] **(a)** (delete) tachar **(b)** (disqualify) (BrE) ‹*doctor/lawyer*› prohibirle* el ejercicio de la profesión a

■ **strike out**
  I [*v + adv*] **to ~ out** (AT sb/sth) arremeter (CONTRA algn/algo)
  II [*v + o + adv, v + adv + o*] (remove from list) tachar

■ **strike up** 1 [*v + adv + o*] **(a)** (begin) ‹*conversation*› entablar; ‹*friendship*› trabar, entablar **(b)** (start to play) ‹*tune*› empezar* a tocar
  2 [*v + adv*] «*band*» empezar* a tocar

strike² *n* 1 (stoppage) huelga *f*, paro *m* (esp AmL); **to be on ~** estar* en *or* de huelga, estar* en *or* de paro (esp AmL); **to come out** *o* **go (out) on ~** ir* a la huelga, declararse en huelga, ir* al paro (esp AmL), declararse en paro (esp AmL); **hunger ~** huelga de hambre 2 (find) descubrimiento *m* 3 (attack) ataque *m*

strikebreaker /'straɪk,breɪkər ‖'straɪk,breɪkə(r)/ *n* rompehuelgas *mf*

striker /'straɪkər ‖'straɪkə(r)/ *n* 1 (Lab Rel) huelguista *mf* 2 (in soccer) artillero, -ra *m,f*, ariete *mf*

striking /'straɪkɪŋ/ *adj* ‹*resemblance/similarity*› sorprendente, asombroso; ‹*color*› llamativo; **a ~ woman** una mujer muy atractiva

string¹ /strɪŋ/ *n* 1 **(a)** (cord, length of cord) cordel *m*, bramante *m* (Esp), mecate *m* (AmC, Méx, Ven), pita *f* (Andes), cáñamo *m* (Andes), piolín *m* (RPl) **(b)** (on apron) cinta *f*; (on puppet) hilo *m*; **no ~s attached** sin compromisos, sin condiciones
  2 **(a)** (on instrument) cuerda *f* **(b)** (on racket) cuerda *f* **(c)** **strings** *pl* (Mus) cuerdas *fpl*
  3 **(a)** (set — of pearls, beads) sarta *f*, hilo *m*; (— of ···>

S

onions, garlic) ristra f **(b)** (series — of people)
sucesión f; (— of vehicles) fila f; (— of events) serie
f; (— of curses, complaints, lies) sarta f

string² (*past & past p* **strung**) *vt* **1** (suspend)
colgar* **2** ⟨*guitar/racket/bow*⟩ encordar*,
ponerle* (las) cuerdas a; ⟨*beads/pearls*⟩ ensartar,
enhebrar
■ **string along** (colloq) [*v + o + adv*] (mislead)
tomarle el pelo a (fam) ⟨*dando esperanzas falsas*⟩
■ **string together** [*v + o + adv, v + adv + o*]
⟨*thoughts*⟩ coordinar, hilar; **she could barely ∼ a
sentence together** apenas podía hilar una frase

string bean *n* ▶ RUNNER BEAN

stringed /strɪŋd/ *adj* ⟨*instrument*⟩ de cuerda

stringent /'strɪndʒənt/ *adj* riguroso, estricto

strip¹ /strɪp/ -pp- *vt* **1** (a) (remove covering from)
⟨*bed*⟩ deshacer*, quitar la ropa de; ⟨*wood/
furniture*⟩ quitarle la pintura (*or* el barniz *etc*) a,
decapar; **to ∼ sb** (naked) desnudar a algn **(b)**
(remove contents from) ⟨*room/house*⟩ vaciar*
2 (Auto, Tech) ∼ **(down)** desmontar
■ ∼ *vi* desnudarse, desvestirse*
■ **strip off** [*v + o + adv, v + adv + o*] ⟨*wallpaper/
paint*⟩ quitar; ⟨*leaves*⟩ arrancar*

strip² *n* **1** (of leather, cloth, paper) tira f; (of metal)
tira f, cinta f; (of land) franja f **2** (BrE Sport) (*no
pl*) equipo m

strip cartoon *n* (BrE) historieta f, tira f
cómica

stripe /straɪp/ *n* raya f, lista f

striped /straɪpt/ *adj* a *or* de rayas, rayado,
listado

strip: ∼ **lighting** *n* (BrE) luz f fluorescente;
∼**-search** /'strɪp'sɜːrtʃ ‖'strɪp'sɜːtʃ/ *vt* hacer*
desnudar y registrar

strive /straɪv/ *vi* (*past* **strove** *or* **strived**;
past p **striven** /'strɪvən/) **to ∼ FOR** *o* **AFTER sth**
luchar *or* esforzarse* por alcanzar algo; **to ∼ to +
INF** esforzarse* POR + INF

strobe (light) /strəʊb/ *n* luz f estroboscópica

strode /strəʊd/ *past of* STRIDE¹

stroke¹ /strəʊk/ *n* **1** (Sport) (a) (in ball games)
golpe m **(b)** (in swimming — movement) brazada f;
(— style) estilo m **(c)** (in rowing — movement) palada
f, remada f
2 (a) (blow) golpe m **(b)** (of clock) campanada f
3 (a) (of thin brush) pincelada f; (of thick brush)
brochazo m; (of pen, pencil) trazo m **(b)** (oblique,
slash) barra f, diagonal f
4 (a) (action, feat) golpe m; **not to do a ∼ of work**
no hacer* absolutamente nada **(b)** (instance): **a ∼
of luck** un golpe de suerte
5 (Med) ataque m de apoplejía, derrame m
cerebral
6 (caress) caricia f

stroke² *vt* acariciar

stroll¹ /strəʊl/ *vi* pasear(se), dar* un paseo

stroll² *n* paseo m; **to have** *o* **go for a ∼** dar* un
paseo

stroller /'strəʊlər ‖'strəʊlə(r)/ *n* **1** (person)
paseante *mf* **2** (pushchair) (esp AmE) sillita f (de
paseo), cochecito m, carreola f (Méx)

strong¹ /strɔːŋ ‖strɒŋ/ *adj* **stronger**
/'strɔːŋɡər ‖'strɒŋɡə(r)/, **strongest** /'strɔːŋɡəst
‖'strɒŋɡɪst/ **1** (a) (physically powerful) ⟨*person/

arm*⟩ fuerte **(b)** (healthy, sound) ⟨*heart/lungs*⟩
fuerte, sano; ⟨*constitution*⟩ robusto **(c)** (firm)
⟨*character/leader*⟩ fuerte
2 (a) (solid) ⟨*material/construction*⟩ fuerte **(b)**
(powerful) ⟨*army/economy*⟩ fuerte **(c)** ⟨*current/
wind*⟩ fuerte
3 (a) (deeply held) ⟨*views/faith/support*⟩ firme **(b)**
(forceful) ⟨*protest*⟩ enérgico; ⟨*argument/evidence*⟩
de peso
4 (definite) (a) ⟨*tendency/resemblance*⟩ marcado;
⟨*candidate*⟩ con muchas posibilidades **(b)**
⟨*features*⟩ marcado
5 (good) ⟨*team*⟩ fuerte; ⟨*cast*⟩ sólido; **∼ point**
punto m fuerte; **she's a ∼ swimmer** es una buena
nadadora
6 (a) (concentrated) ⟨*color/light*⟩ fuerte, intenso;
⟨*tea/coffee*⟩ cargado; ⟨*solution*⟩ concentrado **(b)**
(pungent) ⟨*smell/flavor*⟩ fuerte **(c)** (unacceptable)
⟨*language*⟩ fuerte
7 (in number) (*no comp*): **an army ten thousand ∼**
un ejército de diez mil hombres

strong² *adv*: **to be going ∼** ⟨⟨*car/machine*⟩⟩
marchar bien; ⟨⟨*organization*⟩⟩ ir* *or* marchar
viento en popa; **he's still going ∼** ⟨⟨*old person*⟩⟩
sigue (estando) en plena forma

strong: ∼**box** *n* caja f fuerte *or* de caudales;
∼**hold** *n* (fortress) fortaleza f, bastión m; (center of
support) bastión m, baluarte m

strongly /'strɔːŋli ‖'strɒŋli/ *adv* **1** (a)
(powerfully) fuerte, con fuerza **(b)** (sturdily) ⟨*made/
welded*⟩ sólidamente **2** (a) (deeply, ardently)
totalmente; **it's something I feel very ∼ about** es
algo que me parece sumamente importante **(b)**
(forcefully) ⟨*protest/criticize*⟩ enérgicamente; **I ∼
advise you not to sell** te recomiendo con
insistencia que no vendas

strong: ∼ **room** *n* cámara f acorazada;
∼**-willed** /'strɔːŋ'wɪld ‖,strɒŋ'wɪld/ *adj*
(determined) tenaz; (obstinate) terco, tozudo

strove /strəʊv/ *past of* STRIVE

struck /strʌk/ *past & past p of* STRIKE¹

structural /'strʌktʃərəl/ *adj* estructural

structure¹ /'strʌktʃər ‖'strʌktʃə(r)/ *n* (a)
(composition, organization) estructura f **(b)** (thing
constructed) construcción f

structure² *vt* estructurar

struggle¹ /'strʌɡəl/ *n* (a) (against opponent)
lucha f; (physical) refriega f; **to put up a ∼** luchar,
oponer* resistencia **(b)** (against difficulties) lucha f;
it's a ∼ to make ends meet cuesta mucho llegar a
fin de mes

struggle² *vi* **1** (a) (thrash around) forcejear **(b)**
(contend, strive) luchar; **she had to ∼ to support
her family** tuvo que luchar para mantener a su
familia; **to ∼** ⟨AGAINST/WITH sth⟩ luchar ⟨CONTRA
algo⟩; **to ∼ FOR sth** luchar por algo **(c)** (be in
difficulties) pasar apuros **2** (move with difficulty) (+
adv compl): **he ∼d up the hill** subió penosamente
la cuesta; **he ∼d to his feet** se levantó con gran
dificultad

strum /strʌm/ *vt* -mm- ⟨*guitar/tune*⟩ rasguear

strung /strʌŋ/ *past & past p of* STRING²

strut¹ /strʌt/ *vi* -tt- (+ *adv compl*): **to ∼ around**
o **about** pavonearse

strut² *n* (Const) tornapunta f, puntal m

stub¹ /stʌb/ *n* (a) (of candle, pencil) cabo m; (of

cigarette) colilla f, pucho m (AmL fam) **(b)** (of check) talón m (AmL), matriz f (Esp); (of ticket) contraseña f, resguardo m (Esp)

stub² **-bb-** vt: to ∼ one's toe darse* en el dedo (del pie)

■ **stub out** [v + o + adv, v + adv + o] ⟨cigarette⟩ apagar*

stubble /'stʌbəl/ n **(a)** (Agr) rastrojo m **(b)** (of beard): he had three days' ∼ on his chin tenía una barba de tres días

stubborn /'stʌbərn ‖'stʌbən/ adj **(a)** ⟨person/ nature⟩ (obstinate) terco, testarudo; (resolute) tenaz, tesonero; ⟨refusal/insistence⟩ pertinaz **(b)** ⟨cold/ weeds⟩ pertinaz, persistente; ⟨stain⟩ rebelde

stuck¹ /stʌk/ past & past p of STICK²

stuck² adj **(pred) (a)** (unable to move): the drawer is ∼ el cajón se ha atascado; the door is ∼ la puerta se ha atrancado; she's ∼ at home with the kids all day está todo el día metida en la casa con los niños **(b)** (at a loss) atascado; I got ∼ on the second question me quedé atascado en la segunda pregunta **(c)** (burdened) (colloq): I was ∼ with the bill me tocó pagar la cuenta, me cargaron el muerto (fam); I got ∼ with Bob all evening tuve que aguantar a Bob toda la noche

stuck-up /stʌk'ʌp/ adj (colloq) estirado (fam)

stud¹ /stʌd/ n **1** **(a)** (nail, knob) tachuela f **(b)** (earring) arete m or (Esp) pendiente m (en forma de bolita) **(c)** (for collar, shirtfront) gemelo m (para cuello o pechera de camisa) **2** (male animal) semental m

stud² vt **-dd-** (usu pass) (with studs) tachonar; the sky was ∼ded with stars el cielo estaba tachonado de estrellas (liter)

student /'stu:dnt ‖'stju:dnt/ n (at university) estudiante mf; (at school) (esp AmE) alumno, -na m,f; a medical ∼ un/una estudiante de medicina; (before n) ∼ driver (AmE) persona que está aprendiendo a conducir; ∼ nurse estudiante mf de enfermería

student union n (association) asociación f de estudiantes; (building) centro estudiantil en el campus

studio /'stu:diəʊ ‖'stju:diəʊ/ n **(a)** (Art, Mus, Phot) estudio m **(b)** (Cin, Rad, TV) estudio m **(c)** ∼ (**apartment** o BrE also) **flat** estudio m

studious /'stu:diəs ‖'stju:diəs/ adj estudioso, aplicado

study¹ /'stʌdi/ n (pl **-dies**) **1** (act, process of learning) estudio m **2** **studies** pl **(a)** (work of student) estudios mpl **(b)** (academic discipline): business studies empresariado m or (Esp) empresariales fpl; social studies estudios vinculados a las relaciones sociales que comprenden cursos de historia, sociología y otras asignaturas afines **3** (room) estudio m **4** (investigation, examination) estudio m **5** (Art, Liter, Mus) estudio m

study² **-dies, -dying, -died** vt **(a)** (at school, university) estudiar **(b)** (investigate, research into) estudiar **(c)** (examine, scrutinize) estudiar

■ ∼ vi estudiar; she's ∼ing to be a doctor/lawyer estudia medicina/derecho

stuff¹ /stʌf/ n **1** (colloq) **(a)** (substance, matter): what's this ∼ called? ¿cómo se llama esto or (fam) esta cosa? **(b)** (miscellaneous items) cosas fpl; (personal items) cosas fpl, bártulos mpl; (junk,

rubbish) cachivaches mpl; and ∼ like that y cosas de esas; what sort of ∼ does he write? ¿qué tipo de cosa(s) escribe? **2** (nonsense, excuse) (colloq): surely you don't believe all that ∼ he tells you? tú no te creerás todo lo que te cuenta ¿no?

stuff² vt **1** **(a)** (fill) ⟨quilt/mattress/toy⟩ rellenar; ⟨hole⟩ tapar; the drawer was ∼ed with clothes el cajón estaba atiborrado de ropa; to ∼ oneself/ one's face (colloq) darse* un atracón (fam), ponerse* morado or ciego (Esp fam) **(b)** (Culin) rellenar **(c)** (in taxidermy) disecar* **2** **(a)** (thrust) to ∼ sth INTO sth meter algo EN algo **(b)** (put) (colloq) poner*

stuffed /stʌft/ adj **(a)** (in taxidermy) disecado; (toy) de peluche **(b)** ⟨pepper/tomatoes⟩ relleno

stuffing /'stʌfɪŋ/ n relleno m

stuffy /'stʌfi/ adj **-fier, -fiest** **1** **(a)** ⟨air⟩ viciado; it's ∼ in here está muy cargado el ambiente **(b)** ⟨nose⟩ tapado **2** (colloq) ⟨person⟩ acartonado, estirado (fam); ⟨organization⟩ convencional

stumble /'stʌmbəl/ vi **(a)** (trip) tropezar*, dar* un traspié **(b)** (in speech) atrancarse*; he ∼d over the long words se atrancaba la lengua con las palabras largas

■ **stumble across** ▶ STUMBLE ON

■ **stumble on, stumble upon** [v + prep + o] dar* con, encontrar*

stumbling block /'stʌmblɪŋ/ n escollo m

stump¹ /stʌmp/ n (of tree) tocón m, cepa f; (of limb) muñón m; (of pencil, candle) cabo m

stump² vt (colloq) (often pass): the problem has me ∼ed el problema me tiene perplejo; to be ∼ed for an answer no saber qué contestar

stun /stʌn/ vt **-nn-** **(a)** (make unconscious) dejar sin sentido; (daze) aturdir **(b)** (amaze) dejar atónito or (fam) helado; (shock) dejar anonadado

stung /stʌŋ/ past & past p of STING²

stunk /stʌŋk/ past p of STINK²

stunned /stʌnd/ adj **(a)** (unconscious) sin sentido; (dazed) aturdido **(b)** (shocked, amazed) ⟨expression⟩ de asombro; he was ∼ when they told him se quedó atónito or (fam) helado cuando se lo dijeron

stunning /'stʌnɪŋ/ adj ⟨success/performance⟩ sensacional; ⟨person/dress⟩ despampanante

stunt¹ /stʌnt/ n **1** (feat of daring) proeza f; she does all her own ∼s (Cin, TV) hace todas las escenas peligrosas ella misma; (before n) ∼ man/ woman especialista mf **2** (hoax, trick) truco m, maniobra f; (publicity ∼) ardid m publicitario

stunt² vt detener*, atrofiar

stunted /'stʌntəd ‖'stʌntɪd/ adj ⟨growth/ development⟩ atrofiado; ⟨tree/body⟩ raquítico

stupefy /'stu:pəfaɪ ‖'stju:pɪfaɪ/ vt **-fies, -fying, -fied** (usu pass) dejar estupefacto

stupendous /stu:'pendəs ‖stju:'pendəs/ adj (colloq) ⟨effort/strength⟩ tremendo; ⟨success⟩ formidable

stupid /'stu:pəd ‖'stju:pɪd/ adj (foolish) tonto (fam); (unintelligent) estúpido

stupidity /stu:'pɪdəti ‖stju:'pɪdəti/ n estupidez f, tontería f

stupor /'stu:pər ‖'stju:pə(r)/ n (Med) estupor m; (lethargy) aletargamiento m; in a drunken ∼ en un sopor etílico (frml o hum)

S

sturdy /ˈstɜːrdi ‖ˈstɜːdi/ adj **-dier, -diest**
⟨build/legs/figure⟩ robusto, macizo; ⟨furniture/
bicycle⟩ sólido y resistente

stutter¹ /ˈstʌtər ‖ˈstʌtə(r)/ n tartamudeo m

stutter² vi tartamudear
■ ~ vt balbucear, decir* tartamudeando

St Valentine's Day ▸ VALENTINE'S DAY

sty /staɪ/ n (pl **sties**) **(a)** (pig~) pocilga f,
chiquero m (AmL) **(b)** ▸ STYE

stye /staɪ/ n (pl **sties** or **styes**) orzuelo m

style /staɪl/ n 1 (a) (manner of acting) estilo m;
telling lies is not my ~ decir mentiras no va
conmigo **(b)** (Art, Lit, Mus) estilo m 2 (elegance)
estilo m; to live/travel in ~ vivir/viajar a lo
grande 3 (a) (type, model) diseño m, modelo m
(b) (fashion) moda f; to be in ~ estar* de moda **(c)**
(hair ~) peinado m

-style /staɪl/ suff: American~ al estilo
americano, a la americana

stylish /ˈstaɪlɪʃ/ adj ⟨furniture/clothes/decor⟩
con mucho estilo; ⟨person⟩ con clase or estilo,
estiloso (AmL fam); ⟨resort/restaurant⟩ elegante

stylist /ˈstaɪlɪst ‖ˈstaɪlɪst/ n (hair ~) estilista mf

stylistic /staɪˈlɪstɪk/ adj estilístico

stylized /ˈstaɪlaɪzd/ adj estilizado

stylus /ˈstaɪləs/ n (pl **-li** or **-luses**) aguja f,
púa f (RPl)

Styrofoam® /ˈstaɪrəfəʊm/ n (AmE) espuma f de
poliestireno

suave /swɑːv/ adj suaver, suavest ⟨voice⟩
engolado; ⟨man⟩ elegante y desenvuelto

sub /sʌb/ n (colloq) **(a)** (substitute) suplente mf,
sustituto, -ta m,f **(b)** (submarine) submarino m **(c)**
subs pl (subscription) cuota f

subconscious¹ /ˌsʌbˈkɑːntʃəs ‖ˌsʌbˈkɒnʃəs/
adj subconsciente

subconscious² n the ~ el subconsciente

subcontract /ˌsʌbˈkɑːntrækt ‖ˌsʌbkənˈtrækt/
vt subcontratar

subcontractor /sʌbˈkɑːntræktər
‖ˌsʌbkənˈtræktə(r)/ n subcontratista mf

subdivide /ˈsʌbdəvaɪd ‖ˌsʌbdɪˈvaɪd/ vt
subdividir

subdivision /ˈsʌbdəˈvɪʒən ‖ˌsʌbdɪˈvɪʒən/ n
subdivisión f

subdue /səbˈduː ‖səbˈdjuː/ vt **(a)** (bring under
control) ⟨person⟩ someter*, dominar **(b)** (vanquish)
(liter) sojuzgar* (liter)

subdued /səbˈduːd ‖səbˈdjuːd/ adj ⟨lighting/
color⟩ tenue, apagado; ⟨person/atmosphere⟩
apagado

subheading /ˈsʌbˌhedɪŋ/ n subtítulo m

subject¹ /ˈsʌbdʒɪkt/ n 1 (topic) tema m; to
change the ~ cambiar de tema 2 (discipline)
asignatura f, materia f (esp AmL), ramo m (Chi)
3 (Pol) súbdito, -ta m,f 4 (Ling) sujeto m

subject² /ˈsʌbdʒɪkt/ adj 1 (owing obedience)
⟨people/nation⟩ sometido 2 (a) (liable, prone) to be
~ TO sth ⟨to change/delay⟩ estar* sujeto A algo,

ser* susceptible DE algo; ⟨to flooding⟩ estar*
expuesto A algo **(b)** (conditional upon) to be ~ TO
sth estar* sujeto A algo

subject³ /səbˈdʒekt/ vt to ~ sth/sb TO sth
someter algo/a algn A algo

subject index n índice m de materias

subjective /səbˈdʒektɪv/ adj subjetivo

subject matter n (theme) tema m; (content)
contenido m

subjugate /ˈsʌbdʒəgeɪt ‖ˈsʌbdʒʊgeɪt/ vt
subyugar*

subjunctive¹ /səbˈdʒʌŋktɪv/ n subjuntivo m

subjunctive² adj subjuntivo

sublet /ˈsʌbˈlet/ vt/i ⟨pres p -**letting**; past &
past p -**let**⟩ subarrendar*

sublime /səˈblaɪm/ adj sublime

submachine gun /ˈsʌbməˈʃiːn/ n metralleta
f

submarine /ˈsʌbməˈriːn/ n submarino m

submerge /səbˈmɜːrdʒ ‖səbˈmɜːdʒ/ vt **(a)**
(cover, flood) sumergir* **(b)** (plunge) to ~ sth IN sth
sumergir* algo EN algo
■ ~ vi sumergirse*

submission /səbˈmɪʃən/ n 1 (surrender)
sumisión f 2 (plan, proposal) propuesta f

submissive /səbˈmɪsɪv/ adj sumiso

submit /səbˈmɪt/ -**tt**- vt 1 ⟨claim/report/
application⟩ presentar 2 (subject) to ~ sb TO sth
someter a algn A algo 3 (contend) sostener*
■ ~ vi rendirse*

subnormal /ˈsʌbˈnɔːrməl ‖ˈsʌbˈnɔːməl/ adj por
debajo de lo normal; ⟨person⟩ retrasado,
subnormal

subordinate¹ /səˈbɔːrdnət ‖səˈbɔːdɪnət/ adj
subordinado

subordinate² n subordinado, -da m,f

subscribe /səbˈskraɪb/ vi 1 (buy) to ~ (TO
sth) ⟨to magazine/newspaper⟩ suscribirse* (A
algo) 2 (support) to ~ TO sth suscribir* algo
(frml); I ~ to the view that ... yo soy de la opinión
de que ...

subscriber /səbˈskraɪbər ‖səbˈskraɪbə(r)/ n
(to paper, magazine) suscriptor, -tora m,f

subscription /səbˈskrɪpʃən/ n **(a)** (to magazine)
suscripción f; (for theatrical events) abono m **(b)**
(membership fees) (BrE) cuota f

subsequent /ˈsʌbsɪkwənt/ adj (before n)
posterior, subsiguiente

subsequently /ˈsʌbsɪkwəntli/ adv
posteriormente

subservient /səbˈsɜːrviənt ‖səbˈsɜːviənt/ adj
servil

subside /səbˈsaɪd/ vi 1 «land/road/
foundations» hundirse 2 (abate) «storm/wind»
amainar; «floods/swelling» decrecer*, bajar;
«excitement» decaer*; «anger» calmarse,
pasarse

subsidence /səbˈsaɪdn̩s, ˈsʌbsədn̩s
‖səbˈsaɪdn̩s, ˈsʌbsɪdəns/ n hundimiento m

AmC	América Central	Arg	Argentina	Cu	Cuba
AmL	América Latina	Bol	Bolivia	Ec	Ecuador
AmS	América del Sur	Chi	Chile	Esp	España
Andes	Región andina	CS	Cono Sur	Méx	México

Per	Perú
RPl	Río de la Plata
Ur	Uruguay
Ven	Venezuela

subsidiary¹ /səb'sɪdieri ‖səb'sɪdiəri/ *adj* ⟨*role/interest*⟩ secundario; ~ **subject** materia *f* complementaria

subsidiary² *n* (*pl* **-ries**) (Busn) filial *f*

subsidize /'sʌbsədaɪz ‖'sʌbsɪdaɪz/ *vt* subvencionar, subsidiar (AmL)

subsidy /'sʌbsədi ‖'sʌbsɪdi/ *n* (*pl* **-dies**) subvención *f*, subsidio *m*

subsist /səb'sɪst/ *vi* subsistir

subsistence /səb'sɪstəns/ *n* subsistencia *f*; (*before n*) ⟨*farming*⟩ de subsistencia; ~ **wage** sueldo *m* de hambre; **to live at ~ level** vivir con lo justo para subsistir

substance /'sʌbstəns/ *n* **1** (type of matter) sustancia *f* **2** **(a)** (solid quality, content) sustancia *f*; (of book) enjundia *f*, sustancia *f* **(b)** (foundation) fundamento *m* **(c) in ~** en lo esencial

substandard /'sʌb'stændərd ‖,sʌb'stændəd/ *adj* ⟨*goods/clothes*⟩ de calidad inferior

substantial /səb'stæntʃəl ‖səb'stænʃəl/ *adj* **1** **(a)** ⟨*amount/income/loan*⟩ considerable, importante **(b)** ⟨*changes/difference*⟩ sustancial; ⟨*contribution*⟩ importante **2** **(a)** (sturdy, solid) ⟨*furniture/building*⟩ sólido **(b)** (nourishing, filling) ⟨*meal*⟩ sustancioso

substantiate /səb'stæntʃieɪt ‖səb'stænʃieɪt/ *vt* ⟨*rumors/story/statement*⟩ confirmar, corroborar; **can you ~ these accusations?** ¿puede probar estas acusaciones?

substation /'sʌbsteɪʃən/ *n* (AmE) estafeta *f* de correos

substitute¹ /'sʌbstətuːt ‖'sʌbstɪtjuːt/ *n* **(a)** (thing) ~ (**FOR** sth) sucedáneo *m* (**DE** algo); **sugar** ~ sucedáneo *m* del azúcar; **there's no ~ for experience** nada puede sustituir a la experiencia **(b)** (person) sustituto, -ta *m,f*, reemplazo *m*, suplente *mf*

substitute² *vt* sustituir*, reemplazar*

substitute teacher *n* (AmE) (profesor, -sora *m,f*) suplente *mf*

substitution /sʌbstə'tuːʃən ‖,sʌbstɪ'tjuːʃən/ *n* sustitución *f*

subterfuge /'sʌbtərfjuːdʒ ‖'sʌbtəfjuːdʒ/ *n* subterfugio *m*

subterranean /'sʌbtə'remiən/ *adj* subterráneo

subtitle¹ /'sʌb,taɪtl/ *n* subtítulo *m*

subtitle² *vt* (*usu pass*) subtitular

subtle /'sʌtl/ *adj* **subtler** /'sʌtlər ‖'sʌtlə(r)/, **subtlest** /'sʌtləst ‖'sʌtlɪst/ **(a)** (delicate, elusive) ⟨*fragrance*⟩ sutil **(b)** (not obvious) ⟨*difference/ distinction/hint*⟩ sutil; ⟨*change*⟩ imperceptible **(c)** (tactful) (colloq) delicado

subtlety /'sʌtlti/ *n* (*pl* **-ties**) **(a)** (delicacy, elusiveness) sutileza *f* **(b)** (tact, finesse) delicadeza *f*; **to lack ~** ser* poco delicado

subtly /'sʌtli/ *adv* **(a)** (delicately, elusively) sutilmente **(b)** (tactfully) con delicadeza

subtotal /'sʌbtəʊtl/ *n* subtotal *m*, total *m* parcial

subtract /səb'trækt/ *vt* **to ~ sth** (**FROM** sth) restar algo (**DE** algo)

subtraction /səb'trækʃən/ *n* resta *f*, sustracción *f* (fml)

suburb /'sʌbɜːrb ‖'sʌbɜːb/ *n* barrio *m* or (Méx)

colonia *f* residencial de las afueras; **the ~s** los barrios periféricos *or* de las afueras (de la ciudad)

suburban /sə'bɜːrbən ‖sə'bɜːbən/ *adj* ⟨*area*⟩ suburbano; ⟨*shopping mall*⟩ de las afueras

suburbia /sə'bɜːrbiə ‖sə'bɜːbiə/ *n zonas residenciales de las afueras de una ciudad*

subversive /səb'vɜːrsɪv ‖səb'vɜːsɪv/ *adj* subversivo

subway /'sʌbweɪ/ *n* **1** (AmE Rail) metro *m*, subterráneo *m* (RPI) **2** (BrE) (for pedestrians) pasaje *m* subterráneo

succeed /sək'siːd/ *vi* **1** (have success) ⟨*plan*⟩ dar* resultado, surtir efecto; **she tried to persuade him, but did not ~** intentó convencerlo pero no lo consiguió; **he's ~ed in all that he's done** ha tenido éxito en todo lo que ha hecho; **~ in life** triunfar en la vida; **he finally ~ed in passing the exam** al final logró aprobar el examen **2 to ~** (**TO** sth): **he ~ed to the throne** subió al trono; **to ~ to a title** heredar un título ■ ~ *vt* suceder; **who ~ed him?** ¿quién lo sucedió?

succeeding /sək'siːdɪŋ/ *adj* (*before n*) subsiguiente

success /sək'ses/ *n* éxito *m*; **to be a ~** ser* un éxito; **without ~** sin (ningún) éxito

successful /sək'sesfəl/ *adj* ⟨*person*⟩ de éxito, exitoso (AmL); **the ~ applicant for the job** el candidato que obtenga el puesto; **to be ~ in life** triunfar en la vida

successfully /sək'sesfəli/ *adv* satisfactoriamente

succession /sək'seʃən/ *n* **1** **(a)** (act of following) sucesión *f*; **for 6 years in ~** durante seis años consecutivos; **in rapid ~** uno tras otro **(b)** (series) sucesión *f* **2** (to office, rank) sucesión *f*

successive /sək'sesɪv/ *adj* (*before n*) consecutivo

successor /sək'sesər ‖sək'sesə(r)/ *n* sucesor, -sora *m,f*

succinct /sək'sɪŋkt/ *adj* sucinto, conciso

succulent /'sʌkjələnt ‖'sʌkjʊlənt/ *adj* suculento

succumb /sə'kʌm/ *vi* **to ~** (**TO** sth) sucumbir (**A** algo)

such¹ /sʌtʃ/ *adj* **1** **(a)** (emphasizing degree, extent) tal (+ *noun*); tan (+ *adj*); **I woke up with ~ a headache** me levanté con tal dolor de cabeza ...; **I've got ~ a lot of work to do** tengo tanto (trabajo) que hacer; **I've never heard ~ nonsense** nunca he oído semejante estupidez **(b)** (*with clauses of result or purpose*) **such ...** (**that**) tal/tan ... que **(c)** (*in comparisons*) **such ... as** tan ... como

2 **(a)** (of this, that kind) tal; **~ children are known as ...** a dichos *or* a tales niños se los conoce como ...; **there's no ~ thing as the perfect crime** el crimen perfecto no existe; **I said no ~ thing!** ¡yo no dije tal cosa! **(b)** (unspecified) tal; **the letter tells you to go to ~ a house on ~ a date** la carta te dice que vayas a tal casa en tal fecha

such² *pron* **1** **(a)** (of the indicated kind) tal; **~ were her last words** tales fueron sus últimas palabras **(b)** **~ as** como; **many modern inventions, ~ as radar ...** muchos inventos modernos, (tales) como el radar ... **(c) as such** como tal/tales **2** (indicating lack of quantity, quality): ⋯⋖

the evidence, ∼ as it is, seems to ... las pocas pruebas que hay parecen ... **3** (of such a kind, extent, degree) **such that** tal ... que

such: ∼**-and-**∼ *adj* tal (o cual); **we were told to get** ∼**-and-**∼ **a book** nos dijeron que compráramos tal (o cual) libro; ∼**like** *pron* (colloq) (of things) cosas por el estilo; (of people) gente por el estilo

suck /sʌk/ *vt* **(a)** «*person*» ‹*thumb/candy*› chupar; ‹*liquid*› (through a straw) sorber; «*vacuum cleaner*» aspirar; «*pump*» succionar, aspirar; «*insect*» ‹*blood/nectar*› chupar **(b)** (pull, draw) (+ *adv compl*) arrastrar; **she was** ∼**ed under by the current** la corriente se la tragó
 ■ ∼ *vi* **1** «*person*» chupar; **to** ∼ **AT/ON sth** chupar algo **2** (be objectionable) (AmE sl): **the movie really** ∼**s** la película es una mierda (vulg)
 ■ **suck in** [*v* + *o* + *adv*, *v* + *adv* + *o*] ‹*air/breath*› tomar

sucker /'sʌkər ‖ 'sʌkə(r)/ *n* **1** (colloq) (fool) (pej) imbécil *mf*; **to be a** ∼ **for punishment** ser* un masoquista **2** (suction device — on animal, plant) ventosa *f*; (— made of rubber) (BrE) ventosa *f* **3** (Bot) (shoot) chupón *m*, mamón *m*

suckle /'sʌkəl/ *vt* amamantar, darle* de mamar a
 ■ ∼ *vi* mamar

suction /'sʌkʃən/ *n* succión *f*; (before *n*) ∼ **cup** ventosa *f*

Sudan /suːˈdɑːn/ *n* (the) ∼ (el) Sudán

Sudanese /ˌsuːdṇˈiːz ‖ ˌsuːdɑːˈniːz/ *adj* sudanés

sudden /'sʌdṇ/ *adj* **(a)** (rushed) repentino, súbito; (unexpected) imprevisto, inesperado; **all of a** ∼ de repente, de pronto **(b)** (abrupt) ‹*movement*› brusco

suddenly /'sʌdṇli/ *adv* **(a)** (unexpectedly) de repente, de pronto **(b)** (abruptly) bruscamente

suds /sʌdz/ *pl n* espuma *f* de jabón

sue /suː ‖ suː, sjuː/ *vt* **to** ∼ **sb** (**FOR sth**) demandar a algn (POR algo)
 ■ ∼ *vi* (Law) entablar una demanda, poner* pleito (Esp)

suede /sweɪd/ *n* ante *m*, gamuza *f*

suet /'suːət ‖ 'suːɪt, 'sjuːɪt/ *n* sebo *m*, grasa *f* de pella

suffer /'sʌfər ‖ 'sʌfə(r)/ *vt* **(a)** (undergo) ‹*injury/damage/loss*› sufrir; ‹*pain*› padecer*, sufrir **(b)** (endure) aguantar, tolerar
 ■ ∼ *vi* **(a)** (experience pain, difficulty) sufrir **(b)** (be affected, deteriorate) «*health/eyesight*» resentirse*; «*business/relationship*» verse* afectado, resentirse* **(c)** (be afflicted) **to** ∼ **FROM sth** sufrir *or* (fml) padecer* DE algo

sufferer /'sʌfərər ‖ 'sʌfərə(r)/ *n* ∼**s from arthritis, arthritis** ∼**s** quienes sufren de artritis, los artríticos

suffering /'sʌfərɪŋ/ *n* sufrimiento *m*

suffice /səˈfaɪs/ *vi* (fml) bastar, ser* suficiente

sufficient /səˈfɪʃənt/ *adj* suficiente, bastante

sufficiently /səˈfɪʃəntli/ *adv* lo suficientemente

suffix /'sʌfɪks/ *n* sufijo *m*

suffocate /'sʌfəkeɪt/ *vt* asfixiar, ahogar*
 ■ ∼ *vi* asfixiarse*, ahogarse*

suffocating /'sʌfəkeɪtɪŋ/ *adj* ‹*smoke/routine*› asfixiante; ‹*heat*› sofocante

suffocation /ˌsʌfəˈkeɪʃən/ *n* asfixia *f*

suffrage /'sʌfrɪdʒ/ *n* sufragio *m*

sugar /'ʃʊɡər ‖ 'ʃʊɡə(r)/ *n* azúcar *m or f*; (before *n*) ∼ **bowl** azucarero *m*, azucarera *f* (esp AmL); ∼ **cube** *o* **lump** terrón *m* de azúcar

sugar: ∼ **beet** *n* remolacha *f* azucarera *or* (Méx) betabel *m* blanco; ∼ **cane** *n* caña *f* de azúcar

sugary /'ʃʊɡəri/ *adj* ‹*drink/taste*› dulce, azucarado **(b)** ‹*tones/smile*› meloso, almibarado

suggest /səɡˈdʒest ‖ səˈdʒest/ *vt* **1 (a)** (propose) sugerir*; **to** ∼ **sth TO sb** sugerirle* algo A algn; **to** ∼**-ING** sugerir* + *subj*, sugerir* QUE (+ *subj*); **to** ∼ **TO sb THAT** sugerirle* a algn QUE (+ *subj*) **(b)** (offer for consideration): **can you** ∼ **a possible source for this rumor?** ¿se le ocurre quién puede haber empezado este rumor? **(c)** (imply, insinuate) insinuar*; **are you** ∼**ing (that) my son is a thief?** ¿insinúa usted que mi hijo es un ladrón? **2** (indicate, point to) indicar* **3** (evoke, bring to mind) sugerir*

suggestion /səɡˈdʒestʃən ‖ səˈdʒestʃən/ *n* **1 (a)** (proposal) sugerencia *f*; **to make a** ∼ hacer* una sugerencia; **have you any** ∼**s for speeding up the process?** ¿se le ocurre algo para acelerar el proceso? **(b)** (explanation, theory) teoría *f* **(c)** (insinuation) insinuación *f* **2** (indication, hint) indicio *m* **3** (Psych) sugestión *f*

suggestive /səɡˈdʒestɪv ‖ səˈdʒestɪv/ *adj* **1** ‹*gesture/laugh*› insinuante, provocativo **2** (pred) **to be** ∼ **OF sth (a)** (indicative) parecer* indicar algo **(b)** (reminiscent) hacer* pensar EN algo, evocar* algo

suicidal /ˌsuːəˈsaɪdl ‖ ˌsuːɪˈsaɪdl, ˌsjuː-/ *adj* suicida

suicide /'suːəsaɪd ‖ 'suːɪsaɪd, 'sjuː-/ *n* (act) suicidio *m*; **to commit** ∼ suicidarse; (before *n*) ‹*attempt/pact*› de suicidio; ‹*mission/bombing*› suicida; ∼ **note** carta *f* de despedida de un suicida

suit¹ /suːt ‖ suːt, sjuːt/ *n* **1** (Clothing) (male) traje *m*, terno (AmS); (female) traje *m* (de chaqueta), traje *m* sastre **2** (Law) juicio *m*, pleito *m* **3** (in cards) palo *m*; **to follow** ∼ seguir* su (*or* nuestro *etc*) ejemplo

suit² *vt* **1** (be convenient to, please) venirle* bien a, convenirle* a; **to** ∼ **oneself** hacer* lo que uno quiere; ∼ **yourself!** ¡haz lo que quieras! **2 (a)** (be appropriate, good for): **the job doesn't** ∼ **him** el trabajo no es para él *or* no le va **(b)** (look good on) «*hairstyle/dress*» quedarle *or* (esp Esp) irle* bien a; *see also* SUITED **3** (adapt) **to** ∼ **sth TO sth/sb** adaptar algo A algo/algn

suitable /'suːtəbəl ‖ 'suːtəbəl, 'sjuː-/ *adj* **(a)** (appropriate) apropiado, adecuado; **(to be)** ∼ **FOR sb/sth/-ING** (ser*) apropiado *or* adecuado PARA algn/algo/+ INF **(b)** (acceptable, proper) apropiado **(c)** (convenient) conveniente

suitably /'suːtəbli ‖ 'suːtəbli, 'sjuː-/ *adv* ‹*qualified*› adecuadamente; ‹*dressed/equipped*› apropiadamente

suitcase /'suːtkeɪs ‖ 'suːtkeɪs, 'sjuː-/ *n* maleta *f*, valija *f* (RPl), petaca *f* (Méx)

suite /swiːt/ *n* **(a)** (of rooms) suite *f* **(b)** (of furniture) juego *m* **(c)** (Mus) suite *f*

suited /'suːtəd ‖ 'suːtɪd, 'sjuː-/ *adj* (pred) **to be** ∼ **TO sth** «*thing*» ser* apropiado *or* adecuado PARA algo; **I'm not** ∼ **to this type of work** no sirvo para este tipo de trabajo; **they are very well** ∼ **(to each other)** están hechos el uno para el otro

suitor /'su:tər ‖'su:tə(r), 'sju:-/ n ⟨dated⟩ pretendiente m

sulfur, (BrE) **sulphur** /'sʌlfər ‖'sʌlfə(r)/ n azufre m

sulk /sʌlk/ vi enfurruñarse

sulky /'sʌlki/ adj **-kier, -kiest** ⟨child⟩ con tendencia a enfurruñarse; ⟨look/reply⟩ malhumorado

sullen /'sʌlən/ adj hosco, huraño

sultan /'sʌltn̩/ n sultán m

sultana /sʌl'tænə ‖sʌl'tɑ:nə/ n ⟨Culin⟩ pasa f sultana or de Esmirna

sultry /'sʌltri/ adj **-trier, -triest** ⟨climate/ day⟩ bochornoso **(b)** ⟨voice/smile/person⟩ seductor

sum /sʌm/ n **1** (calculation — in general) cuenta f; (— addition) suma f, adición f (frml) **2** (total, aggregate) suma f, total m **3** (of money) suma f or cantidad f (de dinero)

■ **sum up: -mm-** **1** [v + o + adv, v + adv + o] **(a)** (summarize) ⟨discussion/report⟩ resumir **(b)** (assess) ⟨person⟩ catalogar*; **she quickly** ∼**med up the situation** enseguida se hizo una composición de lugar **2** [v + adv] **(a)** (summarize) recapitular; **to** ∼ **up** (as linker) resumiendo, en resumen **(b)** (Law) recapitular

summarize /'sʌməraɪz/ vt resumir

summary¹ /'sʌməri/ n (pl **-ries**) resumen m

summary² adj ⟨dismissal⟩ inmediato; ⟨trial/ judgment⟩ sumario

summer /'sʌmər ‖'sʌmə(r)/ n verano m; **in (the)** ∼ en (el) verano; (before n) ⟨weather/ clothes/vacation⟩ de verano; ∼ **camp** (in US) colonia f de vacaciones

summer: ∼**house** n cenador m; ∼ **school** n (in US) clases fpl de verano (gen de repaso); (in UK) curso m de verano; ∼**time** n verano m, estío m (liter); ∼ **time** n (BrE) horario m de verano

summery /'sʌməri/ adj veraniego, de verano

summing-up /'sʌmɪŋ'ʌp/ n (pl **summings-up**) recapitulación f

summit /'sʌmət ‖'sʌmɪt/ n **1** (of mountain, career) cumbre f, cima f **2** ∼ **(conference)** (conferencia f) cumbre f

summon /'sʌmən/ vt **(a)** (send for) ⟨servant/ waiter⟩ llamar, mandar llamar (AmL); ⟨police/ doctor⟩ llamar; ⟨help/reinforcements⟩ pedir*; ⟨meeting/parliament⟩ convocar* **(b)** (Law) ⟨witness/defendant⟩ citar, emplazar* **(c)** ▶ SUMMON UP

■ **summon up** [v + adv + o] **(a)** (gather): **he** ∼**ed up the courage to ask her** se armó de valor para preguntárselo; **I couldn't even** ∼ **up the strength to get up the stairs** ni siquiera pude reunir fuerzas para subir la escalera **(b)** (call up) ⟨thoughts/memories⟩ evocar*

summons¹ /'sʌmənz/ n (pl **-monses**) **(a)** (Law) citación f, citatorio m (Méx) **(b)** (for help etc) llamamiento m, llamado m (AmL)

summons² vt (Law) citar, emplazar*

sumptuous /'sʌmptʃuəs ‖'sʌmptʃʊəs/ adj ⟨fabric/color⟩ suntuoso; ⟨mansion/decor⟩ lujoso

sun¹ /sʌn/ n sol m; **under the** ∼: **I've tried everything under the** ∼ he probado de todo

sun² v refl **-nn-**: **to** ∼ **oneself** tomar el sol or (CS tb) tomar sol, asolearse (AmL)

sun: ∼**bathe** vi tomar el sol or (CS tb) tomar sol, asolearse (AmL); ∼**beam** n rayo m de sol; ∼**bed** n cama f solar; ∼**block** n filtro m solar; ∼**burn** n quemadura f de sol; ∼**burned** /'sʌnbɜ:rnd ‖'sʌnbɜ:nd/, (BrE also) ∼**burnt** /'sʌnbɜ:rnt ‖'sʌnbɜ:nt/ adj **(a)** (painfully) quemado por el sol **(b)** (brown) bronceado, tostado, quemado (AmL), moreno (Esp), asoleado (Méx)

sundae /'sʌndeɪ/ n sundae m (helado con fruta, crema, jarabe etc)

Sunday /'sʌndeɪ, '-di/ n domingo m; (before n) ∼ **school** sesiones dominicales de catequesis para niños; see also MONDAY

sun: ∼**dial** n reloj m de sol; ∼**down** n (no art) puesta f de(l) sol; ∼**dress** n vestido m de tirantes, solera f (CS)

sundries /'sʌndriz/ pl n **(a)** (goods) artículos mpl diversos **(b)** (expenses) gastos mpl varios

sundry¹ /'sʌndri/ adj varios, diversos

sundry² pron: **all and** ∼ todos sin excepción, todo el mundo

sunflower /'sʌnflaʊr ‖'sʌnflaʊə(r)/ n girasol m; (before n) ∼ **oil** aceite m de girasol; ∼ **seed** semilla f de girasol, pipa f (Esp)

sung /sʌŋ/ past p of SING

sunglasses /'sʌnˌglæsəz ‖'sʌnˌglɑ:sɪz/ pl n gafas fpl or (esp AmL) lentes mpl or anteojos mpl de sol

sunk¹ /sʌŋk/ past p of SINK¹

sunk² adj (pred) **(a)** (in trouble) (colloq) **to be** ∼ estar* perdido **(b)** (immersed) **to be** ∼ **IN sth** ⟨in depression/gloom⟩ estar* sumido EN algo (liter)

sunken /'sʌŋkən/ adj **(a)** (before n) ⟨ship/ treasure⟩ hundido, sumergido **(b)** (before n) ⟨garden/patio⟩ a nivel más bajo **(c)** (hollow) ⟨eyes/ cheeks⟩ hundido

sun: ∼ **lamp** n lámpara f de rayos ultravioletas; ∼**light** n sol m, luz f del sol; ∼**lit** adj soleado

sunny /'sʌni/ adj **-nier, -niest (a)** ⟨day⟩ de sol; ⟨room/garden⟩ soleado; **it's** ∼ **today** hoy hace sol **(b)** (good-humored) alegre

sun: ∼**rise** n salida f del sol; ∼**roof** n techo m corredizo; ∼**screen** n filtro m solar; ∼**set** n puesta f de(l) sol; **at** ∼**set** al atardecer, a la caída de la tarde; ∼**shine** n sol m; ∼**spot** n **(a)** (Astron) mancha f solar **(b)** (resort) (colloq) lugar de veraneo con mucho sol; ∼**stroke** n insolación f; ∼**tan** n bronceado m, moreno m (Esp); **to get a** ∼**tan** broncearse, tostarse*, quemarse (AmL); (before n) ⟨lotion⟩ bronceador; ∼**trap** n: lugar muy soleado y resguardado

super /'su:pər ‖'su:pə(r)/ adj (colloq) genial (fam), súper adj inv (fam)

superb /sʊ'pɜ:rb ‖su:'pɜ:b/ adj magnífico, espléndido

superbug /'su:pərbʌg ‖'su:pəbʌg/ n microbio m multiresistente

supercilious /ˌsu:pər'sɪliəs ‖ˌsu:pə'sɪliəs/ adj desdeñoso

superficial /ˌsu:pər'fɪʃəl ‖ˌsu:pə'fɪʃəl/ adj superficial

superfluous /su:'pɜ:rfluəs ‖su:'pɜ:fluəs/ adj superfluo

superglue¹ /'su:pərglu: ‖'su:pəglu:/ n cola f
de contacto, superglue m (Esp)

superglue² vt pegar* con cola de contacto,
pegar* con superglue (Esp)

superhighway /'su:pər'haɪweɪ
‖'su:pə,haɪweɪ/ n **(a)** (AmE Auto) autopista f **(b)**
(Comput): **the information** ~ la autopista de la
comunicación

superhuman /'su:pər'hju:mən
‖,su:pə'hju:mən/ adj sobrehumano

superimpose /'su:pərɪm'pəʊz/ vt superponer*

superintend /'su:pərɪn'tend/ vt supervisar

superintendent /'su:pərɪn'tendənt/ n **(a)**
(person in charge — of maintenance, hostel, swimming
pool) encargado, -da m,f; (— of building) (AmE)
portero, -ra m,f, (— of institution) director, -tora m,f
(b) (police officer) (in US) superintendente mf (jefe
de un departamento de policía); (in UK) comisario,
-ria m,f de policía

superior¹ /sʊ'pɪriər ‖su:'pɪəriə(r)/ adj **1** **(a)**
(better) **to be** ~ (TO sth/sb) ser* superior (A algo/
algn), ser* mejor (QUE algo/algn) **(b)** (above
average) ⟨workmanship/writer⟩ de gran calidad
2 (arrogant) ⟨tone/smile⟩ de superioridad; **he's so**
~ se da unos aires de superioridad **3** ⟨rank⟩
superior; **his** ~ **officer** su superior

superior² n superior m

superiority /sʊ'pɪri'ɔ:rəti ‖su:,pɪəri'ɒrəti/ n
superioridad f

superlative¹ /sʊ'pɜ:rlətɪv ‖su:'pɜ:lətɪv/ adj
inigualable, excepcional

superlative² n superlativo m

superman /'su:pərmæn ‖'su:pəmæn/ n (pl
-men /-men/) superhombre m

supermarket /'su:pər,mɑ:rkət ‖'su:pə,mɑ:kɪt/
n supermercado m, autoservicio m

supernatural /'su:pər'nætʃərəl
‖,su:pə'nætʃərəl/ adj sobrenatural

superpower /'su:pərpaʊər ‖'su:pəpaʊə(r)/ n
superpotencia f

supersede /'su:pər'si:d ‖,su:pə'si:d/ vt (often
pass) reemplazar*, sustituir*

supersonic /'su:pər'sɑ:nɪk ‖,su:pə'sɒnɪk/ adj
supersónico

superstar /'su:pərstɑ:r ‖'su:pəstɑ:(r)/ n
superestrella f, gran estrella f

superstition /'su:pər'stɪʃən ‖,su:pə'stɪʃən/ n
superstición f

superstitious /'su:pər'stɪʃəs ‖,su:pə'stɪʃəs/
adj supersticioso

superstore /'su:pərstɔ:r ‖'su:pəstɔ:(r)/ n (BrE)
hipermercado m

supervise /'su:pərvaɪz ‖'su:pəvaɪz/ vt **(a)**
⟨project/staff⟩ supervisar **(b)** (watch over) vigilar

supervision /'su:pər'vɪʒən ‖,su:pə'vɪʒən/ n
supervisión f

supervisor /'su:pərvaɪzər ‖'su:pəvaɪzə(r)/ n
supervisor, -sora m,f

supper /'sʌpər ‖'sʌpə(r)/ n cena f (ligera),
comida f (ligera) (esp AmL); **to have** ~ cenar,
comer (esp AmL)

supplant /sə'plænt ‖sə'plɑ:nt/ vt sustituir*,
reemplazar*

supple /'sʌpəl/ adj **-pler** /-plər ‖-plə(r)/,
-plest /-pləst ‖-plɪst/ ⟨body/fingers⟩ ágil;
⟨leather⟩ fino y flexible, suave

supplement¹ /'sʌpləmənt ‖'sʌplɪmənt/ n
1 (addition to diet, income) complemento m **2** **(a)**
(additional part published separately) suplemento m **(b)**
(section of newspaper — separate) suplemento m; (—
inserted) separata f

supplement² /'sʌpləmənt ‖ 'sʌplɪment/ vt
⟨diet/income⟩ complementar; ⟨report⟩ completar

supplementary /'sʌplə'mentəri
‖,sʌplɪ'mentəri/ adj suplementario

supplier /sə'plaɪər ‖sə'plaɪə(r)/ n (Busn)
proveedor, -dora m,f, abastecedor, -dora m,f

supply¹ /sə'plaɪ/ n (pl **-plies**) **1** (provision)
suministro m; **the water/electricity** ~ el
suministro de agua/electricidad; **the law of** ~ **and
demand** la ley de la oferta y la demanda **2** (stock,
store): **food supplies are running low** se están
agotando las provisiones or los víveres or (Mil) los
pertrechos; **we only have a month's** ~ **of coal left**
solo nos queda carbón para un mes; (Busn) las
existencias de carbón solo van a durar un mes;
to be in short ~ escasear

supply² vt **-plies, -plying, -plied** **1** **(a)**
(provide, furnish) ⟨electricity/gas⟩ suministrar;
⟨goods⟩ suministrar, abastecer* or proveer* de;
⟨evidence/information⟩ proporcionar, facilitar **(b)**
⟨retailer/manufacturer⟩ abastecer*; **to** ~ **sb WITH
sth** ⟨with equipment⟩ proveer* a algn DE algo;
(Busn) abastecer* a algn DE algo, suministrarle
algo A algn; ⟨with information⟩ facilitar or
proporcionarle algo A algn **2** (meet) (frml)
⟨demand/need⟩ satisfacer*

supply teacher n (BrE) (profesor, -sora m,f)
suplente mf

support¹ /sə'pɔ:rt ‖sə'pɔ:t/ vt **1** (hold up)
⟨bridge/structure⟩ sostener*; **the chair couldn't** ~
his weight la silla no pudo aguantar or resistir su
peso **2** **(a)** (maintain, sustain) ⟨family⟩ mantener*;
to ~ **oneself** ganarse la vida **(b)** (Comput) admitir
3 **(a)** (back) ⟨cause/motion⟩ apoyar; **what team
do you** ~? ¿de qué equipo eres (hincha)? **(b)**
(back up) apoyar **4** (corroborate) ⟨theory⟩ respaldar,
confirmar

support² n **1** **(a)** (of structure) soporte m **(b)**
(physical): **to lean on sb for** ~ apoyarse en algn
(para sostenerse) **2** **(a)** (financial) ayuda f
(económica), apoyo m (económico) **(b)** (person)
sostén m **3** (backing, encouragement) apoyo m
4 (Mil) apoyo m, refuerzo m **5** **in support of** (as
prep) en apoyo de

support band n grupo m telonero

supporter /sə'pɔ:rtər ‖sə'pɔ:tə(r)/ n **(a)**
(adherent) partidario, -ria m,f **(b)** (Sport) hincha mf

supporting /səˈpɔːtɪŋ ‖səˈpɔːtɪŋ/ adj (before n) ⟨role/actor⟩ secundario; ~ **act** número m telonero

supportive /səˈpɔːtɪv ‖səˈpɔːtɪv/ adj: she's been very ~ me (or lo etc) ha apoyado mucho

suppose /səˈpəʊz/ vt **1** (a) (assume, imagine) suponer*, imaginarse; ~ **he phones and you're not in** ¿y si llama y tú no estás?; I ~ **so** supongo or me imagino que sí; I ~ **not** supongo que no or no creo (b) (believe, think) creer*; **what do you** ~ **he'll do?** ¿tú qué crees que hará?
2 to be supposed to + INF (a) (indicating obligation, expectation): I'm ~d **to start work at nine** se supone que tengo que empezar a trabajar a las nueve; **aren't you** ~d **to be at home?** ¿tú no tendrías que estar en casa? (b) (indicating intention): **what's that** ~d **to be?** ¿y eso qué se supone que es?; **what's that** ~d **to mean?** ¿y qué quieres (or quieren etc) decir con eso, (si se puede saber)? (c) (indicating general opinion): **it's** ~d **to be a very interesting book** dicen que es un libro muy interesante

supposing /səˈpəʊzɪŋ/ conj (a) (expressing hypothesis) suponiendo que; ~ **she agrees, will they let us go?** suponiendo que ella esté de acuerdo ¿nos dejarán ir? (b) (introducing suggestion) ¿y si … ?

supposition /ˌsʌpəˈzɪʃən/ n suposición f

suppress /səˈpres/ vt (a) ⟨anger/laughter⟩ contener*; ⟨feelings⟩ reprimir (b) ⟨facts/evidence/ truth⟩ ocultar (c) ⟨revolt⟩ sofocar*; ⟨organization⟩ suprimir

suppression /səˈpreʃən/ n (a) (of feelings) represión f (b) (of evidence) ocultación f (c) (of revolt) represión f

supremacy /səˈpreməsi ‖suːˈpreməsi, sjuː-/ n supremacía f

supreme /suːˈpriːm ‖suːˈpriːm, sjuː-/ adj supremo

Supreme Court n the ~ ~ el Tribunal Supremo or (esp AmL) la Corte Suprema (de Justicia)

surcharge /ˈsɜːtʃɑːdʒ ‖ˈsɜːtʃɑːdʒ/ n recargo m

sure¹ /ʃʊr ‖ʃʊə(r), ʃɔː(r)/ adj **surer, surest**
1 (convinced) (pred) seguro; **to be** ~ **ABOUT sth** estar* seguro DE algo; I'm **not** ~ I **agree with you** no sé si estoy de acuerdo contigo; I'm **not** ~ **who/ why/what** … no sé muy bien quién/por qué/qué …; **to be** ~ **OF sth** estar* seguro DE algo/algn; I **want to be** ~ **of getting there on time** quiero asegurarme de que voy a llegar a tiempo; **to be** ~ **of oneself** (convinced one is right) estar* seguro; (self-confident) ser* seguro de sí mismo
2 (certain): **one thing is** ~: **he's lying** lo que está claro or lo que es seguro es que está mintiendo; **it's** ~ **to rain** seguro que llueve; **to make** ~ **of sth** asegurarse de algo; **make** ~ **(that) you're not late** no vayas a llegar tarde
3 (accurate, reliable) ⟨remedy/method⟩ seguro; ⟨judgment/aim⟩ certero; ⟨indication⟩ claro; ⟨ground⟩ seguro
4 (in phrases) for sure: **we don't know anything for** ~ no sabemos nada seguro or con seguridad; **we'll win for** ~ seguro que ganamos; **to be sure** (admittedly) (indep) por cierto

sure² adv **1** (colloq) (as intensifier): **she** ~ **is clever, she's** ~ **clever** ¡qué lista es!, ¡si será lista!;

do you like it? — I ~ **do!** ¿te gusta? — ¡ya lo creo!
2 (of course) por supuesto, claro **3 sure enough** efectivamente, en efecto

sure: ~**fire** adj (before n) ⟨method⟩ segurísimo, infalible; ~**footed** /ˈʃʊrfʊtəd ‖ˌʃʊəˈfʊtɪd, ˌʃɔːˈfʊtɪd/ adj ⟨goat/cat⟩ de pie firme

surely /ˈʃʊrli ‖ˈʃʊəli, ˈʃɔːli/ adv **1** (a) (expressing conviction): ~ **the real problem is** … el verdadero problema, digo yo or me parece a mí, es …; ~ **she doesn't mean that!** ¡no puede ser que lo diga en serio! (b) (expressing uncertainty): **he must be mistaken,** ~? tiene que estar equivocado ¿no? (c) (expressing disbelief): ~ **you don't believe that!** ¡no te creerás eso!; ~ **not!** ¡no es posible! or ¡no puede ser! **2** (undoubtedly, certainly) seguramente, sin duda **3** (gladly, willingly) por supuesto, desde luego

surf¹ /sɜːf ‖sɜːf/ n (a) (waves) olas fpl (rompientes); (swell) oleaje m (b) (foam) espuma f

surf² vi hacer* surf or surfing
■ ~ vt (Comput) explorar, navegar* en

surface¹ /ˈsɜːfəs ‖ˈsɜːfəs/ n **1** (a) (of solid, land) superficie f; (before n) ⟨wound/mark⟩ superficial; ⟨resemblance⟩ superficial (b) (of liquid, sea) superficie f (c) **on the surface** (superficially) en apariencia **2** (Math) ~ **(area)** superficie f, área f

surface² vi ⟨⟨diver/submarine⟩⟩ salir* a la superficie; ⟨⟨problems/difficulties⟩⟩ aflorar, aparecer*
■ ~ vt ⟨road⟩ revestir*, recubrir*; (with asphalt) asfaltar

surfboard /ˈsɜːfbɔːd ‖ˈsɜːfbɔːd/ n tabla f de surf or de surfing

surfeit /ˈsɜːfət ‖ˈsɜːfɪt/ n (liter) **a** ~ **OF sth** un exceso or (liter) una plétora DE algo

surfer /ˈsɜːfər ‖ˈsɜːfə(r)/ n surfista mf

surfing /ˈsɜːfɪŋ ‖ˈsɜːfɪŋ/ n surf m, surfing m

surge¹ /sɜːdʒ ‖sɜːdʒ/ n (in demand, sales) aumento m; **a** ~ **of people** una oleada de gente; **we felt a new** ~ **of hope** sentimos renacer nuestras esperanzas

surge² vi ⟨⟨wave⟩⟩ levantarse; ⟨⟨sea⟩⟩ hincharse; **the crowd** ~**d out through the gates** la gente salió en tropel por las puertas; **anger/ hatred** ~**d up inside her** la ira/el odio la invadió; **to** ~ **ahead of sb** adelantársele a algn

surgeon /ˈsɜːdʒən ‖ˈsɜːdʒən/ n cirujano, -na m,f

surgery /ˈsɜːdʒəri ‖ˈsɜːdʒəri/ n (pl **-ries**) **1** (science) cirugía f **2** (BrE) (a) (room) consultorio m, consulta f (b) (consultation period of doctor) consulta f; (before n) ⟨times/hours⟩ de consulta

surgical /ˈsɜːdʒɪkəl ‖ˈsɜːdʒɪkəl/ adj ⟨instruments/treatment⟩ quirúrgico; ⟨stocking/ appliance⟩ ortopédico

surgical spirit n (BrE) alcohol m (de 90°)

surly /ˈsɜːrli ‖ˈsɜːli/ adj **-lier, -liest** hosco

surmise /sərˈmaɪz ‖səˈmaɪz/ vt (fml) conjeturar (fml)

surmount /sərˈmaʊnt ‖səˈmaʊnt/ vt superar

surname /ˈsɜːrneɪm ‖ˈsɜːneɪm/ n apellido m

surpass /sərˈpæs ‖səˈpɑːs/ vt superar

surplus¹ /ˈsɜːrpləs ‖ˈsɜːpləs/ n (pl **-es**) (of produce, stock) excedente m; (of funds) superávit m

S

surplus² *adj* ⟨goods/stocks⟩ excedente

surprise¹ /sə'praɪz/ *n* sorpresa *f*; **to my ~** para mi sorpresa; **to take sb by ~** sorprender a algn, pillar *or* (esp Esp) coger* a algn desprevenido; (*before n*) ⟨gift/visit/attack⟩ sorpresa *adj inv*

surprise² *vt* (a) (astonish) sorprender (b) (catch unawares) sorprender, pillar *or* agarrar *or* (esp Esp) coger* desprevenido

surprised /sə'praɪzd/ *adj* ⟨look⟩ sorprendido, de sorpresa; **I was so ~** me quedé tan sorprendido; **I'm ~ about** *o* **at that** eso me sorprende mucho; **I'm ~ (THAT)** ... me sorprende *or* me extraña QUE ... (+ *subj*)

surprising /sə'praɪzɪŋ/ *adj* sorprendente

surprisingly /sə'praɪzɪŋli/ *adv* (a) ⟨quiet/near/good⟩ sorprendentemente (b) (*indep*): **~, she feels no resentment** no está resentida, lo cual es sorprendente

surreal /sə'riːəl/ *adj* surrealista

surrealism /sə'riːəlɪzəm/ *n* surrealismo *m*

surrealist /sə'riːəlɪst/ *n* surrealista *mf*; (*before n*) ⟨painter/poem⟩ surrealista

surrender¹ /sə'rendər ‖sə'rendə(r)/ *vt* (a) (Mil) rendir*, entregar* (b) ⟨document/ticket⟩ entregar* (c) (relinquish) ⟨right/claim⟩ renunciar a
■ **~** *vi* rendirse*; **to ~ TO sb** entregarse* A algn

surrender² *n* (a) (capitulation) rendición *f*, capitulación *f* (b) (*frml*) (*no pl*) (of passport, document) entrega *f*

surreptitious /ˌsʌrəp'tɪʃəs/ *adj* furtivo, subrepticio

surrogate¹ /'sʌrəgət/ *n* (*frml*) sustituto *m*

surrogate² *adj* ⟨material⟩ sucedáneo; **~ mother** madre *f* suplente *or* de alquiler

surround¹ /sə'raʊnd/ *vt* (a) (encircle) ⟨place/person⟩ rodear; **the house is ~ed by trees** la casa está rodeada de árboles (b) (Mil) rodear, cercar*

surround² *n* marco *m*

surrounding /sə'raʊndɪŋ/ *adj* (*before n*) ⟨countryside/area⟩ de alrededor

surroundings /sə'raʊndɪŋz/ *pl n* (a) (of town, village) alrededores *mpl* (b) (environment) ambiente *m*

surveillance /sər'veɪləns ‖sə'veɪləns/ *n* vigilancia *f*

survey¹ /'sɜːrveɪ ‖'sɜːveɪ/ *n* ① (a) (of land) inspección *f*, reconocimiento *m*; (for mapping) medición *f* (b) (of building) inspección *f*, peritaje *m*, peritación *f*; (written report) informe *m* del perito, peritaje *m*, peritación *f* ② (overall view) visión *f* general ③ (investigation) estudio *m*; (poll) encuesta *f*, sondeo *m*

survey² /sər'veɪ ‖sə'veɪ/ *vt* ① (a) ⟨land/region⟩ (measure) medir*; (inspect) inspeccionar, reconocer* (b) ⟨building⟩ inspeccionar, llevar a cabo un peritaje de ② (a) (look at) contemplar, mirar (b) (view, consider) ⟨situation/plan/prospects⟩ examinar, analizar* ③ (question) ⟨group⟩ encuestar, hacer* un sondeo de

surveyor /sər'veɪər ‖sə'veɪə(r)/ *n* (a) (of land) agrimensor, -sora *m,f*, topógrafo, -fa *m,f* (b) (of building) perito, -ta *m,f*

survival /sər'vaɪvəl ‖sə'vaɪvəl/ *n* (continued existence) sobrevivencia *f*, supervivencia *f*

survive /sər'vaɪv ‖sə'vaɪv/ *vi* sobrevivir; **her last surviving descendant** su último descendiente vivo; **I can just ~ on $100 a week** con 100 dólares semanales apenas me alcanza para vivir
■ **~** *vt* ① ⟨accident/crash⟩ salir* con vida de; ⟨war/earthquake⟩ sobrevivir a; ⟨experience⟩ superar ② (outlive) ⟨person⟩ sobrevivir

survivor /sər'vaɪvər ‖sə'vaɪvə(r)/ *n* superviviente *mf*, sobreviviente *mf*

susceptible /sə'septəbəl/ *adj* **~ TO sth** ⟨to colds/infections⟩ propenso A algo; **he's ~ to a bit of flattery** se le puede persuadir halagándolo

suspect¹ /sə'spekt/ *vt* ① (a) (believe guilty) ⟨person⟩ sospechar de; **we ~ him of lying** sospechamos que miente (b) (doubt, mistrust) ⟨sincerity/probity⟩ dudar de, tener* dudas acerca de ② (a) (believe to exist): **they ~ nothing** no sospechan nada; **arson is not ~ed** no existen sospechas de que el incendio haya sido provocado (b) **suspected** *past p*: **a ~ed fracture** una posible fractura; **the ~ed murderer** el presunto asesino ③ (think probable) **to ~ (THAT)** imaginarse QUE

suspect² /'sʌspekt/ *n* sospechoso, -sa *m,f*

suspect³ /'sʌspekt/ *adj* ⟨package/behavior⟩ sospechoso; ⟨document/evidence⟩ de dudosa autenticidad

suspend /sə'spend/ *vt* ① ⟨payment/work⟩ suspender ② (debar, ban) suspender; ⟨student⟩ expulsar temporariamente, suspender (AmL) ③ (hang) (*often pass*) suspender

suspended sentence *n*: pena de prisión que no se cumple a menos que el delincuente reincida

suspenders /sə'spendərz ‖sə'spendəz/ *pl n* (*sometimes sing*) ① (braces) (AmE) tirantes *mpl* or (RPl) tiradores *mpl* or (Chi) suspensores *mpl* or (Col) cargaderas *fpl* ② (for stockings, socks) (BrE) ligas *fpl*

suspense /sə'spens/ *n* (in literary work, movie) suspenso *m* or (Esp) suspense *m*; **to keep sb in ~** mantener* a algn sobre ascuas

suspension /sə'spenʃən/ *n* ① (cessation) suspensión *f* ② (banning, withdrawal) suspensión *f*; (of student) expulsión *f* temporaria, suspensión *f* (AmL) ③ (hanging, being hung) suspensión *f* ④ (Auto) suspensión *f*

suspension: ~ bridge *n* puente *m* colgante; **~ points** *pl n* (AmE) puntos *mpl* suspensivos

suspicion /sə'spɪʃən/ *n* (belief) sospecha *f*; (mistrust) desconfianza *f*, recelo *m*; **he's under ~** está bajo sospecha

suspicious /sə'spɪʃəs/ *adj* (a) (mistrustful) desconfiado, suspicaz; **to be ~ OF/ABOUT sb/sth** desconfiar* DE algn/algo (b) (arousing suspicion) ⟨actions/movements⟩ sospechoso

suspiciously /sə'spɪʃəsli/ *adv* (a) (mistrustfully) ⟨regard/watch⟩ con desconfianza, con recelo (b) (arousing suspicion) ⟨act⟩ sospechosamente

sustain /sə'steɪn/ *vt* (a) ⟨life⟩ preservar, sustentar; ⟨hope/interest⟩ mantener*; ⟨pretense/conversation⟩ mantener*; ⟨effort⟩ sostener* (b) (suffer) ⟨injury/loss/defeat⟩ sufrir

sustainable /sə'steɪnəbəl/ *adj* sostenible

sustained /sə'steɪnd/ *adj* ⟨efforts⟩ sostenido

sustenance /'sʌstənəns/ *n* alimento *m*, sustento *m*

SW (= southwest) SO

swab¹ /swɑːb ‖swɒb/ n **(a)** (of cotton, gauze) hisopo *m* húmedo **(b)** (specimen) muestra *f*, frotis *m*

swab² vt **-bb-** to ~ **(down)** ‹deck› lavar, limpiar

swagger /'swæɡər ‖'swæɡə(r)/ vi caminar or andar* con aire arrogante

Swahili /swɑː'hiːli ‖swə'hiːli/ n swahili *m*, suajili *m*

swallow¹ /'swɑːləʊ ‖'swɒləʊ/ n **1** (Zool) golondrina *f* **2** (gulp) trago *m*

swallow² vt **1** ‹food/drink› tragar* **2** ‹insult/ taunts› tragarse* (fam); **that's a bit hard to ~** eso no hay quien se lo trague (fam) **3** ▶ SWALLOW UP
■ ~ vi tragar*
■ **swallow up** [v + o + adv, v + adv + o] **(a)** (use up) ‹money/time› consumir, tragarse* (fam), comerse (fam) **(b)** (cause to disappear) tragarse*

swam /swæm/ past of SWIM¹

swamp¹ /swɑːmp ‖swɒmp/ n pantano *m*, ciénaga *f*; (of sea water) marisma *f*, ciénaga *f*

swamp² vt **(a)** (with water) ‹land› anegar*, inundar **(b)** (overwhelm) (often pass): they were ~ed by offers of help los abrumaron con ofertas de ayuda; **I'm absolutely ~ed with work** estoy inundada de trabajo

swan /swɑːn ‖swɒn/ n cisne *m*

swanky /'swæŋki/ adj **-kier, -kiest** (colloq) **(a)** (boastful) (pej) ‹person› fanfarrón (fam) **(b)** (classy) chic adj inv, pijo (Esp fam), pituco (CS fam), posudo (Col fam), popoff adj inv (Méx fam)

swap¹ /swɑːp ‖swɒp/ n (colloq) cambio *m*, trueque *m*

swap² vt **-pp-** ‹possessions/ideas› intercambiar; **to ~ sth FOR sth** cambiar algo POR algo

swarm¹ /swɔːrm ‖swɔːm/ n enjambre *m*

swarm² vi «bees» enjambrar; **the flies ~ed around the meat** las moscas revoloteaban alrededor de la carne; **the beaches were ~ing with tourists** las playas eran un hormiguero de turistas

swarthy /'swɔːrði ‖'swɔːði/ adj **-thier, -thiest** moreno

swastika /'swɑːstɪkə ‖'swɒstɪkə/ n svástica *f*, esvástica *f*, suástica *f*, cruz *f* gamada

swat /swɑːt ‖swɒt/ vt **-tt-** ‹insect› matar (con matamoscas, periódico etc)

sway¹ /sweɪ/ n to hold ~ «ideas» prevalecer*; «leader» ejercer* dominio

sway² vi «branch/tree» balancearse; (gently) mecerse*; «tower/building» bambolearse
■ ~ vt **1** (influence) ‹person/crowd› influir* en **2** (move) ‹hips› menear, bambolear

swear /swer ‖sweə(r)/ past; past p **sworn** vt ‹allegiance/fidelity/revenge› jurar; **I could have sworn I left it there** hubiera jurado que lo dejé ahí
■ ~ vi **(a)** (vow) jurar; **but I couldn't ~ to it** pero no podría jurarlo **(b)** (curse) decir* palabrotas, soltar* tacos (Esp fam), mentar* madres (Méx fam); **to ~ AT sb** insultar a algn (usando palabrotas)
■ **swear by** [v + prep + o] ‹gadget› ser* un entusiasta de; ‹remedy› tenerle* una fe ciega a
■ **swear in** [v + o + adv, v + adv + o] ‹jury/ witness/president› tomarle juramento a, juramentar

swearword /'swerwɜːrd ‖'sweəwɜːd/ n palabrota *f*, mala palabra *f*, taco *m* (Esp)

sweat¹ /swet/ n (perspiration) sudor *m*, transpiración *f*; **I broke out in a cold ~** me vino un sudor frío

sweat² vi (past & past p **sweated** or (AmE also) **sweat**) sudar, transpirar

sweater /'swetər ‖'swetə(r)/ n suéter *m*, pulóver *m*, jersey *m* (Esp), chompa *f* (Per)

sweat: ~**shirt** n sudadera *f*, camiseta *f* gruesa; ~**shop** n: fábrica donde se explota a los trabajadores; ~**suit** n (AmE) equipo *m* (de deportes), chándal *m* (Esp), pants *mpl* (Méx)

sweaty /'sweti/ adj **-tier, -tiest** sudado, transpirado

swede /swiːd/ n (esp BrE) nabo *m* sueco

Swede /swiːd/ n sueco, -ca *m,f*

Sweden /'swiːdn/ n Suecia *f*

Swedish¹ /'swiːdɪʃ/ adj sueco

Swedish² n **(a)** (language) sueco *m* **(b)** (people) (+ pl vb) **the ~** los suecos

sweep¹ /swiːp/ n **1** **(a)** (movement): **with a ~ of his arm** con un amplio movimiento del brazo **(b)** (curve — of road, river) curva *f* **(c)** (range) (no pl) alcance *m*, extensión *f* **2** (chimney ~) deshollinador, -dora *m,f*

sweep² (past & pp **swept**) vt **1** **(a)** (clean) ‹floor/path› barrer; ‹chimney› deshollinar **(b)** (remove) ‹leaves/dirt› barrer; ‹mines› barrer; **to ~ sth under the rug** o (BrE) **carpet** correr un velo sobre algo
2 (touch lightly, brush) ‹surface› rozar*
3 **(a)** (pass over, across) «storm» azotar, barrer; **the epidemic is ~ing the country** la epidemia se extiende como un reguero de pólvora por el país **(b)** (remove by force) «sea/tide» arrastrar
4 **(a)** (scan) recorrer **(b)** (search) ‹area› peinar
■ ~ vi **1** (+ adv compl) (move proudly): **she swept into the room** entró majestuosamente en la habitación
2 (+ adv compl) **(a)** (spread): **fire swept through the hotel** el fuego se propagó por todo el hotel **(b)** (extend): **the path ~s down to the road** el sendero baja describiendo una curva hasta la carretera
■ **sweep aside** [v + o + adv, v + adv + o] ‹object› apartar; ‹opposition/doubts› desechar
■ **sweep away** [v + o + adv, v + adv + o] **(a)** (carry away) «flood/storm» arrastrar **(b)** (abolish) erradicar*
■ **sweep up** **1** [v + adv] (clear up) barrer, limpiar
2 [v + o + adv, v + adv + o] **(a)** (clear up) ‹dust/ leaves› barrer y recoger* **(b)** (gather up) ‹belongings/bags› recoger*

sweeper /'swiːpər ‖'swiːpə(r)/ n **(a)** (road~) barrendero, -ra *m,f*, barredor, -dora *m,f* (Per) **(b)** (carpet ~) cepillo *m* mecánico

sweeping /'swiːpɪŋ/ adj/ adj ‹movement› amplio; ‹gesture› dramático, histriónico **(b)** (indiscriminate) (pej): **that's rather a ~ statement, isn't it?** ¿no estás generalizando demasiado? **(c)** (far-reaching) ‹reforms/changes› radical; ‹powers› amplio

sweet¹ /swiːt/ adj **-er, -est** **1** ‹taste› dulce **2** ‹wine/sherry› dulce **3** (fresh, wholesome) ‹smell› agradable **4** **(a)** (pleasant, gratifying) ‹sounds/voice/ music› dulce, melodioso **(b)** (kind, lovable) ‹nature/ ⋯⋗

temper/smile⟩ dulce; **she's a very ~ person** es un encanto (de persona); **it was very ~ of her to offer** fue un detalle que se ofreciese **(c)** *(attractive)* ⟨*baby/puppy*⟩ rico (fam), mono (fam), amoroso (AmL fam)

sweet² *n* ⎵1⎵ *(item of confectionery)* (BrE) caramelo *m or* (AmL exc RPl) dulce *m* ⎵2⎵ *(dessert)* (BrE) postre *m* ⎵3⎵ **sweets** *pl (sugary food)* (AmE) dulces *mpl*

sweet: ~-and-sour /'swiːtn̩'saʊr ‖ˌswiːtn̩'saʊə(r)/ *adj (before n)* agridulce; **~corn** *n* maíz *m* tierno, elote *m* (Méx), choclo *m* (AmS), jojoto *m* (Ven)

sweeten /'swiːtn̩/ *vt* **(a)** ⟨*drink/dish*⟩ endulzar* **(b)** ⟨*air/breath*⟩ refrescar*

sweetener /'swiːtnər ‖'swiːtnə(r)/ *n* (Culin) endulzante *m*; *(artificial)* edulcorante *m*

sweet: ~heart /'swiːthɑːrt ‖'swiːthɑːt/ *n* **(a)** *(lover, darling)* novio, -via *m,f*, enamorado, -da *m,f* **(b)** *(colloq) (as form of address)* (mi) amor; ~ **potato** *n* boniato *m*, batata *f*, camote *m* (Andes, Méx); **~shop** *n* (BrE) tienda *f* de golosinas; **~talk** *vt (colloq)* engatusar (fam), camelar (Esp fam)

swell¹ /swel/ *(past p* **swollen** *or* (AmE esp) **swelled)** *vi* ⎵1⎵ ⟨*wood/sails/ankles*⟩ hincharse; «*river/stream*» crecer*, subir ⎵2⎵ *(increase)* «*population/crowd*» crecer*, aumentar
■ ~ *vt* ⎵1⎵ *(increase in size)* ⟨*body/joint/features*⟩ hinchar; ⟨*sails*⟩ hinchar; ⟨*river*⟩ hacer* crecer *or* subir ⎵2⎵ *(increase in number, volume)* ⟨*population/ total/funds*⟩ aumentar
■ **swell up** [*v + adv*] hincharse

swell² *n* **(a)** *(of sea)* oleaje *m* **(b)** *(surge, movement)* oleada *f*

swell³ *adj (fine, excellent)* (AmE colloq) fenomenal (fam), bárbaro (fam)

swelling /'swelɪŋ/ *n* hinchazón *f*

sweltering /'sweltərɪŋ/ *adj* sofocante

swept /swept/ *past & past p of* SWEEP²

swerve /swɜːrv ‖swɜːv/ *vi* ⟨*vehicle/driver/ horse*⟩ virar bruscamente

swift¹ /swɪft/ *adj* **-er, -est** ⟨*runner/movement/ animal*⟩ veloz, rápido; ⟨*reply/reaction/denial*⟩ rápido

swift² *n* vencejo *m*

swiftly /'swɪftli/ *adv (rapidly)* rápidamente, con rapidez; *(promptly)* con prontitud *or* rapidez

swig¹ /swɪg/ *n (colloq)* trago *m*

swig² *vt* **-gg-** *(colloq)* tomar, beber

swill¹ /swɪl/ *n* comida *f* para cerdos

swill² *vt* ⎵1⎵ *(wash, rinse)* **to ~ sth out** ⟨*cups/pans*⟩ lavar/enjuagar* algo ⎵2⎵ *(drink) (colloq & pej)* ⟨*beer*⟩ tomar *or* beber *(a grandes tragos)*

swim¹ /swɪm/ *(pres p* **swimming**; *past* **swam**; *past p* **swum**) *vi* ⎵1⎵ «*person/animal/ fish*» nadar; **to go ~ming** ir* a nadar; **he swam across the river** cruzó el río nadando *or* a nado ⎵2⎵ *(be immersed, overflowing) (usu in -ing form)* **to ~**

IN sth nadar *or* flotar **EN** algo ⎵3⎵ *(of blurred, confused perceptions)* dar* vueltas; **my head was ~ming** la cabeza me daba vueltas
■ ~ *vt* ⟨*length*⟩ nadar, hacer*; ⟨*river*⟩ cruzar* a nado

swim² *n*: **to go for a ~** ir* a nadar; **to have a ~** nadar, bañarse, darse* un baño

swimmer /'swɪmər ‖'swɪmə(r)/ *n* nadador, -dora *m,f*

swimming /'swɪmɪŋ/ *n* natación *f*; *(before n)* **~ cap** gorro *m or* gorra *f* (de baño)

swimming: ~ bath *n*, **~ baths** *pl n* (BrE) piscina *f* cubierta, alberca *f* techada (Méx), pileta *f* cubierta (RPl); **~ costume** *n* (BrE) ▸ SWIMSUIT; **~ pool** *n* piscina *f*, alberca *f* (Méx), pileta *f* (RPl); **~ trunks** *pl n* ▸ TRUNK 4

swimsuit /'swɪmsuːt ‖'swɪmsuːt, -sjuːt/ *n* traje *m* de baño, bañador *m* (Esp), malla *f* (de baño) (RPl)

swindle¹ /'swɪndl/ *n* estafa *f*, timo *m* (fam)

swindle² *vt* estafar, timar

swindler /'swɪndlər ‖'swɪndlə(r)/ *n* estafador, -dora *m,f*, timador, -dora *m,f*

swine /swaɪn/ *n* **(a)** *(pl ~)* *(pig, hog)* cerdo *m* **(b)** *(pl ~s)* *(contemptible person)* (colloq) cerdo, -da *m,f* (fam), canalla *mf*

swing¹ /swɪŋ/ *(past & past p* **swung**) *vi* ⎵1⎵ *(hang, dangle)* balancearse; *(on a swing)* columpiarse *or* (RPl) hamacarse*; «*pendulum*» oscilar
⎵2⎵ **(a)** *(move on pivot)* mecerse*; **the door swung open/shut** la puerta se abrió/se cerró **(b)** *(turn)* girar *or* (*describiendo una curva*); **the ball swung away** la pelota salió desviada
⎵3⎵ *(shift, change)* «*opinion/mood*» cambiar, oscilar
■ ~ *vt* ⎵1⎵ *(move to and fro)* ⟨*arms/legs*⟩ balancear; ⟨*object on rope*⟩ hacer* oscilar; **to ~ one's hips** contonearse, contonear *or* menear las caderas
⎵2⎵ *(wave, brandish)* ⟨*club/hammer*⟩ blandir
⎵3⎵ *(shift)* ⟨*vote*⟩ inclinar
■ **swing around,** (BrE also) **swing round** ⎵1⎵ [*v + adv*] ⟨*vehicle*⟩ dar* un viraje, girar *or* virar (en redondo); **she swung around to face me** giró sobre sus talones para darme la cara
⎵2⎵ [*v + o + adv*] ⟨*car/boat*⟩ hacer* girar en redondo

swing² *n* ⎵1⎵ **(a)** *(movement)* oscilación *f*, vaivén *m* **(b)** *(blow, stroke)* golpe *m*; *(in golf, boxing)* swing *m*; **to take a ~ at sb/sth** intentar darle a algn/algo
⎵2⎵ **(a)** *(shift)* cambio *m*; **a ~ in public opinion** un cambio en la opinión pública **(b)** *(Pol)* viraje *m*
⎵3⎵ **(a)** *(rhythm, vitality)*: **to be in full ~** estar* en pleno desarrollo; **the party was in full ~** la fiesta estaba ya muy animada; **to get into the ~ of sth** agarrarle el ritmo *or* (Esp) cogerle* el tranquillo a algo **(b)** *(Mus)* swing *m*
⎵4⎵ *(Leisure)* columpio *m or* (RPl) hamaca *f*

swing: ~ bin *n* cubo *m or* (CS) tacho *m or* (Méx) bote *m or* (Col) caneca *f or* (Ven) tobo *m* de la basura *(con tapa de vaivén)*; **~ bridge** *n* puente *m* giratorio; **~ door** *n* puerta *f* (de) vaivén

AmC América Central
AmL América Latina
AmS América del Sur
Andes Región andina
Arg Argentina
Bol Bolivia
Chi Chile
CS Cono Sur
Cu Cuba
Ec Ecuador
Esp España
Méx México
Per Perú
RPl Río de la Plata
Ur Uruguay
Ven Venezuela

swinging door /ˈswɪŋɪŋ/ n (AmE) ▶ SWING DOOR

swipe¹ /swaɪp/ n (colloq) golpe m

swipe² vt (colloq) **1** (hit) darle* (un golpe) a **2** (steal) afanarse (arg), volarse* (Méx fam)

swipe card n tarjeta f de plástico con banda magnética

swirl¹ /swɜːrl ‖swɜːl/ n (of water, dust, people) remolino m; (of smoke) voluta f, espiral f

swirl² vi «water/dust/paper» arremolinarse; «dancers/skirts» girar

swish /swɪʃ/ n (a) (of cane) silbido m (b) (of water) rumor m, susurro m (c) (of skirt) frufrú m

Swiss¹ /swɪs/ adj suizo

Swiss² n (pl ~) suizo, -za m,f

switch¹ /swɪtʃ/ vt **1** (a) (change) cambiar de; to ~ channels cambiar de canal; my appointment has been ~ed to Tuesday me cambiaron la cita al martes (b) (exchange) ‹suitcases/roles› intercambiar

2 (shunt) (AmE Rail) cambiar de vía

■ ~ vi cambiar; I ~ed to Channel Four cambié al Canal Cuatro; we've ~ed from electricity to gas hemos empezado a usar gas en lugar de electricidad

■ **switch off 1** [v + o + adv, v + adv + o] ‹light/TV/heating› apagar*; ‹gas/electricity/water› cortar, desconectar

2 [v + adv] ‹light/machine/heating› apagarse*

■ **switch on 1** [v + o + adv, v + adv + o] (esp BrE) ‹light/heating/television› encender*, prender (AmL)

2 [v + adv] ‹light/heating/machine›
encenderse*, prenderse (AmL)

■ **switch over** [v + adv] (a) (change) to ~ over TO sth cambiar A algo (b) (change channels) cambiar de canal (c) (exchange positions, roles) cambiar

switch² n **1** (a) (Elec) interruptor m, llave f (de encendido/de la luz) (b) (AmE Rail) agujas fpl **2** (exchange) intercambio m, trueque m

switchboard n centralita f, conmutador m (AmL); (before n) ~ **operator** telefonista mf

Switzerland /ˈswɪtsərlənd ‖ˈswɪtsələnd/ n Suiza f

swivel /ˈswɪvəl/, (BrE) **-ll-** vi girar
■ ~ vt hacer* girar

swivel chair n silla f giratoria

swollen¹ /ˈswəʊlən/ past p of SWELL¹

swollen² adj ‹ankle/knee/joints› hinchado; ‹gland› inflamado; ~ **with pride** henchido de orgullo; **the river was** ~ el río iba crecido

swoon /swuːn/ vi (a) (show rapture) to ~ (OVER sb) derretirse* (POR algn) (b) (faint) (arch or liter) desvanecerse*

swoop¹ /swuːp/ vi «bird of prey» abatirse; «police» llevar a cabo una redada

swoop² n (of bird, aircraft) descenso m en picada or (Esp) en picado; (by police) redada f; **in one fell** ~ de una sola vez, de un tirón (fam)

swop /swɑːp ‖swɒp/ vt/n ▶ SWAP¹,²

sword /sɔːrd ‖sɔːd/ n espada f

sword: ~**fish** n (pl ~**fish** or ~**fishes**) pez m espada; ~**sman** /ˈsɔːrdzmən ‖ˈsɔːdzmən/ n (pl -**men** /-mən/) espadachín m, espada m

swore /swɔːr ‖swɔː(r)/ past of SWEAR

sworn¹ /swɔːrn ‖swɔːn/ past p of SWEAR

sworn² adj (before n) **1** ‹enemy› declarado, acérrimo **2** ‹statement› jurado

swot¹ /swɑːt ‖swɒt/ n (BrE colloq & pej) matado, -da m,f or (Col) pilo, -la m,f or (Chi) mateo, -tea m,f or (Per) chancón, -cona m,f or (RPl) traga mf or (Esp) empollón, -llona m,f (fam & pey)

swot² vi -tt- (BrE colloq) estudiar como loco (fam), empollar (Esp fam), matearse (Chi fam), chancar* (Per arg), tragar* (RPl fam)

swum /swʌm/ past p of SWIM¹

swung /swʌŋ/ past & past p of SWING¹

sycamore /ˈsɪkəmɔːr ‖ˈsɪkəmɔː(r)/ n ~ (**maple**) plátano m (falso), sicómoro m, sicomoro m

sycophantic /ˌsɪkəˈfæntɪk/ adj adulador

syllable /ˈsɪləbəl/ n sílaba f

syllabus /ˈsɪləbəs/ n (pl -**buses**) plan m de estudios; (of a particular subject) programa m

symbol /ˈsɪmbəl/ n símbolo m

symbolic /sɪmˈbɑːlɪk ‖sɪmˈbɒlɪk/ adj simbólico; to be ~ OF sth simbolizar* algo

symbolism /ˈsɪmbəlɪzəm/ n simbolismo m

symbolize /ˈsɪmbəlaɪz/ vt simbolizar*

symmetrical /səˈmetrɪkəl ‖sɪˈmetrɪkəl/ adj simétrico

symmetry /ˈsɪmətri/ n simetría f

sympathetic /ˌsɪmpəˈθetɪk/ adj **1** (understanding) comprensivo; he was most ~ o toward me when my wife died me dio todo su apoyo y comprensión cuando murió mi mujer **2** (approving) ‹response/view› favorable; ‹audience› bien dispuesto, receptivo

sympathetically /ˌsɪmpəˈθetɪkli/ adv (a) (with understanding) ‹listen/consider/respond› con comprensión (b) (showing pity) con compasión

sympathize /ˈsɪmpəθaɪz/ vi (a) (commiserate): I ~ with him lo compadezco (b) (understand) to ~ (WITH sth/sb) comprender or entender* (algo/a algn)

sympathizer /ˈsɪmpəθaɪzər ‖ˈsɪmpəθaɪzə(r)/ n simpatizante mf, partidario, -ria m,f

sympathy /ˈsɪmpəθi/ n (pl -**thies**) **1** (a) (pity) compasión f, lástima f (b) (condolences) (often pl): you have my deepest ~ le acompaño en el sentimiento (fr hecha), mi más sentido pésame (fr hecha) **2** (a) (support, approval): to come out in ~ with sb (Lab Rel) declararse en huelga en solidaridad con algn (b) **sympathies** pl (loyalty, leanings) simpatías fpl

symphony /ˈsɪmfəni/ n (pl -**nies**) sinfonía f; (before n) ~ **orchestra** orquesta f sinfónica

symptom /ˈsɪmptəm/ n síntoma m

symptomatic /ˌsɪmptəˈmætɪk/ adj ~ (OF sth) sintomático (DE algo)

synagogue /ˈsɪnəgɑːg ‖ˈsɪnəgɒg/ n sinagoga f

synchronize /ˈsɪŋkrənaɪz/ vt sincronizar*

syndicate /ˈsɪndəkət ‖ˈsɪndɪkət/ n (a) (group, cartel) agrupación f; a crime ~ una organización mafiosa (b) (in US) (Journ, TV) agencia f de distribución periodística

syndrome /ˈsɪndrəʊm/ n síndrome m

synonymous /səˈnɑːnəməs ‖sɪˈnɒnɪməs/ adj ‹terms/phrases› sinónimo; ‹ideas› análogo; to be ~ WITH sth ser* sinónimo DE algo

synopsis /sə'nɒːpsəs ‖sɪ'nɒpsɪs/ n (pl **-opses** /-siːz/) sinopsis f

syntax /'sɪntæks/ n sintaxis f

synthesis /'sɪnθəsəs ‖'sɪnθəsɪs/ n (pl **-theses** /-θəsiːz/) síntesis f

synthesize /'sɪnθəsaɪz/ vt sintetizar*

synthesizer /'sɪnθəsaɪzər ‖'sɪnθəsaɪzə(r)/ n sintetizador m

synthetic¹ /sɪn'θetɪk/ adj sintético

synthetic² n fibra f sintética, tejido m sintético

syphilis /'sɪfələs ‖'sɪfɪlɪs/ n sífilis f

syphon n/vt /'saɪfən/ ▶ SIPHON

Syria /'sɪriə/ n Siria f

Syrian /'sɪriən/ adj sirio

syringe /sə'rɪndʒ ‖sɪ'rɪndʒ/ n jeringa f, jeringuilla f

syrup /'sɜːrəp, 'sɪ- ‖'sɪrəp/ n (a) (Culin) (sugar solution) almíbar m; (with other ingredients) jarabe m, sirope m (b) (medicine) jarabe m

system /'sɪstəm/ n 1 (ordered structure) sistema m, método m 2 (a) (technical, mechanical) sistema m (b) (Comput) sistema m 3 (Anat, Physiol): the digestive ~ el aparato digestivo; the nervous ~ el sistema nervioso; to get sth out of one's ~ desahogarse* 4 (establishment, status quo): the ~ el sistema

systematic /ˌsɪstə'mætɪk/ adj sistemático

systematically /ˌsɪstə'mætɪkli/ adv sistemáticamente

systems analyst n analista mf de sistemas

Tt

T, t /tiː/ n T, t f

tab /tæb/ n 1 (a) (flap) lengüeta f (b) (label on clothing) etiqueta f 2 (account, bill) (colloq) cuenta f; to keep ~s on sth/sb tener* algo/a algn controlado 3 (on typewriter, word processor) tabulador m

tabby /'tæbi/ (pl **-bies**), **tabby cat** n gato atigrado, gata atigrada m,f

tab key n tecla f de tabulación

table /'teɪbəl/ n 1 (piece of furniture) mesa f; (before n) ~ football (BrE) futbolín m, taca-taca m (Chi), metegol m (Arg), futbolito m (Ur); ~ mat (mantelito m) individual m 2 (list) tabla f; multiplication o (used by children) times ~s tablas de multiplicar

table: ~**cloth** n mantel m; ~**spoon** n (utensil) cuchara f grande or de servir; (measure) cucharada f (grande)

tablet /'tæblət ‖'tæblɪt/ n (a) (pill) pastilla f, comprimido m (b) (commemorative, of stone) lápida f

table tennis n ping-pong m, tenis m de mesa

tabloid /'tæblɔɪd/ n tabloide m (formato de periódicos utilizado por la prensa popular)

taboo /tə'buː/ adj tabú adj inv

tabulate /'tæbjəleɪt ‖'tæbjʊleɪt/ vt tabular

tacit /'tæsət ‖'tæsɪt/ adj tácito

taciturn /'tæsətɜːrn ‖'tæsɪtɜːn/ adj taciturno

tack¹ /tæk/ n (a) (nail) tachuela f (b) (Naut) bordada f (c) (stitch) (BrE) puntada f; (seam) hilván m (d) (Equ) arreos mpl, aperos mpl (AmL)

tack² vt 1 (nail) ⟨carpet⟩ ~ down clavar con tachuelas 2 (stitch) (BrE) hilvanar
■ ~ vi (Naut) dar* bordadas
■ ~ **tack on** [v + o + adv, v + adv + o] agregar*, añadir

tackle¹ /'tækəl/ n 1 (equipment): sports ~ equipo m de deporte; fishing ~ aparejo m or

avíos mpl de pesca 2 (Sport) (in rugby, US football) placaje m, tacle m (AmL); (in soccer) entrada f fuerte 3 (Naut) aparejo m, polea f

tackle² vt 1 (a) (come to grips with) ⟨problem⟩ enfrentar, abordar; ⟨subject⟩ tratar; ⟨task⟩ abordar (b) (confront) ⟨intruder/colleague⟩ enfrentar, enfrentarse con 2 (Sport) (in rugby, US football) placar*, taclear (AmL); (in soccer) entrarle a

tacky /'tæki/ adj **tackier, tackiest** 1 (cheap, tawdry) chabacano, hortera (Esp fam), naco (Méx fam), lobo (Col fam), rasca (Chi fam), mersa (RPl fam) 2 (sticky) pegajoso

tact /tækt/ n tacto m

tactful /'tæktfəl/ adj ⟨person⟩ de mucho tacto; ⟨question/reply⟩ diplomático

tactfully /'tæktfəli/ adv con mucho tacto

tactic /'tæktɪk/ n táctica f

tactical /'tæktɪkəl/ adj táctico

tactics /'tæktɪks/ n (Mil) (+ sing or pl vb) táctica f

tactless /'tæktləs ‖'tæktlɪs/ adj poco diplomático

tadpole /'tædpəʊl/ n renacuajo m

Tadzhikistan /tɑːˌdʒɪkɪr'stɑːn// n Tayiquistán m

taffeta /'tæfətə ‖'tæfɪtə/ n tafetán m

taffy /'tæfi/ n (AmE) caramelo m masticable

tag /tæg/ n 1 (label) etiqueta f (atada) 2 (Ling) coletilla f; (before n) ~ question coletilla interrogativa
■ **tag on: -gg-** [v + o + adv, v + adv + o] agregar*, añadir

Tahiti /tə'hiːti/ n Tahití m

tail¹ /teɪl/ n (a) (of horse, fish, bird) cola f; (of dog, pig) rabo m, cola f (b) (of plane, kite) cola f; (of shirt, coat) faldón m; see also TAILS 1

tail² vt (follow) ⟨suspect⟩ seguir*
■ **tail off** [v + adv] (a) ⟨⟨demand⟩⟩ disminuir*, mermar (b) ⟨⟨sound/words⟩⟩ apagarse*

tail: **~back** *n* (BrE) caravana *f*, cola *f* (*debido a un embotellamiento*); **~coat** *n* frac *m*; **~ end** *n*: **the ~ end** (of film, concert) el final, los últimos minutos; (of procession) la cola; **~light** *n* luz *f* trasera

tailor¹ /'teɪlər ‖ 'teɪlə(r)/ *n* sastre *m*

tailor² *vt* **1** (Clothing) **(a)** (make) confeccionar **(b) tailored** *past p* (*before n*) (fitted) entallado; (lined, structured etc) armado **2** (adapt) adaptar

tailor-made /'teɪlər'meɪd ‖ ,teɪlə'meɪd/ *adj* **(a)** ⟨*suit*⟩ hecho a (la) medida **(b)** ⟨*product/plan*⟩ a la medida de sus (*or* nuestras *etc*) necesidades

tailpipe /'teɪlpaɪp/ *n* (AmE Auto) tubo *m or* (RPl) caño *m* de escape

tails /teɪlz/ *n* **1** (tailcoat) (+ *pl vb*) frac *m* **2** (on coin) (+ *sing vb*) cruz *f*, sello *m* (Andes, Ven), sol *m* (Méx), ceca *f* (Arg)

taint /teɪnt/ *vt* **(a)** ⟨*meat/water*⟩ contaminar **(b)** ⟨*name/reputation*⟩ mancillar (liter), deshonrar

Taiwan /'taɪ'wɑːn/ *n* Taiwán *m*

take¹ /teɪk/ (*past* **took**; *past p* **taken**) *vt*
I (carry, lead, drive) llevar; **~ an umbrella** lleva un paraguas
II **1** **(a)** ⟨*train/plane/bus/taxi/elevator*⟩ tomar, coger* (esp Esp) **(b)** ⟨*road/turning*⟩ tomar, agarrar (esp AmL), coger* (esp Esp); **~ a left** (turn) (BrE) dobla a la izquierda **(c)** ⟨*bend*⟩ tomar, coger* (esp Esp); ⟨*fence*⟩ saltar
2 **(a)** (grasp, seize) tomar, agarrar (esp AmL), coger* (esp Esp); ⟨*opportunity*⟩ aprovechar; **she took the knife from him** le quitó el cuchillo **(b)** (take charge of): **may I ~ your coat?** ¿me permite el abrigo? **(c)** (occupy): **~ a seat** siéntese, tome asiento (frml); **this chair is ~n** esta silla está ocupada
3 (remove, steal) ⟨*wallet/purse*⟩ llevarse
4 to be **~n ill** caer* enfermo
5 **(a)** (capture) ⟨*town/position*⟩ tomar; ⟨*pawn/piece*⟩ comer **(b)** (win) ⟨*prize/title*⟩ llevarse, hacerse* con; ⟨*game/set*⟩ ganar **(c)** (receive as profit) hacer*, sacar*
6 ⟨*medicine/drugs*⟩ tomar; **I don't ~ sugar in my coffee** no le pongo azúcar al café
7 **(a)** (buy, order) llevar(se); **I'll ~ this pair** (me) llevo este par **(b)** (rent) alquilar, coger* (Esp)
III **1** (of time) «*job/task*» llevar; «*process*» tardar; «*person/letter*» tardar, demorar(se) (AmL); **the flight ~s two hours** el vuelo dura dos horas; **it took me a long time to do it** me llevó mucho tiempo hacerlo
2 (need): **it ~s courage to do a thing like that** hay que tener *or* hace falta valor para hacer algo así; **it took four men to lift it** se necesitaron cuatro hombres para levantarlo
3 **(a)** (wear): **what size shoes do you ~?** ¿qué número calzas?; **she ~s a 14** usa la talla *or* (RPl) el talle 14 **(b)** (Ling) construirse* con, regir*
IV **1** (accept) ⟨*money/bribes/job*⟩ aceptar; **do you ~ checks?** ¿aceptan cheques?; **~ it from me** hazme caso
2 **(a)** (hold, accommodate): **it ~s/will ~ 42 liters** tiene una capacidad de 42 litros; **we can ~ up to 50 passengers** tenemos cabida para un máximo de 50 pasajeros **(b)** ⟨*patients/pupils*⟩ admitir, tomar
3 **(a)** (withstand, suffer) ⟨*strain/weight*⟩ aguantar; ⟨*beating*⟩ recibir **(b)** (tolerate, endure) aguantar; **he**

can't ~ a joke no sabe aceptar una broma **(c)** (bear): **she's ~n it very badly/well** lo lleva muy mal/bien; *see also* HEART 2, 3
4 **(a)** (understand, interpret) tomarse; **don't ~ it personally** no te lo tomes como algo personal; **I ~ it you didn't like him much** por lo que veo no te cayó muy bien **(b)** (consider) (*in imperative*) mirar; **~ Japan, for example** mira el caso del Japón, por ejemplo
V **1** ⟨*steps/measures*⟩ tomar; ⟨*exercise*⟩ hacer*; **to ~ a step forward** dar* un paso adelante
2 (Educ) **(a)** (teach) (BrE) darle* clase a **(b)** (learn) ⟨*subject*⟩ estudiar, hacer*; ⟨*course*⟩ hacer*; **to ~ an exam** hacer* *or* dar* *or* (CS) rendir* *or* (Méx) tomar un examen, examinarse (Esp)
3 **(a)** (record) ⟨*measurements/temperature*⟩ tomar **(b)** (write down) ⟨*notes*⟩ tomar
4 (adopt): **he ~s the view that ...** opina que ..., es de la opinión de que ...; *see also* LIKING A, OFFENSE 2B, SHAPE¹ 1A *etc*
■ **~** *vi* **(a)** «*cutting*» prender **(b)** «*dye*» agarrar (esp AmL), coger* (esp Esp)
■ **take aback** [*v + o + adv*] (*usu pass*) sorprender
■ **take after** [*v + prep + o*] salir* a, parecerse* a; **he ~s after his father** salió a su padre, se parece a su padre
■ **take along** [*v + o + adv, v + adv + o*] llevar
■ **take apart** [*v + o + adv*] **(a)** (dismantle) desmontar **(b)** (show weakness of) ⟨*argument*⟩ desbaratar
■ **take around,** (BrE) **take round** [*v + o + prep + o*] ⟨*house/estate*⟩ mostrar*, enseñar (esp Esp)
■ **take aside** [*v + o + adv*] llevar aparte *or* a un lado
■ **take away**
I [*v + o + adv, v + adv + o*] **(a)** (carry, lead away) ⟨*person/object*⟩ llevarse **(b)** (remove, confiscate) ⟨*possession*⟩ quitar; **to ~ sth away FROM sb** quitarle algo A algn **(c)** (erase, obliterate): **this will ~ the pain away** con esto se te pasará el dolor; **this will ~ the taste away** esto te quitará el sabor de la boca
II [*v + adv + o*] (BrE) ⟨*food*⟩ llevar
■ **take back** **1** [*v + o + adv, v + adv + o*] **(a)** (return) devolver* **(b)** (repossess) llevarse **(c)** (accept back): **she wouldn't ~ back the money she'd lent me** no quiso que le devolviera el dinero que me había prestado **(d)** (withdraw, retract) ⟨*statement*⟩ retirar
2 [*v + o + adv*] (in time): **it ~s me back to my childhood** me transporta a mi niñez
■ **take down** [*v + o + adv, v + adv + o*] **(a)** ⟨*decorations/notice*⟩ quitar **(b)** (dismantle) desmontar **(c)** ⟨*name/address*⟩ apuntar, anotar
■ **take home** [*v + adv + o*]: **she ~s home less than £600** su sueldo neto *or* líquido es de menos de 600 libras
■ **take in**
I [*v + o + adv, v + adv + o*] **1** (move indoors) meter (dentro), entrar (esp AmS)
2 (give home to) ⟨*orphan*⟩ recoger*; ⟨*lodger*⟩ alojar
3 (grasp) ⟨*information*⟩ asimilar
4 (make narrower) ⟨*dress/waist*⟩ meterle *or* tomarle a
II [*v + o + adv*] (deceive) engañar
III [*v + adv + o*] **(a)** (include) ⟨*areas/topics*⟩ incluir*, abarcar* **(b)** (visit) visitar, incluir* (*en el recorrido*)

■ **take off**

I [v + o + adv, v + adv + o] [v + o + prep + o] **1** (detach, remove) quitar, sacar*; **to ~ off one's clothes** quitarse or (esp AmL) sacarse* la ropa **2** (a) (cut off) cortar (b) (deduct) descontar* **3** (have free): **she's ~n the morning off (from) work** se ha tomado la mañana libre

II [v + adv] (a) «*aircraft/pilot*» despegar*, decolar (AmL); «*flight*» salir* (b) (succeed) «*career*» tomar vuelo (c) (depart) largarse* (fam), irse*

III [v + o + adv] [v + o + prep + o] **1** (remove) quitar, sacar* (esp AmL); **~ your hands off me!** ¡quítame las manos de encima! **2** (take away from) (colloq) quitar, sacar* (CS)

■ **take on** **1** [v + o + adv, v + adv + o] (a) (employ) «*staff*» contratar, tomar (esp AmL) (b) (undertake) «*work*» encargarse* de, hacerse* cargo de; «*responsibility*» asumir (c) (tackle) «*opponent*» enfrentarse a **2** [v + adv + o] (acquire) «*expression*» adoptar; «*appearance*» adquirir*

■ **take out**

I [v + o + adv, v + adv + o] **1** (a) (remove physically) sacar*; **to ~ it out of sb** «*fight/race*» dejar a algn rendido (b) (exclude) eliminar (c) (transport) sacar* (d) (AmE) «*food*» llevar **2** (withdraw) «*money*» sacar* **3** (produce) «*gun/wallet*» sacar*

II [v + o + adv, v + adv + o] (a) (extract) «*tooth/appendix*» sacar* (b) (obtain) «*insurance/permit*» sacar*

III [v + o + adv] (accompany, conduct): **he'd like to ~ her out** le gustaría invitarla a salir; **she took me out to dinner** me llevó a cenar

■ **take out on** [v + o + adv + prep + o]: **to ~ it out on sb** desquitarse con algn

■ **take over** **1** [v + adv] (a) (assume control) «*political party*» asumir el poder; **he will ~ over as managing director** asumirá el cargo de director ejecutivo; **to ~ over FROM sb** sustituir* a algn; (in shift work) relevar a algn (b) (seize control) hacerse* con el poder **2** [v + o + adv + o] «*responsibility/role*» asumir; «*job*» hacerse* cargo de; «*company*» absorber

■ **take round** (BrE) ▶ TAKE AROUND

■ **take to** [v + prep + o] (a) (develop liking for): **she took to teaching immediately** enseguida le tomó gusto a la enseñanza; **I didn't ~ to him** no me cayó muy bien (b) (form habit of): **to ~ to drink** darse* a la bebida; **to ~ to -ING** darle* a algn POR + INF

■ **take up**

I [v + o + adv, v + adv + o] **1** (a) (pick up) tomar (b) (accept) «*offer/challenge*» aceptar (c) (adopt) «*cause*» hacer* suyo (or mío etc) (d) (begin): **he's ~n up pottery** ha empezado a hacer cerámica **2** (lift) «*carpet/floorboards*» levantar **3** (a) (continue) «*story*» seguir*, continuar*; «*conversation*» reanudar (b) (issue/point) tratar ; (pursue) volver* a **4** (shorten) «*skirt*» acortar; «*hem*» subir

II [v + adv + o] **1** (use up) «*time*» llevar; «*space*» ocupar **2** (move into) «*position*» tomar

■ **take up on** [v + o + adv + prep + o] (a) (take person at word): **I may well ~ you up on that** a lo mejor te tomo la palabra or te acepto el ofrecimiento (b) (challenge): **I must ~ you up on that** sobre eso discrepo con usted

take² n (Cin) toma f

takeaway¹ /ˈteɪkəweɪ/ adj (BrE) «*meal/pizza*» para llevar; «*restaurant*» de comida para llevar

takeaway² n (BrE) (a) (restaurant) restaurante m de comida para llevar (b) (meal) comida f preparada

take-home pay /ˈteɪkhəʊm/ n sueldo m neto

taken¹ /ˈteɪkən/ past p of TAKE¹

taken² adj (pred) **to be ~ WITH sth/sb: I was quite ~ with him** me cayó muy bien; **they were very ~ with the house** quedaron encantados con la casa

takeoff /ˈteɪkɔːf ‖ ˈteɪkɒf/ n (a) (Aviat) despegue m, decolaje m (AmL) (b) (imitation) (colloq) parodia f

takeout¹ /ˈteɪkaʊt/ adj (AmE) «*meal*» para llevar; «*restaurant*» de comida para llevar

takeout² n (AmE) comida f preparada

takeover /ˈteɪkəʊvər ‖ ˈteɪkəʊvə(r)/ n (a) (Govt) toma f del poder (b) (Busn) absorción f, adquisición f (de una empresa por otra); (before n) ~ **bid** oferta f pública de adquisición or de compra, OPA f

takings /ˈteɪkɪŋz/ n pl (BrE Busn) recaudación f; (at box office) taquilla f, entrada f

talc /tælk/ n polvos mpl de talco, talco m (AmL)

talcum powder /ˈtælkəm/ n polvos mpl de talco

tale /teɪl/ n cuento m, relato m; **to tell ~s** contar* chismes or cuentos

talent /ˈtælənt/ n (a) (aptitude, skill) talento m (b) (talented people) gente f con talento

talented /ˈtæləntəd ‖ ˈtæləntɪd/ adj talentoso, de talento

talisman /ˈtælɪsmən ‖ ˈtælɪzmən/ n (pl ~s) talismán m

talk¹ /tɔːk/ vi **1** (speak) hablar; (converse) hablar, platicar* (esp AmC, Méx); **to ~ ABOUT sb/sth** hablar de algn/algo; **to ~ OF sth/-ING** hablar DE algo/DE + INF; **to ~ TO sb** hablar CON algn; **he was ~ing to Jane** estaba hablando con Jane; **are you ~ing to me ?** ¿me hablas a mí?; **we're not ~ing to each other** no nos hablamos; **to ~ WITH sb** hablar CON algn **2** (a) (have discussion) hablar; **we need to ~** tenemos que hablar; **to ~ ABOUT sth** discutir algo (b) (give talk) **to ~ ABOUT/ON sth** hablar DE/ SOBRE algo

■ ~ vt **1** (speak) (colloq): **to ~ business** hablar de negocios; **don't ~ nonsense!** ¡no digas tonterías! **2** (argue, persuade) **to ~ sb INTO/OUT OF sth/-ING** convencer* a algn DE QUE/DE QUE NO (+ subj)

■ **talk down to** [v + adv + prep + o] hablarle en tono condescendiente a

■ **talk over** [v + o + adv, v + adv + o] discutir

talk² n **1** **(a)** (conversation) conversación f; **I had a long ~ with him** estuve hablando or (AmC, Méx tb) platicando un rato largo con él **(b)** (lecture) charla f **(c)** **talks** pl (negotiations) conversaciones fpl **2** (words) (colloq & pej) palabrería f (fam & pey)

talkative /'tɔːkətɪv/ adj conversador, hablador

talker /'tɔːkər ‖ 'tɔːkə(r)/ n hablador, -dora m,f

talking /'tɔːkɪŋ/: **~ point** n tema m de conversación; **~-to** n (pl **-tos**) (colloq): **to give sb a good ~-to** leerle* la cartilla a algn (fam)

talk show n programa m de entrevistas

tall /tɔːl/ adj **-er, -est** alto; **how ~ are you?** ¿cuánto mides?; **he's nearly 6 feet ~** mide casi 6 pies

tall story, tall tale n cuento m chino (fam)

tally¹ /'tæli/ n (pl **-lies**) cuenta f

tally² vi **-lies, -lying, -lied** coincidir, cuadrar

Talmud /'tælmʊd/ n **the ~** el Talmud

talon /'tælən/ n garra f

tambourine /ˌtæmbə'riːn/ n pandereta f

tame¹ /teɪm/ adj **tamer, tamest** **(a)** ⟨animal⟩ (by nature) manso, dócil; (tamed) domado, domesticado **(b)** (unexciting) ⟨show/story⟩ insulso, insípido

tame² vt ⟨wild animal⟩ domar; ⟨stray⟩ domesticar*

Tamil /'tæməl ‖ 'tæmɪl/ n **(a)** (person) tamil mf, tamul mf **(b)** (language) tamul m

tamper with /'tæmpər ‖ 'tæmpə(r)/ v + o + adv, v + adv + o ⟨engine/controls⟩ tocar*; ⟨figures⟩ alterar

tampon /'tæmpɑːn ‖ 'tæmpɒn/ n tampón m

tan¹ /tæn/ **-nn-** vt **1** ⟨leather/hide⟩ curtir **2** «sun» ⟨body/skin⟩ broncear, tostar*
■ ~ vi broncearse, quemarse (AmL)

tan² n (on skin) bronceado m, moreno m (esp Esp)

tan³ adj habano

tandem /'tændəm/ n tándem m

tang /tæŋ/ n (strong taste) sabor m fuerte; (sharp taste) acidez f; (smell) olor m penetrante

tangent /'tændʒənt/ n tangente f; **to go o fly off at o on a ~** irse* por las ramas

tangerine /ˌtændʒə'riːn/ n mandarina f, tangerina f

tangible /'tændʒəbəl/ adj tangible

tangle¹ /'tæŋɡəl/ vt enredar, enmarañar; **to get ~d (up)** enredarse
■ **tangle up** [v + o + adv, v + adv + o] enredar, enmarañar

tangle² n (of threads, hair) enredo m, maraña f, embrollo m; (of weeds) maraña f

tangled /'tæŋɡəld/ adj enredado

tango /'tæŋɡəʊ/ n (pl **-gos**) tango m

tank /tæŋk/ n **1** (for liquid, gas) depósito m, tanque m; (on trucks, rail wagons) cisterna f; (Auto) tanque m, depósito m **2** (Mil) tanque m, carro m de combate

tankard /'tæŋkərd ‖ 'tæŋkəd/ n jarra f

tanker /'tæŋkər ‖ 'tæŋkə(r)/ n **(a)** (ship) buque m cisterna or tanque **(b)** (truck) camión m cisterna

tanned /tænd/ adj bronceado, moreno

Tannoy® /'tænɔɪ/ n (BrE) sistema m de megafonía

tantalizing /'tæntlaɪzɪŋ ‖ 'tæntəlaɪzɪŋ/ adj tentador

tantamount /'tæntəmaʊnt/ adj **to be ~ TO sth** equivaler* A algo

tantrum /'tæntrəm/ n berrinche m, rabieta f; **Jack had o threw a ~** a Jack le dio un berrinche, Jack hizo un berrinche (Méx)

Tanzania /ˌtænzə'niːə/ n Tanzania f, Tanzanía f

Tanzanian /ˌtænzə'niːən/ adj tanzano

tap¹ /tæp/ n **1** **(a)** (for water) (BrE) llave f or (Esp) grifo m or (RPl) canilla f or (Per) caño m or (AmC) paja f or (AmC, Ven) chorro m **(b)** (gas ~) llave f del gas **(c)** (on barrel) espita f **2** (light blow) toque m, golpecito m **3** ▶ TAP DANCING

tap² **-pp-** vt **1** (strike lightly) dar* un toque or golpecito en **2** **(a)** ⟨tree⟩ sangrar **(b)** ⟨resources/reserves⟩ explotar **3** ⟨telephone⟩ intervenir*, pinchar (fam); ⟨conversation⟩ interceptar
■ ~ vi **(a)** (strike lightly) **to ~ AT/ON sth** dar* toques or golpecitos EN algo **(b)** (make tapping sound) dar* golpecitos, tamborilear

tap dancing n claqué m

tape¹ /teɪp/ n **1** **(a)** (of paper, cloth) cinta f **(b)** (adhesive) cinta f adhesiva; (Med) esparadrapo m; see also MASKING TAPE, SCOTCH TAPE® etc **(c)** (Sport) cinta f de llegada **(d)** ▶ TAPE MEASURE **2** (Audio, Comput, Video) cinta f

tape² vt (record) grabar

tape: **~ deck** n platina f, pletina f; **~ measure** n cinta f métrica, metro m

taper vi afilarse, estrecharse
■ ~ vt afilar, estrechar
■ **taper off** [v + adv] **(a)** «enthusiasm» decaer*; «demand/sales» disminuir* **(b)** ▶ TAPER vi

tape: **~-record** /'teɪprɪ'kɔːrd ‖ 'teɪprɪkɔːd/ vt grabar; **~ recorder** n grabador m, grabadora f; (for cassette format) grabador m, grabadora f, casete m (Esp)

tapestry /'tæpəstri/ n (pl **-tries**) **(a)** (wall hanging) tapiz m **(b)** (art form) tapicería f

tapeworm /'teɪpwɜːrm ‖ 'teɪpwɜːm/ n (lombriz f) solitaria f, tenia f

tar¹ /tɑːr ‖ tɑː(r)/ n alquitrán m

tar² vt **-rr-** ⟨road/fence⟩ alquitranar; ⟨roof⟩ impermeabilizar* (con alquitrán)

target¹ /'tɑːrɡət ‖ 'tɑːɡɪt/ n **1** **(a)** (thing aimed at) blanco m; (Mil) objetivo m; (board) (Sport) diana f **(b)** (of criticism) blanco m **2** (objective, goal) objetivo m; **to be on ~** ir* de acuerdo a lo previsto (or al plan de trabajo etc); (before n) ⟨date/figure⟩ fijado; ⟨market⟩ objetivo adj inv

target² vt **(a)** (select as target): **the company is ~ing the small investor** la empresa está intentando captar al pequeño inversor **(b)** (direct) ⟨advertising⟩ dirigir*; **to ~ benefits at those most in need** concentrar la ayuda a los más necesitados

target practice n prácticas fpl del tiro

tariff /'tærəf ‖ 'tærɪf/ n **1** (price list) (BrE) tarifa f **2** (Tax) arancel m (aduanero)

tarmac /'tɑːrmæk ‖ 'tɑːmæk/ n **(a)** **tarmac**® (AmE) (tar mixture) asfalto m **(b)** (surface — in airport, racetrack) pista f; (— on road) asfalto m

Tarmac® n (BrE) ▶ TARMAC A

t

tarnish /'tɑːrnɪʃ ‖'tɑːnɪʃ/ vt (a) ⟨silver⟩ deslustrar (b) ⟨reputation/name⟩ empañar

tarot card /'tærəʊ/ n carta f de tarot

tarpaulin /tɑːr'pɔːlən ‖tɑː'pɔːlɪn/ n (a) (sheet) lona f (b) (material) lona f impermeabilizada

tarragon /'tærəgən/ n estragón m

tart¹ /tɑːrt ‖tɑːt/ n **1** (Culin) (large) tarta f; (individual) tartaleta f **2** (promiscuous woman) (colloq) fulana f (fam), puta f (vulg)

tart² adj (a) ⟨taste/apple⟩ ácido, agrio (b) ⟨remark⟩ cortante, áspero

tartan /'tɑːrtn̩ ‖'tɑːtn̩/ n (a) (cloth) tela f escocesa or de cuadros escoceses (b) (pattern) tartán m

tartar /'tɑːrtər ‖'tɑːtə(r)/ n (Dent) sarro m

task /tæsk ‖tɑːsk/ n tarea f; **to take sb to ~** llamarle la atención or leerle* la cartilla a algn

tassel /'tæsəl/ n borla f

taste¹ /teɪst/ n **1** (a) (flavor) sabor m, gusto m (b) (sense) gusto m **2** (no pl) (sample, small amount): **can I have a ~ of your ice cream?** ¿me dejas probar tu helado?; **we got a ~ of what was to come** fue un anticipo de lo que nos esperaba **3** (liking) gusto m; **to be to one's ~** ser* de su (or mi etc) gusto **4** (judgment) gusto m; **in good/bad ~** de buen/mal gusto

taste² vt (a) (test flavor of) ⟨food/wine⟩ probar* (b) (test quality of) ⟨food⟩ degustar; ⟨wine⟩ catar (c) (perceive flavor): **you can ~ the sherry in it** sabe a jerez, le siento gusto a jerez (AmL) (d) (experience) ⟨freedom⟩ conocer*

■ ~ vi saber*; **to ~ OF sth** saber* A algo

taste bud n papila f gustativa

tasteful /'teɪstfəl/ adj de buen gusto

tastefully /'teɪstfəli/ adv con (buen) gusto

tasteless /'teɪstləs ‖'teɪstlɪs/ adj (a) (flavorless) insípido, soso, desabrido (b) (in bad taste) de mal gusto

tasty /'teɪsti/ adj **-tier, -tiest** sabroso, apetitoso

tattered /'tætərd ‖'tætəd/ adj ⟨clothes⟩ hecho jirones; ⟨pride/image⟩ destrozado

tatters /'tætərz ‖'tætəz/ pl n: **to be in ~** ⟨⟨clothes⟩⟩ estar* hecho jirones

tattoo¹ /tæ'tuː/ n (pl **-toos**) **1** (picture) tatuaje m **2** (display) espectáculo militar con música

tattoo² vt **-toos, -tooing, -tooed** tatuar*

tatty /'tæti/ adj **-tier, -tiest** (BrE colloq) ⟨clothes/shoes⟩ gastado, estropeado; ⟨furniture⟩ estropeado

taught /tɔːt/ past & past p of TEACH

taunt¹ /tɔːnt/ vt provocar* mediante burlas

taunt² n (insult) insulto m; (jibe) pulla f

Taurus /'tɔːrəs/ n (a) (sign) (no art) Tauro (b) (person) Tauro or tauro mf, taurino -na m,f

taut /tɔːt/ adj ⟨rope/sail⟩ tenso, tirante; ⟨skin⟩ tirante

tavern /'tævərn ‖'tævən/ n taberna f

tawdry /'tɔːdri/ adj **-drier, -driest** ⟨jewelry/ decorations⟩ de oropel; ⟨decor⟩ de mal gusto

tawny /'tɔːni/ adj **-nier, -niest** leonado, pardo rojizo adj inv

tawny owl n cárabo m, antillo m

tax¹ /tæks/ n (individual charge) impuesto m, tributo m (frml); (in general) impuestos mpl; (before n) **the ~ year** (in UK) el año or ejercicio fiscal

tax² vt **1** ⟨company/goods/earnings⟩ gravar; **we're being ~ed too highly** nos están cobrando demasiado en impuestos **2** (strain) ⟨resources/ health⟩ poner* a prueba

taxable /'tæksəbəl/ adj ⟨goods⟩ sujeto a impuestos; **~ income** ingresos mpl gravables, ≈ base f imponible

taxation /tæk'seɪʃən/ n (taxes) impuestos mpl, cargas fpl fiscales; (system) sistema m or régimen m tributario or fiscal

tax: ~ collector n recaudador, -dora m,f de impuestos; **~ evasion** n evasión f fiscal or de impuestos; (large scale) fraude m fiscal; **~-free** /'tæks'friː/ adj libre de impuestos; **~ haven** n paraíso m fiscal

taxi¹ /'tæksi/ n (pl **~s**) taxi m; (before n) **~ driver** taxista mf

taxi² vi **taxies, taxiing** or **taxying, taxied** (Aviat) rodar* por la pista de despegue/de aterrizaje, carretear (AmL)

taxidermy /'tæksədɜːrmi ‖'tæksɪdɜːmi/ n taxidermia f

taxing /'tæksɪŋ/ adj ⟨problem⟩ difícil, complicado; ⟨job⟩ (mentally) que exige mucho

tax: ~man /'tæksmæn/ (pl **-men** /-men/) n (colloq) **the ~man** Hacienda f, el fisco; **~payer** /'peɪər ‖'peɪə(r)/ n contribuyente mf; **~ return** n declaración f de la renta or (esp AmL) de impuestos

TB n = tuberculosis

tbs, tbsp = tablespoon(s)

te /tiː/ n (BrE Mus) si m

tea /tiː/ n **1** (drink, leaves, plant) té m **2** (meal) (a) (in the afternoon) té m, merienda f (b) (evening) (BrE) cena f, comida f (AmL)

tea bag n bolsita f de té

teach /tiːtʃ/ (past & past p **taught**) vt ⟨subject⟩ dar* clases de, enseñar; ⟨course⟩ dar*, impartir (frml); **to ~ sb to + INF** enseñarle a algn a + INF; **who ~es you?** ¿quién te da clase?; **to ~ school** (AmE) dar* clase(s) en un colegio

■ ~ vi dar* clase(s)

teacher /'tiːtʃər ‖'tiːtʃə(r)/ n profesor, -sora m,f, docente mf (frml), enseñante mf (period); (primary school ~) maestro, -tra m,f

teacher: ~s college n (AmE) (for primary education) escuela f normal; (for secondary education) instituto m de profesorado; **~ training** n formación f pedagógica or de profesorado; (before n) **~ training college** (BrE) ▶ ~S COLLEGE

tea chest n caja f de embalaje (utilizada en mudanzas)

teaching /'tiːtʃɪŋ/ n **1** (profession) enseñanza f, docencia f **2** (doctrine) (often pl) enseñanza f

teaching practice n (BrE) práctica f docente

tea: ~ cloth n (BrE) ▶ TEA TOWEL; **~ cozy,** (BrE) **~ cosy** n cubretetera m; **~cup** n taza f de té

teak /tiːk/ n (madera f de) teca f

tealeaf /'tiːliːf/ n (pl **-leaves**) hoja f de té

team /tiːm/ n (a) (of players, workers) equipo m; (before n) it was a ~ effort fue un trabajo de equipo (b) (of horses) tiro m; (of oxen) yunta f

team: ~mate n compañero, -ra m,f de equipo; ~ spirit n espíritu m de equipo

teamster /ˈtiːmstər ‖ ˈtiːmstə(r)/ n (AmE) camionero, -ra m,f

teamwork /ˈtiːmwɜːrk ‖ ˈtiːmwɜːk/ n trabajo m or labor f de equipo

tea: ~ party n té m; ~pot n tetera f

tear¹ n [1] /tɪr ‖ tɪə(r)/ lágrima f; to be in ~s estar* llorando [2] /ter ‖ teə(r)/ rotura f; (rip, slash) desgarrón m, rasgón m; see also WEAR¹ 1B

tear² /ter ‖ teə(r)/ (past tore; past p torn) vt (a) ⟨cloth/paper⟩ romper*, rasgar*; I tore open the letter abrí la carta (rasgando el sobre); to ~ sth to pieces o bits o shreds ⟨cloth/paper⟩ hacer* algo pedazos; ⟨play/essay⟩ hacer* algo pedazos or trizas or (fam) polvo; ⟨argument⟩ echar algo por tierra (b) (divide) (usu pass) dividir; he was torn between ... and ... se debatía entre ... y ... (c) (remove forcibly) to ~ sth FROM sth arrancar* algo DE algo
■ ~ vi [1] ⟨cloth/paper⟩ romperse*, rasgarse* [2] (rush) (+ adv compl): to ~ along ir* a toda velocidad
■ **tear apart** [v + o + adv] desgarrar
■ **tear down** [v + o + adv, v + adv + o] tirar abajo
■ **tear off** [v + o + adv, v + adv + o] arrancar*
■ **tear out** [v + o + adv, v + adv + o] arrancar*
■ **tear up** [v + o + adv, v + adv + o] romper*

teardrop /ˈtɪrdrɑːp ‖ ˈtɪədrɒp/ n lágrima f

tearful /ˈtɪrfəl ‖ ˈtɪəfəl/ adj ⟨look/expression⟩ lloroso; ⟨farewell⟩ triste, emotivo

tear gas /ˈtɪrgæs ‖ ˈtɪəgæs/ n gas m lacrimógeno

tearoom /ˈtiːruːm, -rʊm/ n salón m de té

tease /tiːz/ vt tomarle el pelo a (fam); (cruelly) burlarse or reírse de

tea: ~ service, ~ set n juego m de té; ~shop n (esp BrE) ► TEAROOM; ~spoon n (a) (spoon) cucharita f, cucharilla f (b) (quantity) cucharadita f, ~ strainer n colador m (pequeño)

teat /tiːt/ n (a) (Zool) tetilla f (b) (of feeding bottle) (BrE) ► NIPPLE B

tea: ~time n (of afternoon snack) la hora del té, ≈ la hora de merendar; (of evening meal) (BrE) la hora de cenar or (AmL tb) de comer; ~ towel n (BrE) paño m or trapo m de cocina

technical /ˈteknɪkəl/ adj técnico

technical college n (in UK) escuela f politécnica, ≈ instituto m de formación profesional (en Esp)

technicality /ˌteknɪˈkæləti/ n (pl -ties) (detail) detalle m técnico

technically /ˈteknɪkli/ adv técnicamente; (indep) desde el punto de vista técnico

technician /tekˈnɪʃən/ n técnico mf, técnico, -ca m,f

technique /tekˈniːk/ n técnica f

technological /ˌteknəˈlɑːdʒɪkəl ‖ ˌteknəˈlɒdʒɪkəl/ adj tecnológico

technology /tekˈnɑːlədʒi ‖ tekˈnɒlədʒi/ n (pl -gies) tecnología f

teddy bear /ˈtedi/ n osito m de peluche

tedious /ˈtiːdiəs/ adj tedioso

tedium /ˈtiːdiəm/ n tedio m

teem /tiːm/ vi to ~ WITH sth: the forest is ~ing with birds el bosque está repleto de pájaros; the streets were ~ing with people las calles hervían de gente

teenage /ˈtiːneɪdʒ/ adj ⟨girl/boy⟩ adolescente; ⟨fashions⟩ juvenil, para adolescentes

teenager /ˈtiːneɪdʒər ‖ ˈtiːneɪdʒə(r)/ n adolescente mf

teens /tiːnz/ pl n adolescencia f

tee shirt /ˈtiː/ n ► T-SHIRT

teeter /ˈtiːtər ‖ ˈtiːtə(r)/ vi «person» tambalearse

teeth /tiːθ/ pl of TOOTH

teethe /tiːð/ vi: she's teething le están saliendo los dientes

teething troubles /ˈtiːðɪŋ/ pl n problemas mpl iniciales

teetotal /ˈtiːˈtəʊtl/ adj abstemio

teetotaler, (BrE) **teetotaller** /ˈtiːˈtəʊtlər ‖ ˈtiːˈtəʊtlə(r)/ n abstemio, -mia m,f

TEFL /ˈtefəl/ n (BrE) (= teaching English as a foreign language) enseñanza del inglés como lengua extranjera

tel (= telephone number) Tel., fono (CS)

telebanking /ˈteliˌbæŋkɪŋ/ n telebanca f

telecommunications /ˈtelikəˌmjuːnəˈkeɪʃənz ‖ ˌtelikəˌmjuːnɪˈkeɪʃənz/ n telecomunicaciones fpl

telegram /ˈteləgræm ‖ ˈteligræm/ n telegrama m

telegraph /ˈteləgræf ‖ ˈteligrɑːf/ n (a) (method) telégrafo m; (before n) ⟨wire/cable⟩ telegráfico; ~ pole poste m telegráfico (b) (message) telegrama m, despacho m telegráfico

telemarketing /ˈteliˌmɑːrkətɪŋ ‖ ˈteliˌmɑːkɪtɪŋ/ n telemarketing m, teletienda f

telepathic /ˌteləˈpæθɪk ‖ ˌtelɪˈpæθɪk/ adj ⟨message⟩ telepático; ⟨person⟩ con telepatía, telépata

telepathy /təˈlepəθi/ n telepatía f

telephone¹ /ˈteləfəʊn ‖ ˈtelɪfəʊn/ n teléfono m; (before n) ⟨message/line⟩ telefónico; ~ number (número m de) teléfono m; ~ operator telefonista mf; see also PHONE¹

telephone² vt telefonear, llamar por teléfono a

telephone: ~ booth, (BrE) ~ box n cabina f telefónica or de teléfonos; ~ directory n guía f telefónica or de teléfonos; ~ exchange n central f telefónica or de teléfonos

telephonist /təˈlefənəst ‖ təˈlefənɪst/ n (BrE) telefonista mf

telesales /ˈteliseɪlz/ pl n televentas fpl

telescope /ˈteləskəʊp ‖ ˈtelɪskəʊp/ n telescopio m

telescopic /ˌteləˈskɑːpɪk ‖ ˌtelɪˈskɒpɪk/ adj telescópico

teleshopping /ˈteliˌʃɑːpɪŋ ‖ ˈteliˌʃɒpɪŋ/ n compra(s) f(pl) por teléfono

teletext /ˈtelitekst/ n teletex(to) m, videotex(to) m

televise /ˈteləvaɪz ‖ ˈtelɪvaɪz/ vt televisar

television /'telǝvɪʒǝn ‖'telɪvɪʒǝn/ n (a) (medium, industry) televisión f; on or por (la) televisión; (before n) ~ **licence** (in UK) impuesto y licencia que debe obtenerse para poder usar un receptor de televisión (b) ~ (**set**) televisor m

telex /'teleks/ n télex m

tell /tel/ (past & past p **told**) vt **1** (inform, reveal) decir*; he was told that ... le dijeron que ...; could you ~ me the way to the station? ¿me podría decir cómo se llega a la estación? **2** (recount, relate) ⟨joke/story⟩ contar*; she's told me all about you me ha hablado mucho de ti; ~ us about Lima cuéntanos cómo es Lima (or qué tal se fue en Lima etc) **3** (instruct, warn) decir*; to ~ sb to + INF decirle* a algn QUE (+ subj) **4** (a) (ascertain, know): I could ~ from her voice that ... noté por la voz que ...; to ~ the time decir la hora (b) (distinguish) to ~ sth/sb (FROM sth/sb) distinguir* algo/a algn (DE algo/algn); I can't ~ the difference yo no veo or no noto ninguna diferencia **5**: all told en total
■ ~ vi **1** (reveal): promise you won't ~? ¿prometes que no se lo vas a contar or decir a nadie?; to ~ ON sb (TO sb) (colloq) acusar a algn (A or CON algn) **2** (know) saber*; you never can ~ nunca se sabe **3** (count, have an effect): her age is beginning to ~ se le está empezando a notar la edad
■ **tell apart** [v + o + adv] distinguir*
■ **tell off** [v + o + adv, v + adv + o] (colloq) regañar, reñir* (esp Esp), retar (CS), resondrar (Per), rezongar* (AmC, Ur)

teller /'telǝr ‖'telǝ(r)/ n (in bank) cajero, -ra m,f

telling /'telɪŋ/ adj ⟨sign/remark⟩ revelador

telltale¹ /'telteɪl/ adj (before n) revelador

telltale² n (person) (colloq) soplón, -plona m,f (fam), acusete mf (fam)

temp /temp/ n empleado, -da m,f eventual or temporal

temper¹ /'tempǝr ‖'tempǝ(r)/ n (a) (no pl) (mood) humor m; (temperament, disposition) carácter m, genio m; to have a bad ~ tener* mal genio (b) (rage): to be in a ~ estar* furioso or hecho una furia (c) (composure): to lose one's ~ perder* los estribos

temper² vt (a) (moderate) ⟨criticism⟩ atenuar* (b) (Metall) templar

temperament /'tempramǝnt/ n temperamento m

temperamental /temprǝ'mentl/ adj ⟨person⟩ temperamental

temperance /'tempǝrǝns/ n (a) (moderation) (frml) templanza f (frml), moderación f (b) (alcohol avoidance) abstinencia f de bebidas; (before n) ⟨movement⟩ antialcohólico

temperate /'tempǝrǝt/ adj templado

temperature /'temprǝtʃǝr ‖'temprǝtʃǝ(r)/ n (a) (Phys) temperatura f (b) (Med) (reading on thermometer) temperatura f; (abnormally high reading)

fiebre f, temperatura f (CS); to have o run a ~ tener* fiebre or (CS) temperatura; to take sb's ~ tomarle la temperatura a algn

tempest /'tempǝst ‖'tempɪst/ n (liter) tempestad f (liter)

tempestuous /tem'pestʃuǝs ‖tem'pestjuǝs/ adj (a) ⟨relationship⟩ tempestuoso (b) ⟨sea⟩ (liter) tempestuoso (liter)

temple /'tempǝl/ n **1** (Relig) templo m **2** (Anat) sien f

tempo /'tempǝʊ/ n (pl **-pos** or **-pi** /-pi/) ritmo m; (Mus) tempo m

temporal /'tempǝrǝl/ adj temporal

temporarily /'tempǝ'rerǝli ‖'tempǝrǝrɪli/ adj temporalmente, temporariamente (AmL)

temporary /'tempǝreri ‖'tempǝrǝri/ adj ⟨accommodation/arrangement⟩ temporal, provisional; ⟨job/work/worker⟩ eventual, temporal

tempt /tempt/ vt (often pass) tentar*

temptation /temp'teɪʃǝn/ n tentación f

tempting /'temptɪŋ/ adj tentador

ten¹ /ten/ n diez m; see also FOUR¹

ten² adj diez adj inv

tenable /'tenǝbǝl/ adj defendible

tenacious /tǝ'neɪʃǝs ‖tɪ'neɪʃǝs/ adj tenaz

tenacity /tǝ'næsǝti ‖tɪ'næsǝti/ n tenacidad f

tenancy /'tenǝnsi/ n (pl **-cies**) (holding, possession) tenencia f

tenant /'tenǝnt/ n inquilino, -na m,f, arrendatario, -ria m,f

tend /tend/ vi **1** (have tendency, be inclined) tender*; to ~ to + INF tender* A + INF **2** (attend) to ~ TO sth/sb ocuparse DE algo/algn
■ ~ vt ⟨sheep⟩ cuidar (de), ocuparse de; ⟨victims⟩ cuidar (de), atender*; ⟨garden/grave⟩ ocuparse de

tendency /'tendǝnsi/ n (pl **-cies**) tendencia f; (Med) propensión f, tendencia f

tender¹ /'tendǝr ‖'tendǝ(r)/ adj (a) (sensitive) ⟨spot⟩ sensible; ⟨age⟩ tierno (b) ⟨meat⟩ tierno (c) (loving) tierno

tender² n (a) (Busn) (offer) propuesta f, oferta f (b) (legal ~) moneda f de curso legal

tender³ vt (frml) ⟨resignation⟩ presentar, ofrecer*

tenderize /'tendǝraɪz/ vt ⟨meat⟩ ablandar

tenderly /'tendǝrli ‖'tendǝli/ adv tiernamente, con ternura

tendon /'tendǝn/ n tendón m

tendril /'tendrǝl ‖'tendrɪl/ n zarcillo m

tenet /'tenǝt ‖'tenɪt/ n principio m

tenfold /'tenfǝʊld/ adj/adv ► -FOLD

Tenn = Tennessee

tennis /'tenǝs ‖'tenɪs/ n tenis m; (before n) ~ **court** cancha f or (Esp) pista f de tenis; ~ **player** tenista mf; ~ **racket** raqueta f de tenis

tenor¹ /'tenǝr ‖'tenǝ(r)/ n **1** (Mus) tenor m **2** (frml) (sense) tenor m

AmC	América Central	Arg	Argentina	Cu	Cuba	Per	Perú
AmL	América Latina	Bol	Bolivia	Ec	Ecuador	RPI	Río de la Plata
AmS	América del Sur	Chi	Chile	Esp	España	Ur	Uruguay
Andes	Región andina	CS	Cono Sur	Méx	México	Ven	Venezuela

tenor² *adj* (*before n*) ⟨*voice*⟩ de tenor; ⟨*saxophone*⟩ tenor

ten: ~**pin bowling** *n* (BrE) ▶ ~PINS; ~**pins** *n* (+ *sing vb*) (AmE) bolos *mpl*, bowling *m*

tense¹ /tens/ *adj* (a) ⟨*situation/person*⟩ tenso (b) (taut) tenso, tirante

tense² *vt* ⟨*muscles*⟩ poner* tenso, tensar
■ **tense up** [*v + adv*] (colloq) ponerse* tenso

tense³ *n* (Ling) tiempo *m*

tension /'tentʃən/ *n* (a) (of situation) tensión *f*, tirantez *f* (b) (felt by person) tensión *f* (c) (between two parties) conflicto *m* 2 (tautness) tensión *f* 3 (Elec) tensión *f*

tent /tent/ *n* tienda *f* (de campaña), carpa *f* (AmL)

tentacle /'tentɪkəl ‖'tentəkəl/ *n* tentáculo *m*

tentative /'tentətɪv/ *adj* (a) ⟨*plan*⟩ provisional, provisorio (AmS); ⟨*offer*⟩ tentativo (b) ⟨*person*⟩ indeciso

tenterhooks /'tentərhʊks ‖'tentəhʊks/ *pl n*: **to be on** ~ estar* en *or* sobre ascuas

tenth¹ /tenθ/ *adj* décimo

tenth² *adv* en décimo lugar

tenth³ *n* (Math) décimo *m*; (part) décima parte *f*

tenuous /'tenjuəs/ *adj* ⟨*claim*⟩ poco fundado; ⟨*link*⟩ indirecto

tenure /'tenjər ‖'tenjə(r)/ *n* (a) (of property, land) tenencia *f* (b) (period of office) ejercicio *m*, ocupación *f*

tepid /'tepəd ‖'tepɪd/ *adj* tibio

term¹ /tɜːrm ‖tɜːm/ *n*
I 1 (word) término *m* 2 (a) (period) período *m*, periodo *m*; ~ **of** *o* (AmE also) **in office** mandato *m*; **in the short/long** ~ a corto/largo plazo (b) (Educ) trimestre *m*
II terms *pl* 1 (conditions) condiciones *fpl*; **to come to** ~**s with sth** aceptar algo 2 (relations): **to be on good/bad** ~**s with sb** estar* en buenas/malas relaciones con algn 3 (a) (sense): **in financial** ~**s** desde el punto de vista financiero; **in real** ~**s** en términos reales (b) **in terms of: in** ~**s of efficiency** en cuanto a eficiencia

term² *vt* calificar* de

terminal¹ /'tɜːrmənl ‖'tɜːmɪnl/ *adj* ⟨*illness*⟩ terminal; ⟨*patient*⟩ (en fase) terminal, desahuciado

terminal² *n* (a) (Transp) (at airport) terminal *f*; **bus** ~ terminal *f* de autobuses (b) (Comput) terminal *m* (c) (Elec) terminal *m*

terminally /'tɜːrmənəli ‖'tɜːmɪnəli/ *adv*: **he's** ~ **ill** está en fase terminal, está desahuciado

terminate /'tɜːrməneɪt ‖'tɜːmɪneɪt/ *vt* (frml) ⟨*relationship*⟩ poner* fin a; ⟨*contract*⟩ poner* término a; ⟨*employee*⟩ (AmE) despedir*, cesar (frml *or* period); ⟨*pregnancy*⟩ interrumpir
■ ~ *vi* «*lease/relationship*» terminarse; **this train** ~**s here** este es el final del recorrido de este tren

termination /ˌtɜːrmə'neɪʃən ‖ˌtɜːmɪ'neɪʃən/ *n* (a) (of contract) (frml) terminación *f* (b) (Med): ~ **of pregnancy** interrupción *f* del embarazo

terminology /ˌtɜːrmə'nɑːlədʒi ‖ˌtɜːmɪ'nɒlədʒi/ *n* (*pl* **-gies**) terminología *f*

terminus /'tɜːrmənəs ‖'tɜːmɪnəs/ *n* (*pl* **-nuses** *or* **-ni** /-niː, -naɪ ‖-naɪ/) (of buses) terminal *f*; (of trains) estación *f* terminal

termite /'tɜːrmaɪt ‖'tɜːmaɪt/ *n* termita *f*

terrace /'terəs ‖'terəs, 'terɪs/ *n* (a) (patio) terraza *f* (b) (balcony) (AmE) terraza *f* (c) (on hillside) terraza *f* (d) (row of houses) (BrE) *hilera de casas adosadas*

terraced /'terəst ‖'terəst, 'terɪst/ *adj* (a) ⟨*hillside/slope*⟩ en terrazas *or* bancales (b) ⟨*house*⟩ (BrE) adosado (*en una hilera de casas uniformes*)

terrain /te'reɪn/ *n* terreno *m*

terrestrial /tə'restriəl/ *adj* terrestre

terrible /'terəbəl/ *adj* espantoso, atroz

terribly /'terəbli/ *adv* ⟨*suffer*⟩ terriblemente; ⟨*sing/act*⟩ terriblemente mal

terrier /'teriər ‖'teriə(r)/ *n* terrier *mf*

terrific /tə'rɪfɪk/ *adj* (a) (enormous) (colloq) tremendo, increíble; ⟨*argument*⟩ espantoso (b) (very good) (colloq) estupendo, genial (fam)

terrified /'terəfaɪd ‖'terɪfaɪd/ *adj* ⟨*crowd*⟩ aterrorizado, aterrado; **to be** ~ **of sth/sb** tenerle* terror *or* pánico a algo/algn

terrify /'terəfaɪ ‖'terɪfaɪ/ *vt* **-fies, -fying, -fied** aterrorizar*

terrifying /'terəfaɪɪŋ ‖'terɪfaɪɪŋ/ *adj* aterrador

territorial /ˌterə'tɔːriəl ‖ˌterɪ'tɔːriəl/ *adj* territorial

territory /'terətɔːri ‖'terɪtəri, -tri/ *n* (*pl* **-ries**) territorio *m*

terror /'terər ‖'terə(r)/ *n* terror *m*; **they fled in** ~ huyeron aterrorizados *or* despavoridos

terrorism /'terərɪzəm/ *n* terrorismo *m*

terrorist /'terərəst ‖'terərɪst/ *n* terrorista *mf*

terrorize /'terəraɪz/ *vt* aterrorizar*, tener* atemorizado

terse /tɜːrs ‖tɜːs/ *adj* seco, lacónico

test¹ /test/ *n* (a) (Educ) prueba *f*, (multiple-choice type) test *m* (b) (of machine, drug) prueba *f*; (*before n*) ⟨*run/flight*⟩ experimental, de prueba (c) (of blood, urine) análisis *m*; (for hearing, eyes) examen *m*

test² *vt* (a) ⟨*student/class*⟩ examinar, hacerle* una prueba a; ⟨*knowledge/skill*⟩ evaluar* (b) ⟨*product*⟩ probar*, poner* a prueba (c) ⟨*friendship/endurance*⟩ poner* a prueba (d) ⟨*blood/urine*⟩ analizar*; ⟨*sight/hearing*⟩ examinar; ⟨*hypothesis*⟩ comprobar*

testament /'testəmənt/ *n* 1 (will) testamento *m* 2 **Testament** (Bib): **the Old/New T**~ el Antiguo/Nuevo Testamento

test: ~ **case** *n*: *caso que siente jurisprudencia*; ~ **drive** *n* (Auto) prueba *f* de circulación en carretera

testicle /'testɪkəl/ *n* testículo *m*

testify /'testəfaɪ ‖'testɪfaɪ/ *vi* **-fies, -fying, -fied** (Law frml) prestar declaración, testificar*; **to** ~ **to sth** declarar *or* testificar* algo

testimonial /ˌtestə'məʊniəl ‖ˌtestɪ'məʊniəl/ *n* recomendación *f*

testimony /'testəməʊni ‖'testɪməni/ *n* (*pl* **-nies**) (Law) declaración *f*, testimonio *m*

testing¹ /'testɪŋ/ *n* pruebas *fpl*

testing² *adj* duro, arduo

test: ~ **match** *n* (Sport) partido *m* internacional; ~ **paper** *n* (Educ) examen *m*, prueba *f*; ~ **pilot** *n* piloto *mf* de pruebas; ~ **tube** *n* probeta *f*, tubo *m* de ensayo; (*before n*) ~**-tube baby** niño, -ña *m,f* probeta

tetanus /'tetnəs/ n tétano(s) m

tether¹ /'teðər ‖'teðə(r)/ n soga f

tether² vt atar, amarrar

Tex = **Texas**

text /tekst/ n texto m

textbook /'tekstbʊk/ n libro m de texto

textile /'tekstaɪl/ n textil m

textual /'tekstʃuəl ‖'tekstjuəl/ adj textual

texture /'tekstʃər ‖'tekstʃə(r)/ n textura f

Thai¹ /taɪ/ adj tailandés

Thai² n **(a)** (person) tailandés, -desa m,f **(b)** (language) tailandés m

Thailand /'taɪlænd/ n Tailandia f

Thames /temz/ n the ~ el Támesis

than¹ /ðæn, weak form ðən/ conj **(a)** (in comparisons) que; (with quantity) de; **I'm feeling better ~ I was** me siento mejor que antes; **more ~ $25** más de 25 dólares; **the situation is worse ~ we thought** la situación es peor de lo que pensábamos **(b)** (with alternatives): **I'd rather walk ~ go by bus** prefiero ir a pie a tomar el autobús **(c)** (when) cuando; **no sooner had I sat down ~ the bell rang** apenas me había sentado cuando sonó el timbre

than² prep (in comparisons) que; (with quantity) de

thank /θæŋk/ vt **to ~ sb (FOR sth)** darle* las gracias a algn (POR algo), agradecerle* (algo) a algn; **~ God/heaven(s)** menos mal, gracias a Dios; see also THANK YOU

thankful /'θæŋkfəl/ adj ⟨look/smile⟩ de agradecimiento, agradecido

thankfully /'θæŋkfəli/ adv (indep) menos mal, gracias a Dios

thankless /'θæŋkləs ‖'θæŋklɪs/ adj ingrato

thanks /θæŋks/ pl n **(a)** (expression of gratitude) agradecimiento m **(b)** (as interj) ~! ¡gracias!; **~ very much** o **a lot!** ¡muchas gracias!; **many ~** muchas gracias **(c)** thanks to gracias a

Thanksgiving (Day) /'θæŋksgɪvɪŋ/ n (in US) el día de Acción de Gracias

thank you interj ¡gracias!; **~ very much** muchas gracias; **to say ~** dar* las gracias; **~ ~ for coming/your help** gracias por venir/tu ayuda

that¹ /ðæt/ pron **①** (pl **those**) (demonstrative) ese, esa; (neuter) eso; **those** esos, esas; (to refer to sth more distant or to the remote past) aquel, aquélla; (neuter) aquello; **those** aquellos, aquellas; **~'s wonderful!** ¡es maravilloso!; **those who have been less fortunate** los que no han tenido tanta suerte **②** (in phrases) **at that** (moreover) además; (thereupon): **at ~ they all burst out laughing** al oír (or ver etc) eso, todos se echaron a reír; **that is** es decir; **that's it**: **~'s it for today** eso es todo por hoy; **now lift your left arm: ~'s it!** ahora levanta el brazo izquierdo ¡eso es! or ¡ahí está!; **~'s it: I've had enough!** ¡se acabó! ¡ya no aguanto más! **③** /ðət, strong form ðæt/ (relative) que; **it wasn't Helen (~) you saw** no fue a Helen a quien viste, no fue a Helen que viste (AmL)

that² /ðæt/ adj (pl **those**) ese, esa; **those** esos, esas; (to refer to sth more distant, to the remote past) aquel, aquella; **those** aquellos, aquellas

that³ /ðət, strong form ðæt/ conj que; **she said (~) ... dijo que ...; the news ~ our team had won** la noticia de que nuestro equipo había ganado

that⁴ /ðæt/ adv tan; **he can't be all ~ stupid** no es posible que sea tan tonto

thatched /θætʃt/ adj ⟨roof⟩ de paja (or de juncos etc)or (AmS) de quincha; ⟨cottage⟩ con el tejado de paja (or de juncos etc), quinchado (AmS)

thaw¹ /θɔː/ vi «snow/ice» derretirse*, fundirse; «frozen food» descongelarse; «relations» hacerse* más cordial
■ ~ vt ⟨frozen food⟩ descongelar

thaw² n (Meteo, Pol) deshielo m

the¹ /before vowel ðɪ, ðiː; before consonant ðə, strong form ðiː/ def art **①** (sing) el, la; (pl) los, las **②** (a) (with names): **Henry ~ First** Enrique primero; **~ Smiths** los Smith **(b)** (in abstractions, generalizations) (+ sing vb): **~ impossible** lo imposible; **~ young** los jóvenes **③** (per): **they sell it by ~ square foot** lo venden por pie cuadrado; **I get paid by ~ hour** me pagan por hora

the² /before vowel ðɪ; before consonant ðə/ adv (+ comp) (as conj) cuanto; **~ more you have, ~ more you want** cuanto más tienes, más quieres; **~ sooner, ~ better** cuanto antes, mejor

theater, (BrE) **theatre** /'θiːətər ‖'θɪətə(r)/ n **①** (a) (building) teatro m **(b)** (theatrical world) **the ~** el teatro **②** (movie ~) (AmE) cine m

theatrical /θiˈætrɪkəl/ adj teatral

theft /θeft/ n robo m

their /ðer ‖ðeə(r)/ adj
■ **Note** The translation su agrees in number with the noun which it modifies; their is translated by su, sus, depending on what follows: their father/mother su padre/madre; their books/magazines sus libros/revistas.
(a) (sing) su; (pl) sus; **he cut off ~ heads** les cortó la cabeza **(b)** (belonging to indefinite person) (sing) su; (pl) sus; **whoever called didn't leave ~ number** la persona que ha llamado no dejó su teléfono

theirs /ðerz ‖ðeəz/ pron
■ **Note** The translation suyo reflects the gender and number of the noun it is standing for; theirs is translated by el suyo, la suya, los suyos, las suyas, depending on what is being referred to.
(sing) suyo, -ya; (pl) suyos, -yas; **~ is blue** el suyo/la suya or el/la de ellos es azul; **a friend of ~** un amigo suyo or de ellos

them /ðem, weak form ðəm/ pron **①** (a) (as direct object) los, las; (referring to people) los or (Esp tb) les, las; **where did you buy ~?** ¿dónde los/las compraste?; **he has two sons, do you know ~?** tiene dos hijos ¿los or (Esp tb) les conoces? **(b)** (as indirect object) les; (with direct object pronoun present) se; **I lent ~ some money** les presté dinero **(c)** (after preposition) ellos, ellas **②** (emphatic use) ellos, ellas; **that'll be ~** deben de ser ellos **③** (indefinite person): **if anyone calls, tell ~ that ...** si llama alguien, dile que ...

theme /θiːm/ n tema m; (before n) **~ park** parque m temático; **~ song** tema m musical; (of TV program) (AmE) música f de un programa

themselves /ðəmˈselvz/ pron **(a)** (reflexive): **they bought ~ a new car** se compraron otro coche; **they only think of ~** solo piensan en sí

mismos; they were by ∼ estaban solos/solas **(b)** (emphatic) ellos mismos, ellas mismas **(c)** (normal selves): **the children aren't** ∼ los niños no son los de siempre **(d)** (indefinite person or persons): **if anyone's interested they can find out for** ∼ si a alguien le interesa, puede averiguarlo por sí mismo

then¹ /ðen/ *adv* **1 (a)** (at that time) entonces **(b)** (in those days) en aquel entonces **2** (*after prep*): **by** ∼ para entonces; **from** ∼ **on** a partir de ese momento, desde entonces; **(up) until** *o* **till** ∼ hasta entonces **3 (a)** (next, afterward) después, luego **(b)** (in those circumstances) entonces **(c)** (besides, in addition) además **4** (in that case) entonces; **you do it,** ∼**!** ¡hazlo tú, entonces! **5 then again** (*as linker*) también

then² *adj* (*before n*) entonces; **the** ∼ **leader** el entonces líder

theologian /ˈθiəˈləʊdʒən/ *n* teólogo, -ga *m,f*

theological /ˈθiəˈlɑːdʒɪkəl ‖ˌθiəˈlɒdʒɪkəl/ *adj* teológico

theology /θiˈɑːlədʒi ‖θiˈɒlədʒi/ *n* (*pl* **-gies**) teología *f*

theorem /ˈθiərəm/ *n* teorema *m*

theoretical /ˈθiəˈretɪkəl/ *adj* teórico

theorize /ˈθiəraɪz/ *vi* especular, teorizar*

theory /ˈθiəri/ *n* (*pl* **-ries**) teoría *f*

therapeutic /ˈθerəˈpjuːtɪk/ *adj* terapéutico

therapist /ˈθerəpəst ‖ˈθerəpɪst/ *n* terapeuta *mf*

therapy /ˈθerəpi/ *n* (*pl* **-pies**) terapia *f*

there¹ /ðer ‖ðeə(r)/ *adv* **1 (a)** (close to person being addressed) ahí; (further away) allí, ahí (esp AmL); (less precise, further) allá; **up/down** ∼ arriba/abajo **(b) there and then** (*decide*) en ese mismo momento; **they mended it for me** ∼ **and then** me lo arreglaron en el acto **2** (calling attention to sth): ∼ **you are** (giving sth) aquí tiene; ∼ **go my chances of promotion!** ¡adiós ascenso! **3** (present): **all his friends were** ∼ estaban todos sus amigos; **is Tony** ∼**?** ¿está Tony?; **who's** ∼**?** (at the door) ¿quién es?; (in the dark) ¿quién anda ahí? **4** (*as interj*) ∼**!** **that's the last of the boxes** ¡listo! esa es la última caja; ∼**,** ∼**, don't cry!** vamos, no llores

there² /ðer, *weak form* ðər ‖ðeə(r), *weak form* ðə(r)/ *pron*: **there is/are** hay; **there was** había/ hubo; **there will be** habrá

there: ∼about /ˈðerəbaʊt ‖ˈðeərəbaʊt/ *adv* (AmE) ▶ ∼ABOUTS; **∼abouts** /ˈðerəbaʊts ‖ˈðeərəbaʊts/ *adv* **(a)** (near that figure, time) por ahí **(b)** (in that vicinity) por allí; **∼after** /ðerˈæftər ‖ðeərˈɑːftə(r)/ *adv* (fml) a partir de entonces; **∼by** /ˈðerˈbaɪ ‖ˈðeəˈbaɪ, ˈðeəbaɪ/ *adv* (fml) de ese modo, así; **∼fore** /ˈðerfɔːr ‖ˈðeəfɔː(r)/ *adv* por lo tanto, por consiguiente

there's /ðerz, *weak form* ðərz ‖ðeəz, *weak form* ðəz/ **(a)** = **there is (b)** = **there has**

thermal /ˈθɜːrməl ‖ˈθɜːməl/ *adj* **(a)** (*stream/bath*) termal **(b)** (*underwear/glove*) térmico

thermometer /θərˈmɑːmətər ‖θəˈmɒmɪtə(r)/ *n* termómetro *m*

Thermos® (**flask**) /ˈθɜːrməs ‖ˈθɜːməs/, (AmE also) **thermos** (**bottle**) *n* termo *m*

thermostat /ˈθɜːrməstæt ‖ˈθɜːməstæt/ *n* termostato *m*

thesaurus /θɪˈsɔːrəs/ *n* (*pl* **-ruses** *or* **-ri** /-raɪ/) diccionario *m* ideológico *or* de ideas afines, tesauro *m*

these /ðiːz/ *pl of* THIS¹,²

thesis /ˈθiːsəs ‖ˈθiːsɪs/ *n* (*pl* **-ses** /-siːz/) tesis *f*; (shorter) tesina *f*

they /ðeɪ/ *pron*

■ Note Although *ellos* and *ellas* are given as translations of *they*, they are in practice used only for emphasis, or to avoid ambiguity: *they went to the theater* fueron al teatro; *they did it* ellos *or* ellas lo hicieron.

(a) (pl of he, she, it) ellos, ellas **(b)** (indefinite person or persons): ∼**'ve dug up the road** han levantado la calle

they'd /ðeɪd/ **(a)** = **they would (b)** = **they had**

they'll /ðeɪl/ = **they will**

they're /ðer, *weak form* ðər ‖ðeə(r), *weak form* ðə(r)/ = **they are**

they've /ðeɪv/ = **they have**

thick /θɪk/ *adj* **-er, -est** **1 (a)** (*layer/book/sweater*) grueso, gordo (fam); (*line*) grueso; **it's 5cm** ∼ tiene 5cm de espesor *or* de grosor **(b)** (*sauce/paint*) espeso **(c)** (*fog/smoke*) espeso, denso; (*fur*) tupido; (*beard/eyebrows*) poblado; **through** ∼ **and thin** tanto en las duras como en las maduras **2** (colloq) (stupid) burro (fam), corto (fam)

thicken /ˈθɪkən/ *vt* (*sauce/paint*) espesar
■ ∼ *vi* «*sauce/paint*» espesar(se); «*fog*» hacerse* más espeso *or* denso

thicket /ˈθɪkət/ *n* matorral *m*

thickly /ˈθɪkli/ *adv* **(a)** (in a thick layer): **spread the jam** ∼ pon una capa gruesa de mermelada **(b)** (densely) (*populated*) densamente

thickness /ˈθɪknəs ‖ˈθɪknɪs/ *n* (of fabric, wire) grosor *m*; (of paper, wood, wall) espesor *m*, grosor *m*

thick: ∼set /ˈθɪkˈset/ *adj* fornido; **∼-skinned** /ˈθɪkˈskɪnd/ *adj* insensible

thief /θiːf/ *n* (*pl* **thieves** /θiːvz/) ladrón, -drona *m,f*

thigh /θaɪ/ *n* muslo *m*

thimble /ˈθɪmbəl/ *n* dedal *m*

thin¹ /θɪn/ *adj* **-nn-** **1 (a)** (*layer/slice*) delgado, fino **(b)** (*person*) delgado, flaco; (*waist*) delgado **2 (a)** (*soup/sauce*) claro, poco espeso **(b)** (*hair*) ralo

thin² *vt* **-nn-** (*paint*) diluir*, rebajar; (*sauce*) aclarar, hacer* menos espeso
■ ∼ *vi*: **his hair is** ∼**ning** está perdiendo pelo

thing /θɪŋ/ *n* **1** (physical object) cosa *f* **2** (non-material) cosa *f*; **the same** ∼ **happened to me** a mí me pasó lo mismo; **it's a good** ∼ (that) **... menos mal que ...; the last** ∼ **I expected** lo que menos me imaginaba; **he hadn't done a** ∼ no había hecho absolutamente nada; **it's just one of those** ∼**s** son cosas que pasan **3** (affair, matter) asunto *m*; **I'm fed up with the whole** ∼ estoy harto del asunto **4 the thing (a)** (that which, what) lo que **(b)** (what is needed): **I've got just the** ∼ **for you** tengo exactamente lo que necesitas *or* lo que te hace falta **(c)** (crucial point, factor): **the** ∼ **is, ...** resulta que *or* el caso es que *or* lo que pasa es que ... **5 things** *pl* **(a)** (belongings, equipment) cosas *fpl* ⋯▷

(b) (matters, the situation) cosas *fpl*; **if ~s don't improve** si las cosas no mejoran; **how's ~s?** (colloq) ¿qué tal? (fam)

6 (person, creature): **you poor ~!** ¡pobrecito!; **you lucky ~!** ¡qué suerte tienes!

7 (preference, fad) (colloq): **it's not my ~** no es lo mío

8 (in expressions of time): **first ~ (in the morning)** a primera hora (de la mañana)

thingamabob /'θɪŋəmɑːb ‖ 'θɪŋəməbɒb/, **thingamajig** /-dʒɪg/ *n* (colloq) cosa *f*, chisme *m* (Esp, Méx fam), coso *m* (AmS fam), vaina *f* (Col, Per, Ven fam)

think /θɪŋk/ (*past & past p* **thought**) *vi* **1** (use one's mind) pensar*; **to ~ ABOUT sth** pensar* EN algo; (consider) pensar* algo; **to ~ OF sth/sb** pensar* EN algo/algn; **I hadn't thought of that** no se me había ocurrido eso

2 (intend, plan) **to ~ of -ING** pensar* + INF

3 (a) (find, come up with): **can you ~ of anything better?** ¿se te ocurre algo mejor? **(b)** (remember) **to ~ OF sth** acordarse* DE algo; **I can't ~ of his name** no me puedo acordar de su nombre

4 (have opinion): **to ~ highly of sb** tener* muy buena opinión de algn; **he ~s a lot of you** te aprecia mucho

■ ~ *vt* **1** (reflect, ponder) pensar*; **~ what that would cost** piensa (en) lo que costaría; **that's wrong, I thought to myself** eso está mal — pensé para mí *or* para mis adentros; **I didn't ~ to look there** no se me ocurrió mirar allí

2 (a) (suppose, imagine, expect) pensar*; **I thought you knew** pensé que lo sabías; **I can't ~ why he refused** no me explico por qué se negó **(b)** (indicating intention): **we thought we'd eat out tonight** esta noche tenemos pensado salir a cenar

3 (believe) creer*; **I ~ so** creo que sí *or* me parece que sí; **I don't think so** creo que no *or* me parece que no; **I thought as much** ya me parecía *or* ya me lo imaginaba

■ **think ahead** [*v + adv*]: **you have to ~ ahead** hay que ser previsor

■ **think back** [*v + adv*] (reflect) recordar*; **~ back** haz memoria; **to ~ back TO sth** acordarse* DE algo

■ **think out** [*v + o + adv, v + adv + o*] pensar *or* planear cuidadosamente; **a well thought-out proposal** una propuesta bien elaborada

■ **think over** [*v + o + adv*] pensar*

■ **think through** [*v + o + adv, v + adv + o*] ⟨project⟩ planear detenidamente; ⟨idea⟩ considerar detenidamente

■ **think up** [*v + o + adv, v + adv + o*] ⟨excuse⟩ inventar; ⟨slogan⟩ idear

thinker /'θɪŋkər ‖ 'θɪŋkə(r)/ *n* pensador, -dora *m,f*

thinking /'θɪŋkɪŋ/ *n* ideas *fpl*, pensamiento *m*; **to my (way of) ~** a mi modo de ver, en mi opinión; **good ~!** ¡buena idea!

think tank *n* gabinete *m* estratégico

thinly /'θɪnli/ *adv* **(a)** ⟨slice⟩ en rebanadas finas **(b)** (sparsely): **~ populated** poco poblado

thinner /'θɪnər ‖ 'θɪnə(r)/ *n* disolvente *m*, diluyente *m*

third¹ /θɜːrd ‖θɜːd/ *adj* tercero

■ **Note** The usual translation of *third*, *tercero*, becomes *tercer* when it precedes a masculine singular noun.
---

third² *adv* **(a)** (in position, time, order) en tercer lugar **(b)** (thirdly) en tercer lugar **(c)** (*with superl*): **the ~ highest mountain** la tercera montaña en altura

third³ *n* **1 (a)** (Math) tercio *m* **(b)** (part) tercera parte *f*, tercio *m* **(c)** (Mus) tercera *f* **2** **~ (gear)** (Auto) (*no art*) tercera *f*

third-class /'θɜːrd'klæs ‖θɜːd'klɑːs/ *adj* (*pred* **~ class**) **(a)** (inferior) de tercera **(b)** ⟨mail⟩ (in US) de franqueo económico

thirdly /'θɜːrdli ‖ 'θɜːdli/ *adv* (*indep*) en tercer lugar

third: ~ party insurance *n* seguro *m* contra terceros; **T~ World** *n* the **T~ World** el Tercer Mundo; (*before n*) ⟨nation⟩ tercermundista

thirst /θɜːrst ‖θɜːst/ *n* sed *f*

thirsty /'θɜːrsti ‖ 'θɜːsti/ *adj* **-tier, -tiest** ⟨person/animal⟩ que tiene sed; **to be ~** tener* sed

thirteen /'θɜːr'tiːn ‖θɜː'tiːn/ *adj/n* trece *adj inv/m*; *see also* FOUR¹

thirteenth¹ /'θɜːr'tiːnθ ‖θɜː'tiːnθ/ *adj* decimotercero; (before masculine singular nouns) decimotercer

thirteenth² *adv* en decimotercer lugar

thirteenth³ *n* (Math) treceavo *m*; (part) treceava parte *f*

thirtieth¹ /'θɜːrtiəθ ‖ 'θɜːtiəθ/ *adj* trigésimo

thirtieth² *adv* en trigésimo lugar

thirtieth³ *n* (Math) treintavo *m*; (part) treintava *or* trigésima parte *f*

thirty /'θɜːrti ‖ 'θɜːti/ *adj/n* treinta *adj inv/m*; *see also* FOUR¹

this¹ /ðɪs/ *pron* (*pl* **these**) este, -ta; (*neuter*) esto; **these** estos, -tas; **what is ~?** ¿qué es esto?; **~ is John** (on photo) este es John; (introducing) **te presento a John**; **is ~ where you work?** ¿aquí es donde trabajas?; **~ is Jack Smith** (on telephone) habla Jack Smith, soy Jack Smith

this² *adj* (*pl* **these**) este, -ta; (*pl*) estos, -tas; **look at ~ tree/house** mira este árbol/esta casa; **I like these ones** me gustan estos/estas

this³ *adv*: **it's ~ big** es así de grande; **now we've come ~ far ...** ya que hemos venido hasta aquí ...

thistle /'θɪsəl/ *n* cardo *m*

thong /θɔːŋ ‖ θɒŋ/ *n* **(a)** (leather strip) correa *f* **(b)** (sandal) (AmE) chancla *f*, chancleta *f*

thorn /θɔːrn ‖θɔːn/ *n* espina *f*

thorny /'θɔːrni ‖ 'θɔːni/ *adj* **-nier, -niest** ⟨plant⟩ espinoso; ⟨problem/issue⟩ espinoso, peliagudo

thorough /'θɜːrəʊ ‖ 'θʌrə/ *adj* ⟨person⟩ concienzudo, cuidadoso; ⟨search/investigation⟩ riguroso

thoroughbred /'θɜːrəbred ‖'θʌrəbred/ adj ⟨horse⟩ de pura sangre, de raza

thoroughfare /'θərəfer ‖'θʌrəfeə(r)/ n **(a)** (street) (liter) calle f, vía f **(b)** (public road) vía f pública

thoroughly /'θɜːrəli ‖'θʌrəli/ adv **(a)** ⟨wash/clean⟩ a fondo, a conciencia; ⟨research⟩ rigurosamente; ⟨examine⟩ minuciosamente **(b)** (completely) ⟨understand⟩ perfectamente; **we ~ enjoyed ourselves** nos divertimos muchísimo

those /ðəʊz/ pl of THAT adj, pron 1

though¹ /ðəʊ/ conj aunque

though² adv: **it's easy, ~, to understand their feelings** sin embargo, es fácil comprender sus sentimientos; **the course is difficult; it's interesting, ~** el curso es difícil, pero es interesante

thought¹ /θɔːt/ past & past p of THINK¹

thought² n **1** **(a)** (intellectual activity) pensamiento m **(b)** (deliberation): **after much ~** tras mucho pensarlo **2** **(a)** (reflection) pensamiento m; **what are your ~s on the matter?** ¿tú qué opinas al respecto?; **on second ~(s)** pensándolo bien **(b)** (idea) idea f; **I've just had a ~** se me acaba de ocurrir una idea; **the ~ never even entered my head** ni se me pasó por la cabeza

thoughtful /'θɔːtfəl/ adj **(a)** (kind) atento, amable; (considerate) considerado **(b)** (pensive) pensativo, meditabundo

thoughtfully /'θɔːtfəli/ adv pensativamente

thoughtless /'θɔːtləs ‖'θɔːtlɪs/ adj desconsiderado

thought-provoking /'θɔːtprə,vəʊkɪŋ/ adj que hace pensar or reflexionar

thousand /'θaʊznd/ n mil m

thousandth¹ /'θaʊzndθ/ adj milésimo

thousandth² adv en milésimo lugar

thousandth³ n (Math) milésimo m; (part) milésima parte f

thrash /θræʃ/ vt golpear; (as punishment) azotar; **darle* una paliza a**
■ ~ vi: ~ **(around** o **about)** revolverse*, retorcerse*; (in mud, water) revolcarse*
■ **thrash out** [v + o + adv, v + adv + o] ⟨problem⟩ discutir, tratar de resolver

thrashing /'θræʃɪŋ/ n paliza f, zurra f

thread¹ /θred/ n **(a)** (filament) hilo m; (of plot, conversation) hilo m **(b)** (of screw) rosca f, filete m

thread² vt ⟨needle⟩ enhebrar; ⟨bead⟩ ensartar

threadbare /'θredber ‖'θredbeə(r)/ adj gastado, raído

threat /θret/ n amenaza f; **to be under ~** «way of life» verse* amenazado; «factory» estar* bajo amenaza de cierre

threaten /'θretn/ vt **(a)** ⟨person/stability⟩ amenazar*; **to ~ sb WITH sth** amenazar* a algn CON algo **(b)** (give warning of) ⟨action/violence⟩ amenazar* con
■ ~ vi amenazar*

threatening /'θretnɪŋ/ adj amenazador

three /θriː/ adj/n tres adj inv/m; see also FOUR¹

three: ~-dimensional /'θriːdə'mentʃnəl, -daɪ- ‖'θriːdaɪ'menʃənl, -dɪ-/ adj tridimensional; **~fold** adj/adv ▸ -FOLD; **~-piece** /'θriː'piːs/ adj

(before n): **~-piece suit** traje m con chaleco, terno m; **~-piece suite** juego m de living (de sofá y dos sillones) (AmL), tresillo m (Esp)

three-quarters¹ /'θriː'kwɔːrtərz ‖'θriː'kwɔːtəz/ pron las tres cuartas partes

three-quarters² adv: **it's ~ full** contiene el 75% or las tres cuartas partes de su capacidad

threshold /'θreʃhəʊld/ n **(a)** (doorway) umbral m; **to be on the ~ of sth** estar* en el umbral or a las puertas de algo **(b)** (of pain) umbral m

threw /θruː/ past of THROW¹

thrift /θrɪft/ n economía f, ahorro m; (before n) **~ shop** (esp AmE) tienda que vende artículos de segunda mano con fines benéficos

thrifty /'θrɪfti/ adj **-tier, -tiest** económico, ahorrativo

thrill¹ /θrɪl/ n (excitement) emoción f; **it was a real ~** fue verdaderamente emocionante

thrill² vt emocionar

thrilled /θrɪld/ adj (pred) **to be ~ (ABOUT/WITH sth)** estar* contentísimo or (fam) chocho (CON algo); **to be ~ to + INF: she was really ~ to meet him** le encantó or (Esp tb) le hizo muchísima ilusión conocerlo

thriller /'θrɪlər ‖'θrɪlə(r)/ n novela f/película f de misterio or de suspenso or (Esp) de suspense

thrilling /'θrɪlɪŋ/ adj emocionante

thrive /θraɪv/ vi (past **thrived** or (liter) **throve**; past p **thrived**) «business/town» prosperar; «plant» crecer* con fuerza

thriving /'θraɪvɪŋ/ adj (before n) ⟨business/town⟩ próspero

throat /θrəʊt/ n garganta f; (neck) cuello m

throb /θrɑːb ‖θrɒb/ vi **-bb-** **(a)** «heart/pulse» latir con fuerza; «engine» vibrar **(b)** (with pain): **his leg was ~bing** tenía un dolor punzante en la pierna

throes /θrəʊz/ pl n (death ~) agonía f; **to be in one's death ~** agonizar*, estar agonizando

thrombosis /θrɑːm'bəʊsəs ‖θrɒm'bəʊsɪs/ n (pl **-ses** /-siːz/) trombosis f

throne /θrəʊn/ n trono m

throng /θrɔːŋ ‖θrɒŋ/ n muchedumbre f

throttle¹ /'θrɑːtl ‖'θrɒtl/ vt ahogar*, estrangular

throttle² n **(a)** (Auto) acelerador m (que se acciona con la mano) **(b)** (pedal) acelerador m

through¹ /θruː/ prep **1** **(a)** (from one side to the other) por; **it went right ~ the wall** atravesó la pared de lado a lado; **to hear sth ~ sth** oír* algo a través de algo; **we drove ~ Munich** atravesamos Munich (en coche) **(b)** (past, beyond) **to be ~ sth** haber* pasado algo **2** **(a)** (in time): **we worked ~ the night** trabajamos durante toda la noche; **half-way ~ his speech** en medio de su discurso; **~ the centuries** a través de los siglos **(b)** (until and including) (AmE): **Tuesday ~ Thursday** de martes a jueves; **October ~ December** desde octubre hasta diciembre inclusive **3** (by): **she spoke ~ an interpreter** habló a través de un intérprete; **I heard about it ~ a friend** me enteré a través de or por un amigo

through² adv **1** (from one side to the other): **it sped ~ without stopping** pasó a toda velocidad sin parar; **the red paint shows ~** se nota la ···⟶

pintura roja que hay debajo; *see also* GET, PULL,
PUT *etc* THROUGH **2** (completely): **wet** ~ mojado
hasta los huesos

through³ *adj* **1** (Transp) *(before n) ⟨train/route⟩*
directo; ~ **traffic** tráfico *m* de paso; **❷** **no through
road** calle sin salida **2** (finished) (colloq) *⟨pred⟩*: **to
be** ~ **WITH sb/sth** haber* terminado CON algn/
algo

throughout¹ /θruː'aʊt/ *prep* **1** (all over): ~
Europe en toda Europa **2** (in time): ~ **the
weekend** (durante) todo el fin de semana; ~ **his
career** a lo largo de toda su carrera

throughout² *adv* **(a)** *⟨decorated/carpeted⟩*
totalmente **(b)** (in time) desde el principio hasta el
fin

throughway /'θruːweɪ/ *n* (AmE) autopista *f*

throve /θrəʊv/ *past of* THRIVE

throw¹ /θrəʊ/ *(past* **threw**; *past p* **thrown**) *vt*
1 (a) *⟨ball/stone⟩* tirar, aventar* (Col, Méx, Per);
⟨grenade/javelin⟩ lanzar* **(b)** *⟨dice⟩* echar, tirar
2 (send, propel) *(+ adv compl)*: **to** ~ **sb into jail**
meter a algn preso *or* en la cárcel; **to** ~ **oneself
into a task** meterse de lleno en una tarea
3 *⟨horse⟩ ⟨rider⟩* desmontar, tirar
4 (disconcert) desconcertar*
5 (have, hold) *⟨party⟩* hacer*, dar*
■ **throw away** *[v + o + adv, v + adv + o]* **(a)**
(discard) *⟨can/paper⟩* tirar (a la basura), botar (a
la basura) (AmL exc RPl) **(b)** (waste) *⟨money⟩* tirar,
botar (AmL exc RPl)
■ **throw back** *[v + o + adv, v + adv + o]* **(a)**
⟨ball⟩ devolver* **(b)** (pull back) *⟨curtains⟩*
(des)correr; *⟨bedclothes⟩* echar atrás
■ **throw off** *[v + o + adv, v + adv + o]* **(a)**
⟨jacket/hat⟩ quitarse *⟨rápidamente⟩* **(b)** *⟨illness/
habit⟩* quitarse; *⟨pursuer⟩* despistar
■ **throw out** *[v + o + adv, v + adv + o]* **(a)**
(discard) tirar (a la basura), botar (a la basura)
(AmL exc RPl) **(b)** *⟨bill/proposal⟩* rechazar **(c)**
⟨person⟩ echar
■ **throw together** *[v + o + adv, v + adv + o]*
⟨meal/plan⟩ improvisar
■ **throw up**
I *[v + adv + o]* **1** (raise) *⟨hands⟩* levantar *or*
alzar* *⟨rápidamente⟩*
2 (bring to light) *⟨facts⟩* revelar (la existencia de)
II *[v + adv]* (vomit) (colloq) devolver*, arrojar

throw² *n* **1 (a)** (of ball) tiro *m*; (of javelin, discus)
lanzamiento *m* **(b)** (of dice) tirada *f*, lance *m*
2 (AmE) **(a)** (bedspread) cubrecama *m* **(b)** (shawl)
chal (*m*), echarpe (*m*)

thrown /θrəʊn/ *past p of* THROW¹

thrush /θrʌʃ/ *n* **1** (bird) tordo *m*, zorzal *m*
2 (Med) aftas *fpl*

thrust¹ /θrʌst/ *vt* *(past & past p* **thrust**) (push)
empujar; (push out) sacar*; **to** ~ **out one's chest**
sacar* pecho; **she** ~ **the book at me** me tendió el
libro bruscamente; **he** ~ **his hands into his
pockets** se metió las manos en los bolsillos; **to** ~
sth INTO sth *⟨knife/sword⟩* clavar algo EN algo

thrust² *n* **1 (a)** (with sword) estocada *f* **(b)**
(push) empujón *m* **(c)** (attack, advance) ofensiva *f*
2 (impetus) empuje *m*, fuerza *f*

thruway /'θruːweɪ/ *n* (AmE) autopista *f*

thud /θʌd/ *n* ruido *m* sordo

thug /θʌg/ *n* matón *m*

thumb¹ /θʌm/ *n* pulgar *m*

thumb² *vt* : **I** ~**ed a lift home** me fui a casa a
dedo (fam)

thumbtack /'θʌmtæk/ *n* (AmE) tachuela *f*,
chinche *m* (Andes), chinche *f* (AmC, Méx, RPl),
chincheta *f* (Esp)

thump¹ /θʌmp/ *n* (sound, blow) golpazo *m*

thump² *vt* golpear

thunder¹ /'θʌndər ‖ 'θʌndə(r)/ *n* **(a)** (Meteo)
truenos *mpl* **(b)** (*no pl*) (sound — of traffic)
estruendo *m*

thunder² *vi* (move loudly): **the train** ~**ed through
the station** el tren pasó por la estación con gran
estruendo
■ ~ *vt* (shout): **get out! he** ~**ed** —¡fuera de aquí! —
bramó *or* rugió

thunder: ~**bolt** *n* rayo *m*; ~**storm** *n*
tormenta *f* eléctrica

thundery /'θʌndəri/ *adj* tormentoso

Thursday /'θɜːrzdeɪ, -di ‖ 'θɜːzdeɪ, -di/ *n* jueves
m; *see also* MONDAY

thus /ðʌs/ *adv* **1** (in this way) (frml) así, de este
modo **2** (consequently) (*as linker*) por lo tanto, por
consiguiente (frml)

thwart /θwɔːrt ‖ θwɔːt/ *vt* *⟨plan/attempt⟩*
frustrar

thyme /taɪm/ *n* tomillo *m*

thyroid (gland) /'θaɪrɔɪd/ *n* tiroides *f*,
glándula *f* tiroidea

ti /tiː/ *n* (Mus) si *m*

tiara /ti'ɑːrə/ *n* diadema *f*

Tibet /tɪ'bet/ *n* el Tíbet

Tibetan¹ /tɪ'betn/ *adj* tibetano

Tibetan² *n* **(a)** (person) tibetano, -na *m,f* **(b)**
(language) tibetano *m*

tic /tɪk/ *n* tic *m*

tick¹ /tɪk/ *n* **1** (sound) tic *m* **2** (Zool) garrapata
f **3** (mark) (BrE) marca *f*, tic *m*, palomita *f* (Méx),
visto *m* (Esp)

tick² *vi* «*clock/watch*» hacer* tictac
■ ~ *vt* (BrE) marcar* (con *un visto o una palomita
etc*)
■ **tick over** *[v + adv]* «*engine*» marchar al
ralentí

ticket /'tɪkət ‖ 'tɪkɪt/ *n* **1** (for bus, train) boleto *m*
or (Esp) billete *m*; (for plane) pasaje *m or* (Esp)
billete *m*; (for theater, museum) entrada *f*; (for
baggage, coat) ticket *m*; *(before n)* ~ **collector**
revisor, -sora *m,f*, ~ **office** (Transp) mostrador *m*
(*or* ventanilla *f etc*) de venta de pasajes (*or*
billetes *etc*); (Theat) taquilla *f*, boletería *f* (AmL)
2 (label) etiqueta *f*

tickle /'tɪkəl/ *vt* hacerle* cosquillas a
■ ~ *vi* «*wool/beard*» picar*

ticklish /'tɪklɪʃ/ *adj*: **to be** ~ tener* cosquillas,
ser* cosquilloso *or* (Méx) cosquilludo

tidal /'taɪdl/ *adj* con régimen de marea

tidal wave *n* maremoto *m*

tidbit /'tɪdbɪt/ *n* (AmE) ▶ TITBIT

tide /taɪd/ *n* **1** (Geog) marea *f*; **the** ~ **is in/out** la
marea está alta/baja; **high/low** ~ marea alta/baja
2 (movement) corriente *f*; (of violence) oleada *f*
■ **tide over** *[v + o + adv]*: **this should** ~ **us over
until next month** nos arreglaremos con esto hasta
el próximo mes

tidily /'taɪdli ‖ 'taɪdɪli/ *adv* ordenadamente,
prolijamente (RPl)

tidiness /'taɪdɪnəs ‖'taɪdɪnɪs/ n orden m,
prolijidad f (RPl)

tidy¹ /'taɪdi/ adj **tidier, tidiest** ordenado,
prolijo (RPl)

tidy² **tidies, tidying, tidied** vt arreglar,
ordenar

■ **tidy up** ⬜1 [v + o + adv, v + adv + o] ⟨room/
desk⟩ ordenar, arreglar; ⟨toys⟩ ordenar, recoger*
⬜2 [v + adv] ordenar

tie¹ /taɪ/ n ⬜1 (Clothing) corbata f ⬜2 (a) (bond)
lazo m, vínculo m (b) (obligation, constraint) atadura
f; **family** ~**s** obligaciones fpl familiares ⬜3 (Sport)
(equal score) empate m

tie² **ties, tying, tied** vt ⬜1 (a) (make) ⟨knot/
bow⟩ hacer* (b) (fasten) atar, amarrar (AmL exc
RPl) ⬜2 (restrict) ⟨person⟩ atar ⬜3 (Games, Sport)
⟨game⟩ empatar

■ ~ vi ⬜1 (fasten) atarse ⬜2 (draw) «teams»
empatar

■ **tie in** [v + adv] **to** ~ **in** (WITH sth) concordar*
or cuadrar (CON algo)

■ **tie up** [v + o + adv, v + adv + o] (a) ⟨parcel/
animal⟩ atar, amarrar (AmL exc RPl) (b) **to be ~d
up** (busy) estar* ocupado (c) **to be ~d up WITH
sth** (connected) estar* ligado A or relacionado CON
algo

tie: ~**break** n ▶ ~BREAKER a; ~**breaker** n
(a) (in tennis) muerte f súbita (b) (in quiz game)
pregunta f de desempate; ~**pin** n alfiler m de
corbata

tier /tɪr ‖'tɪə(r)/ n (a) (layer) hilera f superpuesta
(b) (of cake) piso m (c) (in hierarchy) escalón m

tiger /'taɪgər ‖'taɪgə(r)/ n (pl ~**s** or ~) tigre m

tight¹ /taɪt/ adj **-er, -est** ⬜1 (a) (fitting closely)
⟨dress/skirt⟩ ajustado, ceñido; (if uncomfortable)
apretado (b) ⟨knot⟩ apretado (c) (stiff) ⟨screw/lid⟩
apretado, duro (d) ⟨schedule⟩ apretado; ⟨budget⟩
limitado ⬜2 (strict) ⟨security/control⟩ estricto
⬜3 (taut) ⟨cord/thread⟩ tirante, tenso ⬜4 (colloq) (a)
(mean) ▶ TIGHTFISTED (b) (drunk) (pred) borracho,
como una cuba (fam)

tight² adv: hold ~! ¡agárrate bien or fuerte!;
screw the lid on ~ aprieta bien el tapón; **sleep**
~! ¡que duermas bien!

tighten /'taɪtn/ vt (a) ⟨nut/bolt/knot⟩ apretar*;
⟨rope⟩ tensar; **to** ~ **one's belt** apretarse* el
cinturón (b) ⟨regulations⟩ hacer* más estricto or
rígido

■ **tighten up** [v + o + adv, v + adv + o] ⟨laws/
rules⟩ hacer* más estricto; **to** ~ **up security**
reforzar* las medidas de seguridad

tight: ~**fisted** /'taɪt'fɪstəd ‖,taɪt'fɪstɪd/ adj
(colloq) agarrado (fam), amarrete (AmS fam);
~**fitting** /'taɪt'fɪtɪŋ/ adj ⟨jeans⟩ ajustado, ceñido

tightly /'taɪtli/ adv ⟨hold/grip⟩ fuerte; ~
fastened fuertemente atado

tightrope /'taɪtrəʊp/ n cuerda f floja; (before n)
~ **walker** funámbulo, -la m,f, equilibrista mf

tights /taɪts/ pl n (a) (for ballet etc) malla(s) f(pl),
leotardo(s) m(pl) (b) (BrE) ▶ PANTYHOSE

tile¹ /taɪl/ n (a) (for floor) baldosa f, losa f; (for
wall) azulejo m (b) (for roof) teja f

tile² vt ⟨floor⟩ embaldosar; ⟨wall⟩ revestir* de
azulejos, azulejar, alicatar (Esp); ⟨roof⟩ tejar

till¹ /tɪl/ conj/prep ▶ UNTIL¹,²

till² n caja f (registradora)

till³ vt cultivar, labrar

tiller /'tɪlər ‖'tɪlə(r)/ n (Naut) caña f or barra f
del timón

tilt¹ /tɪlt/ vt inclinar

■ ~ vi inclinarse

tilt² n inclinación f

timber /'tɪmbər ‖'tɪmbə(r)/ n (a) (material)
madera f (para construcción) (b) (trees) árboles
mpl (madereros) (c) (beam) viga f, madero m

time¹ /taɪm/ n

I ⬜1 (past, present, future) tiempo m; **at this point o
moment in** ~ en este momento, en el momento
presente; (before n) ⟨travel⟩ en el tiempo; ~
machine máquina f del tiempo

⬜2 (time available, necessary for sth) tiempo m; **to
make** ~ **for sth** hacer(se)* or encontrar* tiempo
para algo; **just take your** ~ tómate todo el tiempo
que necesites or quieras

⬜3 (no pl) (period — of days, months, years) tiempo
m; (— of hours) rato m; **that was a long** ~ **ago** eso
fue hace mucho (tiempo); **in an hour's/ten years'**
~ dentro de una hora/diez años; **for the** ~ **being**
por el momento, de momento

⬜4 (in phrases) **all the time** (constantly)
constantemente; (the whole period) todo el tiempo;
in time (early enough) a tiempo; (eventually) con el
tiempo; **in good time** con tiempo; **in no time** (at
all) rapidísimo, en un abrir y cerrar de ojos

⬜5 (with respect to work): **to take** o (BrE also) **have** ~
off tomarse tiempo libre

⬜6 (epoch, age) (often pl) época f, tiempo m; **in
former** ~**s** antiguamente; **in** ~**s to come** en el
futuro, en tiempos venideros; **to be behind the**
~**s** ser* anticuado, estar* desfasado

II ⬜1 ⬜1 (a) (by clock) hora f; **what** ~ **is it?** o **what's
the** ~**?** ¿qué hora es? (b) (of event) hora f; **we
have to arrange a** ~ **for the next meeting** tenemos
que fijar una fecha y hora para la próxima
reunión; **it's** ~ **you left** o **you were leaving** es
hora de que te vayas

⬜2 (point in time): **at this** ~ **of (the) year** en esta
época del año; **at this** ~ **of night** a estas horas de
la noche; **at all** ~**s** siempre; **it'll be dark by the** ~
we get there (para) cuando lleguemos ya estará
oscuro

⬜3 (instance, occasion) vez f; **let's try one more** ~
probemos otra vez or una vez más; **nine** ~**s out
of ten** en el noventa por ciento de los casos

⬜4 (in phrases) **about time: it's about** ~ **someone
told him** ya es hora or ya va siendo hora de que
alguien se lo diga; **about** ~ **(too)!** ¡ya era hora!; **at
a time:** **four at a** ~ de cuatro en cuatro, de a
cuatro (AmL); **I can only do one thing at a** ~ solo
puedo hacer una cosa a la or por vez; **at the same
time** (simultaneously) al mismo tiempo; (however) (as
linker) al mismo tiempo, de todas formas; **at
times** a veces; **every** o **each time** (as conj)
(whenever) cada vez; **from time to time** de vez en
cuando; **on time** (on schedule): **the buses never run
on** ~ los autobuses casi nunca pasan a su hora
or puntualmente; **she's never on** ~ nunca llega
temprano, siempre llega tarde

⬜5 (experience): **to have a good/bad/hard** ~
pasarlo bien/mal/muy mal; **have a good** ~! ¡que
te diviertas (or que se diviertan etc)!, ¡que lo
pases (or pasen etc) bien!

⬜6 (Mus) compás m; (before n) ~ **signature** llave f
de tiempo

⬜7 **times** pl (Math): **it's four** ~**s bigger** es cuatro
veces más grande

t

time² vt (Sport) cronometrar; **I've ∼d how long it takes me** he calculado cuánto tiempo me lleva

time: ∼ bomb n bomba f de tiempo or de relojería; **∼-consuming** /kən'suːmɪŋ/ ‖kən'sjuːmɪŋ/ adj que lleva mucho tiempo; **∼keeper** n (a) (Sport) cronometrador, -dora m,f (b) (worker) (BrE): **to be a good/bad ∼keeper** ser* puntual/impuntual

timeless /'taɪmləs ‖'taɪmlɪs/ adj (liter) eterno

time limit n plazo m

timely /'taɪmli/ adj **-lier, -liest** oportuno

timer /'taɪmər ‖'taɪmə(r)/ n temporizador m; (of oven, video etc) reloj m (automático)

times /taɪmz/ prep: **3 ∼ 4 is 12** 3 (multiplicado) por 4 son 12; ▶ FOUR¹

time: ∼saving adj que ahorra tiempo; **∼scale** n escala f de tiempo; **∼share** n (property) multipropiedad f; **∼sheet** n hoja f de asistencia; **∼table** n (a) (Transp) horario m (b) (esp BrE Educ) horario m (c) (schedule, programme) agenda f

timid /'tɪməd ‖'tɪmɪd/ adj tímido; ‹animal› huraño

timidly /'tɪmədli ‖'tɪmɪdli/ adv tímidamente, con timidez

timing /'taɪmɪŋ/ n (choice of time): **the ∼ of the action was disastrous** la acción fue de lo más inoportuna; **that was good ∼: we've just arrived** calculaste muy bien el tiempo: acabamos de llegar

tin /tɪn/ n ①(a) (metal) estaño m (b) (tinplate) (hoja)lata f, (before n) ‹soldier› de plomo ② (can) (esp BrE) lata f or (Esp tb) bote m (de conservas, bebidas etc)

tinfoil /'tɪnfɔɪl/ n (made of tin) papel m de estaño; (made of aluminium) papel m de aluminio

tinge¹ /tɪndʒ/ n (a) (of color) tinte m, matiz m (b) (hint, trace) dejo m, matiz m

tinge² vt (usu pass) (color) **to be ∼d WITH sth** estar* matizado DE algo

tingle /'tɪŋɡəl/ vi: **it makes your skin ∼** te hace sentir un cosquilleo or hormigueo en la piel

tingling /'tɪŋɡlɪŋ/ n cosquilleo m, hormigueo m

tinker /'tɪŋkər ‖'tɪŋkə(r)/ vi **to ∼ WITH sth** hacerle* pequeños ajustes A algo; (pej) juguetear CON algo

tinkle vi ‹bell/glass› tintinear

tinned /tɪnd/ adj (BrE) enlatado, en or de lata

tin: ∼ opener n (BrE) abrelatas m; **∼plate** n hojalata f

tint¹ /tɪnt/ n (a) (of color) tinte m, matiz m; (color) tono m (b) (for hair) tintura f, tinte m

tint² vt teñir*

tinted /'tɪntəd ‖'tɪntɪd/ adj ‹glass› coloreado; ‹lenses› con un tinte; ‹hair› teñido

tiny /'taɪni/ adj **tinier, tiniest** minúsculo, diminuto

tip¹ /tɪp/ n ①(end, extremity) punta f, (of stick, umbrella) contera f, regatón m; (filter ∼) filtro m; **to be standing on the ∼s of one's toes** estar* de

puntillas or (CS) en puntas de pie; **on the ∼ of one's tongue** en la punta de la lengua ② (helpful hint) consejo m (práctico) ③ (gratuity) propina f ④ (BrE) (rubbish dump) vertedero m (de basuras)

tip² -pp- vt ① (give gratuity to) darle* (una) propina a ② (a) (tilt) inclinar (b) (pour, throw) tirar
■ **tip off** [v + o + adv, v + adv + o] ‹police/criminal› avisar(le a), pasarle el dato a (CS), darle* un chivatazo a (Esp fam)
■ **tip over** ① [v + o + adv, v + adv + o] volcar* ② [v + adv] caerse*

tipped /tɪpt/ adj ‹cigarette› con filtro

tiptoe¹ /'tɪptəʊ/ vi **-toes, -toeing, -toed** caminar or (esp Esp) andar* de puntillas

tiptoe² n: **on ∼** de puntillas

tiptop /'tɪp'tɑːp ‖,tɪp'tɒp/ adj de primera, excelente; **in ∼ condition** en excelente estado

tirade /taɪ'reɪd/ n diatriba f

tire¹ /taɪr ‖'taɪə(r)/ vt cansar
■ ∼ vi (a) (become weary) cansarse (b) (become bored) **to ∼ OF sth/sb/-ING** cansarse DE algo/algn/ + INF
■ **tire out** [v + o + adv, v + adv + o] agotar

tire², (BrE) **tyre** /taɪr ‖'taɪə(r)/ n neumático m, llanta f (AmL)

tired /taɪrd ‖'taɪəd/ adj (a) (weary) cansado; **to get ∼** cansarse (b) (fed up) **to be ∼ OF sth/sb/-ING** estar* cansado DE algo/algn/ + INF

tiredness /'taɪrdnəs ‖'taɪədnɪs/ n cansancio m

tireless /'taɪrləs ‖'taɪəlɪs/ adj ‹person› infatigable, incansable; ‹patience/efforts› inagotable

tiresome /'taɪrsəm ‖'taɪəsəm/ adj ‹person› pesado; ‹task› tedioso

tiring /'taɪrɪŋ ‖'taɪərɪŋ/ adj cansador (AmS), cansado (AmC, Esp, Méx)

tissue /'tɪʃuː ‖'tɪʃuː, 'tɪsjuː/ n ① (Anat, Bot) tejido m ② (a) (paper handkerchief) pañuelo m de papel, Kleenex® m (b) (∼ paper) papel m de seda

tit /tɪt/ n ① (Zool) paro m ② (sl) (breast) teta f (fam)

titbit /'tɪtbɪt/ n (a) (of food) exquisitez f (b) (of gossip) chisme m

tit for tat /tæt/ n: **it was ∼ ∼ ∼** fue ojo por ojo, diente por diente

title /'taɪtl/ n ① (of creative work) título m ② (a) (status) tratamiento m (como Sr, Sra, Dr etc) (b) (noble rank) título m (nobiliario or de nobleza) (c) (Sport) título m ③ (Law) (right of ownership) derecho m

title: ∼ deed n (usu pl) título m de propiedad; **∼holder** n campeón, -peona m,f; **∼ page** n portada f, carátula f

titter /'tɪtər ‖'tɪtə(r)/ vi reírse* disimuladamente

tittle-tattle /'tɪtl,tætl/ n (colloq) chismes mpl

titular /'tɪtʃələr ‖'tɪtjʊlə(r)/ adj nominal

T-junction /'tiː,dʒʌŋkʃən/ n (BrE) cruce m (en forma de T)

TN = Tennessee

to¹ /tuː, *weak form* tə/ *prep* **1** **(a)** (indicating destination) a; **you can wear it ~ the wedding** puedes ponértelo para la boda **(b)** (indicating direction) hacia; **move a little ~ the right** córrete un poco hacia la derecha **(c)** (indicating position) a; **~ the left/right of sth** a la izquierda/derecha de algo **2** **(a)** (as far as) hasta; **she can count ~ 10** sabe contar hasta 10 **(b)** (until) hasta; **I can't stay ~ the end** no puedo quedarme hasta el final; *see also* FROM 5

3 **(a)** (showing indirect object): **give it ~ me** dámelo; **I gave it ~ Rachel** se lo di a Rachel; **what did you say ~ him/them?** ¿qué le/les dijiste?; **I was talking ~ myself** estaba hablando solo **(b)** (in dedications): **~ Paul with love from Jane** para Paul, con cariño de Jane

4 (indicating proportion, relation): **how many ounces are there ~ the pound?** ¿cuántas onzas hay en una libra?; **Barcelona won by two goals ~ one** Barcelona ganó por dos (goles) a uno; **there's a 10 ~ 1 chance of ...** hay una probabilidad de uno en 10 de ...

5 (producing): **~ my horror ...** para mi horror ...

6 (indicating belonging) de; **the key ~ the front door** la llave de la puerta principal

7 (telling time) (BrE): **ten ~ three** las tres menos diez, diez para las tres (AmL exc RPI)

to² /tə/ (*in infinitives*) **1** **(a)** **~ sing/fear/leave** cantar/temer/partir (in order to) para; **I do it ~ save money** lo hago para ahorrar dinero **2** (*after adj or n*): **it's easy ~ do** es fácil de hacer; **you're too young ~ drink wine** eres demasiado joven para beber vino; **she was the first ~ arrive** fue la primera en llegar; **she has a lot ~ do** tiene mucho que hacer

to³ /tuː/ *adv* (shut): **I pulled the door ~** cerré la puerta

toad /təʊd/ *n* sapo *m*

toadstool /ˈtəʊdstuːl/ *n* hongo *m* (*no comestible*)

to and fro /frəʊ/ *adv* de un lado a otro

toast¹ /təʊst/ *n* **1** (bread) tostadas *fpl*, pan *m* tostado; **a piece of ~** una tostada *or* (Chi, Méx) un pan tostado; (*before n*) **~ rack** portatostadas *m* **2** (tribute) brindis *m*; **we drank a ~ to him** brindamos por él

toast² *vt* **1** (Culin) tostar* **2** (drink tribute to) ⟨*person/success*⟩ brindar por

toaster /ˈtəʊstər ‖ ˈtəʊstə(r)/ *n* tostadora *f* (eléctrica), tostador *m*

tobacco /təˈbækəʊ/ *n* (*pl* **-cos** *or* **-coes**) tabaco *m*

tobacconist /təˈbækənəst ‖ təˈbækənɪst/ *n*: *expendedor de tabaco, cigarrillos y artículos para el fumador,* ≈ estanquero, -ra *m,f* (*en Esp*); **~'s** (shop) tabaquería *f*, tienda *f* de artículos para fumador, ≈ estanco *m* (*en Esp*)

-to-be /təˈbiː/ *suff*: **father~/husband~** futuro padre/esposo

toboggan /təˈbɑːgən ‖ təˈbɒgən/ *n* trineo *m*, tobogán *m*

today¹ /təˈdeɪ/ *adv* **(a)** (this day) hoy **(b)** (nowadays) hoy (en) día, actualmente

today² *n* (*no art*) **(a)** (this day) hoy *adv*; (as) **from ~** a partir de hoy *or* del día de hoy **(b)** (present age) hoy *adv*, hoy (en) día

toddler /ˈtɑːdlər ‖ ˈtɒdlə(r)/ *n* niño pequeño, niña pequeña *m,f* (*entre un año y dos años y medio de edad*)

to-do /təˈduː/ *n* (colloq) (*no pl*) lío *m*, jaleo *m*

toe¹ /təʊ/ *n* dedo *m* (*del pie*); **big ~** dedo *m* gordo (del pie); **to be on one's ~s** estar* *or* mantenerse* alerta

toe² *vt*: **to ~ the line** acatar la disciplina

toenail *n* uña *f* (*del pie*)

toffee /ˈtɑːfi ‖ ˈtɒfi/ *n* toffee *m* (*golosina hecha con azúcar y mantequilla*)

toffee-nosed /ˈtɑːfiˈnəʊzd ‖ ˈtɒfiˌnəʊzd/ *adj* (BrE colloq) estirado (fam)

tofu /ˈtəʊfuː/ *n* tofu *m*, queso *m* de soya (AmL) *or* (Esp) soja

toga /ˈtəʊgə/ *n* toga *f*

together /təˈgeðər ‖ təˈgeðə(r)/ *adv* **(a)** : **they went ~** fueron juntos/juntas; **we left them alone ~** los dejamos solos a los dos; **all ~ now!** ¡todos (juntos *or* a la vez)! **(b)** **together with** junto con

toil¹ /tɔɪl/ *n* (liter) trabajo *m* duro

toil² *vi* (liter) trabajar duro

toilet /ˈtɔɪlət ‖ ˈtɔɪlɪt/ *n* **1** (room) baño *m* (esp AmL), servicio *m* (esp Esp), váter *m* (Esp); (bowl) water *m or* (Esp) váter *m*, inodoro *m*; (*before n*) **~ paper** papel *m* higiénico; **~ roll** rollo *m* de papel higiénico **2** (washing and dressing) (*before n*) **~ soap** jabón *m* de tocador; **~ water** agua *f*‡ de colonia

toiletries /ˈtɔɪlətriz ‖ ˈtɔɪlɪtriz/ *pl n* artículos *mpl* de tocador *or* de perfumería

token¹ /ˈtəʊkən/ *n* **1** (expression, indication): **a small ~ of gratitude** un pequeño obsequio como muestra *or* prueba de agradecimiento; **as a ~ of respect** en señal de respeto; **by the same ~** de igual modo **2** **(a)** (coin) ficha *f* **(b)** (voucher) (BrE) vale *m*; (given as present) vale *m*, cheque-regalo *m*

token² *adj* (before n, no comp) ⟨*fine/gesture*⟩ simbólico

told /təʊld/ *past & past p of* TELL

tolerable /ˈtɑːlərəbəl ‖ ˈtɒlərəbəl/ *adj* **(a)** (endurable) tolerable **(b)** (passable) pasable

tolerance /ˈtɑːlərəns ‖ ˈtɒlərəns/ *n* tolerancia *f*

tolerant /ˈtɑːlərənt ‖ ˈtɒlərənt/ *adj* tolerante

tolerate /ˈtɑːləreɪt ‖ ˈtɒləreɪt/ *vt* **(a)** ⟨*attitude/behavior*⟩ tolerar **(b)** ⟨*person/pain/noise*⟩ soportar, aguantar

toleration /ˌtɑːləˈreɪʃən ‖ ˌtɒləˈreɪʃən/ *n* tolerancia *f*

toll¹ /təʊl/ *n* **(a)** (Transp) peaje *m*, cuota *f* (Méx); (*before n*) **~ call** (AmE) llamada *f* interurbana, conferencia *f* (Esp); **~ road** carretera *f* de peaje *or* (Méx) de cuota **(b)** (cost, damage): **the climate took a ~ on his health** el clima le afectó la salud

toll² *vi* tocar*, doblar

toll: **~booth** *n* cabina *f* de peaje; **~bridge** *n* puente *m* de peaje *or* (Méx) de cuota; **~-free** /ˈtəʊlˈfriː/ *adj* (AmE) gratuito

tomato /təˈmeɪtəʊ ‖ təˈmɑːtəʊ/ *n* (*pl* **-toes**) tomate *m or* (Méx) jitomate *m*

tomb /tuːm/ *n* tumba *f*, sepulcro *m*

tomboy /ˈtɑːmbɔɪ ‖ ˈtɒmbɔɪ/ *n* niña *f* poco femenina, machona *f* (RPI), machetona *f* (Méx), varonera *f* (Arg)

tombstone /ˈtuːmstəʊn/ *n* lápida *f*

tomcat /'tɑːmkæt ‖'tɒmkæt/ n gato m (macho)

tome /təʊm/ n (hum) libro m, librote m

tomorrow¹ /təˈmɔːrəʊ, təˈmɑːrəʊ/ adv mañana; ~ **morning** mañana por la mañana, mañana en la mañana (AmL); **the day after** ~ pasado mañana

tomorrow² n (no art) **(a)** (day after today) mañana adv **(b)** (future) mañana m

tom-tom /'tɑːmtɑːm ‖'tɒmtɒm/ n tam-tam m

ton /tʌn/ n **1** (unit of weight) tonelada f (EEUU: 907kg., RU: 1.016kg.); **this suitcase weighs a** ~ (colloq) esta maleta pesa una tonelada (fam) **2** (large amount) (colloq) (usually pl): ~**s of people/ work** montones mpl de gente/trabajo (fam)

tone¹ /təʊn/ n **1** **(a)** (quality of sound, voice) tono m **(b) tones** pl (sound) sonido m; (voice) voz f **(c)** (Telec) señal f (sonora) **2** (shade) tono m, tonalidad f **3** **(a)** (mood, style) tono m **(b)** (standard, level) nivel m **4** (Mus) (interval) tono m

tone² vt ⟨muscles/skin⟩ tonificar*
■ **tone down** [v + o + adv, v + adv + o] ⟨language⟩ moderar; ⟨color⟩ atenuar*

tone-deaf /'təʊn'def/ adj: **to be** ~ no tener* oído (musical)

tongs /tɑːŋz, tɔːŋz ‖tɒŋz/ pl n tenacillas fpl

tongue /tʌŋ/ n **(a)** (Anat) lengua f; **to say sth** ~ **in cheek** decir* algo medio burlándose or medio en broma **(b)** (language) lengua f

tongue: ~**-tied** /taɪd/ adj tímido, cohibido; ~ **twister** n trabalenguas m

tonic /'tɑːnɪk ‖'tɒnɪk/ n **(a)** (pick-me-up) tónico m **(b)** ~ **(water)** (agua f+) tónica f

tonight¹ /təˈnaɪt/ adv esta noche

tonight² n (no art) esta noche f

tonne /tʌn/ n tonelada f (métrica)

tonsil /'tɑːnsəl ‖'tɒnsəl/ n amígdala f

tonsillitis /ˌtɑːnsəˈlaɪtəs ‖ˌtɒnsɪˈlaɪtɪs/ n amigdalitis f

too /tuː/ adv **1** (excessively) demasiado; **there were** ~ **many people/cars** había demasiada gente/demasiados coches; **that's** ~ **difficult for her to understand** es demasiado difícil para que lo entienda **2** (as well) también **3** (very) muy; **I'm not** ~ **sure** no estoy muy seguro

took /tʊk/ past of TAKE¹

tool /tuːl/ n (instrument) instrumento m; (workman's etc) herramienta f; **garden** ~**s** herramientas fpl or utensilios mpl de jardinería

tool: ~**bar** n (Comput) barra f de herramientas; ~**box** n caja f de herramientas; ~**kit** n juego m de herramientas; ~**shed** n cobertizo m (para herramientas)

toot¹ /tuːt/ n bocinazo m

toot² vi ⟨driver⟩ tocar* la bocina or el claxon, pitar
■ ~ vt ⟨car horn⟩ tocar*

tooth /tuːθ/ n (pl **teeth**) **(a)** (of person, animal) diente m; (molar) muela f; **front teeth** dientes mpl de adelante; **back teeth** muelas fpl; **to grit one's teeth** aguantarse; (lit) apretar* los dientes; **to have a sweet** ~ ser* goloso; **to lie through one's teeth** mentir* descaradamente; (before n) ~ **decay** caries f dental **(b)** (of zip, saw, gear) diente m; (of comb) púa f, diente m

tooth: ~**ache** n dolor m de muelas; ~**brush** n cepillo m de dientes; ~**paste** n dentífrico m,

pasta f dentífrica or de dientes; ~**pick** n palillo m (de dientes), escarbadientes m, mondadientes m

top¹ /tɑːp ‖tɒp/ n **1** **(a)** (highest part) parte f superior or de arriba; (of mountain) cima f, cumbre f; (of tree) copa f; (of page) parte f superior; **from** ~ **to bottom** de arriba abajo; **at the** ~ **of one's voice** a voz en cuello or en grito, a grito pelado (fam) **(b)** (BrE) (of road) final m **2** (highest rank, position): **she came** ~ **of the class** sacó la mejor nota de la clase; **at the** ~ **of the league** (Dep) a la cabeza de la liga **3** (table) ~ tablero m **4** (Clothing): **a blue** ~ una blusa (or un suéter or un top etc) azul **5** **on top** (as adv) encima, arriba; **to come out on** ~ salir* ganando **6** **on top of** (as prep) encima de; **and on** ~ **of it all** o on ~ **of all that, ...** y encima or para colmo, ... **7** (of jar, box) tapa f, tapón m (Esp); (of pen) capuchón m; **to blow one's** ~ (colloq) explotar (fam) **8** (spinning ~) trompo m, peonza f

top² adj (before n) **1** **(a)** ⟨layer/shelf⟩ de arriba, superior; ⟨note⟩ más alto; **on the** ~ **floor** en el último piso; **the** ~ **left-hand corner of the page** la esquina superior izquierda de la página **(b)** ⟨speed/temperature⟩ máximo, tope **2** **(a)** (best): **to be** ~ **quality** ser* de primera calidad; **the service is** ~ **class** el servicio es de primera **(b)** (in ranked order): **our** ~ **priority** nuestra prioridad absoluta **(c)** (leading, senior) ⟨scientists/chefs⟩ más destacado; **the** ~ **jobs** los mejores puestos

top³ -pp- vt **1** (exceed, surpass) superar; **to** ~ **it all** para coronarlo, para colmo **2** (cover) ~**ped with cheese** con queso por encima
■ **top up** [v + o + adv, v + adv + o] ⟨glass⟩ llenar; ⟨battery⟩ (Auto) cargar*; ⟨income⟩ suplementar

topaz /'təʊpæz/ n topacio m

top: ~ **hat** n sombrero m de copa; ~**-heavy** /'tɑːp'hevi ‖ˌtɒp'hevi/ adj ⟨structure⟩ inestable (por ser muy pesado en su parte superior)

topic /'tɑːpɪk ‖'tɒpɪk/ n tema m

topical /'tɑːpɪkəl ‖'tɒpɪkəl/ adj de interés actual, de actualidad

topless /'tɑːpləs ‖'tɒplɪs/ adj topless

top-level /'tɑːp'levəl ‖ˌtɒp'levəl/ adj (before n) ⟨talks⟩ de alto nivel

topography /təˈpɑːgrəfi ‖təˈpɒgrəfi/ n topografía f

topping /'tɑːpɪŋ ‖'tɒpɪŋ/ n: **ice-cream with chocolate** ~ helado con (salsa de) chocolate por encima

topple /'tɑːpəl ‖'tɒpəl/ vi caerse*
■ ~ vt **(a)** ⟨government/dictator⟩ derrocar*, derribar **(b)** (overturn) volcar*

top: ~**-ranking** /'tɑːp'ræŋkɪŋ ‖ˌtɒp'ræŋkɪŋ/ adj (before n) de alto nivel; ~**-secret** /'tɑːp'siːkrət ‖ˌtɒp'siːkrɪt/ adj (pred ~ **secret**) secreto, reservado; ~**soil** n capa superior del suelo

topsy-turvy /'tɑːpsi'tɜːrvi ‖ˌtɒpsi'tɜːvi/ adj (colloq) ⟨room⟩ desordenado, patas (para) arriba (fam)

Torah /'tɔːrə/ n **the** ~ la or el Torá

torch /tɔːtʃ ‖tɔːtʃ/ *n* **(a)** (flame) antorcha *f*, tea *f* **(b)** (electric) (BrE) linterna *f*

torchlight /ˈtɔːtʃlaɪt ‖ˈtɔːtʃlaɪt/ *n*: **by ~** a la luz de la(s) antorcha(s); *(before n)* ⟨*procession*⟩ con antorchas

tore /tɔːr ‖tɔː(r)/ *past of* TEAR²

torment¹ /ˈtɔːrment ‖ˈtɔːment/ *n* tormento *m*

torment² /tɔːrˈment ‖tɔːˈment/ *vt* atormentar, torturar; (tease) martirizar*

torn /tɔːrn ‖tɔːn/ *past p of* TEAR²

tornado /tɔːrˈneɪdəʊ ‖tɔːˈneɪdəʊ/ *n* (*pl* **-does** *or* **-dos**) tornado *m*

torpedo¹ /tɔːrˈpiːdəʊ ‖tɔːˈpiːdəʊ/ *n* (*pl* **-does**) (Mil) torpedo *m*

torpedo² *vt* **-does, -doing, -doed** torpedear

torpor /ˈtɔːrpər ‖ˈtɔːpə(r)/ *n* (frml) letargo *m*, sopor *m*

torrent /ˈtɔːrənt ‖ˈtɒrənt/ *n* torrente *m*

torrential /tɔːˈrentʃəl ‖təˈrenʃəl/ *adj* torrencial

torrid /ˈtɔːrəd ‖ˈtɒrɪd/ *adj* ⟨*heat*⟩ tórrido; ⟨*affair*⟩ apasionado

torso /ˈtɔːrsəʊ ‖ˈtɔːsəʊ/ *n* (*pl* **-sos**) torso *m*

tortoise /ˈtɔːrtəs ‖ˈtɔːtəs/ *n* tortuga *f*

tortoiseshell¹ /ˈtɔːrtəʃel, -təsʃel ‖ˈtɔːtəsʃel, ˈtɔːtəʃel/ *n* (material) carey *m*, concha *f*

tortoiseshell² *adj* (color) de color carey; ⟨*cat*⟩ pardo

tortuous /ˈtɔːrtʃuəs ‖ˈtɔːtjʊəs/ *adj* tortuoso, sinuoso

torture¹ /ˈtɔːrtʃər ‖ˈtɔːtʃə(r)/ *n* tortura *f*

torture² *vt* ⟨*person/animal*⟩ torturar; **she was ~d by doubts** las dudas la atormentaban

Tory /ˈtɔːri/ *n* (*pl* **Tories**) (in UK) tory *mf*

toss¹ /tɔːs ‖tɒs/ *n* **(a)** (throw) lanzamiento *m*; **with a ~ of his head** con un movimiento brusco de la cabeza **(b)** (of coin): **to win/lose the ~** ganar/perder* jugándoselo a cara o cruz (*or* sello *etc*)

toss² *vt* **(a)** (throw) ⟨*ball*⟩ tirar, lanzar*, aventar* (Col, Méx, Per); ⟨*pancake*⟩ darle* la vuelta a (*lanzándolo al aire*); **let's ~ a coin** echémoslo a cara o cruz *or* (Andes, Ven) a cara o sello *or* (Arg) a cara o ceca *or* (Méx) a águila o sol **(b)** (agitate) ⟨*boat*⟩ sacudir, zarandear **(c)** ⟨*salad*⟩ mezclar
■ ~ *vi* ⟨*boat*⟩ dar* bandazos; **to ~ and turn** dar* vueltas (*en la cama*)

tot /tɑːt ‖tɒt/ *n* **(a)** (young child) pequeño, -ña *m,f*, chiquito, -ta *m,f* (esp AmL) **(b)** (of alcohol) copita *f*
■ **tot up** **-tt-** [*v + o + adv, v + adv + o*] (colloq) sumar

total¹ /ˈtəʊtl̩/ *adj* total; ⟨*failure*⟩ rotundo

total² *n* total *m*

total³ *vt*, (BrE) **-ll-** **(a)** (amount to) ascender* *or* elevarse a un total de **(b)** (add up) totalizar*

totalitarian /təʊˈtælətˈteriən ‖ˌtəʊtælɪˈteəriən/ *adj* totalitario

totally /ˈtəʊtl̩i ‖ˈtəʊtəli/ *adv* totalmente, completamente

tote /təʊt/ *vt* (esp AmE colloq) ⟨*weapons*⟩ llevar

totem pole /ˈtəʊtəm/ *n* tótem *m*

totter /ˈtɑːtər ‖ˈtɒtə(r)/ *vi* tambalearse

touch¹ /tʌtʃ/ *n* **1** **(a)** (sense) tacto *m* **(b)** (physical contact): **at the ~ of a button** con solo tocar un botón **2** (small amount, degree — of humor, irony) dejo *m*, toque *m*; (— of paint) toque *m*; (— of

salt) pizca *f* **3** (detail) detalle *m*; **to add o put the final o finishing ~es to sth** darle* los últimos toques a algo **4** (communication): **to get/keep o stay in ~ with sb** ponerse*/mantenerse* en contacto con algn; **I lost ~ with her** perdí el contacto con ella

touch² *vt* **1** **(a)** (be in physical contact with) tocar*; **my feet don't ~ the bottom** (of pool) no hago pie, no toco fondo **(b)** (brush, graze) rozar*, tocar*
2 **(a)** (affect, concern) afectar **(b)** (move emotionally): **he was ~ed by her kindness** su amabilidad lo enterneció *or* le llegó al alma; **I was very ~ed** me emocioné
■ ~ *vi* **(a)** (with finger, hand) tocar* **(b)** «*hands*» rozarse*; «*wires*» tocarse*
■ **touch down** [*v + adv*] (on land) aterrizar*, tomar tierra; (on moon) alunizar*
■ **touch on** [*v + prep + o*] ⟨*subject*⟩ tocar*, mencionar
■ **touch up** [*v + o + adv, v + adv + o*] ⟨*photograph/painting*⟩ retocar*

touch: **~-and-go** *adj*: **I passed the exam, but it was ~-and-go** aprobé el examen, pero por poco; **how is the patient? — it's ~-and-go at the moment** ¿cómo está el paciente? — en situación crítica; **~down** *n* (on land) aterrizaje *m*; (on moon) alunizaje *m*

touching /ˈtʌtʃɪŋ/ *adj* enternecedor, conmovedor

touch: **~line** *n* línea *f* de banda; **~-type** *vi* mecanografiar* al tacto

touchy /ˈtʌtʃi/ *adj* **-chier, -chiest** ⟨*person*⟩ susceptible; ⟨*subject*⟩ delicado

tough /tʌf/ *adj* **-er, -est** **1** **(a)** (strong, hard-wearing) ⟨*fabric/clothing*⟩ resistente, fuerte **(b)** ⟨*meat*⟩ duro **2** ⟨*person*⟩ **(a)** (resilient) fuerte **(b)** (aggressive, violent) bravucón **3** **(a)** (strict) ⟨*boss/teacher*⟩ severo; ⟨*policy/discipline*⟩ duro **(b)** ⟨*exam/decision*⟩ difícil

toughen /ˈtʌfən/ ~ **(up)** *vt* **(a)** ⟨*muscles*⟩ endurecer*; ⟨*material*⟩ hacer* más fuerte *or* resistente **(b)** ⟨*person*⟩ hacer* más fuerte

toupee /tuːˈpeɪ ‖ˈtuːpeɪ/ *n* peluquín *m*, tupé *m*

tour¹ /tʊr ‖tʊə(r), tɔː(r)/ *n* **(a)** (by bus, car) viaje *m*, gira *f*; (of castle, museum) visita *f*; (of town) visita *f* turística, recorrido *m* turístico; *(before n)* **~ guide** guía *mf* de turismo *or* (Méx) de turistas **(b)** (official visit) (to country, region) gira *f*, viaje *m*; (of factory, hospital) visita *f* **(c)** (Mus, Sport, Theat) gira *f*, tournée *f*; **to be/go on ~** estar*/ir* de gira

tour² *vt* **(a)** ⟨*country/area*⟩ recorrer, viajar por **(b)** (visit officially) visitar **(c)** (Mus, Sport, Theat) ir* de gira *or* hacer* una gira por

tourism /ˈtʊrɪzəm ‖ˈtʊərɪzəm, ˈtɔː-/ *n* turismo *m*

tourist /ˈtʊrəst ‖ˈtʊərɪst, ˈtɔː-/ *n* turista *mf*; *(before n)* **~ guide** (book) guía *f* turística; (person) guía *mf* de turismo *or* (Méx) de turistas; **the ~ industry** el turismo, la industria del turismo; **~ office** oficina *f* de (información y) turismo

tournament /ˈtʊrnəmənt ‖ˈtɔːnəmənt/ *n* torneo *m*

tourniquet /ˈtʊrnɪkət ‖ˈtʊənɪkeɪ/ *n* torniquete *m*

tousled /ˈtaʊzəld/ *adj* despeinado, alborotado

tout /taʊt/ vi: **to ~ for customers** andar* a la caza de clientes

tow¹ /təʊ/ n remolque m; **to give sb a ~** remolcar* a algn

tow² vt remolcar*, llevar a remolque; **they ~ed the car away** se llevaron el coche a remolque

toward /tɔːrd ‖təˈwɔːd/, (esp BrE) **towards** /tɔːrdz ‖təˈwɔːdz/ prep **1** (in the direction of) hacia **2** (as contribution): **she gave us $100 ~ it** nos dio 100 dólares como contribución **3** (regarding) para con, hacia; **your attitude ~ them** tu actitud para con or hacia ellos

towel¹ /ˈtaʊəl/ n toalla f; (before n) **~ bar** o (BrE) **rail** toallero m (de barra)

towel² vt, (BrE) **-ll-** secar* con toalla

toweling, (BrE) **towelling** /ˈtaʊəlɪŋ/ n (tela f de) toalla f, felpa f

tower /ˈtaʊər ‖ˈtaʊə(r)/ n torre f
■ **tower above, tower over** [v + prep + o] ⟨building⟩ descollar* sobre; ⟨person⟩ destacar* sobre

tower block n (BrE) (residential) edificio m or bloque m de apartamentos or (AmL tb) de departamentos or (Esp tb) de pisos, torre f

towering /ˈtaʊərɪŋ/ adj (before n) **(a)** ⟨building⟩ altísimo **(b)** ⟨genius⟩ destacado

town /taʊn/ n (in general) ciudad f; (smaller) pueblo m, población f; **to go to ~ on sth** tirar la casa por la ventana; (before n) **~ center** o (BrE) **centre** centro m de la ciudad

town: ~ clerk n (in US) funcionario encargado de llevar los registros de nacimientos, defunciones etc; **~ council** n (in UK) ayuntamiento m, municipio m, municipalidad f; **~ crier** /ˈkraɪər ‖ˈkraɪə(r)/ n pregonero m; **~ hall** n ayuntamiento m, municipio m; **~ planner** n urbanista mf; **~ planning** n urbanismo m

township /ˈtaʊnʃɪp/ n **(a)** (in US) (Govt) municipio m, municipalidad m, ayuntamiento m **(b)** (in South Africa) distrito m segregado

tow: ~path n camino m de sirga; **~rope** n (Naut) sirga f; (Auto) cuerda f or cable m de remolque; **~ truck** n grúa f

toxic /ˈtɑːksɪk ‖ˈtɒksɪk/ adj tóxico

toxin /ˈtɑːksən ‖ˈtɒksɪn/ n toxina f

toy¹ /tɔɪ/ n juguete m
■ **toy with** [v + prep + o] ⟨pen/food⟩ juguetear con; ⟨idea/possibility⟩ darle* vueltas a

toy² adj **(a)** ⟨car/gun⟩ de juguete **(b)** (miniature) enano

toyshop /ˈtɔɪʃɑːp ‖ˈtɔɪʃɒp/ n juguetería f

trace¹ /treɪs/ n **(a)** (indication) señal f, indicio m, rastro m **(b)** (small amount): **~s of poison** rastros de veneno

trace² vt **1 (a)** ⟨criminal/witness⟩ localizar*, ubicar* (AmL) **(b)** ⟨fault/malfunction⟩ descubrir* **2 (a)** (on tracing paper) calcar* **(b)** ⟨line/outline⟩ trazar*

tracing paper /ˈtreɪsɪŋ/ n papel m de calco or de calcar

track¹ /træk/ n **1** (mark) pista f, huellas fpl; **to**

throw sb off the ~ despistar a algn; **to keep/lose ~ of the conversation** seguir*/perder* el hilo de la conversación; **I lost all ~ of the time** no me di cuenta de la hora
2 (a) (road, path) camino m, sendero m **(b) to be on the right/wrong ~** estar* bien/mal encaminado, ir* por buen/mal camino
3 (race ~) pista f; (before n) **~ events** atletismo m en pista
4 (track events) (AmE) atletismo m en pista
5 (Rail) **(a)** (way) vía f (férrea) **(b)** (rails etc) vías fpl
6 (song, piece of music) tema m, pieza f

track² vt seguirle* la pista a, rastrear
■ **track down** [v + o + adv, v + adv + o] ⟨criminal/lost object⟩ localizar*

trackball /ˈtrækbɔːl/ n (Comput) ratón m de bola

tracker /ˈtrækər ‖ˈtrækə(r)/ n rastreador, -dora m,f; (before n) **~ dog** perro m rastreador

tracking /ˈtrækɪŋ/ n (AmE Educ) división del alumnado en grupos de acuerdo al nivel académico

track: ~ record n historial m, antecedentes mpl; **~suit** n equipo m (de deportes), chándal m (Esp), pants mpl (Méx), buzo m (Chi, Per), sudadera f (Col)

tract /trækt/ n **1** (of land, sea) extensión f **2** (Anat) tracto m **3** (short treatise) tratado m breve

traction /ˈtrækʃən/ n **(a)** (Mech Eng, Med) tracción f **(b)** (grip) agarre m, adherencia f

tractor /ˈtræktər ‖ˈtræktə(r)/ n (Agr) tractor m

trade¹ /treɪd/ n **(a)** (buying, selling) comercio m **(b)** (business, industry) industria f **(c)** (skilled occupation) oficio m **(d)** (people in particular trade): **the ~** el gremio

trade² vi (buy, sell) comerciar
■ vt ⟨blows/insults⟩ intercambiar; **to ~ sth FOR sth** cambiar or canjear algo POR algo
■ **trade in** [v + o + adv, v + adv + o] entregar* como parte del pago

trade: ~mark n **(a)** (symbol, name) marca f (de fábrica) **(b)** (distinctive characteristic) sello m característico; **~ name** n nombre m comercial

trader /ˈtreɪdər ‖ˈtreɪdə(r)/ n comerciante mf

trade: ~ secret n secreto m comercial; **~sman** /ˈtreɪdzmən/ n (pl **-men** /-mən/) **(a)** (shopkeeper) (dated) comerciante m, tendero m **(b)** (deliveryman) proveedor m; **~ union** n sindicato m, gremio m (CS, Per); (before n) ⟨leader⟩ sindical, sindicalista, gremial (AmL)

trading /ˈtreɪdɪŋ/ n **(a)** (in goods) comercio m, actividad f or movimiento m comercial **(b)** (on stock exchange) contratación f, operaciones fpl (bursátiles)

tradition /trəˈdɪʃən/ n tradición f

traditional /trəˈdɪʃnəl ‖trəˈdɪʃənl/ adj tradicional

traffic /ˈtræfɪk/ n **1** (vehicles) tráfico m,

919

traffic calming ⋯⟶ transition ⋯

circulación f, tránsito m (esp AmL) **2** (goods, people transported) tránsito m **3** (trafficking) tráfico m

■ **traffic in**: **-ck-** [v + prep + o] traficar* en

traffic: ∼ **calming** /ˈkɑːmɪŋ/ n (before n): ∼ calming measures medidas fpl para reducir la velocidad del tráfico; ∼ **circle** n (AmE) rotonda f, glorieta f; ∼ **island** n isla f peatonal; ∼ **jam** n embotellamiento m, atasco m

trafficker /ˈtræfɪkər ‖ ˈtræfɪkə(r)/ n traficante mf

traffic: ∼ **light** n (often pl) semáforo m; ∼ **warden** n (in UK) persona que controla el estacionamiento de vehículos en las ciudades

tragedy /ˈtrædʒədi/ n (pl **-dies**) tragedia f

tragic /ˈtrædʒɪk/ adj trágico

tragicomedy /ˌtrædʒɪˈkɑːmədi ‖ ˌtrædʒɪˈkɒmədi/ n tragicomedia f

trail¹ /treɪl/ n (a) (left by animal, person) huellas fpl, rastro m; **to be on the** ∼ **of sb/sth** seguir* la pista de algn/algo, seguirle* la pista a algn/algo (b) (path) sendero m, senda f

trail² vt **1** (drag) arrastrar **2** (follow) seguir* la pista de, seguirle* la pista a, rastrear
■ ∼ vi **1** (drag) arrastrar **2** (lag behind) ir* a la zaga **3** «plant» trepar
■ **trail away, trail off** [v + adv] irse* apagando

trailer /ˈtreɪlər ‖ ˈtreɪlə(r)/ n **1** (a) (for boats, equipment) remolque m (b) (house ∼) (AmE) caravana f, tráiler m (AmL), casa f rodante (CS, Ven), cámper f (Chi, Méx), rulot f (Esp) **2** (Cin, TV) avance(s) m(pl) or (Esp tb) tráiler m or (CS) sinopsis f

train¹ /treɪn/ n **1** (Rail) tren m; (before n) ∼ **driver** (BrE) maquinista mf; ∼ **set** ferrocarril m de juguete **2** (a) (of servants) séquito m (b) (of events) serie f; **to lose one's** ∼ **of thought** perder* el hilo (de las ideas) **3** (of dress, robe) cola f

train² vt **1** (a) (instruct) «athlete» entrenar; «soldier» adiestrar; «animal» (to perform tricks etc) amaestrar, adiestrar; «employee» capacitar; «teacher» formar (b) «voice/ear» educar* (c) «plant» guiar* **2** (aim) **to** ∼ **sth on sth/sb** «gun» apuntarle A algo/algn con algo
■ ∼ vi (a) «nurse/musician» estudiar (b) (Sport) entrenar(se)

trained /treɪnd/ adj (a) «worker» calificado (esp AmL), cualificado (Esp); «teacher» titulado, diplomado; **a highly** ∼ **army** un ejército muy bien adiestrado (b) «dog» entrenado (c) «voice» educado

trainee /treɪˈniː/ n (a) (in a trade) aprendiz, -diza m,f; (before n) ∼ **manager** empleado que está haciendo prácticas de gerencia (b) (AmE Mil) recluta mf

trainer /ˈtreɪnər ‖ ˈtreɪnə(r)/ n **1** (of athletes) entrenador, -dora m,f; (of performing animals) amaestrador, -dora m,f, adiestrador, -dora m,f **2** (training shoe) (BrE colloq) zapatilla f de deporte, tenis m

training /ˈtreɪnɪŋ/ n (a) (instruction) capacitación f (b) (Sport) entrenamiento m

traipse /treɪps/ vi (colloq) (+ adv compl): **I** ∼**d all over town** me pateé (fam) toda la ciudad

trait /treɪt/ n rasgo m

traitor /ˈtreɪtər ‖ ˈtreɪtə(r)/ n traidor, -dora m,f

tram /træm/ n (BrE Transp) tranvía m

tramp¹ /træmp/ vi (+ adv compl) **to** ∼ **(along)** caminar or marchar (pesadamente)

tramp² n vagabundo, -da m,f

trample /ˈtræmpəl/ vt pisotear; **they were** ∼**d to death** murieron aplastados
■ ∼ vi **to** ∼ **ON sth** pisotear algo

trampoline /ˈtræmpəliːn/ n trampolín m, cama f elástica

trance /træns ‖ trɑːns/ n trance m

tranquil /ˈtræŋkwəl ‖ ˈtræŋkwɪl/ adj tranquilo

tranquility, (BrE) **tranquillity** /træŋˈkwɪləti/ n (of place, atmosphere) paz f, tranquilidad f; (of person) calma f, serenidad f

tranquilize, (BrE) **tranquillize** /ˈtræŋkwəlaɪz ‖ ˈtræŋkwɪlaɪz/ vt sedar, dar* un sedante a

tranquilizer, (BrE) **tranquillizer** /ˈtræŋkwəlaɪzər ‖ ˈtræŋkwɪlaɪzə(r)/ n sedante m, tranquilizante m

transaction /trænzˈækʃən/ n transacción f, operación f

transatlantic /ˈtrænzətˈlæntɪk/ adj transatlántico

transcend /trænˈsend/ vt (fml) (a) (go beyond) «boundaries» ir* más allá de, trascender* (b) (overcome) superar

transcribe /trænˈskraɪb/ vt transcribir*

transcript /ˈtrænskrɪpt/ n transcripción f

transcription /trænˈskrɪpʃən/ n transcripción f

transfer¹ /trænsˈfɜːr ‖ trænsˈfɜː(r)/ vt **-rr-** (a) «funds/account» transferir* (b) «property/right» transferir*, traspasar, transmitir (c) «call» pasar (d) «employee/prisoner» trasladar; «player» (esp BrE) traspasar

transfer² /ˈtrænsfɜːr ‖ ˈtrænsfɜː(r)/ n **1** (a) (Fin, Law) transferencia f (b) (of employee) traslado m; (of player) (esp BrE) traspaso m (c) (of passengers) transbordo m **2** (design) calcomanía f

transferable /trænsˈfɜːrəbəl/ adj transferible; **not** ∼ intransferible

transferal /trænsˈfɜːrəl/ n (AmE) ▶ TRANSFER² 1 A, B

transfix /trænsˈfɪks/ vt (usu pass) paralizar*

transform /trænsˈfɔːrm ‖ trænsˈfɔːm/ vt transformar

transformation /ˈtrænsfərˈmeɪʃən ‖ ˌtrænsfəˈmeɪʃən/ n transformación f

transformer /trænsˈfɔːrmər ‖ trænsˈfɔːmə(r)/ n transformador m

transfusion /trænsˈfjuːʒən/ n transfusión f

transgress /trænsˈgres ‖ trænzˈgres/ vt (fml) (a) «law» transgredir (fml) (b) (go beyond) exceder, sobrepasar
■ ∼ vi pecar*

transient /ˈtrænziənt, ˈtrænʃənt ‖ ˈtrænziənt/ adj pasajero, fugaz

transistor /trænˈzɪstər, -ˈsɪstər ‖ trænˈzɪstə(r), -ˈsɪstə(r)/ n (a) (Electron) transistor m (b) (∼ radio) (esp BrE) transistor m, radio f or (AmL exc CS) radio m a transistores

transit /ˈtrænsət, -zət ‖ ˈtrænzɪt, -sɪt/ n tránsito m; **passengers in** ∼ pasajeros mpl en or de tránsito; **it was lost in** ∼ se perdió en el viaje

transition /trænˈzɪʃən/ n transición f

transitional /træn'zɪʃnəl ‖træn'zɪʃənl/ *adj* ⟨stage/period⟩ de transición

transitive /'trænsətɪv/ *adj* transitivo

translate /træns'leɪt/ *vt/i* traducir*

translation /træns'leɪʃən/ *n* traducción *f*

translator /træns'leɪtər ‖træns'leɪtə(r)/ *n* traductor, -tora *m,f*

transmission /trænz'mɪʃən/ *n* transmisión *f*

transmit /trænz'mɪt/ *vt* **-tt-** transmitir

transmitter /'trænzmɪtər ‖trænz'mɪtə(r)/ *n* transmisor *m*

transparency /træns'pærənsi/ *n* (*pl* **-cies**) (Phot) transparencia *f*, diapositiva *f*

transparent /træns'pærənt/ *adj* transparente

transpire /træn'spaɪr ‖træn'spaɪə(r)/ *vi* **1** (a) (become apparent): **it ∼d that ...** resultó que ... (b) (happen) ocurrir, suceder **2** (Biol, Bot) transpirar

transplant[1] /træns'plænt ‖træns'plɑːnt/ *vt* (Hort, Med) trasplantar

transplant[2] /'trænsplænt ‖'trænsplɑːnt/ *n* (Med) trasplante *m*

transport[1] /'trænspɔrt ‖'trænspɔːt/ *n* transporte *m*

transport[2] /træns'pɔrt ‖træns'pɔːt/ *vt* transportar

transportation /'trænspər'teɪʃən ‖,trænspɔː'teɪʃən/ *n* transporte *m*

transpose /træns'pəʊz/ *vt* trasponer*, transponer*

transvestite /trænz'vestaɪt/ *n* travestido *m*, travesti *m*, travestí *n*

trap[1] /træp/ *n* trampa *f*

trap[2] *vt* **-pp-** (a) ⟨animal⟩ cazar* (con trampa) (b) (cut off, catch) ⟨often pass⟩ atrapar; **he was ∼ped in the car** quedó atrapado en el coche

trapdoor, trap door /træp'dɔːr ‖'træpdɔː(r)/ trampilla *f*

trapeze /træ'piːz, trə- ‖trə'piːz/ *n* trapecio *m*

trapper /'træpər ‖'træpə(r)/ *n* trampero, -ra *m,f*

trappings /'træpɪŋz/ *pl n* (a) (paraphernalia): **all the ∼ of success** los símbolos del éxito (b) (of horse) arreos *mpl*, jaeces *mpl*

trash[1] /træʃ/ *n* (a) (refuse) (AmE) basura *f*; (before n) **∼ bag** bolsa *f* de la basura; **∼ can** cubo *m or* (CS, Per) tacho *m or* (Méx) bote *m or* (Col) caneca *f or* (Ven) tobo *m* de la basura (b) (worthless stuff) basura *f* (c) (worthless people) (AmE colloq) escoria *f*

trash[2] *vt* (AmE) (a) (dispose of) botar (a la basura) (AmL exc RPl), tirar (a la basura) (Esp, RPl) (b) (criticize) (colloq) ⟨movie/book⟩ poner* por los suelos *or* por el suelo; ⟨person⟩ despellejar (fam)

trashman /'træʃmæn/ *n* (*pl* **-men** /-men/) (AmE) basurero *m*

trashy /'træʃi/ *adj* **-shier, -shiest** ⟨souvenir⟩ barato, de porquería (fam); ⟨movie/magazine⟩ malo

trauma /'trɔːmə/ *n* (*pl* **-mas**) trauma *m*

traumatic /trɔː'mætɪk/ *adj* traumático, traumatizante

travel[1] /'trævəl/, (BrE) **-ll-** *vi* **1** (make journey) viajar **2** (move, go) «vehicle» desplazarse*, ir*; «light/waves» propagarse*

■ ∼ *vt* ⟨country/world⟩ viajar por, recorrer; ⟨road/distance⟩ recorrer

travel[2] *n* (before n) ⟨company/brochure⟩ de viajes

travel: ∼ agency *n* agencia *f* de viajes; **∼ agent** *n* agente *mf* de viajes; **∼ agent's** agencia *f* de viajes

traveler, (BrE) **-ll-** /'trævlər ‖'trævlə(r)/ *n* (a) viajero, -ra *m,f* (b) (itinerant person) (BrE) *persona que ha adoptado el estilo de vida errante de los gitanos*

traveler's check, (BrE) **traveller's cheque** *n* cheque *m* de viaje *or* de viajero

traveling[1], (BrE) **-ll-** /'trævlɪŋ/ *n* (before n) **∼ expenses** gastos *mpl* de viaje

traveling[2], (BrE) **-ll-** *adj* (a) ⟨clothes/companion⟩ de viaje (b) (itinerant) ambulante; **∼ salesman** viajante *m*

travel: ∼sick /'trævəlsɪk/ *adj* (BrE) mareado; **to get ∼** marearse; **∼ sickness** *n* (BrE) mareo *m*; (before n) ⟨pills⟩ para el mareo

trawl /trɔːl/ *vi* hacer* pesca de arrastre

trawler /'trɔːlər ‖'trɔːlə(r)/ *n* barca *f* pesquera (*utilizada para hacer pesca de arrastre*), bou *m*

tray /treɪ/ *n* bandeja *f*

treacherous /'tretʃərəs/ *adj* ⟨person⟩ traicionero, traidor; ⟨sea/current⟩ traicionero

treachery /'tretʃəri/ *n* (*pl* **-ries**) traición *f*

treacle /'triːkəl/ *n* (esp BrE) melaza *f*

tread[1] /tred/ (*past* **trod**; *past p* **trodden** *or* **trod**) *vi* pisar; **to ∼ in sth** pisar algo; **to ∼ carefully** *o* warily andarse* con cuidado *or* con pie(s) de plomo

■ ∼ *vt*: **she trod the earth down** apisonó la tierra; **to ∼ grapes** pisar uvas; **to ∼ water** flotar (*en posición vertical*)

■ **tread on** [*v* + *prep* + *o*] (esp BrE) pisar

tread[2] *n* **1** (step, footfall) paso *m*; (steps) pasos *mpl* **2** (on tire) banda *f* de rodamiento

treadle /'tredl/ *n* pedal *m*

treason /'triːzn/ *n* traición *f*

treasure[1] /'treʒər ‖'treʒə(r)/ *n* (a) (hoard of wealth) tesoros *mpl* (b) (sth valuable, prized) tesoro *m*; (before n) **∼ hunt** (Games) búsqueda *f* del tesoro

treasure[2] *vt* (a) (value greatly): **thank you for the book, I shall always ∼ it** gracias por el libro, lo guardaré como algo muy especial (b) **treasured** *adj* ⟨possession⟩ preciado

treasurer /'treʒərər ‖'treʒərə(r)/ *n* tesorero, -ra *m,f*

treasury /'treʒəri/ *n* (*pl* **-ries**) (a) (public funds) erario *m*, tesoro *m* (b) **the Treasury** *o* **the treasury** el fisco, la hacienda pública, el tesoro (público); **Department of the T∼** (in US) Departamento *m* del Tesoro (*de los Estados Unidos*), ≈ministerio *m* de Hacienda

treat[1] /triːt/ *vt* (a) (+ adv compl) ⟨person/animal⟩ tratar; **you seem to ∼ this whole thing as a joke** pareces tomarte a broma todo esto (b) (process) tratar (c) (deal with) (frml) ⟨subject⟩ tratar (d) (Med) ⟨patient/disease⟩ tratar (e) (entertain): **I'm ∼ing you** te invito yo; **I ∼ed myself to a new dress** me di el gusto de comprarme un vestido nuevo

treat² n gusto m; **I bought myself an ice cream as** o **for a ~** me compré un helado para darme (un) gusto

treatise /'tri:təs ‖'tri:tɪs, -ɪz/ n tratado m

treatment /'tri:tmənt/ n **(a)** (of person, animal, object) trato m; (of subject) tratamiento m **(b)** (of waste) tratamiento m **(c)** (Med) tratamiento m

treaty /'tri:ti/ n (pl **-ties**) tratado m

treble¹ /'trebəl/ n **(a)** (singer) tiple mf; (voice) voz f de tiple **(b)** (Audio) agudos mpl

treble² vt triplicar*
∎ **~** vi triplicarse*

treble³ adj **1** (threefold) triple **2** (before n) (Mus) de tiple or soprano

treble clef n clave f de sol

tree /tri:/ n árbol m; (before n) **~ trunk** tronco m

tree: ~-lined adj (before n) bordeado de árboles, arbolado; **~top** n copa f de árbol

trek¹ /trek/ n (hike) caminata f; **it's quite a ~ to the shops** hay un buen paseo hasta llegar a las tiendas

trek² vi **-kk-** caminar; **to go ~king** hacer* senderismo

trellis /'treləs ‖'trelɪs/ n enrejado m, espaldera f

tremble /'trembəl/ vi temblar*

tremendous /trɪ'mendəs/ adj **(a)** (great, huge) tremendo **(b)** (very good) formidable

tremendously /trɪ'mendəsli/ adv tremendamente

tremor /'tremər ‖'tremə(r)/ n **(a)** (quiver) temblor m **(b)** (earth ~) temblor m (de tierra), seísmo m, sismo m (AmL)

trench /trentʃ/ n zanja f; (Mil) trinchera f

trench coat n trinchera f

trend /trend/ n **(a)** (pattern, tendency) tendencia f **(b)** (fashion) moda f

trendy /'trendi/ adj **-dier, -diest** moderno

trepidation /trepə'deɪʃən ‖,trepɪ'deɪʃən/ n (frml) (fear) temor m (frml); (anxiety) inquietud f

trespass /'trespəs/ vi (Law) entrar sin autorización en propiedad ajena

trespasser /'trespəsər ‖'trespəsə(r)/ n intruso, -sa m,f; ❺ **trespassers will be prosecuted** ≈prohibido el paso

tress /tres/ n (liter) **(a)** (lock of hair) mechón m **(b) tresses** pl (hair) cabellera f (liter), cabellos mpl

trestle /'tresəl/ n caballete m

trial¹ /'traɪəl/ n **1** (Law) **(a)** (court hearing) proceso m, juicio m **(b)** (judgment) juicio m; **a fair ~** un juicio imparcial; **to be on ~ for murder** estar* siendo procesado por asesinato **2** (test) prueba f; **clinical ~** ensayo m clínico; **on ~** a prueba; **by ~ and error** por ensayo y error **3** (trouble) **~s and tribulations** tribulaciones fpl **4** (Sport) (usu pl) prueba f de selección

trial² adj ⟨period/flight⟩ de prueba; **~ offer** oferta f especial (para promover un producto nuevo); **~ run** prueba f

triangle /'traɪæŋgəl/ n (Math, Mus) triángulo m

triangular /traɪ'æŋgjələr ‖traɪ'æŋgjʊlə(r)/ adj triangular

tribal /'traɪbəl/ adj tribal

tribe /traɪb/ n tribu f

tribesman /'traɪbzmən/ n (pl **-men** /-mən/) miembro m de una tribu

tribunal /traɪ'bju:nl/ n (court) tribunal m

tributary /'trɪbjətəri ‖'trɪbjʊtəri/ n (pl **-ries**) afluente m, río m tributario

tribute /'trɪbju:t/ n **1** (acknowledgment) homenaje m, tributo m (AmL); **to pay ~ to sb/sth** rendir* homenaje or (AmL tb) tributo a algn/algo **2** (payment) tributo m

triceps /'traɪseps/ n (pl **~**) tríceps m

trick¹ /trɪk/ n **1** **(a)** (ruse) trampa f, ardid m; (before n) **~ photography** trucaje m; **a ~ question** una pregunta con trampa **(b)** (prank, joke) broma f, jugarreta f **2** (feat, skilful act) truco m; **to do card ~s** hacer* trucos con las cartas **3** (in card games) baza f

trick² vt engañar

trickle¹ /'trɪkəl/ vi (+ adv compl) **(a)** «liquid»: **sweat ~d down his forehead** le corrían gotas de sudor por la frente **(b)** (arrive, go): **letters are still trickling in** todavía se está recibiendo alguna que otra carta

trickle² n hilo m

trickster /'trɪkstər ‖'trɪkstə(r)/ n embaucador, -dora m,f

tricky /'trɪki/ adj **trickier, trickiest** **(a)** (difficult) ⟨task/problem⟩ difícil, peliagudo, que tiene sus bemoles **(b)** (sensitive) ⟨matter/problem⟩ delicado

tricycle /'traɪsɪkəl/ n triciclo m

trifle /'traɪfəl/ n **1** **(a)** (trivial thing) nimiedad f **(b)** (small amount) (no pl) insignificancia f **2** (Culin) postre de bizcocho, jerez, crema y frutas
∎ **trifle with** [v + prep + o] jugar* con

trifling /'traɪflɪŋ/ adj insignificante, sin importancia

trigger¹ /'trɪgər ‖'trɪgə(r)/ n gatillo m

trigger² vt **~ (off)** ⟨reaction/response⟩ provocar*

trill /trɪl/ n **(a)** (in music, of birdsong) trino m **(b)** (Ling) vibración f

trilogy /'trɪlədʒi/ n (pl **-gies**) trilogía f

trim¹ /trɪm/ adj **-mm-** **(a)** (slim) esbelto, estilizado **(b)** (neat) ⟨uniform/suit⟩ elegante

trim² n **1** (good condition): **to be in (good) ~** estar* en buen estado or en buenas condiciones **2** (cut) recorte m

trim³ vt **-mm-** **1** (cut) recortar **2** (decorate): **~med with velvet** con adornos de terciopelo; (round edge) ribeteado de terciopelo

trimester /traɪ'mestər ‖traɪ'mestə(r)/ n (AmE) trimestre m

trimming /'trɪmɪŋ/ n **1** (on clothes) adorno m; (along edges) ribete m **2 trimmings** pl (offcuts) recortes mpl

Trinidad /'trɪnədæd ‖'trɪnɪdæd/ n Trinidad f; **~ and Tobago** Trinidad y Tobago

Trinity /'trɪnəti/ n **the (Holy) ~** la (Santísima) Trinidad

trinket /'trɪŋkət ‖'trɪŋkɪt/ n chuchería f, baratija f

trio /'tri:əʊ/ n trío m

trip¹ /trɪp/ n **1** (journey) viaje m; (excursion) excursión f; (outing) salida f; **she's going on a ~** ⋯⋗

to Japan se va de viaje al Japón; **a ~ to the zoo** una visita al zoológico **2** (stumble, fall) tropezón *m*, traspié *m*

trip² **-pp-** *vi* tropezar*
■ **~** *vt* **~ (up)** hacerle* una zancadilla a
■ **trip over** [*v + adv*] tropezar* y caerse*

tripe /traɪp/ *n* **(a)** (Culin) mondongo *m* (AmS), callos *mpl* (Esp), pancita *f* (Méx) **(b)** (nonsense) (colloq) paparruchas *fpl* (fam)

triple¹ /ˈtrɪpəl/ *adj* triple

triple² *adv*: **~ the amount** el triple

triple³ *vt* triplicar*
■ **~** *vi* triplicarse*

triple jump *n* triple salto *m* (de longitud)

triplet /ˈtrɪplət ‖ ˈtrɪplɪt/ *n* trillizo, -za *m,f*

triplicate /ˈtrɪplɪkət ‖ ˈtrɪplɪkət/ *n*: **in ~** por triplicado

tripod /ˈtraɪpɑːd ‖ ˈtraɪpɒd/ *n* trípode *m*

trite /traɪt/ *adj* **triter, tritest** trillado

triumph¹ /ˈtraɪəmf ‖ ˈtraɪʌmf/ *n* triunfo *m*

triumph² *vi* triunfar

triumphal /traɪˈʌmfəl/ *adj* triunfal

triumphant /traɪˈʌmfənt/ *adj* ⟨troops/team⟩ triunfador; ⟨moment/entry⟩ triunfal; ⟨smile⟩ de triunfo, triunfal

trivia /ˈtrɪviə/ *pl n* trivialidades *fpl*, nimiedades *fpl*

trivial /ˈtrɪviəl/ *adj* ⟨events/concerns⟩ trivial; ⟨sum/details⟩ insignificante, nimio

triviality /trɪviˈæləti/ *n* (*pl* **-ties**) trivialidad *f*

trivialize /ˈtrɪviəlaɪz/ *vt* trivializar*

trod /trɑːd ‖ trɒd/ *past and past p of* TREAD¹

trodden /ˈtrɑːdn̩ ‖ ˈtrɒdn̩/ *past p of* TREAD¹

trolley /ˈtrɑːli ‖ ˈtrɒli/ *n* **1** **(a)** (**~ bus**) trolebús *m* **(b)** (**~ car**) (AmE) tranvía *m* **2** (BrE) (for food, drink) carrito *m*, mesa *f* rodante; (at airport, in supermarket, in hospital) carrito *m*

trombone /trɑːmˈbəʊn ‖ trɒmˈbəʊn/ *n* trombón *m*

troop¹ /truːp/ *n* **1** (unit) compañía *f*; (of cavalry) escuadrón *m* **2 troops** *pl*: **our ~s** nuestras tropas; **500 ~s** 500 soldados

troop² *vi* (+ *adv compl*): **to ~ in/out** entrar/ salir* en tropel *or* en masa

trooper /ˈtruːpər ‖ ˈtruːpə(r)/ *n* **(a)** (cavalryman) soldado *m* de caballería **(b)** (state police officer) (AmE) agente *mf*

trophy /ˈtrəʊfi/ *n* (*pl* **-phies**) trofeo *m*

tropic /ˈtrɑːpɪk ‖ ˈtrɒpɪk/ *n* **(a)** (line) trópico *m*; **the T~ of Cancer/Capricorn** el trópico de Cáncer/ Capricornio **(b) tropics** *pl* (area) **the ~s** el trópico

tropical /ˈtrɑːpɪkəl ‖ ˈtrɒpɪkəl/ *adj* tropical

trot¹ /trɑːt ‖ trɒt/ *n* (*no pl*) trote *m*; **on the ~** (BrE colloq): **four nights on the ~** cuatro noches seguidas

trot² **-tt-** *vi* trotar
■ **trot out** [*v + o + adv, v + adv + o*] ⟨excuses/ clichés⟩ salir* con; ⟨facts⟩ recitar de memoria

trouble¹ /ˈtrʌbəl/ *n* **1** (problems, difficulties) problemas *mpl*; (particular problem) problema *m*; **to get into ~** meterse en problemas *or* en líos; **to have ~ with sb/sth** tener* problemas con algn/ algo; **what's the ~?** ¿qué pasa?
2 (effort) molestia *f*; **I don't want to put you to any ~** no quiero ocasionarle ninguna molestia; **to go to the ~ of doing sth, to take the ~ to do sth** molestarse en hacer algo
3 (strife, unrest) (*often pl*): **the ~s in Northern Ireland** los disturbios de Irlanda del Norte; **to look for ~** buscar* camorra; (*before n*) **~ spot** punto *m* conflictivo

trouble² *vt* **(a)** (worry) preocupar **(b)** (bother) molestar; **I'm sorry to ~ you** perdone *or* disculpe la molestia

troubled /ˈtrʌbəld/ *adj* **(a)** ⟨person⟩ preocupado, atribulado; ⟨look⟩ de preocupación **(b)** (strife-torn) (journ) aquejado de problemas

trouble: ~maker *n* alborotador, -dora *m,f*; **~shooter** /ˈʃuːtər ‖ ˈʃuːtə(r)/ *n* (within company) persona que se envía a resolver problemas, crisis *etc*; (mediator) mediador, -dora *m,f*

troublesome /ˈtrʌbəlsəm/ *adj* problemático

trough /trɔːf ‖ trɒf/ *n* **1** (for water) abrevadero *m*, bebedero *m*; (for feed) comedero *m* **2** (Geog) hoya *f*, depresión *f*

troupe /truːp/ *n* (Theat) compañía *f* teatral; (in circus) troupe *f*

trousers /ˈtraʊzərz ‖ ˈtraʊzəz/ *pl n* pantalón *m*, pantalones *mpl*; **a pair of ~** un pantalón, unos pantalones, un par de pantalones

trouser suit *n* (BrE) traje *m* pantalón, traje *m* de chaqueta y pantalón

trousseau /ˈtruːsəʊ/ *n* (*pl* **-x** *or* **-s** /-z/) ajuar *m*

trout /traʊt/ *n* (*pl* **trout** *or* Zool **trouts**) trucha *f*

trowel /ˈtraʊəl/ *n* (Const) paleta *f*, llana *f*; (for gardening) desplantador *m*, palita *f*

truancy /ˈtruːənsi/ *n* ausentismo *m* *or* (Esp) absentismo *m* escolar

truant /ˈtruːənt/ *n*: **to play ~** faltar a clase, hacer* novillos *or* (Méx) irse* de pinta *or* (RPl) hacerse* la rata *or* la rabona *or* (Per) la vaca *or* (Chi) hacer* la cimarra *or* (Col) capar clase (fam)

truce /truːs/ *n* tregua *f*

truck /trʌk/ *n* **1** **(a)** (vehicle) camión *m*; (*before n*) **~ driver** camionero, -ra *m,f* (BrE Rail) furgón *m*, vagón *m* **2** (vegetables, fruit) (AmE) productos *mpl* de la huerta; (*before n*) **~ farm** huerta *f*

trucker /ˈtrʌkər ‖ ˈtrʌkə(r)/ *n* (AmE) camionero, -ra *m,f*, transportista *mf*

trucking /ˈtrʌkɪŋ/ *n* (AmE) transporte *m* por carretera

truculent /ˈtrʌkjələnt ‖ ˈtrʌkjʊlənt/ *adj* malhumorado y agresivo

trudge /trʌdʒ/ *vi* caminar con dificultad

true¹ /truː/ *adj* **truer, truest** **1** **(a)** (consistent with fact, reality) ⟨story⟩ verídico; **to be ~** ser*

cierto, ser* verdad; **to come** ~ hacerse* realidad;
to hold ~ ser* válido **(b)** (accurate) *(before n)*
‹account› verídico **2** (real, actual, genuine) *(before
n) ‹purpose/courage›* verdadero; *‹friend›*
auténtico, de verdad; ~ **north** el norte geográfico;
it's ~ **love** es amor de verdad **3** (faithful) fiel; ~
TO sth/sb fiel A algo/algn **4** (Tech) *‹pred›*: **to be**
~ *«wall»* estar* a plomo; *«beam»* estar* a nivel

true² *n*: to be out of ~ no estar* a plomo

true: ~**-life** /'tru:'laɪf/ *adj* (journ) *(before n)*
‹story› verídico; ~**-to-life** /'tru:tə'laɪf/ *adj ‹pred*
~ **to life)** *‹novel/film›* realista; *‹situation›*
verosímil

truffle /'trʌfəl/ *n* trufa *f*

truly /'tru:li/ *adv* verdaderamente, realmente;
‹grateful› sinceramente, verdaderamente; **yours**
~ (Corresp) cordiales saludos

trump /trʌmp/ *n* **(a)** ~ **(card)** (Games) triunfo
m; (resource, weapon) baza *f* **(b) trumps** *pl* (suit)
triunfo *m*

trumped-up /'trʌmpt'ʌp/ *adj (before n)* falso,
fabricado

trumpet /'trʌmpət ‖'trʌmpɪt/ *n* trompeta *f*

trumpeter /'trʌmpətər ‖'trʌmpɪtə(r)/ *n*
trompetista *mf*, trompeta *mf*

truncheon /'trʌntʃən/ *n* (esp BrE) porra *f*,
cachiporra *f*

trunk /trʌŋk/ *n* **1 (a)** (of tree) tronco *m* **(b)**
(torso) tronco *m* **2** (of elephant) trompa *f* **3 (a)**
(box) baúl *m* **(b)** (of car) (AmE) maletero *m*
4 trunks *pl* (Clothing) (for swimming) traje *m* de
baño *or* (Esp tb) bañador *m* (*de hombre)*

truss /trʌs/ *vt* atar
■ **truss up** [*v + o + adv, v + adv + o*] atar

trust¹ /trʌst/ *n* **1 (a)** (confidence, faith) confianza
f **(b)** (responsibility): **a position of** ~ un puesto de
confianza *or* responsabilidad **2** (Fin) **(a)** (money,
property) fondo *m* de inversiones **(b)** (institution)
fundación *f* **(c)** (custody) (Law) fideicomiso *m*

trust² *vt* **1** (have confidence in) *‹person›* confiar*
en, tener* confianza en; (in negative sentences)
fiarse* de; **he can't be** ~**ed** no es de fiar; **to** ~ **sb
WITH sth** confiarle* algo A algn **2** (hope, assume)
(fml) esperar
■ ~ *vi* **to** ~ **IN sb/sth** confiar* *or* tener* confianza
EN algn/algo

trusted /'trʌstəd ‖'trʌstɪd/ *adj (before n)* leal,
de confianza

trustee /trʌs'ti:/ *n* **(a)** (of money, property)
fideicomisario, -ria *m,f*, fiduciario, -ria *m,f* **(b)** (of
institution) miembro *m* del consejo de
administración

trust fund *n* fondo *m* fiduciario *or* de
fideicomiso

trusting /'trʌstɪŋ/ *adj* confiado

trustworthy /'trʌst,wɜːrði ‖'trʌst,wɜːði/ *adj*
‹colleague/child› digno de confianza; *‹account/
witness›* fidedigno

truth /tru:θ/ *n (pl* ~**s** /tru:ðz/) **(a)** verdad *f*; (of
account, story) veracidad *f* **(b)** (fact) verdad *f*

truthful /'tru:θfəl/ *adj ‹person›* que dice la
verdad, veraz; *‹answer›* veraz

try¹ /traɪ/ *n (pl* **tries)** **1** (attempt) intento *m*,
tentativa *f* **2** (in rugby) ensayo *m*

try² **tries, trying, tried** *vt* **1 (a)** (attempt)
intentar; **to** ~ **to + INF** tratar DE + INF, intentar +

INF; ~ **not to forget** procura no olvidarte **(b)**
(attempt to operate): **he tried all the windows** probó a
abrir todas las ventanas
2 (a) *‹product/technique/food›* probar*; ~ **some**
pruébalo, prueba un poquito **(b)** (have recourse to):
I'll ~ **his work number** voy a probar a llamarlo al
trabajo
3 (test, strain) *‹courage/patience›* poner* a prueba
4 to ~ **one's luck at sth** probar* suerte con algo
5 (Law) *‹person›* procesar, juzgar*; **to** ~ **sb FOR
sth** juzgar* a algn POR algo
■ ~ *vi* (make attempt) intentar, probar; (make effort)
esforzarse*; **you must** ~ **harder** tienes que
esforzarte más
■ **try on** [*v + o + adv, v + adv + o*] probarse*
■ **try out** [*v + o + adv, v + adv + o*] *‹product/
method›* probar*; *‹employee/player›* probar*,
poner* a prueba; **to** ~ **sth out ON sb** probar* algo
CON algn

trying /'traɪɪŋ/ *adj ‹day/experience›* duro

tsar /zɑːr ‖zɑː(r)/ *n* zar *m*

T-shirt /'tiː.ʃɜːrt ‖'tiː.ʃɜːt/ *n* camiseta *f*

tsp = **teaspoon(s)**

tub /tʌb/ *n* **(a)** (for holding liquids) cuba *f*; (for
washing clothes) tina *f* **(b)** (bath~) bañera *f*, tina *f*
(AmL) **(c)** (for ice cream) envase *m (gen de plástico)*,
tarrina *f* (Esp)

tuba /'tuːbə ‖'tjuːbə/ *n* tuba *f*

tubby /'tʌbi/ *adj* **-bier, -biest** (colloq)
rechoncho (fam)

tube /tuːb ‖tjuːb/ *n* **1** (pipe, container) tubo *m*
2 (television) (esp AmE colloq): **the** ~ la tele (fam)
3 (BrE Transp colloq): **the** ~ el metro, el subte (Arg)

tuber /'tuːbər ‖'tjuːbə(r)/ *n* (Bot) tubérculo *m*

tuberculosis /tʊ'bɜːrkjə'ləʊsəs
‖tjuː,bɜːkjʊ'ləʊsɪs/ *n* tuberculosis *f*

tubing /'tuːbɪŋ ‖'tjuːbɪŋ/ *n* tubería *f*

tubular /'tuːbjələr ‖'tjuːbjʊlə(r)/ *adj* tubular

TUC *n* (in UK) = **Trades Union Congress**

tuck¹ /tʌk/ *n* (fold, pleat) jareta *f*, alforza *f* (CS)

tuck² *vt* meter; **he** ~**ed the blanket under the
mattress** metió bien la manta debajo del colchón
■ **tuck in** [*v + adv*] **(a)** (eat) (colloq) ponerse* a
comer, atacar* (fam) **2** [*v + o + adv, v + adv + o*]
(a) *‹sheet›* meter; ~ **your shirt in** métete la
camisa por dentro (de los pantalones) **(b)** *‹child›*
arropar
■ **tuck up** [*v + o + adv*] **to** ~ **sb up (in bed)**
arropar a algn en la cama)

tuckered out /'tʌkərd ‖'tʌkəd/ *adj* (AmE
colloq) *(pred)* molido (fam), hecho polvo (fam)

Tuesday /'tuːzdeɪ, -di ‖'tjuːzdeɪ, -di/ *n* martes
m; see also MONDAY

tuft /tʌft/ *n* **(a)** (of hair) mechón *m*; (on top of head)
copete *m* **(b)** (of grass) mata *f*

tug¹ /tʌg/ **-gg-** *vt* tirar de, jalar (de) (AmL exc
CS)
■ ~ *vi* **to** ~ **AT sth** tirar DE algo, jalar (DE) algo
(AmL exc CS)

tug² *n* **1** (pull) tirón *m*, jalón *m* (AmL exc CS)
2 (Naut) remolcador *m*

tug of war *n: juego de tira y afloja con una
cuerda*

tuition /tʊ'ɪʃən ‖tjuː'ɪʃən/ *n* **(a)** (instruction) (fml)
~ **(IN sth)** clases *fpl* (DE algo); **private** ~ clases
fpl particulares **(b)** (fees) matrícula *f*

tulip /'tuːləp ‖'tjuːlɪp/ n tulipán m

tumble¹ /'tʌmbəl/ n (fall) caída f

tumble² vi **1** (fall) caerse* **2** (roll, turn) «*acrobat*» dar* volteretas

tumble: ~**down** adj (before n) en ruinas; ~ **dryer** /'tʌmbəl'draɪər ‖'tʌmbəlˌdraɪə(r)/ n secadora f

tumbler /'tʌmblər ‖'tʌmblə(r)/ n (glass) vaso m (de lados rectos)

tummy /'tʌmi/ n (pl **-mies**) (used to or by children) barriga f (fam), pancita f (fam), tripita f (fam)

tumor, (BrE) **tumour** /'tuːmər ‖'tjuːmə(r)/ n tumor m

tumult /'tuːmʌlt ‖'tjuːmʌlt/ n tumulto m

tumultuous /tʊ'mʌltʃʊəs ‖tjʊ'mʌltjʊəs/ adj «*applause*» apoteósico; «*protest*» tumultuoso

tuna /'tuːnə ‖'tjuːnə/ n (pl ~ or ~**s**) atún m

tundra /'tʌndrə/ n tundra f

tune¹ /tuːn ‖tjuːn/ n (a) (melody) melodía f; (piece) canción f, tonada f; **to change one's** ~ cambiar de parecer (b) (correct pitch): **to be in/out of** ~ estar* afinado/desafinado

tune² vt (a) (Mus) afinar (b) (Auto) poner* a punto, afinar (c) (Rad, TV) sintonizar*
■ **tune in** [v + adv] **to** ~ **in** **TO** sth sintonizar* (CON) algo

tuneful /'tuːnfəl ‖'tjuːnfəl/ adj melódico

tuner /'tuːnər ‖'tjuːnə(r)/ n (a) (piano ~) (Mus) afinador, -dora m,f, de pianos (b) (Rad) sintonizador m

tunic /'tuːnɪk ‖'tjuːnɪk/ n (a) (of military uniform) guerrera f (b) (in ancient Rome) túnica f

tuning fork /'tuːnɪŋ ‖'tjuːnɪŋ/ n diapasón m

Tunisia /tuː'niːʒə ‖tjuː'nɪziə/ n Túnez m

Tunisian /tuː'niːʒən ‖tjuː'nɪziən/ adj tunecino

tunnel¹ /'tʌnl̩/ n túnel m; (in mine) galería f, socavón m

tunnel², (BrE) vi **-ll-** abrir* or hacer* un túnel

turban /'tɜːrbən ‖'tɜːbən/ n turbante m

turbid /'tɜːrbəd ‖'tɜːbɪd/ adj turbio

turbine /'tɜːrbən, -baɪn ‖'tɜːbaɪn/ n turbina f

turbo /'tɜːrbəʊ ‖'tɜːbəʊ/ n turbocompresor m, turbo m

turbulence /'tɜːrbjələns ‖'tɜːbjʊləns/ n turbulencia f

turbulent /'tɜːrbjələnt ‖'tɜːbjʊlənt/ adj turbulento

tureen /tjʊ'riːn, tə- ‖tjʊə'riːn/ n sopera f

turf¹ /tɜːrf ‖tɜːf/ n (pl ~**s** or **turves**) (a) (grass) césped m (b) (square of grass) (esp BrE) tepe m

turf² vt «*garden*» encespedar, colocar* tepes en

turgid /'tɜːrdʒəd ‖'tɜːdʒɪd/ adj «*prose*» ampuloso

Turk /tɜːrk ‖tɜːk/ n turco, -ca m,f

turkey /'tɜːrki ‖'tɜːki/ n (pl ~**s**) pavo m, guajolote m (Méx)

Turkey /'tɜːrki ‖'tɜːki/ n Turquía f

Turkish¹ /'tɜːrkɪʃ ‖'tɜːkɪʃ/ adj turco

Turkish² n turco m

Turkish: ~ **bath** n baño m turco; ~ **delight** n delicia f turca (dulce gelatinoso recubierto de azúcar)

Turkmenistan /ˌtɜːrkmenɪ'stɑːn ‖ˌtɜːkmenɪ'stɑːn/ n Turkmenistán m

turmeric /'tɜːrmərɪk ‖'tɜːmərɪk/ n cúrcuma f

turmoil /'tɜːrmɔɪl ‖'tɜːmɔɪl/ n confusión f

turn¹ /tɜːrn ‖tɜːn/ n **1** (a) (rotation) vuelta f; **the meat was done to a** ~ la carne estaba hecha a la perfección, la carne estaba en su punto justo (b) (change of direction) vuelta f, giro m (c) (bend) curva f (d) (change, alteration): **this dramatic** ~ **of events** este dramático giro de los acontecimientos; **to take a** ~ **for the better** empezar* a mejorar; **to take a** ~ **for the worse** empeorar*, ponerse* peor; **the** ~ **of the century** el final del siglo (y el principio del siguiente) **2** (place in sequence): **whose** ~ **is it?** ¿a quién le toca?; **I think it's my** ~ creo que me toca; **to take** ~**s** o **to take it in** ~(**s**). turnarse **3** (service): **to do sb a good** ~ hacerle* un favor a algn **4** (bout of illness): **he had a funny** ~ le dio un ataque (or un mareo etc)

turn² vt **1** (rotate) ‹knob/wheel/key› (hacer*) girar **2** (change position, direction of) ‹head› volver*, voltear (AmL exc RPl); **she** ~**ed her back on them** les volvió or les dio la espalda, les volteó la espalda (AmL exc RPl); **the nurse** ~**ed her onto her side** la enfermera la puso de lado; **3** (reverse) ‹mattress/omelette› darle* la vuelta a, voltear (AmL exc CS), dar* vuelta (CS); ‹page› pasar, volver*, dar* vuelta (CS) **4** (a) (go around) ‹corner› dar* la vuelta a, dar* vuelta (CS) (b) (pass): **she's just** ~**ed 16** acaba de cumplir (los) 16 **5** (change, transform) volver*; **to** ~ sth **TO/INTO** sth transformar or convertir* algo en algo **6** (shape — on lathe) tornear; (— on potter's wheel) hacer*
■ ~ vi **1** (rotate) «handle/wheel» girar, dar* vuelta(s) **2** (a) (to face in different direction) «person» volverse*, darse* la vuelta, voltearse (AmL exc CS), darse* vuelta (CS); «car» dar* la vuelta, dar* vuelta (CS); **he** ~**ed onto his side** se volvió or se puso de lado (b) (change course, direction): **to** ~ **into a side street** meterse en una calle lateral; **to** ~ **left/right** girar or doblar or torcer* a la izquierda/derecha (c) (curve) «road/river» torcer* **3** (a) (focus on): **to** ~ **to another subject** pasar a otro tema; **his mind** ~**ed to thoughts of escape** se puso a pensar en escaparse (b) (have recourse to): **to** ~ **to sb** (for protection, advice) recurrir a algn; **to** ~ **to drink** darse* a la bebida **4** (a) (become): **his face** ~**ed red** se le puso la cara colorada; **her hair had** ~**ed gray** había encanecido (b) (be transformed) **to** ~ **INTO/TO** sth convertirse* **EN** algo (c) (change) «luck/weather/tide» cambiar (d) (go sour) «milk» agriarse* **5** (when reading): ~ **to page 19** vayan a la página 19
■ **turn against** [v + o + prep + o]: **she** ~**ed them against me** los puso en mi contra
■ **turn around,** (BrE also) **turn round 1** [v + adv] darse* la vuelta, volverse*, voltearse (AmL exc CS), darse* vuelta (CS) **2** [v + o + adv] darle* la vuelta a, voltear (AmL exc CS), dar* vuelta (CS)

■ **turn aside** [*v + adv*] darse* la vuelta,
voltearse (AmL exc CS), darse* vuelta (CS)
■ **turn away** 1 [*v + adv*] apartarse
　2 [*v + o + adv, v + adv + o*] **(a)** 〈*head/face*〉
volver*, voltear (AmL exc RPl), dar* vuelta (CS);
he ~ed his eyes away apartó la mirada **(b)** 〈send
away〉 〈*business*〉 no aceptar; **the doorman ~ed
them away** el portero no los dejó entrar
■ **turn back** 1 [*v + adv*] 〈go back〉 volver*,
regresar
　2 [*v + o + adv, v + adv + o*]: **they ~ed back at
the border** en la frontera lo hicieron regresar
■ **turn down** [*v + o + adv, v + adv + o*] **(a)** 〈fold
back〉 doblar **(b)** 〈diminish〉 〈*heating/volume/
temperature*〉 bajar **(c)** 〈reject〉 〈*offer/candidate*〉
rechazar*
■ **turn in** 1 [*v + adv*] 〈go to bed〉 (colloq)
acostarse*
　2 [*v + o + adv, v + adv + o*] 〈hand in, over〉
entregar*
■ **turn off** 1 [*v + o + adv, v + adv + o*] 〈*light/
radio/heating*〉 apagar*; 〈*faucet*〉 cerrar*; 〈*water*〉
cortar
　2 [*v + adv*] **(a)** 〈from road〉 doblar **(b)** 〈switch off〉
apagarse*
■ **turn on** 1 [*v + o + adv, v + adv + o*] **(a)**
〈*light/television/oven*〉 encender*, prender (AmL);
〈*faucet*〉 abrir* **(b)** 〈excite〉 (colloq) gustar; 〈sexually〉
excitar
　2 [*v + prep + o*] 〈attack〉 atacar*
■ **turn out** 1 [*v + o + adv, v + adv + o*] **(a)**
〈switch off〉 〈*light*〉 apagar* **(b)** 〈empty〉 〈*pockets/
cupboard*〉 vaciar*
　2 [*v + adv + o*] 〈produce〉 sacar*
　3 [*v + o + adv, v + adv + o*] 〈force to leave〉 echar
　4 [*v + adv*] **(a)** 〈attend〉: **several thousand ~ed
out to welcome the Pope** varios miles de
personas acudieron *or* fueron/vinieron a recibir
al Papa **(b)** 〈result, prove〉: **everything ~ed out well**
todo salió bien
■ **turn over** 1 [*v + o + adv*] **(a)** 〈flip, reverse〉
darle* la vuelta a, voltear (AmL exc CS), dar*
vuelta (CS); 〈*soil*〉 remover*; 〈*idea*〉 darle* vueltas
a **(b)** 〈Auto〉 〈*engine*〉 hacer* funcionar
　2 [*v + o + adv, v + adv + o*] 〈hand over〉 entregar*
　3 [*v + adv + o*] 〈*page*〉 pasar, volver*, dar*
vuelta (CS)
　4 [*v + adv*] 〈onto other side〉 darse* la vuelta,
darse* vuelta (CS); 〈*car*〉 volcarse*
■ **turn round** (esp BrE) ▶ TURN AROUND
■ **turn up** 1 [*v + o + adv, v + adv + o*] **(a)**
〈*collar*〉 levantarse, subirse **(b)** 〈shorten〉 〈*trousers*〉
acortar; 〈*hem*〉 subir **(c)** 〈increase〉 〈*oven/volume*〉
subir; 〈*radio*〉 subir el volumen de
　2 [*v + adv*] (colloq) **(a)** 〈be found〉 《*sth lost*》
aparecer* **(b)** 〈arrive〉 (BrE) llegar*; **she didn't ~
up** no apareció
turn: **~about, ~around** *n* giro *m*, cambio *m*;
~coat *n* renegado, -da *m,f*
turned-up /'tɜːrnd'ʌp ‖,tɜːnd'ʌp/ *adj* 〈*nose*〉
respingón, respingado (AmL)
turning /'tɜːrnɪŋ ‖'tɜːnɪŋ/ *n* 〈in town〉 bocacalle *f*;
we've missed the ~ nos hemos pasado la calle (*or*
carretera *etc*)
turning point *n* momento *m* decisivo *or*
crucial
turnip /'tɜːrnəp ‖'tɜːnɪp/ *n* nabo *m*
turn: **~out** *n* 〈at election〉 número *m* de votantes;
〈at public spectacle〉 número *m* de asistentes;

~over *n* 1 **(a)** 〈volume of business, sales〉
facturación *f* **(b)** 〈of stock〉 rotación *f* **(c)** 〈of staff〉
movimiento *m*; 2 〈Culin〉 empanada *f* (esp AmL),
empanadilla *f* (esp Esp); **~pike** *n* (AmE) autopista
f de peaje *or* (Méx) de cuota; **~ signal** *n* (AmE)
intermitente *m* direccional *f* (Col, Méx),
señalizador *m* (de viraje) (Chi); **~stile** *n*
torniquete *m*; **~ table** *n* 〈Audio〉 〈platter〉 plato *m*;
〈deck〉 platina *f*, tornamesa *f or m* (AmL); **~up** *n*
(a) 〈hem〉 dobladillo *m* **(b)** 〈on trousers〉 (BrE) vuelta
f or (RPl) botamanga *f or* (Chi) bastilla *f or* (Méx)
valenciana *f*
turpentine /'tɜːrpəntaɪn ‖'tɜːpəntaɪn/ *n*
aguarrás *m*, trementina *f*
turquoise /'tɜːrkwɔɪz ‖'tɜːkwɔɪz/ *adj* (azul)
turquesa *adj inv*
turret /'tɜːrət ‖'tʌrɪt/ *n* torrecilla *f*
turtle /'tɜːrtl ‖'tɜːtl/ *n* **(a)** 〈marine reptile〉 tortuga
f marina *or* de mar **(b)** (AmE) 〈tortoise〉 tortuga *f*
turtleneck /'tɜːrtlnek ‖'tɜːtlnek/ *n* **(a)** **~
(collar)** cuello *m* alto **(b)** **~ (sweater)** suéter
m de cuello vuelto
turves /tɜːrvz ‖tɜːvz/ *pl of* TURF[1]
tusk /tʌsk/ *n* colmillo *m*
tussle /'tʌsəl/ *n* pelea *f*, lucha *f*
tut /tʌt/ *vi* **-tt-** chasquear la lengua
tutor /'tuːtər ‖'tjuːtə(r)/ *n* profesor, -sora *m,f*
particular
tutorial /tuː'tɔːriəl ‖tjuː'tɔːriəl/ *n*: clase
individual o con un pequeño número de
estudiantes
tutu /'tuːtuː/ *n* (*pl* **~s**) tutú *m*
tuxedo /tʌk'siːdəʊ/ *n* (*pl* **-dos** *or* **-does**)
(AmE) esmoquin *m*, smoking *m*
TV *n* (= **television**) televisión *f*, tele *f* (fam), TV
f
twang /twæŋ/ *n* 〈of guitar〉 tañido *m*; 〈of voice,
accent〉: **his voice has a nasal ~** tiene la voz
gangosa
tweak /twiːk/ *vt* pellizcar* (*retorciendo*)
twee /twiː/ *adj* (BrE) cursi
tweed /twiːd/ *n* (Tex) tweed *m*
tweet /twiːt/ *vi* piar*, gorjear
tweezers /'twiːzərz ‖'twiːzəz/ *pl n* pinza(s)
f(pl)
twelfth[1] /twelfθ/ *adj* duodécimo
twelfth[2] *adv* en duodécimo lugar
twelfth[3] *n* (Math) doceavo *m*; 〈part〉 doceava
parte *f*
Twelfth Night *n* Noche *f* de Reyes
twelve /twelv/ *adj/n* doce *adj inv/m*; **~
(o'clock)** **midnight/noon** las doce de la noche/del
mediodía; *see also* FOUR[1]
twentieth[1] /'twentiəθ/ *adj* vigésimo
twentieth[2] *adv* en vigésimo lugar
twentieth[3] *n* (Math) veinteavo *m*; 〈part〉
veinteava *or* vigésima parte *f*
twenty /'twenti/ *adj/n* veinte *adj inv/m*; *see
also* FOUR[1]
twenty-first[1] /'twenti'fɜːrst ‖,twenti'fɜːst/ *adj*
vigesimoprimero
twenty-first[2] *adv* en vigesimoprimer lugar
twice /twaɪs/ *adv* dos veces; **~ a year** dos veces
por año; **to think ~** pensarlo* dos veces; **~ three
is six** dos por tres es (igual a) seis; **I've got ~ as
many as you** yo tengo el doble que tú
twiddle /'twɪdl/ *vt* (hacer*) girar

■ ~ *vi* to ~ WITH sth juguetear CON algo

twig /twɪg/ *n* ramita *f*

twilight /'twaɪlaɪt/ *n* **(a)** (dusk) crepúsculo *m* **(b)** (half-light) penumbra *f* **(c)** (period of decline) (liter) crepúsculo *m* (liter)

twin¹ /twɪn/ *n* mellizo, -za *m,f*, gemelo, -la *m,f* (esp Esp); **identical ~s** gemelos idénticos *or* (téc) univitelinos, gemelos (AmL)

twin² *adj* **(a)** ⟨*brother/sister*⟩ mellizo, gemelo (esp Esp) **(b)** (paired): ~ **beds** camas *fpl* gemelas

twin³ *vt* **-nn-** (BrE) (*usu pass*) to be ~ned WITH sth estar* hermanado CON algo

twine¹ /twaɪn/ *n* cordel *m*, bramante *m* (Esp), cáñamo *m* (Andes), mecate *m* (AmC, Méx, Ven)

twine² *vi* to ~ AROUND sth enroscarse* ALREDEDOR DE algo

twinge /twɪndʒ/ *n* **(a)** (of pain) punzada *f*, puntada *f* (CS); (of remorse) puntada *f*

twinkle¹ /'twɪŋkəl/ *n* **(a)** (of lights, stars) centelleo *m*, titilar *m* **(b)** (in eye) brillo *m*

twinkle² *vi* **(a)** «*light/star*» titilar, centellear **(b)** «*eyes*» brillar

twinkling /'twɪŋklɪŋ/ *n*: **in the ~ of an eye** en un abrir y cerrar de ojos

twirl /twɜrl ‖twɜːl/ *vt* ⟨*cane/baton*⟩ (hacer*) girar
■ ~ *vi* «*baton*» girar; to ~ around girar

twist¹ /twɪst/ *vt* **1** **(a)** (screw, coil) retorcer*; to ~ sth AROUND sth enrollar *or* enroscar* algo ALREDEDOR DE algo **(b)** (turn) ⟨*handle/knob*⟩ girar **2** **(a)** (distort) retorcer* **(b)** (sprain) torcer* **(c)** (alter, pervert) ⟨*words*⟩ tergiversar; ⟨*meaning*⟩ torcer*
■ ~ *vi* **(a)** (wind, coil) «*rope/wire*» enrollarse, enroscarse*; «*road/river*» serpentear **(b)** (turn, rotate) girar

twist² *n* **1** **(a)** (bend — in wire, rope) vuelta *f*, onda *f*; (— in road) recodo *m*, vuelta *f* **(b)** (turning movement) giro *m* **(c)** **a ~ of lemon** una rodajita de limón (*retorcida*) **2** (in story, events) giro *m* inesperado **3** (dance) twist *m*

twisted /'twɪstəd ‖'twɪstɪd/ *adj* retorcido

twister /'twɪstər ‖'twɪstə(r)/ *n* (AmE colloq) tornado *m*

twit /twɪt/ *n* (BrE colloq) imbécil *mf*

twitch¹ /twɪtʃ/ *vi* «*tail/nose*» moverse*

twitch² *n* tic *m*

twitter /'twɪtər ‖'twɪtə(r)/ *vi* **(a)** «*birds*» gorjear **(b)** «*person*» parlotear, cotorrear (fam)

two¹ /tuː/ *n* dos *m*; ~ **by** ~ (liter) de dos en dos, de a dos (AmL); **to put ~ and ~ together** atar cabos; *see also* FOUR¹

two² *adj* dos *adj inv*

two: ~**-bit** *adj* (AmE) (before n) (colloq) de tres al

cuarto (fam); ~**-dimensional** /'tuːdə'mentʃnəl, -daɪ- ‖,tuːdɪ'menʃən/, -daɪ-/ *adj* bidimensional; ~**-edged** /'tuː'edʒd/ *adj* de doble filo; ~**-faced** /'tuː'feɪst/ *adj* (colloq) falso, doble (Andes, Ven fam); ~**-fold** *adj/adv* ▶ -FOLD; ~**-pence** /'tʌpəns/ *n* dos peniques *mpl*; ~**-piece** *adj* ⟨*swimsuit*⟩ de dos piezas; ~**-piece suit** traje *m or* (Col) vestido *m* de dos piezas, ambo *m* (CS); ~**-seater** /'tuː'siːtər ‖,tuː'siːtə(r)/ *n* biplaza

twosome /'tuːsəm/ *n* (pair) pareja *f*

two: ~**-time** *vt* (colloq) (be unfaithful to) ponerle* *or* meterle los cuernos a (fam); (double-cross) engañar; ~**-tone** *adj* de dos tonos; ~**-way** /'tuː'weɪ/ *adj* ⟨*traffic/street*⟩ de doble sentido *or* dirección; ⟨*agreement*⟩ bilateral; ~**-way radio** aparato *m* emisor y receptor

TX = **Texas**

tycoon /taɪ'kuːn/ *n* magnate *mf*

tympani /'tɪmpəni/ *pl n* timbales *mpl*

type¹ /taɪp/ *n* **1** **(a)** (sort, kind) tipo *m*; **it's a ~ of ...** (in descriptions, definitions) es una especie de ... **(b)** (typical example) tipo *m*, ejemplo *m* típico; (stereotype) estereotipo *m* **2** (Print) (characters) tipo *m* (de imprenta)

type² *vt/i* escribir* a máquina, tipear (AmS)

type: ~**cast** *vt* (*past & past p* **-cast**) ⟨*actor*⟩ encasillar (*en cierto tipo de papel*); ~**face** *n* tipo *m* (de imprenta), (tipo *m* de) caracteres *mpl*, (tipo *m* de) letra *f*; ~**script** *n* texto *m* mecanografiado, manuscrito *m* (de una obra, novela etc); ~**set** *vt* (*pres p* **-setting**; *past & past p* **-set**) componer*; ~**setter** /'taɪpsetər ‖'taɪpsetə(r)/ *n* (person) cajista *mf*, componedor, -dora *m,f*; ~**write** (*past* **-wrote**; *past p* **-written**) *vt* (*usu pass*) escribir* a máquina, mecanografiar*; ~**writer** *n* máquina *f* de escribir

typhoid (**fever**) /'taɪfɔɪd/ *n* (fiebre *f*) tifoidea 7*typhoon* /'taɪ'fuːn/ *n* tifón *m*

typical /'tɪpɪkəl/ *adj* típico

typically /'tɪpɪkli/ *adv* típicamente

typify /'tɪpəfaɪ ‖'tɪpɪfaɪ/ *vt* **-fies, -fying, -fied** tipificar*

typing /'taɪpɪŋ/ *n* mecanografía *f*; (before n) ⟨*error*⟩ de máquina; ⟨*lesson*⟩ de mecanografía

typist /'taɪpəst ‖'taɪpɪst/ *n* mecanógrafo, -fa *m,f*, dactilógrafo, -fa *m,f*

typography /taɪ'pɒɡrəfi ‖taɪ'pɒɡrəfi/ *n* tipografía *f*

tyrannical /tə'rænɪkəl ‖tɪ'rænɪkəl/ *adj* tiránico

tyranny /'tɪrəni/ *n* tiranía *f*

tyrant /'taɪrənt/ *n* tirano, -na *m,f*

tyre /taɪr ‖'taɪə(r)/ *n* (BrE) ▶ TIRE²

U u

U, u /juː/ *n* U, u *f*

U (in UK) (Cin) (= **universal**) apta para todo
público (AmL), todos los públicos (Esp)

U, u /juː/ *n* U, u *f*

ubiquitous /juːˈbɪkwətəs ‖juːˈbɪkwɪtəs/ *adj*
omnipresente (frml), ubicuo (liter)

udder /ˈʌdər ‖ˈʌdə(r)/ *n* ubre *f*

UFO *n* (= **unidentified flying object**) ovni
m, OVNI *m*

Uganda /juːˈɡændə/ *n* Uganda *f*

Ugandan /juːˈɡændən/ *adj* ugandés

ugly /ˈʌɡli/ *adj* **uglier, ugliest** feo

UHT *adj* (BrE) (= **ultra high temperature**)
UHT, UAT (AmL), uperizado (Esp)

UK *n* (= **United Kingdom**) RU *m*

Ukraine /juːˈkreɪn/ *n* Ucrania *f*

Ukrainian¹ /juːˈkreɪniən/ *adj* ucraniano,
ucranio

Ukrainian² *n* **(a)** (person) ucraniano, -na *m,f*,
ucranio, -nia *m,f* **(b)** (language) ucraniano *m*,
ucranio *m*

ulcer /ˈʌlsər ‖ˈʌlsə(r)/ *n* (internal) úlcera *f*;
(external) llaga *f*; **a mouth ~** una llaga en la boca

ulterior /ʌlˈtɪriər ‖ʌlˈtɪəriə(r)/ *adj* oculto; **~
motive** segunda intención *f*, motivo *m* oculto

ultimata /ˈʌltəˈmeɪtə ‖ˌʌltɪˈmeɪtə/ *pl of*
ULTIMATUM

ultimate¹ /ˈʌltəmət ‖ˈʌltɪmət/ *adj* **1** (eventual)
⟨aim/destination⟩ final **2** **(a)** (utmost, supreme)
⟨sacrifice⟩ máximo, supremo **(b)** (most sophisticated)
(journ): **the ~ sound system** lo último en sistemas
de sonido, el no va más en sistemas de sonido
(fam)

ultimate² *n*: **the ~ in sth** lo último en algo, el
no va más en algo (fam)

ultimately /ˈʌltəmətli ‖ˈʌltɪmətli/ *adv* **(a)**
(finally) en última instancia **(b)** (in the long run) a la
larga

ultimatum /ˈʌltəˈmeɪtəm ‖ˌʌltɪˈmeɪtəm/ *n* (*pl*
-tums *or* **-ta**) ultimátum *m*

ultra- /ˈʌltrə/ *pref* ultra-, super- (fam)

ultrasonic /ˈʌltrəˈsɑːnɪk ‖ˌʌltrəˈsɒnɪk/ *adj*
ultrasónico

ultrasound /ˈʌltrəsaʊnd/ *n* **(a)** (Phys)
ultrasonido *m* **(b)** (Med) ecografía *f*

ultraviolet /ˈʌltrəˈvaɪələt/ *adj* ultravioleta *adj
inv*

umbilical cord /əmˈbɪlɪkəl ‖ʌmˈbɪlɪkəl/ *n*
cordón *m* umbilical

umbrage /ˈʌmbrɪdʒ/ *n*: **to take ~ (AT sth)**
ofenderse *or* sentirse* agraviado (POR algo)

umbrella /ʌmˈbrelə/ *n* (*pl* **-las**) paraguas *m*

umpire /ˈʌmpaɪr ‖ˈʌmpaɪə(r)/ *n* árbitro, -tra
m,f; (in baseball) umpire *mf*

umpteen /ˈʌmpˈtiːn/ *adj* (colloq) tropecientos
(fam), miles *or* un millón de

umpteenth /ˈʌmpˈtiːnθ/ *adj* (colloq) enésimo;
for the ~ time por enésima vez

un- /ˈʌn/ *pref* in-, des-, no, sin, poco; *see
individual words*

UN *n* (= **United Nations**) ONU *f*

unable /ʌnˈeɪbəl/ *adj* (*pred*) **to be ~ to + INF** no
poder* + INF

unabridged /ˈʌnəˈbrɪdʒd/ *adj* íntegro

unacceptable /ˈʌnəkˈseptəbəl/ *adj* ⟨conduct/
standard⟩ inaceptable, inadmisible; ⟨terms/
conditions⟩ inadmisible

unaccompanied /ˈʌnəˈkʌmpənid/ *adj* **(a)**
⟨luggage⟩ no acompañado; ⟨person⟩ solo **(b)** (Mus)
⟨singing⟩ sin acompañamiento; ⟨instrument⟩ solo

unaccounted for
/ˈʌnəˈkaʊntəd‖ˌʌnəˈkaʊntɪd/ *adj* (*pred*): **the rest
of the money is ~ ~** no se han dado
explicaciones sobre qué sucedió con el resto del
dinero; **the others are still ~ ~** los otros siguen
sin aparecer

unaccustomed /ˈʌnəˈkʌstəmd/ *adj* **(a)**
(unusual) desacostumbrado, poco habitual **(b)**
(unused) **to be ~ TO sth/-ING** no estar*
acostumbrado A algo/+ INF

unadventurous /ˈʌnədˈventʃərəs/ *adj* poco
atrevido *or* audaz

unaffected /ˈʌnəˈfektəd ‖ˌʌnəˈfektɪd/ *adj* **(a)**
(sincere, natural) ⟨person⟩ natural, sencillo **(b)** (not
damaged, hurt) no afectado

unaided /ʌnˈeɪdəd ‖ʌnˈeɪdɪd/ *adj* sin ayuda

unambitious /ˈʌnæmˈbɪʃəs/ *adj* poco
ambicioso

unanimous /juːˈnænəməs ‖juːˈnænɪməs/ *adj*
unánime

unanimously /juːˈnænəməsli ‖juːˈnænɪməsli/
adv ⟨vote/state⟩ unánimemente; ⟨elect⟩ por
unanimidad

unanswered /ʌnˈænsərd ‖ʌnˈɑːnsəd/ *adj*
⟨question/letter⟩ sin contestar

unappetizing /ʌnˈæpətaɪzɪŋ/ *adj* ⟨dish/smell⟩
poco apetitoso; ⟨prospect⟩ poco apetecible

unappreciative /ˈʌnəˈpriːʃətɪv/ *adj* ⟨person⟩
ingrato, desagradecido

unapproachable /ˈʌnəˈprəʊtʃəbəl/ *adj*
⟨person⟩ inabordable, poco accesible *or* asequible

unarmed /ʌnˈɑːrmd ‖ʌnˈɑːmd/ *adj* ⟨person⟩
desarmado; ⟨combat⟩ sin armas

unassisted /ˈʌnəˈsɪstəd ‖ˌʌnəˈsɪstɪd/ *adj* sin
ayuda

unassuming /ˈʌnəˈsuːmɪŋ ‖ˌʌnəˈsjuːmɪŋ/ *adj*
sencillo, sin pretensiones

unattached /ˈʌnəˈtætʃt/ *adj* **(a)** (not affiliated)
independiente **(b)** (not married) sin ataduras

unattended /ˈʌnəˈtendəd ‖ˌʌnəˈtendɪd/ *adj*
(*usu pred*) **(a)** (unwatched, unsupervised): **to leave sb
~** dejar a algn solo; **don't leave your luggage ~**
vigile su equipaje en todo momento **(b)** (not dealt
with) desatendido

unattractive /ˈʌnəˈtræktɪv/ *adj* poco
atractivo

unauthorized /ˈʌnˈɔːθəraɪzd/ adj no autorizado

unavailable /ˈʌnəˈveɪləbəl/ adj: that number is ~ ese número está desconectado (or averiado etc); he is ~ for comment no desea hacer ningún comentario

unavoidable /ˈʌnəˈvɔɪdəbəl/ adj inevitable

unavoidably /ˈʌnəˈvɔɪdəbli/ adv: I was ~ delayed no pude evitar llegar retrasado

unaware /ˈʌnəˈweə(r)/ adj (a) (not conscious) (pred) to be ~ OF sth ignorar algo, no ser* consciente DE algo (b) (naive): politically ~ sin conciencia política

unawares /ˈʌnəˈwerz ‖ ˌʌnəˈweəz/ adv: to catch o take sb ~ agarrar or (esp Esp) coger* a algn desprevenido

unbalanced /ˈʌnˈbælənst/ adj (a) ⟨diet/composition⟩ desequilibrado (b) (mentally) desequilibrado, trastornado

unbearable /ˈʌnˈberəbəl ‖ ʌnˈbeərəbəl/ adj insoportable, inaguantable

unbeatable /ˈʌnˈbiːtəbəl/ adj ⟨team⟩ invencible; ⟨quality/value⟩ insuperable; ⟨price⟩ imbatible

unbeaten /ˈʌnˈbiːtn̩/ adj ⟨champion/army⟩ invicto; ⟨record⟩ insuperado

unbeknown /ˈʌnbɪˈnəʊn/, **unbeknownst** /-ˈnəʊnst/ adv (liter): ~ to me/her sin saberlo yo/ella

unbelievable /ˈʌnbəˈliːvəbəl ‖ ˌʌnbɪˈliːvəbəl/ adj increíble

unbelievably /ˈʌnbəˈliːvəbli ‖ ˌʌnbɪˈliːvəbli/ adv increíblemente

unbelieving /ˈʌnbəˈliːvɪŋ ‖ ˌʌnbɪˈliːvɪŋ/ adj ⟨smile/look⟩ de incredulidad

unbending /ˈʌnˈbendɪŋ/ adj ⟨person/attitude⟩ inflexible; ⟨determination⟩ firme

unbiased /ˈʌnˈbaɪəst/ adj imparcial, objetivo

unblock /ˈʌnˈblɑːk ‖ ʌnˈblɒk/ vt desatascar*, destapar (AmL)

unbolt /ˈʌnˈbəʊlt/ vt ⟨gate/door⟩ descorrer el pestillo or cerrojo de

unborn /ˈʌnˈbɔːrn ‖ ʌnˈbɔːn/ adj ⟨child⟩ que todavía no ha nacido

unbreakable /ˈʌnˈbreɪkəbəl/ adj irrompible

unbridled /ˈʌnˈbraɪdl̩d/ adj desenfrenado

unbroken /ˈʌnˈbrəʊkən/ adj intacto, en perfecto estado; ⟨silence/run⟩ ininterrumpido

unbuckle /ˈʌnˈbʌkəl/ vt desabrochar

unbutton /ˈʌnˈbʌtn̩/ vt desabotonar, desabrochar

uncalled-for /ˈʌnˈkɔːldfɔːr ‖ ʌnˈkɔːldfɔː(r)/ adj ⟨criticism/remark⟩ fuera de lugar

uncanny /ˈʌnˈkæni/ adj raro, extraño

uncaring /ˈʌnˈkerɪŋ ‖ ʌnˈkeərɪŋ/ adj indiferente

unceremonious /ˈʌnˈserəˈməʊniəs ‖ ˌʌnˌserɪˈməʊniəs/ adj brusco, poco ceremonioso

uncertain /ˈʌnˈsɜːrtn̩ ‖ ʌnˈsɜːtn̩/ adj **1** (a) (unsure) (pred) to be ~ ABOUT/OF sth no estar* seguro DE algo (b) (hesitant) vacilante **2** ⟨prospects/future⟩ incierto **3** (vague): in no ~ terms muy claramente, inequívocamente

uncertainty /ˈʌnˈsɜːrtn̩ti ‖ ʌnˈsɜːtn̩ti/ n incertidumbre f

unchanged /ˈʌnˈtʃeɪndʒd/ adj (usu pred): she was quite ~ no había cambiado para nada; the ceremony has remained ~ for centuries la ceremonia se ha celebrado de la misma forma durante siglos

uncharacteristic /ˈʌnˈkærəktəˈrɪstɪk/ adj desacostumbrado, inusitado

uncharitable /ˈʌnˈtʃærətəbəl ‖ ʌnˈtʃærɪtəbəl/ adj ⟨act/remark⟩ poco caritativo

unchecked /ˈʌnˈtʃekt/ adj libre, sin obstáculos

uncivilized /ˈʌnˈsɪvəlaɪzd ‖ ʌnˈsɪvɪlaɪzd/ adj incivilizado

uncle /ˈʌŋkəl/ n tío m

unclean /ˈʌnˈkliːn/ adj impuro

unclear /ˈʌnˈklɪr ‖ ʌnˈklɪə(r)/ adj poco claro, confuso; he was ~ about his reasons for doing it no dio una explicación muy clara de sus motivos

uncoil /ˈʌnˈkɔɪl/ vi desenroscarse*

uncomfortable /ˈʌnˈkʌmfərtəbəl ‖ ʌnˈkʌmftəbəl/ adj incómodo

uncommon /ˈʌnˈkɑːmən ‖ ʌnˈkɒmən/ adj poco común or frecuente

uncommunicative /ˈʌnkəˈmjuːnəkeɪtɪv ‖ ˌʌnkəˈmjuːnɪkətɪv/ adj poco comunicativo

uncomplaining /ˈʌnkəmˈpleɪnɪŋ/ adj resignado

uncomplicated /ˈʌnˈkɑːmpləkeɪtəd ‖ ʌnˈkɒmplɪkeɪtɪd/ adj sin complicaciones; ⟨character/style⟩ poco complicado

uncompromising /ˈʌnˈkɑːmprəmaɪzɪŋ ‖ ʌnˈkɒmprəmaɪzɪŋ/ adj inflexible, intransigente

unconcerned /ˈʌnkənˈsɜːrnd ‖ ˌʌnkənˈsɜːnd/ adj indiferente

unconditional /ˈʌnkənˈdɪʃnəl ‖ ˌʌnkənˈdɪʃənl/ adj incondicional

unconnected /ˈʌnkəˈnektəd ‖ ˌʌnkəˈnektɪd/ adj (unrelated) sin conexión; these incidents are completely ~ estos incidentes no guardan ninguna relación (entre sí)

unconscious¹ /ˈʌnˈkɑːntʃəs ‖ ʌnˈkɒnʃəs/ adj **1** (Med) inconsciente **2** (unaware) (pred) to be ~ OF sth no ser* consciente DE algo **3** (Psych) inconsciente

unconscious² n the ~ el inconsciente

unconsciously /ˈʌnˈkɑːntʃəsli ‖ ʌnˈkɒnʃəsli/ adv inconscientemente

uncontested /ˈʌnkənˈtestəd ‖ ˌʌnkənˈtestɪd/ adj ⟨will⟩ no impugnado; ⟨leader⟩ indiscutible

uncontrollable /ˈʌnkənˈtrəʊləbəl/ adj ⟨trembling⟩ incontrolable; ⟨urge⟩ irresistible, irrefrenable; ⟨laughter⟩ incontenible

uncontrolled /ˈʌnkənˈtrəʊld/ adj incontrolado

unconventional /ˈʌnkənˈventʃnəl ‖ ˌʌnkənˈvenʃənl/ adj poco convencional

unconvinced /ˈʌnkənˈvɪnst/ adj: I'm still ~ aún no estoy muy convencida

unconvincing /ˈʌnkənˈvɪnsɪŋ/ adj poco convincente

uncoordinated /ˈʌnkəʊˈɔːrdneɪtəd ‖ ˌʌnkəʊˈɔːdɪneɪtɪd/ adj ⟨person⟩ falto de coordinación; ⟨movements⟩ no coordinado

uncork /ˈʌnˈkɔːrk ‖ ʌnˈkɔːk/ vt descorchar

uncorroborated /'ʌnkə'rɑ:bəreɪtəd ‖,ʌnkə'rɒbəreɪtɪd/ *adj* no confirmado, no corroborado

uncouth /ʌn'ku:θ/ *adj* zafio, burdo

uncover /'ʌn'kʌvər ‖ʌn'kʌvə(r)/ *vt* **(a)** (remove covering of) destapar **(b)** (expose) ‹*scandal/plot*› revelar, sacar* a la luz

unctuous /'ʌŋktʃuəs ‖'ʌŋktjuəs/ *adj* empalagoso

uncultivated /'ʌn'kʌltəveɪtəd ‖ʌn'kʌltɪveɪtɪd/ *adj* ‹*land/mind*› sin cultivar

uncurl /'ʌn'kɜ:rl ‖ʌn'kɜ:l/ *vt* desenrollar ■ ~ *vi* «*snake*» desenroscarse*

uncut /'ʌn'kʌt/ *adj* [1] **(a)** ‹*grass/hedge*› sin cortar **(b)** ‹*diamond/gem*› sin tallar, en bruto; ‹*stone/marble*› sin labrar [2] (unabridged) íntegro, completo

undamaged /'ʌn'dæmɪdʒd/ *adj* intacto

undaunted /'ʌn'dɔ:ntəd ‖ʌn'dɔ:ntɪd/ *adj* impertérrito

undecided /'ʌndɪ'saɪdəd ‖,ʌndɪ'saɪdɪd/ *adj* **(a)** (wavering) (*usu pred*) indeciso **(b)** ‹*matter*› pendiente, no resuelto

undefeated /'ʌndɪ'fi:təd ‖,ʌndɪ'fi:tɪd/ *adj* invicto

undemanding /'ʌndɪ'mændɪŋ ‖,ʌndɪ'mɑ:ndɪŋ/ *adj* cómodo, que exige poco; ‹*person*› poco exigente

undeniable /'ʌndɪ'naɪəbəl/ *adj* innegable

undeniably /'ʌndɪ'naɪəbli/ *adv* sin lugar a dudas

under¹ /'ʌndər ‖'ʌndə(r)/ *prep* **(a)** (beneath) debajo de, abajo de (AmL) **(b)** (less than) menos de **(c)** ‹*name/heading*› bajo **(d)** ‹*government/authority*› bajo; **he has 20 people ~ him** tiene 20 personas a su mando **(e)** (according to) según

under² *adv* [1] (less) menos; **it will cost $10 or ~** costará 10 dólares como mucho [2] (under water): **they pushed him ~** lo empujaron debajo del agua

under- /'ʌndər/ *pref* **(a)** (below, lower): the **~mentioned** los abajo mencionados **(b)** (less than proper): **they are ~represented on the committee** no tienen la representación que les corresponde en la comisión **(c)** (of lesser rank) sub-; **~manager** subgerente *m*

under: **~age** /'ʌndər'eɪdʒ/ *adj* (*before n*) ‹*person*› menor de edad; **~arm** *adj* (*before n*) (Sport) sin levantar el brazo por encima del hombro; **~carriage** *n* tren *m* de aterrizaje; **~charge** /'ʌndər'tʃɑ:rdʒ ‖,ʌndə'tʃɑ:dʒ/ *vt* cobrarle de menos a; **~coat,** (AmE also) **~coating** *n* [1] **(a)** (paint) pintura *f* base **(b)** (coating) primera mano *f* de pintura; [2] (AmE Auto) tratamiento *m* anticorrosivo del chasis; **~cover** /'ʌndər'kʌvər ‖,ʌndə'kʌvə(r)/ *adj* secreto; **~current** *n* **(a)** (of discontent) trasfondo *m*, corriente *f* subyacente **(b)** (of water) contracorriente *f*; **~cut** /'ʌndər'kʌt ‖,ʌndə'kʌt/ *vt* (*pres p* **-cutting**; *past & past p* **-cut**) ‹*competitor*› vender más barato que; **~developed** /'ʌndərdɪ'veləpt ‖,ʌndədɪ'veləpt/ *adj* poco desarrollado; ‹*nation*› subdesarrollado; **~done** /'ʌndər'dʌn ‖,ʌndə'dʌn/ *adj* ‹*meat*› poco cocido, poco hecho (Esp); **~estimate** /'ʌndər'estəmeɪt ‖,ʌndə'estɪmeɪt/ *vt* **(a)** (guess too low): **they ~estimated the cost** calcularon el costo en menos de lo que correspondía **(b)**

(underrate) subestimar; **~fed** /'ʌndər'fed ‖,ʌndə'fed/ *adj* subalimentado; **~foot** /'ʌndər'fʊt ‖,ʌndə'fʊt/ *adv* debajo de los pies; **~go** /'ʌndər'gəʊ ‖,ʌndə'gəʊ/ *vt* (*3rd pers sing pres* **-goes**; *pres p* **-going**; *past* **-went**; *past p* **-gone**) ‹*change/hardship*› sufrir; **he is ~going treatment** está en tratamiento; **~graduate** /'ʌndər'grædʒuət ‖,ʌndə'grædʒuət/ *n* estudiante universitario, -ria *m,f* (*de licenciatura*); (*before n*) ‹*course/student*› universitario

underground¹ /'ʌndərgraʊnd ‖'ʌndəgraʊnd/ *adj* (*before n*) subterráneo; ‹*organization*› clandestino

underground² /'ʌndər'graʊnd ‖,ʌndə'graʊnd/ *adv* bajo tierra

underground³ /'ʌndərgraʊnd ‖'ʌndəgraʊnd/ *n* [1] *also* **Underground** (BrE Transp) metro *m*, subterráneo *m* (RPl) [2] (secret organization) movimiento *m* clandestino

under: **~growth** *n* maleza *f*, monte *m* bajo; **~hand** /'ʌndər'hænd ‖,ʌndə'hænd/, **~handed** /'ʌndər'hændəd ‖,ʌndə'hændɪd/ *adj* ‹*person*› solapado; ‹*method/dealings*› poco limpio; **~lie** /'ʌndər'laɪ ‖,ʌndə'laɪ/ *vt* (*3rd pers sing pres* **-lies**; *pres p* **-lying**; *past* **-lay**; *past p* **-lain**) subyacer* a; **~line** *vt* subrayar; **~lying** /'ʌndər'laɪŋ ‖,ʌndə'laɪŋ/ *adj* (*before n*) subyacente; **~manned** /'ʌndər'mænd ‖,ʌndə'mænd/ *adj* ‹*factory*› con personal *or* con mano de obra insuficiente; **~mine** /'ʌndər'maɪn ‖,ʌndə'maɪn/ *vt* ‹*health/strength*› minar; ‹*authority*› quitar

underneath¹ /'ʌndər'ni:θ ‖,ʌndə'ni:θ/ *prep* debajo de, abajo de (AmL)

underneath² *adv* debajo, abajo; ‹*dig/crawl*› por debajo, por abajo

under: **~nourished** /'ʌndər'nɜ:rɪʃt ‖,ʌndə'nʌrɪʃt/ *adj* desnutrido; **~paid** /'ʌndər'peɪd ‖,ʌndə'peɪd/ *adj* mal pagado; **~pants** *pl n* calzoncillos *mpl*, calzones *mpl* (Méx); **~pass** *n* (for traffic) paso *m* inferior; **pedestrian ~pass** pasaje *m* subterráneo; **~privileged** /'ʌndər'prɪvəlɪdʒd ‖,ʌndə'prɪvəlɪdʒd/ *adj* desfavorecido; **~rate** /'ʌndər'reɪt ‖,ʌndə'reɪt/ *vt* **(a)** ‹*ability/opponent*› subestimar **(b)** **~rated** *past p* ‹*writer/play*› no debidamente apreciado *or* valorado; **~secretary** /'ʌndər'sekrəteri ‖,ʌndə'sekrətri/ *n* subsecretario, -ria *m,f*; **~sell** *vt* (*past & past p* **-sold**) ‹*competitor*› vender más barato que; **~shirt** *n* (AmE) camiseta *f* (interior); **~shorts** *pl n* (AmE) calzoncillos *mpl* (*en forma de pantalón corto*); **~side** *n* parte *f* inferior *or* de abajo; **~skirt** *n* enagua(s) *f(pl)*, viso *m*, fondo *m* (Méx); **~sold** /'ʌndər'səʊld ‖,ʌndə'səʊld/ *past and past p of* UNDERSELL; **~staffed** /'ʌndər'stæft ‖,ʌndə'stɑ:ft/ *adj*: **to be ~staffed** estar* muy escaso *or* falto de personal

understand /'ʌndər'stænd ‖,ʌndə'stænd/ (*past & past p* **-stood**) *vt* [1] **(a)** (grasp meaning of) entender* **(b)** (sympathize, empathize with) comprender, entender* [2] (believe, infer): **I ~ you play tennis** tengo entendido que juega al tenis ■ ~ *vi* entender*, comprender

understandable /'ʌndər'stændəbəl ‖,ʌndə'stændəbəl/ *adj* comprensible

understanding¹ /'ʌndər'stændɪŋ ‖,ʌndə'stændɪŋ/ *n* [1] **(a)** (grasp) entendimiento ⋯⟫

m **(b)** (interpretation) interpretación *f* **(c)** (sympathy) comprensión *f* **2** (agreement, arrangement) acuerdo *m*; **we had an ~ that ...** habíamos convenido que ... **3** **on the ~ that** bien entendido que

understanding² *adj* comprensivo

understatement /'ʌndərˈsteɪtmənt ‖ 'ʌndəˈsteɪtmənt/ *n*: **to say it wasn't well attended is an ~** decir que no estuvo muy concurrido es quedarse corto

understood¹ /'ʌndərˈstʊd ‖ ,ʌndəˈstʊd/ *past & past p of* UNDERSTAND

understood² *adj* (assumed): **expenses will be paid, that's ~** se sobreentiende que nos (*or* les *etc*) pagarán los gastos

under: **~study** *n* suplente *mf*, sobresaliente *mf*; **~take** /'ʌndərˈteɪk ‖ ,ʌndəˈteɪk/ *vt* (*past* **-took**; *past p* **-taken**) **(a)** ⟨responsibility⟩ asumir; ⟨obligation⟩ contraer*; ⟨task⟩ emprender **(b)** **to ~take to + INF** comprometerse A + INF; **~taker** /'ʌndərˈteɪkər ‖ 'ʌndəˌteɪkə(r)/ *n* ▶ MORTICIAN; **~taking** /'ʌndərˈteɪkɪŋ ‖ ,ʌndəˈteɪkɪŋ/ *n* **(a)** (task) empresa *f*, tarea *f* **(b)** (promise) promesa *f*; **~tone** *n* **(a)** (low voice): **to speak in an ~tone** hablar en voz baja **(b)** (hint) trasfondo *m*; **~took** /'ʌndərˈtʊk ‖ ,ʌndəˈtʊk/ *past of* ~TAKE; **~value** /'ʌndərˈvælju: ‖ ,ʌndəˈvælju:/ *vt* ⟨goods⟩ subvalorar; ⟨person/ skill⟩ subvalorar

underwater¹ /'ʌndərˈwɔːtər ‖ ,ʌndəˈwɔːtə(r)/ *adj* submarino

underwater² *adv* debajo del agua

under: **~wear** *n* ropa *f* interior; **~weight** /'ʌndərˈweɪt ‖ ,ʌndəˈweɪt/ *adj* ⟨person/baby⟩ de peso más bajo que el normal; **~went** /'ʌndərˈwent ‖ ,ʌndəˈwent/ *past of* UNDERGO; **~world** *n* **(a)** (Myth) **the ~world** el infierno, el averno (liter) **(b)** (criminals): **the ~world** el hampa, los bajos fondos; **~write** /'ʌndərˈraɪt ‖ ,ʌndəˈraɪt/ *vt* (*past* **-wrote**; *past p* **-written**) **(a)** (in insurance) asegurar **(b)** (guarantee financially) ⟨project/venture⟩ financiar

undeserving /'ʌndɪrˈzɜːrvɪŋ ‖ ,ʌndɪˈzɜːvɪŋ/ *adj* ⟨person⟩ de poco mérito; ⟨cause⟩ poco meritorio

undesirable /'ʌndɪrˈzaɪrəbəl ‖ ,ʌndɪˈzaɪərəbəl/ *adj* ⟨consequence⟩ no deseado; ⟨person⟩ indeseable

undeveloped /'ʌndɪrˈveləpt/ *adj* ⟨resources/ region⟩ sin explotar

undid /'ʌnˈdɪd/ *past of* UNDO

undignified /'ʌnˈdɪgnəfaɪd ‖ ʌnˈdɪgnɪfaɪd/ *adj* **(a)** (lacking modesty) indecoroso **(b)** (inappropriate to status) poco digno

undisciplined /'ʌnˈdɪsəplənd ‖ ,ʌnˈdɪsɪplɪnd/ *adj* indisciplinado

undiscovered /'ʌndɪsˈkʌvərd ‖ ,ʌndɪsˈkʌvəd/ *adj* (not found) no descubierto; (unknown) desconocido

undisguised /'ʌndɪsˈgaɪzd/ *adj* manifiesto, abierto

undisputed /'ʌndɪrˈspjuːtəd ‖ ,ʌndɪrˈspjuːtɪd/ *adj* ⟨champion/leader⟩ indiscutido; ⟨facts⟩ innegable

undivided /'ʌndɪrˈvaɪdəd ‖ ,ʌndɪˈvaɪdɪd/ *adj*: **you have my ~ attention** tienes toda mi atención

undo /'ʌnˈduː/ *vt* (*3rd pers sing pres* **-does**; *pres p* **-doing**; *past* **-did**; *past p* **-done**) ⟨button/ jacket⟩ desabrochar; ⟨zipper⟩ abrir*; ⟨knot/parcel⟩ desatar, deshacer*; ⟨shoelaces⟩ desatar, desamarrar (AmL exc RPl)

undone /'ʌnˈdʌn/ *adj* ⟨pred⟩ **(a)** (unfastened) desatado, desamarrado (AmL exc RPl) **(b)** (not started) sin empezar; (unfinished) sin terminar

undoubtedly /ʌnˈdaʊtədli ‖ ʌnˈdaʊtɪdli/ *adv* indudablemente, sin duda

undress /ʌnˈdres/ *vt* desvestir*, desnudar; **to get ~ed** desvestirse*, desnudarse

undue /'ʌnˈduː ‖ ʌnˈdjuː/ *adj* ⟨before n⟩ excesivo, demasiado

unduly /'ʌnˈduːli ‖ ʌnˈdjuːli/ *adv* excesivamente, demasiado

unearth /ʌnˈɜːrθ ‖ ʌnˈɜːθ/ *vt* **(a)** ⟨remains⟩ desenterrar* **(b)** ⟨fact/document⟩ descubrir*

unearthly /ʌnˈɜːrθli ‖ ʌnˈɜːθli/ *adj* **-lier, -liest** sobrenatural; **at this ~ hour** a estas horas (intempestivas)

unease /ʌnˈiːz/ *n* (nervousness) inquietud *f*, (tension, discontent) malestar *m*

uneasy /ʌnˈiːzi/ *adj* **-sier, -siest** **(a)** (anxious, troubled) inquieto, preocupado **(b)** (awkward, constrained) ⟨laugh/silence⟩ incómodo, molesto

uneconomical /'ʌnˌekəˈnɑːmɪkḷ, -'iːkə- ‖ ,ʌn,iːkəˈnɒmɪkəl, -,ek-/ *adj* poco económico

uneducated /'ʌnˈedʒəkeɪtəd ‖ ʌnˈedjʊkeɪtɪd/ *adj* sin educación, inculto

unemotional /'ʌnɪˈməʊʃnəl ‖ ,ʌnɪˈməʊʃənl/ *adj* ⟨person⟩ indiferente; ⟨account/report⟩ objetivo

unemployable /'ʌnɪmˈplɔɪəbəl/ *adj* inempleable

unemployed /'ʌnɪmˈplɔɪd/ *adj* ⟨person⟩ desempleado, parado (Esp), en paro (Esp), cesante (Chi)

unemployment /'ʌnɪmˈplɔɪmənt/ *n* (being out of work) desempleo *m*, paro *m* (Esp), cesantía *f* (Chi); ⟨before n⟩ **~ benefit** *o* (AmE also) **compensation** subsidio *m* de desempleo, paro *m* (Esp), subsidio *m* de cesantía (Chi)

unending /ʌnˈendɪŋ/ *adj* interminable, sin fin

unenthusiastic /'ʌnɪnˈθuːziˈæstɪk ‖ ,ʌnɪnˌθjuːziˈæstɪk/ *adj* poco entusiasta

unenviable /ʌnˈenviəbəl/ *adj* nada envidiable

unequal /ʌnˈiːkwəl/ *adj* desigual

UNESCO /juːˈneskəʊ/ *n* (*no art*) (= **United Nations Educational, Scientific and Cultural Organization**) la UNESCO

unethical /ʌnˈeθɪkəl/ *adj* inmoral, poco ético

uneven /ʌnˈiːvən/ *adj* **1** **(a)** (not straight) torcido **(b)** (not level) ⟨surface⟩ desigual, irregular, disparejo (AmL); ⟨ground⟩ desnivelado, desigual, disparejo (AmL) **2** ⟨color/paint⟩ poco uniforme, disparejo (AmL) **3** (unequal) ⟨widths/lengths/ contest⟩ desigual

· ·

AmC	América Central	Arg	Argentina	Cu	Cuba
AmL	América Latina	Bol	Bolivia	Ec	Ecuador
AmS	América del Sur	Chi	Chile	Esp	España
Andes	Región andina	CS	Cono Sur	Méx	México

Per	Perú
RPl	Río de la Plata
Ur	Uruguay
Ven	Venezuela

uneventful /ˌʌnɪˈventfəl/ *adj* ⟨journey⟩ sin incidentes; ⟨day⟩ tranquilo; ⟨life⟩ sin acontecimientos de nota

unexciting /ˌʌnɪkˈsaɪtɪŋ/ *adj* ⟨prospect/job⟩ poco estimulante; ⟨food⟩ insulso, poco apetitoso

unexpected /ˌʌnɪkˈspektəd ‖ˌʌnɪkˈspektɪd/ *adj* ⟨reaction/visitor⟩ inesperado; ⟨result/delay⟩ imprevisto

unexpectedly /ˌʌnɪkˈspektədli ‖ˌʌnɪkˈspektɪdli/ *adv* ⟨arrive⟩ de improviso; ⟨happen⟩ de forma imprevista

unexploded /ˌʌnɪkˈspləʊdəd/ *adj* sin detonar

unexplored /ˌʌnɪkˈsplɔːrd ‖ˌʌnɪksˈplɔːd/ *adj* inexplorado

unfailing /ʌnˈfeɪlɪŋ/ *adj* ⟨optimism⟩ indefectible, a toda prueba; ⟨interest/support⟩ constante

unfair /ʌnˈfer ‖ʌnˈfeə(r)/ *adj* ⟨treatment/ decision⟩ injusto; ⟨competition⟩ desleal; ⟨dismissal⟩ improcedente, injustificado; **it was ~ of him to blame you** fue injusto que te echara la culpa a ti

unfairly /ʌnˈferli ‖ʌnˈfeəli/ *adj* injustamente

unfaithful /ʌnˈfeɪθfəl/ *adj* ⟨spouse/lover⟩ infiel; ⟨follower⟩ desleal

unfamiliar /ˌʌnfəˈmɪljər ‖ˌʌnfəˈmɪliə(r)/ *adj* ⟨face/surroundings⟩ desconocido, nuevo

unfashionable /ʌnˈfæʃnəbəl/ *adj* fuera de moda

unfasten /ʌnˈfæsn ‖ʌnˈfɑːsn/ *vt* ⟨seat belt/ button⟩ desabrochar; ⟨knot⟩ deshacer*, desatar

unfavorable, (BrE) **unfavourable** /ʌnˈfeɪvrəbəl/ *adj* desfavorable

unfinished /ʌnˈfɪnɪʃt/ *adj* sin terminar, inacabado

unfit /ʌnˈfɪt/ *adj* **(a)** (unsuitable) ⟨mother⟩ inepto, incapaz; **he was ~ for the job** no estaba capacitado para el trabajo; **~ for human consumption** no apto para el consumo **(b)** (physically): **I'm ~** no estoy en forma, estoy fuera de forma

unflagging /ʌnˈflægɪŋ/ *adj* ⟨energy/ enthusiasm⟩ inagotable; ⟨interest⟩ sostenido

unflattering /ʌnˈflætərɪŋ/ *adj* ⟨remark/ description⟩ poco halagüeño; ⟨dress⟩ poco favorecedor

unfold /ʌnˈfəʊld/ *vt* ⟨tablecloth/map⟩ desdoblar, extender*; ⟨wings⟩ desplegar*
■ ~ *vi* **(a)** «flower/leaf» abrirse*; «wings» desplegarse* **(b)** «story/events» desarrollarse; «scene» extenderse*

unforeseen /ˌʌnfɔːrˈsiːn ‖ˌʌnfɔːˈsiːn/ *adj* imprevisto

unforgettable /ˌʌnfərˈgetəbəl ‖ˌʌnfəˈgetəbəl/ *adj* inolvidable

unforgivable /ˌʌnfərˈgɪvəbəl ‖ˌʌnfəˈgɪvəbəl/ *adj* imperdonable

unfortunate /ʌnˈfɔːrtʃnət ‖ʌnˈfɔːtʃənət/ *adj* desafortunado; **he has been very ~** ha tenido muy mala suerte

unfortunately /ʌnˈfɔːrtʃnətli ‖ʌnˈfɔːtʃənətli/ *adv* (indep) lamentablemente, desafortunadamente; (stronger) desgraciadamente, por desgracia

unfounded /ʌnˈfaʊndəd ‖ʌnˈfaʊndɪd/ *adj* infundado

unfriendly /ʌnˈfrendli/ *adj* **-lier, -liest** poco amistoso; (stronger) antipático

unfulfilled /ˌʌnfʊlˈfɪld/ *adj* ⟨ambition/hope⟩ frustrado; ⟨prophecy⟩ no cumplido

unfurl /ʌnˈfɜːrl ‖ʌnˈfɜːl/ *vt* desplegar*

unfurnished /ʌnˈfɜːrnɪʃt ‖ʌnˈfɜːnɪʃt/ *adj* sin amueblar

ungainly /ʌnˈgeɪnli/ *adj* desgarbado

ungracious /ʌnˈgreɪʃəs/ *adj* descortés

ungrateful /ʌnˈgreɪtfəl/ *adj* desagradecido, ingrato, malagradecido

unguarded /ʌnˈgɑːrdəd ‖ʌnˈgɑːdɪd/ *adj* (incautious): **in an ~ moment** en un momento de descuido

unhappily /ʌnˈhæpəli ‖ʌnˈhæpɪli/ *adv* **(a)** ⟨sigh⟩ tristemente, con tristeza **(b)** (unfortunately) (indep) lamentablemente

unhappiness /ʌnˈhæpɪnəs ‖ʌnˈhæpɪnɪs/ *n* infelicidad *f*; (stronger) desdicha *f*; (sadness) tristeza *f*

unhappy /ʌnˈhæpi/ *adj* **-pier, -piest (a)** (sad) ⟨childhood⟩ infeliz; (stronger) desgraciado, desdichado **(b)** (worried) (pred): **I was ~ about the children being left alone** me preocupaba or inquietaba que los niños se quedaran solos **(c)** (discontented) (pred) **to be ~ ABOUT sth** no estar* contento CON algo

unharmed /ʌnˈhɑːrmd ‖ʌnˈhɑːmd/ *adj*: **he escaped ~** salió or resultó ileso

unhealthy /ʌnˈhelθi/ *adj* **-thier, -thiest (a)** ⟨person⟩ de mala salud; ⟨complexion⟩ enfermizo; ⟨climate⟩ poco saludable, insalubre, malsano **(b)** ⟨interest/obsession⟩ malsano

unheard of /ʌnˈhɜːrdəːv ‖ʌnˈhɜːdəv/ *adj* insólito

unhelpful /ʌnˈhelpfəl/ *adj* ⟨assistant/secretary⟩ poco servicial; **he was most ~** no se mostró nada dispuesto a ayudar

unhinge /ʌnˈhɪndʒ/ *vt* ⟨person/mind⟩ trastornar

unhurt /ʌnˈhɜːrt ‖ʌnˈhɜːt/ *adj* ileso; **to escape ~** salir* or resultar ileso

unhygienic /ˌʌnhaɪˈdʒiːnɪk/ *adj* antihigiénico

UNICEF /ˈjuːnɪsef/ *n* (no art) (= **United Nations International Children's Emergency Fund**) UNICEF *m or f*

unicorn /ˈjuːnəkɔːrn ‖ˈjuːnɪkɔːn/ *n* unicornio *m*

unidentified /ˌʌnaɪˈdentəfaɪd ‖ˌʌnaɪˈdentɪfaɪd/ *adj* no identificado; **~ flying object** objeto *m* volador or (Esp) volante no identificado

unification /ˌjuːnəfəˈkeɪʃən ‖ˌjuːnɪfɪˈkeɪʃən/ *n* unificación *f*

uniform¹ /ˈjuːnəfɔːrm ‖ˈjuːnɪfɔːm/ *n* uniforme *m*

uniform² *adj* ⟨color/length⟩ uniforme; ⟨temperature/speed⟩ constante

uniformity /ˌjuːnəˈfɔːrməti ‖ˌjuːnɪˈfɔːməti/ *n* uniformidad *f*

unify /ˈjuːnəfaɪ ‖ˈjuːnɪfaɪ/ *vt* **-fies, -fying, -fied** unir

unilateral /ˌjuːnɪˈlætərəl/ *adj* unilateral

unimaginable /ˌʌnəˈmædʒənəbəl ‖ˌʌnɪˈmædʒɪnəbəl/ *adj* inimaginable

unimaginative /ˌʌnɪˈmædʒənətɪv ‖ ˌʌnɪˈmædʒɪnətɪv/ adj ‹person› poco imaginativo; ‹story/design› falto de imaginación

unimportant /ˌʌnɪmˈpɔːrtn̩t ‖ ˌʌnɪmˈpɔːtn̩t/ adj ‹matter/detail› sin importancia

uninhabited /ˌʌnɪnˈhæbətəd ‖ ˌʌnɪnˈhæbɪtɪd/ adj ‹house› deshabitado; ‹region/island› despoblado

uninhibited /ˌʌnɪnˈhɪbətəd ‖ ˌʌnɪnˈhɪbɪtɪd/ adj desinhibido, desenfadado

unintelligent /ˌʌnɪnˈtelədʒənt ‖ ˌʌnɪnˈtelɪdʒənt/ adj poco inteligente

unintelligible /ˌʌnɪnˈtelədʒəbəl ‖ ˌʌnɪnˈtelɪdʒəbəl/ adj ininteligible

unintentional /ˌʌnɪnˈtentʃn̩əl ‖ ˌʌnɪnˈtenʃn̩l/ adj involuntario, no deliberado

unintentionally /ˌʌnɪnˈtentʃn̩əli ‖ ˌʌnɪnˈtenʃn̩əli/ adv involuntariamente, sin querer

uninterested /ʌnˈɪntrəstəd ‖ ʌnˈɪntrestɪd/ adj indiferente

uninteresting /ʌnˈɪntrəstɪŋ/ adj ‹topic› sin interés; ‹person› poco interesante

uninvited /ˌʌnɪnˈvaɪtəd ‖ ˌʌnɪnˈvaɪtɪd/ adj: they came ~ vinieron sin que nadie los invitara

uninviting /ˌʌnɪnˈvaɪtɪŋ/ adj ‹appearance› poco atractivo; ‹food› poco apetitoso

union /ˈjuːnjən/ n **1** (act, state) unión f **2** (Lab Rel) sindicato m, gremio m (CS, Per); (before n) ‹official/movement› sindical, gremial (CS, Per); ~ card carné m de afiliado **3** (at college, university) asociación f or federación f de estudiantes

unionize /ˈjuːnjənaɪz/ vt sindicalizar* (esp AmL), sindicar* (esp Esp)

Union Jack n bandera f del Reino Unido

unique /juˈniːk/ adj ‹no comp› único

unisex /ˈjuːnəseks ‖ ˈjuːnɪseks/ adj unisex adj inv

unison /ˈjuːnəsən ‖ ˈjuːnɪsən/ n: in ~ al unísono

unit /ˈjuːnət ‖ ˈjuːnɪt/ n **1** (a) (item) (Busn) unidad f (b) (of furniture) módulo m **2** (group) (Mil) unidad f **3** (of measurement) unidad f **4** (Educ) (in course) módulo m

unite /juˈnaɪt ‖ juːˈnaɪt/ vt unir
■ ~ vi unirse

united /juˈnaɪtəd ‖ juːˈnaɪtɪd/ adj unido

united: U~ Arab Emirates /ˈemɪrəts ‖ ˈemɪərəts/ pl n the U~ Arab Emirates los Emiratos Árabes Unidos; **U~ Kingdom** n the U~ Kingdom el Reino Unido; **U~ Nations (Organization)** n (+ sing o pl vb) the U~ Nations (organization) (la Organización de) las Naciones Unidas; **U~ States** n (usu + sing vb) the U~ States los Estados Unidos; **U~ States of America** n (usu + sing vb) the U~ States of America los Estados Unidos de América

unity /ˈjuːnəti/ n (pl -ties) unidad f

universal /ˌjuːnəˈvɜːrsəl ‖ ˌjuːnɪˈvɜːsəl/ adj (a) (general) general (b) (worldwide) universal (c) (all-purpose, versatile) ‹adaptor› universal

universally /ˌjuːnəˈvɜːrsəli ‖ ˌjuːnɪˈvɜːsəli/ adv ‹known/admired› mundialmente, universalmente

universe /ˈjuːnəvɜːrs ‖ ˈjuːnɪvɜːs/ n universo m

university /ˌjuːnəˈvɜːrsəti ‖ ˌjuːnɪˈvɜːsəti/ n (pl -ties) universidad f; (before n) ‹town/life› universitario

unjust /ʌnˈdʒʌst/ adj injusto

unjustified /ʌnˈdʒʌstəfaɪd ‖ ʌnˈdʒʌstɪfaɪd/ adj injustificado

unkempt /ʌnˈkempt/ adj ‹appearance› descuidado, desarreglado; ‹hair› despeinado

unkind /ʌnˈkaɪnd/ adj **-er, -est** (unpleasant) poco amable; (cruel) cruel, malo; ‹remark› hiriente

unknown¹ /ʌnˈnəʊn/ adj desconocido

unknown² n (a) (phenomenon) the ~ lo desconocido (b) (person) desconocido, -da m,f

unknown³ adv: ~ to her sin ella saberlo

unlawful /ʌnˈlɔːfəl/ adj ‹conduct› ilegal; ‹possession› ilícito

unleaded /ʌnˈledəd ‖ ʌnˈledɪd/ adj sin plomo

unleash /ʌnˈliːʃ/ vt ‹dog› soltar*, desatar; ‹anger/imagination› dar(le)* rienda suelta a; ‹war› desencadenar

unless /ʌnˈles, ən-/ conj a no ser que (+ subj), a menos que (+ subj)

unlike /ʌnˈlaɪk/ prep (a) (not similar to) diferente or distinto de (b) (untypical of): **it's ~ you to be so optimistic** tú no sueles ser tan optimista (c) (in contrast to) a diferencia de

unlikely /ʌnˈlaɪkli/ adj **-lier, liest** (a) (improbable) ‹outcome/victory› improbable, poco probable (b) (far-fetched) ‹story/explanation› inverosímil (c) (odd, unexpected) insólito

unlimited /ʌnˈlɪmətəd ‖ ʌnˈlɪmɪtɪd/ adj ilimitado

unlined /ʌnˈlaɪnd/ adj (a) ‹paper› sin pautar (b) ‹dress/jacket› sin forro

unlisted /ʌnˈlɪstəd ‖ ʌnˈlɪstɪd/ adj (AmE Telec) que no figura en la guía telefónica

unlit /ʌnˈlɪt/ adj ‹road› sin luz, sin alumbrado

unload /ʌnˈləʊd/ vt/i descargar*

unlock /ʌnˈlɑːk ‖ ʌnˈlɒk/ vt abrir* (algo que está cerrado con llave)

unlucky /ʌnˈlʌki/ adj **unluckier, unluckiest** ‹person› sin suerte, desafortunado; ‹day› funesto, de mala suerte; ‹object› que trae mala suerte; **to be ~** tener* mala suerte

unmanageable /ʌnˈmænɪdʒəbəl/ adj ‹child/horse› rebelde; ‹hair› rebelde

unmanned /ʌnˈmænd/ adj ‹vehicle/rocket› sin tripulación; ‹space flight› no tripulado

unmarried /ʌnˈmærid/ adj soltero

unmask /ʌnˈmæsk ‖ ʌnˈmɑːsk/ vt desenmascarar

unmentionable /ʌnˈmentʃn̩əbəl ‖ ʌnˈmenʃənəbəl/ adj inmencionable, innombrable

unmistakable /ˌʌnməˈsteɪkəbəl ‖ ˌʌnmɪˈsteɪkəbəl/ adj inconfundible; ‹proof› inequívoco

unnamed /ʌnˈneɪmd/ adj no identificado

unnatural /ʌnˈnætʃərəl/ adj (a) (unusual) poco natural or normal (b) (awkward, affected) ‹smile› poco natural (c) (against nature) (fml) antinatural

unnecessarily /ˌʌnnesəˈserəli ‖ ˌʌnnesəˈserɪli, ˌʌnˈnesəserɪli/ adv innecesariamente

933

unnecessary /ˌʌn'nesəseri ‖ ʌn'nesəsəri/ *adj*
innecesario

unnerve /ˌʌn'nɜːrv ‖ ʌn'nɜːv/ *vt* poner*
nervioso, turbar (liter)

unnerving /ˌʌn'nɜːrvɪŋ ‖ ʌn'nɜːvɪŋ/ *adj*
desconcertante, que pone nervioso

unnoticed /ˌʌn'nəʊtəst ‖ ʌn'nəʊtɪst/ *adj*
(*pred*): **to go ~** pasar desapercibido *or*
inadvertido

unobtainable /ˌʌnəb'teɪnəbəl/ *adj* imposible
de conseguir

unobtrusive /ˌʌnəb'truːsɪv/ *adj* discreto

unoccupied /ˌʌn'ɑːkjəpaɪd ‖ ʌn'ɒkjʊpaɪd/ *adj*
(a) ⟨*seat/toilet*⟩ desocupado, libre; ⟨*house*⟩
deshabitado, desocupado **(b)** (Mil) no ocupado

unofficial /ˌʌnə'fɪʃəl/ *adj* no oficial

unofficially /ˌʌnə'fɪʃəli/ *adv* extraoficialmente

unopened /ˌʌn'əʊpənd/ *adj* sin abrir

unopposed /ˌʌnə'pəʊzd/ *adj* sin oposición

unoriginal /ˌʌnə'rɪdʒənl/ *adj* poco original, sin
originalidad

unorthodox /ˌʌn'ɔːrθədɑːks ‖ ʌn'ɔːθədɒks/ *adj*
poco ortodoxo

unpack /ˌʌn'pæk/ *vt* ⟨*bags*⟩ sacar* las cosas de,
desempacar* (AmL); ⟨*suitcase*⟩ deshacer*,
desempacar* (AmL)
■ ~ *vi* deshacer* las maletas, desempacar* (AmL)

unpaid /ˌʌn'peɪd/ *adj* ⟨*work*⟩ no retribuido, no
remunerado; ⟨*leave*⟩ sin sueldo; ⟨*debt*⟩ pendiente,
no liquidado

unpalatable /ˌʌn'pælətəbəl/ *adj* **(a)** ⟨*food/
drink*⟩ de sabor desagradable **(b)** ⟨*fact/truth*⟩
desagradable, difícil de digerir

unparalleled /ˌʌn'pærəleld/ *adj* ⟨*success/
achievement*⟩ sin paralelo, sin parangón;
⟨*disaster*⟩ sin precedentes; ⟨*beauty*⟩ incomparable

unperturbed /ˌʌnpər'tɜːrbd ‖ ʌnpə'tɜːbd/ *adj*
impasible, impertérrito; **she carried on ~** siguió
sin inmutarse

unpleasant /ˌʌn'pleznt/ *adj* desagradable

unplug /ˌʌn'plʌg/ *vt* **-gg-** desenchufar,
desconectar

unpopular /ˌʌn'pɑːpjələr ‖ ʌn'pɒpjʊlə(r)/ *adj*
impopular; **he is ~ with everybody** le cae muy
mal a todo el mundo

unprecedented /ˌʌn'presədentəd
‖ ʌn'presɪdentɪd/ *adj* ⟨*success/hostility*⟩ sin
precedentes; ⟨*decision*⟩ inaudito

unpredictable /ˌʌnprɪ'dɪktəbəl/ *adj* ⟨*result/
weather*⟩ imprevisible; **she's very ~** nunca se
sabe cómo va a reaccionar

unprepared /ˌʌnprɪ'perd ‖ ʌnprɪ'peəd/ *adj* **(a)**
(not ready) (*pred*) **to be ~** no estar* preparado **(b)**
(not expecting) (*pred*) **to be ~ FOR sth** no esperar
algo

unprepossessing /ˌʌnpriːpə'zesɪŋ/ *adj* poco
atractivo

unprincipled /ˌʌn'prɪnsəpəld/ *adj* sin
escrúpulos *or* principios

unproductive /ˌʌnprə'dʌktɪv/ *adj* ⟨*meeting*⟩
infructuoso

unprofessional /ˌʌnprə'feʃnəl
‖ ʌnprə'feʃnl/ *adj* poco profesional

unprofitable /ˌʌn'prɑːfətəbəl ‖ ʌn'prɒfɪtəbəl/
adj no rentable

unprotected /ˌʌnprə'tektəd ‖ ʌnprə'tektɪd/
adj sin protección; ⟨*sex*⟩ sin el uso de
preservativos

unproven /ˌʌn'pruːvən/ *adj* ⟨*theory*⟩ (que está)
por demostrar *or* probar

unpublished /ˌʌn'pʌblɪʃt/ *adj* inédito, no
publicado

unpunished /ˌʌn'pʌnɪʃt/ *adj*: **to go ~**
«*person*» quedar sin castigo; «*crime*» quedar
impune

unqualified /ˌʌn'kwɑːləfaɪd ‖ ʌn'kwɒlɪfaɪd/ *adj*
1 (complete, total) ⟨*approval*⟩ incondicional;
⟨*disaster*⟩ absoluto; ⟨*success/failure*⟩ rotundo
2 (without qualifications) ⟨*teacher/nurse*⟩ sin
titulación *or* título, no titulado; ⟨*staff*⟩ no
calificado *or* (Esp) cualificado

unquestionable /ˌʌn'kwestʃənəbəl/ *adj*
⟨*sincerity/loyalty*⟩ incuestionable, innegable

unquestioning /ˌʌn'kwestʃənɪŋ/ *adj*
⟨*obedience/faith*⟩ ciego; ⟨*loyalty*⟩ incondicional

unravel /ˌʌn'rævəl/ *vt*, (BrE) **-ll-** **(a)** ⟨*threads/
string*⟩ desenredar **(b)** ⟨*mystery*⟩ desentrañar

unreadable /ˌʌn'riːdəbəl/ *adj* **(a)**
⟨*handwriting*⟩ ilegible **(b)** ⟨*novel*⟩ muy difícil de
leer

unrealistic /ˌʌnriːə'lɪstɪk ‖ ʌnrɪə'lɪstɪk/ *adj*
⟨*expectations*⟩ poco realista; **it's ~ to expect that**
no es realista esperar eso

unreasonable /ˌʌn'riːznəbəl/ *adj* ⟨*person*⟩
poco razonable, irrazonable; ⟨*demand/price*⟩
excesivo, poco razonable

unrecognizable /ˌʌn'rekəgnaɪzəbəl/ *adj*
irreconocible

unrefined /ˌʌnrɪ'faɪnd/ *adj* ⟨*flour/sugar*⟩ sin
refinar, no refinado; ⟨*gold*⟩ en estado bruto;
⟨*person*⟩ poco refinado; **~ oil** crudo *m*

unrelated /ˌʌnrɪ'leɪtəd ‖ ʌnrɪ'leɪtɪd/ *adj* ⟨*facts/
events*⟩ no relacionados (entre sí)

unreliable /ˌʌnrɪ'laɪəbəl/ *adj* ⟨*person*⟩
informal; ⟨*information*⟩ poco fidedigno; ⟨*weather*⟩
variable

unrepeatable /ˌʌnrɪ'piːtəbəl/ *adj* irrepetible

unrepentant /ˌʌnrɪ'pentnt/ *adj* impenitente

unreported /ˌʌnrɪ'pɔːrtəd ‖ ʌnrɪ'pɔːtɪd/ *adj*
⟨*crime*⟩ no denunciado

unrepresentative /ˌʌnreprə'zentətɪv/ *adj*
poco representativo

unrequited /ˌʌnrɪ'kwaɪtəd ‖ ʌnrɪ'kwaɪtɪd/ *adj*
⟨*love*⟩ no correspondido

unresolved /ˌʌnrɪ'zɑːlvd ‖ ʌnrɪ'zɒlvd/ *adj* no
resuelto

unresponsive /ˌʌnrɪ'spɑːnsɪv ‖ ʌnrɪ'spɒnsɪv/
adj ⟨*audience/expression*⟩ indiferente; ⟨*pupil*⟩ que
no responde

unrest /ˌʌn'rest/ *n* (Pol) descontento *m*, malestar
m; (active) disturbios *mpl*

unrestricted /ˌʌnrɪ'strɪktəd ‖ ʌnrɪ'strɪktɪd/
adj ilimitado

unrewarded /ˌʌnrɪ'wɔːrdəd ‖ ʌnrɪ'wɔːdɪd/ *adj*
no recompensado

unripe /ˌʌn'raɪp/ *adj* verde, que no está maduro

unrivaled, (BrE) **unrivalled** /ˌʌn'raɪvəld/ *adj*
incomparable, inigualable

unroll /ˌʌn'rəʊl/ *vt* desenrollar

unruffled /ˌʌn'rʌfəld/ *adj* **(a)** (undisturbed)
⟨*manner*⟩ sereno **(b)** (smooth) liso

u

unruly /ʌn'ruːli/ adj **-lier, -liest** ⟨class⟩ indisciplinado, difícil de controlar; ⟨conduct⟩ rebelde; ⟨child⟩ revoltoso

unsafe /ʌn'seɪf/ adj inseguro

unsaid /ʌn'sed/ adj: **to leave sth ~** callar(se) algo, no decir* algo

unsalted /ʌn'sɔːltəd ‖ ʌn'sɔːltɪd/ adj sin sal

unsatisfactory /ʌn'sætəs'fæktri ‖ ˌʌnsætɪs'fæktəri/ adj insatisfactorio; ⟨explanation⟩ poco convincente

unsatisfying /ʌn'sætəsfaɪɪŋ ‖ ʌn'sætɪsfaɪɪŋ/ adj ⟨meal⟩ que no llena or satisface; ⟨job⟩ poco gratificante; ⟨ending⟩ decepcionante

unsavory, (BrE) **unsavoury** /ʌn'seɪvəri/ adj desagradable

unscathed /ʌn'skeɪðd/ adj (pred) (unhurt) ileso; (of reputation etc) indemne

unscented /ʌn'sentəd ‖ ʌn'sentɪd/ adj sin perfume

unscheduled /ʌn'skedʒuːld ‖ ʌn'ʃedjuːld/ adj no programado, no previsto

unscientific /ʌn'saɪən'tɪfɪk/ adj falto de rigor científico

unscrew /ʌn'skruː/ vt ⟨screw/panel⟩ destornillar, desatornillar; ⟨lid⟩ desenroscar*

unscrupulous /ʌn'skruːpjələs ‖ ʌn'skruːpjuləs/ adj inescrupuloso

unseat /ʌn'siːt/ vt (a) ⟨rider⟩ desmontar (b) ⟨government⟩ derribar

unseen /ʌn'siːn/ adj (a) (invisible) ⟨danger/obstacle⟩ oculto (b) (unnoticed) sin ser visto

unselfish /ʌn'selfɪʃ/ adj ⟨person⟩ nada egoísta; ⟨act⟩ desinteresado

unsentimental /ʌn'sentə'mentḷ ‖ ˌʌnsentɪ'mentḷ/ adj ⟨person/outlook⟩ poco sentimental

unsettle /ʌn'setḷ/ vt ⟨plans⟩ alterar; ⟨situation⟩ desestabilizar*; **the question clearly ~d him** la pregunta lo desconcertó visiblemente

unsettled /ʌn'setḷd/ adj **1** (a) (troubled) ⟨period⟩ agitado; ⟨childhood⟩ poco estable (b) ⟨weather⟩ inestable **2** (undecided) ⟨issue/dispute⟩ pendiente (de resolución), sin resolver; ⟨future⟩ incierto

unsettling /ʌn'setḷɪŋ/ adj inquietante; ⟨effect⟩ desestabilizador

unshakable, unshakeable /ʌn'ʃeɪkəbəl/ adj inquebrantable

unshaven /ʌn'ʃeɪvən/ adj sin afeitar, sin rasurar (esp Méx)

unsightly /ʌn'saɪtli/ adj **-lier, -liest** feo, antiestético

unsigned /ʌn'saɪnd/ adj sin firmar

unskilled /ʌn'skɪld/ adj ⟨worker⟩ no calificado or (Esp) cualificado; ⟨work⟩ no especializado

unsociable /ʌn'səʊʃəbəl/ adj insociable, poco sociable

unsold /ʌn'səʊld/ adj no vendido

unsolicited /ˌʌnsə'lɪsətəd ‖ ˌʌnsə'lɪsɪtɪd/ adj que no se ha pedido or solicitado

unsolved /ʌn'sɑːlvd ‖ ʌn'sɒlvd/ adj no resuelto

unsophisticated /ˌʌnsə'fɪstəkeɪtəd ‖ ˌʌnsə'fɪstɪkeɪtɪd/ adj ⟨person⟩ sencillo; ⟨tastes/technology⟩ simple, poco sofisticado

unspeakable /ʌn'spiːkəbəl/ adj ⟨evil⟩ incalificable, atroz; ⟨joy⟩ indescriptible

unspecified /ʌn'spesəfaɪd ‖ ʌn'spesɪfaɪd/ adj no especificado

unspoiled /ʌn'spɔɪld/, (BrE also) **unspoilt** /ʌn'spɔɪlt/ adj ⟨countryside⟩ que conserva su belleza natural

unspoken /ʌn'spəʊkən/ adj ⟨agreement⟩ tácito; ⟨wish⟩ no expresado

unstable /ʌn'steɪbəl/ adj inestable; ⟨prices⟩ variable

unsteadily /ʌn'stedli ‖ ʌn'stedɪli/ adv de modo inseguro or vacilante

unsteady /ʌn'stedi/ adj ⟨chair/ladder⟩ inestable, poco firme; ⟨walk/step⟩ vacilante, inseguro

unstick /ʌn'stɪk/ vt (past & past p **unstuck**) despegar*, quitar

unstuck /ʌn'stʌk/ adj despegado; **to come ~** despegarse*

unsuccessful /ˌʌnsək'sesfəl/ adj ⟨attempt⟩ infructuoso, fallido; **they were ~ in their attempt** fracasaron en su intento

unsuccessfully /ˌʌnsək'sesfəli/ adv en vano, sin éxito

unsuitable /ʌn'suːtəbəl/ adj ⟨clothing⟩ poco apropiado or adecuado; ⟨candidate⟩ poco idóneo; ⟨time⟩ inconveniente

unsuited /ʌn'suːtəd ‖ ʌn'suːtɪd/ adj (pred) **she is ~ to this work** no sirve para este trabajo; **they are completely ~** son totalmente incompatibles

unsure /ʌn'ʃʊr ‖ ʌn'ʃʊə(r), ʌn'ʃɔː(r)/ adj inseguro, indeciso; **to be ~ of oneself** estar* or sentirse* inseguro de sí mismo

unsurpassed /ˌʌnsər'pæst ‖ ˌʌnsə'pɑːst/ adj ⟨beauty/mastery⟩ sin igual, sin par (liter)

unsuspecting /ˌʌnsə'spektɪŋ/ adj desprevenido; **to be ~** no sospechar nada

unsweetened /ʌn'swiːtnd/ adj (without sugar) sin azúcar; (without sweeteners) sin edulcorantes

unsympathetic /ʌn'sɪmpə'θetɪk/ adj (a) (showing no sympathy) ⟨person/attitude⟩ indiferente, poco comprensivo (b) (unfavorable) ⟨account⟩ adverso, desfavorable; **she was ~ to our cause** no veía nuestra causa con simpatía

unsystematic /ʌn'sɪstə'mætɪk/ adj poco sistemático

untamed /ʌn'teɪmd/ adj ⟨animal⟩ sin domar; ⟨wilderness/forests⟩ virgen, agreste

untangle /ʌn'tæŋgəl/ vt desenredar, desenmarañar; ⟨mystery⟩ desentrañar

untapped /ʌn'tæpt/ adj sin explotar

untenable /ʌn'tenəbəl/ adj (fml) insostenible

untended /ʌn'tendəd ‖ ʌn'tendɪd/ adj ⟨garden⟩ descuidado; ⟨patient⟩ desatendido

unthinkable /ʌnˈθɪŋkəbəl/ *adj* inconcebible, inimaginable

untidy /ʌnˈtaɪdi/ *adj* **-dier, -diest** ⟨*room/desk/ person*⟩ desordenado; ⟨*appearance*⟩ descuidado, desprolijo (RPl); ⟨*writing/schoolwork*⟩ descuidado, desprolijo (RPl)

untie /ʌnˈtaɪ/ *vt* **unties, untying, untied** ⟨*knot*⟩ desatar; ⟨*shoelaces*⟩ desatar, desamarrar (AmL exc RPl); ⟨*animal*⟩ soltar*, desatar, desamarrar (AmL exc RPl)

until¹ /ʌnˈtɪl, ənˈtɪl/ *conj* hasta que

■ **Note** When used as a conjunction in positive sentences expressing the future, *until* is translated by *hasta que + subjunctive*: *we'll stay here until Carol comes back* nos quedaremos aquí hasta que llegue Carol.In negative sentences *no* is used optionally before the verb: *he won't be satisfied until they give him his money back* no estará satisfecho hasta que (no) le devuelvan su dinero.

until² *prep* hasta

untimely /ʌnˈtaɪmli/ *adj* **(a)** ⟨*death/end*⟩ prematuro **(b)** ⟨*arrival*⟩ inoportuno, intempestivo

untold /ʌnˈtəʊld/ *adj* ⟨*before n*⟩ ⟨*wealth/sums*⟩ incalculable; ⟨*misery/pleasures*⟩ indecible, inenarrable

untouched /ʌnˈtʌtʃt/ *adj* **(a)** (not handled) intacto, sin tocar; **he left his food ~** no probó la comida **(b)** (safe, unharmed) intacto

untoward /ʌnˈtɔːrd , ˌʌntəˈwɔːrd ‖ˌʌntəˈwɔːd/ *adj* (frml) perjudicial, adverso; **I hope nothing ~ has happened** espero que no haya pasado nada (que haya que lamentar)

untrained /ʌnˈtreɪnd/ *adj* falto de formación *or* capacitación; ⟨*teacher*⟩ sin título; **to the ~ eye/ ear …** para el (ojo/oído de) quien no es experto …

untreated /ʌnˈtriːtəd ‖ʌnˈtriːtɪd/ *adj* ⟨*sewage/ waste*⟩ sin tratar *or* procesar

untried /ʌnˈtraɪd/ *adj* **(a)** (not tested) ⟨*method*⟩ no probado **(b)** (Law) ⟨*case*⟩ no sometido a juicio

untroubled /ʌnˈtrʌbəld/ *adj* tranquilo

untrue /ʌnˈtruː/ *adj* falso; **it is ~ (to say) that …** es falso *or* no es cierto que …

untrustworthy /ʌnˈtrʌst͵wɜːrði ‖ʌnˈtrʌst͵wɜːði/ *adj* ⟨*person*⟩ de poca confianza; ⟨*source*⟩ no fidedigno

untruthful /ʌnˈtruːθfəl/ *adj* ⟨*account/answer*⟩ falso; ⟨*person*⟩ falso, mentiroso

unusual /ʌnˈjuːʒuəl/ *adj* poco corriente *or* común, fuera de lo corriente *or* común, inusual; **with ~ frankness** con inusitada *or* insólita franqueza; **did you notice anything ~ about him?** ¿le notaste algo raro *or* fuera de lo normal?

unusually /ʌnˈjuːʒuəli/ *adv* excepcionalmente, inusitadamente; **she was ~ talkative** estaba más conversadora que de costumbre

unveil /ʌnˈveɪl/ *vt* descubrir*, develar (AmL)

unwanted /ʌnˈwɔːntəd ‖ʌnˈwɒntɪd/ *adj* ⟨*pregnancy/child*⟩ no deseado; ⟨*object*⟩ superfluo

unwarranted /ʌnˈwɔːrəntəd ‖ʌnˈwɒrəntɪd/ *adj* injustificado

unwavering /ʌnˈweɪvərɪŋ/ *adj* ⟨*loyalty/belief*⟩ inquebrantable; ⟨*determination*⟩ férreo

unwelcome /ʌnˈwelkəm/ *adj* ⟨*visit*⟩ inoportuno; ⟨*guest*⟩ inoportuno, poco grato; ⟨*news*⟩ poco grato

unwell /ʌnˈwel/ *adj* mal

unwholesome /ʌnˈhəʊlsəm/ *adj* ⟨*diet/ climate*⟩ poco sano *or* saludable; ⟨*smell/person*⟩ desagradable

unwieldy /ʌnˈwiːldi/ *adj* **-dier, -diest** pesado y difícil de manejar

unwilling /ʌnˈwɪlɪŋ/ *adj* mal dispuesto; **to be ~ to + INF** no querer* + INF, no estar* dispuesto a + INF

unwillingly /ʌnˈwɪlɪŋli/ *adv* de mala gana, a regañadientes

unwind /ʌnˈwaɪnd/ (*past & past p* **unwound** /ʌnˈwaʊnd/) *vt* desenrollar
■ **~** *vi* (colloq) relajarse

unwise /ʌnˈwaɪz/ *adj* poco prudente *or* sensato; **it would be ~ of you to do that** hacer eso no sería sensato

unwitting /ʌnˈwɪtɪŋ/ *adj* involuntario

unwittingly /ʌnˈwɪtɪŋli/ *adv* sin ser consciente (de ello), sin darse* cuenta

unworthy /ʌnˈwɜːrði ‖ʌnˈwɜːði/ *adj* **-thier, -thiest** indigno; **to be ~ to + INF** no ser* digno DE + INF

unwound /ʌnˈwaʊnd/ *past & past p of* UNWIND

unwrap /ʌnˈræp/ *vt* **-pp-** desenvolver*

unwritten /ʌnˈrɪtn/ *adj* ⟨*rule*⟩ no escrito; ⟨*agreement*⟩ verbal, de palabra

unyielding /ʌnˈjiːldɪŋ/ *adj* ⟨*person*⟩ inflexible; ⟨*opposition*⟩ implacable

up¹ /ʌp/ *adv*
I **1** (in upward direction): **~ a bit … left a bit** un poco más arriba … un poco a la izquierda; **we saw them on the way ~** los vimos cuando subíamos; **from the waist ~** desde la cintura para arriba
2 (a) (of position) arriba; **~ here/there** aquí/allí arriba; **300ft ~** a una altura de 300 pies **(b)** (upstairs, on upper floor): **I'll be ~ in a minute** subiré en un minuto **(c)** (raised): **with the blinds ~** con las persianas levantadas *or* subidas; **face ~** boca arriba
3 (a) (upright): **the nurse helped him ~** la enfermera lo ayudó a sentarse **(b)** (out of bed): **they're not ~ yet** todavía no se han levantado
4 (of numbers, intensity): **she had the volume ~ high** tenía el volumen muy alto; **from $25/the age of 11 ~** a partir de 25 dólares/de los 11 años
5 (at or to another place): **the path ~ to the house** el sendero hasta la casa
6 (in position, erected): **is the tent ~?** ¿ya han armado la tienda *or* (AmL) la carpa?; **the shelves are ~** los estantes están colocados *or* puestos
7 (going on) (colloq): **what's ~ with you?** ¿a ti qué te pasa?; **what's ~?** (what's the matter?) ¿qué pasa?; (as greeting) (AmE) ¿qué hay? (colloq)
8 (finished): **your time is ~** se te ha acabado el tiempo
9 (Sport) (ahead in competition): **they're two goals ~** van ganando por dos goles; **to be one ~ on sb** tener* una ventaja sobre algn
II (*in phrases*) **1** **up against (a)** (next to) contra **(b)** (confronted by): **you don't know what you're ~ against** no sabes a lo que te enfrentas
2 **up and down (a)** (vertically): **to jump ~ and down** dar* saltos; **to look sb ~ and down** mirar a algn de arriba abajo **(b)** (back and forth) de arriba abajo

···⊱

3 up till *o* until hasta

III up to **1** (as far as, as much as) hasta; ∼ to here/now hasta aquí/ahora

2 (a) (equal to): it isn't ∼ to the usual standard no es del alto nivel al que estamos acostumbrados; ▶ COME UP TO B **(b)** (capable of): she's not ∼ to the job no tiene las condiciones necesarias para el trabajo; I'm not ∼ to going out no me siente con fuerzas (como) para salir

3 (depending on): that's ∼ to you eso depende de ti; it's not ∼ to me to decide no me corresponde a mí decidir

4 to be ∼ to sth (colloq): they're ∼ to something (planning) están tramando algo, se traen algo entre manos; (doing) están haciendo algo; what have you been ∼ to lately? ¿en qué has andado últimamente?

up² *prep* **1 (a)** (in upward direction): to go ∼ the stairs/hill subir la escalera/colina **(b)** (at higher level): 80ft ∼ the cliff a 80 pies del pie del acantilado **2 (a)** (along): to go ∼ the river ir* por el río; she walked ∼ and down the room iba de un lado a otro de la habitación **(b)** (further along): it's just ∼ the road está un poco más allá *or* adelante

up³ *n*: ∼s and downs (of life) vicisitudes *fpl*; (of marriage) altibajos *mpl*

up: ∼-and-coming /ˌʌpən'kʌmɪŋ/ *adj (before n)*: an ∼-and-coming actor un actor que promete; **∼beat** *adj* (colloq) optimista; **∼braid** /ʌp'breɪd/ *vt* (frml) reprender, reconvenir* (frml); **∼bringing** /'ʌpˌbrɪŋɪŋ/ *n (no pl)* educación *f*; **∼coming** /'ʌp'kʌmɪŋ/ *adj (before n)* próximo, que se acerca

update¹ /ʌp'deɪt/ *vt* poner* al día

update² /'ʌpdeɪt/ *n*: to give sb an ∼ on sth poner* a algn al corriente *or* al tanto de algo

up: ∼end /ʌp'end/ *vt* poner* vertical, parar (AmL); **∼front** /'ʌp'frʌnt/ *adv* por adelantado; **∼grade** *vt* **(a)** ⟨*employee*⟩ elevar de categoría; ⟨*job*⟩ elevar la categoría de **(b)** (improve) ⟨*facilities*⟩ mejorar

upheaval /ʌp'hiːvəl/ *n* trastorno *m*; (social, political) agitación *f*

up: ∼held /ʌp'held/ *past & past p of* ∼HOLD; **∼hill** /'ʌp'hɪl/ *adv* cuesta arriba, en subida; **∼hold** /ʌp'həʊld/ *vt* (*past & past p* ∼held) **(a)** ⟨*tradition*⟩ conservar; ⟨*principle*⟩ mantener* **(b)** (Law) ⟨*decision/verdict*⟩ confirmar

upholster /ʌp'həʊlstər ‖ʌp'həʊlstə(r)/ *vt* tapizar*

upholstery /ʌp'həʊlstəri/ *n* **(a)** (stuffing, springs) relleno *m*; (covers) tapizado *m* **(b)** (craft, trade) tapicería *f*

up: ∼keep *n* (running, maintenance) mantenimiento *m*; (costs) gastos *mpl* de mantenimiento; **∼lift** /ʌp'lɪft/ *vt* elevar; **∼lifting** /ʌp'lɪftɪŋ/ *adj* (spiritually) que eleva el espíritu; (emotionally) que levanta el ánimo; **∼load** /ʌp'ləʊd/ *vt* (Comput) cargar*, subir

upmarket¹ /'ʌp'mɑːrkət ‖ˌʌp'mɑːkɪt/ *adj* de categoría, para gente pudiente

upmarket² *adv*: to go ∼ subir de categoría

upon /ə'pɑːn ‖ə'pɒn/ *prep* (frml) **(a)** (on) sobre; ∼ -ING al + INF **(b)** (indicating large numbers): thousands ∼ thousands miles y miles

upper /'ʌpər ‖'ʌpə(r)/ *adj (before n)* **1 (a)**

(spatially, numerically) superior; ⟨*lip*⟩ superior, de arriba **(b)** (in rank, importance) superior, más elevado **2** (Geog) alto; the U∼ Danube el alto Danubio

upper: ∼ class *n* clase *f* alta; **∼-class** /'ʌpər'klæs ‖ˌʌpə'klɑːs/ *adj* de clase alta; **∼most** *adj* más alto

upright /'ʌpraɪt/ *adj* **(a)** ⟨*post/position*⟩ vertical; to place/stand sth ∼ colocar*/poner* algo de pie *or* vertical **(b)** ⟨*citizen*⟩ recto

up: ∼rising *n* levantamiento *m*, alzamiento *m*; **∼river** /'ʌp'rɪvər ‖ˌʌp'rɪvə(r)/ *adv* río arriba; **∼roar** *n* (noise, chaos) tumulto *m*, alboroto *m*; (outcry) protesta *f* airada; **∼root** /ʌp'ruːt/ *vt* ⟨*plant*⟩ arrancar* de raíz, desarraigar* (téc); ⟨*person*⟩ desarraigar*

upset¹ /'ʌp'set/ *adj* **1** (unhappy, hurt) disgustado; (distressed) alterado; (offended) ofendido; (disappointed) desilusionado **2** (Med): I have an ∼ stomach estoy *or* ando mal del estómago, estoy descompuesto (del estómago) (esp AmL)

upset² /'ʌp'set/ *vt* (*pres p* upsetting; *past & past p* upset) **1** (hurt) disgustar; (distress) alterar, afectar; (offend) ofender **2** (make ill): it ∼s my stomach me cae mal, me sienta mal (al estómago) **3** ⟨*plans/calculations*⟩ desbaratar, trastornar

upset³ /'ʌpset/ *n* **1 (a)** (upheaval) trastorno *m* **(b)** (emotional trouble) disgusto *m* **2** (Med): to have a stomach ∼ estar* mal *or* (esp AmL) descompuesto del estómago

upshot /'ʌpʃɑːt ‖'ʌpʃɒt/ *n*: the ∼ of it all is that ... lo que resulta de todo esto es que ...

upside down /'ʌpsaɪd/ *adj* al revés (con la parte de arriba abajo); to turn sth ∼ ∼ poner* algo boca abajo; ⟨*theory/world*⟩ revolucionar algo

upstage /'ʌp'steɪdʒ/ *vt* eclipsar

upstairs /'ʌp'sterz ‖ˌʌp'steəz/ *adv* arriba; to go ∼ subir

up: ∼start *n* advenedizo, -za *m,f*; **∼state** /'ʌp'steɪt/ *adv* (AmE): he lives ∼state vive en el norte del estado (fuera de la capital); **∼stream** /'ʌp'striːm/ *adv* río o corriente arriba; **∼surge** *n* ⟨*of/in violence*⟩ recrudecimiento *m*; ⟨*in demand*⟩ aumento *m*; **∼take** *n*: to be quick on the ∼take agarrar *or* (esp Esp) coger* las cosas al vuelo; **∼tight** /'ʌp'taɪt/ *adj* (colloq) nervioso, tenso; **∼-to-date** /'ʌptə'deɪt/ *adj* (pred ∼ to date) al día, actualizado

uptown¹ /'ʌp'taʊn/ *adj* (AmE) que va hacia el norte/hacia el distrito residencial (de la ciudad)

uptown² *adv* (AmE): they live/went ∼ viven en/ fueron hacia el norte/hacia el distrito residencial de la ciudad

up: ∼turn *n* (in demand, production) repunte *m*, mejora *f*; **∼turned** /'ʌp'tɜːrnd ‖ˌʌp'tɜːnd/ *adj* ⟨*nose*⟩ respingón, respingado (AmL); ⟨*table*⟩ boca abajo, patas arriba; ⟨*car/crate*⟩ volcado

upward¹ /'ʌpwərd ‖'ʌpwəd/ *adj (before n)* ⟨*direction*⟩ hacia arriba; ⟨*movement*⟩ ascendente; ⟨*tendency*⟩ al alza

upward², (esp BrE) **upwards** /-z/ *adv* ⟨*climb/ look*⟩ hacia arriba; face ∼ boca arriba

upwardly mobile /'ʌpwərdli ‖'ʌpwədli/ *adj* de movilidad social ascendente

uranium /jʊ'reɪmiəm/ *n* uranio *m*

Uranus /'jʊərənəs, jʊə'reɪnəs/ *n* Urano *m*

urban /'ɜːrbən ‖'ɜːbən/ *adj* urbano

urbane /ɜːr'beɪn ‖ɜː'beɪm/ *adj* (frml) fino y cortés, urbano (frml)

urchin /'ɜːrtʃən ‖'ɜːtʃɪn/ *n* golfillo, -lla *m,f*, pilluelo, -la *m,f*

Urdu /'ʊrdu ‖'ʊədu:/ *n* urdu *m*

urge¹ /'ɜːrdʒ ‖ɜːdʒ/ *n* (wish, whim) ganas *fpl*; (creative, sexual) impulso *m*

urge² *vt* instar (frml); (entreat) pedir* con insistencia; **to ~ sb to + INF** instar a algn A QUE (+ *subj*) (frml), pedirle* a algn con insistencia QUE (+ *subj*)
■ **urge on** [*v* + *o* + *adv*] animar, alentar*; ⟨*horse*⟩ espolear

urgency /'ɜːrdʒənsi ‖'ɜːdʒənsi/ *n* urgencia *f*

urgent /'ɜːrdʒənt ‖'ɜːdʒənt/ *adj* ⟨*matter/case*⟩ urgente; ⟨*tone*⟩ apremiante

urgently /'ɜːrdʒəntli ‖'ɜːdʒəntli/ *adv* urgentemente, con urgencia

urinal /'jʊrənl̩ ‖jʊə'raɪnl̩/ *n* (place) urinario *m*; (receptacle) orinal *m*

urinate /'jʊrəneɪt ‖'jʊərɪneɪt/ *vi* (frml) orinar

urine /'jʊrən ‖'jʊərɪn/ *n* orina *f*

urn /ɜːrn ‖ɜːn/ *n* **(a)** (vase) urna *f* **(b)** (for ashes) urna *f* funeraria **(c)** (for tea, coffee) *recipiente grande para hacer o mantener caliente té, café etc*

Uruguay /'jʊrəgwaɪ ‖'jʊərəgwaɪ/ *n* Uruguay *m*

Uruguayan¹ /'jʊrə'gwaɪən ‖'jʊərə'gwaɪən/ *adj* uruguayo

Uruguayan² *n* uruguayo, -ya *m,f*

us /ʌs, *weak form* əs/ *pron* ☐1 **(a)** (as direct object) nos; **they helped ~** nos ayudaron **(b)** (as indirect object) nos; **he gave ~ the book** nos dio el libro; **he gave it to ~** nos lo dio **(c)** (after preposition) nosotros, -tras; **there were four of ~** éramos cuatro ☐2 (emphatic use) nosotros, -tras; **it was ~** fuimos nosotros

US *n* (+ *sing vb*) EEUU, EE UU, EE.UU.

USA *n* **(a)** (= **United States of America**) EEUU, EE UU, EE.UU. **(b)** (= **United States Army**) ejército *m* estadounidense *or* de los EEUU

usable, useable /'juːzəbəl/ *adj* utilizable

USAF *n* (= **United States Air Force**) la Fuerza Aérea de los EEUU

usage /'juːsɪdʒ/ *n* (Ling) uso *m*

use¹ /juːs/ *n* ☐1 (of machine, substance, method, word) uso *m*, empleo *m*, utilización *f*; **to be in ~** «*machine*» estar* funcionando *or* en funcionamiento; «*word*» emplearse, usarse; **to make ~ of sth** usar algo, hacer* uso de algo; **to put sth to good ~** hacer* buen uso de algo ☐2 (application, function) uso *m* ☐3 (usefulness): **to be of ~ to sb** serle* útil *or* de utilidad a algn, servirle* a algn; **these scissors aren't much ~** estas tijeras no sirven para nada; **it's no ~** es inútil, no hay manera, no hay caso (AmL); **what's the ~ (of -ING)?** ¿de qué sirve (+ INF)?, ¿qué sentido tiene (+ INF)? ☐4 (right to use): **to have the ~ of sb's car** poder* usar el coche de algn

use² /juːz/ *vt* ☐1 **(a)** (for task, purpose) usar; **to ~ sth AS sth** usar algo DE *or* COMO algo **(b)** (avail oneself of) ⟨*service/facilities*⟩ utilizar*, usar, hacer*

uso de; **may I ~ your phone?** ¿puedo hacer una llamada *or* llamar por teléfono?; **may I ~ your toilet?** ¿puedo pasar *or* ir al baño? ☐2 (do with) (colloq): **I could ~ a drink** no me vendría mal un trago ☐3 (consume) ⟨*food/fuel*⟩ consumir, usar ☐4 (manipulate, exploit) (pej) utilizar*, usar (esp AmL)
■ **~** *v mod* /juːs/ (*in neg, interrog sentences*): **I didn't ~ to visit them very often** no solía visitarlos muy a menudo; **where did you ~ to live?** ¿dónde vivías?; *see also* USED²
■ **use up** [*v* + *o* + *adv*, *v* + *adv* + *o*] ⟨*supplies/strength*⟩ agotar, consumir; ⟨*leftovers*⟩ usar

useable *adj* ► USABLE

used¹ *adj* ☐1 /juːzd/ ⟨*needle/stamp/car*⟩ usado ☐2 /juːst/ (accustomed) ⟨*pred*⟩ **to be ~ TO sth/-ING** estar* acostumbrado A algo/+ INF; **to get ~ TO sth/-ING** acostumbrarse A algo/+ INF

used² /juːst/ *v mod* (indicating former state, habit) (*only in past*) **~ to (+ INF): there ~ to be** (antes) había; **I ~ to work in that shop** (antes) trabajaba en esa tienda; *see also* USE² *v mod*

useful /'juːsfəl/ *adj* útil; **to come in ~** (BrE) ser* útil, venir* bien

useless /'juːsləs ‖'juːslɪs/ *adj* **(a)** (ineffective) inútil; **these scissors are ~** estas tijeras no sirven para nada **(b)** (not capable) (colloq) ⟨*person*⟩ inútil, negado (fam)

user /'juːzər ‖'juːzə(r)/ *n* usuario, -ria *m,f*; **drug ~** consumidor, -dora *m,f* de drogas

user-friendly /'juːzər'frendli ‖ juːzə'frendli/ *adj* fácil de usar *or* de utilizar

usher¹ /'ʌʃər ‖'ʌʃə(r)/ *n* **(a)** (Cin, Theat) acomodador, -dora *m,f* **(b)** (at wedding) *persona allegada a los novios que se encarga de recibir y sentar a los invitados en la iglesia*

usher² *vt*: **to ~ sb to her/his seat** conducir* a algn hasta su asiento; **he ~ed her into the room** la hizo pasar a la habitación
■ **usher in** [*v* + *o* + *adv*, *v* + *adv* + *o*] ⟨*person*⟩ hacer* pasar; ⟨*new era*⟩ marcar* el comienzo de

usherette /'ʌʃə'ret/ *n* acomodadora *f*

USN *n* = **United States Navy**

USS = **United States ship**

USSR *n* (= **Union of Soviet Socialist Republics**) URSS *f*

usual /'juːʒuəl/ *adj* ⟨*method/response*⟩ acostumbrado, habitual, usual; ⟨*time/place*⟩ de siempre, de costumbre; ⟨*clothes*⟩ de costumbre; **as ~** como de costumbre

usually /'juːʒuəli/ *adv* normalmente, usualmente; **what do you ~ do in the evenings?** ¿qué sueles hacer por las noches?

usurp /jʊ'sɜːrp ‖juː'zɜːp/ *vt* (frml) usurpar

UT = **Utah**

utensil /juː'tensəl ‖juː'tensɪl/ *n* utensilio *m*

uterus /'juːtərəs/ *n* (*pl* **-teri** /-təraɪ/ *or* **-teruses**) útero *m*, matriz *f*

utility /juː'tɪləti/ *n* (*pl* **-ties**) (public service ~) empresa *f* de servicio público

utility room *n*: *cuarto para lavar y planchar*

utilize /'juːtl̩aɪz ‖'juːtɪlaɪz/ *vt* (frml) utilizar*

utmost¹ /'ʌtməʊst/ *adj* ⟨*before n*⟩ mayor, sumo; **with the ~ care** con el mayor cuidado, con sumo cuidado; **of the ~ importance** de suma importancia

utmost² *n*: to do one's ~ (to + INF) esforzarse* al máximo *or* hacer* todo lo posible (PARA + INF)

utopia, Utopia /juːˈtəʊpɪə/ *n* (*pl* **-as**) utopía *f*

utter¹ /ˈʌtər ‖ ˈʌtə(r)/ *adj* (*as intensifier*) completo, total

utter² *vt* ⟨*word*⟩ decir*, pronunciar; ⟨*cry*⟩ dar*

utterly /ˈʌtərli ‖ ˈʌtəli/ *adv* (*as intensifier*) completamente, totalmente

U-turn /ˈjuːtɜːrn ‖ ˈjuːtɜːn/ *n* cambio *m* de sentido; **to make** (AmE) *o* (BrE) **do a** ~ cambiar de sentido

Uzbekistan /ˈʊzbekɪˈstɑːn/ *n* Uzbekistán *m*

Vv

V, v /viː/ *n* V, v *f*

v 1 ▶ vs 2 (*pl* **vv**) (Bib, Lit) = **verse** 3 (colloq) (= **very**) muy

V (Elec) (= **volt(s)**) V ⟨*read as: voltio(s)*⟩

VA *n* = **Virginia**

vacancy /ˈveɪkənsi/ *n* (*pl* **-cies**) **(a)** (job) vacante *f*; ⓢ **vacancies** ofertas de trabajo **(b)** (in hotel) habitación *f* libre

vacant /ˈveɪkənt/ *adj* 1 **(a)** ⟨*building/ premises*⟩ desocupado **(b)** ⟨*post*⟩ vacante **(c)** ⟨*room*⟩ disponible, libre; ⟨*seat/space*⟩ libre 2 (blank) ⟨*look/expression*⟩ ausente

vacate /ˈveɪkeɪt ‖ verˈkeɪt, vəˈ-/ *vt* (frml) ⟨*building*⟩ desocupar, desalojar; ⟨*seat/room*⟩ dejar libre; ⟨*job/post*⟩ abandonar, dejar

vacation¹ /verˈkeɪʃən/ *n* (esp AmE) (from work) vacaciones *fpl*, licencia *f* (Col, Méx, RPl); (from studies) vacaciones *fpl*; **to go/be on** ~ irse*/estar* de vacaciones

vacation² *vi* (AmE) pasar las vacaciones, vacacionar (Méx)

vacationer /verˈkeɪʃnər ‖ vəˈkeɪʃənə(r)/, **vacationist** /-ʃnəst ‖ -ʃənɪst/ *n* (AmE) turista *mf*; (in summer) veraneante *mf*

vaccinate /ˈvæksəneɪt ‖ ˈvæksɪneɪt/ *vt* vacunar

vaccination /ˌvæksəˈneɪʃən ‖ ˌvæksɪˈneɪʃən/ *n* vacunación *f*

vaccine /vækˈsiːn ‖ ˈvæksiːn/ *n* vacuna *f*

vacillate /ˈvæsəleɪt/ *vi* (hesitate) vacilar; (sway) oscilar

vacuum¹ /ˈvækjuəm, -juːm/ *n* vacío *m*; (*before n*) ~ **pump** bomba *f* neumática

vacuum² *vi* pasar la aspiradora, aspirar (AmL)

vacuum: ~ **bottle** *n* (AmE) termo *m*; ~ **cleaner** *n* aspiradora *f*; ~ **flask** *n* termo *m*

vagabond /ˈvæɡəbɑːnd ‖ ˈvæɡəbɒnd/ *n* vagabundo, -da *m,f*

vagina /vəˈdʒaɪnə/ *n* vagina *f*

vagrant /ˈveɪɡrənt/ *n* vagabundo, -da *m,f*

vague /veɪɡ/ *adj* **vaguer**, **vaguest** **(a)** (imprecise, unclear) ⟨*term/wording/concept*⟩ impreciso, vago **(b)** (indistinct) ⟨*outline*⟩ borroso **(c)** (absentminded) ⟨*expression*⟩ distraído; ⟨*person*⟩ distraído, despistado

vaguely /ˈveɪɡli/ *adv* **(a)** (in imprecise, unclear way) ⟨*explain/remember*⟩ vagamente; ⟨*answer/define*⟩ con vaguedad *or* imprecisión; ⟨*suspicious/ ridiculous*⟩ ligeramente; **he looks** ~ **like his father** tiene un ligero parecido con *or* a su padre **(b)** (absentmindedly) distraídamente

vain /veɪn/ *adj* **-er, -est** 1 (self-admiring) vanidoso 2 (*before n, no comp*) **(a)** ⟨*attempt*⟩ vano; ⟨*hope/belief*⟩ vano **(b)** ⟨*promise/words*⟩ vano **(c) in vain** en vano, vanamente

vainly /ˈveɪnli/ *adv* (uselessly) en vano, vanamente

valentine /ˈvæləntaɪn/ *n* **(a)** (card) *tarjeta de tono humorístico y/o amoroso que se envía anónimamente el día de San Valentín* **(b)** *also* **Valentine** (person) enamorado, -da *m,f*

Valentine's Day /ˈvæləntaɪmz/ *n* el día de San Valentín, el día de los enamorados

valet /ˈvælət, ˈvæleɪ ‖ ˈvæleɪ, ˈvælɪt/ *n* **(a)** (servant) ayuda *m* de cámara **(b)** (in hotel) mozo *m* de hotel

valiant /ˈvæljənt/ *adj* ⟨*hero/deed*⟩ valiente, valeroso; ⟨*attempt*⟩ valeroso

valid /ˈvæləd ‖ ˈvælɪd/ *adj* válido

validate /ˈvælədeɪt ‖ ˈvælɪdeɪt/ *vt* **(a)** (frml) ⟨*theory*⟩ dar* validez a, validar (frml) **(b)** (Law) ⟨*contract/document*⟩ validar

valley /ˈvæli/ *n* (*pl* **-leys**) valle *m*

valor, (BrE) **valour** /ˈvælər ‖ ˈvælə(r)/ *n* (frml *o* liter) valor *m*, valentía *f*

valuable /ˈvæljuəbəl/ *adj* valioso; ⟨*time*⟩ precioso

valuables /ˈvæljuəbəlz/ *pl n* objetos *mpl* de valor

valuation /ˌvæljuˈeɪʃən/ *n* valoración *f*, tasación *f*, avalúo *m* (AmL)

value¹ /ˈvæljuː/ *n* 1 (worth) valor *m* 2 **values** (standards) valores *mpl*

value² *vt* **(a)** (Fin) ⟨*assets/property*⟩ tasar, valorar, avaluar* (AmL) **(b)** (regard highly) ⟨*friendship/advice*⟩ valorar, apreciar; ⟨*freedom/ privacy*⟩ valorar

value-added tax /'vælju:'ædəd
‖,vælju:'ædɪd/ *n* impuesto *m* al valor agregado
or (Esp) sobre el valor añadido

valve /vælv/ *n* válvula *f*; (on musical instrument)
pistón *m*

vampire /'væmpaɪr ‖'væmpaɪə(r)/ *n* vampiro
m

van /væn/ *n* **(a)** (Auto) furgoneta *f*, camioneta *f*
(b) (BrE Rail) furgón *m*

vandal /'vændl/ *n* vándalo *m*

vandalism /'vændlɪzəm/ *n* vandalismo *m*

vandalize /'vændlaɪz/ *vt* destrozar*

vanguard /'vængɑːrd ‖'vængɑːd/ *n*
vanguardia *f*

vanilla /və'nɪlə/ *n* vainilla *f*

vanish /'vænɪʃ/ *vi* desaparecer*

vanity /'vænəti/ *n* (*pl* **-ties**) **(a)** (about
appearance) vanidad *f* **(b)** (pride) orgullo *m*,
vanidad *f*

vanity case *n* neceser *m*

vanquish /'væŋkwɪʃ/ *vt* (liter) vencer*

vantage point /'væntɪdʒ ‖'vɑːntɪdʒ/ *n*
posición *f* ventajosa; (for view) mirador *m*

vapor, (BrE) **vapour** /'veɪpər ‖'veɪpə(r)/ *n* (on
glass) vaho *m*; (steam) vapor *m*

vaporize /'veɪpəraɪz/ *vi* evaporarse,
vaporizarse*

vapour *n* (BrE) ▶ VAPOR

variable /'veriəbəl ‖'veəriəbəl/ *adj* variable

variance /'veriəns ‖'veəriəns/ *n*: **to be at ∼
with sth** no estar* de acuerdo con algo, discrepar
de algo

variant /'veriənt ‖'veəriənt/ *n* variante *f*

variation /'veri'eɪʃən ‖,veəri'eɪʃən/ *n*
variación *f*

varicose veins /'værəkəʊs ‖'værɪkəʊs/ *pl n*
varices *fpl*, várices *fpl* (esp AmL)

varied /'verid ‖'veərid/ *adj* variado

variegated /'verɪgeɪtəd ‖'veərɪgeɪtɪd/ *adj*
abigarrado, multicolor

variety /və'raɪəti/ *n* (*pl* **-ties**) **(a)** (diversity)
variedad *f*, diversidad *f* **(b)** (assortment) ∼ **or sth:
it comes in a ∼ of shades** viene en varios colores
(c) (sort) clase *f*

variety show *n* espectáculo *m* de variedades

various /'veriəs ‖'veəriəs/ *adj* **(a)** (several)
(*before n, no comp*) varios **(b)** (different, diverse)
diferentes, diversos

varnish¹ /'vɑːrnɪʃ ‖'vɑːnɪʃ/ *n* barniz *m*; (for
nails) (BrE) esmalte *m*

varnish² *vt* barnizar*; **to ∼ one's nails** (BrE)
pintarse las uñas

vary /'veri ‖'veəri/, **varies, varying, varied**
vi **(a)** (change, fluctuate) variar*; **the temperature
varies between …** la temperatura oscila entre …
(b) (differ) «*standards/prices*» variar*
■ ∼ *vt* variar*; «*diet*» dar* variedad a

vase /veɪs, veɪz ‖vɑːz/ *n* (for flowers) florero *m*;
(ornament) jarrón *m*

vasectomy /və'sektəmi/ *n* (*pl* **-mies**)
vasectomía *f*

Vaseline® /'væsəliːn/ *n* vaselina *f*

vast /væst ‖vɑːst/ *adj* (*size/wealth*) inmenso,
enorme; (*area*) vasto, extenso; (*knowledge*) vasto

vastly /'væstli ‖'vɑːstli/ *adv* infinitamente

vat /væt/ *n* cuba *f*, tanque *m*

VAT *n* (= **value-added tax**) IVA *m*

Vatican /'vætɪkən/ *n* **the ∼** el Vaticano

Vatican City *n* Ciudad *f* del Vaticano

vault¹ /vɔːlt/ *n* ①① **(a)** (strongroom) cámara *f*
acorazada, bóveda *f* de seguridad (AmL) **(b)** (crypt)
cripta *f* ②② (Archit) bóveda *f*

vault² *vi/t* saltar (*apoyándose en algo*)

VCR *n* = **videocassette recorder**

VD *n* = **venereal disease**

VDT *n* (esp AmE) = **visual display terminal**

VDU *n* = **visual display unit**

've /əv/ = **have**

veal /viːl/ *n* ternera *f* (*de animal muy joven y de
carne pálida*)

VE-Day /'viːiːdeɪ/ *n*: *día de la victoria aliada en
Europa en la segunda guerra mundial*

veer /vɪr ‖vɪə(r)/ *vi* «*vehicle/horse*» dar* un
viraje, virar; «*wind*» cambiar de dirección; **the
road ∼s to the left** el camino tuerce *or* se desvía
hacia la izquierda

vegan /'viːgən/ *n* vegetariano estricto,
vegetariana estricta *m,f*

vegetable /'vedʒtəbəl/ *n* **(a)** (Culin) verdura *f*;
fresh/frozen/canned ∼s verdura fresca/
congelada/enlatada **(b)** (plant) vegetal *m*; (*before
n*) (*oil/fats*) vegetal

vegetarian¹ /'vedʒə'teriən ‖,vedʒɪ'teəriən/ *n*
vegetariano, -na *m,f*

vegetarian² *adj* vegetariano

vegetate /'vedʒəteɪt ‖'vedʒɪteɪt/ *vi* vegetar

vegetation /'vedʒə'teɪʃən ‖,vedʒɪ'teɪʃən/ *n*
vegetación *f*

vehement /'viːəmənt/ *adj* vehemente

vehemently /'viːəməntli/ *adv* con
vehemencia, vehementemente

vehicle /'viːəkəl/ *n* vehículo *m*

veil¹ /veɪl/ *n* velo *m*

veil² *vt* (cover with a veil): **to ∼ one's face** taparse
or cubrirse* con un velo, velarse (liter)

veiled /veɪld/ *adj* (*threat/insult*) velado

vein /veɪn/ *n* ①① (Anat, Bot, Zool) vena *f* ②② **(a)** (of
ore, mineral) veta *f*, filón *m*, vena *f* **(b)** (in marble)
veta *f* ③③ (*no pl*) (mood, style) vena *f*

velocity /və'lɑːsəti ‖və'lɒsəti/ *n* (*pl* **-ties**)
velocidad *f*

velvet /'velvət ‖'velvɪt/ *n* terciopelo *m*

vendetta /ven'detə/ *n* vendetta *f*

vending machine /'vendɪŋ/ *n* máquina *f*
expendedora

vendor /'vendər ‖'vendə(r)/ *n* (Busn, Law)
vendedor, -dora *m,f*

veneer /və'nɪr ‖vɪ'nɪə(r)/ *n* (of wood, gold)
enchapado *m*, chapa *f*

venerate /'venəreɪt/ *vt* venerar, reverenciar

venereal disease /və'nɪriəl ‖və'nɪəriəl/ *n*
enfermedad *f* venérea

Venetian blind /və'niːʃən/ *n* persiana *f*
veneciana *or* de lamas

Venezuela /'venə'zweɪlə ‖,venɪ'zweɪlə/ *n*
Venezuela *f*

Venezuelan¹ /'venə'zweɪlən ‖,venɪ'zweɪlən/
adj venezolano

Venezuelan² *n* venezolano, -na *m,f*

vengeance /'vendʒəns/ n venganza f; **with a ∼** (colloq) de verdad or con ganas

vengeful /'vendʒfəl/ adj vengativo

venison /'venəsən ‖'venɪsən/ n (carne f de) venado m

venom /'venəm/ n **(a)** (Zool) veneno m **(b)** (malice) ponzoña f, veneno m

venomous /'venəməs/ adj ‹snake/spider› venenoso; ‹look/words› ponzoñoso

vent¹ /vent/ n **(a)** (in building, tunnel) (conducto m de) ventilación f; (in chimney, furnace) tiro m **(b)** (air ∼) (shaft) respiradero m; (grille) rejilla f de ventilación

vent² vt descargar*; **she ∼ed her anger on the children** descargó su ira sobre los niños

ventilate /'ventleɪt ‖'ventɪleɪt/ vt ventilar

ventilation /ventl'eɪʃən ‖,ventɪ'leɪʃən/ n ventilación f; (system) sistema m de ventilación

ventilator /'ventleɪtər ‖'ventɪleɪtə(r)/ n (Med) respirador m (artificial)

ventriloquist /ven'trɪləkwəst ‖ven'trɪləkwɪst/ n ventrílocuo, -cua m,f

venture¹ /'ventʃər ‖'ventʃə(r)/ n (Busn) empresa f

venture² vi atreverse; **to ∼ out** (atreverse a) salir*
■ ∼ vt ‹opinion/guess› aventurar

venue /'venjuː/ n (for concert) lugar m de actuación; (for conference, Olympics) sede f

Venus /'viːnəs/ n Venus m

veranda, verandah /və'rændə/ n galería f

verb /vɜːrb ‖vɜːb/ n verbo m

verbal /'vɜːrbəl ‖'vɜːbəl/ adj verbal

verbatim /vər'beɪtəm ‖vɜː'beɪtɪm/ adv al pie de la letra

verbose /vər'bəʊs ‖vɜː'bəʊs/ adj ampuloso, verboso

verdict /'vɜːrdɪkt ‖'vɜːdɪkt/ n **(a)** (Law) veredicto m **(b)** (opinion) opinión f

verge /vɜːrdʒ ‖vɜːdʒ/ n ⚊ **(a)** (border) (BrE) borde m **(b) to be on the ∼ of tears** estar* al borde de las lágrimas; **to be on the ∼ of -ING** estar* a punto de + INF ⚋ (of road) (BrE) arcén m
■ **verge on** [v + prep + o] rayar en

verification /ˌverəfə'keɪʃən ‖,verɪfɪ'keɪʃən/ n **(a)** (confirmation) confirmación f **(b)** (checking) verificación f

verify /'verəfaɪ ‖'verɪfaɪ/ vt **-fies, -fying, -fied (a)** (confirm) confirmar **(b)** (check) ‹fact/statement› verificar*

veritable /'verətəbəl ‖'verɪtəbəl/ adj (frml or hum) auténtico, verdadero

vermin /'vɜːrmən ‖'vɜːmɪn/ n (pl ∼) (animals) alimañas fpl; (insects) bichos mpl

vernacular /vər'nækjələr ‖və'nækjʊlə(r)/ n (native language) lengua f vernácula; (local speech) habla f; local

verruca /və'ruːkə/ n verruga f

versatile /'vɜːrsət̬l ‖'vɜːsətaɪl/ adj ‹person› polifacético, versátil; ‹tool› versátil; ‹mind› flexible

versatility /ˌvɜːrsə'tɪləti ‖,vɜːsə'tɪləti/ n versatilidad f

verse /vɜːrs ‖vɜːs/ n ⚊ (poetry) verso m ⚋ **(a)** (short poem) verso m, rima f **(b)** (stanza) estrofa f **(c)** (in Bible) versículo m

versed /vɜːrst ‖vɜːst/ adj (pred): **to be well ∼ in sth** ser* muy versado en algo

version /'vɜːrʒən ‖'vɜːʃən/ n versión f

versus /'vɜːrsəs ‖'vɜːsəs/ prep (Law) contra; (Sport) contra, versus

vertebra /'vɜːrtəbrə ‖'vɜːtəbrə/ n (pl **-bras** or **-brae** /-breɪ/) vértebra f

vertebrate /'vɜːrtəbrət ‖'vɜːtɪbrət/ n vertebrado m

vertical /'vɜːrtɪkəl ‖'vɜːtɪkəl/ adj vertical

vertigo /'vɜːrtɪgəʊ ‖'vɜːtɪgəʊ/ n vértigo m

verve /vɜːrv ‖vɜːv/ n brío m

very¹ /'veri/ adv **(a)** (extremely) muy; **she's ∼ tall** es muy alta; (more emphatic) es altísima; **it was ∼ hot** hacía mucho calor **(b)** (in phrases) very much ‹like/enjoy› mucho; **thank you ∼ much** muchas gracias **(c)** (emphatic): **the ∼ next day** precisamente al día siguiente; **at the ∼ least** como mínimo

very² adj (before n) **(a)** (exact, precise) mismo; **for that ∼ reason** por esa misma razón, por eso mismo **(b)** (actual) mismo; **its ∼ existence is threatened** su misma existencia se halla amenazada **(c)** (mere, sheer) solo, mero; **the ∼ mention of her name** la sola or mera mención de su nombre

vespers /'vespərz ‖'vespəz/ pl n vísperas fpl

vessel /'vesəl/ n ⚊ (Naut frml) navío m (frml), nave f (liter) ⚋ (receptacle) (frml) recipiente m; (drinking ∼) vasija f ⚌ (Anat, Bot) vaso m

vest /vest/ n **(a)** (waistcoat) (AmE) chaleco m **(b)** (undergarment) (BrE) camiseta f

vested interest /'vestəd ‖'vestɪd/ n **to have a ∼ in -ING/sth** tener* gran interés en + INF/algo

vestige /'vestɪdʒ/ n vestigio m

vestry /'vestri/ n (pl **-tries**) sacristía f

vet¹ /vet/ n ⚊ (veterinarian) veterinario, -ria m,f ⚋ (veteran) (AmE colloq) veterano, -na m,f

vet² vt **-tt-** ‹applicant› someter a investigación; ‹application› examinar

veteran /'vetərən/ n **(a)** (of war) veterano, -na m,f de guerra **(b)** (experienced person) veterano, -na m,f

veteran: ∼ car n (BrE) coche m antiguo (fabricado antes de 1919); **V∼s Day** /'vetərənz/ n (in US) día m del Armisticio

veterinarian /ˌvetərə'neriən ‖,vetərɪ'neəriən/ n (AmE) médico veterinario, médica veterinaria m,f

veterinary /'vetərəneri ‖'vetrɪm[...]ri/ adj veterinario; **∼ surgeon** (BrE frml) médico veterinario, médica veterinaria m,f

veto¹ /'viːtəʊ/ n (pl **vetoes**) veto m

veto² vt **vetoes, vetoing, vetoed** vetar

vex /veks/ vt **(a)** (annoy) irritar, sacar* de quicio **(b)** (worry, puzzle) desconcertar*

vexed /vekst/ adj **(a)** (annoyed) ‹expression/tone› irritado; **to be ∼** estar* enojado (esp AmL), estar* enfadado (esp Esp) **(b)** (worried, puzzled) desconcertado

VHF (= **very high frequency**) VHF

via /'vaɪə, 'viːə ‖'vaɪə/ *prep* **(a)** (by way of) vía **(b)** (by means of) a través de

viable /'vaɪəbəl/ *adj* viable

viaduct /'vaɪədʌkt/ *n* viaducto *m*

vibrant /'vaɪbrənt/ *adj* **(a)** ‹color› vibrante; ‹atmosphere› efervescente **(b)** (resonant) ‹voice› vibrante

vibrate /'vaɪbreɪt ‖vaɪ'breɪt/ *vi* vibrar

vibration /vaɪ'breɪʃən/ *n* vibración *f*

vicar /'vɪkər ‖'vɪkə(r)/ *n* párroco *m*

vicarage /'vɪkərɪdʒ/ *n* vicaría *f*, casa *f* del párroco

vicarious /vɪ'keriəs ‖vɪ'keəriəs/ *adj* indirecto

vice /vaɪs/ *n* **1** (wickedness) vicio *m* **2** (BrE) ▶ VISE

vice- /vaɪs/ *pref* vice-

vice: ~ **president** *n* vicepresidente, -ta *m,f*; ~ **versa** /'vaɪsi'vɜːrsə, 'vaɪs'vɜːrsə ‖,vaɪsi'vɜːsə, ,vaɪs'vɜːsə/ *adv* viceversa

vicinity /vɪ'sɪnəti/ *n* (frml) inmediaciones *fpl*

vicious /'vɪʃəs/ *adj* **(a)** (savage, violent) ‹dog› fiero; ‹criminal› despiadado; ‹attack› feroz, salvaje; ‹crime› atroz **(b)** (malicious) ‹rumor› malicioso

vicious circle *n* círculo *m* vicioso

viciously /'vɪʃəsli/ *adv* brutalmente, ferozmente

victim /'vɪktəm ‖'vɪktɪm/ *n* víctima *f*; **the flood** ~**s** los damnificados por las inundaciones

victimize /'vɪktəmaɪz ‖'vɪktɪmaɪz/ *vt* victimizar*

victor /'vɪktər ‖'vɪktə(r)/ *n* vencedor, -dora *m,f*

Victorian /vɪk'tɔːriən/ *adj* victoriano

victorious /vɪk'tɔːriəs/ *adj* ‹army› victorioso; ‹team› vencedor

victory /'vɪktəri/ *n* (*pl* **-ries**) victoria *f*, triunfo *m*; (Mil) victoria *f*

video¹ /'vɪdiəʊ/ *n* (*pl* **videos**) video *m or* (Esp) vídeo *m*; (*before n*) ~ **camera** videocámara *f*; ~ **recorder** aparato *m* de video *or* (Esp) vídeo

video² *vt* **videoes, videoing, videoed** grabar

video: ~**cassette** /'vɪdiəʊkə'set/ *n* videocasete *m*; (*before n*) ~**cassette recorder** magnetoscopio *m*, video *m or* (Esp) vídeo *m*; ~ **game** *n* videojuego *m*

Vienna /vi'enə/ *n* Viena *f*

Vietnam /'viːet'nɑːm, -næm ‖vjet'næm/ *n* Vietnam *m*

Vietnamese¹ /vi'etnə'miːz ‖,vɪetnə'miːz/ *adj* vietnamita

Vietnamese² *n* (*pl* ~) **(a)** (person) vietnamita *mf* **(b)** (language) vietnamita *m*

view¹ /vjuː/ *n* **1** **(a)** (sight) vista *f*; **in full** ~ **of sb** a la vista de algn **(b)** (range of vision): **we had a good** ~ **of the stage** veíamos muy bien el escenario **2** (scene, vista) vista *f* **3** (opinion, attitude) opinión *f*, parecer *m*; **in my** ~ en mi opinión, a mi modo de ver **4** (plan, intention): **with a** ~ **to** ~**ING** con vistas a + INF **5** (*in phrases*) **in view of** en vista de; **on view: to be on** ~ (to the public) exponerse* (al público)

view² *vt* **(a)** ‹sights/scene› ver*, mirar **(b)** (inspect) ‹property› ver* **(c)** (regard) ver*, considerar

viewer /'vjuːər ‖'vjuːə(r)/ *n* **(a)** (person) telespectador, -dora *m,f*, televidente *mf* **(b)** (for slides) visionadora *f*

view: ~**finder** /'vjuː'faɪndər ‖'vjuːˌfaɪndə(r)/ *n* visor *m*; ~**point** *n* punto *m* de vista

vigil /'vɪdʒəl ‖'vɪdʒɪl/ *n* **(a)** (watch) (liter *or* journ) vela *f*; **to keep a** ~ **over sth** velar sobre algo **(b)** (Relig) vigilia *f*

vigilance /'vɪdʒələns ‖'vɪdʒɪləns/ *n* vigilancia *f*

vigilant /'vɪdʒələnt ‖'vɪdʒɪlənt/ *adj* alerta, vigilante

vigilante /'vɪdʒə'lænti ‖,vɪdʒɪ'lænti/ *n* vigilante, -ta *m,f*

vigor, (BrE) **vigour** /'vɪgər ‖'vɪgə(r)/ *n* vigor *m*

vigorous /'vɪgərəs/ *adj* enérgico; ‹growth› vigoroso

vigorously /'vɪgərəsli/ *adv* enérgicamente; ‹deny› rotundamente

vigour *n* (BrE) ▶ VIGOR

Viking /'vaɪkɪŋ/ *n* vikingo, -ga *m,f*

vile /vaɪl/ *adj* **viler, vilest (a)** (despicable) (liter) vil (liter) **(b)** (colloq) ‹taste/food› vomitivo (fam), asqueroso; ‹color/weather› horrible

villa /'vɪlə/ *n* **(a)** (Hist) villa *f* **(b)** (holiday house) chalet *m*

village /'vɪlɪdʒ/ *n* (large) pueblo *m*; (small) aldea *f*

villager /'vɪlədʒər ‖'vɪlɪdʒə(r)/ *n* (of large village) vecino, -na *m,f or* habitante *mf* del pueblo; (of small village) aldeano, -na *m,f*

villain /'vɪlən/ *n* **(a)** (in fiction) villano, -na *m,f* **(b)** (criminal) (BrE sl) maleante *mf*

vinaigrette /'vɪnɪ'gret/ *n* vinagreta *f*

vindicate /'vɪndəkeɪt ‖'vɪndɪkeɪt/ *vt* (frml) (justify) ‹action› justificar*; ‹assertion› confirmar; ‹right› reivindicar*

vindictive /vɪn'dɪktɪv/ *adj* vengativo

vine /vaɪn/ *n* (grape~) (on ground) vid *f*; (climbing) parra *f*

vinegar /'vɪnɪgər ‖'vɪnɪgə(r)/ *n* vinagre *m*

vineyard /'vɪnjərd, -jɑːrd ‖'vɪnjəd, -jɑːd/ *n* viñedo *m*, viña *f*

vintage¹ /'vɪntɪdʒ/ *n* **(a)** (wine, year) cosecha *f* **(b)** (harvest, season) vendimia *f*

vintage² *adj* (*before n, no comp*) **(a)** ‹wine› añejo **(b)** (outstanding) ‹year/performance› excelente

vintage car *n* (esp BrE) coche *m* antiguo (fabricado entre 1919 y 1930)

vinyl /'vaɪnl/ *n* vinilo *m*

viola /vi'əʊlə/ *n* (Mus) viola *f*

violate /'vaɪəleɪt/ *vt* **1** ‹agreement/rights› violar; ‹ban› desobedecer* **2** ‹shrine/grave› profanar

violation /'vaɪə'leɪʃən/ *n* violación *f*

violence /'vaɪələns/ *n* violencia *f*

violent /'vaɪələnt/ *adj* **(a)** ‹person/behavior› violento **(b)** (strong, forceful) ‹storm/explosion› violento, fuerte; **he has a** ~ **temper** tiene muy mal genio

violently /'vaɪələntli/ *adv* violentamente

violet /'vaɪələt/ *n* **(a)** (Bot) violeta *f* **(b)** (color) violeta *m*; (*before n*) violeta *adj inv*

violin /'vaɪə'lɪn/ *n* violín *m*

V

violinist /'vaɪə'lɪnəst ‖,vaɪə'lɪnɪst/ n violinista mf

VIP n (colloq) (= **very important person**) VIP mf

viper /'vaɪpər ‖'vaɪpə(r)/ n víbora f

virgin¹ /'vɜːrdʒən ‖'vɜːdʒɪn/ n virgen f

virgin² adj ⟨forest⟩ virgen; ⟨snow⟩ intacto

virginity /vər'dʒɪnəti ‖və'dʒɪnɪti/ n virginidad f; **to lose one's ∼** perder* la virginidad

Virgo /'vɜːrgəʊ ‖'vɜːgəʊ/ n (pl **-gos**) (a) (sign) (no art) Virgo (b) (person) Virgo or virgo mf

virile /'vɪrəl ‖'vɪraɪl/ adj viril

virtual /'vɜːrtʃuəl ‖'vɜːtʃʊəl, 'vɜːtʃʊəl/ adj (before n) [1] (near total): traffic is at a ∼ standstill el tráfico está prácticamente paralizado [2] (Comput, Opt) virtual

virtually /'vɜːrtʃuəli ‖'vɜːtʃʊəli, 'vɜːtʃʊəli/ adv prácticamente, casi

virtue /'vɜːrtʃuː ‖'vɜːtʃuː, 'vɜːtʃuː/ n (a) (moral excellence) virtud f (b) (advantage) ventaja f (c) **by virtue of** (as prep) en virtud de

virtuoso /vɜːrtʃu'əʊsəʊ ‖,vɜːtʃju'əʊsəʊ, ,vɜːtʃʊ'əʊsəʊ/ n (pl **-sos** or **-si** /-si/) virtuoso, -sa m,f

virtuous /'vɜːrtʃuəs ‖'vɜːtʃʊəs, 'vɜːtʃʊəs/ adj virtuoso

virulent /'vɪrələnt, 'vɪrjə- ‖'vɪrʊlənt, 'vɪrjʊ-/ adj virulento

virus /'vaɪrəs ‖'vaɪərəs/ n (pl ∼**es**) (Med, Comput) virus m

virus checker n (Comput) programa m antivirus

visa /'viːzə/ n (pl **-s**) visado m, visa f (AmL)

vis-à-vis /'viːzə'viː ‖,viːzɑː'viː/ prep con respecto a, respecto de

viscose /'vɪskəʊs/ n viscosilla f

viscount /'vaɪkaʊnt/ n vizconde m

viscous /'vɪskəs/ adj viscoso

vise, (BrE) **vice** /vaɪs/ n torno m or tornillo m de banco

visibility /'vɪzə'bɪləti/ n visibilidad f

visible /'vɪzəbəl/ adj visible; ⟨sign/improvement⟩ evidente

visibly /'vɪzəbli/ adv visiblemente

vision /'vɪʒən/ n [1] (a) (faculty of sight) visión f, vista f (b) (visibility) visibilidad f [2] (imagination, foresight) visión f (de futuro) [3] (dreamlike revelation) visión f

visionary /'vɪʒəneri ‖'vɪʒənri/ n (pl **-ries**) visionario, -ria m,f

visit¹ /'vɪzət ‖'vɪzɪt/ n visita f; **to pay a ∼ to sb** hacerle* una visita a algn

visit² vt visitar
■ ∼ vi hacer* una visita; (stay) estar* de visita

visitor /'vɪzətər ‖'vɪzɪtə(r)/ n (to museum, town etc) visitante mf; (to person's home) visita f

visitor center n (AmE) centro m de informaciones

visor /'vaɪzər ‖'vaɪzə(r)/ n visera f

vista /'vɪstə/ n vista f

visual /'vɪʒuəl/ adj visual; ∼ **display unit** pantalla f, monitor m

visualize /'vɪʒuəlaɪz/ vt (a) (picture mentally) imaginarse, visualizar* (b) (expect) prever*

vital /'vaɪtl/ adj (a) (essential) esencial, fundamental (b) ⟨factor/issue⟩ decisivo, de vital importancia (c) ⟨organ/function⟩ vital

vitality /vaɪ'tæləti/ n vitalidad f

vitamin /'vaɪtəmən ‖'vɪtəmɪn, 'vaɪt-/ n vitamina f; (before n) ∼ **pill** o **tablet** vitamina f

vivacious /və'veɪʃəs ‖vɪ'veɪʃəs/ adj vivaz

vivid /'vɪvəd ‖'vɪvɪd/ adj (a) ⟨color⟩ vivo (b) ⟨account/dream⟩ vívido (c) ⟨imagination⟩ rico

vividly /'vɪvədli ‖'vɪvɪdli/ adv (a) ⟨colored⟩ vistosamente (b) ⟨describe⟩ vívidamente, gráficamente

vivisection /'vɪvə'sekʃən ‖,vɪvɪ'sekʃən/ n vivisección f

vixen /'vɪksən/ n (Zool) zorra f, raposa f

viz /vɪz/ adv a saber

VJ-Day /'viː'dʒeɪdeɪ/ n: día de la victoria aliada sobre el Japón

V-neck /'viːnek/, (BrE also) **V-necked** /'viːnekt/ adj de escote or cuello en pico, de escote en V

vocabulary /vəʊ'kæbjələri ‖vəʊ'kæbjʊləri/ n (pl **-ries**) vocabulario m

vocal /'vəʊkəl/ adj vocal

vocal cords pl n cuerdas fpl vocales

vocalist /'vəʊkələst ‖'vəʊkəlɪst/ n cantante mf

vocation /vəʊ'keɪʃən/ n vocación f

vodka /'vɑːdkə ‖'vɒdkə/ n vodka m

vogue /vəʊg/ n moda f

voice¹ /vɔɪs/ n voz f

voice² vt expresar

voice mail n audiomensajería f, correo m de voz

void¹ /vɔɪd/ n vacío m

void² adj [1] (liter) (pred) **to be ∼ oʀ sth** estar* desprovisto de algo [2] (Law) nulo, inválido

vol (pl **vols**) (= **volume**) vol., t.

volatile /'vɑːlətl ‖'vɒlətaɪl/ adj (a) (Chem) volátil (b) ⟨person/personality⟩ imprevisible (c) ⟨situation⟩ volátil

volcanic /vɑːl'kænɪk ‖vɒl'kænɪk/ adj volcánico

volcano /vɑːl'keɪnəʊ ‖vɒl'keɪməʊ/ n (pl **-noes** or **-nos**) volcán m

volition /vəʊ'lɪʃən ‖və'lɪʃən/ n (frml) volición f (frml); **of one's own ∼** por voluntad propia, (de) motu proprio

volley¹ /'vɑːli ‖'vɒli/ n [1] (of shots) descarga f (cerrada) [2] (Sport) volea f

volley² vt/i volear

volleyball /'vɑːlibɔːl ‖'vɒlibɔːl/ n vóleibol m, balonvolea m

volt /vəʊlt/ n voltio m

voltage /'vəʊltɪdʒ/ n voltaje m

volume /'vɑːljuːm ‖'vɒljuːm/ *n* **1** (Phys) (of a body) volumen *m*; (of container) capacidad *f* **2** (amount) cantidad *f*, volumen *m*; (of business, trade) volumen *m* **3** (of sound) volumen *m* **4** (book) tomo *m*, volumen *m*

voluminous /və'luːmənəs ‖və'luːmɪnəs/ *adj* **(a)** ⟨*blouse/skirt*⟩ amplísimo **(b)** ⟨*correspondence*⟩ voluminoso

voluntarily /'vɑːlənterəli ‖'vɒləntrɪli/ *adv* voluntariamente, por voluntad propia

voluntary /'vɑːlənteri ‖'vɒləntri/ *adj* **1** (unforced) voluntario; ∼ **redundancy** (BrE) baja *f* incentivada **2** (unpaid) ⟨*work*⟩ voluntario; ⟨*organization*⟩ de beneficencia

volunteer¹ /ˌvɑːlən'tɪr ‖ˌvɒlən'tɪər/ *n* voluntario, -ria *m,f*

volunteer² *vt* ofrecer*
■ ∼ *vi* ofrecerse*; **to** ∼ **to** + INF ofrecerse* A + INF

voluptuous /və'lʌptʃuəs/ *adj* voluptuoso

vomit¹ /'vɑːmət ‖'vɒmɪt/ *vi/t* vomitar

vomit² *n* vómito *m*

voodoo /'vuːduː/ *n* vudú *m*

voracious /vɔː'reɪʃəs ‖və'reɪʃəs/ *adj* voraz

vote¹ /vəʊt/ *n* **1** **(a)** (ballot cast) voto *m* **(b)** (right to vote) **the** ∼ el sufragio, el derecho de *or* al voto **2** (act) votación *f*; **to take a** ∼ **on sth** someter algo a votación

vote² *vi* votar; **to** ∼ **FOR sb** votar POR *or* A algn; **to** ∼ **ON sth** someter algo a votación; **to** ∼ **FOR/ AGAINST sth** votar A FAVOR DE/EN CONTRA DE algo

■ ∼ *vt* **1** **(a)** (support, choose) votar por, votar **(b)** (elect) elegir* por votación **2** (decide) **to** ∼ **to** + INF votar POR + INF
■ **vote in** [*v* + *o* + *adv, v* + *adv* + *o*] elegir* (*por votación*)

voter /'vəʊtər ‖'vəʊtə(r)/ *n* votante *mf*

voting /'vəʊtɪŋ/ *n* votación *f*

vouch /vaʊtʃ/ *vi* **to** ∼ **FOR sb** responder POR algn

voucher /'vaʊtʃər ‖'vaʊtʃə(r)/ *n* (cash substitute) vale *m*

vow¹ /vaʊ/ *n* voto *m*, promesa *f*

vow² *vt* jurar, hacer* voto de (frml)

vowel /'vaʊəl/ *n* vocal *f*

voyage /'vɔɪdʒ/ *n* viaje *m*; (overseas) travesía *f*

voyager /'vɔɪədʒər ‖'vɔɪdʒə(r)/ *n* (liter) viajero, -ra *m,f*; (by sea) navegante *mf*

voyeur /vwɑː'jɜːr, 'vɔɪ- ‖vwɑː'jɜː(r), 'vɔɪ-/ *n* voyeur *mf*

vs = **versus**

VT, Vt = **Vermont**

vulgar /'vʌlgər ‖'vʌlgə(r)/ *adj* **(a)** (coarse) ⟨*person/remark*⟩ grosero, ordinario, vulgar **(b)** (tasteless) de mal gusto, ordinario

vulgarity /vʌl'gærəti/ *n* **(a)** (coarseness) ordinariez *f*, grosería *f*, vulgaridad *f* **(b)** (tastelessness) mal gusto *m*, chabacanería *f*

vulnerable /'vʌlnərəbəl/ *adj* vulnerable

vulture /'vʌltʃər ‖'vʌltʃə(r)/ *n* buitre *m*; (turkey ∼) gallinazo *m*, zopilote *m* (AmC, Méx)

vv = **verses**

Ww

W, w /'dʌbəljuː/ *n* W, w *f*

W (a) (Elec) (= **watt(s)**) W **(b)** (Geog) (= **west**) O

WA = **Washington**

wad /wɑːd ‖wɒd/ *n* (roll, bundle — of bills, notes) fajo *m*; (— of papers) montón *m*, tambache *m* (Méx); (— tied together) lío *m*

waddle /'wɑːdl̩ ‖'wɒdl̩/ *vi* ⟨⟨*person*⟩⟩ caminar *or* andar* como un pato; ⟨⟨*duck*⟩⟩ caminar balanceándose

wade /weɪd/ *vi* caminar (*por el agua, barro etc*)
■ **wade through** [*v* + *prep* + *o*] (colloq) leerse* (*algo difícil, largo, aburrido etc*)

wader /'weɪdər ‖'weɪdə(r)/ *n* **(a)** (Zool) ave *f*‡ zancuda **(b)** **waders** *pl* (Clothing) botas *fpl* de pescador

wading pool /'weɪdɪŋ/ *n* (AmE) piscina *f or* (Méx) alberca *f* inflable (*para niños*)

wafer /'weɪfər ‖'weɪfə(r)/ *n* **(a)** (Culin) galleta *f* de barquillo, oblea *f* **(b)** (Relig) hostia *f*

wafer-thin /'weɪfər'θɪn ‖ˌweɪfə'θɪn/ *adj* finísimo

waffle¹ /'wɑːfəl ‖'wɒfəl/ *n* **1** (Culin) wafle *m* (AmL), gofre *m* (Esp) **2** (nonsense) (BrE pej) palabrería *f*; (in essay, exam) paja *f* (fam)

waffle² *vi* (esp BrE) hablar sin decir nada; (in essay, exam) meter paja (fam), payar (RPl)

waft /wɑːft ‖'wɒft/ *vi* (+ *adv compl*): **the smell of coffee that ∼ed from the kitchen** el olor a café que venía de la cocina

wag /wæg/ -**gg**- *vt* ⟨*tail*⟩ menear
■ ∼ *vi* ⟨⟨*tail*⟩⟩ menearse, moverse*

wage¹ /weɪdʒ/ *n* (rate of pay) sueldo *m*; **wages** (actual money) sueldo *m*, paga *f*

wage² *vt*: **to** ∼ **war** hacer* la guerra

wager¹ /'weɪdʒər ‖'weɪdʒə(r)/ *n* apuesta *f*

wager² *vt* apostar*

waggon *n* (BrE) ▶ WAGON

wagon /'wægən/ *n* **1** (drawn by animals) carro *m*; (covered) carromato *m* **2** **(a)** (delivery truck) (AmE) furgoneta *f or* camioneta *f* de reparto **(b)** (BrE Rail) vagón *m* de mercancías

waif /weɪf/ *n* (liter) persona o animal sin hogar

wail¹ /weɪl/ *vi* ⟨⟨*person*⟩⟩ llorar; ⟨⟨*siren/ bagpipes*⟩⟩ gemir*; ⟨⟨*wind*⟩⟩ aullar*

wail² *n* gemido *m*

waist /weɪst/ n (of body) cintura f; (of garment) talle m

waist: ~band n pretina f, cinturilla f; ~coat n (esp BrE) chaleco m; ~line n (of garment) talle m; (of body) cintura f

wait¹ /weɪt/ vi [1] esperar; **we'll have to ~ and see** habrá que esperar a ver qué pasa; **I can't ~ to see his face** me muero de ganas de ver la cara que pone; **to ~ FOR sth/sb** esperar algo/a algn; **to ~ FOR sb/sth to + INF** esperar (A) QUE algn/algo (+ subj) [2] (serve) **to ~ ON sb** atender* a algn
■ ~ vt [1] (await) esperar; **you have to ~ your turn** tienes que esperar (a) que te toque [2] (serve): **to ~ table** (AmE) servir* a la mesa
■ **wait up** [v + adv] (not go to bed) **to ~ up (FOR sb)** esperar (A algn) levantado

wait² n (no pl) espera f; **to lie in ~ for sb/sth** estar* al acecho de algn/algo

waiter /'weɪtər ‖'weɪtə(r)/ n camarero m, mesero m (AmL), mozo m (Col, CS), mesonero m (Ven)

waiting /'weɪtɪŋ/: **~ list** n lista f de espera; **~ room** n sala f de espera

waitress /'weɪtrəs ‖'weɪtrɪs/ n camarera f, mesera f (AmL), moza f (Col, CS), mesonera f (Ven)

waive /weɪv/ vt (frml) **(a)** (not apply) ⟨rule⟩ no aplicar*; ⟨condition⟩ no exigir* **(b)** (renounce) ⟨right/privilege⟩ renunciar a

wake¹ /weɪk/ (past **woke**; past p **woken**) vt despertar*; see also WAKE UP 1
■ ~ vi despertar*, despertarse*
■ **wake up** [1] [v + o + adv, v + adv + o] despertar* [2] [v + adv] (become awake) despertarse*; **~ up!** ¡despiértate!; (pay attention) ¡espabílate!, ¡despabílate!; **to ~ up to sth** ⟨to danger/fact⟩ darse* cuenta de algo

wake² n [1] (of ship) estela f; **the hurricane left a trail of destruction in its ~** el huracán dejó una estela de destrucción a su paso [2] (for dead person) velatorio m

Wales /weɪlz/ n (el país de) Gales

walk¹ /wɔːk/ vi [1] (go by foot) caminar, andar* (esp Esp); (in a leisurely way) pasear; **he ~ed down/up the steps** bajó/subió los peldaños; **to ~ in/out** entrar/salir*; **to ~ up to sb** acercarse* a algn [2] (not use bus, car, etc) ir* a pie
■ ~ vt [1] (go along) ⟨hills/path⟩ recorrer [2] **(a)** (take for walk) ⟨dog⟩ pasear, sacar* a pasear **(b)** (accompany) acompañar
■ **walk away** [v + adv] alejarse
■ **walk into** [v + prep + o] **(a)** (enter) ⟨room/building⟩ entrar en, entrar a (AmL) **(b)** (fall into) ⟨trap⟩ caer* en **(c)** (collide with) darse* contra
■ **walk off** [1] [v + adv] (go away) irse*, marcharse (esp Esp) [2] [v + o + adv, v + adv + o]: **we went out to ~ off our lunch** salimos a dar un paseo para bajar la comida
■ **walk out** [v + adv] (Lab Rel) abandonar el trabajo (como media reivindicatoria)
■ **walk out on** [v + adv + prep + o] ⟨lover/family⟩ dejar, abandonar
■ **walk over** [v + prep + o] (colloq): **don't let him ~ all over you** no te dejes pisotear (por él)

walk² n [1] (leisurely) paseo m; (long) caminata f; **to go for a ~** ir* a pasear or a dar un paseo, ir* a caminar (esp AmL); **it's five minutes' o a**

five-minute ~ from here está a cinco minutos de aquí a pie [2] (path) (esp AmE) camino m [3] (gait) manera f de caminar or andar; see also WALK OF LIFE

walker /'wɔːkər ‖'wɔːkə(r)/ n **(a)** (sb that walks): **to be a fast/slow ~** caminar or andar* rápido/despacio **(b)** (hiker) excursionista mf

walkie-talkie /'wɔːki'tɔːki/ n walkie-talkie m

walk-in /'wɔːkɪn/ adj: **~ closet** vestidor m

walking¹ /'wɔːkɪŋ/ n: **I do a lot of ~** yo camino or ando mucho; (before n) ⟨tour⟩ a pie; **is it within ~ distance?** ¿se puede ir a pie?

walking² adj: **she's a ~ encyclopedia** (hum) es una enciclopedia ambulante (hum); **he's a ~ miracle** vive de milagro

walking stick n bastón m

Walkman® /'wɔːkmən/ n (pl **-mans** /-mənz/) walkman® m

walk: **~ of life** n: **people from all ~s of life** gente de todas las profesiones y condiciones sociales; **~on** (before n) ~on part (Theat) papel m de figurante; (Cin) papel m de extra; **~out** n (from talks, meeting) retirada en señal de protesta; (strike) abandono del trabajo como medida reivindicatoria; **~over** n (victory by default) walkover m (victoria por la no comparecencia del contrincante); (easy victory) (colloq) paseo m (fam); **~way** n (bridge) puente m, pasarela f; (passageway) pasillo m; (path) sendero m

wall /wɔːl/ n [1] **(a)** (freestanding) muro m; (of castle, city) muralla f; **garden ~** tapia f, muro m **(b)** (barrier) barrera f; **a ~ of fire** una barrera de fuego [2] (of building, room) pared f, muralla f (Chi); (before n) **~ chart** gráfico m mural; **~ painting** mural m [3] (of stomach, artery) pared f
■ **wall off** [v + o + adv, v + adv + o] separar con un muro or una pared or una tapia
■ **wall up** [v + o + adv, v + adv + o] ⟨doorway/window⟩ tapiar; ⟨person/body⟩ emparedar

walled /wɔːld/ adj ⟨city⟩ amurallado; ⟨garden⟩ tapiado

wallet /'wɑːlət ‖'wɒlɪt/ n **(a)** (for money) cartera f, billetera f **(b)** (folder) carpeta f

wallflower /'wɔːlflaʊr ‖'wɔːlflaʊə(r)/ n [1] (Bot) alhelí m [2] (person) (colloq): **she was always a ~** nunca la sacaban a bailar, siempre planchaba (Bol, CS fam), siempre comía pavo (Col fam)

wallop /'wɑːləp ‖'wɒləp/ vt (colloq) darle* una paliza a

wallow /'wɑːləʊ ‖'wɒləʊ/ vi **(a)** (bathe) ⟨animal⟩ revolcarse* **(b)** (delight): **to ~ in self-pity** regodearse en la autocompasión

wall: **~paper** n papel m pintado, tapiz m de empapelar (Méx, Ven); **W~ Street** n Wall Street (centro financiero de los EEUU); **~-to-~ carpet** /'wɔːltə'wɔːl/ n alfombra f de pared a pared, moqueta f (Esp), moquette f (RPl)

walnut /'wɔːlnʌt/ n **(a)** (nut) nuez f, nuez f de Castilla (Méx) **(b)** **~ (tree)** nogal m **(c)** (wood) nogal m

walrus /'wɔːlrəs/ n (pl **~es** or **~**) morsa f

waltz¹ /wɔːls, wɔːlts/ n vals m

waltz² vi valsar, valsear

wan /wɑːn ‖wɒn/ adj **(a)** (pallid) ⟨face/complexion⟩ pálido **(b)** ⟨smile⟩ lánguido

wand /wɑ:nd ‖wɒnd/ n (of sorcerer, conjurer) varita f mágica

wander¹ /'wɑ:ndər ‖'wɒndə(r)/ vi (a) (+ adv compl) (walk — in a leisurely way) pasear; (— aimlessly) deambular, vagar* **(b)** (stray): **don't let the children ~ away from the car** no dejes que los niños se alejen del coche; **don't let your mind ~!** ¡no te distraigas!

wander² n (esp BrE) (no pl) vuelta f, paseo m

wanderer /'wɑ:ndərər ‖'wɒndərə(r)/ n trotamundos mf

wanderings /'wɑ:ndərɪŋz ‖'wɒndərɪŋz/ pl n correrías fpl

wanderlust /'wɑ:ndərlʌst ‖'wɒndəlʌst/ n ansias fpl de conocer mundo

wane¹ /weɪn/ vi **(a)** «moon» menguar* **(b)** «interest/popularity» decaer*, disminuir* **(c)** **waning** pres p «moon» menguante; «interest/ popularity/influence» decreciente

wane² n: **to be on the ~** «moon» estar* menguando; «popularity» estar* decayendo or disminuyendo

wangle /'wæŋɡəl/ vt (colloq) agenciarse (fam)

want¹ /wɒnt ‖wɒnt/ vt **1** **(a)** (require, desire) querer*; **to ~ to + INF** querer* + INF; **to ~ sb/sth to + INF** querer* que algn/algo (+ subj) **(b)** «police» buscar*; **☻ wanted** se busca **(c)** (as price for sth) pedir* **(d)** «person» (sexually) desear **2** (need) necesitar; **☻ gardener wanted** se necesita or se precisa jardinero; **you ~ to see a doctor** tienes que ver a un médico;
■ **~** vi (lack) (usu with neg): **you/they will ~ for nothing** no te/les faltará nada

want² n **1** (requirement, need) necesidad f **2** (lack, absence) falta f, carencia f (frml); **for ~ of sth** a falta de algo; **for ~ of a better word** por así decirlo **3** (destitution, penury) miseria f

wanted /'wɒntəd ‖'wɒntɪd/ adj «criminal/ terrorist» buscado (por la policía); see also WANT¹ 1B

wanton /'wɒntn̩ ‖'wɒntən/ adj **(a)** (willful) sin sentido, gratuito **(b)** (licentious) licencioso

war /wɔ:r ‖wɔ:(r)/ n guerra f; **to be at ~ with sb/sth** estar* en guerra con algn/algo; **the ~ on crime** la lucha contra la delincuencia; (before n) **~ memorial** monumento m a los caídos

warble /'wɔ:rbəl ‖'wɔ:bəl/ vi trinar, gorjear

ward /wɔ:rd ‖wɔ:d/ n **1** (in hospital) sala f **2** (person) pupilo, -la m,f
■ **ward off** [v + adv + o] «attack» rechazar*; «blow» desviar*; «danger» conjurar; «illness» protegerse* contra

warden /'wɔ:rdn̩ ‖'wɔ:dn̩/ n (of castle, museum) guardián, -diana m,f; (of hostel, home) encargado, -da m,f; (of university, college) rector, -tora m,f; (church~) coadjutor m; (fire ~) (AmE) encargado, -da m,f de la lucha contra incendios; (game ~) guardabosque(s) mf; (of prison) (AmE) director, -tora m,f (de una cárcel)

warder /'wɔ:rdər ‖'wɔ:də(r)/ n (BrE) celador, -dora m,f (de una cárcel)

wardrobe /'wɔ:rdrəʊb ‖'wɔ:drəʊb/ n **(a)** (clothes cupboard) armario m, ropero m (esp AmL) **(b)** (set of clothes) guardarropa m, vestuario m

warehouse /'werhaʊs ‖'weəhaʊs/ n depósito m, almacén m, bodega f (Chi, Col, Méx)

wares /werz ‖weəz/ pl n mercancía(s) f(pl), mercadería(s) f(pl) (AmS)

war: ~fare n guerra f; **~head** n cabeza f, ojiva f

warily /'werəli ‖'weərɪli/ adv con cautela, cautelosamente

warlike /'wɔ:rlaɪk ‖'wɔ:laɪk/ adj guerrero

warm¹ /wɔ:rm ‖wɔ:m/ adj **-er, -est** **1** «water/day» tibio, templado; «climate/wind» cálido; **the ~est room in the house** la habitación más caliente de la casa; **I'm lovely and ~ now** estoy muy calentito ahora; **~ clothes** ropa f de abrigo or (RPl, Ven tb) abrigada or (Andes, Méx tb) abrigadora; **to get ~** «person» entrar en calor, calentarse*; «room» calentarse* **2** **(a)** (affectionate, cordial) «person» cariñoso; «welcome» caluroso **(b)** «color/atmosphere» cálido **3** (fresh) «scent/trail» reciente, fresco

warm² vt calentar*
■ **~** vi **(a)** (become hotter) calentarse* **(b)** (become affectionate) **to ~ TO o TOWARD sb: we soon ~ed to** o **toward her** pronto se ganó nuestra simpatía
■ **warm over** [v + o + adv, v + adv + o] (AmE Culin) calentar*
■ **warm up** **1** [v + adv] **(a)** (become warmer) «place/food» calentarse*; «person» entrar en calor **(b)** «engine/apparatus» calentarse* **(c)** (become lively) «party/match» animarse **(d)** (for action) «athlete» hacer* ejercicios de calentamiento **2** [v + o + adv, v + adv + o] **(a)** (heat) «food/place» calentar* **(b)** «engine/ apparatus» calentar* **(c)** (make lively) animar

warm: ~-blooded /'wɔ:rm'blʌdəd ‖,wɔ:m'blʌdɪd/ adj «animal» de sangre caliente; **~-hearted** /'wɔ:rm'hɑ:rtəd ‖,wɔ:m'hɑ:tɪd/ adj afectuoso

warmly /'wɔ:rmli ‖'wɔ:mli/ adv «congratulate/ welcome» calurosamente; «smile» afectuosamente

warmth /wɔ:rmθ ‖wɔ:mθ/ n **(a)** (heat) calor m **(b)** (of welcome) lo caluroso **(c)** (of color, atmosphere) calidez f

warm-up /'wɔ:rmʌp ‖'wɔ:mʌp/ n (exercise) ejercicio m de calentamiento; (practice) (pre)calentamiento m

warn /wɔ:rn ‖wɔ:n/ vt **(a)** (admonish) advertir*; **we had been ~ed not to go** nos habían advertido que no fuéramos **(b)** (inform, advise) avisar, advertir*; **we were ~ed against swimming in the river** nos advirtieron que era peligroso nadar en el río

warning /'wɔ:rnɪŋ ‖'wɔ:nɪŋ/ n **(a)** (advice, threat) advertencia f **(b)** (prior notice) aviso m; **they arrived without ~** llegaron sin avisar or sin previo aviso

warp /wɔ:rp ‖wɔ:p/ vt «wood/metal» alabear

warped /wɔ:rpt ‖wɔ:pt/ adj «timber/metal» alabeado; «record» combado; «mind/sense of humor» retorcido

warplane /'wɔ:rpleɪn ‖'wɔ:pleɪn/ n avión m de combate

warrant¹ /'wɔ:rənt ‖'wɒrənt/ n (written authorization) (Law) orden f judicial; (search ~) orden f de registro or (AmL tb) de allanamiento; **to have a ~ for sb's arrest** tener* una orden de arresto contra algn

warrant² vt **1** (justify) justificar* **2** (guarantee) (often pass) garantizar*

W

warranty /'wɔːrənti ‖'wɒrənti/ n (pl **-ties**) garantía f

warren /'wɔːrən ‖'wɒrən/ n (Zool) madriguera f (de conejos), conejera f

warring /'wɔːrɪŋ/ adj (before n) ‹countries/ tribes› en guerra; ‹factions› enfrentado

warrior /'wɔːrjər ‖'wɒriə(r)/ n guerrero, -ra m,f

Warsaw /'wɔːrsɔː ‖'wɔːsɔː/ n Varsovia f

warship /'wɔːrʃɪp ‖'wɔːʃɪp/ n buque m de guerra

wart /wɔːrt ‖wɔːt/ n verruga f

war: ~**time** n: in ~**time** en tiempo de guerra; ~**torn** adj devastado por la guerra

wary /'weri ‖'weəri/ adj **warier, wariest** cauteloso; to be ~ OF sb/sth no fiarse* DE algn/ algo

was /wɑːz, weak form wəz ‖wɒz, weak form wəz/ past of BE

wash[1] /wɔːʃ ‖wɒʃ/ n [1] (a) (act): to have a ~ lavarse; I'll give the car a ~ voy a lavar el coche, voy a darle una lavada al coche (AmL) (b) (in washing machine) lavado m; your shirt is in the ~ tu camisa está lavándose [2] (left by boat, plane) estela f

wash[2] vt [1] (clean) ‹shirt/car/fruit› lavar; ‹floor› fregar*, lavar (esp AmL); to ~ one's face/hair lavarse la cara/la cabeza or el pelo; to ~ the dishes fregar* or lavar los platos [2] (carry away) (+ adv compl): the body had been ~ed ashore by the tide la corriente había arrastrado el cuerpo hasta la orilla; see also WASH AWAY, WASH UP

■ ~ vi (a) (clean oneself) lavarse (b) (do dishes) lavar, fregar* (c) (do laundry) «washing machine/ person» lavar (la ropa), hacer* la colada (Esp)

■ **wash away** [v + o + adv, v + adv + o] (a) (carry away) llevarse (b) (cleanse) ‹dirt› quitar (lavando)

■ **wash down** [v + o + adv, v + adv + o] (a) (clean) ‹paintwork/wall› lavar (b) (accompany) (colloq): a plate of pasta ~ed down with the local wine un plato de pasta acompañado del vino de la región

■ **wash out** [1] [v + o + adv, v + adv + o] ‹sink/ cloth› (clean) lavar; (rinse) enjuagar* [2] [v + adv] (disappear): the stain will ~ out la mancha saldrá or se quitará al lavarlo

■ **wash up** [1] [v + adv] (a) (wash oneself) (AmE) lavarse (b) (wash dishes) (BrE) lavar los platos, fregar* (los platos) [2] [v + o + adv, v + adv + o] (a) (deposit) (usu pass) to be ~ed up ‹body/wreckage› ser* traído por la corriente (b) ‹dishes› (BrE) lavar, fregar*

Wash = Washington

washable /'wɔːʃəbəl ‖'wɒʃəbəl/ adj lavable

wash: ~**basin** n (BrE) ▶ ~BOWL; ~**bowl** n (AmE) (a) (in modern bathroom) lavabo m, lavamanos m, lavatorio m (CS), pileta f (RPl) (b) (bowl) palangana f, jofaina f, lavatorio m (Chi, Per); ~**cloth** n (AmE) toallita f (para lavarse), ≈ manopla f

washed-out /'wɔːʃt'aʊt ‖,wɒʃt'aʊt/ adj (pred **washed out**) (a) ‹fabric› descolorido; ‹color› pálido, lavado (RPl fam) (b) (exhausted) rendido

washer /'wɔːʃər ‖'wɒʃə(r)/ n [1] (Tech) (ring) arandela f; (— on faucet) arandela f, junta f, suela f universal, cuerito m (CS fam), empaque m (Col, Ven) [2] ▶ WASHING MACHINE

washing /'wɔːʃɪŋ ‖'wɒʃɪŋ/ n (a) (laundry — dirty) ropa f para lavar; (— clean) ropa f lavada; to do the ~ lavar la ropa, hacer* la colada (Esp) (b) (act) lavado m

washing: ~ **line** n (BrE) cuerda f para tender la ropa; ~ **machine** n máquina f de lavar, lavadora f, lavarropas m (RPl); ~ **powder** n (esp BrE) jabón m en polvo, detergente m; ~**-up** /'wɔːʃɪŋ'ʌp ‖,wɒʃɪŋ'ʌp/ n (BrE): to do the ~**-up** lavar los platos, fregar* (los platos); (before n) ~**-up liquid** lavavajillas m

wash: ~**out** n (failure) (colloq) desastre m (fam); ~**room** n baño(s) m(pl), servicios mpl (esp Esp)

wasn't /'wɑːznt ‖'wɒznt/ = **was not**

wasp /wɑːsp ‖wɒsp/ n avispa f

WASP /wɑːsp ‖wɒsp/ n (esp AmE) (= **white Anglo-Saxon Protestant**) persona de la clase privilegiada de los EEUU, blanca, anglosajona y protestante

waspish /'wɑːspɪʃ ‖'wɒspɪʃ/ adj sardónico

wastage /'weɪstɪdʒ/ n: there is too much ~ of raw material se desperdicia demasiada materia prima; **natural** ~ (of workforce) bajas fpl vegetativas

waste[1] /weɪst/ n [1] (of fuel, materials) desperdicio m; a ~ of time una pérdida de tiempo; it's a ~ of money es tirar el dinero; to go to ~ «talent» desperdiciarse; «food» echarse a perder [2] (a) (refuse) residuos mpl (b) (surplus matter) material m sobrante [3] **wastes** (pl): the deserted ~s of Antarctica las desiertas inmensidades de la Antártica

waste[2] vt [1] ‹talents/efforts› desperdiciar; ‹money/electricity› despilfarrar; ‹food› tirar; ‹time› perder*; ‹space› desaprovechar [2] **wasted** past p (a) (misused, futile) ‹time/ money› perdido; ‹opportunity/space› desperdiciado; ‹effort› inútil (b) (shrunken) ‹body› debilitado; ‹limb› atrofiado

■ **waste away** [v + adv] «person/body» consumirse; «muscle» atrofiarse

waste[3] adj [1] ‹ground› (barren) yermo; (not cultivated) baldío; to lay ~ (to) sth arrasar algo [2] ‹material/matter› de desecho

waste: ~**basket** n (esp AmE) ▶ WASTE-PAPER BASKET; ~ **disposal unit** n triturador m or trituradora f de desperdicios

wasteful /'weɪstfəl/ adj ‹person› despilfarrador; ‹method› poco económico

waste: ~**land** n (often pl) (barren land) páramo m, tierra f yerma or baldía; (uncultivated land) erial m; ~ **paper** n papel m sobrante; ~**paper basket**, ~**-paper bin** /'weɪst'peɪpər ‖,weɪst'peɪpə(r)/ n papelera f, papelero m (CS); ~ **pipe** n tubo m de desagüe

AmC	América Central	Arg	Argentina	Cu	Cuba	Per	Perú
AmL	América Latina	Bol	Bolivia	Ec	Ecuador	RPl	Río de la Plata
AmS	América del Sur	Chi	Chile	Esp	España	Ur	Uruguay
Andes	Región andina	CS	Cono Sur	Méx	México	Ven	Venezuela

watch¹ /wɑːtʃ ‖wɒtʃ/ *n* **1** (timepiece) reloj *m* (*de pulsera/de bolsillo*); (*before n*) ~ **band** *o* (BrE) **strap** correa *f* de reloj **2** (observation) vigilancia *f*; **to keep** ~ hacer* guardia **3** **(a)** (period of time) guardia *f* **(b)** (individual) guardia *m/f*; (group) guardia *f*

watch² *vt* **1** ‹*person/expression*› observar; ‹*movie/game*› mirar; **to** ~ **television** ver* televisión; **we** ~**ed the sun go down** miramos la puesta de sol

2 (a) (keep under observation) ‹*suspect/house*› vigilar **(b)** (look after) ‹*luggage/children*› cuidar **(c)** (pay attention to) mirar (con atención) **3** (be careful of) ‹*diet/weight*› vigilar, tener* cuidado con; ~ **it!** (colloq) ¡cuidado!

■ ~ *vi* (look on) mirar

■ **watch out** [*v + adv*] **(a)** (be careful) tener* cuidado; ~ **out!** ¡(ten) cuidado!, ¡ojo! (fam), ¡abusado! Méx fam) **(b)** (look carefully) estarse* atento; ~ **out for spelling mistakes** estáte atento por si hay faltas de ortografía

■ **watch over** [*v + prep + o*] ‹*patient/child*› cuidar (de); ‹*safety/interests*› velar por

watchdog /'wɑːtʃdɔːg ‖'wɒtʃdɒg/ *n* (dog) perro *m* guardián; (group) organismo *m* de control

watchful /'wɑːtʃfəl ‖'wɒtʃfəl/ *adj* vigilante

watch: ~**maker** *n* relojero, -ra *m,f*; ~**man** /'wɑːtʃmən ‖'wɒtʃmən/ *n* (*pl* **-men** /mən/) vigilante *m*; ~**tower** *n* atalaya *f*, torre *f* de vigilancia

water¹ /'wɔːtər ‖'wɔːtə(r)/ *n* **1** agua *f*‡; **to be/ lie under** ~ estar*/quedar inundado; **high/low** ~ marea *f* alta/baja; **to pass** ~ (frml & euph) orinar, hacer* aguas menores (euph); **to hold** ~ tenerse* en pie; (*before n*) ‹*bird/plant*› acuático; ~ **sports** deportes *mpl* acuáticos **2 waters** *pl* (of sea, river) aguas *fpl*

water² *vi*: **her eyes began to** ~ empezaron a llorarle los ojos; **his mouth** ~**ed se** le hizo agua la boca (AmL), se le hizo la boca agua (Esp)

■ ~ *vt* ‹*plant/garden/land*› regar*; ‹*livestock*› dar* de beber a

■ **water down** [*v + o + adv, v + adv + o*] ‹*liquid/mixture*› diluir*; ‹*wine/beer*› aguar

water: ~ **bed** *n* cama *f* de agua; ~ **bottle** *n* cantimplora *f*; ~**color,** (BrE) ~**colour** *n* acuarela *f*; ~**cress** *n* berro *m*; ~**fall** *n* cascada *f*, salto *m* de agua; (large) catarata *f*; ~**front** *n* (beside lake, river) zona *f* de una ciudad que bordea un lago o río; (docks) (esp AmE) muelles *mpl*

watering can /'wɔːtərɪŋ/ *n* regadera *f*

water: ~ **lily** *n* nenúfar *m*; ~**logged** /'wɔːtərlɔːgd ‖'wɔːtəlɒgd/ *adj* ‹*land/soil*› anegado, inundado; ‹*shoes*› empapado; ~**mark** *n* filigrana *f*; ~**melon** *n* sandía *f*; ~ **mill** *n* molino *m* de agua; ~ **parting** *n* (AmE) ▶ WATERSHED A

waterproof¹ /'wɔːtərpruːf ‖'wɔːtəpruːf/ *adj* ‹*fabric*› impermeable; ‹*mascara*› a prueba de agua; ‹*watch*› sumergible

waterproof² *n* (esp BrE) prenda *f* impermeable

waterproof³ *vt* impermeabilizar*

water: ~**-resistant** *adj* impermeabilizado, hidrófugo; ~**shed** *n* (Geog) **(a)** (divide) (línea *f*) divisoria *f* de aguas **(b)** (drainage basin) (AmE) cuenca *f*; ~**-ski** *vi* **-skis, -skiing, -skied** hacer* esquí acuático; ~**-skiing** *n* esquí *m* acuático; ~ **table** *n* nivel *m* freático; ~**tight**

adj ‹*seal/container*› hermético; ‹*boat*› estanco; ‹*argument*› irrebatible, sin fisuras; ‹*alibi*› a toda prueba; ~**way** *n* (river) vía *f* fluvial; (canal) vía *f* *or* canal *m* navegable; ~ **wheel** *n* (for driving machinery) rueda *f* hidráulica; (for raising water) noria *f*; ~ **wings** *pl n* flotadores *mpl* (*que se colocan en los brazos*)

watery /'wɔːtəri/ *adj* **(a)** (of, like water) acuoso **(b)** ‹*beer/gravy*› aguado **(c)** ‹*eyes*› lloroso

watt /wɑːt ‖wɒt/ *n* vatio *m*

wave¹ /weɪv/ *n* **1 (a)** (of water) ola *f* **(b)** (in hair) onda *f* **(c)** (Phys) onda *f* **2** (surge, movement) oleada *f* **3** (gesture): **she gave them a** ~ les hizo adiós/los saludó con la mano

wave² *vt* **1 (a)** (shake, swing) ‹*handkerchief/ flag*› agitar; **to** ~ **sth around** agitar algo; **she** ~**d goodbye to him** le hizo adiós con la mano **(b)** (direct) (+ *adv compl*): **the policeman** ~**d us on** el policía nos hizo señas para que or de que siguiéramos adelante

2 (curl) ‹*hair*› marcar*, ondular

■ ~ *vi* **1** (signal): **he** ~**d when he saw us** nos saludó con la mano al vernos; **to** ~ **AT** *o* **TO sb** (to say goodbye) hacerle* adiós A algn con la mano; (in greeting) saludar a algn con la mano

2 (sway, flutter) «*corn/trees*» agitarse; «*flag*» ondear

■ **wave aside** [*v + o + adv, v + adv + o*] **(a)** (with hand): **he** ~**d me aside** me hizo señas para que me hiciera a un lado **(b)** ‹*arguments/attempts*› rechazar

wave: ~**band** *n* banda *f* de frecuencia; ~**length** *n* longitud *f* de onda

waver /'weɪvər ‖'weɪvə(r)/ *vi* **1** (falter) «*person*» flaquear; «*faith*» tambalearse **2** (be indecisive) titubear

wavy /'weɪvi/ *adj* **wavier, waviest** ondulado

wax¹ /wæks/ *n* cera *f*; (ear~) cera *f* (de los oídos), cerumen *m*; (sealing ~) lacre *m*

wax² *vt* **(a)** (treat with wax) ‹*floor/table/skis*› encerar **(b)** (to remove hair) depilar con cera

■ ~ *vi* «*moon*» crecer*; **his popularity** ~**ed and waned** su popularidad sufrió muchos altibajos

waxworks /'wækswɜːrks ‖'wækswɜːks/ *n* (*pl* ~**works**) (+ *sing or pl vb*) museo *m* de cera

way¹ /weɪ/ *n*

I 1 (a) (route) camino *m*; **the** ~ **back** el camino de vuelta; **the** ~ **in/out** la entrada/salida; **it's difficult to find one's** ~ **around this town** es difícil orientarse en esta ciudad; **can you find your** ~ **there by yourself?** ¿sabes ir solo?; **I can drop the package off on my** ~ de paso puedo dejar el paquete; **which** ~ **did you come?** ¿por dónde viniste?; **which** ~ **did he go?** ¿por dónde fue?; (following sb) ¿por dónde se fue?; **could you tell me the** ~ **to the city center?** ¿me podría decir por dónde se va al centro (de la ciudad)?; **on my** ~ **to work** de camino al trabajo; **the doctor is on her** ~ la doctora ya va para allí/viene para aquí; **I'll tell you on the** ~ te lo cuento por el camino; **I don't know the** ~ **up/down** no sé por dónde se sube/se baja; **to lead the** ~ ir* delante; **to lose one's** ~ perderse*; **there is no** ~ **around it** no hay otra solución; **to go out of one's** ~ (make a detour) desviarse* del camino; (make special effort): **they went out of their** ~ **to be helpful** se desviaron por ayudar **(b)** (road, path) camino *m*, senda *f*   **·····❖**

[2] (passage, space): **to be/get in the ~** estorbar; **to stand in the ~: they stood in our ~** nos impidieron el paso; **I couldn't see it, she was standing in my ~** no podía verlo, ella me tapaba (la vista); **I won't stand in your ~** no seré yo quien te lo impida; **(get) out of the ~!** ¡hazte a un lado!; **to move sth out of the ~** quitar algo de en medio; **to keep out of sb's ~** rehuir* a algn
[3] (direction): **it's that ~** es en esa dirección, es por ahí; **this ~!** ¡por aquí!; **we didn't know which ~ to go** no sabíamos por dónde ir; **this ~ and that** de un lado a otro; **we're both going the same ~** vamos para el mismo lado; **look the other ~!** ¡mira para otro lado!; **whichever ~ you look at it, it's a disaster** es un desastre, lo mires por donde lo mires; **the other ~ around** al revés; **which ~ up should it be?** ¿cuál es la parte de arriba?; **to split sth three ~s** dividir algo en tres partes; **every which ~** (AmE) para todos lados; **to go sb's ~: are you going my ~?** ¿vas en mi misma dirección?; **the decision went our ~** se decidió en nuestro favor; **~ to go!** (AmE colloq) ¡así se hace!
[4] (distance) (no pl): **there's only a short ~ to go now** ya falta poco para llegar; **it's a long ~ from here to Rio** Río queda muy lejos de aquí; **he's come a long ~** ha venido de muy lejos; **we've come a long ~ since those days** hemos evolucionado mucho desde entonces; **a little goes a long ~** un poco cunde or (AmL fib) rinde mucho; **we had to walk all the ~ up** tuvimos que subir a pie hasta arriba

II [1] (method, means) forma *f*, manera *f*, modo *m*; **there's no ~ of crossing the border without a passport** es imposible cruzar la frontera sin pasaporte; **it doesn't matter to me one ~ or the other** me da igual una cosa u otra; **all right, we'll do it your ~** muy bien, lo haremos a tu manera; **to do sth the hard/easy ~** hacer* algo de manera difícil/fácil; **to have it both ~s** querer* todo, querer* la chancha y los cinco reales or los veinte** (RPl fam); **you can't have it both ~s** tienes que elegir entre una cosa u otra
[2] (manner) manera *f*, modo *m*, forma *f*; **in a subtle ~** de manera or modo or forma sutil; **he's in a bad ~** está muy mal; **that's the ~ it goes** así son las cosas, así es la vida; **it looks that ~** así or eso parece; **this ~ it's better for everyone** así es mejor para todos; **the ~ I see it** tal y como yo lo veo; **to have a ~ with ...: to have a ~ with children/animals** saber* cómo tratar a los niños/tener* mano con los animales; **to have a ~ with words** tener* mucha facilidad de palabra
[3] (a) (custom, characteristic): **the ~s of our people** las costumbres de nuestro pueblo; **he has a ~ of making people feel at ease** sabe hacer que la gente se sienta cómoda; **to be set in one's ~s** estar* muy acostumbrado a hacer las cosas de cierta manera (b) (wish, will): **to get/have one's (own) ~** salirse* con la suya (or *más etc*)
[4] (feature, respect) sentido *m*, aspecto *m*; **in a ~, it's like losing an old friend** de alguna manera or en cierta forma es como perder a un viejo amigo; **our product is in no ~ inferior to theirs** nuestro producto no es de ninguna manera inferior al suyo

III (in phrases) [1] **by the way** (indep) a propósito, por cierto
[2] **by way of** (as prep) (a) (via) vía, pasando por (b) (to serve as) a modo or manera de

[3] **in the way of** (as regards) (as prep): **don't expect too much in the ~ of help** en cuanto a ayuda, no esperes mucho
[4] **no way** (colloq): **no ~ is he going to do it** de ninguna manera lo va a hacer (fam); **no ~!** ¡ni hablar! (fam)
[5] **to give way (a)** (break, collapse) «*ice/rope/cable*» romperse*; «*floor*» hundirse **(b)** (succumb, give in) **to give ~ TO sth** ‹*to threats/blackmail*› ceder A or ANTE algo **(c)** (BrE Transp) **to give ~ (TO sb/sth)** ceder el paso (A algn/algo) **(d)** (be replaced, superseded by) **to give ~ TO sth** dejar or dar* paso A algo
[6] **under way: to get under ~** ponerse* en marcha; **an investigation is under ~** se está llevando a cabo una investigación

way² *adv* (colloq): **~ back in February** allá por febrero; **~ behind** muy por detrás; **they were ~ out in their calculations** se equivocaron en mucho en los cálculos; **~ past midnight** mucho después de la medianoche; **~ and away** (as intensifier) (AmE) con mucho, lejos (AmL fam)

way: **~lay** /'weɪleɪ/ *vt* (past & past p **~laid**) abordar; **~-out** /'weɪ'aʊt/ *adj* (pred ~ **up**) (colloq) ultramoderno, estrambótico (fam); **~s and means** *pl n* **~s and means (OF -ING)** métodos *mpl* (DE + INF)

we /wiː, *weak form* wi/ *pron*

■ **Note** Although *pron nosotros* and *nosotras* are given as translations of *we*, in practice they are used only for emphasis: *we went to the theater* fuimos al teatro; *we did it* nosotros or nosotras lo hicimos.

nosotros, -tras; **~ English** nosotros los ingleses

weak /wiːk/ *adj* **-er, -est** [1] **(a)** ‹*person/muscles/economy*› débil; ‹*structure*› poco sólido, endeble; ‹*handshake*› flojo; **to have a ~ heart** sufrir del corazón; **to grow ~** debilitarse **(b)** (ineffectual) ‹*character/leader*› débil [2] **(a)** (not competent) ‹*student/performance*› flojo **(b)** (not convincing) ‹*argument/excuse*› poco convincente [3] (diluted) ‹*coffee/tea*› poco cargado; ‹*beer*› suave; ‹*solution*› diluido

weaken /'wiːkən/ *vt* debilitar
■ *vi* «*person/animal*» (physically) debilitarse; «*resolve*» flaquear; «*power*» debilitarse; (relent) ceder

weakling /'wiːklɪŋ/ *n* alfeñique *m*

weakly /'wiːkli/ *adv* ‹*say*› con voz débil; **he struggled ~ and then gave in** se rindió sin apenas oponer resistencia

weakness /'wiːknəs ‖ 'wiːknɪs/ *n* [1] **(a)** (of body, defenses) debilidad *f*; (of structure, material) falta *f* de solidez, endeblez *f*; (of argument) pobreza *f* **(b)** (ineffectualness) falta *f* de carácter [2] **(a)** (weak point — in structure, policy) punto *m* débil; (— in character) flaqueza *f*, punto *m* débil **(b)** (liking) debilidad *f*; **to have a ~ for sth** tener* debilidad por algo

weak-willed /'wiːk'wɪld/ *adj* ‹*person*› de poca (fuerza de) voluntad; **to be ~** tener* poca fuerza de voluntad

weal /wiːl/ *n* verdugón *m* (de un golpe dado con una cuerda, correa etc)

wealth /welθ/ *n* [1] riqueza *f* [2] (large quantity): **a ~ of sth** abundancia *f* de algo

wealthy /'welθi/ *adj* **-thier, -thiest** ‹*person/family*› adinerado, rico; ‹*nation/area*› rico

wean /wiːn/ vt ⟨baby/young⟩ destetar; **to ~ sb OFF sth**: **we ~ed him off drugs** conseguimos que dejara las drogas, conseguimos desengancharle de las drogas (Esp)

weapon /'wepən/ n arma f‡

weaponry /'wepənri/ n armamento m

wear¹ /wer ‖ weə(r)/ n **1** **(a)** (use): **I've had a lot of ~ out of these shoes** les he dado mucho uso a estos zapatos; **carpets that stand hard ~** alfombras que resisten el uso constante **(b)** (damage) desgaste m; **~ and tear** uso m or desgaste natural **2** **(a)** (wearing of clothes): **clothes for evening ~** ropa para la noche **(b)** (clothing) ropa f; **children's ~** ropa de niños

wear² (past **wore**; past p **worn**) vt **1** **(a)** (at specific moment) ⟨clothes/jewelry/watch/makeup⟩ llevar; ⟨glasses⟩ llevar (puesto), usar; ⟨green/black⟩ vestir* de; **what perfume are you ~ing?** ¿qué perfume llevas? **(b)** (usually) ⟨clothes⟩ usar, ponerse*, ⟨glasses⟩ llevar, usar; ⟨makeup/perfume/earrings⟩ usar; **he ~s size 44 shoes** calza (el) 44; **she ~s her hair in a ponytail** se peina con cola de caballo **2** (through use): **the step had been worn smooth** el peldaño se había alisado con el uso; **she's worn holes in the soles** se le han agujereado las suelas
■ ~ vi **1** (through use) ⟨collar/carpet/brakes⟩ gastarse; **to ~ thin** (lit: through use) ⟨cloth/metal⟩ gastarse; ⟨joke⟩ perder* la gracia
2 (last) (+ adv compl) durar; **to ~ well** ⟨cloth/clothes⟩ durar mucho; ⟨person⟩ conservarse bien
■ **wear away** **1** [v + o + adv, v + adv + o] (erode) ⟨rock⟩ desgastar; ⟨pattern/inscription⟩ borrar
2 [v + adv] (become eroded) ⟨rock⟩ desgastarse; ⟨inscription⟩ borrarse
■ **wear down** **1** [v + o + adv, v + adv + o] **(a)** (by friction) ⟨heel/pencil⟩ gastar **(b)** (weaken) ⟨resistance⟩ menoscabar; ⟨person⟩ agotar
2 [v + adv] ⟨heel/tread⟩ gastarse
■ **wear off** [v + adv] **(a)** (be removed) ⟨paint⟩ quitarse **(b)** (disappear) ⟨distress/numbness⟩ pasarse
■ **wear on** [v + adv] ⟨winter/years⟩ pasar (lentamente); ⟨meeting/drought⟩ continuar*
■ **wear out** **1** [v + o + adv, v + adv + o] **(a)** (through use) ⟨shoes/carpet/batteries⟩ gastar **(b)** (exhaust) ⟨person⟩ agotar
2 [v + adv] (through use) ⟨shoes/towel/batteries⟩ gastarse
■ **wear through** [v + adv] (get hole in) ⟨soles/cloth⟩ agujerearse

wearily /'wɪrəli ‖ 'wɪərɪli/ adv ⟨walk/move⟩ cansinamente; **he sighed ~** suspiró cansado

weary¹ /'wɪri ‖ 'wɪərɪ/ adj **-rier**, **-riest** ⟨person/legs⟩ cansado; ⟨sigh⟩ de cansancio; **to be ~ OF sth/-ING** estar* cansado or harto DE algo/+ INF

weary² vt **-ries**, **-rying**, **-ried** **(a)** (tire) cansar **(b)** (annoy) hartar, cansar

weasel /'wiːzəl/ n (Zool) comadreja f

weather¹ /'weðər ‖ 'weðə(r)/ n tiempo m; **what's the ~ like?** ¿cómo está el tiempo?, ¿qué tiempo hace?; **you can't go out in this ~** no puedes salir con este tiempo; (before n) ⟨map/chart⟩ meteorológico; **~ forecast** pronóstico m del tiempo

weather² vt **(a)** (wear) ⟨rocks⟩ erosionar; ⟨surface⟩ desgastar; ⟨skin/face⟩ curtir **(b)** ⟨wood⟩ secar*
■ ~ vi ⟨rock⟩ erosionarse; ⟨surface⟩ desgastarse

weather: **~beaten** adj ⟨face/sailor⟩ curtido; ⟨walls/rocks⟩ azotado por los elementos; **~cock** n veleta f

weathered /'weðərd ‖ 'weðəd/ adj ⟨rocks/brick/stone⟩ erosionado (por la acción de los elementos); ⟨wood⟩ curado

weather: **~man** /'weðərmæn ‖ 'weðəmæn/ n (pl **-men** /-men/) hombre que transmite el pronóstico del tiempo por radio o televisión; **~proof** adj impermeable; **~ vane** /veɪn/ n veleta f

weave /wiːv/ vt (past **wove**; past p **woven**) **(a)** ⟨cloth/mat⟩ tejer (en telar); ⟨basket/web⟩ tejer; ⟨story/plot⟩ tejer **(b)** (thread together) ⟨threads/branches/straw⟩ entretejer
■ ~ vi **1** (past **wove**; past p **woven**) (make cloth, baskets) tejer **2** (past **wove** or **weaved**; past p **woven** or **weaved**) ⟨road⟩ serpentear; ⟨person⟩ zigzaguear

weaver /'wiːvər ‖ 'wiːvə(r)/ n tejedor, -dora m,f

weaving /'wiːvɪŋ/ n (of cloth) tejido m

web /web/ n **(a)** (spider's ~) telaraña f **(b)** ⟨of intrigue⟩ una red de intriga (Comput): **World Wide ~** telaraña f mundial

webbed /webd/ adj palmeado

web: **W~ page** n (Comput) página f web; **W~ site** n (Comput) sitio m web

wed /wed/ vt (past & past p **wedded** or **wed**) (marry) ⟨gallant or journ⟩ ⟨man/woman⟩ casarse con

we'd /wiːd/ **(a)** = **we had** **(b)** = **we would**

wedding /'wedɪŋ/ n **(a)** (ceremony) boda f, casamiento m, matrimonio m (AmS exc RPl); **to have a church/civil** (AmE) o (BrE) **registry-office ~** casarse por la iglesia or (RPl) por iglesia/por lo civil or (Per, RPl, Ven) por civil or (Chi, Méx) por el civil; (before n) **~ dress** vestido m or traje m de novia; **~ ring** alianza f, anillo m de boda, argolla f (de matrimonio) (Chi) **(b)** (anniversary): **silver/golden ~** bodas fpl de plata/oro

wedge¹ /wedʒ/ n **(a)** (for securing) cuña f **(b)** (for splitting) cuña f **(c)** (shape): **a ~ of cake** un trozo grande de pastel

wedge² vt **(a)** (secure): **to ~ a door open** ponerle* una cuña a una puerta para que no se cierre **(b)** (squeeze) meter (a presión)

Wednesday /'wenzdeɪ, -di/ n miércoles m; see also MONDAY

wee¹ /wiː/ adj (small) (esp Scot, IrE) pequeño, chico (esp AmL); **in the ~ small hours** (AmE also) **the ~ hours** a las altas horas de la madrugada

wee² n (BrE colloq): **to have** o **do a ~** hacer* pis or pipí (fam), hacer* del uno (Méx, Per fam)

weed¹ /wiːd/ n **(a)** (Hort) hierbajo m, mala hierba f, yuyo m (RPl), maleza f (AmL) **(b)** (aquatic growth) algas fpl

weed² vt deshierbar, desherbar*, desmalezar* (AmL), sacar* los yuyos de (RPl)
■ **weed out** [v + o + adv, v + adv + o] **(a)** (Hort) quitar **(b)** ⟨errors/items⟩ eliminar; ⟨applicants⟩ eliminar

weedkiller /'wiːdˌkɪlər ‖ 'wiːdˌkɪlə(r)/ n herbicida m

W

weedy /'wiːdi/ adj **-dier, -diest (a)** (lanky) (AmE) larguirucho (fam) **(b)** (feeble, puny) (BrE colloq) enclenque

week /wiːk/ n **(a)** (7 days) semana f; **once a ~** una vez por semana *or* a la semana; **we get paid by the ~** nos pagan semanalmente; **(on) Tuesday ~ o** (BrE also) **a ~ on Tuesday** el martes que viene no, el otro; **she arrived a ~ (ago) yesterday** ayer hizo una semana que llegó **(b)** (working days): **I never go out in o during the ~** nunca salgo los días de semana

week: ~day n día m de semana; **~end** /'wiːkend ‖ wiːkˈend/ n fin m de semana; **what are you doing on o** (BrE) **at the ~?** ¿qué vas a hacer el fin de semana?

weekly¹ /'wiːkli/ adj semanal

weekly² adv semanalmente; **we get paid ~** nos pagan por semana

weekly³ n (pl **weeklies**) semanario m

weep /wiːp/ vi (past & past p **wept**) **1** (cry) llorar **2** (exude liquid) «wound/eye» supurar

weeping willow /'wiːpɪŋ/ n sauce m llorón

weepy /'wiːpi/ adj **-pier, -piest** (colloq) **1 (a)** «person»: **to feel ~** tener* ganas de llorar **(b)** «film/play» que hace llorar, cebollento (Chi fam) **2** «eye» lloroso

weigh /weɪ/ vt **1** «person/load/food» pesar; **to ~ oneself** pesarse
2 (consider) «factors/arguments/evidence» sopesar; **to ~ one's words** medir* sus (or mis etc) palabras
■ **~** vi (measure in weight) «person/load/food» pesar; **how much o what do you ~?** ¿cuánto pesás?; **your inexperience will ~ against you** tu falta de experiencia será un factor en tu contra
■ **weigh down** [v + o + adv, v + adv + o] **(a)** (impose weight on): **the bag was ~ing me down** la bolsa me pesaba mucho; **trees ~ed down with fruit** árboles cargados de fruta **(b)** (depress) abrumar **(c)** ▶ WEIGHT DOWN
■ **weigh on** [v + prep + o]: **it still ~ed heavily on her conscience** todavía sentía un gran cargo de conciencia; **it's been ~ing heavily on my mind** me ha estado preocupando
■ **weigh out** [v + o + adv, v + adv + o] pesar
■ **weigh up** [v + o + adv, v + adv + o] «situation» considerar; «pros and cons» sopesar; «person» evaluar*

weight¹ /weɪt/ n **1** (mass, heaviness) peso m; **the bag is 5kg in ~** la bolsa pesa 5kg; **you mustn't lift heavy ~s** no debe levantar cosas pesadas; **that has taken a ~ off my mind** eso me ha sacado un peso de encima; **to pull one's ~: John isn't pulling his ~** John no trabaja como debería **2** (importance, value) peso m **3 (a)** (unit) peso m; **~s and measures** pesos y medidas **(b)** (for scales, clocks) pesa f **(c)** (Sport) peso f; **(before n) ~ training** entrenamiento m con pesas

weight² vt (make heavier) darle* peso a; «fishing net» lastrar

weight down [v + o + adv, v + adv + o] **(a)** «tarpaulin/papers» sujetar con algo pesado **(b)** «body» (to make it sink) ponerle* un lastre a

weightless /'weɪtləs ‖ 'weɪtlɪs/ adj ingrávido

weight: ~lifter /'weɪt,lɪftər ‖ 'weɪt,lɪftə(r)/ n levantador, -dora m,f de pesas, pesista mf (Andes), halterófilo, -la m,f; **~lifting** /'weɪt,lɪftɪŋ/ n levantamiento m de pesas, halterofilia f

weighty /'weɪti/ adj **-tier, -tiest** «argument» de peso; «matter» importante

weir /wɪr ‖ wɪə(r)/ n presa f

weird /wɪrd ‖ wɪəd/ adj **-er, -est (a)** (strange) (colloq) raro, extraño **(b)** (unearthly) «apparition/figure» misterioso

welcome¹ /'welkəm/ interj bienvenido

welcome² adj **(a)** (gladly received) «guest» bienvenido; «change/news» grato **(b)** (freely permitted): **you're ~ to use the phone** el teléfono está a tu disposición; **you're ~ to these books** puedes llevarte estos libros, si quieres **(c)** (responding to thanks): **you're ~!** ¡de nada!, ¡no hay de qué!

welcome³ vt (greet) darle* la bienvenida a; (receive): **we would ~ any advice you can give us** le agradeceríamos cualquier consejo que pudiera darnos

welcome⁴ n bienvenida f

welcoming /'welkəmɪŋ/ adj **(a)** «ceremony/delegation» de bienvenida **(b)** «smile/hug» acogedor; **the little bar looked very ~** el barcito parecía muy acogedor

weld /weld/ vt/i soldar*

welfare /'welfer ‖ 'welfeə(r)/ n **1** (well-being) bienestar m **2** (Soc Adm) **(a)** (assistance) asistencia f social **(b)** (payment) (AmE) prestaciones fpl sociales

welfare state n estado m de bienestar

well¹ /wel/ adv (comp **better**; superl **best**) **1** (to high standard, satisfactorily) «sing/write/work» bien; **he's doing very ~** le van muy bien las cosas; **~ done!** ¡así se hace!, ¡muy bien!; **to go ~** «performance/operation» salir* bien
2 (thoroughly) «wash/dry/know» bien; **it was ~ worth the effort** realmente valió la pena; **~ and truly** (colloq): **he was ~ and truly drunk** estaba pero bien borracho
3 (a) (considerably) (no comp) bastante; **until ~ into the next century** hasta bien entrado el siglo que viene **(b)** (with justification): **you may ~ ask!** ¡muy buena pregunta!; **she couldn't very ~ deny it** ¿cómo iba a negarlo?
4 (advantageously) «marry» bien; **to do ~ to + INF** hacer* bien en + INF, deber + INF; **to do ~ out of sth** salir* bien parado de algo
5 (in phrases) **(a) as well** (in addition) también **(b) as well as** (in addition to) además de **(c) may/might as well: now you've told him, you may o might as ~ give it to him!** ahora que se lo has dicho dáselo ¿total?

well² adj (comp **better**; superl **best**) **1** (healthy) bien; **how are you? — I'm very ~, thank you** ¿cómo estás? — muy bien, gracias; **get**

W

~ **soon!** ¡que te mejores! **2** (pleasing, satisfactory) bien; **it's all very ~ for him to talk, but ...** él podrá decir todo lo que quiera pero ... **3** **as well: it would be as ~ to keep this quiet** mejor no decir nada de esto; **it's just as ~ I've got some money with me** menos mal que llevo dinero encima

well³ interj **1** (a) (introducing/continuing topic, sentence) bueno, bien (b) (expressing hesitation): **do you like it? — well ... ¿te gusta?** — pues or (esp AmL) este ... **2** (a) (expressing surprise): **~, ~, ~! look who's here!** ¡vaya, vaya! ¡mira quién está aquí! (b) (expressing indignation) bueno (c) (dismissively) ¡bah! (d) (expressing resignation) bueno **3** (expressing expectation): **~? who won?** bueno ¿y quién ganó?

well⁴ n (for water, oil, gas) pozo m
■ **well up** [v + adv] «water» brotar, manar; **tears ~ed up in his eyes** los ojos se le llenaron de lágrimas

well- /'wel/ pref bien

we'll /wiːl/ = **we will**

well: ~-balanced /'wel'bælənst/ adj (pred ~ **balanced**) ‹person› equilibrado; ‹diet› equilibrado, balanceado; **~-behaved** /'welbɪ'heɪvd/ adj (pred ~ **behaved**) ‹child› que se porta bien, bueno; ‹dog› obediente; **~-being** /'wel'biːɪŋ/ n bienestar m; **~-disposed** /'weldɪ'spəʊzd/ adj (pred ~ **disposed**) dispuesto a colaborar (or ayudar etc); **~-done** /'wel'dʌn/ adj (pred ~ **done**) (Culin) bien cocido or (Esp) muy hecho; **~-dressed** /'wel'drest/ adj (pred ~ **dressed**) bien vestido; **~-educated** /'wel'edʒəkeɪtəd ‖ wel'edjʊkeɪtɪd/ adj (pred ~ **educated**) culto; **~-founded** /'wel'faʊndəd ‖ wel'faʊndɪd/ adj (pred ~ **founded**) bien fundado; **~-groomed** /'wel'gruːmd/ adj (pred ~ **groomed**) ‹person› bien arreglado; ‹hair› bien peinado; ‹horse/garden› bien cuidado; **~-informed** /'welɪn'fɔːrmd ‖ welɪn'fɔːmd/ adj bien informado

wellington (boot) /'welɪŋtən/ n (a) (short boot) (AmE) botín m, bota f (corta) (b) (gumboot) (BrE) bota f de goma or de agua or de lluvia, catiusca f (Esp)

well: ~-kept /'wel'kept/ adj (pred ~ **kept**) (a) ‹house/lawns› bien cuidado (b) ‹secret› bien guardado; **~-known** /'wel'nəʊn/ adj (pred ~ **known**) ‹person› conocido, famoso; **it is ~ known that ...** es bien sabido que ...; **~-mannered** /'wel'mænərd ‖ wel'mænəd/ adj (pred ~ **mannered**) de buenos modales, educado; **~-meaning** /'wel'miːnɪŋ/ adj (pred ~ **meaning**) ‹person› bienintencionado; **he's ~ meaning, but ...** lo hace con la mejor intención, pero ...; **~-off** /'wel'ɔːf ‖ wel'ɒf/ adj (pred ~ **off**) adinerado; **~-read** /'wel'red/ adj (pred ~ **read**) culto; **~-to-do** /'weltə'duː/ adj ‹businessman/family› adinerado; **~-wisher** /'wel͵wɪʃər ‖ 'wel͵wɪʃə(r)/ n: **she received lots of cards from ~-wishers** recibió muchas tarjetas en que le deseaban una pronta recuperación (or mucha felicidad etc); **~-worn** /'wel'wɔːrn ‖ wel'wɔːn/ adj (pred ~ **worn**) ‹coat/carpet› muy gastado; ‹phrase› muy trillado

Welsh¹ /welʃ/ adj galés

Welsh² n (a) (language) galés m (b) (people) (+ pl vb) **the ~** los galeses

Welshman /'welʃmən/ n (pl **-men** /-mən/) galés m

welt /welt/ n (weal) verdugón m

went /went/ past of GO¹

wept /wept/ past & past p of WEEP

were /wɜːr ‖ wɜː(r), weak form wər ‖ wə(r)/ (a) 2nd pers sing past ind of BE (b) 1st, 2nd & 3rd pers pl past ind of BE (c) subjunctive of BE

we're /wɪr ‖ wɪə(r)/ = **we are**

weren't /wɜːrnt ‖ wɜːnt/ = **were not**

west¹ /west/ n **1** (point of the compass, direction) oeste m; **the ~, the W~** (region) el oeste **2** **the West** (the Occident) (el) Occidente m; (Pol, Hist) el Oeste

west² adj (before n) oeste adj inv, occidental; ‹wind› del oeste

west³ adv al oeste

westbound /'westbaʊnd/ adj que va (or iba etc) hacia el or en dirección oeste

westerly /'westərli ‖ 'westəli/ adj ‹wind› del oeste; **in a ~ direction** hacia el oeste, en dirección oeste

western¹ /'westərn ‖ 'westən/ adj (a) (Geog) oeste adj inv, del oeste, occidental; **the ~ areas of the country** las zonas oeste or occidentales del país (b) (occidental) (Geog, Pol) occidental

western² n western m, película f (or novela f etc) del Oeste or de vaqueros

Westerner, westerner /'westərnər ‖ 'westənə(r)/ n occidental mf

westernized /'westərnaɪzd ‖ 'westənaɪzd/ adj occidentalizado

west: W~ Indian adj antillano; (in UK) afroantillano; **W~ Indies** /'ɪndiz/ pl n **the W~ Indies** las Antillas

westward¹ /'westwərd ‖ 'westwəd/ adj (before n): **in a ~ direction** hacia el oeste, en dirección oeste

westward², (BrE) **westwards** /-z/ adv hacia el oeste

wet¹ /wet/ adj **-tt-** (a) (moist) ‹floor/grass/clothes› mojado; (damp) húmedo; ‹concrete/plaster› blando; **❺ wet paint** pintura fresca or (Esp tb) ojo, pinta; **to get ~** mojarse (b) (rainy) ‹weather/day› lluvioso

wet² vt (pres p **wetting**; past & past p **wet** or **wetted**) mojar; (dampen) humedecer*; **to ~ the bed** mojar la cama; **to ~ oneself** orinarse, hacerse* pipí (encima) (fam)

wet: ~ blanket n (colloq) aguafiestas mf (fam); **~ suit** n traje m de neopreno or de neopreno

we've /wiːv/ = **we have**

whack¹ /hwæk ‖ wæk/ n (blow) golpe m; (sound) ¡zas!

whack² vt golpear, aporrear; ‹person› pegarle* a

whale /hweɪl ‖ weɪl/ n **1** (pl **~s** or **~**) (Zool) ballena f **2** (colloq) (as intensifier): **we had a ~ of a time** lo pasamos bomba or genial (fam)

wharf /hwɔːrf ‖ wɔːf/ n (pl **wharves** /hwɔːrvz ‖ wɔːvz/) muelle m, embarcadero m

what¹ /hwɑːt ‖ wɒt/ pron **1** (in questions) qué; **~'s that?** ¿qué es eso?; **~'s the problem?** ¿cuál es el problema?; **~'s 'I don't understand' in Russian?** ¿cómo se dice 'no entiendo' en ruso? **2** (in phrases) **or what?** (colloq) ¿o qué?; **so what?** ⋯❖

¿y qué?; **what about: but ~ about the children?** y los niños ¿qué?; **you know Julie's boyfriend? — yes, ~ about him?** ¿conoces al novio de Julie? — sí ¿por qué?; **what ... for:** ~**'s this button for?** ¿para qué es este botón?; ~ **are you complaining for?** ¿por qué te quejas?; **what if:** ~ **if she finds out?** ¿y si se entera?; **what's-her/-his-name** (colloq): **go and ask** ~**'s-her-name next door** ve y pregúntale a la de al lado ¿cómo se llama? **3** **(a)** (in indirect speech) qué; **she knows** ~ **to do** ella sabe qué hacer; **I still don't know** ~**'s ~ in the office** aún no sé cómo funcionan las cosas en la oficina; **(I'll) tell you** ~, ... mira, ... **(b)** (relative use) lo que; **they did** ~ **they could** hicieron lo que pudieron

what² *adj* **1** **(a)** (in questions) qué; ~ **color are the walls?** ¿de qué color son las paredes? **(b)** (in indirect speech) qué; **she didn't know** ~ **color to choose** no sabía qué color elegir **2** (in exclamations) qué; ~ **a surprise!** ¡qué sorpresa!; ~ **a lot of people!** ¡cuánta gente!

whatever¹ /hwɑːˈtevər ‖ wɒtˈevə(r)/ *pron* **1** (in questions, exclamations) qué; ~ **is she doing?** ¿qué (es lo que) está haciendo? **2** **(a)** (no matter what): ~ **you do, don't laugh!** hagas lo que hagas ¡no te vayas a reír!; **he talked about percentiles,** ~ **they are** habló de percentiles, que no tengo ni idea de qué son **(b)** (all that): **they let him do** ~ **he likes** lo dejan hacer todo lo que quiere; ~ **you say** lo que tú digas, como quieras

whatever² *adj* **(a)** (no matter what): **don't give up,** ~ **doubts you may have** no renuncies, tengas las dudas que tengas; **all people, of** ~ **race or creed** todos, cualquiera sea su raza o credo **(b)** (any): ~ **changes are necessary** los cambios que sean necesarios

whatever³ *adv* (as intensifier): **none/nothing** ~ ninguno/nada en absoluto

wheat /hwiːt ‖ wiːt/ *n* trigo *m*

wheatgerm /ˈhwiːtdʒɜːrm ‖ ˈwiːtdʒɜːm/ *n* germen *m* de trigo

wheedle /ˈhwiːdl ‖ ˈwiːdl/ *vt* **to** ~ **sth OUT OF sb** sonsacarle* algo a algn

wheel¹ /hwiːl ‖ wiːl/ *n* **1** **(a)** (of vehicle) rueda *f* **(b)** (potter's ~) torno *m* **2** (steering ~ — of car) volante *m*; (— of ship) timón *m*; **at the** ~ (of car) al volante; (of ship) al timón

wheel² *vt* ⟨bicycle/wheelchair⟩ empujar; ⟨person⟩ llevar (en silla de ruedas etc)
■ ~ *vi* **(a)** (turn suddenly) ~ (**around** *o* (BrE) **round**) «person» girar sobre sus (or mis etc) talones **(b)** (circle) dar* vueltas; «birds» revolotear

wheel: ~**barrow** *n* carretilla *f*; ~**chair** *n* silla *f* de ruedas; ~ **clamp** *n* cepo *m*

wheeling and dealing /ˈhwiːlɪŋənˈdiːlɪŋ ‖ ˈwiːlɪŋənˈdiːlɪŋ/ *n* (colloq) tejemanejes *mpl* (fam)

wheeze /hwiːz ‖ wiːz/ *vi* «person» respirar con dificultad (produciendo un sonido sibilante como los asmáticos); «machine» resollar*

when¹ /hwen ‖ wen/ *adv*

■ **Note** When used as a conjunction in sentences expressing the future, *when* is translated by *cuando* + *subjunctive:* we'll speak to Carol when she gets back hablaremos con Carol cuando vuelva.

1 (in questions, indirect questions) cuándo; **that was** ~ **I realized that ...** fue entonces cuando *or* (esp AmL tb) que me di cuenta de que ...; **say** ~! di

cuándo **2** (as relative): **the year** ~ **we got married** el año en que nos casamos; **in December,** ~ **we were on holiday** en diciembre, cuando estábamos de vacaciones

when² *conj* **1** **(a)** (temporal sense) cuando; **I'll ask him** ~ **I see him** se lo preguntaré cuando lo vea **(b)** (if) si, cuando **2** **(a)** (since, considering that) si, cuando **(b)** (although) cuando; **he said he was 18** ~ **in fact he's only 15** dijo que tenía 18 años cuando en realidad solo tiene 15

when³ *pron* cuándo; ~ **do you have to be in London by?** ¿para cuándo tienes que estar en Londres?

whenever /hwenˈevər ‖ wenˈevə(r)/ *conj* **(a)** (every time that) siempre que; ~ **I hear that song I think of Spain** siempre que *or* cada vez que escucho esa canción, me acuerdo de España **(b)** (at whatever time): **we'll go** ~ **you're ready** saldremos cuando estés listo

where¹ /hwer ‖ weə(r)/ *adv* dónde; (indicating direction) adónde, dónde; ~**'s Lewes?** ¿dónde está Lewes?; ~ **are you taking me?** ¿(a)dónde me llevan?; ~ **are you from?** ¿de dónde eres?

where² *conj* **(a)** donde; (indicating direction) adonde, donde **(b)** (in cases where) cuando; ~ **appropriate** cuando *or* allí donde sea apropiado

whereabouts¹ /ˈhwerəˈbaʊts ‖ ˌweərəˈbaʊts/ *adv*: ~ **in Austria do you live?** ¿en qué parte de Austria vives?

whereabouts² /ˈhwerəbaʊts ‖ ˈweərəbaʊts/ *n* (+ *sing or pl vb*) paradero *m*

whereas /hwerˈæz ‖ weərˈæz/ *conj* mientras que

whereby /hwerˈbaɪ ‖ weəˈbaɪ/ *pron* (frml): **a system** ~ **payments are made automatically** un sistema por *or* según el cual los pagos se efectúan automáticamente

wherever¹ /hwerˈevər ‖ weərˈevə(r)/ *adv* **(a)** (in questions) dónde **(b)** (no matter where) (colloq) en cualquier parte *or* lado

wherever² *conj*: **you can use your card** ~ **you see this sign** puede usar su tarjeta (en cualquier establecimiento) donde vea este símbolo; ~ **he goes, I'll go too** vaya donde vaya, yo iré tambien; **you can sit** ~ **you like** puedes sentarte donde quieras

wherewithal /ˈhwerwɪðɔːl ‖ ˈweəwɪðɔːl/ *n* **the** ~ los medios; **we don't have the** ~ **to do this** no tenemos los recursos para hacer esto

whet /hwet ‖ wet/ *vt* **-tt-** ⟨interest/curiosity⟩ estimular; **the walk** ~**ted our appetites** la caminata nos abrió el apetito

whether /ˈhweðər ‖ ˈweðə(r)/ *conj*: **tell me** ~ **you need us or not** *o* ~ **or not you need us** dime si nos necesitas o no; **I doubt** ~ **he knew** dudo que lo supiera; ~ **you like it or not** te guste o no te guste

whey /hweɪ ‖ weɪ/ *n* suero *m* (de la leche)

which¹ /hwɪtʃ ‖ wɪtʃ/ *pron* **1** **(a)** (in questions) (sing) cuál; (pl) cuáles **(b)** (in indirect use) cuál; **I can never remember** ~ **is** ~ nunca recuerdo cuál es cuál **2** (as relative): **the parcel** ~ **arrived this morning** el paquete que llegó esta mañana; **the newspaper in** ~ **the article appeared** el diario en el que *or* en el cual apareció el artículo

which² *adj* **1** (in questions) (sing) qué, cuál; (pl) qué, cuáles **2** (as relative): **we arrived at two, by ~ time they had gone** llegamos a las dos y para entonces ya se habían ido; **in ~ case** en cuyo caso

whichever¹ /wɪtʃˈevər ‖ wɪtʃˈevə(r)/ *pron* **(a)** (no matter which): **there are several options, but ~ you choose ...** hay varias opciones, pero elijas la que elijas *or* cualquiera que elijas ... **(b)** (the one, ones that): **buy ~ is cheaper** compra el que sea más barato

whichever² *adj* **(a)** (no matter which): **~ party is in power** sea cual sea *or* cualquiera que sea el partido que esté en el poder **(b)** (any that): **you can write about ~ subject you know best** puedes escribir sobre el tema que mejor conozcas, sea cual sea *or* fuere

while¹ /hwaɪl ‖ waɪl/ *conj* **1** (in time) mientras; **they don't drink ~ on duty** no beben cuando están de guardia **2** (though) aunque **3** (whereas) mientras que

■ **while away** [*v + adv + o, v + o + adv*]: **we had a game of chess to ~ away the time** jugamos una partida de ajedrez para pasar el rato

while² *n*: **wait a ~** (a few days, weeks) espera un tiempo; (a few minutes, hours) espera un rato; (a very short period) espera un ratito *or* un momentito; **it's been a good ~ since we had any rain** hace bastante (tiempo) que no llueve; **he was here a little ~ ago** hace un ratito estaba aquí; **(every) once in a ~** de vez en cuando

whilst /hwaɪlst ‖ waɪlst/ *conj* (BrE) ▶ WHILE¹

whim /hwɪm ‖ wɪm/ *n* capricho *m*

whimper¹ /ˈhwɪmpər ‖ ˈwɪmpə(r)/ *vi* gimotear

whimper² *n* quejido *m*

whimsical /ˈhwɪmzɪkəl ‖ ˈwɪmzɪkəl/ *adj* ⟨person⟩ caprichoso; ⟨mood⟩ voluble

whine¹ /hwaɪn ‖ waɪn/ *vi* **(a)** «dog» aullar*; «person» gemir*; «child» lloriquear **(b)** (complain) (pej) quejarse

whine² *n* (of dog) aullido *m*; (of person) quejido *m*; (of engine) chirrido *m*; (of bullet) silbido *m*

whinny /ˈhwɪni ‖ ˈwɪni/ *vi* (3rd pers sing pres **whinnies**; pres p **whinnying**; past & past p **whinnied**) «horse» relinchar

whip¹ /hwɪp ‖ wɪp/ *n* (in horse riding) fusta *f*, fuete *m* (AmL exc CS); (of tamer) látigo *m*; (for punishment) azote *m*

whip² -pp- *vt* **1** **(a)** (lash) ⟨horse⟩ pegarle* a (con la fusta), fustigar*; ⟨person⟩ azotar; ⟨child⟩ darle* una paliza a **(b)** (beat) ⟨egg whites⟩ batir; ⟨cream⟩ batir *or* (Esp) montar; **~ped cream** crema *f* batida *or* (Esp) nata *f* montada **2** (take quickly) (+ adv compl): **she ~ped out her notebook** sacó rápidamente la libreta

■ **whip up** [*v + o + adv, v + adv + o*] **1** **(a)** (arouse) ⟨trouble/unrest⟩ provocar*; ⟨hatred⟩ fomentar; ⟨support⟩ conseguir* **(b)** (incite) ⟨crowd⟩ incitar **(c)** «wind» ⟨sea/waves⟩ agitar; ⟨dust⟩ levantar **2** **(a)** (beat, whisk) ⟨egg whites⟩ batir; ⟨cream⟩ batir, montar (Esp) **(b)** (prepare hurriedly) (colloq) ⟨meal⟩ improvisar

whip: ~lash injury *n* (Med) traumatismo *m* cervical; **~-round** *n* (BrE colloq) colecta *f*, vaca *f* (AmL fam)

whir, (BrE) **whirr** /hwɜːr ‖ wɜː(r)/ *vi* -rr- «machine/propellers» runrunear, zumbar

whirl¹ /hwɜːrl ‖ wɜːl/ *vi* **(a)** (spin) «person» girar, dar* vueltas; «leaves/dust» arremolinarse **(b)** (move fast) (+ adv compl): **he ~ed around** se dio media vuelta rápidamente

■ **~** *vt* (+ adv compl) hacer* girar

whirl² *n* (turn) giro *m*, vuelta *f*; (of dust) remolino *m*; **my head was in a ~** la cabeza me daba vueltas

whirl: ~pool *n* vorágine *f*, remolino *m*; **~wind** *n* torbellino *m*; (before it) **a ~wind romance** un idilio arrollador

whirr /hwɜːr ‖ wɜː(r)/ *vi* ▶ WHIR

whisk¹ /hwɪsk ‖ wɪsk/ *vt* **1** (Culin) batir **2** (convey quickly) (+ adv compl): **she was ~ed off to a meeting** se la llevaron a una reunión a toda prisa; **he ~ed away the plates** retiró los platos rápidamente

whisk² *n* (Culin) batidor *m*

whisker /ˈhwɪskər ‖ ˈwɪskə(r)/ *n* **1** **(a)** (single hair) pelo *m* (de la barba) **(b)** (narrow margin) (no pl) pelo *m* **2 whiskers** pl (of animal) bigotes *mpl*

whiskey /ˈhwɪski ‖ ˈwɪski/ *n* (pl **-keys**) whisky *m*, güisqui *m* (esp americano o irlandés)

whisky /ˈhwɪski ‖ ˈwɪski/ *n* (pl **-kies**) whisky *m*, güisqui *m* (esp escocés)

whisper¹ /ˈhwɪspər ‖ ˈwɪspə(r)/ *vi* **(a)** «person» cuchichear **(b)** (liter) «wind/leaves» susurrar (liter)

■ **~** *vt* ⟨remark/words⟩ susurrar

whisper² *n* **(a)** (soft voice) susurro *m*; **yes, he said in a ~** —sí —susurró **(b)** (rumor) rumor *m*

whistle¹ /ˈhwɪsəl ‖ ˈwɪsəl/ *vi* «person/kettle/wind» silbar; (loudly) chiflar; «referee» pitar; «train» pitar

■ **~** *vt* ⟨tune⟩ silbar

whistle² *n* **(a)** (instrument) silbato *m*, pito *m* **(b)** (sound — made with mouth) silbido *m*; (loud) chiflido *m*; (— made by referee's whistle) silbato *m*, pitido *m*; (— of kettle, wind, bullet) silbido *m*

white¹ /hwaɪt ‖ waɪt/ *adj* **-er, -est (a)** ⟨paint/cat/bread/wine/chocolate⟩ blanco; «coffee/tea» con leche; **she had a ~ wedding** se casó de blanco; **he went ~** se puso blanco **(b)** (Caucasian) blanco

white² *n* **1** (color) blanco *m* **2** *also* **White** (person) blanco, -ca *m,f* **3** **(a)** (of egg) clara *f* **(b)** (of eye) blanco *m*

white: ~ bait *n* morralla *f*, chanquetes *mpl* (Esp), cornalitos *mpl* (Arg), majuga *f* (Ur); **~-collar** /ˈhwaɪtˈkɑːlər ‖ ˌwaɪtˈkɒlə(r)/ *adj* ⟨worker/job⟩ no manual; (clerical) de oficina; **~ elephant** *n* (building, project) elefante *m* blanco; (object) objeto superfluo; **~ gasoline**, **~ gas** *n* (AmE) gasolina *f or* (Andes) bencina *f or* (RPl) nafta *f* sin plomo; **~-hot** /ˈhwaɪtˈhɑːt ‖ ˌwaɪtˈhɒt/ *adj* ⟨metal⟩ al rojo blanco; **W~ House** *n* **the W~ House** la Casa Blanca; **~ lie** *n* mentira *f* piadosa

whiten /ˈhwaɪtn̩ ‖ ˈwaɪtn̩/ *vt* blanquear

white: ~ sauce *n* salsa *f* blanca o bechamel; **~ spirit** *n* (BrE) espíritu *m* de petróleo (usado como sustituto del aguarrás)

whitewash¹ /ˈhwaɪtwɔːʃ ‖ ˈwaɪtwɒʃ/ *n* **1** (Const) cal *f* **2** (defeat) (colloq) paliza *f* (fam)

whitewash² *vt* ⟨wall/building⟩ blanquear, encalar, enjalbegar*

whiting /ˈhwaɪtɪŋ ‖ ˈwaɪtɪŋ/ *n* (pl **~s** or **~**) pescadilla *f*

Whitsun /'hwɪtsən ‖'wɪtsən/ n (esp BrE) Pentecostés f

whittle /'hwɪtl̩ ‖'wɪtl̩/ vt tallar
■ **whittle away** [v + o + adv, v + adv + o] ⟨funds/resources⟩ ir* mermando; ⟨influence⟩ ir* reduciendo; ⟨rights⟩ ir* menoscabando
■ **whittle down** [v + o + adv, v + adv + o] ⟨expenses⟩ recortar; ⟨applicants⟩ reducir* el numero de

whiz, whizz /hwɪz ‖wɪz/ vi **-zz-** (+ adv compl): to ~ by «bullet/arrow/car» pasar zumbando; I ~zed through my homework hice los deberes zumbando or a toda velocidad

whiz kid, whizz kid n (colloq) lince m (fam)

who /hu:/ pron **1** (a) (in questions) (sing) quién; (pl) quiénes; ~ **are you writing to?** ¿a quién le estás escribiendo? (b) (in indirect questions) quién; I **don't know** ~ **you're talking about** no sé de quién estás hablando **2** (as relative): **the boy** ~ **won the prize** el chico que ganó el premio; **there are blankets for those** ~ **want them** hay mantas para quienes quieran

WHO n (= World Health Organization) OMS f

who'd /hu:d/ (a) = **who had** (b) = **who would**

whodunit, whodunnit /,hu:'dʌnɪt ‖,hu:'dʌnɪt/ n (colloq) novela f policíaca

whoever /hu:'evər ‖hu:'evə(r)/ pron (a) (no matter who): **she's not coming in here,** ~ **she is** aquí no entra, quien quiera que sea; ~ **you ask** se lo preguntes a quien se lo preguntes (b) (the one, ones who): ~ **did this must be insane** quienquiera que haya hecho esto debe (de) estar loco; **I'll invite** ~ **I like** voy a invitar a quien (se) me dé la gana (c) (in questions) quién

whole¹ /həʊl/ adj **1** (entire) (before n, no comp): **there's a** ~ **bottle left** queda una botella entera; **the** ~ **truth** toda la verdad; **I'm fed up with the** ~ **affair** estoy harto del asunto **2** (pred) (in one piece) entero

whole² n (a) (integral unit) todo m; **the** ~ **of sth**: **a threat to the** ~ **of mankind** una amenaza para toda la humanidad (b) (in phrases) **as a whole**: **this will affect Europe as a** ~ esto va a afectar a Europa en su totalidad; **on the whole** (indep) en general

wholehearted /həʊl'hɑ:rtəd ‖,həʊl'hɑ:tɪd/ adj ⟨approval⟩ sin reservas; ⟨support⟩ incondicional

wholeheartedly /həʊl'hɑ:rtədli ‖,həʊl'hɑ:tɪdli/ adv ⟨approve/support⟩ sin reservas

whole: ~**meal** adj (BrE) integral; ~ **note** n (AmE) semibreve f, redonda f

wholesale¹ /'həʊlseɪl/ adj (a) (Busn) (before n) al por mayor (b) ⟨destruction/slaughter⟩ sistemático

wholesale² adv (a) (Busn) ⟨buy/sell⟩ al por mayor (b) (on a large scale) de modo general

wholesaler /'həʊlseɪlər ‖'həʊlseɪlə(r)/ n mayorista mf

wholesome /'həʊlsəm/ adj (a) (healthy) ⟨food/climate⟩ sano (b) (morally good) ⟨image⟩ de persona sana

wholewheat /'həʊlhwiːt ‖'həʊlwiːt/ adj integral

who'll /hu:l/ = **who will**

wholly /'həʊlli/ adv totalmente

whom /hu:m/ pron (frml) (a) (in questions): ~ **did you visit?** ¿a quién visitaste? (b) (as relative): **the cousin** ~ **I mentioned earlier** el primo que or a quien mencioné antes; **the girls, both of** ~ **could dance** las chicas, que ambas sabían bailar

whooping cough /'hu:pɪŋ/ n tos f convulsa or convulsiva

whoops /hwʊps ‖wʊps/ interj ¡ay!, ¡epa! (AmS fam), ¡híjole! (Méx fam)

whore /hoːr ‖hoː(r)/ n (pej) puta f (vulg & pey)

who's /hu:z/ (a) = **who is** (b) = **who has**

whose¹ /hu:z/ pron (sing) de quién; (pl) de quiénes

whose² adj (a) (in questions) (sing) de quién; (pl) de quiénes (b) (as relative) (sing) cuyo; (pl) cuyos

who've /hu:v/ = **who have**

why¹ /hwaɪ ‖waɪ/ adv por qué; ~ **not?** ¿por qué no?; ~ **don't you apply for the post?** ¿por qué no solicitas el puesto?; **this is** ~ **the attempt failed** fue por esto que el intento fracasó; **the reason** ~ **he couldn't attend** la razón por la cual no pudo asistir

why² interj ¡vaya!

why³ n porqué m

WI = **Wisconsin**

wick /wɪk/ n mecha f

wicked /'wɪkəd ‖'wɪkɪd/ adj **-er, -est** (a) (evil) ⟨person⟩ malvado, malo; ⟨thought⟩ malo; ⟨lie⟩ infame (b) (vicious) ⟨blow⟩ malintencionado (c) (mischievous) ⟨grin/laugh⟩ travieso

wicker /'wɪkər ‖'wɪkə(r)/ n mimbre m

wickerwork /'wɪkərwɜːrk ‖'wɪkəwɜːk/ n (a) (articles) artículos mpl de mimbre (b) ▶ WICKER

wicket /'wɪkət ‖'wɪkɪt/ n **1** (in cricket) (stumps and bails) palos mpl **2** (window) (AmE) ventanilla f

wide¹ /waɪd/ adj **wider, widest 1** (in dimension) ⟨river/feet/trousers⟩ ancho; ⟨gap⟩ grande; ⟨desert/ocean⟩ vasto; **it's two meters** ~ tiene or mide dos metros de ancho **2** (in extent, range) ⟨experience/powers/area⟩ amplio; **a** ~ **variety of things** una gran variedad de cosas **3** (off target) ⟨ball/shot⟩ desviado; ~ **of sth** lejos DE algo; ▶ MARK¹ 4

wide² adv **wider, widest** ~ **apart: with your feet** ~ **apart** con los pies bien separados; ~ **awake: to be** ~ **awake** estar* completamente espabilado or despierto; **open** ~! abra bien la boca; ~ **open: you left the door** ~ **open** dejaste la puerta abierta de par en par

wide-angle lens /'waɪd'æŋgəl/ n granangular m

widely /'waɪdli/ adv (a) (extensively): **she is very**

AmC	América Central	Arg	Argentina	Cu	Cuba	Per	Perú
AmL	América Latina	Bol	Bolivia	Ec	Ecuador	RPI	Río de la Plata
AmS	América del Sur	Chi	Chile	Esp	España	Ur	Uruguay
Andes	Región andina	CS	Cono Sur	Méx	México	Ven	Venezuela

~ traveled ha viajado mucho; **it was ~ publicized** se le dio mucha publicidad **(b)** (commonly): **a ~ held view** una opinión muy extendida **(c)** (to a large degree) ⟨*vary*⟩ mucho

widen /'waɪdn̩/ *vt* ⟨*road/entrance*⟩ ensanchar; ⟨*range/debate/scope*⟩ ampliar*
■ ~ *vi* «*road/tunnel*» ensancharse

wide: ~-ranging /'waɪd'reɪndʒɪŋ/ *adj* ⟨*powers/ curriculum*⟩ amplio; ⟨*interests*⟩ variado; ⟨*effects*⟩ de gran alcance; **~-screen** /'waɪd'skriːn/ *adj* para pantalla ancha; **~spread** *adj* ⟨*custom/ belief*⟩ extendido

widget /'wɪdʒət ‖'wɪdʒɪt/ *n* (colloq) aparato *m*, artilugio *m*, chisme *m* (Esp fam)

widow¹ /'wɪdəʊ/ *n* viuda *f*

widow² *vt*: **to be ~ed** enviudar, quedar viudo

widower /'wɪdəʊər ‖'wɪdəʊə(r)/ *n* viudo *m*

width /wɪdθ/ *n* **(a)** (measurement) ancho *m*, anchura *f*; **what ~ is the cloth?** ¿qué ancho tiene la tela? **(b)** (in swimming pool) ancho *m*

wield /wiːld/ *vt* ⟨*sword*⟩ blandir*; ⟨*power/ authority*⟩ ejercer*

wife /waɪf/ *n* (*pl* **wives**) esposa *f*, mujer *f*

wig /wɪg/ *n* peluca *f*

wiggle /'wɪgəl/ *vt* ⟨*toes*⟩ mover*; ⟨*hips*⟩ contonear

wild¹ /waɪld/ *adj* **-er, -est** **1** **(a)** ⟨*animal*⟩ salvaje; ⟨*plant/flower*⟩ silvestre; ⟨*vegetation*⟩ agreste **(b)** (uncivilized) ⟨*tribe*⟩ salvaje **(c)** (desolate) ⟨*country*⟩ agreste **2** **(a)** (unruly) ⟨*party/lifestyle*⟩ desenfrenado **(b)** (random, uncontrolled) ⟨*attempt*⟩ desesperado; **a ~ guess** una conjetura hecha totalmente al azar **(c)** ⟨*allegation/exaggeration*⟩ absurdo **3** **(a)** (violent) (liter) ⟨*sea/waters*⟩ embravecido, proceloso (liter); ⟨*wind*⟩ fuertísimo, furioso (liter) **(b)** (frantic) ⟨*excitement/dancing*⟩ desenfrenado; ⟨*shouting*⟩ desaforado; ⟨*appearance/stare*⟩ de loco; **her perfume was driving him ~** su perfume lo estaba enloqueciendo **(c)** (enthusiastic) (colloq) (*pred*) **to be ~ ABOUT sth: I'm not ~ about the idea** la idea no me enloquece **(d)** (angry) (colloq) (*pred*): **it makes me ~** me saca de quicio

wild² *adv*: **these flowers grow ~** estas flores son silvestres; **to run ~: these kids have been allowed to run ~** a estos niños los han criado como salvajes; **the garden has run ~** la maleza ha invadido el jardín

wild³ *n* **the ~: an opportunity to observe these animals in the ~** una oportunidad de observar estos animales en libertad

wild: ~ boar *n* jabalí *m*; **~ card** *n* (Comput) comodín *m*; **~cat** /'waɪldkæt/ *n* (*pl* **~cats** or **~cat**) (European) gato *m* montés; (bobcat) (esp AmE) lince *m*

wilderness /'wɪldərnəs ‖'wɪldənɪs/ *n* **(a)** (wasteland) páramo *m*; (jungle) jungla *f* **(b)** (undeveloped land) (AmE) parque *m* natural

wild: ~fire *n* (AmE) fuego *m* arrasador; **to spread like ~fire** (also BrE) extenderse* como un reguero de pólvora; **~-goose chase** /'waɪld'guːs/ *n*: **I'm not going into town again on another ~-goose chase** no pienso ir otra vez al centro a perder el tiempo para nada; **~life** *n* fauna *f* y flora *f*

wildly /'waɪldli/ *adv* **1** **(a)** (frantically) ⟨*kick/ struggle/rush*⟩ como (un) loco **(b)** (violently) ⟨*rage/ blow*⟩ con furia **2** **(a)** (in undisciplined fashion) ⟨*live*⟩ desordenadamente **(b)** (haphazardly, randomly) ⟨*shoot/guess*⟩ a lo loco **3** (extremely): **~ funny** comiquísimo; **~ inaccurate estimates** cálculos absolutamente errados

Wild West *n* **the ~** el Lejano Oeste; (*before n*) ⟨*adventure/story*⟩ del oeste

wiles /waɪlz/ *pl n* artimañas *fpl*

wilful *adj* (BrE) ▶ WILLFUL

will¹ /wɪl/ *v mod*

───────────────
■ **Note** When translating *will* into Spanish, the future tense is not always the first option. *Ir + a + infinitive* is common in Latin American countries. For examples, see the entry below.
───────────────

(*past* **would**) ['LL *es la contracción de* WILL, WON'T *de* WILL NOT *y* 'LL'VE *de* WILL HAVE]
1 (talking about the future): **he'll come on Friday** vendrá el viernes, va a venir el viernes; **he said he would come on Friday** dijo que vendría *or* iba a venir el viernes; **at the end of this month, he'll have been working here for a year** este fin de mes hará un año que trabaja aquí; **I won't let you down** no te fallaré **2** **(a)** (expressing willingness): **~ o would you do me a favor?** ¿quieres hacerme un favor?; **she won't tell us what happened** no nos quiere decir qué pasó **(b)** (in orders, invitations): **be quiet, ~ you!** cállate, ¿quieres?; **~ you have a drink?** ¿quieres tomar algo? **3** (expressing conjecture): **won't they be having lunch now?** ¿no estarán comiendo ahora?; **that would have been in 1947** eso debe (de) haber sido en 1947 **4** **(a)** (indicating habit, characteristic): **I'll watch anything on television** yo soy capaz de mirar cualquier cosa en la televisión; **he'd get drunk every Saturday** se emborrachaba todos los sábados **(b)** (indicating capability): **this door won't shut** esta puerta no cierra *or* no quiere cerrar
■ ~ *vt* (*past & past p* **willed**) **1** **(a)** (urge, try to cause): **I was ~ing her to get the answer right** estaba deseando con todas mis fuerzas que diera la respuesta correcta **(b)** (desire, ordain) (frml) «*God*» disponer*, querer* **2** (bequeath) legar*

will² *n* **1** **(a)** (faculty) voluntad *f* **(b)** (willpower) voluntad *f*; **to lose the ~ to live** perder* las ansias de vivir **(c)** (desire, intention) voluntad *f*; **patients may come and go at ~** los pacientes pueden entrar y salir a voluntad; ▶ FREE WILL **2** (testament) testamento *m*

willful, (BrE) **wilful** /'wɪlfəl/ *adj* **1** (deliberate) ⟨*misconduct/neglect*⟩ intencionado; ⟨*damage*⟩ causado con premeditación **2** (obstinate) ⟨*person*⟩ terco

willing /'wɪlɪŋ/ *adj* **(a)** (eager, compliant) ⟨*before n*⟩ ⟨*servant/worker*⟩ servicial **(b)** (inclined) (*pred*) **to be ~ to + INF** estar* dispuesto A + INF

willingly /'wɪlɪŋli/ *adv* (gladly) con gusto; (readily, freely) por voluntad propia

willingness /'wɪlɪŋnəs ‖'wɪlɪŋnɪs/ *n* buena voluntad *f*, buena disposición *f*

willow /'wɪləʊ/ *n* sauce *m*

willpower /'wɪlpaʊər ‖'wɪlpaʊə(r)/ *n* (fuerza *f* de) voluntad *f*

W

willy-nilly /'wılı'nılı/ adv (a) (haphazardly) de cualquier manera (b) (like it or not) sea como sea

wilt /wılt/ vi «plant/flower» ponerse* mustio, marchitarse

wily /'waılı/ adj **wilier, wiliest** astuto

win¹ /wın/ (pres p **winning**; past & past p **won**) vt **1** (gain) «prize/title» ganar; «support» conseguir*; «fame/recognition/affection» ganarse; «scholarship/promotion/contract» conseguir* **2** (be victorious in) «war/race/bet/election» ganar
■ ~ vi ganar
■ **win over,** (BrE also) **win round** [v + o + adv, v + adv + o] conquistarse a

win² n victoria f, triunfo m

wince /wıns/ vi hacer* un gesto de dolor; (shudder) estremecerse*

winch¹ /wıntʃ/ n cabrestante m, torno m

winch² vt: levantar con un torno o cabrestante

wind¹ /wınd/ n **1** (Meteo) viento m; **to get ~ of sth** enterarse de algo; (before n) ~ **power** energía f eólica **2** (in bowels) gases mpl **3** (breath) aliento m **4** (Mus): **the ~** los instrumentos de viento; (before n) ~ **instrument** instrumento m de viento

wind² vt
I /wınd/ (a) «exertion» dejar sin aliento; «blow» cortarle la respiración a (b) «baby» sacarle* el aire a (fam)
II /waınd/ (past & past p **wound** /waʊnd/) **1** (coil) «yarn/wool» ovillar; **to ~ sth around o** (esp BrE) **round sth** enroscar* algo ALREDEDOR DE algo; **to ~ sth into a ball** hacer* un ovillo con algo; **to ~ the film on** (hacer*) correr la película **2** (a) (turn) «handle» hacer* girar, darle* vueltas a; «clock/watch» darle* cuerda a (b) (hoist, pull) levantar
■ ~ vi /waınd/ (past & past p **wound** /waʊnd/) (a) «river/road» serpentear (b) **winding** pres p «river/road» sinuoso, serpenteante
■ **wind down** **1** [v + o + adv, v + adv + o] «window» (Auto) bajar; «production/trade» reducir* paulatinamente
2 [v + adv] (colloq) relajarse
■ **wind up** **1** [v + o + adv, v + adv + o] (a) (tighten spring) «watch/toy» darle* cuerda a (b) (bring to conclusion) «meeting/speech» cerrar* (c) (close down) «company» cerrar*, liquidar
2 [v + o + adv] (colloq) (make angry) torear, darle* manija a (RPl fam); (tease) tomarle el pelo a (fam)
3 [v + adv] (end up, find oneself) (colloq) terminar, acabar (b) (conclude) «speaker» concluir*, terminar

wind /wınd/: ~**fall** n (a) (fruit) fruta caída del árbol (b) (unexpected benefit): **the $100 prize was a nice little ~fall** el premio de 100 dólares le (or me etc) cayó como llovido del cielo; ~**mill** n molino m de viento

window /'wındəʊ/ n **1** (a) (of building) ventana f; (of car) ventanilla f; (of shop) vitrina f (AmL), vidriera f (AmL), escaparate m (esp Esp); **to fly/go out (of) the ~** «plans» venirse* abajo, desbaratarse; «hopes» desvanecerse* (b) (sales counter) ventanilla f **2** (Comput) ventana f, recuadro m

window: ~ **box** n jardinera f, ~ **cleaner** n (product) limpiacristales m, limpiavidrios m (esp AmL); (person) limpiacristales mf, limpiavidrios mf (esp AmL); ~ **dressing** n (in shop) vitrinismo m (AmL), vidrierismo m (AmL), escaparatismo m

(esp Esp); ~ **ledge** n alféizar m or repisa f de la ventana; ~**pane** n vidrio m or (Esp) cristal m (de una ventana); ~ **seat** n (in train, plane) asiento m junto a la ventanilla; ~**shop** vi -**pp**-: **to go ~shopping** ir* a mirar vitrinas or vidrieras or (esp Esp) escaparates; ~**sill** n alféizar m or repisa f de la ventana

wind /wınd/: ~**pipe** n tráquea f; ~**screen** n (BrE) ▶ ~SHIELD; ~**shield** n (AmE) parabrisas m; (before n) ~**shield wiper** limpiaparabrisas m, limpiador m (Méx); ~**surfer** n (person) tablista mf, surfista mf; (board) tabla f de windsurf; ~**surfing** n windsurf m, windsurfing m, surf m a vela; ~**swept** adj «beach/plain» azotado por el viento; «person» despeinado; «hair» alborotado

windy /'wındı/ adj -**dier, -diest** «day/weather» ventoso, de viento; **it's ~** hace viento

wine /waın/ n (a) (beverage) vino m; (before n) ~ **cellar** bodega f, ~ **list** carta f de vinos; ~ **rack** botellero m; ~ **waiter** sommelier m, sumiller m (b) (color) rojo m granate; (before n) rojo granate adj inv

wine: ~ **and dine** vt agasajar (con una comida); ~ **bar** n bar m (especializado en vinos); ~ **glass** n copa f de vino; ~**growing** n viticultura f; (before n) «area/region» vinícola; «country» productor de vino; ~**tasting** /'waın,teıstıŋ/ n (a) (act, skill) cata f or catadura f de vinos (b) (event) degustación f de vinos

wing /wıŋ/ n **1** (Zool) ala f; **2** (Aviat) ala f; **3** (BrE Auto) guardabarros m or (Méx) salpicadera f or (Chi, Per) tapabarros m **4** (Pol) ala f; **5** (of building) ala f; **6 wings** pl (Theat) **the ~s** los bastidores

wingspan /'wıŋspæn/ n envergadura f

wink¹ /wıŋk/ n guiño m, guiñada f; **to give sb a ~** guiñarle el ojo a algn; **not to get a ~ of sleep** no pegar* (el or un) ojo

wink² vi (a) «person» guiñar el ojo (b) (flash) «light» parpadear

winner /'wınər ‖'wınə(r)/ n ganador, -dora m,f

winning /'wınıŋ/ adj (a) (victorious) (before n) «candidate/team» ganador; «goal/shot» de la victoria (b) (appealing) «smile/personality» encantador

winning post n (poste m de) llegada f

winnings /'wınıŋz/ pl n ganancias fpl (obtenidas en el juego)

winter /'wıntər ‖'wıntə(r)/ n invierno m; **in (the) ~** en invierno; (before n) «weather» invernal; ~ **sports** deportes mpl de invierno

wintertime /'wıntərtaım ‖'wıntətaım/ n invierno m

wintry /'wıntrı/ adj -**trier, -triest** invernal

wipe¹ /waıp/ n (a) (action): **give the table a ~ with a damp cloth** pásale un trapo húmedo a la mesa (b) (cloth) toallita f

wipe² vt «floor/table» limpiar, pasarle un trapo a; «dishes» secar*; ~ **your nose** límpiate la nariz
■ ~ vi (dry dishes) secar*
■ **wipe away** [v + o + adv, v + adv + o] «tears» secar*; «memory» borrar
■ **wipe off** [v + o + adv, v + adv + o] (a) (remove) «mud/oil» limpiar (b) (erase) «recording» borrar
■ **wipe out** [v + o + adv, v + adv + o] (a) (clean) limpiar, pasarle un trapo a (b) (destroy, eradicate)

⟨species/population⟩ exterminar; ⟨resistance⟩ acabar con; ⟨disease⟩ erradicar*; ⟨army⟩ aniquilar **(c)** (erase) ⟨writing/memory⟩ borrar
■ **wipe up** [v + o + adv, v + adv + o] limpiar

wire¹ /waɪr ‖'waɪə(r)/ n **1 (a)** (metal strand) alambre m; (before n) ~ **fence** alambrada f, alambrado m (AmL) **(b)** (fencing, mesh) alambrada f, alambrado m (AmL) **(c)** (finishing line) (AmE): **the** ~ la línea de llegada, la meta **2 (a)** (Elec, Telec) cable m **(b)** (telegram) (colloq) telegrama m

wire² vt (Elec): **to be** ~**d to sth** estar* conectado a algo

wire: ~ **cutters** /'kʌtərz ‖'kʌtəz/ pl n cortaalambres m, pinzas fpl de corte (Méx); (large) cizalla(s) f(pl); ~**walker** n (AmE) equilibrista mf, funámbulo, -la m,f; ~ **wool** n ▶ STEEL WOOL

wiring /'waɪrɪŋ ‖'waɪərɪŋ/ n (Elec) cableado m, instalación f eléctrica

wiry /'waɪri ‖'waɪəri/ adj **wirier, wiriest (a)** ⟨person⟩ enjuto y nervudo **(b)** ⟨hair⟩ áspero

Wis = **Wisconsin**

wisdom /'wɪzdəm/ n sabiduría f

wisdom tooth n muela f del juicio

wise /waɪz/ adj **wiser, wisest (a)** (prudent) ⟨person⟩ prudente; ⟨choice/decision⟩ acertado **(b)** (learned, experienced) sabio; **to be none the** ~**r.** I'm none the ~**r** sigo sin entender **(c)** (aware) (colloq) **to be** ~ **TO sth/sb: I'm** ~ **to him/his tricks** lo conozco muy bien/le conozco las mañas
■ **wise up** (colloq) [v + adv] (d)espabilarse, avivarse (AmL fam), apiolarse (RPI fam)

-wise /waɪz/ suff **(a)** (with reference to): **price**~/ **weather**~ en lo que respecta al precio/tiempo **(b)** (in particular way): **length**~ a lo largo

wisecrack n broma f, chiste m

wisely /'waɪzli/ adv sabiamente

wish¹ /wɪʃ/ n **(a)** (desire) deseo m; **to make a** ~ pedir* un deseo; **they got married against my** ~**es** se casaron en contra de mi voluntad **(b)** **wishes** pl (greetings): **give your mother my best** ~**es** dale a tu madre muchos recuerdos de mi parte, cariños a tu madre (AmL); **best** ~**es, Jack** saludos or un abrazo de Jack

wish² vt **(a)** (desire fervently) desear; **to** ~ **sth ON sb** desearle algo A algn; **I** ~ **I were rich** ¡ojalá fuera rico!; **she** ~**ed she hadn't told him** lamentó habérselo dicho; **I** ~ **you wouldn't say things like that** me disgusta mucho que digas esas cosas **(b)** (want) (frml) desear (frml) **(c)** (want for sb) desear; ~ **me luck!** ¡deséame suerte!; **to** ~ **sb good night** darle* las buenas noches a algn
■ ~ vi **(a)** (make magic wish) pedir* un deseo **(b)** (want, desire): **if you** ~ como quieras

wishful thinking /'wɪʃfəl/ n: **do you know for sure that they're leaving or is it just** ~ ~**?** ¿sabes a ciencia cierta que se van o es simplemente lo que tú querrías?

wisp /wɪsp/ n (of smoke) voluta f; (of hair) mechón m

wispy /'wɪspi/ adj **-pier, -piest** ⟨cloud⟩ tenue; ⟨hair⟩ ralo

wistful /'wɪstfəl/ adj ⟨smile/thought⟩ nostálgico

wit /wɪt/ n **1** (often pl) (intelligence) inteligencia f; (ingenuity) ingenio m; **to be at one's** ~**s' end** estar* desesperado **2** (humor) ingenio m

witch /wɪtʃ/ n bruja f

witch: ~**craft** n brujería f, hechicería f; ~ **doctor** n hechicero m, brujo m

with /wɪð, wɪθ/ prep
■ **Note** When the translation con is followed by the pronouns mi, ti, and sí, it combines with them to form conmigo, contigo, and consigo: **come with me** ven conmigo; **take it with you** llévalo contigo; **he had his dog with him** tenía el perro consigo.

1 (a) (in the company of) con; **she went** ~ **him/them/me/you** fue con él/con ellos/conmigo/ contigo **(b)** (member, employee, client etc of) en; **I've been banking** ~ **them for years** hace años que tengo cuenta en ese banco
2 (in descriptions): **the shirt is black** ~ **white stripes** la camisa es negra a or con rayas blancas; **the man** ~ **the beard** el hombre de barba; **a tall woman** ~ **long hair** una mujer alta con el pelo largo or de pelo largo; **he is married,** ~ **three children** está casado y tiene tres hijos
3 (a) (indicating manner) con; **the proposal was greeted** ~ **derision** la propuesta fue recibida con burlas **(b)** (by means of, using) con; **she ate it** ~ **her fingers** lo comió con la mano **(c)** (as a result of): **trembling** ~ **fright** temblando de miedo

withdraw /wɪð'drɔː/ (past **-drew;** past p **-drawn**) vt **1 (a)** (recall, remove) ⟨troops/ representative⟩ retirar; ⟨hand/arm⟩ retirar; ⟨coin/ note⟩ retirar de la circulación; ⟨product⟩ retirar de la venta **(b)** ⟨money/cash⟩ retirar, sacar* **2 (a)** (cancel, discontinue) ⟨support/funding⟩ retirar; ⟨permission⟩ cancelar; **they threatened to** ~ **their labor** amenazaron con ir a la huelga **(b)** (rescind) ⟨application/charges⟩ retirar; ⟨demand⟩ renunciar a **(c)** (retract) ⟨statement/allegation⟩ retirar
■ ~ vi **(a)** «troops/competitor/candidate» retirarse **(b)** (socially) recluirse*; (psychologically) retraerse*

withdrawal /wɪð'drɔːəl/ n **1** (of troops, team, representative) retirada f; (of coinage) retirada f de la circulación; (of product) retirada f de la venta **2** (of support, funding) retirada f, retiro m (AmL); (of application, nomination, competitor) retirada f **3** (Psych) retraimiento m **4** (of cash) retirada f, retiro m (AmL) **5** (from drugs) abandono m; (before n) ~ **symptoms** síndrome m de abstinencia

withdrawn¹ /wɪð'drɔːn/ past p of WITHDRAW

withdrawn² adj retraído

withdrew /wɪð'druː/ past of WITHDRAW

wither /'wɪðər ‖'wɪðə(r)/ vi «plant/flower» marchitarse; «limb» atrofiarse

withered /'wɪðərd ‖'wɪðəd/ adj ⟨plant/flower⟩ marchito, mustio; ⟨limb⟩ atrofiado

withering /'wɪðərɪŋ/ adj **(a)** ⟨heat⟩ abrasador **(b)** ⟨look⟩ fulminante

withhold /wɪθ'həʊld ‖wɪð'həʊld/ vt (past & past p **-held**) ⟨payment/funds⟩ retener*; ⟨truth⟩ ocultar; ⟨consent⟩ negar*; ⟨information⟩ no revelar

within¹ /wɪð'ɪn/ prep **1** (inside) dentro de; ~ **a radius of 20 miles** en un radio de 20 millas **2** (indicating nearness) a; **we were** ~ **150m of the summit** estábamos a 150m de la cumbre **3** (in less than): ~ **the time allotted** dentro del tiempo establecido; **they'll be here** ~ **an hour** estarán aquí en menos de una hora

within² adv (arch or liter) dentro

without /wɪð'aʊt/ *prep* sin; **do it ~ cheating** hazlo sin hacer trampas

withstand /wɪð'stænd/ *vt* (*past & past p* **-stood**) resistir; ⟨*heat/pain*⟩ soportar

witness¹ /'wɪtnəs ‖'wɪtnɪs/ *n* **1** (person) testigo *mf*; (*before n*) **~ stand** *o* (BrE) **box** estrado *m* **2** (testimony, evidence) **to be ~ TO sth** ser* testimonio DE algo

witness² *vt* **(a)** (observe) ⟨*change/event*⟩ ser* testigo de; ⟨*crime/accident*⟩ presenciar **(b)** (authenticate) (Law) ⟨*signature*⟩ atestiguar*; ⟨*will*⟩ atestiguar* la firma de

witticism /'wɪtəsɪzəm ‖'wɪtɪsɪzəm/ *n* agudeza *f*; (in conversation) salida *f*

witty /'wɪti/ *adj* **-tier, -tiest** ⟨*person*⟩ ingenioso; (funny) gracioso; ⟨*answer/remark*⟩ ingenioso

wives /waɪvz/ *pl of* WIFE

wizard /'wɪzərd ‖'wɪzəd/ *n* mago *m*, brujo *m*

wizened /'wɪznd/ *adj* (wrinkled) arrugado; (withered) marchito

wk = **week**

wobble /'wɑːbəl ‖'wɒbəl/ *vi* **(a)** (tremble) «*jelly*» temblar* **(b)** (sway, waver) «*cyclist*» bambolearse; «*wheel*» bailar; «*chair*» tambalearse

wobbly /'wɑːbli ‖'wɒbli/ *adj* **-blier, -bliest** **(a)** ⟨*voice*⟩ tembloroso **(b)** ⟨*wheel/tooth*⟩ flojo; ⟨*table/chair*⟩ poco firme, que se tambalea; **my legs are ~** me tiemblan las piernas

woe /wəʊ/ *n* **(a)** (sorrow) congoja *f* (liter), aflicción *f*; **~ betide you if you lose it!** ¡pobre de ti *or* ay de ti si lo pierdes! **(b) woes** *pl* (afflictions) males *mpl*

woeful /'wəʊfəl/ *adj* **(a)** (deplorable) ⟨*neglect/ ignorance*⟩ lamentable **(b)** (sorrowful) (liter) ⟨*person*⟩ acongojado (liter); ⟨*expression*⟩ desconsolado

woke /wəʊk/ *past of* WAKE¹

woken /'wəʊkən/ *past p of* WAKE¹

wolf¹ /wʊlf/ *n* (*pl* **wolves**) (Zool) lobo *m*

wolf² *vt* ~ (**down**) devorar(se)

wolves /wʊlvz/ *pl of* WOLF¹

woman /'wʊmən/ *n* (*pl* **women**) mujer *f*; (*before n*) **a ~ lawyer** una abogada; **a ~ friend of mine** una amiga mía

womanizer /'wʊmənaɪzər ‖'wʊmənaɪzə(r)/ *n* mujeriego *m*

womanly /'wʊmənli/ *adj* femenino

womb /wuːm/ *n* útero *m*, matriz *f*

women /'wɪmɪn/ *pl of* WOMAN

women's room *n* (AmE) baño *m or* (Esp) servicios *mpl* de damas *or* señoras

won /wʌn/ *past & past p of* WIN¹

wonder¹ /'wʌndər ‖'wʌndə(r)/ *n* **1** (awe, curiosity) asombro *m* **2** (marvel, miracle) maravilla *f*; **no ~ you feel tired!** ¡no me extraña que estés cansado!

wonder² *vi* **(a)** (ponder, speculate): **why do you ask? — oh, I was just ~ing** ¿por qué preguntas?

— por nada **(b)** (marvel, be surprised) maravillarse; **I ~ at your patience** me maravilla la paciencia que tienes

■ ~ *vt* **(a)** (ask oneself) preguntarse; **I ~ if** *o* **whether he'll be there** me pregunto si estará **(b)** (be amazed): **I ~ (that) she didn't fire you on the spot** me sorprende que no te haya echado inmediatamente

wonder³ *adj* (*before n*) ⟨*drug/cure*⟩ milagroso

wonderful /'wʌndərfəl ‖'wʌndəfəl/ *adj* maravilloso

wonderfully /'wʌndərfli ‖'wʌndəfəli/ *adv* maravillosamente, de maravilla

wont /wɑːnt ‖wəʊnt/ *n* (liter or hum) costumbre *f*; **as is her ~** como tiene por costumbre

won't /wəʊnt/ = **will not**

woo /wuː/ *vt* (woman) cortejar*; ⟨*customers/ investors*⟩ atraer*; ⟨*voters*⟩ buscar* el apoyo de

wood /wʊd/ *n* **1** (material) madera *f*; (firewood) leña *f* **2** (wooded area) (*often pl*) bosque *m* **3** (in golf) palo *m* de madera

wooded /'wʊdəd ‖'wʊdɪd/ *adj* boscoso

wooden /'wʊdn/ *adj* **(a)** (made of wood) de madera; **~ leg** pata *f* de palo (fam) **(b)** (stiff) ⟨*expression*⟩ rígido; ⟨*performance*⟩ acartonado

wood: **~land** /'wʊdlənd/ *n* (*often pl*) bosque *m*; **~louse** *n* (*pl* **-lice**) cochinilla *f*, chanchito *m* (Andes, CS fam); **~pecker** /'wʊd,pekər ‖'wʊd,pekə(r)/ *n* pájaro *m* carpintero, pico *m* (barreno *or* carpintero); **~pigeon** *n* paloma *f* torcaz; **~pile** *n* (AmE) montón *m* de leña; **~shed** *n* leñera *f*; **~wind** /'wʊdwɪnd/ *n* (*pl* **~wind** *or* **~winds**) **the ~wind(s)** los instrumentos de viento de madera; **~work** *n* **(a)** (wooden fittings) carpintería *f* **(b)** (BrE) ▶ **~WORKING; ~working** *n* (AmE) (carpentry) carpintería *f*; (cabinet making) ebanistería *f*; (craftwork) artesanía *f* en madera; **~worm** *n* (*pl* **~worm**) **(a)** (larva) carcoma *f* **(b)** (infestation): **the table's full of ~worm** la mesa está llena de carcoma *or* está toda carcomida

woody /'wʊdi/ *adj* **-dier, -diest** leñoso

woof /wʊf/ (colloq) ladrido *m*; **~ ~!** ¡guau guau!

wool /wʊl/ *n* lana *f*

woolen, (BrE) **woollen** /'wʊlən/ *adj* de lana

woolens, (BrE) **woollens** /'wʊlənz/ *pl n* (Clothes) prendas *fpl* de lana

wooly, (BrE) **woolly** /'wʊli/ *adj* **-lier, -liest** **(a)** ⟨*hat/sweater*⟩ de lana **(b)** (unclear) ⟨*thinking/ argument*⟩ vago, impreciso

word¹ /wɜːrd ‖wɜːd/ *n* **1** (term, expression) palabra *f*; **what's the German ~ for 'dog'?** ¿cómo se dice 'perro' en alemán?; **in other ~s** (introducing a reformulation) es decir; **to be lost for ~s** no encontrar* palabras **2** (thing said) palabra *f*; **a ~ of advice** un consejo; **I can't hear a ~ you're saying** no te oigo nada; **I don't believe a ~ of it** no me lo creo; **by ~ of mouth: the news spread by ~ of mouth** la noticia se fue transmitiendo de boca en boca; **the last ~:**

to have the last ∼ tener* la última palabra; **the last ∼ in computers** la última palabra en computadoras; *to eat one's ∼s*: **I was forced to eat my ∼s** me tuve que tragar lo que había dicho; *to have a ∼ with sb about sth* hablar con algn de *or* sobre algo; *to have ∼s with sb* tener* unas palabras con algn; ▶ MINCE¹

3 (assurance) (*no pl*) palabra *f*; **to keep/give one's ∼** cumplir/dar* su (*or* mi *etc*) palabra; **you can take my ∼ for it** te lo aseguro; *to take sb at her/his ∼* tomarle la palabra a algn

4 **(a)** (news, message): **there is still no ∼ of survivors** todavía no se sabe si hay supervivientes; **∼ has it that …** corre la noticia *or* el rumor de que … **(b)** (instruction): **if you need a hand just say the ∼** si quieres que te ayude no tienes más que pedirlo; **to give the ∼ (to + INF)** dar* la orden (de + INF)

5 **words** *pl* **(a)** (lyrics) letra *f* **(b)** (Theat): **he forgot his ∼s** se le olvidó lo que tenía que decir

word² *vt* ⟨document/letter⟩ redactar; ⟨question⟩ formular

word for word *adv* ⟨repeat/copy⟩ palabra por palabra; ⟨translate⟩ literalmente

wording /'wɜːrdɪŋ ‖'wɜːdɪŋ/ *n* (of paragraph, letter) redacción *f*; (of question) formulación *f*

word: ∼ processing *n* tratamiento *m or* procesamiento *m* de textos; **∼ processor** /'prɑːsesər, 'prəʊ- ‖'prəʊsesə(r)/ *n* procesador *m* de textos

wordy /'wɜːrdi ‖'wɜːdi/ *adj* **-dier, -diest** verboso

wore /wɔːr ‖wɔː(r)/ *past of* WEAR²

work¹ /wɜːrk ‖wɜːk/ *n* **1** (labor, tasks) trabajo *m*; **she put a lot of ∼ into it** puso mucho esfuerzo en ello; **it's hard ∼ digging** cavar es muy duro **2** (employment) trabajo *m*; **to go to ∼** ir* a trabajar *or* al trabajo

3 (*in phrases*) **at work:** **he's at ∼** está en el trabajo, está en la oficina (*or* la fábrica *etc*); **they were hard at ∼** estaban muy ocupados trabajando; **off work: she was off ∼ for a month after the accident** después del accidente estuvo un mes sin trabajar; **he took a day off ∼** se tomó un día libre; **out of work: to be out of ∼** estar* sin trabajo *or* desocupado *or* desempleado *or* (Chi tb) cesante, estar* parado (Esp); (*before n*) **out-of-work** desocupado, desempleado, parado (Esp), cesante (Chi)

4 **(a)** (product, single item) obra *f*; **a ∼ of art** una obra de arte **(b)** (output) trabajo *m*; **a piece of ∼** un trabajo; **it was the ∼ of a professional** era obra de un profesional; *see also* WORKS

work² *vi* **1** ⟨person⟩ trabajar; **I ∼ as a receptionist** trabajo de recepcionista; **to ∼ hard** trabajar mucho *or* duro; **to ∼ FOR sb** trabajar PARA algn; **to ∼ in oils** pintar al óleo, trabajar con óleos; **he's ∼ing on his car** está arreglando el coche; **scientists are ∼ing on a cure** los científicos están intentando encontrar una cura; **to ∼ UNDER sb** trabajar bajo la dirección de algn **2** **(a)** (operate, function) «machine/system» funcionar; «drug/person» actuar*; **it ∼s both ways: you have to make an effort too, you know: it ∼s both ways** tú también tienes que hacer el esfuerzo, ¿sabes? funciona igual *or* (esp AmL)

parejo para los dos **(b)** (have required effect) «drug/plan/method» surtir efecto; **try it, it might ∼** pruébalo, quizás resulte

■ ∼ *vt* **1** **(a)** (force to work) hacer* trabajar; **to ∼ oneself to death** matarse trabajando **(b)** (exploit) ⟨land/soil⟩ trabajar; ⟨mine⟩ explotar **(c)** ⟨nightclubs/casinos⟩ trabajar en **(d)** (pay for by working): **he ∼ed his passage to Australia** se costeó el pasaje a Australia trabajando en el barco **2** (cause to operate): **do you know how to ∼ the machine?** ¿sabes manejar la máquina?; **this lever ∼s the sprinkler system** esta palanca acciona el sistema de riego **3** **(a)** (move gradually, manipulate) (+ *adv compl*): **∼ the brush into the corners** mete bien el cepillo en los rincones; **to ∼ one's way: we ∼ed our way toward the exit** nos abrimos camino hacia la salida; **she ∼ed her way to the top of her profession** trabajó hasta llegar a la cima de su profesión **(b)** (shape, fashion) ⟨clay/metal⟩ trabajar; ⟨dough⟩ sobar **4** **(a)** (*past & past p* **worked** *or* **wrought**) (bring about) ⟨miracle⟩ hacer*; *see also* WROUGHT **(b)** (arrange) (colloq) arreglar

■ **work off** [*v* + *o* + *adv*, *v* + *adv* + *o*] **(a)** (get rid of): **you can ∼ off a few kilos in the gym** puede rebajar algunos kilos en el gimnasio **(b)** ⟨debt⟩ amortizar*, pagar* (*trabajando*)

■ **work out**
I [*v* + *adv*] **1** **(a)** (turn out) salir*, resultar; **it ∼s out at $75 a head** sale (a) 75 dólares por cabeza **(b)** (be successful) «plan» salir* bien **2** (train, exercise) (Sport) hacer* ejercicio
II [*v* + *o* + *adv*, *v* + *adv* + *o*] **1** **(a)** (solve) ⟨sum⟩ hacer*; ⟨riddle/puzzle⟩ resolver* **(b)** (find, calculate) ⟨percentage/probability⟩ calcular; **have you ∼ed out the answer?** ¿lo has resuelto? **(c)** (understand) entender* **2** (devise, determine) ⟨solution/procedure⟩ idear; ⟨plan⟩ elaborar

■ **work up** [*v* + *o* + *adv*, *v* + *adv* + *o*] **(a)** (stimulate): **they had ∼ed up an appetite** se les había abierto el apetito; **I couldn't ∼ up much enthusiasm** no me entusiasmaba demasiado **(b)** (excite, arouse): **she gets very ∼ed up about it** se pone como loca; **they had been ∼ed up into a frenzy** los habían puesto frenéticos, los habían exaltado

workable /'wɜːrkəbəl ‖'wɜːkəbəl/ *adj* ⟨arrangement/solution⟩ factible

work: ∼bench *n* banco *m* de trabajo; **∼day** *n* **(a)** (part of day) jornada *f* laboral **(b)** (weekday) día *m* hábil *or* laborable *or* laboral *or* de trabajo

worker /'wɜːrkər ‖'wɜːkə(r)/ *n* **(a)** trabajador, -dora *m,f*; **he's a good/slow ∼** trabaja bien/lentamente **(b)** (ant, bee) obrera *f*

work: ∼ experience *n* experiencia *f* laboral; **∼ force** *n* (of nation) población *f* activa; (of company) personal *m*, plantilla *f* (Esp)

working /'wɜːrkɪŋ ‖'wɜːkɪŋ/ *adj* (*before n*) **1** **(a)** ⟨mother/parent⟩ que trabaja; **∼ population** población *f* activa **(b)** ⟨hours/conditions⟩ de trabajo; **we have a good ∼ relationship** trabajamos muy bien juntos **2** **(a)** (capable of operating): **it's in perfect ∼ order** funciona perfectamente **(b)** (suitable for working with) ⟨hypothesis⟩ de trabajo; **I have a ∼ knowledge of Russian** tengo conocimientos básicos de ruso

W

working: ~ **class** *n* (*sometimes pl*) the ~ class(es) la clase obrera *or* trabajadora; ~**-class** /'wɜːkɪŋ'klæs ‖,wɜːŋ'klɑːs/ *adj* ⟨*person*⟩ de clase obrera *or* trabajadora; ⟨*area*⟩ obrero; ~ **day** *n* **(a)** (weekday) día *m* hábil *or* laborable *or* de trabajo **(b)** ▶ WORKDAY A; ~ **party** *n* equipo *m* de trabajo

workings /'wɜːkɪŋz ‖'wɜːkɪŋz/ *pl n* (of machine) funcionamiento *m*

work: ~**load** *n* (volumen *m* de) trabajo *m*; ~**man** /'wɜːkmən ‖'wɜːkmən/ *n* (*pl* **-men** /-mən/) obrero *m*

workmanlike /'wɜːkmənlaɪk ‖'wɜːkmənlaɪk/ *adj* eficiente, profesional

workmanship /'wɜːkmənʃɪp ‖'wɜːkmənʃɪp/ *n* (of craftsman) trabajo *m*; (of object) factura *f*

work: ~**out** *n* sesión *f* de ejercicios *or* gimnasia; ~**place** *n* lugar *m* de trabajo

works /wɜːks ‖wɜːks/ *n* [1] (actions) (liter) (+ *pl vb*) obras *fpl* [2] (engineering operations) (+ *pl vb*) obras *fpl*; road ~ obras viales [3] (factory) (+ *sing or pl vb*) fábrica *f* [4] (mechanism) (+ *pl vb*) mecanismo *m*

work: ~**shop** *n* taller *m*; ~**station** *n* (Comput) terminal *m* de trabajo; ~**surface** *n* **(a)** (area) superficie *f* de trabajo **(b)** ▶ ~TOP; ~**top** *n* encimera *f*, mesada *f* (RPl)

world /wɜːld ‖wɜːld/ *n* [1] (earth) mundo *m*; the longest bridge in the ~ el puente más largo del mundo; **to see the** ~ ver* mundo; (*it's a*) *small* ~! el mundo es un pañuelo, ¡qué pequeño *or* (AmL) chico es el mundo!; *to be out of this* ~ «*food/music*» ser* increíble; *to have the best of both* ~s tener* todas las ventajas; (*before n*) ⟨*economy/peace*⟩ mundial; ⟨*politics/trade*⟩ internacional [2] **(a)** (people generally) mundo *m*; **what is the** ~ **coming to?** ¿adónde vamos a ir a parar? **(b)** (society): **they've gone up in the** ~ han prosperado mucho (*or* hecho fortuna *etc*); **a woman/man of the** ~ una mujer/un hombre de mundo [3] (specific period, group) mundo *m*; **the art** ~ el mundo del arte [4] (*as intensifier*): **we are** ~s **apart** no tenemos nada que ver; **it did her a** ~ **of good** le hizo la mar de bien; **he thinks the** ~ **of her** tiene un altísimo concepto de ella; **to have all the time in the** ~ tener* todo el tiempo del mundo; **without a care in the** ~ sin ninguna preocupación [5] (Relig): **this/the other** ~ este/el otro mundo

world: W~ **Bank** *n* the W~ Bank el Banco Mundial; ~ **champion** *n* campeón, -peona *m,f* mundial; W~ **Cup** *n* the W~ Cup el Mundial, la Copa del Mundo; ~**-famous** /'wɜːld'feɪməs ‖,wɜːld'feɪməs/ *adj* mundialmente famoso

worldly /'wɜːldli ‖'wɜːldli/ *adj* **(a)** ⟨*goods*⟩ material; ⟨*desires*⟩ mundano **(b)** ⟨*person*⟩ de mucho mundo; ⟨*manner/charm*⟩ sofisticado

worldly-wise /'wɜːldli'waɪz ‖,wɜːldli'waɪz/ *adj* de mucho mundo

world: ~ **record** *n* récord *m or* marca *f* mundial; W~ **Series** *n* (in US baseball) the W~ Series la Serie Mundial, el campeonato mundial de béisbol; W~ **War** *n* guerra *f* mundial; **the First/Second** W~ **War,** W~ **War I/II** la primera/ segunda Guerra Mundial

worldwide¹ /'wɜːld'waɪd ‖,wɜːld'waɪd/ *adj* mundial

worldwide² *adv* ⟨*travel*⟩ por todo el mundo

World Wide Web *n* telaraña *f* mundial

worm¹ /wɜːrm ‖wɜːm/ *n* **(a)** (earth~) gusano *m*, lombriz *f* (de tierra) **(b)** (maggot) gusano *m* **(c)** **worms** *pl* (Med) lombrices *fpl*

worm² *vt* (Vet Sci) ⟨*dog/cat*⟩ desparasitar

worn¹ /wɔːrn ‖wɔːn/ *past p of* WEAR²

worn² *adj* ⟨*tire/clothes*⟩ gastado; ⟨*carpet*⟩ raído; ⟨*flagstones/steps*⟩ desgastado

worn-out /'wɔːrn'aʊt ‖,wɔːn'aʊt/ *adj* (*pred* **worn out**) **(a)** ⟨*shoes/clothes*⟩ muy gastado **(b)** (exhausted) rendido

worried /'wɜːrid ‖'wʌrid/ *adj* ⟨*look/voice*⟩ de preocupación; ⟨*person*⟩ preocupado; **to get** ~ preocuparse, inquietarse; **to be** ~ ABOUT sb/sth estar* preocupado POR algn/algo

worrier /'wɜːriər ‖'wʌriə(r)/ *n*: **she's such a** ~ se preocupa *or* se angustia tanto por todo

worry¹ /'wɜːri ‖'wʌri/ *n* (*pl* **-ries**) preocupación *f*

worry² **-ries, -rying, -ried** *vt* [1] (trouble) preocupar, inquietar [2] «*dog*» ⟨*sheep*⟩ acosar
■ ~ *vi* preocuparse, inquietarse; **to** ~ ABOUT sth/ sb preocuparse POR algo/algn

worrying /'wɜːriɪŋ ‖'wʌriɪŋ/ *adj* inquietante, preocupante

worse¹ /wɜːrs ‖wɜːs/ *adj* (*comp of* BAD¹) peor; **to get** ~ empeorar; (sicker) ponerse* peor; **things are getting** ~ **and** ~ las cosas van de mal en peor; **to make things** ~, **it started snowing** por si fuera poco, empezó a nevar

worse² *adv* (*comp of* BADLY) peor

worse³ *n* the ~ el (*or* la *etc*) peor; **a change for the** ~ un cambio para mal

worsen /'wɜːrsn ‖'wɜːsn/ *vi/t* empeorar

worse-off /'wɜːrsɒf ‖,wɜːs'ɒf/ *adj* (*pred* **worse off**) **(a)** (financially) en peor posición económica **(b)** (emotionally, physically) (*pred*) peor

worship¹ /'wɜːrʃəp ‖'wɜːʃɪp/ *n* [1] (Relig) culto *m*, adoración *f* [2] **Worship** (as title): **Your/His** W~ (of magistrate) Su Señoría; (of mayor) el señor alcalde

worship² *vt*, (BrE) **-pp-** ⟨*God*⟩ adorar; ⟨*success/ wealth*⟩ rendir* culto a; ⟨*hero*⟩ idolatrar

worshipper /'wɜːrʃəpər ‖'wɜːʃɪpə(r)/ *n* (Relig) fiel *m*

worst¹ /wɜːrst ‖wɜːst/ *adj* (*superl of* BAD¹) peor; **he's the** ~ **student in the class** es el peor alumno de la clase; ~ **of all** lo peor de todo

worst² *adv* (*superl of* BADLY): **she did (the)** ~ (**of all**) **in both exams** le fue peor que a nadie en los dos exámenes

worst³ *n* [1] the ~ **(a)** (+ *sing vb*) lo peor; **his sister brings out the** ~ **in him** cuando está con su hermana está peor que nunca; *if (the)* ~ *comes to (the)* ~ en el peor de los casos **(b)** (+ *pl vb*) los peores [2] **(a) at worst** en el peor de los casos **(b)** at her/his/its worst: **I'm at my** ~ **in the morning** la mañana es mi peor momento del día; **this is racism at its** ~ esto es racismo de la peor especie

worth¹ /wɜːrθ ‖wɜːθ/ *adj* (*pred*) **(a)** (equal in value to) **to be** ~ valer*; **it cost 300 dólares, but it was** ~ **the money** costó $300, pero valió la pena; **goods** ~ **£5,000 were stolen** robaron mercancías por valor de 5.000 libras; **this is my opinion, for what it's** ~ esta es mi opinión, si es que a

alguien le interesa **(b)** (worthy of): **it's ∼ a try** vale
la pena intentarlo; **that's ∼ knowing** es bueno
saberlo; **don't argue with them, it isn't ∼ it** no
discutas con ellos, no vale or no merece la pena

worth² n **(a)** (equivalent): **$2,000 dollars' ∼ of
furniture** muebles por valor de 2.000 dólares; **I've
had my money's ∼ out of this car** le he sacado
mucho jugo a este coche (fam) **(b)** (of thing) valor
m; (of person) valía f

worthless /'wɜːrθləs ‖'wɜːθlɪs/ adj ⟨object⟩ sin
ningún valor; ⟨person⟩ despreciable; **to be ∼** no
tener* ningún valor, no valer* nada

worthwhile /wɜːrθ'hwaɪl ‖wɜːθ'waɪl/ adj
⟨enterprise/project⟩ que vale la pena

worthy /'wɜːrði ‖'wɜːði/ adj **-thier, -thiest**
[1] (appropriate, equal) ⟨opponent/successor⟩ digno; **to
be ∼ OF sth/sb** ser* digno DE algo/algn [2] (good,
estimable) ⟨person⟩ respetable; **a ∼ cause** una
buena causa

would /wʊd/ v mod

■ **Note** When *would* + a verb in English is used to
form the conditional tense, it is translated by the
conditional tense in Spanish.When *would* + a verb in
English is used to express habitual activity in the past,
it is translated by the imperfect tense in Spanish.For
examples of this use, see the entry below.

['D *es la contracción de* WOULD, WOULDN'T *de*
WOULD NOT *y* 'D'VE *de* WOULD HAVE] [1] *past of*
WILL¹
[2] (in conditional sentences): **I ∼ if I could** lo haría si
pudiera; **if I had known, I ∼n't have come** si lo
hubiera sabido no habría or no hubiera venido
[3] (expressing wishes): **I wish you'd stop pestering
me!** ¡deja de fastidiarme por Dios!
[4] (in requests, invitations): **∼ you type this for me
please?** ¿me haría el favor de pasar esto a
máquina?; **∼ you like to come with us? — I'd love
to** ¿quieres venir con nosotros? — me encantaría

would-be /'wʊdbiː/ adj (before n): **a ∼ star/
poet** un aspirante a estrella/poeta

wouldn't /'wʊdn̩t/ = would not

would've /'wʊdəv/ = would have

wound¹ /wuːnd/ n herida f

wound² /wuːnd/ vt/i herir*

wound³ /waʊnd/ past & past p of WIND² vt II, vi

wounded /'wuːndəd ‖'wuːndɪd/ adj ⟨soldier/
animal/pride⟩ herido; ⟨look/tone⟩ dolido

wove /wəʊv/ past of WEAVE

woven /'wəʊvən/ past p of WEAVE

WP n **(a)** = **word processor** **(b)** = **word
processing**

wpm (= **words per minute**) palabras por
minuto

wrangle¹ /'ræŋgəl/ vi discutir, reñir*

wrangle² n altercado m, riña f

wrap¹ /ræp/ **-pp-** vt **(a)** (cover) ⟨parcel/gift⟩
WRAP¹ vt A **(b)** (wind, entwine): **she ∼ped a shawl
about her** se envolvió en un chal

■ **wrap up** [1] [v + o + adv, v + adv + o] **(a)** ▶
WRAP¹ vt A **(b)** (complete) (colloq) ⟨order/sale⟩
conseguir*; ⟨deal⟩ cerrar* **(c)** (conclude) (colloq)
⟨meeting⟩ dar* fin a **(d)** (engross) (colloq) **to be
∼ped up in sth: she's totally ∼ped up in her
work** no piensa más que en su trabajo, vive para
su trabajo [2] [v + adv] (dress warmly) abrigarse*

wrap² n **(a)** (shawl) chal m, pañoleta f **(b)** (robe)
(AmE) bata f, salto m de cama (CS)

wraparound /'ræpəraʊnd/ adj ⟨skirt/dress⟩
cruzado

wrapper /'ræpər ‖'ræpə(r)/ n envoltorio m,
envoltura f

wrapping /'ræpɪŋ/ n envoltorio m, envoltura f

wrapping paper n (plain) papel m de
envolver; (decorative) papel m de regalo

wrath /ræθ ‖rɒθ/ n (liter) cólera f, ira f

wreak /riːk/ vt (liter) ⟨destruction/chaos⟩
sembrar*; **to ∼ havoc** causar estragos

wreath /riːθ/ n corona f

wreck¹ /rek/ n [1] (ship) restos mpl del
naufragio; (vehicle) restos mpl del avión (or tren
etc) siniestrado [2] (sth, so ruined): **the attack left
him a physical ∼** el ataque lo dejó hecho una
ruina; **he's a nervous ∼** tiene los nervios
destrozados

wreck² vt **(a)** ⟨ship⟩ provocar* el naufragio de;
⟨train⟩ hacer* descarrilar; ⟨car⟩ destrozar* **(b)**
(damage) destrozar* **(c)** (demolish) (AmE) ⟨house/
building⟩ demoler* **(d)** (spoil, ruin) ⟨plans/chances⟩
echar por tierra; ⟨marriage/happiness⟩ destrozar*

wreckage /'rekɪdʒ/ n (of plane, car, ship) restos
mpl; (of house) ruinas fpl

wrecker /'rekər ‖'rekə(r)/ n (AmE) **(a)**
(demolition worker) obrero m de derribo or
derribo **(b)** (car dismantler) desguazador m or (Méx)
deshuesador m

wren /ren/ n (Zool) carrizo m

wrench¹ /rentʃ/ vt **(a)** (pull) arrancar*; **to ∼
oneself away** soltarse* de un tirón or (AmE exc CS)
de un jalón **(b)** (sprain) ⟨muscle⟩ desgarrarse*;
⟨joint⟩ dislocarse*

wrench² n [1] **(a)** (twist, pull) tirón m, jalón m
(AmE exc CS) **(b)** (emotional pain) dolor m (causado
por una separación) [2] (adjustable ∼) llave f
inglesa; see also MONKEY WRENCH

wrest /rest/ vt **to ∼ sth FROM sb** arrancarle*
algo A algn

wrestle /'resəl/ vi **(a)** (Sport) luchar **(b)** (grapple)
to ∼ WITH sb forcejear CON algn; **to ∼ WITH sth**
batallar CON algo

wrestler /'reslər ‖'reslə(r)/ n luchador, -dora
m,f

wrestling /'reslɪŋ/ n lucha f

wretch /retʃ/ n (liter) **(a)** (unfortunate person)
desdichado, -da m,f, infeliz mf **(b)** (despicable
person) desgraciado, -da m,f

wretched /'retʃəd ‖'retʃɪd/ adj **(a)** (abject,
pitiable) ⟨existence/creature⟩ desdichado **(b)** (very
bad) (colloq) ⟨weather⟩ horrible; **to feel ∼** sentirse*
muy mal

wriggle /'rɪgəl/ vi (move) retorcerse*; **the
children ∼d in their seats** los niños se movían
inquietos en sus asientos

■ **wriggle out of** [v + adv + prep + o] ⟨dress/
jeans⟩ quitarse (con dificultad); **don't try to ∼ out
of it!** ¡no trates de escabullirte!

wring /rɪŋ/ (past & past p **wrung**) vt [1] **(a)**
⟨cloth/garment⟩ escurrir, retorcer* **(b)** **to ∼ sth
FROM/OUT OF sb** ⟨confession/information⟩
arrancarle* algo A algn [2] ⟨neck⟩ retorcer*   ⋯⟶

W

■ **wring out** [*v* + *o* + *adv*, *v* + *adv* + *o*] ①《*cloth/ swimsuit*》 retorcer*, escurrir ②《*water*》 escurrir; 《*truth/money*》 sacar*

wrinkle¹ /'rɪŋkəl/ *n* arruga *f*

wrinkle² *vi* «*skin/garment*» arrugarse*

wrinkled /'rɪŋkəld/ *adj* arrugado

wrinkly /'rɪŋkli/ *adj* **-klier, -kliest** (colloq) arrugado

wrist /rɪst/ *n* (Anat) muñeca *f*

wrist: ~**band** *n* (bracelet) pulsera *f*; (strap) correa *f*; (sweatband) muñequera *f*; ~**watch** *n* reloj *m* (de) pulsera

writ /rɪt/ *n* (Law) orden *f or* mandato *m* judicial

write /raɪt/ (*past* **wrote**; *past p* **written**) *vt* **(a)** (put in writing) escribir*; **I wrote him a letter** le escribí una carta; **to ~ sb a check** *o* (BrE) **cheque** extenderle* *or* hacerle* un cheque a algn **(b)** (write letter to) (AmE) escribirle* a
■ ~ *vi* escribir*; **to ~ TO sb** escribirle* A algn
■ **write back** [*v* + *adv*] **to ~ back** (**TO sb**) contestar(le A algn)
■ **write down** [*v* + *o* + *adv*, *v* + *adv* + *o*] anotar
■ **write off** [*v* + *adv*] ① **to ~ off FOR sth: she wrote off for a form** escribió pidiendo que le mandaran un formulario
② [*v* + *o* + *adv*, *v* + *adv* + *o*] **(a)** (consider beyond repair) 《*vehicle*》 declarar siniestro total **(b)** (damage beyond repair) (BrE) destrozar* **(c)** (consider a failure, disregard) 《*marriage/project*》 dar* por perdido **(d)** 《*debt*》 cancelar
■ **write out** [*v* + *o* + *adv*, *v* + *adv* + *o*] **(a)** (write fully, copy) escribir* **(b)** (complete, fill out) 《*prescription*》 escribir*; 《*check/receipt*》 hacer*, extender* (frml)
■ **write up** [*v* + *o* + *adv*, *v* + *adv* + *o*] 《*report/ notes*》 pasar en *or* (Esp) a limpio; 《*experiment*》 redactar un informe sobre

write-off /'raɪtɔːf ‖'raɪtɒf/ *n*: **the car was a ~** el coche fue declarado un siniestro total

writer /'raɪtər ‖'raɪtə(r)/ *n* (author) escritor, -tora *m,f*; **the ~ of the letter** el autor de la carta; **~'s cramp** calambre *m* (*que da por escribir mucho*)

write-up /'raɪtʌp/ *n* (colloq) (review) crítica *f*, reseña *f*; (report) artículo *m*

writhe /raɪð/ *vi* «*snake*» retorcerse*; **to ~ in agony** retorcerse* de dolor

writing /'raɪtɪŋ/ *n* **(a)** (script) escritura *f* **(b)** (written material): **the ~'s rather blurred** la letra está algo borrosa; **in ~** por escrito; (*before n*) **~ desk** escritorio *m*; **~ pad** bloc *m*; **~ paper** papel *m* de carta **(c)** (BrE) (handwriting) letra *f* **(d)** (act of composing): **~ takes up a lot of my time** paso mucho tiempo escribiendo **(e)** (written composition) literatura *f* **(f) writings** *pl*: **the ~s of Swift** la obra de Swift

written¹ /'rɪtn/ *past p of* WRITE

written² *adj* 《*examination/language*》 escrito; **~ permission** permiso *m* por escrito

wrong¹ /rɔːŋ ‖rɒŋ/ *adj* ① **(a)** (incorrect, inappropriate) 《*answer*》 equivocado, incorrecto; **you've given me the ~ change** se ha equivocado al darme el cambio; **we've taken the ~ bus** nos hemos equivocado de autobús; **he went in the ~ direction** tomó *or* (esp Esp) cogió para dónde no debía; **I did it the ~ way** lo hice mal; **this is the ~ time to mention the subject** este no es (el) momento oportuno para mencionar el tema; **she always says the ~ thing** siempre dice lo que no debe; **the picture is the ~ way up** el cuadro está al revés; **you've got your T-shirt on the ~ way round** llevas la camiseta al *or* del revés; **I'm the ~ person to ask** no soy la persona indicada para contestar esa pregunta **(b)** (mistaken) (*pred*) **to be ~** estar* equivocado; **I was ~ about her** la había juzgado mal
② (morally): **stealing is ~** robar está mal; **you were ~ to shout at her like that** no debiste haberle gritado así, estuviste mal en gritarle así; **I haven't done anything ~** no he hecho nada malo; **what's ~ with that?** ¿qué hay de malo en eso?
③ (amiss) (*pred*): **what's ~?** ¿qué pasa?; **there's something ~ with her/with the lock** algo le pasa/ algo le pasa a la cerradura; **there's nothing ~ with your heart** su corazón está perfectamente bien

wrong² *adv* 《*answer*》 mal, incorrectamente; **I did it all ~** lo hice todo mal; **to go ~** «*machinery*» estropearse, descomponerse* (AmL); «*plans*» salir* mal, fallar

wrong³ *n* **(a)** (immoral action) mal *m*; (injustice) injusticia *f*; **he can do no ~** para ella, es incapaz de hacer nada malo; **to be in the ~** estar* equivocado **(b)** (Law) agravio *m*

wrong⁴ *vt* (frml): **she had been ~ed by her family** su familia había sido muy injusta con ella

wrong: ~**doer** /'rɔːŋduːər ‖'rɒŋduːə(r)/ *n* malhechor, -chora *m,f*; ~**doing** *n*: **she was punished for her ~** la castigaron por sus fechorías

wrongful /'rɔːŋfəl ‖'rɒŋfəl/ *adj* 《*accusation/ punishment*》 injusto

wrongly /'rɔːŋli ‖'rɒŋli/ *adv* 《*spell/pronounce*》 mal, incorrectamente; 《*believe/assume*》 equivocadamente; 《*accuse*》 injustamente

wrote /rəʊt/ *past of* WRITE

wrought /rɔːt/ (*past & past p of* WORK² *vt* 4A) (frml *or* liter) 《*the devastation* ~ **by the war** los estragos causados por la guerra

wrought iron *n* hierro *m* forjado

wrung /rʌŋ/ *past & past p of* WRING

wry /raɪ/ *adj* **wrier, wriest** 《*smile/laugh/joke*》 irónico; **to make a ~ face** torcer* el gesto

WV, W Va = **West Virginia**

WWW *n* (= **World Wide Web**) WWW

WY, Wyo = **Wyoming**

W

Xx

X, x /eks/ *n* **(a)** (letter) X, x *f* **(b)** (Cin) (in US) prohibida para menores de 18 años

xenophobia /ˈzenəˈfəʊbiə/ *n* xenofobia *f*

xenophobic /ˌzenəˈfəʊbɪk/ *adj* xenófobo

xerox /ˈzɪrɑːks, ˈze-‖ˈzɪərɒks/ *vt* fotocopiar, xerografiar*

XL = **extra large**

Xmas /ˈkrɪsməs, ˈeksməs/ *n* Navidad *f*

X-rated /ˈeksˈreɪtəd ‖ˌeksˈreɪtɪd/ *adj* (BrE) ⟨film⟩ solo para adultos, clasificado X (Esp)

X-ray¹, x-ray /ˈeksreɪ/ *n* **(a)** (ray) rayo *m* X **(b)** (photograph) radiografía *f*; **I had a chest ~** me hicieron *or* me sacaron una radiografía de tórax

X-ray², x-ray *vt* hacer* *or* sacar* una radiografía de

xylophone /ˈzaɪləfəʊn/ *n* xilofón *m*, xilófono *m*

Yy

Y, y /waɪ/ *n* Y, y *f*

yacht /jɑːt ‖jɒt/ *n* **(a)** (sailing boat — large) velero *m*, yate *m*; (— small) balandro *m*; (*before n*) **~ club** club *m* náutico; **~ race** regata *f* **(b)** (pleasure cruiser) yate *m*

yachting /ˈjɑːtɪŋ ‖ˈjɒtɪŋ/ *n* navegación *f* a vela

yak /jæk/ *n* yac *m*, yak *m*

yam /jæm/ *n* **(a)** (plant, vegetable) ñame *m* **(b)** (AmE) ▶ SWEET POTATO

yank /jæŋk/ *vt* tirar de, jalar de (AmL exc CS)

Yank /jæŋk/ *n* (BrE colloq & often pej) ▶ YANKEE C

Yankee /ˈjæŋki/ *n* **(a)** (Hist) yanqui *mf* **(b)** (sb from Northern US) (AmE colloq) norteño, -ña *m,f* **(c)** (US citizen) (colloq; in BrE often pej) yanqui *mf* (fam & pey), gringo, -ga *m,f* (fam & pey)

yap¹ /jæp/ *vi* **-pp-** ladrar (*con ladridos agudos*)

yap² *n* ladrido *m* (*agudo*)

yard /jɑːrd ‖jɑːd/ *n* **1 (a)** (of school, prison) patio *m* **(b)** (of house) (BrE) patio *m*; (garden) (AmE) jardín *m* **(c)** (stock~) corral *m* **2** (boat~, ship~) astillero *m* **3** (measure) yarda *f* (0,91m)

yardstick /ˈjɑːrdstɪk ‖ˈjɑːdstɪk/ *n* criterio *m*

yarn /jɑːrn ‖jɑːn/ *n* **1** (Tex) hilo *m* **2** (tale) (colloq) historia *f*

yawn¹ /jɔːn/ *vi* bostezar*

yawn² *n* bostezo *m*

yawning /ˈjɔːnɪŋ/ *adj* (*before n*) enorme

yd (*pl* **yd** *or* **yds**) = **yard**

yeah /jeə/ *interj* (colloq) sí

year /jɪr ‖jɪə(r)/ *n* **1** (period of time) año *m*; **all (the) ~ round** todo el año; **by the ~ 2000** para el año 2000; **over the ~s** I've grown accustomed to it con el tiempo *or* con los años me he ido acostumbrando; **~ after ~/~ in, ~ out** año tras año; **I'm 12 ~s old** tengo doce años **2** **years** *pl* (a long time): **I haven't seen him for ~s** hace años que no lo veo; **~s ago,** there was a church here años atrás, aquí había una iglesia **3** (Educ) curso *m*, año *m*

-year /jɪr ‖jɪe(r)/ *suff*: **a third~ student** un estudiante de tercer año *or* de tercero

yearly¹ /ˈjɪrli ‖ˈjɪəli/ *adj* anual; **on a ~ basis** cada año

yearly² *adv* cada año; **twice ~** dos veces al *or* por año

yearn /jɜːrn ‖jɜːn/ *vi* **to ~ to +** INF anhelar + INF; **to ~ FOR sth** añorar algo

yearning /ˈjɜːrnɪŋ ‖ˈjɜːnɪŋ/ *n* **~ FOR sth/to +** INF anhelo *m* or ansia *f*‡ DE algo/+ INF

-year-old /ˈjərˈəʊld ‖ˈjɪərˈəʊld/ *suff*: **a thirty-two~ woman** una mujer de treinta y dos años; **a six~** un niño/una niña de seis años

yeast /jiːst/ *n* levadura *f*

yell¹ /jel/ *vi/t* gritar

yell² *n* grito *m*

yellow¹ /ˈjeləʊ/ *adj* amarillo; ⟨hair⟩ muy rubio *or* (Méx) güero *or* (Col) mono *or* (Ven) catire; ⟨traffic light⟩ (AmE) amarillo, ámbar *adj inv*

yellow² *n* **(a)** (color) amarillo *m* **(b)** (signal) (AmE) luz *f* amarilla

yellow³ *vi* ponerse* amarillo

yellow: ~ fever *n* fiebre *f* amarilla; **~ pages,** (BrE) **~ Pages®** *pl n* páginas *fpl* amarillas

yelp¹ /jelp/ *vi* dar* un gañido *or* aullido

yelp² *n* gañido *m*, aullido *m*

Yemen /ˈjemən/ *n* Yemen *m*

yen /jen/ *n* **1** (longing) (colloq) (*no pl*) **to have a ~ to +** INF morirse* de ganas DE + INF (fam) **2** (*pl* **~**) (Fin) yen *m*

yes¹ /jes/ *interj* sí; **are you ready? — ~, I am** ¿estás listo? — sí; **you didn't tell me — ~, I did!** no me lo dijiste — ¡sí que te lo dije!

yes² *n* (*pl* **~es**) sí *m*

yes-man /ˈjesmæn/ *n* (*pl* **-men** /-men/) (pej): **he's a ~** es de los que dicen amén a todo

yesterday¹ /ˈjestərdeɪ, -di ‖ˈjestədeɪ, -di/ *adv* ···⟡

ayer; **~ morning** ayer por la mañana, ayer en la mañana (AmL), ayer a la mañana *or* de mañana (RPl)

yesterday² *n*: **~ was a busy day** ayer fue un día de mucha actividad; **the day before ~** anteayer

yet¹ /jet/ *adv* **1** **(a)** (up to this or that time, till now) *(with neg)* todavía, aún; **I haven't eaten** *o* (AmE also) **I didn't eat ~** todavía *or* aún no he comido, todavía no comí (RPl); **as ~** aún, todavía **(b)** (now, so soon) *(with neg)* todavía **(c)** (thus far) *(after superl)*: **it's his best book ~** es el mejor libro que ha escrito hasta ahora

2 (by now, already) *(with interrog)* ya; **has she decided** *o* (AmE also) **did she decide ~?** ¿ya se ha decidido?, ¿ya se decidió? (AmL)

3 (still) todavía, aún

4 (eventually, in spite of everything): **we may win ~** todavía podemos ganar

5 *(as intensifier)* **(a)** (even) *(with comp)* aún, todavía; **the story becomes ~ more complicated** el cuento se complica aún *or* todavía más **(b)** (in addition, besides): **~ more problems** más problemas aún; **we had to go back ~ again** tuvimos que volver otra vez más (aún)

6 (but, nevertheless) *(as linker)* sin embargo

yet² *conj* pero

yew /juː/ *n* tejo *m*

Yiddish /ˈjɪdɪʃ/ *n* yidish *m*, yiddish *m*

yield¹ /jiːld/ *vt* **1** (surrender) *(position/territory)* ceder; **to ~ one's right of way** (AmE Transp) ceder el paso **2** *(crop/fruit/mineral/oil)* producir*; *(results)* dar*

■ **~** *vi* **1** **(a)** (give way) ceder **(b)** (give priority): **Ⓢ yield** (AmE) ceda el paso **2** *(ground/ice)* ceder

yield² *n* rendimiento *m*

YMCA *n* (= **Young Men's Christian Association**) YMCA *f*, Asociación *f* Cristiana de Jóvenes

yodel /ˈjəʊdəl/ *vi*, (BrE) **-ll-** cantar al estilo tirolés

yoga /ˈjəʊgə/ *n* yoga *m*

yoghurt, yoghourt, yogurt /ˈjəʊgərt ‖ˈjɒgət/ *n* yogur *m*, yoghourt *m*

yoke¹ /jəʊk/ *n* **(a)** (for oxen, horses) yugo *m* **(b)** (burden, bondage) yugo *m*

yoke² *vt* *(oxen)* uncir*

yokel /ˈjəʊkəl/ *n* (*pej* or hum) pueblerino, -na *m,f or* (Méx) indio, -dia *m,f or* (Col) montañero, -ra *m,f or* (RPl) pajuerano, -na *m,f or* (Chi) huaso, -sa *m,f* (pey *o* hum)

yolk /jəʊk/ *n* yema *f* (de huevo)

yonder /ˈjɑːndər ‖ˈjɒndə(r)/ *adv* (poet *or* dial) allá

you /juː/ *pron* **1** (sing) **(a)** (as subject — familiar) tú, vos (AmC, RPl); (— formal) usted; **~ liar!** ¡mentiroso! **(b)** (as direct object — familiar) te; (— formal, masculine) lo, le (Esp); (— formal, feminine) la **(c)** (as indirect object — familiar) te; (— formal) le; (— with direct object pronoun present) se; **I told ~** te dije/ le dije; **I gave it to ~** te lo dije/se lo di **(d)** (after prep — familiar) ti, vos (AmC, RPl); (— formal) usted

2 (pl) **(a)** (as subject, after preposition — familiar) vosotros (AmL), vosotros, -tras (Esp); (— formal) ustedes; **be quiet, ~ two** ustedes dos: ¡cállense!, vosotros dos: ¡callaos! (Esp) **(b)** (as direct object — familiar) los, las (AmL), os (Esp); (— formal, masculine)

los, les (Esp); (— formal, feminine) las **(c)** (as indirect object — familiar) les (AmL), os (Esp); (— formal) les; (— with direct object pronoun present) se; **I gave ~ the book** les *or* (Esp tb) os di el libro; **I gave it to ~** se *or* (Esp tb) os lo di

3 (one) **(a)** (as subject): **~ can't do that here** aquí no se puede hacer eso, aquí uno no puede hacer eso, no puedes hacer eso aquí (Esp) **(b)** (as direct object): **people stop ~ in the street and ask for money** la gente lo para a uno en la calle y le pide dinero, la gente te para en la calle y te pide dinero (Esp) **(c)** (as indirect object): **they can cause ~ a lot of trouble** le pueden a uno crear muchos problemas, te pueden crear muchos problemas (Esp)

you'd /juːd/ **(a)** = **you had** **(b)** = **you would**

you'll /juːl/ = **you will**

young¹ /jʌŋ/ *adj* **younger** /ˈjʌŋgər ‖ˈjʌŋgə(r)/, **youngest** /ˈjʌŋgəst ‖ˈjʌŋgɪst/ **(a)** *(animal/ person)* joven; **I have a ~er brother** tengo un hermano menor; **she is four years ~er than me** tiene cuatro años menos que yo; **a ~ man/woman** un/una joven; **a ~ lady** una señorita, una chica joven; **~ people** la gente joven, los jóvenes, la juventud; **to marry ~** casarse joven **(b)** *(appearance/manner/complexion)* juvenil

young² *pl n* (animals) crías *fpl*

youngster /ˈjʌŋstər ‖ˈjʌŋstə(r)/ *n* chico, -ca *m,f*

your /jʊr, *weak form* jər ‖jɔː(r), *weak form* jʊə(r)/ *adj*

■ **Note** The translations *tu* and *su* agree in number with the noun which they modify; they appear as *tu, tus, su, sus*, depending on what follows: *your father/ mother* tu padre/madre *or* su padre/madre; *your books/magazines* tus libros/revistas *or* sus libros/ revistas. The translation *vuestro* agrees in number and gender with the noun which it modifies; it appears as *vuestro, vuestra, vuestros, vuestras*, depending on what follows: *your father/mother* vuestro padre/ vuestra madre; *your books/magazines* vuestros libros/ vuestras revistas.

(a) (belonging to one person) *(sing, familiar)* tu; *(pl, familiar)* tus; *(sing, formal)* su; *(pl, formal)* sus; **wash ~ hands** lávate/lávese las manos **(b)** (belonging to more than one person) *(sing, familiar)* su (AmL), vuestro, -tra (Esp); *(pl, familiar)* sus (AmL), vuestros, -tras (Esp); *(sing, formal)* su; *(pl, formal)* sus; **put ~ shoes on** pónganse *or* (Esp) pone(r)os los zapatos **(c)** (one's): **if ~ name begins with A ...** si tu/su nombre empieza con A ...; **you have to take ~ shoes off in a mosque** hay que quitarse los zapatos en una mezquita

you're /jʊər ‖jʊə(r), jɔː(r)/ = **you are**

yours /jʊrz ‖jɔːz/ *pron*

■ **Note** The three translations of *yours* reflects the gender and number of the noun they are standing for; *yours* is translated by *tuyo, tuya, tuyos, tuyas, suyo, suya, suyos, suyas, vuestro, vuestra, vuestros, vuestras*, depending on the meaning being translated, and what is being referred to.

(a) (belonging to one person) *(sing, familiar)* tuyo, -ya; *(pl, familiar)* tuyos, -yas; *(sing, formal)* suyo, -ya; *(pl, formal)* suyos, -yas; **~ is here** el tuyo/la tuya/el suyo/la suya está aquí; **a friend of ~** un amigo tuyo/suyo **(b)** (belonging to more than one person) *(sing, formal)* suyo, -ya; *(pl, formal)*

suyos, -yas; (*sing, familiar*) suyo, -ya (AmL),
vuestro, -tra (Esp); (*pl, familiar*) suyos, -yas
(AmL), vuestros, -tras (Esp); **~ are here, children**
los suyos *or* los de ustedes están aquí, niños
(AmL), los vuestros están aquí, niños (Esp); **is he a
friend of ~?** ¿es amigo de ustedes *or* suyo *or*
(Esp) vuestro? **(c)** (Corresp): **~, Daniel** un abrazo,
Daniel

yourself /jər'self ‖jɔː'self/ *pron* **(a)** (reflexive):
describe ~ (formal) descríbase; (familiar) descríbete;
stop thinking about ~ (formal) deje de pensar en sí
mismo; (familiar) deja de pensar en ti mismo; **by ~**
solo/sola **(b)** (emphatic use) (formal) usted mismo,
usted misma; (familiar) tú mismo, tú misma; **you're
a musician ~, I hear** usted también es *or*
(*familiar*) tú también eres músico, tengo
entendido **(c)** (normal self): **just be ~** compórtate
con naturalidad; **you're not ~ today** hoy no eres
el/la de siempre **(d)** (oneself) uno mismo, una
misma

yourselves /jər'selvz ‖jɔː'selvz/ *pron* **(a)**
(reflexive): **behave ~!** ¡pórtense bien! (AmL),
¡porta(r)os bien! (Esp); **by ~** solos/solas **(b)**
(emphatic use) (formal) ustedes mismos/mismas;
(familiar) ustedes mismos/mismas *or* (Esp) vosotros
mismos/vosotras mismas **(c)** (normal selves): **just
be ~** compórtense *or* (Esp) comporta(r)os con
naturalidad

youth /juːθ/ *n* (*pl* **youths** /juːðz/) **1** (early life)
juventud *f* **2** (young people) (+ *sing or pl vb*)
juventud *f*; (*before n*) (*movement/orchestra*)
juvenil; **~ club** club *m* de jóvenes **3** (young man)
(frml) joven *m*

youthful /'juːθfəl/ *adj* ‹*enthusiasm/manner*›
juvenil; ‹*folly/ignorance*› de juventud

youth hostel *n* albergue *m* juvenil *or* de la
juventud

you've /juːv/ = **you have**

yowl /jaʊl/ *vi* «*person*» dar* alaridos; «*dog*»
aullar*; «*cat*» maullar*

yo-yo /'jəʊjəʊ/ *n* yo-yo *m*

yr (*pl* **yrs**) = **year**

Yugoslav /'juːgəʊˈslɑːv ‖'juːgəsˌlɑːv/ *adj/n* ▶
YUGOSLAVIAN[1,2]

Yugoslavia /ˌjuːgəʊˈslɑːviə ‖ˌjuːgəˈslɑːviə/ *n*
(Hist) Yugoslavia *f*

Yugoslavian[1] /ˌjuːgəʊˈslɑːviən
‖ˌjuːgəˈslɑːviən/ *adj* (Hist) yugoslavo

Yugoslavian[2] *n* (Hist) yugoslavo, -va *m,f*

yuppie, yuppy /'jʌpi/ *n* (*pl* **-pies**) (colloq)
yuppy *mf* (fam)

YWCA *n* (= **Young Women's Christian
Association**) YWCA *f*, Asociación *f* de Jóvenes
Cristianas

Zz

Z, z /ziː ‖zed/ *n* Z, z *f*

Zaire /zɑːˈiːr ‖zɑːˈiːə(r)/ *n* Zaire *m*

Zairean /zɑːˈiːriən ‖zɑːˈiːəriən/ *adj* zaireño

Zambia /'zæmbiə/ *n* Zambia *f*

Zambian /'zæmbiən/ *adj* zambiano

zany /'zeɪni/ *adj* **zanier, zaniest** (colloq)
‹*person*› chiflado (fam); ‹*adventure*› loco

zap /zæp/ *vt* **-pp- (a)** (defeat, blast) (colloq) liquidar
(fam) **(b)** (Comput) eliminar, borrar

zeal /ziːl/ *n* (Pol, Relig) fervor *m*, celo *m*

zealot /'zelət/ *n* (fanatic) fanático, -ca *m,f*

zealous /'zeləs/ *adj* ‹*follower*› ferviente;
‹*worker*› que pone gran celo en su trabajo

zebra /'ziːbrə ‖'zebrə, ziː-/ *n* (*pl* **-bras** *or* **-bra**)
cebra *f*

zebra crossing *n* (BrE) paso *m* de cebra

zee /ziː/, (BrE) **zed** /zed/ *n* zeta *f*

zenith /'ziːnəθ ‖'zenɪθ/ *n* (Astron) cenit *m*, zenit
m; **at the ~ of her popularity** en el cenit *or* el
apogeo de su popularidad

zero[1] /'zɪrəʊ, 'ziː- ‖'zɪərəʊ/ *n* (*pl* **zeros** *or*
zeroes) cero *m*; **the temperature fell below ~** la
temperatura bajó de los cero grados; (*before n*) **~
hour** hora *f* cero

zero[2] *adj* cero *adj inv*; **~ degrees centigrade**
cero grados centígrados

zest /zest/ *n* entusiasmo *m*

zigzag[1] /'zɪgzæg/ *n* zigzag *m*

zigzag[2] *vi* **-gg-** zigzaguear

zilch /zɪltʃ/ *n* (sl) nada de nada

Zimbabwe /zɪmˈbɑːbwi, -weɪ/ *n* Zimbabwe *m*,
Zimbabue *m*

Zimbabwean /zɪmˈbɑːbwiən/ *adj*
zimbabuense, de Zimbabwe

zinc /zɪŋk/ *n* cinc *m*, zinc *m*

Zionism /'zaɪənɪzəm/ *n* sionismo *m*

Zionist /'zaɪənəst ‖'zaɪənɪst/ *adj* sionista

zip[1] /zɪp/ *n* **1** (vigor) (colloq) garra *f* (fam)
2 (fastener) (BrE) ▶ ZIPPER

zip[2] **-pp-** *vt* ‹*pocket/bag*› cerrar* la cremallera
(*or* el cierre *etc*) de
■ **~** *vi* **1** (with zipper): **the suitcase ~s open/shut**
la maleta se abre/cierra con cremallera (*or* cierre
etc) **2** (move fast) (colloq): **we ~ped through the
work** (nos) despachamos el trabajo en un
santiamén (fam)
■ **zip up** [*v* + *o* + *adv*, *v* + *adv* + *o*] ‹*bag*› cerrar*

zip: ~ code *n* (AmE) código *m* postal; **~
fastener** *n* (BrE) ▶ ZIPPER[1]; **~-on** *adj* (*before n*)
‹*hood/lining*› que se puede quitar, desmontable

zipper[1] /'zɪpər ‖'zɪpə(r)/ *n* (AmE) cremallera *f*,
cierre *m* (AmL), zíper *m* (AmC, Méx, Ven), cierre *m*
relámpago (RPl) *or* (Chi) eclair

zipper[2] *vt* (AmE) ▶ ZIP[2] *vt*

zodiac /'zəʊdiæk/ *n* **the ~** el zodíaco *or* zodiaco

zombie /'zɑːmbi ‖'zɒmbi/ *n* zombie *mf*

zone /zəʊn/ n **(a)** (area) zona f; time ~ huso m
horario **(b)** (AmE) distrito m

zoo /zuː/ n (pl **zoos**) zoológico m, zoo m (esp
Esp)

zoologist /zəʊˈɑːlədʒəst ‖ zəʊˈɒlədʒɪst, zuː/ n
zoólogo, -ga m,f

zoology /zəʊˈɑːlədʒi ‖ zəʊˈɒlədʒi, zuː/ n zoología
f

zoom¹ /zuːm/ n **1** (sound) (no pl) zumbido m
2 ~ **(lens)** (Cin, Phot, TV) teleobjetivo m, zoom
m

zoom² vi (move fast) (colloq) (+ adv compl): to ~
along/past ir*/pasar zumbando (fam)
■ **zoom in** [v + adv] to ~ in (ON sth/sb) hacer*
un zoom in (SOBRE algo/algn) (acercar
rápidamente una imagen usando un teleobjetivo)

zucchini /zʊˈkiːni/ n (pl ~ or ~**s**) (AmE)
calabacín m, calabacita f (Méx), zapallito m (largo
or italiano) (CS)

Zulu¹ /ˈzuːluː/ adj zulú

Zulu² n **(a)** (person) zulú mf **(b)** (language) zulú m

Spanish verb tables

1 Guide to Verb Tables

Every Spanish verb entry in the dictionary is cross-referred to one of the conjugation models shown in the following tables. The reference is given in square brackets immediately after the headword.

All the simple tenses are shown for **hablar** [A1], **meter** [E1], and **partir** [I1], the conjugation models for regular -**ar**, -**er**, and -**ir** verbs. For other verbs only the irregular tenses are given.

Compound tenses are not listed in the tables. The perfect tenses are formed with the relevant tense of the auxiliary **haber** and the past participle:

- Le *he hablado* de ti
- Lamento que *se haya ofendido*
- El profesor nos *había visto*
- Cuando *hubo terminado* de hablar, ...

- Para entonces ya *habremos terminado*
- Si lo *hubiera sabido*, *habría llamado*

The continuous tenses are formed with the relevant tense of the auxiliary **estar** and the present participle:

- *Estoy estudiando* el problema
- Cuando llegó, *estábamos cerrando*
- *Estuvieron esperando* mucho tiempo
- ¿*Han estado hablando* de mí?

Other verbs such as **andar**, **ir**, and **venir** can also be used as auxiliaries to express different nuances of meaning:

- *Andaba diciendo* que ...
- A medida que lo *fui conociendo*...
- ¿Por qué no *te vas vistiendo*?
- Hace mucho tiempo que te lo *vengo diciendo*

2 Verbs ending in -ar

A1 hablar

gerundio (gerund)	participio pasado (past participle)	indicativo (indicative)			
hablando	hablado	presente (present)	imperfecto (imperfect)	pretérito indefinido (past simple)	futuro (future)
		hablo	hablaba	hablé	hablaré
		hablas	hablabas	hablaste	hablarás
		habla	hablaba	habló	hablará
		hablamos	hablábamos	hablamos	hablaremos
		habláis	hablabais	hablasteis	hablaréis
		hablan	hablaban	hablaron	hablarán

condicional (conditional)	subjuntivo (subjunctive)			imperativo (imperative)
	presente (present)	imperfecto (imperfect)	futuro (future)	
hablaría	hable	hablara*	hablare	
hablarías	hables	hablaras	hablares	habla
hablaría	hable	hablara	hablare	hable
hablaríamos	hablemos	habláramos	habláremos	hablemos
hablaríais	habléis	hablarais	hablareis	hablad
hablarían	hablen	hablaran	hablaren	hablen

* all –**ar** verbs have an alternative form in which the –**ara** is replaced by –**ase**, e.g. hablase, hablases, hablase, hablásemos, hablaseis, hablasen

2 Verbs ending in -ar continued

A2 sacar

indicativo pretérito indefinido	subjuntivo presente	imperativo
saqué	saque	
sacaste	saques	saca
sacó	saque	saque
sacamos	saquemos	saquemos
sacasteis	saquéis	sacad
sacaron	saquen	saquen

A3 pagar

indicativo pretérito indefinido	subjuntivo presente	imperativo
pagué	pague	
pagaste	pagues	paga
pagó	pague	pague
pagamos	paguemos	paguemos
pagasteis	paguéis	pagad
pagaron	paguen	paguen

A4 cazar

indicativo pretérito indefinido	subjuntivo presente	imperativo
cacé	cace	
cazaste	caces	caza
cazó	cace	cace
cazamos	cacemos	cacemos
cazasteis	cacéis	cazad
cazaron	cacen	cacen

A5 pensar

indicativo presente	pretérito indefinido	subjuntivo presente	imperativo
pienso	pensé, etc	piense	
piensas		pienses	piensa
piensa		piense	piense
pensamos		pensemos	pensemos
pensáis		penséis	pensad
piensan		piensen	piensen

A6 empezar

indicativo presente	pretérito indefinido	subjuntivo presente	imperativo
empiezo	empecé	empiece	
empiezas	empezaste	empieces	empieza
empieza	empezó	empiece	empiece
empezamos	empezamos	empecemos	empecemos
empezáis	empezasteis	empecéis	empezad
empiezan	empezaron	empiecen	empiecen

A7 regar

indicativo presente	pretérito indefinido	subjuntivo presente	imperativo
riego	regué	riegue	
riegas	regaste	riegues	riega
riega	regó	riegue	riegue
regamos	regamos	reguemos	reguemos
regáis	regasteis	reguéis	regad
riegan	regaron	rieguen	rieguen

A8 rogar

indicativo presente	pretérito indefinido	subjuntivo presente	imperativo
ruego	rogué	ruegue	
ruegas	rogaste	ruegues	ruega
ruega	rogó	ruegue	ruegue
rogamos	rogamos	roguemos	roguemos
rogáis	rogasteis	roguéis	rogad
ruegan	rogaron	rueguen	rueguen

A9 volcar

indicativo presente	pretérito indefinido	subjuntivo presente	imperativo
vuelco	volqué	vuelque	
vuelcas	volcaste	vuelques	vuelca
vuelca	volcó	vuelque	vuelque
volcamos	volcamos	volquemos	volquemos
volcáis	volcasteis	volquéis	volcad
vuelcan	volcaron	vuelquen	vuelquen

A10 contar

indicativo presente	pretérito indefinido	subjuntivo presente	imperativo
cuento	conté, etc	cuente	
cuentas		cuentes	cuenta
cuenta		cuente	cuente
contamos		contemos	contemos
contáis		contéis	contad
cuentan		cuenten	cuenten

A11 forzar

indicativo presente	pretérito indefinido	subjuntivo presente	imperativo
fuerzo	forcé	fuerce	
fuerzas	forzaste	fuerces	fuerza
fuerza	forzó	fuerce	fuerce
forzamos	forzamos	forcemos	forcemos
forzáis	forzasteis	forcéis	forzad
fuerzan	forzaron	fuercen	fuercen

2 Verbs ending in -ar continued

A12 degollar

indicativo		subjuntivo	imperativo
presente	pretérito indefinido	presente	
degüello	degollé, etc	degüelle	
degüellas		degüelles	degüella
degüella		degüelle	degüelle
degollamos		degollemos	degollemos
degolláis		degolléis	degollad
degüellan		degüellen	degüellen

A13 avergonzar

indicativo		subjuntivo	imperativo
presente	pretérito indefinido	presente	
avergüenzo	avergoncé	avergüence	
avergüenzas	avergonzaste	avergüences	avergüenza
avergüenza	avergonzó	avergüence	avergüence
avergonzamos	avergonzamos	avergoncemos	avergoncemos
avergonzáis	avergonzasteis	avergoncéis	avergonzad
avergüenzan	avergonzaron	avergüencen	avergüencen

A14 desosar

indicativo		subjuntivo	imperativo
presente	pretérito indefinido	presente	
deshueso	desosé, etc	deshuese	
deshuesas		deshueses	deshuesa
deshuesa		deshuese	deshuese
desosamos		desosemos	desosemos
desosáis		desoséis	desosad
deshuesan		deshuesen	deshuesen

A15 jugar

indicativo		subjuntivo	imperativo
presente	pretérito indefinido	presente	
juego	jugué	juegue	
juegas	jugaste	juegues	juega
juega	jugó	juegue	juegue
jugamos	jugamos	juguemos	juguemos
jugáis	jugasteis	juguéis	jugad
juegan	jugaron	jueguen	jueguen

A16 averiguar

indicativo	subjuntivo	imperativo
pretérito indefinido	presente	
averigüé	averigüe	
averiguaste	averigües	averigua
averiguó	averigüe	averigüe
averiguamos	averigüemos	averigüemos
averiguasteis	averigüéis	averiguad
averiguaron	averigüen	averigüen

A17 vaciar

indicativo		subjuntivo	imperativo
presente	pretérito indefinido	presente	
vacío	vacié, etc	vacíe	
vacías		vacíes	vacía
vacía		vacíe	vacíe
vaciamos		vaciemos	vaciemos
vaciáis		vaciéis	vaciad
vacían		vacíen	vacíen

A18 actuar

indicativo		subjuntivo	imperativo
presente	pretérito indefinido	presente	
actúo	actué, etc	actúe	
actúas		actúes	actúa
actúa		actúe	actúe
actuamos		actuemos	actuemos
actuáis		actuéis	actuad
actúan		actúen	actúen

A19 aislar

indicativo		subjuntivo	imperativo
presente	pretérito indefinido	presente	
aíslo	aislé, etc	aísle	
aíslas		aísles	aísla
aísla		aísle	aísle
aislamos		aislemos	aislemos
aisláis		aisléis	aislad
aíslan		aíslen	aíslen

A20 ahincar

indicativo		subjuntivo	imperativo
presente	pretérito indefinido	presente	
ahínco	ahinqué	ahínque	
ahíncas	ahincaste	ahínques	ahínca
ahínca	ahincó	ahínque	ahínque
ahincamos	ahincamos	ahinquemos	ahinquemos
ahincáis	ahincasteis	ahinquéis	ahincad
ahíncan	ahincaron	ahínquen	ahínquen

A21 arcaizar

indicativo		subjuntivo	imperativo
presente	pretérito indefinido	presente	
arcaízo	arcaicé	arcaíce	
arcaízas	arcaizaste	arcaíces	arcaíza
arcaíza	arcaizó	arcaíce	arcaíce
arcaizamos	arcaizamos	arcaicemos	arcaicemos
arcaizáis	arcaizasteis	arcaicéis	arcaizad
arcaízan	arcaizaron	arcaícen	arcaícen

Spanish verb tables

2 Verbs ending in -ar continued

A22 cabrahigar

indicativo		subjuntivo	imperativo
presente	pretérito indefinido	presente	
cabrahígo	cabrahigué	cabrahígue	
cabrahígas	cabrahigaste	cabrahígues	cabrahíga
cabrahíga	cabrahigó	cabrahígue	cabrahígue
cabrahigamos	cabrahigamos	cabrahiguemos	cabrahiguemos
cabrahigáis	cabrahigasteis	cabrahiguéis	cabrahigad
cabrahígan	cabrahigaron	cabrahíguen	cabrahíguen

A23 aunar

indicativo		subjuntivo	imperativo
presente	pretérito indefinido	presente	
aúno	auné, etc	aúne	
aúnas		aúnes	aúna
aúna		aúne	aúne
aunamos		aunemos	aunemos
aunáis		aunéis	aunad
aúnan		aúnen	aúnen

A24 andar

indicativo	subjuntivo
pretérito indefinido	imperfecto
anduve	anduviera
anduviste	anduvieras
anduvo	anduviera
anduvimos	anduviéramos
anduvisteis	anduvierais
anduvieron	anduvieran

A25 dar

indicativo		subjuntivo	
presente	pretérito indefinido	presente	imperfecto
doy	di	dé	diera
das	diste	des	dieras
da	dio	dé	diera
damos	dimos	demos	diéramos
dais	disteis	deis	dierais
dan	dieron	den	dieran

A26 errar

indicativo	subjuntivo	imperativo
presente	presente	
yerro	yerre	
yerras	yerres	yerra
yerra	yerre	yerre
erramos	erremos	erremos
erráis	erréis	errad
yerran	yerren	yerren

A27 estar

gerundio	participio pasado	indicativo			
		presente	imperfecto	pretérito indefinido	futuro
estando	estado	estoy	estaba	estuve	estaré
		estás	estabas	estuviste	estarás
		está	estaba	estuvo	estará
		estamos	estábamos	estuvimos	estaremos
		estáis	estabais	estuvisteis	estaréis
		están	estaban	estuvieron	estarán

condicional	subjuntivo		imperativo
	presente	imperfecto	
estaría	esté	estuviera	
estarías	estés	estuvieras	está
estaría	esté	estuviera	esté
estaríamos	estemos	estuviéramos	estemos
estaríais	estéis	estuvierais	estad
estarían	estén	estuvieran	estén

. . . .

3 Verbs ending in -er

E1 meter

gerundio (gerund)	participio pasado (past participle)	indicativo (indicative)			
		presente (present)	*imperfecto (imperfect)*	*pretérito indefinido (past simple)*	*futuro (future)*
metiendo	metido	meto	metía	metí	meteré
		metes	metías	metiste	meterás
		mete	metía	metió	meterá
		metemos	metíamos	metimos	meteremos
		metéis	metíais	metisteis	meteréis
		meten	metían	metieron	meterán

condicional (conditional)	subjuntivo (subjunctive)			imperativo (imperative)
	presente (present)	*imperfecto (imperfect)*	*futuro (future)*	
metería	meta	metiera*	metiere	
meterías	metas	metieras	metieres	mete
metería	meta	metiera	metiere	meta
meteríamos	metamos	metiéramos	metiéremos	metamos
meteríais	metáis	metierais	metiereis	meted
meterían	metan	metieran	metieren	metan

* all –er verbs have an alternative form in which –era is replaced by –ese, e.g. metiese, metieses, metiese, metiésemos, metieseis, metiesen

E2 vencer

indicativo		subjuntivo	imperativo
presente	*pretérito indefinido*	*presente*	
venzo	vencí, etc	venza	
vences		venzas	vence
vence		venza	venza
vencemos		venzamos	venzamos
vencéis		venzáis	venced
vencen		venzan	venzan

E3 conocer

indicativo		subjuntivo	imperativo
presente	*pretérito indefinido*	*presente*	
conozco	conocí, etc	conozca	
conoces		conozcas	conoce
conoce		conozca	conozca
conocemos		conozcamos	conozcamos
conocéis		conozcáis	conoced
conocen		conozcan	conozcan

3 Verbs ending in -er continued

E4 placer

indicativo		subjuntivo			imperativo
presente	pretérito indefinido	presente	imperfecto	futuro	
plazco	plací	plazca	placiera	placiere	
places	placiste	plazcas	placieras	placieres	place
place	plació[1]	plazca[3]	placiera[4]	placiere[5]	plazca
placemos	placimos	plazcamos	placiéramos	placiéremos	plazcamos
placéis	placisteis	plazcáis	placierais	placiereis	placed
placen	placieron[2]	plazcan	placieran	placieren	plazcan

alternative forms, applicable only to the verb 'placer':
[1]plugo; [2]pluguieron; [3]plega or plegue; [4]pluguiera or pluguiese; [5]pluguiere.

E5 yacer

indicativo		subjuntivo	imperativo
presente	pretérito indefinido	presente	
yazco[1]	yací, etc	yazca[2]	
yaces		yazcas	yace[3]
yace		yazca	yazca
yacemos		yazcamos	yazcamos
yacéis		yazcáis	yaced
yacen		yazcan	yazcan

[1]alternative forms: yazgo or yago; [2]alternative conjugations: yazga, yazgas, etc or yaga, yagas, etc.
[3]alternative conjugations: yaz, yazga or yaga, yazgamos or yagamos, yaced, yazgan or yagan.

E6 coger

indicativo		subjuntivo	imperativo
presente	pretérito indefinido	presente	
cojo	cogí, etc	coja	
coges		cojas	coge
coge		coja	coja
cogemos		cojamos	cojamos
cogéis		cojáis	coged
cogen		cojan	cojan

E7 atañer

gerundio	indicativo	subjuntivo
pretérito	imperfecto indefinido	
atañendo	atañí	atañera
	atañiste	atañeras
	atañó	atañera
	atañimos	atañéramos
	atañisteis	atañerais
	atañeron	atañeran

E8 entender

indicativo		subjuntivo	imperativo
presente	pretérito indefinido	presente	
entiendo	entendí	entienda	
entiendes	entendiste	entiendas	entiende
entiende	entendió	entienda	entienda
entendemos	entendimos	entendamos	entendamos
entendéis	entendisteis	entendáis	entended
entienden	entendieron	entiendan	entiendan

E9 mover

indicativo		subjuntivo	imperativo
presente	pretérito indefinido	presente	
muevo	moví, etc	mueva	
mueves		muevas	mueve
mueve		mueva	mueva
movemos		movamos	movamos
movéis		mováis	moved
mueven		muevan	muevan

3 Verbs ending in -er continued

E10 torcer

indicativo		subjuntivo	imperativo
presente	pretérito indefinido	presente	
tuerzo	torcí, etc	tuerza	
tuerces		tuerzas	tuerce
tuerce		tuerza	tuerza
torcemos		torzamos	torzamos
torcéis		torzáis	torced
tuercen		tuerzan	tuerzan

E11 volver

participio pasado	indicativo		subjuntivo	imperativo
presente	presente	pretérito indefinido		
vuelto	vuelvo	volví, etc	vuelva	
	vuelves		vuelvas	vuelve
	vuelve		vuelva	vuelva
	volvemos		volvamos	volvamos
	volvéis		volváis	volved
	vuelven		vuelvan	vuelvan

E12 oler

indicativo		subjuntivo	imperativo
presente	pretérito indefinido	presente	
huelo	olí, etc	huela	
hueles		huelas	huele
huele		huela	huela
olemos		olamos	olamos
oléis		oláis	oled
huelen		huelan	huelan

E13 leer

gerundio	indicativo	subjuntivo
	pretérito indefinido	imperfecto
leyendo	leí	leyera
	leíste	leyeras
	leyó	leyera
	leímos	leyéramos
	leísteis	leyerais
	leyeron	leyeran

E14 proveer

participio pasado	indicativo	subjuntivo
	pretérito indefinido	imperfecto
provisto	proveí	proveyera
	proveiste	proveyeras
	proveyó	proveyera
	proveímos	proveyéramos
	proveísteis	proveyerais
	proveyeron	proveyeran

3 Verbs ending in -er continued

E15 caber

indicativo				condicional	subjuntivo		imperativo
presente	imperfecto	pretérito indefinido	futuro		presente	imperfecto	
quepo	cabía	cupe	cabré	cabría	quepa	cupiera	
cabes	cabías	cupiste	cabrás	cabrías	quepas	cupieras	cabe
cabe	cabía	cupo	cabrá	cabría	quepa	cupiera	quepa
cabemos	cabíamos	cupimos	cabremos	cabríamos	quepamos	cupiéramos	quepamos
cabéis	cabíais	cupisteis	cabréis	cabríais	quepáis	cupierais	cabed
caben	cabían	cupieron	cabrán	cabrían	quepan	cupieran	quepan

E16 caer

gerundio	participio pasado	indicativo			subjuntivo		imperativo
		presente	imperfecto	pretérito indefinido	presente	imperfecto	
cayendo	caído	caigo	caía	caí	caiga	cayera	
		caes	caías	caíste	caigas	cayeras	cae
		cae	caía	cayó	caiga	cayera	caiga
		caemos	caíamos	caímos	caigamos	cayéramos	caigamos
		caéis	caíais	caísteis	caigáis	cayerais	caed
		caen	caían	cayeron	caigan	cayeran	caigan

E17 haber

indicativo				condicional	subjuntivo		imperativo
presente	imperfecto	pretérito indefinido	futuro		presente	imperfecto	
he	había	hube	habré	habría	haya	hubiera	
has	habías	hubiste	habrás	habrías	hayas	hubieras	he
ha	había	hubo	habrá	habría	haya	hubiera	haya
hemos	habíamos	hubimos	habremos	habríamos	hayamos	hubiéramos	hayamos
habéis	habíais	hubisteis	habréis	habríais	hayáis	hubierais	habed
han	habían	hubieron	habrán	habrían	hayan	hubieran	hayan

E18 hacer

participio pasado	indicativo			condicional	subjuntivo		imperativo
	presente	pretérito indefinido	futuro		presente	imperfecto	
hecho	hago	hice	haré	haría	haga	hiciera	
	haces	hiciste	harás	harías	hagas	hicieras	haz
	hace	hizo	hará	haría	haga	hiciera	haga
	hacemos	hicimos	haremos	haríamos	hagamos	hiciéramos	hagamos
	hacéis	hicisteis	haréis	haríais	hagáis	hicierais	haced
	hacen	hicieron	harán	harían	hagan	hicieran	hagan

3 Verbs ending in -er continued

E19 rehacer

participio pasado	indicativo			condicional	subjuntivo		imperativo
	presente	pretérito indefinido	futuro		presente	imperfecto	
rehecho	rehago	rehíce	reharé	reharía	rehaga	rehiciera	
	rehaces	rehiciste	reharás	reharías	rehagas	rehicieras	rehaz
	rehace	rehízo	rehará	reharía	rehaga	rehiciera	rehaga
	rehacemos	rehicimos	reharemos	reharíamos	rehagamos	rehiciéramos	rehagamos
	rehacéis	rehicisteis	reharéis	reharíais	rehagáis	rehicierais	rehaced
	rehacen	rehicieron	reharán	reharían	rehagan	rehicieran	rehagan

E20 satisfacer

indicativo			condicional	subjuntivo		imperativo
presente	pretérito indefinido	futuro		presente	imperfecto	
satisfago	satisfice	satisfaré	satisfaría	satisfaga	satisficiera	
satisfaces	satisficiste	satisfarás	satisfarías	satisfagas	satisficieras	satisfaz[1]
satisface	satisfizo	satisfará	satisfaría	satisfaga	satisficiera	satisfaga
satisfacemos	satisficimos	satisfaremos	satisfaríamos	satisfagamos	satisficiéramos	satisfagamos
satisfacéis	satisficisteis	satisfaréis	satisfaríais	satisfagáis	satisficierais	satisfaced
satisfacen	satisficieron	satisfarán	satisfarían	satisfagan	satisficieran	satisfagan

[1]alternative form: satisface

E21 poder

gerundio	participio pasado
pudiendo	podido

indicativo			condicional	subjuntivo		imperativo
presente	pretérito indefinido	futuro		presente	imperfecto	
puedo	pude	podré	podría	pueda	pudiera	
puedes	pudiste	podrás	podrías	puedas	pudieras	puede
puede	pudo	podrá	podría	pueda	pudiera	pueda
podemos	pudimos	podremos	podríamos	podamos	pudiéramos	podamos
podéis	pudisteis	podréis	podríais	podáis	pudierais	poded
pueden	pudieron	podrán	podrían	puedan	pudieran	puedan

E22 poner

participio pasado	indicativo			condicional	subjuntivo		imperativo
	presente	pretérito indefinido	futuro		presente	imperfecto	
puesto	pongo	puse	pondré	pondría	ponga	pusiera	
	pones	pusiste	pondrás	pondrías	pongas	pusieras	pon
	pone	puso	pondrá	pondría	ponga	pusiera	ponga
	ponemos	pusimos	pondremos	pondríamos	pongamos	pusiéramos	pongamos
	ponéis	pusisteis	pondréis	pondríais	pongáis	pusierais	poned
	ponen	pusieron	pondrán	pondrían	pongan	pusieran	pongan

3 Verbs ending in -er continued

E23 traer

gerundio	participio pasado	indicativo		subjuntivo		imperativo
		presente	*pretérito indefinido*	*presente*	*imperfecto*	
trayendo	traído	traigo	traje	traiga	trajera	
		traes	trajiste	traigas	trajeras	trae
		trae	trajo	traiga	trajera	traiga
		traemos	trajimos	traigamos	trajéramos	traigamos
		traéis	trajisteis	traigáis	trajerais	traed
		traen	trajeron	traigan	trajeran	traigan

E24 querer

indicativo				condicional	subjuntivo		imperativo
presente	*imperfecto*	*pretérito indefinido*	*futuro*		*presente*	*imperfecto*	
quiero	quería	quise	querré	querría	quiera	quisiera	
quieres	querías	quisiste	querrás	querrías	quieras	quisieras	quiere
quiere	quería	quiso	querrá	querría	quiera	quisiera	quiera
queremos	queríamos	quisimos	querremos	querríamos	queramos	quisiéramos	queramos
queréis	queríais	quisisteis	querréis	querríais	queráis	quisierais	quered
quieren	querían	quisieron	querrán	querrían	quieran	quisieran	quieran

E25 saber

indicativo			condicional	subjuntivo		imperativo
presente	*pretérito indefinido*	*futuro*		*presente*	*imperfecto*	
sé	supe	sabré	sabría	sepa	supiera	
sabes	supiste	sabrás	sabrías	sepas	supieras	sabe
sabe	supo	sabrá	sabría	sepa	supiera	sepa
sabemos	supimos	sabremos	sabríamos	sepamos	supiéramos	sepamos
sabéis	supisteis	sabréis	sabríais	sepáis	supierais	sabed
saben	supieron	sabrán	sabrían	sepan	supieran	sepan

E26 ser

gerundio	participio pasado	indicativo			
		presente	*imperfecto*	*pretérito indefinido*	*futuro*
siendo	sido	soy	era	fui	seré
		eres	eras	fuiste	serás
		es	era	fue	será
		somos	éramos	fuimos	seremos
		sois	erais	fuisteis	seréis
		son	eran	fueron	serán

condicional	subjuntivo			imperativo
	presente	*imperfecto*	*futuro*	
sería	sea	fuera	fuere	
serías	seas	fueras	fueres	sé
sería	sea	fuera	fuere	sea
seríamos	seamos	fuéramos	fuéremos	seamos
seríais	seáis	fuerais	fuereis	sed
serían	sean	fueran	fueren	sean

• •

3 Verbs ending in -er continued

E27 tener

| indicativo | | | condicional | subjuntivo | | imperativo |
presente	pretérito indefinido	futuro		presente	imperfecto	
tengo	tuve	tendré	tendría	tenga	tuviera	
tienes	tuviste	tendrás	tendrías	tengas	tuvieras	ten
tiene	tuvo	tendrá	tendría	tenga	tuviera	tenga
tenemos	tuvimos	tendremos	tendríamos	tengamos	tuviéramos	tengamos
tenéis	tuvisteis	tendréis	tendríais	tengáis	tuvierais	tened
tienen	tuvieron	tendrán	tendrían	tengan	tuvieran	tengan

E28 valer

| indicativo | | | condicional | subjuntivo | | imperativo |
presente	pretérito indefinido	futuro		presente	imperfecto	
valgo	valí	valdré	valdría	valga	valiera	
vales	valiste	valdrás	valdrías	valgas	valieras	vale
vale	valió	valdrá	valdría	valga	valiera	valga
valemos	valimos	valdremos	valdríamos	valgamos	valiéramos	valgamos
valéis	valisteis	valdréis	valdríais	valgáis	valierais	valed
valen	valieron	valdrán	valdrían	valgan	valieran	valgan

E29 ver

| participio pasado | indicativo | | | subjuntivo | imperativo |
	presente	imperfecto	pretérito indefinido	presente	
visto	veo	veía	vi	vea	
	ves	veías	viste	veas	ve
	ve	veía	vio	vea	vea
	vemos	veíamos	vimos	veamos	veamos
	veis	veíais	visteis	veáis	ved
	ven	veían	vieron	vean	vean

E30 romper

participio pasado

roto

E31 verter

| gerundio | indicativo | | subjuntivo | imperativo |
	presente	pretérito indefinido	imperfecto	
vertiendo[1]	vierto	vertí	vertiera[4]	
	viertes	vertiste	vertieras	vierte
	vierte	vertió[2]	vertiera	vierta
	vertemos	vertimos	vertiéramos	vertamos
	vertéis	vertisteis	vertierais	verted
	vierten	vertieron[3]	vertieran	viertan

alternative forms: [1]virtiendo; [2]virtió; [3]virtieron; [4]virtiera, virtieras, etc.

- -

4 Verbs ending in -ir

I1 partir

gerundio (gerund)	participio pasado (past participle)	indicativo (indicative)			
		presente (present)	imperfecto (imperfect)	pretérito indefinido (past simple)	futuro (future)
partiendo	partido				
		parto	partía	partí	partiré
		partes	partías	partiste	partirás
		parte	partía	partió	partirá
		partimos	partíamos	partimos	partiremos
		partís	partíais	partisteis	partiréis
		parten	partían	partieron	partirán

condicional (conditional)	subjuntivo (subjunctive)			imperativo (imperative)
	presente (present)	imperfecto (imperfect)	futuro (future)	
partiría	parta	partiera*	partiere	
partirías	partas	partieras	partieres	parte
partiría	parta	partiera	partiere	parta
partiríamos	partamos	partiéramos	partiéremos	partamos
partiríais	partáis	partierais	partiereis	partid
partirían	partan	partieran	partieren	partan

* all -ir verbs have an alternative form in which -era is replaced by -ese, e.g. partiese, partieses, partiese, partiésemos, partieseis, partiesen

I2 distinguir

indicativo		subjuntivo	imperativo
presente	pretérito indefinido	presente	
distingo	distinguí,	distinga	
distingues	etc	distingas	distingue
distingue		distinga	distinga
distinguimos		distingamos	distingamos
distinguís		distingáis	distinguid
distinguen		distingan	distingan

I3 delinquir

indicativo		subjuntivo	imperativo
presente	pretérito indefinido	presente	
delinco	delinquí,	delinca	
delinques	etc	delincas	delinque
delinque		delinca	delinca
delinquimos		delincamos	delincamos
delinquís		delincáis	delinquid
delinquen		delincan	delincan

I4 zurcir

indicativo		subjuntivo	imperativo
presente	pretérito indefinido	presente	
zurzo	zurcí, etc	zurza	
zurces		zurzas	zurce
zurce		zurza	zurza
zurcimos		zurzamos	zurzamos
zurcís		zurzáis	zurcid
zurcen		zurzan	zurzan

I5 lucir

indicativo		subjuntivo	imperativo
presente	pretérito indefinido	presente	
luzco	lucí, etc	luzca	
luces		luzcas	luce
luce		luzca	luzca
lucimos		luzcamos	luzcamos
lucís		luzcáis	lucid
lucen		luzcan	luzcan

4 Verbs ending in -ir continued

16 reducir

indicativo		subjuntivo		imperativo
presente	pretérito indefinido	presente	imperfecto	
reduzco	reduje	reduzca	redujera	
reduces	redujiste	reduzcas	redujeras	reduce
reduce	redujo	reduzca	redujera	reduzca
reducimos	redujimos	reduzcamos	redujéramos	reduzcamos
reducís	redujisteis	reduzcáis	redujerais	reducid
reducen	redujeron	reduzcan	redujeran	reduzcan

17 dirigir

indicativo		subjuntivo	imperativo
presente	pretérito indefinido	presente	
dirijo	dirigí, etc	dirija	
diriges		dirijas	dirige
dirige		dirija	dirija
dirigimos		dirijamos	dirijamos
dirigís		dirijáis	dirigid
dirigen		dirijan	dirijan

18 regir

indicativo		subjuntivo	imperativo
presente	pretérito indefinido	presente	
rijo	regí, etc	rija	
riges		rijas	rige
rige		rija	rija
regimos		rijamos	rijamos
regís		rijáis	regid
rigen		rijan	rijan

19 gruñir

gerundio	indicativo	subjuntivo
	pretérito indefinido	imperfecto
gruñendo	gruñí	gruñera
	gruñiste	gruñeras
	gruñó	gruñera
	gruñimos	gruñéramos
	gruñisteis	gruñerais
	gruñeron	gruñeran

110 asir

indicativo		subjuntivo	imperativo
presente	pretérito indefinido	presente	
asgo	así, etc	asga	
ases		asgas	ase
ase		asga	asga
asimos		asgamos	asgamos
asís		asgáis	asid
asen		asgan	asgan

111 sentir

gerundio	participio pasado	indicativo		subjuntivo		imperativo
		presente	pretérito indefinido	presente	imperfecto	
sintiendo	sentido	siento	sentí	sienta	sintiera	
		sientes	sentiste	sientas	sintieras	siente
		siente	sintió	sienta	sintiera	sienta
		sentimos	sentimos	sintamos	sintiéramos	sintamos
		sentís	sentisteis	sintáis	sintierais	sentid
		sienten	sintieron	sientan	sintieran	sientan

112 concernir

indicativo		subjuntivo	imperativo
presente	pretérito indefinido	presente	
concierno	concerní, etc	concierna	
conciernes		conciernas	concierne
concierne		concierna	concierna
concernimos		concernamos	concernamos
concernís		concernáis	concernid
conciernen		conciernan	conciernan

113 adquirir

indicativo		subjuntivo	imperativo
presente	pretérito indefinido	presente	
adquiero	adquirí, etc	adquiera	
adquieres		adquieras	adquiere
adquiere		adquiera	adquiera
adquirimos		adquiramos	adquiramos
adquirís		adquiráis	adquirid
adquieren		adquieran	adquieran

. . . .

4 Verbs ending in -ir continued

I14 pedir

gerundio	participio pasado	indicativo		subjuntivo		imperativo
		presente	*pretérito indefinido*	*presente*	*imperfecto*	
pidiendo	pedido	pido	pedí	pida	pidiera	
		pides	pediste	pidas	pidieras	pide
		pide	pidió	pida	pidiera	pida
		pedimos	pedimos	pidamos	pidiéramos	pidamos
		pedís	pedisteis	pidáis	pidierais	pedid
		piden	pidieron	pidas	pidieran	pidan

I15 ceñir

gerundio	participio pasado	indicativo			subjuntivo		imperativo
		presente	*imperfecto*	*pretérito indefinido*	*presente*	*imperfecto*	
ciñendo	ceñido	ciño	ceñía	ceñí	ciña	ciñera	
		ciñes	ceñías	ceñiste	ciñas	ciñeras	ciñe
		ciñe	ceñía	ciñó	ciña	ciñera	ciña
		ceñimos	ceñíamos	ceñimos	ciñamos	ciñéramos	ciñamos
		ceñís	ceñíais	ceñisteis	ciñáis	ciñerais	ceñid
		ciñen	ceñían	ciñeron	ciñan	ciñeran	ciñan

I16 dormir

gerundio	participio pasado	indicativo		subjuntivo		imperativo
		presente	*pretérito indefinido*	*presente*	*imperfecto*	
durmiendo	dormido	duermo	dormí	duerma	durmiera	
		duermes	dormiste	duermas	durmieras	duerme
		duerme	durmió	duerma	durmiera	duerma
		dormimos	dormimos	durmamos	durmiéramos	durmamos
		dormís	dormisteis	durmáis	durmierais	dormid
		duermen	durmieron	duerman	durmieran	duerman

I17 embaír

gerundio	indicativo	subjuntivo
	pretérito indefinido	*imperfecto*
embayendo	embaí	embayera
	embaíste	embayeras
	embayó	embayera
	embaímos	embayéramos
	embaísteis	embayerais
	embayeron	embayeran

. . . .

4 Verbs ending in -ir continued

I18 reír

gerundio	participio pasado
riendo	reído

indicativo				condicional	subjuntivo		imperativo
presente	imperfecto	pretérito indefinido	futuro		presente	imperfecto	
río	reía	reí	reiré	reiría	ría	riera	
ríes	reías	reíste	reirás	reirías	rías	rieras	ríe
ríe	reía	rio	reirá	reiría	ría	riera	ría
reímos	reíamos	reímos	reiremos	reiríamos	riamos	riéramos	riamos
reís	reíais	reísteis	reiréis	reiríais	riáis	rierais	reíd
ríen	reían	rieron	reirán	reirían	rían	rieran	rían

I19 argüir

gerundio	participio pasado	indicativo			subjuntivo		imperativo
		presente	imperfecto	pretérito indefinido	presente	imperfecto	
arguyendo	argüido	arguyo	argüía, etc	argüí	arguya	arguyera	
		arguyes		argüiste	arguyas	arguyeras	arguye
		arguye		arguyó	arguya	arguyera	arguya
		argüimos		argüimos	arguyamos	arguyéramos	arguyamos
		argüís		argüisteis	arguyáis	arguyerais	argüid
		arguyen		arguyeron	arguyan	arguyeran	arguyan

I20 huir

gerundio	participio pasado	indicativo			subjuntivo		imperativo
		presente	imperfecto	pretérito indefinido	presente	imperfecto	
huyendo	huido	huyo	huía, etc	huí	huya	huyera	
		huyes		huiste	huyas	huyeras	huye
		huye		huyó	huya	huyera	huya
		huimos		huimos	huyamos	huyéramos	huyamos
		huís		huisteis	huyáis	huyerais	huid
		huyen		huyeron	huyan	huyeran	huyan

I21 rehuir

indicativo		subjuntivo	imperativo
presente	pretérito indefinido	presente	
rehúyo	rehuí, etc	rehúya	
rehúyes		rehúyas	rehúye
rehúye		rehúya	rehúya
rehuimos		rehuyamos	rehuyamos
rehuís		rehuyáis	rehuid
rehúyen		rehúyan	rehúyan

I22 prohibir

indicativo		subjuntivo	imperativo
presente	pretérito indefinido	presente	
prohíbo	prohibí, etc	prohíba	
prohíbes		prohíbas	prohíbe
prohíbe		prohíba	prohíba
prohibimos		prohibamos	prohibamos
prohibís		prohibáis	prohibid
prohíben		prohíban	prohíban

4 Verbs ending in -ir continued

123 reunir

indicativo		subjuntivo	imperativo
presente	pretérito indefinido	presente	
reúno	reuní, etc	reúna	
reúnes		reúnas	reúne
reúne		reúna	reúna
reunimos		reunamos	reunamos
reunís		reunáis	reunid
reúnen		reúnan	reúnan

124 decir

gerundio	participio pasado
diciendo	dicho

indicativo				condicional	subjuntivo		imperativo
presente	imperfecto	pretérito indefinido	futuro		presente	imperfecto	
digo	decía	dije	diré	diría	diga	dijera	
dices	decías	dijiste	dirás	dirías	digas	dijeras	di
dice	decía	dijo	dirá	diría	diga	dijera	diga
decimos	decíamos	dijimos	diremos	diríamos	digamos	dijéramos	digamos
decís	decíais	dijisteis	diréis	diríais	digáis	dijerais	decid
dicen	decían	dijeron	dirán	dirían	digan	dijeran	digan

125 bendecir

gerundio	participio pasado
bendiciendo	bendecido

indicativo			condicional	subjuntivo		imperativo
presente	pretérito indefinido	futuro		presente	imperfecto	
bendigo	bendije	bendeciré	bendeciría	bendiga	bendijera	
bendices	bendijiste	bendecirás	bendecirías	bendigas	bendijeras	bendice
bendice	bendijo	bendecirá	bendeciría	bendiga	bendijera	bendiga
bendecimos	bendijimos	bendeciremos	bendeciríamos	bendigamos	bendijéramos	bendigamos
bendecís	bendijisteis	bendeciréis	bendeciríais	bendigáis	bendijerais	bendecid
bendicen	bendijeron	bendecirán	bendecirían	bendigan	bendijeran	bendigan

126 erguir

gerundio	indicativo		subjuntivo		imperativo
	presente	pretérito indefinido	presente	imperfecto	
irguiendo	yergo[1]	erguí	yerga[2]	irguiera	
	yergues	erguiste	yergas	irguieras	yergue[3]
	yergue	irguió	yerga	irguiera	yerga
	erguimos	erguimos	yergamos	irguiéramos	yergamos
	erguís	erguisteis	yergáis	irguierais	erguid
	yerguen	irguieron	yergan	irguieran	yergan

[1]alternative conjugation: irgo, irgues, irgue, erguimos, erguís, irguen; [2]alternative conjugation: irga, irgas, irga, irgamos, irgáis, irgan; [3]alternative conjugation: irgue, irga, irgamos, erguid, irgan.

4 Verbs ending in -ir continued

127 ir

gerundio	participio pasado	indicativo			
		presente	imperfecto	pretérito indefinido	futuro
yendo	ido	voy	iba	fui	iré
		vas	ibas	fuiste	irás
		va	iba	fue	irá
		vamos	íbamos	fuimos	iremos
		vais	ibais	fuisteis	iréis
		van	iban	fueron	irán

condicional	subjuntivo			imperativo
	presente	imperfecto	futuro	
iría	vaya	fuera	fuere	
irías	vayas	fueras	fueres	ve
iría	vaya	fuera	fuere	vaya
iríamos	vayamos	fuéramos	fuéremos	vayamos
iríais	vayáis	fuerais	fuereis	id
irían	vayan	fueran	fueren	vayan

128 oír

gerundio	participio pasado
oyendo	oído

indicativo				condicional	subjuntivo		imperativo
presente	imperfecto	pretérito	futuro		presente	imperfecto	indefinido
oigo	oía	oí	oiré	oiría	oiga	oyera	
oyes	oías	oíste	oirás	oirías	oigas	oyeras	oye
oye	oía	oyó	oirá	oiría	oiga	oyera	oiga
oímos	oíamos	oímos	oiremos	oiríamos	oigamos	oyéramos	oigamos
oís	oíais	oísteis	oiréis	oiríais	oigáis	oyerais	oíd
oyen	oían	oyeron	oirán	oirían	oigan	oyeran	oigan

129 salir

indicativo			condicional	subjuntivo		imperativo
presente	pretérito indefinido	futuro		presente	imperfecto	
salgo	salí, etc	saldré	saldría	salga	saliera	
sales		saldrás	saldrías	salgas	salieras	sal
sale		saldrá	saldría	salga	saliera	salga
salimos		saldremos	saldríamos	salgamos	saliéramos	salgamos
salís		saldréis	saldríais	salgáis	salierais	salid
salen		saldrán	saldrían	salgan	salieran	salgan

130 seguir

indicativo		subjuntivo		imperativo
presente	pretérito indefinido	presente	imperfecto	
sigo	seguí	siga	siguiera	
sigues	seguiste	sigas	siguieras	sigue
sigue	siguió	siga	siguiera	siga
seguimos	seguimos	sigamos	siguiéramos	sigamos
seguís	seguisteis	sigáis	siguierais	seguid
siguen	siguieron	sigan	siguieran	sigan

. . . .

4 Verbs ending in -ir continued

131 venir

gerundio	indicativo			condicional	subjuntivo		imperativo
	presente	*pretérito indefinido*	*futuro*		*presente*	*imperfecto*	
viniendo	vengo	vine	vendré	vendría	venga	viniera	
	vienes	viniste	vendrás	vendrías	vengas	vinieras	ven
	viene	vino	vendrá	vendría	venga	viniera	venga
	venimos	vinimos	vendremos	vendríamos	vengamos	viniéramos	vengamos
	venís	vinisteis	vendréis	vendríais	vengáis	vinierais	venid
	vienen	vinieron	vendrán	vendrían	vengan	vinieran	vengan

132 abolir

This is a regular verb but in the present indicative it is only used in the first and second person plural.

133 abrir

participio pasado

abierto

134 escribir

participio pasado

escrito

135 freír

gerundio	participio pasado	indicativo		subjuntivo		imperativo
		presente	*pretérito indefinido*	*presente*	*imperfecto*	
friendo	frito	frío	freí	fría	friera	
		fríes	freíste	frías	frieras	fríe
		fríe	frió	fría	friera	fría
		freímos	freímos	friamos	friéramos	friamos
		freís	freísteis	friáis	frierais	freíd
		fríen	frieron	frían	frieran	frían

136 imprimir

participio pasado

impreso

137 morir

gerundio	participio pasado	indicativo		subjuntivo	
		presente	*pretérito indefinido*	*presente*	*imperfecto*
muriendo	muerto	muero	morí	muera	muriera
		mueres	moriste	mueras	murieras
		muere	murió	muera	muriera
		morimos	morimos	muramos	muriéramos
		morís	moristeis	muráis	murierais
		mueren	murieron	mueran	murieran

138 pudrir

infinitivo	participio pasado
pudrir, podrir	podrido

All other forms are regular and are derived from the infinitive pudrir e.g. pudro, pudres, etc.

Los verbos irregulares ingleses

Las formas irregulares que solo se usan en algunas acepciones se indican con un asterisco (e.g. *abode*).

La información completa acerca del uso, la pronunciación, etc., de cada verbo se encontrará en el artículo correspondiente.

infinitive/ *infinitivo*	past tense/ *pretérito*	past participle/ *participio pasado*	infinitive/ *infinitivo*	past tense/ *pretérito*	past participle/ *participio pasado*
abide	abided, *abode	abided, *abode	deal	dealt	dealt
arise	arose	arisen	dig	dug	dug
awake	awoke	awoken	dive	dived, (AmE also) dove	dived
be	was/were	been			
bear	bore	borne	do	did	done
beat	beat	beaten	draw	drew	drawn
become	became	become	dream	dreamed, (BrE also) dreamt	dreamed, (BrE also) dreamt
befall	befell	befallen			
beget	begot, (arch) begat	begotten			
begin	began	begun	drink	drank	drunk
behold	beheld	beheld	drive	drove	driven
bend	bent	bent	dwell	dwelt, dwelled	dwelt, dwelled
beseech	beseeched, besought	beseeched, besought	eat	ate	eaten
			fall	fell	fallen
beset	beset	beset	feed	fed	fed
bet	bet	bet	feel	felt	felt
bid	*bade, bid	*bidden, bid	fight	fought	fought
bind	bound	bound	find	found	found
bite	bit	bitten	flee	fled	fled
bleed	bled	bled	fling	flung	flung
bless	blessed	blessed, (arch) blest	floodlight	floodlit	floodlit
			fly	flew	flown
blow	blew	blown, *blowed	forbid	forbade, forbad	forbidden
break	broke	broken	forecast	forecast, forecasted	forecast, forecasted
breed	bred	bred			
bring	brought	brought	foresee	foresaw	foreseen
broadcast	broadcast	broadcast	foretell	foretold	foretold
browbeat	browbeat	browbeaten	forget	forgot	forgotten
build	built	built	forgive	forgave	forgiven
burn	burned, burnt	burned, burnt	forsake	forsook	forsaken
bust	busted, (BrE also) bust	busted, (BrE also) bust	freeze	froze	frozen
			get	got	got, (AmE also) gotten
buy	bought	bought	give	gave	given
cast	cast	cast	go	went	gone
catch	caught	caught	grind	ground	ground
choose	chose	chosen	grow	grew	grown
cling	clung	clung	hang	*hung, *hanged	*hung, *hanged
come	came	come	have	had	had
cost	*cost, *costed	*cost, *costed	hear	heard	heard
creep	crept	crept	hew	hewed	hewn, hewed
crow	crowed	crowed	hide	hid	hidden, (arch) hid
cut	cut	cut			

Los verbos irregulares ingleses

infinitive/ *infinitivo*	past tense/ *pretérito*	past participle/ *participio pasado*	infinitive/ *infinitivo*	past tense/ *pretérito*	past participle/ *participio pasado*
hit	hit	hit	outshine	outshone	outshone
hold	held	held	overbid	overbid	overbid
hurt	hurt	hurt	overcome	overcame	overcome
inlay	inlaid	inlaid	overdo	overdid	overdone
input	input, inputted	input, inputted	overdraw	overdrew	overdrawn
interweave	interwove, interweaved	interwoven, interweaved	overeat	overate	overeaten
			overfly	overflew	overflown
keep	kept	kept	overhang	overhung	overhung
kneel	kneeled, knelt	kneeled, knelt	overhear	overheard	overheard
knit	knitted, *knit	knitted, *knit	overlay	overlaid	overlaid
know	knew	known	overlie	overlay	overlain
lay	laid	laid	overpay	overpaid	overpaid
lead	led	led	override	overrode	overridden
lean	leaned, (BrE also) leant	leaned, (BrE also) leant	overrun	overran	overrun
			oversee	oversaw	overseen
			overshoot	overshot	overshot
leap	leaped, (BrE also) leapt	leaped, (BrE also) leapt	oversleep	overslept	overslept
			overtake	overtook	overtaken
learn	learned, (BrE also) learnt	learned, (BrE also) learnt	overthrow	overthrew	overthrown
			partake	partook	partaken
leave	left	left	pay	paid	paid
lend	lent	lent	plead	pleaded, (AmE also) pled	pleaded, (AmE also) pled
let	let	let			
lie (yacer etc)	lay	lain	prove	proved	proved, proven
light	lighted, lit	lighted, lit	put	put	put
lose	lost	lost	quit	quit, quitted	quit, quitted
make	made	made	read /riːd/	read /red/	read /red/
mean	meant	meant	rend	rent	rent
meet	met	met	rid	rid	rid
miscast	miscast	miscast	ride	rode	ridden
misdeal	misdealt	misdealt	ring	rang	rung
mishear	misheard	misheard	rise	rose	risen
mishit	mishit	mishit	run	ran	run
mislay	mislaid	mislaid	saw	sawed	sawed, (esp BrE) sawn
mislead	misled	misled			
misread /ˌmɪsˈriːd/	misread /ˌmɪsˈred/	misread /ˌmɪsˈred/	say	said	said
			see	saw	seen
misspell	misspelled, (BrE also) misspelt	misspelled, (BrE also) misspelt	seek	sought	sought
			sell	sold	sold
			send	sent	sent
misspend	misspent	misspent	set	set	set
mistake	mistook	mistaken	sew	sewed	sewn, sewed
misunderstand	misunderstood	misunderstood	shake	shook	shaken
mow	mowed	mown, mowed	shear	sheared	*shorn, *sheared
outbid	outbid	outbid, (AmE also) outbidden	shed	shed	shed
			shine	*shone, *shined	*shone, *shined
			shit	shit, shat	shit, shat
outdo	outdid	outdone	shoe	shod	shod
outfight	outfought	outfought	shoot	shot	shot
outgrow	outgrew	outgrown	show	showed	shown, showed
outlay	outlaid	outlaid	shrink	shrank, shrunk	shrunk, shrunken
output	output, outputted	output, outputted	shut	shut	shut
outrun	outran	outrun	sing	sang	sung
outsell	outsold	outsold	sink	sank	sunk

Los verbos irregulares ingleses

infinitive/ infinitivo	past tense/ pretérito	past participle/ participio pasado	infinitive/ infinitivo	past tense/ pretérito	past participle/ participio pasado
sit	sat	sat	swim	swam	swum
slay	slew	slain	swing	swung	swung
sleep	slept	slept	take	took	taken
slide	slid	slid	teach	taught	taught
sling	slung	slung	tear	tore	torn
slink	slunk	slunk	tell	told	told
slit	slit	slit	think	thought	thought
smell	smelled, (BrE also) smelt	smelled, (BrE also) smelt	thrive	thrived, (liter) throve	thrived, (arch) thriven
			throw	threw	thrown
sow	sowed	sowed, sown	thrust	thrust	thrust
speak	spoke	spoken	tread	trod	trodden, trod
speed	*sped, *speeded	*sped, *speeded	typecast	typecast	typecast
spell	spelled, (BrE also) spelt	spelled, (BrE also) spelt	typeset	typeset	typeset
			typewrite	typewrote	typewritten
spend	spent	spent	undercut	undercut	undercut
spill	spilled, spilt	spilled, spilt	undergo	underwent	undergone
spin	spun, (arch) span	spun	underlie	underlay	underlain
			undersell	undersold	undersold
spit	spat, (esp AmE) spit	spat, (esp AmE) spit	understand	understood	understood
			undertake	undertook	undertaken
split	split	split	undo	undid	undone
spoil	spoiled, (BrE also) spoilt	spoiled, (BrE also) spoilt	unstick	unstuck	unstuck
			unwind	unwound	unwound
spread	spread	spread	uphold	upheld	upheld
spring	sprang, (AmE also) sprung	sprung	upset	upset	upset
			wake	woke	woken
			waylay	waylaid	waylaid
			wear	wore	worn
stand	stood	stood	weave	wove, *weaved	woven, *weaved
steal	stole	stolen	wed	wedded, wed	wedded, wed
stick	stuck	stuck	weep	wept	wept
sting	stung	stung	wet	wet, wetted	wet, wetted
stink	stank, stunk	stunk	win	won	won
strew	strewed	strewn, strewed	wind (dar cuerda etc)	wound	wound
stride	strode	stridden			
strike	struck	struck	withdraw	withdrew	withdrawn
string	strung	strung	withhold	withheld	withheld
strive	strove	striven	withstand	withstood	withstood
sublet	sublet	sublet	work	worked, *wrought	worked, *wrought
swear	swore	sworn			
sweat	sweated, (AmE also) sweat	sweated, (AmE also) sweat	wring	wrung	wrung
			write	wrote	written
sweep	swept	swept			
swell	swelled	swollen, (esp AmE) swelled			

Glosario de términos gramaticales

Abreviatura Representación de una palabra de una manera más corta por una o varias de sus letras: Sr. = Mr

Acento Mayor énfasis al pronunciar una determinada sílaba dentro de una palabra y representación gráfica (tilde) de dicho énfasis: ca*sa*; ca*fé*

Adjetivo Palabra que califica o determina a un sustantivo: un lápiz *rojo* = a *red* pencil, *mi* casa = *my* house

Adverbio Palabra que modifica a un verbo, a un adjetivo o a otro adverbio: corrió *rápidamente* = he ran *quickly*; *muy* bonito = *very* pretty; canta *muy* mal = she sings *very* badly

Agente El que ejecuta la acción del verbo: *el perro* ladra = *the dog* barks; fue descubierta por *Colón* = it was discovered by *Columbus*

Aguda Tratándose de palabras, que llevan el acento en la última sílaba: infor*mar*, re*vés*, ca*mión*

Apócope Pérdida o supresión de uno o más sonidos al final de una palabra: **algún** (alguno), **tan** (tanto)

Artículo Palabra que va antepuesta al sustantivo e indica su género y su número

Artículo definido Es el que se antepone a un sustantivo que ya nos es conocido: el/la/los/las = the

Artículo indefinido Es el que se antepone a un sustantivo que no conocemos de antemano: un/una = a/an

Aumentativo Palabra formada con un sufijo que indica aumento: grand*ote*; cabez*azo*; simpl*ón*

Cardinal Tratándose de números, que expresan la cantidad entera de elementos de un conjunto: **ocho/nueve/diez** = eight/nine/ten

Comparativo Adjetivo, adverbio o conjunción que expresa una comparación. De superioridad: **más … (que)** = more … (than). De inferioridad: **menos … (que)** = less … (than). De igualdad: **tan/tanto … como** = as … as

Complemento directo Ver **Objeto directo**

Complemento indirecto Ver **Objeto indirecto**

Complemento circunstancial Completa el significado de un verbo, expresando una circunstancia de la acción: compré un libro *ayer* = I bought a book *yesterday*

Condicional Tiempo verbal que expresa una acción como posible si algo ocurre: **iría** = he/she/it would go; **comeríamos** = we would eat

Concordancia Correspondencia del género y el número de un adjetivo con los de un sustantivo y del número y la persona del verbo con el sujeto de una oración: ga*to* ne*gro*; l*os* niñ*os* español*es*; mi marido y yo habla*mos* inglés; Pedro y Juan gana*ron*

Conjugación Serie ordenada de las formas que toma un verbo para expresar modo, tiempo, número y persona y cada uno de los tres tipos de verbos en que se dividen, según la terminación del infinitivo: **ar, - er, -ir**

Conjunción Palabra que une dos oraciones o dos elementos de una oración: **y** = and; **porque** = because

Contracción Unión de dos palabras en una sola: **al** (a + el); **del** (de + el)

Demostrativo Tratándose de adjetivos y pronombres, que muestran o señalan algo o a alguien: *esta* mesa = *this* table; *ésta* es mi hermana = *this* is my sister

Diéresis Signo que indica que debe pronunciarse la vocal 'u' de las sílabas 'güe' y 'güi': cig*üe*ña; ping*üi*no

Diminutivo Palabra que se forma con un sufijo que indica menor tamaño, poca importancia o valor afectivo: perr*ito*; doctor*cillo*; abuel*ita*

Esdrújula Palabra que lleva el acento (tilde) en la antepenúltima sílaba: *trá*fico

Estilo directo El que consiste en narrar lo que se ha dicho citando textualmente las palabras del hablante: me dijo: ¡cállate! = he said: be quiet!

Estilo indirecto El que consiste en narrar lo que se ha dicho sin citar textualmente las palabras del hablante: me dijo que me callara = he told me to be quiet

Femenino Género que se aplica a los seres del sexo femenino y el que se atribuye a las cosas por la terminación (-a) o por el uso: la mujer; la perra; la página; la cruz

Frase Unidad dentro de una oración, que tiene sentido y que no tiene verbo

Futuro Tiempo verbal que sitúa la acción en un momento futuro: **llegará tarde** = he will arrive late

Género Una de las tres categorías gramaticales de los sustantivos, adjetivos, artículos y pronombres: masculino, femenino y neutro

Gentilicio Expresa el lugar de origen o la nacionalidad: **londinense** = Londoner; **español** = Spanish

Gerundio Forma verbal que presenta la acción en proceso de ejecución. En español acaba en -ando o -iendo: habl*ando*; com*iendo* y en inglés en -ing: speak*ing*

Grave Tratándose de palabras, que llevan el acento en la penúltima sílaba: *exa*men; *dé*bil

Imperativo Modo verbal que expresa una orden, un mandato o una petición: ¡ven aquí! = come here!

Imperfecto Tiempo verbal que indica una acción pasada sin que se dé idea de su comienzo o final o una acción pasada habitual: los Niños jugaban = the children were playing; iba allí todos los lunes = I used to go/I went there every Monday

Indicativo Modo verbal en el que la acción del verbo se considera como un hecho sin aportar otro tipo de matices: no tengo hambre = I'm not hungry

Infinitivo Forma no personal del verbo que se construye añadiendo la terminación -ar, -er, ir, a la raíz: cant*ar* = to sing

Interjección Palabra o expresión exclamativa que expresa una impresión repentina de sorpresa, dolor, alegría, ira etc. o que sirve para llamar la atención: ¡caramba! = good heavens!; ¡ay! = ouch!

Interrogativo Adjetivo, adverbio o pronombre que pregunta algo o acerca de alguien: ¿qué? = what?; ¿cuánto? = how much?; ¿quién? = who?

Locución Combinación fija de dos o más palabras cuyo sentido no es el resultado de la suma de los significados de sus miembros. Equivale con frecuencia a un adjetivo, un adverbio o una preposición: de balde = for free

Masculino Género que se aplica a los seres del sexo masculino y el que se atribuye a las cosas por su terminación (-o) o por el uso: el hombre; el perro; el pelo; el árbol

Modo Conjunto de determinadas formas de un verbo que manifiesta la actitud del hablante respecto de lo que está diciendo, diferente según se trate del modo indicativo, modo subjuntivo o modo imperativo.

Negativo Que contiene un adverbio de negación

Neutro Uno de los tres géneros del español, que no es ni masculino ni femenino: eso es lo bueno de esto = that's the good thing about this

Nombre Ver **Sustantivo**

Nombre propio Es el que se aplica a una persona, lugar, institución, etc., y se escribe con mayúscula: Juan, España, London

No numerable Se aplica a los sustantivos que no se pueden contar y que por lo tanto no se usan en plural: tristeza = sadness; solidaridad = solidarity

Numerable Se aplica a los sustantivos que se pueden contar, o sea, que se pueden usar en singular o en plural: una, dos, tres casas etc. = one, two, three houses etc

Número Indica si un elemento es singular o plural

Objeto Palabra o conjunto de palabras que designa a la persona, el animal o la cosa sobre la que recae la acción del verbo

Objeto directo Es aquel sobre el que recae directamente la acción del verbo: compré un libro = I bought a book

Objeto indirecto Es aquel sobre el que recae indirectamente la acción del verbo: le escribí una carta a mi madre = I wrote a letter to my mother

Oración Conjunto de palabras que tiene un sentido gramatical completo, con sujeto y predicado y que se puede comprender sin necesidad de otras explicaciones o referencias.

Oración subordinada es la que depende de la principal, a la que completa o determina: quiero que estudies

Ordinal Tratándose de números, que indican el orden o la colocación en una serie, como primero = first; quinto = fifth; undécimo = eleventh

Parte de la oración Cada uno de los términos gramaticales con los que se designa la función que una palabra desempeña en una oración: sustantivo, verbo, adjetivo, etc., son todos partes de la oración

Participio pasado Parte del verbo que se utiliza para formar tiempos compuestos, expresando una acción acabada. Se utiliza también como adjetivo: he terminado = I have finished; un producto terminado = a finished product

Pasiva Ver **Voz pasiva**

Pasiva refleja Oración con significado pasivo que se forma con el pronombre 'se' y el verbo en tercera persona en voz activa y sin agente expreso: se construyeron muchas casas = many houses were built

Persona Cualquiera de los tres grupos de pronombres personales y de las formas verbales que designan al individuo que habla o primera persona (p.ej. yo/I); al individuo al que se habla o segunda persona (p.ej. tú o Ud/you); al individuo del cual se habla o tercera persona (p.ej. él o ella/he o she)

Plural Número de los sustantivos, adjetivos etc., cuando se refieren a más de una cosa o persona: las casas = the houses

Posesivo Tratándose de pronombres (p.ej. mío/tuyo = mine/yours) o de adjetivos (p.ej. mi/tu = my/your), que indican pertenencia o posesión

Glosario de términos gramaticales

Predicado Parte de la oración que dice algo del sujeto y cuyo núcleo es el verbo: **Ana** *estudia mucho* = Ana *studies a lot*

Prefijo Letra o grupo de letras que se antepone a una palabra y que modifica su sentido: *i*legible; *ante*sala

Preposición Palabra invariable que establece una relación entre dos palabras en una oración: **con** = with; **sin** = without

Presente Tiempo verbal que indica que algo sucede en el momento en que se habla: *abro* **la puerta** = I *open* the door

Pretérito Tiempo verbal que indica que la acción ya ha ocurrido o pertenece al pasado.

Pretérito imperfecto ver **Imperfecto**

Pretérito indefinido Tiempo simple que indica una acción pasada completa y acabada: **se despertó** = he woke up

Pretérito perfecto Tiempo compuesto que indica que una acción, comenzada en el pasado, dura hasta el presente o tiene efectos todavía o bien que sucedió inmediatamente antes del momento presente: **he aprendido mucho/ha salido** = I have learnt a lot/he has gone out

Pretérito pluscuamperfecto Tiempo compuesto que indica una acción pasada y terminada, anterior a otra también pasada: **se había marchado** = he had left

Pronombre Palabra que sustituye o determina a un sustantivo o nombre: p.ej. **él/ella** = he/she; **alguien** = someone; **el mío/la mía** = mine

Pronombre personal Es el que se refiere a una persona o a una cosa: p.ej. **yo/tú/usted** etc.= I/you etc; **me/te** = me/you etc.

Pronombre reflexivo Es el que representa al sujeto y es parte de un verbo pronominal: **me/te/se/nos/os/se**

Pronombre relativo Es el que representa en una oración subordinada a una persona o a una cosa mencionada en la principal: **el hombre** *que* **nos visitó** = the man *who* visited us

Raíz Parte de una palabra que es común a todas las de la misma familia: *com*- es la raíz de *com*eré y *com*ida

Singular Número de los sustantivos, adjetivos etc., cuando se refieren a una sola persona o cosa: **la casa** = the house

Sintagma Sección, dentro de una oración, que constituye una unidad aislable

Sobresdrújula Tratándose de palabras, que llevan el acento en la sílaba anterior a la antepenúltima: *tí*ramelo

Subjuntivo Modo verbal que expresa idea de duda, posibilidad, deseo etc., y que se usa especialmente en oraciones subordinadas: **espero que** *venga* = I hope he will come; **si** *fuera* **posible** = if *it was* o *were* possible

Sufijo Letra o grupo de letras que se añade a una palabra o a su raíz para formar otra palabra:

cafe*tera* frute*ría*; cas*ita*

Sujeto Palabra o conjunto de palabras que designa a la persona, el animal o la cosa que realiza la acción del verbo: *Inés* **estudia geografía** = *Inés* studies geography; **el mío corre más rápido** = *mine* runs faster

Superlativo Grado máximo de significación de un adjetivo o de un adverbio: **la casa más pequeña de la calle** = the smallest house in the street; **muchísimo** = very much

Sustantivo Palabra que nombra a las personas o a las cosas materiales e inmateriales: **silla** = chair

Sustantivo colectivo Es el que en singular se refiere a un conjunto, p.ej: **ejército, rebaño**

Sustantivo compuesto Es el que está formado de dos palabras, p.ej: **aeropuerto (aero + puerto)** = airport

Terminación Letra o conjunto de letras que siguen a la raíz de un vocablo para formar tiempos verbales, el plural de los sustantivos, diminutivos, etc.

Verbo Palabra o conjunto de palabras que describe una acción o un estado: **Los niños están jugando** = the children are playing

Verbo auxiliar Es el que se une a otro para formar los tiempos compuestos o para expresar distintos matices, p.ej.: **haber, estar, poder**: *he* **comido** = I *have* eaten

Verbo impersonal Es el que no admite sujeto, p.ej.: **llover: está lloviendo** = it is raining

Verbo intransitivo Es el que no tiene complemento u objeto directo: **murió repentinamente** = he died suddenly

Verbo irregular Es el que no sigue un modelo sistemático, sino que tiene su propias formas individuales de conjugación

Verbo pronominal Es el que se conjuga en todas sus formas con los pronombres **me/te/se/os/se**, p.ej. **equivocarse**

Verbo reflexivo Es el verbo pronominal que expresa una acción que es realizada y recibida por su propio sujeto: **se lavó** = he washed himself

Verbo recíproco Es el verbo pronominal cuya acción se intercambia entre dos o más sujetos y recae sobre todos ellos, p.ej. **besarse: Pedro y Ana se besaron** = Pedro and Ana kissed each other

Verbo regular Es aquél cuya conjugación se ajusta a la de los verbos que se toman como modelo

Voz activa Indica que el sujeto del verbo es el agente de la acción: **Pedro besa a Ana**

Voz pasiva Indica que el sujeto recibe la acción del verbo y el agente se introduce por la preposición "por", no es muy usual en español: **Ana** *es besada* **por Pedro**

Glossary of grammatical terms

Abbreviation A shortened form of a word or phrase: **Mr = Sr.**

Absolute use The use of a transitive verb without an expressed object, as in: **I didn't** *realize*

Active In the active form the subject of the verb performs the action: **Pedro** *kisses* **Ana =** **Pedro** *besa* **a Ana**

Adjective A word describing a noun: **a** *red* **pencil = un lápiz** *rojo*; *my* **house = mi casa**

Adverb A word that describes or changes the meaning of a verb, an adjective, or another adverb: **he ran** *quickly* **= corrió** *rápidamente*; *very* **pretty =** *muy* **bonito; she sings** *very* **badly = canta** *muy* **mal**

Apocope The omission of the final sound of a word, as in Spanish **algún** (alguno), **tan** (tanto)

Article The definite article, **the =** **el/la/los/las**, and indefinite article, **a/an =** **un/una**

Attributive An adjective or noun is attributive when it is used directly before a noun: **a** *good* **wine = un** *buen* **vino;** *business* **hours = horas** *de oficina*

Auxiliary verb A verb used with another verb to form compound tenses, as English **be, do,** and **have: I** *have* **eaten =** *he* **comido; he** *was* **sleeping =** *estaba* **durmiendo**

Cardinal number A whole number representing a quantity: **one/two/three =** **uno/dos/tres**

Clause A self-contained section of a sentence that contains a subject and a verb

Collective noun A noun that is singular in form but refers to a group of individual persons or things, e.g. **royalty, government**

Collocate A word that regularly occurs with another; in Spanish, **libro** is a typical collocate of the verb **leer.**

Comparative The form of an adjective or adverb that makes it "more": **smaller = más pequeño; better = mejor**

Compound An adjective, noun, or verb formed from two or more separate words: **self-confident (self + confident) = seguro de sí mismo; airmail (air + mail) = correo aéreo; outdo (out + do) = superar**

Conditional tense A tense of a verb that expresses what might happen if something else occurred: **he would go = iría**

Conjugation Variation of the form of a verb to show tense, person, mood, etc

Conjunction A word used to join clauses together: **and = y; because = porque**

Countable noun A noun that can form a plural and, in the singular, can be used with the indefinite article, e.g. **a book, two books**

Definite article: the = **el/la/los/las**

Demonstrative adjective An adjective indicating the person or thing referred to: *this* **table =** *esta* **mesa**

Demonstrative pronoun A pronoun indicating the person or thing referred to: *this* **is my sister =** *ésta* **es mi hermana**

Direct object The noun or pronoun directly affected by the verb: **I bought** *a book* **= compré** *un libro*

Direct speech A speaker's actual words or the use of these in writing: **he said:** *be quiet!* **= dijo: ¡cállense!**

Elliptical Having a word or words omitted, especially where the sense can be guessed from the context

Ending Letters added to the stem of verbs to show tense, and to nouns to show plurality

Feminine One of the genders in Spanish, applied to nouns, pronouns, adjectives, and articles: **la casa blanca = the white house; ella = she**

Future tense The tense of a verb that refers to something that will happen in the future: **he** *will arrive* **late =** *llegará* **tarde**

Gender Spanish nouns, pronouns, adjectives, and articles almost all fall into two genders, masculine and feminine; in addition, Spanish uses the neuter pronouns **esto, eso,** and **aquello,** and the neuter article **lo**

Gerund The part of a verb used in Spanish to form continuous tenses: **muriendo = dying; cantando = singing**

Imperative A form of a verb that expresses a command: **come here! = ¡ven aquí!**

Imperfect tense The tense of a verb that refers to an uncompleted or a habitual action in the past: **the children** *were playing* **= los niños** *jugaban*; **I** *went/used to go* **there every Monday =** *iba* **allí todos los lunes**

Impersonal verb A verb in English used only with **it: it is raining = está lloviendo**

Indefinite article a/an = un/una

Indefinite pronoun A pronoun that does not identify a specific person or object: **one, something**

Indicative form The form of a verb used when making a statement of fact or asking questions of fact: **I'm not hungry** = **no tengo hambre**

Indirect object The noun or pronoun indirectly affected by the verb, at which the direct object is aimed: **I wrote a letter *to my mother*** = **le escribí una carta *a mi madre***

Indirect speech A report of what someone has said which does not reproduce the exact words: **she said that they had gone out** = **dijo que habían salido; he told me to be quiet** = **me dijo que me callara**

Infinitive The basic part of a verb: **to sing** = **cantar**

Inflect To change the ending or form of a word to show its tense or its grammatical relation to other words: **gone** and **went** are inflected forms of **to go**

Interjection A sound, word, or remark expressing a strong feeling such as anger, fear, or joy, or attracting attention: **¡ouch!** = **¡ay!; good heavens!** = **¡Dios mío!**

Interrogative An adjective, adverb, or pronoun that asks a question: **what?** = **¿qué?; how much?** = **¿cuánto?; who?** = **¿quién?**

Intransitive verb A verb that does not have a direct object: **he died suddenly** = **murió repentinamente**

Invariable noun A noun that has the same form in the plural as the singular: **sheep, species**

Irregular verb A verb that does not follow one of the set patterns and has its own individual forms, e.g. English **to be**, Spanish **ser**

Masculine One of the genders in Spanish applied to nouns, pronouns, adjectives, and articles: **el perro negro** = **the black dog; él= he**

Modal verb A verb that is used with another verb to express necessity or possibility, e.g. **might, should, will**

Mood A category of verb use, expressing fact (indicative), command (imperative), or wish or conditionality (subjunctive)

Negative expressing refusal or denial

Neuter One of the genders in Spanish, used only in the pronouns **esto, eso,** and **aquello,** and the article **lo**

Noun A word that names a person or a thing

Number The state of being either singular or plural

Object The word or words naming the person or thing acted upon by a verb or preposition: **John studies *geography*** = **John estudia *geografía***

Ordinal number A number that shows a person's or thing's position in a series: **first** = **primero**

Part of speech A grammatical term for the function of a word; noun, verb, adjective, etc, are parts of speech.

Passive In the passive form the subject of the verb experiences the action rather than performs it – common in English, but not in Spanish: **Ana *is kissed by* Pedro** = **Ana *es besada por* Pedro**

Past participle The part of a verb used to form past tenses: **she had *gone*** = **había *ido***

Perfect tense The tense of the verb that refers to an event that has taken place in a period of time that includes the present: **I have eaten** = **he comido**

Person Any of the three groups of personal pronouns and forms taken by verbs; the **first person** (e.g. **I/yo**) refers to the person(s) speaking, the **second person** (e.g. **you/tú**) refers to the person(s) spoken to; the **third person** (e.g. **he/él**) refers to the persons spoken about

Personal pronoun A pronoun that refers to a person or thing: **I/he/she** = **yo/él/ella**

Phrasal verb A verb in English combined with a preposition or an adverb to have a particular meaning: **run away** = **huir; go past** = **pasar**

Phrase A self-contained section of a sentence that does not contain a full verb

Pluperfect tense The tense of a verb that refers to something that happened before a particular point in the past: **he had left** = **había salido**

Plural Of nouns etc, referring to more than one: **the houses** = **las casas**

Possessive adjective An adjective that shows possession, belonging to someone or something: **my/your** = **mi/tu**

Possessive pronoun A pronoun that shows possession, belonging to someone or something: **mine/yours** = **mío/tuyo**

Postpositive Placed after the word to which it relates, such as "in stock" in the phrase **items in stock**

Predicative An adjective is predicative when it comes after a verb such as **be** or **become: she is beautiful** = **es hermosa**

Prefix A letter or group of letters added to the beginning of a word to change its meaning: **im**possible = **im**posible, **un**lucky =**des**afortunado

Preposition A word that stands in front of a noun or pronoun, relating it to the rest of the sentence: **with** = **con; without** = **sin**

Present participle The part of a verb that in English ends in –ing, and is used in forming continuous tenses: **doing** = **haciendo**

Present tense The tense of a verb that refers to something happening now: I *open* the door = *abro* la puerta

Preterite tense A simple tense referring to a completed action in the past: I *did* it yesterday = lo *hice* ayer

Pronominal verb A Spanish verb conjugated using the pronouns me, te, se, nos, and os, in which the pronoun refers to the subject of the verb: **(yo) me equivoqué = I was wrong.** A subgroup of these verbs are **Reflexive verbs**

Pronoun A word that stands instead of a noun: he/she = él/ella ; someone = alguien; mine = el mío/la mía

Proper noun A name of a person, place, institution, etc, in English written with a capital letter at the start: **Spain, the Atlantic, London, Juan, Madrid** are all proper nouns.

Reflexive pronoun A pronoun that refers back to the subject of the clause in which it is used: myself = me; themselves = se

Reflexive verb A verb whose object is the same as its subject; in Spanish, it is used with a reflexive pronoun: **he washed himself = se lavó**

Regular verb A verb that follows a set pattern in its different forms

Relative pronoun A pronoun that introduces a subordinate clause, relating to a person or thing mentioned in the main clause: **the man** *who* **visited us = el hombre** *que* **nos visitó**

Reported speech Another name for **Indirect speech**

Sentence A sequence of words, with a subject and a verb, that can stand on their own to make a statement, ask a question, or give a command

Singular Of nouns etc, referring to just one: the house = la casa

Stem The part of a word to which endings are added: **care** is the stem of **careful** and **careless**; in Spanish **cuidado** is the stem of **cuidadoso.**

Subject In a clause or sentence, the noun or pronoun that causes the action of the verb: *John* studies geography = *John* estudia geografía

Subjunctive A verb form that is used to express wishes or conditionality: **long** *live* **the King! = ¡***viva* **el Rey!; if it** *was* **or** *were* **possible = si** *fuera* **posible**

Subordinate clause A clause which adds information to the main clause of a sentence but cannot be used as a sentence by itself, e.g. **she answered the phone** *when it rang*

Suffix A letter or group of letters joined to the end of a word to make another word, e.g. quick*ly* = rápida*mente*

Superlative The form of an adjective or adverb that makes it "most": **the smallest = la más pequeña; the best = el mejor**

Tense The form of a verb that tells when the action takes place: present, future, imperfect, perfect, pluperfect are all tenses.

Transitive verb A verb that is used with a direct object: **she** *read* **the book =** *leyó* **el libro**

Uncountable noun A noun that cannot form a plural in ordinary usage and is not used with the indefinite article: **china, luggage**

Verb A word or group of words that describes an action: **the children** *are playing* **= los niños** *están jugando*

Numbers / Números

zero	0	cero	
one (first)	1	uno (primero)	
two (second)	2	dos (segundo)	
three (third)	3	tres (tercero)	
four (fourth)	4	cuatro (cuarto)	
five (fifth)	5	cinco (quinto)	
six (sixth)	6	seis (sexto)	
seven (seventh)	7	siete (séptimo)	
eight (eighth)	8	ocho (octavo)	
nine (ninth)	9	nueve (noveno)	
ten (tenth)	10	diez (décimo)	
eleven (eleventh)	11	once (undécimo)	
twelve (twelfth)	12	doce (duodécimo)	
thirteen (thirteenth)	13	trece (decimotercero)	
fourteen (fourteenth)	14	catorce (decimocuarto)	
fifteen (fifteenth)	15	quince (decimoquinto)	
sixteen (sixteenth)	16	dieciséis (decimosexto)	
seventeen (seventeenth)	17	diecisiete (decimoséptimo)	
eighteen (eighteenth)	18	dieciocho (decimoctavo)	
nineteen (nineteenth)	19	diecinueve (decimonoveno)	
twenty (twentieth)	20	veinte (vigésimo)	
twenty-one (twenty-first)	21	veintiuno (vigésimo primero)	
twenty-two (twenty-second)	22	veintidós (vigésimo segundo)	
twenty-three (twenty-third)	23	veintitrés (vigésimo tercero)	
twenty-four (twenty-fourth)	24	veinticuatro (vigésimo cuarto)	

twenty-five (twenty-fifth)	25	veinticinco (vigésimo quinto)
thirty (thirtieth)	30	treinta (trigésimo)
thirty-one (thirty-first)	31	treinta y uno (trigésimo primero)
forty (fortieth)	40	cuarenta (cuadragésimo)
fifty (fiftieth)	50	cincuenta (quincuagésimo)
sixty (sixtieth)	60	sesenta (sexagésimo)
seventy (seventieth)	70	setenta (septuagésimo)
eighty (eightieth)	80	ochenta (octogésimo)
ninety (ninetieth)	90	noventa (nonagésimo)
a/one hundred (hundredth)	100	cien (centésimo)
two hundred (two hundredth)	200	doscientos (ducentésimo)
three hundred (three hundredth)	300	trescientos (tricentésimo)
five hundred (five hundredth)	500	quinientos (quingentésimo)
seven hundred (seven hundredth)	700	setecientos (septingentésimo)
nine hundred (nine hundredth)	900	novecientos (noningentésimo)
a/one thousand (thousandth)	1000	mil (milésimo)
a/one million (millionth)	1,000,000	un millón (millonésimo)

Weights and measures / Pesos y medidas

1 Longitud / Length

Conversión / *Conversion*

Millas a kilómetros . . . .*Miles to kilometers*
Dividir por 5 y multiplicar por 8 . . . .*Divide by 5 and multiply by 8*

Kilómetros a millas . . . .*Kilometers to miles*
Dividir por 8 y multiplicar por 5 . . . .*Divide by 8 and multiply by 5*

Sistema métrico / *metric system*	Sistema estadounidense y británico / *US/UK system*
10 milímetros . . . . = 1 centímetro *10 millimeters* . . . .= *1 centimeter*	. . . .= 0.394 inch
100 centímetros . . . . . .= 1 metro *100 centimeters* . . . . . .= *1 meter*	. . . .= 39.4 inches/1.094 yards
1.000 metros . . . .= 1 kilómetro *1,000 meters* . . . .= *1 kilometer*	. . . . .= 0.6214 mile . . . . .= $\frac{5}{8}$ *mile*

US/UK system / *Sistema estadounidense* y británico	Metric system / *Sistema métrico*
1 inch . . . . *1 pulgada*	= 25.4 mm
12 inches . . . .= 1 foot . . . . = *1 pie*	= 30.48 cm
3 feet . . . .= 1 yard . . . . = *1 yarda*	= 0.914 m
1,760 yards . . . .= 1 mile . . . . = *1 milla*	= 1.609 km

· ·

2 Volumen / Volume

Sistema métrico / metric system	Sistema estadounidense y británico / US/UK system
	1 centímetro . . . .= 0.06 cubic inches
	cúbico
	1 cubic centimeter
1.000 000 centímetros = 1 metro cúbico . . .= 35.714 cubic feet	= 1.307 cubic yards
cúbicos	
1,000,000 cubic = 1 cubic meter	
centimeters	

US/UK system / Sistema estadounidense y británico	Metric system / Sistema métrico
	1 cubic inch . . . . . .= 16,38 cm^3
	1 pulgada cúbica
1,728 cubic inches . . . .= 1 cubic foot . . . . . .= 0,028 m^3	= 1 pie cúbico
27 cubic feet . . . .= 1 cubic yard . . . . .= 0,764 m^3	= 1 yarda cúbica

3 Capacidad / Capacity

Sistema métrico / metric system	Sistema estadounidense y británico / US/UK system
10 mililitros . . . .= 1 centilitro	
10 milliliters . . . .= 1 centiliter	
10 centilitros . . . .= 1 decilitros	
10 centiliters . . . .= 1 deciliter	
10 decilitros . . . .= 1 litro . . . .= 2.1 US pints	
10 deciliters . . . .= 1 liter . . . .= 1.76 UK pints	
	= 0.264 US gallons
	= 0.22 UK gallons

US/UK system / Sistema estadounidense y británico	Metric system / Sistema métrico
	1 fluid ounce . . . . . .= 2,95 centilitros
	1 onza fluida
16 fluid ounces . . . .= 1 pint . . . .= 0,47 litros	= 1 pinta
2 pints . . . .= 1 quart . . . .= 0,946 litros	= 1 cuarto
4 quarts . . . .= 1 gallon . . . .= 3,785 litros	= 1 galón

Weights and measures / Pesos y medidas

US/UK system / Sistema estadounidense y británico	Metric system / Sistema métrico
1 fluid ounce / 1 onza fluida	= 2,84 centilitros
20 fluid ounces = 1 pint / = 1 pinta	= 0,568 litros
2 pints = 1 quart / = 1 cuarto	=1,136 litros
4 quarts = 1 gallon / = 1 galón	= 4,546 litros

4 Peso / Weight

Sistema métrico / metric system	Sistema estadounidense y británico / US/UK system
10 miligramos = 1 centigramo / 10 milligrams = 1 centigram	
100 centigramos = 1 gramo / 100 centigrams = 1 gram	= 0.0352 ounces
1.000 gramos = 1 kilo(gramo) / 1,000 grams = 1 kilo(gram)	= 2.205 pounds
1.000 kilogramos = 1 tonelada / 1,000 kilograms = 1 metric ton / = 1 tonne	= 0.9842 tons

US/UK system / Sistema estadounidense y británico	Metric system / Sistema métrico
= 1 ounce / = 1 onza	= 28,35 gramos
16 ounces = 1 pound / = 1 libra	= 0,454 kilogramos
14 pounds = 1 stone*	= 6,35 kilogramos
112 pounds = 1 hundredweight	= 50,8 kilogramos
20 hundredweight = 1 ton	= 1,016 kilogramos
2000 pounds = 1 short ton	= 0,907 toneladas
2,240 pounds = 1 long ton	= 1,016 toneladas

* En EEUU el peso de una persona se suele expresar en libras y no en 'stone'
She weighs 129 pounds (US)
She weighs 9 stone 3 pounds (UK)